P9-AFP-918

THE FIFTY RADICALS 五十部首

Fifty Radicals. Most of the 214 radicals (Kanghsi) stand on the left or the top and thus fall under the initials. Fifty of the most common radicals are taken, designated A, B, C, D. All the rest (uncommon radicals) are thrown together with the split characters, marked 10S, 41S, 93S, etc.

When the usually left radicals do not stand at the left, but are shifted elsewhere, they do not count as radicals. Thus 警 comes under 廾 (20), not under 言 (60A); 漿 comes under 乚 (21), not under 水. 康熙 214 部首，取其常用者 50，其餘盡倂爲 S 類. 部首必在上形，不在上形者，仍爲 S 類. 警上形廾 (20)，不在言部，漿上形乚 (21)，不在水部.

五 十 部 首

	NS	A	B	C	D	S		NS	A	B	C	D	S
10	十	扌	木	牛	車	SPLIT CHARACTERS	51	厂	厂	馬			SPLIT CHARACTERS
11	土	土					52	尸	尸	門			
20	廾	廾	革				60	亠	言				
21	乚	卜	山				61	广	疒				
22	丨	忄	巾	米	虫		62	宀	穴				
31	丅	玉	石	酉	雨		63	丶	氵	礻	衤	戶	
32	フ	阝					81	人	金	食			
40	口	口	⻊				90	丿	禾				
41	図	日	目	貝	皿		91	丿	亻	彳	犭	火	
42	冈	月	骨				92	𠂉	竹	角	魚		
50	乛	弓					93	ㄑ	女	糸			

Remarks on Top and Bottom Forms

(1) The written form is standard: 示衣戶 are considered 礻衤户 (63); 眞 is considered 真 (10); 兪 is considered 俞 (00); 令 is considered 令 (63). 檢字以楷書爲主.

(2) 図冈 are containers: 図 (41) includes 西酉由甘國; 冈 (42) includes 月再内同兩丹凡. 外殼爲主.

(3) 口 (40) includes the modified forms 凸凹 and 巨. 口(40) 包括凸凹及巨.

(4) 丨丨 丿丨 (22) includes multiple vertical tops 北兄川悲世帶 and multiple vertical bottoms 川非兼弗肅齊. 凡多數豎筆屬 22.

(5) 厂厂 are 51 and 51A; 尸尸 are 52 and 52A. 厂厂爲 51 及 51A；尸尸爲 52 及 52A.

(6) 乛 (50) includes 匃毋乃鳥. 乛 (50) 包括匃毋乃鳥.

(7) Top of stroke is taken as top: 勹 𠂉 (𠂉 92), 几 (冂 42). Bottom of stroke is taken as bottom: 勹 (フ 32), 勹 (乛 50), 力 (乛 50), 几 (乚 70). 同一筆之上形爲上，下形爲下.

(8) Uncertain forms 筆形不定者：不丕 (丨 22) 彑彑 (勹 92)
兼兼 (丨 22) 負負 (乛 50)
豕 (丿 91) 畚畚 (勹 92)

(9) ノ (90 千兵受與) is a short horizontal stroke; but 彡 (91 亻 彳犭 豕火九白鳥) is a vertical slant. ノ (90) 是短硺筆；彡 (91) 是通常撇筆.

(10) Consult the illustrative examples with all variations (Table of Initials and Finals, see end paper at back). 參見封底內頁上下形舉例表.

當代漢英詞典

林語堂

Dr. Lin is an M.A. from Harvard, and Doctor of Philology from Leipzig. He was professor of English philology at the Peking National University. In 1948, he was chief of the Section of Arts and Letters at UNESCO. He made his name as founder and editor of three influential Chinese literary fortnightlies, the famous *Lunyu*, the *Jenchienshih* and the *Yuchoufeng*. Since 1935, he has written exclusively in English over 30 works, many of which are internationally known best-sellers, notably *The Importance of Living*, *My Country and My People* and *Wisdom of China and India* and his monumental trilogy *Moment in Peking*, *A Leaf in the Storm* and *The Vermilion Gate*. He is also inventor of a Chinese typewriter, with 8,000 characters and a 64-key keyboard. At 77, he has given us this *Chinese-English Dictionary* which he considers his lifework.

背頁中文由香港中文大學校長李卓敏博士題

The Chinese calligraphy overleaf was written by Dr. Choh-Ming Li, Vice-Chancellor of The Chinese University of Hong Kong.

Lin Yutang's

CHINESE-ENGLISH DICTIONARY OF MODERN USAGE

LIBRARY
JUL 18 1973
UNIVERSITY OF THE PACIFIC

LIN, Yutang. Chinese-English dictionary of modern usage. Chinese University of Hong Kong (dist. by McGraw-Hill), 1973 (c1972). 1720p tab 72-3899. 39.50. SBN 07-099695-4

CHOICE *SEPT. '73*
Reference

The chief selling point of this dictionary, apart from the splendid paper and printing, is the fact that it is the first work of its kind since 1931. The lexical updating is welcome; the lexicographical innovations of the editor, Lin Yutang, are less welcome. Why yet another system for ordering Chinese characters, the Instant Index System of Lin's own invention? Why National Romanization instead of the Yale system, which most users know, or the Mainland system, which most users will have soon to learn? The most welcome innovation, in the editor's own words, "modern linguistic treatment," turns out to be little more than assignment of the same old inexact definitions of Chinese words to grammatical form classes. Lip service alone has been paid to the principle of showing the phylogeny of the widely varying meanings of a single word. Definitions of particles, however, are fuller than in Mathews and, as noted above, 40 years of new words and meanings are, hopefully, recorded. Libraries should buy the book; individuals may sensibly hesitate.

Ref
PL
1455
L75

57

The Chinese University of Hong Kong
1972

Copyright © 1972
The Chinese University of Hong Kong

All rights reserved

No part of this publication may be reproduced, stored in a retrieval system, or transmitted, in any form or by any means, electronic, mechanical, photocopying, recording, or otherwise, without the prior written permission of the Publisher.

The Instant Index System is copyrighted by Dr. Lin Yutang. Use is forbidden except by consent of the Author.

Library of Congress Card No. 72-3899
ISBN 07-099695-4

LIBRARY
JUL 18 1973
UNIVERSITY OF THE PACIFIC
268514
Ref
PL
1455
L75

版權所有　翻印必究

林語堂

當代漢英詞典

編著者　林語堂
出版者　香港中文大學詞典部
發行者　香港中文大學
印刷者　研究社印刷株式會社（日本）
總經售　美國 McGraw-Hill 圖書公司

Distributed by McGraw-Hill, Inc.
Printed by Kenkyusha Printing Co., Ltd.
Tokyo, Japan.

CONTENTS

序言

過去一百年來,坊間所見到的漢英詞典只有兩冊是在國際間流行通用的。第一冊出版於一八九二年,是由翟理斯 (Herbert A. Giles) 編的漢英詞典 (Chinese-English Dictionary);四十年後,在一九三二年,麥氏 (R. H. Mathews) 出版了另一冊「麥氏漢英大辭典」(*Mathews, Chinese-English Dictionary*)。這兩本詞典都由居留於中國的外籍傳教士所編,在當時雖然是重要的工具書,可是時至今日,從社會變遷及學術發展的觀點說來,都不足以應付我們的需要。

二十世紀的下半葉,由於政治和社會的巨大變化,大家都覺得國與國之間,人民與人民之間實在需要更透徹的瞭解和溝通,這種需要,在使用英國語文的國家與人民及使用中國語文的國家與人民之間,尤爲殷切。理由很簡單:英文一向被認爲國際語言之一,而中國人佔有世界人口四份之一以上。在這種情形之下,出版一部適應現時代的漢英詞典,用以詮釋新出現的名詞和字彙,實爲當務之急。

以前漢英詞典一向以解釋意義爲主旨,實在不合我們的要求。例如坊間的漢英詞典多將「廢鐵」解爲 "old iron," 殊覺可笑,因爲正確的譯法應爲 "scrap iron"。換句話說,一部好詞典,在翻譯時必須盡可能採用最接近原文,同時又最合乎本國語法習慣的語言文字,好像順手拈來一樣。

最接近原文而又合乎本國語言習慣的譯法,有時是可遇而不可求的,也可以說是翻譯的最高境界。在處理語系相接近像英、法、德等語言時,能够傳神達意已經相當困難,而處理語言和文化傳統根本上迥然不同的中文和英文,其困難更不待言。在翻譯時,原文和譯文每字每句都要銖兩悉稱是絕無可能的,不過一個爐火純青的譯者卻往往可以使兩種語言達到最接近的境界。

那麼,誰來承擔此項重任呢?把「啼笑皆非」這樣美妙的中文譯作 "neither crying nor laughing is proper" 未嘗不可,祇是譯文並不是道地的英文，多少帶點中文的味道。倘若這句成語是一個書名時，又有那一個譯法比 "Between Tears and Laughter" 更恰當呢？這種傳神達意的翻譯，若不是從事者有精通漢英語文的才具，又怎能譯得如此恰到好處？所以一定要有一位非但精通中英兩國語言，而且對文字的敏感和表現的能力有天生的才能，方能勝任編纂當代漢英詞典的重責。把「啼笑皆非」譯成 "Between Tears and Laughter," 同時兼具這兩個條件的不是別人，就是蜚聲國際的名作家林語堂博士。

林語堂博士曾在德國萊比錫大學專攻文字學和語言學，並獲博士學位。他曾創辦了中國第一本以幽默見稱風行全國的中文雜誌；他也是唯一以英文寫作了多冊暢銷的文學作品的中國籍作家。他的英文著述，大部份已輾轉譯成許多他國文字，相信無數心儀林語堂博士的讀者，一定同意這項艱鉅的任務，理應由他擔當。

在一九六五年底，香港中文大學成立兩年之後，林語堂博士由美抵港。其時他正努力推介自創的中文打字機，同時念念不忘完成他終生的抱負，就是編纂一部新的並且是適應現時代需要的漢英詞典。經過商談後，我們決定傾全力於實現詞典的編纂計劃。在一九六七年春，林語堂博士即受聘爲中文大學的研究教授，親自主理詞典的翻譯工作。至於資料的收集、查核、抄寫和彙編的工作，則由各助手分勞。自那時開始，林博士日以繼夜的埋頭工作。一九七一年春，全部原稿始告完竣。

中文大學的預算中並沒有一筆經費可供詞典計劃之用，只得借重外界人士的資助。對是項工作鼎力支持的，計有太古輪船有限公司，利希慎置業有限公司和星系報業有限公司，各慷慨捐助港幣十萬元，使我們得到莫大的鼓勵。其後，金山輪船公司和讀者文摘亦加以贊助。至於詞典完成後印刷和發行工作的費用，則有賴於恒生銀行有限公司的優待墊借。同時中文大學成立了一個監理會，由大學校董利榮森先生和利國偉議員悉心指導，俾使工作得以順利進行。今天這詞典計劃得以美滿完成，相信所有資助我們的友好會引以爲慰。

詞典部的主任潘光迥博士和他的助理及顧問多人，除了從事校訂印製工作外，並編成一套英文索引，使這部詞典具有漢英及英漢詞典的雙重功能，更形完備。

沒有一部詞典敢誇稱是十全十美的，這一部自不能例外，但我們深信它將是迄今爲止最完善的漢英詞典。因此，我謹代表中文大學中國文化研究所將這部鉅著呈獻給學術界，著作界和從事文化交流的工作人士。

一九七一年聖誕節

香港中文大學校長

李卓敏 識

當代漢英詞典緣起

編一部中文詞典,以仿牛津簡明字典,是我數十載的夙願。民國三十三年,書成,共六十餘冊,由家兄憾廬及海戈先生編成。抗戰初發,燬於兵火,僅餘帶走美國之十三冊。三十年來常懷此志,民國五十五年,退隱臺北,七載辛勤,始償素願,爰舉大旨如左。

國語必有詳確紀載國語的詞書,這個觀念與字書完全不同;中國字書,一概以字為本位,不以語文中之詞為本位。所以到現在,還沒有由現代語言學觀點編成的一本中國語文詞典的專書。西方的英文、法文「字典」,都是以那些的國語為本體,凡國語中的詞的用法及文法詞類,及其變化,都紀載詳盡。我國的詞書,如「辭源」、「辭海」,雖然以詞為單位,內容却偏於百科全書性質,未能就詞論詞,研究其在句中之文法地位及變化,也不能於單音組及數音組綴合所成之詞,加以整理及分析。中國語言中平常的字,如「如果」,「倘使」,「一下子」就不屑列入。朱駿聲以「說文通訓定聲」獨具隻眼,能辨明詞意之孳乳,遂能於六書之「轉注」加以新解釋,以「長成」之「長」與「家長」之「長」,「命令」之「令」與「縣令」之「令」(段氏「假借」之例)認為轉注。因為他通達音聲之理,所以能注重語言中之音聲,通其語音之轉變,而超出說文研究字形的範圍。

中國向來無國語,因國語尙未統一,經五十年來國語統一會諸公(如吳稚暉、黎錦熙等)的高瞻遠矚,不斷的討論,始定北平話為國語。一九三二年「國音常用字彙」,一九四七年「中華新韻」頒布出版,而後讀音始有統一的標準。又跟着一九一八年頒布的注音字母各處推行,始有今日普遍承認之國語與讀音。又自從文學革命以來,以白話為文學工具,教育部乃成立中國大辭典編纂處,經三十年之搜集材料始由汪怡主編「國語辭典」,在抗戰期間由一九三七年出版第一冊,至一九四五年出版第四冊,而後我們可以說中國國語有一部詳盡準確的詞書。對於已往的白話文學(詩、詞、曲及明淸小說)及現代北平國音所有的材料都已有系統的記錄。這是開山的工作，前人篳路藍縷之功，我們後學乃受其賜。所以我方敢夢想做一本更合時代的漢英詞典。

(1) 範圍——本書的範圍，凡當代國語中通用的辭語，報紙，雜誌及書籍可以見到的，一概列入。現在國語基本文法是白話的，但文言中傳下來不少豐富的辭彙，已經混成一片。所謂文言與白話的區分並無嚴格的畛域。今日報章所見，文言與白話的成份各不同，但是白話既成了國人的文學工具，必定要吸收古代詩文中丰富的、煆煉過的、多含蓄的意象。如「集思廣益」、「欲速則不達」、「飛黃騰達」、「通宵達旦」，及「不即不離」，已為教育界文人所通用的成語，絕非用白話所能達意。如今「而立之年」已成陳跡，士子亦不屑引用，認爲炫弄而已。但是「不即不離」，以白話翻譯，已經失其傳神之用。文言中許多常用的辭語，如「心許其人」，「其貌不揚」，還是通用的文雅詞語。因為有了這些三千年煆煉下來的辭語、所以今日的語文，傳神達意之妙，可以媲美英文、法文。凡這些辭語，都應該成為國語的一部份，在這詞典都應該收入。

一國的語文，必應時而變。如「超音速」，「原子能」是以前沒有的。我們細讀一九七〇年十一月十二日的「中央日報」經濟部長的話，就明白西洋所有的詞語，我們都有了。他說：「今日的中國要積極發展高級化及現代化的基本關鍵工業」，「改善投資環境」，「探勘大陸礁層的石油資源」，而「由輕油裂解的設備，年產乙稀廿萬噸以上」。這種思想比前精確多了，與古文「雞有五德」，思想文字，全不同了。現代語文、英文、法文所能表出，我們也能表出。

(2) 定辭——定辭是本書的基要工作，目的爲定單音組及多音組的辭語 (WORDS) 及其文法詞類。國語有多少辭語，到現在無人曉得。這個悲慘的局面，是作者發憤負起重大責任的原因。

以前的字書，忽略「詞」的形成及其詞類。文言是多單音組的，現代的國語決不是，因為在文字上，我們已有部首的分別，如「鬍、湖、糊、蝴」，不受同音字的困擾。在口語上，一定須解決這個困擾，所以鬍成鬍子、糊成漿糊、蝴成蝴蝶、虎成老虎、月稱月亮、日稱太陽。因為意思明瞭，是語言第一條通則，多音組的辭語自然而然演化出來。

今日的國語，八成是多音組的，文言之單音字必定加上一音。例如通常的助動詞及介詞：

能——能够　將——將要　但——但是　或——或者
可——可以　需——需要　雖——雖然　如——如果
必——必須　應——應該　且——而且　倘——倘使

我們文化思想的字就是多音辭。如問題、答案、會議、議論、相信、懷疑、服從、決定、研討、夢想、推敲、推測、推動、推舉、贊成、反對等，不一而足。所以，辭不定，就意象不明，學者捉摸不定。重字有沉重一義，而不能不舉出嚴重(時局、病勢)、隆重(典禮)、穩重、厚重(人品)。相反的「輕」一字，孳乳成為輕浮(人品—形容詞)，輕鬆(一下—動詞)，輕易(不可告人—狀詞)。輕慢(鄙薄)是他動詞，輕薄是形容詞，或作他動詞用(給他輕薄一頓)。沒有這些多音組的辭，我們只能說粗鄙光滑滑的字了。

(3) 情景——由以上所述，我們可知國語中，辭語有情景的限制，用處各有不同，或他地可能用，此地不能用。凡語言都始於「情景」，最平常如打電話叫對方不要掛起來，英文為「wait a minute」，法文為「ne quittez pas」，德文為「ein Augenblick」，情景同而文字不同。這種情景的限制，必一一標出。

本書中(AC)卽指經書，史記，漢書，六朝古文的古義，現在並不通行。在這部詞典，古義從簡，不過聊備一格而已，且不必舉例。

(MC)卽指中古白話，是已往白話文學，唐詩、宋詞、元曲及明清小說，所有過去的白話，現在並不通用，出處可查國語詞典。

(LL)指文言與白話相對。由古文中提煉出來之辭語，雖然或出詩、書、易，但已渾成國語之一部。但文言辭語不宜亂用，否則行文時，多古僻字句。

(Dial.)指方言辭語及用法。

此外很多辭語，用處用地都有情景的限制。如(court.)限於禮貌稱呼時用之。

(Sl.) 即指俚語。此外，還有譏諷 (satir.)，戲謔 (facet.)，輕鄙 (derog.)，漫罵 (abuse)，鄙俚 (vulgar)，文雅 (litr.) 等用法，合時用之，則得宜。

(Coll.) 指口語，在口語上用之，行文則難登大雅之堂。

(4) 傳神——白居易說得好：「感人心者，莫先乎情，莫始乎言，莫切乎聲，莫深乎義……，上自聖賢，下至愚騃，微及豚魚，幽及鬼神，群分而氣同，形異而情一。未有聲入而不應，情交而不感者」(與元稹書)。他獨得千古之祕，深知語言發乎情景，而寄托音聲，始由音聲生出意義。語言不但達意，且可傳神。傳神必有其地其時，故又曰：「文章合為時而著，詩歌合為事而作。」文章詩歌，都有感人作用，必得其地，必得其事，必得其情，必得其景，然後感人也深。故本書於辭語之用處，三致意焉。

一九七一年十二月十二日

林　語　堂

Instant Index System

上下形檢字法

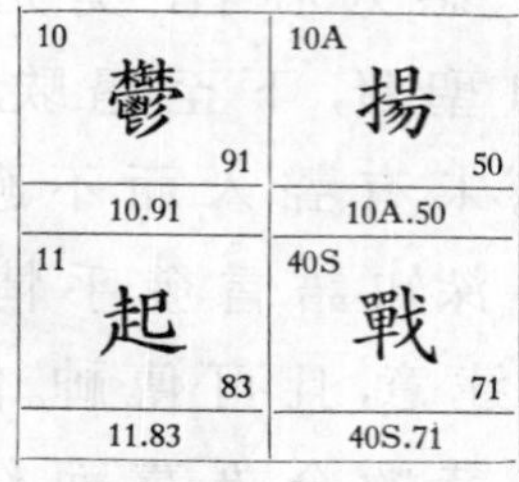

10
鬱
91
10.91
10A
揚
50
10A.50
11
起
83
11.83
40S
戰
71
40S.71

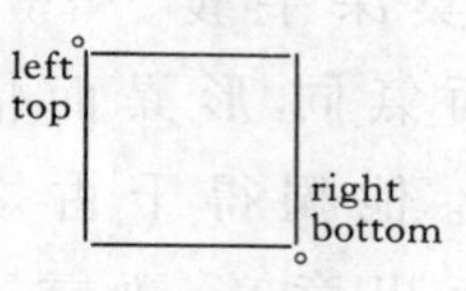

了	十	廿	三	四	五	六	七	八	九千
00 亅	10 十	20 廾	30 一	40 口	50 ㇕	60 亠	70 乚	80 八	90 ㇀
01 小 02 長	11 土 12 ナ	21 ⺊ 22 丨	31 丁 32 フ	41 図 42 冈	51 厂 52 戶	61 广 62 六 63 丶	71 弋 72 心	81 人 82 乂 83 乀	91 丿 92 ⺈ 93 く

凡字依其左上形及右下形分類。漢字通常之上形及下形共三十三個，分爲十類，配以數目。即漢字自然形體以便記憶：

亅	十	卄	一	口	㇕	亠	乚	八	彡
(了)	(十)	(廿)	(三)	(四)	(五)	(六)	(七)	(八)	(九千)
00	10	20	30	40	50	60	70	80	90

(一) 上形即最高字形，下形即最低字形。不論筆順，只看高低。

中、光、由之上形是丨 22

我、成之下形是弋 71

道之上形八 80，下形乀 83

(二) 字分左右旁，可以截開者謂之 S；不分左右旁，不可截開者謂之 NS。

羊義 (NS)　　詳祥羢 (S)

基其 (NS)　　祺淇期 (S)

楚起 (NS)　　松樹地 (S)

舊有部首見於左上者，取其常用五十個，分爲 A、B、C、D，其餘盡併入爲 S。見五十部首表 (封面內頁)。

(三) 同類之字 (同四個號碼)，依其餘部上形，分別先後。

鋁 81A.40–4 (餘部呂上形口 4)

鎔 81A.40–6 (餘部容上形亠 6)

鎗 81A.40–8 (餘部倉上形八 8)

說　明

(1) 字體依楷書寫體爲主。示衣戶即礻衤户 (63)，眞即真 (10)，兪即俞 (00)，令即令 (63)。

(2) 図 41 取外殼，包括西、酉、由、甘、国等字。

冈 42 取外殼，包括月、冉、咼、同、兩等字。

(3) 刂 丿 22 包括多數之丨，上形如北、兆、川、悲、世、帶，下形如川、非、兼、弗、肅、齊。
(4) 口 40 包括變形凸凹及巳。
(5) 厂厂都是 51；尸 尸都是 52；
刂川都是 22。
(6) ㄱ包括匈、母。
(7) 同一字形，上形取其上端，ク欠 (𠂉 92) 几，(冈 42)；下形取其下端，ㄅ (フ 32)，勹 (ㄱ 50)，力 (ㄱ 50)，几 (乚 70)。
(8) 異體不定者，定一體爲主：

不丆 (丨 22)　乢乢 (𠂉 92)
兼兼 (丨 22)　負負 (𠂉 92)
畨 畨 (𠂉 92)

(9) ㇀ (90) 與丿 (91) 之分：㇀ (90) (千兵受與) 是橫磙筆，丿 (91) (亻彳犭火九白鳥) 是通常撇筆。
(10) 各上下形之變形及其舉例，見封面內頁。

FOREWORD

Among the several Chinese-English dictionaries now available, there are two that have stood out as basic works in the last one hundred years or so. One is the *Chinese-English Dictionary* by Herbert A. Giles, published eighty years ago in 1892; and the other, the more familiar *Chinese-English Dictionary* by R. H. Mathews about forty years later in 1932. Both authors were English missionaries in China. While each of these two basic works served well the needs of its day, neither could continue to meet the demands of recent social and technological change.

The social and political changes taking place in the latter half of the twentieth century have brought to the fore the pressing need for much better understanding and communication than ever before between the English-speaking peoples who speak and write a language generally accepted as an international medium of communication and the Chinese-speaking and Chinese-reading people who constitute over one-quarter, if not one-third, of humanity. In this context a new Chinese-English dictionary, which takes into account new usages and expressions, is urgently needed.

A Chinese-English dictionary is no longer satisfactory if it is merely explanatory in nature, as has always been the case. To render "廢鐵" into "old iron," as is found in many existing Chinese-English dictionaries today, comes close to being ridiculous, for the proper rendering is obviously "scrap iron." In other words a good Chinese-English dictionary should present as adequately as possible an "idiomatic equivalence" of words and expressions between the two languages.

This "idiomatic equivalence," probably the highest form of translation, is difficult enough between different languages of cultures of more or less similar origin, say, English and French or German. But these difficulties are multiplied where one is concerned with languages of totally different cultural origin, as with Chinese and English. Admittedly, such an equivalence is not possible for every word or expression under any circumstances; nevertheless, the nearest approach to equivalence can be made if, and only if, the author is thoroughly at home in both the languages he is dealing with.

Who would be the person to undertake the task? The expression "啼笑皆非" is of good Chinese usage and may be rendered as "neither crying nor laughing is proper." That is a perfectly acceptable translation, although the latter expression is certainly not idiomatic usage in English, but rather Chinese-English. Using the expression as the title of a book, who would think of a better rendering in English than "Between Tears and Laughter"? Would anyone not thoroughly versed in both languages be able to come up with such a precise and idiomatic "translation"? Would not the one who possesses such talent be the best candidate for compiling the kind of Chinese-English dictionary that is needed today? That person is the world-renowned author, Dr. Lin Yutang.

Dr. Lin received his degree of Doctor of Philology at the University of Leipzig. He is the first Chinese who founded a Chinese-language literary magazine known for its wit and humour, each issue of which was eagerly awaited by a truly nation-wide reading public in China. He is also the only Chinese thus far who has produced a number of best-selling literary works in English for the English-speaking world, many of which have been translated into other languages. It would be very difficult to find someone else who could match Dr. Lin's qualifications as the one person to compile a completely new Chinese-English dictionary. A man of such prominence naturally has his share of critics as well as followers. In this instance, however, Dr. Lin's unique qualification is beyond question.

It was in late 1965, about two years after the establishment of The Chinese University, that Dr. Lin called on me in Hong Kong when he came from the United States. He was at that time as interested in promoting his invention of a Chinese-language typewriter as in fulfilling his life-long ambition to compile a new Chinese-English dictionary as a lasting contribution to knowledge. We settled on the latter. As a result Dr. Lin was appointed Research Professor of the University in the spring of 1967. The arrangement committed him to doing the "translation" personally, leaving to his assistants only the work of collecting data, checking, copying and filing. Since then, he had labored day in and day out for four years until the completion of the manuscript in the spring of 1971.

The project, including Dr. Lin's appointment, could not be financed from the University budget, and had to be funded by outside sources who shared my faith in the very conception of it. Thus it was Butterfield & Swire (H.K.) Ltd., Lee Hysan Estate Co. Ltd., and Sin Poh Amalgamated (H.K.) Ltd.—each contributing HK$100,000—that enabled the project to get started in 1967. Later, both the Island Navigation Corporation and the

Reader's Digest Association gave additional support. At the last stage, the work of printing and distribution was, on the one hand, financed through arrangements with the Hang Seng Bank Ltd., and, on the other, very much guided by Mr. J. S. Lee and Hon. Q. W. Lee, both members of the governing Council of the University, at great personal expense of time and effort. I am sure all these generous donors and supporters will derive immense satisfaction from the fact that their faith in the project has now been rewarded.

Dr. Francis K. Pan, Director of the Project from the beginning, has been assisted by a hard-working staff and a number of able consultants. The office was responsible, among other things, for compiling an English index, which, by the very nature of "idiomatic equivalence," renders the volume as much an English-Chinese dictionary as it is a Chinese-English dictionary.

No work of this kind can ever be claimed to be perfect, and this volume makes no such claim. But we do believe it will be found to be the best of its kind thus far. It gives me great pleasure to present it to both the academic world and the general public as a contribution from the Institute of Chinese Studies of The Chinese University of Hong Kong to scholarship, to knowledge, and to cultural exchange.

Choh-Ming Li
Vice-Chancellor

Christmas Day, 1971

INTRODUCTION

The idea of compiling a dictionary of the modern Chinese national language has engrossed my attention for decades. The need for a comprehensive and linguistically adequate dictionary of a modern language is obvious, but in the case of Chinese, the compiler of a Chinese dictionary is confronted with the first question: which Chinese language, the classical or the vernacular, does one intend to record? and what is the object of this study, the written Chinese characters or the living spoken tongue? Naturally, the fascinating Chinese characters, so rich and interesting in themselves, almost always distract the lexicographer's attention to the neglect of the spoken language as language. I have always maintained that the Chinese living tongue should be treated as such as one of the modern languages, whether it was written with the Chinese characters or not.

This was not possible forty or fifty years ago. The literary or classical language was the established written medium, and the study of this classical medium was a scholar's occupation *par excellence*. The spoken tongue existed in the form of many more less extensive dialects; there was no standard spoken Chinese. And if one wanted to, there was no adequate romanization system which could serve as an intelligible reading text, for lack of hyphenation and tonal marks and any way of recording integrated polysyllabic words. No national language could be a combination of alphabet and arithmetic, which was the Wade system: *Wu² lun⁴ na³ i¹ keh⁴ kuo² chia¹ bu⁴ neng² yung⁴ wei² er² shih⁴ so³ yung⁴ tzu⁴ mu³ chia¹ shang⁴ suan⁴ shu⁴ di⁴ chih⁴ tu⁴*. The Wade was an excellent system for phonetic notation, but must be unintelligible in any running script since it never indicates where a word begins or ends. It merely registers the sounds of characters as characters. However, since the literary revolution of 1917, introducing the *paihua* vernacular as the written medium, and with the continuous efforts of societies and committees for standardization of the national language of the last fifty years, the national language, or *guoryuu*, has slowly come into its own. Through long years of debate and discussion, the Peiping tongue has been established as the standard *guoryuu* or "national language." Standard pronunciation for the characters was officially established by the publication of the 國音常用字彙 in 1932, and the promulgation of the 中華新韻 in 1947. Most important of all, the great *Dictionary of the National Language* (*Guoryuu Tsyrdiaan*) 國語詞典 (appearing in 4 vols. 1937–1945) compiled by Wang Yi (汪怡) and his staff, may be said to be the first comprehensive dictionary that recorded the spoken language scientifically and adequately. It shows a bias towards Peking colloquialisms, but gives examples of the spoken tongue dating back to Sung poems, Yuan dramas and Ming novels. The present editor would not have attempted this *Chinese-English Dictionary* if the data were not available in Wang Yi's *Dictionary of the National Language*.*

The Scope. The scope of the present dictionary is accurately defined by its title, *A Chinese-English Dictionary of Modern Usage*. It includes all words and phrases that a modern reader is likely to encounter with in reading modern newspapers, magazines and books. The Chinese national language of today is vernacular in basic grammatical structure, but draws heavily on the past literary tongue in vocabulary. It is not the raw and somewhat bald *patois* of a Peking peasant, but is a literary man's intercourse as well.

The distinction between *wenyen* and *paihua* (classical and vernacular) is not a hard and fast one.

* This appears now in Commercial Press edition, still in 4 vols., Taiwan, but with minor abridgements is available in a convenient one-volume reprint, Commercial Press, Hong Kong, under the name 漢語詞典. The first volume of this *Guoryuu Tsyrdiaan* was published in 1937 and the last in 1945, thus covering exactly the years of the war with Japan. A second edition was pubished in 1947. (Officially the work was compiled by 中國大辭典編纂處).

In today's writing, the proportion between literary and vernacular varies, but it is understood that as the *paihua* becomes the written medium, it must absorb the rich, cultivated expressions, images and ideas, so rich and terse in ancient prose and poetry. Thus 集思廣益 (benefit by sharing opinions), 欲速則不達 (make haste slowly), 飛黃騰達 (rise rapidly in career or social position), 通宵達旦 (the whole night), and 中流砥柱 (pillar of strength) cannot be expressed by wordy circumlocutions in the colloquial medium. The pedantic allusions like 而立之年 have been shamed into disuse, but 運籌帷幄 (draw strategic plans with tallies in a tent) has still subtle connotations and associations that are lost in vernacular substitutes. Literary usage of many common words still serves a purpose; thus 心許其人 is a cultivated expression for "give one's heart to some one"; 其貌不揚 is still a good refined phrase for remarking that a person is ugly. Because of this literary heritage of three thousand years, the Chinese spoken language is as subtly expressive and rich in nuances as English or French. All such expressive literary phrases which are likely to become part and parcel of the Chinese national tongue come within the scope of the present dictionary.

Language changes with the changes in man's thoughts. It is seldom realized that, reflecting the great increase of modern terms, it is possible now to express almost every Western term by its Chinese equivalent. Thus modern Chinese is closer to the Westerner in thinking than formerly, and if a foreign student is familiar with the Chinese equivalents of modern terms (like 超音速 for "supersonic speed" and 原子能 for "atomic power"), it would be quite easy to write or talk in Chinese, once the sentence patterns are mastered. Thus one reads in Taipei newspapers (*Central Daily News*, November 12, 1970) that the Minister of Economic Affairs had declared that in order "to meet fierce competition in the international market" (面對國際激烈競爭) the government will "actively develop" (積極發展) in the direction of "sophistication and modernization" (高級化及現代化) and expand the "fundamental and key industries (基本及關鍵工業), will improve the investment climate" (改善投資環境), that it is planned to "explore continental shelf deposits" (探勘大陸礁層的石油資源) and that in "petro-chemicals" (石油化學品), the Chinese Petroleum Corporation will have a "light oil cracking plant" (輕油裂解的設備) with "a capacity of over 200,000 tons of annual production of polyethylene" (年產乙烯廿萬噸以上), etc. The Chinese scholar's thinking promises to be more and more precise, as this goes on. This sounds a far cry from saying the "rooster has five virtues" (鷄有五德)—that living symbol of polygamous society. The newspapers bristle with terms like *weekends* (週末), *cowboy pants* (牛仔褲), *astronauts* (太空人), *satellites* (人造衛星), *lunar modules* (登月艙), and *intercontinental ballistic missiles* (洲際彈道飛彈).

It is for this reason that today the word *guoryuu* (國語 national language) has a wider connotation than *paihua* (白話). It is in this medium that all newspaper editorials are written. To pick at random, today's editorial (Jan. 3, 1971) in *China Times* begins like this: 中華民國六十年代初期，國際間之姑息逆流仍可能出現某種程度的高潮 ("At the opening of the seventh decade of the Republic of China, the counter-current of appeasement in international relations may still possibly appear as a rising tide of a certain degree.")

The levels of speech. Such being the case, the present dictionary finds it necessary to distinguish the levels of speech. One comes across phrases and expressions in books which may or may not be used in modern colloquial.

(AC) indicates Ancient Chinese. This covers all usages found in ancient writing, especially the classics and 史記 and 漢書, that are *not* current, and would sound bookish and abstruse in modern writing. Some of these meanings are rare and quite different from modern meanings of the same words. In the *Dictionary of Modern Usage*, the treatment of AC is cursory, not always provided with examples.

(MC) indicates Middle Chinese. This category covers usages in Tang poetry, Yuan dramas and novels of Ming and Ching Dynasties that reflected the spoken tongue of past days. The sources are usually given in Wang Yi's *Guoryuu Tsyrdiaan*, but omitted here.

(LL) indicates literary language or *wenyen.* This comprises many expressions from AC sources, which have become part and parcel of the literary language. This indication is a warning not to use it freely in modern speech. It would sound pedantic and slightly archaic like the Puritan's *thou* and *thee.*

Since this is a dictionary of modern usage, current words need no special indication.

(*Dial.*) indicates a dialect colloquialism. The pronunciation of 和 ("with") as *hahn*, allowed by the official lists, must still be regarded as a dialect of the northern environs of Peking, and cannot be said to represent the national language. The editor also takes exception to the pronunciation of 期 (學期, 星期) in the first tone, although it is rapidly gaining ground in Taiwan today. The two pronunciations for 和, *her* and *hahn*, and for 期, *chi* and *chir*, are both given by the standard pronunciation books, but owing to the adoption of the dialect sounds used in matrices with Chinese phonetic notation for schoolbooks, the effect is overwhelming on the younger generation.

(*Court.*) is an important indication of words and phrases used in courteous address. Other levels of speech indicated are *sl.* (slang), *satir.* (satirical,) *facet.* (facetious), *contempt.* (contemptuous), *abuse, derog.* (derogatory), *vulgar*, and *litr.* (literary), indicating when the usage of a word may or may not be appropriate. (*Coll.*) colloquial signifies that the expression is quite in order in speech, but not quite acceptable in writing except in describing dialogues.

Word Determination: *Monosyllabism and polysyllablism.* One of the basic tasks the present dictionary sets itself is to determine what are the Chinese words for the first time, and record their pronunciation as integrated polysyllabic units, and their parts of speech. I do not know what are the Chinese words (as distinct from characters) and how many there are, and nobody does. It is this grievous state of things that motivates the author to undertake this gigantic work. It is based on the obvious fact that modern Chinese is largely polysyllabic and that nothing is gained by ignoring this fact; rather its recognition would greatly facilitate the acquiring of a vocabulary: thus *durlih* as "independent" and *syshiaang* as "thinking."

It is natural that all previous Chinese dictionaries centering upon the characters as units of learning should neglect to note the formation of a word as a grammatical unit and did not give its part of speech. It is also true that the classical language was largely monosyllabic, but this is certainly untrue of modern Chinese. For in the classical language, the character *hur* 鬍 for "whiskers" precludes it from confusion with the other *hur's*, but in the spoken language it becomes immediately necessary to add a syllable and say *hurtse* to avoid confusion with "a lake" or "paste." The word for "but," *dahn*, is perfectly clear in the written language 但, but in the spoken language one may be tempted to ask "what *dahn*—an egg? a hen's egg or duck's egg?" or a "bullet" or "mild in flavor"; so one says *dahnshyh* and all ambiguity is cleared up. For the law of intelligibility is the first law of any spoken language. The avoidance of homonyms was done in writing by adding a radical: 湖 (lake) for *hur* of water, 糊 (paste) for *hur* with rice radical and 鬍 (*whiskers*) for *hur* with the hair radical. In the spoken language one says *jianghur* for "paste" and *hurtse* for "whiskers." Thus the vernacular creates the bisyllabic *yuehliahng* for the "moon" which does not necessarily refer to the moonlight, but to the more or less bright, round disc in the sky.

Eighty percent of words in the spoken tongue are bisyllabic. The overwhelming character of polysyllabism in modern Chinese must be apparent to everyone. It is easy to compile a list where the monosyllabism of *wenyen* is expanded by adding a syllable in the vernacular. In the following list, even in the common auxiliaries and conjunctions, the original monosyllabic word in *wenyen*, acquires another syllable in *paihua*.

能 =	能够	can	但 =	但是	but
可 =	可以	may	雖 =	雖然	although
必 =	必須	must	且 =	而且	furthermore
將 =	將要	will	或 =	或者	perhaps
需 =	需要	need	如 =	如果	if
應 =	應該	should	倘 =	倘使	if

It is merely necessary to enumerate some of the most common words about our mental processes and cultural activities, all of a bisyllabic character, to realize this essential character of our everyday language:

問題 problem	否決 reject (proposal)	推動 propel
答案 answer	選舉 elect, -tion	推翻 overthrow
會議 conference	提議 propose, -sal	推舉 elect
討論 discuss, -ion	附議 second (motion)	推算 calculate
相信 believe	棄權 abstain	審核 examine officially (accounts)
懷疑 doubt	研討 study (problem)	彈劾 impeach
爭辯 argue	夢想 dream	贊成 approve
服從 obey	推敲 ponder (meaning)	反對 oppose
決定 decide	推測 conjecture	etc., etc.

It is desperately necessary for any student of the Chinese language, Chinese or foreign, to have such words listed as words in a dictionary and recognized. Thus it helps no one to have the character 重 *juhng* explained as meaning "heavy, important" and leave unrecorded such important words as 嚴重 "grave, serious" (situation), 隆重 "august" (ceremony), 穩重 "steady" (character), 沉重 "heavy" (weight). Or, the opposite word 輕 *ching* forms concepts which can only be expressed by bisyllabic words: 輕浮 adj., "frivolous, volatile" (character), 輕鬆 v.i., "relax" (a moment), 輕易 adv., "lightly, without due consideration" (give out information), 輕慢 v.t., show disrespect to (person), 輕薄 adj., "frivolous" (young man) or v.t., to "make coarse remarks about" (a girl), etc. Without such a vocabulary, one must talk only in bald monosyllables.

The recognition that many Chinese words are polysyllabic has great implications. First, it blows away the academic myth that romanization of Chinese is impossible or would be unintelligible, a view held by many eminent sinologs. The collection of words in the present dictionary gives evidence of how few the homonyms are in the Chinese language. (There may be many John Smiths in the N.Y. Telephone Directory; the chances of two persons called John Frederick Smith must be few; and the chances of two persons called John Waynsworth Smith are practically *nil*). Secondly, freed from preoccupation with the monosyllabic characters, it is seen clearly that the Chinese language has a grammar, and the words have each a part of speech or several parts of speech, as in any other language. It is difficult to assign part of speech to half a word like *sheng* (生), which could be *live*, *life*, *living*, *bear*, *born*, *uncooked* or a *person;* there can be no question that a complete word containing the syllable *sheng* like *shiansheng* (先生 teacher) is a noun, *shengcherng* (生成 born) is an adjective, *shenghuor* (生活 life) is again a noun, *shengde* (生的 uncooked) again an adjective. It is hoped that with the determination and recording of words as such, Chinese grammar, or study of relationships of words in a sentence, can begin. "In a language such as Latin or German," says Bernhard Karlgren, "a reader who knows his grammar and who has a dictionary should be able to find out what every sentence means. . . . In Chinese grammatical analysis is of much less help. The only thing which really helps is experience . . . a feeling for how the Chinese make up their sentences," (*The Chinese Language*, 1949, p. 59). Karlgren equates grammatical analysis with "a well-developed sense of guessing." W. Simon found it necessary even to ask the elementary question: Has the Chinese Language Parts of Speech? (*Transactions of the Philological Society*, London, 1937). We are forced to assert that the Chinese language has grammar, or laws of syntactical relationships; that every word has a part of speech defining its function in a grammatical sentence. It is hoped that we may get away from the quagmire of learned confusion, and assert with a boyish confidence that a "teacher," *shiansheng*, is a noun in Chinese as in English or Eskimo, and that *chairs, tables, pancake, stoves, ice* are also nouns in the "inscrutable" Chinese language.

Hyphenation. Polysyllabic words gain a visual individuality and are much easier to recognize when they are spelled as words without hyphen, thus: "*Shanghai*" instead of *Shang-Hai*, and "Taipei" instead of *Tai-Pei*, and "Piccadilly" instead of Pic-Ca-Dil-Ly. Conceptually, the writing of Chinese words in unconnected separate syllables inflicts untold loss in time and energy on the learner, if not a gratuitous insult on his intelligence.

In determining words, the problem often comes up as to what extent the two syllables are bound together, and whether a hyphen is called for or not. It is a problem common to all languages. In this respect, English dictionaries often vary among themselves: "basketball" and "volleyball" are spelled as one word in *New World Webster's* but hyphenated in *New Century* and in *Pocket Oxford*. The same variation may be observed in such words as "fire-brick" (*Century*), "firebrick" (*Webster's*) and "fire brick" (*POD*); or in "fire engine" (*Webster's*), "fire-engine" (*Century, POD*). Generally the older a word is, the more tightly bound it is felt to be, as *fireplace, firearms, fireworms* and *firebrand*. In German, the writing of separate words together is quite common: thus *Landesversicherungsgesellschaft* (Land Insurance Company).

In this dictionary words are spelled together when it is felt they are tightly bound together, like *tzyhyour* (freedom), *durlih* (independent, -ce), *guorjia* (state), *perngyoou* (friend). One never takes the syllables apart.

A hyphen is used in the following cases:

(a) When a transitive vb. is followed by a noun (v.t.+n.) to make an intransitive vb., as 走路 *tzoou-luh*, 讀書 *dur-shu*. Obviously one can take them apart and say 我走我的路, 你讀你的書, yet 讀書 or 走路, "walking," "studying," are v.i. themselves.

(b) Vb. complements which are advv. or prepositions like English, "come upon," "come around" "come out," 走出來, 走上去 are hyphenated; *tzoou-chulair, tzoou-shahngchyuh*.

(c) The adv. 不 which precedes vbb.: thus 不肯, 不要, 不得不, *buh-keeng, bur-yuah, buh-der-buh*.

(d) Abstract nn. made up of two opposite adjj; thus 快慢 (degree of speed), 長短 (length), 高低 (height) are hyphenated as *kuaih-mahn, charng-duaan, gau-di*.

(e) It is highly recommended that more literary four-word phrases which have to be read together to be understood should also be hyphenated; as 高瞻遠矚, 深思熟慮. The hyphenation indicates that when read as a phrase, they will be understood even aurally.

In this dictionary, the vocabulary under each character includes both hyphenated and unhyphenated words and rarely also phrases, (marked "phr."), arranged alphabetically under the first character. But often words are also found under their last character which help to illustrate the usage. Thus under 舞 (dance) will be found the words for *jazz, tango, rock-'n'-roll*, and under 曲 (song) will be found the words for *serenade, popular song*.

The romanization and index system for locating words are explained separately.

I am happy that the task which I set out to do has been completed, and that the rich Chinese national language, the *guoryuu*, has at last been given a modern linguistic treatment. (1) For the first time, Chinese words, whether monosyllabic or polysyllabic, are listed as words and their grammatical functions—their parts of speech, or how they fit into a sentence structure—have been determined. (2) Their meanings, primary and derivative, have been related and organized, so that each entry makes a readable whole. (3) Its basic principle is contextual semantics, the subtle, imperceptible changes of meaning due to context. Examples of usage are not just illustrations of a given definition; they are rather the raw material of language from which the meanings and nuances derive. The context always modifies the meanings. (4) It shows the streams of allusions and usages which have been deposited through the past and entered into the structure of the modern living language. It gives a cursory glance at these archaic deposits only so far as they may still be encountered with. It gives also the usages of earlier vernacular, such as are found in Tang poems, Sung *tsyr*, Yuan dramas and Ming novels. (5) Contrary to previous practice, the language as it is spoken is given prime importance. Its simple and often colorful phrases and expressions are regarded as expressive as any superannuated literary metaphors. A healthy feeling for language calls for simple expressions. A glance at the entries for 可, 不, 頭 and 爾 will show how these common words are tumbled about in the daily language. Many such common expressions as 些兒, 些兒個, 些小, 些些, 些須, 些許 have never been carefully noted; so with 一扠 a width measure between outstretched thumb and finger, or 平頭數 a round number, or 掖 (pronounced *ye* in first tone) as 掖在懷裏 to tuck something under the blouse, or 勒 (pronounced *lei* in the first tone) in 勒死 to strangle some one to death. (6) Lastly, in words with modified pronunciations in certain definite combinations, it always indicates such variations so that the student may know exactly when these are to be used.

It remains to acknowledge my debt to all who have helped make the realization of this project possible. First of all, the success of this undertaking is due to Dr. Choh-ming Li, Vice-Chancellor of The Chinese University of Hong Kong, whose vision and enthusiastic support enabled the work to be carried to its fruition. Mr. L. Z. Yuan (袁倫仁) of The Asia Foundation, himself an accomplished bilingual scholar, and a guiding spirit in intercultural exchange, was an important influence in promoting the dictionary project. Mr. J. S. Lee (利榮森), by his personal donations and his hearty interest in this dictionary, did more than anyone else to see the project through from beginning to the end. The whole project was sponsored by the Chinese University of Hong Kong.

My thanks are due to Mr. Durham S. F. Chen (陳石孚), Chief Assistant Editor, for his invaluable help and suggestions, and to Mr. Ma Chi-shen (馬驥伸) and Miss Huang Chao-heng (黃肇珩), Assistant Chinese Editors, who did the analysis and organization of word meanings, and selection and addition of material, with their expert knowledge of Peking colloquial and current as well as ancient Chinese. Dr. Francis K. Pan (潘光迥) and Mr. Stephen Soong (宋淇) were good enough to read through the manuscripts while the book was going through the press; I appreciate the very high quality of their suggestions for improvement, which are incorporated in the dictionary. Miss Shih Pei-ying (施佩英) helped making the numerical index and romanized index with consummate accuracy.

Special thanks are due to Miss Francesca Shou-ching Chen (陳守荊), my secretary, whose superb intelligence and meticulous attention to details in the editorial work lightened my work greatly. I am also blessed with having the presence of my wife (廖翠鳳) and presiding spirit, whose gentle guidance and feminine touch created a home of love and peace for my work through all these years.

Professors Chiang Wan-hsüan (江萬煊), of National Taiwan University, Lu Hsiao-kwang (呂曉光), Mr. Ma Hsieh-hsi (馬爕熙), and Mr. Wu Yi-chou (武憶舟) of Soochow University, Prof. Chu Chien-min (朱建民) of National Chengchi University, Miss Ch'iu Ch'i-ming (裘啟明) of Central Trust of China, and conductor Teng Chang-kuo (鄧昌國) have all helped as consultants in their respective fields of medicine, law, international relations, finance and music. I alone am responsible for the final form in which such technical terms appear in this dictionary. For the pronunciation of characters I follow completely the *Guoryuu Tsyrdiaan*. I have also relied heavily on Bernard E. Read's *Chinese Medicinal Plants from the Pen Ts'ao Kang Mu* (published by the *Peking History Bulletin*, 3rd ed., 1936), especially for the common English names of trees and vegetables.

Translation is an art. No pains have been spared to make the English renderings as close to the Chinese original as possible, especially with regard to its context and usage rather than its literal meaning. Where a literal meaning would help to make it clearer, it is supplied in addition to the rendering. There may be errors of commission and omission in a book of this size. The author will be grateful to have any such oversight pointed out.

Jan. 3, 1971

Lin Yutang

HOW TO USE THE DICTIONARY

A. Romanization and Pronunciation: the Simplified Romatzyh.
B. The Instant Index. (inside front cover)
C. The Numerical Index, the Romanization Index and the English Index.
D. Abbreviations and Symbols.

A. Romanization and Pronunciation: the Simplified Romatzyh.

Any spoken language which can be aurally understood when spoken is equally understandable when transcribed and read; if it is not, the fault is in the sound transcription. The more exact the transcription, the clearer it is for the reader. The Guoryuu Romatzyh (GR) is intended as such an exact transcription system. The romanization system here used is the official Guoryuu Romatzyh, promulgated in 1928, now simplified. It has a built-in tonal system, doing away with all diacritical marks. It means a lot to have a *typable* yet simple and exact romanization for the foreign student of the Chinese language and to have at one stroke telegraph, teletype and all means of telecommunication available by writing in this system. Type it, telegraph it and if desired, computerize it.

(1) This built-in tonal system is simple, without the sophistications and modifications of the official GR.

1st tone—a	e	i	o	an	ang
2nd tone—ar	er	ir	or	arn	arng
3rd tone—aa	ee	ii	oo	aan	aang
4th tone—ah	eh	ih	oh	ahn	ahng

Thus, simply without exceptions: the 1st tone—without mark; the 2nd tone—add *r* after vowel; the 3rd tone—double main vowel; the 4th tone—add *h* after vowel. With the diphthongs, double the main vowel in the 3rd tone, thus: *iaa, iee, ioou, aau, oou, aai, eei.*

It may be called the "Basic" GR.*

(2) For clearer division of syllables, the rule is every syllable begins with a consonant, and if it begins with *u-* or *i-*, *u* becomes *w* and *i* becomes *y*. So we have *wa, wei, wen, wan*, and *ya, you, yen, yau*. Standing alone, *i* becomes *yi*, *u* becomes *wu*. A, o, u cannot begin a second syllable, but must be preceded by a hyphen, thus: *si-an, shi-ou*. Any consonant between two syllables belongs to the second syllble: thus, *sutou, jiinshehn, taihkung*.

(3) (') is used to indicate unaccented syllables, like (.) in the Chinese phonetic script. Thus *mar'fan* (troublesome) means *fan* is unaccented and of indeterminate tone, although it is spelled like the 1st tone.

* The writer was a co-worker on the official GR and first proposed the basic form (*a-ar-aa-ah*) and its modifications like *ae* for *aai*, *ao* for *aau*, *ay* for *aih*, and the *y-e-ih* and *w-o-uh* series finally incorporated in the Guoryuu Romatzyh. This was in 1923–4. It is still the ideal. After years of trial, however, it is felt such changes are sometimes confusing to the learner (as *iou-you-eou-iouh* and *uei-wei-oei-uey*). Therefore I have returned to the simpler basic pattern. The regular *Guoryuu Romatzyh* spellings are given in the Taiwan edition of *Guoryuu Tzyrdiaan.* I have also to return to the basic pattern in the dictionary in order to get a simpler alphabetic order, instead of separating *iou, you, eou* and *iouh* wide apart.

As it is, the simplified Guoryuu and the Yale system show little difference except Yale always writes *sya*, *chyan*, *nya* for *sia*, *chian*, *nia* and *swa*, *chwan*, *swa* for *sua*, *chuan*, *sua*, whereas the Guoryuu reserves *w* and *y* for the initial position. Where Wade uses *ih* and *ŭ* (*shih*, *szŭ*), Guoryuu uses *y* for both (*shy*, *sy*) and Yale uses *r* (*shr*), and *dz*, *tsz*, *sz*. Guoryuu alone uses *el* (*'l*) for Wade and Yale *er*.

SIMPLIFIED NATIONAL ROMANIZATION 簡化國語羅馬字

ㄅ b	ㄉ d	ㄍ g	ㄐㄓ j	ㄗ tz	1st tone —
ㄆ p	ㄊ t	ㄎ k	ㄑㄔ ch	ㄘ ts	2nd tone r
ㄇ m	ㄋ n	ㄏ h	ㄒㄕ sh	ㄙ s	3rd tone double vowel
ㄈ f	ㄌ l		ㄖ r		4th tone h

ㄚ	ㄝ	ㄜ	ㄛ	ㄧ	ㄨ	ㄩ	(知,資)元音	ㄦ	·輕聲之前
a	-e	e	o	i(yi)	u(wu)	yu	y	el	'l,
ar		er	or	ir	ur	yur	yr	erl	'fan
aa		ee	oo	ii	uu	yuu	yy	eel	'yoou,
ah		eh	oh	ih	uh	yuh	yh	ehl	etc.

ㄞ	ㄟ	ㄠ	ㄡ	ㄢ	ㄤ	ㄣ	ㄥ
ai	ei	au	ou	an	ang	en	eng
air	eir	aur	our	arn	arng	ern	erng
aai	eei	aau	oou	aan	aang	een	eeng
aih	eih	auh	ouh	ahn	ahng	ehn	ehng
ㄧㄚ	ㄧㄝ	ㄧㄠ	ㄧㄡ	ㄧㄢ	ㄧㄤ	ㄧㄣ	ㄧㄥ
ia	ie	iau	iou	ian	iang	in(yi-)	ing
iar	ier	iaur	iour	iarn	iarng	irn	irng
iaa	iee	iaau	ioou	iaan	iaang	iin	iing
iah	ieh	iauh	iouh	iahn	iahng	ihn	ihng
ㄨㄚ	ㄨㄟ	ㄨㄞ	ㄨㄛ	ㄨㄢ	ㄨㄤ	ㄨㄣ	ㄨㄥ
ua	uei	uai	uo	uan	uang	un(wen)	ung(weng)
uar	ueir	uair	uor	uarn	uarng	urn	urng
uaa	ueei	uaai	uoo	uaan	uaang	uun	uung
uah	ueih	uaih	uoh	uahn	uahng	uhn	uhng
	ㄩㄝ			ㄩㄢ		ㄩㄣ	ㄩㄥ
	yue			yuan		yun	yung
	yuer			yuarn		yurn	yurng
	yuee			yuaan		yuun	yuung
	yueh			yuahn		yuhn	yuhng

i, u at initial position:
Simple vowel:
i, in- > yi, yin-
u, un- > wu, wun-
Diphthongs:
ia-, ie-, io-
> ya-, ye-, yo-
ua-, ue-, uo-
> wa-, we-, wo-

yu=ü (ㄩ)
ei =English ā (ㄟ)
y alone=Wade ih, ŭ
e alone=Eng. er (ㄜ)

INITIALS

Labials	ㄅ ㄆ ㄇ ㄈ	b	p	m	f	伯	潑	墨	佛
Dentals	ㄉ ㄊ ㄋ ㄌ	d	t	n	l	德	特	訥	肋
Gutturals	ㄍ ㄎ ㄏ	g	k	h		格	客	赫	
Palatals	ㄐ ㄑ ㄒ	j	ch	sh		基	欺	希	
Retroflexes	ㄓ ㄔ ㄕ ㄖ	j	ch	sh	r	知	痴	詩	日
Dental sibilants	ㄗ ㄘ ㄙ	tz	ts	s		資	雌	思	

Wade				*Guoryuu*				*Yale*			
p	p'	m	f	b	p	m	f	b	p	m	f
t	t'	n	l	d	t	n	l	d	t	n	l
k	k'	h		g	k	h		g	k	h	
ch	ch'	hs		j	ch	sh		j	ch	s	
ch	ch'	sh	j	j	ch	sh	r	j	ch	sh	r
ts	ts'	s		tz	ts	s		dz	ts	s	

The well-established p-p', t-t', k-k' and ch-ch' of Wade system is the common and prevailing one. But it is voted out 3–1, and substituted by the b-p, d-t, g-k, j-ch series in the Guoryuu, Yale and Latin system of Peking.

FINALS

ㄚ a	ㄛ o	ㄜ e	ㄦ el	啊	喔	婀	兒
ㄞ ai	ㄟ ei	ㄠ au	ㄡ ou	哀	欸	熬	歐
ㄢ an	ㄣ en	ㄤ ang	ㄥ eng	安	恩	昂	(哼)
ㄧ i	ㄨ u	ㄩ yu		衣	烏	迂	

	Wade	*Guoryuu*	*Yale*
(1)	*ia, ie, iu,* etc. (*i* before vowels)	*-ia, -ie, -iou,* etc. *ya, ye, you* (initial)	*-ya, -ye, -you,* etc.
(2)	*ua, uo, ue,* etc. (*i* before vowels)	*-ua, -uo, -ue,* etc. *wa, wo, wen* (initial)	*-wa, -wo, -we,* etc.
(3)	ü üan üeh yün	yu yuan yue yun	yu ywan ywe yun
(4)	ao	au	au
(5)	eh (ieh, üeh) erh	e (ie, yue) el	e er
(6)	lo, so, tso mo, no, p, p'o	luo, suo, tsuo mo, nuo, bo, po	lwo, swo, dzwo mwo, nwo, bwo, pwo
(7)	chih, shih (after retroflex)	jy, shy	jr, shr
(8)	tsŭ, ts'ŭ, szŭ (after dental sibilant)	tzy, tsy, sy	dz, tsz, sz

PRONUNCIATION

The vowels a, e, i, o, u have the regular continental values, as in *Roma*, *Venezia*, *Mussolini*, not the English.

The palatal *ji*, *chi*, *shi* (Wade *chi*, *ch'i*, *hsi*) always come before *i* and *yu* (ü); the retroflex *j*, *sh*, *sh* always come before *a*, *o*, *u*. Therefore they are written alike without distinction. The Peking pronunciation of the retroflexes is made with the lips pronouncedly extended, whereas the palatal series is made with the lips drawn back. People not from Peking usually fail to make extended lips so pronounced.

The (Wade) *shih* and *szŭ* are usually difficult for foreigners to reproduce. Here they are written *shy* (師) and *sy*(思). In *shy*, say *hush*, *sh-sh-sh* and vocalize it without changing tongue position. In *sy*, say *s-s-s*, *z-z-z* and vocalize it without changing tongue position.

The English b, d, g, j are only the nearest approximations to unaspirated p, t, k, ch. (Thus: *Jungguor* for 中國). The correct pronunciation of the unaspirated stops is found in French, thus: *Paris*, *tu*, *quatre* and in English sp, st, sk: contrast *pain* and *Spain*, *tick* and *stick*, *tongue* and *stung*. To achieve a pronunciation without foreign student, learn this French p, t, k. B, d, g are voiced, French p, t, k are voiceless. If one has to pronounce *Jungguor*, it is best not to voice the *j* too clearly.

TONES

A tone is an integral part of a Chinese syllable. A mistake in tones in speaking Chinese makes it at once unintelligible, just as in English pronunciation of *cor'rect* as *'cor-rect*. Chinese speech moves in tonal rhythms. Therefore in written Chinese, the tonal marks are essential; they cannot be optional, dropped or added as an afterthought, at the risk of confusion.

Wade	*Guoryuu*	*Yale*
a^1	a	a (calling)
a^2	ar	á (asking)
a^3	aa	ǎ (deliberating)
a^4	ah	à (abrupt)

This is exemplified in the dialogue:

"John (calling), are you coming (questioning)?"
"Well (deliberating), yes (abrupt)."

In English, tonal difference is heard in *cad* and *cat*, *head* and *hat*, *food* and *foot*, *card* and *cart* (vowels before voiced and voiceless consonants).

The third tone is slow, deliberate and pitched low. Since Chinese speech moves in tonal rhythms (rise and fall), two successive third-tone syllables are awkward, ⌣ ⌣. Instinctively, speakers of *guoryuu* change the first third-tone syllable into the second tone, thus making a smoother undulation ∼. *Laautzyy* ⌣ ⌣ becomes Laurtzyy ∼. This is the so-called "tone sandhi." This dictionary always indicates this change. (In long English words with secondary accents, the same alternation of accented and unaccented syllables also serves a rhythmic purpose: ′drasti″cally, de″libe′ration.

THE EL ('L) TRANSFORMATIONS

In English, vowels before *r* are altered in quality and timber. In *serious*, the long *e* becomes lower [i] and an [ə] sound is added before *r* [siəriəs]. In *various*, the long *a* becomes [ɛ].

Something similar is true of the influence of the *el* (*'l*) finals.

(1) *an* > *a'l*, *uan* > *ua'l*
(2) *ai* also > *a'l*
(3) *i* > *ie'l*
(4) *ue* > *ue'l*
(5) *y* > *e'l*

ng'l remains *ng'l*; the *ng* is not dropped, but the whole syllable becomes nasalized.

The pronunciation of the 'l-words is a characteristic and charming feature of the Peking language. It is part of the national standard, but other provincials get by without it.

B. The Instant Index System

The Instant Index System and all relevant remarks on actual application will be found in the end paper inside the front cover.

C. The Numerical Index, the Romanized Index and the English Index

Numerical Index (p. xxxiii) In front of the body of the dictionary is a numerical index of the characters which is useful to locate any character. The reader will find it useful to get familiar with this numerical index and its actual application.

In case where the character can belong under one or another index number, both are given, with cross reference to the number under which it may be found. The cross number is marked with an asterisk. Thus: 革 is found under 20.10, where a cross-reference is made to *22.10 in the numerical index.

The numerical index also indicates by a circle left of a character that it is included among the 3000 common characters selected by the Chinese Press Association, a member of the World Press Association (IPI). The Chinese Press Association adopted this list in November, 1970 and recommends that all Chinese language newspapers all over the world voluntarily restrict the use of characters to this number.

The **Romanized Index** (p. 1483) is provided for those who know the sound and wish to find the character. It will be seen that as far as possible, the characters with the same "phonetic" (right-hand) component are grouped together, to facilitate learning of the characters. It is most useful when a writer is not quite sure with what "radical" a character is formed.

English Index (p. 1539) to increase the usefulness of the dictionary, an English Index supplement has been added at the end of the book. In fact, this serves as an English-Chinese Dictionary. The numbers refer to the page, column and line. Thus 281–B15 means page 281, column B, line 15. Every page in this dictionary contains three columns, 1st, 2nd and 3rd, designated as A, B, C respectively.

D. Abbreviations and Symbols

abbr.	abbreviation
AC	Ancient Chinese
allu.	allusion
anc.	Ancient, -ly
arch.	archaic
astron.	astronomy
bot.	botany
biol.	biology
Budd.	Buddhism
callig.	calligraphy
cen.	century
chem.	chemistry
Chin.	Chinese
Christ.	Christian
cogn.	cognate
coll.	colloquial
comb.	combination
comm.	commercial
comp.	compound
complim.	complimentary
Confu.	Confucian, -ism
contempt.	contemptuous
court.	courteous
derog.	derogatory
dial.	dialect
dist.	distinguish from
dyn.	dynasty
econ.	economics
Eng.	English
equiv.	equivalent to
err.	erroneous
esp.	especially

euphem.	euphemism
excl.	exclamation
facet.	facetious
fig.	figurative 引伸
fin. part.	final particle
Fr.	French
gen.	general
geog.	geography
geol.	geology
geom.	geometry
Ger.	German
gram.	grammar
interch.	interchangeable with 通
joc.	jocular
lit.	literally
litr.	literary
LL	literary language
math.	mathematics
mech.	mechanics
med.	medicine
MC	Middle Chinese (earlier vernacular found in poems, plays and novels)
mil.	military
min.	mineralogy
modn.	modern
mus.	music
myth.	mythology
NS	"not split" characters
obs.	obsolete
occa.	occasionally
oft.	often
opp.	opposed to
orig.	originally
p.p.	past participle
phil.	philosophy
phr.	phrase
phys.	physics
physiol.	physiology
poet.	poetic
pop.	popular
pr.	pronunciation
pres. p.	present participle
psych.	psychology
re. pr.	reading pronunciation
rel.	religion
related	related to
rhet.	rhetorical
S	"split" characters
Sanskr.	Sanskrit
satir.	satirical
sl.	slang
s.o.	some one
spec.	specifically
sp. pr.	spoken pronunciation
s.t.	something
translit.	transliteration （譯音）
u.f.	used for 假借（古文）
usu.	usually
var.	variant
vulg.	vulgar
vern.	vernacular
wd.	word
wr.	written
zoo.	zoology
△	cross-reference.
↑	see above
↓	see below

* Modified pronunciation in indicated context (**shau*)
' Precedes an unaccented syllable (*mar'fan*)
: Followed by example of definition

NUMERICAL INDEX OF CHARACTER

NOTICE

1. "*" Indicates variants, almost all given in the dictionary itself, but a few are given in this index only.
2. The 3,000 common characters selected by the Chinese International Press Institute (IPI) are indicated by a circle ("○").
3. When several characters in this group are too many, as in some NS characters, they are distinguished by the bottom forms in bracket. Thus in the group 10.01, (小) for 未, 來, 東, (木) for 森, 槖, (糸) for 索, 素, 紮.
4. Triangle "△" indicates variant characters.

注　　意

1. "*" 號指異體字。 索引中異體字通常見於詞典； 但有少數別體字雖不見於詞典，爲讀者便利，索引中特別表出。
2. "○" 號指中文報業協會所選定常見之三千字，希望世界各中文報紙儘量推行。
3. 不分左右之字，若同一號碼，依下形分類排列。例如第 10.01 段中，未、來、東，下形同爲小，森、槖，下形同爲木，索、素、紮，下形同爲糸。
4. "△" 表示異體字。

10.00 (十/亅)
(亅)○才
○事
(寸)○寸
○專
(子)○李
孛
(手) 挈
掣
○擊
○攀

10.01 (十/小)
(儿) 朮
朮
○未
○末
○朱
耒
○來
○東
○柬
○束
棗
(木)○木
○森
槧
槖
櫜
柰
(示) 禁
(糸)○索
○素
△紮
○紫
絜
○繫
纛

10.02 (十/水)
(水)○求
泰
滕
(衣)○表
○喪
裘
○襲
○製
○囊

10.10 (十/十)
○十
○本
丰
○車
○轟
○幸
(牛)○牛
犇
犛
犨

10.11 (十/土)
○生
埜
塹
○釐

10.20 (十/卄)
卉

10.21 (十/乚)
鬮

10.22 (十/亅)
○韭
鼐

10.30 (十/一)
△丗
○直
矗
○查
彗
○整
鹽
(金) 鏊
鏨

10.32 (十/フ)
○麥
梦

10.40 (十/口)
○古
○杏
○告
○哲
(言)○誓
謦
(石) 砉
磬

10.41 (十/図)
(日) 杳
沓
晳
○暫
曺
晳
(図) 眚
啚

10.42 (十/冈)
○甫
○青
○南

10.50 (十/ㄱ)
○毒
棼
㽙
鷔

10.63 (十/丶)
○杰
熬
鰲

10.70 (十/乚)
(乚)○七
乜
屯
鼇
(儿)○先
○克
剋
梵
氅
麓

10.72 (十/心)
恝
○惠
○想
○慧
慙
懋

10.80 (十/八)
○真
○責
賁
賚
贅
○贊
賣

10.81 (十/人)
(大)○契
嫢
樊
(火)○焚
燓

10.82 (十/乂)
(乂)○支
△麦
皷

10.83 (十/～)
(人)○楚
踅
疐
(辶) 迍
○述
选
○翅
○速
○造
逋
○逝
逑
○連
遊
遨
(麥) 麩 *10S.81
○麪 *10S.50
△麵 *10S.41
麴 *10S.50

10.91 (十/ノ)
○鬱

10.93 (十/く)
(厶)△长
(女)○妻
婪
嫠
(虫) 蛰
蛰
螯
蠹

10A.00 (扌/亅)
-1○持
搏
搏
擣
掎
-2○撐

-3 捯
○打
抒
-4 △捌
-5 擣
捫
撊
○擱
○攔
-6 擰
-8 撙
揄
-9 捋
○掙
拊

10A.01 (扌/小)

-1 ○抹
揀
捺
撩
-2 ○搽
-3 摽
揉
搡
搎
-4 ○操
-6 ○掠
○擦
○探
-9 ○採
攃

10A.02 (扌/⺊)

-1 捄
攮
-2 ○據
-5 ○振
搌
-6 攘
-8 捸
-9 掭
掾

10A.10 (扌/十)

-1 ○抖
擀

○捧
攆
-2 ○掉
○拌
-3 扞
(捍)
抨
撢
○攝
-4 撣
○揖
○擇
-5 擗
-6 捽
○摔
○揮
-9 扦
捭
摧

10A.11 (扌/土)

-1 ○挫
○擡
-2 ○攤
○摧
-3 攉
-4 攞
-5 擢
捱
○握
-6 扗
○撞
○擁
搉
搴
-8 拴
-9 △捶
○推

10A.20 (扌/卄)

-5 摒
-8 揜
-9 ○拼
擤
△拚

10A.21 (扌/乚)

-1 摏
-2 揕
○拙
-5 ○掘
○拒
摳
揠
擓
-9 ○搖
插
搯
掐

10A.22 (扌/丨)

-1 ○掛
-2 ○撕
扑
抻
○排
○拂
-3 揶
抔
-4 ○押
-5 挪
○掃
-6 抃
○擠
○搾
-8 搛
○擲
-9 ○抑
○折
-9 ○拆
挿

10A.30 (扌/一)

-1 揸
搕
-2 ○扯
△挡
-3 ○扛
掗
○拯
-4 △担
搵

捏
(揑)
-5 ○扭
擥
-6 ○拉
○擅
揎
○控
-8 搓
撿
捡

10A.32 (扌/フ)

-9 抮

10A.40 (扌/口)

-1 拮
-2 掿
○搭
拈
-3 ○拓
-4 ○扣
撂
-5 ○招
△据
捃
-6 掊
掂
搪
挌
-8 ○拾
○捨
○搶
-9 ○括
△抬
○擔

10A.41 (扌/図)

-1 搢
-2 ○描
拑
○措
○指
○揩
○抽
○擋
-3 摺

擂
-4 捆
摑
-5 摺
-6 揞
揊
攊
-9 播
○拍
揩

10A.42 (扌/冈)

-1 ○捕
-2 搆
揹
捎
揣
○攜
-3 擩
捅
-4 ○捐
搰
-6 搞
○摘
擿
掮
-8 搠
掄
擒
-9 撟

10A.50 (扌/ㄱ)

-1 拷
-2 ○擄
△攄
擕
-3 扔
-4 ○拐
拇
○揭
○揚
搨
-5 搦
-6 搒
搧
-8 ○扮

-9 撝
摀
○搗
○拘
掬
○掏
搊
拗
撈

10A.63 (扌/丶)

-2 攩
-6 摭
-8 拎
△扲
-9 撫
撚

10A.70 (扌/乚)

-1 ○撓
○拋
○掩
○捲
-2 ○扎
○批
○挑
-4 挹
○擺
-5 扼
攬
○把
-6 ○抗
○攏
○挖
攛
-9 ○托
搋
撬
○攪
扢
○拖
○抱
△执
挽
攙
捲

10A.71 (扌/弋)

-5 抿
-7 ○找
拭
拽
-9 ○抵

10A.72 (扌/心)

-4 揌
摁
-7 撼
-8 捻

10A.80 (扌/八)

-1 攢
擷
-2 ○拱
捵
-4 ○損
○摜
-5 ○撰
-6 ○擴
擯
-8 ○扒

10A.81 (扌/人)

-1 揳
○扶
○挾
○揍
-2 ○摸
○撲
△拟
-3 揆
-5 撅
擫
-6 捩
-8 撳
○撿
-9 ○掀
揪
○抉
○換
○挨

10A.82 (扌/乂)

-1 ○技
○拔

–2 ○撒
○拔
○搜
撇
擞
–3 ○擾
扠
掇
○撥
–4 撮
攫
投
–5 △报
–6 抆
○撤
–8 撥
–9 ○扳
○授
○援
○搬

10A.83 (扌/乛)
–1 ○捷
撻
–2 ○擬
–4 ○捉
○提
擿
–6 掖
–9 ○抓
○挺
搥

10A.91 (扌/ノ)
–2 ○抄
–6 抄
△扩
–9 摻

10A.93 (扌/く)
–2 摟
–3 △抎
搔
–4 攖
△摆
–6 ○接
○按

–9 捼
搽

10B.00 (木/亅)
○木 *10.01
–1 ○村
○材
梈
○樹
檮
○椅
–2 構
–3 杅
○柯
栵
杼
–5 枒
○橱
檲
○欄
–6 楟
檸
–8 樽
揄
–9 桴
桁
榭

10B.01 (木/小)
–1 ○林
○株
○楝
梀
榛
–3 ○杯 *10B.22
○標
–4 ○棵
–6 檁
棕
–9 櫟

10B.02 (木/⺊)
–2 檬
棣
–5 棖
○根
–8 ○樣

–9 椽
橡

10B.10 (木/十)
–1 ○棒
–2 樺
○棹
–3 ○杆
枰
–4 ○楫
○桿
–5 樨
–6 ○梓
○樟
–9 欅
椑
榫
杵
槲

10B.11 (木/土)
–1 ○杜
○桂
○檯
–2 ○權
槿
–3 ○枉
桎
槤
–4 桯
欐
–5 櫂
–6 ○柱
橦
–8 栓
–9 棰
椎
○榷

10B.20 (木/艹)
–2 橯

10B.21 (木/乚)
–1 ○椿
–2 棋
柚
–5 柜
榧

○櫃
○框
○柩
樞
–9 桕
稻

10B.22 (木/丨)
–1 梆
–2 朴
–3 ○榔
○杯
–4 柙
–6 柿
槨
○榨
榔
–8 ○梯
–9 ○析
○柝
○柳
○棉
柞
櫛

10B.30 (木/一)
–1 ○植
楂
榼
–2 櫨
櫨
–3 ○桓
杠
椏
○極
榅
橙
–4 櫺
–5 檻
櫪
–6 ○檀
楦
椌
–8 槎

10B.32 (木/フ)
–2 朽

–9 橯

10B.40 (木/口)
–1 ○枯
○梏
桔
–2 楷
–3 柘
梧
栖
櫺
–4 梠
–6 ○棺
○榕
○槍
–8 栝
–9 △枱
枷
○格
櫓

10B.41 (木/囗)
–1 檣
楮
○椿
–2 ○柑
○槽
樀
○楷
○柚
○檔
–3 △栢
△栖
檑
–4 ○相
梱
–5 楣
–6 櫧
–8 ○檜
–9 楯
○榴
○柏
櫓

10B.42 (木/冈)
–1 楠
–2 ○構

○梢
–3 槅
柄
○桶
○橘
橢
欄
–4 ○桐
柵
○棚
–6 槁
–8 檎
枘
–9 ○橋
樵
栴

10B.50 (木/コ)
–1 栲
–3 ○朽
檮
–4 ○楞
楞
○楊
○榻
櫻
栩
–5 枋
–6 ○榜
–8 枌
–9 ○梅
椈
枸
枸
杓

10B.63 (木/丶)
–9 ○樵

10B.70 (木/乚)
–1 栳
橈
棬
–2 ○枇
○札
桄
○桃

(儿) –3 杌
欖
–4 梲
○棍
○楓
–5 欖
杷
○杷
–6 ○杭
○梳
櫬
櫳
△椀
柁
–8 棁
–9 栀
橇
○枕
○概
槐
枹
桅

10B.71 (木/弋)
–7 ○械
○棧
棫
槭
–9 柢
○機

10B.80 (木/八)
–1 櫝
–2 ○棋
横
楨
–3 槓
–4 枳
–6 ○櫝

10B.81 (木/人)
–1 杕
–2 楔
–2 ○模
○樸
–5 橛
–6 ○核

-8 ○檢
-9 楸
10B.82 (木/乂)
-1 ○枝
○杖
-2 椒
椶
-3 ○梗
○橄
杈
-6 ○校
-8 △杈
-9 ○板
梗
檄
○枚
梭
楥
10B.83 (木/～)
-9 樅
梃
槌
10B.91 (木/ノ)
-1 彬
-2 ○杪
-6 桫
-9 ○杉
△桥
10B.93 (木/く)
-1 ○棲
-2 ○樓
-3 △枟
-4 櫻
-6 桉
-8 ○松
△桧
楡
-9 桜
10C.00 (牛/亅)
-1 ○特
犄
10C.11 (牛/土)
-1 ○牲
○牡
10C.30 (牛/一)
-3 牼
10C.40 (牛/口)
-1 牯
-3 牾
10C.42 (牛/冈)
-6 犒
10C.50 (牛/㇆)
-5 牣
-9 ○物
10C.70 (牛/乚)
-1 犙
-2 牝
○牠
10C.71 (牛/弋)
-8 ○犧
-9 ○牴
10C.80 (牛/八)
-1 犢
10C.82 (牛/乂)
-9 牧
10C.83 (牛/～)
-2 犍
10D.00 (車/亅)
-1 轉
-3 軻
-8 ○輸
10D.01 (車/小)
-3 輮
-9 轢
10D.02 (車/卜)
-1 轅
-4 轘
-5 輾
10D.10 (車/十)
-2 轔
-3 ○軒
-4 ○輯
10D.11 (車/土)
-3 輊
-8 輇
10D.20 (車/廾)
-9 軿
10D.22 (車/丨)
-9 斬
10D.30 (車/一)
-2 轤
-3 ○輕
-5 轣
10D.40 (車/口)
-5 軺
-6 ○轄
-9 輅
10D.41 (車/図)
-2 ○軸
-3 ○輻
-9 ○輜
10D.42 (車/冈)
-1 ○輔
-3 ○輛
-8 ○輪
-9 ○轎
輷
10D.50 (車/㇆)
-5 軔
-9 輷
10D.70 (車/乚)
-2 ○軋
-3 軏
○軱
-5 軛
-6 轆
-9 輗
○軌
輓
10D.71 (車/弋)
-7 軾
10D.72 (車/心)
-7 轗
10D.81 (車/人)
-1 軼
輳
-9 ○軟
10D.82 (車/乂)
-3 輟
輙
-6 轍
較
10D.91 (車/ノ)
-5 轇
-8 軫
10D.93 (車/く)
-8 轜
10S.00 (十[s]/亅)
-1 ○博
-2 ○剌
○刺
○制
剳
-3 耔
-9 ○靜
10S.01 (十[s]/小)
-1 ○棘
-5 耨
-8 榦
10S.02 (十[s]/卜)
-2 ○隸
10S.10 (十[s]/十)
-2 ○韓
-8 ○幹
斡
10S.11 (十[s]/土)
-1 牲
10S.20 (十[s]/廾)
-2 ○耕
10S.22 (十[s]/丨)
-3 ○邦
△邨
鄹
10S.40 (十[s]/口)
-4 耜
10S.41 (十[s]/図)
-2 麯
-3 △麵
10S.42 (十[s]/冈)
-4 ○胡
○朝
耦
10S.50 (十[s]/㇆)
-3 ○麪
-4 ○甥
勑
鶘
-5 ○切
-6 耪
-8 ○翰
-9 ○協
○勅
勃
勣
鳷
鴣
鶄
鵲
麴
10S.70 (十[s]/乚)
-1 兢
-3 △甎
-4 靚
-5 耙
-9 耗
○乾
艳
10S.71 (十[s]/弋)
-7 戟
10S.80 (十[s]/八)
-3 ○頓
○顛
-5 ○頼
10S.81 (十[s]/人)
-1 麸
△献
-9 ○款 *11S.81
歎
10S.82 (十[s]/乂)
-3 穫
-5 蝦
-9 ○故
敖
敕
○救
○敷
10S.83 (十[s]/～)
-6 靛
10S.93 (十[s]/く)
-2 耬
-3 耘
11.00 (土/亅)
(寸)○寺
○壽
○孝
○赤
(手) 摯
11.01 (土/小)
縶
(木) 槖
11.02 (土/卜)
○袁
11.10 (土/十)
(十)○幸
○埠 *11A.10
韋
鞏
(耳)○聲
11.11 (土/土)
○土
○士
圭
○墊
(至)○臺
臺
11.21 (土/乚)
罄
11.22 (土/丨)
△幇
○幫
11.30 (土/一)
(皿) 盍
盞
△塩
△壹
(亞)○壺
壼
11.40 (土/口)
(口)○吉
○喜
嚞
○嘉
(石) 磬
(言) 謦
11.41 (土/図)
(日)○者
耆
馨
(図) 瞽
11.50 (土/㇆)
○考
耉
○勢
翥
鷙
11.63 (土/丶)
○煮
○熱
熹
熹
鼕
11.70 (土/乚)
(乚)○老
(儿)○堯
翹
壳
耄
11.71 (土/弋)
(栽)○栽
○載
-4 哉
○戴
-6 ○裁
-8 㦸
-9 戕
○截
11.72 (土/心)
○志
恚
懿
11.80 (土/八)
○賣
贅
11.81 (土/人)
(大) 奊

11.83 (土/〜)
逹
○達
○遠
遶
○走
(赱) 趬
趲
-2 ○赴
赳
○趙
○趟
-3 趔
○趣
-4 趄
○趧
趮
-5 超
趯
○起
-6 趑
-7 ○越
-8 ○趁
-9 趍
○趨
趫

11.91 (土/ノ)
△声

11.93 (土/く)
○去
盩
蟄
(ム) 蠹

11A.00 (土/亅)
-3 圩
坷
-4 塒
-9 埒
坿

11A.01 (土/小)
-2 堞
-3 ○坏 *11A.22
垛

11A.02 (土/k)
-5 垠
-6 壕
○壞
○壤

11A.10 (土/十)
-3 ○坪
-5 墀
-9 埤
埠

11A.11 (土/土)
-1 墪
-3 垤
堙
-4 ○埋
-6 壅
塞
-9 埵
○堆

11A.21 (土/乚)
-2 ○堪
-5 埳
堰
堀

11A.22 (土/丨)
-2 ○坤
圤
-3 ○坏
-5 ○却
埽
-9 圻
○圳

11A.30 (土/一)
-1 埴
(埴)
-2 ○址
墟
壚
塏
-3 ○垣
○坯
-4 ○坦
-6 ○垃
○壇
-9 坵

11A.40 (土/口)
-2 ○塔
-6 ○培
○塘
-9 ○垢

11A.41 (土/図)
-1 △墻
○堵
-2 坩
-8 ○增
-9 墦

11A.42 (土/冈)
-1 埔
-3 壖
○壩
○壻
-4 坍
垌
堋
-6 墉
-9 埆

11A.50 (土/㇆)
-1 ○垮
-2 ○墈
-3 圬
-4 場
○場
○塌
-6 ○坊
-9 塢
○均
坳

11A.63 (土/丶)
-9 壎

11A.70 (土/乚)
-1 墝
-2 ○地
-5 塊
圮
圯
-6 ○坑
○境
坨
垞
壠
-9 垷
○塊
垝

11A.71 (土/弋)
-7 ○城
○域
堿
-9 坻

11A.72 (土/心)
-7 壏
-8 埝

11A.80 (土/八)
-1 ○墳
-2 ○填
-4 垻
-6 壙
塓

11A.81 (土/人)
-1 塽
-6 垓
-9 堠
墺
坎
块
埃

11A.82 (土/乂)
-2 ○坡
-3 埂
○圾
-4 墁
-6 墩
-9 坂

11A.83 (土/〜)
-4 ○堤
-9 埏

11A.93 (土/く)
-3 △坛
塿
-4 壜

11S.00 ($土^s$/亅)
-1 ○封
○赫
-2 △刲
封

11S.02 ($土^s$/k)
-2 ○隸

11S.22 ($土^s$/丨)
-2 ○卦
-3 郝
○都
-5 却

11S.40 ($土^s$/口)
-1 喆
-3 嚞
-6 赯

11S.41 ($土^s$/図)
-1 赭

11S.50 ($土^s$/㇆)
-4 堨
-9 ○劫
(刧, 刼, 刲)

11S.70 ($土^s$/乚)
-4 ○覩
覩
-9 ○執

11S.72 ($土^s$/心)
-6 懿

11S.80 ($土^s$/八)
-3 頡

11S.81 ($土^s$/人)
-9 ○款

11S.82 ($土^s$/乂)
-1 ○鼓
-4 轂
彀
殼
○穀
縠
鷇
觳
-5 赧
○報
-9 ○赦
○教 *82S.82

11S.91 ($土^s$/ノ)
-9 ○彭

12.00 (ナ/亅)
○存
○奇
○拳
○奪
△寿

12.01 (ナ/小)
○奈
○秦

12.02 (ナ/k)
○泰
豢

12.10 (ナ/十)
○奉
夆
輦

12.11 (ナ/土)
○在
奎

12.20 (ナ/廾)
○奔

12.21 (ナ/乚)
春

12.22 (ナ/丨)
○布
奩

12.30 (ナ/一)
○左
盋
盇
盔

12.32 (ナ/フ)
奓

12.40 (ナ/口)
○右

12.41 (ナ/図)
○春
○奢
○替
昚
○眷
○奮

12.42 (ナ/冈)
有
○有

12.50 (ナ/㇆)
夸
○券
夯

12.63 (ナ/丶)
叅

12.70 (ナ/乚)
奄
○卷
○尤
尪
尷
尬
尨
尥

12.72 (ナ/心)
惷

12.80 (ナ/八)
○真 *10.80
△賛

12.81 (ナ/人)
○犬
○大
○太
猋
○夫
夬 *91.81
央 *91.81
○失
夷
○夾
○爽
奭
○灰
○奏

12.82 (ナ/乂)
○丈
○友
○吏

12.83 (ナ/〜)
迶
遼
迭

12.93 (ナ/く)
○套
○蠢
12S.00 (ナ^s/亅)
–2 刳
制
12S.11 (ナ^s/土)
–9 ○雄
12S.22 (ナ^s/丨)
–3 郁
12S.50 (ナ^s/フ)
–5 翃
–9 鶴
鶾
12S.70 (ナ^s/乚)
–4 ○規
飆
–9 匏
12S.80 (ナ^s/八)
–3 頬
12S.81 (ナ^s/人)
–1 △献
–9 歆
12S.82 (ナ^s/乂)
–1 皷
12S.83 (ナ^s/～)
–9 瓠
20.00 (艹/亅)
擎
20.01 (艹/小)
○某
綦
△栄 *91.01
棊
檠
20.02 (艹/ﾄ)
○恭
20.10 (艹/十)
○革
20.11 (艹/土)
○基
堇 *20A.11
20.20 (艹/艹)
○井

20.21 (艹/乚)
○廿
○世 *21.21
○甚
20.22 (艹/丨)
○帶 *22.22
20.40 (艹/口)
警
(石) 碁
20.41 (艹/図)
○甘
○昔
○曹
20.42 (艹/冈)
春
20.50 (艹/フ)
○驚
20.63 (艹/、)
○燕
20.70 (艹/乚)
○巷
20.72 (艹/心)
懃
戁
20.80 (艹/八)
○共
○其
黄
20.83 (艹/～)
遘
○遭
20A.00 (艹/亅)
–1 葶
蓴
△莠
葑
△荐
–2 ○蔣
–3 芓
○苛
○茅
–4 蒔
摹
–5 蕁
○芽
蕁
○蔚
○蘭
藺
–6 葶
苧
○薄
–9 荸
○莉
苻
○荷
蘅
孽
薊
嫥

20A.01 (艹/小)
–1 茉
茱
萊
蓁
–2 ○葉
–3 ○蒜
蕬
蔯
–4 △菓
–5 蘖
–6 △蔴
蕖
○藻
藳
蘂
–8 荼
○茶
荼
蒤
–9 ○菜
葆
蘗
蘖
○蔡
○蘇
○藥

20A.02 (艹/ﾄ)
–3 蔡
–4 ○慕
○藤
–5 莨
–6 蓑
蘘
○蒙
莨
–9 蕬
藜
蒃
20A.10 (艹/十)
–1 芈
苯
蘀
–2 葦
–3 苹
茸
○華
蕈
–4 葺
○草
蕐
–5 薜
–6 莘
萃
葷
○萍
–9 芊
萆
葎
蓒
○薛
蘚
20A.11 (艹/土)
–1 臺
–2 ○莊
堇
–3 △墊
藿
○薩
–4 ○墓
蘿

–6 蕹
–8 荃
–9 董
蘳
荏
蘿
20A.20 (艹/艹)
–1 ○莽
–3 ○葬
20A.21 (艹/乚)
–2 莯
茁
–3 菡
–5 蓞
苣
–6 ○芒
○茫
–9 ○舊
20A.22 (艹/丨)
–2 ○菲
茀
○蕭
–3 茉
–4 蘄
○幕
–5 △苐
△莭
–6 ○芾
蒂
△蓆
○薪
薺
蘼
–8 蒹
○芥
–9 芹
茆
蒒
薌
20A.30 (艹/一)
–1 ○蓋
–2 芷
蒞
韮

蘆
藎
–3 △荳
○薑
苤
莖
蕹
–4 苴
–5 藍
–6 虀
萱
菹
–9 莅
葒
○蘊
20A.32 (艹/フ)
–4 萝
○夢
–8 苓
20A.40 (艹/口)
–1 ○苦
荅
○若
–2 苫
–4 莒
–5 菖
茗
–6 ○菩
蘑
△莒
菅
○蓉
○落
–8 ○蒼
荅
–9 茄
蓓
○茗
落
茹
○菇
苔
20A.41 (艹/図)
–1 ○藉

○著
蓍
蔷
–3 蒀
茜
蕾
菖
–4 ○薯
○暮
苜
曹
苗
茼
○茵
○菌
–6 ○蓄
藷
蓿
○藩
薈
–8
–9 ○蕃
蕕
菑
20A.42 (艹/冈)
–1 菁
○葫
蒲
○藕
–2 苒
–3 薷
–4 ○萌
○萬
蕳
萵
藺
–6 蒿
蒲
○萹
–8 芮
蒴
–9 蕎
藊
蒨
蓨

20A.50 (卄/㇇)
-1 葝
-3 蔫
-4 蕁
葛
藒
莓
募
-5 芎
蒻
-6 ○芳
蒡
蒟
○藹
○薦
藭
○蕩
△劳
-8 ○芬
蓊
-9 ○莠
荔
△苏
蔦
蘤
莓
芍
○茍
苟
○蔔
○菊
○葡
○蘜
△葯

20A.52 (卄/尸)
-6 △芦

20A.63 (卄/丶)
-1 爇
-3 蘸
○蒸
-6 △菸
○蕉
-8 苶
-9 ○薫

○蕉
○蕪

20A.70 (卄/乚)
-1 葹
蕘
△菴
-3 芫
○蔬
-4 莧
蕢
蕘
芃
-5 菟
芑
○芭
-6 ○荒
蘢
莞
蔻
○范
-9 芼
○藐
○花
艽
葩
蓖
蒐
○苞
苑
蒓

20A.71 (卄/弋)
-4 蕺
蔑
-7 ○茂
葳
蒧
○藏
-9 茋
莪

20A.72 (卄/心)
-1 蕙
惹
-4 葸
-6 薏

芯
蕊
苾
-9 蔥

20A.80 (卄/八)
-1 蕢
-2 萁
○蘋
蕡
-3 黃 *20.80
蘈
-5 蕻

20A.81 (卄/人)
-1 蔌
芙
莢
萸
-2 苡
-3 葵
-4 ○莫
-5 蕨
-6 蔟
蒺
茨
-9 萩
○英
萸
茯
荻
芡

20A.82 (卄/乂)
-1 菱
茇
-2 菽
莜
蔽
藪
虁
-3 茷
-4 ○蔓
蕞
芟
菔
-5 葭

-6 茭
○護 *60A.82
菠
蘐 *63A.82
-8 艾
-9 蓤
○穫 *90A.82
○薇
○獲 *91C.82
蘹 *92S.82

20A.83 (卄/～)
-1 蓮
-2 蘧
蕿
-3 蓫
蓰
菰
-4 ○邁
薹
-6 ○芝
-9 莛
蓏
蔙
○蓬

20A.91 (卄/ノ)
-5 蓼
-6 ○莎

20A.93 (卄/く)
-1 萋
菘
○藝
-2 蕒
-3 △芸
蕓
-3 △蔭
-4 薑
-9 荽
○萎
○茲 *80.93

20B.00 (革/亅)
-3 靪

20B.01 (革/小)
-1 靺

20B.10 (革/十)
革 *22.10
-2 靽

20B.11 (革/土)
-1 ○鞋
-2 鞺
-4 鞓

20B.22 (革/丨)
-5 靷
-9 靳

20B.30 (革/一)
-3 韁

20B.41 (革/囗)
-8 鞧

20B.42 (革/冈)
-2 鞘
韛

20B.50 (革/㇇)
-2 韉
-4 鞨
-5 靭
-6 鞤
-9 ○勒
○鞠
鞫
靿

20B.70 (革/乚)
-2 鞉
-5 靶
-9 靴
鞄
鞔

20B.71 (革/弋)
-2 韄

20B.81 (革/人)
-9 鞦
鞅

20B.82 (革/乂)
-3 靸
-9 ○鞭

20B.83 (革/～)
-2 韃
-3 韆

20B.93 (革/く)
-6 鞍

20S.00 (卄ˢ/亅)
-2 荊
剳
蒯
劐

20S.02 (卄ˢ/k)
-5 ○艱

20S.10 (卄ˢ/十)
-1 ○斟
斠

20S.11 (卄ˢ/土)
-9 ○難

20S.22 (卄ˢ/丨)
-3 邯
鄞
-9 ○斯
斳

20S.42 (卄ˢ/冈)
-4 ○期

20S.50 (卄ˢ/㇇)
-9 ○勘
○勤
○勱
○勸
鶘
鸛

20S.70 (卄ˢ/乚)
-4 覲
○覲
○觀

20S.71 (卄ˢ/弋)
-7 ○戡

20S.80 (卄ˢ/八)
-3 顢
顴

20S.81 (卄ˢ/人)
-9 ○欺
△歎
○歡

20S.82 (卄ˢ/乂)
-9 ○散
○敬

20S.91 (卄ˢ/ノ)
-2 尠

21.00 (ㄴㅏ/亅)
孽

21.01 (ㄴㅏ/小)
嶪
嶫
祟
○崇
○嶸
彙 *92.01

21.02 (ㄴㅏ/k)
○裝
○嵾
象 *92.02

21.10 (ㄴㅏ/十)
○岸
○峯
崒
嵂

21.11 (ㄴㅏ/土)
○崖
崔

21.21 (ㄴㅏ/ㄴ)
○山
○出
○幽
豳
○世
○凶

21.22 (ㄴㅏ/丨)
爿
嶄
巋

21.30 (ㄴㅏ/一)
○豈
○豐

21.32 (ㄴㅏ/フ)
岑

21.40 (ㄴㅏ/口)
△岩
岧

21.41 (ㄴㅏ/囟)
(日) 旹

○醬

21.42 (ㄴㅏ/冈)
△峃
○嵛
△崗
○崩
嵩

21.70 (ㄴㅏ/ㄴ)
(ㄷ) 匕 *21A.70
比 *21A.70
岜
崑
嶇
(儿)△兇
兕 *40.70
嵐
嵬
巍
嶢 *92.70

21.71 (ㄴㅏ/乁)
崴
(乀)△峩

21.72 (ㄴㅏ/心)
崽

21.80 (ㄴㅏ/八)
○眞 *10.80
○巔
貰
○嶺

21.81 (ㄴㅏ/人)
○以 *21S.81
○炭
裝
○獎
○嶽
○嵌
嶔

21.82 (ㄴㅏ/乂)
岌
○巖

21.83 (ㄴㅏ/〜)
遄
嶷

21.93 (ㄴㅏ/く)
崧
蚩
蟼

21A.00 (ㅏ/亅)
虖

21A.01 (ㅏ/小)
○桌
○柴
粲
○紫

21A.02 (ㅏ/ｋ)
○餐

21A.10 (ㅏ/十)
○卓
罩

21A.11 (ㅏ/土)
壑

21A.21 (ㅏ/ㄴ)
○虐
○鹵

21A.22 (ㅏ/丨)
○卡

21A.30 (ㅏ/一)
○上
○止
○些
虗
○虛
○盧

21A.40 (ㅏ/口)
○占
訾

21A.41 (ㅏ/図)
(日)○旨
○皆
(目) 眥
睿
○督
(図) 卣
○鹵

21A.42 (ㅏ/冈)
○肯
○膚

胔

21A.50 (ㅏ/ㄱ)
△与
(匇)
△虜

21A.63 (ㅏ/丶)
(灬)△点

21A.70 (ㅏ/ㄴ)
匕
比 *21S.70
○虎
彪

21A.71 (ㅏ/乁)
○歲

21A.72 (ㅏ/心)
志
惄
○慮
毖

21A.80 (ㅏ/八)
○貞
眞 *10.80
貲

21A.81 (ㅏ/人)
虞

21A.82 (ㅏ/乂)
支
○虔

21A.83 (ㅏ/〜)
○處
逌
逭
遽

21A.91 (ㅏ/ノ)
○步

21B.00 (山/亅)
–1 ○峙
崎
–9 ○崢
(子)○孽 *21.00

21B.01 (山/小)
–9 嵊
嶸
(木) 櫱 *21.01

櫱 *21.01

21B.10 (山/十)
–2 嶙
–6 嶂
–9 ○峰

21B.21 (山/ㄴ)
–2 嵁
–5 ○嶇
崛

21B.22 (山/丨)
–1 嶄
–4 岬

21B.30 (山/一)
–3 嶝
–6 崆
–8 嵯

21B.40 (山/口)
–1 岵
–8 峪

21B.41 (山/図)
–2 岫
–8 嶒
–9 嶓

21B.42 (山/冈)
–2 峭
–4 嵎
峒
–9 嶠

21B.50 (山/ㄱ)
–9 峋

21B.70 (山/ㄴ)
–1 嶢
崦
–4 崐
(ㄴ) 岜 *21.70
–9 屹
巉

21B.71 (山/乁)
–2 巇
–5 岷
–9 ○峨

21B.80 (山/八)
–9 ○嶼

21B.81 (山/人)
–1 ○峽
–2 巘
–8 嶮

21B.82 (山/乂)
–1 岐
崚
–9 岅
峻

21B.93 (山/く)
–2 嵫

21S.00 (ㄴㅏ^{s}/亅)
–1 齮
–2 剴
○劇
劇
–9 ○將

21S.01 (ㄴㅏ^{s}/小)
–1 △牀

21S.02 (ㄴㅏ^{s}/ｋ)
–5 齦

21S.10 (ㄴㅏ^{s}/十)
–2 ○肆
–8 牂

21S.11 (ㄴㅏ^{s}/土)
–1 ○壯
–5 齷
齷
–9 ○雌

21S.21 (ㄴㅏ^{s}/ㄴ)
–5 歫

21S.22 (ㄴㅏ^{s}/丨)
–2 △艸 *22.22
–3 鄷
–5 帰
–8 齡
齡
鱶
–9 ○斷
斷
斷

21S.30 (ㄴㅏ^{s}/一)
–1 豔
–4 齟

21S.40 (ㄴㅏ^{s}/口)
–3 齬
–5 齠

21S.41 (ㄴㅏ^{s}/図)
–1 ○牆

21S.42 (ㄴㅏ^{s}/冈)
–4 齵
–9 齲

21S.50 (ㄴㅏ^{s}/ㄱ)
–3 ○虧
–4 齶
–9 齣
鴇
鸕
勱

21S.63 (ㄴㅏ^{s}/丶)
–8 ○齡

21S.70 (ㄴㅏ^{s}/ㄴ)
–2 ○比
○此
齜
齜
△乩
–3 甗
–4 覘
覬
覷
○凱
–9 齕
齙
齯
○艷

21S.71 (ㄴㅏ^{s}/乁)
–7 △战
戕
○戲
鹹

21S.80 (ㄴㅏ^{s}/八)
–3 ○頃
潁
穎
△頴
潁
○頻

○顛 *10S.80
顗
顱

21S.81 (ㄴㅏ^{s}/人)
–1 ○狀
○猷
○獻
–8 鹼
以
–9 △欵 *11S.81
(款)
欽
歔

21S.82 (ㄴㅏ^{s}/乂)
–1 ○歧
战
–2 戲
–3 ○叔
叡
–6 皺
–9 ○收 *22S.82

21S.83 (ㄴㅏ^{s}/〜)
–3 ○疑
–4 齯

21S.93 (ㄴㅏ^{s}/く)
–9 ○妝

22.00 (丨/亅)
○掌
(子)△學

22.01 (丨/小)
小
(小)○米
○棠
○業
祟 *21.01

22.02 (丨/ｋ)
○水
△氷
淼
○農
○裳
斐
○蒙 *20A.02

22.10 (丨/十)
○半
聿
韋
丵 *20A.10
輩

22.11 (丨/土)
○坐
○堂
○雀

22.20 (丨/卄)
○弊

22.21 (丨/乚)
○山 *21.21
○出 *21.21
○幽 *21.21
豳 *21.21
○世 *21.21

22.22 (丨/丨)
(丨)○卜
○巾
○中
○串
○申
肅
○常
○幣
○帯
(川)○川
○州
○卅
冊
卝
丱
△艸
○非
○弗

22.30 (丨/一)
韭
(ヨ)△当
○晝
○畫
(皿)盅
○盡
蟲
(金)○鑿
○豐 *21.30

22.41 (丨/図)
(日)沓
○書
○嘗
(図)△甞
○省
瞥
○當
○由
○曲

22.42 (丨/冈)
(月)○肖
冑
冉
○背
(冈)○尚
黹

22.50 (丨/ㄱ)
○劣
彎
翡

22.63 (丨/丶)
○黨
鱉

22.70 (丨/乚)
○北
兆
乜
○也
○光
甇
○甈
甖

22.72 (丨/心)
○忠
○患
○悲
懋
懟

22.80 (丨/八)
○典
○共 *20.80
冀
○糞
(貝)○貴
○費
貫
賞

22.81 (丨/人)
○尖

22.82 (丨/乂)
○皮
○叟
斐
○叢
叢

22.83 (丨/⺄)
遘
迆
○逃
迪
○建
○迷
○逍
○逮
○違
○遣
○遺
遴
蹩

22.91 (丨/ノ)
○少

22.93 (丨/く)
(女) 婁
(虫) 虫
蟲
蛬
(ム) 尝

22A.00 (忄/亅)
-1 悖
忖
愽
○恃
-4 惻
-5 憫
-6 惇
-8 ○愉
-9 悧
悸
惸

22A.01 (忄/小)
-1 忱
悚
愫
-3 慄
-4 ○憬
-6 懍

22A.02 (忄/k)
-5 ○悵
○恨
-6 ○懷
○慷
悢

22A.10 (忄/十)
-1 ○悻
-2 ○悼
○憐
-3 怦
懾
-4 憚
○悍
懌
-6 悴
惲
-9 忤
懈

22A.11 (忄/土)
-1 ○性
-2 ○懂
△懽
-3 ○怪
-4 惺
○懼
-5 慳
-6 ○憧
-9 ○惟
○惶

22A.21 (忄/乚)
-5 恇
慪
愜
-6 ○忙
-9 慆

22A.22 (忄/丨)
-1 ○慚
○怖
-2 ○忡
悱
怫
-3 怀
-6 忭
懠
-8 悌
△慊
悕
-9 △忻
怍

22A.30 (忄/一)
-2 愷
-3 怔
○恆
-4 怛
慍
-5 忸
-6 悾
-9 ○恤

22A.40 (忄/口)
-1 怙
-2 怗
-3 ○悟
-6 ○惦
-8 ○恰
○愴
-9 恬
恪
怡

22A.41 (忄/図)
-2 懵
○惜
-3 愊
恓
愐
-4 悃
慖
-5 慴
-6 愔
-8 憎
-9 惛
○怕
○惱

22A.42 (忄/冈)
-1 ○情
○惰
-2 惴
○悄
惝
-3 ○懦
-4 悁
恫
○惆
惘
-6 慵

22A.50 (忄/ㄱ)
-4 愕
愣
○惕
愒
-5 △忉
-9 怮
慟
恂
○悔

22A.63 (忄/丶)
-9 ○憔
憮

22A.70 (忄/乚)
-1 ○惓
-2 ○慌
○恍
恌
-4 悒
-5 怩
○慨
-6 伉
○惋
-8 ○悅
-9 ○忱
○愧
愾

22A.71 (忄/弋)
-7 慽
○懺

22A.72 (忄/心)
-6 ○憶
-7 ○憾
-9 ○惚

22A.80 (忄/八)
-1 ○慎
○憤
○懶
-2 惧
憒
-4 ○慣
△惧

22A.81 (忄/人)
-1 ○恢
-3 愞
-4 ○悞
-5 懨
-9 愀
○快
怏
懊

22A.82 (忄/乂)
-1 忮
悛
-3 惙
-4 ○慢
-9 愎
慍
悛

22A.83 (忄/⺄)
-1 憶
慥

22A.91 (忄/ノ)
-5 憀
-9 ○慘

22A.93 (忄/く)
-1 ○悽
○怯
-8 忪

△愉

22B.00 (巾/亅)
-1 幬

22B.02 (巾/卜)
-2 幪
-5 ○帳

22B.10 (巾/十)
-2 幃
-6 ○幛

22B.11 (巾/土)
-5 幄
-6 幢
-9 帷

22B.20 (巾/卄)
-9 帲

22B.40 (巾/口)
-2 帖
-8 帢
-9 幨

22B.41 (巾/図)
-3 ○幅
-4 ○帽
幗
-9 幡
○帕

22B.70 (巾/ㄴ)
-4 幌
○帆
-8 帨

22B.71 (巾/弋)
-6 ○幟

22B.80 (巾/八)
-1 幘
-2 幀

22B.81 (巾/人)
-1 帙
-2 幞
-6 幎

22B.82 (巾/乂)
-2 帔
-4 幔

22C.00 (米/亅)
-3 籽

22C.01 (米/小)
-3 糅
-6 粽

22C.02 (米/卜)
-5 粻
-6 △粮
糠

22C.10 (米/十)
-1 料
-6 粹
-9 粺

22C.11 (米/土)
-4 ○糧
-6 △粧

22C.30 (米/一)
-4 ○粗
-6 ○粒

22C.40 (米/口)
-2 粘
-6 ○糖

22C.41 (米/図)
-2 ○糟
-4 糰
-9 粕
糌

22C.42 (米/冈)
-1 ○精
○糊
-2 糒
-3 ○糯
糈
-5 糲

22C.50 (米/ㄱ)
-8 ○粉

22C.63 (米/、)
-8 ○糕

22C.70 (米/ㄴ)
-2 粃
-5 粑

22C.81 (米/人)
-2 ○糢
-9 糗

22C.82 (米/乂)
-2 糉
-9 粄

22C.83 (米/〜)
-1 ○糙

22C.91 (米/ノ)
-9 糝

22C.93 (米/く)
-5 糨
-8 糍
-9 △粄

22D.00 (虫/亅)
-1 蝲
-5 蚜
-6 蝣
-9 蜉
蜊

22D.01 (虫)
-1 ○蛛
蠑
-2 ○蝶
-3 螵
-4 ○蜾
螺
-8 蜍

22D.02 (虫/卜)
-2 蠓
-6 蠔
蜋

22D.10 (虫/十)
-1 ○蚌
蚪
-3 蟫
-4 蟬
-6 蜶
-9 蝌
蜂
△蠏
蛘

22D.11 (虫/土)
-1 ○蛙
-2 ○蝗
-3 蛭
蟶
-6 ○蛀
-9 ○蝗

22D.20 (虫/卄)
-2 ○蟒

22D.21 (虫/ㄴ)
-6 虻

22D.22 (虫/丨)
-1 蜥
-2 蚪
-3 虾
-5 蚓
-6 蠐
螂
-8 蚧
-9 螄
蚱

22D.30 (虫/一)
-2 螘
-3 虹
蜢
-4 蛆
-9 蚯

22D.40 (虫/口)
-1 蛄
-6 螗
-8 蟮
蛤
-9 蜘
蟾

22D.41 (虫/図)
-2 蚶
蜡
螬
蚰
蛐
-3 蝠
-4 蛔
蟈
-8 蝤
-9 蟠

22D.42 (虫/冈)
-1 ○蜻
蛸
蝻
○蝴
-3 蠕

蛹
-4 蜎
蛢
蜩
蜠
蝸
-5 蠣
-6 螭
蝙
-8 蚋

22D.50 (虫/ㄱ)
-4 蜴
蝎
蠋
-5 螞
-6 螃
-8 蚡

22D.63 (虫/、)
-8 蛉

22D.70 (虫/ㄴ)
-1 蟯
蜷
蚘
-2 虬
虵
蚍
蛦
-4 蜆
○蠅
-6 蛇
○蛯
蜿
-8 蛻
蟯
-9 蜺
蛇
○蠟

22D.71 (虫/弋)
-2 蠛
-7 蜮
-8 ○蟻
-9 ○蛾
蟣

22D.72 (虫/心)
-1 蟪
-9 蟋

22D.80 (虫/八)
-2 蜞
蟥
-6 蠙
螟

22D.81 (虫/人)
-1 蚨
蛺
-2 螟
-3 蝡
-4 蜈
蠍

22D.82 (虫/乂)
-1 蚑
-2 蠖
-5 ○蝦
-6 ○蚊
蛟
-9 蝮

22D.83 (虫/〜)
-1 蜨
-9 ○蜓
蜒

22D.91 (虫/ノ)
-1 蟛

22D.93 (虫/く)
-2 螻
-8 蚣

22S.00 (|^{s}/亅)
-1 ○對
-2 剉
削
○劃
判 *91S.00

22S.10 (|^{s}/十)
-2 韡
-6 ○輝

22S.11 (|^{s}/土)
-1 △壯
-5 耀

22S.21 (|^{s}/ㄴ)
-9 韜

22S.22 (|^{s}/丨)
-2 卝 *22.22
-3 ○鄰
酆 *21S.22
-8 齡 *21S.63

22S.30 (|^{s}/一)
-1 豔 *21S.30
-4 韞

22S.41 (|^{s}/図)
-4 旧

22S.42 (|^{s}/冈)
-1 黼

22S.50 (|^{s}/ㄱ)
-4 ○暢
-5 韌
-9 鸛
勸 *21S.50

22S.70 (|^{s}/ㄴ)
-2 ○北 *22.70
○兆 *22.70
-4 靦
-9 皰
艴

22S.71 (|^{s}/弋)
-2 韤

22S.80 (|^{s}/八)
-3 ○順
○頗
○頪
類
纇

22S.82 (|^{s}/乂)
-1 黻
-9 ○收
○敝
○敞
○數

30.00 (一/亅)
亍

30.01 (一/小)
○示

30.30 (一/一)
○一
○二
○三
○豆
亙 *31.30
30.42 (一/冈)
鬲
30.50 (一/ㄱ)
(ㄱ)△亏
30.70 (一/乚)
○元
黿
○麗
30.83 (一/～)
远
逗
○逼
邇
30.93 (一/く)
○云
30S.00 (一s/亅)
-2 刓
○副
30S.01 (一s/小)
-3 △祘
30S.22 (一s/丨)
-3 鄜
30S.30 (一s/一)
-3 豇
30S.42 (一s/冈)
-3 △丽
30S.50 (一s/ㄱ)
-5 翮
-9 鸝
30S.70 (一s/乚)
-6 豌
-9 ○魂
30S.71 (一/弋)
-7 戠
30S.80 (一s/八)
-3 ○頑
○頭

30S.82 (一s/乂)
-1 豉
30S.93 (一s/く)
-2 融
31.00 (丅/亅)
○丁
○于
○可
○哥
△覇
31.01 (丅/小)
○不 *31.22
丕
(小)△乐
栗
△琹
纍
○票
○粟
31.02 (丅/k)
汞
泵
豖
○裂
○聚
饕
31.10 (丅/十)
○干
○平
覃
鞏
○耳
聶
31.11 (丅/土)
○王
○玉
○至
○型
垩
○聖
壐
31.20 (丅/廾)
○弄

31.21 (丅/乚)
(凵)○函
△画
31.22 (丅/丨)
○不
○下
冪
31.30 (丅/一)
○工
○五
○互
亙
丕
○正
歪
巫
○亞
盂
△盃
罶
31.32 (丅/フ)
○歹
○琴
31.40 (丅/口)
○否
○吾
△啓
(石)○石
○碧
磊
31.41 (丅/図)
○百
(日)○晉
○西
覀
○面
(図)△覃
31.42 (丅/冈)
○而
○再
○雨
○丙
○兩
甭

(冈) 鬲
○爾
△覇
31.50 (丅/ㄱ)
△万
○丐
○焉
粤
覊
31.63 (丅/丶)
○烈
31.70 (丅/乚)
无
○瓦
瓩
瓸
(儿) 兀
虺
○死
○覓
31.71 (丅/弋)
戞
31.72 (丅/心)
忑
恧
○恐
○惡
憨
瑟
31.80 (丅/八)
○頁
○貢
○賈
31.81 (丅/人)
○天
奭
叕
31.82 (丅/乂)
○更
○夏
○憂
○覆
覈

31.83 (丅/～)
(辶) 迂
迺
△还
○逦
逕
○逐
○遷
邐
(人) 登
尠
31.91 (丅/ノ)
○歹 *31.32
31.93 (丅/く)
要
○要
○娶
蚕
登
31A.00 (王/亅)
-1 琦
-3 玎
珂
-8 瑜
-9 琤
珩
31A.01 (王/小)
-1 琳
○珠
-2 璨
-4 璪
璟
-6 琛
-9 球
璅
31A.02 (王/k)
-1 ○球
-2 璩
-3 琢
-4 ○環
-6 瓌
琅
-9 璬

31A.10 (王/十)
-1 琫
-2 瑋
璘
-3 玕
珥
-6 璋
31A.11 (王/土)
-1 珪
-2 瑾
璀
-3 珏
-4 ○理
-6 斑
-9 ○班
31A.21 (王/乚)
-9 瑤
31A.22 (王/丨)
-3 玔
-6 瑯
31A.30 (王/一)
-8 瑳
31A.40 (王/口)
-2 玷
-4 璐
-8 琀
瑲
-9 珞
31A.41 (王/図)
-2 璿
瑺
-3 璠
-4 瑁
-9 珀
瑙
31A.42 (王/冈)
-1 瑚
-2 ○瑞
-4 珊
琱
-6 ○璃
31A.50 (王/ㄱ)
-1 璹
-5 瑪

-9 琇
31A.63 (王/丶)
-8 玲
31A.70 (王/乚)
-2 珧
琥
-3 ○玩
-4 琨
○現
珮
-5 玘
-6 ○琉
瓏
琬
-9 瑰
31A.71 (王/弋)
-5 珉
-7 琖
瑊
-9 玳
璣
31A.72 (王/心)
-9 璁
31A.80 (王/八)
-1 瑱
(瑱)
瓚
-2 琪
璜
瑣
-3 瑻
-9 璵
31A.81 (王/人)
-2 瑛
璞
-9 玦
△玖
31A.82 (王/乂)
-2 玻
-5 瑕
-9 ○玫
瓊
31A.83 (王/～)
-6 璇

-9 瑽
31A.91 (王/ノ)
-5 璆
-8 ○珍
31A.93 (王/く)
-1 珐
-4 瓔
-8 瑜
31B.00 (石/亅)
-1 ○磚
-3 硎
-4 ○碍
-5 砑
31B.01 (石/小)
-1 ○硃
-2 ○碟
-3 磙
-9 磔
礫
31B.02 (石/k)
-5 ○碾
-6 硠
-9 ○碌
31B.10 (石/十)
-2 ○磷
-3 砰
-6 ○碎
-9 ○碑
31B.11 (石/土)
-1 硅
-9 碓
○確
31B.20 (石/廿)
-3 ○研
31B.21 (石/ㄴ)
-2 碮
-5 砸
31B.22 (石/丨)
-2 砷
-6 碲
-9 斫
砟
31B.30 (石/一)
-1 碴

磕
-3 硜
磴
-8 碰
磋
31B.32 (石/フ)
-2 硚
-9 矽
31B.40 (石/口)
-2 砧
-9 硌
31B.41 (石/囚)
-2 磠
-3 礝
-9 磻
硇
31B.42 (石/冈)
-2 硝
-4 碉
硼
-5 礪
-9 确
31B.50 (石/ㄱ)
-1 砌
碡
-4 碭
碣
-5 ○碼
-6 ○磅
31B.63 (石/丶)
-9 ○礁
31B.70 (石/ㄴ)
-1 磽
-2 砒
-4 ○硯
-5 砨
-6 ○硫
○碗
-9 砬
○砲
31B.71 (石/乚)
-7 ○碱
-9 砥
磯

31B.80 (石/八)
-1 磧
-2 ○磺
○碘
-3 ○碩
-6 ○礦
31B.81 (石/人)
-1 硤
-2 碶
-9 砍
31B.82 (石/乂)
-2 ○破
-3 ○硬
-5 △礟
○礮
-9 礉
31B.83 (石/～)
-1 ○礎
-2 △礙
-6 碇
-9 砭
31B.91 (石/ノ)
-2 △砂
-9 磣
31B.93 (石/く)
-1 砝
-8 ○磁
31C.00 (酉/亅)
-1 酎
酵
-3 酊
-6 酧
醇
-9 酹
醽
31C.01 (酉/小)
-3 醥
-6 醾
-8 酴
-9 酥
31C.02 (酉/k)
-2 醵
醲
-6 ○釀

-9 醁
31C.10 (酉/十)
-3 醰
-6 ○醉
31C.11 (酉/土)
-2 醛
-4 ○醒
31C.21 (酉/ㄴ)
-2 酗
31C.22 (酉/丨)
-2 ○酬
-6 醡
醾
-9 酢
31C.30 (酉/一)
-1 醘
-2 醴
-4 ○醞
-6 醯
-8 醶
31C.40 (酉/口)
-1 酤
○酷
-3 醹
-6 醅
-9 酪
酩
31C.41 (酉/囚)
-2 ○酣
○醋
-6 醑
31C.42 (酉/冈)
-1 酺
醐
31C.50 (酉/ㄱ)
-9 ○酌
31C.63 (酉/丶)
-9 醺
醮
31C.70 (酉/乚)
-1 醃
-5 配
-6 酡
-9 酖

○醜
31C.71 (酉/七)
-7 醎
31C.81 (酉/人)
-2 醭
31C.82 (酉/乂)
-3 醙
醱
醳
-4 酘
-9 ○酸
31C.83 (酉/～)
-4 醍
31C.91 (酉/ノ)
-5 醪
31D.00 (雨/亅)
-3 雩
31D.01 (雨/小)
-1 ○霖
31D.02 (雨/k)
-4 霢
-5 ○震
31D.10 (雨/十)
-5 霹
31D.11 (雨/土)
-6 霪
-9 霾
○霍
31D.22 (雨/丨)
-2 霏
-6 霽
霈
零 *31D.63
31D.30 (雨/一)
-4 ○靈
-5 ○雪
靂
31D.40 (雨/口)
-4 霝
○露
-6 霑
31D.41 (雨/囚)
-1 ○霜
-4 ○雷

31D.42 (雨/冈)
-2 ○霸
霄
-3 ○需
31D.50 (雨/ㄱ)
-3 雩
○霧
(ㄱ)△ -5 霚
-6 雱
靄
霶
-8 雰
-9 霉
31D.63 (雨/丶)
-8 ○零
31D.70 (雨/乚)
-4 ○電
-8 霓
雹
31D.81 (雨/人)
-2 霙
31D.82 (雨/乂)
-2 霰
-5 霞
-6 雯
31D.83 (雨/～)
-9 霆
31D.93 (雨/く)
-3 雲
-6 雾
31S.00 (丅^{s}/亅)
-1 ○耐
-2 ○列
○刑
刵
○到
△剅
剄
剽
(亅)△ 斫
-9 殍
31S.01 (丅^{s}/小)
-1 ○殊
臻

31S.02 (丅^{s}/k)
-8 △殘
31S.10 (丅^{s}/十)
-4 殫
31S.11 (丅^{s}/土)
-2 殣
31S.22 (丅^{s}/丨)
-2 殢
-3 邛
邗
邢
邳
郅
耶
鄢
-8 豨
-9 ○聊
○聯
31S.30 (丅^{s}/一)
-1 殖
殪
-2 △耻
-3 ○殭
殛
-4 殂
31S.40 (丅^{s}/口)
-9 聒
殆
31S.41 (丅^{s}/囚)
-1 △豬
31S.42 (丅^{s}/冈)
-2 聃
31S.50 (丅^{s}/ㄱ)
-2 ○聘
-3 ○巧
-9 ○功
勁
勔
殉
殤
31S.63 (丅^{s}/丶)
-8 聆
-9 △聰

31S.70 (丅ˢ/乚)
-3 甄
-4 覡
靦
覶
飄
-5 豝
-9 耽

31S.71 (丅ˢ/弋)
-6 ○職
-7 ○殘
○殲

31S.72 (丅ˢ/心)
-1 ○聽
-6 ○恥
-9 聰

31S.80 (丅ˢ/八)
-1 殨
-2 聵
-3 ○頂
○項
頊
○頸
-4 ○殞
-6 ○殯

31S.81 (丅ˢ/人)
-8 ○殮
(大)△联
-9 殀
○殃
○耿
○歌
△聨

31S.82 (丅ˢ/乂)
-3 ○取
-5 豭
-9 ○歿
○攻
○政
○致
△攷
○敢
嫛

31S.83 (丅ˢ/〜)
-9 瓢

31S.91 (丅ˢ/ノ)
-8 殄
-9 ○形
彭

32.00 (フ/亅)
○了
孑
孓
○予
矛
○子
(子)○孕
○承

32.01 (フ/小)
○朶
○柔
○桑
[illegible]

32.02 (フ/k)
○承 *32.00
隳

32.11 (フ/土)
(土)△圣
○墮
○墜

32.22 (フ/丨)
鼐

32.30 (フ/一)
○丞
○亟
○孟
○盈
○登
鍪
○叠

32.41 (フ/図)
晉
(図)△函

32.42 (フ/冈)
胥
甬
矞

32.50 (フ/ㄱ)
○乃
○勇
鶩
騖
鷩

32.63 (フ/丶)
烝

32.70 (フ/乚)
○乙
虱
○飛
巹
○凳

32.72 (フ/心)
恿

32.80 (フ/八)
負

32.81 (フ/人)
癸

32.82 (フ/乂)
○又
○叉
○及
○發

32.83 (フ/〜)
○疋
○迅
○通
○遜

32.93 (フ/く)
(女) 婺
(虫) 蚤
○蛋
蝥
蟊
蝨

32A.00 (阝/亅)
-3 ○阿
-8 險
-9 ○附

32A.01 (阝/小)
-1 ○陳
-2 ○隙
-8 ○除
-9 ○際

32A.02 (阝/k)
-4 隈
-5 ○限
-8 ○隊

32A.10 (阝/十)
-1 ○陣
-2 ○隣
-6 ○障
-9 阡
陴
○降

32A.11 (阝/土)
-1 ○陸
-2 陛
-3 陻
-9 陞
陲
隍
○隆

32A.20 (阝/廾)
-2 阱

32A.21 (阝/乚)
-3 ○陋
-9 ○陷

32A.22 (阝/丨)
-6 隮
-9 阼

32A.30 (阝/一)
-2 阯
-3 陘
-4 ○阻
-8 隘

32A.40 (阝/口)
-2 阽
-6 ○陪

32A.41 (阝/図)
-2 ○階
-3 ○陌

32A.42 (阝/冈)
-1 隋
-3 ○隔
-4 隅

32A.50 (阝/ㄱ)
-4 ○陽
-6 ○防
-9 ○陶
隖

32A.63 (阝/丶)
-4 隰

32A.70 (阝/乚)
-3 阮
-5 阨
-6 隴
陀
阬
院
-9 隗
阣

32A.72 (阝/心)
-9 ○隱

32A.80 (阝/八)
-2 隫
-4 隕

32A.81 (阝/人)
-1 陜
-8 ○險
-9 隩

32A.82 (阝/乂)
-1 陵
-2 陂
-3 陬
-9 阪

32A.83 (阝/〜)
-1 陡
○隨
-4 ○隄
-8 ○隧

32A.91 (阝/ノ)
-2 陟

32A.93 (阝/く)
-8 ○陰
險

32S.00 (フˢ/亅)
-1 △对
-2 剢
剟
-3 孖

32S.01 (フˢ/小)
-1 △疎
-9 ○孫

32S.02 (フˢ/k)
-5 △艰
-9 ○豫

32S.11 (フˢ/土)
-9 △难

32S.22 (フˢ/丨)
-3 ○鄧

32S.32 (フˢ/フ)
-8 矜

32S.42 (フˢ/冈)
-3 ○孺

32S.50 (フˢ/ㄱ)
-9 ○務
鶩
△劝
△鸡

32S.70 (フˢ/乚)
-2 ○孔
-6 ○疏
-9 毹

32S.71 (フˢ/弋)
-7 △戏
戲

32S.80 (フˢ/八)
-3 ○預
頹

32S.81 (フˢ/人)
-6 ○孩
-9 △欢

32S.82 (フˢ/乂)
-2 敠
-3 △双
-9 孜

32S.83 (フˢ/〜)
-9 飞
○孤

40.01 (口/亅)
(木)○呆

40.02 (口/k)
饕

40.10 (口/十)
○單
斝

40.11 (口/土)
○呈

40.21 (口/乚)
○咢

40.22 (口/丨)
吊

40.40 (口/口)
○口
囗
凸
凹
○呂
○品
碞
○器
嚚
囂

40.41 (口/図)
△啚

40.50 (口/ㄱ)
○另
△号
○罵 *41D.50
鷶

40.63 (口/丶)
喣

40.70 (口/乚)
○兄
○邑
黾
兕
○咒
鼉

40.80 (口/八)
○只
○員

40.81 (口/人)
○吳
○哭

40.82 (口/乂)
○嚴

40.83 (口/〜)
○足
逞

40.93 (口/く)
(ム)△虽

40A.00 (口/亅)
–1 吋
喇
囀
哮
嚇
–2 嘑
–3 叮
吁
呵
咧
○啊
–5 ○呀
囒
–6 哼
啍
嚀
–8 ○喻
–9 ○呼
嚼
○咐
喝

40A.01 (口/小)
–1 ○味
嗦
嗉
噤
嘹
–2 嚹
喋
咪
–3 嘌
嗓
–4 噪
–6 嘛
–9 咻

40A.02 (口/k)
–1 囔
–2 噱

噥
–3 啄
–4 喂
–5 哏
–6 嚎
囔
△咏
–9 喙

40A.10 (口/十)
–1 叶
–2 吽
唪
○叫
嘩
–3 囁
–4 嚗
–6 啐
–9 啤
嗥

40A.11 (口/土)
–1 ○吐
哇
–3 咥
–4 囉
○哩
嚜
–5 喔
–9 唾
○唯
喤

40A.20 (口/廾)
–3 哶
–8 嗱

40A.21 (口/乚)
–1 囓
–2 咄
–5 哑
嘔
–9 啿
啗

40A.22 (口/丨)
–1 嘟
–2 嘶
呻

嘯
○啡
–3 吓
–4 呷
–5 ○叩
哪
–6 ○啼
啷
–8 嗛
唏
–9 唧
咋
○啣

40A.30 (口/一)
–1 ○啦
喳
嗤
嗑
噎
–2 嘘
–3 哐
唔
呸
○哑
–4 嗢
咀
–5 嚦
–6 喧
–8 嗟
唫
–9 噬

40A.32 (口/フ)
–4 啰
–8 ○吟
–9 哆

40A.40 (口/口)
–1 咕
咭
嘻
–2 喏
嗒
呫
–3 唔
–6 唁

喀
嗐
–8 ○哈
哈
啥
嗆
–9 ○咖
咯
哈

40A.41 (口/囟)
–1 ○嗜
–2 喈
△嚐
嘈
喵
咁
噹
–3 哂
–4 ○咽
○唱
嘓
–6 喑
–8 噌
噲
–9 噆
咱
咱
嚕
嚕

40A.42 (口/冈)
–1 哺
喃
○嘲
–2 啨
哨
○嘴
○喘
嗃
–3 嗝
嚅
–4 喟
喁
啁
喎

–5 △噣
–6 唷
–8 噙
呐
–9 △响

40A.50 (口/ㄱ)
–1 咵
–2 噶
嘞
–4 ○喝
噣
嘐
–5 叼
叨
嗨
○嗎
△囑
–6 嗙
嗨
–8 ○吩
嗡
嗡
–9 ○嗚
○鳴
嘮
○吻
啕
呦
喲

40A.63 (口/丶)
–2 嚥
–6 嗻
–9 噍
咚
嘸

40A.70 (口/乚)
–1 嘵
唵
–2 呲
唬
叱
咷
–3 叽
○吼

–4 △呪
–5 呃
○呢
○吧
–6 吭
嘵
○嚨
咤
–9 吒
噢
嘅
吪
○吃
咆
吮
嚥

40A.71 (口/弋)
–2 嚱
–3 嘎
–7 喊
嘁
–9 哦
嚱

40A.72 (口/心)
–6 噫
–8 △唸
–9 嗯

40A.80 (口/八)
–1 嘖
○噴
△嚬
囋
–2 ○哄
嗔
嗩
–4 唄
–8 叭

40A.81 (口/人)
–1 ○嗽
△喫
吠
咦
–2 噗
嘆

–5 噘
–6 ○咳
嗾
噉
唳
–8 唉
△叺
–9 ○嗅
○喉
啾
啖
○吹
○喚
○唉

40A.82 (口/乂)
–1 吱
嗷
–2 哎
嚄
–3 ○哽
嗄
噉
○吸
啜
–4 嘬
–5 唚
–6 ○咬
啵
–9 嗳
嗷
呶
唆

40A.83 (口/〜)
–1 啑
嚏
唗
–9 呱

40A.91 (口/ノ)
–2 ○吵
–5 嘐
–6 唦
嗲
–9 咿

40A.93 (口/く)
-1 呿
-2 囈
嗤
嘍
-4 嚶
-6 咳
-8 喩
-9 吆

40B.00 (足/亅)
-1 躊
踦
-2 躪
蹐
-6 躕
○跡
-8 蹲
踰
-9 跗

40B.01 (足/小)
-2 蹀
-3 踩
蹂
-4 躁
踝
-6 △踪
-9 躒

40B.02 (足/k)
-5 ○跟
踀
-6 踉

40B.10 (足/十)
-2 踔
-3 躡
-4 蹕
-5 躃

40B.11 (足/土)
-1 跬
-2 蹚
-5 ○躍
-6 躔
-9 踵

40B.20 (足/廾)
-3 跰

40B.21 (足/乚)
-5 ○距
-9 蹈

40B.22 (足/丨)
-6 ○蹄
躋
-8 躑

40B.30 (足/一)
-1 踏
-2 跓
-3 蹬
踁
-8 蹉

40B.40 (足/口)
-3 跖
-5 踞
-6 踣
-8 蹌
-9 跏
○路
踋

40B.41 (足/囟)
-2 躇
蹧
○踏
-3 跴
-8 蹭
-9 蹯

40B.42 (足/冈)
-2 蹣
踹
蹦
-3 踊
-4 蹣
-6 蹁
-9 踽
蹻

40B.50 (足/ㄱ)
-1 ○跨
-3 ○踴
-4 ○踼
蹋
躅
-5 踻

-9 趵

40B.63 (足/丶)
-6 蹠

40B.70 (足/乚)
-1 跣
蹺
踡
-2 跐
○跳
-3 躩
-6 蹴
跎
躝
-9 ○跑
跪
躐
踬

40B.71 (足/弋)
-7 踆
○踐

40B.72 (足/心)
-5 踠

40B.80 (足/八)
-1 躦
蹟
-8 趴
-9 躓

40B.81 (足/人)
-1 跌
趺
-2 蹼
-5 蹶
-9 蹊
趹

40B.82 (足/乂)
-1 跂
跋
-2 踙
蹴
跛
-3 趿
-6 跤
踱
躞

40B.83 (足/〜)
-1 躂
-4 踶
-9 ○蹤
蹝

40B.93 (足/く)
-6 踜
-8 踰

40S.00 (口ˢ/亅)
-2 ○別
△别

40S.01 (口ˢ/小)
-4 △槑

40S.02 (口ˢ/k)
-5 鼹

40S.11 (口ˢ/土)
-9 ○雖

40S.22 (口ˢ/丨)
-3 郢
鄂
○鄙

40S.50 (口ˢ/ㄱ)
-5 ○嗣
-9 鴞
鶻
鶚
○勛

40S.70 (口ˢ/乚)
-2 ○號

40S.71 (口ˢ/弋)
-7 戢
○戰

40S.80 (口ˢ/八)
-3 顎

40S.81 (口ˢ/人)
-1 ○獸

41.01 (囟/小)
○果
○累
○景
△県
△纍

41.02 (囟/k)
○暴

○畏
○晨
曩

41.10 (囟/十)
○早
○旱
○畢
○暈

41.11 (囟/土)
○里
○星
○量
○墅
○墨
○壘
瞿

41.20 (囟/廾)
○昇

41.21 (囟/乚)
罌
罍

41.22 (囟/丨)
○甲
畀
○昂
○界
○鼎

41.30 (囟/一)
○旦
昱
○盟
○疊

41.40 (囟/口)
(口)△畧
晷

41.41 (囟/囟)
(日)○日
○曰
○昌
○晶
○暑
(目)○冒
○目
(田)○田
-1

毌
○因
○困
○囤
○固
囿
○圃
圉
圊
○圈
○園
○團
-2 ○圍
-3 囝
圄
圂
-4 △回
○圓
○圖
圜
-7 ○國
-8 囚
圇
圙
○四
-9 囮
囫
囡
△図
圝

41.42 (囟/冈)
冐
○胃
禺

41.50 (囟/ㄱ)
○毋
○母
○男
○勗
○易
○曷
曻

41.63 (囟/丶)
○黑

煦
○照
△默 *41S.81
△點 *41S.40

41.70 (囟/乚)
(儿) 皃
○見
○昆
晃
晁
冕
(乚) 鼂
矍
毘

41.71 (囟/弋)
晟

41.72 (囟/心)
○思
○恩
慁
○愚
偲
○懸

41.80 (囟/八)
○具
○異
○貝
○貫
贔

41.81 (囟/人)
昃
昊

41.82 (囟/乂)
旻
○曼
○最
矍

41.83 (囟/〜)
○迴
○遇
○遏
遢
遲
逿

○是
匙
尟
韙
○題
[illegible]
41.93 (図/く)
晏
嬰
曇
△県
41A.00 (日/亅)
-1 ○時
△时
41A.01 (日/小)
-1 昧
-6 晾
41A.02 (日/k)
-2 ○曚
-4 ○曝
41A.10 (日/十)
-2 曄
-6 晬
暉
41A.11 (日/土)
-3 ○旺
-5 曜
-6 曈
41A.21 (日/ㄴ)
-5 暱
41A.22 (日/丨)
-1 晰
-8 晞
-9 昕
△昨
41A.30 (日/一)
-1 曀
-6 暄
41A.40 (日/口)
-3 ○晤
-5 ○昭
41A.41 (日/図)
-3 △晒
-4 ○曙
-6 ○暗
41A.42 (日/冈)
-1 晡
○晴
-4 ○明
-9 昫
41A.50 (日/ㄱ)
-4 暘
-6 昉
-9 晦
41A.63 (日/、)
-9 曛
41A.70 (日/ㄴ)
-1 ○曉
晻
-3 ○曬
-5 昵
-6 ○曨
-9 ○晚
41A.71 (日/弋)
-8 ○曦
41A.80 (日/八)
-6 ○曠
暝
41A.81 (日/人)
-2 暵
-3 暌
暎
-9 ○映
41A.82 (日/乂)
-5 ○暇
-6 暾
-9 ○暖
曖
41A.91 (日/ノ)
-6 旷
41B.00 (目/亅)
-3 盱
-5 瞯
矙
-9 ○睜
41B.01 (目/小)
-1 ○眛
睞
○瞭
-2 眯
-3 眎
瞟
-9 睬
41B.02 (目/k)
-2 ○矇
-5 ○眼
-9 眽
睩
41B.10 (目/十)
-2 瞵
-6 睟
-9 ○瞬
睥
眸
41B.11 (目/土)
-1 ○睦
-2 瞠
-3 矐
-5 睚
-6 瞳
-9 ○睡
睢
41B.21 (目/ㄴ)
-5 眶
瞘
41B.22 (目/丨)
-8 睇
41B.30 (目/一)
-1 瞌
-3 瞪
41B.32 (目/フ)
-9 眵
41B.40 (目/口)
-6 ○瞎
-9 眙
○瞻
41B.41 (目/図)
-1 ○睹
-2 ○瞄
-4 ○睏
41B.42 (目/冈)
-1 ○睛
-2 ○瞞
-4 △眀
41B.50 (目/ㄱ)
-3 眄
-5 ○矚
-8 ○盼
盻
41B.63 (目/、)
-9 ○瞧
41B.70 (目/ㄴ)
-1 盹
-2 眦
○眺
-4 睍
-6 ○矓
-9 眊
睨
眈
41B.71 (目/弋)
-5 ○眠
41B.80 (目/八)
-2 瞋
○瞶
-6 矉
○瞑
41B.81 (目/人)
-3 睽
-9 瞅
41B.82 (目/乂)
-3 瞰
41B.83 (目/～)
-1 睫
-2 瞇
-9 眨
41B.91 (目/ノ)
-2 ○眇
41B.93 (目/く)
-2 瞜
-6 眩
41C.00 (貝/亅)
-1 ○財
賻
-2 ○則
-6 ○貯
41C.01 (貝/小)
-8 賒
41C.02 (貝/k)
-1 賕
-5 ○賑
○賬
41C.11 (貝/土)
-6 ○賍
41C.22 (貝/丨)
-8 ○賺
41C.30 (貝/一)
-2 贐
-9 △賉
41C.40 (貝/口)
-2 ○貼
-6 ○賠
-9 ○賂
○贍
○貽
41C.41 (貝/図)
-1 賭
-4 賵
-8 ○贈
41C.42 (貝/冈)
-1 ○賄
-2 ○購
-4 賙
41C.50 (貝/ㄱ)
-4 ○賜
41C.63 (貝/、)
-5 賥
41C.70 (貝/ㄴ)
-4 貺
41C.71 (貝/弋)
-7 ○賊
○賦
○賤
○贓
41C.80 (貝/八)
-1 ○贖
41C.81 (貝/人)
-6 賅
41C.82 (貝/乂)
-9 ○販
○敗
41C.83 (貝/～)
-9 ○貶
41D.00 (皿/亅)
-2 羇
-5 罽
-6 ○罰
-9 罦
41D.02 (皿/k)
-9 △[illegible]
41D.10 (皿/十)
-1 罼
-2 ○罩
41D.11 (皿/土)
-1 罣
-2 ○罹
-9 ○羅
41D.22 (皿/丨)
-2 ○罪
-3 罘
41D.30 (皿/一)
-1 ○置
-3 罡
41D.32 (皿/フ)
(ク) -9 △罗
41D.40 (皿/口)
-1 罟
-6 詈
41D.41 (皿/図)
-1 ○署
-8 罾
-9 罶
41D.50 (皿/ㄱ)
-2 ○羈
-5 罵
-9 ○蜀
41D.63 (皿/、)
-9 羆
41D.70 (皿/ㄴ)
-1 罨
-9 ○罷
41D.80 (皿/八)
-4 ○買
41D.83 (皿/～)
-2 遝
-3 ○還
-9 △邏
41D.93 (皿/く)
-1 △罢
41S.00 (図^{s}/亅)
-1 畸
疇
-2 剔
-3 町
○野
41S.01 (図^{s}/小)
-1 黥
-9 ○縣
41S.10 (図^{s}/十)
-2 ○畔
41S.11 (図^{s}/土)
-1 畦
-9 睢
41S.21 (図^{s}/ㄴ)
-2 黜
黮
41S.32 (図^{s}/フ)
-8 黔
-9 ○黟
41S.40 (図^{s}/口)
-1 黠
-2 ○點
-9 ○略
41S.41 (図^{s}/図)
-6 黯
41S.50 (図^{s}/ㄱ)
-9 ○助
勖
昀
黝
鵬
○鴨
鶡
鸛
鷃
41S.70 (図^{s}/ㄴ)
-2 毗

-6 ○晼
-9 氍

41S.80 (図ˢ/八)
-1 黷
-3 ○顆
顋
顒
顥
○顯

41S.81 (図ˢ/人)
-1 昳
○默
-9 ○歇

41S.82 (図ˢ/乂)
-9 畋
畯
斁

41S.91 (図ˢ/ノ)
-8 畛
-9 ○影
黪

42.30 (冈/一)
○皿
○且

42.40 (冈/口)
凸 *40.40
凹 *40.40

42.42 (冈/冈)
○月
○骨
○丹
○冊
○用
网
○同
○周
○岡
罔
咼

42.50 (冈/ㄱ)
(冈)○回

42.70 (冈/乚)
○几
○凡
甩
夙
凬
兕 *40.70
凨
凰
鳳
鼂
○風
(颩) -1 颷
-2 颭
颼
-3 ○飃
-4 颶
颺
-9 ○颳
○颱

42.82 (冈/乂)
殳

42.83 (冈/⺈)
迵
○週
○過
遯

42.93 (冈/く)
蜸

42A.00 (月/亅)
-1 肘
膊
脖
膞
-2 刖
-6 ○腑
-9 脬
胕

42A.01 (月/小)
-1 膝
膝
臊

42A.02 (月/⺊)
-1 ○膝
滕
-2 ○朦
○膿
-3 豚
-5 ○脹
-6 △脉
-9 ○脈
腺

42A.10 (月/十)
-2 膵
○胖
-3 ○肝
-8 肸
-9 脾

42A.11 (月/土)
-1 ○肚
睦
-2 臛
脞
○膛
-4 ○腥
臞
-6 臃
膣
-9 ○腫

42A.20 (月/廾)
-8 胼

42A.21 (月/乚)
-2 腨

42A.22 (月/丨)
-2 胇
腓
-4 胛
-6 ○肺
臍
-8 ○腳
-9 胙

42A.30 (月/一)
-2 臚
-3 肛
胚
脛
-4 △胆
膃
-6 膻
腔

42A.40 (月/口)
-1 ○膽
-6 膪
-8 ○膳
-9 胳
脳
○膾
○胎

42A.41 (月/図)
-2 △腊
○脂
-3 腷
腼
-4 胭
-6 腤
-8 ○膾
-9 膰
○腦

42A.42 (月/冈)
-1 脯
腩
-3 膈
-4 ○朋
胴
腡
-8 肭

42A.50 (月/ㄱ)
-1 胯
○勝
○騰
-4 膠
○腸
○鵬
-6 肪
○膀
-8 肣
-9 ○肋
脇
朐
○胸

42A.63 (月/丶)
-2 臙
-6 膴

42A.70 (月/乚)
-1 肫
腌
-2 胱
-3 肊
-4 ○肌
-5 ○肥
胞
-6 ○朧
脘
○腕
-8 ○脫
-9 肐
○胞
脆
臘

42A.71 (月/弋)
-2 ○臟
-7 ○膩
-9 胝

42A.72 (月/心)
-4 腮
-6 臆

42A.80 (月/八)
-1 臢
△臢
-2 腆
-6 臏

42A.81 (月/人)
-1 胰
膆
-2 ○膜
-8 朕
臉
-9 腴

42A.82 (月/乂)
-1 ○肢
臌
胈
-4 ○股
-5 ○服
-9 ○腹
朘

42A.83 (月/⺈)
-2 腱
-5 ○腿
-6 腋
腚

42A.91 (月/ノ)
-1 ○膨
-5 ○膠
-8 胗

42A.93 (月/く)
-1 胠
肱
膢
膡
-3 ○腰
-8 △脍

42B.00 (骨/亅)
-1 髆

42B.01 (骨/小)
-4 髁

42B.10 (骨/十)
-9 髀

42B.20 (骨/廾)
-2 ○髒

42B.30 (骨/一)
-2 ○體

42B.40 (骨/口)
-1 骷
-6 髂
-9 骼

42B.50 (骨/ㄱ)
-1 骻
-4 髑
-6 髈

42B.70 (骨/乚)
-1 髐
-6 ○骯
-9 骫
骴

42B.71 (骨/弋)
-9 骶

42B.80 (骨/八)
-6 髕

42B.81 (骨/人)
-6 骸

42B.82 (骨/乂)
-2 骹
-3 骾
-4 骰

42B.83 (骨/⺈)
-1 ○髓

42B.93 (骨/く)
-2 髏

42S.00 (冈ˢ/亅)
-2 ○删
○剛
剮

42S.11 (冈ˢ/土)
-9 ○雕

42S.42 (冈ˢ/冈)
-4 硼

42S.50 (冈ˢ/ㄱ)
-9 鵰

42S.82 (冈ˢ/乂)
-2 艭

42S.91 (冈ˢ/ノ)
-9 彤
○彫

50.00 (ㄱ/亅)
○尋

50.01 (ㄱ/小)
(木)○彙

50.10 (ㄱ/十)
○翠
翬

50.11 (ㄱ/土)
翟

50.20 (ㄱ/廾)
羿

50.21 (ㄱ/乚)
卍

50.22 (ㄱ/丨)
○弔
○彗

50.30 (ㄱ/一)
○丑
○翌

50.40 (ㄱ/口)
○召
50.41 (ㄱ/囚)
○習
50.42 (ㄱ/冈)
鬻
50.50 (ㄱ/ㄱ)
刁
○刀
○刃
○弓
○司
50.70 (ㄱ/ㄴ)
虱 *32.70
兕
○兎
50.72 (ㄱ/心)
○忌
○忍
50.80 (ㄱ/八)
○翼
負
50.81 (ㄱ/人)
△灵
50.83 (ㄱ/〜)
迢
逮
50.93 (ㄱ/く)
翏
50A.01 (弓/小)
-9 △弥
50A.02 (弓/k)
-5 ○張
50A.10 (弓/十)
-3 弭
-4 ○彈
50A.21 (弓/ㄴ)
-5 彄
50A.22 (弓/丨)
-2 ○引
50A.30 (弓/一)
-3 彊
50A.42 (弓/冈)
-3 ○彌
-4 弸
50A.50 (弓/ㄱ)
-2 ○粥
-3 弼
50A.70 (弓/ㄴ)
-2 ○弛
-5 弝
50A.80 (弓/八)
-6 彍
50A.82 (弓/乂)
-2 弢
50A.83 (弓/〜)
-9 弧
50A.93 (弓/く)
-6 ○弦
-9 ○弘
○強
50S.10 (ㄱ^{s}/十)
-8 △群
50S.22 (ㄱ^{s}/丨)
-3 ○那
○邵
50S.30 (ㄱ^{s}/一)
-3 ○疆
50S.50 (ㄱ^{s}/ㄱ)
-5 ○羽
○弱
-9 劭
鸐
50S.70 (ㄱ^{s}/ㄴ)
-3 翫
50S.71 (ㄱ^{s}/弋)
-7 戮
戳
50S.82 (ㄱ^{s}/乂)
-9 ○改 *52S.82
51.00 (ㄏ/亅)
鬥 *52B.00
○牙
鬎
鬡
鬁
鬋
鬖
(手) 擥
51.01 (ㄏ/小)
○緊
縏
鬃
鬆
51.02 (ㄏ/k)
○長
鬢
51.11 (ㄏ/土)
○堅
51.21 (ㄏ/ㄴ)
(匚) -1 匭
匱
-2 匵
匿
匝
匜
○臣
○匪
○匡
-3 叵
-4 匣
○區
-5 ○巨
-6 匹
○匾
○匯
-8 匳
-9 △医
○匠
匹
51.22 (ㄏ/丨)
△鬅
鬍
51.30 (ㄏ/一)
△竪
○豎
鑒
○鑒
○監
△鹽
○鹽
51.40 (ㄏ/口)
髻
髺
51.41 (ㄏ/囚)
腎
○醫
51.42 (ㄏ/冈)
○腎
髯
(髯)
鬅
○鬍
51.50 (ㄏ/ㄱ)
○馬
△髩
髫
鬗
髴
51.63 (ㄏ/丶)
熙
黳
51.70 (ㄏ/ㄴ)
(ㄴ) 髢
髦
髭
鬈
鬣
(儿) 髡
○覽
51.72 (ㄏ/心)
慝
51.80 (ㄏ/八)
○賢
鬒
○鬚
鬢
51.82 (ㄏ/乂)
○髮
鬘
51.83 (ㄏ/〜)
迓
51.93 (ㄏ/く)
○鬆
○蠶
51A.00 (厂/亅)
-1 △厨
-3 ○辱
△厨
-4 ○厚
擘
△厠
50A.01 (厂/小)
-9 ○原
51A.02 (厂/k)
-3 ○辰
-4 蜃
51A.10 (厂/十)
-9 廨
51A.11 (厂/土)
-1 厓
-2 厘
-4 ○壓
-9 ○雁
51A.22 (厂/丨)
-2 厮
-4 △所
51A.30 (厂/一)
-9 ○歷
51A.40 (厂/口)
-3 ○唇
51A.41 (厂/囚)
-2 厝
-4 靨
-9 ○曆
51A.42 (厂/冈)
-2 ○厲
-3 △脣
51A.50 (厂/ㄱ)
-3 厉
-9 △鴈
51A.63 (厂/丶)
-4 黶
51A.70 (厂/ㄴ)
-1 厐
-4 魘
-5 ○厄
-6 △龎
51A.72 (厂/心)
-3 △廳
-9 愿
51A.80 (厂/八)
-9 贋
51A.81 (厂/人)
-4 ○厭
-8 厥
(人) 仄
-9 灰
51A.82 (厂/乂)
-2 △廠
-3 △厦
51A.91 (厂/ノ)
-5 厂
51A.93 (厂/く)
-3 㕓
51B.00 (馬/亅)
-1 ○騎
-9 駙
51B.01 (馬/小)
-3 驃
-4 騾
51B.02 (馬/k)
-3 驟
-6 驤
51B.10 (馬/十)
-2 驊
-4 驛
-6 騂
51B.11 (馬/土)
-2 驩
-6 ○駐
-9 騅
51B.20 (馬/廾)
-9 駢
51B.21 (馬/ㄴ)
-5 ○驅
駆
51B.22 (馬/丨)
-2 驌
○馴
騑
-3 騸
-9 △驕
51B.30 (馬/一)
-2 驢
-4 駔
51B.40 (馬/口)
-1 驍
-9 駱
駘
51B.41 (馬/囚)
-4 駟
駰
-9 騮
51B.42 (馬/冈)
-4 駉
-6 ○騙
-9 驕
51B.50 (馬/ㄱ)
-2 騯
-6 騸
-9 駒
騶
51B.52 (馬/戶)
-6 駁
51B.70 (馬/ㄴ)
-1 驍
-2 ○馳
-3 驪
-6 駝
51B.72 (馬/心)
-8 △験
-9 驄
51B.80 (馬/八)
-2 騏
驥
51B.81 (馬/人)
-1 馱
-6 駭
-8 ○驗
-9 騤
51B.82 (馬/乂)
-3 馭
-5 駸
-8 駮
-9 ○駛

駿
51B.91 (馬/ノ)
-9 駗
51B.93 (馬/く)
-3 騷
51S.00 (厂s/亅)
-2 厰
(鬧)
-1 鬧 *52B.00
-2 鬨 *52B.00
-3 鬪 *52B.00
-4 ○鬬 *52B.00
-5 鬥 *52B.00
-6 ○鬧 *52B.00
-9 鬩 *52B.00
鬮 *52B.00
51S.10 (厂s/十)
-2 ○肆
51S.11 (厂s/土)
-9 ○雅
51S.22 (厂s/丨)
-2 ○卧
-3 ○邪
鄖
51S.40 (厂s/口)
-9 ○臨
51S.50 (厂s/ㄱ)
-9 劻
○勵
鴉
鷗
51S.70 (厂s/乚)
-3 甌
51S.80 (厂s/八)
-1 頣
-3 頤
○願
51S.81 (厂s/人)
-8 臥 *51S.22
-9 ○歐
51S.82 (厂s/乂)
-2 毆
-4 毆
52.00 (尸/亅)
擘
52.01 (尸/小)
檗
檗
52.02 (尸/k)
艮
襞
52.10 (尸/十)
○羣
52.11 (尸/土)
○壁
○璧
52.20 (尸/廾)
(廾)△昪
52.40 (尸/口)
(口) 㠯
○君
○譬
52.41 (尸/囟)
○眉
(日) 昬
𧨾
52.42 (尸/冈)
○臂
臀
52.50 (尸/ㄱ)
○劈
鷿
52.70 (尸/乚)
○己
○已
巳
○巴
甓
52.71 (尸/弋)
○民
52.72 (尸/心)
愍
○慰
52.80 (尸/八)
巽
52.81 (尸/人)
熨
52.83 (尸/〜)
○退
遐
○選
○避
躄
52.91 (尸/ノ)
○尸
尹
52.93 (尸/く)
嬖
52A.00 (戸/亅)
(屛)
-3 屙
孱
52A.01 (戸/小)
-2 ○屎
-6 屪
-9 屧
52A.02 (戸/k)
-2 ○展
○尿
52A.10 (戸/十)
-2 犀
-8 屖
52A.11 (戸/土)
-3 ○屋
52A.20 (戸/廾)
-9 ○屛
52A.21 (戸/乚)
-1 ○屆
-2 ○屈
-9 屜
52A.22 (戸/丨)
-4 屌
52A.30 (戸/一)
-4 △昼
52A.40 (戸/口)
-1 ○居
52A.41 (戸/囟)
-1 ○屠
-2 屇
-8 ○層
52A.42 (戸/冈)
-2 ○屑
-9 △属
52A.50 (戸/ㄱ)
-2 ○屬
-5 ○局
52A.63 (戸/丶)
-6 △尽
52A.70 (戸/乚)
-2 ○屁
○尼
-3 △屍
-9 ○尾
尻
52A.80 (戸/八)
-4 屭
-6 屄
52A.82 (戸/乂)
-9 屐
履
52A.83 (戸/〜)
-2 ○遲
-4 咫
-5 ○尺
-9 屣
屣
52A.91 (戸/ノ)
-5 戸
52A.93 (戸/く)
-2 ○屢
-9 屨
52B.00 (𠁣/亅)
(閇)
-1 ○閉
閇
△閑
○闌
○閨
○闔
闥
閎
閹
闚
-2 閧
閧
闓
闐
閫
闈
闠
-3 門
鬪
閈
閏
開
閒
閾
闃
-4 ○問
閪
閰
○闌
○鬬
○間
闆
闞
闤
闡
闒
○閞
-5 ○門
鬥
○闖
○闢
-6 鬧
閔
閡
闇
闍
閼
閬
○闊
○悶
閟
-7 閾
-8 閡
○閲
鬩
○閃
△閤
-9 闅
闍
闃
○閥
○閤
○閻
闢
○關
闟
52S.00 (尸s/亅)
-1 ○尉
-2 ○刷
52S.10 (尸s/十)
-6 辟
52S.22 (尸s/丨)
-3 郡
-5 ○即
52S.50 (尸s/ㄱ)
-9 鳰
鷳
52S.70 (尸s/乚)
-4 覞
-5 ○既
52S.82 (尸s/乂)
-4 ○殿
-9 ○改
60.00 (亠/亅)
○亦
亨
○享
○亭
(手) 挛
(子)△孪
60.01 (亠/小)
(小)○京
亶
稟
亵
(木) 栾
○棄
桒
稾
60.02 (亠/k)
襲
○豪
饔
○衣
(衣)
-1 ○褻
-2 ○衷
-3 衺
-4 ○哀
○衰
褭
○裏
○裹
○襄
-5 褱
-8 衮
-9 袤
袁
褒
△褒
○褎
60.10 (亠/十)
○辛
○卒
(十) 𢆉
○章
○率
○牽
○聾
60.11 (亠/土)
(王)○主
○望
○產
(土) 堃
○童
○塾
壅
○壟
雍
60.20 (亠/廾)
弈
(廾) 弁
60.21 (亠/乚)
○亡
△峦
饕
60.22 (亠/丨)
卞

○市
○帝
△廉 *61.22
○齊
齋
齎
齏

60.30 (亠/一)
○立
亶
銮

60.40 (亠/口)
○言
○客
啻
礱

60.41 (亠/囟)
○盲
○音
○畜

60.42 (亠/冈)
肓
○育
膂
○膏
○高
○商
○裔
(冈)△斋
△离
离

60.50 (亠/ㄱ)
○方
○旁
△弯
(𠂉)△鸢
鹜
旁

60.63 (亠/、)
○烹
○熟

60.70 (亠/乚)
(乚) 亳
○毫

甕
(儿) 亢
○充
兖
○亮
○竟
兗
竟
羸
羸
○羸

60.72 (亠/心)
○忘
○意
△恋
憝
懿

60.80 (亠/八)
○六
龔

60.81 (亠/人)
亥
奕

60.82 (亠/乂)
○文
○交
△変

60.83 (亠/𠃋)
○夜
(人) 甏
(辶)△迹
○這
○遊
○適

60.91 (亠/丿)
彦

60.93 (亠/く)
(女)○妄
○妾
娈
(厶)○玄
△蛮
蝱
螽

60A.00 (言/亅)
−1 ○討
○詩
譸
−3 ○訂
訏
訶
△詞
−5 ○訝
讕
譋
諄
−6 ○諭
−8 ○諍
−9 ○謝

60A.01 (言/小)
−1 諫
誄
○誅
−2 ○謀
諜
譟
−4 ○課
−6 ○諒

60A.02 (言/k)
−3 詠
−6 ○讓
○詠

60A.10 (言/十)
−1 ○計
−2 ○譁
○諱
−3 訐
○評
○譚
−4 ○譯
−6 誶
諢
−8 ○詳
−9 ○許

60A.11 (言/土)
−2 △讙
○謹
−6 ○註

−8 詮
−9 ○誰
誑

60A.21 (言/乚)
−2 諶
訕
詘
謔
−5 ○詎
誆
謳
−9 諂
○諂
○謠

60A.22 (言/丨)
−2 ○訃
○訓
○誹
−6 ○諦
−8 ○謙
−9 ○訴
○詐

60A.30 (言/一)
−3 訌
△証
○誣
○證
−4 詛
−6 誼
○誼
謐
−8 謚

60A.40 (言/口)
−1 詁
誥
詰
−2 ○諾
−3 ○語
−5 ○詔
−6 ○諮
−9 ○話
詬
譫
詒

60A.41 (言/囟)
−1 ○諸
−2 ○詣
○諧
−6 諳
譖
−8 ○譜
−9 譖

60A.42 (言/冈)
−1 諵
○請
−2 ○講
誚
−3 ○誦
諝
譎
−4 ○謂
誷
○調
−6 謫
諞
−8 ○論
訥

60A.50 (言/ㄱ)
−1 ○誇
−4 諤
○謁
−5 訒
○詞
詡
−6 ○訪
○謗
−8 讑
−9 ○誘
譌
○詢
詾
○誨
謅

60A.63 (言/、)
−2 讖
讜
−9 譙

60A.70 (言/乚)
−1 譊
詵
−2 ○謊
謔
訑
−3 ○訊
−4 諷
−5 ○記
−6 ○詫
−8 ○說
−9 ○託
訛
○訖
詭
讒

60A.71 (言/弋)
−6 ○識
−7 ○試
○誠
○誡
讖
−8 ○議
−9 詆
○譏

60A.72 (言/心)
−1 ○誌
−3 讔
−5 ○認
−8 諗

60A.80 (言/八)
−1 ○讚
○讀
−5 譔

60A.81 (言/人)
−1 詼
−2 謨
○讞
−4 ○誤
−6 ○該
−9 ○訣
諛
○談
誒

60A.82 (言/乂)
−2 護
詖
−3 諏
−4 謾
諼
○設
−6 譈
−8 △議
−9 諼
詉

60A.83 (言/𠃋)
−2 ○謎
○譴
−4 諟
−6 謫
−9 ○誕

60A.91 (言/丿)
−5 ○謬
−6 ○諺
−8 ○診

60A.93 (言/く)
−8 ○訟
△諭
−9 諉

60S.00 (亠ˢ/亅)
−2 △刘
○刻
剅
○剖
剷
○劑
爛
−5 爛
−6 竚
−9 旖

60S.01 (亠ˢ/小)
−1 竦
○辣

60S.02 (亠ˢ/k)
−9 ○旅

60S.10 (亠ˢ/十)
−6 ○辯
−9 ○瓣
○辨

○辦
辮
60S.11 (亠^{s}/土)
-9 旌
○雜
○離
60S.22 (亠^{s}/丨)
-3 ○郊
○部
郭
-9 旂
旆
○新
60S.30 (亠^{s}/一)
-6 竝
-9 旜
60S.40 (亠^{s}/口)
-2 ○站
-5 韶
60S.41 (亠^{s}/図)
-9 旛
60S.42 (亠^{s}/冈)
-1 ○靖
-2 ○端
-6 媥
-9 旃
60S.50 (亠^{s}/ㄱ)
-4 ○竭
-5 翊
-9 ○劾
○効
勍
勷
△韵
鶉
鷁
60S.63 (亠^{s}/丶)
-8 ○於
60S.70 (亠^{s}/乚)
-1 ○就
-2 ○龍
-3 瓿
-4 ○親
颯
-6 ○競
-9 ○施
旎
旋
○孰
旒
旒
○氈
60S.71 (亠^{s}/弋)
-5 ○氓
-7 斌
60S.80 (亠^{s}/八)
-3 頏
頞
○顏
○顫
○韻
-9 ○旗
贛
60S.81 (亠^{s}/人)
-9 △欬
○畝
○族
歆
竢
60S.82 (亠^{s}/乂)
-2 ○敲
皻
-4 ○毅
-9 ○放
○效
○敦
○竣
○敵
60S.83 (亠^{s}/〜)
-9 ○旋
瓤
60S.91 (亠^{s}/ノ)
-2 妙
-9 ○彰
60S.93 (亠^{s}/く)
-1 竑
(ム) -9 畆
61.00 (广/亅)
-1 ○摩
○廚
-2 㕑
-3 ○序
-4 ○廁
-9 ○府
61.01 (广/小)
-1 ○床
○麻
糜
縻
-2 穈
-6 廩
-9 麻
61.02 (广/⺊)
-2 ○康
61.10 (广/十)
-1 ○庫
-2 廱
-8 庠
-9 庳
廨
61.11 (广/土)
-1 △庄
-2 廛
○座
○塵
麈
-4 壥
61.22 (广/丨)
-1 靡
-2 ○席
○廝
-6 廓
廊
-8 ○廉
61.30 (广/一)
-2 ○廬
鏖
-6 ○应
61.40 (广/口)
-1 ○磨
-2 ○店
○唐
廫
61.41 (广/図)
-1 ○廂
-2 廧
(図) △庙
61.42 (广/冈)
-1 ○廟
-2 ○庸
-4 ○庽
-9 ○腐
○膺
61.50 (广/ㄱ)
-2 鴈
-9 ○鷹
61.63 (广/丶)
-2 ○庶
麃
-8 △庻
-9 廡
61.70 (广/乚)
-1 麾
○魔
彪
○庵
-2 庇
庀
鹿
麤
麅
麂
麑
麀
-6 ○龐
-9 庖
廐
61.71 (广/弋)
-9 ○底
61.72 (广/心)
-3 ○廳
-9 ○應
61.80 (广/八)
-2 ○廣
廎
-9 賡
61.81 (广/人)
-2 ○㢊
-9 ○庚
庾
61.82 (广/乂)
-1 庋
△废
-2 ○度
○廠
○慶
廋
-3 ○廈
○廢
-9 廄
61.83 (广/〜)
-2 ○遮
-9 ○庭
61.91 (广/ノ)
-5 ○廖
61.93 (广/く)
-1 ○麼
-3 廕
-9 △広
61A.00 (疒/亅)
-1 瘌
痔
-3 疔
疴
痾
㾐
-5 𤸷
-8 ○瘉
-9 ○痢
61A.01 (疒/小)
-1 痳
痲
○療
-4 瘭
-9 瘵
61A.02 (疒/⺊)
-3 瘃
-4 瘯
-5 ○痕
-8 ○癢
61A.10 (疒/十)
-4 癉
-5 ○癖
-6 瘁
○瘴
-8 △痒
-9 痺
○癬
61A.11 (疒/土)
-1 痓
-2 ○癱
-3 㾬
癃
-4 癯
-8 ○痊
-9 癰
61A.21 (疒/乚)
-2 ○瘧
疝
-4 ○癌
61A.22 (疒/丨)
-2 疿
痱
-4 痹
-8 疥
-9 痄
癤
61A.30 (疒/一)
-3 ○痘
疰
○症
痙
-4 疸
瘟
疽
-5 癧
-8 瘥
61A.40 (疒/口)
-2 瘩
痁
-3 痞
-8 ○瘡
-9 痂
△痴
61A.41 (疒/図)
-1 瘏
-2 痏
-4 痼
-6 瘖
-9 瘤
61A.42 (疒/冈)
-1 痡
-2 癘
-3 ○病
○痛
-4 痌
痭
-5 瘺
-9 瘠
瘸
癑
61A.50 (疒/ㄱ)
-4 瘍
-9 ○癆
痀
痗
61A.63 (疒/丶)
-6 瘀
-9 ○疼
61A.70 (疒/乚)
-1 疣
-2 疵
-4 ○瘋
-5 疤
痆
-9 疙
○疱
61A.71 (疒/弋)
-9 疷
61A.72 (疒/心)
-1 痣
-3 ○癮
-8 △癒
61A.80 (疒/八)
-1 癩
-2 癲

61A.81 (疒/人)
-1 痍
-2 瘼
-9 ○瘓
瘊
○痰
瘐
○疚
○疾

61A.82 (疒/乂)
-2 ○疲
○瘦
-3 △癈
-4 ○疫
-5 瘕
癜
-9 瘢
○癥
瘘

61A.83 (疒/〜)
-2 ○癡

61A.91 (疒/ノ)
-5 瘳
-6 痧
-8 疹

61A.93 (疒/く)
-2 瘻
-4 癭
-6 痃
-8 △瘉
-9 瘘

61S.00 (广ˢ/亅)
-2 廁

61S.10 (广ˢ/十)
-2 ○麟

61S.22 (广ˢ/丨)
-3 鄜
鄘
鄺

61S.50 (广ˢ/ㄱ)
-9 鷓
鷓

61S.80 (广ˢ/八)
-2 ○麒

62.00 (宀/亅)
-1 ○守
○寄
-2 搴
-3 ○宇
○字
-6 ○寧

62.01 (宀/小)
-1 ○宋
寮
-2 寨
○寐
-3 ○宗
-9 寀
○察
○案

62.02 (宀/ｋ)
-2 褰
-3 ○家
冢
-4 寰
-5 宸

62.10 (宀/十)
-1 ○牢
○軍
-6 ○宰
-8 ○罕
(十) -9 搴

62.11 (宀/土)
-2 ○塞
-3 △宝
○室

62.21 (宀/乚)
-3 寤
-5 ○宦
-6 ○密

62.22 (宀/丨)
-2 冪
-4 幂
幂

62.30 (宀/一)
-3 ○宣
-4 ○宜

62.40 (宀/口)
-1 ○害
-2 謇
寤
-3 宕
-4 ○官
○宮
-5 宭
-8 容
-9 ○客

62.41 (宀/図)
-2 ○宙
-3 ○富
-9 ○宿
○審

62.42 (宀/冈)
-1 ○宥
-2 ○宵
-4 ○寓
-6 △寗
-9 寯

62.50 (宀/ㄱ)
-2 騫
-3 ○寡
-9 ○寫

62.63 (宀/丶)
-2 ○寒

62.70 (宀/乚)
-2 ○寬
○它
-3 ○完
○冠
○寇
-5 ○冤
-6 ○寵
-9 ○宅
宂
宄
△宛

62.72 (宀/心)
-1 ○憲
-6 宓
-9 窸

62.80 (宀/八)
-2 ○賽
寘
-3 ○寅
○賓
△寶
-4 ○冥
○實
(八) 寘
-8 ○穴
-9 △实

62.81 (宀/人)
-2 ○寞
-9 灾

62.82 (宀/乂)
-2 ○寂
○寢
-3 冣
-6 寖
-9 変

62.83 (宀/〜)
-1 寁
-1 ○運
-2 蹇
-3 ○定
-4 逭

62.91 (宀/ノ)
-5 寥

62.93 (宀/く)
-1 ○宏
-4 ○宴
-6 ○蜜
-9 ○安

62A.00 (穴/亅)
-5 ○穿
-8 窬

62A.01 (穴/小)
-4 窠

62A.10 (穴/十)
-6 窣

62A.11 (穴/土)
-3 ○窒
窿
-6 窪

62A.20 (穴/卄)
-2 穽

62A.21 (穴/乚)
-5 ○窟
-9 窖

62A.22 (穴/丨)
-2 帘
-9 ○窄

62A.30 (穴/一)
-3 ○空

62A.32 (穴/フ)
-9 穸

62A.40 (穴/口)
-5 窘

62A.41 (穴/図)
-4 窅
-6 窨
-9 ○窗

62A.42 (穴/冈)
-4 ○窩
-9 ○竊

62A.50 (穴/ㄱ)
-1 窃
-5 穹
-9 ○窮
窈
窵

62A.63 (穴/丶)
-8 窯

62A.70 (穴/乚)
-1 窀
○竈
○窺
-2 窕
-9 竄
○究

62A.72 (穴/心)
(心) -9 △窓
△窻

62A.80 (穴/八)
-1 竇

62A.81 (穴/人)
-1 窾
○突

62A.82 (穴/乂)
-9 竅

62A.83 (穴/〜)
-8 邃
-9 窆
窳

62A.93 (穴/く)
-2 窶
-8 窬

62S.00 (宀ˢ/亅)
-2 剜
○割

62S.22 (宀ˢ/丨)
-3 鄆

62S.40 (宀ˢ/口)
-8 豁

62S.80 (宀ˢ/八)
-3 ○額

62S.82 (宀ˢ/乂)
-2 鞁

63.00 (丶/亅)
斈
(子) 学

63.01 (丶/小)
(木) △柒
○染
○梁
○渠
(米) ○粱
粢
粢
(糸) 縏

63.02 (丶/ｋ)
○永
○良
裟

63.10 (丶/十)
○斗
○準
○肇

63.11 (丶/土)
○塗

63.30 (丶/一)
○盜
○盪

63.40 (丶/口)
○咨
啓 *63D.40
(言) △誉

63.41 (丶/図)
(図) △峃

63.50 (丶/ㄱ)
(ㄱ) △门

63.63 (丶/丶)
鯊

63.70 (丶/乚)
○瓷
△凴
(儿) △覚

63.72 (丶/心)
○心 *72.72
○必 *72.72
恣
懣
○憑
懑
瀿

63.80 (丶/八)
○資

63.81 (丶/人)
○溦

63.82 (丶/乂)
△雙

63.83 (丶/〜)
○之
祁

63.91 (丶/ノ)
○戸

63.93 (丶/く)
○姿
娑
○婆

63A.00 (氵/亅)
-1 浡
溥
澍
○濤
-3 汀

○汙
○河
洌
洌
-4 ○測
-5 潯
溽
涮
○潺
○潤
△潤 *52B.00
澗
瀾
-6 淳
○游
濘
-8 湔
○渝
-9 ○浮
○淨
瀏
漪

63A.01 (氵/小)
-1 ○湅
○沐
沬
○沫
沭
○淋
洙
○潔
溱
潦
-3 溧
潥
○漂
-4 ○澡
-5 ○源
-6 ○涼
澟
凛
淙
○深
-8 涂

-9 ○滌
滁
濼

63A.02 (氵/⺊)
-1 ○漆
-2 ○濃
○濛
○冰
-3 涿
-4 ○瀑
-5 ○漲
-6 ○滾
濠
瀼
○泳
○浪
-8 漾
滄
(滄)
-9 ○派
○添
渌

63A.10 (氵/十)
-1 ○汁
澣
-2 淖
泮
○津
潾
-3 ○汗
洱
○潭
-4 ○澤
-5 澼
-6 淬
○漳
滸
○滓
渾
-8 ○洋
-9 湃
洚

63A.11 (氵/土)
-2 ○灌

○灘
-3 ○汪
湮
○溼
-4 涅
-5 濯
○涯
渥
-6 ○注
潼
-9 ○淫
淮
淮
瀅

63A.20 (氵/廿)
-2 漭
-9 洴
(洴)
濞

63A.21 (氵/乚)
-2 湛
汕
泄
-3 涵
-5 △滙 *51.21
滙
-9 ○滔

63A.22 (氵/丨)
-1 ○浙
淅
○漸
-2 ○瀟
澌
澌
○沖
(沖)
沛
○沸
○洲
○淵
○滯
-3 泲
-6 沭
○沛

濂
○濟
-8 ○泠 *63A.63
○涕
-9 沂

63A.30 (氵/一)
-1 渣
淕
-2 沚
瀣
瀘
灃
灩
澧
-3 ○江
泜
洹
涇
○澄
-4 ○溫
沮
-5 澀
○濫
瀝
-6 ○泣
澶
涳
渲
-8 淦
溢
溢
-9 洫
湦 *63A.11
湴

63A.32 (氵/フ)
-2 涔
-9 汐

63A.40 (氵/口)
-1 ○沽
○浩
渚
-2 ○沾
-4 ○沿
-5 ○沼

-6 涪
溏
○溶
-8 ○浴
○洽
滄
-9 ○活
○洛
澹
洳
冶
○治

63A.41 (氵/図)
-1 ○湘
渚
-2 泔
漕
○滷
濬
○油
-3 △洒
○酒
湎
潴
-4 汩
泪
泗
泅
洄
涸
澗
-5 ○湄
-6 ○瀋
湆
-8 澮
-9 ○潛
○溜
○潘
○泊
湶
淄

63A.42 (氵/冈)
-1 ○清
清

○浦
淯
○湖
潸
○潮
-2 ○滿
○溝
湍
○消
淌
-3 湎
濡
灞
涌
-4 ○涓
洞
○洞
○凋
渦
○滑
-5 ○瀰
○漏
-6 漓
○滴
-8 ○溯
○淪
淪
○淆
汭

63A.50 (氵/ㄱ)
-1 渤
○瀚
沏
-3 △汚
污
汅
○鴻
泐
○湧
-4 ○渴
○湯
○濁
-5 ○溺
○馮

-6 滂
○瀉
-8 汾
滃
-9 渴
澇
洵
○洶
○淘
○海
○灣

63A.63 (氵/丶)
-4 △濕
-6 淤
-8 泠
○冷
-9 ○漁

63A.70 (氵/乚)
-1 沌
○洗
○澆
○淹
-2 ○港
泚
○池
洮
灩
-3 沅
○灑
汎
-4 ○況
△況
浥
○混
○汎
淝
澠
-5 △氾
汜
○泥
-6 沆
○流
瀧
瀛

漉
沱
浣
○漚
△沉
-9 氿
○洸
○漑
汔
○汽
○泡
浼
63A.71 (氵/弋)
-4 濺
-5 泯
-7 ○洩
○淺
淢
○滅
○滅
63A.72 (氵/心)
-2 濾
滮
-6 沁
泌
-8 淰
63A.80 (氵/八)
-1 瀆
瀆
滇
瀨
漬
-2 ○洪
淇
淟
潢
湞
瀕
○潰
-4 灝
-6 ○演
○濱
溟
瀠
-8 汃
-9 浜
63A.81 (氵/人)
-1 ○漱
○汰
涑
浹
○湊
-2 ○漠
○漢
-6 ○淚
-8 渼
-9 渙
○沃
湫
○溪
溴
○澳
○決
泱
洑
○淡
濮
○次
湊
63A.82 (氵/乂)
-1 ○淩
-2 濩
○淑
潊
○波
溲
-3 汊
汲
○潑
-4 ○漫
-5 ○浸
○澱
-6 汶
○潵
○渡
-8 潋
-9 湲
○激
○沒
○浚
63A.83 (氵/乛)
-1 漣
-2 ○凝
-6 ○液
○漩
淀
-9 ○泛
○涎
63A.91 (氵/ノ)
-1 ○澎
-2 ○涉
○沙
-4 ○渺
-5 漻
-6 △沪
-8 沴
-9 汐 *63A.32
○滲
63A.93 (氵/く)
-1 ○淒
○淞
○法
-5 泓
-6 泫
瀘
-8 △渝
○滋
-9 ○汝
63B.00 (礻/亅)
-1 ○禱
△祷
63B.01 (礻/小)
-2 祼
63B.02 (礻/阝)
-6 禳
-9 ○祿
63B.10 (礻/十)
-4 禪
-8 ○祥
63B.11 (礻/土)
-1 ○社
-3 禋
63B.22 (礻/丨)
-2 ○神
-3 祁
-9 ○祈
祚
63B.30 (礻/一)
-2 祉
○禮
-4 ○祖
63B.40 (礻/口)
-1 祜
○禧
○祐
63B.41 (礻/囗)
-2 禣
-3 ○福
63B.42 (礻/冈)
-3 禰
-4 ○禍
63B.50 (礻/㇆)
-5 ○祠
禡
63B.70 (礻/乚)
-2 △礼
祧
-4 ○祝
○視
-5 ○祀
63B.71 (礻/弋)
-9 祇
祗
禨
63B.72 (礻/心)
-6 △祕
63B.80 (礻/八)
-1 禛
-2 祺
禎
63B.81 (礻/人)
-1 禊
-3 祆
祅
63B.82 (礻/乂)
-1 祓
63B.93 (礻/く)
-1 祛
63C.00 (衤/亅)
-1 襻
-5 褥
襉
襴
63C.01 (衤/小)
-1 袜
襟
-4 裸
-9 褓
△襍
63C.02 (衤/阝)
-1 裱
-2 襛
-4 襮
-5 裉
63C.10 (衤/十)
-2 褘
-6 ○褲
褌
-9 裨
63C.11 (衤/土)
-4 裎
△裡
-9 衽
63C.22 (衤/丨)
-1 △褂
-6 褯
63C.30 (衤/一)
-4 袓
-5 襤
63C.32 (衤/フ)
-8 衿
63C.40 (衤/口)
-2 褡
-5 △裙
裾
-8 ○裕
袷
-9 襜
63C.41 (衤/囗)
-1 褚
-2 ○袖
襠
-4 袒
裀
-5 褶
63C.42 (衤/冈)
-1 ○補
-2 褙
-3 襦
-6 褊
褵
-8 衲
63C.50 (衤/㇆)
-1 △袴
-4 裼
褐
褟
-5 ○初
63C.70 (衤/乚)
-4 裩
襬
-6 ○襯
-9 ○褫
袍
裷
63C.71 (衤/弋)
-2 ○襪
-9 △衹
63C.81 (衤/人)
-1 裌
-2 襆
-8 襝
-9 袄
袂
袱
襖
63C.82 (衤/乂)
-2 ○被
-3 衩
裰
襏
-9 ○複
63C.83 (衤/乛)
-1 褳
-5 ○褪
63C.91 (衤/ノ)
-8 袗
-9 ○衫
63C.93 (衤/く)
-1 袪
-2 褸
-5 襁
63D.01 (戶/小)
棨 *63.01
綮 *63.01
63D.02 (戶/阝)
-6 扆
63D.10 (戶/十)
-6 戽
肇 *63.10
63D.11 (戶/土)
-9 ○扉
63D.22 (戶/丨)
-2 屏
63D.40 (戶/口)
-9 △啓 *63S.82
63D.42 (戶/冈)
-4 ○肩
○扁
扃
63D.50 (戶/㇆)
-5 ○扇
-6 ○房
63D.70 (戶/乚)
-4 扈
63D.81 (戶/人)
-1 戾
63D.83 (戶/乛)
-4 ○遍
63D.91 (戶/ノ)
-5 ○戶
63S.22 (丶ˢ/丨)
-3 ○郎
63S.42 (丶ˢ/冈)
-4 ○朗

63S.50 (、^{s}/ㄱ)
–5 翩
63S.80 (、^{s}/ㅅ)
–3 ○顧
63S.82 (、^{s}/乂)
–9 △啟
70.70 (ㄴ/ㄴ)
(ㄴ) ○七 *10.70
匕 *21A.70
70S.22 (ㄴ^{s}/丨)
–3 △邨 *10S.22
70S.50 (ㄴ^{s}/ㄱ)
–9 鴇 *21S.50
70S.70 (ㄴ^{s}/ㄴ)
–2 ○比 *21S.70
71.30 (乜/一)
盞
○盛
71.42 (乜/冈)
屩
71.50 (乜/ㄱ)
鳶
71.71 (乜/乜)
(弋) 弋
(戈) ○戈
△弌
△弎
戎
○戒
○式
○或
彧
忒
曳
○武
○戔
△貳
(戊) 戊
戍
戌
○成
咸
威
○戚
臧
○感
71.72 (乜/心)
慼
惑
71.83 (乜/〜)
蹵
71S.00 (乜^{s}/亅)
–2 ○划
剗
71S.50 (乜^{s}/ㄱ)
–9 鵡
71S.80 (乜^{s}/ㅅ)
–3 顣
72.72 (心/心)
(心) ○心
○必
80.00 (ㅅ/亅)
○前
○兼 *80.22
○尊
孳
○導
80.01 (ㅅ/小)
槊
80.02 (ㅅ/k)
○養
80.10 (ㅅ/十)
○羊
80.11 (ㅅ/土)
坌
塑
80.20 (ㅅ/卄)
○并
80.21 (ㅅ/ㄴ)
岔
80.22 (ㅅ/丨)
△竒
丫
○弟
△斧
(リ) △养
○兼
○爺
80.30 (ㅅ/一)
○並
△竝
○差
○羞
○釜
(皿) ○盆
○益
△盖
80.32 (ㅅ/フ)
○爹
80.40 (ㅅ/口)
(口) ○谷
○善
△谷 *92A.40
80.41 (ㅅ/図)
○首
○曾
○普
○着
○酋
80.50 (ㅅ/ㄱ)
○分
兮
○翁
剪
翦
鷟
80.63 (ㅅ/、)
羔
○煎
△羔 *80.22
羹 *12.63
80.70 (ㅅ/ㄴ)
○爸
○兌
羌
兓
羛 *63.70
80.71 (ㅅ/乜)
○義
羲
80.72 (ㅅ/心)
○忿
○恙
○慈
○慾
愬
80.80 (ㅅ/ㅅ)
○八
○貧
80.81 (ㅅ/人)
(大) △关
○美
(人) △美
○奠
○羨
羹
80.82 (ㅅ/乂)
○父
80.83 (ㅅ/〜)
○送
○逆
遡
○迸
○道
○遂
遒
○遵
80.93 (ㅅ/く)
○公
姜
(ム) △会
○兹
80S.00 (ㅅ^{s}/亅)
–2 ○剃
80S.22 (ㅅ^{s}/丨)
–3 邠
△郤
○鄭
鄯
–5 ○郤
80S.30 (ㅅ^{s}/一)
–6 羶
80S.42 (ㅅ^{s}/冈)
–4 朔
80S.50 (ㅅ^{s}/ㄱ)
–4 羯
羈
–5 翂
○翔
–9 鶒
鴿
鷁
鵜
80S.63 (ㅅ^{s}/、)
–8 羚
80S.70 (ㅅ^{s}/ㄴ)
–3 ○瓶
甌
–5 羓
80S.71 (ㅅ^{s}/乜)
–7 ○羢
羬
–9 羝
80S.80 (ㅅ^{s}/ㅅ)
–3 ○頒
○頌
80S.81 (ㅅ^{s}/人)
–1 ○猷
–9 ○欲
○歉
80S.82 (ㅅ^{s}/乂)
–4 羖
81.00 (人/亅)
○俞
○拿
81.01 (人/小)
佘
○余
81.02 (人/k)
汆
○食
衾
81.10 (人/十)
○傘
81.11 (人/土)
○全
81.21 (人/ㄴ)
(ㄴ) 匹
81.22 (人/丨)
△个
○介
○命
令 *81.63
81.30 (人/一)
△仝
○企
○金
鑫
○盒
龕
81.32 (人/フ)
○今
81.40 (人/口)
○合
○含
○舍
○倉
81.41 (人/図)
畬
○會
81.42 (人/冈)
○內
○肉
离
○禽
侖
81.50 (人/ㄱ)
翕
81.63 (人/、)
○令
81.70 (人/ㄴ)
龕
岔
81.72 (人/心)
○念
愈
忩
81.80 (人/ㅅ)
○貪
81.81 (人/人)
○人
○入
△从
众
僉
81.83 (人/〜)
○途
△逾
81.93 (人/く)
△兪
81A.00 (金/亅)
–1 鏄
○鑄
錡
–2 鑮
鏘
釗
–3 釕
釘
鉤
鋼
鍘
–4 鍘
鋝
–5 鍆
鐗
錭
鑭
–8 鐏
鐘
鑰
–9 錚
81A.01 (金/小)
–1 銖
鍊
錸
鐐
鐐
–3 鏢
–4 錁
–6 鑔
–9 鎳
鑠
81A.02 (金/k)
–1 △銾
–2 鑢
–4 鐶
–5 ○銀

−6 鈫
鎄
○鑲
鋃
鎵
−9 ○錄

81A.10 (金/十)
−1 ○針
鉢
−3 鉺
鑷
−4 銲
鐸
−6 ○鋅
−9 鋒

81A.11 (金/土)
−1 釷
−2 鑵
銼
鏜
−3 鈺
−4 ○鑼
鋰
−5 鏗
−6 鏟
○鐘
−8 ○銓
−9 ○鍾
錘
錐
鍠

81A.20 (金/廾)
−1 鉼

81A.21 (金/乚)
−2 鋩
−5 ○鉅
鉕
−9 鍤

81A.22 (金/丨)
−1 鉓
−2 △鈡
釙
鉡
釧

○鏽
−3 釬
−4 鉀
−6 鐮
鍗
(碲)
鈰
−8 銻
鈴 *81A.63
−9 釿
○錦

81A.30 (金/一)
−2 鑪
鎧
−3 鉦
錳
鐙
−4 鉭
鉏
−5 鈕
△鑑
−8 鎰

81A.32 (金/フ)
−4 鏐
−8 鈐

81A.40 (金/口)
−1 鈷
鋯
−2 鎝
鍩
−4 釦
○鋁
○鉛
−5 ○鋸
−6 鎔
錇
−8 鉿
△鎗
−9 銛
○銘
鉻
鉫

81A.41 (金/囗)
−1 鍺

−2 錨
鉗
○錯
鍇
鈾
鐺
−3 鐳
−4 鈿
鉬
銦
錮
−5 鎇
−8 鐠
−9 鉑
鐂
鎦

81A.42 (金/冂)
−1 ○鋪
銪
−2 銷
−3 鎘
鐍
−4 ○銅
○鋼
○鍋
−6 鎬
鏑
鏞
−8 ○錀
鈉
−9 鐫

81A.50 (金/ㄱ)
−1 銬
−3 鈣
釢
−4 鎶
○錫
鐲
鋤
−5 鋦
−6 鈁
○鎊
−9 △銹
鎢

○釣
○鈞
銁
○鉤
鋂
鐒

81A.63 (金/丶)
−2 钂
−6 鑣
−8 ○鈴
−9 鐎

81A.70 (金/乚)
−1 鈍
銑
鐃
銠
−2 銧
銚
釓
鈚
−3 釔
−4 釩
−5 鈀
鈮
−6 鈧
鉈
銃
○鏡
鑞
−8 銳
−9 銫
鉋
鑱
鑞

81A.71 (金/弋)
−1 ○鐵
−7 鉞
○錢
鉽
鍼
鑯
−9 鋨

81A.72 (金/心)
−2 鑢

−4 鍶
−6 鐿
鉍

81A.80 (金/八)
−1 ○鑽
−2 ○鎮
○鎖
鐨
−4 鋇
−6 鑌
△鑛
−9 鑕

81A.81 (金/人)
−1 鍥
銕
鈦
鈇
△鉄
鋏
−2 鏷
−6 鏃
−8 鎂
−9 ○欽
欽
鍬

81A.82 (金/乂)
−1 鈸
−2 鈙
鑊
鈹
−3 釵
−4 鏝
−5 鋟
−6 鉸
○鍍
−8 鐓
−9 鍰
鑁
鍛

81A.83 (金/〜)
−1 鏈
−2 鍵
−6 鏇
錠

−9 鋌
鎚

81A.91 (金/ノ)
−2 ○鈔
−9 釤

81A.93 (金/く)
−2 鎡
鏤
−5 鎓
−6 鉣
−9 銩
鈫

81B.00 (食/亅)
−1 餑
餺

81B.01 (食/小)
−1 餗
−4 餜
−8 ○餘

81B.02 (食/阝)
−4 ○餵
−5 餦

81A.10 (食/十)
−3 餌

81B.11 (食/土)
−2 饉
−9 ○飪

81B.20 (食/廾)
−8 ○餅

81B.21 (食/乚)
−2 飿
−9 餡

81B.22 (食/丨)
−3 飦
−6 飥
−9 ○飾

81B.30 (食/一)
−3 飷
−6 饘
−8 饈

81B.40 (食/口)
−6 饎
○館
−8 △饍

−9 餂
飴

81B.41 (食/囗)
−9 餾

81B.42 (食/冂)
−1 餔
餬
−8 餚
−9 ○餉

81B.50 (食/ㄱ)
−4 餳
餲
−5 飼
−9 ○飭

81B.63 (食/丶)
−8 △餻

81B.70 (食/乚)
−1 飩
饒
−4 餛
△飢
−9 餽
○飽
餼
饞

81B.71 (食/弋)
−7 ○餞
−9 ○餓
○饑

81B.72 (食/心)
−6 飶

81B.81 (食/八)
−2 饋
−5 饌

81B.81 (食/人)
−2 饃
−9 飫
餱
○飲

81B.82 (食/乂)
−2 餿
−4 饅
−6 餃
−9 ○飯

餕

81B.93 (食/く)
–2 ○蝕
–9 餒
餧

81S.00 (人ˢ/亅)
–2 ○創
剏
○劍
–3 ○舒

81S.01 (人ˢ/小)
–9 穌

81S.10 (人ˢ/十)
–1 ○斜

81S.11 (人ˢ/土)
–5 糴

81S.22 (人ˢ/丨)
–3 郤

81S.30 (人ˢ/一)
–4 俎

81S.40 (人ˢ/口)
–6 舘

81S.42 (人ˢ/冈)
–1 △舖

81S.50 (人ˢ/㇆)
–5 △劒
劔
–9 鴒
○鴿

81S.70 (人ˢ/乚)
–3 瓴
–4 覦
–9 毹

81S.71 (人ˢ/弋)
–7 戧

81S.80 (人ˢ/八)
–3 ○領
頷
顩

81S.81 (人ˢ/人)
–8 △从
–9 歛
欽
歙

81S.82 (人ˢ/乂)
–2 敍
–3 ○敘
–9 斂

82.21 (乂/乚)
凶 *21.21

82.22 (乂/丨)
○希

82.42 (乂/冈)
肴

82.70 (乂/乚)
○兇 *21.70

82.82 (乂/乂)
爻
○爻
爻

82S.00 (乂ˢ/亅)
–2 刈
刹

82S.22 (乂ˢ/丨)
–3 郄
郗

82S.71 (乂ˢ/弋)
–7 弑

82S.81 (乂ˢ/人)
–9 欷

82S.82 (乂ˢ/乂)
–4 ○殺
殽
–9 教

90.00 (㇒/亅)
○手
(手)○舉
○乎
○爭
豸 *91.00
○孚
○季
○學
○爵

90.01 (㇒/小)
○禾
(木)○采
○棃
(小)○系
○秉
○乘

90.02 (㇒/⺊)
忝
黍
○黎

90.10 (㇒/十)
○千
(十)秊
○犂
○舜
△舉

90.11 (㇒/土)
壬
○垂
○重

90.20 (㇒/卄)
升
△并 *91.20
昇

90.21 (㇒/乚)
臼
岳
臿
舀

90.22 (㇒/丨)
○斤
○斥
乓
○乖
–1 △帋
△帮
○幫
(リ)△乔

90.30 (㇒/一)
○丘
盥
垂
疊
鍪

90.40 (㇒/口)
○后
○舌
○吞
嚳
礐
嚳

90.41 (㇒/囚)
(日)○昏
○香
(目)○看
○盾
(囚)○留
番

90.42 (㇒/冈)
○禹
○喬

90.50 (㇒/㇆)
○秀
(力)○舅
釁
舄
○爲
△鵞
鶖
鷽

90.63 (㇒/丶)
乒
熏
△勳 *90S.50
黧
黨

90.70 (㇒/乚)
(乚)卮
甃
(儿)禿
○兒
○覓
○覺
○毛
(毛)–1 毬
–2 毽
–6 △氈
–7 毧
–8 氌
–9 ○毯
毺
毳
(儿)○兎
毵
(乚)○鼠
(鼠)–1 鼢
–2 鼬
–3 鼩
鼯
–5 鼴
鼦
–6 鼫
–8 鼬
–9 鼷
兜

90.71 (㇒/弋)
○氏
○我

90.72 (㇒/心)
○悉
○愁
○愍
○憩
○懇 *91.72

90.80 (㇒/八)
○兵
○與
△舆
興
輿
○貿
○質
釁

90.81 (㇒/人)
○夭
奚
爨

90.82 (㇒/乂)
○反
○受
爰
○愛

90.83 (㇒/乀)
(乀)○乏
○爪
爬
○瓜
廷
○延
(辶)返
迁
○近
○迎
适
逅
○透
逶
遁
○遞
遛
○遙 *92.83
邈 *91.83

90.91 (㇒/ノ)
乓

90.93 (㇒/く)
○丢
(厶)蚕 *31.93
○妥
○委

90A.00 (禾/亅)
–2 ○利

90A.01 (禾/小)
–1 秫
秣
稞
–4 稞
–9 △称

90A.02 (禾/⺊)
–2 穠
–6 穰
穅
稼
稂

90A.10 (禾/十)
–1 ○科
–3 秤
稈
–4 稗
–5 稗
–9 稗

90A.11 (禾/土)
–1 稑
–4 ○程
–9 種
○稚

90A.21 (禾/乚)
–1 稆
–2 秈
–9 ○稻

90A.22 (禾/丨)
–2 秭
–8 稊
○稀

90A.30 (禾/一)
–4 ○租

90A.32 (禾/フ)
–9 移

90A.40 (禾/口)
–4 ○和

90A.41 (禾/囚)
–1 穡
稽
–2 稭

90A.42 (禾/冈)
–2 ○稍
–3 穤
–4 稠
–6 ○稿
–9 ○稱

90A.63 (禾/丶)
–6 穮
–9 穛

90A.70 (禾/乚)
–2 秕
–6 秔
–8 ○稅

90A.71 (禾/弋)
–2 ○穢
–9 秪

90A.72 (禾/心)
–1 ○穗
–6 ○秘
–8 稔
–9 ○穩

90A.80 (禾/八)
-1 ○積
-2 稹
90A.81 (禾/人)
-1 ○秩
-3 稉
-9 ○秋
○秧
90A.82 (禾/乂)
-1 稜
-2 ○穫
-4 稷
90A.91 (禾/ノ)
-2 ○秒
-9 ○穆
90A.93 (禾/く)
-3 秐
-9 ○私
90S.00 (ーˢ/亅)
-2 ○刋
刮
○剩
劉
-5 ○孵
-8 掰
掎
90S.02 (ーˢ/丬)
-9 舔
90S.10 (ーˢ/十)
-3 ○拜
-4 ○釋
-6 △辞
辫
○辭
90S.11 (ーˢ/土)
-9 ○雞
90S.22 (ーˢ/丨)
-3 ○邱
○邸
郛
○郵
鄱
-5 印
○印

卯
○卵
-9 ○卿
○所
斲
斵
○邦 *10S.22
90S.40 (ーˢ/口)
-2 ○黏
-8 谿
90S.41 (ーˢ/図)
-2 ○甜
釉
90S.50 (ーˢ/ㄱ)
-5 ○翻
-9 ○動
鵰
○鵾
△鷄
○勳
90S.70 (ーˢ/乚)
-2 ○乳
○亂
虢
-3 黐 *90S.50
-4 飆 *92S.70
-9 ○魏
90S.71 (ーˢ/七)
-9 舐
90S.72 (ーˢ/心)
-6 謐
90S.80 (ーˢ/八)
-3 頎
○頹
90S.81 (ーˢ/人)
-9 ○欣
歃
歟
90S.82 (ーˢ/乂)
-4 ○段
○殷
○毀
-9 馥

90S.91 (ーˢ/ノ)
-9 ○彩
91.00 (ノ/亅)
○身
豸
91.01 (ノ/小)
(亅) 糸
(木)○架
梟
梟
○集
槃
槩
○棨
(小)○禦
縈
91.02 (ノ/丬)
(水)○泉
衆
滎
(衣)○袋
袈
裊
91.10 (ノ/十)
(十) 卆
皁
○卑
阜
隼
臯
臯
犖
犨
○聳
91.11 (ノ/土)
○皇
○堡
○墾
塋
○瑩
91.20 (ノ/廾)
弃
○鼻

91.21 (ノ/乚)
(山) 岱
島
嶨
91.22 (ノ/丨)
彳
○川 *22.22
○州 *22.22
○弗 *22.22
○片
○帛
91.30 (ノ/一)
○血
盇
○暨
○盤
91.40 (ノ/口)
○售
○營
○磐
○譽
91.41 (ノ/図)
○白
○自
○囟
旮
囱
-9 △临
91.42 (ノ/冈)
○內 *81.42
○肉 *81.42
○向
甪
○舟
○脊
○脅
雋
91.50 (ノ/ㄱ)
○粵
(力)○力
△办
○勞
○島
△為

(灬)○駕
○烏
○鳥
鴦
○鶯
91.63 (ノ/丶)
○焦
黛
91.70 (ノ/乚)
(乚)○皂
煢
(九)○九
○丸
○旭
馗
(儿)○兜 *90.70
△凭
凫
凣
○鬼
(魁)-2 魈
魅
魃
○魁
魎
魍
魑
魊
魋
○兆 *22.70
91.72 (ノ/心)
偬
恁
息
恖
悠
您
愆
慫
○懥
○懲
懇
91.80 (ノ/八)
(八)△兴

○貨
○賀
○貸
○賃
91.81 (ノ/人)
○央
臾
△头
(大)○臭
奧
(火)○火
○炎
熒
煲
91.82 (ノ/乂)
○史
○隻
燮
○雙
91.83 (ノ/⺃)
(人) 氽
(辶) 迦
○迫
逈
○追
○進
遑
○邀
○邊
○边
○逃 *22.83
○逛
○逖
△迩
邈
91.93 (ノ/く)
(女) 嫛
(厶) 么
○盤
○螢
蠹 *51.93
91A.00 (亻/亅)
-1 ○付
傅

○傳
○侍
○儔
○倚
-3 ○仃
○何
○例
○倒
○仔
-4 ○側
-5 ○們
-6 ○停
○俯
○佇
-8 ○倫
-9 ○俐
○俘
91A.01 (亻/小)
-1 ○休
△体 *91A.10
侏
俫
倷
○僚
○僄
-3 ○保
-4 ○係
-9 ○你
○倏
○條
○傑
○傺
91A.02 (亻/丬)
-1 俅
○俵
-2 ○儂
-4 ○儇
○假
-5 ○倀
-6 ○依
○傢
○假
-9 ○像

91A.10 (亻/十)
-1 ○什
○件
△体
○倖
○俸
-2 倬
○伴
○偉
-3 伻
-5 ○僻
-6 倅
-8 佯
-9 △仟
○俾
仵
侔

91A.11 (亻/土)
-1 ○仕
○佳
-2 ○僅
儺
○催
-3 ○侄
-4 儸
俚
-6 ○住
○隹
△僮
△僱
-9 ○任

91A.20 (亻/廾)
-9 ○併

91A.21 (亻/乚)
-2 ○仙
-5 佢
偃
傴
倔
-9 傜

91A.22 (亻/丨)
-1 ○佈
-2 仆
○仲
○伸
○佛
俳
-6 侪
儕
-8 △价
-9 ○仰
○作
△侨

91A.30 (亻/一)
-1 ○值
○佐
-2 ○儘
-3 ○仁
仨
○僵
○伍
佂
伾
-4 ○但
-6 ○位
倥

91A.32 (亻/フ)
-9 ○侈

91A.40 (亻/口)
-1 ○估
僖
○佑
偌
-2 △佔
-4 ○侶
-5 倨
-6 ○信
○倍
倌
-8 ○俗
佮
傖
-9 伽
儋
(言) 讐

91A.41 (亻/図)
-2 ○借
○偕
-3 偪
△佰
價
-4 ○倡
○佃
○偏
○個
-6 ○儲
-8 ○僧
儈
-9 ○伯
△俻
偺
-9 僣

91A.42 (亻/冈)
-1 倩
侑
-2 ○備
俏
○倘
-3 ○倆
○儒
俑
-4 ○偶
△佣
侗
倜
-6 ○傭
○偏
侑
-8 ○倫
-9 ○僑
俑
儁
△脩

91A.50 (亻/ㄱ)
-1 鵂
侉
-2 僔
-3 ○仍
-4 偈
-5 仞
伺
偈
-6 ○仿
○傍
-8 ○份
-9 ○僞
仂
僗
佝
○侮
傷
儵
○傷

91A.63 (亻/丶)
-2 儻
-5 △侭
-8 伶
-9 佟
儵
儵

91A.70 (亻/乚)
-1 僥
俺
○倦
-2 仳
○化
○他
佻
-3 △儷
△僊
-4 侃
俔
○佩
-6 ○伉
僦
佗
侘
-9 ○倪
○仇
○傀
仡
俛

91A.71 (亻/弋)
-1 儀
-7 ○代
○伐
-8 ○儀
-9 ○低
○俄

91A.72 (亻/心)
-4 偲
-6 ○億
伈
-9 傯

91A.80 (亻/八)
-1 ○債
債
儹
-2 ○供
○偵
○傾
○償
-3 ○價
-4 ○俱
-6 儐

91A.81 (亻/人)
-1 ○伏
○佚
佚
○俠
-2 儆
○似
○僕
-3 ○侯
○候
-8 ○儉
-9 ○伙
倏
倐
俟

91A.82 (亻/乂)
-1 伎
○做
傲
○仗
○使
-2 儆
俶
○僂
○佊
-3 ○便
○優
-4 儼
-5 ○侵
○假
-6 佼
△倣
△傚
-8 △仪
-9 儌
○攸
○俊

91A.83 (亻/〜)
-1 僆
-2 儗
○健
-4 ○促

91A.91 (亻/ノ)
-5 ○伊
-9 ○修

91A.93 (亻/く)
-2 僂
-6 佞
-8 侩
-9 倭

91B.00 (彳/亅)
-1 ○術
衕
○待
○街
-2 ○衖
衟
○衞
-3 ○行
衎
○衙
-4 ○得
衢
衕
-6 衚
衍
-8 ○衜
-9 ○衝
○衡

91B.01 (彳/小)
-1 徠
-8 ○徐

91B.02 (彳/⺊)
-5 ○很

91B.10 (彳/十)
-2 ○律
-8 徉

91B.11 (彳/土)
-6 ○往
-9 徨

91B.21 (彳/乚)
-9 徭

91B.22 (彳/丨)
-2 △彿
○徘
-9 ○御

91B.30 (彳/一)
-3 ○征
徑
徂
-4 徂

91B.41 (彳/図)
-4 ○徊
-9 ○循

91B.42 (彳/冈)
-2 徜
-6 ○徧

91B.50 (彳/ㄱ)
-6 △彷
徬
-9 徇

91B.72 (彳/心)
-1 ○德

91B.81 (彳/人)
-9 徯

91B.82 (彳/乂)
-2 ○微
○徵
○徽
○黴
○彼
-4 ○役
-6 ○徹
-9 徼

○復
○後

91B.83 (彳/〜)
-1 ○徒
-2 徙
-8 ○從

91C.00 (犭/亅)
-1 猘
猗
-6 狩
○獰
-9 猁
猙

91C.01 (犭/小)
-1 獉
獠
-3 猱
猻

91C.02 (犭/k)
-1 猿
-4 猥
-5 ○狠
-6 ○狼

91C.10 (犭/十)
-3 犴
-6 猝
獐
-9 猈
獬

91C.11 (犭/土)
-2 狴
-3 ○狂
-4 猩
狸 *91S.11

91C.22 (犭/丨)
-2 狒
-4 狎
-9 獅

91C.30 (犭/一)
-3 狉
○猛
-4 狙
-5 狃

91C.40 (犭/口)
-6 狺
-8 猞

91C.41 (犭/図)
-1 ○猪
-2 ○猫
-4 ○猖
-8 ○猶
獪

91C.42 (犭/冈)
-1 ○猜
猢
-3 獳
獮
-4 狷
猬
○猾
-5 獼
-9 獢

91C.50 (犭/ㄱ)
-4 ○獨
-9 ○狗
狥

91C.70 (犭/乚)
-1 犹
-2 猇
-5 犯
-6 犺
獍
-9 猊
○獵

91C.71 (犭/弋)
-7 狘

91C.80 (犭/八)
-1 獺
-4 狽
-6 獱

91C.81 (犭/人)
-1 ○狹
-5 獗
-6 ○獄
-9 ○狄
○猴

91C.82 (犭/乂)
-2 ○獲
-6 ○狡
-9 猨
狻

91C.83 (犭/〜)
-9 ○狐

91C.93 (犭/く)
(ム) -2 △独
-8 狯

91D.00 (火/亅)
(亅) △灯
-5 焞
燜
○爛
-9 爝

91D.01 (火/小)
-1 ○煉
燎
-2 ○煤
○燦
煠
-3 煣
-4 ○燥
-9 烌
爍

91D.02 (火/k)
-4 ○爆
煨
-6 烺

91D.10 (火/十)
-2 燁
煒
燐
-6 焠
煇
-8 烊
-9 烽

91D.11 (火/土)
-1 △灶
-3 △煙
-5 △燿
-6 炷
-9 ○煌

91D.21 (火/乚)
-5 ○炬
-9 ○焰

91D.22 (火/丨)
-9 炘
○炸

91D.30 (火/一)
-2 ○爐
爈
-3 烜
○燈
-4 煜
-6 煊

91D.40 (火/口)
-1 熺
-3 焐
-5 炤
-6 焙
○熔
-8 熗
-9 烙

91D.41 (火/図)
-4 ○烟
-5 熠
-8 燴
-9 燔

91D.42 (火/冈)
-3 ○炳
-4 烔
熇
-8 煸

91D.50 (火/ㄱ)
-1 烤
-4 煬
○燭
-6 熵
-9 灼

91D.63 (火/丶)
-5 烬
-9 燻
燋
○燃

91D.70 (火/乚)
-1 ○燒
-4 焜
-6 炕
爖
-9 ○炮

91D.71 (火/弋)
-6 ○熾

91D.72 (火/心)
-9 ○熄

91D.80 (火/八)
-2 ○烘
-3 ○煩

91D.81 (火/人)
-2 熯
-9 炊
燠
○炊
○煥

91D.82 (火/乂)
-6 燉
-9 △煖
○燬
煅

91D.83 (火/〜)
-8 燧

91D.91 (火/ノ)
-2 ○炒
-6 炉

91D.93 (火/く)
-2 烛
-6 炫
-8 烩

91S.00 (ノ^{s}/亅)
-1 ○射
豺
-2 ○判
剣
劓
-3 舸
-9 爵

91S.01 (ノ^{s}/小)
-2 牒
-3 躲
-9 貅
-9 △繇

91S.02 (ノ^{s}/k)
-1 艭
-2 艨
-9 △衇

91S.10 (ノ^{s}/十)
-1 躰
-2 衅
-3 衈
鼾
豻
-9 ○牌
皞

91S.11 (ノ^{s}/土)
-2 貛
-4 貍
-6 艟
艠

91S.21 (ノ^{s}/乚)
-2 舢
-5 ○軀
-9 舾

91S.22 (ノ^{s}/丨)
-2 丱 *22.22
○非 *22.22
○弗 *22.22
○帥
-3 ○邦 *10S.22
△師
郯
郫
鄔
-5 △衄
○卽
○歸
-9 舴

91S.30 (ノ^{s}/一)
-2 皚
艫
-3 舡
艋
-5 衃
归
艞
○艦

91S.40 (ノ^{s}/口)
-1 ○皓
-4 ○加
○船
-5 貂
-8 ○艙
-9 貉

91S.41 (ノ^{s}/図)
-1 艢
-2 舳
-2 △貓
-3 貊
-9 皤
○舶
艪

91S.42 (ノ^{s}/冈)
-2 艄
舺
貒
-6 艑

91S.50 (ノ^{s}/ㄱ)
-2 艕
-5 ○躬
衂
翱
-6 舫
膀
-9 ○的
豹
鳩
鴂
鴝
○鶴
鶺
鷦

91S.63 (ノ^{s}/丶)
-6 皫
-8 舲

91S.70 (ノ^{s}/乚)
-5 ○旣
-6 ○航
○舵
皖
鮀

-9 胤
○貌
貎
○魄
鮑
鮠
鰓

91S.71 (ノs/弋)
-2 巇
○賤
-8 艤
-9 䑙

91S.72 (ノs/心)
-4 鰓
-9 △腮

91S.80 (ノs/八)
-1 ○牘
-3 頎
○須
○順 *22.80
頤
顛

91S.81 (ノs/人)
-9 欸

91S.82 (ノs/乂)
-2 ○艘
-4 ○般
-6 皎
-9 皈
○叛
○版
舨
皦

91S.83 (ノs/乛)
-9 ○艇

91S.93 (ノs/く)
-6 舷

92.00 (⺈/亅)
(亅)○争

92.01 (⺈/小)
(木) 桀
○彙
△条
渠

(小)△尔
○祭
○繁

92.02 (⺈/k)
彔
彖
○象

92.10 (⺈/十)
○午
○年
○舞

92.11 (⺈/土)
生

92.20 (⺈/艹)
彝

92.21 (⺈/乚)
缶

92.22 (⺈/丨)
乍

92.30 (⺈/一)
盎
盌

92.32 (⺈/フ)
○夕
○多

92.40 (⺈/口)
○名
○各
咎
○詹
詹

92.41 (⺈/図)
昝
習
○智
○魯

92.42 (⺈/冈)
○角
△胃

92.50 (⺈/ㄱ)
○每
鴛
(勹) -1 匍
匐

-2 芻
-3 匐
-4 ○句
○旬
甸
勹
-6 勺
匀
匃
訇
-8 ○匈
-9 ○勾
○勿
○匆

92.63 (⺈/丶)
○冬
炰
焦
○魚
○無
○然
○煞
鰲
鱻

92.70 (⺈/乚)
(乚)○乞
○包
○危
○色
○免
○勉
毚
龜
(气) -1 氪
○氣
-2 氙
氟
-3 氩
○氫
氖
-4 氤
氳
-6 氦
氨

-8 ○氛
○氧
氝
-9 氮
氯
氡

92.72 (⺈/心)
○忽
△怱
○怎
○急
○怨

92.80 (⺈/八)
貟
○負 *50.80

92.81 (⺈/人)
○久
奐
○欠
(大)○矢
(大)△疾
灸
炙

92.82 (⺈/乂)
○攵
△发
复

92.83 (⺈/乛)
迩
○迄
迤
迮
迮
迻
逄
○逢
逯
○逸
○遙
邂
(人)△処

92.93 (⺈/く)
蝨
○蟹

蠡
蠭

92A.00 (竹/亅)
-1 ○等
○籌
-3 竽
-5 ○筲
-6 ○簾 *92A.22
○簿
-8 ○箭
-9 箣
箏
○符

92A.01 (竹/小)
-1 ○策
-3 箕
○築
-4 纂

92A.02 (竹/k)
-4 簑
-6 簣
-8 籙
-9 ○篆

92A.10 (竹/十)
-1 ○笨
籜
-2 ○筆
-3 ○竿
簟
-4 簞
箪
-9 箄
篺

92A.11 (竹/土)
-1 笙
-4 ○籮
-5 籗
-6 ○籬
-8 筌
-9 箠
篁

92A.20 (竹/艹)
-3 ○筭
筓

-4 ○算
箅

92A.21 (竹/匕)
-1 箷
-5 笸
○筐
篋
篚

92A.22 (竹/丨)
-2 ○第
簫
-3 節
-5 ○第
箒
-6 ○簾
-9 ○節
篩

92A.30 (竹/一)
-1 箏
-2 篪
-3 笁
筮
-4 笪
-5 簋
籃
-6 笠
箜

92A.32 (竹/フ)
-4 箩
-9 簃

92A.40 (竹/口)
-2 箸
-4 筥
-5 笤
-6 ○管
-8 ○答
-9 笳
○簷
筈

92A.41 (竹/図)
-1 箝
籀
○箱
○籍

箸
-2 ○笛
簹
-4 △箇
箘
-6 箔
-9 簪

92A.42 (竹/冈)
-1 筲
-3 箾
-4 ○筒
-6 篙
篱
○篇
-8 籥

92A.50 (竹/ㄱ)
-1 筠
-4 筋
筯
-5 笥
○篤
-9 竻
笏
笱
○筍

92A.63 (竹/丶)
-8 笭

92A.70 (竹/乚)
-1 箢
範
笓
-2 筅
-3 筑
-4 筧
篸
-5 ○笆
-6 ○籠
簏
筅
-9 △笔
篪
篦
筦

92A.71 (竹/弋)
-4 筬

-5 筤
-7 △箋
箴
-8 籤
-9 筏
92A.80 (竹/八)
-1 簀
籟
-2 箕
簧
簣
篢
-8 ○籲
92A.81 (竹/人)
-1 筴
簌
-2 ○筷
-6 簇
-8 ○簽
-9 ○笑
篌
92A.82 (竹/乂)
-2 簸
-3 笈
-6 笅
箥
-9 筱
篘
92A.83 (竹/〜)
-1 篚
篴
-2 籧
-9 笊
筳
○筵
籩
○篷
92A.91 (竹/ノ)
-5 △笄
92A.93 (竹/く)
-2 簍
-4 篡
92B.00 (角/亅)
-1 觭
92B.01 (角/小)
-1 觫
92B.02 (角/⺊)
-1 觩
92B.10 (角/十)
-1 斛
-4 觶
-5 ○解
92B.42 (角/冈)
-2 觿
92B.50 (角/⺄)
-4 ○觸
-9 觔
觴
92B.70 (角/乚)
-2 觥
92B.71 (角/弋)
-9 觝
92B.83 (角/〜)
-9 觚
92C.00 (魚/亅)
-4 鮬
鯽
-5 鰣
-8 鱒
-9 鮒
92C.01 (魚/小)
-2 鰈
-3 鰾
-6 ○鯨
-9 ○穌
蘇
92C.02 (魚/⺊)
-4 鰥
92C.10 (魚/十)
-2 ○鱗
-3 鱘
-4 鱓
-8 ○鮮
92C.11 (魚/土)
-1 鮭
-4 鯉
-9 鰉
92C.22 (魚/丨)
-6 鯖
-8 鰜
-9 鯽
鮓
92C.30 (魚/一)
-2 鱸
鱧
-3 鱷
鱺
-4 鰛
-6 鱣
92C.40 (魚/口)
-2 鮎
-8 鱔
-9 鮐
92C.41 (魚/囟)
-1 鰭
-4 鯧
-8 鱠
92C.42 (魚/冈)
-1 鯖
鮪
-4 鯛
-6 鯿
92C.50 (魚/⺄)
-4 鰐
-6 魴
92C.70 (魚/乚)
-1 魷
-3 魟
-4 鯤
-6 鮀
-9 鯢
鮑
92C.72 (魚/心)
-4 鰓
92C.81 (魚/人)
-5 鱖
-9 鰍
92C.82 (魚/乂)
-1 鯪
鮁
-3 鯁
鯫
鱍
鰻
-4 鮫
-6 魬
-9 鰒
92C.83 (魚/〜)
-1 鰱
92S.00 (⺈s/亅)
-2 ○刎
刨
剝
劄
鑄
劓
-8 鐏
-9 ○竹
92S.01 (⺈s/小)
-9 繇
92S.02 (⺈s/⺊)
-8 飧
92S.10 (⺈s/十)
-1 舛
缽
-3 罈
92S.11 (⺈s/土)
-2 矬
○罐
-9 雉
雒
雛
92S.20 (⺈s/卄)
-8 缾
92S.21 (⺈s/⺄)
-5 ○矩
92S.22 (⺈s/丨)
-2 ○外
-3 郈
鄒
-5 卸
矧
-9 △矫
92S.30 (⺈s/一)
-2 罏
-3 ○缸
○短
92S.32 (⺈s/フ)
-9 △够
92S.40 (⺈s/口)
-4 ○知
92S.41 (⺈s/囟)
-8 矰
92S.42 (⺈s/冈)
-9 矯
92S.50 (⺈s/⺄)
-9 劬
○夠
鴝
鴿
92S.70 (⺈s/乚)
-4 飆
-6 毓
92S.81 (⺈s/人)
-9 ○缺
飲
92S.82 (⺈s/乂)
-2 ○皺
矱 *20A.82
-9 敏
○敏
92S.93 (⺈s/く)
-9 ○矮
93.00 (く/亅)
孥
拏
孿
攣
93.01 (く/小)
梟
○巢
絮
○樂
欒
93.02 (く/⺊)
絫
饗
93.10 (く/十)
牟
牟
93.20 (く/廾)
弁
93.21 (く/乚)
轡
93.22 (く/丨)
帑
帤
93.30 (く/一)
鑾
93.40 (く/口)
△台
砮
轡
93.41 (く/囟)
畚
○響
93.42 (く/冈)
○嚮
欒
93.50 (く/⺄)
弩
○努
駑
○彎
鷥
○鸞
93.63 (く/丶)
○熊
93.70 (く/乚)
○允
邕
93.71 (く/弋)
○幾
畿
93.72 (く/心)
○怠
○怒
○恕
○態
○戀
93.80 (く/八)
(貝) △貟
93.81 (く/人)
○矣
○災
炱
93.82 (く/乂)
○變
93.83 (く/〜)
○巡
迨
逡
邋
93.91 (く/ノ)
○參
93.93 (く/く)
厶
○幺
○女
△姦
孌
○蠻
93A.00 (女/亅)
-3 ○好
婀
-5 嫺
-6 婷
-8 媮
93A.01 (女/小)
-1 ○妹
姝
-2 ○媒
媟
-3 ○嫖
-9 △妳
93A.02 (女/⺊)
-1 婊
-4 嬛
-5 娠
-6 △孃
嫁
○娘
93A.10 (女/十)
-2 婥
-3 ○奸
-4 嫜

-9 婢

93A.11 (女/土)

-1 ○姓
○娃
-3 △姪
-4 娌
-9 妊

93A.20 (女/廾)

-3 姸
-8 婷
-9 姘

93A.21 (女/L)

-5 姬
嫗
嫟

93A.22 (女/丨)

-2 外
△姊
○婦
嫺
-5 娜
○婦
-8 娣
○嫌
-9 △娇

93A.30 (女/一)

-3 婭
-4 媪
○姐
○妞
-5 嬗

93A.32 (女/フ)

-8 妗

93A.40 (女/口)

-1 ○姑
○嬉
-3 ○姤
-4 ○如
-9 ○始

93A.41 (女/図)

-1 嫱
-2 妯
-3 ○孀
-4 ○娼
娼
○姻
-5 ○媚
-6 ○嬸
-9 ○婚

93A.42 (女/冈)

-2 媾
姌
-3 嬭
△婿
-4 ○娟
姍
媧
-6 ○嫡
-9 ○嬌

93A.50 (女/ㄱ)

-1 姱
-2 娉
-3 嫣
○奶
-4 姆
-5 嫋
○媽
-6 妨
-9 嫣
妁

93A.63 (女/丶)

-9 嫵

93A.70 (女/L)

-1 ○姥
嬈
-2 妣
○她
○姚
-5 妃
妮
娓
-6 姹
婉
-9 奼
婗
媿
婎
娩
媿

93A.71 (女/弋)

-7 娬
-9 ○娥

93A.72 (女/心)

-9 ○媳

93A.80 (女/八)

-1 嬾
-5 媜
-6 嬪

93A.81 (女/人)

-1 ○姨
-2 姒
-4 ○娛
-6 ○嫉
-9 ○妖

93A.82 (女/乂)

-1 ○妓
○嫩
-2 嬓
○嫂
-3 ○奴
-4 嫚
-6 ○姣
姣
-9 ○媛
○嫒

93A.91 (女/ノ)

-2 ○妙
-5 嫪
-9 △妒

93A.93 (女/く)

-2 嬶
-3 嫛
-6 嬷

93B.00 (糸/亅)

-1 紂
縛
綧
綺
-3 紆
紓
縟
-9 絎

93B.01 (糸/小)

-1 ○練
繚
-3 縹
-4 繰
纅
-6 紵
綜
-9 ○綵
緣
○絲
纖
纙

93B.02 (糸/k)

-1 綠
-4 繯
-6 繯
-9 ○線
○綠
○緣

93B.10 (糸/十)

-2 縴
綽
絆
緯
-4 ○緝
繹
-6 綷
縴
-9 絳

93B.11 (糸/土)

-3 絰
絟
-4 纆
-6 ○纏
-9 紝
△維

93B.21 (糸/L)

-2 絀
緪
○繼
-9 縚

93B.22 (糸/丨)

-1 ○綁
-2 ○糾
○紳
紼
○繡
緋
-6 ○締
-8 綈
縑
絺
○綿

93B.30 (糸/一)

-2 纑
緪
-3 繮
○紅
○經
-4 縕
○組
-5 紐
-8 縊

93B.40 (糸/口)

-1 ○結
-5 ○紹
-6 綰
-8 ○繕
綌
○給
-9 ○絡
綹
紿

93B.41 (糸/図)

-1 緗
緒
-2 紬
紺
-3 ○緬
縉
-4 ○細
絪
緉
縉
-5 縉
-6 ○縮
-8 緧
繒
○繪
-9 繙
緇

93B.42 (糸/冈)

-2 綃
○繃
-3 繻
-4 ○絹
綗
○綢
○綱
○網
○繃
-6 縞
縭
○編
-8 ○綸
○納
-9 繑

93B.50 (糸/ㄱ)

-1 綺
-5 ○紉
-6 ○紡
-8 ○紛
-9 ○約
絢
綯
縐
△綉

93B.63 (糸/丶)

-9 ○終

93B.70 (糸/L)

-1 ○純
○繞
綣
-2 紕
糺
絖
-4 緄
○繩
-5 ○紀
○絕
○纜
-6 ○統
紽
-9 紈
紇
絁
△纔

93B.71 (糸/弋)

-6 ○織
-7 縔
○絨
△綫
○緘
○纖
-9 ○紙

93B.72 (糸/心)

-1 繐
-4 緦
-9 ○總

93B.80 (糸/八)

-1 ○績
纘
○續
-2 縝
繢
-6 纊
繽

93B.81 (糸/人)

-1 △絨

93B.82 (糸/乂)

-1 綾
紱
-2 繳
-3 綆
緅
○緻
○級
○綴
-4 縵
-5 緌
-6 ○紋
○絞
-9 緩
○緞
○緩
緶

○繳

93B.83 (糸/〜)
-1 縫
-2 繿
-4 緹
-6 綻
-9 縋

○縦
○縫

93B.91 (糸/ノ)
-2○紗
-4○緲
-5 繆
-8 紾

93B.93 (糸/く)
-1 紘
-2○縷
-3 紜
-4 纓
-5 繈
-6○紘

-8△絵
-9○綏
綉

93S.00 (くs/亅)
-2○剿

93S.11 (くs/土)
-9 雝

93S.22 (くs/丨)
-3 郶
△鄙
-9 鄉

93S.50 (くs/ㄱ)
-5○幻
△勦

-9○幼
△勦

93S.63 (くs/、)
(灬)△ 絲 -9

93S.70 (くs/乚)
-2○能
-9 毵

93S.81 (くs/人)
-9 欸

93S.82 (くs/乂)
-2 皴

LIN YUTANG'S CHINESE-ENGLISH DICTIONARY OF MODERN USAGE

SECTION 10

§ 10.00 (十/亅)

才 10.00

tsair.

N. (1) Ability, aptitude, natural gift: 才能, 才幹, 才力, etc. *-nerng*, *-gahn*, *-lih* ↓; 文才, 詩才 literary, poetic gift. (2) Person in regard to capability, personality, character: 人才 useful person; 沒有人才 lacking in capable men; 幹才 practical ability, person with such ability; 天才 genius; 奴才 (contempt.) slave; 蠢才 (abuse) dullard, idiot, imbecile; 大才小用 an able man given a small job; 英才, 高才 great talent; 小有才 (person) gifted with a fair degree of cleverness, possesses certain but limited abilities; 才難 really able men are difficult to come by; (closely related 材 timber, 10B.00).

Adv. (1) (Emphatic assertion, similar to German *doch*) indeed: 那我才不怕 I'm certainly not afraid of that; 那才妙了 would indeed be fun (if it should happen); 你才是我所喜歡的人 you (not anybody else) are the one I love. (2) Just, just now (in place of awkward character 纔): 剛才 just now; 才晴又雨 sky has just cleared and now it rains again; 才要開飯客人來了 just as we were sitting down to dinner, a guest appeared.

才氣 *tsairchih* (*-'chi*), n., rich talent, brilliance of mind.

才情 *tsairchirng*, n., great ability, esp. litr. aptitude.

才調 *tsairdiauh*, n., see *-chih* ↑.

才分 *tsairfehn*, n., inborn ability.

才幹 *tsairgahn* (*-'gan*), n., practical ability.

才華 *tsairhuar*, n., see *-chih* ↑.

才智 *tsairjyh*, n., wisdom and ability.

才具 *tsairjyuh*, n., aptitude, capability (of person).

才力 *tsairlih*, n., force of personality, spirit.

才略 *tsairlyueh*, n., resourcefulness, political ability.

才貌 *tsairmauh*, n., personal appearance as reflecting ability.

才名 *tsair-mirng*, n., literary reputation.

才能 *tsairnerng*, n., natural gift, talent, litr. or practical ability.

才人 *tsairrern*, n., talented scholar.

才士 *tsairshyh*, n., good scholars.

才學 *tsairshyuer* (*-'shyue*), n., ability and learning, person's scholarship.

才思 *tsairsy*, n., brilliance in writing.

才藻 *tsairtzaau*, n., see *-sy* ↑.

才子 *tsairtzyy*, n., (1) brilliant writer; (2) 才子佳人小說 popular romance with a handsome scholar and a pretty girl.

才悟 *tsair-wuh*, n., aptitude for understanding.

才穎 *tsir-yiing*, n., intellectual brilliance.

才媛 *tsair-yuarn*, n., a gifted maiden.

事 10.00

shyh.

N. (1) Affair, business, matter: 事務, 事件, 事情 *-wuh*[2], *-jiahn*, *-chirng* ↓; affair: 這件事 this affair, this business; 國事, 家事 national, family affairs; 人事 personnel (problems); 公事, 私事 public, private affairs; 萬事 all: 萬事如意 have all one's wishes; 風流韻事 a romantic affair, a scholar's gathering; 事不干己 the affair does not concern one; 事急, 事忙 matter is urgent, business is pressing; 事半功倍 half the work with double results; 事倍功半 twice the work with half of results. (2) Fact, event, happening: 事實 *-shyr* ↓; 事與願違 events do not happen as one wishes; 事過境遷 events have passed and times have changed; 事出有因 this happens not without reason; 事前, 事後 before, after the event; 喜事 happy event (wedding, celebration); 喪事 funeral; 紅白事 happy and unhappy events; 事故, 事端 *-guh*, *-duan* ↓. (3) Trouble, accident, undesirable event: 出事 have an accident (in travel); 肇事 cause trouble, a row; 事變 *-biahn* ↓; 平安無事 all is

亅	小	⺊	十	土	𠂇	卄	ㄴ卜	丨	一	丁	乛	口	区	冈	𠃌	厂	尸	亠	广	宀	丶	乚	弋	心	八	人	乂	〜	㇀	丿丿	𠂉	く
00	01	02	10	11	12	20	21	22	30	31	32	40	41	42	50	51	52	60	61	62	63	70	71	72	80	81	82	83	90	91	92	93

well; 多事之秋 year of many troubles; 大事化爲小事, 小事化爲無事 reduce a big trouble into a small one, and a small one into nothing; 省事 save trouble; 費事 takes a lot of doing; 少管閒事 don't meddle in others' affairs; 造謠生事 cause trouble by spreading rumors; 惹事生非 be meddlesome; 了事 close a dispute, lawsuit; 息事寧人 stop dispute and live and let live; 舉事, 起事 start rebellion; 事到如今 things have come to such a pass that. (4) Matter in gen., matters: 這是怎麽一回事 what is all this? 醫事 medical matters; 政事 politics, government; 軍事 military matters or affairs; 任事 take charge of matters; 史事 historical matters; 軼事, 趣事 anecdotes; 房事 sexual intercourse; 月事 menstruation. (5) Oft. part of title: 董事, 理事 board directors; 監事 supervisor; 幹事 executive officer, secretary or manager; 推事 judge; 通事 formerly, official interpreter of foreign language; 領事 consul; 執事 (LL) oft. used in letters like 先生 you, sir; 管事 men in charge; 縣知事 county magistrate.

V.i. & t. (1) To do: 不事農商 will not take up farming or a trade; 不事生產 does not attend to business or hold a job; 從事教育 devote oneself to education; 無所事事 do nothing all day. (2) To serve: 事親, 事君 serve parents, ruler.

事變 *shyhbiahn*, n., sudden turn of events (rebellion, *coup d'état*, etc.).

事情 *shyhchirng*, n., (1) course of events, story; (2) (-'*ching*) affair, event: 這件事情 this affair; 沒有事情 nothing has happened; 有什麽事情 what is up?

事權 *shyhchyuarn*, n., duties and responsibilities (of an official), legal power in a case.

事端 *shyhduan*, n., an event, a dispute: 引起事端 causes disputes.

事故(兒) *shyhguh('l)*, n., an affair; some trouble.

事蹟 *shyhji*[1], n., record of events; a person's activities.

事機 *shyhji*[2], n., crux of a situation, happenings behind the scenes.

事件 *shyhjiahn*, n., an event, an item of business: 這些事件交給你 you will take charge of these several items; 事件發生 something happens.

事主 *shyhjuu*, n., party in an accident dealing or lawsuit.

事兒 *shyh'l*, n., see -*chirng* ↑.

事例 *shyhlih*, n., case history, case law.

事略 *shyhlyueh*, n., brief biographical sketch.

事項 *shyhshiahng*, n., item of business, see -*jiahn* ↑.

事先 *shyh-shian*, adv., prior to event. ⌈events.

事勢 *shyhshyh*[1], n., trend of

事事 *shyhshyh*[2], pron., everything: 事事小心 be careful in everything.

事實 *shyshyr*, n., fact: 事實如此 that is the fact; 事實上 --*shahng*, adv., as a matter of fact, factually (impossible, etc.).

事畜 *shyhshyuh*, v.i., (LL) to serve (parents) and raise (children).

事態 *shyhtaih*, n., the look of things, situation, circumstances.

事體 *shyhtii*, n., business (important, unimportant): 事體簡單, 複雜 matter is simple, complicated.

事物 *shyhwuh*[1], n., things, articles, objects: 各種事物 different things (coats, umbrellas, etc.).

事務 *shyhwuh*[2], n., business, business duties, gen. affairs; 事務員 (also wr. 庶務) man in business office in charge of business side (outings, arrangements, etc.); 事務所 business office (as of lawyer, doctor).

事樣兒 *shyhyahng'l*, n., look or appearance of things: 成什麽事樣兒 what will it look like?

事業 *shyhyeh*, n., (1) a man's business or life work, career; (2) business enterprise: 公共事業 a public enterprise.

事宜 *shyhyir*, n., (official) event, case, subject dealt with.

事由 *shyhyour*, n., story (of event, dispute, etc.); 事由兒 --'*l*, n., some kind of work or event: 什麽事由兒他也做 he'll take up any kind of work.

寸 10.00

tsuhn.

N. An inch (cf. 吋 English inch): 三寸丁 a three-inch nail, (fig.) a pint-sized person; 三寸金蓮 81.30; 方寸 square inch, also heart: 方寸已亂 my heart is already upset; 立方寸 cubic inch; 公寸 decimeter; 尺寸 dimensions of anything; 尺有所短, 寸有所長 every man has his strong and weak points.

Adj. (1) Very small in amount: 手無寸鐵 a man unarmed ("not a scrap of metal"); 寸步難行 cannot walk a step; 寸土寸地 a wisp of territory; 寸絲不掛 totally nude; 寸腸 my little thoughts or feelings; 寸紙 a short note; 寸刻, 寸隙, 寸晷 even a brief moment (must be utilized); 寸功 humble achievement or service; 寸進 small progress; 寸草不留 complete devastation of land. (2) (Coll.) just right, right moment: 他來得眞寸 he comes just at the right time.

寸衷 *tsuhnjung*, n., (LL) my heart, innermost feelings.

寸口 *tsuhnkoou*, n., (Chin. med.) a person's pulse on the wrist.

寸心 *tsuhnshin*, n., see -*jung* ↑.

寸田 *tsuhntiarn*, n., the heart (from 心田).

寸子 *tsuhntz*, n., (Chin. opera) false sole worn by actress.

寸陰 *tsuhnyin*, n., a few minutes, a very short time (to be valued for study and not squandered.)

專 10.00

juan.

N. (1) A surname. (2) Short for

專門學校, see 專門 *-mern*↓: 商專 commercial college; 體專 college of physical culture; 大專 universities and technical schools.

V.t. To monopolize, take possession alone: 專美 monopolize credit, enjoy credit alone; 專權, 專政 *-chyuarn, -jehng*↓; 專掌其事 take charge of matter alone.

Adj. & adv. (1) Concentrated, devoted: 用心不專 is not devoted to one thing: 專心, 專誠, 專一, 專專 *-shin, -cherng, -yi, -juan*↓. (2) Special, -ly confined to one subject or area: 專長, 專利 *-charng, -lih*↓; 專門, 專科 *-mern, -ke*↓; 專家 *-jia*↓; 專攻歷史 specialize in history; 專精, 專擅 be specially good at some field; 專對他一人說 talk specially to him along; 專此 (end of letter) the above is what I write about specially; 專望 I wait or hope specially; 專差, 專足 by special messenger; 專用綫 lines for special use, private line; 專律 special laws; 專條 special clause. (3) Arbitrary, high-handed, tyrannical: 專橫, 專制 *-hehng, -jyh*↓; 自專 arbitrary, willful.

專差 *juanchai*, adv., by special messenger.
專長 *juancharng*, v.i. & n., to specialize in, be good specially at (oratory, criticism, etc.); a specialty: 那是他的專長 that is his specialty.
專車 *juanche*, n., special car or train.
專誠 *juancherng*, adv., specially: 專誠拜訪 make a special trip to call on s. o.; 專誠奉復 write a reply specially.
專寵 *juanchuung*, v.i., monopolize ruler's favor.
專權 *juanchyuarn*, (1) n., full power to do s. t.; (2) v.i., to become absolute head of government.
專電 *juandiahn*, n., special or direct telegram.
專斷 *juanduahn*, adj., arbitrary (in decisions).
專橫 *juanhehng*, adj., arbitrary, intolerant, overbearing.
專政 *juanjehng*, n., autocracy.
專征 *juanjeng*, v.i., formerly, to enjoy full powers in the field for all military decisions.
專家 *juanjia*, n., a specialist.
專專 *juanjuan*, adv., specially: 專專對他吩咐 specially told him (to do s.t.).
專制 *juanjyh*, n., absolute monarchy; dictatorship; tyrannical government.
專科 *juanke*, n., special department or subject; 專科學校 technical or professional school or college.
專閫 *juankuun*, n., formerly, an army commander with full powers in his jurisdiction.
專欄 *juanlarn*, n., (newspaper) column, feature.
專利 *juanlih*, n., monopoly in trade, patent.
專賣 *juanmaih*, n., ditto.
專門 *juanmern*, (1) n. & adj., a specialized science; a specialty; 專門學校 a technological or professional school or college; (2) adv., specially: 專門與我作對 obsessed in opposing me.
專命 *juanmihng*, adv., formerly, without waiting for orders from above.
專名 *juanmirng*, n., (gram.) proper noun.
專任 *juanrehn*, v.t., specially appointed to take full charge of (department, case, affair, etc.); adj. & n., full-time job, opp. 兼任 concurrent.
專人 *juanrern*, adv., by special messenger.
專擅 *juanshahn*, v.t., specialize in, be especially good at (playing flute, etc.); take things into one's own hands, act without authorization from superior.
專心 *juanshin*, adv., with concentration, devoted purpose.
專修 *juanshiou*, v.i., to specialize in study: 英文專修學校 school of English, or specially for English only.
專使 *juanshyy*, n., special emissary of government.
專司 *juansy*, v.t., see *-rehn*↑.
專才 *juantsair*, n., specialist, person specially good at s.t.
專祠 *juantsyr*, n., temple specially in honor of s.o.
專業 *juanyeh*, n., special vocation.
專一 *juanyi*, adv., with single mind and purpose.
專員 *juanyuarn*, n., an official ("specialist") attached to some ministry for a temporary or nominal job.

李 10.00

lii.

N. (1) (*-tz*) (Bot.) the plum, *Prunus salicina*: 桃李 peaches and plums, (fig.) one's students: 桃李滿天下 with students all over the world; 李代桃僵 (orig. allu.) two persons suffering for one another, (now) girl replaces another as wife; 瓜田李下 or 李下之嫌 be found in a suspicious position. (2) A surname.

孛 10.00

beih (**bor*).

N. 孛星 a comet.

Adv. (**bor*) U.f. 勃 suddenly.

挈 10.00

chieh.

V.t. To take by the hand, to lift or lead by hand: 提挈 to lift or carry, (fig.) 提綱挈領 to give the main points (like "drawing a net in by its main lines and taking a

亅	小	𠂉	十	土	𠂇	廾	乚	丨	一	丅	乛	口	囚	冈	冂	厂	尸	亠	广	宀	丶	乚	弋	心	八	人	乂	𠂆	乛	丿	𠂉	𡿨
00	01	02	10	11	12	20	21	22	30	31	32	40	41	42	50	51	52	60	61	62	63	70	71	72	80	81	82	83	90	91	92	93

挈 掣 擊 攀 朩 朮 未

coat by its collar"); 挈眷南下 bring one's family south; 挈出紅塵 lead a person away from this mortal life; 挈缾之知 (AC) trivial knowledge.

挈挈 *chiehchieh*, adj., (AC) in a hurry.

挈領 *chiehliing*, v.t., (1) to bring, lead (children, family); (2) 提綱挈領, see V.t. ↑.

掣 10.00

cheh.

V.t. (1) To pull, to hinder by pulling back: 掣後腿 hinder progress by "pulling leg"; 掣肘 *-joou* ↓. (2) To strike like lightning: 風馳電掣 to pass or strike swiftly like the wind or lightning.

掣肘 *cheh-joou*, v.i., to tug at elbow to prevent action.

掣曳 *chehyih*, v.t., to drag along.

擊 10.00

jir.

V.t. (1) To strike, hit: 擊罐 to beat a drinking cup and sing; 擊柝 (of night watchmen) beat the rattle and go the rounds; 擊楫 to vow to bring peace to the country (allu. to the story of 祖逖); 擊筑 to strike the strings of an ancient lute; 擊鼓 to strike a drum; 擊鉢催詩 celebration of festive occasions by poets writing poems within set time limits; 拳擊 boxing; 敲擊 to pound, to hammer; 打擊 to beat, to strike a heavy blow; 重重一擊 give (s.o.) a pounding; 棒擊 hit with a stick or club; 技擊 to fence; 搏擊 to wrestle, engage in hand-fight scuffle; 槍擊 to shoot; 轟擊 bombard with guns or from the air, (fig.) criticize severely; 擊沈 to bombard and sink (a ship); 擊落敵機 to down an enemy plane; 擊節 *-jier*; 擊賞 *-shaang* ↓. (2) To combat, to fight: 攻擊 to attack, also attack, criticize in writing; 游擊 to wage guerrilla warfare; 打游擊 (now also) sponge meals on friends; 游擊戰爭 guerrilla warfare; 突擊 mount a sudden attack; 襲擊 make a surprise raid; 擊敗 defeat; 聲東擊西 feign attack on the east and strike on the west. (3) Come in contact with: 目擊 see with one's own eyes.

擊節 *jirjier*, v.i. & t., as in 擊節稱賞 to clap and applaud.

擊賞 *jirshaang*, v.t., ditto.

擊刺 *jirtsyh*, v.t., (1) stab with a sword; (2) (of troops) fight with swords and spears.

攀 10.00

pan.

V.i. & t. (1) To climb: 攀鞍上馬 mount a horse, (lit.) mount by clasping saddle; 攀附(權貴) attach oneself to (persons in power) as a means of securing promotion; 攀龍附鳳 (LL) attach oneself to dragon and phoenix, with similar meaning; 攀高親 to marry into rich, well-known family; 高攀 try to make friends with those higher-up; 攀不上 dare not, be unworthy to seek connections with (persons); 攀桂 (LL) formerly, to succeed in civil examinations ("win the laurel"); 攀折 *-jer* ↓; 攀花折柳 phr., to philander. (2) To implicate (accomplice) at court by accused: 攀他一口 make such statements, also 攀供.

攀纏 *pancharn*, v.t., to keep annoying by inappropriate talk, request.

攀親 *pan-chin*, v.i., to betroth, discuss betrothal.

攀登 *pandeng*, v.i., climb up.

攀折 *panjer*, v.t., break branches: 不准攀折 do not pick flowers, break branches.

攀緣 *panyuarn*[1], v.i., (Budd.) be distracted by material world, like monkeys swinging from branch to branch.

攀援 *panyuarn*[2], n., seek help from those on top.

攀輿 *parn-yur*, v.i., to surround carriage of departing magistrate in affectionate farewell.

§10.01 (十/小)

朩 10.01

pihn.

V.t. Peel off the bark of hemp (麻).

朮 10.01

jur.

N. (Bot.) 白▵朮 91.41.

未 10.01

weih.

N. (1) Number 8 in duodecimal cycle, see Appendix A. (2) 未時 1:00–3:00 p.m.

Adv. (1) Not, yet, have not yet (contrast 不 do not, will not): 未曾 *-tserng* ↓; 未能 have not been able to; 尚未過目 have not seen it yet; 未遇 failed to see him on visit; 未嫁 not yet married; 未成年 under age, or a minor; 和約未成 negotiations have not yet been concluded; 未老先衰 old before one's age; 未之前聞 never heard of it; 未之有也 there never was such a thing. (2) (LL) at the end of a sentence, equals "or not?": 寒梅著花未 have the plum flowers come to bud yet?

未便 *weih-biahn*, phr., it's not convenient to.

未必 *weih-bih*, phr., is not sure (to, that), not definitely (usu. conjecture): 未必來 is not sure to come; 未必看見這件 (s.o.) may not have seen this letter.

未嘗 *weihcharng*, adv., never: 未嘗對他說過 never told him; used in double negative: 未嘗不是 can't say that it is wrong, it is quite right, see *-tserng*↓.

未定草 *weih-dihng-tsaau*, n., author's manuscripts which are not final, also 未定稿.

未冠 *weihguahn*, adj., (AC) not yet mature, before the "capping ceremony" (冠禮).

未遑 *weih-huarng*, phr., have not had time to (do): 未遑執筆 have not had the time to write you a letter.

未婚妻 *weihhun-chi*, n., fiancée.

未幾 *weihjii*, adv., (1) soon after, in a short time; (2) (LL) not much or many (＝無幾).

未經 *weih-jing*, phr., have not yet (gone through): 未經閱過 have not read it yet.

未及 *weih-jir*, phr., not in time for, have not had time to; have not had time (to prepare, to answer your letter, etc.).

未知數 *weih-jy-shuh*, n., an unknown quantity or number.

未來 *weihlair*, n., the future, time to come; 未來的 adj., future (luck, etc.).

未了 *weih-liaau*, adj., unfinished (business).

未免 *weihmiaan*, adv., (1) can't say that it isn't (tactful expression for "is"): 未免過份 is rather too presumptuous; (2) could not help: 未免答他兩句 could not help saying a word or two in reply; 未免多情 could not help being sentimental.

未能 *weihnerng*, adv., could not: 未能免俗 phr., (court.) have to follow the customs.

未然 *weih-rarn*, adj. & n., before event, before it happens: 防患於未然 prevent trouble before it happens.

未入流 *weih-ruhliour*, adj., out of the run; (of writers) not yet known or recognized.

未若 *weih-ruoh*, phr., it would be better to (sell it, recognize its existence, etc.).

未悉 *weih-shi*, phr., (in letters) do not know (how you are, etc.), ＝未知.

未詳 *weih-shiarng*, phr., is not expressly stated, not told: 情形未詳 do not know the details.

未遂 *weih sueih*, phr., (plan, wish) not realized or fulfilled.

未曾 *weihtserng*, adv., never: 未曾見過 never saw, have never seen.

未完 *weih-warn*, phr., not yet finished.

未亡人 *weih-warng-rern*, n., widow in self-reference (person who is due to die but "hasn't yet").

未央 *weih-yang*, phr., (the night) is not far spent yet.

未有 *weih-yoou*, phr., there never was: 未有如此作法 it was never done like this.

末 10.01

moh.

N. (1) Last part (versus 本 foundation): 本末 beginning and end: 物有本末, 事有終始 there is a proper sequence of foundation and end-results, of first and last things; 德者本也, 財者末也 character is the foundation and wealth follows; 本末倒置 put first things last or last things first. (2) Dust, powder (oft. *-tz*, *-'l*): 粉筆末(兒) chalk powder; 麵包末兒 bread crumbs; 茶葉末 tea-leaves dust; 藥末 medical powder. (3) Name of old man's role in Chin. drama.

Adj. (1) Last in time: 末了 at the end; 末班車 the last train or bus; 末年 the last years of a period; 末葉 the last generations of family, last part of century or dynasty; 末流, 末代 last generations. (2) Last in place: 末座, 末位, 末席 the lowest seats at table. (3) Last in importance: 末技, 末藝 small arts; 末策, 末計 the last resort after other methods fail; 末議 insignificant criticism, (modest) my humble views; 末官 (modest) your humble servant, self-reference of official to superior.

末後 *mohhouh*, adv., later, after that.

末減 *mohjiaan*, v.t., commute sentence, lighten punishment.

末節 *mohjier*, n., unimportant details.

末了(兒) *mohliaau* (*'l*), adv., at the end.

末流 *mohliour*, n., later and usually corrupted stage of movement.

末路 *mohluh*, n., the end, death (of plans).

末命 *mohmihng*, n., last will (oral).

末末了 *mohmohliaau*, adv., at the very end.

末日 *mohryh*, n., the Judgment Day.

末梢 *mohshau*, n., small end, extremity; 末梢神經 nerve endings, peripheral nerves.

末世 *mohshyh*, adj., last or declining years; 末世論 *--luhn*, n., eschatology.

末學 *mohshyuer*, n., shallow scholar, -ship: 末學後進 the younger superficial students; (oft. modest) one's own scholarship.

末俗 *mohsur*, n., (derog.) modern customs; latter-day fashions or fads; decadent ways.

末尾 *mohweei*, n., end (of event, thing).

末業 *mohyeh*, n., lower professions (traditionally, commerce and industry).

朱 10.01

ju.

朱 耒 來

N. A surname.

Adj. Vermilion, scarlet: 朱唇皓齒 red lips and white teeth; 傅粉塗朱 facial make-up of powder and rouge; 近朱者赤 phr. (fig.) be influenced by close association.

朱陳 *ju-cherng*, phr., 結朱陳之好 marriage of two families, from AC allu., the clans 朱 and 陳 traditionally married into each other.

朱黃 *ju-huarng*, n., "yellow and red" colors used in revising or correcting text—hence the work of correction.

朱紅 *juhurng*, adj., scarlet, vermilion, a shade paler than 大紅 deep red.

朱槿 *jujiin*, n., (bot.) red hibiscus (=扶$^{\Delta}$桑 10A.81), described as similar to the mulberry.

朱欒 *juluarn*, n., (LL) the pomelo (=文旦).

朱鷺 *juluh*, n., (zoo.) a crane with white pinkish body, *Nipponia nippon*.

朱輪 *julurn*, n., red carriage wheels of noble or rich family, see *-shyuan*↓.

朱門 *jumern*, n., "vermilion gate," (fig.) a rich mansion: 朱門酒肉臭 (allu.) meat is allowed to spoil in rich men's homes (while wayfarers die of cold).

朱墨 *jumoh*, n., red ink (made of cinnabar): 朱墨套印 bicolor printing in black and red.

朱儒 *jurur*, n., see 侏$^{\Delta}$儒 91A.01.

朱砂 *jusha*, n., cinnabar, used as red ink and medicine.

朱軒 *jushyuan*, n., red-painted carriage of the noblemen.

朱紫 *jutzyy*, n., the noblemen and those of high official rank (in vermilion and purple costume).

朱顏 *juyarn*, n., pink face, referring (1) to beautiful women, (2) to youth or in 朱顏皓髮 healthy old age.

朱殷 *juyin*, adj., (AC) deep red.

耒 10.01

leei.

N. A plough: 耒耜 ploughs and plowshares; 耒耨 plough and rake.

來 10.01

lair (**laih*).

[Pop. 来]

N. A surname.

V.i. & t. (1) Come: 來往 *-waang* ↓; 往來 exchange of visits, goods, gifts, etc.; 來來往往 come and go; 來而不往 not to pay a return call on s.o.; 歸去來兮 (LL) I am homeward bound; 魂兮歸來 (LL) may the spirit of the deceased come back to us! 來回 *-hueir*↓; 跑來跑去 be ever coming and going; 來到 *-dauh*, 來臨 *-lirn*↓; 前來領獎 come forward to receive a prize or award; 不來也好 it's just as well that s.o. hasn't come; 過來吧 come over here; 來呀, 來吧 come, come; 眉來眼去 exchange glances between them. (2) V.i., do: 來得及 can be done, there is time enough; 來不及 cannot be done, time won't allow it; 來一下 come and try it; 你來 you come and try; 你來不來 will you join us? 不來了 won't do it, won't come, give up; 胡來, 亂來, 瞎來 you are making a mess of it; 白來 wasted one's time in coming; 照樣再來一回 let's do it over again; 別來這一套 don't give me that! 慢來, 慢慢來 do it slowly, take your time; 來來 *-'lai*↓; 這樣一來, 這一來 by so doing, in this way. (3) V.t., bring, let's do (s.t.): 來酒, 來飯 bring some wine, rice; 來他五斤 let me have five catties; 來八圈 (of mahjong) let's play eight rounds; 來兩盤 (of chess) let's play a couple of games. (4) (**laih*) (Interch. 徠) v.t., to comfort, encourage (s.o.) to come over to one's side.

Vb. complement. (1) Used after vb. to complement its meaning: (a) be able to, be worth: 說不上來 don't know how to say it, don't remember it now; 辦不來 be unable to do it; 買不來 be unable to buy it; 搶不來 be unable to get it by fair means or foul; 趕不起來 be unable to finish it in time; 做不來 don't know how to do it; 合得來 be able to get along with (s.o.); (b) be worth the effort or money; 花得來 be worth the money; 花不來 be not worth it. (2) Expressing an action begun: 颳起風來 a wind starts blowing; 鬧出事來 have got into trouble; 打起架來 a fight has broken out; 提起筆來 take up a pen to write. (3) Having the sense of "having done!": 你同誰吵嘴來 with whom are you quarrelling? 你剛才說什麼來 what were you saying just then? (4) Oft. equiv. Eng. "to": 看來, 想來, 說來, 聽來好笑 it's ridiculous to see it, to think of it, to speak of it, to hear it; 說來話長 it's a long story to tell. (5) Expressing direction toward speaker: 走過來 come over here; 拿張紙來 bring a piece of paper; 上來 please come up; 下來 please come down. (6) With 去 (一來一去) having the sense of "over," "about," "in both directions": 唸來唸去 read it over and over again; 想來想去 after thinking it over; 寫來寫去 write it over and over again. (7) Used as a final particle: 盍歸乎來 (AC) why not come home? 你這是何苦來 why have you done such an abominable thing? 爲的什麼來 what have you come or done such a thing for?

Adj. (1) Future, later on: 來年 *-niarn*, 來日 *-ryh*↓; 來春 next spring; 來月 next month; 來歲 next year; 來世 *-shyh*^{2}, 來生 *-sheng*↓. (2) (Of person or thing) coming, incoming: 來人 *-rern*, 來使 *-shyy*, 來者 *-jee*↓; 來函, 來札, 來翰 your letter; 來意 *-yih*↓; 來情去意 mutual expressions of affection; 來勢 *-shyh*^{4}↓; 送往迎來 be busy welcoming and bidding good-bye to friends.

Adv. (1) About, approximately:

三十來歲 about 30 years old; 十來個 approximately ten or so; 尺來長 about one foot long. (2) As (big, small, etc.) as: 你色膽有天來大 your daring in sex exploits is fantastic ("big as the sky").

Special formations. (1) Forming words meaning "since," "originally": 本來, 原來 original(ly); 由來 since. (2) Part of n. denoting time: 近來 recent(ly); 將來, 未來 in the future; 後來 later on; 日來 the other day; 以來, 而來 since then; 從來, 向來 usually, in the past. (3) Adv. conj., in order to, so that, to: 唱個歌來湊熱鬧 sing us a song (in order) to make the party more lively (equiv. 以 in LL); 開口來說話 open one's mind and (to) talk. (4) In enumeration: 一來, 二來, 三來 firstly, secondly, thirdly.

來賓 *lairbin*, (1) n., guest(s); (2) v.i., (AC) come as guest(s).

來禽 *lairchirn*, n., (bot.) the apple, *Pirus malus* var. *tomentosa* (also 林檎).

來去 *lairchyuh*, n., (1) a round trip; (2) distance between two places; (3) friendly contacts and intercourse.

來到 *lair-dauh*, v.i., arrive at, come to (place).

來得 *lair'de*, v.i., as usual followed by a complement: (1) have the capacity for, be able to: 他很來得一兩杯 he is able to drink quite a few cups; (2) act or speak with great force: 你這一句話來得利害 your words are most telling; 這一招兒來得好 this move (parry)of yours is well aimed; (3) happen, come: 來得不巧 happens at the wrong (unfortunate) moment.

來頓瓶 *lairdun pirng*, n., a Leyden jar or vial.

來附 *lair-fuh*¹, v.i., submit as vassal state.

來復 *lair-fuh*², n., a seven-day cycle (as used in the *Book of Change*); 來復鎗 a rifle (translit. also 來福槍).

來服 *lairfur*, n., (bot. MC) the turnip (also 萊服)=modn. 蘿▵蔔 *luor'bo*, 20A.11

來稿 *lair-gaau*, n., manuscript submitted to an editor.

來歸 *lairguei*, v.i. & t., (1) (AC) (of women) be married into husband's home; (2) submit as vassal; (3) return, come home.

來亨雞 *lairhengji*, n., the Leghorn.

來回(兒) *lairhueir(-huer'l)*, n., return: 打來回 make a return trip; 來回一趟 ditto; 一個來回 a return trip; 來回來去的 ever coming and going; 來回票 a return ticket.

來朝 (1) *lairjau*, n., (AC) tomorrow; (2) *lairchaur*, v.i., (LL) come to pay homage or tribute.

來著 *lair'je*, aux. vb., expressing a continuing or completed action: 他說甚麽來著 what has he been saying? 聽見說你認得他來著 it's said that you know him.

來者 *lairjee*, n., (1) anything in the future: 來者猶可追 (AC) the future is yet for oneself to shape or mold; (2) anyone who has come: 來者不善, 善者不來 (AC) those who have come are not friendly, those who are friendly have not come; 來者不拒 all comers welcome.

來件 *lairjiahn*, n., incoming communication or other articles received.

來今 *lairjin*, n., days to come.

來客 *lairkeh*, n., guests, visitors.

來來 *lair'lai*, v. t., try to do (s.t.): 他做的不好, 你來來看 if he doesn't know how to do it, you come and try.

來歷 *lairlih*, n., a person's background, career.

來臨 *lairlirn*, (1) v.i., come, arrive; (2) n., advent, arrival.

來路 *lairluh*, n., (1) see *-lih*↑; (2) anything from abroad: 來路貨 imported goods.

來龍 *lairlurng*, n., (geomancy) a hill exerting a decisive influence (in selecting a site for a building or grave): 來龍去脈 a sequence of events, cause and effect.

來牟 *lairmour*, n., (AC) wheat and barley.

來年 *lairniarn*, n., next year.

來派 *lairpaih*, n., onset, first symptoms (of a disease): 這病的來派可不輕: the disease comes with serious first symptoms.

來人 *lairrern*, n., (1) a messenger, bearer of note; (2) in 來人兒 middleman in business deals or employment service.

來日 *lairryh*, n., (1) tomorrow; (2) the future: 來日方長 there are many days yet to provide for or think about; 來日大難 difficult days are ahead.

來生 *lairsheng*, n., future life.

來手 *lairshoou*, n., the bearer of a letter: 請交來手帶下 please give to the bearer.

來示 *lairshyh*¹, n., (court.) your letter or note (same as 來諭).

來世 *lairshyh*², n., (1) later generations; (2) future life.

來事 *lairshyh*³, n., future events.

來勢 *lairshyh*⁴, n., (1) manner of approaching enemy, landslide, etc.: 來勢洶洶 break in in full fury, also come to look for trouble; (2) onset, first symptoms (of a disease).

來使 *lairshyy*, n., a messenger; representative from another country.

來頭(兒) *lairtou('l)*, n., (1) position or social status: 大有來頭 very influential socially or politically; 來頭不小 not to be taken lightly; 此馬來頭大 this person has influential backing; (2) fun in doing anything: 這種賭博還有甚麽來頭兒 what's the fun with this kind of gambling?

來茲 *lairtz*, n., (LL) the future.

來往 (1) *lairwaang*, v.i., come and go: 來往奔波 ceaselessly come and go; (2) *lair'wang*, n., friendly intercourse: 您和他有來往麽 do you have dealings with him? 常來常往 frequently see each other; 來往文件 correspondence, communication.

來意 *lair-yih*, n., purpose of one's coming.

亅	小	⺊	十	土	ナ	卄	𠃊ト	丨	一	丅	フ	口	囗	冈	㇆	厂	尸	亠	广	宀	丶	乚	弋	心	八	人	乂	乛	一	丿丨	𠂉	く
00	01	02	10	11	12	20	21	22	30	31	32	40	41	42	50	51	52	60	61	62	63	70	71	72	80	81	82	83	90	91	92	93

來儀 *lair-yir*, phr., (AC) arrival of phoenixes as a good omen for the country: 鳳凰來儀.

來由 *lairyour*, n., (also wr. 來繇) (1) cause: 我尋思著甚來由 I've tried to find out its cause; (2) background: 問起他的來由 asked where he had come from or purpose of his visit; 沒來由 without rhyme or reason, (person) of unknown identity.

來源 *lairyuarn*, n., origin, source (of water, news, word).

東 10.01

dung.

N. & adj. (1) The east, eastern: 東方 east; 東邊 east side; 遠東 the Far East: 近東 Middle East; 東半球 Eastern Hemisphere; 東風過耳 (advice) unheeded; 東山再起 (of politician) to stage a comeback (allu.); 東施效顰 (allu.) ugly woman (東施) trying to imitate famous beauty (西施) knitting her brows. (2) Host, landlord, owner: 房東 landlord; 股東 shareholder; 作東 be host of dinner; 東道, 東兒, 東家 *-dauh*, *-'l*, *-jia*↓. (3) (MC) toilet, latrine in 東廁, 東司. (4) A surname.

Adv. 東行 going east; oft. coupled with 西 west, describing confusion, on all sides: 東倒西歪, 東零西亂 lying on all sides; 東一個, 西一個 lying here and there, spread everywhere; 東一拳, 西一腳 a blow here, a kick there; 東不成, 西不就 cannot or will not accept post and be without job; 東塗西抹 draw paint everywhere; 東食西宿 without definite place for board or lodging; 東拉西扯 (of talk) rambling, incoherent, disorderly; 東奔西走 going in all directions for s.t.; 東張西望 to look in all directions.

東北 *dungbeei*, n., northeast, usu. reference to Manchuria.

東邊 *dungbian*, adj., east side, on the east.

東牀 *dungchuarng*, n., son-in-law: 東牀快婿, 坦腹東牀 (allu.).

東道 *dungdauh*, n., host for party: 做東道, also 東道主.

東丁 *dungding*, n., jingling sound.

東都 *dungdu*, n., Loyang in Suhng Dyn.

東方 *dungfang*, n., (1) the east, the Orient: 東方文化 oriental culture; (2) a surname.

東宮 *dunggung*, n., the crown prince; his residence; also empress in East Palace.

東家 *dungjia*, n., (1) landlord, house owner; (2) the person whom one serves as tutor, secretary or domestic help; (3) eastern neighbor.

東京 *Dungjing*, n., Tokyo; 東京灣 Gulf of Tonkin, also Tokyo Bay.

東兒 *dung'l*, n., host for party.

東南亞 *Dungnarnyaa*, n., Southeast Asia; 東南亞公約組織 Southeast Asia Treaty Organization (SEATO).

東三省 *Dungsansheeng*, n., Manchuria.

東西 *dungshi*, n., (1) east and west; (2) (*dung'shi*) a thing: 很多東西 many things; 什麼東西 what, what things; 你是什麼東西 (abusive) what are you anyway? 不是東西 a rascal, scoundrel.

東廁 *dungtseh*, n., latrine.

東亞 *Dungyaa*, n., East Asia.

東洋 *Dungyarng*, n., Japan; 東洋人 Japanese; 東洋車 rickshaw, also called 人力車 jinrickshaw.

東瀛 *Dungyirng*, n., Japan.

柬 10.01

jiaan.

N. (Interch. 簡) a written note, calling cards: 喜柬 invitation to a wedding; 柬帖, 名柬 a visiting card; 請柬 a formal invitation; 紅柬 formerly, red visiting cards; 禮柬 a card sent with presents; 庚柬, 媒柬 betrothal card giving the name of the betrothed and the year, month, day, and hour of his (her) birth.

V.t. (Interch. 揀) select, choose.

束 10.01

shuh.

N. (1) A bundle, bale, bunch: 一束花 a bunch of flowers; 一束草 a bundle of straw; 束芻, 束脩 *-chur*, *-shiou*↓. (2) A surname.

V.t. To tie, tie up, keep immobile, put away: 束縛 *-fur*↓; 束髮 to tie up hair; 束手 *-shoou*↓; 束之高閣 to shelve a matter (put it away unheeded); 拘束 exercise rigid control over, not free; 管束, 約束 control, put restraint (on children); 結束 conclude (matter, discussion).

束帛 *shuh-bor*, v.i., (AC) ancient rite of betrothal, the bridegroom giving a roll of silks.

束芻 *shuh-chur*, n., a bundle of grass in sacrifice at grave.

束髮 *shuh-faa*, v.i., tie up the hair; (AC) ceremony of capping boy on maturity.

束縛 *shuhfur*, v.t. & adj. & n., constraint, rigid control: 不受束縛 will not submit to control.

束躬 *shuh-gung*, v.i., (LL) exercise self-control in conduct.

束裝 *shuh-juang*, v.i., as in 束裝就道 to pack up for journey.

束身 *shuh-shen*, v.i., see *-gung*↑.

束脩 *shuh-shiou*, n., a teacher's salary—in Confucius' time, a parcel of dried meat (脩).

束手 *shuh-shoou*, v.i., to fold one's hands in gesture of hopelessness: 束手待斃 wait helplessly for death; 羣醫束手 the doctors can do nothing to help.

束胸 *shuh-shyung*, n., a brassiere.

束腰 *shuh-yau*, (1) n., a girdle; (2) v.t., to girdle the waist.

棗 10.01

tzaau.

N. (Bot.) the date tree or its fruit: 棗子 *-'tz*; 棗兒 *-'l*↓; 蜜棗 preserved dates; 紅棗, 黑棗 red, black dates.

棗核兒 *tzaauher'l*, n., date-stones; 棗核檳榔 see *-'l*↓; 棗核兒桃 a kind of slender peach; shaped like date-stones.
棗紅 *tzaauhurng*, n., red like dates (also 棗兒紅).
棗兒 *tzaau'l*, n., dates; 棗兒 or 棗核兒檳榔 the betel nut; 棗兒糕 steamed cake with dates.
棗泥 *tzaaunir('l)*, n., date paste.
棗仁 *tzaaurern*, n., kernel of dates.
棗糖兒色 *tzaautarng'l-shaai*, n., reddish-brown.

木 10.01

muh.

N. (1) Wood: 木已成舟 too late to change. (2) Trees, timber: 樹木 trees; 林木 forest; 木皮 bark; 木屑 sawdust, wood chips; 木桶, 木橋wooden pail, bridge, etc.; 木刻, 木雕 wood carving, carved of wood; 木偶, 木像 wooden idol, figure; 木偶戲 puppet show; 木紋, 木理 wood grain; 木行 timber shop, etc. (3) One of five elements 五行, the element of growth and expansion. (4) The planet 木星 Jupiter; 木曜日 Friday. (5) A surname.

Adj. (1) Wooden. (2) Insensitive: 木了, 麻木(了) benumbed, paralyzed; 木訥 *-nah*↓; 木頭木腦 blockhead, stupid; 木立 stand like a post; 木雕泥塑 (person like) clay or wooden statue, blockhead.

木板 *muhbaan*, n., wooden board, plank; 木板畫 woodcut.
木半夏 *muh-bahnshiah*, n., (bot.) wild cherry.
木本 *muhbeen*, n., trees (a classification as dist. from grass 艸本)
木鼈 *muhbie*, n., (bot.) *Momordica*, a tropical fruit.
木筆 *muhbii*, n., magnolia, also called 辛夷.
木廠 *muhchaang*, n., timber mill.
木材 *muhchair*, n., timber.
木強 *muhchiarng*, adj., stiff, insensitive, also wr. 木彊.
木器 *muh-chih*, n., wooden vessels, wooden furniture.
木蠹蛾 *muhduh-er*, n., (zoo.) a moth which eats into trees, *Cossus lignipera*.
木鐸 *muhduor*, n., (AC) a bell with wooden clapper, used for communal signal.
木耳 *muh-eel*, n., edible tree fungus.
木筏 *muhfar*, n., wooden raft.
木芙蓉 *muh-furrurng*, n., (bot.) hibiscus.
木瓜 *muhgua*, n., papaya.
木管樂器 *muhguaan yuehchih*, n., wood-wind instruments.
木工 *muhgung*, n., carpenter.
木札 *muhjar*, n., slips of wood.
木雞 *muhji*, n., (AC) insensate like a wooden chicken.
木屐(子) *muhji ('tz)*, n., wooden sandals.
木匠 *muhjiahng*, n., carpenter.
木焦油 *muhjiauyour*, n., (chem.) wood tar.
木槿 *muhjiin*, n., hibiscus.
木精 *muhjing*, n., wood alcohol.
木樁 *muhjuang*, n., wooden pile.
木主 *muhjuu*, n., spirit tablet＝神主.
木刻 *muhkeh*, n. & adj., wood-carved (object); wood carving; woodcut.
木蠟 *muhlah*, n., wood wax, Japan wax.
木蘭 *muhlarn*[1], n., magnolia; name of famous girl impersonating as man soldier, celebrated in song and drama; 木蘭花(慢) name of melodic form in Suhng poetry.
木藍 *muhlarn*[2], n., indigo dye stuff, made from 馬棘 *Indigofera tinctoria*.
木料 *muhliauh*, n., timber.
木馬 *muhmaa*, n., wooden horse (gymnastics).
木棉 *muhmiarn*, n., cotton.
木乃伊 *muhnaaiyi*, n., mummy.
木訥 *muhnah*, adj., silent, slow of speech.
木牛流馬 *muhniour liourmaa*, n., military transport vehicles, with control mechanism, credited to 諸葛亮 around 220 A.D.
木偶 *muh-oou*, n., wooden figure; a blockhead, puppet; 木偶戲 a puppet show.
木排(兒) *muhpair(-pai'l)*, n., raft.
木芍藥 *muh-shauryauh*, n., (MC) peonia.
木犀 *muh'shi*, n., (bot.) cassia.
木香 *muhshiang*, n., putchuck, an incense of Cambodia; 木香花 n., banksia rose.
木星 *muhshing*, n., planet Jupiter.
木梳 *muhshu*, n., comb.
木蝨 *muhshy*, n., wood louse, bedbug.
木樨 *muhshyu*, n., (bot.) the cassia; 木樨肉 scrambled egg; 木樨湯 egg soup (from gen. Peking custom to avoid the word 蛋 *dahn*).
木炭 *muhtahn*, n., charcoal.
木頭 *muh'tou*, n., wood, wood block; blockhead.
木叢 *muhtsurng*, n., copse, wood, grove.
木賊 *muhtzer*, n., a short, stiff grass, used for polishing wood.
木作 *muhtzuoh*, n., carpentry.
木魚 *muhyur*, n., wooden fish used for beating rhythm during Buddhist incantations.
木俑 *muhyuung*, n., (AC) wooden idol.

森 10.01

sen.

N. Forest: 森林 *-lirn*↓.

Adj. (1) In close rows as trees in forest: 森羅 *-luor*↓; in close rows. (2) Dark: 陰森 dark in dealings, cunning; 黑森森 very

棗 木 森

dark; 森然 see-*yarn*↓. (3) Severe: 森嚴 -*yarn*↓.

Adv. (LL) rising or growing closely: 森豎, 森聳 (buildings, trees) rising closely together or in a row; 森列 displayed, stacked closely (weapons, armed soldiers, monuments, etc.).

森林 *senlirn*, n., forest, cultivated or wild.

森羅 *senluor*, adj., formidable: 森羅萬象 in formidable array; 森羅殿 palace of the King of Hell =閻羅殿.

森森 *sensen*, adj. & adv., dark, close, thick (vegetation): 黑森森 frightfully dark.

森嚴 *senyarn*, adj., (laws, regulations) severe.

森鬱 *senyuh*, adj., thickly overgrown.

槧 10.01

chiahn.

N. & v.t. Engraving on wood-block; 宋槧 a Suhng (wood-block) edition.

橐 10.01

tuor.

N. A hollow bag open on both ends, dist. 囊 closed on one end.

橐筆 *tuorbii*, phr., formerly, poor scholar with a bag of books and a pen stuck in hair, symbolic of writing profession.

橐駝 *tuortuor*[1], n., camel; a hunchback.

橐橐 *tuortuor*[2], adj., click-clack, sound of footsteps.

橐籥 *tuoryueh*, n., a (pair of) bellows.

櫜 10.01

gau.

N. (AC) case or bag for bows and arrows.

V.t. (AC) to put away in bag.

柰 10.01

naih.

N. A crab apple.

Adv. (Corrupt var. of 奈 12.01).

禁 10.01

jihn (**jin*).

N. (1) Royal residence: 宮禁 palace grounds; 紫禁城 the Forbidden City in Peking; 禁城 -*cherng*↓, 禁苑 -*yuahn*↓; 禁中 imperial quarters; 禁衛軍 -*weihjyun*↓. (2) Sorcery, witchcraft.

V.t. (1) Prohibit, forbid: 禁止 -*jyy*, 禁令 -*lihng*↓; 違禁 illegal acts; 違禁品 n. & adj., contraband; 禁制 -*jyh*↓; 禁屠 days on which no meat is sold; 禁烟, 禁賭, 禁娼 ban on opium-smoking, gambling, prostitution; 禁酒 (U. S. history) Prohibition; 嚴禁 strictly forbid(den); 開禁 lifting of a ban; 禁運 trade embargo; 禁地 forbidden ground; 難禁 difficult (impossible) to suppress; 不禁 cannot help it; 情不自禁 cannot control oneself (one's own feelings). (2) Take into custody, imprison: 監禁 throw into prison; 囚禁 imprison, incarcerate; 禁閉 -*bih*, 禁錮 -*guh*, 禁卒 -*tzur*, 禁子 -*tz*↓. (3) To taboo: 禁忌 -*jih*↓. (4) (**jin*) Be able to withstand or endure: 禁得起, 禁不起(住) can, cannot stand.

Adj. & adv. (**jin*) Durable, -bly: 禁穿 (of clothes) to wear well; 禁用 long-lasting, serviceable for a long time; 禁燒 (of fuel) slow-burning.

禁閉 *jihnbih*, v.t., to jail, lock up, detain.

禁城 *jihncherng*, n., palace grounds; 紫禁城 the Forbidden City in Peking.

禁地 *jihndih*, n., forbidden ground.

禁方 *jihnfang*, n., a secret formula or prescription.

禁錮 *jihnguh*, v.t., (1) imprison; (2) (AC) debar from holding office.

禁菓 *jihn-guoo*, n., the forbidden fruit.

禁忌 *jihnjih*, n. & v.i., taboos (in food, superstition).

禁制 *jihnjyh*, v.t., restrict, prohibit, forbid, ban.

禁軍 *jihnjyun*, n., short for 禁衛軍 -*weihjyun*↓.

禁止 *jihnjyy*, v.t., forbid, prohibit, ban: 禁止吸烟 "no smoking."

禁例 *jihnlih*, n., an official ban or restraint.

禁令 *jihnlihng*, n., legal restriction or ban.

禁臠 *jihnluarn*, n., (LL) the "forbidden fruit," much desired but inaccessible woman.

禁書 *jihn-shu*, n., an officially banned book.

禁土 *jihn-tuu*, n., (astrology) days on which all ground-digging is forbidden.

禁子 *jihntz*, n., a jailer.

禁卒 *jihntzur*, n., ditto.

禁網 *jihn-waang*, n., network of legal restrictions.

禁衛軍 *jihnweih-jyun*, n., imperial guards.

禁夜 *jihnyieh*, v.i. & n., (declare) a curfew.

禁掖 *jihn-yih*, n., palace grounds.

禁苑 *jihn-yuahn*, n., imperial gardens.

禁慾 *jihn-yuh*, v.i., suppress sensual passion; 禁慾主義 asceticism.

索 10.01

suoo.

N. (1) (*-tz*) A rope: 鐵索 iron cable: 索頭 *-tour*↓. (2) A surname.

V.t. (1) To search, try to get: 拔索 ditto; 索求, 索解 *-chiour*, *-jiee* ↓; 索取 *-chyuu*↓. (2) To demand (payment): 索欠, 索薪 *-chiahn*, *-shin*↓.

Vb. aux. (MC) must (=須): 這數年索是 (=須是) 辛苦也 these last few years must be hard indeed; 你索教 (=須使) 意兒温存 you must try to be gentle; 不索 (=不須) 生嗔 don't be angry.

Adj. Lonely, depressed: 索然 *-rarn*↓; 離羣索居 live alone, cut off from society.

Adv. (**suor*) 索性 *-shihng*↓.

索欠 *suoo-chiahn*, v.i., to demand pay.
索求 *suoochiour*, v.t., to seek (person, job, etc.).
索取 *suorchyuu*, v.i., try to get, obtain.
索合 *suooher*, aux. vb., (MC) must (=須當).
索解 *suor jiee*, phr., requires explanation.
索落 *suooluoh*, v.t., (coll.) to berate (person).
索寞 *suoomoh*, adj., lonely, bored, depressed (also wr. 索莫, 索漠).
索賠 *suoopeir*, v.t., claim.
索然 *suoorarn*, adj., (1) dull, uninteresting: 索然無味; (2) quiet, isolated: 牙門索然 (AC) commandant's office is quiet, without callers; (3) depressed: 索然出涕 (AC) depressed and shed tears.
索性 **suorshihng*, adj., (1) straight-tempered; (2) (**suor-*) adv., may just as well, simply, without further ado: 索性給了他 might just as well make it a gift to him; 索性走了 left without further trouble.
索薪 *suoo-shin*, phr., to demand payment of salary in arrears.
索是 *suooshyh*, aux. vb., (MC) must be.
索索 *suorsuoo*, adj., (1) a rustle, whispering sound; (2) (AC) frightened, startled; (3) bored, see *-rarn*↑.
索頭 *suootour*, n., end of a rope.
索要 *suooyauh*, v.t., to demand (money, etc.).
索引 *suoryiin*[1], n., an index: 書名索引 title index; 作者索引 author index, etc.
索隱 *suor-yiin*[2], phr., (1) 探賾索隱 (AC) to search for hidden meanings; (2) 索隱行怪 to look for the abstruse and behave eccentrically.

素 10.01

suh

N. (1) White silk; (LL) a letter; 縞素 white of mourning. (2) Vegetarian food: 吃素, 茹素 be vegetarian; 素食 *-shyr*↓. (3) Element, factor: 原素 chemical element; factor in situation.

Adj. (1) White, color of mourning: 素服 *-fur*↓; 素車白馬 white horse and unadorned carriage used at funeral; 素手 *-shoou*↓; 素月 the bright moon. (2) Simple, unadorned: 樸素 (person) simple, without ostentation of any kind; 素質 *-jyr*↓; 素服, 素位, 素餐 *-fur*, *-weih*, *-tsan*↓. (3) Usual, habitual, present and past: 素望 usual, habitual reputation; 素願 lifelong wish; 素行 *-shirng*, 素交 *-jiau*↓; 素風 habitual manner. (4) Vegetarian, opp. 葷 *hun*, meat: 素火腿 ham made of bean curd; 素麵 noodles with vegetarian garnish; 素油 *-your*↓; 素席 *-shir*[1]↓. (5) Poor: 寒素 (family) poor; 無奈自己手頭兒素 unfortunately have no money.

Adv. Usually, in the past, heretofore: 平素 ditto; 素來, 素日, 素昔 *-lair*, *-ryh*, *-shir*[2]↓; 素不相識 didn't know him before; 素不通信 haven't written each other before; 素稱 has been known to be; 素識 have known (person) for a long time; 素知 I have known always.

素常 *suhcharng*, adv., usually (comes to office punctually, etc.).
素秋 *suhchiou*, n., autumn.
素琴 *suh-chirn*, n., a stringed instrument without strings—typical of 陶淵明 Taur Yuanmirng's easy, simple nature.
素尺 *suhchyy*, n., (LL) a letter.
素封 *suhfeng*, adj., (AC) rich without ranks.
素服 *suhfur*, n., (1) white dress; (2) white of mourning.
素交 *suhjiau*, n., long-known friend.
素節 *suhjier*, n., (1) habitual conduct; (2) personal integrity; (3) (LL, rare) autumn season.
素淨 *suhjihng*, adj., simple and neat (dress).
素志 *suhjyh*, n., life ambition.
素質 *suhjyr*, n., (1) innate quality (of material) or character; (2) white background.
素來 *suhlair*, adv., see *-charng*↑.
素練 *suhliahn*, n., (LL) waterfall (coming down like a sheet of white silk).
素描 *suhmiaur*, v.i. & n., to sketch, a sketch (painting); delineate (character in novel).
素朴 *suhpur*, adj., simple, unadorned (also wr. 素樸).
素日 *suhryh*, adv., usually, in the past, see *-charng*↑.
素性 *suhshihng*, n., one's nature, temperament.
素馨 *suhshin*[1], n., jasmine.
素心 *suhshin*[2], n., one's simple, habitual nature; 素心人 person of simple character; 素心蘭 *--larn*, n., a kind of orchid with undotted petals.
素席 *suhshir*[1], n., a vegetarian meal.
素昔 *suhshir*[2], adv., here to fore.
素行 *suhshirng*, n., habitual conduct.
素手 *suh-shoou*, (1) n., white hand; (2) adj, empty-handed.
素(因)數 *suh(yin) shuh*, n., (math.) prime (factor) number.
素事 *suhshyh*[1], n., funeral affairs.

素 紮 紥 絜 繫 纛 求

素識 *suhshyh*[2], n., old acquaintance.

素食 *suhshyr*, n. & v.i., (1) (be) vegetarian; (2) (AC) eat without work, see *-tsan*↓.

素菜 *suhtsaih*, n., vegetarian dish.

素餐 *suhtsan*, v.i., hold sinecure job.

素族 *suhtzur*, n., (come from) common folks without rank.

素王 *suhwarng*, n., the uncrowned king—Confucius.

素位 *suh-weih*, phr., 素其位而行 (AC) act according to one's status or station in life.

素養 *suhyaang*, n., cultivated manners or poise; cultivation of learning.

素油 *suhyour*, n., vegetable oil.

素願 *suhyuahn*, n., (my) cherished ambition or wish.

素約 *suh-yue*, n., long-standing promise.

紮 10.01

jar (**tza*).

N. A bundle (of flowers, etc.).

V.t. (1) To tie up, pack up: 紮裹 *-'guo*↓; 包紮, 用繩子紮起來 to pack with strings, tape, rope. (2) (**tza*) 紮住, 紮緊 tie up fast; 紮燈, 紮風箏 make paper lantern, kite, with string; 紮辮子 make a queue. (3) To pitch (tent, camp): 紮營, 紮寨 *-yirng*, *-jaih*↓.

紮裹 *jar'guo*, v.i., (coll.) adjust girdle and shoes; tidy up.

紮寨 **tzarjaih*, v.i., pitch tent, to encamp (usu. of brigands).

紮門 **tzar-mern*, v.i., to stand guard at gate.

紮營 **tzaryirng*, v.i., (of army units) set up base camp.

紥 10.01

jar (**tza*).

[Var. of 紮]

絜 10.01

shier (**jier*).

Adj. (**jier*) U. f. 潔 63A.01.

絜矩 *shierjyuu*, v.i., follow the golden rule: 絜矩之道 the principle of reciprocity.

繫 10.01

shih (**jih*).

[Cf. related 係 91A.01, 系 90.01]

V.t. (1) To tie up, around (also **jih*): 繫絆, 繫囚 *-bahn*, *-chiour*↓. (2) To remember in mind: 繫掛, 繫懷 *-guah*, *-huair*↓. (3) To be in contact: 聯繫 to contact (person), 取聯繫 get in contact.

繫絆 *shihbahn* (**jih-*), n., a stumbling rope across roadway (＝羈絆); a burden, added responsibility, what impedes movement.

繫囚 *shih-chiour* (**jih-*), n., a prisoner in fetters.

繫掛 *shihguah*, v.t., to be concerned with, think always of (person perhaps in need).

繫懷 *shih-huair*, v.i. & t., to have constantly on one's mind.

繫戀 *shihliahn*, v.i. & t., ditto.

繫念 *shihniahn*, v.i. & t., ditto.

繫腰 *shihyau*, n., (MC) a girdle.

纛 10.01

dauh (or *dur*).

N. Big square army banner.

§10.02 (十/ｋ)

求 10.02

chiour.

N. A surname.

V.i. & t. (1) To beg for, to seek or look for, to demand: 要求 to demand; 苛求 to demand too much (of person) or criticize by severe standards; 求索 to seek for; 求偶 seek for life mate; 求婚, 求人 *-hun*, *-rern*↓; 求職, 求事 seek for job; 求才 look for real talents; 反求諸己 to look for cause of failure in oneself; 求治 (the people) yearn for peace, (ruler) tries to put country in order; 求之不得 just what one wished for; 可遇而不可求 s.t. unique which may come by chance but not by diligent search; 供過於求 supply exceeds demand; 求漿得酒 get more than that one was looking for; 求田問舍 to busy oneself with business deals and have no higher ambition in life, looking for a site for a permanent home. (2) To beg, request, pray for: 求乞, 求化, 求情 *-chii*, *-huah*, *-chirng*↓; 求你, 求求你 I beg you; 求借 beg to borrow; 求見 beg for an interview; 求子, 求雨 pray for the birth of a son, for rain; 求生不得, 求死未能 can neither live nor die—utter misery; 有求必應 (of god, gentleman) never refuses a request. (3) Set one's mind to, try to: 力求上進 try to make progress in studies; 不求有功, 只求無過 dare not hope for great accomplishment, but only to be free from mistakes; 力求 try very hard to; 求名, 求利 set one's mind to obtain fame, wealth; 刻意求工 try to do one's best (in writing, workmanship); (oft. ＋adj.); 求速, 求簡 try to be efficient, simple; 求備, 求全 *-beih*, *-chyuarn*↓.

求備 *chiour-beih*, phr., to ask for perfection: 毋求備於一人 don't

ask for perfection in any man.

求成 *chiour-cherng*, phr., hope for success.

求籤 *chiour-chian*, v.i., to pray and draw divination sticks at temple.

求乞 *chiourchii*, v.i. & t., to ask s.o. for s.t. (help, pardon, etc.).

求親 *chiourchin*, v.i., (1) to ask for marriage between two families; (2) to ask for help from relatives.

求情 *chiourchirng*, v.i., to ask for special consideration, make appeal as friend or for friend.

求全 *chiourchyuarn*, v.i., to ask for perfection: 萬事莫求全 don't ask for perfection; 求全之毀 (AC) one tries one's best and still gets criticized for it; see 委曲求全 90.93.

求貸 *chiourdaih*, v.i., to ask for loan.

求和 *chiourher*, v.i., to beg for peace by offering surrender.

求化 *chiourhuah*, v.i., (Budd.) to ask for subscriptions.

求凰 *chiour-huarng*, v.i., a man looking for a life mate.

求婚 *chiourhun*, v.i., ask for a girl's hand.

求積法 *chiourji-faa*, n., (math.) mensuration.

求假 *chiour-jiah*, phr., to ask for leave of absence.

求教 *chiour-jiauh*, v.i., (court.) to ask for advice (cf. 請教 60A.42).

求救 *chiour-jiouh*, phr., to cry (ask) for help.

求牡 *chiour-muu*, v.i., (AC) as in 雉鳴求其牡 a female pheasant calls for mate, (fig.) a girl courts a boy.

求饒 *chiour-raur*, v.i., to ask for pardon.

求人 *chiour-rern*, phr., (1) to ask others for help; (2) to look for talents.

求容 *chiour-rurng*, phr., ask to be permitted to stay, also to be pardoned for slight oversights.

求仙 *chiour-shian*, phr., seek to meet with (Taoist) immortals.

求心力 *chiourshinlih*, n., (phys.) centripetal force.

求學 *chiour-shyuer*, v.i., to go to school or college for further studies; try to improve oneself in studies.

桼 10.02

chi.

[Var. of 漆 63A.02; dist. 黍]

漦 10.02

lir.

N. Saliva: 龍漦 (myth.) dragon's saliva (symbol of dyn.'s downfall).

V.i. (AC) to flow downstream.

表 10.02

biaau.

N. (1) Outside, surface, contrasted with 裏 *lii*, inside: 表裏相應 front attack helped by people inside the city; 表裏爲奸 conspiracy with people working inside; 表裏如一 conformity of profession and conduct; 溢於言表 (feeling) shows between the lines, in overtones; 出了意表(之外) beyond expectations, unexpectedly; 表面 *-miahn*↓. (2) External appearance: 儀表不凡 handsome looks; 虛有其表 deceptively handsome, good in appearance only. (3) Memorial to emperor: 表章, 表奏, 奏表. (4) Chart, graph, any chart for consultation, meter, watch: 手表 wrist watch; 鐘表 clock and watch (also wr. 鐘錶); 計程表 taximeter; 溫度表 thermometer; 氣壓表 barometer; 電表, 水表 power, water meter; 一覽表 general chart; 圖表 chart; 表格 *-ger*↓. (5) Memorial tablet: 紀功表, 碑表. (6) Cousin on mother's side, contrasted with 堂 on father's side: 表妹, 弟 cousin sister, brother; 表親 mother's relatives; 中表 first cousin, child of father's sister or mother's brother.

V.t. To show, manifest, bring to surface, mention: 表同情 show sympathy: 略表寸心 just to show my gratitude, remembrance; 表過不提 merely mention by the way; 表達, 表示, 表明 *-dar*, *-shyh*, *-mirng*, etc.↓; 表汗 bring about perspiration.

表白 *biaaubair*, v.t., express (real feelings, intentions, usu. under clouded circumstances).

表情 *biaauchirng*, v.i., & n., (of actors) express feelings, such performance or expression.

表尺 *biaurchyy*, n., gun sight.

表達 *biaaudar*, v.t., express (ideas, feelings).

表格 *biaauger*, n., blank form; chart.

表彰 *biaaujang*[1], v.t., commend (work); publicize (good works).

表章 *biaaujang*[2], n., memorial to emperor.

表記 *biaaujih*, n., a mark; souvenir, mark of remembrance.

表決 *biaaujyuer*, v.t., decide by vote: 付表決 put to the vote.

表殼兒 *biaauker'l*, n., cover of watch.

表禮 *biaurlii*[1], n., gift at first meeting.

表裏 *biaurlii*[2], n., outside and inside.

表蒙子 *biaaumerngtz*, n., (dial.) watch cover.

表面 *biaaumiahn*, n. & adj., outside, surface; on the outside, superficial: 由表面觀之 look at on the surface; 當表面 as a front; 表面上 *--shahng*, adj. & adv., superficial, -ly: 表面上的進步, 朋友 superficial progress, friends; 表面化 *--huah*, v.i., come to the surface (of hidden feelings, currents).

表明 *biaaumirng*, v.t. & n., ex-

求 桼 漦 表

亅	小	⺊	十	土	ナ	卄	凵卜	丨	一	丅	フ	口	区	冈	㇕	⺁	尸	亠	广	亠	丶	乚	弋	心	八	人	乂	㇏	㇀	㇓	㇗	く
00	01	02	10	11	12	20	21	22	30	31	32	40	41	42	50	51	52	60	61	62	63	70	71	72	80	81	82	83	90	91	92	93

press, demonstrate (friendship, etc.), give expression to: 表明奸情 show up conspiracy, hypocrisy.

表皮 *biaaupir*, n., (biol.) epidermis; (bot.) bark, outer layer.

表瓤(兒) *biaaurarng('l)*, n., inside mechanism of watch (瓤=meat of melon).

表現 *biaaushiahn*, v.t., give evidence of, show (work, results), demonstrate (ability).

表象 *biau-shiahng*[1], n., signs (of heavens, approval, etc.).

表相 *biau-shiahng*[2], n., external appearance.

表率 *biaaushuaih*, n., model, personal example for others.

表示 *biaaushyh*, v.t., show, express, demonstrate: 表示同意, 反對 express consent, disagreement; 表示樂觀 show optimism.

表土 *biaurtuu*, n., (geol.) top layer of soil.

表字 *biaautzyh*, n., secondary personal name=別號.

表演 *biauryaan*, v.t. & n., perform (-ance).

表揚 *biaauyarng*, v.t., give public recognition.

喪 10.02

sahng (**sang*).
[Pop. 丧]

N. (**sang*) (1) A funeral: 喪事 ditto; 出喪 hold funeral procession; 送喪 partake in above; 弔喪 attend funeral. (2) Mourning: 居喪 be in mourning; 國喪 national mourning; 囚首喪面 with disheveled hair and dismal looks; 喪聲歪氣 (of servants) dismal and lazy.

V.t. (*sahng*) To lose (life, parents, country): 喪命 *-mihng*↓; 喪妻, 喪偶 lose one's wife (through death); 喪家狗 as tray dog (homeless), (fig.) dismal, crestfallen appearance; 如喪考妣 wearing a funeral face as if newly bereft of both parents.

Adj. (**sahng*) Downcast, outcast: 喪氣 *-chih*↓; 頹喪 downcast, given up hope, dismal.

喪榜 **sangbaang*, n., white notice of funeral in home.

喪謗 *sahng'bang*, v.t., to blaspheme; to revile, slander.

喪氣 *sahngchih*, adj., (1) downcast, frustrated; (2) (*-'chi*) adj., unlucky.

喪膽 *sahng-daan*, v.i., to lose heart.

喪服 **sangfur*, n., funeral costume.

喪國 *sahng-guor*, v.i., to lose one's country to conqueror, see one's country subjugated.

喪家 **sang-jia* (*-'jia*), n., family of deceased.

喪祭 **sangjih*, n., funeral sacrifices.

喪主 **sang-juu*, n., eldest son during a parent's funeral or eldest grandson in absence of eldest son.

喪種 **sangjuung*, n., a corruption of *-juu*↑.

喪志 *sahng-jyh*, v.i., to lose ambition: 玩物喪志 be a playboy without ambitions.

喪居 **sangjyu*, v.i., live in mourning.

喪亂 **sahngluahn*, n., (AC) war and turmoil.

喪門 **sangmern*, n., bereft family; 喪門鬼 an evil spirit in charge of death (Death with a sickle).

喪命 *sahng-mihng*, v.i., to die, esp. during war and turmoil.

喪明 *sahng-mirng*, v.i., (1) become blind; (2) (AC allu. to father who) mourns the death of his son.

喪煞 **sangshah*, n., return of the ghost of deceased to his home for a last look.

喪身 *sahng-shen*, v.i., to lose one's life (in accident, through drowning, incurring punishment, etc.).

喪心 *sahng-shin*, phr., 喪心病狂 seized with crazy ideas, losing all balance of judgment.

喪師 *sahng-shy*, v.i., be defeated in battle.

喪事 **sangshyh*, n., funeral affair.

喪失 *sahngshyr*, v.i., to lose (a wallet, ambition, etc.).

喪頭 **sangtour*, n., a slight nodding of head, less than usual, made by one in mourning.

裘 10.02

chiour.

N. (1) A surname. (2) A fur coat: 皮裘, 裘衣 ditto; 狐裘 a fox coat; 輕裘肥馬 (AC) rich style of living ("light fur and well-fed horses"); 裘馬 ditto; 裘蔽金盡 (allu.) short of living expenses abroad ("coat tattered, gold gone"); 箕[A]裘 92A.80; 裘葛 change from fur to linen—passing of one year; 裘褐 simple gown of hempen material.

辳 10.02

nurng.
[Arch. of 農 22.02]

製 10.02

jyh.

V.t. To cut and make (dresses), to make (shoes, movies, clocks), to manufacture: 土製 home-made; 製成 make into (utensils); 鐵製, 銅製, 皮製 made of iron, copper, leather; 製紙 paper-making; 製片 make (produce) films; 製圖 make charts or blueprints; 製版 set up (printing) plates; 仿製 make copy after ancient model; 複製 make duplicates; 製法 method for making; 製藥 make medical pills, powder or lotion; 製品 product.

製片 *jyhpiahn*, n., film producer.

製造 *jyhtzauh*, v.t. & n., manufacture: 日本製造 made in Japan.

製作 *jyhtzuoh*, v.t., to create; manufacture.

囊 10.02

narng.

N. (1) A bag, case, sack, purse: 皮囊 a leather case; 革囊 ditto; 行囊 travelling bag; 背囊 knapsack; 被囊 sleeping bag; 囊空如洗 without a penny in one's purse; 探囊取物 things which one can readily lay hands on, easily, as easy as picking one's own pocket; 阮囊羞澀 (allu.) lacking sufficient funds to meet necessary expenses; 囊中物 things already in the bag; 囊中穎 talent is bound to make its mark (as point of awl in pocket) 錦囊妙計 have s.t. up one's sleeve; 酒囊飯袋 "wine bag and rice basket"—(derog.) a glutton and a drunk, a good-for-nothing. (2) A surname.

V.t. To put in a bag: 囊括 *-gua* ↓; 囊螢映雪 (allu.) to study hard in spite of poverty (lit., to read by the light of bagged fireflies or the reflected light of snow).

囊膗 *narngchuaih*, n., (also *nang-*) pork near the pig's nipples.

囊括 *narnggua*, v.t., to bag (wealth, etc.): 囊括一切 sweep up everything.

§10.10 (十/十)

十 10.10

shyr.

N. & adj. Ten: 十多個, 十來個 over ten (pieces); 十多歲, 十來歲 over ten (of age); 幾十個 several tens or dozens; 百十來個 over hundred (pieces); 十二使徒 the Twelve Disciples; 十八羅漢 the eighteen Lohans (Arahats); 女大十八變 a growing girl changes a great deal, how a teenage girl changes from year to year; 十八般武藝 various skills in boxing, fighting with sword, spear, etc.; 十三經 the Thirteen Classics, see 經 93B.30; 十有八九 eight or nine out of ten; 十無二三 less than two or three out of ten; 十分之一 one-tenth; 十一 (a) eleven, (b) one-tenth; 十成, 十分 *-cherng*, *-fen* ↓; 十室九空 almost all (nine-tenths) houses empty after raid; 十拿九穩 almost (nine-tenths) certain, 90 percent sure; 十羊九牧 nine shepherds for ten sheep—more officials than residents; 十目所視, 十手所指 (AC) all eyes see it and all fingers point to it—useless to hide; 十年樹木, 百年樹人 it takes ten years to grow a tree and a hundred years to bring up a generation of good men—long-term plan.

Adj. & adv. Complete: 十全十美 perfect (beauty, character); 十足 *-tzur* ↓.

十成(兒) *shyrcherng('l)*, adj., hundred per cent (gold content, etc.): 有十成把握 hundred per cent certain.

十全 *shyrchyuarn*, adj., perfect, all complete (happiness, etc.).

十冬(臘月) *shyrdung*, n., the winter months (10th, 11th and 12th).

十二 *shyr-eh (sh-eh)*, adj., twelve: 十二分抱歉, 滿意 hundred per cent ("120%") sorry, satisfied; 十二宮 the twelve constellations of the zodiac; 十二指腸 *--jyy charng*, n., the duodenum; 十二時 the twelve two-hour periods, 子, 丑, 寅, 卯 (see Appendix A); 十二小時 twelve hours; 十二屬 *--shuu*, 十二肖 *--shiauh*, the twelve animals corresponding to twelve-year cycle (see Appendix A).

十方 *shyrfang*, n., (Budd.) the ten directions, north, south, east, west, four intermediate and above, below.

十分 *shyrfen*, adj. & adv., (1) hundred per cent (satisfied, pleased, etc.); (2) tenth part: 十分之一, 之三 one-tenth, three-tenths.

十個頭兒 *shyr'getour'l*, adv., (coll.) very, extremely: 天氣十個頭兒的冷 bitterly cold.

十胡 *shyrhur*, n., name of card game (also wr. 十湖).

十進法 *shyrjihnfaa*, n., the decimal system; the metric system.

十錦 *shyrjiin*, adj., (dish) garnished with various ingredients: 十錦大鍋 casserole with different meat and vegetable contents.

十惡 *shyr-oh*, n., (1) the ten cardinal sins; (2) (law) 十惡不赦 formerly, ten unpardonable crimes, including rebellion and other not well-defined items, as lack of filial piety, of harmony in family relationships, lack of righteousness, of humanity, etc.; beyond redemption.

十項運動 *shyr shiang yuhnduhng*, n., decathlon.

十足 *shyr tzur*, adj., hundred per cent (pleased, arrogant, etc.): 十足赤金 24-karat gold; 十足洋奴 completely denationalized person, subservient to foreigners.

十字(兒) *shyrtzyh (-tzeh'l)*, n. & adj., cross-shaped like letter +: 十字架 the Christian cross; 十字街 or 街口 crossroads; 十字軍 the Crusades; 十字火 cross fire; 紅十字會 the Red Cross.

十姊妹 *shyr tzyymeih*, n., (1) (zoo.) a kind of small singing birds, *Uroloncha domestica*; (2) (bot.) a plant of rose family, *Rosa multiflora*; (3) certain sisterhoods of Kwangtung, in which girls prefer independent work and pledge never to marry.

十月 *shyr-yueh*, n., October; 十月革命 *--germihng*, October Revolution (the Russian Revolution in 1917).

本 10.10

been.

本

N. adjunct. A volume: 一本書 a book.

N. (1) Stem, root of plants: 艸本 grass family; 木本 plants with stiff trunks; 本草綱目 classical Chinese *Materia Medica*, a treatise on medicinal plants. (2) Foundation of things: 本末倒置, 捨本逐末 attend to the superficials and neglect the essentials; 事有本末 (AC) there is distinction of the basic essentials and the periphery. (3) Origins: 源源本本 (trace) from the origins; 細說本末 recount the development from the beginning; see 本源 *-yuarn*↓; 忘本 (derog.) forget one's ancestry or ancestral tradition. (4) Capital (vs. interest), capital investment: 資本 capital in gen.; 本利 capital and interest; 不够本, 虧本, 賠本, 折本 lose money, cannot cover cost; 小本, 無本 small, inadequate capital; see 本錢 *-chiarn*↓. (5) Edition, manuscript copy: 原刻本 original edition; 抄本 manuscript copy; 臨本 copy of calligraphy or painting; 拓本, 搨本 rubbings from stone inscriptions; 奏本 memorial to emperor; see 本兒, 本子 *-'l*, *-tz*↓.

Adj. (1) This, the present, our: 本日, 本月, 本週, 本年 this day, month, week, year; 本埠, 市 local (mail), this city; 本國, 本省 our country, this or our province; 本鄉 or 本鄉土兒 our (one's) local district; 本校 our school; 本號 our shop; 本人 *-rern*↓; 本土 native (products, etc.). (2) Original: 本籍 one's ancestral district; 本意 original meaning or intention; 本義 original meaning.

Adv. Originally, indicating what is not, but should be (short for 本來): 本(來) 應該如此 should have been so anyway, similarly 本應, 本該, 本當; 本(來) 不如此 originally it was not so; 本屬, 本是, 本可 originally belong, should be, might; 本可合併討論 (the two problems) could have been discussed together.

本部 *beenbuh*, n., headquarters, as 參謀本部 military staff headquarters.

本錢 *beenchiarn*, n., capital investment, layout, sometimes display of a person's stock in trade, as physical charms of an attractive woman.

本地 *beendih*, n., & adj., native place or people, local; 本地人, 話 local people, dialect; 本地出產 local product.

本分 *beenfehn*, n., duty.

本工兒 *beengung'l*, n., (coll.) what is one's duty.

本行 *beenharng*, n., (1) one's own profession: 這是我本行 this is my line; (2) our firm.

本家 *beenjia*, n., same clan or family: 本家兒 (a) same clan; (b) the family of bride, groom or deceased, etc. on occasions (wedding, funeral, accident, etc.): 新娘本家 bride's family.

本金 *beenjin*, n., =*-chiarn*↑.

本州 *beenjou*, n., (1) Honshu, Japan's largest island; (2) this district.

本主兒 *bernjuu'l*, n., (law) rightful owner; person involved on certain occasions.

本質 *beenjyr*, n., innate character (of metal, children), essential character (of teachings).

本旨 *beenjyy*, n., main purpose, tenet.

本兒 *bee'l*, n., (1) capital (money); (2) a copy, volume.

本來 *beenlair*, adv. & adj., originally, as a matter of fact: 本來不該他的事 (this matter) should not concern him; 本來面目 real (unmasked), original appearance or character.

本利 *been-lih*, n., capital and interest; 本利和 total of capital and interest.

本領 *bernliing*, n., skill, skillful ability.

本論 *beenluhn*, n., main tenet.

本命年 *beenmihng-niarn*, n., recurrent year in the twelve-year cycle, of the same animal (rat, cow, etc.) as one's year of birth.

本末 *beenmoh*, n., beginning and end, see N. 1↑; 紀△事本末 93B.70.

本能 *been-nerng*, n., instinct, born ability.

本票 *beenpiauh*, n., promissory note; 銀行本票 cashier's check; 質押本票 collateral note; 動產抵押本票 cognovit note.

本人 *beenrern*, n., the person himself (applicant, plaintiff, etc.); (court.) I, myself=鄙△人 40S.22.

本色 *beenseh*, n., true color: 英雄本色 true color of a hero; natural color; 本色兒 --*'l*, n., unstained, undyed color of article.

本身 *beenshen*, n., self, person himself: 本身品行 person's own conduct (apart from his preachings); itself (民族本身 the nation itself).

本生 *beensheng*, adj., natural: 本生父母 one's real, natural parents.

本性 *beenshihng*, n., man's natural character, what is born in man.

本心 *beenshin*, n., true intention; conscience: 非出於本心 was forced by others, not one's free will.

本息 *been-shir*, n., capital and interest (息=利息).

本師 *beenshy*, n., one's master (in trade, religion).

本事 *beenshyh*, n. (1) *bernliing*↑; (2) resumé of story in plays, movies.

本題 *beentir*, n., subject (of discussion).

本子 *beentz*, n., volume, edition, version, see N. 5↑.

本字 *beentzyh*, n., the formal or early form of character, as opposed to later forms.

本問 *beenwehn*, v.i., (arch.) investigate, question (=盤問).

本位 *beenweih*, n., basis, basic unit: 金本位, 銀本位 gold, silver standard of currency; 本位主義 working for self as motive; 本位工作 one's proper duty.

本務 *beenwuh*, n., proper duty.

本業 *beenyeh*, n., one's main profession; original profession.

本願 *beenyuahn*, n., true, real desire.

本源 *beenyuarn*, n., origins.

丰 10.10

feng.

[Var. of 豐 21.30]

Adj. Good-looking, handsome, full and round.

丰標 *fengbiau*, n., looks, appearance.

丰容 *fengrurng*, n., (court. to ladies) your face.

丰神 *fengshern*, n., handsome looks.

丰態 *fengtaih*, n., demeanor.

丰采 *fengtsaai*, n., personal appearance: 一瞻丰采 (court.) to have a look at person's beautiful appearance, i.e., to meet personally.

丰姿 *fengtzy*, n., handsome or pretty looks, demeanor (oft. of ladies).

丰儀 *fengyir*, n., esteemed personality.

丰韻 *fengyuhn*, n., personal charm.

車 10.10

che (re. pr. **jyu*).

N. (1) A vehicle: 車輛 *-liahng* ↓; 汽車 an automobile, a motor car; 火車 a railway train: 火車頭 a locomotive; 馬車 a chariot, a carriage; 牛車 an ox cart; 手車 a handcart; 雞公車 (Szechuan dial.) a wheelbarrow; 戰車 chariot; 坦克車 a tank; 轎車 a sedan; 腳踏車, 自行車 a bicycle; 摩托車, 機車 a motorcycle; 電車 a tramcar, streetcar; 貨車 a motor truck, a lorry, a freight car; 旅行車 a station wagon; 油車 a tank truck; 跑車 a sport(s) car; 校車 school bus; 救火車 a fire engine; 救護車 an ambulance; 靈車 a hearse; 警車 a police van; 專車 a special car (train); 客車 a railway coach; 洋車, 人力車, 黃包車 a rickshaw; 三輪車 a pedicab, a tricycle; 餐車, 飯車 a dining car, a diner; 臥車 a sleeping car, a sleeper, Pullman (car); 花車 floats: 花車遊行 a float parade; 駕車, 開車 drive a car; 乘車, 坐車, 搭車 go by car (train); 上車 board a car (train); 下車 alight from a car (train); 車載斗量 immense quantities; 車水馬龍 heavy traffic on street ("an endless stream of horses and carriages"); 車匠 a wheelwright; 趕車的 a carter; 開車的 a car driver, chauffeur; 車禍 traffic accident; 車笠之盟 true friendship. (2) Any device which operates with the help of wheels: 紡車 a spinning wheel; 吊車 a crane; 滑車 a pulley; 風車 a windmill; 衣車 (Cantonese dial.) a sewing machine; 水車 a water cart, a water wheel, a wooden treadmill for lifting water. (3) (**jyu*) A surname. (4) A pawn in chess, the "chariot."

V.t. (1) Carry in a cart: 車煤, 車米 to cart away coal, rice. (2) To lift (water): 車水 do this by means of a water wheel. (3) To shape (things) on a lathe.

車把 *chebaa*, n., the handle bars of a bicycle or rickshaw.

車前 *chechiarn*[1], n., (bot.) the plantain, *Plantago major* var. *asiatica*.

車錢 *che-chiarn*[2], n., money paid for hiring a car (cart, rickshaw, etc.).

車牀 *che-chuarng*, n., a turner's lathe.

車道 *che-dauh*, n., a driveway.

車燈 *che-deng*, n., the headlight of an automobile or motorcycle, a bicycle lamp.

車墊(子) *che-diahn(tz)*, n., car cushions.

車費 *che-feih*, n., cartage, car fare, car hire.

車夫 *che'fu*, n., a carter, a cart driver; also chauffeur.

車轂轆 *chegu'lu*, n., car wheels: 車轂轆話 the same words repeated again and again; 車轂轆圓 (sp. pr. *-yuahn*) a children's game in which they join hands to form a circle and dance and sing.

車行 *che-harng*, n., (1) a place where carts may be bought or hired; (2) a garage; (3) a car dealer's.

車後喘 *che-houh-chuaan*, n., (sl.) part of retinue running after a carriage—a lackey.

車長 *chejaang*, n., the conductor of a train.

車站 *chejahn*, n., (1) a railway station; (2) a bus stop.

車照 *che-jauh*, n., a car license.

車轍 *che-jer*, n., (1) a rut made by a passing vehicle; (2) a driveway or track for cars.

車腳錢 *che-jiaau'chian*, n., fee paid for the delivery of goods.

車架 *che-jiah*, n., a lathe.

車駕 **jyujiah*, n., carriage.

車磔 **jyujier*, n., (AC) formerly, dismemberment of a person by making carts pull in different directions.

車騎 **jyujih*, n., (1) carriages and horses; (2) formerly, title of a military commander.

車軸 *che-jour*, n., the axle.

車捐 *che-jyuan*, n., a vehicle license fee.

車鍊 *che-liahn*, n., the roller chain of a bicycle, the tire chain of an automobile

車輛 *che-liahng*, n., vehicles, carriages, carts, cars, esp. in traffic.

車裂 **jyu-lieh*, n., (=車磔 *-jier* ↑).

車輪(兒)(子) *che-lurn(-luer'l)(tz)*, n., car wheels: 車輪會 a group of persons who take turns to invite one another to dinner; 車輪戰 formerly, a fight in which several persons take turns to engage one opponent in combat to tire him out.

車馬 *che-maa*, n., carriages and horses: 門前冷落車馬稀 the house was deserted and there were few callers; 車馬費 travel allowance.

車幔 *che-mahn*, n., the curtain of a carriage.

車門(兒) *che-mern (-mer'l)*, n., side doors of a motor vehicle or carriage.

車牌 *che-pair*, n., the number plate of a vehicle.

車棚 *che-perng*[1], n., a shed for vehicles.

車篷(子) *che-perng*[2]*(tz)*, n., the awning of a cart.

車票 *che-piauh*, n., a train or bus ticket.

車皮 *che-pir*, n., (railway) unloaded rolling stock.

車身 *che-shen*, n., the body of a car or carriage.

車箱 *che-shiang*, n., (1) compartments of a railway train; (2) railway coaches; 車箱兒 (a) the inside of a car or carriage; (b) the boot (trunk) of an automobile.

車胎 *che-tai*, n., car tires.

車頭 *che-tour*, n., a train locomotive.

車僮 *che-turng*, n., attendants on a railway train.

車子 (1) **jyutz*, n., formerly, a cart driver; (2) (*chetz*) a cart, carriage, wagon.

車資 *che-tzy*, n., car fare.

車帷 *che-weir*[1], n., see *-mahn* ↑.

車圍(子) *cheweir*[2]*(tz)*, n., the cloth hood of a carriage.

車沿兒 *che-yar'l*, n., the edge of a carriage.

車轅(兒)(子) *che-yuarn(-yuar'l)(tz)*, n., the shafts of a cart or carriage.

轟 10.10

hung.

V.i. & t. (1) To explode or make noise of explosion: 雷轟 the thunder strikes. (2) To attack by bomb, shell or by violence: 炮轟, 轟擊 shell (enemy position); 他在議會上轟市長 he attacked the mayor in the Assembly; 寫文章轟他 attack him in writing; 轟走 show s.o. the door, run a person out of town; 轟出去 drive (person) out; 轟沉 to shell and sink (a boat).

Adj. A booming noise: see 轟轟 *-hung* ↓.

轟動 *hungduhng*, v.i. & t., as in 轟動一時 cause a sensation; 轟動全國 make a sensation all over the country.

轟轟 *hunghung*, adj., descriptive of big, booming noise: 轟轟烈烈 with a heroic determination or in a sensational manner.

轟炸 *hungjah*, v.t., to bomb (a place).

轟擊 *hungjir*, v.t., to shell by artillery.

轟然 *hungrarn*, adj. & adv., with booming noise.

辜 10.10

gu.

N. (1) A crime, a criminal offense. (2) A surname.

V.i. Be ungrateful: 辜負 *-'fuh*, 辜恩 *-en* ↓.

Adj. Guilty: 無辜 innocent, free from guilt.

辜恩 *gu-en*, v.i., show ingratitude for favors or kindnesses received.

辜負 *gu'fuh*, v.t., be ungrateful to (person, his good intentions): 辜負朋友 to fail a friend; 辜負父母 fail one's parents for their solicitude, expectations (also wr. 孤負).

牛 10.10

niour.

N. (1) (Zoo.) cattle: 牛頭馬面 (Chin. myth.) messenger boy of Hell; 牛鬼蛇神 (of things) supernatural, (of a person's appearance) ugly, (now) bad elements; 牛頭不對馬嘴 (of speech or action) incongruous; 水牛 water buffalo; 黃牛 common yellow cow or ox, also illegal agent for tickets or crossing forbidden territory; 乳牛 milk cow; 母牛 cow. (2) (Astron.) Sagittarius, one of the twenty-eight Chinese zodiac constellations. (3) A surname.

牛蒡 *niourbahng*, n., (bot.) burdock, *Arctium lappa*.

牛扁 *niourbiaan*, n., (bot.) *Aconitum lycoctonum*.

牛鼻子 *niourbirtz*, n., (牛鼻子老道) (derog.) formerly, old Taoist.

牛脖子 *niourbortz*, n., person obstinate like cattle.

牛車 *niour-che*, n., ox cart.

牛氣 *niour'chi*, adj., arrogant.

牛刀 *niourdau*, n., butcher's knife: 割雞焉用牛刀 (lit.) why use a butcher's chopper to kill a chicken?—making unnecessarily great efforts to do trivial things; wasting of talent on trivials; 牛刀小試 (fig.) (of person of great potentials) give a little inkling of what one is capable of.

牛痘 *niourdouh*, n., vaccine against smallpox.

牛頓 *Niourduhn*, n., Sir Isaac Newton.

牛犢子 *niourdurtz*, n., a calf.

牛耳 *niour-eel*, n., the ears of an ox or cow: 執牛耳 (AC) to "hold the cow's ear" before slaughter for blood sacrifice—an honor reserved for leader during conference of states—hence to be acknowledged leader.

牛黃 *niourhuarng*, n., (Chin. med.) bile juice from the body of a diseased ox, congealed, and used for the cure of infant cramps.

牛角 *niour-jiaau*, n., ox horn.

牛勁 *niour-jihn*, n., as in (1) 一身牛勁 as strong as an ox; (2) 犯了牛勁 obstinate like an ox.

牛津 *Niourjin*, n., Oxford.

牛酒 *niour-jioou*, n., (lit.) beef and wine; (fig.) gifts for soldiers at the front.

牛郎 *niourlarng*, (1) n., a cowboy; (2) n., one of the Chinese zodiac constellations: 牛郎織女 the Cowboy and the Spinning Maid, two constellations, the separated lovers in Chinese mythology.

牛酪 *niourluoh*, n., cheese, yogurt.

牛馬 *niour-maa*, (1) n., cattle and horses; (2) v.i., slave for others: 莫為兒孫作牛馬 do not slave for your children.

牛毛 *niourmaur*, n. (1), ox hair;

(2) innumerable: 多如牛毛 innumerable as ox hair; 牛毛細雨 fine drizzling rain.

牛蝱 *niourmarng*, n., (zoo.) horsefly, gadfly (also wr. 虻).

牛奶 *niournaai*, n., cow's milk; 牛奶糖 butter candy, toffee.

牛排 *niourpair*[1], n., beefsteak.

牛(兒)牌 *niour('l)pair*[2], n., set of playing cards made of cattle bone (also called 骨牌).

牛扒 *niourpar*, n., beefsteak.

牛皮 *niourpir*, (1) n., ox hide, leather: 牛皮靴 leather boots; 牛皮帶 leather belt; (2) gross exaggeration: 牛皮大王 person given to gross exaggerations: 吹牛皮 to brag; 牛皮紙 brown packing paper; 牛皮糖 a kind of chewing candy, also one who persists in forcing his attentions on others.

牛肉 *niourrouh*, n., beef.

牛乳 *niourruu*, n., cow's milk, see *-naai*↑.

牛膝 *niour'shi*, n., (bot.) hyssop.

牛性 *niour-shihng*, n., obstinacy.

牛溲 *niour sou*, n., in 牛溲馬勃 two lowly plants—worthless trifles.

牛子眼(兒) *niour'tz-yaan(-yaa'l)*, n., a tumor-like growth on the eyeball obstructing eyesight.

牛瘟 *niour-wen*, n., rinderpest.

牛衣 *niour-yi*, n., cattle blanket.

牛疫 *niour-yih*, n., cattle plague.

牛飲 *niour-yiin*, n., unrestrained drinking bout (lit., "drinking like a cow").

牛蠅 *niouryirng*, n., (zoo.) gadfly.

牛油 *niouryour*, n., butter.

犇 10.10

ben.

[Var. of 奔 12.20]

犛 10.10

lir (also *maur*).

N. (Zoo.) the yak.

聱 10.10

aur.

聱牙 *aur-yar*, phr., (1) in 詰屈聱牙 (of ancient writings) full of characters that are difficult to make out and pronounce, descriptive of foreign sounds, unpronounceable, crotchety writing; (2) twisting (old trunks); rough (experience).

§ 10.11 (十/土)

生 10.11

sheng.

N. (1) Life: 生命 *-mihng*↓; 生活 *-huor*↓; 舍生取義 sacrifice life for honor; 輕生 risk one's life; 起死回生 (of good doctors) effect a miraculous cure; 救生圈 lifebelt; 養生 cultivate health. (2) Lifetime, life span: 一生 whole life; 半生 half one's life (struggling, etc.); 此生, 今生 this present life or incarnation; 來生 future life; 生生世世 generation after generation; 生時 when one was alive; 殘生 the remaining years of one's life; 偷生 keep alive without serious ambition or purpose; 再生, 重生 next incarnation, also rebirth; 永生 eternal life, also 常生. (3) Living beings: 生靈 *-lirng*↓; 衆生, 羣生 all animal kingdom; 畜生 the beasts; 殺生 kill animate beings; 放生 (Budd.) buy fish and turtle and keep them alive in a pond (called 放生池). (4) A living: 謀生, 營生 make a living; 生活, 生計, 生涯 *-huor*, *-jih*[2], *-yar*↓. (5) Student, pupil, scholar: 儒生 Confucian scholar; 書生 a scholar, a pedant: 書生之見 pedantic views; 學生, 生徒 student, also apprentice; 先生 teacher, also "Mr." (placed after surname), also (polite and friendly) after personal name; 生員 *-yuarn*↓; 門生 formerly, personal student or pupil of a master, also successful candidate *vis-à-vis* the examiner; 男生, 女生 boy, girl student; 小生, 晚生 self-reference of student, esp. in letter to teacher; 畢業生 graduate student. (6) Male actor, opp. 旦 *dahn*, actress.

V.i. & t. (1) Happen, occur: 生起 *-chii*↓; 發生 v.i., (s.t.) happens, or v.t., produce (accident). (2) Produce, give birth to: 出生 be born; 出生年月 date of birth; 生下了男孩 give birth to a boy; 生育, 生殖 *-yuh*, *-jyr*↓; 生財, 生產 *-tsair*, *-chaan*↓; 生聚 *-jyuh*↓; 胎生 viviparous, -ity; 卵生 oviparous, ovipara, -ity, those that produce offspring by eggs; 接生 midwifery. (3) Create (accident, trouble, etc.): 生事, 生出事來 cause trouble; 生花樣 make difficulties; 節外生枝 bring up unnecessary ramifications; 無事生非 make uncalled-for trouble. (4) Be born (handsome, stupid, etc.), to grow: 生得很漂亮 grow up beautiful; 生得矮 be born short; 生長, 生成 *-jaang*, *-cherng*↓.

Adj. (1) Raw, uncooked (meat, fruit), not processed (iron, copper, silk, oil, etc.): 生菜 uncooked, fresh vegetable; 生油 *-your*↓; unripe: 蘋果生得很 the apple is still quite unripe; 生地 one's birthplace, a strange place, a piece of uncultivated land; 生書, 生課 a new, yet untaught lesson. (2) Crude, inexperienced, not smooth, not well learned: 生澀, 生硬 *-seh*[2], *-yihng*↓; 生手 *-shoou*↓. (3) Strange, unfamiliar: 生人, 生客 *-rern*, *-keh*[1]↓; 面生, 陌生 (face) not seen before; 生字 new, unlearned character. (4) Alive:

生 生擒 capture alive; 生呑活剝 interpret text, passage crudely without real understanding ("eat it alive"); 生拉硬拽 do arm-twisting, force s.o. to do s.t.

Adv. (1) Keenly in 生恐, 生怕 *-kuung, -pah*↓; 生疼 keenly painful; 活生生 very much alive. (2) Abruptly, rudely, by force: 生把他拉下來 pull him down by force; 硬生生 abruptly. (3) Used as adv. ending: 好生走路 walk carefully; 偏生 unfortunately; 偏生我又不會 unfortunately, I don't know how; 怎生 how: 不知怎生是好 don't know what to do (esp. in MC＝怎麽, also wr. 作麽生).

生變 *sheng-biahn*, v.i., trouble arises (mutiny, etc.).

生病 *shengbihng*, v.i., fall ill.

生產 *shengchaan*, v.i. & t. & n., (1) produce, production: 生產過剩 overproduction; 生產力 productivity; 生產率 rate of production; 生產費 cost of production; 生產量 volume of production; (2) give birth to children.

生辰 *shengchern*, n., birthday.

生成 *shengcherng*, adj., born (clever, stubborn, etc.).

生前 *sheng-chiarn*, adv., while person was living.

生氣 *shengchih*, (1) v.i., to get angry; (2) n., vitality (of vegetation, writing, also pr. (-*'chi*).

生起 *sheng-chii*, v.t., to bring about.

生芻 *sheng-chur*, n., hay; (allu.) offering at grave, funeral gift.

生全 *sheng-chyuarn*, v. i., return alive, survive.

生趣 *shengchyuh*, n., as in 有生趣 (writing) has lively interest; full of vitality.

生齒 *sheng-chyy*, n., population: 生齒過剩 overpopulation.

生動 *shengduhng*, adj., moving: 氣韻生動 (painting) has rhythmic vitality.

生發 *shengfa*, v.i., produce (profit).

生髮油 *shengfaa-your*, n., hair oil.

生番 *sheng-fan*, n., savage, cannibal; savage tribe.

生分 *sheng'fen*, adj., (person) not intimate enough, not well known to one: 不生分 quite familiar with each other.

生根 *sheng-gen*, v.i., take root (habit, studies).

生花 *sheng-hua*, phr., 生花之筆, 筆生花 gifted pen, a rich style (Li Po dreamed that his "pen grew blossoms").

生還 *sheng-huarn*, phr., return alive.

生貨 *sheng-huoh*, n., raw goods, material.

生火 *sheng-huoo*, v.i., to light a fire.

生活 *shenghuor* (1) n., life, living, profession: 生活維艱 it is hard making a living; 做生活 make a living; 吃生活 (Shanghai dialect) get a beating; 生活費 living expenses, cost of living; 生活力 vitality; 生活素 vitamin (also 維他命); (2) v.i., to live: 民非水火不能生活 man cannot live without fire and water.

生虎子 *shenghuu'tz*, n., (sl.) an inexperienced hand.

生長 *shengjaang*, v.i., (1) (plants) grow; (2) (the young) grow up: 生長得不錯 grow up quite handsome.

生機 *sheng-ji*, n., spring of vitality, a new lease of life.

生薑 *shengjiang*, n., raw ginger.

生忌 *sheng-jih*[1], n., birthday of a deceased person.

生計 *sheng-jih*[2], n., living, means of livelihood, profession.

生就(的) *shengjiouh('de)*, adj., born one way or another (nervous, suspicious, etc.).

生知 *sheng-jy*, n., (AC) those who are born wise.

生殖 *shengjyr*, (1) v.i., (plants) grow, multiply; (2) v.i. & n., (men) reproduce, multiply, reproduction; 生殖器 sexual organs (male and female).

生聚 *shengjyuh*, v.i., (AC, LL of a nation) grow in population.

生客 *sheng-keh*[1], n., a stranger.

生尅 *sheng-keh*[2], v.i., mutually accelerate, reinforce, or counteract, neutralize; phr. in 五行 (the five movements): 生 accelerate, 尅 counteract (木生火, 火尅金 "wood" accelerates "fire," and "fire" is inimical to "metal").

生口 *shengkoou*, n., (1) domestic animals (usu. wr. 牲口); (2) (AC) war prisoners.

生壙 *shengkuahng*, n., tomb erected by person or for oneself, while living.

生恐 *shengkuung*, v.i., to fear, be afraid, see *-pah*↓.

生來 *shenglair*, adj., see *-jiouh, -cherng*↑.

生冷 *shengleeng*, adj., cold (in style, approach); n., (Chin. med.) cold dishes, cold drinks, fruits.

生臉兒 *sheng-liaa'l*, n., a stranger.

生憐 *shengliarn*, v.t., to love (child, helpless or small being).

生料 *shengliauh*, n., dry goods; 生料廠 timber shop.

生利 *sheng-lih*, v.i., (capital) bears interest; (business) makes profit.

生力軍 *shenglih-jyun*, n., (mil.) fresh reinforcement.

生理 *shenglii*, n., (1) 生理學 physiology: 生理化學 physiological chemistry; 生理學家 physiologist; (2) (dial.) business; (3) 料無生理 it is feared s.o. will not live.

生靈 *shenglirng*, n., all living things: 生靈塗炭 the people's life destroyed, all life decimated.

生路 *shengluh*, n., way out: 無生路 no way out or chance of escape; 另謀生路 find another way of living.

生龍(活虎) *sheng-lurng*, phr., 生龍活虎 (of fighter or painting) extremely forceful or vivid.

生煤 *sheng-meir*, n., unburnt coal.

生命 *shengmihng*, n., life: 生命之保障 protection of life; 生命保險 life insurance.

生民 *shengmirn*, n., (LL) the people, mankind: 生民以來 since creation of mankind.

生母 *shengmuu*, n., one's own mother.

生怕 *shengpah*, v.i., to fear, be afraid, lest: 生怕來不及 afraid it is too late; 生怕他不答應 afraid that he will not consent.

生平 *shengpirng*, adv. phr., all one's life; usually: 生平不好酒 usually (one) does not drink or never drinks.

生人 *shengrern*, n., a stranger.

生日 *sheng(')ryh*, n., birthday.

生色 *shengseh*[1], (1) v.i., add color or luster (to gathering), come alive; (2) adj., distinctive (performance).

生澀 *shengseh*[2], adj., crude, faulty (knowledge), lacking in fluency (in reading).

生身 *shengshen*, n., as in 生身父母 parents who give you birth; the (Mongolian) one who has not had smallpox.

生生 *shengsheng*, adv., (1) generation after generation: 生生世世 ditto; (2) well and healthy: 生生憂慮出病來 get sick from sheer worry (for a healthy person); 好生生的怎麽就死了 how could he die so suddenly—he was looking so well? 生生不息 life and growth in nature, continuous reproduction (of plants and animals).

生肖 *shengshiauh*, n., the year of the animal in which one was born: 十二生肖 (the year of the) rat, ox, tiger, rabbit, dragon, snake, horse, lamb, monkey, chicken, dog, pig—corresponding to the duodecimal cycle 子丑寅卯, etc.; see Appendix A.

生隙 *shengshih*, v.i., cause friction (between people).

生性 *shengshihng*, (1) n., one's born nature (violent, gentle, etc.); (2) (*-'shing*) adj., aloof, solitary in nature: 他有點兒生性 he does not get along well with people.

生心 *sheng-shin*, v.i., (AC) begin to feel disloyal.

生息 *sheng-shir*, v.i., (1) (money) bear interest; (2) (of animal herds) multiply.

生手(兒) *sheng-shoou('l)*, n., an inexperienced hand.

生受 *shengshouh*, v.i., (esp. MC) to suffer: 不好生受 difficult to bear; (MC) 生受你 (=modn. 難爲你) thanks for the trouble.

生疏 *shengshu*, adj., (1) (of friends) having less contact, getting more distant; (2) (piano playing, sleight-of-hand, etc.) having not played for a long time, getting rusty.

生水 *sheng-shueei*, n., unboiled water; fresh water.

生事 *sheng-shyh*, v.i., to cause trouble.

生石灰 *sheng-shyrhuei*, n., (chem.) calcium oxide.

生死 *sheng-syy*, phr., life and death: 生死關頭 grave crisis between life and death; 生死之交 a friend until death.

生態學 *shengtaih-shyuer*, n., ecology, study of environmental influence on living beings.

生鐵 *sheng-tiee*, n., pig iron, cast iron.

生菜 *sheng-tsaih*, n., (1) uncooked or fresh vegetable; (2) lettuce.

生財 *sheng-tsair*, v.i., to make money. ⌈-al.

生存 *shengtsurn*, v.i. & n., survive,

生祠 *sheng-tsyr*, n., temple to one still living.

生疼 *shengtuhng*, (1) adj., very painful; (2) v.t., to love dearly.

生徒 *shengtur*, n., disciple; pupil of private school; apprentice.

生子 *sheng-tzyy*, v.i., to give birth to a son.

生物 *shengwuh*, n., living creatures or plants; 生物學 *--shyuer*, biology; 生物化學 biochemistry.

生養 *shengyaang*, v.i., (of parents) give birth to and bring up children.

生涯 *shengyar*, n., see *-jih*[2] ↑.

生業 *shengyeh*, n., business: 不治生業 does not attend to business or hold a job.

生意 *shengyih*, n., (1) prospect of living or survival; (2) (*-yih* or *-'yi*) a business or business deal: 做生意 run a business (shop, etc.); (*-'yi*) a crooked deal; 生意口 *--koou*, n., words of a petty dealer, not to be trusted; business man's ways or know-how; 生意經 *--jing*, business sense, business expertise.

生硬 *shengyihng*, adj., not smooth, not polished, crude (writing), rigid, stern, stiff.

生油 *shengyour*, n., (1) peanut oil; (2) unrefined oil.

生員 *shengyuarn*, n., formerly, students.

生育 *shengyuh*, v.t. & n., give birth to and raise (children); growth (of population); 生育能力 fertility.

埜 10.11

yee.

[Arch. of 野 41S.00]

塹 10.11

chiahn.

N. A trench, moat: 天塹 natural terrain for defense.

塹壕 *chiahnhaur*, n., city moats; trench.

釐 10.11

lir (**shi*).

N. (1) One thousandth of a Chinese 尺 foot. (2) One hundredth of a 畝 *mow*. (3) One thousandth of a 兩 *liang* or tael; see Appendix C. (4) (Rate of interest) one tenth of one per cent: 月息四釐 a monthly interest of 0.4 per cent; 年息四釐 an annual interest of four per cent. (5) Short for 釐金: 釐金, 釐捐, 釐卡 *-jin*, *-jyuan*, *-chiaa* ↓. (6) (Interch. 禧 **shi*) happiness: 恭祝新釐 a Happy New Year!

V.t. To regulate, rectify: 允釐百工 (AC) regulate the different offices; 釐定, 釐正 *-dihng*, *-jehng* ↓.

釐卡 *lirchiaa*, n., see *-jin* ↓.

釐定 *lir-dihng*, v.t., to work out

or draw up (rules, regulations, etc.), also 釐訂.
釐革 *lir-ger*, v.t., to reform, readjust (old practices, rules, etc.).
釐正 *lir-jehng*, v.t., to correct, amend, edit (texts, drafts, etc.).
釐金 *lirjin*, n., an internal tax on the transit of goods (formerly, spelled "likin").
釐捐 *lir-jyuan*, n., (=釐金 *-jin*↑).
釐剔 *lir-tih*, v.t., to strike out, expunge (anything superfluous).

§10.20 (十/卄)

卉 10.20

hueih.

N. 花卉 flowers and grass, plants in gen. flora (in painting).

Adj. Plentiful.

§10.21 (十/乚)

齧 10.21

nieh.
[Var. 嚙; pop. 囓]

N. (AC) a dent in a sword.

V.t. (1) Bite: 齧臂 bite one's arm, as a pledge; (of a man and a woman) as a pledge of love. (2) Erode, as water erodes a bank.

§10.22 (十/丨)

靠 10.22

kauh.

V.i. & t. (1) To rely on: 倚靠, 依靠 to depend on (s.o.); 無依無靠 no one to support for living, quite alone; 靠天吃飯 without visible means of support; 靠此爲生 depend on this for a living; 靠自己 depend on oneself; 靠别人 depend on others; 可靠 dependable; 不可靠 not dependable; see 靠得住, 靠不住 *-derjuh*, *-burjuh*↓. (2) To lean on: 靠着 leaning on; 靠在一起 huddle together.

Prep. Near, along, toward, by: 靠近 *-jihn*↓; 靠岸 alongshore; 靠牆 toward or by the wall; 靠海 (city) on the coast; 靠邊兒走 walk on the side (not in the middle); 靠右邊走 walk on the right; 背靠背 (sleeping, sitting) back to back; 靠山吃山, 靠水吃水 on the mountain one lives by mountain products, near the water one lives by the products of the sea or river.

靠背 *kauhbeih*, n., back of chair; (Chin. opera) armor; 靠背老生 (opera) military officer in armor.
靠不住 *kauhburjuh*, adj., undependable.
靠常兒 *kauhcharng'l*, adj., (coll.) long lasting, wearing well.
靠旗 *kauhchir*, n., (Chin. opera) pennant on back of military officer.
靠得住 *kauhderjuh*, adj., dependable.
靠枕 *kauhjeen*, n., hard cushion used as arm rest on couch.
靠近 *kauhjihn*, adj. & prep., near: 靠近那邊 near that side.
靠賴 *kauhlaih*, v.t., depend on (s.o.).
靠攏 *kauhluung*, v.i. & t., lean toward; 靠攏份子 opportunist elements.
靠山(兒) *kauhshan(-sha'l)*, n., person for political or financial backing.
靠手 *kauhshoou*, n., arm rest.
靠子 *kauh'tz*, n., hard cushion for arm or back support: 車靠子 (in cart).
靠托 *kauhtuo*, v.t., depend on (s.o. to do s.t.).
靠椅 *kauhyii*, n., easy chair; lounge chair.

鼒 10.22

tzy.

N. (AC) a tripod tapering off towards the top.

§10.30 (十/一)

査 10.30

shyh.
[Pop. of 世 22.21]

直 10.30

jyr.
[Usu. wr. 直]

V.t. To straighten up or out: 直其冤 to redress a wrong done to s.o.; 直直腰兒 stretch (body) a bit.

Adj. (1) Erect, vertical, straight, not crooked: 垂直 perpendicular, hang straight; 直上 straight up; 直上直下 perpendicular; 伸直腿 stretch legs straight; 直挺挺, 直蹶蹶 straight and stiff (in erect or prostrate position); 直勾勾, 直瞪瞪 stare bluntly, scared stiff; 筆直 very straight; 曲直 the right and wrong of parties in quarrel. (2) Straight and honest: 正直 fair and honest; 忠直 loyal; 直道 *-dauh*² ↓. (3) Straight forward: 直脾氣 straight temper: 直性 *-shihng*↓; 剛直 honorable, inflexible, incorruptible; 直心眼兒 forthright (person); 直漢 an honest fellow; 坦直, 率直 frank, candid, straight forward (confession, admission); 說直話 give a straight talk; 直爽 *-shuaang*↓. (4) On duty: 直日

(=値日) day on duty.

Adv. (1) Straight, directly: 直達 go straight or directly; 直視 look straight; 秉筆直書 write the truth without fear or favor; 直言, 直說 talk straight; 直打直 in a straight manner; 直前, 直向前往 go straightforward; 直陳 to present (facts) straight. (2) Continuously: 一直走 go without stop; 一直說 (or 哭) 下去 talk (or cry) on and on; 直去直來 go and come back without stopover; 直等一個人 keep waiting (without stop) for a person; 直到 (conj.) until: 直到日入 until sundown; 直到今日 until today. (3) Just, only, indeed: 直是 be indeed, be just (a shadow, a phantasy, a joke, etc.); 直須 need only to (ask him direct, etc.); 直不百步耳 (孟子) (of a retreating army retreating fifty paces) only difference is that it did not retreat a hundred paces.

直筆 *jyr-bii*, phr., record historical events without fear or favor.
直腸 *jyrcharng*, n., the rectum.
直臣 *jyrchern*, n., an outspoken minister. ⌈until.
直到 *jyrdauh*[1], prep. & conj.,
直道 *jyrdauh*[2], adj. & n., honest, straight dealing, the straight and narrow path.
直點兒 *jyrdiaa'l*, adv., (apologize, etc.) continuously, repeatedly without stop.
直裰 *jyr-duor*, n., (of jacket or ancient robe) open with line of buttons straight down the center.
直根 *jyrgen*, n., (bot.) axial root.
直觀 *jyrguan*, n., intuition, intuitive perception, see *-jyuer* ↓.
直躬 *jyrgung*, phr., (LL) see *-dauh*[2] ↑. ⌈honest fellow.
直棍兒 *jyrguoh'l*, n., (pop.) an
直講 *jyrjiaang*, n., formerly, a lecturer at government college (國子監).
直角 *jyrjiaau*, n., (math.) right angle; 直角柱 right prism; 直角錐 right pyramid; 直角體 a cuboid; 直角三角形 right-angled triangle.
直諫 *jyr-jiahn*, phr., to advise or admonish emperor at risk of latter's wrath.
直接 *jyrjier*[1], adj. & adv., direct, -ly; 直接民權 rights of referendum and recall; 直接教授法 direct method of teaching modern language.
直捷 *jyrjier*[2], adj., direct (communication, line): 直捷 (or 直截) 了當 phr., simple and direct (opp. beating about the bush).
直徑 *jyrjihng*, n., (math.) diameter.
直己 *jyr-jii*, phr., see *-dauh*[2] ↑.
直致 *jyrjyh*, (1) adj., straight, without wavering; (2) adv., until, so that.
直覺 *jyrjyuer*, n., intuition.
直諒 *jyrliahng*, adj., (AC) right and honorable (persons).
直隸 *Jyrlih*, n., formerly, name for Hopei Province.
直溜 *jyr'liou*, adj., very smooth and straight. ⌈current.
直流 *jyrliour*, n., (phys.) direct
直脈 *jyrmoh*, (1) adj., (bot.) straight-veined; (2) n., direct line of descent, see *-shih* ↓.
直聲 *jyrsheng*, (1) n., reputation for honesty; (2) phr., (cry) aloud. ⌈(or 直昇).
直升機 *jyrshengji*, n., helicopter
直線 *jyrshiahn*, n., (math.) straight line, or right line.
直轄 *jyr-shiar*, adj., under direct jurisdiction of central government. ⌈tives).
直系 *jyrshih*, n., direct line (rela-
直性(兒)(子) *jyrshihng('l)(tz)*, adj., forthright (character).
直受兒 *jyr-shouh'l*, phr., to receive gifts without giving in return.
直爽 *jyrshuaang*, adj., outspoken, straightforward, forthright.
直率 *jyrshuaih*, adj., ditto.
直譯 *jyr-yih*, v.t. & n., (to render) literal translation.
直喻 *jyryuh*, n., simile.

矗 10.30

chuh.

Adj. & adv. Perpendicular: 矗立 stand erect; 直矗矗 very straight, straight up.

查 10.30

char(**ja*).

N. (**ja*) A surname.

V.t. (1) To investigate, audit, check, find out, inspect: 檢查 to inspect (luggage), have physical checkup; 調查 to investigate; 盤查 investigate thoroughly, cross-examine; 清查 examine accounts; 查收 (in letter) please receive; 查照 *-jauh* ↓; 查看, 查察 look into; 明查暗訪 investigate (crime); 查班 inspect class; 查賬 *-jahng* ↓; 查字典 look up dictionary; 查對無訛 formula for okaying accounts; 查戶口 check residents; take census. (2) In opening paragraph relating findings: have gone into the matter and found that. . . .

查辦 *charbahn*, v.i., to investigate and prosecute (case, person).
查抄 *charchau*, v.t., to confiscate (property; lit.,"take inventory").
查點 *chardiaan*, v.t., check (inventory) item by item.
查封 *charfeng*, v.t., to confiscate and seal up (property, goods).
查核 *charher*, v.t., to examine (accounts). ⌈counts.
查賬 *charjahng*, v.i., examine ac-
查照 *charjauh*, v.i., (in official communications among equals) am submitting for your attention: 查照辦理 please consider and act accordingly.
查禁 *charjihn*, v.i., search for violations of ban (smuggled goods, etc.).
查究 *charjiouh*, v.i., to investigate, follow up (a case): 查究辦理 investigate and act accordingly; 查究原因 find out the cause.
查考 *charkaau*, v.t., look up for reference, data.

查勘 *charkahn*, v.t., to investigate on the spot.

查明 *char-mirng*, v.t., to find out: 查明眞相 find out the true facts.

查哨 *charshauh*, v.t., search passengers at sentry point.

查驗 *charyahn*, v.t., to check up (physical conditions); inspect (goods).

查閱 *charyueh*, v.t., read (report, correspondence).

彗 10.30

hueih.

N. (1) A broomstick. (2) 彗星 a comet.

整 10.30

jeeng.

V.t. To put to order; to adjust: 整理, 整頓 *-lii*, *-duhn* ↓; 整衣冠 to adjust hat and dress; 整裝就道 dress up and prepare for journey (also 整旆); 整裝待命 ready to move at short notice in full array; 整好 put in good shape; 別把他整壞了 don't spoil it, trying to fix it; 整隊, 整旅 put army unit in good shape; also the whole unit, see Adj. 2 ↓; to discipline, see 整肅 *-shuh²* ↓.

Adj. (1) Neat, tidy, orderly: 整齊, 整潔 *-'chir*, *-jier* ↓; 齊整 tidy. (2) Whole, not divided: 完整 intact; 整個兒, 整數 *-geh'l*, *-shuh¹* ↓; 整日整夜 whole day and night; 整夜不眠 did not sleep the whole night; 整塊給他 give him the whole piece; 整句唸出來 read the whole sentence; 說不出一句整話 cannot say a complete sentence; 整院子都聽見你叫了 the whole courtyard heard your scream.

整編 *jeengbian*, v.t., to reorganize (army).

整齊 *jeeng'chir*, adj., tidy, orderly, well-arranged (group or row), forming a complete set.

整飭 *jeengchyh*, adj., clean and orderly, sharply disciplined (conduct): 軍容整飭 in fine battle array.

整頓 *jeengduhn*, v.t., to put to order, to restore to good shape: 整頓學風 restore good order among the students.

整風 *jeeng-feng*, v.t., (in Communist China) to rectify atmosphere of schools, party, etc.

整個兒 *jeenggeh'l*, adv., the whole piece or lot; completely (fail, destroyed, etc.).

整整 *jerngjeeng*, (1) adv., exactly: 整整一百元 exactly $100; (2) adj., as in 整整齊齊 very neat and orderly, see *-'chir* ↑.

整潔 *jeengjier*, adj., clean and neat.

整莊 *jeeng'juang*, n., the whole amount.

整治 (1) *jeengjyh*, v.t., see *-lii* ↓; (2) (*'jy*) to prepare (food), mend (clothing); (3) to teach a lesson, punish: 我總得整治他.

整兒 *jeeng'l*, n., round number.

整臉子 *jerng-liaantz*, n., person habitually wearing a severe countenance.

整理 *jernglii*, v.t., to put to order (accounts), tidy up (room, appearance), shape up, revise (material for book).

整容 *jeengrurng*, v.i., to dress up, esp. to shave.

整日 *jeengryh*, adv., the whole day; 整日價 ditto.

整天 *jeengtian*, adv., the whole day: 一整天.

整形 *jeengshirng*, n., orthopedics: 整形手術 plastic surgery.

整數 *jeengshuh¹*, n., a whole number, integral.

整肅 *jeengshuh²*, v.t.,(in communist China) to purge; also shortened to 整: 整他一下 to discipline him.

整體 *jerngtii*, n., the whole; 整體化 integrate, integration.

盬 10.30

guu.

N. A pot: (沙) 盬子 an earthen pot (related 鍋子 *guotz*).

鏊 10.30

aur.

N. (AC) a flat iron plate for making cakes.

鏨 10.30

tzahn.

N. A small chisel; engraving tool.

V.t. Engrave, carve: 鏨花 carve flowers; 鏨字 engrave characters.

鏨刀 *tzahndau*, n., a graving knife.

鏨子 *tzahn'tz*, n., (1) a small chisel; (2) a graving tool.

鏨菜 *tzahntsaih*, n., (bot.) *Leonurus macranthus*.

§10.32 (十/フ)

麥 10.32

maih (sp. pr.); *moh* (re. pr.).

N. (1) Wheat, (oft. *-tz*): 大麥 barley; 小麥 wheat; 油麥, 燕麥 oats; 蕎麥, 烏麥 buckwheat. (2) A surname.

麥餅 *maihbiing*, n., wheaten cake.

麥碴兒 *maihchar'l*, n., potato grown on wheat field after wheat crop.

麥場 *maihcharng*, n., thrashing floor for wheat.

麥秋 *maih-chiou*, n., wheat harvest in 4th or 5th lunar month.

麥冬 *maih-dung*, n., see *-merndung*↓.

麥蛾 *maih-er*, n., a moth that feeds on wheat, *Gelechia cerealella.*

麥麩子 *maihfurtz*, n., chaff, bran.

麥糊 *meih-hur*, n., oatmeal.

麥角(菌) *maihjiaau(jyuhn)*, n., ergot, a wheat disease, caused by *Claviceps purpurea*, a fungus.

麥酒 *maihjioou*, n., beer (usu. 啤酒 *-pir*).

麥克風 *maihkehfeng*, n., (translit.) microphone.

麥浪 *maih-lahng*, n., waves of billowing wheat field caused by breeze.

麥芒 *maih-marng*, n., the awn (bristly fibers) of wheat, or prickly wheat sheaf.

麥門東 *maihmerndung*, n., (bot.) a plant of leek family, *Liriope graminfolia*, much used as herb medicine.

麥苗 *maih-miaur*, n., wheat seedling.

麥片 *maih-piahn*, n., oatmeal.

麥信風 *maihshihn-feng*, n., the northeast wind in 5th lunar month.

麥穗兒 *maih-sueh'l*, n., (1) ears of wheat; (2) lambskin with long hair resembling ears of grain.

麥子 *maihtz*, n., wheat or barley.

麥牙糖 *maihyar-tarng*, n., malt sugar.

梦 10.32

mehng.

[Abbr. of 夢 20A.32-4]

§10.40 (十/口)

古 10.40

guu.

N. (1) Time long past: 遠古 time immemorial; 上古(史), 中古(史) ancient, medieval times (history); 古往今來 from ancient to modern times. (2) Ancient artifacts, relics of the past: 考古 to study ancient relics; 考古學(家) archeology, archeologist. (3) A particular style of painting or pottery of the past: 仿古 in the style of an ancient master or period; 法古 (painting) imitate an ancient master; (of political or social institutions) follow an ancient practice. (4) The ancient people: 疑古 to doubt the ancients; 思古, 懷古 nostalgia, thinking of the past; 作古 (of person) passed away, died (joined the ancients). (5) A surname.

Adj. (1) Old, ancient, classic, old-fashioned: 古代 *-daih*, 古人 *-rern*, 古物 *-wuh*↓; 古錢, 古畫, 古籍 ancient coins, paintings, books; 古裝 old-fashioned binding or dress; 古妝 in ancient costume; 古語, 古諺 an old saying, proverb; 古井無波 (usu. of women) have no more sexual desire, (lit., "not a ripple in an ancient well"); 古色古香 (of ancient objects of art) having antique flavor; 古雅 *-yaa*↓; 古法 time-honored methods. (2) (Of persons or things) different from the gen. accepted norm: 古怪 *-'guaih*, 古板 *-baan*↓.

古板 *gurbaan*, adj., (1) ultraconservative, single-track-minded; unaccommodating; (2) old-fashioned, out-of-date.

古刹 *guuchah*, n., an ancient temple.

古代 *guu-daih*, n., ancient times.

古道 *guu-dauh*, (1) adj., kind, considerate, generous (lit., "acting like a gentleman of old"): 古道熱腸 considerate and warmhearted; (2) n., ancient rules and methods; (3) n., ancient road.

古典 *gurdiaan*, n. & adj., classic, classical: 古典主義 classicism; 古典派 classicist; 古典音樂 classical music.

古董(兒) *gurduung('l)*, n., curios, antiques (also wr. 骨董).

古方 *guu-fang*, n., (1) an ancient medical recipe; (2) old methods or ways of doing things.

古風 *guu-feng*, n., (1) ancient manners, customs and habits; (2) ancient style poetry.

古怪 *guu'guaih*, adj., peculiar, eccentric, exotic: 希奇古怪 strange and eccentric.

古跡 *guuji*, n., historic monuments, sites.

古記兒 *guujieh'l*, n., ancient events or incidents: 聽古記兒 listen to a storyteller telling old stories.

古今 *guujin*, n., ancient and modern times.

古老 *gurlaau*, adj., old-fashioned, outmoded.

古來 *guulair*, adv., since ancient times.

古樸 *gurpuu*, adj., (of manners) simple and plain, uncontaminated by modern fads.

古人 *guurern*, n., (1) the ancients; (2) a person who has passed away.

古稀 *guushi*, adj., seventy years old: 古稀老人 an old man aged three score and ten; 年近古稀 approaching seventy in age.

古昔 *guushir*, adj., of old, in times gone by.

古學 *guushyeur*, n., ancient learning, knowledge of the classic.

古時 *guushyr*, n., ancient times.

古訓 *guushyuhn*, n., (1) ancient maxims or precepts; (2) ancient meanings of words.

古銅 *guuturng*, n., (1) ancient bronze works; (2) the color of ancient bronzes.

古玩 *gurwaan*, n., curios.

古文 *guuwern*, n., (1) archaic script of Jou period; (2) 古文學派 a school of Confucian classicists believing in the authenticity of parts of classics doubted by 今文派; (3) the classic style of writing.

古物 *guuwuh*, n., (1) ancient relics; (2) ancient objects of art.

古雅 *guryaa*, adj., with a classic touch and in the best taste.

杏 告 哲 誓

杏 10.40

shihng.

N. Apricot: 杏仁 almond, see *-rern*↓.

杏脯 *shihngfuu*, n., preserved apricot.

杏乾兒 *shihngga'l*, n., dried apricot.

杏花 *shihnghua*, n., apricot flower; 杏花村 oft. used to describe a spring rustic scene.

杏黃 *shihnghuarng*, adj., apricot yellow.

杏臉 *shihngliaan*, n., oval face of girl or woman.

杏林 *shihnglirn*, n., (allu., rare) medical doctor.

杏仁 *shihngrern*, n., almond; 杏仁兒茶 almond cream; 杏仁兒粉 almond powder; 杏仁精 almond essence; 杏仁水 almond drink.

杏壇 *shihngtarn*, n., school platform, the teaching rostrum; orig. the apricot grove where Confucius taught.

杏眼 *shihng-yaan*, n., woman's apricot-like eyes.

杏靨 *shihngyeh*, n., a woman's oval face; see *-liaan*↑.

告 10.40

gauh (**guh*).

N. A declaration, announcement: 文告 statement by ruler or superior; 通告 public notice; 廣告 advertisement; 告白 *-bair*↓.

V.t. (1) Tell, inform, announce: (LL) 告我, (vern.) 告訴我 tell me; 報告 v.i. & n., (to, a) report to a superior; 告密 give secret information against s.o., see 告密 *-mih*↓. (2) Oft. used in the sense of "be" or "reported to be" in certain phrr.: 告罄 be exhausted: 存貨告罄 all our stock has been exhausted; 告乏 be tired or exhausted; 告捷 *-jier*² ↓; 告終, 告成, 告竣 be completed, see *-jung*, *-cherng*, *-jyuhn*↓. (3) Sue, accuse: 告訴 *-suh*↓; 告發 *-fa*↓; 告他一狀 file a suit against him; 原告 the plaintiff; 被告 the defendant. (4) Ask for: 告老 *-laau*↓; 告假 *-jiah*↓; 告退 *-tueih*↓; 告病 ask for sick leave, be sick; 告貸 *-daih*↓; 告幫 *-bang*↓; 告饒 ask for pardon; 自告奮勇 offer one's free services. (5) (**guh*) In 忠告 tell s.o. honestly what one thinks (also *gauh*); 告朔 (AC) ancient sacrifice at ancestral temple.

告白 *gauhbair*, n., a public notice.

告幫 *gahbang*, v.i., ask for financial assistance.

告窆 *gauhbiaan*, n., an obituary notice.

告便(兒) *gauhbiahn(-biah'l)*, v.i., (1) bid good-bye to friends for a short leave of absence; (2) go to the toilet.

告別 *gauhbier*, v.i., take leave.

告稟 *gauhbiing*, v.i., to file a petition, to request from superior.

告成 *gaucherng*, v.t., announce the completion of s.t. important: 大功告成 the great task has been (reported) completed.

告貸 *gauhdaih*, v.i., make a request for a loan, borrow money: 告貸無門 nowhere to borrow money.

告發 *gauhfa*, v.t., formally inform court of a crime committed, lodge complaint.

告假 *gauhjiah*, v.i., ask for leave of absence.

告誡 *gaujieh*, v.t., warn, enjoin, admonish.

告訐 *gauhjier*¹, v.i., inform against s.o.

告捷 *gauhjier*², v.i. & t., announce victory, be victorious.

告警 *gauhjiing*, v.i., to sound an alarm, give report of danger.

告急 *gauhjir*, v.i., make an emergency request for help.

告狀 *gauhjuahng*, v.t. & n., to sue at court; text of formal complaint.

告終 *gauhjung*, v.i., be completed.

告知 *gauhjy*, v.i. & t., tell, inform, notify.

告竣 *gauhjyuhn*, see *-jung*↑.

告老 *gauhlaau*, v.i., retire from age.

告密 *gauhmih*, v.i., give secret information against s.o.

告擾 *gauhraau*, v.i., to thank one's host for his hospitality, a phr. used on taking leave: 告擾了.

告示 *gauh'shy*, n., a public announcement.

告訴 *gauhsuh*, v.t., (1) (law) bring a suit against s.o.: 告訴乃論 a case will be taken cognizance of by the court only if s.o. files a suit; (2) (*gauh'su*) tell, inform: 我告訴你 I tell you; 不能告訴你 I can't tell you.

告辭 *gauhtsyr*, v.i., bid good-bye, take leave.

告退 *gauhtueih*, v.i., ask to be excused from meeting; resign from office.

告罪 *gauhtzueih*, v.i., (court.) please excuse me for any unintentional offense; 告無罪 can say I have a clear conscience, have done my best.

哲 10.40

jer.

N. (1) Wisdom: 哲學, 哲理 *-shyuer*, *-lii*↓. (2) Sage, wise man: 聖哲 the sages.

Adj. Wise: 明哲 discreet; 明哲保身 keep out of harm by discretion.

哲理 *jerlii*, n., philosophy, philosophical principle.

哲人 *jerrern*, n., a wise man, the sage master.

哲學 *jershyuer*, n., philosophy; 哲學家 philosopher.

哲嗣 *jer-syh*, n., (court.) your son.

誓 10.40

shyh.

N. An oath, a pledge: 誓願, 誓言, 誓約 *-yuahn*, *-yarn*, *-yue*↓; 宣誓

take oath in public; 立誓, 起誓, 發誓 take an oath; 背誓, 違誓 break one's pledge.

V.i. & t. To swear: 誓不兩立 swear that one of the two must be destroyed; 誓不甘休 swear to fight to the finish; 誓死不屈 swear to die rather than submit; 誓必 swear to.

誓詞 *shyhtsyr*, n., text of oath.
誓言 *shyhyarn*, n., a pledge.
誓願 *shyhyuahn*, v.i., to swear before God; n., a pledge.
誓約 *shyhyue*, v.i. & n., (to make) a pledge (of alliance, marriage, etc.).

謷 10.40

aur.

V.t. To deride, clamor: 謷謷.

Adj. (AC) magnificent: 謷乎大哉.

砉 10.40

huoh.

Adj. (AC) sound of crashing.

礬 10.40

farn.

N. Alum: 明礬, 白礬 alum; 皂礬, 青礬 copperas, ferrous sulphate.

礬紙 *farnjyy*, n., sized paper (for painting).
礬石 *farnshyr*, n., (min.) alum shale.
礬土 *farntuu*, n., (min.) alumina.

§ 10.41 (十/図)

杳 10.41

yaau (also *miaau*).

Adj. (1) Deeply hidden: 杳冥, 杳遠 *-mirng*, *-yuaan*↓. (2) Dark, silent: 杳然 *-rarn*↓; 杳無音信 completely not heard from; 杳杳無踪 left without a trace; 杳如黃鶴 (LL) gone like the yellow stork.

杳冥 *yaaumirng*, adj., dark and fathomless.
杳然 *yaaurarn*, adj., without any sound.
杳遠 *yauryuaan*, adj., far distant.

昚 10.41

chun.

[Anc. var. of 春 12.41]

晳 10.41

shi.

Adj. (1) Clear (=晰 41A.22). (2) White (u.f. 皙).

暫 10.41

jahn (re. pr. *tzahn*).

[Related 漸 63A. 22]

Adj. & adv. (1) Temporary, for the time being: 暫且, 暫時 *-chiee*, *-shyr*↓; 暫定 temporarily decide(d); 暫住 stop at place for a while; 暫用, 暫借 use, borrow, for a short period; 暫緩 postpone for the moment; 暫不施行 hold up measure for the present. (2) (AC) suddenly: 暫面 suddenly see one's face.

暫且 *jahnchiee*, adv., for the time being.
暫時 *jahnshyr*, adv., ditto.

曺 10.41

tsaur.

[Form of callig. of 曹 20.41]

晢 10.41

shi.

[Var. 皙]

Adj. (1) (Of human skin) white: 白皙, 白皙皙 very white. (2) Clear (var. of 晰 41A.22).

眚 10.41

sheeng.

N. (AC) (1) (med.) eye cataract. (2) Unfortunate mistakes: 除眚 eliminate errors, malpractices; 眚災 (AC) calamities.

嗇 10.41

seh.

Adj. Miserly, stingy: 吝嗇 ditto.

§ 10.42 (十/冈)

甫 10.42

fuu.

N. (1) A man's courtesy name 字: 台甫 (court.) your personal name. (2) (Court.) 尊甫 your father = 父.

Adv. (LL) Just: 甫至, 甫畢 just arrived, just closed (meeting); 甫能 be just able to; 甫識 just begin to know.

青 10.42

ching.

N. (1) (LL) bamboo strip, formerly used for writing: 青簡 such bamboo strip; 青史 *-shyy*↓; 殺青 completion of a book or film production; 汗青 prepared bamboo strip for writing ("sweated bamboo," i.e., heated bamboo to drive out moisture, also called 汗簡). (2) Green pastures: 青兒 *-'l*↓.

Adj. (1) Green, greenish, sometimes blue; cf. 青綠, 青翠 *-lyuh, -tsueih*↓; 青虛虛 very green; 青山綠水 green hills and blue waters; 青天 the blue sky; 臉色發青 sallow, greenish complexion; 青腫 bluish swelling on skin; 青出於藍而勝於藍 pupil excels teacher ("green comes from blue but excels blue"); 不管青紅皂白 phr., irrespective of right or wrong in dispute ("green, red, black or white"). (2) Not ripe: 青梅, 青杏 green prune, apricot; 橘子還青呢 the orange is not ripe yet; 青黃不接 food shortage between two harvests, gap between generations or any gap in succession. (3) Young: 年青 (of person) young, immature; 他很年青 he is very young; 青春, 青年 *-chun, -niarn*↓. (4) Black, dark, greyish: 青牛, 青狐 black ox, black fox; 青驪, 青馬 grey horse; 藏青 dark, heavy blue; 石青 dark green; 佛青 purplish black; 青素 black and white (clothing); 青絲 black hair. (5) Gracious: 青眼 (the black of eye) sympathetic look, dist. 白眼 (white of eye) look of disdain; 青覽, 青鑒, 青及 (in letters) for your gracious perusal; 青眼, 青睞 *-yaan, -laih*↓; 垂青 show favor to (person), kindly look or consideration.

青錢 *chingchiarn*, n., coins of copper or copper alloys.

青青 *chingching*, adj., green (grass).

青春 *chingchun*, adj. & n., (1) young, period of youth: 青春時代 years of one's youth; 青春期 puberty; (2) age (in asking of a youth): 你青春幾何 how young (i.e., old) are you?

青蟲 *chingchurng*, n., a caterpillar.

青雀 *chingchyueh*, n., a small singing bird, *Eophona personata.*

青黛 *chingdaih*, n., a Chinese medicine made from scum on indigo, for external use.

青燈 *chingdeng*, n., an oil lamp, esp. in temple.

青豆 *chingdouh*, n., green beans in gen.

青蛾 *chinger*, n., moth; (LL) (fig.) eyebrow (resembling moth's feelers).

青礬 *chingfarn*, n., ferrous sulphate.

青蜂 *chingfeng*, n., a kind of wasp, *Stilbum amethyslinum.*

青蚨 *chingfur*, n., (LL) money, cash.

青蛤 *chingger*, n., a kind of edible clam (=蛤蜊).

青光眼 *chingguang-yaan*, n., (Chin. med.) glaucoma (cf. *-marng*↓).

青宮 *chinggung*, n., (LL) residence of crown prince.

青果 *chingguoo*, n., (1) the olive; (2) fresh fruit; 青果公會 fruit-dealers' association.

青蒿 *chinghau*, n., (bot.) *Artemisia apiacea.*

青花 *chinghua*, n., (1) fine grains on ink stone; (2) flower design on porcelain.

青花魚 *chinghuayur*, n., a fish, *Scomber japonicus.*

青灰 *chinghuei*, n., greenish lime.

青簡 *chingjiaan*, n., (LL) books in gen. (簡 being bamboo strips).

青椒 *chingjiau*[1], n., green pepper.

青鮫 *chingjiau*[2], n., a ferocious sea fish, *Isuropsis glauca.*

青金 *chingjin*[1], n., lead or tin.

青衿(襟) *chingjin*[2], n., (LL) students, youth (from students' dress in classical times).

青竹絲 *chingjursy*, n., a small, green, poisonous snake.

青稞 *chingke*, n., a variety of wheat grown in high plateaus of Tibet and Chin. Turkestan.

青兒 *ching'l*, n., (1) green pasture, green fields: 逛青兒 take a walk in the countryside; 放青兒 to pasture cows, sheep; (2) seedlings in field: 看青兒 watch seedlings against birds; (3) (coll.) egg white.

青欖 *chinglaan*, n., olive.

青睞 *chinglaih*, n., (LL) your gracious look or consideration.

青帘 *chingliarn*[1], n., sign of wine shop.

青蓮 *chingliarn*[2], n., lotus, (fig.) Buddha's eyes.

青藜 *chinglir*, n., walking stick.

青蛉 *chinglirng*, n., a dragonfly.

青鱗魚 *chinglirnyur*, n., herring.

青樓 *chinglour*, n., (LL) a sing-song house; a brothel.

青鸞 *chingluarn*, n., a bird with many bright colors, related to 鳳 42.70.

青螺 *chingluor*, n., a kind of clam, *Acmaea schrenckii.*

青龍 *chinglurng*, n., (1) dragon, as a symbol of good omen; (2) the left side (opp. 白虎 the right side).

青綠 *chinglyuh*, n., green color: 青綠山水 landscape painting of northern school with fine lines and bluish-green colors; 青山綠水 beautiful country scene ("green mountains and blue waters").

青盲 *chingmarng*, n., amaurosis, due to optic nerve, but without organic trouble; color blind; see *-guang-yaan*↑.

青茅 *chingmaur*, n., (bot.) *Miscanthus tinctorius*, a grass whose stem and leaves are used for yellow dye.

青梅 *chingmeir*[1], n., green prunes: 青梅竹馬 the games of childhood, hence, the period when a boy and girl grew up together.

青黴 *chingmeir*[2], n., a green mold, penicillium; 青黴素 ditto.

青苗 *chingmiaur*, n., system of farmers' loan at planting time, to be returned at harvest, instituted in 1069 A.D. by 王安石, (also called 青苗錢).

青目 *chingmuh*, see *-yaan* ↓.

青囊 *chingnarng*, n., geomancy (from a book on geomancy 青囊經).

青鳥 *chingniaau*, n. (myth.) bird messenger of Fairy God-Mother 西王母; (LL) messenger; *The Blue Bird* by Maurice Maeterlinck.

青年 *chingniarn*, n. & adj., youth; youthful; 青年期 adolescence; 青年會 Y.M.C.A.; 青年商會 Junior Chamber of Commerce; 青年節 Youth Day.

青女 *chingnyuu*, n., the goddess of frost.

青盼 *chingpahn*, n., your gracious look or consideration.

青皮 *chingpir*, n., (1) a tree, *Ilex macropoda*; (2) orange peel, used in medicine; (3) (coll.) a ne'er-do-well, an eccentric or impertinent fellow.

青苹 *chingpirng*, n., duckweed.

青紗障(帳) *chingshajahng*, n., (in Manchuria) tall growing Indian corn, sorghum, etc., convenient for hiding of rebels.

青衫 *chingshan*, n., (1) plain dress; (2) see *-yi* ↓.

青蝦 *chingshia*, n., shrimp; prawn.

青士 *chingshyh*, n., (LL) bamboo.

青石 *chingshyr*, n., granite; also *Lapis lazuli*.

青史 *chingshyy*, n., history: 青史留名 have a niche in history, leave one's name to posterity.

青蒜 *chingsuahn*, n., leek.

青絲 *chingsy*, n., black hair: 斬斷青絲 shave off one's hair to enter monastery.

青苔 *chingtair*, n., moss, lichens.

青天 *chingtian*, n., (1) the clear, blue sky: 青天白日 in broad daylight; (2) as symbol of justice: 重見青天 regain freedom, freed from prison; formerly, address to judge: 青天大人.

青頭菌 *chingtour-jyuhn*, n., a mushroom, *Lactaris hatsudake*.

青菜 *chingtsaih*, n., fresh vegetables in gen.

青翠 *chingtsueih*, adj., beautiful green (garden, etc.).

青葱 *chingtsung*, (1) adj., ditto; (2) n., onion.

青瓷 *chingtsyr*[1], n., pure pale-green porcelain, much valued.

青詞 *chingtsyr*[2], n., Taoist prayer, written on special paper.

青桐 *chingturng*[1], n., the *wurturng* (梧A桐 10A.40).

青銅 *chingturng*[2], n., bronze; 青銅時代 the Bronze Age; 青銅器 bronze vessels.

青紫 *chingtzyy*, adj. & n., (1) purple and blue (bruise); (2) ancient officials of high rank (dressed in purple and green).

青蛙 *chingwa*, n., the common frog.

青眼 *chingyaan*, v.t., look on with favor or pleasure, dist. 白眼 show white of eye in disdain.

青陽 *chingyarng*[1], n., (LL) springtime.

青楊 *chingyarng*[2], n., a kind of willow, *Salix thunbergiana* (also called 楊).

青衣 *chingyi*, n., (1) (AC) servant, maid; (2) plain informal dress: 青衣小帽; (3) (AC) green robes worn in spring; (4) (Chin. opera) role of simple good young woman (dressed in black, specializing in singing).

青熒 *chingyirng*[1], adj., shining (of lamp light, jade).

青蠅 *chingyirng*[2], n., green flies, *Lucilia caecar* (also called 金蠅).

青玉 *chingyuh*, n., sapphire (=藍寶石).

青魚 *chingyur*, n., a carp-like fish.

青雲 *chingyurn*, n., the region of clouds: (a) symbolic of great official career or literary rank; 直上青雲 hit the highest literary honors; and (b) symbolic of retirement to nature.

南 10.42

narn.

N. (1) The south: 南方 *-fang* ↓; 南面 *-miahn* ↓; 南轅北轍 to head for the wrong direction, diametrically opposite; 天南地北 (of friends or relatives) be separated far and wide. (2) The southern parts of a country: 南腔北調 (of speech) talk with mixed accents; 北人南相 a northerner with the looks of a southerner. (3) A surname.

Adv. Southward: 南巡 (or kings) make an inspection trip in the south; 南奔 escape southward; 南投 go southward; 南行 ditto; 南下 go down south.

南半球 *Narnbahnchiour*, n., the Southern Hemisphere.

南北朝 *Narnbeei-chaur*, n., era of the Southern and Northern Dyns., 420–589 A.D.

南方 *narnfang*, n., (1) (of direction) the south: 在南方 in the south; 面向南方 facing the south; (2) the southern parts of a country: 南方人 a southerner; 南方女郎 a girl from the south.

南非 *Narn-Fei*, n., South Africa; 南非聯邦 *Nam-Fei Liarnbang*, Union of South Africa; Republic of South Africa since 1961.

南瓜 *narngua*, n., (bot.) the pumpkin, *Cucurbita pepo*.

南瓜子兒 *narn'guatzee'l*, n., pumpkin seeds.

南國 *narnguor*, n., the south in general: 南國佳人 a beauty from the south.

南回歸線 *Narn-hueir-guei-shiahn*, n., the Tropic of Capricorn.

南貨 *narnhuoh*, n., (orig.) products from southern China; now, any native product, foodstuff, ham, etc.

南胡 *narnhur*, n., a kind of musical instrument.

南鍼 *narnjen*, n., (also 南針) a

compass, (fig.) a guide or guideline, abbr. from 指南針.

南箕 *narnji*, n., as in 南箕北斗 (lit.) the Sagittarius and the Dipper; (fig.) nominal things without any practical use.

南京 *Narnjing*, n., Nanking.

南極 *Narnjir*, n., (geog.) the South Pole; 南極圈 the Antarctic Circle; 南極洲 Antartica.

南燭 *narnjur*, n., (bot.) (also 南天燭) *Andromeda ovalifolia*.

南柯 *narnke*, n., in 南柯一夢 (allu.) an imaginary or empty dream, symbolic of man's life.

南美 *Narn-Meei*, n., South America.

南面 *narnmiahn*, n., (1) the south; (2) (AC) a king or emperor: 南面稱王 to ascend the throne (from ancient practice that all kings sat facing the south in holding audience).

南無 *narmor* (-'*mo*), v.t., (Sanskrit) *Namo*, take refuge in (the Buddha, the dharma or the sangha).

南山壽 *narnshan-shouh*, phr., 壽比南山 many, many happy returns of the day (lit., "as long-lived as Mt. Nanshan").

南斯拉夫 *Narn-Sylafu*, n., Yugoslavia.

南天竹 *narntianjur*, n., (bot.) *Nandia domestica*.

南腿 *narntueei*, n., a kind of ham produced in southern China.

南緯 *narnweei*, n., (geog.) southern latitudes.

南洋 *Narnyarng*, n., the South Seas; 南洋羣島 the South Sea Islands.

§10.50（十/ㄱ）

毒 10.50

dur.

N. Poison: 有毒 be poisonous; 中毒 (*juhng-*) get poisoned; 下毒 put poison in (drink); 服毒 commit suicide by poison; 流毒 deleterious effect, harm to society; 消毒 to disinfect, sterilize; 解毒 counteract poison; 解毒藥 antidote.

V.t. To poison: 毒殺, 毒死, 毒斃 poison to death; 毒害 to harm gravely, persecute to death.

Adj. & adv. (1) Poisonous: 毒蟲, 毒蛇 poisonous insect, snake; 毒牙, 毒刺 poison fangs, poisonous sting; 毒箭, 毒酒 poisoned arrow, wine. (2) Malicious, murderous, with hate or intention to harm: (下) 毒手 use murderous means; 毒計 dastardly plan to hurt or persecute; 毒心 murderous heart; 狠毒心腸 cruel heart; 毒恨 bitter hate; 惡毒 evil, cruel; 毒打 beat mercilessly; 毒罵 revile, rail at madly.

毒氣 *durchih*, n., poisonous gas.

毒著兒 *durjau'l*, n., a murderous plan.

毒質 *durjyr*, n., poisonous material, element.

毒辣 *durlah*, adj., murderous, cruel, devilish (plan).

毒砂 *dursha*, n., (min.) arsenopyrite.

毒素 *dursuh*, n., toxin.

毒血症 *durshyuehjehng*, n., toxemia.

毒瓦斯 *dur waasy*, n., poison gas.

毒藥 *duryauh*, n., poison.

棼 10.50

fern.

N. (1) (AC) cross beams on roof. (2) A kind of hemp cloth.

Adj. Confusing, tangled.

𠩺 10.50

lir.

V.t. To scrape with a knife.

驁 10.50

aur.

N. A steed, charger; an uncontrollable wild horse, mustang.

Adj. Unruly, uncontrollable, proud: 桀驁 violent-tempered; 驁放 proud and disdainful of conventions.

§10.63（十/丶）

杰 10.63

jier.

[Var. of 傑 91A.01]

熬 10.63

aur (**au*).

V.i. & t. (1) To stew (beef, vegetable), decoct (medicine), simmer (gruel) and make thick soup. (2) To suffer (as in Eng. "stew in one's own juice"): 熬不過苦刑 could endure no longer the tortures; 熬過這一夜 (of dying patient) pull through this night; 熬夜, 熬眼皮子 to go without sleep the whole night; 熬枯受淡 drag through a monotonous life.

Adj. (**au*) Worried, despondent: 今天他熬了 he is in a bad mood today; 熬心, 熬惱 *-shin*, *-naau* ↓; 熬頭, 熬喳兒 *-'tou*, *-char'l* ↓.

熬熬 *aur-aur*, adj., (AC) discontented, clamorous (＝嗷嗷).

熬喳兒 **auchar'l*, adj., depressed, indifferent to everything.

熬煎 *aurjian*, v.i. & t., to endure, drag through unhappy days: 怕家眷受熬煎 afraid that one's family will live through hard days.

熬煉 *aurliahn*, v.t., to let (person, body) go through hard training.

熬惱 **aunaau*, adj., irritated, vexed.

熬審 *aur-sheen*, v.t., to apply third degree.

熬心 **aushin*, adj., see *-naau*↑.

熬刑 *aur-shirng*, v.t., to endure tortures by court, police.

熬頭 **au'tou* ,n., mental torment; 心裏這一分熬頭 this torment, anguish in my heart; 熬頭兒 reward for long hardships and patience; 將來有個熬頭兒 will be well rewarded (for present suffering).

熬油(兒) *aur-your('l)*, v.i., to waste lamp oil by not sleeping at night.

鰲 10.63

aur.
[Pop. of 鼇 10.70]

§ 10.70 (十/乚)

七 10.70

chi (*chir* before 4th tone (h) and unaccented syllable).

N. A seventh day after death, when sacrifice is offered until seven times seven days (forty-ninth) is over; 七七 forty-ninth day; 頭七 the first seventh; 三七 the third seventh, etc.

Adj. Seven, seven times; 七擒七放 (allu.) 諸葛亮七擒孟獲 Juker Liahng subjugated a native chief by capturing him and releasing him seven times; 七十二 a round number; 七十二行 every one of the seventy-two professions; 出七 an impossible number in dice where the maximum is six, hence a miracle: 說出七來也不行 even a miracle won't make (s.o.) budge; 他可貧出七來了 he is down to the last cent; 七…八… higgledy-piggledy, pellmell; 七大八小, 七長八短 of uneven size; 七顛八倒 totter in any and all directions; 亂七八糟, 七零八落 all a hideous mess; 七扭八歪 (of things) in a state of great disorder: 七楞八瓣 of most uneven size and formation; 七手八腳 to serve hand and foot; 七上八下 (or 落) in a mental flurry of indecision; 七嘴八舌, 七言八語 all talking in confusion or offering different opinions; 七拼八湊 to scrape together; 七折八扣 not pay up full amount; 七通八達 (of location) reaching out in all directions; 七老八十 in one's seventies.

七寶 *chibaau*, n., (Budd.) seven kinds of gems (and other explanations): 七寶樓臺 tower of seven jewels.

七七 *chichi*, n., (1) the seven times seven days after death, see N.↑; (2) the seventh day of seventh lunar month, see *-shih*↓; 七七事變 July 7, 1937, the outbreak of Sino-Japanese War.

七巧(板) *chichiaau(baan)*, n., (1) see *-shih*↓; (2) the magic square, cut into seven pieces, which could be arranged in many different shapes, an educational puzzle.

七竅 *chi-chiauh*, phr., the seven apertures of human face (eyes, ears, nostrils and mouth): 七竅流血 bleeding from nose and mouth, etc.; 七竅生烟 fumigate with anger.

七情 *chi chirng*, phr., the normal human emotions of joy, anger, sorrow, fear, love, hate and desire.

七出 *chi-chu*, phr., formerly, the seven valid reasons for divorce: (1) barrenness, (2) adultery, (3) disrespect to parents-in-law, (4) wicked tongue, (5) theft, (6) jealousy and (7) heinous disease.

七尺 *chi-chyy*, phr., 七尺之軀 the human adult body, seven "foot" 尺 in ancient measure (a foot being perhaps seven modern inches).

七古 *chi-guu*, n., see *-yarn*↓.

七件事 *chi-jiahn-shyh*, phr., the seven household needs: 柴 fuel, 米 rice, 油 oil, 鹽 salt, 醬 sauce, 醋 vinegar, 茶 tea.

七絕 *chijyuer*, n., see *-yarn -shy*↓.

七律 *chilyuh*, n., see *-yarn -shy*↓.

七色 *chi seh*, n., the seven colors of spectrum or rainbow.

七聲 *chi sheng*, phr., the seven-tone scale of music: 宮, 商, 角, 徵, 羽 (pentatonic) plus 變徵 *fa* and 變宮 *ti*.

七香 *chi shiang*, n., a mixture of seven spices.

七絃 *chi-shiarn*, n., the seven-stringed instrument.

七夕 *chishih*, n., the festival of the seventh day of seventh month, celebrating the annual reunion of lovers, the Cowherd and the Spinster, two stars in heaven, also called 乞巧.

七星 *chi-shing*, n., (astron.) the Great Dipper; 七星板 a panel in coffin carved with design of the Great Dipper.

七條 *chitiaur*, n., Buddhist cassock: 七條袈裟.

七言詩 *chiyarn-shy*, n., a poetic form of seven syllables to a line; 七律 such poem of eight lines with prescribed tonal pattern; 七絕 of four lines with prescribed tonal pattern; 七古 poem of seven syllables to a line, without tonal prescription and of any number of lines.

七曜 *chi-yauh*, n., the seven days of the week, named after the sun (Sunday), the moon (Monday) and five planets (Mars, Mercury, Jupiter, Venus and Saturn).

七音 *chi-yin*, n., (1) (phonetics) the seven classes of consonants; 脣 labial, 舌 lingual, 牙 back teeth, 齒 dental, 喉 guttural, 半舌 lateral and 半齒 dental sibilant; (2) see *-sheng*↑.

乜 屯 鼇 先

乜 10.70

shern.

[Abbr. of 甚 20.21]

屯 10.70

turn (**jun, *churn*).

N. (1) (*-tz, -'l*) A small hamlet. (2) (**churn*) Anc. place name.

V.t. (1) To hoard, stock up for sale: 屯貨 stock up goods; 屯糧 (mil.) stock up food supplies; gather, accumulate, 屯聚, 屯積 *-jyuh, -ji* ↓. (2) To station soldiers at place for defense: 屯兵.

Adj. (**jun*) (In AC compp. only) 屯剝 (*-bo*), 屯否 (*-pii*), 屯難 (*-nahn*), 屯質 (*-jyh*), 屯坎 (*-kaan*), all meaning encountering hard knocks in life, buffeted.

屯堡 *turnbaau*, n., military outpost.

屯積 *turnji*, v.t., to store up (gold, goods, food supplies).

屯聚 *turnjyuh*, v.i., (of people) flock together, form a crowd (at a place).

屯墾 *turnkeen*, v.i., open up frontier land.

屯糧 *turnliarng*, v.i. & n., store(d) up food supplies (chiefly rice); sometimes farm tax on colonizing farmers.

屯田 *turntiarn*, v.i. & n., to station soldiers on borders, making them raise their own food.

鼇 10.70

aur.

[Pop. 鰲]

N. A big sea turtle; oft. a stone turtle supporting a tablet and associated with Hanlin Academy 翰林院: 獨佔鼇頭 to come out first in national civil examinations as 狀元.

先 10.70

shian (**shiahn*).

N. (1) Place ahead, time before: 在你之先 ahead of you; 未開始之先 before it began; see 先前 *-chiarn* ↓. (2) A surname.

V.t. (1) To precede: 先意承志 do things before one is told. (2) (pr. **shiahn* in AC classics) To go before, precede: 知所先後 to know what should precede, and what follow; 先己後人 put self before others; 先下手爲強 advantage for striking first.

Adj. (1) Ahead in place, before in time, opp. 後 behind: 先路 road ahead, those leading; 先例 *-lih* ↓. (2) The deceased, the late (uncle, mother, husband, wife, etc.): 先大夫, 先府君 my (our) late father; 先秦 pre-Chirn period. (3) Pertaining to past ages: 先聖, 先賢, 先哲, 先輩 *-shehng, -shiarn, -jer, -beih* ↓. (4) Of prime importance or prior in importance: 先要 *-yauh* ↓.

Adv. First, before (other things): 我先吃了 I have eaten already (ahead of dinner hour); first: 你先去 or 在先, you go first; 以先, 之先; (used after vb.) before: 未去之先 before he went away; 先發制人 (mil.) the advantage of initiative or initial attack, also in social or political fights; 先禮後兵 first a courteous exchange of words, then war; 先入爲主 the first speaker has the advantage to instil certain notions; 先入之見 prejudice; 先花後果 "first flower, then fruit"—first have daughters, then sons; 先錢後酒 first pay, then deliver goods; 先斬後奏 (general) empowered to kill first then report later; 先親後不改 the form of address of a relative does not change if a new relationship develops; 先憂後樂 first labor, then enjoy later; 先天下之憂而憂, 後天下之樂而樂 a leader should plan and worry ahead of the people, and enjoy the fruits after the people.

先輩 *shianbeih*, n., the elder generation.

先妣 *shianbii*, n., my deceased mother.

先前 *shianchiarn*, adv., in times before: 先前不這樣 it was not so before.

先期 *shianchir*, (1) adv., beforehand: 先期通知他 inform him beforehand; (2) in earlier period.

先驅 *shianchyu*, n., pioneer, vanguard.

先達 *shiandar*, n., the elder leaders, leaders of the past generation, see *-shehng, -shiarn* ↓.

先導 *shiandauh*, n., pioneer; guide, leader setting example for others.

先德 *shiander*, n., (1) the respected elders; (2) (court.) another's ancestors.

先鋒 *shianfeng*, n., vanguard; leader of a movement.

先河 *shianher*, n., (LL) beginnings, breaking of path for others to follow (as the sea can be traced back to the rivers).

先後 *shianhouh*, (1) adv., successively: 先後到會 (guests) come in succession; (2) n., order of precedence.

先兆 *shianjauh*, n., omen, foreboding of what is to come.

先正 *shianjehng*, n., see *-shiarn* ↓.

先哲 *shianjer*, n., wise men of the past.

先見 *shianjiahn*, n., foresight, vision: 先見之明 the ability to discern what is coming.

先進 *shianjihn*, n., the forerunners: 先進國家 the countries that have progressed ahead.

先知 *shianjy*, n., prophet, seer.

先決 *shianjyuer*[1], adj., first to be determined: 先決問題, 條件 problem, terms, to be decided first, precondition.

先覺 *shianjyuer*[2], n., prophet: 先知先覺 phr., see *-jy* ↑.

先君 *shianjyun*, n., my late father; 令先君 your late father.

先考 *shiankaau*, n., deceased father; cf. 先妣 *-bii* ↑.

先烈 ***shianlieh***, n., the martyrs of the past.

先例 ***shianlih***, n., a precedent: 古無先例 unprecedented in history.

先令 ***shianlihng***, n., (translit.) a shilling.

先民 ***shianmirn***, n., ancestors of a race, primitive forbears.

先人 ***shianrern***, n., ancestors.

先容 ***shianrurng***, v.i., to speak for person before one contacts or sees person on business: 爲我先容 speak for me first.

先聖 ***shianshehng***, n., sages of the past.

先生 ***shian'sheng***, n., (1) teacher; (2) Mr. (used after surname) 林先生 Mr. Lin (or after personal name, which is also courteous among friends and acquaintances: 克強先生); 某某先生夫人 Mr. & Mrs. So-and-so; (3) a court. address to scholars, elders: 諸位先生 gentlemen (opening address); (4) as address to literate profession: 賬房先生 Mr. treasurer; 風水先生 necromancer; 星相先生 astrologer; (5) a singsong girl: 小先生 non-adult girl; 大先生 adult girl; (6) reference to husband: 我的, 他的先生不在家 my, her, husband is not at home; (7) (in Yuarn Dyn.) a Taoist priest.

先聲 ***shiansheng***, n., first signs, herald, precursor (to an event or change).

先賢 ***shianshiarn***, n., wise men; scholars of the past.

先行 ***shianshirng***, adv., first: 先行試辦 try first this arrangement.

先手 ***shianshoou***, n., the first by turn or in action.

先師 ***shianshy***, n., teacher or master of the past: 至聖大成先師孔子 Confucius, the ultimate teacher and master.

先世 ***shianshyh¹***, n., former generations.

先事 ***shianshyh²***, adv., first: 先事宣傳 begin first with publicity, propaganda.

先是 ***shianshyh³***, adv., (LL) to go back to the beginning (introducing background of story).

先室 ***shianshyh⁴***, n., my late wife.

先識 ***shianshyh⁵***, n., foresight.

先緒 ***shianshyuh***, n., ancestral heritage.

先史 ***shianshyy***, adj., prehistoric: 先史時代 prehistoric times.

先天 ***shiantian***, n., (1) born constitution, physique or mental energy; (2) instinctive, inborn, innate (kindness); (3) 先天性 adj. & n., (disease) congenital.

先頭 ***shiantour***, adv., (1) at first: 先頭他不知道 at first he did not know; (2) formerly.

先策 ***shiantseh***, v.t., to foretell, predict (outcome).

先慈 ***shiantsyr***, n., my deceased mother.

先澤 ***shiantzer***, n., benefits from one's ancestor(s).

先子 ***shiantzyy***, n., (AC) a deceased father, or ancestor or uncle.

先王 ***shianwarng***, n., (AC) the great kings of past dynasties; 三代先王 refers to the great kings of early periods: 禹, 湯, 文王, 武王 of 夏, 商, 周 Dyns.

先務 ***shian-wuh***, phr., 先務之急 first things first.

先嚴 ***shianyarn***, n., my deceased father.

先要 ***shianyauh***, n., first essentials.

先引 ***shianyiin***, n., guide (who leads the way).

先塋 ***shianyirng***, n., ancestral graveyard.

克 10.70

keh.

N. Gram, weight unit: 毫克, 厘克, 克, 千克(公斤) milligram, centigram, gram, kilogram.

Aux. vb. (AC, LL) can=modn. 能: 不克分身 cannot leave here; 克勤克儉 have capacity for industry and thrift; 克紹箕裘 can carry on father's tradition; 弗克如願 could not have it as one wished; 克享 can enjoy; 克當 be worthy; 克堪 be worthy to receive.

V.t. To overcome, conquer: 克難 overcome difficulty, crisis; 柔能克剛 softness can overcome strength; 克私, 克欲 overcome selfishness, desires; 克己, 克制, 克服, 克復 *-jii*, *-jyh*, *-fur*, *-fuh* ↓.

Adj. The very (day): 克日, 克期完成 finish the very day, on set date (also wr. 剋).

克復 ***kehfuh***, v.t., recover (lost territory).

克服 ***kehfur***, v.t., overcome (difficulty, opposition).

克家 ***kehjia***, adj., (AC) be worthy to carry on family fortune; 克家子 such worthy son.

克己 ***kehjii***, adj., unselfish, or v.i., overcome selfishness; (in business sales) sacrifice, cheap; self-denial.

克制 ***kehjyh***, v.t., overcome (feelings, desires), rule over (territory).

克拉 ***kehla***, n., (translit.) carat unit of weight (also wr. 卡剌特).

剋 10.70

keh.

[Var. 尅]

V.t. (1) Cut down, reduce, see 剋扣 *-kouh* ↓. (2) Overcome, work against: 剋制, 剋服; see 克 10.70; 相生相剋 (*yin* and *yarng*) reinforce or counteract each other; 剋夫, 剋妻 (fortunetelling) destined to mourn husband's or wife's death. (3) As var. of 刻 to carve; 苛剋 (=苛刻) mean and cruel.

剋期 ***kehchi***, phr., on set date (oft. in mil. orders).

剋扣 *kehkouh*, v.t., have illegal "cut": 剋扣軍餉 take illegal cut on soldiers' pay.

梵 10.70

jahn.

Adj. (1) Buddhist: 梵宮, 梵刹, 梵宇 Buddhist temple; 梵師 Buddhist monk; 梵嫂 Buddhist monk's wife (facet.). (2) Sanskrit: 梵文, 梵字 Sanskrit script, language; 梵語 Sanskrit language.

梵唄 *fahnbeih*, n., Buddhist song, singing.

梵蒂岡 *fahndihgang*, n., the Vatican, also 梵諦岡.

梵國 *fahnguor*, n., India.

梵衆 *fahnjuhng*, n., Buddhist monks.

梵志 *fahnjyh*, n., Brahma.

梵天 *fahntian*, n., one of the three heavens or heavenly states; 大梵天 the highest abode of 梵王 *-warng* ↓.

梵王 *fahnwarng*, n., (Budd.) the King of Heaven.

梵亞玲 *fahnyahlirng*, n., (translit.) violin, usu. called 小提琴.

梵音 *fahnyin*, n., the sound of Buddhist incantations.

氂 10.70

lir (**maur*).

N. (1) Yak's tail. (2) Long curly hair. (3) The yak (＝犛) 氂鍼 *lirjen*, n., (Chin. med.) a needle broader at one end.

麓 10.70

luh.

N. Foothill: 山麓; 南麓 (北麓) foothill on south (north) side.

§10.72 (十/心)

恝 10.72

jiar.

V.t. Neglect, pay no attention to: 恝置 ignore.

Adj. Without care or worry: 恝然 indifferent, unconcerned.

惠 10.72

hueih.

N. (1) Kindness, compassion, grace: 仁惠. (2) Favor, gift: 恩惠 s.o.'s kindness, generosity; 施惠 give gifts, charity; 受惠, 蒙惠 (court.) be favored with (kindness, gift, letter, etc.). (3) A surname.

V.t. Give: 見惠一票 kindly present me with a vote; 惠我良多 (LL) have received your many favors.

Adj. Kind, generous: 惠音 your kind letter; 惠政 benevolent policy; 惠聲 reputation for kindness; 惠風 mild air or breeze; 惠而不費 phr., a kind act which does not cost much.

Adv. Kindly, graciously, be so kind as to: 惠賜, 惠贈 (court.) so kind as to give; 惠臨, 惠然肯來 honor (me) with your presence; 惠顧 (court. of prospective customer) graciously come to our shop, to patronize; 惠存 (court.) keep as souvenir.

想 10.72

shiaang.

N. A thought, thinking, speculation: 思想 thought, ideas; 幻想 imagination, fantasy, daydream; 構想 speculation, imagination, plan for (novel, etc.); 妄想 crazy or absurd idea(s); 異想天開 phr., have strange, fantastic ideas; 理想 ideal: 理想主義(者) idealism (-t); 想法 viewpoints; 感想 thoughts and impressions after reading a book, visiting a country, see also V.i. & t. ↓.

V.i. & t. (1) To think, speculate, suppose: 我想 I think; 別想, 休想 don't think that; 想來想去 turn over in one's mind, see 想來 *-lair* ↓; 想開了 to put s.t. out of mind, stop worrying, take it easy; 想不開 keep on worrying, commit suicide, cannot put out of one's mind; 想通了, 想不通 have found, cannot find a way out, a suitable solution (to a problem); 想當然耳 just a conjecture; 想入非非 have daydreams, fantastic ideas, improper thoughts. (2) To think of, to remember (oft. followed by adv., 到, 起): 虧你想得到 how good of you to think of it; 想不到她會離開我 never thought she would leave me; 想家 be homesick; 想得好苦 long for s.o.; 想我母親 am thinking of my mother; 回想 remember, recall (a past event), think back (of old days); 想錢 think of, be preoccupied with money; 想個事做 think of s.t. to do; 想點辦法 think of some way to do it; 想起一件事 suddenly remember one thing. (3) To wish, have a mind to: 我想去 I want to go; 想不去 don't want to go; 想要 *-yauh* ↓; 我想到別處去 I am thinking of going elsewhere. (4) Short for "I think," "I suppose": 想是車誤點了 I think the train is late; 想必有緣故 I think there must be a reason; 想有問題 I am afraid there might be some hitch; 想他不肯 I believe he will not consent.

想碴兒 *shiaang-char'l*, phr., to ruminate (over past errors, events).

想起 *shiaang-chii*, n., recall (some past event, or s.t. forgotten).

想著 *shiaang'je*, v.i. & t., pres. p. of 想 in all senses, see V.i. & t. ↑:

我想著他 I am always thinking of him; 想著去又想著不去 thinking of going one moment, and not going the next.

想見 *shiaang-jiahn*, v.i., (1) (LL) imagine: 想見其爲人 imagine what he was like; (2) wish to see (s.o.).

想來 *shiaang-lair*, phr., after thinking, I suppose, I imagine: 想來是家裏有人病了 I suppose somebody at home is sick; 想來眞不應該 when I come to think of it, I really should not have done it.

想念 *shiaangniahn*, v.t., remember, long for (person, home).

想像 *shiaangshiahng*, v.i. & n., to imagine, -tion: 想像力 imaginative power; 想像文學 imaginative literature.

想頭 *shiaang'tou*, n., (1) a thought, idea (＝念頭): 你有這些想頭 you have such ideas; (2) hope, wish: 沒想頭 (the matter) is hopeless, there's no more use thinking.

想望 *shiaangwahng*, v.i., (1) to hope to, that; (2) (LL) admire: 天下想望風采 you are the admiration of the world.

想要 *shiaang yauh*, phr., want to, feel like: 想要回家 want to go home.

慧 10.72

hueih.

N. (1) Wisdom: 智慧 ditto. (2) (Budd.) intelligence, latent or developed in man, for knowledge of God: 慧心 wisdom-mind, see 慧心, 慧劍, 慧根, 慧眼 *-shin*, *-jiahn*, *-gen*, *-yaan*↓.

Adj. Intelligent: 聰慧 bright, (mind, child); 靈慧, 黠慧 quick in understanding; 秀外慧中 (usu. of child, girl) pretty and intelligent; 淑慧 bright and good (woman).

慧根 *hueihgen*, n., (Budd.) born, latent intelligence for understanding God or religious enlightenment.

慧劍 *heihjiahn*, n., (Budd.) the sword of wisdom which cuts through the illusions of material world.

慧心 *hueihshin*, n., (Budd.) the enlightened mind, wisdom.

慧眼 *hueihyaan*, n., (Budd.) the eye of wisdom, religious insight; (complim.) your penetrating insight.

慙 10.72

tsarn.

[Var. of 慚 22A. 22]

懋 10.72

mouh (*mauh*).

V.i. & t. (1) Reward with money, rank, etc.: 懋賞, 懋庸. (2) (AC) try hard, endeavor: 維時懋哉 do your duty well!

Adj. Splendid, worthy: 懋業, 績, 功 splendid achievement; 懋典 impressive ceremony.

懋遷 *mouhchian*, n. & v.i., trade, barter＝貿△易 90.80.

§10.80 (十/八)

真 10.80

jen.

[Oft. printed 眞]

N. (1) A surname. (2) (Taoist) the true, original, unspoiled character of man: 全真, 葆真 keep the original character; 真人, 真君 *-rern*, *-jyun*↓.

Adj. Real, genuine, true: 真實, 真確 *-shyr*, *-chyueh*↓; (opp. to 僞,假) 真僞 *-weih*↓; 真假 *-jiaa*↓; 這玉是真的 this jade is genuine; 真的事實 real, true facts; 真情, 真迹 *-chirng*, *-ji*↓; 真面目 the real or close view of person or thing, dist. hearsay or reputation; 真知灼見 insight won from close knowledge of subject; 真善美 (nn.) the true, the good and the beautiful; 失真 (of portrait, copy) not true to life or to original; 天真 innocent, naive; 認真 earnest; 寫真, 傳真 portrait; 寫真 also (Japanese) photograph; 逼真 lifelike.

Adv. Really, truly: 真正 *-jehng*↓; 真箇 *-geh*↓; 他真了不起 he is really marvellous; 真的那麽厲害 is he really that capable or ruthless? 你真行 you are really wonderful; 真大膽, 聰明, etc. really daring, clever.

真切 *jenchieh*, adj., realistic, close to life (description); earnest (appeal).

真情 *jenchirng*, n., (1) the real facts of a situation; (2) genuine feeling: 真情實意 out of genuine friendship.

真除 *jen-chur*, v.t., to give real post, not merely rank to person: 真除部長 confirm as regular minister (person who has been "acting" only).

真詮 *jenchyuarn*, n., the real meaning of text or teaching.

真確 *jenchyueh*, adj., true, not false (facts, opinion).

真諦 *jen-dih*, n., (Budd.) true meaning of teaching or doctrine.

真箇 *jengeh*, adv., (esp. MC) really (＝真的): 真箇銷魂 (of woman) really captivating; really surrender in love.

真箇的 *jenger'de*, adv., ditto.

真果 *jenguoo*, n., (bot.) true fruit.
真正 *jenjehng*, adv., really, truly.
真迹 *jen-ji*, n., real handwriting of famous men (not reproduction).
真假 *jen-jiaa*, n., question of truth in story ("true" or "false").
真珠 *jenju*, n., pearl (usu. wr. 珍珠).
真君 *jenjyun*, n., (Taoist) title of immortal or fairy.
真空 *jenkung*, n., (phys.) vacuum; 真空管 vacuum tube.
真理 *jenlii*, n., truth (religious, scientific).
真皮 *jenpir*, n., (physiol.) real skin, dermis, dist. epidermis.
真人 *jenrern*, n., (Taoist) a perfect man, an immortal.
真如 *jenrur*, n., (Budd.) the unconditioned, unchanging reality, dist. changing form and appearance.
真相 *jen-shiahng*, n., real condition or aspect of situation.
真性 *jen-shihng*, n., the real nature, natural character of man and animals.
真心 *jen-shin*, n., real feeling; adv., genuinely, sincerely: 真心信佛 genuinely believe in Buddhism.
真書 *jen-shu*, n., another name for 楷書 the formal script of characters.
真率 *jenshuaih*, adj., genuine, forthright, without affectations.
真實 *jenshyr*, adj. & adv. & n., true, -ly, real, -ly, factual, -ly, (facts, opinions, feelings, etc.).
真宰 *jentzaai*, n., true lord of the universe (莊子).
真贓 *jen-tzang*, n., factual evidence (loot, etc.) of burglars.
真妄 *jen-wahng*, n., (Budd.) reality and illusion.
真偽 *jen-weih*, n., question of truth (of story).
真贋 *jen-yahn*, n., question of genuineness (of painting, etc.).
真元 *jenyuarn*, n., (Taoist) vital spirit of man.

責 10.80

tzer.

N. One's duty, responsibility: 責任 *-rehn* ↓; 責任心 sense of responsibility; 責任感 moral obligation; 責無旁貸 duty-bound; 敷衍塞責 do things perfunctorily; 職責 official responsibility; 負責 be responsible, have sense of responsibility.

V.t. (1) To blame, condemn, censure: 責詰, 詰責 chide, rebuke; 責問 take to task; 責難 *-narn* ↓; 責讓 to reprimand, to lash out at; 責言 words of censure. (2) (AC) to demand, ask for: 責賂于鄭 demand tribute from Jehng. (3) Punish: 責罰 *-far* ↓; 責罵 chide, revile; 責備 *-beih* ↓; 責打 *-daa* ↓; 杖責 flog with a cane; 笞責 flog with a bamboo stick; 痛責 scold severely; 譴責 lash out at, make verbal attacks on; 自責 reproach oneself.

責備 *tzerbeih*, v.t., (1) expect too much of (another): 求全責備 take to task severly, expect (people) to be saints; (2) to rebuke, reprimand.
責成 *tzercherng*, v.t., entrust a task to (s.o.).
責打 *tzerdaa*, v.t., (LL) mete out corporeal punishment to, punish by flogging.
責罰 *tzerfar*(-'*fa*), v.t., punish (a child, pupil).
責分 *tzerfehn*, n., one's bounden duty.
責難 *tzernarn*, v.t., (1) to call upon (s.o.) to make superhuman efforts; (2) (*-nahn*) rebuke severely: 受人責難 be taken to task (censured).
責任 *tzerrehn*, n., (1) one's duty, responsibility; (2) one's moral or legal obligation; 責任準備金 liability reserve funds.
責善 *tzershahn*, v.t., expect the best of (s.o.): 父子之間不責善 between father and son there is no room for sermonizing.
責望 *tzerwahng*, v.i., cause misgivings between friends by expecting too much of each other.

賁 10.80

ben (**bih*).

[Cogn. of 奔, 濆]

V.i. (AC) Flee, dash (=奔) 賁軍 fleeing troops: 虎△賁 21A.70 (*ben*) brave like "dashing tiger."

Adj. (**bih*) Shining.

賁賁 *benben*, adj., (AC) making chattering noises (of birds).
賁臨 **bihlin*, v.i., (LL & court.) condescend and attend my humble dinner=光臨.

賚 10.80

laih.

N. A surname.

V.t. 賚品 a gift.

贅 10.80

jueih.

N. (1) (AC) a pawn. (2) Appendage, what is extra: 贅疣, 贅瘤 *-your*, *-liour*^{2} ↓. (3) A son-in-law who marries into bride's family and takes her family name. (4) To be married into brides home and take her name, see N. 3 ↑.

V.i. & t. (1) (AC) to pawn, also to offer oneself as hostage: 贅子 (AC) to sell son as slave. (2) To hang like an appendage: 這孩子贅着我 this child hangs on to me everywhere. (3) (AC) 贅聚 to assemble, meet. (4) To say what is not necessary, to talk incessantly or repetitiously: 不贅 (in letters) will stop here (and you will understand the rest).

Adj. & adv. Extra, supernumerary: 贅言, 贅詞, 贅述 *-yarn, -tsyr, -shuh*↓; 累贅 wordy, repetitious.

贅旒 *jueihliour*[1], n., (AC) a figurehead, a mere adornment.
贅瘤 *jueihliour*[2], n., a goiter, a thing of no purpose, unneeded thing.
贅述 *jueihshuh*, v.i., in 不必贅述 it's unnecessary to go into details.
贅壻 *jueihshyuh*, n., see N. 3↑.
贅詞 *jueihtsyr*, n., unnecessary talk.
贅言 *jueihyarn*, n., see *-tsyr*↑.
贅疣 *jueihyour*, n., see *-liour*[2]↑.

贊 10.80

tzahn.

N. A literary eulogy.

V.t. (1) Help, assist, support: 贊助 to support (plan, program) morally or financially; 贊理, 贊襄 assist (person) with a task; 贊翼 serve as an assistant to (person). (2) Praise, laud: 贊美 *-meei*↓; 贊歎 to praise highly; 贊賞 appreciate (a job well done, a work of art); 稱贊 speak well of; 贊許 endorse, approve; 贊揚 speak favorably of, sing the praises of; 贊頌 laud to the skies. (3) Agree with, assent to: 贊同 be in agreement with, approve of (action, proposal); 贊成 *-cherng*↓. (4) Assist in a ceremony: 贊禮 *-lii*↓; 徧贊賓客 to greet all guests.

贊成 *tzahncherng*, v.t., (1) to approve: 我不贊成 I do not approve; to second (s.o.'s proposal, motion) during discussion or debate; (2) help (s.o.) to succeed.
贊禮 *tzahnlii*, v.i., serve as a program announcer; 贊禮人 a master of ceremonies.
贊美 *tzahnmeei*, v.t., to praise: 贊美上帝 praise God; 贊美詩 n., hymn.

賷 10.80

ji.
[Var. 齎]

N. & v.t. A gift, to give.

§10.81 (十/人)

契 10.81

chih (**chieh*).
[Var. 栔]

N. A written agreement, a deed: see 契約 *-yue*↓; 地契, 田契, 房契 title deed of land, farm, house; 租契 lease contract: 文契 written contract.

Adj. Sworn: 契兄弟 sworn brother; 契父, 契母 *-fuh, -muu*↓.

V.t. (1) To match, to be attached closely as friend: 相契 get along together beautifully; 契友 close friend; 契合 *-her*↓. (2) (LL) to bite, bite off: 契臂之交 (lit.) "bite shoulder"—sworn friend; 契斷 to bite off. (3) (**chieh*) To carve: 契舟求劍 (=刻契) to carve on gunwale of moving boat, marking where a sword was dropped—foolish undertaking; 契闊 *-kuoh*↓. (4) Adopted (father, mother, brother).

契契 *chihchih*, adv., (AC) sorrowfully.
契丹 *chihdan*, n., the Kitan tribe (ruled China 907–1115 A.D.).
契父 *chihfuh*, n., adopted father.
契合 *chihher*, (1) v.i., agree, match together; (2) adj., intimate, suitable, friendly.
契箭 *chih-jiahn*, n., (AC) military order, in form of an arrow.
契券 *chih-jyuahn*, n., contractual agreement, deed of sale or ownership.
契據 *chihjyuh*, n., written contract, papers of agreement.
契紙 *chihjyy*, n., a title deed.
契闊 **chieihkuoh*, adj., (LL) separated: 契闊三年 absence of three years; 契闊之情 remembrance during absence.
契母 *chihmuu*, n., adopted mother.
契女 *chihnyuu*, n., adopted daughter.
契税 *chihshueih*, n., tax on landownership registration.
契兄弟 *chihshyungdih*, n., sworn brothers.
契子 *chihtzyy*, n., adopted son.
契尾(子) *chihwei('tz)*, n., formerly, landownership registration paper.
契文 *chihwern*, n., (1) text of agreement; (2) bone inscriptions of Shang Dyn., being earliest known forms of writing.
契印 *chihyihn*, n., official seal stamped on agreement.
契約 *chihyue*, n., a written contract.

獒 10.81

aur.

N. A mastiff, a large fierce dog.

樊 10.81

farn.

N. (1) A surname. (2) Bird cage.

樊籠 *farnluung*, n., bird cage;

(fig.) deadening confinement in art, literature.

樊然 *farn-rarn*, adj., (LL) confusing.

焚 10.81

fern.

V.i. & t. (LL) Burn (=vern. 燒 *shau*): 焚毀 destroy by fire; 焚斃 burn (-ed) to death; 焚掠, 焚劫 (of troops and bandits) burn houses and loot; 焚稿 burn manuscripts; 焚香 burn incense and pray at temple; 焚琴煮鶴 (derog.) burn famous string instrument for fuel and cook crane for meat, vandalism, offence against culture; 焚書坑儒 burning of books and burying Confucianists alive in ravine by 秦始皇 in 213–212 B.C.; 焚膏繼晷 "burn midnight oil" in hard study; 玩火自焚 play with fire, burn one's fingers; 焚溺 fire and drowning flood, symbol of people's misery under oppression.

焚燒 *fernshau*, v.i. & t., to burn.

僰 10.81

Bor.

N. *Bor* (or 僰人 *Bor-rern*), an aboriginal tribe in Southwest China.

§ 10.82 (十/乂)

支 10.82

jy.

N. adjunct. A stick (u.f. 枝): 一支蠟燭 one candle; hence, candle power: 五十支光 fifty candle-power; number of threads per inch in gauze or silk material.

N. (1) A surname. (2) A branch office, branch line, a branch of family (related 枝 10A. 82): 支部 branch office; 支店, 支行 local office; 支隊 an army column; 支線 branch telegraphic or railway line (opp. 幹線 trunk line); 支流 tributary, branch of river; 宗支, 支脈 branch of family; 本支 same branch of family; 支路 feeder road, branch of road. (3) U.f. 肢 limbs: 支解, 支骸 *-jiee*, *-hair* ↓. (4) 地支 the duodecimal cycle for counting years, days and hours: 子, 丑, 寅, 卯, 辰, 巳, 午, 未, 申, 酉, 戌, 亥 used in conjunction with the decimal cycle 天干; see Appendix A.

V.t. (1) To disburse, pay out: 支付, 支出 *-fuh*, *-chu* ↓; 支撥 pay (a certain sum); 支給 pay to (person, etc.); 開支 expenditures, disbursements; 收支相抵 (平衡) balance of income and expenditures. (2) To receive, get payment: 支取 *-chyuu* ↓; 支款, 支錢 take out cash; 支借 borrow on account; 預支 prepay, (receive) advance payment; 透支 overdraw, overdraft; 停支 stop payment; 濫支 improperly disburse. (3) To support: 支持, 支撐, 支援 *-chyr*, *-cheng*, *-yuaan* ↓; 支不住 or 支(持)不住 cannot hold back (onslaught), cannot hold up against (illness); 支鍋瓦兒 a three-legged support of iron or brick for round cauldrons. (4) To send about, to order, to control: 支使, 支配 *-'shy*, *-peih* ↓; 支嘴兒 to order others about while not moving oneself; 把他支走 send him away.

Adj. Disperse: 支離 *-lir* ↓.

支撐 *jycheng*, v.t., to prop up, to hold up a collapsing or collapsible structure: 支撐門面 to maintain the front or show.

支氣管 *jychih-guaan*, n., bronchi; 支氣管炎 bronchitis.

支出 *jy-chu*, v.t., to pay out, take out (sum); n., outlay, expenses, expenditures.

支絀 *jychuh*, adj., short of money.

支持 *jychyr*(-'*chy*), v.t., to support (leader, cause, campaign, theory, etc.).

支取 *jychyuu*, v.t., to draw out (money).

支點 *jydiaan*, n., (phys.) fulcrum.

支對 *jydueih*, v.t., (LL) to reply to question.

支費 *jyfeih*, n., expenses.

支付 *jyfuh*, v.t., to disburse; to take out (sum.).

支骸 *jyhair*, n., human limbs and skeleton (=肢骸).

支招兒 *jyjau'l*, v.i., (coll.) to help to plan.

支解 *jyjiee*, v.t., (AC) to dismember (criminal) as form of punishment.

支節 *jyjier*, n., detail: 支節問題 problems of detail (also wr. 枝).

支樁 *jyjuang*, v.i., (coll.) to stall an argument, to give non-committal reply.

支柱 *jyjuh*, n., a propor supporting pillar.

支楞 *jy'leng*, v.t., to prick up (one's ears).

支離 *jylir*, adj., broken up, piecemeal: 支離散亂 all jumbled up; 支離破碎 all broken up, (of arguments) occupied with unimportant details; 言語支離 give ambiguous statements.

支爐兒 *jylur'l*, n., an earthen pan with holes, used over oven for baking cakes.

支派 *jypaih*, n., branch of family or school of thought.

支配 *jypeih*(-'*pei*), v.t., (1) to allot (money, manpower), to have (time) available for service, to control, regulate (nation, resources, etc.).

支票 *jypiauh*, n., a check payable: 空頭支票 rubber check, overdrawn check without coverage in deposits; 保付支票 certified check; 櫃臺支票 counter check.

支庶 *jyshuh*, n., the collateral branches of family.

支屬 *jyshuu*, n., relatives from branches of family.

支使 *jy'shy*, v.t., to control: 爲他所支使 be controlled by him.

支吾 *jywur*(-'*wu*), v.i., to prevaricate, to stall with words: 你用話支吾他 make excuses with words to hold off s.o.; (AC) to resist (＝枝梧).

支應 jyyihng(-'ying), v.t., (1) to control (receipts and disbursements); (2) to keep on the lookout; (3) see *-wur*↑.

支移 *jyyir*[1], v.i., to transfer fund for another purpose where it is needed.

支頤 *jy-yir*[2], phr., to rest chin in palm or cheek in hand.

支援 *jyyuaan*, v.t., to support with money needed or send military reinforcements.

支用 *jy-yuhng*, v.i. & t., to defray expenses.

麦 10.82

maih.

[Pop. of 麥 10.32]

菠 10.82

tsurng.

[Var. of 叢 22.82]

§10.83 (十/〜)

楚 10.83

chuu.

N. (1) (AC) a thistle. (2) A punishing rod: 夏楚 (LL) spanking, spanking rod. (3) Name of ancient kingdom, roughly modern Hupei: 楚材晉用 (allu.) a great person given important post by another country; 楚弓楚得 (楚人失弓，楚人得之) (AC) the King of *Chuu* lost a bow and gave up the search, contenting himself with the thought that it was most probably found by one of his countrymen and therefore not a loss. (4) A surname.

Adj. (1) Painful: 痛楚 pain, -ful; 苦楚 (also v.t. & n.) a distress, distressed, to distress; 酸楚 pitiful, sad. (2) Neat, clear: 清楚 clear; 楚楚 *-chuu*↓.

楚囚 *chuuchiour*, n., (allu.) a held prisoner, man in difficult straits.

楚楚 *churchuu*, adj., (1) bright and clear; (2) luxuriant; (3) 楚楚可憐 delicate and touching (girl); 楚楚動人 delicate and attractive.

楚服 *chuufur*, n., (AC) full formal dress.

楚歌 *chuu-ge*, phr., 四面楚歌 (allu.) surrounded on all sides by enemy (who sang "the Songs of *Chuu*").

楚腰 *chuuyau*, n., slender waist—from allu., the King of *Chuu* loved women with slender waistline.

踅 10.83

shyuer (**chyh*).

V.i. (1) To go around, whirl around. (2) (**chyh*) (AC) to limp on one foot.

踅轉 *shyuerjuaan*, v.i., to go around (hill, etc.).

踅溜風 *shyuer'liufeng*, v.i., a whirlwind.

踅探 *shyuertahn*, v.i., to go around from house to house.

蹇 10.83

jyh.

V.i. Totter (related 躓 40B.80).

迍 10.83

jun.

迍邅 *junjan*, v.i., (AC) move forward with difficulty.

述 10.83

shuh.

V.t. (1) To transmit, hand down: 述而不作 "I pass on (the ancient culture) and do not create" (Confucius). (2) To narrate, to compose, express in writing: 敍述 to narrate, tell (what has happened, origin of conflicts, etc.); 述人之言 (LL) tell what s.o. said; 口述 dictate (book, speech) and have s.o. record it (筆錄); 陳述 to present (a case, reasons for action), to tell (story); 著述, 述作 to write (books); 論述 to discuss (subjects); 行述 biographical sketch (of deceased).

述職 *shuhjy*, v.i., to return to capital and report.

述作 *shuhtzuoh*, v.t. & n., to write; writings.

选 10.83

shyuaan.

[Abbr. of 選 52.83]

翅 10.83

chyh.

亅	小	⺊	十	土	ナ	廾	ㄩ	丨	一	丅	フ	口	区	冈	㇆	厂	尸	亠	广	宀	丶	乚	弋	心	八	人	乂	〜	㇀	儿	㇀	〈
00	01	02	10	11	12	20	21	22	30	31	32	40	41	42	50	51	52	60	61	62	63	70	71	72	80	81	82	83	90	91	92	93

N. (1) ('*l*) Wings: 振翅, 展翅 flap wings. (2) (-*tz*) Fins, esp. 魚翅 sharks' fins.

翅 膀 *chyhbaang*, n., wings (of chicken, etc.).

翅 果 *chyhguoo*, n., (bot.) winged seed vessels.

速 10.83

suh.

V.t. To invite (s.o.): 不速之客 a guest who comes uninvited.

Adj. & adv. Quick, -ly, rapid, -ly: 迅速, 快速 quickly: 快速公路 freeway; 火速, 神速 as quickly as possible; 高速 supra-speed (highway); 加速 go faster, accelerate; 速爲辦理 do it quickly; 速度, 速率 -*duh*, -*lyuh*↓.

速 成 *suh-cherng*, v.i. & adj., do hurriedly, cram: 速成科 a short course (in subject).

速 度 *suhduh*, n., speed, velocity; 速度計 (astron.) accelerometer.

速 駕 *suhjiah*, adv., (invitation) to come early, start early on journey.

速 記 *suhjih*, n., shorthand, stenography; 速記員 stenographer.

速 客 *suh-keh*, v.i., to send servant to beg guest to come.

速 率 *suhlyuh*, n., velocity, see -*duh*↑.

速 香 *suhshiang*, n., perfume from gum of tropical trees.

速 寫 *suhshiee*, v.i. & n., (painting) sketch.

造 10.83

tzauh (**tsauh*).

N. (1) One of the parties (to a contract, dispute, lawsuit): 兩造 both parties. (2) Era, epoch, period: 末造 in the latter days. (3) (Also **tsauh*) achievements, accomplishments: (AC) 小子有造 the young man has made a name for himself; 造詣 -*yih*², 造就 -*jiouh*↓; 高造 higher studies; 深造 higher specialized training.

V.t. (1) Establish, set up, build: 造邦 build up a nation, nation-building; 建造 construct; 營造 ditto; 承造 enter into a contract to build; 造屋, 造橋, 造船 build a house, bridge, ship; 修造 repair. (2) Make, shape, manufacture, produce: 人造的 man-made, artificial; 人造花 artificial flowers; 造句子 make sentences; 造作 -*tzuoh*↓; 改造 reform, reshape, remodel, reconstruct; 天造的 natural; 自造 made by oneself; 造孽 -*nieh*, 造反 -*faan*↓; 造福人羣 confer benefits on society (one's fellow-men), be a benefactor of mankind; 創造 create; 製造 manufacture. (3) Fabricate: 造謠 -*yaur*↓; 造謠言 spread rumors; 造言 (AC) ditto; 捏造 fabricate, invent (a story, an alibi); 僞造 forge, falsify. (4) Begin, commence, start: 造端 make a beginning; 造肇 make a start, get under way; 造始 come into being. (5) (Also **tsauh*) go to: 造府 call at your home; 造訪 pay a visit to; 造請 go to invite. (6) Prepare (report, etc.): 造報, 造具 -*bauh*, -*jyuh*↓.

造 報 *tzauh-bauh*, v.i., compile a report on funds expended.

造 反 *tzauh-faan*, v.t., (1) to revolt, rebel: 造反了 this is rebellion! (2) (of children) be noisy.

造 福 *tzauh-fur*, v.t., to benefit.

造 化 *tzauhhuah*, n., (1) the Creator, God; (2) (**tzauh'hua*) fortune: 我們也沒有這麽大的造化 we have no such good fortune, are not so lucky.

造 就 *tzauhjiouh*, v.t., (1) (sp. pr. '*jiou*) help (a promising person) to succeed in life; (2) visit with; (3) n., accomplishments.

造 具 *tzauhjyuh*, v.t., compile (tables, reports).

造 林 *tzauhlirn*, v.i. & n., afforest (-ation).

造 命 *tzauh mihng*, v.i., (LL) be the master of one's or other people's fate.

造 魔 *tzauh-mor*, v.i., talk like a false prophet, rumor monger.

造 孽 *tzauh-nieh*, v.i., do evil, to sin (also wr. 造業); (fig.) to do s.t. execrable.

造 像 *tzauhshiahng*, n., (1) a statue of the Buddha or of a god; (2) a photographic portrait; (3) v.i., to make a statue.

造 形 藝 術 *tzauhshirng yihshuh*, n., plastic arts.

造 士 *tzauhshyh*, n., (LL) an accomplished scholar.

造 次 **tsauhtsyh*, adv., abruptly, quickly, without too much care.

造 罪 *tzauh-tzueh*, v.i., to sin, esp. against the gods.

造 作 *tzauhtzuoh*, (1) v.t., make, manufacture; (2) adj., artificial, labored; (3) as in 矯揉造作 falsify, -fied, done for effect.

造 謠 *tzauh-yaur*, v.i., fabricate rumors.

造 意 *tzauhyih*¹, n., concept, -tion of a piece of art or writing.

造 詣 *tzauhyih*², (1) n., scholastic attainments; (2) v.t., call on, visit with.

逋 10.83

bu.

[Dist. 捕 10A. 42]

V.i. & t. (1) To flee: 逋債 flee creditors. (2) Owe, evade: 逋租 fail to pay rent; 逋欠, 逋負 fail to pay debt.

逋 逃 *butaur*, v.i., flee from justice; 逋逃藪 asylum for refugees.

逋 竄 *butsuahn*, v.i., run away from justice.

逋 亡 *buwarng*, v.i., flee from justice.

逝 10.83

shyh.

V.i. (1) To pass away, to flow on (as water, time): 逝水 flowing water; 日月逝矣 months and days have passed; 光陰飛逝 time flies, passes on. (2) To die: 逝世 *-shyh*↓; 逝沒, 長逝, 仙逝 (LL) pass away; 偕逝 die together.

逝止 *shyh-jyy*, v.i., (AC) stop or pass on.

逝世 *shyh-shyh*, v.i., to pass away from this world.

逑 10.83

chiour.

N. (AC) life mate: 君子好逑 a gentleman's good mate.

連 10.83

liarn.

[Dist. 聯 same pr.="unite"; 連="continue"; interch. 鏈]

N. (1) A surname. (2) (Mil.) a company: see 連長 *-jaang*↓; 砲兵連 artillery corps. (3) (AC) iron chain (u.f. 鏈).

V.i. & t. Join, continue: 相連 join or be joined together, continuous; 連續, 連天 *-shyuh*, *-tian*↓; 連着 continued, -ing, -uous; 連着班兒 one after another, continuously, in a row; 連着不停 without stop; 連三併四, 接二連三 continuously, one after another.

Adj. & adv. Continuous, -ly, joined: 連年, 連日, 連天 year after year, day after day; 連連 continuous, -ly; see 連緜, 連續 *-miarn*, *-shyuh*↓; 兵連禍結 continuous wars and turmoil; 連篇累牘 pages and pages (of persiflage); 連署 sign joint signatures; 連記法 *-jih-faa*↓; 連名 (write letter, statement) with joint signatures; in comb. 連…帶: 連踢帶打 both kick and hit (a person); 連本帶利 both capital and interest.

Adv. Even: 連看都不一看 won't even take a look; 連理都不理 won't even pay any attention.

Prep. Even (used like 將, 把, 給 preceding objective n. or pron. and, like the above, making the vb. follow the object): 連你在內 that includes you, too; 連他一同去 go together, with him included; usu. in comb. 連…也, or 連…都; 連話都不會說 can't even talk; 連水也不喝 won't even take water; 連自己兒女也殺了 killed even one's own children; 連你也不是 you, too, will be blamed for this.

連璧 *liarn bih*, phr., (of two good things) combined together.

連城 *liarn-cherng*, n., a series of towns: 價同連城 very valuable, commanding a high price (worth a couple of towns together).

連翹 *liarnchiaur* (*-chiauh*), n., (bot.) forsythia.

連氣兒 *liarn-chieh'l*, adv., in a fit of determination, anger, etc.: 一連氣兒告了三天假 asked for three days' leave straight; 一連氣跑了三里路 ran for a mile at one stretch.

連串(兒) *liarn-chuahn*(*-chuah'l*), n., a whole series (of disasters, mishaps).

連帶 *liarndaih*, adj., connected: 連帶關係 (two events) are connected.

連號 *liarn-hauh*, n., (1) consecutive numbers; (2) formerly, firms of same owner; (3) the hyphen.

連合 *liarnher*, v.i. & adj., combine(d), join (efforts, pieces together); cf. 聯[A]合 unite(d), 31S.22.

連環 *liarnhuarn*, n., a chain of rings linked together: 連環計 strategy of making A cause B, B cause C, etc.); 連環圖 comic strips.

連長 *liarnjaang*, n., company captian.

連接 *liarnjie*, v.i. & adj., (happen) together, one after another: 連接見四個客人 receive four visitors in succession.

連結 *liarnjier*, v.i., to bind, join up together (threads, clues, societies).

連記法 *liarnjih-faa*, n., system of booking accounts in parallel columns.

連珠 *liarnju*, adj., joined like a string: 連珠炮 a string of firecrackers; 連珠箭 a volley of arrows.

連綴 *liarnjueh*, v.i., join together (pieces) to form a whole.

連累 *liarn'lei*, v.t., to cause or bring trouble to another: 連累了你 cause you inconvenience.

連連 *liarnliarn*, adv., continuously, in succession: 連連點頭 nod repeatedly.

連理 *liarnlii*, adj., in 連理枝 two trees with a joined branch; (fig.) marital love.

連絡 *liarnluoh*, v.i. & t., as in 連絡某人 or 同他連絡 get in touch with (s.o.), keep in contact with, strengthen connections, (usu. 聯絡 preferred): 連絡官 liaison officer.

連忙 *liarnmarng*, adv., quickly, without hesitation.

連緜 *liarnmiarn*, adj., continuous, -ly: 連緜不斷 without stop or break.

連年 *liarn-niarn*, adv., year after year.

連篇 *liarn pian*, phr., whole essay, whole pages: 白字連篇 full of "misspelled" or incorrect forms of words; 連篇累牘 whole pages (of trite, insipid talk).

連票 *liarn piauh*, n., coupon.

連譜 *liarn-puu*, n., person regarded as same branch (同宗) of clan (同姓).

連任 *liarn-rehn*, v.i., serve second term of office.

連日 *liarn-ryh*, adv., day after day (it rains, etc.).

連心 *liarn-shin*, adj., deeply attached to one another.

連手 *liarn-shoou*, v.i., take concerted action; (gambling) gang up to cheat.

連書 *liarnshu*, v.i., to write two or more syllables of a word together (as in Chin. alphabet 注音字母): 詞類連書 such practice, so-called because the part of speech (詞類) then becomes clear.

連署 *liarn-shuu*, v.i., sign jointly.

連市 *liarnshyh*, v.i., to keep shop, business open on holidays.

連史紙 *liarnshyr-jyy*, n., a fine-quality paper, designed for letters, scrolls.

連續 *liarnshyuh*, adj. & adv., continuous, -ly: 連續下雨 rains continuously; 連續犯 repeated offender.

連鎖 *liarnsuoo*, adj., linked together: 連鎖關係 causally related; 連鎖反應 chain reaction.

連臺 *liarntair*, n., (1) "continuous" theatrical performance; (2) 打幾個連臺 work several shifts in succession.

連天 *liarn-tian*, adj. & adv., (1) for days: 連天陰雨 rainy for days; (2) "touching the sky"; 叫苦連天 cry to heavens; 喊聲連天(=震天) screams pierce the sky; 大水連天 the flood reaches the horizon.

連詞 *liarntsyr*, n., conjunction.

連坐 *liarn-tzuoh*, v.i., be punished as accomplice in crime.

連延 *liarnyarn*, v.i. & adj., stretch on, spread (as mountain range).

連夜 *liarn-yieh*, adv., (1) the very same night; (2) all night.

連姻 *liarnyin*, n., relation by marriage.

連語 *liarnyuu*, n., a polysyllabic word, a compound word.

遊 10.83

your.

[Pop. of 遊 60.83]

遨 10.83

aur.

遨遊 *auryour*, v.i., to roam about at pleasure, spend one's time in idle pursuits.

麸 10.83

fu.

See 麸 10S.81.

麪 10.83

miahn.

See 麪 10S.50.

麵 10.83

miahn.

See 麪 10S.50.

麴 10.83

chyur.

See 麴 10S.50.

§ 10.91 (十/ノ)

鬱 10.91

yuh.

[Var. 鬰, 欝]

N. A surname.

Adj. (1) Dense (forest): 鬱勃 *-bor* ↓; 鬱沉沉 very dense or deep. (2) Melancholy, pent up, repressed in feeling: 鬱悶, 鬱紆, 鬱伊 *-mehn, -yu, -yi* ↓.

鬱勃 *yuhbor*, adj., dense (growth).

鬱結 *yuhjier*, adj., tied up, tangled up, depressed in feeling.

鬱金 *yuhjin*, n., (bot.) a fragrant herb, *Curoma longa*; also 鬱金香 tulip.

鬱積 *yuhjir*, adj., tangled up, see *-jier* ↑.

鬱悶 *yuhmehn*, adj., depressed, melancholy.

鬱塞 *yuhseh*, adj., see *-jier* ↑.

鬱陶 *yuhtaur*, adj., (AC) longing, anguished.

鬱伊 *yuhyi*, adj., melancholy, depressed.

鬱邑 *yuhyih*, adj., ditto (also wr. 鬱悒).

鬱紆 *yuhyu*, adj., ditto.

鬱郁 *yuhyuh*[1], adj., fragrant.

鬱燠 *yuhyuh*[2], adj., (1) hot, murky (weather); (2) melancholy.

§ 10.93 (十/く)

长 10.93

charng.

[Pop. of 長 51.02]

妻 10.93

chi (**chih*).

N. A wife: 妻女 wife and daughter(s); 妻帑, 妻孥 (AC) wife and children; 妻小, 妻兒老小 wife and family; 妻黨 wife's relations (esp. those influential politically); 妻弟 wife's brother; 賢妻良母 ideal type of womanhood as an understanding wife and loving mother; 妻財 money that bride brought with her.

V.t. (**chih*) (AC) to marry a girl to (a person): 以其兄之女妻之 married his brother's daughter to him.

妻舅 *chijiouh*, n., wife's brother.

妻室 *chishyh*, n., wife (and home).
妻子 *chitzyy*, n., (1) wife; (2) wife and children: 妻離子散 family broken up.

婪 10.93

larn.

N. Greed, avarice.

Adj. Greedy, avaricious: 貪婪.

婪酣 *larnhan*, adj., gluttonous.
婪婪 *larnlarn*, adj., insatiably greedy.
婪尾春 *larnweeichun*, n., (=芍藥) (AC) the peony, the last of all flowers in spring; 婪尾酒 --*jioou*, n., (AC) the last cup of wine passed around among friends at a drinking party (also 籃尾酒, 闌尾酒).

嫠 10.93

lir.

N. A widow.

嫠婦 *lirfuh*, n., (LL) widow.
嫠節 *lirjier*, n., (LL) chaste widowhood.

蜇 10.93

jer.

N. 海蜇 jellyfish; pressed and dried variety, usu. served cold on table.

V.t. (MC) bite (by insect) (cf. 螫 11.93).

蛰 10.93

jyr.

[Abbr. of 蟄 11.93]

螯 10.93

aur.

N. A crab's nippers: 持螯把酒 enjoy a cup of wine eating crabs.

蠹 10.93

duh.

[Var. of 蠧, 螙]

N. Insects that eat into clothing, books: 蠹魚 *-yur*↓; 書蠹 bookworm; 蠹吏 officials who fatten themselves on national treasury.

V.t. 蠹國害民 to eat up public funds and prey upon the people.

蠹魚 *duhyur*, n., cloth-eating or book-eating insect, silverfish.

SECTION 10A

§ 10A.00 (扌/亅)

持 10A.00-1

chyr.

V.i. & t. (1) To hold (pen, knife, etc.): 持筆 hold a pen . . . write; 持贈 to present gift with both hands. (2) To hold fast, hold the ground, sustain: 把持 to monopolize (position, power); 相持不下 both hold their grounds, neither yielding. (3) To manage, maintain: 主持 to head some undertaking; 持家, 主持家政 manage the home, household; 維持 maintain, keep s.t. going; 維持場面 maintain the front; 保持 maintain (status, distance), guard (treasure, tradition); 支持, 扶持 sustain, support (person to stand up, tottering regime, etc.). (4) To hold by force: 劫持 hold for ransom; 挾持 control s.o. in one's power (as emperor by warlord).

持法 *chyr-faa*, v.i., maintain the law: 持法森嚴 administer sharp justice.
持服 *chyrfur*, v.i., resign and stay at home during parents' mourning of three years.
持更 *chyr-geng*, v.i., keep night watch by sounding drum at intervals.
持衡 *chyr-herng*, (1) v.i., (LL) maintain standard by criticism of events, personalities; (2) adj., balanced (criticism).
持齋 *chyr-jai*, v.i., keep vegetarian fast.
持正 *chyr-jehng*, v.i., support what is right.
持家 *chyr-jia*, v.i., (1) run a household; (2) maintain family

fortune and status.

持戒 *chyr-jieh*, v.i., (Budd.) observe monastic rules.

持節 *chyr-jier*, v.i., be sent abroad as ambassador (see 節 92A.22).

持久 *chyrjioou*, v.i., hold out long, last: 不能持久 this will not last; 持久戰 protracted warfare, war of endurance.

持重 *chyrjuhng*, v.i., act with gravity, not flighty or frivolous: 老成持重 experienced and steady (person).

持祿 *chyr-luh*, v.i., hold sinecure jobs.

持論 *chyr-luhn*, v.i., hold views: 持論公平 hold impartial views.

持滿 *chyrmaan*, v.i., be proud of oneself or of success.

持平 *chyr-pirng*, v.i., hold just views: 持平之論 a balanced view.

持身 *chyrshen*, v.i., conduct oneself (properly).

持行 *chyrshirng*, v.i. & n., (Budd.) conduct.

持續 *chyrshyuh*, v.i., carry on.

持養 *chyryaang*, v.i., take good care (of health), cultivate spiritual regimen.

持盈 *chyr-yirng*, v.i., maintain a good luck or success: 持盈保泰 maintain good luck by restraint.

搏 10A.00-1

bor.

[Dist. 摶]

V.t. To strike, pounce upon, attack physically, catch (prey): 搏影 beat at shadows (cf. 捕[A]風捉影 10A.42); 搏手 (AC) slap one's hand helplessly; 搏膺 (AC), beat one's chest=modn. 拍胸; 肉搏 hand-to-hand fight.

搏鬭 *bordouh*, n., physical fight; fisticuffs.

搏風 *borfeng*, n., cornice work under eaves.

摶 10A.00-1

tuarn.

V.t. (AC) to knead (rice, etc.); to turn s.t. round.

擣 10A.00-1

daau.

[Var. 搗 10A.50]

V.t. To pound: 擣衣 washing clothing by beating it on stone slab; 擣米 hull rice in mortar; beat (enemy).

擣虛 *daaushyu*, v.i., attack enemy at his weakest.

掎 10A.00-1

jii.

V.t. Drag, pull: see compp. ↓.

掎摭 *jii-jer*, v.t., draw near and take in one's hand: 掎摭星宿 reach up for the stars; 掎摭病利 distinguish between advantages and disadvantages.

掎角 *jii-jyuer*, v.i., (of troops) be deployed for attack from different sides.

撐 10A.00-2

cheng.

[Var. 牚, 撑]

V.i. & t. (1) To prop up, to support from under: 支撐 ditto; 撐住 *-juh*↓; 撐場面 to maintain the front or appearance: 撐起枕頭來 fill out the pillow (with cotton wool). (2) To punt a boat: 撐竿, 撐篙 punting pole; 撐搖 to work the sweeps of a boat. (3) To stretch tight, to burst: 肚子撐的慌 stomach is bursting; 撐病了 sick with bursting pressure, breakdown due to overwork; 把門都撐破了 (crowd) bursts open the door.

撐竿 *chenggan*, n., a punting pole; 撐竿跳(高) pole vault.

撐住 *cheng-juh*, v.t., to set up with props: 撐不住 cannot hold it up.

撐住 *cheng-juu*, v.t., to prop from under.

撐拒 *chengjyuh*, v.t., to prop against.

撐開 *cheng-kai* (*'kai*), v.t., to push open.

捯 10A.00-3

daur.

[Dist. 倒 91A.00]

V.t. Pick up thread: 這案子已捯出點頭緒來 have found certain clues in this case; 捯線 draw in thread in flying kite.

捯氣(兒) *daurchih* (*-chieh'l*), v.i., talk garrulously; feel short of breath.

捯飭 *daur'chy*, v.i., (of woman) touch up appearance: 捯飭捯飭 doll up a little.

打 10A.00-3

daa.

N. A dozen (eggs, etc.).

V.i. & t. (1) To strike (a bell): 鐘打一下 the clock strikes one; 打鈴 press a bell. (2) To fight: 打架, 打仗 *-jiah*, *-jahng*↓; 打嘴吧 give a slap on the mouth. (3) Hunt, fetch, purchase: 打魚 to fish, esp. as a profession; 打獵 to hunt; 打油, 打酒 to purchase some oil, wine; 打柴 to cut wood (from the mountain); 打洗臉水 fetch a basin of water; 打水 to fetch water; 打冰 to fetch ice from frozen river. (4) To make article by weaving, plaiting, knitting or forging: 打毛衣 knit a sweater; 打辮子 plait a queue; 打一把刀 (blacksmith) make or shape a knife; 打金鐲子, 銀筷子 have a gold bracelet, silver chopsticks made. (5) To do or make some kind of action, to send, put through, put on, etc.: 打電話 make a telephone call; 打電報 send a telegram: 打游擊 fight a guerrilla war, hit and run in different directions, also (fig.) obtain benefits by various means; 打成一片 to merge with, to become a harmonious whole, to be in line; 打主意 make a decision; 打招呼 say "hello" on the street; 打噴嚏 make a sneeze; 打個照面 meet person face to face; 打稿, 打底子 make a draft; 打官司 file or get into a lawsuit; 打合同 make a contract; 打官腔, 打官話 put person off by talking formalities as an excuse ("we are not allowed to, etc."); see compp. & phrr. (6) To play (games, mahjong, etc.): 打牌 *-pair*↓; 打跟斗 turn a somersault; 打彈子 play billiard; 打鞦韆 sit on swing; 打燈謎 guess riddles as party game. (7) To carry: 打旗子 carry a flag; 打著傘 carry an umbrella opened; 打燈籠 carry a lantern lighted.

Prep. From: 打什麼地方來的 where does one come from? 打那兒說起 where am I to begin (telling a story)?

打熬 *daa-aur*, v.i., to harden body through endurance; to endure.

打靶(子) *dar-baa(tz)*, phr., practise shooting; engage in target practice.

打擺子 *dar-baaitz*, phr., have an attack of malaria.

打扮 *daabahn*, v.i. & n., make up, to dress: 她打扮的很美 she dresses very prettily.

打包 *daa-bau*, n. & v.i., packing; to pack.

打奔兒 *daa-be'l*, v.i., to make a slip in recital.

打扁兒 *daa-biaa'l*, v.i., to lose appetite, (patient) to have difficulty in swallowing.

打邊鼓 *daa-bianguu*, v.i., to spread or circulate praise of actor, etc.

打補子 *dar-buutz*, v.i., (person) to be used as a substitute.

打吵子 *dar-chaautz*, v.i., to make a row, create a lot of noise.

打喳喳 *daa-cha'cha*, v.i., to talk in whisper.

打岔 *daachah*, v.i., to interrupt a conversation; to talk off the mark.

打茶圍 *daa-char-weir*, v.i., to have a visit or round of visits in brothels and have tea.

打搶 *darchiaang*, v.i., to loot.

打千(兒) *daa-chian(-chia'l)*, v.i., to make a greeting by dipping the body, hands at the sides.

打錢 *daa-chiarn*, phr., (1) place money on table for bet; (2) (acrobats) to collect cash from onlookers; (3) to collect debts.

打前失 *daa-chiarn'shy*, v.i., (esp. horse) to trip, to stumble.

打旗兒的 *daa-chier'l'de*, n., (Chin. opera) foot soldiers and retinue.

打氣 *daa-chih*, v.t., (1) to inflate (tire); (2) to boost morale.

打起 *dar-chii*, v.t., to lift up: 打起精神 to buck up, brace up energy.

打秋風 *daa-chiou-feng*, phr., to obtain gifts of money (as by sending obituary notices around to mere acquaintances), to collect tips on occasions (lit., "have a windfall").

打抽豐 *daa-chou-feng*, phr., ditto.

打出手兒 *daa-chu-shoou'l*, phr., (Chin. opera) throw weapons back and forth on stage (also called 過傢伙).

打拳 *daa-chyuarn*, v.i., to box as sport.

打趣 *daa-chyuh*, v.i., to make fun, indulge in raillery.

打倒 *dar-daau*, phr., to overthrow (regime); (in slogans) "down with."

打當 *daadang*, v.i. & t., to put in order, to pack up.

打道 *daa-dauh*, v.i., to open the way.

打點 *dar'dian*, (1) v.t., to pack up (luggage); (2) to ask a third party to speak on one's behalf, usu. implying sending bribes.

打疊 *daadier*, v.i., to arrange (things) in order.

打地攤兒 *daa-dih-ta'l*, phr., to fall down flat on ground.

打短兒 *dar-duaa'l*, phr., to pick up odd jobs for living; to appear in jacket and trousers.

打動 *daaduhng*, v.t., to strike, to arouse: 給這番話打動了 was struck or roused to action by these words.

打賭 *darduu*, v.i., to bet, wager.

打盹(兒) *dar-duun(-duee'l)*, v.i., to take a nap, to doze off.

打發 *daa'fa*, v.i. & t., (1) to send (s.o. to go); (2) to dismiss (personnel); (3) to send (person) away by yielding to request or by force.

打高空 *daa-gau-kung*, phr., to embellish narrative or rumors.

打嗝(兒) *daager ('l)*, v.i., to hiccup.

打躬 *daa-gung*, v.i., to make a deep bow.

打鼓 *dar-guu*, v.i., to beat the drum: 心裏直在打鼓 have "butterflies in the stomach"—of excitement.

打滾(兒) *darguun(-guee'l)*, v.i., to frolic, roll on the ground.

打哈哈 *daa-ha'ha*, v.i., to laugh out loud; to make fun.

打鼾 *daa-han*, v.i., to snore.

打夯 *daahang*, v.i., to drill piles in construction (from rhythmic cries of workmen "*hang-ah!*")

打晃兒 *daa-huahng'l*, v.i., to sway one's body before falling down.

打諢 *daa-huhn*, v.i., to indulge in raillery, to mock in fun.

打夥 *darhuoo*, v.i., to pool resources, joint make a enterprise.

打火機 *dar-huoo-ji*, n., lighter.

打戰 *daajahn*, v.i., to shiver; to engage in war.

打仗 *daajahng*, v.i., to fight each other; to fight a war.

打針 *daa-jen*, v.i., to have an injection.

打攪 *darjiaau*, v.t., to disturb; (court.) to trouble (person), to take person's time.

打架 *daajiah*, v.i., to fight, engage in a broil.

打價兒 *daa-jiah'l*, v.i., to haggle.

打尖 *daajian*, v.i., to have a snack and rest during journey.

打交道 *daajiau'dau*, v.i., do s.t. as a social act or for friendship's sake.

打醮 *daa-jiauh*, v.i., say (Taoist, Budd.) mass for departed souls.

打刦 *daajier*, v.i., to loot.

打緊 *darjiin*, (1) v.i., as in 不打緊 does not matter, of no importance; (2) adj., critical, urgent.

打更 *daajing*, v.i., to patrol streets at night and announce the watches (1 to 5) of the night.

打擊 *daajir*, n., a setback blow, v.t., to deal a blow.

打轉兒 *daajuah'l*, v.i., to turn round and round.

打住 *daa-juh*, v.i., to stop; (oft. vocative) "stop!"

打開 *daa-kai* (-*'kai*), v.i., to open up.

打撈 *daalau*, v.i., to draw dragnet for recovering things in water.

打雷 *daaleir*, v.i., to thunder (as "it thunders").

打量 *daaliahng*, v.i., conjecture.

打罵 *daa-mah*, v.i., to beat and scold (person).

打抹 *darmoo*, v.t., to wipe (shoes, dust).

打鬧 *daanauh*, v.i., to make a row, create trouble.

打牌 *daa-pair*, v.i., to play cards.

打耙 *daapar*, v.i., (coll.) to change one's mind.

打破 *daapoh*, v.t., to break: 打破紀錄 break records; 打破迷信 destroy superstitions.

打擾 *derraau*, v.t., see *-jiaau* ↑

打閃 *darshaan*, v.i., lightning flashes.

打閒 *daashiarn*, v.i., to be unemployed.

打消 *daashiau*, v.t., to cancel, withdraw (a decision, etc.).

打手 *darshoou*, n., a bodyguard, employed for committing violence (throwing people out, etc.).

打旋兒 *daashyuarn'l*, v.i., to turn round and round.

打算 *daasuahn*, v.i., intend, have a mind to: 你打算怎麽樣 what do you intend to do?

打算盤 *daa-suahn'pan*, v.i., to calculate costs or gains.

打探 *daatahn*, v.t., to find out.

打胎 *daa-tai*, phr., to cause abortion.

打鐵的 *dartiee'de*, n., a blacksmith.

打挺兒 *dartiing'l*, v.t., to stand up straight in gesture of defiance.

打聽 *daa'ting*, v.i. & t., to find out (news, happenings).

打從 *daatsurng*, prep., from, (to come) from.

打退 *daatueih*, v.t., to defeat troops, to send rolling back.

打通 *daa-tung*, v.t., to break through (hindrances): 打通關節 to bribe officials in charge.

打雜(兒) *daatzar('l)*, v.i. & n., serve as handy man, run errands.

打嘴 *dar-tzueei*, v.i., to give a slap in the face; (fig.) to break one's promise, to lose "face."

打坐 *daatzuoh*, v.i., (Budd.) to go into meditations; to sit in crossed-leg position as physical regimen.

打總兒 *dartzuung'l*, adv., altogether.

打字 *daatzyh*, v.i., to type; 打字員 *--yuan*, n., typist; 打字機 *--ji*, n., typewriter.

打圍 *daa-weir*, v.i., to hunt.

打樣(兒)(子) *daayahng('l)(tz)*, n., printer's proof; construction model.

打牙兒 *daa-yar'l*, v.i., chat at people's expense.

打噎 *daa-ye*, v.i., to hiccup.

打油詩 *daa-your-shy*, n., a light poem, satiric poetry (similar to limerick).

抒 10A.00-3

shu.

V.t. (1) To pour out, give relief, unburden (feelings): 抒情, 抒意 *-chirng*, *-yih* ↓. (2) To untie, straighten (difficulties): 抒難 *-nahn* ↓, (related 紓 to relax).

抒情 *shuchirng*, v.i., to express feelings, sentiments: 抒情詩 lyric poetry.

抒難 *shu-nahn*, v.i., to allay troubles, settle difficulties, give relief (also wr. 紓難).

抒念 *shu-niahn*, v.i., allay friend's anxiety.

抒意 *shu-yih*, v.i., to express thoughts, ideas.

捌 10A.00-4

ba.

[Var. of 扒]

N. "Spelling out" of character for 八, used in checks to avoid mistakes.

V.t. To pull apart, break: 捌開＝擘開.

挦 10A.00-5

shyurn.

V.t. To take hold of, to pick (hair).

挦扯 *shyurnchee*, v.t., to get hold of (some trifle, minor defect, (also wr. 挦撦).

捫 10A.00-5

mern.

V.t. Touch, feel by hand: 捫心自問 examine one's own conscience; 捫心無愧 honestly feel I have not done anything wrong; 捫蝨而談

(allu.) attitude of complete informality during conversation ("while scratching for lice on body").

捫搎 *mern'sun*, v.i., feel by hand, grope.

撋 10A.00–5

ruarn.

V.t. (1) Demolish, destroy. (2) Rub with both hands.

擱 10A.00–5

ge.

V.t. (1) To place, lay, keep, preserve: 擱在桌子上 put on the table; 擱在冰箱裏 keep (s.t.) in the refrigerator; 這屋子太小，擱不下這麽多東西 the room is too small for so many things; 擱好 place in a safe place; 大熱天魚和肉都擱不住的 fish and meat won't keep on very hot days; 把這些文件給我擱起來 please file these papers for me. (2) To postpone, shelve, delay, put aside: 事還沒辦完，怎麽能擱得下呢 how can you put it aside, as it isn't finished yet? 擱置 *-jyh*, 擱淺 *-chiaan*, 擱筆 *-bii*↓; 耽擱 to delay; 延擱 postpone.

擱筆 *ge-bii*, v.i., (of writers) stop writing either temporarily or for good (lit., "put down the pen").

擱淺 *ge-chiaan*, v.i., (of ships) run aground, (fig.) held up by some obstacle.

擱置 *gejyh*, v.t., to put in place, put off.

攔 10A.00–5

larn.

V.t. To bar, separate, cut off, hinder, obstruct: 遮攔 to screen, cut off from; 阻攔 hinder, obstruct; 攔住 stop, hold back; 攔不了 cannot be stopped or held back; 攔着 hinder or bar; 攔擋 *-daang*, 攔阻 *-tzuu*, 攔截 *-jier*, 攔開 *-kai*↓; 攔門 bar the gateway; 攔路 bar the road; 攔街阻路 obstruct traffic; 攔路虎 a highwayman; 攔門牆兒 just talk for form's sake (not to be taken seriously); 攔勸 *-chyuahn*↓; 攔腰抱住 hold (s.o.) by the waist, usu. from behind.

攔勸 *larnchyuahn*, v.t., dissuade from.

攔擋 *larndaang*, v.t., restrain (s.o.), stop, persuade not to.

攔櫃 *larngueih*, n., a shop counter.

攔截 *larnjier*, v.t., (=闌截) intercept, hinder, cut off.

攔開 *larn-kai*, v.t., break off 「(fight).

攔阻 *larntzuu*, v.t., hinder, obstruct.

擰 10A.00–6

nirng (**niing*, **nihng*).

V.t. (1) To wring, pinch: 擰手巾 wring out the towel; 擰乾 wring (s.t.) dry; 擰他的嘴 pinch his lips (threat to s.o. thought to have lied); 擰腿 pinch (s.o.'s) leg. (2) 擰眉瞪眼, 擰眉立目 (lit.) raise one's eyebrows and stare in anger. (3) (**niing*) To wrench, twist or pull violently: 擰開門鎖 wrench a locked door open.

Adj. (1) (**niing*) Wrong, mistaken: 擰了 make mistake, make a correction; (n.,) 擰兒 a difference of opinion: 他們倆有點擰兒. (2) (**nihng*) 擰性 stubborn by nature; 擰種 such a stubborn fellow!

擰簧 **niinghuarng*, v.i. & t., make a mistake; to spoil s.t. by mistake.

擰葱 **niingtsung*, v.i., ditto.

撙 10A.00–8

tzuun.

V.i. & t. Economize.

撙節 *tzuunjier*, v.i. & t., economize, cut down expenses.

撙省 *tzuun'sheng*, v.i. & t., ditto.

揄 10A.00–8

yur (**your*).

V.t., (1) To lift, raise. (2) Flap (long sleeves). (3) (**your*) 或舂或揄 (AC) some pound the rice in mortar and some winnow it.

揄揚 *yuryarng*, v.t., to praise, make known s.o.'s merits.

捋 10A.00–9

leh (**lyuu*, **luo*).

V.t. (1) Pick, take. (2) Stroke, rub hands (also **lyuu*): 捋鬍鬚 stroke one's beard and whiskers; 捋虎鬚 pluck the tiger's whiskers; (fig.) be foolhardy, do (s.t.) to offend the powerful; 摩捋 rub one's own hands. (3) (**luo*) Pinch, squeeze off: 捋樹葉兒 rub and crush leaves; 捋汗 wipe off sweat; 捋胳膊 pinch and rub the arms; 捋奶 to milk (cow) by pinching and squeezing nipples.

掙 10A.00-9

jeng (**jehng*).

V.i. (1) To struggle to free oneself or s.t., to stretch, push and pull: 掙開 free oneself or s.t. from tangle; 掙壞了 tear by too much pulling; 掙扎 *-jar*↓. (2) (**jehng*) To earn, to obtain by struggle or effort: 掙錢, 掙命 *-chiarn*, *-mihng*↓; 掙來的 it is earned (not given).

掙錢 **jehng-chiarn*, v.i., to earn money: 掙多少錢 how much have you earned?

掙扎 *jengjar*, n. & v.i., (to) struggle (for goal); to suffer privations and hardships in order to reach goal.

掙命(兒) **jehngmihng('l)*, v.i., make a life-and-death struggle.

拊 10A.00-9

fuu.

[Cf. 撫 10A.63]

V.t. (1) To strike, slap, beat: 拊手, 拊掌 (大笑) slap hands (and laugh), also wr. 撫; 拊心, 拊膺 beat one's chest; 拊髀 (LL) slap one's thigh; 拊背扼喉 (AC) (of strategic post) have a squeeze hold on enemy ("slap back and strangle throat"). (2) (Var. of 撫) 拊循 to pat in a comforting gesture.

§10A.01 (扌/小)

抹 10A.01-1

moo (**moh*).

[Cogn. 摸 *mo*, 10A.81]

V.t. (1) To brush off, wipe clean, wipe off: 抹抹桌椅 wipe tables and chairs; 抹掉灰塵 dust off; 抹眼淚, 鼻涕 wipe off tears, mucus; 抹了良心 ignore conscience, be ruthless; 抹零兒 wipe off decimals, forget the small change. (2) To smear, apply on: 抹粉 apply powder; 塗脂抹粉 apply facial make-up; 抹泥 (**moh*) smear mud; 抹水泥 (**moh*) apply cement; 抹稀泥 soften a person's anger by gentle words; 抹了一鼻子灰 get an awkward rebuff; 山抹微雲 (**moh*) the hills touched with a wisp of clouds. (3) To play (mahjong): 抹骨牌 (running hand over the pieces). (4) (*moo* or **moh*) To straighten one's face: 抹下臉來. (5) (**moh*) To turn: 抹頭進屋裏去 turned one's head and went in; 抹過林子 turn past a grove; 轉彎抹角 turn at different corners.

抹(了)脖子 *moo ('le) bortz*, phr., (facet.) commit suicide.

抹布 *moobuh*, n., dishcloth, rag for wiping tables.

抹膩 *moo'ni*, adj., very neat and precise.

抹殺 *moosha*, v.t., annihilate: 抹殺事實 ignore or suppress certain facts (also wr. 抹煞, 抹摋).

抹香鯨 *mohshiangjing*, n., big whale, *Physeter macrocephalus*, so named on account of ambergris 龍涎香, aromatic substance found in its intestines.

抹胸 **mohshyung*, n., formerly, woman's vest for pressing down and concealing breasts.

抹子 *mootz*, n., mason's spade for applying mortar.

揀 10A.01-1

jiaan.

V.t. (1) Choose, select: 揀擇 choose, pick out; 揀派 select and appoint; 揀選 select, choose for office; 挑揀 select, pick out; 揀好的 choose the best, select a good one (the better ones). (2) (Interch. 撿) pick up, gather: 撿起來 pick (s.t.) up; 撿到(來)的 (of things) obtained without working for it, acquired through luck; 揀柴 gather firewood; 揀破爛的 a ragpicker; 揀煤渣 pick unburnt coal from cinders; 揀香煙頭 make a living by picking cigaret ends; 揀到便宜 get the better of a bargain.

捺 10A.01-1

nah.

N. (Chin. callig.) a slanting downward stroke towards the right.

V.t. To press with force: 捺印 put the seal on (a document, etc.); 按捺 restrain, keep (s.t.) down with force; 捺指印 take fingerprints.

捺悉 *nahseh*, n., a set of clapping boards, used for marking rhythm, esp. in monologue story telling (大鼓), also called 檀板 sandalwood boards.

撩 10A.01-1

liaur (**liau*).

V.t. (1) Take or stir lightly: 撩動肝火 stir up s.o.'s anger ("bile fire"); 撩動春情 stir up love in young person; 撩情 *-chirng*↓; 撩醒 wake up; 撩戰 challenge to battle; 撩撥, 撩逗 *-bo*, *-douh*↓. (2) (**liau*) To lift up (dress, skirt, curtain): 撩開, 撩起衣裳; to sprinkle water with fingers: 撩水. (3) (**liau*) To throw a quick glance: 輕輕撩了他一眼.

撩撥 *liaurbo*, v.i., to incite to trouble; to stir up sentiments.

撩情 *liaur-chirng*, v.i., to flirt.

撩逗 *liaurdouh*, v.i., see *-bo*↑.

撩亂 *liaurluahn*, adj., in confusion.

撩人 *liaurren*, adj., stirring, moving.

搽 10A.01-2

char (also *tsa*).

V.i. & t. To wipe, rub, smear, apply: 搽起來 rub off s.t.; 搽布 rag for wiping; 搽口紅, 搽胭脂 put on lipstick or rouge; 搽藥膏 apply ointment to skin (also wr. 擦).

摽 10A.01-3

biau (*biauh, *piaau).
[Var. of 標 in 摽牌, 摽幟]

V.i. & t. (1) (*piaau) (AC) dismiss with a hand gesture. (2) (*biauh) (Coll.) lock together: 他們倆摽着胳膊走 they walk locked arm in arm; 兩條腿摽得很緊 the two legs locked tight together; (coll.) snuggle close.

摽梅 **piaaumeir*, phr., (AC) marriageable age of girls.
摽牌 *biaupair*, n., rattan shield, ancient weapon of defense.

揉 10A.01-3

rour.

V.t. (1) Rub: 揉揉眼睛 rub one's eyes; 揉一揉 rub gently; 揉出淚來 cause tears to flow by too much rubbing; 揉搽 to massage. (2) Knead: 揉麵 knead dough; 揉成一團 to roll into a mass by kneading; 揉碎 crush into pieces with hands.

Adj. Mixed, mingled, confused: 揉雜 disordered, jumbled, intermingled.

揉兒舖 *rour'l-puh*, n., a second-hand goods shop dealing in jewels.
揉輪 *rour-lurn*, v.i., bend wood and shape it into wheels.
揉搓 *rour'tsuo*, v.t., (1) to roll between hands; (2) to play with, make fun of, put through trials and tribulations.

搡 10A.01-3

saang.

V.t. To push: 被人搡了一交 was pushed and fell down.

搎 10A.01-3

sun.

V.i. See 捫^A搎 10A.00.

操 10A.01-4

tsau (*tsauh).

N. (1) (Also *tsauh) integrity, moral principle in person's conduct: 操守, 操行, 操節 *-shoou -shihng, -jier*↓; 志操 a person's stern principles. (2) Drill, exercise: 兵操, 軍操 military drill; 閱操 review troops; 體操 physical exercise. (3) A song played on 琴 *chirn*. (4) Name of famous historical person 曹操 (pr. *tsauh).

V.t. (1) To hold (weapon, moral principle): 操刀, 操劍 to hold a knife, sword; 操戈 *-ge*↓; 操持, 操守 *-chyr, -shoou*↓. (2) To run (a boat, a firm), to control: 操縱 *-tzuhng*↓. (3) To carry a profession: 操業 ditto; 操醫業 practice medicine; 操作 *-tzuoh*↓. (4) To drill (troops), exercise (body): 操演, 操練 *-yaan, -liahn*↓. (5) To speak a certain language: 操英語 speak English.

操場 *tsauchaang*, n., drill ground.
操切 *tsauchieh*, v.i., to be over-fastidious, control too tightly.
操琴 *tsau-chirn*, v.i., play on *chirn* instrument.
操持 *tsauchyr* (-'*chy*), v.t., to manage (business, shop); to control or guide (conduct).
操券 *tsau-chyuahn*, v.i., "hold the card"—be sure to succeed.
操戈 *tsau-ge*, v.i., "hold spear": 同室操戈 internecine fight.
操觚 *tsau-gu*, v.i., (LL) (1) to write (AC 觚=a strip for writing); (2) practise a profession or craft.
操勞 *tsaulaur*, v.i., to work hard at domestic chores, to labor intensively.
操練 *tsauliahn* (-'*lian*), v.t. & n., to drill, a drill.
操履 *tsaulyuu*, n., upright personal conduct.
操神 *tsaushern*, v.i., to tax the mind or energy.
操行 *tsaushihng* (*tsauh-), n., moral conduct.
操心 *tsaushin*, v.i., (1) to worry; (2) to harbor certain ideas.
操守 *tsaushoou* (*tsauh-), n., a person's moral principles, personal integrity.
操縱 *tsautzuhng*, v.i. & t., to control (another's movements): 受人操縱 be controlled by others; pull the lines (as in marionette); manipulate, control (stock market, etc.).
操作 *tsautzuoh*, (1) n., work, esp. manual or household work; (2) v.t., operate, manipulate, handle (process, machine, etc.).
操演 *tsau-yaan* (-'*yan*), n. & v. i., (hold) military exercise; athletic practice, etc.

撩 搽 摽 揉 搡 搎 操

亅	小	𠂔	十	土	𠂇	卄	𠃊	丨	一	丅	𠃍	口	区	冈	𠃌	厂	尸	亠	广	宀	丶	乚	弋	心	八	人	乂	𠂊	𠂉	丿	𠂉	く
00	01	02	10	11	12	20	21	22	30	31	32	40	41	42	50	51	52	60	61	62	63	70	71	72	80	81	82	83	90	91	92	93

掠 擦 探 採 攥

掠 10A.01-6

lyueh.

N. The long left slanting stroke in calligraphy.

V.i. & t. (1) To ransack, sack; rob: 掠食 hunt for food; 掠人 capture and take away inhabitants; 掠地 take away territory; 掠奪, 掠取, 劫掠, 搶掠 to rob; 不敢掠美 dare not conceal debt to another author or previous work—acknowledge such debt. (2) To pass quickly: 掠過, 掠面一過 pass lightly like wind, brush past. (3) To lash: 掠笞 lash (s.o.) with whip.

擦 10A.01-6

tsa.

V.i. & t. (1) To rub, wipe as with rag, mop, polish: 擦鞋 to polish shoes; 擦槍 clean rifle; 擦銅油 copper polish; 摩擦 v.i. & n., friction, have differences of opinion with each other; 擦汗 wipe perspiration; 拭擦 clean and polish (table, etc.). (2) To bruise (skin): 擦破了皮; (*tsaa*) to scrape, grate (carrot, etc.). (3) To brush past: 擦身而過 ditto. (4) To apply (powder, rouge, ointment, color, etc.): 擦背 to massage (back of body).

擦布 *tsabuh*, n., a wiper, rag for wiping.
擦牀兒 **tsaachuarng'l*, n., kitchen utensil for grating potatoes, etc.
擦黑兒 *tsahe'l*, adv., about or toward dusk.
擦擦 *tsatsa*, adj., descriptive of scraping sounds.

探 10A.01-6

tahn.

N. (*-tz*) Detective, esp. private agent: 偵探, 密探 detective, spy.

V.t. (1) Look for, investigate (bottom, origins): 探深淺 take soundings; 探本, 探原 trace to origins, make a fundamental study; 探湯 thrust hand to feel boiling water—dangerous thing to do; 探隱, 探頤索隱 delve into secret facts or principles; 探驪得珠 writing which brings out important points from a mass of facts. (2) Spy on, look in: 探一探 go and take a look; 探探虛實 try to find out the true situation; 探穴 explore cave; 探頭探腦 pop in to look without being seen; 探知, 探悉 ascertain, find out that; 探身子 bend over to look below (e.g., at a well); 探囊取物 delve into pocket to fish out s.t.—easy thing to do; 探求, 探究, 探討 *-chiour, -jiouh, -taau*, ↓. (3) To visit, pay a call: 探親, 探友 visit relatives, friends; 探喪 visit family of bereaved; 探病 visit the sick; 探訪 *-faang* ↓.

探求 *tahnchiour*, v.t., investigate, find out.
探春 *tahnchun*, v.i., make a spring outing.
探訪 *tahnfaang*, v.t., find out (news, situation); 探訪員 reporter.
探戈 *tahn'ge*, n. & v.i., (translit.) tango.
探海燈 *tahnhaaideng*, n., searchlight, see *-jauhdeng* ↓.
探花 *tahn'hua*, n., number three in former national civil examinations.
探照燈 *tahnjauhdeng*, n., searchlight.
探究 *tahnjiouh*, v.t. & n., investigate, -tion.
探險 *tahnshiaan*, n. & v.i., adventure, explore, -ation (e.g., Arctic regions).
探悉 *tahn-shir*, v.i. & t., ascertain, find out that.
探試 *tahnshyh*, v.t., try to find out (person's opinions, etc.).
探詢 *tahnshyurn*, v.t., see *-wehn* ↓.
探討 *tahntaau*, v.i. & n., study, investigate, -tion.
探聽 *tahnting*, v.i. & t., find out (news, situation): 探聽情形, 消息.
探測 *tahntseh*, v.t. & n., probe into, probings; conjecture.
探子 *tahn'tz*, n., private spy.
探望 *tahnwahng*, v.t., visit (old friends, relatives).
探問 *tahnwehn*, v.t., find out (news, facts).

採 10A.01-9

tsaai.

V.t. (1) (Interch. 采) to pluck, gather, collect (flowers, mulberries, tea), mine for (minerals). (2) To select, adopt: 採擇, 採取, 採用 *-tzer, -chyuu, -yuhng* ↓.

採辦 *tsaaibahn*, v.t., to purchase shop supplies, (as tea, herbs, cloth) by careful selection.
採補 *tsairbuu*, v.t., (Taoist) short for 採陰補陽 borrow feminine force to strengthen male health by sleeping with women.
採取 *tsairchyuu*, v.t., adopt (policy, system, method).
採訪 *tsairfaang*, v.t., gather (news) as reporter.
採購 *tsaaigouh*, v.t., to procure (machinery, raw materials, office supplies).
採摘 *tsaaijer*, v.t., pick, select for use.
採擷 *tsaaijie*, v.t., ditto.
採集 *tsaaijir*, v.t., to collect (samples, specimens, material for writing, etc.).
採礦 *tsaai-kuahng*, v.i., to mine for minerals.
採買 *tsairmaai*, v.t., see *-bahn* ↑.
採納 *tsaainah*, v.t., to adopt, take in (advice).
採選 *tsairshyuaan*, v.t., select and purchase, see *-bahn* ↑.
採擇 *tsaaitzer*, v.t., to select for use, to adopt (method, name, etc.).
採用 *tsaaiyuhng*, v.t., to adopt (method, system, etc.) for use.

攥 10A.01-9

tzuahn.

A

V.t. Grasp, clutch: 一把攥住他的手 caught hold of his hand; 攥在手心裏 clasp in hand.

§ 10A.02 (扌/⺊)

捄 10A.02-1

jiouh.

[Var. of 救 10S.82]

攮 10A.02-1

naang.

V.t. (1) To repel: 推攮 to ward off. (2) To stab: 攮他一刀 give him a stab; 攮死人 stab (s.o.) to death.

攮子 *naangtz*, n., a dagger.

據 10A.02-2

jyuh.

N. Proof, evidence: 收據 receipt; 字據 written evidence; 證據 testimony, proof; 確據 irrefutable evidence; 實據 factual proof; 憑據, 根據 proof, testimony, evidence; 契據 written agreements (contracts).

V.t. (1) Base or be based on: 據理力爭 argue on the basis of reason; 據實報告 make a factual report; 據說 *-shuo*↓; 依據 rely on; 根據 on the basis of; 據云 it is said that; 據此 *-tsyy*↓; 據他說法 according to what he says; 據我看來 as I see it. (2) Take possession of: 佔據 occupy, take hold

B

of, lay hands on; 盤據 seize illegally and entrench oneself in; 據有 *-yoou*↓; 據爲己有 appropriate to oneself (what rightfully belongs to another).

據點 *jyuh-diaan*, n., a base for action.

據說 *jyuh-shuo*, phr., it is said that . . . .

據此 *jyuh-tsyy*, adv., on these grounds, for this reason, therefore, hence.

據有 *jyuh-yoou*, v.t., take possession of.

振 10A.02-5

jehn (**jen*).

V.i. & t. (1) To rise, move up, move to action: 振作, 振興 *-tzuoh, -shing*↓; 一蹶不振 fall, never to rise again. (2) To relieve (famine, etc.): 振濟, 振救 *-jih, -jiouh*↓. (3) To raise, to take up: 振翎, 振翅 flap (bird's) wings to rise; 振衣 to lift up and put on garment, 振臂, 振筆 *-beih, -bii*↓; 振兵 to strengthen army for action; 振旅 to call army to order after battle, esp. after victory to return. (4) To shake: 威振天下 s.o.'s power shakes the world.

Prep. From: 振古以來 since the ancient times.

振臂 *jehn-beih*, v.i., raise arm in call for action: 振臂一呼.

振筆 *jehn-bii*, v.i., take up pen: 振筆直書 take up pen and write rapidly.

振起 *jehn-chii*, v.t., to restore spirit: 振起精神 put forth fresh energy.

振動 *jehnduhng*, v.i. & n., (1) vibrate, -tion; (2) to cause to shake.

振奮 *jehnfehn*, v.i., to bestir oneself: 振奮精神 put forth new

C

energy.

振幅 *jehnfur*, n., (phys.) amplitude of vibration.

振振 **jenjen*, adj., (AC) kind, generous; impressive-looking; 振振有詞 with eloquence (argumentatively).

振濟 *jehnjih*, v.t., to relieve (famine, flood victims; also wr. 賑).

振救 *jehnjiouh*, v.t., to relieve, help (those in distress); to rescue from predicament.

振興 *jehnshing*, v.t., to develop (industries, etc.).

振作 *jehntzuoh*, v.i., to determine to make good, feel heartened.

搌 10A.02-5

jaan.

V.i. To wipe lightly; to lay on lightly (as a blotting paper, to soak up extra ink): 輕輕搌一搌.

搌布 *jaan-buh*, n., cloth used in wiping and cleaning.

攘 10A.02-6

raang (**rarng*).

V.t. (1) (**rarng*) Take away by force, plunder, loot: 攘竊 steal, pilfer, swipe; 攘奪 pillage, sack, rob; 攘善 *-shahn*↓. (2) (**rarng*) Get rid of, free from: 攘夷狄 drive out the barbarian invaders; 攘除 discard, reject, cast out; 攘災 ward off misfortune (disaster, calamity); 攘詬 rehabilitate one's good name, cleanse oneself of dishonor; 攘外 resist foreign aggression (encroachments).

Adj. & adv. In a state of confusion: 天下攘攘, 皆爲利往 (AC) all the hustle and bustle in the world is only for money; 熙熙攘

攘 (LL) streams of people busily coming and going.

攘臂 *rarngbih*, v.i., bestir oneself to action.

攘塲 *rarng-charng*, phr., (of farmers) strew fields with grain and return home after harvesting.

攘袂 *rarng-meih*, v.i., roll up one's sleeves and be ready for action.

攘善 *rarng-shahn*, phr., appropriate to oneself credit (honor) rightfully due to s.o. else.

攘袖 *rarng-shiouh*, v.i., roll up one's sleeves.

攘羊 *rarng-yarng*, phr., keep a neighbor's stray sheep for oneself.

㩒 10A.02-8

chihn.

[Var. of 撳 10A.81]

掭 10A.02-9

tiahn.

V.t. (1) To dip (brush) in ink: 掭筆, 掭墨. (2) To raise wick in oil lamp: 掭燈.

掾 10A.02-9

yuahn.

N. (LL) minor official or officer.

§ 10A.10 (扌/十)

抖 10A.10-1

doou.

V.i. & t. (1) Shake up, give a shake: 把這張毯子抖一抖 give this blanket a shake; 打抖 tremble from cold. (2) To wake up, put up energy: 抖擻 *-soou* ↓; to succeed in staging comeback: 這下子他可抖起來了 this time he has made good; 抖機靈 (or 伶) 兒 use one's wits. (3) To play certain toy: 抖空竹, 抖空鐘 to suspend string around axis of carved bamboo disk and whirl it by hand, causing the bamboo to make a steady whirling sound.

抖翻 *doou'fan*, v.i., dig up old stories to discredit s.o.: 抖翻老底 also wr. 兜翻.

抖攬 *dourlaan*, v.i. & t., to solicit business: 抖攬生意; 抖攬詞訟 try to get lawsuits as a huckster; also wr. 兜攬.

抖摟 *doou'lou*, v.i. & t., to shake off (dust, contents) in a blanket; to dig up (scandals).

抖擻 *doursoou*, v.t., arouse spirit, pick up energy: 抖擻精神起來 pull oneself together and do things; 抖擻灰土 shake off dust; 抖抖擻擻 or 抖抖縮縮的 adv., cringing, trembling with fear or embarrassment.

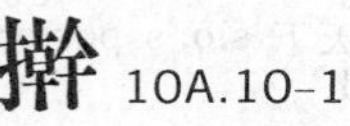

擀 10A.10-1

gaan.

V.t. To stretch (s.t.) with the hand: 擀麵 to roll out dough; 擀麵皮 to roll out dough wrappings; 擀麵杖 (棍) a rolling pin; 擀氈 flatten out a piece of rug: 皮襖都擀氈了 fur coat has been shaken smooth.

捧 10A.10-1

peeng.

[Cogn. of 奉]

V.t. (1) Hold up with both hands: 捧水飲 drink from cupped hands; 把東西捧住 hold up article to prevent toppling; 捧心 (AC) allu. to famous beauty 西施 suffering from *Angina pectoris*, covering chest with hands, imitated by ugly women; 捧日 (LL) show loyalty to emperor. (2) Serve with both hands: 捧茶, 捧藥 serve tea, medicine. (3) To pay public tribute to actor, applaud in public: 把他捧到天上 applaud person to the skies; 捧得太高 praise person too highly; 捧臭腳 lick one's boots, see 捧塲 *-charng* ↓. (4) Holding with two hands as gesture of respect: 捧讀, 捧誦 read your letter held in two hands.

捧塲 *peengcharng*, v.t., to pay tribute to actor or public person, usu. with idea of building up popularity: 請捧塲 please give me support or patronage.

捧腹 *peeng-fuh*, v.i., have a belly laugh (with hands holding the sides).

攆 10A.10-1

niaan.

V.t. To drive away, pursue: 攆走, 攆出去 drive (s.o.) away, esp. fire a servant; 攆上去 pull up to.

掉 10A.10-2

diauh.

V.i. & t. (1) To turn about, turn sideways, wag: 掉過來 turn over or around; 掉背臉兒 turn face away; 掉頭 shake or turn one's head; 掉頭不顧 turn away and leave; 掉臂而去 part hands and separate; 掉尾巴 wag tail; 尾大不掉 litr. phr., tail is wagging the dog. (2) To change from one to another: 掉手 change hands; 掉腳 change shoes from foot to foot; 掉車頭 change locomotive, or direction of; 掉換, 掉包 *-huahn*, *-bau*↓. (3) To drop down, to lose: 掉下來 drop down; 掉色 lose color, fade; 掉魂兒 (coll.) lose one's wits; 掉價兒 decrease in price, value or prestige. (4) To play or show off for effect: 掉槍花 play tricks or make moves to deceive; 掉書袋 "shake book bag"—to fill writing with quotations, just to parade learning; 掉文舞墨 write showy style; 掉舌頭 talk garrulously; 掉歪 *-wai*↓.

Vb. Complement. Off, signifying loss: 丟掉, 失掉 lose; 吃掉, 殺掉 eat off, kill off; 賣不掉 cannot sell off, dispose of in trade.

掉包 *diauhbau*, v.i., replace s.t. valuable with a worthless one.

掉換 *diauhhuahn*, v.i. & t., exchange, change one for another: 掉換地位 change places.

掉舌 *diauhsher*, v.i., chatter, stir up ill will between others by loose gossip.

掉歪 *diauhwai*, adj., naughty, mischievous.

拌 10A.10–2

bahn (**pahn*).

V.t. Stir and mix (mustard, etc.): 拌一拌 mix; 涼拌豆腐 bean curd served cold with bits of onion, etc.; 拌勻 mix even.

拌棄 **pahnchih*, v.t., abandon (err. for 拚).

拌蒜 *bahnsuahn*, v.i., walk knock-kneed, bandy-legged; (fig.) meet constant frustrations; n. & adj., gauche, gaucherie, clumsy, -siness.

拌嘴 *bahntzueei*, v.i. & n., bicker, have little quarrels or exchange heated remarks＝吵嘴.

扞(捍) 10A.10–3

hahn.

V.t. To defend by force: see 扞衞 *-weih*↓; 扞拒 resist by force; 扞禦 resist (invader).

扞蔽 *hahnbih*, n., (AC) bufferstate.

扞格 *hahnger*, adj., incompatible, ill-fitting: 扞格不入 do not mesh, (ideas) mutually conflict.

扞拒 *hahnjyuh*, v.t., to resist (force, invasion).

扞衞 *hahnweih*, v.t., to defend: 扞衞國家 defend the country.

扞禦 *hahnyuh*, v.t., resist (invader).

抨 10A.10–3

peng.

V.t. Criticize, attack verbally.

抨劾 *pengheh*, v.t., (of legislature) move for censure (of person).

抨擊 *pengjir*, v.t., make attack, accusations on (person, measures).

抨彈 *pengtarn*, v.t., see *-heh*↑.

撢 10A.10–3

daan.

[U.f. 探 10A.01]

攝 10A.10–3

sheh (**nieh*).

V.t. (1) To gather up (skirts going up steps): to grab 攝取 *-chyuu*↓; 勾攝 to hook up; to attract by magnetic force (related 吸); 攝力 *-lih*↓; (fig.) to photograph ("grab image") 攝影 *-yiing*↓. (2) To act as regent or deputy: 攝政 *-jehng*↓; 攝任, 攝篆 to act as deputy; 兼攝 to act concurrently as deputy or acting officer. (3) To conserve (life, energy): 攝生, 攝護, 攝衞 *-sheng*, *-huh*, *-weih*↓. (4) (**nieh*) To pacify: 鎮攝.

攝取 *sheh-chyuu*, v.t., to absorb, assimilate (nutrition, food), take between the fingers.

攝護 *shehhuh*, v.t., to conserve energy, life force; 攝護腺 the prostate gland.

攝政 *shehjehng*, n., (also 攝政王) prince regent.

攝力 *sheh-lih*, n., magnetic force.

攝理 *shehlii*, v.i., to be acting officer.

攝生 *sheh-sheng*, v.i. & n., the art of conserving life energy.

攝行 *sheh-shirng*, v.i., to act in some capacity.

攝氏表 *shehshyh-biaau*, n., Celsius thermometer, centigrade.

攝衞 *shehweih*, v.i., see *-sheng*↑.

攝影 *shehyiing*, v.i. & n., photograph, -y; 攝影機 camera (also 照相機); 攝影師 photographer, cameraman.

撣 10A.10–4

daan.

N. (*-tz*) Duster: 鷄毛撣子 feather duster.

V.t. (1) To dust: 撣衣, 撣鞋 wipe dust off clothing, shoes; 撣灰 beat off dust. (2) U.f. 探 pr. *tahn*, to pry into.

揖 10A.10–4

yi.

V.i. & t. (1) To make a bow; to bow to (person): 作揖 ditto; 揖客

掉 拌 扞 捍 抨 撢 攝 撣 揖

亅	小	⺊	十	土	ナ	卄	𠃊	丨	一	丁	フ	口	区	冈	丆	厂	尸	亠	广	宀	丶	乚	弋	心	八	人	乂	乛	一	丿	𠂉	く
00	01	02	10	11	12	20	21	22	30	31	32	40	41	42	50	51	52	60	61	62	63	70	71	72	80	81	82	83	90	91	92	93

bow to a visitor. (2) (AC) u.f. 輯 to put together.

揖讓 *yi-rahng*, v.i., (1) to bow and concede; to observe courtesy in gen.; (2) (AC) to yield the throne to a worthy successor, and not to one's son.

擇 10A.10-4

tzer (*jair, coll.).

V.t. (1) Select, choose: 選擇 pick and choose; 擇選 choose from among many; 擇配 choose a spouse; 擇偶 ditto; 擇婿 select a husband for one's daughter; 擇親 make marriage arrangements for one's children; 擇對 *-dueih*↓; 擇人而事 choose a master (prince) to serve; 擇之而歸 ditto; 擇鄰 pick a suitable place to live in, esp. for the rearing of one's children; 擇交 *-jiau*↓; 擇優 choose the best there is; 擇善固執 find out what is good and hold fast to it; 擇期 pick a date (for marriage, burial, business venture); 擇日子 ditto; 擇吉(開張) choose an auspicious day to start a business; 擇肥而噬 to victimize the rich. (2) Differentiate: 牛羊何擇焉 (AC) why differentiate between cattle and sheep?

擇不開 *jair'bukai, v.i., (1) cannot be separated: 他們倆是擇不開的一對兒 the two of them are an inseparable pair; (2) cannot get away: 我忙得一點兒功夫擇不開 I'm so busy that I can't tear myself away for a moment.
擇對 *tzer-dueih*, (1) v.i., choose a spouse; (2) (*-'duei) v.t., make a careful choice of: 擇對好了日子 choose an auspicious day.
擇乾淨兒 *jair-ganjihng'l, v.i., shirk one's responsibility.
擇交 *tzer-jiau*, v.i., choose friends carefully.
擇毛兒 *jair-maur'l, phr., find fault with; fault-finding, captious, cavilling, carping.
擇木 *tzer-muh*, v.i., (lit.) (of birds) choose a tree to nestle in, (fig.) choose a master to serve.
擇席 *jair-shir, v.i., be choosy about the bed in which one sleeps.
擇手貨 *jair'shou-huoh, n., inferior goods left over unsold.
擇食 *jair-shyr (tzer-), v.i., be particular about the food one eats: 饑不擇食 when one is hungry, one will eat anything given him.
擇刺 *jair-tsyh, v.i., pick fish bones; (fig.) remove misunderstandings.

擗 10A.10-5

pih.

V.t. To break open; to pound, see 擗踊 *-yuung*↓.

擗摽 *pihbiau*, v.i., (AC) be frightened.
擗踊 *pihyuung*, v.i., to pound the heart and stamp the ground as expression of sorrow at parents' funeral.

捽 10A.10-6

tzur (sp. pr. *tsuor).

V.t. (1) To grasp, clutch, grip: 捽髮 grasp by the hair. (2) (*tsuor) To pull up: 捽草 pull up grass (weeds). (3) Be in conflict with: 戎夏交捽 the barbarian tribes and China oft. came into open conflict.

摔 10A.10-6

shuai.

[Related 甩 *shuaai*, 42.70]

V.t. To throw down, fling down (s.t.): 摔在地上 dash it to the ground; 摔東西 throw s.t. with force; 摔破, 摔碎 dashed to pieces; 摔掉 *-diauh*↓.

V.i. To trip, be thrown down: 摔下來 thrown as from a horse or cart; 摔倒 *-daau*↓; 摔跟頭, 摔跤 *-gen'tou, -jiau*↓; 摔死了 fallen dead.

摔打 *shuaidaa*, v.i., receive hard knocks: 在外頭摔打過 went through the rough and tumble of life—experienced hardships; 摔打咂拉 *--tzarlar*, adj., tough (person), letting nothing stand in the way.
摔倒 *shuai-daau*, v.i., be thrown down, slip down.
摔掉 *shuai-diauh*, v.t., cast away.
摔跟頭 *shuaigen'tou*, v.i., fall head over heels.
摔簧 *shuai-huarng*, v.i., make innuendoes.
摔角 *shuai-jiaau*, n. & v.i., wrestle.
摔跤 *shuai-jiau*, v.i., (1) to trip and fall down: 摔一跤; (2) to wrestle.
摔牌 *shuai-pair*, v.i., lose face (lit., "throw cards down").
摔砲(兒) *shuaipauh('l)*, n., toy cracker which explodes on being thrown to the ground.
摔盆兒 *shuai-per'l*, n., custom for the son of deceased to dash an earthen basin to pieces before starting funeral procession.
摔喪 *shuai-sang*, n., ditto, also 摔喪盆子.
摔讚兒 *shuai-tzah'l*, v.i., (coll.) to grumble.

揮 10A.10-6

huei.

V.i. & t. (1) To brandish (a sword, whip), to brush, make a light or rapid stroke: 揮手而別 wave hand on departure; 揮汗成雨 (great number of troops) brushing their sweat drops makes it look like rain; 揮淚 flick a tear; 揮毫 to write; 揮拳 lift a fist to fight; 指揮 to direct (troop movements, a concert, course of action). (2) To squander: 揮金如

土 squander money like dust.

揮發 *hueifa*, v.i., to vaporize, volatize; 揮發油 volatile oil.
揮翰 *hueihahn*, v.i., to write (brandish the pen).
揮毫 *hueihaur*, v.i., ditto.
揮霍 *heihuoh*, v.i. & t., to squander money, spend lavishly.
揮灑 *hueisaa*, v.i., to write or paint freely.
揮散 *hueisaan*, v.i., to evaporate, vaporize, to dissipate (wealth).

扦 10A.10-9

chian.

N. (*-tz*) A wooden pick or iron poker for poking into sacks, etc.: 牙扦 toothpick, also wr. 籤 92A.71; 煙扦子 a wire-like appliance for cleaning pipe bowl.

V.i. To poke at or into.

扦脚 *chian-jiaau*, v.i., to pedicure (also called 修脚).
扦手 *chianshoou*, n., formerly, customs inspector (who pokes at sacks of goods).

捭 10A.10-9

baai.

V.t. Open.

捭闔 *baaiher*, phr., open and close as in 縱^A^橫捭闔 93B.83.

⿰扌隼 10A.10-9

suun.

[Var. of 榫 10B.10]

§10A.11 (扌/土)

挫 10A.11-1

tsuoh.

V.t. (1) To chop down, break down: 挫折 *-jer* ↓. (2) To frustrate, be frustrated.

挫折 *tsuohjer*, v.t. & n., frustrate, -ed, -tion.
挫磨 *tsuoh'mo*, v.t., to persecute (person) by daily scolding, ridicule, etc.
挫辱 *tsuohruh*, v.t., to humiliate (person).

擡 10A.11-1

tair.

[Pop. 抬]

V.t. To lift up, raise (table, etc.): 擡著頭 lift up one's head, see 擡頭 *-tour* ↓; 擡價 raise price; 擡出去 carry it out; 擡起來 lift up; 擡不動 cannot lift up; 擡身 straighten up from bending position; 擡手擡脚 gesticulate; 高擡貴手 phr., used in asking for pardon, more tips, or higher pay; 擡扛, 扛擡 carry s.t. heavy with hands on shoulders or the back; 擡轎子 carry a sedan chair, (gambling) gang up on a player; 擡高身價 put higher value on oneself.

擡槓 *tairgahng*, v.i., to wrangle, quarrel, argue for argument's sake.
擡肩 *tair-jian*, n., a tailor's term, width from armpit to middle of back.
擡舉 *tair'jyu*, v.t., encourage by words or deeds, to help by promoting: 不識擡舉 not worth, do not appreciate, such help.
擡頭 *tair-tour*, v.i., (1) raise one's head: 擡頭一看 raise one's head and look; 永遠不能擡頭 doomed to an inferior status; 擡頭紋 lines on forehead; (2) rule in documents to begin new line above margin on mentioning superior's or king's name; (3) become firmer (in stock prices).

攤 10A.11-2

tan.

N. adjunct. A collection of liquid: 一攤水, 一攤泥 a pool of water, mud.

N. (*-tz*, *-'l*) A stall, booth, mat on sidewalk displaying goods for sale: 香煙攤 cigarette booth; 測字攤 fortuneteller's booth; 菓子攤 fruit stall; 擺攤 spread out goods for sale in booth or (排地攤) on mat.

V.t. (1) To spread out: 攤開 spread out; 攤一攤, 攤攤看 spread out and see; 攤位 assign seats; 攤牌 *-pair* ↓. (2) To distribute: 攤還, 攤償 *-huarn*, *-charng* ↓; 分攤責任 distribute responsibility; 攤認, 攤派 *-rehn*, *-paih* ↓.

攤償 *tancharng*, v.t., to pay back (debt) by installment.
攤販 *tanfahn*, n., stall keeper; seller on sidewalks.
攤還 *tanhuarn*, v.i. & t., to pay back by installment.
攤簧 *tanhuarng*, n., a form of storytelling in rhymes at teahouses, partly sung (also wr. 灘).
攤黃菜 *tanhuarngtsaih*, n., scrambled eggs (from Peking custom of avoiding word 卵 "egg").
攤派 *tanpaih*, v.t., assign contributions, work.
攤牌 *tanpair*, v.i. & n., make a showdown (lay cards on the table).

揮 扦 捭 ⿰扌隼 挫 擡 攤

亅	小	⺀	十	土	ナ	廾	⺊	丨	一	丅	フ	口	区	冈	ㄱ	厂	尸	亠	广	宀	丶	乚	弋	心	八	人	乂	乛	丿	丿	𠂉	く
00	01	02	10	11	12	20	21	22	30	31	32	40	41	42	50	51	52	60	61	62	63	70	71	72	80	81	82	83	90	91	92	93

攤 摧 擢 攞 擢 捱 握 拄 撞 擁

攤認 *tanrehn*, v.i. & t., to pledge contribution individually to gen. fund.

攤銷 *tanshiau*, v.t., amortization; also distribute sales.

摧 10A.11-2

tsue.

[Dist. 推 10A.11, 催 91A.11]

V.t. To smash, destroy: 摧枯拉朽 smash (enemy) easily like breaking dry branches: 摧殘, 摧陷, 摧毀 *-tsarn, -shiahn, -hueei*↓

摧毀 *tsuehueei*, v.t., to destroy, smash to pieces, wreck (buildings, enemy power, etc.).

摧陷 *tsueshiahn*, v.t., destroy (enemy city, army): 摧陷廓清 exterminate, destroy, uproot entirely (evil systems) and clear the ground.

摧殘 *tsuetsarn*, v.t., to trample down (life, ideas), tyrannize over, destroy wantonly.

摧頹 *tsuetueir*, v.i., (1) to falter (=蹉跎 40B.30); (2) to decay.

擢 10A.11-3

huoh.

V.t. To pick: 挑三擢四 to pick and choose.

攞 10A.11-4

luo.

V.t. (Vern.) to lift up, tuck up (end of gown or trousers).

擢 10A.11-5

juor.

V.t. (1) To select and promote: 擢升, 擢用 *-sheng, -yuhng*↓; 拔擢人才 to pick out and promote talents. (2) To pull out: 擢髮難數 (transgressions, etc.) too numerous to count (like "pulling out a tuft of hair" and trying to count it).

Adj. Tall, erect (trees): 擢木千尋 trees hundreds of feet tall.

擢第 *juordih*, v.i., to pass the civil examinations.

擢升 *juorsheng*, v.t., promote specially (not by routine).

擢秀 *juorshiouh*, adj., (1) outstanding (talent, character); (2) luxuriant (plant).

擢用 *juoryuhng*, v.t., promote specially in government service.

捱 10A.11-5

air.

[Interch. 挨 *air*, see 10A.81]

握 10A.11-5

woh.

N. To grasp, take by the hand: 握手, 握管 *-shoou, -guaan*↓; 握筆, see 握管 *-guaan*↓; 握住 hold in grasp; 掌握 to control, manage; 把握 firm control, full confidence; 在握 in control; 大權在握 hold real power in one's hand.

握別 *woh-bier*, v.i., part with a hand grasp.

握管 *woh-guaan*, v.i., to write (hold the pen).

握手 *woh-shoou*, v.i., shake hands.

拄 10A.11-6

juu.

V.i. & t. To rest on support: 拄杖而走 went leaning on a cane; 拄頤 rest chin in hand.

撞 10A.11-6

juahng (re. pr. also *chuarng*).

V.t. (1) To collide, strike with force, knock (down): 撞車, 撞船 cars, ships, collide; 撞上 knock against; 船撞沉了 ship sinks from collision; 飛機撞山 an airplane hits a peak; 撞壞 destroyed by knocking; 撞倒 to fell (a tree); 相撞 collide with each other; 冲撞 bump into: 言語上冲撞起來 to get into argument, exchange words. (2) Find, meet unexpectedly: 撞見 bump into (person); 撞鬼 encounter a ghost, also run around in distraction.

Adj. 撞鼻 rebuffed.

撞壁 *juahngbih*, adj., up against a blind wall.

撞球 *juahngchiour*, n., billiard (also called 檯球).

撞歸 *juahngguei*, n., a method of division in using abacus.

撞見 *juahng-jiahn*, v.t., to encounter, run into, meet or discover by chance.

撞客 *juahngkeh*, n., formerly, a person possessed by the devil.

撞凌 *juahnglirng*, v.i., to break ice by icebreaker.

撞木鐘 *juahng muhjung*, phr., (coll.) to swindle.

撞騙 *juahngpiahn*, v.i., to swindle.

擁 10A.11-6

yuung (also *yung*).

V.t. (1) To embrace: 擁抱 *-bauh*↓; to hold: 擁篲 hold a broomstick. (2) To support (leader): 擁護, 擁戴 *-huh, -daih*↓. (3) To jostle, pack tight: 擁擠 *-jii*↓. (4) To heave, dash forward in swarm or group: 一擁而上 dash

A

up, jostle up; 擁上來 (crowd) push and egg forward.

擁抱 *yuungbauh*, v.t., embrace each other.

擁戴 *yuungdaih*, v.t., to support and adore (leader).

擁遏 *yuung-eh*, v.t., to obstruct; p.p., blocked up.

擁護 *yuunghuh*, v.t., to support (leader, candidate).

擁擠 *yurngjii*, adj., crowded.

擁塞 *yuungseh*, v.t., to obstruct; p.p., blocked up.

搉 10A.11-6

chyueh.

V.i. & t. (1) To strike (part of body). (2) To discuss: 商搉 discuss, -ion.

搴 10A.11-6

sai.

V.t. To tuck s.t. in or under (as pocket, mattress).

拴 10A.11-8

shuan.

V.i. & t. To tie (horse) to a post, to tie with rope: 拴住 fasten with rope; see compp.↓; 拴塞, 血管拴塞 clotting of blood vessel, thrombosis.

拴插 *shuan'cha*, v.i., to look after food and clothing of child.

拴車 *shuan-che*, v.i., to provide carts and carriages.

拴縛 *shuanfur*, v.t., to tie up (s.t.) usu. with rope.

拴扣兒 *shuan-kouh'l*, v.i., (1) to

B

tie a knot; (2) try to alienate friends.

拴束 *shuanshuh*, v.t., see *-fur*↑.

拴娃娃 *shuan-war'wa*, v.t., (woman) take a wooden doll home after praying to goddess of fertility.

捶 10A.11-9

chueir.

N. (*-tz*) A stick for beating: 鼓捶子 drumstick (cf. 鎚 81A.83, 槌 10B.83 and 搥 10A.83).

V.t. To pommel, pound, cudgel (person): 捶他一拳 pommel him with a fist.

推 10A.11-9

tuei.

V.t. (1) To push, push open, push down, push on: 推開 push away, 推去 push out; 把他推推搡搡 (*saang*) 到廊下 push and pull him to the corridor; 推門 push door open; 推車 push cart; 推動 to propel, give impetus to; 推動力 motivation force, force of propulsion; 順水推舟 go with the current, take advantage of favorable trend; 推波助瀾 follow and hasten movement of waves—to aggravate dispute by third party, add to quarrel; 推陳出新 (biol.) assimilation, process of change, make renovations; 推開天窗說亮話 talk frankly without hedging about (pun on 亮 meaning "clear" and "daylight"); 寒暑相推 the seasonal changes hurry on. (2) Push away offer, or step back in favor of s.o. else: 推讓 *-rahng*↓. (3) Push forward, promote, elect, recommend: 推爲第一 regard as No. 1; 推他做首 choose him as leader; 推賢與能 select the capa-

C

ble men and put them in power; 推薦, 推舉, 推崇, 推許 *-jiahn*, *-jyuu*, *-churng*, *-shyuu*↓. (4) Reject, make excuse, give as reason or pretext: 推病不去 did not go on pretext of illness; 推故 give as an excuse or reason. (5) Shake off, shirk, refuse: 推卸, 推諉, 推託, 推辭 *-shieh*, *-weei*, *-tuo*, *-tsyr*↓; 推乾淨兒, 推個一乾二淨 push all blame on others; 推開責任 shake off all responsibility; 推到別人身上 put the blame on others; 推作 (推爲) 不知 pretend not to know; 推三阻四, 推來推去 make all sorts of excuses; 半推半就 (of woman) half refusing and half yielding. (6) Trace origins, investigate, deduce, calculate: 推原 trace origins; 推究 (原因) investigate, study causes; 推其故 find out the cause; 推敲, 推測 *-chiau*, *-tseh*↓; 因一推十 deduce ten from one; 以此類推 and so on (one can deduce the rest from this); 推己及人 "place yourself in another's place"—do unto others what you would do unto yourself; 推心置腹 show the greatest consideration or confidence (treat s.o. as yourself). (7) Certain actions: 推牌九 to play dominoes; 推光 rub and polish (wood surface); 推地板 polish floor.

推鉋(子) *tueibauh(tz)*, n., carpenter's plane.

推背 *tuei-beih*, n., Chin. massage; 推背圖 the name of a pop. book of prophecy.

推步 *tuei-buh*, v.i., (LL) make astronomical calculations.

推誠 *tuei-cherng*, phr., open one's heart to another, as sincere friend: 推誠相與.

推敲 *tueichiau*, v.t., try to find out, to fathom (meaning, cause).

推求 *tueichiour*, v.t., to reason out.

推崇 *tueichurng*, v.t., to worship, admire, acknowledge as leader.

推卻 *tuei-chyueh*, v.i., reject, shirk (responsibility).

推倒 *tuei-daau*, v.t., (1) to overthrow; (2) to push down.

擁 搉 搴 拴 捶 推

亅	小	⺊	十	土	ナ	卄	𠂤	丨	一	丁	フ	口	囗	冂	刁	厂	尸	亠	广	宀	丶	乚	弋	心	八	人	乂	乛	亻	丿	𠂉	く
00	01	02	10	11	12	20	21	22	30	31	32	40	41	42	50	51	52	60	61	62	63	70	71	72	80	81	82	83	90	91	92	93

推宕 *tueidahng*, v.i., procrastinate (also 拖宕).
推戴 *tueidaih*, v.t., acclaim as leader.
推定 *tuei-dihng*, v.i., (1) predict outcome; (2) elect or nominate s.o. for office.
推斷 *tueiduahn*, v.i., predict.
推度 *tueiduh*, v.i., conjecture.
推恩 *tuei-en*, v.i., extend favors, kindness.
推翻 *tueifan*, v.t., to overthrow (government, previous theory).
推服 *tueifur*, v.t., admire, consider as better than oneself.
推廣 *tueiguaang*, v.t., to extend, expand (area, sales, etc.).
推故 *tuei-guh*, v.i., give as reason or pretext.
推轂 *tuei-guu*, v.t., recommend for high post.
推薦 *tueijiahn*, v.t., to recommend (person).
推進 *tueijihn*, v.t., to push forward, propel; 推進機 propeller.
推究 *tueijiouh*, v.i. & t., conjecture, figure out (reason, principles, etc.), make a careful study of.
推重 *tueijuhng*, v.t., regard with respect, place importance upon (person).
推舉 *tueijyuu*, v.t., to elect person to post; to recommend.
推類 *tueileih*, (or 類推) v.i., reason by analogy: 推類至盡 push to logical extreme.
推理 *tueilii*, v.i., to reason logically, study the reason.
推論 *tueiluhn*, n., conclusion; reasoning.
推磨 *tueimoh*, v.i., turn the grindstone; (fig.) pass the bucket, shirk duty.
推拏 *tueinar*, v.i. & n., (Chin. med.) a kind of massage, kneading and rubbing.
推念 *tueiniahn*, v.i., think of s.o. distant or past.
推排 *tueipair*, v.i., (MC) see -*chiau* ↑.
推讓 *tueirahng*, v.i., courteously ask s.o. to precede or take post.
推想 *tueishiaang*, v.i., imagine, reckon (s.o. must have arrived, etc.).
推銷 *tueishiau*, v.t., promote sales of; 推銷員 salesman.
推卸 *tueishieh*, v.t., to evade, to shove off (duty etc.), be irresponsible.
推行 *tueishirng*, v.t., promote (system, ideas), carry into effect (new laws, practices).
推事 *tueishyh*, n., a judge.
推選 *tueishyuaan*, v.t., elect (person).
推許 *tueishyuu*, v.t., praise, esp. by s.o. above, commend favorably by superior.
推算 *tueisuahn*, v.i. & t., reckon (dates, etc.); predict (future).
推測 *tueitseh*, v.i. & t., calculate, conjecture.
推辭 *tueitsyr*, v.i. & t., decline (offer).
推託 *tueituo*, v.i., & t., give reasons, excuses, for not doing.
推輓 *tueiwaan*, v.t., (LL) recommend, urge forward (lit., "push and pull carriage").
推諉 *tueiweei*, v.i. & t., shirk (responsibility).
推問 *tueiwehn*, v.i. & t., investigate, interrogate.
推延 *tueiyarn*, v.i., delay, procrastinate.
推移 *tueiyir*, v.i., change or move round (as the seasons).
推原 *tuei-yuarn*, v.i., find out reason, or cause.

§10A.20 (扌/廾)

摒 10A.20-5

bihng.
[Var. 擯]

V.t. Remove (obstacles); cast aside: 摒開 move away, see compp. ↓.

摒棄 *bihngchih*, v.t., abandon, cast aside (old friends, honors, family).
摒除 *bihngchur*, v.t. remove (prejudices 成見); overcome (obstacles 障礙).
摒擋 *bihngdahng*, v.t., clean up and put in order (as before departure): 摒擋一切 get everything ready.
摒絕 *bihngjyuer*, v.t., cut loose entirely.

揜 10A.20-8

yaan.
[Var. of 掩 10A.70]

拼 10A.20-9

pin.
[Dist. 拚 *pahn*, see *pinmihng* ↓]

V.t. Assemble, put together, throw all in: 拼命 -*mihng* ↓; to spell: 拼音 -*yin* ↓.

拼法 *pinfaa*, v.t. & n., see -*yin* ↓.
拼命 *pinmihng*, v.i., do everything to (even at the risk of life): 拼命工作, 讀書 work, study very hard (neglecting health); 和他拼命 fight him with all one has got; 拼老命 fight regardless of life or death (in this sense, also 拚△命 10A.20).
拼音 *pinyin*, v.t. & n., spell, -ing: 這字怎樣拼法 how do you spell this word?

擤 10A.20-9

shiing.

V.t. 擤鼻子 blow the nose.

拚 10A.20-9

pahn (coll. also *pan*).
[Dist. 拼 10A.20]

V.t. Abandon, discard.

拚棄 *pahnchih*, v.t., to abandon

(person, thing).

拚命 *pahnmihng*, v.i., (lit.) risk life to, i.e., to try very hard to: 拚命讀書, 做生意 to study, or keep business, with heart and soul; also 拼^Δ命 *pingmihng*, 10A.20.

§ 10A.21 (扌/乚)

舂 10A.21-1

chung.

V.t. To strike at; to pound (wall, etc.).

揕 10A.21-2

jehn.

V.t. (AC) to stab.

拙 10A.21-2

juor.

Adj. (1) Stupid, dull: 笨拙 ditto; 口拙 slow of speech; 拙眼 *-yaan* ↓. (2) (Court., self-deprecating) my ("stupid"): 拙見 my opinion; 拙著 my book or essay; 拙荊 my wife; 恕我眼拙 I beg to differ ("excuse my stupid view").

拙笨 *juorbehn*, adj., stupid.
拙筆 *juorbii*, n., (Chin. painting) spontaneous unadorned lines.
拙工 *juorgung*, n., (AC) coarse workman.
拙荊 *juorjing*, n., (court.) my wife.
拙劣 *juorlieh*, adj., inferior, execrable (work).
拙實 *juor'shy*, adj., solidly built.
拙眼 *juor-yaan*, n., (LL) common, philistine view: 觀人如觀玉, 拙眼喜譏評 judging character is like judging jade, the uninformed like to criticize.

掘 10A.21-5

jyuer.

V.t. Dig, excavate: 掘地, 掘井 dig the earth, a well; 挖掘 scoop (dig) out; 掘穿 make a hole, as in a wall, by digging; 掘坑 dig a pit; 發掘 excavate, -tion, to discover, exploit: 發掘人材 to discover talents; 採掘 to mine (ores); 掘土機 a bulldozer.

拒 10A.21-5

jyuh.

V.t. (1) Resist, oppose: 抗拒 to offer resistance to; 拒敵 repel or resist the enemy; 拒守 *-shoou* ↓. (2) Refuse, decline to accept: 拒絕 *-jyuer* ↓; 拒捕 resist arrest; 來者不拒 all are welcome, none will be turned away.

拒冬 *jyuhdung*, n., (bot.) the caper spurge, mole plant.
拒付 *jyuhfuh*, v.i., go on default, refuse payment.
拒絕 *jyuhjyuer*, v.t., to reject (request, etc.), to refuse to do.
拒守 *jyuhshoou*, v.t., to guard, defend against enemy attack.

摳 10A.21-5

kou.

V.t. (1) To pick (s.t. as from pocket): 摳不出來 cannot get it out; 摳鼻孔 to pick the nose. (2) To follow up clue, to fish out details: 他遇到一個問題, 總愛死摳 he wants to get all the details when he comes to a problem. (3) To lift up (dress): 摳衣升堂 lift up skirt or dress as one enters the hall.

摳摟 *kou'lou*, adj., sunken: 眼睛摳摟兒 the eyes are sunken (as from lack of sleep).
摳門兒 *koumer'l*, n., a miser: 這個人眞是摳門兒 he is really a miser.

揠 10A.21-5

yah.

V.t. (AC) to pull up: 揠苗助長 (AC) to pull up seedling in mistaken hope of helping it to grow.

擓 10A.21-5

kuaai.

V.t. 擓癢 to scratch an itch.

搖 10A.21-9

yaur.

V.i. & t. To shake, quake, wag, flutter: 搖動 *-duhng* ↓; 搖來搖去 to rock (as a cradle), to swing (as pendulum); 搖頭, 搖首 shake one's head; 搖尾 to wag (dog's tail); 搖尾乞憐 to beg like a dog; 搖唇鼓舌, see 搖舌 *-sher* ↓; 搖手, 搖首 *-shoou*[1,2] ↓; oft. coupled with 晃 *-'huang* and 擺 *-baai* ↓; 搖旗吶喊 to wave the flag and shout, oft. said of political followers; 搖身一變 shake and be transformed by magic.

搖擺 *yaurbaai*, v.i., to stagger, to walk with a swinging gait: 搖搖擺擺 walk thus, esp. with an air of importance; 搖頭擺尾 waggling tail to please the master.

搖板 *yaurbaan*, n., (Chin. opera) a continuing slow rhythm without definite beat (also called 散板).

搖錢樹 *yaur-chiarn-shuh*, n., a "money tree" which sheds coins upon shaking—a singsong girl bringing lots of income for madam.

搖船 *yaur-chuarn*, v.i., to row a boat.

搖動 *yaurduhng*, v.i. & t., (1) to cause to move by touch or pull; (2) to be pried loose, to lose stability of position (also 動搖); to wave.

搖滾舞 *yaurgurn-wuu*, n., rock-and-roll dance.

搖撼 *yaur'han*, v.t., to shake (branches), to cause displacement.

搖晃 *yaur'huang*, v.i., (of flags) to flutter, sway; to walk with swaying motion, oft. with cultivated air of importance: 搖兒晃兒 (*-huaang*) 的 walking with affected swing and sway.

搖會 *yaurhueh*, n., an old-style mutual loan club, the monthly sum going to highest bidder of interest.

搖籃(兒) *yaurlarn(-lar'l)*, n., a cradle.

搖舌 *yaur-sher*, v.i., to wag one's tongue, to talk glibly.

搖手(兒) *yaur-shoou*[1]*('l)*, v.i., to make a hand motion showing disapproval.

搖首 *yaur-shoou*[2], v.i., to shake one's head in disapproval.

搖攤 *yaurtan*, n., a gambling game played with four dice in a bowl; the game being to guess the total number being a multiple of four (4), or any remainder (1, 2, or 3).

搖頭(兒) *yaur-tour('l)*, v.i., to shake one's head in disapproval.

搖搖 *yauryaur*, adj. & adv., shaky, -ily.

搖曳 *yauryih*, v.i., to flutter in the wind, to walk with a swing.

搖椅 *yauryii*, n., a rocking chair.

插 10A.21-9

cha.

[Var. 挿]

V.t. (1) To insert, stick in: 插進去 stick in (flower in vase, pole in ground, etc.); 插花 *-hua* ↓; 插翅 (or 翼) stick on wings (which cannot help escape); 插話, 插一句話 to interrupt, to insert a remark; 插圖 *-tur* ↓: 插圖弄計 set up a trap; 插標 esp. 插草標 put a tag of straw showing s.t. is for sale; 插天 (high peaks) seem to stick into the sky; 插柳成蔭 do s.t. which brings results without effort and easily; 插科打諢 (Chin. opera) insert dialogue for comic relief.

插板 *chabaan*, n., formerly, plank to double-secure city gate; door bar; 插板兒 (coll.) close up business ("board up" shop).

插班 *cha-ban*, v.i., to put new student in grade according to his ability.

插釵 *cha-chai*, v.i., to formalize marriage engagement, see *-dihng* ↓.

插曲 *chachyuu*, n., (mus.) an interlude, intermezzo, episode.

插戴 *chadaih*, v.i., (1) see *-dihng* ↓; (2) n., what one wears (hat, girdle, hair decorations, etc.).

插單 *cha-dan*, v.i., (of monk) take up abode in monastery.

插定 *cha-dihng*, v.i., to formalize marriage engagement of girl.

插關兒 *chagua'l*, n., door bar.

插花 *cha-hua*, v.i., (1) to insert flower (on hair, in vase); (2) arrange flowers in vase, (Japanese) *ikebana*; (3) to pay land tax in a county other than the one where it is due.

插話 *cha-huah*[1], v.i., to interrupt in speech.

插畫 *cha-huah*[2], n., an illustration in book.

插腳 *chajiaau*, n., a foothold, a place to rest one's foot.

插架 *chajiah*, n., a bamboo book shelf, wall shelf.

插枝 *chajy*, v.i., to plant (willows, etc.) by sticking branch in soil.

插句 *chajyuh*, n., an inserted remark, insertion.

插口 *chakoou*, v.i., to put in a word, to interrupt speech, also *-tzuee* ↓.

插屏(兒) *chapirng('l)*, n., a standing screen (with marble, or painting); a partition or wall frame for painting.

插入 *cha-ruh*, v.i., to insert; to add remark.

插身 *cha-shen*, v.i., to gain a place (in group).

插消 *chashiau*, n., electric plug.

插手 *cha-shoou*, v.i., to meddle, lay hands on.

插頭 *cha-tour*, n., electric plug.

插圖 *cha-tur*, n., illustration in book.

插嘴 *cha-tzuee*, v.i., to put in a word, to interrupt speech, also *-koou* ↑.

插足 *cha-tzur*, v.i., to gain a place (in group).

插秧 *cha-yang*, v.i., to transplant rice seedlings.

搯 10A.21-9

tau.

V.t. (1) To take out (as from pocket): 搯出來 take out from pocket, also wr. 掏; 搯 (or 掏) 腰包 pay out money, oft. unwillingly, take out pocketbook; 搯錢 take out cash. (2) To clean up: 搯 (or 淘, 掏) 井, 水溝 clean out a well, a sewer; 搯耳朵 pick the ears.

掐 10A.21-9

chia.

[Dist. 搯 *tau*]

V.t. (1) To gather with the hand

(cogn. 夾 *jiar*): 把東西掐在一起 gather the things together with fingers; 把紙掐在一起 nip the papers together with paper nip; 把頭髮掐起來 gather up one's hair; 手裏掐着一把青菜 holding or grasping a bunch of vegetables in his hand. (2) To pinch, nip: 掐他一把 pinch (s. o.); 掐得好痛 give a painful pinch; 掐斷了 break off with hand; 掐花 break off a flower from stem; 掐頭去尾 to nip off unwanted parts (of vegetables, etc.). (3) To choke: 掐住了, 掐喉嚨 to choke, be choked in the throat; 掐死了 choked to death. (4) To bend fingers in counting: 掐算, 掐指一算, 掐弄 count by fingers.

掐把 *chiaba*, v.t., to pinch, hurt by pinching; (fig.) to treat harshly.

掐尖兒 *chiajiae'l*, v.i., (1) to nip off young branches for better growth of plants; (2) 掐尖兒, 掐尖落鈔 make illegal profit, nip off profits for oneself.

掐訣 *chiajyuer*, v.i., (Taoist) to make finger gestures during incantations.

§ 10A.22 (扌/丨)

掛 10A.22-1

guah.

[Interch. 挂]

V.t. (1) Hang up, suspend: 懸掛 hang (pictures, scrolls, etc.) on the wall; 高掛 hang high up; 掛起來 have (s.t.) hung up; 掛上 ditto, pin up; 掛羊頭, 賣狗肉 carry high-sounding but misleading names (lit., "hang a sheep's head as shop sign and sell dog meat"); 掛幌子 (of shops) put up a signboard to advertise goods, give oneself away: 他剛才準是喝了酒, 臉上都掛幌子了 he must have had a drink or two a moment ago, for his face shows it. (2) Put on record, register: 掛名 *-mirng*, 掛賬 *-jahng*, 掛號 *-hauh* ↓; 掛一漏萬 (author's apologetic phrase) I may have left out many important facts, cases. (3) Have or keep in mind, remember: 記掛 think of; 掛念 *-niahn* ↓; 掛在心上 keep in mind; 牽掛 be concerned about; 掛慮 be anxious about; 掛懷 *-huair* ↓.

掛礙 *guah-aih*, n., a hindrance, impediment; v.i., to be concerned.

掛欠 *guahchiahn*, v.i., charge to one's account.

掛齒 *guah-chyy*, v.t., (LL) to mention, refer to (lit., "hang on one's teeth"): 何足掛齒 don't mention it.

掛單 *guah-dan*, v.i., (of Buddhist priest) put up at a temple for a short stay.

掛鈎 *guahgou*, n., (of railway cars) the coupling links.

掛冠 *guah-guan*, v.i., (of official) resign from office (lit., "hang up the official hat"): 掛冠而去 resign and go home.

掛號 *guah-hauh*, v.t., to register (at school, hospital, etc.); 掛號信 a registered letter.

掛懷 *guahhuair*, v.t., be ever thinking of, bear in mind.

掛火(兒) *guahhuoo('l)*, v.i., (coll.) be furious.

掛紅 *guah-hurng*, v.i., hang up a red banner on festive occasions.

掛賬 *guah-jahng*, v.t., charge to one's account.

掛僵(兒) *guahjiang('l)*, v.i., be humiliated and burst into a fury.

掛勁(兒) *guahjihn(-jiehl)*, v.i., be furious, see *-huoo* ↑.

掛樁 *guahjuang*, v.t., to shadow s.o. before arresting him.

掛鐘 *guahjung*, n., a wall clock.

掛累 *guahleei*, v.t., implicate, involve s.o. in trouble.

掛零(兒) *guahlirng('l)*, adj., odd, with a little extra: 他已經五十掛零了 he is over fifty ("fifty plus").

掛麵 *guahmiahn*, n., noodles made by hanging dough-strings to dry on a frame.

掛名(兒) *guah-mirng('l)*, v.i., hold a position in name but not in fact: 掛名差事 a sinecure.

掛念 *guahniahn*, v.t., be ever thinking of, bear in mind.

掛屏兒 *guahpirng'l*, n., a hung picture used as wall decoration.

掛孝 *guah-shiauh*, v.i., wear mourning.

掛心 *guahshin*, v.i., be concerned about.

掛錫 *guahshir*, v.i., (of Buddhist priest) put up in a temple for the night (from "hang the pewter staff").

掛帥 *guah-shuaih*, v.t. & n., (1) be appointed a commanding general; (2) such appointment.

掛失 *guah-shy*, v.t., give notice of the loss of (bank checks, important papers, etc.).

掛彩 *guah-tsaai*, v.i., (1) hang up red ribbons on festive occasions, see *-hurng* ↑; (2) (of soldiers) be wounded in action.

掛圖 *guah-tur*, n., a wall map or chart.

掛味兒 *guahweh'l*, adj., (of singing or food) pleasing to the ear or palate, pleasant to listen to or to eat.

撕 10A.22-2

sy.

V.t. (1) To tear: 撕開 tear open; 撕裂, 撕碎 tear to pieces; 撕破 break, scratch (skin, cover) by hand, claws. (2) (Coll.) to cut a piece of material at a shop: 到布舖撕半匹綢子來 please go and buy ("cut") half a bolt of silk for me.

撕打 *sydaa*, v.i., engage in fisticuffs.

撕羅(擄) *sy'luo*, v.t., (1) to break up (a fight); (2) to deal with some difficult matter; to disentangle (affair); (3) to romp and play with (person).

撕旁岔兒 *sy-parngchah'l*, v.i., to beat about the bush, evade question and confuse issue.

撕票(兒) *sy-piauh('l)*, v.i., to kill kidnapped person (票 person kidnapped and held for ransom, see 綁△票 93B.22).

扑 10A.22-2

pu.

N. (AC) the teacher's rod.

V.t. & i. Var. of 撲 10A.81.

抻 10A.22-2

shehn (also *chen*).

V.t. To pull, stretch: 把這張紙抻開 stretch out this piece of paper.

排 10A.22-2

pair.

N. (1) Row: 第一, 前, 後排 first, front, back row; 一排一排的人 rows of people. (2) An army unit, platoon: 排長 *-jaang*↓. (3) A volley, a string of shots, cartridges: 一排鎗, 子彈.

V.t. (1) To set, arrange in order, in a row or formation: 排得緊 arrange closely; 並排 arrange alongside; 排列 *-lieh*↓; 排開 spread out, also break off scuffle; 排起來 set up (objects) for show; 排着 arranged for show, showing in place; 安排 set in proper place; 排隊 form in line; 排隊遊行 parade; 排班 arrange teams for turns of work; 排陣 deploy troops; 排陣勢 in battle formation; 排龍△門陣 60S.70; 排飯, 排桌子 set table; 排位 set seating order at table; 排(八)卦 arrange the eight diagrams; 排版 compose type; 排頭排尾 set or stand first, last; 安△排 62.93. (2) To push out, dispel: 排悶 dispel boredom; 排除 to exclude, to push aside, to overcome; 排難解紛 mediate disputes; 排山倒海 overwhelm by hordes of troops (like crushing waves); 排沙簡金 sift sand for gold, (fig.) sift minutely, also 披沙揀金. (3) To campaign against: 排外運動 anti-foreign movement; 排俄, 排華 anti-Russian, anti-Chinese, etc.; 編△排 93B.42. (4) 排戲 to cast, rehearse or present play.

排筆 *pairbii*, n., a form of multiple brushes used in painting.

排杈兒 *pairchah'l*, n., a kind of latticework in window; a crisp, fluffy eatable made of flour.

排場 *paircharng*, adj., impressive-looking (of dress, feasts, gatherings).

排球 *pairchiour*, n., volleyball.

排斥 *pairchyh*[1], v.t., to boycott, attack, discard, condemn (foreign goods, influence, school of thought).

排翅 *pairchyh*[2], n., whole-piece sharks' fin, as different from loose ends.

排骨 *pairguu(-'guu)*, n., pork ribs.

排行 *pairharng*, n., seniority among brothers, sisters: 排行第五 No. 5.

排長 *pairjaang*, n., lieutenant.

排解 *pairjiee*, v.t., mediate.

排擠 *pairjii*, v.t., team up against, boycott (goods), squeeze out (person).

排列 *pairlieh*, v.t., arrange (objects, persons) in order.

排律 *pairlyuh*, n., a form of Tarng poetry, with at least three antithetical couplets (see 律△詩 91B.10).

排門(兒) *pairmern(-mer'l)*, adv., (sell) door to door.

排比 *pairpii*, v.t., to arrange in order (for comparison); to criticize (people, faults); n., (rhetoric) parallel construction.

排簫 *pairshiau*, n., a form of ancient panpipes.

排洩(泄) *pairshieh*, v.t., execrete, let off (anger, excrement); 排洩物 n., excrement; 排洩器 n., stool, organ for draining fluid.

排水量 *paishueei-liahng*, n., (of ships) displacement.

排揎 *pairshyuan*, v.t., to make satirical remarks about (person), humiliate by scoffing.

排闥而入 *pair-tah-erl-ruh*, phr., (LL) break into room unceremoniously.

排子車 *pairtzy-che*, n., large handcart used for house removal.

拂 10A.22-2

fur (**bih*).

N. (*-tz*) A duster.

V.i. & t. (1) Brush, brush off: 拂塵, 拂灰 brush off dust, ashes; 拂淚而別 wipe tears and leave; 拂桌子 to dust table; 拂抹 clean up; 拂拭 *-shyh*↓. (2) To touch lightly as light breeze: 春風拂面 the spring wind caresses the cheeks; 拂曉, 拂晨 *-shiaau*, *-chern*[1]↓. (3) To make a rapid sweeping motion: 拂袖而去 giving a sweeping jerk with (his) sleeves, (he) left; 拂衣而去 ditto, leave abruptly; 拂衣 shake the clothing. (4) To cross one's wishes, to defy: 拂盛意 disobey your warm friendly wishes; 拂輿情 defy public sentiment; 拂逆, 拂意 *-nih*, *-yih*↓. (5) (AC) (**bih*) 拂士 (AC) straight-speaking advisors.

拂晨 *furchern*[1], adv., at daybreak.

拂塵 *furchern*[2], v.i., (LL) shake off the dust of journey, give welcome dinner, more commonly 洗塵.

拂拂 *furfur*, adv., flapping.

拂戾 *furlih*, adj. disobedient, unruly.

拂逆 *furnih*, v.t., ditto: 不敢拂逆

你的好意 dare not but obey your wishes.
拂曉 *furshiaau*, adv., at break of day.
拂手 *furshoou*, n., a duster.
拂拭 *furshyh*, v.t., brush clean (a mirror, etc.).
拂子介 *furtzyyjieh*, n., Portuguese man-of-war, sponge-like creature, *Hyalomena sieboldi*.
拂意 *fur-yih*, v.i., go against wishes; feel one's wishes thwarted.

揶 10A.22-3

yer.

揶揄 *yeryur*, v.t., to deride, tease, taunt (person).

抔 10A.22-3

pour.

V.t. & n. To hold, catch (soil) by cupped hands (抔土); drink from cupped hands (抔水而飲).

押 10A.22-4

ya (**yar*).

V.t. (1) To pawn, mortgage: 抵押 v.t. & n., (put up) security for loan; 典押 v.t. & n., mortgage. (2) To detain by police, to guard or watch from behind: 扣押, 押起來 to detain person; 看押 keep under detention; 押解, 押送 *-jieh*, *-suhng* ↓; 押到警察局 escort (suspect) to the police station; 押車 to accompany and guard goods in cart; 押尾 *-weei* ↓. (3) To affix signature: 簽押 attach signature to contract; 畫押 make a sign in lieu of signature for the illiterate; 花押 affix private mark (some kind of monogram) at the end. (4) U.f. 壓 51A.11, (a) press down, repress; (b) to shelve (a paper) for later attention.

押標金 *yabiaujin*, n., bond for a bid.
押契 *ya-chih*, n., a mortgage deed.
押牀 *yachuarng*, n., formerly, a torture bed, to which prisoner was fastened, (cf. Procrustean bed).
押當 *yadahng*, v.i. & t., to pawn (s.t.).
押抵 *yadii*, v.t., to mortgage, use as security for loan (also 抵押).
押發 *yafa*, v.t., to send away (prisoner) under guard, see *-suhng* ↓.
押縫 **yar-fehng*, v.t., formerly, to sign on last and/or first page of old manuscript as testimonial.
押封 *yafeng*, v.t., to seal and attach (property).
押號 *ya-hauh*, n., a private mark as signature.
押後 *ya-houh*, v.i., to defer; to remand (in law).
押滙 *yahueih*, n., a bill of exchange.
押賬 *ya-jahng*, v.i. & n., (use as) security for loan.
押解 *yajieh*, v.t., to send away (prisoner, goods) under guard.
押金 *yajin*, n., deposit, security money.
押質 *yajyh*, v.t. & n., to pawn, mortgage.
押款 *yakuaan*, v.i. & t., to borrow money with security.
押歲 *ya-sueih*, n., a New Year gift esp. for children (usu. wr. 壓歲).
押送 *yasuhng*, v.t., to send away under guard.
押頭(兒) *ya'tou('l)*, n., (1) security, collateral; (2) (MC) officer in charge of prisoner being transported.
押租 *ya-tzu*, n., deposit for rent.
押字 **yar-tzyh*, n., signature.
押尾 **yar-weei*, n., (1) see *-fehng* ↑; (2) v.i., to bring up the rear.
押運 *yayuhn*[1], v.t., to transport goods under guard.
押韻 *ya-yuhn*[2], v.i., to rhyme (verse).

挪 10A.22-5

nuor.

V.t. To move, transfer: 挪動, 挪借, 挪用 *-duhng*, *-jieh*, *-yuhng* ↓; 挪騷窩兒 an infant baby's first visit after birth to the outside world, which must be the home of its maternal grandmother; 挪開 draw apart, move away.

挪動 *nuorduhng*, v.t., move (furniture, etc.) to another place; touch, dislocate.
挪借 *nuorjieh*, v.t., apply funds temporarily for some other use.
挪威 *Nuorwei*, n., Norway.
挪用 *nuoryuhng*, v.t., see *-jieh* ↑; 挪用公款 appropriate public funds for personal use.

掃 10A.22-5

saau (**sauh*).
[Usu. wr. 掃]

N. (**sauh*) (1) (*-tz*) A broom. (2) Special bags of willow branches, framed by bamboo, for building dykes; mattress used in dyke construction.

V.t. (1) To sweep (floor): 打掃, 清掃 ditto; 灑掃 spray and sweep; gen. clean up room; 灑掃應對 cleaning up room and good manners in replying to questions as part of child's education. (2) To sweep clean, or sweep off: 掃除 *-chur* ↓; 掃數 *-shuh* ↓; 掃射 to strafe; 掃田刮地 do menial work; 掃蕩 *-dahng* ↓. (3) To paint the eyebrow: 淡掃蛾眉朝至尊 went to see the emperor

亅	小	⺊	十	土	ナ	卄	凵	丨	一	丅	フ	口	区	冈	㇆	厂	尸	亠	广	宀	丶	乚	弋	心	八	人	乂	㇀	一	丿丿	㇓	〈
00	01	02	10	11	12	20	21	22	30	31	32	40	41	42	50	51	52	60	61	62	63	70	71	72	80	81	82	83	90	91	92	93

with touched-up eyebrow—without heavy rouge; see 掃眉 *-meir* ↓. (4) To take in in a sweeping glance: 眉目裏掃人 saw at glance.

掃把 **sauhbaa*, n., a broomstick.
掃邊 *saaubian*, n., minor role in Chin. opera.
掃晴娘(兒) *saauchirng-niarng('l)*, n., a cut-paper figure of woman with a broom, put under eaves to pray for clearing up of skies.
掃除 *saauchur*, v.t., to sweep away (obstacles).
掃蕩 *saaudahng*, v.t., to clean up, to wipe out, to map up (all enemy).
掃地 *saau-dih*, v.i., to sweep the floor; 斯文掃地 the cultural tradition topples over.
掃房 *saau-farng*, v.i., make gen. house-cleaning.
掃軌 *saur gueei*, phr., (AC) sweep off, i.e., obliterate the tracks, to show there have been no (political) visitors.
掃海 *saur-haai*, v.i., sweep off mines in sea.
掃帚 *sauh'jou*, n., a broomstick. 掃帚星 *--shing*, n., a comet.
掃雷艇 *saauleir-ting*, n., mine sweeper.
掃臉 *saur-liaan*, v.i., to "lose face": 掃臉的事 a disgraceful affair.
掃眉 *saau-meir*, phr., 掃眉才子 a girl poet or author ("scholar with picked eyebrows").
掃墓 *saau-muh*, v.i., visit grave on 清明 *Chingmirng* day.
掃平 *saau-pirng*, v.t., to squelch, quash (rebellion).
掃興 *saaushihng* (*sauh-*), v.i., feel disappointed; adj., disappointing.
掃數 *saaushuh*, adv., the whole amount (repaid, etc.).
掃榻 *saau-tah*, v.i., (LL) to welcome visitor ("sweep the mat").
掃堂腿 *saautarngtueei*, n., a move in boxing, stretch leg on floor to topple opponent.
掃聽 *saau'ting*, v.i., to pick up, fish for, news (=打聽).
掃營兒 *saau-yirng'l*, adv., (coll.) see *-shuh* ↑.

扑 10A.22-6

biahn.

V.i. (LL) show happiness: 扑掌 clap applause; 扑舞, 扑躍 jump and dance for joy.

擠 10A.22-6

jii.

V.t. To crowd, push against, exert pressure on: 擁擠 crowd together; 擠死了 be squeezed to death; 擠擠插插 jammed with people; 擠滿 be filled to overflowing, overcrowded; 擠上前去 push to the front; 擠進去 to force a passage through; 擠來擠去 push about; 排擠 discriminate against; 擠奶 to milk an animal; 擠水 wring out water; 擠古眼兒 make grimaces; 擠眉弄眼 ditto; 擠對 *-dueir*, 擠陷 *-shiahn* ↓.

擠對 *jii'duei*, v.t., to force (s.o.'s) hand, embarrass.
擠兌 *jiidueih*, v.i. & n., run on a bank.
擠陷 *jiishiahn*, v.t., plot to cause (s.o.'s) downfall.

搾 10A.22-6

jah.

[Var. 榨]

V.i. & t. (1) To squeeze (tax, money): 搾取 *-chyuu* ↓. (2) To press (wine, juice): 壓搾 to press (juice), also to squeeze (money) by pressure, to oppress (people).

搾牀 *jahchuarng*, n., wine press, oil press and the like.
搾取 *jahchyuu*, v.t., to obtain (money) by political pressure, or tyranny.
搾菜 *jahtsaih*, n., a kind of pickled vegetable root, much used for flavoring.

搛 10A.22-8

jian.

V.t. Pick up with a forked instrument: 搛菜 pick up food with chopsticks, help guest to some food.

擲 10A.22-8

jyr.

N. A throw: 千金一擲 a thousand dollars at a throw (of dice); 孤注一擲 stake everything on it.

V.t. To throw (ball, spear, dice, rock, etc.): 擲下, 擲去 throw away; 擲還 (court. in letter) please return (borrowed book, etc.); 擲中 (*-juhng*) hit by throwing; 擲鐵球 put the shot 擲鐵餅 throw the discus; 擲標槍 throw javelin.

擲老羊 *jyr-laau-yarng*, phr., a dice game.
擲骰子 *jyr-shaai'tz*, phr., to throw dice (also wr. 擲色子).
擲梭 *jyr-suo*, phr., a passing of loom shuttle, (fig.) the quick passing of time.
擲采 *jyr-tsaai*, phr., see *-shaai'tz*.

抑 10A.22-9

yih.

V.t. (1) To stop, block, hinder, repress: 抑強扶弱 restrain the powerful and help the weak; 抑制, 抑止 *-jyh*, *-jyy* ↓; 抑割 (AC) abandon, cut off. (2) (AC) to bend (head); to concede.

Conj. (LL) or, or else (somewhat rhet.): 人歟, 抑鬼耶 is it a human being or is it a ghost? 不知乎, 抑不爲乎 didn't he know, or didn't he want to do it? 抑或 *-huoh*↓; 抑且 *-chiee*↓.

抑且 *yihchiee*, conj., furthermore, besides.

抑糴 *yih-dir*, v.i., compulsorily buy grain from the people at reduced prices.

抑或 *yihhuoh*, conj., or else, or perhaps (rhet.).

抑制 *yihjyh*, v.t., to repress (desire, rebellion, etc.); 抑制劑 n., depressant, sedative.

抑止 *yihjyy*, v.t., to stop; suppress.

抑勒 *yihleh*, v.t., to restrain by force, to suppress.

抑搔 *yihsau*, v.i., (AC) to massage (parents) and scratch itches for them.

抑塞 *yihseh*, (LL) (1) v.i. & t., to block progress; (2) adj. or p.p., (drain) blocked; (people) hindered from rising to top.

抑損 *yihsuun*, (1) v.t., (LL) to restrain (excesses); (2) v.i., to minimize oneself, be modest.

抑揚 *yihyarng*, (1) adj., rising and falling (of tones, rhythm); (2) n., praise and blame; (3) adj., drifting aimlessly.

抑抑 *yihyih*, adj., (AC) meticulously correct (manners).

折 10A.22-9

jer (**sher*, **je*).

N. (1) A bend, a twist: 曲^{A}折 22.41. (2) Discount: 七折 30% discount; 六折 40% discount; 折頭 *-'tou*↓. (3) An act in Yuarn drama. (4) A surname.

V.i. & t. (1) To break off: 折斷 *-duahn*↓; 攀折花木 to break off flowers and branches; 折柳, 折桂 *-lioou*, *-gueih*↓; 折骨 break a bone; 折簡 open a letter; 折券 burn I. O. U. (act of generosity). (2) (**sher*) Break: 棍子折了 the cane is broken in two. (3) To pronounce verdict, to judge: 折獄 *-yuh*↓. (4) To die young: 夭折, 早折. (5) (*jer* or **sher*) To lose money in business: 虧折 ditto; 折損, 折本 *-suun*, *-been*↓; 折耗 depreciate in value. (6) To admire (person): 心折 admire person's superior ability; 折服 *-fur*^{1}↓. (7) To discount, sell at lower rate, convert property into cash: 不折不扣 no discount, also completely (true, etc.); 折半 50% discount; 折變, 折賣 to sell property, *-biahn*, *-maih*↓; 折合, 折賬 *-her*, *-jahng*↓. (8) To humiliate: 折磨, 折辱 *-'mor*, *-ruh*^{2}↓. (9) (**je*) To toss about: 折跟頭 turn somersault: 折過兒 turn over; 折餅, 折騰, 折籮 *-biing*, *-teng*, *-luor*↓. (10) To cool (liquid) by pouring into another cup successively. (11) To turn back: 折回 *-hueir*↓; 折入 turn into another street.

折半 *jer-bahn*, v.i., to sell at half price.

折北 *jerbeei*, v.i., be defeated.

折本 *jerbeen* (**sher-*), v.i., sell below cost.

折變 *jerbiahn*, v.i., (1) to sell property to pay debt; (2) (in Suhng Dyn.) to pay tax by equivalent value in some other goods.

折餅 **jebiing*, v.i., to toss about in bed (as in colic, like "turning over cake" in oven).

折衝 *jerchung*, v.i., to blunt enemy attack: 折衝樽俎 to conduct diplomatic negotiations (樽俎 "over wine and meat" dinners).

折斷 *jerduahn*, v.t., to break in two.

折服 *jerfur*^{1}, v.i., to admit defeat, admit another's superiority (also wr. 折伏).

折福 *jer-fur*^{2}, v.i., to be extravagant or enjoy inordinately (lit., "overdraw on reserve of happiness").

折乾兒 *jergan*(*-ga'l*), v.i., to give gifts of cash instead of articles.

折桂 *jer-gueih*, v.t., to pass the degree in civil examinations ("break the laurel branch" like Eng. "win the laurel wreath").

折合 *jerher*, v.t., to be worth (thirty dollars, etc.) after discount or according to exchange rates.

折回 *jerhueir*, v.t., to turn back on the road.

折賬 *jer-jahng*, v.i., to pay by goods in lieu of cash.

折屐 *jer-ji*, phr., (allu.) joy of receiving a great friend—"break the wooden clogs" over a threshold in the rush of welcome.

折價 *jer-jiah*, v.i., mark down price; make cheap sale.

折節 *jer-jier*, v.i., (1) to lower or humiliate oneself; (2) to change one's beliefs or loyalties.

折中 *jerjung*, v.i., to compromise; 折中辦法 a compromise (also wr. 折衷).

折枝 *jer-jy*, v.i., (1) to paint only two or three branches in a painting; (2) 爲長者折枝 (allu.) s.t. very easy to do.

折扣 *jer'kouh*, n., discount: 多少折扣 what is the discount?

折柳 *jer-lioou*, v.i., (allu.) "break a willow branch" when parting with friend.

折籮 **je-luor*, n., leftover of a banquet, collected in a basket, chop suey.

折賣 *jer'maih*, v.i., to sell property to pay debt (=變賣), see 折 V.i. & t. 7↑.

折磨 *jermor*, v.i. & n., (or 磨折) a series of mishaps, hardships or slow torture by mistress: 經過了這場折磨 after the series of persecutions.

折入 *jerruh*^{1}, v.i., (1) turn into another street; (2) recovered capital at discount.

折辱 *jerruh*^{2}, v.t. & n., humiliate, -ed, -tion.

折煞 *jer'sha*, v.t., (or 折殺) break the luck: 你折煞我 you overwhelm me with more than what I deserve, see *-fur*^{2}↑.

折射 *jersheh*, v.t. & n., (phys.)

refract, -tion.

折現 *jer-shiahn*[1], phr., convert into cash.

折線 *jershiahn*[2], n., (math.) broken line.

折受 *jershouh*[1], v.t., see *-fur*[2] ↑.

折壽 *jer-shouh*[2], phr., to do s.t. (such as overindulgence) which cuts short a man's normal span of life; enjoy now, pay later.

折水 *jershueei*, n., discount in exchange.

折損 *jersuun*, v.t. & n., to damage, a damage (in property, flowers in garden, reputation, etc.).

折騰 **je'teng*, v.i. & t., (1) to toss about; (2) indulge or spend freely: 他把上萬家當都折騰了 he has squandered away a fortune of over ten thousand dollars.

折頭 *jer'tou*, n., discount, discount for commission agent.

折腰 *jer-yau*, phr., to "bend one's waist": 不能爲五斗米折腰(陶淵明) cannot make curtsies for the salary of five bushels of rice—sick of official life.

折獄 *jer-yuh*, phr., to decide a legal case: 片言可以折獄 (AC) can settle a case at court with a few simple words.

拆 10A.22-9

cheh (sp. pr. **cheh* or *chai* both allowable).

V.i. & t. (1) (**cheh*) To tear apart, break up: 拆信, 拆封 open letter, envelope; 拆開來看 open (letter, package) and see; 拆裂 split up. (2) (**chai*) To break up, tear down, wreck (house): 拆房子 tear down house; 拆臺 *-tair* ↓; 拆平 to level (building); 拆毁 *-hueei* ↓. (3) (*cheh*) To break up and analyze, dissect: 拆字, 拆辯 *-tzyh*, *-biahn* ↓.

拆白黨 *chaibairdaang* (*cheh-ber-*), n., gang of swindlers, oft. practising confidence game: 女拆白 woman swindler.

拆辯 **chehbiahn*, v.i., (MC) to argue law case.

拆穿 **chai-chuan*, v.t., reveal (secret, motive): 拆穿西洋景(鏡) destroy illusory setup, expose trickery.

拆毁 **chehhueei*, v.t., to destroy, tear down (bridge, etc.), dismantle (house).

拆貨 **chaihuoh*, v.i., deal in the business of wrecking (houses, etc.) and selling broken-up timber, tiles, etc.

拆開 **cheh-kai*, v.t., break open (letter); take things apart to study.

拆爛汚 **chailahnwu*, v.i., to do things lousily and leave a mess.

拆票 **chai-piauh*, v.i., formerly, settle transfer of accounts between local banks morning and noon.

拆散 **cheh-saan*, v.t., break up (family, mother and son).

拆梢 **chaishau*, v.i., (Shanghai dial.) to swindle.

拆洗 *chaishii*, v.t., take off and wash (bed sheets, etc.).

拆息 **chaishir*, v.i. & n., (pay) daily interest on loan.

拆臺 **chai-tair*, v.i., (lit.) tear down stage—to expose or otherwise do harm to a program: 別拆我的臺 do not undermine what I am doing.

拆字 **chehtzyh*, v.i., (fortune-telling) dissect components of character to give an esoteric meaning.

揷 10A.22-9

cha.

[Pop. of 插 10A.21]

§ 10A.30 (扌/一)

揸 10A.30-1

ja.

V.i. & t. To grasp by hand: 揸得穩, 揸緊 grasp tight; 揸爛, 揸碎 crush by hand.

搕 10A.30-1

ke.

V.i. & t. To knock, hit: 搕扁 to flatten; 搕碎 smash to pieces; (cf. 磕 31B.30).

扯 10A.30-2

chee.

V.i. & t. (1) To pull (apart, off): 扯破了, 扯壞了, 扯爛 to pull about and spoil, break by pulling and fumbling; 扯開嘴巴 open mouth wide; 扯開嗓子 speak or sing out loud; 扯住袖子 pull by the sleeve; 扯住不放 grab (person) and will not let go; 扯鈴 pull the bell; 扯衣領 grab by the collar; 扯頭髮 pull by the hair; 扯上扯下 pull up and down; 東拉西扯 talk incoherently, also put together (money, etc.) from different sources or do patch work in writing. (2) To tear (off, apart): 扯碎 tear to pieces; 撕扯 crumble up and tear (paper); 扯票 *-piauh* ↓. (3) To hoist (sail, flag). (4) To involve by talk, to ramble in all directions, to lie: 牽扯的人太多 involve too many persons (in scandal); 扯拉 *-la* ↓; 拉拉扯扯 or 扯扯拉拉 pull and push, ramble in talk; 扯東扯西 ditto. (5) To gossip, talk irresponsibly, to lie: 扯謊 *-huaang* ↓; 瞎扯, 胡扯, 亂扯 gabble, gossip irresponsibly.

扯倒 *cher-daau*, v.i., quit: 倘不願意, 扯倒罷休 if you don't like it, you can just quit.

扯淡 *cheedahn*, v.i., talk idly.

扯謊 *cherhuaang*, v.i., to lie: 不用扯謊 don't lie to me.

扯拉 *cheela*, v.t., involve (person) in talk: 扯拉上人 (or 別人) mention names, involve others.

A B C

扯落 *chee'luo*, v.i., as in 心愛的人扯落着你 (MC) s.o. who loves you will not let you go.
扯票 *chee-piauh*, phr., (1) destroy (a ballot, ticket); (2) (coll.) kill kidnapped person when ransom is not paid.
扯臊 *cheesauh*, v.i., should be ashamed, shame on you! talk nonsense.
扯手 *chershoou*, n., the reins.

挡 10A.30-2

daang, dahng.
[Pop. of 擋 10A.41]

扛 10A.30-3

gang (**karng*).

V.t. (1) Lift up, heave (a heavy object with both hands or by two or more persons at the same time): 力能扛鼎 so strong as to be able to lift up a tripod. (2) (**karng*) Carry on the shoulders: 扛東西, 扛在肩膀上 carry on one's shoulders. (3) (**karng*) Answer back.

扛叉的 **karngcha'de*, n., a person who protects prostitutes from molestation.
扛夫 **karngfu*, n., a worker employed to carry loads on shoulders.
扛肩兒的 **karngjial'de*, n., a porter who carries heavy objects on back.
扛頭 **karngtour*, v.i., to throw one's head up in a gesture of disdain, said esp. of proud prostitutes.

揠 10A.30-3

yah.

V.t. To hold, grasp fast, to hold and shake.

揠把 *yah'ba*, v.t., (MC) to have in one's grasp or firm control.
揠擺 *yahbaai*, v.t., (MC) ditto.

拯 10A.30-3

jeeng.

V.t. To rescue from fire or flood: 拯救 *-jiouh*↓; to save (souls).

拯救 *jeengjiouh*, v.t., to rescue, aid, relieve (the distressed); to save from sin.
拯恤 *jeengshyuh*, v.t., to give relief (to the poor).

担 10A.30-4

dan, dahn.
[Pop. of 擔 10A.40]

搵 10A.30-4

wehn.

V.t. To press down with knuckles: 搵淚, see 抆△淚 10A.82.

捏 10A.30-4

nie.
[Var. of 揑, 捏; cf. 湼]

V.t. (1) Seize, take hold of, pinch, apply pressure with hands, strangle: 捏(一)把汗 be seized with fear or deep concern; 捏着 hold between fingers; 捏着鼻子 suffer patiently and silently; 捏着頭皮 ditto; 捏住了 have finally caught (s.t.); 捏手捏腳 do things stealthily; 捏神捏鬼 plan behind (s.o.'s) back; 捏他的腿 pinch his leg; 捏他一把 give him a pinch; 捏死 strangle (s.o.) to death. (2) Knead with the fingers, mold: 捏塑 *-suh*↓; 捏泥人 make an earthen figurine; 捏麵團 knead dough; 捏一撮土 knead a pinch of earth; 捏一把泥 knead a handful of mud. (3) Fabricate, trump up: 捏造 *-tzauh*↓; 捏報 *-bauh*↓; 拿捏 hesitant, wavering.

捏報 *niebauh*, v.t., make a false report.
捏病 *nie-bihng*, v.i., feign sickness.
捏告 *niegauh*, v.t., accuse (s.o.) falsely.
捏咕 *nie'gu*, v.t., reconcile, mediate, bring together (＝撮合).
捏合 *nieher*, v.t., (1) reconcile, mediate; (2) flirt with, have illicit sexual relations with.
捏弄 *nie'nuhng*, v.t., (1) fabricate, trump up; (2) reconcile, mediate; manipulate.
捏陷 *nieshiahn*, v.t., implicate (s.o.) by groundless accusations.
捏酸 *niesuan*, v.i., to carry on with pompous air or affected scholar's gait, to strut.
捏塑 *niesuh*, v.t., to mold (clay figures).
捏詞 *nietsyr*, v.t., make a false statement, tell a lie.
捏造 *nietzauh*, v.t., fabricate, trump up.

扭 10A.30-5

nioou.

丨	小	⺊	十	土	𠂇	廾	乚	丨	一	丁	乛	口	囗	冈	冂	厂	尸	亠	广	宀	丶	乚	弋	心	八	人	乂	乛	乛	丿	⺈	く
00	01	02	10	11	12	20	21	22	30	31	32	40	41	42	50	51	52	60	61	62	63	70	71	72	80	81	82	83	90	91	92	93

扭 **V.t.** (1) Twist, wrench, turn round, sprain: 扭送 seize and turn over to (police, etc.); 扭打 to tussle, wrestle; 扭結 to tussle together; 扭斷 wrench off; 扭開 break (s.t.) open by force; 扭筋 sprain (ankle, wrist, etc.); 扭傷 sprain; 扭壞 (of human body) sprain, (of things) damage by manipulation; 扭了脖子 have one's neck sprained; 扭過臉 turn one's face away; 扭頭 turn one's head; 扭乾 wring (s.t.) dry; 扭曲作直 (lit.) "turn (s.t.) crooked straight"—(fig.) turn black into white. (2) (Of bodily movement) swing from side to side: 扭捏 wriggle; 扭腰 wriggle one's waist; 扭屁股, 扭臀 wriggle one's buttocks.

Adj. & adv. 扭扭捏捏 bashful; 扭股兒糖 in a twisting or wriggling manner; 扭扭搭搭 swinging from side to side.

扭轉 *nioujuaan*, v.t., turn round: 扭轉頭去 turn round your head; 扭轉劣勢 to check deteriorating conditions; 扭轉大局 save a critical situation; 扭轉乾坤 save a country or the world from disaster; 扭轉心腸 make (s.o.) change his mind.

扭扭舞 *niourniourwuu*, n., rock-and-roll.

搵 10A.30–5

laan.

[Var. of 攬 10A.70]

拉 10A.30–6

la (**lar*, **laa*).

V.i. & t. (1) To pull, drag, draw: 拉扯 *-chee*↓; 拉拉扯扯 pull and drag this way and that; 拉過來 pull (s.t.) over here; 拉出去 drag (s.t. or s.o.) out; 拉長方臉兒 pull a long face; 拉的下臉來 can pull a long face; 拉不下臉來 embarrassed; 拉開 *-kai*↓; 拉下窗簾 pull down the blinds; 拉縴 *-chiahn*, 拉倒 *-daau*, 拉運 *-yuhn*, 拉曳 *-yih*↓; 拖拉 drag on or out; 拉鈴 pull the bell rope; 拉緊(些) draw (s.t.) tight(er); 拉近 *-jihn*↓; 拉長 pull or make (s.t.) longer, (fig.) cause (conversation, speech, or a piece of writing) to be tediously long; 拉幕 draw the curtain; 拉線 pull the wires; 拉線人 a wirepuller; 拉攏 *-'lung*↓; 拉關係 try to draw close to (s.o.), (lit.) "draw relations with s.o."; 拉馬 *-maa*↓; 拉家帶口 bear family burdens; 拉鋸 *-jyuh*↓; 拉胡琴 play the Chin. fiddle; 拉提琴 play a violin; 拉風箏 fly kite; 拉網 draw a net in; 拉車 pull cart; 拉板車 pull a handcart; 拉洋車 pull a rickshaw; 拉車的 a rickshaw puller; 拉硬弓 force (s.o.) to do (s.t.) against his will; 拉大片(兒), 拉洋片 run a peep show. (2) To hold: 手拉手 hold one another's hand; 拉手 *-shoou*↓; 一把拉住不放 hold and won't let go; 拉他一把 give him a helping hand. (3) To solicit: 拉買賣, 拉生意, 拉主道 solicit business; 拉客 solicit customers, said esp. of street-walkers; 拉票 solicit votes; 拉股 solicit shareholders. (4) To recruit, impress, look for: 拉角 recruit actors for play; 拉人 recruit men for service; 拉伕, 拉夫 *-fu*↓; 拉替身兒 look for (s.o.) to be the scapegoat for oneself. (5) To cut, amputate, eliminate, move bowels: 拉掉 (surg.) amputate (any diseased part of the body); 摧枯拉朽 (AC) (of obstacles easily overcome) like tearing down dried-up trees or buildings in decay; 拉屎 *-shyy*, 拉尿 *-niauh*², 拉稀 *-shi*↓; 拉了一褲子 wet one's underwear; 拉肚子 have loose bowels; 拉不出來 have difficulty in moving one's bowels; 還沒拉完 have not yet finished moving one's bowels; 拉了兩天 have had loose bowels for two days in succession. (6) To borrow or owe money: 拉賬 *-jahng*, 拉空 *-kuhng*↓; 拉一屁股債 owe a mountain of debts; 拉饑荒 *-jihuang*↓; 東拉西扯 owe debts all around, see *-chee*↓. (7) To leave behind, leave undone: 拉在後面 (of runners or cars) leave (s.o.) behind; 拉後勾兒 let (s.t.) remain unfinished with a view to its possible continuation later on; 拉長線(兒) leave (s.t.) for future decision. (8) To talk or gossip: 拉不斷, 扯不斷 talk on and on without end; 拉短兒 talk behind s.o.'s back; 拉舌頭, 拉老婆舌頭 (or 舌液) to gossip. (9) (**lar*) (Var. 剌) cut into two, slash (**lar*).

拉巴 *la'ba*¹, v.t., pull and drag (=拉扯).

拉拔 *la'ba*², v.t., promote a person's career, help advance (person).

拉絆 *la'ban*, v.t., hamper, obstruct.

拉叉 *lacha* (sp. pr. *lachah*), v.i., (of limbs, branches) extend in all directions.

拉塲 *la-chaang*, n., (of supporting actors in Chin. opera) intentional prolongation of time on stage to wait for the appearance of the leading actor or actress; 拉塲子 acrobatic and other shows in market place.

拉岔 *lachah*, n., a kind of card game played for money.

拉長 *la-charng*, v.i. & t., to prolong (business, voice).

拉扯 *lachee*, v.t., (1) pull and drag; (2) (*la'che*) involve other persons by loose talk; give a helping hand to; help and support (s.o.); (3) (*-chee'l*) to even up, stretch even.

拉縴 *lachiahn*, v.t., (1) (of boat going upstream) pull the tow-rope; (2) (fig.) act as a go-between (also --兒).

拉抽屜(兒) *lachou'ti*(*-'tie'l*), v.i., pull out desk drawer; (fig.) go back on one's word; make seesaw action.

拉持 *la'chy*, v.t., (dial.) bring (s.o.) up.

拉倒 *ladaau*, v.t., (1) pull down; (2) (coll.) forget about it: 這件事我看還是拉倒罷!

拉答 *ladar*, adj., untidy, slovenly (of composition, furniture, etc.).

拉丁 *Lading*, n. & adj., (translit.) Latin (also wr. 臘丁).

拉夫 *lafu*, v.t., press men for

military or coolie service.

拉忽 *laa'hu*, adj., (1) careless, negligent; (2) stupid, foolish, muddle-headed.

拉火 *lahuoo*, n., fuse used for ancient-type cannon.

拉賬 *la-jahng*, v.t., buy things on credit.

拉饑荒 *la-jihuang*, v.t., (coll.) run short of money.

拉角 *lajiaau*, v.t., recruit supporters or players.

拉架 *la-jiah*, v.t., mediate between two persons quarrelling or fighting.

拉近 *la-jihn*, v.t., draw nearer.

拉鋸 *lajyuh*, v.t., (1) cut with a saw; (2) make seesaw movements: 拉鋸戰 (fight) a seesaw battle.

拉開 *la-kai*, v.t., (1) pull or draw (s.t.) open or apart; (2) (fighters) draw apart.

拉跨 *lakuah*, v.i., limp, walk lamely or unevenly.

拉空 *la-kuhng*, v.i., run into debt.

拉了 *la'le*, (1) v.t., take off (boots, necktie); (2) v.i., acknowledge defeat.

拉鍊 *laliahn*, n., zipper.

拉攏 *la'lung*, v.t., draw (s.o.) over to one's side, draw persons with different views together.

拉馬 *lamaa*, v.i., act as a pimp (also 拉皮條).

拉溺 *la-niauh*[1], v.i., to pass water.

拉尿 *la-niauh*[2], v.i., ditto.

拉弄 *la'nung*, v.t. & n., (1) pull apart: 這本書被你拉弄散了 you have pulled the book apart; (2) wear and tear: 這件衣裳不禁拉弄 this dress cannot stand wear and tear.

拉皮條 *lapir'tiaur*, v.i., act as a pimp (also 拉皮條縴 ---*chiahn*).

拉皮子 *lapirtz*, v.i., be thick-skinned or unashamed.

拉薩 *Lasa*, n., Lhasa, the capital city of Tibet.

拉颯 *lasah*, n. & adj., (MC & Soochow dial.) dirt, -ty, garbage (var. of 垃圾, *lehseh*).

拉稀 *lashi*, v.i., (1) have loose bowels; (2) (coll.) acknowledge defeat.

拉手(兒) *la-shoou('l)*, v.t., (1) hold hands; (2) shake hands; (3) join hands: 人家倆人一拉手，就把你給毀了 when they two work together, you are done for.

拉屎 *la-shyy*, v.t., move bowels.

拉鎖子 *lasuootz*, n., (in embroidery) setting contour of flower patterns.

拉絲 *lasy*, adj., (1) (of action) hesitating: 人家決不拉絲，說走就走 they never hesitate and, if they agree to go, will go right away; (2) (of speech) long-winded: 說的簡捷脆快，並不拉絲 what (he) said was perfectly clear-cut and not long-winded.

拉遢 *lar'ta*, adj., dirty, untidy.

拉雜 *latzar*, adj. & adv., untidy, confused, (of room, etc.): 拉雜書來 write at random.

拉晚兒 *lawaa'l*, v.i., (of persons) be a night owl; (2) (of ricksaw puller) work at night.

拉曳 *layih*, v.t., drag along, trail (skirts).

拉運 *layuhn*, v.t., transport by handcarts.

擅 10A.30-6

shahn.

V.i. (1) To arrogate to oneself, to claim arbitrarily: 擅兵, 擅權 *-bing*, *-chyuarn*↓. (2) To make special claim to: 專擅 to be law unto oneself, also to excel in some specialty; 不敢擅美 dare not claim all credit to oneself.

Adv. Arbitrarily: 擅自作主 act arbitrarily; 擅敢 dare without permission (open letters, etc.); 擅便 *-biahn*↓.

擅便 *shahnbiahn*, adv., arbitrarily: 擅便行事 act arbitrarily.

擅兵 *shahn-bing*, phr., (of governors) hold independent military power.

擅場 *shahn-chaang*, v.i., to excel in some field.

擅長 *shahncharng*, v.i. & n., to excel; one's speciality (in some field).

擅權 *shahn-chyuarn*, v.i., to hold absolute power, to hold power illegally (as eunuchs in certain periods).

擅國 *shahn-guor*, v.i., (AC) to rule country as sovereign.

擅利 *shahn-lih*, v.i., to enjoy monopoly in trade.

擅命 *shahn-mihng*, phr., to arrogate power to oneself, be *de facto* ruler.

揎 10A.30-6

shyuan.

V.i. To roll up sleeves: 揎拳擄袖 roll up sleeves and raise fists to fight; 揎擊 to hit with bare fists.

控 10A.30-6

kuhng.

V.t. To accuse at court: 控告, 控訴 *-gauh*, *-suh*↓. (2) To subject to control, to curb (horse): 控制 *-jyh*↓. (3) (AC) to draw a bow: 控弦. (4) (AC) to fall upon the ground: 控于地.

控告 *kuhnggauh*, (1) v.t., to complain, accuse; (2) n., a complaint.

控制 *kuhngjyh*, (1) v.t., to keep in control: 控制不了 cannot control; (2) n., control: 受他控制 under his control and direction; 控制艙 (astron.) service module.

控訴 *kuhngsuh*, v.t. & n., see *-gauh*↑.

控御 *kuhngyuh*, v.t., to control and direct.

搓 搤 捦 拶 拮 搙 搭

搓 10A.30-8

tsuo.

[Related 擦 10A.01, 挫 10A.11, 銼 81A.11, 磋 31B.30]

V.i. & t. To rub or roll with hand: 搓揉 *-rour* ↓; 搓繩子 roll a rope; 搓作一團 roll into a ball; 搓紙△捻兒 93B.71.

搓板兒 *tsuobaa'l*, n., washing board.

搓腳石 *tsuo-jiaau-shyr*, n., stone near gate for wiping shoes.

搓弄 *tsuo'nung* (sp. pr. also *tsuor-*), v.i. & t., to rub s.t. between hands.

搓揉 *tsuorour*, v.i. & t., ditto.

搓碎 *tsouo-sueih*, v.t., rub into powder or bits.

搤 10A.30-8

eh.

[Var. of 扼 10A.70]

捦 10A.30-8

chirn.

V.t. (1) To grasp by hand. (2) To seize enemy (var. of 擒).

§ 10A.32 (扌/フ)

拶 10A.32-9

tzar (also *tzaan*).

V.t. To press, squeeze hard, to subject to pressure.

拶指 *tzarjyy* (*tzarn-*), v.i., press fingers between sticks as a form of torture.

拶子 *tzaan'tz*, n., such instruments of torture.

§ 10A.40 (扌/口)

拮 10A.40-1

jier.

拮据 *jierjyu*, (1) n., a sore hand; (2) adj., lacking financial resources: 手頭拮据 broke, short of funds.

拮抗筋 *jierkahngjin*, n., (physiol.) antagonistic muscles (opp. 協同筋 synergistic muscles).

搙 10A.40-2

nuoh.

[Related 搦 10A.50 in 搦戰]

V.t. To hold in hand, grasp: 手搙雙斧 (MC) holding a battle-axe in each hand; 搙戰廝殺 (MC) challenge to fight.

搭 10A.40-2

da.

N. adjunct. (MC) 三五搭人家 three or four houses.

N. Linking stroke in same character or adjacent characters in calligraphy.

V.i. & t. (1) To put up, put together: 搭棚, 戲臺, 浮橋 put up a shed, a temporary theatrical stage, a pontoon bridge; 搭彩 put up festoons; see 搭架子 *-jiahtz* ↓. (2) To join up, attach to: 搭幫, 搭夥, 搭伴 travel with others in same vehicle, esp. 搭船, 搭車 go aboard a boat, a car, thus 搭客 (be) a passenger; 搭姘頭 (and dial. 搭夥計) man and woman live together without marriage; 張弓搭箭 attach arrow to bow; 衣服搭在竹竿上 hang laundry on bamboo pole; 牽搭, 勾搭 to induce attachment to, work in collusion with s.o.; 搭朋友 attach or attract s.o. as friend; 搭錯線 (Cantonese phr.) cross wire, wrong number (in telephoning). (3) To make certain gestures: 搭把手, 搭架子 *-barshoou, -jiahtz* ↓. (4) To copulate: 搭配 ditto.

搭把手 *da barshoou*, phr., as in 請您搭把手兒, 幫我一下 please give me a hand.

搭包 *da'bau*, n., waistband outside jacket, used for carrying things (also wr. 褡△包 63C.40).

搭膊 *da'bo*, n., (MC) see *-'bau* ↑.

搭補 *dabuu*, v.t., to make up what is needed or missing.

搭搭腳 *dadajiaau*, v.i., (1) to rest one's feet; (2) *-jiaau'l* ↓.

搭話 *da-huah*, v.i., strike up a conversation with s.o.

搭夥 *da-huoo*, v.i., travel with others; join up with party.

搭着 *da'je*, phr., in addition: 搭着他老子逼他念書 besides, his father forced him to study.

搭架子 *da-jiahtz*, v.i., (fig.) put on airs; (lit.) put up scaffolding.

搭腳兒 *da-jiaau'l*, v.i., take vehicle to rest one's legs.

搭街坊 *da jie'fang*, v.i., be neighbors.

搭界 *da-jieh*, v.i., be adjacent.

搭救 *dajiouh*, v.t., to rescue (s.o. in distress).

搭住 *dajuh*, v.i., take up lodging: 和人搭住 share house with s.o.

搭桌 *da-juo*, v.i., (formerly of theatrical troupe) give performance for relief.

搭拉 *da'la*, v.i., hang down: 搭拉下來; 搭拉尾巴 *--yii'ba*, hang tail (of dog); 搭拉貨 *--huoh*, bad or damaged goods (also wr. 耷拉).

搭撒 *dasa*, v.i., (eyelids) droop.

搭訕著 *dashahn'je*, adv., (reply, leave) in a listless or embarrassed manner.

搭手 *dashoou*, n., tumor around shoulder blades; accomplice in swindle, gambling, etc.

搭載 *da-tzaih*, v.i., go on boat or car as additional passenger.

拈 10A.40-2

niarn (**niaan*).

V.t. (1) To take or pick up s.t. with one's fingers: 拈弄 examine, fondle s.t. in hand; 拈香 (rel.) burn incense sticks before the altar; 拈鬚 stroke one's beard; 拈花惹草 have many love affairs; 拈筆 pick up the pen to write; (2) (**niaan*) (Interch. 捻) roll up s.t. with one's fingers or between palms.

拈鬮 *niarn-jiou*, v.t., draw lots.

拈酸 *niarnsuan*, v.t., be jealous.

拓 10A.40-3

tuoh (**tah*).

V.i. & t. (1) To expand (territory, etc.): 開拓, 拓地, 拓荒 develop waste land; 拓邊 develop frontier regions, expand boundary. (2) Push (object) with hand. (3) (**tah*) To make rubbings of inscriptions: 這幅碑帖拓得很好 this rubbing of inscription is well done.

拓本 **tahbeen*, n., a rubbing, esp. of ancient inscription, (the rubbing itself could be ancient and therefore important).

拓撲學 *tuohbur-shyuer*, n., (math.) topology.

拓荒 *tuohhuang*, v.t., to develop waste land.

拓展 *tuohjaan*, v.i. & t., to develop, expand (business, industry).

拓殖 *tuohjyr*, v.t., to colonize.

拓落 *tuohluoh*, adj., in hard luck, unsuccessful in career.

扣 10A.40-4

kouh.

N. (1) A knot: 扣子, 扣兒 *-tz*, *-'l*↓; 鈕扣 cloth button; 花扣 decorative button; 鞋扣 shoe buckle; 打了死扣 a knot that does not get loose by itself; 絲絲入扣 (of novels, fine reasoning) all threads neatly tied up, closely knit. (2) A bunch, bundle: 一扣線 a bundle of thread; 一扣文書 a sheaf of documents, letters.

V.t. (1) To tie up, together, button up: 扣緊 tie up well; 把衣服扣好 button up dress; 扣在一起 tie up together; 扣馬 (=牽馬) lead horse on strap. (2) To arrest: 扣押, 扣留 *-ya*, *-liour*↓; 把這人扣起來 arrest this person; 把行車執照扣下來 take away driving license. (3) To discount, deduct, take off, hold back part or whole: 扣除 *-chur*↓; 回扣 discount for agent; 扣底子 (coll.) ditto; 扣錢 deduct money; 扣薪水 deduct part of salary; 扣分數 deduct school marks; 剋扣 illegally deduct (soldier's pay, ration). (4) Cover on top: 扣着瓦蓋 cover with roof tiles; 把碗扣在盤子上 turn bowl over on the plate; 扣在我頭上 put (unpleasant duty) on my shoulder. (5) To strike, knock: (interch. 叩門) 扣門 knock at door; 扣舷 knock on boat's side (for rhythm while singing); 扣其背 slap one's back.

扣除 *kouhchur*, v.t., to deduct (expenses, etc.).

扣兒 *kouh'l*, n., a knot.

扣留 *kouhliour*, v.t., detain (person, car, etc.).

扣肉 *kouhrouh*, n., a Szechuan specialty, a dish of richly seasoned steamed pork.

扣頭 *kouh'tou*, n., discount on price.

扣子 *kouh'tz*, n., (1) a knot; (2) a knot or bottleneck in affairs; (3) suspense at end of chapter in novels.

扣押 *kouhya*, v.t., to detain (person).

撂 10A.40-4

liauh.

V.t. (1) To drop: 把東西撂下來 drop things on the ground; 撂手不管 wash one's hands of the matter; 太太死了, 撂下兩個孩子 the mother died, leaving two children behind. (2) (Coll.) die, pop. 撂了.

撂地 *liauhdih*, v.i., show acrobatic skill in open spaces (also called 拉場).

撂跤 *liauhjiau*, v.i., a form of wrestling.

招 10A.40-5

jau.

N. (1) One move in boxing (hold, thrust, catch, counterblow, etc.): 招 or 招數 *-shuh*↓; 這一招眞厲害 that was a beautiful move (strike, parry, etc.); 妙招, 巧招 beautiful move; 絕招 (boxing) master blow, against which there is no defense. (2) (AC) target.

V.i. & t. (1) To beckon: 以手招之 beckon him to come; 招之則來, 麾之則去 at beck and call. (2) To enlist, invite to be member, enlist soldiers: 招兵, 招募, 招安 *-bing*, *-muh*, *-an*↓; enlist students

亅	小	⺊	十	土	ナ	廾	ㄴ	丨	一	丅	フ	口	区	冈	㇆	厂	尸	亠	广	宀	丶	乚	七	心	八	人	乂	一	ノ	リ	⺅	く
00	01	02	10	11	12	20	21	22	30	31	32	40	41	42	50	51	52	60	61	62	63	70	71	72	80	81	82	83	90	91	92	93

招 招生 *-sheng*↓; 招女婿 to take in a son-in-law to bear bride's clan name, rather than marry her out, see 招親 *-chin*↓; 招友作春遊 invite a friend to a spring outing; 招會員 enlist new members; 招租 (house) to let. (3) To incite, incur, to court disaster: 招災, 招禍 *-tzai, -huoh*↓; to provoke laughter, contempt: 招笑 (招人笑), 招瞪, 招打 *-shiauh, -dehng, -daa*↓; incite hatred, etc.: 招怨 *-yuahn*↓; 滿招損 (AC) pride leads to loss or downfall. (4) To provoke, flirt with: 招惹 *-'re*↓; 別再招他了 don't provoke him again; 招蜂引蝶 (of women) flirt with men. (5) To receive (guests, customers), extend (business, clientele): 招生意 to get new customers; 招呼, 招徠, 招攬 *-hu, -lai, -laan*↓. (6) To confess: 不打自招 make a confession, admit fault freely or unintentionally; 招供, 招認 *-gung, -rehn*↓. (7) To infect: 這病可招人 (coll.) this disease is infectious. (8) (AC) to tie up: 既入其苙, 又從而招之 (AC) after they have got (the pig) into pen, they begin to tie it up.

招安 *jau-an*, v.t., see *-fuu*↓.

招標 *jaubiau*, v.i., invite bids (for contract).

招兵 *jau-bing*, v.i., to recruit men for army, enlist men for armed forces: 招兵買馬 prepare for war; to expand a fighting force.

招承 *jaucherng*, v.i., to confess, own to (act).

招親 *jau-chin*, v.i., (1) to look for or take son-in-law who will marry into bride's family (taking her family name and living with her family); (2) (in vern. literature) to elope.

招打 *jau-daa*, v.i., to invite or deserve a spanking.

招待 *jau'daih*, (1) n., reception of guest (attentive, negligent, etc.): 招待不週 (pardon us for) any lack of attention; (2) v.i. & t., to receive guests, visitors: 恕不招待女客 sorry we don't receive lady guests; (3) to serve, look after: 好好的招待他 look after him well; 這店夥不會招待客人 this shop employee does not know how to serve customers; 招待員 steward or usher; 女招待 stewardess; 招待所 reception room or house, clubhouse for members.

招瞪 *jau-dehng*, v.i., "invite stare"—be annoying.

招風耳 *jaufeng-eel*, n., projecting ears.

招撫 *jaufuu*, v.t., to pacify rebellious area by offering amnesty.

招供 *jaugung*, v.i. & n., to confess; a confession, affidavit.

招股 *jau-guu*, v.i., offer shares to public.

招呼 *jauhu*, v.i., (1) to invite (able men at court); (2) *jau'hu*, (a) to acknowledge acquaintance on the road: 打招呼 say "hello"; (b) look after, take care of (child in public square, etc.); (c) get into a fight: 他們倆招呼上了 (coll.) they have started fighting; (d) call: 有人招呼你 s.o. is calling you; (e) instruct s.o. to do s.t.; (f) take care lest: 招呼頭上的磚頭掉下來 take care lest the brick overhead drops down.

招禍 *jau-huoh*, v.t., to invite disaster.

招魂 *jau-hurn*, v.i., (1) (AC) "call the soul back" when s.o. is dying, by going up the roof, facing the north and crying his name three times; (2) to call the soul back of s.o. who died abroad unburied, into an empty coffin prepared with his shoes and dress for proper burial; 招魂旛 formerly, a pennant before the coffin.

招展 *jaujaan*, v.i., to float in the wind (as a flag): 花枝招展 flower branches move, or a lady's hair decorations move as she passes by.

招架 *jaujiah*, v.i., (1) to parry a blow, come out and offer combat: 招架不住 cannot sustain the blows; (2) receive guests, see *-daih*, (2)↑; (3) (MC) to confess, (see *-rehn*↓): 他若欺心不架時 if he is dishonest and will not admit . . . .

招咎 *jau-jiouh*, v.i., give cause for blame or disaster.

招集 *jau'jir*, v.t., to assemble (men, members); call for conference.

招贅 *jaujueih*, v.i., see *-chin*↑.

招致 *jaujyh*, v.t., to invite (learned men) to serve at court or college.

招考 *jaukaau*, v.i. & n., (give) entrance examination.

招兒 *jau'l*, n., (1) (coll.) plan or strategy: 你出的好招兒 you have suggested a good plan; (2) posted bill, a signboard: 招貼, 招牌 *-tie, -'pair*↓.

招攬 *jaulaan*, v.t., (1) to invite (able men); (2) to extend business by securing new customers: 招攬生意.

招徠 *jaulai*, v.t., see *-jyh*↑.

招領 *jauliing*, v.t., to take home (lost child, dog, article) by presenting oneself as owner; advertise for owner of lost thing.

招募 *jaumuh*, v.t., to enlist men for army or other form of service.

招牌 *jau'pair*, n., a shop signboard; established trademark or trade name: 好招牌 a name or person enjoying popularity.

招盤 *jauparn*, v.i., to sell shop and contents to prospective buyer.

招惹 *jau're*, v.t., to provoke (person, resentment).

招認 *jaurehn*, v.i., to confess (crime); to claim (lost articles).

招生 *jau-sheng*, v.i., to hold entrance examinations, see *-kaau*↑.

招笑(兒) *jau-shiauh('l)*, v.i., to invite or provoke laughter: 你說話眞招笑兒 what you say is laughable.

招手兒 *jau-shoou'l*, v.i., to beckon with the hand.

招數 *jaushuh*, n., one move in boxing, see N. 1↑.

招說 *jau-shuo*, v.i., be annoying (as a too restless child).

招事 *jau-shyh*, v.i., cause trouble by reckless words or action.

招討 *jautaau*, v.t., to suppress (rebels) by force and calling for surrender.

招貼 *jautie*, n., bills on wall, billboards.

招提 *jautir*, n., (Budd.) a monastery; the Sangha or Buddhist Church (corruption from 拓鬬

提舍 Sanskr.—Katurdisa).

招子 *jautz*, n., (1) bills on walls; (2) shop sign.

招災 *jau-tzai*, v.i., to invite calamity.

招租 *jau-tzu*, v.i., (house) to let.

招眼 *jauyaan*, adj., conspicuous; 招眼毒 *--dur*, v.i., cause jealousy.

招邀 *jauyau*, v.t., to invite (to party, etc.).

招搖 *jauyaur*, v.i., show off, attract too much attention: 招搖(而)過市 pass along the streets dressed to attract attention; 招搖撞騙 to swindle by false pretenses.

招引 *jau'yiin*, v.i., see *-jyh*↑.

招怨 *jau-yuahn*, v.i., to cause hatred by reckless words or behavior.

据 10A.40-5

jyu.

[Pop. of 據 *jyuh* 10A.02]

拮据 *jierjyu*, adj., short of money.

捃 10A.40-5

jyuhn.

V.t. (LL) choose, select, see compp.↓.

捃華 *jyuhnhuar*, v.i., extract the essence, select the most essential points.

捃摭 *jyuhnjyr*, v.t., collect, gather (quotations, etc.).

捃拾 *jyuhnshyr*, v.t., ditto.

掊 10A.40-6

pour, *poou*.

V.t. (1) To attack physically: 掊擊 give blows, attack physically or verbally. (2) U.f. 抔 to cup (soil) in hand. (3) U.f. 裒 to gather, haul: 掊克 levy heavy taxes from people.

掂 10A.40-6

dian.

[Anc. var. 敁]

V.i. & t. To weigh in the hand, to estimate: 掂一掂有多重 weigh in hand and see how heavy it is; 掂斤播兩 to argue about little details (also wr. 掂兩).

掂對 *diandueih*, v.i., estimate and consider relative importance.

掂敠 *dianduo*, v.i., to estimate weight of s.t. held in hand; estimate and consider relative importance (also wr. 敁敠).

掂過兒 *dianguoh'l*, v.i., enumerate s.o.'s mistakes: 掂十來個過兒 has repeatedly mentioned some mistakes a dozen times.

掂算 *diansuahn*, v.i., estimate, calculate (costs, etc.).

搪 10A.40-6

tarng.

V.t. (1) To block: 搪差使 fulfill assignment nominally; 搪饑餓 stop hunger by eating s.t.; 搪賬 evade payment of debts; 再搪幾天 delay for a few days; 搪不住風雨 cannot keep out wind and rain; see 搪塞 *-seh*↓. (2) (MC) 搪酒吃 ask for wine.

搪塞 *tarngseh*, v.t., fulfill assignment nominally, use evasive answers.

搪瓷 *tarngtsyr*, n., enamelware.

搪突 *tarngtur*, v.t., see 唐突 61.40.

揢 10A.40-6

ker.

V.i. & t. (1) To catch in hand: 手裏揢着一大把錢 holds a lot of cash in his hand; catch, get stuck: 揢住他的喉嚨 s.t. caught in his throat; 抽屜揢住了, 打不開 drawer gets stuck. (2) To make difficulties for (person): 故意揢人 embarrass person on purpose.

拾 10A.40-8

shyr (**sheh*, **shy*).

V.t. (1) To pick up: 拾起來 pick it up; 拾人牙慧, 拾人唾餘 (contempt.) pick up what others say or write; 拾物招領 articles found, owner please contact; 拾金不昧 return money found; 拾級 (**sheh-jir*) 而登 mount up a flight of steps; 拾遺 *-yir*↓; 如俛拾芥 (AC) as easy as to pick dirt from the floor (芥 s.t. insignificant). (2) To gather: 揀拾 select and gather; 拾取 *-chyuu*↓; 收拾 put (room, objects) in order. (3) To turn (things) about: 拾翻 *-'fan*↓.

拾取 *shyrchyuu*, v.t., (1) collect, gather: 拾取風光月色 (LL) to take in and enjoy the air and the moon; (2) to pick up from the ground.

拾掇 *shyr'duo*, v.t., (1) to assemble and put to order; (2) to gather (sundry things, quotations); (3) to punish: 非拾掇拾掇他不可 must teach him a lesson.

拾翻 **shy'fan*, v.t., to turn upside down: 把一抽屜的東西都拾翻亂了 has turned over the contents of the drawer.

拾漏(兒)(子) *shyrlouh('l)(tz)*, v.i., to find a chance to pick up some money.

拾沒 *shyr'mo*, adj., (MC)＝什麼, 甚麽 what?

拾笑兒 *shyr-shiauh'l*, v.i., to join in laughter.

拾遺 *shyryir*, n. & v.i., (1) (to make) a supplement of omissions in some work; (2) to pick up lost articles.

捨 10A.40-8

shee.

V.t. (1) To part with (what is dear): 難分難捨 (of lovers) find it difficult to tear apart; 割捨 cut off (what is dear); 捨掉 abandon, forsake; 捨得, 捨不得 *-'de, -buh-der* ↓; 捨命 *-mihng* ↓; 捨死忘生 risk one's life for some worthy cause; 捨身救人 sacrifice one's life to save others; 捨生取義 prefer honor to life; 捨近取遠 go for the abstruse and forget the obvious; 捨己從人 give up one's own views and follow others. (2) To give alms: 捨粥, 捨飯 to give gruel or rice to the poor; 施捨 give alms, contribute to a monastery.

捨不得 *shee-buh-der*, v.t., loath to give up: 捨不得去 unwilling to go; 捨不得放 unwilling to let go.

捨棄 *sheechih*, v.t., to abandon (lover), cut out (bad habits), give up (one's contention).

捨得 *shee'de*, v.i., (1) be willing to give up or away: 捨得一個假期 sacrifice a holiday (for some work); (2) can be parted with; see *-buh-der* ↑.

捨哥兒 *shee'ge'l*, n., (coll.) a hapless and friendless person.

捨著 *shee'je*, v.i., (MC) forced to part with s.t.: 捨著還了他十兩金子 had to return him ten ounces of gold.

捨命 *shee-mihng*, adv., at the risk of one's life (＝拼命).

捨身 *shee-shen*, v.i., (Budd. & gen.) risk one's life to (save others, country).

搶 10A.40-8

chiaang (**chiang*).

V.i. & t. (1) To rob, loot, take by violence: 搶奪, 搶掠 *-duor, -lyueh* ↓; 搶親 capture bride from bride's family for wedding (by those too poor to pay for ceremony), see 搶婚 *-hun* ↓; 搶東西 scramble for things in a riot or fracas; 搶來的 obtained by loot or scramble. (2) To wrangle for first place: 搶先 compete in being the first to; 搶前發言 (several persons) try to speak first; 搶盡鏡頭 phr., steal the spotlight; 搶出風頭 try to outshine others. (3) To rush in an emergency: 搶上幾步 rush forward a few steps; 搶修河隄 rush to repair dykes; 搶購物品 rush to buy up things (anticipating higher prices, etc.); 搶救 *-jiouh* ↓. (4) To bruise: 搶破皮 bruise skin. (5) To sharpen (knives, scissors). (6) (**chiang*) To brave: 搶風 brave the wind; 搶鋒陷陣 to smash into enemy ranks. (7) (**chiang* or **chuaang*) 頭搶地 knock head on the ground.

搶案 *chiaang-ahn*, n., a case of robbery.

搶背 *chiaangbeih*, v.i., (old opera) a way of somersault landing on one's back.

搶白 *chiaangbor*, v.t., berate (person) openly, cut short abruptly: 被他搶白了一頓 was cut short by him rudely, berated.

搶奪 *chiaangduor*, v.i. & t., to loot; to wrangle for (profit, power, territory).

搶鋒 *chiaangfeng*, v.i., (callig.) a stroke made by reversing tip of brush, dist. 順鋒.

搶購 *chiaanggouh*, v.t., to rush to buy, anticipating scarcity.

搶婚 *chiaang-hun*, v.i., to kidnap or carry off a woman and marry her.

搶紅 *chiaanghurng*, n., a form of dice game.

搶劫 *chiaangjier*, v.t., to rob, commit robbery.

搶救 *chiaangjiouh*, v.t., rush to save (from fire, flood).

搶掠(略) *chiaanglyueh*, v.t., to loot (town, village).

搶嘴 *chiarngtzueei*, v.t., (several persons) shout and talk in confusion.

括 10A.40-9

gua (also *kuoh*).

V.t. (1) Include, enclose, embrace, comprise: 包括 consist of; 總括 to sum up; 囊括 bag everything, monopolize. (2) Scrape up or together: 搜括 ransack, be carpetbagger. (3) To tie, fasten: 括髮 (AC) bind up the hair with hemp as a symbol of mourning.

括搭 *gua'da*, v.t., as in 括搭着臉 pull a long face.

括號 *guahauh*, n., brackets or parentheses (also 括弧).

括弧 *guahur*, n., (＝括號), see *hauh* ↑.

抬 10A.40-9

tair.

[Pop. of 擡 10A.11]

擔 10A.40-9

dan (as vb.), **dahn* (as n.).

[Pop. 担]

N. (1) (**dahn*) (*-tz*) A carrier load, two units on ends of pole carried on shoulder: 一擔菜, 米 such a load of vegetables, rice; 擔擔子 *dan*dahntz*, carry a load; 扁擔, 擔杆 carrying pole. (2) A picul, unit of measure.

V.t. (1) Carry, bear (lit. & fig.): 擔水, 米 carry water, rice; 擔水向河頭賣 carry coal to Newcastle; 擔得動, 不動 can or cannot, lift up and carry; 擔得起, 不起 can, cannot bear responsibility, oft. 擔當, 擔待 (得起, 不起) *-dang*, *-daih* ↓; take blame for: 擔錯, 擔不是 take blame for mistakes; 擔是不擔錯 will take credit for what is right, but not bear blame for mistakes; 擔處分 will bear responsibility if s.t. fails. (2) Suffer, endure: 擔風, 擔險 endure hardships of weather, risks; 擔驚 bear the worries, be exposed to fears; 擔心 *-shin* ↓.

擔 保 *danbaau*, v.t. & n., guarantee: 擔保你沒事 guarantee you will not be in trouble; 擔保人 be guarantor.

擔 承 *dancherng*, v.t., shoulder up responsibility: 擔承責任, see *-dang*, *-daih* ↓.

擔 待 *dandaih*, v.t., 擔: see V.t. 1↑; 擔待 (擔起, 不起) can, cannot bear responsibility (also 擔當 *-dang*).

擔 負 *danfuh*, v.t., carry (burden, responsibility).

擔 擱 *dan'ge*, v.i. & t., delay: 擔擱一件事 cause s.t. to be delayed; usu. wr. 躭擱, 耽擱.

擔 荷 *dahnheh*, v.t. & n., (carry) burden.

擔 架 牀 *danjiah-chuarng*, n., stretcher.

擔 任 *danrehn*, v.t., fill (post), take charge of (responsibility): 擔任賬項 take charge of accounts; 擔任秘書 act as secretary.

擔 心 *danshin*, v.i., worry, be worried: 不必擔心 don't worry.

擔 憂 *danyou*, v.i., be worried.

§ 10A.41 (扌/図)

揞 10A.41-1

jy.

V.t. Var. of 支; 揞起來＝支起來; 揞頤 (＝支頤) cheek in hand.

描 10A.41-2

miaur.

V.i. & t. Portray, describe: 描像 depict portrait; 細描 depict in fine detail.

描 畫 *miaurhuah*, n. & v.i. & t., depict by words or painting; trace (painting, design).

描 金 *miaurjin*, adj., (of furniture) painted with gold lines.

描 摹 *miaurmor*, v.t., describe by words or painting.

描 寫 *miaurshiee*, v.t. & n., describe, description: 描寫人物 delineation of characters in fiction.

拑 10A.41-2

chiarn.

[Interch. 鉗 81A.21]

措 10A.41-2

tsuoh.

V.i. & t. (1) To handle, put in place, dispose of properly: 措辭 *-tsyr* ↓; put in execution: 措置, 措施 *-jyh*, *-shy* ↓; 措手 *-shoou* ↓; 手足無措, 不知所措 do not know what to do; 籌措 to manage, make preparations, esp. secure funds. (2) (AC) abandon: 學之弗能, 弗措也 if you find s.t. difficult to learn, do not give up.

措 大 *tsuohdah*, n., (contempt. also 窮措大) a penniless fellow.

措 置 *tsuohjyh*, v.i. & t. & n., execute (affairs), -tion: 措置失宜 mismanagement.

措 手 *tsuohshoou*, v.i., to handle: 無所措手 do not know what to do ("lay hands on"); 措手不及 too late to do anything about it.

措 施 *tsuohshy*, n., manner or measures of execution (of plans, policies).

措 辭 *tsuoh-tsyr*, (1) n., the wording (of statement); (2) v.i., to word (a text, a complaint, etc.).

措 意 *tsuoh-yih*, v.i., to pay attention to (matter): 不甚措意 do not pay much attention.

指 10A.41-2

jyy.

N. Finger: 指頭 *-'tou* ↓; 拇指 thumb; 食指 index finger; 中指 middle finger; 無名指 ring finger; 小指 little finger; 腳指 toe; 指甲 *-'jia* ↓ 屈指可數 can count on the fingers of a hand; 指不勝屈 too many to count (on the fingers); 食指浩繁 many mouths to feed; 染指 have a finger in the pie; 彈指間 at the snap of a finger, instantly.

V.i. & t. (1) To point at, point to: 指着 pointing at; 向前指 point forward; 指手畫腳, 指天畫地 point right and left, gesticulate wildly; 指天誓日 swear by the heaven and sun as witness; 十手所指 target of public accusation. (2) To point out, indicate, to show, demonstrate: 指示, 指明, 指點, 指導 *-shyh*[1], *-mirng*[2], *-diaan*,

指 揩 抽

-dauh↓; 指桑罵槐, 指雞罵狗 scold, abuse person by ostensibly pointing to s.o. else; 指東説西 make concealed reference to s.t.; 指鹿爲馬 (AC allu.) a trick by ancient premier 趙高 to demand absolute agreement by pointing at a deer and calling it a horse and killing those who disagreed. (3) To count on s.t.: 指望 -'wahng↓; 就指着這點錢度日 depend on this money for expenses; 指日可成 can finish in a few days (on definite date). (4) (Var. of 旨) aim at: 指趣, 指要, 指歸 -chyuh, -yauh, -guei↓.

指標 *jyybiau*, n., an index sign; (math.) characteristic.

指斥 *jyychyh*, v.t., to censure (person, act), denounce, blame.

指趣 *jyychyuh*, n., essential idea (旨趣 preferred).

指導 *jyydauh*, v.t., to guide, advise (person).

指點 *jyrdiaan*(-'*dian*), v.t., to point out (mistakes, pitfalls), to advise, give guidance; 指點兒 -*diaa'l*, (pop.) point out and identify criminal by witness.

指定 *jyydihng*, v.t., assign (date, person).

指歸 *jyyguei*, n., concourse where all points meet; main drift or tenet.

指顧 *jyyguh*, phr., as in 指顧間 in a short while, before you turn your back.

指骨 *jyrguu*, n., finger bones, phalange.

指畫 *jyyhuah*, n., finger painting, with fingers in place of brush.

指環 *jyyhuarn*, n., ring (on finger).

指揮 *jyyhuei*¹, (1) v.t., to direct (as with sword on battlefield); to conduct (performance); to command (a big army); (2) n., 指揮官 commanding officer; 總指揮 commander in chief; 指揮刀 officer's sword; 指揮 conductor; 指揮棒 conductor's baton; 指揮艙 (astron.) command module.

指麾 *jyyhuei*², v.t., to direct (as with a flag on battlefield); see -*huei*¹↑.

指掌 *jyr-jaang*, phr., usu. in 瞭如指掌 clear like pointing at a palm; 易如指掌 easy as pointing at a palm.

指摘 *jyyjer*, v.t., point out (faults).

指甲 *jyy'jia*, n., fingernails; 指甲套兒 fingernail protector; 指甲草 balsam, used for dyeing fingernails; 指甲油 nail polish.

指教 *jyyjiauh*, v.t., instruct, advise, oft. used courteously to ask for opinion: 請你多多指教.

指囷 *jyy jyun*, phr., (AC, allu.) help friend in need.

指令 *jyylihng*, v.t. & n., to issue government order to party concerned; such issue.

指迷 *jyy-mir*, phr., 指迷津 help one realize one's error ("point out the ferry").

指名 *jyy-mirng*¹, phr., with direct mention of person's name (in accusation, etc.).

指明 *jyymirng*², v.t., to demonstrate (correct, incorrect points), point out, indicate.

指摹 *jyymor*, n., fingerprint (also wr. 指模), see -*yihn*↓.

指南 *jyynarn*, n., a guidebook (to place, language, subject.); 指南針 mariner's compass.

指書 *jyy-shu*, n., writing with finger in place of brush; cf. -*huah*↑.

指數 *jyyshuh*, n., (math.) exponent, index; index number.

指示 *jyyshyh*¹, n. & v.t., an instruction, see -*jiauh*↑; advise, instruct (way to do it).

指事 *jyyshyh*², n., one of the six principles (see 六ᐞ書 60.80) of formation of Chin. characters —a compound pictograph, as 上下 "above" "below."

指使 *jyrshyy*, v.t., to direct, esp. behind the scene; to instigate.

指算 *jyysuahn*, n., counting by fingers; use of abacus.

指沓 *jyytah*, n., thimble (also wr. 揸).

指頭 *jyy'tou*, n., finger; 指頭肚兒 base joint of finger which slightly bulges out.

指責 *jyytzer*, v.t., see -*chyh*↑.

指望 *jyy'wahng*, v.i., to hope: 指望成功 hope for, look forward to, success; 指望兒子成家立業 look forward to the time when (the son) will marry and settle down; 指望兒 one's hope.

指紋 *jyywern*, n., fingerprint; 指紋學 dactylography.

指要 *jyy-yauh*, n., outline, essentials (of a subject).

指印 *jyy-yihn*, n., fingerprint, see -*wern*↑.

指引 *jyryiin*, n. & v.t., guidance; to guide.

揩 10A.41-2

kai (*ka).

V.i. & t. Wipe (face, tears, window, table).

揩油 *kai-your* (*ka-*), v.i. & t., to sponge, get s.t. from friend free (such as meal, trip, articles): 揩他的油 sponge on him.

抽 10A.41-2

chou.

V.i. & t. (1) To draw in many senses: 抽烟 to smoke; 抽水 to pump water; 抽籤 -*chian*↓; 抽刀, 抽劍 draw a knife, sword; 抽血 draw blood (for blood test); 抽膿 drain the pus; 抽鼻兒 blow the nose. (2) To take part or percentage from a lot: 抽税 -*shueih*↓; 抽丁 -*ding*↓; 抽二成 take 20%; 抽+vb. to take random sample or draw lots by turn: 抽換, 抽選 -*huahn*, -*shyuaan*↓. (3) To put forth: 抽芽 put forth sprouts: 抽絲 draw out thread (as cocoon). (4) To lash, beat: 抽他一下 give him a lash, as with whip. (5) To have spasms: 抽筋, 抽瘋 -*jin*, -*feng*¹↓. (6) To gasp, sob: 抽抽噎噎 to sob; 抽氣 -*chih*↓. (7) Drive (ball) in tennis and table-tennis.

抽查 *chou-char*, v.t., to inspect by random samples.

抽籤(兒) *chou-chian*(-*chia'l*), v.i., to draw lots; to draw divination

A

sticks before Buddha.

抽氣 *chou-chih*, v.i., to gasp; 抽氣機 air pump.

抽抽(兒) *chou'chou('l)*, v.i., (1) to shrink: 越抽抽越小 shrink smaller and smaller; (2) 抽抽噎噎, 抽抽搭搭 to sob intermittently.

抽出 *chou-chu*, v.t., (1) to draw out (as from casing, drawer); (2) to select from a lot.

抽搭 *chou'da*, v.i., make intermittent sobs; also 抽抽搭搭.

抽打 *choudaa*, (1) v.t., to whip (s.o.); (2) (*'da*) to beat clothing to remove dust.

抽丁 *chou-ding*, v.i., to conscript men for government service.

抽斗 *choudoou*, n., (shanghai dial.) a drawer (=-*'ti*↓).

抽分 *choufen*, n., a percentage, commission fee or discount; formerly, levy on commercial goods.

抽瘋 *choufeng*[1], (1) n., spasms, cramps; (2) v.i., (abusive) behave abominably.

抽豐 *choufeng*[2], v.t., take a cut on purchase, etc.: 打抽豐 try to get a cut or get gifts, money from master.

抽個兒 *chou-geh'l*, v.i., to dilute or otherwise reduce value of package.

抽換 *chouhuahn*, v.t., to replace parts of a whole.

抽筋(兒) *chou-jin(-jie'l)*, v.i., to have spasms.

抽縐(兒) *chou'jou('l)*, v.i., to shrivel up.

抽考 *chou-kaau*, v.i., to make sample examinations.

抽空兒 *chou-kuhng'l*, v.i., take advantage of any free time (to write letters, etc.).

抽冷子 *chouleengtz*, adv., to strike at unexpected moment, unexpectedly.

抽身 *chou-shen*, v.i., to leave the place: 抽身不得 cannot leave place to do s.t. else.

抽象 *choushiahng*, adj., abstract: 抽象名詞 abstract nouns; 抽象畫 abstract painting.

抽閒 *chou-shiarn*, v.i., see -*kuhng'l* ↑.

抽水 *chou-shueei*, v.i., (1) to pump water; (2) to take a percentage (as in gambling house.); 抽水機 a water pump; 抽水馬桶 flush toilet.

B

抽稅 *chou shueih*, v.i., to levy tax.

抽選 *choushyuaan*, v.t., to select from a lot.

抽屜 *chou'ti*, n., a desk drawer.

抽條 *chou-tiaur*, v.i., to dilute or otherwise reduce the contents of package.

抽頭兒 *choutour'l*, v.i. & n., (the banker in gambling) takes a percentage.

抽簪 *choutzan*, v.i., (LL) to resign from office (remove a hairpin which was symbol of an official).

抽演 *chouyaan*, v.t., (LL) to amplify (meaning).

抽烟 *chou-yan*, v.i., to smoke.

抽印本 *chouyihn-been*, n., reprint of magazine article.

擋 10A.41-2

daang (*dahng*).

[Pop. var. 擋]

N. 擋箭牌 shield; pretext.

V.t. (1) (*daang*) Block off, ward off (blow): 擋住; 擋路 block off road, to hold up, to hold back; 擋橫, 擋駕; see 擋 10A.63. (2) (*dahng*) See 摒[Δ]擋 10A.20.

搢 10A.41-3

jihn.

V.t. (AC) (1) To stick into. (2) To shake.

搢紳 *jihnshen*, n., the officialdom, the gentry (lit., "tablet and sash"); 搢紳錄 --*luh*, an official (social) register (also 縉紳).

C

擂 10A.41-3

leir.

N. Pestle: 擂鉢 motar and pestle; 擂搥 pestle for pounding.

V.t. To beat: 擂鼓 beat a drum; 擂鼓篩鑼 make a fuss about trifles; 擂磚 (of beggars) beat one's breast with a brick to arouse pity.

擂臺 *leihtair*, n., a stage on which challenge fights of boxing are fought: 打擂臺 a challenge fight between two boxers.

捆 10A.41-4

kuun.

N. (-*tz*, *'l*) A bundle (of hemp, firewood, beddings, etc.).

V.t. (1) To tie into a bundle, to bind, tie up, truss up (person). (2) (AC) 捆屨 to make hemp sandals.

摑 10A.41-4

guor.

V.t. To slap, to box the ears: 摑他一掌 give him a slap on the face; 掌摑 ditto.

摺 10A.41-5

jer.

N. (1) A folder, a folded brochure: 摺子 -*tz*↓; 存摺 or 存款摺 a passbook for bank deposits; 奏摺 a

抽
擋
搢
擂
捆
摑
摺

亅	小	⺊	十	土	ナ	廾	乚	丨	一	丅	乛	口	図	冈	𠃌	厂	尸	亠	广	宀	丶	乚	弋	心	八	人	乂	乛	𠂉	丿	𠂉	く
00	01	02	10	11	12	20	21	22	30	31	32	40	41	42	50	51	52	60	61	62	63	70	71	72	80	81	82	83	90	91	92	93

memorial to the throne. (2) A folding mark, a fold: 摺兒 -'l↓.

V.t. To fold or fold up: 摺紙 to fold paper.

摺尺 *jerchyy*, n., a folding rule.
摺刀 *jerdau*, n., a folding knife, pocket knife.
摺疊 *jerdier*, v.t. & n., to fold several times, a manifold.
摺兒 *jer'l*, n., a fold, folding: 打摺兒 make fold; 有摺兒 has a folding mark.
摺扇 *jershahn*, n., a folding fan.
摺子 *jertz*, n., (1) a folded booklet, like a passbook, which opens up as a continuous page; (2) a folding mark; (3) 奏摺 a memorial.
摺奏 *jertzouh*, n., a memorial to the throne.

揞 10A.41-6

aan.

[Related 按 10A.93]

V.i. & t. To press firmly with hand (as in rubbing ointment); cover up, as with plaster.

搐 10A.41-6

chuh (*chou*).

V.i. (Of muscles) to twitch: 抽搐 have muscular spasms.

攟 10A.41-6

jyuhn.

V.t. To gather, collect (material; interch. 捃).

播 10A.41-9

boh.

V.i. & t. (1) To cast, sow, broadcast, make known abroad, spread: 播種 sow seeds by scattering; 播道 spread gospel; 傳△播 91A.00 spread religion, disseminate ideas, news; 廣△播 61.80 broadcast; 轉播 relay broadcast; 收播 receive broadcast. (2) Move about, see 播遷 -*chian*↓.

播遷 *bohchian*, v.i., (of peoples, clans) migrate.
播蕩 *bohdahng*, v.i., wander about, cf. 簸△盪 92A.82.
播放 *bohfahng*, v.t., broadcast (news, etc.) on the air.
播種機 *bohjueng-ji*, n., machine for sowing seeds.
播弄 *bohluhng*, v.t., esp. in 播弄是非 spread unfounded rumors.
播送 *bohsuhng*, v.t., broadcast news.
播影 *bohyihng*, v.t., broadcast on television.
播音 *bohyin*, v.i., broadcast on the air; 播音劇 --*jyuh*, n., radio plays; 播音員 --*yuarn*, n., announcer.

拍 10A.41-9

pai (occa. *paih*, **poh*).

N. (Mus.) A beat: 一拍, 兩拍, 拍節.

V.i. & t. (1) To beat, clap, tap lightly: 拍(巴)掌, 拍手 clap hands in applause or to keep rhythm; 拍門 knock at door; 拍桌子 strike the table in anger; 拍案 -*ahn*↓. (2) To take certain actions: 拍照 to take a photo; 拍電 to send a telegram; 拍球 to play ball game; 拍老腔兒 to play the old tune, i.e., to talk like a Dutch uncle. In many cases interch. with 打.

拍案 *pai-ahn*, v.i., (LL) strike table in joy, surprise, anger; 拍案驚奇 name of collection of short stories.
拍板 *paibaan*, n., musical clapping board for indicating rhythm; such rhythm created; v.i., to beat time.
拍打 *paidaa*, v.i., tap lightly.
拍花子 *paihuatz*, n., (dial.) swindler supposed to kidnap children by narcotic.
拍節 *paijier*, n., time rhythm: 拍節稱賞 clap hands in appreciation; 拍節器 n., metronome.
拍馬(屁) *paimaa*(*pih*), v.t., (coll., vulgar) to flatter (person): 拍他的馬屁 flatter him.
拍賣 *paimaih*, n. & v.i., auction, sell by auction.
拍子 *paitz*, n., (mus.) a beat.
拍網子 *paiwaangtz*, n., snare for birds; (fig.) swindle in confidence game by showing off wealth.

揝 10A.41-9

tzuahn.

V.t. (＝攥) Lay hold of: 揝拳頭 clench one's fist; 揝不住 slip away from grasp; 揝着筆 grip a pen.

§10A.42 (扌/冈)

捕 10A.42-1

buu.

V.t. Catch: 捕盜, 魚, 鳥, 蛇 catch thieves, fish, birds, snakes; 捕食 (of birds and animals) prey for food; 捕生 hunt animals as a living; 捕風捉影 catch at shadows, make accusations on hearsay.

捕蟲網 *buuchurng-waang*, n., net for catching insects.

捕房 *buufarng*, n., police station, from 巡捕 *shyurn-*, police.

捕獲 *buu-huoh*, v.t., succeed in catching (thieves, booty).

捕鯨船 *buu-jing-chuarn*, n., whaler (ship).

捕快 *buukuaih*, n., formerly, constable (sheriff) for catching criminals.

捕手 *burshoou*, n., (baseball) the catcher.

捕頭 *buutour*, n., formerly, head constable.

捕役 *buuyih*, n., constable.

捕蠅紙 *buu-yirng-jyy*, n., fly-paper.

搆 10A.42-2

gouh.

V.t. (1) To pull, haul, drag: 搆不着 cannot reach it. (2) Var. of 構 10B.42.

捎 10A.42-2

kehn.

V.i. & t. To force, to use means or subterfuge to make one do s.t.: 捎勒 force (contribution); 捎留 force one to stay; 捎阻 obstruct; 捎贖 force ransom; 這孩子, 好捎人 this child bothers and begs until he gets what he wants.

捎 10A.42-2

shau (**shauh*).

V.i. & t. (1) To brush against: 横捎 brush past; 被老鷹捎了一翅膀 the eagle's wing brushed against (it). (2) (Coll.) to bring along, carry: 捎信, 捎個信兒來 bring along a message or letter; 捎帶 *-daih* ↓. (3) (**shauh*) To catch raindrops: 這落地窗會捎雨 this French window will get wet in case of rain. (4) (**shauh*) To glance at: 往後捎着點 give a quick glance back. (5) (**shauh*) See 捎色, 捎馬子 *-shaai*, *-maatz* ↓.

捎帶 *shau(')daih*, (1) v.t., to bring or carry along (an article); (2) 捎帶着 adv., while one is on it; 這件事他捎帶着就辦了 he will do it while on the job (without special effort); 捎帶腳兒逛公園 took a stroll in the park while on the way (to an invitation).

捎間(兒) *shaujian(-jia'l)*, n., a backroom, usu. connected with parlor and smaller.

捎馬子 *shauhmaatz*, *n.*, a saddlebag.

捎色 *shauh-shaai*, v.i., to fade in color.

揣 10A.42-2

chuaai.

V.i. & t. To estimate, calculate, reckon: 揣度, 揣摩, 揣測 *-duoh*, *-'mor*, *-tseh* ↓.

揣度 *chuaaiduoh*, v.i. & t., to reckon (another's motive), to conjecture.

揣骨 *chuair-guu*, v.i., to read character and tell fortune by studying person's bone structure.

揣摩 *chuaai'mor*, v.i., (1) see *-duoh* ↑; (2) to study intensively a sentence and elicit its meaning.

揣測 *chuaaitseh*, v.i., see *-duoh* ↑.

擕 10A.42-2

shi (sp. pr. *shier*).

[Pop. 携, 攜, 擕]

V.t. (1) To carry by the hand, to bring: 擕款潛逃 abscond with funds; 提擕 to help a younger man; 擕眷同行 travel with one's family; 擕帶 *-daih* ↓. (2) Join hands, see 擕手 *-shoou* ↓. (3) (AC) turn away from person in loyalty: 擕貳 *-ehl* ↓.

擕帶 *shidaih*, v.t., to carry (s.t.) on body or on journey (luggage, etc.).

擕貳 *shi-ehl*, v.i., (AC) to show disloyalty at heart.

擕手 *shi-shoou*, v.i., (1) to join hands: 擕手同行 walk hand in hand; (2) (of factions) join hands in cooperation.

擩 10A.42-3

ruh.

V.t. (LL) Immerse, moisten.

捅 10A.42-3

tuung.

V.t. (coll.) To poke, stir up, shove: 捅馬峰窩 stir up a hornets' nest; 捅樓子 (coll.) stir up trouble; 捅出禍來 ditto; 捅破, 捅穿 poke a hole, poke through; 捅他一刀 stab him, to cut or slash; 捅窟窿 poke a hole, (fig.) incur debt.

捅球 *tuungchiour*, v.i. & n., (coll.) (to play) billiard.

捐 10A.42-4

jyuan.

亅	小	⺊	十	土	ナ	廾	⺊	丨	一	丅	フ	口	区	冈	㇆	厂	尸	亠	广	宀	丶	乚	七	心	八	人	乂	乛	一	リ	⺊	く
00	01	02	10	11	12	20	21	22	30	31	32	40	41	42	50	51	52	60	61	62	63	70	71	72	80	81	82	83	90	91	92	93

捐 搰 搞 摘 摛 掮 搠

N. A temporary or special tax: 稅捐 taxes, duties; 房捐 a special tax on houses.

V.i. & t. (1) Donate, contribute: 捐助 *-juh*, 捐輸 *-shu*, 捐款 *-kuaan*↓; 樂捐 voluntary contribution; 捐錢 donate money; 募捐 launch a financial drive, solicit funds; 捐血 to donate blood. (2) Purchase an official appointment: 捐班 *-ban*, 捐納 *-nah*↓. (3) Cast away: 捐棄 *-chih*↓.

捐班(兒) *jyuanban(-ba'l)*, n., formerly, a title or post purchased with money.

捐棄 *jyuanchih*, v.t., throw away, get rid of.

捐軀 *jyuan-chyu*, v.i., die for a worthy cause or one's country.

捐館 *jyuanguaan*, v.i., (litr. euphem.) die ("leave one's abode for good").

捐助 *jyuanjuh*, v.t., make financial contributions to.

捐款 *jyuankuaan*, v.i. & n., contribute money, money contributed.

捐納 *jyuannah*, v.i., purchase an office or title.

捐生 *jyuan-sheng*, v.i., to sacrifice one's life.

捐輸 *jyuanshu*, v.i., make financial contributions to the government.

捐稅 *jyuansueih*, n., duties and taxes.

捐冊 *jyuantseh*, n., a book listing contributors and their contributions.

捐貲 *jyuantzy*, n., donate funds (also wr. 資).

搰 10A.42-4

hur.

[Related 掘 10A.21]

V.t. To dig: 狐埋狐搰 a fox buries things and again digs them up—change one's mind constantly.

搰摟 *hur'lu*, v.i. & t., (coll.) to rub tenderly (baby's skin, etc., also wr. 胡嚕).

搞 10A.42-6

gaau.

V.i. & t. (1) (Vern.) do, be engaged in (some task), carry out, busy oneself with, eke out a living; to play (tricks): 搞得不壞 be doing quite well, can make a decent living; 近來搞得怎麽樣 how have you been doing lately? 這幾天搞些什麽 what have you been busying with in the last few days? 搞了半天也沒搞好 have been trying to fix s.t. up for a long time but have not succeeded; 他又在搞鬼 he is again playing one of his tricks; 搞錢 make money; 搞政治 to play politics; 搞花樣 to play tricks, cheat, deceive; 搞不通 can never make sense of s.t.; 搞不清 perplexed, to wonder; 搞報紙 run a newspaper. (2) Disrupt, stir up, demoralize, make a mess of: 這消息搞得人心不安 the news has had the effect of demoralizing the people, has made people jittery; 被你搞亂了 you've disrupted everything.

搞垮 *gaurkuaa*, v.t., to destroy, to disrupt, overthrow (s.o. in position).

摘 10A.42-6

jer (sp. pr. **jai*).

V.t. (1) To pick (flowers, fruit) with hand, to take down: 摘下來 pick off (flowers); 摘帽 to take off hat; 摘招牌 "take down shop's signboard"—greatly damage reputation; 摘紗帽, 摘頂戴 deprive official of rank (used like "defrock" a priest); 摘印 to take away the official seal—deprive of post. (2) To select, make excerpt extract: 文摘 a digest, collection of selected articles; 摘錄, 摘要, 摘由, 摘選 *-luh*, *-yauh*, *-your*, *-shyuaan*↓. (3) (Re. pr. only) to point out, specify (mistakes): 指摘 point out (mistakes); 摘發 make charges (of crimes). (4) (Sp. pr. only) to borrow: 摘借 *-jieh*↓.

摘借 **jaijieh*, v.i., to borrow from various sources.

摘錄 *jerluh*, v.t. & n., to record excerpts (of speech, etc.).

摘選 **jairshyuaan* (*jer-*), v.t. & n., (to make) selections.

摘要 *jeryauh*, n. & v.t., digest (of book, articles).

摘由(兒) *jeryour('l)*, n., a résumé or digest of official communication prepared for superior.

摛 10A.42-6

chy.

V.i. To brandish (pen), flourish.

摛翰 *chyhahn*, v.i., (LL) to brandish a pen, to write.

摛詞 *chytsyr*, v.i., (LL) to weave an ornate passage.

摛藻 *chytzaau*, n., (LL) writing with a flourish.

掮 10A.42-6

chiarn.

V.t. To carry (rifle, load, etc.) on the shoulder; 掮木梢 (Shanghai dial.) be made a fool of.

掮客 *chiarnkeh*, n., a broker.

搠 10A.42-8

shuoh.

V.t. (1) To stab as with spear. (2) To apply (mud, color), cf. 塑 80.11.

掄 10A.42–8

lurn (**lun*).

V.i. & t. (1) (**lun*) To flourish, swing (a sword, staff, etc.): 掄拳 (boxing) make a circular movement before striking blow. (2) To select: 掄才 (or 材) select talent (for office). (3) Squander (money).

擒 10A.42–8

chirn.

V.t. To seize (as bird of prey), to capture (culprit, enemy): 生擒活捉 to capture alive; 擒賊先擒王 destroy the leader and the gang will collapse; 就擒 submit to arrest.

擒捉 *chirnjuo*, v.t., to seize (thief, etc.).

擒拿 *chirnnar*, v.t., to arrest (culprit).

擒縱 *chirntzuhng*, v.t., as in 擒縱自如 arrest and release at will—in perfect control of situation.

撟 10A.42–9

jiauh (**jiaau*).

V.i. & t. (1) (**jiaau*) U.f. 矯 92S.42. (2) (**jiauh*) To lift up, raise, curl up: see compp.↓.

撟捷 *jiauhjieir*, v.i. & adj., agile, alert and nimble.

撟舌 *jiauhsher*, v.i., be struck dumb, tongue-tied.

§ 10A.50 (扌/乛)

拷 10A.50–1

kaau.

V.t. Beat up (prisoner).

拷貝 *kaaubeih*, n., (translit.) copy, a film print; 拷貝筆 copy pencil.

拷打 *kaurdaa*, n. & v.t., subject (prisoner) to third degree, beat up (prisoner). 「↓.

拷訊 *kaaushyuhn*, v.t., see *-wehn*

拷問 *kaauwehn*, v.t., cross-examine, including torture.

擄 10A.50–2

luu (also *luoo*).

V.t. To capture (prisoners): 擄獲 capture (prisoners, booty).

擄掠 *luulyueh*, v.t., to take captives and ransack (city, people).

據 10A.50–2

jyuh.

[Pop. of 據 10A.02]

攜 10A.50–2

shi (sp. pr. *sher*).

[Var. of 攜, 携; pop. of 攜]

扔 10A.50–3

reng (also *reeng*).

V.t. (1) Throw away, cast aside: 扔過去 hurl over; 扔石子 throw stones; 扔球 (ball games) pitch (throw) the ball; 用完卽扔 discard after using. (2) Abandon, leave behind: 他扔下我走了 he went away without taking me along; 那些行李還在外面扔着呢 the baggage is still lying about abandoned; 扔崩 to desert, forsake; 扔在街上 leave on the street; 扔開 leave on one side; 扔掉了 have discarded; 扔棄 get rid of.

拐 10A.50–4

guaai.

N. Var. of 枴 10B.50.

V.i. & t. (1) V.t., obtain (s.t.) by fraud, to cheat, to swindle: 拐騙, 拐帶, 拐賣 *-piahn*, *-daih*, *-maih*↓; 拐走了不少東西 have absconded with many things. (2) V.i., to act like an Indian giver: 送他點禮, 倒拐回來許多東西 gave him some small gift and brought home a number of return gifts. (3) V.i., make turns in walking: see 拐彎兒 *-wa'l*↓: 拐彎兒抹角兒 follow the turns of the path; 拐來拐去 turn this way and that; 拐過來, 拐過去 ditto; 向左拐 turn to the left; 右拐彎 turn to the right; 拐回來 turn back.

拐帶 *guaaidaih*, v.t., to kidnap (a person) or abscond with (s.t.) valuable.

拐孤 *guaai'gu*, adj., odd, whimsical: 那人脾氣很拐孤 that man

捌 掄 擒 撟 拷 擄 據 攜 扔 拐

亅	小	⺊	十	土	ナ	卄	⺊	丨	一	丅	フ	口	区	冈	㇆	厂	尸	亠	广	宀	丶	乚	弋	心	八	人	乂	乛	一	ノ	㇀	く
00	01	02	10	11	12	20	21	22	30	31	32	40	41	42	50	51	52	60	61	62	63	70	71	72	80	81	82	83	90	91	92	93

is rather peculiar.

拐杖 *guaaijahng*, n., a walking stick, cane.

拐角兒 *guairjiaau'l*, (1) v.i., make just one turn; (2) adj., situated at the corner: 拐角兒上那家店舖 the shop just around the street corner.

拐賣 *guaaimaih*, v.t., kidnap (s.o.) or abscond with (s.t.) for sale.

拐騙 *guaaipiahn*, v.t., to swindle.

拐子 *guaaitz*, n., a kidnaper.

拐彎兒 *guaaiwa'l*, adj., (1) making turns in walking; (2) where the road turns; (3) speaking indirectly or hinting: 這個人說話總愛拐彎兒抹角兒的 the man will always beat around the bush; (4) (of numbers) more than: 這本新書比那本舊的貴兩倍還要拐彎兒 the new book costs more than double the old one.

拇 10A.50-4

muu.

N. Thumb: 拇指 *-jyy*.

揭 10A.50-4

jie.

N. A surname.

V.t. (1) Hoist, raise, lift: 揭開鍋蓋 lift up the pot cover; 揭竿 *-gan* ↓. (2) Proclaim, announce: 揭櫫 *-ju*, 揭曉 *-shiaau* ↓. (3) Expose, disclose, uncover, unveil: 揭露 *-luh*, 揭穿 *-chuan*, 揭開 *-'kai*, 揭破 *-poh* ↓.

揭榜 *jiebaang*, v.i., announce the results of an examination.

揭白 *jie-bair*, v.i., draw the likeness of a dead person's facial appearance.

揭裱 *jiebiaau*, v.t., take off from old mount and mount anew (scrolls).

揭穿 *jiechuan*, v.t., bare, expose (secret).

揭短(兒) *jie-duaan(-duaa'l)*, v.i., expose s.o.'s weaknesses.

揭發 *jiefa*, v.t., to disclose, to reveal (secret, scandal).

揭竿 *jiegan*, v.i., to revolt, rebel: 揭竿而起 (allu.) raise the standard of revolt (with "bamboo poles" even without arms); 揭竿起義 ditto.

揭根子 *jiegentz*, phr., expose (friend's secrets).

揭櫫 *jieju*, v.t., proclaim, announce, publish.

揭開 *jie'kai*, v.t., uncover, unseal, tear open.

揭露 *jieluh*, v.t., announce (results of lottery, etc.), publish (scandals, etc.) in newspapers.

揭幕 *jiemuh*, v.i., inaugurate, unveil a new building, monument, theater, etc. ("raise the curtain"); (fig.) come into being, get under way.

揭破 *jiepoh*, v.t., see *-chuan* ↑.

揭曉 *jieshiaau*, v.t., publish, announce (the results of an examination).

揭示 *jieshyh*, v.t., to post a notice, publicly announce.

揭挑 *jie'tiaau*, v.i., see *-duaan* ↑.

揭帖 *jietiee*, (1) v.t., see *-shyh* ↑; (2) n., a written note: 匿名揭帖 an anonymous letter or poster, usu. of a slanderous nature.

揚 10A.50-4

yarng.

N. (AC) battle-axe.

V.i. & t. (1) To hoist (sail, flag). (2) To wave, flutter, stir: 揚手 wave hand; 飄揚 flutter in the wind; 揚湯止沸 stir the soup to stop boiling—a temporary redress; 揚眉吐氣 a feeling of exaltation upon fulfillment; 揚塵 kick up dust. (3) To spread abroad, make known: 宣揚 publicize, propagate (faith, beliefs); 發揚(光大), 宏揚 to further develop or expand (idea, thoughts); 張揚 to publicize.

Adj. Loud, showy: 趾高氣揚 strut about, head in the clouds, give oneself airs; 揚聲 a loud voice.

揚長 *yarng-charng*, phr., 揚長而去 to shake the sleeves and go away haughtily—sail out of the room.

揚氣 *yarng'chi*, adj., smug, self-satisfied.

揚搉 *yarngchyueh*, v.t., (LL) as in 揚搉古今 make a cursory review of the past and the present.

揚厲 *yarnglih*, adj., arrogant.

揚名 *yarng-mirng*, phr., spread fame.

揚聲 *yarng-sheng*, phr., raise one's voice; 揚聲器 loud-speaker.

揚威 *yarng-wei*, phr., 耀武揚威 to parade military prowess.

揚言 *yarng-yarn*, v.i., to announce openly what often is untrue.

揚揚 *yarngyarng*, adj., self-satisfied.

搨 10A.50-4

tah (**ta*).

[Var. 拓; dist. 塌, 榻]

N. & v.t. (1) To make rubbings of calligraphy from stone or metal inscriptions; usu. 搨本 such rubbings. (2) (**ta*) 衣裳搨了汗 dress sticks from perspiration.

搦 10A.50-5

nuoh.

V.t. (1) (AC) to restrain: 搦秦起趙 hold Chirn's power in check and encourage Jauh. (2) To get hold of, take in hand: 搦管 (＝執筆) take up a pen to write; 搦棹 take up the oars to row. (3) To challenge: 搦戰 challenge to fight.

搒 10A.50-6

behng.

V.t. 標搒 *biaubehng*, to praise (person) in public (cogn. 標△榜 *biaubaang* 10B.01).

搧 10A.50-6

shan.

V.i. & t. (1) To give a slap on face. (2) To fan up (see compp. under 扇 63D.50 and 煽 91D.50).

扮 10A.50-8

bahn.

V.i. & t. (1) To dress up, make up: 打扮, 裝扮 dress up. (2) To play role in drama: 扮男(裝), 扮女(裝) play male, female role; 扮作 in the disguise of, play role of; play role of person in drama, as 扮張飛.

扮裝 *bahnjuang*, v.t., wear make-up of person in opera.
扮相 *bahnshiahng*, n., the make-up for an acting role.
扮戲 *bahn-shih*, v.i., to present play in public.
扮演 *bahnyaan*, v.t., to perform (play, role).

撝 10A.50-9

huei.

V.i. Rare var. of 麾.

Adj. 撝謙 (AC) sincere and humble.

摀 10A.50-9

wuu.

V.t. (1) (Coll.) to cover up: 摀耳朵 cover one's ears; 摀上眼睛 cover up one's eyes; 摀不住 cannot be covered up. (2) (Coll.) wrap up (tea, pickles, etc.) air-tight for preserving flavor: 豆豉摀起來 keep preserved black beans tightly in jar. (3) (Sl.) put in prison: 摀起來.

摀蓋 *wuugaih*, v.t., (coll.) to cover up, to keep secret.

搗 10A.50-9

daau.

[Pop. of 擣 10A.00]

V.i. & t. To pound, beat with stick or pestle: 搗蒜 pound leek into pulp; 搗米 hull rice; 搗汁 crush out the juice; 搗爛, 搗碎 pound into pulp; 搗虛 attack enemy at his weakest.

搗蛋 *daaudahn*, v.i., to make trouble.
搗鬼 *daurgueei*, v.i., play tricks.
搗亂 *daauluahn*, v.i., cause disturbance; create nuisance; 搗亂份子 disturbing elements (in group).
搗騰 *daau'teng*, v.i., turn upside down.

拘 10A.50-9

jyu.

V.i. & t. (1) Arrest, seize: 拘捕 *-buu*, 拘押 *-ya*, 拘拿 *-nar*, 拘留 *-liour*↓. (2) Restrain, restrict, limit the freedom of: 不拘 without restraint, no matter what, regardless: 不拘形式 disregard formalities; 拘束 *-shuh*↓. (3) V.i., hesitate: 拘忌 *-jih*↓.

Adj. Subject to restraint: 拘謹 *-jiin*↓; 拘拘縮縮 timid, timorous, spiritless; 拘泥 *-nir*↓; 拘禮 *-lii*↓.

拘捕 *jyubuu*, v.t., arrest, take into custody.
拘牽 *jyuchian*, v.t., put limitations on.
拘管 *jyu(')guaan*, v.t., arrest and put under surveillance.
拘介 *jyujieh*, adj., (LL) (of conduct) scrupulously correct.
拘忌 *jyujih*, v.i., hesitate out of scruples.
拘謹 *jyujiin*, adj., (of persons) cautious, modest, diffident, reserved.
拘住 *jyu-juh*, (1) v.i. & t., seize, catch; (2) p.p., tied down by forms.
拘執 *jyujyr*, (1) adj., stubborn; (2) v.t., to arrest.
拘拘 *jyujyu*, adj., (1) sticking to rules, formalistic; (2) (AC) hunchbacked; (3) 拘拘小數 a small amount.
拘禮 *jyu-lii*, v.i., be bound by formalities, stand on ceremony.
拘留 *jyuliour*, v.t., detain (a person) on minor charges.
拘攣 *jyulyuarn* (-'*lyuan*), (1) n., cramps, spasms; (2) v.t., restrain, restrict the freedom of; 拘攣兒 -'*lyua'l*, adj., cramped; forming ringlets or coils (of hair).
拘縻 *jyumir*, v.t., put under restraint.
拘拿 *jyunar*, v.t., see *-buu*↑.
拘泥 *jyunir*, v.i. & adj., (be) formalistic, sticking to the rules.
拘票 *jyu-piauh*, n., a warrant for arrest.
拘束 *jyushuh* (-'*su*), (1) v.t., restrain, restrict the freedom of; (2) adj., (of persons) awkward, timid, shy, not at ease.
拘提 *jyutir*, v.t., summon (defendant) to appear before court;

arrest and keep under detention.

拘押 *jyuya*, v.t., take into custody.

拘役 *jyuyih*, n., imprisonment, a prison term.

掬 10A.50-9

jyur.

N. What can be held by putting two hands together: 一掬之淚 a handful of tears.

V.t. Take (scoop) up with both hands: 掬水 cup one's hands to hold water; 笑容可掬 beaming with a broad smile.

掏 10A.50-9

tau.

[Cf. 搯 10A.21]

V.t. Take out with hand: 掏腰包 make money payment, oft. unwillingly, take out pocketbook; 掏錢 take out money; 掏心窩子的 confide one's secrets to another, telling s.t. usu. not revealed to others.

掏摸 *taumo*, v.t., to steal, obtain by underhand means: 掏摸幾個錢來 beg or borrow some money.

搊 10A.50-9

chou.

V.t. (MC) to pluck a stringed instrument.

搊搜 *chousoou*, adj., (MC) ugly in looks or temper.

搊彈詞 *choutarntsyr*, n., (MC) a song sung to a plucked instrument.

拗 10A.50-9

auh (**aau*, **yuh*, **yauh*, **niouh*).

V.t. (1) (**aau*) To break (branches). (2) (**yauh*) 拗口 *-koou*↓.

Adj. (**yuh*, **yauh*, sp. pr. **niouh*) Stubborn, recalcitrant: 違拗 defy (orders, law), defiant; 拗強, 拗性 *-chiarng*, *-shihng*↓.

拗彆 *auh'bie*, v.i., (coll.) to get into a quarrel.

拗強 *auhchiarng*, adj., stubborn.

拗口 **yauhkoou*, v.i., be difficult to pronounce, to lisp, otherwise pronounce defective sounds; 拗口令 a tongue-twister (rhyme, like "she sells seashells").

拗怒 **yuhnuh*, v.i., to suppress anger.

拗性 **niouhshihng* (-'*shing*), adj., stubborn.

撈 10A.50-9

laur (sp. pr. *lau*).

V.t. To drag for (s.t.) in water, dredge for: 撈摸 grope for; 混水撈魚 to fish in troubled waters; 打撈 salvage; 大海撈針 look for a needle in a haystack; 撈本兒 recoup money lost in gambling; 撈一把 (coll.) to reap some profit; 有機會就撈他一筆大錢 make a fast buck, if given the chance.

撈毛的 *laumaur'de*, n., (old usage) manservant in a house of ill fame.

撈什子 *laurshyrtz*, n., (=牢什子) an eyesore, anything disagreeable or abominable.

§10A.63 (扌/丶)

擋 10A.63-2

daang.

[Pop. var. of 攩]

V.t. To parry (a blow), shield off, ward off (cogn. 搪 *tarng*, 10A.40): 抵擋 meet, counter (attack); 擋住 successfully ward off; 擋橫兒 stop a bully.

擋戧 *daangchiahng*, v.i., support against criticism or attack.

擋駕 *daangjiah*, v.i., refuse to see visitor, also a courtesy to express unworthiness of receiving call.

擋膜兒 *daang'mo'l*, n., an obstructing cover.

摭 10A.63-6

jyr.

V.t. To pick, gather.

摭拾 *jyrshyr*, v.t., pick, collect (samples, gossip, anecdotes, phrases).

拎 10A.63-8

ling.

[Interch. 擰; usu. printed 拎]

V.t. (Coll.) to lift or carry by hand, esp. by bent fingers: 提拎菜籃 carry a basket in one's hand; 拎著, 拎東西.

扵 10A.63-8

yur.

[Pop. of 於 60S.63]

撫 10A.63–9

fuu.

N. (1) Pacification: 勦撫兼施 quash revolts both by force and pacification measures. (2) Part of title of governor in Mirng and Manchu times: 督撫, 巡撫 military governor (cf. 總督 civil governor), hence 撫臺, 撫院, 撫軍 as term of address.

V.t. (1) To fondle, stroke, to touch lovingly: 撫琴, 撫劍 touch string instrument, stroke sword; 撫掌 clasp hand; 撫躬自問 (LL) examine one's own conscience; 撫棺大哭 weep with hand stroking coffin; 撫孤松 fondle a lone pine tree; 撫今追昔 evoke memories of the past while living in the present. (2) Touch with the idea of comforting, soothe by hand: 撫孤 embrace or nurse orphan; to foster, bring up to maturity, see 撫養, 撫育 *-yaang*, *-yuh* ↓; to soothe, comfort; 撫慰, 撫卹 *-weih*, *-shyuh* ↓. (3) To pacify: 撫綏, 撫靖, 安撫 pacify a country by justice.

撫摩 *fuumor*, v.t., fondle (baby, object of art).
撫卹 *fuushyuh*, v.t., comfort the bereaved; 撫卹金 fund for relief of family of deceased.
撫綏 *fuusuei*, v.t., bring peace and justice to country.
撫慰 *fuuweih*, v.t., to comfort (person in trouble).
撫養 *furyaang*, 撫育 *fuuyuh*, v.t., bring to maturity, esp. orphan: 撫育成人.

撚 10A.63–9

niaan.

[Pop. 捻 10A.72]

V.t. (1) To pick up s.t. with one's fingers: 撚起來 pick (s.t.) up; 撚香 (rel.) burn incense sticks before the altar; 撚灰 pick up ashes. (2) To play with s.t. with fingers, roll up s.t. with fingers: 撚指間 in a short moment—at the snap of one's fingers; 撚鬚 stroke one's beard; 撚錢 spin a coin; 撚酸 be jealous of, said esp. of women.

---

§ 10A.70 (扌/乚)

撓 10A.70–1

naur.

[Cf. 擾 *raau*, 10A.82]

V.t. (1) Disturb, interrupt, interfere: 撓亂 create confusion in; 撓擾 interfere with. (2) Scratch: 撓頭 scratch the head, hence (of hair) dishevelled; 撓癢癢兒 scratch an itch. (3) Be cowed, submit to superior force: 撓屈 be cowed into submission; 不屈不撓 refuse to be cowed or submit; 百折不撓 never yield in spite of reverses; 撓折 destroy or force to yield; 撓敗 be defeated, frustrated.

拋 10A.70–1

pau.

[Common var. 抛]

V.t. (1) To throw, cast: 抛石頭 throw stones; 抛磚引玉 "throw stones and bring back jade," i.e., (of writings) a hope that my crude remarks may draw forth others by abler men; 抛網 cast net; 抛錨 cast anchor, (of cars) get stuck midway; 抛繡球 throw embroidered ball to select suitor; 抛頭露面 phr., (of woman) expose herself in public. (2) Cast away, abandon, esp. 抛棄 *-chih* ↓.

抛棄 *pauchih*, v.t., abandon (family, responsibility, etc.).
抛躲 *pauduor*, v.t., (MC) abandon (lover).
抛費 *paufeih*, v.i., spend extravagantly.
抛荒 *pauhuang*, v.t., neglect (studies), be neglected.
抛擲 *paujer*, v.i., to toss, haul.
抛空(頭) *paukung(tour)*, v.i., speculate (on stocks); to sell short.
抛盤(兒) *pauparn (-par'l)*, v.i., (comm.) sell short (stocks, commodities); to give a quotation.
抛閃 *paushaan*, v.t. (MC) abandon.
抛射 *pausheh*, v.i. & t., shoot by sling.
抛售 *paushouh*, v.t. & n., sell out at low prices; clearance sale.
抛堶 *pautuor*, n., (AC) an anc. game consisting of throwing bricks or stones.

掩 10A.70–1

yaan.

V.i. & t. (1) To cover up: 遮掩 ditto; 掩蓋 *-gaih* ↓; 掩人耳目 to cover up story; 掩鼻 cover nostrils to avoid stink; 掩泣 to weep silently; 掩口 cover mouth in laughter or keep silent; 掩耳不聞 turn a deaf ear; 掩耳盜鈴 to steal a bell while covering one's ears—self-deception. (2) (Mil.) to cover own troops: 掩護 *-huh* ↓. (3) To shut: 掩卷 close the book; 掩門, 掩戶 close the door; 半掩 (door) half shut. (4) To ambush and attack: 掩擊 *-jir*, 掩殺 *-sha* ↓.

掩蔽 *yaanbih*, v.t., to cover up

(mistakes).
掩 蓋 *yarngaih*, v.t., ditto.
掩 護 *yaanhuh*, v.t., (mil.) (1) to cover one's units by tactical move or by artillery barrage; (2) to camouflage, take cover.
掩 擊 *yaanjir*, v.t., to waylay.
掩 埋 *yaanmair*, v.t., to bury (corpse).
掩 殺 *yaansha*, v.t., waylay and kill.
掩 襲 *yaanshir*, v.t., to attack from the flank or by silent, forced march, make surprise attack on enemy.
掩 飾 *yaanshyh*, v.t., to cover up (mistakes, misconduct, etc.).
掩 藏 *yaantsarng*, v.t., to hide.

捲 10A.70-1

jyuaan.

N. A roll, a reel: 烟捲 cigarets; 膠捲 a roll of photographic film; 幾捲電影片 several reels of cinema film; 一捲鈔票 a wad of bank notes; 行李捲 a travelling bag; 花捲 a steamed roll.

V.t. (1) Roll up, gather, snatch: 捲地皮 *-dihpir* ↓; 捲逃 *-taur* ↓; 捲土重來 (usu. of politicians) to stage a comeback; 捲入漩渦 be embroiled (in a dispute, quarrel, fight), be implicated (in an affair); 捲起來 roll up (sleeves, a blind, a painting); 捲上 ditto; 席捲 gobble up (all enemy territory) in war, win (all the money) in gambling, carry off (all the top prizes) in a contest; 風捲殘雲 (of gourmand) eat up all the dishes at one sitting, make a clean sweep of all opposition, meet with no resistance. (2) Scold, rebuke: 捲罵 *-mah* ↓.

捲 包 (兒) *jyuaan-bau('l)*, v.i., abscond with everything.
捲 尺 *jyuarn-chyy*, n., a tape (line).
捲 單 *jyuaan-dan*, v.i., (of monks) leave monastery *en masse*.
捲 地 皮 *jyuaan-dihpir*, v.i., (of official) enrich oneself by corrupt means, (lit., "roll up the land" and carry it home).
捲 髮 *jyuarnfaa*, v.i., to curl one's hair.
捲 簾 格 *jyuaanliarn-ger*, n., one form of riddle standing for a phrase to be read backwards, (as a screen is rolled upwards).
捲 罵 *jyuaanmah*, v.t., (MC) rebuke, scold, abuse (also 捲 used alone).
捲 棚 *jyuaanperng*, n., an awning that can be rolled up.
捲 鋪 蓋 *jyuaanpu'gai*, v.i., resign from office; get fired ("pack up").
捲 心 菜 *jyuaanshin-tsaih*, n., the cabbage.
捲 堂 *jyuaantarng*, v.i., (1) (MC) (of students) go on strike; (2) (of monks) leave monastery *en masse.*
捲 逃 *jyuaantaur*, v.i., abscond with valuables.
捲 子 *jyuaantz*, n., a roll (of bedding, articles).
捲 烟 *jyuaanyan*, n., cigarets, esp. cigaret rolled by hand.
捲 葉 蛾 *jyuaanyeh-er*, n., (zoo.) *Cacaecia crataegan.*

扎 10A.70-2

ja (**jar*, **jaa*).

V. (1) To pierce, prick or irritate by sharp point: 扎眼, 札心, 扎手, 扎耳 *-yaan, -shin, -shoou, -eel* ↓; 札耳朶眼兒 pierce ear for ear-rings; 札耳朶. (2) To embroider: 扎花兒 to embroider designs. (3) 扎猛子 *-meengtz* ↓. (4) (**jar*) To struggle: 扎掙 *-'jeng* ↓. (5) To open up: 扎手舞腳 swing arms and legs, stand or sit restlessly; 扎乎 *-'hu* ↓. (6) (**jaa*) To stop: 扎住 stop moving. (7) (**jar*) To tie up, var. of 紮 10.01.

Adj. (1) Broad: 扎腦門兒 broad-headed. (2) Widespread, open: 扎煞, 扎勒扎煞 *-'sha, -lejasha* ↓.

扎 耳 *ja-eel*, adj., grates on the ears, irritating to the ears: 這話聽着很扎耳朶 such words grate on my ears.
扎 根 *jargen*, v.i., take root (in s.t.).
扎 乎 *ja'hu*, v.i., (coll.) to show off: 剛剛有幾個錢就札乎起來了 (he) has just made a little money and immediately begins to show off.
扎 針 *jajen*, v.i., to puncture skin with special needle in acupuncture.
扎 掙 **jar'jeng*, v.i., to maintain, struggle to maintain, under difficult circumstances: 扎掙不住 cannot keep up or maintain (certain situation).
扎 空 槍 *ja-kungchiang*, phr., "fire a blank shot," to buy on margin, deal in speculative venture.
扎 勒 扎 煞 *ja'lejasha*, adj., widespread: 這棵樹扎勒扎煞的不好搬運 this tree, with its branches stretching out in all directions, is not easy to move.
扎 猛 子 *jameengtz*, v.i., (coll.) to swim fast head under water.
扎 蓬 棵 *ja'pengke*, phr., (coll.) wear dishevelled hair.
扎 煞 *ja'sha*, v.t., spread wide-open: 她扎煞兩隻手 she spreads her two hands; see *-'lejasha* ↑.
扎 心 *ja-shin*, phr., "prick the heart": 這話聽着實在扎心 such words prick one's heart, cf. *-eel* ↑.
扎 手 *ja-shoou*, phr., "prick the hand"—(of affair) difficult to handle.
扎 實 *ja'shy*, adj., well in hand, firm, solidly planned or controlled.
扎 眼 *ja-yaan*, phr., "irritate the eyes"—attract one's attention by strangeness or conspicuous dress, etc.

批 10A.70-2

pi.

N. (1) Lot, load, shipment (of goods); group (of people): 這批人 these people; 這批學生 this group of students; 一批貨 a shipment of goods; 一大批 a big lot; 分批寄到 send in separate lots. (2) Annotation, marginal comment in books: 眉批, 頂批 comment on top of page; 旁批 written comments on side of page; 硃批 comment in red ink.

V.t. (1) To slap: 批頰 slap one's face; 批嘴巴子 slap on the face. (2) To slice as with knife: 批逆鱗 "slice against fish scales," i.e., rub one the wrong way and incur anger; 批卻導窾 make penetrating criticism (like carving joints by skillful butcher); 批亢擣虛 attack enemy at his weak spots. (3) To comment: 批八字 to make astrologer's comment; make official comments on documents: 批駁, 批回, 批准 *-bor*, *-hueir*, *-juun* ↓. (4) To correct papers, annotate texts, see 批註 *-juh* ↓.

批 駁 *pibor*, v.t., reject (official request or communication with adverse comment).

批 單 *pidan*, n., bill of sale.

批 發 *pifaa*, v.i. & n., wholesale: 批發生意 wholesale business; 批發商 wholesale dealer; 批發價 wholesale price.

批 改 *pigaai*, v.t., correct (school papers, drafts).

批 回 *pihueir*, v.i., reject or send (request, petition) back with comments.

批 註 *pijuh*, v.i., to annotate with comments.

批 准 *pijuun*, v.t., officially approve, grant (request, proposal).

批 判 *pipahn*, v.t., judge (case), give official judgment: 某某學説之批判 a critique of certain theories.

批 評 *pipirng*, v.t. & n., criticise (-ism); 文學批評 literary criticism.

批 首 *pishoou*, v.i., (MC) to rank first among candidates.

批 閱 *piyueh*, v.t., read or see official document, with remarks.

挑 10A.70–2

tiau (**tiaau*).

N. (*-tz*, *'l*) A load (of fruit, etc.) carried with a pole on shoulder.

V.t. (1) To carry with a pole on the shoulder (by one person; 擔 *dan* by two persons): 挑水的 water carrier; 挑不動, 不起 cannot carry it. (2) Select, pick out: 挑好的 choose the good ones; 挑便宜 try to drive a good bargain; 挑好日子 choose a propitious day; 挑三擢四, 挑么挑六 pick and choose—fussy. (3) Pick fault: 挑毛病, 挑錯, 挑不是 try to find fault; 挑字眼兒 pick bones with person; 挑鼻子 ditto; 挑剔, 挑刺, 挑眼 *-'tih*, *-tsyh*, *-yaan*, ↓. (4) To prick, adjust lightly: 挑疔 prick, lance a boil; 挑痧 to pinch certain ligaments on neck as remedy for sunstroke. (5) (**tiaau*) Lift up: 挑燈 raise wick of oil lamp; 挑簾子 lift up bamboo curtain or screen; 挑眉毛 pick eyebrow. (6) (**tiaau*) To provoke, incite, stir up: 挑動 incite to action; 挑情, 挑戰, 挑撥 *-chirng*, *-jahn*, *-bo*, etc. ↓.

挑 撥 **tiaaubo*, v.t., to instigate (person), incite (hatred, suspicion): 挑撥是非 to cause alienation between friends by spreading rumors, etc.

挑 情 **tiaauchirng*, v.i., to dally with (girl), to incite sexual passion.

挑 取 *tiauchyuu*, v.t., to pick, choose (s.t. or s.o.).

挑 鬭 **tiaaudouh*, v.t., challenge to a fight; (MC) dally.

挑 動 **tiaauduhng*, v.i., see *-bo* ↑.

挑 費 **tiaaufeih* (*-'fei*), n., daily expenses.

挑 夫 *tiaufu*, n., carrier (of baggage, water, etc.), see V.t. 1.

挑 花 (兒) *tiauhua('l)*, v.i. & n., needle point (lace, embroidery).

挑 戰 **tiaau-jahn*, v.t., challenge, challenge to battle.

挑 揀 *tiaujiaan*, v.t., choose (best fruit, goods).

挑 賣 *tiaumaih*, v.i. & t., peddle, be pedlar.

挑 弄 **tiaaunuhng*, v.t., see *-bo* ↑; tease.

挑 戲 **tiaaushih*, v.t., dally with, tease (girls).

挑 釁 **tiaaushihn*, v.i., make an act of provocation.

挑 選 *tiaushyuaan*, v.i., choose the best.

挑 唆 **tiaausuo* (*-'suo*), v.t., instigate (to fight), try to alienate (friends).

挑 達 *tiautah*, adj., restless, agile, dexterous (also wr. 跳踢, 佻傞).

挑 剔 *tiau'tih*, v.i. & t., (1) to pick fault; (2) (callig.) make an abrupt, upward stroke.

挑 刺 (兒) *tiau-tsyh* (*-tseh'l*), v.i., to pick fault.

挑 眼 *tiau-yaan*, v.i., to pick fault.

挹 10A.70–4

yih.

V.t. (1) To ladle out (liquid, money). (2) To draw forward.

挹 注 *yihjuh*, v.i., to "ladle out and into," to combine and equalize resources, to shift funds to meet temporary needs.

擺 10A.70–4

baai.

[Pop. 摆; cogn. 排 *pair*]

N. Pendulum, esp. 鐘擺 clock pendulum.

V.t. (1) To shake, wag: 擺頭擺手 shake hand, head as signal; 擺尾巴 wag tail. (2) Shake off, shake loose: 擺不開 cannot shake off business in hand; 擺撥常務 get away from routine business. (3) Jostle, shake up, manipulate: 擺佈 *-buh*, 擺弄 *-luhng* ↓. (4) Arrange, set in order, esp. table, etc.: 擺列 arrange in order; 擺陣 (mil.) fall in, deploy in formations; 擺龍門陣 (Szechuan coll.) make leisurely conversation; 擺飯 set table; 擺酒 give dinner to honor s.o.; 擺請兒 (coll.) give dinner to settle disputes; 擺台 set table for Western style dinner; 擺供 set up sacrifices at altar; 擺設兒 *bai'she'l*, n., display (of art objects), interior decorations. (5) Set up for show: 擺樣子, 擺場面 just show off; 擺 (空) 架子 pose for effect, put up airs, be stuck up, arrogant; 擺譜兒 try to appear rich and elegant, try to impress.

擺佈 *baaibuh*, v.t., manage s.o., put s.o. in place, manhandle or dispose of s.o. at will.

擺搭 *baai'da*, v.i., swing, rock.

擺渡 *baaiduh*, n., ferry, ferry boat.

擺針(兒) *baaijen(-je'l)*, n., pointer as in scales; pendulum.

擺開 *baai-kai*, v.t., put (affairs) on the side.

擺弄 *baailuhng*, v.t., as in 擺弄(人家) trick, persecute or play with s.o.; palpitate: 此藥吃下去,心中擺弄 heart palpitates after taking this medicine.

擺忙 *baaimarng*, v.i., bustle about, be foolishly busy: 你安靜一會兒罷, 別擺忙了.

擺脫 *baituo*, v.i. & t., get rid of, get away from (duties, pressure, etc.).

扼 10A.70–5

eh.

N. U.f. 軛 10D.70, harness shaft.

V.t. (1) To strangle (throat): 扼虎 strangle a tiger. (2) To take firm hold of: 扼守 *-shoou* ↓; 扼腕 *-wahn* ↓.

Adj. Essential, salient: 扼要 *-yauh* ↓.

扼吭 *ehharng*, v.i., to choke, suffocate.

扼制 *ehjyh*, v.t., to keep under control by force.

扼守 *ehshoou*, v.t., to guard (strategic point).

扼腕 *eh-wahn*, v.i., to wring one's wrists in sorrow or despair.

扼要 *ehyauh*, adj. & adv. & n., (the) essential(ly), salient points as in summary: 請扼要的說一遍 tell us the essential points.

攬 10A.70–5

laan.

[Equiv. 擥, 擥]

V.t. (1) Take hold of, grasp, exercise control over: 總攬權綱 hold the reins of government; 攬城郭之兵 command all troops in the city and its suburbs; 攬鏡自照 hold up a mirror to look at one's own reflection; 攬筆 take up a pen to write; 攬轡 hold the reins. (2) To round up (talents): 延攬人才. (3) To contract sales by district or quantity: 攬貨 *-huoh* ↓; 攬得了 be able to obtain business deal; 包攬, 承攬 to contract for; 兜攬 solicit (business).

攬契 *laanchih*, n., written guarantee given by a shipper undertaking to ship goods; cargo receipt.

攬權 *laanchyuarn*, v.t., seize or extend (political) power.

攬取 *laanchyuu*, v.t., take hold of.

攬單 *laandan*, n., see *-chih* ↑.

攬貨 *laanhuoh*, v.t., undertake to ship or market goods.

攬頭 *laantour*, n., (1) contractor; (2) gen. term for shipping company.

攬總(兒) *lanrtzuung('l)*, v.t., assemble together.

把 10A.70–5

baa (coll. also **baai*, **bah*).

N. adjunct. (1) Used before objects with handles or things to take hold of: 一把刀, 一把傘, 一把茶壺 a knife, an umbrella, a teapot; 一把椅子 a chair. (2) A handful of: 一把蔴繩, 頭髮, 花生, 沙 a handful of hemp, hair, peanuts, soil or sand; a neat lot of (given reasons, etc.).

N. 把子, 把兒 **bahtz*, **bah'l*, a handle; 刀把兒, 槍把兒 knife handle, gun butt; 把兒缸子 teacup with handle; 把兒鏡子 hand mirror.

Adj. About, used after numbers or measures: 百把個人 about a hundred persons: 一年把日子, about a year long; 一點把鐘 about an hour.

V.t. (1) Hold, hold in hand: 把手 hold hands; 把卷 hold book in hand (read); 把盞 or 把酒 hold cup in hand (and drink). (2) Guard, watch, keep: 把門 guard door, gate; 把風 be on the lookout (of thieves' colleague); 把舵 be at the rudder or steering wheel in ship. (3) Use s.t. as, regard as: 把來做洋傘用 use as substitute for umbrella; 把來恫嚇人 use it to threaten people; 把他當一回事 take, regard the matter seriously. (4) To assist child in natural functions: 把屎, 把尿. (5) (MC) to give: 一向沒把得你 have not given it you so far.

Prep. (Coll. also **baai*) used before direct object, followed by v.t. (把＋object＋v.t.): 把門關上 close the door; similarly, 把人殺死, 把錢搶走 kill a man and rob his money; 把故事講完了 finish telling the story; 把錢看得太重 think too much of money; 把東西丟了 lose s.t.; 把事情忘了 forget s.t.

把臂 *baa-bih*, phr., holding arms (meeting of friends).

把柄 *baabihng* (-'*bing*), n., evidence that can be got hold of in lawsuits, arguments.

把鼻 *baabir*, n., cue, or clue, esp. 沒把鼻 without any clue.

把持 *baachyr*, v.t., monopolize,

keep control of (situation, post, power): 把持不定 undecided, wavering. 「house.

把家 *baa-jia*, v.i., (MC) keep

把捉 *baajuo*, v.t., get hold of, put finger on, be sure about (person, truths): 把捉不定 difficult to assess.

把口兒 *baakoou'l*, n., entrance to alley.

把攬 *barlaan*, v.t., to monopolyze, control.

把牢 *baalaur*, adj., safe and secure, dependable.

把袂 *baa-meih*, phr., holding sleeves, i.e., in loving friendship.

把戲 *baashih*, n., jugglery; (derog.) action to fool people, or for show, cheap trick.

把兄弟 *baashiungdih*, n., sworn brother.

把守 *barshoou*[1], v.i., guard (entrance).

把手 *bar-shoou*[2], phr., hand in hand.

把式 *baashyh*, n., special artist or performer (劍把式, 車把式, 花兒把式 in sword play, carriage driving, horticulture): 打△把式(勢) 10A.00, practise boxing gestures.

把素 *baa-suh*, v.i., (Budd.) keep vegetarian vow.

把子 *baatz*, n., a group of (thieves); sworn brotherhood; (拜把子, be sworn thus); vulg. for 靶△子 20B.70.

把玩 *barwaan*, v.t., fondle (toys, jade, etc.).

把穩 *barween*, v.i. & t., be sure about, be firm, play safe.

把握 *baawo*, n., confidence about future venture: 有把握 have confidence in dealing with s.t.; 毫無把握 have no confidence at all.

把晤 *baawuh*, v.i., meet and talk personally (of friends).

抗 10A.70-6

kahng.

N. A surname.

V.t. (1) To resist (force, pressure, enemy): 抗敵 resist enemy; 抗拒 resist, stand up against (invasion, force); 抗戰 *-jahn*↓; 抗日戰爭 war of resistance against Japan; 抗衛, 抗禦 defend (country) against aggression. (2) To defy: 抗命 defy order; 違抗 act against, defy (rule, order); 抗稅 (抗糧) refuse to pay tax (rice tax). (3) To take stand against, protest: 抗議, 抗論 *-yih*, *-luhn*↓; 對抗 stand against. (4) To stand as equal: 抗衡, 抗禮 *-herng*, *-lii*↓. (5) To carry thing on shoulder: 抗物, 抗東西, 抗一袋米 carry things, a bag of rice on shoulders. (6) (Vern.) to hide away: 把這包東西抗起來 hide away this package.

Adj. (Interch. 亢) high, upright: 抗直 (=亢直) upright; 抗節, 抗志 upright character.

抗毒素 *kahng-dur-suh*, n., antitoxin.

抗告 *kahnggauh*, v.i. & t., to lodge complaint against (s.o.) at court.

抗衡 *gahngherng*, v.t., (LL) match, be equal to: 與之抗衡 match another (in prestige, ability, etc.).

抗戰 *kahngjahn*, n., war against aggression; specifically the war against Japan, 1937–45.

抗禮 *kahnglii*, phr., 分庭抗禮 (AC) (of rulers, diplomats) meet as equals.

抗論 *kahngluhn*, v.i. & n., (make) brave defense against opposite view: 抗論時世 make frank criticism of the times.

抗熱板 *kahngreh-baan*, n., (astron.) heat shield.

抗生素 *kahngsheng-suh*, n., antibiotics.

抗濕紙 *kahngshy-jyy*, n., waterproof paper.

抗體 *kahngtii*, n., (med.) immune bodies, antibodies.

抗足 *kahngtzur*, phr., stand on tiptoe: 翹首抗足 (AC) "crane one's neck and stand on tiptoe" in admiration.

抗議 *kahngyih*, v.i. & t. & n., protest: 提出抗議 lodge a formal protest.

抗原 *kahngyuarn*, n., (med.) antigen (also 抗體原).

攏 10A.70-6

luung (**lurng*).

V.i. & t. (1) To gather up: 合攏, 聚攏 gather together; 攏頭髮 gather up hair. (2) To come alongside: 攏岸 (ship) lie alongside; 靠攏 to take side, to affiliate; (of person) go over to Communists. (3) (**lurng*) To make a light tap on pipa string.

挖 10A.70-6

wa (**war*).

N. (**war*) 耳挖子 an ear pick.

V.t. (1) To dig (earth, a hole, a well). (2) To pick (nose, ear): 挖角兒 to lure away star performers from rival companies; 挖花 a game similar to mahjong.

挖墊 *wadiahn*, n., formerly, a decorative cushion.

挖苦 *wa'ku*, v.t., to disparage (person) by innuendoes; to needle (person).

攛 10A.70-6

tsuan.

V.i. & t. (1) To throw (s.t.) away. (2) To do a hurried job: 事前不弄, 臨時現攛 do a thing hurriedly at the last moment; 攛趕 (子活)

-gaan↓. (3) See 擹掇 *-'duo*↓.

擹掇 *tsuan'duo*, v.t., to instigate s.o. to do s.t.

擹趕 *tsuangaan*, v.i., to do hurriedly: 擹趕子活 a hurried job.

擹弄 *tsuan'nung*, v.t., see *-'duo*↑ (=撮弄).

托 10A.70–9

tuo.

N. (*-tz, 'l*) (1) Small tray or support for utensils: 茶托(兒) tea saucer; 托盤, 托子 *-parn, -'tz*↓. (2) Lining for collar, fur, etc.: 托裏 ditto; 托領 *-liing*↓.

V.t. (1) To hold or hold up s.t. on palm of hand, to support from under: 托在手裏 hold s.t. on open palm; 托塔天王 a Taoist god who held a pagoda in his open hand; 托着走 go about holding s.t. resting on open hand; 托起來 lift up from under; 托着盤子 holding tray in hand; 托着下巴 rest chin in hand; 托腮 rest cheek in hand. (2) Put lining in: 托一層紙(布) to line with paper (cloth); 襯托出來 serve as contrast (such as supporting cast, flower arrangements). (3) To entrust s.t. to another, to rely on, to request a favor (interch 託): 托你一件事 I want to ask you to do s.t.; 把這件事交托你 I entrust this matter to you; 拜托, 求托, 請托 (common var. 託) request a favor; 托人情 ask s.o.'s favor; 托人說好話 ask s.o. to put in a nice word; 依托, 托賴 rely on; 托孤 entrust orphan to (friend); 托兒所 *-erl-suoo*↓; 托身(托足)之處 a place for a living, or to live in; 寄托 to give form to feelings, ambitions, through poetry, etc. (4) To give as pretext: 托病不見 refuse to see visitor on pretext of illness; 托故不來 fail to show up on some pretext.

托鉢 *tuobo*, v.i., (沿門托鉢) (of mendicant monks) to beg for alms (with "alms bowl in hand").

托地 *tuodih*, adv., (MC) suddenly: 托地跳將過去 (=突然).

托兒所 *tuo-erl-suoo*, n., day nursery, where working mothers can deposit their children for the day.

托賴 *tuolaih*, v.t., (MC) thanks to (=modn. 托庇).

托領 *tuoliing*, n., stiffing material for collar.

托墨 *tuomoh*, adj., (of writing paper) support ink well.

托盤 *tuoparn*, n., a tray.

托子 *tuo'tz*, n., a tray support.

搋 10A.70–9

chuai.

V.i. & t. (1) To stick away: 搋在身上 to stick or carry s.t. in bosom; 搋手兒 to fold one's arms inside sleeves; 搋起來 hide s.t. in bosom. (2) To knead: 搋麵 knead dough.

撬 10A.70–9

chiauh (**chiau*).

V.t. (1) To pry (with lever, crowbar): 撬開, 撬起來 pry open, up; 撬門, 撬鎖 to pry, open door, lock; 把這個人撬走了 deprive this person of his post; 撬用 to borrow or "lift" (a person) from another place. (2) (**chiau*) To lift up, to curl up (as a plank).

攪 10A.70–9

jiaau (**gaau*).

V.i. & t. (1) (**gaau*) (Also wr. 搞) v.i., make mischief: 瞎攪 to fool around; 胡攪 make a mess of s.t. (2) V.t., disturb, agitate, stir, shake: 攪亂 create confusion in; 攪混 throw into disorder; 攪局 cause trouble, uncertainty; 打攪 interrupt, break in upon, impose upon (s.o.'s) hospitality; 攪和 to blend, to stir or mix well; 攪拌 ditto; 攪動 to shake up; 攪勻 mix evenly.

扢 10A.70–9

shih.

V.i. (AC) to dance for joy: 扢然 dancing about.

拖 10A.70–9

tuo.

V.i. & t. (1) To drag, pull: 拖人出去 drag person out of house; 拖過來, 拖過去 drag about; 衣服拖在地上 skirt trails on the floor; 拖拖拉拉 drag and pull; 拖曳 ditto; 拖車 *-che*↓; 拖船 pull boat (against current) by worker on bank; 拖拉機 tractor; drag person into business; 別拖着我 don't drag me in; 拖着母親 child drags mother about; 拖泥帶水 diffuse, irrelevant talk, not clear-cut; 拖人下水 drag s.o. down to one's own level of crime or misery; 拖地板 mop the floor. (2) To delay, prolong: 別拖了 don't delay any more; 拖得太久了 this has been dragging on for too long; 拖長 prolong (meeting, speech); 拖時間 delay, play for time; 拖了一屁股(一身)債 burdened down with debts; 拖延, 拖宕 *-yarn, -dahng*, etc.↓.

拖車 *tuoche*, (1) n., trailer; (2) v.i., to pull cart.

拖欠 *tuochiahn*, v.t., be in debt, bear debt.

拖牀(兒) *tuochuarng('l)*, n., sledge.

拖宕 *tuodahng*, v.i., delay, drag on.

拖累 *tuoleei*, v.t., involve another person in financial loss, or court proceedings.

拖露 *tuoluh* (also *tu'lu* in Peking coll.), v.i., hang down.
拖鞋 *tuoshier*, n., slippers.
拖沓 *tuotah*, adj., not clear-cut, troublesome in dealings.
拖延 *tuoyarn*, v.t., procrastinate.
拖油瓶 *tuo-your-pirng*, n., children of preceding marriage living with mother in second marriage.

抱 10A.70-9

bauh.

N. (1) A surname. (2) A fathom (embraced by two outstretched arms), as a measure of a tree trunk's circumference (=圍).

V.t. (1) To carry in breast, to embrace, to make an enclosing gesture, to hold with both arms: 抱小孩 carry a child in arms; 抱火柴 carry a bundle of firewood; 抱薪救火 phr., add fuel to the fire; 抱空窩 be left out on a limb; 抱火盆兒, 抱砂鍋 or 抱瓦罐 be beggar; 抱雪向火 phr., do thankless task; 平時不燒香, 臨時抱佛腳 neglect one's prayers in times of peace, then embrace the Buddha's feet in a crisis; 抱粗腿 (coll.) be hanger-on of the rich and powerful; 抱頭鼠竄 flee with arms covering one's head; 抱頭痛哭 cry in one another's arms; 抱孫子 to have a grandson born. (2) To adopt a baby: 這小孩是抱來養的 or 抱養的 this child is an adopted one. (3) To nourish a grudge, hope, etc. in one's heart: 抱恨終天 harbor an eternal sorrow (regret); 抱委屈 feel injured; 抱憾, 抱怨, 抱負 *-hahn*, *-yuahn*, *-fuh*↓; 懷抱 one's ambition; 抱定決心, 主意 hold firmly a determination, decision; 抱着一腔熱誠 be filled with enthusiasm; 抱着希望 entertain a hope; 抱樂觀, 抱悲觀 be optimistic, pessimistic; 抱不平 feel injustice done to another and wish to help; 抱殘守缺 phr., be a stickler for ancient ways and things, be a traditionalist; 抱關擊柝 (AC) serve as gatekeeper and night watchman. (4) To carry on, burdened with: 抱病; 抱痛西河 phr., suffer sorrow of losing one's son; 抱恙工作 carry on work while sick. (5) To fit nicely: 抱腳兒 (shoes) fit the feet nicely; 抱身兒 (dress) fit nicely.

抱冰 *bauh-bing*, v.i., (AC) train oneself to endure hardships.
抱歉 *bauchiahn*, v.i., feel sorry, apologetic: 抱歉得很 I am so sorry.
抱屈 *bauhchyu*, v.i., feel being wronged.
抱牘 *bauh-dur*, v.i., (LL) be in charge of documents.
抱負 *baufuh*, n., ambition: 抱負不凡 have great life ambition.
抱憾 *bauh-hahn*, v.i., have a secret regret (for life 終身).
抱恨 *bauh-hehn*, v.i., ditto.
抱火盆的 *bauh huoopern'de*, n., (coll.) beggar.
抱柱 *bauh-juh*, v.i., (LL) be faithful to death (allu. to lover who held on to a bridge pile during rising tide and died rather than quit rendezvous); 抱柱對兒 n., pair of couplet inscribed on curved panels fitting round posts.
抱愧 *bauhkueih*, v.i., feel ashamed.
抱念 *bauh-niahn*, v.t., remember or think of (person).
抱罪 *bauhtzueih*, v.i., feel guilty.
抱窩 *bauh-wo*, v.i., (of hen) sit on eggs.
抱養 *bauhyaang*, v.i., raise another's child.
抱恙 *bauh yahng*, see V.t. 4↑.
抱腰 *bauh-yau*, v.t., (coll.) support, assist, usu. with money.
抱怨 *bauhyuahn*, v.i., keep grudge against (person); v.t., 抱怨某人 blame s.o.

执 10A.70-9

jyr.

[Pop. of 執 11S.70]

挽 10A.70-9

waan.

V.t. (1) To pull (a bow, a cart): 挽回, 挽救 *-hueir*, *-jiouh*↓. (2) U.f. 輓 elegy: 挽歌. (3) To fold up: 挽袖子 fold sleeves; 挽扣兒 to button up.

挽回 *waanhueir*, v.t., to save (a dangerous situation): 無可挽回 beyond any help, irretrievable.
挽救 *waanjiouh*, v.t., ditto.
挽留 *waanliour*, v.t., to persuade (person) not to resign.
挽手 *warn-shoou*, phr., hold hands.

攙 10A.70-9

chan.

V.t. (1) To support or assist (person) gently while standing or walking: 攙扶 *-fur*↓; 攙起來 assist to get up from sitting position; 攙著他 supporting him. (2) To mix, blend (materials): 攙水 add water; 攙假, 攙雜 *-jiaa*, *-tzar*↓.

攙親 *chan-chin*, v.i., to assist bride to come down from sedan chair.
攙放 *chanfahng*, v.t., to mix in other ingredients.
攙扶 *chanfur*, v.t., to assist (aged or invalid) to walk.
攙合 *chan'her*, v.t., to mix, blend with other materials (also 摻合).
攙夥 *chan'huoo*, v.t., to mix up (cards, chess pieces).
攙假 *chanjiaa*, v.t., to adulterate (medicine, lotion).
攙雜 *chantzar*, v.t., to mix in

攙 撧 抿 找 拭 拽 抵

other things; p.p., adulterated. 攙嘴 *chan tzueei*, v.i., to interrupt while others are speaking.

撧 10A.70-9

jyue.

V.t. (1) Break in two: 撧開 break open; 撧斷 break in two. (2) Massage a person who has lost consciousness to revive him: 撧過來 revive s.o. by such means. (3) Embarrass (s.o.) in his face.

§10A.71 (扌/弋)

抿 10A.71-5

miin.

N. (*-tz*) A small hair brush.

V.i. & t. (1) To smooth by hand, to brush: 抿頭 smooth over the forehead; 抿髮 brush the hair. (2) To pucker in smile: 抿嘴兒(而)笑.

找 10A.71-7

jaau.

V.t. (1) To look for: 找尋 *-'shyun* ↓; 找遍了 have looked for everywhere; 找不到 cannot find; 找出來 find out; 東找西找 look for in all directions; 找人 look for missing person or one with unknown address; 找幫手, 找替身 look for help, substitute; 找差事 look for job; 找出路 look for way out or job with a future; 找門路 look for approach to an important person; 找死 *-syy* ↓. (2) Invite: 找打, 找罵 ask for a spanking, scolding; 找麻煩 asking for unnecessary trouble; 找對頭 ready to risk a fight. (3) To get the balance of change: 找錢 ditto; 找補 *-buu* ↓; 不用找了 never mind the change. (4) See person responsible: 有事找我 I shall be responsible if anything happens.

找病 *jaau-bihng*, v.i., to invite trouble.

找補 *jaurbuu*, v.i., get balance due in cash.

找碴兒 *jaau-char'l*, v.i., to pick quarrel.

找塲 *jaau-charng*, v.i., try to save one's face.

找縫子 *jaau-fehng'tz*, v.i., look for opening for attack, look for pretext.

找轍 *jaau-jer*, v.i., to explain away former mistake.

找落兒 *jaau-lauh'l*, v.i., look for a steady job.

找面子 *jaau-miahn'tz*, v.i., try to save face.

找細兒 *jaau-shieh'l*, v.i., try to better one's work.

找尋 *jaau'shyun*, v.i., to search for (s.t. or person).

找死 *jaur syy*, phr., (contempt.) 你來找死 this is your end (I warn you).

找頭 *jaau'tou*, n., the change due at a purchase.

拭 10A.71-7

shyh.

V.t. To wipe (table, floor); wipe off (tear).

拽 10A.71-7

*juaih (*yeh).*

V.t. (1) To twist (another's arm): 拽胳膊兒 have arm muscles strained; 拽着 twisted; 把門拽上 twist the doorknob shut. (2) To knock, throw (ball): 把球拽過去 knock the ball over to the opponent's side. (3) (**yeh*) To trail (garment), pull, drag (s.t.).

抵 10A.71-9

*dii (*jyy).*

V.i. & t. (1) To resist, deny: 抵不住 cannot hold against; 抵抗, 抵賴, 抵當, 抵制 *-kahng, -laih, -daang, -jyh* ↓. (2) To serve as compensation, collateral: 抵補, 抵押, 抵消 *-buu, -ya, -shiau* ↓; 抵命 to pay for life with life. (3) To reach, arrive at: esp. 抵達 *-dar* ↓; 抵美 arrive at the United States; 抵任 arrive at post for duty. (4) Point out: 抵瑕蹈隙 (LL) point out flaws. (5) (**jyy*) To tap: 抵掌而談 chat leisurely ("tapping the palm").

抵補 *dirbuu*, n., compensation.

抵償 *diicharng*, v.i. & t., to compensate for loss.

抵觸 *diichuh*, v.i. & t., conflict with: 相抵觸, also wr. 牴.

抵當 *dirdaang*, v.t., (1) to resist, also wr. 抵擋; (2) *diidahng*, to mortgage.

抵達 *diidar*, v.t., reach (place): 抵達英國 arrive in England.

抵掌 *dirjaang*, v.i., in 抵掌而談 have a close, intimate talk ("tapping hands"); also pr. *jyrjaang*.

抵制 *diijyh*, v.i. & t., to boycott.

抵抗 *diikahng*, v.t., offer resistance, oppose, boycott: 抵抗日貨 boycott Japanese goods; 抵抗侵略 resist aggression.

抵賴 *diilaih*, v.i., refuse to admit (guilt).

抵銷(消) *diishiau*, v.i., as in 相抵銷 cancel out each other.

抵死 *dirsyy*, adv., stubbornly "until death," to the end: 抵死不從, 抵死不承認 refuse to submit, admit, even unto death; 抵死醉了 be dead drunk.

抵牾 *dirwuu*, v.i., (LL) conflict with, see *-chuh* ↑.

抵押 *diiya*, v.i. & n., (offer as) collateral; 抵押品 collateral for loan.

§10A.72 (扌/心)

揌 10A.72-4

sai.

[Var. of 塞 *sai*, 62.11, and of 㩙 10A.11]

摁 10A.72-4

ehn.

V.t. (1) To press (button) by hand (related 按 *ahn*, 10A.93). (2) To keep out of publicity: 這件事多虧你給摁住了 thank you for keeping this affair from the public.

撼 10A.72-7

hahn.

V.t. To shake (branches, mountains): 撼天地，山河 (powerful enough) to shake the skies and land.

撼動 *hahnduhng*, v.t., to move: 撼動人心 to move one's heart, to shake people's faith.

捻 10A.72-8

niaan.

N. A twisted or rolled shape: 紙捻(兒) a twist of paper, used to light oil lamp, tobacco pipe, etc.; 麻捻(兒) a string or rope made of flax; 燈捻(兒) wick for oil lamp; 藥捻(子) a medicated roll inserted into abscess.

V.t. To pick up (s.t.) with fingers, twist (s.t.) with fingers: 捻指間 happen in no time as only at the snap of one's fingers; 捻紙捻 roll a piece of paper into a long and slender form, see N.↑; 捻線 roll thread into a pointed shape.

捻捻轉兒 *niaan'nianjuah'l*, n., a top which, when turned by hand, spins round and round.

§10A.80 (扌/八)

攢 10A.80-1

tzaan (**tsuarn*).

V.t. (1) To save, accumulate: 攢錢 *-chiarn*↓. (2) (**tsuarn*) To come or bring together: 攢毆 surround and beat up (s.o.).

攢拌兒 **tsuarnbah'l*, phr., ganging up on s.o.
攢錢 *tzaanchiarn*, v.i., (1) to save money; (2) (**tsuarn-*) to chip in.
攢盒 **tsuarnher*, n., a box with partitions for assorted candies and nuts.
攢眉 **tsuarnmeir*, v.i., to knit one's brows.
攢餡兒 **tsuarnshiah'l*, n., a kind of steamed dumpling with assorted stuffing.
攢簇 **tsuarntsuh*, v.i., to crowd together.

擷 10A.80-1

shier (also *jier*).

V.t. (1) To pick: 擷取精華 to pick the best. (2) To hold (flowers, etc.) in the lap.

拱 10A.80-2

guung.

N. An arch: 拱門 *-mern*, 拱道 *-dauh*↓; 拱圓屋頂 an arched roof, a dome; 拱橋 an arched bridge.

V.t. (1) Encircle, to span with the hands: 拱手 *-shoou*↓; 拱別 take leave by saluting with both hands folded and raised in front; 拱衛 *-weih*↓. (2) To push up imperceptibly from below, to curl up: 新出的芽兒把土都拱起來了 the young shoots have pushed the soil up.

拱道 *guungdauh*, n., an archway.
拱門 *guungmern*, n., an arched entrance.
拱手 *gurngshoou*, v.t., to salute with the hands folded.
拱衛 *guungweih*, v.t., to garrison, to guard.

抻 10A.80-2

chen.

V.t. To draw out s.t. flexible: 把他抻出來 draw it out; 抻麵 see *-miahn*↓.

抻練 *chen-liahn*, v.t., to embarrass, put (s.o.) on the spot (by difficult questions).
抻麵 *chen-miahn*, n., a kind of noodles made by pulling out dough and not by slicing.

損 10A.80-4

suun.

V.i. & t. (1) To decrease: 減損 ditto; 損益 *-yih*↓; 損壽 to shorten one's life (by enjoying more than one's share). (2) To lose, damage: 損失 *-shy* ↓; 虧損 to lose money in trade; 損陰壞德, 損陰騭 (Budd.) to sin and thus have to pay for it later; 損傷, 損壞, 損害 *-shang*, *-huaih*, *-haih* ↓. (3) To criticize, deride or smear (person): 損人利己 to hurt s.o. for one's own benefits; 你別損人了 don't deride others.

Adj. (1) Mean or cruel in criticism: 這話眞損透了 it is really being mean to say so; 這法子眞損到家 this is too mean. (2) (Chin. med.) debilitated, weakened from long illness.

損到家 *suun-dauhjia*, phr., (1) minimum: 損到家的價錢 minimum price (i.e., at cost); (2) really mean or cruel.

損德 *suun-der*, phr., wicked, unconscionable, what will damage one in final reckoning.

損根子 *suun-gentz*, n., wicked person.

損骨頭 *suun-gur'tou*, n., ditto.

損害 *suunhaih*, v.t. & n., to damage, a damage (to reputation, business, etc.).

損壞 *suunhuaih*, v.t., to break, damage (reputation, furniture, etc.).

損傷 *suunshang*, v.t., to hurt, be hurt.

損失 *suunshy* (-'*shy*), v.i. & n., lose (in business, bargain, reputation); loss.

損事(兒) *suunshyh*(*-sheh'l*), n., s.t. underhand, wicked.

損條子 *suuntiaur'tz*, n., words of vituperation: 直給他上損條子 gave him a string of invectives.

損益 *suunyih*, n., addition and taking off, readjustment: 有所損益 there have been some readjustments.

損友 *surn-yoou*, n., (LL) a bad friend with demoralizing influence.

攢 10A.80-4

guahn.

V.i. & t. Throw down: see 攢交 *-jiau* ↓.

攢交 *guahnjiau*, v.i. & n., wrestling to make opponent fall down.

撰 10A.80-5

juahn.

V.t. To compose, compile, write (book, essay): 撰文, 撰稿 to write (essay, etc.); 撰著, 撰述 *-juh*, *-shuh* ↓; 編撰 to compile, edit (magazine, dictionary); 杜撰 to invent, concoct (story); 撰安 (end of letter to writer) your "literary" health.

撰著 *juahnjuh*, n. & v.t., literary works; to write (book, essay).

撰述 *juahnshuh*, n. & v.t., ditto.

撰次 *juahntsyh*, v.t., to compile.

擴 10A.80-6

kuoh.

[Related 廓 61.22]

V.i. & t. To enlarge, expand, see compp. ↓.

擴充 *kuohchung*, v.t., to expand (meaning, sphere, program, building, etc.).

擴大 *kuohdah*, v.i. & t., to enlarge (sphere, etc.).

擴展 *kuohjaan*, v.i. & t., to develop, expand (business, industry, etc.).

擴張 *kuohjang*, v.i. & t., to expand, broaden.

擴散 *kuohsahn*, v.t., (of gases or liquids) mix and blend together.

擯 10A.80-6

bihn.

V.t. Abandon, reject.

擯斥 *bihncheh*, v.t., dismiss with scolding

擯棄 *bihnchih*, v.t., abandon, discard (wife, lover, family, official post, etc.): 擯棄一切 set aside everything.

擯黜 *bihnchu*, v.t., degrade, send to remote post.

擯除 *bihnchur*, v.t., cast aside: 擯除障碍, 成見 remove, overcome obstacles, prejudices.

扒 10A.80-8

par (**ba*).

V.i. & t. (1) (**ba*) To climb, grip: 扒得高, 跌得重 the higher one climbs, the heavier the fall (danger of keeping high position); 扒牆上 catch hold of top of wall; 沒扒頭兒 nothing to catch hold of. (2) (**ba*) To rob, strip, peel, pull apart: 扒皮 peel (an orange) (cogn. 剝 92S.00); 把衣扒脫了 strip one's clothing. (3) To dig up; crawl; flop down: 扒下 "lie down," used in asking child to lie down and sleep.

扒船 *parchuarn*, n., fast rowboat, formerly, of Cantonese navy.

扒餻 *pargau*, n., a kind of pudding, made of buckwheat flour.

扒灰 *parhuei*, v.i. & n., (commit) incest between father- and daughter-in-law (pretext of "cleaning up ashes" in the kitchen).

扒豁子 *parhuohtz*, v.i., to spoil one's plan by revealing secrets, pointing out flaws.

扒拉 **ba'la*, v.i., separate, move rapidly as in operating the abacus: 扒拉兩口飯 pr. *par'la* or **ba'la*, shove rice rapidly into mouth (eat hurriedly).

扒犁 *par'li*, n., ice sledge used in northern Manchuria.

扒皮鬼(兒) **bapirgueei* (*-gue'l*), n., skinny person, ghostly (appearance).

扒山虎(兒) *par shan huu*(*'l*), n.,

(bot.) a kind of ivy.
扒手 *parshoou*, n., pickpocket.
扒載 *par-tzaih*, v.t., jettison cargo.

§ 10A.81 (扌/人)

揳 10A.81-1

shie.

V.i. To wedge in (see 楔 10B.81).

扶 10A.81-1

fur.

V.i. & t. (1) To hold up, support: 扶(他)起來 help him up; 扶着, 扶住 leaning on (cane, etc.); 扶牀而立 stand leaning on bed; 扶杖 lean on a stick; 扶老攜幼 supporting the old and carrying the young, come in a throng; 扶疾, 扶病而行 go burdened with sickness, despite sickness. (2) To carry from under: 扶靈, 扶柩, 扶櫬 act as pallbearer; 扶乩, 扶鸞 *-ji*, *-luarn*↓. (3) To help, lend support to: 扶危 help those in distress, bolster up tottering structure; 扶植 nurse and strengthen (a plant), (fig.) help to stand up, bring (young) to maturity.

扶持 *furchyr*, v.t., support (a cause, the church), give support to.
扶正 *furjehng*, v.t., recognize as wife proper (e.g., concubine after wife's death).
扶乩 *furji*, v.i. & n., planchette.
扶助 *furjuh*, v.t., to help (s.o.), succor.
扶老 *furlaau*, (1) n., old man's walking stick; (2) v.i., to support the old.
扶鸞 *furluarn*, n., see *-ji*↑.
扶桑 *Fursang*, n., mythic island, usu. interpreted as Japan.
扶手(板) *furshoou* (*baan*), n., armrest; 扶手椅 *-yii*, armchair.
扶疏 *furshu*, adj., (of foliage) luxuriant (枝葉扶疏).
扶侍 *furshyh*, v.t., serve, attend to, also wr. 服侍.
扶梯 *furti*, n., staircase, ladder, esp. hand ladder.
扶養 *furyaang*, v.i. & t., bring up (child) to maturity.
扶搖 *furyaur*, (1) n., (AC) a typhoon; (2) v.i., climb swaying upwards: 扶搖直上 be promoted quickly in official career.
扶掖 *furyeh*, v.t., support, help (young people).

挾 10A.81-1

shier (also *shiar*; **jiar*).
[Dist. 狹, 俠]

V.t. (1) To hold under the armpit: 挾泰山以超北海 (also pr. **jiar*) (AC) carry Tai mountain under the armpit and leap across the North Sea—obviously impossible undertaking; 挾一個書袋 carry a satchel under the arm; to carry concealed: 挾帶 *-daih*↓. (2) To carry or nurse a grudge: 挾嫌, 挾恨, 挾仇 *-shiarn*, *-hehn*, *-chour*↓. (3) Carry a badge, rely on some protection or privilege: 挾貴自重 proud of being in high position; 挾長 take liberties of being an older man; 挾義誅伐 attack s.o. in the name of justice; 挾勢 *-shyh*↓. (4) To rule in the name of: 挾天子以令諸侯 to give orders to the feudal princes in the name of the emperor (who existed in name only).

挾仇 *shierchour*, v.i. & adv., nursing an enmity, harboring an old wrong.
挾持 *shierchyy*, v.i., to force, coerce to do one's bidding.
挾帶 *shierdaih*, v.t., carry under arms; entail with.
挾恨 *shierhehn*, v.i. & adv., harboring a grudge, hatred.
挾擊 *shierjir*, v.t., to outflank, attack from the flank.
挾制 *shierjyh*, v.t., force s.o. into doing one's bidding.
挾嫌 *shiershiarn*, v.i. & adv., carrying a grudge against s.o.
挾勢 *shiershyh*, v.i., to rely on, take advantage of, one's power.
挾怨 *shieryuahn*, v.i., see *-hehn*↑.

揍 10A.81-1

tzouh.

V.t. (1) Hit, strike, beat: 揍人 beat up a person; 揍死他 finish him off; 挨揍 take a beating; 揍屁股 administer a smack on the buttocks; 揍他一頓 beat him up. (2) Break, smash: 不留神把茶碗揍了 smashed the teacup through carelessness.

摸 10A.81-2

mo (**mau*, **mor*).
[Dist. 摹 *mor* 20A.00]

V.i. & t. (1) To grope for, feel by groping motion, rub gently: 摸臉 gently feel (child's) face; 摸摸她的手 gently feel her hand; (coll. **mau*) 混水摸魚 fish in troubled waters. (2) (Fig.) search for, try to get at: 摸不着門兒 cannot find the proper approach; 摸不清 cannot understand what it is all about; 摸不着頭緒 cannot find the key or order in the whole thing; 這個人一天到晚到處摸錢 his fellow is trying all the time and everywhere to get at some money.

摸底 **maudii*, v.i., get at the bot-

扒 揳 扶 挾 揍 摸

亅	小	卜	十	土	ナ	卄	凵	丨	一	丁	フ	口	囗	冂	乛	厂	尸	亠	广	宀	丶	乚	七	心	八	人	乂	㇀	一	丿	㇖	く
00	01	02	10	11	12	20	21	22	30	31	32	40	41	42	50	51	52	60	61	62	63	70	71	72	80	81	82	83	90	91	92	93

tom (of things).

摸骨相 *mo-gurshiahng*, v.i., a way of telling a person's fortune by feeling his bones.

摸黑兒 **mau-he'l*, v.i., walk in the dark. ⌈10B.81.

摸稜 **morlirng*, adj., see 模[A]稜

摸瞎兒 **mau-shia'l*, v.i., (1) to grope one's way about, as a blind man; (2) try all sorts of ways and fail.

摸索 *mosuo*, v.i., (1) grope for; (2) dawdle, potter about.

撲 10A.81-2

pu.

[Var. 扑]

V.i. & t. (1) Assault, rush toward: 撲上來 lurch forward (esp. toward opponent). (2) Various forms of wrestling movements: 相撲, 撲交 come to grips; 撲倒, 撲跌 fall, fell (person) to the ground; 撲個空 overreach oneself, see 撲空 *-kung* ↓. (3) Strike, beat, flop, catch with a sudden movement: 撲殺此獠 "beat the beast to death" (allu. to brutal saying of Empress Wu Tseh-tien); 撲蠅 swat fly; 撲蝶 catch butterfly with a quick flop. (4) Touch lightly, tap: 撲面 tap face with powder; 清風撲面而來 the gentle breeze brushes against one's face; 清香撲鼻 a sweet scent assails the nostrils. (4) In combb. 噗噗, 噗通, 噗落 describing sudden, light movement, see *-pu*, *-tung*, *-luoh* ↓.

撲嗤(兒) *puchy* (*-che'l*), adv., descriptive of burst of laughter, or guffaw.

撲的 *pu-de*, adv., suddenly.

撲燈蛾(子) *pudeng-er*(*tz*), n., moth ("beating at lamp").

撲蝶會 *pu-dier-hueih*, n., butterfly-catching contest, on the Flower Festival (花朝), being 12th of 2nd month in lunar calendar.

撲地 *pudih*, adj. & adv., (1) all over the ground; (2) suddenly: 撲地落下來 suddenly drops to the ground.

撲兒 *pu-erl*, n., powder puff (粉撲兒 *feen--*).

撲虎兒 *pu-huu'l*, v.i., throw body forward, lurch forward.

撲救 *pujiouh*, v.i., fight fire.

撲克 *pu'ke*, n., (translit.) poker.

撲空 *pu-kung*, v.i., (oft. 撲個空) miss a punch; (fig.) be left holding the bag, fail to get what one wants.

撲鹿(撲漉) *puluh*, v.i., ditto.

撲落 *puluoh*, v.i., scatter around.

撲滿 *pumaan*, n., clay coin bank, "broken when filled."

撲忙子 *pu-marngtz*, v.i., bustle about nothing.

撲撲 *pupu*, adv., descriptive of palpitation: 撲撲的心頭跳.

撲簌簌 *pu-shu-shu*, adv., gushing forth (tears).

撲朔迷離 *pushuoh mirlir*, adj., whirling, confusing the eye.

撲騰 *puterng*, v.i., leap up, leap awkwardly; try to magnify (s.t.); n., show-off affair.

撲通 *putung*, adv., descriptive of sound of s.t. dropping into water.

扒 10A.81-2

nii.

[Pop. of 擬 10A.83]

揆 10A.81-3

kueir (also *kueei*).

N. (1) Formerly, the premier, see 揆席 *-shir* ↓, now (LL) also used of chief ministers of state. (2) Measure: 其揆一也 (AC) by the same measure or standard. (3) Important affairs: 百揆 all the state matters.

V.t. To conjecture, see 揆度 *-duoh* ↓.

揆度 *kueirduoh*, v.t., to calculate; conjecture.

揆席 *kueirshir*, n., (LL) formerly, the premier.

撅 10A.81-5

jyue.

V.t. (1) Raise: 撅尾巴 (of birds or animals) stick up the tail. (2) = 撧 10A.70. (3) Dig. (4) To attack.

擛 10A.81-5

yeh.

[Var. of 擪 51A.00]

捩 10A.81-6

lieh.

V.i. To twist (s.t.) with the hand: 轉捩點 (of writing) where one makes a turn; a twist in callig.; a turning point.

撳 10A.81-8

chihn.

[Related 揿]

V.t. To press: 撳鈕, 撳鈴 press a button, a bell; 撳喇叭 toot horn.

撿 10A.81-8

jiaan.

V.t. (1) U.f. 檢 10B.81, to inspect. (2) Pick up: 撿起來 pick up (from the ground); 撿破爛 a ragpicker. (3) Obtain by sheer luck: 這條命是撿來的 I saved my neck by mere chance.

掀 10A.81-9

shian.

V.t. (1) To raise up, lift up (curtain, pot cover, etc.): 掀鬚 to brush beard upwards in play. (2) To expose, reveal: 掀人罪狀 expose a man's crime; 掀他老底兒 reveal his past.

掀起 *shian-chii*, v.t., to lift up, cause, to bring about (big wave or movement).

掀動 *shianduhng*, v.t., raise a tumult: 掀動風波 raise a crisis.

掀腫 *shianjuung*, v.i., to swell up (of skin).

掀開 *shian'kai*, v.t., to open (book, cover, curtain).

掀掀 *shianshian*, adj. (MC) standing straight up.

掀騰 *shian'teng*, v.i. & t. & adj., (be) in a tumult.

掀天 *shian-tian*, v.i. & adj., (1) cause a big change in affairs: 掀天事業 a revolutionary undertaking; 掀天動地 sensational; world-shaking (event); (2) 海浪掀天 waves heave to the skies; 鼓樂掀 (or 喧) 天 a great din of drums and pipes ("heavens shake" with the noises of music).

揪 10A.81-9

jiou.

V.t. To hold fast, clutch, grasp: 揪住, 揪着 clench, lay hold of, seize; 揪他的辮子 get hold of his queue; 揪耳朵 pinch s.o.'s ear; 把他從牀上揪起來 drag him from his bed; 揪心 (s.t.) breaks the heart (as to touch savings).

揪心 *jioushin*, adj., to feel nervous.

抉 10A.81-9

jyuer.

V.t. (1) Choose (between), select (from): see compp.↓. (2) Pluck out: 抉目 gouge out the eyes; 抉首 cut off the head.

抉摘 *jyuerjer*, v.i., choose the best.

抉剔 *jyuerti*, v.t., pick out and dispose of.

抉擇 *jyuertzer*, v.i., make a choice from alternatives.

換 10A.81-9

huahn.

V.i. & t. To change: 換姓, 換名 change one's surname, personal name; 換衣服 change dress; 換地方 change place; 換錢 to change (dollars into cents, etc.); 換班 change shifts for duty; 替換 to substitute; 對換, 交換 to exchange, change (seats, etc.) with each other; 包換 guarantee to take back goods for exchange if unsatisfactory; 換回去 change it back; 換命的交情, 換下心來 become bosom friends; see 換帖 *-tiee*↓; 換言之, 換句話說 in other words; 換湯不換藥 make a superficial change.

換季 *huahnjih*, v.i., to change dress proper for the season.

換帖 *huahn-tiee*, v.i., be sworn brothers by exchange of papers bearing name, surname, year of birth, horoscope, etc.

換樣 (子) *huahnyahng(tz)*, v.i., (of person) change character or behavior; (of articles) change shape (due to misuse, temperature, etc.).

挨 10A.81-9

ai (**air*).

[Interch. 捱 when pr. **air*]

V.i. & t. (1) (**air*) To stand or go close by: 挨著牆走 walk along the wall; 挨牆靠壁 hug close to the wall; 挨肩, 挨近 *-jian, -jihn*↓. (2) To push, rub, jostle (in, out): 挨過去 jostle into a room; 挨擠, 挨揍, 挨摻 *-jii, -tzouh, -tzar*↓; 挨挨 *-ai*, 挨親兒 *-chie'l*↓. (3) (**air*) To suffer (beating, scolding): 挨打, 挨罵 *-daa, -mah*↓; endure silently (hunger, etc.): 挨冷受凍 endure the cold; 挨餓 *-eh*↓. (4) To go one by one or in order: 挨次, 挨門 *-tsyh, -mern*↓; 挨家兒打聽 go from house to house to find out news. (5) (**air*) To wait, bide one's time, delay: 再挨兩天 let's wait another two days; 挨過月底就好了 wait till the end of the month, then it will be all right.

挨挨兒 *ai'a'l*, v.i., to delay: 這筆賬再往後挨挨兒 delay this payment till later.

挨挨 *ai-ai*, v.i., to jostle together: 挨挨搶搶 *--chiarng chiaang*, 挨挨摻摻 *--tzar tzar*, 挨挨蹭蹭 *--tsehng tsehng*, to crowd together.

挨親兒 *ai-chie'l*, v.i., (a form of showing affection, said of a child) rub its face against mother's body or one whom he loves.

挨打 *ai-daa* (**air-*) v.i., to suffer beating.

挨餓 *ai-eh* (**air-*), v.i., to endure hunger.

挨光 *ai-guang*, v.i., (MC, sl.) to have illicit relations with opposite sex.

挨著 *ai'je* (**air-*), (1) part., hugging close to: 挨著路邊 hugging to the roadside; (2) adv., one by one: 一個挨著一個過去 pass by one by one.

挨肩 *ai-jian* (**air-*), adv., rubbing shoulders with: 挨肩擦膀

挨 技 拔 撒

go in a jostling crowd, also 挨肩兒 (*-jia'l*).

挨近 *ai-jihn* (**air-*), (1) adj., close by; (2) to come close to (person).

挨擠 *aijii*, v.i., to jostle together.

挨靠(兒) *aikauh('l)*, v.t., to depend on (person) for support.

挨罵 *ai-mah* (**air-*) v.i., receive scolding.

挨門(兒) *ai-mern(-mer'l)*, adv., door-to-door (canvass, deliver, etc.).

挨磨 *aimor*, v.i., to wait patiently for s.t. to happen, to linger around; v.t., to grind s.t.

挨鬧 *ainauh*, adj., (of crowd) jostling and noisy.

挨排 *aipair*, v.i., (MC) arrange.

挨人兒 *ai-rer'l*, v.i., to cohabit (also 挨親家兒), see *-guang* ↑.

挨噌 *ai-tseng*, v.i., receive scolding.

挨次 *aitsyh*, adv., in good order, one by one.

挨推 *aitueei*, v.i. & t., to delay (matter).

挨拶 *aitzar*, v.i., to jostle together.

挨揍 *ai-tzouh* (**air-*), v.i., see *-daa* ↑.

挨晚兒 *aiwaa'l*, adv., toward dusk.

§ 10A.82 (扌/乂)

技 10A.82-1

jih.

N. Ability, skill: 技倆 tricks; 技藝 *-yih*, 技能 *-nerng* ↓; 末技, 小技 minor skills; 雕蟲小技 (contempt.) a precious or purely decorative style of writing; 絕技 incomparable skill; a blow against which there is no defence.

技巧 *jihchiaau*, adj. & n., dexterity, -trous, ingenuity, -nuous.

技工 *jihgung*, n., a mechanic.

技正 *jihjehng*, n., a senior specialist, foreman; see *-shyh* ↓.

技擊 *jihjir*, n., boxing, pugilism.

技能 *jihnerng*, n., specialized skill, ability.

技術 *jihshuh*, n., technique; 技術人員 technical personnel.

技師 *jihshy*, n., a technical expert.

技士 *jihshyh*, n., a junior specialist, see *-jehng* ↑.

技癢 *jih-yaang*, phr., to itch for a chance to show off.

技藝 *jihyih*, n., (1) mechanical arts; (2) expert skill.

拔 10A.82-1

bar.

[Dist. 祓 63B.82, 跋 40B.82]

V.t. (1) To pull out, pluck, raise, move: 拔出 pull out; 拔釘, 艸, 門閂, 毛 pull out a nail, weeds, door bolt, hair; 拔牙 to extract teeth; 拔腿 to take to one's heels; 拔不出腿來 cannot get off from pressing duties; 拔來報往 phr., exchange visits, have frequent contacts; 拔虎鬚 pull tiger's whiskers (twist lion's tail); 拔幟 capture enemy's colors; 拔營 strike camp; 拔樹尋根 trace to very roots; 拔茅連茹 phr., (LL) promote good men who will bring in their associates; 拔本塞源 (AC) phr., abandon source, (MC) clear up source and restore purity. (2) Draw: 拔毒 draw out poison (pr. *baa dur* in Peking dial.); 拔了短籌 draw a poor lot, i.e., be short-lived; 拔十得五 get fifty percent. (3) Select, promote, place ahead, pay out of order: 拔付, 拔還 pay, repay first; 選拔 select candidates, talent; 拔擢, 拔尤 select and promote the best; 拔薦 *-jiahn* ↓; 名拔前茅 phr., come out among the first in examinations or with honors; 出乎其類, 拔乎其萃 phr., be distinguished from one's kind, be among the select best, see 拔萃 *-tsueih* ↓; 拔親 update wedding on account of scheduled funeral. (4) Rise from: 拔地而出 rise straight from the ground (of rock formations, etc.); hence 海拔 degrees above sea level. (5) Capture (city, fort 拔城, 寨). (6) To cool s.t. by water or ice: 拔一拔.

拔白 *barbair*, n., (MC) daybreak.

拔步 *bar-buh*, v.i., to march forward, move forward quickly.

拔闖 *barchuahng*, v.i., step in and defend person being bullied.

拔除 *bar-chur*, v.t., eradicate.

拔羣 *bar-chyurn*, adj., outstanding.

拔貢 *barguhng*, n., government fellow, fellowship, selected from districts in Manchu Dyn., see 貢生 31.80.

拔河 *bar-her*, v.i. & n., tug-of-war.

拔火罐兒 *barhuooguah'l*, n., small funnel over casserole to help draw charcoal fire.

拔薦 *barjiahn*, v.t., recommend for post or promote ahead of others.

拔脯(兒) *bar-pur('l)*, n., man who stands straight (forward looking); 拔脯子 *--tz*, v.i., stick chest out as challenging attitude.

拔撒 *barsha*, v.i. & t., (MC) separate.

拔身 *bar-shen*, v.i., get away (from pressing duties).

拔舌地獄 *bar-sher dihyuh*, n., (Budd.) hell where tongues are split; "you will go to such hell" said of person with vicious tongue.

拔絲(山藥) *barsy (shanyau)*, n., sugar-coated potato served red hot when sugar can be drawn out in threads; same with lotus-seeds, etc.

拔萃 *bartsueih*, adj., outstanding, among the select best.

撒 10A.82-2

sa (**saa*).

V.i. & t. (1) To let go, let out, release: 撒放 *-fahng* ↓; 撒手, or 撒開手 let go the hand, also wash hands of matter, 撒手(兒) *-shoou('l)* ↓; 撒氣 deflate tire; 撒

線 let out string in kite-flying; 撒溺, 撒糞 *-niauh, -fehn*↓. (2) To act in a spoiled, silly, joking or drunken manner: 撒嬌 *-jiau*↓; 撒風撒痴, 撒嬌撒痴 to act spoiled (esp. woman); 撒賴, 撒潑 *-laih, -po*↓; 撒酒風兒 to yell, shout when drunk; 撒科 *-ke*↓. (3) (**saa*) (Interch. 灑 63A.70, 洒 63A.41) to cast (sand, seeds), spray (fluid); 撒網 cast a net, see *-waang*↓; 撒豆成兵 (myth.) cast beans on ground which are transformed by magic into soldiers.

撒氣 *sa-chih*, v.t., to deflate; vent anger.

撒旦 *Sadahn*, n., (translit.) Satan.

撒對兒 *sa-duoh'l*, v.i., to challenge, antagonize, offend.

撒放 *safahng*, v.t., to let go, to spray (fluid, particles).

撒糞 *sa-fehn*, v.i., to ease bowels, also (abuse) talk rubbish.

撒和 **saa'he*, v.i., take a stroll: 撒和撒和一下 ditto; to trot (horse).

撒歡兒 *sa-hua'l*, v.i., to romp about (as a cat).

撒謊 *sa-huaang*, v.i., to tell a lie, a fib.

撒帳 **saa-jahng*, v.i., formerly, a wedding custom, after the ceremonies were over, with bride and groom seated on bed, coins and fruit were thrown by guests.

撒姦 *sajian*, v.i., indulge in cunning, play dirty trick.

撒嬌(兒) *sajiau('l)*, v.i., (lady) to act in pettishly charming manner, act spoiled, to pout, also 撒嬌撒痴 act like spoiled child.

撒極 *sajir*, v.i., driven to extremities (and commit suicide).

撒種 *sar-juung*, v.i., to sow seeds.

撒開 *sa-kai*, v.i. & t., to let: 撒開了手 wash one's hands of the matter, disclaim further interest.

撒科 *sa-ke*, v.i., as in 撒科打諢 *--daa-huhn*, (Chin. theater) to introduce comic remarks in dialogue.

撒賴 *salaih*, v.i., to lie and cheat, speak falsehood to clear oneself and hurt others.

撒馬 *sa-maa*, v.i., to let go the reins and gallop.

撒漫 **saamahn*, v.t., to spend freely; to spoil (s.t.) by a hasty word.

撒溺 *sa-niauh*, v.i., to urinate.

撒潑 *sapo*, adj. & adv., vile-tempered (woman), given to scolding others.

撒然 **saararn*, adv., (MC) abruptly (awakened).

撒散 **saa'san*, v.t., to distribute (handbills, etc.); to spend lavishly.

撒鞋 **saashier*, n., slippers (also wr. 靸鞋); a special kind of workman's slippers with cloth sole and leather top.

撒手(兒) *sa-shoou('l)*, v.i., wash one's hands of the matter; 撒手鐧 the climaxing act, one's specialty; 撒手塵寰 to pass away.

撒薰香 *saa shyuhnshiang*, phr., to indulge in smearing tactics.

撒尿 *sa-suei* (also *-niauh*), v.i., to urinate.

撒村 *sa-tsun*, v.i., to use vulgar language, act like a country bumpkin.

撒腿 *sa-tueei*, v.i., to beat it as fast as one can, disappear sheepishly from scene.

撒嘴 *sa-tzueei*, v.i., to release a bite.

撒網 *sa-waang*, v.i., cast net; (fig.) to give a party on occasion of wedding, funeral, etc., in the hope of collecting presents.

撒鴨子 *sa-yatz*, v.i., see *-tueei*↑.

撒野 *sa'yee*, v.i., to get rude, bumptious.

撒囈症 *sayih-jehng*, n., sleepwalking, also habit of talking in sleep, somnambulism.

披 10A.82-2

pi (also *pei* in certain vern. phrr.)

Vb. (1) To open, lay open: 披心, 披肝露膽, 披瀝肝膽 lay open my heart (to urge, give honest advice or show loyalty); 披露 publish, cause to be published (article); 披襟 (fig. or lit.) bare breast. (2) To spread out, flutter, disperse: 披髮, 披頭散髮 (*pi* or *pei*) wear hair dishevelled; 披沙揀金 sift sand for gold, sift carefully. (3) To put on, wear: 披衣而起 throw on gown and rise; 披甲 put on armor; 披麻帶孝 in deep mourning; 披枷帶鎖 in cangue and shackles; 披星戴月 journey or work under stars and moon in the night. (4) To open and read: 披覽, 披誦 scan or read book, roll, letter.

披風 *pifeng*, n., ancient lady's cloak.

披拂 *pifur* (*pei-*), adj., moving in the wind.

披掛 *pi-guah* (*pei-*), adj., in military attire.

披紅 *pi-hurng* (*pei-*), adj., covered with red sashes on festive occasions.

披肩 *pijian*, n., woman's shoulder-piece; stole.

披離 *pilir*, adj., (LL) luxurious (growth of foliage).

披披 *pipi*, adj., (LL) trailing, blowing about (of girdles, willows).

披片兒 *peipiah'l*, v.i., be a beggar.

披頭 *pitour*, n., Beatles: 披頭士, 披頭四.

披緇 *pi-tzy*, v.i., (LL) wear black, i.e., become monk.

搜 10A.82-2

sou.

V.t. To search, ransack: 搜索 *-suoo*↓; 搜購 collect, select for purchase.

搜捕 *soubuu*, v.t., search and arrest (criminal).

搜查 *souchar*, v.t., to search (house, etc.).
搜求 *souchiour* (also *-'chiou*), v.t., to hunt for (evidence, etc.).
搜括 *sougua*, v.t., to loot (valuables, etc.), take away by force.
搜檢 *soujiaan*, v.t., to search for (illegal goods).
搜緝 *soujih*, v.t., to issue warrant for escaped (convicts, etc.).
搜集 *soujir*, v.t., to collect (articles, rare editions, stamps, ores).
搜看 *soukahn*, v.t., (MC) to inspect (place).
搜羅 *sou'luor* (*-'lou*), v.t., to collect from various sources.
搜拿 *sounar*, v.t., see *-buu* ↑.
搜尋 *soushyurn* (also *-'shyun*), v.t., to search.
搜索 *sousuoo*, v.t., to search (hidden articles, etc.).
搜討 *soutaau*, v.t., to examine and study (doctrines, etc.).
搜剔 *souti*, v.t., to pick, select; to weed out (textual errors).

撇 10A.82–2

pie (**piee*).

N. (**piee*) A slanting stroke in calligraphy, like the first stroke in 人, 千.

V.t. (1) Cast aside, leave behind, often with complement: 撇下, 撇開: 撇下一妻三子 leave behind one wife and three children; 撇不開 cannot shove aside (duties, etc.). (2) To skim oil or matter from surface of liquid: 撇油 *-your* ↓. (3) (**piee*) As in 撇嘴 to draw down corners of lips in contempt, or in a child about to cry; 撇齒拉嘴 phr., making a contemptuous expression.

撇棄 *piechih*, v.t., abandon.
撇清 *pieching*, v.i., disengage oneself, pretend to be uninvolved.
撇蘭 pr. *piee-larn*, n. & v.i., a game in which each person chooses the leaf of a drawn orchid, determining sum to be contributed, covered and unseen.
撇漾 *pieyahng*, v.t., (MC) abandon and drift apart.
撇油兒 *pieyour'l*, v.i., have a finger in the pie, grease one's palm.

擻 10A.82–2

soou.

V.i. & t. (1) To flap (clothing) free of dust: 抖ᐞ擻 10A.10. (2) To tremble, flutter: 擻抖抖地顫 trembling, shivering.

擾 10A.82–3

raau.

V.t. (1) Disturb, trouble: 擾動 to stir, shake, agitate; 擾亂 *-luahn* ↓; 擾攘 cause utter confusion; 擾擾 in disorder, confusion; 騷擾 create disturbances, make trouble; 喧擾 noisy confusion, hubbub; 擾害 endanger; 紛擾 in a state of confusion, disorderly. (2) Be guest to: 奉擾 "thank you for your hospitality"; 我擾你一頓吧 may I have potluck with you? 叨擾, 打擾 have the honor to be your guest, enjoy your hospitality; 擾聒 impose on your kindness; 煩擾 cause you so much inconvenience, trouble you so much.

擾亂 *raauluahn*, v.t., make a mess of, trouble, disturb.

扠 10A.82–3

cha (**jaa*).

N. (**jaa*) A length, see V.i. 2 ↓.

V.i. (1) To place arms akimbo: 扠腰. (2) (**jaa*) To measure length with stretched thumb and middle finger.

掇 10A.82–3

duor.

[Dist. 綴]

V.t. To pick up, to pluck (leaves from stems, vegetables).

掇弄 *duornuhng*, v.t., arrange, rearrange nicely (as with finger).
掇拾 *duorshyr*, v.t., pick up: 掇拾章句 stud composition with picked up phrases.

撥 10A.82–3

bo.

N. (1) A handful (of earth, ashes, powder). (2) (AC) cord for pulling hearse＝紼 93B.22. (3) (AC) a kind of ladies' hair ornament.

V.t. (1) To stir with hand or stick: 撥土, 灰 stir dust, ashes; to move (switch, etc.) with a slight finger movement; 撥表針 move watch hand; 撥動 *-duhng* ↓ 撥算盤 tick off beads on abacus; poke fire, see 撥火棍 *-huoo-guhn* ↓; 撥開 poke aside, spread out; 撥歸一邊 set on one side. (2) To dispel, push aside (curtain): 撥開雲霧見青天 (or 撥雲見日) clear the clouds and see the sky, (fig.) remove cloud of suspicion, redress wrong and restore justice; 撥亂反正 dispel chaos and restore peace. (3) To assign, set aside: 撥兵 despatch troops; 撥項 transfer a sum; 撥一筆款 set aside a sum.

撥動 *boduhng*, v.t., move by finger (hour hand), turn (a switch).
撥發 *bofa*, v.t. & n., pay out, transfer (funds).
撥火棍 *bohuoo-guhn*, n., poker for fireplace.
撥腳 *bojiaau*, v.i., fell (a person) by placing leg across opponent's, a boxer's movement.

撥剌 *bolah*, n., noise of striking fins, 扒 also 扒Δ拉 10A.80; noise of twanging bow.

撥浪鼓 *bolanggu*, n., ＝波Δ浪鼓 63A.82.

撥弄 *boluhng*, v.t., as in 撥弄是非 stir up trouble by gossip, rumors; fiddle with.

撮 10A.82-4

tsuo.

N. (1) A handful, small quantity. (2) A milliliter.

V.t. (1) To pick up or hold (dust, powder) between fingers. (2) To put together: 撮合 *-her* ↓.

撮鳥 *tsuodiaau*, n., (MC vulg., abuse) weakling for sexual purposes.

撮合 *tsuoher* (*-'he*), v.t., to bring two parties together, esp. for matrimonial alliance; 撮合山 matchmaker.

撮口 *tsuokoou*, adj., (Chin. phonetics) the sound "yu" (Wade: "ü") as in 玉, 越, 圓 *yuh, yueh, yuarn.*

撮弄 *tsuo-'luhng* (*-'lung*), v.t., (1) to make fun of (person); (2) to manipulate, instigate (to riot, rebellion, etc.); (3) n., (MC) acrobatic shows and the like.

撮土 *tsuotuu*, (1) n., (contempt.) a small country (cf. 蕞Δ爾 20A.82); (2) v.i., to gather soil with hand.

撮要 *tsuoyauh*[1], n., summary (of speech, etc.); elementary outline (of subject).

撮藥 *tsuoyauh*[2], v.i., (Chin. med.) to fill out a prescription.

攫 10A.82-4

jyuer.

V.t. Catch with claws, jump upon and seize: 攫取 seize and carry off; 攫捕 to grasp, as with claws; 攫奪 rob (goods); 攫而食之 catch and eat it.

投 10A.82-4

tour.

V.i. & t. (1) To throw, cast away, fling (s.t.); 投石 throw stone; 投炸彈 throw bomb; 投竿, 投綸 cast line in angling; throw down: 投筆(翰)從戎 throw down the pen and join the army; 投袂而別 whisk one's sleeves and depart; 投簪 throw down official job; 投戈 lay down the arms; 投鞭斷流 if the soldiers threw their whips into the river, it would be enough to stem the current—fig. of size of troops; 投鼠忌器 throw s.t. at a rat, but afraid to break the vase—caution in taking action; 投桃報李 exchange gifts between lovers, friends; 投擲, 投棄 *-jyr, -chih* ↓. (2) Project an image: 投影 cast reflection in water; 投射 *-sheh* ↓. (3) Throw oneself: 投水, 投海, 投河 jump into water to drown oneself; 投火 jump into fire, also throw s.t. into fire; 投荒 *-huang* ↓; 投繯 hang oneself (繯＝noose); 自投羅網 walk into trap; 投入軍隊 join the army, enlist; 投敵, 投降 surrender to enemy; 投胎 (of spirit) enter the womb, be born again (as another person). (4) To submit, send in, deliver: 投書, 投函, 投郵 send letter; 投稿 submit article to publisher; 投刺, 投名片, 投帖 send in one's card; 投考 apply for entrance examination; 投告, 投官 surrender or report to police; 投稟 send in petition; 投票, 投資 *-piauh, -tzy* ↓. (5) Seek shelter, stop over: 投入懷抱 find comfort and warmth in embrace (of church, country); 投親 go and stay with relatives; 投店 stop over at inn; 投門路 ask friend to help get job; 投靠, 投宿 *-kauh, -suh* ↓. (6) Fit into, be attracted toward: 意氣(氣味, 臭味)相投 friends attracted to each other by common tastes: 投簧 be mutually compatible, fit into; 投其所好 cater to person's pleasures, tastes; 投機 *-ji* ↓.

投案 *tour-ahn*, v.i., (of party involved) report to court, surrender oneself to police.

投奔 *tourbehn*, v.i. & t., seek shelter (in country, place), esp. return to freedom: 投奔自由 escape to freedom.

投標 *tourbiau*, v.i., submit bid for contract.

投誠 *tourcherng*, v.t., surrender to, switch loyalty to.

投棄 *tourchih*[1], v.t., abandon, throw away.

投契 *tourchih*[2], v.i., feel attracted toward each other, get along well.

投親 *tourchin*, v.i., go and stay with relative (usu. as dependent).

投遞 *tourdih*, v.t., deliver (letter, gift).

投稿 *tour-gaau*, v.i., submit manuscripts.

投戈 *tourge*, v.i., lay down arms.

投合 *tourher*, v.i., (talks, persons) agree with each other.

投荒 *tourhuang*, v.i., send, go away to distant regions.

投壺 *tourhur*, n. & v.i., ancient game of throwing arrows into vases, described in 禮記.

投機 *tourji*, v.i., (1) play opportunist: 投機份子 opportunist; 投機取巧 take advantage of the moment; (2) speculate on stocks; (3) get along well: 他們談得很投機 they are having a very interesting talk together; 話不投機 dissidence of opinion in talks, resulting in estrangement.

投杼 *tourjuh*, phr., "leave the loom", (allu.) mother of good Confucianist unbelieving when first told of her son being murderer, but believing it on third

A

time—influence of rumor and gossip.

投擲 *tourjyr*, v.t., to throw, cast (stone, etc.).

投止 *tourjyy*, v.i., stop over for the night.

投考 *tourkaau*, v.i., apply for entrance examination, register and take part in any examination.

投靠 *tourkauh*, v.t., to go and live (with person) as dependent.

投老 *tourlaau*, v.i., (MC) retire for old age.

投明 *tourmirng*, (1) adv., toward dawn; (2) 棄暗投明 (of bandits, rebels) give oneself up to the government.

投暮 *tourmuh*, adv., (MC) toward dusk.

投票 *tourpiauh*, v.i., cast vote.

投射 *toursheh*, v.i., to project.

投生 *toursheng*, v.i., be reincarnated (as another person).

投轄 *tourshiar*, phr., (AC allu.) "cut off axle" as a way of asking and insisting friend not to depart.

投降 *tourshiarng*, v.i., to surrender: 無條件投降 unconditional surrender.

投首 *tourshoou*[1], v.i., report to police, admit guilt.

投手 *tourshoou*[2], n., (baseball) pitcher.

投順 *tourshuhn*, v.t., see *-cherng* ↑.

投宿 *toursuh*, v.i., stop over (at inn) for the night.

投胎 *tourtai*, v.i., be reincarnated.

投子 *tourtz*, n., dice (＝骰子).

投資 *tourtzy*, v.i., to invest.

报 10A.82-5

bauh.

[Abbr. of 報 11S.82]

抆 10A.82-6

wehn.

V.t. To wipe off (tears): 抆淚 a

B

literary convention for prescribed degree of sorrow in obituary notices apparently wiping tears more energetically for close cousins (by pressing knuckles on eye socket) than 拭淚 merely brushing or flicking tears away for more distant cousins, cf. 搵 10A.30.

撤 10A.82-6

cheh.

[Cf. 徹, 澈]

V.t. (1) To take away, remove, withdraw: 撤退, 撤換, 撤銷, etc. *-tueih*, *-huahn*, *-shiau* ↓; 撤回 to withdraw, to retract; remove from office: 撤職, 撤差 *-jyr*, *-chai* ↓; 撤水 pump off water; 撤火 remove heating arrangements when cold season is over. (2) To counteract: 酸撤鹹 the sour counteracts the salty flavor.

撤保 *cheh-baau*, v.i., withdraw or cease guaranteeship.

撤兵 *cheh-bing*, v.i., withdraw soldiers.

撤差 *cheh-chai*, v.i., remove from office.

撤懲 *chehcherng*, v.t., remove from office and punish (person).

撤出 *cheh-chu*, v.t., to withdraw, remove (soldiers) from place.

撤除 *cheh-chur*, v.t., to remove (obstacles, etc.).

撤防 *cheh-farng*, v.i., withdraw garrison or security arrangements.

撤廢 *chehfeih*, v.t., abolish (old rules).

撤換 *chehhuahn*, v.t., to replace (with new articles, troops, positions).

撤職 *cheh-jyr*, v.t., dismiss from office: 把他撤職; 撤了職 (p.p.) dismissed.

撤任 *cheh-rehn*, v.t., ditto.

撤銷 *chehshiau*, v.t., cancel (arrangement), invalidate (guarantee), withdraw (offer).

撤席 *cheh-shir*, v.i., terminate dinner, clear off dinner table.

C

撤退 *chehtueih*, v.i. & t., retreat, order (troops) to retreat from place.

撤脱 *cheh-tuo*, v.i., get away (from appointments, etc.).

搬 10A.82-8

sah.

V.t. (AC) to kill with edge of hand.

扳 10A.82-9

ban.

V.t. Pull (bar, switch, gear shift): 扳不動 cannot pull (in, out); 扳過來 pull it over.

扳指兒 *banjee'l*, n., heavy ring, orig. protecting archer's finger (also wr. 搬指兒).

扳機 *ban-ji*, n., the switch bar.

扳罾 *bantzehng*, n., fishing net supported and operated by long poles.

授 10A.82-9

shouh.

[Related 受 90.82]

V.t. (1) To give (to person): usu. 授予, 授與 *-yuu* ↓; 授受 *-shouh* ↓. (2) To teach, pass on to future generation: 講授 teach (a subject); 教^Δ^授 82S.82, v.t., to teach; n., a professor; 傳授 pass on oral tradition (classical interpretation, secret formula). (3) To invest (person) in office.

授課 *shouh-keh*, phr., give lessons.

授命 *shouh-mihng*, phr., 見危授命 (AC) willing to sacrifice life in case of danger.

授首 *shouh-shoou*, v.i., (AC) be beheaded.

授受 *shouh-shouh*, v.i., to pass (objects) from hand to hand: 私相授受 pass money between hands in bribery; 男女授受不親 (AC) it is improper for man and woman to hold each other's hands, pass objects from hand to hand.

授室 *shouh-shyh*, v.t., to take in a bride; (AC) to accept daughter-in-law in formal ceremony.

授時 *shouh-shyr*, phr., (AC) to give official calendar of year's seasons.

授業 *shouh-yeh*, v.i., (LL) to teach (cf. 受業 to be pupil).

授意 *shouh-yih*, v.i., to suggest idea behind scenes to (person) for action.

授與 *shouh-yuu*, phr., to give to: 授與勳章 to award medal.

援 10A.82–9

yuarn.

N. Aid: 美援 American foreign aid; 內援, 外援 domestic, foreign help, ally.

V.t. (1) To lift by hand, to aid: 援助, 援救 *-juh, -jiouh*↓; 援溺 to rescue a drowning or drowned man; 擧賢援能 to promote able men. (2) To stretch a hand, hold (hand, pen): 援手 *-shoou*↓; 援筆 take up the pen. (3) To cite (example, precedent): 援例, 援據 *-lih, -jyuh*↓.

援隊 *yuarn-dueih*, n., (mil.) support unit.

援照 *yuarnjauh*, prep., according to rules precedents.

援救 *yuarnjiouh*, v.t., to rescue.

援助 *yuarnjuh*, v.t., to help, succor (the needy).

援據 *yuarnjyuh*, prep., in accordance with.

援軍 *yuarn-jyun*, n., rescue troops.

援例 *yuarn-lih*, adv., according to precedent.

援手 *yuarn-shoou*, v.i., to give a hand, to help.

援引 *yuarnyiin*, v.t., (1) to cite (examples); (2) to help promote (friends to position).

搬 10A.82–9

ban.

V.i. & t. Move (furniture, luggage): 搬家 move to another house; 搬出去 take away (usu. heavy object); 搬到那裏去 where are you moving or taking (the things) to? 搬來搬去 move back and forth; 搬磚砸腳 phr., one's own doing (drop brick on one's own foot); 搬弄是非 phr., carry tales.

搬不倒兒 *ban'budaau'l*, n., doll that always rights itself up=不倒翁.

搬塲 *bancharng*, n. & v.i., house removal.

搬指兒 *ban'jee'l*, n., heavy finger ring, orig. for protection of archer's finger.

搬配 *banpeih*, adj., be well-matched in marriage (also wr. 般配, 班配).

搬子 *bantz*, n., bottle opener; a wrench.

搬演 *banyaan*, v.t., =扮^Δ演 10A.50.

搬運 *banyuhn*, n. & v.t., transport (goods, luggage); 搬運費 *--feih*, transportation charges.

§10A.83 (扌/乛)

捷 10A.83–1

jier.

N. (1) Victory, triumph, conquest: 大捷 an overwhelming victory; 奏捷 to score a victory; 連捷 score one victory after another. (2) A surname.

V.t. Be victorious or successful (in war, examination, games, etc.).

Adj. Fast, quick, nimble, smart: 捷足先得(登) victory to the swift-footed; 捷徑 *-jihng*↓; 快捷, 迅捷 fast, quick, fleet, speedy; 敏捷 nimble, agile, quick-witted: 文思敏捷 (of writer) ability to think and write fast; 便捷 convenient, handy.

捷報 *jierbauh*, n., (1) tidings of military victory; (2) formerly, news of a person's success in government examinations.

捷徑 *jierjihng*, n., (lit. & fig.) a short cut.

捷給 *jierjii*, adj., having quick wits, ready at making repartees.

捷口 *jier-koou*, adj., clever of speech.

捷黠 *jiershiar*, adj., crafty.

捷書 *jier-shu*, n., a victory bulletin.

捷才 *jiertsair*, n., ready wits, quickness of mind.

撻 10A.83–1

tah.

V.t. To whip: 鞭撻, 撻罰 punish (enemy), whip in fig. sense.

撻伐 *tahfa*, v.t., (AC) invade (neighbors): 大張撻伐 declare war on a country to punish its iniquities.

擬 10A.83–2

nii.

擬 捉 提

[Pop. 拟]

V.t. (1) To guess, estimate: 擬度 *-duh*↓; 擬料 *-liauh*↓. (2) To draft (a letter, resolution, document): 擬就 have drafted (a document, etc.), is already drafted; 擬妥 ditto; 擬稿 to draft a document; 草擬 to draft; 擬訂 to draft, to draw up; 擬定 *-dihng*↓; 擬具 *-jyuh*↓. (3) To intend to, have a mind to: 擬於明日啟行 intend to leave tomorrow; 不擬 do not intend to; 擬將 plan to; 擬請 intend to ask (for leave, etc.); 擬辦 intend to do (s.t.); 虛擬 to make a supposition. (4) Compare, draw comparison: 比擬 compare (s.t., s.o.) with another; 相擬 draw an analogy between two things or persons. (5) To consciously imitate, to follow manner or style: 摹擬 carefully copy anc. painting; 擬唐人作 done in the manner or style of Tarng poets.

擬曲 *nirchyuu*, n., a mime; words of song by s.o.

擬尺蠖 *niichyyhuoh*, n., (zoo.) *Plusia festucae*.

擬定 *niidihng*, v.i., to propose, draft (a plan, date); to plan to do s.t.

擬度 *niiduh*, v.t., think over, conjecture.

擬古 *nii-guu*, v.t., imitate the style of ancient writers.

擬具 *niijyuh*, v.t., to draw up (practical measures, a plan).

擬人法 *niirern-faa*, n., personification.

擬料 *niiliauh*, v.t., suppose, conjecture.

擬態 *nii-taih*, n., mimicry.

擬議 *nii-yih*, v.t., (1) consider and comment; (2) make proposals or recommendations.

捉 10A.83-4

juo.

V.t. (1) To clutch: 捉筆 to wield the pen; 捉刀 *-dau*↓; 一沐三捉髮 (allu.) to tie up hair three times during a bath in order to see callers—busy, attentive in government affairs; 捉襟見肘 cannot make the ends meet; 捉迷藏 play hide-and-seek. (2) To catch (rat), arrest (thief): 捉拿, 捕捉 ditto; 捉姦 catch adultery in the act.

捉鼻 *juo-bir*, v.i., (LL) hold one's nose in contempt.

捉刀 *juodau*, v.t., to write examination papers, etc., by other than true candidate or writer (allu.: 曹操 held a knife watching while s.o. wrote for him).

捉弄 *juoluhng*, v.t., to play trick upon (s.o.).

捉狹 *juoshiar*, adj. & adv., mischievous, calculating; 捉狹鬼 (abuse) nasty, mean fellow.

提 10A.83-4

tir (*di).

V.t. (1) To carry or lift by the hand, lift up: 提起來 lift up by hand; 提開 take (s.t.) away, put aside; 提不動 cannot lift it; 提菜籃, 提燈籠 carry basket, lantern; 提高, 提掇, 提攜, 提拔, 提升 *-gau, -duoh,- shi, -bar, -sheng*↓; 提筆 take up pen (and write); 提款, 提項 draw out money; 提鞋 pull on shoes; 提腕 write with wrist not touching desk; 提心吊膽 breathless with fear, worry; 提心在口 have one's heart in one's mouth (exactly as in English); 提手躡腳的走 walk on tiptoe; 耳提面命 (of teacher, parent) give personal advice constantly (耳提=pulling ear); 提綱挈領 give main outline (of facts, principles). (2) To mention, bring up for discussion, refer to: usu. 提起, 提到, 提出, 提及; 提起這件事 mention this affair; 提出條件 state conditions (for peace, etc.); 提出意見 express one's opinion, ideas; 提出證據 bring forth proofs; 提出訴訟 bring suit to court; 別提了, 不要提起 don't bring this up; 提到這件事 refer to this matter; 提到我沒有 did he mention me? (3) Guide, promote, lead: 提攜, 提拔 promote, see *-shi, -bar*↓; 提率軍隊 lead troops; 提倡, 提調 *-chahng, diauh*↓. (4) Extract: 提取 extract (oil, etc.); 提煉, 提淨, 提舉 *-liahn, -jihng, -jyuu*↓. (5) Of law action, bring out and bring to court: 提解, 提押 send over, deliver (convict); 提送 send over; 提審, 提問, 提究, 提質 bring out accused and cross-examine in court.

提案 *tir-ahn*, n., proposition, resolution to be discussed.

提拔 *tirbar*, v.t., (1) specially promote to office, promote as a special consideration; (2) (-'*ba*) (coll.) remind: 如我忘了, 請提拔我一聲 please remind me in case I forget (=*-shiing*↓).

提包 *tirbau*, n., handbag.

提撥 *tirbor*, v.t., to appropriate.

提補 *tirbuu*, v.t., select and fill (post).

提倡 *tirchahng*, v.i. & n., promote, sponsor (new movement, styles, physical culture, etc.); promotion.

提成 *tir-cherng*, v.i., take a percentage.

提前 *tirchiarn*, v.t., advance in date; adv., ahead: 提前考試 take examination ahead of schedule; v.i., as in 提前清償 payment in advance.

提挈 *tirchieh*, v.t., help, lead, guide, see *-shi*↓.

提起 *tir-chii*, v.t., (1) mention, bring up: 別再提起這事 don't bring this up again, see *-chu*↓; (2) 提起精神 put forth more energy, refresh one's mind; (3) 提起公訴 to initiate public prosecution.

提親 *tir-chin*, v.i., bring up proposal of marriage.

提琴 *tirchirn*, n., violin (小提琴); 中提琴 viola; 大提琴 cello; 低音提琴 double bass.

提出 *tirchu*, v.t., propose, bring up: 提出意見, 問題, 議案, 訴訟, 條件 bring up idea, question, resolution, lawsuit, condition, etc.

提取 *tirchyuu*, v.t., extract (oil,

etc.); come specially to bring (certain article); draw (money) from bank.

提袋 *tirdaih*, n., handbag.

提單 *tirdan*, n., bill of lading, invoice.

提到 *tir-dauh*, v.t., mention, refer to.

提燈會 *tirdeng-hueih*, n., lantern festival.

提點 *tirdiaan*, v.i., remind.

提調 *tirdiauh*, v.t., supervise (troops); select, appoint, and assign (officers, troops).

提督 *tirdu*, n., former title of provincial commander in chief (水師提督, etc.).

提掇 *tirduoh*, v.t., to help (younger people) by guidance, promotion, see *-bar* ↑, *-shi* ↓.

提防 *tirfarng* (**di'fang*), v.t., guard against (enemy, attack, flood, infiltration, etc.).

提高 *tir-gau*, v.t., elevate (standard), increase (attention, cautionary measures), heighten: 提高警覺 heighten vigilance.

提供 *tirgung*, v.t., contribute: 提供節目 "program is brought to you by."

提盒(兒) *tirher('l)*, n., carrying case (for food, presents).

提貨單 *tirhuohdan*, n., invoice for taking delivery; 提貨摺 passbook for taking delivery.

提壺 *tirhur*, (1) n., name of bird; (2) v.i., to carry wine pot.

提淨 *tirjihng*, v.t., refine (oil, extract).

提及 *tir-jir*, v.t., mention, refer to.

提舉 *tirjyuu*, v.t., promote (person).

提款 *tir-kuaan*, v.t., withdraw money from bank.

提籃(兒) *tirlarn(-lar'l)*, n., a light basket (for vegetables, etc.).

提煉 *tirliahn*, v.t., refine, extract (oil, chemical from ores).

提梁(兒) *tirliarng('l)*, n., part (bridge, handle) used for lifting (cover, basket).

提溜 **diliou*, v.t., carry lightly in hand or with fingers: 提留着心 make one uneasy.

提名 *tir-mirng*, v.t., nominate (person for election, appointment).

提偶戲 *tir-ooushih*, n., marionette usu. called 傀儡戲 *kueirleei shih*.

提票 *tirpiauh*, n., warrant for arrest.

提審 *tirsheen*, v.i., hold hearing at 「court.

提攝 *tirsheh*, v.i., (Taoist) arouse, excite certain bodily energies.

提升 *tirsheng*, v.t., promote in rank.

提神 *tirshern*, v.i., refresh oneself; put on one's guard.

提攜 *tirshi*[1], v.t., to guide and help (younger people).

提撕 *tirshi*[2], v.t., (1) wake up, put on one's guard; (2) help and guide (the young), see *-chieh* ↑.

提箱 *tirshiang*, n., suitcase.

提醒 *tirshiing*, v.t., remind; alert (person) to danger.

提示 *tirshyh*, v.t., point out, give advice (to younger people).

提學使 *tirshyuershyy*, n., former commissioner of education.

提訴 *tir-suh*, v.i., bring up lawsuit. 「court.

提堂 *tir-tarng*, v.i., to bring to

提提 *tirtir*, adj., as in (AC) 好人提提 gentleman is poised and at ease; descriptive of flying.

提頭兒 *tirtour'l*, v.i., (1) introductory remarks; (2) worth talking: 這個人沒個大提頭兒 this man is not worth talking about.

提要 *tiryauh*, n., *résumé*, brief summary.

提議 *tir-yih*, n., proposal, resolution brought for discussion.

提運 *tiryuhn*, v.t. & n., transport, -tation.

撾 10A.83-4

jua.

V.t. To knock at (door, branch).

掖 10A.83-6

yih (also *yeh*; **ye*).

N. (1) Armpit (interch. 腋 42A.83). (2) Side: 宮掖, 掖庭 side palaces: 掖門 side gate of palace; 掖垣 side wall.

V.t. (1) To hold up by the arms ("armpit"): 扶掖 to support elder person). (2) (**ye*) To fold up: 掖袖子 fold up sleeves; 把衣襟掖起來 gather skirt up. (3) (**ye*) To tuck away: 把錢掖在懷裏 to tuck away money in bosom.

抓 10A.83-9

jua (sp. pr. *jau*).

V.t. (1) To scratch: 抓癢 scratch an itch; 抓撓 *-nau* ↓; 抓破臉兒 (coll.) openly break relations (lit., "scratch face till it bleeds" or "come to blows"); 抓耳撓腮 twisting ears and beards in pondering. (2) To clutch, grab, to get or get at indiscriminately: 抓住 to clutch fast; 抓取 to grab at; 抓一劑藥 to buy a lot of prescribed herbs; 抓錢 to grab money, in a hurry to get rich; 抓不起來 too soft to be lifted; 抓大頭 a game of picking lines leading to covered numbers (for pooling money), in which the 大頭 pays more than the others; 抓尖兒賣快 show avid attentions to s.o. to curry favor; 抓工夫 (coll.) steal time for idling. (3) To catch, arrest (thief).

抓碴兒 *juachar'l*, v.i., make use as pretext.

抓哏 *juagern*, v.i., (in Chin. drama) make *ad lib* jokes.

抓會 *juahueih*, n., a club in which subscribers pay a certain amount monthly, the sum going to the person who shakes out the best dice.

抓鬮兒 *jua-jiou'l*, v.i., draw lots.

抓周兒 *juajou'l*, v.i., on child's first anniversary, different objects (abacus, writing brush, etc.) are placed before baby to see which article it tries to grab, indicating future inclination.

抓局 *jua-jyur*, v.i., to make a raid on gambling den.

抓撓 *jua'nau*, v.t., (1) to scratch (itch); (2) to scramble, clutch and grab: 別抓撓東西 don't scramble a set of things; (3) to struggle, clamber: 他們兩人抓撓起來了 the two begin to clutch at each other; (4) to hustle, make hastily: 幫他們抓撓飯 help them hurry up the meal; 抓抓撓撓 adv., hurriedly: 抓抓撓撓把飯吃了 finished the meal hurriedly; (5) 抓撓兒 n., a children's game of bending and unbending fingers.

抓瞎 *juashia*, v.i., act in a flurried or confused manner.

抓彩 *jua-tsaai*, v.i. & n., to raffle; a raffle.

抓早兒 *jua-tzaau'l*, adv., get up early (to start journey, etc.).

挺 10A.83–9

tiing.

[Cf. 梃 10B.83, 鋌 81A.83]

V.i. & t. (1) To stick up or out, to bulge or protrude, to straighten: 挺着肚子 protrude belly; 挺胸, 挺起胸膛 stick out chest, stand straight in gesture of self-confidence; 挺起腰板兒 stand up as a man; 挺身而出 stand up and volunteer to help; to raise: 挺劍而起 flash a sword and stand up. (2) To stand up against, to stick it out, to sustain: 他挺不住了 he cannot stand (pain, suffering) any more; 這場病眞挺過去了 he succeeded in pulling through the illness; 這個人好硬挺 this man can stand through a lot; 挺刑 suffer corporeal punishment without flinching. (3) (Of market price) be firm, go up: 上挺.

Adj. (1) Erect, firm: 直挺挺的 rigorously straight, 挺直, 挺立 *-jyr*, *-lih* ↓. (2) Distinguished, standing out: 挺然不羣 be distinguished from fellowmen; 挺拔, 挺秀 *-bar*, *-shiouh* ↓.

Adv. (1) (Coll.) rather, pretty: 挺好 quite good; 挺大, 挺長 pretty big, long; 挺嚴 rather stiff. (2) Forward: 挺進 go forward.

挺拔 *tiingbar*, adj., independent, outstanding.

挺覺 *tiingjiauh*, v.i., (MC) *-shy* ↓.

挺直 *tiingjyr*, adj., rigorously straight.

挺立 *tiinglih*, v.i., stand erect.

挺秀 *tiingshiouh*, adj., distinguished in talent, handsome.

挺屍 *tiingshy*, v.i., (facet.) lie stiff in bed, like a corpse.

搥 10A.83–9

chueir.

[Cf. 槌 10B.83]

V.t. (1) To beat with a stick or fist: 搥胸 beat upon the breast; 搥打 to buffet or pommel (person), lay on blows; 搥鼓 to beat drum; 搥他一頓 give him a beating. (2) To give a series of rapid gentle taps in massage: 搥肩, 搥背, 搥腰 massage or tap the shoulder, back, waist.

§10A.91 (扌/ノ)

抄 10A.91–2

chau.

V.i. & t. (1) To copy (also wr. 鈔): 抄寫, 抄本 *-shiee*, *-been* ↓; 抄錄 *-luh* ↓; 手抄 to copy by hand; 手抄本 a hand copy; to plagiarize: 抄襲 *-shir* ↓; 文抄公 (sarcastic) a plagiarist. (2) To invade, loot, strike (army): 抄掠 *-lyueh* ↓. (3) To outflank, take a short cut: 抄小路, 抄近路 take a short cut. (4) To confiscate: 抄家, 抄沒 *-jia*, *-moh* ↓. (5) To whip out: 抄起一根棍子 whip out a bar. (6) To parboil vegetable (cf. 炒 *chaau*).

抄本 *chaubeen*, n., a hand copy of an original.

抄掇 *chauduor*, v.i., to piece together copied material—not original writing; to plagiarize, see *-shir* ↓.

抄家 *chau-jia*, v.i., formerly, to confiscate entire family property.

抄紙 *chau-jyy*, v.i., a way of paper making.

抄錄 *chauluh*, v.t., to make a copy (of record, document, etc.): 抄錄下來.

抄掠 *chaulyueh*, v.t., to loot and harass (territory).

抄沒 *chaumoh*, v.t., to confiscate.

抄寫 *chaushiee*, v.i., to make hand copy.

抄襲 *chaushir*, v.t., (1) to plagiarize; (2) to outflank (enemy).

抄手兒 *chau-shoou'l*, v.i., (MC) to cross one's arms (cf. 叉[A]手 32.82).

抄事 *chaushyh*, n., formerly, a clerk.

抄胥 *chau-shyu*, n., (MC) one engaged for making copies (also wr. 鈔).

抄 10A.91–2

suo.

V.t. (1) To rub gently, to stroke fondly: 摩抄 ditto. (2) 挓抄 (pr. *ja'sha*) wide open.

扩 10A.91–6

kuoh.

[Abbr. of 擴 10A.80]

摻 10A.91–9

chan (*shan, *shaan).

V.t. (1) (AC *shaan*) hold (hand). (2) To seep in: 摻水 add water to mixture; 摻入 mix, blend with (related 滲 63A.91, *shahn*).

Adj. (AC *shan*) 摻摻女手 lady's slender hands.

§ 10A.93 (扌/く)

摟 10A.93-2

lou (*lour*, *loou*).

V.t. (1) (*loou*, re. pr. *lour*) To embrace: 摟的好緊 embrace tightly; 摟在一起 embrace each other. (2) (*lou*) Solicit business, contract to do certain services: 摟包兒 -*bau'l*, 摟攬 -*laan*, 摟貨 -*huoh*↓. (3) Hold up, pick up: 摟起來 pick up pieces from the ground; 摟衣裳 hold up the lower part of a long gown; 摟起裙子 hold up the skirts. (4) Obtain money by fair means or foul: 摟錢 -*chiarn*↓; 摟他一票 made a fast buck; 摟了一大筆錢 make a pile; 摟了不少 made a small fortune.

摟抱 *looubauh, v.t., hold (s.o.) in one's arms.

摟包兒(匠) *loubau'l(jiahng)*, n., (1) one who solicits business; (2) a firm for hiring day laborer.

摟錢 *lou-chiarn*, v.i., extort money by force.

摟貨 *lou-huoh*, v.t., act as commission agent in selling goods.

摟攬 *loulaan*, v.t., to contract to do certain services (=包攬).

摟算 *lousuahn*, v.t., to check an account.

摟頭 *loutour*, adv., head on: 摟頭就是一棍，把他打倒 felled him with a blow head-on.

抎 10A.93-3

shahn.

[Pop. of 擅 10A.30]

搔 10A.93-3

sau.

V.t. (1) To rub gently (skin), to scratch (itch): 搔癢 -*yaang*↓; 搔爬 -*par*↓. (2) U.f. 騷 to be restless: 搔動 -*duhng*↓.

搔動 *sauduhng*, v.i., (=騷動) to swirl in commotion, become restless.

搔爬 *saupar*, v.t., to scratch (itch).

搔擾 *sauraau*, (1) v.t., to loot, despoil (land); (2) adj., (land, people) disrupted, restless.

搔首 *sau-shoou*, v.i., to scratch the head in thinking: 搔首踟躕 ditto; 搔首弄姿 (of woman) to giggle and flirt, see -*tour*↓.

搔頭 *sau-tour*, v.i., (1) ditto; (2) n., an article of woman's hair decoration.

搔癢 *sau-yaang*, v.i., to scratch an itch.

攖 10A.93-4

ying.

V.t. (LL) to ruffle, irritate, challenge: 攖其鋒 to blunt enemy force; 虎負隅，莫之敢攖 no one dare to challenge a tiger at bay; 攖人心 to disturb men's hearts.

摆 10A.93-4

baai.

[Abbr. of 擺 10A.70]

接 10A.93-6

jie.

V.t. (1) Come close to, approximate: 接觸 -*chuh*, 接界 -*jieh*, 接近 -*jihn*, 接境 -*jihng*, 接壤 -*raang*↓; 直接 direct, directly; 間接 indirectly. (2) Accept, pick up, take over: 接收 -*shou*, 接受 -*shouh*↓; 接過來 stretch out hand to receive; 接納 accept (gifts, advice), receive (visitors); 交接 have contacts, social dealings; 接任 assume office; 接取 take what is held out to one. (3) Join, continue, unite: 接辦 -*bahn*↓; 接不上 cannot be connected, unable to continue; 接不上氣來 out of breath; 接連 -*liarn*↓; 接二連三 continuously; 接起來 join, unite, piece together; 接骨 -*guu*↓; 接合 -*her*↓; 移花接木 (of plants) to graft, (fig.) to resort to dishonest practices, to palm off the spurious for the genuine; 接續 -(')*shyuh*↓; 接班 take one's turn on duty. (4) Take hold of, catch: 接着 -'*je*↓; 接好了 catch and hold it firmly; 接球 (in football or basketball) to catch the ball, (in tennis) to return a served ball. (5) To welcome, receive, meet (guests, visitors): 接待 -*daih*, 接風 -*feng*↓; 迎接 to welcome (with open arms); 應接 to usher in or receive guests: 應接不暇 play host to a constant stream of callers; 接財神 ceremony held on the 5th day of the lunar New Year featuring the home-coming of the God of Good Fortune.

接辦 *jiebahn*, v.t., take up and continue to carry out (an unfinished task).

接觸 *jiechuh*, v.t., to touch, come into contact with; n., a contact.

接充 *jiechung*, v.i., take up a job vacated by a predecessor.

接待 *jiedaih*, v.t., receive (guests, visitors).

接風 *jie-feng*, v.i., give a reception

in honor of some newly arrived person.

接管 *jieguaan*, v.t., take over the management or administration.

接骨 *jieguu*, v.i., to set broken bones; 接骨眼兒 *-'guyaal*, n., a suitable occasion, an opportune moment.

接合 *jieher*, v.t., to fuse, combine, join together, link.

接著 *jie'je*, adv., right after: 接著第三者來了 a third party came right after.

接見 *jiejiahn*, v.t., receive (guests, visitors).

接界 *jiejieh*, v.t., to border on, be contiguous to.

接濟 *jiejih*, v.t., give relief to, offer financial or material assistance to.

接近 *jiejihn*, v.t., (1) approximate, approach; (2) on intimate terms with.

接境 *jiejihng*, v.t., to border on, see *-jieh* ↑.

接踵 *jiejuung*, v.i., come in crowds ("one on the heels of another").

接客 *jiekeh*, v.i., (1) (of hotel boys) extend welcome to tourists at railway stations, wharves, etc.; (2) (of prostitutes) sleep with patrons.

接連 *jieliarn*, v.t., join together, connect, be adjacent to, adjoin.

接力 *jielih*, v.t. & n., relay (race): 接力賽跑.

接壤 *jieraang*, v.t., be adjacent to, contiguous.

接生 *jiesheng*, v.i. & n., (to practice) midwifery.

接膝 *jieshi*, v.i., (of friends) sit close to each other ("knee to knee").

接線生 *jieshiahn-sheng*, n., a telephone (switchboard) operator.

接洽 *jieshiar*, v.t., discuss (business), deal with (person, affairs).

接收 *jieshou*, v.t., take over (duties), as from predecessor in office.

接受 *jieshouh*, v.t., receive (honors, awards, gifts, advice).

接手 *jie-shoou*, (1) v.i., take up matters left unfinished by predecessor; (2) (*jie'shou*) n., assistant.

接續 *jie(')shyuh*, v.i. & t., join on, continue (story, article).

接頭 *jietour*, (1) v.t., deal with, contact with (person), see *-shiar* ↑; (2) adj., be in contact: 此事我全不接頭 I know nothing about it at all; (3) n., joints (also 接頭兒).

接吻 *jieween*, v.i. & t. & n., (to) kiss.

接物 *jiewuh*, v.i., come into relations with other people: 待人接物 the way one conducts oneself in relation to others.

接應 *jie(')yihng*, v.t., render assistance or support to.

接引 *jieyiin*, v.t., to lead the way for, serve as a guide to, conduct, guide.

按 10A.93-6

ahn.

V.i. & t. (1) To put hand on: 按劍 to put hand on sword. (2) To press down: 手指一按 press with finger; 按鈴 press the bell; 按鈕 press a button; 按箱蓋 press down trunk cover; (fig.) to repress, keep down by force; 按住, 按不住 keep down by hand, cannot keep s.t. down; 按捺 *-nah* ↓; 按轡 draw up a horse; 按兵 *-bing* ↓. (3) To make legal investigation: 按察, 按問 *-char*, *-wehn* ↓. (4) To comment, make an editor's or author's comment: 編者按 editor's note, comment; 按語 *-yuu* ↓.

Prep. (1) According to: 按照 *-jauh* ↓; 按規矩 according to regulations or customs; 按理 *-lii* ↓; 按圖索驥 locate s.t. by a plan or chart; 按步(部)就班 go each according to his duties, proceed in order. (2) By, one by one: 按戶 (go round) door by door; 按次序 (proceed) in order; 按月交款 pay by the month; 按期清還 repay according to schedule.

按兵 *ahn-bing*, phr., 按兵不動 keep back army from battle.

按察 *ahnchar*, v.t., to investigate court cases; 按察使 formerly, inspector of justice (idea similar to circuit court).

按成(兒) *ahn-cherng('l)*, adv., proportionately (＝按成分).

按蹻 *ahnchiau*, v.i., (AC) to massage.

按堵 *ahnduu*, v.i., (AC) to settle down, return to normal (also 安堵).

按照 *ahnjauh*, prep., according to (regulations, etc.).

按酒 *ahnjioou*, n., (MC) snacks or things to go with wine.

按治 *ahnjyh*, v.i. & t., to cross-examine.

按理 *ahn-lii*, phr., according to reason; according to established principles (one should be punished, but now need not, etc.)

按脈 *ahn-moh*, v.i., feel the pulse.

按摩 *ahnmor*, v.i., give massage.

按納(捺) *ahnnah*, v.t., to repress anger, restrain: 按捺不住 could not restrain any longer.

按鈕 *ahn-nioou*, v.i., press a button.

按説 *ahnshuo*, phr., (＝按理説) according to reason, see *-lii* ↑.

按次 *ahntsyh*, adv., in good order or sequence.

按問 *ahnwehn*, v.t., to cross-examine (person).

按壓 *ahnya*, v.t., to hold back (a document, report, decision) in bureaucratic tradition.

按語 *ahnyuu*, n., a comment (by author, editor).

挼 10A.93-9

nuor (re. pr. *ruor*).

V.t. To stroke with hands.

挼挲 *nuorsuo*, v.t., stroke gently.

挼搓 *nuortsuo*, v.t., stroke and rub.

捼 10A.93-9

nuor.

V.t. (1) (MC) to push, destroy. (2) (Var. of 挼) to stroke with hands, see 挼 10A.93.

A B C

SECTION 10B

§ 10B.00 (木/亅)

村 10B.00-1

tsun.

[Var. 邨]

N. A village, hamlet: 村莊, 村落 *-juang*, *-luoh* ↓; 鄉村 country place, village; 農村 village, countryside; 村夫, 村子 *-fu*, *-tzyy* ↓.

V.t. (coll.) To scold, berate: 村了幾句 give a little scolding; 撒村 to curse in vulgar language.

Adj. Uncouth, countrified, coarse (person, manners): 村氣, 村話 *-chih*, *-huah* ↓

村氣 *tsunchih*, n., as in 有村氣 have the air of a country lad.

村夫 *tsunfu*, n., country lad, rustic person: 村夫俗子 uneducated person; 村夫子 n., (contempt.) village schoolmaster, person of narrow knowledge.

村姑(兒) *tsungu('l)*, n., a country lass or girl.

村話 *tsun-huah*, n., vulgar talk; also words of scolding.

村長 *tsunjaang*, n., chief of village.

村莊 *tsunjuang*, n., a farmstead; a village.

村兒 *tsun'l*, n., a country lad.

村落 *tsunluoh*, n., a hamlet.

村女 *tsunnyuu*, n., a country girl.

村人 *tsunrern*, n., a villager, a country bumpkin.

村塾 *tsun-shur*, n., village school.

村墟 *tsun-shyu*, n., village fairgrounds.

村學究 *tsunshyuerjiou*, n., (contempt.) a person of little learning and narrow views, village schoolmaster.

村子 *tsuntzyy*, n., (1) a small village; (2) country lad.

村塢 *tsunwuh*, n., village settlement.

材 10B.00-1

tsair.

N. (1) Timber: 木材 ditto; hence symbolic of good or bad timber, useful or useless talent; 成材, 不成材 (person) useful, useless in society. (2) Material: 材料 *-liauh* ↓; 教材 teaching material. (3) Interch. 才 talent: 才△能, 才△器 10.00; 人材＝人才. (4) Natural bent: 因材施教 educate a person according to his natural ability. (5) Short for 棺材 coffin.

材器 *tsairchih*, n., person's usefulness, practical ability (also wr. 才).

材幹 *tsairgahn*, n., practical or administrative ability.

材料 *tsairliauh* (-'*liau*), n., material (of cloth, construction, for writing, research).

材木 *tsairmuh*, n., timber.

材能 *tsairnerng*, n., natural ability (also wr. 才能).

材人 *tsairrern*, n., able man (＝才人).

材士 *tsairshyh*, n., able scholars (＝才士).

桲 10B.00-1

bor.

N. See 榲△桲 10B.30.

樹 10B.00-1

shuh.

N. A tree: 樹木 ditto; 大樹 a big tree; 喬樹 a tall tree; 樹叢 a grove, thicket; 樹葉, 樹根, 樹枝 *-yeh*, *-gen*, *-jy*^{2} ↓; 樹頂上, 樹梢 treetop; 栽樹, 種樹, 植樹 to plant trees: 植樹節 Arbor Day, March 12; 樹倒猢猻散 monkeys disperse when tree falls—members run away when family or institution falls.

V.t. To set up, to plant: 樹立 *-lih* ↓; 樹之以桑 plant field with mulberries; 樹名 earn a reputation for oneself; 樹威 make oneself respected, feared; 建樹 to establish, achieve (permanent results); (fig.) plant seeds of (hatred, love, etc.): 樹恩, 樹怨 *-en*, *-yuahn* ↓; 樹人, 樹德 *-rern*, *-der* ↓; 樹黨 form a party or clique.

樹本 *shuh-been*, v.i., lay foundation for future growth.

樹杈(兒)(子) *shuhchah ('l)(tz)*, n., branches.

樹蟲子 *shuhchurngtz*, n., poachers who steal timber.

樹德 *shuh-der*, v.i., to leave good work.

樹恩 *shuh-en*, v.i., to cement relationships by giving favors.

樹幹 *shuhgahn*, n., tree trunk.

樹根(兒)(子) *shuhgen(-ge'l)(tz)*, n., tree stump, root; 樹根頭 where the tree stands.

樹掛 *shuhguah*, n., icicles.

樹行子 *shuhhahngtz*, n., even sets or rows of trees.

樹介 *shuhjieh*, n., see *-guah* ↑ (also wr. 樹嫁, 樹稼).

樹樁子 *shuhjuangtz*, n., tree stump.

樹脂 *shuh-jy*^{1}, n., resin.

樹枝 *shuh-jy*^{2}, n., tree branches, boughs.

樹懶 *shuhlaan*, n., (zoo.) the sloth.

樹立 *shuhlih*, v.i. & t., to establish (name, organization); to stand up, be independent.

樹林(兒)(子) *shuhlirn(-lier'l)('tz)*, n., forest, woods.

樹杪 *shuh-miaau*, n., see *-shau* ↓.

村 材 桲 樹

亅	小	⺊	十	土	ナ	廾	𠃊	丨	一	丅	フ	口	区	冈	㇆	厂	尸	亠	广	宀	丶	乚	弋	心	八	人	乂	乛	㇀	丿	⺈	く
00	01	02	10	11	12	20	21	22	30	31	32	40	41	42	50	51	52	60	61	62	63	70	71	72	80	81	82	83	90	91	92	93

樹末 *shuh-moh*, n., tip of tree.
樹木 *shuhmuh*, n., tree in gen.
樹皮 *shuh-pir*, n., bark.
樹人 *shuh-rern*, v.i., to nurture, bring up men of ability: 百年樹人 takes a hundred years to nurture a generation of good men.
樹梢 *shuh-shau*, n., treetop.
樹心 *shuh-shin*, n., pith.
樹梃(兒) *shuh-tiing('l)*, n., see -*gahn*↑.
樹栽子 *shuh-tzaitz*, n., sapling.
樹葉 *shuh-yeh*, n., tree leaves.
樹藝 *shuhyih*, v.t., to sow and cultivate.
樹蔭 *shuh-yihn*, n., tree shade.
樹陰 *shuh-yin*, n., shade under a tree.
樹怨 *shuh-yuahn*, v.i., to sow seeds of hatred.

檮 10B.00-1

taur.

檮杌 *taur-wuh*, n., (AC) a fabulous fierce beast with a man's face, tiger's paws, and boar's tusks, which never runs away from fight; (AC) a legendary incorrigible vile son of a ruler; (AC) name of the annals of Chuu 楚 kingdom.

椅 10B.00-1

yii.

N. (1) (-*tz*) A chair: 沙發椅 sofa; 交椅 armchair; 躺椅 lounge chair, *chaise longue*; 太師椅 lounge chair with planks for footrest. (2) (Bot.) 椅梓 the catalpa, *Idesia polycarpa*.

樽 10B.00-2

bor.

樽櫨 *borlur*, n., (AC) cornice.

杅 10B.00-3

yur.

N. (AC) a drinking vessel, a bathtub.

柯 10B.00-3

ke.

N. (1) (AC) axe-handle. (2) A bough, heavy branch. (3) Name of a tree, *Pasania cuspidata*. (4) A surname.

栵 10B.00-3

lih.

N. (1) A kind of chestnut tree. (2) (AC) trees growing in a row.

杼 10B.00-3

juh.

[Dist. 抒, 紓]

N. Weaving machine, loom: 機杼.

枒 10B.00-5

yar.

N. Forked branches: 枒杈.

橱 10B.00-5

chur.

[Var. 櫥]

N. (-*tz*, -'*l*) A cabinet, wardrobe: 書橱 bookcase; 菜橱 pantry cabinet; 貨橱 case or series of shelves for storing goods.

橱櫃 *churgueih*, n., cabinet, sideboard.

櫚 10B.00-5

lyur.

N. (1) A palm. (2) (AC) name of hardwood tree, similar to sandalwood.

欄 10B.00-5

larn.

N. (1) An enclosure for domestic animals: 牛欄 stockade; 馬欄 a stable. (2) A wooden fence: 柵欄 palisades, a railing of posts; 欄杆 -*gan*↓. (3) 專欄 special column (in periodicals).

欄杆 *larngan*, n., (1) a railing: 木欄杆, 鐵欄杆 a wooden, iron railing; (2) trimming for women's dress.
欄櫃 *larngueih*, n., a shop counter.
欄楯 *larnshuun*, n., (=欄杆↑) a railing, of which the vertical pieces are known as 欄 and the horizontal pieces as 楯.

楟 10B.00-6

tirng.

N. The birch leaf pear, *Pirus betulaefolia* (also 棠梨).

檸 10B.00-6

nirng.

檸 檬 *nirngmerng*, n., (bot.) lemon.

樽 10B.00-8

tzun.

N. A wine goblet (commonly wr. 尊).

榆 10B.00-8

yur.

N. The elm tree.

榆 錢 *yurchiarn*, n., elm seeds or pods (hanging down in pods like strings of cash).
榆 莢 *yurjiar*, n., ditto.
榆 樹 *yurshuh*, n., the elm tree.

桴 10B.00-9

fur.

N. Wooden raft; drum stick (var. 枹 pr. *fu*); 桴鼓相應 noise of war drums around; 桴思 var. of 罘^Δ罳 41D.22.

桁 10B.00-9

herng (**harng*, **hahng*).

N. (1) The crossbeam of a house. (2) (**harng*) A heavy wooden bar used in torture. (3) (**hahng*) A clothes tree.

榭 10B.00-9

shieh.

N. A hall on terrace, oft. open on three sides: 樓榭 towers and terrace halls.

§10B.01 (木/小)

林 10B.01-1

lirn.

N. (1) A surname. (2) A forest, wood: 森林 jungle; 叢林 copse, grove; 竹林 bamboo grove; 林泉 woods and stream, symbol of retirement to countryside; 林壑 rocks and trees, wild nature for enjoyment; 歸隱林下 retire from official life; 綠林豪傑 "green wood" bandits or boxers, heroes of the forest, Robin Hoods. (3) Forest as symbolic of multitude or group: 儒林 the Confucian scholars esp. in biographical section of dynastic histories; 士林 scholarly circles, the scholars' world; 碑林 collection of stone inscriptions; 杏^Δ林 10.40; used as modifier: 林立 "stand like a forest"; 學堂林立 schools spring up like mushrooms.

林 薄 *lirnbor*, n., wild jungle, heavy underbrush (sometimes bandits' hide-out).
林 產 *lirnchaan*, n., products of forest; timber.
林 場 *lirnchaang*, n., forestry station.
林 檎 *lirnchirn*, n., (bot.) kind of crab apple, *Pirus malus* (also called 沙果).
林 肯 *Linkeen*, n., Abraham Lincoln.
林 莽 *lirnmaang*, n., wild jungle.
林 木 *lirnmuh*, n., timber, wood; forest.
林 藪 *lirnsoou*, n., woods and jungle.

株 10B.01-1

ju.

N. adjunct. Used only of trees: 三株樹 three trees; 兩株梅 two plum trees.

N. & v.i. & t. A tree root above the ground; 株守, 株連 *-shoou*, *-liarn* ↓.

株 連 *juliarn*, v.i., to implicate associates or relatives (of criminal case, involving others besides original culprit).
株 戮 *juluh*, v.t., kill or be killed because of connection with criminal case.
株 守 *jushoou*, v.t., usu. in 守株待兔 wait at tree hole for the reappearance of the hare—hence 株守 to keep (narrow or bigoted views) and resist change, as 株守成法.

棟 10B.01-1

duhng.

N. adjunct. 一棟房屋 a house.

N. Beams of roof: 棟折榱崩 beams and rafters are broken, (fig.) of downfall of state.

棟 梁 *duhngliarng*, n., (fig.) the pillars of state.
棟 宇 *duhngyuu*, n., building, mansion.

樽 榆 桴 桁 榭 林 株 棟

亅	小	⺊	十	土	𠂇	卄	⺊	丨	一	丁	乛	口	区	冈	乛	厂	尸	亠	广	宀	丶	乚	弋	心	八	人	乂	一	一	丿	𠂉	く
00	01	02	10	11	12	20	21	22	30	31	32	40	41	42	50	51	52	60	61	62	63	70	71	72	80	81	82	83	90	91	92	93

楝 10B.01-1

liahn.

N. (Bot.) persian lilac, Chinaberry, *Melia japonica.*

榛 10B.01-1

jen.

N. (1) The hazel tree. (2) Underbrush.

Adj. Overgrown with brushwood: 榛莽 thick underbrush; 榛榛 overgrown, wild; 榛狉未改 appearance of primitive jungle.

榛栗 *jenlih*, n., a kind of nut. (=橡栗).
榛子 *jentz*, n., hazelnut.
榛蕪 *jenwur*, adj. & n., wild underbrush; (fig.) of lowly people.

標 10B.01-3

biau.

N. (1) Mark, label; 商標 trademark; 音標 phonetic notation; 標識, 標誌, 標記 a marking, what serves to mark (ownership, identity); 浮標 buoy or other marking at sea; 路標 road signal. (2) Banner, esp. as prize at contests: 奪得錦標 capture the banner. (3) Standard, target: 目標 aim, target; 標準, 標的 *-juun, -dih*↓. (4) Public commercial bidding: 投標 partake at public bidding for contract; 得標 receive contract at bidding. (5) Symptom, outside appearance: 治標不治本 to cure the symptoms, not the disease, hence used of temporary remedies of relief in medicine or social problems. (6) A regiment in Manchu Dyn.

V.t. (1) To mark: 標名 mark name, give name to; 標明 mark clearly. (2) To receive contract at bidding: 被他標到了 he won at the bidding.

標榜 *biaubaang*, v.t., give favorable publicity to: 互相標榜 (esp. of writers) gain popularity by mutual compliments.
標本 *biaubeen*, n., (bot.) specimen.
標籤 *biauchian*, n., price tag.
標槍 *biauchiang*, n., javelin.
標點 *biaudiaan*, n. & v.t., punctuate (-tion); 標點符號 punctuation marks.
標的 *biaudih*, n., declared object, target to strive for: 訴之標的 subject matter of court action.
標封 *biaufeng*, v.i. & t., sealed with labels.
標竿 *biaugan*, n., marking pole.
標高 *biaugau*, n., (survey) vertical distance.
標格 *biauger*, n., model to imitate.
標購 *biaugouh*, v.t., buy at public bidding.
標價 *biaujiah*, v.t. & n., to mark price, marked price.
標準 *biaujuun*, n. & adj., model (husband, citizen), standard (of behavior, temperature): 不合(不够)標準 not up to standard, disqualified; 標準太高 the standard is set too high; 漫無標準 without consistent standard.
標致 *biaujyh*, adj., handsome (of person, dress), also wr. 標緻.
標買 *biaumaai*, v.t., see *-gouh*↑.
標賣 *biaumaih*, n., sell at marked price or at public bidding.
標牌 *biaupair*, n., see 摽△牌 10A.01.
標題 *biautir*, n., subject (of essay, etc.); 標題音樂 program music.
標語 *biauyuu*, n., slogan.

棵 10B.01-4

ke.

N. adjunct. 一棵樹 a tree; 一棵白菜 a head of cabbage.

檁 10B.01-6

liin.

N. A cross rafter on roof.

棕 10B.01-6

tzung.
[Var. 椶]

N. The palm tree: 棕繩 coir rope.

棕竹 *tzungjur*, n., (bot.) *Rhapis humilis.*
棕櫚 *tzunglyuu*, n., (bot.) the palm tree, *Trachycarpus excelsa.*
棕色 *tzungseh*, adj. & n., brown (color).
棕簑 *tzungsuo*, n., coir raincoat.

櫟 10B.01-9

lih.

N. (Bot.) chestnut-leaved oak, *Quercus serrata.*

櫟散 *lihsaan*, n., useless timber or person.
櫟樗 *lihshu*, n., (1) chestnut oak and ailanthus; (2) useless timber or person.

§10B.02 (木/卜)

檬 10B.02-2

merng.

檬果 *mernguoo*, n., mango (also wr. 芒果).

棣 根 根 樣

棣 10B.02-2

dih.

N. (1) A plant of plum family: 常棣, 棠棣 *Prunus japonica*. (2) (LL) used as elegant var. of 弟: 學棣, 仁棣 (from allu. to 唐棣 Duke Jou's poem to his brothers).

V.i. (AC, rare) 棣通 relate to each other (possibly u.f. 隸).

棣棣 *dihdih*, adj., (AC) poised, dignified.

棣鄂(萼) *dih-eh*, n., love of brothers, from allu. to ancient poem 唐棣之華 celebrating brothers' reunion.

棣書 *dihshu*, n., a style of Chin. calligraphy.

棣棠 *dihtarng*, n., (bot.) *Kerria japonica*.

根 10B.02-5

cherng.

N. A doorjamb.

V.t. To touch: 根撥 (MC) to spread out (ashes, as with a stick) 棖觸 (AC) to touch (a crawling insect, etc.).

根 10B.02-5

gen.

N. adjunct. A long thin piece: 幾根粉筆, 幾根頭髮 several pieces of chalk, strands of hair; 一根竹竿 a bamboo pole; 一根草 a stalk of grass.

N. (1) Roots: 樹根 roots of a tree; 根深蒂固 deeply or firmly rooted; 根生土長 indigenous, native-born; root of a growth: 鬚根, 髮根 root of whiskers, hair. (2) The bottom of things: 刨根問底 inquire into the root of the matter; 刨根兒 ditto; 歸根 phr., in the end (fail, succeed, etc.). (3) (Math.) the radical, the radical sign (√); 立方根 cube root. (4) (Chem.) the radical, radical symbol (R). (5) (Linguistics) 字根 or 語根 root from which a word is derived.

根本 *genbeen*, (1) n., root, bottom, foundation; (2) adj. & adv., basic(ally): 根本問題 a basic problem; 這件事根本就不對 the thing is basically wrong; (3) adj., honorable, reputable: 根本人家兒 a decent family; (4) adv., utterly, entirely, completely: 根本不知 don't know it at all; 根本沒有這回事 it's utterly unfounded.

根除 *genchur*, v.t., exterminate, uproot (social evils); effect cure (of disease).

根底(兒) *gendii(-diee'l)*, n., (1) the basis, the why and wherefore of a thing (also 根兒底兒, 根兒裏); as adv. phr., basically; (2) the foundation of a thing; (3) background learning, early training: 他的根底很好 he has good scholastic training; (4) one's material possessions: 他頗有根底 he is quite well-to-do.

根荄 *gengai*, n., (LL) roots of trees and grasses.

根基 *genji*, n., (1) foundation; (2) *-'ji*, character, grounding: 此人沒根基 this man does not have a sound character or grounding.

根腳 *gen'jiau*, n., foundation.

根莖 *genjing*, n., (bot.) rhizomes.

根究 *genjiouh*, v.t., to probe to the bottom of, make a thorough investigation into.

根治 *genjyh*, v.t., (1) find a basic cure for (disease); (2) find a basic solution for (social ills).

根絕 *genjyuer*, v.t., exterminate, stop entirely (habit).

根據 *genjyuh*, n., (1) a basis, authority, evidence; (2) source of statement; (3) prep., according to: 根據法律 according to law; 根據他的意見 according to his opinion; 根據地 *--dih*, n., (a) (mil.) a base of operations; (b) a robbers' den.

根苗 *genmiaur*, n., roots and shoots, beginnings.

根性 *genshihng*, n., one's born nature: 劣根性 inveterate bad nature.

根由 *genyour*, n., origin (of event, dispute, etc.).

根源 *genyuarn*, n., source, foundation.

樣 10B.02-8

yahng.

N. (1) (*-tz*, *-'l*) Shape, form, figure, pattern: 怎樣 how; 我不怎樣 I am feeling all right; 圖樣 pattern, blueprint, illustration; 打樣 draw a blueprint, make construction design; 花樣: 出了花樣 (of events) take unexpected turns; 式樣 form (of shoes, hat, fashion, etc.); 同樣 same: 同樣的 in the same way; 走樣 out of shape, (copy) different from original shape; 成樣, 像樣 adj., presentable; 太不像樣 (成樣) getting out of bounds; 裝模作樣 to affect a show (of kindness, modesty, etc.). (2) Kind, class: 樣樣 every kind, all kinds: 樣樣都會 can do everything; 多樣 many kinds; 各式各樣 every kind of (hats, people, etc.). (3) Sample (of goods, art work, etc.): 抽樣 take a sample. (4) Proof: 校樣 read proof.

樣本 *yahng-been*, n., a sample copy.

樣冊子兒 *yahngchaaitz'l*, n., book of patterns (for dress, etc.).

樣張 *yahng-jang*, n., a sample sheet.

樣品 *yahng-piin*, n., sample goods.

樣式 *yahng'shy*, n., form (of

亅	小	⺊	十	土	ナ	廾	𠃊⺊	丨	一	丅	フ	口	囗	冂	㇆	厂	尸	亠	广	宀	丶	乚	弋	心	八	人	乂	乛	ノ	刂	⺈	く
00	01	02	10	11	12	20	21	22	30	31	32	40	41	42	50	51	52	60	61	62	63	70	71	72	80	81	82	83	90	91	92	93

shoes), style (of dress), manner (of person).

樣樣 *yahngyahng*, n., everything: 樣樣宗宗 every class and kind.

椽 10B.02-9

chuarn.

N. A house beam: 如椽之筆 a powerful pen; a brush for writing big characters.

橡 10B.02-9

shiahng.

N. (1) The rubber tree: 橡皮樹 *-pirshuh* ↓. (2) The chestnut-leaved oak, *Quercus serrata* (= 櫟).

橡膠 *shiahngjiau*, n., rubber gum; 橡膠園 rubber plantation.
橡皮 *shiahngpir*, n., (1) rubber: 人造橡皮 synthetic rubber; 橡皮樹 rubber tree; (2) rubber eraser; 橡皮膏 court plaster.
橡樹 *shiahngshuh*, n., (bot.) the chestnut oak.
橡實 *shiahngshyr*, n., acorns.

§10B.10 (木/十)

棒 10B.10-1

bahng.

N. (1) Stick, staff, policeman's truncheon, baseball bat: 木棒, 鐵棒 wooden, iron, staff; 電棒 flashlight; 球棒 ball bat (cricket, baseball). (2) Blow with a stick: 打他一棒 give him a blow; 迎頭一棒 give a front blow with stick; 棒頭出孝子 spare the rod and spoil the child. (In sense of flogging, cf. 榜 pr. *behng*, 10B.50).

Adj. (Coll.) smart, handsome, good to look at (of acrobatic skill), excellent (of class work, health): 他的身體眞棒 he is physically very strong, in tiptop form.

棒棒雞 *bahngbahngji*, n., cold spiced chicken in Szechuan style.
棒冰 *bahngbing*, n., ice-cream stick, usu. sherbet stick.
棒球 *bahngchiour*, n., baseball.
棒瘡 *bahng-chuang*, n., wounds, marks from blows.
棒槌 *bahng'chuei*, n., wooden slat for beating clothes in laundary.
棒喝 *bahngheh*, n., (orig. Budd.) a blow and a shout to waken one from error, esp. 當頭棒喝 direct sharp warning.
棒糖 *bahngtarng*, n., (usu. 棒棒糖) candy stick; ice cream stick.
棒子 *bahngtz*, n., (1) short heavy baton; (2) maize; (3) flour from maize.

樺 10B.10-2

huah.

N. A kind of birch, *Betula alba* var. *vulgaris.*

棹 10B.10-2

juo (**jauh*).

N. (1) Var. of 桌 21A.01. (2) Var. of 櫂 (**jauh*) 10B.11.

杆 10B.10-3

gan.

[Cf. 桿]

N. A shaft, pole: 旗杆 a flagpole; 電杆 pole for power line; 欄杆 a railing, balustrade; 桅杆 a mast; 秤杆 the beam of a steelyard.

杆子 *gantz*, n., (1) a pole, rod; (2) a gang of robbers of thieves: 杆子頭(兒) the head of such a gang.

枰 10B.10-3

pirng.

[Dist. 秤]

N. Chess game.

楫 10B.10-4

jir.

N. An oar or paddle: 舟楫 boats; (fig.) (LL) a minister of state who helps tide over a crisis.

桿 10B.10-4

gaan.

N. adjunct. 一桿槍 a rifle or pistol.

N. (1) A wooden stick, club or cudgel: 桿棒 a wooden staff; 桿子 a wooden rod; 桿兒 ditto, a symbol of authority wielded by the head beggar; 桿兒上的 beggar chief. (2) A pole as a unit of measure, equal to 16.5 feet or one rod (cf. 杆 10B.10).

桿秤 *gaanchehng*, n., beam scales.
桿錐 *gaanjuei*, n., a screwdriver.
桿菌 *gaanjyuhn*, n., (med.) rod-shaped bacteria.

梩 10B.10-5

shi.

N. See 木△梩 10.01.

梓 10B.10-6

tzyy.

N. (1) The catalpa. (2) Wood-engraving: 梓匠 a wood engraver, a carpenter; 梓人 *-rern*↓; 付梓 (of books) send to the press. (3) Native district: 梓里, 桑梓 one's native village, place where one was born and brought up.

梓器 *tzyychih*, n., a coffin.
梓宮 *tzyygung*, n., the royal coffin.
梓人 *tzyyrern*, n., (AC) a carpenter, an architect.

樟 10B.10-6

jang.

N. The camphor tree.

樟腦 *jangnaau*, n., camphor; 樟腦油 oil of camphor; 樟腦精 essence of camphor.
樟蠶 *jangtsarn*, n., (zoo.) wild silkworm.

櫸 10B.10-9

jyuu.

N. (Bot.) a tree of the elm family, *Zelkawa accuminata.*

椑 10B.10-9

bei (**pir*).

N. (**pir*) (AC) a round wine vessel.

Adj. (AC) oval.

椑柹 *beishyh*, n., a small variety of persimmon.

榫 10B.10-9

suun.

N. (*-tz*, *'l*) A tenon.

榫頭 *suun'tou*, n., (1) a tenon; (2) a plug, projection (for socket) in machinery.
榫眼 *surnyaan*, n., a mortise.

杵 10B.10-9

chuu.

N. (1) A pestle. (2) A big staff: 鐵杵 iron staff (a weapon); 鐵杵磨成繡花針 long, persistent practice makes perfect (as in practising the pen). (3) A wooden club, slat, esp. used for beating laundry.

V.t. To point (a gun), poke (finger): 拿指頭杵他一下 poke him with a finger.

槲 10B.10-9

hur.

N. (Bot.) the big leaf oak, *Quercus dentata.*

§10B.11 (木/土)

杜 10B.11-1

duh.

N. (1) A kind of pear, see 杜梨 *-lir*↓. (2) A surname.

V.t. To shut out, prevent (cogn. 堵): 杜門謝客 close the gate and shut out visitors, live in complete seclusion; 杜口不言 shut up, keeping silence; 防微杜漸 guard against gradual creeping corruption or malpractice; 杜塞, 杜絕 *-seh*, *-tzueir*↓.

杜衡 *duhherng*, n. (bot.) *Asarum blumei.*
杜撰 *duhjuahn*, v.i., fabricate (story).
杜仲 *duhjuhng*, n., (bot.) *Eucommia ulmoides.*
杜鵑 *duhjyuan*, n., (1) azalea, a flowering plant; (2) a bird, the cuckoo, also called 杜宇, 子規, 思歸, 子巂.
杜絕 *duhjyuer*, v.t., completely eradicate.
杜梨 *duhlir*, n., (bot.) a kind of small pear (also 杜棠梨 *duhtarnglir*).
杜賣 *duhmaih*, v.t., sell outright irrevocably.
杜若 *duhruoh*, n., (bot.) *Pollia japonica.*
杜塞 *duhseh*, v.t., to stop up.
杜松 *duhsung*, n., the common juniper, *Juniperus communis* or the needle juniper, *Juniperus rigida.*
杜宇 *duhyuu*, n., see *-jyuan* (2)↑.

桂 10B.11-1

gueih.

N. (1) (Bot.) the cassia or laurel:

肉桂 the cinnamon bark. (2) A surname.

桂冠 *gueihguan*, n., a garland made of laurel blossoms: 桂冠詩人 a poet laureate.

桂宮 *gueihgung*, n., (LL) the moon (where one imagines seeing the shadow of a laurel tree).

桂花 *gueihhua*, n., cassia or laurel blossoms, *Cinnamomum Cassia*.

桂枝 *gueihjy*, n., cinnamon barks.

桂窟 *gueihku*, n., (AC) the moon, see *-gung* ↑.

桂輪 *gueilurn*, n., (AC) ditto.

桂皮 *gueihpir*, n., (herb med.) cinnamon bark.

桂子 *gueihtzyy*, n., euphem. for a friend's son: 桂子蘭孫 same for a friend's descendants.

桂圓 *gueihyuarn*, n., dried longans (龍[A]眼 60S.70).

桂月 *gueihyueh*, n., the 8th lunar month.

檯 10B.11-1

tair.

[Pop. 枱]

N. (*-tz*) Table: 寫字檯 desk; 櫃檯 shop counter, hotel reception desk; 轉檯子 (bar girl) change over to another table.

檯布 *tairbuh*, n., tablecloth.

檯球 *tairchiour*, n., billiard; (sometimes) ping-pong.

權 10B.11-2

chyuarn.

N. (1) (AC) Chin. steelyard for measuring weight; 權衡 *-herng* ↓. (2) Power, (law) right, influence: 權柄, 權力, 權利, 權限 *-bihng*, *-lih*[1], *-lih*[2], *-shiahn* ↓; 政權 political power; 君權 monarchical power; 民權 people's rights; 人權 human rights; 當權 in power; 有權, 無權 has, has no, power; 特權 special rights and privileges; 主權 sovereign rights, sovereignty; 極權 absolute power, dictatorial powers, totalitarian rule; 弄權 jockey for political power; 攬權 to grab power, be in the saddle; 大權旁落 chief loses power to those under him; 權傾人主 (of high minister) hold actually more power than the king; 選舉權 the right to vote; 立法權 legislative power. (3) Expediency as against 經 basic principles: 權宜, 權變, 權術 *-yir*, *-biahn*, *-shuh* ↓. (4) Anc. var. of 顴 cheekbone. (5) A surname.

V.t. To weigh, judge importance: 權衡輕重 judge the comparative importance; 權子母 to invest capital for interest.

Adj. Powerful: 權臣 powerful ministers.

Adv. For the present: 權且代理 act as deputy for the time being.

權變 *chyuarnbiahn*, n., expediency: 權變多謀 resourceful.

權柄 *chyuarn'bihng* (-'*bing*), n., (political) power: 權柄在手 hold power in one's hand.

權且 *chyuarnchiee*, adv., for the time being.

權度 *chyuarnduh* v.t., to estimate (importance, strength, length, etc.).

權槩 *chyuarngaih*, v.i., see *-liarng* ↓.

權骨 *chyuarn'gu*, n., (AC) cheekbone (modn. 顴骨).

權貴 *chyuarn-gueih*, n., the powerful persons at court; the nobility.

權衡 *chyuarnherng*, (1) v.t., judge or weigh (importance, etc.); (2) n., the balance of power, the center of gravity in politics.

權詐 *chyuarnjah*, adj., crafty, deceitful; resourceful.

權軸 *chyuarnjur*, n., (LL) (lit.) the axis of power.

權量 *chyuarnliarng*, v.t., to weigh (importance).

權利 *chyuarnlih*[1], n., (1) right, privilege: 自由權 or 自由的權利 the right to freedom; 說話的權利 the right of speech; (2) power and influence: 爭權奪利 fight for power and privilege; 權利能力 legal capacity.

權力 *chyuarnlih*[2], n., power, actual power to do things: 權力很大 hold great power.

權謀 *chyuarnmour*, n., political strategy, resourceful tactics.

權能 *chyuarnnerng*, n., the power or ability to do things: 權能劃分 separation of powers and authorities.

權限 *chyuarnshiahn*, n., legal power: 超過他的權限 exceeds his power as limited by law.

權幸 *chyuarnshihng*, n., favorites of the king.

權術 *chyuarnshuh*[1], n., strategy; the art of political maneuvering.

權數 *chyuarnshuh*[2], n., ditto.

權勢 *chyuarnshyh*, n., political power and influence.

權時 *chyuarnshyr*, adj., expedient: 權時之計 a measure of expediency.

權威 *chyuarnwei*, n., (1) authority, -ties: 權威人士, 權威方面 the authorities; (2) authority on certain subjects: 史學權威 authority on history.

權益 *chyuarnyih*, n., (law) rights of ownership.

權宜 *chyuarnyir*, adj., expedient, measure of expediency.

槿 10B.11-2

jiin (also *jihn*).

N. The common hibiscus: 木槿 shrubby althaea.

枉 10B.11-3

waang.

V.t. (1) To bend, cause to deviate from straight line, right path or justice: 枉屈 *-chyu*[1]↓; 枉法 *-faa*↓;

枉尺直尋 (AC) bend in small places (尺 foot) and straight in total (尋 ten feet).

Adj. Bent, crooked: 矯枉過正 overdo in rectifying behavior—hence 矯枉 be hypocritical; 枉己正人 rectify others and forget oneself.

Adv. (1) (Court.) condescend to: 枉顧, 枉駕 *-guh, -jiah* ↓. (2) Vainly: 枉費, 枉然 *-feih, -rarn* ↓. (3) Unjustly: 枉死 *-syy* ↓.

枉屈 *waangchyu*[1], v.t., to wrong (person), be unjust to.
枉曲 *waangchyu*[2], adj., bent, crooked, warped.
枉道 *waang-dauh*, phr., 枉道而事人 (AC) to please a superior by immoral ways.
枉斷 *waang-duahn*, v.i., to decide unfairly.
枉法 *warng-faa*, phr., to circumvent the law.
枉費 *waangfeih*, v.t., esp. in 枉費心機 to wreck one's brains without results.
枉顧 *waangguh*, v.t., (court.) condescend to visit (my shop).
枉駕 *waangjiah*, v.t., (court.) condescend to come to my place.
枉結 *waangjier*, v.t., (AC) condescend to befriend.
枉橈 *waangnaur*, v.i., (AC) fail to carry out justice.
枉然 *waangrarn*, adv., (struggle, die) in vain.
枉死 *warngsyy*, v.i., (condemned to) die unjustly.

桎 10B.11-3

jyh.

N. Shackles: 桎梏 *-guh* ↓.

V.t. To shackle; (AC) obstruct: 不桎 not obstructed.

桎梏 *jyhguh*, n., (hand) fetters and foot) shackles; also (fig.) v.t. & n., bind, prevent from action.

檉 10B.11-3

cheng.

N. (Bot.) varieties of willow: 檉柳.

桯 10B.11-4

ting.

N. Footstool near bed: 桯凳.

欏 10B.11-4

luor.

N. See 桫△欏 10B.91.

櫂 10B.11-5

jauh.

N. (1) An oar: 鼓櫂而進 row the boat forward. (2) (LL) a boat: 歸櫂 boat returning home; 櫂歌 boatman's song.

柱 10B.11-6

juh.

N. (1) (*-tz*) A pillar, post: 庭柱 portico columns; 臺柱 important actors in troupe; (fig.) mainstay of a group or movement. (2) Peg for adjusting string on music instrument.

柱石 *juhshyr*, n., stone pillar; (fig.) pillar of strength.

橦 10B.11-6

turng.

N. A tree in Yunnan whose flower petals can be made into cloth, hence 橦布.

栓 10B.11-8

shuan.

N. (1) A bolt: a door bolt (also wr. 閂). (2) A stopper; a lock at hydrant.

V.t. To bolt (door, etc.).

栓塞 *shuarnseh*, n., (1) occlusion, a bolt; (2) (med.) embolism.

棰 10B.11-9

chueir.

N. A rod, cane for caning (also wr. 箠).

椎 10B.11-9

juei (also *chueir*).
[Dist. 錐 an awl]

N. Wooden knocker, truncheon (dist. 錐 81A.11).

V.t. To strike, hit with a weapon.

推 椎 [木莽] 椿 椹 柮 柜 榧 櫃 框 柩 樞

椎 輪 *jueilurn*, n., (AC) unfinished wheel without spokes; (fig.) s.t. begun and not yet in completed stage.
椎 魯 *jueiluu*, adj., (LL) stupid (person).
椎 剽 *jueipiauh*, v.t., (AC) kill and rob.
椎 子 *jueitz*, n., a hammer.

榷 10B.11-9

chyueh.

N. A log used as footbridge.

N. & v.t. (1) Tax. (2) Monopoly: 榷鹽, 榷酤 salt, wine monopoly; 榷利 monopoly.

§ 10B.20 (木/卄)

[木莽] 10B.20-2

maang.

[木莽] 果 *marngguoo*, n., mango (common form 芒果).

§ 10B.21 (木/乚)

椿 10B.21-1

juang.

N. adjunct. 一椿事 one affair; 椿椿事都要我們做 we have to do everything.

N. (*-tz*) A pile driven into the ground: 拴牛椿 a pole for tying up cattle; 打椿 to drive a pile, set up row of stakes.

椹 10B.21-2

jen (**shehn*).

N. (1) Chopping block for execution (var. of 砧): 椹板 see 砧^Δ板 31B.40. (2) (**shehn*) The berry of mulberry.

柮 10B.21-2

duoh.

N. 榾柮 logs.

柜 10B.21-5

jyuu (**gueih*).

N. (1) Wicker material for basket. (2) Abbr. for 櫸 10B.10. (3) Abbr. for 櫃 a box, cabinet.

榧 10B.21-5

feei.
[Var. 棐]

N. A species of yew, *Torreya nucifera.*

榧 子 *feeitz*, n., (1) the nut of *feei*; (2) snap one's finger: 給你榧子吃呢 "thumb one's nose at."

櫃 10B.21-5

gueih.

N. A container for storing clothes, books, chinaware, money, etc.: 衣櫃 a wardrobe; 櫃子 a cupboard; 櫃兒 a chest; 櫃櫥 a showcase; 木櫃 wooden chest; 貨櫃 (shipping) a container: 貨櫃運輸 shipping by container; 貨櫃化 containerization; 鐵櫃 iron safe, file cabinet; 書櫃 a bookcase; 掌櫃的 a shop owner; 內掌櫃 a shop owner's wife; 押櫃 a deposit as guarantee.

櫃 房 *gueihfarng*, n., cashier, cashier's office.
櫃 面 兒 *gueihmiah'l*, n., a shop counter.
櫃 上 *gueihshahng*, (1) n., a shop cashier, hotel desk; (2) adj., inside the shop.

框 10B.21-5

kuahng.

N. (1) 門框 doorjamb, doorpost. (2) 鏡框子, 眼鏡框兒 frame of picture, eyeglasses.

柩 10B.21-5

jiouh.

N. A coffin containing a corpse: 靈柩 a casket, a bier, a coffin; 柩車 a hearse; 運柩 transport a coffin; 送柩 to escort a coffin to the burial ground.

樞 10B.21-5

shu.

N. (1) Door hinge. Hence, (2) axis of power, strategic position upon which affairs hinge: 中樞 central government, central authority, such as Cabinet, Privy Council; 樞衡, 樞要 *-herng*, *-yauh* ↓.

樞 奧 *shu-auh*, adj. & n., Privy Council, see *-mih* ↓.
樞 臣 *shu-chern*, n., (LL) high ministers of state.

樞衡 *shuherng*, n. & v.t., balance or axis of power; to hold the balance of power, to be at the helm of government.

樞機 *shuji*, n., (1) the hinge, (fig.) axis, helm; the highest positions of power; (2) as in 樞機主教 (Catholic) cardinal.

樞近 *shujihn*, adj., position close to the imperial court.

樞軸 *shujur* (*-jour*), n., axis of power. 「government.

樞路 *shuluh*, n., central posts of

樞密 *shumih*, n., state secret; highest Privy Council; 樞密使 --*shyy*, n., formerly, Privy Councillor.

樞紐 *shunioou*, n., the hinge upon which other things turn or hang, basic determining factor.

樞務 *shuwuh*, n., affairs of state; premier's duties.

樞要 *shuyauh*, n., the seat of political power.

桕 10B.21-9

jiouh.

N. (Bot.) the tallow tree (also 烏^Δ 桕 91.50).

槄 10B.21-9

tau.

N. (Bot.) a tree, *Mallotus japonicus*, also known as 山楸.

§ 10B.22 (木/丨)

梆 10B.22-1

bang.

N. In 梆子 *-tz* ↓.

梆兒頭 *bang'ltour*, n., an insect with protruding head; person with protruding forehead.

梆子 *bangtz*, n., bamboo tube or wooden slat used for beating time or announcing watch of night; 梆子腔 --*chiang*, music or opera in Shensi, marked by use of *bangtz*, also called 秦腔.

朴 10B.22-2

pur (also *poh*).

[Var. of 樸 10B.81]

N. A surname.

Adj. Simple, honest, unadorned, of sturdy character. For compounds, see 樸 10B.81.

朴刀 *purdau*, n., (mil.) a kind of knife.

朴硝 **pohshiau*, n., (chem.) sodium sulfate or Glauber's salt; • for other compp., see 樸 10B.81.

椰 10B.22-3

yer.

N. The cocoanut palm: 椰子 cocoanut; 椰肉 meat of cocoanut.

椰花酒 *yerhua-jioou*, n., toddy, arrack.

椰菜 *yertsaih*, n., cole; 花椰菜 cauliflower; 嫩椰菜 Savoy cabbage.

杯 10B.22-3

bei.

[Var. 盃, AC 桮]

N. Cup (also 杯子): 酒杯 wine cup; 茶杯 teacup; 杯酒 (a cup of wine) banquet; 杯酒之歡 pleasure of a banquet; 杯中物 wine; 杯盤狼藉 stacks of cups and dishes, scene of big dinner; 杯弓蛇影 see serpent's image in wine cup, atmosphere of fear and admonition (feast of Nebuchadnezzar); 杯水車薪 to squelch the fire of a cartload of firewoods with one cup of water (entirely inadequate means).

杯葛 *beiger*, v.t., (translit.) to boycott.

柙 10B.22-4

shiar.

N. (1) (AC) beast's cage. (2) (AC) scabbard.

柿 10B.22-6

shyh.

N. (*-tz*) The persimmon: 柿餅 preserved persimmon; 柿霜 ditto ("frosted").

椁 10B.22-6

guoo.

[Var. 槨]

N. An outer coffin.

樞 桕 槄 梆 朴 椰 杯 柙 柿 椁

亅	小	卜	十	土	ナ	廾	ㄴ	丨	一	丅	フ	口	区	冈	ㄱ	厂	尸	亠	广	宀	丶	乚	弋	心	八	人	乂	一	㇀	丿	ㅗ	く
00	01	02	10	11	12	20	21	22	30	31	32	40	41	42	50	51	52	60	61	62	63	70	71	72	80	81	82	83	90	91	92	93

榨 10B.22-6

jah.

[Pop. var. 搾 10A.22]

椰 10B.22-6

larng.

[Var. 桹]

N. A tall tree: 桄椰 *Arenga saccharifera*; 檳椰 the areca palm or betel nut; 鳴椰 to beat the stern of a fishing boat with rod as a means to drive fish (also 鳴桹).

Adj. 椰椰 descriptive of the sound produced by beating wood against wood.

椰頭 *larng'tou*, n., a hammer.

梯 10B.22-8

ti.

N. A ladder, stairs, steps: 天梯 long ladder; 雲梯 ladder for scaling city walls; 樓梯 staircase; 電梯 elevator, lift; 安全梯 fire escape; 軟梯, 繩梯 rope ladder; 板梯 stepladder.

梯氣 *tichih*, adj., (MC) very intimate: 梯氣酒, 梯氣話; see *-jii*↓.
梯衝 *tichung*, n., scaling ladder for attacking city walls.
梯航 *ti-harng*, phr., (LL) short for 梯山航海 "scaling mountains and crossing seas"—long, arduous voyage.
梯階 *tijie*, n., steps of ladder; elements ("first steps") in subject (French, painting, etc.).
梯己 *tijii*, (1) n., secret savings (of housewife, etc.); (2) adj., very partial, confidential (probably standing for 體己): 梯己話 confidential talk; 梯己人 a confidant(e); (3) adv., personally: 梯己送路 send off personally.
梯形 *tishirng*, n., (math.) trapezoid; staggered arrangement (of timetable). 「fields.
梯田 *ti-tiarn*, n., terraced (rice)
梯次 *titsyh*, n., turn, term: 第幾梯次 (first, second, etc.) turn; term (of military training).

析 10B.22-9

shi.

V.i. & t. (1) To break up (unit), cut or tear apart: 剖析 to dissect (word meaning); for members of a family to break up and live separately: 析居, 析爨 *-jyu*, *-tsuahn*, etc.↓. (2) To analyze, dissect (meaning, problem): 分析 analyze, -lysis; 解析 analyze meaning; 析疑, 析義 *-yir*, *-yih*↓.

析產 *shi-chaan*, v.i., (brothers) divide common property.
析箸 *shi-juh*, v.i., see *-tsuahn*↓.
析居 *shi-jyu*, v.i., (brothers, husband and wife) to live separately. 「(var. 淅淅).
析析 *shishi*, adj., rustling sound
析爨 *shitsuahn*, v.i., to set up separate kitchens.
析煙 *shi-yan* v.i., see *-tsuahn*↑.
析義 *shi-yih*, v.i., to analyze and explain meaning of text.
析疑 *shi-yir*, v.i., to dispel doubts (in problems of authorship, text, etc.).

柝 10B.22-9

tuoh.

N. Watchman's knocker or plaque, sounded to mark hour of night.

柳 10B.22-9

lioou.

[Anc. var. 栁, 桺]

N. (1) A surname. (2) The willow, much used in Chin. poetry: 柳枝 soft willow branch; 楊柳 a variety of willow used as symbol of feminine delicacy: 柳腰 soft waistline; 柳眉 arch eyebrows; 柳眼 long, slender eyes; in comb. with 花 signifying courtesans and their life; 尋花問柳 go round singsong houses; 花柳病 venereal disease; 花街柳巷 redlight district.

柳穿魚 *lioouchuanyur*, n., (bot.) a grass, *Linaria japonica*.
柳線 *liooushiahn*, n., the long, swaying branches of willows ("threads").
柳絮 *liooushyuh*, n., willow catkins floating in air like "cotton" (絮).
柳芽兒 *lioouyar'l*, n., young willow sprouts.
柳條 *liooutiaur*, n., willow branch; 柳條包, 柳條箱 basket made of willow branches.

棉 10B.22-9

miarn.

N. Cotton: 棉花, 棉布, 棉線 *-hua*, *-buh*, *-shiahn*↓.

Adj. Cotton padded: 棉襖, 棉褲 *-aau*, *-kuh*↓.

棉襖 *miarn-aau*, n., cotton-padded jacket.
棉被 *miarnbeih*, n., cotton-padded quilt.
棉薄 *miarnbor*, adj., meager, trivial (strength, contribution, etc.).
棉布 *miarnbuh*, n., cotton cloth.
棉花 *miarnhua*, n., cotton plant; cotton; 棉花火藥 guncotton; 淨棉花 cleaned cotton, free from seeds.
棉織品 *miarnjy-piin*, n., cotton textiles. 「paper.
棉紙 *miarnjyy*, n., a soft writing

棉褲 *miarn-kuh*, n., cotton-padded pants.
棉袍 *miarnpaur*, n., cotton-padded gown.
棉紗 *miarnsha*, n., cotton yarn; 棉紗廠 cotton mill.
棉線(綫) *miarnshiahn*, n., cotton thread.
棉屑 *miarnshieh*, n., cotton waste.
棉絮 *miarnshyuh*, n., waste cotton.
棉子 *miarntz*, n., cotton seeds; 棉子油 cotton-seed oil.
棉衣 *miarnyi*, n., cotton or cotton-padded jacket.

柞 10B.22-9

tzuoh (**tzer*).

N. An evergreen shrub, *Quercus serrata.*

V.i. (**tzer*) To fell trees.

柞木 *tzuohmuh*, n., (bot.) *Myroxylon racemosum.*
柞蠶 *tzuohtsarn*, n., wild silkworm; 柞蠶絲 silk from wild silkworm.

櫛 10B.22-9

jier.

N. A fine-toothed comb: 侍執巾櫛 serve as a wife or concubine (attend to bath and hairdress).

V.i. (1) To comb hair: 櫛髮 dress one's hair; 櫛風沐雨 expose oneself to the winds and rains in travel.

櫛比 *jier-bii*, adj., as in 鱗次櫛比 (houses) close together in a row, in serrated formation.

§10B.30 (木/一)

植 10B.30-1

jyr.

[Usu. printed 植]

N. Plant: 植物 *-wuh*↓.

V.i. (1) To plant, to cultivate: 栽植 to plant; 栽花植木 to plant flowers and trees; 培植 to raise (plant), to educate and train (youth); 移植 to transplant: 心臟移植 heart transplantation. (2) To establish: 植基 establish foundation; 植黨 *-daang*↓. (3) (AC) 植杖而耘 planted his stick and started weeding. (4) (AC) 植耳 prick up one's ears.

植黨 *jyy-daang*, phr., 植黨營私 form political cliques.
植物 *jyrwuh*, n., plants; 植物學 botany; 植物園 botanical garden.

楂 10B.30-1

char (**ja*).

N. (1) A raft (var. of 槎). (2) (*ja*) 山楂 (also wr. 樝) a kind of hawthorn; its red, sour berry.

榼 10B.30-1

keh.

N. (AC) a wine goblet; a box or basket.

樝 10B.30-2

ja.

[Var. of 楂 10B.30↑]

櫨 10B.30-2

lur.

N. (1) Square supporting block between roof and beam. (2) (Bot.) Hungarian fustic, *Rhus cotinus*, related to lacquer tree.

桓 10B.30-3

huarn.

N. A surname.

杠 10B.30-3

gang (**gahng*).

N. (1) A flagstaff. (2) A small bridge: 徒杠 (AC) a footbridge. (3) (**gahng*) Var. of 槓 10B.80.

椏 10B.30-3

ya.

N. Forked branch: 椏杈, 椏枝 ditto.

極 10B.30-3

jir.

N. (1) The ridge beam of a build-

棉 柞 櫛 植 楂 榼 樝 櫨 桓 杠 椏 極

ing. (2) The throne: 登極 ascend the throne, become king. (3) The utmost point: 四極 the four corners of the earth; 八極 farthest points of the universe. (4) The Poles of the earth: 北極, 南極 the North, South Pole; 陰極, 陽極 (of electric currents) the cathode, anode. (5) The Absolute: 太極 (Chin. cosmogony) the condition as it existed before the creation of the world; 太極拳 a form of boxing emphasizing slow, circular movements.

V.t. Reach the end of, push to extremes: 極力 *-lih*↓; 極盡心力 put one's body and soul into a task, work to the best of one's ability.

Adj. Utmost, final, furthest: 無極 limitless; 無所不用其極 to resort to extreme measures, unscrupulous; 終極 the ultimate end.

Adv. Very, to the highest degree: 極大, 極小 the biggest, smallest; 極好, 極壞 the best, the worst; 極多, 極少 maximum, minimum amount; 極美, 極醜 prettiest, ugliest; 極難, 極易 hardest, easiest; 極表同情 most sympathetic; 極爲讚美 praise to the skies.

極其 *jir-chir*, adv., very, to the fullest measure.
極處 *jir-chuh*, n., the farthest point.
極圈 *jirchyuan*, n., (geog.) the polar circle: 北極圈 the Arctic Circle; 南極圈 the Antarctic Circle.
極點 *jirdiaan*, n., the farthest point, extremities: 達於極點 to the utmost point or the highest degree; 壞到極點 thoroughly wicked.
極地 *jirdih*, n., the polar region.
極頂 *jirdiing*, n., zenith.
極端 *jirduan*, (1) n., extreme points, ends, or limits of a thing: 走極端 go to extremes; (2) adj., extreme, radical: 極端手段 extreme measures; 極端思想 radical thoughts; (3) adv., extraordinarily, very: 極端不好 indescribably bad; 極端可恨 most hateful; 極端可愛 most lovable; 極端理想 highly idealistic.
極度 *jirduh*, adj. & adv., extreme (ly), ultimate(ly), intemperate (ly), up to the breaking point.
極峯 *jirfeng*, n., the highest executive officer of a country.
極光 *jirguang*, n., the aurora australis, aurora borealis.
極致 *jirjyh*, n., highest achievements.
極樂 *jirleh*, adj., blissful, happiest: 極樂世界 paradise, condition of perfect happiness.
極力 *jir-lih*, v.i., do one's best, exert the greatest effort.
極目 *jir-muh*, adv., as far as the eye can see: 極目四望 take a panoramic view from some vantage point.
極品 *jirpiin*, n., (of artistic works, food, etc.) the best of its kind.
極限 *jir-shiahn*, n., (1) farthest confines: 最大極限 maximum limits; (2) (math.) a limit.
極行 *jirshihng*, n., exemplary conduct, virtuous behavior, excellences, best qualities.
極刑 *jir-shirng*, n., extreme punishment, death penalty.
極選 *jir-shyuaan*, n. & adj., ultimate best.

楹 10B.30–3

yirng.

N. (1) A house beam (also used as n. adjunct: 一楹房間 one room; 三楹房間 three rooms). (2) A pillar: 楹聯 literary couplet on pillar or wall.

橙 10B.30–3

cherng (sp. pr. **chern*).

N. (1) orange. (2) 橙黃 orange color.

榅 10B.30–4

wen.

榅桲 *wenbor*, n., a papaya-like fruit that makes good jelly, *Cydonia oblongs*.

檻 10B.30–5

jiahn (**kaan*).

N. (1) A railing, bars, an enclosure: 獸檻 a cage for animals; 檻車 an enclosed cart for prisoners. (2) (**kaan*) Threshold, a doorsill: (Shanghai dial.) 門檻很精 clever and smart and not easily duped, know all the tricks of a trade.

櫪 10B.30–5

lih.

N. (1) A stable: 老驥伏櫪, 志在千里 (lit.) a veteran thoroughbred, while tied to its stable, still dreams of the wilds, (fig.) a man of action, temporarily lying low, has yet ambitions unfulfilled. (2) (Var. of 櫟) *Quercus serrata*. (3) Mats on which silkworms are raised.

檀 10B.30–6

tarn.

N. (1) A surname. (2) Sandalwood of red-brownish color: 柴檀木 red sandalwood; 檀口櫻脣 cherry lips and sandalwood mouth (of woman; here 檀 refers to fragrance, see 檀香 *-shiang*↓).

檀板 *tarnbaan*, n., hardwood

plaque used for keeping rhythm in Chin. opera.

檀香 *tarnshiang*, n., also 檀香木 sandalwood; 檀香爐 sandalwood censer; 檀香山 Honolulu, Hawaii.

檀越 *tarnyueih*, n., (Budd.) almsgiver; donor to temples.

楦 10B.30-6

shyuahn.

N. Shoemaker's last for shaping shoes; 鞋楦, 楦子, 楦頭.

椌 10B.30-6

chiang.

N. (AC) name of anc. wood-wind instrument; 秦椌 *chirnchiang*, song style of Shensi district (also wr. 秦腔).

槎 10B.30-8

char.

N. A raft (on river, sea).

§ 10B.32 (木/フ)

梣 10B.32-2

chern.

N. (Bot.) a tree, *Fraxinus bungeana* var. *pubbinervis* (in med. known as 秦皮).

桚 10B.32-9

tzar.

[Var. of 拶 10A.32]

§ 10B.40 (木/口)

枯 10B.40-1

ku.

V.i. Dry up, dried up: 樹木枯了 tree has dried up; see Adj.↓; 榮枯 prosperity and decline.

Adj. (1) Dry, withered: 枯木逢春, 枯樹生花 a dried up tree comes to life again; 枯骨 dry bones; 枯槁, 枯萎, 枯謝 *-gaau, -weei, -shieh*↓; dried up (of thoughts, springs): 枯井 dried up well; 搜索枯腸 rack one's brains for some ideas to write on; thin: 枯瘦, 枯寂 *-shouh, -jir*[1]↓. (2) Poor, impoverished, desolate: 枯窘 hard up; 枯坐 sit idly without anything to do.

枯凋 *kudiau*, adj., see *-shieh*↓.
枯礬 *kufarn*, n., dry, flaky alum.
枯槁 *kugaau*, adj., dried up (of trees, facial appearance), lifeless (composition).
枯乾 *kugan*, adj., dry (branches, fruit).
枯涸 *kuher*, adj., dried up (pools).
枯候 *kuhouh*, v.i., to wait interminably.
枯竭 *kujier*, adj., dried up (springs of water, of thought).
枯寂 *kujir*[1], adj., lonely.
枯瘠 *kujir*[2], adj., emaciated.
枯窘 *kujyuung*, adj., impoverished, without money or fresh ideas.
枯謝 *kushieh*, adj., (of flowers) withered.
枯瘦 *kushouh*, adj., emaciated.
枯燥 *kutzauh*, adj., (of weather, place) dry; (of composition) lifeless: 枯燥無味 dull and boring, uninteresting dry-as-dust.
枯萎 *kuweei*, adj., dried up.
枯葉蝶 *kuyeh dier*, n., (zoo.) *Gastropacha quercifolia*, an insect which feeds on and destroys leaf sprouts (also 枯葉蛾).

梏 10B.40-1

guh.

N. Manacles, fetters: 桎梏 handcuffs and shackles, fetters.

V.t. To fetter.

桔 10B.40-1

jier (*jyur).

N. (1) 桔梗 (bot.) The balloon flower, kikio root, *Platycodon grandiflorus*. (2) (*jyur) A simplified form of 橘.

楛 10B.40-2

huh.

N. (AC) a wood used for arrows.

柘 10B.40-3

jeh.

N. (1) A hardwood tree, whose leaves are used for feeding silkworms in place of mulberry and whose bark is used as yellow pigment. (2) (AC) u.f. 蔗＝甘蔗[△] 20A.63: 柘漿 sugar cane juice.

柘黃 *jehhuarng*, n., yellow dye from *jeh* tree.
柘榴 *jehliour*, n., pomegranate (usu. 石榴).
柘蠶 *jehtsarn*, n., silkworms fed on *jeh* leaves; silk spun is called 柘絲 *jeh* silk.

梧 10B.40–3

wur.

梧檟 *wur-jiaa*, n., (AC) two trees producing good timber.
梧桐 *wurtung* (-'*tung*), (bot.) the kolanut, the Chin. plane tree, *Sterculia platanifolia*.

桮 10B.40–3

bei.

[Var. of 杯 10B.01]

櫺 10B.40–3

lirng.

N. (1) Lattice window. (2) Cornice work.

梠 10B.40–4

lyuu.

N. (Door) lintel.

棺 10B.40–6

guan.

N. A coffin: 棺材 *-tsair*, 棺木 *-muh* ↓; 棺槨 inner and outer coffins; 開棺驗屍 disinterment of a corpse for autopsy.

棺罩 *guanjauh*, n., a funeral pall.
棺木 *guanmuh*, n., a coffin.
棺材 *guantsair*, n., ditto; 棺材板 *--baan*, (1) wooden planks used in making coffins; (2) a coffin made of thin wooden planks; 棺材瓤子 (abusive) an old wreck fit for the coffin (lit., "coffin-stuffing").

榕 10B.40–6

rurng.

N. The banyan: 榕樹 ditto; 榕厦 the shaded area covered by a banyan tree.

槍 10B.40–8

chiang.

N. (1) A spear, lance, javelin: 長槍大戟 long spears and halberds; 刀槍不入 (magic) proof against spear thrusts and sword cuts; 槍頭 spearhead; 槍尖 point of spear; 投槍 throw a javelin. (2) A tube-shaped thing: 烟槍 opium pipe. (3) A gun, rifle, pistol (interch. 鎗): 手槍 pistol, etc., see 鎗 81A.40.

V.t. To substitute for another during tests: 槍替, 槍手 *-tih*, *-shoou* ↓.

槍笆 *chiangba*, n., a spiked fence of wood or bamboo.
槍斃 *chiangbih*, v.t., to execute (criminal) by shooting; to shoot (person) to death.
槍決 *chiangjyuer*, v.t., ditto.
槍籬 *chianglir*, n., see *-ba* ↑.
槍手 *chiangshoou*, n., (1) a sharpshooter; (2) a gunman; (3) (-'*shoou*) a substitute during examinations on false pretenses.
槍替 *chiangtih*, v.t., to act as subtitute under false pretense.

栝 10B.40–9

gua.

N. (1) (AC) the juniper. (2) (AC) the pointed end of an arrow. (3) (AC) firewood.

栝樓 *gualour*, n., (bot.) a kind of melon, *Trichosanthes japonica*.

枱 10B.40–9

tair.

[Pop. of 檯 10B.11]

枷 10B.40–9

jia.

N. The cangue: 帶枷 (of prisoners) confine in a cangue.

枷板兒 *jiabaa'l*, adj., in an awkward fix: 套上枷板兒了 in a bad fix; 受枷板兒氣 placed between the devil and the deep sea.
枷號 *jiahauh*, n., formerly, parade a prisoner in a cangue.
枷鎖 *jiasuoo*, n., fetters, shackles.

格 10B.40–9

ger.

N. (1) Form, shape, standard, qualifications: 格式 *-shyh*, 格局 *-jyur*, 格律 *-lyuh*, 格度 *-duh* ↓; 資格 qualifications; 合格 qualified; 格外 *-waih* ↓. (2) Style, character: 獨創一格 original in style or design; 品格 a person's character; 人格 moral character; 格調, 格言 *-diauh, -yarn*↓. (3) A pattern, frame, ruled lines: 橫格紙 paper with horizontal ruled lines; 花格布 checkered fabrics; 畫格子 to draw ruled lines; 窗格 a window lattice; 格子 *-tz*↓. (4) A surname.

V.t. (1) Resist, hinder, obstruct, impede: 阻格 be an impediment to; 格格不入 (of persons) cannot get along with one another, (of things) cannot fit one another; 格於規定 be barred by regulations; 格開 separate one from another; 間 (*jiahn*) 格 (to, a) partition, divide into compartments; 扞格 impede, obstruct; cannot fit in. (2) To fight: 格鬬 *-douh*↓; 格殺勿論 capture and summarily execute. (3) To correct, put to right: 格非 rectify what is morally wrong. (4) To probe to the bottom, study carefully: 格物 *-wuh*, 格致 *-jyh*↓.

格調 *gerdiauh*, n., a style: 特殊格調 a special style.
格鬬 *gerdouh*, n. & v.i., (engage in) fisticuffs, a free-for-all.
格度 *gerduh*, n., standard.
格致 *gerjyh*, (1) phr., 格物致知 to study the phenomena of nature in order to acquire knowledge; (2) n., old name of natural sciences, esp. physics.
格局 *gerjyur*, n., the general layout, situation.
格律 *gerlyuh*, n., set rules.
格式 *gershyh*, n., a standardized form, style, pattern.
格子 *gertz*, n., a trellis, a lattice, a pattern.
格外 *gerwaih*, adv., exceptionally: 格外小心 be especially careful.
格物 *gerwuh*, v.i., study the phenomena of nature.
格言 *geryarn*, n., proverbs, maxims, axioms.

檐 10B.40-9

yarn.

[Var. of 簷 92A.40]

§ 10B.41 (木/図)

檣 10B.41-1

chiarng.

N. A mast; yardarm: 桅檣 ship masts.

楮 10B.41-1

chuu.

N. (1) The mulberry, whose bark is made into paper. (2) (U.f. 紙) paper, esp. paper money burnt for the dead: 楮錢, 楮鏹 *-chiarn, -chiarng*↓.

楮幣 *chuubih*, n., (Suhng Dyn.) paper money.
楮錢 *chuuchiarn*, n., paper money burnt for the dead.
楮鏹 *chuuchiarng*, n., ditto.
楮葉 *chuuyeh*, n., (AC) jade mulberry leaf, resembling real leaf—hence 莫辨楮葉 cannot distinguish between real and imitation.

椿 10B.41-1

chun.

N. Fragrant cedar, (also called 香椿) *Cedrela chinensis*; symbol of father: 椿萱 *-shyuan*↓; symbol of long life: 椿齡, 椿壽 long life; 臭椿 *Ailanthus glandulosa.*

椿萱 *chunshyuan*, n., father and mother (萱 symbol of mother, 20A.30): 椿萱並茂 both parents alive and well.

柑 10B.41-2

gan.

N. (Bot.) 蜜柑 the tangerine.

槽 10B.41-2

tsaur.

N. (1) A trough, manger (for water, animal feed); a wine vat; watertank: 跳槽 "feed in another's manger," "jump on another bandwagon"—inconstancy in love affairs, esp. among visitors of prostitutes. (2) A rabbet plane, joint in woodwork; a rabbet: 槽縫, 槽線 line of rabbet joint; 不合槽 won't fit in groove. (3) A section in lattice window.

槽碓 *tsaur-dueih*, n., a mortar for husking rice by waterpower.
槽坊 *tsaurfarng*, n., a distillery.
槽糕 *tsaurgau*, n., cake made with molds (dist. 糟糕 *tzau-*, 22C.41).
槽兒 *tsaur'l*, n., (1) a depression in surface; (2) wine waiter.
槽櫪 *tsaurlih*, n., a stable.
槽刨 *tsaur-paur*, n., a rabbet plane.
槽子 *tsaurtz*, n., (1) trough, manger; (2) a depression in surface.
槽牙 *tsaur-yar*, n., a molar (tooth).

樐 楷 柚 檔 栢 栖 槠 相

樐 10B.41-2

luu.
[Var. 櫓 10B.41]

楷 10B.41-2

kaai.

N. (1) (Callig.) 楷書 formal style, (opp. 草書 cursive script, 行書 running script): 正楷 correct, carefully delineated style; 大楷, 小楷 such lettering of different sizes; 楷法 style of this script. (2) Model form, see 楷模, 楷範 *-mor*, *-fahn* ↓. (3) (AC) name of a tree (also pr. *jie*).

楷範 *kaaifahn*, n., see *-mor* ↓.
楷模 *kaaimor*, n., model for others (in conduct, etc.).
楷書 *kaaishu*, n., see N. ↑ (also called 眞書).
楷則 *kaaitzer*, n., see *-mor* ↑.

柚 10B.41-2

youh.

N. The pomelo.

檔 10B.41-2

dahng (also *daang*).

N. Shelf; door frame; esp. files: 歸檔 return to the files; 檔案 *-ahn* ↓.

檔案 *dahng-ahn*, n., archives: 內府檔案 palace archives.
檔期 *dahngchir*, n., scheduled dates for showing of films.
檔子 *dahngtz*, n. adjunct, 一檔子事 (=一件事) an affair; 一檔子人 a group of persons.

栢 10B.41-3

baai.
[Var. 柏 ↓]

栖 10B.41-3

shi (*chi*).

V.i. Var. 棲 to roost, perch, see 10B.93.

栖栖 *shishi*, adj., (AC) vexed, rushing about (also 栖栖皇皇; also wr. 恓 22A.41).

槠 10B.41-3

leir.

N. Stone missiles or wooden beams used by defenders of cities against enemy attack: 槠木 wooden beams swinging from city wall to attack the enemy below.

相 10B.41-4

shiang (**shiahng*).

N. (**shiahng*) (1) A surname. (2) Appearance, looks: 相貌 *-mauh* ↓; 醜相 ugly looks; 怪相 strange, disgusting appearance; 無相 (Budd.) beyond material distinction or material reality; 本相 real inner self; 眞相 real situation. (3) (Fortunetelling) physiognomy as indicative of destiny: 凶相 face indicating violence, also ill luck. (4) Portrait (interch. 像), photograph: 相片 *-piahn* ↓; 照相 n. & v.t., photograph. (5) (AC) prime minister: 丞相, 宰相, 首相, 相國 ditto; 拜相 (emperor) makes s.o. prime minister. (6) (Phys.) phase: 相律 phase rule.

V.t. (**shiahng*) (1) To size up by appearance: 端相 observe carefully; 相女婿 to look at prospective son-in-law for approval; 相地, 相宅 practise geomancy, look at gen. outlay of land as influencing luck; 相馬 look at a horse's physical build. (2) To watch for opportunity: 相機 *-ji* ↓; 相機 or 相時而動 watch for the proper moment for action. (3) To read person's physiognomy, esp. face and hand reading: 相面, 相術, 相法 *-miahn*, *-shuh*, *-faa* ↓; 相命 *-mihng*, 相士 *-shyh*[2] ↓; 星相 astrology. (4) To assist (usu. the emperor, ruler): 相夫敎子 (of wife) assist husband and bring up children. (5) To bless: 吉人天相 God protects the good men.

Adv. Mutually, each other, together (oft. used like a prefix to vbb., with the sense "with"): 相勸 to reason with, persuade; 相會, 相聚 to meet together; 相對 face with; 相告 tell (speak with) another person; 相煩 to bother (person); 相罵, 相打 scold, fight each other; 相爭 wrangle with each other; 相助 help each other; 相敬如賓 (of couple) treat each other with respect ("like guests"); 相生相尅 (of 五行 the states of motion) mutually reinforce or neutralize; 相映成趣 gain by contrast; 相提並論 to be mentioned in the same breath, regarded in same category; 相形見拙 lose by comparison; 相得 *-der* ↓; 不相上下 about equal; 實不相瞞 I am telling you the truth; 相犯 interfere with each other; 相商 discuss together; 相托, 相囑 to ask a person to do s.t., etc.

相安 *shiang-an*, v.i., live together peacefully: 相安無事.
相比 *shiangbii*, v.i., compare with each other.
相差 *shiangchah*, v.i., to differ, to deviate: 相差不遠 not much difference between the two.
相稱 *shiangchehn*, v.i., fit together, pair off nicely.
相成 *shiangcherng*, v.i., to help complement, be complementary in action.

相切 *shiangchieh*, v.i., (lines) cross each other; (surfaces) come into contact.

相親 **shiahngchin*, (1) v.i., to look over prospective bride; (2) (*shiang-*) adj., intimate, fond of each other.

相傳 *shiangchuarn*, v.i., (1) pass from generation to generation; (2) it is rumored, the story goes.

相處 *shiangchuu*, v.i., live or work together (well, badly).

相持 *shiangchyr*, v.i., both parties will not give in.

相去 *shiangchyuh*[1], v.i., both differ, see *-chah* ↑.

相覷 *shiangchyuh*[2], v.i., look at each other with silent understanding: 面面相覷 the audience look at each other in surprise.

相當 *shiangdang*, v.i. & adj., (1) proper, appropriate (compensation, etc.); (2) 相當于 is equal to (dismissal, etc.); 相當的 fairly (expensive, etc.).

相等 *shiangdeen*, (1) adj., equal: 相等於 be equal to; (2) n., equivalent, equal amount, number.

相得 *shiangder*, v.i., get along well: 相得益彰 each improves by association with the other.

相對 *shiangdueih*, adj., (1) opposite, facing each other; (2) as in 相對的 relative, opp. 絕對的 absolute; 相對論 theory of relativity; 相對基金 counterpart fund.

相法 **shiahngfaa*, n., the art of fortunetelling by reading faces.

相反 *shiangfaan*, v.i., to be opposite, contrary: 正正相反 exactly the opposite; 相反的 adv., contrariwise, on the contrary.

相仿 *shiangfaang*, v.i., resemble, look like.

相風 **shiahngfeng*, n., formerly, weathercock, weather vane, a device for telling wind direction (also called 相風竿, 相風烏).

相符 *shiangfur*, v.i., agree with (orig. signature, etc.): 名實相符, 名符其實 reality corresponds with claims or title.

相干 *shianggan*, v.i., have to do with: 這事與你毫不相干 this has nothing to do with you.

相關 *shiangguan*, v.i., see *-gan* ↑.

相公 **shiahnggung*, n., (1) Your Excellency, formerly, address to prime minister; (2) (*-'gung*) (a) young master of a noble house or handsome young man (in vern. literature); (b) a pederast: 相公堂子 house of pederasts.

相好 *shianghaau*, v.i., be fond of each other; 相好的人 good friend or a mistress.

相會 *shianghueih*, v.i., to meet together: 後期相會 meet again.

相互 *shianghuh*, adv., mutually (help, envy, etc.) each other.

相機 **shiahngji*, phr., watch for right time for action.

相見 *shiangjiahn*, v.i., to meet personally: 相見恨晚 regret we didn't meet sooner.

相將 *shiangjiang*, adv., together, in each other's company.

相交 *shiangjiau*, v.i., (1) (lines) cross each other; (2) make friends with each other: 相交甚厚 they are very good friends.

相較 *shiangjiauh*, v.i., compare with: 兩件相較 compare the two.

相偕 *shiangjie*, adv., together (go away, etc.).

相繼 *shiangjih*, v.i., follow one another: 相繼死亡 die one after another.

相近 *shiangjihn*, adj., close by, nearly alike: 住得相近 live nearby; 相近的朋友 close friend.

相助 *shiangjuh*, v.i., help each other.

相知 *shiangjy*, v.i. & n., to know a person really well; a very close friend.

相看 *shiangkan*, (1) v.i., look at each other; (2) (**shiahng'kan*) v.t., to size up (prospective son-in-law, etc.) by looking.

相連 *shiangliarn*, v.i., connect together.

相貌 **shiahngmauh*, n., gen. looks, personal appearance.

相面 **shiahng-miahn*, v.i., read faces.

相命 *shiahngmihng*, v.i. & n., fortunetelling.

相配 *shiangpeih*, v.i., (1) to match each other (as shoes and dress); (2) to mate, pair off.

相片 **shiahngpiahn*, n., a photograph, esp., a print.

相撲 *shiangpu*, v.i., to wrestle together.

相人 **shiahngrern*, v.i., to read person's character.

相若 *shiangruoh*, adj., similar, like each other.

相如 *shiangrur*, adj. & v.i., like, resemble each other.

相善 *shiangshahn*, v.i., be fond of each other (as friends), be familiar with each other.

相聲(兒) **shiahng'sheng('l)*, n., ventriloquist: 對口相聲 witty dialogue by professional performers on stage.

相向 *shiangshiahng*[1], v.i., face each other.

相像 *shiangshiahng*[2], v.i., resemble.

相匣子 **shiahngshiartz*, n., (Peking pop.) a camera.

相信 *shiangshihn*, v.i. & t., believe: 相信不會錯的 I believe it is the right thing; 相信他 believe him; 不能相信 cannot believe.

相形 *shiangshirng*, phr., (1) 相形見絀 lose by comparison; (2) (**shiahng-*) see *-miahn*, *-faa* ↑.

相術 **shiahngshuh*, n., see *-faa* ↑.

相識 *shiangshyh*, (1) v.i., be acquainted with; (2) n., an acquaintance.

相士 *shiahgshyh*, n., fortuneteller.

相思 *shiangsy*, v.i., be lovesick; 相思病 n., lovesickness; 苦相思 deep longing; 兩地相思 longing of parted lovers; 相思子 the gram, a tree, *Abrus precatorius*, producing red beans (紅豆) which are used as lovers' souvenirs, see also 紅^Δ豆 93B.30.

相似 *shiangsyh*, v.i., resemble each other.

相投 *shiangtour*, v.i., fit in well: 意氣相投 (persons) have the same likes and dislikes.

相同 *shiangturng*, v.i., be alike, be the same (opinion, view of things).

亅	小	⺊	十	土	ナ	廾	卝	丨	一	丅	乛	口	図	冈	冂	厂	尸	亠	广	亠	丶	乚	七	心	八	人	㐅	乛	乛	リ	𠂉	く
00	01	02	10	11	12	20	21	22	30	31	32	40	41	42	50	51	52	60	61	62	63	70	71	72	80	81	82	83	90	91	92	93

相 左 *shiangtzuoo*, v.i., (1) diverge, disagree (in opinion); (2) cross one another's way.

相 違 *shiangweei*, v.i., (1) be parted; (2) disagree in opinion.

相 沿 *shiangyarn*, v.i., come down from earlier times: 相沿已久 (custom) has been so for a long time.

相 羊 *shiangyarng*, v.i., (AC) wander, roam about (also wr. 相佯).

相依 *shiangyi*, v.i., depend on each other: 母子相依爲命 the mother and son share their life together.

相 印 *shiangyihn*, (1) v.i., to bear each other out: 心心相印 their hearts are like one; (2) (**shiahng*-) n., premier's seal i.e., (carry on) premier's work.

相 應 *shiangying*, (1) v.i., (in official documents) it is proper that (this be communicated, etc.); (2) (-*yihng*) (a) v.i., to act in response; (b) adj., proper: 嫁得相應的人家 (in vern. literature) marry into a proper family.

相 宜 *shiangyir*, adj., (1) fitting and proper; (2) agreeable (weather, etc.): 氣候不相宜 the weather does not agree with a person.

相 友 *shiangyoou*, v.i., be friends ⌈together.

相 與 *shiangyuu*, (1) v.i., live or work together: 很難相與 difficult to live with or work with (person); (2) adv., together (climb mountains, laugh, etc.).

梱 10B.41-4

kuun.

N. (AC) doorjamb.

楣 10B.41-5

meir.

N. (1) Lintel, esp. 門楣 lintel; (fig.) the house: 有辱門楣 a disgrace to the house. (2) A cross beam under roof.

櫧 10B.41-6

ju.

N. (Bot.) the sweet oak, *Quercus glauca* whose timber can be used for making boats, beams; hence 櫧材 good timber, pillar of strength.

檜 10B.41-8

kuaih (also *gueih*).

N. (Bot.) Chinese cypress, juniper.

楯 10B.41-9

shuun.

N. (1) Horizontal piece in balcony. (2) Shield, u.f. 盾 90.41.

榴 10B.41-9

liour.

[Var. 橊]

N. Short for 石榴 pomegranate: 榴火 when pomegranates are in full bloom ("afire").

榴 彈 *liourdahn*, n., grenade, usu. 手榴彈 hand grenade.

榴 霰 彈 *liourshiahndahn*, n., shrapnel.

柏 10B.41-9

baai (*bor*).

[Var. 栢]

N. (1) Cypress, cedar; trees of the cypress family (扁^Δ柏 63D.42, 檜^Δ柏 10B.41, 羅^Δ漢柏 41D.11). (2) A surname.

柏 酒 *borjiour*, n., wine treated with juniper leaves for flavor.

柏 林 *Bohlirn*, n., Berlin.

柏 油 *baaiyour*, n., (1) asphalt; (2) pitch, gum.

櫓 10B.41-9

luu.

N. (1) A scull or sweep for propelling boats. (2) (AC) a big shield. (3) (AC) a turret tower on city wall.

§10B.42 (木/冈)

楠 10B.42-1

narn.

[Var. of 枏, 柟]

N. (Bot.) *Machilus nanmu*, usu. 楠木 a fine hardwood oft. used for furniture.

構 10B.42-2

gouh.

N. A structure, building, piece of literary work: 佳構 a good piece of writing; 宏構, 巨構 a magnificent building or a great literary work; 華構 a stately mansion; 構造 -*tzauh*↓; 結構 (of novel or art work) structure, composition.

V.t. (1) Build, construct: 構成 build into (a pavilion, a play). (2) To plan, project: 構思 -*sy*, 構想 -*shiaang*↓; 構亂 plan a rebellion.

構 梢 槅 柄 桶 橘 椭 欛 桐

構兵 *gouhbing*, v.i., to wage war.

構想 *gouhshiaang*, v.i., imagine; n., creative imagination, concept of structure in litr. work; work, see *-sy*↓.

構陷 *gouhshiahn*, v.t., implicate (s.o.) in crimes.

構釁 *gouhshihn*, v.i., to provoke, to engender enmity between states.

構思 *gouhsy*, v.t., (of writer) draw up a mental outline, think hard.

構圖 *gouhtur*, v.i., draw up a blueprint, make a sketch of a painting, (photography) compose a picture before releasing the shutter.

構造 *gouhtzauh*, n. & v.t., construct(ion), build(ing); 構造式 (chem.) constitutional formula.

構怨 *gouhyuahn*, v.t., see *-shihn*↑.

梢 10B.42-2

shau.

N. (1) Top of tree: 樹梢 ditto; 柳梢 top of willow; 梢頭 *-tour*↓. (2) Tip, tail end: 鞭梢, 辮梢 tip of whip, of queue; 末梢, 收梢 end of affair; 沒下梢 (story) stops without ending, do not hear further about it. (3) A boat rudder (cf. 艄 91S.42): 梢公, 梢婆, 梢子 *-gung*, *-por*, *-tz*↓.

梢公 *shaugung*, n., (MC) boatman.

梢婆 *shaupor*, n., (MC) boatwoman.

梢梢 *shaushau*, adj., sousing, whistling, rustling sound of wind.

梢頭 *shautour*, n., (MC & poet.) top of tree; end (of street, things).

梢子 *shautz*, n., (1) long, slender end, tip; (2) a boatman; (3) a hand-rotated small drum (toy); (4) (dial.) short pants.

槅 10B.42-3

ger.

[Dist. 隔 32A.42]

N. A yoke for harnessing animals.

柄 10B.42-3

bihng (*biing).

N. (1) Handle (of axe, knife): 葉柄 stem of leaf; 槍柄 butt, stock of gun. (2) Control: 權柄 official power; 執國柄 be in control of government, be chief minister. (3) Target: 笑柄, 話柄 butt of jokes, material for gossip; see 把△柄 10A.70.

V.t. (*biing) (LL, rare) 柄政 be in control of government (秉 preferred, 90.01).

柄臣 *bihngchern*, n., (AC, rare) chief policy-making minister.

柄眼類 *bihngyaanleih*, n., (biol.) animals with eyes resting on projecting stems, such as snails.

桶 10B.42-3

tuung.

N. (*-tz*) Wooden pail, container: 水桶 water bucket; 糞桶, 馬桶 commode; 飯桶 rice jar or pail, (fig. abusive) a useless person, a good-for-nothing.

橘 10B.42-3

jyur.

N. The orange: 橘子 an orange, a tangerine; 橘化爲枳 phrase showing the important influence of environment (deterioration of orange species in another climate).

橘紅 *jyur-hurng*, n., (1) (Chin. med.) dried orange peel; (2) orange red.

橘絡 *jyurluoh*, n., (Chin. med.) the dried fibers of the orange.

椭 10B.42-3

tuoo.

Adj. Oval-shaped: 椭圓.

欛 10B.42-3

bah.

N. (Obs.) handle (var. of 把 in 把△柄 pr. *bahbihng*, 10B.70).

桐 10B.42-4

turng.

N. (1) Name given to various trees, esp. 梧桐 *Firmiana platanifolia*, the Chin. parasol tree, loved for its shade: 桐樹 *Paulownia tomentosa*; 桐油樹 *Aleurites cordata*, the wood-oil tree valued for its oil, the tung oil (桐油) used in paint. (2) Name of a town in Anhuei: 桐城; 桐城派 a school of writing known for austere simplicity.

桐子 *turngtz*, n., fruit of wood-oil tree.

桐油 *turngyour*, n., viscid *tung* oil, used in paint.

柵 棚 槁 檎 枘 橋 槜 栴 栲 朽

柵 10B.42-4

jah (also *shahn*).

N. A palisade, a series of upright posts across a street; window bars: 鐵柵 iron bars across door or window; 木柵 series of wooden stakes to fence off a place.

柵壘 *jahleei*, n., a stockade.
柵欄兒 *jahlar'l*, n., wooden fence consisting of upright posts across a street; 大柵欄兒 name of two streets in Peking (also pr. *-shalar'l*).
柵門 *jahmern*, n., a fence gate across a street.
柵塘 *jahtarng*, n., a fenced-off pond.

棚 10B.42-4

perng.
[Cogn. of 篷 92A.83]

N. (1) (*-tz, 'l*) A mat shed: 搭棚兒 build such mat shed; 草棚, 竹棚 rush shed, bamboo shed. (2) Booth: 茶棚 open teahouse, tea booth. (3) Awning, tent: 帳棚 tent; 天棚, 涼棚 awning, esp. for summer.

槁 10B.42-6

gaau.
[Dist. 稿, 搞]

N. Dry or withered tree.

V.i. To wither.

Adj. (Of wood) rotten, dry: 槁木死灰 unfeeling, lifeless like a piece of dry wood or cold ashes; 形容枯槁 an emaciated, dried-up appearance.

檎 10B.42-8

chirn.

N. See 林▵檎 10B.01.

枘 10B.42-8

rueih.

N. A piece of wood cut to fit into a socket: 枘鑿 (of persons) cannot see eye to eye, incongruous, incompatible ("round peg in a square hole").

橋 10B.42-9

chiaur.

N. (*-'l*) A bridge: 橋梁 *-liarng* ↓; 吊橋 suspension bridge, also drawbridge; 浮橋 pontoon bridge; 鵲▵橋 20S.50; 橋過丢柺 throw away staff after passing bridge—forget benefactor; 橋洞, 橋空 arch under bridge.

Adj. (AC) var. of 喬 high, tall (tree).

橋墩 *chiaurdun*, n., bridge pier, earthern or stone structure under bridge.
橋梁 *chiaurliarng*, n., (lit. & fig.) bridge.
橋牌 *chiaurpair*, n., game of 「bridge.
橋頭堡 *chiaurtourbaau*, n., (mil.) a bridgehead; a salient point in battle line.
橋堍 *chiaurtuh*, n., ramp or earthern embankment leading to bridge.
橋梓 *chiaurtzyy*, n., (LL) father and son (橋 being a tall tree and 梓 a short one).

槜 10B.42-9

tzueih.

N. A kind of plum tree.

栴 10B.42-9

jan.

N. Sandalwood: 栴檀.

§10B.50 (木/ㄱ)

栲 10B.50-1

kaau.

N. (Bot.) mangrove.

栲栳 *kaurlaau*, n., (AC) wooden or bamboo basket.

朽 10B.50-3

shioou.

V.i. To decay.

Adj. Decayed, rotten: 朽木不可雕 one cannot carve on rotten wood—intractable person; 朽材 bad timber (in self-deprecation); 老朽 (contempt.) a worthless old man, also adj., old and useless; 不朽 immortal (name), immortality.

朽敗 *shiooubaih*, adj., corrupt, decayed (structure).
朽蠹 *shioouduh*, v.i., (of hoarded grain) spoilt from insects or moisture.
朽腐 *shiooufuh*, adj., rotten, rotting: 朽腐復化爲神奇 (莊子) (AC) the corruptible again becomes mysterious life.
朽爛 *shioulahn*, adj., decayed, rotten (meat, fruit, etc.).
朽邁 *shiooumaih*, adj., (of a per-

son) old and useless.

樗 10B.50-3

shu.

N. (Bot.) the stinking cedar, a tree of useless timber, *Ailanthus altissima*, commonly known as 臭椿, hence 樗櫟之材 timber of ailanthus and chestnut oak—useless person.

樗 蒲 *shupur*, n., an ancient dice game (also wr. 蒱).
樗 散 *shusaan*, adj., (LL) (person) unemployed, ignored by the world.
樗 材 *shu-tsair*, n., (LL) useless person.

枴 10B.50-4

guaai.

N. (1) An old man's staff. (2) The anklebone.

枴 棒 *guaaibahng*, n., a staff, club, stick.
枴 棍 *guaaiguhn*, n., a walking stick, cane.
枴 杖 *guaaijahng*, n., ditto.
枴 子 *guaaitz*, n., pop. term for the anklebone.

枵 10B.50-4

shiau.

Adj. Empty, dried up: 枵木 dried-up tree trunk; 枵腹 empty stomach; 枵腹從公 to attend office on an empty stomach, i.e., on starvation salary.

枵 然 *shiaurarn*, adj., (AC) big.

楊 10B.50-4

yarng.

N. (1) The poplar, aspen: 白楊 white poplars; 赤楊 the alder; 黃楊木 boxwood. (2) The willow: 楊柳 *-lioou* ↓. (3) A surname.

楊 花 *yarnghua*, n., willow catkins: 水性楊花 said of an inconstant woman; 楊花蘿蔔 a kind of turnip.
楊 枝 *yarngjy*, n., tender willow branch, used for cleaning teeth (of Hindu origin): 楊枝淨水 for brushing teeth in morning.
楊 柳 *yarnglioou*, n., (1) the willow and aspen (the aspen with flattened leafstalks that tremble in the breeze and the willow known as "weeping willow" with soft hanging stems); (2) the willows.
楊 櫨 *yarnglur*, n., (bot.) *Diervilla japonica*, a flowering brush.
楊 梅 *yarngmeir*, n., the arbutus, the wild strawberry tree, *Myrica rubra*, its berries; 楊梅瘡 --*chuang*, syphilitic sores.
楊 桃 *yarngtaur*, n., (bot.) the carambola.
楊 桐 *yarngturng*, n., (bot.) *Eurya ochnacea*.

榻 10B.50-4

tah.

N. Couch, bed: 臥榻, 睡榻, 床榻 bed; 籐榻 rattan bed.

榻 榻 米 *tahta'mi*, n., (Japanese) bedstead usu. provided with mattress; a measure of living space equal to about 18 sq. ft.

楞 10B.50-4

lerng (**lehng*).
[Var. 稜 90A.80 (*lerng*) angle, corner, also pop. var. 愣 22A.50 (**lehng*) stunned, stupid]

栩 10B.50-5

shyuu.

N. (AC) chestnut oak.

Adj. 栩栩如生, 栩然 (of descriptions) alive, like real life.

枋 10B.50-6

fang (**bihng*).

N. (1) A tree, used in making timber for boats. (2) 蘇枋 a tree in East Indies, used for dye. (3) (**bihng*) (AC) var. of 柄 authority.

榜 10B.50-6

baang (**behng*).

N. (1) A wooden panel over gate or top part of tablet: 榜額 *-eh* ↓. (2) Published list announcing successful candidates at civil examinations: 榜上題名 name was on the list; 放榜, 開榜 announce such list; 榜示, 揭榜 make such announcement; 同榜 graduates of the same class or year in civil examinations. (3) Model: 榜樣 *-yahng* ↓; 標ᐞ榜 10B.01. (4) (**behng*) A small boat, esp. pleasure boat. (5) (**behng*) A rowboat.

V.t. (*behng*) Interch. 棒 to flog: 榜掠, 榜笞 *-lyueh*, *-chy* ↓.

榜 箠 **behngchueir*, n. & v.t., flogging.
榜 楚 **behngchuu*, v.t., flogging.
榜 笞 **behngchy*, n. & v.t., ditto.
榜 額 *baang-eh*, n., top part of tablet.
榜 歌 **behng-ge*, n., boat song.
榜 掠 *behnglyueh*, n. & v.t., flogging, whipping.
榜 女 *behngnyuu*, n., boat maid.
榜 牌 *baangpair*, n., public notice, announcement.
榜 人 **behngrern*, n., boatman.
榜 帖 *barngtiee*, n., document announcing list of successful graduates; any public announcement.
榜 眼 *barngyaan*, n., No. 2 at palace examinations ("on bull's-eye").
榜 様 *baangyahng*, n., (1) model for others; (2) pattern.

枌 10B.50-8

fern.

N. (AC) a variety of elm (枌榆) with white bark.

梅 10B.50-9

meir.

N. (1) Plum; prune: 酸梅 sour plum; 烏梅 black plum; 楊梅 arbutus, wild strawberry; 臘梅 yellow plum loved for its flowers; 妻梅子鶴 allu. to Suhng poet-bachelor 林和靖, a great lover of plum flowers and storks. (2) A surname.

梅 毒 *meirdur*, n., syphilis.
梅花 *meirhua*, n., the plum flower; five-petalled pattern; 梅花大鼓 a form of monologue storytelling, accompanied by drum-beats and musical instruments.
梅 香 *meirshiang*, n., common name for maidservant, esp. on stage.
梅 天 (=霉天) *meir-tian*, n., the rainy (moldy) season, from the 5th lunar month, also called 黃霉天.
梅 雨 *meiryuu*, n., see *-tian* ↑.

椈 10B.50-9

jyur.

N. The cypress, the cedar.

枸 10B.50-9

goou(**jyuu*).

枸 杞 *gourchii* (also *jyur-*), n., (bot.) *Lycium chinensis*, Chin. wolfberry, matrimony vine.
枸 骨 *gourguu*, n., (bot.) the holly, *Osmanthus aquifolium*.
枸 櫞 **jyuuyuarn*, n., (bot.) citron, *Citrus medica* sub-sp. *limonum*.

栒 10B.50-9

shyurn.

N. (AC) horizontal bar of rack on which musical stones were suspended.

杓 10B.50-9

shaur.
[Var. of 勺 92.50]

§10B.63 (木/丶)

樵 10B.63-9

chiaur.

N. (1) Woodcutter: 樵夫, 樵戶, 樵客 woodcutter; 樵歌 woodcutter's song; 樵隱 retire and live like a woodcutter; 樵蘇 gather wood and grass for fuel. (2) Wood gathered from mountains: 採樵 to gather firewood.

樵 夫 *chiaurfu*, n., woodcutter.
樵 戶 *chiaurhuh*, n., ditto.

§10B.70 (木/ㄴ)

栳 10B.70-1

laau.

N. 栲栳 Wickerwork, wicker basket.

橈 10B.70-1

naur (**raur*).

N. (1) A piece of bent or twisted wood. (2) (**raur*) An oar, a paddle.

V.i. & t. (1) V.t., (AC) weaken: 謀橈某人之權 plot to weaken s.o.'s power or influence. (2) (AC) scatter: 橈萬物者莫疾乎風 nothing scatters things about so quickly as the wind. (3) V.i., (AC) become bent, twisted: 棟橈 the beam has become bent.

棬 10B.70-1

chyuan.

N. (AC) a plate or tray or woven wicker or cane: 桑戶棬樞 (AC) door posts of mulberry and door hinge of bent wood—extreme poverty.

枇 10B.70-2

pir.

枇杷 *pirpar*, (sp. pr. *pir'pa, pi'pa*), n., loquat, a fruit: 枇杷門巷 redlight district.

札 10B.70-2

jar.

N. (1) (AC) bamboo strip for writing. (2) A note, correspondence: 信札，書札 a letter; 大札，寶札，尊札，華札 (court.) your letter; 簡札 a short note. (3) Formerly, official communication from superior to inferior: 札委 appoint, direct officially; 札文 such communication; 札行 send orders to inferior.

札裹 *jar'guo*, phr., (var. of 扎裹) to tidy up dress and shoes.

札記 *jarjih*, n. & v.i., sundry notes and comments, a collection of notes and comments in book form; to note down, make a note (oft. wr. 劄記).

桄 10B.70-2

guang (**guahng*).

N. (1) (Bot.) 桄榔 *-larng*↓. (2) (**guahng*) Rungs of a ladder, wooden crosspieces of a hand loom or a boat. (3) (**guahng*) A ball of string, a strand of thread.

桄榔 *guanglarng*, n., (bot.) *Arenga saccharifera.*

桃 10B.70-2

taur.

N. (*-tz, -'l*) Peach: 桃樹，桃花 peach tree, flower; 人面桃花相映紅 allu. to blooming young girl; 桃弧棘矢 bow of peach wood and arrow of thistle, anciently used to avert evil influences; 桃園結義 allu. to three heroes of *Three Kingdoms* forming a pact of friendship to death.

桃蟲 *taurchurng*, n., the eastern wren, *Troglodytes fumigatus* (also known as 鷦鷯).

桃脯 *taurfuu*, n., preserved peach; a sweetmeat looking like glazed peach.

桃符 *taurfur*, n., peachwood charm, painted with demons hung over doors to ward off evil spirits, term now used of New Year scrolls pasted on sides of doors.

桃花 *taurhua*, n., peach flower; 桃花石 *--shyr*, a peach-colored stone much valued; 桃花癬 skin affection on girl's face; 桃花汛 spring flood in Yellow River area; (交) 桃花運 luck in love, romance; 桃花源 see *-yuarn*↓.

桃紅 *taurhurng*, adj., pink color.

桃金孃 *taurjinniarng*, n., (bot.) downy rose myrtle, *Rhodomyrtus tomentosa.*

桃膠 *taur-jiau*, n., peach gum.

桃仁(兒) *taurrern(-rer'l)*, n., the meat of peach nut.

桃瓤(兒) *taurrarng('l)*, n., meat of peach fruit.

桃枝 *taurjy*, n., also called 桃枝竹 a kind of bamboo.

桃李 *taur-lie*, n., students: 桃李滿天下 (of well-known teachers) have students all over the world; 桃李不言，下自成蹊 peaches and plums do not have to talk, yet the world beats a path to them —natural attraction; 桃李年 a girl's blooming age.

桃色 *taurseh*, n., peach color; symbolic of romance: 桃色新聞 newspaper stories of love and sex; 桃色案件 crimes of passion.

桃絲竹 *taursyjur*, n., a kind of bamboo.

桃源 *tauryuarn*, n., "peach spring," allu. to story of a fisherman finding an Arcadia cut off from the world; hence 世外桃源 Arcadia, Shangrila, haven of peace and simple living.

杌 10B.70-3

wuh.

N. (1) A bare tree. (2) A stool.

杌凳(兒) *wuhdehng('l)*, n., a footstool.

杌隉 *wuhnieh*, adj., (LL) uneasy.

杌子 *wuhtz*, n., see *-dehng*↑.

櫈 10B.70-3

dehng.

[Var. 凳 32.70]

柷 10B.70-4

juh.

N. (AC) an anc. musical instrument; a square wooden tray.

棍 10B.70-4

guhn.

N. (1) A stick, cudgel: 棍子 *-tz* ↓; 棍兒 a rod; 棍棒 *-bahng* ↓; 軍棍 formerly, wooden or bamboo rods used in the army for corporeal punishment; 銅棍, 鐵棍, 木棍 brass, iron, wood rod. (2) A scoundrel: 光棍 a bachelor, also rascal; 惡棍 a villain; 棍徒 *-tur* ↓.

棍 棒 *guhnbahng*, n., (1) sticks and clubs; (2) (gymnastics) Indian clubs.

棍 騙 *guhnpiahn*, v.t., to swindle.

棍 徒 *guhntur*, n., a villain, rowdy, ruffian.

棍 子 *guhntz*, n., a stick, club, baton.

楓 10B.70-4

feng.

N. Maple: 楓葉 maple leaves (red); 丹楓 red maple.

欖 10B.70-5

laan.

N. 橄欖 the olive.

杞 10B.70-5

chii.

N. (1) A surname. (2) Name of anc. country, dwelled by descendants of *shiah* 夏 Dyn.: 杞人憂天 (abbr. into 杞憂) (allu.) a man of 杞 worried that the sky might fall down—superfluous worry. (3) A kind of willow; see compp. ↓.

杞 柳 *chirlioou*, n., (AC) a kind of willow.

杞 梓 *chirtzyy*, n., a kind of fine wood, good for making woodblocks for printing; see 梓 10B.10.

杷 10B.70-5

par.

N. See 枇^杷 10B.70 ↑.

杭 10B.70-6

harng.

N. (1) 杭州 Hangchow, name of city: 上有天堂, 下有蘇杭 above there's heaven, below there are Soochow and Hangchow. (2) A surname.

梳 10B.70-6

shu.

N. (-*tz*) A comb: 木梳 ditto; cf. 篦 fine comb, 92A.70.

V.t. To comb: 梳頭 *-tour* ↓; 爬梳史實 comb out the historical data.

梳 齒 *shu-chyy*, n., comb teeth.

梳 裹 *shuguoo*, v.i., (MC) to comb hair and tie turban.

梳 粧 *shujuang*, n. & v.i., hairdressing, ladies' make-up; 梳粧臺 dressing table.

梳 攏 *shu'lung*, v.i., (of young girl raised in singsong house) formally receives a man in bed for the first time (also wr. 梳籠, 梳弄).

梳 洗 *shushii*, v.i., wash face and comb hair.

梳 頭 *shu-tour*, v.i., to dress hair in top coil (of both men and ladies); to dress hair.

櫬 10B.70-6

chehn.

N. Coffin.

櫳 10B.70-6

lurng.

N. (-*tz*) A cage, a pen, set of bars: 窗櫳 window with bars: 門櫳子 horizontal bars across door.

椀 10B.70-6

waan.

[Var. of 碗 31B.70]

柁 10B.70-6

duoh (**tuor*).

N. (1) Pop. of 舵 helm. (2) (**tuor*) Big beam in Chin. house.

棁 10B.70-8

juor.

N. (AC) a joist, short support connecting beams.

梔 10B.70-9

jy.

N. The gardenia: 梔子 or 黃梔

seeds of gardenia which produce a yellow dye.

橇 10B.70-9

tsueih (also *chiau*).

N. A sledge, sleigh.

枕 10B.70-9

jeen (*jehn).

N. (1) Pillow: 枕頭 *-tour*↓; 枕邊言 curtain advice; 告枕頭狀 wife's complaints against person; 同牀共枕 (of couple) share the same bed; 枕席 *-shir*↓; 枕冷衾寒 loneliness in bed; 綉花枕頭 person good only in looks ("embroidered pillow"); 空氣枕 air pillow; 枕中書, 枕中秘 secret book not to be seen by others. (2) Crossboard at back of carriage (also wr. 軫): 枕木 *-muh*↓.

V.t. (*jehn) To use as pillow: 枕枕頭 rest head on the pillow; 曲肱而枕之 (AC) to crook one's arm for head support during sleep; 枕着椅背 to incline on back of chair; 枕戈待旦 (in mil. campaign) to sleep with "weapon as pillow," i.e., without undress; 枕流漱石 or 枕石漱流 to enjoy rocks and stream (to "pillow one's head on stream" or "on rock"); 枕塊 to mourn for death of parents ("to pillow on clod" at grave site).

枕簟 *jeen-diahn*, n., see *-shir*↓.
枕骨 *jern-guu*, n., back part of skull, the occiput.
枕巾 *jeenjin*, n., pillow cover.
枕藉 **jehnjir*, adj., lying on top of each other (of corpses in battlefield); lying in disorder.
枕木 *jeenmuh*, n., sleepers supporting railway track.
枕席 *jeen-shir*, n., "pillow and mat"—symbol of bed: 枕席之間 while in bed; 枕席未安 cannot afford to sleep peacefully——situation not settled yet; 以荐枕席 (LL) to go to bed with lover.
枕套 *jeen-tauh*, n., pillowcase.
枕頭 *jeen'tour*, n., pillow.

概 10B.70-9

gaih.
[Var. 槩]

N. (1) A T-shaped wooden piece used to level off grain in a measure. (2) Manner of carrying and conducting oneself: 氣概 bearing, deportment; 節概 upright conduct. (3) Landscape, scenery: 勝概 excellent view. (4) General outline: 概略 *-lyueh*, 概要 *-yauh*↓; 梗概 essentials, an abridged summary.

V.t. (1) Exemplify, typify: 即此一端, 可概其餘 this single item will suffice to typify all the rest. (2) Generalize: 概括 *-kuoh*↓.

Adj. General: 概論 *-luhn*, 概況 *-kuahng*↓; 概算 a rough estimate.

Adv. 概 or 一概 all, without exception; 概不賒欠 no credit allowed to anybody, always cash; 概作罷論 let no more be said about it altogether; 概不作答 no reply will be given to any correspondence; 概而言之 generally speaking; 可以概見 generally evident; 概覽 viewed in gen.

概觀 *gaihguan*, n., a general view, a bird's-eye view.
概況 *gaihkuahng*, n., general condition or situation.
概括 *gaihkuoh*, v.t. & n., generalize, generalization: 概括起來 to summarize.
概論 *gaihluhn*, n., a general outline, an introduction (to subject), statement of basic principles.
概略 *gaihlyueh*, n., a summary outline.
概念 *gaihniahn*, n., a concept.
概要 *gaihyauh*, n., essentials; elements (of science), outline (of history).

槐 10B.70-9

huair.

N. (Bot.) the locust (tree), *Sophora japonica*: 洋槐 the ash tree.

枹 10B.70-9

fu (*fur*).

V.t. (AC) to beat drum.

桅 10B.70-9

weir.

N. Ship's mast: 桅桿, 船桅 ditto; 雙桅, 三桅船 boat of two, three masts; 主桅 mainmast; 前桅 foremast; 後桅, 尾桅 mizzenmast; 桅頂 masthead; 桅繩 stays; 桅梯 (ship's) shrouds.

§ 10B.71 (木/弋)

械 10B.71-7

shieh (also *jieh*).

N. (1) Military weapons: 軍械

械 棧 椷 槭 柢 機

weapons and ammunition; 械鬭 *-douh*↓. (2) Instruments: 器械, 機械 ditto. (3) Fetters and shackles: 械繫 *-shih*↓.

械 鬭 *shiehdouh*, n., a fight with weapons, esp. in clan fights.

械 繫 *shiehshih*, v.t., bind with fetters, chain.

棧 10B.71-7

jahn.

N. (1) Storehouse: 棧房 *-farng*↓; 棧費 storage fee. (2) 客棧 an inn; 馬棧, 羊棧 a stable (for horses, sheep). (3) A plank way: 棧道 *-dauh*↓.

棧 橋 *jahnchiaur*, n., bridge or plank way built into the sea.

棧 單 *jahndan*, n., storage receipt for goods.

棧 道 *jahndauh*, n., plank way, esp. those built on sides of cliffs for army.

棧 房 *jahnfarng*, n., storehouse, warehouse, godown.

棧 閣 *jahnger*, n., see *-dauh*↑.

椷 10B.71-7

jian.

N. (1) A letter, an envelope. (2) A wooden box.

槭 10B.71-7

tzur.

N. (Bot.) *Acer palmatum.*

柢 10B.71-9

dii.

N. (AC) root; bottom.

機 10B.71-9

ji.

[Abbr. 机]

N. (1) Short for mechanical contrivances: 機械 *-shieh*, 機器 *-chih*↓; 蒸汽機 a steam engine; 發電機 a dynamo, power generator; 電機 electrical engineering; 電機工程師 electrical engineer; 照相機 camera; 電視機 a television set; 收音機 a radio receiver; 飛機 an airplane; 機艙 aircraft passenger compartment; 機翼 aircraft wings; 機身 the fuselage of an airplane; 機製 machine-made; 機織 woven by machinery. (2) An opportune moment, suitable occasion: 機會 *-hueih*, 機遇 *-yuh*↓; 時機 a timely opportunity: 時機成熟 time is propitious; 投機 speculate, -tion; 投機家 speculator; 話不投機半句多 it's a sheer waste of breath to talk to s.o. with whom one can't see eye to eye; 機緣 *-yuarn*↓; 天賜良機 a godsend; 機不可失 a golden opportunity not to be missed; 有機可乘 an opportunity to be taken advantage of; 乘機, 趁機 make hay while the sun shines; 見機而作 take advantage of an opportunity that comes one's way; 隨機應變 decide according to changing situtation, use discretion; 待機而作 wait for an opportune moment to act; 一線生機 a ray of hope; 相機行事 act when the time is opportune. (3) S.t. to be kept secret or difficult to fathom: 機密 *-mih*↓; 事機 a secretly hatched plan of action: 事機不密, 事機洩漏 the plot has prematurely leaked out; 天機不可洩漏 keep this to yourself, mum's the word; 神機 dark secrets (lit., "divine will unknown to man"): 神機妙算 ability to divine the unknown; 靈機 inspiration: 靈機一動 seized by a sudden impulse, or inspiration.

Adj. (1) Secret, confidential: 機務 *-wuh*^{2}, 機要 *-yauh*↓. (2) Cunning, clever, skillful, crafty: 機巧 *-chiaau*, 機智 *-jyh*, 機悟 *-wuh*^{1}↓; 心機 crafty, -iness, tricky, -ery; 機警 *-jiing*↓.

機 變 *jibiahn*, adj., (1) flexible, adaptable; (2) crafty, tricky.

機 場 *jichaang*, n., airfield, airport.

機 車 *jiche*, n., motorcycle.

機 巧 *jichiaau*, adj., skillful, cunning.

機 器 *jichih*, n., (1) a machine, machinery, engine; (2) a person who follows orders blindly and mechanically: 機器人 *--rern*, an automaton; 機器脚踏車 *--jiaautahche*, motorcycle.

機 動 *jiduhng*, adj., mobile, motorized; 機動性 flexibility, mobility.

機 房 *jifarng*, n., an engine room.

機 鋒 *jifeng*, n., sharp edge or point of argument: 鬬機鋒 to match wits.

機 構 *jigouh*, n., an organization, a government agency, a civic body.

機 關 *jiguan* (-'*guan*), n., (1) a public or private organization, a government agency; (2) a mechanical contrivance; (3) a ruse, an artifice, a strategem; 機關車 *--che*, a railway locomotive; 機關槍 *--chiang*, a machine gun.

機 會 *jihueih*, n., an opportunity, favorable circumstances, opening, break: 機會均等 equality of opportunity; 大好機會 a golden opportunity; 機會主義(者) opportunism(-nist).

機 詐 *jijah*, adj., tricky, treacherous.

機 件 *jijiahn*, n., parts of a machine.

機 警 *jijiing*, adj., astute, sharp, shrewd, alert, vigilant.

機 軸 *jijour*, n., vitally important or key positions (lit., "axle"): 據機軸 occupy high government posts.

機 杼 *jijuh*, n., (1) the shuttle of a loom; (2) thoughts and ideas in writing: 文章須自出機杼 a writer should have his own original ideas. 「wit(ty).

機智 *jijyh*, adj. & n., tactful(ness),

機括 *jikuoh*, n., a mechanical contrivance, a trigger or catch.

機伶 *ji'ling*, adj., (1) shrewd, clever, smart and quick (also 機靈); (2) astonished, stunned: 嚇得他一機伶 he was amazed, taken aback.

機密 *jimih*, n., classified information, important affairs of State.

機敏 *jimiin*, adj., clever, skillful, quick-witted.

機謀 *jimour*, n., a plan of action for emergencies.

機能 *jinerng*, n., functions (of a human organ, etc.)

機鈕 *jinioou*, n., a trigger, button in machine.

機先 *ji-shian*, v.i., take anticipatory action.

機械 *jishieh*, n., (1) an engine, a mechanical contrivance; (2) a robot; (3) adj., mechanical-minded; 機械化 *--huah*, n., mechanization; 機械工程 *--gungcherng*, n., mechanical engineering.

機心 *jishin*, n., a mind given to deception or trickery.

機師 *jishy*, n., (1) an engineer; (2) an airplane pilot.

機體 *jitii*, n., an organism.

機悟 *jiwuh*[1], adj., discerning, quick-witted.

機務 *jiwuh*[2], n., (1) important matters, classified information; (2) mechanical works.

機要 *jiyauh*, adj. & n., confidential (matter), classified information: 機要秘書 confidential secretary.

機宜 *jiyir*, n., guidelines, gen. principles of action: 請示機宜 ask for directives from one's superior.

機油 *jiyour*, n., lubricant.

機緣 *jiyuarn*, n., a chance occurrence leading to happy results.

機遇 *jiyuh*, n., a chance happening, an opportunity: 機遇率 *--lyuh*, n., (math.) probability.

機運 *jiyuhn*, n., a spell of good fortune.

§10B.80 (木/八)

橨 10B.80-1

dur.

N. Cabinet, wardrobe; casket.

棋 10B.80-2

chir.

[Anc. var. 棊; pop. 碁]

N. A game of chess, go, checkers, draughts and similar games: 下棋, 下一盤棋, 賽棋, 圍棋 to play any of these games; 象棋 Chin. chess, similar to Western chess; 圍棋 "*go*" in Japanese, with 324 squares played with black and white pieces; 跳棋 draughts or checkers; 棋子, 棋盤, 棋譜 *-tzyy*, *-parn*, *-puu*↓; 棋布, 棋列 to set out in some formation (as stars); 棋峙 (AC) to match in power as rivals (as in *Three Kingdoms*); 棋戰 a chess match; 棋聖 national champion at chess.

棋局 *chirjyur*, n., (1) chess pattern of men in certain positions; (2) a game of chess.

棋盤 *chirparn*, n., a chessboard.

棋品 *chirpiin*, n., character or grade of chess player.

棋譜 *chirpuu*, n., manual of chess with illustrations of different stratagems.

棋子(兒) *chirtzyy(-tzee'l)*, n., chess pieces, chessmen; draughtsmen; a kind of small dumplings, looking like chess pieces.

橫 10B.80-2

herng (**hehng*).

N. (1) A horizontal bar. (2) A horizontal stroke. (3) Width. (4) A surname.

V.t. (1) To set or wear across: 橫劍 hold sword crosswise; 腰橫玉帶 wear a jade girdle across the waist. (2) To stiffen up and bear responsibility: 這件有他橫起來, 我們不必管 he has taken this up, so we needn't bother.

Adj. & adv. (1) Across, horizontal, sideways: 橫渡 ferry or sail across; 橫放 lay down horizontally; 橫斜 (flower branches) leaning across and downward; 橫斷山脈 a mountain range which cuts across area; 橫斷面 a cross section (of a tree, ship, etc.); 橫行 walk sideways (as crab); 橫貫公路 the cross-island highway, east-west highway, opp. 縱貫 north-south; 橫擋路中 stand across the road; 玉體橫陳 her body lying stretched across the bed; 橫列 arranged in a row; opp. 豎 or 直 straight down, hence 橫豎 crisscross, see *-shuh*↓. (2) (**hehng*) Violent, cross, cruel, tyrannical: 他忽然橫起來 he suddenly became cross (flared up); 你不要這麼橫 don't be so cross; 橫虎虎的 excited and angry; 橫話 violent words; 橫眼 a sidelong belligerant look, glower; 處士橫議 (AC) the scholars indulged in free criticism; 橫行霸道 act against law and reason, like a tyrant; 蠻橫 overbearing, arrogant; 橫暴, 橫逆 *-bauh*, *-nih*↓. (3) (**hehng*) By accident: 橫死 die an unnatural death; 橫禍 unexpected disaster; 橫事 ditto. (4) (**hehng*) Illegal: 發橫財 get rich illegally, making a windfall.

橫暴 **hehngbauh*, adj., cruel, tyrannical: 橫征暴斂 levy exorbitant taxes.

横 楨 槓 枳 檳 杕 楔 模

橫波 *herngbo*, n., (phys.) transverse wave.

橫笛 *herngdir*, n., the flute.

橫反 *herngfaan*, v.i., (coll. of children) too mischievous.

橫膈膜 *hernggermor*, n., (physiol.) the diaphragm.

橫兒 *herng'l*, n., (coll.) see -*'pi* ↓.

橫楣子 *herngmeirtz*, n., the lintel, the cross top of doors or windows.

橫逆 **hehngnih*, n., rebellious, disobedient, lawless.

橫披 *herng'pi*, n., a horizontal scroll.

橫肉 *herng-rouh*, n., as in 一臉橫肉 ugly, pugnacious looks.

橫痃 *herngshiarn*, n., (med.) chancre.

橫豎 *herngshuh*, adv., either way, in either case: 橫豎我不來了 anyway I am not coming; oft. in phr., meaning crisscross: 橫七豎八, 橫三豎四 spread all across in confusion; 橫衝直撞 to run amuck, (of vehicle or person) collide right and left.

楨 10B.80-2

jen (also *jeng*).

N. Hardwood: 楨幹 (AC) hardwood structure used in building walls; (fig.) pillar of strength.

槓 10B.80-3

gahng.

N. (1) A crowbar: 槓桿 -*gaan* ↓; 擡槓 to quarrel, dispute. (2) A carrying pole, a wooden or iron bar: 槓子 -*tz* ↓; 單槓 an iron bar on posts for gymnastic exercises; 雙槓 parallel bars. (3) A straight line on page, for underlining or deletion.

V.i. & t. (1) V.t., sharpen (knives, razors, etc.): 槓刀 -*dau* ↓. (2) V.i., be aggressive and fond of picking quarrels with others: 他又跟我槓上子 he is again picking on me.

槓刀 *gahngdau*, v.t., sharpen knives or razors: 槓刀布 a strop, formerly, a canvas strap for sharpening razors.

槓房 *gahngfarng*, n., an old-fashioned funeral parlor.

槓夫 *gahngfu*, n., professional coffin bearers.

槓桿 *gahnggaan*, n., a lever.

槓頭 *gahngtour*, n., (1) a quarrelsome person; (2) head of coffin bearers, see -*fu* ↑.

槓子 *gahngtz*, n., (1) a carrying-pole; (2) (gymnastics) an iron or wooden bar: 盤槓子 take gymnastic exercises on bars.

枳 10B.80-4

jyy.

N. (1) Brambles. (2) A kind of orange with thick skin and thin pulp: 橘逾淮而爲枳 the orange is changed into a *jyy* north of Huai River—the influence of environment.

枳殼 *jyychyueh*, n., dried orange peel, used as medicine.

枳棘 *jyyjir*, n., hedge thorn.

枳椇 **jirjyuu*, n., (bot.) *Hovenia dulcis*.

枳實 *jyyshyr*, n., dried orange including pulp, used in medicine.

檳 10B.80-6

bin (also *bing*).

檳榔 *bin'larng* (*bing-*), n., areca-nut palm, betel nut; also 檳子 *bintz*, areca nut.

§10B.81 (木/人)

杕 10B.81-1

dih.

Adj. (AC) standing alone.

楔 10B.81-1

shieh (also *shie*).

N. (1) (AC) a doorjamb. (2) (-*tz*) A wedge: 楔形文字 cuniform writing. (3) 楔子 an interlude or inserted scene in Yuarn drama, usu. limited to only four acts; also a prelude in a novel.

V.t. To wedge: 楔住 to put a wedge in to fasten; 楔起來 to stabilize by means of a wedge.

模 10B.81-2

mor (**mur*).

[Var. 摹 in sense of copy, imitate]

N. Standard, pattern: 模型, 模範 -*shirng*, -*fahn* ↓.

V.t. To copy, imitate: 模擬, 模仿 -*nii*, -*faang* ↓.

Adj. 模糊 -*hur* ↓.

模仿 *morfaang*, v.t., to copy (master, person) esp. in painting, conduct; to model after (s.o.).

模範 *morfahn*, n., standard, model (such as ideal gentlemen): 模範小學, 監獄, 軍隊, 夫婦 model school, prison, troops, couple.

模糊 *morhur*, adj., blurred, unclear, hazy (also 模模糊糊): 模

模 樸 橛 核 檢

糊不清 unclear (print, etc.), also wr. 糢糊.

模楷 *morkaai*, n., see *-fahn*↑.

模稜 *morlirng*, adj., esp. in 模稜兩可 ambiguous, unclear (attitude), fence-sitting, ready to accept either course.

模擬 *mornii*, (1) v.t., consciously imitate (ancient masters, etc.); (2) n., imitation (such as poll tests): 模擬考試 unofficial test to test results; a mock test.

模型 *morshirng*, n., pattern, model (of machine, buildings, etc.).

模特兒 *morteh'l*, n., model for painters, photographers, building model, etc.

模子 **murtz*, n., mold from which engine parts, pastry are made; a die.

模樣(兒) **muryahng* (*-yah'l*), n., shape, esp. woman's figure: 一模一樣 exactly alike.

樸 10B.81-2

pur.

N. (1) Uncarved wood, symbolic of original nature of man (Taoist). (2) (Bot.) *Aphananthe aspera*, a plant whose dried leaves are used for polishing metal, woodwork.

Adj. Simple, unadorned, honest: 民風淳樸, 樸厚 the people are simple and honest, unspoiled; 簡樸 simple (living, furniture); 樸素 *-suh*[1]↓.

樸鈍 *purduhn*, adj., stupid, slow-witted.

樸拙 *purjuor*, adj., uncouth (manners), straightforward.

樸質 *purjyr*, adj., unadorned, unsophisticated.

樸馬 *pur-maa*, n., (AC) unbroken horse.

樸實 *pur'shyr*, adj., simple, direct honest: 樸樸實實(兒) adv., directly, in simple, direct way.

樸學 *purshyuer*, n., name of scholastic tendency (Manchu Dyn.) devoted to philological research and spurning speculative philosophy.

樸素 *pursuh*[1], adj., (of dress, customs, way of living) simple.

樸樕 *pursuh*[2], n., (AC) brush, underwood.

樸野 *puryee*, adj., uncouth.

橛 10B.81-5

jyuer.

N. (1) A small wooden stake: 橛子 wooden posts; 橛兒 ditto. (2) A bit for a horse. (3) A piece of broken wood. (4) A piece of anything round and straight: 一橛粉筆 a piece of chalk.

核 10B.81-6

her.

N. (1) (-'l) Nut, kernel (of peach, date, etc.). (2) A lump, an incrustation: 肺結核 tuberculosis. (3) Short for 核子 nucleus, see 核子 *-tzyy*↓.

V.t. To investigate, verify, estimate, pass upon, officially consider: 考核, 查核 investigate; 核辦 officially consider and carry out, see many compp.↓.

核辦 *herbahn*, v.i. & t., officially consider and carry out.

核定 *herdihng*, v.i. & t., pass on (budget).

核對 *herdueih*, v.i., to check (figures, proof).

核奪 *herduor*, v.i. officially consider and decide.

核價 *herjiah*, n., appraisal.

核計 *herjih*, v.i. & t., officially assess, calculate.

核准 *herjuun*, v.i. & t., officially approve.

核心 *hershin*, n., nucleus, core: 核心人物 the key personnel.

核實 *hershyr*, v.t., to verify (accounts, report).

核算 *hersuahn*, v.i. & t., estimate, calculate.

核酸 *hersuan*, n., (chem.) nucleic acid.

核桃 *her'tau*, n., walnut.

核子 *hertzyy*, n., (phys.) nucleus; 核子戰 nuclear bomb; 核子戰爭 nuclear war; 核子武器 nuelear weapons; 核子俱樂部 the Nuclear Powers forming a so-called Nuclear Club; 核子能發電廠 nuclear power station; 核子爆炸 nuclear explosion; 熱核子彈 thermonuclear bomb; 核子潛艇 nuclear submarine; 核子勒索 nuclear blackmail; 熱核子武器 thermonuclear weapons; 核子大國 Nuclear Powers; 核子反應 nuclear reaction.

檢 10B.81-8

jiaan.

N. (1) A book label. (2) A rule, model, pattern: 先自爲檢式儀表 first set oneself up as an example for others to follow.

V.t. (1) To check, restrain, restrict: 檢點 *-diaan*, 檢束 *-shuh*↓. (2) Examine, inspect: 檢定 *-dihng*, 檢校 *-jiauh*, 檢驗 *-yahn*, 檢查 *-char*[1]↓.

檢波器 *jiaanbochih*, n., (phys.) a detector.

檢查 *jiaanchar*[1], v.t., inspect (luggage, passport, identity card, etc.): 衛生(清潔)檢查 health (sanitation) inspection.

檢察 *jiaanchar*[2], v.t., prosecute; 檢察官 public prosecutor; 檢察長 chief prosecutor; attorney general.

檢點 *jiarndiaan*, (1) n., formerly, commander of the imperial guard; (2) v.t., pay close attention to (conduct), carefully check over.

檢定 *jiaandihng*, v.t., examine and certify (quality of commodities, purity of seeds): 檢定考試 evaluate a candidate's qualifications.

檢校 *jiaanjiauh*, v.t., to check up on.

檢擧 *jiarnjyuu*, v.t., to impeach, ferret out and openly denounce (irregularities, illegal acts, misconduct).

檢修 *jiaanshiu*, v.t., to revise.

檢束 *jiaanshuh*, v.t., regulate, restrain (conduct).

檢討 *jiarntaau*, v.t., discuss thoroughly, to review: 檢討得失(利弊) review the merits and demerits.

檢字 *jiaantzyh*, (1) v.i., find a character in a dictionary; (2) n., list of characters arranged for ready identification: 檢字表 such a table, index.

檢驗 *jiaanyahn*, v.t., inspect and examine (troops, weapons and ammunition, training, etc.): 檢驗吏 an inspecting officer, inspector.

檢疫 *jiaanyih*, n. & v.t., quarantine; 檢疫法 (交通檢疫) quarantine.

檢閱 *jiaanyueih*, v.t., inspect or review (troops, a fleet, aircraft, honor guard).

楸 10B.81-9

chiou.

N. (Bot.) the catalpa.

楸枰 *chioupirng*, n., a chessboard of catalpa wood.

§ 10B.82 (木/乂)

枝 10B.82-1

jy.

N. adjunct. A slender piece: 一枝筆 a pen, brush; 一枝花 a flower spray.

N. (1) (*-tz*, *'l*) Branch: 樹枝 tree branch; 枝幹 branch and stem; 枝條, 枝葉 *-tiaur*, *-yeh*↓; 枝頭, 枝梢 top of branches; 節外生枝 proliferate issues and problems; see 枝節 *-jiee*↓. (2) A job or post: 求得一枝棲 hope to get a job (like a wandering bird looking for a branch to rest on). (3) (**chir*) (U.f. 歧) 枝指 *-jyy*↓.

V.t. U.f. 支 in 枝持, 枝撑 see 支^持, 支^撑 10.82.

枝針 *jyjen*, n., pine needles and the like.

枝節 *jyjiee*, n. & adj., proliferation; 枝節問題 side issues, minor problems.

枝指 **chirjyy*, n., an extra thumb.

枝條 *jytiaur*, n., soft, overhanging branches.

枝辭 *jy-tsyr*, n., (AC) quibble, prevarication.

枝葉 *jy-yeh*, n., branches and leaves, describing growth of trees, and of families, also gen. look of trees: 枝葉扶疏 trees with branches spread out gracefully.

杖 10B.82-1

jahng.

N. (1) A walking staff, cane: 禪杖 monk's staff, sometimes credited with power of saving souls; 錫杖 monk's travelling staff, associated with monk's travels and whereabouts, see 錫 81A.50; the mourning staff, see 杖期 *-ji*↓; (AC) staff as privilege of old age: 五十杖於家, 六十杖於鄉, 七十杖於國, 八十杖於朝 (禮記) at 50, privileged to carry cane in house, at 60 in the village, at 70 in the capital, at 80 at the royal court—hence the phrr. 杖鄉, 杖國, 杖朝. (2) Punishment by flogging: 杖刑 ditto.

V.i. (1) To walk with a staff, see N. 1↑. (2) To flog: 杖打 punish by flogging; 杖責 ditto; 杖三十 flog thirty strokes. (3) To use staff in mourning, see 杖期 *-ji*↓. (4) U.f. 仗 91A.82, to rely on, to hold: 杖劍, 杖策 hold a sword, a whip.

杖期 *jahngji*, v.i. & n., degree of mourning for one year period; classical regulation on use of staff during mourning (用杖) or not to use staff (不用杖), according to prescribed and (Confucianist) codified degree of sorrow (on the assumption that the deeply stricken mourner cannot walk without a staff); 不杖期 one-year mourning without use of staff observed by husband for death of wife if parents are living, but 杖期 or 服杖期 leaning on the staff if parents are dead, etc.

杖履 *jahng-lyuu*, phr., the privilege of the aged to use staff (see N. 1) and not take off shoes in house.

杖頭錢 *jahngtourchiarn*, n., money for buying drink hung on top of walking cane (allu.).

椒 10B.82-2

jiau.

N. (1) Spice plants: 花椒 pepper; 胡椒 black pepper; 辣椒 hot pepper; 秦椒 Chinese pepper, *Xanthoxylum piperitum*; 蜀椒 Szechuan or Japanese pepper; 番椒 *Capsicum annuum*. (2) A mountain peak or top of hill: (AC) 菊散芳於山椒 fragrance of chrysanthemums pervades the hilltop. (3) A surname.

椒房 *jiaufarng*, n., the private apartment of the queen (also 椒屋, 椒殿).

椒粉 *jiaufeen*, n., ground pepper (also 椒末 *jiaumoh*).

椒酒 *jiaujioou*, n., wine spiced with peppers.

椒蘭 *jiaularn*, n., (1) fragrance like that of spices and orchids; (2) a deceitful flatterer; (3) queen's relatives.

椒庭 *jiautirng*, n., palace grounds, the imperial or royal court.

椶 10B.82-2

tzung.

[Var. 棕 10B.01]

梗 10B.82-3

geeng.

N. (1) The stem of a plant: 枝梗 stem and branches; 花梗子 the stem of a flower; 茶葉梗兒 tea stalks. (2) An outline: 梗概 *-gaih* ↓.

V.t. (1) Hinder, obstruct: 阻梗 meet with obstruction; 梗塞 *-seh* ↓; 作梗, 爲梗 stand in the way of, to obstruct. (2) (Of thorny plants) to prick. (3) Straighten: 梗著脖子 to stiffen one's neck, i.e., ready to face any possible difficulties or obstacles.

Adj. (1) Obstinate, stubborn: 強梗 firm and stubborn; 頑梗 obstinate; 直梗梗的 blunt; 梗性子 obstinacy. (2) Upright: 梗直 *-jyr* ↓.

梗概 *geenggaih*, n., a general summary.

梗直 *geengjyr*, adj., honest, straightforward.

梗塞 *geengseh*, v.t., obstruct, impede, hinder.

橄 10B.82-3

gaan.

橄欖 *garnlaan*, n., (bot.) olive, (also 青果): 橄欖樹 the olive tree; 橄欖油 olive oil; 橄欖球 ball used in Rugby.

杈 10B.82-3

cha (also coll. *chah*).

[Cf. 扠]

N. (1) Forked branches: (*-tz*, *'l*) logs or spikes stacked together to block roads, *cheval-de-frise*; 樹杈子 forked branches. (2) Pitchfork. (3) Ancient fork for attack and defense.

杈桿兒 *chagaa'l*, n., protector of prostitutes, also (derog.) protector.

杈枒 *chayar*, n., forked branches.

校 10B.82-6

shiauh (**jiauh*).

N. (1) A school, college, academy: 校長, 校舍 *-jaang*, *-sheh* ↓; 校規 school regulations; 校醫 school physician; 校警 school guards; 校歌 school song; 母校 alma mater; 女校 girls' school; 軍校 military academy; 警校 police training school (cf. 學△院 90.00, 大△學 12.81). (2) A military and naval rank, below 將 and above 尉: 上校 colonel; 中校 lieutenant colonel; 少校 major; 將校 general and field officers; 校官 military officers: 校官學校 military officers' academy.

V.i. (**jiauh*) (1) To contest: 校塲 *-chaang* ↓. (2) To revise: 校閱 *-yueh* ↓; 校對 *-dueih* ↓; 校正 correct (textual errors); 校稿 to proofread; 二校, 三校 second, third proof. (3) To collate, compare critically: 校勘, 校讐, 校訂 *-kan*, *-chour*, *-dihng* ↓.

校塲 **jiauhchaang*, n., drill ground.

校讐 **jiauhchour*, v.i. & t., compare texts, see *-kan* ↓; to proofread.

校訂 **jiauhdihng*, v.t., editorially revise.

校對 **jiauhdueih*, v.t., to proofread.

校董 *shiauhduung*, n., board of directors of school.

校風 *shiauhfeng*, n., prevailing morals of a school.

校長 *shiauhjaang*, n., president (of university, college); principal of school.

校勘 **jiauhkan*, v.t., to collate, compare texts to establish correct version.

校舍 *shiauhsheh*, n., school buildings.

校書 **jiauhshu*, n., (LL, allu.) a high-class singsong girl.

校友會 *shiauhyoou hueih*, n., alumni association.

校閱 **jiauhyueh*, v.t., to revise; to go over (script), to review (troops).

权 10B.82-8

chyuarn.

[Abbr. of 權 10B.11]

板 10B.82-9

baan.

[Dist. 版; sometimes var. of 版]

N. (1) A piece of board, a plank; board in wood-block printing (usu. 版). (2) A flat piece: 石板, 紙板 of stone, cardboard. (3) Things made of board: 地板 wooden floor; 黑板 blackboard; 樓板 wooden floor of upper story; 壽板 coffin; 天花板 ceiling; 麪板 flour board; 切菜板 chopping board; 板上釘釘 (*dihng ding*) phr., make firm, unchangeable decision; 奏板 memorial tablet in imperial audience.

V.i. Pull tight, in 板着臉 pull a long face.

Adj. Stiff: 古板 stiffly traditional, opposed to change; 板板六十四 stiff, mechanical (interpretation); 板套, 呆板, 刻板 going by rules, letter of law, inflexible, mechanical; 板執不通 phr. be stickler for rules; 老板 boss (var. of 老闆).

板本 *barnbeen*, n., edition of books, cf. 版 91S.82.
板橋 *baanchiaur*, n., small wooden bridge (of planks).
板蕩 *baandahng*, adj., & n., (AC) social confusion and chaos.
板凳 *baandehng*, n., bench.
板斧 *barnfuu*, n., broad axe.
板畫 *baanhuah*, n., wood-block painting.
板滯 *baanjyh*, adj., inflexible, opposed to change, slow-moving.
板兒 *baa'l*, n., board.
板擦(兒) *baantsa('l)*, n., brush for applying whitewash.
板子 *baantz*, n., (1) edition (pop. for 版); (2) flogging board.
板屋 *baanwu*, n., house constructed of wooden boards.
板鴨 *baanya*, n., dried pressed duck preserved in oil.
板眼 *barnyaan*, n., musical beat.
板魚 *baanyur*, n., the flounder (fish).

梗 10B.82-9

piarn.

N. Name of a tree, now also called 黃梗木.

檄 10B.82-9

shir.

N. (AC) 檄 or 檄文 an official public declaration, addressed to junior officers and people, usu. on starting a campaign.

枚 10B.82-9

meir.

N. adjunct. A countable piece: 一枚銅版, 三枚李子 one copper coin, three plums; 猜枚 a game of guessing numbers.

N. (1) (AC) stem: 伐其條枚 cut down its branches and stems. (2) Piece of stick used as mouth gag: 銜枚疾走 (army) hastening with mouth gags esp. in night attacks. (3) A surname.

枚卜 *meirbuu*, phr., (AC) 枚卜功臣 cast lot among ministers.
枚擧 *meirjyuu*, v.t., enumerate, esp. 不勝枚擧 too many to enumerate piece by piece.
枚枚 *meirmeir*, adj., (AC) abundant growth (of fruit).

梭 10B.82-9

suo.

N. The shuttle: 穿梭 move to and fro like a shuttle: 穿梭轟炸 shuttle bombing; 日月如梭 time passes quickly.

梭布 *suobuh*, n., native cloth.
梭(兒)胡 *suo('l)hur*, n., a kind of card game.
梭巡 *suoshyurn*, v.i., to patrol back and forth.
梭梭 *suosuo*, adv., (eyes) shifting like the shuttle.
梭子 *suotz*, n., a shuttle; 梭子米 a small and long-shaped kind of rice; 梭子蟹 a shuttle-shaped crab; 梭子魚 a fish, *Sphyreena pinguis*.

楥 10B.82-9

shyuahn.

[Var. of 楦 10B.30]

§ 10B.83 (木/〜)

樅 10B.83-9

tsung.

N. (Bot.) a tree of pine family, *Abies firma*.

梃 10B.83-9

tiing.

[Dist. 挺 10A.83]

N. (1) A wooden stick, a club. (2) (-'*l*) A stem of wood or bamboo: 木梃, 竹梃.

Adj. Straightforword; erect (var. of 挺 10A.83).

槌 10B.83-9

chueir.

N. A wooden stick, truncheon for beating: 棒槌, 木槌 ditto; 鼓槌 drumstick.

V.t. U.f. 搥 10A.83.

槌球 *chueir-chiour*, n., croquet.

§10B.91 (木/ノ)

彬 10B.91-1

bin.

N. A surname.

Adj. Having both appearance (文) and substance (質), handsome and solid in character, usu. in comp. 彬彬 *-bin*↓.

彬彬 *binbin*, adj., handsome and solid: 彬彬有禮 well-mannered.

彬蔚 *binweih*, adj., (LL) handsome, festive, attractively dressed up.

杪 10B.91-2

miaau.

[Dist. 秒 90A.91]

N. End; tip, top (of trees): 歲杪, 月杪 (LL) end of year, month.

桫 10B.91-6

suo.

桫欏 *suoluor*, n., (bot.) (1) the horse chestnut; (2) *Cyathea spinulosa* (cf. 娑^Δ^羅 63.02).

杉 10B.91-9

shan (sp. pr. also *sha*).

N. Pine, fir; pinewood.

杉杆子 *shangantz*, n., sliced pinewood as construction material.

杉篙 *shagau*, n., see *-gantz*↑; 杉篙尖子 (facet.) a tall and slender person.

杉海苔 *shanhaaitair*, n., (bot.) a seaweed, *Gigartina tenella*.

杉錦 *shanjiin*, n., fine-quality pine.

杉木 *shamuh*, n., pine timber, deal.

桥 10B.91-9

chiaur.

[Abbr. of 橋 10B.42]

§10B.93 (木/く)

棲 10B.93-1

chi (also *shi*).

[Var. 栖]

V.i. (1) To roost, to stop for rest: 鳥棲樹上 a bird alights or roosts on a tree; 兩棲動物 amphibious animal; 棲息, 棲止 *-shir*, *-jyy*↓; (fig.) to make one's home; 棲身 *-shen*↓. (2) Interch. 悽 disconsolate, see 悽^Δ^惶, 悽^Δ^惻 22A.93.

棲遁 *chiduhn*, v.i., to live in retirement.

棲苴 *chijyu*, n., floating weeds.

棲止 *chijyy*, v.i., to stop and rest in (place).

棲身 *chi-shen*, v.i., to dwell, obtain shelter.

棲息 *chishir*, v.i., to dwell, dwell for rest.

棲宿 *chisuh*, v.i., see *-shir*↑.

樓 10B.93-2

lour.

N. (1) A storied building: 樓房 *-farng*↓; 洋樓 a foreign-style building; 樓閣 *-ger*↓; 酒樓 a restaurant, a wine shop; 茶樓 a teahouse; 玉樓 a magnificent mansion; 小樓 a small attic; 紅樓 a red-painted building, also women's quarters; 青樓 a brothel; 花樓, 彩樓 a temporary platform decorated with festoons for celebration; 樓臺, 樓廂, 樓梯, 樓板 *-tair*, *-shiang*, *-ti*, *-baan*, ↓; 一樓, 二樓 1st, 2nd floor in U.S.A., 2nd, 3rd floor in Britain; 十層樓 a ten-storied building; 摩天高樓 a skyscraper; 高樓大厦 tall buildings, big mansions; 樓頂 *-diing*, 樓底(下) *-dii*(*shiah*)↓; 一樓一底 a two-storied building. (2) A structure with an upper deck: 樓車 *-jyu*↓, 樓船 *-chuarn*↓; 牌樓 a stone or wooden arch or archway either permanent or temporary; 城樓 gate tower; 城門樓 ditto; 望樓 watchtower, a lookout. (3) A surname.

樓板 *lourbaan*, n., flooring of an upper storey.

樓船 *lourchuarn*, n., formerly, a ship with an upper deck.

樓底(下) *lourdii*(*shiah*), n., downstairs, the ground floor.

樓頂 *lourdiing*, n., the upper stories, upstairs; the top of a tall building.

樓房 *lourfarng*, n., a storied building.

樓閣 *lourger*, n., a tower for enjoying distant views, often with partitions thrown open.

樓車 *lourjyu*, n., a chariot with a turret.

樓櫓 *lourluu*, n., a movable wooden watchtower (also wr. 樓樐).

樓上 *lourshahng*, n., upstairs.

樓下 *lourshiah*, n., downstairs.

樓廂 *lourshiang*, n., a box on second floor in theater.

樓臺 *lourtair*, n., a terrace, a stage for theatrical performances.

樓梯 *lourti*, n., a staircase, ladder.

樓座 *lourtzuoh*, n., (seats in) the gallery or balcony of a theater.

枟 10B.93-3

tarn.

[Abbr. of 檀 10B.30]

櫻 10B.93-4

ying.

N. The cherry: 櫻桃, 櫻花 *-taur, hua*↓; 櫻口, 櫻唇 cherry lips.

櫻貝 *yingbeih*, n., (zoo.) a sea shell, *Tellina nitidula*.

櫻花 *yinghua*, n., cherry blossoms.

櫻桃 *yingtaur* (-'*tau*), n., the cherry tree, its fruit.

櫻草 *yingtsaau*, n., (bot.) the primrose, *Primula cortusoidea*.

桉 10B.93-6

ahn.

N. (1) The eucalyptus. (2) Var. of 案 62.01.

松 10B.93-8

sung.

N. The pine, fir tree, symbol of integrity (節操) because it endures cold: 松筠 pine and bamboo as symbols of integrity; with the crane 松鶴 symbols of long life; 松喬 reference to 赤松子 and 王子喬 two Taoists, symbols of long life, and of Taoist recluse; 松竹梅 (friendship) 歲寒三友, pine, bamboo, plum blossom (three durable plants of winter).

松板 *sungbaan*, n., deal board.

松柏 *sungboh*, n., the pine and the cypress—the conifers.

松楸 *sung-chiou*, n., the pine and the catalpa—trees planted on graveyard; hence the graveyard.

松球 *sungchiour*, n., pine cones, fir cones.

松花 *sung'hua*, n., preserved egg (its jelly showing patterns of pine needles); 松花兒 n., pine cones.

松黃 *sunghuarng*, n., pine flowers with yellow pollen.

松活 *sunghuor*, n., artificial men, deer, pavilion, etc., made with pine branches, burned for the dead.

松針 *sungjen*, n., pine needles.

松雞 *sungji*, n., (zoo.) the hazel grouse.

松膠 *sungjiau*, n., pine resin.

松節油 *sungjieryour*, n., turpentine.

松脂 *sungjy*, n., resin, pitch, (chem.) colophony (also called 松膏, 松香); 松脂油 resin oil.

松菌 *sungjyuhn*, n., edible thick mushroom grown under pines.

松蘿 *sungluor*, n., (bot.) (1) pine lichen; (2) a tea produced in Anhuei.

松毛 *sungmaur*, n., pine needles, see *-jen*↑.

松明 *sungmirng*, n., resin, resinous pine branch which serves as torch.

松木 *sung'muh* (-'*mu*), n., pine wood, deal.

松瓤 *sungrarng*, n., see *-rern*↓.

松仁(兒) *sungrern*(*-rer'l*), n., pine seeds.

松茸 *sungrurng*, n., see *-jyuhn*↑.

松香 *sungshiang*, n., pine resin.

松樹 *sungshuh*, n., the pine tree (with many varieties).

松鼠(兒) *sungshuu*('*l*), n., the squirrel.

松蕈 *sungshyuhn*, n., see *-jyuhn*↑.

松塔(兒) *sungtaa*('*l*), n., pine cones, fir cones.

松濤 *sung-taur*, phr., whistling wind through pine forest, compared to sea waves.

松子(兒) *sungtzyy*(*-tzee'l*), n., pine seeds, also called 松仁 *-rern*↑.

松煙墨 *sungyanmoh*, n., best ink cake made from pine soot.

桧 10B.93-8

kuaih.

[Abbr. of 檜 10B.41]

楡 10B.93-8

yur.

[Printed form of 榆 10B.00]

桵 10B.93-9

rueei.

N. A thorny shrub.

SECTION 10C

§ 10C.00 (牛/丿)

特 10C.00-1

teh.

N. (1) (AC) bull. (2) (AC) spouse, mate.

Adj. Especial, special, exceptional: usu. 特別, 特殊 *-bier*, *-shu*↓; 特價 special price; 特權 special privilege; 特稿 special write-up, see many compp.↓; unusual, distinguished: 特色, 特點, 特長 specialty, special features; 特立獨行 noteworthy conduct and independent character.

Adv. Especially, specially: oft. 特別, 特地 *-bier*, *-dih*↓; 特 used alone, common in LL and official writing: 特派, 特遣 send, appoint especially; 特命 appoint by presidential mandate; 特准, 特赦 give special permission, pardon by special decree; at end of correspondence: 特此函達, 奉告, 通知 you are hereby notified, informed, of the above; 大錯特錯 grievously mistaken.

Conj. But (=但), except that: 特不能超出範圍 except that the limit must be observed; only: 特一時失檢 only a momentary oversight; 不特, 非特 not only.

特別 *tehbier*, adj. & adv., special, -ly: 特別費用, 開支 special expenses; 特別理由 special reason; 特別快車 special express; 特別掛號 special delivery; 特別通融 make a special exception.

特別市 *tehbier-shyh*, n., special municipality under direct central control.

特產 *techaan*, n., special product of locality.

特長 *techarng*, n., specialty, special aptitude.

特出 *techu*, adj., outstanding: 特出人才 such talent.

特點 *tehdiaan*, n., characteristic, special features or traits.

特地 *tehdih*, adv., specially: 特地爲這件事來 came specially for this purpose.

特徵 *tehjeng*, n., characteristic (of class, species, symptoms).

特種 *tehjuung*, n., special kind, brand, breed.

特製 *teh-jyh*, n., specially made, made to order.

特質 *tehjyr*, n., characteristic, special quality.

特刊 *teh-kan*, n., special issue (of bulletin, etc.).

特派員 *tehpaih-yuarn*, n., special delegate, emissary.

特任 *tehrehn*, n., appoint by presidential order; 特任官 official of this rank.

特色 *tehseh*, n., specialty, unique, exceptional quality.

特效藥 *tehshiauh-yauh*, n., especially effective medicine for disease.

特寫 *tehshiee*, n., feature article or column in newspapers.

特殊 *tehshu*, adj., distinguished (merits, etc.); special (treatment, honor, privilege) different from others.

特許 *tehshyuu*, v.t. & n., (by) special permission.

特使 *tehshyy*, n., special envoy, emissary.

特爲 *tehweir*, adv., specially (do, provide s.t.); (*-weih*) specially for.

特務 *tehwuh*, n., security police in charge of (counter) espionage.

特意 *teh-yih*[1], adv., purposely.

特異 *tehyih*[2], adj., distinguished, exceptional.

特約 *tehyue*, adj., by special appointment or assignment.

犄 10C.00-1

ji.

N. See 犄角 *-jiau*↓.

犄角 *ji-jiau*, n., the horns of an ox: 犄角之勢 (cf. troops) so deployed as to be able to render instant mutual assistance; (cf. var. 觭 92B.00).

§ 10C.11 (牛/土)

牲 10C.11-1

sheng.

N. Domesticated animal: 牲畜 ditto; 犧牲 (AC) sacrifice of cow, hog and sheep, now n. & v.t., sacrifice in gen.

牲口 *shengkoou*, n., domesticated animal (donkey, cattle, hog, etc.).

牡 10C.11-1

muu (also *mouu*).

N. (1) Male of animal: 牡牛 ox (cf. 母牛 with same pr. but indicating reverse sex, cow; cf. 牝 female, 10C.70). (2) (AC) door bolt.

牡丹 *muudan* (*muu'dan*), n., peony.

牡蒿 *muuhau*, n., (bot.) *Artemisia japonica.*

牡荊 *muujing*, n., (bot.) *Vitex negundo*, cane, thornstick.

牼 牯 牾 犒 牣 物 牻

牡蠣 *muulih*, n., oyster, also called 蠣黃.

§ 10C.30 (牛/一)

牼 10C.30–3

keng.

N. Calf-bone of cows.

§ 10C.40 (牛/口)

牯 10C.40–1

guu.

N. (AC) (1) The cow. (2) A castrated bull.

牾 10C.40–3

wuu.

V.t. See 牴ᴬ牾 10C.71.

§ 10C.42 (牛/同)

犒 10C.42–6

kauh.

V.t. 犒軍 to comfort soldiers with gifts or money.

犒勞 *kauh'lau*, v.t., (1) to comfort (troops) with gifts of money, food, etc.; (2) (吃) 犒勞 (have) extra food for employees on designated days.

犒賞 *kauhshaang*, v.t. & n., (give) gifts, gratuities to troops or workers as encouragement.

§ 10C.50 (牛/乛)

牣 10C.50–5

rehn.

Adj. (1) Full of, plentiful: 於牣魚躍 (AC) schools of fish happily swimming in the pond. (2) (U.f. 韌) pliable but strong.

物 10C.50–9

wuh.

N. (1) A thing, matter, things in gen.: 無物 nothing; 他物 some other things; 物極則反 things always revert or reverse themselves after reaching an extreme; 物腐蟲生 worms invest decayed matter, (fig.) of decadent organization; 物換星移 things or aspects of things have changed; 物質, 物產, 物品 *-jyr*, *-chaan*, *-piin* ↓; 植物 plants; 動物 animals; 人物 human figures in painting, types of character: 這種人物 this kind of person; 文物 cultural objects or institutions. (2) The outside or material world versus 我 the self: 物累 material cares and worries; 遊心物外 let the mind soar free from the material things; 物我兩忘 (Taoist contemplation) become unaware of both the self and the outside world. (3) The public: 物議, 物論 *-yih²*, *-luhn* ↓; 物望 *-wahng* ↓.

物產 *wuhchaan*, n., native products.

物情 *wuhchirng*, n., the condition of things.

物故 *wuhguh*, v.i., (LL) to die.

物候 *wuhhouh*, n., the season of things, quality of fruit, vegetable according to the seasons.

物化 *wuhhuah*, v.i., (LL) to die; spec. (Taoist) pass away and become spirit.

物華 *wuhhuar*, n., (LL) the beautiful nature.

物價 *wuhjiah*, n., prices: 物價指數 price index.

物件(兒) *wuhjiahn(-jiah'l)*, n., a thing, an article.

物主 *wuh-juu*, n., owner of article.

物質 *wuhjyr*, n., matter; 物質主義 materialism.

物料 *wuhliauh*, n., raw material.

物力 *wuhlih*, n., economic or material strength.

物理 *wuhlii*, n., physics; 物理科學 physical science; 物理治療法 physiotherapy.

物論 *wuhluhn*, n., public criticism.

物品 *wuhpiin*, n., wares, goods, products, articles: 貴重物品 valuable articles.

物色 *wuhseh*, (1) n., color or quality of goods; (2) (-'*se*), v.t., to look for (able, qualified men, special products).

物事 *wuhshyh*, n., matter, thing, event, affair (also 事物): 任何物事 any kind of matter.

物體 *wuhtii*, n., form and state of matter; material body: 天球之物體 material body of stars.

物資 *wuhtzy*, n., natural resources.

物望 *wuhwahng*, n., a person's prestige.

物物 *wuhwuh*, adv., everything: 物物交換 exchange article by article.

物役 *wuh-yih¹*, n., (LL) the slave of material cares and ambitions.

物議 *wuhyih²*, n., public criticism.

物宜 *wuhyir*, n., (AC) what is proper to each one.

§ 10C.70 (牛/乚)

牻 10C.70–1

marng.

N. (AC) black and white cow.

牻牛兒 *marngniour'l*, n., (bot.) geranium.

牝 10C.70-2

pihn.

N. (1) Female of species contrasted with 牡 *muu* 10C.11 (applied not to men, only to animals; applicable to birds, but less frequently; cf. 雌^Δ雄 21S.11): 牝雞司晨 a hen trying to cry cock-a-doodle-doo, reverse of husband being head of the family; 求之於牝牡驪黃之外 judge not by material aspects of things. (2) (AC) the valley, symbol of *yin* (female) principle. (3) The hole in lock, made to receive the corresponding male (the key).

牝期 *pihnchir*, n., (of animals) in heat.
牝戶 *pihnhuh*, n., vagina ＝陰戶.

牠 10C.70-2

tuo (**ta*; **'te when unaccented*). [Var. 它 62.70]

Pron. Modern invented character (cf. 她 93A.70) to represent Eng. "it". Theoretical pr. *tuo*, actually spoken *ta*.

§10C.71 (牛/弋)

犧 10C.71-8

shi.

N. Sacrificial offerings, see 犧牲 *-sheng* ↓

犧牲 *shisheng*, (1) n., sacrificial offerings of cows, pigs, etc.; a sacrifice (of interest, etc.); (2) v.t., to sacrifice: 犧牲自己 sacrifice oneself; 爲國犧牲 sacrifice oneself for the country.
犧尊 *shitzun*, n., an anc. wooden wine vessel in shape of an ox with hole on back.

牴 10C.71-9

dii.

[Var. 觝; cogn. 抵 10A.71]

V.t. Conflict: 抵^Δ觸, 抵^Δ牾 conflict, 10A.71.

§10C.80 (牛/八)

犢 10C.80-1

dur

N. (*tz*, *'l*) Calf: 舐犢(情深) mother love ("licking calf"); 初生之犢不怕虎 new-born calf is not afraid of tiger.

犢鼻褌 *durbirkun*, n., breeches, knee-length pants, embroidered knee apron.
犢子 *durtz*, n., calf; also (coll.) little child.

§10C.82 (牛/乂)

牧 10C.82-9

muh.

N. (1) Shepherd, cowherd. (2) Local magistrate: 州牧 (LL) formerly, district magistrate. (3) A surname.

V.t. To tend (sheep, cow, etc.), lead to pasture: 牧牛, 牧羊 look after cattle, sheep; 畜牧 raise cattle or sheep as industry: 遊牧 nomad's way of life; 牧民 look after people like a shepherd.

牧場 *muhchaang*, n., cattle ranch; shepherd's pasture land.
牧者 *muhjee*, n., shepherd.
牧師 *muhshy*, n., Christian pastor.
牧童 *muhturng*, n., shepherd boy; usu. buffalo boy.
牧圉 *muhyuu*, n., (AC) horse breeder.

§10C.83 (牛/〜)

犍 10C.83-2

jian.

N. A castrated bull.

犍爲 *jianweir*, n., a county in Szechuan Province.

SECTION 10D

§10D.00 (車/丿)

轉 10D.00-1

juaan (**juahn*).

V.i. & t. (1) To turn round, to revolve: 旋轉 revolve: 地球旋轉 the earth revolves; 輾轉 round and round: 輾轉送到 (a letter) is delivered after passing through several hands; 轉圈 make circle; 轉磨 *-mor*↓. (2) To change direction, alter condition: 向左轉 turn left; 轉彎 *-wan*↓; 轉變, 轉移, 轉向 *-biahn, -yir, -shiahng*↓; 轉上, 轉出, 轉進 send up, out, in; 轉去 send s.t. off; 回轉心意, 回心轉意 change one's mind; 轉危爲安 carry over the crisis; 轉敗爲勝 turn defeat into victory: 轉禍爲福 turn bad luck into a blessing; 隨風轉舵 change course of action according to the wind—"see which way the wind blows." (3) To transfer, pass on: 轉運 *-yuhn*↓; 轉賣, 轉讓 *-maih, -rahng*↓; 轉徙 *-shii*↓.

Adv. Used freely before another vb., in sense "on," "round": 轉交, 轉達, 轉致, 轉遞, 轉送 please forward (letter); 轉告 please tell the other party; 轉飭 please give order to subordinate (department); see 轉相 *-shiang*↓; 宛^轉 62.70.

轉背 *juaanbeih*, adv., as soon as one turns one's back.

轉變 *juaanbiahn*, n. & v.i., a change for the better or worse (political situation, patient's condition, etc.), to change (direction, plan).

轉播 *juaanboh*, n. & v.t., relay (broadcast).

轉補 *juaanbuu*, v.t., to transfer (official post).

轉道 *juaan-dauh*, n., formerly, official route of shipping of food.

轉動 *juaanduhng*, v.i., (1) (of machine) to revolve; (2) to turn about (bodily): 不能轉動 cannot turn or move about.

轉轂 *juarnguu*, n. & v.i., formerly, land transport.

轉化 *juaanhuah*, n. & v.i., change in gen.; react chemically.

轉圜 *juaanhuarn*, v.i., (1) to go around; (2) to save situation by going about or speaking to s.o.

轉折 *juaanjer*, v.i. & n., (have) turn of road, plot or events; 轉折點 *--diaan*, n., turning point.

轉機 *juaanji*, n., a change for the better (patient's condition, any deplorable condition).

轉嫁 *juaanjiah*, v.i. & t., (1) to remarry; (2) 轉嫁租稅 to shift tax burden, as from taxpayer to consumer.

轉燭 *juaan-jur*, phr., 萬事如轉燭 (MC) events change kaleidoscopically.

轉捩點 *juaanlih-diaan*, n., critical point.

轉錄 *juaanluh*, n. & v.t., reprint.

轉賣 *juaanmaih*, v.t., to sell to third party.

轉面子 *juaan-miahn'tz*, phr., recover one's "face."

轉磨 **juahnmor*, v.i., feel lost, confused ("mill around").

轉念 *juaan-niahn*, adv., as in 轉念間 in a short while, before you know it.

轉盼 *juaan-pahn*, v.i., (1) ditto; (2) cast side glances.

轉蓬 *juaan-perng*, phr., to float about in a shiftless way, like a leaf blown about.

轉讓 *juaanrahng*, v.t & n., to sell out (shop, house) to next buyer; to transfer; such transfer.

轉生 *juaansheng*, v.i., to be born in next incarnation (as dog, donkey, another human being, etc.).

轉向 *juaan-shiahng* (**juahn-*), v.i., to change directions.

轉相 *juaanshiang*, adv., each other by turn: 轉相仿效 copy each other; 轉相警告 warn each other in turn.

轉徙 *juarnshii*, v.i., to migrate, resettle in new place.

轉心 **juahn-shin*, v.i., to change one's mind or attitude.

轉手 *juarn-shoou*, (1) v.i., to pass on to another; (2) adv., in a moment: 轉手成空 lose all quickly; 轉手變卦 change one's mind in a short moment.

轉瞬 *juaanshuhn*, adv., in the twinkling of an eye, quickly.

轉世 *juaan-shyh*, v.i., see *-sheng* ↑.

轉學 *juaan-shyuer*, v.i., to transfer to another school.

轉漕 *juaantsaur*, v.i., formerly, be in charge of canal transport.

轉側 *juaantseh*, (1) v.i., toss about in bed; (2) adv., before you turn your back.

轉託 *juaantuo*, v.i., to request through a third person.

轉彎 *juaan-wan* (coll. **juahn-*), v.i., to turn a corner (of road) (also 轉彎兒 *-wa'l*) to turn (right, left): 轉個彎兒 make a turn; 轉彎抹角 or 轉彎子 beat about the bush, deviously; 不要轉彎子罵人 don't make oblique remarks.

轉眼 *juarn-yaan*, adv., in the twinkling of an eye.

轉移 *juaanyir*, v.i., to change, shift (direction, plan); n., what hinges upon.

轉運 *juaanyuhn*, v.i. & n., transport, -tation, forwarding; 轉運公司 transport company.

軻 10D.00-3

ke.

N. (1) Personal name of Mencius (孟軻). (2) Axle between two wheels.

輸 10D.00-8

shu.

[Usu. printed 輸]

V.i. & t. & n. (1) To transport, -ation: 運輸 ditto; 輸出, 輸入 *-chu, -ruh*↓; 輸運 *-yuhn*↓. (2) To pay (tribute, tax), to contribute, give, offer: 輪將, 輪納 *-jiang, -nah* ↓; offer loyalty, heart, etc.: 輪誠 *-cherng* ↓. (3) To conduct: 輪尿管, 輪卵管, 輪精管 *-niauh-guaan, -luarn-guaan, -jing-guaan* ↓.

V.i. To lose at gamble, be beaten: 輪贏 *-yirng* ↓; 輪虧, 輪家 *-kuei, -'jia* ↓; 輪錢 lose money in gamble; 他輪了 he lost, is beaten; 輪給他 lost to him; 錢都賭輪了 lost all money at gamble; 認輪, 不認輪 admit, do not admit defeat; 輪不得他那一雙眼 (MC) cannot deceive his eyes.

輪誠 *shucherng*, v.i., (1) offer loyalty to; (2) admit defeat and go over to the other side.

輪情 *shu-chirng*, v.i., to report secretly or secrets, sometimes to enemy.

輪出 *shu-chu*, n. & v.i. & t., export: 輪出稅 export duty; 輪出額 volume of exports; 輪出商(行) export firm; 輪出機 output unit in computer.

輪着兒 *shujau'l*, n., a wrong move.

輪家(兒) *shu'jia('l)*, n., the loser.

輪將 *shujiang*, v.t., to transport, see *-suhng* ↓.

輪精管 *shujing-guaan*, n., sperm duct, *vas deferens*.

輪注 *shujuh*, v.t. & n., infuse (-sion).

輪捐 *shujyuan*, v.t., to pay (tax); to contribute (to charity).

輪虧 *shukuei*, v.i., to lose at battle or gamble.

輪卵管 *shuluarn-guaan*, n., the oviduct, the Fallopian tube.

輪納 *shunah*, v.t., to pay (taxes).

輪尿管 *shuniauh-guaan*, n., the urethra.

輪入 *shu-ruh*, n. & v.t., import, to import; 輪入機 input unit in computer.

輪血 *shu-shyueh*, v.i., to make blood transfusion.

輪送 *shusuhng*, v.i. & t., to send over, to transport to.

輪嘴 *shu-tzueei*, v.i., (1) to admit defeat in argument; (2) not live up to one's word.

輪眼 *shu-yaan*, v.i., to make a mistake in judgment.

輪贏 *shu-yirng*, n., gain or loss, gain and loss.

輪運 *shuyuhn*, v.i. & t., & n., transport (-ation).

§ 10D.01 (車/小)

輮 10D.01-3

rour.

N. The outer rim of a wheel.

V.t. Interch. 揉.

轢 10D.01-9

lih.

V.i. & t. (1) To roll over (s.t.) by cart. (2) To bully by force: 欺轢. (3) (AC) to scrape pan with spoon.

§ 10D.02 (車/⺊)

轅 10D.02-1

yuarn.

N. (1) The shafts of a cart or carriage; 轅下駒 (fig.) person tied down to duties. (2) Office of magistrate, governor, general: 轅門 ditto, esp. where horses are unharnessed; 行轅 field headquarters, etc.; stops.

轘 10D.02-4

huahn.

N. Anc. execution by tearing body apart with several carts.

輾 10D.02-5

*jaan(*niaan).*

V.i. (1) To roll: 輾轉 *-juaan* ↓. (2) (**niaan*) U.f. 碾 to crush with roller.

輾轉 *jaanjuaan*, v.i., (1) toss about: 輾轉反側 toss about (in bed); 輾轉難忘 cannot forget, keep thinking in mind; (2) from person to person: 輾轉相告 (story) passes from mouth to mouth.

§ 10D.10 (車/十)

轔 10D.10-2

lirn.

轔轢 *lirnlih*, v.t., crush over (as by carts); trample upon.

轔轔 *lirnlirn*, n., rattle of carriage.

軒 10D.10-3

shyuan.

N. (1) (AC) a chariot, a cart higher in front than back. (2) An open hall, corridor or pavil-

丿	小	⺊	十	土	ナ	廾	ㄴ	丨	一	丁	フ	口	囗	冈	コ	厂	尸	亠	广	宀	丶	乚	弋	心	八	人	乂	⺈	一	冖	ノ	く
00	01	02	10	11	12	20	21	22	30	31	32	40	41	42	50	51	52	60	61	62	63	70	71	72	80	81	82	83	90	91	92	93

ion: 軒檻 railing on balcony. (3) A studio, a scholar's den, small room: 茶軒 a tea room; 書軒 a study, studio.

Adj. (1) High, lofty, airy: 軒朗, 軒豁, 軒昂 *-laang, -huoh, -arng* ↓; 軒擧, 軒翥 fly aloft. (2) Self-pleased, merry: 軒然自得, 軒軒然 self-pleased, holding head high; 軒眉吐氣 an air of pride and satisfaction (eyebrows high and sniffing pleasantly"); 軒渠 *-chyur* ↓

軒昂 *shyuan-arng*, adj., proud, aspiring, tall: 志氣軒昂 aiming high in life.
軒敞 *shyuanchaang*, adj., open and airy (room).
軒騫 *shyuanchian*, adj., soaring aloft.
軒渠 *shyuanchyur*, v.i. & adj., to laugh; laughing, merry.
軒豁 *shyuanhuoh*, adj., see *-laang* ↓.
軒駕 *shyuan-jiah*, phr., imperial carriage, imperial going about.
軒輊 *shyuanjyh*, adj. & n., different, difference: 未嘗軒輊於其間 no difference between them (from 軒 the front high part of cart and 輊 the low back part).
軒擧 *shyuanjyuu*, adj., as in 風神軒擧 (LL) a distinguished air (of person).
軒朗 *shyuanlaang*, adj., (room) bright and airy, sunny.
軒冕 *shyuanmiaan*, n., gen. nobility (from their caps and carriages), including the emperor.
軒闢 *shyuanpih*, adj., see *-laang* ↑.
軒然 *shyuanrarn*, adj., (1) laughing (manner): 軒然大笑; (2) 軒然大波 a big, crushing wave; (fig.) a crisis.
軒秀 *shyuanshiouh*, adj., eminent, distinguished, superior.
軒爽 *shyuanshuaang*, adj., bright and airy (room).
軒軒 *shyuanshyuan*, adj., & adv., proud, self-pleased: 軒軒自得.
軒掖 *shyuanyih*, n., (LL) forbidden grounds of palace.
軒轅 *shyuanyuarn*, n., the Yellow Emperor; hence 軒岐 (combination of 軒轅 and 岐伯) the fathers of medicine.

輯 10D.10–4

jir.

V.t. Collect, gather together: 輯錄 *-luh*, 輯要 *-yauh* ↓; 編輯 edit(or); 剪輯 compile from clippings.

Adj. (LL) peaceful, harmonious: 輯睦 *-muh*[1]; 輯寧 *-nirng* ↓.

輯錄 *jirluh*, v.t., compile, edit.
輯睦 *jirmuh*[1], adj., tranquil, harmonious.
輯穆 *jirmuh*[2], adj., ditto.
輯寧 *jirnirng*, adj., peaceful, harmonious.
輯要 *jiryauh*, (1) n., an abstract, summary; a selection; (of books, articles); (2) v.i., summarize the essential ideas (of a book, etc.).

§ 10D.11 (車/土)

輊 10D.11–3

jyh.

N. & adj. See 軒△輊 10D.10.

軨 10D.11–8

chyuarn.

N. U.f. 銓 81A.11.

§ 10D.20 (車/廿)

輧 10D.20–9

pirng.

N. (AC) covered wagon.

§ 10D.22 (車/丨)

斬 10D.22–9

jaan.

V.t. (1) To cut off (branches, etc.), cut in two: 斬斷 cut in two; 斬草除根 (fig.) to eradicate, root out (bandits, etc.); 快刀斬亂麻 cut the Gordian knot; 斬釘截鐵 shows firm determination ("cut through nail"); 五世而斬 (AC, of ancestors' benefits) stop at the fifth generation. (2) To execute: 斬首 *-shoou* ↓; 斬立決 sentence to be beheaded immediately.

斬決 *jaanjyuer*, v.t., to execute (criminal).
斬首 *jarn-shoou*, v.t., to behead.
斬衰 *jaantsuei*, v.i., (in extreme mourning prescribed for death of parents) wear merely cut but unhemmed hemp cloth.

§ 10D.30 (車/一)

轤 10D.30–2

lur.

N. See 轆△轤 10D.70, pulley.

輕 10D.30–3

ching.

V.t. (LL) to slight, regard lightly: 輕之 slight a person or thing; 輕其言 regard his words as of no importance; 輕敵 underestimate enemy; 文人(好)相輕 writers like to disparage one another; 輕財重義 regard money lightly and enthusiastic over a public cause; 輕生 take one's life lightly; 輕慢, 輕視, 輕忽 *-mahn*, *-shyh*, *-hu* ↓.

Adj. (1) Light in weight or importance: 很輕, 輕的 light; 輕飄飄的, 輕嫋嫋 very light, feather-light; 輕於鴻毛 (death) could be entirely of no significance; 身輕如燕 light as a swallow; 輕事重報 exaggerate the importance in report; 減輕負擔 lighten responsibility; 輕刑, 輕載 light punishment, load; 輕典 (LL) easy, tolerant laws; 輕症 slight illness; 輕汗 slight sweat; 關係非輕 grave in consequences or implications; 輕裘緩帶 "soft fur and loose girdles"—soft living. (2) Airy, fast: 輕快, 輕捷 *-kuaih*, *-jier* ↓. (3) Cheap, frivolous, flippant, silly: 輕薄, 輕佻, 輕狂, 輕浮 *-bor*, *-tiaur*, *-kuarng*, *-fur* ↓; 輕口薄舌 flippant, like to say nasty things about people. (4) Easy: 輕而易舉 easy to undertake: 輕易 *-yih* ↓.

Adv. Lightly, softly: 輕吹, 輕奏 play softly in music; 輕敲 tap softly; 輕輕 *-ching* ↓; 輕舉妄動 act rashly; 輕諾寡信 who promises too lightly is seldom able to live up to his words; 輕信謠言 listen indiscriminately to rumors; 輕妝 have a simple make-up.

輕便 *chingbiahn*, adj., easy and convenient, portable, (luggage) light; 輕便車, 輕便鐵路 narrow-gage cars, railways.

輕薄 *chingbor*, (1) v.t., to insult: 她被流氓輕薄了一頓 she was insulted with coarse language by a group of ruffians; (2) adj., cheaply critical, flippant: 輕薄少年 coarse, vulgar youth; (3) flirtatious, frivolous: 輕薄子(兒) playboy, fickle lover.

輕巧 *chingchiaau*, adj., (1) agile, skillful; (2) delicate, well-made (gadget, etc.); (3) light, portable.

輕氣 *chingchih*, n., hydrogen (also wr. 氫氣); 輕氣球 a balloon.

輕輕(兒)(的) *chingching('l)('de)*, adv., lightly, softly (tap a door, lay s.t. on floor); (talk) softly; (tell him) gently.

輕粉 *chingfeen*, n., calomel.

輕肥 *ching-feir*, phr., (LL) from 輕裘肥馬 soft furs and well-fed horses—luxurious living.

輕浮 *chingfur*, adj., frivolous, ill-mannered, flighty.

輕工業 *ching-gungyeh*, phr., light industry.

輕寒 *chingharn*, adj., cool, mildly cold.

輕忽 *chinghu*, (1) v.t., to slight, ignore; (2) adj., flighty.

輕賤 *chingjiahn*, (1) adj., vulgar, cheap (work, position); (2) v.t., to despise.

輕捷 *chingjier*, adj., fast, agile.

輕騎 *ching-jih*, phr., light-armed cavalry; advance on horseback.

輕金屬 *chingjin shuu*, n., (chem.) light metals.

輕重(兒) *ching-juhng('l)*, n., "light and heavy"—weight, importance: 較量輕重 compare the importance ("weight"); 不知輕重 have no appreciation of thing's importance.

輕車 *ching-jyu*, phr., (1) a light, swift chariot; (2) any light cart: 輕車簡從 travel with light luggage and few attendants (for quick movements); 輕車熟路, 駕輕就熟 make easy progress from experience (familiarity with the route).

輕舉 *ching-jyuu*, phr., (1) (LL) (Taoist) to go up to heaven bodily; (2) 輕舉妄動 see Adv. ↑.

輕快 *chingkuaih*, adj., (1) fast, easy to handle (carriage, etc.); (2) 價錢輕快 price has eased off; 天氣冷的輕快 (also pr. *chirng'kuai*) weather has become milder.

輕狂 *chingkuarng*, adj., rash, reckless.

輕慢 *chingmahn*, (1) v.t., to slight (person); (2) adj., rude.

輕蔑 *chingmieh*, v.t., to despise.

輕年 *chingniarn*, adj., (MC) young (var. of 年輕, 青年).

輕炮 *ching pauh*, n., light artillery.

輕剽(僄) *chingpiau*, adj., see *-tiaur* ↓.

輕身 *ching shen*, phr., (1) to travel light; (2) see *-sheng*[1] ↓.

輕生 *ching-sheng*[1], phr., take one's life lightly (commit suicide).

輕聲 *chingsheng*[2], (1) n., untoned or unaccented (syllable), marked by preceding ('), as 先生 *shian-'sheng*, *-'sheng*; (2) adv., in a light voice.

輕爽 *chingshuaang*, adj., light and comfortable; (of writing) with a light touch.

輕率 *chingshuaih*, adj. & adv., light-minded, -ly.

輕視 *chingshyh*, v.t., to despise.

輕石 *chingshyr*, n., (min.) pumice stone; slag or cinder-like lava.

輕鬆 *ching'sung*, adj., (of style, conversation, speech) light, with a light touch; relaxed (vein).

輕佻 *chingtiaur*, adj., frivolous (also 輕窕 *-tiaau*).

輕脆 *chingtsueih*, adj., brittle (biscuit, etc.).

輕微 *chingweir*, adj., slight (accomplishment), light (task); piddling (loss, profit).

輕易 *chingyih*, (1) adj., easy to do; (2) adv., light-mindedly: 輕易舉兵 rashly start a war; 他不輕易來 he does not come without important reason; 不輕易動怒 he does not get angry without good reason.

輕盈 *chingyirng*, adj., lissome, lithe: 輕盈體態 a soft, well-rounded figure.

轣 10D.30-5

lih.

轣轆 *lihluh*, n., pulley for drawing buckets from well.

軺
轄
輅
軸
輻
輜
輔
輛

§10D.40 (車/口)

軺 10D.40-5

yaur.

N. (AC) a light horse cart.

轄 10D.40-6

shiar.

V.t. To govern (place, people), have jurisdiction over: 管轄, 統轄 rule over (territory, people); 直轄 direct jurisdiction; 省轄市 city under control of provincial government.

轄區 *shiar-chyu*, n., area under jurisdiction.
轄境 *shiar-jiing*, n., ditto.
轄治 *shiar-jyh*, n. & v.t., rule, control, govern.

輅 10D.40-9

luh.

N. (AC) a chariot.

§10D.41 (車/冈)

軸 10D.41-2

jur (sp. pr. **jour*).

N. (1) (*-tz*) Axle of wheels. (2) Roller of scrolls of painting or calligraphy: 畫軸, 卷軸 roller for scrolls. (3) Axis of geometry, of the earth, of mechanics and of power: 當軸 the authority that be; 軸心 *-shin* ↓. (4) 軸子 (**jouhtz*) in Chin. opera, the last but one selection or scene is called 壓軸子 (*ya--*), and the last, the most important, is called 大軸子 (*dah--*). (5) U.f. 舳 in 舳△艫 91S.41.

軸心 *jurshin*, n., axis; 軸心國 the Axis.

輻 10D.41-3

fur.

N. Axis of wheel.

輻射 *fursheh*, v.i. & n., radiate, -tion (of light, energy); 輻射式 radial pattern; 輻射塵 radioactive fallout; 輻射線 radioactive ray.
輻凑 *furtsouh*, v.i., converge (of traffic, population)

輜 10D.41-9

tzy.

N. A covered wagon: 輜車 *-jyu* ↓; 輜軿 *-pirng* ↓.

輜重 *tzyjuhng*, n., baggage, impedimenta, military supplies; 輜重兵 army service corps.
輜車 *tzyjyu* (*-che*), n., (AC) (1) a covered wagon; (2) a baggage cart.
輜軿 *tzypirng*, n., (AC) a covered wagon.

§10D.42 (車/冈)

輔 10D.42-2

fuu.

N. (1) Side poles of cart acting as wheel guard. (2) (AC) official assistant. (3) (AC) as var. of 酺 cheek and jowl; 輔車 *-jyu* ↓. (4) Territory surrounding capital: 畿輔. (5) Place name. (6) A surname.

V.i. & t. To assist, collaborate, guide, help: 以友輔仁 friendship as a help to right conduct; 相輔而行 two courses of action are complementary to each other; 匡輔 to help, assist (ruler) in conduct of affairs; 輔導, 輔助, 輔佐 *-dauh, -juh, -tzuoo* ↓.

Adj. Subsidiary: 輔幣 *-bih*[2] ↓.

輔弼 *fuubih*[1], n., (LL) prime minister.
輔幣 *fuubih*[2], n., subsidiary coins.
輔導 *fuudauh* (*-daau*), v.i. & t. & n., to guide, facilitate, counsel; 輔導委員會 advisory counsel; adj., advisory.
輔助 *fuujuh*, n. & v.t., help, assist (with money, counsel).
輔治 *fuujyh*, v.i., help in government.
輔車 *fuujyu*, n., (AC) as in 輔車相依 rely on one another as wheel guard and cart or (in another explanation) as cheek and jowl.
輔相 *fuushiahng*, (1) v.i., to act as guide counsel; (2) n., (LL) minister of state.
輔行 *fuushirng*, n., (AC) assistant.
輔佐 *furtzuoo*, n., assistant; 輔佐人 (law) legal counsel or representative.
輔衛 *fuuweih*, v.t. & n., to guide and protect, guard.
輔音 *fuuyin*, n., consonant, cf. 元△音 vowel, 30.70.

輛 10D.42-3

liahng.

N. & n. adjunct. 車輛甚多 heavy traffic; 一輛汽車 one motorcar; 三輛馬車 three carriages.

A

輪 10D.42-8

lurn.

N. (1) A wheel or wheel-like object: 車輪 cart or car wheel; 飛輪 flywheel; 滑輪 pulley; 齒輪 cogwheel; 日輪, 月輪 the sun, moon (disc); 一輪紅日, 一輪明月 a red sun, a bright moon. (2) A surname.

V.i. (1) To take turns: 輪流, 輪班 *-liour*, *-ban* ↓; 輪到你了 it is your turn now; 輪不到我 (of good chance) I shall not have the chance (others ahead of me); 輪姦 to rape by turns. (2) To turn: 輪轉 *-juaan*, 輪廻 *-hueir* ↓.

Adj. 美輪美奐 phr., (AC of building) magnificent, sumptuous.

輪班 *lurn-ban*, v.i., be on duty by turns.
輪掣 *lurncheh*, n., a brake.
輪船 *lurnchuarn*, n., steamer, steamboat, steamship.
輪渡 *lurnduh*, n., steam ferry.
輪番 *lurnfan*, v.i., see *-ban* ↑.
輪換 *lurnhuahn*, v.i., go by turns: 輪換次序 (math.) cyclic order; 輪換排列 cyclic permutation.
輪廻 *lurnhueir*, n., (1) (Budd.) transmigration of souls; (2) eternal cycle of birth and death.
輪軸 *lurnjour*, n., axle.
輪轉 *lurnjuaan*, v.i., to turn (like a wheel); 輪轉印刷機 *--yihnshua-ji*, n., cylinder-press.
輪值 *lurnjyr*, v.i., to be on duty by turns.
輪廓 *lurnkuoh*, n., outline, contour; general layout or main outline (without details).
輪流 *lurnliour*, v.i., take turns.
輪生葉 *lurnsheng yeh*, n., (bot.) verticillate leaf, arranged in verticils.
輪旋曲 *lurnshyuarn-chuu*, n., (mus.) rondo.
輪胎 *lurntai*, n., a tire.
輪作法 *lurntzuoh-faa*, n., (agriculture) rotational cropping (to

B

conserve soil).

轎 10D.42-9

jiauh.

N. A sedan chair, palanquin: 轎子 *-tz* ↓; 花轎 a bridal sedan chair; 轎車 *-che* ↓; 坐轎(子), 擡轎(子) ride in, carry a sedan chair, (sl.) be gypped by professional card sharpers; 上轎 enter a sedan chair.

轎班 *jiauban*, n., chair bearers.
轎車 *jiauhche*, n., (1) a covered cart drawn by donkey; (2) a sedan; (British) saloon car.
轎夫 *jiauhfu*, n., chair bearers.
轎子 *jiauhtz*, n., a palanquin, a sedan chair.

輈 10D.42-9

jou.

輈張 *joujang*, adj., (AC) (1) flurried; (2) insolent.

§ 10D.50 (車/乛)

軔 10D.50-5

rehn.

N. (1) A piece of wood serving as a brake to halt a carriage: 發軔 start going, beginning. (2) (U.f. 仞) an anc. measure of varying lengths: 掘井九軔 dig a well several score feet deep.

C

V.t. To stop, block, bar: 遂以頭軔乘輿輪 (AC) then he put his head against the wheel of the imperial carriage to halt it.

輷 10D.50-9

hung.

N. Sound of rolling carriage.

§ 10D.70 (車/乚)

軋 10D.70-2

yah (*gar*).

V.t. (1) To crush by weight or pressure: 軋碎 crush into small pieces; 互相傾軋 (colleagues in office) try to fight each other for power; 軋棉花 to gin cotton. (2) (*gar*) (Shanghai dial.) hitch up: 軋姘頭 cohabit with man or woman.

軋花機 *yah-hua-ji*, n., a cotton gin.
軋轢 *yahlih*, v.t., to crush.
軋碾 *yahniaan*, v.t., to crush by roller.
軋票口 *yahpiauhkoou*, n., wicket.
軋軋 *yah-yah*, adj., descriptive of click-clack sound.

軏 10D.70-3

yueh.

N. A crossbar in carriage hitched to two parallel bars for guiding direction.

輪 轎 輈 軔 輷 軋 軏

亅	小	⺊	十	土	ナ	廾	凵	丨	一	丅	フ	口	囗	冈	丁	厂	尸	亠	广	宀	丶	乚	弋	心	八	人	乂	一	丿	𠂉	く
00	01	02	10	11	12	20	21	22	30	31	32	40	41	42	50	51	52	60	61	62	63	70	71	72	80	81	82	83	90	91	92	93

輒 10D.70

jer.

[Var. 輙; dist. 轍]

N. (AC) stepping board on anc. cart.

Adv. (LL) usually, often: 輒難之 often took issue with him; 輒以爲是 usually approve; 動輒得咎 usually blamed for every move.

軛 10D.70-5

eh.

N. Harness shafts.

轆 10D.70-6

luh.

轆 轤 *luhlur*, n., a pulley, a windlass for hauling up water.

輗 10D.70-9

nir.

N. The crossbar at the end of a carriage pole.

輗 軏 *niryueh*, n., essential parts of a carriage for alignment of wheels and changing direction without which it cannot move, hence, (fig.) a man's vital convictions.

軌 10D.70-9

gueei.

N. (1) The distance between the wheels of a carriage: 軌距 the gauge. (2) A rut, track, path: 軌轍 *-jer* ↓; 同出一軌 of an identical nature, similar in measurement; 軌道 *-dauh* ↓; 納入正軌 guide into normal path or procedure; 鐵軌 steel rails; 路軌 a rut, railway track; 出軌 derail, be off course; 雙軌 double-tracked. (3) Planetary orbit. (4) General rules, regulations: 軌則 *-tzer*, 軌物 *-wuh*, 軌度 *-duh*, 軌範 *-fahn* ↓; 圖謀不軌 engage in illegal activities, to plot an uprising or rebellion; 軌外行動 unlawful, irregular activities.

軌 道 *gueeidauh*, n., (1) steel rails, a railway track; (2) a planetary orbit; (3) proper course of doing things: 上軌道 on the right track.

軌 度 *gueeiduh*, n., laws, statutes.

軌 範 *gueeifahn*, n., norm, standard, criterion.

軌 轍 *gueeijer*, n., (1) a rut; (2) past events.

軌 條 *gueeitiaur*, n., steel rails.

軌 則 *gueeitzer*, n., laws, regulations.

軌 物 *gueeiwuh*, n., (LL) ditto.

輓 10D.70-9

waan.

V.i. To pull (hearse): hence 輓歌 elegy, *-ge* ↓; to offer condolence.

Adj. U.f. 晚: 輓近 lately.

輓 對 *waandueih*, n., elegiac couplet offered in condolence of the departed, usu. eulogy.

輓 歌 *waange*, n., elegy.

輓 聯 *waanliarn*, n., an elegiac couplet, see *-dueih* ↑.

輓 輸 *waanshu*, v.t., (AC) transport by cart.

輓 詩 *waanshy*, n., elegiac poem.

輓 詞 *waantsyr*, n., elegiac prose-poem.

§10D.71 (車/弋)

軾 10D.71-7

shyh.

N. A horizontal bar in front of carriage for armrest: 憑軾 resting on the front bar (to write poetry).

§10D.72 (車/心)

轗 10D.72-7

kaan.

轗 坷 *kaanke*, n., see 坎^A坷 11A.81.

§10D.81 (車/人)

軼 10D.81-9

yih.

V.t. (1) To excel: 軼羣 *-chyurn* ↓. (2) (AC) 侵軼 to encircle (enemy).

V.i. & adj. (Be) lost, missing: 軼事, 軼聞 *-shyh*, *-wern* ↓; 軼才 extraordinary gifts, superlative talent (interch. 逸).

軼 羣 *yih-chyurn*, phr., to excel, stand above the rest.

軼 倫 *yih-lurn*, phr., see *-chyurn* ↑.

軼 事 *yihshyh*, n., anecdotes, usu. of a famous person.

軼 聞 *yihwern*, n., ditto.

輳 10D.81-9

tsouh.

V.i. To concentrate around one point, as spokes on axis: 輻輳 (cars) crowd together, jam in traffic.

軟 10D.81-9

ruaan.

[Pop. form of 輭]

Adj. (1) Soft, yielding, flexible, weak, gentle (opp. 硬 hard, tough, rigid, strong, harsh): 軟硬 soft or hard, gentle or harsh; 軟皮塞兒 the cork of a bottle; 軟木塞(兒) ditto; 軟皮 soft leather (skin); 軟性 *-shihng*↓; 軟不叮噹 soft, smooth, fluffy; 軟勒咕唧 soft to the touch; 柔軟 easily bent, flexible, pliable: 柔軟體操 calisthenics; 軟和 comfortable, cosy, soft and tender: 軟和話兒 soft words; 軟語 soft speech, words gently spoken; 軟聲 soft-spoken voice; 軟美 charming; 軟纏,軟磨兒 cajole, coax; 軟熟 weak-kneed, having no backbone; 軟袷襖 a lined silk jacket; 軟牀 a stretcher; 軟梯 a rope ladder; 軟糖 soft, gelatinous candies, sweetmeats; 軟(殼)蛋 soft-shelled eggs; 軟筋 a kind of gluten of wheat of thin consistence; 軟弱 *-ruoh*↓; 軟綿綿 velvety,feathery; 軟答刺 weak and flabby; 軟兀刺 flaccid; 軟揣揣 timid, shy, coy; 軟善 weak from being too good and kind; 軟膿包 coward(ly); 軟不喫, 硬不喫 (of persons) would neither listen to reason nor bow to force; 軟硬不喫 ditto; 喫硬不喫軟 understand only the language of force; 喫軟不喫硬 can be persuaded by reason but not be cowed by force; 軟硬兼施 bring both force and reason to bear; 欺軟怕硬 meek towards the brutal and brutal towards the meek; 心(腸)軟 tenderhearted, softhearted; 耳軟 be easily swayed by others; 手軟 (lit.) lacking in muscular strength, (fig.) haven't enough courage to do s.t. cruel; 腳軟 can hardly stand up or walk; 喫軟飯 (of men) live on the earnings of a woman; 軟功(夫) tactics of persuasion; 碰了一個軟釘子 meet with a polite refusal (gentle rebuff). (2) Deficient, insufficient: 菜軟 few good dishes to eat; 戲碼兒軟 (of Peking opera) an unattractive program.

軟半 *ruaan-bahn*, adj., less than one half.

軟刀子 *ruaan-dau'tz*, n., killing of people by a slow and imperceptible process or means.

軟風 *ruaan-feng*, n., (1) a light breeze; (2) (meteorology) winds with a velocity of 1.5–3.4 meters per second.

軟膏 *ruaangau*, n., ointment.

軟骨 *ruarnguu*, n., (physiol.) cartilage.

軟化 *ruaanhuah*, v.i. & t. & n., (lit. & fig.) soften(ing).

軟炸 *ruaan-jar*, v.t., (cooking) to fry without overdoing it.

軟腳 *ruarn-jiaau*, v.i., (MC) give a dinner party of welcome to s.o. back from journey; 軟腳病 (med.) beriberi.

軟禁 *ruaan-jihn*, v.t., keep under detention, usu. in person's house.

軟脂酸 *ruaanjy-suan*, n., (chem.) the palmitic acid.

軟口蓋 *ruarn-koougaih*, n., (physiol.) the soft palate.

軟款 *ruarnkuaan*, adj., shy, coy, bashful.

軟片 *ruaan-piahn*, n., photographic film.

軟弱 *ruaanruoh*, adj., (1) (sp. pr. *-'ruo*) made of inferior material; (2) (*-'ruo*) weak, sickly; (3) easily influenced.

軟繩 *ruaansherng*, n., (acrobatics) a tightrope: 踩軟繩 walking on tightrope.

軟性 *ruaanshihng*, adj., of an amusing or non-serious nature, (of books, plays, music) light; 軟性下疳 *--shiahgan*, n., (med.) soft chancre.

軟刑 *ruaan-shirng*, n., soft, refined torture.

軟水 *ruarn-shueei*, n., (chem.) soft water.

軟鐵 *ruarn-tiee*, n., soft iron.

軟體動物 *ruarntii duhngwuh*, n., (zoo.) mollusk.

軟子 *ruaan'tz*, n., basket or other container for holding things: 刨軟子 calculate the net weight by subtracting the weight of container.

軟棗(兒) *ruarn-tzaau('l)*, n., a kind of dates produced in Mukden.

軟玉 *ruaan-yuh*, n., (min.) nephrite.

§ 10D.82 (車/乂)

輟 10D.82-3

chuoh.

V.i. To stop (work, project, studies): 中輟 stop half way; 輟學 drop out from school; 輟工 stop work, lay down tools; 輟耕 to pause and reflect between farm work.

輒 10D.82-3

jer.

[Pop. of 輙 10D.70]

轍 10D.82-6

cheh (*jer*).

N. (1) Cart track: 轍環天下 (LL) travels cover the whole world.

轍 較 轇 軫 輸 博

(2) (*jer) Avenue of approach: 沒轍 lost track, no traces. (3) 轍兒 (*jer'l) (Chin. music) tone. (4) 找轍 (*jer) look for excuse to cover up.

較 10D.82-6

jiauh.

Adj. Clear.

Adv. More (＝更): 較高, 較低 higher, lower; 較好, 較長, 較短 better, longer, shorter; 較遠, 較近 farther, nearer; 比較 v.t., to compare, see 比 21S.70, adv., comparatively; 計較 to dispute: 別和他計較 to let him have his way.

較眞兒 *jiauhje'l*, adv., in earnest (＝認眞), earnestly.

較勁兒 *jiauhjihe'l*, v.i., (1) to match strength; (2) to get worse, aggravate: 你越說, 他越較勁兒 the more you talk to him, the worse he behaves.

較量 *jiauh'liahng* (-'*liang*), v.i., (1) to match, to compare (strength, skill); (2) to contest: 較量高下 to contest and see who is better or stronger. 「clear.

較然 *jiauhrarn*, adj., explicit,

§10D.91 (車/ノ)

 10D.91-5

jiou.

轇轕 *jiouger*, n., complications, misunderstandings (also wr. 糾葛).

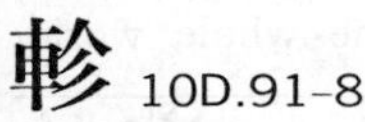

jeen.

N. (1) Cross board at rear of carriage; 車軫 carriage in gen. (2) Peg for tuning stringed instrument.

V.i. To turn about in mind, to think about constantly, esp. in compassion: 軫念時艱 to bear in mind the troubles of the country, see compp.↓.

Adj. (1) In great throngs: 殷殷軫軫 (AC) ditto. (2) 軫石 (AC) square rocks.

軫悼 *jeendauh*, v.t., to sorrow over (the dead), to mourn the loss.

軫懷 *jeenhuair*, v.t., to remember with sorrow.

軫慕 *jeenmuh*, v.t., to remember fondly.

軫念 *jeenniahn* v.t., to remember constantly.

軫惜 *jeenshir* v.t., to feel compassionate toward.

軫恤 *jeenshyuh*, v.t., ditto.

§10D.93 (車/く)

輸 10D.93-8

shu.

[Printed form of 輸 10D.00]

SECTION 10S

§10S.00 (十ˢ/亅)

博 10S.00-1

bor.

V.i. & t. (1) To gamble: 賭博 ditto. (2) Win with good luck (popularity, reputation) honestly or by artifice: 博得美名 win a good name; 博得一官半職 obtain with luck some post with the government. (3) Broaden: (AC) 博我以文 broadens me with literature; 博文約禮 (motto of the Chinese University of Hong Kong) broad learning and proper conduct.

Adj. & adv. Broad, learned, well-read, esp. 廣博 broad in learning, knowledge or territory; 淵博 broad and deep (in learning, philosophy); 博大 *-dah*↓; 博施濟衆 phr., interested in charities; 博洽多聞 phr., knowledgeable, well-informed, conversant; 博覽羣書 be well read, has read many books; 博古通今 conversant with ancient and modern learning.

博愛 *bor-aih*, n. & adj., love, love for all.

博大 *bordah*, adj., great (of scholarship, personality).

博達 *bordar*, adj., ditto; showing deep mastery.

博徒 *bor-dur*, n., gambler.

博局 *bor-jyur*, n., gambling party.

博覽會 *borlaanhueih*, n., (international) exposition; (art) exhibition.

博浪鼓 *borlangguu*, n., ＝波ᐞ浪鼓 63A.82.

博士 *borshyh*, n., doctor of philosophy, medicine, law, etc.; one of several academic honors from Hahn to Sueir Dyns., as 五經博士, 太常博士; 博士買驢 a Ph.

D. buying a donkey, i.e., a lot of academic jargon; 茶博士 tea connoisseur.

博學 *borshyuer*, adj., learned; 博學鴻儒 a rank for great scholars in Chienlung's time.

博物 *borwuh*, n., nature studies; 博物館 *--guaan*, museum.

博奕 *boryih*, n., (AC) gambling and chess.

刺 10S.00-2

tsyh.

[Dist. 刺↓]

N. (1) (-'*l*) Thorns. (2) Small fish bones. (3) A name card: 名刺 ditto; 投刺 send in a visiting card.

V.t. (1) To stab (person, to death), hence to assassinate: 刺死; 刺殺 -'*sha*; 刺客 -*keh*↓. (2) To prick, irritate: 刺耳, 刺骨 -*eel*, -*guu*[2]↓. (3) To prod: 刺探, 刺擧 -*tahn*, -*jyuu*↓. (4) To satirize: 譏刺, 諷刺 ditto. (5) To embroider: 刺繡 -*shiouh*↓.

刺刀 *tsyhdau*, n., bayonet.

刺耳 *tsyh-eel*, adj., irritating to the ear.

刺蛾 *tsyh-er*, n., (zoo.) *Monema flavescens*, a harmful insect (also called 刺蟲蛾, 雀甕蛾).

刺股 *tsyh-guu*[1], phr., (AC allu.) "prick one's thigh" to prevent oneself from falling into sleep—extreme diligence at studies.

刺骨 *tsyh-guu*[2], phr., cut to the bones (hatred, biting wind).

刺槐 *tsyhhuair*, n., (bot.) acacia, *Robinia pseudacacia* (also called 洋槐).

刺激 *tsyhji* (-'*ji*), n. & v.t., bitter experience, emotional upset; to stimulate, -tion: 受刺激 was upset; 刺激劑 a stimulant.

刺戟 *tsyh'jii*, v.t., see -*ji*↑.

刺擧 *tsyhjyuu*, v.t., formerly, to investigate (crime) and bring up for prosecution.

刺客 *tsyhkeh* (-'*ke*), n., an assassin.

刺口 *tsyh-koou*, n., (MC) as in 刺口論事 make intrepid remark, open criticisms.

刺兒頭 *tsyh'ltour*, n., (sl.) a knave, "tough customer," a person hard to deal with.

刺撓 *tsyh'nau*, v.t., to prick, irritate (skin); (p.p.) irritated, itchy.

刺配 *tsyhpeih*, v.t., brand and banish.

刺殺 *tsyh'sha*, v.t., to assassinate (person).

刺繡 *tsyhshiouh*, n., embroidery.

刺史 *tsyhshyy*, n., formerly, district magistrate.

刺探 *tsyhtahn*, v.t., to detect, pry (into case).

刺刺 *tsyhtsyh*, adj., garrulous: 刺刺不休 gabble on and on.

刺桐 *tsyhturng*, n., (bot.) the colanut, a tree of *Sterculia* family.

刺字 *tsyh-tzyh*, v.t., to brand convict (on face or arm); to tattoo.

刺蝟 *tsyhweih*, n., the hedgehog, porcupine.

刺癢 *tsyhyaang*, adj., itchy.

刺 10S.00-2

lah (**lar*).

[Dist. 刺↑]

V.t. (**lar*) To slash, cut (also wr. 揦): 刺開 cut open with a sharp knife; 刺破 cut slits in (a fabric, dress, etc.); 刺玻璃 cut a piece of glass.

Adj. (1) Perverse, rebellious: 無乖刺之心 (AC) with no rebellious intentions. (2) Descriptive of certain sounds: 刮刺刺 ('*la*) a slashing sound, as that made with a whip.

刺子 *lahtz*, n., (1) a person hard-hearted by nature; (2) (old usage) a glass bottle (also 揦子, **lartz*).

刺闒 *lar'ta*, adj., dirty, untidy, slovenly (=邋遢).

制 10S.00-2

jyh.

N. (1) System (of laws, regulations, rites and rituals, education): 制度 -*duh*↓; 學制 educational system; 軍制 army system; 建制 set up system. (2) Three years of mourning for parents.

V.t. (1) To create, establish: 制作, 制定 -*tzuoh*, -*dihng*↓. (2) To control: 制裁 -*tsair*↓; 制慾 control passions; 統制 unify control; 管制 control, have charge of (traffic, people, etc.); 專制 dictatorship, absolute monarchy, despotism; 限制 n. & v.t., limit; 節制 bring under control: 節制生育 birth control; 自制 self-control; 抵制 resist, boycott.

Adj. (1) Standard, standardized: 制幣, 制錢 -*bih*, -*chiarn*↓; 制服 -*fur*[2]↓. (2) Imperial: 制誥, 制詔 -*gauh*, -*jauh*↓.

制幣 *jyubih*, n., standard currency.

制錢(兒) *jyhchiarn*(-*chiar'l*), n., formerly, copper coins of standard content.

制定 *jyhdihng*, v.t., to set up (rules, rites, etc.).

制度 *jyhduh*, n., system (of laws, promotion, examination, degrees, etc.).

制伏 *jyhfur*[1], v.t., to subdue.

制服 *jyhfur*[2], n., (1) uniform; (2) formerly, dress of mourning for parents.

制誥 *jyhgauh*, n., sacrificial prayer.

制詔 *jyhjauh*, n., imperial decree.

制擧 *jyhjyuu*, n., orig. civil

亅	小	⺊	十	土	ナ	卄	ト	丨	一	丅	フ	口	区	冈	㇆	厂	尸	亠	广	宀	丶	乚	七	心	八	人	乂	一	乛	丿	𠂉	く
00	01	02	10	11	12	20	21	22	30	31	32	40	41	42	50	51	52	60	61	62	63	70	71	72	80	81	82	83	90	91	92	93

service examinations under emperor's supervision (殿試); later civil examinations in gen.

制止 *jyhjyy*, v.t., to stop (riot, dissension, etc.).

制科 *jyhke*, n., see *-jyuu* ↑.

制禮 *jyh-lii*, v.i., to set up rites and ceremonies.

制勝 *jyhshehng*, v.i. & t., to overcome, come out victorious.

制限 *jyhshiahn*[1], v.i., to limit (number of persons, etc.).

制憲 *jyh-shiahn*[2], v.i., to write, establish constitution.

制使 *jyhshyy*, n., formerly, imperial emissary.

制裁 *jyhtsair*, v.t., to impose sanction on (aggressor), bring under control, control by law.

制策 *jyhtzeh*, n., formerly, examination by emperor on current political topics.

制作 *jyhtzuoh*, n., creation (of arts, music, etc.).

制藝 *jyhyih*, n., formerly, examination papers by stereotype formulas (八股).

劃 10S.00-2

huoh.

Adj. (AC) sound of crashing (var. of 砉).

耔 10S.00-3

tzyy.

V.i. To bank up the roots of seedlings.

靜 10S.00-9

jihng.

Adj. & adv. (1) Motionless, static, passive (opp. 動 mobile, dynamic, active): 動靜 active and passive, dynamic and static, also a person's movements; 靜臥 lie motionless; 靜伏 lie low; 靜觀 contemplate, watch from the sidelines; 靜修 (Cath.) retreat, also 避靜. (2) Silent, quiet: 靜悄悄 quiet(ly), silent(ly); 寂靜 silent, quiet, still, noiseless; 沈靜 taciturn, reticent; 夜深人靜 in the dead of night. (3) Peaceful, calm, tranquil: 靜謐 quiet and peaceful. (4) Chaste: 貞靜 modest and chaste.

靜便 *jihng'bian*, adj., quiet, peaceful.

靜鞭 *jihng-bian*, n., formerly, a whip which was cracked to enforce silence wherever the emperor passed.

靜電 *jihng-diahn*, n., static electricity.

靜止 *jihngjyy*, adj., static, stationary, motionless.

靜脈 *jihngmoh*[1], n., (physiol.) veins; 靜脈注射 intravenous injection.

靜默 *jihngmoh*[2], adj., silent, speechless, noiseless.

靜僻 *jihngpih*, adj., quiet and secluded.

靜心 *jihng-shin*, n., a quiet mind.

靜坐 *jihngtzuoh*, n., the practice of sitting motionless and meditating — a form of physical regimen.

靜物 *jihngwuh*, n., (painting & photography) still life.

靜養 *jihngyaang*, v.i., (of the sick or aged) take a complete rest.

§ 10S.01 (十S/小)

棘 10S.01-1

jir.

N. The jujube tree, thorny brambles.

Adj. (1) Urgent: 孔棘 (=孔急) (LL) requiring prompt action or attention. (2) (LL) sterile (land): 棘者欲肥 apply manure to make barren land fertile.

棘楚 *jir-chuu*, n., (LL) thorns, brambles. 「thorns.

棘針 *jir-jen*, n., thorny branches;

棘林 *jir-lirn*, n., (AC) a law court, so called because it was usu. held under trees.

棘人 *jir-rern*, n., (LL) a person recently bereaved of his father or mother.

棘心 *jir-shin*, n., (AC allu.) a son's heart.

棘手 *jir-shoou*, adj., difficult, thorny (affair).

棘闈 *jir-weir*, n., formerly, an examination hall.

耨 10S.01-5

nouh.

[Var. 鎒]

N. A rake.

V.t. To weed: 耕耨 to plough and hoe.

榦 10S.01-8

gahn(**harn*).

[Dist. 幹]

N. (1) A tree trunk. (2) 楨榦 (LL) the posts and boards used in making walls, (fig.) the mainstay. (3) (**harn*) 井榦 a well curb.

§ 10S.02 (十S/⺊)

隸 10S.02-2

lih.

N. (1) One of the ancient styles of Chinese calligraphy, precursor to modern 楷書: 隸書 such style; 隸字 characters written in such style; 隸漢 such style of the Hahn Dyn. (2) A lowly person: 奴隸 (制度) slave(ry); 隸人 (AC) a convict sentenced to hard labor.

V.t. Attached to: 隸屬 belonging to, under the jurisdiction of; 隸於 belong to; 附隸 attached to.

§ 10S.10 (十^{s}/十)

韓 10S.10-2

harn.

N. (1) A surname. (2) (AC) a well curb. (3) 韓國 Korea: 北韓, 南韓 North, South Korea; 韓戰 the Korean War.

幹 10S.10-8

gahn.

N. (1) The trunk of a tree, stem: 樹幹 tree trunk; 枝幹 trunk and branches; 箭幹 shaft of arrow. (2) The trunk of the human body: 軀幹. (3) Power, ability: 才幹 talent, ability.

V.t. Do, work, attend to (business): 幹什麽 what are you doing? see 幹麽 *-mar* ↓; 幹不了 I can't manage it; 不幹了 I wash my hands of it all; 苦幹 work hard at (s.t.); 硬幹 continue to do (s.t.) in spite of opposition or difficulties; 幹到底 see (s.t.) through; 幹得過兒 be worth doing; 幹活兒 work for a living; 幹上了 be determined to do (s.t.); keep at (s.t.) without relenting; persistently criticize or annoy (s.o.).

Adj. Able, capable: 能幹 be capable of; 幹練, 幹才 *-liahn, -tsair* ↓.

幹部 *gahnbuh*, n., cadres, staff, rank and file: 中級幹部 middle-rank staff.
幹勁 *gahnjihng*, n., gusto, zeal.
幹了 *gahnliaau*, adj., (1) finished with; (2) (*gahn'le*) spoiled, made a mess of.
幹練 *gahnliahn*, adj., capable and well-experienced.
幹麽 *gahnmar*, adv., (1) why: 你幹麽不走 why didn't you leave? (2) what are you doing? (oft. shortened to *gah-*).
幹線 *gahnshiahn*, n., (of railway, highway) the trunk line.
幹事 *gahnshyh*, (1) n., (*-'shy*) manager, secretary; (2) v.t., manage affairs.
幹頭兒 *gahn'tou'l*, n., what makes a thing worth doing: 這件事沒甚麽幹頭兒 the thing is not worth doing.
幹才 *gahntsair*, n., (1) a talented individual; (2) ability.
幹員 *gahnyuarn*, n., a capable member of the staff.

斡 10S.10-8

woh (**guaan*).
[Dist. 幹 *gahn* ↑]

V.i. (1) To turn, turn round. (2) (**guaan*) U.f. 管 (AC) to control.

斡轉 *wohjuaan*, v.i., see *-shyuarn* ↓.
斡旋 *wohshyuarn*, v.i., to bring around (disputing parties).
斡運 *wohyuhn*, v.t., to transport over.

§ 10S.11 (十/土)

甡 10S.11-1

shen.

Adj. (AC) numerous, abundant.

§ 10S.20 (十^{s}/廾)

耕 10S.20-2

geng (sp. pr. *jing*).

V.i. & t. (1) V.t., to plough (fields): 耕田 *-tiarn*, 耕種 *-juhng* ↓; 耕者有其田 land to the tillers; 農耕 farming, tilling of fields; 耕牧 farming and pasturing; 耕牛 farm cattle; 耕具 farming tools or implements; 耕事 farm work. (2) V.i., make a living: 筆耕, 舌耕 earn one's living by writing, by teaching.

耕地 *geng-dih*, n., farmland, cultivated fields.
耕稼 *gengjiah*, n., farming, agriculture.
耕種 *gengjuhng*, v.t., to plough and sow, to work on the farm.
耕織 *geng-jy*, n., farming and and weaving: 男耕女織 men tilling the farm and women weaving — former division of labor.
耕田 *geng-tiarn*, v.i., to till fields, engage in farming.
耕作 *gengtzuoh*, v.i., do farm work.
耕耘 *gengyurn*, v.t., to plough and weed; to cultivate.

§10S.22 (十ˢ/丨)

邦 10S.22–3

bang.

N. (1) (LL) country, state: 邦家＝國家; 邦人＝國人 people of a country; 邦彥 the *élite* of a country; 友邦 friendly country, -tries; 鄰邦 neighboring country, -tries; 聯邦 confederation; 邦交 diplomatic relations between countries. (2) (AC) feudal state (cogn. of 封).

邨 10S.22–3

tsun.

[Var. of 村 10B.00]

鄞 10S.22–3

chi.

N. Name of river in Szechuan.

§10S.40 (十ˢ/口)

耜 10S.40–4

syh.

N. A plough: 耒耜.

§10S.41 (十ˢ/図)

麯 10S.41–2

chyur.

[See var. 麴 10S.50]

麪 10S.41–3

miahn.

[Pop. 麵 10.83]

N. Noodles, see var. 麫 10S.50.

§10S.42 (十ˢ/冈)

胡 10S.42–4

hur.

N. (1) Northern tribes, including Tartars, Mongols, Turkics: 胡狄 *-dir* ↓; 五胡亂華 the five northern tribes invaded and occupied North China in 4th, 5th and 6th centuries. (2) A surname.

Adv. (1) (AC) why (＝modn. 何): 胡不歸 why not go (come) home; 胡以, 胡爲 *-yii*, *-weir* ↓; 作此胡爲, 此胡爲者 what is this for? (2) Without law, order or reason, recklessly, blindly, foolishly: 胡花 spend money foolishly; 胡來, 胡搞 *-lair*, *-gaau* ↓; 胡亂, 胡鬧 *-luahn*, *-nauh*↓; 胡說 *-shuo*↓; oft. coupled with 亂: 胡思亂想 let mind wander, entertain foolish ideas; 胡言亂語 talk foolishly; 胡作非爲 commit foolish acts.

胡柴 *hurchair*, v.i., (MC) for 胡說 talk foolishly.

胡纏 *hurcharn*, v.i. & t., persist in arguing or criticizing endlessly, pursue (girl) in annoying manner.

胡琴(兒) *hurchirn* (-'*chie'l*), n., string instrument used in Peking opera.

胡蝶 *hurdier*, n., (＝蝴蝶) butterfly.

胡狄 *hurdir*, n., northern tribesmen.

胡豆 *hurdouh*, n., (bot.) horse bean, broad bean (also called 蠶豆).

胡蜂 *hurfeng*, n., (zoo.) a kind of wasp, *Vespa ducalis*.

胡搞 *hurgaau*, v.i. & t., make a mess of (things), act without plan or proper knowledge.

胡瓜 *hurgua*, n., (bot.) a variety of cucumber, *Cucumis sativus* (also called 黃瓜).

胡笳 *hurjia*, n., a reed pipe used by Tartars and other northern tribes.

胡攪 *hurjiaau*, n. & v.i., (1) tomfoolery, create a disorder; (2) (also pr. *-gaau*) see *-gaau* ↑.

胡椒 *hurjiau*, n., pepper.

胡來 *hur-lair*, v.i., act unreasonably or thoughtlessly.

胡裏胡塗 *hur'li-hur'tu*, adv., in disorderly fashion (also wr. 糊裏).

胡嚕 *hur'lu*, v.i., (1) to soothe child by rubbing where it is hurt; (2) to make a crashing noise: 胡魯倒地下去 send crashing to the ground; (3) fuss about, muddle through: 八下裏橫胡嚕著 muddle through (too many concurrent jobs).

胡亂 *hurluahn*, adv., anyhow, carelessly: 胡亂過一夜 pass the night without proper sleep; 胡亂吃下去 eat a meal without thinking.

胡蘿蔔 *hurluor'bo*, n., (bot.) the carrot.

胡盧 *hurlur*, v.i., as in 胡盧大笑 roar with laughter.

胡嚨 *hurlurng*, n., the throat (also called 喉嚨 *hour-*).

胡虜 *hurluu*, n., (contempt.) northern barbarians.

胡麻 *hurmar*, n., (bot.) linseed, sesame.

胡鬧 *hurnauh*, v.i., commit tomfoolery, make irresponsible talk or action.

胡哨 *hurshauh*, n., a whistle call.

胡說 *hurshuo*, v.t., talk nonsense, rubbish: 胡說八道 ditto; 信口胡說 talk recklessly.

胡蒜 *hursuahn*, n., garlic and leeks.

胡荽 *hursuei*, n., (bot.) coriander, an aromatic plant.

胡桃 *hurtaur*, n., the walnut.

胡梯 *hurtir*, n., a ladder (also 扶梯 *fur-*).

胡同 *hurtuhng*, n., a *hutung*, an alley in Peiping (also wr. 衚衕).

胡塗 *hurtur*[1] (-'*tu*), adj. & adv.,

(1) muddle-headed, slow-witted; (2) haphazardly, slipshod: 胡塗了事 wind up a case or finish a job carelessly.

胡突 *hurtur*[2], adv., see *-tur*[1] ↑.

胡謅 *hurtzou*, v.i., talk nonsense, rubbish, fabricate (stories).

胡爲 *hurweir*, adv., (LL) why: 胡爲至此 why brought to this pass?

胡以 *huryii*, adv., why: 胡以如此 why so, why this?

朝 10S.42-4

chaur (**jau*).

N. (1) (**jau*) Morning: 朝夕 *-shih* ↓; 朝陽 the morning sun; 朝露 morning dew; 人生若朝露 human life is evanescent, "like the morning dew"; 朝菌 (fig.) short span of life; 朝暮人 an old man whose days are numbered; 朝不保夕 anything may happen any time; 朝發夕至 distance easily covered in a day's travel; 朝秦暮楚 (of person) change one's loyalty constantly; 朝三暮四 contradict one's own words, fickle, undecided in mind; 朝乾夕惕 (AC) laboring day and night; 朝陽鳴鳳 "phoenix crying in morning sun"—said of minister who spoke out boldly against misrule. (2) (**jau*) Day: 今朝, 明朝 today, tomorrow; 朝朝暮暮 morning and night. (3) Dynasty: 秦朝, 漢朝 Chirn, Hahn Dyn.; 朝代 *-daih* ↓. (4) The court, the government: 朝廷 *-tirng* ↓; 朝政 the state of government; 朝野 people in and out of government, i.e., the whole nation; 朝官, 朝貴 government officials; 滿朝文武 all the civilian and military officers at court. (5) Court audience: 朝服, 朝帽, 朝鞋 court dress, hat, boots; 朝珠 beads worn at court; 朝儀 court etiquette.

V.i. & t. To be received by the emperor: 朝見, 朝覲 ditto; 朝參, 朝謁 ditto; also go on pilgrimage to worship: 朝聖, 朝山 *-shehng*, *-shan* ↓.

Prep. Facing: 坐南朝北 (of house) facing north; 朝東面走 go toward the east; 朝後退 go backwards, retreat; 兩腳朝天 lie or fall down with legs pointing up.

朝拜 *chaurbaih*, v.t., worship, make obeisance (to God, ruler).

朝氣 **jauchih*(-'*chi*) n., spirit of youth and progress, on the upturn ("air of morning").

朝代 *chaurdaih*, n., a dynasty.

朝綱 *chaurgang*, n., governmental structure and discipline: 朝綱大振 the government was set in good order.

朝考 *chaurkaau*, n., (of successful candidates 進士) personal interview with emperor, after which appointments were made.

朝山 *chaur-shan*, n. & v.i., (to make) a pilgrimage.

朝聖 *chaurshehng*, v.i., ditto.

朝夕 **jaushih*, adv., (1) morning and night: 朝夕思慕 think of person morning and night; (2) in a short while.

朝市 *chaurshyh*, n., (LL) field of struggle for power and wealth.

朝廷 *chaurtirng*, n., (1) the royal or imperial court; (2) royal government; (3) the ruler himself: 朝廷的旨意 the wish of the court (or ruler).

朝陽 **jauyarng*, n., the morning sun; east side of mountain.

耦 10S.42-4

oou.

N. (1) A plough. (2) A team of two, a match, an equal: 齊大非耦也 the Kingdom Chir is too powerful to be our partner in marriage.

Adj. U.f. 偶 even (number).

§ 10S.50 (十^{S}/ㄱ)

麪 10S.50-3

miahn.

[Var. 麵, 麵, 麪]

N. (1) Flour, dough: 白麪 wheat flour (白麪兒 heroin). (2) Vermicelli: 切麪 freshly made vermicelli; 掛麪 dried vermicelli. (3) Noodles: 湯麪 noodles in soup; 涼拌麪 noodles served with cold sauce; 炒麪 fried noodles, ("chow mein" in the U.S.); 滷麪 noodles served with sauce; 湯麪 soup with noodles, noodle soup.

麪板 *miahnbaan*, n., board for rolling dough.

麪包 *miahnbau*, n., bread; 烤麪包 toast; 麪包樹 *--shuh*, bread fruit tree.

麪茶 *miahnchar*, n., flour, with boiling water, served with pepper, salt and sesame sauce.

麪起餅 *miahnchirbiing*, n., leavened wheat cake, also called 發麪餅 *faamiahnbiing*.

麪牀 *miahnchuarng*, n., board for rolling dough, see *-baan* ↑.

麪粉 *miahnfeen*, n., wheat flour; 麪粉廠 flour mill.

麪糊 *miahnhur*, n., flour paste; 麪糊團 *--tuarn*, n., a ball of dough, a wishy-washy person.

麪杖 *miahnjahng*, n., rolling pin.

麪筋 *miahnjin*, n., gluten.

麪兒 *miahn'l*, n., noodles.

麪片(兒) *miahnpiahn* (*-piah'l*), n., dough strips.

麪食 *miahnshyr*, n., gen. term for noodles, vermicelli and similar eatables made of flour, such as wonton.

麪條 *miahntiaur*, n., noodles, strips of noodles.

麪魚兒 *miahnyur'l*, n., dough cut up in form of small fish.

甥 10S.50-4

sheng.

N. (1) Sister's child (nephew or niece): 外甥(女) ditto. (2) (AC) various nephews and nieces, cousins of lower generation.

甥兒 *sheng-erl*, n., nephew, sister's son.

甥女 *shengnyuu*, n., niece, sister's daughter.

甥媳婦 *sheng-shirfuh*, n., nephew's wife.

甥婿 *shengshyuh*, n., niece's husband; also son-in-law.

甥孫 *shengsun*, n., grandnephew, -niece.

耡 10S.50-4

chur.

[Var. of 鋤 80A.50]

鶘 10S.50-4

hur.

N. See 鵜[A]鶘 80.50.

切 10S.50-5

chieh (*chie).

V.i. (1) 切脉 To feel the pulse. (2) (**chie*) To cut (paper, fish, meat, melon, etc.): 切斷 cut in two; 切開 cut open; 切片 cut into slices; 切平 cut even; 切成碎兒 cut into bits.

Adj. & adv. (1) Close, -ly, fitting, to the point: 切中(時弊, 要害) hit closely the shortcomings, hit the nail on the head; 不切事, 不切實際 (opinions, remarks) unrealistic, not practicable, not correspond to reality; 切鄰 (MC) close neighbor; 切膚之痛 sorrow hits home, or sorrow like cutting one's flesh: 切身, 切己, 切近 *-shen*, *-jii*, *-jihn*↓; 親切 warm and sincere; 關切 be concerned about (person, affair); 密切注意 watch closely. (2) Firmly: 切勸 sincerely persuade or dissuade, firmly advise; 切諫 firmly advise (ruler) against; 切責 severely charge (with duty), reprimand. (3) Urgent, -ly, be careful to, carefully: 迫切 urgent; see 切切 *-chieh*↓; used imperatively, be sure to: 切記 be sure to remember; 切勿忘記 must never forget; 切不可 must never; 切囑 (this is my) most urgent advice; 切望 I hope sincerely, urgently.

切切 *chiehchieh*, adv., (1) (in imperative sentence) please do, be sure to: 切切記住 be sure to remember; 切切毋違 be sure not to disobey; (2) descriptive of sorrow: 淒淒切切, 切切而哀 plaintive, mournfully; of small whispering sounds: 小弦切切如私語 the small strings seem like whispering; (AC) of careful work or demeanor: 切切偲偲; of fondness: 切切故鄉情 fondly remember home distict.

切齒 *chieh-chyy*, v.i., grind one's teeth in hatred.

切當 *chiehdahng*, adj., (of remarks, procedures) very appropriate, to the point.

切點 *chiehdiaan*, n., (math.) point of contact.

切斷* *chieduahn*, v.t., to amputate (leg, etc.).

切糕 **chie-gau*, n., a kind of pudding made of glutinous rice, dates, etc., cut and sold in small pieces.

切骨 *chiehguu*, phr., (1) hate to the bones; (2) (wind) cutting ("into the bones").

切合 *chiehher*, adj., (opinion) fitting, apt; v.t., fit: 切合事實 correspond to the facts.

切角 *chihjiaau*, n., (math.) angle of contact.

切近 *chiehjihn*, adj., close at home, close to reality.

切己 *chiehjii*, adj., very close, personal (relationships).

切口 *chiehkoou*, n., secret language of underground gangs.

切麵 **chie-miahn*, n., vermicelli made by cutting with knife.

切身 *chieh-shen*, adj., close, personal, intimate (problems, relations): 切身之痛 sorrow which hits close at home.

切線 *chieshiahn*, n., (math.) a tangent.

切實 *chiehshyr*, adj., practical, actual (work), opp. dilatory (talk), also 切切實實 in earnest, really (get down to work).

切磋 **chietsuo*, v.i., to study and learn by mutual discussion (from allu. 如切如磋 "like cutting and grinding" stones).

切音 *chiehyin*, v.i. & n., system of spelling out sound by *faanchieh* 反切 confluent consonants and syllabary.

切圓 *chiehyuarn*, n., (math.) tangent circles.

切韻 *chiehyuhn*, n., syllabary or rhyme classification of characters; name of rhyme book around 600 A.D. used as dictionary.

耪 10S.50-6

paang.

V.t. To cultivate land: 耪地.

翰 10S.50-8

hahn.

N. (1) The writing brush. (2) The "pen" as symbol of literary work: 文翰 literature; 詞翰 poetry. (3) (Polite) letters of correspondence: 來翰, 華翰 your letter; 芳翰 (lady's) letter.

翰林 *hahnlirn*, n., (1) usu. spelled

Hanlin, (翰林院) the Hanlin College or Imperial Academy; (2) a Hanlin academician, awarded from group of *jihnshyh* (進士).

翰墨 *hahnmoh*, n., the work of writing, literary production ("ink and brush").

翰苑 *hahnyuahn*, n., The Hanlin Academy, see *-lirn* ↑.

協 10S.50-9

shier.

V.t. (1) To cooperate: 協力, 協同 *-lih*, *-turng* ↓. (2) To try to reach agreement: 協商, 協議 *-shang*, *-yih* ↓. (3) To assist: 協助, 協理 *-juh*, *-lii* ↓.

Adj. Cooperative, amicable: 協和 *-her* ↓.

協定 *shierdihng*, (1) v.t., to negotiate for settlement as a treaty: 協定計畫 to reach agreement for a plan; (2) n., a formal agreement or understanding between nations, less formal in procedure than a 條約 treaty.

協和 *shierher*, (1) adj., amicable; (2) v.t. to cement relationships: 協和萬邦 to make all nations live together peacefully.

協會 *shierhueih*, n., an association for some common objective or of some trade.

協助 *shierjuh*, n. & v.t., assistance; to assist.

協句 *shier-jyuh*, n., see 叶△韻 40A.10.

協力 *shierlih*, adv., pulling together: 同心協力 unite all efforts for common purpose.

協理 *shierlii*, (1) n., assistant manager; (2) v.i. & t., to assist in management.

協商 *shiershang*, v.t., to meet and discuss together.

協調 *shiertiaur*, v.t., to adjust to each other, to readjust (relationships, etc.).

協同 *shierturng*, adv., working together or with (another person).

協統 *shiertuung*, n., (Manchu Dyn.) commander of a brigade.

協贊 *shiertzahn*, v.t., to assist (in affair or duty).

協議 *shieryih*, v.i. & t., to discuss, negotiate.

協約 *shieryue*, n., a diplomatic agreement; a trade treaty; 協約國 allies, member nations of a treaty.

協韻 *shieryuhn*, v.i., see 叶△韻 40A.10.

勅 10S.50-9

chyh.

[Anc. var. 敕 10S.82]

勃 10S.50-9

bor.

Adj. & adv. Sudden (-ly), rising: 勃騰騰 (MC) very angry.

勃勃 *borbor*, adj., thriving, alive, full of vitality.

勃姑 *borgu*, n., (var. 鵓鴣) wood-pigeon.

勃荷 *bor'ho*, n., (=薄△荷 20A.00) mint.

勃蘭地 *borlarndih*, n., brandy.

勃羅斯 *borluorsy*, n., (translit.) blues.

勃然 *bor-rarn*, adj. & adv., sudden (-ly): 勃然變色 turning red in the face, angry.

勃谿 *borshi*, v.i., (LL) quarrel (esp. among in-laws).

勣 10S.50-9

ji.

N. (Interch. 績 93B.80) merit, conduct deserving of rewards.

鳷 10S.50-9

jy.

鳷鵲 *jychyueh*, n., a singing bird, *Garrulus lidthi*, which can be trained to talk.

鴣 10S.50-9

gu.

N. 鷓鴣, see 鵓△鴣 10S.50 ↓.

鵓 10S.50-9

bor.

鵓鴿 *borge*, n., (coll.) pigeon (pop. wr. 白鴿).

鵓鴣 *borgu*, n., (zoo.) wood pigeon.

鵠 10S.50-9

hur (**guu*).

N. (1) (Zoo.) a species of crane, as symbol of standing still or waiting: 鵠立 to stand still like a crane; 鵠候 to wait like a crane, (court.) to await (your reply); 鵠望 to crane one's neck and hope. (2) (**guu*) An arrow target.

鵠的 **guudih*, n., an arrow target, goal (of struggle, ambition).

麴 10S.50-9

chyur.

[Var. 麯, 麹]

翰 協 勅 勃 勣 鳷 鴣 鵓 鵠 麴

亅	小	⺊	十	土	ナ	廾	𠃊	丨	一	丅	フ	口	区	冈	ㄱ	厂	尸	亠	广	宀	丶	乚	弋	心	八	人	乂	𠂉	一	丿	𠂉	〈
00	01	02	10	11	12	20	21	22	30	31	32	40	41	42	50	51	52	60	61	62	63	70	71	72	80	81	82	83	90	91	92	93

麴 兢 甎 靚 耙 耗 乾

N. (1) A surname. (2) Yeast (pop. called 酒母 "mother of wine"). (3) Liquor: 麴監 *-jahn*; 麴車 *-jyu* ↓.

麴塵 *chyurchern*, n., foamy yeast that appears on surface of fermenting liquor.
麴監 *chyur jiahn*, n., formerly, officer in charge of wine.
麴車 *chyurjyu*, n., (MC) wine cart.
麴菌 *chyurjyuhn*, n., the yeast plant.
麴黴 *chyurmeir*, n., ditto.
麴櫱 *chyurnieh*, n., (1) yeast; (2) wines and liquors.
麴院 *chyuryuahn*, n., distillery, brewery.

§ 10S.70 (十^{s}/乚)

兢 10S.70-1

jing.
[Dist. 競 60S.70]

Adj. Cautious, wary, fearful: 戰戰兢兢 fearful of hidden perils, watchful of possible pitfalls; 兢兢業業 cautious and attentive, constantly on one's guard.

甎 10S.70-3

juan.

N. A brick, tile: 花甎 designed tiles; 甎地 tiled floor; 甎牆 brick wall; 甎房 a brick house; 空心甎 insulated tile; 甎窰 brick kiln; 敲門甎 a means to finding favor with influential persons, open sesame, key to understanding.

甎頭 *juan'tou*, n., a brick.
甎瓦 *juanwaa*, n., a brick; debris of broken tiles.

靚 10S.70-4

jihng.

Adj. (1) (Of woman) painted: 靚妝 smartly dressed. (2) (Cantonese dial.) beautiful (girl, woman).

耙 10S.70-5

par.
[Var. 筢, 鈀]

V.t. To rake, gather (garbage, hay, weeds): 耙草 rake weeds.

N. A rake, usu. 耙子 *-'tz* ↓.

耙耡 *parchur*, n. & v.t., a harrow, to plough with a harrow.
耙子 *par'tz*, n., a rake: 找不到耙子 (fig.) cannot find the proper approach.

耗 10S.70-9

hauh.

N. Bad news: 音耗 ditto; 噩耗 shocking news (of s.o.'s death).

V.i. & t. To waste away: 耗盡, 耗光, 耗乾 spend all; 耗日子, 耗時間 to waste time.

Adj. Bad (crops): (AC) 年之豐耗 year of good or bad crops.

耗費 *hauhfeih*, v.i., spend (with reference to cost): 耗費甚大 cost a lot; to waste (time, energy).
耗減 *hauhjiaan*, v.i., lose in value, depreciate.
耗子 *hauhtz*, n., (coll.) a rat, mouse.

乾 10S.70-9

gan (**chiarn*).

N. (1) (**chiarn*) The first of the eight diagrams (八卦), denoting the principle of heaven, the sovereign, the male and strength (cf. 坤 11A.22); see compp. ↓. (2) Dry, preserved meat, fruit: 牛肉乾 treated and preserved beef; 豆腐乾 partially dehydrated bean curd; 餅乾 biscuit. (3) (**chiarn*) A surname.

V.t. (1) (Coll.) to scold: 我又乾了他一頓 I gave him a scolding. (2) To cold-shoulder (person): 把咱們又乾起來了 gave us again the cold shoulder; 乾着他, 別理他 leave him in the cold, ignore him.

Adj. (1) Dry: 乾巴 *-'ba* ↓; 擦乾 wipe dry; 晒乾 to sun dry, sun-dried; 乾淨 *-jihng* ↓; 乾柴烈火 (youth and girl) caught in passion; 乾裂, 乾旱 *-lieh, -hahn* ↓. (2) Dried up: 喝乾了 drink up all in a glass; 乾杯 *-bei* ↓; 井水乾了 well has dried up; 乾電池 dry battery. (3) Finished, cleaned out: 輸乾了 cleaned out in gambling, see 乾淨 *-jihng* ↓. (4) Adopted (relation) not related by blood: 乾爹 adopted father; 乾兄弟, 乾姊妹 adopted brothers, sisters; see 乾爹, 乾媽, 乾兒(子), 乾娘 *-die, -ma, -er(tzyy), -niarng* ↓ etc. (5) Cash in place of gift: 乾禮 *-lii* ↓; 折乾 give gifts in cash.

Adv. (1) In vain: 乾着急 exasperated and anxious and can do nothing about it; 乾瞪眼 stare helplessly; 乾擱臺 fail to turn up for appointment. (2) Without tears or other liquids: 乾咳 a dry cough (without phlegm); 乾哭, 乾嚎, 乾號 howling without tears; 乾嘔 vomit and throw up nothing; 借乾舖 borrow a bed for the night in singsong house ("without moisture"). (3) Only, with nothing else: 乾憑這點本事 (person) has only this bit of skill; 乾靠你一份薪水 depend only on your salary (for household expenses).

乾巴 *gan'ba('l)*, adj., dried up (lake bottom): 乾巴巴的 all dry and hard; 乾巴疵裂 tough and coarse (person, thing).

乾爸 *ganba*, n., see *-die*↓.

乾綳兒 *ganbeh'l*, (1) n., a kind of baked cake; (2) adj., very dry.

乾杯 *ganbei*, v.i., bottoms up.

乾貝 *ganbeih*, n., dried, preserved edible ligaments of a species of clam, *Altrina japonica* (also wr. 干貝, cf. 江^Δ瑤柱 63A.30).

乾癟 *ganbiee*, n., dry and cracked, (of person) thin, skinny, emaciated: 乾癟臭虫 (Shanghai dial.) person without a cent.

乾冰 *ganbing*, n., artificial ice-block.

乾乾 (1) **chiarnchiarn*, v.i., (AC, LL) to strive ceaselessly; (2) *gan-gan*, adj., 乾乾淨淨 see *-jihng*↓; 乾乾兒的 empty-handed (to visit without presents).

乾親 *ganchin*, n., adopted relative.

乾道 **chiarndauh*, n., the male principle, principle of action.

乾爹 *gandie*, n., adopted father.

乾兒(子) *gan-er(tzyy)*, n., adopted son.

乾飯 *ganfahn*, n., usu. cooked rice as dist. 稀飯 gruel or congee.

乾粉 *ganfeen*, n., dry 粉條 (vermicelli made from bean flour, not yet soaked in water).

乾綱 **chiarngang*, n., the sovereign's power; (facet.) husband's power: 乾綱大振 (不振) husband reestablishes his power vis-a-vis his wife (be henpecked).

乾果 *ganguoo*, n., dried or preserved fruit.

乾旱 *ganhahn*, n., drought.

乾涸 *ganher*, adj., dried up (water, also finances).

乾宅 **chiarnjair*, n., (LL) bridegroom's family (used during wedding).

乾淨 *ganjihng*, adj., (1) clean (room, dress); (2) cleaned up: 輸乾淨了 (cash) all cleaned up at gambling; 乾乾淨淨, 一乾二淨 all finished, cleared up without remainder.

乾渴 *gankee*, adj., very thirsty.

乾枯 *ganku*, adj., dried up (leaves, ideas).

乾坤 **chiarnkun*, n., (1) the principles of heaven and earth or male and female; (2) the universe; (3) husband-and-wife relationship.

乾酪 *ganlauh*, n., cheese.

乾糧 *gan'liarng*, n., (1) not perishable foodstuff, such as grains, bean; (2) dehydrated food, army food supplies or those that can be carried on a long foot journey.

乾裂 *ganlieh*, adj., (wood, soil) dry and cracked.

乾禮(兒) *ganlii(-liee'l)*, n., cash gifts: 送乾禮兒 give cash on festive occasions.

乾餾 *ganliouh*, v.i., (chem.) dry distillation.

乾媽 *ganma*, n., adopted mother.

乾麵 *ganmiahn*, n., flour.

乾沒 *ganmoh*, v.t., confiscate, appropriate what is not one's own.

乾娘 *ganniarng*, n., adopted mother.

乾女兒 *gannyuu'l*, n., adopted daughter.

乾熱 *ganreh*, n. & adj., dry heat; (weather) scorching hot.

乾象 **chiarnshiahng*, n., heaven, as symbol of *chiarn* principle.

乾笑 *ganshiauh*, v.i., to make a forced smile.

乾洗 *ganshii*, v.i., dry-clean.

乾薪 *ganshin*, n., sinecure: 拿乾薪 draw salary without work.

乾瘦 *ganshouh*, adj., shrivelled, haggard (appearance).

乾癬 *ganshyuaan*, n., ringworm skin disease, with discolored patches covered with scales.

乾血癆 *ganshyuehlaur*, n., (Chin. med.) amenorrhoea; anemia.

乾絲 *gansy*, n., fine shreds of bean curd.

乾苔 *gantair*, n., (bot.) enteromorpha.

乾菜 *gantsaih*, n., (1) various kinds of pickled or sun-dried vegetables; (2) a meal served without soup.

乾脆 *gantsueih*, (1) adj., straightfoward: 他做人很乾脆 he is very straightforward; (2) adv., simply and without hesitation or mincing words: 他説話乾脆 he does not beat about the bush; 不如乾脆把這筆賬勾掉 it would be simpler to write it off as bad debt; 乾脆就做吧 do it then without further discussion; (3) adj., (food) crisp: 又乾又脆.

乾攢 *gantzaan*, adj., very thrifty, trying every way to save.

乾造 **chiarntzauh*, n., (fortune-telling) a man's horoscope.

乾燥 *gantzauh*, adj., (weather) dry; 乾燥劑 (chem.) dryer, substance which absorbs moisture; 乾燥器 (chem.) desiccator.

乾曜 **chiarnyauh*, n., (LL) the sun.

乾咽 *ganyeh*, v.i., to sob.

乾元 **chiarnyuarn*, n., heaven.

艳 10S.70-9

yahn.

[Pop. of 豔 22S.30]

---

§ 10S.71 (十^S/乀)

戟 10S.71-7

jii.

N. A lance, a halberd.

戟指 *jiijyy*, v.t., to point one's fingers at (another) and revile him.

戟門 *jiimern*, n., (AC) a high official's residence ("a house with lances").

戟手 *jiishoou*, v.t., see *-jyy*↑.

§ 10S.80 (十^{S}/八)

頓 10S.80–3

duhn.

N. adjunct. What takes place at one time (like a bout, meal, etc.): 一頓飯 one meal; 一頓惡打 (or 罵) a good thrashing or tongue lashing.

N. A pause (in music, reading); a stamping (in dance); a pause of the brush with silent pressure in calligraphy.

V.i. & t. (1) To make a meaningful pause as in calligraphy: 頓筆 make caesura or period, a pause for breath in reading or writing; 停頓 (affairs) draw to a stop, at a standstill. (2) To nod: 頓首 make ceremonious nod; 頓足 to stamp one's foot as in regret. (3) To place or arrange for rest: 安頓 put (person, object) in a restful or safe place.

Adj. Frustrated, meeting with difficulties: 困頓 unsuccessful in career; 委頓 dispirited, downhearted.

Adv. Suddenly: 頓改前非 suddenly reform oneself; 頓悟 suddenly realize (the truth), (Zen) awakening in a flash of insight.

頓號 *duhnhauh*, n., the caesura sign "、" placed between several proper names, as different from comma.
頓躓 *duhnjyh*, v.i., falter; meet many mishaps.
頓首 *duhnshoou*, v.i., make ceremonious nod, bow.
頓時 *duhnshyr*, adv., at once, immediately, in a short space.
頓挫 *duhntsuoh*, v.i., sustain delays, obstacles.

顚 10S.80–3

dian.
[Usu. printed 顛]

N. Top, peak (＝巓); (AC) forehead of horse: 有馬白顚; 顚末 beginning and end (of story).

V.i. (1) To totter, fall, tumble (see compp.); to turn upside down, see 顚倒 *-daau*↓; 顚來覆去 totter, roll over, change story frequently; to roll down: 石顚下來 stone rolls down. (2) To trot: 馬顚得穩 horse trots steadily; 大顚小顚 fast and slow trot.

Adj. Mentally deranged (＝癲): 顚狂 ditto; 瘋顚 insane.

顚簸 *dianboo*, v.i., to rock, roll sideways.
顚倒 *diandaau*, (1) v.i. & t., turn upside down: 顚倒是非, 黑白 distort facts, give false account of the true facts; (2) adj., upside down, confused: 顚三倒四, 七顚八倒 all in confusion; 心神顚倒 utterly confused, unable to think straight; 顚顚倒倒 tottering; 顚鸞倒鳳 in sexual embrace.
顚覆 *dianfuh*, v.i., to totter, turn over like a sinking ship; (v.t.) to overthrow (government).
顚躓 *dianjyh*, v.t., falter and fall.
顚兒 *dian'l*, v.i., (coll.) run away, escape, decamp.
顚連 *dianliarn*, v.i., totter and about to fall, falter.
顚沛 *dianpeih*, v.i., see *-liarn*↑.
顚撲 *dianpu*, phr., 顚撲不破 (truth, theory) stands despite time and argument.
顚癇 *dianshiarn*, n., epilepsy.
顚眴 *dianshyuahn*, n., ditto.
顚危 *dianweir*, adj., (of regime) tottering.
顚越 *dianyueh*, v.i., (LL) make false steps, falter and fall.

賴 10S.80–5

laih.

N. (1) A surname. (2) (Var. for 癩) scabies; leprosy. (3) 無賴之徒 shiftless person, vagabond; 百無聊賴 utterly bored or helpless.

V.t. (1) Rely or depend on, have (s.t.) as last resort: 倚賴, 依賴, 仰賴, 托賴 depend on (s.o., s.t.) for support; 賴仗 *-jahng*[2]↓; 賴得(有)此耳 thanks to s.t. for support or as last resort; 賴衣求食 depend on others for a living. (2) Deny, repudiate, accuse (s.o.) else falsely: 賴債 *-jaih*, 賴賬 *-jahng*[1], 賴婚 *-hun*↓; 賴掉 deny all knowledge of or connection with; 賴不了 cannot be denied or repudiated; 誣賴, 訛賴 falsely accuse; 賴別人 lay the blame on others; 大家都賴他偷東西 everybody accuses him of being a thief. (3) Drag on: 拖賴 purposely keep on putting off (payment, etc.); 賴不過去 cannot be settled simply by dragging on without decision.

賴婚 *laih-hun*, v.t., repudiate a marriage contract.
賴賬 *laih-jahng*[1], v.t., repudiate debt.
賴仗 *laihjahng*[2], v.t., be dependent on (s.o.) for support.
賴債 *laih-jaih*, v.t., repudiate debt.
賴臉 *laihliaan*, v.i., be shameless: 嘻皮賴臉.
賴磨子 *laihmortz*, n., a sly and shameless person: 耍賴磨子 play a little trick on s.o.
賴皮 *laihpir*, adj., shameless: 賴皮賴骨 be utterly shameless; 他眞賴皮 he is thoroughly shameless.
賴學 *laih-shyuer*, v.i., play truant.
賴詞兒 *laihtser'l*, n., a false accusation, a pack of lies.
賴子 *laihtz*, n., a rogue (＝無賴).

§ 10S.81 (十^{S}/人)

麩 10S.81–1

fu.

N. (*-tz*) Bran.

麩金 *fu-jin*, n., gold dust.

麩料 *fu-liauh*, n., bran mixed with black beans as cattle or horse feed.
麩皮 *fu-pir*, n., bran chaff.
麩炭火 *futahn-huoo*, n., warm, well-banked fire, as in hand-warmer stove.

献 10S.81–1

shiahn.
[Pop. of 獻 21S.81]

款 10S.81–9

kuaan.
[Var. of 款 11.81]

歕 10S.81–9

pen.
[Var. of 噴 40A.80]

§ 10S.82 (十^{s}/乂)

耰 10S.82–3

you.

N. A rake.

嘏 10S.82–5

*guu (*jiaa).*

N. (LL) (1) felicity, prosperity, blessing. (2) Birthday felicitations: 祝嘏.

Adj. (**jiaa*, rare) Immense, faraway, distant.

故 10S.82–9

guh.

N. (1) Cause, reason: 緣故, 原故 underlying cause or reason; 何故 why? 非有他故 there's no other reason; 無故 without cause or reason. (2) An event, incident, happening: 事故 an incident; 變故 a mishap, unfortunate event, esp. death of one's father or mother; 故故由兒 (coll.) what is taking place: 他們鬧甚麽故故由兒哪 what are they fussing about?

V.i. Die, pass away: 病故 die of illness; 亡故 pass away; 物故, 身故 ditto; 已故 have died, deceased.

Adj. (1) Old, ancient, of long standing: 故國 *-guor*↓; 故事 *-shyh*↓; 故都, 故宮 ancient capital, palace; 故交 an old friend; 故知 *-jy*, 故人 *-rern*, 故舊 *-jiouh*↓; 故步自封 ultraconservative and self-satisfied; 故態復萌 revert to one's old way of life, said of bad habits; 故居, 故址 old homestead, site; 故土 one's native land. (2) U.f. 固 41.41.

Adv. Purposely, intentionally: 故意 *-yih*↓; 明知故犯 commit an offense knowingly; 故作不知 pretend not to be aware of.

Conj. Therefore, consequently, hence: 故不能來 therefore I could not come; 是故 for this reason; 故爾 *-eel*↓; 故而 *-erl*, 故此 *-tsyy*↓.

故常 *guhcharng*, adj., the same, normal.
故道 *guh-dauh*, n., (1) an old path or road; (2) a time-honored method.
故我 *guh-ee*, (re. pr.) pron., my old self: 依然故我 I am still my old self.
故爾 *guh-eel*, adv., therefore, hence.
故而 *guherl*, adv., ditto.
故國 *guhguor*, n., (1) an ancient land; (2) one's fatherland: 故國之思 nostalgia for one's native land; (3) one's native district.
故障 *guhjahng*, n., a hindrance, obstacle, hitch: 機器發生故障 there is some engine trouble.
故轍 *guhjer*, n., (lit. & fig.) an old rut.
故家 *guhjia*, n., an old family, esp. of well-known status: 故家子 a young man from such a family.
故舊 *guhjiouh*, n., a close friend of many years' standing.
故知 *guhjy*, n., ditto.
故智 *guhjyh*, n., an old trick.
故老 *guhlaau*, n., an elder of town, village.
故里 *guhlii*, n., one's native village.
故人 *guhrern*, n., (1) (litr. & poet.) an old friend; (2) one's former wife.
故殺 *guh-sha*, n., a premeditated murder.
故鄉 *guhshiang*, n., one's home town.
故事 *gushyh*, n., (1) an old story: 故事重演 repetition of s.t. that has happened before; (2) (*guh'shyh*) a story: 兒童故事 stories for children; 民間故事 folk tales; (3) (*guh'shyh*) an incident (usu. 事故).
故實 *guhshyr*, n., anecdotes.
故此 *guhtsyy*, adv., for this reason, on this account.
故吾 *guhwuu*, pron., my old self, see *-ee*↑.
故意 *guhyih*, n. & adv., (1) n., an old friend's goodwill: 十觴亦不醉, 感子故意長 so grateful for your hospitality, I have downed ten goblets and not got tipsy; (2) adv., on purpose: 故意不回答 purposely did not give a reply.

敖 10S.82–9

aur.

V.i. (AC) u.f. 遨 to ramble, play about: 敖遊, 敖戲 *-your*, *-shih*↓.

Adj. (AC) scorching, see 敖然 *-rarn*↓.

敖敖 *auraur*, adj., (AC) tall, towering: 碩人敖敖.
敖盪 *aurdahng*, v.i., to frisk or play about, to idle away one's time.
敖然 *aurrarn*, adj., (AC) scorching hot.
敖戲 *aurshih*, v.i., see *-dahng*↑.
敖遊 *auryour*, v.i., see *-dahng*↑.

敕 10S.82-9

chyh.

N. (1) An imperial decree. (2) Taoist magic order given to demons and spirits.

V.i. U.f. 飭 81B.50.

救 10S.82-9

jiouh.

V.t. (1) To stop, prevent: 汝弗能救與 can't you prevent it? (2) To help, assist: 救命 *-mihng*, 救護 *-huh*, 救援 *-yuarn*↓; 援救 rescue from peril; 搭救 give a helping hand; 拯救 extend assistance to; 急救 give first aid; 救國救民 save the country and people from an impending danger; 救災 relieve victims of disaster; 救治 *-jyh*↓; 救苦救難 help people in distress.

救兵 *jiouh-bing*, n., reinforcements, a relief column.
救度 *jiouhduh*, n., (Budd.) salvation.
救護 *jiouhhuh*, v.t., give first aid to (wounded); 救護車 an ambulance.
救火 *jiouh-huoo*, v.t., put out a fire; 救火車 a fire engine.
救濟 *jiouhjih*, n. & v.t., (give) relief (to); 救濟院 a poorhouse.
救急 *jiouhjir*, v.i., relieve (people in) urgent need; 救急車 ambulance.
救助 *jiouhjuh*, v.t., to help, assist (the poor, the needy).
救主 *Jiouhjuu*, n., the Savior.
救治 *jiouhjyh*, v.t., to remedy.
救命 *jiouhmihng*, v.i., (1) save s.o.'s life, as one about to drown; (2) to cry "Help! help!"
救生 *jiousheng*, v.i., to rescue people in danger of drowning; 救生船 a lifeboat; 救生圈 a life buoy; 救生衣 a lifesaving jacket; 救生員 a lifeguard.
救星 *jiouhshing* (-'*shing*), n., a national savior.
救世主 *Jiouhshyh-juu*, n., the Savior.
救時 *jiouh-shyr*, v.i., to turn the tide of the times.
救亡 *jiouhwarng*, v.i., help one's country tide over a period of national crisis.
救藥 *jiouh-yauh*, n., a remedy; v.t., to remedy (situation): 不可救藥 (of sickness) incurable, (of situation) beyond remedying, irreversible, (of persons) incorrigible.
救援 *jiouhyuarn*, n. & v.t., (render) assistance (to s.o. in distress).

敷 10S.82-9

fu.

V.i. & t. (1) To apply: 敷粉, 藥 apply powder, medical ointment or powder; 敷一敷 rub a little with ointment; 外敷 external application. (2) (AC) to spread (v.i. & t.): 敷放, 敷布, 敷施 to spread (culture, etc.); 敷告天下 make public to the world; 敷宣, 敷揚 publicize, promote (teachings). (3) To lay before one: 敷奏 explain in letter to king; 敷陳, 敷設 *-chern*, *-sheh*↓. (4) To suffice: 敷用 suffice for expenses; 不敷 insufficient; 入不敷出 income cannot cover expenses.

敷陳 *fuchern*, v.i. & t., to outline in orderly fashion.
敷設 *fusheh*, v.t., lay, arrange in order (decorations, etc.), lay (railroads).
敷演 *fuyaan*[1], v.t., show, perform, develop (story, etc.); dist. 衍.
敷衍 *fuyaan*[2], v.i., go through the motions without sincerity: 和他敷衍一下 do necessary courteous things; 敷衍了事 do the routine things superficially and have done with it.

§ 10S.83 (十^{s}/～)

靛 10S.83-6

diahn.

N. Indigo, indigo (blue) color: 洋靛 Prussian blue.

靛白 *diahnbair*, n., indigo white.
靛青 *diahnching*, n., see *-larn*↓.
靛花 *diahn-hua*, n., scum on indigo tank.
靛藍 *diahnlarn*, n., indigo blue.

§ 10S.93 (十^{s}/〈)

耬 10S.93-2

lour.

耬車 *lourche*, n., a plowlike implement for sowing grain.

耘 10S.93-3

yurn.

V.i. & t. To weed (grass).

SECTION 11

§11.00 (土/丿)

寺 11.00

syh.

N. (1) Formerly, a govenment bureau, as 大理寺, 太常寺. (2) A religious temple, a monastery: 寺院 *-yuahn* ↓. (3) A palace attendant: 寺人 *-rern* ↓.

寺主 *syhjuu*, n., abbot.
寺庫 *syhkuh*, n., formerly, a pawnshop near a temple.
寺人 *syhrern*, n., palace attendant; a eunuch.
寺舍 *syhsheh*, n., temple building.
寺院 *syhyuahn*, n., temple; cloister.

壽 11.00

shouh.
[Var. 夀; pop. 寿]

N. (1) Age of person: 壽命 *-mihng* ↓; 長壽 longevity; 壽比南山 formula of birthday congratulations ("may you live as long as the southern mountain"—allu.); 以介眉壽 (AC) to pray for long life; 壽終正寢 pass away peacefully; 人壽保險 life insurance. (2) Birthday celebration: 壽誕, 壽辰 *-dahn, -chern* ↓; 壽酒, 壽麵 birthday wine, noodles; 壽桃 *-taur* ↓; 壽星, 壽婆 *-shing, -por* ↓; 祝壽, 上壽 to drink a toast to long life. (3) Burial or having to do with burial: 壽板, 壽器, 壽衣 *-baan, -chih, -yi* ↓. (4) A surname.

V.i. & t. (1) To toast to one's long life: 祝壽, 爲某人祝壽 ditto. (2) To bring long life and blessings to people: 壽世 (said of doctors); 壽民 (AC) to bring benefits to the people.

壽板 *shouh-baan*, n., coffin.
壽辰 *shouhchern*, n., birthday: 五十壽辰 fiftieth birthday.
壽器 *shouh-chih*, n., (euphem.) coffin, oft. bought and kept during one's lifetime.
壽誕 *shouhdahn*, n., birthday anniversary.
壽紀 *shouhjih*, n., person's age.
壽豈 *shouhkaai*, adj., (AC) enjoying long life and happiness (豈 u.f. 愷 happiness, harmony).
壽考 *shouhkaau*, n., long life.
壽命 *shouhmihng*, n., person's life span: 壽命不長 (will) die young.
壽母 *shouhmuu*, n., (AC) aged mother.
壽屏 *shouhpirng*, n., birthday scrolls on which are written congratulatory messages or poems; a folding screen, engraved with many forms of the letter 壽.
壽婆 *shouhpor*, n., wife of 壽星 *-shing* ↓.
壽險 *shouhshiaan*, n., short for 人壽保險 life insurance.
壽星 *shouhshing*, n., (1) (court.) person whose birthday is being celebrated; (2) the god of longevity (sp. pr. *-'shing*) (also called 壽星老兒) distinguished by having abnormally high forehead.
壽數 *shouhshuh*, n., person's destined age.
壽穴 *shouhshyueh*, n., graveyard built during one's lifetime.
壽序 *shoushyuh*, n., (LL) message of congratulations on birthday.
壽算 *shousuahn*, n., see *-shuh* ↑.
壽桃 *shouh-taur*, n., birthday peach; peach-colored breadroll associated with birthday dinner.
壽頭 *shouhtour*, n., (Shanghai dial.) a nitwit, a sucker.
壽材 *shouhtsair*, n., coffin made during one's lifetime.
壽藏 *shouhtzahng*, n., (AC) graveyard, see *-shyueh* ↑.
壽文 *shouhwern*, n., message of birthday congratulations.
壽衣 *shouh-yi*, n., burial costume prepared during lifetime.
壽域 *shouh-yuh*, n., (LL) burial place.

孝 11.00

shiauh.

N. Mourning, esp. for parents (see Adj.): 守孝, 穿孝, 戴孝 observe mourning; 正在孝中 be in mourning period; 孝滿, 脱孝 mourning is over; 重孝 double mourning; 孝袍, 孝衣掛子 mourning garment; 孝服, 孝帽 mourning dress, cap; 孝幔 curtain before coffin.

Adj. Filial, obedient (son): 孝子, 孝友 *-tzyy, -yoou* ↓; 孝敬, 孝養 (vbb.) *-jihng, -yaang* ↓.

孝道 *shiauhdauh*, n., Confucian doctrine of filial piety.
孝婦 *shiauhfuh*, n., (1) a good, filial woman; (2) a woman in mourning.
孝家 *shiauh'jia*, n., person in mourning: 我們姑娘是孝家 the young mistress is in (family of) mourning.
孝敬 *shiauhjihng*, v.t., (1) to present eatables, etc. (to parents, elders): 這是我孝敬祖母的 this is my present to grandmother; (2) to serve with love and respect.
孝廉 *shiauhliarn*, n., formerly, term for "*jyuurern*" (舉人), scholar of second degree.
孝男 *shiauhnarn*, n., the surviving son, important person at funeral (used also in self-reference; cf. *-nyuu* ↓).
孝女 *shiauhnyuu*, n., (1) surviving daughter, daughter in mourn-

ing; (2) a well-behaved daughter.

孝行 *shiauhshihng*, n., filial conduct.

孝心 *shiauh-shin*, n., filial piety, love toward parents.

孝順 *shiauh'shuhn*, (1) adj., (of children) obedient, loving (to parents); (2) v.t., obey (parents).

孝思 *shiauh-sy*, n., heart of filial piety.

孝堂 *shiauh-tarng*, n., (1) parlor in which the coffin is laid; (2) the white curtain in front of coffin or hall.

孝弟 *shiauhtih*, adj., Confucian prime virtues of being dutiful son and brother (弟 also wr. 悌).

孝慈 *shiauhtsyr*, adj., kind (on the part of those above) and obedient (those below).

孝子 *shiauhtzyy*, n., (1) a good, obedient or worthy son; (2) a son in mourning (=*-narn*↑).

孝養 *shiauhyaang*, v.t., (1) to serve (parents) with all material needs; (2) (Budd.) say masses with offerings for parents.

孝友 *shiauhyoou*, adj., being a good son and good friend, obedient, loving and friendly.

赤 11.00

chyh.

Adj. (1) Red color: 赤豆 *-douh*↓; 赤金, 赤色 *-jin*, *-seh*↓; 面紅耳赤 emotionally excited, face reddens to the ears; 赤紅臉 a red face. (2) Communistic, "Red": 赤化 *-huah*↓; 赤俄 Soviet Russia, Red Russia. (3) Bare, naked: 赤手空拳 barehanded; 赤貧 *-pirn*↓; 赤地 bare, sun-scorched land; 赤口白舌 tawdry squabble over nothing; 赤裸, 赤膊 *-luoo*, *-bor*↓; 赤裸裸, 赤條條, 赤條精光 completely naked; 赤背, 赤身 *-beih*, *-shen*↓. (4) Sincere: 赤誠, 赤心 *-cherng*, *-shin*↓.

赤背 *chyh-beih*, adj., bareback.

赤膊 *chyhbor*, adj., naked.

赤誠 *chyhcherng*, n., loyalty of heart.

赤膽 *chyhdaan*, adj. & n., brave, valiant; also sincerity, loyalty.

赤帶 *chyhdaih*, n., (med.) leucorrhoea.

赤道 *chyhdauh*, n., the equator.

赤豆 *chyhdouh*, n., red lentils.

赤化 *chyhhuah*, adj., communistic, "Red"; v.t., communize, sovietize.

赤腳 *chyhjiaau*, adj. & adv., barefooted.

赤金 *chyhjin*, n., (1) pure gold; (2) (AC) copper.

赤楝蛇 *chyhliahn-sher*, n., a brown snake, non-poisonous, *Tropidonotus tigrinus.*

赤痢 *chyhlih*, n., dysentry, with traces of blood.

赤裸 *chyhluoo*, adj., naked (body, description): 赤裸裸 nakedly, completely revealed.

赤貧 *chyhpirn*, adj., penniless.

赤色 *chyhseh*, adj., (1) red color; (2) Communist.

赤身 *chyhshen*, adj., (1) as in 赤身裸體 naked; (2) (travel, adventure) single-handed.

赤心 *chyhshin*, n., *-cherng*↑.

赤手 *chyhshoou*, adv., with barehands.

赤血球 *chyh-shyueh-chiour*, n., red corpuscles.

赤松 *chyhsung*, n., a giant pine, *Pinus densiflora.*

赤足 *chyhtzur*, adj. & adv., barefooted, see *-jiaau*↑.

赤字 *chyhtzyh*, n., (of accounts) red lettering, deficit, in the red.

赤子 *chyhtzyy*, n., the child; 赤子之心 the innocent heart of a child.

赤楊 *chyhyarng*, n., (bot.) (1) the alder, of birch family, *Alnus japonica*; (2) *Tamarix chinensis* (檉柳).

摯 11.00

jyh.

N. A surname.

Adj. (1) Sincere, close: 親摯 warm (friend); 摯友 close friend.

§11.01 (土/小)

縶 11.01

jyr.

V.t. (1) To tie up, hamper with rope or chain. (2) To fetter, shackle (prisoner). (3) 縶維 (AC) to collect and keep (men of talent).

槖 11.01

tuoh.

[Var. of 橐 10.01]

§11.02 (土/k)

袁 11.02

yuarn.

[Callig. form 袁]

N. A surname.

§11.10 (土/十)

幸 11.10

shihng.

N. (1) Luck, good luck: 幸福, 幸運 *-fur*, *-yuhn*↓; 有幸 lucky; 三生有幸 thrice blessed, luck for three incarnations. (2) A surname.

V.t. (Of emperor) (1) visit (a place); 臨幸 condescend to pay a visit; 巡幸 make an imperial tour. (2) Sleep with (a woman): 幸某妃 (or 臨幸) slept with certain lady-in-waiting (possibility of having a son by her); to have as favorite: 寵幸 show special favor to (lady or minister); hence 幸臣 *-chern*↓. (3) To wish well: 幸其早成 wish him early success; 幸災樂禍 to gloat over s.o.'s disaster; 所幸得以脱禍 so happy to learn that s.o. has escaped an accident; 慶幸 to congratulate.

Adj. Lucky, fortunate: 不幸 unfortunate; 人生有幸有不幸 some people are lucky, some not; 不幸 adj. & adv., unfortunate, -ly.

Adv. (1) Kindly, please: 幸勿推卻 please be kind enough not to decline. (2) Fortunately: 幸而, 幸虧 *-erl, -kuei*↓; 幸得 ditto; 幸得是你 luckily it was you; 幸得原諒 fortunately you forgave me; 幸已脱險 happily or luckily (person) is out of danger; 幸告完成 happily it is completed; 不幸給他瞧見 unfortunately he saw it; 不幸而言中 if unfortunately what I predict should come about.

幸臣 *shihng-chern*, n., court favorite.

幸而 *shihngerl*, adv., luckily: 幸而是你 luckily it is you and not s.o. else.

幸福 *shihngfur*, n., good luck, blessing, happiness: 人生的幸福 happiness of life.

幸虧 *shihngkuei*, adv., fortunately: 幸虧他早有準備 fortunately he was well prepared.

幸免 *shihngmiaan*, v.i., to escape (punishment, accident): 難得幸免 will be difficult to escape the consequences.

幸甚 *shihng-shehn*, phr., (a common phrase placed at the end of request): 請從速示知,幸甚 please reply as soon as possible—this is my request ("it will make me very happy").

幸位 *shihng-weih*, n., an undeserved high position.

幸運 *shihngyuhn*, n., good luck; 幸運兒 lucky person; "lucky dog."

鞤 11.10

bang.
[Var. 幫]

N. Stiff side of boots.

鼙 11.10

pir.

N. Mil. drum.

鼙鼓 *pirguu*, n., drum used in battle, call to battle.

聲 11.10

sheng.
[Abbr. 声]

N. (1) Noise, person's voice: 發聲 make a noise; 不出聲 make no noise, keep quiet (during dialogue); 大聲, 高聲 loud voice; 大聲疾呼 to shout at the top of one's voice; 聲淚俱下 make pitiful plea; 聲音笑貌 person's voice and expression; 力竭聲嘶 exhausted from effort ("voice hoarse"). (2) Used in counting cries: 說一聲, 哭一聲 cry between the words; 一聲炮響 one crack of gun or firecrackers; 三聲大砲 a three-gun salute. (3) Tone: 四聲the four tones: 1. 陰平; 2. 陽平; 3. 上; 4. 去; the 入聲 orig. with final *p, t, k, h*, has disappeared in many dialects, including that of Peking and is not recognized in national Chinese); 聲母, 聲韻, 聲調 *-muu, -yuhn, -diauh*↓; 有聲有色 very impressive; 聲色, 聲容 *-seh, -rurng*↓. (4) Reputation: 名聲 ditto; 聲名, 聲價, 聲譽 *-mirng*[1], *-jiah, -yuh*↓.

V.i. Declare, announce: 聲東擊西 "announce east and strike west"—mil. feint; 聲言, 聲明, 聲張, 聲請 *-yarn, -mirng*[2], *-jang, -chiing*↓; 不聲不響 quietly without attracting notice.

聲稱 *shengcheng*, v.i., to announce (that), declare (one's intentions).

聲氣 *sheng-chih*, n., spiritual or physical relations: 聲氣相投 (from 同聲相應, 同氣相求) having spiritual affinity (of friends); communication: 通聲氣 keep in contact with each other, esp. in secret.

聲請 *shengchiing*, v.i. & t., to make open request, apply for.

聲帶 *shengdaih*, n., vocal cord; sound track.

聲調(兒) *shengdiauh('l)*, n., (1) melody in writing, music; (2) word tone or sentence tone; tone of speaking.

聲符 *shengfur*, n., phonetic notation.

聲喚 *shenghuahn*, v.i., (MC) to shout, call aloud.

聲華 *shenghuar*, adj., (LL) popular and well-known; 聲華客 (LL) popular writer.

聲張 *shengjang*, v.i., to make known: 不要聲張 hush-hush, do not make a noise.

聲價 *shengjiah*, n., personal good reputation, social esteem.

聲妓 *sheng-jih*, n., (LL) singsong girl.

聲浪 *sheng-lahng*, n., sound waves.

聲律 *sheng-lyuh*, n., laws of rhythm in writing.

聲門 *shengmern*, n., (physiol.) the glottis.

聲名 *shengmirng*[1], n., reputation, fame.

聲明 *shengmirng*[2], v.i. & n., to declare (intentions, etc.); a declaration (of purpose, etc.), public statement.

聲母 *shengmuu*, n., a consonant, opp. 韻母 vowel or syllabary.

聲納 *shengnah*, n., sonar.

聲喏 *sheng-ree*, v.i., (MC) say "Yes, sir!"

聲容 *shengrurng*, n., voice and expression.

聲色 *sheng-seh*, n., (1) carnal pleasures, song and women; (2) voice and countenance of person: 聲色俱厲 severe in voice and countenance.

聲息 *sheng-shir*, n., (1) noise, news heard from; (2) 聲息相通 see *-chih* ↑.

聲述 *sheng-shuh*, v.t., to tell, narrate (what happened).

聲說 *shengshuo*, v.i., to declare, announce.

聲勢 *sheng-shyh*, n., threatening force (of striking army); domineering posture or position.

聲學 *shengshyuer*, n., acoustics.

聲望 *shengwahng*, n., person's prestige, reputation.

聲問 *shengwehn*, n., (AC) news (=modn. 音問).

聲威 *sheng-wei*, n., prestige, domineering power.

聲聞 *sheng-wern*, phr., be reputed to: 聲聞過情 (AC) to enjoy higher reputation than is justified.

聲言 *shengyarn*, v.i., to announce, declare.

聲音 *shengyin*, n., person's voice; noise.

聲援 *shengyuarn*, v.i., come openly to the rescue (troops); declare to be on the side of.

聲樂 *sheng-yueh*, n., vocal music, opp. 器樂 instrumental music; 聲樂家 *--jia*, n., vocalist.

聲譽 *shengyuh*, n., personal prestige, reputation.

聲韻 *shengyuhn*, n., (1) tone and melody of writing; (2) the historical study of vowels and consonants.

§11.11 (土/土)

土 11.11

tuu.

N. (1) Land: 國土 national territory; 疆土 ditto; 故土 home country; 守土有責 be responsible for guarding land from enemy; 皇天后土 Heaven and Earth (personified); 土地 *-dih* ↓. (2) Soil, earth: 泥土 clay, mud; 沙土 sandy soil; 沃土 fertile soil; 黃土 yellow soil; 三合土 Chin. cement; 土崩瓦解 complete collapse, disintegration of authority or government structure; 土牛木馬 or 土雞瓦狗 shape without soul, completely useless persons. (3) Euphem. for opium: 運土 transportation of opium for profit; 煙土 opium. (4) Clay musical instrument. (5) One of the Five Elements (五行之一) or five modes of motion. (6) A surname.

Adj. (1) Native, local, of or from the country: 土產 *-chaan* ↓; forming many compp. meaning local, native, aboriginal, like 土風, 土豪, 土人, 土布 see *-feng²*, *-haur*, *-rern*, *-buh*, etc ↓. (2) Earthen, made of earth: 土瓶 earthen jar; 土城 earthen city wall. (3) Uncouth, crude, rude, stubborn; 土性, 土氣 *-shihng*, *-chih*, etc. ↓; 他打扮得好土 he dresses like a country bumpkin; 土頭土腦 bumptious, stupid and uncouth.

土包 *tuubau*, n., (1) (*-tz*) a coarse person, country bumpkin; (2) a pack of earth.

土豹 *tuu-bauh*, n., a kind of wild cat, also called 猞猁孫 *shehli sun*.

土鱉 *tuu-bie*, n., a kind of ground insect (also known as 地鱉).

土兵 *tuu-bing*, n., local troops or recruits.

土撥鼠 *tuubor-shuu*, n., the marmot.

土布 *tuu-buh*, n., homespun, coarse local cloth.

土產 *turchaan*, n., local product or produce.

土娼 *tuu-chang*, n., local prostitute.

土常山 *tuu-charngshan*, n., (bot.) hydrangea.

土城 *tuu-cherng*, n., city wall made of clay or adobe.

土氣 *tuuchih*, adj., rustic, lacking refinement, crass: 土氣十足, also 土裡土氣.

土地 *tuudih*, n., land: 土地改革 land reform; 土地稅 land tax; 土地銀行 land bank; (*-'di*) earth god in charge of farms and vegetation: 土地神 earth god; 土地爺 ditto; 土地廟 earth god's temple.

土堆 *tuu-duei*, n., heap of earth, soil.

土遁 *tuu-duhn*, v.i., (myth, certain spirits capable of) disappearing into the earth and becoming invisible.

土耳其 *tureelchir*, n., Turkey.

土法 *tur-faa*, n., local or native method of production.

土方 *tuu-fang*, n., recipe of folk medicine.

土匪 *turfeei*, n., bandit.

土蜂 *tuufeng¹*, n., a kind of wasp, *Discolia vittifrons*.

土風 *tuufeng²*, n., local custom; 土風舞 local or aboriginal dance.

土官 *tuu-guan*, n., formerly, border chief sanctioned by the Chin. government, see *-sy* ↓.

土棍 *tuuguhn*, n., village bully, ruffian.

土共 *tuu-guhng*, n., local communists.

土豪 *tuuhaur*, n., the local rich and influential class, esp. 土豪劣紳 phr., local oppressive rich gentry.

土花 *tuuhua*, n., discolorations of antiques long buried underground.

土話 *tuuhuah*, n., *patois*, dialect.

土貨 *tuuhuoh*, n., product of local industry; local produce.

土芥 *tuu-jieh*, n., (LL) trifles.

土著 *tuujuh*, n., aborigines (also pr. *tuujuor*).

土螽 *tuujung*, n., an insect, *Criotettix bispinosus*.

土炕 *tuukahng*, n., the *kang*, a built-in earthen bed in North China.

土老兒 *tur-laau'l*, n., country bumpkin.

土饅頭 *tuu-marn'tou*, n., (sarcastic) grave ("earthen bun").

土脈 *tuu-moh*, n., veins of land, geologic strata.

土末兒 *tuu-moh'l*, n., powder of tea leaves.

土木 *tuumuh*, n., construction

activity; 土木工程 civil engineering.
土偶 *tuu-oou*, n., clay idol.
土坯 *tuu-pi*, n., unburnt brick.
土壤 *turraang*, n., soil; land.
土人 *tuurern*, n., aborigines, natives.
土色 *tuu-seh*, n. & adj., ashen color.
土山(子) *tuu-shan(tz)*, n., hill without rocks.
土性 *tuushihng*, n., coarse, bumptious character.
土星 *tuushing*, n., (astron.) Saturn.
土虛子 *tuushyutz*, n., see *-guhn*↑.
土俗 *tuusur*, n., local custom.
土司 *tuusy*, n., border government in charge of dealings with border tribes.
土賊 *tuutzer*, n., see *-feei*↑.
土作 *tuu-tzuoh*, n., mason's and carpenter's work.
土物 *tuu-wuh*, n., local product.
土藥 *tuu-yauh*, n., native recipe, native medicine; domestic opium, dist. 洋藥 imported opium.
土曜日 *tuuyauh-ryh*, n., Saturday.
土音 *tuu-yin*, n., dialect accent.
土儀 *tuu-yir*, n., gift of native products.
土語 *turyuu*, n., local, native language.

士 11.11

shyh.

N. (1) Scholar, the intelligentsia: 士子, 士人 *-tzyy*, *-rern*↓; gen. term of polite reference: 男士 gentleman; 女士 gen. term equiv. "Miss" attached to surname (張女士) or personal name (玉華女士); 士林, 士流, 士族 *-lirn*, *-liour*, *-tzur²*↓. (2) Soldier: 士兵, 兵士 ditto; 上士, 中士, 下士 staff sergeant, sergeant, corporal; 壯士, 勇士 warrior, brave fighter; 甲士 soldiers bearing arms (lit. "shields"). (3) 士 a pawn, name of a chessman in Chin. chess.

士兵 *shyhbing*, n., private, soldier.
士氣 *shyh-chih*, n., morale of the educated class or of the army.
士大夫 *shyhdahfu*, n., (1) the intelligentsia, literati, gentry; (2) the men or officers of rank.
士多 *shyhduo*, n., store, usually grocery store (translit. Cantonese).
士官 *shyhguan*, n., the officials.
士君子 *shyh-jyuntzyy*, n., the intelligentsia, educated class; a gentleman.
士類 *shyh-leih*, n., scholars as a class.
士禮 *shyh-lii*, n., rites and rituals.
士流 *shyh-liour*, n., the scholar class, literary circles.
士林 *shyhlirn*, n., literary circles.
士民 *shyhmirn*, n., (LL) the people, including scholars.
士敏土 *shyhmirntuu*, n., cement (translit., also called 水泥).
士女 *shyh-nyuu*, n., (1) boys and girls; (2) 士女畫 painting of human figures (also wr. 仕女).
士人 *shyhrern*, n., a scholar, an educated man.
士行 *shyh-shihng*, n., conduct of scholars.
士庶 *shyhshuh*, n., the common people.
士卒 *shyhtzur¹*, n., army privates.
士族 *shyh-tzur²*, n., family of scholars.
士子 *shyhtzyy*, n., student, scholar.
士伍 *shyhwuu*, n., rank and file of soldiers.

圭 11.11

guei.

N. (1) (AC) a piece of jade for ceremonial occasions: 圭璋 *-jang*↓. (2) A dry measure equal to one hundred thousandth part of 升.

圭表 *gueibiaau*, n., (1) (AC) a sundial; (2) a person of exemplary character.
圭竇 *gueidouh*, n., (LL) a poor man's den.
圭璋 *gueijang*, n., high-quality jade, (of persons) noble character.
圭角 *gueijiaau*, n., (1) sharp corner of a piece of jade; (2) (of persons) correct and honest behavior and principles.
圭臬 *gueinieh*, n., an exemplary model: 奉爲圭臬 take as one's model.

墊 11.11

diahn.

N. Cushion: 椅墊 chair cushion; 牀墊, 褥墊 mattress, etc.

V.i. & t. (1) To raise or make even by cushion. (2) To advance money for need: 墊多少錢 advance so much money; 墊一墊 pay for first by s.o.,; 先墊, 代墊 ditto. (3) 墊沒 (LL) (of land) to sink down.

墊隘 *diahn-aih*, adj. & n., low, damp hole.
墊被 *diahnbeih*, n., mattress: 被人當墊被 serve as steppingstone, be exploited as expendable.
墊喘兒 *diahnchuaa'l*, n., serve as outlet for anger with others.
墊戲 *diahnshih*, n., preliminary performance before the big play proper.

臺 11.11

tair.

[Common pop. 台; var. 臺]

N. (1) A platform, stage: 臺上 on the stage; 上臺, 下臺 go on stage, come off stage, (fig.) of political ins and outs; 講臺 speaking platform; 戲臺 theatrical stage; 砲臺 fort; 氣象臺 meteorological station; 天文臺, 觀象臺 astronomical observatory; 司令臺, 閱兵臺 commander's platform, reviewing stand; 月臺 railway platform; terrace: 陽臺, 晒臺 terrace; 亭臺 pavilions and terraces; 臺榭 terraces and open halls; 近水樓臺 terrace and pavilion near water—convenient access; 債臺高築 (fig.) pile of debts; 燭臺 candle-stand. (2) Term of respect in 憲臺 governor; 撫臺 military governor; 道臺 intendant of circuit. (See also 台 compp. 93.40).

臺北 *Tairbeei*, n., Taipei.
臺球 *tairchiour*, n., billiard (usu. wr. 台球).
臺地 *tairdih*, n., tableland, plateau.
臺階(兒) *tairjie(-jie'l)*, n., steps; steppingstone, a chance to change position during negotiations.
臺簾(兒) *tairliarn(-liar'l)*, n., curtain on stage.
臺門 *tairmern*, n., gate tower of palaces.
臺盤 *tairparn*, n., stage: 上不得臺盤 not good enough to appear in high society.
臺灣 *Tairwan*, n., Formosa, Taiwan.

耋 11.11

dier.

N. (AC) old people over seventy or eighty.

§11.21 (土/乚)

罄 11.21

chihng.

V.t. To exhaust, use up: 罄竹難書 (of a man's sins, misdemeanors) too numerous to inscribe on all bamboo strips.

Adj. Exhausted, used up: 告罄 (s.t. like money, rice) is all used up.

罄竭 *chihngjier*, adj., finished, exhausted (funds, etc.).
罄然 *chihngrarn*, adj., (AC) tidy, neat.
罄身(兒) *chihng-shen('l)*, adj., (MC) stripped of clothing.

§11.22 (土/丨)

幇 11.22

bang.

[Abbr. of 幫 11.22↓]

幫 11.22

bang.

[Original and printed form, usu. contracted to 幇 and esp. 帮 as pop. var.]

N. (1) Gang, group: 這幫人 this kind of people; 一幫人 a group of people; 這幫貨 this shipment of goods. (2) 青幫紅幫, 青紅幫 former underground gang of tightly organized ruffians, ne'er-do-wells; member of such gang; 在幫 be member of gang. (3) Upright side of boots (also wr. 幚): 鞋幫; side wall of ditch: 溝幫.

V.i. Help, assist, usu. 幫助 *-juh*, 幫忙 *-marng*↓.

幫辦 *bangbahn*, n., assistant; v.i., assist in managing.
幫補 *bangbuu*, v.i., help out with money.
幫襯 *bangchehn*, v.i., serve as contrast in design.
幫腔 *bang-chiang*, v.i., give support to person by speaking during discussions.
幫錢 *bang-chiarn*, v.i., help out with money.
幫拳 *bang-chyuarn*, v.i., help one of the fighters.
幫工 *bang-gung*, n., work assistant.
幫夥 *banghuoo*, n., shop assistant.
幫助 *bangjuh*, n. & v.t., help: 得了不少幫助 got no little help.
幫兒 *bang'l*, n., gang, see N. 2↑.
幫忙 *bangmarng*, n. & v.t., (to) help: 越幫越忙 phr., futile help; 謝謝你幫忙 thank you for your help.
幫箱 *bang-shiang*, n., gifts or contributions to bride.
幫閑 *bangshiarn*, v.i., (derog.) be troublemaker, give advice from having nothing to do (usu. of friends, dependents of the rich).
幫手 *bangshoou*, n., assistant; accomplice.
幫兇 *bangshyung*, n. & v.i., assist in crime or bullying.
幫貼 *bangtie*, v.t., subsidize.
幫湊 *bangtsouh*, v.i. & t., contribute money.
幫子 *bangtz*, n., see N.↑; 白菜幫子 outside part of cabbage (dist. homonym 梆ᐞ子 10B.22).
幫嘴 *bangtzueei(-tzuue'l)*, v.i., speak in support of person.

§11.30 (土/一)

盍 11.30

her.

[Related 曷 41.50]

Adv. (1) (AC) why not (何不, 曷不): 盍各言爾志 (AC) why not tell me each of his ambition in life? 盍興乎來 (AC) why not rise up (in revolt), come and join us? (2) (AC) why: 盍令不行 why is order not obeyed?

盩 11.30

jou.

盩厔 *joujy*, n., name of a 縣 in Shensi.

塩 11.30

yarn.
[Pop. of 鹽 51.30]

壹 11.30

yi.

Adj. One (esp. as " spelling out " of Arabic numeral "1").

壺 11.30

hur.

N. (-'*l*) A pot: 酒壺 wine pot; 茶壺 teapot; 咖啡壺 coffee pot; 鼻烟壺 (oft. *hur'l*) snuff bottle; 尿壺 chamber pot; 瓷壺 porcelain pot; 銅壺 copper pot.

壺 盧 *hurlur*, n., a gourd, calabash (also wr. 葫蘆).

壼 11.30

kuun.
[Dist. 壺 11.30]

N. Alley inside palace: 壼政 rule by empress (cf. 閫 52B.00).

§ 11.40 (土/口)

吉 11.40

jir.

N. (1) Good luck, favorable omen: 卜吉凶 consult oracles of good or bad omen. (2) A surname.

Adj. (1) Happy, propitious, lucky, auspicious: 吉利 *-lih*, 吉慶 *-chihng*, 吉祥 *-shiarng*[1] ↓. (2) Good: 吉士 *-shyh*[1] ↓; 吉人天相 Heaven keeps the good out of harm's way. (3) Empty: 交吉 lease on property.

吉 貝 *jirbeih*, n., (bot.) Malabar kapok (silk-cotton tree) (also 木棉, 古貝).

吉 卜 賽 *jirbuusaih*, n., (translit.) Gypsies.

吉 器 *jir-chih*, n., sacrificial vessels.

吉 慶 *jir-chihng*, n., a joyous or happy occasion.

吉 期 *jir-chir*, n., wedding day.

吉 旦 *jir-dahn*, n., an auspicious day.

吉 地 *jir-dih*, n., a suitable burial ground.

吉 服 *jir-fur*, n., (1) (AC) a formal dress; (2) (AC) a sacrificial robe.

吉 光 *jirguang*, n., (AC) a mythical animal: 吉光片羽 fragments of an ancient literary or artistic work ("a few feathers of 吉光").

吉 兆 *jir-jauh*, n., a good omen.

吉 徵 *jir-jeng*, n., ＝吉兆↑.

吉 利 *jirlih*, adj., lucky, auspicious: 大吉大利 the most favorable auspices; 取個吉利兒 for the sake of good luck.

吉 禮 *jir-lii*, n., ceremonies (birthday, wedding, etc.).

吉 普 車 *jirpuuche*, n., (translit.) a jeep.

吉 人 *jir-rern*, n., a good and virtuous man.

吉 夕 *jir-shih*, n., wedding night.

吉 祥 *jirshiarng*[1] (-'*shiang*), n. & adj., luck(y), good luck.

吉 羊 *jirshiarng*[2], n. & adj., (AC) interch. 吉祥 *-shiarng*[1] ↑.

吉 席 *jir-shir*, n., (court.) phrase used in congratulatory messages to bridegroom.

吉 士 *jir-shyh*[1], n., (AC) a good and virtuous person.

吉 事 *jir-shyh*[2], n., ceremonial rites.

吉 屋 *jir-wu*, n., ("lucky house") phrase used in advertisement: 吉屋出租 house for rent.

喜 11.40

shii.

N. (1) Happiness, joy: 報喜 report on birth of a son, getting a degree, etc.; 恭喜, 道喜, 賀喜 to congratulate, -tions; 喜, 怒, 哀, 樂 joy, anger, sorrow and happiness; 雙喜 wedding. (2) Expecting a child: 有喜 (a woman) is expecting; 害喜 show symptoms of early pregnancy (morning sickness, etc.).

V.i. (1) To like, be fond of: 喜歡 -'*huan* ↓; 喜愛, 喜好 *-aih*, *-hauh* ↓; 喜新厭舊 be fickle lover, abandon the old for the new; 好大喜功 like to do grandiose things to impress people; 喜客 like to have visitors and friends; 喜賭 love gambling; 喜帶高帽 like empty titles and honors. (2) To feel happy: 可喜 likeable, (adv.) luckily; 可喜可賀 to be congratulated; see Adj. ↓.

Adj. (1) Happy, pleased: 喜出望外 pleased beyond one's expectations; 喜孜孜, 喜氣洋洋 filled with gayety; 歡天喜地 overjoyed; 喜色 a happy expression on one's face; 喜從天降 a sudden unexpected happy event; 喜事 *-shyh* ↓. (2) Concerning expectation of a child: 喜病 pregnancy, a "happy kind of illness." (3) Concerning wedding: 喜帖 card of announcement of a wedding or birthday celebration; 喜轎 bridal sedan chair; 喜堂 hall for wedding ceremony.

喜愛 *shii-aih*, v.t., to like, to love (child, swimming, detective story, etc.).

喜慶 *shii-chihng*, n., celebration of some happy event (wedding, etc.).

喜鵲 *shii-chyueh*, n., the magpie, supposed to forecast good news.

喜房 *shii-fang*, n., (1) wedding chamber; (2) a dressing room for the bride to retire during ceremony and dinner.

喜果 *shir-guoo*, n., red painted eggs, presented to friends on third day of birth of baby, also on wedding.

喜好 *shiihauh*, v.t., to love or like (skating, detective films, etc.).

喜歡 *shii'huan*, (1) v.t., to like or love (person, game); (2) adj., pleased: 他很喜歡 he is very pleased.

喜帳 *shii-jahng*, n., a long silk scroll to be hung on wall during some celebration, containing words of felicitations.

喜敬 *shiijihng*, n. & v.t., a gift on occasion; to present such gift.

喜劇 *shiijyuh*, n., comedy.

喜脈 *shii-moh*, n., pulsebeat indicating pregnancy.

喜娘 *shii-niarng*, n., a semi-professional woman attendant serving as bride's counsel on different steps of procedure.

喜容(兒) *shii-rurng('l)*, n., (1) a happy look; (2) portrait of person done while living.

喜事 *shii-shyh*, (1) n., happy occasions (birthdays, weddings, etc.); (2) v.t., to love to meddle.

喜悅 *shiiyueh*, adj., pleased.

嗸 11.40

aur.
[Var. of 嗷 40A.82]

嘉 11.40

jia.
[Cf. 佳 91A.11]

N. (AC) blessing.

V.t. Commend, admire, approve, laud: 嘉獎 *-jiaang*, 嘉納 *-nah*, 嘉許 *-shyuu*, 嘉勉 *-miaan*↓; 可嘉 deserve commendation.

Adj. Good, blessed, auspicious: 嘉會 auspicious occasion; 嘉年華會 (translit.) carnival: 嘉禮 *-lii*↓; 嘉名 good name, reputation; 嘉言懿行 wise words and exemplary conduct.

嘉賓 *jia bin*, n., highly welcome guests.

嘉穀 *jiaguu*, n., (euphem.) paddy rice.

嘉禾 *jiaher*, n., (euphem.) an ear of growing grain; 嘉禾章 formerly, a government decoration.

嘉惠 *jiahueih*, v.t., to benefit: 嘉惠後學, 嘉惠士林 benefit young students, the scholars.

嘉獎 *jiajiaang*, v.t., to praise or reward (s.o.) by superiors.

嘉重 *jiajuhng*, v.t., look upon with favor, commend highly.

嘉貺 *jia-kuahng*, n., (court.) highly valued gifts.

嘉禮 *jialii*, n., wedding, marriage ceremony.

嘉勉 *jiamiaan*, v.t., urge (s.o.) to greater efforts with words of encouragement.

嘉謨 *jiamor*, n., sage counsel, also *-your*↓.

嘉納 *jianah*, v.t., accept (views, suggestions, advice).

嘉釀 *jia-niahng*, n., vintage or quality wine.

嘉耦 *jia-oou*[1], n., a happily married couple.

嘉偶 *jiaoou*[2], n., ditto.

嘉尚 *jiashahng*, v.t. & adj., commend(able), praise (worthy).

嘉羞 *jia-shiou*, n., (food) delicacies.

嘉許 *jiashyuu*, v.t., show appreciation for, be pleased with, praise by superior.

嘉歲 *jia-sueih*, n., year of bumper harvest.

嘉餚 *jia-yaur*, n., choice food, dainty dishes.

嘉猷 *jiayour*, n., see *-mor*↑.

磬 11.40

chihng.

N. (1) An L-shaped musical stone, suspended from above, with a definite pitch; hence 磬折 hunchbacked like an L-shaped musical stone. (2) A metal piece in temples suspended and struck as signal for dinner, prayer service, etc.

Adj. Empty, u. f. 罄 11.21.

磬口梅 *chihngkoou-meir*, n., a kind of plum.

磬控 *chihngkuhng*, v.t., (AC) tighten or relax reins on a horse.

謦 11.40

chihng.

謦欬 *chihngkaih*, v.i., (AC) to make noise or make a lot of noise: 久違謦欬 (LL) have not heard from you for a long time.

§11.41 (土/図)

者 11.41

jee (oft. *-'je*, unaccented).
[Gen. pop. 者 without dot]

N. A surname.

Fin. part. 告夫二三子者 (AC) am telling a few of you disciples; used in Yuarn drama, indicating actor's movements: 左右放了他

者 set him free (said in an order).

Pron. (1) Person(s) who (used like "-er" in "worker," "reporter"): 記者 reporter; 作者, 讀者 writer, reader; 死者 those who are dead, he who is dead; 長者 an elder; (except in regular words like 記者, 讀者, 長者 above) oft. pr. *'je*: 來者 those who come, also bearer of this letter; 來者不拒 all visitors are welcome; 老者少者 the old and the young; 大者, 小者 the big and the small; 佳者, 劣者 the good and the bad; 近者遠者 those near by and those from afar; 賢者不惑 the wise man has no perplexities; 能者 (or 賢者) 多勞 (complim.) the able ones are always busy; 愚而自用者 those who are ignorant and do not know it. (2) Denoting a portion: 事其大夫之賢者 serve the wise one among the lords; 友士之仁者 befriend the real persons among the scholars. (3) (LL) oft. coupled with 也 in . . . 者, . . . 也 this word . . . means . . . : 庠者, 養也, the word 庠 (high school) means to cultivate; 校者, 敎也 this word 校 (school) means to teach. (4) "What is": 敬啟者 what I want to say is this (regular opening in letter); 再者 "another thing" (regular formula, equiv. "P. S." in letters); 所要者 what is important is that (preceding a clause).

Adj. (MC in vern. literature) this, these: 者賊無賴 this bastard is devoid of shame; 者箇 this one.

Excl. (MC vern.) 者, 者 "yes, yes!" (also wr. 嗻).

耆 11.41

chir.

N. (LL) an old man, over sixty or seventy.

Adj. (1) (LL) elderly, venerable. (2) (AC) brave.

耆艾 *chir-aih*, n., (LL) old people.

耆舊 *chirjiouh*, n., (LL) old people, of the elder generation.

耆老 *chirlaau*, n., people of elder generation. 「scholar.

耆儒 *chirrur*, n., old respected

耆碩 *chirshyr*, n., respectable old people, old scholar.

耆宿 *chirsuh*, n., see *-rur* ↑.

馨 11.41

shin (also *shing*).

Adj. & n. (1) Fragrant, -ce: 馨香禱祝 this I pray with burning of incense; 芳馨 fragrance. (2) (Anc. dial.) such, like in 寧馨兒 such a (bright) child; 爾馨語 such talk (preserved in Shanghai dial. as 那馨 *na-hang*).

瞽 11.41

guu.

N. A blind person.

Adj. (1) Blind: 瞽者 a blind person. (2) (LL) stupid, absurd: 瞽說, 瞽言 absurdities, foolish gossip; 瞽議 foolish discussions.

§11.50 (土/㇆)

考 11.50

kaau.

[Sometimes u.f. 攷]

N. (1) Deceased father or grandfather: 考妣 deceased father and mother, esp. on tombstones; 先考 deceased father; 先祖考 deceased grandfather: 顯考 the late illustrious father; 如喪考妣 (contempt.) wear a miserable face, as if at parents' graves. (2) Old age: 壽考 longevity.

V.i. & t. To test, examine: 招考 hold entrance examinations; 應考 take examinations; 月考, 大考 monthly test, year-end examinations; 考中 (pr. *juhng*), 考取, 考上了 pass examination; 聯考 national examinations for entrance to colleges; 主考, 考官 formerly, chief examiner at civil examinations; 監考 to supervise, -sor, at examinations; 考場, 考院 examination hall; 考題 subject of examination; 考卷 examination papers. (2) To investigate (the past, for errors): 考古, 考核, 考證, 考訂, 考察, 考據 *-guu, -her, -jehng, -dihng, -char*[2], *-jyuh* ↓; 參考 reference, look up reference; 查無可考 no evidence available.

考查 *kaauchar*[1], v.t., investigate, study (facts, conditions).

考察 *kaauchar*[2] v.t., investigate, study: 考察教育 (工業) study conditions of education (industry) at a place usu. foreign; 考察團 group of people sent abroad to study conditions and progress (industrial, educational) mission.

考求 *kaauchiour*, v.i. & t., study (conditions, origin, relations): 考求病原 study cause of disease.

考勤 *kaauchirn*, v.i., to grade work of individuals in organizations.

考訂 *kaaudihng*, v.i. & t., study and settle problems of age, authorship, textual differences; research on scientific problems.

考古 *kaurguu*, n. & v.i., archaeology, do archaeological work; 考古家 archaeologist; 考古學 the science of archaeology.

考核 (覈) *kaauher*, v.t., officially examine and pass on (results,

亅	小	⺊	十	土	ナ	廾	㔾	丨	一	丅	フ	口	囚	冈	㇆	厂	尸	亠	广	宀	丶	乚	弋	心	八	人	乂	乛	丿	𠂉	く
00	01	02	10	11	12	20	21	22	30	31	32	40	41	42	50	51	52	60	61	62	63	70	71	72	80	81	82	83	90	91	92	93

plans, reports, budgets).

考證 *kaaujehng*, v.i. & n., (do) research, study of data, higher textual criticism.

考績 *kaauji*, v.i. & n., examine (-ation) at end of semester or year; grades given.

考校 *kaaujiauh*, v.i., research and compare (texts, variations, etc.).

考究 *kaaujiouh*, (1) v.i., examine carefully: 考究原因 study cause; (2) adj., (-'*jiou*) fastidious, careful; 穿得很考究 dresses very carefully; 考究吃 be a gourmet.

考據 *kaaujyuh*, v.i. & n., see -*jehng* ↑.

考慮 *kaaulyuh*, v.i. & t., consider, weigh (problem in mind): 正在考慮 is considering (a decision), is being considered; 未曾考慮 not yet considered.

考試 *kaaushyh*, v.i. & t. & n., examine (-ations), tests; 考試院 one of the five *yuan* or branch of Chin. government in charge of examinations for civil service.

考選 *kaurshyuaan*, v.i., select by examination.

考問 *kaauwehn*, v.i. & t., discuss problems of knowledge by interrogation, cf. 拷ᴬ問 10A.50.

考驗 *kaauyahn*, v.i. & t. & n., test: 經不起考驗 cannot stand the test (of time); 時代考驗青年 the age is putting the young men to the test.

考語 *kauryuu* (-'*yu*), n., remark giving opinion on test paper; written comments showing approbation or disapproval.

耇 11.50

goou.

Adj. Old and haggard.

勢 11.50

shyh.

N. (1) Force, power: 勢力 -*lih*[1] ↓; 權勢 power of position; 威勢 pomp and power; 勢燄薰天 one's position and power dominate the world ("flame darkens the sky"); 趨炎附勢 cater to those in power; 仗勢 rely on the protection of s.o. in power; 狗仗人勢 said of servant ("dog") bullying others because of master's power and position. (2) Direction and force of movement: 火勢 the way fire spreads; 水勢 the force and direction of the current; 手勢 hand gesture, way of striking; 姿勢 posture, grace of movement (standing, walking, sitting). (3) Situation in combat: 得勢 successful, gains advantage in combat; 勢均力敵 their strength and advantage of situation match each other; 勢窮力竭 in a deplorable plight and powerless; 攻勢, 兵勢 force of attacking army; 勢如破竹 smashes into enemy territory "like splitting bamboo"—without effort. (4) Situation in gen.: 情勢, 形勢 situation, the way things look; 地勢, 山勢 the lay of the land, mountains; 事勢, 大勢 the trend of events; 乘勢, 趁勢 take advantage of situation; 大勢不佳 situation deplorable, not tenable; 勢難兼顧 situation is such one cannot look after both at the same time; 勢不兩立 one of the two must be destroyed; 勢成騎虎 in the position of one riding a tiger—unable to get down and dangerous to go on; 勢所必至 is bound to come; 勢將, 勢必 it will, it certainly will, by force of circumstances. (5) (LL) male genitals: 去其勢 to castrate.

勢力 *shyhlih*[1], n., (1) force of strike; (2) political influence or influence of riches: 勢力範圍 sphere of influence.

勢利 *shyhlih*[2], adj., snobbish; 勢利眼 snobbery, judging people by wealth and power.

勢派(兒) *shyhpaih*(-*pah'l*), n., style of personality; pomp and circumstance.

勢頭 *shyhtour*, n., prestige, power, the way things look.

勢要 *shyh-yauh*, n., those in power.

 11.50

juh.

V.i. (AC) fly aloft.

鷙 11.50

jyh.

N. A vulture.

Adj. Ferocious.

§11.63 (土/丶)

煮 11.63

juu.

V.t. To cook, spec. to boil or stew: 煮飯 cook rice; 煮茗 make tea; 煮藥 stew medicine; 清煮 boil in water without garnish; 煮爛了 boiled very soft; 煮熟了 done in cooking; 煮老了 overdone in boiling; 煮豆燃萁 (allu.) boil beans with beanstalks—reference to fight among brothers; 煮鶴焚琴 reference to rich vulgarian who cooked the crane for meat and burned a stringed instrument for fuel—inappreciative of art or beauty.

熱 11.63

reh.

Adj. (1) Hot (opp. 冷 cold): 冷熱(無常) (lit.) (of weather) marked by sudden changes in temperature, (fig.) (blowing) hot and cold; 炎熱 sweltering; 悶熱 sultry; 躁熱 sizzling; 熱浪 a hot wave in summer; 熱天(兒) hot weather; 大熱天 a very hot day; 熱兒 hot, summer heat; 好熱 terribly hot; 熱死(了) unbearably hot, die of sunstroke; 熱昏了頭 (lit.) faint from overexposure to heat, (fig.) become muddle-headed through overexcitement; 熱呼呼的 very hot; 熱烘烘的 red-hot; 熱剌忽喇 (of the human skin) burning-hot; 熱騰騰 steaming-hot (coffee, tea, rice); 滾熱 boiling-hot; 熱飯, 熱湯, 熱菜 rice, soup, meat (fish, vegetable) served hot; 熱湯兒麵 noodles in soup; 熱一熱 put in (over) cooker to heat; 加熱 to heat; 熱炕 a brick-bed that can be warmed by a fire from below in winter; 熱泉 hot springs; 熱霧 hot, steamy vapors; 受熱 heat stroke; 傳熱 to conduct heat; 發熱 give off heat, have (run) a fever. (2) Showing warmth of feeling: 熱心 *-shin*↓; 熱腸 enthusiastic, zealous, ardent, sincere; 熱心腸(兒) ditto; 熱誠 *-cherng*↓; 熱忱 zeal, enthusiasm; 熱望 intense longing, desire; 熱愛 ardent love; 熱情 *-chirng*↓; 熱烈 *-lieh*↓; 熱狂 fanatic; 狂熱 fanaticism; 熱淚盈眶 eyes glistening with hot tears; 打得火熱 (of two persons) passionately attached to each other; 熾熱 passionate, sincere, enthusiastic, hearty; 熱熟 on very familiar terms; 親熱 on very intimate terms, closely attached to one another; 親爹熱娘 loving parents. (3) Restless: 熱中 *-jung*↓; 熱剌剌 (*lah*) 的 anxious, restive, impatient.

Adv. Immediately: 趁熱 do s.t. right away: 趁熱打鐵 strike while the iron is hot; 又不趁熱趕將去 haven't gone there at once.

熱痺 *reh-bih*, n., (bot.) heat rigor.
熱病 *reh-bihng*, n., any disease causing a fever.
熱誠 *rehcherng*, adj., ＝熱心 *-shin*↓.
熱氣 *reh-chih*, n., hot air, short-lived enthusiasm.
熱情 *rehchirng*, n., passionate feelings or love, fervor, ardor.
熱帶 *rehdaih*, n., (geog.) the torrid zone, the tropics; 熱帶魚 *--yur*, n., tropical fish.
熱電 *reh-diahn*, n., (phy.) thermoelectricity.
熱度 *rehduh*, n., temperature: 五分鐘熱度 short-lived enthusiasm.
熱毒 *rehdur*, n., (Chin. med.) carbuncles.
熱和 *reh'huo*, adj., (1) giving off a moderate degree of heat; (2) friendly, genial; (3) affectionate.
熱着 *reh'jau*, v.i., fall victim to heatstroke.
熱中 *rehjung*, (1) adj., restless, restive, impatient; (2) v.t., to hanker for (official preferment).
熱客 *reh-keh*, n., (1) a sycophant, a toady, a servile flatterer; (2) a frequent caller; (3) formerly, a man infatuated with a prostitute.
熱量 *reh-liahng*, n., (phys.) quantity of heat measured in calories.
熱烈 *rehlieh*, adj., (of feelings) warm, passionate, fervent, ardent.
熱力 *reh-lih*, n., thermodynamic energy; 熱力學 thermodynamics.
熱門(兒) *reh-mern(-mer'l)*, n. & adj., (1) n., any commodity in great demand; (2) adj., popular: 熱門人物 persons who make front-page news; 熱門音樂 popular music, musical hit.
熱鬧 *reh'nau*, adj., (1) jolly (party, celebrations); (2) noisy, boisterous; 熱鬧兒 (a) a noisy fun in which many people take part; (b) stage shows and stunts: 他家辦生日, 有甚麽熱鬧兒沒有 is there any interesting show at the birthday celebrations in his house? (c) merrymaking: 咱們大家湊個熱鬧兒吧 let's have some fun together!
熱喪 *reh-sang*, v.i., be newly bereaved of one's parent.
熱線 *rehshiahn*, n., hot line (telephone line between White House and Kremlin).
熱孝 *reh-shiauh*, adj., in mourning.
熱心 *rehshin*, adj., enthusiastic, ardent, zealous, earnest.
熱水瓶 *rehshueei-pirng*, n., hot water bottle, thermos flask.
熱血 *reh-shyueh*, adj., (1) red-blooded, high-spirited; (2) warm-blooded, as mammals and birds (opp. 冷血 cold-blooded, as fishes and reptiles).
熱學 *reh-shyuer*, n., (phys.) thermotics, the science of heat.
熱罨法 *rehyarnfaa*, n., (med.) hot compress (also 溫罨法).

熹 11.63

shi.

[Var. 熺]

Adj. (1) (AC) warm; hot. (2) (AC) prosperous (cf. 熙): 熹盛.

熹微 *shiweir*, adj., diffuse (light of daybreak).

燾 11.63

taur (also *dauh*).

V.t. (1) (AC) cover like a canopy (var. 幬). (2) (AC) cast light over: 無不覆燾 (中庸) all fall under the canopy (of moral laws).

鼕 11.63

dung.

Adj. 鼕鼕 *dungdung*, descriptive of sound of gongs, drums.

§11.70 (土/乚)

老 11.70

laau.

N. (1) Abbr. for Laotse, the founder of Taoism: 老莊 Laotse and Chuangtse; 佛老 Buddhism and Taoism; 黃老 (之術) the art of government according to the principle of inaction ascribed to 黃帝 (Huangti) and Laotse. (2) The old people: 老幼 the young and the old; 一家老少 all members of family; 敬老尊賢 honor the aged and the wise. (3) Old age: 養老 pension or support for old age; 告老 retire on old age. (4) Familiar term of respect for elderly people, usu. prefixed by a character chosen from the personal name: thus, 張石湖 would be 石老; 此老 (familiarly referring to) a grown-up. (5) A surname.

V.i. (1) (AC) retire from official service. (2) Become old: 老去 have become old; 一年年地老起來了 show signs of age year by year. (3) To honor the aged: 老吾老以及人之老 to honor the aged of other people, as we honor our own.

Adj. (1) Old in age: 老人 *-rern*; 老翁 *-weng*; 老年人 *-niarnrern*; 老叟 *-soou*; 老媼 *-aau*; 老嫗 *-yuh*↓; 老先生 an old gentleman; 你老人家 (affectionately to old people) you; 老公公 a venerable old man, also formerly, a eunuch; 老婆婆 an old lady; 老嬤嬤 an old maidservant; 老夫人 an old lady of higher rank than oneself; 老丈人 father-in-law; 老前輩 one's senior in age or position; 老一輩 the older generation; 老一代 ditto; 老輩 *-beih*↓; 老氣橫秋 (derog.) showing self-importance of the aged; 倚老賣老 capitalize on being advanced in age; 老當益壯 more vigorous with age; 老淚縱橫 weep unashamedly (said of old people); 老景淒涼 a lonely, dreary life in old age; 老蚌生珠 (of old woman long past the childbearing age) give birth to a child; 老牛舐犢 dote on one's children; 老牛破車 an old cow pulling a rickety cart. (2) Shameless, thick-skinned: 老着臉(皮) doing s.t. without showing embarrassment. (3) Experienced: 老行家 an old hand; 老把勢 a person skilled in some craft or technique; 老手 *-shoou*, 老將 *-jiahng*↓; 老於此道 well-experienced in this matter; 老吏 an experienced judge; 老馬識途 (of experienced people) know the ropes; 老驥伏櫪 able men tied down to a routine post; 老謀深算 make every move only after mature deliberation. (3) Of many years' standing, lasting for many years: 老交情 friend(ship) of long standing; 老世交 friend(ship) for many generations; 老相好 old sweetheart; 老相識 an old acquaintance; 老主顧, 老客人, 老顧客 an old customer; 老毛病 a chronic ailment, an inveterate habit; 老家人 an old employee; 老街坊 old neighbors; 老鄰居 ditto; 老朋友, 老同學, 老同事 old friend, schoolmate, colleague; 老仇敵, 老對頭 long-standing enemy; 老尺, 老秤 old measure of length, weight; 老酒 (vintage) wine; 老式樣, 老方式, 老樣(子)(兒) old-fashioned; 老規矩 traditional rules; 老花樣, 老方法 old methods; 老題材 a stale topic or subject; 老故事 an often-told tale; 老貨兒 old stuff. (4) Adj. adjunct denoting respect, familiarity or without special meaning: 老伯, 老大哥, 老大妞 (court.) my dear uncle, elder brother, sister; 老兄 *-shyung*↓; 老弟 *-dih*↓; 老賢侄, 老侄 my good nephew (vocative); 老張, 老李 old Chang, Li, as terms of endearment or familiarity; 老大 *-dah*↓; 老二 (of brothers, sisters, or close friends) the number two; 老妹子, 老兄弟 my dear younger sister, brother; 老鄉 *-shiang*↓; 老雕 the hawk, the vulture; 老鷹 *-ying*↓; 老虎 *-huu*↓; 老鼠 *-shuu*↓; 老天(爺) *-tian(yer)*↓; 老拳 fists: 飽以老拳 give (s.o.) a sound beating. (5) (Derog.) useless, decrepit, old fashioned: 老怪物 an old eccentric; 老廢物 a good-for-nothing; 老背晦, 老糊塗 a senile person, senility; 老不死 a person who has outlived his usefulness; 老不修 an old debauchee; 老八板兒 an obstinate conformist; 老古板 an ultra-conservative; 老古董 (derog.) a museum piece; 老頑固 a bigot, a die-hard; 老腐敗 decadent, old and useless; 老派兒 *-paih'l*↓; 老面皮 *-miahnpir*↓; 老臉皮 thick-skinned. (6) Hardened (opp. 嫩 tender): 老筍 tough bamboo shoots; 老豆腐 hardened bean curd; 鷄子(牛肉)老了 the chicken (beef) is overdone or too tough; 炸老一點 please have it well-done; 老油條 well fried fritters of twisted dough, (fig.) a hard-boiled and slippery person (=老油子 *-yourtz*↓). (7) Steady, trustworthy: 老實 *-shyr*↓; 老成 *-cherng*↓; 老聲老氣 speaking with a steady voice; 聲音蒼老 sure and steady in intonation. (8) (Peking dial.) youngest: 老兒子, 老妹妹 the youngest son, sister; also see 老子 *-tz*↓; 老么 *-yau*↓. (9) (Of color) dark, deep: 老綠 deep green; 老紅 dark red; 老色 a deep color.

老媼 ***laur-aau***, n., an old woman, esp. servant.

老板 ***laurbaan***[1], n., (1) the owner of a shop or store; (2) (court.) a businessman; (3) (court.) an actor; (4) an old edition of Chinese books printed from woodblock; 老板娘 (Shanghai dial.) the wife of a shop owner.

老闆 ***laurbaan***[2], n., the owner of a shop or store (=老板 (1)↑).

老鴇子 ***laurbaau(tz)***, n., a procuress (=鴇母), woman keeper of prostitutes.

老伴(兒) ***laaubahn*** (***-bah'l***), n., the husband or wife of an old couple.

老梆子 ***laaubangtz***, n., (abusive) old duffer, doddering old fool (also 老梆殼).

老本 ***laurbeen***, n., the trunk or main stem of a tree; 老本兒 (a) the capital invested in some enterprise; (b) an old edition.

老輩(兒) *laaubeih* (*-beh'l*), n., (1) a person of higher rank than oneself; (2) the older generation.

老綳 *laau'beng*, adj., old (incrusted scar); (2) experienced and steady person.

老表 *laurbiaau*, n., a cousin, the son of one's uncle or aunt.

老病 *laau-bihng*, (1) adj., old and sick; (2) n., a chronic ailment, an inveterate habit.

老兵 *laaubing*, n., an old soldier: 文藝界一老兵 a veteran in literary circles.

老伯 *laaubor*, n., uncle, (court.) a friend of one's father or father of one's friend.

老巢 *laau-chaur*, n., a robber's den.

老秤 *laau-chehng*, n., the old steelyard or scale, now not in general use.

老成 *laaucherng*, adj., (of person) well-experienced and steady; (2) (of style of writing) showing easy command of words.

老搶兒 *laurchiaang'l*, n., (coll.) a robber, bandit, also 老千(dial.) a swindler.

老氣 *laauchih*, adj., (1) 老氣橫秋 self-important, pompously conceited; (2) (of dress) old fashioned; (3) (of color) plain or dark.

老親 *laau-chin*, n., (1) parents; (2) relatives of long standing.

老膗 *laauchuaih*, n., (1) fat as opposed to muscles; (2) a fatty.

老處女 *laau-chuhnyuu*, n., a spinster, an old maid.

老大 *laaudah*, n., (1) a person of advanced age; (2) the eldest brother; (3) a gangster leader; 老大的 *--'de*, adv., very, extremely, exceedingly: 心裏老大的不願意 extremely unwilling.

老旦 *laau-dahn*, n., (Chin. opera) actor playing the part of an old woman.

老呆 *laaudai*, n., a fool, a simpleton (also wr. 老獃).

老到 *laaudauh*¹, adj., experienced and trustworthy; (of style) masterly.

老道 *laaudauh*², n., a Toaist priest (in address or self-reference).

老爹 *laaudie*, n., (1) one's father; (2) (court. address) venerable elderly person.

老底 *laurdii*, n., (1) ground one relies for upon support: 我心裏有老底, 所以一點不害怕 I was not a bit afraid, for I knew I was on firm ground; (2) one's past or background, esp. weaknesses: 你的老底全在我心裏那 I know your past only too well! 老底兒(子) *-diee'l* (*-tz*) n., (a) the family estate; (b) the status of one's family.

老弟 *laaudih*, n., (1) (vocative) my dear younger brother; (2) (vocative) my dear friend, a term used by a teacher to address his pupil (esp. formal or in correspondence).

老斗 *laurdoou*, n., formerly, an actor's or actress's lover.

老兒 *laau'el*, n., (usu. MC) an old man.

老佛爺 *laaufor'ye*, n., (1) (Budd.) popular name for the Buddha; (2) (Manchu court.) the queen mother or the emperor's father.

老夫 *laaufu*, n., (1) my old self, a term used by old men; (2) old husband; 老夫子 *--tzyy*, n., (a) formerly, tutor in a private school; (b) formerly, a bureaucrat.

老婦 *laaufuh*, n., (1) my old self, a term used by old women; (2) an old woman.

老趕 *laurgaan*, (1) n., a person utterly ignorant and innocent; (2) adj., ignorant, bungling and ridiculous.

老乾 *laau'gan*, adj., (of dress and general appearance) plain and simple: 打扮的很老乾 dresses very simply; 老乾兒 formerly, a woman servant.

老哥 *laauge*, n., my elder brother, also used among friends.

老根兒 *laauge'l*, n., see *-dii* ↑.

老鴰 *laau'gua*, n., pop. name for the crow.

老姑兒 *laaugu'l*, n., (Peking dial.) the youngest aunt (also 老娘兒); 老姑娘 (a) (pr. *-'gu'niang*) (Peking dial.) the youngest daughter; (b) (pr. *-gu'niang*) a spinster, an old maid.

老公 *laaugung*, n., (1) an old man; pop. name for husband; (2) (pr. *-'gung*) a eunuch: 老公公 *laaugung'gung*, n., Santa Claus.

老好子 *laurhaautz*, n., a good-natured person.

老漢 *laau-hahn*, n., (1) an old chap; (2) (used by an old man in self-reference).

老花眼 *laauhua-yaan*, n., (med.) farsightedness: 老花眼鏡 glasses for the farsighted.

老話兒 *laauhuah'l*, n., (1) what has happened in bygone days; (2) an old expression: 說句老話兒 to use an old phrase.

老猾 *laauhuar*, adj., as in 老猾巨奸 old, crafty person, great hypocrite.

老貨 *laauhuoh*, n., (contempt.) old fellow.

老虎 *laurhuu*, n., the tiger; 老虎攤兒 a stall where faked objects, esp. of art, are palmed off as genuine; 老虎鉗 a vise; 老虎豆 a kind of spotted beans (also 老皮豆); 老虎眼 a kind of sour date.

老丈 *laaujahng*, n., (court.) a venerable gentleman.

老者 *laurjee*, n., the old, an elderly person.

老家 *laaujia*, n., (1) one's old home, home town; (2) (vulg.) the nether world: 送你回老家 I'll send you to hell; 老家子 (pop.) the sparrow.

老將 *laaujiahng*, n., (1) an old officer; (2) a veteran: 球壇老將 a veteran ballplayer.

老酒 *laurjioou*, n., vintage wine, esp. that made in Shaoshing.

老舊 *laaujiouh*, adj., old and worn-out, old-fashioned.

老鷄頭 *laaujitour*, n., (bot.) the foxnut, pop. name for *Euryale ferox*.

老準兒 *laurjuoo'l*, n., (1) a firm and unshakable resolution; (2) see *-dii* ↑.

老拙 *jaaujuor*, n., (1) (term of

老 self-disparagement used by an old person) "my clumsy self"; (2) see *-tsu'l* ↓.

老直 *laaujyr*, n., an honest and frank person.

老辣 *laaulah*, (1) adj., efficient but unscrupulous; (2) n., such person.

老來 *laaulai*, adv., in one's old age: 老來貧 live in poverty in old age; 老來少 old in age but young at heart; 老來俏 (of woman) becomes prettier as one gets older.

老郎神 *Laaularng-shern*, n., formerly, the god of actors.

老老 *laau'lau*, n., (＝姥姥) (1) maternal grandmother; (2) a midwife.

老臉 *laurliaan*, (1) adj., shameless (also 老臉皮); (2) n., (Chin. opera) an actor with a painted face, generally, a heroic character (another name for 花臉).

老練 *laauliahn*, adj., having rich and varied experience.

老例(兒) *laaulih(-lieh'l)*, n., an old precedent: 照老例辦 follow the old precedent.

老琉璃 *laauliour'li*, n., pop. name for the dragonfly.

老媽(子)(兒) *laauma(tz)('l)*, n., a maidservant, usu. middle-aged.

老邁 *laaumaih*, adj., advanced in age.

老眊 *laaumauh*[1], adj., (1) dim-sighted; (2) ＝老耄↓.

老耄 *laaumauh*[2], adj., senile, enfeebled through age.

老面皮 *laaumiahnpir*, n., a shameless person.

老命 *laaumihng*, n., (coll.) one's life: 拚了這條老命 I'll fight with all my life; 要你老命 I'll finish you off.

老衲 *laaunah*, n., (self-reference) an old monk.

老娘兒 *laauniar'l*, n., (Peking dial.) the youngest aunt.

老年人 *laauniarn-rern*, n., a person of advanced age.

老娘 *laauniarng*, n., (1) one's mother (sometimes in self-reference) your mother; (2) (*-'niang*) a midwife; (North China) maternal grandmother; 老娘婆 *--por*, n., a midwife.

老奴 *laaunur*, n., (1) (old usage) an old servant; (term of self-disparagement) your old servant; (2) (derog. reference to) an old man.

老派兒 *laaupaih'l*, n., an old-fashioned person; a conservative.

老牌(兒)(子) *laaupair(-par'l)(tz)*, n., (of goods) an old and well-known brand.

老婆 *laau'po*, n., (coll.) wife: 老婆孩子 wife and children; 討老婆 marry a wife; 老婆兒 *-por'l*, n., (a) an elderly woman; (b) one's wife; (c) a maidservant.

老圃 *laurpuu*, n., (AC) an experienced gardener.

老譜兒 *laurpuu'l*, n., traditional rules or methods.

老人 *laaurern*, n., (a) an old man or woman; (b) parents; 老人班 the old folks; 入了老人班 have joined the ranks of the aged; 老人家 (1) (court.) one's own or another person's parents; 我們老人家, 你們老人家 our, your parents; (2) (court.) a venerable old man: 你老人家.

老弱 *laau-rouh*, adj. & n., (1) aged and weak: 老弱殘兵 remanents of a rabble army; (2) the old and the young in gen.

老少年 *laaushauhniarn*, n., (1) (bot.) another name for the red amaranth (紅莧); (2) a young head on old shoulders.

老身 *laaushen*, n., an elderly man or woman referring to self.

老生 *laausheng*, n., (1) a scholar of an advanced age; (2) (opera) an elderly character.

老鄉 *laaushiang*, n., (1) a person from the same country, province, town, etc. as oneself; (2) my dear sir! (term used in addressing a stranger).

老朽 *laaushiou*, n., (1) an old and useless person; (2) (term of self-disparagement) my old and worthless self.

老手(兒) *laurshoou('l)*, n., a person with rich experience: 個中老手 an old hand in . . . .

老壽星 *laaushoushing*, n., (1) (court.) a venerable old man or woman, esp. at birthday or wedding parties; (2) an idol with the likeness of an old man.

老鼠 *laurshuu*, n., the mouse, rat.

老師 *laaushy*, n., (1) (court.) a teacher; (2) formerly, a term of respect as applied by the examinees to the examiner; (3) a teacher; 老師傅 (a) an Islamic church officer; (b) a master craftsman in any craft.

老式 *laaushyh*, adj. & n., (1) old style or method; (2) the original form.

老實 *laaushyr*, (1) n., an honest and trustworthy person; (2) adj., (pr. *-'shy*) prudent and reliable; simple-minded and guileless; silent and unobtrusive.

老兄 *laaushyung*, n., (1) my own humble self (used by an elder brother in self-reference); (2) my dear friend.

老叟 *laur-soou*, n., (LL) an old man.

老宿 *laau-suh*, n., a high priest, a revered scholar.

老胎 *laau'tai*, n., the youngest among blood relations of same or younger generation (also 老台).

老態 *laautaih*, n., the manners of an aged person: 老態龍鍾 doddering old age; old men's manners or appearance.

老太太 *laautaih'tai*, n., (1) the mother of one's employer; (2) one's own mother or the mother of another person; (3) a term of respect for an old lady; (4) an old woman: 老太婆 (coll.) an old woman.

老太爺 *laautaihyer*, n., (1) the father of one's employer; (2) one's own father or the father of another person; (3) a term of respect for an old gentleman.

老饕 *laautau*, n., a glutton.

老天(爺) *laautian(yer)*, n., Heaven personified: (1) 我的老天 my God! good heavens! (2) 老天有眼 there is divine justice after all!

老頭(兒) *laautour('l)*, n., (1) an aged person; (2) one's own father or the father of another person, a rather informal and familiar term, see *-tourtz* ↓; 老頭兒樂 *---leh*, n., (a) (bot.) a kind of melon, so called probably because of its tenderness so much liked by the elderly people; (b) a kind of winter shoes with cotton padding; 老頭子 *-tourtz*, n., (a) (contempt.) an old fellow; (b) (familiar) one's hubby or "old man"; (c) a gangster leader.

老傖 *laautsang*, n., (contempt.) a worthless fellow.

老醋 *laautsuh*, n., old vinegar.

老粗兒 *laautsu'l*, n., a roughneck, a bumptious fellow.

老葱 *laautsung*, n., (bot.) big onions (opp. 小葱).

老子 *laautz*, n., (1) (familiar) daddy; (2) "your dad," meaning the speaker himself, a term used to show contempt for the one spoken to; (3) (pr. *-tzyy*) 老子 Laotse the philosopher.

老早 *laurtzaau*, adv., very early: 老早起來 got up very early; long ago: 那信老早寄出去了 that letter was posted long ago.

老祖兒 *laautzuu'l*, n., great-grandfather; 老祖宗 sometimes used of grandparents with great respect.

老總(兒) *laurtzuung('l)*, n., (1) the boss; (2) (court.) formerly, any soldier in uniform.

老翁 *laauweng*, n., (1) (poet.) an old man; (2) father.

老物 *laauwuh*, n., (contempt.) the old fool.

老鴉 *laauya*, n., the crow (=烏鴉).

老醃兒 *laauya'l*, n., (1) anything salted and preserved; (2) salted eggs.

老么 *laauyau*, n., (of brothers, sisters or close friends) the youngest one.

老謠 *laauyaur*, n., a rumor, hearsay, gossip.

老爺 *laau'ye*, n., (1) (court.) formerly, any government official or a member of the gentry; (2) formerly, the master (opp. 僕人 a servant); (3) (court.) formerly, husband; (4) (familiar) maternal grandfather; (5) pop. name for the god 關羽 (關老爺); 老爺子 (--'*tz*,) (a) one's father; (b) "dad," a respectful form of address to elder persons; (c) (court.) any old man; 老爺兒 (--'*l*), pop. name for the sun; 老爺車 jalopy.

老鷹 *laauying*, n., the eagle.

老營兒 *laauyirng'l*, n., (orig.) a barracks or headquarters; base of operations of bandits.

老油子 *laauyourtz*, n., (contempt.) an "old fox."

老遠 *lauryuaan*, adj. & adv., from afar.

老嫗 *laauyuh*, n., an old woman.

老運 *laauyuhn*, n., (horoscope) good luck in one's old age: 老運亨通 have good luck in old age; 走老運 be lucky in old age.

堯 11.70

yaur.

N. Name of idealized emperor (2357–2255 B.C.).

翹 11.70

chiaur(**chiauh*).

N. (1) (AC) tail feather. (2) (AC) a woman's hair decoration.

V.t. To lift up, to turn up: 翹首 to crane one's neck; 翹首而望 lift up one's head in hope; 翹足而待 curl up one's leg and wait—anticipate arriving in a short while; 翹舌頭 curl up one's tongue.

V.i. (**chiauh*) To stick up, bend upwards, curl up: 板凳兩頭翹起來 bench curls up at both ends; 頭髮翹起來 hair sticks up; 翹嘴巴 to pout (in displeasure).

Adj. (1) Bent, upturned: 晒翹了 (a board) warped from exposure to the sun. (2) (**chiauh*) See *-biahntz* ↓.

翹辮子 **chiauhbiahntz*, v.i., (sl.) to kick the bucket, die ("queue curled up").

翹翹 *chiaurchiaur*, adj., (AC) (1) tall; (2) hanging dangerously; (3) (LL) distinguished: 翹翹人才 distinguished, talented man.

翹企 *chiaurchih*, v.i., to hope ("on tiptoe"), see *-wahng* ↓.

翹楚 *chiaurchuu*, adj., outstanding (men, talents).

翹關 *chiaurguan*, v.i., (AC) a contest of lifting weights.

翹棱 *chiaur'leng*, v.i., become warped from exposure.

翹秀 *chiaurshiouh*, adj., see *-chuu* ↑.

翹思 *chiaursy*, v.i., to remember (person) from a distance.

翹材 *chiaur-tsair*, n., outstanding talent.

翹望 *chiaurwahng*, v.i., to hope earnestly.

壳 11.70

chiauh.

[Var. of 殼 11S.82]

耄 11.70

mauh.

Adj. Very old (person, age), senile: 老耄 senile; 老耄之年, 耄齡, 耄期 senile age, also venerable age.

耄耋 *mauhdier*, adj., (AC) very advanced in age (耋 over 70, 耄 over 80 or 90).

耄耄 *mauhmauh*, adj., old and shrivelled in appearance.

§ 11.71 (土/弋)

栽 11.71

tzai.

栽 載 哉 戴 裁

V.i. & t. (1) V.i., tumble, trip, fall: 栽跟頭 *-gen'tou*↓; 栽倒 fall down; 栽折了腿 fell and broke one's leg; 栽破頭 tripped and received cuts on the head. (2) V.t., to plant: 栽培 *-peir*, 栽植 *-jyr*↓; 栽種 to sow, plant, raise; 栽秧 transplant rice seedlings; 栽花, 栽樹 to plant flowers, trees; 栽上 put in ground to grow; 栽不活 (of trees, flowers) fail to grow.

栽跟頭 *tzaigen'tou*, v.i., (1) have a fall; (2) fail and expose oneself to public ridicule.

栽植 *tzaijyr*, v.t., ＝栽培 *-peir*↓.

栽排 *tzaipair*, v.t., (MC) pave the way for.

栽培 *tzaipeir*, v.t., (1) (of plants) cultivate; (2) (of men) educate, train; (3) select for service: 受栽培 be taken under s.o.'s wing, brought up and given opportunity for education.

栽絨 *tzairurng*, n., a kind of fabric topped with velvet woven into it, generally used, as material for cushion, covering, etc.

栽贓 *tzai-tzang*, v.i., to "plant" a stolen article with s.o. else to frame him.

載 11.71

tzaih (**tzaai*).

N. (**tzaai*) A year: 一年半載 six months or a year; 千載難逢 only once in a lifetime.

V.t. (1) Transport, convey from one place to another: 裝載 to load (goods); 載運 transport by vehicle; 載重 *-juhng*↓; 超載 overload(ed); 載滿 be fully loaded; 滿載而歸 return with a full load of presents (honors, booty); 載人(客), 載貨(物) carry passengers, goods; 載貨量 payload (shipping); 載到 convey to (a place); 載多少 how much does (a cart, boat) hold or carry? 載不了 cannot hold (carry) so much. (2) Put on record, write down: 紀載 put in writing; 登載 publish in newspaper (magazine); 載明 to state clearly in writing; 載入 enter (an item) in a list, make an entry of; 失載 fail to be recorded; 刊載 be duly recorded; 載於何書 in which book does this appear? (3) Be full of: 載道 *-dauh*↓. (4) Receive: 載福 be blessed.

Adv. (1) (U.f. 再) again, once more: 載拜 "yours respectfully," as a polite complimentary close to letters. (2) Then: 載戢干戈 then fighting will cease.

Particle Often used in pairs to indicate parallel action or sequence: 載沉載浮 (of a sailing boat) bobbing up and down; 載馳載驅 (of a carriage) darting and dashing; 載歌載舞 now singing, now dancing; 載飛載止 (of a bird) flying awhile, alighting to rest awhile; 載清載濁 (of currents) sometimes clear, sometimes muddy.

載道 *tzaih-dauh*, v.i. & adv., (1) v.i., (of litr. works) moralize; (2) adv., everywhere: 怨聲載道 voices of discontent can be heard all over.

載貨證券 *tzaihhuoh jehngchyuahn*, n., bill of lading.

載記 *tzaihjih*, n., historical records, accounts of past events.

載籍 *tzaihjir*, n., books, written works.

載重 *tzaihjuhng*, n., (of a vehicle) capacity to carry weight.

哉 11.71

tzaih.

Particle. (1) (LL) final particle at end of questions: 何哉 why? wherefore? 不亦快哉 isn't that delightful? 何足道哉 that's nothing, why mention it? 天何言哉 does Heaven ever speak? (2) Used in exclamations: 嗚呼哀哉 Oh! what a pity! alas! 大哉孔子 great indeed was Confucius!

戴 11.71

daih.

N. A surname.

V.t. To wear on top, as a hat, or spectacles, gloves, costume, jewelry, ring, etc.: 戴高帽 be given titles and social distinctions, unduly flatter s.o.; 給他戴高帽 play upon his vanity with high praises; 戴綠帽 be a cuckold; 戴盆望天 to look at the sky under a basin—work blindly; 戴月披星 go to work in the field before dawn and come home after dark or journey during the night; 不共戴天 cannot share the same sky with murderer of one's father. (2) (Fig.) 擁戴 support as leader; 愛戴 love and support (leader); 感恩戴德 bear a debt of gratitude for past kindness.

戴勝 *daihsheng*, n., the bird hoopoe.

裁 11.71

tsair.

N. Form: 體裁 form and style of writing; 身裁 person's figure.

V.t. (1) To cut: 裁縫 tailor ("cut and sew"); 剪裁 to trim tree, cut things into shape; 裁衣 to cut a dress; to cut and trim lines; 裁詩 write poems. (2) To cut out, reduce (armament, guards, staff, budget): 裁併, 裁撤, 裁汰, 裁減 *-bihng, -cheh, -taih, -jiaan*²↓; 裁員 reduce staff; 裁兵 *-bing*↓. (3) To judge, make decision: 鑒裁, 尊裁 your discerning decision; 裁奪, 裁度, 裁決 *-duor, -duoh, -jyuer*↓. (4) To kill in 自裁 take one's own life.

裁併 *tsairbihng*, v.t., reduce (administrative units) and combine into one.

裁兵 *tsairbing*, v.i. & n., disarm, disarmament.
裁撤 *tsaircheh*, v.t., abolish (post), withdraw (troops).
裁成 *tsaircherng*, v.t., (AC, of Nature) to give form to all life.
裁處 *tsairchuu*, v.t., to cut down and dispose of (unneeded items).
裁答 *tsairdar*, v.i., to compose letter of reply.
裁斷 *tsairduahn*, v.i., to exercise judgment, decide.
裁度 *tsairduoh*, v.i. & t., to weigh and decide.
裁奪 *tsairduor*, v.i. & t., to make decision.
裁縫 *tsair'ferng*, n., tailor, dressmaker.
裁剪 *tsairjiaan*[1], v.t., (1) to cut (paper, cloth) into certain shape; (2) to trim (trees), cut and give form (to book, essays, etc.).
裁減 *tsairjiaan*[2], v.t., to cut down (budget, conscription).
裁軍 *tsairjuun*, n., disarmament.
裁決 *tsairjyuer*, v.i., to make decision.
裁可 *tsairkee*, v.t., (LL) to approve officially.
裁量 *tsairliarng*, v.i. & t., see *-duor* ↑.
裁判 *tsairpahn*, v.t., to hand down court decision, to pass sentence; 裁判司 magistracy; 裁判員 umpire.
裁排 *tsairpair*, v.t., (MC) to arrange (matter), make possible.
裁汰 *tsairtaih*, v.t., eliminate (unnecessary staff, expenses); to liquidate, cause to become extinct.
裁衣 *tsair-yi*, v.i., to make dress.
裁員 *tsair-yuarn*, v.i., to reduce employees.

胾 11.71

tzyh.

N. (AC) minced meat.

烖 11.71

tzai.

[Anc. var. of 災 93.81]

截 11.71

jier.

N. A section, segment, division: 一截 one piece; 半截 half; 兩截 two pieces; 上半截, 下半截 the upper, lower half; 這一大截子 such a big chunk; 這半截兒 this little slice.

V.t. (1) To cut in two: 截斷 *-duahn* ↓; 截長補短 even up scarcity and superabundance ("cut off from the long to add to the short"). (2) Intercept, stop, block: 截住 -(')*ju* ↓.

Adv. Distinctly, clearly: 截然 *-rarn* ↓.

截斷 *jierduahn*, v.t., sever, split, cut off: 截斷後路 cut off retreat.
截奪 *jierduor*. v.t., intercept and rob.
截獲 *jierhuoh*, v.t., intercept and seize.
截住 *jier(')ju*, (1) v.i., to stop short: 話到這裏突然截住 suddenly stopped short at this point; (2) v.t., intercept: 截住他 block him halfway; 截住一輛車 have intercepted a car.
截止 *jierjyy*, v.i., come to an end: 報名截止 registration has ended.
截開 *jier-kai*, v.t., cut open.
截留 *jierliour*, v.t., keep for one's own use what is intended for others.
截然 *jierrarn*, adv., clearly, sharply: 截然不同 entirely different.

§ 11.72 (土/心)

志 11.72

jyh.

N. (1) Will, determination, ambition: 志氣, 志向 *-'chih*, *-'shiahng*; 立志 form determination to forge ahead; 立志不嫁 determine not to marry a husband; 有志于此 take a deep interest in this; 大志 high ambition, great determination; 得志 be a success (in politics, society); 躊躇滿志 elated with success. (2) Historical record (interch. 誌): 風土志 record of a district, its landscape and custom; 人物志 biographical notes and data; 府志, 州志, 縣志 district history of *fuu*, *jou* or *shiahn*, giving geography, history, historical personalities, customs and other sociological data; 三國志 History of the Three Kingdoms (220–264 A.D.), 通^志 32.83.

V.i. (AC) be devoted to: 志於學 devoted to studies.

志氣 *jyh'chih*, n., great determination, personal ambition.
志趣 *jyhchyuh*, n., devotion (to some subject).
志怪 *jyh-guaih*, n., book of supernatural stories.
志節 *jyhjier*, n., firm principles (against temptations).
志量 *jyhliahng*, n., capacity for great undertaking (persistence, staunch overcoming of obstacles, etc.).
志略 *jyhlyueh*, n., (1) determination and plan (略＝謀略); (2) outline of events.
志乘 *jyhshehng*, n., local histories.
志向 *jyh'shiahng*, n., a man's life ambition.
志行 *jyhshihng*, n., personal ambition and conduct.

志書 *jyhshu*, n., local, district or provincial histories, giving topography, history, personages, products and custom, see N. 2↑.

志士 *jyhshyh*, n., an up-and-coming scholar: 仁人志士 kind and upright man.

志學 *jyh-shyuer*, adj., devoted to studies.

志操 *jyhtsau*, n., personal integrity.

志願 *jyhyuahn*, n., a man's wish in life; a pledge to do s.t.; 志願軍 volunteer (corps); 志願書 written application and pledge (to join some unit).

恚 11.72

hueih.

N. & adj. (LL) anger: 恚憤; 既愧且恚 shamed and angered.

慤 11.72

chyueh.

Adj. (LL) sincere: 誠慤.

§11.80 (土/八)

賣 11.80

maih.

V.t. (1) To sell: 賣出 sell out, opp. 賣進 buy in; 賣不出, 不了 cannot dispose of by selling; 賣不着 will not sell at low price; 賣與(給)某人 sell to s.o.; 賣價 selling price; 賣方 selling party in contract; 出賣 set for sale; 出賣朋友 betray friends ("friendship for sale"); 賣友求榮 sell, betray friends to obtain promotion; 賣國 *-guor*↓; 賣臉 *-liaan*↓; 拍賣 (sell at) auction; 轉賣 sell to another party; 非賣品 not for sale; 賣妻鬻子 sell wife and children; 賣官鬻爵 sell official posts for a consideration; 賣字號 policy of maintaining good will of customers by refusing to sell inferior goods; 賣刀買犢, 賣劍買牛 beat swords into ploughshares; 賣李鑽核 sell plums without kernel (making planting impossible)—a mean trick. (2) Be paid for in certain professions: 賣文 (爲生) write for a living; 賣胳臂 "sell muscles," i.e., make a living by manual labor; 賣藝不賣身 (of singsong profession) sell art but not body; 賣臉不賣身 sell looks, but not body; 賣技 be professional artist; 賣淫 be prostitute; 賣唱 be professional singer; 賣笑 "sell smiles," be prostitute; 賣眼 attract by coquettish looks, glances; 賣人口 engage in white slave traffic. (3) Show off: esp. 賣弄 *-luhng*↓; 賣風情, 賣風流, 賣俏 flirt; 賣乖 show off cleverness, good behavior; 賣人情 do s.t. for good will; 賣恩 sell favors in politics in return for support; 賣派頭, 賣本事 show off skill; 賣野人頭 (derog.) exaggerate for show-off; 賣氣力, 賣勁(兒) put in extra energy in work; 賣(個)破綻 feint in combat to attract a thrust by opponent; 賣名 show off for publicity; 賣舌, 賣嘴 show off forensic skill, indulge in clever talk.

賣卜 *maihbuu*, v.i., be fortuneteller.

賣唱(兒)的 *maichahng('l) -de*, n., professional (girl) singer at teahouse, etc.

賣呆(獃)(兒) *maihdai(-da'l)*, v.i., (1) pretend not to understand, assume cloak of ignorance; (2) as in 倚門賣呆 (of woman) idle at house door.

賣底 *maih-dii*, phr., betray secret.

賣放 *maih-fahng*, phr., receive bribe and free prisoner.

賣國 *maihguor*, v.i., be traitor; 賣國賊 n., (abusive) traitor.

賣主 *maihjuu*, n., seller.

賣絕 *maihjyueir*, n., sell outright, not on mortgage.

賣臉 *maih-liaan*, v.i., (1) disregard loss of face, take insults, etc.; (2) (of singsong artist) sell looks, not body.

賣弄 *maihluhng*, v.t., to show off skill, see V.t. 3↑.

賣嚷嚷兒 *maih-rarngraang'l*, v.i., tell everybody (about affair, a scandal, grudge).

贄 11.80

jyh.

N. Ceremonial offering.

贄見 *jyhjiahn*, v.i., to make first visit or meeting with presents: 贄見禮 such gifts.

贄敬 *jyhjihng*, n., formerly, gift to teacher, similar to tuition.

§11.81 (土/人)

賣 11.81

maih.

[Callig. form of 賣 11.80]

§11.83 (土/〜)

逵 11.83

kueir.

N. (AC) a thoroughfare where many roads converge.

達 11.83

dar.

N. (1) Success: 富貴利達 riches, honor and success. (2) A surname.

V.i. & t. (1) (Largely LL) to mature in thinking, comprehend: 通達 be wise, mature, reach full comprehension; 達道 comprehend the truth; 達於事理 be understanding and amenable to reason, understand human affairs; 賜也達 (AC) Syh is very intelligent, Syh understands. (2) Reach goal, to progress: 達於海 (stream) reaches the sea; (LL) 達乎四境 reach all parts of the country; 自天子達於庶人 from the emperor down to the common man; 欲速則不達 fail in goal by being hasty; 通宵達旦 whole night until dawn; oft. 達到 *-dauh*, reach, to attain: 達到目的 reach goal; 君子上達, 小人下達 the gentleman progresses upward, the small man progresses downward. (3) To express (idea) to reach person by writing: 特此函達 communicate the above; 上達天聽 reach the emperor's ears; 達意, 表達意思 express one's thoughts; 辭達而已矣 all one asks of writing is that the idea be expressed (adequately); 不達意 (writing) does not express what the writer wishes to say.

Adj. (1) Having the quality of thorough comprehension: 明達 wise, comprehending. (2) (AC) successful: 達則兼善天下 in success, one tries to benefit others; 發達 prosper in business, become prominent; 達官 highly-placed official. (3) (AC) 達道 right path, main road (to virtue). (4) (**tah*) In 挑[△]達 10A.70.

達觀 *darguan*, adj., detached (point of view), having broad perspective, not easily upset, optimistic.
達賴喇嘛 *Darlaih La'ma*, n., Dalai Lama.
達摩 *Darmor*, n., Bodhidharma, who introduced the Chan (Zen) sect to China, in 6th Cen.
達姆彈 *darmuudahn*, n., dumdum bullet.
達人 *darrern*, n., a very wise man.
達士 *darshyh*[1], n., great scholar.
達識 *darshyh*[2], n., superior understanding.
達子 *dartz*, n., Tartars.
達因 *daryin*, (phys.) a dyne, unit of force that moves one gram of mass one centimeter per second.

遠 11.83

yuaan (**yuahn*).
[Var. 逺, abbr. 远]

V.t. (**yuahn*) To keep away from: 遠小人 keep away from the mean and selfish characters; 遠庖廚 (AC) keep away from the kitchen (to enjoy food).

Adj. & adv. Distant, far away in time or space: 遠行, 遠程 distant journey; 遠途, 遠路 a long journey; 遠事 long past event; 遠客 a guest from distant place; 遠走高飛 to slip away to distant place; 遠涉重洋 sail across the seas; 遠交近攻 phr., policy of attacking near-by neighbor and maintaining friendly relations with more distant nations; 差得遠 far inferior; 老遠 very far; 遠年, 遠期 *-niarn*, *-chir* ↓. (2) Distant in relationship: 遠親, 遠房 *-chin*, *-farng* ↓; 疏遠 vb. & adj., remote, cool (friendship), to cool off (toward person). (3) Farsighted, profound, permanent: 深遠 profound (meaning); 遠見 farsighted (view, policy); 遠景 prospect, outlook, distant view; 遠大 *-dah* ↓; 長遠 farsighted (plan); 久遠 permanent (plan); 高瞻遠矚 farsighted, take a long view.

遠避 *yuaan-bih*, v.i., avoid and keep far away from.
遠親 *yuaan-chin*, n., distant relative.
遠期 *yuaan-chir*, adj., long-term.
遠處 *yuaan-chuh*, n., distant place.
遠大 *yuaandah*, adj., great, broad (plan, policy, view of things).
遠道兒 *yuaan-dauh'l*, adv., from a distant place.
遠地點 *yuaandih-diaan*, n., (astron.) apogee.
遠東 *Yuaandung*, n., the Far East.
遠方 *yuaan-fang*, adj., & n., distant, -ce.
遠房 *yuaan-farng* (-'*fang*), n., a distant branch of family.
遠見 *yuaanjiahn*, n., farsightedness.
遠近 *yuaan-jihn*, adv., far and near.
遠支(兒) *yuaan-jy*(*-je'l*), n., see *-farng* ↑.
遠志 *yuaanjyh*, n., (1) a great ambition; (2) (bot.) Japanese senega, a medical herb, *Polygala japonica*.
遠兒 *yuaa'l*, n., distance: 多麼遠兒 how far is it?
遠略 *yuaan-lyueh*, n., some great plan.
遠慮 *yuaan-lyuh*, n., great foresight.
遠謀 *yuaan-mour*, n., see *-lyueh* ↑.
遠年 *yuaan-niarn*, adj. & adv., long ago.
遠日點 *yuaanryh-diaan*, n., aphelion.
遠限 *yuaan-shiahn*, n., a distant time limit.
遠心力 *yuaan-shin-lih*, n., (phys.) centrifugal force (commonly 離心力).
遠識 *yuaanshyh*, n., great foresight.
遠視眼 *yuaanshyh-yaan*, adj. & n., farsighted (in eye vision), hypermetropia.
遠孫 *yuaan-sun*, n., distant progeny.
遠圖 *yuaantur*, n., see *-lyueh* ↑.
遠祖 *yuarn-tzuu*, n., distant ancestor.
遠因 *yuaan-yin*, n., remote cause.
遠遊 *yuaan-your*, v.i., to travel to distant countries.
遠遠(兒)的 *yuarnyuaan*(*-yuaa'l*)-

'de, (coll. also *yuaanyuan*), adv., from a distance.

遶 11.83

rauh.

V.t. (U.f. 繞) surround, encircle.

走 11.83

tzoou.

V.i. (1) Go, walk: 行走 go on foot; 走路 ditto; 向前走 go straight ahead; 走道兒 a sidewalk, footpath; go by foot, a corridor; 走來走去 come and go, go and fro, back and forth; 走進走出 go in and out; 走得快, 走得慢 go quickly, slowly; 走累了 tired by walking; 走倦了 ditto; 走去了 have gone away; 走不動 can't go, be unable to move; 走不慣 unaccustomed to walking; 走岔了 gone astray; 走下坡 down the slope, on the decline; 走迷了路 gone off the right track; 走脫 separated and lost contact; 走過一遭 go round once; 走攏 draw near to, approach; 競走 foot race; 走失 lose one's way; 走走 -'*tzou*↓; 走溜兒 stroll back and forth; 走趟趟兒 ditto; 走南闖北 roam all over the country; 走遍天下 travel all over the world; 走黑道兒 walk in the dark at night; 走黑道兒的 a thief, a burglar; 走索 (acrobatics) walk the tightrope; 走軟繩 ditto; 走讀生 a student attending a day school; 飛沙走石 "flying sand and rolling pebbles," said of violent windstorms; 走馬看花 take only a passing glance (at things, a new city, etc.); 走投(頭)無路 poor and utterly helpless ("with no one to depend on"). (2) Escape, run away, make off: 敗走 (of troops) be routed and retreat; 棄甲曳兵而走 (of troops) abandon arms and quit fighting. (3) Make a trip: 走訪 go to make a call; 走見 go to interview; 走候 go to pay one's respects (to a friend). (4) Leak out: 走風, 走話 betray a secret; 走漏 *-louh*↓; 走嘴 make an unguarded utterance. (5) Incur loss: 走味兒 (of food, wine, tobacco) become stale, lose flavor; 走顏色 discolor; 走樣 *-yahng*↓; 走板 (of singing) be out of tune; 走板兒 behave improperly; 走跡 (of houses, furniture) be out of shape with the lapse of time; 走高了腳 be puffed up with pride and behave abnormally. (6) Take one's leave, depart: 走開 go away; 他走了 he has left; 走不了 be unable to leave; 走不得 should not go; 走不脫 be unable to tear oneself away.

Pron. One's humble self: 下走 (MC) "your humble servant."

走背運 *tzoou-beihyuhn*, phr., have back luck (also 走背字兒).

走鏢 *tzoou-biau*, v.i., formerly, serve as a bodyguard on a journey.

走筆 *tzour-bii*, v.i., take the pen in hand and write.

走不開 *tzoou'bukai*, v.i., (1) be unable to tear oneself away; (2) (of alleys) be too narrow to allow easy passage: 胡同兒太窄, 走不開車 the alley is too narrow for carts to go through.

走禽 *tzoouchirn*, n., birds that can only walk and not fly, as the ostrich, turkey.

走動 *tzoouduhng(-dung)*, v.i., (1) have social intercourse with friends, be socially active; (2) take a stroll: 走動走動; (3) (northern dial.) move one's bowels.

走肚子 *tzoou-duh'tz*, v.i., have loose bowels.

走舸 *tzour-gee*, n., (MC) a fast-sailing boat.

走狗 *tzourgoou*, n., (1) a hound; (2) (contempt.) a person running errands for another ("a running dog").

走好運 *tzour-haauyuhn*, phr., have a spell of good luck.

走會 *tzoou-hueih*, v.i., to stage shows at religious festivals.

走貨 *tzoou-huoh*, v.i., transport goods (from one place to another).

走火 *tzour-huoo*, v.i., (1) short-circuited; (2) (of firearms) to fire accidentally.

走着瞧 *tzoou-je-chiaur*, phr., (of an undertaking) try and see how it works.

走之兒 *tzooujee'l*, n., the radical 辵 wr. as 辶; index No. "83."

走摺 *tzoou-jer*, n., (business) a cashbook.

走江湖 *tzoou-jiang'hu*, phr., (of acrobats, dancers, singers) go from place to place to stage shows for a living.

走集 *tzoou-jir*, n., (AC) a point of convergence.

走局 *tzooujyur*, n., =走會 *-hueih*↑.

走廊 *tzoolarng*, n., a veranda, corridor: 波蘭走廊 (history) the Polish Corridor.

走了困 *tzoou'lekuhn*, v.i. & n., be unable to sleep, insomnia.

走漏 *tzooulouh*, (1) v.i., engage in smuggling; (2) v.t., leak out: 走漏風聲 leak out a secret.

走馬 *tzourmaa*, (1) v.i., to dash past on horseback, (fig.) fast, swiftly; (2) n., a horse for riding in journeys, not for racing; 走馬(兒)燈 a lantern with rotating shadows; 走馬牙疳 an acute gumboil.

走內線 *tzoou neihshiahn*, phr., bring influence to bear on s.o. through his close relatives.

走票 *tzoou-piauh*, n., a show staged by amateurs.

走散 *tzoou-sahn*, v.i., (1) (of a crowd) disperse; (2) lose contact with companion.

走扇 *tzoou-shahn*, adj., (of door panels) unable to close properly.

走解 *tzoou-shieh*, v.i., do stunts on horseback.

走斜道兒 *tzoou shierdauh'l*, phr., patronize brothels.

走心經 *tzoou shin'jing*, phr., keep s.t. constantly in mind.

走獸 *tzooushouh*, n., animals, beasts (opp. 飛禽 birds).

走水 *tzourshueei*, (1) v.i., to catch fire; (2) n., (-'*shuei*) a narrow band overhanging a curtain or other drapery.

走私 *tzoousy*, v.i. & n., smuggle, -ing.

走走 *tzoou'tzou*, v.i., (1) go for a stroll; (2) come or go in a gen. sense: 到我這裏走走 come to see me; 到他那裏走走 drop in on him.

走卒 *tzooutzur*, n., an errand boy, a non-commissioned officer or foot soldier.

走無常 *tzoou-wurcharng*, n., a person claiming to be able to communicate with departed souls (pop. 走陰差).

走樣 *tzoouyahng*, v.i., (1) be out of shape; (2) (of conduct) fail to conform to the norm.

走陽 *tzoouyarng*, n., (med.) an involuntary discharge of semen.

走油 *tzoouyour*, v.i. & t., (1) (of varnished furniture) lose luster; (2) to fry (fish, meat); (3) (of oily substance) to dry up; 走油子 (of plaster) oozing with oil.

趬 11.83

chiau.

V.i. To lift: 蹺足 put one's leg up (as on bed), also wr. 蹻 40A.42, 翹 11.70.

Adv. (Walking) nimbly, agilely.

趲 11.83

tzaan.

V.i. & t. Hasten, do in a hurry: 趲課程 to cram one's lessons; 趲造 speed up construction (of a house, road, boat); 趲路, 趲行, 趲程 travel by forced march.

趲足 *tzaantzur*, n., savings: 頗自有些趲足 have a good deal of savings (cf. 攢△錢 10A.80).

赴 11.83

fuh.

V.t. (1) Attend: 赴席, 赴宴, 赴會 attend dinner party, meeting; 赴約 go to an engagement; 赴任 arrive at post to assume duty; 赴試 go to take part in examinations; 以全力赴之 do s.t. with all resources in command. (2) Go to: 赴英, 美 go to England, America. (3) Attend to, usu. s.t. difficult or dangerous: 赴難 *-nahn*, go and help face the situation; 共赴國難 play citizen's part when nation calls; 赴義 take up stand and be martyr if necessary; 赴敵 go to the front of battle; 赴湯蹈火 go through fire and water.

赳 11.83

jioou.

Adj. Valiant, gallant: 赳赳武夫 a soldier of dauntless courage.

趙 11.83

jauh.

N. (1) Name of an anc. country; 原璧歸趙, 奉趙 (allu.) return article to owner. (2) A surname.

趟 11.83

tahng.

N. One round trip: 走一趟 go over once; 走了好幾趟 have made serveral trips; 一趟又一趟 time and again.

趟子 *tahngtz*, n., as in 趟子車, 趟子驢 cart or donkey for hire on specific trips.

趔 11.83

lieh.

趔趄 *liehjyu*, (1) n. & v.i., tumble: 打的那丫頭一個趔趄 hit the maid until she fell backward; (2) adj., (coll.) awkward, inexperienced in handling.

趣 11.83

chyuh (**tsuh*).

N. ('*l*) Interest, what attracts or holds one's attention: 有趣兒 (s.t.) is interesting (as a book, play, article, subject); 沒趣兒 uninteresting; 湊趣兒 join in the fun; 沒趣 a rebuff: 自討沒趣 he asked for it (rebuff); 異趣 (different people have) different tastes in life; 養趣 cultivate taste or love of what is good; 不知趣 (person) dull, prosaic; 了無生趣 lose all interest in life; 志趣 interest or motive in life; 旨趣 main object.

V.i. (**tsuh*) To hurry: 趣裝 (LL) hurriedly prepare for jounrey.

Adj. Interesting: 趣事, 趣聞 interesting news or anecdotes; 趣話, 趣語 an interesting saying or story; 趣劇 an amusing play, comedy.

趣向 *chyuhshiahng*, n., one's ambition, inclination.

趣味 *chyuhweih*, n., interest of or in subject.

A

趄 11.83

jyu.

V.i. Hold oneself back: 趑趄 hesitate to advance; 趔趄 stumble backward, see 趔 11.83↑; 趄避 evade meeting face to face.

趕 11.83

gaan.

[Abbr. 赶]

V.i. & t. (1) V.i., to rush from one place to another, hurry on or up, catch up with s.t. or s.o., rush to do or make s.t.: 趕上 *-shahng* ↓; 趕得及 have plenty of time to get s.t. done; 趕路 *-luh*, 趕考 *-kaau* ↓; 連夜趕到城裡來 hurried to the city overnight; 趕不上時代 cannot catch up with the times; 功課趕不上了 cannot catch up with the lessons. (2) V.t., compare with, be a match for: 這女孩子那裡趕得上你 how can this girl compare with you? (3) V.t., increase the pace of: 趕工 try to get the work done faster; 趕活 *-huor* ↓; 趕寫(文章等) dash off (a piece of writing, etc.); 趕拍電影 shoot a movie to beat a deadline; 趕死了人 be overworked and dead tired; 趕得我筋疲力盡 I am utterly exhausted from the pace of work. (4) V.t., drive away, expel: 趕走, 趕開 drive away; 趕散 disperse; 趕出去 show (s.o.) the door, kick out; 趕進籠子裡 (of domestic animals) herd into the pens; 趕盡殺絕 drive away and exterminate every one (of the enemy). (5) V.t., to drive (cart, donkey, etc.); to herd (cattle, sheep, ducks, etc.). (6) To hurry (s.o.): 趕着他 hurry him.

Adv. Swiftly, quickly: 趕快 *-kuaih*, 趕忙 *-marng*, 趕緊 *-jiin* ↓.

Prep. 趕早(兒) *-tzaau('l)* ↓; 趕機會 take advantage of an opportune moment; till, until: 趕明兒 (wait) until another day; 趕回來, 趕以後再商量 let's discuss it upon your return, later.

B

趕場 *gaan-charng*, v.i., see *-jir* ↓.

趕車的 *gaanche'de*, n., a cart driver.

趕趁 *gaanchehn*, v.i., take advantage of an opportunity to do business.

趕檔子 *gaandahngtz*, v.i., (1) sell goods or stage open-air shows at a market place; (2) to fish in troubled waters.

趕到 *gaan-dauh*, (1) v.t., catch up with, overtake; (2) prep., until: 趕到明天 wait until tomorrow.

趕汗 *gaan-hahn*, v.i., to induce perspiration.

趕猴兒 *gaan-hour'l*, n., a game of chance played with three dice.

趕會 *gaan-hueih*, v.i., attend a religious festival and fair held at a temple.

趕活 *gaanhuor*, v.t., get work done as soon as possible.

趕着 *gaan-je*, adv. phr., (1) in a hurry: 趕着做活 work at a forced pace; 趕着作親 in a hurry to get married; (2) v.t., coincide with: 正趕着放假的時候 just coincided with the holidays; (3) pursue and overtake.

趕緊 *garnjiin*, adv., quickly: 趕緊離開此地 quickly get away from here.

趕集 *gaan-jir*, v.i., go to a village fair to buy or sell goods (also 趕場).

趕考 *garn-kaau*, v.i., formerly, go on a voyage to take civil examinations.

趕快 *gaankuaih*, adv., quickly, see *-jiin* ↑.

趕碌 *gaan'lu*, v.t., (1) cause (s.o.) to hurry up: 你別趕碌我了, 我這就走 please don't press me, I'll go right away; (2) drive (s.o.) into a corner: 不要把人趕碌急了 don't drive others into a corner.

趕路 *gaanluh*, v.i., travel on foot; go by land.

趕忙 *gaanmarng*, adv., quickly, in a hurry.

趕上 *gaan-shahng*, v.t., (1) catch or be in time for: 趕不上車了 won't be able to catch the bus or train; 正趕上吃飯的時候 be just in time for lunch; (2) overtake: 敵人趕上來了 the enemy is about to overtake us; (3) to match: 他的學問趕得上你 he knows as much as you do.

C

趕趟(兒) *gaan-tahng('l)*, v.i., be in time for s.t.: 趕不上趟(兒) be late for some occasion or schedule.

趕早(兒) *garntzaau('l)*, adv., as early as possible.

趕嘴 *garn-tzueei*, v.i., be an uninvited guest at dinner, take potluck at a friend's.

趕網兒 *garn-waang'l*, v.i., to sacrifice oneself for the benefit of s.o. else.

趮 11.83

tzauh.

[Var. of 躁 40B.01]

超 11.83

chau.

V.i. & t. (1) (AC) to jump over, cross over: 超度 *-'duh* ↓; 超乘 (AC) jump aboard cart. (2) To surpass, exceed: 超過 *-guoh* ↓; 超凡 *-farn* ↓; 超羣 surpass one's fellows; 超乎 *-'hu* ↓.

Adj. Super-, extra-, superior: 超越, 超級 *-yueh, -jir* ↓; 超重 overweight; 超載 overload; 超量 extra capacity; 超速 extra speed; see many compp. ↓.

超拔 *chaubar*, (1) adj., outstanding (personality); (2) v.t., (Budd.) to save from sin or hell.

超遷 *chauchian*, v.t., formerly, to promote, be promoted, by special order and not routine.

超羣 *chauchyurn*, adj., as in 超群絕倫 far surpassing one's fellows.

超等 *chaudeeng*, adj. & n., superior grade (of goods, students); outstanding, eminent.

超度 *chau'duh*, v.t., (Budd.) to save from sin, esp. to say mass for deceased person: 超度衆生 to save mankind from the sea of misery which is life.

超凡 *chaufarn*, phr., as in 超凡入聖 to overcome the material desires and attain sainthood.

超格 *chauger*, (1) adj., extra-grade; (2) adv., as in 超格任用 promote a person specially and not by rank of service.

超過 *chauguoh*, v.t., to surpass, exceed (normal number, expectations, etc.).

超乎 *chau'hu*, v.t., goes beyond.

超忽 *chauhu*, adj., (LL) far distant.

超豁 *chauhuoh*, v.t., to exempt, pardon (from duty, punishment).

超級 *chaujir*, adj., super (quality); 超級強國 a superpower; 超級市場 supermarket.

超卓 *chaujuor*, adj., eminent.

超絕 *chaujyuer*, adj., unequalled, unexcelled.

超倫 *chaulurn*, adj., (LL) above the average.

超然 *chaurarn*, adj., detached, free, not involved, independent in point of view.

超人 *chaurern*, n., superman.

超升 *chausheng*[1], v.t., see *-chian* ↑.

超生 *chausheng*[2], v.t., (usu. beg to) spare life.

超脫 *chautuor*, adj., see *-rarn* ↑.

超逸 *chauyih*, adj., free, disentangled.

超音速 *chauyin-shuh*, adj., & n., supersonic speed.

超越 *chauyueh*, v.t. & adj., to surpass, excel; surpassing, above the normal.

趯 11.83

tih.

N. The upward cut in calligraphy ("㇀").

Adj. 趯趯 (AC) jumping about (like crickets).

起 11.83

chii.

N. (1) Group: 一起客人 one group of visitors who come together; 又一起亂兵 another group of stray soldiers. (2) A happening, a batch, a time: 一日數起 several happenings or times on one day; 第幾起 which batch, time; 第二起 the second batch, time.

V.i. & t. (1) To stand up, get up: 起滿坐滿 standing room also full; 起牀 get up from bed; 黎明而起, 雞鳴而起 rise at dawn, at cock-a-doodle-do; 起猛了 get up too early; 起早睡晚 early to rise and late to bed; 起個大早 rise very early; (of patients) get well and leave bed; 一病不起 fell ill and never recovered; 起色, 起席 *-seh, -shir*[2] ↓. (2) To rise, or cause to rise, to start (s.t.): 不起作用 cause no reaction; 興起 rise and do s.t. (as protest, revolt); 起風 the wind rises; 起火 to light, start, a fire; 起了壞心, 起了邪念 start idea of doing s.t. wicked, evil thought; 起予者商也 (AC) it is Shang who opens my mind (＝啟); 起疑 *-yir* ↓; 起疙瘩, 起紅點, 起泡 have, start a boil, a rash, a blister. (3) To begin or start: 起頭, 起初, 起始, 起先, *-tour, -chu, -shyy, -shian* ↓; 起句 opening sentence; 起訖 opening and conclusion, from ... to ... ; 起承轉合 the four movements in a formal essay—opening theme, follow-up expansion or clarification, further development and conclusion; to start counting, interest, periodic payment: 起算, 起息, 起租 *-suahn, -shir*[1], *-tzu* ↓. (4) To rise in height or value: 起伏 the ups and downs of a cycle, the rise and fall; 起落 ebb and flow (of tides), rise and fall (of waves, prices); 起價 *-jiah* ↓. (5) To call into office: 起用 promote (person) from temporary obscurity. (6) To build a house: 起房子 ditto; 茅屋臨江起 a hut stands on the river bank. (7) To unload, to remove, to take up from a vault: 起貨 to unload from shop; 起贓 to unearth or discover booty in hiding place; 把地下銀子起出來 to send for silver from the vault; 起油 to take off oil stains from clothing; 起瓶蓋 take off cap from bottle or tin. (8) To buy, provide a ticket: 起票 buy a ticket; 起行李票 get ticket for luggage; 起卓 monk leaves temple or gets travel ticket to other monasteries.

Vb. suffix. A detachable suffix with the sense of "up": 提起這件事 to mention this matter; 提不起來 cannot lift up; 說起 to bring up a subject in talk; 想起, 想起來 think of; 想起妙計 think up a fine plan; 蓋起房子 to build up a house; 擔當不起 cannot bear responsibility; 看他不起 look down upon him; 做起這件事 start up this affair.

Prep. From ... on: 起這兒剪下來 cut (with scissors) from here; 從明天起, 你就別來了 from tomorrow on, you need not come again; 從前面算起 counting from the front; 從一算起 counting from one on; 從何說起 how should I begin the story?

起壩(霸) *chiibah*, v.i., (Chin. opera, of mil. officers) to adjust helmet and armor on entrance on stage.

起病 *chii-bihng*, v.i., to give a present to sick person to celebrate recovery: 送他一雙鞋給他起病 give him a pair of shoes as celebration.

起兵 *chii-bing*, v.i., to rise in revolt; to make preparations for hostilities (on enemy).

起程 *chii-cherng*, v.i., to start on journey.

A

起

起訖 *chii-chih*, n., opening and conclusion; from starting point to stop.

起初 *chiichu*, adv., at first, at the beginning.

起翅 *chii-chyh*, v.i., (of birds) start (flapping wings) to fly away.

起打 *chir-daa*, v.i., (Chin. opera) to start a sham fight.

起點 *chir-diaan*, n., starting point.

起端 *chii-duan*, n., beginning (of event, quarrel).

起飛 *chiifei*, (1) v.i. & n., (airplanes) take off, depart, -ture; (2) n., quick progress, flying start: 經濟起飛 economic takeoff.

起復 *chiifuh*, v.i. & t., formerly, to resume official life and duties after parents' mourning period is over, cf. *-yuhng*↓.

起稿 *chir-gaau*, v.i., to draft (document, paper): 起草稿, 起稿子.

起根兒 *chii-ge'l*, adv. phr., to begin with, fundamentally.

起工 *chii-gung*, v.i., begin construction or other operation.

起鍋伙(兒) *chii-guo'huo('l)*, v.i., (coll.) to have mess together with fellow workers (also wr. 夥兒).

起旱 *chii-hahn*, v.i., take an overland route, to start foot journey.

起花 *chiihua* (sp. pr. also *chir'hua*), n., a fireworks unit tied around a pole and fired in succession.

起鬨 *chii-huhng*, v.i., start a fight (among members of group).

起火 *chir-huoo*, v.i., (1) to start a fire (disaster); (2) to fume, become enraged: 起火冒油 ditto.

起家 *chiijia*, (1) v.i., to build up a family fortune; (2) n., background of a person (such as family, origins).

起價 *chii-jiah*, (1) v.i., to rise in price; (2) n., the minimum price.

起見 *chiijiahn*, n., purpose or motive for certain action: 爲什麽起見 for what purpose or motive?

起轎 *chii-jiauh*, v.i., to start trip in sedan chair.

起解 *chiijieh*, v.i., to start sending prisoner away under escort.

B

起勁 *chii-jihng*[1], (1) adv., (perform) with zest and vigor; (2) adj., elated, excited.

起敬 *chii-jihng*[2], v.i., show respect (for person): 肅立起敬 show respect by standing up.

起更 *chii-jing*, v.i. & n., the beginning of any of the five watches of the night, see 更 31.82.

起急 *chiijir*, v.i., get impatient, get exasperated.

起住 *chii-juh*, n. & v.i., movement and rest; (callig.) way of starting a stroke and pausing in middle or end.

起重機 *chiijuhng-ji*, n., a derrick, a crane for lifting load.

起居 *chii-jyu*, n., daily life or living: 起居安吉 (I hope) you are doing well; 起居無恙 in good health; 起居注 notes on daily life (of emperor).

起止 *chir-jyy*, n., beginning and end of period or era.

起開 *chii-kai*, v.i., (coll.) go away: 你起開這裏 get away from here!

起課 *chii-keh*, v.i., start session in divination.

起來 *chii-lair*, (1) v.i., get up from bed; get up, arise; (2) vb. suffix, up: 拿起來 take up; 扛起來 carry up on shoulder; 檢(拈)起來 pick up; has meaning of "when" or "done": 唱起來很好聽 sounds beautiful when sung, or when s.o. sings; 走起來不方便 (a dress) is not easy for walking or when walking (too tight); 看起來事情不妙 it seems ("when seen") we are in for some trouble, this matter will not be pretty; 說起來話長 it's a long story to tell (when told).

起立 *chii-lih*[1], v.i., to get on one's feet, stand up as respect.

起利 *chii-lih*[2], v.i., to start bearing interest.

起落 *chii-luoh*, v.i. & n., to be up and down; ups and downs (of prices).

起碼(兒) *chir-maa('l)*, adv., as the minimum, at the least; 起碼貨 cheapest goods; 最起碼條件 minimum conditions, requirements. 「anchor.

起錨 *chii-maur*, v.i., to weigh

起麵 *chii-miahn*, n., (AC) fermented (flour, cake).

C

起名(子) *chii-mirng(tz)*, v.i., be given personal name: 他起名叫 he (a child) is named. . . .

起膩 *chiinih*, v.i., be coying, sticky, annoying (child, etc.).

起色 *chii-seh*, v.i., get better (in illness), pick up (in business).

起身 *chii-shen*, v.i., to start a journey; to get up in the morning: 起身砲 (lit.) fireworks on departure; (fig.) an official gives promotions to staff before he leaves post.

起小兒 *chir-shiaau'l*, phr., from childhood: 他起小兒身體就強壯 he was healthy from childhood.

起先 *chiishian*, adv., at first (he did not approve, etc.).

起釁 *chii-shihn*, v.i., to start hostilities, conflicts.

起興 *chii-shihng*, v.i. & n., (in poems) be inspired by s.t.; the inspiration.

起息 *chii-shir*[1], v.i., start to bear interest, see *-lih*[2]↑.

起席 *chii-shir*[2], v.i., to leave table during meal or conference: 大家起席了 all the guests have left the dining table.

起行 *chiishirng*, v.i., to start on journey.

起手 *chirshoou*, v.i., to begin (work, operation, scuffle); 起手兒 adv., at first.

起事 *chii-shyh*[1], v.i., to start rebellion or revolution, see *-yih*[1]↓.

起誓 *chii-shyh*[2], v.i., to swear, make an oath.

起始 *chirshyy*, n., the beginning: 凡事起始難 all things are difficult at the start.

起算 *chii-suahn*, v.i., start counting (days, numbers, etc.), counting from.

起訴 *chii-suh*, v.i., lodge complaint at court.

起死 *chir-syy*, phr., 起死回生 (of physicians) bring back to life and health.

起頭(兒) *chiitour ('l)*, adv., at first, in the beginnings.

起草 *chir-tsaau*, v.i., to draft, see *-gaau*↑.

起土 *chir-tuu*, v.i., (coll.) to take private profit: 經理辦事不要起土 a manager should not take private profit in business.

起子 *chiitz*, n., (1) a screwdriver; (2) a can opener; (3) yeast.

起租 *chii-tzu*, phr., start paying rent (from date).

起坐(兒) *chii-tzuoh('l)*, phr., to rise from seat as form of respect: 這人連起坐兒都沒有 this man doesn't know manners, even to get up to receive guests.

起卧 *chii-woh*, v.i., (proper time for) rising and going to bed.

起舞 *chirwuu*, v.i., to rise and dance in a happy mood.

起眼 *chir-yaan*, v.i., attract attention: 不起眼 (page make-up, advertisement) does not attract attention.

起夜 *chii-yeh*, v.i., to get up at night and relieve nature.

起義 *chii-yih*[1], v.i., to start revolution: 武昌起義 the Wuchang Uprising in 1911.

起意 *chii-yih*[2], v.i. & n., (have) idea (to do s.t.).

起因 *chiiyin*, n., cause (of quarrel, war, etc.).

起疑 *chii-yir*, v.i. & v.t., begin to suspect.

起原 *chiiyuarn*, v.i. & n., originate origins (of events, clan, etc.) (also wr. 源).

起用 *chii-yuhng*, v.t., to raise (person) to office.

趑 11.83

tzy.

趑趄 *tzychyu*, v.i. & adj., shilly-shally.

越 11.83

yueh.

N. (1) Name of anc. kingdom. (2) 越南 Vietnam; 越戰越南化 Vietnamization of the Vietnam War.

V.t. To exceed, go over, surpass (limit, number, time), transgress (boundary): 超越 to stand above (a group, norm); 越出範圍 exceed the limits (of one's powers, etc.); 隕越 to commit transgression or dereliction of duty; 越獄 escape from prison; 越界, 越境 *-jieh, -jihng*, 越分 *-fehn* ↓.

Adj. Superior, excellent in 優越, superior in character, results, etc.

Adv. More and more, the more (=LL 愈): 越來越壞 getting worse and worse; 越想越氣 the more one thinks about it, the madder one gets.

越期 *yueh-chir*, adj. & adv., passing time limit.

越權 *yueh-chyuarn*, adj. & adv., exceeding one's powers.

越發 *yuehfa*, adv., more and more: 長得越發漂亮 grows prettier and prettier.

越法 *yueh-faa*, adj. & adv., transgressing the law, illegal(-ly).

越分 *yueh-fehn*, adj. & adv., above one's status, undue (demands), unjustified (desires).

越軌 *yueh-gueei*, adj. & adv., (conduct, etc.) beyond bounds or contrary to regulations.

越過 *yueh-guoh*, v.t., surpass, pass over (crest, etc.), cross (rails), pass by (house).

越界 *yueh-jieh*, adj. & adv., outside legitimate territory or boundary.

越境 *yueh-jihng*, adj. & adv., ditto.

越級 *yueh-jir*, adv., (appeal) over the head of direct superior.

越禮 *yueh-lii*, adj., indecorous (conduct).

越南 *Yuehnarn*, n., Vietnam.

越年 *yueh-niarn*, adv., the following year.

越日 *yueh-ryh*, adv., the next day.

越俎 *yueh-tzuu*, phr., 越俎代庖 to do what is not in one's department (kitchen assistant taking place of the *chef*).

越野賽跑 *yuehyee saihpaau*, n., cross country race.

越越 *yuehyueh*, adv., (AC) easily, lightly; making sound of flapping or slobbering.

趁 11.83

chehn.

[Pop. 趂]

V.t. (1) To take advantage of (opportunity, occasion, time, convenience, wind in sailing): forming phrr., indicating "while" (convenient, you are at it, etc.), see 趁早, 趁便 *-tzaau, -biahn*, etc. ↓; 趁他還未來, 我先告訴你 I am telling you first before he arrives; 趁風揚帆 hoist the sail while the wind is good; 趁火打劫 take advantage of a conflagration to loot—fish in troubled waters; 趁年輕時候 take advantge of youthful years to (learn, etc.); 趁時候, 趁機會 take advantage of the time, opportunity. (2) To attend: 趁墟, 趁集 attend the village fair (cf. 趕 11.83). (3) To take a boat: 趁船 (also 乘船). (4) To earn money: 趁錢 (related to 賺[A]錢 41C.22). (5) To fulfill (wish): 趁心, 趁願 *-shin, -yuahn* ↓ (=稱).

趁便 *chehn-biahn*, adv., while convenient; without extra trouble.

趁好 *chehnhaau*, adv., opportunely.

趁口 *chehn-koou*, adv., as in 趁口胡說 speak thoughtlessly (=信口).

趁亮(兒) *chehnliahng('l)*, adv., (travel) while there is yet sunlight.

趁熱(兒) *chen-reh('l)*, adv., (eat) while food is hot, strike while iron is hot.

趁社 *chehn-sheh*, v.i., to attend religious festival.

趁心 *chehn-shin*, v.i., have as one wishes: (=稱心如意).

趁勢 *chehn-shyh*, adv., taking advantage of situation (as pursue enemy while on the run).

趁食 *chehn-shyr*, v.i., (MC) make a living (related 賺 41C.22).

趁此 *chehn-tsyy*, adv., taking advantage of the present.

趁早(兒) *chehn-tzaau('l)*, adv., while there's yet time.

趁願 *chehn-yuahn*, v.i., to have wish fulfilled.

趍 11.83

chyu.

[Pop. of 趨 11.83 ↓]

趨 11.83

chyu.

V.i. (1) To run forward: 亦步亦趨 be assiduous follower (follow the pace, quick or slow). (2) Polite way of expressing "to come forward on the double" as sign of respect: 趨謁, 趨晤, 趨前致候 come to pay respects; 趨奉, 趨承, 趨拜 *-fehng*, *-cherng*, *-baih* ↓. (3) To lean toward or be attracted by power, fashion, etc.: 趨時 *-shyr* ↓; 趨炎附勢, 趨炎附熱 be a snob who plays up to those in power; 大勢所趨 the general trend of things.

趨拜 *chyubaih*, v.i., go and pay respects.

趨避 *chyubih*, v.i., to step behind or keep away from company of officials or of men in case of women.

趨承 *chyucherng*, v.i., to do one's bidding or do everything to please (a master).

趨奉 *chyufehng*, v.i., ditto.

趨風 *chyu-feng*, v.i., (AC) march fast against the wind.

趨附 *chyufuh*, v.t., to attach oneself as subordinate to official: 趨附權貴 be a hanger-on of high officials.

趨吉 *chyujir*, v.i., as in 避凶趨吉 (fortunetelling) conduct oneself so as to avoid impending trouble and seek good luck.

趨利 *chyu-lih*, v.i., concentrate on making profits.

趨向 *chyushiahng*, n., directional trend; ambition, what one is seeking after.

趨勢 *chyushyh*, (1) n., trend, tendency (of world events, etc.); (2) v.i., be a snob.

趨時 *chyushyr*, adj. & v.i., fashionable; to follow the fashion or the crowd.

趨庭 *chyutirng*, v.i., a father's instructions, allu. from Confucius' son (鯉趨而過庭) who received instructions when passing through a courtyard.

趫 11.83

chiaur.

[Sometimes interch. 蹻]

N. Stilts: 踹高趫 walk on stilts.

Adj. Fleet-footed; brave.

趫才 *chiaurtsair*, adj. & n., fleet-footed (person).

§11.91 (土/ノ)

声 11.91

sheng.

[Abbr. of 聲 11.10]

§11.93 (土/く)

去 11.93

chyuh.

N. 去聲 The fourth tone in Mandarin speech, represented consistently by letter "h" after vowel in present dictionary (in some systems represented by diacritical mark "\").

V.i. (1) To go to a place, to leave, depart: 來來去去 coming and going; 去不了 unable to go; 去不去 will go or won't go? 去不得 mustn't go; 去不起 cannot afford to go (to expensive hotel); 美國去不成了 the hope to go to the U.S. cannot be realized; 去他的 let him go (about his business); 去你的 go your way (I am not stopping you); 去留 the choice between staying or quitting; 去路 a way out. (2) Be apart: 相去不遠 not far from each other.

V.t. (1) To drop (habits, office), drive away (heat, cold), leave (country): 去掉 throw away; 去不掉 cannot remove (stain); 去火 reduce combustion in body system; 去病 drive away illness; 去邪 (Chin. med.) reduce poison in system; 壞習慣老去不了 an old habit is difficult to drop; 去泰去甚 avoid excesses, extravagance; 去官, 去職 resign from office; 去任 leave when term expires. (2) In Chin. opera, to play the role of: 他去甚麼角色 what role is he given to play? 去王寶釧 plays Lady Precious Stream.

Infin. part. Used like Eng. infinitive particle "to": 回家去吃飯 go home and ("to") have supper; 拿錢去養家, 去玩 take money to support his family, to have a good time.

Adj. Past: 去年, 去歲 last year; 去今來 (Budd.) the past, present and future; 去事 past events; 去日 days in the past.

Adv. Off, on, away: 信口說去 just talk on; 說來說去 after so much talk (on and on); 讓他哭去 let him cry on; 進去 go in; 做去 just go ahead and do it.

Prep. From: 去包裹裏取些碎銀子

took some bits of silver from the parcel.

去處 *chyuhchuh*, n., (1) a place: 荒涼去處 a solitary place; (2) s.t. on the record: 他平生沒有得罪人的去處 from his record he never seems to have offended any one; (3) place gone to: 不知去處 do not know where one has gone to.

去得(過兒) *chyuh'de(guo'l)*, phr., (1) presentable, passable, good enough: 他模樣倒還去得 or 去得過兒 or 過得去 his looks are not so bad; (2) worth a visit.

去就 *chyuh-jiouh*, n., the moral principle of when to stay in office and when to resign—important in Confucianism: 以去就爭 threat to leave if one's idea is not taken.

去了 *chyuh'le*, adv., far too: 人數多了去了 far too many people; 屋子大了去了 the house is far too big.

去聲 *chyuhsheng*, n., the fourth tone, see N. ↑.

去向 *chyuhshiahng*[1], n., direction: 不知去向 do not know where one is gone.

去項(兒) *chyuh-shiahng*[2]*('l)*, n., items of expense.

去世 *chyuhshyh*, v.i., (person) to pass away.

螫 11.93

(re. pr.) *shyh*; (sp. pr.) *je*.

V.t. (Of insect) to sting: 被馬蜂螫了一下 was stung by a wasp; 螫人 sting persons.

蟄 11.93

jyr (sp. pr. *jer*).

V.i. To hibernate: 出蟄 come out of hibernation; 蟄雷 thunderclap in spring, when chrysalis awakes; 驚^蟄 20.50.

蟄伏 *jyrfur*, v.i., to hibernate; to lie low.

蟄蟄 *jyrjyr*, adj., (AC) thriving in a peaceful community.

蟄居 *jyrjyu*, v.i., to live in retirement, away from publicity.

蠧 11.93

duh.

[Var. of 蠹 10.93]

SECTION 11A

§11A.00 (土/丿)

圩 11A.00-3

yur (also *weir*).

N. A field boundary for protecting water; such embanked field: 圩田.

坷 11A.00-3

kee.

Adj. See 坎^坷 11A.81.

塒 11A.00-4

shyr.

N. A chicken roost.

埒 11A.00-9

leh.

N. An enclosure, a dike, an embankment: 馬埒 an enclosure for horses; 水埒 a dike; 界埒, 埒丘 ditto.

V.t. To equal, be comparable to: 富埒王侯 as rich as princes and dukes; 相埒 are comparable to each other (in ability, strength, riches).

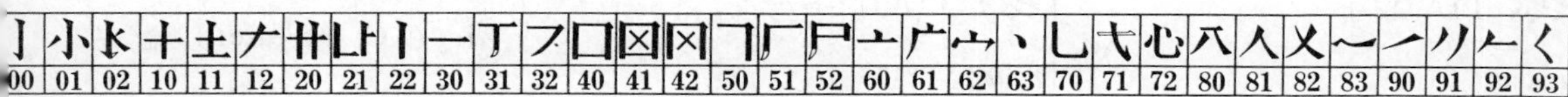

坿 11A.00-9

fuh.

[Anc. var. of 附 32B.00]

V.i. & t. To add, increase, esp. 坿益.

§11A.01 (土/小)

堞 11A.01-2

dier.

N. Parapet.

垛 11A.01-3

*duoo (*duoh).*

N. (1) Some mud construction: 城垛口 a battlement; 門垛子. (2) (**duoh*) Target: 箭垛 archery target. (3) (**duoh*) Heap: 灰垛, 草垛 a heap of ashes, hay.

V.t. (**duoh*) Pile up (ashes, straw, firewood).

§11A.02 (土/k)

垠 11A.02-5

yirn.

N. (1) Boundary, river bank. (2) Limit: 無垠 limitless.

壕 11A.02-6

haur.

N. A trench; a moat: 防空壕 an air shelter.

壕溝 *haurgou*, n., a trench, a ditch.

壞 11A.02-6

huaih.

V.t. (Oft. as past participle) spoil, -ed, destroy, -ed: 壞了 spoiled, also an excl. of bad news; 壞了大事 to spoil an important affair; usu. 破壞 to spoil (plan); 損壞 destroy, damage (reputation, house); 毀壞 destroy (building, faith, good name); 打壞 to break (kettle, watch, etc.); 摔壞 break by dashing to the ground.

Adj. (1) Bad (book, student, teacher, system, etc.), wicked (thought, motive, person): 壞人 bad man; 壞坯子, 壞蛋 *-pitz*, *-dahn*↓; 壞東西 (derog.) bad person or thing; 壞骨頭 (abusive) "bad egg"; 壞嘎嘎兒 a "bad egg"; 壞良心 evil intent, malice; 壞念頭 wicked idea; 壞品行 bad conduct; etc. (2) Ill, aching: 肚子壞了 a bad stomach; 吃壞了 ill from eating; 壞水 *-shueei*↓.

壞鈔 *huaihchau*, n., (MC) to go to expenses (=modn. 破鈔).

壞處 *huaihchuh*, n., bad points, defect, shortcoming.

壞蛋 *huaihdahn*, n., a "bad egg," a villain.

壞坯子 *huaihpitz*, n., a "bad egg," a lout, an oaf.

壞水(兒) *huaihshueei(-shuee'l)*, n., secret, evil conspiracy: 到處灑壞水兒 spread evil ideas.

壞血病 *huaihshyueh bihng*, n., scurvy.

壤 11A.02-6

raang.

N. Loam, earth, soil: 土壤 soil; 壤地 territory; 平壤 level land; 沃壤 fertile land, rich soil; 天壤 heaven and earth: 天壤之別 an immeasurably vast difference; 接壤 with territory adjacent to one another, territorial propinquity.

Adj. (1) (AC interch. 穰) rich, plentiful, bounteous. (2) (AC interch. 攘) disorderly, in confusion.

壤土 *rarngtuu*, n., loamy soil.

§11A.10 (土/十)

坪 11A.10-3

pirng.

N. (1) A flat piece of ground: 草坪 meadow; 停機坪 parking area for airplanes. (2) A Japanese measure of area, used in Taiwan, =roughly 6×6 ft.; 建坪 area of construction, floor space.

墀 11A.10-5

chyr.

N. (LL) steps leading up to temple or palace: 玉墀, 丹墀 palace steps (described as "jade," "vermilion").

埤 11A.10-9

*pir (*bih, pih).*

N. Low wall.

V.i. (AC) increase: 埤益.

Adj. (**bih*) Low, damp (ground).

埤垷 **pihnir*, n., (AC) small peepholes in city wall, cf. 睥△睨 to look down upon, 41B.10.

埠 11A.10-9

buh.

N. Port, port city: 本埠 this port; 外埠 foreign ports.

埠頭 *buhtour*, n., port.

§11A.11 (土/土)

埁 11A.11-1

cherng.

[Var. of 塍 42A.11]

垤 11A.11-3

dier.

N. (AC) little molehill, mound thrown up by ants; small mound.

堙 11A.11-3

yin.

[Interch. 陻; cogn. 淹 63A.70]

V.t. To block up (river) (interch. 湮).

堙滅 *yinmieh*, v.i., to vanish, sunk down and be forgotten (also wr. 湮).

埋 11A.11-4

mair.

V.t. Bury: 埋葬 *-tzahng* ↓; 埋香, 埋玉 bury a beautiful woman; (fig.) conceal: 埋名 "bury" one's name (live unknown) in some obscure place; 埋沒 "bury" one's talent, see 埋沒, 埋伏 *-moh, -'fu* ↓; 埋憂 "bury" one's sorrow by some distraction.

埋伏 *mair'fu*, n. & v.i. & t., (to) ambush; keep under cover.

埋根 *mairgen*, v.i., prepare the ground for future action.

埋蠱 *mairguu*[1], v.i., to bury figurine or charm under victim's bed—a form of witchery.

埋骨 *mairguu*[2], v.i., to die: 埋骨沙場, 異域 to die on the battlefield, in foreign country.

埋沒 *mairmoh*, v.t., to bury; (fig.) fail to bring to public notice: 埋沒好漢 let a good man pass unnoticed.

埋頭 *mairtour*, v.i., to work intensely: 埋頭苦幹, 埋頭讀書.

埋藏 *mairtsarng*, v.t., to bury (object), hide away.

埋葬 *mairtzahng*, v.t., to bury.

埋怨 *mair'yuahn*, v.i. & t., conceive grudge against person; put blame on (person).

壅 11A.11-6

yuung.

[Var. of 壅 60.11]

塞 11A.11-6

sai.

V.t. To push in (s.t. under mattress, etc.); to put stopper on bottle (also wr. 塞 and 揌).

埵 11A.11-9

duoo.

[Related 垛]

N. (1) (AC) hard clay. (2) Cluster (of grapes).

V.t. (AC) stack up (bricks, etc.).

堆 11A.11-9

duei (**tzuei*).

N. A heap, pile: 一堆一堆 in heaps, heaps of; 一堆土 a heap of earth; 土堆, 糞堆 heap of earth, manure.

V.t. (**tzuei*) Pile up: 堆 (*tzuei*) 成一堆 (*duei*) make a heap; 堆起來 pile up; 堆金積玉 great wealth, amass a fortune.

堆砌 *dueichih*, v.i., pile, esp. piling up of phrases and allusions in composition, like piling up bricks (as against simple style).

堆垛兒 *duei'duo'l*, n., a pile, things gathered together to form a heap.

堆房 *duei'fang*, n., storehouse, storeroom.

堆肥 *dueifeir*, n., compost, manure mixture for fertilizing.

堆花(兒) *dueihua('l)*, n., padded flowers made of satin.

堆紅 *dueihurng*, n., raised flowers on red lacquer ware.

堆棧 *dueijahn*, n., warehouse.

堆積 *dueiji*, v.i. & n., accumulate (-tion); v.t., to pile up (wealth, jewelry, waste).

堆絹 *dueijyuahn*, n., colored silk-padded flowers and figures on screens, etc.

§ 11A.21 (土/乚)

堪 11A.21-2

kan.

[Abbr. 墈]

V.i. & t. (1) Be worth (—ing, or n.), be worthy of, equal to task: 堪以告慰 I am glad to inform you (of writer's health, progress); 堪用 good enough for use, usable; 堪當 worthy of task, responsibility; 堪任 equal to task or office; 前途堪虞 the prospect can cause worry. (2) 不堪 cannot endure, unbearable, extremely: 不堪其憂 causes unbearable worry; 不堪設想 dare not imagine (prospect); 不堪回首 too sad to reflect (on past); 破爛不堪 (of house) extremely broken down; 那堪 (in questions) how can one bear=不堪: 那堪回首=不堪回首; 情何以堪 how can one endure (the thought, idea, situation)?

堪布 *kanbuh*, n., a lama priest or head officer.
堪堪 *kankan*, adv., about to: 堪堪病死 about to die of illness.
堪輿 *kanyur*, n., necromancy, science of influence of landscape on human destiny; geomancy, the magic art of choosing building or burial sites.

埳 11A.21-5

kaan.

[Interch. 坎 11A.81]

堰 11A.21-5

yahn.

N. An earthen dike, embankment.

堀 11A.21-5

ku.

[Interch. 窟 62C.21]

§ 11A.22 (土/丨)

坤 11A.22-2

kun.

[Arch. 堃]

N. One of the eight diagrams, denoting the earth, the *yin*, the feminine, see *baguah* 八卦 80.80; 乾坤 heaven and earth, the universe.

Adj. Feminine, of woman: 坤範 exemplary woman; 坤德 feminine virtues; 坤鞋 female shoes; see compp.↓.

坤宅 *kunjair*, n., (formerly LL), the bride's family.
坤角 *kunjiaau*, n., an actress.
坤軸 *kunjour*, n., axis of the earth.
坤伶 *kunlirng*, n., an actress.
坤戲 *kunshih*, n., a play by an entirely female cast.
坤造 *kuntzauh*, n., (fortunetelling) horoscope of a woman.
坤輿 *kunyur*, n., (LL) the earth: 坤輿之學 (formerly) geography.

圤 11A.22-2

yarn.

[Pop. of 鹽 51.30]

坏 11A.22-3

peir.

[Also. pop. of 壞]

N. (1) Small hill. (2) Unfired earthenware (var. of 坯 11A.30).

V. t. (AC) to stop holes in wall.

却 11A.22-5

chyueh.

[Pop. of 卻 80S.22]

埽 11A.22-5

saau.

[Var. of 掃 10A.22]

圻 11A.22-9

chir.

N. A boundary.

圳 11A.22-9

chour (also *tzuhn*).

N. A ditch along farm fields; a small brook.

§ 11A.30 (土/一)

埴 11A.30-1

jyr.

[Usu. printed 埴]

N. Clayey soil, which is unproductive.

埴壚 *jyrluu*, n., clayey and loose soil.
埴土 *jyrtuu*, n., clayey soil.

址 11A.30-2

jyy.

N. Grounds, address, site: 住址 location; 地址 (mail) address; 校址 school compound, campus; 社址 club grounds; 廠址 factory site.

墟 11A.30-2

shyu.

N. (1) Plains, hilly countryside. (2) Devastated countryside; 殷墟 the old plains of Yin (Shang) Dyn.; 廢墟 ruins (of city, settlement). (3) A hamlet: 墟里, 墟落 *-lii*, *-luoh* ↓.

V. t. (AC) to devastate, to level (city, temple) to the ground.

墟里 *shyulii*, n., hamlet.
墟落 *shyuluoh*, n., ditto.
墟墓 *shyumuh*, n., burial grounds.
墟市 *shyushyh*, n., village fair grounds.

壚 11A.30-2

lur.

N. (1) Black earth: 黃壚 yellow soil, grave. (2) Var. of 爐 and 鑪 stove.

塏 11A.30-2

kaai.

N. High, dry land.

垣 11A.30-3

yuarn.

N. (1) (LL) a wall: 城垣 city wall; 省垣 provincial capital. (2) (Astron.) area of a constellation. (3) A surname.

坯 11A.30-3

pei (also *pi*).

N. Moulded or shaped but unfired earthenware: 坯子 ditto.

坦 11A.30-4

taan.

Adj. Level, open and flat: 坦途 open, straight path; 平坦 flat, smooth; 君子坦蕩蕩 (Confucius) "a gentleman is open and poised"; 坦腹東牀 be son-in-law, ("lie in bed with bare belly"—from allu.).

坦白 *taanbor* (or *-bair*), (1) adj., frank, straightforward: 坦白的對你講 I tell you frankly; (2) v. i., confess one's own guilt in communist meeting.
坦直 *taanjyr*, adj., straightforward.
坦克車 *taankehche*, n., (mil.) (translit.) a tank.
坦然 *taanrarn*, adj., calm, unperturbed, undisturbed: 坦然自若 completely at ease.
坦率 *taanshuaih*, adj., open, straightforward.

垃 11A.30-6

leh.

N. 垃圾 *-seh*, garbage (also wr. 拉圾).

壇 11A.30-6

tarn.

N. (1) Altar: 醮壇 temporary altar for prayer; 設壇 set up altar; 天壇, 地壇 altar to Heaven, to Earth. (2) Forum: 講壇 speaking platform; 論壇 tribune, forum for discussion, used as name of magazines and newspapers. (3) Corresponding to "circles": 文壇, 劇壇, 影壇 literary, dramatic, movie circles. (4) 花壇 raised flower bed.

壇場 *tarncharng*, n., area of the sacrificial altar.
壇坫 *tarndiahn*, n., (AC) sacrificial altar for taking oath set up during conference of states; hence symbol of diplomacy.

坵 11A.30-9

chiou.

[Var. of 丘 90.30]

§ 11A.40 (土/口)

塔 11A.40-2

taa.

N. ('*l*) Pagoda: 寶塔 Buddhist pagoda; 燈塔 lighthouse; 塔灰 cobwebs and dirt under ceiling.

培 塘 垢 墻 堵 坩 增

培 11A.40-6

peir (**poou*).

Vb. To cover (plants) and nourish with soil: 培植, 培養 *-jyr*, *-yaang* ↓; 栽ᴬ培 11.71.

培植 *peirjyr*, v.t., plant, and nourish (trees), educate, train (persons) for special abilities (培植人材).
培塿 **pourloou* n., (MC) small hillock (var. 部婁).
培養 *peiryaang*, v.t., see *-jyr* ↑.
培育 *peiryuh*, v.t., ditto.
培壅 *peiryuung*, v.t., plant and cover with soil.

塘 11A.40-6

tarng.

N. (1) Embankment: 海塘 seawall; 河塘 river embankment. (2) Pond: 魚塘 fishpond; 池塘 pond.

垢 11A.40-9

gouh.

N. (LL) dirt, filth, stains: 塵垢 dust and dirt; 污垢 dirty marks; 無垢 pure, flawless; 藏污納垢 a place where the worst elements of society are assembled; 忍辱含垢 silently endure all the disgrace and humiliations.

Adj. Dirty, filthy, stained: 蓬首垢面 with unkempt hair and an unwashed face.

垢膩 *gouhnih*, n., deposits of sweat, oil on the skin.
垢泥 *gouhnir*, n., see *-nih* ↑.

§11A.41 (土/図)

墻 11A.41-1

chiarng.

N. A wall (usu. wr. 牆).

堵 11A.41-1

duu.

[Var. of 睹]

N. (1) Wall, section of wall. (2) A surname.

V.t. To block up (hole in wall, embankment): stop up, shut up, see 堵嘴 *-tzueei* ↓; 堵死 stop up completely (a doorway); 堵着 blocked up.

堵牆 *duuchiarng*, n., low wall.
堵喪 *duu'sang*, v.t., offend (person) by rude remark.
堵塞 *duuseh*, v.t., stop (leaks, holes).
堵心 *duushin*, v.i., feel badly, frustrated.
堵嘴 *durtzueei*, v.i., (1) to shut up, silence (argument); (2) to silence witness, etc. by money or other inducement.

坩 11A.41-2

gan.

N. Earthenware, an earthware vessel.

坩堝 *ganguo*, n., (chem.) a crucible: 坩堝鍊鋼法 the crucible process; 坩堝鋼 crucible steel.

增 11A.41-8

tzeng.

V.i. & t. Add to, increase: 增加 *-jia* ↓; 增減 add or subtract; 增多 become more numerous; 增補 fill up gaps, supply deficiencies; 增福 be more blessed; 增壽 have a longer span of life, enjoy longevity; 增德 grow in moral stature; 增價 hike prices; 增高 become taller, heighten; 增援 reinforce troops; 增兵 send reinforcements; 增強 strengthen; 增大 enlarge, expand; 增廣 broaden, extend; 增刪 add and delete; 倍增 to double in amount; 突增 increase all of a sudden.

增產 *tzeng-chaan*, v.t., to boost (industrial, agricultural) production.
增光 *tzeng-guang*, v.i., add honor, glory, luster.
增長 *tzengjaang*, v.i. & t., grow (in size, bulk), become larger; wax, thrive; to increase (knowledge, experience).
增加 *tzengjia*, v.i. & t., to increase (burden, responsibility, appropriations), add to (expenses, worries, pleasures); (populations) increase.
增進 *tzengjihn*, v.i. & t. develop (skills, technical know-how); cultivate (friendship), improve (relations, mutual understanding).
增值 *tzengjyr*[1], v.i., to increase in value: 土地增值稅 land increment tax.
增殖 *tzengjyr*[2], v.i., propagate, procreate, reproduce.
增刊 *tzengkan*, n., a (weekly, literary) supplement of newspaper.
增損 *tzeng-suun*, v.t., to increase or decrease, add or subtract.
增添 *tzengtian*, v.t., ＝增加 *-jia* ↑.
增益 *tzengyih*, v.i., add s.t. more to the original stock.

A

墦 11A.41-9

arn.

N. (AC) Grave: 墦祭 sacrifice at the graves.

§11A.42 (土/冈)

埔 11A.42-1

buu(*puu*).
[Dist. 浦 63A.42]

N. Port or river area: 黃ᐞ埔 20.80 place name.

壖 11A.42-3

ruarn.

N. A stretch of open space outside the city wall or along a river.

壩 11A.42-3

bah.
[Var. 覇; pop. 垻]

N. Embankment: 打壩 build embankment.

壻 11A.42-3

shyuh.
[Var. of 婿 93A.42]

B

坍 11A.42-4

tan.

V.i. Collapse: 坍下來 collapse; 坍了半截 half collapse; 坍倒 crumble down.

坍 台 *tan-tair*, v.i., be humiliated; draw out props: 坍我的台 undermine what I am trying to do.

坰 11A.42-4

jyung.
[Var. 垌]

N. Wild uncultivated land: 坰牧 the wilds; 坰野 ditto.

堋 11A.42-4

behng(**perng*).

N. (**perng*) (AC) target.

V.t. (AC) bury in grave.

墉 11A.42-6

yurng (also *yung*).

N. (1) An adobe wall. (2) A very small walled town.

埆 11A.42-9

chyueh.
[Var. of 确 31B.42]

C

§11A.50 (土/ㄱ)

垮 11A.50-1

kuaa.

V.i. To collapse: 牆垮了 wall has collapsed; 打垮了 be routed; 拖垮了 wear down by attrition, pull down; 賠垮了 become bankrupt through business losses; 病垮了 become a physical wreck through long illness; 累垮了 exhausted from overwork; 他身體垮了 his health is failing.

垮 台 *kuaatair*, v.i., to collapse, to step down from office, to lose high position: 他垮台了 has lost official position, see 臺 11.11.

墈 11A.50-2

kahn.

N. Dangerous cliffside.

圬 11A.50-3

wu.
[Var. 杇]

V.t. To plaster (wall), whitewash: 圬者, 圬人 plasterer; 圬鏝 a trowel used for plastering.

場 11A.50-4

yih.
[Dist. 塲]

N. (AC) border region; field

boundary.

場 11A.50-4

charng (sp. pr. *chaang*).
[Var. 塲]

N. adjunct. A passing scene: 一場好戲 a good play; 一場春夢 a spring dream; 一場比賽 one contest.

N. (1) Field, open space, hall, place of congregation: 廣場 square, plaza, in city; 操場 athletic field; 球場 tennis field, baseball field, etc.; 跑馬場 racecourse; 空場 open space; 靶場 archery grounds, rifle range; 溜冰場 skating rink; 戰場 battlefield; 會場 place of meeting, assembly hall; 舞場 dance hall; 飛機場 airport; 市場 market place; 商場 emporium, market; 鹽場 salt-beds; 漁場 fishing grounds, fish nursery; 林場 tree plantation, logging station, forestry station; 實驗農場 experimental farm; 場圃 nursery for flowers, vegetable farm. (2) A scene in drama, a place in action: 第三場 scene III; 上場, 下場 exit and entrance on stage; see also N. Adjunct ↑; 在場 s.o. is present, on the scene; 當場抓到 caught on the spot; 誤場 late for contest or arranged meeting; 出場 appear on the scene; 臨場 at time of (closing battle, examinations); 大鬧一場 create a big scene; 哭叫一場 have a bout of yelling and weeping; 排場 put up a show, or (adj.) showy, ostentatious; 道場 a Taoist mass of prayers, etc.; 官場 official life or circles, officialdom.

場合 *charngher*, n., a bout in fighting, jousting; a scene or situation: 在那個場合 in that situation or context.
場面 *charngmiahn*, n., (1) public appearance: 維持場面 s.t. for appearance's sake; (2) scope: 場面很大 a big scope or size and quality of meeting.
場所 *charngsuoo*, n., place of meeting or assembly.
場子 *chaangtz*, n., a public place for amusements.

塌 11A.50-4

ta.

V.i. To collapse, sink or bend downward: 房子塌下去 house collapses; 倒塌, 塌倒 ditto; 垂頭塌翼 downcast, dejected, head bent and wings drooping; see esp. 塌台 *-tair* ↓; 塌鼻子 a flat nose; 塌鼻梁 a nose with broken bridge; 塌天大禍 a disaster like the heavens falling down.

塌架 *ta-jiah*, v.i., collapse (of house, affairs; 架＝scaffolding).
塌中 *tajung*, v.i., (of opera singer) voice breaks from insufficient breath.
塌颯 *tasah*, v.i., feel frustrated.
塌陷 *tashiahn*, v.i., collapse, give way (pavement, bridge, etc.).
塌實 *ta'shy*, adj., at ease: 我心裏不塌實 do not feel at ease; 塌實着說 to tell the truth, to be quite honest.
塌台 *ta-tair*, v.i. & t., ruin or spoil a show, undermine a build-up: 請不要塌我的台 please do not undermine what I am hoping to do.
塌塌兒 *ta'ta'l*, n., (Manchu) a small house.
塌秧兒 *tayang'l* v.i., droop (of grass); (fig.) feel crestfallen.

坊 11A.50-6

fang (*'fang*).

N. (1) Streets, city quarter: 街坊 (*-'fang*) the streets; 坊市 the streets and markets; 坊間 in the streets, city quarters. (2) Memorial arch: 牌坊; 貞節坊 chastity arch; 節孝坊 arch of chastity and filial piety. (3) Shop, mill: 染坊 shop, mill where cloth is dyed; 磨坊 (*-'fang*) flour mill; 油坊 oil press.

坊本 *fangbeen*, n., trade edition of book.
坊門 *fangmern*, n., gate of an alley (can be closed at night).
坊廂 *fangshiang*, n., (MC) divisions of city area into precincts: 坊 inside city and 廂 near city gate.

塢 11A.50-9

wuh.
[Var. of 隖]

N. A cove, recess or depressed area: 船塢 a dockyard; 村塢 depressed or back areas of village.

均 11A.50-9

jyun (**yuhn*).

N. (1) A potter's wheel. (2) Name of an anc. measure. (3) An anc. musical instrument. (4) (**yuhn*) (＝韻) Rhyme.

Adj. & adv. (1) Equal(ly), fair(ly): 均派 *-paih*, 均平 *-pirng* ↓; 平均 (on) an average, equally; 均買均賣 fair dealing in business; 均分 *-fen*, 均等 *-deeng*, 均攤 *-tan*, 均衡 *-herng* ↓; 均霑 to share equally; 均產 equal distribution of wealth (property); 均權 equality of rights; 均勢 *-shyh* ↓; 均一 *-yi*[1], 均勻 *-(')yurn* ↓. (2) All, both: 均可 all, both, will do.

均等 *jyundeeng*, adv., on an equal footing.
均分 *jyunfen*, v.t., divide equally.
均衡 *jyunherng*, adj., well balanced.
均派 *jyunpaih*, v.t., apportion (burden, work) equally.
均平 *jyunpirng*, adv., on the

average; adj., even, balanced.

均勢 *jyun-shyh*, n., balance of power.

均攤 *jyun-tan*, v.t., share (work) equally.

均一 *jyunyi*[1], adj. & adv., uniform (ly), equal(ly).

均壹 *jyunyi*[2], adv., with concentrated effort.

均勻 *jyun(')yurn*, adj. & adv., even (distribution), smooth (binding, etc.).

坳 11A.50-9

au (also *auh*).

[Var. 垇, related 窪 62A.11]

N. A depression, a hollow in ground: 坳堂 (AC) a hollow in the yard; 坳塘 a small pond.

§ 11A.63 (土/丶)

壎 11A.63-9

shyun (also *shyuan*).

N. Anc. ocarina, made of clay; 壎篪 (allu.) harmony of brothers, see 篪 92A.70.

§ 11A.70 (土/乚)

墝 11A.70-1

chiau.

Adj. (Of land) rocky, unproductive (var. of 磽).

地 11A.70-2

dih.

Part. (*'de*) Particle: 忽地 suddenly; 特地 specially; a modern substitute for 的, equiv. to Eng. "-ly," affected by some writers: 偷偷地 stealthily; 慢慢地 slowly; 不聲不響地 (in place of 的) silently.

N. (1) The Earth: 天地 heaven and earth; 地球 the earth. (2) Ground, land: 地上, 地下 on the ground, underground; 田地 field; 空地 vacant land; 耕地, 荒地 cultivated, uncultivated land; 草地 lawn, pasture land; 不毛之地 land which does not grow anything; 地皮 land, real estate; 土地 land (in real estate value). (3) Place, locality, territory: 地帶, 地區 district; 殖民地 colony; 佔領地 occupied territory; 此地 here, this place. (4) Situation, position: 地位 situation; 易地則皆然 change places and everybody would act in the same way. (5) Base: 見地 point of view; 心地 heart, disposition (broad, narrow, selfish, etc.); 白地黑字 black letters on white, put down in black and white.

地板 *dihbaan*, n., wooden floor.

地保 *dihbaau*, n., local constable, responsible for law and order among residents of locality.

地柏 *dihbor*, n., (bot.) plant of cypress family, *Selaginella kraussiana.*

地步 *dihbuh*, n., (1) situation; (2) free space, esp. room for movement or retreat: 留地步 leave (s.o.) room for staying on or retreat.

地產 *dihchaan* n., real estate: 地產生意 real estate business.

地錢 *dihchiarn*, n., (bot.) *Marchantia polymorpha.*

地殼 *dihchiauh*, n., (geol.) earth-crust.

地契 *dihchih*, n., title deeds for land.

地球 *dihchiour*, n., the earth; 地球儀 *--yir*, n., globe model.

地權 *dihchyuarn*, n., right to land, landownership: 平均地權 equalization of land rights, as advocated by Dr. Sun Yat-sen.

地膽 *dihdaan*, n., (zoo.) an insect with bulging belly, *Meloe coarctatus.*

地帶 *dihdaih*, n., district, region.

地道 *dihdauh*, n., (1) tunnel, underground passage; (2) also pr. *dih'dau*, adv., thoroughly, (=道地).

地點 *dihdiaan*, n., locality (good, bad, convenient).

地丁 *dihding*, n., formerly, term denoting land tax and labor levy.

地段 *dihduahn*, n., district, region, section of city.

地動 *dihduhng*, n., earthquake (also 地震 *-jehn* ↓).

地方 *dihfang*, n. & adj., local, locality: 地方行政 local administration; 地方色彩 local color; 地方自治 local self-government; 地方時 local time; 地方法院 district court (pr. *dih'fang*) =地保 constable, see *-baau* ↑.

地膚 *dihfu*, n., (bot.) *Kochia scoparia.*

地府 *dihfuu*, n., Hades, netherworld.

地根兒 *dihge'l*, adv., at heart (unwilling, etc.), also wr. 底.

地瓜 *dihgua*, n., potato (cf. Fr. *pomme de terre*).

地棍 *dihguhn*, n., local ruffian, see *-pii* ↓.

地花菜 *dihhua-tsaih*, n., (bot.) *Patrinia palmata.*

地黃 *dihhuarng*, n., (bot.) *Rehmannia lutea*, whose root is used as Chin. medicine (also known as 熟地).

地震 *dihjehn*, n., earthquake; 地震計 *--jih*, seismograph.

地基 *dihji*, n., foundation (of building).

地價稅 *dihjiahsueih*, n., land tax.

地窖 *dihjiauh*, n., cellar, basement.

地界 *dihjieh*, n., boundary.

地錦 *dihjiin*, n., (bot.) a creeper

plant, *Quinaria tricuspidata*.

地軸 *dih-jour*, n., axis of earth's rotation.

地中海 *Dijung-haai*, n., the Mediterranean.

地主 *dihjuu*, n., landlord: 盡地主之誼 exercise hospitality toward visitor.

地支 *dihjy*, n., the duodecimal cycle, beginning with 子, 丑, 寅, 卯, cf. 天^Δ干 31.81, see Appendix A.

地志(誌) *dihjyh*, n., district history (including geography, famous sons, historic sites).

地質學 *dihjyr-shyuer*, n., geology; 地質時代 geologic age, period.

地址 *dihjyy*, n., address.

地炕 *dihkahng*, n., earthen bed heated from underneath in North China.

地牢 *dihlaur*, n., dungeon.

地雷 *dihleir*, n., land mine.

地力 *dihlih*¹, n., land productivity.

地利 *dihlih*², n., (1) military advantage in terrain; (2) see 力 *-lih*¹↑.

地栗 *dihlih*³, n., water chestnut.

地理(學) *dihlii-shyuer*, n., geography.

地龍 *dihlurng*, n., earthworm.

地黴素 *dihmeirsuh*, n., terramycin.

地面 *dihmiahn*, n., ground surface; area.

地脈 *dihmoh*, n., layout of strata in the land; underground rivers.

地盤 *dihparn*, n., surrounding land of building; region marked out as operating ground for bandits, warlords.

地痞 *dihpii*, n., "scars of the land"—local ruffians who prey on the residents.

地皮 *dihpir*, n., land regarded as estate.

地平面 *dihpirngmiahn*, n., horizontal plane; 地平線 *--shiahn*, horizon.

地舖 *dihpuh*, n., bed space on the floor.

地熱 *dihreh*, n., subterranean heat.

地上莖 *dihshahng-jing*, n., (bot.) aerial stem of plant.

地下 *dihshiah*, adj. & n., underground (train, organization, work); 地下莖 *--jing*, subterranean stem of plant; 地下水 *--shueei*, ground water; 地下組織 underground organisation.

地線 *dihshiahn*, n., ground wire.

地峽 *dihshiar*, n., isthmus.

地心 *dihshin*, n., center of earth; 地心吸力 *--shihlih*, gravitation of the earth.

地形 *dihshirng*, n., topography.

地勢 *dihshyh*, n., topography, layout of land.

地史學 *dihshyy-shyuer*, n., historical geology.

地毯 *dihtaan*, n., carpet.

地攤(兒) *dihtan (-ta'l)*, n., from 擺地攤 sell articles displayed on side walk floor.

地頭 *dihtour*, n., place, locality: 地頭鬼 local ruffians who operate with outside gang; 地頭蛇 local gangsters who feed on population.

地蠶 *dihtsarn*, n., (bot.) Chin. artichoke, *Stachys sieboidi*; 地蠶蛾 *--er*, (zoo.) insect pest on beans, *Mamestra brassicae*.

地層 *dihtserng*, n., geologic strata.

地磁 *dihtsyr*, n., terrestrial magnetism.

地圖 *dihtur*, n., map.

地位 *dihweih*, n., social position.

地衣 *dihyi*, n., lichens.

地窨子 *dihyihntz*, n., cellar, basement.

地域 *dihyuh*¹, n., territory.

地獄 *dihyuh*², n., hell.

地榆 *dihyur*¹, n., the garden burnet, *Sanguisorba offinalis*.

地輿 *dihyur*², n., (LL) geography.

堍 11A.70-5

tuh.

N. Ramp leading to a bridge.

圮 11A.70-5

pii.

Adj. (1) Broken down (of buildings, walls): 傾圮 falling apart; 圮毀 (LL) destroyed. (2) stopped up: 圮滯 (LL) stopped up; 圮地 rubbles or unpassable area.

圯 11A.70-5

yir.

N. (AC) bridge.

坑 11A.70-6

keng.

N. A pit, a sunken hole in ground: 土坑 a sunken pit; 糞坑, 茅坑 sunken construction for manure, country-style water closet over an open pit; 煤坑 coal pit; 泥坑 quagmire; 水坑 pool of water; 火坑 fire pit; 跳火坑 undertake an impossible task, accept an extremely delicate job (likened to "jumping into a fire pit"); 墜入火坑 sink into prostitution; 跳出火坑 get out of prostitution or slave traffic.

V.t. (1) To bury; to bury alive: 焚書坑儒 (of 秦始皇) burned books and buried Confucian scholars alive in gully. (2) Bring disaster, entrap in misery: 坑其民 (AC) bring disaster to his people; 坑害 brutally destroy; 坑人 *-rern*↓.

坑道 *kengdauh*, n., (mil.) underground tunnel.

坑坑窪窪 *kengkengwawa*, adj., (of road surface) full of bumps and holes.

坑兒 *keng'l*, n., a depression, a pit; see *-tz*↓.

坑騙 *kengpiahn*, v.t., to cheat by trickery, to swindle.

坑人 *kengrern*, v.i., (1) to lay trap for people; (2) to cause endless trouble: 你可把我坑苦了 you have got me into a fix; 這麽做, 可坑死人了 it will kill me to do it this way; 才坑人哪 what a setup!

坑子 *kengtz*, n., (1) a pit, a small hole; (2) village water closet set up over an open pit.

境 11A.70-6

jihng.

N. (1) Boundary, border, territory under jurisdiction: 邊境 the frontier; 出境, 入境 exit from, entry into, a country; 境域 *-yuh* ↓; 越境 to cross the border, trespass; 離境 depart(ure) from a country (city); 國境 national territory. (2) Fortune, good or bad: 順境 good fortune, prosperity; 逆境 bad fortune, adversity; 處境 personal circumstances: 處境困難 in an awkward predicament, in a bad fix. (3) Condition, situation: 佳境 a favorable situation: 漸入佳境 is getting more and more enjoyable; 險境 a dangerous situation; 環境 environment; 境況 *-kuahng*, 境遇 *-yuh*[1] ↓. (4) 進境 progress: 學有進境 have made some progress in studies.

境地 *jihngdih*, n., territory under jurisdiction.
境界 *jihngjieh*, n., (1) boundaries; (2) position, location; (3) condition, state of affairs, circumstance; (4) atmosphere of poetry.
境況 *jihngkuahng*, n., personal circumstances.
境遇 *jihngyuh*[1], n., a person's fortune, good or bad, personal circumstances.
境域 *jihngyuh*[2], n., territory.

坨 11A.70-6

tuor.

N. A mound, roundish mass: 鹽坨 mound of salt in salt fields; 秤坨 metal weight for steelyards.

坨 11A.70-6

char.

N. A small mound.

壠 11A.70-9

luung.

[Var. of 壟 60.11]

垷 11A.70-9

nir.

N. See 埤⁴垷 11A.10.

塊 11A.70-9

kuaih.

N. adjunct. A piece (mostly a broken, divided or cut solid part): 一塊石頭, 鐵 a piece of rock, iron; 一塊布, 肉 a piece of cloth, a slice of meat; 一塊糖 a piece of candy, a cube of sugar; 一塊豆腐 a piece of bean curd; 一塊地 a plot of land.

N. A broken solid piece: 碎塊 broken bits; 布塊 piece cloth, any cut of cloth; 大塊, 小塊 a big, small piece.

Adj. 塊然 standing apart or alone.

垝 11A.70-9

gueei.

Adj. Dilapidated, ruined: 垝垣 a wall fallen into ruin.

§11A.71 (土/弋)

城 11A.71-7

cherng.

N. City, town: 城市 *-shyh*, 城郭 *-guo* ↓; 城下之盟 capitulate to the enemy, treaty signed below the city wall to avert destruction; 城狐社鼠 city foxes and rats in temples — corrupt officials and gentry (educated rascals) who prey upon the common people.

城牆 *cherngchiarng*, n., city wall.
城池 *cherngchyr*, n., city wall and moat—the city defense.
城圈兒 *cherngchyuah'l*, n., the city enclosure.
城闕 *cherngchyueh*, n., gate tower.
城堞 *cherngdier*, n., battlements, parapets on city wall.
城垛口 *cherngduoo'kou*, n., battlements; projected corners on city wall.
城府 *cherngfuu*, n., (1) see *-shyh* ↓; (2) prejudices: 城府甚深 deep prejudices; 胸無城府 quite open-minded.
城根(兒) *chernggen(-ge'l)*, n., area directly adjacent to city wall.
城郭 *cherng-guo*, n., city wall and 郭 outer city wall—city defense.
城濠 *chernghaur*, n., moat around city.
城河 *chernghe*, n., ditto.
城隍 *chernghuarng*, (1) see *-chyr* ↑; (2) (also *-'huang*) the justices in Hades presiding over fate of the souls.
城樓 *chernglour*, n., city tower.
城門 *cherngmern*, n., city gate: 城門洞兒 the gate shaped like a tunnel because of the thickness of the wall; 城門樓子 gate tower; 城門臉兒 area just outside city gate.
城市 *cherngshyh*, n., the city, as opp. the country 鄉下.
城頭 *cherngtour*, n., the top of city wall.

域 堿 坻 壈 埝 墳 塡 垻 壙 塓 塽

域 11A.71-7

yuh.

N. Land, territory, district: 疆域 national territory; 異域 foreign, strange country; 絕域 remote isolated territory; 西域 Turkestan; 域外 outside China; 域中 inside the country; 領域 jurisidictional territory.

堿 11A.71-7

jiaan.

[Var. of 鹼 22S.71 alkali]

坻 11A.71-9

chyr (**dii*).

N. (1) (AC) sandbars. (2) (**dii*) (AC) a slope: 隴坻 slope in fields.

§11A.72 (土/心)

壈 11A.72-7

kaan.

壈 坷 *karnkee*, adj., (var. of ᐞ坎坷) meeting hard luck, frustrated.

埝 11A.72-8

niahn.

N. Earthen embankment for flood prevention.

§11A.80 (土/八)

墳 11A.80-1

fern (**fehn*).

N. Grave, usu. in form of a mound: 墳地 graveyard, cemetery; 墳山 hill cemetery; 墳圈子 graveyard enclosure; 墳頭兒 front of grave mound; 墳少爺 (facet.) cemetery caretaker.

V.i. Bulge up: 墳起, also pr. **fehn.*

Adj. Bulging.

墳 典 *ferndiaan*, n., (LL) referring to 三墳五典 early lost books on oracles, etc.
墳 地 *ferndih*, n., grave site.
墳 墓 *fernmuh*, n., grave.
墳 山 *fernshan*, n., public cemetery on hill ground.

塡 11A.80-2

tiarn.

V.t. To fill up: 塡空 fill hole, blank; 塡平 fill up and make even (road); 塡餡兒 fill with stuffing, (fig.) serve as expendable; 塡表 fill blank form; 塡滿, 塡飽 feed to the full; 塡鴨 forced feeding of duck for rapid growth; cram information into student's head as one form of "education"; 塡還 pay back (debt).

Adj. See 塡塡 -*tiarn* ↓.

塡 補 *tiarnbuu*, v.t., fill a vacancy.
塡 地 *tiarndih*, n., land reclaimed from sea or river.
塡 發 *tiarnfa*, v.t., fill in printed form and issue (certificate, etc.).
塡 房 *tiarnfang*, n., second wife after first wife's death.
塡 海 *tiarn-haai*, v.i., & n. reclaim, -ation.
塡 註 *tiarn-juh*, v.t., add notes.
塡 空 *tiarn-kung*, v.i., fill in what is needed, whether competent or not.
塡 塞 *tiarnseh*, v.t., fulfill (obligation) as a matter of form.
塡 寫 *tiarnshiee*, v.i., copy in, fill a form.
塡 塡 *tiarntiarn*, adj., (AC) thunderous, rumbling in sound; heavy-stepped; full.
塡 詞 *tiarntsyr*, v.i., to write words to given melody, to write 詞 a form of poem with definite song pattern.

垻 11A.80-4

bah.

[Pop. of 壩]

壙 11A.80-6

kuahng.

N. (1) Grave. (2) Prairies.

Adj. (AC) var. of 曠 open, empty.

塓 11A.80-6

mih.

V.t. (AC) to plaster (wall).

§11A.81 (土/人)

塽 11A.81-1

shuaang.

N. A high wide-open ground.

垓 11A.81-6

gai.

N. (1) Distant lands: 垓極 (LL) the farthest corners of the country. (2) A boundary or frontier: 垓限 utmost limits, frontier regions. (3) One hundred million.

堠 11A.81-9

houh.

N. A watchtower, or outpost; a milestone.

墺 11A.81-9

auh.

N. Bay land, bay strip.

坎 11A.81-9

kaan.

N. (1) A pit, hole, trap in ground: 坎坑, 坎穴 *-keng, -shyuer* ↓; 心坎 feeling at bottom of the heart. (2) One of the eight diagrams, denoting water, hidden danger; see *baguah* 八卦 80.80. (3) Sound of beating, chopping, see 坎坎 *-kaan* ↓.

Adj. In danger, in distress: 坎坷, 坎兒 *-kee, -'l* ↓.

坎窞 *kaandahn*, n., pitfall, snare.

坎肩兒 *kaanjia'l*, n., vest, waistcoat.

坎坎 *karnkaan*, n., (1) (AC) sound of drumbeats; sound of chopping wood; (2) (AC) empty (stomach); (3) (MC) meeting hardships, see *-kee* ↓.

坎坷 *karnkee*, adj., meeting hard luck, frustrated, (also wr. 坎軻).

坎坑 *kaankeng*, n., hole, pit in the ground.

坎兒 *kaa'l*, (1) n., obstruction on road; (2) uneven surface.

坎壈 *karnlaan*, adj., see *-kee* ↑.

坎穴 *kaanshyuer*, n., a cave, an underground hole.

垁 11A.81-9

kuaih.

[Pop. of 塊 11A.70]

埃 11A.81-9

ai.

N. (1) Dust: 塵埃 dust. (2) Short for 埃及 Egypt.

---

§ 11A.82 (土/乂)

坡 11A.82-2

po.

N. (*-tz, 'l*) A slope: 山坡 foothill slope; 斜坡 slanting ground; 上, 下坡 to go up or down slope.

埂 11A.82-3

geeng.

N. (1) A hole, depression in ground. (2) 田埂 a footpath in the fields.

圾 11A.82-3

jir (**seh*).

N. (**seh*) 垃圾 (*lehseh*) garbage, refuse.

Adj. (U.f. 岌 21.82) perilous, dangerous.

墁 11A.82-4

mahn.

N. Spate for applying plaster (*-tz*), (=鏝).

V.t. To plaster (wall); to pave: 墁地 pave floor (with bricks).

墩 11A.82-6

dun.

N. (1) A small mound. (2) (*-tz*) Thick chopping board or block.

坂 11A.82-9

baan.

[Var. 阪]

N. Hill slope.

---

§ 11A.83 (土/〜)

堤 11A.83-4

tir.

[Var. of 隄 32A.83]

埏 11A.83–9

yarn (**shan*).

N. (1) (AC) a walk leading to grave. (2) (**shan*) Molded clay tile.

V.t. (**shan*) See 埏埴 *-jyr* ↓.

埏 埴 **shanjyr*, v.i., (potter) mix water with clay to shape molds.

§ 11A.93 (土/く)

坛 11A.93–3

tarn.
[Abbr. of 壇 11A.30]

埂 11A.93–3

ruarn.

N. (1) Lands close to the edge of a river: 河埂, 水埂 riparian land. (2) Fields outside the city wall. (3) Empty spaces outside the palace or imperial shrine.

壜 11A.93–4

tarn.
[Related 墰, 罈, 罎]

N. (*-tz*) An earthen wine jar, jug: 壜子肉 pork stewed in earthen jar over slow fire.

SECTION 11S

§ 11S.00 (土^{S}/丿)

封 11S.00–1

feng.
[Cogn. 邦 10S.22]

N. adjunct. 一封信 one letter, see N. ↓.

N. (1) A surname. (2) Package, parcel: 一封銀子 one package of silver; 信封 envelope. (3) Tip: 賞 封 tip; 門封 tip to gate keeper.

V.t. (1) Establish fiefdoms for nobles, princes: 封建 *-jiahn* ↓; 太公封於齊 Duke Tai was made prince of Chir; 封侯, 封相 create duke, appoint prime minister; 封爵 create noble; 封誥, 封贈 grant titles to deceased parents of high officials so that sacrifices may be made due to rank; grant posthumous honors: 封君 *-jyun* ↓; 封神 deify, canonize; 封禪 *-shahn* ↓. (2) To seal, close up: 封了 is sealed already; 封上 seal up; 封送, 封寄, 封上 seal and send to (person); 封存, 封貯 seal up for storage or safekeeping; 封火 to bank up fire; 封關 close up for customs, (bank) holiday; 封門 (大吉) seal up for New Year holidays; 封河 rivers freeze stopping traffic; 封臺, 封箱 theaters stop performance for period near New Year; 封印 *-yihn* ↓; 查封 confiscate, attach property (with official seal over door); 密封 seal up (letter) completely; 故步自封 limit one's own progress. (3) Heap earth over mound: 封土, 封墓, 封樹.

Adj. (AC) big: 封豕長蛇 big hogs and long snakes, (fig.) rapacious person; 封狐 (AC) big fox.

封 拜 *fengbaih*, v.t., create (nobles), confer (ranks, posts).

封 閉 *fengbih*, v.t., seal up, close up (harbor, river traffic).

封 建 *fengjiahn*, n. & adj., feudalism; 封建制度 feudal system; 封建社會, 思想 feudalistic society, ideas.

封 疆 *fengjiang*, n., border provinces; 封疆大臣 (大吏) governors, commanders of border-provinces.

封 禁 *fengjihn*, n. & v.t., blockade (seaport 海口), see *-suoo* ↓; shut up and prevent access: 封禁地 ground closed to public.

封 殖 *fengjyr*, v.t., (1) bank up earth around trees; foster; (2) (AC) 厚自封殖 amass wealth.

封 君 *fengjyun*, n., deceased father or ranked official (given posthumous title).

封 蠟 *fenglah*, n., sealing wax.

封 面 *fengmiahn*, n., cover (of book, magazine).

封 皮 *fengpir*, n., outside cover.

封 賞 *fengshaang*, v.t., give tips.

封 禪 *fengshahn*, n., grand ceremony of worship of heaven on mountain top (Taishan) to pray and say thanks for peace and prosperity.

封 神 榜 *Fengshernbaang*, n., a classical novel of chin. gods and heroes.

封 守 *fengshoou*, v.t., guard (defense posts).

封 鎖 *fengsuoo*, n. & v.t., (mil.) blockade; seal up (treasure, etc.): 封鎖貨幣 blocked currency.

封 套 *fengtauh*, n., folder, large envelope, enclosing case for protection.

封 條 *fengtiaur*, n., official slip of paper pasted over door, cover, to prevent opening (as in bond).

封 翁 *fengweng*, n., see *-jyun* ↑.

封 邑 *fengyih*, n., a manor estate granted by a monarch.

封 印 *fengyihn*, n.& v.i., custom of closing up office for New Year by locking up seal.

赫 11S.00–2

heh.

Adj. (1) Resplendent, brilliant, splendid, awe-inspiring. (2) Bright, flaming red.

赫赫 *hehheh*, adj., majestic, awe-inspiring: 赫赫有名 far-famed, illustrious. 「surname.

赫連 *Hehliarn*, n., a compound

赫然 *hehrarn*, adj. & adv., flaming, stunning, overwhelming in appearance: 赫然震怒 in flaming anger.

赫烜 *hehshyuan*, adj., radiant, impressive, marvellous to behold.

刦 11S.00-2

jier.

[Var. of 劫 11S.50]

刲 11S.00-2

kuei.

V.t. (AC) to cut, to slice off.

§ 11S.02 (土^S/ㄎ)

隸 11S.02-2

lih.

[Var. of 隸 10S.02]

§ 11S.22 (土^S/丨)

卦 11S.22-2

guah.

N. (AC) symbols used in divination: see 八^{A}卦 80.80 the Eight Diagrams; 卦攤兒 a fortune-teller's stall; 占卦 to consult *baguah* oracles.

郝 11S.22-3

haau (re. pr. *heh*).

N. A surname.

都 11S.22-3

du (*dou).

N. (1) Metropolis, capital: 京都 national capital; 省都 provincial capital; 建都, 遷都 establish, move capital; 首都 national capital, most important city; 陪都 second capital; 都下, 都中 at the capital; 都城, 都會 *-cherng, -hueih* ↓. (2) City: 都市, 都邑 *-shyh, -yih* ↓.

Adj. (AC) elegant, handsome: 麗都, 都麗 handsome (building, person, etc.); 都雅 *-yaa* ↓.

Adv. (*du* or **dou*) All: 都來了 all have come, have all come; 我都要 I want all of it; 都 (是) 因爲你 all because of you; 都拿去 take all of it; 都是我的不是 it's all my mistake; 大都 mostly.

都察院 *ducharyuahn*, n., formerly, Court of Censors; 都老爺 address or reference to court censor.

都城 *ducherng*, n., capital city.

都督 *duduh*, n., formerly, military governor of province.

都會 *duhueih*, n., metropolis.

都麗 *dulih*, adj., handsome, elegant.

都門 *dumern*, n., the capital.

都市 *dushyh*, n., urban area, city.

都統 *dutuung*, n., see *-duh* ↑.

都尉 *duweih*, n., formerly, captain, commander.

都雅 *duyaa*, adj., (LL) elegant, refined-looking.

都邑 *duyih*, n., metropolitan city.

郤 11S.22-5

chyueh

[Pop. of 卻 80S.22]

§ 11S.40 (土^S/口)

喆 11S.40-1

jer.

[Var. of 哲 10.40]

嚭 11S.40-3

pii.

N. (AC) a personal name.

Adj. Big.

赯 11S.40-6

tarng.

N. Purple, purple-brown (complexion).

§ 11S.41 (土/図)

赭 11S.41–1

jee

Adj. Brown sepia or reddish-brown in color: 赭色 ditto; 赭堊 reddish clay; 赭衣 (AC) convict's dress; 赭面 face painted reddish.

赭黃 *jeehuarng*, n., yellow ocher (ochre), a clay of reddish-brown or sepia color, used as pigment, see *-shyr* ↓.

赭石 *jeeshyr*, n., (min.) hematite, earth containing iron ore, used as pigment.

§ 11S.50 (土^{S}/乛)

朅 11S.50–4

chieh.

Adj. (AC) strong, powerful (body).

V.i. To go: 來朅 (AC) turn around; 朅休 (AC) go and stop.

劫 11S.50–9

jier.

[Var. of 刼 11S.00]

N. Disaster, misfortune: 大劫, 浩劫 a calamity; 在劫難逃 there is no escape from one's fate; 萬劫不復 everlasting perdition; 劫後餘生 lucky survivor from a holocaust; 劫難 *-nahn* ↓; 生死劫 fateful crisis, a matter of life and death.

V.t. (1) Take by force: 劫道 *-dauh*[1], 劫盜 *-dauh*[2] ↓; 路劫 hold up (a person) to rob him; 洗劫 pillage, plunder; 劫奪 *-'duo* ↓; 劫營 launch a surprise attack on enemy camp; 劫寨 rush an enemy fortress; 劫牢 force open a prison to free the prisoners; 打劫 to loot. (2) Coerce: 劫制 *-jyh*, 劫持 *-chyr* ↓.

劫騎 *jierchir*, v.t., to hijack.

劫持 *jierchyr*, v.t., force one's hand, take as hostage, kidnap.

劫道 *jierdauh*[1], n., highway robbery.

劫盜 *jierdauh*[2], n., (1) robbers, bandits; (2) robbery, banditry.

劫奪 *jier'duo*, v.t., to loot, plunder, rob.

劫灰 *jierhuei*, n., ruins of destruction.

劫機 *jierji*, v.i., to hijack a plane.

劫制 *jierjyh*, v.t., coerce to compel obedience.

劫掠 *jierlyueh*[1], v.t., rob, plunder, loot.

劫略 *jierlyueh*[2], v.t., ditto.

劫盟 *jiermern*, v.t., force to sign a treaty under duress.

劫難 *jiernahn*, n., a fateful calamity.

劫數 *jiershuh*, n., an inexorable fate.

劫運 *jieryuh*, n., an inescapable fate: 劫運難逃 impossible to escape one's doom.

劫餘 *jieryur*, n., the aftermath of a natural or man-made disaster.

§ 11S.70 (土^{S}/乚)

覩 11S.70–4

duu.

[Var. 睹]

V.t. To witness, see with own eyes: 目覩 to witness (some event, situation); 有目共覩 plain for everybody to see for himself: 覩而不見 saw (bodily) but did not see; 覩此情形 seeing such (pitiful) situation.

覿 11S.70–4

dir.

V.t. Meet personally: 覿面, 覿過面 have met; 覿面相失 met personally without knowing identity.

執 11S.70–9

jyr.

N. 父執 father's friends.

V.t. (1) To hold in hand: 執筆, 執(教)鞭 *-bii, -bian* ↓; 執馬鞭 hold a whip; 執手 hold hands; 執手同行 walking together, hand in hand; 執手爲禮 shake hands (=握手); 執牛耳 (AC) "hold the ears of the cow" to be slaughtered in sacrifice during conclusion of treaty — a privilege of the head of the alliance; hence to be the acknowledged leader (in business, industry, etc.); 執其兩端 "hold both ends" — examine opposing views; 執干戈衛社稷 take up arms to defend the state; 捕執 to arrest. (2) To keep: 執中, 允執厥中 (AC, LL) keep to the center, or golden mean, unbiased; 執兩用中 (LL) listen to both sides and choose the middle course. (3) To carry out, to execute (laws, regulations): 執行 *-shirng* ↓; 執法, 執政 *-faa, -jehng* ↓; 執炊 attend to the kitchen; 執獄 act as judge. (4) To persist: 執迷不悟 persist in error; 執一 hold on to one course, not give up or deviate; 固執己見 persist in one's opinion; 執意 *-yih* ↓.

Adj. Stubborn: 固執 stubborn; 執意, 執拗, 執著 *-yih, -auh, -juor* ↓; 偏執 (a) adj., biassed, (b) v.t., insist on (one's opinion).

執拗 *jyr-auh*, adj., stubborn, headstrong.

執鞭 *jyr-bian*, phr., (1) to be carriage driver ("hold the whip"); (2) to be teacher: 執教鞭 ("hold the rod").

執筆 *jyr-bii*, v.i., to draft public statement, to take down minutes of conference (by one skilled in the use of the pen).

執法 *jyr-faa*, v.i., to execute the law; to execute person.

執紼 *jyr-fur*, v.i., to hold a staff wrapped in white paper in the funeral procession.

執掌 *jyrjaang*, n., duties, functions (of an official); v.t., to administer (government, education, secretariat, etc.).

執照 *jyrjauh(-'jau)*, n., a license (for driver, tradesman, etc.).

執政 *jyrjehng*, (1) n., head of government; (2) v.i., to head the government.

執教 *jyr-jiauh*, v.i., to teach (at certain school).

執著 *jyrjuor*, v.i., (Budd.) to persist in error.

執柯 *jyr-ke*, phr., (AC) to be matchmaker.

執禮 *jyr-lii*, v.i., to observe the formalities (of wedding, master-pupil relationship, etc.).

執行 *jyrshirng*, v.t., to execute (law, resolutions); 執行委員會 executive committee.

執事 *jyrshyh*, n., (1) (LL) one on the staff of organization; (2) formerly, court. address like 先生, 兄台 in letters; (3) (-'*shy*) paraphernalia of a funeral procession.

執業 *jyryeh*, (1) n., profession; (2) v.i., to be student (受業) of a master.

執意 *jyryih*, v.i., insist on doing s.t.

執友 *jyryoou*, n., friends of the same circle.

§11S.72 (土^{S}/心)

懿 11S.72-6

yih.

Adj. (1) (LL) (of character, esp. woman's) good, benign, virtuous, moral, worthy. (2) (AC) deep (basket).

Excl. (AC) alas! (u.f. 噫).

懿德 *yih-der*, n., woman's worthy or meritorious character.

懿範 *yih-fahn*, n., exemplary character.

懿旨 *yih-jyy*, n., command or wish of empress or empress-mother.

懿行 *yihshirng*, n., woman's virtuous conduct.

§11S.80 (土^{S}/八)

頡 11S.80-3

shier (also *jier*).

V.i. To fly upwards.

頡頏 *shierharng*, v.i. & t., (1) to rival: 互相頡頏 to rival each other; (2) to fly up and down.

§11S.81 (土^{S}/人)

款 11S.81-9

kuaan,

[Var. 欵; pop. 欵]

N. (1) A clause, item: 條款, treaty clause; 款目, 款項 *-muh*, *-shiahng*↓. (2) Fund, money: 募款, 籌款 raise money; 撥款 appropriate funds, allot money (for some purpose); 款額, 款子 *-er*, *-tz*↓; 公款 public funds; 借款 a loan; 存款 deposit, money on hand; 賠款 reparations, indemnity; 進款 income. (3) Manner: 款式 *-shyh*↓. (4) Signature on scroll or inscription: 題款 ditto; 上款, 下款 the inscription (to person) and the signature in a scroll.

V.t. (1) To take care of guests: 款待 *-daih*↓; 款客 give reception to guest. (2) (AC) to knock at gates: 款關, 款門.

Adj. & adv. (1) Sincerely: 款誠 sincere heart; 款留 cordially invite to stay; 款服 (LL) sincerely pay homage to: 款附 (LL) sincerely submit as vassal state; 款交 (LL) true friendship; 款語 (LL) intimate talk. (2) Slow, leisurely: 款步 *-buh*↓.

款步 *kuaanbuh*, adv., in slow, leisurely steps, in a stroll.

款洽 *kuaanchiah*, adj., cordial (relationship).

款曲 *kuaanchyu*, n., innermost feelings: 一敍款曲 to have a hearty talk (after long absence).

款待 *kuaandaih*, v.t., to receive, look after (guest): 慇勤款待 receive most cordially.

款冬 *kuaandung*, n., (bot.) *Petasites japonicus* (also wr. 款東).

款額 *kuaan-er*, n., a sum.

款費 *kuaanfeih*, n., expenses.

款伏 *kuaanfur*, v.t., (of accused) plead guilty.

款接 *kuaanjie*, v.t., to receive, welcome (guest, friend).

款識 *kuaanjyh*, n., signature or inscription on scroll, bronze or stone.

款款 *kuarnkuaan*, adv., leisurely: 款款而來.

款兒 *kuaan'l*, n., (1) see *-jyh*↑; (2) manner: 小姐款兒 (coll.) manner of a young lady.

款密 *kuaanmih*, adj., intimate.

款目 *kuaanmuh*, n., an item, esp. in accounts; a clause in agreement.

款項 *kuaanshiahng*, n., (1) see

-*muh*↑; (2) (-'*shiang*) a definite sum.

款式 *kuaanshyh*, (1) n., style: 蘇州款式 Soochow style (of hair, dress); (2) (-'*shyh*) adj., stylish.

款子 *kuaantz*, n., a sum: 這筆款子 this sum.

款要 *kuaanyauh*, n., (LL) true feelings.

§ 11S.82 (土^{s}/乂)

鼓 11S.82-1

guu.

N. (1) A drum: 大鼓, 小鼓 big, small drum; 鑼鼓喧天 noise created by gongs and drums; 定音鼓 tympani. (2) The beating of a drum as a unit measure of time: 五鼓 the fifth and last night-watch.

V.t. (1) To beat, strike, sound: 鼓掌 -*jaang*↓; 鼓翼 (of birds) beat wings; 鼓瑟吹笙 celebration of weddings or birthdays by playing lutes and blowing pipe instruments. (2) Stir up, rouse to action, incite, instigate: 鼓動 -'*duhng*, 鼓舞 -*wuu*, 鼓吹 -*chuei*, 鼓勵 -'*lih*↓; 鼓足幹勁 to go all out, to put forth one's energy. (3) 鼓着嘴 to pout one's lips.

Adj. Bulging, swelling: 鼓鼓囊囊 (of things fully stuffed) bulging out.

鼓吹 *guuchuei*, v.t., (1) promote and encourage (a movement); (2) promote by publicity.

鼓搗 *gurdau*, v.t., (Peip. pr. also *gur'dau*) incite, rouse to action.

鼓動 *guu'duhng*, v.t., instigate, incite: 鼓動學潮, 鼓動罷工 stir up a student demonstration, a labor strike.

鼓腹 *guufuh*, v.i., (1) be good at nothing but eating and loafing; (2) 鼓腹而歌 to beat one's belly to keep time in singing—allu. peace at time of Emperor Yao.

鼓惑 *guu'huoh*, v.t., incite to rebellion; lure into various popular sects or beliefs.

鼓掌 *gurjaang*, v.i. & t., clap hands, applaud.

鼓脹 *guujahng*, n., (med.) tympanites, distention of the belly region (also wr. 臌脹).

鼓姬 *guuji*, n., (LL) a songstress who sings to the accompaniment of a drum.

鼓鑄 *guujuh*, v.i., to mint coins by melting metals.

鼓角 *guu-jyuer*, n., (AC) a drum and horn used in the army much like the modern bugle.

鼓兒詞 *guu'l tsyr*, n., a pop. form of entertainment consisting of singing accompanied by the beating of drums (cf. 大△鼓 31.81).

鼓勵 *guu'lih*, v.t., encourage: 鼓勵後進 give encouragement to the younger generation.

鼓樓 *guu-lour*, n., a drum tower.

鼓膜 *guumor*, n., (physiol.) the tympanic membrane.

鼓盆 *guu-pern*, n., the death of one's wife (lit., "to beat an earthen basin," which Chuangtzu the philosopher did at the time of his wife's death).

鼓鼙 *guupir*, n., military affairs or maneuvers.

鼓舌 *guusher*, v.i., speak evil of others, argue speciously, to gossip, babble.

鼓手 *gurshoou*, n., a drummer.

鼓譟 *guutzauh*, v.i., argue noisily, create a commotion (also 鼓噪).

鼓舞 *gurwuu*, (1) v.t., instigate, cause (trouble); (2) v.t., encourage; (3) 歡欣鼓舞 v.i., dance for joy.

轂 11S.82-4

gu.

N. The nave or hub of a wheel: 轂擊肩摩 with jamming vehicles and pedestrians; 轂下 (AC) the imperial capital; 推轂 (allu.) put in a word for (s.o.), recommend highly (lit., "push s.o.'s vehicle").

轂轆 *gu'lu*, n., wheels; 轂轆兒 *gu'lu'l*, (a) a small wheel, a pulley; (b) a segment of anything cylindrical: 一轂轆兒香腸, 一轂轆粉筆 a piece of sausage, chalk.

彀 11S.82-4

gouh.

N. Shooting range: 入其彀中 within shooting range, (fig.) fall under trap or come under control.

V.i. To draw a bow to the full.

Adj. & adv. (Var. 够, 夠) adequate(ly), enough, sufficient(ly).

殼 11S.82-4

chueh (sp. pr. **ker* and **chiauh*). [Var. 殻]

N. (-*tz*, '*l*) Shell (of fruit and shellfish): 硬殼 hard shell; 花生殼 peanut shell; 甲殼 turtle shell; 外殼 outer shell; 子彈殼 artillery shell; 帶殼炒蝦 fried shrimp with shell on.

殼斗 *chuehdoou*, n., (bot.) *cupule*.

殼菜 *chuehtsaih*, n., (zoo.) mussel, a shellfish, *Mytilus crassitesta*.

殼物 *chuehwuh*, n., shellfish in gen.

穀 11S.82-4

guu.

N. (1) Grain, corn, cereals: 五穀

five major grains, of which, however, one list differs from another; 百穀 grains in gen.; 穀物 corn; 穀物條例 (Eng. history) the Corn Laws; 穀類 cereals as a class; 穀子 *-tz* ↓; 稻穀 paddy rice. (2) A surname.

V.t. (1) (AC) give food to, provide food for: 以穀我士女 in order to provide food for our men and women. (2) (AC) give notice of, notify: 穀喪 notify friends of s.o.'s death.

Adj. (1) (AC) (of persons) good, well-meaning: 既富方穀 one will be good after he has become rich; 不穀 (self-deprecatory) I, your unworthy prince. (2) Alive, living: (LL) 穀則異室，死則同穴 living separately during lifetime but buried in the same grave after death.

穀場 *gurchaang*, n., a threshing floor.
穀蟲 *guuchurng*, n., the weevil.
穀道 *guudauh*, n., the rectum.
穀旦 *guudahn*, n., a lucky day.
穀蛾 *guu-er*, n., (zoo.) *Tinea granella*.
穀風 *guufeng*, n., (AC) the east wind (＝谷風).
穀穀 *gurguu*, n., the cooing of 「birds.
穀種 *gurjuung*, n., seed corn.
穀梁 *guuliarng*, n., a two-character surname; 穀梁傳 one of the three expansions of Confucius' *Spring and Autumn Annals*.
穀田 *guutiarn*, n., rice fields.
穀倉 *guutsang*, n., granary.
穀子 *guutz*, n., (1) unhulled rice; (2) millet.
穀雨 *guryuu*, n., one of the twenty-four terms into which a year is divided (about April 20th–May 4th), see Appendix B.

縠 11S.82-4

hur.

N. Crepe.

鷇 11S.82-4

kouh.

N. Fledgeling; 鷇音 chirping of fledgelings.

觳 11S.82-4

hur.

N. (1) (AC) an ancient container. (2) (AC) thin, poor, lean.

觳觫 *hursuh*, adj., trembling from fear: 觳觫屏營 (LL) in fear and trembling.

赧 11S.82-5

naan.

Adj. Blushing.

赧然 *naanrarn*, adj. & adv., shamefaced, -ly.
赧顏 *naanyarn*, adj., shamefaced.

報 11S.82-5

bauh.

N. (1) Periodical, newspaper, news bulletin: 日報 daily; 晚報 evening paper; 畫報 pictorial magazine; 週報 weekly; 小報 tabloid paper. (2) Any kind of report: 情報 intelligence (bureau, department); 邸報 special newsletter from capital, official bulletin; 戰報 war bulletin; 報告 *-gauh* ↓. (3) (Budd.) retribution, God's reward and punishment (果^A報 41.01): 善有善報，惡有惡報 there is (heavenly) justice in this world; 現報 retribution before our eyes.

V. i. & t. (1) To report: 報名 register (for school, organization); 報到 report arrival; 報信 report news; 報喪 obituary; 報喜 announce happy news, such as birth of child; 報稅, 報關 pay tax, pay customs duties; 報苦窮兒 (of well-to-do people) pretend poverty, make such (false) complaints; 報功 report achievement (victory, etc.) to claim credit; 報警 report to the police, report emergency crisis. (2) To show vengeance or gratitude: 報(私)仇 revenge for (private) grudge; 報仇雪恨 revenge and wipe out standing grudge (against s.o.); 無以爲報 do not know how to compensate (person) for help; 報父母養育之恩 make oneself worthy of parents' care and upbringing; 報德 recompense for kindness; 報謝 *-shieh* ↓; 報國 serve the country worthily; often 報答 *-dar* ↓.

報案 *bauh-ahn*, v.i., register complaints at court; submit official report on case.
報罷 *bauhbah*, v.i., (1) fail in civil examinations; (2) be rejected (of minister's suggestion to emperor).
報差 *bauhchai*, n. delivery boy of newspapers.
報償 *bauhcharng*, n. & v.t., monetary reward; make amends for deficit.
報酬 *bauhchour*, n. & v.t., remunerate (-tion).
報單 *bauhdan*, n., report, esp., customs declaration.
報答 *bauhdar*, n. & v. t., pay back debt of gratitude: 報答盛意.
報導 *bauhdauh*[1], (sp. pr. *-dauu*), n. & v. t., report, such as news, intelligence: 報導經過 report on

what happened; 新聞報導 newspaper report.

報到 *bauhdauh*², v. i., report for 「duty.

報端 *bauhduan*, n., the papers.

報販 *bauhfahn*, n., news dealer, esp. seller of papers on the streets.

報廢 *bauhfeih*, v. i., announce invalidated check in paper; be declared worthless (of person, old car): 這部車子報廢了.

報復 *bauhfuh*, n. & v. i., revenge; (MC) report (to person).

報告 *bauhgauh*, n. & v. i. & t., a report, to report, often preceding verbal communication to superior; 報告書 written report; 報告文學 --*wernshyuer*, reportage.

報館 *bauhguaan*, n., newspaper 「office.

報關行 *bauhguan-harng*, n., agent for clearing customs.

報章 *bauhjang*, n., newspapers in gen.

報界 *bauhjieh*, n., the press: 報界同仁 gentlemen of the press.

報考 *bauh-kaau*, v. i., register for examinations.

報馬 *bauhmaa*, n., (MC) special messenger; intelligence man.

報命 *bauh-mihng*, n., report on return from duty.

報名 *bauh-mirng*, v. i., register for school, etc.

報幕 *bauhmuh*, n., screen or stage announcement concerning story, production, etc.: 報幕人 --*rern*, announcer.

報盤兒的 *bauhpar'l-de*, n., employee of commercial firms charged with report on current prices.

報屁股 *bauh-pih'gu*, n., (coll.) supplement of newspaper; back page of papers.

報聘 *bauhpihn*, n. & v. i., (to) return visit of country representative to thank for earlier visit of another country's dignitary.

報人 *bauh-rern*, n., member of the press (editor, etc.).

報賽 *bauhsaih*, n., festival celebrating good crops, also called 報歲 *-sueih*.

報曉 *bauhshiaau*, n. & v. i., cry cock-a-doodle-doo ("announce dawn").

報銷 *bauhshiau*, n. & v. i., (make) financial report; register loss (of article).

報効 *bauhshiauh*, n. & v.i., (render) service in gratitude, more esp. monetary gift for official favors.

報謝 *bauhshieh*, v. i. & t., to pay debt of gratitude.

報歲 *bauh-sueih*, n., see *-saih* ↑.

報頭 *bauh-tour*, n., column giving publisher's name, address, etc. in newspaper.

報子 *bauhtz*, n., wall posters, esp. announcement of theatrical performances.

報務 *bauhwuh*, n., affairs concerning the press, esp. telegraph.

報業 *bauhyeh*, n., the press as a 「profession.

報應 *bauhyihng*, n., retribution.

報怨 *bauh-yuahn*, n. & v. i., vengeance, revenge.

赦 11S.82-9

sheh.

V. t. To pardon (crime, criminal): 大赦 general amnesty; 特赦 special pardon; 赦書 decree for pardon.

赦免 *shehmiaan*, v. t., to forgive (person, son).

赦罪 *shehtzuei*, n., forgiveness of sins; v.t., to pardon punishment.

教 11S.82-9

jiauh (**jiau*).

[Pop. var. of 教 82S.82]

§11S.91 (土^{S}/ノ)

彭 11S.91-9

perng.

N. A place name; a surname: 彭祖 Chinese Methuselah; hence 彭聃 Perngjuu and Laotse, symbols of great old age: 彭殤 Perngjuu and the demised infant; 齊彭殤 to regard great age and infant death as the same (Chuangtse's theory of relativity); 彭公案 a collection of detective stories, centered on Judge Perng.

彭亨 *pernghen*g, adj., big-bellied; self-important.

彭彭 *perngperng*, adj., (AC) busy (of traffic): 行人彭彭 a great congregation of people; 四牡彭彭 handsome four horses (of a noble's carriage).

彭澤 *Perng-tzer*, n., name of county.

SECTION 12

§ 12.00 (ナ/亅)

存 12.00

tsurn.

V.i. (1) To exist, to be, remain in a place: 存在 *-tzaih* ↓; 生存 survive, -al; 存亡, 存歿 *-warng, -moh* ↓. (2) Remain on account: 結存 balance; 僅存 only so much remains.

V. t. (1) To deposit money in bank: 存放, 存款 *-fahng, -kuaan*↓; 存單, 存摺 *-dan, -jer* ↓; 存庫 *-kuh* ↓ 存戶 *-huh* ↓. (2) To keep in mind, to send remembrance to friend: 惠存 signature on photograph presented to friend, "for you to keep"; 存慰, 存問, 存候, 存勞 to send remembrance, *-weih, -wehn, -houh, -laur* ↓; 存心, 存意 have intention, *-shin, -yih* ↓; 存疑 entertain doubt, *-yir* ↓. (3) To leave for safekeeping: 寄存 leave at friend's place for safekeeping; 寄存銀行 deposit in a bank; 保存 to preserve (art works, tradition).

Adj. Remaining (food, water): 存貨 inventory of merchandise.

存案 *tsurn-ahn*, v. i., register officially for the record.
存查 *tsurnchar*, v. t., to keep in the files for future reference.
存儲 *tsurnchuu*, v.t., to deposit in bank; to hoard up (also 存貯).
存單 *tsurndan*, n., receipt for deposit.
存放 *tsurnfahng*, v. t., to deposit in bank, to place for safekeeping.
存撫 *tsurnfuu*, v.i., to send regards to people in distress, to comfort.
存根 *tsurngen*, n., check stub, counterfoil.
存候 *tsurnhouh*, v.t., to send regards.
存戶 *tsurnhuh*, n., depositor or an account at bank.
存貨 *tsurnhuoh*, n., remaining goods.
存活 *tsurnhuor*, v.i. & t., to survive, to keep alive.
存摺 *tsurnjer*, n., deposit or savings book.
存記 *tsurnjih*, v.i., to register officially for future reference (as applicant, etc.).
存注 *tsurnjuh*, v.i., (LL) see *-jyuahn* ↓.
存眷 *tsurnjyuahn*, v.i., (LL) to keep for remembrance, remember (friend).
存庫 *tsurnkuh*, n. & v.i., treasury, vault; to keep in vault.
存款 *tsurnkuaan*, n., amount deposited; credit balance.
存勞 *tsurnlaur*, v.t., to send remembrance, send gifts for remembrance, to comfort (soldiers).
存錄 *tsurnluh*, v.t., to record for future reference.
存歿 *tsurn-moh*, phr., question of remaining in existence or not, of life or death.
存身 *tsurn-shen*, v.i., to preserve one's life or health; to survive.
存神 *tsurn-shern*, v.i., to recuperate, store up energy.
存項 *tsurnshiahng* (-'*shiang*), n., credit balance.
存省 *tsurnshiing*, v.i., to keep and consider.
存心 *tsurn-shin*, adv., have intention in mind: 存心不良 have wicked intentions.
存息 *tsurn-shir*, n., interest on deposits.
存視 *tsurnshyh*, v.t., to pay calls or respects.
存恤 *tsurnshyuh*, v.t., to comfort (the distressed).
存在 *tsurntzaih*, v.i. & n., exist, -ence: 存在主義(者) existentialism (-list).
存亡 *tsurn-warng*, n., question of survival or not.
存問 *tsurnwehn*, v.i., to pay respects, ask after health.
存慰 *tsurnweih*, v.i., to send comforting message.
存養 *tsurnyaang*, v.i., to cultivate mind and preserve its original good nature.
存意 *tsurn-yih*, adv., see *-shin* ↑.
存疑 *tsurnyir*, v.i., to show doubt, leave a question mark.

奇 12.00

chir (**ji.*).

V.t. (LL) to consider as odd or interesting: 奇之 was struck by it.

Adj. (1) Strange, unusual, remarkable: 奇怪 *-guaih* ↓; oft. with 怪: 奇形怪狀 strange sight, badly dressed appearance; 奇裝異服 strange, unusual or exotic dress; 希奇古怪 strange, odd; 千奇百怪 many strange, unusual things; 奇男子, 奇女子 remarkable man, girl; 奇士 a remarkable man; 奇珍, 奇寶 very rare and valuable objects; 奇貨可居 waiting to sell s.t. valuable at a high price, set a high price and hold back; 希奇 strange, rare; 暗暗稱奇 silently admire s.t. rare; 傳奇 a romance, (MC) short story or play. (2) Surprising, unexpected: 奇兵 a surprise military move; 奇襲 surprise attack; 奇謀, 奇計 surprising move or stratagem; 奇禍 unexpected disaster; 奇辱, 奇恥 terrible humiliation; 奇説 strange talk or theory; 奇事 unusual happening; 奇逢 strange meeting of person; 奇緣 *-yuarn* ↓. (3) Enormous, marvellous: 奇觀, 奇功 *-guan, -gung* ↓. (4) (**ji*) Odd in number: 奇偶, 奇數, 奇零 *-oou, -shuh, -lirng* ↓; 奇日 on odd days (1, 3, 5, etc.).

Adv. (LL) marvellously, extremely: 奇大 extremely huge; 奇驗 (of medicine) marvellously effective; 價錢奇貴 or 奇昂

A

奇
拳
奪
寿
奈

prices are extremely high.

奇巧 *chirchiaau*, adj., clever (story, plot), cleverly made (jewelry, gadget.)

奇怪 *chirguaih*, adj., strange (phenomena, ideas): 奇奇怪怪 very strange, odd.

奇觀 *chir-guan*, n., an imposing, impressive sight (landscape, etc.).

奇功 *chir-gung*, n., distinguished service, outstanding achievement.

奇蹟 *chir-ji*, n., a miracle.

奇技 *chir-jih*, n., some rare skill (acrobatic, etc.).

奇儁 *chirjyuhn*, adj., (of persons) rare, distinguished.

奇零 **jilirng*, adj. & n., odd lots, remainders.

奇門 *chir-mern*, n., (Taoist magic) the art of becoming invisible (also called 遁甲).

奇妙 *chirmiauh*, adj., wonderful, marvellous: 奇妙莫測 mysterious and hard to guess.

奇偶(耦) **ji-oou*, phr., odd and even.

奇人 *chirrern*, n., an eccentric fellow.

奇羨 **jishiahn*, n., (LL) net gain.

奇數 **jishuh*, n., an odd number.

奇特 *chirteh*, adj., striking, unusual (story, event, conduct, etc.).

奇才 *chir-tsair*, n., a remarkable talent (also wr. 材).

奇偉 *chirweei*, adj., great and wonderful.

奇贏 **ji-yirng*, n., small gains.

奇緣 *chiryuarn*, n., strange encounters; a romance.

奇遇 *chir-yuh*, n., a fortuitous, usu. lucky encounter.

拳 12.00

chyuarn.

N. A fist: 拳頭 -'*tou*↓; 拳打腳踢, 拳足交加 to strike and kick; 拳來腳去 give tit for tat, exchange blows; 給他一拳 give him a blow with the fist; 握拳 close a fist; 打拳 to box; 太極拳 see 12.81.

B

拳棒 *chyuarn-bahng*, n., fighting with fist and staff.

拳曲 *chyuarnchyu*, v. i., to curl up.

拳拳 *chyuarnchyuarn*, adv., always keeping in mind.

拳匪 *chyarnfeei*, n., boxers: 拳匪之亂 the Boxer Rebellion of 1900.

拳腳 *chyuarn-jiaau*, n., fights with hand strikes and kicks.

拳擊 *chyuarnjir*, v. t., to punch with fist, to box (jaw, etc.).

拳跼 *chyuarnjyur*, adj., hemmed in, frustrated.

拳賽 *chyuarn-saih*, n., boxing match.

拳術 *chyuarn-shuh*, n., the art of boxing.

拳師 *chyuarn-shy*, n., a boxer, master in boxing.

拳頭 *chyuarn'tou*, n., (1) blow by fist; (2) boxing.

拳勇 *chyuarnyuung*, n., a good boxer.

奪 12.00

duor.

V.t. (1) To rob, take by force: 強奪 take by force; 劫奪, 搶奪 rob; 爭奪 fight for (s. t.); 爭權奪位 fight for power; 勿奪其時 (AC) do not take away people's time for planting and harvest: 匹夫不可奪志 (Mencius) a common man should have an unswerving goal or ambition; 奪寵 (of mistress) snatch master's favors from rival. (2) To force one's way; break out: 奪門而入 force way into house; 奪眶而出 (tears) break out (cannot be kept back). (3) To capture (prizes): 奪得錦標 capture prize (banner); 奪彩 capture prize. (4) To stun by shock: 驚魂奪魄 to be shocked, frightened out of wits; 奪氣 unnerve person; 光耀奪目 so bright that it dazzles the eye—dazzlingly beautiful.

奪情 *duorchirng*, v. i., do violence

C

to human nature; fail to observe parent's death.

奪取 *duorchyuu*, v. t., to rob, take (prize, objects) after struggle.

奪佔 *duorjahn*, v. t., take possession of (s. t.) illegally.

奪職 *duorjyy*, v. t., deprive (s.o.) of office.

寿 12.00

shouh.

[Pop. of 壽 11.00]

§12.01 (ナ/小)

奈 12.01

naih.

V. i. To bear, stand: 奈不過, 奈不住糾纏不休 could not stand the constant bother; see adv. 無奈, 怎奈 and comp. 奈何 -*her*↓.

Adv. To one's regret, however, despite all: 奈 or 無奈人多口雜, 説不上去 however, there were so many voices speaking, I could not get a word in; 奈援軍不至 to one's regret the allied troops failed to show up; cannot be helped: 怎奈 how can it be helped? 怎奈他不答應 despite everything he just refused; used of a forlorn situation: 怎奈晚來風急 alas! the wind is blowing fast tonight!

奈煩 *naihfarn*, v. t., (=耐煩) bear, endure: 不奈煩 bored, restless.

奈何 *naihher*, (1) adv., why, for what reason: 奈何不跟我説話 why refuse to talk to me? 奈何騙你母親 why deceive your mother? (2) (detachable v.t.), esp. in negative form, to make difficulties for (person): 不能奈我何 or 奈何我 could not do anything to me; 不能奈何他 or 奈何他不得 could not take measures against him; (3) 無奈 or 無奈的, 沒奈何 or 無可奈何 a helpless situation; hence adj., "helpless," "sad," "forlorn": 奈何天 sad, helpless days; 奈何橋 bridge to Hell where the deceased spirits have to pass.

秦 12.01

chirn.

N. Name of state (897–221 B.C.), before it became name of Dynasty (221–207 B.C.): 秦楚 (LL) great distance as between 秦 and 楚; 秦晉 two neighboring states (in Shensi, Shansi); 結秦晉之好 marriage between two families (royalty of two states traditionally intermarried); 秦贅 (LL) husband marries into wife's family, supposed to originate in 秦; 哭秦庭 (allu.) cry at the court of Chirn begging for troops to fight invading enemy.

秦腔 *chirnchiang*, n., Shensi songs.

秦箏 *chirnjeng*, n., an ancient musical instrument with 12 or 13 strings, of 秦 origin.

秦椒 *chirnjiau*, n., red pepper or capsicum.

秦鏡 *chirnjihng*, n., mirror supposed to look into a man's heart —penetrating insight.

秦篆 *chirnjuahn*, n., a form of script of 秦 Dyn. (＝小篆); simplified from 大篆.

秦樓 *chirnlour*, n., as in 秦樓楚館 house of courtesans with wining and dining.

§ 12.02 (ナ/⺊)

泰 12.02

taih.

N. (1) Name of a trigram in 八卦 *paguah* 80.80. (2) Thai, see 泰國 *-guor* ↓. (3) A surname.

Adj. (1) Peaceful, calm, healthy: 國泰民安 a contented people living in a country at peace: 天地交泰 celestial and terrestrial forces in harmony, i.e. peaceful and prosperous times; 康泰 in good health; 泰然自若 calm, unperturbed; 泰適 comfortable; 泰而不驕 poised but not arrogant, see 2. (2) Arrogant: 驕泰 proud and arrogant; 泰侈 extravagant. (3) (Var. of 太) great, grand, too: 泰半, 泰古, 泰初, see 太 12.81.

泰斗 *taihdoou*, n., leading scholar of the times (short for 泰山北斗, to which all look up to).

泰國 *Taihguor*, n., Thailand.

泰然 *taihrarn*, adj., poised, unperturbed.

泰山 *Taihshan*, n., the sacred mountain associated with Confucius; (fig.) a thing of great weight or import: 死重於泰山, 輕於鴻毛 death could be of great import or without significance; (facet.) father-in-law.

泰西 *taishi*, n.; the West, the Occident.

泰水 *taishueei*, n., (facet.) mother-in-law, cf. *-shan* ↑.

泰晤士報 *Taihwuhshyh Pauh*, n., The Times (London, N.Y.).

豢 12.02

huahn.

N. Domesticated animals.

V.t. To feed (animals): 豢養.

§ 12.10 (ナ/十)

奉 12.10

fehng.

[Cogn. 捧 10A.10]

V.i. & t. (1) Receive or proffer from below, quite freely attached to vbb. esp. in correspondence, with the sense "I beg to," "I have the honor to": 奉懇, 奉求, 奉禱 I beg, pray; 奉託 I request, entrust; 奉復 I reply; 奉陳, 奉達, 奉告 beg to inform you; 奉請, 奉候 offer best wishes; 奉勸 venture to persuade you; 奉獻 beg to present (s.t.); 奉還, 奉陪, 奉送 *-huarn*, *-peir*, *-suhng* ↓. (2) Generally to receive, keep, obey (orders, laws): 奉旨 by imperial decree; 奉公守法 carry out official duties and observe the laws; 奉職 carry out duties; 奉使 carry out mission; 奉命, 奉行 *-mihng*, *-shirng* ↓; 等因奉此 "etcetera, therefore"—formula in official documents for passing on communication from superior, after quote, followed by 相應函達 I dutifully pass on information, without commitment or assuming responsibility. (3) To serve, attend to comforts of parents: 侍奉父母, 晨昏, see 奉養 *-yaang* ↓.

奉安 *fehng-an*, n., ceremony of burial of empress.

奉承 *fehngcherng* (*fehng*'-), v.t., to serve with particular attention; to get into the good graces of (superior).

奉還 *fehnghuarn*, n., (court.) to return (article).

奉命 *fehng-mihng*, v.i., to follow

orders, instructions.

奉陪 *fehnpeir*, v.i., have the honor of keeping company; accept invitation to come.

奉行 *fehngshirng*, v.i., carry out orders: 奉行故事 do s.t. as a matter of form.

奉送 *fehngsuhng*, v.t., have the honor to send.

奉養 *fehngyaang*, v.t., to look after parents in their old age.

奄 12.10

da.

N. Big ear.

奄拉 *da'la*, adj., hanging down like big ear lobe (also wr. 搭[Δ]拉 10A.40).

輦 12.10

niaan.

N. (1) A hand-drawn carriage. (2) (AC) imperial carriage.

V.t. To transport by carriage.

§12.11 (ナ/土)

在 12.11

tzaih.

V.i. & t. (1) V.i., exist, live, remain: 存在(主義) exist (-entialism); 留在那兒 stay (remain) there; 在不在 be alive or dead, at home or not; 在世 (of persons) live; 在堂 (of parents) remain alive; 父母在 both parents are living; 在室 (of women) be not yet married. (2) V.t., be at, in, on: 在上 is above; 在桌上 is on the table; 在桌下 is under the table; 在其中 is in the middle; 在外,在內 *-waih, -neih* ↓; 在下位而不憂 not sorry for being placed in a subordinate position; 在家出家 one who, though retaining family ties, observes all the monastic rules; 在官言官 from the strictly official point of view; 在朝 (of politicians) be in power; 在野 (of politicians) be in opposition: 在野黨 the Opposition, a minority political party; 在位 (of a monarch) to reign ("on the throne"): 在位五十年 reigned for 50 years; 在職 be in active service; 在學 attend school; 在望 within sight, within reach; 在福中不知福 unmindful of the happy life one is blessed with; 在劫難逃 impossible to escape. (3) (Importance, meaning) lies in, rests in: 事情關鍵在此 the crux of the matter is this; 在止於至善 (it) lies in the attainment of moral perfection. (4) Be in a certain condition (in the act of): 在逃 be at large; 在押 in custody; 在握 in hand; 在手 ditto; 在喪 in mourning. (5) Be present: 在場 be present at the scene; 在座 be among the audience. (6) Be in certain category of class: 在所不免 is (one of those things) unavoidable; 在所不究 is (in the class) forgivable, will not be prosecuted; 在不可知之數 is one of those things that are yet uncertain.

Prep. (1) In: 在夢中 in a dream; 在夜裏 in the evening (night); 在某種情況之下 in a certain circumstance. (2) According to: 在你(我)看 from your (my) point of view, as you (I) see it.

在案 *tzaih-ahn*, phr., (case) is the subject of a previous communication; (person) is on the police record.

在幫 *tzaih-bang*, phr., be a member of a secret society.

在陳 *tzaih Chern*, phr., be in financial straits (allu. to the story of Confucius suffering from food shortage in the country of Chern).

在旗 *tzaih-Chir*, phr., be a member of a Manchu "banner"—one of the army corps that conquered China and their descendants.

在處 *tzaihchuh*, adv., everywhere.

在公 *tzaih-gung*, v.i. & adj., (LL) (be) on duty: 夙夜在公 attend office morning and night.

在行 *tzaihharng*, adj., experienced, adept, conversant.

在後 *tzaihhouh*, adv., behind; later on.

在乎 *tzaih-huh*(-'*hu*), (1) v.t., (importance, etc.) lie in, rest with: 這個人的長處,就在乎他肯說老實話 this man's strength lies in his readiness to tell the truth; (2) v.i., be interested; 不在乎 not concerned: 他滿不在乎 he is totally unconcerned.

在家 *tzaihjia.*, (1) n., (Budd.) live at home, not in monastery (opp. 出家 one who has left home and become a monk or nun); (2) adv., at home.

在教 *tzaih-jiauh*, phr., be a believer in Islamism.

在疚 *tzaih-jiouh*, v.i. & adj., (AC) (be) in bereavement.

在卽 *tzaihjir*, adj., forthcoming, fast approaching: 考試在卽 examinations are near at hand.

在莒 *tzaih Jyuu*, phr., living in exile (as a political refugee) allu. to the story of 齊桓公 biding his time at Jyuu.

在理兒 *tzaihlie'l*, n., a member of a 17th cen. secret semireligious society (理教) dedicated to the overthrow of the Manchu Dyn.

在理 *tzaihlii*, phr., according to reason.

在內 *tzai-neih*, adj., included: 小賬在內 tips included.

在苫 *tzaihshan*, adj., newly bereaved of father or mother.

在下 *tzaihshiah*, (1) adv., below; (2) pron., I, your humble servant.

在先 *tzaihshian*, adv., (1) beforehand; (2) formerly, previously.

在心 *tzaih-shin*, v.i. & adj., (be) attentive, alert, on the watch.

在昔 *tzaishir*, adv., once upon a time, formerly, in former times, in times past.

在事 *tzaih-shyh*, v.i., be in charge (of s.t.).

在在 *tzaihtzaih*, adv., everywhere, in all directions.

在外 *tzaih-waih*, adj. & adv., (1) outside; (2) away from home; (3) excluded: 小賬在外 excluding tips.

在意 *tzaihyih*, v.i. & adj., (be) careful, attentive: 不在意 not concerned.

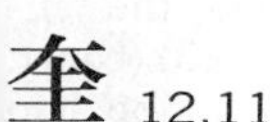 12.11

kueir.

N. (1) Name of a constellation: 奎星閣 temple to the God of Literature (see 魁△ 91.70). (2) A surname.

§ 12.20 (ナ/卄)

奔 12.20

ben.

[AC var. 犇]

V.i. (1) Run, flee, rush about, rush to, gallop (of cattle, horses): 奔來奔去 rushing about; 奔牛, 奔馬 fleeing cattle, horses in stampede; 奔流 rushing torrent; 奔向自由 flee for freedom; 戎師大奔 (AC) the troops fled. (2) Elope: 淫奔 elope for love.

奔北 *benbeei*, v.i., flee in defeat.

奔波 *benbo*, v.i., rush about, bustle and hustle.

奔泉 *ben-chuarn*, n., gushing spring.

奔馳 *benchyr*, v.i., =*-bo*↑.

奔放 *benefahng*, adj., free, bold and unrestrained (style of writing).

奔競 *benjihng*, v.i., campaign for election.

奔逐 *benjur*, v.t., chase after (wealth, ambition, etc.).

奔雷 *benleir*, n., thunderbolt.

奔忙 *benmarng*, v.i., bustle about.

奔命 *benmihng*, v.i., usu. 疲於奔命 tired from rushing around on official business.

奔跑 *benpaau*, v.i., rush, dash.

奔喪 *bensang*, v.i., hurry back for (parents') funeral.

奔星 *benshing*, n., shooting star (rare) =流星.

奔竄 *bentsuahn*, v.i., flee and hide.

奔走 *bentzoou*, v.i., to rush about on business; esp. to serve under, take orders from s.o., as 在大人門下奔走.

奔軼 *benyih*[1], v.i., usu. 奔軼絕塵 soar in freedom (of art, thought) like a flying horse leaving no trace.

奔逸 *benyih*[2], v.i., ditto.

§ 12.21 (ナ/ㄴ)

舂 12.21

chung.

V.t. To pound rice or herbs with mortar and pestle: 舂米.

§ 12.22 (ナ/丨)

布 12.22

buh.

N. Cloth, usu. of cotton, also used generally of textiles: 布褂, 布袍 cotton jacket, gown; 布衣 *-yi*↓; 布簾 padded cotton door screen used in the north; 布鞋, 布襪 cotton shoes, cotton socks; 檯布 tablecloth; 尿布 diaper, etc.; 布鼓雷門 phr., make a fool of oneself by foolish display.

V. i. & t. (1) To spread, publish, make known (sometimes also wr. 佈): 宣布 announce; 公布 publish (statutes, lists of candidates, etc.); 散布謠言 spread gossip; 傳布聖道 spread gospel; 布種 sow seeds. (2) To set or plan: 布網 cast or drop net, set snares; 布局 plan strategy, structure of story, composition of painting; 布棋局 make plan of moves in chess; 布陣 deploy troops; 布防 deploy patrols; 布白 plan blank spaces in painting.

布帛 *buhbor*, n., cottons and silks.

布袋 *buhdaih*, n., jute bags, calico sack; 布袋戲 marionette play.

布丁 *buhding*, n., pudding.

布爾喬亞 *buh-erl-chiaur-yah*, n., bourgeois.

布爾施維黨 *Buh-erlshyweir Daang*, n., Bolsheviks.

布告 *buhgauh*, n., public notice; v. i., make public announcement: 布告天下 make known to the world.

布景 *buhjiing* (also wr. 佈景), n., set, backdrop for scenes in plays; background of landscape, paintings.

布置 (also 佈) *buhjyh*, v.t. & n., to arrange, -ment; interior decor, garden arrangement; placing of troops in strategic places, of characters and plot in play, etc.

布疋 *buhpii*, n., cotton cloth, piece goods.

布施 *buhshy*, v. i., (Budd.) give charities, donate to religious causes.

布衣 *buhyi*, n., "cloth gown," as symbol of scholar not in government: 布衣之交 friends in days of simple life.

奩 12.22

liarn.

[Var. 匳 51.21]

§ 12.30 (ナ/一)

左 12.30

tzuoo.

N. A surname.

V. t. (U.f. 佐) assist: 左證 *-jehng*, 左驗 *-yahn* ↓.

Adj. (1) Left (opp. 右 right): 左面 *-miahn*, 左邊 *-'bian*, 左方 *-fang*, 左右 *-youh* ↓; 左思右想 turn over in one's mind; 左宜右有 talented and capable; 左右逢源 resourceful; 不爲左右袒 refuse to take sides in a quarrel or fight, remain strictly neutral; 左右開弓 give s.o. a box on both ears, (Chin. boxing) hit with both hands, kick with both feet; 左右兩(爲)難 caught in a dilemma; 左鄰右舍 next-door neighbors; 左顧右盼 glancing left and right; 左支右吾 equivocate, prevaricate. (2) To the east of person or thing facing south: 山左 Shantung Province, so-called because it lies to the east of Mt. Taiharng; 江左 region east of the Yangtze River. (3) Unorthodox: 左道 *-dauh* ↓. (4) Clumsy, awkward (cf. Fr. "*gauche*"). (5) Wrong, contrary to: 你想左了 you are mistaken; 意見相左 cannot see eye to eye. (6) Queer, odd, stubborn, bigoted: 左性子 *-shihng-tz*; 左見 *-jiahn* ↓.

左邊(兒) *tzuoo'bian* (*-'bia'l*), adj. & adv., on the left (-handed) side, to the left (of a point of reference).

左不過 *tzuoo'bu-guoh*, adv., anyway, anyhow, in any event.

左不是 *tzuoo'bushyh*, adv., ditto.

左遷 *tzuoochian*, v. i., (of an official) be demoted, degraded.

左契 *tzuoochih*, n., *-chyuahn* ↓.

左傾 *tzuooching*, v. i., & adj., (be) inclined to the left, leftist: 左傾分子 the leftists.

左券 *tzuoochyuahn*, n., a bond, contract, agreement: 持(操)左券 be confident (of succeeding in an undertaking).

左道 *tzuoodauh*, n., (1) heterodoxy, heresy; (2) sorcery, witchcraft: 旁門左道 black magic.

左方 *tzuoo-fang*, n., the left (-hand) side (of anything).

左顧 *tzuoo-guh*, v. i., (1) to look to the left; (2) condescend to call on s.o.

左證 *tzuoojehng*, n., evidence (of guilt, innocence), proof (of fact, good faith).

左見 *tzuoojiahn*, n., prejudice, bias.

左計 *tzuoo-jih*, n., an impractical plan (scheme).

左近 *tzuoojihn*, adv., in the neighborhood (vicinity), not far away, nearby.

左轉 *tzuor-juaan*, v. i., turn to the left.

左傳 *Tuoojuahn* (usu. wr. *Tso Chuan*), n., the famous commentary by Tsu Chiu Ming on *The Spring and Autumn Annals.*

左面 *tzuoo-miahn*, n., the left (-hand) side, page (of an open book).

左派 *tzuoo-paih*, n., (1) the leftists; (2) the left wing (of party, group) (opp. 右派).

左撇捩 *tzuor-piee-lieh*, adj., left-handed, as in writing, holding tennis racket or throwing balls.

左脾氣 *tzuoo-pir'chi*, n., (of a person) peculiar, odd, eccentric temperament.

左衽 *tzuoo-rehn*, phr., (AC) following the barbarian custom of fastening garment on the left side.

左人 *tzuoorern*, n., a compound surname.

左嗓子 *tzuor saangtz*, phr., voice that sounds off key.

左性 *tzuoo'shihng*, adj., pigheaded, obstinate: 左性子 *--tz*, ditto.

左行 *tzuoo-shirng*, adj., (writing) from left to right.

左手 *tzuor-shoou*[1], n., (1) the left hand; (2) the left-hand side.

左首 *tzuor-shoou*[2], n., the left side.

左袒 *tzuortaan*, v. t., to side with (s.o.) in a dispute.

左側 *tzuootseh*, n., the left side.

左驗 *tzuooyahn*, n., a witness (of incident).

左翼 *tzuoo-yih*, n., (1) the left wing of an army, an airplane; (2) the left wing of a party or group.

左右 *tzuoo-youh*, (1) n., the left and right sides; (2) the entourage of an official; (3) (court. opening of letter) "to be laid before your desk"; (4) v.t., serve as adviser to; (5) adv., pros and cons; (6) anyway: 左右你要去那兒 you have to go there anyway; (7) nearby, not far away; 分左右兒 place according to rank or seniority; 左右手 one's right-hand man; 左右翼 both wings of an army, an airplane.

盋 12.30

bo.

[Var. 鉢 81A.10]

N. A shallow bowl.

盇 12.30

her.

[Anc. var. of 盍 11.30]

盔 12.30

kuei.

N. A helmet: 盔甲 helmet and armor.

§ 12.32 (ナ/フ)

奓 12.32

ja.

V. t. (AC) to open (door, wing).

§ 12.40 (ナ/ロ)

右 12.40

youh.

N. A surname.

V. t. (1) To favor: 右文 (of ruler) to patronize literature and the arts; 右武 interested in building up military power. (2) (AC) u.f. 佑 to help, bless, take one's side.

Adj. (1) Right (hand, side). (2) In Chin. books, the right side= the above: 右第十三章 the above is Chapter Thirteen. (3) The west side: 山右 west of the mountain; 江右 west of the river. (4) Formerly, the right being the seat of honor (now the left): 無出其右 no one can be placed higher than he—no one excels him. (5) Politically on the right, conservative: 右傾 *-ching* ↓.

右邊(兒) *youhbian(-bia'l)*, n., the right side.

右傾 *youhching*, adj., politically inclined to the right or conservative side, opp. 左傾分子 the leftists, see *-paih* ↓.

右券 *youhchyuahn*, n., the right half of ancient contract or lease with seal riding the dividing line (see 左[A]券 12.30).

右派 *youhpaih*, n., rightist elements or section, see *-ching* ↑.

右姓 *youhshihng*, n., as in 強宗右姓 (AC) houses of nobility.

右行 *youh-shirng*, adj., going from right to left (as in Chinese books).

右手 *youhshoou*, n., the right hand.

右翼 *youhyih*, n., (1) (mil.) the right wing; (2) the rightist section or faction.

§ 12.41 (ナ/図)

春 12.41

chun.

N. (1) Spring: 春天, 春季 *-tian, -jih* ↓; 新春, 陽春, 開春 New Year season; 立春 Feb. 4th or 5th; 春日 spring day; 春遊 spring outing; 春裝 spring dress or fashion; 春氣 an air of vitality and growth; 春景, 春色, 春光 the beauties of spring; 春風化雨 stimulating influence of teacher compared to spring atmosphere; 春霖, 春雨 spring showers; 春汛 spring flood; 春夢了無痕 vanishes like a spring dream; 春忙, 春事 farmer's planting activities; 春樹暮雲 (allu.) remembrance of a friend; 春寒料峭 slight spring chill; 春蘭秋菊 each in its season ("spring orchid, autumn chrysanthemum"); 春花秋實, 春露秋霜 the progression of seasons; 春秋 *-chiou* ↓. (2) (In Tarng writings) wine: 玉壺買春 buy wine. (3) Sentiment of love, romance: 有女懷春 (AC) there's a girl in love; 春宮, 春畫 *-gung, -huah* ↓; 春情, 春意 *-chirng, -yih* ↓; 貓叫春 a cat's caterwauling courtship. (4) Life, vitality: 大地回春 the earth in spring; 妙手回春 (of physician) bring back life to patient. (5) Age: 青春 youth; 青春時候 time of youth; 春秋 *-chiou* ↓.

春餅 *chunbiing*, n., "spring roll" —a roll with various stuffing, see *-jyuaan* ↓.

春秋 *chunchiou*, n., (1) (LL, court.) age: 春秋幾何 what is your venerable age? (2) name of Annals written by Confucius and one of the classics with implied condemnation of usurpations, murder, incest, etc.; 春秋三傳 the three records elucidating Confucius' Annals (左傳, 公羊傳, 穀梁傳); (3) period covered by the Annals, 722–481 B.C. (242 years); (4) (AC) name of many books and annals (as 呂氏春秋, 晏子春秋)

春情 *chunchirng*, n., stirring of love or desire.

春凳 *chundehng*, n., a lounge chair with extended footrests.

春分 *chunfen*, n., vernal equinox.

春宮 *chungung*, n., pornography.

春畫 *chunhuah*, n., ditto.

春暉 *chunhuei*, n., light of spring, oft. parental love.

春假 *chunjiah*, n., spring holiday.

春節 *chunjier*, n., spring season; spring festival.

春季 *chunjih*, n., spring season.

春酒 *chunjioou*, n., (1) wine made in spring and matured in winter; (2) New Year banquet.

春捲 *chunjyuaan*, n., "spring roll," see *-biing* ↑.

春困 *chun-kuhn*, n., moodiness in spring, spring fever.

春聯(兒) *chunliarn* (*-liar'l*), n., New Year couplets (red and pasted on door panels).

春羅 *chunluor*, n., a kind of thin silk.

春牛 *chunniour*, n., an ox made of clay, paper or straw, beaten (打春牛) at beginning of planting season.

春曉 *chun-shiaau*, n., spring morn.

春宵 *chun-shiau*, n., spring night and its pleasures.

春禊 *chun-shih*, n., a "cleansing" festival in spring by waterside.

春心 *chunshin*, n., see *-chirng* ↑:

春 奢 替 昚 眷 奮

春心已動 sexual desire is aroused.

春天 *chuntian*, n., springtime.

春條兒 *chuntiaur'l*, n., see *-liar'l* ↑.

春藥 *chunyauh*, n., aphrodisiac.

春意 *chunyih*, n., see *-chirng* ↑.

奢 12.41

she.

N. A surname.

Adj. Extravagant: 奢侈, 奢華, 奢靡 *-chyy*, *-huar*, *-mii* ↓; wild (hope): 奢望, 奢願 *-wahng*, *-yuahn* ↓; exaggerated: 奢言, 奢語 extravagant talk.

奢侈 *she(')chyy*, adj., extravagant with money; living in luxury; 奢侈品 *--piin*, n., luxury goods.

奢華 *she(')huar*, adj., luxurious (living, dress).

奢遮 *sheje*, adj., (MC) ostentatious, sensational.

奢靡 *shemii*, adj., see *-chyy* ↑.

奢想 *sheshiaang*, v. i., think wishfully.

奢泰 *shetaih*, adj., extravagant with money, see *-chyy* ↑ (also wr. 汰).

奢望 *shewahng*, v. i. & n., (entertain) wild hope, extravagant wish.

奢願 *sheyuahn*, n., ditto.

替 12.41

tih.

V. t. (1) Substitute, change: usu. 替代, 替換 *-daih*, *-huahn* ↓: 頂替 be substitute; 冒名頂替 act as fraudulent substitute for person; 更替 change, take turns. (2) V.i. & n., decline: 歷代興替 rise and fall of dynasties; 衰替 (or 退) decline. (3) V.t., (AC) discontinue, supersede: 勿替敬典 do not discontinue ancient institutions.

Prep. For, on behalf of, in place of: 替人受罪 suffer for another; 我替你去 I will go in your place, on your behalf.

替代 *tihdaih*, v. t. & n., substitute, act as substitute.

替工 *tihgung*, n., temporary substitute workman.

替換 *tihhuahn*, v. t., change, exchange (goods bought, etc.): 可以替換 may be exchanged.

替另 *tihlihng*, adv., in addition, separately: 我替另再給你錢 I will pay you extra (also pr. *tir-*).

替身(兒) *tihshen(-she'l)*, n., substitute: 找替身 find a substitute (for work).

替手 *tihshoou*, n., ditto.

替死鬼 *tihsyr-gueei*, n., person made to suffer for another's mistake.

昚 12.41

shehn.

[Anc. var. of 愼 22A.80]

眷 12.41

jyuahn.

N. Relatives, members of the same family: 家眷 one's wife and children; 軍眷 dependents of soldiers or offiicers; 親眷 relatives; 寶眷 (court.) your wife and family; 眷屬 *-shuu*, 眷口 *-koou* ↓.

V. t. Take a deep interest in, show affection for, love: 眷念 *-niahn* ↓; 眷懷 *-huair* ↓; 眷眷 *-jyuahn* ↓; 眷佑 *-youh* ↓; 眷戀 *-liahn* ↓; 眷顧 *-guh* ↓; 眷注 *-juh* ↓; 眷愛 *-aih* ↓; see many compp. ↓.

眷愛 *jyuahn-aih*, v. t., to love, have affection for subordinate.

眷顧 *jyuahnguh*, v. t., to regard with tenderness, take interest in (subordinate's) welfare.

眷懷 *jyuahnhuair*, v. t., (of friend or relative) have fond memories of, keep constantly in mind.

眷注 *jyuahnjuh*, v. t., think of with tenderness.

眷眷 *jyuahnjyuahn*, adv., ever thinking of.

眷口 *jyuahnkoou*, n., the members of a family.

眷戀 *jyuahnliahn*, v. t., love dearly, unwilling to part with (official post).

眷念 *jyuahnniahn*, v. t., have tender thoughts of.

眷屬 *jyuahnshuu*, n., wife and children, dependents.

眷佑 *jyuahnyouh*, v. t., protect, bless.

奮 12.41

fehn.

v. i. Resolve to, put forth energy to: 奮發 *-fa* ↓; 奮勉 *-miaan* ↓; 奮起 make a rigorous start; 奮不顧身 set one's mind to, regardless of personal danger; 興奮 excited, elated.

V.t., Brush energetically; 奮臂, 奮袂 roll up sleeves, (call for revolt, etc.).

Adv. Energetically, with force and spirit; 奮鬬 *-douh* ↓; 奮擊 attack with vigor.

奮鬬 *fehndouh*, v.i., make a vigorous fight; struggle hard (to succeed).

奮發 *fehnfa*, v.i., make high resolve to succeed: 奮發有爲 resolve to do some great things; 奮發圖強 strive to make country strong.

奮志 *fehn-jyh*, v. i., set one's mind to.

奮力 *fehn-lih*, adv., with energy, force (to study, etc.).

奮勉 *fehnmiaan*, v. i., try with great determination.

奮然 *fehn-rarn*, adv., with determination and spirit.

奮勇 *fehnyuung*, v.i., strive, fight bravely: 自告奮勇 volunteer for some special duty.

§ 12.42 (ナ/冈)

冇 12.42

moou.

Adv. (Cantonese dial.) have not: 無.

有 12.42

yoou.

N. (1) Being: 有生於無 being comes from not being. (2) A surname.

V.i. & t. (1) To have; there is (are), opp. 沒 or 沒有 there is (are) not: 那有,豈有 how can there be? 豈有此理 how unreasonable! 有了 I have it! 所有 all there is; 有生必有死 just as there is life, so there must also be death; oft. 有…有: 有始有終 finish what is started; 有名有姓 has both name and surname (clear identity); 有來有去 there is exchange of calls, gifts; 有聲有色 quite vivid, alive; 有條有理 very clear and precise; oft. coupled with negative word 無, 沒: 有頭無尾 leave s.t. half done, start off but never finish; 有眼無珠 having eyes without pupils (cf. "having eyes, see not")—blind; 有備無患 be prepared and you won't be sorry; 有教無類 with education there is no distinction between classes or races of men; 有則改之, 無則加勉 to correct mistakes if you have committed them, and to avoid if you have not. (2) To possess, own: 爲而不有 (老子) to do s.t. but not claim possession: 所有權 right of ownership; 公有 owned by public; 私有, 己有 privately owned; 國有 state-owned (railways, etc.); 民有 owned by private capital; forms many phrr. with words denoting strength, skill, etc.: 有氣力 possesses strength; 有骨頭 has backbone; 有手段 possesses tact; 有把握 has confidence; 有根底 has background training, etc. (3) (Court.) in phrr. expressing causing trouble: 有勞, 有累, 有惹 sorry to have caused so much trouble; 有等 thank person for waiting; 有僭 apologize for taking a higher seat at table; 有請 send for s.o.'s presence. (4) To be betrothed, married, pregnant: 有了人家了 (girl) is already betrothed; 有室 (man) is already married; 有身, 有喜 *-shen*, *-shii* ↓. (5) There are many: 有日 (LL) and 有日子了 (vern.) many days already: 有歲數了 well-advanced in age; 開設有年 founded many years ago.

Adj. Abundant, wealthy: 富有 rich; 大有之年 an abundant year.

Conj. (LL) pr. *youh*, used like "又": 三十有五 thirty-five; 十有五年 fifteen years.

有邦 *yoou-bang*, n., (AC) the feudal princes.

有邊兒 *yoou-bia'l*, phr., contains an inkling, a vague outline, adumbrations: 兩個人商議已經有邊兒了 the negotiations are taking shape.

有不是 *yoou-buh'shy*, phr., be in the wrong; also in case s.t. is wrong: 有不是找我 if anything is wrong, come to me.

有產階級 *yourchaan jiejir*, n., the propertied class; bourgeoisie.

有碴兒 *yoou-char'l*, phr., have a grudge.

有成(兒) *yoou-cherng('l)*, phr., there is some hope.

有錢 *yoou-chiarn*, adj., rich.

有頃 *your-chiing*, adv., (LL) after a while.

有期徒刑 *yoouchir turshirng*, phr., a sentence to hard labor for a specified period.

有情 *yoou-chirng*, (1) adj., warm, affectionate; (2) n., 有情人 lovers.

有趣(兒) *yoouchyuh* (*-chyueh'l*) adj., interesting.

有袋類 *yooudaihleih*, n., (zoo.) *Marsupialia*.

有的 *yoou'de*, pron. & adj., some: 有的來, 有的不來 some will come and some will not; 有的人 some people; 有的時候 sometimes; 有的地方 some places; 有的是 there is no lack of it.

有底 *your-dii*, phr., 有裏有底, 並不害怕 is familiar with (the problem, proposal) and is not afraid.

有毒 *yoou-dur*, adj., poisonous.

有分 *yoou-fehn*, phr., have a proper share (of benefit, responsibility): 他很有分兒 (coll.) he has powerful connections.

有服 *yoou-fur*, phr., (LL) be in mourning: 有服的 a kinship that requires keeping of mourning.

有哏 *yoougern*, adj., comical, witty.

有鉤條蟲 *yoougoutiau-churng*, n., (zoo.) tapeworm, *Taenia solium*.

有恆 *yoou-herng*, adj., having persistence, permanence.

有後 *yoou-houh*, phr., leave progeny after death, opp. 無後 without progeny.

有奇 *yoou-ji*, phr., (LL) and over: 百元有奇 one hundred odd dollars.

有價 *yooujiah*, adj., marketable; 有價證券 marketable security.

有間 *yoou-jiahn*, phr., (LL) (1) after a while; (2) there is a wavering of loyalty; (3) there is a difference; (4) (AC) (illness) is getting better.

有加利 *yooujialih*, n., (bot.) eucalyptus.

有機的 *yoouji'de*, adj., (chem.) organic: 有機酸 organic acids; 有機體 organism; 有機物 organic matter; 有機化合物 organic compounds; 有機化學 organic chemistry.

有勁 *yoou-jihn*, adj., strong, powerful.

有酒 *your-jioou*, phr., (coll.) gotten drunk.

有準兒 *your-juee'l*, adj., (1) having definite goal; (2) definite; (3) firm, resolute; also 有準頭

有來 *yoou-lair*, adv., (MC, at the end of a sentence) already.

有落兒 *yoou-lauh'l*, phr., have a dependable living.

有臉 *your-liaan*, phr., have the honor ("face"): 有臉的人 person with good social status.

有理 *your-lii*[1], adj., reasonable.

有禮(兒) *your-lii*[2]*(-liee'l)*, adj., as in 彬彬有禮 polite, courteous, good-mannered.

有零 *yoou-lirng*, phr., and odd: 八百有零 800 odd.

有門兒 *yoou-mer'l*, phr., know the ropes, be on the right track.

有面兒 *yoou-miah'l*, phr., know how to keep up appearances.

有名 *yoou-mirng*, adj., famous, well-known, renowned.

有染 *your-raan*, phr., has had illicit intercourse with man or woman.

有如 *yoou-rur*, phr., for example.

有日 *yoou-ryh*, adv., (vern. 有日子) (1) many days: 有日子沒會面了 we haven't seen each other for many days; 還有日子呢 there are good many days yet—a long way off; (2) a definite date set: 喜事有日子沒有 is the date set for the wedding?

有身 *yoou-shen*, adj., pregnant, expecting.

有生 *yoou-sheng*, adv., as in 有生以來 from birth, since life began.

有限 *yoou-shiahn*, adj., limited; 有限公司 a limited stock company; 有限責任 limited liability.

有閑 *yoou-shiarn*, adj., possessing leisure, leisurely (life): 有閑階級 the leisure class.

有孝 *yoou-shiauh*[1], adj., be in mourning for parents.

有效 *yoou-shiauh*[2], adj., efficacious.

有些(兒) *yoou-shie(-shie'l)*, adj. & pron., a few, several, some: 有些人 some people; 有些不對 s.t. is wrong.

有隙 *yoou-shih*, phr., having a grudge.

有喜 *your-shii*, adj., expecting a child.

有心 *yoou-shin*, adv., purposely, having the intention to; 有心人 a good-hearted person; 有心胸 possessing ambition, courage, generosity; 有心眼兒 (person) of calculating type.

有形 *yoou-shirng*, adj., visible, opp. 無形 invisible.

有數 *yoou-shuh*, adj., (1) (AC) destined, fated; (2) (AC) in good form: 登降有數 ascend and descend in form; (3) the best: 有數的人才 among the best; 有數兒 best, rare; limited number (of books, etc.); 肚裏有數兒 know very well in one's heart.

有事 *yoou-shyh*,[1] phr., (1) (AC) celebrate some great occasion; (2) be occupied; (3) come across some untoward accident.

有識 *yoou-shyh*[2], adj., possessed of understanding, insight.

有時 *yoou-shyr*, adv., sometimes.

有司 *yoou-sy*, n., official, judge officer in charge.

有蹄類 *your-tii-leih*, n., (zoo.) *Ungulata.*

有味兒 *yoouweh'l*, adj., good-flavored (food), pleasing (music, writing).

有爲 *yoou-weir*, phr., can accomplish great things, promising.

有意 *yoou-yih*, adv., intentionally, have intention to (harass, cause trouble, etc.).

有因(兒) *yoou-yin(-ye'l)*, phr., 事出有因 there is a reason for it.

有緣 *yoou-yuarn*, phr., have the luck; (love affair) decreed from above, (marriage) "made in heaven."

有餘 *yoou-yur*, adj., enough and 「to spare.

§ 12.50 (ナ/乛)

夸 12.50

kua.

Adj. (1) (LL) extravagant: 夸誕 boastful (cf. 誇 60A.50). (2) (AC) big. (3) (AC) handsome: 夸容 (var. of 姱 93A.50).

券 12.50

chyuahn.

[Var. 劵]

N. (1) Certificate, ticket: 債券 certificate of debt; 公債券 government bond; 證券交易 stock exchange; 獎券 lottery ticket, certificate of award; 禮券 a gift certificate (on occasions): 入場券 ticket for admission; 贈券 certificate for buying more goods at department stores. (2) Title deeds, lease certificate: 契券, 券契.

夯 12.50

hang.

N. (1) Piles as foundation: 打夯 drive piles; 夯歌 song of construction workers as they drive piles. (2) A dam of piles and mud, sand and pebbles.

V.t. To lift up: 擡夯 to lift and carry uttering *hang* sound as one goes.

夯漢 *hanghahn*, n., carrier, laborer who carries loads on shoulder.

夯貨 *hanghuoh*, n., a husky but 「stupid person.

§ 12.63 (ナ/丶)

12.63

shiaang.

[See 鯗 80.63]

§ 12.70 (ナ/乚)

奄 12.70

yaan (**yan*).

Adj. (1) (**yan*) U.f. 閹 castrated, 52B.00. (2) Feeble (related 㦽).

Adv. Completely: 奄有四方 conquer the whole world.

奄忽 *yaanhu*, adv., in a short time.
奄息 **yanshir*, v.i., to stop for rest.
奄奄 **yanyan*, adj., hard of breath: 奄奄一息 barely perceptible breathing.

卷 12.70

jyuahn(**juaan*, **chyuarn*).

N. (1) Anything that can be rolled up and unrolled: 卷軸 *-jour*↓; 卷帙 *-jyh*↓; 畫卷 a scroll of paintings; 書卷 books: 有書卷氣 bookish, learned, (of writings) academic ("smacking of books"); 手不釋卷 studious, ever studying. (2) Chapters or volumes of a book: 第一卷 chapter (volume) one; 一共五卷 five volumes in all; 上下卷 first, second volume. (3) An examination paper: 卷紙 *-jyy*↓; 考卷 quiz paper; 問卷 question paper; 交卷 (of student) hand in examination paper, finish an assignment: 交卷主義 perfunctory performance, such an attitude; 交白卷 failure to answer the questions in an examination or to carry out a given task. (4) Documents, records: 卷宗 *-tzung*↓; 文卷 official papers; 案卷 archives. (5) (＝捲) A roll, a reel.

V.t. (**jyuaan*) (＝捲) Roll up, curl up.

Adj. (**chyuarn*) Curly: 卷髮 *-faa*↓.

卷柏 *jyuarnbaai*, n., (bot.) *Selaginella involvens*.
卷卷 **chyuarnchyuaan*, adj., earnest, sincere (interch. 拳拳).
卷丹 **jyuaandan*, n., (bot.) the tiger lily, *Lilium tigrinum* (also 虎皮百合).
卷髮 **chyuarnfaa*, v. i., curl one's hair; n., curly hair.
卷軸 *jyuahnjour*, n., a scroll.
卷帙 *jyuahnjyh*, n., books, volumes.
卷紙 *jyuahnjyy*, n., paper for use in examinations.
卷舌 **jyuaan-sher*, adj., tongue-tied; 卷舌音 the Peiping retroflex *j, ch, sh, r* sound.
卷鬚 **jyuaan-shyu*, n., tendrils.
卷子 *jyuahntz*, n., (1) a scroll; (2) an examination paper.
卷幘 **jyuaantzer*, n., formerly, a boy's rolled-up turban.
卷宗 *jyuahntzung*, n., office files, archives, folders.
卷尾猿 **jyuarnweei-yuarn*, n., (zoo.) *Cebus capucinus*.

尤 12.70

your.

N. (1) (AC) mistake: 言寡尤 few mistakes in speech. (2) Blame: 招尤 cause criticism. (3) A surname.

V. t. To blame: 怨天尤人 blame heaven or blame other people.

Adj. Strange, peculiar: 尤異, 尤物 *-yih*, *-wuh*↓; 無恥之尤 most shameless of all.

Adv. Particularly, especially: 尤其 *-chir*↓; 尤甚 especially bad; 尤佳 especially good; 尤是 especially; 尤非 especially not; 尤可怪 particularly to be deplored; 尤不宜 particularly should not.

尤其 *yourchir*, adv., especially.
尤物 *yourwuh*, n., a bewitching female, *femme fatable*.
尤異 *youryih*, adj., strange.

尪 12.70

wang.

[Var. of 尫 80.70]

尷 12.70

gan.

[Anc. var. 尲]

尷尬 *gangah* (also pr. *jianjieh*), adj., (1) difficult to cope with; (2) embarrassing, embarrassed: 事情有點尷尬 the situation is embarrassing; (3) not very respectable (method, affair).

尬 12.70

gah(also *jieh*).

Adj. See 尷尬 12.70.

尨 12.70

parng (**marng*, **merng*).

[Interch. 厖, 庬]

N. (**marng*) (AC) shaggy type of dog.

Adj. (Of dogs) of mixed colors.

尨茸 *merngrurng*, adj., shaggy.

炈 12.70

liauh.

炈蹶子 *liauhchyueetz*, v. i., (of horses, mules) kick; (fig.) (of person) defy, kick back.

§ 12.72 (ナ/心)

惷 12.72

chuun.
[Var. 蠢 12.93]

§ 12.80 (ナ/八)

真 12.80

jen.
[Var. of 眞 21.80; cf. 10.80]

賛 12.80

tzahn.
[Pop. of 贊 10.80]

§ 12.81 (ナ/人)

犬 12.81

chyuaan.

N. (1) (LL) dog (vern. 狗): 犬牙相錯 jigsaw outline; 鷹犬 hawks and hounds, (fig.) underlings of the powerful who harass the people; 獵犬 hunting dog, hound; 聲色犬馬之樂 the material pleasures of song and women, hunting and racing; 效犬馬之勞 (court. of oneself) to serve one faithfully; 犬彘 pigs and dogs: 犬彘食人食 (AC) the dogs and pigs eat like their masters ——— of corrupt aristocracy. (2) 小犬 (formerly court.) my son, see 犬子 *-tzyy*↓.

犬齒 *chyuaanchyy*, n., canine teeth.

犬子 *chyuaantzyy*, n., (formerly court.) my son ("little dog"), also 小犬.

犬于兒 *chyuaanyue'l*, n., "reverse dog radical," 犭, in dictionaries, also called 反犬旁.

大 12.81

dah (*re. pr* **daih*).

N. (1) (Coll.) a penny: 不值一個大 not worth a penny. (2) A surname.

Adj. (1) Big, large, great: 大人 *-rern*↓; 大陸 *-luh*↓; 大路 highway, main road; 大門 the gate; 大樓 a tall building; 大大小小 the big and the small—all considered; 大而無當 phr., big, impractical (plan), big and burdensome ("white elephant"). (2) The eldest (brother, uncle, aunt, cousin, etc.): 大房 eldest branch of family; senior of same rank: 大姑 (子) senior sister of wife; 大舅 (子) senior brother of wife. (3) (Oft. in address) honored, esteemed: 大爺, 大老爺 *-yer*, *-laau'ye*↓; 大法官 Grand justice; 大札 your gracious letter; 大作 your great composition; 大駕 your "carriage," i. e., your arrival; 大名 great reputation; 名山大川 well-known mountains and rivers; self-given appellation: 大唐 the Great Tarng Empire; 大清 the Great Ching (Manchu) Dyn. (4) Important: 大人物 the V. I. P.s; 大事 important occasion or event; 大處着眼 pay attention to the important points.

Adv. (1) Generally: 大凡, 大概, 大抵, 大致 *-farn*, *-gaih*, *-dii*, *-jyh*↓. (2) Further ahead or behind: 大前天 two days before yesterday; 大後天 two days after tomorrow; 大前年 two years before last; 大後年 two years after next; 大後兒(個) next to next behind. (3) Greatly (angered, pleased, etc.): 大謬 greatly mistaken; 大不爲然 greatly disapprove. (4) Completely: 大晴 (the sky is) completely clear; 大亮 it's day already. (5) Showily, pompously, oft. 大……大: 大模大樣 (大模厮樣兒) in an open or showy manner; 大搖大擺 take big, swinging steps; 大手大腳 spend extravagantly; 大庭廣衆 in broad daylight, in front of everybody; 大天白日 in broad daylight; 大書特書 it is clearly written; 大言不慚 to talk big; 大言欺人 to exaggerate; 大躍進 (phr.) great leap forward.

大寶 *dah-baau*, n., (LL) the throne.

大拜 *dah-baih*, v. i., formerly, (emperor) make person prime minister.

大班 *dahban*, n., compradore, Taipan.

大本營 *dah-been-yirng*, n., general headquarters.

大便 *dahbiahn*, v. i., answer nature's call; to evacuate bowels.

大辟 *dah-bih*, n., crime punishable by death.

大比 *dah-bii*, n., formerly, provincial civil service examinations.

大鼻子 *dahbirtz*, n., (derog.) a Russian ("big-nosed").

大白 (1) *dah-bor*, n., a wine cup: 浮一大白 drink a cup (to celebrate); (2) (*-bair*) 眞相大白 the facts are clear now.

大不列顚 *Dah-buh-lieh-dian*, n., Great Britain.

大不了 *dah'buliaau*, phr., 沒什麽大不了的事情 it's nothing

frightening, nothing to worry about.

大氅 *dahchaang*, n., overcoat of old type.

大腸 *dahcharng*, n., (physiol.) the colon.

大成 *dahcherng*, n., great consummation; a compendium; 集大成 composition which embodies contributions of previous scholars.

大千 *dah-chian*, n., (Budd.) a universe of many universes (大千世界)

大蟲 *dah-churng*, n., (coll.) a tiger.

大大咧咧 *dah'dalielie*, adv., haughtily.

大大落落兒 *dah'daluohluo'l*, adv., in dignified manner (also pr. *--lulu'l*).

大膽 *dahdaan*, adj. & adv., with determination without fear or hesitation: 大膽做去 do it without hesitation.

大典 *dah-diaan*, n., an august ceremony.

大抵 *dahdii*, adv., mostly.

大豆 *dahdouh*, n., the soybean (also called 黃豆).

大動脈 *dah-duhng-moh*, n., the aorta.

大方 *dahfang*, (1) n., experts, connoisseurs: 貽笑大方 be laughed at by those who know; (2) adj., generous with money, not stingy; (3) (appear or walk) with proud bearing.

大凡 *dahfarn*, adv., mostly, generally.

大分 *dah-fehn*, n., (LL) person's destined years to live.

大夫 **daihfu*, n., a physician, doctor: 陳大夫 Dr. Chen.

大婦 *dah-fuh*^{1}, n., (LL) the wife.

大副 *dahfuh*^{2}, n., (nautical) the mate.

大概 *dahgaih*, adv., in general, most probably.

大綱 *dahgang*, n., outline (of program, plan), the elements (of political science, etc.).

大褂(兒) *dahguah'l*, n., unlined long gown: 藍布大褂 blue cotton gown.

大觀 *dahguan*, n., as in 洋洋大觀 an impressive array (of exhibits, buildings, etc.).

大歸 *dah-guei*, v.i., formerly, a divorced woman returns to her mother's home for good.

大故 *dah-guh*, n., parents' funeral.

大公 *dahgung*, adj., (1) impartial: 大公無私; (2) n., impartiality; Catholicity.

大鼓書 *dah-guu-shu*, n., monologue storytelling in rhythmic language, accompanied by a hand drum.

大海 *dahhaai*, n., (1) a wide-mouthed bowl or wine cup; (2) the sea.

大亨 *dahheng*, n., (coll.) (slightly derog.) a big merchant.

大花臉 *dah-hua-liaan*, n., (Chin. opera) a male role of dignified type.

大話 *dahhuah*, n., exaggeration: 說大話 to exaggerate.

大黃 *dahhuarng*, n., (bot.) rhubarb; *Rheum officinale*.

大會 *dahhueih*, n., a conference, assembly meeting.

大丈夫 *dahjahngfu*, n., (AC, LL) a gentleman, a man of character or real worth.

大家 *dahjia*, n., (1) all, all people: 大家唱 let's all sing together; (2) master of an art of craft; (3) 大家閨秀 woman from a cultured family.

大解 *dahjiee*, v.i., see *-biahn*↑.

大節 *dah-jier*, n., matter of honor, principles: 大節無虧 firm in matters of honor (apart from personal weakness).

大靜脈 *dah-jihng-moh*, n., the great vein carrying blood of the body to the heart.

大戟 *dahjii*, n., (bot.) spurge; *Euphorbia pekinensis*.

大襟(兒) *dahjin(-jie'l)*, n., the right-hand flap of Chinese gown where it is buttoned.

大軸子 *dah-jouh'tz*, n., (Chin. opera) the last act.

大篆 *dahjuahn*, n., Chinese script in time of Confucius, before 小篆 was introduced in Chirn 秦 Dyn.

大著 *dah-juh*, n., (court.) your book.

大衆 *dahjuhng*, n., (1) the people; (2) the masses: 大衆文學 literature for the masses; 大衆化 to popularize or simplify (writing); 大衆傳播 mass communication; 大衆傳播工具 mass media.

大致 *dahjyh*, adv., on the whole (acceptable, etc.), with a few exceptions.

大吉 *dahjyi*, n., great luck, fortune.

大覺 *dahjyuer*, n., (Budd.) the great awakening.

大局 *dahjyur*, n., general situation.

大旨 *dah-jyy*^{1}, n., general theme (of book, teaching).

大指 *dahjyy*^{2}, n., the thumb (also called 拇指).

大塊 *dah-kuaih*, n., (1) the earth; (2) the universe.

大魁 *dah-kueir*, n., the champion in national examinations.

大老爺 *dahlaau'ye*, n., formerly, address of city magistrate.

大剌剌的 *dahlahlahde*, adj. & adv., pompous, -ly.

大斂 *dah-liahn*, n., formal laying-in of body in coffin.

大量 *dah-liahng*, adv., in great quantities, in volume: 大量生產 mass production.

大禮服 *dah-lii-fur*, n., formal dress.

大理石 *dahliishyr*, n., marble.

大陸 *dahluh*, n., the mainland; continent: 大陸礁層 continental shelf.

大落落 *dahluohluoh*, adj., impressive, pompous.

大羅天 *dahluortian*, n., the fairyland.

大略 *dahlyueh*, (1) adv., generally; (2) n., the gist of things; (3) 雄才大略 (person's) great talent.

大麥 *dahmaih*, n., barley.

大麻 *dahmar*, n., hemp; marijuana, *Cannabis sativa*.

大麻蠅 *dahmaryirng*, n., a large variety of flies feeding on refuse.

大帽子 *dah-mauh'tz*, n., a formal hat in Manchu Dyn.; pressure from some influential person.

A B C

大 太

大面 *dahmiahn*, n., (Chin. opera) a male role, see *-hualiaa('l)*↑; 大面皮兒 the surface, on the surface; 大面兒上 ditto, also in public.

大米 *dahmii*, n., rice.

大名 *dah-mirng*, n., a great name, reputation; your name.

大腦 *dahnaau*, n., cerebrum.

大內 *dahneih*, n., imperial palace.

大逆 *dahnih*, phr., 大逆不道 treason.

大牌 *dahpair*, n., (1) trump card; (2) popular (movie actress, doctor, etc.).

大稔 *dah-reen*, n., (year of) bumper crops.

大人 *dahrern*, n., (1) a grown-up person; (2) formerly, a mandarin; (3) a term of respect in addressing a judge or any high official; 大人物 *--wuh*, n., great personage.

大撒巴掌兒 *dahsaba'jang'l*, phr., to let things take their own course, leave a free hand.

大赦 *dahsheh*, n., general amnesty.

大乘 *dahshehng*, n., (Budd.) Mahayana doctrine or school, opp. 小乘 Hinayana.

大西洋 *Dah-shi-yarng*, n., the Atlantic Ocean; 大西洋憲章 The Atlantic Charter (1941).

大小 *dah-shiaau*, n., size (of hat, shoes, etc.): 一般大小 of the same size.

大祥 *dah-shiarng*, n., celebration when period of mourning for parents is over.

大寫 *dahshiee*, n., capital (in spelling, printing).

大帥 *dahshuaih*, n., commander in chief, also term of addressing military governors in Manchu Dyn.

大數 *dahshuh*, n., man's destiny, fate, esp. number of years to live.

大師 *dahshy*, n., (1) the master, a term of respect among scholars; (2) a Budd. monk or abbot; 大師傅 common address to a cook, also a monk.

大勢 *dahshyh*, n., general trend of events, general situation.

大學 *dahshyuer*, n., (1) a university; (2) one of the Confucian *Four Books*, the "Great Learning."

大熊座 *dah-shyurng-tzuoh*, n., the Great Bear constellation.

大使 *dahshyy*, n., an ambassador; 大使館 embassy.

大蒜 *dahsuahn*, n., garlic.

大餐 *dahtsan*, n., dinner; 大餐廳 dining hall.

大腿 *dahtueei*, n., the thigh.

大同 *dahturng*, n., as in 世界大同 Confucius' dream of a world commonwealth—a Utopia, opp. 小康 the well-organized human society.

大統 *dahtuung*, n., an emperor's rule, imperial house.

大自然 *dah-tzyh-rarn*, n., the world of Nature, natural phenomena.

大我 *dah-woo*, phr., the greater self, the spiritual self, opp. 小我 the material self.

大無畏 *dah-wur-weih*, adj., fearless.

大雅 *dahyaa*, n., beautiful form and culture: 不登大雅之堂 unqualified to take its place in the higher circles; 無傷大雅 unimportant defects.

大樣 dahyahng, n., full-page proof (in typesetting).

大洋 *dahyarng*, n., (1) the ocean; (2) a dollar: 大洋千元 $1,000.

大洋洲 *Dah-yarng-jou*, n., Oceania.

大要 *dahyauh*, n., the important points, an outline of essentials.

大爺 *dahyer*, n., uncle; eldest among elders.

大衣 *dahyi*, n., overcoat.

大意 *dahyih*[1] (*-'yi*), (1) n., gist of thought, idea; (2) adj., careless: 不可大意 don't be too sure or neglect to provide against the unexpected.

大義 *dahyih*[2], n., (1) the principle of right and wrong: 深明大義 know where one's loyalty belongs; (2) general idea.

大元帥 *dah-yuarn-shuaih*, n., generalissimo.

太 12.81

taih.

Adj. Great, grand, used in many titles and addresses of elder generation, like Eng. "grandparent," "Grand Master", thus 太太, 太祖 *-'tai*, *-tzuu*, etc.↓; 太子 *-tzyy*↓; 太上皇 *-shahng-huarng*↓; 太老爺 grandfather, formerly, address of magistrate ("Your Honor"); 太老伯 great uncle; 太師 *-shy*↓.

Adv. Too: 太好, 太壞 too good, bad; 太甚 too much; 太不成話 (of action or speech) beyond all limits; 太不像樣 too awful; 太無禮 too rude, blunt.

太保 *taihbaau*, n., (1) formerly, Grand Tutor to crown prince; (2) juvenile delinquent (see *-meih*↓).

太半 *taihbahn*, n., the greater half (=大半).

太初 *taihchu*, n., the beginning of the world; 太初時候 primordial times; 太初物質 primordial matter.

太阿 (泰阿) *taih-e*, n., famous sword: 太阿倒持 surrender power to subordinate (hold sword backward).

太夫人 *taihfurern*, n., (court.) your mother.

太羹 *taihgeng*, n., (AC) soup offering in sacrifices.

太公 *taihgung*, n., terms used variously for great-grandfather, grandfather, greatly esteemed elder.

太古 *taihguu*, adj. & n., primordial (times).

太和 *taihher*, n., grand harmony (of *yin* and *yang*).

太后 *taihhouh*, n., mother of emperor, empress dowager.

太監 *taihjian(-jiahn)*, n., eunuch.

太極拳 *taihjirchyuarn*, n., a kind of boxing or gymnastics, consisting of slow, circular movements with breath control.

太極圖 *taihjirtur*, n., diagram of cosmological scheme (Suhng Dyn.).

太空 *taihkung*, n., outer space; 太空人 astronaut; 太空船 space ship; 太空時代 space age; 太空裝 fashion modelled after astronauts; 太空法 space law; 太空站 space stations; 太空總署

U.S. National Aeronautics and Space Administration (NASA).

太牢 *taihlaur*, n., sacrifices consisting of ox, sheep and pig.

太妹 *taihmeih*, n., female juvenile delinquent (cf. *-bau*↑).

太廟 *taihmiauh*, n., Royal Ancestral Temple.

太平 *taihpirng*(*-'ping*), n., peace, world peace; 太平洋 Pacific Ocean; 太平鼓 a kind of drum, used in spring outings; 太平門 fire exit in theaters; 太平梯 fire escape stairs; 太平花 a kind of fireworks; a flowering plant.

太婆 *taihpor*, n., great-grandmother.

太上皇 *taihshahng-huarng*, n., retired father of emperor; a too powerful person, not the titular ruler.

太守 *taihshouh*, n., formerly, prefect.

太師 *taishy*, n., n., Grand Tutor; 太師椅 wooden lounge chair.

太虛 *taihshyu*, n., interstellar space.

太學 *taihshyuer*, n., formerly, imperial university.

太史 *taihshyy*, n., court historian; 太史公 reference to 司馬遷 *Symaa Chian*, author of 史記.

太歲 *taihsueih*, n., star god presiding over the year; star Jupiter: 太歲頭上動土 extreme folly of offending the powerful.

太太 *taih'tai*, n., Mrs.: 李太太, 張太太, etc.; used without surname, servant's address of mistress of the house; 老太太 usu. mother of master or mistress, also old woman.

太祖 *taihtzuu*, n., first founder of dynasty.

太子 *taihtzyy*, n., crown prince.

太陽 *taih'yang*(*-yarng*), n., the sun; 太陽系 solar system; (太)陽曆 Gregorian calendar; 太陽穴 the temples (of head); 太陽膏 headache ointment plastered over temples; 太陽燈 sun lamp; 太陽能電池板 solar panel (astron.); 太陽神 Apollo, also wr. 阿波羅.

太醫 *taihyi*, n., imperial physician.

太乙 *taihyii*, n., primordial unity of *yin* and *yang*.

太陰 *taihyin*, n., the moon; (太)陰曆 lunar calendar, commonly 陰曆.

猋 12.81

biau.

[More modn. var. 飇 see 42.70]

N. (AC) Storm.

Adj. (AC) Dashing, speeding fast.

夫 12.81

fu as n., man, husband; *fur* (LL) in all other parts of speech.

Fin. part. (LL) in questions and exclamations, indicating deep feeling: 逝者如斯夫 things pass away like this! oft. with 矣: 有矣夫 there is such a thing; 吾已矣夫 it is time for me to stop; with 也: 莫吾知也夫 alas, no one understands me!

Adj. (LL demonstrative adj. & pron.) this, that, these, those: 夫人不言 this man does not talk; 賊夫人之子 you are spoiling this man's son; 夫三子者之言 what those three people say; 今夫地, 今夫水 now this earth, this water.

Adv. & conj. (LL beginning sentences and opening generalizations) now, as regards: 夫仁者 now (as regards) 仁; 夫道若大路然 now the Way (Tao) is like a broad highway; 夫何憂何懼 now what is there to worry about? 夫如此, 夫如是 only so; 夫豈不知 now don't I (doesn't he) know? 夫既如此 now that it is so; that being so; 夫唯不爭, 故 . . . it is because he does not contend, therefore . . . ; with 且 in 且夫 moreover; with 今 in 今夫 now (introducing generalization).

Prep. (LL) than, at, with: 視夫前者 compared with the former.

N. Pr. *fu*. (1) Man, like Eng. "working man," "fisherman," or "-er" in "worker" "farmer": 漁夫 fisherman; 農夫 farmer; 販夫 pedlar; 車夫 driver, chauffeur; 馬夫 driver of horse carriage; 轎夫 sedan chair bearer; 挑夫 porter; 厨夫 cook; 凡夫 ordinary person; 匹夫 an ordinary individual; 夫役 servants; 征夫 wayfarer; 老夫 old man (oft. speaking of oneself). (2) Husband: 丈夫 husband, see 夫君, 夫主 *-jyun, -juu*↓; 夫黨 husband's people; 夫兄弟 husband's brothers; 夫婦, 夫妻, 夫家 *-fuh, -chi, -jia*↓; 未婚夫 fiancé, see 大△夫, 大△丈夫 12.81.

夫妻 *fu-chi*, n., husband and wife: 夫妻反目, 不和 quarrel between husband and wife.

夫婦 *fu-fuh*, n., husband and wife: 夫婦偕老 husband and wife live together till old age; 夫婦好合, 夫唱婦隨 harmony between husband and wife; see *-chi*↑.

夫家 *fu-jia*, n., husband's family.

夫己氏 *fujii-shyh*, n., (AC) a certain person (purposely vague)＝某.

夫主 *fujuu*, n., husband (as head of family).

夫君 *fujyun*, n., husband (litr. term of reference).

夫馬 *fumaa*, n., official retinue; servants; 夫馬費 entertainment expenses.

夫人 *furern* (*fu'ren*), n., madam, Mrs., gen. term of reference for wife in polished society: 張夫人 Mrs. Chang; 如夫人 concubine; 竹夫人 bamboo footrest, "Dutch wife."

夫婿 *fushyuh*, n., husband.

夫子 (1) *futzyy*, n., (LL) teacher, master: 孔夫子 Confucius,

Master Kung; elderly scholar; (2) *fu'tz*, n., common laborer (also wr. 伕子).

夫役 *fuyih*, n., servants.

失 12.81

shy.

N. (1) Mistake, error: 過失 ditto. (2) Failure, loss, opp. 得 success, gain: 一得一失 a gain here, a loss there; 得失相抵 gains are offset by losses; 萬無一失 guarantee complete success.

V. i. & t. (1) To lose (s.t.), to miss (chance): 失落 *-luoh*↓; 遺失, 丟失, 失去 to lose (s.t.); 失了 have lost; 失物 *-wuh*[1]↓; 失面子 lose face; 失名譽 lose a good name; 失和氣 spoil friendship; 失禮貌 commit a breach of etiquette; 失去聯絡 lose contact; 失而復得 lost and found again; 失之東隅, 收之桑榆 what is lost in the morning is made up in the evening; 交臂失之 to lose (opportunity or s.t.) close at hand; 失之毫釐, 謬以千里 a minimal error or deviation results in wide divergence; 坐失良機 watch a golden chance slip by; see many compp.: 失傳, 失名, 失時, 失業 *-chuarn*, *-mirng*[2], *-shyr*[1], *-yeh*, etc.↓. (2) As verbal prefix, equal to Eng. "mis-", "mal-" in "misdeed," "malpractice": see 失政, 失言, 失察 *-jehng*, *-yarn*, *-char*, etc.↓; or oft. equiv. "in-," "im-": as 失當, 失宜 inappropriate, from 當 and 宜 appropriate.

失敗 *shybaih*, v. i. & n., to fail (in attempt, experiment), be defeated; a failure: 成功與失敗 success and failure; 失敗者 one who has failed; 失敗主義 defeatism.

失察 *shychar*, v. i., to make mistake from oversight: 一時失察 a momentary oversight.

失常 *shycharng*, adj., abnormal: 神經失常 mentally abnormal, unduly depressed (=反常, opp. 正常).

失氣 *shychih*, adj., frustrated, deeply disappointed, deflated.

失出 *shy-chu*, v. i., (law) to err in too light penalty or fail to give any penalty at all; cf. 失入 *-ruh*↓.

失傳 *shy-chuarn*, v. i., (of anc. art, book, medical formula) lost through the generations.

失寵 *shy-chuung*, v. i., fall into disfavor.

失卻 *shy-chyueh*, v. t., to lose (=失去, 失了).

失當 *shydahng*, adj. & adv., inappropriate: 處置失當 (affair) badly handled.

失單 *shy-dan*, n., list of lost property.

失盜 *shydauh*, v. i., to be burglarized.

失德 *shyder*, v. i., (1) to do s.t. very cruel or inhuman or reprehensible; (2) (Taoist) to lose original character of man: 失德然後義 (老子) one talks of "righteousness" after losing original character of man.

失掉 *shydiauh*[1], v. t., to lose (=失去).

失調 *shy-diauh*[2], adj., (1) (mus.) out of tune; (2) (*-tiaur*) upset, unbalanced: 飲食失調 have improper or unbalanced food.

失度 *shyduh*, adj. & adv., excessive, -ly, irregular, -ly, immoderate, -ly.

失和 *shy-her*, v. i., (two friends) quarrel, have differences of opinion.

失候 *shy-houh*, v. i., (1) (of food) suffer from faulty timing; (2) (court.) to be absent when s.o. calls (=失迎); (3) 失候起居 (court.) to fail to keep up correspondence.

失怙 *shy-huh*, v. i., to lose father (when young).

失火 *shy-huoo*, v. i., to have fire accident, (house) catch fire.

失魂 *shy-hurn*, phr., frightened or stricken (by sorrow), out of wits.

失著 *shyjau*, n., a wrong, mistaken step; bad move in chess.

失政 *shyjehng*, n., misgovernment.

失眞 *shy-jen*, v. i., (photograph, portrait) lose expression, not true to life.

失機 *shy-ji*, v. i., to miss a chance or commit a vital mistake in mil. or other matters.

失檢 *shy-jiaan*, v. i., see *-char*↑.

失腳 *shy-jiaau*, v. i., to slip on the ground.

失節 *shy-jier*, v. i., to lose integrity or chastity; be disloyal to ruler, country or husband.

失計 *shy-jih*, n., a mistaken move.

失敬 *shy-jihng*, v. i., (court.) to fail in courtesy, etiquette.

失主 *shyjuu*, n., the owner of lost property.

失職 *shy-jyr*, v. i., to be delinquent in duty.

失據 *shy-jyuh*, phr., (mil.) to lose base of support.

失口 *shy-koou*, v. i., see *-yarn*↓.

失戀 *shy-liahn*, v. i., to be disappointed in love.

失利 *shy-lih*, v. i., to be defeated; to lose in business.

失禮 *shy-lii*, v. i., commit a breach of etiquette.

失落 *shyluoh*, v. t., to lose (opportunity, handkerchief, etc.).

失眠 *shymiarn*, v. i., suffer from insomnia.

失滅 *shymieh*, v. i., (things) disappear, vanish; (fire) be extinguished; v. t., to lose (things).

失迷 *shymir*, v. i., be lost on the way.

失明 *shy-mirng*[1], v. i., become blind.

失名 *shy-mirng*[2], v.i., name unknown.

失黏 *shy-niarn*, v. i., (LL) have mistakes in tones in a poem.

失陪 *shypeir*, v. i., (court.) take leave: 我失陪了 excuse me (for leaving).

失人 *shy-rern*, v. i., fail to recognize a good man: 可與言而不與之言, 失人 to fail to speak to one worth speaking to is to miss a good person.

失入 *shy-ruh*, v. i., (law) to impose improper or improperly heavy penalty; cf. *-chu*↑.

失容 *shy-rurng*, v. i., see *-seh*↓.

失散 *shysahn*, v. i., scatter, disperse.

失色 *shy-seh*, v. i., to change countenance for fear, disgrace.

失閃 *shy'shan*, v. i., have a mishap.

失愼 *shy-shehn*, v. i., (1) to make a

slip, be careless; (2) (house) to catch fire.

失身 *shy-shen*, v. i., to lose virginity (with a man).

失聲 *shy-sheng*, v. i., (voice) caught: 失聲而哭 lose control and cry out loud.

失神 *shy-shern*, v. i., be inattentive in moments: 一失神就出錯誤 the slightest lack of attention results in errors.

失陷 *shyshiahn*, v. i., (of towns, territory) be lost to the enemy.

失效 *shy-shiauh*[1], v. i., become not valid; (med.) lose efficacy.

失笑 *shy-shiauh*[2], v. i., break into laughter.

失信 *shy-shihn*, v. i., to fail in promise.

失心瘋 *shy-shin-feng*, n., (MC) a mania, being out of one's mind; amnesia.

失修 *shy-shiou*, v. i., (1) make a mistake in conduct; (2) (of old structures) suffer from neglected repairs.

失手 *shy-shoou*[1], v. i., make a slip of the hand (and drop s.t.).

失守 *shy-shoou*[2], v. i., (of towns, territory) fall into enemy's hand.

失事 *shyshyh*[1], v. i., (1) to run into trouble, catastrophe (fire, accident, etc.); (2) to make a mistake in handling or management.

失恃 *shy-shyh*[2], v. i., (AC, LL) to lose one's mother; cf. *-huh* ↑.

失勢 *shy-shyh*[3], v. i., (1) to lose support; (2) to be in disgrace or out of power.

失時 *shy-shyr*[1], v. i., to lose an opportunity offered by the times.

失實 *shy-shyr*[2], v. i., (report) be inaccurate.

失學 *shy-shyuer*, v. i., to be forced to drop out of school (from poverty).

失算 *shy-suahn*, n., mistaken move or decision.

失態 *shy-taih*, adj., rude in behavior.

失策 *shy-tseh*, v. i., make a wrong decision.

失措 *shy-tsuoh*, v. i., make a mistake, mismanage.

失辭 *shy-tsyr*, v. i., to use wrong or discourteous words.

失脱 *shy'tuo*, v. i., (article) be lost.

失踪 *shy-tzung*, v. i., (person) to disappear ("lose traces").

失足 *shy-tzur*, v. i., take a wrong step: 一失足成千古恨 a wrong step taken results in eternal regret.

失望 *shy-wahng*, v. i., be disappointed: 令人失望 be disappointing.

失物 *shy-wuh*[1], n., lost articles.

失誤 *shy-wuh*[2], n., a mistake.

失言 *shy-yarn*, v. i., to say s.t. which should not be said.

失業 *shy-yeh*, v. i., be unemployed.

失意 *shy-yih*, adj., disappointed: 情場失意 disappointed in love.

失宜 *shy-yir*[1], adj., improper (conduct, speech).

失儀 *shy-yir*[2], v. i., see *-lii* ↑.

失迎 *shy-yirng*, v. i., (court.) fail in meeting when friend arrives or in hospitality.

失約 *shy-yue*, v. i., (1) to fail to meet appointment; (2) to break promise.

失語症 *shy-yuu-jehng*, n., loss of power of speech.

夷 12.81

yir.

N. (1) Anc. barbarian tribe on east border, any border or foreign tribe: 夷狄 border tribes in gen., spec. on east (夷) and north (狄); 蠻夷 border tribes on the south; 外夷 foreign tribes. (2) U.f. 痍 wound. (3) Anc. ploughlike implement.

V.t. (1) To pacify, to squash (rebellion). (2) To level: 夷爲平地 to raze (houses, cities) to the ground. (3) To annihilate (whole families) as punishment for serious offences.

Adj. (1) Level (ground): 化險爲夷 (fig.) pass through a dangerous crisis safely. (2) (AC) calm, contented (cf. 怡 22A.40). (3) (AC) much: 降福孔夷 give very many blessings.

夷簡 *yirjiaan*, adj., (AC) simple (way of life).

夷戮 *yirluh*, v.t., to slaughter, sentence to death.

夷滅 *yirmieh*, v.t., to wipe out (tribe, family).

夷俟 *yirsyh*, v.i., (AC) to squat.

夷由 *yiryour*[1], adj., (AC) undecided.

夷猶 *yiryour*[2], adj., (1) undecided, see *-your*[1] ↑; (2) leisurely.

夾 12.81

jiar (**jia, *jiah*).

N. (1) Tweezers, pincers, pliers: 夾子 *-'tz* ↓; 火夾 fire tongs. (2) A small case, boards for keeping things in place: 信夾 a case for holding letters, a letter clip; 書夾 book ends; 紙夾 a paper clip. (3) A fastener: 髮夾 hairpins; 衣夾 dress hanger, clothes rack; 領帶夾 tiepin.

V. t. (1) To press, squeeze, compress: 夾持 *-chyr* ↓; 夾起來 pick up (as with chopsticks); 用筷子夾 pick up with chopsticks; 夾心麵包 sandwiches; 夾鼻眼鏡 pince-nez; 夾尾巴 (狗) (of dogs) put the tail between the legs, (fig.) act like a coward. (2) Intermix: 夾七夾八 to foul up; 夾雜 *-tzar* ↓.

Adj. Furnished with a lining: 夾衣, 夾襖, 夾褲 a lined coat, jacket, trousers; 夾大衣 a spring overcoat.

夾板 **jiabaan*, n., (1) thin boards for holding things together; (2) an instrument of torture:

亅	小	⺊	十	土	ナ	廾	⺃	丨	一	丅	フ	口	区	冈	冂	厂	尸	亠	广	宀	丶	乚	弋	心	八	人	乂	乛	丿	リ	ノ	く
00	01	02	10	11	12	20	21	22	30	31	32	40	41	42	50	51	52	60	61	62	63	70	71	72	80	81	82	83	90	91	92	93

上夾板 (lit. & fig.) put on the rack; (3) 三夾板 plywood.

夾壁牆兒 *jiabih-chiarng'l*, n., an impossible fix, a predicament: 他掉在夾壁牆裏了 he finds himself between the devil and the deep sea.

夾氣傷寒 *jiarchih shangharn*, n., pop. term for typhoid.

夾持 *jiarchyr*, v. t., hold in between, press on both sides.

夾袋 *jiardaih*[1], n., anything one keeps for the rainy day: 夾袋人物 persons whom one can implicitly trust and share responsibilities with.

夾帶 *jiardaih*[2], (1) n., contraband (goods); (2) v.t., to bring in illegally notes by students during examination.

夾道 *jiardauh*, n., a narrow passageway.

夾棍 *jiarguhn*, n., formerly, an instrument of torture, a rack.

夾攻 *jiargung*, v. t. & n., (make) a pincers movement against (the enemy).

夾間兒 **jiajiah'l*, n., space in between two things (also 兩夾間兒).

夾擊 *jiarjir*, v. t., to attack from both flanks.

夾注 *jiarjuh*, n., (printing) interlinear notes: 夾注號 parentheses, brackets.

夾竹桃 **jiahjur-taur*, n., (bot.) sweetscented oleander, *Nerium odorum*.

夾生 **jiah'sheng*, adj., not thoroughly cooked, underdone: 這飯煮夾生了 the rice is not well cooked. 「food.

夾餡兒 **jiashiah'l*, n., stuffed

夾彩 *jiartsair*, n., (of pottery, porcelain) the second coating of color.

夾子 **jia'tz*, n., (1) tongs, pincers, pliers, forceps; (2) a wallet, a billfold, a purse.

夾雜 *jiartzar*, (1) v. t., mix up, blend; (2) adj., mixed up, confused, impure.

爽 12.81

shuaang.

V. i. (1) To fail in promise: 爽約, 爽信 *-yue*, *-shihn* ↓. (2) To err, to lose: 爽失 *-shy* ↓.

Adj. (1) Exhilarating (air): 爽快 *-kuaih* ↓; 爽朗, 爽氣 *-laang*, *-chih* ↓; 秋高氣爽 dry, crisp air of autumn. (2) High-spirited, forthright: 豪爽, 英爽 generous, genial (spirit); 爽直, 爽快 *-jyr*, *-kuaih* ↓.

爽氣 *shuaangchih*, (1) adj., (person) generous, simple and direct; (2) n., spirit of geniality; also cold, crisp air.

爽慧 *shuaanghueih*, adj., intelligent, quick in understanding.

爽直 *shuaangjyr*, adj., straightforward.

爽口 *shuarng-koou*, adj., pleasing to the palate.

爽快 *shuaangkuaih* (-'*kuai*), adj., (1) feeling fine, comfortable, happy; (2) generous (with money, tips, etc.).

爽朗 *shuarnglaang*, adj., (climate) crisp and dry.

爽利 *shuaang*(')*lih*, n., (dial.) see *-shihng* ↓.

爽然 *shuaangrarn*, adj., waking up in. 爽然自失 it dawned upon me that I had been wrong.

爽神 *shuaangshern*, adj., very refreshing.

爽信 *shuaang-shihn*, v. i., to fail to keep one's promise.

爽性 *shuaangshihng*, adv., (since s.t. is so) might as well . . . (=索性): 既然應允, 爽性來個痛快 since you have already promised, might just well make it a big affair.

爽心 *shuaang-shin*, adj., entertaining, refreshing, gay.

爽爽 *shuarngshuaang*, adj., distinctive, outstanding.

爽失 *shuaangshy*, n., failure, error, mistake.

爽脆 *shuaangtsueih*, adj., forthright, quick and simple (in negotiations, etc.).

爽約 *shuaang-yue*, v. i., to fail in promise, appointment, to breach contract.

奭 12.81

shyh.

Adj. (AC) red, angry, full.

灰 12.81

huei.

N. (1) (-'l) Ashes: 煙灰 cigarette ashes; 煤灰, 骨灰 ashes from stove, bones; 劫灰 (fig.) what is left after looting; 死灰復燃 cold ashes burn again—the buried past comes alive again, defeated rebels stage a comeback. (2) Lime (=石灰). (3) Dust: 灰土, 灰沙 *-tuu*, *-sha* ↓; 灰頭土腦 head covered with dust, also a blockhead. (4) The grey color.

Adj. (1) Grey in color: 灰白, 灰色 *-bair*, *-seh* ↓. (2) Disheartened: 心灰意冷 very much discouraged; 萬念俱灰 all hopes dashed to pieces, tired of earthly life; 灰心 *-shin* ↓.

灰白 *hueibair*, adj., grey, greyish-white, ashen (colored); 灰白質 grey matter in brains. 「etc.).

灰塵 *hueichern*, n., dust (on table,

灰分 *hueifehn*, n., (bot.) inorganic matter in plants (found in ashes).

灰燼 *hueijihn*, n., ashes.

灰滅 *hueimieh*, v. i., to vanish (of hopes, dreams, etc.).

灰棚(兒) *hueiperng*('*l*), n., plastered mud hut (also called 灰房 opp. brick houses).

灰色 *hueiseh*, adj., (1) grey in color; (2) of unclear or ambiguous attitude or belief.

灰沙 *hueisha*, n., dust, sand dust.

灰心 *huei-shin*, v. i. & adj., (feel) discouraged, disappointed, lose interest: 他灰心了 he is disheartened or 灰了心 ready to give up.

灰鼠 *hueishuu*, n., the squirrel.

灰膛 *huei-tarng*, n., ash pan in stove.

灰槽子 *huei-tsaur'tz*, n., old-fashioned wooden ash box for pipe tobacco.

灰土 *hueituu*, n., dust, mud.

奏 12.81

tzouh.

V. i. & t. (1) To play music: 奏樂 ditto; 奏琴 play the piano; 奏鼓 beat the drum; 演奏 give a musical performance; 和奏 to play in harmony; 合奏 to play together, as a band or orchestra; 獨奏 (give) a solo; 彈奏 play (piano, violin); 二重奏 duet; 三重奏 trio; 吹奏 play (a wind in strument). (2) Memorialize the emperor: 奏摺, 奏疏, 奏章, 奏本 *-jer, -shu, -jang, -been*↓; a memorial to the throne; 奏草, 奏稿 a draft memorial: 奏對 (of ministers) to answer questions at an audience with the emperor; 陳奏, 面奏, 上奏 memorialize the throne in person; 先斬後奏 (a general empowered to) execute person on the spot without prior approval from the court.

奏案 *tzouh-ahn*, n., formerly, a matter laid before and approved by the throne.

奏本 *tzouhbeen*, n., a memorial to ruler.

奏刀 *tzouh-dau*, v. t., (LL) to cut (meat) with butcher's knife.

奏功 *tzouh-gung*, v. i., be successful in undertaking.

奏章 *tzouhjang*, n., a memorial to ruler.

奏摺 *tzouhjer*, n., a memorial to the throne.

奏捷 *tzouh-jier*, v. i., (1) be victorious (in war); (2) to report news of victory to government.

奏技 *tzouh-jih*, v. i., (of acrobats, singers, dancers) to stage a performance.

奏凱 *tzouh-kaai*, v. i., be victorious in war.

奏效 *tzouh-shiauh*, v. i., to show results.

奏疏 *tzouhshu*, n., a memorial to ruler.

奏參 *tzouh-tsan*, v. t., impeach (an official) by means of a memorial to the throne.

奏議 *tzouhyih*, n., (1) memorandum on current national affairs submitted to the ruler; (2) a memorial to the throne.

§ 12.82 (ナ/乂)

丈 12.82

jahng.

N. (1) Length of ten feet: 丈二金剛 a Buddhist statue twelve feet high, hence 摸不著頭腦 (a pun) "cannot reach to the head" —cannot make head or tail of; 丈六金身 a tall Buddhist idol. (2) An older relative or person: 丈夫, 丈人, 丈母 *-fu, -rern, -muu*↓; 老丈, 老丈人 respectful address to elder person; 方丈 abbot; 國丈 elder statesman; 嶽丈, 岳丈 father-in-law.

V. t. To measure land: 丈量 *-liarng*↓.

丈夫 *jahngfu*, n., (1) a husband; (2) a man: 大丈夫 a man of honor, an upright, fearless person.

丈量 *jahngliarng*, v. t., to survey land, establish dimensions of land officially.

丈母 *jahngmuu*, n., mother-in-law; (AC) elderly woman; 丈母娘 mother-in-law.

丈人 *jahngrern*, n., father-in-law; (AC) elderly person; 丈人峯 (court.) father-in-law; 丈人行 a person of elder generation.

友 12.82

yoou.

N. (1) A friend: 朋友 ditto; 好友, 良友 good friends; 老友, 舊友 old friends; 密友 close friends; 親友 friends and relatives; 賭友, 酒友 gambling, drinking companions; 交友 make friends. (2) Member of guild, class, school, profession: 教友, 校友, 級友 member of same church, school, class; affected reference to worker: 工友 "my labor friend"; 小朋友 *cliché* for school children and kindergarten kids.

V. t. (LL) 友其人 to befriend (person); 友之 become his friend.

Adj. Kind, friendly allied: 友邦 friendly country; 友軍 allied troops; 友黨 political parties maintaining friendly relations with one another.

友愛 *yoou-aih*, (1) v. t., to be good friends with; to be kind to (brothers); (2) adj., kind, amiable.

友邦 *yooubang*, n., allied country, country maintaining friendly relations.

友情 *yoouchirng*, n., friendship.

友好 *yourhaau*, n., good friends.

友朋 *yourperng*, n., friends.

友人 *yoourern*, n., a friend.

友善 *yooushahn*, v. t. & adj., to cultivate good relationships with, friendly.

友生 *yoousheng*, n., (AC) friend.

友誼 *yoouyih*, n., friendship.

吏 12.82

lih.

N. An official, a government clerk: 官吏 officialdom; 吏議 ministerial recommendations;

吏治 *-jyh*↓.

吏部 *lihbuh*, n., formerly, the Ministry of the Interior, in charge of the appointment, promotion, and dismissal of officials.
吏治 *lihjyh*, n., administration (good, bad) of officials.
吏目 *lihmuh*, n., government clerks, minor officers.
吏員 *lihyuarn*, n., a minor official.

§ 12.83 (ㄊ/ㄧ)

迍 12.83

behn.
[Cogn. 奔 in 奔命 12.20]

遼 12.83

liaur.

N. (1) Name of Liao tribe in Inner Mongolia, 契丹 Kitan Tartars 901–1125 A.D.. (2) Name of river.

Adj. Distant, broad (interch. 寥 see 62.91).

遼東半島 *Liaurdung Bahndaau*, n., the Liaotung Peninsula.
遼隔 *liaurger*, adj., distantly apart.
遼闊 *liaurkuoh*[1], adj., broad (of desert, ocean) (also wr. 寥).
遼廓 *liaurkuoh*[2], adj., ditto.
遼朗 *liaurlaang*, adj., serene.
遼遼 *liaurliaur*, adj., very distant.
遼落 *liaurluoh*, adj., distant, stretching a great distance.
遼寧 *Liaurnirng*, n., a province in Manchuria.
遼遠 *liauryuaan*, adj., distant.

迭 12.83

dier.

Adv. (1) Repeatedly: 迭奉大札 repeatedly received your letters; 迭經催請 have asked (him) several times, to hurry up. (2) 不迭 without stop.

迭次 *diertsyh*, adv., repeatedly, again and again.

§ 12.93 (ㄊ/ㄑ)

套 12.93

tauh.

N. adjunct. A set, series: 這一套衣服 this coat and pants, dress ensemble; 一套麻匠牌子 a set of mahjong; 一套東西 an odd lot of things.

N. (1) (*-tz*, *'l*) Cover, covering case: 枕套 pillowcase; 被套 bedding; 椅套 slip cover for chairs; 手套 gloves; 套鞋 *-shier*↓; 外套 overcoat; 套衣, 套褲 *-yi*, *-kuh*↓; 封套 envelope, folder; 筆套 case for writing brush; 書套 cloth case for a set of books; 信套 big envelope. (2) Set: 整套傢具 a whole set of furniture; 套房, 套版, 套杯 *-farng*, *-baan*, *-bei*↓. (3) Trick, trap: 圈套 a trap; 落套, 落了套中 fall into trap. (4) *Cliché*, formula: 俗套, 老套 (derog.) same old things, hackneyed phrases or statements; 客套, 虛套 empty, routine compliments; 老是這一套 the same old things too often repeated.

V. t. (1) Fit over, slip over (as gloves, slip covers): 套上去, 套進去 put into cover; 從頭上套下來 slip overhead (as pullovers); 套白狼 strangle from the back; 套半車 of widow with children remarrying. (2) To harness: 套車 to get cart ready; 套馬 to harness horse to cart, to lasso horse. (3) To trick into talking: 套口供, 套出來 trick accused into confession or admitting details; 套頭裹腦 blindfold person. (4) Bring close, attach: 套上交情, 套拉攏 succeed in establishing friendship; 套近 hang around, become close to (person); 套紅 to add red coloring. (5) Copy: 套樣 copy model; 套用成語 use hackneyed formulas; 套別人的話 borrow other's phrases.

套版 *tauhbaan*, n., colored plates, ancient color wood-block printing, see *-sehbaan*↓.
套杯 *tauhbei*, n., a set of cups, one inside another.
套氣 *tauh'chih*, n., formality (=客氣).
套房 *tauhfarng*, n., suite of rooms, hotel suite.
套話 *tauhhuah*, n., conventionalities: 話裏套話 loaded questions.
套環兒 *tauhhuar'l*, n., pretzel-like eatable; a set of connected rings.
套滙 *tauhhueih*, n., arbitrage.
套價 *tauhjiah*, n., cross rate.
套間 *tauhjian*, n., small side room adjacent to main room, see *-farng*↑.
套褲 *tauhkuh*, n., leg sheaths or over trousers without hips that are tied over trousers.
套連 *tauhliarn*, v. i., connect up by ties.
套禮 *tauhlii*, n., conventional courtesies.
套色版 *tauhsehbaan*, n., anc. colored woodblocks; such printing.
套鞋 *tauhshier*, n., galoshes, rubbers.
套數 *tauhshuh*, n., (Yuan Dyn.) opera text without dialogues.
套索 *tauhsuoo*, n., lasso.
套衣 *tauhyi*, n., outer garment.

蠢 12.93

chuun.

Adj. (1) Stupid: 蠢材, 蠢貨, 蠢笨 *-tsair*, *-huoh*, *-behn*↓; 蠢東西 (abuse) silly ass. (2) Extremely fat, torpid. (3) 蠢蠢 stirring, wriggling: 蠢蠢欲動 (of person) restless and about to start some move.

蠢笨 *chuunbehn*, n., (1) stupid; (2) awkward with hand movement.

蠢貨 *chuunhuoh*, n., (abuse) silly fellow.

蠢材 *chuuntsair*, n., dull wit, nincompoop.

SECTION 12S

§ 12S.00 (ナS/亅)

刳 12S.00-2

ku.

V. t. To hew, plane: 刳木爲舟 (AC) hew a tree trunk and shape it into a canoe.

剞 12S.00-2

ji.

N. A carving or engraving knife.

V.t. To carve (wood block).

§ 12S.11 (ナS/土)

雄 12S.11-9

shyurng.

N. (1) A hero, champion: 英雄 hero, conqueror, (also adj.) heroic; 一世之雄 champion, first man, of his generation. (2) A powerful and rich man: 豪雄 ditto.

V. t. (Coll.) to shout or threaten with words: 拿話雄人 to intimidate with words.

Adj. (1) Male of species, orig. of birds: 雄雞, 雄鳥 a cock, a male bird; later also of beasts (bull, stallion, male pig, etc.) and of flowers, see 雄蕊 *-rueei*↓; opp. to 雌 female, oft. in phr., 雌雄 "female and male"; 一決雌雄 see who is the stronger; see another set of words for male and female in 牝, 牡 10C.70, 10C.11. (2) Brave, valiant, strong: 雄壯 *-juahng*↓; 雄糾糾 very strong and handsome; 雄師, 雄兵 strong, mighty army; 雄將 a brave general; 雄風 (AC) strong wind. (3) Superior: 爭雄 see who is superior, to vie for supremacy; 稱雄 to be recognized as the master (among countries); 逞雄 to rely on superior power. (4) Great, solid: 雄圖 *-tur*↓; 雄才大略 great talent, capable of doing great things; 雄厚 *-houh*↓.

Adv. Greatly, heroically, skillfully: 雄辯 *-biahn*↓; 雄飛 fly or soar aloft; 雄斷 make a heroic or skillful decision; 雄張 expand greatly.

雄辯 *shyurng-biahn*, phr., eloquence of speech, make skillful defense of case: 事實勝於雄辯 facts speak louder than words.

雄氣 *shyurngchih*, n., (AC) a spirited appearance.

雄兒 *shyurng-er'l*, n.,(MC) a hero.

雄藩 *shyurng-farn*, phr., powerful governors or feudal princes (Tang Dyn.).

雄豪 *shyurnghaur*, (1) n., the powerful men of a locality or time; (2) valiant (person).

雄厚 *shyurnghouh*, adj., solid (wealth).

雄花 *shyurng-hua*, n., (bot.) male (barren) flowers.

雄黃 *shyurnghuarng*, n., (min.) realgar, flowers of sulphur: 雄黃酒 wine containing flowers of sulphur, said to cure snake bites, etc.

雄渾 *shyurnghurn*, adj., (of callig., prose) powerful, rich and satisfying.

雄長 *shyurngjaang*, n., (LL) an acknowledged master of a generation.

雄鎮 *shyurng-jehn*, n., a strategic stronghold.

雄健 *shyurngjiahn*, adj., see *-juahng* ↓.

亅	小	卜	十	土	ナ	廾	ㅏ	丨	一	丁	フ	口	区	冈	㇆	厂	尸	亠	广	宀	丶	乚	乁	心	八	人	乂	乀	ノ	リ	⺊	く
00	01	02	10	11	12	20	21	22	30	31	32	40	41	42	50	51	52	60	61	62	63	70	71	72	80	81	82	83	90	91	92	93

雄壯 *shyurngjuahng*, adj., stalwart (body), massive (financial power), impressive looking (person, army).

雄蕊 *shyurngrueei*, n., stamens.

雄勝 *shyurng-shehng*, n. & adj., strategic place.

雄心 *shyurng-shin*, n., life ambition: 雄心未死 still full of ambition, not willing to give up.

雄雄 *shyurngshyurng*, adj., (AC) resplendent.

雄圖 *shyurng-tur*, n., (LL) great plans (also 鴻圖).

雄姿 *shyurngtzy*, n., handsome appearance.

雄偉 *shyurngweei*, adj., stately, magnificent, valiant, impressive.

§ 12S.22 (ナˢ/丨)

郁 12S.22-3

yuh.

N. A surname.

Adj. (1) Rich in aroma. (2) Cultured: 郁郁 *-yuh*↓.

郁馥 *yuhfuh*, adj., rich in fragrance.

郁烈 *yuhlieh*, adj., sharp-smelling (liquor), pungent.

郁李 *yuhlii*, n., a prune, *Prunus japonica*.

郁郁 *yuhyuh*, adj., (1) as in 郁郁乎文哉 (AC) splendid in cultural attainments; (2) suffused with fragrance.

§ 12S.50 (ナˢ/ㄱ)

翃 12S.50-5

hurng.

Adv. Descriptive of humming of insects.

鶬 12S.50-9

an.

鶬鶉 *anchurn* (-'*chun*), n., the quail.

鶉 12S.50-9

liaur.

N. See 鵪鶉 91S.50.

§ 12S.70 (ナˢ/乚)

規 12S.70-4

guei.

N. (1) Rules, regulations: 法規 laws and ordinances; 官規 rules of official conduct; 陋規 corrupt practices, illegal exactions, irregularities; 規例 *-lih*, 規範 *-fahn*, 規章 *-jang*, 規條 *-tiaur*, 規則 *-tzer*, 規程 *-cherng*, 規矩 *-jyuh*↓; 墨守成規 stick to precedents; 常規 normal regulations; 門規 family rules; 教規 religious rules; 校規 school rules; 犯規, 違規 violate the rules. (2) Instrument for drawing circles: 圓規 a pair of compasses; 半圓規 protractor. (3) Specifications: 規格.

V. t. (1) To order, ordain, direct: 規勸 *-chyuahn*, 規諫 *-jiahn*, 規定 *-dihng*↓; 規過 persuade (s. o.) to follow the right path. (2) To plan: 規畫 *-huah*↓.

Adj. Orderly, systematic: 規矩 *-jyuh*↓; 規規矩矩 (of persons) polite, law-abiding, (of conduct) unexceptionable; 規行矩步 strictly upright and correct (in behavior).

規避 *gueibih*, v. t., evade (duties, responsibilities, etc); also evade meeting person of opposite sex.

規程 *gueicherng*, n., rules, regulations, by-laws.

規勸 *gueichyuahn*, v. t., admonish.

規定 *gueidihng*, (1) v. t., regulate, prescribe; (2) n., rules, regulations.

規範 *gueifahn*, (1) n., a norm, criterion; (2) v. t., regulate by laws or rules.

規費 *gueifeih*, n., customary payments or dues, fees.

規復 *gueifuh*, v. t. & n., restore to norm, rehabilitate, -tion.

規畫 *gueihuah*, v. t. & n., to plan; planning.

規章 *gueijang*, n., rules, regulations, by-laws.

規正 *gueijehng*, v. t., admonish.

規諫 *gueijiahn*, v. t., remonstrate with (one's superior).

規戒 *gueijieh*, v. t., warn, reprove, admonish.

規矩 *gueijyuh* (-*jyu*), n., & adj., (1) a pair of compasses and T square; (2) a custom, an established practice: 照規矩辦 follow the customary practice; (3) adj., behaving properly, acting correctly: 守規矩 obedient to discipline, well-behaved; 這人很規矩 the man is well-behaved.

規例 *gueilih*, n., precedents established practices.

規律 *gueilyuh*, n., rules, statutes.

規模 *guei'mor*, n., scope, scale, magnitude: 規模不小 by no means a small scale; 很有規模 of a respectable size or magnitude.

規條 *gueitiaur*, n., detailed rules or provisions for gen. observance.

規則 *gueitzer*, n., rules, regulations, prescribed procedure.

規約 *gueiyue*, n., a written agreement.

飆 12S.70-4

biau.

N. Storm, hurricane, usu. 飆風.

匏 12S.70-9

paur.

N. Bottle-shaped gourd; one of eight categories of ancient music, using gourd shell as resonance box.

匏瓜 *paurgua*, n., gourd, calabash.
匏繫 *paurshih*, n., (LL allu.) hanging gourd shell, a useless or unemployed person.
匏尊 *paurtzun*, n., (AC) gourd shell as wine cup.

§ 12S.80 (ナˢ/八)

頰 12S.80-3

jiar.

N. The jaw, the cheeks: 臉頰 cheeks; 掌頰 give (s. o.) a slap on the face, box the ear; 批頰 ditto; 腮頰 the jaws.

頰骨 *jiar-guu*, n., the cheekbone.

§ 12S.81 (ナˢ/人)

献 12S.81-1

shiahn.
[Pop. of 獻 21S.81]

欹 12S.81-9

yi.
[Interch. 猗 91C.00]

§ 12S.82 (ナˢ/乂)

攲 12S.82-1

chi.

V.i. To lean to one side: 傾攲 ditto; 攲器 a lopsided vessel apt to lean over.

§ 12S.83 (ナˢ/⌒)

瓠 12S.83-9

huh.

N. (1) Gourd, calabash. (2) An ancient surname.

瓠果 *huhguoo*, n., gourd, calabash.
瓠落 *huhluoh*, adj., (AC) useless.
瓠犀 *huhshi*, n., melon seeds: 齒如瓠犀 (AC) beautiful and even teeth (of women), like a row of melon seeds.

SECTION 20

§ 20.00 (卄/亅)

擎 20.00

chirng.

V. i. & t. To hold arms up high, as to receive s. t.: 擎受 extend arms to receive; 擎拳 brandish a closed first aloft; 擎起 hold s. t. up; 擎槍 to present arms.

擎手 *chirngshoou*, v. i., (1) to hold arms up; (2) to "hold," i. e., stop movement.
擎天柱 *chirngtian-juh*, n., a pillar of strength ("supporting sky").

§ 20.01 (卄/小)

某 20.01

moou.

Pron. & adj. Pronominal adjective denoting indeterminate, unspecified person or thing, like "a certain," "Mr. X": 某人, 地 a certain person, place; 某年, 月 a certain year, month; 某種 a certain kind; 某些人 certain persons; 王某張某 a certain Mr. Wang, Mr. Chang; pron., (AC) 某在斯, 某在斯 (showing to a blind person) who is here and who is here; (LL) sometimes used (court.) in place of "I"; 某不敢同意 I cannot agree.

綦 20.01

chir.

N. A surname; straps for sandals.

Adv. (LL) very: 綦繁 very complicated; 綦重 very heavy; 綦嚴 very severe.

綦綺 *chirchii*, n., a textile with crisscross surface.
綦巾 *chirjin*, n., (AC) woman's greenish scarf.

荣 20.01

rurng.
[Abbr. of 榮 91.01]

棊 20.01

chir.
[Anc. var. of 棋 10B.80]

檠 20.01

chirng.

N. (1) 燈檠 lamp stand; a plate with leg supports. (2) 檠柎 (AC) device for holding crossbow in position.

§ 20.02 (卄/k)

恭 20.02

gung.

N. (1) A surname. (2) Feces: 出恭 to move bowels; 恭桶 *-tuung* ↓.

V. t. To reverence, to respect: 恭維 *-'wei* ↓.

Adj. & adv. Polite(ly), respectful(ly): 恭敬 *-'jihng* ↓; 恭賀 felicitate, congratulate; 恭祝 ditto; 恭候 patiently wait to welcome; 恭請 cordially invite; 恭送 solemnly bid (s. o.) Godspeed; 恭順 *-shuhn* ↓; 恭本 *-'ben* ↓;

恭本 *gung'ben*, adj., serious (in deportment), earnest: 恭本正傳 to talk in all seriousness, not jokingly.
恭敬 *gung'jihng*, v. t. & adj., (1) v. t., to respect; (2) adj., respectful.
恭人 *gungrern*, n., formerly, wives of high officials.
恭喜 *gungshii*, n. & v. t., (1) congratulate (-tions); (2) work, (hold) an appointment: 您在那裡恭喜 where are you working?
恭順 *gungshuhn*, v. i. & adj., (be) submissive, complaisant.
恭桶 *gungtuung*, n., a commode.
恭維 *gung'wei*, v. t., to wish (luck, health) to praise; 不敢恭維 "dare not sing praises of"——an understatement for condemning s.t. bad.

§ 20.10 (卄/十)

革 20.10

*ger(*jir)*

N. (1) Animal hides without hair: 毛革 furs and hides; 皮革 leather; 革囊 a leather case or bag; 革履 leather shoes; 兵革 weapons of war, also gen. warfare; 老革 (coll.) an aged soldier; 膚革 the human skin. (2) A musical instrument made of leather, spec. a drum. (3) A surname.

V. t. Remove, get rid of, dismiss, change, reform: 革命 *-mihng* ↓; 革面洗心 (of a person with a past) become a new man, start life anew; 革心 to change one's heart; 革退 to dismiss; 革員 to cut the number of employees; 革除 *-chur*, 革職 *-jyr* ↓; 革新 *-shin* ↓; 改革 to reform; 變革 replace the old with the new; 興革 introduce reforms; 革故鼎新 discard the old ways of life in favor of the new; 沿革 origins and development of an institution.

Adj. (*jir) (LL) critical, dangerous (＝急): 疾革 (of illness) in a critical stage; 病革 ditto.

革除 *gerchur*, v. t., expel, dismiss, get rid of.
革職 *ger-jyr*, v. t., to dismiss, be dismissed, from office.
革命 *germihng*, (1) n., revolution: 革命黨, 革命軍 a revolutionary party, army; 革命家 a revolutionist; (2) v. i., to revolt, overthrow the established authorities;
革新 *gershin*, v. i., & t. to reform, innovate, change for the better.

§ 20.11 (卄/土)

基 20.11

ji.

N. (1) The foundation or base of buildings: 奠基 to lay the foundation stone; 基石 cornerstone; 基層 *-tserng* ↓. (2) (Chem.) radicals. (3) Basis: 基本 *-been* ↓; 根基 groundwork, roots.

Prep. According to, for: 基於 according to; 基此理由 for this reason.

基本 *jibeen*, n., basis, fundamentals; adj., basic (education, etc.).

基礎 *jichuu* (-'*chu*), n., (lit. & fig.) a foundation.
基調 *jidiauh*, n., (1) central theme; (2) (music) the keynote.
基地 *jidih*, n., (mil.) base of operations.
基督 *jidu*, n., Christ; 基督教 Christianity; 基督徒 a Christian; 基督會 (rel.) Church of Christ.
基多 *Jiduo*, n., Quito, the capital of Ecuador.
基爾特 *ji-eel-teh* n., (translit.) guild.
基輔 *Jifuu*, n., Kiev.
基金 *jijin*, n., an endowment fund: 洛氏基金, 福特基金 the Rockefeller, Ford Foundation.
基準 *jijuun*, n., (1) criteria; (2) (math.) postulates.
基址 *jijyy*[1], n., a building site, base.
基趾 *jijyy*[2], n., a basis on which anything rests.
基線 *jishiahn*, n., (math.) a base line.
基數 *jishuh*, n., (1) (math.) the basic numbers from one to nine; (2) (math.) a constant figure on which later terms of a series are calculated.
基層 *jitserng*, n., the basic unit, grassroots, the lowest level, substratum.
基業 *jiyeh*, n., an empire built up by the founder of a dynasty or of a business enterprise, the family estate, an heirloom.
基音 *jiyin*, n., (phys.) a fundamental (tone) (opp. 諧音 harmonics).

堇 20.11

jiin (also *jihn*).
[U.f. 僅 91A.11, only; pop of 堇 20A.11]

§ 20.20 (卄/卄)

井 20.20

jiing.

N. (1) A well: 井水 well water; 井闌 -*larn*↓; 井口 the mouth of a well; 井水不犯河水 none may encroach upon the precincts of another; 投井, 跳井 drown oneself in a well; 枯井 a dried-up well; 鹽井, 油井 salt wells, oil wells; 鑿井 well-digging. (2) An ancient system of farming and land distribution: 井田 -*tiarn*↓. (3) A surname.

井拔涼 *jiing'baliarng*, n., cool fresh water from a well.
井底蛙 *jirng-dii-wa*, n., a person with a limited outlook ("a frog living at the bottom of a well").
井井 *jirngjiing*, adj., neat, tidy, well-arranged: 井井有條 in an orderly manner.
井臼 *jiingjiouh*, n., domestic work, household management("drawing water and pounding rice").
井闌 *jiinglarn*, n., (1) well curb; (2) (AC) scaffolding for attacking city walls.
井然 *jiingrarn*, adj., well arranged, in good order, tidy.
井臺兒 *jiingtar'l*, n., a raised platform by the side of a well.
井田 *jiingtiarn*, n., an ancient system of cutting farm land into nine squares in the pattern of character 井, the center square being communal farm, the surrounding eight private.
井蛙 *jiing-wa*, n., see -*dii-wa*↑.
井窩子 *jiingwotz*, n., formerly, a place near a well where sellers of well water lived in Peiping.
井鹽 *jiingyarn*, n., salt from salt wells.

§ 20.21 (卄/乚)

廿 20.21

niahn.
[Usu. wr. 廿]

N. The number twenty (also wr. 念 81.72): 念載 or 廿載 twenty years.

甚 20.21

shehn (*shern, *sher).

Adj. (1) (*shern) What, what kind: 甚麽 -'*mo*↓; 甚樣 -*yahng*↓; 甚般 -*ban*↓; short for 甚麽: 甚人, 甚事, 甚地 what person, business, place; 甚時, 甚日 what time, day. (2) (AC) fast (related 迅): 甚風, 甚雨 fast-driving wind, rain; 甚口 fast talker.

Adv. Very, very much, quite: 甚好, 甚佳, 甚善 very good; 甚壞, 甚惡 very bad; 甚大, 甚小 very big, very small; 甚多, 甚少 very much or many, very little or few, etc.; 甚可疑 very suspicious; 甚不壞 not bad indeed; oft. in comb. 甚爲, 甚是 instead of 甚 for rhythmic reason; thus 甚是可疑, 甚是不壞; 甚是可人 very lovable; 甚有道理 (term of approval) quite right; 太甚 too much; 欺人太甚 has gone too far in insult or injury; 莫爲已甚 don't drive s. o. into a corner.

甚般 *shernban*, adj. & adv., (MC) how (solitary, sad, etc.)=modn. 怎般.
甚處 *shern-chuh*, adv., where.
甚的 *shern'de*, n., (short for 甚麽的) what: 這柬帖說個甚的 what does this note say? 管他作(做)甚 what do you care to bother

about it?

甚而 *shehn-erl*, adv., even, go so far as to: 甚而打起來 even came to blows.

甚至 *shehnjyh*, adv., see *-erl*, ↑: 甚至趕他出門 even throw him out of the house: also 甚至於 go so far as to.

甚麽 *sher'mo* (weak form of *shern'mo*, also *shyr'mo*, wr. 什麽) pron. & adj., (1) what: 你作甚麽 or 甚麽事 what are you doing? 甚麽人, 甚麽地方 what man (who), what place (where); 甚麽意思 what do you (does it) mean? (2) any, anything: 想甚麽, 説甚麽 say whatever comes to mind; 沒有甚麽不好 do not see anything wrong with it; (3) some or other: 不知誰説甚麽話 I do not know who said something or other (to offend him); 甚麽姓張的 a certain Mr. 張; 忽然看見一個甚麽妖怪 suddenly we saw a I-do-not-know-what monster; 甚麽様 *--yahng*, adj. & adv., what kind of (animal, dress, etc.).

甚恁底 *shernrehn'dii*, adv., (MC) ＝甚怎的, 甚麽的 what, see *-'mo* ↑, *-yahng* ↓.

甚日 **shernryh*, n., what day.

甚是 *shehn-shyh*, adv., very＝甚, see 甚 Adv. ↑; identical with 甚爲 *-weir* ↓.

甚時 *shernshyr*, n., what time.

甚爲 *shehn weir*, phr., very, identical with 甚, see Adv. ↑: 甚爲不恭 very impolite.

甚様 *shern-yahng*, adj., what kind (short for 甚麽様) see *-'mo* ↑.

§ 20.40 (廿/口)

警 20.40

jiing.

N. (1) Short for 警察 the police: 刑警 criminal police; 法警 judicial police; 警方 the police authorities; 報警 report to the police; 警棍 police baton; 警探 *-tahn* ↓; 巡警 a policeman; 税警 customs police; 警官 *-guan* ↓; 警界 police circles. (2) Short for 警報, an alarm signal: 火警 fire alarm; 邊警 alarm of a border raid; 聞警 learning of an alarm.

V. t. (1) Guard against, garrison: 警備 *-beih* ↓. (2) Warn, admonish: 警告 *-gauh*, 警戒 *-jieh*, 警世 *-shyh* ↓; 以警將來 serve as a warning for the future. (3) To alert: 警惕 *-tih*, 警悟 *-wuh*[1], 警覺 *-jyuer* ↓.

Adj. (1) Alert, vigilant: 機警 show vigilance, on the alert. (2) To the point, apropos, apposite: 警句 *-jyuh*, 警語 *-yuu*, 警策 *-tseh* ↓.

警報 *jiingbauh*, n. & v. i., (to sound) an alarm (of fire, raid).

警備 *jiingbeih*, v. t., to garrison: 警備部隊 garrison forces; 警備司令部 Garrison Command.

警標 *jiing-biau*, n., a beacon, a lighthouse, a buoy.

警蹕 *jiingbih*, n., a temporary curfew imposed on roads where the emperor passed.

警察 *jiingchar*, n., the police, policemen: 警察局 police station or department.

警犬 *jirngchyuaan*, n., a police dog.

警笛 *jiing-dir*, n., a police whistle.

警動 *jiingduhng*, v. t., arouse, attract attention of.

警告 *jiinggauh*, v. t., warn, put on guard, caution.

警官 *jiingguan*, n., a police officer.

警鼓 *jirng-guu*, n., an alarm drum.

警號 *jiinghauh*, n., a warning signal.

警長 *jirngjaang*, n., a police chief.

警章 *jiingjang*, n., police regulations.

警枕 *jirng-jeen*, n., a piece of hard wood used as a pillow to keep the sleeper from sleeping too soundly.

警角 *jirng-jiaau*, n., a military bugle.

警戒 *jiingjieh*, (1) v. i., hold oneself ready to meet enemy moves; (2) v.t., warn, caution: 警戒色 (zoo.) a warning color of insects.

警鐘 *jiing-jung*, n., an alarm bell.

警覺 *jiingjyuer*, n., vigilance: 提高警覺 maintain a high degree of vigilance.

警句 *jiingjyuh*, n., a sparkling sentence.

警鈴 *jiinglirng*, n., a siren, an electric alarm.

警人 *jiingrern*, adj., exciting, fascinating.

警信 *jiingshihn*, n., a warning signal.

警醒 *jirngshiing*, adj., sleeping lightly, keeping alert.

警世 *jiing-shyh*, v. i., serve as a warning to the world at large.

警探 *jiingtahn*, n., a police detective.

警惕 *jiingtih*, v. i., be extra cautious, alert.

警策 *jiingtseh*, n., (of literary works) startling or revealing passages.

警衛 *jiingweih*, n., guards, troops on duty to protect (a city, military camp).

警悟 *jiingwuh*[1], v. i., sharply aware (to dangers ahead, one's past mistakes, etc.).

警務 *jiingwuh*[2], n., police affairs.

警員 *jiingyuarn*, n., policemen.

警語 *jirngyuu*, n., see *-jyuh* ↑.

碁 20.40

chir.

[Var. of 棋 10B.80]

§ 20.41 (廿/囚)

甘 20.41

gan.

N. A surname.

V. t. (1) Be willing to, pleased,

contented or satisfied with: 心甘情願 of one's free will; 不甘 unwilling; 心有未甘 be somewhat dissatisfied; 自甘退讓 be prepared to give way to s. o. else; 甘願 *-yuahn*, 甘心 *-shin*↓. (2) Be fond of: 甘酒嗜音 be fond of wine and music.

Adj. & adv. Sweet(ly), pleasant(ly): 甘美 *-meei*, 甘味 *-weih*↓; 甘甜 sweet; 甘芳 fragrant; 甘睡 a sweet sleep; 甘言 sweet, deceptive words; 甘苦 *-kuu*↓; 甘棠 a wild, small pear; 甘棠遺愛 (allu.) sweet memories left behind by a popular official after his retirement.

甘地 *Gandih*, n., Mohandas Karamchand Gandhi, the Mahatma, 1869–1948.

甘汞 *ganguung*, n., (chem.) calomel.

甘蔗 *gan'jeh*, n., sugar cane.

甘蕉 *ganjiau*, n., (bot.) the banana, *Sapientum*.

甘菊 *ganjyur*, n., (bot.) camomile, *Chrysanthemum sinense*.

甘旨 *ganjyy*, n., delicacies.

甘苦 *gan-kuu*, n., (1) prosperity and adversity, joys and pains: 同甘共苦, 甘苦與共 share with s.o. both prosperity and adversity; (2) as in 個中甘苦 the taste (experiences) of life; 甘苦自知 one knows best what one has gone through with.

甘藍 *ganlarn*, n., (bot.) *Brassica oleracea*, and its derivatives the cauliflower, Brussels sprouts, and kale.

甘霖 *ganlirn*, n., timely rain after a long drought.

甘露 *ganluh*, n., (1) the sweet dew; (2) (fig.) benefits from the ruler.

甘美 *ganmeei*, adj., pleasant to the taste, sweet and tasty.

甘心 *ganshin*, v. i. & adj., (be) pleased, willing: 甘心情願 be of one's free will; 死也甘心 be willing even if one had to die for it; 死不甘心 die with regret (wrong unavenged); 甘心樂意 be perfectly happy.

甘休 *ganshiou*, v. t., be willing to let go or give up (lawsuit, quarrel) (also wr. 干休).

甘藷 *ganshuh*, n., (bot.) the sweet potato (also 香薯, 山芋).

甘薯 *ganshuu*, n., (=甘藷↑) see *-shuh*↑.

甘遂 *gansueih*, n., (bot.) Siebold's spurge.

甘草 *gantsaau*, n., (bot.) *Glycyrrhiza glabra*, licorice; (Chin. med.) the dried root of licorice used as an expectorant or laxative or for other purposes.

甘味 *ganweih*, n., (1) sweet flavor; (2) appetite for food: 食不甘味 has no appetite for food (in deep sorrow).

甘油 *ganyour*, n., (chem.) glycerine, glycerole.

甘願 *ganyuahn*, adj. & adv., willing, -ly, of one's own accord.

昔 20.41

shir.

N. (1) Ancient times or days: 古昔 in ancient days; 夙昔, 往昔 in the early days. (2) (AC, u. f. 夕) night: 通昔不寐 could not sleep all night.

Adj. Past (days, years), ancient, see compp.↓.

昔者 *shir-jee*, adv. phr., (LL) in former days.

昔酒 *shir-jioou*, n., wine of old vintage.

昔年 *shir-niarn*, adv., in years past.

昔人 *shir-rern*, n., the ancient people.

昔日 *shir-ryh*, adv., in former days, in the early days.

昔時 *shir-shyr*, adv., in former times.

曹 20.41

tsaur.

[Abbr. 曺]

N. (1) A surname. (2) (LL, AC) plural particle (=vern. 們): 吾曹, 爾曹, 彼曹 we, you, they; 兒曹 you children; (AC) group (of beasts). (3) Staff: 部曹, 官曹 ministry officials, staff; 六曹 the six ministries; 功曹 officers on duty; 賊曹 rebels, bandits; (MC) police department; 陰曹, 天曹 officials in the nether world. (4) Shift of duty: 分曹 different shifts of work. (5) U. f. 造, 兩曹 two parties in lawsuit (=兩造). (6) U.f. 槽 stables.

§20.42 (廿/冈)

朞 20.42

ji.

N. A full year: 朞年 a full year; 朞服 one year's mourning.

§20.50 (廿/ㄱ)

驚 20.50

jing.

V. i. & t. To frighten, startle, (p.p.) feel frightened: 驚怕 *-pah*, 驚駭 *-haih*, 驚慌 *-huang*↓; 驚天動地 world-shaking; 驚弓之鳥 a once-bitten person; 驚走 frightened away; 大驚 be astounded, frightened; 吃驚 get a fright, give a start; 可驚 startling,

亅	小	卜	十	土	ナ	廿	㔾	丨	一	丅	フ	口	図	冈	ㄱ	厂	尸	亠	广	宀	丶	乚	弋	心	八	人	乂	乛	丆	丿丿	𠂉	く
00	01	02	10	11	12	20	21	22	30	31	32	40	41	42	50	51	52	60	61	62	63	70	71	72	80	81	82	83	90	91	92	93

frightening, alarming; 又驚又喜 be pleasantly surprised; 心驚肉跳 nerve-racking, make one's flesh creep; 這匹馬驚了 the horse has bolted.

Adj. Violent, furious, fierce: 驚風駭浪 tempestuous winds and waves; 驚湍 rapid currents; 驚濤 raging waves.

驚奇 *jingchir*, (1) v. i., show surprise, astonishment; (2) shocking (event).
驚倒 *jingdaau*, v. i., fall down from fright.
驚動 *jing'duhng* (*-'dung*), v. t., (1) to trouble, disturb; (2) startle: 這個消息,驚動了全城的人 this news created a sensation in the city.
驚愕 *jihg-eh*, v. i., be startled, surprised, taken aback.
驚風 *jingfeng*, n., (1) (Chin. med.) spasms, convulsions esp. in children; (2) furious winds.
驚服 *jingfur*, v. i., be overawed.
驚怪 *jingguaih*, v. i., see *-chir*↑.
驚閨 *jingguei*, n., a pedler's rattle used to draw prospective buyers' attention; 驚閨葉 *--yeh*, a string of small metal sheets used as a rattle by knife-sharpeners to draw people's attention.
驚汗 *jinghahn*, v. i., to sweat from fright.
驚駭 *jinghaih*, v. i., be scared, terrified, frightened.
驚慌 *jinghuang*, v. i., be alarmed, startled.
驚惶 *jinghuarng*, v. i., be taken by surprise: 驚惶失措 be paralyzed by fear.
驚魂 *jinghurn*, n., the state of being terrified, frightened: 驚魂甫定 have hardly recovered from a recent shock.
驚鴻 *jinghurng*, n., as in 翩若驚鴻 (of woman) as graceful as a frightened swan; a beautiful woman: 驚鴻一瞥 barely catch a glimpse of a passing beauty.
驚蟄 *jingjer*, n., one of the 24 solar terms in a year, usu. falling on March 5 or 6; see Appendix B.
驚悸 *jingjih*, v. i., be alarmed, startled.

驚恐 *jingkuung*, v. i., be scared, terrified, frightened.
驚怕 *jingpah*, v. t., to fear, be afraid.
驚擾 *jingraau*, v. t., to trouble, disturb, bother.
驚人 *jingrern*, adj., astonishing, amazing, surprising, shocking, frightening: 驚人之筆 extraordinarily forceful phrases.
驚醒 *jingshiing*, (1) v. i. & t., (pr. *jingshiing*) wake up or cause to wake up; (2) (pr. *jing'shing*) adj., sleeping lightly and easily roused.
驚心 *jingshin*, adj., shocking, terrifying, dreadful: 驚心動魄 hair-raising, struck with fright or horror.
驚歎 *jingtahn*, v. i., exclaim in surprise: 驚歎號 *--hauh*, n., the exclamation mark (!).
驚堂木 *jingtarngmuh*, n., a gravel used by judge in court.
驚座 *jingtzuoh*, v. i., give a shock to the audience: 語驚四座 his words electrified his listeners.
驚訝 *jingyah*, v. i., be surprised, alarmed.
驚異 *jingyih*, v. i., be astonished, astounded, feel curious, strange, extraordinary.
驚疑 *jingyir*, v. i., be bewildered, feel doubtful, be apprehensive.

§20.63 (廾/丶)

燕 20.63

yahn(**yan*).

N. (1) (*-tz*) The swallow, the martin, swift: 燕巢幕上 the swallow makes its nest in a tent—not aware of its danger. (2) Short for 燕窩 *-wo*↓: 南燕 edible swallow's nest from the south; 官燕 the best kind of swallow's nest. (3) (**yan*) (a) Name of anc. kingdom where Peiping is: 燕京 *-jing*↓; (b) a surname.

Adj. At ease, relaxed, happy: 新婚燕爾 happy wedding; 燕安, 燕居 *-an*, *-jyu*↓.

燕安 *yahn-an*, adj., at home relaxed, peaceful.
燕蝙蝠 *yahn-biaanfur*, n., (dial.) the bat.
燕雀兒 *yahnchiaau'l*, n., the mountain finch.
燕好 *yahnhaau*, adj., (AC, LL) enjoying marital happiness.
燕剪 *yahnjiaan*, n., swallow's tail (shaped like scissors).
燕京 *Yenjing*, n., ancient name of Peiping (Peking).
燕居 *yahnjyu*, phr., to live at home (when one is by oneself).
燕麥 *yahnmaih*, n., wild oats.
燕享 *yahnshiaang*, v.i., to enjoy offering of food (also wr. 燕饗, 宴饗).
燕私 *yahnsy*, v.i., (AC) to enjoy private life, rest at home.
燕菜 *yahntsaih*, n., see *-wo*↓.
燕子花 *yahntz-hua*, n., (bot.) the iris.
燕婉 *yahnwaan*, adj., (AC) friendly.
燕尾服 *yahnweeifur*, n., swallow-tailed (coat).
燕窩 *yahnwo*, n., edible bird's-nest, nest of cliff swallow, regarded a delicacy.
燕翼 *yahnyih*, phr.,(AC) plan and provision for children and grandchildren.
燕樂 *yahnyueh*, (1) n., (a) (AC) music at ceremonial banquet; (b) (MC) (**yan*) music introduced from northwest; (2) (*-leh*) v.i., to dine and wine (also wr. 宴樂).

§20.70 (廾/ㄴ)

巷 20.70

shiahng.

N. (*-tz*, *'l*) Alleyway, alley: 大街小巷 streets and alleys; 狹巷 a narrow alley; 黑巷 a dark alley; 陋巷 (living in) a narrow lane; 萬

人空巷 the whole town turns out to see some great event; 街頭巷尾 in street corners, (gossip) in the streets; 巷議 public gossip; 巷戰 battle in the streets; 巷遇 meet in an alley.

巷口 *shiahng-koou*, n., exit or entrance to alley.

巷陌 *shiahng-moh*, n., streets and alleys, alleyway.

§ 20.72 (廿/心)

勲 20.72

chirn.

Adj. & adv. Earnest, -ly (see 勤 20S.50, Adj.).

戁 20.72

naan.

Adj. (AC) (1) ashamed. (2) Reverend, respectful.

§ 20.80 (廿/八)

共 20.80

guhng.

N. Short for Communist (Party): 共黨 a Communist, the Communist Party; 中共, 俄共 the Chinese, Russian Communist Party; 共諜 Communist agents; 反共 anti-Communist.

V. t. To share (s. t.) with (s. o.): 休戚與共 share joy and sorrow; 同甘共苦 share prosperity and adversity; 與朋友共 share (s. t.) with one's friends.

Adj. (1) Common, joint, mutual, collective: 共同 *-turng* ↓; 共有 joint possession; 共管 joint management or control: 國際共管 international control; 共濟 (會) (society for) mutual assistance; 共存 coexistence; 共榮 co-prosperity: 東亞共榮圈 East Asia Co-prosperity Sphere; 共享 enjoy in common. (2) Total: 共計 the sum total; 總共, 合共, 一共 the total amount.

Adv. Together: 共事 work together as colleagues; 同舟共濟 people in the same boat (should) help each other; 同生共死 live and die together.

共產 *guhngchaan*, adj., Communist: 共產黨 a Communist (Party); 共產主義 Communism; 共產國際 Communist International (Comintern); 共產集團 Communist bloc.

共棲 *guhngchi*, n., (biol.) symbiosis (also 共生).

共軛角 *guhng-eh-jiaau*, n., (math.) conjugate angles.

共犯 *guhngfahn*, n., an accomplice.

共和 *guhngher*, adj., republican; 共和國 *--guor*, n., a republic; 共和黨 the Republican Party.

共鳴 *guhngmirng*, n., (1) (phys.) sympathetic vibration or resonance; (2) sympathy, sympathetic understanding: 他這種表現, 引起了共鳴 his action has aroused much sympathy.

共生 *guhngsheng*, n., (biol.) symbiosis (also 共棲 ↑).

共性 *guhng-shihng*, n., common traits or characteristics.

共同 *guhngturng*, (1) adj., common, collective, joint: 共同興趣, 共同目標 common interests, goal; 共同努力, 共同奮鬪 collective or joint efforts, endeavors; 採取共同行動 take united or concerted action; 共同負責 joint responsibility; 共同市場 Common Market; (2) adv., together: 共同生活 live together as husband and wife.

其 20.80

chir(-**ji*).

Fin. part. (*'ji*) (AC) interrogative particle: 夜如何其, 夜未央 How is the night? It is not dawn yet.

Pron. (1) (Possessive pron.) his, her, its, their: 其子 his son; 其貌不揚 his face is ugly; 其心可誅 his motive is execrable; 不得其門而入 could not find its entrance or proper approach. (2) In Chinese sentence construction: (a) the use of 其 as "its" often follows a n. clause, which describes the antecedent first: 鳥之將死, 其鳴也哀 when a bird is dying, its cry is pitiful; 周雖舊邦, 其命維新 although Chou is an old country, its destiny (mandate) is new; (b) "its" is used often to denote place or time: 其先 in the beginning; 其前 in front of it; 其後 later, or behind. (3) That: 其何以堪 can one stand that? 其奈我何 can I be stopped by that?

Adj. (1) (Demonstrative) that: 其人其事 that man and that business; 其父其子 a chip off the old block. (2) (AC) 其 often stands for "it is", following directly the antecedent n.: 北風其涼 the north wind——it's cold; 雨雪其雱 it snows——and it is heavy snow.

Adv. & Conj. (1) (Interrogative) 其...乎 can it be...? (=豈乎...): 一之爲甚, 其可再乎 once is bad enough, must it happen a second time? (2) (Optative) or: 誠愛趙乎, 其憎趙乎 does he really love the Jauh country, or rather doesn't he hate it? (3) (Emphatic) indeed: 然乎, 不其然乎 is it so? is it not so? 才難, 不其然乎 talent is rare to come by, isn't it so indeed? (4) (Imperative) in an order, like English "let": 其以沛爲朕沐邑 let Paih be designated as my resort town; 其各凜遵 let all obey this order carefully; 其毋 let not.

其間 *chirjian*, prep. phr. & n., (relationship) in between; that interval; the inside (aspect).

其中 *chirjung*, prep. phr. & n., among (a group); inside (a situation).

其內 *chirneih*, n. & adv. phr., inside: 車錢也在其內 (or 在內) transportation expenses included.

其實 *chirshyr*, adv. phr., in reality, as a matter of fact.

其他 *chirta* (coll. *-tuo*), phr., and others, often 及其他 and others; the other (persons, things): 其他作品 and other works.

其次 *chirtsyh*, n. & adv., next in importance: 費用還在其次 money expenses are a minor consideration.

其外 *chirwaih*, n. & adv. phr., outside, extra (persons, things) =此外: 其外概不收費 but for this there are no charges.

其餘 *chiryur*, n. & adj., the remaining, the rest: 擧一以概其餘 just mention one example which serves for the rest.

黃 20.80

huarng.

N. (1) A surname. (2) The yellow color. (3) Short for personal and place names: 炎黃子孫 descendants of 神農 and 黃帝 the Yellow Emperor, see 黃帝 *-dih* ↓; 黃老 Taoism of Yellow Emperor and Laotse; 岐黃 for 岐伯 and Yellow Emperor, reputed fathers of medicine; 皮黃 (for 西皮 and 二黃) place names in Hupei where present Peking opera music originated. (4) Certain animal products: 蛋黃 egg yolk; 蟹黃 roe of crabs; 牛黃 (Chin. med.) product from diseased cow livers for treating nervous diseases of children.

Adj. (1) Yellow; 面黃肌瘦 (person's face) thin and colorless; 黃葉 brown leaves of autumn; 青黃不接 gap between two harvests causing starvation, also gap between new and old; 杏黃 apricot-yellow; 牙黃 ivory-yellow; 籐黃 gamboge (much used in Chinese printing): 草黃 straw-colored; yellow as color of emperor; 黃榜 imperial edict; 黃袍 the imperial robe; 黃馬褂 the Yellow Jacket, rank conferred by emperor; 黃帶子 Yellow Girdle, Manchu nobility. (2) Yellow race: 黃種 yellow race; 黃禍 the Yellow Peril. (3) Catering to sex interest (orig. borrowed from "yellow journalism", now used more widely): 黃色新聞 sex stories in papers; yellow journalism; 黃色小說 sexy novels; 這部小說好黃 this novel is very sexy (also of films); 這人說話太黃 this man's talk is very indecent. (4) Spoiled, withered: 明日黃花 "a withered flower of yesterday"—topic no longer of interest; 這個買賣 (這副牌) 眼看要黃 this business (hand of cards) is about to fail (end in a draw).

黃柏 *huarngbaai*, n., pop. form of 黃檗 *-boh* ↓.

黃包車 *huarngbauche*, n., rickshaw.

黃表紙 *huarngbiaurjyy*, n., yellow paper for prayer to the gods.

黃病 *huarngbihng*, n., jaundice (=黃疸病).

黃檗 *huarngboh*, n., (bot.) the yellow bark, *Phellodendron amurense*; name of a Zen master in Tarng Dynasty (黃檗禪師).

黃白 *huarng-bor*, phr., gold and silver; 黃白術 alchemy.

黃錢(兒) *huarngchiarn*(*-chiar'l*), n., paper-money for burning before gods.

黃芪 *huarngchir*[1], n., pop. form of 黃耆 *-chir*[2] ↓.

黃耆 *huarngchir*[2], n., (Chin. med.) the yellow vetch, much valued as gen. tonic, *Astragalus hoantchy*.

黃芩 *huarngchirn*, n., (bot.) the skullcap, a plant, *Scutellaria baikalensis*.

黃泉 *huarngchyuarn*, n., the grave; the nether world.

黃疸 *huarngdaan*, n., jaundice.

黃道 *huarngdauh*, n., (astron.) the ecliptic; 黃道帶 the zodiac; 黃道吉日 a lucky day; 黃道光 zodiacal light.

黃碘 *huarngdiaan*, n., (chem.) iodoform.

黃帝 *Huarngdih*, n., the Yellow Emperor, a legendary ruler, synonymous with the father of Chinese civilization (2698–2598 B.C.).

黃豆 *huarngdouh*, n., soybean (also called 大豆); 黃豆牙 common bean sprout.

黃獨 *huarngdur*, n., a name for yam (potato).

黃髮 *huarngfaa*, n., an old man: 黃髮垂髫 old and young.

黃風 *huarngfeng*[1], n., sandstorm from Mongolian deserts.

黃蜂 *huarngfeng*[2], n., wasps, hornet.

黃瓜 *huarnggua*, n., cucumber (also called 胡瓜).

黃海 *Huarnghaai*, n., the Yellow Sea.

黃河 *Huarngher*, n., the Yellow River.

黃花 *huarnghua*, n., another name for 菊花 chrysanthemum; 明日黃花 out-of-date news; 黃花女兒 an old spinster.

黃花岡 *Huarng hua-gang*, n., a place near Canton where the 72 martyrs of the Chinese Revolution lost their lives.

黃花魚 *huarnghuayur*, n., (zoo.) croacher (also called 黃魚, 石首魚), *Seiaena schlegeli*, much valued for its blubber (known as 魚肚).

黃昏 *huarnghun*, n., sunset, dusk.

黃薑 *huarngjiang*, n., turmeric.

黃教 *huarngjiauh*, n., Yellow Lamaism.

黃金 *huarngjin*[1] n., gold; 黃金時代 the Golden Age.

黃巾 *huarngjin*[2] n., Yellow Turbans, a rebel movement at close of Hahn Dyn.

黃精 *huarngjing*, n., (bot.) the deer bamboo, *Polygonatum giganteum*.

黃酒 *huarngjioou*, n., a rice wine, also known as 紹興 *Shaoshing*.

黃鐘 *huarngjung*, n., one of the twelve bells determining musical scale in anc. China.

黃種 *huarngjuung*, n., the yellow race.

黃口 *huarngkoou*, n., infant: 黃口孺子 (derog.) immature person.

黃蠟 *huarnglah*, n., beeswax.

黃曆 *huarng'li*, n., (coll.) almanac.

黃連 *huarngliarn*, n., (bot.) the golden thread, a plant, *Coptis japonica*, known for its bitter taste; 啞子吃黃蓮 a dumb person eats this bitter plant—be a silent victim.

黃粱夢 *huarngliarng mehng*, n., (allu.) a tale like Rip van Winkle—signifying vanishing of dream or of time; disillusionment; a vanished dream.

黃流 *huarngliour*, n., (AC) wine.

黃鸝 *huarnglir*, n., the golden oriole (also called 黃鶯).

黃燐 *huarnglirn*, n., yellow phosphorus.

黃落 *huarngluoh*, v. i., (of plants, leaves) turn brown and fall off.

黃櫨 *huarnglur*, n., (bot.) the Hungarian fustic tree, *Rhus cotinus*.

黃毛(兒)丫頭 *huarngmaur('l)ya'tou*, n., (contempt. or facet.) a witless young girl.

黃梅 *huarngmeir*, n., (1) the apricot; (2) the yellow plum flower; 黃梅天 rainy season about time of summer solstice.

黃門 *huarngmern*, n., (1) a palace gate; (2) a eunuch: 黃門官, 黃門監 eunuch in charge of inner palaces.

黃米 *huarngmii*, n., millet (=黍).

黃鳥 *huarngniaau*, n., the oriole.

黃牛 *huarngniour*, (1) n., the common ox; (2) n., professional guide or contact man for illicit purposes; 色情黃牛 procurator of girls; 電影黃牛 movie ticket scalper; (3) v. i., to fail to show up at appointment: 又黃牛了 again fail to show up.

黃胖兒 *huarngpahng'l*, n., a portly person with yellow skin.

黃袍 *huarngpaur*, n., (1) imperial robe; (2) robe worn by Buddhist monks of certain ranks and sects.

黃浦 *Huarngpuu*, n., military academy known as Whompoa Academy in Kwangtung.

黃熱病 *huarngreh-bihng*, n., (med.) yellow fever.

黃砂 *huarngsha*, n., loess, see 「*-tuu*↓.

黃心樹 *huarngshinshuh*, n., a tree of magnolia family.

黃水瘡 *huarngshueei-chuang*, n., 「eczema.

黃鼠 *huarngshuu*, n., a desert rat; 黃鼠狼 *--larng*, n., skunk, weasel.

黃蜀葵 *huarngshuukueir*, n., (bot.) the okra, or lady's finger, a flower.

黃絁 *huarngshy*, n., Taoist priest's robe of coarse silk.

黃血鹽 *huarngshyueh-yarn*, n., (chem.) yellow prussiate of potash.

黃湯(子) *huarngtang(tz)*, n., (pop. and derog.) wine.

黃琮 *huarngtsurng*, n., a kind of yellow jade, used in sacrificial vessels.

黃銅 *huarngturng*, n., brass.

黃土 *huarngtuu*, n., loess.

黃芽菜 *huarngyar tsaih*, n., sprout of celery cabbage, grown in darkened basement.

黃楊 *huarngyarng*, n., boxwood.

黃鶯 *huarngying*, n., the golden oriole.

黃鼬 *huarngyouh*, n., a kind of 「skunk.

黃油 *huarngyour*, n., butter.

黃玉 *huarngyuh*, n., (min.) topaz or chrysolite.

黃魚 *huarngyur*, n., (1)=黃花魚 see *-huayur*↑; (2) (sl.) passengers taken in freight trucks during the war.

§20.83 (廿/〜)

遘 20.83

gouh.

V. t. (AC) to meet 邂遘 come across one another accidentally.

遭 20.83

tzau.

N. (1) A time, an occasion: 一遭 once; 遭兒 *-'l*↓. (2) (Of movement) a turn: 周遭 make a full circle, go round and round; 多繞幾遭 make a few more rounds.

V. t. Meet with, come across: 遭受(打擊) suffer (blows); 遭報 take the consequences of one's action; 遭遇 *-yuh*, 遭逢 *-ferng*, 遭際 *-jih*, 遭難 *-nahn*, 遭殃 *-yang*↓; 遭災 meet with disaster; 連遭災變 come upon a series of misfortunes; 遭回祿 have one's house burnt down (回祿 god of fire); 遭劫 have a spell of bad luck: 遭累 be implicated in s.t. for which one is not responsible, suffer loss on account of s.o. else.

遭逢 *tzauferng*, v. t., (1) come across, to meet (a powerful person); (2) have (misfortune, etc.).

遭際 *tzaujih*, n., happenings, esp. unhappy circumstances.

遭兒 *tzau'l*, n., (1) a time, an occasion; (2) (of movement) a full circle, a complete turn.

遭難 *tzau-nahn*, v. i., come to grief, meet with misfortune (ill luck).

遭瘟 *tzau-wen*, v. i., suffer misfortune, have bad luck.

遭殃 *tzau-yang*, v. i., meet with calamity.

遭遇 *tzauyuh*, v. t., =遭逢 *-ferng*↑.

SECTION 20A

§ 20A.00 (艹/丿)

荸 20A.00–1

bir (also *bor*).

荸薺 *bir'chi*, n., water chestnut.

蓴 20A.00–1

churn.
[Var. 莼]

N. (Bot.) water mallow, *Brasenia purpurea*: 蓴羹鱸膾 mallow soup and minced eel (allu. remembrance of food at home town); hence 蓴鱸之思 homesickness.

等 20A.00–1

deeng.
[Abbr. of 等 92A.00]

葑 20A.00–1

feng.

N. (1) Rape turnip. (2) Tangled roots.

葑菲 *fengfeei*, n., (AC allu.) some good in every man (some plants have tangled roots, but useful stems).

荐 20A.00–1

jiahn.

N. & v. t. Interch. 薦 20A.50.

Adv. Again and again, often: 荐饑 crop failure year after year; 荐仍 frequently, repeatedly, time after time.

蔣 20A.00–2

jiaang.

N. A surname.

芋 20A.00–3

yuh.

N. Taro: 芋頭, 芋奶 ditto: 山芋, 洋芋, 洋山芋 potato.

苛 20A.00–3

ke (*her).

Adj. & adv. Harsh, undesirably severe (government, taxes, laws): 苛政 tyrannical government; 苛政猛於虎 "a tyrannical government is more to be feared than tigers"——Confucius; 苛捐雜稅 multifarious taxes; 苛責, 苛評 harsh, petty criticism; 苛罰 severe punishment; 苛待 harsh treatment (of inferiors); 苛疾 severe illness; see 苛求, 苛刻 *-chiour*, *-keh* ↓.

V. t. (**her*) (AC) disturb, harass (border).

苛求 *kechiour*, v. i. & t., expect, demand too much from people.
苛刻 *kekeh*, adj., mean and exacting, ungenerous, parsimonious.
苛性 *keshihng*, adj., (chem.) caustic.

茅 20A.00–3

maur.

N. Reed, rush, grass used to make sheds: 茅店, 茅屋 grass shed; 茅茨土階 (LL) grass roof and earthen steps; 茅舍, 茅廬 humble thatched house, (court. & LL) my humble living quarters.

茅房 *maur'fang*, n., gen. toilet, privy.
茅栗 *maurlih*, n., a kind of hazelnut.
茅蒲 *maurpur*, n., (AC) farmer's straw hat.
茅塞 *maur-seh*, n., (LL & court.) (my) lack of understanding: 頓開茅塞 am suddenly enlightened (by your words).
茅蕈 *maurshyuhn*, n., a kind of edible mushroom, *Hydnum olidum*.
茅司, 茅厠 *maur'sy*, n., village-style privy, also wr. 毛厠.
茅土 *maurtuu*, n., (AC) fiefdom.

蒔 20A.00–4

shyr.

V.t. (AC) to transplant seedlings into field.

蒔蘿 *shyrluor*, n., (bot.) the dill, *Anethum graveolens*.

摹 20A.00–4

mor (**meh*).
[Interch. 模 esp. in artistic work]

V. t. To copy; consciously imitate: 臨摹 copy ancient painting, calligraphy, inscription

51S.40; 摹古 make copy of antique art; 摹刻 copy antique version; 摹寫 copy ancient calligraphy; 摹擬 consciously imitate.

摹本 *morbeen*, n., (1) wood-block copy made after ancient wood block; (2) (**mehbeen*) name of silk fabric.

摹印 *moryihn*, n., a seal-script style after Chirn Dyn. models.

蕁 20A.00–5

shyurn.

蕁麻 *shyurnmar*, n., (bot.) a shrub of the nettle family, poisonous to the touch, *Urtica thunbergiana*; 蕁麻疹 (med.) urticaria, hives.

芽 20A.00–5

yar.

N. (1) (-'*l*, -*tz*) Sprout, shoot, bud: 豆芽 bean sprout: 發芽, 冒芽 to bud; 萌芽 (fig.) to sprout up, to bud forth, have a small beginning; 月芽 the crescent moon. (2) Outcroppings of ores: 銀芽 croppings of silver ores.

芽胞 *yar-bau*, n., (bot.) spore.

芽茶 *yar-char*, n., tea made from tender buds. 「on trees.

芽甲 *yar-jiaa*, n., budding leaves

芽韮 *yar-jioou*, n., leek sprout, pale yellowish. 「(also 豆芽菜).

芽菜 *yartsaih*, n., bean sprouts

蓐 20A.00–5

ruh.

N. A mat for bedding: 牀蓐 bedding; 坐蓐 (of pregnant woman) lie in.

蓐瘡 *ruhchuang*, n., (1) bedsores; (2) infantile boils.

蓐婦 *ruh-fuh*, n., a midwife (also 蓐母).

蓐食 *ruh-shyr*, v. i., (AC) have breakfast in bed.

蔚 20A.00–5

weih.

Adj. (1) (Vegetation) thick, luxuriant: 蔚茂 ditto; 蔚藍 deep blue. (2) Impressive: 蔚然 -*rarn*↓; 蔚成大觀 makes an impressive sight.

蔚茂 *weihmauh*, adj., luxuriant (growth).

蔚然 *weihrarn*, adj., impressive-looking.

蘭 20A.00–5

larn.

N. (1) (Bot.) the orchild. (2) A surname. (3) Fragrance, elegance, refinement, moral excellence: 蘭交 -*jiau*, 蘭艾 -*aih*↓; 蘭因絮果 the vicissitudes of life; 蘭摧玉折 premature death of a virtuous or gifted individual; 蘭薰桂馥 (lit.) as fragrant as orchids and cassia, (fig.) a man's beautiful moral influence; 蘭形棘心 appearances are deceptive (lit., "appearance of orchid and heart of thistle").

蘭艾 *larn-aih*, n., orchid and artemisia; the virtuous vs. the ignoble.

蘭秋 *larnchiou*, n., (LL) the seventh lunar month.

蘭閨 *larnguei*, n., (LL) a lady's boudoir.

蘭桂 *larn-gueih*, n., orchids and cassia; (fig.) (complim.) beautiful descendants, progeny, offspring.

蘭花 *larnhua*, n., the orchid (flower).

蘭兆 *larnjauh*, n., a good omen auguring the birth of a son.

蘭交 *larnjiau*, n., intimate friendship between like-minded individuals.

蘭芝 *larnjy*, n., the orchid flower, symbolic of high-minded individuals.

蘭夢 *larnmehng*, n., ＝蘭兆 -*jauh*↑.

蘭盆 *larnpeen*, n., (1) (Budd.) (盂蘭盆會) the Feast of All Souls held on the 15th day of the 7th lunar month, with floating lanterns or candles on water, for the deliverance of hungry ghosts; (2) a basin, a bathtub.

蘭譜 *larnpuu*, n., (1) books on orchidology or the painting of orchids; (2) the genealogical records of sworn brothers, each of whom keeps a copy.

蘭若 *larnree*, n., (1) (bot.) Chinese and Japanese thoroughwort, *Eupatorium chinensis* and *japonica*; (2) (Budd.) monastery, a hermit's cell.

蘭麝 *larnsheh*, n., sweet fragrance.

蘭香 *larnshiang*, n., (bot.) the sweet basil, *Ocimum basilicum* (also 羅勒, 香菜).

蘭臭 *larnshiouh*, adj., like-minded, on very intimate terms with s.o. (lit., "agreeably fragrant").

蘭孫 *larnsun*, n., (LL) (court.) grandchildren.

蘭草 *larntsaau*, n., (bot.) *Eupatorium chinensis*, a gen. name for orchid-like plants.

蘭澤 *larntzer*, n., (1) orchid pomade or ointment; (2) 蘭草 -*tsaau*↑; (3) 蘭香 -*shiang*↑.

蘭蕕 *larnyour*, n., orchids and *Caryopteris divaricata*, a foul-

摹 蕁 芽 蓐 蔚 蘭

smelling water plant; (fig.) a man of noble versus one of ignoble character.

蘭玉 *larnyuh*, n., (1) orchids and jade as symbols of young men's good conduct; (2) as symbols of female chastity.

藺 20A.00-5

lihn.

N. A surname.

葶 20A.00-6

tirng.

葶藶 *tirnglih*, n., a kind of grass, *Draba nemorosa* var. *hebecarpa*.
葶薴 *tirngnirng*, n., a poisonous plant.

苧 20A.00-6

juh.

N. Ramie, an Asiatic hemp-producing plant.

苧麻 *juhmar*, n., ramie fibre or cloth made from it, linen: 苧麻裙 linen skirt.

薄 20A.00-6

bor (coll. **baur*).
[Dist. 簿 92A.00]

N. (1) (AC) reed screen. (2) (AC) thicket. (3) A surname.

V.t. (LL) To slight (person); to rebuke (conduct), see 薄待 *-daih* ↓.

Adj. (1) (**baur*) Thin (paper, soup): 薄鬆鬆 very thin; 薄怯怯 (of clothing) very thin, inadequate in cold. (2) Weak, poor, mean, stingy: 薄言 (輕言) light-tongued, given to gossip; 薄弱 *-ruoh* ↓, 薄行 *-shihng*[1] ↓; 薄田, 薄土 stingy, unproductive soil; 薄命 poor, unlucky life; 薄俗, 風俗鄙薄 stingy, selfish character of a locality; 淺薄 superficial, 浮薄 ditto; 待遇不薄 remuneration is not bad, is fair; 輕薄 v.t., behave in ungentlemanly manner to ladies; adj., coarse, vulgar (behavior). (3) (Court.) my little, my humble: 薄物 my humble gifts; 薄技 small skill; 薄宦 small post. (4) (AC) broad: 薄海＝普海 all seas, the world over.

Adv. (Court.) slightly: 薄具禮物, offer slight or humbly offer, gifts; 薄有研究 (modest) have made a little study.

Conj. (AC, rare, with undetermined meaning, perhaps similar to) just, and so: 薄伐玁狁 and invade the Huns; 薄澣我衣 will just wash my clothes; 薄言采之 and we picked them.

薄餅 **baurbiing*, n., varieties of rolls containing various stuffing; a form of egg roll.
薄薄 *borbor*, adj., (1) thin, dilute (of wine); (2) (AC) very broad (of land).
薄曲 *borchyuu*, n.,(AC) frame for keeping silkworms.
薄待 *bordaih*, v.t., to slight, ill-treat (person), be cold toward (person).
薄夫 *borfu*, n.,(AC) mean person.
薄荷 **boh'ho*, n., mint; 薄荷油 menthol.
薄遽 *borjyuh*, adv., (AC) suddenly.
薄陋 *borlouh*, adj., uncouth, common, paltry.
薄落 *borluoh*, adj., (MC) in poor circumstances (of person).
薄暮 *bormuh*, n., sundown.
薄媚 *bor-meih*, adj., with simple charm (of ladies); n., (MC) name of song.
薄呢 *bornir*, n., light serge.
薄片 *borpiahn*, n., thin slice.
薄弱 *bor-ruoh*, adj., weak in strength.
薄曉 *borshiaau*, n., (AC) daybreak＝破曉.
薄相 *borshiahng*, adj., (MC) playful, capricious (fate); cogn. of modn. Soochow 白相 to play about in city.
薄行 *bor-shihng*[1], n., unruly, unfaithful, rash conduct.
薄倖 *borshihng*[2], adj., fickle, esp. 薄倖郎 fickle (man) lover.

莩 20A.00-9

fur (**piaau*).

N. (1) Thin membrane inside rush stalk; see 葭[A]莩 20A.82. (2) (**piaau*) 餓莩 dead bodies of those starved to death, (var. of 殍 31S.00).

莉 20A.00-9

lih.

N. See 茉[A]莉 20A.01.

苻 20A.00-9

fur.
[Dist. 符 92A.00]

N. (1) A surname. (2) A kind of grass of rush family.

荷 20A.00-9

her (**heh*).

N. The lotus, water lily: 荷花, 荷蓮 *-hua*, *-liarn* ↓; 荷葉 lotus leaves, used for flavor and for wrapping food for steaming (cf. 蓮 20A.83).

V. t. (*heh) To carry on the shoulder, to receive gratefully, to bear burden of gratitude: 荷鋤, 荷擔 to carry a hoe, a load, on the shoulder; 荷槍實彈 (of soldiers, riot squads) carry loaded guns; 荷蒙, 荷賜 (court.) receive (award, letter, kindness, etc.); 荷賞 receive award or gratuity; hence 感荷, 拜荷 receive with gratitude; 是荷, 爲荷 (form in letter) the above would be a great kindness or is my request.

荷包(兒) *her'bau'l*, n., wallet; 荷包牡丹 (bot.) *Dicentra spectabilis*, "wallet peony," so called because of resemblance.
荷錢 *herchiarn*, n., young sprouts of lotus leaves.
荷爾蒙 *her-eel-merng*, n., (translit.) hormone: 男性荷爾蒙 testerone; 女性荷爾蒙 estrogen.
荷負 *hehfuh*, n. & v.t., a burden, to bear burden.
荷花(兒) *herhua('l)*, n., the lotus flower; 荷花大少 (*shauh*) a playboy in spring who cannot afford good clothing in winter; cf. *-liarn* ↓.
荷蘭 *Herlarn*, n., Holland.
荷蘭水 *herlarn-shueei*, n., aereated water.
荷蓮 *herliarn*, n., the lotus (also called 芙蕖).
荷葉 *heryeh*, n., lotus leaf; 荷葉粥 rice congee, cooked while covered with a lotus leaf for flavor; 荷葉肉 a pack of steamed glutinous rice with pork, wrapped in lotus leaf.

蘅 20A.00-9

herng.

N. The plant *Asarum blumei* (also 杜[A]蘅 10B.11).

孽 20A.00-9

nieh.

[Pop. var. 孼]

N. (1) A wicked demon. (2) Son born of a concubine: 孤臣孽子 a minister without support at court and a concubine-born prince fallen from grace, sometimes used of s.o. nobly espousing a lost cause. (3) Seed of evil: 作孽, 造孽 do misdeeds, be the seed of evil, bring disaster down upon oneself or others, sow the seeds of destruction; 天作孽, 猶可爲, 自作孽, 不可活 if disasters come from nature, s.t. can be done to counter them; but if they are of one's own making, one is done for.

孽障 *niehjahng*, n., retribution for evil one has committed; wicked children born to one for evils one is supposed to have committed, (var. 業障); (Budd.) karmic obstruction.

葪 20A.00-9

jih.

N. (1) (Bot.) Thistles, *Cirsium*. (2) A surname. (3) Formerly, a place name in Peiping.

薅 20A.00-9

hau.

V.t. To weed, to pick off: 薅下幾根頭髮 pick off a few hairs.

§ 20A.01 (廿/小)

茉 20A.01-1

moh.

茉莉 *mohlih*, n., (bot.) jasmin(e).

茱 20A.01-1

ju.

茱萸 *juyur*, n., (bot.) a plant of several unidentified varieties, one of which is called "edible" (食茱萸).

萊 20A.01-1

lair.

N. (1) (Bot.) (=藜) the pigweed, or goosefoot, *Chenopodium album*. (2) Wild grass: 草萊 fields overgrown with grass. (3) A surname.

萊菔 *lairfur*, n., (bot.) (MC) turnip (=modn. 蘿蔔).
萊衣 *lairyi*, n., (AC allu.) a multicolored dress (of 老萊子).

蓁 20A.01-1

jen (*chirn).

N. (Bot.) 蓁椒 (*chirnjiau), the Chin. pepper or fagara.

Adj. Underbrush: 蓁莽, 蓁蓁

蓁 葉 蒜 蓀 蔯 菓 蘗 蔴 蕖 藻 藁 蘂 苶

overgrown underbrush (also wr. 蓁蓁榛榛).

葉 20A.01-2

yeh (**sheh*).

N. (1) A leaf (of plant): 楓葉, 紅葉 maple leaf; 荷葉 lotus leaf; 葉落歸根 what comes from the soil will return to the soil; 葉落知秋 or 一葉知秋 one falling leaf is indicative of the coming of autumn—everything is part of a whole; (fig.) of a boat in landscape: 一葉扁舟. (2) A petal: 千葉 a composite flower (of many petals). (3) U. f. 頁 a leaf in a book. (4) (Related to 世) a generation: 中葉 (=中世) middle of a dynasty; 末葉 end of a century, regime, or dynasty. (5) A surname. (6) (**sheh*) (Related to 世) name of a county: 葉縣.

葉柄 *yehbiing*, n., (bot.) petiole.
葉黃素 *yehhuarng-suh*, n., (bot.) xanthophyll.
葉針 *yehjen*, n., (bot.) needle (as pine needle).
葉尖 *yehjian*, n., (bot.) apex of leaf.
葉筋 *yehjin*, n., leaf veins.
葉綠素 *yehluh-suh*, n., (bot.) chlorophyll.
葉脈 *yehmoh*, n., leaf veins.
葉肉 *yehrouh*, n., (bot.) mesophyll.
葉身 *yehshen*, n., (bot.) leaf blade.
葉序 *yehshyuh*, n., (bot.) leaf cycle.
葉子 *yehtz*, n., a leaf; 葉子戲 game of cards; 葉子烟 formerly, cut leaf tobacco for pipe.

蒜 20A.01-3

suahn.

N. Garlic: 叩頭如搗蒜 make a rapid succession of *kowtows* on the ground (like "crushing garlic").

蒜瓣兒 *suahnbah'l*, n., quarters of head of garlic.
蒜辮子 *suahnbiahntz*, n., a bunch of garlic stalks.
蒜毫兒 *suahnhaur'l*, n., young garlic shoots.
蒜苗 *suahnmiaur*, n., edible center of garlic flower.
蒜泥兒 *suahnnier'l*, n., mashed garlic.
蒜薹 *suahntair*, n., see *-miaur* ↑.
蒜條 *suahntiaur*, n., filigree; 蒜條金 gold threads; 蒜條鐲子 filigree bracelet.
蒜頭兒 *suahntour'l*, n., head of garlic.

蓀 20A.01-3

sun.

N. (AC) an aromatic plant.

蔯 20A.01-3

chern.

N. See 茵▵蔯 20A.41.

菓 20A.01-4

guoo.

N. Fruit (pop. of 果, see 果 41.01).

蘗 20A.01-5

boh.

[Var. 檗; dist. 蘖 *nieh*, 20A.01]

N. In 貢蘗 (commonly wr. 貢柏) (bot.) *Phellodendron amurense*, a dwarf plant; 黃蘗 name of Zen Sect and master.

蔴 20A.01-6

mar.

[Pop. of 麻 61.01, signifying hemp, flax]

蕖 20A.01-6

chyur.

N. See 芙▵蕖 20A.81.

藻 20A.01-6

tzaau.

N. (1) Waterweeds: 紅藻, 綠藻 reddish, green weeds; 海藻 seaweeds. (2) Literary elegance: 詞藻 elegant language; 文藻 well-turned phrases; 藻思 ideas expressed in refined language.

藻井 *tzaurjiing*, n., (AC) a painted squares in ceiling.
藻飾 *tzaaushyh*, n., embellishments with phrases in writing.

藁 20A.01-6

gaau.

[Var. of 稿 90A.42]

蘂 20A.01-6

rueei.

[Var. of 蕊 20A.72]

苶 20A.01-8

nier.

Adj. (AC) tired and weary, worn-out.

茶 20A.01-8

char.

N. Tea: 茶樹 tea plant; 茶花 *-hua*↓; 茶葉 tea (leaves); the drink made from tea: 吃茶, 飲茶 take tea; 品茶 drink tea and enjoy or sample its flavor; 綠茶, 紅茶 green, red, tea; 香茶 scented tea; 清茶 simple, pure tea; 小ᐞ種茶 22.01; 茶敍 (hold) a tea party, have a talk over a cup of tea; 茶會, 茶杯 *-hueih, -bei*↓, etc.; 採茶 pick tea; 烹茶 make tea; 焙茶 prepare tea leaves by slow baking process; 淡茶, 濃茶 weak, strong tea.

茶杯 *charbei*, n., teacup.
茶錢 *charchiarn*, n., tip to servant.
茶器 *char-chih*, n., tea set, tea utensils.
茶青 *charching*, adj., tea-green color, brownish-green.
茶匙(兒) *charchyr(-cher'l)*, n., teaspoon, teaspoonful.
茶點 *chardiaan*, n., pastry, cookies, etc. served with tea at party.
茶底(兒)(子) *chardii (-diee'l) (tz)*, n., dregs of tea.
茶鼎 *chardiing*, n., special pan for making tea.
茶飯 *charfahn*, n., gen. food and drinks: 茶飯無心 have no time or appetite for food and drinks.
茶坊 *charfang*, n., teahouse.
茶房 *char'fang*, n., waiter, steward on ship.
茶缸子 *chargangtz*, n., a wide large bowl for tea.
茶館 *charguaan*, n., teahouse.
茶果 *charguoo*, n., tea and fruit (fresh or glazed).
茶褐色 *charher seh*, adj., dark brownish green.
茶花 *charhua*, n., the camellia.
茶話會 *charhuahhueih*, n., see *-hueih*↓.
茶會 *charhueih*, n., a tea reception.
茶戶 *charhuh*, n., a tea merchant.
茶几(兒) *charji (-jie'l)*, n., a tea side table, teapoy.
茶金 *charjin*, n., present of money at betrothal.
茶晶 *charjing*, n., quartz the color of dark tea.
茶磚 *charjuan*, n., tea bricks.
茶盅 *charjung*, n., small teacup.
茶棹(兒) *charjuo'l*, n., tea table.
茶質 *charjyr*, n., theine, caffeine.
茶居 *charjyu*, n., see *-guaan*↑.
茶具 *charjyuh*, n., tea vessels, tea service.
茶菊 *charjyur*, n., a species of aster, camomile (also called 甘菊).
茶課 *char-keh*, n., tea tax.
茶寮 *charliaur*, n., tea booth.
茶樓 *charlour*, n., teahouse.
茶滷 *charluu*, n., tea concentrate.
茶梅 *charmeir*, n., (bot.) the *Thea sasanqua*, of camellia family.
茶麪子 *charmiahntz*, n., a preparation of tea flour, which makes a pasty drink with boiling water.
茶末 *charmoh*, n., tea dust.
茶棚 *charperng*, n., tea booth.
茶毗 *charpir*, n. & v. i., (Budd.) cremation, from Sanskr. *Jhapita*.
茶色 *charseh*, adj., dark brownish-green color.
茶筅 *charshiaan*, n., small brush for cleaning tea utensil.
茶水錢 *charshueei-chiarn*, n., see *-chiarn*↑.
茶稅 *char-shueih*, n., tea tax.
茶室 *charshyh*, n., a tearoom.
茶食 *charshyr*, n., cookies, etc. served with tea.
茶肆 *charsyh*, n., a tea shop.
茶攤兒 *charta'l*, n., tea booth.
茶湯 *chartang*, n., (1) gen. non-alcoholic drinks served to guests; (2) a drink of millet flour and sugar.
茶腿 *chartueei*, n., best-grade ham.
茶托(兒)(子) *chartuo('l) (tz)*, n., tea saucer.
茶資 *chartzy*, n., pocket money.
茶碗 *charwaan*, n., large teacup.
茶葉 *charyeh*, n., tea leaves.
茶油 *charyour*, n., oil from seeds of tall tea plants, used in hair-dressing.
茶園 *charyuarn*, n., tea garden, formerly, opera theater.

荼 20A.01-8

tur.

[Dist. 茶 *char*, 20A.01↑]

N. (1) A kind of bitter weed; symbolic of bitterness: 如火如荼 phr., descriptive of blazing powerful army or of things growing vigorously. (2) Rush with white flowers.

荼毒 *turdur*, v.t., persecute, cause suffering (to people).
荼蓼 *turliaau*, n., kind of bitter weed, symbolic of bitter life.
荼蘼 *turmir*, n., rose leaf raspberry, *Rubus commersoni*.

棻 20A.01-8

fen.

N. A wood known for its perfume.

菜 20A.01-9

tsaih

N. (1) Vegetable: 菜蔬 *-shu*↓; 鹹菜 salted vegetable; 青菜, 生菜 fresh vegetable; 白菜 cabbage; 滷菜 pickled or marinated vegetable; 菜湯 vegetable soup; name used by vegetarian monks to eat taboo food, as 溜黃菜 egg omelette. (2) A dish, item or course in menu (whether of meat or vegetable):

菜 葆 蘖 蘗 蔡 蘇 藥

三樣菜 three dishes of meat or vegetable to go with rice; hence food, dinner: 菜好不好 is the dinner all right? 西菜, 中菜 Western, Chin. food; 素菜 vegetarian food; 葷菜 meat dish.

菜包子 *tsaihbautz*, n., (lit.) vegetable dumpling; (fig.) (abuse) nincompoop, idiot.
菜場 *tsaihchaang*, n., (food) market.
菜青 *tsaihching*, adj., dull green.
菜畦 *tsaih-chir*, n., vegetable plot or patch.
菜牀兒(子) *tsaih-chuarng'l (tz)*, n., shelf for raw vegetables as in shops.
菜單(兒)(子) *tsaihdan (-da'l) ('tz)*, n., menu, bill of fare.
菜刀 *tsaih-dau*, n., chopper for kitchen use.
菜豆 *tsaihdouh*, n., kidney bean.
菜墩子 *tsaihduntz*, n., kitchen chopping board.
菜瓜 *tsaihgua*, n., a cucumber, usu. served cooked, also pickled.
菜貨 *tsaihhuoh*, n., a simpleton.
菜牛 *tsaih-niour*, n., cattle raised for beef.
菜色 *tsaihseh*, n., famished, colorless complexion.
菜蔬 *tsaihshu*, n., vegetable in gen.
菜市 *tsaihshyh*, n., food market, also 菜市場.
菜攤(兒)(子) *tsaihtan(-ta'l)(tz)*, n., booth for vegetables.
菜子 *tsaihtzyy*, n., vegetable seeds.
菜油 *tsaihyour*, n., vegetable oil, colza oil, rapeseed.
菜園 *tsaihyuarn*, n., vegetable garden.

葆 20A.01-9

baau.

N. Ornamental parasol in: 羽葆 made of feather; 翟葆 made of pheasant feather; 頭如蓬葆 with shaggy hair.

V. t. (AC) keep, preserve: 葆光, 葆眞 preserve light of original nature.

蘖 20A.01-9

nieh.

[Var. 櫱; dist. 蘗]

N. New shoot from an old stump.

蘗 20A.01-9

nieh.

[Dist. 蘖]

N. Yeast for wine-making.

蔡 20A.01-9

tsaih.

N. (1) A surname. (2) An anc. state.

蘇 20A.01-9

su.

N. (1) A surname. (2) Abbr. for 蘇州 Soochow: 蘇綉 Soochow embroidery; 蘇杭 Soochow and Hangchow. (3) Part of name for province 江蘇 Kiangsu, (abbr. in 蘇省: 蘇浙 Kiangsu and Chekiang). (4) Abbr. for Soviet: 蘇俄, 蘇聯 *-eh, -liarn* ↓.

V. i. & t. (1) Interch. 甦, wake up, revive. (2) To relieve, recover: 以蘇民困 to relieve the people's distress.

蘇白 *Su-bair*, n., Soochow dialect.
蘇打 *sudar*, n., (translit.) soda.
蘇俄 *Su-eh*, n., Soviet Russia.
蘇枋 *sufang*, n., (bot.) sapanwood, whose juice is used as red pigment.
蘇格蘭 *Sugerlarn*, n., Scotland.
蘇合香 *suher-shiang*, n., (bot.) rose-storax, made from *Liquidambar orientalis*.
蘇活 *suhuor*, v. i., to revive.
蘇州碼(兒)(子) *Sujou-maa('l) (tz)*, n., pop. numerals used gen. in accounts: 〡, 〢, 〣, 〤, 〥, 〦, 〧, 〨, 〩 (standing for 1, 2, 3, 4, 5, 6, 7, 8, and 9).
蘇聯 *Suliarn*, n., the Union of Soviet Socialist Republics (USSR).
蘇麻 *sumar*, n., (bot.) a kind of bamboo, *Perilla ocimoides*.
蘇木 *sumuh*, n., see *-fang* ↑.
蘇軟 *suruaan*, adj., (legs, arms) go soft (also wr. 甦).
蘇醒 *sushiing*, v. i., wake up (also wr. 甦).
蘇息 *sushir*, v. i., to rest, recuperate.
蘇子 *sutzyy*, n., see *-mar* ↑; 蘇子油 lamp oil from *-mar* ↑.
蘇維埃 *Suweir-ai*, n., Soviet.
蘇彝士河 *Suyirshyh-her*, n., the Suez Canal.

藥 20A.01-9

yauh (re. pr. *yueh*).

N. (1) Medicine: 服藥 take medicine; 配藥 fill a prescription; 照方抓藥 have prescription filled at pharmacy; 補藥 tonic; 麻藥 anesthetic, narcotic; 毒藥 poison; 草藥 herb medicine; 膏藥 plasters; 良藥苦口 good advice, like medicine, is hard to take; 得占勿藥 happily recovered from illness. (2) Certain chemicals: 火藥, 炸藥 explosive; 農藥 insecticide; 銲藥 solder.

V. t. (1) To cure: 不可救藥 beyond cure, hopeless. (2) To poison: 藥老鼠 to poison rats.

藥叉 *yauhcha*, n., (Budd.) a ferocious demon that flies by

night (from Sanskr. *yaksha*, also wr. 夜叉).

藥單 *yauh'dan*, n., a prescription.

藥店 *yauhdiahn*, n., pharmacy, drugstore.

藥鼎 *yauh-diing*, n., (Taoist) crucible for making pill of immortality.

藥餌 *yauh-eel*, n., medicine and tonic.

藥方(兒)(子) *yauhfang('l)(tz)* n., a prescription, medical recipe.

藥房 *yauhfarng*, n., pharmacy, drugstore.

藥粉 *yauhfeen*, n., powder medicine.

藥膏(兒)(子) *yauhgau('l)(-tz)* n., medical ointment.

藥衡 *yauhherng*, n., pharmacist scales.

藥渣(子) *yauhja(tz)*, n., dregs from medical concoctions.

藥針 *yauhjen*, n., hyperdemic needle.

藥箭 *yauh-jiahn*, n., poisoned arrow.

藥劑 *yauhjih*, n., a prescription, recipe; 藥劑子 dose of medicine (large, small).

藥酒 *yauhjioou*, n., tonic wine.

藥珠 *yauh-ju*, n., small commercial pearls which pulverized are used as medicine.

藥局(子) *yauhjyur(tz)*, n., formerly, wholesaler of herb medicine, a drugstore.

藥科 *yauhke*, n., the study of pharmacy.

藥力 *yauh'lih*, n., potency of medicine.

藥理學 *yauhliishyuer*, n., pharmacology (also 藥物學 *yauhwuh-shyuer* ↓).

藥籠 *yauhlurng*, n., medicine box: 藥籠中物 things which may be needed any time, like household medicine chest.

藥麵(兒)(子) *yauhmiahn(-miah'l)(tz)*, n., medical powders.

藥棉(花) *yauhmiarn('hua)*, n., antiseptic cotton.

藥末(兒) *yauhmoh('l)*, n., medical powder.

藥捻兒 *yauhniaa'l*, n., (1) fuse; (2) a paper roll of medicine inserted into sores, etc. (also 藥捻子).

藥碾子 *yauhniaantz*, n., roller for crushing medicine.

藥片(兒) *yauhpiahn(-piah'l)*, n., a tablet of medicine.

藥品 *yauhpiin*, n., medicine in gen.

藥舖 *yauhpuh*, n., a pharmacist shop.

藥散 *yauhsaan*, n., medical powder.

藥線 *yauhshiahn*, n., fuse for explosives.

藥性 *yauhshihng*, n., characteristic effect of a medicine: 藥性氣 smell of medicine or medical herbs.

藥水(兒) *yauhshueei(-shuee'l)*, n., liquid medicine, lotion: 咳嗽藥水 a cough mixture or syrup; 藥水針 hypodermic needle.

藥師 *yauhshy*, n., (1) pharmacist in charge of filling prescriptions; (2) expert gatherer of herbs from nature.

藥石 *yauhshyr*, n., medicine and acupuncture: 藥石無效 all medicines tried and found useless; 藥石之言 unpleasant but needed advice.

藥學 *yauhshyuer*, n., the science of pharmacy.

藥死 *yauh'syy*, v. t., to poison to death.

藥膛 *yauh-tarng*[1], n., compartment for gunpowder in old-style guns.

藥糖 *yauhtarng*[2], n., medicated gums.

藥草 *yauhtsaau*, n., medical ⌈herbs.

藥材 *yauh'tsair*, n., ditto.

藥(肥)皂 *yauh(feir)tzauh*, n., medicated soap.

藥丸(兒)(子) *yauhwarn(-war'l)(tz)*, n., pill of medicine.

藥味 *yauhweih*, n., medical ingredients in a prescription; 藥味兒 taste or flavor of medicine.

藥喂的 *yauhweih'de*, adj., (weapons) soaked in poison.

藥物 *yauhwuh*, n., medicine; 藥物學 pharmacology.

藥言 *yauh-yarn*, n., (LL) bitter advice.

藥衣子 *yauh-yitz*, n., coating for ⌈pills.

藥引子 *yauh-yiintz*, n., ingredients in Chin. concoction to help in the efficacy of principal medicine.

藥胰子 *yauh-yirtz*, n., medicated soap.

§20A.02 (艹/卜)

蔟 20A.02-3

tsurng.

[Var. of 叢 22.82]

慕 20A.02-4

muh.

[Bottom 小＝心]

N. & v.t. Admiration, longing: 愛慕, 思慕 love; 仰慕, 仰慕之情, 嚮慕, 欣慕 love and admiration; 羨慕 admire and envy; 慕名而來 phr., have come, attracted by one's fame; 慕義 love of seeking the truth.

慕容 *Muhyurng*, n., surname of northern 鮮卑 tribe.

藤 20A.02-4

terng.

[Commonly wr. 籐]

N. (1) Creeper plant in gen., rattan, cane (used in furniture): 長春藤 ivy; 紫藤 wistaria; 藤椅, 藤桌, 藤牀, 藤席 cane (or rattan), chair, table, bed, mat; 藤肉 split rattan. (2) Vine: 瓜藤 melon vine; 葡萄藤, 蕃薯藤 grapevine, potato vine; 爬藤

藥 蔟 慕 藤

亅	小	卜	十	土	ナ	卄	ㄩ	丨	一	丅	フ	口	囗	冂	ㄱ	厂	尸	亠	广	宀	丶	乚	弋	心	八	人	乂	⌒	一	ノ	𠂉	く
00	01	02	10	11	12	20	21	22	30	31	32	40	41	42	50	51	52	60	61	62	63	70	71	72	80	81	82	83	90	91	92	93

creeper; 葛藤 complications, entanglements of affairs.

藤鞭 *terngbian*, n., cane for caning schoolboys.
藤黃 *ternghuarng*, n., (bot.) gamboge, gum from *Garcinia morella*, much used in Chin. painting.
藤蘿 *ternglour*, n., (bot.) plants of creeper family, like wistaria.
藤牌 *terngpair*, n., rattan shield.
藤條 *terngtiaur*, n., see *-bian*↑.
藤子 *terngtz*, n., rattan.

茛 20A.02-5

gehn.

N. See 毛△茛 90.70 *Ranunculus acer* var. *japonicus*, the tall buttercup or bitter crowfoot.

蓑 20A.02-6

suo.

N. A raincoat made of various kinds of leaves, hemp fibre, etc.: 蓑衣.

蘘 20A.02-6

rarng.

N. 蘘荷 (bot.) mioga ginger, *Zingiber mioga*.

蒙 20A.02-6

merng.

N. (1) In childhood ignorance, see Adj.↓. (2) A surname.

V. t. (1) To cover: 蒙上一層 cover with a layer; 蒙頭大睡 sleep soundly with face covered under sheets; 蒙頭蓋面 with face covered or veiled; 蒙面大盜 robber in a mask. (2) Hoodwink: 受蒙蔽 see *-bih*↓; 欺蒙 deceive. (3) Encounter, come under, receive: 蒙難 meet a fatal accident; 蒙塵 a king flees in trouble ("be covered with dust"); 西子蒙不潔 (AC) when a beauty's good name was smeared; 蒙冤 be unjustly accused; 蒙恩 (court.) receive superior's favor; 承蒙不棄 you have so kindly (favored me with . . .); 蒙教 be favored with advice.

Adj. Untutored (state), in childhood ignorance: 愚蒙 mentally not developed; 啟蒙時代 early period of enlightenment (in philosophy or child's development); 蒙求 elementary course; see 蒙童 *-turng*↓.

蒙蔽 *merngbih*, v. t., hoodwink: 爲物欲所蒙蔽 (mind) be clouded by material desires.
蒙館 *mernggaan*, n., formerly, elementary school.
蒙古 *Mernguu*, n. & adj., Mongolia; 蒙古包 *--bau*, n., Mongol tent; 蒙古症 Mongolism.
蒙汗藥 *mernghahn-yauh*, n., sleeping drug.
蒙混 *merngguhn*, v. i., deceive by assuming similar appearance.
蒙籠(蘢) *mernglurng*, adj., covered with vegetation.
蒙昧 *merngmeih*, adj., ignorant.
蒙蒙 *merngmerng*, adj., (1) luxuriant (growth); (2) ignorant, unknowing.
蒙茸 *merngrurng*, adj., hairy, furry; growing profusely (of plants).
蒙童 *merngturng*, n., children.
蒙養 *merngyaang*, n., process of tutoring or developing children's mind.

莨 20A.02-6

larng.

N. (Bot.) see 狼△尾草 91C.02; 薯莨 a creeping plant whose roots are good for dyeing.

莨菪 *lahng dahng*, n., (bot.) the henbane, *Hyoscyamus niger*.

菾 20A.02-9

tiarn.

N. The leaf beet, *Beta vulgaris* (=甜菜).

藜 20A.02-9

lir.
[Var. 蔾]

N. (Bot.) lamb's-quarters, goosefoot, *Chenopodium album*.

藜蘆 *lirlur*, n., (bot.) black false hellebore, *Veratrum nigrum*.

菉 20A.02-9

luh(**lyuh*).

N. (1) A kind of bamboo. (2) (**lyuh*) Var. for 綠△豆 93B.02.

§ 20A.10 (艹/十)

芈 20A.10-1

mie (re. pr. *mii*).
[Cogn. 哔, 咩]

N. & v. i. (1) Bleating of lamb. (2) (**mii*) (AC) a surname.

苯 20A.10-1

been.

N. (Chem.) benzene.

蘀 20A.10-1

tuoh.

N. (1) Fallen barks and leaves. (2) Interch. 籜 92A.10.

葦 20A.10-2

weei.

N. Reed, rush.

葦箔 *weei-baur*, n., a coarse reed matting used as frame for pouring mortar on house roof.
葦席 *weei-shir*, n., reed mat.
葦塘 *weei-tarng*, n., rush pond.
葦櫻 *weeiying*, n., Japanese cherry tree, *Prunus yedoensis*.

苹 20A.10-3

pirng.
[Dist. 萍]

N. (AC) a plant of rush family.

苹苹 *pirngpirng*, adj., luxuriant (of grass, brush).

茸 20A.10-3

rurng(**ruung*).
[Dist. 葺]

N. (1) 鹿茸 the budding antlers of the deer. (2) (**ruung*) Down or fine hair (*=毧).

Adj. (1) (Also **ruung*), (of grass) having just sprouted: 茸茸 luxuriant. (2) Disorderly, confused.

茸兒 *rurng'l*, n., (coll.) an embryonic egg.
茸母 *rurngmuu*, n., (bot.) the cudweed, *Gnaphalium multiceps*.
茸闒 *rurngtah*, adj., (1) of inferior quality, cheap, mediocre; (2) mean, lowly.

華 20A.10-3

huar(**huah*).

N. (1) China: 華夏 (LL) China; 中華 China; 中華民國 the Republic of China. (2) Glory, halo, diffuse light: 光華, 榮華 glory; 月華 diffused moonlight. (3) The course of time, esp. prime of youth: 年華逝水 time passes like water; 芳華虛度 youth vainly passes away; 韶華 the prime of youth. (4) Essence: 精華 the cream (of writing), the best passages or pieces. (5) (**huah*) A surname.

Adj. (1) Chinese: 華語, 華文 Chinese language; 華英辭典 Chinese-English dictionary; 華洋 Chinese and foreign; 華胄, 華裔 (LL) Chinese descent; 華族 Chinese race; 華籍 Chinese citizenship; 華商 Chinese merchant; 華僑 *-chiaur*↓. (2) Flowery, resplendent, decorative, bedecked: 華美, 華麗, 華貴 *-meei*, *-lih*, *-gueih*↓; 華服, 華屋 beautiful dress, house; 華構 beautiful structure; 豪華 rich, resplendent, gorgeous; 奢華 luxurious; 繁華 prosperous, gay (city life). (3) Used in compliments, illustrious: 華誕, 華壽, see *-dahn*, *-shouh*↓; 華譽 illustrious fame. (4) Empty, showy: 華而不實 showy and not substantial; 華言巧語 flowery words; 浮華 superficial. (5) (LL) greyish: 華髮 greyish hair; 華首, 華顛 a hoary head.

華表 *huarbiaau*, n., a commemorative tablet, a stone pillar by a grave.
華僑 *huarchiaur*, n., overseas Chinese, Chinese abroad: 華僑子弟 children of Chinese abroad.
華誕 *huardahn*, (1) n., (court.) birthday; (2) adj., superficial and unreliable.
華蓋 *huargaih*, n., parasol or shade over cart or bier.
華貴 *huargueih*, adj., stylish (dress).
華翰 *huarhahn*, n., (court.) your letter.
華札 *huarjar*, n., ditto.
華麗 *huarlih*, adj., gorgeous, resplendent.
華美 *huarmeei*, adj., beautiful.
華年 *huarniarn*, n., youth.
華沙 *Huarsha*, n., Warsaw.
華山 *Huahshan*, n., the Huah Mountain in Shensi.
華盛頓 *Huarshehngduhn*, n., Washington.
華壽 *huarshouh*, n., (court.) birthday.
華飾 *huarshyh*, n. & adj., decorative, decorated, -tion.
華氏表 *huarshyh biaau*, n., Fahrenheit thermometer.
華胥 *Huashyu*, n., (allu.) land of dreams.
華簪 *huartzan*, adj., as in 華簪之家 nobleman's family.
華宗 *huartzung*, n., (court.) of the same clan.
華族 *huartzur*, n. & adj., (of) Chinese race.
華耀 *huaryauh*, adj., glorious.
華腴 *huaryur*, adj., soft living.

蕈 20A.10-3

shyuhn(also *shihn*).

葺 **N.** Fungus (related 菌 *jyuhn*, 20A.41).

草

葺 20A.10-4

chih.

N. Grass roof for hut: 葺屋 grass-covered hut.

V. t. (1) To repair: 葺牆 repair wall; 修葺 repair (house). (2) To arrange in layers (as roof tiles).

草 20A.10-4

tsaau.
[Var. 艸]

N. (1) Grass: 草木 *-muh*↓; 草卉, 花草 flowers and underbush; 草叢 underbush; 打草驚蛇 frighten away thieves by raising a scare; 斬草除根 uproot s. t., destroy root and all; 拔草 to weed (a ground); 野草閒花 girls or women to be picked up; grassland: 草野, 草莽 *-yee, -maang*↓; 草頭露 like dew on the grass—evanescent. (2) Straw: 草帽, 草鞋, 草蓆 *-mauh, -shier, -shir*↓ (3) Rapid, cursive style of writing: 草書 *-shu*↓; 大草 highly cursive writing; 行草 semi-cursive style usual in letters or any informal writing; 章ᐞ草 60.10. (4) A draft: 起草 make a draft (of statement or any writing).

V. t. To draft (statement, etc.); hence also to pioneer s. t.: 草創, 草制 *-chuahng, -jyh*[1]↓.

Adj. Drafted, not final: 草稿, 草案 *-gaau -ahn*↓.

Adv. (1) Hastily: 草具 hastily prepare (letter, etc.). (2) Slipshod, crude, careless: 潦草, 粗草 rough, careless (writing, work). (3) Female of species: 草驢 female donkey; 草雞 *-ji*↓; 草馬 mare.

草案 *tsaau-ahn*, n., a draft (of resolution, proposal); a drafted plan.

草包 *tsaaubau*, n., (abuse) dullard, imbecile, one who is liable to spoil things.

草本 *tsaurbeen*, n., (1) draft copy; (2) (bot.) a grass, herb.

草標兒 *tsaaubiau'l*, n., a wisp of straw marking s. t. for sale: 插草標兒 mark s. t. to be sold in market.

草鄙 *tsaurbii*, adj., rustic, uneducated (person).

草蜻蛉 *tsaauchinglirng*, n., a grass insect, *Chrysopa perla*.

草創 *tsaauchuahng*, v. i. & t., (1) to pioneer, start (s. t.); (2) (AC) to draft (document).

草底兒 *tsaurdiee'l*, n., handwritten draft, original.

草地 *tsaaudih*, n., lawn, grassy plot.

草稿 *tsaurgaau*, n., preliminary draft (of essay, etc.).

草雞 *tsaauji*, n., a hen; (fig.) a chicken-hearted person.

草菅 *tsaurjian*, v.t., as in 草菅人命 to have complete disregard for human life—slaughter people.

草芥 *tsaaujieh*, n., insignificant trifle.

草螽 *tsaaujung*, n., an insect, *Conocephalus thumbergi*.

草蜘蛛 *tsaaujyju*[2], n., a small spider, *Agalena limbata*.

草制 *tsaaujyh*[1], v. t., see *-chuahng* (2)↑.

草蛭 *tsaaujyh*[2], n., a kind of leech, *Haemadipsa japonica*.

草紙 *tsaur-jyy*, n., toilet paper.

草寇 *tsaaukouh*, n., (AC) robbers, brigand.

草萊 *tsaaulair*, n., wasteland, primitive land or jungle.

草蘭 *tsaaularn*, n., a species of orchid, *Cymbidium*.

草料 *tsaauliauh*, n., hay, fodder.

草廬 *tsaaulur*, n., a grass hut, matshed.

草綠 *tsaaulyuh*, n., color of grass.

草履蟲 *tsaurlyuu-churng*, n., (zoo.) a primitive worm, *Paramaecium caudatum*.

草莽 *tsaurmaang*, n., see *-lair*↑.

草帽(兒) *tsaaumauh('l)*, n., straw hat.

草茅 *tsaaumaur*, n., lowly or rustic condition of life.

草昧 *tsaaumeih*, n., primeval times.

草棉 *tsaaumiarn*, n., (bot.) common cotton.

草木 *tsaaumuh*, n., vegetation in gen.; 草木灰 ashes from grass stalks, used as fertilizer.

草坪 *tsaaupirng*, n., a lawn, a stretch of grassland.

草上飛 *tsaaushahngfei*, n., formerly, a fast rowboat on the Grand Canal.

草上霜 *tsaaushahng-shuang*, n., a rare lamb skin, so called from the pearl-like white curls at the top.

草寫 *tsaurshiee*, v. t., to write hastily or in hasty style.

草鞋 *tsaaushier*, n., straw sandal; 草鞋錢 tip demanded of people by official couriers, or petty officers.

草蓆 *tsaau-shir*, n., straw mat.

草書 *tsaaushu*, n., cursive, rapid style of writing, marked by tendency to join strokes and economy of lines.

草率 *tsaaushuaih*, adv., careless, slipshod, slovenly (in work).

草市 *tsaaushyh*, n., village market.

草石蠶 *tsaaushyrtsarn*, n., (bot.) *Stachys sieboldi*.

草酸 *tsaausuan*, n., (chem.) oxalic acid.

草堂 *tsaautarng*, n., (real or alleged) "grass abode"—scholar's residence.

草草 *tsaurtsaau*, adv., (finish s.t.) roughly, without due care.

草刺兒 *tsaautseh'l*, n., see *-jieh*↑.

草蹙 *tsaautsuh*, adv., see *-tsaau*↑.

草次 *tsaautsyh*, adv., (AC) carelessly (=造次); (2) on the grass, in open air.

草賊 *tsaautzeir*, n., *-kouh*↑.

草澤 *tsaautzer*, n., life in the open: 起於草澤 rustic origins.

草字 *tsaautzyh*, n., see *-shu*↑.

草字頭兒 *tsaautzyhtour'l*, n., the "grass" radical "艹"; index No. 20A.

草藥 *tsaauyauh*, n., herb medicine.

草野 *tsaauyee*, n., country life of common people; the people at large (opp. 朝廷 the court).

草原 *tsaauyuarn*, n., steppe, prairie.

蓽 20A.10-4

bih.

N. (LL) (bot.) rush: 蓽門圭竇 rush hut, a poor man's house; 蓽(篳)路(露)藍縷(蔞) phr., pioneering work (cutting swaths in jungle).

蓽茇 *bihbar*, n., (bot.) (MC) translit. of pepper (also wr. 蓽撥).

薜 20A.10-5

*bih (*boh).*

[Dist. 薛 20A.10]

N. (**boh*) A medicinal aromatic herb, pop. name 當歸.

薜荔 *bihlih*, n., (bot.) *Ficus pumila*, also called 薜蘿 *-luor*.

薜暴 *bohpuh*, n. & v.i., a crack in earthenware, (AC) to crack.

莘 20A.10-6

shen (also *shin*).

Adj. (1) (AC) long. (2) Numerous: 莘莘學子 numerous students.

萃 20A.10-6

tsueih.

N. A bush: 出類拔萃 be head and shoulders above others, stand out among equals; 拔乎其萃 ditto.

V. i. To assemble: 薈△萃 20A.41, ditto; 萃於一堂 (all the friends, schoolmates, socialites) were gathered at the place.

Adj. Luxuriant (grass).

葷 20A.10-6

hun.

N. & adj. (1) Meat as food, contrasted with 素 vegetable: 吃葷 nonvegetarian; 葷菜 a meat dish. (2) Adj., sharp-smelling: 葷辛 *-shin*↓. (3) Adj., sexy, indecent: 葷小説 sexy novel; 葷笑話 dirty jokes; 説葷話 talk filth.

葷辛 *hunshin*, adj., sharp-smelling (like garlic, etc.).

葷腥 *hunshing*, n. & adj., meat in food, contrasted with vegetable.

葷油 *hunyour*, n., animal fat in cooking.

萍 20A.10-6

pirng.

N. Duckweed, symbol of floating existence: 萍水相逢 casual, temporary meeting; 萍蹤靡定 person's uncertain movements, constant travel.

萍蓬草 *pirngperngtsaau*, n., (bot.) *Nuphar japonicum*.

芊 20A.10-9

chian.

Adj. (Of pastures) lush, green.

芊芊 *chianchian*, adj., lush (vegetation): 草色芊芊 ditto, also wr. 仟, 阡.

芊緜 *chianmiarn*, adj., lush, brightly green, also wr. 芊眠.

萆 20A.10-9

bih.

[Var. of 蔽, 蓖]

萆薢 *bihshieh*, n., a medicinal herb.

葎 20A.10-9

lyuh.

N. (Bot.) the wild hop, *Humulus japonicus* (also called 勒草, 拉拉藤).

蔊 20A.10-9

haan.

N. (Bot.) nasturtium, a flowering vegetable, *Nasturtium montanum*.

薛 20A.10-9

shyue.

N. (1) A surname. (2) The name of an anc. feudal state.

蘚 20A.10-9

shiaan.

蓽 薜 莘 萃 葷 萍 芊 萆 葎 蔊 薛 蘚

N. Moss, lichen: 蘚痕 marks made by moss on rocks, steps, etc.; 蘚斑 patches of lichen; 蘚帽 calyptra of mosses.

§20A.11 (艹/土)

薹 20A.11-1

tair.

N. (Bot.) sedge, *Cyperus rotundus*; 薹笠 rain hat made of sedge.

莊 20A.11-2

juang.
[Pop. 壯]

N. (1) A village, hamlet, a homestead: 村莊 a village: 田莊 farms, usu. of considerable dimensions; 王家莊 Mr. Wang's farmland—— 家莊, sometimes used as name of hamlet. (2) A villa: 山莊, 別莊 a country villa. (3) A shop: 錢莊 money shop, old-style local bank; 布莊 shop for clothing materials; 綢緞莊 silk shop; 飯莊 restaurant; 莊口 *-koou*↓. (4) Banker at gambling: 莊家 *-'jia*↓; 做莊, 坐莊 be banker by turn. (5) A surname.

Adj. Solemn: 莊重 *-juhng*↓; 莊肅 *-suh*↓; 莊嚴 *-yarn*↓; 莊語, 莊論 (LL) serious talk, discussion (not joking).

莊戶 *juanghuh*, n., (reference or self-reference in North China) farmer.

莊家 *juang'jia*, n., (1) country house; (2) banker at gambling table.

莊稼 *juangjiah* (*-'jia*), n., farm goods, crops, farm work: 種莊稼 plant different grains, beans for food, 莊稼地 farmland; 莊稼活 farm work; 莊稼老兒 (coll.) old farmer; 莊稼漢 (coll.) farmer.

莊重 *juangjuhng*, adj., solemn (ceremony); serious, decorous (demeanor): 莊重點兒 be serious (opp. facetious).

莊客 *juangkeh*, n., tenant farmer.

莊口 *juangkoou*, n., (coll.) market for goods.

莊肅 *juangsuh*, adj., solemn (ceremony, gathering).

莊田 *juangtiarn*, n., farms of fairly big size.

莊頭 *juang'tou*, n., chief of hired farm lands, head of tenant farmers (佃戶).

莊子 (1) *Juangtzyy*, n., name of philosopher about 300 B. C.; (2) (*'tz*) a homestead, hamlet.

莊嚴 *juangyarn*, adj., solemn, august, oft. used in Budd. worship.

莊園 *juangyuarn*, n., manor, private park, domain, estate.

菫 20A.11-2

jiin.

N. (1) (Bot.) the celery, *Apium graveolens.* (2) The wild aconite.

葬 20A.11-3

tzahng.
[Var. 葬]

藿 20A.11-3

huoh.

N. (1) (Bot.) 藿香 betony, mint herb. (2) 荳藿 bean leaves.

薩 20A.11-3

sah.

N. (1) A surname. (2) Short for 菩薩 bodhisattva.

墓 20A.11-4

muh.

N. Tomb, grave: 古墓 ancient tomb; 陵墓 emperor's mausoleum; 祭墓 sacrifice at the grave; 掃墓 festival at 清明 for visiting grave; 盗墓 steal treasures in tombs; 諛墓 "flatter the grave," eulogy on memorial tablet; 墓木已拱 the trees on graveyard are already grown tall, i.e., deceased long ago.

墓碑 *muhbei*, n., tombstone.

墓表 *muhbiaau*, n., memorial tablet at grave.

墓道 *muhdauh*, n., paved front leading to grave.

墓地 *muhdih*, n., graveyard.

墓碣 *muhjier*, n., memorial tablet.

墓誌銘 *muhjyhmirng*, n., biographical sketch engraved on memorial tablet; such composition.

墓門 *muhmern*, n., door of tomb.

墓穴 *muhshyuuh*, n., grave.

墓園 *muhyuarn*, n., cemetery ground.

蘿 20A.11-4

luor.

蘿蔔 *luorbo*, n., turnip (also 蘿菔): 蘿蔔糕 turnip pudding.

蘿藦 *luormoh*, n., (bot.) *Metaplexis stauntoni*, whose flower seeds can be used for cotton and in making ink pads.

蕹 20A.11-6

yung.

N. 蕹菜 A common vegetable, usu. grown in water, *Ipomoea aquatica.*

荃 20A.11-8

chyuarn.

N. (1) (AC) an aromatic plant. (2) (LL) used in phr., 荃察, 荃鑒, 荃諒 (in correspondence) your esteemed consideration.

董 20A.11-9

duung.

N. (1) A surname. (2) Short for 董事 *-shyh*↓; 校董 board of directors of a school; 商董 board of directors of chamber of commerce: 紳董 the gentry. (3) Curio in 古董.

V.t. Direct, supervise: 理董其事 supervise, manage the affairs; 董其成 see that it is completed.

董事 *duungshyh*, n., member of board of directors; 董事會 board of directors; 董事長 chairman of the board.

薶 20A.11-9

mair.

[Var. of 埋 11A.11, to bury]

荏 20A.11-9

reen.

N. (1) A kind of bean: 荏菽 *-shuu*↓. (2) (Bot.) *Perilla ocimoides,* a mint-smelling herb (= 紫蘇).

Adj. & adv. Soft(ly): 荏染 soft, yielding; 荏弱 delicate, weak.

荏胡麻 *reenhurmar,* n., (bot.) *Perilla ocimoides.*

荏苒 *rernraan,* adv., gradually, little by little (time passes).

荏菽 *rern-shuu,*n., (1) large beans; (2) the garden pea, *Pisum sativum.*

荏桐 *reen-turng,* n., (bot.) wood oil tree, *Aleurites cordata* (also 罌子桐).

荏油 *reen-your,* n., (1) oil extracted from *Perilla ocimoides;* (2) the tung oil.

薙 20A.11-9

tih.

V. t. (1) To weed: 薙草. (2) To shave: 薙髮 (=剃 80S.00).

§20A.20 (艹/艹)

莽 20A.20-1

maang.

N. (1) Thick underbrush: 草莽 wild jungle. (2) A poisonous plant, *Illicium anisatum.*

Adj. (1) Rude, coarse (of person): 鹵莽 rash, reckless. (2) Wild, limitless, see 莽蕩 *-dahng*↓.

Adv. Recklessly: 莽撞 dash or drive recklessly.

莽蕩 *maangdahng,* n., wild, limitless (prairie).

莽夫 *maangfu,* n., a bumptious fellow.

莽漢 *maanghahn,* n., see *-fu*↑.

莽莽 *marngmaang,* adj., deep (of forest, foliage).

莽蒼 *maangtsang,* adj., color of wide, wild country, also 莽莽蒼蒼.

葬 20A.20-3

tzahng.

[Var. 塟]

V. t. Bury, inter: 葬埋 *-mair*↓; 埋葬 bury (the dead); 葬了 be buried; 葬身魚腹 be drowned; 死無葬身之地(所) die an ignominious death, die a beggar (an outcast); 土葬, 海葬 bury (person) in the ground, the sea; 火葬 cremate; 合葬 (of two or more persons) lie in the same tomb; 厚葬 (薄葬) (give s.o.) an elaborate (simple) funeral; 遷葬 give (the dead) a second burial (at a different site); 葬禮 funeral rites; 送葬 to escort a funeral; 葬花 bury flower petals (allu. to the story of 林黛玉); 葬玉埋香 lay a beauty to rest.

葬埋 *tzahngmair,* v. t., entomb, bury, inter, lay to rest.

葬送 *tzahngsuhng,* v. t., to ruin (one's future, hopes).

§20A.21 (艹/乚)

葚 20A.21-2

shehn (also *rehn*).

N. Berry of mulberry tree.

茁 20A.21-2

juor.

Adj. (Of vegetation) thriving: 茁茁, 茁壯 healthy and strong.

菡 20A.21-3

hahn.

菡萏 *hahndahn*, n., (LL) another name for lotus (荷ᐞ花 20A.00).

萏 20A.21-5

dahn.

N. See 菡ᐞ萏 20A.21↑.

苣 20A.21-5

jyuh.

N. (Bot.) 萵苣 the lettuce.

芒 20A.21-6

marng.

N. (1) The awn of wheat; a spike, any sharp point: 光芒 ray of light; 鋒芒 sharp point or edge of weapon, (fig.) of argument, cutting edge; 鋒ᐞ芒太露 81A.10; 芒刺在背 in most uncomfortable position, like "having prickles on the back." (2) A surname.

芒果 *marngguoo*, n., mango.
芒種 *marngjuhng*, n., term in lunar calendar, about June 7 or 8, see Appendix B.
芒芒 *marngmarng*, adj., (1) (AC) expansive, far and wide; cf. modn. form 茫茫 20A.21↑; (2) (AC) tired, exhausted; (3) blindly.
芒硝 *marngshiau*, n., (chem.) sodium sulphate.
芒鞋 *marngshier*, n., straw sandals.

茫 20A.21-6

marng.

Adj. (1) Widespread, far and wide: 茫茫大海 great, big sea; 白茫茫 an expanse of white. (2) Lost, uncomprehending; 茫無頭緒 completely at sea; 茫無界限 without any guidelines; see compp.↓.

茫昧 *marngmeih*, adj., uncomprehending, hoodwinked.
茫然 *marng-rarn*, adj., unseeing, not knowing what to do: 茫然無知 not knowing a thing.

舊 20A.21-9

jiouh.
[Abbr. 旧]

N. Friendship: 與之有舊 have long-standing friendship with him.

Adj. Old (opp. 新 new), former, past: 陳舊 old, antiquated, outmoded; 腐舊 worn-out, decayed; 破舊 broken-down, tattered (clothing); 舊曆 *-lih*↓; 舊教 Catholicism (opp. 新教 Protestantism); 舊派 conservative, old-fashioned (people); 舊瓶裝新酒 new wine in old bottles; 棄舊迎新 replace the old with the new; 除舊佈新 ring out the old, ring in the new; 舊日 *-ryh*, 舊地 *-dih*↓; 舊居 one's former dwelling house; 舊遊之地 old haunts; 舊部 *-buh*, 舊故 *-guh*, 舊觀 *-guan*, 舊好 *-haau*, 舊情 *-chirng*↓; 舊事 *-shyh*¹↓; 舊業 family estate, old studies, an old pursuit; 舊例 old precedents; 舊調重彈 to repeat the same old tunes; 依舊 as of old; 仍舊, 照舊 as usual; 守舊 conservative (-minded), old-fashioned.

舊案 *jiouh-ahn*, n., (1) old archives, historical records; (2) a past event; (3) a dead issue; (4) an outstanding legal suit.
舊部 *jiouh-buh*, n., former subordinates, troops formerly under one's command.
舊情 *jiouh-chirng*, n., (1) former friendship; (2) former condition or state.
舊地 *jiouh-dih*, n., (1) an old site; (2) old haunts.
舊都 *jiouh-du*, n., (1) the former capital; (2) an old metropolis.
舊惡 *jiouh-eh*, n., wicked deeds of the past, old grievances: 不念舊惡 forget old grudges.
舊觀 *jiouh-guan*, n., a thing's original form or appearance.
舊故 *jiouh-guh*, n., old friends or associates.
舊好 *jiouh-haau*, n., an old "pal."
舊恨 *jiouh-hehn*, n., remorse, regrets: 舊恨新愁 heart-breaking regrets and sad memories, old and new.
舊家 *jiouhjia*, n., an old (respected) family.
舊交 *jiouh-jiau*, n., old friends (-ship).
舊金山 *Jiouhjinshan*, n., San Francisco.
舊曆 *jiouhlih*, n., (1) the Lunar Calendar: 舊曆年 the Lunar New Year; (2) (of calendar) the Old Style.
舊年 *jiouhniarn*, n., (1) last year; (2) the Lunar New Year.
舊日 *jiouh-ryh*, (1) n., the old days; (2) adv., formerly.
舊書 *jiouh-shu*, n., (1) old or secondhand books; (2) classical works.
舊事 *jiouh-shyh*¹, n., an old matter.
舊式 *jiouhshyh*², adj., old-styled; n., old style.
舊學 *jiouh-shyuer*, n., the classical learning, as opposed to modn. scientific knowledge.
舊俗 *jiouh-sur*, n., old customs, folklore.

舊族 *jiouhtzur*, n., an old well-known family.

舊友 *jiouh-yoou*, n., a friend of long standing, former associates.

舊約 *Jiouhyue*, n., the Old Testament.

舊雨 *jiouh-yuu*, n., an old friend or customer: 舊雨新知 (business) clients, old and new (from allu. in Tu Fu: 舊雨來, 今雨不來).

§ 20A.22 (卄/丨)

菲 20A.22-2

feei.

N. 菲律賓 The Philippines.

Adj. (1) (Court. LL) unworthy, humble: 菲禮, 菲敬, 菲儀 my humble gift; 菲酌 my humble dinner; 菲點 small tea; 菲才 my unworthy talent. (2) (AC) Fragrant: 菲菲.

菲薄 *feeibor*, adj., (court.) unworthy, small (gift, etc.): 妄自菲薄 (one should not) underestimate oneself.

茀 20A.22-2

fur.

N. (1) (AC) good luck: 福. (2) (AC) cart screen.

Adj. (AC) bushy, tangled (of grass).

茀茀 *furfur*, adj., (AC) vigorous.

蕭 20A.22-2

shiau.

N. A surname: 蕭規曹隨 the successor 曹參 merely followed rules set up by previous minister 蕭何 in Hahn Dyn.

Adj. Desolate, dejected, disconsolate, see most compp.↓: 蕭晨 a gloomy morning.

蕭艾 *shiau-aih*, n., (AC) common grass.

蕭牆 *shiauchiarng*, n., (LL) nearby at home: 禍起蕭牆 trouble breaks out at home.

蕭斧 *shiaufuu*, n., (AC) axe.

蕭齋 *shiaujai*, n., (LL) (1) studio; (2) a Buddhist temple, see *-shyh*↓.

蕭然 *shiaurarn*, adj., (1) desolate: 環堵蕭然 the walls are quite bare; (2) detached, unhampered: 蕭然物外 (man's spirit) untrammeled by worldly affairs.

蕭灑 *shiausaa*, adj., free, emancipated, unhampered by conventions; (person, writing) spirited, wayward, forthright; pure, noble.

蕭散 *shiausaan*, v. i. & adj., disperse, -d, scattered, thinning out.

蕭颯 *shiausah*, adj., chilly (autumn air).

蕭騷 *shiausau*, adj., see *-tiaur*↓.

蕭瑟 *shiauseh*, adj., (1) disconsolate, gloomy; (2) (business) dull.

蕭森 *shiausen*, adj., bare (wintry landscape).

蕭閒 *shiaushiarn*, adj., leisurely and at ease (also 消閒).

蕭蕭 *shiaushiau*, adj., whistling (wind), whinnying (horse).

蕭疎 *shiaushu*, adj., (of trees, leaves) sparse and graceful.

蕭寺 *shiaushyh*, n., (LL. allu.) Buddhist temple.

蕭索 *shiausuoo* (-'*suo*), adj., poverty-stricken, lonely (cf. 蕭瑟 *-seh*↑).

蕭條 *shiautiaur*, n., (business) very dull, (family) on the go-down, (gen. conditions) depressed, lonely, forsaken.

苿 20A.22-3

four.

苿苢 *fouryii*, n., (bot.)=車前草 the plantain.

蘄 20A.22-4

chir.

N. (Bot.), 蘄草 see 當^歸 22.41.

V.i. & t. To beg (var. of 祈 63B.22).

蘄艾 *chir aih*, n., (bot.) see 當^歸 22.41.

蘄春 *Chirchun*, n., a district in Hupeh.

蘄竹 *chirjur*, n., (bot.) a species of fine bamboo produced at *-chun*↑.

蘄蛇 *chirsher*, n., a mottled grey poisonous snake found at *-chun*↑.

幕 20A.22-4

muh.

N. (1) Curtain, tent; 幕天席地 picnic party in the open; general's or governor's office, hence 幕下 advisors "under the tent"; 幕客, 幕府, 幕僚 *-keh*, *-fuu*, *-liaur*, etc.↓. (2) Session: 開幕, 閉幕 open, close session; 揭幕 raise curtain on scene; 落幕 curtain down. (3) Scene in play:

第三幕 scene three. (4) Cinema screen: 銀幕, 字幕 flash on screen containing words; 幕後 backstage; 幕後人物 man behind the scene, backing. (5) 煙幕 smoke screen. (6) 鐵幕 iron curtain.

幕賓 *muhbin*, n., high official's house guest and advisor.
幕府 *muhfuu*, n., governor's or general's office.
幕客 *muhkeh*, n., see *-bin* ↑.
幕僚 *muhliaur*, see *-bin* ↑.
幕友 *muhyoou*, n., high official's guest or friend advisor.

苐 20A.22-5

dih.
[Abbr. of 第 92A.22]

莭 20A.22-5

jier.
[Abbr. of 節 92A.22]

芾 20A.22-6

feih (**fur*).

N. (**fur*) (AC) leather kneecap in ceremonial dress; (AC) 蔽芾 *bihfeih*, very small.

芾芾 **furfur*, adj., (AC) luxuriant (of plants).

蒂 20A.22-6

dih.
[Var. 蔕]

N. Calyx, base of flower, stem: 根深蒂固 deeply rooted (of social customs); 瓜熟蒂落 when melon is ripe, it breaks from the stem—full maturity; 並蒂 two flowers growing from same base—symbol of marital luck.

蒂芥 *dihjieh*, n., some slight misunderstanding; also 芥蒂.

蓆 20A.22-6

shir.

N. (*-tz*) A mat (oft. abbr. 席 61.22): 草蓆 a straw mat; 竹蓆 a mat of split bamboo; 枕蓆 "pillow and mat"—conjugal bed.

薪 20A.22-6

shin.

N. (1) Fuel, firewood: 米珠薪桂 high food prices ("rice like pearl, fuel like cinnamon"); 負薪請罪 be contrite and ask for pardon, (allu.) carry firewood (rod) and ask to be spanked; 薪傳 carry the fire of learning from teacher to pupil. (2) Salary: 薪金, 薪俸 *-jin, -fehng* ↓.

薪俸 *shinfehng*, n., salary.
薪火 *shin-huoo*, n., (1) torch; (2) the torch of learning handed from teacher to pupil.
薪金 *shinjin*, n., salary.
薪水 *shinshueei*, n., ditto.

薺 20A.22-6

jih (**chir*).

N. (1) Thorns, puncture vines. (2) 薺菜 (bot.) shepherd's-purse. (3) (**chir*) 荸薺 water chestnut.

蘼 20A.22-6

mir.

蘼蕪 *mirmuu*, n., (bot.) *Gracilaria confervoides*.

蒹 20A.22-8

jian.

N. The common reed, *Phragmites communis*; 蒹葭 ditto.

芥 20A.22-8

jieh.

N. (Bot.) the mustard; (fig.) thing of little or no value, a trifle: 草芥 rubbish, worthless stuff; 芥舟 a tiny little boat; 芥末 *-moh* ↓.

芥蒂 *jiehdih*[1], n., a misunderstanding, unpleasant memories: 心存芥蒂 bear s.o. a grudge, feelings of resentment.
芥蔕 *jiehdih*[2], n., ditto.
芥藍菜 *jiehlarntsaih*, n., the Chin. kale.
芥末 *jiehmoh*, n., ground mustard.
芥菜 *jiehtsaih*, n., the mustard plant, leaf mustard; 芥菜頭 *--tour*, n., mustard root, oft. pickled.
芥子 *jiehtzyy*, n., a mustard seed, a very small thing: 納須彌於芥子 a universe inside a mustard seed (cf. the atomic structure); 芥子泥 *--nir*, a mustard plaster.

芹 20A.22-9

chirn.

N. Celery: 芹獻, 芹曝 "offering

of celery, of warm sunshine," (allu.) my humble present (oft. of advice); 掇芹 (LL) formerly, be successful in obtaining 1st degree of 秀才 *shiouhtsair*; 芹藻之德 (LL) my flimsy worth.

芹菜 *chirntsaih*, n., celery.

茆 20A.22-9

maau.

N. (Bot.) an edible vegetable, *Brasenia schreberi* =蓴菜.

蒒 20A.22-9

shy.

N. (Bot.) the sedge, whose seeds are edible.

薌 20A.22-9

shiang.

N. (Rare, LL) fragrance (=香).

§20A.30 (卄/一)

蓋 20A.30-1

gaih.

[Pop. 盖, arch. 葢]

N. (1) A protective cover: 壺蓋, 盒蓋 the lid of a pot, box; 蓋子 *-tz*↓; 蓋兒 ditto; 舖蓋 quilt, bedding. (2) (AC) an umbrella. (3) A surname.

V.t. (1) To provide with a cover, to shield: 掩蓋, 遮蓋 cover up; 覆蓋 cover physically; 蓋掩 cover with earth, hay, etc.; 蓋住 have s.t. covered up; 蓋上 put a cover on; 蓋起來 cover or be covered up; 蓋被 cover with a quilt; 蓋棺論定 a man's merits or demerits can be finally judged only after his death, usu. said of public men; 欲蓋彌彰 the more one tries to cover up one's faults, the more they are exposed to public view. (2) Surpass, excel: 他的武藝把別人都蓋下去了 he excels all others in feats of strength; 蓋世, 蓋代 *-shyh*, *-daih*↓. (3) Build, construct: 蓋房子, 蓋屋 build a house; 蓋造 construct (a building, etc.); 蓋瓦 cover with tiles; 加蓋一層 add another storey to a building. (4) To seal, affix a seal to: 蓋章 put one's personal chop on; 蓋印, 蓋關防 affix an official seal on a document; 蓋戳 to stamp; 蓋手印 take finger-prints.

Conj. (AC & LL) for, oft. used as initial particle, introducing a generalization: 蓋聞 for I've heard it said that; 蓋天下萬物之萌生, 靡不有死 for nothing lives which doesn't die; stating an admission: 蓋有之矣 it is possible that such cases exist; 蓋難言也 it is difficult to say (I admit, I allow); 蓋因 it is because.

蓋代 *gaihdaih*, adj., superior to the generation: 蓋代英雄 greatest hero of generation, see *-shyh*↓.

蓋火 *gaihhuoo*, n., a stove's iron cover with small holes on top.

蓋盅(兒) *gaihjung('l)*, n., teacup with a cover.

蓋面兒 *gaih-miah'l*, adj., ostensibly plausible (also 蓋面子): 蓋面兒的話 argument for covering up.

蓋世 *gaihshyh*, adj., rising above all others: 蓋世無雙 (of things or persons) without a match, peerless; 蓋世英雄, the greatest hero; see *-daih*↑.

蓋頭 *gail-tour*, n., a bridal veil.

蓋藏 *gaihtsarng*, n. & v. t., things hoarded up; to hoard up.

蓋子 *gaihtz*, n., (1) a cover (of pot, etc.); (2) the outer shell of crustaceans.

蓋碗 *gaihwaan*, n., a covered bowl or dish.

芷 20A.30-2

jyy.

N. 白芷 (bot.) the angelica, a spicy plant; 芷若 (白芷 and 杜芷) both fragrant plants.

蕋 20A.30-2

rueei.

[Pop. of 蕊 20A.72]

韮 20A.30-2

jioou.

[Var. of 韭 22.30]

蘆 20A.30-2

lur.

[Abbr. 芦]

N. (Bot.) reed, rush.

蘆花 *lurhua*, n., fluffy ends of reed, also called 蘆絮 *-shuh.*

蘆薈 *lurhueih*, n., aloe.

蘆粟 *lursuh*, n., sweet sorghum.

蘆筍 *lursuun*, n., asparagus.

蘆葦 *lurweei*, n., reed.

芹 茆 蒒 薌 蓋 芷 蕋 韮 蘆

亅	小	⺊	十	土	ナ	廾	⺊	丨	一	丅	フ	口	区	冈	冂	厂	尸	亠	广	宀	丶	乚	弋	心	八	人	乂	一	ノ	丿	⺊	く
00	01	02	10	11	12	20	21	22	30	31	32	40	41	42	50	51	52	60	61	62	63	70	71	72	80	81	82	83	90	91	92	93

藎荳薑苤莖薤苴藍虀萱

藎 20A.30-2

jihn.

N. (Bot.) *Arthraxon ciliare.*

Adj. Patriotic and loyal: 王之藎臣 the king's loyal minister.

荳 20A.30-3

douh.

[Var. for 豆 30.30]

薑 20A.30-3

jiang.

N. (bot.) Ginger.

薑黃 *jianghuarng*, n., turmeric: 薑黃試紙 turmeric paper.

苤 20A.30-3

piee (also *pii*).

苤藍 *piee'lan*, n., (bot.) a vegetable, *Brassica campestris* (＝蔓青).

莖 20A.30-3

jing.

N. A stem, the stalk of a plant: 玉莖 (affected circumlocution) the penis.

薤 20A.30-3

shieh.

N. Shallots; scallions; 薤露 a classic dirge or funeral song.

苴 20A.30-4

jyu.

N. (1) A pack, package, packet: 苞苴 bribes (wrapped up in a bundle). (2) The female plant of the nettle hemp: 苴麻 *-mar*, 苴布 *-buh* ↓.

苴布 *jyubuh*, n., coarse cloth.
苴麻 *jyumar*, n., the female plant of the hemp.

藍 20A.30-5

larn.

[Dist. 籃 92A.30]

N. (1) (Bot.) the indigo plant. (2) (Abbr. of 伽藍) (Budd.) a monastery or convent. (3) A surname.

Adj. Blue.

藍寶石 *larn-baaushyr*, n., (min.) sapphire.
藍本 *larnbeen*, n., an original manuscript or publication from which copies are made, a model for copying.
藍青 *larnching*, adj., (1) dark, indigo blue; (2) (of speech) 藍青官話 corrupt Mandarin.
藍靛(澱) *larndiahn*, n., indigo blue (also 靛青, 藍靛).
藍菊 *larnjyur*, n., (bot.) the common China aster, *Callistephus chinensis* (also 翠菊).
藍縷 *larnlyuu*, adj., (of clothes) tattered, torn and ragged (also 襤褸, 藍褸): 篳路藍縷, 蓽露藍蔞 be a trail blazer or pioneer in opening up virgin lands; the pioneering spirit.
藍皮書 *larnpirshu*, n., official blue book, so called from its blue cover.
藍衫 *larnshan*, n., (MC) a scholar having passed the first degree government examination under the Mirng monarchy, so called from the blue gown he was entitled to wear (＝秀才).
藍田 *larntiarn*, n., name of county in Shensi Province noted for its jades: 藍田生玉 children born of great parents; 藍田種玉 cause to be pregnant, usu. said of illicit sexual relations.
藍菜 *larntsaih*, n., (bot.) the cabbage, *Brassica oleracea* (also 甘藍).
藍圖 *larntur*, n., a blueprint.
藍輿 *larnyur*, n., (1) a light carriage; (2) a bamboo sedan chair.

虀 20A.30-6

ji.

N. (1) Interch. 齏 60.30. (2) Pickles.

虀鹽 *jiyarn*, n., vegetable diet ("eating only pickles and salt").

萱 20A.30-6

shyuan.

[Var. 萲]

N. A day lily, *Hemerocallis flava*, whose flower petals are edible (also called 金針菜); (a) as symbol of motherhood from AC allu., as 椿 10B.41 is symbolic allu. to father: 椿萱並茂 both father and mother are in good health; see 萱堂 *-tarng* ↓; (b) as symbol of relief from sorrow (also called 忘憂草): 萱草忘憂.

萱堂 *shyuantarng*, n., (LL, court.) mother, your mother.

菹 20A.30-6

jyu.

N. (1) Pickles. (2) A swamp overgrown with grass. (3) Mince, hash: 菹醢 kill (s.o.) and make his flesh into mincemeat.

莅 20A.30-9

lih.

[Var. 蒞, 涖]

V. t. Come to, arrive at, reach: 莅盟 (AC) attend an international conference, (of friends) keep a rendezvous.

葒 20A.30-9

hurng.

N. (Bot.) 葒草 the prince's feather, *Polygonum orientale.*

蘊 20A.30-9

yuhn.

[Usu.. 縕]

N. (1) A water plant. (2) Hidden bottom: 底蘊 the bottom of affairs.

V.t. (1) To collect, to hide. (2) (AC) to make a bonfire.

蘊藉 *yuhnjieh*, adj., see 醞 31C.30.
蘊結 *yuhnjier*, v.i., to be pent up, oppressed at heart.
蘊蓄 *yuhnshyuh*, v.i. & t., to hoard, save (money).
蘊藏 *yuhntsarng*, v.i. & t., ditto.
蘊藻 *yuhntzaau*, n., watercress and the like; decorations on house beams or in writing.

§20A.32 (卄/フ)

萝 20A.32-4

luor.

[Abbr. of 蘿 20A.11]

夢 20A.32-4

mehng.

[Abbr. 梦]

N. & v. i. & t. To dream; oft. 夢見 *mehng-jiahn* (s. t. or s. o.); oft. 做夢 have a dream; 他在做夢 he is dreaming (planning s. t. impossible); 夢中 in a dream; 夢鄉 dreamland; 夢遊 dream of travelling; 夢熊 (AC) dream of a bear, omen of having a boy; 夢虺 (AC) dream of a serpent, omen of having a daughter; 夢魂顛倒 deeply in love; 迷夢 foolish dream; 如夢初醒 like wakening from a dream; (蝴)蝶[Δ]夢, butterfly dream, 22D.01; 一塲噩夢 all like a bad dream; 一塲幻夢 all like a dream; 夢筆生花 dream of being a successful writer.

夢話 *mehnghuah*, n., talking in a dream; nonsense.
夢幻 *mehnghuan*, n., in 夢幻泡影 like a dream and a bubble's shadow; illusion (of life).
夢兆 *mehng-jauh*, n., dream omen.
夢境 *mehng-jihng*, n., dream world.
夢蘭 *mehnglarn*, n., (LL) dream of an orchid (allu.)—be pregnant.
夢夢 *mehngmehng*, adj., unaware, uncomprehending, cf. 懵懵 22A.41.
夢寐 *mehngmeih*, n., in sleep: 夢寐不忘 remember always, even in sleep; 夢寐以求 try to find (solution) even in sleep.
夢想 *mehngshiaang*, v. i. & t., hope and dream, have illusions: 別夢想 don't have any foolish idea (to be s. t.); 夢想不倒 never dreamt, it was a complete surprise.
夢魘 *mehngyaan*, n., nightmare.
夢遺 *mehngyir*, n., nocturnal emission.

芩 20A.32-8

chirn.

N. (Bot.) 黄芩 the skullcap, *Scuttelaria biacalensis.*

§20A.40 (卄/口)

苦 20A.40-1

kuu.

V. i. Suffer from: 苦熱, (苦夏) suffer from the heat, (summer heat); 苦雨 troubled by too much rain; 苦于 suffer from: 苦于奔命 suffer from dashing about on duties.

Adj. (1) Bitter (lit. & fig.), hard, unlucky, painful: 苦味 bitter taste; 苦酒 bitters; 苦盡甘來 sweet are the fruits of labor (cf. "sweet are the uses of adversity"), luck turns after hardship; 同甘共苦 share good luck and ill (husband and wife); 苦命, 命苦 hard luck; 痛苦 painful, causing suffering; 苦不堪言 suffer unspeakably; 苦樂 joy and sorrow; 苦中作樂 enjoy life though hard up; 艱▵苦 20S.02, difficult (struggle); 過苦日子 be hard up; 苦過 ditto; 苦生意, 苦買賣 business with very thin profits; 苦活兒 poorly paid living; 苦差 job with hard work and poor pay. (2) Hardworking: 辛苦, 苦辛 do hard work (to make a living, etc.); 勞苦 to labor hard, see 勞▵苦 91.50; 苦力, 苦工 *-lih, -gung* ↓; 下苦功 work hard (at lessons, etc.).

Adv. Hard, energetically: 苦幹 work hard; 苦讀, 苦學 study hard; 苦勸 try one's best to persuade, convince; 苦口婆心 phr., ditto; 苦諫 earnest admonitions; 苦追 try hard to catch up with s. o.; 苦留 try hard to ask s.o. to stay; 苦戰, 苦鬪 fight bitterly; 苦打 ditto, beat up terribly.

苦處 *kuuchuh*, n., personal difficulty not always understood: 這是我的苦處 this is my difficulty.

苦楚 *kurchuu*, n. & v. t., persecute (person): 苦楚自己 torture oneself unnecessarily; n., misery; pain, sorrow.

苦窮 *kuuchyurng*, adj., desperately poor, usu. said of oneself to stave off friends who come to borrow.

苦瓜 *kuugua*, n., (bot.) bitter gourd, *Momordica charanta*.

苦工 *kuugung*, n., hard labor, coolie: 做苦工.

苦海 *kurhaai*, n., (Budd., said of human life) a sea of woes: 苦海無邊 the endless sea of tribulations; 脱離苦海 to escape from the human world of woes and find salvation.

苦節 *kuujier*, n., severe self-discipline, self-denial.

苦衷 *kuujung*, n., real kind intentions, usually not expressed: 你不明白我的苦衷 you do not realize my motives; 訴苦衷 explain one's motives.

苦竹 *kuujur*, n., (bot.) Japanese timber bamboo, *Phyllostachys bambusoides*.

苦主 *kur-juu*, n., relative of victim in a murder case.

苦汁 *kuujy*, n., (chem.) bittern.

苦口 *kurkoou*, (1) adj., bitter in taste; (2) as in 苦口(勸他), 苦口婆心 remonstrate earnestly and kindly.

苦苦 *kurkuu*, adv., hard, strenuously: 苦苦相勸 remonstrate earnestly; 苦苦追求 try hard to gain (some object).

苦力 *kuulih*, n., coolie (special word in colonies for miners, porters, sedan chair carriers, etc.), manual laborer.

苦蕒 *kuumai* (Peking dial. also *chyuu'-*), the sow thistle, *Lactuca denticulata*.

苦惱 *kurnaau*, n. & adj., distress, misery; miserable (affair).

苦難 *kuunahn*, n., distress, trials and tribulations: 人生的苦難 the trials of life.

苦人 *kuurern*, n., poor man; hand laborer.

苦肉計 *kuurouh-jih*, n., a confidence game, a trick to gain s.t. by showing self-sacrifice in the beginning.

苦參 *kuushen*, n., (bot.) *Sophora flavescens*, a plant used as insecticide.

苦相 *kuushiahng*, n., face of misery; physiognomy of hard luck.

苦笑 *kuushiauh*, v. i. & n., (force) a bitter smile.

苦心 *kuushin*, adv., with patience and enduring resolve: 苦心孤詣 notable achievement after persistent work.

苦刑 *kuushirng*[1], n., torture, third degree.

苦行 *kuushirng*[2], n., (monk's) life of self-denial and mortification.

苦水 *kurshueei*, n., "hard" water; water in some wells not fit for drinking (cf. 甜▵水 90S.21); 苦水子 (coll.) medicinal potion.

苦死 *kursyy*, (1) adv., (=苦苦): as in 你苦死要來 you were determined to come regardless . .; (2) adj., very miserable; (3) phr., in the worst circumstances: 苦死了每天也要給你兩頓飯吃 have to provide you two meals a day despite everything.

苦頭(兒) *kuutour('l)*, (1) adj., mildly bitter: 井裏的水是苦頭的 this well water is slightly bitter; (2) n., as in 吃苦頭 experience hardship, suffer loss; 給他一點苦頭吃 give him a lesson.

苦菜 *kuutsaih*, n., (bot.) a term denoting various vegetables with mildly bitter taste, including *Sonchus oleraceus*.

苦痛 *kuutuhng*, n. & adj., pain, -ful: 心中苦痛 heartache; 苦痛不堪 suffer extremely.

苦土 *kurtuu*, n., (chem.) magnesia; 煆苦土 calcined magnesia.

苦子 *kuutz*, n., see *-tour* (2) ↑.

苦業 *kuuyeh*, n., (Budd.) normal sufferings of human life.

苦窳 *kuryuu*, adj., (of industrial products) coarse, crude, of poor quality.

莕 20A.40-1

shihng.

N. (Bot.) the floating heart, or fringed water lily, *Limnanthemum nymphoides*.

若 20A.40-1

ruoh.

N. (1) (**ree*) 蘭若 (Budd.) a monastery, hermitage (from Sanskr. *aranya*); 般若 (Budd.) understanding, wisdom (from Sanskr. *prajna*). (2) A surname.

Pron. (LL, AC) you, your: 若輩 *-beih* ↓; 若屬 (pl.) you; 若曹 ditto; 若父 your father.

V. i. Seem, appear to: 若合符節 seem to fit to a T; 若無其事 as if nothing had occurred.

Adj. Such, like, similar: 若而人 such kind of persons; 不若人 unlike, no match for, others; 相若 similar to: 年相若 of the same age; 君子哉若人 such a person is truly a gentleman; 若大旱之望雨也 it's like longing for rain during a drought; 宛若天仙

divinely beautiful ("looks like a heavenly fairy").

Adv. Seemingly, partly, in uncommitted manner: 若有若無 not much, if any; (of misty landscape) faintly discernible; 若隱若現 partly hidden and partly visible; 若卽若離 (of relations between persons) lukewarm, half-hearted, (between lovers) partly accepting, partly rejecting.

Prep. As, like: 視若仇敵 regard as enemy; 待之若上賓 treat s.o. as an honored guest; 視若父兄 as dearly beloved as father and brother; 若喪家之狗 like a stray dog.

Conj. (1) If, as if, in case: 倘若 if, supposing; 若使 *-shyy*↓; 若有所失 feel lost; 若有所思 as if deep in thought; 若將就木 as though about to die; 若己推而內之溝中 as if oneself had pushed them into the gutters; 若不早圖 if no attempt is made early enough to forestall it; 若果立之 if he is made king; 若有甲兵之事 in case war should come; 若其 in case; 若果 in case that; 若非 unless. (2) Both ... and ...: 若老若幼 both old and young. (3) Than: 莫若 nothing better than: 止謗莫若自修 nothing stops gossip as correcting one's own ways.

若輩 *ruoh-beih*, pron., (1) (pl.) you; (2) such people.
若夫 *ruoh-fur*, prep., as to.
若干 *ruohgan*, (1) n., a certain amount; (2) adj., how much or many?
若箇 *ruohgeh*, pron., (1) that one (also 若個); (2) how much or many?
若何 *ruohher*, adv., (1) how then? (2) what then?
若榴 *ruohliour*, n., (bot.) (AC) the pomegranate.
若鷺 *ruohluh*, n., (zoo.) the pond smelt.
若木 *ruohmuh*, n., (AC) a legendary tree supposed to grow where the sun sets.
若若 *ruohruoh*, adj., (AC) dangling, overhanging.
若是 *ruohshyh*, conj., if, supposing: 若是乎 so, thus, in such a way, to such an extent.
若許 *ruohshyuu*, adj., so much or many.
若使 *ruohshyy*, conj., if, supposing.
若爲 *ruohweir*, adv., if, if it is.
若言 *ruohyarn*, n., (1) words of this kind; (2) (AC) candid words.
若英 *ruohying*, n., (1) the flower of 若木 *-muh*↑; (2) *Pollia japonica*.

苫 20A.40-2

shan.

N. Grass mat: 苫塊 *-kuaih*↓.

V. t. To cover (hut) with hay.

苫塊 *shan-kuaih*, phr., (LL) to observe parent's mourning by sleeping on grass mat on ground (苫) and using clod (塊) as pillow, now used only as litr. convention "at the grass mat" (so claimed)—in mourning.

莒 20A.40-4

jyuu.

N. (1) A fibrous plant like the hemp. (2) The taro. (3) The name of an anc. principality: 毋忘在莒 (allu.) a reminder not to forget the national humiliation but to recover the lost territory.

苣 20A.40-5

yii.

[Var. of 苡 20A.81]

苕 20A.40-5

tiaur.

N. A rush plant, whose stems can be used for broomstick.

菩 20A.40-6

pur.

N. Name of aromatic plant.

菩薩 *pur'sa*, n., (Budd.) Bodhisattva; 小菩薩 doll, term of endearment for baby; 菩薩蠻 *--marn*, name of melody; 菩薩心腸 a great kind heart; 菩薩低眉 kind face.
菩提 *purtir*, n., (Budd.) the bodhi tree; true awakening.

蘑 20A.40-6

mor.

V. i. & t. (Coll.) occa. var. of 磨 61.40 in the sense of wearing out person by persistent annoying.

蘑菇 (菰) *mor'gu*, n., a kind of edible mushroom.

营 20A.40-6

yirng.

[Abbr. of 營 91.40]

菅 蓉 落

菅 20A.40-6

jian.

N. (Bot.) *Themeda forskali*: 草菅人命 have scant regard for human life, kill off people ("like rooting out wild grass").

蓉 20A.40-6

rurng.

N. 芙蓉 the hibiscus.

落 20A.40-6

luoh (**lauh* in many coll. usages).

N. (1) A settlement, division, place where people congregate: 部落 a tribe; 村落 a village; 下落 whereabouts: 下落不明, 不知下落 whereabouts unknown; 告一段落 (of affairs) a chapter has been concluded, a stage of development closed. (2) A lot: 一落兒 (*yir lauh'l*) 書, 一落兒碟子 a stack of books, dishes. (3) A hedge: 籬落.

V.i. & t. (1) To shed, drop down, off: 落葉 shed leaves; 落花, 落英 fallen petals; 打得落花流水 route the enemy completely; 落日 setting sun; 落下來 drop down; 落淚 shed tears; 落雨, 落雪 it rains, snows; 落膽 lose heart, frightened out of one's wits; 落髮 drop off hair, hair falls; 落髮爲僧 shave one's head and become a monk; 落胎 have, or cause, an abortion; 落湯雞 drenched through, like chicken drenched and about to be feathered; 落湯螃蟹 helpless like crab in steaming pot; 落井(穽)下石 to throw rocks in after a man has fallen into well (trap)—strike man when he is down; 落水 (of person, ship) go into the water, (woman) become prostitute. (2) (Pr. **lauh* or *luoh*) fall, come down on: 落在地上 drop to the ground; 鳥落在房上 bird alights on the roof; 落第六名 name comes out in sixth place; 名落孫山 (phr. allu.) fail in civil examination—name comes out behind the last name, that of Sun Shan; see 落第, 落選 *-dih*^{2}, *-shyuaan*↓. (3) (As vb. suffix or as adv.) off, down: 脱落 shed off: 失落 lose (a handkerchief, watch); 遺落 drop out (by mistake); 降落 descend; 墜落 sink into, drop down, degenerate; 殂落, 隕落 die, fallen upon bad times, unsuccessful, withered; 衰落 declined; 凋落 withered; 淪落 degenerate; 流落 drift about without fixed profession; 沒落 (of fame, movement) die out, be forgotten, decline. (4) To drop out by mistake: 落了一個字 a word has been dropped out; 落禮兒 a mistake or oversight in courtesy; 落神 be absent-minded. (5) To result in, end up in: 落圈套 fall into trap; 這封信落到他手 this letter has fallen into his hand; 落空 (plans, endeavors) end up in nothing; 落難 get into trouble, in distress; (**lauh*) receive comment: 落褒貶 receive criticism; 落不是 be condemned, criticised as wrong; 落好兒 receive favorable comment; 除開消以外落了幾塊錢 made a few dollars after expenses; 落了不少油水 made a lot on the side as commission. (6) To set (ink, brush in writting, painting): 落筆 to set pen on paper in given manner or style; 落墨 set ink; 落款 (**lauh*) to put signature to scroll, including artist's name and that of recipient possibly also date; 落賬 (*lauh*) enter item in account. (7) To stay, stop over: 落棧 (coll.) stop at an inn for the night; 落脚兒 (coll.) stop for a rest; 落炕 sick confined to bed. (8) (**lauh*) To drop down, drop out: 落價 come down in price; to fade: 落色 fade in color; (*luoh*) to drop out of elections, army, tests, see 落選, 落伍, 落第 *-shyuaan*, *-wuu*, *-dih*^{2}↓; drop behind, 落後 *-houh*.↓.

Adj. (1) Scarce, scattered, thinned out: 零落, 疏落 scattered; 零零落落 bits here and there; 寥落 thinly populated.

Adv. See V. i. & t. 3↑

落榜 *luohbaang*, v.i., formerly, fail in civil examinations.

落成 *luohcherng*, v.i., (of buildings) completed: 落成典禮 inauguration ceremony of new building.

落地 *luohdih*^{1}, (1) be born: 落地爲兄弟 are born brothers; (2) (**lauh dih*) touching the ground: 落地燈 floor lamp; 落地窗 French window; 落地式收音機 cabinet or console type radio set (as against desk type).

落第 *luohdih*^{2}, v. i., fail in civil examinations.

落後 *luoh-houh*, v. i., fall behind in work; adj., behind times (in thinking), backward: 落後國家 underdeveloped countries.

落花生 *luohhuasheng*, n., peanut.

落荒 *luohhuang*, n., take to the wilds: 落荒而逃 be a fugitive from justice.

落價 **lauhjiah*^{1}, v. i., come down in price.

落架 **lauhjiah*^{2}, v. i., (of family) fall apart, decline.

落葵 *luohkueir*, n., (bot.) malaba nightshade, *Basella rubra*.

落空 *luohkung*, v. i., end up in nothing, suffer loss.

落落 *luohluoh*, adj., as in 落落大方 very poised and dignified; 落落寡合 socially aloof; 零零落落 in piecemeal fashion.

落寞 *luohmoh*, adj., (1) aloof, alone; (2) off and on, in piecemeal fashion.

落腮鬍(子) *luohsai hur*(*tz*), n., whiskers on cheeks.

落選 *luohshyuaan*, v. i., fail to be elected or in competitive examinations.

落體 *luoh-tii*, n., (phys.) a falling body.

落草 *luohtsaau*(**lauh-*), v. i., to join the bandits: 落草爲寇 turn to banditry.

落魄 *luohtuoh* (also pr. *-poh*, wr. also 落泊 *-poh*), adj., (1) down and out, be a failure, downhearted; (2) (*-tuoh* usu. wr. 落拓), unconventional, going one's own way.

落子 *lauhtz, (1) as in 落子館兒 equiv. to cheap amusement park where singing, vaudeville shows are given; (2) means of living: 窮得都沒落子了 without means of subsistence.

落伍 *luohwuu*, v. i., drop behind others, become outdated, see *-houh*↑.

落葉樹 *luohyeh shuh*, n., deciduous trees.

蒼 20A.40-8

tsang.

N. The sky above: 上蒼 the sky, heaven (oft. personified).

Adj. (1) Blue (sky, sea). (2) Green (grass, vegetation). (3) Grey (beard, temples), old: 蒼老 *-laau*↓. (4) Black or deep grey (eagles, flies): 蒼蠅, 蒼鷹, 蒼龍, 蒼鷺 *-'ying*, *-ying*, *-lurng*, *-luh*↓; cf. 青 10.42 for confusion of colors.

蒼白 *tsangbair*, adj., pale (complexion).

蒼穹 *tsangchyurng*, n., (LL) the blue sky, firmament.

蒼耳 *tsang-eel*, n., the burweed.

蒼朮 *tsangjur*, n., a medicinal herb, *Atractylis lancea*, var. *ovata*.

蒼老 *tsanglaau*, adj., (1) old, weathered (appearance), weak and split (voice); (2) masterly, thoroughly mature (calligraphy).

蒼鷺 *tsangluh*, n., the grey stork, *Ardea cinerea*.

蒼龍 *tsanglurng*, n., black dragon.

蒼茫 *tsangmarng*, adj., diffused, misty, indistinct (night sky).

蒼生 *tsangsheng*, n., (LL) the younger generation; all living mankind, the people at large.

蒼苔 *tsangtair*, n., lichen.

蒼天 *tsangtian*, n., heaven (oft. personified).

蒼頭 *tsangtour*, n., (AC) black-turbaned servants, also foot soldiers.

蒼蒼 *tsangtsang*, adj., (1) dark green; (2) grey (hair, beard); (3) old, weathered.

蒼鷹 *tsangying*, n., the eagle.

蒼蠅 *tsang'ying*, n., the common fly; 蒼蠅刷兒 a fly swat.

荅 20A.40-8

da.

[Abbr. of 答 92A.40]

茄 20A.40-9

chier (*jia).

N. (1) (*-tz*) The eggplant: 茄袋 a wallet, shaped like eggplant; 番茄 tomato. (2) (*jia) The lotus stalk.

蓓 20A.40-9

beih.

N. A bud, only in comp.↓.

蓓蕾 *beihleei*, n., flower bud.

茗 20A.40-9

mirng (*miing*).

N. (LL) tea (=vern. 茶): 品茗 sample or critically enjoy tea; 茗坊, 茗肆 teasample or house; 茗圃 tea field, plantation.

茖 20A.40-9

ger.

N. (Bot.) 茖葱 the wild or long-root onion, *Allium victorialis*.

茹 20A.40-9

rur (also *ruh*).

N. (1) Roots attached to the crown of a plant: 拔茅連茹 pull up the rushes with their roots. (2) Vegetable food in gen. (3) A surname.

V.t. Eat: 茹苦 suffer ("taste bitterness"); 茹荼 ditto; 茹葷 eat meats; 茹素 practise vegetarianism; 貪茹 to swallow greedily, to gorge oneself; 茹毛飲血 live the life of a savage ("eat animal flesh raw and drink its blood").

Adj. Rotten and foul-smelling: 茹魚 putrid fish.

茹筆 *rur-bii*, v.i., lick writing brush into shape.

茹痛 *rurtuhng*, v.i., suffer, endure, put up with, bear up under (pains).

菇 20A.40-9

gu.

N. (Bot.) 蘑菇, 草菇 edible mushrooms; 香菇, 冬菇 varieties of fine mushroom.

苔 20A.40-9

tair (*tai).

苔 藉 著

N. (1) Moss, lichens: 青苔 moss; 苔梅 moss-covered plum tree; 苔紙 paper made from moss; 苔錢 small discs of lichens; 苔茵 carpet of moss. (2) (*tai*) Whitish coating (fur) on tongue: 舌苔.

苔砌 *tair-chih*, n., mossy steps.
苔痕 *tair-hern*, n., mossy growths (with footprints).
苔癬 *tairshiaan*, n., lichens.
苔菜 *tairtsaih*, n., (bot.) *Corydalis incisa*.
苔衣 *tairyi*, n., a spread of lichens.

§20A.41 (艹/図)

藉 20A.41-1

jieh (**jir*).

N. (1) (**jir*) A mattress. (2) (**jir*) Reliance, basis: 憑藉. (3) A surname.

V.t. (1) (**jir*) Sit or lie on: 藉藉 *-jir*↓; 狼藉 scattered about, lying here and there; 枕藉 piled up (plates after dinner, dead and wounded after battle). (2) To make use of (=借): 藉此 take advantage of (event, situation, pretext); 藉以 in order to (satisfy demands, seek distraction, get notoriety, etc.).

藉端 *jieh-duan*, v.t., make a pretext.
藉故 *jieh-guh*, v.t., give as an excuse.
藉藉 **jirjir*, adj., in a state of utter confusion, scattered here and there; wide spread.
藉重 *jiehjuhng*, v.t., depend on for support or assistance.
藉口 *jieh-koou*, phr., on the pretext of.
藉手 *jieh-shoou*, v.t., do through the hands of another.
藉詞 *jieh-tsyr*, (1) v.t., give as an excuse; (2) phr., on the pretext that.
藉資 *jieh-tzy*, v.t., avail oneself of, take advantage of.

著 20A.41-1

juh (**juor*, **jau*, **jaur*, **je*).

[Common var. 着, in all senses except "compose," "well-known"]

N. (1) Written works: 著述 author's works, writings; 名著 famous works. (2) (**juor*) A move in chess or any move (political, etc.): 這一著很出色 this is a brilliant move. (3) (**jau*) A plan, strategy: 高著, 妙著 brilliant strategy; a move in chess: 著數 *-shuh*↓.

V.t. (1) To compose, write (books): 著書 write books; 著書立說 to write and propound ideas. (2) (**juor*) To touch, put one's hand on, apply, make a (chess) move; to put on (dress); to make different moves: 著棋 play chess; 著力, 著手 *-lih, -shoou*↓; 著意, 著色 *-yih, -seh*↓. (3) (**juor*) To send s.o.: 著人去辦 send s.o. to do it. (4) (**jau*) To catch, be affected by contact (with heat, cold): 著風, 著涼 *-feng, -liarng*↓; 著雨 wetted by rain; 著水 wetted by water; 著慌, 著急 *-huarng, -jir*↓; and a special variation (**jaur*)—catch (fire): 著火 catch fire, also 火著了 fire begins to burn. (5) (**jaur*) To put out effort, to hit, strike at some point: 著用 *-yuhng*, 著眼 *-yaan*↓; 著一把手兒 lend a hand (to help); 著三不著兩 unable to attend to all at same time.

Adj. (1) Well-known: 著名 *-mirng*↓; 卓著 outstanding. (2) (**juor*) 著實 *-shyr*↓.

Adv. (1) (**jaur*, accented) Used after vb. to indicate a hit: 找著了 have found it; 打著了 have hit it (target); 猜著了 have guessed correctly; (*-'je*) when unaccented, see 2↓. (2) (**je*, unaccented) Used like inflexional ending, pres. part. "-ing," indicating continuing process, 坐著等他 sit and wait (lit., "wait sitting") for him; 站著寫信 write a letter standing up; 看著他來 watching him come; 拉著手走路 walk holding hands; or like p.p. in sense of "hit": 得著了 have got it; 買著了 have already bought; 找著了 have found it.

著處 **juorchuh*, adv., (MC) everywhere (=逐處).
著風 **jaufeng*, v. i., to catch cold, see *-liarng*↓.
逐花 **juor-hua*, v. i., (of flower tree) blossoms.
著慌 **jauhuarng*, v. i., become nervous, tense.
著火 **jaur-huoo*, v. i., catch fire.
著績 *juhji*, n., well-known results, accomplishments.
著急 **jaujir*, v. i., become nervous, anxious, agitated.
著重兒 **jaujuhng'l*, v. i., (of illness) become serious, take a bad turn.
著涼 **jauliarng*, v. i., catch cold.
著力 **juor-lih*, v. i., to put forth effort (to do things).
著落 **juorluoh* (**jaur-*), n., (1) whereabouts: 不知著落 do not know where he went to; (2) a satisfactory result or settlement: 沒有著落 without known results.
著忙 **jaumarng*, v. i., to hurry, hustle, see *-huarng*↑.
著名 *juhmirng*, adj., well-known.
著色 **juor-seh*, v. i., to apply color.
著手 **juorshoou*, v. i., to begin (to write, build, etc.): 還沒著手 have not begun yet.
著述 *juhshuh*, v. i. & n., write (books, essays): 著述豐富 has many books to his name.
著數 **jaushuh*, n., (1) a move in chess; (2) a move in pugilism (also wr. 招數)
著實 **juor-shyr*, adv., really (do s. t.), not in perfunctory manner.
著作 *juhtzuoh*, n., (a person's) works, writings; artistic products (as sculpture); 著作人, 著作家 author; 著作權 copyright.
著眼 **jaur-yaan*, v. i., fix attention on (object); 著眼點 points

to be attended to.

著意 *juor-yih, v.i., (1) be attracted by (person); (2) concentrate (on work).

著用 *jauryuhng, v.t., be needed, useful.

蓍 20A.41-1

shy.

N. A plant whose stalks were used in divination: 蓍龜 the *shy*-stalks and the tortoise-shell used in divination.

薔 20A.41-1

chiarng.

薔薇 *chiarngweir*, n., a rambler rose (cf. 玫△瑰 31A.82); 薔薇露 rose water; a kind of wine; 薔薇硝 a rose powder; 薔薇水 rose water; 薔薇輝石 n., (min.) rhodonite.

葍 20A.41-3

fur.

N. (AC) weed.

茜 20A.41-3

chiahn.

Adj. Red.

茜草 *chiahntsaau*, n., (bot.) a grass whose root is used as red pigment, *Rubia cordifolia*.

蕾 20A.41-3

leei.

N. A flower bud: 蓓蕾.

菖 20A.41-4

chang.

菖蒲 *changpur*, n., (bot.) the sweet flag or iris: 白菖蒲 ditto; 菖蒲酒 calamus wine; 菖蒲棒兒 stem of sweet flag; 石菖蒲 dwarf calamus, trained for flower arrangement.

薯 20A.41-4

shuu.

[Var. 藷]

N. A potato, yam: 白薯, 紅薯 sweet potato; 馬鈴薯 common potato; 大薯, 薯芋 yam (also called 山藥)—usage differs in dialects.

暮 20A.41-4

muh.

N. The dusk, sundown: 薄暮 toward sundown; 暮夜 *-yeh*↓; 旦暮 morning and night, see 旦 41.30; 朝朝暮暮 morning and night; 暮鼓晨鐘 evening drum and morning bell of monastery, daily call to religious life.

Adj. Twilight, dusk, declining: 暮年, 暮氣 *-niarn, -chih*↓; end of season: 暮春, 暮夏, 暮秋 last month of spring, summer, autumn; 歲聿其暮 (AC) the year is drawing to its close.

暮氣 *muh-chih*, n., spirit of decline: 暮氣沉沉 opp. 朝△氣 10S.42.

暮景 *muh-jiing*, n., sunset view or atmosphere.

暮年 *muh-niarn*, n., declining years.

暮生兒 *muh'sheng'l*, n., child born after father's death=遺腹子.

暮歲 *muh-shueih*, n., the end of the year; declining years.

暮夜 *muh-yeh*, n., night; 暮夜金 bribe money ("paid at night").

苜 20A.41-4

muh.

苜蓿 *muhsuh*, n., (bot.) clover, *Medicago denticulata*.

瞢 20A.41-4

merng.

[Cogn. 懵 22A.41]

Adj. Obscure; dim-sighted.

瞢騰 *merngterng*, adj., half drunk (cf. 矇△矓 41B.02).

苗 20A.41-4

miaur.

N. (1) Sprouts, seedling: 苗而不秀 corn which does not bear grain; 幼苗 young sprout; 豆苗 edible sprout of peas in the pot; 麥苗 wheat seedling; 樹苗 plant seedling for transplanting; 苗裔 *-yih*↓. (2) 火苗 pilot flame. (3) 礦苗 outcrops of mineral deposits. (4) Name of aboriginal tribes in southwest China: 苗族, 苗人, 苗子 the "Miaotse"; 熟苗 Miaotse under Chinese control or influence; 生苗 not under such influence.

苗兒 *miaur'l*, n., as in 苕帚苗兒 *tiaur'sou*—the fine, thin fibres of a broom.
苗條 *miaur'tiau*, adj., slender: 身段苗條 (lady) has a slender figure.
苗頭(兒) *miau'tou'l*, n., early beginning, clues, some visible results: 這件事已經有苗頭了 we have begun to see some visible results or clues; 這人很有苗頭 this man knows what he is doing.
苗裔 *miauryih*, n., progeny.
苗胤 *miauryihn*, n., ditto.

茴 20A.41-4

hueir.

茴香 *hueirshiang*, n., (bot.) 小茴香 sweet fennel; 大茴香 star-aniseed.

茵 20A.41-4

yin.

N. (AC) a coverlet, mattress: 草茵 (fig.) a carpet of grass, lawn.

茵陳蒿 *yinchern-hau*, n., (bot.) *Artemisia capillaris.*
茵芋 *yinyuh*, n., (bot.) *Skimmia japonica.*

菌 20A.41-4

jyuhn.

N. (1) (Also 蕈) the mushroom: fungus. (2) (Short for 細菌) germs, bacteria.

菌花 *jyuhnhua*, n., patterned mildew.
菌類 *jyuhnleih*, n., (bot.) fungi.

蓄 20A.41-6

shyuh.

V. t. (1) To save, hoard up: 積蓄 to save, have savings; 蓄積 *-jir* ↓. (2) To keep for a long time: 蓄志, 蓄意 *-jyh, -yih* ↓. (3) To let hair grow long after leaving monastic vow: 蓄髮.

蓄艾 *shyuh-aih*, phr., (AC allu.) be prepared to meet emergencies; keep talented men for future use.
蓄電池 *shyuhdiahn-chyr*, n., (electricity) a condenser, capacitor battery.
蓄恨 *shyuh-hehn*, v. i., to nurse a hatred, bear grudge.
蓄積 *shyuhjir*, v. i., to hoard, save up (money, property).
蓄志 *shyuh-jyh*, v. i., keep an ambition, determine (to do s. t.).
蓄謀 *shyuh-mour*, v. i., conceive, without revealing, a plan, plot in secret.
蓄念 *shyuh-niahn*, v. i., harbor an idea (to do).
蓄銳 *shyuh-rueih*, phr., as in 養精蓄銳 train an excellent army in preparation for war.
蓄泄 *shyuh-shieh*, phr., dam up and let off.
蓄養 *shyuhyaang*, v. t., to raise (cattle, etc.).
蓄意 *shyuh-yih*, v. i., see *-niahn* ↑.
蓄疑 *shyuh-yir*, v. i., to harbor suspicion.
蓄怨 *shyuh-yuahn*, v. i., see *-hehn* ↑.

藷 20A.41-6

ju (**shuu*).

N. (1) 藷蔗 (AC) sugar cane. (2) (**shuu*) Potato (usu. wr. 薯 as in 白薯, 紅薯).

蓿 20A.41-6

suh.

N. See 苜蓿 20A.41.

藩 20A.41-6

farn.

N. (1) Fence. (2) Outlying post, authority or province protecting border: 屏藩 border defense authority, protectorate.

藩國 *farnguor*, n., feudatory state, governed by prince of royal house.
藩鎮 *farnjehn*, n., commander of outlying province.
藩籬 *farnlir*, n., fence, hedge; (fig.) boundary: 打破藩籬 break through hedging-in traditions.
藩屏 *farnpirng*, n., governorships in outlying provinces, also 屏藩.
藩屬 *farnshuu*, n., protectorate.
藩司(臺) *farnsy(-tair)*, n., Mirng Dyn. commissioner ＝布政使.

薈 20A.41-8

hueih.

Adj. Abundant.

薈萃 *hueihtsueih*, v. i., assemble: 薈萃一堂 a distinguished gathering.
薈蔚 *hueihweih*, adj., abundant

(vegetation), massive (clouds).

蕃 20A.41-9

farn.

[Dist. 藩 20A.41]

Adj. (1) Used as var. of 番 "foreign" in 番椒, 番薯, 番國, see 90.41 adj. & compp. (2) Luxurious, thriving, multiplying fast.

蕃昌 *farnchang*, adj., flourishing, proliferous.
蕃殖 *farnjyr*, v.i., grow well, multiply fast.
蕃茂 *farnmouh*, adj., luxuriant, rank (vegetation).
蕃息 *farshir*, v. i., multiply quickly (plants, animals).
蕃庶 *farnshuh*, adj., numerous (progeny).
蕃滋 *farntzy*, v. i., multiply.
蕃衍 *farnyaan*, v. i., spread (of plants, descendants).
蕃育 *farnyuh*, v. i., multiply (descendants).

蕕 20A.41-9

your.

N. (LL) a stinking grass; (fig.) stinking personality: 薰蕕 the good and the bad.

菑 20A.41-9

tzy (**tzai*).

N. (1) (AC) a piece of newly cultivated land: 菑畬 farm land that has been cultivated for one or two years. (2) (**tzai*) (Interch. 災) a natural disaster: 無菑無害 free from any visitations of nature or calamity.

V. t. To hoe, to weed.

§20A.42 (卄/冈)

菁 20A.42-1

jing.

N. (1) Flower of the leek family. (2) Reeds.

菁華 *jinghuar*, n., essence, quintessence, the best part of anything (=精華).
菁菁 *jingjing*, adj., luxuriant, lush.

葫 20A.42-1

hur.

葫蘆 *hurlur* (-'*lu*), n., the bottle gourd; dried shell of bottle gourd, used for holding medicine: 葫蘆裏賣藥讓你猜 guess what's in the gourd; hence 悶葫蘆 a puzzling matter; 葫蘆兒 embroidered bag of spices worn by children on 5th lunar month for warding off infectious influence; 冰糖葫蘆兒 sugar-coated crab apple.
葫蒜 *hursuahn*, n., garlic and leeks (also wr. 胡蒜).
葫荽 *hursuei*, n., coriander (also wr. 胡荽).

蒱 20A.42-1

pur.

N. 摴蒱 kind of dice gambling.

藕 20A.42-1

oou.

N. Arrowroot, bulbous root of the lotus: 藕斷絲連 a section of arrowroot is separated, but the clinging fibre remains——of lovers separated by force but their love lingers on; relations that cannot be entirely severed.

藕棒兒 *oubahng'l*, n., rootstock of lotus, oft. fig. of woman's or child's white arms.
藕粉 *ourfeen*, n., arrowroot.
藕覆 *ooufuh*, n., formerly, ankle cover for woman with bound foot.
藕合 *oou'her*, adj., purplish-blue (color).
藕荷 *oouher*, adj., ditto.
藕花 *oouhua*, n., lotus flower.
藕灰 *oouhuei*, adj., greyish lilac (color).
藕節(兒)(子) *oujier* (*-jier'l*)(*tz*), n., root fibres between joints of arrowroot, used in Chin. med.
藕零兒 *oulirng'l*, n., preserved slices of sugar-treated arrowroot.
藕色 *oouseh*, adj., pale pink color.
藕絲 *oousy*, n., fibres of lotus root or lotus flower stem; its color, pale lilac.

苒 20A.42-2

raan.

苒苒 *rarnraan*, adj., (of grasses) luxuriant, lush.
苒荏 *rarnreen*, adj., (of time) passing imperceptibly (also 荏苒).
苒弱 *raanruoh*, adj., (of flowers) drooping.

薷 萌 萬

薷 20A.42-3

rur.

N. (Bot.) (＝木耳 the Jew's ear, *Auricularia Auricula-Judae*).

萌 20A.42-4

merng.

V. i. & n. To bud, to sprout; buds, sprouts; (fig.) put forth new life, revive: 故態復萌 old habits come back again; (LL) germinate (thoughts, plans): 萌動, 萌生.

萌兆 *merng-jauh*, n., first signs of.
萌黎 *mernglir*, n., (AC)＝氓黎, the common people.
萌芽 *merng-yar*, n. & v. i., sprout, to sprout (lit. & fig.): 萌芽時代 early beginnings, early period.

萬 20A.42-4

wahn.

N. & adj. Ten thousand, used as a unit of counting: 百萬 million; 千萬 ten million; 萬萬 or 億 hundred million; 十萬萬 billion; 萬倍 ten thousand fold; 萬把 about ten thousand; used in sense of "all," "myriads": 萬般, 萬象 *-ban*, *-shiahng*↓; 萬民, 萬人 *-mirn*, *-rern*↓; 萬邦, 萬國 *-bang*, *-guor*↓; 萬能 *-nerng*↓; 萬目睽睽 all eyes centered on (s. t.); 萬衆一心 all united in one purpose; 萬家燈火 a myriad lights in the valley; 萬劫不復 doomed eternally; 萬籟俱寂 all sounds of nature stopped—complete silence of the night.

Adv. Completely, a thousand times, under all circumstances: 萬難, 萬全 *-narn*, *-chyuarn*↓; 萬幸 *-shihng*[1]↓; oft. coupled with negative: 千萬別忘記 under no circumstances forget; 萬無此理 certainly cannot be true; 萬不能 positively cannot; 萬不肯 positively unwilling; 萬不及 far inferior to; 萬勿推辭 please do not say "no"; 萬不可說 should under no circumstances tell; 萬無一失 cannot fail under any circumstances; 萬一, 萬萬 *-yi*, *-wahn*↓.

萬安 *wahn-an*, (1) phr., (MC) do not worry: 你萬安, 沒的事 don't worry, it is not true; (2) see *-chyuarn*↓.
萬把 *wahn'ba*, adj., about ten thousand.
萬般 *wahn-ban*, (1) n., all, all kinds, all classes; (2) adv., extremely, to the last degree: 萬般無奈 absolutely bored.
萬邦 *wahnbang*, phr., all nations.
萬千 *wahn-chian*, adj., numberless, thousands and tens of thousands; 萬紫千紅 innumerable flowers of purple and red.
萬全 *wahn-chyuarn*, adj., completely safe (plan).
萬端 *wahn-duan*, n., innumerable (affairs, ways, manners).
萬方 *wahn-fang*, adv., (1) by all sorts of methods (try to please, etc.); (2) in all countries (unsettled, etc.); (3) incomparably: 儀態萬方 distinguished air of elegance and coquetry.
萬分 *wahn-fen*, adv., a thousand times (regret, ashamed), completely (satisfied).
萬福 *wahn-fur*, phr., (1) wishing you all happiness—a formula like "good luck"; (2) 道萬福 formerly, a form of greeting by women, hands holding to sides of jacket.
萬貫 *wahn-guahn*, n., formerly, ten million cash (貫 a string of 1,000 cash); 萬貫家私 a millionaire.
萬國 *wahn-guor*, adj., international: 萬國博覽會 international exposition; 萬國公法 international law (now usu. 國際); 萬國郵政聯盟 Universal Postal Union (UPU).
萬古 *wahn-guu*, adv., eternally: 萬古常新 eternally new; 萬古流芳 will be remembered throughout the ages.
萬花筒 *wahn-hua-tuung*, n., kaleidoscope.
萬化 *wahn-huah*, n., (LL) all creation.
萬彙 *wahn-hueih*, n., all categories; see *-leih*↓.
萬機 (幾) *wahn-ji*, n., myriad affairs of the state attended to by the ruler (also wr. 萬幾).
萬劫 *wahn-jier*, n., (Budd.) all ages, eternity (劫 Sanskr. *kalpa*, an aeon).
萬急 *wahn-jir*, adj., most urgent (telegram, etc.).
萬狀 *wahn-juahng*, n., all kinds, shapes, manners; as adv., 危急萬狀 extremely critical.
萬鈞 *wahn-jyun*, n., a superhuman load (a weight of 300,000 catties).
萬類 *wahnleih*, n., all categories; esp. birds and beasts of the creation.
萬里長城 *Wahn-li-charng-cherng*, n., the Great Wall.
萬里侯 *wahnlii-hour*, n., (AC) governor of a great territory.
萬民 *wahnmirn*, n., the common people; 萬民傘 a souvenir parasol given to departing magistrate, with inscribed silk strips.
萬難 *wahn-narn*, adj., extremely difficult (to deal with); certainly cannot (consent, follow, etc.).
萬能 *wahn-nerng*, adj., all-powerful: 科學萬能 science can do anything.
萬年 *wahnniarn*, n., ten thousand years, also (AC) "Long live"; see *-sueih*↓; 萬年青 (bot.) a tough evergreen which requires very little attention, *Rhodea japonica*; 萬年曆 calendar good for any future year.
萬人 *wahn-rern*, n., a myriad people; 萬人坑 mass grave; 萬人敵 warrior who could fight his way out and take on any challenger.
萬乘 *wahn-shehng*, n., as in 萬乘之主(之尊) an emperor (of "ten thousand chariots").
萬象 *wahn-shiahng*, n., all things of the universe.
萬幸 *wahnshihng*[1], adj., unusually lucky.
萬姓 *wahn-shihng*[2], n., all the people, ("myriad clans").
萬壽 *wahnshouh*, n., as in 萬壽無疆 "long live for ever"—a form of greeting for birthdays; 萬壽菊

(bot.) *Tagetes erecta.*

萬事通 ***wahn-shyh-tung***, n., jack of all trades, expert at none.

萬歲 ***wahnsueih***, n., (1) "Long live" (Japanese "banzai"); 萬歲 or 萬歲爺 (court. address) "His Majesty."

萬萬 ***wahnwahn***, adv., absolutely (not to forget, etc.); with negative: 萬萬不可 positively do not.

萬勿 ***wahn-wuh***[1], phr., positively do not (lose it!).

萬物 ***wahnwuh***[2], n., the creation, all living things.

萬無 ***wahn-wur***, phr., positively, absolutely no: 萬無一失 not a chance of an error.

萬一 ***wahnyi***, (1) adv., just in case ("one in ten thousand"): 萬一他不來 just in case he does not come; (2) n., contingency: 準備萬一 provide for such an eventuality.

萬應藥 ***wahngyihngyauh***, n., panacea.

萬有 ***wahn-yoou***, adj., all-comprehending, universal: 萬有引力 universal gravitation; 萬有皆靈説 animism.

茼 20A.42-4

turng.

茼蒿 ***turnghau***, n., the (edible) garland chrysanthemum, *Chrysanthemum coronarium.*

萵 20A.42-4

wo.

萵苣 ***wojyuh***, n., lettuce.

萵笋 ***wosuun***, n., a kind of vegetable, related to lettuce, eaten raw or cooked.

繭 20A.42-4

jiaan.

N. (1) The cocoon of the silkworm or other insects: 繭綢 pongee of wild silk; 作繭自縛 do s.t. which, unintentionally, results in restricting one's own freedom of action ("make a cocoon to shut oneself in"). (2) (Interch. 趼) blisters and calluses on the feet: 重繭, 老繭 calloused skin on the feet.

蒿 20A.42-6

hau.

N. Different varieties of artemisia, including wormwood: 蒿目時艱 phr., (AC) to survey the world with concern, to look with anxiety at the world's ills.

蒿里 ***Haulii***, n., orig. a town near Taishan; (allu.) where departed souls are said to return to.

蒲 20A.42-6

pur.

N. (1) Kinds of rush: 蒲席 rush mat; 蒲墊 rush cushion; 蒲輪 (MC) wheel wrapped with rush for comfort; 蒲柳之姿 (of female sex) frail beauty; 香蒲 *Typha japonica*, a water plant used for pungent aroma; see also 菖^A蒲 20A.41; short for 蒲葵 *-kueir* ↓, a kind of palm. (2) Name of place. (3) A surname.

蒲包 ***purbau***, n., generally used for wallet, pocket book; anciently, package of scented herbs or package of gifts wrapped in 蒲 palm leaves.

蒲鞭 ***purbian***, n., whip made of palm stem, used for mild punishment.

蒲伏 ***purfur***, v.i., var. of 匍^A伏 92.50, crawl.

蒲公英 ***purgungying***, a garden grass with small yellow flowers.

蒲劍 ***purjiahn***, n., a sword-shaped bag of aromatic herbs hung on doorposts on Dragon Boat Festival for warding off insects (and "evil spirits").

蒲節 ***pur-jier***, n., the fifth day of fifth lunar month, Dragon Boat Festival.

蒲葵 ***purkueir***, n., a kind of palm, whose leaves are used for making fans.

蒲扇(兒) ***purshahn (-shah'l)***, n., palm leaf fan, made from *-kueir* ↑.

蒲團 ***purtuarn***, n., rush prayer-mat.

蒲月 ***puryueh***, n., the fifth month of lunar calendar.

萹 20A.42-6

pian.

[Common var. in fast script of 篇]

萹蓄 ***pianshyuh***, n., (bot.) *Polygonum aviculare*, a flowering plant used as herb (also called 萹竹).

芮 20A.42-8

rueih.

N. (1) Name of an anc. principality. (2) The edge of a body of water. (3) Thongs of a shield. (4) A surname.

Adj. Small, tiny.

芮稻 *rueih-dauh*, n., a rice variety which ripens in late autumn.
芮芮 *rueihrueih*, adj., (AC) (of grass blades) slender.

蒴 20A.42-8

shuoh.

N. (Bot.) a capsule of seeds.

蒴藋 *shuohdiauh*, n., (bot.) the Chin. elder (also called 接骨草); 木蒴藋 the red elderberry.

蕎 20A.42-9

chiaur.

N. Buckwheat; see 蕎麥 *-maih* ↓.

蕎巴 *chiaurba*, n., buckwheat cake.
蕎麥 *chiaurmaih* (-'*mai*), buckwheat; 蕎麥麪 buckwheat flour.

稨 20A.42-9

biaan.

[Var. of 扁 63D.42]

蒨 20A.42-9

chiahn.

N. & adj. Var. of 茜 20A.41.

蒨蒨 *chiahnchiahn*, adj., (AC) (1) bright-colored; (2) with beautiful smile; (3) lush (vegetation).

蓨 20A.42-9

shiou.

蓨酸 *shiousuan*, n., (chem.) oxalic acid (＝草酸).

§ 20A.50 (卄/ㄱ)

葧 20A.50-1

bor.

N. A plant of rush family, *Artemisia stelleriana*, of the rush family (also u. f. 孛 10.00, and 勃 10S.50).

蔫 20A.50-3

nian.

Adj. (1) (Of flowers and grass) faded, withered: 太陽把花都晒蔫了 the flowers have become withered under the scorching sun. (2) (Of person) despondent, depressed.

Adv. Silently, quietly, stealthily: 蔫蔫兒的, 蔫不咭兒 silently, quietly; 蔫溜兒 escape stealthily; 蔫出溜兒的 get away stealthily.

蔫甘 *nian'gan*, adj., good-natured and gentle.
蔫拱兒 *nianguung'l*, v.t., instigate or incite secretly.
蔫土匪 *niantufeei*, n., sly hypocrite, honest-faced crook (also 蔫頭匪類).

萼 20A.50-4

eh.

[Var. 蕚]

N. Calyx of flower: 花萼.

葛 20A.50-4

ger.

N. (1)(Bot.) the *ke* hemp, *Pueraria Thunbergiana*: 葛布 a coarse, yellowish hemp cloth; 葛巾 a kerchief made of such cloth; 葛衣 a dress made of such cloth; 葛籐 creepers, tendrils, (fig.) complications, difficulties; 瓜葛 creeping vines, (fig.) complicated relations; 糾葛 quarrels, disputes. (2) A surname.

驀 20A.50-4

moh.

V. t. (AC) to mount a horse.

Adj. (AC) Atop.

Adv. Suddenly, see 驀然, 驀地 *-rarn, -dih* ↓.

驀然, 驀地 *mohrarn, -dih*, adv., (MC) suddenly.

莓 20A.50-4

meir.

[Var. of 苺, 20A.50 ↓]

募 20A.50-4

muh.

V. t. Enlist (soldiers): 募兵, 招募 try to enlist soldiers; 募捐 raise (funds); 募役 enlist labor, or military force.

募化 *muhhuah*, v. i., collect contributions for monastery (also 化緣).
募捐 *muhjyuan*, v. i., raise (funds).
募緣 *muhyuarn*, v. i., see *-huah* ↑.

芎 20A.50-5

chyung (also *chyurng*).

芎藭 *chyungchyurng*, n., a Chin. herb, *Conioselinum univitatum.*

蒻 20A.50-5

ruoh.

N. A water plant.

芳 20A.50-6

fang.

N. Perfume, good name: 流芳百世 leave a good name for posterity.

Adj. (1) Perfumed: 芳味, 芳香 fragrance; see 芳草, 芳蘭 *-tsaau, -larn* ↓; 芳辰 beautiful day, morning. (2) In court. phrr., more nearly akin to Eng. "elegant," "esteemed": 芳儀, 芳範 your esteemed presence; 芳翰, 芳札 your esteemed letter; 芳蹤 your whereabouts. (3) (Court. & litr.) reference to things connected with ladies: 芳名 your (her) name; 芳齡 your (her) age; 芳心已碎 lady's heart is broken; 得親芳澤 be admitted to lady's intimate presence, bodily contact; 芳卿 elegant address to ladies (very litr.).

芳菲 *fangfei*, adj., (LL) fragrant.
芳馥 *fangfuh*, adj., ditto.
芳華 *fanghuar*, adj. & n., young, blooming years.
芳蘭 *fanglarn*, phr., fragrant orchid, symbolic of gentleman's beautiful character.
芳香 *fangshiang*, adj., & n., fragrant, -ce.
芳草 *fangtsaau*, n., scented flowers, (LL) symbol of righteous gentlemen.

蒡 20A.50-6

bahng.

N. See 牛蒡 10.10.

蒟 20A.50-6

jyuu.

N. (1) 蒟蒻 (bot.) the elephant's foot, *Amorphaphalus konjac.* (2) 蒟醬 the betel pepper.

藹 20A.50-6

aai.

Adj. (1) Luxuriant. (2) Gentle, easy to approach.

藹藹 *air-aai*, adj., (LL) luxuriant (forest), numerous (guests).
藹甘 *aai'gan*, adj., sweet and pleasant in manner of speech.
藹和 *aai'he*, adj., gentle, amiable.
藹然 *aairarn*, adj., ditto.

薦 20A.50-6

jiahn.

N. (1) Feed, fodder. (2) A straw mattress. (3) Food and wine offered as sacrifice: 薦羞 *-shiou* ↓.

V. t. (1) To sacrifice to the gods: 薦酒 *-jioou* ↓. (2) Recommend for service: 薦舉 *-jyuu*, 薦拔 *-bar* ↓; 薦賢 recommend good and able men; 舉薦 nominate for appointment; 推薦 recommend for employment; 自薦 recommend oneself.

Adv. Repeatedly=饑饉薦 (or 荐) 臻 famine came repeatedly.

薦拔 *jiahnbar*, v. t., select and recommend for official preferment.
薦骨 *jiahn-guu*, n., (physiol.) the sacrum, sacral vertebrae.
薦章 *jiahnjang*, n., a memorial to the throne recommending s.o. for official preferment.
薦枕席 *jiahn jeenshir*, phr., (of woman) to sleep with, become a wife or concubine to (a man).
薦酒 *jiahn-jioou*, v. i., to offer wine to the gods or departed ancestors.
薦擢 *jiahnjuor*, v. t., recommend for official service.
薦主 *jiahnjuu*, n., an employment agent.
薦居 *jiahn-jyu*, v. i., (of pastoral people) migrate from place to place in search of water and grass.
薦舉 *jiahnjyuu*, v. t., recommend for promotion.
薦派 *jiahnpaih*, v. t., recommend for employment.
薦任 *jiahnrehn*, v. t., (of low-ranking officials) be appointed upon recommendation by a minister.
薦新 *jiahnshin*, (1) n., a seasonal sacrifice in which new products of the earth are offered to the gods or departed ancestors; (2)

v. i., make such sacrifice.

薦羞 *jiahnshiou*, n., offer of food and wine to the gods or departed ancestors.

薦頭 *jiahntour*, n., an employment agent: 薦頭行 an employment agency.

薦引 *jiahnyiin*, v. t., see *-jyuu* ↑.

藭 20A.50-6

chyurng.

N. See 芎ᴬ藭 20A.50.

蕩 20A.50-6

dahng.

V. i. & t. (1) To waft, drift over water: 蕩船 to drift or sit in rowboat; 蕩漾 *-yahng* ↓; hence be agitated: 震蕩, 搖蕩; be shaky: 心蕩, 蕩氣廻腸 agitated in mind; drift away; 蕩析, 蕩產 whittle away family fortune, become bankrupt; 蕩沒 be submerged. (2) To wash away: 蕩滌. (3) Subdue, quell rebellion: 掃蕩, 蕩平, 蕩寇 suppress rebels.

Adj. (1) (AC) great, vast, plain: 蕩蕩 *-dahng* ↓. (2) Dissolute, licentious: 蕩檢踰閑 licentious in conduct; 蕩子, 蕩婦 *-tzyy*, *-fuh* ↓.

蕩產 *dahngchaan*, v.i., become bankrupt.

蕩蕩 *dahngdahng*, adj., (AC) vast, great, straight: 君子坦蕩蕩 a gentleman is calm and poised; 蕩蕩悠悠 drift along.

蕩滌 *dahngdir*, v. t., cleanse, wash away.

蕩婦 *dahngfuh*, n., dissolute woman.

蕩平 *dahngpirng*, v. t., quell (rebellion).

蕩然 *dahngrarn*, adj., as in 蕩然無存 all gone, dissipated.

蕩析 *dahngshi*, v.i., become separated (of family, friends).

蕩子 *dahngtzyy*, n., vagabond, a drifter.

蕩漾 *dahngyahng*, v.i., drift along; be agitated.

劳 20A.50-6

laur, *lauh*.

[Abbr. of 勞 91.50]

芬 20A.50-8

fen.

[Cogn. 芳; var. of 紛 93B.50.]

Adj. (LL) fragrant, of delicate aroma.

芬芳 *fenfang*, adj., fragrant.

芬菲 *fenfei*, adj., (flowers) of beautiful scent.

芬芬 *fenfen*, adj., fragrant, scented: confusingly abundant.

芬馥 *fenfuh*, adj., scented, rich in fragrance.

芬華 *fenhuar*, adj., blooming, beautiful.

芬郁 *fenyuh*, adj., richly scented.

蓊 20A.50-8

weeng.

Adj. Thick, fast-growing (vegetation).

莠 20A.50-9

yoou (also *youh*).

N. Weeds, tares; (fig.) the undesirable elements: 良莠不齊 (of a group) uneven, some good and some bad.

荔 20A.50-9

lih.

荔枝 *lihjy* (-'*jy*), n., (bot.) Litchi, a subtropical fruit of South China.

苏 20A.50-9

su.

[Abbr. of 蘇 20A.01]

蔦 20A.50-9

niaau.

蔦蘿 *niaauluor*, (1) n., (bot.) *Quamoclit vulgaris*; (2) n., 蔦與女蘿 *Ribes ambiguum* and *Usnea plicata*; (fig.) brothers, sisters, and other relatives interrelated and dependent upon one another.

蘤 20A.50-9

huar.

[Arch. of 花 20A.70]

莓 20A.50-9

meir.

N. 草莓 (*tsaaumeir*) strawberry, blackberry, etc.

莓苔 *meirtair*, n., moss, lichen.

芍 苟 苟 荀 菊 葡 蔔 葯 芦 爇 蘸

芍 20A.50-9

shaur (re. pr. *shuoh*)

N. 芍藥 *shauryauh* (also *-'yau*), re. pr. *shuohyueh*, a flower plant whose flower resembles the peony (牡丹) in color and size, *Paeonia albiflora*.

苟 20A.50-9

goou.

N. A surname.

Adj. Negligent, frivolous, careless, heedless: 苟且 *-chiee* ↓; 一絲不苟 meticulously attentive; 不苟言笑 discreet in speech and manner.

Adv. (1) Just, merely, barely: 苟全性命 barely manage to survive, remain alive; 苟延殘喘 just manage, to remain alive for a little while to prolong one's feeble existence, to eke out a meagre life. (2) Indiscriminately: 苟且, 苟得, 苟取 *-chiee, -der, -chyuu* ↓.

Conj. If, if indeed: 苟非其人 if it's not the right man; 苟能如此 if it could be so; 苟志於仁矣 (AC) if indeed one is set on the pursuit of manhood; 苟不然 if it is not so; 苟非 if it were not that . . ., unless there be.

苟安 *goou-an*, v.i., (=苟且偷安) live in a fool's paradise, seek temporary peace.

苟且 *gourchiee*, adj., (1) negligent, careless (in work); (2) disregarding principles, temporizing: 苟且偷生 live on just for sake of remaining alive 苟且偷安 see *-an* ↑; (3) lax in morals, see *-her* ↓.

苟取 *gourchyuu*, adj., unscrupulous in accepting gifts, benefits.

苟得 *goouder*, n., illicit gains: 臨財勿苟得 be careful where the money comes from.

苟合 *goouher*, v.i., (1) to ally oneself for the sake of convenience; (2) have illicit sexual relations.

苟活 *goouhuor*, v.i., just to remain alive at the sacrifice of principles or honor.

苟簡 *gourjiaan*, adj., slipshod.

苟免 *gourmiaan*, v.t., evade: 臨難勿苟免 do not compromise when confronted with personal danger.

苟存 *gootsurn*, v.i., just manage to live an animal existence.

苟同 *goouturng*, v.i., agree for agreement's sake: 不敢苟同 dare not agree with you in such a serious matter.

荀 20A.50-9

shyurn.

N. A surname.

萄 20A.50-9

taur.

N. See 葡^Δ萄 20A.50 ↓.

菊 20A.50-9

jyur.

N. The chrysanthemum.

葡 20A.50-9

pur.

葡萄 *purtaur* (also *pur'tau*), n., grapes; 葡萄乾 raisin; 葡萄酒 port wine; 葡萄糖 glucose.

葡萄牙 *Purtauryar*, n., Portugal.

蔔 20A.50-9

bor.

N. See 蘿^Δ蔔 20A.11.

葯 20A.50-9

yauh (also *yueh*).

[Pop. of 藥 medicine, 20A.01]

§ 20A.52 (廾/尸)

芦 20A.52-6

lur.

[Abbr. of 蘆 20A.30]

§ 20A.63 (廾/丶)

爇 20A.63-1

ruoh (also *reh*).

V. t. Set fire to, burn.

蘸 20A.63-3

jahn.

[Related 沾 63A.40; dist. 醮

亅	小	⺊	十	土	ナ	廾	㇄⺊	丨	一	丅	フ	口	区	冈	㇕	厂	尸	亠	广	宀	丶	乚	弋	心	八	人	乂	一	乛	ノ	𠂉	く
00	01	02	10	11	12	20	21	22	30	31	32	40	41	42	50	51	52	60	61	62	63	70	71	72	80	81	82	83	90	91	92	93

31C.63]

V. t. To dip s. t. in liquid.

蒸 20A.63-3

jeng.

N. (1) (AC) 以薪以蒸 with firewood and kindling. (2) U. f. 烝 (AC) winter sacrifice.

V. t. To steam (rice, bread, chicken, etc.).

Adj. U. f. 烝 many (people).

蒸汽(氣) *jengchih*, n., steam, vapor.
蒸發 *jengfa*, v.i. & t., evaporate, ferment with heat.
蒸蒸 *jengjeng*, adv., as in 蒸蒸日上 (of developing industry, scholarship) make rapid progress.
蒸餾 *jengliouh*, v. t., to distil; 蒸餾水 distilled water.
蒸籠 *jengluung* (or *lurng*), n., a bamboo case used for steaming food; double-boiler.
蒸民 *jengmirn*, n., (AC) the common people.
蒸溽 *jengruh*, adj., humid and hot (summer days).
蒸庶 *jengshuh*, n., see *-mirn*↑.
蒸暑 *jengshuu*, n., steaming hot summer.
蒸食 *jengshyr*, n., steamed food (rolls, 包子 etc.).
蒸騰 *jengterng*, v. i., (of vapor) go up.
蒸鬱 *jengyuh*, adj., damp, soggy, muggy.

菸 20A.63-6

yan.

[Var. of 烟 91D.41 in 菸岬, 菸葉]

蔗 20A.63-6

jeh.

N. Sugar cane: 甘蔗 ditto; 蔗汁 sugar cane juice; 蔗糖 cane sugar; 蔗酒 wine made from fermented sugar cane juice.

苓 20A.63-8

lirng.

[Usu. wr. 苓]

苓耳 *lirngeel*, n., (bot.) the cocklebur, *Xanthium strumarium* (also called 卷耳).

薰 20A.63-9

shyun.

[More commonly used than var. 燻 90.63]

N. An aromatic plant.

V. t. To smoke(d) (fish, meat); (fig.) to exert slow, transforming influence, like processing of curing meat: 薰陶, 薰染 *-taur*, *-raan*↓; 利慾薰心 mind overcome by greed.

Adj. Mild: 薰風 gentle warm breeze, *-feng*↓.

薰風 *shyunfeng*, n., (AC) influence of benign government.
薰腐 *shyunfuu*, n., punishment by castration, see 腐△刑 61.42.
薰蒸 *shyunjeng*, v. t., to steam (food) with special flavors.
薰沐 *shyunmuh*, v. i., to take bath and burn incense in preparation of solemn prayer.
薰染 *shyunraan*, v. t., to stain, to color; (fig.) to form habits or influence character by environment or example: 爲風俗所薰染.
薰陶 *shyuntaur*, v. t., to transform character by daily example, like the slow influence of curing meat.
薰草 *shyuntsaau*, n., (bot.) an aromatic grass, *Coumarouna odorata* (common name: 佩蘭).

蕉 20A.63-9

jiau.

N. (1) The banana: 芭蕉, 香蕉 bananas. (2) Untreated hemp. (3) The plantain.

蕉布 *jiaubuh*, n., linen made from the fibers of hemp.
蕉葛 *jiauger*, n., linen made from the fibers of the plantain.
蕉扇 *jiaushahn*, n., a palm leaf fan.
蕉葉 *jiauyeh*, n., (1) plantain leaves; (2) a shallow wineglass.

蕪 20A.63-9

wur.

Adj. Gone to seed, shabby: 荒蕪 ditto, unattended to; 蕪穢, 蕪雜 *-hueih*, *-tzar*↓.

蕪穢 *wurhueih*, adj., (garden) unattended to, gone to seed.
蕪菁 *wurjing*, n., a vegetable with bulbous root like turnip, *Brassica campestris*.
蕪雜 *wurtzar*, adj., untidy, uncultivated (garden), good and bad mixed together.

§ 20A.70 (卄/匕)

菢 20A.70-1

bauh.

V. i. (AC) (of bird) sit on eggs.

蕘 20A.70-1

raur.

N. (1) Firewood: 芻蕘 a woodcutter. (2) 蕘花 (bot.) *Wisktroemia japonica*. (3) (Bot.) the bird rape or rape turnip, *Brassica campestris*.

菴 20A.70-1

an.

[Var. of 庵 61.70]

芫 20A.70-3

yuarn.

N. (Bot.) *Daphne genkwa*, a flowering plant poisonous to fish.

芫青 *yuarnching*, n., (zoo.) *Lytta vesicatoria*, a beetle—dried and used as med.

芫花 *yuarnhua*, n., see N.↑.

芫荽 *yuarnsuei* (-'*suei*), n., coriander, a spice (also called 胡荽, 香菜).

蔬 20A.70-3

shu (also *su*).

N. Vegetable(s): 菜蔬 ditto; 蔬菜 *-tsaih*↓; 蔬飯, 蔬食 *-fahn*, *-shyr*↓; 蔬糲 *-lih*↓; 蔬果 vegetable and fruit.

蔬飯 *shu-fahn*, n., see *-tsaih*↓.

蔬糲 *shulih*, n., coarse rice and vegetable for meal.

蔬食 *shushyr*, n., meal with vegetable, but no meat.

蔬菜 *shutsaih*, n., vegetables.

莧 20A.70-4

shiahn.

N. (Bot.) the amaranth (red, white, purple, etc.), a vegetable; 馬齒莧 purslane.

甍 20A.70-4

merng.

N. Rafters under the roof: 甍棟 rafters and beams.

薨 20A.70-4

hung.

V. i. (AC) to die (usu. only of the feudal princes).

Adj. 薨薨 buzzing sound of flies, etc.

芃 20A.70-4

perng.

芃芃 *perngperng*, adj., luxuriant (of grass), (AC var. of 蓬蓬).

菟 20A.70-5

tuh.

[Var. 兔]

N. (Bot.) dodder.

菟裘 *tuhchiour*, n., (AC) name of town; allu. serves as reference to place of retirement from office.

菟葵 *tuhkueir*, n., (1) (bot.) the winter aconite; (2) (zoo.) the sea anemone.

菟絲子 *tuhsy(tz)*, n., (bot.) dodder, *Cuscuta japonica*.

芑 20A.70-5

chii.

芑實 *chiishyr*, n., (Chin. med.), Job's-tears, *Coix lacryma*.

芑菜 *chiitsaih*, n., (Chin. med.) *Rehmannia lutea* (=地黃).

芭 20A.70-5

ba.

N. A fragrant plant; rush.

芭蕉 *bajiau*, n., banana; 芭蕉布 cloth made of banana fibres; 芭蕉扇, 芭蕉葉(兒) palm leaf fan, cf. 蒲△葵 20A.42.

芭蕾舞 *baleir-wuu*, n., ballet; 芭蕾女角 ballerina.

芭籬 *balir*, n., (var. 笆籬, 芭犂, 芭黎) hedgerow of underbrush or bamboo, also 籬笆.

芭芒 *bamarng*, n., plantain, used in hedges.

芭茅 *bamaur*, n., see *-marng*↑.

芭棚 *baperng*, n., mat shed.

荒 20A.70-6

huang.

N. A desert, wasteland: 八荒 the border lands; 開荒, 拓荒 open up primitive place; 大荒 a big waste-

蕘 菴 芫 蔬 莧 甍 薨 芃 菟 芑 芭 荒

亅	小	⺊	十	土	ナ	卄	㇄丨	丨	一	丁	フ	口	区	冈	冂	厂	尸	亠	广	宀	丶	乚	弋	心	八	人	乂	⺈	一	丿	⺊	く
00	01	02	10	11	12	20	21	22	30	31	32	40	41	42	50	51	52	60	61	62	63	70	71	72	80	81	82	83	90	91	92	93

land; 荒地, 荒野 *-dih, -yee*↓.

V.t. To abandon, neglect (one's garden): 荒廢學業 neglect one's studies.

Adj. (1) Lean, famine (year): 荒年 *-niarn*↓. (2) Fantastic, absurd: 荒誕, 荒謬, 荒唐 *-dahn, -miouh, -tarng*↓.

荒誕 *huangdahn*, adj., fantastic, unbelievable, absurd (idea, theory): 荒誕不經 ditto.
荒地 *huang-dih*, n., a wasteland.
荒廢 *huangfeih*, adj., neglected (estate, garden, studies).
荒郊 *huangjiau*, n., wild countryside.
荒涼 *huangliarng* (-*'liang*), adj., desolate.
荒謬 *huangmiouh*, adj., absurd (statement) (also pr. -*'niouh*): 荒謬絕倫 absolutely preposterous.
荒年 *huang-niarn*, n., a famine year.
荒僻 *huangpih*, adj., deserted, out-of-the-way (district).
荒疏 *huangshu*, adj., neglected.
荒唐 *huangtarng*, adj., (1) grossly exaggerated; (2) licentious, on a spree.
荒蕪 *huangwur*, adj., overgrown with underbrush.
荒野 *huangyee*, n., a deserted or wild countryside.
荒淫 *huangyirn*, adj., given to sexual pleasures.

蘢 20A.70-6

lurng.

蘢葱 *lurngtsung*, adj., (of wood) luxuriant and green.

莞 20A.70-6

waan (**guan, *wan*).

N. (1) (**guan*) (Bot.) a long-stemmed water grass, *Scirpus lacustris*. (2) U. f. 豌 the garden pea. (3) (**guan*) A surname.

Adv. 莞爾而笑 give a soft smile.

蔻 20A.70-6

kouh.

N. 豆蔻 (荳蔻) cardamon, see 蔻仁 *-rern*↓; 豆蔻年華 an adolescent girl, sweet sixteen.

蔻丹 *kouhdan*, n., nail polish.
蔻仁 *kouhrern*, n., nutmeg, cardamon seeds.

范 20A.70-6

fahn.

N. A surname (sometimes u. f. 範 92A.70).

芼 20A.70-9

mauh.

N. (AC) a vegetable: 芼羹 a vegetable soup.

V. t. (AC) to pick (flower, vegetable).

藐 20A.70-9

miaau.
[Cogn. 渺]

V. t. Disregard, ignore, look down upon: 藐法 disregard the law; 藐之 to slight a person.

Adj. Very small; small and distant, cf. 眇 41B.91; 渺 63A.91.

藐忽 *miaauhu*, v. t., disregard.
藐小 *miaurshiaau*, adj., very small.
藐視 *miaau-shyh*, v. t., look down upon (person); disregard (laws, regulations).

花 20A.70-9

hua.

N. (1) Flower: 鮮花 fresh flowers; 鳥語花香 birds' twitter and fragrance of flowers—an idyllic scene; 花圃, 花盆 *-puu, -pern*↓; 花店 florist; 花市 flower market; 開花 to flower, to blossom; 花容月貌, 花貌, 花顏 beautiful face of woman; 花朝月夕 beautiful days and nights with moon and flowers; 賞花 to see and enjoy flowers; 花木, 花卉, 花草 *-muh, -hueih*^{2}*, -tsaau*↓; for pistils and stamens, calyx, pollen, stem, see 花鬚, 花苞, 花粉, 花梗 *-shyu, -bau, -feen, -geeng*↓. (2) Symbol of women: 花國, 花界 circle of courtesans; 花國 also world of flowers; 名花有主 a famous courtesan or a socially prominent beauty is married; 野草閑花 women of easy virtue, paramours; 解語花 (allu.) a beautiful and understanding woman, ("a talking flower"); 家花那有野花香 a mistress is better than a wife; 花案兒 lawsuit concerning romance or illicit love; 花柳, 花酒 *-lioou, -jioou*↓. (3) Smallpox: 天花 ditto; 種花, 種天花 vaccination. (4) Bits: 葱花 bits of onion. (5) A surname.

V.t. To spend: 花錢 to spend money; 花冤枉錢 waste money without results; 花不起 cannot afford to buy or spend; 花不來 the price is not right, does not pay; 花費, 花消 *-feih, -'shiau*↓.

Adj. (1) Flowery, floral, of many colors: 花布 *-buh*^{1}↓; 花紙 papers with designs; 花衣服 multicolored dress; 花團錦簇 company of gorgeously dressed ladies; 花枝招展 decorated headdress; 花紅

柳絲 a profusion of garden flowers or pretty ladies. (2) Pertaining to luxury, profligate: 花花世界 world of sensual pleasures, the demimonde; 花花公子 playboy; 花和尚 profligate monk; 花天酒地 world of wine and women. (3) Blurred, unclear: 眼睛花 dim-sighted; 頭昏眼花 dizzy; 眼花撩亂 dazzled (by sight of things). (4) False, flowery without substance: 花帳 false accounts; 花言巧語 flowery, deceiving words.

花瓣兒 *huabahn* (*-bah'l*), n., flower petals.

花白 *huabair*, (1) adj., (of hair) greyish-white; (2) v.t., (MC) to rebuke, use strong, rude language against (s.o.)

花苞 *haubau*, n., (bot.) calyx.

花邊 *huabian*(*-bia'l*), n., lace, lace work; 花邊新聞 news or miscellany of human interest; tidbits, news in box.

花布 *huabuh*[1], n., printed calico.

花部 *huabuh*[2], n., (in Manchu Dyn.) department of opera and folk music except 崑曲 (which is 雅部 or "literary" opera).

花茶 *huachar*, n., perfumed tea, such as 香片.

花車 *huache*, n., a decorated car in parade, a float.

花扦兒 *huachia'l* n., cut flowers for vase.

花鎗 *huachiang*[1], n., a short spear.

花腔(兒) *huachiang*[2]*('l)*, n., (1) opera airs with long-drawn passages; (2) (mus.) coloratura.

花牆(兒)(子) *huachiarng('l)('tz)*, n., crenelated wall.

花青 *huaching*, n., indigo, a painting color.

花旗 *huachir*, n., the United States of America ("flowery flag"); 花旗橘子 American ("Sunkist") oranges; 花旗鈔票 American dollar bill, greenbacks.

花船 *huachuarn*, n., decorated houseboat with women entertainers.

花池子 *huachyrtz*, n., see *-puu* ↓.

花圈 *huachyuan*, n., a (1) wreath; (2) garland.

花拳 *huachyuarn*, n., shadow-boxing, showy boxing of no practical use.

花搭着 *hua'daje*, adj., checkered, also 花花搭搭 variegated.

花旦 *huadahn*, n., (Peking opera) a role portraying young, pretty woman.

花燈 *huadeng*, n., decorative paper lantern.

花鈿 *huadiahn*, n., hair decorations of women.

花彫 *huadiau*, n., first-class Shaoshing 紹興 wine.

花朵 *huaduoo*, n., a blossom; a cluster of flowers.

花房 *huafarng*, n., greenhouse, conservatory.

花粉 *huafeen*, n., (1) pollen; (2) cosmetics; 花粉錢 pin money.

花費 *huafeih*, v.i. & t. & n., to spend money, to cost; the cost.

花崗石 *huagaang-shyr*, n., granite.

花梗(兒) *huageeng('l)*, n., a flower stalk, or peduncle.

花咕朵(兒) *huagu'duo('l)*, n., (coll.) flower bud.

花瓜 *huagua*, n., cucumber, esp. for pickling; chopped-up appearance: 臉上打得花瓜似的 face was all cut up.

花冠 *huaguan*, n., (1) (bot.) the corolla; (2) a garland.

花鼓(戲) *huaguu(shih)*, n., a form of monologue entertainment, narrating a story to the accompaniment of a small drum.

花活 *huahour*, n., (1) carpenter's fine carving; (2) 耍花活 to swindle.

花黃 *huahuarng*, n., an anc. cosmetic, from yellow flowers, rubbed on women's forehead.

花會 *huahueih*[1], n., (1) a popular game of numbers for gambling; (2) a flower fair.

花卉 *huahueih*[2], n., vegetation in gen.; flowers, also as special subject of painting.

花戶 *huahuh*, n., a florist.

花紅 *huahurng*, n., (1) tips, gratuities; (2) bonus.

花障(兒) *huajahng('l)*, n., a hedge-row with flowers.

花枝(兒) *huaje'l*, n., a flower twig: 長得花枝兒似的 has grown up as pretty as flower.

花甲 *huajiaa*, n., the cycle of sixty years: 年逾花甲 over sixty years of age.

花(兒)匠 *hua('l)jiahng*, n., horticulturist, gardener.

花箋 *huajian*, n., letter paper with designs in lighter shade.

花椒 *huajiau*, n., wild pepper grown in West China.

花轎 *hua-jiauh*, n., decorated wedding sedan chair.

花街 *hua-jie*, n., as in 花街柳巷 redlight district.

花界 *hua-jieh*, n., the world of singsong girls.

花鏡 *huajihng*, n., eyeglasses for old people (from 眼花 dimmed eyesight).

花酒 *huajioou*, n., dinner parties with girl entertainers; also wine made from flowers.

花招(兒) *huajuau('l)*, n., showy fight on stage (also 花着兒).

花燭 *huajur*, n., (1) wedding: 花燭之夜 wedding night; 洞房花燭夜 ditto; 花燭夫妻 legally married couples; (2) fancy candles for celebration.

花種兒 *huajuung'l*, n., flower seeds.

花捲(兒) *huajyuaa('l)*, n., a roll (fancy bread).

花捐 *hua-jyuan*, n., tax on sing-song houses.

花棵(兒)(子) *huake('l)('tz)*, n., a small flowering plant, a sapling.

花魁 *huakueir*, n., (1) the winter plum (梅當花魁); (2) (MC) the most popular courtesan.

花兒洞子 *hualduhng'tz*, n., a hothouse.

花兒毒 *hualdur*, n., poison from smallpox (天花).

花籃(兒) *hualarn*(*-lar'l*), n., floral basket (used as tribute on occasions); a flower basket.

花郎 *hualarng*, n., (MC) a male beggar.

花蕾 *hualeir*, n., flower bud.

花臉 *hualiaan*, n., (Chin. opera) a male character (＝淨): 大花臉

principal male character; 二花臉 supporting male character; 小花臉 clown (names from masks).

花柳 *hualioou*, n., ("flowers and willows") prostitutes; 殘花敗柳 a hag; 花街柳巷 see *-jie*↑; 花柳病 venereal disease.

花梨木 *hualir-muh*, n., rosewood.

花翎 *halirng*, n., (Manchu Dyn.) peacock feathers on official caps.

花露水 *hualuh shueei*, n., *eau de cologne*, a perfumed toilet water, essence of flowers.

花蝱 *huamerng*, n., a small bee-like insect, *Eristalis tenax*.

花面 *huamiahn*, n., see *-liaan*↑.

花蜜 *huamih*, n., honey.

花名 *huamirng*, n., (formerly, in official documents) person's legal name; 花名冊 list of names; 花名兒 (a) name of flower; (b) professional name of courtesan.

花木 *huamuh*, n., flowers and trees in gen.

花鳥 *hua-niaau*, n., flowers and birds, a special branch in Chin. painting.

花娘 *huaniarng*, n., (MC) a prostitute.

花炮 *huapauh*, n., fireworks.

花盆 *huapern*, n., flowerpot.

花瓶(兒) *huapirng('l)*, n., flower vase; (facet.) a girl secretary in office kept for her looks rather than work.

花圃 *huapuu*, n., a flower nusery.

花蕊 *huarueei*, n., the pistils and stamens of a flower; a flower.

花衫 *huashan*, n., (Chin. opera) a female role, including 青衣, 花旦.

花稍 *hua'shau*, adj., (1) (coll.) pretty; (2) romantic; fond of opposite sex.

花生 *huasheng*, n., peanut: 花生米, 花生仁 meat of peanut; 花生油 peanut oil; 花生糖 peanut bar or candy.

花神 *huashern*, n., the Goddess of Flowers.

花項 *huashiahng*, n., item of expense: 沒有甚麼花項, 要不了這麼多錢 there is no occasion to spend; I don't need so much money.

花消 *hua'shiau*, n., expenses (see V. t.↑).

花心兒 *huashie'l*, n., center of flower.

花信 *huashihn*, n., (1) news of certain flowers in bloom; (2) 花信之年 (of women) twenty-four years of age.

花事 *huashyh*, n., the business of planting, enjoying flowers in spring.

花石 *huashyr*, n., marble.

花鬚 *huashyu*, n., pistils and stamens.

花序 *huashyuh*[1], n., (bot.) inflorescence, the order of development of a flower.

花絮 *huashyuh*[2], n., topics for gossip, human interest side lights, also 花花絮絮 different side lights.

花壇 *huatarn*[1], n., flower terrace.

花罈(兒) *huatarn*[2] *(-tar'l)*, n., an acrobatic show featuring the skillful manipulation of earthen pots.

花廳(兒) *huating('l)*, n., parlor.

花莛兒 *huatirng'l*, n., flower stalk.

花頭 *hua'tou*, n., trumped-up tricks: 出花頭 resort to trickery, cf. *-yahng*↓; 花頭兒 cut flower without long stem and leaves.

花草 *huatsaau*, n., flowers and grass in gen., also such paintings.

花叢 *huatsurng*, n., a flower bush.

花托 *huatuo*, n., (bot.) floral receptacle, the torus.

花子 *hua'tz*, n., (coll.) beggar (also 叫化子).

花籽兒 *huatzee'l*, n., flower seeds.

花字兒 *huatzeh'l*, n., added words in opera arias for sound effect.

花王 *huawarng*, n., "the king of flowers," the peony (牡丹).

花紋 *huawern*, n., pattern or texture of cloth; wood grain.

花眼 *huayaan*, adj., dimmed vision of old people, farsighted, hypermetropia.

花樣 *huayahng*, n., pattern, design (of dress): 花樣翻新 innovations of style; ways and forms in performance; 許多花樣 many variations; 不知又要弄出甚麼花樣 do not know what next he will do.

花秧兒 *huayang'l*, n., flower sapling.

花押 *huayar*, n., signature in contracts, etc.

花椰菜 *huayertsaih*, n., cauliflower.

花園 *huayuarn*, n., garden, also 花苑 *-yuaan*.

芄 20A.70–9

warn.

芄蘭 *warnlarn*, n., (bot.) name of plant, *Metaplexis stauntoni*.

葩 20A.70–9

pa.

N. Flower: 葩卉＝花卉; 葩實 flower seeds.

Adj. (AC) in bloom; flowering, blossoming.

蓖 20A.70–9

bih.

蓖麻 *bihmar*, n., (bot.) castor oil plant, *Ricinus communis*, 蓖麻油 castor oil.

蒐 20A.70–9

sou.

V. t. (1) To collect (related 搜): see compp.↓. (2) (AC) to hold spring or autumn hunt.

蒐集 *soujir*, v. t., to collect (anecdotes, proofs, samples).

蒐羅 *souluor (-'luo)*, v. i., ditto.

蒐索 *sousuoo*, v. t., to search (also wr. 搜).

苞 20A.70-9

bau.

N. (1) A kind of rush, used for mats. (2) The calyx of a flower: 含苞未放 in early puberty, still a virgin (in calyx); 開苞 deflorate (virgin); to blossom.

Adj. (AC) luxurant, thick (growth): 竹苞松茂 phr., symbolizing prosperity of family.

苞蟲 *bauchurng*, n., insect parasite which hurts rice plant.
苞苴 *baujyu*, n., bribery.
苞稂 *baularng*, n., (AC) wild bush, undergrowth.
苞木 *baumuh*, n., bamboo.
苞桑 *bausang*, adj., (AC) firmly bound.
苞筍 *bausuun*, n., one kind of bamboo shoot (=冬筍).

苑 20A.70-9

yuahn (**yuarn*)

N. (1) (LL) mansion, garden home: 宮苑 palace and garden. (2) A collection of art, writing: 文苑 literature as a branch of writing; 藝苑 the fine arts as a creative field. (3) (**yuarn*) A surname.

蒓 20A.70-9

churn.
[Var. of 蓴 20A.00]

§ 20A.71 (廾/弋)

蕺 20A.71-4

jir.

N. 蕺菜 (bot.) a grass, *Houttuynia cordata.*

蔑 20A.71-4

mieh.
[Dist. 篾 92A.71]

V. t. To belittle: 侮蔑 treat cheaply, insult.

Adj. Little, small: 蔑賤 lowly.

Adv. (AC) not: 蔑以 (=無以): 蔑以復加 could not be surpassed.

蔑棄 *mieh-chih*, n., abandon, cast off, disregard.
蔑視 *mieh-shyh*, v. t., to disregard, ignore (fact, person).

茂 20A.71-7

mouh (or *mauh*).

Adj. (1) Luxuriant, thick (forest, leaves): 茂林修竹 thick forest and tall bamboos. (2) Talented: see 茂才 *-tsair* ↓.

茂密 *mouhmih*, adj., thick, heavy (growth of trees); handsome, brilliant (style, thought, content).
茂年 *mouh-niarn*, n., vigorous years, youth.
茂盛 *mouhshehng*, adj., luxuriant, plentiful (foliage, etc.).
茂才 *mouh-tsair*, n., (1) talented scholar; (2) synonoym for 秀ᐞ才 90.50, B. A. degree.

葳 20A.71-7

wei.

葳蕤 *weirueir*, (1) adj., (plants) hanging down in clusters; (2) n., (bot.) Solomon's seal, *Polygonatum officinale.*

蒇 20A.71-7

chaan.

V.i. & t. See comp.↓

蒇事 *chaanshyh*, v.i., to finish, be completed.

藏 20A.71-7

tsarng (**tzahng*).

N. (**tzahng*) (1) Thibet (Tibet) (西藏): 藏葡萄 Tibetan grapes; 藏青果 Tibetan olives; 藏藍, 藏青 *-larn, -ching* ↓. (2) A treasure vault: 庫藏, 寶藏 ditto. (3) Collection of Buddhist or Taoist sutras: 大藏, 大藏經 or 藏經 the *Tripitaka*, the whole collection of Budd. sutras; 三藏法師, see 玄ᐞ奘 60.93. (4) U.f. 臟 42A.71, entrails.

V.t. (1) To hide, conceal. (2) To keep a collection of (books); to keep (beautiful girls); nurse (hatred, etc.): 藏嬌, 藏怒 *-jiau, -nuh*↓.

藏青 **tzahngching*, adj., (Tibetan) deep dark blue.

藏 茋 莪 蕙 惹 葸 薏 芯 蕊

藏鋒 *tsarng-feng*, v.i., (1) (callig.) to conceal brush point in writing by turning up before descent, turning right before left, etc.; (2) to sheathe one's talent; refrain from outspoken attack.

藏鉤 *tsarng-gou*, n., an ancient game to guess in whose hand an object is.

藏奸 *tsarng-jian*, v.i., to conceal a traitor.

藏嬌 *tsarng-jiau*, phr., 金屋藏嬌 live with one's young wife in a plush apartment, keep a mistress in a love nest.

藏拙 *tsarng-juor*, v.i., (court.) conceal my weakness, lack of talent, etc.

藏藍 **tzahnglarn*, adj., Tibetan blue, slightly purplish.

藏矇歌兒 *tsarngmerngee'l*, n., game of hide-and-seek (also 藏矇格兒, 藏貓兒).

藏怒 *tsarng-nuh*, v.i., harbor a hatred, anger.

藏身 *tsarng-shen*, v.i., to hide oneself.

藏書 *tsarngshu*, (1) v.i., to collect books; (2) n., person's collection of books; 藏書樓 library.

藏私 *tsarngsy*, v.i., to hide s.t. illegally.

藏掖(兒) *tsarngye(-ye'l)*, n., (coll.) s.t. hidden; hiding place.

茋 20A.71-9

chir.

N. See 黃^A茋 20.80

莪 20A.71-9

er.

莪蒿 *erhau*, n., (bot.) a species of artemisia.

§ 20A.72 (艹/心)

蕙 20A.72-1

hueih.

N. A species of orchid (oft. 蘭蕙): symbolic of purity, beauty or fragrance; 蘭質蕙心, 蕙質蘭心 pure heart and spirit.

惹 20A.72-1

ree.

V. t. Stir up, incite, tease, annoy: 惹不得 not to be taunted (vexed, annoyed, irritated); 我不敢惹他 I dare not offend him; 這個人不能惹(不好惹) this person must not be offended; 惹事 *-shyh*↓; 惹出事來 have brought trouble on one's own head; 惹是非 stir up ill will (misunderstanding); 惹是生(招)非 ditto; 惹亂子(兒) do mischief, cause trouble, commit misdemeanor (crime); 惹禍 *-huoh*↓; 惹火燒身 burn one's own fingers; 惹人笑 lay oneself open to ridicule; 惹人注意 make oneself conspicuous; 惹嫌 incur dislike, provoke disgust; 惹厭 *-yahn*↓; 惹氣, 惹怒 provoke (s.o.) to anger; 惹惱 annoy, tease, make angry; 惹不起 dare not provoke to anger, cannot be stirred up; 別惹她 don't tease (annoy, provoke) her; 惹草拈花 sow one's wild oats, have promiscuous relations with women; 引惹 incite, provoke; 招惹 tempt, allure, entice.

惹起 *rer-chii*, v. t., (1) draw (attention); (2) stir up, provoke, incite (trouble, dispute).

惹得 *ree'de*, v. t., perpetrate, incite, provoke.

惹禍 *ree-huoh*, v. i., bring calamity (misfortune) on oneself (others).

惹事 *ree-shyh*, v. i., cause trouble.

惹厭 *ree-yahn*, v. i., invite dislike (disgust, resentment).

葸 20A.72-4

shii.

Adj. Overcautious, timid, worried about small things: 畏葸 ditto.

薏 20A.72-6

yih.

N. See 薏苡 *-yii*↓.

薏米 *yihmii*, n., seed of Job's-tears, see *-yii*↓.

薏仁米 *yih'renmii*, n., ditto (also 薏仁).

薏苡 *yihyii*, n., (bot.) Job's-tears, *Coix lacryma*, also u. f. pearl barley.

芯 20A.72-6

shin (**shihn*).

N. (1) Lamp pith (=燈心草); 蠟芯兒 candle wick. (2) Tongue: 芯子 (**shihntz*); 蛇芯子 (coll.) snake's tongue; 羊芯子 lamb's tongue.

蕊 20A.72-6

rueei.

N. (1) Flower buds: 發蕊 put forth buds. (2) Reproductive organs of flowers: 雌蕊 pistil; 雄蕊 stamens; (花) 蕊兒 stamens and pistils.

Adj. (Of plants) growing in clusters.

蕊柱 *rueeijuh*, n., (bot.) a style (part of the pistil).

苾 20A.72-6

bih.

N. & adj. Fragrance, -nt: 香苾 ditto.

苾苾 *bihbih*., adj., fragrant, nice-smelling.
苾勃 *bihbor*, adj., bursting with fragrance.
苾芻 *bihchur*, n., nun, translit. of Sanskr. *bhiksuni*, (usu. wr. 比丘尼); also a fragrant plant, emblem of monastic life.

葱 20A.72-9

tsung.
[Var. 蔥]

N. Onion; scallion: 洋葱 the common onion; 胡葱 shallot (cf. 蒜 garlic).

葱白 *tsungbor*, adj., very pale green; 葱白兒 white base of onion.
葱花(兒) *tsunghua('l)*, n., chopped onions.
葱黄 *tsunghuarng*, adj., yellowish green.
葱鬍子 *tsunghurtz*, n., beard-like roots of onions, beard stud on man's face.
葱蘢 *tsunglurng*, adj., luxuriantly green.
葱綠 *tsunglyuh*, adj., pale yellowish green.
葱頭 *tsungtour*, n., the common round onion.
葱翠 *tsungtsueih*, adj., see -*lurng* ↑.
葱葱 *tsungtsung*, adj., (grass) green, luxuriant.

§ 20A.80 (艹/八)

蕡 20A.80-1

fern.

N. (AC) hemp seeds.

Adj. (AC) Abundant, bearing much fruit.

萁 20A.80-2

chir.

N. Beanstalk.

蘋 20A.80-2

pirn (**pirng*).

N. (Bot.) a flowering plant, *Marsilia quadrifolia*.

蘋果 **pirngguuo*, n., apple; 蘋果臉 --*liaan*, cheeks like an apple; 蘋果綠 --*lyuh*, color of unripe apple (green), name of type of porcelain; 蘋果酸 --*suan*, n., (chem.) malic acid.

蕢 20A.80-2

kueih.

N. (1) Edible amaranth with reddish stalks. (2) A surname.

黃 20A.80-3

huarng.
[See 20.80]

蕷 20A.80-3

yuh.

N. See 薯^Δ^蕷 20A.41.

蕻 20A.80-5

huhng.

N. See 雪^Δ^裏蕻 31D.30.

§ 20A.81 (艹/人)

蔌 20A.81-1

suh.

N. A vegetable.

Adj. 蔌蔌 soughing (wind).

芙 20A.81-1

fur.

芙蕖 *furchyur*, n., the lotus; lotus fully opened, cf. 菡^Δ^萏 20A.21.
芙蓉 *furrurng*, n., lotus; 木芙蓉 a flowering tree of the hibiscus family, also called 芙蓉; 芙蓉面 a pretty face; 芙蓉鳥 a song bird like canary(金絲雀), *Serinus canarius*; 阿芙蓉 (litr.) opium.

亅	小	⺊	十	土	𠂇	廾	𠃊	丨	一	丅	乛	口	囗	冂	乛	厂	尸	亠	广	宀	丶	乚	弋	心	八	人	乂	乀	丿	刂	𠂉	く
00	01	02	10	11	12	20	21	22	30	31	32	40	41	42	50	51	52	60	61	62	63	70	71	72	80	81	82	83	90	91	92	93

莢 荑 苡 葵 莫 蕨 蔟 蒺 茨 萩 英

莢 20A.81-1

jiar.

N. Pods of leguminous plants: 豆莢 bean pods; 皂莢 pods of the Chin. honey locust; 莢果 leguminous seeds.

荑 20A.81-1

tir (**yir*).

N. (1) (AC) sprouts (of grass). (2) Tares (var. of 稊 90A.22).

V. t. (**yir*) (AC, LL) to weed.

苡 20A.81-2

yii.

[Var. of 薏 20A.72]

葵 20A.81-3

kueir.

N. (1) The sunflower: 向日葵. (2) Any plant of the family of mallows (hollyhock, marsh mallow, okra, etc.). (3) 蒲葵 palm, Chin. fan, *Livistonis chinensis.*

葵傾 *kueir-ching*, v.i., to incline in loyalty to person, as the sunflower follows the sun's direction.
葵瓜子 *kueir-guatzyy*, n., edible sunflower seeds.
葵藿 *kueirhuoh*, n., (inferiors in self-deprecation) cheap, worthless things.
葵扇 *kueirshahn*, n., palm leaf fan.

莫 20A.81-4

moh.

N. (Rare) u. f. 暮 *muh*, late afternoon, late year.

Adv. Not, be not, do not (imperative mood, but more often subjunctive) in combination 莫不, 莫非 "might it not be" in sense of conjecture: 莫說 don't say that; 莫要這樣 do not be like this; 莫管, 莫教 (MC) do not let (s. t. happen); 莫不是, 莫不成 could it be that? unless it be (his fault); 莫過(於) nothing is better than: 學問莫過於某君 no better scholar than Mr. X; 莫大於 nothing is greater, more important than; 哀莫大於心死 the greatest pity is the death of the human heart (Mencius), see following special phrases.

莫非 *mohfei*, phr., unless it be: 莫非是他 perhaps it is he; 莫非是他錯了 perhaps it was his mistake; 普天之下, 莫非王土 all this territory belongs to the king.
莫怪 *moh guaih*, phr., it is not surprising that (the child will not eat, having eaten already): 莫怪人家這樣說你 so that is why people say this of you; 請莫怪 (modest) please do not blame me.
莫名 *moh mirng*, phr., difficult to express: 莫名其妙 (not 莫明) difficult to guess what it is all about; 感戴莫名 do not know how to express my gratitude.
莫逆 *moh-nih*, adj., in 莫逆之交 friend with complete mutual understanding.
莫若 *moh ruoh*, 莫如 *moh rur*, conj. phr., nothing better than, it would be better to: 莫如回去, 和他絕交 it is better to go home, to break relations with him; 以爲天下莫己若也 (LL) thinks he has no equal in this world.
莫須有 *moh-shyu-yoou*, phr., famous decision of collaborator 秦檜 who had the great general 岳飛 killed by announcing these three words (三字獄) "it is unnecessary" to proffer charges or prove anything.

蕨 20A.81-5

jyuer.

N. (Bot.) common bracken, female fern.

蔟 20A.81-6

tsuh.

[Var. of 簇 92A.81]

蒺 20A.81-6

jir.

N. 蒺藜 (bot.) thorns, the puncture vine.

茨 20A.81-6

tsyr.

N. (1) Thatched hut. (2) (Bot.) a grass, *Tribulus terrestris.*

V. t. (AC) to fill up with mud.

萩 20A.81-9

chiou.

N. (1) (Bot.) a kind of rush. (2) Var. of 楸 the catalpa.

英 20A.81-9

ying.

N. (1) Petals: 落英繽紛 fallen petals lie in profusion. (2) The select, the best (see Adj.): 羣英 gathering of stars, heroes, etc. (3) Short for 英格蘭 England, 英吉利 English; 英美 England and the U.S. (4) A surname.

Adj. (1) Heroic, outstanding: 英豪, 英雄 *-haur*, *-shyurng*↓; 英武 *-wuu*↓; 英挺, 英拔 *-tiing*, *-bar*↓. (2) Bright, brilliant: 英才 brilliant student; 英明, 英俊 *-mirng*, *-jyuhn*↓.

英拔 *yingbar*, adj., distinguished, outstanding (man).
英氣 *ying-chih*, n., heroic spirit, fearless courage.
英發 *yingfa*, adj., (LL) distinctive, brilliant.
英格蘭 *Yinggelarn*, n., England.
英國 *Yingguor*, n., England.
英豪 *yinghaur*, adj. & n., heroic; hero.
英華 *yinghuar*, (1) n., exuberance; (2) Anglo-Chinese (college, etc.).
英吉利 *Yingjirlih*, adj., English.
英俊 *yingjyuhn*, adj., handsome, brilliant; n., such men.
英靈 *yinglirng*, n., (1) fine spirit; atmosphere of hills and waters as affecting human character; (2) (court.) departed soul.
英髦 *yingmaur*, adj., see *-jyuhn*↑.
英美法 *Ying-Meei faa*, n., Anglo-American Law.
英明 *yingmirng*, adj., astute, wise, enlightened (ruler).
英年 *yingniarn*, n., youth.
英挺 *yingtiing*, adj., select, brilliant.
英雄 *yingshyurng* (*-'shyung*), n., hero: 英雄所見略同 great minds think alike.
英偉 *yingweei*, adj., tall and handsome.
英文 *Yingwern*, n., English.
英物 *ying-wuh*, n., (LL, rare) a genius.
英武 *yingwuu*, adj., martial (appearance, spirit).
英英 *yingying*, adj., (LL) brilliant (clouds, family), resounding (voice).
英語 *Yingyuu*, n., the English language.
英勇 *yingyuung*, adj., heroic, brave, stalwart.

荑 20A.81-9

yur.

N. See 茱^Δ^荑 20A.01.

茯 20A.81-9

fur.

茯苓 *furlirng*, n., (bot.) China Root, a large edible fungus growing on fir roots; 茯苓糕 a white delicacy made from 茯苓.

荻 20A.81-9

dir.

N. A kind of reed: 荻筆 reed stem used as pen to write on ashes.

芡 20A.81-9

chiahn.

芡粉 *chiahnfeen*, n., sauce made of a mixture of bean powder, arrowroot and caltrop.
芡實 *chiahnshyr*, n., the foxnut, *Euryale ferox*; edible seeds of this plant.

§ 20A.82 (卄/乂)

菱 20A.82-1

lirng.

N. A kind of caltrop (water chestnut) of irregular shapes with pointed ends (cf. round-shaped 荸^Δ^薺 20A.00).

菱角 *lirng'jiau*, n., caltrop; its edible nut.
菱苦土 *lirngkurtuu*, n., (min.) magnesite.
菱錳鑛 *lirngmeengkuahng*, n., (min.) rhodochrosite.
菱面體 *lirngmiahntii*, n., (math.) rhombohedron.
菱鋅鑛 *lirngshinkuahng*, n., (min.) smithsonite.
菱形 *lirngshirng*, n., (math.) rhombus.
菱鐵鑛 *lirngtieekuahng*, n., (min.) siderite.

茇 20A.82-1

bar.

N. Roots of grass (茇舍 *-sheh*, huts so covered for roof).

菽 20A.82-2

shur.

N. Beans: 菽水承歡 poor but filial (serve parents with simple meals); 不辨菽麥 ignorant of common things ("cannot tell wheat from beans").

莜 20A.82-2

chiaur.

[Var. of 蓨 20A.42]

蔽 20A.82-2

bih.

V.t. (1) (LL) Cover, spread over: 衣不蔽體 be in rags (clothing cannot cover the body); 野花蔽野 the country is covered with wild flowers; 蔽於讒 (of king) deceived by sycophant attendants; as var. of 閉 in 蔽月羞花 (of woman's beauty which "shames the flowers"). (2) Block, cloud, hide from view: 蔽月 (clouds) hide the moon; 烏雲蔽日 (fig.) bad ministers surround the emperor; 蔽風雨 shelter from wind and rain; 蔽賢 (LL) block the way of the good ministers; 物欲所蔽 (of the heart) clouded by material desires; 蒙蔽 hoodwink; 受人蒙蔽 (of ruler) kept in ignorance. (3) To sum up: 一言以蔽之 in one word.

蔽障 *bihjahng*, v.t. & n., to keep in obscurity; obstacle to faith or clear vision.

蔽塞 *bihseh*, v. t. block (understanding, channels of thinking); p.p., blocked.

藪 20A.82-2

soou.

N. (1) Jungle, thicket: 盜賊淵藪 thieves' den, lair. (2) A lake; wild country.

夔 20A.82-2

kueir.

N. (AC) a one-legged monster in fable.

夔夔 *kueirkueir*, adj., awe-struck, in fear.

夔龍 *kueirlurng*, n., an animal of lizard type in anc. bronzes.

芨 20A.82-3

jir.

N. (1) (Bot.) *Bletilla hyacinthina*, 白芨. (2) Another name for 菫草 the Chin. elder, *Sambucus javanica.*

蔓 20A.82-4

mahn (**marn*; re. pr. **wahn*).

N. Vine, ivy: 瓜蔓 (**wahn*) melon vine.

蔓青 **marn'ching*, n., (bot.) the rape-turnip.

蔓脚類 *mahnjiaau-leih*, n., (bot.) plants of the creeper type, *Cirripedia*, also 蔓生植物.

蔓延, 蔓衍 *mahnyarn, mahnyaan*, v. i., grow and spread (vine, disease, bad customs); adj., widespread, also wr. 曼, 漫.

蕞 20A.82-4

tzueih.

Adj. Little small, tiny: 蕞爾小邦 a tiny kingdom (state).

芟 20A.82-4

shan.

N. A big sickle.

V. t. To weed (grass, field), to weed out (evil, undesirable elements), cf. 刪 42S.00.

菔 20A.82-4

fur (or *bor*).

N. 萊菔 *lairfur*, turnip (var. for 蘿蔔 *luorbor*).

葭 20A.82-5

jia.

N. (1) (Bot.) a bulrush or reed. (2) (Interch. 笳) a flute.

葭莩 *jiafur*, n., (1) the membrane of a reed stem (as in reed type); (2) distant relatives (i.e., very "thin").

茭 20A.82-6

jiau.

N. (1) (Bot.) water bamboo, Indian rice, *Zizania aquatica* (also known as 菰). (2) Hay, fodder.

茭白 *jiaubair*, n., young shoots of *Zizania aquatica*.

茭米 *jiaumii*, n., Indian rice.

菠 20A.82-6

bo (*bor*).

N. 菠菜 *botsaih* (*bor-*), or 菠稜菜 *Bolerng-tsaih*, n., spinach.

艾 20A.82-8

aih (**yih*).

N. (1) Mugwort, artemisia or mint, used for cauterization or as counterirritant: 艾炷, 艾絨 *-juh, -rurng*↓. (2) Person over fifty years of age. (3) A surname.

V. i. (1) To end, be spent: 夜未艾 the night is young yet: 方興未艾 on the upward surge. (2) (AC) to nurture, protect: 保艾爾後 protect your offspring.

Adj. (1) 少艾 (AC) the young and handsome. (2) (AC) grey-haired, over fifty of age.

艾焙 *aihbeih*, c. i., to cauterize with end of artemisia, see *-juh, -rurng*↓; (fig.) (MC) 受艾焙 to suffer.
艾蒿 *aihhau*, n., (bot.) artemisia.
艾火 *aih-huoo*, n., lighted end of artemisia for cautering.
艾虎 *aih-huu*, n., formerly, a bag of mint herb for warding off infectious insects, worn on 5th day of 5th lunar month.
艾豭 *aih-jia*, n., (AC) old male pig.
艾炷 *aih-juh*, n., stick of artemisia, used for cauterizing.
艾絨(兒)(子) *aihrurng('l)('tz)*, n., tuft of artemisia, used for cauterizing and for making inkpad for Chin. seals.

蔆 20A.82-9

lerng.

N. See 菠Δ蔆 20A.82.

薇 20A.82-9

weir.

N. (1) A plant, *Osmunda regalis* var. *japonica*. (2) 薔Δ薇 20A.41.

§ 20A.83 (廾/乛)

蓮 20A.83-1

liarn.

N. (1) Lotus, water lily＝蓮花 *-hua*↓. (2) Buddha's seat and symbol of purity. (3) The bound feet: 三寸金蓮 three-inch bound feet. (4) 西番蓮 the passion-flower, dahlia.

蓮步 *liarn-buh* n., mincing steps of bound feet, from 步步蓮花 allu. 5th cen. prince whose favorite dancing girl left prints of lotus flower from her soles.
蓮房 *liarnfarng*, n., see *-perng*↓.
蓮鈎 *liarngou*, n., small bound feet with shoes turning up like a crescent.
蓮花 *liarnhua*, n., lotus flower: 蓮花池 lotus pond; 蓮花(兒)燈 lotus-shaped lantern; 蓮花白 a liqueur; 蓮花落 a popular song or melody.
蓮炬 *liarn-jyuh*, n., festive candles.
蓮蓬 *liarnperng*, n., lotus seed-pod, (fig.) a big fat person; 蓮蓬子兒 see *-tzyy*↓.
蓮肉 *liarnrouh*, n., edible lotus seed (its "meat").
蓮心 *liarnshin*, n., heart of lotus seed.
蓮實 *liarnshyr*, n., lotus seed (see *-rouh*↑).
蓮臺 *liarntair*, n., Buddha's seat in the form of lotus flower.
蓮座 *liarntzuoh*, n., see *-tair*↑.
蓮子 *liarntzyy*, n., lotus seed, a delicacy.

蘧 20A.83-2

chyur.

N. A surname.

Adj. (AC) frightened, (interch. 瞿).

蘧蘧 *chyurchyur*, adj., (1) as in (AC) 蘧蘧然周也 (waked up to find that) I am 莊周 myself, real and alive; (2) high up.
蘧廬 *chyurlur*, n., (AC) humble home, dwelling place.
蘧麥 *chyurmaih*, n., see 瞿Δ麥 41.11.

薿 20A.83-2

nii.

Adj. Growing vigorously, luxuriant, flourishing: 黍稷薿薿 (AC) how vigorously the millet grows!

蓫 20A.83-3

jur.

N. (Bot.) the yellow dock, *Rumex japonicus* (also called 羊蹄).

蕤 20A.83-3

rueir.

N. A thick growth of bushes, a thicket.

Adj. (Of flowers) drooping.

菰 20A.83-3

gu.

N. (1) (Bot.) Asian wild rice, *Zizania aquatica*. (2) Var. of 菇 mushrooms.

邁 20A.83-4

maih.

V. i. (Dial.) pass: 邁過去 pass by; advance: 邁不開步 unable to take a step.

Adj. Old: 老邁 advanced in age; 年高老邁 reach venerable age.

Adv. Advancing firmly, forward: 邁進 steadily pushing forward; 邁大步走 taking large firm steps.

邁步(兒) *maihbuh('l)*, v. i., move forward.
邁方步(兒) *maihfangbuh('l)*, v. i., take slow, swinging steps (often seen on stage).
邁邁 *maihmaih*, adv., (AC) as in 視我邁邁 looked at me coolly, in slighting manner.

躉 20A.83-4

duun.

N. & v.t. & adv. Wholesale: 躉買, 躉 buy wholesale; 躉賣, 售 sell wholesale.

躉船 *duunchuarn* (also *dun-*), n., a warehouse boat, or boat warehouse.
躉批 *duunpi*, v.t., sell wholesale; n., whole lot.

芝 20A.83-6

jy.

N. (1) A fabulous plant of fairyland: 靈芝, 瑞芝 described as a mushroom with purplish stalk, good omen of long life. (2) Orchid=芝蘭 noted for fragrance and color; hence litr. symbol of fragrance, the gentleman, high character, see 芝蘭, 芝艾 *-larn*, *-aih* ↓, (cf. 芷). (3) Sesame: 芝麻 *-'ma* ↓.

芝艾 *jy-aih*, n., select flower and common grass: 芝艾俱焚 the good perishes with the bad.
芝蘭 *jylarn*, n., a kind of orchid: (a) fragrance of saintly character: 如入芝蘭之室 pervading uplifting character of a moral gentleman; (b) in praise of another's children: 芝蘭子弟; (c) in praise of high-minded friendship: 芝蘭氣味.
芝麻 *jy'ma*, n., sesame (also wr. 芝蔴) the plant or its seed; 芝麻細 insignificant amount or detail; 芝麻油 sesame oil; 芝麻醬 sesame sauce or paste.
芝眉 *jy-meir*, n., (LL court.) your distinguished appearance.
芝顏 *jy-yarn*, n., ditto (oft. used in letters): 得睹芝顏 (LL) was able to see you.

莛 20A.83-9

tirng.

N. Stem of grass.

蓏 20A.83-9

luoo.

N. Different kinds of melon.

蓰 20A.83-9

shii.

N. (AC) five-fold increase.

蓬 20A.83-9

perng.
[Dist. 篷]

N. (Bot.) *Erigeron acris*, also called 飛蓬, a grass, oft. used figuratively of s.t. tangled, dishevelled (hair): 蓬首蓬頭, 蓬髮, (AC) 蓬葆 dishevelled hair; 蓬頭垢面, unkempt appearance, dishevelled hair and dirty face; in sense of thatched hut, (fig.) of humble house: 蓬室, 蓬戶, 蓬門 house with grass mat door or window; 篳門蓬戶 grass hut; 蓬篳生輝 my humble house is honored with your visit; 蓬生麻中不扶自立 AC allu., influence of good society, like grass growing straight in a hemp field; (fig.) of s.t. blown about by the wind like thistle: 蓬轉 flying about; 蓬累而行 (AC) wandering about with bag and baggage.

蓬勃 *perngbor*, adj., rising, growing fast, viable: as 蓬勃氣象 a sense of luxuriant growth, vitality, also 蓬蓬勃勃.
蓬蒿 *pernghau*, n., (bot.) grass of the rush family; wild underbrush.
蓬顆 *perngkee*, n., (AC) mud bricks.
蓬萊 *Pernglair*, n., a fabled Fairy Isle on the China Sea.
蓬虆 *pernglei r*, n., (bot.) *Rubus thunbergii*, a plant of the rose family.
蓬蓬 *perngperng*, adj., luxuriant; booming (sound of wind).
蓬茸 *perngrurng*, adj., luxuriant, tangled (of grass).
蓬砂 *perngsha*, n., borax, commonly wr. 硼砂.
蓬鬆 *perngsung*, adj., fluffy (of hair, etc.).

§20A.91 (艹/ノ)

 20A.91-5

liaau (**luh*).

N. (Bot.) smartweed, *Polygonum*.

蓼莪 **luh-er*, n., name of ode in *Book of Poetry*, expressing remembrance of deceased parents.
蓼藍 *liaaularn*, n., (bot.) indigo, whose leaves are used for dyeing.
蓼蓼 **luhluh*, n., (AC) luxuriant.

莎 20A.91-6

suo (**sha*).

N. A kind of sedge grass: 莎草.

莎鷄 **shaji*, n., variously interpreted: (a) (AC) a species of grasshopper; (b) a species of cicada (=紡織娘) *Mecopoda niponensis*.
莎士比亞 **Shashyhbiryaa*, n., Shakespeare.
莎草 *suotsaau*, n., (bot.) a kind of sedge, *Cyperus rotundus*

§20A.93 (艹/く)

萋 20A.93-1

chi.

Adj. (AC) (1) thriving (plants). (2) Rumbling (clouds). (3) 萋萋, see 淒Δ淒 63A.93.

菘 20A.93-1

sung.

N. Celery cabbage, *Brassica chinensis* (=白菜).

藝 20A.93-1

yih.

[Anc. var. 埶]

N. (1) Art, fine arts, skill: 藝術 *-shuh*↓; 文藝 literature, literary art: 六Δ藝 60.80; 手藝 handicraft; 工藝 artisan's craft; 園藝 horticulture; 技藝 technical skill. (2) (AC) horticulture.

藝妓 *yihjih*, n., (Japan) geisha, girl artist of song and dance.
藝林 *yih-lirn*, n., the fine arts; the artistic and literary circles; a collection of creative works.
藝名 *yih-mirng*, n., artist's stage name.
藝能 *yihnerng*, n., artistic ability.
藝人 *yihrern*, n., artist.
藝術 *yihshuh*, n., art, creative art (sculpture, music, poetry, architecture, etc.); 藝術家 an artist.
藝徒 *yihytur*, n., apprentice, artisan.
藝文 *yih-wern*, n., literature and the arts.
藝苑 *yihyuahn*, n., see *-lirn*↑.
藝員 *yihyuarn*, n., artisan, any member of artistic profession.

蔞 20A.93-2

lour.

蔞蒿 *lourhau*, n., (bot.) the beach wormwood, *Artemisia stelleriana* (=白蒿).

芸 20A.93-3

yurn.

N. The rue, a strongly scented herb used for keeping moths away from books, hence 芸閣 a study; 芸籤 bookmark; 芸帙 casing for books.

V. t. U. f. 耘, to weed garden.

芸蒿 *yurnhau*, n., the rue.
芸香 *yurnshiang*, n., see N.↑.
芸芸 *yurnyurn*, adj., numerous: 芸芸衆生 the multitudes.

蕓 20A.93-3

yurn.

蕓薹 *yurntair*, n., a kind of cabbage, *Brassica campestris*.

蔭 20A.93-3

yihn.

N. (1) Shade, shelter: 樹蔭 tree shade. (2) Material benefit or inheritance from ancestor (interch. 廕 61.93): 餘蔭 benefit, blessing from ancestor.

蔭庇 *yihnbih*, v.t. & n., to bring under protection or patronage; spiritual or material protection of ancestor.
蔭蔚 *yihnweih*, adj., shady, cool.
蔭翳 *yihnyih*, adj., ditto.
蔭鬱 *yihnyuh*, adj., heavily shaded by trees.

蠆 20A.93-4

chaih.

N. (LL) a kind of scorpion: 蠆尾 tail sting of scorpion; 蜂蠆 wasps and scorpions—(fig.) deadly, poisonous things.

荽 20A.93–9

suei.

N. Coriander (a spice): 芫荽 ditto.

萎 20A.93–9

wei.

V. i. (Flowers) wilt; (fig.) 哲人其萎 the philosopher is aging, passing away; 萎縮 atrophy.

茲 20A.93–9

tzy.

[see 茲 80.93]

SECTION 20B

§ 20B.00 (革/亅)

靪 20B.00–3

ding.

V. t. To re-sole a shoe.

§ 20B.01 (革/小)

靺 20B.01–1

moh.

N. Stockings, socks, (var. 韈, 襪).

§ 20B.10 (革/十)

靽 20B.10–2

bahn.

[Var. of 絆 93B.10]

§ 20B.11 (革/土)

鞋 20B.11–1

shier.

N. (*-tz*) Shoes: 皮鞋 leather shoes; 布鞋 cloth shoes; 草鞋 straw sandals; 拖鞋 slippers; 球鞋 tennis shoes; 高跟鞋 high-heeled shoes.

鞋幫(兒) *shierbang('l)*, n., the sides of shoes.
鞋拔子 *shierbar(tz)*, n., a shoehorn.
鞋撐 *shiercheng*, n., a shoe tree.
鞋帶 *shierdaih*, n., shoelace, shoestring.
鞋底(子)(兒) *shierdii(tz) (diee'l)*, n., shoe sole.
鞋跟 *shiergen*, n., the heel of a shoe.
鞋後跟 *shierhouhgen*, n., the back part of shoe, above the heel.
鞋匠 *shierjiahng*, n., cobbler, shoemaker.
鞋臉(兒) *shierliaan (-liaa'l)*, n., the front top of shoes.
鞋面 *shiermiahn*, n., the shoe top.
鞋舌 *shiersher*, n., the shoe flap.
鞋刷(兒)(子) *shiershua('l)(tz)*, n., shoe brush.
鞋楦(頭)(子) *shier-shyuahn(tour)(tz)*, n., shoe tree.
鞋油 *shieryour*, n., shoeshine, shoe cream.

鞺 20B.11–2

tang.

N. Noise of drums; also 鞺鞳.

鞓 20B.11–4

ting.

N. Leather belt or sash.

§ 20B.22 (革/丨)

靷 20B.22–5

yiin.

N. A leather strap for pulling cart.

靳 20B.22-9

jihn.

N. (1) Trappings under the neck of a horse. (2) A surname.

V. i. & t. (1) V. i., be parsimonious: 靳惜 be reluctant to part with. (2) V. t., (AC) to ridicule.

§20B.30 (革/一)

韁 20B.30-3

jiang.
[Var. of 繮 93B.30]

§20B.41 (革/図)

鞧 20B.41-8

chiou.

N. Leather strap on flanks of horse (also wr. 鞦 see 20B.81).

§20B.42 (革/冈)

鞘 20B.42-2

chiauh.

N. A scabbard.

鞴 20B.42-2

beih.

V. t. (AC) to drive a horse (鞴馬).

§20B.50 (革/ㄱ)

韉 20B.50-2

jian.

N. A saddle cloth.

鞨 20B.50-4

her.

N. (AC) rough sandal.

靭 20B.50-5

rehn.
[Var. of 韌 22S.50]

鞤 20B.50-6

bang.
[Var. of 幫 11.10]

勒 20B.50-9

leh (**lei*).

N. (1) Bridle. (2) A horizontal stroke in Chin. callig. (3) Ribs (var. of 肋). (4) A surname.

V. t. (1) (AC) to command, exercise control over: 親勒六軍 took personal command of the army. (2) (勒+vb.) to force s.o. to do s.t.: 勒索 *-suoo*, 勒捐 *-jyuan*, 勒借 *-jieh*, 勒贖 *-shur* ↓. (3) Carve, inscribe: 勒石, 勒碑 inscribe on a stone tablet. (4) (**lei*) Tighten: 勒死 strangle to death; 勒緊褲(腰)帶 tighten one's belt.

勒逼 *lehbi*, v. t., force (s. o.) to do (s. t.) against his will.
勒兵 *leh-bing*, v. t., order a temporary halt of the army's advance.
勒交 *leh-jiau*, v. t., force (s. o.) to hand over (money, person or thing).
勒借 *lehjieh*, v. t., compel (s. o.) to lend oneself money.
勒住 *lehjuh*, v. t., stop, halt by pulling in reins.
勒捐 *lehjyuan*, v. t., compel (s. o.) to make monetary contributions.
勒揹 **lei'ken*, v. t., (MC) (1) extort; (2) force (s. o.) to do (s. t.) against his will; (3) restrain, control.
勒令 *lehlihng*, v. t., to order: 勒令退學 order (a student) to leave school; 勒令停職 order (s. o.'s) dismissal from office; 勒令自盡 order (s. o.) to commit suicide.
勒馬 *leh-maa*, v. t., rein in a horse: 懸崖勒馬 (lit.) rein in one's horse at the edge of a cliff, (fig.) avoid danger before it is too late.
勒派 *lehpaih*, v. t., levy (money) by compulsion.
勒限 *lehshiahn*, v. t., fix an arbitrary time limit for (s. o.) to do (s. t.).
勒贖 *lehshur*, v. t., hold for ransom.
勒索 *lehsuoo*, v. t., extort (money, food, etc.).
勒草 *lehtsaau*, *n.*, (bot.) the wild hop, *Humulus japonicus* (=葎).
勒魚 *lehyur*, n., (zoo.) *Ilisha elongata*, the white or long-finned herring.

靳 韁 鞧 鞘 鞴 韉 鞨 靭 鞤 勒

亅	小	㇏	十	土	ナ	廾	𠃊	丨	一	丅	フ	口	図	冈	ㄱ	厂	尸	亠	广	宀	丶	乚	乀	心	八	人	乂	⌒	乛	ノ丿	㇘	く
00	01	02	10	11	12	20	21	22	30	31	32	40	41	42	50	51	52	60	61	62	63	70	71	72	80	81	82	83	90	91	92	93

鞠 鞫 鞠 鞦 靶 靴 鞄 鞔 韈 鞦 鞅

鞠 20B.50-9

jyur.

N. (1) 鞠球 formerly, a football. (2) A surname.

V.t. (1) Bend: 鞠躬 *-gung* ↓. (2) Bring up, rear: 鞠養 *-yaang*, 鞠育 *-yuh* ↓. (3) (U.f. 鞫) interrogate (prisoners).

Adj. Young, childish: 鞠子 a young lad.

鞠部 *jyurbuh*, n., an operatic troupe.
鞠藭 *jyurchyurng*, n., (bot.) the hemlock parsley, *Conioselinum univitatum*, (also wr. 芎藭).
鞠躬 *jyurgung*, v.t., to bow ("bend the body"): 鞠躬盡瘁 tire oneself out in official duties.
鞠養 *jyuryaang*, v.t., bring up (children), rear.
鞠育 *jyuryuh*, v. t., ditto.

鞫 20B.50-9

jyur.
[Dist. 鞠]

V. t. Interrogate (prisoner), make a thorough investigation of: 鞫訊 put (prisoner) on trial; 鞫治 try (s.o.) in court and sentence him; 鞫實 conduct a thorough inquiry into a case.

鞠 20B.50-9

yauh.

N. The stem of boots, stockings: 靴鞠 stiff stem of boots; 高鞠靴 high boots; 短鞠襪子 socks.

§ 20B.70 (革/乚)

鞉 20B.70-2

taur.
[Var. 鼗 22.82]

靶 20B.70-5

baa.

N. 靶子 *baatz*, target; 把靶子 archery or rifle practice; 靶子場 rifle range.

靴 20B.70-9

shyue.
[Anc. var. 鞾]

N. (*-tz*) High boots: 雨靴 waterproof boots; 馬靴 riding boots; 隔靴搔癢 scratch an itch across the boots——to talk way off the mark.

靴袍 *shyuepaur*, n., formerly, long gown worn with boots on formal occasions.
靴筩 *shyuetuung*, n., the leg of the boot.
靴鞠 *shyueyauh*, n., neck of boot where it bends near the ankle.
靴掖子 *shyueyehtz*, n., pocketbook carried inside a boot.

鞄 20B.70-9

baur (also *pau*).

N. & v.t. Soft leather; to soften leather.

鞔 20B.70-9

marn.

V. t. (AC) fasten skin on (drum).

§ 20B.71 (革/七)

韈 20B.71-2

wah.
[Var. of 襪 63C.71]

§ 20B.81 (革/人)

鞦 20B.81-9

chiou.
[Var. of 緧, 鞧]

N. A leather strap.

鞦韆 *chiouchian*, n., the swing (a children's or ladies' pastime; preferable var. 秋千).

鞅 20B.81-9

yaang (also *yang*).

N. Halter strap: 鞅掌 (AC, LL) busy with public affairs.

§ 20B.82 (革/乂)

靸 20B.82-3

ta (**saa*).

靸拉 *ta'la*, v. t., to pull, drag, esp. in trailing slippers; also wr. 趿.

靸鞋 **sarshiee*, n., a kind of cloth shoes, with cloth soles, used by laborers; children's shoes; (MC) sandals.

鞭 20B.82-9

bian.

N. (1) Whip: 馬鞭 horsewhip; usu. 鞭子 *biantz*; 執鞭之士 (AC) horseman, carriage driver; 鞭長莫及 phr., beyond one's ability to help, i. e., out of reach. (2) (AC) bamboo whip; metal chain as weapon. (3) The rod as symbol of teacher: 執教鞭 be a teacher (at such a school).

V. t. To whip, flog: 鞭打, 鞭箠; 鞭打棍捶 beat up with sticks and whips.

鞭辟 *bianbih*, v. t., urge forward by severity, whip forward: 鞭辟入裏 phr., demolish (a writer, writing) by penetrating criticism.

鞭春 *bianchun*, phr., see *-tuuniour* ↓.

鞭笞 *bianchyr*, v. t. & n., flog (-ging).

鞭炮 *bianpauh*, n., string of firecrackers.

鞭扑 *bianpuh*, v. t., submit (person) to flogging.

鞭撻 *biantah*, v. t., whip, whip into submission (of countries); (MC) drive (person) about.

鞭策 *biantseh*, v. t., whip, drive (person, oneself) forward.

鞭土牛 *bian tuuniour*, phr., anc. spring ceremony of beating earthen ox, also called 打春 "beating the spring."

§ 20B.83 (革/乛)

鞬 20B.83-2

jian.

N. A leather case for bow and arrows: 鞬櫜干戈 (AC) turn to peaceful pursuits ("put swords and spears in storage").

韆 20B.83-3

chian.

N. See 鞦$^{\Delta}$韆 20B.81.

§ 20B.93 (革/く)

鞍 20B.93-6

an.

N. (*-tz*) Saddle.

SECTION 20S

§ 20S.00 (廾^{S}/亅)

荆 20S.00-2

jing.

[Var. of 荊]

N. (1) Thorns, brambles. (2) A rod for flogging: 負荆請罪 apologize for wrongdoing. (3) One's own wife, from 荆釵 *-chai* ↓: 拙荆, 山荆 my wife; 荆婦 *-fuh*, 荆室 *-shyh* ↓. (4) A surname. (5) 荆州 Jinggou, in Hupei.

荆釵 *jingchai*, n., as in 荆釵布裙 a woman's plain dress ("thorns as hairpin and skirt made of coarse cloth").

荆柴 *jingchair*, n., poor man's cottage.

荆婦 *jingfuh*, n., my wife.

荆芥 *jingjieh*, n., (bot.) *Nepeta japonica*.

荆棘 *jingjir*, n. & adj., thorns, -y: 荆棘叢生 beset with difficulties.

荆人 *jingrern*, n., see *-fuh* ↑.

荆室 *jingshyh*, n., ditto.

剳 20S.00-2

jar.

[Related 劄 92S.00]

蒯 20S.00-2

kuaai.

N. (1) (Bot.) a rush: 蒯屨 rush sandals; 蒯蓆 rush mat. (2) A surname.

劐 20S.00-2

huo.

V.t. To slit open (a fish's belly).

§20S.02 (卄^{s}/k)

艱 20S.02-5

jian.

N. & adj. (1) Difficult(y), hard (ship): 艱難 *-nan*, 艱苦 *-kuu* ↓. (2) Bereavement, particularly of parent(s): 丁艱 bereaved of parents.

艱貞 *jianjen*, adj., loyal through thick and thin.
艱鉅 *jianjyuh*, adj., herculean (task), difficult to surmount.
艱困 *jiankuhn*, adj., vexing, difficult (work, circumstances).
艱苦 *jiankuu*, n. & adj., hard (-ships), arduous (labor).
艱難 *jiannarn*, n. & adj., difficult(y).
艱澀 *jianseh*, adj., (of roads) difficult to traverse, (of written works) hard to comprehend, (of writers) slow with one's pen, (of food or drinks) bitter and harsh.
艱深 *jianshen*, adj., (of written works) abstruse.
艱險 *jianshiaan*, adj., difficult and dangerous, perilous.
艱辛 *jianshin*, n. & adj., see *-kuu* ↑.
艱危 *jianweir*, adj., hazardous, critical (times).
艱虞 *jianyur*, n., difficulties, worries.

§20S.10 (卄^{s}/十)

斟 20S.10-1

jen.

V. t. (1) To pour wine or tea into cup: 斟酒, 斟茶 pour wine, tea; 斟滿 pour a cup full. (2) To gauge or consider course and extent of action: 斟酌 *-juor* ↓; 斟量, 斟議, 細斟 carefully consider.

斟酌 *jenjuor*, v. i. & t., to consider carefully, deliberate (course of action): 斟酌情形辦理 act after full consideration of actual situation.

斠 20S.10-1

jiauh.

N. A strickle; a grain measure.

V. t. (1) To level a measure of grain with a strickle. (2) To measure (grain).

§20S.11 (卄^{s}/土)

難 20S.11-9

narn (**nahn*).

N. (**nahn*) Calamity, disaster, difficulty, hindrance, impediment: 國難 national crisis; 大難不死 escape from death in a great catastrophe; 災難 natural disaster; 患難(之交) (friends in) adversity; 遇難 die a tragic death; 逃難 take refuge in a safe place; 冒險犯難 run risks to overcome obstacles; 克難 overcome diffculties; 難民 *-mirn* ↓; 難胞 *-bau* ↓; 臨難 on the verge of death, at the most critical moment; 落難 fallen upon evil days, in dire circumstances.

V. t. (**nahn*) (1) Make difficult, confront with obstacles: 難住了 be confounded, stymied in argument; 難不住 cannot confound by argument. (2) To ask, discuss, rebuke: 問難 have discussion with (s. o.) on doubtful points; 責難 to rebuke, find fault with.

Adj. Not easy, hard, difficult: 難以 *-yii* ↓; 難乎爲繼 difficult to follow up brilliant example of predecessor; 艱難 hard to do, hard up, difficult; 困難 (*kuhn-'nan*) difficult, -ty (of work, questions, etc.); 難上加難 doubly difficult; 難能可貴 (of things or actions) exceptionably commendable; 難兄難弟 (of brothers) equally brilliant or talented; 難纏 hard to get along with; 難產 *-chaan* ↓; 難處 *-chuu* ↓; 難說話兒 difficult to talk with or deal with; 難題 *-tir* ↓; 難關 *-guan* ↓; 難事 a difficult matter or job; 難字 an unfamiliar word; 難色 reluctant looks; 面有難色 appear to be reluctant; difficult to: 難買難賣 a hard bargain; 難懂 hard to understand; 難明 hard to be clear about; 難容 hard to put up with, inexcusable.

Adv. (1) Scarcely, hardly, oft. with negative sense: 難免 hardly escape=cannot escape, see 難免 *-miaan* ↓; 難堪 *-kan* ↓; 難怪 little wonder that; 難得 *-der*, 難保 *-baau* ↓; 難憑 undependable; 空口難憑 oral promise is not enough; 難忍 unbearable; 難耐 difficult to endure; 難受 *-shouh* ↓; 難說 difficult to say, also "you don't mean to say"; 難道 *-dauh* ↓. (2) *Narn*+vbb. forming adjj., meaning "bad": 難聽, 難看, 難吃, 難聞 not good to hear, look at, eat, smell, see *-ting*, *-kahn*, *-chy*, *-wern* ↓.

難保 *narnbaau*, v. i., difficult to ensure (success) or to say for sure: 難保他不透漏秘密 difficult to guarantee that he will not leak out the secret.

難胞 *nahn-bau, n., fellow citizen(s) in distress, (euphem.) refugees.

難產 *narnchaan*, n., (of childbirth) difficult labor.

難處 *narnchuu* (1) adj., difficult to deal with, or get along with; (2) (-'*chu*) n., difficulties; (3) (*nahn'chu*) n., disaster, predicament: 大家都在難處 everybody is in an awkward predicament.

難吃 *narnchy*, adj., unpalatable (food).

難道 *narndauh*, v. i., could be, used in rhetorical questions: 難道說 could it be said that . . .? you don't mean to say; 難道是 could it possibly be that . . .?

難得 *narnder*, adj. phr., hard to get, hard to meet with or come by, rare, exceptionally fine: 這個人很難得 (praise) difficult to find one like him or to replace him.

難關 *narnguan*, n., a critical situation, crisis: 過 or 度過難關 pass through crisis.

難過 *narnguoh*, adj., (1) uncomfortable: 肚子有點難過 feeling somewhat uncomfortable in the stomach; (2) in straitened circumstances: 日子難過 being in desperate straits, hard up; (3) distressed: 心裏很難過 feeling very uncomfortable, very sorry.

難看 *narnkahn*, adj., ugly, disgraceful-looking (appearance).

難堪 *narnkan*, adj., unbearable: 令人難堪 embarrassing to people.

難免 *narnmiaan*, v.i., cannot help: 難免失望 could not help feeling disappointed.

難民 *nahnmirn*, n., refugees.

難受 *narnshouh*, adj., (1) unbearable: (2) distressed, anguished.

難聽 *narnting*, adj., unpleasant (music, sound); embarrassing (remark), repulsive (words).

難題 *narntir* (*nahntir*), n., a difficult topic to write on, a hard nut to crack; a difficult problem.

難爲 *narn'wei*, v. t., (1) make it difficult for (s. o.), embarrass: 你別再難爲他了 don't you ever embarrass him again; (2) thank (s. o.) for any trouble: 難爲你跑了大半天替我拿來 thank you so much for spending so much time to bring it to me; 難爲了你 thank you so much for the trouble; (3) express sympathy to (s. o.) for anything unfortunate: 難爲你受了這許多誤解 it is hard on you to have been so much misunderstood; (4) v. i., express appreciation: 這麼冷天，難爲你想著來 you have been so good to think of coming in such cold weather.

難爲情 *narnweirchirng*, v. i., be shy: 他怕難爲情不敢開口 he is too shy to speak out.

難聞 *narnwern*, adj., ill-smelling, stinking.

難以 *narn-yii*, adj., hard to, not easy to: 難以相信 unbelievable (lit., difficult to believe); 難以決定 hard to dicide; 難以出口 too embarrassing to say it.

§20S.22 (廿S/丨)

邯 20S.22-3

harn.

邯鄲 *Harndan*, n., (AC) capital of Chao, famous for its beautiful women.

鄞 20S.22-3

yirn.

N. 鄞縣 name of a county (＝寧波 Ningpo).

斯 20S.22-9

sy.

N. A surname.

Pron. & adj. (LL) this: 斯人，斯土 this person, this land; 生於斯 was born here; 如斯 like this (＝如此).

Adv. & conj. Then: 有目斯能視 having eyes, then one can see.

斯文 *sywern*, (1) adj., cultured, refined (person); (2) n., the educated class: 斯文敗類 person who is a disgrace to the educated class; (3) a national tradition of cultured: 天之未喪斯文 if God does not wish this cultural tradition to perish.

斮 20S.22-9

juor.

V. t. (AC) to chop; to scrape off (fish scales).

§20S.42 (廿S/冈)

期 20S.42-4

chir (dial. **chi*; **ji*).

N. (1) A period of time: 時期已到 time is drawing near, also it is time; 期日 or 日期 date set; 定期 fixed period: 定期刊物 periodical; 週期 weekly; 學期 school semester; 假期 holidays; 期約 dated appointment; 期會 regular meeting (every Wednesday, etc.); 期滿 or 滿期 period expires; 到期 at the appointed time, time set or time of maturity; 延期 extend time limit; 過期 past expiration of date; 後會有期 we'll meet again. (2) (*ji) A year: 期年, 期服 -niarn, -fur ↓.

V.i. & t. To hope, expect, wait: 期望, 期待, 期許 -wahng, -daih, -shyuu ↓; 勝利可期 victory may be expected; 以期 in order that . . . may: 以期完成 in order that it may be completed; 期+vb., hope to.

期期 *chirchir*, adv., (AC) allu. to an example of stuttering: 期期以爲不可 (LL) just won't do.
期待 *chirdaih*, v.i. & t., to wait in hope.
期服 **jifur*, n., one-year mourning; 期又三月 in mourning one year and three months.
期貨 *chirhuoh*, n., goods promised to be delivered on fixed date.
期間 *chirjian*, n., period.
期考 *chirkaau*, n., semester examinations.
期刊 *chirkan*, n., a periodical (weekly, etc.).
期年 **jiniarn*, adv., one year.
期票 *chirpiauh*, n., time draft, post-dated check.
期限 *chirshiahn*, n., a limit of time.
期許 *chirshyuu*, v.i., expect to, be expected to.
期望 *chirwahng*, v.i. & t., to hope +vb. or n.
期頤 *chiryir*, adj., (LL of person) a hundred years old.
期月 **jiyueh*, adv. (AC) one year, or month: 期月可也 a year or so will do; 不能期月守也 cannot maintain it for a month.

§ 20S.50 (卄S/ㄱ)

勘 20S.50-9

kahn (**kan*).

V. t. (1) To examine officially and pass judgement: 察勘 examine on the spot; 勘問, 推勘 cross-examine; 勘斷 determine officially; 勘破 discover (mistakes) under examination. (2) (**kan*) To proofread: 校勘, 校勘記 notes on variants in texts; 勘正, 勘誤 to proofread, correct printing errors.

勘察 *kahnchar*, v. t., examine on the spot; investigate (facts).
勘度 *kahnduh*, v. t., see -*liarng* ↑.
勘合 *kahnher*, v. t., to match part of official seal with another document for authenticity, esp. in mil. orders.
勘量 *kahnliarng*, v. t., survey (land).
勘測 *kahntseh*, v.t., see -*liarng* ↑.
勘誤 *kahnwuh* (**kan*-), v.i. & n., amend errors in text; such amendments; 勘誤表 errata, list of corrections of error.
勘驗 *kahnyahn*, v. t., to examine on the spot (land); perform autopsy.

勤 20S.50-9

chirn.

N. Department of work, its worker: 勤務 -*wuh* ↓; 內勤 office work; 外勤 field work involving running around; 出勤 go out on field duty; 值勤 during hours of duty; 聯勤總部 Combined Service Forces General Headquarters.

V. t. Be diligent at: 勤政 diligently attending to government affairs; 勤民 diligently attend to people's welfare; 勤王 -*warng* ↓.

Adj. & adv. (1) Diligent, industrious, hard-working: 勤學 study hard. (2) Attentive, earnest, anxious to please: 殷勤, 獻殷勤 to court a lady, to do everything to please (also wr. 慇懃).

勤惰 *chirn-duoh*, n., degree of hard work or laziness.
勤儉 *chirn-jiaan* (-*jiahn*), adj. & n., industry and thrift; hard-working and thrifty.
勤謹 *chirnjiin*, adj., dutiful and careful in work.
勤懇 *chirnkeen*, adj., earnest and assiduous.
勤快 *chirnkuaih*, adj., efficient (at work).
勤苦 *chirnkuu*, adj., hard-working, sparing no energy, diligent.
勤勞 *chirnlaur*, adj., hard-working, busy, indefatigable.
勤力 *chirnlih*, adj., diligent, industrious.
勤勉 *chirnmiaan*, adj., earnest (at work).
勤王 *chirn warng*, phr., to serve the royal house; to send troops to support king when the latter is in trouble.
勤務 *chirnwuh*, n., military logistic support; ground crew for air force; person so employed; 勤務兵 an orderly in army.

勱 20S.50-9

maih.

V. i. To strive forward (related 邁 20A.83).

勸 20S.50-9

chyuahn.

V. i. & t. (1) To persuade: 勸不了, 勸不動 cannot persuade (s. o.); 把他們勸開 break up fight, quarrel between them; 勸勸他 try to persuade him; 勸慰 to comfort one in distress or anger; 勸善, 勸人爲善 exhort one to go the right way, to do good; 勸戒, 勸告 -*jieh*, -*gauh* ↓. (2) To encourage: 勸勉 -*miaan* ↓.

勸酬 *chyuahnchour*, v. i., urge to drink, gather for drink.
勸導 *chyuahndaau*, v. i., & t., to urge, exhort.

勸告 *chyuahngauh*, v. t., to exhort by friend, teacher or government, to persuade by gentle advice; n., exhortation.

勸和 *chyuahnher*, v. t., to offer services for reconcilliation.

勸化 *chyuahn-huah*, v. i., (1) to urge one to do good; to convert others; (2) to solicit contributions for temple.

勸誨 *chyuahn-hueei*, v. i. & t., to teach, exhort.

勸架 *chyuahn-jiah*[1], see *-her* ↑.

勸駕 *chyuahn-jiah*[2], v. t., to help persuade one to accept invitation or post.

勸諫 *chyuahnjiahn*, v. t., to advise and admonish against.

勸戒 *chyuahnjieh*, v. i. & t., to exhort against (lawlessness, smoke, drink, etc.).

勸進 *chyuahnjihn*, v.i., formerly, (associates or ministers) make formal appeal for s. o. to mount the throne.

勸酒 *chyuahn-jioou*, v. i., urge to ⌈drink.

勸捐 *chyuahn-jyuan*, v. i., to solicit contributions.

勸勉 *chyuahnmiaan*, v. i. & t., to urge and encourage.

勸募 *chyuahn-muh*, v. i., see *-jyuan* ↑.

勸說 *chyuahn-shuo*, v. t., try to persuade (s. o.).

勸世 *chyuahn-shyh*, v. i., gen. homily on morals.

勸誘 *chyuahn-youh*, v. t., to win over by gentle persuasion.

鵲 20S.50–9

chyueh (also *chiaau*).

N. The magpie: 喜鵲 the magpie whose cry is supposed to bring good news; 鵲巢鳩佔 phr., allu., the turtledove occupies magpie's nest——take what is not one's own; 鵲笑鳩舞 great joy among the people.

鵲報 *chyueh-bauh*, n., harbinger of joy.

鵲橋 *chyueh-chiaur*, n., (myth.) on 7th day of 7th lunar month, the magpies spread their wings together to form a bridge, enabling the lovers in heaven (cowherd and spinster) to meet that night, see 織△女 93B.71.

鵲起 *chyueh-chii*, n., (AC) (of reputation) to rise rapidly.

鵲豆 *chyuehdouh*, n., (bot.) a flat bean, *Dolichos cultratus*.

鵲鏡 *chyuehjihng*, n., anc. bronze mirror with magpie design on back.

鸛 20S.50–9

guahn.

N. (Zoo.) the crane, the stork.

---

§20S.70 (卄S/ㄴ)

覯 20S.70–4

gouh.

V.t. (AC) to see.

覲 20S.70–4

jiin (also *jihn*).

V. t. Have an audience with (a ruler): 朝覲, 覲見 be formally received (by a sovereign).

觀 20S.70–4

guan (**guahn*).

N. (1) View, sight, range of vision: 壯觀 a grand view; 奇觀 a spectacular sight; 洋洋大觀 an imposing array of anything; 美觀 aesthetic beauty, beautiful or attractive looks. (2) A mental concept, notion, idea: 主觀, 客觀 subjective, -ity, objective, -ity; 觀念 *-niahn*, 觀點 *-diaan* ↓; 樂觀 optimism; 悲觀 pessimism; 達觀 freedom from worldly worries, supreme unconcern for fame, honor or riches, detachment, spiritual serenity; 作如是觀 let the matter be viewed in this light. (3) (**guahn*) A Taoist temple: 道觀. (4) (**guahn*, rare) An open-air terrace.

V. t. Behold, observe: 觀看 take a look at; 觀覽 *-laan*, 觀賞 *-shaang* ↓; 參觀 to visit (school, hospital), inspect; 縱觀 make a gen. observation of (universe, gen. situation); 觀觀 to watch silently, (Budd.) meditation on life; 旁觀 to watch from the sidelines; 袖手旁觀 look on with folded arms; 明若觀火 very clear-sighted as viewing a fire, also very clear; 觀光 *-guang* ↓.

觀察 *guanchar*, (1) v. t., to look into, observe, -ation: 據我觀察 according to my observation; 政治觀察家 a political observer; 觀察員 an observer (at conference); (2) n., formerly, a district superintendent.

觀點 *guandiaan*, n., standpoint, point of view: 觀點不同 difference in viewpoint.

觀風 *guanfeng*, v. i., (1) look for an opportunity to do s. t.; (2) observe the custom and habits of a country or locality; (3) formerly, to set questions to government students, as indication of standards; (4) stand watch for s. t.: 我這裏與你兩個觀風 I'll be keeping watch here for you two (also 把風).

觀感 *guangaan*, n., observations and comments.

觀光 *guanguang*, v. t., (1) visit as a

tourist, make sight-seeing trip; (2) make a tour: 觀光客 tourist; 觀光事業 the tourist business.

觀 瞻 *guanjan*, n., (of things) outward appearance: 有礙觀瞻 to present an ugly or unpleasant appearance; 觀瞻所在 concerns appearance to visitors.

觀 衆 *guanjuhng*, n., the audience.

觀 止 *guanjyy*, n., the last word of perfection: 歎爲觀止 what perfection! nothing could be better!

觀 覽 *guanlaan*, v. i. & t., to view at leisure (a book, art, landscape).

觀 摩 *guanmor*, v. t., to study and fondle (works of art).

觀 念 *guanniahn*, n., an idea, notion, concept: 舊觀念 old ideas; 新觀念 new ideas.

觀 賞 *guanshaang*, v. t., to enjoy by sight (view, flower, art, literature).

觀 象 *guanshiahng*, v. i., make astronomical observations; 觀象臺 observatory.

觀 測 *guantseh*, v. t., prognosticate through careful observation.

觀 望 *guanwahng*, v. i., (1) take a wait-and-see attitude; (2) be hesitant.

觀 音 *Guanyin*, n., (Budd.) the Goddess of Mercy (usu. spelled Kwanyin): 觀音菩薩 the Kwanyin boddhisattva; 美的像觀音似的 as beautiful as the Goddess of Mercy; 觀音兜 (*dou*), formerly, a woman's soft, warm shawl reaching down to the shoulders, (lit.) a cowl like that worn by the Goddess of Mercy; 觀音粉 --*feen*, n., a white clayish substance oft. used by people as food during famine (also called 觀音土).

§ 20S.71 (廿^{S}/弋)

戡 20S.71-7

kan.

V.t. To quell (rebellion): 戡平, 戡亂 restore peace and order in rebellious districts, pacify country.

§ 20S.80 (廿^{S}/八)

顢 20S.80-3

marn (sp. pr. *man*).

顢 頇 *marnhan*, adj. & adv., thoughtless, -ly, sometimes shameless, -ly; stupid and confused, also 顢裏顢頇 *marn'li*--.

顴 20S.80-3

chyuarn.

N. Cheekbone.

§ 20S.81 (廿^{S}/人)

欺 20S.81-9

chi.

V. i. & t. (1) To cheat (person): 欺騙, 欺詐 *-piahn, -jah*, etc. ↓; 自欺欺人 to cheat oneself and others, to believe one's own lies; 欺世盜名 win popularity by cheap means, unsound scholarship. (2) To bully, humiliate, browbeat: 欺負 *-fu* ↓; 欺善怕惡, 欺軟怕硬 to be a bully.

欺 負 *chi'fu*, v.t., to take advantage of (people); to browbeat, humiliate.

欺 和 *chi'huo*, v.i., to knit (brows): 眉毛眼睛都欺和到一塊兒 one's brows and eyes screw up together.

欺 誑 *chikuarng*, v.t., to cheat.

欺 詐 *chijah*, (1) v.t., to cheat; (2) adj., deceitful.

欺 陵 *chilirng*, v.t., to browbeat.

欺 謾 *chimarn*, v.t. & adj., see *-merng* ↓.

欺 矇 *chimerng*, v.t. & adj., cheat, -ing, deceitful.

欺 騙 *chipiahn*, v.t., to cheat.

欺 心 *chishin*, adj., dishonest.

欺 罔 *chiwaang*, v.t. & adj., to cheat, deceitful.

欺 侮 *chiwuu*, v. t., to browbeat, humiliate.

欺 壓 *chiya*, v. t., see *-wuu* ↑.

歎 20S.81-9

tahn.

[Interch. 嘆 40S.81]

V. i. Sigh (in despair or admiration): 歎一口氣 give a sigh; 長歎 give a deep sigh; 哀歎, 悲歎 sigh in sorrow; 感歎 feel deeply about s. t.; 歎惜, 歎惋 regret; 歎羨, 讚歎, 歎服 give sigh of admiration; 可歎 alas!

歎 氣 *tahn-chih*, n. & v. i., (give) a sigh.

歎 號 *tahn-hauh*, n., (punctuation) exclamation mark.

歎 賞 *tahnshaang*, v. t., to admire.

歎 息 *tahnshir*, v. i., sigh, sigh audibly: 長歎息 give a long sigh.

歎 詞 *tahntsyr*, n., (gram.) exclamation.

歡 20S.81-9

huan.

N. (1) Joy, see 歡樂 *-leh* ↓. (2) Love, esp. sexual union: 偷歡 secret lovers' union; 尋歡, 貪歡 seek joys of lovers' union; 求歡 ask for sexual union. (3) A surname.

V. i. & t. (1) (LL) to love: 男歡女愛 man and woman in passion of love; to like as favorite: 所歡 be favorite, lover. (2) To enjoy: 歡喜 *-shii* ↓.

Adj. & adv. Joyful, *-ly*, happy, -ily: 歡欣, 歡樂, 歡笑 *-shin*, *-leh*, *-shiauh* ↓; 歡天喜地 overjoyed; 歡宴 dinner on some happy occasion; 歡聚, 歡敘 happy reunion, also meet happily together.

歡忭 *huanbiahn*[1], adj., (LL) happy, overjoyed.

歡抃 *huanbiahn*[2], v. i., clap hands for joy.

歡呼 *huanhu*, v. i., shout, cheer: 歡呼萬歲 shout *banzai*.

歡會 *huanhueih*, n., a happy reunion.

歡虎兒 *huanhuu'l*, n., (coll.) "happy cub" (of children jumping about): 這個小孩子歡虎兒似的 this child is as happy and gay as a puppy.

歡樂 *huanleh*, adj., happy, delighted, enjoying oneself.

歡龍 *huanlurng*, n., (coll.) "happy dragon"——frolicsome child, see *-huu'l* ↑.

歡笑 *huanshiauh*, v. i., laugh heartily.

歡喜 *huanshii*, (1) adj., happy, delighted; (2) v. t., to like a person: 我歡喜她 I like her——euphem. for "I love her"; 歡喜錢兒 tips to servants on celebrations; 歡喜佛 (Lama Budd.) image of spirits in sexual embrace, understood as a god subjugating a demon.

歡心 *huanshin*[1], (1) adj., joyful; (2) v. t., to love (person); (3) n., love.

歡欣 *huanshin*[2], adj., to be exultant: 歡欣鼓舞 dance for joy.

歡敘 *huanshyuh*, v. i. & n., (meet for) happy reunion.

歡送 *huansuhng*, v. t., to give send-off party; 歡送會 farewell party.

歡迎 *huanyirng*, v. t., to welcome (person, new publication, criticism, etc.): 受人歡迎 (of magazine, book) is well-liked, popular.

歡悅 *huanyueh*[1], adj., pleased.

歡躍 *huanyueh*[2], v. i., jump for joy.

歡娛 *huanyur*, v. i., to enjoy oneself.

§ 20S.82 (卄[S]/乂)

散 20S.82-9

sahn (**saan*).

N. (**saan*) Medicinal powder (cf. 丹, 膏, 丸).

V.i. & t. (1) (*sahn* or **saan*) Spread out, scatter: 散開 (clouds, crowd) disperse; 人散了 people have gone away, left meeting; 分散 scatter about; 聚散 (friends, relatives) separation and reunion. (2) Dismiss, stop (meeting, etc.): 散會, 會散了 meeting adjourned; 散學 after school; 戲散了 play has ended and people are coming out; 散工 work hours terminated; 散坐 formula inviting guests to leave table after dinner.

Adj. (1) (**saan*) Scattered, dispersed, not in group: 散卒, 散兵 stray soldiers after defeat; 散帙 odd volumes; 散散落落 scattered about; 散漫 *-mahn* ↓. (2) (**saan*) Relaxed, carefree: 散逸, 散蕩 *-yih*, *-dahng* ↓; 閒散 free, relaxed (time); 散人 a person not harnessed with duties; 散才, 散儒 (AC) unconventional scholar. (3) (**saan*) Random, unclassified, without rank: 散職 *-jyr* ↓; 散座兒 orchestra seats in theater, opp. 包廂 box seats.

散兵線 **saanbing-shiahn*, v. i. & n., (mil.) to defile, march in single file or in files; defilade.

散佈 *sahnbuh*[1], v.t., scatter (gossip, etc.).

散步 *sahnbuh*[2], v.i., to take a stroll, also 散散步.

散場 *sahnchaang*, v.i., play ends and people file out.

散曲 **sarnchyuu*, n., (Yuarn Dyn.) plays containing songs without dialogue.

散淡 **saandahn*, v.i., to relax, have a recreation: 散淡散淡一下 (MC) (also wr. 散誕).

散蕩 **saandahng*, v.i., see *-dahn* ↑.

散髮 *sahnfaa* (*sarn-*), v.i., to wear dishevelled hair.

散光 *sahnguang* (sp. pr. **saan-*), adj., astigmatic (lens).

散逛 **saan'guang*, v.i., take a stroll.

散花 *sahn-hua*, v.i., to display textile flowers in Buddhist ceremony.

散話 **saanhuah*, n., idle talk.

散鬨 *sahnhuhng*, v.t., to break up in disagreement.

散夥 *sahn-huoo*, v.i., to break up partnership.

散職 *saanjyr*, n., official post without much work.

散開 *sahn-kai*, v.i., to spread out, disperse.

散落 *sahnluoh*, v.i., (friends) disperse.

散漫 *sahnmahn* (**saan-*), adj., (thoughts) scattered, untidy, (writing) not tightly composed.

散悶(兒) *sahnmehn*(*-meh'l*) (also **saan-*), v.i., to have a recreation or distraction.

散散的 *sarnsaan'de*, (1) adv., leisurely, random; (2) v.i., 散散兒, 散散心 to relax, take a stroll, have a change (distraction, etc.).

散沙 **saan-sha*, n., scattered sands; (fig.) 一盤散沙 lacking spirit of cooperation.

散仙 **saanshian*, n., (Taoist) immortals without given post in heaven.

散心 *sahnshin*(**saan-*), v.i., to relax by stroll or change of place, also 散散的 *sarnsaan'de* ↑.

散失 *sahnshy*, adj., get lost.

散學館 *saanshyuer-guaan*, n., formerly, private school.

散攤子 *sahntantz*, v.i., (coll.) break up, see *-huoo* ↑.

散做 *saantzuoh*, v.i., work for hire by the day (of workman, musician).
散卒 *saantzur*, n., stray soldiers after defeat.
散文 **saanwern*, n., prose; 散文詩 prose poem, free verse.
散逸 *saanyih*, adj., carefree.

敬 20S.82-9

jihng.

N. (1) A gift, a present: 喜敬 a wedding present, usu. in cash; 茶敬 a money gift ("for buying tea"); 贄敬 a cash present to a teacher; 節敬 gifts presented to friends on festivals; 脈敬 (LL) fee paid to a doctor. (2) A surname.

V. t. (1) To offer as a present: 敬酒 toast s.o.'s health; 敬茶 serve tea to guest; 敬煙 offer cigarettes; 敬香 burn incense at temple; 回敬 propose a toast in return. (2) Show respect to: 致敬 pay respects to; 禮敬 show deference to; 敬老, 敬長, 敬師 respect the old, one's elders, teachers; 敬神 to sacrifice to the gods; 敬鬼神而遠之 to act correctly to nasty people and keep them at arm's length; 敬業樂羣 study diligently and benefit by the company of friends; 失敬 fail to show due respect to; 可敬 (be) worthy of respect, respectable, venerable; 大不敬 guilty of serious disrespect, misdemeanor.

Adv. Solemnly, seriously, respectfully: 敬奉 *-fehng*, 敬獻 *-shiahng*, 敬贈 *-tzehng*, 敬重 *-juhng*, 敬仰 *-yaang* ↓; 恭敬 polite(ly); 敬啓, 敬呈, 敬稟 (of letters to superiors) respectfully written by . . .; 敬請, 敬候 (phrr. used in complimentary close) "with best wishes for (your good health)"; 敬告 solemnly (seriously, respectfully) inform; 敬惜 save, economize (time, writing paper); 敬惜字紙 "don't throw away scraps of paper that have been written on" (the Chin. people's respect for the written word).

敬愛 *jihng-aih*, v. t., to love and respect.
敬奉 *jihng-fehng*, v. t., to present (a gift) with compliments; to receive letter or obey instructions from superior.
敬服 *jihng-fur*, v. t., admire and respect.
敬賀 *jihng-heh*, v. t., offer congratulations to, felicitate.
敬祝 *jihng-ju*, v. t., ditto.
敬重 *jihngjuhng*, v. t., to esteem highly, look up to with great respect.
敬禮 *jihng-lii*, n., (1) gifts, presents; (2) ceremonial salutation; (3) respects paid by writer of letter to its recipient.
敬佩 *jihngpeih*, v. t., see *-fur* ↑.
敬獻 *jihng-shiahng*, v. t., to offer (a present) to a superior or elder.
敬謝 *jihng-shieh*, phr., (1) "thank you so much"; (2) "I regret to decline your kind invitation": 敬謝不敏 regret being unable to comply with your request.
敬頌 *jihng-suhng*, phr., "please accept my best wishes."
敬贈 *jihng-tzehng*, v. t., respectfully present(ed).
敬畏 *jihngweih*, v. t., hold in high esteem, to reverence (God).
敬仰 *jihngyaang*, v. t., have the highest admiration for (s.o.).
敬意 *jihngyih*, n., esteem, respects.

§ 20S.91 (卄S/丿)

尠 20S.91-2

shiaan.

[Pop. of 尟 41.83]

SECTION 21

§ 21.00 (ㄴ卜/丨)

孼 21.00

nieh.

[Pop. var. of 孽 20A.00]

N. One born of concubine.

Adj. Born of evil, illegal (offspring): 孼種 illegitimate child (abusive); 孼因 sinful cause; 孼子 child of sin.

§ 21.01 (ㄴ卜/小)

櫱 21.01

nieh.

[Var. of 蘖 20A.01]

N. Sprout from chopped branch.

糱 21.01

nieh.

[Var. of 糵 20A.01]

N. Fermented rice.

祟 21.01

sueih.

[Dist. 崇 21.01]

N. An evil spirit: 作祟 (of devil) possessing (a person); 鬼祟 ghost, evil spirit.

Adj. & adv. 鬼鬼祟祟 (act) secretive, -ly, afraid of being seen.

崇 21.01

churng.

N. A surname.

V. t. To worship, adore: 崇拜, 崇奉 *-baih, -fehng*↓; 尊崇 respect (person, his wishes).

Adj. (LL) high, mighty, worthy of respect: 崇山, 崇崖 high mountain, cliff; 崇論, 崇論宏議 great essay or lofty exposition of point of view.

崇拜 *churngbaih*, n. & v.t., (to) worship, adore (God, a great person).
崇奉 *churngfehng*, v. t., to belong to (a certain church).
崇閎 *churnghurng*, adj., great (scholarship, point of view).
崇朝 *churng-jau*, phr., (AC) all day: 誰謂宋遠，曾不崇朝 who says Suhng is distant? It can be reached in less than a day.
崇敬 *churngjihng*, v. t., to respect, adore (God, person).
崇尚 *churngshahng*, v. t., (1) see *-baih*↑; (2) to believe in, emphasize: 崇尚禮節, 正義 emphasize form, justice.

槳 21.01

jiaang.

N. An oar, a paddle.

彙 21.01

hueih.

[See 92.01]

§21.02 (ㄴㅏ/⺊)

裝 21.02

juang.

N. Dress, outfit, attire: 服裝 dress, clothing; 男裝, 女裝 man's, ladies' outfit; 盛裝, 豔裝 (interch. 粧) in beautiful dress; 行裝 travelling outfit, also preparation for travel; 整裝 prepare, provide or adjust outfit.

V. i. & t. (1) To dress up, trim, decorate: 裝束, 裝飾 *-shuh, -shyh* ↓. (2) To furnish, fit out: 裝配, 裝置 *-peih, -jyh*↓; 裝潢 *-huarng* ↓. (3) To pack, pack up, provide frame, case, etc.: 裝包, 裝箱 *-bau, -shiang*↓; 裝裱 *-biaau*↓; 裝甲 *-jiaa*↓. (4) To load: 裝載, 裝運 *-tzaih, -yuhn*↓. (5) To pretend, disguise: 裝假 *-jiaa*[1]↓; 裝傻, 裝憨兒 *-shaa, -ha'l*↓; 裝 or 假裝不知 pretend not to know; 裝病 pretend illness; 裝門面 put up a front; 裝模作樣 assume airs, make pretense (of hard work, etc.); 裝瘋賣傻 to get away by pretending ignorance; 裝腔, 裝幌子 *-chiang, -huaangtz*↓.

裝扮 *juangbahn*, n. & v. i., attire, array.
裝包 *juangbau*, v. t. & n., to pack, packing.
裝裱 *juangbiaau*, v. t. & n., to mount (a scroll of painting); mounting.
裝腔 *juangchiang*, v.i., to affect certain airs, esp. 裝腔作勢 assume airs of importance.
裝訂 *juangdihng*, n. & v. t., bookbinding; to bind a book.
裝裹 *juang'guo*, n., the burial dress and *ensemble*.
裝憨兒 *juangha'l*, v. i., pretend not to understand.
裝幌子 *juanghuaangtz*, v. i., to put up a front, esp. false front, to put up a show to deceive.
裝潢 *juanghuarng*, n. & v. t., furniture and decorations; (to furnish with) handsome bookbinding.
裝幀 *juangjehng*, n., bookbinding; binding of scroll.
裝假 *juangjiaa*[1], v. t., to pretend.
裝甲 *juangjiaa*[2], v.i., to armor; 裝甲車 *--che*, n., armored car; 裝甲部隊 armored brigade or unit.
裝置 *juangjyh*, v. t. & n., arrange, -ment, set up (of hall, temple, room, etc.).
裝老 *juanglaau*, n., see *-'guo*↑.
裝殮 *juangliahn*, n. & v. i., proper dress up of deceased and laying in coffin.
裝配 *juangpeih*, v. t., to provide with accessories (hearing facilities, etc.); to decorate.
裝傻 *juangshaa*, v. i., pretend not to know or understand; get away thus.
裝箱 *juangshiang*, n. & v. i., case, box; to pack (for shipment).
裝修 *juangshiou*, v. t., to repair (house, clock).
裝束 *juangshuh*, n. & v. i., attire.
裝飾 *juangshyh*, n. & v. t., to decorate, -tion; 裝飾品 decorations.
裝蒜 *juangsuahn*, v. i., (abuse) assume airs, put up false show.
裝載 *juangtzaih*, n. & v.t., a load; to load.
裝么 *juangyau*, v. i., see *-chiang*↑.
裝運 *juangyuhn*, v. t. & n., transport, -ation; 裝運公司 transportation company.

漿 21.02

jiang.

[Cf. 醬 *jiahng*, 21.41]

N. Any thick fluid: 豆漿 bean milk; 泥漿 mud, mire, slush; 漿糊 paste.

V. t. To starch (clothes) after washing.

漿果 *jiangguoo*, n., berries.

彖 21.02

tuahn.

[Var. of 彖 92.02]

§ 21.10 (ㄴㅏ/十)

岸 21.10

ahn.

N. (1) River bank, seashore: 岸上 on the coast; 上岸 go on land from ship; 靠岸 alongshore; 彼岸 (Budd.) that shore of salvation; 回頭是岸 (Budd.) turn back and you are ashore (from sea of sorrows); 泊岸, 隄岸 embankment. (2) (AC) prison (cf. 犴 91C.10).

Adj. Towering.

岸然 *ahnrarn*, adj., impressive: 道貌岸然 looking severe and solemn.

岸幘 *ahn-tzer*, phr., (LL) to wear hat tilted back, revealing forehead.

岸獄 *ahnyuh*, n., (AC) prison (see 犴 91C.10).

峯 21.10

feng.

N. (1) Mountain peaks: 山峯 mountain peaks; 高峯 high peaks; 羣峯 group of mountain peaks; 孤峯 a peak standing alone; 峯嶺, 峯巒 peaks and hill crests. (2) Pointed part: 乳峯 nipple; 駝峯 camel hump; 鼻峯 tip of nose.

崒 21.10

tzur.

V.i. 山冢崒崩 a landslide from the peak.

嵂 21.10

lyuh.

嵂崒 *lyuhtzur*, adj., (of mountains) steep and jagged.

§ 21.11 (ㄴㅏ/土)

崖 21.11

yair.

N. Cliff, cliffside: 斷崖 overhanging cliff; 懸崖勒馬 draw up sharp on brink of catastrophe.

Adj. Steep, towering, rocky.

崖岸 *yair-ahn*, (1) n., steep bank; (2) adj., (LL) rigid, stiff, austere (conduct).

崖谷 *yairguu*, n., ravine.

崖檢 *yairjiaan*, adj., (LL) austere (conduct), stiff (exterior).

崖略 *yairlyueh*, n., outline, essential points.

崖異 *yairyih*, adj., (LL) maintaining a rigid front to be different from others.

崔 21.11

tsuei.

N. A surname.

Adj. (AC) high, towering.

崔崔 *tsueitsuei*, adj., (AC) high, towering.

崔巍 *tsueiweir*, adj., towering (mountain, tall edifice).

§ 21.21 (ㄴㅏ/ㄴ)

山 21.21

shan.

N. (1) A mountain, hill: 上山, 爬山 climb mountain; 山居 to live in the mountains; 山窮水盡 come to a dead end; 山高水長 (fig.) lasting forever; 高山流水 descriptive of lofty music, symbol of lofty character; 山盟海誓 pledge of eternal love; 山水 *-shueei* ↓; 山河 *-her* ↓. (2) Oft. attached to plant or animal names, indicating growing on the hills or wild variety, as 山蝙蝠, 山扁豆; otherwise, of the hills: 山公, 山人, 山胞 *-gung, -rern, -bau* ↓.

山百合 *shanbaaiher*, n., (bot.) a variety of lily.

山胞 *shanbau*, n., polite term of reference to aboriginal mountain tribes in Formosa (胞=同胞).

山崩 *shanbeng*, n., landslide.

山茶 *shanchar*, n., (bot.) wild camelia.

山妻 *shan-chi*[1], n., my rustic wife.

山漆 *shan-chi*[2], n., a kind of lacquer tree, *Rhus Trichocarpa*.

山牆 *shanchiarng*, n., a high wall on the side of a house.

山丘 *shanchiou*, n., (1) a hillock; (2) graveyard.

山川 *shan-chuan*, n., mountains and streams; (fig.) gen. topography.

山雀 *shanchyueh*, n., (zoo.) a small bird which can be trained, *Parus varius.*

山丹 *shandan*, n., the lily, *Lilium concolor*.

山巔 *shandian*, n., mountain peak.

山底兒 *shandiee'l*, n., a type of shoes with sturdy cloth soles for mountain roads.

山地 *shandih*, n., mountainous country, aboriginal area: 山地人 aborigines.

山頂兒 *shandiing'l*, n., mountain peak, hilltop.

山斗 *shan-doou*, n., "the Taih mountain 泰山 and the Dipper 北斗"—symbol of persons looked up to with great respect.

山兜 *shandou*, n., a mountain chair.

山豆根 *shandouhgen*, n., (bot.) *Euchresta japonica*.

山都 *shandu*, n., a species of monkey in South China, *Cynocephalus porcarius*.

山洞 *shanduhng*, n., a cave in the mountains.

山東 *Shandung*, n., Shantung Province.

山阿 *shan-e*, n., a spur or turn in the mountains.

山房 *shanfarng*, n., a lodge, oft. used poetically for studio right in the city.

山峯 *shanfeng*, n., mountain peak.

山腹 *shanfuh*, n., see *-yau*¹ ↓.

山歌 *shange*, n., folk song.

山根 *shangen*, n., (1) foothill; (2) (coll.) back of one's neck; (3) (fortunetelling) the bridge of the nose.

山公 *shangung*, n., (coll.) monkey.

山谷 *shanguu*, n., a valley.

山河 *shanher*, n., (or 河山) general topography, also as symbol of love of one's country: 山河變色 the country has fallen under foreign rule; 還我河山 "return us our country"—war cry for driving out foreign rulers.

山畫眉 *shan-huahmeir*, n., the song thrush.

山貨鋪 *shanhuoh-puh*, n., shop selling rustic articles of wood and bamboo.

山洪 *shanhurng*, n., swollen mountain stream.

山長 *shanjaang*, n., formerly, head of a college (書院).

山楂 *shan'jar*, n., the hill haw; hawberry: 山楂糕 hawberry cake.

山珍 *shanjen*, n., as in 山珍海味 exotic delicacies from mountain and sea.

山雞 *shanji*, n., the ringed pheasant.

山脚 *shanjiaau*, n., the foot or base of a hill.

山薑 *shanjiang*, n., (bot.) *Alpinia japonica*.

山脊 *shanjii*, n., mountain ridge.

山荆 *shanjing*, n., see *-chi*¹ ↑.

山茱萸 *shanjuyur*, n., (bot.) *Cornus officinalis*.

山莊 *shanjuang*, n., a mountain lodge; a country villa.

山君 *shanjyun*, n., (coll.) the tiger, "King of the forests."

山口 *shankoou*, n., a mountain pass.

山嶺 *shanliing*, n., a mountain range.

山林 *shanlirn*, n., forests; symbolic of retreat in the country.

山陵 *shanlirng*, n., (1) a plateau; (2) a royal mausoleum.

山貓 *shanmau*, n., a wildcat, *Felis microtis*.

山門 *shanmern*, n., gate to a monastery.

山民 *shanmirn*, n., (1) oft. assumed poetic title for one supposed to be living in the country, whether so or not; (2) mountain tribe.

山脈 *shanmoh*, n., mountain range.

山柰 *shannaih*, n., (bot.) *Kaempferia galanga*.

山砲 *shanpauh*, n., a howitzer.

山坡(兒)(子) *shanpo('l)('tz)*, n., a slope.

山人 *shanrern*, n., (1) assumed title for recluse, whether so or not; (2) pretentious title of astrologer and others communing with the spirits.

山神 *shanshen*, n., a spirit of the mountain.

山西 *Shanshi*, n., Shansi Province.

山向(兒) *shanshiahng('l)*, n., the facing direction of a grave.

山魈 *shanshiau*, n., the mandrill monkey, *Cynocephalus mormon*.

山系 *shan-shih*, n., mountain system.

山水 *shanshueei*, n., landscape, landscape painting; 山水畫 ditto.

山頹 *shantuei*, phr., 山頹木壞 allu. referring to death of Confucius or a sage.

山頭 *shantour*, n., hilltop.

山兔 *shantuh*, n., the Mongolian hare.

山子石兒 *shantzsher'l*, n., a rockery in Chin. garden.

山嘴 *shantzueei*, n., the spur of a hill.

山隝 *shanwuh*, n., a nook in the hills.

山巖 *shanyarn*, n., a cliff.

山羊 *shanyarng*, n., the goat, *Capra hircus*.

山腰 *shanyau*¹, n., halfway up a hill.

山藥 *shan'yau*², n., the yam.

山野 *shanyee*, n., the countryside.

山園 *shanyuarn*, n., (AC) mausoleum.

山岳 *shanyueh*, n., a sacred mountain, symbol of strength (also wr. 嶽).

山芋 *shanyuh*, n., the sweet potato (also called 地瓜).

山楡 *shanyur*, n., (bot.) a variety of elm.

出 21.21

chu.

V.i. (1) To go out, come out, leave (v.t.), opp. 入 *ruh*, go in, come in: 出入 *-ruh* ↓; 出去, 出來 *-'chyuh*, *-lair* ↓; 出門, 出行, 出外 *-mern*, *-shirng*, *-waih* ↓; 出奔, 出走 *-ben*, *-tzoou* ↓; 出爾反爾 promise and then deny in succession. (2) To appear: 出現, 出沒 *-shiahn*, *-moh* ↓; 雪花六出 snow crystals appear hexagonal. (3) To stand out: 出色 *-seh* ↓; 出類拔萃 stand out among others; 出人頭地 ditto; 出乎意料, 出人

山
出

亅	小	⺊	十	土	ナ	卄	ㄴㅏ	丨	一	丅	フ	口	区	冈	乛	厂	尸	亠	广	宀	丶	乚	乜	心	八	人	乂	冖	乛	刂	𠂉	く
00	01	02	10	11	12	20	21	22	30	31	32	40	41	42	50	51	52	60	61	62	63	70	71	72	80	81	82	83	90	91	92	93

出 意表 go beyond expectations, come as a surprise.

V.t. (1) To produce, issue, beget: 出產, 出品 -'*chaan*, -*piin* ↓; 出於, 出自 come from; 出自山東 (goods) come from Shantung; 出於至情 come from natural affection; 出生 -*sheng*² ↓; 所出 was born by s.o., 愛如己出 love (child) like one's own; 出芽 send forth sprout. (2) To grow (pimples, etc.), to meet with s.t. unpleasant or have it occur: 出痲疹, 出天花 to have measles, smallpox; 出事 -*shyh*⁵ ↓; 出亂子, 出摟子 be found out and run into trouble; 出凶案 have a murder case; 出新聞 get into the papers; 出笑話 become a joke; 出醜 -*choou* ↓. (3) To leave: 出國 go abroad; 出世 (religious attitude) leave the secular world, opp. 入世 take part in human community; 出口 -*koou* ↓; 出門 -*mern* ↓. (4) (Often as vb. prefix, like "outcome," "outpour" in Eng.) to send out, pay out, rent out, etc.: 出錢 provide the money; 出力 -*lih* ↓; 出火, 出氣 -*huoo*, -*chih* ↓; 出納 -*nah* ↓; 出租 rent out; 出讓, 出賣 offer for sale; 支出 pay out; 出妻 to divorce wife; 出兵, 出師 -*bing*, -*shy* ↓.

Adv. Out: 拿出, 取出 take out; 送出 send out; 倒出 pour out; 放出 let out; speak out, etc. (in all cases, 出來 or 出去 is commonly used in place of 出, see 出來, 出去 -*lair*, -'*chyuh* ↓).

出版 *chubaan*, v.t., to publish: ××出版 (s.t.) published by certain company; 出版物 --*wuh*, n., publications.

出榜 *chu-baang*, v.i., publish list of successful candidates at examinations.

出奔 *chuben*, v.i., to leave country as political refugee.

出殯 *chubihn*, v.i., to hold funeral procession.

出兵 *chubing*, v.i., to march army for battle.

出產 *chu'chaan*, (1) v.t., to produce (farm, factory goods); (2) n., production, products.

出岔兒 *chu-chah'l*, v.i., run into trouble.

出差 *chu-chai*, v.i., leave capital on official mission; be sent out on special errand; go on field trip.

出場 *chu-charng*, v.i., to appear on stage or contest field.

出超 *chu-chau*, n., (have) favorable balance of trade; excess of export over import.

出塵 *chu-chern*, (1) v.i., (Budd.) leave the secular world; (2) adj., (writing, ideas) far above the common run.

出妻 *chu-chi*, v.i., to divorce wife.

出錢 *chu-chiarn*, v.i., provide the funds.

出氣 *chu-chih*, v.i., to vent one's spleen.

出奇 *chuchir*, adj. & adv., surprising, -ly: 出奇制勝 win by novelty or by surprise attack: 壞得出奇 surprisingly bad.

出勤 *chu-chirn*, v.i., be sent out on an errand.

出醜 *chuchoou*, v.i., expose one's weak points; (oft. court. self-reference) to perform.

出出着 *chuchu'je*, adj., (house beam, etc.) projecting out.

出處 *chuchuh*, n., (1) (Confu.) some moral principle by which a Confu. scholar joins or resigns from an office; (2) (also -'*chu*) source for litr. allusion or reference.

出圈兒 *chu-chyua'l*, v.i., do s.t. slightly irregular or beyond bounds.

出去 *chu'chyuh*, (1) v.i., go out; (2) (-'*chuchyuh*) adv., out (away from speaker, cf. -*lair*): 說出去不好聽 it will sound bad to have this known; 放不出去 cannot let go.

出缺 *chu-chyue*, v.i., leave a vacancy; specifically die during office.

出倒 *chudaau*, v.i., (coll.) see -*rahng* ↓.

出頂 *chudiing*, v.i., see -*rahng* ↓.

出痘 *chu-douh*, v.i., to have smallpox.

出隊 *chudueih*, v.i., (army units) start off.

出動 *chuduhng*, v.i., (of groups, mil. units) to start out on expedition.

出發 *chufa*, v.i., to start (as on outing); 出發點 point of departure.

出風頭 *chu-feng'tou*, v.i., to show off, gain notoriety.

出婦 *chufuh*, n., (LL) a divorced woman.

出港 *chu-gaang*, v.i., (of goods) leave port for abroad; (of ship) sail from port.

出格 *chu-ger*¹, (1) adj., exceptional; (2) v.i., formerly, to write outside the ruled marking on official paper.

出閣 *chu-ger*², v.i., (of girls) to be married: 已出閣 is already married.

出軌 *chu-gueei*, adj., (1) irregular: 出軌的行動 irregular activities; (2) 火車出軌 derailed.

出恭 *chugung*, v.i., to ease bowels.

出汗 *chu-hahn*, v.i., to perspire.

出號 *chu-hauh*, adj., oversized (shoes, etc.).

出乎 *chu'hu*, phr., come from: 出乎眞心好意 come from the heart, from good intentions.

出花兒 *chu-hua'l*, v.i., have smallpox.

出豁 *chuhuo*, v.i., (1) (MC) to lighten severity of crime (＝開豁); (2) 沒出豁 (MC) have no way out.

出貨 *chu-huoh*, v.i., (1) to produce goods (per day, etc.); (2) to take delivery of goods (as from godown); (3) (AC) to pay money.

出火 *chu-huoo*, v.i., be aflame with desire, anger.

出活 *chu-huor*, v.i., (coll.) produce a great deal (of goods).

出診 *chu-jeen*, v.i., (physicians) visit patients at home.

出疹子 *chu-jeentz*, v.i., to have measles or similar disease.

出陣 *chu-jehn*, v.i., to leave ranks and come out for combat or (Budd.) for meeting people.

出征 *chujeng*, v.i., start on campaign.

出家 *chu-jia*, v.i., to leave family and be a monk or nun: 出家人 --*rern*, n., a monk or nun.

出嫁 *chujiah*¹, v.i., (woman) to be married (out).

出價 *chujiah*², v.i. to bid, opp. 發價 offer.

出尖(兒) *chujian* (-*jia'l*), v.i. & adj., (coll.) well-known (bandit, rascal): 出尖任事 (MC) to take up a difficult or dangerous task.

出教 *chu-jiauh*, v.t., (p.p.) be excommunicated.

出借 *chujieh*, v.t., to lend out.

出結 *chu-jier*, v.i., to give written guarantee of end of dispute.

出繼 *chujih*, v.i. & t., to be legally adopted as son.

出進 *chu-jihn*, n., incoming and outgoing; receipt and expense; difference: 沒甚麼出進 not much difference in comparing two (also 出入).

出境 *chu-jihng*, adv., exit from country: 驅逐出境 expel from country; 出境證 exit permit.

出贅 *chujueih*, v.t., to marry into a family and take bride's family name.

出衆 *chu-juhng*, v.i., to stand out, be outstanding.

出主意 *chu-juu'yi* (*-jur'yi*), phr., to give decision (to do s.t.): 誰出的主意 who made this decision—whose idea is it?

出口 *chukoou*, n., exit; export.

出來 (1) *chulair*, v.i., to come out; come out and intervene; to occur: 這事已經出來 it has occurred already; (2) *chulair* (or *'chulai*), adv., freely attached to vb. to express "out": 説出 or 説出來 to speak out; 拿出 or 拿出來 to take out; 説不出來 cannot say it; 找不出來 cannot find it.

出力 *chulih*, (1) adv., do one's best: 他很出力 he worked very hard (to have s.t. done); (2) v.i., to work hard: 出力做事 work hard; 出力做去 do your best; 出力不討好 do a thankless task.

出溜 *chu'liou*, v.i., to slide along (of snake): 從山坡上出溜 roll down the slope; 打個出溜兒 slip down.

出路 *chuluh*, n., (1) an outlet; (2) a way out; (3) a future (of profession): 出路問題 problem of (a boy's) future; 這裏沒有出路 there is no future (better jobs) here.

出落得 *chu'luo-de*, v.i., grow up into (a beauty, a handsome young man).

出籠 *chu-lurng*, v. i., to have a sale *en masse*; to put paper money into circulation: 就出籠 newly put in circulation.

出馬 *chu-maa*, v.i., (1) formerly, to come out of ranks for combat; (2) to come out and assume post; (3) see *-jeen*↑.

出賣 *chumaih*, v.t., (1) to offer for sale; (2) to sell out (friend, one's soul).

出梅 *chu-meir*, n., the end of the mildew season, when dry season begins (also wr. 出霉).

出門 *chu-mern*, v.i., to go away from home, for short walk or long journey: 出門兒 (*-mer'l*) ditto; n., social parties, such as wedding, funeral; 出門子 (*--tz*) to be married (of woman).

出面 *chu-miahn*, v.i., to appear publicly (in negotiations, as sponsor, etc.): 不出面 to work only behind the scenes.

出名(兒) *chu-mirng('l)*, v.i., (1) ditto; (2) become famous.

出沒 *chu-moh*, v.i., to appear and disappear: 出沒無常 (roving bands) appear unpredictably.

出納 *chunah*, n., cashier; 出納課 cashier's department; 管出納 be cashier.

出品 *chupiin*, n., artistic or manufactured product.

出讓 *churahng*, v.i., to offer (house, shop) for sale.

出入 *chu-ruh*, n., see *-jihn*↑.

出賽 *chusaih*, n. & v.i., exhibit; contest.

出色 *chuseh*, adj., outstanding, distinguished (performer, -mance, talent, etc.).

出山 *chu-shan*, v.i., come out from retirement and join government.

出身 *chu-shen*, (1) v. i., enter career of public service; start such career: 進士出身 started career as scholar of third degree; (2) (*-'shen*) n., a man's scholastic and other records; origins: 出身寒微 came from humble origins.

出聲 *chu-sheng*[1], phr., make a noise.

出生 *chu-sheng*[2], v.i., be born; 出生日期 day and year of birth.

出神 *chu-shern*, v.i., appear occupied in thought, appear wondering.

出險 *chu-shiaan*, (1) phr., escape from disaster, (patient) come out of danger; (2) v.i., (*chu-shiaan*) to have an accident (as a train).

出現 *chushiahn*, v.i., to appear (of comet, ghost, etc.).

出項 *chu'shiahng*, n., item of expense.

出席 *chushir*[1], v.i., to be present at meeting, conference.

出息 *chushir*[2], (1) v.i., bear interest: 出息若干 how much interest does it bear? (2) n., (Budd.) exhalation; (3) (*-'shi*) (a) n., chance to better one's circumstances: 有出息 (兒), 沒出息(兒) (also 不出息) (a person) has ambition, no ambition; (4) n., interest, profit: 出息很大 great profit; (5) 出息得 v.i., see *-'luo-de*↑.

出行 *chushirng*, v.i., go on a long journey.

出首 *chu-shoou*[1], v.i., (1) come out and plead guilty; (2) to come out and lead.

出手 *chu-shoou*[2], (1) v.i., (of manuscript) be completed; (2) v.t., to sell: 不肯出手 will not sell (at poor price) (=脱手); (3) take matter in hand; 出手兒 (a) adv., at first trial (fail, succeed); (b) n., (Chin. opera) way of throwing or passing weapons.

出售 *chushouh*, v. i., to offer for sale.

出水 *chushueei*, v.i., formerly, (of official or sold prostitutes) to be freed from profession.

出師 *chu-shy*, v.i., see *-bing*↑.

出示 *chushyh*[1], v.t., (1) to post notice; (2) to show or exhibit for inspection (a particular article).

出仕 *chushyh*[2], v.i., (LL) to become official, join government.

出世 *chushyh*[3], v.i., (1) see V.t. 3↑; (2) (of Buddha) to be born into this world or appear bodily; to leave the secular world; (3) be born.

出使 *chushyh*[4], v.i., to be sent

亅	小	卜	十	土	ナ	廾	ㄴㅏ	丨	一	丁	フ	口	図	冈	㇆	厂	尸	亠	广	宀	丶	乚	七	心	八	人	乂	乛	㇀	刂	⺊	く
00	01	02	10	11	12	20	21	22	30	31	32	40	41	42	50	51	52	60	61	62	63	70	71	72	80	81	82	83	90	91	92	93

abroad as ambassador, minister or special emissary.

出事 *chushyh*^{5}, v.i., to have an accident occur: 出了事 (euphem.) to have s.o. die in the family.

出血 *chushyueh*, n., hemorrhage.

出堂 *chu-tarng*, v.i., (of coffin) to leave the ceremonial hall.

出挑 *chu'tiau*, v.i., (boy, girl) to grow up beautifully; usu. 出挑得 *--de*.

出涕 *chu-tih*, v.i., (LL) shed tears.

出題 *chu-tir*, v.i., give out or set, subject for examination paper.

出庭 *chu-tirng*, v.i., (judge, persons involved in lawsuit) to appear at court.

出頭 *chutour*, v.i., (1) to be successful in career: 出頭的日子 the day of success; (2) see *-miahn*↑.

出彩 *chu-tsaai*, v.i., (Chin. opera) to appear bleeding.

出材(兒) *chutsair* (*-tsar'l*), adj., outstanding: 不出材的丫頭 a very common slave girl.

出脫 *chutuo*, v.i., (1) to be absolved; (2) to sell: 一千兩便出脫了 will sell for 1,000 ounces; (3) see *-'luo-de*↑.

出土 *chutuu*, v.i., (1) (anc. objects) be excavated; (2) sprout up; (3) 剛出土兒 just born.

出走 *chutzoou*, v.i. flee or go away.

出租 *chutzu*, v.i., for hire, to let.

出外 *chuwaih*, v.i., to go abroad.

出亡 *chuwarng*, v.i., to live as exile or refugee.

出言 *chu-yarn*, v.i., (LL) to speak (coarsely, elegantly, abruptly, etc.).

出洋 *chu-yarng*, v.i., to go abroad ("across the oceans").

出遊 *chuyour*, v.i., to go on a tour.

出月兒 *chuyueh'l*, adv., next month; 出月子 (of women after child delivery) recover normal health and vitality.

幽 21.21

you.

Adj. (1) Quiet, tranquil, serene, secluded: 幽靜, 幽雅 *-jihng*, *-yaa*↓; 幽谷 *-guu*↓. (2) Deep hidden, unconstrained, natural: 幽情 *-chirng*↓; 幽憤 *-fehn*↓. (3) Of the world of spirits: 幽冥 *-mirng*^{2}↓.

幽閉 *youbih*, v. t., (1) to place under house detention; (2) formerly, to cut off ovary as a form of female castration.

幽棲 *youchi*, v. i., to live in seclusion.

幽囚 *you'chiour*, v. t., to cast in prison, incarcerate.

幽期 *youchir*, n., a secret rendezvous.

幽情 *youchirng*, n., one's most deeply felt emotion; innermost thoughts.

幽獨 *youdur*, adj., isolated.

幽憤 *youfehn*, n., suppressed anger or frustration.

幽谷 *youguu*, n., secluded valley.

幽會 *youhueih*, n., a lover's rendezvous.

幽魂 *youhurn*, n., ghost.

幽靜 *youjihng*, adj., secluded, tranquil.

幽居 *youjyu*, v. i., to live in seclusion.

幽蘭 *yoularn*, n., the orchid (which grows in out-of-the-way places)—symbol of content with accomplishment without seeking notoriety.

幽靈 *youlirng*, n., phantom; an evil monster.

幽美 *youmeei*, adj., quietly beautiful, serene.

幽昧 *youmeih*, adj., dark.

幽門 *youmern*, n., (physiol.) the pylorus.

幽眇 *youmiaau* adj., distant, remote, indiscernible.

幽明 *you-mirng*^{1}, n., the world of the living and that of the dead: 幽明異路 the line that separates the living from the dead.

幽冥 *youmirng*^{2}, (1) adj., dark, shadowy; (2) n., (Budd.) Hades.

幽默 *youmoh*, n., (translit.) humor: 幽默感 sense of humor.

幽壤 *youraang*, n., (Budd.) Hades.

幽人 *yourern*, n., (LL) a recluse.

幽深 *youshen*, adj., profound.

幽邃 *yousueih*, adj., deep and impenetrable.

幽思 *yousy*, n., deep, unspoken thoughts.

幽雅 *youyaa*, adj., tranquil and enjoyable, (of a study) quiet and in good taste.

幽咽 *youyeh*, adj., submerged gurgling (water); silently sobbing.

幽幽 *you-you*, adj., (AC) faraway, distant (hills).

豳 21.21

bin.

[Var. 邠]

N. (AC) place name.

世 21.21

shyh.

N. (1) A generation, defined in AC as 30 years: 五世其昌 prosper for five generations; 後世 future generations, posterity; 先世 ancestors or their times. (2) An incarnation or one life: 今世 the present life; 一世 all one's life; 塵世 the material or worldly life; 來世 future life or incarnation; 出世, 入世 (philosophy of) leaving or joining secular life; (religion) other worldliness or active interest in worldly affairs; 世外桃源 a Utopia, beautiful retreat. (3) This world: 世間, 世界 *-jian*, *-jieh*↓; 世上 in this world; 名聞於世 world-famous; 世人 people of this world; 舉世 the whole world; 世運 *-yuhn*↓; 蓋世 world distinguished; 世無其匹 unrivalled in the world; 一世之雄 a hero of the world. (4) Epoch, era: 世代 *-daih*↓; 世紀 *-jih*↓; 近世 modern times or era; 中世 middle period, Middle Ages; 末世 *fin de siècle*, latter part, latter days; 亂世, 盛世 chaotic, peaceful times, restless, prosperous period; 當世 contemporary, of those times. (5) Experience of human society: 世道日衰 the ways of the world go from bad to worse; 世態炎涼

A

fickleness of human friendships ("blow hot and cold"); 世風日下 the world is declining in its moral values; 人情世故 the ways of the world; 世故, 世俗 *-guh, -sur*↓; 世面, 世情 *-miahn, -chirng*↓; 不識世務 inexperienced in society; 處世 how to get along in this world.

Adj. For generations (of friends): 世交, 世誼 *-jiau, -yih*↓; address of friends connected through family relations; thus 世伯, 世叔, 世兄, etc. uncle, brother who are friends of the family or clan.

世伯 *shyhbor*, n., uncle who is friend of one's family or member of clan.

世情 *shyhchirng*, n., the ways of the world.

世仇 *shyhchour*, n., a feud between families.

世傳 *shyhchuarn*, adj., known or transmitted for generations.

世代 *shyhdaih*, n., (1) a generation; (2) an epoch or era; (3) adv., for generations: 世代書香 a family of scholars for generations.

世道 *shyhdauh*, n., the morals of a nation or the world.

世弟 *shyhdih*, n., son of father's friend, younger than oneself.

世法 *shyhfaa*, n., fashions, custom of the times.

世故 *shyhguh*, n., the ways of the world: 不懂人情世故 inexperienced in life; 世故甚深 or 甚知世故 well versed in art of dealing with people.

世好 *shyhhaau*, (1) n., friends for generations; (2) (*-hauh*) n., fashions, vogue of the times.

世家 *shyhjia*, n., (1) a noble family; (2) a family politically influential for generations; (3) (AC) biography of men connected with noble families.

世間 *shyhjian*, n., the world, the present life: 世間上 in this world.

世交 *shyhjiau*, n., long-standing friendship between two families.

B

世界 *shyhjieh*, n., the universe, the world: 世界大戰 world war; 世界和平 world peace; 世界大同 the world a commonwealth (Confu. ideal); 世界觀 *Weltanschauung*; 科學世界 the scientific world; 兒童世界 the children's world; 滿世界 (*'*-jei*) the whole world; 世界衛生組織 World Health Organization (WHO); 世界糧食方案 World Food Program (UN); 世界人權宣言 Universal Declaration of Human Rights (1948).

世紀 *shyhjih*, n., century.

世及 *shyh-jir*, phr., (AC) handed down from generation to generation, hereditary.

世胄 *shyh-jouh*, n., hereditary nobleman.

世主 *shyh-juu*, n., (LL) ruler of the times.

世姪 *shyhjyr*¹, n., a close friend's son.

世職 *shyh-jyr*², n., hereditary title.

世路 *shyh-luh*, n., the ways of the world (usu. untrustworthy).

世論 *shyhluhn*, n., (1) philosophy dealing with human world, as opp. Budd.; (2) current criticism.

世面 *shyh(')miahn*, n., higher-class society: 沒見過世面 has never known higher society.

世人 *shyhrern*, n., the people of the world.

世上 *shyh-shahng*, adv., in this world.

世系 *shyhshih*, n., genealogy.

世襲 *shyhshir*, adj., hereditary (rank, post).

世叔 *shyhshur*, n., a younger friend of one's father.

世世 *shyhshyh*¹, adv., from generation to generation.

世事 *shyhshyh*², n., the current affairs, affairs of the world.

世兄 *shyhshyung*, n., (court. address) son of one's friend or teacher.

世俗 *shyhsur*, n., (1) customs, manners of a place; (2) (Budd. or Christianity) those outside the church, non-believer.

世統 *shyhtuung*, n., see *-shih*↑.

C

世澤 *shyh-tzer*, n., the benefits, privileges handed down from ancestors.

世尊 *shyhtzun*, n., (Budd.) devotees' name for Buddha (the Revered One of the World).

世族 *shyhtzur*, n., a family politically influential for generations.

世子 *shyhtzyy*, n., the princes, sons of the emperor except the crown prince.

世務 *shyhwuh*, n., worldly affairs.

世業 *shyh-yeh*, n., (1) hereditary profession in the family; (2) inherited property.

世誼 *shyhyih*, n., long-standing friendship between two families.

世緣 *shyhyuarn*, n., secular ties and business.

世運 *shyhyuhn*, n., (1) the course of events, rise and fall of nations; (2) the Olympic Games (from 世界運動大會).

凶 21.21

shyung.

[Interch. 兇 in sense "fierce," "crime"]

N. (1) Culprit: 凶犯, 凶手 *-fahn, -shoou*↓; 正凶 chief culprit (dist. accomplice); 疑凶 suspect, person suspected of crime. (2) Murder: 行凶 commit murder.

Adj. (1) Bad, sad, unlucky, unfortunate (event): 凶兆 *-jauh*↓; 吉凶未卜 do not know whether it will turn out good or bad (patient's life uncertain); 凶宅 unlucky house where occupant dies or meets other mishaps; 凶耗, 凶信 bad news (as of person's death); 凶門 *-mern*↓. (2) (Year) of bad crops: 凶年, 凶歲 *-niarn, -sueih*↓. (3) Fierce, ferocious: 凶焰 flame of violence; 凶象 look of violence; 凶聲 sounds of fights or battle; 來勢甚凶 enemy advances in great strength; 凶狠, 凶悍, 凶猛 *-heen, -hahn, -meeng*

↓. (4) Wicked, brutal: 他太凶了 he is too brutal; 凶惡, 凶徒, 凶暴 *-eh, -tur, -bauh* ↓; 凶地 (AC) a bad country with bad customs.

Adv. Horribly, fearfully: 病得很凶 is extremely or dangerously ill; 鬧得太凶了 in a fearful mess; 凶終 (friendship, alliance) end disastrously, (of person) die an unnatural death.

凶暴 *shyungbauh*, adj., brutal, cruel (tyrant).

凶氣 *shyungchih*[1], n., a ferocious mien.

凶器 *shyung-chih*[2], n., (1) (AC) military weapons (lit., "weapons of evil"); (2) weapons involved in murder (knife, pistol, etc.); (3) funeral appurtenances (including coffin).

凶渠 *shyung-chyur*, n., gang leaders.

凶惡 *shyung-eh*, adj., brutish, fearful, ferocious.

凶犯 *shyungfahn*, n., culprit in murder case.

凶服 *shyung-fur*, n., mourning dress.

凶悍 *shyunghahn*, adj., ferocious-looking.

凶耗 *shyung-hauh*, n., bad news; news of s.o.'s death.

凶狠 *shyungheen*, adj., warlike, cruel, merciless.

凶兆 *shyung jauh*, n., a bad omen.

凶具 *shyungjyuh*, n., coffin.

凶禮 *shyung-lii*, n., funeral ceremony.

凶猛 *shyungmeeng*, adj., fierce, brutish.

凶門 *shyung-mern*, n., white festoon outside door of family during funeral ceremony.

凶年 *shyungniarn*, n., year of bad crops or famine.

凶殺 *shyungsha*, v., t., to murder (s o.).

凶煞 *shyungshah*, n, evil luck, causing illness, death, etc.

凶神 *shyung-shern*, n., evil spirit, said to take possession of person: 凶神附體 be possessed by a demon.

凶險 *shyungshiaan*, adj., extremely hazardous, dangerous.

凶信 *shyung-shihn*, n., bad news; news of death.

凶手 *shyungshoou*, n., murderer, culprit.

凶事 *shyungshyh*, n., (1) funeral affairs; (2) news of murder or near-murder; (3) (AC) war.

凶歲 *shyungsueih*, n., see *-niarn* ↑.

凶死 *shyung-syy*, n., death by violence.

凶殘 *shyungtsarn*, adj., bloodthirsty, merciless, ruthless.

凶徒 *shyungtur*, n., a villain, cutthroat.

§21.22 (ㄴㅏ/ㅣ)

爿 21.22

chiarng (**bahn*).

N. (1) A radical (used for phonetic value in 壯, 牀, 牆, etc.). (2) Half of a tree trunk (graphically opposite of 片 91.22). (3)(**bahn*, Shanghai dial.) 一爿商店 a shop front.

嶄 21.22

jaan (**chaan*).

Adj. (1) 嶄新 brand-new. (2) Var. of 巉 (also **charn*), see compp. ↓.

嶄然 **charnrarn*, adj., rising steeply.

嶄巖 **charnyarn*, adj., (of peaks) steep, (rocks) overhanging.

巋 21.22

kuei.

Adj. (1) (Of hills) in a row. (2) Standing alone: 巋然獨存 standing alone immutable.

§21.30 (ㄴㅏ/—)

豈 21.30

chii (**kaai*).

Adv. An interrogative particle used for positive assertion, meaning "how" (=could not): 豈能 how could; 豈有 how could it be? 豈有此理 how could such a thing be possible?—it is absurd; 豈可如此 how could this be allowed?—should not be allowed; oft. with 不, 無 is it not (=it is): 豈不重複 would it not be redundant? 豈不容易 wouldn't it be easy? 豈不知 doesn't(he) know? oft. goes with final particle 乎 or 哉: 豈不危乎 (or 哉) would it not be dangerous; 豈敢, 豈止 *-gaan, -jyy* ↓.

Adj. (**kaai*) (AC) 豈弟 friendly; 豈樂 peaceful and happy (also wr. 愷, 凱).

豈但 *chiidahn*, adv., not only: 豈但 . . . 而且 not only . . . but also.

豈敢 *chirgaan*, adv., would not dare: 他豈敢欺騙她 he would not dare to cheat her; (as a court. phr.) I am unworthy (of such compliment): 豈敢, 豈敢!

豈止 *chiijyy*, adv. phr., not only (but further than that); similarly 豈只 not only … alone.

豐 21.30

feng.

[Pop. 丰 10.10, which has also separate meanings]

N. (1) Name of a trigram in 八卦 *paguah*, 80.80. (2) A surname.

Adj. Abundant, plentiful, full, solid: 豐衣足食 dress and feed well; rich (harvest): 豐收, 豐登, 豐稔 good harvest; 豐年 year of good crops, also years of youth; round and healthy: 豐潤 good, healthy complexion; 豐肌 plump; 豐腴 plump, well-fed.

豐富 *fengfuh*, adj., rich (wealth, material things); vigorous (energy).
豐厚 *fenghouh*, adj., rich, plentiful (dinner, financial strength).
豐滿 *fengmaan*, adj., plentiful; (ladies' figure) full and round.
豐盛 *fengshehng*, n. & adj., plenty, -teous, prosperous, -ity (of dinner, vegetation, products).
豐足 *fengtzur*, adj. & n., adequate, sufficient, -cy.
豐盈 *fengyirng*, adj., plump and full (face, body); full (granary).

§21.32 (ㄴㅏ/フ)

岑 21.32

tsern.

N. A surname.

Adj. Suggestive of hill regions, see compp.↓; 岑樓 sharp and slender tower.

岑寂 *tsernjir*, adj., quiet, far removed from the hustle of life.
岑岑 *tserntsern*, adj., (LL) dizzy (cf. 涔 63A.32).
岑翳 *tsernyih*, n., (LL) mountainous region covered with dense forest.

§21.40 (ㄴㅏ/口)

岩 21.40

yarn.

N. (1) (LL) Interch. 巖 cliffside 21.82. (2) Rocks: 岩石 *-shyr*↓; 火成岩 igneous rocks; 水成岩 aqueous or sedimentary rocks; 變質岩 metamorphic rocks.

岩壁 *yarnbih*, n., (1) a cliff; (2) (geol.) a dike.
岩牀 *yarnchuarng*, n., (geol.) intrusive sheet.
岩基 *yarnji*, n., (geol.) batholith.
岩漿 *yarnjiang*, n., (geol.) magma, molten rock.
岩流 *yarnliour*, n., (geol.) flow.
岩脈 *yarnmoh*, n., (geol.) rock vein, vein.
岩盤 *yarnparn*, n., (geol.) laccolith.
岩石 *yarnshyr*, n., rocks; 岩石學 petrology.
岩層 *yarntserng*, n., rock strata.
岩鹽 *yarnyarn*, n., rock salt.

岧 21.40

tiaur.

Adj. (AC) high (mountains).

§21.41 (ㄴㅏ/図)

眚 21.41

shyr.

[Arch. of 時 41A.00]

醬 21.41

jiahng.

N. (1) A sauce, condiment: 豆瓣醬 bean sauce; 辣醬 a hot sauce; 醬油 *-your*↓; 醬菜 pickled vegetables; 醬肉 meat cooked in soy sauce; 醬瓜 pickled cucumbers; 醬園 a soy or condiment shop. (2) Any jamlike or paste-like substance: 菓醬 fruit jam; 肉醬 minced meat; 番茄醬 tomato sauce, ketchup; 芝麻醬 sesame sauce or paste.

醬色 *jiahngseh*, adj., dark, reddish brown.
醬紫 *jiahngtzyy*, adj., deep purple.
醬油 *jiahngyour*, n., bean sauce, soya sauce.

§21.42 (ㄴㅏ/冈)

耑 21.42

juan.

[Var. of 專 10.00, esp. in letters: 耑此＝專此]

崙 21.42

lurn.

N. See 崑△崙 21.70.

崗 21.42

gang (also *gaang*).

N. (1) Pop. of 岡. (2) A guard post; an office or post: 守崗位 stay

崗 崩 嵩 岂 崑 鬯 兇 嵐 嵬 巍 兕 崴 峩

at post of duties; 站崗 on patrol duty.

崩 21.42

beng.

V. i. (1) Collapse (of houses): 山崩 landslide; 雪崩 avalanche. (2) Crack and fall: 崩了一角 one corner cracks open. (3) (AC) (of emperor) pass away: 駕崩.

崩症 *bengjehng*, n., see 血^崩症 91.30.
崩口 *bengkoou*, n., crack, hole made by cracking.
崩潰 *bengkueih*, n. & v. i., collapse (of houses, army).
崩裂 *benglieh*, n. & v. i., crack.
崩坍 *bengtan*, n. & v. i., collapse, fall down (of buildings).

嵩 21.42

sung.

Adj. & adv. High up: 嵩呼 (LL) cry "hurrah."

嵩山 *Sungshan*, n., name of high mountain in Honan.
嵩嶽 *Sungyueh*, n., a high mountain, also *-shan* ↑.

§21.70 (ㄴㅏ/ㄴ)

岂 21.70

chii.
[Abbr. of 豈 21.30]

崑 21.70

kun.
[Var. 崐]

崑腔 *kunchiang*, n., music and opera of 崑山, see *-chyuu* ↓.
崑曲 *kunchyuu*, n., form of opera developed at 崑山 ↓.
崑崙 *Kunlurn*, n., the Kunlun Mountains in Chinese Turkestan.
崑山 *Kunshan*, n., name of district near Shanghai.

鬯 21.70

chahng.

N. (1) A sacrificial wine. (2) A bow case.

Adj. (Interch. 暢 22S.50) straight and clear.

兇 21.70

shyung.
[Var. of 凶]

N. & adj. In sense of "crime," "fierce," see 凶 21.21.

兇懼 *shyungjyuh*, adj., perturbed and afraid, upset.
兇兇 *shyungshyung*, adj., clamorous (also wr. 訩).

嵐 21.70

larn.

N. Vapor, haze on hillside: 嵐氣 misty hill atmosphere; 曉嵐 morning mist; 夕嵐 evening mist; 山嵐 mountain mists.

嵬 21.70

weir.

Adj. High, rugged (cf. 巍 21.70).

嵬峨 *weir-er*, adj., lofty.
嵬嵬 *weirweir*[1], adj., ditto.
嵬巍 *weirweir*[2], adj., ditto.
嵬嶷 *weiryir*, adj., ditto.

巍 21.70

weir.

Adj. Lofty, mighty, impressive.

巍峩 *weir-er*, adj., tall and rugged (also wr. 嵬峩).
巍巍 *weirweir*, adj., ditto (also wr. 嵬嵬).

兕 21.70

jyh.
[See 兕 92.70]

§21.71 (ㄴㅏ/弋)

崴 21.71

weir.
[Var. of 嵬 in 嵬峩]

峩 21.71

er.
[Var. of 峨 21B.71]

§ 21.72 (ㄴㅏ/心)

崽 21.72

tzaai.

N. The young of animals: 下崽子 (of animals) to litter; 西崽 (contempt.) a Chinese employee of a foreign firm ("a Westerner's underling"); 崽子 *-tzyy* ↓.

崽子 *tzairtzyy* (sp. pr. *tzaai'tz*), n., (1) a child; (2) a pederast, also used as term of abuse.

§ 21.80 (ㄴㅏ/八)

眞 21.80

ien.

[See 眞 10.80]

巔 21.80

dian.

N. Summit of hill, top of tree: 山巔, 樹巔.

貰 21.80

hyh.

V. i. & t. (1) To hire out, rent out (house, vehicle). (2) To take (s.t. such as wine) on credit. (3) (AC) to pardon: 貰赦.

嶺 21.80

liing.

N. Mountain range, mountain pass: 爬山越嶺 over hills and mountains; 分水嶺 watershed.

嶺南 *liingnarn*, n., Kwangtung—"south" of mountain range (大庾嶺).

§ 21.81 (ㄴㅏ/人)

炭 21.81

tahn.

[In chem., the var. 碳 31B.81 for carbon is oft. used]

N. (1) Charcoal: 木炭 charcoal from wood; 煤炭 coal; 石炭 anthracites; 炭盆 charcoal basin. (2) (Chem.) carbon (oft. wr. 碳): 炭質 *-jyr* ↓; for 炭化, see 碳$^{\Delta}$酸 31B.81.

炭筆 *tahnbii*, n., carbon pencil.
炭氣 *tahn-chih*, n., (chem.) carbon dioxide.
炭化 *tahnhuah*[1], v.i., see 碳$^{\Delta}$化 31B.81.
炭畫 *tahnhuah*[2], n., charcoal drawing.
炭灰 *tahnhuei*, n., ashes.
炭精 *tahnjing*, n., pure carbon.
炭質 *tahnjyr*, n., (chem.) carbon.
炭紙 *tahnjyy*, n., carbon paper (also called 炭精紙).
炭坑 *tahnkeng*, n., coal pit.
炭簍子 *tahn-loou'tz*, n., (coll.) as in 給他一個炭簍子 give him a high (empty) title (＝戴高帽子).
炭酸 *tahnsuan*, n., see 碳$^{\Delta}$酸 31B.81.
炭田 *tahn-tiarn*, n., coal field.
炭層 *tahn-tserng*, n., coal bed.
炭氧氣 *tahnyaang chih*, n., carbonic acid gas.
炭油 *tahnyour*, n., coal tar.

奘 21.81

tzahng (**juaang*).

Adj. (1) Big, powerfully-built (person). (2) (**juaang*) Large-sized (related 壯): 奘粗 stout, thick, coarse; 奘的細的 the strong (stout) and the weak (slender).

獎 21.81

jiaang.

N. A prize, a reward (opp. 懲 punishment): 獎券 *-chyuahn*[2] ↓; 中獎 draw a winning number; 得獎 win a prize; 大獎 a big prize; 末獎 the smallest prize; 特獎, 頭獎 special, first prize; 抽獎 to draw prizes; 摸獎 ditto; 贈獎 offer prizes; 附獎 a consolation prize; 有獎徵答 offer of prizes for correct answers.

V. t. (1) To praise, commend, laud, extol: 獎勉 *-miaan*, 獎進 *-jihn*, 獎勸 *-chyuahn*[1], 獎許 *-shyuu* ↓; 過獎 overpraise. (2) Give award to: 獎品 *-piin*, 獎勵 *-lih*, 獎金 *-jin*, 獎章 *-jang*, 獎狀 *-juahng*, 獎賞 *-shaang* ↓; 授獎, 頒獎 make awards; 領獎 accept awards. (3) Give financial assistance to: 獎助 *-juh*, 獎掖 *-yih* ↓; 獎學金 scholarships.

獎勸 *jiaangchyuahn*[1], v.t., encourage by rewards.
獎券 *jiaangchyuahn*[2], n., a lottery ticket.
獎章 *jiaangjang*, n., a medal award, a decoration.
獎進 *jiaangjihn*, v. t., recommend for promotion.
獎金 *jiaangjin*, n., a cash award.
獎狀 *jiaangjuahng*, n., a citation.
獎助 *jiaangjuh*, v. t., provide for financial assistance, to subsidize.
獎勵 *jiaanglih*, v. t., commend,

praise, encourage by rewards.

奬勉 *jiarngmiaan*, v. t., speak approvingly of.

奬牌 *jiaangpair*, n., a gold, silver or bronze medal or plaque given as award. ⌈prize.

奬品 *jiarngpiin*, n., an award, a

奬賞 *jiarngshaang*, v.t. & n., (make) cash or other awards to (person).

奬飾 *jiaangshyh*, v. t. & n., to decorate, -ation.

奬許 *jiarngshyuu*, v.t., give praise (by superior).

奬掖 *jiaangyih*, v. t., encourage (youth) by active assistance.

奬譽 *jiaangyuh*, v. t., to give recognition (by superior).

嶽 21.81

yueh.

N. A high or sacred mountain: 山嶽 high mountain; 嶽立 standing immovable.

嵌 21.81

chian (also *chiahn, kahn*).

V. t. To set (stone in jewelry), to inlay as decoration: 嵌鑲 to inlay pieces as decoration (in earrings, etc.).

Adj. See 嵌巉 *-charn* ↓.

嵌巉 *chiancharn*, adj., (LL) (of mountains) rocky, rugged.

嶔 21.81

chin.

嶔崟 *chinyirn*, adj., (LL) descriptive of high mountain.

§21.82 (ㄴㅏ/乂)

岌 21.82

jir.

Adj. (Of mountains) lofty, towering: 岌岌可危 precarious, in imminent danger of falling down.

巖 21.82

yarn.

[Var. 岩 21.40]

N. (1) A hill cave, a grotto: 巖穴, 巖洞 *-shyueh, -duhng* ↓. (2) A cliff, a precipice; oft. site of a temple: 巖居穴處 (of recluses) dwell in mountain caves.

Adj. Precipitous: 巖牆 a precipitous wall.

巖洞 *yarnduhng*, n., a mountain cave.

巖穴 *yarnshyueh*, n., ditto.

§21.83 (ㄴㅏ/へ)

遄 21.83

chuarn.

Adv. (LL) fast: 遄行, 遄返 quickly go, come back.

嶷 21.83

yir (*nih).

N. 九嶷 name of mountain.

Adj. (*nih) 嶷岌 (LL) steep, towering (mountain); 嶷嶷 (LL) growing luxuriantly, thriving (crops).

§21.93 (ㄴㅏ/ㄑ)

崧 21.93

sung.

[Interch. 嵩 21.42]

蚩 21.93

chy.

Adj. (AC) ignorant, uncouth (people): 蚩蚩 ditto; 蚩拙 uneducated and stupid.

蚩尤 *Chyyour*, n., mythological warrior engaged in fight with the Yellow Emperor 黃[A]帝 20.80.

螿 21.93

jiang.

N. A kind of cicada.

SECTION 21A

§21A.00 (⺊/亅)

虖 21A.00

hu.

[AC var. of 乎; interch. 呼]

§21A.01 (⺊/小)

桌 21A.01

juo.

N. (1) (*-tz*) A table, desk: 桌子 ditto; 辦公桌 office desk; 書桌 desk in study; 飯桌 dining table; 圓桌 round table; 圓桌武士 round table knights; 桌面子 table top; 桌燈 table lamp. (2) A table at dinner: 開幾桌 how many tables? 幾桌客人 how many tables of guests? 同桌 sit at the same table.

柴 21A.01

chair.

N. (1) Firewood, fire sticks, unhewn timber: 打柴, 砍柴 gather, cut wood for fuel; 劈柴 v.t. & n. to split firewood, such split wood; 火柴 matches; 木柴 firewood; 骨瘦如柴 thin like a skeleton. (2) A surname.

柴扉 *chair-fei,* n., humble cottage door.

柴禾 *chair'her,* n., (MC) fuel.

柴火 *chairhuoo,* n., fuel.

柴胡 *chairhur,* n., (bot.) sickle-leaved hare's ear, an herb, *Bupleurum falcatum.*

柴雞 *chairji,* n., a species of chicken.

柴荊 *chair-jing,* n., humble cottage.

柴門 *chair-mern,* n., house door made of unhewn wood.

柴米 *chair-mii,* n., rice and fuel, the household essentials.

柴木 *chairmuh,* n., lower-grade wood, good for fuel.

柴薪 *chairshin,* n., firewood.

柴水 *chair-shueei,* n., fuel and water—basic household needs.

柴油 *chairyour,* n., diesel oil; 柴油機 diesel engine.

粲 21A.01

tsahn.

N. (1) (AC) polished ice. (2) A smile: 以博一粲 win a smile from you.

Adj. & adv. (1) Bright, illumined. (2) Smiling.

粲然 *tsahnrarn,* adj. & adv., (1) bright, -ly; (2) laughingly, smilingly.

粲粲 *tsahntsahn,* adj., bright, illumined, heart-warming.

紫 21A.01

tzyy.

N. & adj. Purple: 紫色 the purple color; 紫花 purple flowers; 紫紅 purple-red; 紫糖(膛)色兒 (of the human complexion) swarthy; 紫葡萄 European grapes; 臉色發紫 with a frightened look; 紅得發紫 at the height of one's power and influence, enjoying great popularity.

紫斑病 *tzyybanbing,* n., purpura.

紫貝 *tzyybeih,* n., (zoo.) *Cypraea macula.*

紫氣 *tzyychih,* n., an auspicious atmosphere.

紫闕 *tzyychyueh,* n., (1) the royal palace; (2) fairyland.

紫萼 *tzyy-eh,* n., (bot.) *Hosta coerulea.*

紫羔(兒) *tzyygau('l),* n., purplish-dark fur.

紫姑 *Tzyygu,* n., a legendary goddess supposed to be the patroness of sericulture.

紫毫 *tzyyhaur,* n., a writing brush made of brownish rabbit hair.

紫河車 *tzyyherche,* n., (1) the placenta; (2) (bot.) *Paris polyphylla.*

紫薑 *tzyyjiang,* n., young ginger shoots.

紫膠 *tzyyjiau,* n., sealing wax (usu. called 火漆).

紫禁 *tzyyjihn,* n., palace grounds: 紫禁城 the Forbidden City in Peking.

紫菫 *tzyrjiin,* n., (bot.) *Corydalis incisa.*

紫金 *tzyyjin,* n., gold of the best quality.

紫荊 *tzyyjing,* n., (bot.) the Judas tree or red bud, *Cercis chinensis.*

紫竹 *tzyyjur,* n., (bot.) *Bambusa nana,* var. *gracillima.*

紫羅蘭 *tzyyluorlarn,* n., (bot.) the violet.

紫陌 *tzyymoh,* n., (LL) roads leading to the national capital.

紫茉莉 *tzyymohlih,* n., (bot.) *Mirabilis jalapa.*

紫泥 *tzyynir,* n., purple sealing wax; 紫泥書 a royal edict.

紫杉 *tzyysha,* n., (bot.) *Taxus cuspidata.*

紫參 *tzyyshen,* n., (bot.) *Polygonum tenuicaule.*

紫水晶 *tzyr-shueeijing,* n., (min.) amethyst.

紫蘇 *tzyysu,* n., (bot.) *Perilla nankinensis.*

紫檀 *tzyytarn,* n., (bot.) the red sandalwood.

紫藤 *tzyyterng,* n., (bot.) the wistaria.

紫草 *tzyrtsaau*, n., (bot.) *Lithospermum officinale*, var. *erythrorhiron*.
紫菜 *tzyytsaih*, n., (bot.) the laver, edible purple seaweeds.
紫銅 *tzyyturng*, n., bronze.
紫藏 *tzyytzahng*, n., purple Tibetan incense.
紫外線 *tzyywaih-shiahn*, n., ultraviolet ray.
紫薇 *tzyyweir*, n., (bot.) the crape myrtle, *Lagerstroemia indica*.
紫雲英 *tzyyyurnyin*, n., (bot.) the milk vetch, *Astragalus sinicus*.

§21A.02 (⊦/ｋ)

餐 21A.02

tsan.
[Var. 湌]

N. A meal, dinner: 早餐, 午餐, 晚餐 breakfast, lunch, supper; 中餐, 西餐 Chinese, Western dinner; 每餐 every meal; 餐後 after meal (take pills); 進餐 serve dinner; 餐室, 餐間, 餐廳 dining room, hall; 餐桌 dining table; 餐巾 table napkin; 餐具 table service (plates, etc.).

V.t. To dine: 飽餐 eat one's fill; 餐風宿露 ("eat wind and sleep dew") hardships of travel without shelter.

§21A.10 (⊦/十)

卓 21A.10

juor.

N. A surname.

Adj. Eminent, outstanding, unexcelled: 卓絕, 卓越 *-jyuer, -yuer* ↓; 卓識, 卓見 *-shyh, -jiahn* ↓.

Adv. Erect: 卓立 *-lih* ↓.

卓奪 *juorduor*, n., (court. in letters) your discerning decision.
卓爾 *juor-eel*, adj., outstanding, eminent, standing alone.
卓見 *juorjiahn*, n., distinguished opinion, also wr. 灼見.
卓著 *juorjuoh*, adj., eminent, well-known.
卓卓 *juorjuor*, adj., outstanding, distinguished.
卓絕 *juorjyuer*, adj., singular, unsurpassed: 卓絕千古 unprecedented, unmatched past or present.
卓立 *juorlih*, adj., outstanding; standing erect, apart from others.
卓犖 *juorluoh*, adj., (AC) unsurpassed, eminent (also wr. 卓躒).
卓然 *juorrarn*, adj., standing apart, superior: 成效卓然 distinguished results.
卓錫 *juorshir*, n., (court.) a monk's residence (錫＝錫杖 81A.50).
卓殊 *jourshu*, adj., distinguished, unusual (character, accomplishments).
卓識 *juorshyh*, n., superior insight or judgment.
卓裁 *juortsair*, n., (court.) your decision.
卓午 *juorwuu*, n., (MC) midnoon.
卓異 *juoryih*, adj., see *-shu* ↑.
卓越 *jouryueh*, adj., unusual, superior.

顰 21A.10

pirn.

Adj. With knitted eyebrows: 東施效顰 phr., allu. to ugly woman (東施) trying to imitate a beauty (西施), famous for her knitted eyebrows, by knitting hers.

§21A.11 (⊦/土)

壑 21A.11

huoh.

N. Ravine, abyss, a depressed ground: 溝壑 gutters; 林壑之勝 the beauties of woods and ravines; 深壑 deep abyss.

§21A.21 (⊦/∟)

虐 21A.21

nyueh.

N. (AC) disaster, calamity, catastrophe; oppression.

Adj. & adv. Cruel(ly), oppressive (ly): 暴虐 tyrannical and cruel.

虐待 *nyuehdaih*, v. t., ill-treat, persecute (people, servants).
虐政 *nyuehjehng*, n., tyranny, misgovernment.

齒 21A.21

chyy.

N. (1) Tooth: 牙齒 ditto; 門齒 front teeth; 犬齒 canine teeth, also (descriptive) jagged, uneven; 臼齒 molar; 乳齒 milk teeth; 齒蠹 tooth decay; 齒痕, 齒印 tooth marks of biting; 切齒 gnash teeth with hatred; 不敢啟齒 dare not mention subject; 何足掛齒 not worth talking about; 露齒而笑 to grin; 齒亡舌存 the soft and flexible lasts longer than the hard; 沒齒不忘 shall not forget till death; 齒決 (AC) bite off with teeth.

(2) Gear, teeth of appliances: 輪齒 gear, cogs; 鋸齒, 梳齒 teeth of a saw, a comb; 齒輪, 齒軌 *-lurn*, *-gueei*↓. (3) Age, seniority: 序齒 seat guests according to seniority; 馬齒已長 (fig.) (self-derogatory) one is old.

V. i. (1) To mention: 不屑齒及 not worth mentioning. (2) To arrange; to regard as same class: 齒列 arrange in a row; 齒錄 to list in order; 不齒人類, 不以人齒之 (contempt.) do not regard as a human being.

齒腔 *chyychiang*, n., pulp cavity of tooth.

齒根 *chyygen*, n., root of tooth.

齒冠 *chyyguan*, n., tooth crown.

齒軌 *chyrgueei*, n., rack rail.

齒寒 *chyy-harn*, phr., see 脣亡齒寒 51A.42.

齒及 *chyy-jir*, phr., 何足齒及 not worth mentioning.

齒擊 *chyh-jir*, phr., teeth chatter.

齒質 *chyyjyr*, n., dentine.

齒冷 *chyrleeng*, v.i., snigger at: 令人齒冷 invite contempt.

齒列 *chyylieh*, v.i., regard as same class.

齒錄 *chyy-luh*, v.t., to register in proper class, pass examinations.

齒輪 *chyylurn*, n., wheel gear.

齒次 *chyytsyh*, n., order according to seniority.

齒吻 *chyr-ween*, n., lips and teeth.

齒音 *chyyyin*[1], n., (phonetics) dental sibilant (*ts*, *tz*, *s*, etc.).

齒齦 *chyyyin*[2], n., gum (of teeth).

§21A.22 (⺊/丨)

卡 21A.22

kaa (**chiaa*, **chiar*).

N. (1) Card: 卡片 *-piahn*↓. (2) (**chiaa*) Pincers, see 卡子 *-tz*↓.

V.t. (1) (**chiar*) To wedge in: 把茶几卡在兩把椅子中間 put a tea table between two chairs. (2) (**chiar* or **chiaa*) To choke, be choked: 魚骨卡住了喉嚨 a fishbone sticks in the throat; 卡住了, 卡着了 to wedge in, to be stuck in the throat; 卡死了 be choked to death; 他卡着了, 卡了一下 he gets choked.

卡賓槍 *kaabin-chiang*, n., (translit.) a carbine.

卡癶 *kaa'bo*, adj., bow-legged: 卡癶着腿兒往前走 walks bow-legged; 卡癶襠 (*-'bodang*) n., place between the thighs.

卡車 *kaache*, n., cart, truck.

卡介苗 *kaajiehmiaur*, n., (med.) BCG vaccine (abbr. for Bacillus Calmette-Guerin).

卡剌特 *kaalahteh*, n., (translit.) a carat.

卡路里 *kaaluhlii*, n., (translit.) calorie.

卡倫 *kaalurn*, n., formerly, a Mongolian border post (also called 邊臺).

卡片 *kaapiahn*, n., a card (as name card, postcard, card catalogue).

卡通 *kaatung*, n., (translit.) cartoon.

卡子 **chiaa'tz*, n., (1) toll, post for domestic duty: 卡口, 關卡 such station for collecting duty; (2) patrol: 下卡子, 撒卡子 set patrols; (3) pincers, also hairpin (髮卡).

§21A.30 (⺊/一)

上 21A.30

shahng (**shaang*).

N. (1) Top, summit: 山上, 屋上 top of hill, roof, see Prep.↓. (2) The superior, oft. the emperor: 上不悅 the emperor was displeased; 皇上 the emperor, ruler, (vocative) my Lord; 上頭, 上面, 上方 *-tour*, *-miahn*, *-fang*↓; 上帝 *-dih*↓. (3) (**shaang*) The third tone: 上聲. (4) (**shaang*) One of the pitches in pentatonic scale.

V.i. & t. (1) To go up, mount (mountain, wall): 上船, 上車 go aboard ship, car. (2) To go to: 上來, 上去 *-lair*, *-chyuh*↓; 上天津 go to Tientsin; 上京 go to Capital; 上城 go to city; 上飯店, 上影院 go to restaurant, cinema; 上街 go out (to shop, for a stroll); 上課 go to class; 上學 go to school; 上班 go on duty; 上法院 go to court; 上路 start on journey; 上墳 visit the grave; 上臺 to appear on stage, see 臺 20.11; 上牀 to go to bed, also to put dying person on another bed. (3) Appear on scene or enter category: 上市 (vegetables, etc.) be in season, appear on market; 上水 to go up the river; 上燈時候 time to light lamps; 上貨 replenish supplies; 戲館剛上人兒 people are just coming in to the theater; 上年紀, 上歲數兒 getting old; 上千上萬 run to thousands and tens of thousands; 上冬 when winter sets in. (4) To present: 上菜 serve food on table; 上書 write to a superior; 上奏 present memorial; 某某上 or 敬上 at end of letters added to signature ("presented by so-and-so"); 上條陳 make written recommendations to superior, present an official request. (5) To affix, apply, place in position: 上門窗 fix windows and doors in new building; 上板兒 to close window before closing up shop; 上梁 place beam on house being built; 上刺刀 fix bayonet; 上鞋底 fix sole on shoe being made; 上領子 affix collar on dress being made; 上顏色 to apply color; 上漆 to apply lacquer; 上糞 apply fertilizer to field; 上捐, 上稅 to pay tax on goods; 不上心念書 does not apply one's mind to

上 school lessons; 請你上眼瞧 please use your eyesight and look. (6) To wind up (clock, watch, machine); 上鍊 -*liahn*, to chain up.

Adj. (1) Upper, first, best (opp. 下 lower): 上等 first-class (goods, etc.); 上級 upper grade in school or army; 上品 the first grade (of goods); 上策, 上計 the best plan; 上上 A 1, the very best; 上下 -*shiah* ↓; 最上 topmost. (2) Above, previous, last: 上月 last month; 上篇 first chapter or chapter above; 上回, 上次 the last time (I saw him, etc.).

Adv. Up, often 上來; 說不上 not worthy to speak of; 攀上 to climb up; 拉上 or 上來 pull up; 拉上我 involve me by mentioning; 飛上 fly up; 走上來 come forward, approach; 追上, 趕上 or 上來 catch up; 趕不上 fail to catch, miss (train, meeting).

Prep. (Used after nn.) above, over, oft. 上, 以上 or 之上; 三十以上, 三百以上 over thirty, three hundred; 在其上 is above it; 路上 on the road; 船上 on the boat; 地上 on the ground; 席上 at table, during dinner; 書上 in the book; often forms prepositional phr.; 表面上 superficially, on the surface; 心裏上 in one's heart; 口頭上 orally (promise, etc.).

上輩(兒)(子) *shahng-beih ('l, tz)*, n., the elders of the family, the older generation.

上邊(兒) *shahng'bian(-bia'l)*, n. & adj., above; servants' or subordinates' reference to master(s).

上幣 *shahng-bih*, n., (AC) gold as currency.

上賓 *shahng-bin*, (1) n., guest of honor; (2) (AC) v. i., (of emperor) to die.

上部 *shahng-buh*, n., upper part, esp. of body.

上場 *shahng-chaang*, v. i., appear on scene, market or stage: 上場門兒 entrance and exit on stage.

上朝 *shahng-chaur*, v. i., go to imperial audience, go to court duty.

上秤 *shahng-chehng*, v. i., to put on the scale and weigh.

上前(兒) *shahng-chiarn(-chiar'l)*, v. i., to come forward.

上去 *shahng-chyuh*, (1) v. i., to go up: 上不去 cannot go up; (2) adv., up: 掛上去 hang up; 拉上去 pull up.

上當 *shahng-dahng*, v. i., to fall into trap.

上代 *shahngdaih*, n., (1) the earliest historical times; (2) the ancestors.

上達 *shahng-dar*, v.i., (1) (AC) to develop spiritually; (2) to reach the ears of the ruler.

上等 *shahngdeeng*, adj. & n., first-class, superior grade.

上德 *shahng-der*, n., (Laotse) the highest character.

上吊 *shahng-diauh*, v. i., to hang oneself.

上帝 *Shahngdih*, n., (AC and modn. term for) God.

上端 *shahngduan*, n., the top end; what is mentioned above.

上凍 *shahng-duhng*, v. i., (of river) to freeze.

上顎 *shahng-eh*, n., roof of mouth.

上方 *shahng-fang*, n., (1) the place above; (2) the celestial realm.

上礬 *shahng-farn*, v. i., apply alum to "size" paper for painting.

上房 *shahng-farng*, n., master's quarters, main rooms of Chinese courtyard.

上風 *shahng-feng*[1], n., point of vantage: 佔上風 stand at advantage, on the windward side.

上峯 *shahng-feng*[2], n., (LL) official superiors, the top people in bureaucracy.

上趕着 *shahnggaan'je*, v. i., hurry forward to please s. o.: 上趕着叫老伯 hurried forward and called "uncle!"

上崗兒 *shahng-gaang'l*, v. i., (derog.) to sit at honored seat.

上鉤 *shahng-gou*, v. i., (of fish) take the bait; (also fig.) be entrapped.

上官 *shahng-guan*, n., (1) official directly in charge or higher-up; (2) a compound surname.

上工 *shahng-gung*, v.i., (1) report for work on given date; (2) (Chin. med.) the best skill in diagnosis.

上國 *shahngguor*, n., term used to refer to conquering nation by conquered (cf. 勝^國 42A.50).

上古 *shahng-guu*, n., primordial times.

上海 *Shahnghaai*, n., Shanghai.

上好 *shahng-haau*, adj., the best (quality).

上畫兒 *shahng-huah'l*, v.i., (of landscape) be a subject for painting, to go into painting.

上皇 *shahng-huarng*, n., emperor's father, already retired, also 太上皇.

上會 *shahng-hueih*, v. i. & n., (to attend or form) temporary association for mutual loan money, decided monthly by highest bidder for interest, or by dice.

上回 *shahng-hueir*, adv., the last or previous time.

上戶 *shahng-huh*, n., rich landlords.

上火(兒) *shahng-huoo('l)*, v. i., to get angry, inflamed with anger.

上賬 *shahng-jahng*, v. i., to record in the account book.

上陣 *shahng-jehn*, v. i., to go to battle; (fig.) have dispute: 這孩子不聽話, 他母親天天和他上陣 the mother has daily rows with the child who would not listen.

上家 *shahng-jia*, n., the person on one's left at drinking or gamble.

上尖兒 *shahngjia'l*, v. i., make a heapful (of rice, etc.) in bowl.

上焦 *shahngjiau*, n., see 三^焦 30.30; 上焦熱 (Chin. med.) symptoms including irregular pulse, dizziness, inflammation of the eye, dry thirst, etc.

上界 *shahng-jieh*, n., the upper region of heaven.

上計 *shahng-jih*, n., the best plan.

上進 *shahngjihn*[1], v. i., to go forward, make progress esp. in studies; 上進心 n., desire to advance.

上勁 *shahng-jihn*[2], v.i., do s. t. energetically, go full steam ahead.

上緊 *shahng-jiin*, adv., quickly and without delay.

上九 *shahng-jioou*, n., (1) the ninth day of ninth lunar month; (2) (AC) the 29th day of each lunar month (9th being 中九 and 19th the 下九).

上裝 *shahng-juang*, v. i., fully dress up (as actor or bride).

上知 *shahng-jyh*, n., (AC) man of

highest intelligence.

上客 *shahng-keh*, n., the most honored or esteemed guest.

上口 *shahng-koou*, adv., (read) fluently; 上口字 *--tzyh*, n., (in Peking opera) words pronounced with archaic vowels (thus 知, 朱 pr. as *ji*, *jyu*).

上款(兒) *shahng-kuaan(-kuaa'l)*, n., the line of dedication on scroll, usu. on right, as against the signature, 下款 usu. on left.

上來 *shahnglair*, v. i., come up.

上列 *shahng-lieh*, adj., above-mentioned or listed.

上流 *shahngliour*, adj., (1) first-rate (scholars, etc.); upper-class (society); (2) n., upper stream.

上落 *shahngluoh*, v. t., (MC) to rebuke, take issue with (person).

上略 *shahng-lyueh*, phr., the top or preceding part omitted.

上門(兒) *shahng-mern(-mer'l)*, v.i., (1) come to person's house (to collect debt, etc.); (2) to lock the door for the night.

上面(兒) *shahng'mian(-'mia'l)*, n., one's master or superior; adv., above, on the surface.

上年 *shahng-niarn*, n. & adv., last year.

上皮 *shahng-pir*, n., (physiol.) epidermis; (bot.) outer bark of trees.

上人 *shahng-rern*, n., (court. address) monk.

上日 *shahng-ryh*, n., (AC) the first day of month; (LL) a beautiful or festive day.

上腮 *shahngsai*, n., upper jaw.

上色 (1) *shahng-shaai*, v. i., to apply color (to furniture); distinguished; 不上色 not distinguished or successful; (2) (*-seh*) n., the best grade; (AC) a beauty.

上上 *shahng-shahng*, adj., top grade, A 1; 上上月, 上上星期 month, week before last; 上上下下 high and low (agree, praise, etc.).

上乘 *shahng-shehng*, adj., best, exquisite (goods, writing); (Budd.) *mahayana*(＝大乘).

上身 *shahng-shen*, n., upper part of body: 上身兒 also a short jacket; 上身 also v. i.＝鬼上身 *gueei--*, possessed.

上昇 *shahng-sheng*, v. i., go up skywards.

上下 *shahng-shiah*, (1) prep., (after a number) or thereabouts: 三十上下 about thirty; (2) v. i., to differ: 不相上下 match equally; 上下其手 change wording in legal document to alter meaning slightly by changing emphasis; 上上下下 to go up and down, both high and low; (3) adj., high and low, above and below; up and down; (4) first and second characters in inquiring or mentioning name of ancestor or monk.

上像 *shahng-shiahng*, adj., (of person) photogenic: 不上像 not photogenic.

上香 *shahng-shiang*, v. i., go to temple to pray, esp. on pilgrimage.

上弦 *shahngshiarn*, (1) n., second quarter of moon or lunar month; (2) v. i., to wind up spring (in watches, etc.).

上庠 *shahngshiarng*[1], n., (AC) college of elders.

上詳 *shahng-shiarng*[2], v. i., to report to superior.

上鞋 *shahng-shier*, v. i., formerly, to fix cloth soles to new shoes.

上行 *shahng-shirng*, v. i., (of boats, carts) going upstream or toward city or place; opp. 下行 going away from.

上手 *shahngshoou*[1], (1) n., the predecessor; one's superior; (2) v. i., to get in one's hand, to get (victim, fish on hook).

上首 *shahng-shoou*[2], n., the honored one; the leader, boss.

上壽 *shahng-shouh*, (1) adj., having reached highest grade of longevity (AC 100 or 120 yrs.); (2) v. i., to drink a toast for longevity.

上書 *shahng-shu*[1], v. i., to write to ruler or high official.

上疏 *shahng-shu*[2], v. i., to submit memorial to emperor.

上士 *shahng-shyh*[1], n., (1) (AC) best kind of scholar; (2) (modn.) first-class sergeant.

上世 *shahng-shyh*[2], n., primeval times; earliest historical periods.

上選 *shahng-shyuaan*, n. & adj., select or choice (goods, scholars).

上學 *shahng-shyuer*, v. i., go to school.

上旬 *shahng-shyurn*, n., the first ten days of the month.

上算 *shahng-suahn*, adj., it pays to (do s. t.): 不上算 does not pay to do it.

上訴 *shahng-suh*, v. i., to appeal to higher court.

上司 *shahng'sy*, n., one's official superior.

上台 *shahng-tair*[1], v. i., to go on the stage; (fig.) (of officials) to come into power, be appointed as premier, minister.

上檯 *shahng-tair*[2], v. i., to make a parade of bride's trousseau on the streets, including jewels, beddings, etc.

上堂 *shahng-tang*, v.i., to go up the hall, also to go to class.

上湯 *shahng-tarng*, n., formerly, soup served at end of feast, when tips were given and guests rose.

上套兒 *shahng-tauh'l*, v. i., to fall into trap.

上天 *shahng-tian*, (1) n., the sky above, oft. personified, upper space; (2) v. i., go up to heaven.

上體 *shahng-tii*, n., upper part of body.

上頭 *shahngtour*, (1) v. i., (AC) ceremony of coming of age for boys and girls; (2) pron. & prep., (*'tou*) those above, above.

上蒼 *shahng-tsang*, n., the blue sky, oft. personified.

上操 *shahng-tsau*, v. i., go to drill.

上策 *shahng-tseh*, n., the best plan.

上次 *shahng-tsyh*, n. & adv., the previous time, last (time).

上竈 *shahng-tzauh*, v. i., serve in the kitchen.

上座 *shahng-tzuoh*, (1) n., the seat of honor; (2) v. i., to begin Buddhist mass; 上座兒 customers begin to come into restaurant.

上
止
些

上足 *shahng-tzur*, n., (1) able student, see 高$^{\triangle}$足 60.42; (2) (AC) superior horses.

上祖 *shahng-tzuu*, n., remote ancestor.

上梓 *shahng-tzyy*, v. i., (of books) go to press (lit., "carved on wood block").

上位 *shahng-weih*, n., top seat: 在上位 (AC) when serving as ruler.

上文 *shahng-wern*[1], n., the preceding context.

上聞 *shahng-wern*[2], v. i., (LL) formerly, to write to imperial court.

上屋 *shahng-wu*, n., the upper rooms of a courtyard.

上午 *shahngwuu*, n., morning, the forenoon.

上壓力 *shahng-yalih*, n., upward pressure, opp. 下壓力 downward pressure.

上眼 *shahng-yaan*[1], v.i., to look at intently: 看不上眼 spurn, disdain, hold in contempt.

上演 *shahng-yaan*[2], v.i., give a public performance.

上言 *shahng-yarn*, v. i., (LL) respectfully submit (request, etc.).

上夜 *shahng-yeh*[1], v.i., (of watchman) be on night duty, to watch the night.

上葉 *shahngyeh*[2], n., (LL) former times (葉=代).

上衣 *shahng-yi*, n., outer garment.

上映 *shahng-yihng*, v. i., to exhibit (films); also (movie, film) now showing.

上癮 *shahng-yiin*, v. i., to form habit (in use of narcotics, etc.); adj., addicted.

上游 *shahng-your*, n., the upper stream.

上苑 *shahng-yuahn*, n., imperial garden.

上元 *shahng-yuarn*, n., the 15th day of lunar first month, a lantern festival.

上月 *shahng-yueh*, n., last month.

上諭 *shahng-yuh*, n., imperial decree.

止 21A.30

jyy.

Fin. part. (AC) 百室盈止,婦子寧止 all the rooms are full and the womenfolk are content.

N. 容止 a person's demeanor; 人而無止 (AC) if a man does not have proper appearance; 擧止 stature, gait, bodily movements: 擧止大方 the dignified movements of a gentleman.

V. i. & t. (1) V. i., to stop: 停止 (work, etc.) stops; 截止 cut short; 中止 stop halfway; 止住了 has stopped; 流個不止 flow without stop; 適可而止 do not overdo a thing, play it just right; 禁止, 阻止 to forbid, obstruct. (2) V. t., to stop s.t., (as bleeding, cough, thirst, hunger, gossip, pain, itch, anger, etc.): 止戈爲武 (AC) to disarm military prowess (from an ancient explanation of the character 武 as consisting of "stop" and "arms"); 望梅止渴 (AC allu.) tell the army there are prunes ahead so as to stop their thirst—wishful thinking. (3) To stop over at a place: 止宿 *-suh* ↓; to have as final goal; 止于至善 (AC) to aim at absolute perfection. (4) (AC) to arrive: 莅止.

Adj. Still (water): 止水不波 still water does not have ripples—dead to the sins of the flesh; 心如止水 a mind tranquil as still waters.

Adv. U. f. 只 only: 止是 (=只是) only thing is; 止得 (=只得) only have to.

止步 *jyy-buh*, phr., as in (1) 遊人止步 a formula "loiterers not permitted"; (2) 請止步 a formula asking host not to trouble to accompany departing guest further.

止風 *jyy-feng*, phr., (Chin. med.) stop arthritic pain.

止觀 *jyyguan*, phr., (Budd.) maintain mental calm while observing the universe—a sect emphasizing mental discipline.

止境 *jyyjihng*(*-'jing*), n., the destination, ultimate goal: 學無止境 there is no end to learning.

止血 *jyyshyueh*, v. i., to stop bleeding.

止宿 *jyysuh*, v.i., to stop over for the night.

止痛劑 *jyytuhng-jih*, n., analgesic.

些 21A.30

shie (**suoh*)

Fin. part. (**suoh*) (AC) only in 楚辭 poetry) particle expressing regret: 何爲四方些 "why wander about?"

Adj. (1) Few, a few, indicating plural number: 一些 or often contracted to just 些, a few, limited to countable nn. (books, persons, chairs), while 一點兒 a little is used for countable and uncountable nn. (water, oil, strength); 一些書, 一些人, 一些椅子, but 加點水, 添點油, 出點力量 (also see sense 2); 些微, 些須, 些許 *-weir, -shyu, -shyuu* ↓, 有些 some, few; 有些人 some people; 有些時候 sometimes; 有些不同, 有些兩樣 there's some difference; 好些 quite a few; 好些人 quite a few people. (2) Used after 這, 那 as indicating plural: 這些 these; 那些 those.

Adv. A little: 多些, 少些 a little more, a little less; 方便些 a little more convenient; 好聽些 sounds a little better.

些箇 *shie'ge*, (1) adv., (MC) a little (=些兒): 滿縣人都讓他些箇 all the people in the district deferred to him a bit, do not quite measure up to him; (2) pron., 這些箇, 那些箇 these, those.

些兒 *shie'l*, (1) adv., a little, a bit: 些兒來時, 已成不救 if he had come a little later, it would have been too late; 不害些兒怕 (=一點不害怕) am not a bit afraid; (2) n., 些兒短不得 won't take a little less—must have the amount; also 些兒箇 adv. & n., a little, a few, a bit: 你曉事些兒

箇 you'd better know a little what you are doing.

些少 *shieshaau*, (1) adj. & adv., a little (time, attention, etc.): 有些少不便 there's some inconvenience; (2) n., 給我些少 give me a little.

些小 *shieshiaau*, (1) adj. & adv., a little, just a little; (2) n., 懂得些小 know just a little.

些些 *shieshie*, adj. & adv., a little: 有些些似外翁 a little resembles his maternal grandfather; 窗兒外雨些些 some light rain outside the window.

些時 *shieshyr*, adv., a little while.

些須 *shieshyu*, adj. & adv., some, few, a little: 些須懂得 understand a little.

些許 *shieshyuu*, adj. & adv., see *-shyu* ↑: 些許禮物 just some little present; 些許小事 just some small matter.

些子(兒) *shietz('l)*, adj. & adv., (MC) a little.

些微 *shieweir*, adj. & adv., a little: 些微銀子 a little money; 些微不同 some slight difference.

虗 21A.30

shyu.

[Var. of 虛 21A.30↓]

虛 21A.30

shyu.

N. (1) The sky, the empyrean: 太虛 the great void, outer space; 凌虛 soar to the skies. (2) A vulnerable, not defended, point: 乘虛而入 (the enemy) enter, taking advantage of the unpreparedness.

V. t. To reserve space: 虛左(虛位)以待 reserve the honored post for s. o. competent.

Adj. (1) Empty, unoccupied, void: 空虛 empty; 虛空 *-kung*↓; 虛無縹渺 (talk which is) abstruse, vague, insubstantial; 膝下猶虛 (of married couple) still childless. (2) Vain, nominal: 虛名虛利 reputation and material wealth, regarded as vain; 虛文 *-wern*↓; 虛銜, 虛號 nominal title; 虛言, 虛辭 vain words, promises; 虛談 twaddle, "gas." (3) Humble, open-minded: 謙虛 modest; 虛心, 虛懷, 虛冲 *-shin*, *-huair*, *-chung*↓. (4) Timid: 膽虛 timid, frightened; 心虛 (contrast 虛心 above) have a guilty conscience. (5) Weak: 虛弱 *-ruoh*↓; 體虛 body is weakened. (6) False, insubstantial, worthless: 虛僞 *-weih*↓; 不知虛實 do not know whether it is true or false; 虛情假意 hypocritical show of cordiality; 虛與委蛇 pretend to have interest and sympathy; 虛報 make a false report (of funds); 虛謗 malign gossip; 虛詐 *-jah*↓.

Adv. (1) Vainly, without truth, substance or result: 虛度光陰 waste time; 彈無虛發 no shot was wasted; 虛有其表 (of man) good looks without substantial ability or virility; 虛張聲勢 make pretenses (of wealth, power); 虛應故事 do s. t. for form's sake only; 這位等於虛設 the post exists nominally only; 虛耗公帑 waste public funds; 虛費 sundry, unnecessary expenses. (2) Based on imagination rather than reality: 虛設, 虛想, 虛構, 虛擬 *-sheh*, *-shiaang*, *-gouh*, *-nii*↓.

虛白 *shyu-bor*[1], phr., 虛室生白 (AC) light of meditation in an empty house.

虛薄 *shyubor*[2], adj., thin, insubstantial (provisions, character).

虛怯 *shyuchieh*, adj., timid.

虛器 *shyuchih*, n., (AC) ability without power.

虛冲 *shyuchung*, adj., open-minded and modest.

虛誕 *shyudahn*, adj., given to exaggeration, exaggerated, fantastic.

虛浮 *shyufur*, adj., flighty, superficial (opinions).

虛構 *shyugouh*, adj. & n., purely imaginative, -tion.

虛恭 *shyugung*, adj., (1) modest, retiring; (2) 出虛恭 let off gas, from 出恭 regular bowel movement.

虛喝 *shyuheh*, v. i., to threaten with words.

虛幻 *shyuhuahn*, adj., vain, vainglorious; (Budd.) illusive, false (appearance of sensuous experience).

虛懷 *shyuhuair*, adj., modest, open-minded: 虛懷若谷 (Taoist) receptive heart "like the valley," free from pride and prejudices.

虛火 *shyuhuoo*, n., (1)(Chin. med.) fever or nervous heart from gen. weakness: 虛火上升 easily get excited, irascible; (2) (contempt.) (rely on) s.o. else's power or influence.

虛詐 *shyujah*, adj., deceitful, tricky.

虛假 *shyujiaa*, adj., deceitful, false, hypocritical, also 虛虛假假.

虛竭 *shyujier*, adj., exhausted (vitality, funds).

虛靜 *shyujihng*, adj., quiet and passionless.

虛己 *shyujii*, adj., not self-opinionated, ready to listen to advice.

虛驚 *shyujing*, v.i. & n., (to experience) a false alarm: 受了虛驚 received a shock; 飽受虛驚 suffer from nervous fears.

虛衷 *shyujung*, adj., open-minded, willing to take advice; modest.

虛曠 *shyukuahng*, adj., broad and open (country).

虛空 *shyukung*, n., (1) the upper space; (2) (Budd.) void, emptiness of the material world, also adj., unreal, insubstantial.

虛勞 *shyulaur*, n., (Chin. med.) gen. debility.

虛面子 *shyumiahntz*, n., insincere gesture of politeness, formal hospitality or friendship.

虛靡 *shyumii*, v. t., to waste (time, funds).

亅	小	⺊	十	土	ナ	卄	⺊	丨	一	丁	フ	口	区	冈	㇆	厂	尸	亠	广	宀	丶	乚	七	心	八	人	乂	⺈	一	刂	⺈	く
00	01	02	10	11	12	20	21	22	30	31	32	40	41	42	50	51	52	60	61	62	63	70	71	72	80	81	82	83	90	91	92	93

虛名 *shyu-mirng*, n., (1) hollow reputation; (2) nominal office, title or rank.

虛擬 *shyunii*, v. i. & t. & n., conjecture, hypothetical supposition.

虛牝 *shyupihn*, n., empty valley: 虛牝光陰 waste good time.

虛弱 *shyuruoh*, adj., debilitated (health), lacking in vitality.

虛榮 *shyururng*, n., vainglory: 虛榮心 vanity, love of vainglory.

虛設 *shyusheh*, adj., nominal (title, position).

虛聲 *shyusheng*, (1) adj. & adv., making exaggerated reports; (2) n., false reports (of victory, etc.).

虛想 *shyushiaang*, n. & v.i., imagine, -ation, a mere wish.

虛線 *shyushiahn*, n., dotted line.

虛像 *shyushiahng*, n., (phys.) virtual image.

虛邪 adj., (1) *shyushier*, debilitated; (2) (*-shyur*＝虛徐) leisurely.

虛心 *shyu-shin*, adj., not self-opinionated, ready to take advice.

虛數 *shyushuh*, n., (math.) imaginary number.

虛實 *shyu-shyr*, n., truth or opposite of a matter: 探聽軍中虛實 spy on enemy's true conditions or plans. 「talk.

虛頭 *shyutour*, n., (coll.) empty

虛辭 *shyutsyr*, n., subterfuge, irrelevant talk.

虛脫 *shyutuo*, n. & v.i., (med.) physical collapse from gen. debility, to be in such symptom.

虛足 *shyutzur*, n., (zoo.) pseudopodia.

虛字 *shyutzyh*, n., (Chin. gram.) functional words (conj., adv., exclamation) versus 實字 substantive words (n. & pron.).

虛妄 *shyuwahng*, adj., absurd, ostentatious and fake.

虛僞 *shyuweih*, adj. & n., false, -ness; hypocritical, -crisy.

虛文 *shyu-wern*, n., routine formalities: 虛文縟節 empty forms, rituals.

虛無 *shyuwur*, adj. & n., unreal, -ity; 虛無主義 nihilism.

虛言 *shyu-yarn*, n., empty talk.

虛譽 *shyu-yuh*, n., fame without substance.

盧 21A.30

lur.

N. (1) (AC) a vessel; a hound. (2) A surname.

Adj. (AC) black color: 呼盧喝雉 (LL) to gamble (shouting for black and red as at crab game).

盧比 *Lurbii*, n., rupee.

盧布 *Lurbuh*, n., rouble.

盧森堡 *Lursenbaau*, n., Luxemberg.

---

§21A.40 (卜/口)

占 21A.40

jan (**jahn*).

V. i. & t. (1) To practise divination: 占卜, 占卦, 占星 *-buu, -guah, -shing* ↓; 早占勿藥 phr., already recovered from illness ("as foretold by divination"), wish you a speedy recovery. (2) To versify: 口占一絕 repeated a verse just composed. (3) (**jahn*) (Interch. 佔) to occupy (place): 占領, 占有, 占先 *-liing, -yoou, -shian* ↓.

占卜 *janbuu*, v. i. & t., to practise divination.

占斷 *janduahn*, v. t., to determine or find out by divination: 占斷吉凶 find out good or bad luck.

占卦 *janguah*, v. i. & n., (to make) divination by 八卦 or arrangement of the eight diagrams; see 八[4]卦 *baguah*, 80.80.

占據 **jahnjyuh*, v. t., to occupy illegally or by force.

占課 *jankeh*, v. i., see *-guah* ↑.

占領 **jahnliing*, v. t., see *-jyuh* ↑.

占先 **jahnshian*, v. i., to occupy before others, to pre-empt.

占星 *janshing*, v. i., to divine by astrology.

占驗 *janyahn*, n., confirmation of oracle.

占有 **jahnyoou*, v. t., *-jyuh* ↑.

訾 21A.40

tzyy.

N. (AC) fault of s.o.

V. t. (1) Criticize: 訾短 point out s.o.'s shortcomings; 訾毀 detract (s.o.) behind his back; 訾病 criticize severely; 訾議 take (s.o.) to task. (2) (AC) to measure: 訾粟而稅 pay taxes in kind.

Adj. (AC) poor or inferior quality: 訾食者不肥 one brought up on poor food can't be physically strong.

---

§21A.41 (卜/図)

旨 21A.41

jyy.

N. (1) Main idea, aim: 宗旨 aim; 意旨 a man's desire or aim in some undertaking; 遵從意旨 obey s. o.'s desire; 本旨, 主旨, 大旨 main idea or purpose (of book, organization); 要旨 essential point(s); 旨趣 *-chyuh* ↓. (2) Imperial decree: 聖旨 ditto; 請旨 ask for His Majesty's desire; 奉旨 by His Majesty's decree.

Adj. (LL) beautiful (words), delicious (food, smell): 旨哉斯言 how true, how beautiful these words; 旨酒 fine wine; 美旨, 甘旨 delicious food.

旨趣 *jyychyuh*, n., essential idea, purport (in speech, teachings).

旨蓄 *jyyshyuh*, n., (AC) store of good food.

旨意 *jyy-yi*, n., (1) a sovereign's

desire expressed or not; (2) essential purport.

皆 21A.41

jie.

Pron. Everybody, all: 皆大歡喜 (orig. Budd.) satisfaction of everybody concerned; 四海之內皆兄弟也 within the four seas all men are brothers.

Adv. (LL) all: 皆失 all lost; 盡皆 all without exception; 皆然 all like this: 皆因 all because.

眥 21A.41

tzyh.

[Var. 眦]

N. The socket of the eye: 目眥欲裂 with a fiery look (as if one's eyes would "pop out").

V.i. Stare with an angry look: 睚眥 look at s.o. in anger; 睚眥必報 would not let any one get away even with a hostile look.

睿 21A.41

rueih.

Adj. (1) Gifted with a keen insight, astute, sagacious, perspicacious: 睿知 *-jyh*↓; 睿哲 *-jer*↓. (2) Referring to things belonging to or done by the sovereign: 睿藻 works written by the emperor.

睿哲 *rueihjer*, adj., (LL) divinely wise, saintly.

睿知 *rueihjyh*, n., (LL) (1) keen perception; (2) the rational faculty.

督 21A.41

du.

N. & v. t. (1) Supervise, oversee, direct: 監督 direct, -tor, see many compp.↓; forming names of many offices: 總督 governor of province; 都督 governor; 督撫 civil (總督) and military (巡撫) governors; 督憲, 督堂 court. address of governor; 督戰 to direct campaign; 督課 to inspect work done. (2) (AC) middle seam of jacket.

督辦 *dubahn*, n., director, director general (of railway administration, iron works, etc.).

督察 *duchar*, n., inspector, inspector general (of customs, tax administration, etc.); v. t., to inspect and supervise.

督飭 *duchyh*, v. t., supervise and direct.

督軍 *dujyun*, n., (early Republican days) governor of one or more provinces.

督理 *dulii*, v. t., supervise.

督率 *dushuaih*, v. t., lead (troops, followers).

督師 *dushy*, n., commander appointed by court to take overall charge of campaign.

督學 *dushyuer*, n., educational commissioner or inspector.

督促 *dutsuh*, v. t., to hurry, speed up (work, construction, etc.).

督責 *dutzer*, v. i. & t., closely supervise (work, worker, student).

卣 21A.41

yoou.

N. An ancient wine vessel.

鹵 21A.41

luu.

N. (1) Rock salt; natural salt on land. (2) (AC) big shield.

V.t. Used as var. of 擄 to capture.

Adj. Coarse, rash, stupid: 粗鹵 (of person) rash, coarse; 鹵漢 coarse person. (In this sense oft. wr. 魯).

鹵簿 *luubuh*, n., (1) (AC) protocol in imperial procession; (2) (AC) bodyguard of nobility.

鹵地 *luudih*, n., alkaline soil.

鹵獲 *luuhuoh*, v.t., to capture in battle.

鹵鹼 *lurjiaan*, n., alkalis.

鹵掠 *luulyueh*, v.t., to capture and loot.

鹵莽 *lurmaang*, adj., as in 鹵莽滅裂 (of person) reckless, rash (also 魯莽).

鹵素 *luusuh*, n., (chem.) halogens (fluorine, chlorine, bromine and iodine).

鹵鹽 *luuyarn*, n., natural salt.

§ 21A.42 (⺊/冈)

肯 21A.42

keen (also *keeng*).

[Archaic var. 肎, 肻]

V. i. & aux. Be willing(to): 肯不肯 are you willing, will you? 他肯嗎 is he willing? 不肯來 is not willing to come, will not come; 肯吃苦, 肯做事 is willing to work hard, to take up things.

肯綮 *keenchihng*, n., meat joints; (fig.) critical or important juncture, essential points.

肯定 *keendihng*, adj., (1) affirmative, as opp. 否定 negative (answer, vote); (2) positive, determined (resolve, attitude).

膚 21A.42

fu.

N. Human skin: (vern.) 皮膚髮膚 hair and skin; 切膚之痛 hurt in most intimately close manner; 膚受之愬 (AC) rumor or smear which hurts intimately; 不膚撓 (AC) do not flinch from blows.

Adj. (1) Skin-deep: 膚淺 -*chiaan* ↓. (2) Vague, superficial, see 膚泛, 膚廓 -*fahn*, -*guor* ↓. (3) great, admirable: 膚功 (AC) great achievement; 膚敏 (AC) handsome and agile of body.

膚淺 *fuchiaan*, adj., superficial, "skin-deep" (of knowledge, discussion).

膚泛 *fufahn*, adj., vague (cf. 浮^△^泛 63A.00).

膚廓 *fuguor*, adj., (LL) grandiloquent, impractical.

胔 21A.42

tzyh.

N. (AC) (1) Dried bones of birds or animals. (2) Putrid meat.

§ 21A.50 (⺊/㇆)

与(㸚) 21A.50

yuu.

[Abbr. of 與 90.80]

虜 21A.50

luu (also *luoo*).

N. Captive: 俘虜 war prisoner.

V.t. To capture (var. of 擄 10A.50).

§ 21A.63 (⺊/丶)

点 21A.63

diaan.

[Pop. for 點 41S.40]

§ 21A.70 (⺊/乚)

匕 21A.70

bii.

N. (1) (AC) spoon. (2) Arrowhead.

匕首 *birshoou*, n., short sword, bayonet: 圖窮而匕首見 come to open hostility after subterfuges fail.

虎 21A.70

huu.

N. (1) Tiger: 老虎 tiger (not necessarily "old"); 猛虎 a fierce tiger; 如虎添翼 lend support to rebel ("like adding wing to tiger"); 虎頭捉虱, 虎頭抓蒼蠅 try to catch lice, flies, on tiger's head . . . unwise provocation; 捋(or 拔) 虎鬚 "twist tiger's whiskers"—twist lion's tail; 勢成騎虎, 騎虎難下 like riding on tiger—afraid to go on and unable to get down; 不入虎穴, 焉得虎子 the only way to catch tiger cubs is to go into tiger's den—take necessary risk; 虎毒不食兒 even a beast does not eat its young; 爲虎作倀^△^ 91A.02; 虎口 (a) a dangerous spot, (b) (fortune-telling) area between thumb and index finger; 虎口餘生 narrowly escape from danger; 虎步 a great warrior's firm strides like the tiger's; 虎背熊腰 (a person) of a stocky and imposing build, boxer's sinuous posture; 虎視眈眈 cast covetous eyes on; 虎頭虎腦 (person's) appearance of strength; 踏虎尾, 虎尾春冰 like treading on tiger's tail or spring ice; 虎頭蛇尾 (of affairs) a brave beginning and weak ending. (2) Tiger as symbol of ferocity or bravery: 虎而冠 a vindictive person (tiger in a human cap); 虎將 a brave general; 虎帳 general's tent; 虎臣 brave ministers; 虎士 brave fighter; 虎狼之性 voracious, violent nature; 虎威 fear-inspiring prowess. (3) A surname.

虎榜 *hurbaang*, n., announcement of successful military graduates.

虎賁 *huuben*, n., (AC) a brave warriors.

虎蹲砲 *huudun-pauh*, n., (1) a short-barreled mortar; (2) an ancient catapult.

虎耳草 *hureeltsaau*, n., (bot.) the saxifrage.

虎符 *huufur*, n., a general's seal.

虎掌 *hurjaang*, n., (bot.) a poisonous plant, the jack-in-the-pulpit.

虎帳 *huujahng*, n., a general's tent.

虎列拉 *huuliehla*, n., (translit.) cholera, now usu. called 霍亂.

虎皮豆兒 *huupirdouh'l*, n., (1) a kind of black spotted bean; (2) an insect resembling (1).

虎穴 *huu-shier*, n., tiger's den, esp. 虎穴龍潭 a hazardous spot.

虎鬚 *huushyu*, n., (1) tiger's whiskers; (2) lamp pith.

虎頭拍 *huu'tourpai*, n., words to scare (person).

虎頭牌 *huutourpair*, n., a sign of magistrate's office to "keep off."
虎刺 *huutsyh*, n., (bot.) the barberry, *Damnacanthus indicus*.
虎子 *huutzyy*, n., a tiger cub.

彪 21A.70

biau.

N. (1) Tiger's stripes. (2) (AC) Young tiger. (3) A surname.

Adj. Tiger-like: 彪形 martial-looking and handsome.

彪炳 *biaubiing*, adj., shining, glorious (achievement).
彪蒙 *biau-merng*, v. i., (arch.) develop the mind.
彪子 *biautz*, n., frolicsome creature; 半彪子 crude, immature person.

§ 21A.71 (⺊/乁)

歲 21A.71

sueih.
[Abbr. 岁]

N. (1) Year: 歲歲 or 歲歲年年 from year to year; 歲出, 歲入, 歲收 as adj., annual, see -*chu*, -*ruh*, -*shou* ↓; 歲杪, 歲尾 -*miaau*, -*weei* ↓; 歲晚, 歲闌, 歲暮 late in the year, the year drawing to its close; 歲寒三友 "three friends in winter"—the pine, the bamboo and the plum; 隔歲 the following year; 客歲, 去歲 last year; 新歲 the new year; 凶歲, 豐歲 a year of bad, good, crops. (2) Year of age: 年歲 ditto; 歲數 -'*shuh* ↓; 幾歲 how old (are you?); 五十歲 is fifty years old; . . . 萬歲 long live . . . ! 千歲 long live (the prince); 週歲 first birthday, first anniversary.

歲出 *sueih-chu*, n., annual expenditure.
歲除 *sueih-chur*, n., New Year's Eve.
歲俸 *sueih-fehng*, n., annual salary.
歲費 *sueih-feih*, n., annual expenditure.
歲功 *sueih-gung*, n., (AC) annual harvest.
歲華 *sueihhuar*, n., the procession of the seasons.
歲朝 *sueihjau*, n., (AC) New Year's Day.
歲計 *sueih-jih*, n., annual budget.
歲君 *sueihjyun*, n., a constellation in power for a certain year.
歲杪 *sueih-miaau*, n., year's end.
歲入 *sueih-ruh*, n., annual revenue, income.
歲星 *sueihshing*, n., the planet Jupiter which marks the twelve-year cycle.
歲首 *sueih-shoou*, n., year's beginning.
歲收 *sueihshou*, n., annual income; annual harvest.
歲數(兒) *sueih'shu('l)*, n., a person's age: 多少歲數 how many years of age?
歲時 *sueihshyr*, n., the procession of the seasons.
歲尾 *sueih-weei*, n., year's end.
歲月 *sueih-yueh*, n., the years and months—the passing of time: 歲月無情 time and tide wait for no man.
歲運 *sueih-yuhn*, n., person's luck during a certain year.

§ 21A.72 (⺊/心)

忐 21A.72

taan.

忐忑 *taanteh*, adj., uneasy: 心中忐忑 ("up and down"), 忐忑不安 uneasy at heart.

惄 21A.72

nih.

Adj. (AC) sad: 惄焉如擣 (AC) my heart is greatly disturbed (lit., "pounding").

慮 21A.72

lyuh.

N. & v.i. & t. (1) Be concerned, worry: 慮及 concerned about (future); 憂慮, 愁慮 worry, fear for; 疑慮 worry in uncertainty; 遠慮 be concerned about distant future, also n., farsightedness, forethought; 無慮數百 may well run into hundreds. (2) Plan, consider: 考慮: 他答應要考慮 he promised to consider; 謀慮, 計慮 plan and consider (future); 深謀遠慮 great foresight and plan for the future; 焦慮 worrying anxiously.

毖 21A.72

bih.

V. i. & t. (AC) (1) provide against: 而毖後患 provide against future troubles. (2) Take trouble to, be concerned.

Adj. (AC) flowing, gushing (spring).

§ 21A.80 (⺊/八)

貞 21A.80

jen (also *jeng*).

N. & v. t. Divination, to divine: 貞卜文字 oracle characters.

Adj. (1) Chaste: 貞節 *-jier* ↓; 貞婦 chaste woman; 貞女 chaste girl; 守貞 keep one's virginity. (2) Loyal: 忠貞 faithful, loyal (minister, etc.). (3) Hard (wood): 貞木 *-muh* ↓.

貞白 *jenbair*, adj., chaste, of unsullied character.
貞固 *jenguh*, adj., of unswerving loyalty.
貞節 *jen-jier*[1], (1) adj. & n., (chaste) virginity (貞) and widowhood (節): 貞節觀念 the concept of chastity; see 節 92A.22; (2) n., integrity in men.
貞潔 *jenjier*[2], adj., (of maiden) pure and chaste.
貞烈 *jenlieh*, adj., willing to commit suicide out of loyalty of love; n., such woman or maiden.
貞木 *jenmuh*, n., hardwood, symbolic of men of integrity or loyalty.
貞淑 *jenshur*, adj., (of woman) pure and intelligent.
貞操 *jentsau*, n., (1) feminine purity of character, chastity; (2) man's faith or integrity.

貲 21A.80

tzy.

N. (1) Riches, wealth. (2) A limited amount: 所損不貲, 損失不貲 suffer no small amount of damage.

§ 21A.81 (卜/人)

虞 21A.81

yur.

N. (1) A matter of concern, error, danger: 之虞 danger of (drowning, fire, etc.); 無虞 without any accident; 不虞 accident: 有什麽不虞發生 if anything untoward should happen. (2) Name of regime of Emperor Shuhn 舜 (2255–2205 B.C.), see Appendix D. (3) A surname.

V.i. To worry: 堪虞 justify worry, may well happen.

Adj. Happy, contented.

§ 21A.82 (卜/乂)

攴 21A.82

pu.

[One of the radicals, modern form 攵, appearing on right side of character, usually pertaining to some form of action, in characters like 收 receive, 放 let go, 攷 examine, 數 count, etc.]

V. i. & t. (AC) Strike, tap lightly.

虔 21A.82

chiarn.

[Cogn. 謹]

V. t. (AC) to rob.

Adj. Devout, sincere, see compp. ↓.

虔誠 *chiarncherng*, adj., pious, devout (believer).
虔虔 *chiarnchiarn*, adj. & adv., reverent, -ly, worshipful, -ly
虔敬 *chiarnjihng*, adj. & adv., reverent, -ly.
虔恪 *chiarnkeh*, adj., earnest, pious.
虔婆 *chiarnpor*, n., (coll., abusive) vixen, old hag, procuress.
虔心 *chiarnshin*, adj., devout.

§ 21A.83 (卜/乀)

處 21A.83

chuh (**chuu* as vb.).

N. (1) A place: 處處, 到處, 四處, 各處 everywhere; 何處 where; 此處 here; 他處, 別處 another place; 敝處 my humble home; 處所 *-suoo* ↓. (2) Point, often used for ending of abstract nn.: 難處 difficulty; 疑處, 不同處 point of doubt, of difference; 長處, 短處 one's good point, shortcoming; 好處, 壞處 good and bad points. (3) Bureau, office, department, section: 警務處 police department; 衛生處 department of sanitation; 情報處 information service; 辦事處 office; 報名處 registration office; 收費處 cashier's office; 處長, 處主任 department chief.

V. i. & t. (**chuu*) (1) To live, stay: 獨處 to live alone; 處約 live in poverty; 處境困難 live in difficult circumstances; 處在, 處於 be placed in (situation); 處於死地 to send (person) to his doom. (2) To conduct, carry on, deal with: 處身 conduct oneself; 處世 carry on or deal with the world; 處世之道 a way of life; 相處, 共處 (two people) carry on, get along (well, not well); 處不來 cannot carry on. (3) To manage, deal with; 處理, 處置, 處事 *-lii*, *-jyh*[2], *-shyh*[2] ↓. (4) To punish: 處刑, 處治, 處分, 處死 *-shirng*, *-jyh*[1], *-fehn*, *-syy* ↓.

處處 *chuhchuh*, adv., everywhere.
處斷 **chuuduahn*, v. t., to decide on difficult problem.
處方 *chuufang*, n. & v. i., prescription; to prescribe.
處罰 **chuufar*, v. t., to punish.
處分 **chuu'fehn*, v. t., ditto: 受處分 be punished. 「(criminal).
處斬 **churjaan*, v. t., to execute
處境 **chuujihng*, (1) n., circumstances; (2) v. t., be placed in situation.

處治 *chuujyh¹*, v. t., to punish.

處置 *chuujyh²*, (1) v. t., to dispose of, to arrange, settle (matter): 處置得好 well dealt with; 怎樣處置 how to deal with (this matter)? (2) n., settlement.

處決 *chuujyuer*, v. t., (1) to execute (criminal); (2) to decide (matter).

處理 *churlii*, v. t., see *-jyh²* ↑.

處女 *chur-nyuu*, n., a virgin; 處女膜 the hymen; 處女地 virgin soil; 處女作 (作品) first work of an author; 處女航 maiden voyage (of ship).

處刑 *chuushirng*, v. t., to punish: 處極刑 sentence to death.

處士 *chuushyh¹*, n., a retired scholar.

處事 *chuu-shyh²*, v. t., deal with affairs.

處所 *chuhsuoo*, n., dwelling place.

處死 *chursyy*, v. t., sentence to death.

處子 *churtzyy*, n., (1) see *-nyuu* ↑; (2) (AC) see *-shyh¹* ↑.

處窩子 *chuu'wotz*, n., one shut up away from society.

逌 21A.83

your.

Adj. & adv. (Related 攸, 悠) (LL) spontaneously: 逌然, 逌爾 smiling, -ly, contented, -ly.

逭 21A.83

jen (also *jeng*).
[Var. of 偵 91A.80]

遽 21A.83

jyuh.

Adj. Trembling, embarrassed, fearful: 惶遽 shaking with fear; 駭遽 frightened, astonished, amazed; 遽色 *-seh* ↓.

Adv. Suddenly: 遽然 *-rarn* ↓; 遽爾 *-eel* ↓.

遽爾 *jyuh-eel*, adv., suddenly, unexpectedly, all at once.

遽然 *jyuhrarn*, adv., ditto.

遽色 *jyuh-seh*, n., an air of astonishment, bewilderment.

§ 21A.91 (卜/ノ)

步 21A.91

buh.

N. (1) Step: part of many compp. in 快步 quick step; 徐步, 慢步 slow, leisurely steps; 散步 stroll; 信步 carefree stroll whither the foot leads; 徒步 go on foot; 止步, 留步 go no further; 請止步 phr., asking host to stop seeing guest to the gate; 起步 start in race; 步步高陞 rise step by step; 寸步難行 in difficult pass; 進步 progress; 退步 retrogress. (2) Path: 國步艱難 the national path is beset with troubles; 地[Δ]步 11A.70. (3) An ancient measure, length of a step (6 ancient "feet"). (4) A surname.

V.i. & t. (1) To stroll: 步下山坡 (LL) walk down the slope; 步月 (LL) stroll in moonlight. (2) To follow in footsteps: 步其後塵 follow in another's footsteps; 亦步亦趨 to follow slavishly. (3) Set the pace: 獨步一時 (LL) set the pace for the generation.

步兵 *buhbing*, n., infantry.

步步高 *buhbuhgau*, n., (coll.) ladder, many-tiered shelf.

步步搖 *buhbuhyaur*, n., ancient woman's hair decoration, "bobbing at every step."

步程計 *buh-cherng-jih*, n., pedometer.

步鎗 *buhchiang*, n., rifle.

步調 *buhdiauh*, n., path and pace: 步調相同 move in the same pattern.

步隊 *buhdueih*, n., troops in command, var. of 部隊.

步伐 *buhfar*, n., (mil.) movement of troop formations: 步伐整齊 move in beautiful formations.

步弓 *buh-gung*, n., an ancient wooden fork-like device for marking length of a step.

步號 *buh-hauh*, n., (mil.) infantry signals.

步障 *buhjahng*, n., portable large silk screen sheltering court ladies from public view.

步履 *buhlyuu*, n., walking gait, a man's movements.

步輦 *buhniaan*, n., formerly, royal carriage pulled by attendants.

步哨 *buhshauh*, n., security patrol guarding road along route of important persons: 放步哨 set up such patrols.

步行 *buhshirng*, n. & v.i., walk on foot.

步驟 *buhtzouh*, n., steps, plan of procedure.

步從 *buhtzuhng*, n., retinue.

步足 *buhtzur*, n., ambulacral feet of starfish, etc. (also 步腳).

步武 *buhwuu*, v.t., imitate predecessor.

亅	小	⺊	十	土	ナ	卄	𠃊卜	丨	一	丁	フ	口	区	冈	㇆	厂	尸	亠	广	宀	丶	乚	弋	心	八	人	乂	〜	ノ	ノ丨	⺊	く
00	01	02	10	11	12	20	21	22	30	31	32	40	41	42	50	51	52	60	61	62	63	70	71	72	80	81	82	83	90	91	92	93

SECTION 21B

§21B.00 (山/亅)

峙 21B.00-1

jyh.

V. i. To stand up: 雄峙 tower high above others; 對峙 stand up against, to rival.

崎 21B.00-1

chir (also *chi*).

崎嶇 *chichyu*, adj., (1) (of mountain paths) uneven, rough; (2) having difficulties on the way.

崢 21B.00-9

jeng (also *cherng*).

崢嶸 *jengrurng* (*cherng-hurng*), adj., (of mountain, ravines) steep, awe-inspiring; (persons) outstanding; (MC, rarely of weather) bitingly cold.

§21B.01 (山/小)

嵊 21B.01-9

shehng.

N. 嵊縣 name of county in Chekiang Province.

嶸 21B.01-9

rurng.

Adj. 崢嶸 (1) (Of mountains) lofty, towering. (2) (Of persons) talented, gifted: 頭角崢嶸 (of a young man) showing extraordinary gifts, see 崢 21B.00↑.

§21B.10 (山/十)

嶙 21B.10-2

lirn.

嶙嶙 *lirnlirn*, adj., jagged (of peaks).

嶙峋 *lirnsyurn*, adj., craggy, jagged (peak formations): 瘦骨嶙峋 bony appearance (of horses).

嶂 21B.10-6

jahng.

N. Mountain barrier.

峰 21B.10-9

feng.

[Var. of 峯 21.10]

§21B.21 (山/乚)

嵁 21B.21-2

kan.

嵁巖 *kanyarn*, adj., rough, jagged (mountain roads, peaks).

嶇 21B.21-5

chyu.

N. See 崎[Δ]嶇 21B.00.

崛 21B.21-5

jyuer.

Adj. Towering: 崛起 rising high in the sky, standing out prominently; also v.i., rise from the ranks or humble origins.

§21B.22 (山/丨)

嶃 21B.22-1

charn.

[Var. of 嶄 21.22]

岬 21B.22-4

jiaa.

N. (1) A defile, passageway between mountains. (2) A cape, promontory, headland.

§21B.30 (山/一)

嶝 21B.30-3

dehng.

N. Hill path.

崆 21B.30-6

kung.

崆峒 *Kungduhng*, n., name of a mountain.

嵯 21B.30-8

tsuor.

嵯峨 *tsuor-er*, adj., towering (mountain).

§21B.40 (山/口)

岵 21B.40-1

huh.

N. (AC) a grassy hill.

峪 21B.40-8

yuh.

N. An enclosed valley.

§21B.41 (山/囗)

岫 21B.41-2

shiouh.

N. (1) A mountain peak, esp. a cleft between peaks: 雲無心以出岫 the cloud emerges from between the peaks without intent or purpose. (2) (AC) a mountain cave.

嶒 21B.41-8

tserng.

嶒嶸 *tserngyirng*, adj., (mountains) high, towering.

嶓 21B.41-9

bo.

N. Name of a mountain.

§21B.42 (山/冈)

峭 21B.42-2

chiauh.

Adj. (1) Rugged (cliffs, peaks): 陡峭 steep; 峭峻 perpendicular; 峭壁 cliffside. (2) Severe, harsh in temperament: 嚴峭 severe (laws), 峭刻,峭厲 *-keh*, *-lih*² ↓. (3) Chilly, cutting: 峭風 cutting winds; 峭寒, 料峭 chilly.

峭拔 *chiauhbar*, adj., (of mountain peaks) rising sharply; (callig.) powerful, angular in strokes.

峭薄 *chiauhbor*, adj., mean and cutting.

峭覈 *chiauhher*, adj., (AC) harsh, uncompromising.

峭急 *chiauhjir*, adj., harsh-tempered.

峭直 *chiauhjyr*, adj., (temper, words) straightforward, rude.

峭刻 *chiauhkeh*, adj., severe (criticism, temper).

峭麗 *chiauhlih*¹, adj., strange and beautiful.

峭厲 *chiauhlih*², adj., stern in countenance.

嵎 21B.42-4

yur.

N. (1) A hill recess: 負嵎 (tiger) at bay. (2) Sometimes interch. 隅 corner.

峒 21B.42-4

turng.

N. (1) Name of mountain: 崆^峒 21B.30. (2) Var. of 洞 pr. *duhng*.

嶠 21B.42-9

jiauh.

N. A high mountain with pointed peaks.

嶝 崆 嵯 岵 峪 岫 嶒 嶓 峭 嵎 峒 嶠

亅	小	⺊	十	土	ナ	卄	丄	丨	一	丅	フ	口	囗	冈	𠃌	厂	尸	亠	广	亠	丶	乚	弋	心	八	人	乂	一	一	ノ	㇀	く
00	01	02	10	11	12	20	21	22	30	31	32	40	41	42	50	51	52	60	61	62	63	70	71	72	80	81	82	83	90	91	92	93

峋 嶢 崦 崐 屹 巉 巇 岷 峨 嶼 峽 巘 嶮

§21B.50 (山/冂)

峋 21B.50-9

shyurn.

Adj. See 嶙峋 21B.10.

§21B.70 (山/乚)

嶢 21B.70-1

yaur.

嶢 崎 *yaurchir*, adj., ragged, rough (mountain roads).

嶢 嶢 *yauryaur*, adj., (1) rising straight up; (2) straightforward, upright (character).

崦 21B.70-1

yan.

N. 崦嵫 (1) Name of a mountain in Kansu Province. (2) The western region where the sun sets: 日薄崦嵫 in the evening of one's life.

崐 21B.70-4

kun.

[Var. of 崑 21.70]

屹 21B.70-9

yih.

Adj. (Mountains) towering, high and massive: 屹立(不動) standing mighty, immovable.

巉 21B.70-9

charn.

Adj. (LL) steep, jagged.

巉 巉 *charncharn*, adj., (LL) steep.

巉 岏 *charnwarn*, adj., (LL) sharp, pointed (peaks).

巉 巖 *charnyarn*, adj., (LL) steep, jagged.

§21B.71 (山/弋)

巇 21B.71-2

shi.

N. A crack, crevice: 巇隙.

Adj. Dangerous: 山路巇嶮 dangerous mountain paths.

岷 21B.71-5

mirn.

N. Name of a mountain, river.

峨 21B.71-9

er.

[Var. 峩]

Adj. (1) (LL) High, tall: 峨冠, 峨冕 tall hat. (2) Steep, jagged (cliff): 嵯峨 ditto.

峨 峨 *er-er*, adj., (1) tall; (2) (AC) tall and impressive (appearance).

峨 嵋 *Ermeir*, n., Omei, name of mountain in Szechuan.

峨 然 *errarn*, adj., (LL) tall, towering.

§21B.80 (山/八)

嶼 21B.80-9

yuu.

N. An island: 島嶼 group of islands.

§21B.81 (山/人)

峽 21B.81-1

shiar.

N. A gorge; a sharp ravine: 三峽 the Yangtse Gorges; 巫峽 a famous gorge on Szechuan border.

巘 21B.81-2

yaan.

N. (AC) mountain peak.

嶮 21B.81-8

shiaan.

嶮 巇 *shiaanshi*, adj., steep, difficult (path).

§ 21B.82 (山/乂)

岐 21B.82-1

chir.

N. (1) Name of a mountain. (2) A surname.

Adj. Branching off (var. of 歧, see 歧△路, 歧△視 21S.82).

岐黃 *chirhuarng*, n., (AC) the practice of medicine from 岐伯 and 黃帝 (mythical) fathers of medicine.

岐嶷 *chirnih*, adj., (AC) thriving.

崚 21B.82-1

lerng.

崚嶒 *lerngtserng*, adj., steep, rugged (hill), also 嶒崚.

岅 21B.82-9

baan.

[Var. of 坂]

峻 21B.82-9

jyuhn.

Adj. (1) High, towering, great, rising sharply: 峻坂 *-baan* ↓; 崇山峻嶺 high mountains and towering peaks; 峻宇 huge mansion; 峻峭 *-chiauh*, 峻直 *-jyr* ↓; 險峻 dangerous (terrain); 峻德 *-der*, 峻節 *-jier* ↓. (2) Headlong, rash, precipitate, impetuous: 峻急 *-jir* ↓. (3) Strict, rigid, stern: 峻密 *-mih*, 峻法 *-faa*, 峻刻 *-keh* ↓; 峻拒 flat refusal, sternly turn down.

峻坂 *jyuhn-baan*, n., steep mountain slope.

峻峭 *jyuhnchiauh*, adj., (1) (of mountain, cliff) precipitous; (2) ＝峻刻 *-keh* ↓.

峻切 *jyuhnchieh*, adj., strict, rigorous.

峻德 *jyuhn-der*, n., great virtue.

峻法 *jyuhn-faa*, n., harsh and rigid laws.

峻節 *jyuhnjier*, n., nobility of character.

峻急 *jyuhnjir*, adj., (1) intolerant, bigoted, headstrong, dogged; (2) (of currents) swirling, rushing headlong, flowing swiftly.

峻直 *jyuhnjyr*, adj., strict and upright (character).

峻刻 *jyuhnkeh*, adj., harsh, unrelenting, stern.

峻酷 *jyuhnkuh*, adj., cruelly oppressive.

峻厲 *jyuhnlih*, adj., pitiless, merciless.

峻密 *jyuhnmih*, adj., strict, rigorous, stern, rigid.

§ 21B.93 (山/く)

嵫 21B.93-2

tzy.

N. See 崦△嵫 21B.70.

SECTION 21S

§ 21S.00 (乚卜ˢ/亅)

齮 21S.00-1

yii.

齮齕 *yiiher*, v.i. & t., (AC) to chew between the teeth; (fig.) to squeeze out able men out of jealousy.

剴 21S.00-2

kaai.

Adj. Thorough.

剴切 *kaaichie*, adj., as in 剴切詳盡 thorough and exhaustive (explanation).

劇 21S.00-2

jyuh (also *jir*).

N. (1) The drama, a stage show: 演劇 put on (take part in) a play; 劇場 *-chaang* ↓; 劇中人 dramatic characters; 戲劇 a dramatic work; 平劇 the Peking opera; 話劇 a stage play; 歌劇 an opera; 歌舞劇 a musical comedy; 劇情 *-chirng* ↓; 獨幕劇 an one-act play; 電視劇 television drama; 廣播劇 radio drama; 喜劇 a comedy; 悲劇 a tragedy; 鬧劇 opera bouffe, melodrama; 趣劇 ditto; 劇本 *-been* ↓; 慘劇 a tragic incident; 滑稽劇 farce. (2) A surname.

Adj. & adv. Extreme(ly), severe (ly), serious(ly): 劇盜, 劇賊 notorious robbers; 劇寇 notorious bandits; 劇藥 potent drugs; 劇飲 drink an inordinate amount of liquor; 劇毒 *-dur*, 劇烈 *-lieh* ↓; 劇鬥 violent fisticuffs; 病劇 seriously ill; 日劇 become more serious day by day.

劇本 *jyuhbeen*, n., a play in written form.
劇塲 *jyuhchaang*, n., a theater.
劇情 *jyuhchirng*, n., the dramatic plot.
劇毒 *jyuhdur*, n., deadly poison.
劇烈 *jyuhlieh*, adj., violent (struggle), vigorous, strenuous: 劇烈運動 strenuous exercises.

劌 21S.00-2

gueih.

V. t. To cut, slice.

將 21S.00-9

jiang (**jiahng*, **chiang*).

N. (**jiahng*) A military commander, a general officer: 將領 *-liing*, 將帥 *-shuaih*[1] ↓; 上將 full general; 中將 lieutenant general; 少將 major general; 准將 brigadier general; 大將 a great commander; 驍將, 勇將 a brave, dauntless general; 驕兵悍將 unruly commander and soldiers; 將在外君命有所不受 a field commander must decide even against king's orders; 將材 *-tsair* ↓; 將相本無種 generals and prime ministers are not born but made.

V. i. & t. (1) Move forward, advance: 日就月將 make steady and continual progress. (2) Take, see Prep. below: 將酒來 bring me some wine; 將就 *-jiouh* ↓. (3) (**jiahng*) To command: 將兵 *-bing* ↓; 將將 *-jiahng* ↓. (4) (**chiang*) (AC) ask, appeal for: 將伯 ask for assistance; 將子無怒 please don't be angry with me. (5) Take care of: 將護 *-huh* ↓. (6) Engage in doing: 將事 *-shyh* ↓. (7) (AC) give a send-off to: 百兩將之 (AC) despatch a hundred chariots to escort her. (8) (AC) accompany: 鄭伯將王自圉門入 the Earl of Tseng accompanied the king to enter by the Yumen. (9) (Of the game of chess) to checkmate (the opponent's king). (10) As vb. suffix, begin to: 叫將起來, 怕將起來 begin to scream, to be afraid.

Vb. aux. Will (about to, on the point of, soon): 天將下雨 it's going to rain; 將要 *-yauh* ↓; 卽將 will soon, about to; 不知老之將至 don't know that old age is just around the corner ("will be soon coming"); 將來 *-lair* ↓.

Adv. (1) Just, a moment earlier, a very short time ago: 昨天將到 came only yesterday; 將才 *-tsair*, 將將 *-jiang*, 將次 *-tsyh* ↓. (2) Partly . . . partly . . . : 將信將疑 half believing, half doubting.

Prep. By, with (followed by object and vb., cf. use of 把 10A.70): 將它移開 take this away; 將有餘補不足 take from the rich and give to the poor; 將心比心 judge other person's feelings by one's own; 將功贖罪 redeem sins by good deeds; 將勤補拙 make up for lack of skill with industry; 將錯就錯 make the best of a bad bargain; 將計就計 turn a person's trick against him.

將弁 **jiahngbiahn*, n., military officers in general.
將兵 **jiahng-bing*, v. i., to command troops, cf. *-jiahng* ↓.
將護 *jianghuh*, v. t., take good care of, look after (s.o.) carefully, tend (the sick, injured, or aged).
將將 **jiahngjiahng*, (1) v. i., be the commander of commanders; (2) (*jiang-jiang*) adv., a short while earlier, a moment ago (＝剛剛).
將近 *jiangjihn*, adv., nearly, approximately, about, soon.
將就 *jiangjiouh*, v. i., make do with s.t., to compromise, accept the *fait accompli*.
將種 **jiahng-juung*, n., person born of military forbears.
將軍 *jiangjyun*, n., (1) a general; (2) (AC) loosely any officer.
將指 **jiahngjyy*, n., (1) the middle finger of the hand; (2) the toe.
將來 *jianglair*, (1) n. & adj., (the) future; (2) adv., in the future.
將令 **jiahnglihng*, n., orders issued by a commanding general.
將領 **jiahngliing*, n., high-ranking military leaders.
將略 **jiahnglyueh*, n., military strategy and tactics.
將門 **jiahngmern*, n., the family of a high-ranking military officer.
將攝 *jiangseh*, v. i., to rest and recuperate, convalesce, see *-shir* ↓.
將校 **jiahngshiauh*, n., a collective term for general and field officers.
將息 *jiangshir*, v. i., to rest and recuperate.
將帥 **jiahngshuaih*[1], n., a commanding general.
將率 **jiahngshuaih*[2], n., ditto.
將士 **jiahngshyh*, n., officers and men.
將事 *jiangshyh*, v. i., going to: 將事努力 going to work hard.
將食 *jiangshyr*, v. i., take food, have a meal.
將才 *jiangtsair*, (1) (**jiahngtsair*) n., ＝將材 ↓; (2) (*jiang-*) adv., a moment ago (＝剛才).
將材 **jiahngtsair*, n., a person with all the qualifications of a great general.
將次 *jiangtsyh*, adv., nearly, gradually, slowly.
將佐 **jiahngtzuoo*, n., high-ranking military officers.
將晚 *jiangwaan*, adv., towards evening.
將養 *jiangyaang*, v. i., recuperate, convalesce.
將要 *jiangyauh*, vb. aux., will, be going to: 將要出動, 停止 going to start, stop.

§21S.01 (ㄴㅏs/小)

牀 21S.01-1

chuarng.
[Pop. 床]

N. (1) Bed: 單人牀, 雙人牀 single, double bed: 吊牀 suspended bed, hammock; 牀上安牀 double or treble berths; 疊牀架屋 overstuffed with redundancies; 牀頭金盡 money runs out; 牀笫 *-tzyy*↓. (2) Chassis, support, bench: 車牀 chassis; 機牀 lathe; 琴牀 bench for stringed instrument. (3) (Coll.) coffin before laying-in of body.

牀 鋪 *chuarngpuh*, n., (coll.) bed.
牀 蓐 *chuarngruh*, n., beddings; mattress: 常在牀蓐 be confined to bed.
牀 蝨 *chuarngshy*, n., bedbug.
牀 頭 人 *chuarngtourrern*, n., (coll.) wife.
牀 子 *chuarngtz*, n., shelf for storing goods: 菜牀子, 魚牀子, 羊肉牀子 shop shelf for vegetable, fish, mutton.
牀 笫 *chuarngtzyy*, n., bed, as in Eng. "conjugal bed," intimacies: 牀笫之間 in bed or in it's intimacies.
牀 位 *chuarngweih*, n., berth in ship or train.

§21S.02 (ㄴㅏs/ㅏ)

齦 21S.02-5

yirn.

N. Gum (of teeth).

§21S.10 (ㄴㅏs/十)

肆 21S.10-2

yih.
[Dist. 肆 51S.10]

肄 業 *yihyeh*, v. i., to study in a school or college.

牂 21S.10-8

tzang.

N. (AC) a ewe.

牂 牂 *tzangtzang, adj.*, (AC) thick, dense: 其葉牂牂 so dense is the foliage.

§21S.11 (ㄴㅏs/土)

壯 21S.11-1

juahng.
[Abbr. 壮]

Adj. (1) Robust, strong: 強壯 strong (nation, body); 健壯 strong, healthy; 長得很壯 has a robust body; 壯大 *-dah*↓; 壯盛 *-shehng*↓; 悲壯 strong in adversity, undaunted; 勇壯 brave. (2) In prime of life, youthful: 壯年, 壯夫, 壯士 *-niarn, -fu, -shyh*↓; 少壯 young; 少壯派 the younger group in parties. (3) Unfettered, dauntless, unrestricted: 壯遊, 壯舉 *-your*[1], *-jyuu*↓.

V. t. To strengthen: 以壯觀瞻 to beautify appearance; 以壯行色 to make one feel better on travel (by money gifts).

壯 氣 *juahngchih*, n., brave morale, splendid spirit.
壯 膽 *juahng-daan*, (1) v. i., feel spirited, brave; (2) v. t., to encourage (person): 壯他的膽 give him courage; 壯壯膽 help to encourage.
壯 大 *juahngdah*, adj., (1) robust, stalwart (body); (2) grown-up: 壯大了 has grown up (cf. 長大).
壯 丁 *juahngding*, n., able-bodied men (for recruits).
壯 夫 *juahngfu*, n., able-bodied person, strong person.
壯 觀 *juahngguan*, (1) adj., grand and handsome (building); (2) n., impressive sight.
壯 志 *juahngjyh*, n., life ambition to accomplish s.t.: 壯志未酬身先死 died without accomplishing what he wanted.
壯 舉 *juahngjyuu*, n., a great or impressive undertaking.
壯 烈 *juahnglieh*, adj., courageous (martyrs, patriots).
壯 麗 *juahnglih*, adj., grand-looking, impressive (structure).
壯 美 *juahngmeei*, n., raw, primitive beauty; grandeur (of landscape).
壯 年 *juahngniarn*, n. & adj., prime of life, in one's thirties or forties.
壯 然 *juahngrarn*, adj., forbidding, awe-inspring.
壯 盛 *juahngshehng*, adj., strong (army, nation); youthful, healthy.
壯 士 *juahngshyh*, n., a great fighter, warrior, hero.
壯 圖 *juahng-tur*, phr., a great plan or undertaking.
壯 遊 *juahngyour*[1], v.i., to make extensive, delightful trip.
壯 猷 *juahng-your*[2], phr., see *-tur* ↑.

糶 21S.11-5

tiauh.

V.t. To sell grain (cf. 糴 buy grain, 81S.11): 糶出, 糶糧 sell grain; 平齪 ancient government system for stabilizing grain prices.

齷 21S.11-5

woh.

齷齪 *wohchuoh*, n. & adj., filth, -y, dirt, -y.

雌 21S.11-9

tsy (also *tsyr*).

N. A female, opp. 雄 male (of animals, as cow, lion, fowl, eagle); rarely of persons: "英雌" (facet.) heroine, opp. 英雄 hero; 雌老虎 a tigress, a ferocious woman; 雌威 (of shrew) wife's ferocity.

V.t. To chide, rebuke: 挨雌 (coll.) be rebuked.

Adj. Female, also gentle, small: 知其雄, 守其雌 (老子) possessing strength, but retaining gentleness; 雌聲 a weak, low voice.

雌答 *tsy'da*, v.i., (MC) to scold, chide.

雌花 *tsyhua*, n., (bot.) pistillate flower, see *-rueei* ↓.

雌黃 *tsyhuarng*, (1) n., yellow ochre, used as yellow pigment; hence, (2) v.t., to blot out mistakes and make corrections: hence, 信口雌黃 to make deceitful statements or unfounded charges.

雌兒 *tsyrerl*, (1) n., (coll.) a young lass, young thing; (2) (-'*l*) v.t., to chide (person).

雌蕊 *tsyrueei*, n., (bot.) pistil.

雌雄 *tsy-shyurng*, adj., male or female, oft. 決雌雄 see who is the winner, the stronger.

§21S.21 (ㄴㅏ^{s}/ㄴ)

岠 21S.21-5

jyuh.

[Var. of 距 40B.21]

§21S.22 (ㄴㅏ^{s}/丨)

酆 21S.22-3

feng.

N. (1) Place name in Szechuan; 酆都城 *Fengducherng*, Hades, Inferno. (2) A surname.

帰 21S.22-5

guei.

[Arch. of 歸 91S.22]

齘 21S.22-8

shieh.

N. & v.t. (AC) to grind teeth.

齡 21S.22-8

lirng.

[See 齡 21S.63]

鰜 21S.22-8

jian.

[Var. fo 鹼 21S.81]

斷 21S.22-9

duahn.

[Abbr. 断]

V.t. (1) To cut or break off, snap: 斷手, 指, 臂 cut off hand, finger, arm; 斷髮紋身 (of barbarians) cut hair short and tattoo body; 斷頭 to behead; 斷了 be broken; 不斷(的) continuously; 斷碎 broken to pieces; 斷線風箏 kite with broken line—whereabouts unknown; 斷片 broken part; 斷簡殘編 incomplete parts of ancient scripts; 斷章取義 take out of context to make a deliberate misinterpretation out of context. (2) To discontinue: 斷後 have no progeny; 斷交 break off friendship; 斷氣, 斷魂, 斷炊 *-chih*, *-hurn*, *-tsuei* ↓. (3) To stop, break off habits, practice: 斷煙, 酒 stop smoking, drinking; 斷癮 stop opium-smoking; 斷屠, 斷宰 ban butchery of pigs; 斷乳 be weaned. (4) To decide: 斷定, 決斷, 定斷 ditto; 當機立斷 decide on the spot; 很有決斷 have strong decision; 獨斷獨行 highhanded, arbitrary, imperious, overbearing, decide and act alone; 非常果斷 have determination of character; decide at court and decree: 斷有罪, 無罪 pronounce guilty, not guilty; 斷案 settle lawsuit; 斷押, 償, 罰 decree detention, compensation, fine; 斷吉凶 decide luck by divination.

Vb. suffix. In half, apart, off: 切斷, 割斷, 截斷 cut off (retreat, line); 折斷 break, tear apart (rails, stick); 拉斷 pull and break (thread); 打斷 interrupt (speech, story); 間斷 (*jiahn-*) interrupted, -tion.

Adv. Certainly, absolutely: 斷然, 斷斷 absolutely; 斷然不可 certainly will not be allowed; 斷無此理 certainly could not have happened, could not be; 斷不能 certainly cannot; 斷難相允 certainly will not consent.

斷腸 *duahn-charng*, phr., "break

intestines" (poet.) for extreme sadness, esp. longing for lovers.

斷七 *duahn-chi*, phr., (Budd.) mass on 49th day of death.

斷氣 *duahn-chih*, v.i., draw last breath.

斷除 *duahnchur*, v.t., break off, remove (obstacles, bad habits or customs, etc.).

斷定 *duahn-dihng*, v.i., decide (good, bad, to go, not to go).

斷斷 *duahnduahn*, adv., certainly, absolutely.

斷根 *duahn-gen*, v.i., make real cure of disease, opium-smoking, etc.

斷魂 *duahn-hurn*, phr., (poet.) be forlorn, very sad, feel like a "lost soul."

斷機 *duahn-ji*, n., allu., mother of Mencius cut cloth on loom when child did not study hard.

斷絕 *duahnjyuer*, v.t., cut off definitely: 斷絕後患 remove seeds of future trouble.

斷片 *duahnpiahn*, n. & adj., piecemeal.

斷然 *duahnrarn*, adv., decisively.

斷絃 *duahn-shiarn*, phr., wife's death (like snapping of string on string instrument; cf. 續絃 re-string, i.e., remarry).

斷袖 *duahn-shiouh*, litr. phr., homosexuality.

斷送 *duahnsuhng*, v.t., forfeit: 斷送前程 forfeit career.

斷頭臺 *duahntour-tair*, n., guillotine; 斷頭將軍 allu. general who would rather die than surrender.

斷層 *duahntserng*, n., (geol.) a fault of vein.

斷炊 *duahn-tsuei*, phr., no hot meals (no more rice to cook at home).

斷言 *duahyarn*, v.i. & t., assert, affirm, to make an allegation.

断 21S.22-9

duahn.

[Abbr. of 斷 21S.22↑]

齗 21S.22-9

yirn.

N. (Physiol.) the gum of teeth (var. of 齦 21S.02).

齗齗 *yirnyirn*, adj., argumentative.

§21S.30 (ㄴㅏs/一)

豔 21S.30-1

yahn.

[Pop. 艷]

V.t. To admire greatly: 豔羨 *-shiahn*↓.

Adj. (1) Beauteous, resplendent, bright, dazzlingly beautiful: 豔麗 *-lih*↓; 美豔, 嬌豔 beautiful, enticing, attractive, gorgeous; 鮮豔 fresh and beautiful, bright (colors, flowers). (2) Having to do with love: 豔史 romantic records of personalities; 豔詩, 豔詞 love poetry; 豔歌 love song.

豔麗 *yahnlih*, adj., resplendent, gorgeous.

豔射 *yahnsheh*, adj., dazzling.

豔羨 *yahnshiahn*, v.t., to admire heartily.

豔陽 *yahnyarng*, n., a bright sun or day.

豔遇 *yahnyuh*, n., encounter with a beautiful woman.

齟 21S.30-4

jyuu.

齟齬 *jyuryuu*, adj., (1) (of upper and lower rows of teeth) failing to meet properly; (2) (of persons) holding contradictory views, unable to see eye to eye.

§21S.40 (ㄴㅏs/口)

齬 21S.40-3

yuu.

Adj. See 齟△齬 21S.30.

齠 21S.40-5

tiaur.

[Cogn. 髫]

齠齔 *tiaurchehn*, v.i., to shed the milk teeth; 齠年 young age, about seven or eight.

§21S.41 (ㄴㅏs/図)

牆 21S.41-1

chiarng.

N. A wall: 牆角 corner of wall; 危牆 a toppling wall; 牆隙 a hole in the wall; 牆外漢 an outsider; also 門外漢 layman, not expert; 門△牆 52B.00.

牆壁 *chiarngbih*, n., wall (of house).

牆垛(子) *charngduoo(tz)*, n., battlement on city wall.

亅	小	⺊	十	土	ナ	廾	ㄴㅏ	丨	一	丁	フ	口	図	冈	了	厂	尸	亠	广	宀	丶	乚	弋	心	八	人	乂	乛	一	丿	𠂉	く
00	01	02	10	11	12	20	21	22	30	31	32	40	41	42	50	51	52	60	61	62	63	70	71	72	80	81	82	83	90	91	92	93

牆根(兒) *chianggen(-ge'l)*, n., foot of wall.
牆頭 *chiarngtour*, n., top of wall, (flowers, etc.) over the wall; 牆頭草 (fig.) fence rider, a man without opinions of his own, one who "sees how the wind blows."
牆衣 *chiarngyi*, n., moss on wall.
牆垣 *chiarngyuarn*, n., wall; city wall.
牆宇 *chiarngyuu*, n., (LL) the wall and house tops visible from outside—man's external appearance.

§ 21S.42 (ㄴㅏ^{S}/冈)

齵 21S.42-4

yur (also *our*).

Adj. (AC) having uneven teeth.

齲 21S.42-9

chyuu.

N. & v. i. (AC) 齲齒 tooth decay.

§ 21S.50 (ㄴㅏ^{S}/ㄱ)

虧 21S.50-3

kuei.

N. & v. i. Loss, deficit; to fall short, suffer loss, run into deficit: 虧欠, 虧損, 虧折 *-chiahn*, *-suun*, *-jer*, etc.↓; 吃虧 suffer loss in transaction, be short-changed.

Adj. (1) Short, deficient, not enough to meet normal needs: 腎虧 a run-down kidney, (med.) sexual debility; 血虧 blood deficiency, anemia; 身子虧了, 虛虧 general debility; 心虧 uneasy in conscience; 功虧一簣 (of task, work) just fall short of final completion. (2) Waning, declining: 月虧 moon in partially shaded phase, waning; 盈虧 wax and wane, also (business) profit and loss.

Adv. (1) Luckily: 多虧, 幸虧 luckily; 多虧你幫忙 thanks to your help; 虧得是你 luckily it is you (and not s. o. else); 虧殺 very luckily, owing greatly to. (2) In mocking sense: 虧你 you, of all people: 虧你受教育的人, 還說出這種話 shame on you, an educated person to say such a thing; 虧得他說得出口 he has the cheek to say it (other people would not).

虧本(兒) *kueibeen(-bee'l)*, v.i., to suffer loss in business.
虧欠 *keuichiahn*, (1) n., deficit; (2) v.i., to owe debts in arrears; (3) to go bankrupt, see *-jer*↓.
虧短 *kueiduaan*, v.i., short of due amount.
虧負 *kuei'fuh*, n. & v.i. & t., (1) be deficient in friendship or duties, not quite fair to (person) (cf. 辜負 10.10); (2) to owe (amount, person).
虧耗 *kueihauh*, v.i. & n., to lose money, esp. from extravagant expenditures; such a loss.
虧折 *kueijer*, v.i. & n., (1) suffer (-ing) loss of capital; (2) to fail in business without owing debts.
虧空 *kuei'kuhng*, n. & v.i., loss in business; be short of (amount); 虧空公款 to embezzle, embezzlement.
虧累 *kueileei*, v. t. to involve (others) in loss.
虧心 *kueishin*, v.i. & adj., be remorseful; unconscionable, ungrateful; 虧心人 ungrateful person; 虧心事 ungrateful, unconscionable act.
虧蝕 *kueishyr*, n. & v.i., (1) financial loss; to lose (in business); (2) eclipse of sun or moon.
虧損 *kueisuun*, n. & v.i., loss in business.

鷨 21S.50-4

eh.

[Var. of 腭 42A.50]

齣 21S.50-9

chu.

N. adjunct. An act of a play: 一齣戲 a play.

鴇 21S.50-9

baau.

N. The bustard; procuress, see 鴇母 *baurmuu*↓.

鴇兒 *baau'l*, n., (1) prostitute; (2) procuress.
鴇母 *baurmuu*, n., procuress, madame of brothels.

鸕 21S.50-9

lur.

鸕鷀 *lurtsyr*, n., fishing cormorant.

勩 21S.50-9

yih.

V.i. (AC) to work hard, belabored.

§21S.63 (ㄴㅏ^s/丶)

齡 21S.63-8

lirng.

N. Person's age: 年齡, 遐齡, 高齡 long life, venerable age.

§21S.70 (ㄴㅏ^s/ㄴ)

比 21S.70-2

bii (**bih*).

N. (1) (AC) Metaphor in poetry. (2) Comparison, contest: 無比 incomparable, without compare; 大比 provincial or district civil examinations.

V.t. Compare, oft. 比較: 兩樣相比 compare the two together; 比一比 compare them; 比不得, 比不上 cannot compare with (person, object); 可比 may be compared to, be just like; 難比 it is another matter, not the same as; 比上不足, 比下有餘 worse off than some, better off than many—formula for contentment; 比快, 比高 determine relative speed, height; 比重 *-juhng* ↓.

Adj. (**bih*) Close: 比親, 比鄰 close relative, neighbor; 比年, 比歲 recent years.

Prep. Than: 他比我強 he is better, bigger than I; 比這大得多 much bigger than this one.

Adv. conj. (**bih*) (LL) until, till; 比及 when, by the time; 比來 recently; 比聞, 比見 (LL) recently heard, saw; 比維起居佳吉 (LL) I hope everything goes well with you.

比比 **bihbih*, adv., in 比比皆是: they are everywhere, all like that.
比並 *biibihng*, v.i., compare to.
比丘 *biichiou*, n., Buddhist monk, from Sanskr. *bhiksha*; 比丘尼 *--nir*, n., nun, from Sanskr. *bhiksuni*.
比方 *bii'feng*, adv., for instance; n., a supposition, illustration by example: 比方說 suppose, let us say.
比附 *biifuh*, v.t., (LL) compare by putting things together; append.
比畫 *biihuah*, v.i., (1) make hand gestures; (2) make boxing gestures for warming up; (3) come to blows: 兩人說着說着比畫起來.
比照 *biijauh*, adj. & prep., according to, in accordance with (regular procedure).
比輯 *biiji*, v.t., collate.
比肩 **bihjian*, adv., shoulder to shoulder: 比肩並進 advance thus.
比較 *biijiauh*, v.i., compare; adv., relatively; 比較大, 快 relatively bigger, faster; 比較心理學, 語言學 comparative psychology, linguistics; 比較音樂學 comparative musicology; 比較文學 comparative literature.
比周 **bihjouh*, adj., (LL) close and cordial.
比重 *biijuhng*, n., specific weight or gravity.
比來 **bihlair*, adv., recently.
比例 *biilih*, n., (1) comparison; (2) example: 做比例 as an example; (3) proportion, ratio: 正比例 direct ratio, proportion; 反比例 reverse ratio; 常比例 constant ratio; 比例尺 *--chyy*, scale (of map); 比例規 *--guei*, proportional dividers.
比目魚 *biimuh-yur*, n., sole, flounder.
比擬 *birnii*, n. & v.i., compare to; such comparison.
比熱 *biireh*, n., (phys.) specific heat.
比如 *biirur*, adv., for example; suppose.
比賽 *biisaih*, n. & v.i., contest (athletics, art, etc.).
比手畫腳 *bir-shoou-huah-jiaau*, phr., make lively gestures (while talking).
比翼 *bii-yih*, adv., (fly) wing to wing, inseparable (of lovers, married couple): 比翼雙飛, 比翼鳥 such happy couple.
比喩 *biiyuh*, n., a parable, metaphor, allegory.

此 21S.70-2

tsyy.

Pron. & adj. This (LL, but is largely used in vern. in many common phrr.): 此番, 此次 this time; 此人, 此地, 此時 this person, place, time; 此項 this item; 此種, 此類 this kind; 如此 like this, thus; 因此 for this reason; 故此, 爲此 ditto; 類此, 似此 like this, such; 彼此 each other, mutually; 專此, 特此 (form closing a letter) so I am writing you as above; 此復 this in reply; 此請台安 (form closing letter) I close with best wishes.

Adv. (AC) then: 有人此有土 having popular support, it follows (then) that he will be a ruler of the land (here 此=斯).

此啓 *tsyy chii*, phr., (form closing letter, official tone) the above is my communication.
此道 *tsyy dauh*, phr., this line: 精於此道 is good at this line.
此地 *tsyy-dih*, adv., here.
此番 *tsyy-fan*, adv., this time.
此後 *tsyy-houh*, adv., henceforth.
此間 *tsyy-jian*, adv., here, over here.
此際 *tsyy-jih*, adv., at this time or juncture.
此中 *tsyy-jung*, adv., herein.
此致 *tsyy jyh*, phr., (form closing letter) the above to inform you.
此君 *tsyy-jyun*, n., (1) this person; (2) (LL, allu.) bamboo.

此舉 *tsyr jyuu*, phr., this undertaking.
此刻 *tsyr-keh*, adv., now, this moment.
此若 *tsyyruoh*, adj., (AC, rare) this.
此生 *tsyy-sheng*, n., this life; adv., in this life.
此時 *tsyy-shyr*, adv., now, at present.
此次 *tsyy-tsyh*, adv., this time.
此外 *tsyy-waih*, adv., besides, in addition.

齔 21S.70-2

chehn.

N. Period when child is shedding milk teeth: 童齔 young childhood.

齜 21S.70-2

tzy.

V. i. To snarl: 齜牙 *-yar* ↓.

Adj. (Of teeth) irregular.

齜牙 *tzy-yar*, v. i., (1) to snarl: 齜牙瞪眼 to gnash the teeth and stare in anger; (2) writhe, contort one's face with pain: 齜牙咧嘴 squirm and cry in pain.

乩 21S.70-7

ji.

N. Planchette as in 扶乩 a traditional form of divination whereby the spirit, when invoked, writes characters on a sand pan by means of a stick attached to a horizontal piece supported by two persons serving as mediums.

甗 21S.70-3

yaan.

N. (AC) an ancient double boiler.

覘 21S.70-4

jan.

V. i. & t. To watch: 覘時而動 watch for opportunity; 覘候 watch and wait.

覬 21S.70-4

jih.

V. t. Covet, long for.

覬幸 *jihshihng*, v. t., hope to get (s.t.) by a stroke of good luck.
覬覦 *jihyur*, v. t., covet (another's territory, possessions).

覰 21S.70-4

chyuh.

[Pop. 覷]

V.i. & t. To peep, watch: 覰機會 watch for a chance; 覰著眼看 scrutinize; 覰窺 peep at.

凱 21S.70-4

kaai.

N. & adj. Triumph, triumphant: 凱歌 song of victory; 奏凱 to win victory.

凱撒 *Kaaisa*, n., Caesar, Kaiser.

凱旋 *kaaishyuarn*, v. i., return in triumph; 凱旋門 triumphal arch (esp. *Arc de Triomphe*).

齕 21S.70-9

her.

V. t. (AC) to bite.

齙 21S.70-9

bau (**paur*, re. pr.).

Adj. 齙牙 protruding front teeth.

齯 21S.70-9

nir.

N. 齯齒 tooth that grows in old age.

豔 21S.70-9

yahn.

[Pop. of 豔 21S.30]

§21S.71 (ㄴㅏ^{S}/弋)

战 21S.71-7

jahn.

[Abbr. of 戰 40S.71]

戕 21S.71-7

chiarng.

V. t. To destroy, wound, to kill: 自戕 commit suicide.

戕殺 *chiangsha*, v. t., to kill: 戕殺生民 to butcher the people.
戕傷 *chiangshang*, v. t., to wound (as with knife).
戕賊 *chiangtzer*, v. t., to destroy, injure, damage (growth, talent, material); to kill (life).

戲 21S.71–7

shih.

[Pop. 戱; abbr. 戏]

N. (1) Theater, theatrical shows: 戲劇 *-jyuh*↓; 戲曲 *-chyuu*↓; 京戲 Peking opera: 文明戲 modern drama in modern vernacular; 傀儡戲 puppet show; 影戲 movie; 皮影戲 puppet shadow show; 演戲 to perform a play, performance; 拿手好戲 an opera which is some singer's specialty——hence specialty in gen. (2) S. t. interesting: 有戲可看了 s. t. interesting (e. g., an open break between parties) will turn up. (3) Games, amusement; 遊ᴬ戲 60.83, a game; 逢場作戲 to take part in merely accidental amusement; 調ᴬ戲 60A.42; see 戲弄, 戲謔 *-nuhng*, *-nyueh*↓.

戲本(子) *shihbeen(tz)*, n., text for play or opera.
戲班(兒) *shihban(-ba'l)*, n., a troupe.
戲包袱 *shih-bau'fu*, n., an actor who commands a wide repertory.
戲筆 *shihbii*, n., a "playful stroke of the pen," in rapid sketch.
戲齣兒 *shihchu'l*, n., comics or toys with themes from the theater.
戲曲 *shihchyuu*, n., the theater, theatrical plays.
戲單(兒) *shih-dan(-da'l)*, n., the theatrical bill.
戲法(兒) *shihfaa('l)*, n., magic, sleight-of-hand; (fig.) a trick: 戲法人人會變 tricks in business, politics are common to all——no one's specialty.
戲館子 *shihguantz*, n., formerly, a theater (now usu. 戲院 *-yuahn*↓).
戲劇 *shihjyuh*, n., common term for drama; 戲劇性 dramatic.
戲碼兒 *shihmaa'l*, n., theatrical program.
戲迷 *shihmir*, n., an addict of (Peking) opera.
戲弄 *shihnuhng*, v. t., to mock, tease (person).
戲謔 *shihnyueh*, n. & v. i. & adj., cajolery, making fun of each other; mocking.
戲判 *shih-pahn*, n., an occasional critical opinion, usu. written in fun.
戲評 *shihpirng*, n., dramatic criticism.
戲殺 *shih-sha*, v. t., (LL) to commit manslaughter, without intention and started in fun.
戲衫(子) *shihshan(tz)*, n., stage costume.
戲箱 *shihshiang*, n., actors' trunks containing accessories of play.
戲耍 *shihshuaa*, n. & v. i., playing and joking; to do for fun.
戲臺 *shihtair*, n., the theatrical stage.
戲談 *shihtarn*, n., playful discussion.
戲子 *shihtz*, n., (derog.) an actor.
戲文 *shihwern*, n., (1) a play; (2) text of a play.
戲言 *shihyarn*, n., a joke, a humorous remark.
戲衣 *shihyi*, n., stage costume.
戲院 *shihyuahn*, n., a theater or movie house.
戲園子 *shihyuarntz*, n., formerly, a theater (modn. *-yuahn*↑).

鹹 21S.71–7

shiarn.

Adj. Salty, salted: 鹹鴨蛋 salted duck's egg; 鹹魚 salted fish; 太鹹了 too salty; 鹹津津的 very salty.

鹹肉 *shiarnrouh*, n., salt pork; (Shanghai sl.) low-class call girl; 鹹肉莊 secret brothel.
鹹瀉 *shiarnshieh*, adj., (land, soil) impregnated with salt, barren.
鹹水 *shiarnshueei*, n., salt water; 鹹水妹 (Cantonese sl.) prostitutes patronized exclusively by white men in the ports.
鹹濕 *shiarnshy*, adj., (Cantonese) (lit.) salty and wet; (fig.) indulgent in sex and sexual matters.
鹹菜 *shiarntsaih*, n., salted vegetable; 鹹酸菜 pickled vegetables.

§21S.80 (ㄴ卜S/八)

頃 21S.80–3

chiing (*ching).

N. (1) A land measure: a hundred *moou* 畝, about 15.13 acres; 千頃, 萬頃 a vast expanse (of fields, water, sorrows). (2) A short while, see 頃刻 *-keh*↓.

Adj. (*ching) (AC) leaning, inclining (u.f. 傾).

Adv. Just now: 頃接來信 just received your letter; 頃聞 have just heard; 頃者, 頃之 (LL) just now.

頃久 *chirngjioou*, adv., (AC) a short moment.
頃刻 *chiingkeh*, adv., in a short instant; also 頃刻間, 頃間.

潁 21S.80–3

yiing.

N. Name of river.

戕 戲 鹹 頃 潁

穎 21S.80-3

yiing.
[Interch. 頴]

N. Spike of wheat; a sharp point: 脱穎而出 a good man cannot be kept down as an awl point is bound to stick out of pocket.

Adj. Outstanding, intelligent: 穎秀, 穎悟 *-shiouh, -wuh*↓.

穎 慧 *yirnghueih*, adj., intelligent.
穎 秀 *yiingshiouh*, adj., brilliant (student).
穎 脱 *yiingtuo*, v. i., to distinguish oneself (see N.↑).
穎 悟 *yiingwuh*, adj., quick in understanding.

頴 21S.80-3

yiing.
[Pop. of 穎↑]

䌹 21S.80-3

chyuung.

N. A plant of hemp family.

頻 21S.80-3

pirn.
[Rarely used as var. of 蘋 20A.80, 顰 22.10]

Adj. & adv. (1) Frequent, -ly, often, again and again: 頻送秋波 the girl repeatedly casts a glance in one's direction; continuous: 頻年內亂 continuous civil wars. (2) (AC) in critical condition.

頻 煩 (繁) *pirnfarn*, adj., multifarious, crushing (business, duties).
頻 率 *pirn-lyuh*, n., (phys.) frequency (of waves).
頻 仍 *pirnrerng*, adj., continuous, uninterrupted (civil wars 內亂).

顓 21S.80-3

juan.

Adj. (1) (AC) cautious, honest: 顓 good, honest people. (2) Ignorant: 顓蒙 *-merng*↓.

顓 顓 *juanjuan*, adj., (AC) 顓顓獨居 living alone. ⌈(people).
顓 蒙 *juanmerng*, adj., ignorant
顓 頊 *Juanshyuh*, n., name of an emperor (2514–2436 B.C.), grandson of Yellow Emperor.

顱 21S.80-3

lur.

N. 頭顱 the skull.

§21S.81 (L⊦^{S}/人)

狀 21S.81-1

juahng.

N. (1) Shape, appearance, form, manner: 狀貌 *-mauh*↓; 狀態 *-taih*↓; 形狀 shape; 凶惡之狀 a ferocious manner; 狀如瘋狂 looks like mad; 出言無狀 use rude language. (2) Condition: 狀況 *-kuahng*↓; 情狀 condition (of patient, neighborhood after fire), how one feels (see 情 22A.42). (3) (*-tz*) A letter of appeal to authority, esp. a legal plaint or complaint: 狀詞, 狀子 *-tsyr, -tz*↓; 告狀, 訴狀 to register legal complaint; 具狀 lodge a charge or complaint. (4) Official document: 委任狀 letter of appointment; 獎狀 certificate of award. (5) 行狀 brief biographical sketch of deceased.

V. t. To describe, narrate: 自狀其過 confessed his own mistakes; 不可名狀 indescribable (confusion, etc.).

狀 棍 *juahngguhn*, n., pettifogging lawyer, "shyster."
狀 紙 *juahngjyy*, n., legal-sized paper.
狀 況 *juahngkuahng*, n., condition (of things in school, hospital, of patient), general aspects.
狀 貌 *juahngmauh*, n., a person's looks, appearance.
狀 態 *juahngtaih*, n., manner or appearance; condition of things, see *-kuahng*↑; 戰前狀態 *status quo ante bellum*; 現此狀態 status quo.
狀 頭 *juahngtour*, n., (1) (Yuan Dyn.) plaintiff; (2) coll. for 狀元 *-yuarn*↓.
狀 詞 *juahngtsyr*, n., legal plaint.
狀 子 *juahngtz*, n., ditto.
狀 元 *juahngyuarn*, n., the No. 1 of the national civil examinations; 狀元籌 *--chour*, n., a dice game of 6 dices, so-called because one who throws highest combination 狀元紅 is called 狀元.
狀 語 *juahngyuu*, n., (gram.) adverb (commonly called 副詞); 狀語子句 adverbial clause; 狀語短語 adverbial phrase.

獃 21S.81-1

air (also *dai*).

Adj. (Identical with 呆 40.01) stupid, dull: 獃頭獃腦 tactless, insensible to what is happening in given circumstances.

獃 氣 *airchih* (*dai-*), n., a stupid air or look.
獃 子 *airtz* (*dai-*), n., an idiot.

獻 21S.81-1

shiahn.
[Abbr. 献]

N. 文獻 cultural heritage; historical data, papers, documents, literature.

V. t. To offer up, present to superior: 獻計 present a plan or strategy; 獻俘 present war prisoners to emperor or commander; 獻捷 announce victory; 貢獻 pay tributary goods, also contribute (ideas, suggestions); 供獻 to offer (sacrifices, etc.); 奉獻 to offer, contribute (to church, superior).

獻芹 *shiahn-chirn*, v. i., (LL, court.) to contribute or present an insignificant gift (lit., "celery").
獻醜 *shiahn-choou*, v. i., (derog. or self-depreciating) present (a show, performance); (lit.) "reveal awkwardness," exposes one's weaknesses.
獻馘 *shiahn-guor*, v. i., (AC) present the cut-off left ears of war prisoners or captives.
獻拙 *shiahn-juor*, v. i., see *-choou* ↑.
獻媚 *shiahn-meih*, v. i., to curry favor, fawn upon, cater to.
獻曝 *shiahn-puh*, v. i., (LL, court. allu.) give a sincere but unworthy present ("present sunshine" of one's country).
獻身 *shiahn-shen*, v. i., to dedicate oneself (to cause, country).
獻歲 *shiahn-sueih*, n., (LL) the New Year, year's beginning.
獻替 *shiahn-tih*, phr., (=獻可替否) (AC) persuade to do good and dissuade from evil.
獻辭 *shiahn tsyr*, n., dedication (of a book or at ceremony).
獻贈 *shiahn-tzehng*, n., a contribution (of gift or ideas).

鹼 21S.81-8

jiaan.
[Var. 鹻; pop. 硷]

N. & adj. Alkali(ne): 鹼性 alkaline; 鹼土, 鹼地 such soil; 燒鹼 caustic soda; 鹼水 lye; 汗鹼 sweat stains on underwear; 鹼質 alkalis.

以 21S.81-8

yii.

N. Short for 以色列 Israel (cf. 意 for Italy).

V.i. & t. (1) Do: 可以 vb. aux., may; 視其所以 see what he does. (2) Consider as: 以爲 *-weir*, 以謂 *-weih* ↓. (3) In order to; like Eng. "to", used to introduce infinitive: 以免, 以妨 in order to avoid, prevent; 以備萬一 to provide against any contingency; 以杜後患 to forestall future trouble; 以釋羣疑 to allay doubt in public's mind; 以補所失 to repay the loss; 以救眉急 to answer urgent needs; 以資參考 to provide for reference; 以致身亡 as a result, he died; 以昭信用 to show good faith.

Prep. (Usu.) placed before nn. (1) Giving direction or time sequence: 以上, 以下 above, below; 以東, 以西, 以左, 以右 to the east, west, left, right; 以前, 以後 before, after; 以往 formerly; 以來 since that time; 以外, 以內 excluding, including. (2) Giving cause: 以此, 以此之故, 以故 for this reason; 是以, 所以 therefore; 良有以也 (LL) indeed that was why. (3) With, indicating implement, instrumentality; 以毒攻毒 fight poison with poison; 以德報怨 to return good for evil; 以手加額 place hand over one's forehead (in greeting); 以身作則 make oneself serve as example to others; 以淚洗面 "wash my face with tears" (in extreme misery); 以逸待勞 hold one's position awaiting enemy attack after long march; 以訛傳訛 pass on rumors, incorrect reading, etc.

以便 *yii-biahn*, phr., in order to facilitate (doing): 以便回報, 回家 so that I can make a report, return home.
以前 *yii-chiarn*, adv. & prep., before: 啟程以前 before departure; 以前不是這樣 it was not so before.
以待 *yii-daih*, phr., in order to wait for (what is expected).
以防 *yii-farng*, phr., in order to prevent.
以故 *yii-guh*, adv. & conj., therefore.
以後 *yii-houh*, adv., (1) since (used after vb.); (2) later on, afterwards.
以還 *yii-huarn*, adv., (LL) since (=以來 used after vb.).
以降 *yii-jiahng*, adv., (LL) since (some past date or event), from (event) down.
以致 *yii-jyh*, phr., resulting in (division, destruction, death, etc.); with the result that (I came late, etc.).
以來 *yii-lair*, adv., since, after (doing): 民國以來 since the founding of the Republic.
以免 *yir-miaan*, phr., in order to prevent, forestall.
以內 *yii-neih*, prep. phr. including.
以色列 *Yiisehlieh*, n., Israel.
以上 *yii-shahng*, (1) adv. & prep., above (certain number, age, etc.): 以上所說 what is said above; (2) n., the above (passage).
以下 *yii-shiah*, adv. & prep., below (number, age): 三十以下 below thirty; 以下所說 what follows.
以次 *yii-tsyh*, adv., according to order.
以此 *yir-tsyy*, (1) conj., because of this, therefore; (2) phr., with this (conclude, etc.); (3) accordingly: 以此進行 proceed thus.
以資 *yii-tzy*, phr., to help along (doing); to provide for (refer-

ence, etc.).

以往 *yir-waang*, adj. & adv., former, -ly: 以往的事 past events.

以外 *yii-waih*, (1) phr., excluding; (2) conj., furthermore.

以謂 *yii-weih*, phr., (AC) see *-weir* ↓.

以爲 *yii-weir* (-'*wei*), v.i., regard as, take for (usu. mistakenly): 以爲好人 thought or took s.o. as a good man; 我以爲 I thought (by mistake).

欸 21S.81-9

kuaan.

[Pop. of 款 11S.81]

欤 21S.81-9

yur.

[Abbr. of 歟 90S.81]

歔 21S.81-9

shyu.

V. i. To blow, suck: 歔枯吹生 (AC) blow life into dead plants.

歔欷 *shyushi*[1], v.i., to sob and sniffle; cf. 嘘 40A.30.

歔吸 *shyushi*[2], v.i. & t., to suck in.

§21S.82 (ㄴㅏ^S/ㄨ)

歧 21S.82-1

chir.

Adj. (Of roads and methods) branching off, see 歧路, 歧途 *-luh*, *-tur* ↓; 意見分歧 opinions sharply differ, divided counsel; discriminating, see 歧視 *-shyh* ↓.

歧歧 *chirchir*, adj., (AC) descriptive of flying.

歧出 *chirchu*, v.i., to fork out.

歧路 *chirluh*, n., a forked road: 歧路亡羊 phr., a lamb goes astray on forked road; (fig.) going astray. ⌈stray thoughts.

歧念 *chirniahn*, n., strange ideas,

歧視 *chirshyh*, v.t., to discriminate against (s.o.).

歧途 *chirtur*, n., stray road: 錯入歧途 fall into wrong path; see *-luh* ↑. ⌈ence.

歧異 *chiryih*, n., deviation, differ-

战 21S.82-2

dian.

V.i. 战敠 to weigh (with hand); to estimate the weight of.

戯 21S.82-2

ja.

N. Red blotch (esp. on nose from excessive drinking): 酒戯.

叔 21S.82-3

shur.

N. (1) An uncle younger than father. (2) Husband's younger brother, also 小叔, 叔叔, 叔子. (3) Familiar address of junior member of father's generation.

Adj. (1) Number 3 in sequence of brothers: 伯 1, 仲 2, 叔 or 季 3. (2) The last, latter part: 叔世, 叔季 *-shyh*, *-jih* ↓.

叔伯 *shurbor* (-'*bo*), n., uncles (伯 senior uncle; 叔 junior uncle).

叔父 *shurfuh*, n., paternal uncle who is younger than one's father.

叔公 *shurgung*, n., granduncle; also used by mothers following children's address of uncle.

叔丈(人) *shurjahng*(*rern*), n., wife's uncle.

叔季 *shur-jih*, n., the latter days (of dynasty, empire).

叔舅 *shurjiouh*, n., mother's younger brother. ⌈ew.

叔姪 *shur-jyr*, n., uncle and neph-

叔母 *shurmuu*, n., aunt, wife of junior uncle.

叔婆 *shurpor*, n., grandfather's younger brother's wife.

叔嬸 *shursheen*, n., aunt, wife of junior uncle.

叔叔 *shur'shu*, n., (vocative) uncle; husband's younger brother.

叔世 *shur-shyh*, n., (AC) see *-jih* ↑.

叔子 *shurtz*, n., husband's younger brother (also called 小叔子).

叔祖 *shurtzuu*, n., granduncle.

叔翁 *shurweng*, n., (vocative) granduncle.

叡 21S.82-3

rueih.

Adj. Interch. 睿 21A.41.

皺 21S.82-6

yaau.

[Var. of 咬 40A.82]

§21S.83 (ㄴㅏ^S/〜)

疑 21S.83-3

yir.

V.i. & t. To doubt, suspect: 疑心,

疑惑 *-shin, -huoh*↑; 不疑 doubt not; 無疑的 doubtlessly; 可疑 suspicious, questionable; 見疑 do not enjoy confidence; 多疑 prone to suspect, doubt; 令人生疑 arouse one's suspicion; 猜疑 to suspect; 嫌▲疑 93A.22; 疑信參半 half believe, do not believe entirely; 疑神疑鬼 imagine all sorts of things.

Adj. Unclear, unsettled, undecided: 疑案, 疑義, 疑問 *-ahn, -yih²*, *-wehn*↓; 疑犯 *-fahn*↓.

疑案 *yir-ahn*, n., an unsettled case at court, a mystery case.
疑謗 *yirbahng*, v.i. & t., to smear one's name, be subject to smearing.
疑兵 *yir-bihng*, n., (mil.) a feint to mislead enemy.
疑貳 *yir-ehl*, v.i., become disaffected, of wavering loyalty.
疑犯 *yir fahn*, n., a suspect (in a lawsuit).
疑惑 *yirhuoh*, n., doubt and perplexity; v.i., to be perplexed, to be wondering (what will happen, etc.).
疑忌 *yirjih*, v.t., to be jealous (of person); v., jealousy.
疑懼 *yirjyuh*, v.i. & n., (to live in) doubt and fear.
疑慮 *yirlyuh*, v.i. & t., to be worried, concerned; n., worry, concern.
疑難 *yirnahn*, n., a difficulty, a difficult problem.
疑相 *yir'shiang*, n., misunderstanding or mistake: 弄疑相 (coll.) do s.t. questionable.
疑心 *yirshin*, v.i., to guess, suspect: 我疑心是他 I guess it is he; 絕不疑心 have full confidence; 疑心病 morbid suspicion.
疑似 *yirsyh*, adj., apparently correct but is not, fallacious.
疑團 *yirtuarn*, n., dark shadows of doubt lurking in one's mind.
疑問 *yirwehn*, n., a question in gen.: 有什麽疑問 any questions?
疑意 *yiryih¹*, n., doubt, suspicion in mind.
疑義 *yiryih²*, n., doubtful or inadequately explained meaning of words.
疑影 *yir'ying*, n. shadow of suspicion.
疑獄 *yiryuh*, n., see *-ahn*↑.

齪 21S.83-4

chuoh.

N. & adj. See 齷▲齪 21S.11.

§ 21S.93 (ㄴ卜ˢ/く)

妝 21S.93-9

juang.

[Pop. 粧; var. 娤, 裝]

N. Costume, make-up: 宮妝 palace style; 梳妝 hairdressing; 梳妝臺 dressing table; 新妝 new fashion; 嫁妝 trousseau; 假妝, 化妝 disguise; 濃妝, 豔妝 (of woman) heavy make-up, dressy, beautiful dress; 淡妝, 素妝 simple attire.

V. i. & t. (1) To dress up, adorn, apply make-up: 妝點, 妝扮, 妝飾 *-diaan, -bahn, -shyh*↓. (2) To pretend, disguise (see 裝 21.02).

妝扮 *juangbahn*, v. i. & n., dress (-ing) up, be dressed up.
妝點 *juangdiaan*, n. & v.i., ditto.
妝奩 *juangliarn*, n., (1) trousseau; (2) (rare) cosmetic articles.
妝樓 *juanglour*, n., a lady's boudoir.
妝梳 *juangshu*, n., (=梳妝) hairdressing.
妝飾 *juangshyh*, n. & v.t., decorations; dress up.
妝臺 *juangtair*, n., dressing table.
妝次 *juang-tsyh*, phr., opening formula in letter addressing a lady.

SECTION 22

§ 22.00 (丨/亅)

掌 22.00

jaang.

N. (1) The palm of hand: 巴掌, 手掌 ditto; 腳掌 sole of foot; 拍掌 clap in applause; 擊掌 clap hands as signal; 鼓掌 (audience) clap applause; 孤掌難鳴 one cannot make a clap with one hand—useless without friendly support. (2) (Fig.) as in: 易如反掌 very easy to do ("as turning hand over"); 瞭如指掌 very evident; 掌上明珠 a dearly beloved daughter. (3) Paw, hoof of animal: 熊掌 (edible) bear's paw; 鴨掌 duck's feet; 釘馬掌 put on horseshoe. (4) Paw-like object: 仙人掌 cactus, "prickly pear."

V. i. & t. (1) To slap: 掌頰 slap on the face; 掌嘴 slap across the mouth. (2) To be in charge of, be head of: 掌管, 掌握 *-guaan, -woh*↓; 職掌 a person's duty; 掌家 manage a home; 掌校 to head a school; 掌教 to head a church; 掌政 head a government; 掌案兒的 the employee in butcher shop responsible for chopping; 掌勺兒的 the cook specialising in frying; 掌灶兒的 person in charge of cooking in restaurant; 掌鼓 (person) be in charge of the drum (Chin. opera). (3) To bear, stand: 掌不住笑了 could not help laughing; 強掌住不哭出來 control one's weeping.

掌案 *jaang-ahn*, n., head of bureau of files and records.
掌權 *jaang-chyuarn*, v. i., to have real power.
掌燈 *jaang-deng*, phr., to light a

亅	小	⺊	十	土	ナ	廾	ㄴ卜	丨	一	丅	フ	口	囗	冂	ㄱ	厂	尸	亠	广	宀	丶	乚	弋	心	八	人	乂	⼀	一	ノ	ㄥ	く
00	01	02	10	11	12	20	21	22	30	31	32	40	41	42	50	51	52	60	61	62	63	70	71	72	80	81	82	83	90	91	92	93

lamp: 掌燈的時候 the hour when lamps are lighted.

掌舵 *jaang-duoh*, (1) n., helmsman; (2) v. i., to be at the helm.

掌管 *jarngguaan*, v. t., to have charge of (household, the lights, the official seal, etc.).

掌櫃的 *jaanggueih'de*, n., (1) cashier; (2) the boss, in shop.

掌故 *jaangguh*, n., anecdote in gen.; stories of the past.

掌記 *jaangjih*, n., (1) (AC) historiographer in charge of recording natural phenomena (comets, etc.); (2) secretary in charge of documents and official communications.

掌理 *jarnglii*, v. t., see *-guaan* ↑.

掌扇 *jaangshahn*, n., a big parasol with long handle, used in parades.

掌心 *jaangshin*, n., center of palm of hand; 掌心雷 Taoist magic, reputed to be able to call forth thunder by rubbing palm of hand.

掌紋 *jaangwern*, n., hand lines in palmistry.

掌握 *jaangwoh*, n. & v. t., control, have in control: 掌握時政 in charge of government policy.

學 22.00

shyuer.

[Abbr. of 學 90.00]

§22.01 (丨/小)

小 22.01

shiaau.

N. The young: 老小 the young and old; 妻小 wife and children.

Adj. (1) Small in size: 小舖子 a small store; 小巷 an alley; 小本生意 small business; 小型汽車 small car; 小指 the little finger; 小楷 fine regular characters in small size; 小築 a little villa. (2) Little, unimportant: 小名氣 some little reputation; 小便宜 petty gains; 小聰明 intelligent in small ways, but oft. tricky; 小意思 *-yih'sy* ↓; 小人, 小民 *-rern, -mirn* ↓; 小題大做 much ado about nothing; 小不忍則亂大謀 who cannot take small insults or setbacks is liable to spoil big plans. (3) Minor, junior: 小丫頭, 小么兒 *-ya'tou, -yau'l* ↓; 小弟, 小妹 younger brother, sister; 小孩 *-hair* ↓; 小妻 *-chi*, 小老婆 *-la-au'por* ↓. (4) (In self-deprecation) humble, small: 小僧 used by monk; 小女 my daughter; 小婿 my son-in-law; 小門生 your humble pupil. (5) Lesser: 小年夜, 小除夕 day before New Year's Eve; 小至 day before 冬至 winter solstice; 小重陽 day after 9th day of 9th lunar month.

Adv. A little: 小立, 小坐 stand, sit for a while; 小語 have a little talk; 小別 temporary parting; 小憩, 小息 rest a little; 小看 to despise; 小覷 *-shyh* ↓.

小半(兒) *shiaau-bahn(-bah'l)*, n., the lesser half.

小白臉兒 *shiaau-bair-liaa'l*, n., handsome, fair-complexioned, small and not muscular young man.

小班(兒) *shiaauban(-ba'l)*, n., as in 清吟小班 formerly, first-class courtesan.

小報兒 *shiaaubauh'l*, n., tabloid paper.

小輩 *shiaaubeih*, n., (1) the younger generation, youth; (2) lout.

小便 *shiaaubiahn*, (1) v.i., to urinate; (2) n., urine.

小步(兒) *shiaau-buh('l)*, adv., in leisurely steps.

小產 *shiaurchaan* (*-'chan*), n., abortion.

小腸 *shiaaucharng*, n., the intestines; 小腸氣 (Chin. med.) inflammation of kidneys and testicles (also called 疝氣).

小成 *shiaau-cherng*, n., (AC) completion of 7-year high-school course.

小妻 *shiaau-chi*, n., concubine.

小氣 *shiaau'chi*, adj., narrow-minded, stingy (also wr. 小器).

小巧 *shiaurchiaau*, adj., as in 小巧玲瓏 (small art objects) pretty, cleverly made.

小瞧 *shiaau-chiaur*, v.t., to look down upon.

小竊 *shiaau-chieh*, n., petty thief, burglar.

小青 *shiaauching*, n., (1) (bot.) indigo plant; (2) (MC) maid.

小醜 *shiaur-choou*[1], n., roughnecks.

小丑(兒) *shiaurchoou*[2]*('l)*, n., clown.

小雛兒 *shiaauchur'l*, n., (1) chicken; (2) a dolt, inexperienced youth.

小吃店 *shiaauchy-diahn*, n., snack bar.

小曲 *shiaurchyuu*, n., folk song, ditty.

小大姐 *shiaau-dah-jiee*, n., mature girl servant.

小旦 *shiaaudahn*, n., Chin. opera actress.

小道兒 *shiaau-dauh'l*, n., (1) bypath; (2) irregular or illegal approach.

小的 *shiaau'di*, n., (1) a servant; (2) (*-de*) a young one (also wr. 小底).

小調(兒) *shiaaudiauh('l)*, n., a song, ditty.

小弟 *shiaaudih*, n., (court. in self-reference) younger brother.

小豆 *shiaaudouh*, n., (1) kinds of small beans; (2) kind which turns dark red when cooked; 小豆腐兒 --*'fu'l*, n., a paste mixture of rice, flour and vegetable in North China; 豆兒 minute trifles.

小肚子 *shiaauduhtz* n., region below navel.

小二 *shiaau-ehl*, n., waiter at wine shop or hotel.

小兒 *shiaau-erl*, n., (1) a child; my son; (2) (*-'l*) period of childhood: 從小兒 from childhood; a child, children; 小兒科 n., pediatrics; 小兒麻痺 poliomyelitis= polio, infantile paralysis.

小販 *shiaaufahn*, n., a peddler.

小方脈 *shiaau-fang-moh*, n., pediatrics.

小費 *shiaaufeih*, n., tips, gratuities.

小腹 *shiaaufuh*[1], n., region below

A

navel; see *-duhtz*↑.

小婦 *shiaaufuh*[2], n., see *-chi*↑.

小夫人 *shiaau-furern*, n., concubine.

小哥 *shiaauge*, n., as in 小哥兒們 a group of young men, also 小哥們兒.

小歌劇 *shiaau-ge-jyuh*, n., operetta.

小狗兒的 *shiaurgoou'l'de*, n., affectionate term for children ("puppy").

小姑(兒) *shiaaugu('l)*, n., husband's younger sister (also 小姑子); 小姑娘(兒) young girl.

小褂兒 *shiaauguah'l*, n., light, unlined jacket.

小官(兒) *shiaauguan('l)*, n., minor official; formerly, court. self-reference of official before superior; 小官人 (MC) address for upper-class young man.

小鬼(兒) *shiaur-gueei('l)*, n., (1) "little devil"—intimate reference to mischievous boy (also 小鬼頭); (2) little devils that run errands in Hell.

小功 *shiaau-gung*[1], n., mourning of five months for certain relatives.

小工(兒) *shiaaugung*[2]*('l)*, n., a labor hand (carrying gravel, soil in construction work, etc.).

小鼓 *shiaauguu*, n., a tabor, taborine.

小孩(兒)(子) *shiaauhair('l)(-har'l)(tz)*, n., a child.

小鬟 *shiaauhuarn*, n., a young maidservant.

小夥(子)(兒) *shiaurhuoo (tz) ('l)*, n., able-bodied young man.

小賬 *shiaaujahng*, n., tip for waiters, etc.

小照 *shiaaujauh*, n., (photo) a portrait.

小腳(兒) *shiaur-jiaau('l)*, n., bound feet.

小家子 *shiaaujiatz (-tzyy)*, n., coarse, lower-class person; 小家碧玉 daughter of middle-class family.

小姐 *shiaurjiee*[1], n., an unmarried girl: 廖小姐 Miss Liauh, also used for married professional women.

小解 *shiaurjiee*[2], v.i., to urinate.

B

小節 *shiaaujier*, n., minor points of conduct.

小薊 *shiaaujih*, n., cat thistle.

小己 *shiaurjii*, n., person, individual.

小舅子 *shiaaujiouhtz*, n., wife's younger brother.

小傳 *shiaau-juahn*[1], n., a short biography, biographic sketch.

小篆 *shiaaujuahn*[2], n., anc. script in Chirn and Hahn Dyns., simplified from 大篆.

小註(兒) *shiaaujuh('l)*, n., footnotes.

小君 *shiaaujyun*, n., (AC) wife.

小楷 *shiaurkaai*, n., regular small script.

小看 *shiaaukahn*, v.t., to despise, look down upon.

小開 *shiaaukai*, n., (Shanghai dial.) young boss of a business.

小康 *shiaaukang*, n., (1) as in 小康之家 a well-to-do middle-class family; (2) period of well-organized human society (cf. 大△同 12.81).

小可 *shiaurkee*, adj. & adv., a little.

小老婆 *shiaurlaau'por*, n., (coll.) concubine.

小郎 *shiaaularng*, n., (1) (MC) husband's younger brother; (2) (MC) a young man.

小李 *shiaurlii (-li)*, n., a petty burglar.

小綹 *shiaurlioou*, n., see *-lii*↑.

小零兒 *shiaaulirng'l*, n., change (of coins).

小麥 *shiaaumaih*[1], n., wheat.

小賣 *shiaaumaih*[2], v.t., to peddle (noodles, cold drinks, etc.).

小米兒 *shiaurmiee'l*, n., millet.

小民 *shiaaumirn*, n., humble people; also (in self-reference toward judge) your humble servant.

小名(兒) *shiaaumirng('l)*, n., childhood name at home, different from legal name.

小末 *shiaaumoh*, n., (Chin. opera) minor male role.

小拇指(頭) *shiaau'mujyy('tou)*, n., the little finger.

小腦 *shiaurnaau*, n., (physiol.) cerebellum.

小奶奶(兒) *shiaau'nai'nai('l)*, n., see *-chi*↑.

C

小娘子 *shiaauniarngtz*, n., (MC) a young girl: 小娘們兒 (a) (derog.) young women; (b) concubines.

小妮子 *shiaaunirtz*, n., (1) (coll.) a small girl, girl of teenage; 小妮兒 ditto; (2) a maidservant.

小女 *shiaurnyuu*, n., (court.) my daughter.

小品 *shiaurpiin*, n., also 小品文 belles-lettres, essays, sketches.

小貧 *shiaau-pirn*, adj., (rare) stingy.

小人 *shiaaurern (-'ren)*, n., (1) common people; (2) selfish or mean person; (3) used of oneself in humble intercourse; 小人兒 a clay doll, figurine; 小人兒書 books for children.

小軟兒 *shiaurruaa'l*, n., a defenseless person.

小日子兒 *shiaauryh'tze'l*, n., (1) simple home life: 小日子兒過得不錯 lead a fair simple home life; (2) the bride's day of menstruation ascertained in fixing wedding day.

小嬸(兒)(子) *shiaurshee ('l) (-tz)*, n., younger brother's wife.

小生 *shiaausheng*, n., (1) (court. used in self-reference, by scholars or pupils) your pupil; (2) (Chin. opera) young male actor.

小舌 *shiaausher*, n., (physiol.) the uvula.

小小 *shiaurshiaau*, adj., very small (affair), very young (child): 小小子兒 a young male child.

小相 *shiaaushiahng*[1], n., (AC) assistant.

小像 *shiaaushiahng*[2], n., portrait (＝肖像).

小祥 *shiaaushiarng*, n., first anniversary of parent's death.

小寫 *shiaurshiee*, n., (spelling) small letters, (printing) lower case, "l.c."

小性兒 *shiaaushihng'l*, n., childish temper.

小喜 *shiaurshii*, n., (sl.) abortion.

小心 *shiaaushin (-'shin)*, (1) adj., careful; (2) v.i. & t., take care: 小心燈火 take care of the lights; 玻璃小心 glass—handle gently ("fragile").

小心眼兒 *shiaaushinyaa'l*, adj., narrow-minded, stingy.

小星 *shiaaushing*, n., (LL) concubine.

小數 *shiaaushuh* n., (math.) fraction.

小說(兒) *shiaaushuo('l)*, n., a novel; 小說家 novelist; (AC) writer of anecdotes, stories.

小叔(子) *shiaaushur(tz)*, n., husband's younger brother.

小視 *shiaaushyh*, v, t., to despise (s.o.), regard as of no importance.

小食 *shiaaushyr*[1], n., snacks (noodles, dumplings, etc.).

小時 *shiaaushyr*[2], n., (1) an hour; (2) the young days: 小時候 childhood days.

小雪 *shiaurshyuee*, n., a solar term, see Appendix B.

小學 *shiaaushyuer*, n., (1) elementary school, primary school; (2) study of anc. forms, phonology and meaning of written language.

小兄 *shiaaushyung*, n., (court. self-reference) I, your elder brother.

小廝 *shiaausy*, n., manservant.

小帖兒 *shiaurtiee'l*, n., exchange of bride's and groom's horoscopes written on red paper.

小提琴 *shiaau-tirchirn*, n., violin.

小蹄子 *shiaau-tirtz*, n., (coll., abusive) little wench.

小偷(兒) *shiaau-tou('l)*, n., petty thief.

小菜兒 *shiaautsah'l*, n., (1) small dishes to go with rice; (2) macerated cucumbers, pickles, etc.; (3) (sl.) one browbeaten by others.

小腿 *shiaurtueei*, n., (physiol.) the calf.

小宗 *shiaautzung*, n., (1) branch of younger sons of family, opp. 大宗 eldest branch; (2) Hinayana school.

小卒兒 *shiaautzur'l*, n., foot soldier.

小組 *shiaurtzuu*, n., a section, division: 小組會議 sectional conference, committee or subcommittee meeting.

小組織 *shiaur-tzuu-jy*, n., (Communist, underground) cell.

小字 *shiaautzyh*, n., (1) pet name (=小名 *-mirng* ↑); (2) see *-kaai* ↑.

小子 *shiaurtzyy*, n., (1) child, -ren; (2) court. self-reference; (3) (*-tz*) a boy (sometimes derog. or joc.); a boy servant.

小押(兒) *shiaauya('l)*, n., formerly, loan at usurious interest.

小丫頭 *shiaauya'tou* n., a young maid.

小洋 *shiaau-yarng*, n., formerly, a fraction of a dollar, a dime; cf. 大洋 a dollar.

小么兒 *shiaauyau'l*, n., (coll.) (contempt.) a servant.

小衣 *shiaau-yi*, n., underwear: 小衣兒 formerly, pants.

小夜曲 *shiaau-yieh-chyuu*, n., serenade.

小爺 *shiaauyier*[1], n., young master (of house).

小姨(兒)(子) *shiaauyier*[2]*('l) (-tz)*, n., wife's younger sister; the youngest of maternal aunt.

小意思 *shiaau-yih'syh*, n., a small gift (small token of respect), a mere trifle.

小引 *shiaauryiin*, n., foreword, introduction.

小影 *shiauryiing*, n., portrait, photograph.

小音階 *shiaau-yin-jie*, n., (mus.) minor scale.

小遺 *shiaauyir*, v.i., go to toilet.

小月 *shiaauyueh*, n., lunar month of 29 days; solar calendar month of 30 days.

米 22.01

mii.

N. (1) Rice, husked rice (known as 稻 90A.21 in the fields): 米飯 cooked rice; 白米 white rice; 小米 spiked millet; 爆米 puffed rice; 糯米 glutinous rice; 紅穀米 red rice; 西米 sago; 米珠薪桂 rice and fuel are expensive ("like pearls and cassia") in times of famine; 秈米 common rice; 粳米 japonica rice; 蓬萊米 ditto. (2) Small dried object: 蝦米 dried shrimp; 花生米 peanut.

米粉 *mirfeen*, n., noodles made of rice-flour.

米蛀蟲 *miijuh-churng*, n., rice worm; (fig.) hoarding rice merchant.

米糠 *miikang*, n., rice chaff, bran.

米粒(兒) *miilih (-lieh'l)*, n., grain of rice.

米色 *miiseh*, n., pale brown, buff color.

米湯 *miitang*, n., rice soup; 灌米湯 flatter (a person).

米突 *mii'tu*, n., meter: 米突制 --*jyh*, n., metrical system.

棠 22.01

tarng.

N. A plant: 海棠 the begonia.

棠棣 *tarngdih*, n., see 唐△棣 61.40.

棠梨 *tarnglir*, n., the birch leaf pear, *Pirus betulaefolia.*

業 22.01

yeh.

N. (1) Profession, line of business or industry: 事業 career, a project, an undertaking; 職業 profession, vocation; 本業, 正業 main profession; 副業 a side line, an avocation; 工業 industry; 商業 business, trade, commerce; 農業 agriculture; 實業 industry; 停業 close up shop; 轉業 to change one's occupation; 休業 business closed; 失業 unemployed; 成家立業 have a home and profession. (2) School studies, education: 學業 ditto; 肄業 to study (at some school); 畢業 graduate; 受業 study under (teacher); 修業 to study. (3) Achievement: 功業 ditto; 創業 founding of a house, a dynasty or any permanent institution. (4) Property: 產業 ditto; 賣業 sell property; 業主 *-juu* ↓. (5) (Sanskr. *karma*; Budd.) total accumulation of thoughts and actions which determines or influences person's future: 業障 *-jahng*↓.

V. t. To practise certain profession: 業醫 practise medicine; 業農 be a farmer, etc.

Adv. Already: 業已, 業經 *-yii*, *-jing*↓: 業已病故 already died of illness.

業障 *yehjahng*, n., the burden of sin, which is "obstacle" to one's life (also wr. 孽障); (abuse) a prodigal son, any one constantly causing trouble: 我的業障 seed of my sin, s. o. unwanted and cannot be got rid of.

業經 *yeh-jing*, adv., already (approved, delivered, broken, etc.).

業主 *yeh-juu*, n., owner of property.

業種 *yehjuung*, n. & adj., (abuse) bastard (also wr. 孽種).

業師 *yeh-shy*, n., person's teacher or professional master.

業務 *yeh-wuh*, n., business affairs.

業業 *yeh-yeh*, phr., 兢兢業業 (AC, LL) with great fear and caution.

業已 *yeh-yii*, adv., already, see *-jing*↑.

業餘 *yeh-yur*, adj., outside business or office hours (as clubs for various hobbies), amateur, nonprofessional.

祟 22.01

sueih.

[See 21.01]

---

§22.02 (亅/⺊)

水 22.02

shueei.

N. (1) Water: 鹹水, 淡水 salt, fresh water; 自來水 running water, water from the tap; 井水 well water; 汽水 soda water, sparkling, carbonated water; 蒸溜水 distilled water; 死水 stagnant water; 活水 flowing water; 順水 with the current; 逆水 against the current; 開水, 滾水 boiled water; 茶水 tea and drinks; 山水 landscape, landscape painting; 水中撈月 fish for moon in the water—futile phantasy; 混水摸魚 to fish in troubled waters; 水深火熱 (people) in deep distress, an abyss of suffering; 水乳交融 get along swimmingly with each other, mix well like milk and water; 水到渠成 canal is formed when water comes—s.t. achieved without effort; 水落石出 doubts will clear up when facts are known; 水洩(泄)不通 (of road) so jammed as to be impassable; crowd, audience, tightly packed; 水清無魚 fish do not come when water is too clear—said of ultra-pure official, giving no chance for malpractice; 水漲船高 ship rises with the tide—a person's social rise benefits those related to him. (2) Travel by water, opp. 旱 or 陸 land: 水路, 旱路 (陸路) travel by water, by land; 水陸交通 land and sea communications; 水師 *-shy*[1]↓; 水客 *-keh*↓; 水戰 sea or river battle. (3) Cosmetic lotion, fruit juice: 花露水 *eau de cologne*; 生髮水 hair lotion. (4) Silver content in coins: 貼水, 扣水 discount for inferior coins. (5) Quality: 頭水貨 goods "of the first water" (as said of diamond, artist in Eng.); top quality. (6) A surname.

V. t. To coax (person): 連水帶拍, 把他問的三心二意 by coax and threats made him confused, undecided.

Adj. Transparent, clear or wet like water: 水亮 *-liahng*↓; 水淋淋, 水漴漴 dripping wet; 水汪汪 watery (eyes).

水半球 *shueeibahnchiour*, n., water hemisphere.

水泵 *shueei-beng*, n., water pump.

水表 *shueir-biaau*, n., water meter, water gauge.

水鬢 *shueei-bihn*, n., curl of hair below the temple.

水筆 *shueir-bii*, n., writing brush of fairly stiff quality, kept moist in brass stop when not used.

水玻璃 *shueei-bo'li*, n., (chem.) water glass, sodium or potassium silicate.

水產 *shueir-chaan*, n., marine products (fish, shellfish, etc.).

水汊 *shueei-chah*, n., tributaries, a branch of current.

水蒼玉 *shueeichang-yuh*, n., aquamarine or beryl.

水車 *shueei-che*, n., (1) wheel (for propelling water for the fields from river); (2) water cart; 水車前 (bot.) the dragon's tongue, *Ottelia alismoides* (also called 龍舌草).

水丞 *shueei-cherng*[1], n., see *-juh*↓.

水程 *shueei-cherng*[2], n., watercourse, waterways; voyage.

水成岩 *shueeicherng-yarn*, n., (geol.) aqueous or sedimentary rocks; 水成礦物 n., hydrogen sulphite.

水球 *shueei-chiour*, n., water polo.

水芹 *shueei-chirn*[1], n., celery.

水禽 *shueei-chirn*[2], n., waterfowl.

水池 *shueei-chyr*, n., a pond, pool.

水圈 *shueeichyuan*, n., (geol.) hydrosphere.

水泉 *shueeichyuarn*, n., (water) spring.

水丹 *shueeidan*, n., putty (also called 油灰).

水道 *shueeidauh*, n., waterways; drainage system.

水滴 *shueeidi*, n., (1) drops of water; (2) tiny case or pot for dripping water in ink slab.

水殿 *shueei-diahn*, n., a hall overlooking lake; emperor's houseboat.

水底電線 *shueir-dii diahnshiahn*, n., submarine cable.

水痘(兒) *shueei-douh('l)*, n., chicken pox, varicella.

水碓 *shueei-dueih*, n., mill, powered by water, for hulling rice.

業 祟 水

亅	小	⺊	十	土	ナ	卄	ㄴ卜	丨	一	丅	フ	口	区	冈	ㄱ	厂	尸	亠	广	宀	丶	乚	弋	心	八	人	乂	一	㇀	丿丿	𠂉	く
00	01	02	10	11	12	20	21	22	30	31	32	40	41	42	50	51	52	60	61	62	63	70	71	72	80	81	82	83	90	91	92	93

水

水燉兒 *shueei-duo'l*, n., food warmer, a large bowl containing hot water for keeping food warm (also wr. 水囤兒).

水厄 *shueei-eh*, n., (LL) death by drowning.

水法(兒) *shueei'fa('l)*, n., an ornamental fountain, fountain display.

水粉 *shueir-feen*, n., (1) bean noodle; (2) lady's powder paste.

水分 *shueei-fehn*, n., percentage of water (in cooking); moisture, humidity.

水飛 *shueei-fei*, n., a method of collecting solids (such as cinnabar) by sedimentation.

水肺 *shueei-feih*, n., (zoo.) water lung.

水夫 *shueeifu*, n., water carrier.

水甘草 *shueei-gantsaau*, n., (bot.) *Amsonia elliptica*.

水閣 *shueei-ger*, n., an open hall by the side of water.

水溝 *shueeigou*, n., drains, ditch.

水管 *shueirguaan*, n., water pipe, pipe line; 水管系 *--shih*, n., (zoo.) water-vascular system.

水關 *shueei-guan*, n., water gate.

水光 *shueei-guang*, n., the shining surface of rivers, lakes, sea.

水鬼 *shueirgueei*, n., (1) underwater monster or sprite; (2) (facet.) a frogman.

水工 *shueei-gung*, n., a sailor; one who works on dams, etc.

水郭 *shueei-guo*, n., outer city bordering on the water.

水果 *shueirguoo*, n., fruit in gen.

水國 *shueei-guor*, n., flooded area.

水臌 *shueir-guu*, n., see *-jahng*[1]↓.

水花 *shueei-hua*, n., spray: 水花兒 n., (a) water spray; (b) chicken pox; (c) furs made of sheepskin.

水患 *shueei-huahn*, n., floods.

水滑石 *shueeihuar-shyr*, n., (min.) brucite.

水會 *shueei-hueih*, n., formerly, volunteer fire brigade.

水戽 *shueei-huh*, n., dipper.

水火 *shueir-huoo*, n., water and fire, (AC) the necessities of life; fire and flood disasters: 水火不相容 (of temperament) incompatible, inborn hostility.

水紅 *shueeihurng*, n., pale pink.

水柵 *shueei-jah*, n., a weir.

水戰 *shueei-jahn*, n., naval battle.

水脹 *shueei-jahng*[1], n., dropsy in the belly.

水漲 *shueei-jahng*[2], n., flood tide; v. i., water rises.

水閘 *shueei-jar*, n., floodgate.

水蒸氣 *shueeijeng-chih*, n., steam.

水腳 *shueirjiaau*[1], n., fees for loading, unloading.

水餃(兒) *shueirjiaau*[2]*('l)*, n., Chin. ravioli.

水攪 *shueir-jiaau*[3], n., storms in the skies, rumblings in the sky before rainstorm.

水膠 *shueeijiau*, n., hide glue (also called 黃明膠).

水界 *shueei-jieh*, n., (geol.) hydrosphere.

水鏡 *shueei-jihng*, n., (LL) (1) the moon; (2) (AC) person of intellectual brilliance.

水警察 *shueir-jiingchar*, n., water police, marine police.

水晶(精) *shueeijing*, n., crystal; 水晶包 a bun containing sweetened pork fat; 水晶體 the crystalline lens of the eye; 水晶宮 crystal palace; 水晶鹽 natural salt crystals; 水晶球 crystal ball.

水韭 *shueir-jioou*[1], n., (bot.) a kind of leek, *Isoetes japonica*.

水酒 *shueir-jioou*[2], n., (self-deprecatory) wine offered to guest—"my insipid wine."

水注 *shueei-juh*, n., a tiny pot holding water for ink slab.

水竹葉 *shueei-juryieh*, n., (bot.) *Aneilema keisak*, a water plant.

水準 *shueirjuun*, n., (1) a water level; (2) level (of education, art, magazines, morals, etc.); 水準器 a water gauge, water level; 水準圖 map showing sea level of places.

水蛭 *shueei-jyh*, n., the leech.

水質 *shueeijyr*, n., fluid matter.

水居 *shueei-jyu*, v. i., (men and fish) make one's home on rivers, lakes, waterways.

水蕨 *shueei-jyuer*, n., (bot.) an edible water plant, *Ceratopteris thalictroides*.

水客 *shueei-keh*, n., (1) a boatman; (2) a buyer who travels to obtain shop supplies.

水坑(兒)(子) *shueeikeng('l)('tz)*, n., a pond.

水葵 *shueeikueir*, n., (bot.) the water mallow, *Brasenia purpurea* (=蓴).

水老鴨 *shueir-laauya*, n., pop. name for cormorant.

水蠟蟲 *shueeilah-churng*, n., a wax-producing insect in Szechuan.

水蠟樹 *shueeilah-shuh*, n., (bot.) *Ligustrum ibota*.

水老鼠 *shueei-laurshuu*, n., water rat; beachcomber, waterfront thief, tramp.

水雷 *shueeileir*, n., torpedo; submarine mines; 水雷艇 torpedo boat (also 魚雷艇).

水蓼 *shueirliaau*, n., (bot.) water pepper, *Polygonum hydropiper*.

水亮 *shueeiliahng*, adj., (1) bright and clear (looks); (2) juicy (fruit).

水簾 *shueei-liarn*, n., a screen of water (as in waterfall).

水療 *shueei-liaur*, n., hydrotherapy.

水力 *shueeilih*[1], n., water power: 水力學 hydraulics; 水力電 hydroelectric power; 水力電機 hydroelectric power plant; 水力摩托 hydraulic motor; 水力昇降機 hydraulic elevator; 水力起重機 hydraulic crane.

水利 *shueeilih*[2], n., water conservancy, irrigation: 水利局 conservancy bureau; 水利工程 marine hydraulic engineering.

水禮 *shueir-lii*, n., gifts of fruit and sweetmeats.

水霤 *shueei-liouh*, n., a bamboo, clay or iron pipe, cut open, for guiding rain water down from the eaves.

水流 *shueeiliour*, n., water current.

水漏 *shueei-louh*, n., an (anc.) water clock, clepsydra.

水路 *shueei-luh*[1], n., (1) course of water; (2) voyage.

水陸 *shueei-luh*[2], n., travel by land and water.

水輪 *shueei-lurn*, n., water propeller.

水龍 *shueei-lurng*, n., (1) (coll.) fire engine and its hose; (2) (bot.) *Jussieua repens*; 水龍頭 *--'tou*, n., water tap, hydrant.

水綠 *shueei-lyuh*, n., pale green.

水馬 *shueir-maa*, n., (1) water beetle; (2) (fig.) racing boat on Dragon Boat Festival.

水錳礦 *shueirmeeng-kuahng*, n., (min.) manganite.

水煤氣 *shueei-meirchih*, n., water gas.

A

水門 *shueei-mern*, n., floodgate; 水門汀 cement (translit.), otherwise called 水泥 *-nir* ↓.

水面(兒) *shueei-miahn(-miah'l)*, n., water surface.

水綿 *shueei-miarn*, n., (bot.) *Spirogyra longata* (also called 石衣, 石苔).

水蜜桃 *shueeimih-taur*, n., a juicy variety of peach.

水米 *shueir-mii*, n., the minimum food of rice and water.

水黽 *shueir-miin*, n., (zoo.) *Hydrotrechus remigator*, an insect which lives and moves on water surface.

水脈 *shueei-moh*, n., natural waterways.

水墨畫 *shueeimoh-huah*, n., ink-wash painting.

水磨 *shueei-mor*, n., (1) (*-moh*) water mill; (2) fine work on jade, etc. by grinding with water as lubricant; 水磨調 reference to 崑曲 a variety of opera.

水木作 *shueei-muh-tzuoh*, n., bricklayer and carpenter.

水母 *shueir-muu*, n., (zoo.) jellyfish.

水鳥 *shueir-niaau*, n., waterfowl.

水牛 *shueeiniour*, n., (water) buffalo; 水牛兒 pop. term for snail.

水泥 *shueeinir*, n., cement; 鋼筋水泥 reinforced concrete.

水牌 *shueeipair* (*-'pai*), n., a lacquered board in shops, used like slate for erasable writing.

水泡 *shueeipauh*, n., bubble; blister.

水瓢 *shueei-piaur*, n., calabash or gourd used as dipper.

水皮兒 *shueei-pier'l*, n., (coll.) water surface.

水平 *shueei-pirng*, n., sea level, elevation from the sea; 水平尺 a water level; 水平舵 airplane vane regulating climbing and descent; 水平角 (math.) horizontal angle; 水平面 (math.) horizontal plane; 水平線 horizon; water level, also level (of attainment, etc.).

水波 *shueei-po*, n., ripples of water.

水上飛機 *shueei-shahng feiji*, n., hydroplane.

B

水上運動 *shueei-shahng yuhnduhng*, n., aquatic sports.

水筲 *shueei-shau*, n., water pail.

水蛇 *shueei-sher*, n., water snake; 水蛇腰 waist slightly bent.

水螅 *shueei-shi*, n., (zoo.) hydra.

水險 *shueir-shiaan*[1], n., short for 水上保險 marine insurance.

水蘚 *shueir-shiaan*[2], n., (bot.) *Sphagnum japonicum*.

水仙 *shueeishian*, n., the narcissus.

水鄉 *shueei-shiang*, n., swampy regions, lake areas; (LL) watery kingdom.

水榭 *shueei-shieh*[1], n., see *-ger* ↑.

水瀉 *shueeishieh*[2], n., diarrhoea.

水性 *shueei-shihng*, n., (1) the way water acts or moves: 不習水性 said of inexperienced swimmer; (2) 水性楊花 said of woman of easy virtue (attaches to any one).

水心 *shueei-shin*, phr., center of stream.

水星 *shueeishing*, n., the planet Mercury.

水銹 *shueei-shiouh*, n., water-marks, rust.

水手 *shueirshoou*, n., sailor.

水師 *shueei-shy*[1], n., formerly, the navy.

水蝨 *shueei-shy*[2], n., (zoo.) *Gammarus*, a water louse.

水勢 *shueei-shyh*, n., force of river current.

水蝕 *shueei-shyr*, n., water erosion.

水蘇 *shueeisu*, n., (bot.) rough nettle betony, *Stachys aspera*.

水松 *shueeisung*, n., sea grass, *Codium mucronatum*.

水梭花 *shueeisuo-hua*, n., vegetarian's euphemism for fish.

水塔 *shueir-taa*, n., water tower.

水獺 *shueeitah*, n., (zoo.) the common otter, *Lutra vulgars*.

水苔 *shueeitair*, n., duckweed.

水塘 *shueei-tarng*, n., a pond.

水田 *shueeitiarn*, n., paddy field; 水田衣 Budd. monk's cassock (in pattern of squares like rice fields).

水汀 *shueeiting*, n., steam heating (translit.).

水亭 *shueei-tirng*, n., a pavilion on the water.

C

水頭 *shueei-tour*, n., (1) the crest of the wave; (2) juice of fruit; (3) luster of jade.

水彩(畫) *shueirtsaai(huah)*, n., water color.

水草 *shueir-tsaau*, n., (speaking of nomads) lands where there are water and grass: 逐水草而居 (of nomads) migrate to wherever water and grass are available.

水土 *shueirtuu*, n., climate: 不服水土 climate does not agree with person.

水桶 *shueirtuung*, n., water pail.

水藻 *shueirtzaau*[1], n., algae; water plants in gen.

水蚤 *shueirtzaau*[2], n., *Daphnia*, a tiny insect in water, used as feed for goldfish, etc.

水葬 *shueei-tzahng* n., burial at sea.

水災 *shueei-tzai*, n., flood disaster.

水賊 *shueei-tzeir*, n., a pirate (commonly 海盜).

水鑽(兒) *shueei-tzuahn(-tzuah'l)*, n., name for diamond.

水作坊 *shueeitzuoh'fang*, n., beancurd factory.

水族 *shueeitzur*, n., "denizens of the sea," fishes, turtles and the like; 水族館 aquarium.

水漬 *shueei-tzyh*, adj., as in 水漬貨 water-damaged goods.

水位 *shueei-weih*, n., water level in rivers, lakes.

水文 *shueei-wern*, n., (LL) water ripples (=水紋); 水文地理 hydrology.

水鴨 *shueeiya*, n., wild duck.

水舀子 *shueir-yaautz*, n., dipper.

水瀁液 *shueeiyahng-yeh*, n., (physiol.) aqueous humor.

水壓機 *shueeiyaji*, n., hydraulic press: 水壓昇降機 hydraulic elevator.

水煙 *shueei-yan*, n., water pipe for smoking; such tobacco: 水煙袋 pouch for water pipe tobacco.

水癌 *shueei-yarn*, n., (med.) noma.

水楊 *shueeiyarng*, n., the willow; 水楊梅 *--meir*, n., (bot.) *Geum japonicum*; 水楊酸 *--suan*, n., (chem.) salicylic acid; 水楊酸鈉 sodium salicylate.

水曜日 *shueeiyauh-ryh*, n., (LL)

Wednesday.

水衣 *shueeiyi*, n., moss.

水印(兒) *shueeiyihn(-yeh'l)*, n., watermark; formerly, a shop seal.

水引擎 *shueir-yiinchirng*, n., water engine.

水音(兒) *shueei-yin(-ye'l)*, n., a clear, round voice.

水銀 *shueeiyirn*, n., mercury; 水銀燈 *--deng*, n., mercury-vapor lamp.

水源 *shueei-yuarn*, n., the source of a river.

水月 *shueei-yueh*, n., moon in the water, symbolic of purity: 鏡花水月 beautiful but evanescent dreams; 水月電燈 acetylene lamp; 水月電石 n., carbide of calcium.

水運 *shueei-yuhn*, n., water transport.

氷 22.02

bing.

[Pop. for 冰 63A.02]

淼 22.02

miaau.

Adj. Descriptive of wide expanse of water.

淼漫 *miaaumahn*, adj., overflowing, flooding.

淼茫 *miaaumarng*, adj., ditto.

淼淼 *miaurmiaau*, adj., ditto.

農 22.02

nurng.

[Arch. 蕽]

N. Farming; farmer: 農業, 農夫, 農人 *-yeh*, *-fu*, *-rern*↓; 農閑 slack farming season.

農產 *nurngchaan*, n., farm production, -ducts; 農產量 volume of farm production.

農塲 *nurngchaang*, n., a farm.

農夫 *nurngfu*, n., a farmer.

農婦 *nurngfuh*, n., a farm woman.

農會 *nurnghueih*, n., a farmers' association.

農戶 *nurnghuh*, n., a farm family.

農家 *nurngjia*, n., (1) a family engaged in farming: 農家子 farmer's son; (2) (AC) one of the nine schools of thought in ancient China, students of agriculture.

農具 *nurngjyuh*, n., farm implements.

農科 *nurngke*, n., department of agriculture in a college; agriculture as an academic study.

農曆 *nurnglih*, n., the lunar calendar (lit. "the farmer's calendar," used by Chin. farmers as a guide for sowing and harvesting).

農林 *nurng-lirn*, n., agriculture and forestry.

農忙 *nurng-marng*, *n.*, peak season on a farm.

農民 *nurngmirn*, n., a farmer, the farming population.

農奴 *nurngnur*, n., a serf, a slave working on a farm for the landlord.

農人 *nurngrern*, n., a farmer, the farming population as a whole.

農桑 *nurng-sang*, n., farming and sericulture.

農事 *nurngshyh*, n., farm work.

農時 *nurngshyr*, n., farming season.

農學 *nurngshyuer*, n., science of agriculture.

農田 *nurngtiarn*, n., farm land, farm fields.

農村 *nurngtsun*, n., a village, a rural district.

農作 *nurngtzuoh*, n., farming, cultivation of crops: 農作物 farm produce.

農業 *nurngyeh*, n., agriculture.

農月 *nurngyueh*, n., summer months, busy months for the farmers.

裳 22.02

charng (also *shang*).

N. Skirt: 衣裳 (*-'shang*) dress in gen.

裴 22.02

peir.

N. A surname.

§22.10 (丨/十)

半 22.10

bahn.

N. Half: 一天半, 一天又半 one and half days; 夜半＝半夜 midnight; 薪俸之一半 half one's salary; 大半, 少半(小半) greater, lesser half; 對半 fifty-fifty; 多半 adv., most probably, greater half; 減半 reduce by half.

Adj. (1) Half number, amount or measure: 半小時 half an hour; 半個時辰 half of two-hour period; 半日, 半月, 半元, 半打 half day, half month, half dollar, half dozen; 半生, 半世 half a lifetime, very long time; 半費, 半價 (半折) 50% discount in fees, price; 半途, 半道 midway, 半不道＝半道; 半途而廢 leave off (a task) halfway; 半路出家 without solid foundation or training; 半面之交 (雅) a once-met acquaintance. (2) Not even a little: 半步不能行 cannot move (half) a step; 半籌莫展 could not do a thing. (3) 半…半 half and half: 半懂半不懂 not fully understand; 半推半就 (of woman) half yield and half deny; 半吞半吐 speak with reservation, will not come out with it; 半明半暗 half open, half underhand; 半信半疑 half believe, not quite believe; 半工半讀 work while studying at school; 半青半黃 not quite mature, knowing a subject or lesson half well. (4) 半…不 (combined with opposite): 半新不舊 half-new (dress); 半生不熟 having casual acquaintance; not well learned (lesson); 半死不活 dead-alive.

半百 *bahnbaai*, n., half hundred.

半半路路 *bahnbahn-luhluh*, adv., halfway, midway (also 半半落落).

半包兒 *bahnbau'l*, n., mean trick: 別跟我掏這個半包兒 lay off your dirty trick.

半邊人 *bahnbian-rern*, n., (coll.) widow or widower.

半彪子 *bahnbiautz*, n., heady, young fellow.

半壁 *bahnbih*, n., (of a country) half, a slice of territory.

半大小子 *bahn'da shiaautz*, n., boy in puberty.

半島 *bahndaau*, n., peninsula.

半吊子 *bahndiauhtz*, n., immature person.

半瘋兒 *bahnfeng'l* (*-fe'l*), n., a highly unconventional person, a crank.

半規 *bahnguei*, n., semicircle.

半憨子 *bahnhantz*, n., half-crazy person.

半截劍 *bahnjier-jiahn*, n., small but smart person; 半截兒 *-jier'l*, n., half of a body, a half part; 半截塔 *-taa*, n., a tall, husky person (half a pagoda).

半徑 *bahnjihng*, n., radius.

半斤八兩 *bahnjin-baliaang*, phr., not much to choose between the two.

半中間 *bahn-jungjian*, n., midway, also 半中腰 *--yau*.

半殖民地 *bahn-jyrmirndih*, n., semi-colony.

半開門兒 *bahnkaimer'l*, n., secret prostitute (half-open door), also 半掩門兒.

半開眼兒 *bahn-kaiyaa'l*, n. & adj., pseudo-professional.

半空中 *bahnkungjung*, adv., in, out of the sky.

半拉 *bahn'la*, n., half a piece.

半瓶醋 *bahn-pirng-tsuh*, n., a man with superficial knowledge of a subject.

半晌 *bahnshaang*, n., a long time: 等了你半晌 have been waiting you for a long time.

半身不遂 *bahnshen-buhshueh*, adj., half-paralyzed.

半生 *bahnsheng*, (1) n., half a lifetime; (2) adj., immature, half-cooked.

半夏 *bahnshiah*, n., (bot.) *Pinellia tuberifera*, a medicinal herb.

半夏稻 *bahnshiah-dauh*, n., rice crop harvested in Sept.-Oct.

半仙 *bahnshian*, n., Taoist magician, "half an immortal," fortuneteller; 半仙戲 *--shih*, n., the swing (a sport).

半歇 *bahnshie*, n., see *-shang*↑.

半天 *bahntian*, n., half a day, a very long time.

半子 *bahntzyy*, n., son-in-law.

半夜 *bahnyeih*, n., midnight.

半音階 *bahn-yinjie* n., chromatic scale.

半圓規 *bahn-yuarnguei*, n., protractor.

半語子 *bahn-yuutz*, n., one who stutters.

聿 22.10

yuh.

Part. (AC) then, and then, used in introducing phr. or sentence, (possibly related 亦 already, also): 歲聿云暮 the year is drawing to the close.

韋 22.10

weir.

N. (1) Leather. (2) A radical (having to do with leather). (3) A surname.

韋編 *weir-bian*, n., (AC) leather strap for binding bamboo strips (竹簡, 策冊) the anc. form of books.

輩 22.10

beih.

N. (1) Generation in family: 長輩, 幼輩 elder, younger generation; 後輩, 晚輩 the younger generation; see 輩分 *-'fen*, 輩行 *-harng* ↓. (2) (*-tz*) A lifetime, a very long time: 他這輩子算是完了 he is finished for good; 下輩子 next incarnation, generation; 一輩子吃不完 has enough to live on for life; 那輩子 for a long time, for life. (3) Inner group, familiar circle; 我輩 (LL) we, people of our group; 彼輩 (LL) they, that group; 我輩中人 is one of us; 輩流 or 流輩 (contempt.) group, gang, coterie.

Adv. For generations: 人才輩出, (of a district) give birth to talented men generation after generation.

輩輩兒 *beihbeh'l*, adv., generation after generation.

輩分 *beih'fen*, n., status of a generation in the family.

輩行 *beihharng*, n., seniority of the generation (first, second, etc.).

輩數 *beihshuh*, n., ditto.

§22.11 (丨/土)

坐 22.11

tzuoh.

N. Interch. 座 a seat.

V. i. & t. (1) Sit: 坐下 sit down; 坐定 sit quietly; 坐好, 坐正 sit properly; 坐立不安 feel uneasy, restless, whether sitting or standing; 坐冷板凳 "be put in cold

坐 storage," be given the cold shoulder; 坐紅椅子 be the last of a number of successful candidates (allu. to the practice of making a check (√) with red ink at the end of a list of such candidates); 坐家兒女 an unmarried girl; 坐井觀天 take a narrow view of things, ("see the sky from the bottom of a well"); 如坐針氈 feel extremely uneasy ("like sitting on a pin-cushion"); 坐以待斃 resign oneself to death; 坐以待旦 quietly wait for the day to dawn; 坐失良機 let a golden opportunity slip by; 坐觀成敗 wait to see how s.t. succeeds (which side wins); 坐吃山空 remain at home and "eat away" a whole fortune; 上坐 sit in the seat of honor; 正坐, 端坐 sit upright; 正襟危坐 sit solemnly ("gingerly") as show of respect; 並坐 sit side by side; 靜坐 sit in silence, often as a form of physical or spiritual regimen; 獨坐 sit alone; 告坐 ask leave to sit; 列坐 sit in a row; 打坐 sit in meditation; 請坐 please sit down; 趺坐 sit with crossed legs on the ground; 陪坐 keep s.o. company. (2) Go by, ride in (car, boat, airplane). (3) Go to, arrive at: 坐堂 *-tarng*, 坐殿 *-diahn* ↓. (4) (Of things) fall back from pressure: 這堵牆往後坐了 the wall is beginning to give backwards; 後坐力 (of a gun) recoil. (5) Be accused for crime: 反坐 be punished for unfounded accusation against another; 連坐 be implicated in crime; 坐法 *-faa* ↓.

Prep. Owing to, because of: 坐此解職 for this reason he was relieved of his duties.

坐板瘡 *tzuohbaan-chuang*, n., (med.) sores on the buttocks.

坐禪 *tzuohcharn*, v. i., (Budd.) sit still in Zen meditation.

坐牀 *tzuoh-chuarng*, (1) v. i., (of the bridegroom and bride (be formally seated on the edge of the bed in the bridal room after the wedding ceremony; (2) n., inaugural ceremony of the Dalai or Panchan Lama in Tibet.

坐馳 *tzuohchyr*, phr., (LL) thinking far away, though sitting quietly at home.

坐大 *tzuoh-dah*, v. i., allow s.o. to wax strong (without doing s.t. to prevent it).

坐等兒 *tzuohdeeng'l*, v. t., sit and wait (for s.t. to happen).

坐殿 *tzuoh-diahn*, v. i., see *-tarng* ↓.

坐地 *tzuoh-dih*, (1) v. i., sit on the ground; (2) adv., on the spot: 坐地分贜 divide the booty on the spot; 坐地兒 *--'l*, 坐地窩兒 *--woe'l* phr.: (a) to begin with: 他坐地窩兒就不會 he doesn't know how in the first place; (b) right there and then: 坐地窩兒就辦妥了 had it done right away.

坐蹲兒 *tzuohdue'l* (sp. phr.), v.i., squat on the heels.

坐墩 *tzuohdun*, n., an earthen or procelain stool.

坐法 *tzuoh-faa*, v. i., be punished for crime.

坐館 *tzuoh-guaan*, v. i., (1) formerly, be a tutor in a private school; (2) formerly, serve as a secretary to an official.

坐關 *tzuoh-guan*, phr., (Budd.) shut oneself up to chant the sutras and be lost in contemplation for a fixed period of time.

坐功 *tzuoh-gung*, n., (Taoism) the practice of sitting in silence to meditate.

坐賈 *tzuohguu*, n., a shopkeeper.

坐化 *tzuohhuah*, v. i., (Budd.) die remaining seated cross-legged.

坐帳 *tzuoh-jahng*, v. i., see *-chuarng* ↑.

坐鎮 *tzuohjehn*, v. t., (of a military commander) to garrison (a city, area, district).

坐騎 *tzuohjih*, n., (MC) one's personal mount.

坐莊 *tzuohjuang*, (1) n., formerly, a resident agent for business firms; (2) v. i., be the banker in games of chance.

坐鐘 *tzuohjung*, n., a desk clock.

坐致 *tzuoh-jyh*, v. t., earn (profit) without working for it.

坐具 *tzuoh-jyuh*, n., chairs and benches.

坐科 *tzuoh-ke*, v. i., be apprenticed in an operatic class in one's tender years.

坐客 *tzuohkeh*, n., a passenger on boat, etc. (cf. 行[b]客 91B.00).

坐扣 *tzuohkouh*, v. t., to take deduction (from bill for expenses, etc.).

坐困 *tzuoh-kuhn*, v. i., to find oneself in a helpless situation.

坐兒 *tzuoh'l*, n., (1) a seat (in a theater, teahouse); (2) (coll.) patrons of saloons, bars, teahouses.

坐落 *tzuohluoh*, n., the location of a piece of land (a house).

坐坡 *tzuohpo*, v. i., sit with body leaning backwards: 打坐坡 to sit thus.

坐蓐 *tzuoh-ruh*[1], v. i., (of a woman) be in labor.

坐褥 *tzuohruh*[2], n., cushion (for sitting on).

坐商 *tzuohshang*, n., shopkeeper (opp. 行商 a peddler, traveling trader).

坐性 *tzuoh'shing*, n., ability to sit alone quietly for a long time.

坐席 *tzuoh-shir*, v. i., (of guests) take seats at a dinner party.

坐守 *tzuoh-shoou*, v. i., remain patiently to wait or look after s.t.

坐食 *tzuoh-shyr*[1], v. i., eat without working for one's living.

坐實 *tzuohshyr*[2], adj., (1) solid, firm, strong: 桌子做的很坐實 the table is solidly made; (2) substantiated.

坐索 *tzuoh-suoo*, v. i., remain at s.o.'s to demand payment of debt.

坐討 *tzuoh-taau*, v. i., ditto.

坐堂 *tzuoh-tarng*, v. i., (formerly, of magistrates) sit in court.

坐草 *tzuoh-tsaau*, v. i., see *-ruh*[1] ↑.

坐曹 *tzuoh-tsaur*, v. i., (formerly, of bureaucrats) attend office.

坐次 *tzuoh-tsyh*, n., seating arrangements (for guests).

坐罪 *tzuoh-tzueih*, v. i., be sentenced by court for crime.

坐忘 *tzuoh-wahng*, adj., oblivious of one's surroundings, free from worldly concerns.

坐位 *tzuohweih*, n., a seat.

坐窩兒 *tzuohwo'l*, adv., see *-'dihwo'l* ↑.

坐衙 *tzuoh-yar*, v. i., see *-tarng* ↑.

坐藥 *tzuoh-yauh*, n., (med.) a suppository.

坐夜 *tzuoh-yeh*, v. i., keep vigil in the night, sit up all night.

堂 22.11

tarng.

N. adjunct. A session: 這一堂課 this class (session); 上一堂課 the last class, go to a class (上 used as a v.t.); a set: 一堂瓷器, 木俱 a table set of porcelain, a set of furniture.

N. (1) Hall, main hall: 廳堂 hall; 教堂 church building; 講堂 lecture hall; 課堂 classroom; 佛堂 Buddhist temple; 祠堂 ancestral, temple; 禮堂 assembly hall; 澡堂, 浴堂 bathhouse; 登堂入室 degrees of understanding of master's teachings (堂 guest room; 室 bedroom as more intimate in degree); 堂屋, 堂廡 *-wu*, *-wuu*↓. (2) Hall as symbol of main houses in family system: 父母在堂 parents living; 拜堂 bride and groom perform wedding ceremony in the hall; 五代同堂 five generations living together; 糟糠之妻不下堂 a wife who shared poverty may not be divorced in times of comfort; 令堂 (court.) your mother; 堂兄弟, see Adj↓. (3) Courtroom: 過堂 have a hearing of the case; 公堂 the court; 對簿公堂 confrontation of evidence at court; 升堂, 退堂 open, close court session; 鼓堂 drum beaten for opening, closing court session; 打退堂鼓 (fig.) beat a hasty retreat, withdraw from dispute, signal that situation has drastically changed; 堂諭 court order. (4) In Tarng Dyn. the six ministers, and prime minister: 中堂 (MC) formerly, the prime minister; 堂印 prime minister's seal; 堂案, 堂判 prime minister's communications on cases; 堂食, 堂餐 meals of the cabinet. (5) Guildhall; title of theatrical clubs or troupes; title of "tongs" in Chinatown.

Adj. (1) Open, dignified: 堂堂, 堂皇 *-tarng*, *-huarng*↓. (2) Of same clan: 堂兄弟, 堂姊妹 cousins of same paternal grandfather; 堂的 opp. 表的 cousins on mother's side; 堂族 members of same clan.

堂坳 *tarng-au*, n., damp, low grounds.

堂奥 *tarng-auh*, n., deep, hidden recesses; depths (of teaching).

堂布 *tarngbuh*, n., wipe cloth.

堂構 *tarnggouh*, phr., (AC allu.) son succeeding to father's profession.

堂官 *tarngguan(-'guan)*[1], n., formerly, magistrates and superior officials; (Tarng Dyn.) cabinet ministers.

堂倌 *tarngguan(-'guan)*[2], n., restaurant waiter.

堂花 *tarnghua*, n., flower forced by heat to blossom early.

堂皇 *tarnghuarng*, n., stately, impressive: 堂哉皇哉 ditto; 冠冕堂皇 impressive looking.

堂會 *tarnghueih*, n., communal gathering for celebration.

堂客 *tarng'ke*, n., lady guests.

堂名 *tarngmirng*, n., clan name, usu. named after the clan hall; name of a branch of family when separate hall has been established.

堂上 *tarngshahng*, n., parents; formerly, form of address to magistrates or judges.

堂堂 *tarngtarng*, adj., open, dignified: 堂堂大丈夫 a dignified gentleman; 堂堂正正 open, fair-minded, dignified.

堂頭 *tarngtour*, n., abbot: (coll.) 堂頭和尚 usu. called 方丈 *fang-jahng*.

堂子 *tarngtz*, n., (Shanghai dial.) brothels, courtesans; (Manchu Dyn.) palace temples.

堂屋 *tarngwu*, n., main hall of building.

堂廡 *tarngwuu*, n., buildings and rooms surrounding main hall or temple.

雀 22.11

chyueh (sp. pr. **chiaau*).

N. The common sparrow: 麻雀 ditto.

雀斑 *chyuehban* (sp. pr. *chiaau'-ban*), n. freckles.

雀麥 *chyuehmaih*, n., (bot.) a species of oats.

雀盲 *chyuehmarng*, n., night blindness; 雀盲眼 (**chiaau-'mang-yaan*) one suffering from night blindness, also one whose eyes are narrowed into slits.

雀屏 *chyuehpirng*, n., chosen as son-in-law, from 雀屏中目 (allu.) the one who shoots an arrow through the eye of the carved peacock on a screen.

雀舌 *chyuehsher*, n., a kind of delicate tea leaves.

雀鼠 *chyuehshuu*, n., bickering, from (AC) allu., "pecking and gnawing like birds and rats."

雀躍 *chyuehyueih*, v.i., to be overjoyed ("jump like sparrows").

§ 22.20 (丨/卄)

弊 22.20

bih.

N. Shortcomings, irregularities, corrupt practice, disadvantage: 利與弊 advantages and disadvantages; 興利除弊 clean up the administration; 流弊 (很多流弊) corrupt practice, troubles arising from ill-advised systems; 營私舞弊 corruption in government; 作弊 v.i., to circumvent law for gain; to cheat in examination.

弊病 *bihbihng*, n., corrupt practices; disadvantage(s); frequent troubles, shortcomings (in machine or institution).

弊竇 *bihdouh*, n., (open) door to corruption.

弊端 *bihduan*, n., irregularities, corrupt practices; disadvantage, bad point.

弊害 *bih-haih*, n., undesirable points, ills of system.

§22.21 (丨/乚)

山 22.21

shan.

[See 21.21]

出 22.21

chu.

[See 21.21]

幽 22.21

you.

[See 21.21]

豳 22.21

bin.

[See 21.21]

世 22.21

shyh.

[See 21.21]

§22.22 (丨/丨)

卜 22.22

buu.

N. (1) Divination: 卜卦先生, 賣卜先生 fortuneteller; 求神問卜 pray and consult oracle. (2) A surname.

V. i. & t. (1) To divine: 卜卦, 卜課 *-guah, -keh* ↓. (2) To predict, foretell: 勝負難卜 difficult to tell who will win; 吉凶未卜 cannot predict the outcome, good or bad; 未可預卜 cannot foretell; 未卜先知 to know without consulting oracle. (3) To choose (with or without divination): 卜居 place for residence; 卜鄰 choose neighborhood; 卜宅 choose house or tomb site; 卜老 choose place for retirement; 卜晝卜夜 phr., (AC) day and night without cease.

卜卦 *buuguah*, n. & v.i., divine, divination by the eight diagrams (八*卦 80.80).

卜課 *buukeh*, n. art of divination; a session at the divination.

卜數 *buushuh*, n. & v.i., art of fortunetelling; augur.

卜筮 *buushyh*, v.i. & n., to divine by tortoise shell or straw, now used as gen. term for fortunetelling.

卜算 *buusuahn*, n. & v.i., see *-shuh* ↑.

卜辭 *buutsyr*, n., the oracle as shown on tortoise shell in Shang Dyn.

巾 22.22

jin.

N. (1) A kerchief: 毛巾 a towel; 浴巾 a bath towel; 手巾 a handkerchief; 枕巾 a pillow sham; 圍巾 a scarf; 頭巾 a shawl; 餐巾 a napkin; 絲巾 a silk kerchief; 汗巾 a girdle sash; 巾幗 *-guor*, 巾櫛 *-jier* ↓. (2) A turban.

巾櫛 *jinjier*, n., towel and comb: 侍奉巾櫛 (of woman) wait on with towels and comb—serve as wife or concubine.

巾幗 *jinguor*, n., women in gen., womanhood: 巾幗丈夫 a great woman.

中 22.22

jung (**juhng*).

N. (1) Center, middle, inside: 當中 center; 內中 inside; 居中 in the center; 中間 *-jian* ↓; 中央 *-yang* ↓; 中樞 *-shu* ↓. (2) Middle of time, place, period, area used after n., thus forming what must be called *post*positions, in place of *pre*positions, like "within" "during": 國中, 家中, 校中 in the country, home, school; 之中 in the course of: 說話之中 during the talk; also in area: 吳中 in the *Wur* region; 貞觀中 during the reign *Jenguan*; 局中人 a person involved in the case; 在考慮中 under consideration; 入其圈中 fall inside trap, circle. (3) Short for 中國: 中外人士 Chinese and foreign gentlemen; 中西合璧 Chinese and Western (styles, texts) combined; 中俄關係 relations between China and Russia. (4) Short for 中學: 高中, 初中 senior, junior high school.

V. t. (1) (**juhng*) Hit (target): 中彩, 中獎 win lottery, prize; 中選 win election; 中槍, 中彈 be hit by bullet; 中計, 中的 *-jih, -dih*[1] ↓. (2) Be touched by (weather, poison, etc.): 中暑, 中寒, 中風, 中毒 *-shuu, -harn, -feng, -dur* ↓. (3) Pass examination: 中舉, 中式 *-jyuu -shyh*[3] ↓. (4) To fit taste, liking, be agreeable to: 中聽, 中吃, 中用 *-ting, -chy, -yuhng* ↓; 中肯, 中理 *-keen, -lii* ↓; 中意 *-yih* ↓. (5) As vb. complement like "on" in "hit on," "hook on": 考中 pass examination; 猜中 guess right; 看中了 take a fancy to (object, girl).

Adj. (1) Middle, mid-: 中世紀 the Middle Ages; 中古 mid-ancient period, *-guu*↓; 十九世紀中葉 mid-nineteenth century; 中圈 middle circle; 中立, 中正 *-lih*, *-jehng*[1]↓; 中庸, 中和 *-yung*, *-her* ↓. (2) Medium-grade, mediocre: 中等身材 of medium height; 中等人才 medium or average talent; 中姿 middling looks; 中篇小說 a novelette; 適中 just right; 中產, 中學 *-chaan*, *-shyuer*↓.

Adv. In the middle, halfway: 中斷, 中輟 stop halfway.

中保 *jungbaau*[1], n., guarantor.
中飽 *jungbaau*[2], v. i., to put into personal pocket (accounts); to "squeeze" public funds.
中表 *jungbiaau*, n., first cousin, child of father's sister or mother's brother.
中變 *jungbiahn*, n., unexpected change in events.
中部 *jungbuh*, n., central part (of anything).
中產 *jungchaan*, n., as in 中產階級 the middle class.
中朝 *jungchaur*, n., (1) Chin. court (government); (2) the officialdom: 中朝半爲黨人 (MC) half of the officials are party men.
中秋 *jungchiu*, n., (中秋節) 15th day of the eight month of the lunar calendar, Mid-Autumn Festival.
中吃 **juhngchy*, adj., good to eat, tasty.
中權 *jungchyuarn*, n., (LL) (1) (AC) main army; (2) those in power.
中道 *jungdauh*, (1) n., the middle course: 中道而行 follow the middle course; (2) adv., halfway: 中道而廢 stop halfway.
中點 *jungdiaan*, n., (math.) middle point.
中的 **juhngdih*[1], phr., hit the target.
中第 **juhngdih*[2], v. i., pass the civil examinations.
中斷 *jungduahn*, v. i., break in the middle, break off.
中東 *jungdung*, n. Middle East (Asia).
中毒(兒) **juhngdur('l)*, v. i., be poisoned.
中耳 *jung-eel*, n., (physiol.) the middle ear; 中耳炎 *--yarn*, n., *Otitis media.*
中飯 *jungfahn*, n., lunch, luncheon.
中非 *Jung-Fei*, n., Central Africa.
中費 *jungfeih*, n., agent's fee.
中風 **juhngfeng*, n., a paralytic stroke: 中風不語 paralysed in speech.
中鋒 *jungfeng*, n., (1) (football) center forward; (2) (callig.) the use of the brush point perpendicularly, rather than on a slant.
中耕 *junggeng*, v. i., to till the farm after the sprouts have come up.
中冓 *junggouh*, n., (AC & LL) 中冓之言 gossip about private morals.
中官 *jungguan*, n., (1) eunuch; (2) (AC) the officials.
中宮 *junggung*, n., the empress.
中國 *Jungguor*, n., China; 中國人 *--rern*, n., Chinese.
中古 *jungguu*, n., "mid-ancient" or medieval period (generally 漢晉 Hahn and Jihn Dyns., preceded by 上古時代—terms with fluctuating connotations).
中寒 **juhngharn*, v. i., to catch a cold.
中和 *jungher*, (1) v.t. & adj., moderate, not extreme; (2) n., 中和作用 (chem.) neutralization.
中華 *Junghuar*, n., China; 中華民國 the Republic of China (oft. abbr. ROC).
中悔 *junghueei*, v. i., change one's mind in middle course; regret.
中正 *jungjehng*[1], adj., the central and the upright.
中證 *jungjehng*[2], n., personal witness.
中將 *jungjiahng*, n., (mil.) lieutenant general.
中堅 *jungjian*[1], n., the core; (football) center half back: 中堅分子 the hard-core of a group, party.
中間 *jungjian*[2], n., (1) the inside, the middle between (as alley between houses); (2) in the course of: 說話中間 while speaking; 中間人 *--rern*, n., go-between, agent, mediator.
中節 **juhng-jier*, phr., (1) in rhythm; (2) (AC) not too much of anything, proper and just: 發而皆中節 (emotions) are expressed justly (not repressed).
中計 **juhng-jih*, phr., fall into trap.
中酒 **juhng-jioou*, phr., suffer from over drinking.
中涓 *jungjyuan*, n., (AC) palace eunuchs.
中軍 *jungjyun*, n., formerly, (mil.) central column, main army.
中舉 **juhng-jyuu*, phr., to pass the second degree of 舉人 *juurern* in Imperial Examinations.
中止 *jungjyy*[1], v. i., to stop in the middle.
中指 *jungjyy*[2], n., the middle finger.
中肯 **juhngkeen*, adj., (of remarks) to the point.
中饋 *jungkueih*, n., (AC) as in 主中饋 cooking as wife's job; also later used for "wife."
中立 *junglih*, adj. & n., neutral, -ity: 中立國 neutral country; 武裝中立 armed neutrality.
中理 **juhnglii*, adj., reasonable (=合理).
中流 *jungliour*, (1) n., midstream, river current: 中流砥柱 pillar of strength; (2) adj., middle average: the middle class: 中流社會; 中流人品 average character or looks.
中路 *jungluh*, (1) n., middle of road; (2) adj., mediocre (goods).
中落 *jungluoh*, v. i., (of fortunes) to decline.
中滿 *jungmaan*, adj., (Chin. med.) have a swollen belly.
中美 *Jung-Meei*, (1) n., Central America; (2) phr., China and U. S.
中年 *jungniarn*, n., middle of life, after forty.
中波 *jungpo*, n., (electronics) medium wave.
中人 *jungrern*, n., (1) person of

亅	小	⺊	十	土	𠂇	廾	𠃊	丨	一	丁	𠃌	口	囗	冂	𠃍	厂	尸	亠	广	宀	丶	乚	弋	心	八	人	乂	乛	𠂉	丿	𠂉	𡿨
00	01	02	10	11	12	20	21	22	30	31	32	40	41	42	50	51	52	60	61	62	63	70	71	72	80	81	82	83	90	91	92	93

medium or average grade; (2) (AC) middle class; (3) friends in the palace; eunuchs.

中山 *Jungshan*, n., courtesy name of Dr. Sun Yat-sen (孫逸仙), father of Chinese Republic; (oft. used as name of roads, schools, etc.); 中山裝 style of man's jacket with closed collar without tie.

中傷 **juhng-shang*, v. t., to hurt s. o. by remark; (p. p.) hit by sword or bullet.

中殤 *jungshang*, v. i., (AC) die between 12–15 of age.

中生代 *jungsheng-daih*, n., (geol.) Mesozoic era.

中夏 *jungshiah*, n., (LL) China.

中線 *jungshiahn*, n., (math.) line from apex of triangle to middle of base.

中宵 *jungshiau*, n., middle of the night; midnight.

中校 *jungshiauh*, n., (mil.) lieutenant colonel.

中性 *jungshihng*, n. & adj., neutral, neutral character.

中心 *jungshin*, n., center (of problem, attention, etc.), core (of group, matter), center of related studies, study or service center, etc.: 中心思想 basic idea in philosophic system; 中心軸 central axis; 中心蝕 central eclipse; 中心點 central point.

中興 *jungshing*, n., resurgence, restoration of power after temporary collapse in dynastic rule: 中興名臣 minister who gave a new lease of life to ruling house.

中行 *jungshirng*, n., (AC) one who follows the middle road.

中樞 *jungshu*, n., (lit.) the "axis" of power——the highest council of state; 中樞神經 central nervous system.

中數 *jungshuh*, n., (math.) the median number.

中書省 *jungshusheeng*, n., (Tarng Dyn.) cabinet of ministers.

中暑 **juhngshuu*, n., sunstroke.

中士 *jungshyh*[1], n., (mil.) sergeant.

中世 *jungshyh*[2], n., see *-guu*↑.

中式 *jungshyh*[3], (1) adj., Chin. style; (2) (**juhng-*) v. i., formerly, to pass civil examinations.

中學 *jungshyuer*, n., high school.

中旬 *jungshyurn*, n., the middle ten days of a month.

中使 *jungshyy*, n., palace petty officer, eunuch.

中堂 *jungtarng*, n., a wide scroll hung in center of hall.

中聽 **juhngting*, adj., agreeable to the ear, (words, advice) pleasing to listener.

中材 *jungtsair*, n., men of average quality or stature.

中餐 *jungtsan*, n., (1) midday lunch; (2) Chin. dinner.

中途 *jungtur*, adv., midway.

中子 *jungtzyy*, n., (phys.) neutron.

中尉 *jungweih*, n., (mil.) first lieutenant (少尉 second lieutenant).

中位數 *jungweihshuh*, n., (statistics) the median.

中午 *jungwuu*, n., midday.

中亞 *Jung-Yaa*, n., Central Asia.

中央 *jungyang*, n. & adj., (1) the center; (2) central government; 中央威信 prestige of the national government; 中央情報局 Central Intelligence Agency (CIA); 中央研究院 Academia Sinica.

中夜 *jungyeh*[1], n., the middle of the night.

中葉 *jungyeh*[2], n., middle period (of dyn., century, reign).

中衣 *jungyi*[1], n., underclothing.

中醫 *Jungyi*[2], n., Chin. medicine; Chin. doctor.

中意 **juhngyih*, v. i., (person) takes fancy to (girl), likes: 中意她或他 love her or him.

中元 *jungyuarn*[1], n., the fifteenth of the seventh lunar month.

中原 *Jungyuarn*[2], n., the "central plains" of China, actually the Yellow River valley.

中用 **juhngyuhng*, adj., serviceable, convenient: 不中用了 hopelessly ill.

中庸 *jungyurng*, n., the Doctrine of the Golden Mean, name of a chapter in 禮記 and one of the Four Books in Confu. school.

串 22.22

chuahn.

N. (1) A string (of cash, beads). (2) Relatives: 親串 various kins.

V. i. To conspire, league up to swindle: 串通, 串同 *-tung*, *-turng* ↓; 串供 *-gung* ↓.

V. t. (1) To string up: 串起來. (2) To pass out and in irregularly or freely: 串衚衕兒 peddle things through the alleys of Peiping; 串房沿兒 (landlord) rents out all rooms and himself lives around yard; 串店 to act as salesman from house to house or as minstrel singer in restaurants, see 串店的 *-diahn'de* ↓; 串百家門兒的 see 串門的 *-mern'de* ↓. (3) To take part in play: 串戲 *-shih* ↓; 反串 for man to play female part and woman to play male part. (4) To pour into: 把酒串回瓶子裏 pour wine back into bottle.

串氣 *chuahn-chih*, n., (coll.) asthma.

串店的 *chuahn-diahn'de*, n., itinerant salesman or minstrel singer.

串供 *chuahn-gung*, v.i., (witnesses, parties in lawsuit) to act in collusion.

串轍 *chuahn-jer*, v.i., to make wrong link-up of persons and places.

串疽 *chuahn-jyu*, n., (med.) herpes, *Herpes zoster*, shingles.

串鈴 *chuahn'ling*, n., metal pieces clapped together to attract customers, used by pedlars and itinerant fortunetellers, etc.

串門 *chuahn-mern*, v.i., as in 串門子 *--tz*, to visit different houses and carry gossip; 串門的 *--'de*, n., a gossipper.

串騙 *chuahnpiahn*, v.i., to league up and swindle (s.o.).

串票 *chuahn-piauh*, n., formerly, receipt for land tax.

串皮 *chuahn-pir*, v.i., (effect of medicine) come to the skin surface (as a rash).

串戲 *chuahn-shih*, v.i., (1) to take part in or rehearse a play; (2) to act in play as amateur.

串屜兒 *chuahn-tieh'l*, v.t., to warm up (rolls, buns) by putting in oven for short time.

串通 *chuahntung*, v.t., to conspire with (person) for illegal acts: 串通作弊 ditto.

串同 *chuahnturng*, v.t., ditto.

串子 *chuahntz*, n., (1) a string (of beads, etc.); (2) formerly, receipt for goods in granary or storage.

串演 *chuahnyaan*, v.i., to take part in a play, esp. by amateur.

串秧兒 *chuahnyang'l*, n., hybrid plant or animal.

申 22.22

shen.

N. (1) A letter in the duodecimal cycle see Appendix A. (2) The two-hour period, 3–5 p.m. (3) A surname.

V. i. (1) As prefix to vb., has the force of "ex-," "out-" as in "express," "extend": 申明, 申述, 申說, 申敍 *-mirng*, *-shuh*, *-shuo*, *-shyuh*↓; 申敬, 申謝 *-jihng*, *-shieh*↓. (2) Specifically, prefixed to vb., in submitting communication to official superior: 申請, 申陳, 申奏, 申送, 申文, 申狀 *-chiing*, *-chern*, *-tzouh*, *-suhng*, *-wern*, *-juahng*↓. (3) To repeat orders, instructions to subordinate: 申斥, 申飭 *-chyh*[1], *-chyh*[2]↓; 三令五申 have ordered repeatedly.

申報 *shenbauh*, (1) n., name of the oldest Chin. newspaper in Shanghai; (2) v. t., (a) to report to superior; (b) declare (dutiable goods) to customs officials, (one's income).

申辯 *shenbiahn*, v.i., to plead or rebut in defense.

申補 *shenbuu*, n. & v. i., see *-shueei*↓.

申陳 *shenchern*, v. i., to communicate with superior.

申請 *shenchiing*, v. i., to apply (for permit, etc.), make application; to make official request.

申斥 *shenchyh*[1], v. t., to rebuke (subordinate).

申飭 *shenchyh*[2], v. t., (1) ditto; (2) to instruct (subordinate) to do s.t.

申敕 *shenchyh*[3], v. t., (1) to instruct (subordinate) to do s.t.; (2) to rebuke.

申旦 *shendahn*, adv., (AC) toward daybreak.

申覆 *shenfuh*, v. t., to submit written reply to superior.

申告 *shengauh*, v. t., (1) to instruct officially; (2) to register complaint.

申解 *shenjiee*, v. t., to explain.

申結 *shenjier*, v. i., (LL) to cement friendship.

申敬 *shen-jihng*, v. i., to express respect, high esteem.

申救 *shenjiouh*, v. t., to rescue, help.

申狀 *shen-juahng*, n. & v. i., (send) communication or report to superior.

申明 *shenmirng*, v. t., to make clear, declare (reason for visit, etc.).

申牌 *shenpair*, n., notice of hour, 3–5 p.m.

申申 *shenshen*, & (AC) (1) adj., 申申如也 (of Confucius at home) relaxed; (2) adv., repeatedly: 申申其詈餘 rebuked me again and again.

申憲 *shen-shiahn*, phr., (AC, rare) punish (person) by law.

申詳 *shenshiarng*, v.i., to explain, report to superior in detail.

申謝 *shen-shieh*, v. i., to express thanks (for gifts, kindnesses received).

申水 *shenshueei*, n. & v.i., formerly, (commercial) charge for difference in currency rates (also wr. 升水).

申述 *shenshuh*, v. t., explain (reasons), express (opinions, feelings); to repeat an account, story.

申說 *shenshuo*, v. i., to express (one's feelings), explain (one's difficulties).

申敍 *shenshyuh*, v. i., to narrate (events, condition) to superior.

申訴 *shensuh*, v. t., to explain (one's difficulties), express (complaint).

申送 *shensuhng*, v. t., submit (documents) to superior.

申奏 *shen-tzouh*, v. t., to send official report to court.

申文 *shen-wern*, v. i., to communicate officially (on some case).

申冤 *shenyuan*, v. i., to ask for redress of an injustice (also wr. 伸).

肅 22.22

suh.

[Abbr. 粛]

V.i. & t. (1) To bow (guest) in: 肅客. (2) To send greetings esp. at end of letter: 手肅 greet personally; 敬肅 my greetings; 肅此, 肅復 this I write, reply, respectfully. (3) To clear away (bandits): 肅清 *-ching*↓.

Adj. & adv. Severe, solemn, -ly, respectfully: 肅立 stand solemnly; 肅然, 肅肅 *-rarn*, *-suh*↓; implied silence on solemn occasions: 肅靜 *-jihng*↓.

肅清 *suhching*, v.t., to rid country of (bandits).

肅靜 *suhjihng*, adj., solemnly silent; boards carried by retinue during official procession, meaning "silence."

肅穆 *suhmuh*, adj., respectful and solemn.

肅然 *suhrarn*, adv., respectfully.

肅殺 *suhsha*, adj., (AC) (of autumn) chilling (life, vegetation), now generally wr. 蕭殺 20A.22.

肅爽 *suhshuaang*, n., (AC) name of famous horse (also wr. 驌騻, 驌驦).

肅肅 *suhsuh*, adj. & adv., (1) respectful, -ly, solemn, -ly; (2) (AC) in a hurry (related 速); (3) (AC) descriptive of rustling noise (cf. 簌簌).

常 22.22

charng.

亅	小	⺊	十	土	ナ	卄	凵	丨	一	丁	㇇	口	区	冈	㇆	厂	尸	亠	广	宀	丶	乚	弋	心	八	人	乂	㇀	㇒	丿	㇐	く
00	01	02	10	11	12	20	21	22	30	31	32	40	41	42	50	51	52	60	61	62	63	70	71	72	80	81	82	83	90	91	92	93

A B C

常 幣 帶

N. (1) Norms of conduct: 綱常, 倫常 (Confu.) basic human relationships. (2) A surname.

Adj. & adv. (1) Constant, -ly, permanent, -ly: 生命無常 nothing is permanent in life; 反復無常 change one's mind frequently. (2) Continual, -ly, frequently: 常常 *-charng* ↓; 時常 frequently; 常聽見 often heard; 常見 often saw, seen, etc.; 不常來 seldom comes. (3) Normal, -ly, usual, -ly, regular, -ly: 正常 normal; 反常 abnormal; 常例 *-lih* ↓; 常法, 常規 *-faa*, *-guei* ↓; 通常, 經常, 日常 usual, -ly; 照常, 如常 as usual; 常備軍 *-beihjyun* ↓; 常務 *-wuh* ↓. (4) Common, -ly: 常識 *-shyh*² ↓; 平常 common.

常備兵 *charngbeih-bing*, n., regular, standing army; also 常備軍 *-jyun*.
常產 *charngchaan*, n., property.
常常(兒) *charngcharng('l)*, adv., often, frequently.
常川 *charngchuan*, adv., continually, on a permanent basis (also wr. 長川).
常春籐 *charngchunterng*, n., (bot.) a kind of vine, *Hedera helix*.
常度 *charngduh*, n., frequency.
常法 *charngfaa*, n., norm, regular warp, procedure.
常服 *charngfur*, n., informal dress.
常軌 *charnggueei*, n., regular rules or procedure.
常規 *charngguei*, n., regulations.
常會 *charnghueih*, n., regular meeting (weekly, monthly, etc.); 常會兒 *-hueh'l*, adv., often: 他常會兒來 he often comes.
常見 *charngjiahn*, n., common sense.
常久 *charngjioou*, adv., for a long while: 常久不來了 has not been here for a long time.
常住 *charngjuh*¹, (Budd.) (1) n., resident monk: 常住物 his things; (2) n., temples; (3) adj., eternal, invariable.
常駐 *charngjuh*², adj., (army) permanently stationed.
常恐 *charngkuung*, adv., (Shanghai dial.) fear lest.
常例 *charnglih*, n., regular routine procedure.
常禮 *charnglii*¹, n., regular etiquette; 常禮服 formal dress.
常理 *charnglii*², n., convention, logical thinking.
常綠樹 *charnglyuh-shuh*, n., (bot.) evergreen.
常人 *charng-rern*, n., ordinary people.
常山 *charngshan*, n., (1) name of mountain (＝恆山); (2) (bot.) *Orixa japonica*.
常勝 *charng-shehng*, adj., ever victorious.
常行(兒) *charngshirng('l)*, adv., see *-hueh'l* ↑: 常行兒喝酒 drink frequently.
常數 *charngshuh*, n., (math.) a constant.
常式 *charngshyh*¹, n., the regular form or style.
常識 *charngshyh*², n., elementary knowledge, elements (of science, sanitation, etc.); common sense.
常事 *charng-shyh*³, n., ordinary affairs, a common occurrence.
常祀 *charng-syh*, n., regular sacrifices.
常態 *charng-taih*, n., regular, normal, way or appearance.
常談 *charngtarn*, n., as in 老生常談 moral platitudes.
常溫 *charng-wen*, n., constant temperature.
常務 *charngwuh*, n., as in 常務董事會 standing committee; 常務理事 executive director.
常言 *charng-yarn*, n., proverb: 常言道 as the proverb says.
常業 *charng-yeh*, n., regular profession.

幣 22.22

bih.

N. Currency, coins: 日幣, 英幣, 新台幣 Japanese, English, New Taiwan currency; 法幣 legal tender, also French currency; 輔幣 subsidiary coins; 紙幣 paper currency; 金幣, 銀幣 gold, silver currency.

幣帛 *bih-bor*, n., (AC) gifts of tribute in money and silks.
幣制 *bihjyh*, n., monetary system.

帶 22.22

daih.

N. (1) Belt, girdle, strap (*-tz*): 衣帶 belt of gown, dress; 褲帶 trousers belt or cord; 皮帶 leather belt; 鞋帶 shoelace; 馬肚帶 belly strap for horse. (2) Belt of territory: 溫帶, 熱帶 temperate zone, torrid zone, tropical zone; region: 這帶地方 here, this region; 沿海一帶 the coastal region.

V.t. (1) Carry, take to: 帶刀, 劍, 甲 carry knife, sword, armor; 帶錢 carry money; 帶信, 帶消息 take a letter, message to (place); 帶個好兒 carry greetings to (person): 帶到城裏去 take it to the city. (2) Lead: 帶兵 lead troops; 帶路, 帶道 *-luh*, *-dauh* ↓. (3) Bring up: 你把小孩帶壞了 you have spoiled the child. (4) Involve: 帶累, 連帶 involve person in trouble, lawsuit; 把門帶上 close the door as you go out. (5) Show incidentally, mix with: 面帶笑意, 病容, 愁色 one's face shows smiling mood, sickly countenance, sad expression; 帶口音 (one's speech) shows accent; 連踢帶打 mix kicks with hand blows; 連打帶罵 scold and beat (person) at the same time.

帶案 *daih-ahn*, v.t., subpoena.
帶打 *daihdaa*, v.i., rain fisticuffs; show of combat in Chin. opera.
帶道 *daihdauh*, v.i., see *-luh* ↓.
帶肚子 *daih-duhtz*, (1) v.i., be pregnant; (2) n., secretary (of magistrate) who pays for the job of going along, expecting to profit from squeezing the people.
帶分數 *daih-fenshuh*, n., (math.) mixed fraction.
帶鉤 *daihgou*, n., belt buckle.
帶累 *daihleih*, v.t., involve s.o. in trouble or expense.
帶領 *daihliing*, v.t., be in charge

of (troops).
帶路 *daihluh*, v.i., lead the way, serve as a guide.
帶身子 *daih-shentz*, v.i., be pregnant.
帶下 *daihshiah*, n., leucorrhoea (＝白帶).
帶孝 *daihshiauh*, v.i., wear mourning.
帶手 *daih-shoou*, n., wiping cloth carried by restaurant waiters; 帶手兒 *-shoou'l*, adv., on the way: 帶手兒把門關上 close the door as you go out.
帶頭 *daihtour*, v.i., to lead in action.
帶魚 *daihyur*, n., (zoo.) the hairtail, *Trichiurus chinensis*.

川 22.22

chuan.

N. (1) A river: 山川 lands and waters—landscape, topography; 高山大川 high mountains and big rivers; 百川會於海 all rivers flow into the sea. (2) Short for 四川 Szechuan, a province: 川菜, 川馬 Szechuan cuisine, pony; 川邊 Szechuan border.

V. t. Boiled and served in soup: 川丸子 meat ball soup.

Adv. See 常▵川 22.22.

川穀 *Chuanguu*, n., a kind of Szechuan corn, *Coix agrestis*.
川連 *Chuanliarn*, n., (Chin. med.) ＝黃連 the golden thread, *Coptis japonica*, produced in Szechuan.
川流 *chuan-liour*, n., river current: 川流不息 a continuous flow (of profits, income).
川朴 *Chuanpoh*, n., (Chin. med.) 厚朴 a kind of magnolia of Szechuan, *Magnolia obovata*.
川芎 *Chuanshyung*, n., an aromatic plant, 芎藭, the hemlock parsley, *Conioselinum univitatum*.
川苔 *Chuantair*, n., edible mushroom grown on rocks, in Szechuan.
川資 *chuantz*, n., voyage or journey expense.

州 22.22

jou.

N. (1) Name of an administrative district, consisting of several 縣 *shiahn*: 州治 the district government; 州長, 州牧 formerly, chief magistrate of district. (2) U. f. 洲 continent: 神州＝神洲.

V. i. (AC) 州處 to settle in a place.

州伯 *joubor*, n., (AC) head of one of the nine main divisions (九州) in anc. times.
州官 *jouguan*, n., district magistrate.
州里 *joulii*, n., the gen. countryside: 州里之民 the people in the country.
州閭 *joulyur*, n., (AC) see *-lii* ↑.

卅 22.22

sah.

N. & adj. Thirty (contracted from 三十).

卌 22.22

shih.

N. & adj. (Rare) forty.

卝 22.22

guahn (also *kuahng*).

Adj. (AC) having (child's) hair done up in two side tufts.

丱 22.22

guahn.

N. The two tufts made in dressing a child's hair.

艸 22.22

tsaau.

[Var. of 草 20A.10]

非 22.22

fei.

N. Wrong, wrong-doing, mistake: 文過飾非 try to cover up one's mistakes; 爲非作歹 carry on misdeeds; 無事生非 create problems where none exists; opp. 是: 分別是非 distinguish right and wrong; 沒有是非 do not get involved in disputes, also there is no justice, cf. 是▵非41.83.

V. t. To oppose, criticize, regard as wrong: 非之 (LL) oppose it, condemn it; 非孔, 非十二子 criticize Confu., criticize the twelve schools; 非議, 非難, 非毀, 非笑 *-yih*, *-nahn*, *-hueei*, *-shiauh* ↓.

Adj. & adv. (1) Not, be not; in most cases, 非 has sense of 不是 be not, while 不 stands for "do not" and "be not": 不敢 dare not, but 非敢 it is not that I dare; 非牛非馬 neither fish nor fowl; 非吾同類, 非吾徒也 is not one of us, is not my disciple; 非所望也 is not what I hoped or expected; 非吾所欲 is not what I want; 非出本心 is not one's real intention; 非金屬 nonmetal; 非正式, 非賣品 not formal, not for sale; 非比尋常 is not of the common run; 非同小可 is not trivial matter; 非常 *-charng*↓. (2) Oft. coupled with 卽, if not that, then this: 非大卽小 is either big or small; 非此卽彼 must be one of these two (this or that); 非吃卽喝 is either eating or drinking; 非傷卽死 are either wounded or dead. (3) Oft. coupled with 不, meaning "only": 非他不嫁 will marry noone but him; 非錢不行 cannot do without money; 你非來不可 you simply have to come; 我非打死你不可 I must kill you. (4) Oft. coupled with 無, 莫: 無非 is nothing but (some quarrel about money); 莫非 perhaps (a conjecture); 莫非又有新情人 perhaps he has a new lover; 非君莫屬 only you can fill the post. (5) Not right, not good: 所言非也 you are wrong; 非也 (a LL phr., often used in spoken language) it is not so; 非類 bad character (=匪類); 非計 wrong way of doing it, bad plan; 非時 not the right time; violent: 非刑, 非命 *-shirng, -mihng*↓. (6) In phrr. 非得, 非但, 非僅, 非止, 非獨, 非徒 all meaning "not only"; see under 非得, 非但 *-der, -dahn*↓; 非徒無益, 而又害之 it is not only useless, but does some harm (worse than useless).

非常 *feicharng*, adj. & adv., (1) very: 非常危險, 不高興 very dangerous, displeased; (2) abnormal: 非常行爲 abnormal behavior; (3) extraordinary: 非常時期 extraordinary period.
非但 *feidahn*, adv., not only; variations: 非僅, 非止, 非獨, 非徒, 非特 *-jiin, -jyy, -dur, -tur, -teh*; 非但你一個人 it's not only you alone.
非得 *feider*, adv., (usu. 非得…不可, but sometimes also with 不可 understood) must, it is necessary that: 非得你走一趟 (不可) it is necessary for you to go personally.
非獨 *feidur*, adv., not only.
非法 *feifaa*, adj. & adv., illegal (behavior); illegitimate, unauthorized (action, leaving the campus, etc.).
非分 *feifehn*, adj., improper to one's status: 非分的要求 improper demand.
非非 *feifei*, n., esp. in 想入非非 indulge in phantasy; get fantastic or wayward, incorrect thoughts.
非毀 *feihueei*, v.t., to discredit (person) by critical remarks.
非洲 *Feijou*, n., Africa.
非命 *feimihng*, phr., 死於非命 die unnatural death.
非難 *feinahn (-narn)*, v. i. & t., ask (person) embarrassing questions.
非笑 *feishiauh*, v. t., scoff at, make fun of.
非刑 *feishirng*, n., third degree, illegal torture.
非特 *feiteh*, adv., especially not, not only without; simply have to.
非議 *feiyih*, n. & v. i., hostile opinion, criticism.

弗 22.22

fur.

[Cogn. 不, 匪, 否]

Adv. Not (equiv. 不, only in AC and LL, and in Shanghai dial.): 弗敢=不敢, 弗察=不察, 弗克=不克, 弗能=不能, 弗及=不及, 弗如=不如; 弗思則弗得 without thinking one cannot realize; 何弗思之甚 how thoughtless! 弗豫 indisposed, displeased.

弗弗 *furfur*, adj., (AC) descriptive of floating, flapping motion.

---

§ 22.30 (丨/一)

韭 22.30

jioou.

[Also wr. 韮]

N. (Bot.) the leek.

韭黃 *jioouhuarng*, n., tender, yellowish leek.
韭菜花 *jiooutsaih-hua*, n., the leek flowers.

当 22.30

dang.

[Abbr. of 當 22.41]

晝 22.30

jouh.

N. Daytime, opp. 夜 night: 晝日 ditto; 晝夜 *-yeh*↓; 白晝殺人 kill person in broad daylight; 晝氣惰 (AC) feeling of soldiers at noon tired and relaxed; 晝晦 murky daylight.

晝分 *jouhfen*, n., (AC) noon.
晝夜 *jouh-yeh*, adv., day and night: 晝夜相隨 keep each other's company day and night.

畫 22.30

huah.

[Abbr. 画]

N. (1) Painting, drawing: 圖畫 painting, drawing, illustrations; 字畫, 書畫 calligraphy and painting as twin arts; 油畫 oil painting; 水彩畫 water color; 國畫, 西洋畫 Chinese, Western painting; 壁畫 murals, fresco; 漫畫 cartoon; 詩中有畫, 畫中有詩 (of 王維) there is painting in his poetry, and poetry in his painting; 畫中人 (of lady) as pretty as a picture; 畫報, 畫刊 a pictorial magazine; 畫冊 an album of paintings. (2) A horizontal stroke in calligraphy. (3) A stroke of any kind in writing: 這個字共幾畫 how many strokes in this character?

V.i. & t. (1) To draw (a line, a picture); 繪畫 make a drawing; 畫圖 *-tur* ↓: 畫畫 to paint a painting; 能寫會畫 can write and paint; 畫稿 first sketch; 畫樣子 a rough draft; 畫影圖形 to draw a portrait; 畫餅充饑 to draw a cake and call it a dinner——a Barmecide feast; 畫龍點睛 "to put in the eye pupil in painting a dragon"——the critical touch; 畫蛇添足 paint a snake with feet——superfluous; 畫虎類犬 fail to achieve what one set out to do, unsuccessful attempt in description; 畫鬼易, 畫狗難 easier to paint a ghost than a dog; 畫脂鏤冰 to draw on butter or carve ice——a futile undertaking; 畫法 the technique of painting; 畫神, 畫理 to paint the expression of persons or inner law of things. (2) To draw a line in sense of "divide" (also wr. 劃): 畫界 to draw the boundary; 畫分 divide the line; 畫開 to set aside (a sum of money, duty). (3) To plan: 計畫, 籌畫, 策畫 to plan (as to draw an outline). (4) To put one's signature: 畫諾 to "okay"; 畫到 sign arrival at office; see 畫押, 畫供 *-ya*, *-gung*[1] ↓.

Adj. Painted (boat, girders, hall, etc.).

畫板 *huahbaan*, n., an easel, board for painting.
畫報 *huahbauh*, n., pictorial magazine. ⌈painting.
畫布 *huahbuh*, n., canvas for
畫荻 *huah-dir*, phr., mother's instruction (from Ouyang Shiu's mother who taught him to write by using a rush stalk on the ground).
畫分 *huahfen*, v.t., to divide in parts (also wr. 劃分).
畫供 *huahgung*[1], v.i., to sign affidavit.
畫工 *huahgung*[2], n., a commercial painter.
畫壺兒 *huahhur'l*, n., a snuffbottle with miniature drawing.
畫展 *huah-jaan*, n., art exhibition.
畫家 *huahjia*, n., a painter.
畫架 *huahjiah*, n., an easel, a rack for painting.
畫匠 *huahjiahng*, n., (derog.) commercial artist.
畫境 *huahjihng*, n., the poetic level of painting, a beautiful scene as visualized by the artist.
畫角 *huahjyuer*, n., an anc. horn used in the army like bugle.
畫具 *huahjyuh*, n., painting instruments.
畫刊 *huahkan*, n., a pictorial magazine. ⌈scribble.
畫拉 *huah'la*, v.i., to daub ink,
畫卯 *huahmaau*, v.i., to sign arrival at office (about 7 a.m.).
畫眉 *huahmeir*, (1) n., the grey thrush; (2) v.i., to draw eyebrows.
畫面 *huahmiahn*, n., the gen. appearance of a work of art in respect of light, color, and composition.
畫片兒 *huahpiah'l*, n., small reprints of paintings.
畫屏 *huahpirng*, n., a painted portable screen or partition.
畫譜 *huahpuu*, n., (1) a painting album; (2) book on painting and painters.
畫象 *huahshiahng*, n., portrait.
畫師 *huahshy*, n., (court.) painter.
畫室 *huahshyh*, n., artist's studio.
畫學 *huahshyuer*, n., the study of painting. ⌈for copying.
畫帖 *huahtieh*, n., model painting
畫策 *huahtseh*, n. & v.i., plan.
畫圖 *huahtur*, v.i. & n., paint, -ing, draw, -ing; 畫圖器 T-square, protractor, etc. for drawing designs.
畫押 *huahya*, v.i., to make a sign (esp. by an illiterate) in lieu of signature.
畫一 *huahyi*, v.t. & adj., uniform (order, appearance); definite, unequivocal, standardized.

盅 22.30

jung.

N. (-'l) A small cup: 茶盅 teacup; 酒盅 wine cup; 金盅 golden wine cup.

盡 22.30

jihn.

[Abbr. 尽].

Pron. All: 盡歸我有 all belongs to me; 盡在於此 everything is here; 盡皆 *-jie* ↓.

V. i. & t. (1) V. i., come to an end: 歲盡 the year has come to an end (is ending), year-end; 氣數已盡 s.o.'s spell of good fortune has run out, his days are numbered; 自盡 commit suicide; 盡頭 *-tour* ↓. (2) V. t., to use up completely: 盡力 *-lih* ↓; 竭盡 to the last measure (drop, ounce); 盡心 *-shin* ↓; 盡人事, 聽天命 do one's level best and leave the rest to God's will; 各盡其分 each one doing his part; 盡其所長 give of one's best; 盡其在我 do all in one's power; 盡忠盡孝 be loyal to one's country and filial to one's parents; 盡情 *-chirng* ↓; 鞠躬盡瘁 spare no efforts for the good of the country; 盡節 (of a woman) die in defence of her honor, (of a government official) die for the country; 盡義務 do one's duties, do s.t. without pay; 盡職 faithfully carry out one's duties; 好話説盡, 壞事做盡 a sinner under the guise of a saint; 花盡了身上的錢 spent every cent in one's pocket; 用盡 consumed everything; 出盡全力 made all-out efforts.

Adv. To the highest degree or the utmost limit: 盡善盡美 the best there is, it's perfection itself; 至矣盡矣 the utmost perfection; 仁至義盡 have done everything in one's heart and in one's duty.

盡情 *jihn-chirng*, adv., all, fully: 盡情告訴 tell all.
盡皆 *jihnjie*, adv., one and all,

without a single exception.

盡忠 *jihnjung*, v. i., (1) serve the country faithfully; (2) die for the country.

盡量(兒) *jihnliahng('l)*, adv., to the best of one's ability.

盡力 *jihnlih*, v. i. & adv., do one's utmost, give of one's best; wholeheartedly.

盡命 *jihn-mihng*, adv., to one's utmost.

盡日 *jihnryh*, adv., all day long, the whole day.

盡孝 *jihnshiauh*, v.i., be filial to one's parents.

盡性 *jihnshihng*[1], v. i., fulfill one's nature.

盡興 *jihnshihng*[2], v. i., do s. t. to heart's content.

盡心 *jihnshin*, adv., with all one's heart, soul.

盡數 *jihnshuh*, adv., the whole amount hence, inclusively.

盡頭 *jihntour*, n., the very end.

盡意 *jihnyih*, v. i., (1) give full expression to one's views; (2) see *-chirng* ↑.

蠱 22.30

guu.

N. & v.t. Poison, witchcraft, see compp. ↓.

蠱毒 *guudur*, (1) adj., poisonous; (2) n., a mixture of poisonous insects (snakes, spiders, etc.), used in herb medicine.

蠱惑 *guuhuoh*, v. t., seduce to wrong doing: 蠱惑人心 spread false doctrines to undermine the people's morale.

蠱疾 *guujir*, n., a condition caused by excessive sexual activities.

鑿 22.30

tzuoh (sp. pr. **tzaur*).

N. (1) A chisel: 鑿子 *-tz* ↓. (2) A socket, mortise: 鑿枘 *-rueih* ↓.

V. t. (1) To cut a hole in: 鑿孔, 鑿個眼兒 ditto; 鑿木 to chisel wood; 鑿牙 knock out a person's teeth; 鑿通 bore through; 鑿破 bore open; 鑿開 ditto. (2) To polish (rice). (3) As in 穿鑿附會 make a forced interpretation of text.

Adj. True, accurate, certain: 鑿鑿 *-tzuoh* ↓.

鑿氣 **tzaur'chi*, adj., stubborn, obstinate.

鑿井 *tzuohjiing*, v. i., dig a well.

鑿空 *tzuohkung*, v. i., (1) to open up holes; (2) to read more than what is meant: 穿鑿附(傅)會 make a forced interpretation of text.

鑿木鳥 *tzuohmuh-niaau*, n., the woodpecker (also wr. 啄木鳥).

鑿坏 *tzuohpeir*, v. i., dig a hole in the wall.

鑿枘 *tzuohrueih*, (1) n., mortise and tenon; (2) adj., incompatible, ill-fitting (round peg in a square hole).

鑿子 **tzaur'tz*, n., a chisel.

鑿鑿 *tzuohtzuoh*, adj., (1) bright and clean: 白石鑿鑿 (AC) spotlessly clean are the white pebbles; (2) true, accurate: 言之鑿鑿 said to be indisputable, with definite evidence; 鑿鑿可據 certain and reliable, capable of being proved.

---

§22.41 (丨/図)

沓 22.41

tah.

Adj. Confused; see 沓雜 *-tzar* ↓.

沓杯 *tah-bei*, n., set of cups, one inside another.

沓沓 *tahtah*, adj., (LL) garrulous; (of moving crowd) confusing, hurried.

沓雜 *tahtzar*, adj., confused, mixed.

書 22.41

shu.

N. (1) A book: 圖書 books; 書評 *-pirng* ↓; 盡信書不如無書 (孟子) better not to read at all than to believe all one reads; 書上, 書中 in the book or letter; see compp. ↓. (2) A letter of correspondence: 書信, 書札, 書翰, etc., *-shihn, -jar, -hahn* ↓; 書不盡言 (end of letter) there is more what I want to say but cannot. (3) A certificate, document: 證書 ditto; 診斷書 doctor's certificate of diagnosis; 證婚書, 離婚書 marriage, divorce certificate; 文書 official documents; 説明書 note of instructions (on how to use appliance, medicine, etc.); 申請書 letter of application, etc. (4) Script, style of callig.: 書畫 calligraphy and painting; 楷書 regular, formal style of script; 草書 rapid, cursive style; 行書 running script (halfway between 楷 and 草); 隸書, 八分書 Hahn Dyn. script; 篆書 seal script; 書法 *-faa* ↓. (5) Storytelling in teahouse, such book for storytelling: 説書, 大鼓書 ditto.

V. t. To write: 書寫 *-shiee* ↓; 書此爲誌 I write this as a memorial; 書丹 *-dan* ↓; 書春 to write New Year couplets.

書案 *shu-ahn*, n., writing desk.

書辦 *shu'ban*, n., formerly, clerk in government office.

書包 *shubau*, n., a schoolboy's satchel.

書本(兒) *shubeen(-bee'l)*, n., a volume, a book.

書場 *shuchaang*, n., teahouse where there is professional storytelling.

書差 *shuchai*, n., see *-'ban* ↑.

書城 *shu-cherng*, n., a library with books on all sides.

書簽(兒) *shu-chian(-chia'l)*, n., (1) a book mark; (2) book label pasted on cover.

書篋 *shu-chieh*, n., case or trunk containing books, cf. *-chur, -jiah* ↓.

書契 *shu-chih*, n., (1) (LL) art or invention of writing; (2) commercial papers.

書啟 *shuchii*, n., a piece of correspondence.

書廚 *shu-chur*, n., a bookcase; (facet.) a person who reads but does not digest reading.

書癡 *shu-chy*, n., a bookworm, see *-daitz* ↓.

書獃子 *shu-daitz*, n., a bookworm.

書丹 *shu-dan*, v. i., to write (with red ink) for stone inscription.

書店 *shudiahn*, n., a bookshop, bookstore.

書底兒 *shudiee'l*, n., extent of one's reading, literary background.

書蠹 *shuduh*, n., a bookworm, see *-daitz* ↑.

書牘 *shudur*, n., official correspondence.

書法 *shufaa*, n., art and practice of callig.

書坊 *shufang*, n., a bookshop, esp. old style.

書房 *shufarng*, n., one's study, library.

書槅子 *shuger'tz*, n., a simple bookcase without panels.

書館 *shuguaan*, n., (1) a private school held at home; (2) formerly, a bookshop; 書館兒 a teahouse with professional storytelling (説書).

書櫃 *shugueih*, n., book cabinet.

書翰 *shu-hahn*, n., (LL) letter of correspondence.

書函 *shu-harn*, n., (1) ditto; (2) formerly, sack for letters.

書後 *shu-houh*, n., a postscript, remarks on reading a certain piece of writing.

書狀 *shujahng*, n., written petitions or written statements.

書齋 *shujai*, n., a scholar's study, studio.

書札 *shujar*, n., correspondence, letters.

書跡 *shuji*, n., personal handwriting.

書家 *shujia*, n., a calligraphist.

書柬 (書簡) *shujiaan*, n., (LL) a letter.

書架 (子) *shujiah(tz)*, n., bookcase.

書記 *shujih*, n., a secretary; (LL) official recorder; (AC) records.

書籍 *shu-jir*, n., books in gen.

書傳 *shu-juahn*, n., (AC) books and records; commentary on 尚書 an anc. classic.

書桌 (兒) *shujuo('l)*, n., desk.

書帙 *shu-jyh*, n., casing of books.

書卷 *shujyuahn*, n., book, esp. in anc. form of a scroll: 書卷氣 phr., (of painting, person) air of cultivated refinement.

書局 *shujyur*, n., a publisher, book company.

書口 *shu-koou*, n., book margin, usu. containing page number.

書扣子 *shukouhtz*, n., a critical point in story where the storyteller stops (to collect more cash from listeners).

書庫 *shukuh*, n., a vault for books; a big book collection.

書空 *shu kung*, phr., 咄咄書空 (allu.) make futile gestures in space—in exasperation or frustration.

書吏 *shulih*, n., formerly, government clerk.

書林 *shu-lirn*, n., (LL) "forest of books"—a world of books.

書簏 *shu-luh*, n., wastebasket; (facet.) person who reads but does not understand.

書眉 *shu-meir*, n., upper page margin.

書面 *shumiahn*, n., a written note, which serves as "memo" of an interview.

書目 *shu-muh*, n., bibliography, catalogue of books.

書腦 *shu-naau*, n., the book back, the spine of the binding.

書判 *shu-pahn*, n., the verdict.

書皮(兒) *shu pir(-piel)*, n., book cover.

書評 *shupirng*, n., book review.

書舖 *shupuh*, n., a bookshop.

書生 *shusheng*, n., a student or scholar: 白面書生 scholar inexperienced in affairs of business.

書香 *shu-shiang*, n., "fragrance of books"—surrounding or family of scholars: 書香子弟 children from a scholarly family; 世代書香 family of scholars for generations.

書寫 *shushiee*, v. i. & t., to write.

書信 *shushihn*, n., a letter, correspondence.

書手 *shushoou (-'shou)*, n., copyist, amanuensis.

書肆 *shusyh*, n., (LL) bookshop.

書攤 (兒) (子) *shutan(-ta'l)(tz)*, n., a bookstall.

書套 *shutauh*, n., cardboard casing for books.

書體 *shu-tii*, n., style of callig.

書題 *shutir*, n., title or label of a book.

書冊 *shutseh*[1], n., books in gen.

書策 *shutseh*[2], n., books (anciently written on bamboo strips, also called 簡策).

書僮 *shu-turng*, n., a boy serving in scholar's study.

書筒 *shutuung*, n., formerly, envelope.

書帷 *shuweir*, n., "a curtain of books" surrounding a teacher; heaps of books in which a scholar buries himself.

書業 *shuyeh*, n., the book trade.

書衣 *shuyi*, n., see *-tauh* ↑.

書役 *shuyih*, n., see *-bahn* ↑.

書院 *shuyuahn*, n., a college.

嘗 22.41

charng.

V. t. (1) To taste (also vulg. 嚐): 嘗一嘗 have a taste of food; 嘗味道 taste the flavor; 嘗新 taste fruit, fish that is just in season; 甘苦共嘗 to taste joys and hardships together; 臥薪嘗膽 (allu.) the King of Yueh (越王勾踐) slept on firewood for mattress and had a gall hung over his bed to remind him of the bitterness (gall) of his defeat and prepare for a comeback. (2) To try: 嘗試 *-shyh* ↓.

Aux. vb. Have, have once, had been: 嘗聞 I have heard that; 嘗思 I have thought; 未嘗 have never: 未嘗見他 have never seen him; 未嘗不可, 未嘗不是 double negative used as polite positive:

未嘗不可 it's not impossible=it may be; 未嘗不是辦法 it's not a bad way: it is a good way; 何嘗 did it ever, did I ever=never—a rhetorical interrogative form, but same meaning as 未嘗; 何嘗不可 why impossible?=of course possible.

嘗 試 *charngshyh*, n. & v. i., a trial, have a trial of s. t.

甞 22.41

charng.

[Var. of 嘗 22.41↑]

省 22.41

sheeng (**shiing*).

N. (1) A province: 行省 ditto; 省政府 provincial government; 省長, 省主席 provincial governor; 省治 *-jyh*↓; 省轄 under provincial administration; 省城, 省會, 省垣 *-cherng, -hueih, -yuarn*↓; 省議會 provincial assembly; 省議員 member of above; 省立 founded by provincial government. (2) Formerly, a department of government, as 中書省 (Tarng Dyn.) the cabinet.

V. t. (1) To economize, save (time, money, trouble): 省得 *-'de*↓; 省不少麻煩 save a lot of trouble; 省減 *-jiaan*[1]↓; 省略 *-lyueh*↓; 省事 *-shyh*↓; 省不下, 省不了 cannot spare or go without; 省不了多少錢 does not save much expense; 省吃儉用 to save money on food and expenses. (2) (**shiing*) To examine critically: 省察, 省視 *-char, -shyh*↓; 內省, 反省, 自省 to search oneself for mistakes; 三省吾身 (AC) examine myself three times a day. (3) (**shiing*) To visit: 晨昏定省 attend to parents' comfort on getting up and putting to bed; hence 省親 to visit parents and see how they are; 省墓, 省墳 visit relative's grave. (4) To be conscious: 不省人事 become unconscious, in a state of coma.

Adj. Economical: 儉省 ditto.

省 察 **shiingchar*, v. t., to inspect, review for mistake (an administration), watch (person's conduct); to introspect.

省 城 *sheeng-cherng*, n., provincial capital.

省 錢 *sheeng-chiarn*, v. i., to save.

省 卻 *sheeng-chyueh*, v. t., to drop, omit (item), save (trouble, time).

省 得 *sheeng'de*, v. i., be saved from (the trouble, expense).

省 分 *sheeng'fen*, n., a province.

省 會 *sheenghueih* (1) n., provincial capital; (2) (**shiing-*) v.i. & t., to understand; (MC) to give instructions.

省 減 *sherngjiaan*[1], v.t., to reduce (expenses, work).

省 儉 *sherngjiaan*[2], adj., economical in spending money.

省 治 *sheeng-jyh*, adj., provincial capital.

省 力 *sheeng-lih*, v.i., save energy; adj., labor-saving.

省 略 *sheenglyueh*, (1) v.t., cut off; delete (passage); (2) adj., very brief.

省 下 *sheeng-shiah*, v. t., to save up (so much money, time).

省 心 *sheeng-shin*, v. i., save a lot of bother.

省 事 *sheeng-shyh*, adj., (1) convenient, saving energy, trouble; (2) (**shiing-*) adj., knowing how to behave, tactful.

省 視 **shiingshyh*, v. t., to inspect (area, school, etc.).

省 悟 **shiingwuh*, v. i., to wake up, to realize (also wr. 醒悟).

省 油 燈 *sheengyour-deng*, n., (slang) a man who causes the least trouble ("save-oil lamp").

省 垣 *sheengyuarn*, n., provincial capital.

瞥 22.41

pie.

[Usu. wr. 瞥]

N. A wink, extremely short time, quick glance.

V. t. Glance quickly, catch sight of.

瞥 地 *pieidih*, adv., (MC) suddenly.

瞥 見 *pie-jiahn*, v. t., suddenly see, catch sight of.

瞥 然 *pie-rarn*, adv., suddenly.

瞥 眼 *pie-yaan*, n., extremely short time: 瞥眼過去 pass by quickly (like winking).

當 22.41

dang (**dahng, *daang*).

[Abbr. 当]

N. (**dahng*) (1) Trap, trick: 勾當 (contempt.) business; 上當 fall into trap. (2) Pawn: 贖當 redeem pawn ticket; 當當 (*dahng-dahng*) to pawn object.

Aux. vb. Ought, should: usu. 該當, 應當 ought, should; 罪當死 should die for crime; 早晨當起來 one should get up in the morning; 不當改期 should not postpone date; should in subjunctive use: 當已 should already have (arrived, etc.); 當會 should be able to; 當必 should certainly; 當即 should then; 合當 should, it is proper that; 當斷不斷 fail to act when one should.

V. i. & t. (1) To fill an office, carry duty, bear: 當 (擔當) 責任 bear responsibility; 當不起, 不了, 不得 be not worthy to; 不敢當 you do me too much honor (regular answer to compliment); 當之無愧 to merit the reward, to be deserving; 承當 take up (responsibility); serve in capacity: 當兵 serve as soldier; 當差 as messenger, on errand; 當娼 be prostitute; 當班, 當值 be on duty. (2) Be in charge of: 當國 be in charge of country's affairs (e. g., prime minister); 當家, 當局, 當權 *-jia, -jyur, -chyuarn*↓. (3) Meet, face, match: 當風 face the wind; 當太陽 exposed to the sun; 當 . . . 之時, see Prep.↓; 當仁不讓 in good causes do not lag behind; 豺狼當道 wolf stands astride road, (fig.) bad person in power; 銳不可當 army's attacking power cannot be checked. (4) (Also **dahng*) regard as, take (s. t.) for something else: 當爲上帝 regard (s. o.) as God; (不) 當正經一回事 regard or fail to regard it as serious business; 當玩, 當做玩, 當玩意兒, 當耍兒 regard as a game, not seriously; 當眞 *-jen*↓; 當耳旁風 take advice like passing wind; 死馬當活馬醫 try last resort to save hopeless situation; 當某字解 regard certain character as another character in meaning. (5) (**dahng*) To pawn: 當東西 pawn object. (6) (**daang*) Thought: 我當是誰, 原來是你 it is you, I thought it was somebody else; 你當我是誰 whom did you take me for?

Adj. (1) (*dang, *dahng*) That very (day, year), the same (day, etc.), that, then: 當天 that very day; 當日 that same day, in those days; 當夜, 當夕 that night; 當年 that year; 當時 at that time; 當初, 當代, 當今, 當世 *-chu, -daih, -jin, -shyh*↓. (2) (*dang*) Equal: 相當 equal to, corresponding to; 門當戶對 (of betrothal) two families match in social status. (3) (**dahng*) Fit, proper: 穩當 safe; 妥當, 適當 appropriate; 不當 not appropriate; 的當, 甚當 very appropriate.

Prep. (*dang*) At, in front of: 當 ... 之時 at the time of; 當先, 當後 at the front, at the rear; 當中 at the middle; 當場 right on the spot; 當 (着) 衆人 (面前) in front of everybody; 當衆宣布 announce in public; 當堂畫押 sign affidavit during court session; 當官 before the judge; 當面商量 discuss face to face; 當頭棒喝 (Budd.) give sharp advice for one to wake up from error; 當機立斷 decide on the moment, on the spot.

當差的 *dang-chai'de*, n., employee of the servant class.

當飯 **daangchiahng*, adj., useful, practicable.

當初 *dangchu*, adv., at the beginning, in days past.

當權 *dangchyuarn*, v.i., be in power.

當代 *dangdaih*, adj., contemporary: 當代音樂 contemporary music.

當道 *dang-dauh*, n. & v. i., those in power; be in power; block the road.

當店 **dahngdiahn*, n., pawnshop.

當關 *dang-guan*, n., (officer) in charge of strategic pass.

當歸 *dangguei*, n., (bot.) an aromatic herb, *Ligusticum acutilobum*, root of which being usu. used as med.

當眞 *dangjen* (**dahng-*), (1) v.i., take seriously: 這事不可太當眞 don't take this too seriously; (2) (*dang-*) adv., really: 他當眞走了 he is really gone.

當家 *dang-jia*, v.i., take charge of household affairs; 當家的 n., master or mistress of house; (coll.) wife's reference to husband; business manager of monastery; 當家婆婆, 媳婦 mother-, daughter-in-law in charge of household; 當家(兒)(子) **dahngjia('l)(-tz)*, person of same clan.

當今 *dangjin*, adv., nowadays.

當軸 *dang-jour*, n., person in power.

當中 *dangjung*, n. & adj., middle, in the middle.

當局 *dangjyur*, n., authorities (of school, town, government, etc.): 當局者迷 those closely involved cannot see as clearly as those outside.

當口(兒) *dang'koou('l)*, n., just at the moment.

當兒 *dang'l*, n., ditto.

當量 *dangliahng*, n., (chem.) equivalent.

當路 *dang-luh*, n., see *-dauh*↑.

當罏 *dang-lur*, n., sell wine, be wine attendant for warming up wine, also wr. 盧, 壚.

當面 *dangmiahn*, adv., (order, instruct, communicate) directly, in person.

當票 **dahngpiauh*, n., pawn ticket.

當舖 **dahngpuh*, n., pawnshop.

當然 *dangrarn*, adv., of course.

當心 *dangshin*, adj. & adv., careful, -ly; n., center of chest.

當世 *dangshyh*, n., contemporary.

當事人 *dangshyh-rern*, n., person in charge, parties to a quarrel or lawsuit.

當時 *dangshyr*, adv., at that time.

當選 *dangshyuaan*, v. i., be elected.

當頭人 *dangtourrern*, n., (coll.) wife's reference to husband as head of family.

當槽兒的 *dangtsaur'lde*, n., (dial.) waiter at restaurant.

由 22.41

your.

N. Reason: 原由, 理由 ditto; 事由 story or course of events; 情由 reason, how s. t. happened; 根由 basic cause.

V. t. To let: 由他去 let him do what he likes; 由性兒 *-shihng'l*; 心不由主 lose mental control; 由不得 *-'bu'de*↓, 笑罵由他笑罵 let them talk and criticize all they like.

Prep. From: 由乎, 由於 from; 由於何因 from what cause? 由此, 由是 *-tsyy, -shyh*↓; 由何而起 whence arises this? 由近而遠 from the close-by examples to those far off; 由淺入深 proceed from the simple to the more complex; 經由 via.

由不得 *your'bu'de*, adv., (1) in spite of oneself: 由不得大笑起

當 由

亅	小	⺊	十	土	ナ	卄	上	丨	一	丅	フ	口	図	冈	冂	厂	尸	亠	广	宀	丶	乚	弋	心	八	人	乂	𠂉	一	丿	𠂊	く
00	01	02	10	11	12	20	21	22	30	31	32	40	41	42	50	51	52	60	61	62	63	70	71	72	80	81	82	83	90	91	92	93

來 could not help laughing out loud; (2) beyond one's control: 這事由不得你 this is s. t. you cannot control.

由打 *yourdaa*, adv., since: 由打昨夜 since last night (it has been raining, etc.).

由衷 *yourjung*, adj., from the heart: 言不由衷 talk insincerely; 由衷之言 a talk straight from the heart.

由兒 *your'l*, n., (coll.) reason (= 源由).

由來 *yourlair*, (1) adv., for a long time; (2) n., a person's past record or antecedents.

由性(兒) *yourshihng'l*, v. i., to be wilful.

由是 *yourshyh*, adv., from this, hence: 由是可觀 one can see therefore.

由頭(兒) *your'tou'l*, n., a pretext: 尋出由頭兒來 find a pretext.

由此 *yourtsyy*, adv., hence, see *-shyh*↑: 由此可見 thus it is seen that.

由由 *youryour*, adj., (AC) natural, unaffected.

曲 22.41

chyu (**chyuu*).

N. (**chyuu*) (1) (*-tz, 'l*) A song, esp. one sung on the stage; 歌曲 a song; 曲本, 曲譜, 曲牌, 曲調 *-been, -puu, -pair, -diauh*↓; 作曲 compose melody for song; 度曲 to sing or play melody apart from reading words; 交響曲 symphony; 協奏曲 concerto; 圓舞曲 waltz; 輪旋曲 rondo; 搖籃曲 lullaby; 組曲 suite; 序曲 overture; 奏鳴曲 sonata; 小步舞曲 minuet; 小夜曲 serenade; 幻想曲 fantasia; 狂想曲 rhapsody; 前奏曲 prelude; 練習曲 *étude*; 進行曲 march; 流行曲 popular music. (2) Drama, opera: 戲曲 drama; 宋元戲曲 Suhng and Yuarn drama; 元曲 Yuarn drama (where the songs are the essential parts); 崑曲 Kunshan drama; 北曲, 南曲 northern, southern forms of drama; 雜曲 popular songs, esp. those sung for public entertainment. (3) A nook, recess: 河曲 bend of river; 鄉曲 small town, remote from cities; 鄉曲之士 village schoolmaster; 心曲, 衷曲 inner recesses of the heart; 委曲 a sense of being wronged, usu. not expressed. (4) Private in army: 部曲 rank and file of soldiers. (5) A surname.

Adj. (1) Bent, twisted, curving: 曲曲彎彎, 曲裏拐彎兒 twisting along (alley, etc.); 曲線 *-shiahn*↓; 曲突徙薪 clear up corner of firewoods to prevent fire——take precautionary measures; 曲水 a hidden recess on water; 曲徑通幽 (Chin. architecture) a small path opens up on an enchanting view. (2) Not right, wrong: 曲直, 曲解, 曲庇 *-jyr, -jiee, -bih*↓. (3) In a roundabout way, by special effort: 委曲求全 save the situation by some concessions; 曲全其意 to yield and enable his goal to be achieved; 曲庇, 曲成, 曲赦 *-bih, -cherng, -sheh*↓.

曲本 **chyurbeen*, n., libretto, opera text.

曲庇 *chyubih*, v. t., specially protect, be partial to (s. o.).

曲筆 *chyubii*, v. i., (1) (LL) to gloss over (person's faults), esp. in history writing; to hint merely at (unsavory facts); (2) to distort laws or their interpretation.

曲箔 *chyubor*, n., bamboo frame for cultivating silkworms where silk cocoons are spun.

曲成 *chyucherng*, v. t., to help completion (of a good cause), help a lovers' union.

曲全 *chyuchyuarn*, v. i., make special effort to bring about realization (of plan, goal, etc.).

曲尺 *chyuchyy*, n., carpenter's square.

曲調 **chyuudiauh*, n., melody of song.

曲度 *chyuduh*, n., (math.) curvature.

曲拐 *chyuguaai*, n., a crank (in machine).

曲折 *chyujer*, n., (1) ups and downs in course of events; (2) turns and twists of affairs.

曲解 *chyujiee*, v. t., to misinterpret, to force a wrong interpretation.

曲謹 *chyujiin*, adj., fastidious on details.

曲直 *chyu-jyr*, n., the right and wrong (of a case).

曲領 *chyu-liing*, n., (MC) round collar.

曲率 *chyulyuh*, n., (math.) curvature.

曲面 *chyumiahn*, n., (math.) curved face.

曲撓 *chyunaur*, v. t., (p.p.) wrongly blamed.

曲牌 **chyuupair*, n., name of song or operatic selection on program.

曲譜 **chyurpuu*, n., music notation for songs.

曲蟮 *chyushahn* (re. pr. also **chyur-*), n., (AC) earthworm.

曲赦 *chyusheh*, v. t., pardon by special decree.

曲線 *chyushiahn*, n., (1) (math.) a curve; (2) curve esp. of feminine body: 曲線美 beautiful curves; 曲線板 a curved ruler used by draftsmen.

曲說 *chyushuo*, n., a biassed or forced opinion.

曲士 *chyu-shyh*[1], n., (AC) a philistine, shallow scholar.

曲室 *chyu-shyh*[2], n., (AC) a den or conclave, room for discussion in secret.

曲學 *chyu-shyuer*, n., heretical school, esoteric teachings.

曲意 *chyu-yih*[1], adv., by special or roundabout methods: 曲意求全 make special allowances or concessions to save a situation.

曲藝 *chyuyih*[2], n., the musical arts (of singing, dancing).

曲踊 *chyuyuung*, v. i., (AC) jump up and down in folk dances.

§ 22.42 (丨/冈)

肖 22.42

shiauh.

[Usu. wr. 肖]

肖 胄 冉 背

V. t. & adj. (1) To resemble: 微肖 be somewhat like; 酷肖 strikingly resemble; 畢肖 (of description, portrayal) completely true to life. (2) Be a good son (lit., like parents): 肖子 a filial son; 不肖 n. & adj., bad, a bad son; opp. to 賢 wise: 賢不肖 the wise and the wicked (here intellectual and moral qualities are equated); 不肖子弟 the depraved younger generation.

肖像 *shiauhshiahng*, n., a portrait.
肖似 *shiauhsyh*, adj. & v. t., to resemble, (be) like (person, object).
肖子 *shiauhtzyh*, n., a filial son, a good son, see V. t. 2↑.

胄 22.42

jouh.

N. (1) Armor. (2) (AC) progeny.

胄子 *jouhtzyy*, n., (AC) children, descendants.
胄裔 *jouhyih*, n., distant progeny.

冉 22.42

raan.

N. A surname.

Adv. Little by little, gradually: 冉冉 *-raan*↓; 冉冉上升 go (soar) up slowly; 光陰冉冉 time passes imperceptibly.

冉冉 *rarnraan*, adj. & adv., (1) gradual(ly), imperceptible(ly): 老冉冉其將至兮 it seems old age is slowly catching up with me; (2) (of trees) drooping, hanging downwards; (3) (of clouds) floating about.
冉弱 *raanruoh*, adj., (of plants) drooping (also 苒弱).

背 22.42

beih (**bei* in many vb. senses, carry on the back).
[Var. 悖 in sense of recalcitrant]

N. Body's back, back side: 刀背(兒) back side of knife; 椅背, 靠背 chair back, back cushion; 書背 book back; 鏡背 back of mirror; 駝△背 hunchback 51B.70; 背後 *-houh*↓; 人心之向背 the direction (向 or 背) in which people feel toward this or that regime.

V. i. & t. (1) (**bei*) To carry (burden) on back: 背不動 cannot carry it on back; 背着蔴袋 carrying a hemp sack on back. (2) Turn back on, with back facing, in shadow of, in secret: 背着人, 背人 secretly, without being seen; 背眼兒的地方 where one cannot be seen; 背花陰 in the shadow of flower bush; 背山面水 (of house) fronting water and with hill on the back; 背城借一 make one last stand before the city wall; 背水爲陣 fighting with back to river. (3) Repeat, commit to memory: 能背着 can repeat (whole passage) from memory, (from former custom of turning back on book on teacher's desk during individual recitation); 背不出來 cannot recite; 背書 *-shu*↓. (4) Turn back on treaty, promise: 背約 break treaty; 背卻前言 break one's word; 背盟棄信 violate treaty; 背主 disloyal to master. (5) Abandon: see 背棄 *-chih*↓. (6) Euphem. for parents' death: 父母見背 bereaved (saw back) of parents. (7) To faint, fall unconscious (背過氣了).

Adj. & adv. (1) On reverse side: 背面 reverse; 背後 behind; 背後有人 some one behind you; 背馳, 背道而馳 run in opposite directions, draw further apart. (2) Unlucky: 背時, 背運 unlucky times, fate.

背榜 **beibaang*, v. i., be the last name on list of candidates ("bring up the rear").
背包 **beibau*, n., package carried on back.
背部 *beihbuh*, n., the back (of house, body, etc.).
背棄 *beihchih*, v.t., abandon (family, etc.).
背褡 *beihda*, n., vest.
背帶 *beihdaih*, n., suspenders.
背道 *beihdauh*, n., back path, also 背道而馳, see Adv. 1↑.
背負 *beihfuh*, v.t., carry on the back (load, responsibility).
背旮旯(兒)(子) *beihgalar('l)('tz)*, n., a quiet, hidden corner.
背黑鍋 **bei-hei-guo*, v.i., to take the blame for others.
背後 *beih-houh*, n., back: 在背後 at the back, behind; 山背後 the back side of the mountain.
背花 *beih-hua*, n., game of rolling spears on back; marks of lashing on back.
背剪 *beih-jiaan*, v. i., hands tied on back: 背剪綁了 so tied.
背脊(梁) *beihjii(liarng)*, n., the spine.
背景 *beihjiing*, n., background (of story, scene, politics); social connections: 有背景 has some person backing up; back drop of plays.
背拉 **bei'la*, v. i., mix, beat (egg) to make even.
背累 *beih'leih*, n., financial burdens.
背囊 *beihnarng*, n., knapsack.
背叛 *beihpahn*, v. i. & t. & n., to rebel against; rebellion.
背信 *beih-shihn*, v. i., break one's word.
背心(兒) *beihshin(-shie'l)*, n., vest.
背手 *beih-shoou*, v. i., (also 背着手) hands at the back (as in stroll).
背書 *beih-shu*, v.i., (1) recite lesson from memory; (2) endorse (check).

背誦 *beihsuhng*, v.i. & t., recite from memory.

背錯(兒) **beitsuoh('l)*, v.i., bear blame for others.

背子 *beihtz*, n., (1) stiffening material at back as 紙背子 card board stiffening; (2) (**beitz*) n., stack for carrying burden on back.

背字(兒) *beihtzyh* (*-tzeh'l*), n., bad luck.

背椅 *beihyii*, n., chair with back.

背陰(兒) *beihyin*(*-yie'l*), phr., in the shade.

背泳 *beihyuung*, n., (swimming) backstroke.

尚 22.42

shahng.

N. A surname.

V. t. (1) To value highly: 尚年, 尚齒 to honor old age; 尚賢 to place high value on good and wise men in government. (2) (LL) 尚公主 to marry a princess.

Adv. (1) Yet, still: (vern.) 尚且 *-chiee* ↓; 尚有不少 still many are left; 事尚未成 affair still not yet settled; 尚來得及 still time to do it; 尚未娶 still unmarried; 尚何言哉 what more can one say? (2) Fairly, rather: 尚可 can do fairly; 尚不錯 (=vern. 還不錯) not bad, fair. (3) In court. phr., respectfully (=上): 尚希, 尚祈 I hope or pray; 尚饗 *-shiaang* ↓. (4) (LL) a long time: 由來尚矣 has been like this for a long time.

Conj. Even: 衣食尚不足, 何論其他 one has not even enough to live on, let alone other things.

尚且 *shahngchiee*, adv. & conj., vern. for 尚, even, still, yet, see Adv. ↑.

尚絅 *shahng-jyuung*, phr., 衣錦尚絅 (AC) put on outer garment on top of silk dress.

尚然 *shahngrarn*, adv., still yet, see *-chiee* ↑.

尚饗 *shahng-shiaang*, phr., (at end of sacrificial prayer) may you taste of this offer.

尚書 *Shang-shu*, n., (1) *The Book of History*, also called 書經 *Shu Ching*; (2) (AC, MC) high-ranking official, minister.

尚自 *shahngtzyh*, adv., see *-chiee* ↑.

尚友 *shahng-yoou*, phr., (AC) to regard the ancient authors as friends and try to understand them as persons (Mencius).

尚猶 *shahngyour*, adv., still, yet: 尚猶力弱 still weak, see *-chiee* ↑.

黹 22.42

jyy.

N. & v.i. Embroidery; embroider: 鍼黹 needlework.

---

§ 22.50 (丨/㇆)

劣 22.50

lieh.

Adj. (1) Inferior: 劣等 *-deeng* ↓; 定優劣 to grade (persons, things), superior or inferior; 優勝劣敗 survival of the fittest; 劣貨 inferior quality goods; 劣品 inferior goods, art or person; 劣馬 a nag. (2) Bad: 惡劣, 卑劣, 鄙劣 bad, mean, despicable (conduct, character). (3) Court. in self-reference: 劣兄 my stupid brother.

劣巴 *lieh'ba*, adj., (coll.) green, amateur, inexperienced (also wr. 力巴, 劣把), 劣巴頭 a greenhorn.

劣等 *liehdeeng*, n. & adj., inferior quality: 劣等貨色 (人才) goods (men) of inferior quality.

劣根性 *liehgenshihng*, n., innate wickedness.

劣跡 *liehji*, n., notorious past, record.

劣紳 *liehshen*, n., esp. in 土豪劣紳 local rich and gentry who prey upon the people.

彆 22.50

bieh.

[Cf. 憋 *bie*, 22.72]

彆氣 *biehchih*, adj., silently resentful, depressed.

彆扭 *bieh'nioou*, adj., (1) depressed: 心裏彆扭 feel all wrong; (2) not smooth, ungainly (of art work, writing, etc.); (3) 鬧彆扭 begin to bicker, taunt each other, etc. (also wr. 憋扭).

翡 22.50

feei.

翡翠 *feeitsueih*, n., (1) (bot.) kingfisher, *Halcyon coromanda*; (2) jadeite.

---

§ 22.63 (丨/丶)

黨 22.63

daang.

[Pop. 党]

N. (1) Political party, clique, coterie: 政黨 political party; 以黨治國 rule by political party; 革命黨, 國民黨 revolutionary party, the Kuomintang; 朋黨, 朋黨之爭 political cliques in Hahn and Suhng Dyns.; 黨爭 political fights, see 黨錮 *-guh* ↓. (2) Relatives: 父黨, 母黨 (AC) father's, mother's relatives. (3) A surname.

V.t. To band together, shield: 黨同伐異 have sectional, sectarian, controversies.

黨綱 *daang-gang*, n., party program, organization or discipline.
黨錮 *daang-guh*, n., bitter party fights, esp. Hahn Dyn. 「ship.
黨籍 *daang-jir*, n., party member-
黨魁 *daang-kueir*, n., party leader, bandit chief. 「cliques.
黨派 *daangpaih*, n., parties or
黨人 *daang-rern*, n., member of political party, partisan. 「ber.
黨員 *daang-yuarn*, n., party mem-
黨羽 *darngyuu*, n., underlings; members of thieves' gangs.

鱉 22.63

bie.
[Var. of 鼈 22.70]

§22.70 (丨/乚)

北 22.70

beei (**boh*, **beih*).

N. & adj. The north, northern: 北面 the northern side; 北部, 北方, 北邊 the northern part; 華北 North China; 塞北 *Saihbeei*, Mongolian region; 北門鎖鑰 strategic key to the north; 山東以北 north from Shantung; 北半球 Northern Hemisphere; 北雁南飛 the northern goose flies south.

V.i. (1) (**beih*) (AC) 分北三苗 divide the Three Miao tribes. (2) (**boh*) (AC) 士無反北之心 soldiers do not turn rebellious (=背).

Adv. (1) Northward: 北上 go up north, similarly 北征 campaign in the north; 北狩 (of king) make hunting trip in the north, also (of king) visit the north; 北奔 escape north. (2) Defeated: 敗北. (3) Facing north: 北面稱臣 (*beei* or **boh*) (AC) make obeisance as vassal to king whose throne always faces south (南面).

北朝 *beei-chaur*, n., The Northern Dyns. (396–581 A.D.) esp. 南北朝 The South and North Dyns.
北闕 *beeichyueh*, n., the emperor's court (in the north).
北大西洋公約組織 *Beeidah-Shiyarng Gungyueh Tzuujy*, n., North Atlantic Treaty Organization (NATO).
北道主人 *beeidauh juurern*, n., (LL) the host (=東道).
北斗 *beirdoou*, n., North Star, the pol-estar.
北伐 *beeifar*, n. & v.i., the Northern Expedition; to fight north.
北瓜 *beeigua*, n., a kind of melon.
北回歸線 *beei hueirguei-shiahn*, n., northern latitude 23.51°, line of summer solstice.
北京 *Beeijing*, n., usu. called Peking (now 北平); 北京人 Peking man (anthropology).
北極 *Beeijir*, n., the North Pole, the Arctic; 北極圈 --*chyuan*, Arctic circle; 北極海 --*haai*, the Arctic sea; 北極光 --*guang*, aurora borealis; 北極熊 --*shiurng*, the Polar bear.
北至 *beeijyh*, n., summer solstice.
北里 *beirlii*, n., (LL) red-light district. 「America.
北美洲 *Peir Meeijou*, n., North
北平 *Beeipirng*, n., Peiping (Northern Peace), formerly, Peking (Northern Capital), cf. Nanking (Southern Capital).
北緯 *beirweei*, n., northern latitudes.
北洋 *Beeiyarng*, n., as in 北洋軍閥 name of group of military governors dominating China for three decades until 1927.

兆 22.70

jauh.

N. (1) An omen: 吉兆, 凶兆 good, bad omen; 預兆 an omen, augury or foreshadowing; 兆域 -*yuh* ↓. (2) A number: (a) (less common) one million, or (b) one billion; 億兆 indeterminate="millions" or "milliards"; 兆民 the millions of people. (3) A surname.

兆朕 *jauhjehn*, n., omen, foreboding, augury.
兆頭 *jauh'tou*, n., ditto.
兆域 *jauhyuh*, n., (AC) grave site (determined by augury).

乜 22.70

mie (**nieh*).

N. (1) (**nieh*) A surname. (2) (*mie*) (Cantonese) what?

乜斜 *mie'shie*, v.i., to walk sideways; to glance sideways; 乜斜倦眼 narrow eyes into a slit; 乜乜斜斜 to amble.

也 22.70

yee

Fin. part. (1) (LL) indicating what s.t. is: 兵甲不多, 非國之災也 not to have a strong army is not the real trouble for a nation; oft. 者…也: 仁者人也 *rern* is to be human; 義者宜也 *yih* means to be just; sometimes=modn. 了: 我去也 here I go! (2) Indicating a caesura or break in mid-sentence: 夫子之至於是邦也, 必聞其政 when the Master came to a country, he always tried to find out about its government; 古也, 墓而不墳 in anc. days, a grave was made without a mound.

Adv. (1) Also: 你去, 我也去 you go and I go, too; 我也要去 I want to go also; 不哭也不鬧 (child) neither cries nor makes any trouble; 也就 and so; 也曾 also had; 也有 there also is; 也有道理 also is reasonable; 再也休提 don't mention it again. (2) Used in sentence beginning, like Eng. "might as well": 也罷 might as well call it off, or let it be! 也行, 也好 all right (I agree).

也麽哥 *yeemorge*, fin. part., (MC oft. in Yuarn drama) indeed: 兀的不苦殺人也麽哥 how exasperating indeed! 「maybe.
也許 *yershyuu*, adv., perhaps,
也似 *yeesyh*, part., like: 雪花也似 (=似雪花) 申奏將來 the complaints come like snowflakes.

光 22.70

guang.

N. (1) Light: 燈光 lamplight; 月光 moonlight; 日光 sunlight, sunshine; 夜光 the moon, the firefly, a pearl; 光線 *-shiahn*, 光芒 *-marng*, 光澤 *-tzer*↓; 發光 to shine, emit light; 閃光 (燈) flashlight; 回光反照 the dying flicker of a man's life; 光明 *-mirng*, 光輝 *-huei*↓. (2) Favor, grace: 借光兒 (phr. used in asking for favor) pardon me please! 沾光, 叨光 share in reflected glory. (3) A surname.

v.t. Recover, regain, glorify: 光復 *-fuh*↓; 重光 (of sun or moon) reappear after eclipse, (of territory) be restored; 光前裕後 win praises for one's ancestors and enrich one's posterity; 光宗耀祖 reflect glory on one's ancestors; 光耀門楣 bring honor to the family name; 發揚光大 to glorify, broaden and heighten (a nation's cultural heritage).

Adj. (1) Bright, brilliant, shining: 光亮 *-liahng*↓; 光風霽月 (of a person's character) benign and openhearted (like "a light breeze and clear moon"); 光天化日之下 in broad daylight. (2) Smooth: 光滑 *-huar*↓; 刮垢磨光 make s.t. clean and smooth by scraping and polishing; 光塌塌 bare, without decoration; 光撻撻 shiny and smooth; 光溜溜 ditto, naked; 光溜 slippery; 光潤 sleek. (3) Glorious, bringing honor, gracious: 光臨 *-lirn*, 光降 *-jiahng*↓; 候光 waiting to be honored by your company; 光顧 *-guh*↓; 光寵 be honored; 光榮 *-rurng*↓. (4) With nothing left, everything gone: 當光, 賠光, 輸光, 吃光 with everything pawned, lost in business, gambling, consumed; 光蛋 *-dahn*↓; 光了 nothing left, every cent spent; 精光 naked, penniless; 光光 *-guang*↓; 光炕蓆兒 completely destitute. (5) Naked, nude: 光裸 *-luoo*↓; 光屁股 bare buttocks; 光膀子 bare-armed; 光腳 barefoot(ed); 光腿 barelegged; 光著身子 naked; 光脊梁 barebacked; 脫光 stripped naked; 光眼子 nude; 光眼兒 (usu. of children) without clothes.

Adv. Only, alone: 光剩下他一人在家 he alone remains at home; 光說不做 only talk and don't act.

光板兒 *guangbaa'l*, n., worn-out fur coats showing hide below.
光圈 *guangchyuan*, n., (photography) diaphragm or lens aperture of a camera.
光大 *guangdah*, v.t., to brighten, develop to a higher stage.
光蛋 *guangdahn*, n., a person reduced to destitution: 窮光蛋 a penniless loafer.
光度 *guangduh*, n., (phys.) intensity of light.
光復 *guangfuh*, v.t., recover: 光復失地 regain possession of lost territory; 光復節 Restitution Day, day of restitution of sovereignty.
光桿兒 *guanggaa'l*, n., a bachelor or widower: 窮光桿兒 a poor bachelor; 光桿兒生活 the life of a man without wife and children.
光怪 *guangguaih*, adj., absurd, fantastic: 光怪陸離 grotesque, fantastic.
光光 *guangguang*, adj., (1) bright, shining: 亮光光; (2) smooth: 光光滑滑; (3) not a cent left: 輸得光光的 lost every cent in gambling; (4) naked: 脫得光光 stripped naked.
光顧 *guangguh*, v. t., (1) (court.) to honor with your gracious presence; (2) (court.) (of customers) come to shop.
光棍 *guangguhn*, n., (1) a bachelor (also 光棍兒, 光桿子); (2) a ruffian, desperado; (3) (*-'gun*) a person showing a bold front: 你充甚麽光棍 what are you trying to put on?
光華 *guanghuar*[1], n. & adj., glory, -rious, splendor, -did, replendent. 「smooth.
光滑 *guanghuar*[2], adj., shiny and
光輝 *guanghuei*, (1) n., glory, splendor; (2) adj., glorious, splendid.
光火 *guanghuoo*, v.i. & adj., provoke(d) to anger.
光腳的 *guangjiaau'de*, n., the poor (lit., "persons without shoes to wear"): 光腳的不怕穿鞋的 the poor are not daunted by the rich.
光降 *guangjiahng*, v. i. & t., to honor with your gracious presence.
光景 *guangjiing*, n., (1) circumstances at a given time and place: 光景很難 times are very hard; (2) (*-'jing*) prospects: 光景是要下雨 it's likely to rain.
光兒 *guang'l*, n., (1) dim lights; (2) (=光子) eyeglass lenses.
光亮 *guangliahng*, adj., bright and clear, glossy, shining.
光臨 *guanglirn*, v. i., (court.) honor (me, us) with your gracious presence.
光裸 *guangluoo*, adj., nude, naked.
光芒 *guangmarng*, n., flashes, rays of light: 光芒萬丈 blazing ahead, glorious radiant.
光面兒 *guangmiahn(-miah'l)*, n., a flat, smooth surface.
光明 *guangmirng*, (1) n., glory, brilliance; (2) adj., bright, brilliant, shining, openhearted.
光年 *guang-niarn*, n., (astron.) light year. 「wave.
光波 *guang-po*, n., (phys.) light
光譜 *guang-puu*, n., (phys.) a spectrum. 「-rious.
光榮 *guangrurng*, n. & adj., glory,

光線 *guang-shiahn*, n., ray of light.

光鮮 *guangshian*, adj., fresh and bright.

光手 *guang-shoou*, adj., barehanded.

光學 *guangshyuer*, n., (phys.) optics.

光頭 *guangtour*, adj., (1) close-shaven; (2) bareheaded, uncovered.

光頭兒 *guangtour'l*, n., a kind of cake.

光彩 *guangtsaai*, n., (1) (of lights) brilliance, splendor; (2) glory, honor.

光子 *guangtz*, n., eyeglass lenses.

光澤 *guangtzer*, n., luster.

光耀 *guangyauh*, adj. & n., magnificent, -nce, illustrious, bright, -ness.

光陰 *guangyin*, n., a duration of time: 光陰如箭 time passes fast.

光源 *guang-yuarn*, n., (phys.) light source.

氅 22.70

chaang.

N. Fur coat, overcoat: 大氅 overcoat; 鶴氅 overcoat trimmed with crane's down, associated with 諸葛亮 Juker Liahng.

斃 22.70

bih.

V. i. (LL) die, fall down dead: 自斃 (LL) come to bad end; 束手待斃 helpless, waiting for the end; 槍斃 shoot to death; place against firing squad; 猝斃 die suddenly by violence; 倒斃 fall down dead.

斃命 *bih-mihng*, n., (LL) die, lose one's life.

鼈 22.70

bie.

N. Turtle; term of abuse in 鼈縮頭 a coward (turtle retracts head); (sl.) 鼈蛋 an abuse word like "skunk"; 鼈裙 edible fringe of turtle meat.

§22.72 (丨/心)

忠 22.72

jung.

N. Loyalty (to king, cause, country, friend).

Adj. & adv. Loyal, faithful, steadfast: 盡忠 be faithful to master, ruler or country; 不忠 unfaithful to ruler; 忠於職守 faithful to one's duties; 忠言逆耳 honest advice is hard to take; 忠告 speak from honest motives; 忠款 loyal heart, see 忠誠 *-cherng*↓; see compp.↓.

忠臣 *jungchern*, n., honest and loyal minister.

忠誠 *jungcherng*, (1) n., honest heart; (2) adj., honest, reliable.

忠鯁 *junggeeng*, adj., see *-jyr*↓.

忠厚 *junghouh*, adj., (person) honest and simple.

忠直 *jungjyr*, adj., honest and straightforward.

忠良 *jungliarng*, adj., good and faithful (servant, official).

忠孝 *jungshiauh*, adj. & n., loyal to country and filial to parents, loyalty and filial piety: 忠孝之道 the teachings of loyalty and filial piety.

忠信 *jungshihn*, adj., & n., loyal, -ty, and honest, -y.

忠心 *jungshin*, adj., & n., loyal, -ty (to duty, master).

忠恕 *jungshuh*, adj. & n., honest (-y) and considerate(-tion) of others: 忠恕之道 the Golden Mean, do unto others as you would have others do unto you.

忠實 *jungshyr*, adj., loyal (disciples, employees).

忠義 *jungyih*, n. & adj., standing for faith and right——oft. associated with chivalrous, independent warriors as in 水滸傳, *The Water Margin*, a picaresque novel.

忠勇 *jungyuung*, adj., honest and brave.

患 22.72

huahn.

N. (1) Cause for worry, concern, trouble, disaster: 患難 *-nahn*↓; 災患 disaster; 水患 flood; 禍患 source of disaster (strong neighboring state, seething discontent, etc.); 後患無窮 source of endless trouble; 大患 great trouble: 人之患在好爲人師 the great trouble of most men is that they like to lecture other people——Confucius. (2) A surname.

V. i. & t. (1) To worry about: 患得患失 worry about securing office, then worry about losing it—be too anxious for official promotion. (2) To contract illness: 患病 fall ill; 患處 where it (illness) hurts.

患難 *huahnnahn*, n., troubles, tribulations: 患難之交 a friend who went through difficult times together; 可以共患難 a man who can be trusted in times of trouble.

悲 22.72

bei.

光 氅 斃 鼈 忠 患 悲

亅	小	⺊	十	土	ナ	廾	乚	丨	一	丁	フ	口	囚	冈	㇆	厂	尸	亠	广	宀	丶	乚	弋	心	八	人	乂	㇀	乛	丿	㇓	く
00	01	02	10	11	12	20	21	22	30	31	32	40	41	42	50	51	52	60	61	62	63	70	71	72	80	81	82	83	90	91	92	93

悲 憋 懟 典 冀

N. Sorrow, feeling of sadness: 悲從中來 overcome by feeling of sorrow; 興盡悲來 feeling of sadness follows a bout of pleasure; 悲憤 moved and angered; 悲歡離合 joys and sorrows, separations and reunions in the drama of life; 慈△悲 mercy, 80.72.

V.i. & t. To feel pity: 悲之 (LL) take pity on it (him); feel sorry: 悲憐 *-liarn*↓; 悲天憫人 feeling for universal compassion, cosmic pity.

Adj. & adv. Sad, sadly: 悲鳴 sad cry of animals; 悲啼 moaning; 悲悲切切 sad and touching; 悲歌 somber song; 悲風 moaning wind.

悲哀 *bei-ai*, n. & adj., sorrow, sorrowful, mournful.
悲切 *beichii*, adj., sad and touching.
悲秋 *bei-chiou*, v.i., beautiful feeling of sadness induced by autumn, esp. in sentimental poetry (傷春悲秋).
悲悼 *beidauh*, n. & v.i., (to) sorrow for lost friend.
悲憤 *beifeen*, adj. & n., sad(ness) and anger(ed) (悲憤交集).
悲感 *beigaan*, n., sense of sadness.
悲歌 *beige* n., elegy.
悲觀 *beiguan*, n. & adj., pessimism, -stic.
悲壯 *beijuahng*, adj., stirred by defeat, determine to fight.
悲劇 *beijyuh*, n., tragedy.
悲憐 *beiliarn*, v.t., to take pity on (person).
悲涼 *beiliarng*, adj., desolate.
悲傷 *beishang*, adj., sad, disconsolate, moving, touched (feeling, scene, event).
悲喜劇 *beishii-jyuh*, n., tragicomedy.
悲酸 *beisuan*, adj., moved to tears, wanting to cry; touching, heartbreaking (scene, etc.).
悲田院 *beitiarn-yuahn*, n., (also wr. 卑田院) institution for the poor (with income from grants of land).
悲慘 *beitsaan*, adj., sad and shocking (as death from fire, accident).

憋 22.72

bie (*bieh*).
[Var. 彆]

V. i. & t. (1) To contain smouldering anger: 憋不住 cannot hold anger any longer, ready to burst; 憋着氣 smoulder with resentment; 憋得慌, 憋得難受 depressed, exasperated. (2) To shut up: 憋住不說 hold back one's tongue.

Adj. Hot-tempered: 憋性 impatient.

憋氣 *bie-chih*, v. i. & adj., short of breath, suffocate.
憋悶 *bie-mehn*, adj., bored, depressed.
憋扭 *bieh'niou*, (also wr. 憋拗, 彆扭), v.i., (coll.) be of contrary opinion; 鬧憋扭 getting quarrelsome; ungainly, not smooth (of performance, writing).

懟 22.72

dueih.

N. & v.t. Resentment, hatred; to cause resentment; to hate.

§ 22.80 (丨/八)

典 22.80

diaan.

N. (1) Established or traditional system, institution or laws: 法典 code of laws; 典刑 *-shirng*[1]↓; 國有常典 established laws of country. (2) Model, established standard: 典則 model, standard: 典範 *-fahn*↓. (3) Classic: 經典 the classic; 佛典 Buddhist classic. (4) Dictionary, encyclopaedia: 字典 dictionary; 辭典 dictionary of phrases; 永樂大典 Encyclopaedia (collection) of Emperor Yunglo; 會典 encyclopaedia on institutions of a dyn.; 通典 name of an encyclopaedia (Tarng Dyn.). (5) Literary allusion or reference: 語出何典 what is the allusion to? 典故 *-guh*↓. (6) A surname.

V. t. (1) To mortgage, to pawn: 典業 mortgage property; 典賣, 典當, 典押 *-maih*, *-dahng*, *-ya*↓. (2) To supervise, be in charge of: 典試 act as chief examiner; 典獄 in charge of prison: 典獄官 prison warden.

典奧 *diaan-auh*, adj. & n., profound, profundity.
典常 *diancharng*, n., established laws and customs.
典當 *diaandahng*, v. t., pawn (articles).
典範 *diaanfahn*, n., model to be copied, followed.
典故 *diaanguh*, n., literary reference or allusion.
典章 *diaanjang*, n., cultural establishments (典章文物); anc. institutions.
典籍 *diaanjir*, n., books in gen., esp. anc. works.
典制 *diaanjyh*[1], n., traditional institutions.
典質 *diaanjyh*[2], v. t., to pawn (articles).
典賣 *diaanmaih*, v. t., to mortgage.
典舖 *diaanpuh*, n., pawnshop.
典刑 *diaanshirng*[1], n., laws, esp. penalties: 明正典刑 carry out a capital punishment.
典型 *diaanshirng*[2], n. & adj., model: 典型人物 model personalities.
典守 *diarnshoou*, v.t., to be in charge of (prisons, etc.).
典史 *diaanshyy*, n., district chief of police (Manchu Dyn.).
典押 *diaanya*, n. & v. t., mortgage, used as pledge in loan, pawn.
典雅 *diarnyaa*, adj., refined, cultured (of manners, writing).

冀 22.80

jih.

N. (1) Hopei Province. (2) A surname.

V. i. & t. To hope: 冀得 hope to get; 冀望 look forward to or long for; 希冀 covet or crave for.

糞 22.80

fehn.

N. Manure, dung: 糞壤, 糞堆 dung heaps for manure.

V. t. To apply manure as fertilizer: 糞田.

糞便 *fehnbiahn*, n., feces and urine, excrements (as for medical examination).
糞除 *fehnchur*, v. t., to clean up dirt from place.
糞池 *fehnchyr*, n., septic tank, also 化糞池.
糞門 *fehnmern*, n., anus.
糞土 *fehntuu*, n., dirt, filth: 棄如糞土 cast away like dirt.

貴 22.80

gueih.

N. A surname.

V. t. (1) To esteem highly, to value, to prize: 賤貨而貴德 to despise material goods and respect virtue; 貴耳賤目 rely on hearsay, "trust one's ears rather than one's eyes"; 所貴乎 what makes (s.t.) valued. (2) To honor or love: 下安則貴上 when the people are happy and contented, they will honor the powers that be.

Adj. (1) Expensive, costly: 昂貴 (of prices) high; 貴賤 *-jiahn*↓; 太貴 too costly; 貴得很 very expensive. (2) Honorable, noble: 貴客 *-keh*, 貴族 *-tzur*↓; 顯貴 high-ranking officials; 貴冑 *-jouh*, 貴人 *-rern*↓; 權貴 the politically powerful and influential; 富貴 loaded with riches and honors; 華貴 elegant, magnificent; 高貴 noble and dignified; 尊貴 highly respectable and revered. (3) Precious, of great value: 珍貴 rare and highly valuable; 貴重 *-juhng*↓; 物以稀為貴 a thing is valued in proportion to its rarity; 可貴 esteemable. (4) Honorific: 貴姓 may I know your (honorable) name? 貴庚 *-geng*, 貴處 *-chuh*↓; 貴國, 貴校, 貴局, 貴部 your (honorable) country, school, bureau, ministry; 貴恙 your illness; 貴公子 (address to) a noble young man; 貴价 (court.) your servant; 貴幹 *-gahn*, 貴上 *-shahng*↓.

貴賓 *gueihbin*, n., honored guest, V. I. P.
貴處 *gueihchuh*, idiomatic phr., where do you come from, sir?
貴妃 *gueihfei*, n., (AC) title of a lady-in-waiting, an imperial concubine.
貴幹 *gueihgahn*, n., (court.) your work or business: 有何貴幹 what business have you come here for?
貴庚 *gueihgeng*, idiomatic phr., may I know your (honorable) age?
貴賤 *gueih-jiahn*, adj., (1) (of prices or costs) high or low; (2) (of persons) highly placed or lowly.
貴金屬 *gueihjinshuu*, n., (chem.) noble metals.
貴冑 *gueihjouh*, n., noblemen, princes of the blood.
貴重 *gueihjuhng*, adj., valuable: 貴重物品 valuable articles.
貴客 *gueihkeh*, n., honored guests, V.I.P.s.
貴人 *gueihrern*, n., (1) a high-ranking government official; (2) (AC) title of a female palace official; (3) (fortunetelling) some unknown benefactor.
貴上 *gueihshahng*, v.t., see V.t. 2↓.
貴族 *gueihtzur*, n., a noble family, a noble, the nobility.

費 22.80

feih (**bih*).

N. (1) Fees, expense(s), expenditure: usu. 費用 *-yuhng*↓; 雜費 sundry expenses; 學費 school fees; 車馬費 honorarium for transportation and entertainment expenses; 經費 expenses (very big, etc.), budget for expenditure (inadequate); 每年經費 annual budget, expenditure; 免費 free of charge. (2) (**bih*) Name of place: 費縣. (3) A surname.

V.t. Cost, waste, take a lot of (time, energy) to do: 費工夫, 費時 takes a lot of work, time; 費力 *-lih*↓; 費力不討好 a thankless task; 費了九牛二虎之力 takes a tremendous lot of work to do; 費財 waste a lot of money; 費心機 takes a lot of thinking; 費商量 requires a lot of discussion; 費唇舌 waste a lot of words; 費手腳 troublesome to do; 費解 difficult to explain (takes a lot to); 枉費 (心思, 氣力) waste to no purpose; 耗費, 浪費 waste or spend extravagantly; 白費 to labor in vain; 破費 (court.) cost (you) money (to provide dinner, etc.).

費勁(兒) *feih-jihn(-jieh'l)*, adj. & adv., difficult, (ly), requiring a lot of effort.
費力 *feih-lih*, adj., hard to tackle, requiring work, energy.
費神(心) *feih-shern (-shin)*, adj., (1) requiring attention; (2) formula for thanking beforehand in making request: 費神(心)得很 I thank you beforehand.
費事 *feih-shyh*, adj., troublesome, takes doing.
費菜 *feihtsaih*, n., (bot.) *Sedum kamtschficum*.
費用 *feihyuhng*, n., expenses.

貰 22.80

shyh.

[See 21.80]

賞 22.80

shaang.

N. Award for merit: 奬賞 ditto; 有賞, 懸賞 offer reward (for capture of criminal, etc.); 賞罰 reward and punishment to maintain order in government.

V. i. & t. (1) To bestow (honor, a gift): 賞賜 *-tsyh*, 賞錢 *-chiarn*, 賞格 *-ger*↓; 恩賞 n. & v.i., award by government; 犒賞 n. & v.i., gift to soldiers; 賞臉 to "give" face; 賞臨 to honor one as by presence at dinner; 賞收 (court.) please to accept. (2) To appreciate, enjoy beauty of (flowers, moon, snow): 欣賞 enjoy, appreciate (esp. literature, speech); 鑑賞 critically appreciate.

賞錢 *shaang chiarn*, (1) phr., to give tips; (2) (*-'chian*) n., a tip to servants.

賞格 *shaangger*, n., price put on the head of a wanted criminal, legal reward or promotion for service.

賞光 *shaang-guang*, v.i., to do one the honor (of attending, etc.).

賞鑒 *shaangjiahn*, v. t., to appreciate; to honor one by reading or critical approval.

賞鍾 *shaangjung*, n., (MC) a toast for distinguished services.

賞聲 *shaang-sheng*, n., (=上聲) the third tone.

賞心 *shaang-shin*, v. i., to enjoy oneself (as at wine dinner).

賞識 *shaangshyh*, v. t., to recognize worth (of talent, person); to love or appreciate (writing).

賞賜 *shaangtsyh*, v. t., to bestow (honor, gift) by superior.

賞玩 *shaangwahn*, v. t., to fondle (objects of art); to love and appreciate (moon, flowers).

賞音 *shaangyin*, n., (LL) an understanding friend (cf. 知音).

§ 22.81 (丨/人)

尖 22.81

jian.

N. (1) A sharp point: 筆尖 the point of a pen, a pen nib; 刀尖, 針尖, 槍尖 the point of a knife, needle, spear; 尖端 *-duan*↓; 尖頭 the sharp end; 指尖 finger tips. (2) (Mountain) peak: 頂尖(兒) the best of its kind. (3) Meal by the roadside: 打尖 (dial.)(of travelers) have a bite at a roadside inn.

Adj. Sharp, pointed: 尖銳 *-rueih*, 尖利 *-lih*↓; 很尖 very smart, clever; 尖細 *-shih*, 尖刻 *-keh*, 尖酸 *-suan*↓.

尖兵 *jian-bing*, n., (of troops) advance guard.

尖臍 *jian-chir*, n., male crabs.

尖端 *jianduan*, n., the extreme (highest) point, the pinnacle.

尖尖 *jianjian*, adj., tapering, (sharp-) pointed.

尖刻 *jiankeh*, adj., (of words, speech) sharp, pointed, barbed.

尖利 *jianlih*, adj., sharp (point, person).

尖劈 *jianpi*, n., a wedge.

尖銳 *jianrueih*, adj., (lit. & fig.) sharp, pointed, barbed: 尖銳化 (of situation) becoming increasingly critical, aggravated.

尖細 *jianshih*, adj., fine (workmanship).

尖酸 *jiansuan*, adj., (of words, speech) sarcastic, petty, mean.

尖團 *jiantuarn*, n., (1) male and female crabs; (2) (Chin. opera) 尖團字 differentiated *tz*, *ts* and *j*, *ch* consonants.

§ 22.82 (丨/乂)

皮 22.82

pir.

N. (1) Skin: often 皮膚 *-'fu*↓; oft. 皮子 or 皮兒; 仔細你的皮 threat of flogging; 厚臉皮, 老臉皮 thick-skinned, impudent; 水菓皮 skin of fruit; 剝皮 to skin (animal) also (fig.) (person); 吹牛皮 blow one's own horn; 表皮 epidermis; 眞皮 true skin; 皮包骨 extremely emaciated, skinny; 雞皮鶴髮 old, haggard look; 皮之不存, 毛將焉附 mutually dependent (of neighboring states), usefulness of having a buffer state in between; 皮裏陽秋 (春秋) smooth, well-covered remark or sarcasm. (2) Oft. used with 肉: 皮肉 skin and flesh see 皮肉 *-rouh*↓; 皮裏抽肉 very thin; 皮開肉綻 badly bruised from flogging, skin and flesh torn; 皮笑肉不笑 false smile, skin-deep smile; 又和他皮鬆肉緊的談會子 engage in irrelevant talk. (3) In combnation with 臉 face, denoting facial expression: 嘻皮笑臉 a face full of smiles; 皮臉(兒), 皮臉皮痴, 沒皮沒臉, 死皮賴臉 thick-skinned, unashamed; 嬉皮 hippies. (4) Skin goods, hide, fur: 皮貨 hide, fur business; 豹死留皮 leopard's skin survives his body (of fame); 虎皮, 豹皮, 鹿皮 tiger skin, leopard skin, deerskin; 皮袍子 fur-lined gown; 皮襖 fur-lined jacket. (5) Leather: 皮箱 leather suitcase; 皮夾克, 手套, 椅子 leather jacket, gloves, chair; 皮帶 leather belt; 皮鞭 leather whip, etc. (6) Cover: 書皮, 封皮 book cover. (7) Thin sheet: 鉛皮 lead sheet.

Adj. (1) Thick-skinned: 這小孩子罵皮了; this child no longer cares about scolding; 皮着臉 thick-skinned, unashamed. (2) Naughty: 皮死了, 跳皮 very naughty. (3) Opp. of crisp, no longer crisp (biscuit), leathery in taste.

皮弁 *pirbiahn*, n. (AC) deerskin cap.
皮幣 *pir-bih*, n. (AC) hides and coins, used in gifts, tributes.
皮纏 *pircharn*, v. t., annoy (usu. of children).
皮車 *pirche*, n., Peking term for rickshaw, short for 膠皮車 ("rubber-wheeled cart").
皮氣 *pir'chi*, n.,=脾氣 temper.
皮球 *pirchiour*, n., leather ball (football, etc.).
皮蛋 *pirdahn*, n., chemically treated, preserved egg.
皮袋 *pirdaih*, n., leather bag; (Budd.) physical body, also 皮囊.
皮膚 *pir'fu*, n., skin; 皮膚病 n., skin disease; 皮膚炎 dermatitis.
皮侯 *pir-hour*, n. (AC) archery target.
皮黃 *pir-huarng*, n., Peking opera music, combination of music of two districts 西皮 and 二黃.
皮掌 *pirjaang*, n., front part of sole in mended shoes.
皮匠 *pir-jiahng*, n., shoemaker.
皮膠 *pir-jiau*, n., glue, also 牛皮膠 made from cow hide.
皮重 *pir-juhng*, n., weight including package.
皮脂 *pir-jy*, n., natural oil of skin.
皮紙 *pirjyy*, n., parchment.
皮科(兒) *pirke('l)*, n., joke, joking.
皮臉 *pirliaan*, n., "face" representing man's honor; facial expression: 不喜歡看他那幅皮臉 do not like the look on his face.
皮毛 *pir'maur*, adj. & n., superficial; -ity: 皮毛之見 superficial opinion; 得其皮毛 only learned the superficial things, without the spirit.
皮肉 *pir-rouh*, n., the flesh: 皮肉生涯 *--sheng-yar*, prostitution.
皮下注射 *pir-shiah juh-sheh*, n., subcutaneous injection.
皮相 *pirshiahng*, n., external appearance: 皮相之談 superficial opinion.
皮硝 *pirshiau*, n., tannic acid for treating leather.
皮實 *pir'shyr*, adj., solid, solidly built.
皮條(兒) *pirtiaur('l)*, n., leather strap; 拉皮條 be a pimp.
皮草 *pirtsaau*, n., furs at furriers.
皮桶子 *pirtuungtz*, n., (Peip. coll.) fur goods.

叟 22.82

soou.

N. (LL) old man, an elder; (AC, court. address) elder.

斐 22.82

feei.

N. A surname.

Adj. (LL) handsome: 斐然成章 phr., well-cultivated, in good shape; 斐然可觀 handsome looking, stately (performance, structures).

斐斐 *feirfeei*, adj., (LL) light; well decorated or furnished.

叢 22.82

tsurng (also **tsung*).

N. (1) A bush, shrub: 叢莽 a grove of trees; 叢冢 a group of graves, also multiple graves; 叢帖 collection of callig., rubbings; 叢祠 ancestral temple overgrown with underbush. (2) A surname.

Adj. & adv. In great quantity, multiple: 百病叢生 all kinds of troubles grow up; 萬物叢生 grow in great variety and profusion.

叢薄 *tsurngbor*, n., (LL) a grove, copse.
叢林 *tsurnglirn*, n., woods, forest.
叢莽 *tsurngmaang*, n., see *-bor* ↑; shrubbery.
叢木 *tsurngmuh*, n., underbrush.
叢書 *tsurngshu*, n., a collection of books, a set of books issued in the same format by a publisher; 百科叢書 encyclopaedia; 人人叢書 Everyman's Library.
叢談 *tsurngtarn*, n., talks on random or special subjects: 飲食叢談 talks on food and drinks.

鼗 22.82

taur.

N. A small handdrum with beads striking when rotated.

---

§22.83 (丨/乛)

遘 22.83

gouh.

V.t. (AC) to encounter.

迆 22.83

yii.

[Var. of 迤 92.83]

逃 22.83

taur.

V.i. To flee, escape: 逃去了 has escaped; 逃出去 escape; 逃之夭夭 escaped and is nowhere to be found; 別逃 don't try to run away; 逃不掉 cannot escape from justice; 逃往 abscond to; hide away, keep out of sight, see many compp.↓.

V.t. To escape (famine, war, school class, conscription): 逃荒, 逃難, 逃學, 逃兵 *-huang*, *-nahn*, *-shyuer*, *-bing*, etc.↓; 逃婚 run away from wedding; 逃嫁 (of married woman) elope with another man; 逃世 live the life of a recluse, retire from world; 逃課 play truant; 逃刑 flee from punishment; 逃稅 evasion of tax; escaped: 逃兵, 逃軍 deserter, also fleeing troops; hiding: 在逃 is in hiding.

逃奔 *taurben*, v.i., flee.
逃避 *taurbih*, v.i., shirk (duty); refuse to face (reality 逃避現實).
逃兵 *taurbing*, n., deserter.
逃禪 *taurcharn*, v.i., become Buddhist convert.
逃遁 *taurduhn*, v.i., hide away.
逃犯 *taurfahn*, n., escaped convict.
逃荒 *taurhuang*, v.i., to flee from famine area.
逃婚 *taurhun*, v.i., run away from wedding.
逃命 *taurmihng*, v.i., flee for life.
逃名 *taur-mirng*, v.i., shun publicity.
逃難 *taur-nahn*, v.i., be refugee.
逃匿 *taur-nih*, v.i., escape and hide, keep oneself out of sight.
逃跑 *taurpaau*, v.i., escape, flee, steal away.
逃生 *taursheng*, v.i., flee for life.
逃學 *taur-shyuer*, v.i., play truant.
逃竄 *taur-tsuahn*, v.i., (of bandits, rebel forces) flee elsewhere.
逃脫 *taurtuo*, v.i., succeed in escaping.
逃走 *taurtzoou*, v.i., run away.
逃罪 *taur-tzueih*, v.i., escape from the law.
逃亡 *taurwarng*, v.i., flee from home or country.

迪 22.83

dir.

[Var. 廸]

V.i. & t. To open one's mind, enlighten; to progress.

建 22.83

jiahn.

N. (1) (Peking dial. also *jin*) a lunar month: 大建, 小建 one of 30, 29 days. (2) A surname.

V. t. (1) Establish, set up, erect, found, create: 建都, 建校 to found a capital, a school; 建功 win glory for one's country or any group to which one belongs; 建國 *-guor*, 建立 *-lih*, 建設 *-sheh*↓; 建造 *-tzauh*↓; 增建 make new additional structures; 違建 illegal structures; 再建 reconstruct, build anew; 重建 rehabilitate, rebuild. (2) Overturn: 建瓴 *-lirng*↓.

建白 *jiahn-bor*, v. i., make appeal or recommendations on public affairs.
建朝 *jiahn-chaur*, v.i., found a dynasty.
建國 *jiahn-guor*, v. i., create a new nation.
建基 *jiahn-ji*, v. i., lay the foundations.
建極 *jiahn-jir*, v. i., (of a monarch) ascend the throne.
建築 *jiahnjur*, v. t., build (houses, roads, bridges): 建築物 a building, edifice, structure.
建立 *jiahnlih*, v. t., erect (a monument), build (a church, school, hospital), create (an office, agency, institution).
建瓴 *jiahnlirng*, adj. phr., (AC) as easy as letting spilt water flow down the roof.
建設 *jiahnsheh*, n., new developments, progress; v. t., build up (a business, reputation, armed forces, agriculture, industry); 建設性 adj., constructive; 建設性批評 constructive criticism.
建樹 *jiahnshuh*, v. t., set up, establish; n., achievements.
建造 *jiahntzauh*, v. t., build (house, ship, railroad, highway).
建議 *jiahnyih*, (1) v. i., make recommendations, offer suggestions, give advice; (2) n., a proposal, resolution.
建寅 *jiahnyirn*, n., (AC) the dynastic calendar of Hsia (2205–1766 B.C.) with the month of Yirn (寅) as the first month of the year, see Appendix A.

迷 22.83

mir.

N. Maniac: 影迷, 舞迷, 戲迷 person crazy about movies, dancing, opera.

V. i. & t. (1) To lose one's way: 迷失去向 lose one's bearings; 迷路 *-luh*↓. (2) Enchant, cast under a charm: 被她迷住了 be infatuated with her; 迷人的力量 infatuating, fascinating power; 迷人的心 bewitch person; 迷拐 drug and kidnap; 迷昏了 cast under spell.

Adj. (1) Dazed, befuddled, lost: 昏迷; 迷忽忽 confused in delirium, collapsed and fainted; 昏迷狀態 in a state of coma, unconscious; 迷羊 the lost sheep; 迷糊, 迷亂, 迷惘 *-hur*, *-luahn*, *-maang*↓. (2) Enchanted, drunk with, enamored with: 迷溺 fall into habit of, love deeply (wine, women, gambling). (3) Confusing: 布迷陣 (mil.) deploy troops to confuse the enemy; 迷魂 *-hurn*↓.

迷暗 *mir-ahn*[1], adj., in the dark, difficult to see.
迷岸 *mir-ahn*[2], n., (Budd.) the shore of sensuous error.
迷瞪 *mir'deng*, v. i., become infatuated with s. t., also 迷迷瞪瞪 *mirmir-dengdeng*.
迷宮 *mirgung*, n., labyrinth.
迷糊 *mir'hu*, adj., unclear, blurred (picture, impression); also 迷迷糊糊 *mir'mi-hur'hu*, in a daze, difficult to make out.
迷惑 *mirhuoh*, v. t. & n., temptation, tempting, tempted; to

tempt; mislead, confuse; adj., puzzled.

迷魂 *mirhurn*, adj., enticing; 迷魂湯 (cast, be under) enticing spell; 迷魂藥 --*yauh*, n., a drug to hypnotize a victim.

迷津 *mirjin*, n., wrong path (ferry where one goes astray): 指破迷津 (Budd.) point out where one has gone astray from right path.

迷戀 *mirliahn*, v. t., be drunk, enamored with.

迷離 *mirlir*, adj., confusing, see 撲朔迷離 10A.81.

迷亂 *mirluahn*, adj., confusing, -sed.

迷路 *mirluh*, n., (1) wrong path; (2) inner ear; (3) v. i., have lost one's way.

迷惘 *mirmaang*, adj., lost, confused.

迷蒙精 *mirmerng-jing*, n., chloroform.

迷謬 *mirmiouh*, adj., false (of doctrine, teaching).

迷迷 *mirmir*, adj., unclear, see *-deng*, *-hur* ↑.

迷你 *mirnii*, adj., mini: 迷你裙 miniskirt.

迷笑 *mirshiauh*, n. & v.i., beguiling smile; to smile beguilingly.

迷信 *mirshihn*, (1) n., superstition; (2) v. t., blindly believe.

迷途 *mirtur*, n., the lost way, stray path.

迷醉 *mirtzueih*, v. t., be drunk, fascinated by (new ideas, etc.).

逍 22.83

shiau.

逍遙 *shiauyaur*, v. i., to jaunt; stroll in freedom: 逍遙自在 enjoying freedom, calm and master of oneself; 逍遙法外 (of criminal) go free, at large; adj., carefree; 逍遙遊 n., a carefree journey.

逮 22.83

daih (**daai*).

V.i. & t. (1) Reach: 力不逮也 ability is unequal to the task. (2) (**daai*) Arrest: 把他逮住 arrested him; 逮捕 *dairbuu*, v.t., to arrest.

Prep. Up to, until: 逮於今日 up to now (also wr. 迨).

違 22.83

weir.

V. t. (1) To be separated, absent (used in letters): 久違 have not seen you for a long time; 違教, 睽違 have not seen (person); 自違雅範 since parting ("from your presence"), (court.) since last seeing you. (2) To disobey, defy: 違背 ditto; 違法, 違犯 *-faa*, *fahn* ↓; 違令 *-lihng* ↓. (3) To avoid: 違避 *-bih* ↓. (4) To miss, lose, err: 違失 *-shy* ↓; 違和 *-her* ↓.

違礙 *weir-aih*, v. t., to obstruct; disobey; damage (morals).

違背 *weirbeih*, v. t., to disobey (instructions), violate (treaty): 違背法令 judgement contrary to law or ordinances.

違避 *weirbih*, v. t., to stand aside to avoid s.o.'s presence; to shirk (duty).

違法 *weir-faa*, (1) v. i., break the law; (2) adj., illegal (conduct).

違反 *weirfaan*, v. t., go against, flout (orders).

違犯 *weirfahn*, v. t., break (regulations).

違和 *weir-her*, v. i., (LL) be unwell ("miss harmony").

違章 *weirjang*, v.t. & adj., violate (-ting) rules and regulations.

違禁 *weir-jihn*, v. i. & adj., act against the law, do what is forbidden: 違禁品 --*piin*, n., forbidden goods, contraband.

違抗 *weirkahng*, v. t., to defy (authority, police).

違例 *weur-lih*, adj., against the rules.

違令 *weir-lihng*, v. i. & adj., against the orders.

違理 *weir-lii*, adj., against reason or propriety.

違憲 *weir-shiahn*, adj., unconstitutional.

違心 *weir-shin*, adj., as in 違心之論 statement contrary to one's inner belief.

違失 *weirshy*, n., error, mistake.

違忤 *weirwuu*, v. t., to disobey (wish, etc.).

違言 *weir-yarn*, n., (AC) unreasonable talk; dispute.

違拗 *weiryauh*, v. t., to defy (orders, wish).

違約 *weir-yue*, phr., break contract or treaty.

遣 22.83

chiaan.

V. t. (1) To send (person) to do s. t.: 遣他去 send him to do it; 遣使 *-shyy* ↓. (2) To seek relief from boredom, to relax, have a diversion: 遣興, 遣意, 遣悶 *-shihng*, *-yih*, *-mehn* ↓; 無以自遣 to need but do not have some diversion; 何以遣此 how to pass such a day, night? (3) To send off, send away, to exile: 遣戍 *-shuh* ↓; 遣歸 send s.o. home.

遣奠 *chiaandiahn*, n., libation ceremony on start of funeral procession.

遣發 *chiaanfa*, v.t., send (s.o.) on an errand.

遣懷 *chiaan-huair*, v. i., to relax, have some good fun or pastime.

遣悶 *chiaan-mehn*, v. i., to seek some distraction, escape from boredom.

遣散 *chiaansahn*, v. t., send away (servants, soldiers, etc.); to dismiss from or to terminate service, hence 遣散費 termination pay.

遣興 *chiaan-shihng*, v. i., to versify, write or paint as a pastime or to help celebrate a moment.

遣刑 *chiaan-shirng*, n., (AC) punishment by exile.

遣戍 *chiaanshuh*, v. t., send to exile.

遣使 *chiaan-shyy*, v.t., to send (s.o.) to some place.

遣送 *chiaansuhng*, v. t., to send s. o. to a place: 遣送回國 repatriate (prisoner of war, unwanted person, etc.).

遣意 *chiaanyih*, v. i., express some thought in writing as relaxation, see *-shihng*↑.

遺 22.83

yir (**weih*).

N. Article lost: 路 (道) 不拾遺 no one would keep lost articles found by the roadside; 拾遺 supplement to book, supplying omissions.

V.i. & t. (1) To lose: 遺失 *-shy*↓. (2) To drop out by mistake: 遺漏 *-louh*↓; 夢遺, 遺精 *-jing*↓. (3) To urinate: 小遺 (rare). (4) To bequeath: 遺留 *-liour*, 遺下 *-shiah*↓. (5) (**weih*) (AC, LL) bequeath; send (gift, letter).

Adj. (1) Inherited, handed down: 遺傳, 遺產 *-chuarn*, *-chaan*↓; 遺制 customs handed down from the past. (2) Prefixed to certain words, meaning "mis-": 遺計, 遺策 miscalculated plan, *-jih*, *-tseh*↓.

遺愛 *yir-aih*, n., (AC) long-cherished love: 古之遺愛 beloved persons of the past.

遺產 *yirchaan*, n., inheritance, heritage, legacy.

遺棄 *yirchih*, v.t., to desert (wife, lover, duty).

遺臭 *yir-chouh*, v.i., to leave a name that stinks for ever: 遺臭萬年 to leave a bad name for thousands of years to come.

遺籌 *yir-chour*, n., see *-jih*↓.

遺傳 *yirchuarn*, (1) v.i. & t., to pass on to offspring; to transmit to future generations; (2) n., heredity: 遺傳性 heredity; 遺傳病 hereditary disease; 遺傳因子 gene; 遺傳學 genetics.

遺風 *yir-feng*, n., uplifting influence of s.o. past.

遺腹子 *yirfuhtzyy*, n., son born when father is dead, posthumous son.

遺憾 *yirhahn*, n., a regret, a matter of regret; a flaw in s.t. otherwise perfect.

遺骸 *yir-hair*, n., corpse, esp. of one dying abroad, waiting to be shipped home.

遺恨 *yirhehn*, n., see *-hahn*↑.

遺詔 *yir-jauh*, n., ruler's last will.

遺摺 *yir-jer*, n., a memorial left for emperor when high minister dies.

遺跡 *yir-ji*, (1) n., historic relic, relic of some famous persons; (2) v.i., to lose oneself in retirement: 遺跡江湖 go away from home and roam about the world, retire to lake district.

遺教 *yir-jiauh*, n., advice, teachings left by s.o. past.

遺計 *yir-jih*, n., a miscalculation.

遺精 *yir-jing*, n., nocturnal emission.

遺珠 *yir-ju*, n., (AC) unrecognized talent.

遺囑 *yir-juu*, n., (law) person's last will and testament: 遺囑附加書 codicil.

遺老 *yirlaau*, n., old man of past dynasty or regime; old person mentally living in another age.

遺留 *yirliour*, v.t., to leave behind (children, request, etc.), esp. at death.

遺漏 *yirlouh*, v.t., to omit by mistake; n., an omission.

遺民 *yirmirn*, n., see *-laau*↑.

遺容 *yir-rurng*, n., portrait of s.o. dead.

遺少 *yirshauh*, n., young man mentally like 遺老, see *-laau*↑.

遺下 *yir-shiah*, v.t., to leave behind (children, wife, etc.) at death.

遺像 *yirshiahng*, n., portrait of s.o. dead.

遺書 *yir-shu*, n., (1) dying testament; (2) collected works of a deceased author; (3) books that have generally become extinct.

遺失 *yirshy*, (1) v.i., to commit a mistake; to lose (key, handbag, etc.); (2) n., a mistake.

遺世 *yir-shyh*, phr., (LL) to leave this world: 遺世獨立 cast aside worldly cares and live independently.

遺訓 *yir-shyuhn*, n., dying instructions; advice or teachings left by s.o.

遺矢 *yir-shyy*, v.i., to ease bowels.

遺尿 *yir-suei*, v.i., (LL) to urinate (also pr. *yirniauh*).

遺體 *yir-tii*, n., a person's mortal remains.

遺才 *yir-tsair*, n., scholar who failed in civil examinations; discovered talent.

遺策 *yir-tseh*, n., (1) plan or policy handed down; (2) a miscalculation, see *-jih*↑.

遺贈 *Yirtzehng*, n., bequest; 遺贈產 devise, bequeathed property.

遺族 *yir-tzur*, n., descendants (of a tribe or noted person).

遺忘 *yirwahng* (*-warng*), v.i. & t., to forget.

遺言 *yir-yarn*, n., dying instructions.

遺業 *yiryeh*, n., unfinished work of ancestor, inherited family property.

遴 22.83

lirn.

V. t. To select (talent for post): 遴選.

躄 22.83

bier.

[Var. 蹩]

Adj. Lame.

躄脚 *bierjiaau*, adj., (1) inferior,

cheap in quality; (2) frustrated.

§ 22.91 (丨/丿)

少 22.91

shaau (few, little), **shauh* (youth).

V. i. & t. (1) To find missing: 這屋裏少了幾件東西 a few things are missing in this room; 東西少了 things are missing. (2) To pay less than what is due: 少人的錢還得還人家 what is owed must be made up. (3) To spare, go without: 飯不可少 rice is s. t. we cannot go without; 少了他不成 cannot go without him; 少不得, 少不了 see *-bu-der*, *-bu-liaau* ↓. (4) (AC) look down upon.

Adj. & adv. (1) Few, little, opp. 多 much, many: 很少 very little, few; 太少 too little, too few; 少許 *-shyuu* ↓; 少見 seldom seen, unique, rare: 少見多怪 having seen little, get excited easily; 少來往 have little to do with each other; 少少兒的 just a little; 稀少 very few, rarely seen; 至少 at least; a short moment: 少等 (候), 少待一下 please wait a little; 少頃 *-chiing* ↓; 少息 rest a little, *-shir* ↓. (2) Less, short of measure, inadequate: 短少 short of (money, etc.); 缺少 be in need of (money, a good guide); 你數數錢少了沒有 please count the money and see if the amount is correct; 不多不少 neither more nor less; 十五比十八少了三 15 is 3 less than 18. (3) (In command) equiv. "don't": 少說話 don't talk; 少喫點 don't eat too much; 少管閒事 don't meddle in others' affairs; 少安勿躁 take it easy, don't make a fuss; 少回 (coll.) please don't turn back (to avoid collision). (4) (**shauh*) Young: opp. 老 old: 少年, 少女 *-niarn*, *-nyuu* ↓; 少時, 少日 when one was young; 老少 young and old; 少年老成 an old head on young shoulders; 少不更事 young and inexperienced. (5) (**shauh*) Term attached to mil. rank, as 少將, 少校, 少尉 *-jiahng*, *-shiauh*, *-weih* ↓.

少艾 **shauh-aih*, n., (AC) the young and beautiful.
少白頭 **shauhbairtour*, n., young man with white or grey hair.
少輩兒 **shauhbeh'l*, n., the younger generation of a family.
少不得 *shaau-buh-der*, phr., cannot be avoided; necessary.
少不了 *shaau-buh-liaau*, phr., necessary, indispensable.
少頃 *shaurchiing*, adv., in or after a little while.
少處 *shaau'chu*, phr., 不在少處 (one has spent) not a little amount (also 少數 *shaau'shu*).
少東 **shauhdung*, n., formerly (rare), son of the owner or master.
少婦 **shauhfuh*, n., a young woman.
少腹 **shauhfur*, n., the area below the navel (also called 小腹).
少府 **shauhfuu*, n., (1) (Chin. med.) point in third joint of the small finger; (2) (AC, MC) an official title.
少長 **shauh-jaang*, n., the young ones and their elders.
少掌櫃的 **shauh-jaanggueih'de*, n., son of shop owner.
少間 *shaaujiahn*, adv., after a little while: 疾少間 (AC) after slight recovery from illness.
少將 **shauhjiahng*, n., (mil.) major general.
少壯 **shauhjuahng*, adj. & n., young and able-bodied (persons): 少壯派 the younger group in a political party or other organization.
少刻 *shaaukeh*, adv., in a short moment.
少牢 **shauhlaur*, n., (AC) lamb and pig used in sacrifice.
少禮 *shaur-lii*, phr., (modest) 上回我少禮了 last time I was deficient in manners (failed to attend celebration), cf. 失[△]禮 12.81.
少奶奶 **shauh-naai'nai*, n., address or reference to young mistress of house or to daughter-in-law.
少年 **shauhniarn*, n. & adj., young; young person; 少年的時候 when one is young: 少年人 young people.
少女 **shauhnyuu*, n., a young girl.
少陪 *shaau-peir*, phr., phrase used when begging to be excused: 少陪了.
少小 **shauhshiaau*, adv., as in 少小的時候 when young.
少像 **shauhshiahng*, adj., as in 看起來挺少像的: looking quite young.
少校 **shauhshiauh*, n., (mil.) major.
少息 *shaaushir*, phr., (1) rest a little; (2) (mil.) at ease.
少數(兒) *shaaushuh'l*, n., a small number (of people, things); minority.
少時 *shaaushyr*, phr., (1) after or in a little moment; (2) (**shauh-*) phr., when young.
少選 *shaurshyuaan*, adv., (dial.) in a moment.
少許 *shaurshyuu*, adj. & adv., a little, slightly: 少許不舒服 slightly unwell.
少算 *shaausuahn*, v. i., to reduce price to an old customer.
少停 *shaau-tirng*, adv., after or in a moment.
少頭 *shaau'tou*, n., discount in price.
少子 **shauhtzyy*, n., youngest son.
少微 *shaauwei*, adv., slightly.
少尉 **shauhweih*, n., (mil.) second lieutenant.
少焉 *shaau'yan*, phr., (LL) after a while.
少陽 *shauhyarng*, n., (Chin. physiol.) the liver and the digestive system.
少爺 **shauh'ye*, n., address and reference to son of master, or to young man of upper-class family.
少陰 *shauhyin*, n., (Chin. physiol.) the heart and the kidney.

少有 *shauryoou*, adj., rare: 少有的事情 a rare occurence.

§ 22.93 (丨/く)

婁 22.93

lour.

N. A surname.

虫 22.93

hueei (**churng*).

N. (1) Anc. var. of 虺 31.70. (2) (**churng*) Abbr. of 蟲 22.93; a radical for insects, see 22D.

蟲 22.93

churng.
[Abbr. 虫]

N. Insect, worm: 蟲蝕 worm-eaten; 蟲霜水旱 insect pest, frost, flood and drought, the four calamities for farmers (農民四害); 蟲毒 *-haih*↓; 益蟲, 害蟲 useful, harmful insects; 幼蟲 young insect, larva; 毒蟲 poisonous insect; 微生蟲 bacteria; 生蟲 putrefy and grow worms; 除蟲, 滅蟲 to exterminate insects; 滅蟲粉 insecticide; 蟲魚 insects and fishes, oft. mentioned as a field of Chin. painting; 蟲吃牙 decayed tooth.

蟲白蠟 *churng-bairlah*, n., white wax produced by certain insects.
蟲害 *churnghaih*, n., insect pest.
蟲篆 *churng-juahn*, n., (1) the *juahn* or seal script on anc. bronze; (2) (AC) (fig.) insignificant decorative skill.
蟲豸 *churngjyh*, n., (LL) the insect world; (fig.) (abuse) you vermin!
蟲兒 *churng'l*, n., (1) a worm; (2) (sl.) 我不像是這裏頭的蟲兒 don't take me for one of the inside party.
蟲媒花 *churngmeir-hua*, n., flowers fertilized by insects.
蟲子 *churngtz*, n., a worm; (fig.) 慈善蟲子 one who makes a living by charity organization.
蟲災 *churngtzai*, n., insect pest.
蟲(兒)眼 *churng('l)yaan*, n., hole eaten by insect.

蜚 22.93

feei (**fei*)

N. (AC) cockroach, also called 蟑螂; a grain-eating insect.

V.t. (**fei*) (AC) var. of 飛 to fly.

蜚聲 **feisheng*, adj., be well-known: 蜚聲國際 internationally well-known.
蜚語 **feiyuu*, n., flying, baseless rumors.

尝 22.93

charng.
[Abbr. of 嘗 22.41]

SECTION 22A

§ 22A.00 (忄/亅)

悖 22A.00–1

beih (rarely **bor*).
[Cogn. 背]

Adj. (1) Against, contrary to: 悖禮 (AC) contrary to good form; 悖情 against human nature. (2) Lawless, offensive, violent: 悖出悖入 (or 悖而出者, 亦悖而入) what is obtained illegally will be lost in the same manner; 狂悖 irresponsible and unruly; see compp.↓.

悖晦 *beih-'huei*, (wr. 背晦), adj., in senile decay, confused in thinking.
悖謾 *beihmahn*, adj., insolent.
悖謬 *beihmiouh*, adj., heretical, absurd, morally wrong (opinions).
悖逆 *beihnih*, adj., disloyal (of sons, with strong condemnation); rebellious: 悖逆不道 offensive to all established values.

忖 22A.00–1

tsuun.

V.i. To conjecture what is in another's mind (related 揣 10A.42): 忖度, 忖摸 *-duoh*, *-mo*↓; 忖想 *-shiaang*↓.

忖度 *tsuunduoh*, v.i. & t., to surmise (what another is thinking).
忖量 *tsuun-liarng* (-'liang), v.i. & t., see *-duoh*↑.
忖摸 *tsuun'mo*, v.i. & t., see *-duoh*↑.
忖想 *tsurnshiaang*, v.i., to imagine, wonder.
忖思 *tsuunsy*, v.i., ditto.

慱 22A.00-1

tuarn.

Adj. (AC for modn. 團): 勞心慱慱 my heart is turning round and round with sorrow.

恃 22A.00-1

shyh.

N. (1) (LL) support, esp. of parents: 失恃 lost mother; 慈恃 mother as child's support; 嚴恃 father. (2) A mainstay or support.

V. t. To rely on (s.t.) and step out of bounds: 恃財, 恃勢 rely on wealth, position, to commit s.t.; 恃強 rely on force; 恃衆 rely on multitude; 恃愛, 恃寵 rely on master's or superior's love and indulgence.

惻 22A.00-4

tseh.

V.t. & adj. Feel compassion; compassionate.

惻愴 *tsehchuahng*, adj., saddened at heart.
惻怛 *tsehdar*, adj., (AC) concerned, worried.
惻然 *tsehrarn*, adj., disconsolate, disconcerted.
惻惻 *tsehtseh*, adj., sad, saddened; concerned, worried.
惻隱 *tsehyiin*, adj., merciful, compassionate: 惻隱之心 the sense of mercy.

憫 22A.00-5

miin.

V. i. Feel for people in sorrow or trouble: esp. 憐憫 have pity for; 悲天憫人 cosmic pity, pity for all mankind, broad-hearted kindness.

憫恤 *miinshyuh*, v. i. & t., take pity on (person), feel for fellow being.
憫惻 *miintseh*, v. i. & t., ditto.

惇 22A.00-6

dun.

Adj. Sincere, friendly (cogn. with 敦).

愉 22A.00-8

yur.

Adj. Happy, pleased: 愉快 *-kuaih* ↓; 歡愉 happy; 不愉 (LL) displeased; 愉色 pleasant expression.

愉快 *yurkuaih*, adj., happy, pleased; comfortable.
愉樂 *yurleh*, adj., happy, pleased; n., amusement, distraction.
愉逸 *yuryih*, adv., contented and free.
愉悅 *yuryueh*, adv., pleased.

悧 22A.00-9

lih.

[Var. of 俐 91A.00]

悸 22A.00-9

jih.

V. i. Be fearful, tremble: 心悸 (of heart) palpitate from fear; 驚悸 be shaken with astonishment, be shocked.

悸動 *jihduhng*, v. i., (of heart) palpitate from nervousness.
悸慄 *jihlih*, v. i., tremble with fear.

惸 22A.00-9

chyurng.

Adj. (1) (AC) orphaned, lonely: 惸獨 orphaned; 惸嫠 widow. (2) (AC) 惸惸 depressed (cf. var. 煢 91.70).

---

§ 22A.01 (忄/小)

怵 22A.01-1

chuh.

V.i. To shiver, quiver: 怵惕 *-tih*↓; 驚心怵目 be thoroughly frightened.

Adj. (1) Sad, grieved. (2) Shy: 怵頭, 怵場 *-tour, -chaang*↓.

怵場 *chuhchaang*, adj., (coll.) shy to meet people.
怵迫 *chuhpoh*, v.t., to threaten and induce.
怵然 *chuhrarn*, adj. & adv., in a frightened manner.
怵惕 *chuhtih*, v.i., to tremble, shiver, shudder.
怵頭 *chuhtour*, adj., see *-chaang*↑.

悚 22A.01-1

suung (**surng*).

Adj. & adv. (1) Shivering in fright. (2) (**surng*) (Coll.) chicken-hearted(ly), soft(ly).

悚慄 *suunglih*, v. i., to feel a thrill or shock: 悚慄電影 a thriller movie (like Hitchcock's).
悚然 *suungrarn*, adj., feeling frightened, shivering.

愫 22A.01-1

suh.

N. Sincere feeling: 情愫 person's mood, heart-felt feeling.

慄 22A.01-3

lih.

Adj. & adv. Trembling(ly), cautious(ly): 戰慄 trembling with fear; 慄慄危懼 trembling and fearful.

慄冽 *lihlieh*, adj., cold, chilly (also wr. 溧冽).
慄慄 *lihlih*, adj., (1) fearful; (2) trembling with cold.

憬 22A.01-4

jiing.

V. i. (1) Awaken: 憬然 come to realize; 憬悟 realize what is right and what is wrong. (2) Think vaguely: 憧憬 entertain fond thoughts of.

懍 22A.01-6

liin.

V. i. Tremble with fear.

Adj. Inspiring fear (cf. 凜).

懍慄 *liinlih*, v. i., fear and tremble.
懍懍 *lirnliin*, adj., fearful.
懍然 *liinrarn*, adj., inspiring fear; (of portrait) alive.

§ 22A.02 (忄/㇏)

悵 22A.02-5

chahng.

Adj. Regretful, disappointed: 惆悵 ditto; see compp.↓.

悵悵 *chahngchahng*, adj., (LL) regretfully.
悵然 *chahngrarn*, adj., disappointed: 悵然若失 feel lost.
悵惋 *chahngwaan*, adj., regretful, disappointed, sorry.
悵惘 *chahngwahng*, adj., ditto (also wr. 悵望).

恨 22A.02-5

hehn.

N. Hatred: 懷恨在心 cherish a grudge or hatred; 深仇大恨 great enmity, deep hostility; 長恨歌 Song of Eternal Regret.

V.i. & t. (1) To hate: 恨入骨髓 to hate with all one's soul ("to the marrow"); 恨他 hate him. (2) To be exasperated, anxious: 恨不得 very anxious to: 恨不得插翅歸家 wish only if one could grow wings and fly home; 恨他不肯寫信 be exasperated at his failure to write. (3) To regret: 悔恨 regret deeply (some past event); 可恨 it is regrettable that, also hateful.

Adj. (1) Regretful. (2) Hateful: 恨事 something lamented; 恨人 a frustrated man given to regrets.

懷 22A.02-6

huair.

N. (1) Bosom: 抱在懷中 carry in the bosom, hug; 坐懷不亂 was not disturbed with a woman in his lap; 胸懷 a person's chest or heart, feelings, (fig.) breadth of view, capacity; 掛懷 always on the mind; 不能去懷 cannot forget; 放懷, 開懷暢飲 drink to one's content. (2) A surname.

V. i. & t. (1) To harbor (thought, revenge), cherish, dwell on: 不懷好意, 懷有惡意 do s. t. with malice; 懷有異心 harbor disloyal thoughts; 懷私心 with selfish motives; 懷古, 懷舊 cherish the past; 懷土 (LL) be homesick, think of home; 懷戀 *-liahn*, 懷念 *-niahn*, 懷春 *-chun*↓; 懷恩 remember always with gratitude; 懷恨, 懷怨 *-hehn*, *-yuahn*↓. (2) To carry concealed: 身懷利刃 carrying concealed a sharp knife; 懷璧其罪 (allu.) one's only crime was only to carry a jade; 懷胎, 懷孕, 懷妊 *-tai*, *-yuhn*, *-rehn* (for pregnancy)↓; 懷着他的孩子 conceived his child (in her body). (3) To cause to remember, to win the heart of: 以懷諸侯 to win the loyalty of the feudal princes; 以懷遠方 to win over those in distant lands with kindness; 少者懷之 the young love and admire him.

懷抱 *huairbauh*, n., (1) the breast, embrace: 投他的懷抱 (oft. of homeland) seek its embrace, come home to; (2) one's ambition: 很有一些懷抱 (=抱負 10A.70) entertain great ambitions; 懷抱兒 period of infancy: 這孩子從懷抱兒就愛鬧病 this child has been prone to illness since infancy; (3) v. t., to carry in the breast: 懷抱着小孩.

懷春 *huairchun*, v. i., (AC, LL) be in love: 有女懷春 there is a girl in love.

懷恨 *huair-hehn*, v. i. & t., to hate (person), to harbor grudge against.

懷戀 *huair-liahn*, v. t., to remember fondly always (person, old country).

懷念 *huair-niahn*, v. t., to remember always.

懷妊 *huair-rehn*, v. i., to conceive, be pregnant.

懷柔 *huairrour*, adj., as in 懷柔政策 policy of conciliation, policy of winning over conquered tribes with restraint and kindness.

懷想 *huairshiaang*, v. t., to remember and think about.

懷胎 *huair-tai*, v. i., (woman) to conceive.

懷藏 *huairtsarng*, v. t., to conceal (weapon, jewel, etc.).

懷疑 *huairyir*, n. & v.i. & t., (to) doubt, entertain doubt.

懷憂 *huair-you*, v. i., be concerned, worried.

懷怨 *huair-yuahn*, v. i., harbor a grudge.

懷孕 *huair-yuhn*, v. i., to conceive (child).

慷 22A.02-6

kang (also *kaang*).

[Interch. 忼]

Adj. & adv. Generous (ly).

慷慨 *kaangkaih*, adj. & adv., generous(ly): 這人很慷慨 this man is very generous; 慷慨捐輸 generously contribute funds; 慷慨激昂 (of denouncement, declaration, atmosphere) moving, vehement, excited (over some good cause); 慷慨就義 die a martyr's death, went to his death bravely (also wr. 忼慨).

悢 22A.02-6

liahng.

Adj. 悢悢 (AC) sad (at parting, etc.).

§ 22A.10 (忄/十)

悻 22A.10-1

shihng.

Adj. & adv. 悻悻 gruff, -ly, in surly manner.

悼 22A.10-2

dauh.

V.i. Think of the deceased, mourn the dead: 悼亡 mourn deceased wife or just lose wife; 追悼會 memorial service or ceremony for deceased; 悲悼, 哀悼 (v. i. & adj.) bemoan, feel sad, shocked; 悼念 think of the one who is gone.

憐 22A.10-2

liarn.

V.t. Feel tender toward, be kind towards (poor and helpless): 可憐 (a) pitiful, (b) endearing; 怪可憐, 可憐見 very pitiful, very tender and helpless; see compp.↓.

憐愛 *liarnaih*, v.t., love, esp. tender ones.

憐憫 *liarnmiin*, v.t. & adj., merciful, take pity on.

憐惜 *liarn(')shir*, v.t., feel tender and protective toward (child, etc.).

憐恤 *liarn'shyu*, v.t., to pity; to help (the helpless, orphaned).

怦 22A.10-3

peng.

V. i. (Of heart) palpitate, usu. 怦然心動 palpitating with excitement.

怦怦 *pengpeng*, adj., palpitating with excitement; (AC) keen and straightforward, in excited state.

慴 22A.10-3

jer (also *sheh*).

V. i. To submit in fear: 慴服 *-fur* ↓; 慴于淫威 terrorized by tyranical methods.

慴服 *jerfur*, v. i., submit in fear.

慴慴 *jerjer*, v. i., retreat in fear.

慴息 *jershir*, v. i., hold breath in fear.

憚 22A.10-4

dahn.

V. t. (LL) fear, avoid, shirk: 過則勿憚改 don't be afraid to correct

亅	小	⺗	十	土	ナ	卄	⺊	丨	一	丅	フ	口	区	冈	乛	厂	尸	亠	广	宀	丶	乚	弋	心	八	人	乂	ー	一	丿	𠂉	く
00	01	02	10	11	12	20	21	22	30	31	32	40	41	42	50	51	52	60	61	62	63	70	71	72	80	81	82	83	90	91	92	93

mistakes; 小人無所忌憚 the small man acts without any (moral) restraint; 不憚煩 do not mind all the trouble, take all the trouble.

悍 22A.10-4

hahn.

Adj. (1) Brave, tough (general): 悍銳 brave and well-trained (soldiers); 短小精悍 (of person) small, compactly built, and very capable. (2) Ferocious, vindictive: 悍婦 a ferocious woman; 悍室, 悍妻 a shrew; 凶悍, 強悍 rude, fierce, violent, terrible (enemy, bandit); 悍然不顧 rudely brush aside; 悍藥 medicine of violent nature.

懌 22A.10-4

yih.

Adj. (LL) pleased, happy (=悅).

悴 22A.10-6

tsueih.

Adj. (1) Weary, depressed in appearance: 憔$^{\Delta}$悴 22A.63. (2) (LL) sorrowful.

惲 22A.10-6

yuhn.

N. A surname.

忤 22A.10-9

wuu.

V. t. To defy, disobey (wish, order): 忤物 cannot get along with people; 忤俗 defy custom.

Adj. Defiant, disobedient: 忤逆 *-nih* ↓.

忤 逆 *wuunih*, adj. & n., disobedient, -ce, esp. disobedience to parents, a grave crime formerly punishable by law.

懈 22A.10-9

shieh.

V. i. & adj. To relax, be relaxed; slowed down, diminished: 鬆懈 slow down or slowed down in work; 努力不懈 strive without cease; 夙夜匪懈 morning and night without cease.

懈 怠 *shiehdaih*, v. i. & adj., be idle, idle about, be delinquent in duty.

懈 慢 *shiehmahn*, adj., careless in manners or work.

懈 弛 *shiehshyy*, v. i. & adj., slow down, slowed down.

懈 意 *shiehyih*, v. i. & adj., show slacking of interest; lethargy, -aic; apathy, -hetic.

§ 22A.11 (忄/土)

性 22A.11-1

shihng.

N. (1) In modn. terms, equivalent of *-ness*, *-ity* for expressing abstract notions: 可能性 possibility, from 可能 possible; 複雜性 complexity, from 複雜 complex; 必要性 necessity; 正確性 correctness; 準確性 accuracy; 永久性 permanence; 臨時性 temporary character; 危險性 dangerous character (of disease); 硬性 rigidity, inflexibility; 彈性 flexibility; 爆發性 explosiveness; also for distinguishing types of disease: 急性 acute; 慢性 chronic. (2) Nature, inborn nature: 天命之謂性, 率性之謂道, 修道之謂教 (中庸) "What is God-given is called nature; to follow that nature is called the way; to cultivate the way is called culture"; 性與天道, 不得而聞 Confucius seldom talked about nature and Heaven's way; 性理, 性命 *-lii*, *-mihng* ↓. (3) What is instinctive, inherent: 性能 *-nerng* ↓; 天性, 本性 man's inborn nature, also original nature of man; 出於本性 comes from man's nature; 人性 human nature; 禽獸之性 beastly nature; 獸性 beastliness; 生性如此 one is born like that; 盡人之性 that man may fulfill what is born in him; 盡物之性 that all nature may fulfill the laws of their being; 情性 born nature; 記性 power of memory; 性質 *-jyr* ↓; 性善, 性惡 philosophical argument whether man is born good or born bad; 性欲 instinctive (sexual) desire(s). (4) Sex, sexual desire or impulse: 兩性 the two sexes; 男性 the male sex; 女性 the female sex; 性衝動 the sexual impulse; 性教育 sex education; 性愛, 性病, 性交, 性感 *-aih*, *-bihng*, *-jiau*, *-gaan* ↓. (5) Gender: 陰性, 陽性, 中性 feminine, masculine, neuter gender; 通性 universal gender; also universality. (6) Personal temperament, character, personality: 性情 *-chirng* ↓; 心性 man's heart and character: 心性不良 (man) of bad character; 品性, 德性 character; 性靈, 性格, 性根 *-lirng*, *-ger*, *-gen* ↓; 性子, 性急 *-tz*, *-jir* ↓; 牽$^{\Delta}$性 60.10; 索$^{\Delta}$性 10.01.

性 愛 *shihng-aih*, n., sexual love.

性 別 *shihngbier*, n., sex of man or animal (male or female).

性 病 *shihng-bihng*, n., venereal disease.

性 氣 *shihngchih*[1], n., (MC) personality, temperament: 性氣很烈 of strong temperament; 性氣太壞 of very bad temper or character.

性器 *shihngchih²*, n., sexual organ.

性情 *shihngchirng*, n., (1) a man's temperament (hard, irascible, soft, yielding, etc.); (2) (-'*ching*) bad temper, see *-tz*↓.

性地 *shihngdih*, n., (rare) a man's basic endowment: 性地聰明 by nature intelligent.

性分 *shihngfehn*, n., a man's temperament (good, bad).

性感 *shihnggaan*, (1) n., sex appeal; (2) adj., appealing to sex, sexy: 性感文學 sexy literature; 性感缺乏症 frigidity.

性根 *shihnggen*, n., (Budd.) man's inborn root of character, basic endowment (refined, coarse, intelligent, stupid); 劣根性 or 性根 stupidity, coarseness of nature.

性格 *shihngger*, n., character, personal type, temperament: 性格明星 movie actor or actress specializing in portraying human character; 性格不合 incompatibility of temperament.

性徵 *shihngjeng*, n., characteristics, specific features.

性交 *shihngjiau*, n., sexual intercourse.

性急 *shihngjir*, adj., impatient: 這個人性急得很 this man is very impatient.

性質 *shihngjyr*, n., qualities of material (iron, copper, etc.); character (of a play, novel, propaganda, etc.); nature (of task, work, duties, research, organization).

性理 *shihnglii*, n., the Neo-Confucian philosophy (理學) of human reason and nature.

性靈 *shihnglirng*, n., soul, personality; 性靈文學 school of literature which emphasizes expression of personal views and feelings.

性命 *shihngmihng*, n., (1) life: 性命交關, 性命攸關 a matter of life and death; 摧殘性命 destroy life; (2) (phil.) the study of man's origin and destiny (Neo-Confucian).

性能 *shihngnerng*, n., fitness or capacity for work, capabilities (of machine, camera, airplane), potency (of drug).

性向 *shihngshiahng¹*, n., disposition; 性向測驗 aptitude test.

性相 *shihngshiahng²*, n., (Budd.) nature and manifestations in man.

性子 *shihngtz*, n., (1) temperament: 性子不好 bad temper; (2) anger: 等我性子上來 see when I lose my temper.

性慾 *shihngyuh*, n., sexual desire (also wr. 性欲).

懂 22A.11-2

duung.

V. i. & t. Understand: 懂不懂 do you understand? 我懂了, 懂得 I understand; 你懂得什麽 you know nothing; 懂道理, 懂人情 understand how to behave; 懂門路 know the ropes; 懂人意 (dog, animals) understand master's wishes.

懽 22A.11-2

huan.

[Var. of 歡 20S.81]

怪 22A.11-3

guaih.

N. An evil force: 妖怪 a devil; 鬼怪 a demon; 神怪 a supernatural beings, spirits; 怪物 *-wuh*↓.

V. i. & t. (1) V. i., show surprise or astonishment: 驚怪 be astonished; 可怪 strange and inexplicable; 不足怪 nothing surprising; 難怪 no wonder that; 怪不得 ditto: 怪不得老來找你, 原來是想借錢 no wonder that he often came to see you, for he wanted to borrow money; 莫怪 please don't be surprised. (2) To blame, rebuke: 怪不得他 don't blame him; 不能怪你 you are not to blame; 見怪 be offended; 責怪 to blame and scold; 別怪, 莫怪 please don't be offended.

Adj. Strange, uncanny, abnormal, unusual: 怪事 a strange affair; 怪談 tall tales; 怪人 an eccentric; 怪物 *-wuh*↓; 怪異 *-yih*↓; 奇怪 extraordinary, unusual; 怪癖 *-pih*↓; 怪模怪樣 queer in appearance and manners; 怪誕 *-dahn*↓; 怪現象 a strange phenomenon.

Adv. Very: 怪可憐 so very pitiable; 怪貴的 unusually costly; 怪難看的 extraordinarily ugly.

怪誕 *guaihdahn*, adj., fantastic, unbelievable: 怪誕離奇 unheard-of; 怪誕不經 nonsensical, absurd, (of stories, etc.) tall.

怪道 *guaihdauh*, adv. phr., no wonder that: 原來便是尊翁, 怪道面目相似 so he is your father, no wonder that he looks so much like you.

怪癖 *guaihpih*, n., eccentricity; adj., (of persons) eccentric, odd, queer, self-opinionated.

怪物 *guaihwuh*, n., (1) a monster or monstrosity; (2) an eccentric person.

怪異 *guaihyih*, n., supernatural events.

惺 22A.11-4

shing.

N. Alert, awake.

惺惺 *shingshing*, adj., (1) awake; (2) intelligent: 惺惺惜惺惺 the intelligent ones sympathize with their own kind (when they suffer); (3) 假惺惺 those who pretend, affect (to be friendly, etc.); (4) 常惺惺 (Neo-Confucian) always holding mind alert or free of passion.

惺忪 *shingsung*[1], adj., shadowy, hazy, (like moving shadows): 睡眼惺忪 have a drowsy look.

惺鬆 *shingsung*[2], adj., ditto.

惺悟 *shingwuh*, v.i., become alert, awake to.

懼 22A.11-4

jyuh.

[Pop. 惧]

V.i. & t. To fear, be afraid: 恐懼 fear(ful), dread(ful); 畏懼 be afraid, lose courage, stand in awe of; 懼怕 *-pah* ↓; 懼內 *-neih* ↓.

懼內 *jyuh-neih*, v.i. & adj., (be) henpecked. 「be afraid.

懼怕 *jyuhpah*, v.t., to fear, dread,

慳 22A.11-5

chian.

Adj. (1) Miserly, niggardly. (2) 慳錢 thin worn-out copper coin of low value.

慳吝 *chianlihn*, n., avarice; adj., miserly, niggardly.

慳囊 *chiannarng*, adj., niggardly.

憧 22A.11-6

chung.

Adj. Stupid: 愚憧.

憧憬 *chungjiing*, v. t., to long for greatly, to remember vividly (some dream, distant or past event).

惟 22A.11-9

weir.

V.i. (1) (AC) to think, ponder: 思惟 ditto (also wr. 維). (2) (AC) u.f. 爲 be: 共惟帝臣 serve together as ministers.

Adv. & conj. & prep. (1) Only: 惟一 only one; 惟有 only have; 惟恐 only fear; 惟願 only wish; oft. in form 惟＋object＋是 vb.: 惟命是聽 only listen to orders; 惟汝是問 only you have to answer (for any mistake); 惟我獨尊 terribly self-conceited; 惟心, 惟物 *-shin, -wuh* ↓; 惟理主義 rationalism. (2) Very: 惟妙惟肖 (of painting, portrayal) strikingly true to life.

惟獨 *weirdur*, adv., (1) only; (2) except.

惟心 *weir-shin*, adj., idealistic (phil.); 惟心主義 philosophic idealism (more commonly wr. 唯心).

惟物 *weir-wuh*, adj., materialistic (philosophy); 惟物主義 materialism; 惟物史觀 materialistic interpretation of history (more commonly wr. 唯物).

惟一 *weiryi*, adj., only one: 惟一上帝 only one God; 惟一愛人 one's only love.

惶 22A.11-9

huarng.

Adj. Agitated, flurried.

惶惑 *huarnghouh*, adj., nervous: 惶惑不安 confused and uneasy.

惶惶 *huarnghuarng*, adj., agitated: 人心惶惶 people are agitated, nervous.

惶遽 *huarngjyuh*, adj. & adv., sudden, -ly.

惶恐 *huarngkuung*, adj., in fear: 誠惶誠恐 in fear and tredipation (used in memorial to emperor).

§ 22A.21 (忄/乚)

恇 22A.21-5

kuang.

Adj. Frightened, fearful.

恇怯 *kuangchieh*, adj., (LL) timid.

恇駭 *kuanghaih*, adj., (LL) frightened. 「fearful.

恇懼 *kuangjyuh*, adj., (LL) afraid,

恇擾 *kuangraau*, v.t., (LL) to harass. 「pressed, harassed.

恇勷 *kuangrarng*, adj., (LL) hard

慪 22A.21-5

ouh.

V.i. To antagonize, rouse one's spleen (interch. 嘔 40A.21): 慪氣 set one's blood up, to arouse hostility toward (person).

愜 22A.21-5

chieh.

V.t. & adj. Satisfy, -ing; satisfactory: 愜情, 愜心 satisfying; see 愜意, 愜懷 *-yih, -huair* ↓.

愜當 *chiehdahng*, adj., just right, to the point: 愜當之論 a just remark. 「satisfying, -fied.

愜懷 *chiehhuair*, adj., satisfactory,

愜意 *chiehyih*, adj., pleasing, -sed, satisfying, -fied: 愜意貴當 just, appropriate (remark, opinion).

忙 22A.21-6

marng.

Adj. Busy, pressed with work; bustling, hustling: 忙得很, 忙不過來 very busy; 忙於 to have one's hand full, to be busily engaged in; 不要忙 take it slowly; 忙甚麽 what's the hurry? 急急忙忙 in a great hurry; 忙裏偷閒 take a breathing spell in the midst of pressing affairs; 匆忙 hurried; 慌忙 in a flurry, flustered; 幫忙 help.

忙合 *marng'he*, v.i., to help.
忙亂 *marngluahn*, adj., (affairs) pressing; flurried, disorderly.
忙碌 *marngluh*, adj., busy; also 忙忙碌碌 *marng'mang-luh'lu*.
忙忙叨叨 *marng'mang-tau'tau*, adj., very busy.
忙迫 *marngpoh*, adj., busy, urgent.

慆 22A.21-9

tau.

V. i. & t. (1) (AC) to please: 慆心 gladden one's heart. (2) (AC) cover up: 以樂慆憂 make merry to hide one's sorrows.

Adj. (1) (AC) dissolute: 慆淫 live a licentious life. (2) (AC) doubtful, dubious, uncertain: 天命不慆久矣 long has there been no doubt of Heaven's mandate.

Adv. 慆慆 for a long time: 慆慆不歸 has been away from home for many long years.

§ 22A.22 (忄/丨)

慚 22A.22-1

tsarn.
[Var. 慙]

V.i. & adj. Feel ashamed, shameful: 羞慚 ashamed, shy; 慚色 expression of remorse; 自慚形穢 (court.) ashamed of one's own unworthiness.

慚德 *tsarn-der*, n., (court.) flaw in one's character.
慚愧 *tsarnkueih*, adj., ashamed.
慚怍 *tsarntzuoh*, adj. & n., (LL) (court.) ashamed, -ness.

怖 22A.22-1

buh.

N. Terror, esp. 恐怖 terror; 恐怖政策 policy of terrorism.

V.i. & adj. Fear, afraid: 恐怖 terrorized; 可怖 (LL) terrible, horrifying.

忡 22A.22-2

chung.

Adj. (AC) sad, heavy of heart: 憂心忡忡 ditto.

忡怔 *chungjeng*, adj., (LL) uneasy, distressed.

悱 22A.22-2

feei.

Adj. Smouldering, suppressed (anger, determination): 不悱不發 "Will not explain to one not determined to learn,"—Confucius.

悱悱 *feirfeei*, adj., (AC) desirous but unable to speak out.
悱憤 *feeifehn*, adj., peeved, infuriated, vexed; with firm resolve (to succeed).
悱惻 *feeitseh*, adj., sorry for (people, country).

怫 22A.22-2

fur (**feih*).

Adj. & adv. (1) Depressed. (2) (**feih*) Angry: 怫然 angrily, abruptly.

怀 22A.01-3

huair.
[Abbr. of 懷 22A.02]

忭 22A.22-6

biahn.

Adj. Happy: 歡忭, 欣忭 happy, esp. on occasions.

Adv. Happily: 忭頌, 忭躍 happily celebrate with song, felicitate.

懠 22A.22-6

chir.

Adj. (AC) furious: 天之方懠 Heaven is greatly angered.

悌 22A.22-8

tih.

Adj. Brotherly: 孝悌 being good son and good brother; 愷悌 friendly and courteous.

慊 22A.22–8

chiahn.

Adj. Bashful, uneasy: 慊慊於心 feel uneasy.

悕 22A.22–8

shi.

V.i. (AC) (1) To wish. (2) To grieve.

忻 22A.22–9

shin.
[Related 欣 90S.81]

怍 22A.22–9

tzuoh.

V.i. To turn pale (red), blush.

Adj. Ashamed: 愧怍, 慚怍 embarrassed, abashed; 怍色 an ashamed look; 仰不愧於天, 俯不怍於人 have nothing to be ashamed of before God or man.

§ 22A.30 (忄/一)

愷 22A.30–2

kaai.

N. Rare var. of 凱 victory.

Adj. Gentle, contented: 愷惻, 愷澤 kind, -ness; graciousness.

愷悌 *kaaitih*, adj., (LL) friendly, amiable: (AC) 愷悌君子 amiable gentleman.

怔 22A.30–3

jeng (*leng).

Adj. (1) Afraid, awe-stricken, nonplussed: 怔忪, 怔營 *-jung*, *-yirng* ↓. (2) (*leng) Stunned: 怔住了 stunned speechlees; 發怔 become stunned.

怔忡 *jengchung*, (1) n., (disease) heart palpitation; (2) adj., queasy; melancholic.
怔忪 *jengjung*, adj., (AC) agog with fear.
怔營 *jengyirng*, adj., (LL) trembling in fear.

恆 22A.30–3

herng.
[Pop. 恒]

N. A surname.

Adj. (1) Lasting, enduring: 永恆 lasting, permanent; 恆久, 恆常 *-jioou*, *-chaan* ↓. (2) Persistent: 有恆 has persistence; 恆心 *-shin* ↓. (3) Common: 恆常 usual, common; 恆言 (LL) a common saying; 恆例 ordinary practice; 人之恆情 a common failing, feeling or reaction.

Adv. (LL) often (for vern. 常): 恆念 often think of.

恆產 *herngchaan*, n., real estate, property, land: 有恆產 (AC) have land and property.
恆等式 *herngdeeng-shyh*, n., (math.) identical equation, identity.
恆河 *Hengher*, n., the Ganges: 恆河沙數 innumerable like the sands of the Ganges.
恆勁 *herngjihn*, n., persistent strength or power, staying power, stamina.
恆久 *herngjioou*, adj., endurable, long lasting.
恆心 *herngshin*, n., persistence, constancy of purpose.
恆星 *herngshing*, n., (astron.) fixed star.
恆溫層 *herngwentserng*, n., (geog.) stratosphere, stratum of constant temperature.

怛 22A.30–4

dar.

Adj. (AC) worried, troubled, saddened: 惻^Δ怛 22A.00.

慍 22A.30–4

yuhn.
[Usu. wr. 愠]

N. & v. i. Resentment; resent.

慍恨 *yuhnhehn*, n., resentment.
慍怒 *yuhnnuh*, n., chagrin.
慍容 *yuhn-rurng*, n., face of resentment.
慍色 *yuhn-seh*, n., ditto.

忸 22A.30–5

nyuh (also *nyuu*).

Adj. (1) Bashful. (2) Var. of 狃 91C.30.

忸怩 *nyuhnir* (also *nioou-*), adj., bashful, uneasy.

悾 22A.30-6

kung.

Adj. (1) Simple-minded. (2) Earnest.

恤 22A.30-9

shyuh.

V. t. To take pity on, have consideration for: 憐恤 be kind to (the unfortunate); (see interch. 卹 91S.22.)

§ 22A.40 (忄/口)

怙 22A.40-1

huh.

V.t. (1) To rely on, see 怙恃 *-shyh*↓. (2) To persist in evil: 怙惡不悛 to persist in evil and not repent; 失怙 lose father through death.

怙恃 *huhshyh*, n., (1) backing; (2) (LL) parents' support: 失怙 lose father, 失恃 lose mother.

怗 22A.40-2

*tie (*jan).*

Adj. (1) (*tie*) Submissive, settled (var. of 帖). (2) (**jan*) Sticky (var. of 沾).

怗服 *tiefur*, adj., quiet, submissive.
怗懘 *janjyh*, adj., (AC) sluggish, blocked.

悟 22A.40-3

wuh.

V. i. & t. (1) To understand, realize or perceive (truth, meaning): 悟道 to come to realize truth of teaching. (2) To waken up, to realize mistake: 醒悟, 悔悟 to repent; 執迷不悟 refuse to realize one's error.

Adj. Quick at understanding: 穎悟 brilliant (mind).

悟性 *wuhshihng*, n., (1) power of understanding, of insight; (2) (Neo-Confu.) to realize man's true nature, to find the soul.

惦 22A.40-6

diahn.

V.t. To remember, think of.

惦記 *diahnjih*, v.t., remember (dear one), have constantly in mind.
惦念 *diahnniahn*, v.t., ditto.

恰 22A.40-8

chiah.

Adv. (1) Just, exactly: 恰好, 恰巧, 恰恰 *-haau, -chiaau, -chiah*↓; 恰似, 恰便似 just like; 恰待, 恰待要 was just going to; 恰恁恃 (MC) ditto; 恰如其分, 恰到好處 just right (in wording, criticism). (2) By chance: 恰遇, 恰逢 meet in chance encounter, also happen to be (Sunday); 恰值 happen to be (not at home, holiday). (3) (MC)＝卻 on the contrary.

恰巧 *chiahchiaau*, adv., it happens, happen to: 恰巧他來 he came in by chance, at the right moment.
恰恰 *chiahchiah*, (1) adv., exactly: 恰恰相反 exactly the opposite; 恰恰好 *--haau*↓; (2) n., cha-cha dance; (3) (MC) (birds) twitter.
恰當 *chiahdahng* (-'*dang*), adj., right in degree or extent: 用字恰當 use the right word in writing.
恰好 *chiahhaau*, adv., (1) by luck: 恰好他進來 by luck he just turned up; also 恰恰好; (2) exactly right (dress length, musical performance, etc.).
恰如 *chiahrur*, adv., just like, seems almost like (being home, etc.).
恰似 *chirhsyh*, adv., see *-rur*↑.
恰纔 *chirhtsair*, adv., just now, then: 恰 or 恰纔飲得三杯 just as (I) had drunk three cups.

愴 22A.40-8

chuahng.

Adj. (LL) forlorn, disconsolate.

愴愴 *chuahngchuahng*, adj., disconsolate, heavy-hearted.
愴悢 *chuahngliahng*, adj., ditto.
愴惻 *chuahngtseh*, adj., ditto.

恬 22A.40-9

tiarn.

Adj. Quiet and contented, calm, tranquil, see compp.↓: 恬不爲怪, 恬不知恥 phr., devoid of all sense of shame, regard calmly s.t. reprehensible.

恬澹(淡) *tiarndahn*, adj., quiet: 恬淡生活 simple and contented life.

恬靜 *tiarnjihng*, adj., tranquil (life, place).

恬然 *tiarnrarn*, adj., contented.

恪 22A.40–9

keh (also *chyueh*).

Adv. Respectfully, carefully: 恪遵, 恪守 carefully obey (laws, orders, tradition).

恪愼 *kehshehn*, adj. & adv., careful, -ly, reverent, -ly.

怡 22A.40–9

yir.

N. A surname.

V.t. To relax: 怡情 *-chirng*↓.

Adj. Happy, content.

怡情 *yirchirng*, v. i., to relax, to enjoy.

怡蕩 *yirdahng*, adj., dissolute, given to sensual pleasures.

怡樂 *yirleh*, n., happiness, contentment; adj., enjoying oneself.

怡然 *yirrarn*, adj., content: 怡然自得 happy and contented.

怡色 *yir-seh*, n., a pleasant countenance.

怡聲 *yir-sheng*, phr., 下氣怡聲 with a subdued and soft voice.

怡顏 *yir-yarn*, n., see *-seh*↑.

怡怡 *yiryir*, adj. & adv., pleasant, -ly, contented (manner), -ly.

怡悅 *yiryueh*, v.i. & adj., (feel) pleased.

§ 22A.41 (忄/囟)

懵 22A.41–2

merng, *meeng*.

Adj. Dull, unaware.

懵懂 *merngduung*, adj., unaware, uncomprehending, dull-witted.

懵憒 *merngkueih*, adj., ditto.

懵懵 *merngmerng* or 懵懵憒憒 *--kueihkueih*, adj., ditto.

懵然 *merng-rarn*, adj., as in 懵然無知 completely in the dark.

惜 22A.41–2

shir.

V. i. & t. (1) To love and care, to love tenderly: 愛惜, 憐惜 to be tender and considerate toward (children, orphans, flowers), to love and care for (what is precious); 惜玉憐香 be tender toward pretty girls. (2) To protect with care, to be sparing in use: 珍惜寶物 to keep treasure with loving care; 惜陰, 惜寸陰 to harness one's time, value every spare moment for study; 惜福 not to squander when one has plenty; 惜墨如金 (of a writer, calligrapher, painter) abstemious in his use of ink; 惜指失掌 save a finger and lose the whole hand; 吝惜 parsimonious. (3) To rue (the hour), be distressed: 可惜 it is a pity; 痛惜前非 repent, regret deeply one's past; 惜別 be distressed at parting.

愊 22A.41–3

bih.

Adj. (LL) Depressed, frustrated.

愊憶 (愊臆, 愊抑) *bihyih*, adj., (LL) depressed.

恓 22A.41–3

shi.

恓惶 *shihuarng*, adj., vexed, troubled; also 恓恓惶惶 (also wr. 栖).

愐 22A.41–3

miaan.

愐懷 *miaanhuair*, v. t., think of (commonly 緬 93B.41).

愐㥏 *miaan'tian*, adj., see 腼⁴腆 42A.41.

悃 22A.41–4

kuun.

N. & adj. (LL) sincerity; sincere: 悃誠 sincerity; 謝悃 (my) sincere gratitude.

慁 22A.41–4

huhn.

[Var. of 慁 41.72]

慴 22A.41–5

jer.

V. i. To fear: 慴伏 submit in fear.

愔 22A.41–6

yin.

愔愔 *yinyin*, adj., (AC) contented, amiable.

憎 22A.41-8

tzeng.

N. Hatred: 愛憎 love and hatred, likes and dislikes.

V. t. To hate, detest, abhor: 憎惡 *-wuh* ↓; 憎恨 *-hehn* ↓; 可憎 abominable, hateful, detestable.

憎恨 *tzenghehn*, v. t., hate intensely, abhor.
憎嫉 *tzengjir*, v. t., ditto.
憎嫌 *tzengshiarn(-'shian)*, v. t., scorn, dislike.
憎惡 *tzengwuh*, v. t., detest, loathe.

惛 22A.41-9

hun.

Adj. Var. of 昏 90.41.

怕 22A.41-9

pah.

N. A surname.

V. i. & t. Fear, be afraid, be afraid of: 怕死 afraid of death; 怕老婆 (coll.) be henpecked; 怕得很 be very much afraid; 怕見人 afraid to see people; 怕什麽 what are you afraid of? or, don't be afraid; 怕事 afraid of upsets, such as lawsuits; 怕的是 what I am afraid of is that; 怕不 afraid not=afraid (double negative, like lest it should not): 怕不也還要三四十天功夫 afraid it will take 30–40 days yet; 怕是不成吧 I rather think, I am afraid, it can't be done; also 恐怕, 畏怕, 懼怕 afraid, fear (vb. & n.).

怕人 *pah-rern*, adj., (1) shy; (2) terrifying, shockingly bad.
怕臊 *pahsauh*, adj., bashful.
怕羞 *pahshiou*, adj., ditto.

惱 22A.41-9

naau.

V.i. Be angry, irritated or filled with hatred: 懊惱 be filled with regret or discontent; 惱恨 *-hehn* ↓; 惱怒 *-nuh* ↓.

Adj. Irritated, irritating, vexed, vexing: 惱巴巴 irritated; 惱忿忿地 vexed; 惱人 irritating; 惱人春色 suffering from love in spring; 惱意 feeling of vexation; 煩惱 vexing, vexations; 惱羞成怒 become angry from embarrassment; 苦惱 in a sad, deplorable state.

惱恨 *naauhehn*, v.i., be irritated and filled with hatred.
惱怒 *naaunuh*, v.i., be irritated and angry.

§ 22A.42 (忄/冈)

情 22A.42-1

chirng.

N. (1) Affection, feeling, sentiment: 七情 (喜怒哀懼愛惡欲) the seven passions (joy, anger, sorrow, fear, love, hatred, desire); 心情, 情緒 one's state of mind; 情感 *-gaan* ↓; 感情 personal affection; 友情, 交情 friendship; 親情 natural affection for one's family; 情同手足 (the two) are close like brothers; 情不自禁 in the grip of passion; 情何以堪 too much to bear; 情有所寄 have a center of affection (as a hobby); 人之常情 it's only human, our common humanity; 情見乎辭 the writer's sincerity shines through his words; 文情並茂 beautiful both in sentiments and in their expressions; 情切 heartfelt; 情切切 so passionate among lovers. (2) Circumstances, esp. feelings of those involved, (usu. expressed in Eng. as "condition" or "the facts of the case" but really "condition as felt," see 軍情, 國情, 民情 below): 情形, 情況, 情狀, 情勢 *-'shirng*, *-kuahng*, *-juahng*, *-shyh*[1] ↓; 事情 affair; 實情 true state of things; 內情, 隱情 unknown factors or relations in the case; 情知故犯 deliberate flouting of the law; 知情不報 fail to report the facts; 不知情 (legal) do not know about the case; 軍情 military situation (at the front), army morale; 國情 the state of the nation; 民情 how the people live and feel; 敵情 the condition, facts about the enemy; 情報 *-bauh* ↓; 商情, 行 (*harng*) 情 condition of the market, the behavior of the prices; 劇情 the story of a play or movie, dramatic force; 聲聞過情 the facts do not quite correspond to one's reputation; 情節 *-'jier* ↓. (3) Personal relations esp. as or set against even-handed justice: 徇情 accommodate personal considerations as against the law; 說情, 求情 intercede and ask for leniency or special consideration; 情面 *-miahn*, the personal face; 賣交情 show special favor to a friend; 盛情難卻 difficult to refuse such kindness; 反面無情 turn a cold shoulder, forget old times; 情分, 情義 *-fehn*, *-yih*[2] ↓. (4) Love of the sexes: 愛情 love; 定情 first declaration and acceptance of love; 偷情 have illicit love; 情婦, 情郎, 情侶, 情人 *-fuh*, *-larng*, *-lyuu*, *-rern* ↓; 情投意合 in

情 惰 惴

love with each other; 薄情, 負情, 情變 change one's love; 多情 affectionate, also sentimental; 情深 deep in love or friendship; 色情 sex (appeal, etc.); 奸情, 姦情 adultery; 情殺 crime of passion; 殉情 die in sacrifice to love. (5) Tone, mood, flavor: 情調, 情趣, 情致 *-diauh*, *-chyuh*, *-jyh* ↓.

情愛 *chirng-aih*, n., love (of friends, man and woman).
情報 *chirngbauh*, n., intelligence reports; 情報司 (局) government information office or service; 情報員 information agent.
情弊 *chirngbih*, n., deliberate irregularities, violations of the law.
情塲 *chirngchaang*, n., drama of love as struggle between suitors and lovers: 情塲失意 disappointed in love, jilted.
情腸 *chirngcharng*, n., passion of love.
情趣 *chirngchyuh*, n., the interesting point or aspect; what is intriguing or fascinating.
情調 *chirngdiauh*, n., fervor, sentimental appeal (intense, indifferent, insipid, etc.); tone and mood.
情竇 *chirngdouh*, n., stirrings of sex: 情竇初開 onset of puberty, awakened interest in opposite sex; 情竇未開 before puberty.
情分 *chirngfehn*, n., what one is entitled to in view of personal relationship: 看我們兩人的情分 for friendship's sake.
情婦 *chirngfuh*, n., sweetheart, mistress, paramour, a kept woman.
情感 *chirnggaan*, n., sentiment, emotion, feeling, friendship between two persons.
情甘 *chirnggan*, adj., willing to (=情願 *-yuahn* ↓).
情海 *chirnghaai*, n., the vast, tumultuous sea of love between man and woman.
情話 *chirnghuah*, n., (1) whispers of love, lovers' talk; (2) heartfelt talk.
情懷 *chirnghuair*, n., state of mind (despondent, reminiscent, etc.).
情節 *chirng'jier*, n., plot or details of a story or play.
情景 *chirngjiing*, n., general aspect, how it looks, a general situation.
情急 *chirngjir*, adj., desperate.
情狀 *chirngjuahng*, n., general condition of things (family circumstances, patient's condition, etc.).
情致 *chirngjyh*, n., an enticing situation, see *-chyuh* ↑.
情款 *chirngkuaan*, n., warm personal feelings.
情況 *chirngkuahng*, n., general aspect or condition (of country, finance, health, etc.).
情郎 *chirnglarng*, n., (LL) a girl's lover.
情理 *chirnglii*, n., reason, reasonableness: 不近情理 unreasonable; 天理人情 nature's justice and human feelings.
情侶 *chirnglyuu*, n., love companion, lovers.
情貌 *chirngmauh*, n., (1) touching sincerity; (2) appearance of person as reflecting state of mind.
情面 *chirngmiahn*, n., "face," social obligation, what is due to person in view of social status.
情人(兒) *chirngrern(-rer'l)*, n., lover (male or female), sweetheart.
情性 *chirngshihng*, n., temperament, born nature or character.
情形 *chirng'shirng*, n., gen. condition, situation (of locality, hospital, finance, country): 最近的情形 the recent situation; 情形不對 the situation looks bad.
情書 *chirngshu*, n., love letter.
情勢 *chirngshyh*[1], n., situation, what promises to develop.
情事 *chirngshyh*[2], n., affairs in gen. (=事情).
情實 *chirngshyr*, n., real facts, esp. illegal actions.
情緒 *chirngshyuh*, n., personal feeling, (friendship, etc.); state of mind, mood: 情緒不好 feel depressed; 情緒緊張 feeling tense.
情素 *chirngsuh*, n., one's heart-true feeling (also wr. 愫).
情死 *chirngsyy*, v. i. & n., die of love; a frustrated lover's suicide.
情態 *chirngtaih*, n., demeanor.
情天 *chirngtian*, n., (LL) the vast realm of love.
情田 *chirngtiarn*, n., human feelings, sentiments and desires considered as a "field" to be cultivated, from (AC) 人情以爲田.
情操 *chirngtsau*, n., noble thoughts and feelings.
情網 *chirngwaang*, n., the snares of love.
情僞 *chirng-weih*, n., (1) sincerity and falseness; (2) see *-bih* ↑.
情意 *chirngyih*[1], n., cordiality; love and affection.
情義 *chirngyih*[2], n., love and honor.
情誼 *chirngyih*[3], n., friendship.
情由 *chirngyour*, n., the reason or origin (of disputes, etc.).
情願 *chirngyuahn*, n. willingness; v. i., to wish, want to, be willing to; adj. & adv., willing, -ly, of one's free will.
情欲 *chirngyuh*[1], n., desire, esp. mortal desire.
情慾 *chirngyuh*[2], n., sexual passion, carnal or sensual desire; 放縱情慾 sensualism.

惰 22A.42-1

duoh.

Adj. Lazy: 懶惰 indolent, lazy; be idle, neglect (work).

惰性 *duohshihng*, n., (1) sloth, laziness; (2) (phys.) inertia.

惴 22A.42-2

jueih.

[Dist. 揣]

V.i. (LL) to tremble in fear.

惴惴 *jueihjueih*, adj., trembling: 惴惴不安 ill at ease.
惴懼 *jueihjyuh*, adj., trembling in fear.
惴恐 *jueihkuung*, adj., ditto.
惴慄 *jueihlih*, adj., ditto.

悄 22A.42-2

chiaau.

Adj. & adv. (1) (AC) sorrowful. (2) Silent, -ly, stealthily: 悄默 silent; 悄冥冥 (MC) silently, also 悄悄冥冥; 靜悄悄 descriptive of quietness (such as night, deserted room); 悄窺 stealthily peep at.

悄悄 *chiaurchiaau*, adj. & adv., (1) (AC) silent, -ly; (2) (AC) sorrowful, -ly; 悄悄兒, 悄悄兒地, 悄悄地 silently, stealthily, with as little noise as possible: 悄悄地告訴他 tell him quietly; 悄悄地走過去 walk over quietly.
悄然 *chiaurrarn*, adv., sorrowfully.
悄聲兒 *chiaausheng'l*, adv., in a low voice.

惝 22A.42-2

taang (also *chaang*).

Adj. Disappointed, feeling lost, see compp.↓.

惝怳 *tarnghuaang*, adj., confused, feeling lost: 惝怳迷離.
惝然 *taangrarn*, adj., feeling lost: 惝然若失.

懦 22A.42-3

nuoh.

Adj. Cowardly, weak in character.

懦夫 *nuohfu*, n., a coward.
懦弱 *nuohruoh*, adj., weak in character, incompetent, easily swayed by others.

悁 22A.42-4

jyuahn (**jyuan*).

Adj. (1) (**jyuan*) Angry: 悁忿 irritated, indignant, furious; 悁悁 *-jyuan*↓. (2) Anxious, nervous: 悁急 *-jir*↓.

悁急 *jyuahnjir*, adj., anxious, fretful, restless.
悁悁 **jyuanjyuan*, adj., (1) (LL) worried, fretting, uneasy; (2) (LL) angry, irritable.

恫 22A.42-4

tung (**duhng*).

V. t. (**duhng*) To use threat, see 恫嚇 *-heh*↓.

Adj. (*tung*) Sorrowful: 哀恫 (cf. 痛).

恫嚇 **duhngheh*, v. t., to threaten (also wr. 恫喝).

惆 22A.42-4

chour.

Adj. Sad.

惆悵 *chourchahng*, adj., disappointed, disconsolate.
惆然 *chourrarn*, adj., sad, downcast, heavy-hearted.
惆惋 *chourwaan*, adj., unhappy, miserable about s.t.

惘 22A.42-4

waang.

Adj. Disconcerted: 惘然, 惘惘 ditto; 悵惘 disappointed; 迷惘 perplexed.

慵 22A.42-6

yurng (also *yung*).

Adj. Lazy, idle with implied poetic sense: 賦性疎慵 by nature indolent.

---

§ 22A.50 (忄/ㄱ)

愣 22A.50-4

eh.

Adj. (1) Startled. (2) U.f. 諤 straightforward.

愣愣 *eheh*, adj., startled.
愣然 *ehrarn*, adj., ditto.
愣視 *ehshyh*, v. i., give a startled look.

愣 22A.50-4

lehng (**leng*).

Adj. (1) Be dumbfounded, astonished: 愣住了, 嚇愣了 be stunned speechless; 發愣 become speechless. (2) Foolish, awkward, clumsy, rash, rude: 愣小子 a little fool; 愣頭愣腦, 愣頭膒腦 a blockhead; 愣葱 *-tsung*↓; 愣頭兒青 ditto; 愣愣膒膒 stupid. (3) 愣愣睜睜 sleepy-eyed, 愣眼 (兒) 巴睜 weary and sleepy with eyes half closed.

Adv. Rashly, recklessly: 愣說, 愣辦, 愣要 speak, do, want s. t.

亅	小	⺊	十	土	ナ	卄	𠃊	丨	一	丁	フ	口	区	冈	ㄱ	厂	尸	亠	广	宀	丶	乚	弋	心	八	人	乂	乛	㇀	刂	⺊	く
00	01	02	10	11	12	20	21	22	30	31	32	40	41	42	50	51	52	60	61	62	63	70	71	72	80	81	82	83	90	91	92	93

without thinking of the consequences.

愣兒 *lehng'l*, adj., (1) dumbfounded: 當時一愣兒 was dumbfounded and didn't know what to do; (2) (*leng'l*) confounded through inexperience.
愣葱 *lehngtsung*, n., (coll.) a rash fellow.

惕 22A.50-4

tih.

V. i. Alert, be alert: 警惕, 惕厲, 惕惕 be alert, strive hard.

愒 22A.50-4

chih (*kaih, *heh*).

V. i. (*chih*) (AC) u. f. 憩 rest a little.

V. t. (*heh*) U. f. 喝, 嚇 to frighten.

Adj. (*kaih*) (AC) 玩愒 to be addicted to.

忉 22A.50-5

dau.

Adj. (AC) sad, miserable: 忉忉 (AC) miserable.

恊 22A.50-9

shier.
[Abbr. of 協 10S.50]

慟 22A.50-9

tuhng.

Adv. Bitterly: 慟哭 weep bitterly; 哀慟 feel deeply grieved.

恂 22A.50-9

shyurn.

Adj. (AC) (1) fearful. (2) Honest, careful.

恂達 *shyurndar*, adj., (AC) discerning: 思慮恂達 (AC) discerning in mind.
恂慄 *shyurnlih*, adj., cowering, nervous.
恂目 *shyurnmuh*, adv., (AC) in a wink.
恂恂 *shyurnshyurn*, adj., (AC) honest and respectful.

悔 22A.50-9

hueei.

V. i. & t. To repent, to regret, show remorse: 後悔 to regret, 後悔不及 (LL 悔之晚矣) too late to regret; 悔改, 悔過, 悔恨 *-gaai, -guoh, -hehn* ↓; 悔罪 penance, repent; 痛悔 deeply regret (one's mistake); 懺悔 to repent; 追悔 regret the past; 懊悔 to regret, blame oneself.

悔改 *hueirgaai*, v. i., to repent and reform.
悔過 *hueei-guoh*, v. i., to repent.
悔恨 *hueeihehn*, v. i., to regret deeply (one's mistake).
悔心 *hueeishin*, n., repentance.
悔悟 *hueeiwuh*, v. t., repent and realize (truth).

§ 22A.63 (忄/丶)

憔 22A.63-9

chiaur.

Adj. Weary, worried, see compp. ↓.

憔慮 *chiaurlyuh*, v. i., to worry.
憔悴 *chiaurtsueih*, adj., (1) weary-looking, worn-out, sorrow-laden; (2) distressed.

憮 22A.63-9

wuu.

Adj. (LL) 憮然 disappointed; 憮然興嘆 gave a sign of disappointment.

§ 22A.70 (忄/乚)

惓 22A.70-1

chyuarn.

Adj. 惓惓於懷 constantly remembering at heart.

慌 22A.70-2

huang.

Adj. (1) Frantic, frenzied, hysterical: 心慌意亂 confused and hysterical. (2) Frightened: 恐慌起來, 引起恐慌 arouse fear; 他心慌了, 慌了神兒 he is frightened, becomes frantic. (3) Adj. & adv. complement (pr. *'huang*, also *'heng*) frightfully: 煩得慌 frightfully tedious or occupied; 悶得慌 frightfully bored; 累得慌 extremely tired.

慌惚 *huanghu*, adj., nervous, not with a clear mind: 精神慌惚 in a state of mental confusion, mind does not function clearly (var. of 恍^Δ惚 22A.70).

慌張 *huang'jang*, adj., desperate, frantic, nervous.
慌忙 *huangmarng*, adv., in a great hurry.
慌速 *huangsuh*, adv., hurriedly.

恍 22A.70-2

huaang.

Adj. & adv. Seeming, -ly: 恍如, 恍若, 恍同 feel like; 恍如一塲大夢 feel like it was a dream.

恍惚 *huaanghu*, adj. & adv., (1) illusory (ily), elusive (ly); (2) (of patient's mind) unclear (ly), mixing real and unreal: 精神恍惚 feeling lost (also pr. *'hu*); (3) seemingly (also pr. *'hu*): 我恍惚聽見 I seem to have heard (=彷彿 *faang'fu*).
恍然 *huaangrarn*, adv., (1) suddenly: 恍然大悟 suddenly realize (like coming out of a dream); (2) 恍然若失 feel like having lost bearings.

恌 22A.70-2

tiau.

Adj. (AC) mean unsteady, frivolous; see 佻 91A.70.

悒 22A.70-4

yih.

Adj. Depressed; uneasy.

悒悶 *yihmehn*, adj., depressed.
悒怏 *yihyahng*, adj., (LL) ditto.
悒悒 *yihyih*, adj., (LL) worried, depressed, unhappy.

怩 22A.70-5

nir.

Adj. See 忸[△]怩 22A.30.

忼 22A.70-6

kang (also *kaang*).
[Var. of 慷 22A.02]

惋 22A.70-6

wahn.

V. i. To feel sorry.

惋惜 *wahnshir*, v. i. & t., (1) to feel sorry for; (2) to pity.
惋歎 *wahntahn*, v. i. & t., ditto.

悅 22A.70-8

yueh.

V.t. (1) To please: 悅目, 悅耳, 悅心 please the eye, the ear, the mind; p.p., pleased: 不悅 displeased. (2) To like, be fond of: 悅(女)色 fond of women.

Adj. Happy, glad: 愉悅 ditto.

Adv. Happily: 悅服 submit or be convinced gladly, also 心悅誠服.

悅樂 *yuehleh*, n. & adj., pleasure, pleasant.

慨 22A.70-9

kaai (also *kaih*).
[Dist. 概 10B.70]

V. i. To sigh, regret: 感慨萬千 filled with a thousand regrets.

Adj. & adv. Generous, -ly: 慷慨 generous, big-hearted; 慨允, 慨諾 generously promise.

慨然 *kaairarn* (*kaih-*), adv., generously, without stint.
慨惜 *kaaishir* (*kaih-*), v. i., regret. ⌈with regret.
慨歎 *kaaitahn* (*kaih-*), v. i., sigh

忱 22A.70-9

chern.

N. (LL esp. in letters) heart, feeling: 微忱, 下忱 (modest) my humble feeling (of gratitude, etc.); 熱忱 enthusiasm; 丹忱 loyalty.

愧 22A.70-9

kueih.
[Var. 媿]

V.i. & adj. Feel ashamed, embarrassed by kindness, uneasy, regretful: 慚愧, 羞愧 ashamed; 愧不敢當 embarrassed by undeserved praise or gift; 感愧交集 feel grateful and uneasy at the same time; 愧汗 (LL) perspire from a sense of shame.

愧服 *kueihfur*, v.t., admire (one better than oneself), feel humble toward (person).
愧恨 *kueihhehn*, v.i. & adj., regret, -ful (as for negligence, failure).
愧赧 *kueihnaan*, adj., (LL) ashamed of oneself.
愧恧 *kueihnyuh*, adj., (LL) ditto.
愧心 *kueihshin*, adj., ashamed at heart.

愾 22A.70-9

kaih.

N. Anger, hatred: 同仇敵愾 share hatred of same enemy.

Adj. 愾然 generously (＝慨△然 22A.70).

§22A.71 (忄/七)

慽 22A.71-7

chi.

[Arch. Var. of 慼 71.71]

懺 22A.71-8

chahn.

N. & v.i. Repentance; repent: 拜懺, see 懺禮 *-lii* ↓.

懺七 *chahnchi*, n., (Budd.) saying of mass for the dead on the seventh day and multiple of seventh.

懺悔 *chahnhueei*, v.i., to feel or show repentance.

懺禮 *chahnlii*, n., (Budd.) ceremony of penance or penitence.

懺事 *chahnshyh*, n., ditto.

§22A.72 (忄/心)

憶 22A.72-6

yih.

N. Memory, remembrance: 記憶 ditto.

V. t. (LL) to remember: 憶得, 憶及 remember (s. t.); 憶念 *-niahn* ↓; 懷憶 remember fondly; 憶昔, 憶舊 think of the old days; 長相憶 remembrance for ever.

憶念 *yihniahn*, v.t., to remember (old friends, etc.)

憾 22A.72-7

hahn.

N. Regret: 遺憾 regret over s.t. neglected or uncompleted; 終身遺憾 a regret for life; 缺憾 s.t. missing, a shortcoming, what detracts from perfection; 憾恨 bitter regret; 爲憾, 憾事 a regretful fact or event.

惚 22A.72-9

hu.

Adj. & adv. See 恍△惚 22A.70.

§22A.80 (忄/八)

慎 22A.80-1

shehn.

[Usu. printed 愼]

N. & adj. (1) Carefulness, careful, caution: 慎重 *-juhng* ↓; 謹慎 be careful; 慎莫, 慎勿 careful not to; 慎勿告人 be sure not to tell any one. (2) (Coll.) frightened: 眞慎得慌 was greatly frightened (by tiger's roar, etc.).

慎獨 *shehn-dur*, phr., (LL, Confucian) to be on caution when alone with oneself, referring to secret thoughts, desires.

慎着 *shehn'je*, v. i., to delay, postpone: 作事別慎着 do not postpone things you have to do.

慎重 *shehnjuhng*, adj., careful, cautious: 慎重其事 be very careful, handle with care.

慎終 *shehn-jung*, phr., (Confu.) take great care in making funeral arrangements (including sacrifices), esp. for one's parents.

慎密 *shehnmih*, adj. & adv., with great caution and secrecy.

慎刑 *shehn-shirng*, phr., exercise restraint in punishment of criminals.

慎思 *shehn-sy*, phr., (AC, LL) think deeply.

憤 22A.80-1

fehn.

[Related 忿]

N. & adj. Anger, exasperation, resentment: 憤不欲生 would end life in fit of bitterness; 引起公憤 stir up public indignation; 憤世嫉俗, phr., misanthropic, highly critical of society; 不憤不啟 (Confucius) would not explain unless one is desperately anxious to learn; 發憤 make firm resolve (also wr. 奮); 氣憤 angry.

憤憤 *fehnfehn*, adj, & adv., angrily.

憤恚 *fehnhueih*, adj., deeply resentful.

憤激 *fehnjir*, adj., excited and bitter.

憤慨 *fehnkaai*, adj., excited and bitter (over public injustice).

憤懣 *fehnmehn*, n. & adj., resentment; resentful.

憤惋 *fehnwahn*, adj., angry and sorry.

懶 22A.80-1

laan.

[Var. 嬾]

Adj. Idle, lazy, indolent: 懶惰

-*duoh*↓; 貪懶 unwilling to work; 偷懶 ditto; 好吃懶做 caring for nothing but eating; 懶東西, 懶小子 a lazy fellow; 懶傢伙 ditto; 懶洋洋 spiritless, take everything in a leisurely way; 懶懶的 idly, leisurely.

懶蟲 *laanchurng*, n., (abusive) a lazy person, lazybones.
懶蛋 *laandahn*, n., lazybones.
懶待 *laan'dai*, adj., disinclined to, not in the mood to: 又懶待吃東西 not disposed to eat anything; 懶待理他 won't like to speak to him (see -*'de*↓).
懶怠 *laandaih*, adj., indolent.
懶得 *laan'de*, adj., not disposed or too tired to do anything (=懶待 -*'dai*↑).
懶凳 *laan-dehng*, n., formerly, a bench inside the main entrance of a house.
懶惰 *laanduoh*, adj., lazy, idle.
懶骨頭 *laangur'tou*, n., lazybones.
懶驢愁 *laanlyurchour*, n., a stiff, short whip used by donkey drivers.
懶散 *larnsaan* (also Peking dial. -*'san*), adj., indolent, careless.
懶腰 *laan'yau*, v.i., as in 伸懶腰 to stretch oneself.

㥏 22A.80-2

tiaan.

Adj. (AC) ashamed (cf. 䩄 22S.70, 靦 31S.70).

憒 22A.80-2

kueih.

Adj. Dizzy, staggered, befuddled, unable to think: 昏憒 befuddled, lose all sharp perceptions, stupid.

憒憒 *kueihkueih*, adj., (LL) (1) befuddled; (2) chaotic.

慣 22A.80-4

guahn.

N. Habit, custom: 風俗習慣 customs and habits.

V. t. (Of children) to spoil, be overindulgent to: 慣縱 indulge (a child); 慣壞了 become spoiled; 你太慣着孩子們了 you have spoiled your children; 嬌生慣養 (of children) brought up by indulgent parents.

Adj. Habitual, customary: 慣常 -*charng*↓; 慣例 customary practice; 慣習 accustomed to; an old trick; 慣俗 habitual ways; 慣賊, 慣竊 incorrigible thief; 慣性 -*shihng*↓; 慣犯 a habitual criminal; 看不慣 (of sights) unpleasant, revolting, ugly; 使慣了左手 got used to being left-handed.

慣常 *guahncharng*, adj., customary.
慣性 *guahnshihng*, n., (phys.) inertia.

惧 22A.80-4

jyuh.

[Pop. of 懼 22A.11]

§ 22A.81 (忄/人)

恢 22A.81-1

huei.

V. t. To restore: 恢復 -*fuh*↓.

Adj. Big, strange; see compp.↓.

恢奇 *hueichir*, adj., grand remarkable, big and strange (person, story).
恢誕 *hueidahn*, adj., exaggerated.
恢復 *hueifuh*, v. t., to restore (original shape, health, lost territory): 恢復期 convalescent period.
恢恢 *hueihuei*, adj., large: 天網恢恢 God's justice is all-encompassing.
恢宏 *hueihurng*, adj., generous (attitude).
恢張 *hueijang*, v. i., to expand (prestige, etc.).

愞 22A.81-3

ruaan.

Adj. (AC) cowardly: 坐畏愞棄市 was condemned and executed for cowardice.

悮 22A.81-4

wuh.

[Var. of 誤 60A.80; dist. 娱 93A.81]

懨 22A.81-5

yan.

懨懨 *yanyan*, adj., very feeble, merely lingering in life.

愀 22A.81-9

chiaau (also *jioou*).

懶 㥏 憒 慣 惧 恢 愞 悮 懨 愀

亅	小	⺊	十	土	ナ	卄	𠃊	丨	一	丅	フ	口	区	冈	冂	厂	尸	亠	广	宀	丶	乚	弋	心	八	人	乂	冖	一	丿	𠂉	く
00	01	02	10	11	12	20	21	22	30	31	32	40	41	42	50	51	52	60	61	62	63	70	71	72	80	81	82	83	90	91	92	93

愀然 ***chiaaurarn***, adv., (1) sad-looking; (2) 愀然變色 change one's countenance.

快 22A.81-9

kuaih.

N. 馬快 formerly, a mounted messenger; 捕快 formerly, constable, sheriff deputy.

Adj. & adv. (1) Pleased, elated, joyful: 快樂, 快活, 快意 *-leh, -'huo, -yih*↓; 愉快 happy; 快哉 (LL) how happy! what joy! 拍手稱快 clap hands for joy; 人心大快 the people are overjoyed (as over abolition of bad laws); 心中不快, 不快於心 not pleased; 暢快 thrilling, heartily gratified; 爽快 good and comfortable, also not stingy; 快慰 pleased (to hear news); (乘龍) 快婿 attractive son-in-law. (2) Straight, unrestrained: 快人快語 straight talk from an honest man; 快嘴 *-tzueei*↓. (3) Fast, quick, soon: 快極了 very fast; 快(一)點 be quick! 加快 hurry up! 趕快 quickly; 快些 quicker, please! 快快的 quickly; soon, at once; 快説 please speak out; 快離開吧 better leave here at once; 快完了 will soon be finished; 快到了 shall arrive soon. (4) (Of knife) keen, sharp: 快刀斬亂麻 cut the Gordian knot; 刀鋒極快 knife is very sharp; 磨快了 ground sharp, sharpened; 快剪 sharp scissors.

快板(兒) ***kuaihbaan(-baa'l)***, n., (Chin. music) quick tempo.

快班 ***kuaihban***, n., mounted messenger, footmen: 快班車 express train.

快車 ***kuaihche***, n., railway express.

快當 ***kuaih'dang***, adj., quick and well-done.

快感 ***kuaihgaan***, n., a pleasant sensation, feeling.

快活 ***kuaih'huo***, adj. (1) comfortable and happy; (2) thrilled.

快樂 ***kuaihleh***, n. & adj., pleasure, joy; happy, joyful.

快慢 ***kuaih-mahn***, n., rate of speed.

快門 ***kuaihmern***, n., shutter (of a camera).

快信 ***kuaihshihn***, n., express letter.

快手 ***kuaihshoou***, (1) adj., nimble-handed; (2) n., formerly, officer's messenger.

快事 ***kuaih-shyh***, n., a pleasure, a joyful event.

快艇 ***kuaihtiing***, n., speed boat.

快嘴 ***kuaih-tzueei***, adj., quick-tongued; one who talks without thinking.

快意 ***kuaihyih***, adj., elated: 人生快意的事 a joyful event (e. g., final success).

快 22A.81-9

yahng.

Adj. Sad, disappointed: 快快不樂 unhappy.

懊 22A.81-9

auh.

V. i. & adj. (1) Be discomfited, nervous, worried. (2) Repent, -tant.

懊恨 ***auhhehn***, v. i., to regret bitterly.

懊悔 ***auhhueei***, v. i., to repent.

懊惱 ***auhnaau***, adj., displeased, annoyed.

懊憹 ***auhnaur***, adj., see *-naau*↑.

懊儂 ***auhnurng***, adj., see *-naau*↑.

懊喪 ***auhsahng***, adj., dispirited, downcast.

§ 22A.82 (忄/乂)

忮 22A.82-1

jyh.

V. t. (AC) to envy, be mean: 忮心 envious heart.

忮求 ***jyhchiour***, v. i., to be greedy for s. t.: 不忮不求 (AC) not envious or greedy for what others have.

悽 22A.82-1

lirng.

V. i. & t. (1) To fear: (LL) 悽遽 to fear, fearful. (2) U.f. 憐, take pity, be tender toward.

惙 22A.82-3

chuoh.

Adj. (1) (AC) sad, dejected, mournful: 惙惙, 惙怛 ditto. (2) (AC) exhausted.

慢 22A.82-4

mahn.

Adj. & adv., (1) Slow: 慢點(兒) go slowly; "wait a minute" (said to contradict s. o.), also 且慢; 慢打法器 don't play up the music yet, i. e., don't let people know yet; 慢騰騰 *-'teng'teng*, annoyingly slow, very slowly, see 慢慢的 *-'man-de*↓; 慢工出巧器 or 出細活 slow work means careful work. (2) Careless, -ly, rude, -ly: 慢待, 輕慢 to treat (s.o.) cheaply; 傲慢 proud; 怠慢 (court. of oneself) fail in hospitality, also to neglect (work); 慢藏誨盜 phr., to be careless (of jewels, etc.) is to invite thieves. (3) (MC) don't: 慢道, 慢説=莫道, 莫説 it couldn't be that, somewhat similar to Eng. "you don't say."

慢車 *mahn-che*, n., local train, opp. 快車 express.
慢火 *mahn-huoo*, n., slow fire.
慢驚風 *mahn-jingfeng*, n., (Chin. med.) a children's disease (a mild flu).
慢臉 *mahnliaan*, n., (MC) full, handsome face (=曼 41.82).
慢慢的 *mahn'man-de*, adv., very slowly: 慢慢騰騰 *mahn'man-'teng'teng*, adv., very slowly.
慢世 *mahn-shih*, adj., cynical.
慢性病 *mahnshihng-bihng*, n., chronic disease; 慢性(兒)(子) person of slow temperament, slow in response.
慢條斯理 *mahntiaur-sylii*, adj. & adv., very slowly and imperturbed.

愎 22A.82-9

bih.

Adj. Self-opinionated, stubborn: 剛愎自用 obdurate, unwilling to take advice.

V. t. Reject: 愎諫 reject advice.

怓 22A.82-9

naur.

怓怓 *naurnaur*, v. i. & adj., babble, babbling.

悛 22A.82-9

chyuan.

V. i. To repent: 悛改 to repent one's ways; 悛心 repentance; 悛容 look of repentance.

§ 22A.83 (忄/乛)

懥 22A.83-1

jyh.

Adj. (AC) angry: 忿懥 ditto.

慥 22A.83-1

tzauh (also *tsauh*).

Adv. 慥慥 earnestly, wholeheartedly.

§ 22A.91 (忄/ノ)

憀 22A.91-5

liaur.

Adj. (AC) sad, forlorn.

慘 22A.91-9

tsaan.

Adj. & adv. (1) Miserable, wretched, pitiful: 悲慘, 悽慘 pitiful, miserable. (2) Disastrous: 慘禍 a disatrous happening; 慘殺, 慘遭殺害 was cruelly killed; 慘酷 *-kuh* ↓.

慘案 *tsaan-ahn*, n., a murder case; a tragic political incident: 五卅慘案 the May 30, 1925, incident at Shanghai; 濟南慘案 1928, Tsinan Incident.
慘變 *tsaanbiahn*, n., disastrous turn of events.
慘澹(淡) *tsaandahn*, adj. & adv., (1) dull (atmosphere, color); (2) with strenuous effort: 慘淡經營 build up a business by years of effort and persistence.
慘怛 *tsaandar*, adj., heartbroken, grieved.
慘急 *tsaanjir*, adj., (AC) cruel, ruthless (administration).
慘狀 *tsaan-juahng*, n., a sad sight.
慘沮 *tsaanjyu*, adj., (LL) miserable in heart.
慘劇 *tsaanjyuh*, n., a tragic happening or drama of events.
慘酷 *tsaankuh*, adj., ruthless, merciless, pitiless.
慘綠 *tsaanlyuh*, adj., dull green.
慘然 *tsaanrarn*, adj., sad, saddened, bemoaned.
慘殺 *tsaansha*, v. t., to kill brutally.
慘慘 *tsarntsaan*, adj., dull, somber, melancholy (sky, heart).
慘惻 *tsaantseh*, adj., miserable, wretched.
慘痛 *tsaantuhng*, adj., greatly aggrieved, saddened; also saddening.

§ 22A.93 (忄/く)

悽 22A.93-1

chi.

Adj. Sad, mournful, dolorous; see 淒 63A.93 Adj. 2.

悽悽 *chichi*, adj., sad, desolate.
悽愴 *chichuahng*, adj., in a sad circumstance.
悽惶 *chihuarng*, adj., distressed, forlorn: 悽悽惶惶 rushing about in distress.
悽惻 *chitseh*, adj., (of sounds, feelings) mournful, disconsolate.

悽惘 *chiwaang*, adj., sadly disappointed.
悽婉 *chiwuaan*, adj., (of music) sadly moving.

怯 22A.93-1

chieh (**chyueh*).

Adj. (1) (sp. pr. **chyueh*) Timid, coward, nervous: 膽怯 timid; 怯弱 *-ruoh* ↓; 畏怯 fearful; 怯怯喬喬(僑僑) (MC) timid, bashful; 怯羞 bashful; 怯色 appearance of apprehension; followed by nn., fearful: 怯官, 怯上 afraid of official, superior; 怯生生的 very timid, shy. (2) Uncouth, countrified, awkward like one from the country: 怯頭怯腦, 怯愣兒 (of country bumpkins) lumpish, countrified; 怯口 *-koou* ↓.

怯夫 *chiehfu*, n., (LL) a coward.
怯症 *chiehjehng*, n., (coll.) tuberculosis.
怯口 *chiehkoou*, adj., talking with country (rustic) accent.
怯懦 *chiehnuoh*, adj., timid, faint-hearted.
怯弱 *chiehruoh*, adj., ditto.

忪 22A.93-8

jung.

Adj. See 怔^忪 22A.30; 惺^忪 22A.11.

惀 22A.93-8

yur.

[Printed form of 愉 22A.00]

SECTION 22B

§ 22B.00 (巾/丿)

幬 22B.00-1

dauh (**chour*).

N. & v.t. (1) (AC) cover. (2) (**chour*) u.f. 裯 curtain.

§ 22B.02 (巾/ㄎ)

幪 22B.02-2

merng (**meeng*).

N. See 帡^幪 22B.20.

幪幪 **merngmeeng*, adj., (AC) 麻麥幪幪 the hemp and wheat are beautiful (grow well).

帳 22B.02-5

jahng.

N. (1) (*-tz*) Bed curtain: 蚊帳 mosquito net in bed; 絳帳 (LL) brown curtain—(allu.) room for teaching pupils; 帳飲 to drink in tent (of mil. officers). (2) A tent: 帳棚, 帳幕 *-'perng*, *-muh²* ↓. (3) (Interch. 賬) accounts, account book: 帳目 *-muh¹*, 帳簿 *-buh* ↓; 結帳 give total of balance in accounts; 算帳 reckon accounts, (fig.) to square a grudge; 欠帳 to owe; 借帳 to borrow; 賴帳 to default or delay paying accounts; 流水帳, 日記帳 day-to-day running accounts.

帳簿 *jahngbuh*, n., account book.
帳額 *jahng-er*, n., see *-yarn* ↓.
帳房(兒) *jahngfarng('l)*, n., cashier; cashier's office; bursar.
帳鈎 *jahnggou*, n., curtain hook for holding up curtain.
帳戶 *jahnghuh*, n., bank account; 凍結帳戶 frozen account; 封鎖帳戶 blocked account; 扣留帳戶 attached account.
帳籍 *jahng-jir*, n., see *-buh* ↑.
帳主(兒)(子) *jahngjuu('l)* (*-tz*), n., creditor.
帳落 *jahngluoh*, n., nomad settlement.
帳目 *jahngmuh¹*, n., accounts; itemized bill.
帳幕 *jahngmuh²*, n., tent.
帳棚(蓬) *jahng'perng*, n., tent; matshed.
帳下兒 *jahngshiah'l*, n., soldiers under command; 帳下吏 aide-de-camp.
帳務 *jahng-wuh*, n., accounts in gen.
帳簷 *jahng-yarn*, n., the overhanging fringe of bed curtain.

§ 22B.10 (巾/十)

幃 22B.10-2

weir.

[Dist. 緯 93B.22]

N. (1) Wall curtain (see 帷 22B.11). (2) (AC, rare) spice pouch.

幛 22B.10-6

jahng.

N. A scroll of cloth or silk, hung up on wall or partition, containing congratulations or condolences by friends: 壽幛, 喜幛 congratulatory silk scroll for birthday, wedding; 輓幛 for condolence; 幛光兒 paper cut-out containing characters on such scrolls.

§ 22B.11 (巾/土)

幄 22B.11-5

woh.

N. A tent, curtained place: 帷幄 tent.

幢 22B.11-6

chuarng.

N. adjunct. 一幢房屋 a house.

N. (1) Pennant, pendant streamer: 幢幡, 幢蓋 ditto; standard bearers: 幢隊 pennant carriers in a procession. (2) Cart curtain.

Adj. 幢幢 (of flags, pennants) floating, flapping in the wind.

帷 22B.11-9

weir.

N. Curtain, tent.

帷 薄 *weirbor*, n., (1) curtains and screens; (2) woman's quarters: 帷薄不修 sexually promiscuous at home.
帷 房 *weirfarng*, n., women's quarters.
帷 幕 *weirmuh*, n., military tent.
帷 堂 *weir-tarng*, n., curtained hall for funeral services.
帷 幄 *weirwoh*, n., tent: 運籌帷幄 (AC allu.) map out strategy.

§ 22B.20 (巾/廾)

帲 22B.20-9

pirng.

N. & v. t. (AC) shelter.

帲 幪 *pirngmerng*, n., (AC) shelter, tent.

§ 22B.40 (巾/口)

帖 22B.40-2

tiee (**tie*, **tieh*).

N. (1) (*-tz*, *-'l*) A notice, an invitation card, a brief note: 請帖, 回帖 invitation, return card; 喜帖 wedding invitation; 謝帖 card of thanks; 房帖兒, 招帖 a notice posted on doorways, streets (house for rent, etc.); a brief note; 來帖 your note; 藥一帖 one prescribed dose of medicine. (2) (**tieh*) Model of calligraphy for copying, usu. rubbings from inscriptions: 碑帖, 字帖 (兒) ancient writings on silk. (3) (**tie*) (Tarng, Suhng, Yuarn) civil service examination papers: 括帖.

V.t. & adj. (**tieh*) To lie close to, submit: 帖尾 (of dog) put tail between legs; hence adj., 妥帖 well-placed, settled; 帖服 *-fur* ↓.

帖 耳 **tie-eel*, adj., submissive (cf. 貼耳).
帖 伏 (帖 服) **tiefur*, v. i., (pets) snuggle close, submit; adj., submissive.
帖 子 *tieetz*, n., invitation card.

帢 22B.40-8

chiah.

N. An ancient fatigue cap.

幨 22B.40-9

chan.

幨 帷 *chanweir*, n., formerly, carriage curtains.

§ 22B.41 (巾/図)

幅 22B.41-3

fur.

N. adjunct. Denoting a long strip: 一幅畫 one painting; 一幅對子 a couplet of calligraphy hung on wall; 一幅肖像 a portrait; dist. 副 30S.00 pr. *fuh*, a set.

N. (1) Width of cloth or paper: 全幅 whole piece of material; 單幅, 雙幅 cloth material of single or double width. (2) Hem: 邊幅 hemline, see 91.83.

幅 巾 *furjin*, n., (MC) turban made of whole length of material, also called 幞頭.
幅 員 *furyuarn*, n., territory as shown on maps; size of it.

帽 22B.41-4

mauh.

亅	小	⺊	十	土	ナ	廾	㐄	丨	一	丅	フ	口	図	冈	㇕	厂	尸	亠	广	宀	丶	乚	乀	心	八	人	乂	乛	㇒	刂	⺧	く
00	01	02	10	11	12	20	21	22	30	31	32	40	41	42	50	51	52	60	61	62	63	70	71	72	80	81	82	83	90	91	92	93

N. (1) Hat, cap (*-tz, -'l*): 草帽 straw hat; 禮帽 top hat; 睡帽 night cap; 給他戴高帽 flatter one's vanity by rank, honor; 喜歡戴高帽 love titles and social honors. (2) Cap of pen: 筆帽.

帽花(兒) *mauh-hua'l*, n., decorations, jewels on hat.
帽簷(兒) *mauh-yarn(-yar'l)*, n., hat brim.

幗 22B.41-4

guoo.

N. Women's headgear: 巾幗 the female sex; 巾幗英雄 a heroine.

幡 22B.41-9

fan.
[Var. 旛]

N. Banner, pennant.

幡幡 *fanfan*, adj., (AC) fluttering about.
幡蓋 *fangaih*, n., formerly, portable shade held in procession of idols, dignitaries.
幡兒 *fan'l*, n., a white wand of mourning held by son of deceased.
幡然 *fan-rarn*, adv., abruptly or decisively changing: 幡然改途 repent and change course.

帕 22B.41-9

pah.

N. Kerchief, a piece of cloth carried or worn, in compounds only: 頭帕 turban; 手帕 handkerchief.

帕額 *pah-er*, n., (MC) forehead band, often used by women.
帕腹 *pahfuh*, n., (MC) chestcloth worn by women over breasts.
帕子 *pah'tz*, n., a kerchief, often used for carrying a package: 手帕子 handkerchief.

§22B.70 (巾/匕)

幌 22B.70-4

huaang.

N. (1) Curtain, usu. with *-tz* (幌子). (2) A flag as sign of wineshop. (3) Any specially carved shopsign. (4) Front, window-dressing: 裝幌子 put on airs; 拿這話當幌子 regard what he says as merely window-dressing.

帆 22B.70-4

farn.

N. Sail: 揚帆 hoist sail, set sail; 一帆風順 *bon voyage*.

帆布 *farnbuh*, n., canvas.
帆檣 *farnchiarng*, n., sail mast.
帆船 *farn-chuarn*, n., sail boat.

帨 22B.70-8

shueih.

N. (AC) woman's shawl.

§22B.71 (巾/弋)

幟 22B.71-6

jyh.

N. A flag, a sign: 旗幟 flag, also sign of what stands for: 旗幟鮮明; 獨樹一幟 become an independent school, not a follower of others; 易幟 change flags or allegiance.

§22B.80 (巾/八)

幘 22B.80-1

tzer.

N. A turban: 喪幘 a white turban as a symbol of mourning.

幀 22B.80-2

jehng.

N. A roll (of painting).

§22B.81 (巾/人)

帙 22B.81-1

jyh.

N. A folder of documents, a cardboard casing for Chinese books: 書帙 ditto; 公文一帙 folder file of documents.

幞 22B.81-2

pur.

N. Turban.

幞頭 *purtour*, n., (MC) turban; a turbaned worker.

幎 22B.81-6

mih.

[Var. of 冪 62.22]

§22B.82 (巾/乂)

帔 22B.82-2

peih.

N. Woman's shawl, shoulder-piece, esp. 霞帔, bridal shoulder-piece, cf. 披△肩 10A.82.

幔 22B.82-4

mahn.

N. Curtain (*-tz*): 帷幔 curtain hangings, tent; 布幔 cotton hanging curtain; 障幔 screen.

SECTION 22C

§22C.00 (米/丿)

籽 22C.00-3

tzyy.

N. The seeds of a plant: 種籽 seed; 籽粒 grains of seeds.

§22C.01 (米/小)

糅 22C.01-3

roou (also *niouh*).

V.t. Mix, intermix: 糅合 to form a mixture; 糅雜 mingle, blend, commingle; mixed, disorderly.

粽 22C.01-6

tzuhng (also *juhng*).

[Var. 糉]

N. 粽子 Pyramid-shaped pudding made of glutinous rice wrapped in bamboo leaves.

§22C.02 (米/卜)

粻 22C.02-5

jang.

N. (AC) food.

粮 22C.02-6

liarng.

[Var. 糧 22C.11]

糠 22C.02-6

kang.

N. Chaff (of grain): 糠蘿蔔 (coll.) dry and puffy turnip; 粃糠 chaff, see 糠粃 *-bii* ↓.

糠粃 *kangbii*, n., chaff; riffraff, trash.

糠蝦 *kangshia*, n., (zoo.) the opossum shrimp, *Mysis opossum.*

糠穗 *kangsueih*, n., autumn bent grass, *Agrostis perennaus.*

§22C.10 (米/十)

料 22C.10-1

liauh.

N. (1) Material, raw material: 原料 material for making (utensils, chemicals, etc.); 資料 material for study, data; 衣料 fabrics, clothing material; 木料 timber; 工料 labor and material; 廢料 waste material, scraps; 飲料 drinks; 燃料 fuel (oil, wood, gas); 顏料 dye stuff; 藥料 medicine; 食料 foodstuff; 飼料, 草料 animal feed, fodder, silage; 加料 enriched (food, drink, paint); 單料, 雙料 simple, enriched material. (2) Chin. synthetic jade: 料貨 synthetic jade or glass. (3) A worthless person: 這塊料. (4) Used as n. adjunct: 一料藥方 one prescription.

V. i. (1) To imagine, calculate, reckon, anticipate: see 料想, 料算 *-shiaang*, *-suahn* ↓; 料敵 anticipate what the enemy will do; 逆料, 預料 anticipate beforehand, predict; 難以逆料 difficult to foretell; 料事如神 foretell things accurately ("miraculously"). (2) To look after, take care of: 照料 look after person's welfare, comfort: 照料孩兒 take good care of child.

料峭 *liauhchiauh*, adj., chilly.
料器 *liauhchih*, n., synthetic jade.
料袋 *liauhdaih*, n., (MC) bag for food.
料豆 *liauhdouh*, n., black bean as feed for cattle, horses.
料度 *liauhduoh*, v. i., reckon, imagine, calculate.
料估 *liauh'gu*, v. i., (1) estimate; (2) conjecture.
料貨 *liauhhuoh*, n., synthetic or imitation jade or glass.
料件子 *liauhjiahntz*, v. i., 料件子活 tailor work paid by piece.
料量 *liauhliahng*[1], v. i., calculate; imagine.
料諒 *liauhliahng*[2], v. i., ditto.
料想 *liauhshiaang*, n., a conjecture; v.i., imagine, conjecture.
料算 *liauhsuahn*, v.i. to calculate (date of arrival, etc.)
料子 *liauhtz*, n., material (good, bad) of cloth.

粹 22C.10-6

tsueih.

N. Essence, best or most precious elements: (保存) 國粹 (keep intact) the national cultural heritage; 文粹, 選粹 selected prose; 精粹 essence (of philosophy, writing).

Adj. Select, selected, pure: 純粹 pure, purely (imagination, Chinese, wool, etc.).

粺 22C.10-9

baih.

[Dist. 稗 90A.10]

N. Fine rice.

§ 22C.11 (米/土)

糧 22C.11-4

liarng.

N. (1) Food, nutriment: 乾糧 grain and dry goods, esp. on travel, in the army; 雜糧 miscellaneous cereals, (potatoes, beans, etc.). (2) Farm tax: 田糧 farm land tax; 錢糧 tax as in gen.; 漕[Δ]糧 63A.41.

糧米(兒) *liarngmii(-miie'l)*, n., grain as food: 糧米兒不足 not enough rice to eat.
糧餉 *liarngshiaang*, n., money for food and other supplies in army.
糧食 *liarng'shyr*, n., food, food supply.
糧草 *liarngtsaau*, n., food or fodder in army.

粧 22C.11-6

juang.

[Pop. of 妝 21S.93]

§ 22C.30 (米/一)

粗 22C.30-4

tsu.

Adj. & adv. (1) Rough, -ly, careless, -ly, not thorough: 粗心, 粗通, 粗略 *-shin*, *-tung*, *-lyueh* ↓. (2) Heavy, bulky, wide in diameter, opp. 細 *shih*, small, slender: 粗笨 *-behn*, 粗重 *-juhng* ↓; 粗繩子, 粗線 heavy rope, thread; 粗脖子 stodgy neck; 粗眉大眼 bushy eyebrows and big eyes. (3) Simple, coarse, unrefined, lower-grade: 粗布 coarse cloth; 粗米 brown, unpolished rice; 粗糧食 inferior foodstuff (corn, sorghum, millet instead of rice); 粗菜 simple fare; 粗陋 *-louh* ↓; 粗枝大葉 done in broad strokes or rough outline; 粗聲, 粗嗓子 coarse, heavy voice; 粗人, 粗俗, 粗野 *-rern*, *-sur*, *-yee* ↓.

粗暴 *tsubauh*, adj., (person) coarse, rude.
粗笨 *tsubehn*, adj., heavy, bulky (furniture, luggage); awkward, heavy-handed (stroke in callig., or gen. way of doing things).
粗淺 *tsuchiaan*, adj., superficial (knowledge); elementary.
粗蠢 *tsuchuun*, adj., see *-behn* ↑.
粗大 *tsudah*, adj., bulky.
粗豪 *tsuhaur*, adj., (person) forthright, not urbane.
粗話 *tsuhuah*, n., coarse language, esp. obscene language.
粗活 *tsuhuor*, n., heavy manual labor.
粗壯 *tsujuahng*, adj., robust, sturdy, stout.
粗重 *tsujuhng*, adj., heavy (luggage, work opp. 細輭 what is light and soft).
粗糲 *tsulih*, n., coarse, plain fare.
粗陋 *tsulouh*, adj., ill-mannered, not refined (person); plain (living quarters).
粗魯 *tsuluu* (-'*lu*), adj., stupid, vulgar.
粗略 *tsulyueh*, n. & adj., gen. idea; rough, not detailed.
粗莽 *tsumaang*, adj., rash, boorish (person).
粗人 *tsurern*, n., (1) a boorish, unrefined person; (2) a man good only at heavy work.
粗線條 *tsu-shiahn-tiau*, adj., vulgar, not refined (in manners).
粗細 *tsushih*, n., both light and heavy work; all kinds (of mate-

rial, work, furniture).
粗心 *tsushin*, adj., careless (in work).
粗疎 *tsushu*, adj., careless, overlooking details.
粗率 *tsushuaih* (-'*shuai*), adj., choppy (work), careless, roughly done.
粗實 *tsu'shy*, adj., solid (furniture, box).
粗俗 *tsusur*, adj., vulgar.
粗通 *tsu-tung*, v.i., barely understand (a subject).
粗糙 *tsutsau* (-*tsauh*), adj., rough (work), coarse.
粗躁 *tsutzauh*, adj., hasty, rash (temperament).
粗野 *tsuyee*, adj., vulgar, uncultured.
粗樂 *tsu-yueh*, n., music played with percussion instruments.

粒 22C.30-6

lih.

N. adjunct. A grain, a pill: 十粒葡萄 ten grapes; 一粒鈕扣 a button; 幾粒米 several grains of rice; 一粒藥丸 a pill.

N. A small particle: 碎粒 broken pieces: 細粒 tiny particles; 顆粒 particles, grains; 粒子 specks; 粒兒 ditto; 米粒 grains of rice; 飯粒 grains of cooked rice.

V.i. (AC) have rice as food: 烝民乃粒 then the general masses could have rice to eat.

粒粒 *lihlih, n.*, each grain; hence 粒粒皆辛苦 each grain of rice comes from hard labor, bitter rice.

§ 22C.40 (米/口)

粘 22C.40-2

niarn (or *jan*).
[Var. of 黏 90S.40]

糖 22C.40-6

tarng.

N. Sugar, sugared sweetmeats, candy: 白糖, 精糖 refined sugar; 紅糖 brown sugar; 砂糖 granulated sugar; 塊糖, 方糖 sugar cubes; 冰糖 (crystallized) rock sugar; 蔗糖 cane sugar; 蜜糖 honey; 巧克力糖 chocolates; 麥芽糖 malt sugar; 葡萄糖 glucose; 棉花糖 marshmallow, spun sugar; 糖薑 sugared ginger; 糖瓜(兒) sugared melons; 糖人兒 sugar dolls; 糖葫蘆(兒) sugared plums; 糖耳朵 fried sweetmeat; 糖雜麵兒 fine threads of flour and molasses; 糖兒豆兒 sweetmeats in gen. for children, hence petty favors.

糖果(兒) *tarngguor('l)*, n., sweetmeats in gen.
糖漿 *tarngjiang*, n., syrup.
糖精 *tarngjing*, n., saccharin.
糖汁 *tarngjy*, n., syrup.
糖鑼(兒) *tarngluor('l)*, n., small gong beaten by seller of sweetmeats.
糖蘿蔔 *tarngluor'bo*, n., sugar beet, beetroot.
糖尿病 *tarngniauh-bihng*, n., diabetes.
糖嗓兒 *tarngsaang'l*, n., split voice.
糖稀 *tarngshi*, n., molasses; syrup.
糖霜 *tarngshuang*, n., rock sugar.
糖水 *tarngshueei*, n., syrup.
糖食 *tarngshyr*, n., sweetmeats.
糖槭 *tarngtzur*, n., (bot.) a sugar producing plant, *Acer saccharinum.*
糖子兒 *tarngtzyy'l*, n., small sweetmeats.
糖衣 *tarngyi*, adj., sugar-coated (pills).

§ 22C.41 (米/囟)

糟 22C.41-2

tzau.

N. Dregs: 糟粕 *-poh*↓; 酒糟 fermented grain mash used for sauce or seasoning; 紅(白)糟 such mash with (without) coloring.

V. t. (1) To pickle: 糟發麵兒 dough fermented with yeast and made from glutinous rice; 糟魚, 糟肉 fish, meat treated with fermented grain mash; 糟豆腐 pickled bean curd; 糟鼻子 a drunkard's nose. (2) To waste, spoil, destroy: 糟蹋 *-'ta*, 糟踐 *-'jian*, 糟毀 *-hueei*↓.

Adj. (1) Ruined, spoiled: 糟了 (of things) be made a mess, in terrible shape; 糟透了 what a mess! too bad!completely ruined; 糟不可言 in an indescribable mess. (2) Rotten, decayed: 糟爛 decomposed, putrid; 糟朽 decayed, crumbled, disintegrated; 這些木板糟了 these planks are worn down.

Adv. In a state of confusion: 亂七八糟 at sixes and sevens, topsy-turvy, messy, chaotic; 亂糟糟的 untidy, disordered, out of joint.

糟錢兒 *tzauchiar'l*, n., filthy lucre.
糟糕 *tzaugau*, adj., in a terrible mess, awful, unfortunate.
糟毀 *tzauhueei*, v.t., to damage by rough treatment.
糟踐 *tzau'jian*, v.t., to trample upon.

糟 糰 粕 糌 精

糟糠 *tzaukang*, n., (1) coarse food (of the poor); (2) the woman married to a man before he became prosperous: 糟糠之妻 such a wife.

糟粕 *tzaupoh*, n., (1) (distilling) leftover grains; (2) anything worthless or unwanted, dregs (opp. 精華 essence, quintessence).

糟擾 *tzauraau*, phr., thanks for your hospitality!

糟心 *tzau-shin*, adj., (1) irritating, disagreeable; (2) ＝糟糕 *tzaugau*↑.

糟蹋 *tzau'ta*, v. t., (1) to spoil, ruin; (2) to insult.

糰 22C.41-4

tuarn.

N. Dumpling: 湯糰, 糰子; 麻糰 dumpling with sesame seeds in it.

粕 22C.41-9

poh.

N. See 糟△粕 22C.41↑.

糌 22C.41-9

tzarn.

N. 糌粑 a kind of fried flour blended with tea and butter—staple food of Tibetans.

§22C.42 (米/冈)

精 22C.42-1

jing.

N. (1) Essence, extract: 味精 flavor essence, monosodium glutamate; 咖啡精 instant coffee; 糖精 saccharin; 酒精 alcohol, spirit(s) of wine; 香精 perfume; 精華 *-huar*, 精要 *-yauh*, 精義 *-yih*, 精粹 *-tzueih*↓. (2) Ethereal beings, genie: 妖精 demon, devil, a woman with too much make-up; 精靈 *-lirng*, 精怪 *-guaih*↓; 山精 a gnome, a leprechaun; 狐狸精 (contempt.) a vixen, a spiteful woman, a sexy woman; 蛇精 a snake spirit. (3) Bodily secretion, semen: 精液 *-yeh*, 精子 *-tzyy*, 精巢 *-chaur*↓; 遺精, 流精 involuntary discharge of semen, have a wet dream. (4) Mental or moral attitude: 精神 *-(')shern*, 精力 *-lih*↓.

Adj. (1) Fine (opp. 粗 coarse): 精細 *-shih*, 精巧 *-chiaau*, 精緻 *-jyh*[2], 精美 *-meei*, 精密 *-mih*↓; 精益求精 always endeavoring to do still better. (2) Unmixed, refined: 精純 *-churn*↓; 專精 specializing in. (3) Unclothed, unclad: 精光 *-guang*↓; 精赤條條 naked, nude.

Adv. Very, extremely, exceedingly: 精溼 soaked through; 精窄兒 exceptionally narrow; 精通 *-tung*↓; 精瘦 all skin and bone; 精小 minute, infinitesimal.

精白 *jingbair*, adj., pure and clean.

精兵 *jingbing*, n., crack troops.

精巢 *jingchaur*, n., (physiol.) the spermary, the testicles.

精誠 *jingcherng*, adj., earnest and sincere.

精巧 *jingchiaau*, adj., skillful, delicate, cleverly made.

精氣 *jingchih*, n., (1) (Chin.) the vital principle in man; (2) (Budd., Taoism) vitality, virility.

精勤 *jingchirn*, adj., persevering, industrious, diligent.

精純 *jingchurn*, adj., pure, unalloyed, unmixed.

精蟲 *jingchurng*, n., (physiol.) sperms.

精確 *jingchyueh*, adj., accurate, precise.

精到 *jingdauh*, adj., meticulously exact.

精怪 *jingguaih*, n., evil spirits, ghosts, phantoms, spooks.

精光 *jingguang*, (1) adj., stripped of everything, stark naked; (2) n., vigor.

精工 *jinggung*, adj., & n. (of) fine workmanship.

精悍 *jinghahn*, adj., capable, sharp, vigorous.

精覈 *jingher*, adj., carefully checked.

精華 *jinghuar*, n., essence, the cream or best part.

精進 *jingjihn*, adj., (1) pushing, aggressive, enterprising; (2) vigorous, energetic; (3) (Budd.) making earnest efforts to cultivate virtue and get rid of evil.

精忠 *jingjung*, adj., loyal and patriotic.

精製 *jing-jyh*[1], adj., refined, skillfully made, manufactured by a special process.

精緻 *jingjyh*[2], adj., of fine workmanship, exquisite (art work).

精絕 *jingjyuer*, adj., extraordinarily well done.

精空 *jingkung*, adj., stripped of everything: 一掳精空 looted clean.

精兒 *jing'l*, n., (coll.) an onrush of mother's milk fed to baby: 一個精兒.

精練 *jingliahn*, (1) v.t., to train hard for (boxing, archery, swordsmanship, etc.); (2) adj., (of troops) well-trained.

精良 *jingliarng*, adj., of the highest grade or the best quality; excellent, finest, choicest.

精力 *jinglih*, n., energy, vigor, physical and mental vitality: 精力過人 exceptional vitality.

精靈 *jinglirng*, n., (1) spirits, ghosts; (2) a cunning and tricky person.

精美 *jingmeei*, adj., elegant and refined, of the finest quality.

精妙 *jingmiauh*, adj., ingenious, admirable, skillfully contrived.

精密 *jingmih*, adj., exact, precise.

精敏 *jingmiin*, adj., clever, smart, shrewd.

精明 *jingmirng* (*-'ming*), adj., smart, bright, brilliant: 精明強幹 shrewd and capable.

精囊 *jingnarng*, n., (physiol.) seminal vesicles.

精銳 *jingrueih*, n. & adj., crack (troops).

精舍 *jingsheh*, n., (1) a villa, a scholar's retreat; (2) (Budd.) a monastery or nunnery.

精深 *jingshen*, adj., deep, profound, erudite.

精神 *jingshern* (-'*shen*), n., (1) the spiritual part of a human being; (2) mental faculties; (3) spirit: 民治精神 the democratic spirit; (4) vigor, physical strength: 他作事很有精神 he is full of energy: 精神勞動(者) mental work(er), white-collar worker; 精神生活 spiritual life; 精神勝利 moral victory; 精神分析 psychoanalysis; 精神分裂 schizophrenia; 精神治療 psychotherapy; 精神研究 psychical research; 精神感應 telepathy; 精神病 mental disease; 精神病院 a mental hospital or institution, asylum; 精神鎮定劑 tranquilizer.

精細 *jingshih*, adj., (1) fine, delicate, meticulous; (2) calculating, shrewd, cautious: 精打細算 careful and detailed calculation.

精心 *jingshin*, adj. & adv., wholehearted(ly), done with meticulous care, heart and soul.

精選 *jingshyuaan*, adj., carefully selected or chosen.

精采 *jingtsaai*, n. & adj., (of litr. or artistic works) (the) most interesting, exciting, (features or parts): 精采表演 spirited performance.

精粗 *jingtsu*, n., things of all sorts ("the fine and the coarse").

精通 *jingtung*, adj., expert at, well-versed in.

精粹 *jingtzueih*, n. & adj., (of) the best and finest quality.

精子 *jingtzyy*, n., (physiol.) sperms.

精衛 *jingweih*, n., as in 精衛填海 a mythical bird which tries to fill up the ocean with twigs and pebbles—to fill a sea of regrets.

精微 *jingweir*, adj., deeply thought or perceived (truth).

精研 *jingyarn*[1], v. t., make a deep study (of subject).

精鹽 *jingyarn*[2], n., refined salt, table salt.

精要 *jingyauh*, n., essentials, fundamentals.

精液 *jingyeh*, n., (physiol.) semen; essence.

精一 *jingyi*, adj., single-minded, with only one aim or purpose.

精義 *jing-yih*, n., the essential or fundamental idea.

糊 22C.42-1

hur (**huh*).

N. (1) Paste: 漿糊 (also '*huh*) paste for gluing. (2) Paste-like food: 芝蔴糊 viscous soup of sesame seeds; 麥糊 oatmeal; 鱔魚糊 eel paste.

V.t. 裱糊 To paste up wallpaper, or mounting on scrolls.

Adj. (1) Muddy, unclear: 模糊, 迷糊, 迷迷糊糊 (-*hur* or -'*hu*) misty, unclear. (2) (Of food) overcooked until food turns mushy 燒糊了.

糊口 *hurkoou*, v.i., make a living to feed the family: 足以糊口 enough to keep body and soul together (also wr. 餬).

胡弄 **huh'nung*, v. i., do (s. t.) carelessly.

糊刷 **huhshua*, n., brush used for whitewashing wall or mounting scroll.

糊塗 *hurtur* (-'*tu*) (also 糊裏糊塗 *hur'lihutur*), adj., (1) in a mess, messed up; (2) muddleheaded, careless, stupid: 你這樣糊塗 how can you be so stupid? finish up affair in a slipshod manner (also wr. 胡).

糒 22C.42-2

beih.

N. (AC) Dried rice (for the journey.)

糯 22C.42-3

nuoh.

[Var. 稬, 穤]

N. (Bot.) *Oryza sativa*, var. *glutinosa.*

糯米 *nuohmii*, n., glutinous rice.

糈 22C.42-3

shyuu.

N. Army rations.

糲 22C.42-5

lih.

N. Brown rice: 糲飯 cooked brown rice; 糲粱 coarse food; 布服糲食 live a simple life.

Adj. 粗糲 coarse (food).

§ 22C.50 (米/ㄱ)

粉 22C.50-8

feen.

N. (1) Powder: 牛奶粉 powdered milk; 米粉 rice vermicelli; 麵粉 (wheat) flour; 珠粉 pearl powder (used as medicine); 藕粉 arrowroot; 涼粉 jelly made from agar-agar; 牙粉 dental powder; 肥皂粉 soap powder; 白粉 white powder, chalk. (2) Ladies' face powder: 脂粉 cosmetics; 粉盒 compact; 粉刷 powder brush; 粉撲兒 powder

亅	小	⺊	十	土	ナ	卄	⺊	丨	一	丅	フ	口	囗	冈	ㄱ	厂	尸	亠	广	宀	丶	乚	弋	心	八	人	乂	一	乛	丿	⺈	く
00	01	02	10	11	12	20	21	22	30	31	32	40	41	42	50	51	52	60	61	62	63	70	71	72	80	81	82	83	90	91	92	93

粉 糕 粃 粑 糢 糗 糉 籹 糙

puff; 粉裝兒 formerly, powder box; 粉紙 (a) fine white writing paper; (b) ladies' face powder paper; 粉底 powder foundation; 粉底霜 foundation cream.

V. t. (1) To crush to powder: 粉身碎骨在所不辭 would do anything to pay in gratitude. (2) Cover up, whitewash: 粉飾 *-shyh*↓.

Adj. (1) Powdered, plastered: 粉牆 whitewashed wall; 粉白 white-washed or plastered (wall); 粉白黛綠 stage make-up; 油頭粉面 painted and powdered. (2) Soft as powder: 粉嫩 soft and smooth (skin); 粉紅 *-hurng*↓.

粉本 *fernbeen*, n., chalk sketch for Chin. painting.
粉筆 *fernbii*, n., chalk (for blackboard).
粉黛 *feendaih*, n., cosmetics, esp. stage make-up (white powder and black for eyebrows); ladies in palace or rich homes.
粉蝶 *feendier*, n., kind of butterfly, with white wings.
粉房 *feen-farng*, n., mill for making flour from bean starch.
粉紅 *feenhurng*, adj., rosy, pale pink.
粉箋 *feen-jian*, n., pink letter paper, also used for copying poems.
粉金 *feenjin*, n., powdered gold, mixed with oil, used in painting.
粉末 *feenmoh*[1], n., powder, powdery substance.
粉墨 *feenmoh*[2], n., cosmetics: 粉墨登場 go on stage, also (contempt.) political stage.
粉皮 *feenpir*, n., vermicelli made from bean starch; lambskin without the fur.
粉刷 *feenshua*, v.t., to whitewash and cover up (facts, situation); n., blackboard eraser.
粉飾 *feenshyh*, v.t., to present pleasant appearance, cover up, hide faults: 粉飾太平 present false appearance of peace and prosperity.
粉碎 *feen-sueih*, v.t., crush to pieces.
粉絲 *feensy*, n., vermicelli made from beans.
粉條 *feentiaur*, n., ditto.
粉頭 *feentour*, n., (MC) prostitutes; clowns and villains on stage with daubs of white powder in make-up.
粉刺 *feentsyh*, n., pimples.
粉團 *feentuarn*, n., flour dumplings; 粉團花 (bot.) a flower, *Hydrangea hortensia*.

§22C.63 (米/丶)

糕 22C.63-8

gau.

[Var. 餻]

N. Cakes, pastry: 糕餅 cakes and biscuits; 糕點 pastry; 蛋糕 sponge cakes; 豆沙糕 bean cakes; 綠豆糕 green lentil cakes; 山楂糕 jelly made from hill haws or berries; 雪糕 (Cantonese) ice cream.

§22C.70 (米/乚)

粃 22C.70-2

bii.

[Var. 秕]

粃糠 *biikang*, n., chaff; what is worthless: 粃糠之妻不下堂 a wife who lived in poverty with husband should not be divorced in times of comfort.

粑 22C.70-5

ba.

N. See 糌[Δ]粑 22C.41.

§22C.81 (米/人)

糢 22C.81-2

mor.

糢糊 *mor'hu*, adj., unclear, hazy (memory, impression, print); also wr. 模.

糗 22C.81-9

chioou.

N. (AC) cooked dry food for journey.

§22C.82 (米/乂)

糉 22C.82-2

tzuhng (also *juhng*).

[Var. of 粽 22C.01]

籹 22C.82-9

mii.

[Dist. 枚 10B.82]

V.t. To subjugate (rebellion), esp. 籹平.

§22C.83 (米/〜)

糙 22C.83-1

tsau (also *tsauh*).

A

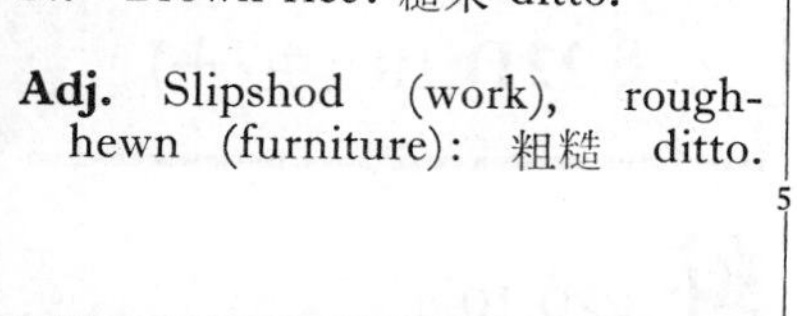

N. Brown rice: 糙米 ditto.

Adj. Slipshod (work), rough-hewn (furniture): 粗糙 ditto.

§ 22C.91 (米/ノ)

糝 22C.91-9

saan.

N. Rice grain.

§ 22C.93 (米/く)

糨 22C.93-5

jiahng.

N. 糨糊, 糨子 Paste (related 醬 21.41 commonly wr. 漿).

糍 22C.93-8

tsyr.

糍粑 *tsyr'ba*, n., a glutinous paste, which can be steamed or fried.

粧 22C.93-9

juang.
[Pop. var. of 妝 21S.93]

N. 粔粧 (AC) a pastry made of fried flour and honey.

B

SECTION 22D

§ 22D.00 (虫/亅)

蝲 22D.00-1

lah.

蝲蛄 *lahgu*, n., (zoo.) *Astacus japonicus.*

蚜 22D.00-5

yar.

N. (Zoo.) an insect kept by ants, *Aphis mali*: 蚜蟲.

蝣 22D.00-6

your.

N. See 蜉^Δ^蝣 22D.00↓.

蜉 22D.00-9

fur.

蜉蝣 *furyour*, n., a kind of insect, *Ephemera strigata*, with life span of only a day.

蜊 22D.00-9

lir.

C

N. See 蛤^Δ^蜊 22D.40.

§ 22D.01 (虫/小)

蛛 22D.01-1

ju.

N. Short for 蜘蛛 spider: 蛛網 spider's web; 蛛絲 spider's thread; 蛛絲馬跡 spider's web and horse's footprint—traces (for detective work).

螓 22D.01-1

chirn.

N. A kind of cicada: 螓首蛾眉 (AC) beautiful women ("cicada hairdo and moth feeler eyebrows").

蝶 22D.01-2

dier.

N. Butterfly, see 蝴^Δ^蝶 22D.42.

螵 22D.01-3

piau.

螵蛸 *piaushiau*, n., bag of grasshopper's eggs.

亅	小	卜	十	土	ナ	廿	⺊	丨	一	丅	フ	口	区	冈	ㄱ	厂	尸	亠	广	宀	丶	乚	弋	心	八	人	乂	⌒	㇀	丿	⺌	く
00	01	02	10	11	12	20	21	22	30	31	32	40	41	42	50	51	52	60	61	62	63	70	71	72	80	81	82	83	90	91	92	93

蜾 22D.01-4

guoo.

N. 蜾蠃 *guorluo*, n., (zoo.) A kind of wasp, *Eumenes pomifomis.*

螺 22D.01-4

luor.

[Anc. var. 蠃]

N. A spiral shellfish, a conch, a snail: 螺殼 *-ker*↓; 田螺 garden snail; 香螺片 edible cartilage cover of conchshell; 螺杯 a shell wine cup.

螺青 *luorching*, n., dark blue color, see *-daih*↓.

螺黛 *luordaih*, n., black for eye pencil.

螺鈿 *luordiahn*, n., lacquerware with imbedded mother-of-pearl.

螺髻 *luorjih*, n., spiral-shaped coil in woman's hairdo.

螺祖 *Luorjur*, n., goddess of sericulture, wife of Huang Dih 黃帝, said to be first to produce silk from silk worms.

螺距 *luorjyuh*, n., pitch or width between threads in screw.

螺殼 *luorker*, n., shell of shellfish.

螺線 *luorshiahn*, n., spiral coil.

螺旋 *luorshyuarn*, n. & adj., spiral, spiral shape: 螺旋柱 spiral column; 螺旋梯 spiral staircase; 螺旋槳 propeller of an airplane, see 螺絲 *-sy*↓.

螺螄 *luor'sy*, n., a kind of small snail.

螺絲 *luorsy*, n., screw: 螺絲釘 screw; 螺絲擺 screwdriver; 螺絲板 spanner; 螺絲鉗 wrench; 螺絲栓, 螺絲公 bolt; 螺絲母, 螺絲帽 nut (for screw); 螺絲蓋 screw top; 螺絲起重機 screw jack; 螺絲鑽 or 螺紋鑽 an auger; 陰螺絲 female thread; 陽螺絲 male thread.

蜍 22D.01-8

chur.

N. See 蟾▵蜍 22D.40, toad.

§ 22D.02 (虫/k)

蠓 22D.02-2

meeng.

N. See 蠛▵蠓 22D.71.

蠔 22D.02-6

haur.

N. Oyster: 蠔油 oyster sauce or oyster oil, a non-greasy common cooking ingredient.

蜋 22D.02-6

larng.

[Var. 螂]

N. A kind of beetle: 蜋蜩 *-tiaur*↓; 螳蜋 the mantis; 蜣蜋 (pr. *liarng*) the dung beetle, *Geotrupes laevistriatus.*

蜋蜩 *larngtiaur*, n., (zoo.) *Melampalta radiator.*

§ 22D.10 (虫/十)

蚌 22D.10-1

*bahng (*behng).*

N. Mother-of-pearl: 老蚌生珠 compliment on man having a son at old age; 鷸▵蚌相爭 32S.50.

蚌埠 **Behngbuh*, n., name of town in Anhwei Province.

蚌珠 *bahngju*, n., pearl.

蚌殼 *banhgker*, n., mother-of-pearl.

蚪 22D.10-1

doou.

N. See 蝌▵蚪 22D.10.

蟫 22D.10-3

tarn.

N. Cloth-destroying moth, silverfish.

蟬 22D.10-4

charn.

N. (1) The cicada. (2) Delicate gauze.

蟬鬢 *charn-bihn*, n., woman's hair-set with framed gauze decorations on side.

蟬聯 *charnliarn*, v.i., continue (to hold office) for another term, to arrive in close succession (like a string of cicadas).

蟬冕 *charn-miaan*, n., ancient hat

with framed gauze.

蟬紗 *charnsha*, n., muslin.

蟬蛻 *charntueih*, n., cicada's molted skin, used in med.; (Taoist) to emancipate oneself from material body, to pass away.

蟬紋 *charnwern*, n., fine lines like those on cicada or dragonfly wings.

蟬衣 *charnyi*, n., see *-tueih*↑.

蟬翼 *charn-yih*, n., cicada's wings, simile for extreme lightness.

蟀 22D.10-6

shuaih (re. pr. *shuoh*).

N. See 蟋△蟀 22D.72.

蝌 22D.10-9

ke.

蝌蚪 *kedoou*, n., tadpole.

蜂 22D.10-9

feng.

N. Bee, wasp: 蜜蜂 honey bee; 胡蜂, 馬蜂 different varieties of wasps; 蜂王 queen bee; 蜂巢, 蜂窩, 蜂房 beehive; 一窩蜂 a swarm of bees, symbolic of an onrushing crowd; 蜂擁而入 (而出) (of crowds) burst, crash in (out); 蜂起 (of bandits) rise like a swarm of bees, i.e., everywhere; 招蜂惹蝶 (of girls) flirt with and attract young men (as flowers attract bees and butterflies).

蜂巢胃 *fengchaur-weih*, n., honeycomb tripe.

蜂糕 *fenggau*, n., a pudding with many holes in it.

蜂蠟 *fenglah*, n., beeswax.

蜂蜜 *fengmih*, n., honey.

蜂鳥 *fengniaau*, n., hummingbird.

蜂窩兒 *fengwo'l*, n., pitted formations as in fermented dough, cakes.

蠏 22D.10-9

shieh.

[Var. of 蟹 92.93]

蛑 22D.10-9

mour.

N. See 蝤△蛑 22D.41.

§ 22D.11 (虫/土)

蛙 22D.11-1

wa.

N. A frog: 井底蛙 a frog in the well—person extremely limited in viewpoint; 蛙式游泳 breast-stroke swimming.

蛙鳴 *wam-irng*, n., croaking of frog.

蛙人 *warern*, n., "frogman"—person specially trained for underwater activities.

螳 22D.11-2

tarng.

N. The praying mantis: usu. 螳螂 *-larng*↓; 螳臂當車 (莊子) overestimating one's own strength, a "mantis trying to stop a cart"; 螳螂捕蟬, 不知黃雀在後 (莊子) mantis seizes the cicada, not knowing the oriole is waiting for the mantis behind.

螳螂 *tarnglarng*, n., the praying mantis.

蛭 22D.11-3

jyh.

N. (Zoo.) the leech: 水蛭 ditto.

蟶 22D.11-3

cheng.

N. (*-tz*) The razor clam.

蛀 22D.11-6

juh.

N. Moth that eats into fabric: 蛀蟲 *-churng*↓.

V. t. (Of insects) eat into; (of tooth) decay: 蟲蛀 be eaten by moth; 蛀爛 destroyed by moth; 蛀齒 a decayed tooth.

蛀蟲 *juhchurng*, n., fabric-eating moth.

蛀蝕 *juhshy*, v. t., eat, be eaten, by moth.

蝗 22D.11-9

huarng.

蟬 蟀 蝌 蜂 蠏 蛑 蛙 螳 蛭 蟶 蛀 蝗

亅	小	⺊	十	土	ナ	卄	⺃	丨	一	丅	フ	口	囗	冂	㇕	厂	尸	亠	广	宀	丶	乚	弋	心	八	人	乂	㇀	丿	⺁	ㄑ
00	01	02	10	11	12	20	21	22	30	31	32	40	41	42	50	51	52	60	61	62	63	70	71	72	80	81	82	83	90	91	92	93

蝗 蟒 虻 蜥 虯 虾 蚓 蠐 螂 蚧 螄 蚱 螘 虹 蜢

N. The locust: 蝗蟲; 蝗災 locust pest.

§ 22D.20 (虫/卄)

蟒 22D.20-2

maang.

N. Boa constrictor; python.

蟒袍 *maangpaur*, n., former official costume of ministers, decorated with gold-thread boa constrictor design.
蟒衣 *maangyi*, n., see *-paur* ↑.

§ 22D.21 (虫/ㄴ)

虻 22D.21-6

merng.
[Abbr. of 蝱 60.93]

§ 22D.22 (虫/丨)

蜥 22D.22-1

shi.

蜥蜴 *shiyih*, n., (zoo.) lizard; 蜥蜴類 (zoo.) *Sauria.*

虯 22D.22-2

chiour.
[Pop. 虬]

Adj. Curly: 虯龍 curling dragon; 虯須, 虯髯 curly beard; 虯蟠 curling and twisting (certain tree roots).

虾 22D.22-3

shiar.
[Abbr. of 蝦 22D.82]

蚓 22D.22-5

yiin.

N. See 蚯△蚓 22D.30.

蠐 22D.22-6

chir.

蠐螬 *chirtsaur*, n., a kind of maggot.

螂 22D.22-6

larng.

N. (1) Var. 蜋 22D.02. (2) 蜣△螂 (pr. *liarng*) 22D.70, 蟑螂.

蚧 22D.22-8

jieh.

N. 蛤蚧 (*gerjieh*) A red-spotted lizard.

螄 22D.22-9

sy.

N. See 螺△螄 22D.01.

蚱 22D.22-9

jah.

蚱蟬 *jahcharn*, n., (zoo.) a kind of cicada, *Cryptotympana pustulata.*
蚱蜢 *jahmeeng*, n., (zoo.) a kind of grasshopper, *Oxya verox.*

§ 22D.30 (虫/一)

螘 22D.30-2

yii.
[Anc. var. of 蟻 ant]

虹 22D.30-3

hurng.

N. The rainbow: 彩虹 many-colored rainbow; 霓虹燈 neon light.

虹橋 *hurngchiaur*, n., arched or camel-back bridge.
虹霓 *hurngnir*, n., rainbow.
虹吸管 *hurngshi-guaan*, n., syphon.
虹彩膜 *hurngtsaaimo*, n., (physiol.) the iris.

蜢 22D.30-3

meeng.

N. See 蚱Δ蜢 22D.22.

蛆 22D.30-4

chyu (**jyu*).

N. Maggots: (fig. and abusive) of another's words compared to maggots: 嚼蛆 talk "tommyrot"; 不知誰下的蛆 do not know who told this stuff and nonsense; 蝍蛆 (**jyu*) a centipede.

蚯 22D.30-9

chiou.

蚯 蚓 *chiouyiin*, n., earthworm.

§ 22D.40 (虫/口)

蛄 22D.40-1

gu.

N. 螻Δ蛄 22D.93, 螻Δ蛄 22D.72, the mole cricket, *Platypleura kaempferi.*

螗 22D.40-6

tarng.

螗 蜩 *tarngtiaur*, n., a kind of cicada.

蟮 22D.40-8

shahn.

N. See 蛐Δ蟮 22D.40, earthworm.

蛤 22D.40-8

ger (**har*).

蛤 蚌 *gerbahng*, n., oysters.
蛤 蚧 *gerjieh*, n., (zoo.) *Phrynosoma.*
蛤 蠣 (蛤蜊) *gerlih*, n., a species of clam.
蛤 蟆 **har'mo*, n., (zoo.) frogs (also wr. 蝦蟆): 癩蛤蟆想吃天鵝肉 (coll. phr.) ugly man hopes to marry a pretty girl.

蜘 22D.40-9

jy.

蜘 蛛 *jyju*, n., spider: 蜘蛛網 spider's net; 蜘蛛抱蛋 (bot.) a plant, *Aspidistra elatior.*

蟾 22D.40-9

charn.

N. (1) The toad, short for 蟾蜍 -*chur* ↓. (2) Dark shadows on the moon, hence the moon, see compp. ↓.

蟾 蜍 *charnchur*, n., the toad, a shadow on the moon, showing a laurel tree and a toad.
蟾 桂 *charngueih*, n., a shadow on the moon, see -*chur* ↑.
蟾 宮 *charngung*, n., the moon ("toad palace," supposed to be a poetic reference): 蟾宮折桂 win the laurel in civil examinations.
蟾 兔 *charntuh*, n., the toad and the hare, shadows on the moon.

§ 22D.41 (虫/図)

蚶 22D.41-2

han.

N. A clam.

蜡 22D.41-2

jah.

[Related to 褚 63C.41 in 褚祭]

螬 22D.41-2

tsaur.

N. See 蠐Δ螬 22D.22.

蚰 22D.41-2

your.

N. 蚰蜒 (Zoo.) *Scutigera*, a kind of centipede.

蛐 22D.41-2

chyur (**chyu*).

N. (1) Earthworm, see 蛐蟮 -'*shan* ↓. (2) Cricket, see 蛐蛐兒 -*chyu'l* ↓.

亅	小	㇎	十	土	ナ	廾	ㆤ	丨	一	丁	乛	口	図	冈	冂	厂	尸	亠	广	宀	丶	乚	七	心	八	人	乂	一	一	丿	𠂉	く
00	01	02	10	11	12	20	21	22	30	31	32	40	41	42	50	51	52	60	61	62	63	70	71	72	80	81	82	83	90	91	92	93

蛐 蝠 蛔 蟈 蝤 蟠 蜻 蛕 蝻 蝴 蠕 蛹 蝟 蚺

蛐蛐兒 *chyuchyu'l*, n., cricket, oft. raised for cricket fights; 蛐蛐罐兒 earthen pot for keeping crickets; 蛐蛐兒罩子 hand net for catching crickets.

蛐蟮 *chyur'shan*, n., earthworm.

蝠 22D.41-3

fur.

N. See 蝙△蝠 22D.42.

蛔 22D.41-4

hueir.

N. The tapeworm: 蛔蟲屬 *-churngshuu*, an intestinal parasite.

蟈 22D.41-4

guo.

N. 螻△蟈 22D.93; see 蟈蟈兒 *-'guo'l*↓.

蟈蟈兒 *guo'guo'l*, n., (zoo.) a large kind of green cricket.

蝤 22D.41-8

chiour.

蝤蠐 *chiourchir*, n., a caterpillar.

蝤蛑 *jioumou*, n., a kind of crab, *Neptunus sp*.

蟠 22D.41-9

parn.

Adj. Bent, curving: 蟠龍 twining dragon; 蟠木 curving tree trunk.

蟠虬紋 *parn-chiour-wern*, n., see *-chy wern*↓.

蟠螭紋 *parnchy wern*, n., (of pillars) with carved curving dragons or lizards.

蟠屈 *parnchyu*, v.i. & adj., twisting (of tree trunks); (of emotions) suppressed.

蟠踞 *parnjyuh*, v.i. & adj., see 盤△踞 91.30.

蟠繞 *parnraur*, v.i. & adj., see 盤△繞 91.30.

蟠桃 *parntaur*, n., a flat, small peach, reputed to be food for Taoist fairies; hence 蟠桃會 the third of third month, birthday of 西王母 Queen Mother of Heaven; (fig.) birthday celebration for aged people.

§ 22D.42 (虫/冈)

蜻 22D.42-1

ching.

蜻蜻 *chingching*, n., a small cicada-like insect.

蜻蛚 *chinglieh*, n., a kind of cricket, *Cyrtoxiphus ritsemae*.

蜻蛉 *chinglirng*, n., an insect very similar to dragonfly, *Libellulidae*.

蜻蜓 *chingtirng*, n., the dragonfly.

蛕 22D.42-1

hueir.

[Var. of 蛔 22D.41]

蝻 22D.42-1

naan (also *narn*).

N. (Zoo.) immature or unfledged locusts.

蝴 22D.42-1

hur.

蝴蝶 *hurdier*, n., butterfly; 蝴蝶花 *--hua*, the iris, *fleur-de-lis*.

蠕 22D.42-3

ruaan (also *rur*).

Adj. (Of small worms) creeping, crawling: 蠕動 wriggling; 蠕蠕 ditto.

蛹 22D.42-3

yuung.

N. Larva.

蝟 22D.42-4

weih.

N. The porcupine: 刺蝟 ditto; 蝟集 (business) pile up ("swarm like porcupines"); 蝟毛而起 (AC) rise up in numbers (in rebellion).

蚺 22D.42-4

rarn.

N. A boa constrictor.

蜩 22D.42-4

tiaur.

N. Cicada (AC for modn. 蟬 22D.10).

蜩螗 *tiaurtarng*, adj., noisy and in confusion: 國事蜩螗 the country is in dire confusion.

蝄 22D.42-4

waang.

N. See 魍ᐞ魎 91.70.

蝸 22D.42-4

gua (also *wa*).

N. 蝸牛 see *-niour* ↓.

蝸角 *guajiaau*, n., (anything small like) a snail's tentacles.
蝸居 *gua-jyu*, v. t., to live cut off from the world.
蝸螺 *gualuor*, n., (zoo.) a shellfish, *Melania libertina* (also 河貝子).
蝸廬 *gualur*, n., (self-deprecatory) one's humble home.
蝸牛 *guaniour*, n., (zoo.) the snail.
蝸舍 *guasheh*, n., see *-lur* ↑.

蠣 22D.42-5

lih.

N. The oyster: see compp. 蠣塘 a pond for oyster culture.

蠣房 *lihfarng*, n., oyster shell.
蠣粉 *lihfeen*, n., oyster shell powder.
蠣黃 *lihhuarng*, n., oyster meat.
蠣奴 *lihnur*, n., (zoo.) the hermit crab.

螭 22D.42-6

chy.

N. A lizard or gargoyle-like ornament, often seen on antiques, pillars: 螭頭 gargoyle-like ornament on temple or palace roofs; 螭紐 carved lizard handle of a cup.

蝙 22D.42-6

bian (also *biaan*).

蝙蝠 *bianfur* (*biaan-*), n., (zoo.) a bat.

蚋 22D.42-8

rueih.
[Var. 蜹]

N. A gnat: 蚊蚋 mosquitoes and gnats, small biting insects.

§ 22D.50 (虫/⺄)

蜴 22D.50-4

yih.

N. See 蜥ᐞ蜴 22D.22.

蝎 22D.50-4

shie (**her*).

N. (1) Pop. var. of 蠍 22D.81, scorpion. (2) (**her*) A wood-destroying moth.

蠋 22D.50-4

jur.

N. A kind of harmful insect.

螞 22D.50-5

maa (**ma, *mah*).

螞蟥 *maahuarng*, n., horseleech (also wr. 馬蟥).
螞蚱 *mah'ja*, n., a kind of locust.
螞螂 *ma'lang*, n., dragonfly.
螞蟻 *maayih*, n., ant (also wr. 馬蟻).

螃 22D.50-6

parng (*baang*).

N. (**baang*) A species of toad.

螃蜞 *parngchir*, n., a small species of crabs.
螃蟹 *parngshieh*, n., crab.

蚡 22D.50-8

fern.

N. Field mouse, a kind of mole, also wr. 鼢.

蜩 蝄 蝸 蠣 螭 蝙 蚋 蜴 蝎 蠋 螞 螃 蚡

亅	小	⺊	十	土	𠂇	廾	𠃊	丨	一	丅	⺄	口	区	冈	ㄱ	厂	尸	亠	广	宀	丶	乚	弋	心	八	人	乂	一	ノ	⺁	𠃋	く
00	01	02	10	11	12	20	21	22	30	31	32	40	41	42	50	51	52	60	61	62	63	70	71	72	80	81	82	83	90	91	92	93

蛉
蟯
蜷
蚘
虯
虵
蚍
蛛
蜆
蠅
蛇

§ 22D.63 (虫/丶)

蛉 22D.63–8

lirng.
[Usu. printed 蛉]

N. See 蜻▵蛉 22D.42; 螟▵蛉 22D.80; 白▵蛉子 91.41.

§ 22D.70 (虫/乚)

蟯 22D.70–1

raur.

N. 蟯蟲 (zoo.) the pinworm, *Oxyuris vermicularis.*

蜷 22D.70–1

chyuarn.

V. i. To curl up like worms.

蜷曲 *chyuarnchyu*, v. i. & adj., to curl up, curling.
蜷伏 *chyuarnfur*, v. i., (of worms) to curl up and sleep.
蜷局 *chyuarnjyur*, adj., (AC) curled up, frustrated.
蜷蜿 *chyuarnwaan*, adj., encircling (like mountain range).

蚘 22D.70–1

hueir.
[Var. of 蛔 22D.41]

虯 22D.70–2

chiour.
[Pop. of 虬 22D.22]

虵 22D.70–2

sher.
[Pop. of 蛇 22D.70]

蚍 22D.70–2

pir.

蚍蜉 *pirfur*, n., a species of big ant: 蚍蜉撼大樹 phr., an ant trying to shake a big tree—futile effort.

蛛 22D.70–2

yaur.

N. A kind of mother-of-pearl.

蜆 22D.70–4

shiaan.

N. (1) A species of small clam, *Corbicula leana.* (2) A small black insect with a red head, which suspends itself by a thread from its mouth; hence the nickname 縊女 "suicide girl."

蠅 22D.70–4

yirng.
[Abbr. 蝇]

N. A fly: 蒼蠅 ditto; 蠅營 -*yirng* ↓.

蠅毒草 *yirngdur-tsaau*, n., (bot.) *Phryma leptoslachya*, whose root contains fluid poisonous to flies.
蠅拂 *yirngfur*, n., a fly swatter.
蠅虎 *yirnghuu*, n., (zoo.) a kind of spider that feeds on flies.
蠅頭 *yirngtour*, adj., petty, very small (profits): 蠅頭小字 very small characters.
蠅營 *yirngyirng*, v. i., to hustle about trying to make some profits.

蛇 22D.70–6

sher (**yir*).
[Pop. 虵]

N. A snake, serpent: 一條蛇 a snake; 毒蛇, 蝮蛇 poisonous snake; 海蛇 sea snake; 水蛇 water snake; 四脚蛇 lizard; 響尾蛇 rattlesnake; 眼鏡蛇 or 毒帽蛇 cobra; 蛇頭鼠尾 sneaky, crafty look; 蛇蠍 snakes and scorpions; 蛇豕 or 封豕長蛇 (AC) wild boars and snakes—fiends of society; 虎頭蛇尾 things which start off big and then end up in nothing; 蛇吞象 (fig.) inordinately greedy, a snake trying to swallow an elephant; 蛇無頭不行 a snake cannot crawl when head is injured—importance of leader; 打草驚蛇 put enemy on guard by premature action; 畫蛇添足 doing what is superfluous ("adding feet to a picture of a snake").

Adj. (**yir*) 蛇蛇 (AC) calmly, leisurely; 委▵蛇 90.93.

蛇牀 *sherchuarng*, n., (bot.) *Cridium japonicum*; 蛇牀子 --*tz*, n., (bot.) *Selinum japonicum* (also called 蛇米, 蛇粟, 蛇蛋果).
蛇符 *sherfur*, n., the slough of a snake.
蛇含 *sherharn*, n., (bot.) *Potentilla kleiniana* (also wr. 蛇銜).
蛇舅母 *sherjiouhmuu*, n., (zoo.) a long-tailed lizard, *Takydromus*

tachydromoides ("snake's maternal uncle's wife").

蛇麻 *shermar*, n., (bot.) hops, *Humulus lupulus*.

蛇矛 *shermaur*, n., as in 丈八蛇矛 an ancient long spear.

蛇苺 *shermeir*, n., (bot.) the Indian strawberry, *Duchesnea indica*.

蛇皮癬 *sherpir-shyuaan*, n., (med.) a skin disease with dry scales.

蛇婆 *sherpor*, n., a sea snake.

蛇葡萄 *sher-purtaur*, n., (bot.) *Ampelopsis heterophylla* or northern fox grape.

蛇行 *sher-shirng*, v. i., to crawl forward: 蛇行而進.

蛇頭瘡 *shertour-chuang*, n., (med.) a whitlow.

蛇蛻 *shertueih*, n., slough of a snake, used as medicine.

蛇足 *sher-tzur*, n., (from 畫蛇添足) s.t. superfluous.

蛇紋石 *sherwern-shyr*, n., (min.) serpentine.

蛇 22D.70-6

jah.

N. (AC) jellyfish (=modn., 水母, 海蜇).

蜿 22D.70-6

wan (also *waan*).

蜿蜒 *wanyarn*, v. i., (boundaries, the Great Wall) to wind around, to stretch over long distance (related 蔓[A]延 20A.82).

蛻 22D.70-8

tueih (*shueih*).

N. Exuviae, shedded skin of insects: 蟬蛻 molted skin of cicada, used as medicine.

V. t. To molt (moult), to shed skin, horn, etc.

蛻變 *tueihbiahn*, v. i., to change (customs, habits, fashions, to mutate).

蜣 22D.70-8

chiang.

蜣螂 *chianglarng*, n., the dung beetle.

蜺 22D.70-9

nir.

N. (1) (Var. of 霓) a rainbow. (2) (Zoo.) a cicada, *Cosmopsaltria opalifera*.

虼 22D.70-9

geh.

虼蚤 *gehtzaau*, n., lice.

蠟 22D.70-9

lah.

[Dist. 臘 42A.70]

N. Wax, a candle: 木蠟 wood-wax; 鯨蠟 ambergris; 蜜蠟 beeswax; 蟲白蠟 white wax produced from wax insects; 蠟燭 *-jur*↓; 洋蠟 ("Western") candle; 蠟淚 *-leih*↓; 味同嚼蠟 insipid like chewing wax.

V. t. To apply wax to (s. t.).

Adj. Yellowish like wax: 蠟梅 *-meir*↓; 面色如蠟 (of face) ashen-colored.

蠟筆 *lahbii*, n., color crayons.

蠟扦(兒) *lahchian* (*-chia'l*), n., candlestick with sharp point.

蠟蟲 *lahchurng*, n., a scale insect which produces wax.

蠟膏 *lahgau*, n., (med.) an ointment made with wax as base.

蠟花 *lahhua*, n., a flower-like formation on a burning candle or snuff.

蠟渣(子) *lahja*(*tz*), n., molten candle, candle drippings: 似蠟渣子黃 (of face) of waxen color.

蠟箋 *lahjian*, n., waxed or sized letter paper (also 蠟紙 *-jyy*↓).

蠟夾子 *lahjiartz*, n., tweezers or scissors for trimming candle-wick.

蠟燭 *lahjur*, n., candle.

蠟炬 *lahjyuh*, n., big candle.

蠟紙 *lahjyy*, n., (1) wax(ed) paper (also 蠟箋 *-jian*↑); (2) stencil.

蠟淚 *lahleih*, n., guttering or dripping of candle (lit., "candle tears").

蠟梅 *lahmeir*, n., (bot.) the winter-sweet, *Calycanthus fragrans* (also wr. 臘梅).

蠟人 *lahrern*, n., wax figure.

蠟像 *lahshiahng*, n., waxworks.

蠟芯兒 *lahshie'l*, n., candlewick.

蠟書 *lahshu*, n., (AC) secret message sealed in a wax-coated ball.

蠟樹 *lahshuh*, n., (bot.) *Ligustrum*, the white wax tree *Lucidum* (another name for 女貞).

蠟石 *lahshyr*, n., (min.) (1) steatite; (2) yellow quartz.

蠟臺 *lahtair*, n., candleholder, candle stand (also 燭臺).

蠟頭兒 *lahtour'l*, n., (1) the stump of a candle; (2) (fig.) anything nearing its end.

蠟坨(兒)(子) *lahtuor*('*l*)(*tz*), n., a lump of wax.

蠟 蠛 蜮 蟻 蛾 蟣 蟪 蟋 蜞 蟥 蠙 螟 蚨

蠟嘴 *lahtzueei*, n., (zoo.) the haw-finch, waxbill.

蠟子 *lahtzyy*¹, n., (1) nest made by wax insects for laying eggs; (2) (min.) a purple precious stone.

蠟滓 *lahtzyy*², n., see 蠟渣 *-ja* ↑.

蠟丸(兒) *lahwarn(-war'l)*, n., a wax-coated pill (of medicine or other things).

蠟油 *lahyour*, n., drips from lighted candle.

§22D.71 (虫/七)

蠛 22D.71-2

mieh.

蠛蠓 *miehmeeng*, n., small flies.

蜮 22D.71-7

yuh.

N. (1) A fabulous creature, said to be like a turtle and blow poisonous sand in man's face, hence 鬼蜮伎倆 devilish tricks. (2) A rice-destroying insect.

蟻 22D.71-8

yii.

N. Ant: 螞蟻 ditto; 蟻附 swarm around like ants; 蟻動 stir about like ants; 蟻合，蟻聚，蟻集 (said usu. of bandits) infest.

蟻垤 *yii-dier*, n., (LL) anthill.

蟻封 *yii-feng*, n., (LL) see *-dier* ↑.

蟻孔 *yir-kuung*, n., ant hole.

蟻民 *yiimirn*, n., formerly, self-reference of common people *vis-à-vis* the magistrate.

蟻穴 *yiishyueh*, n., ant hole, ant's nest.

蟻酸 *yiisuan*, n., (chem.) formic acid.

蛾 22D.71-9

er.

N. (1) (*-tz*) A moth: 蠶蛾 the silkworm moth; 燈蛾 moth attracted by lamp light. (2) Mushroom, fungus: 木蛾 tree fungus.

蛾眉 *ermeir*, n., (1) beautiful eyebrows of woman; (2) a beautiful woman.

蛾眉月 *ermeir-yueh*, n., the crescent moon.

蟣 22D.71-9

jii.

N. (1) A nit. (2) The leech.

§22D.72 (虫/心)

蟪 22D.72-1

hueih.

蟪蛄 *hueihgu*, n., a kind of cicada.

蟋 22D.72-9

shi.

蟋蟀 *shishuaih* (*-shuoh*), n., cricket.

§22D.80 (虫/八)

蜞 22D.80-2

chir.

N. See 蟛△蜞 22D.91.

蟥 22D.80-2

huarng.

N. See 馬△蟥 51.50.

蠙 22D.80-6

bin.

[Var. of 蚌△ 22D.10]

N. (AC) mother-of-pearl (commonly called 蚌 22D.10).

螟 22D.80-6

mirng.

螟蛉 *mirnglirng*, n., various kinds of caterpillars; 螟蛉子 adopted son, from erroneous observation that the wasp carries caterpillars to nest to feed them (really to feed its larvae).

§22D.81 (虫/人)

蚨 22D.81-1

fur.

A

N. A water beetle: 青蚨 (LL) cash, money.

蚨蝶 *furdier*, n., var. for 胡蝶 butterfly.

蛺 22D.81-1

jiar.

N. 蛺蝶 (rare) gen. term for the butterfly.

蟆 22D.81-2

mar.

N. See 蝦ᐞ蟆 22D.82.

蝡 22D.81-3

ruaan.

[Var. of 蠕 22D.42]

蜈 22D.81-4

wur.

蜈蚣 *wurgung* (-'*gung*), n., the centipede.

蠍 22D.81-4

shie.

N. Scorpion.

蠍虎 *shiehuu*, n., a house lizard.

B

蠍子媽 *shietzma*, n., ("scorpion's mother"—a person to be shunned like scorpion.

§ 22D.82 (虫/乂)

蚑 22D.82-1

chir.

N. A kind of insect: 長蚑 (AC) an insect like spider; 蚑行 to crawl like an insect, see 跂 40B.82.

蠖 22D.82-2

huoh.

N. See 尺ᐞ蠖 52.91.

蝦 22D.82-5

shia (**har*).

N. Shrimp: 明蝦 prawn; 龍蝦 lobster.

蝦蛄 *shiagu*, n., the locust shrimp, *Squilla oratoria*.
蝦蟆 **har'ma*, n., a frog, a toad.
蝦米 *shia'mi*, n., dried shrimp.
蝦仁(兒) *shiarern*(-*rer'l*), n., shelled shrimp meat.
蝦鬚 *shia-shyu*, n., shrimp's feelers.
蝦子 *shiatzyy*, n., shrimp roe.

蚊 22D.82-6

wern.

C

N. (-*tz*) Mosquito: 蚊雷 din of mosquitoes; 蚊力 a mosquito's strength—woefully inadequate.

蚊廚 *wernchur*, n., (LL) mosquito net, see -*jahng* ↓.
蚊蟲 *wernchurng*, n., mosquito.
蚊帳 *wernjahng*, n., mosquito net.
蚊母鳥 *wernmur-niaau*, n., a kind of night hawk, *Caprimulgus jotaka*.
蚊母樹 *wernmuu-shuh*, n., (bot.) *Distylium racemosum*, a fine, hard wood.
蚊(子)香 *wern*(*tz*)*shiang*, n., incense for keeping away mosquitoes.

蛟 22D.82-6

jiau.

N. A mythical aquatic animal supposed to be the cause of great floods: 蛟龍之志 a person with great ambitions; 蛟龍得水 happy like dragons in water—in the most congenial surroundings.

蝮 22D.82-9

fuh.

N. Venomous snake, viper.

§ 22D.83 (虫/乀)

蜨 22D.83-1

dier.

[Var. of 蝶 22D.01]

蜓 22D.83-9

tirng.

N. See 蜻ᐞ蜓 22D.42.

蜒 22D.83-9

yarn.

V. i. 蜿蜒 to stretch for miles.

蜒 蚰 *yarnyour*, n., (zoo.) *philomycus*, a kind of snail (also called 蛞蝓, 鼻涕蟲).

§ 22D.91 (虫/ノ)

蟛 22D.91-1

perng.

蟛 蜞 *perngchir*, n., (zoo.) a species of small crabs, *Grapsus sp.*; also wr. 螃蜞 (*parng-*).

§ 22D.93 (虫/く)

螻 22D.93-2

lour.

N. (Zoo.) 螻蛄 *-gu* ↓.

螻 蛄 *lourgu*, n., (zoo.) the mole cricket, *Gryllotalpa africana*.
螻 國 *lourguo*, n., (zoo.) the frog.
螻 蟻 *louryii*, n., (zoo.) mole crickets and ants, hence anything of no significance.

蚣 22D.93-8

gung.

N. (Zoo.) 蜈蚣 the centipede.

SECTION 22S

§ 22S.00 (丨ˢ/亅)

對 22S.00-1

dueih.

N. & n. adjunct. (1) (*'l*) A pair: 一對耳環, 手套 a pair of earrings, gloves; 一對夫妻 a married couple. (2) (*-tz*) A literary couplet, couplet wr. on scrolls: 對聯 *-liarn* ↓; practice of matching character with another, same in category, but opposite in tone (e.g., "heaven" 對 "earth"; "rain" 對 "wind"), known as 對子 *-tz* ↓; 對對子 make such couplet. (3) (*-'l*) Match: 成雙作對, 對對雙雙 pairs of boys and girls, men and women; 配對兒 form couples (in dance, etc.).

V. i. & t. (1) To answer: 對答 answer (vern. usu. 答 alone); 對曰 (LL) answer(ed); 無以爲對 (LL) do not know how to reply; 對答如流 give fluent replies. (2) To face, encounter: 一人對一人 one person against another; 相對 face each other; 反對 oppose; 絕對 absolute(-ly); 對牛彈琴 waste effort, cast pearls before swine; 對症下藥 prescribe specific medicine for illness; oft. used in sense of "facing": 對着這件事 facing (regarding) this situation; 對景傷情 moved by what one sees (dear one gone, etc.); 對月獨酌 drink alone under moon; 對菊賦詩 compose poem facing chrysanthemums; 對面 *-miahn* ↓. (3) Check: 對號頭 check number (of ticket for seats, etc.); 對筆跡 check signature; 對口供 confront witness at court; 對簿, 對證, 對條, 對質 *-buh*, *-jehng*, *-tiaur*, *-jyr*, etc. ↓; 校對 proofreading; 核對 check figures, draft, etc. (4) Agree: 對胃口 agree with stomach; 對縫兒 close fitting of seam; 對勁兒, 對工兒 *-jihn'l*, *-gung'l*. (5) Add water:

對

對點兒水 add a little water. (6) Deal with, in dealings with, treat: 對待人不錯 treat people well, esp. show fairness, behave properly; 對不住 *-bur-juh*, 對不起 *-bur-chii*, regular form for saying "I am sorry"; 對不起朋友 act unworthily to a friend; 對不起他 be less than fair to him; 對得住 (or 起) act worthily (of friend, parents).

Adj. (1) Correct: 對不對 is that correct? 你不對 you are wrong; (不對 as n.) 有什麽不對 (的地方) if there is any mistake. (2) Facing, opposite: 對門 across the street; 對岸 opposite shore. (3) Adv., half, in half: 對半 half; 對開, 對合子 *-kai*, *-hertz* ↓.

Adv. Directly, face to face, together: 對立, 坐 stand, sit opposite each other; 對談, 飲 talk, drink together; 對打 fight each other; 對換 exchange (seats, etc.); 對調 switch posts; 對設 place opposite each other.

Prep. At, for, toward, in regard to (對 or 對於): 對我 (對於我) 沒有什麽不好 for me it is all right; 對他 (對於他) 有大損失 for him, it means a great loss; 對我説 say to me; 對 (於) 這問題 in regard to this problem; 他對我很好 he is very good to me; 對外, 對內 externally, internally; 對外宣傳 propaganda abroad; 對內政策 domestic policy.

對半 *dueihbahn*, n. & adj., half, fifty-fifty.

對白 *dueihbair*, n., dialogue.

對比 *dueihbii*, n., proportionate measure: 成對比 in proportion to.

對簿 *dueihbuh*, v.i., confront s.o. with witness: 對簿公堂 check evidence of both parties at court.

對稱 *dueihchehn*, n. & adj., symmetry, -trical; analogue, one of a pair balanced against or symmetrical with the other.

對答 *dueihda*, n. & v.i., reply to questions, ability to answer questions or carry on conversation.

對待 *dueihdaih*, v.i., treat, deal with (person): 對待下人 treat domestics; 你怎麽對待他 how are you going to deal with him?

對等 *dueihdeeng*, adj., on an equal footing, equal to: 相對等.

對點子 *dueihdiaantz*, v.i., similar in name; coincide.

對調 *dueihdiauh*, v.i., exchange places or posts.

對敵 *dueihdir*, n., opponent; v.i., to oppose, antagonize.

對頂角 *dueihdirngjiaau*, n., (geom.) vertically opposite angles.

對方 *dueihfang*, n., the other party (in negotiations).

對付 *fueih'fu*, v. i., (1) deal with: 讓我來對付他 let me deal with him; 對付局面 deal with situation; (2) do, serve, superficially: 可以對付 good enough; 勉強對付就算了 will serve for the moment.

對光兒 *dueihguang'l*, v. i., fight it out: 讓他們打個對光兒 let them fight it out.

對工兒 *dueihgung'l*, adj., serviceable, serve the purpose.

對過(兒) *dueihguoh('l)*, adv. phr., across the street, face to face.

對合子 *dueihhertz*, adj., half: 對合子的利 a profit of 50%.

對換 *dueihhuahn*, v. i., exchange (goods, seats, etc.).

對仗 *dueihjahng*, n., antithesis in rhetoric; 做對仗, 工對仗 make, good at, parallel, antithetical constructions.

對照 *dueihjauh*, v. i., check against (original, variant version): 互相對照 check one against another; face opposite.

對證 *dueihjehng*, n. & v. i., confrontation of, witnesses at court, confront.

對角線 *dueihjiaau-shiahn*, n., (geom.) diagonal line.

對勁(兒) *dueihjihn('l)*, v. i., get along well: 不對勁兒 do not get along.

對襟(兒) *dueihjin('l)*, n. & adj., Chinese jacket with buttons straight down middle.

對狀 *dueihjuahng*, v. i., confront (party) at court.

對峙 *dueihjyh*, v. i., stand opposite each other (armies, mountains).

對質 *dueihjyr*, v. i., confront at court; cross-examine.

對局 *dueih-jyur*, v.i., play chess.

對抗 *dueihkahng*, v. t., oppose; resist (enemy); v. i., to rival: 與之對抗爭衡 to rival (s. o.) in power, prestige, etc.

對開 *dueihkai*, n., (of paper) folio; v. i., (of vehicles) run in opposite directions. ⌈10B.41.

對口 *dueihkoou*, n., see 對口相聲

對兒 *due'l*, n., a couplet, see *-liarn* ↓; 成對兒 make a pair.

對壘 *dueihleei*, n., opposing camps.

對聯(兒) *dueihliarn(-liar'l)*, n., a pair of scrolls containing a poetic couplet.

對流 *dueihliour*, n., (phys.) convection of heat or electrified particles.

對路子 *dueihluhtz*, adj., appropriate for needs, good for one's purposes.

對門 *dueihmern*, adj., opposite the gate, across the road, (of houses) facing each other.

對面(兒) *dueihmiahn(-miah'l)*, adj., just across, in front.

對偶 *dueih-oou*, v.i., to couple, mate; n., see *-'l* ↑. ⌈court.

對審 *dueihsheen*, v.i., confront at

對蝦 *dueihshia*, n., (zoo.) prawn.

對象 *dueihshiahng*, n., object wooed, pursued or looked for.

對手 *dueihshoou*, n., opponent in contest, equal match: 不是他的對手 not his match.

對數 *dueihshuh*, n., (math.) logarithms; 對數率 modulus; 對數級數 logarithmic series; 對數曲線 logarithmic curve; 對數表 table of logarithm; 對數底 logarithmic base; 對數螺線 logarithmic spiral.

對式 *dueihshyh*, adj., of correct standard, suitable, fitting.

對汛 *dueishyuhn*, v. i., patrol along national borders.

亅	小	⺊	十	土	ナ	廾	𠃊⺊	丨	一	丁	フ	口	区	冈	㇕	厂	尸	亠	广	宀	丶	乚	弋	心	八	人	乂	〜	丿	丿丿	𠂉	く
00	01	02	10	11	12	20	21	22	30	31	32	40	41	42	50	51	52	60	61	62	63	70	71	72	80	81	82	83	90	91	92	93

對條 *dueihtiaur('l)*, n., check, chit for delivering goods.
對頭 *dueihtour*, n., match for person in strength: 不是他的對頭 not his match; enemy, (also pr. *dueih'tou*); match in matrimony.
對策 *dueihtseh*, v. i., formerly, oral test on current topics in civil examinations; proposal to deal with situation.
對子 *dueihtz*, n., literary couplet.
對位法 *dueihweih-faa*, n., (mus.) counterpoint.
對眼 *dueihyaan*, adj., cross-eyed.
對於 *dueih'yu*, prep., in regard to, regarding; see Prep. ↑.

剉 22S.00-2

tsuoh.

V. t. To cut, chop up into fine pieces, (interch. 挫 10A.11).

削 22S.00-2

shyueh (sp. pr. *shiau*).
[Usu. wr. 削]

V. t. (1) To scrape off: 削皮 scrape off skin; 削蘋果 peel an apple; 削鉛筆 sharpen pencil; 削足適履 cut the foot to fit the shoe—Procrustean methods; 削牘 scraped off writing on ancient bamboo strips; 削草 (LL) destroy original draft of official communications as a measure of safety; 削葱 ("cut onions") a lady's slender fingers. (2) To exterminate, deprive: 削除, 削奪 *-chur*, *-duor* ↓; 削減 cut down (budget, force, etc.); 削職 deprive person of office; 削地 cede a piece of territory.

Adj. Steep (cliffside).

削除 *shyueh-chur*, n., deprive one of (rights); cut off (malpractices, etc.).
削奪 *shyuehduor*, n., deprive one of s. t., forcibly take away (power, land, rank).
削髮 *shyueh-faa*, n., shave head (to become monk or nun).
削正 *shyueh-jehng*, v. t., (court.) ask s. o. to mercilessly revise script.
削迹 *shyueh-ji*, v. i., to lead a hide-out life.
削籍 *shyueh-jir*, v. i., dismiss (official) and disqualify him for future office.
削職 *shyueh-jyr*, n., to deprive person of post.
削平 *shyueh-pirng*, v. i., to suppress (a rebellion).
削弱 *shyuehruo*, v.t., to weaken.

劃 22S.00-2

huah.

V.i. & t. To draw a line or boundary, to divide or set apart (also wr. 画): 劃分, 劃開 divide, set apart; 劃入 cause s.t. to be included in, set apart for some account or purpose; 劃界 to mark out boundary; 劃撥 (of bank) transfer funds, pay out; 劃線支票 crossed check; 劃時代的 epoch-making.

劃拉 *huar'la*, v.i., (1) to rub gently (a child); (2) to shove in anyhow: 劃拉入嘴; (3) to scribble or daub hurriedly: 隨便劃拉幾筆 just scribble a few lines.
劃一 *huahyi*, v.t. & adj., (make) uniform (prices), neat and definite; 劃一不二 one-price system, no haggling.

§ 22S.10 (丨ˢ/十)

韡 22S.10-2

weei.

Adj. (AC) bright, luxuriant.

輝 22S.10-6

huei.

N. Glory, splendor: 光輝, 輝光 shining glory.

Adj. Splendid, see compp.↓.

輝煌 *hueihuarng*, adj., glorious, shining (achievements).
輝然 *hueirarn*, adj., bright.
輝耀 *hueiyauh*, v. i., (of name, achievement) to shine (over places); adj., shining.
輝映 *hueiyihng*, v. i., to reflect: 互相輝映 shine by reflected glory, (many lights) increase the brilliant display; also of contemporary great artists, etc.

§ 22S.11 (丨ˢ/土)

壯 22S.11-1

juahng.
[Abbr. of 壯 21S.11]

耀 22S.11-5

yauh.

N. Brightness: 光耀 brightness; 榮耀 honor.

V. i. To shine: 炫耀 to show off, glorify; 誇耀 to magnify, extol; 耀武揚威 put on airs, show one's prowess; 耀目 to dazzle.

Adj. Shining.

A B C

§22S.21 (丨S/乚)

韜 22S.21-9

tau.

N. (1) Scabbard, bow case. (2) Military science in 六韜; hence 韜略, see *-lyueh* ↓.

V.t. Cover up: 韜光, 韜晦 dim the light—Laotse's counsel against being ostentatious.

韜 略 *taulyueh*, n., military tactics.

§22S.22 (丨S/丨)

鄰 22S.22-3

lirn.

N. (1) Neighbor, neighborhood; neighboring country: 四鄰 surrounding neighbors; 近鄰 close neighbors. (2) Lowest self-government unit in village or town, a division of 里.

Adj. Close, adjacent, being neighbor: 鄰國, 鄰邦 neighboring country; 鄰鄉 neighboring village; 鄰舍 next house; 鄰境 neighboring area; 毗鄰 adjacent; 相鄰 close together.

鄰 界 *lirnjieh*, n., frontier, boundary.
鄰 近 *lirnjihn*, adj., close by.
鄰 居 *lirnjyu*, n., neighbor.
鄰 里 *lirnlii*, n., people of the same neighborhood or district.
鄰 人 *lirnrern*, n., neighbor.

§22S.30 (丨S/一)

韞 22S.30-4

yuhn.

V.i. To hide: 韞匵 (AC) to hide one's talent like keeping pearl in casket (also wr. 櫝).

§22S.41 (丨S/図)

旧 22S.41-4

jiouh.

[Abbr. of 舊 20A.21]

§22S.42 (丨S/冈)

黼 22S.42-1

fuu.

黼 黻 *fuufur*, n., square patch on official costume embroidered with white and black axes; 黼黻文章 decorative prose, high-flown prose.

§22S.50 (丨S/ㄱ)

暢 22S.50-4

chahng.

Adj. & adv. (1) Thorough, -ly, free, -ly: 通暢 (style) lucid; 流暢 (style) flowing freely; 暢所欲言 express with zest and gusto; 暢所欲爲 do whatever one wants; 暢飲 drink to heart's content; 暢敍, 暢談 have a great delightful talk together. (2) Delightful, -ly, gratifying, with gusto: 舒暢 relaxed, pleasurable, comfortable; 歡暢 delight, -ed, -ful (occasion, reunion, etc.); 暢懷, 暢適 *-huair*, *-shyh* ↓. (3) Prosperous, doing very well: 暢銷 sells very well; 暢行 spreads widely; 暢旺, 暢茂 *-wahng*, *-mauh* ↓.

暢 達 *chahngdar*, adj., (business) prosperous; (style) expressive.
暢 好 *chahnghaau*, adj., satisfying.
暢 懷 *chahnghuair*, n., gratifying, delightful, -ed.
暢 快 *chahngkuaih*, adj. & adv., (1) straight and quick, without mincing words; (2) relax, -ing, -ed, comfortable, satisfied.
暢 茂 *chahngmauh*, adj., (business, trees) prospering, thriving.
暢 洽 *chahngshiar*, adj., satisfying, cordial (reunion).
暢 適 *chahngshyh*, adj., relaxing, -ed, refreshing, -ed.
暢 旺 *chahngwahng*, adj., *-mauh* ↑.
暢 鬱 *chahngyuh*, adj., *-mauh* ↑.

韌 22S.50-5

rehn.

Adj. Pliable but strong: 堅韌 tough and resilient.

韌 帶 *rehndaih*, n., (physiol.) ligaments.
韌 度 *rehnduh*, n., resilience.
韌 皮 *rehnpir*, n., (bot.) the phloem, bast, tough fibre for making ropes, etc.
韌 性 *rehnshihng*, n., tenacity, flexibility, resilience.

韜 鄰 韞 旧 黼 暢 韌

亅	小	⺊	十	土	ナ	廾	㇄	丨	一	丅	フ	口	図	冈	㇆	厂	尸	亠	广	宀	丶	乚	七	心	八	人	乂	乛	一	ノ	𠂉	く
00	01	02	10	11	12	20	21	22	30	31	32	40	41	42	50	51	52	60	61	62	63	70	71	72	80	81	82	83	90	91	92	93

鷫 22S.50-9

suh.

鷫鷞 *suhshuaang*, n., variously described as a water bird, like the crane, also a mythic bird.

§ 22S.70 (丨^S/ㄴ)

覞 22S.70-4

tiaan.

Adj. Ashamed, see 靦$^\Delta$覞 31S.70.

皰 22S.70-9

pauh.

N. Pimple.

艴 22S.70-9

fur.

Adv. (AC) 艴然不悅 angrily, showing angry countenance; (var. of 怫 22A.22).

§ 22S.71 (丨^S/七)

韈 22S.71-2

wah.

[Anc. var. of 襪 63C.71]

§ 22S.80 (丨^S/八)

順 22S.80-3

shuhn.

V. t. (1) Obey: 順命 *-mihng*↓; 順從 *-tsurng*↓. (2) Follow (bent, direction, wind), go with (general trend): 順理, 順流 *-lii, -liour*↓; 順帶 phr., bring along casually; 順帶一提 mention by the way; 順人情, 順合人意 go with what people feel or desire; 順時俗 follow prevailing customs; 順竿兒爬 fall in with other people's wishes; 順條順理兒, 順順溜溜 smoothly, obediently. (3) To submit, render obedience: 順服 *-fur*↓; 歸順 render obedience to regime or government, opp. 逆 to rise or fight against.

Adj. (1) With a trend, (also prep.) opp. 逆 against: 順風 *-feng*↓; 順路, 順手 *-luh, -shoou*^{2}↓. (2) Satisfactory, doing well, as one desires: 順利 *-lih*↓; 順當, 順適 *-'dang, -shyh*↓; 境遇不順 meet with adverse circumstances.

順把 *shuhnbaa*, adj., obedient: 這個人有點不順把 this man does not always listen to what you say.

順便(兒) *shuhnbiahn(-biah'l)*, adv., conveniently, without extra effort: 順便把這信交他 as you are going there, please take this letter to him.

順差 *shuhncha*, n., favorable balance.

順成 *shuhncherng*, v. i., accomplish s.t. without hindrance.

順情 *shuhn-chirng*, v. i., show respect for what others feel; (philosophy) allow people to fulfill their natural feelings.

順當 *shuhn'dang*, adj., carrying on smoothly.

順道 *shuhndauh*, adv., see *-luh*↓.

順耳 *shuhn-ee*, adj., pleasing to the ear.

順風 *shuhn-feng*, adv., leeward, with the wind; (court. phr.) *bon voyage*; 順風耳 (myth.) one who has magical power of hearing miles away.

順服 *shuhnfur*, v. t., (of people) gladly serve under.

順懷 *shuhn-huair*, adj., following one's heart desires.

順腳兒 *shuhn-jiaau'l*, adv., see *-luh*↓.

順境 *shuhn-jihng*, n., fortunate circumstances.

順職 *shuhn-jyr*, v.i., be dutiful.

順口 *shuhn-koou*, adv., casually: 順口答應 promise without hesitation; 順口兒 --'*l*, adj., (a) ditto; (b) agreeable to taste.

順利 *shuhnlih* (-'*li*), adv., (1) as planned: 順利進行 proceed as planned and without a hitch; (2) (business) doing well.

順理 *shuhnlii*, adj., reasonable and proper: 順理成章 in clear and ordered pattern.

順溜 *shuhn'liou*, adj. & adv., (1) doing well, smooth, -ly; (2) agreeable (temperament).

順流 *shuhn-liour*, adv., with the stream, current.

順路(兒) *shuhnluh('l)*, adv., (doing s.t.) on the way or lying on one's route.

順命 *shuhn-mihng*, v. i., obey orders: 順天命 obey God's will.

順民 *shuhn-mirn*, n., peaceful citizens.

順心 *shuhnshin*, adv., in agreement with what one wants.

順星 *shuhn-shing*, n., sacrifice to the stars on 8th day of first lunar month.

順守 *shuhnshoou*^{1}, v. i., maintain status: 逆取順守 maintain peacefully what was taken by force.

順手(兒) *shuhnshoou*^{2}*('l)*, adv., without extra trouble: 順手牽羊 take s.t. lying within easy reach, profit by special situation.

順水 *shun-shueei*, adv., (1) see *liour*↑; (2) effortlessly, costlessly: 順水推舟 do s. t. without extra effort; 順水人情 a friendly gesture without extra cost to oneself.

順適 *shuhnshyh*, adj., satisfied, happy, satisfactory (situation).

順時 *shuhnshyr*, adv., in its proper time.

順序 *shuhnshyuh*, adj., (1) in proper order or sequence; (2) (-'*shyu*) smooth, successful.
順遂 *shuhnsueih*, adj., smooth, successful (progress, development).
順從 *shuhntsurng*, v. t., to obey (another's wish, order).
順次 *shuhntsyh*, adv., in successive order.
順嘴兒 *shuhn-tzuee'l*, (1) adj., easy to pronounce; (2) (say s.t.) without stopping to think.
順眼 *shuhn-yaan*, adj., easy on the eye: 看不順眼 (things) are disgusting (to look at).
順應 *shuhnyihng*, v. t., to adjust (to changing circumstances).
順運 *shuhn-yuhn*, v. i., to ride the crest of fortune.

頗 22S.80-3

poo (re. pr.); **po* (sp. pr. and in sense of "uneven").

Adj. (**po*) In 偏頗 one-sided.

Adv. Rather: 頗佳 rather good, fair; 頗好 fairly good; 頗多 rather many (much); 頗有出入 present some discrepancies; 頗形 seem rather (embarrassed, etc.); 頗知一二 (modest exp.) seem to know a little; 頗不容易 not exactly easy.

頗奈 *poonaih*, adv., (MC var. of 叵$^{\Delta}$耐 51.21=無奈) unfortunately.
頗頗的 **popo'de*, adv., rather (well-known, etc.).

頮 22S.80-3

hueih.

V. i. (AC) to make facial ablutions.

類 22S.80-3

leih.

N. (1) Class or kind: 類別 -*bier* ↓; 同類 of the same kind or class, fellow beings, fellow creatures; 同類意識 consciousness of kind; 人類 mankind, humanity; 分門別類 be divided into classes and divisions; 物以類聚 birds of the same feather flock together; 類型 -*shirng* ↓. (2) A surname.

Adj. Similar: 相類 look alike; 類似 -*syh* ↓; 不類 different from; 不倫不類 indescribable, messy, below standard.

Adv. Generally: 類多 mostly; 類常 usually; 類不 generally not.

類編 *leihbian*, n., a book of reference arranged according to subject matter.
類別 *leihbier*, n., classification.
類如 *leihrur*, adv. phr., such as, for example.
類型 *leihshirng*, n., type or class.
類書 *leihshu*, n., (LL) encyclopedia.
類似 *leihsyh*, v.t. resemble; adj., similar to.
類次 *leihtsyh*, n., headings; v.t., divide into headings, arrange according to some logical order.
類推 *leihtuei*, v. t., to reason by analogy: 餘可類推 and so forth.

纇 22S.80-3

leih.

N. (1) Entangled silken knots. (2) A flaw: 疵纇 defects; 無纇 flawless, without defects.

Adj. (AC) perverse, wicked, unreasoning.

§ 22S.82 (丨^{s}/乂)

黻 22S.82-1

fur.

N. An embroidery in square pattern on official gowns, see 黼$^{\Delta}$黻 22S.42.

收 22S.82-9

shou.

[Abbr. 収]

V. t. (1) To receive: 收書, 收信 receive letter; 接收 receive (letter), take over charge (of property); 沒收 to confiscate; 收入 -*ruh* ↓; 收據 -*jyuh* ↓; 收支 -*jy* ↓; 收下, 收受 to receive; 收發 receive and dispatch; 收發室 room for incoming and outgoing mails. (2) To collect: 收稅 collect taxes; 收租 collect rent; 收欠, 收債 collect debts; 收買, 收購 -*maai*, -*gouh* ↓; 專收舊貨 buy secondhand goods; 收民心 win over people's support. (3) To keep in safe place, bury, incorporate, incarcerate: 收存, 收留 -*tsurn*, -*liour* ↓; 收養 -*yaang* ↓; 收錄 -*luh* ↓; 收屍 (尸) bury the dead; 收殮, 收葬 -*liahn*[1], -*tzahng* ↓; 收拿, 收捕, 收押 -*nar*, -*buu*, -*ya* ↓. (4) To take back, withdraw, conclude: 收回 -*hueir*, 收復 -*fuh* ↓; 收兵 withdraw troops from battle; 收歸國有 to nationalize (industry); 收淚 stop weeping; 收買賣 close up business; 收工, 收場 -*gung*, -*charng* ↓; 收束 -*shuh* ↓; 收口 -*koou* ↓. (5) To harvest, and n., a harvest: 收成, 收穫 -*cherng*, -*huoh* ↓.

收報機 *shoubauhji*, n., telegraphic receiving set.
收捕 *shoubuu*, v.t., to arrest (person).

亅	小	⺊	十	土	ナ	卄	⺊	丨	一	丁	フ	口	区	冈	ㄱ	厂	尸	亠	广	宀	丶	乚	弋	心	八	人	乂	乛	ノ	〃	⺈	く
00	01	02	10	11	12	20	21	22	30	31	32	40	41	42	50	51	52	60	61	62	63	70	71	72	80	81	82	83	90	91	92	93

收場 *shoucharng* (-'*chang*), n., end, ending (of a play): 沒有好收場 will come to a bad end.

收成 *shoucherng* (-'*cheng*), n., harvest.

收復 *shoufuh*, v.t., to recover (lost territory).

收購 *shougouh*, v.t., to buy up for business (crops, etc.) or collection (jewelry, stamps).

收工 *shougung*, v.i., to finish (work).

收回 *shouhueir*, v.t., (1) to take back; (2) to rescind (order).

收穫 *shouhuoh*, n., harvest; (fig.) results (of study, exploration).

收張 *shou-jang*, phr., close up business.

收監 *shoujian*, v.t., to take into custody, throw into prison.

收驚(兒) *shou-jing*('*l*), phr., formerly, in case of child receiving a shock or in state of coma, take the child's clothing and calling its name in open air, hoping to call back child's frightened soul.

收支 *shou-jy*, n., receipt and expenditure: 收支相等 receipt and expenditure balance; 收支平衡 a balanced budget.

收據 *shoujyuh*, n., a receipt, written note acknowledging money received.

收口(兒) *shoukoou*('*l*), n., a healed or healing wound.

收攬 *shoulaan*, v.t., (1) to have within control; 沒有收攬了 get out of control; (2) 收攬民心 win over the people's support.

收殮 *shouliahn*[1], v.t., to lay (body) in coffin.

收斂 *shouliahn*[2], (1) v.i., to harvest; (2) v.t., to collect (taxes); (3) v.i., to mind one's steps, refrain from rash action; 收斂劑 astringents, medicine for stopping bleeding, loose bowels, etc.

收留 *shouliour* (-'*liou*), v.t., to take in, accept (orphan) for care.

收錄 *shouluh*, v.t., to accept (new students) in register; to include in catalogue or collection of books.

收買 *shoumaai*, v.t., to buy (products), usu. in quantity: 收買人心 try to win popular support.

收沒 *shoumoh*, v.t., to confiscate.

收拿 *shounar*, v.t., to arrest, detain.

收盤 *shouparn*, n., closing price on stock market.

收入 *shouruh*, n. & v.t., receipt or income; to receive income.

收容 *shourung* (-'*rung*), v.t., to provide housing for; 收容所 --*shuoo*, n., house of detention, house for refugees, victims of disaster.

收殺 *shousha*, n., (MC) see -*charng*↑.

收梢 *shoushau*, n., (MC) see -*charng*↑.

收降 *shou-shiarng*, v.i., receive surrender.

收繫 *shoushih*, v.t., see -*buu*↑.

收受 *shoushouh*, v.t., to receive (praise, blame, torture, insult, benefit, gifts, etc.).

收束 *shoushuh*, n. & v.i., ending of story; bring to an end.

收贖 *shoushur*, v.t., formerly, bail out from exile for aged, young, sick, etc.

收拾 *shoushyr* (-'*shy*), v.t., (1) tidy up (room): 不可收拾 unmanageable; (2) (sl.) 收拾他 put s.o. (thieves) out of the way.

收縮 *shousuoh*, v.i. & t., shrink up, curtail (business, deals).

收條(兒) *shoutiaur*('*l*), n., a receipt.

收藏 *shoutsarng*, v.t., to collect and keep (curios, rare editions); 收藏家 -*jia*, n., a collector of art.

收存 *shoutsurn*, v.t., to receive, to keep (money, photograph, book, etc.).

收葬 *shoutzahng*, v.t., to bury (dead).

收尾 *shouweei*, n., ending of affair, story.

收押 *shouya*, v.t., see -*jian*↑.

收養 *shouyaang*, v.t., keep and raise (an orphan).

收益 *shouyih*, n., income, profit.

收益稅 *shouyih-shueih*, n., property or business tax.

收音 *shouyin*, v.i., to receive radio message; 收音機 radio receiver.

敝 22S.82-9

bih.

V. i. & t. (AC) to destroy; wear out.

Adj. (1) Old, tattered, worn-out: 敝衣, 敝屋, tattered clothing, house, see 敝屣 -*shii*↓. (2) Courteous reference to speaker's own: 敝姓 my surname; 敝校, 敝公司, 敝友 my (our) school, firm, friend; 敝處 my place (home); 敝同鄉 person of my home district; 敝帚自珍 phr., "I value my own old broomstick" (court. reference to one's own worthless composition).

敝屣 *bihshii*, n., old shoes, scrap; v. t., to regard as worthless: 敝屣尊榮 turn one's back on worldly honors.

敞 22S.82-9

chaang.

Adj. (1) Broad, phys. spacious: 寬敞 (of room) spacious; 高敞 high and extensive (temple, hall); 敞廳 large hall. (2) Open, not closed: 敞著門 leave door open; 敞著鈕子 unbuttoned; 敞胸, 敞著懷, 敞胸露懷 bare-chested; 敞地兒 open ground or area; 敞篷兒車 cart with open cover. (3) Relaxed: 敞心 relaxed in mind; 敞快 -*kuaih*↓ (related 暢 22S.50).

Adv. Openly, unreservedly: 敞開兒 -*ka'l*↓; 敞笑 give a broad smile.

敞開兒 *chaang-ka'l*, adv., without inhibitions: 敞開兒吃, 敞開兒樂 eat, enjoy, without inhibitions.

敞快 *chaang'kuaih*, adj. & adv., straightforward, relaxed, unreserved.

敞亮 *chaang'liang*, adj., (room) light and spacious.

敞嘴 *charngtzueei*, adj., (嘴敞) unguarded in one's talk.

數 22S.82-9

shuh (**shuu* as vb.; **shuoh*, **suh*,

*tzuh (AC)).

N. (1) Number (of things): 數學 *-shyuer* ↓; 數字, 數目 *-tzyh*, *-muh* ↓; 多數 most, -ly; 大多數 the greater number, majority; 有數兒 I get the idea (have the figures), also limited in number; 來者有數 just a few turned up; 無數 innumerable; 無數的蒼蠅 innumerable flies; 算術級數, 等差級數 arithmetic progression; 幾何級數, 等比級數 geometric progression; 奇數, 偶數 odd, even numbers. (2) Ancient theory and practice of 陰陽五行 *yin-yarng*, as a means of prophecy. (3) Destiny, fate: 氣數 ditto; 定數 predestination; 有定數 it is destined; 劫數 destined disaster or crisis in life; 在不可知之數 is one of those things we cannot be sure about. (4) (AC) 術數 the art of government, also the art of divination. (5) (AC) art: 夫奕之爲數, 小數也 the art of playing chess is a small art (Mencius).

V. t. (1) (**shuu*) To count, enumerate: 計數 ditto; 數一數, 數數看 count it (see if it is correct); 數錢 count the money; 數賬 reckon accounts; 數不清, 數不過來 cannot reckon how many; 數米而炊 "count grains of rice before cooking"—extremely poor; 數貧嘴, 數東瓜道茄子 gabble, twaddle; 數典忘祖 (AC) forget one's ancestors, or ancestral tradition. (2) (**shuu*) Count (as best, etc.): 數他好, 數他壞 (in a group) he ranks the best, the worst; 數他最小 he is the youngest; 數不上 does not count (not important enough); 數得上, 數得着 can count, qualify; 數一數二 count at the top, among the best. (3) (**shuu*) To scold, reprove, rebuke ("enumerate" faults): 數罵, 數落 *-mah*, *-'luoh* ↓. (4) (**shuoh*) Frequent: 朋友數斯疏矣 frequent reproofs among friends cause estrangement. (5) (**suh*) To tell beads: 數珠光.

Adj. (1) Several: 數個 several; 數人 several persons; 三數個 three or four; 數十個 several tens (scores of people, etc.); 數百, 數千 several hundreds, thousands. (2) (**tzuh*) (AC) fine, close (mesh): 數罟不入汚池 a close-meshed net is not let into the ponds (prevent taking small fish).

Adv. (**shuoh*) (LL) repeatedly: 數見不鮮 encountered with many times; 頻數, 數數, 數回 many times.

數額 *shuh-er*, n., number, quantity (of export, etc.).

數著 **shuu'je*, v. i., count as (the best, the ablest, etc.).

數奇 *shuhji*, adj., in for bad luck, ill-starred.

數九 **shur-jioou*, v. i., to start counting every ninth day from winter solstice until 9×9=81 days when winter is over.

數珠兒 **suh-jue'l*, v. i., to tell the beads of rosary.

數中 *shuh-jung*, phr., one in the group (is a young man, etc.).

數兒 *shuh'l*, n., (1) number (of things); (2) 有數兒 I get the idea.

數量 *shuhliahng*, n., quantity, volume, number (of trade, students, etc.).

數落 **shuu'luoh*, v.t., to scold (person).

數碼(兒) *shuhmaa('l)*, n., figures (math., statistical): 1, 2, 3, 4, etc.

數罵 **shuumah*, v. t., to scold ("enumerate" faults).

數目 *shuhmuh*, n., number (of things counted), also amount: 很大的數目 a big sum.

數息 **shuu-shir*, v. i., (in Zen Budd.) count beats in respiration.

數數兒 **shuu-shuh'l*, v. t., to count number.

數學 *shuhshyuer*, n., mathematics.

數字 *shuhtzyh*, n., arithmetic figure(s).

SECTION 30

§ 30.00 (一/亅)

亍 30.00

chuh.

N. (Rare, AC) the right step, cf. 彳 the left step; 彳 and 亍 together forming character 行 to walk.

§ 30.01 (一/小)

示 30.01

shyh.

N. A letter, instructions: 賜示, 來示, 示下 (LL) your letter; 示悉 (來示敬悉) your letter duly received; 回示 your letter of reply; 請示 ask for your instructions.

V. i. & t. (1) To instruct: 訓示, 指示 instruct one what to do; 啟示 to enlighten (mind, person, knowledge). (2) To inform: 告示 n., a public notice; vb., to inform the public; 暗示 vb., to suggest, hint at; n., a hint, suggestion; 明示, 昭示 show to the public, clearly show (one's intentions); 揭示 announce to public. (3) To show, demonstrate: 顯示 show (sincerity, good will, strength); 示意, 示威 *-yih*, *-wei* ↓; 示警, 示儆 to give warning; 示怯, 示弱 show one's weakness lack of courage; 示信 demonstrate one's sincerity. (4) A radical, standing for words having to do with spirits, see 示補兒 *-buu'l* ↓.

示 補 兒 *shyhbuu'l*, n., the radical "ネ" (as in 神, 祈), index No. "63B."

示 範 *shyhfahn*, n. & v. i., a model or demonstration model; demonstrate: 示範農場 demonstration farm.

示 寂 *shyhjir*, v. i., (Buddhist monk) to pass away.

示 衆 *shyh-juhng*, v. i., punish by parading through streets and as warning to others.

示 例 *shyhlih*, n., example.

示 威 *shyhwei*, v. i. & n., demonstrate, -tion: 示威遊行 protest parade.

示 意 *shyhyih*, v. i., give sign (to go ahead, etc.).

§ 30.30 (—/—)

一 30.30

yi.

In sp. pr. **yih* before all tones except the 4th (*-h-*): 一天, 一頭, 一體 (*yihtian, yihtour, yihtii*); **yir* before the 4th tone and before unaccented syllable: 一步, 一次 *yirbuh, yirtsyh*.

Pron. (1) The number one "1" in numbering series (1, 2, 3,): point or item one: 一, 二, 三 also 第一, 第二, 第三 first, second, third; 一則, 二則 firstly, secondly, used in presenting different aspects of a situation; 一月 January; 一二八事變, n., The Shanghai Incident of January 28, 1932; 一 . . . 一 one . . . the other: 一臧一否 (LL) one good and the other bad; 一方面 one aspect only, on the one hand; 一個回合 one bout, one round; 一則以喜, 一則以懼 in one way, it is a cause for joy, in another, a matter of concern (said of parents' age); 不一而足 there are more than one; 一無, 一不 or 一 . . . 不 not one; 一無所知 (person) knows not a thing; 一無足取 not one good thing to be said about it; 一竅不通 an absolute blockhead; 一毛不拔 will not give a cent (to charity), lift a finger to help; 獨一無二 the one and only; 統一 unified control; 合一, 合而爲一 united as one. (2) Once: 一之爲甚, 其可再乎 once is bad enough; 可一不可再 once is forgivable, not twice. (3) One principle: 一以貫之 one principle runs through it all.

Adj. (1) One: 一天, 一人, 一物, one day, one person, one thing; 一一 one by one, see 一意 *-yih*↓; 一神論 monotheism; 一二 or 一兩個 one or two, a couple: 一兩天 a couple of days; 一二十打 one or two dozens; 一二(兩)百 a couple of hundred; 一二朋友 one or two friends; 一來二去 gradually; 一差二錯 one or two mistakes; 一長兩短 should there be some unfortunate happenings; 一五一十 (descriptive) reckoning, enumerating on and on; coupled with 半 meaning inadequately: 一知半解 know only superficially; 一年半載 in a year or so; 一顰一笑 every twinkle and smile; the slightest of facial expression; 一笑置之 dispose it with a smile; 一文不值 to be not worth the paper on which it is written; not worth a cent; 一言難盡 it's a long story (to tell). (2) Each, a: 一桌十人 ten persons a table; 一舉一動 each and every move (is being watched, etc.); 一天三頓飯 three meals a day. (3) Another: 蟬一名知了 another name for cicada is 知了. (4) All, completely: 一心一意 with all one's heart and mind; 一年到頭 all the year round; 一身都是膽 the whole body is one mass of courage; 一律, 一概 *-lyuh, -gaih*↓; 一向 all along, always, consistently, used to; completely, entirely: 一如, 一似 *-rur, -syh*↓; 一塌 *-ta*↓; 一乾二淨 completely cleaned out; 一清二白 completely clear; 一敗塗地 utter failure or defeat, completely wiped out. (5) So, such, to such extent: 一至 *-jyh*[1]↓; 一何愚也 why so foolish? (6) Same, together: 一同 *-turng*↓; 其揆一也 the principles are the same; 一模一樣 look exactly alike; 一家人 (we are) of the same family or clan; 一丘之貉 foxes of the same hole (said of scoundrels "of the same ilk"); 一鼻孔出氣 say exactly the same thing (by collusion); 一視同仁 treat all alike without discrimination.

Adv. (1) Once (like Eng. "once" it is also used as conj.): 一見不忘 once seen, never forgotten; 一失足成千古恨 (of a girl) once she takes a false step, she will regret it eternally; 歲一不登 once the harvest fails (people will starve); 一不做, 二不休 once it is started, go through with it; 一見傾心 fall in love at first sight; 一見如故 feel like old friends at the first meeting; 一望而知 one glance and you know; 一說便知 once said it becomes clear; 一鳴驚人 make one's mark at the first shot, win popularity with the first work; 天氣一冷 the moment the weather gets cold; 一聽見這話 the moment one hears it. (2) A little: 看一看 just have a look; 嘗一嘗 just have a taste (of food); 試一試 have a try at it; 試一試看 try and see; 裏邊一瞧 one swift look inside; 用手一摸 just touch (s. t.) with the hand. (3) 一 . . . 一 alternately: 一張一弛 tense up and relax alternately.

一 般 (兒) *yihban(-ba'l)*, adj. & adv., (1) alike, just as (pretty, disgusting, etc.): 一般模樣 the same appearance; (2) general: 一般人 the common run of men, the average man or men; 一般社會 society in gen.

一 併 *yirbihng*, adv., together, along: 一併帶走 take it along with others.

一 切 *yirchieh*, adj. & adv., all, the whole (contents, members, funds, things).

一 起 (兒) *yihchii(-chie'l)*, adj., (mix, live) together: 常在一起 are always together.

一 齊 *yihchir*, adv., together (go, walk, die, get rich, etc.).

一 旦 *yirda'hn*, adv. & conj., once (s.t. should happen): 一旦死了 should s. o. die one day.

一 道 兒 *yirdauh'l*, adv., (walk, go)

A

together ("same route").

一 得 *yihder*, phr., 愚者千慮, 必有一得 (court.) a stupid person may once in a while have a good idea.

一 點 (兒) *yihdiaan* (*-diaa'l*), adj. & adv. & n., little, just a little, a small amount: 一點兒不怕 not the least bit afraid; 一點兒不錯 absolutely right.

一 定 *yirdihng*, adj. & adv., certain, -ly.

一 丟 點 兒 *yihdioudiaa'l*, adj. & adv. & n., just a tiny bit.

一 堆 兒 *yihdue'l*, (1) n., a heap, a pile (of things); (2) adv., (eat, work) together.

一 概 *yirgaih*, adj. & adv. & n., all, without exception: 一概不准 all forbidden; 一概而論 to lump together.

一 個 個 *yir'gege*, pron., each one, every one.

一 貫 *yirguahn*, adj., consistent (policy).

一 共 *yirguhng*, (1) adv., together (eat at the same table, etc.); (2) n., total amount, number: 一共六個人 altogether six persons.

一 古 腦 兒 *yirgurnaau'l*, adv. & n., altogether the whole lot (stolen, etc.).

一 忽 兒 *yihhu'l*, n., in a short moment.

一 晃 兒 *yihhuaang'l*, n., in a flash.

一 會 兒 *yirhueih* (*-hue'l*), n., in a short moment: 請坐一會兒 sit down for a moment; 一會兒哭, 一會兒笑 cry one moment and laugh the next.

一 回 兒 *yihhuer'l*, adv. & n., ditto.

一 家 *yih-jia*, phr., same family: 咱們是一家人 we are of the same family.

一 己 *yihjii*, adj., personal, private (affairs), opp. 公 public.

一 至 *yirjyh*[1], adv., to such extent: 何以一至於此極 how or why come (fail, suffer) to such extreme?

一 致 *yirjyh*[2], adj. & adv., unanimous, -ly (support, approve, etc.).

一 直 *yihjyr*, adv., consistently (appear, disappear), continually (absent, defiant, etc.).

B

一 刻 *yirkeh*, n. & adv., a moment: 一刻不停 never stop for a moment.

一 塊 兒 *yirkuah'l*, adv., (eat, work) together.

一 溜 烟 兒 *yihliouhyan* (*--ya'l*), adv., (slink) away and disappear (without permission or news).

一 硫 化 *yihliourhua*, n., (chem.) sulfide: 一硫化二銅 cuprous sulfide.

一 零 兒 *yihlirng'l*, n., adv., see *-diaa'l* ↑.

一 弄 兒 *yirluhng'l*, adv., (coll.) the whole lot; altogether.

一 律 *yirlyuh*, adv., all, without exception (stopped, forbidden, etc.).

一 面 *yirmiahn*, (1) n. adjunct, 一面鼓, 一面旗 a drum, a flag; (2) adj. & adv. & n., one-sided (argument, view): 一面之緣 the pleasure of having met once; 獨當一面 (of officeholder) take charge as chief.

一 仍 *yihrerng*, adv., still, as ever, see 仍 91A.50.

一 日 *yirryh*, adv., one day; such a day: 總有一日 there'll be one day when . . . ; 較一日之長 let's see who is the better of the two of us.

一 晌 *yirshaang*, n., a short moment.

一 身 *yih-shen*, phr., whole body: 一身一口 a bachelor living singly.

一 生 *yihsheng*, n. & adv., the whole life, for the past whole life.

一 下 子 *yirshiahtz*, adv., all at once.

一 些 *yihshie*, n., little, a few: 一些著涼 catch a little cold.

一 順 *yihshuhn*, adv., (dial.) see *-jyr* ↑; 一順兒, 一順子 straight (ahead, east, etc.).

一 時 *yihshyr*, adv., for a time, temporarily: 一時疏忽 (apologetic) it was an oversight at that time; 一時不能去 for the time being I cannot get away.

一 似 *yirsyh*, adv., just like (being home, etc.).

一 塌 *yihta*, adv., completely: 一塌糊塗 is in a complete mess; 一塌

C

括子 (Shanghai dial.) completely, the whole amount.

一 頭 *yihtour*, adv., (1) along with s. t. else: 一頭走, 一頭哭 weeps as one walks along; 東一頭西一頭亂跑 run about in all directions; (2) suddenly: 一頭碰見 suddenly met; (3) a whole headful: 一頭珠花 (wears) pearl decorations all over her hair.

一 從 *yirtsurng*, adv., ever since (=自從), also 一自 *-tzyh* ↓.

一 次 *yirtsyh*, adv., one time, once: 頭一次 the first time.

一 同 *yihturng*, adv., (go, work) together.

一 統 *yihtuung*, n., unification (of country); centralization, uniformity (of ideas, beliefs).

一 早 兒 *yihtzaau'l*, adv., in early morning.

一 再 *yirtzaih*, adv., again and again.

一 昨 *yihtzuor*, adv., (LL) yesterday.

一 總 *yirtzuung*, adv. & n., altogether, the whole amount.

一 自 *yirtzyh*, adv., since.

一 往 *yih-waang*, phr., 一往情深 deeply attached (to s. o.).

一 味 (兒) *yirweih* (*-weh'l*) adv., persistently, doggedly: 一味兒讀書 study devotedly; 一味兒玩 just keep on playing; 一味兒與他反對 persistently oppose him.

一 氧 化 *yihyaanghuah*, n., (chem.) monoxide: 一氧化碳 carbon monoxide; 一氧化二氮 nitrogen monoxide.

一 樣 *yiryahng*, adj. & adv., same, just as (convenient, etc.): 還不是一樣 is it not just the same?

一 一 *yihyi*, adv., one by one (count, explain, etc.).

一 意 *yiryih*, adv., (1) with complete devotion, full concentration; (2) stubbornly: 一意孤行 self-opinionated, self-willed.

一 元 論 *yihyuarn-luhn*, n., monism.

一
二 30.30

ehl.

亅	小	卜	十	土	ナ	廾	匕卜	丨	一	丁	フ	口	囟	冈	乛	厂	尸	亠	广	亠	丶	乚	弋	心	八	人	乂	乛	一	丿	𠂉	く
00	01	02	10	11	12	20	21	22	30	31	32	40	41	42	50	51	52	60	61	62	63	70	71	72	80	81	82	83	90	91	92	93

二 **Adj.** (1) Two (cf. 兩 31.42): 二三 *-san*↓; 一二 one or two (days, etc.); 二十, 二百 twenty, two hundred; 十二 twelve; 二倍 double; 不二價 one-price (sales system), 二八 *-ba*↓; (in writing checks, 貳 is used to prevent mistakes, as in spelling out amount). (2) Second: 第二 ditto; 星期二 Tuesday; 第二次 second time; 二房 *-farng*↓; 天下無二 not an equal in the world.

二八 *ehlba*, adj., sixteen (2×8): 二八佳人 a pretty young girl of sweet sixteen; (poet.) also used for sixteenth day of month; (Budd.) sixteen as a full round number: 二八弘規 the full regulations.

二把刀 *ehlbaa-dau*, n., (coll.) second-rate (knowledge of subject).

二半破子 *ehlbahnpohtz*, n., see *-baa-dau*↑.

二百五 *ehlbairwuu*, n., (coll.) a stupid person.

二碴(兒) *ehlchar('l)*, n., a regrowth of hair, of harvest.

二乘冪 *ehlcherngmih*, n., see *-tsyh-fang*↓.

二親 *ehlchin*, n., father and mother.

二重唱 *ehlchurng-chahng*, n., duet; 二重奏 duet performance on piano; 二重奏曲, 二重唱曲 duet for instrument, for voice.

二等 *ehl-deeng*, adj., second-class.

二二忽忽 *ehl-ehl-hu-hu*, adj., perplexed, undecided.

二房 *ehlfarng*, n., concubine.

二房東 *ehl-farngdung*, n., landlady who herself rents room or house from owner.

二副 *ehlfuh*, n., second mate (navigation).

二乎 *ehl'hu*, adj., see *-'leng*↓.

二花臉 *ehl-hualiaan*, n., (Chin. opera) number two in male role (also called 副淨, see 淨 63A.00).

二黃 *ehlhuarng*, n., (Chin. opera) term for popular form of Chin. opera, said to come from 黃陂, 黃岡 Huarngpir and Huarnggang, districts in Hupeh.

二婚兒 *ehl-hue'l*, n., (coll.) woman who marries twice, also 二婚頭.

二混子 *ehl-huhntz*, n., (coll. contempt.) a ne'er-do-well, who finds jobs either too high or too low for him.

二葷鋪 *ehl-hun-puh*, n., a cheap eating place.

二和 *ehl-huoh*, n., second infusion, see *-jian*↓.

二胡 *ehlhur*, n., a stringed instrument, slightly lower in tone than 胡琴 *hurchirn*.

二價 *ehljiah*, phr., usu. 不二價 one-price system.

二煎 *ehljian*, n., second infusion of medical herbs.

二指 *ehljyy*, n., the index finger.

二老 *ehllaau*, n., father and mother.

二來來 *ehllairlair*, adv., all over again.

二藍 *ehllarn*, adj., a color paler than dark blue.

二郎神 *Ehl-larng-shern*, n., a popular Chin. god, good at fighting demons.

二愣 *ehl'leng*, adj., (1) stunned; (2) scared stiff.

二六板 *ehl-liouh-baan*, n., (Chin. opera) name of a rhythm, marked one beat per bar.

二硫化 *ehlliourhuah*, n., (chem.) disulfide: 二硫化碳 carbon disulfide; 二硫化鐵 iron disulfide.

二路腳兒 *ehlluh-jyuer'l*, n., (Chin. opera) secondary role.

二路兒 *ehlluh'l*, adj., second-rate (goods).

二綠 *ehllyuh*, adj., light green.

二氯化汞 *ehllyuhhuah gaang*, n., (chem.) mercuric chloride; 二氯化錫 stannous chloride.

二毛 *ehlmaur*, n., (AC) grey-haired person: 二毛子 (Boxer Uprising) a Chin. working with missionary or white merchant (大毛).

二門(兒)(子) *ehl-mern(-mer'l)(tz)*, n., second gate leading to main court.

二面 *ehl-miahn*, n., (dial.) see *-hualiaan*↑.

二拇指 *ehl'mujyy*, n., index finger.

二難 *ehl-narn*, n., (complim.) unusual brothers (難兄難弟); sometimes also unique host and guest.

二人奪 *ehl-rern-duor*, n., a sword or knife encased in scabbard shaped like walking cane; sword is exposed if s. o. tries to grab it.

二三 *ehl-san*, phr., (1) two or three; (2) (AC) 二三其德 of changeable character.

二色 *ehl-seh*, (1) adj., two-colored; (2) v.i., keep a mistress or commit adultery: 不二色 never know another woman.

二項式 *ehlshiahngshyh*, n., (math.) binomial equation; 二項定理 binomial theorem.

二絃 *ehlshiarn*, n., a stringed instrument, smaller than 老絃.

二姓 *ehl-shihng*, n., (1) two families of different clan names united in marriage; (2) two ruling houses of different surnames.

二性子 *ehlshihng-tz*, n., a bisexual person, hermaphrodite (see *-shirng-rern*↓).

二心 *ehlshin*, n., disloyalty of heart.

二形人 *ehl-shirng-rern*, n., hermaphrodite, a bisexual person.

二水兒 *ehlshuee'l*, n., second hand (cover, shroud, etc.) which has been rented out before.

二豎 *ehl-shuh*, n., (LL) evil spirit responsible for illness (allu. two boys hiding in body).

二碳化 *ehltahnhuah*, n., (chem.) carbide: 二碳化鈣 calcium carbide.

二踢腳 *ehl-ti-jiaau*, n., a double-explosion firecracker.

二體人 *ehl-ti-rern*, n., hermaphrodite, see *-shirng-rern*↑.

二次方 *ehl-tsyh-fang*, n., (math.) square, the product of a number multiplied by itself.

二屋(兒)裡 *ehl-wu('l)'li*, n., as in 說到二屋裏 stray off in discussion.

二五眼 *ehl'wuyaan*, n., person of dubious discrimination or judgment.

二氧化 *ehlyaanghuah*, n., (chem.) dioxide; 二氧化碳 carbon dioxide; 二氧化錳 manganese dioxide; 二氧化硫 sulphur dioxide; 二氧化氫 hydrogen dioxide.

二儀 *ehlyir*, n., heaven and earth.

二元論 *ehlyuarn-luhn*, n., dualism (phil.).

二月 *ehlyueh*, n., Feburary.

A B C

三 30.30

san (**sahn*).

Adj. Three: 第三 number three; 三十, 三十三 thirty, thirty-three; 十三 thirteen; 三分之一 one third; 三倍 threefold; 三次, 三回, 三番 three times (see Adv. ↓), 一問三不知 deny all knowledge of event; coupled with "two," indicating several, a few: 三兩個 two or three; 三言兩語 a few words spoken; 三句不離本行 always the trade talk; 三差兩錯 a few, just a few mistakes; 三長兩短 if s.t. untoward should happen; 三天兩頭 every other day or so; 三心兩意 wavering, undecided; 三窩兩塊 siblings, children of different mothers; coupled with "three": 三三兩兩 (stroll, come in) in twos and threes; coupled with "four": 三番四復 so many times; coupled with "five," several: 三五個人 several persons; 三回五次 repeatedly; 三年五載 in a few years; 三令五申 have repeatedly issued orders (to people); 三上五下 up and down (in intermittent actions); 三下五除二 rapidly sold out (orig. a sentence in teaching abacus); 三五成羣 in odd groups of threes or fives; 三頭六臂 three-headed and six-armed monster, person with exhaustless resources; 三親六眷 all the kinsmen; 三六九等 (coll.) make fine distinctions, calculate costs; 不管三七二十一 3×7=21, i.e., (do s.t.) without further ado; coupled with "eight," multifarious: 三災八難 of a child prone to various illnesses.

Adv. Three times: 三呼萬歲 three cheers of "Long live . . ."; 三緘其口 (AC, allu.) mouth sealed three times, absolute refusal to talk; 三顧茅廬 (AC allu.) a Hahn prince three times called on famous scholar to solicit his help; (**sahn*) 三思而後行 think thrice before acting.

三寶 *san-baau*, phr., (Budd.) the Three Treasures: the Buddha, the dharma, and the church—sacred depository of divine truths.

三瓣(子)嘴兒 *san-bahn(tz)tzue-e'l*, adj., hare-lipped.

三白 *san-bair*, n., ("three whites") the white melon (white in skin, pulp and seeds).

三部曲 *san-buh-chyuu*, n., a trilogy; a musical composition with statement of theme, development and conclusion.

三不知 *san buhjy*, adv. phr., (MC) I don't know how: 三不知逢著貴客 have the pleasure to meet you (visitor) without knowing to whom I owe the honor.

三不朽 *san buhshiou*, phr., the three forms of immortality: 立德 in character, 立言 in words, and 立功 in deeds—influences which will last for ever.

三叉 *san-cha*, adj. & n., forked (road); 三叉路 forked roads (also wr. 三岔).

三青子 *san-chingtz*, n., cunning, irresponsible fellow.

三秋 *san chiou*, phr., (1) (LL) three seasons: 一日不見, 如三秋兮 a day absent from you is like three seasons (or years); (2) (LL) the three months of autumn; (3) (LL) the last month of autumn.

三尺 *san-chyy*, phr., (1) three feet: 三尺童子 a young kid; (2) (AC allu.) laws and statutes, written on three-foot bamboo strips; 三尺水 (LL) a gleaming sword.

三大件兒 *san dah jiah'l*, n., (MC) the fetters, the shackles and the neck lock.

三代 *san-daih*, n., (1) the classical Three Dynasties: 夏 *Shiah* 商 *Shang* and 周 *Jou*; (2) three generations.

三點水兒 *sandiarnshueel*, n., the radical "氵" (water); index No. "63A."

三段論法 *sanduahn luhnfaa*, n., (logic) syllogism.

三對六面 *san-dueih liouh-miahn*, phr., two parties to contract plus one eyewitness.

三冬 *san dung*, phr., three winters.

三多 *san duo*, n., the three blessings: 多福, 多壽, 多男子 luck, longevity and male progeny.

三讀(會) *san dur(hueih)*, phr., third reading in legislative assembly.

三二 *san-ehl*, adj., several.

三分 *san-fen*, adj., thirty percent: 三分人材, 七分打扮 three-tenths natural figure and seven-tenths make-up.

三墳五典 *san-fern wur-diaan*, n., lost anc. books of historical records.

三伏 *san-fur*, n., three periods of ten days each after summer solstice——hottest days.

三竿 *san gan*, phr., 日上三竿 the sun is three poles high——late in the morning.

三綱 *san-gang*, n., (Confu.) the three mainstays ("hawsers") of social order: the relationships of 君臣, 父子, 夫妻 ruler-subject, father-child and husband-wife; 三綱五常 the main principles of social order (五常 plus two other relations: between brothers and friends).

三更 *san-geng* (sp. pr. *-jing*), n., the third watch—midnight.

三光 *san guang*, n., the sun, the moon and stars.

三行兒 *san harng'l*, phr., the cook, the sauce man and the waiter in a restaurant; (Canton) mason, carpenter and blacksmith.

三合(兒)房 *san-her('l)farng*, n., a Chin. courtyard with rooms on three sides (cf. 四^A^合房 41.41).

三合土 *sanhertuu*, n., native cement, made up of lime, sand and soil (also 三和土).

三合油 *sanher-your*, n., sauce made up of sesame oil, soya sauce and vinegar.

三花臉(兒) *sanhualiaan*, n., clown in Chin. opera.

三魂 *san hurn*, phr., 三魂七魄 the three finer spirits and seven baser instincts that motivate human body.

三

亅	小	⺊	十	土	𠂇	卄	卜	丨	一	丅	乛	口	囗	冂	冖	厂	尸	亠	广	宀	丶	乚	弋	心	八	人	乂	乛	丿	丿	𠂉	く
00	01	02	10	11	12	20	21	22	30	31	32	40	41	42	50	51	52	60	61	62	63	70	71	72	80	81	82	83	90	91	92	93

三 三朝 *san-jau*, phr., (1) third day of child's birth; (2) a bride's homecoming on the third day after matrimony.

三正 (1) *san jeng*, phr., the year beginnings of the Three Dynasties: 夏 in 寅 month, 商 in 丑, and 周 in 子; (2) (*-jehng*) (AC) the three regular constituents of heaven, earth and man.

三家村 *san-jia-tsun*, n., a small remote hamlet (of only a few houses).

三甲 *san-jiaa*, n., as in 三甲進士 the three grades of *jihnshyh* degree.

三角 *sanjiaau*, n. & adj., a triangle; triangular; 三角洲 a delta; 三角木 a cleat, a wedge; 三角釘 caltrops, a device of spikes; 三角術, 三角法 trigonometry; 平面三角術 plane trigonometry; 弦面三角術 spherical trigonometry; 三角形 triangle; 二等邊三角形 isosceles triangle; 直角, 直邊三角形 right, equilateral triangles; 鈍角, 銳角三角形 obtuse-angled, acute-angled triangle; 三角(兒)眼 eyes that slope outwards.

三脚櫈(兒) *san-jiaaudehng('l)*, n., three-legged stool.

三脚架 *san-jiaau-jiah*, n., a tripod, a three-legged support for camera.

三脚貓 *san-jiaau mau*, n., an odd fellow, one who may do odd things.

三焦 *san-jiau*, n., (Chin. med.) the three points: 上焦 entrance to stomach, 中焦 the duodenum, and 下焦 entrance to bladder.

三教 *san jiauh*, phr., Confucianism, Taoism and Buddhism.

三節 *san-jier*, phr., the three important festivals of the year: 端午 5th of 5th lunar month, 中秋 mid-autumn, 15th of 8th lunar month, and the New Year.

三節棍 *san-jier-guhn*, n., an anc. weapon, a three-jointed bar.

三晉 *San Jihn*, phr., the anc. state of Jihn 晉, later divided into three states: 趙 Jauh 魏 Weih and 韓 Harn.

三徑 *san jihng*, n., (poet, allu.) a scholar's garden of retreat.

三九 *san-jioou*, phr., (1) (AC) short for 三公九卿 (Hahn Dyn.) three councillors and nine ministers: 三九公宴 state dinner to them; (2) the third nine days (19–27) after winter solstice.

三級跳遠 *san jir tiauh-yuaan*, n., hop, step and jump.

三隻手 *san-jy-shoou*, n., (sl.) a pickpocket.

三隻眼 *san-jy-yaan*, adj., clear-eyed, clear-sighted, "three-eyed"—of one who sees clearly everything that is going on.

三軍 *san jyun*, n., (1) (AC) the army in gen.; (2) the armed forces (the army, navy, and air-force).

三框闌兒 *san-kuarng-lar'l*, n., the radical "匚" ("three-sided frame").

三窟 *san kuh*, phr., 狡兔三窟 "fox's three holes," (fig.) many provisions for cunning escape.

三稜鏡 *san-lerng-jihng*, n., a prism.

三輪兒(車) *san-luer'l(che)*, n., pedicab, three-wheeled cart.

三路兒 *san-luh'l*, adj., third-class.

三昧 *san-meih*, n., (1) (Budd.) purity and calm arising from correct realization (also 三摩地 from Sanskr. "samadhi"); (2) secret, expert knowledge (of poetry, good tea, etc.): 箇中三昧 secrets known only to experts.

三明 *san-mirng*, n., see *-guang* ↑.

三木 *san muh*, n., see *-dah jiah'l* ↑.

三年艾 *san-niarn-aih*, n., (AC allu.) early preparations (against future trouble).

三色 *san seh*, n., the three basic colors: red, yellow and blue.

三生 *san sheng*[1], phr., three incarnations, future, present and past: 三生有幸 lucky indeed.

三牲 *san sheng*[2], n., the sacrifices of pig, sheep and ox.

三鮮 *san-shian*, adj., (soup, etc.) made of three kinds of fresh ingredients.

三弦(兒) *san-shiarn(-shiar'l)*, n., a three-stringed instrument.

三星 *san shing*, n., three stars of luck: 福祿壽 happiness, honor and longevity.

三心兩意 *san-sin-liang-yih*, adj. phr., undecided, hesitant.

三思 **sahn-sy* (*san-*), phr., think thrice (before acting).

三頭 *san tour*, phr., (1) three-headed: 三頭政治 triumvirate; 三頭二面 double-faced, cunning; (2) 三頭兩日 in two or three days; (3) 三頭對案 two parties and witness confront in court.

三才 *san tsair*, phr., the three "geniuses" (life forces): 天, 地, 人 the heaven, the earth and man.

三寸丁 *san-tsuhn ding*, n., (MC) a physically very small man, a "shrimp."

三寸舌 *san-tsuhn sher*, n., the tongue, symbolic of a great talker: 憑我三寸不爛之舌 on the strength of my eloquence.

三從 *san-tsurng*, phr., (Confu. 儀禮) the three "obeys" for women: —obey father at home, obey husband when married, and obey son when husband dies (cf. 四[A]德 41.41).

三塗 *san tur*, phr., (Budd.) 火塗, 刀塗, 血塗 three kinds of punishment in hell, by fire, chopping by knife and tearing apart by beasts.

三字經 *Santzh-jing*, n., formerly, a primary textbook for children, all composed of three word phrases.

三族 *san tzur*, n., (AC) with various interpretations: (1) parents, brothers and wife and children; (2) relatives of father, of mother and of wife (誅三族 all killed in crime against the throne); (3) three generations of grandfather, father and son; (4) brothers of father, of self and of son.

三位一體 *San-weih-yir-tii*, phr., the Christian Trinity.

三五 *san-wuu*, adj., several, three to five (days, etc.); (rare, AC) 15 (3×5): 三五而盈 (the moon) is full on the 15th day of a month.

三陽 *san yarng*, phr., 三陽開泰 the *yang* spirits on the upsurge in spring; surge of good luck.

三一律 *san-yi-lyuh*, n., the dramatic unities of action, time, and place.

三友 *san youu*, phr., three kinds of friends to be sought after: 友

直, 友諒, 友多聞 those that are straight, those that are honest and those that know a great deal; 歲寒三友 the pine, the bamboo, and the winter-sweet.

三元 *san yuarn*, phr., (1) those who come out first in civil examinations at the provincial capital, the national capital and the palace: 鄉試, 會試, 殿試; (2) the 15th day of the first, seventh, and tenth lunar months.

三月 *sanyueh*, n., March.

豆 30.30

douh.

[Var. 荳 is really not needed]

N. (1) Various kinds of beans: 大豆, 黃豆 soybean; 黑豆 black beans, much used as sauce; 扁豆 hyacinth bean; 蠶豆 broad beans; 芸豆 kidney beans; 紅豆 (=相[Δ]思子 10B.41); 荷蘭豆 peas in the pod. (2) Anc. sacrificial vessel.

豆餅 *douhbiing*, n., bean cake, consisting of crushed soybean husks used as fertilizer.

豆青 *douhching*, adj., pea-green.

豆萁 *douhchir*, n., beanstalk.

豆豉 *douhchyy*, n., pickled black bean; black bean sauce.

豆腐 *douh'fu*, n., bean curd: 豆腐乾 treated dehydrated bean curd; 豆腐漿 whey from bean curd, a drink; 豆腐皮 hard substance obtained from bean whey; 豆腐乳 fermented bean curd.

豆羹 *douhgeng*, n., simple fare.

豆醬 *douhjiahng*, also 豆瓣醬 *-bahnjiahng*, n., sauce made from soybean.

豆漿 *douhjiang*, n., see 豆腐漿 under *-fuh*↑.

豆莢 *douhjiar*, n., bean or pea pod.

豆汁 *douhjy*, n., a drink made from ground green peas.

豆蔻 *douhkouh*, n., nutmeg, cardamon; 豆蔻年華 teenage of girls.

豆兒粥 *douh'ljou*, n., porridge made from peas in the pod.

豆綠 *douhlyuh*, adj., pea-green.

豆苗(兒) *douhmiaur('l)*, n., young green sprout from bean.

豆娘子 *douhniarngtz*, n., (zoo.) a small insect, *Agrion quadrigerum.*

豆乳 *douhruu*, n., see 豆腐乳 under *-fuh*↑.

豆沙 *douhsha*, n., bean paste, sweetened and used as stuffing in cakes.

豆象 *douhshiahng*, n., (zoo) a bean-destroying insect, *Bruchus chinensis.*

豆素 *douhsuh*, n., (chem.) legumin.

豆芽(兒) *douhyar('l)*, n., bean sprout.

豆油 *douhyour*, n., soya sauce.

§ 30.42 (一/冈)

鬲 30.42

lih.

N. (AC) a large earthen pot, a large iron tripod.

§ 30.50 (一/㇕)

亏 30.50

kuei.

[Abbr. of 虧 21S.50]

§ 30.70 (一/乚)

元 30.70

yuarn.

N. (1) Dollar (var. 圓), coin: 銅元 a copper coin; 銀元 a dollar; 金元 gold dollar; 美元 American dollar; 拾元 $10, 百元 $100. (2) (Phil.) origin: 一元論, 多元論 monistic, pluralistic universe; 二元論 dualism. (3) (Math.) term. (4) The 元朝 *Yuarn* or Mongol Dyn. (1277–1368 A.D.). (5) The head, chief: 元首, 元戎 *-shoou, -rurng*↓. (6) Vital state, vitality: 復元 recover in health; 還元 come back to life; 元氣 *-chih*↓. (7) A surname.

Adj. (1) The first (day, wife, etc.): 元旦, 元配 *-dahn, -peih*↓; 元元本本 (also wr. 原原) (tell) in detail from very beginning; closely related 原 51A.01. (2) Old, eminent: 元老, 元勳 *-laau, -shyun*↓.

元板 *yuarn-baan*, n., (Chin. opera) one-beat rhythm.

元寶 *yuarnbaau*, n., (1) a coin; (2) a silver ingot of 50 taels.

元本 *yuarnbeen*, n., (1) the origin (also wr. 原); (2) original capital investment; (3) a Yuarn Dyn. edition.

元辰 *yuarnchern*, n., (1) New Year's Day (=元旦); (2) a propitious day.

元氣 *yuarnchih*, n., vitality, vital energy.

元青 *yuarnching*, adj., deep black (also 玄青).

元春 *yuarnchun*, n., New Year.

元旦 *yuarndahn*, n., New Year's Day.

元惡 *yuarn-eh*, n., first or great culprit.

元老 *yuarnlaau*, n., a veteran statesman.

元年 *yuarn-niarn*, n., the first

year: 公曆元年 the year 1 A.D.; 民國元年 first year of the Republic, 1911.

元配 *yuarn-peih*, n., the first wife; also called 德配.

元戎 *yuarnrurng*, n., (1) commander in chief; (2) (AC) chariot.

元色 *yuarnseh*, n., black color, see *-ching* ↑ (also 玄色 as var.).

元宵 *yuarnshiau*, n., (1) the night of 上元 or 15th day of first lunar month; (2) sweet dumplings.

元夕 *yuarnshih*, n., ditto.

元首 *yuarnshoou*, n., chief of state.

元書紙 *yuarnshu-jyy*, n., a kind of writing paper.

元帥 *yuarnshuaih*, n., commander in chief.

元勳 *yuarnshyun*, n., as in 開國元勳 a founding father of a country.

元兇 *yuarn-shyung*, n., chief culprit of rebellion.

元始 *yuarnshyy*, n., beginnings (of history, country, etc.), more commonly wr. 原始.

元素 *yuarnsuh*, n., (chem.) element (also wr. 原素), list of elements, see Appendix F.

元孫 *yuarnsun*, n., great-grandson, see 玄[A]孫 60.93.

元宰 *yuarntzaai*, n., (LL) prime minister.

元夜 *yuarnyeh*, n., see *-shih*, *-shiau* ↑.

元音 *yuarnyin*, n., vowel.

元月 *yuarnyueh*, n., January.

黿 30.70

yuarn.

N. (AC) a giant turtle.

麗 30.70

lih.

N. A surname

V.t. (1) (AC) fasten, tie to: 麗於碑 tied to a stone tablet. (2) (AC) attached to, adhere to: 日月麗乎天 the sun and the moon hang in the firmament; 附麗 connected with, joined to.

Adj. Beautiful, pretty: 華麗 elegant; 美麗 very good-looking, pleasing to the eye; 都麗 resplendent; 豔麗 gorgeous; 綺麗 attractive, beautifully dressed; 秀麗 delicate and graceful.

麗都 *lihdu*, (LL) beautiful, resplendent.

麗質 *lihjyr*, n., as in 天生麗質 a born beauty.

麗人 *lihrern*, n., a beauty.

麗藻 *lihtzaau*, n., elegant phrases, decorative language.

麗澤 *lihtzer*, n., (AC) mutual encouragement and assistance between friends.

§ 30.83 (一/～)

远 30.83

yuaan.

[Abbr. of 遠 11.83]

逗 30.83

douh.

V. i. & t. (1) To tease: 逗着玩兒, 逗樂兒 tease for fun: 逗得他惱了 tease and make him mad. (2) To tarry, stop: 逗留不進 tarry around a place.

逗趣兒 *douhchyuh* (*-chyuee'l*), v. t., tease for fun.

逗點 *douhdiaan*, n., the mark (、) less than a comma (,), indicating breath-group or a succession of proper names.

逗哏兒 *douhger'l*, v.t., see *-chyuh* ↑.

逗留 *douhliour*, v. i., tarry, stop over for a time.

逗弄 *douh'nung*, v. i. & t., induce, provoke, play with.

逗笑兒 *douhshiauh'l*, v. i., try to induce a smile (esp. in child).

逼 30.83

bi (also **bih*).

V. t. (1) Be forced to, compelled: 逼不得已, 逼於無奈 compelled against one's will. (2) Compel s.o. to do s. t.: 逼嫁 compel a girl to marry; 逼姦 rape by force; 逼死 persecute to death; 逼上梁山 force one to join rebels; 逼供 extract confession by force or pressure; 逼令 compel one to, as 逼令改嫁 compel woman to remarry; 逼人太甚 relentless, merciless in forcing demands. (3) Exert pressure for: 逼債 demand quick repayment of debt.

Adj. Close: 逼鄰 very close neighbor; 逼近 *-jihn* ↓.

Adv. Closely: 逼視 examine very closely; 逼肖 resemble very closely.

逼眞 **bihjen* (*bi-*), adj., showing life, vitality, individuality (in portrayal); true to life.

逼近 *bijihn*, adj., right close to.

逼勒 *bileh*, v. t., force by threat or pressure, as 逼勒自殺 force one to commit suicide.

逼迫 *bipoh*, v. t., to force (person) to.

逼狹 *bishiar*, adj., harsh, ungenerous.

逼索 *bisuoo*, v.i. & t., force; obtain (money, repayment) by force.

逼問 *biwehn*, v. t., to question closely.

邐 30.83

lii.

邐迤 *liryii*, adj., (of mountains, sand dunes, etc.) sprawling out in all directions (also 邐迆, 邐倚, 迤儷).

§ 30.93 (一/く)

云 30.93

yurn.

V. i. (1) (AC, LL) to say: 詩云 the *Book of Poetry* says; 人云亦云 say what everybody says (slavishly); oft. used like Eng. "say": 云誰之思 say, whom are you thinking of? (2) To mean: . . . 云然 which is to say, which means; 玉帛云乎哉 do you mean that (rituals) merely mean the presenting of jades and silks?

云爾 *yurn-eel*, n. particle., only, simply: 不思云爾 it is simply lack of thinking; just 徐徐云爾 just slowly.
云何 *yurn-her*, adv., (AC, LL) how, why: 云何不言 why not tell me? 云何不顧而去 why leave without saying good-bye?
云云 *yurnyurn*, phr., and so forth, *et cetera.*

SECTION 30S

§ 30S.00 (—ˢ/亅)

刓 30S.00-2

warn.

V.t. To carve, to slice (wood, bamboo), (cf. 剜 *wan* 62S.00).

副 30S.00-2

fuh.

N. adjunct. A set: 一副耳環 a pair of earrings; 一副眼鏡 a pair of glasses; 一副麻將 a mahjong set; 一副象棋 a set of Chin. chess; 那副臉孔 that face (including set of features), cf. 幅 22B.41.

N. Assistant: 副理 assistant manager; 大副, 二副 first assistant, second assistant, esp. on ship, in kitchen; the mate, second mate in ship.

V.t. Tally: 名副其實 reputation corresponds to reality, also wr. 符.

Adj. (1) Second in office, deputy, vice-: 副總統 vice-president of republic; 副經理 vice-president of firm; 副校長 vice-president of university or school; 副領事 vice-consul; 副議長 vice-chairman of congress; 副淨, 副末 second actor in man's role in Chin. drama; 副將 deputy general; opp. 正, the first, the regular (general, wife, etc.). (2) Subsidiary, incidental, accessory: 副產品 secondary products, by-products; 副作用 side effect of medicine; 副食物 additional, complementary diet.

副本 *fuhbeen*, n., duplicate.
副啓 *fuhchii*, n., postscript.
副官 *fuhguan*, n., *aide-de-camp.*
副張 *fuhjang*, n., duplicate.
副腎 *fuhshehn*, n., adrenal glands.
副手 *fuhshoou*, n., assistant (in surgery, etc.).
副署(會簽) *fuhshuu*, v.i. & t., countersign.
副室 *fuhshyh*, n., (LL) concubine.
副詞 *fuhtsyr*, n., adverb (also called 狀詞).
副業 *fuhyeih*, n., by-line in contrast to main profession.

§ 30S.01 (—ˢ/小)

祘 30S.01-3

suahn.

[Abbr. of 算 92A.20]

§30S.22 (—ˢ/丨)

酈 30S.22-3

lih.

N. A surname.

§ 30S.30 (—ˢ/—)

豇 30S.30-3

jiang.

豇 丽 翮 鸝 豌 魂 戩 頑 頭

N. 豇豆 (bot.) the cowpea, *Vigna sinensis* (also wr. 江豆).

§ 30S.42 (—^{S}/冈)

丽 30S.42-3

lih.

[Abbr. of 麗 30.70]

§ 30S.50 (—^{S}/ㄱ)

翮 30S.50-5

her.

N. Central stem of a feather.

鸝 30S.50-9

lir.

N. (Zoo.) the oriole (also 黃鶯).

§ 30S.70 (—^{S}/ㄴ)

豌 30S.70-6

wan.

豌豆 *wandouh*, n., the garden pea.

魂 30S.70-9

hurn.

N. Soul; the finer spirits of man as dist. 魄 *poh*, the baser spirits or animal forces: 魂靈, 魂魄 *-lirng, -poh*↓; 靈魂 human soul; 鬼魂 spirit of those departed; 魂飛魄散, 失魂落魄 frightened out of one's wits; 魂不附體 "soul departs from body"—severely shocked, upset; 三魂七魄 the three finer spirits and seven animal forces; 銷魂, 黯然銷魂 (poet.) beside oneself, grief-stricken; 招魂 formerly, to call for the soul of dying person to return to the body; 安魂 (med.) to tranquilize the spirit of person suffering from shock.

魂靈 *hurnlirng*, n., soul of departed, ghost.
魂魄 *hurnpoh*, n., psyche, the spirits and animal forces of man.

§ 30S.71 (—^{S}/七)

戩 30S.71-7

jiaan.

N. Bliss, blessedness.

Adj. Full, complete: 戩穀 (AC) perfect happiness.

§ 30S.80 (—^{S}/八)

頑 30S.80-3

warn.

V.t. U.f. 玩 31A.70, to play: 頑耍, 頑意兒 *-shuaa, -yeh'l*↓.

Adj. (1) Mischievous: 頑皮 *-pir*↓. (2) Thick-headed, stupid: 愚頑 ditto (also used of self in modesty); 頑鈍 *-duhn*↓. (3) Stubborn, die-hard, unreformed: 頑梗, 頑固, 頑強 *-geeng, -guh, -chiarng*↓; 頑廉懦立 (from allu. 頑夫廉, 懦夫有立志) the corrupt become honest and the drifters filled with ambition; 頑石點頭 (Budd. allu.) even the rocks nod in approval during preaching.

頑強 *warnchiarng*, adj., stubborn.
頑軀 *warnchyu*, n., (court.) my health.
頑鈍 *warnduhn*, adj., (1) stupid, slow to learn; (2) uneducated, vulgar, coarse.
頑梗 *warngeeng*, adj., recalcitrant.
頑固 *warn'guh*, adj., die-hard, old-fashioned, unprogressive.
頑健 *warnjiahn*, adj., (court. in self-reference) "stupidly" robust.
頑劣 *warnlieh*, adj., cheap, third-rate, low-class.
頑皮 *warnpir* (*-'pi*), adj., (child) mischievous.
頑耍 *warnshuaa*, v.i., to play.
頑癬 *warn-shyuaan*, n., a stubborn skin disease.
頑童 *warnturng*, n., young scamp, scalawag.
頑意兒 *warnyeh'l*, n., s.t. pleasant or interesting, a trick, a plaything: 有什麼頑意兒 is there anything interesting to see? 這是小頑意兒 (court. of one's gift) just a little trifle; 不知這裏頭甚麼頑意兒 don't know what's in it; what's the trick.

頭 30S.80-3

tour.

N. adjunct. A unit or piece of: 兩頭牛 two heads of cattle (cf. 兩條狗, 兩隻雞, etc.); 三頭蒜 three pieces of garlic; 一頭親事 one matrimonial match.

N. (1) (*'l*) Head: 頭上, 頭頂上 overhead; 頭尾 head and tail, beginning and end; 點頭 nod one's head; 探頭探腦 pop in one's head to look; 光頭 uncovered head; 禿頭 bald; 披頭 the Beatles or their hair style; 頭腦, 頭臉, 頭皮 *-naau, -liaan, -pir* ↓; 頭足異處 beheaded, dismembered; 頭不保 life in danger; 頭齊腳不齊 (woman) half dressed up; 頭上腳下 (women's) ensemble, gen. make-up; 頭朝裏 self-centered, egocentric, interested only in oneself, not in others; 頭朝下 crestfallen; 頭拱地 prostrate oneself; 回頭 to turn one's head, by and by: 回頭是岸 to mend one's ways; 掉頭不顧 turn head away in disregard; 出頭, 出人頭地 be honored, distinguished among a group; 拋頭露面 (derog. of woman) show oneself much in the streets; 埋頭苦幹 bury oneself in work; 昏頭昏腦 muddle-headed, absent-minded, too busy to think; 頭昏腦脹 overwhelmed with work; 頭昏眼花 dizzy; 頭昏腦悶 disconcerted; 頭痛, 頭暈 *-tuhng, -yuhn* ↓. (2) Head of group: 工頭 foreman; 頭領, 頭家 *-liing, -jia* ↓. (3) Main thread, line or aspect of work: 分頭進行 proceed each following one assignment; 千頭萬緒 complexities of a situation, innumerable things to do; 頭頭件件 every item; 頭頭是道 clear and convincing presentation (of argument or subject). (4) Side, nearby position: 這頭, 那頭 (*'tou*) this side, end, that side, end; 前頭, 後頭 (*'tou*) the front, rear; 裏頭, 外頭 inside, outside; 兩頭跑 run about at both places; 開頭, 起頭 beginning; 心頭 at heart; 心頭的恨 deep-seated hatred; 床頭 bedside; 床頭人 wife; 案頭 on the desk; 上頭 (quite proper reference to) superior, master; 看風頭 watch how the wind blows; 出風頭 to show off. (5) Forming suffix of a wide variety of words: 沒說頭, 沒講頭 (*'tou*) nothing worth discussing with a person; 沒看頭 (*'tou*), nothing worth seeing; 此馬來頭大 used of persons coming with great backing or influence; 想頭, 念頭 (*'tou*) thought, idea; 甜頭 (給甜頭吃) (*'tou*) give him "presents" or bribe; 苦頭 (吃過苦頭) have tasted some bitter experience; 彩頭 good luck; 霉頭 bad luck; 木頭 (*'tou*) timber, a blockhead; 零頭 odd change, odd pieces; 盡頭 the end; 到頭來 in the end; 空頭 (*'tou*) empty head, brainless; 空頭支票 bounced cheque, dishonored cheque: 做空頭 (stock exchange) buy on margin. (6) Used of men: 老頭(子) old man; 老實頭 (*'tou*) a simpleton; 孱頭 (*'tou*) weak fellow; 丫頭 (*'tour*) maidservant. (7) Used with parts of body: 奶頭 nipple; 舌頭 (*'tou*) tongue; 眉頭 expression in eyebrows; 指頭 finger; 手頭 money at disposal: 有手頭, 手頭寬 have plenty of money to spend.

Adj. First, No. 1: 頭等 first-class; 頭獎 first prize; 頭胎 the first-born; 頭一天, 頭一個 first day, first one, but see 頭年 *-niarn* ↓; 頭條新聞 (phr.) front page news; 頭道, 遭, 次, 回, 陣 first time; 頭挑 the best class of goods; 頭水(兒) *-shueei('l)* ↓.

頭部 *tourbuh*, n., the head: 頭部受傷 sustained a head injury.

頭妻 *tourchi*, n., first wife; legal wife.

頭擋(兒) *tourdaang('l)*, n., headboard on baby crib to ward off draft.

頭等 *tourdeeng*, adj., first-class: 頭等國 first-class Power.

頭頂(上) *tourdiing(shahng)*, n. & adj., overhead.

頭額 *tour-eh*, n., forehead.

頭髮 *tourfaa*, n., hair on human head.

頭風 *tourfeng*, n., headache, migraine.

頭蓋 *tourgaih*, n., cranium; 頭蓋骨 skull; 頭蓋腔 cranial cavity.

頭垢 *tourgouh*, n., dandruff.

頭箍兒 *tourgu'l*, n., Manchu woman's band for gathering up hair.

頭骨 *tourguu*, n., skull.

頭號(兒) *tourhauh('l)*, n., the best, the biggest.

頭昏 *tourhun*, n., headache, dizziness.

頭家 *tourjia*, n., banker or host at gambling party.

頭角 *tourjiaau*, n., in phrr., 初露頭角 (writer) make first appearance; 頭角崢嶸, 嶄然見頭角 (of youth) very promising.

頭尖 *tourjian*, n., (coll.) the very best.

頭巾 *tourjin*, n., scarf for the head, turban; 頭巾氣 bookish air; Neo-Confucian puritanical manner.

頭口 *tourkoou*, n., gen. term for domestic animals (cattle, mules, etc.＝牲口).

頭盔 *tourkuei*, n., helmet.

頭兒 *tour'l*, n., see N.↑ in all senses; 頭兒錢 banker's commission at gambling parties.

頭臉(兒) *tourliaan(-liaa'l)*, n., person's facial appearance.

頭裏 *tourlii*, adv., formerly, at the beginning; in front; beforehand.

頭領 *tourliing*, n., leader, headman.

頭路 *tourluh*, n., (1) clue, main thread; (2) profession, access: 頭路兒 first class (goods).

頭顱 *tourlur*, n., skull.

頭面 *tourmiahn*, n., face: 不露頭面 do not show one's face.

頭目 *tourmuh*, n., foreman, head of group or gang.

頭腦 *tournaau*, n., (1) head, brains: 有頭腦 has a good head; (2) thread, clue: 沒頭沒腦 (case) completely without clue; (3) head of group.

頭年 *tourniarn*, adv., last year.

頭帕 *tourpah*, n., turban.

頭皮 *tourpir*, n., (1) dandruff; (2) skin of head: 打破頭皮 a blow on head causing it to bleed.

頭晌(兒) *tourshaang('l)*, adv., in the forenoon.

頭上 *tourshahng*, adv., above, overhead.

頭銜 *tourshiarn*, n., official rank or title.

頭水(兒) *tourshueei (-shuee'l)*, n., the first and best distillation, best quality (goods); first time used (furniture).

頭蝨 *tourshy*, n., head louse, *Pediculus capitis*.

頭勢 *tourshyh*, n., force (of blow, etc.); tendency.

頭緒 *tourshyuh*, n., order, main threads: 理個頭緒出來 gather the main points, arrange in order.

頭天 *tourtian*, adv., (1) the first day; (2) the day before (cf. 頭一天 the first day).

頭寸 *tourtsuhn*, n., ready cash, cash reserve of bank.

頭痛 *tourtuhng*, n., headache; (also fig.) 偏頭痛 migraine.

頭子 *tourtz*, n., (1) the best; (2) formerly, headman, chieftain.

頭尾 *tour-weei*, n., beginning and end, parts of a connected story; 無頭無尾的故事 one cannot make head or tail of story.

頭影 *touryiing*, n., shadow: 不見你頭影 never saw even a shadow of you.

頭暈 *touryuhn*, adj. & n., dizzy, -ziness.

§ 30S.82 (—ˢ/乂)

豉 30S.82-1

chyy (re. pr. *shyh*).

N. 豆豉 pickled black beans, an ingredient in Chin. cuisine.

§ 30S.93 (—ˢ/く)

融 30S.93-2

rurng.
[Related 溶]

N. (1) 金融 currency, money market. (2) A surname: 祝融 the god of fire; 祝融爲災 there was a fire accident.

V.i. & t. (1) (Of heat) dissipate: 融散 slowly rise and be dissipated. (2) Blend, intermix: 融會 mix (bring) together: 融會貫通 integrated (knowledge), thorough understanding of the inter-relationship between different disciplines; 水乳交融 complete understanding between friends ("blending of water with milk"). (3) Melt, fuse: 初融 thaw; 融化 *-huah*↓; 融解 *-jiee*↓; 融結 combine together.

Adj. (1) Harmonious, agreeable: 融合 *-her*↓; 融和 (of weather) mild, genial; 融洽 *-shiar*↓; 融通 congenial, agreeable, accommodating; 融融 *-rurng*↓. (2) 明而未融 (AC) it has dawned but is not yet broad daylight.

融合 *rurngher*, v. i., blend, mix together.

融化 *rurnghuah*, v. i. & t., melt, fuse, liquefy.

融解 *rurngjiee*, v. i. & t., ditto; 融解點 (phys.) the melting point (also 鎔點); 融解熱 (phys.) heat of fusion.

融融 *rurngrurng*, adj., (1) happy, joyful, cheerful; (2) (of weather) warm, mild.

融洽 *rurngshiar*, adj., (of persons, feelings) mutually agreeable, on friendly terms.

融蝕 *rurng-shyr*, n., erosion of the earth's crust by water.

SECTION 31

§ 31.00 (丁/亅)

丁 31.00

ding (**jeng*).

N. (1) The fourth of the 天干 decimal cycle, see Appendix A; 丁等 Class D; 丁丁卯卯 fastidiously accurate; 丁三確四 very definite. (2) Male adult: 成丁, 未成丁 become, not yet become, adult (formerly, age 16); 添丁 have one more son; 壯丁, 人丁 males of population; esp. males subject to service, or tax in lieu of service; 丁役, 丁口, 丁戶, 丁稅 *-yih*, *-koou*, *-huh*, *-sueih*↓; male domestic or employee: 庖丁 園丁, 門丁 cook, gardener, gatekeeper; 家丁 domestic; 兵丁 soldier. (3) T-shaped: 丁字尺 *-tzyh*[1], *chyy*, etc.↓. (4) Taoist god: 六丁 the gods who fight demons. (5) A surname.

Adj. Descriptive of cling, clang, tinkling sound: 丁冬 *ding-dung*, 丁當 *ding-dang* (also wr. 叮噹); 伐木丁丁 (**jeng-jeng*), (AC) sound of cutting wood.

丁錢 *dingchiarn*, n., poll tax.

丁噹 *ding-dang*, adj., descriptive tinkling sound (cf. 玎ᴬ璫 31A.00).

丁對 *dingdueih*, adj., comfortable, agreeable: 吃得不丁對 food does not agree.

丁賦 *dingfuh*, n., poll tax.

丁戶 *dinghuh*, n., see *-koou*↓.

丁幾 *dingji*, n., tincture (translit.).

丁艱 *dingjian*, v. i., see *-you*↓.

丁祭 *dingjih*, n., spring and autumn sacrifice to Confucius on first 丁 day.

丁口 *dingkoou*, n., male of population.

丁男 *dingnarn*, n., male adult.

丁年 *dingniarn*, n., year of maturity (sixteen).

丁寧 *dingnirn*, v. i., repeat, give repeated, careful instruction (also wr. 叮嚀).

丁香 *dingshiang*, n., lilac; 丁香油 *--your*, oil of clove.

丁稅 *dingsueih*, n., poll tax.

丁字尺 *dingtzyhchyy*, n., T-square; 丁字斧 *--fuu*, n., pickaxe with two ends; 丁字節 *--jier*, n., tube joint at right angle.

丁徭 *dingyaur*, n., poll tax, see *-yih*↓.

丁夜 *dingyeh*, n., the fourth watch of the night.

丁役 *dingyih*, n., military service.

丁銀 *dingyirn*, n., poll tax money.

丁憂 *dingyou*, v. i., be in mourning for parent's death: 丁父憂, 丁母憂.

于 31.00

yur.

N. A surname.

Prep. To, at, with, from, varying with context (var. of 於 see 60S.63) used esp. in constructions with vb.+于+n. or pron. (as 告于人 speak to person, 遇于途 meet on the road, 遷于秦 move to Chirn, 會于河 assemble at the river); indistinguishable from 於 60S.63, except anc. usage has confirmed the following compp. ↓.

于飛 *yurfei*, phr., (LL) 鳳凰于飛 (fig.) of marital happiness.

于歸 *yurguei*, v.i., (LL) (girl) goes and marries, goes to her husband's home.

于思 *yursai*, adj., (LL) descriptive of a thick beard.

于時 *yurshyr*, adv., (LL) in those times.

于役 *yuryih*, v.i., (LL) serve in the army.

可 31.00

kee.

Aux. vb. (1) May, can: 不可, 不可以 may not, must not (vern. usu. 可以 see *-yii*↓): 可想而知 you can imagine; 可有可無 may or may not be needed; 無可無不可 (of Confu.) may or may not do a thing (keep an open mind); 可大可小 flexible; 可進可退 be free to go forward or back out; 可望而不可卽 may see at a distance, but may not approach (of inaccessible person); 可遇而不可求 may come by (s. t.) with luck, but not by searching for it. (2) Expressing doubt, conjecture, question: 你可好 are you well? 這下子他可好了 he must be well by now; 你可知道 do you know? you should know that; 可曾 do you ever: 你可曾聽到 (看到, 想到) have you heard (seen, thought)? (3) Expressing a statement, opinion or point of view (usu. 可不, different from 不可): 那我可不答應 I will not permit that; 時間可不早了 it's late; 可不是嗎 isn't it so? 可把我累死了 the work will kill me (too exhausting); 你可不是一個好人 I don't think you are an honest person; 這個人可不好惹 this person is not easy to handle.

V. i. (LL) 可也 this will do, (you) may; 不知其可也 don't see how this will do; formerly, in official documents, "okay."

Adj. Forming many adjj. with vbb. or nn.=-ible, -able: 可行 practicable, permissible; 可吃, 可食 edible; 可觀 *-guan*, 可愛 *-aih*, 可人 *-rern*, 可惡 *-wuh*, 可恥 *-chyy* ↓; 可教 tractable, promising: 孺子可教 (approval) the young man is worthy to be taught; 面目可憎 a hateful face; 其志可嘉 has laudable ambition; 笑容可掬 with a charming smile; 可恨 regrettable, hateful; 可惱 annoying, irritating; 可氣 provoking (anger); 可敬 worthy of respect; 可嘆 regrettable; see compp.↓.

Adv. (1) About: 年可八十 about eighty years of age; 飲可五六斗 can drink five or six gallons. (2) How (in negative sense): 可堪, 可奈 how can one endure (=cannot endure).

Conj. But, see 可是 *-shyh*↓.

可愛 *kee-aih*, adj., lovable, likeable, darling.

可恥 *kerchyy*, adj., shameful.

可兒 *kee-erl*, adj., charming, pretty (used more of pretty girl than of a lady), also 可人兒.

可風 *keefeng*, adj., exemplary, worthy as an example: 廉潔可風 exemplary honesty.

可否 *kerfoou*, aux. vb., can you or can't you? 可否答應 will you promise? 可否一同走 can I go with you? 未知可否 do not know the outcome yet; 不加可否 refuse to comment.

可怪 *keeguaih*, adj., shocking, singular, strange; phr., it is strange that: 可怪他不留一句話 it is strange that he did not leave a word.

可觀 *keeguan*, adj., (1) worth seeing; (2) sizable: 這數字也就很可觀了 will be quite a respectable sum.

可著 *kee'je*, phr., (1) according to: 可著頭做帽子 make a hat according to head size; (2) in all: 可著這一屋子的人, 也沒有像他那麼難看 there is not one so ugly in all the company present.

可加 *keejia*, n., (bot.) coca, from which cocaine is made, see *-koou* ↓.

可見 *kee jiahn*, phr., one can see therefore: 可見是他 one can see therefore it is he; 可見他從頭就不打算來 you see he never meant to come.

可知 *kee jy*, phr., (1) it must be true then, one can thus see: 他帽子還在這裏, 可知他還沒走 his hat is still here, evidently he has not gone yet; (2) (MC) naturally:

可知你聽不見 of course you cannot hear (him coming), see *-jiahn*↑.

可靠 *keekauh*, adj., reliable, dependable, accurate (report).

可可 *kerkee*, n., (1) cocoa, a drink; (2) adv., 可可(兒)的 just: 可可兒的正要出門 (I met him) just as he was leaving.

可口(兒) *kerkoou('l)*, adj., tasty, good to eat; 可口可樂 *--Keeleh*, n., Coca-Cola.

可蘭經 *Keelarn-jing*, n., the Koran.

可憐 *keeliarn*, (1) adj., small and helpless, very endearing, pitiful: 可憐的很, 怪可憐 very pitiful; (2) v. t., be merciful to (person): 可憐我 please have mercy on me; 可憐蟲 pitiful creature.

可能 *keenerng*, adj. & n., (1) possible, possibility: 有這個可能 there is this possibility; (2) (MC)=可耐 (無奈): 我未成名君未嫁, 可能俱是不如人 I am yet unknown and you are unmarried, unfortunately our lot is so wretched; 可能性 *--shihng*, n., possibility: 可能性很大 there's great possibility.

可念 *keeniahn*, adj., (1) worth remembering; (2) (MC)=可憐 pitiful.

可怕 *keepah*, adj., horrible, terrible (event, person, look, etc.).

可燃性 *keerarnshihng*, n., combustibility.

可人 *keerern*, adj., (of flavor) charming, agreeable; (of person) charming, *sympatico*: 始信淵明是可人 one sees what a charming character Taur Yuanmirng was.

可笑 *keeshiauh*, adj., laughable, ridiculous.

可惜 *keeshir*, adj. & adv., unfortunately: 可惜我不能來 unfortunately (it's a pity) I cannot come; 可惜了兒的 what a pity!

可是 *keeshyh*, (1) v. i., be indeed, be (emphatic): 你那樣可是眞糟 you are simply awful; (2) conj., but: 他雖做不好, 可是已盡力了 it's not very well done, but he has done his best; (3) (in questions) is that right? 我説的可是 is what I say right?

可憎才 *keetzengtsair*, n., (MC) lover ("hateful person" used in reverse meaning, like 冤家 "predestined enemy").

可惡 *keewuh*, adj., wicked, damned, rotten (used in condemnation).

可厭 *keeyahn*, adj., disgusting (person, talk, etc.).

可以 *keryii*, (1) aux. vb., may, can (esp. in vern.): 你可以去, 他不可以 you may go, but he may not; 可以這樣説 one may say so; (2) v. i. & adj., will do, good or bad enough: 這孩子鬧得眞可以 this child has made enough fuss; 可以休矣 enough of it, time to stop; 畫的眞可以 painted pretty well; 可以了 that will do.

可疑 *keeyir*, adj., suspicious (character, circumstance).

哥 31.00

ge.

N. Elder brother: 哥哥 *-'ge*↓; 大哥 eldest brother; 哥子 *-tz*↓.

哥哥 *ge'ge* n., (vocative) (my) elder brother.

哥兒 *ge'l*, n., (1) collective name for all brothers, (vocative) my elder brother, used among close friends: 幾個哥兒 several brothers or close friends; 哥兒倆 the two brothers; 哥兒們 the good fellows; (2) a boy, usu. from a rich family: 公子哥兒 a playboy; 哥兒大爺 a dandy, a coxcomb.

哥羅仿 *geluorfaang*, n., (translit.) chloroform.

哥倫比亞 *Gelurnbiryaa*, n., Columbia; 哥倫比亞大學 Columbia University.

哥倫布 *Gelurnbuh*, n., Columbus.

哥們兒 *ge'me'l*, n., (1) brothers: 老哥們兒 my good old brothers; 哥們兒倆 those two brothers; (2) (term of endearment) my dear brothers.

哥子 *getz*, n., (vocative) (my) elder brother.

嚣 31.00

ji.

[Pop. of 羈 41D.00]

---

§ 31.01 (丅/小)

不 31.01

nieh (*duun)

[Dist. 不]

N. (1) The stump of a tree. (2) (**duun*) 白不 Kaolin, a kind of white clay used for making pottery or porcelain at Chingteh, Kiangsi Province.

乐 31.01

leh.

[Abbr. of 樂 93.01]

栗 31.01

lih.

N. (1) (Bot.) the chestnut tree; 栗子 *-tz*↓; 板栗 chestnuts; 毛栗 ditto; 栗木 *-muh*↓. (2) A surname.

V.i. & t. (1) V.i., (AC interch. 慄) tremble, fearful: 戰戰栗栗 to tremble with fear. (2) V.t., (AC interch. 裂) to split, break into pieces: 栗薪 to split firewood.

Adj. (1) (AC) firm, durable: 縝密以栗 it has a fine and close texture. (2) (AC) dignified: 寬而栗 magnanimous and yet dignified.

栗苞 *lih'bau*, n., (1) the shell of a chestmut (also 栗房); (2) a clenched fist, so called because of its resemblance to a chestnut (also 栗暴).

栗房 *lihfarng*, n., the shell of a chestnut, see -*'bau*↑.

栗烈 *lihlieh*, adj., extremely cold (also wr. 凓冽, 栗冽).

栗碌 *lihluh*, adj., (LL) busily occupied with work: 人事栗碌.

栗木 *lihmuh*, n., the chestnut tree or its wood.

栗色 *lihseh*, adj., reddish brown, chestnut color.

栗鼠 *lihshuu*, n., (=松鼠) the squirrel.

栗子 *lihtz*, n., chestnuts.

琹 31.01

chirn.

[Anc. var. of 琴 31.32]

蘪 31.01

ju.

N. A small wooden pile; 楬蘪 (AC) stick marking burial site.

票 31.01

piauh.

N. (1) Ticket: (入)門票 ticket for admission; 免票, 半票 admission free, at half price; 彩票 lottery ticket; 船票, 車票, 飛機票, 來回票 boat, train, airplane, return ticket. (2) Warrant, certificate, check: 股票 stock certificate; 支票 bank or personal check; 滙票 bank check for transfer of money; 期票 post-dated check; 見票卽付 phr., pay at sight; 傳票 court warrant, court notice to appear. (3) Any official printed slip: 郵票 stamp; 印花票 tax stamp. (4) Ballot, the vote: 票選 election by vote; 廢票 disqualified vote; 投票 cast vote. (5) (Comm.) business deal: 做他一票 make a deal; 一票貨物 a shipment of goods. (6) The kidnapped person: 綁票 to kidnap; 肉票 the kidnapped person; 撕票 kill kidnapped person; 贖票 pay the ransom. (7) Opera singing by amateurs: 玩票 be such amateur.

票布 *piauhbuh*, n., badge of membership in former secret society.

票串 *piauhchuahn*, v. i. & n., be amateur of opera singing.

票額 *piauh-ehl*, n., sum stated on check or certificate.

票房兒 *piauhfarng'l*, n., (1) ticket office; (2) place where opera amateurs (see -*yoou*↓) meet for practice.

票匪 *piauhfeei*, n., kidnapper (or gang).

票根 *piauhgen*, n., stub of check.

票匭 *piauhgueei*, n., ballot box.

票號 *piauhauh*, n., exchange shop; formerly, firm dealing in money exchange and transfer.

票活 *piauh-huor*, n., non-pay work or job.

票莊 *piauhjuang*, n., see -*hauh*↑.

票據 *piauhjyuh*, n., certificate; 商業票據 commercial paper; 票據交換所 clearing house.

票兒 *piauh'l*, n., certificate, ticket.

票面 *piauhmiahn*, n., par value of certificate.

票子 *pauhtz*, n., (1) bill, paper money; (2) notice to appear at court (=傳票); (3) ticket.

票友 *piauh-yoou*, n., amateur in opera singing.

粟 31.01

suh.

N. (1) Unhusked rice. (2) Millet, maize, corn (also called 玉粟). (3) (AC) grain in gen., also used as indication of salary by payment of grain.

粟飯 *suhfahn*, n., meal of maize, corn, or millet, in place of rice course food.

粟米 *suhmii*, n., maize, Indian corn.

§ 31.02 (T/ㄎ)

汞 31.02

guung (also **huhng*).

N. (Chem.) mercury.

泵 31.02

behng.

N. Pump: 水泵 water pump.

泵浦 *behngpuu*, n., (translit.) pump.

豕 31.02

shyy.

N. (AC, LL) pig, hog (modn. 豬 31S.41): 犬豕 (contempt.) dogs and cats; 豕交獸畜 (AC allu.) treat like beasts—to feed a person without love or respect.

豕牢 *shyylaur*, n., pigpen.

豕突 *shyytur*, v.t., (of bandits) infest and harass.

裂 31.02

lieh.

V.i. & t. Crack, split, break open: 分裂 (of parties, region) split up; 四分五裂 fall apart; 裂開 split open; 破裂, 斷裂 break, broken; 斷裂(絕)關係 sever relations; 撕裂 tear apart.

裂帛 *liehbor*, adj., "tear silk": 聲如裂帛 a noise like tearing up silks; (AC) tear silk strips for writing, see 帛 91.22.

裂縫(兒)(子) *liehfehng('l)(tz)*, n., crack in seams, signs of estrangement among friends.

裂膚 *liehfu*, adj., (LL) chapping, freezing cold, enough to "crack skin."

裂鍋 *liehguo*, phr., "break cooking pan," sever relations.

裂痕 *liehhern*, n., see *-fehng* ↑.

裂口(兒)(子) *liehkoou('l)(tz)*, n., open wound, opening of seam.

裂罅 *liehshiah*, n., a break, a leak.

裂紋兒 *liehwer'l*, n., cracks on surface; wrinkle on skin: 她臉上一點裂紋兒都沒有 not even a wrinkle on her face.

聚 31.02

jyuh.

N. A hamlet, village: 聚落 *-luoh* ↓.

V.t. (1) Assemble, come together: 聚攏 *-luung*, 聚合 *-her*, 聚集 *-jir* ↓; 聚精會神 concentrate one's attention and energy on a given task; 聚散 *-sahn* ↓; 聚一聚 enjoy a nice meeting together; 歡聚 have a happy reunion; 完聚, 團聚 a family reunion; 相聚 gather together, meet. (2) Accumulate, amass, pile up: 聚斂 *-liahn* ↓.

聚齊兒 *jyuhchier'l*, v.i., (of persons) assemble, gather together.

聚賭 *jyuh-duu*, v.i., gather together to gamble.

聚光器 *jyuhguangchih*, n., (optics) a condenser.

聚合 *jyuhher*, v.i., come together, assemble. 「a meeting.

聚會 *jyuhhueih*, v.i. & n., (hold)

聚集 *jyuhjir*, v.i., see *-her* ↑.

聚斂 *jyuhliahn*, v.i. & t., (1) collect, amass, accumulate; (2) levy heavy taxes.

聚落 *jyuhluoh*, n., a village or hamlet; settlement.

聚攏 *jyuhluung*, v.t., assemble in one place, meet together.

聚散 *jyuh-sahn*, v.i., (of persons) meet and go away: 人生聚散無常 separation and reunion are part of life.

聚首 *jyuh-shoou*, v.i., (of friends) meet, see one another (cf. *tête-à-tête*).

聚訟 *jyuh-suhng*, v.i., argue back and forth and cannot agree: 聚訟紛紜 ditto.

聚餐 *jyuh-tsan*, v.i. & n., (have) a lunch or dinner party.

聚麀 *jyuh-you*, v.i., commit incest.

餮 31.02

tieh.

N. See 饕餮 40.02.

§ 31.10 (丅/十)

干 31.10

gan.

N. (1) A shield: 干戈 *-ger*, 干城 *-cherng* ↓. (2) Short for 天干 (甲, 乙, 丙, 丁, 戊, 巳, 庚, 辛, 壬, 癸) the decimal cycle of ten characters by which the Chinese reckon their years, see Appendix A; 干支 *-jy* ↓. (3) The edge of a body of water: 江干 a river bank. (4) A surname.

V.t. (1) Offend against: 干犯 *-fahn* ↓. (2) (Related 關) to concern, interfere with: 干預, 干涉, 干係, 干連 *-yuh*³, *-sheh*, *-shih*, *-liarn* ↓; 相干 be concerned with; 與你何干 what has this to do with you? 干你何事 it's none of your business; 干卿底事 ditto; 事不干己 it doesn't concern me; 不干我事 it's none of my concern; 干政 take an active part in politics. (3) Entreat, seek, request: 干求, 干進, 干祿, 干謁 *-chiour*, *-jihn*, *-luh*, *-yeh* ↓.

Adj. (1) 若干 how many? (2) These, those, some: 那干人 those people; 又一干人 another group of people. (3) (Var. of 乾) dried: 豆腐干 dried bean curd.

干貝 *ganbeih*, n., dried meat of tendons of big clams.

干城 *gancherng*, n., (1) defense works, fortifications; (2) soldiers fighting for the country: 國之干城 heroic defenders of the nation.

干求 *ganchiour*, n. & v.t., entreat(y), request: 經不起他一再干求 cannot resist his peristent requests.

干犯 *ganfahn*, v.t., (1) hurt the feelings of; (2) encroach upon; (3) infringe upon (regulations).

干戈 *ganger*, n., (1) shield and spear, weapons of war in gen.; (2) wars, fighting, armed forces: 干戈四起 fighting broke out all over the country; 逞干戈 resort to military might.

干進 *ganjihn*, v.i., seek official preferment.

干支 *ganjy*, n., short for 天干 and 地支 (子, 丑, 寅, 卯, 辰, 巳, 午, 未, 申, 酉, 戌, 亥), the twelve characters by which the Chinese reckon the hours of a day; the combination of one character from 天干 and another from 地支 forms a term by which a year or date is known; the orderly series of such possible combinations yield sixty different terms to designate a cycle of sixty years; when one cycle ends, another begins all over again; see Appendix A.

干連 *ganliarn*, v.t., to implicate,

be implicated in.

干祿 *gan-luh*, v.i., seek official position.

干冒 *ganmauh*, v.t., offend, hurt the feelings of (superior).

干涉 *gansheh*, n. & v.t., (1) take part in (policy); be implicated or involved in; interfere with: 干涉內政 interfere with internal affairs of a nation; (2) (phys.) interference.

干係 *ganshih*, n., relations(hip) (=關係).

干休 *ganshiou*, v.t., give up (a fight, quarrel, etc.): 不肯干休 refuse to stop dispute.

干時 *ganshyr*, v.i., be opportunist, go along with the current trends.

干謁 *ganyeh*, v.t., seek to interview (s.o.) with requests for favors.

干譽 *gan-yuh*¹, v.i., seek popular recognition.

干與 *ganyuh*², v.t., intervene, interfere.

干預 *ganyuh*³, v.t., ditto.

平 31.10

pirng.

N. (1) Short for Peiping: 平劇 Peking opera. (2) The even tone: 陰平, 陽平 first and second tones; 平仄 (*pirng* and *tzeh*) even and uneven tones, basis of Chin. poetic rhythm. (3) Peace: 太平, 和平 peace (in country). (4) Scale, measure of silver: 庫平 Treasury Scale; 關平 Customs silver scale. (5) A surname.

V.t. (1) To pacify, bring peace to: 治國平天下 rule country and unify the world in peace: 平定 subjugate (rebels) and restore peace. (2) To restore to normal: 他的病平復了 his illness is over, has gone back to normal; 物價平落 prices drop to normal. (3) To weigh and pay: 平出十兩銀子 pay out ten ounces of silver.

Adj. (1) Flat: 平地 flat, level ground, see *-dih*↓; 平沙 *-sha*↓; 平底 flat bottom; 平底鞋 low-heeled shoes, opposed to high-heels 高跟鞋; 平視 look on straight level; 平面 *-miahn*↓. (2) Common: 平郵, 平信 ordinary mail; 平常, 平時, 平民 *-charng*, *-shyr*, *-mirn*↓. (3) Balanced, calm: 平心靜氣 phr., calm, -ly; 平心而論 objectively speaking, without emotional bias; 平靜, 平安, 平淡 *-tzihng*, *-an*, *dahn*²↓. (4) Fair, objective: 公平 fair.

平安 *pirng-an*, adj. & n., well, peace, -ful: 身體平安 in good health; 平安無事 all is well; 平安信 letter reporting safe arrival or all is well.

平版 *pirngbaan*, n., offset (printing).

平白 *pirngbair*, adv., without any reason (of insult, quarrel); see *-kung*↓.

平輩(兒) *pirng-beih* (*-beh'l*), n., of same generation (as between brothers, cousins).

平常 *pirngcharng*, adj., ordinary, not distinguished, common; (euphem.) so-so; adv., ordinarily.

平情 *pirngchirng*, adj. & adv., calm: 平情而論 objectively speaking.

平楚 *pirng-chuu*, n., (LL) prairie.

平旦 *pirng-dahn*¹, n., early dawn.

平淡 *pirngdahn*², adj., mild in color; mild-flavored; easy-reading (prose): 平淡無奇 nothing exciting.

平等 *pirngdeeng*, n. & adj., equal, -ity: 男女平等 sexual equality; 平等待遇 equal treatment.

平地 *pirngdih*, (1) n., flat ground; (2) adv., suddenly and without cause or warning: 平地風波, 平地一聲雷 sudden, unexpected trouble, catastrophe; 平地起孤丁 quarrel, trouble without reason.

平定 *pirngdihng*, n. & adj., peaceful; v.t., to conquer: 平定天下 conquer the world.

平糴 *pirngdir*, phr., a measure for stabilization of grain prices by buying grain when it is cheap.

平反 *pirngfaan*, v.i., reverse court sentence, freeing the wrongly condemned.

平方 *pirngfang*, n., (math.) square; 平方尺 *--chye*, square foot; 平方根 *--gen*, square root.

平凡 *pirngfarn*, adj., ordinary, undistinguished, common.

平房 *pirngfarng*, n., one-storied house, bungalow; contrast 樓房 several-storied house.

平分 *pirng-fen*, v.t., divide equally.

平復 *pirngfur*, v.t., quench (rebellion); v.i., recover (from illness); restore (price) to normal.

平光 *pirng-guang*, adj., (of lenses) anastigmatic; glasses not for far- or nearsighted.

平衡 *pirngherng*, n. & adj., equilibrium, -brious; 平衡表 balance sheet (also called 狀況表, 財務狀況表).

平話 *pirnghuah*, n., storyteller's copy at teahouses in Suhng Dyn.

平章 *pirngjang*, v.t., settle (state business); n., usu. 同平章(政)事 prime minister (Tarng Dyn.).

平整 *pirngjeeng*, adj., neat (dress, facial features).

平正 *pirngjehng*, adj., fair, impartial; right proportioned (facial features).

平價 *pring-jiah*, n., low price.

平肩 *pirng-jian*, adj., of equal status.

平交道 *pirngjiau-dauh*, n., level railroad crossing.

平靜 *pringjihng*, adj., quiet, tranquil.

平金 *pirng-jin*, n., gold-thread embroidery.

平準 *pirngjuun*, phr., see *-dir*↑; 平準基金 equalization fund.

平直 *pirngjyr*, adj., straight and even.

平居 *pirngjyu*, adv., see 平日 *-ryh*↓.

平劇 *pringjyuh*, n., Peking opera.

平均 *pirngjyun*, n. & adj., average: 平均分數 average marks; 平均地權 socialistic control of land value.

平康里 *pirngkang-lii*, n., red-light district.

平空 *pirngkung*, adv., suddenly, out of the blue: 平空造謠 create rumor without basis.

平林 *pirnglirn*, n., wood groves on level ground.

平面 *pirngmiahn*, n., flat surface; 平面幾何 plane geometry.

平民 *pirngmirn*, n., common people, the people; 平民教育 popular education.

平明 *pirngmirng*, n., dawn.

平脈 *pirng-moh*, n., (Chin. med.) regular, even pulse.

平年 *pirng-niarn*, n., year which is not leap year.

平平 *pirngpirng*, adj., so-so, ordinary, nothing special.

平人 *pirng-rern*, n., ordinary person; (LL) ordinary free citizen.

平日 *pirngryh*, adv., in the usual course of things, usually.

平色 *pirng-seh*, n., intrinsic value of coins.

平沙 *pirngsha*, n., sand beach: 平沙落雁 wild geese on the beach, (theme for painting).

平射砲 *pirngsheh-pauh*, n., trench mortar.

平身 *pirng-shen*, adj., normal standing position after bowing.

平生 *pirngsheng*, n. & adj., life, lifetime: 平生事業 lifetime work; 平生大事 big event in one's life; adv., in the past.

平西 *pirngshi*, v.i., (of the sun) incline to the west; pacify the western region.

平信 *pirngshihn*, n., ordinary mail.

平昔 *pirngshir*, adv., in the past.

平行 *pirngshirng*, adj., (1) parallel; (2) going together; 平行線支票 crossed cheque.

平手(兒) *pirng-shoou('l)*, n., proper match in prowess, boxing skill.

平順 *pirngshuhn*, adj., going smoothly, well.

平時 *pringshyr*, adv., usually, except on occasions: 平時不用功 usually neglect one's studies.

平素 *pirngsuh*, adv., in the past: 平素的朋友 old friend; 平素不相往來 never were friends before.

平坦 *pirngtaan*, adj., (of roads) level and easy to walk on.

平台 *pirng-tair*, n., terrace.

平天冠 *pirngtian-guan*, n., (MC) emperor's cap with flat top.

平糶 *pirngtiauh*, phr., a measure for stablilization of grain prices by selling grain when the prices are high, cf. *-dir*↑.

平亭 *pirngtirng*, v.t., (MC) judge and settle (case).

平頭 *pirngtour*, adj., (MC) as in 平頭百姓 common people; n., crew cut; 平頭正臉 phr., well-featured (of woman or man); 平頭甲子 full cycle of 60 years; 平頭數 a round number.

平槽 *pirng-tzau*, adj., (of water) filling to the brim.

平穩 *pirngween*, adj., steady, safe, fair (opinion), even, smooth (footsteps, prose).

平文 *pirng-wern*, n., (MC) prose, usu. 散$^{\Delta}$文 20S.82.

平野 *pirngyee*, n., the open suburb, the countryside.

平衍 *pirngyiaan*, n., =平野 *-yee*↑.

平易 *pirngyih*[1], adj., easy to understand (writing): 平易近人 reasonable and simple (of person).

平議 *pirngyih*[2], n., criticism, fair evaluation.

平原 *pirngyuarn*, n., prairie, flat countryside; 平原督郵 (MC) bad liquor.

平月 *pirng-yueih*, n., February of 28 days (not in leap year).

平允 *pirngyuun*, adj., fair, objective.

覃 31.10

tarn.

N. A surname.

V.i. Spread: 覃及 (LL) spread to.

Adj. & adv. Deep(-ly), profound (-ly): 覃思 (LL) deep thought; 覃恩 (LL) deep or broad favor (to people).

鞏 31.10

guung.

N. (1) Name of a county in Honan Province. (2) A surname.

V. t. To fasten with a leather band.

Adj. Strong, solid: 鞏固 *-guh*↓.

鞏固 *guungguh*, (1) v. t., make stronger, strengthen, consolidate, buttress; (2) adj., solid, strong (position).

鞏膜 *guungmor*, n., (physiol.) the sclerotic coat.

耳 31.10

eel.

Fin. part. Only (probably contraction of 而已): 前言戲之耳 I was only joking; also indeed: 且吾所爲者極難耳 besides, what I did was indeed difficult.

N. (1) The ear: 耳朵 *-'duo*↓; 耳孔 *-kung*↓; 掩耳, 充耳不聞 turn a deaf ear to; 傾耳而談 whisper to one's ears; 逆耳 or 不入耳之言 words that offend; 洗耳恭聽 listen respectfully; 東風過耳 in one ear and out the other; 面紅耳赤 blush up to the ears; 耳濡目染 influence of surroundings (what one hears and sees); 耳提面命 personal, daily instruction; 耳鬢斯磨 close association during childhood, rub shoulders; 耳聽八方 extraordinarily alert; 耳鳴 buzzing in the ears (usu. combined with dizziness); 耳沉, 耳背 heavy of hearing; 耳軟(心活) easily influenced by others; 耳生, 耳熟 *-sheng, -shur*↓; 百聞不如一見, 耳聞不如目見 to see once is better than a hundred hearsays; 外耳 external ear; 中耳 middle ear (tympanum); 內耳 inner ear (labyrinth). (2) Side (rooms, handles): 耳房, 耳門 *-fang, -mern*↓; 鼎耳 the ears of a tripod. (3) Fungus, mushroom: 木耳 tree mushroom, "Jew's ear"; 銀耳 white tree fungus.

A

V. t. (LL) to hear: 久耳大名 have heard of your name for a long time.

耳報神 *eel-bauh-shern*, n., (coll.) spy who reports on person's doings.

耳背 *eel-beih*, phr., (MC) heavy of hearing.

耳邊風 *eel-bian-feng*, n., rumor, hearsay; s. t. to be disregarded.

耳脖子 *eelbortz*, n., area below the ears on the neck.

耳沉 *eel-chern*, adj., heavy of hearing.

耳垂(兒) *eel-chueir(-chuer'l)*, n., lower ear lobe.

耳治 *eel-chyr*, phr., (AC) to listen.

耳殼 *eelchyueh*, n., the external ear.

耳璫 *eeldang*, n., earring, esp. pendant type.

耳刀兒 *eeldau'l*, n., name for the radicals "卩" and "阝": 單耳刀兒 "卩" and 雙耳刀兒 "阝."

耳底 *erldii*, n., (1) inner ear; (2) inflammation of the ear (also 耳朵底子).

耳朵 *eel'duo*, n., common vern. for 耳, the ear: 耳朵不靈 hearing is bad; hearing: 耳朵長 good at hearing all news, reports; 耳朵軟 easily influenced by others; 耳朵沉 heavy of hearing; 耳朵帽兒 earflaps; 耳朵眼兒 (a) ear aperture; (b) aperture for earring.

耳耳 *erl-eel*, phr., (LL) only so-so.

耳房 *eelfarng*, n., side room, small annex.

耳糞 *eelfehn*, n., see *-lah* ↓.

耳風 *eel'feng*, n., rumor heard.

耳根 *eelgen*, n., (1) the ear; (2) hearing: 耳根清淨 quiet, no disturbing sounds; 耳根前 in the immediate presence; 耳根底下 ditto; 耳根臺子 base at back of ear.

耳垢 *eelgouh*, n., earwax, see *-lah* ↓.

耳刮(子) *eelgua(tz)*, n., a box on the ear: 打了一耳刮 (also wr. 耳瓜).

耳光(子) *eelguang(-tz)*, n., a box

B

on the ear; also *-gua* ↑.

耳鼓 *erlguu*, n., (physiol.) eardrum.

耳毫 *eelhaur*, n., (in masks or paintings) stiff hair showing from ears, indicating a coarse or warlike character.

耳環 *eelhuarn*, n., earring.

耳機(子) *eelji(tz)*, n., earphone.

耳界 *eeljieh*, n., sounds within hearing distance: 耳界清淨 cosy, quiet, free from noise.

耳珠 *eelju*, n., pearl or similar earring.

耳墜子 *eeljueihtz*, n., pendant earrings.

耳脂 *eeljy*, n., see *-gouh* ↑.

耳科 *eelke*, n., otology, section in hospital specializing on ear troubles: 耳科專家 otologist, ear specialist.

耳孔 *erlkuung*, n., (1) the ear; (2) the ear aperture, external ear canal.

耳蠟 *eellah*, n., earwax, (also *-gouh, -fehn*).

耳力 *eel-lih*, n., hearing power.

耳漏 *eel-louh*, n., otorrhoea, ear inflammation with pus.

耳輪 *eellurn*, n., the earlap, the rim of the ear.

耳聾 *eellurng*, adj., deaf.

耳門 *eelmern*, n., side door.

耳鳴 *eel-mirng*, phr., buzzing in the ears, (tinnitus).

耳目 *eelmuh*, n., (1) sights and sounds: 耳目一新 a pleasant change of atmosphere or appearance of a place; (2) the eyes and ears, i. e., spies set to watch and report on doings: 耳目衆多 too many people in a place watching or listening.

耳衄 *eelnyuh*, n. bleeding in the ear.

耳旁風 *eel-parng-feng*, n., see *-bian-feng* ↑.

耳熱 *eel-reh*, phr., ears flush from excitement, wine.

耳塞(子) *eel'sai(tz)*, n., see *-lah* ↑.

耳生 *eelsheng*, adj., (name, etc.) sounds unfamiliar, cf. *-shur* ↓.

耳順 *eel-shuhn*, (1) adj. phr., sixty years of age (allu. Confucius, when nothing he heard could upset him); (2) pleasing to the

C

ear (of opera singing).

耳熟 *eelshur*, adj., (name) sounds familiar: 耳熟能詳 very familiar, have heard many times.

耳食 *eelshyr*, v. i., to believe all that one hears: 耳食之徒 such people; 耳食不化 hearing without digesting what is heard.

耳學 *eel-shyuer*, phr., learn not directly from books but from what others say.

耳屎 *erlshyy*, n., see *-lah, -fehn* ↑.

耳孫 *eelsun*, n., eighth-generation grandchild.

耳痛 *eeltuhng*, n., earache.

耳子 *eeltz*, n., the ears or side handles of a basin, barrel, incense tray, etc.

耳挖(兒)(子) *eelwar('l)(tz)*, n., an ear pick.

耳聞 *eelwern*, v. i. & t., to hear.

耳衣 *eelyi*, n., earflaps.

耳語 *erlyuu*, n. & v. i., whisper.

聶 31.10

nieh.

N. A surname.

V. t. (AC) whisper (s.t.) to (s.o.).

§ 31.11 (丅/土)

王 31.11

warng (**wahng*).

N. (1) A king; 國王, 君王 ditto; 先王 royal ancestors; 明王 a wise, powerful ruler. (2) (Fig.) best or strongest of its kind: 王者 *-jee* ↓; 獸王 the king of beasts, the lion; 球王 king of baseball (football, etc.); 拳王 boxing champion; 歌王 champion singer, etc. (3) One of princely rank: 親王 a

A

王 玉 prince; 王侯 duke; 郡王 chief of a principality, a minor prince; 王公 *-gung*[1]↓. (4) A surname.

V. t. (1) (**wahng*) To rule over: 王天下 rule over the world; 王此大邦 rule over this big country. (2) 莫不敢來王 (AC) no one dared refuse to come and acknowledge (s. o.) as lord.

Adj. (1) Kingly, royal, opp. 霸 31D.42 tyrannical (rule by force): 王法, 王命 *-faa, -mihng*↓. (2) Potent: 王道 *-dauh*↓. (3) (**wahng*＝旺) Prosperous.

王八 *warng-ba* (*-'ba*), n., (1) a tortoise; (2) (abuse) a cuckold, scoundrel: 王八蛋, 王八羔子 (abuse) son-of-a-bitch; (3) formerly, man servant at brothels.

王霸 *warng-bah*, n., rule (or ruler) by justice (王) and rule (or ruler) by force (霸).

王不留行 *warng-buh-liour-shirng*, n., (bot.) a flowering plant, *Vaccaria vulgaris*.

王城 *warng-cherng*, n., the royal city.

王道 *warng-dauh*, (1) n., the kingly way of government by justice; (2) (*-'dau*) adj., potent (tonic), sharp (flavor).

王度 *warng-duh*, n., kingly generosity, regal heart or manner.

王法 *warng-faa* (*-'fa*), n., the way of the land: 沒王法 defiant of all law and social traditions.

王妃 *warngfei*, n., princess-consort, a rank next to the queen.

王父 *warngfuh*, n., (LL) grandfather.

王府 *warngfuu*, n., a prince's residence.

王綱 *warng-gang*, n., the imperial laws and institutions.

王姑 *warnggu*, n., (LL) grandmother.

王瓜 *warnggua*, n., (1) the cucumber; (2) a kind of small melon.

王公 *warnggung*[1], n., the princes and dukes: 王公大人 the dukes and high ministers, the titled nobility.

王宮 *warnggung*[2], n., a royal palace.

王后 *warnghouh*, n., a queen.

B

王化 *warng-huah*, n., cultural influence of a good king.

王虺 *warng-hueei*, n., (AC) king of serpents.

王章 *warng-jang*, n., royal institutions.

王者 *warngjee*, n., a great king, a royal personality; 王者香 *--shiang*, n., name for the orchid or *Epidendrum*; 王者師 a teacher of kings.

王畿 *warng-ji*, n., the suburbs of the capital.

王考 *warngkaau*, n., deceased grandfather (used esp. on tombstones).

王蓮 *warngliarn*, n., (bot.) *Victoria regia*, a variety of the lotus with huge floating leaves.

王命 *warngmihng*, n., king's order.

王母 *warngmuu*, n., (LL) grandmother; 西王母, see 西 31.41.

王女 *warngnyuu*, n., king's daughter.

王蛇 *warng-sher*, n., a python, a boa constrictor.

王水 *warng-shueei*, n., (chem.) aqua regia, a mixture of nitric and hydrochloric acid, able to dissolve gold and platinum.

王事 *warng-shyh*[1], n., (AC) state affairs.

王室 *warng-shyh*[2], n., the royal house.

王孫 *warngsun*, n., as in 王孫公子 rich men's sons, young noblemen.

王庭 *warng-tirng*, n., the royal court.

王族 *warng-tzur*, n., members of the royal house.

王子 *warngtzyy*, n., (1) a prince; (2) (*-'tz*) (fig.) king of animals: 蜜蜂王子 queen bee.

王爺 *warng'ye*, n., address of a prince, His Royal Highness; a popular god.

王業 *warngyeh*, n., the business of being a great ruler.

玉 31.11

yuh.

N. Jade: 玉石 *-shyr*↓; 寶玉, 美玉

C

jade, precious stones; (fig.) the female body: 玉人 *-rern*↓; 玉殞香消, 玉碎珠沉 death of a woman; 玉減香消 (of woman) emaciated; 亭亭玉立 (woman) stands very straight; 玉潤珠圓 (female singer) rich round voice; 玉容, 玉貌 *-rurng, -mauh*↓; (court. not confined to women) your esteemed: 玉體, 玉趾, 玉照 *-tii, -jyy, -jauh*↓; 玉音 *-yin*↓; 玉覽, 玉展 (letter) for your esteemed perusal; symbolic of purity: 冰清玉潔 pure like jade, clear like ice—chaste appearance or morals; 玉全 *-chyuarn*↓.

玉柏 *yuh-baai*, n., (bot.) a plant, *Lycopodium obscurum*.

玉版 *yuh-baan*, n., a fine-quality writing paper; 玉版魚 *--yur*, n., the sturgeon.

玉帛 *yuh-bor*, n., jade and silks—gifts in anc. China.

玉蟬 *yuhcharn*[1], n., (bot.) a kind of iris, *Iris laevigata* (*Kaempfeir*).

玉蟾 *yuh-charn*[2], n., the moon ("jade toad"—toad representing a shadow on the moon).

玉成 *yuhcherng*, v.i., to help to successful conclusion.

玉全 *yuh-chyuarn*, v.t., to help succeed.

玉闕 *yuh-chyueh*, n., palace of Taoist immortals in heaven.

玉牒 *yuh-dier*, n., (1) genealogy of royal house; (2) prayer at important sacrifice or other documents carved on precious stone.

玉帝 *yuh-dih*, n., Taoist God, "Emperor of Heaven."

玉粳 *yuh-geeng*, n., (fig.) white even teeth of woman.

玉鈎 *yuh-gou*, n., jade hook; (fig.) the crescent moon.

玉環 *yuh-huarn*, n., jade bracelet.

玉壺 *yuh-hur*, n., a jade pot, symbolic of spiritual purity; a jade "hourglass."

玉虎 *yuh-huu*, n., (poet. only) well pulley.

玉照 *yuh-jauh*, n., your portrait, photograph.

玉舟 *yuh-jou*, n., (poet. only) wine cup.

玉筯 *yuh-juh*, n., (1) jade chopsticks; (2) (poet. only) tears.

玉菌 (蕈) *yuh-jyuhn*, n., a kind of

mushroom, *Tricholoma simji*.
玉趾 *yuh-jyy*, n., your presence.
玉蘭 *yuhlarn*, n., magnolia; 玉蘭片 --*piahn*, n., (poet.) dried bamboo shoots.
玉粒 *yuh-lih*, n., (LL) rice ("jade grains").
玉漏 *yuh-louh*, n., hourglass at the palace.
玉樓 *yuh-lour*, phr., 玉樓赴召 (allu.) death of a young poet.
玉露 *yuh-luh*, n., pearly dew.
玉輪 *yuh-lurn*, n., (poet.) the moon.
玉貌 *yuh-mauh*, n., your looks.
玉米 *yuh'mi*, n., maize, corn; 玉米花兒 --*hua'l*, n., popcorn.
玉女 *yuh-nyuu*, n., (Taoist) fairy damsel in land of immortals; (fig.) a pretty girl.
玉盤 *yuh-parn*, n., the moon ("jade plate").
玉髯 *yuh-rarn*, n., (poet.) bean sprouts.
玉人 *yuh-rern*, n., (1) a handsome man or woman; (2) (AC) worker on jade.
玉容 *yuh-rurng*, n., your face, appearance.
玉色 *yuh'shai*, n., jade color—green or bluish-green.
玉璽 *yuh-shii*, n., the imperial seal.
玉樹 *yuh-shuh*, n., (poet.) handsome person.
玉蜀黍 *yuhshurshuu*, n., maize, corn.
玉石 *yuh-shyr*, phr., 玉石俱焚 jade and stone both burned—good men destroyed with the bad.
玉髓 *yuh-sueei*, n., chalcedony.
玉碎 *yuh-sueih*, phr., 寧爲玉碎，毋爲瓦全 die with honor, rather than survive with dishonor.
玉筍 *yuh-suun*, n., (poet.) a woman's fingers, or bound feet.
玉堂 *yuh-tarng*, n., "jade hall"—life of the very rich; name for Hanlin Academy.
玉體 *yuh-tii*, n., (1) (court.) your esteemed health; (2) 玉體橫陳 a woman stretched in bed.
玉葱 *yuh-tsung*, n., (1) (poet.) lady's slender fingers; (2) (bot.) a kind of onion, *Allium cepa*.
玉兔 *yuh-tuh*, n., (poet.) the moon (with shadow of a supposed hare).
玉簪 *yuh-tzan*, n., the tuberose.
玉顏 *yuh-yarn*, n., (litr.) a lady's face.
玉液 *yuh-yeh*, n., (poet.) fine wine.
玉音 *yuh-yin*, n., your esteemed letter, news from you.
玉宇 *yuh-yuu*, n., jade palace.

至 31.11

jyh.

N. The extreme, solstice: 夏至，冬至 summer, winter solstice: 殘酷之至 extreme of cruelty.

V. i. (1) (LL) to arrive, reach: 至於秦 reached state of Chirn; 無微不至 (attention, influence) reaches everywhere; 久候不至 did not turn up after a long waiting. (2) Go so far, to the extent: 竟至 indeed go so far as to; 至於此極 to such an extent; 不至 phr., not to that extent; 不至於此 couldn't be that bad, that cruel, etc.

Adj. (1) Most, greatest, most perfect, most profound: 至言，至行，至聖，至德 -*yarn*, -*shihng*, -*shehng*, -*der*↓. (2) Most sincere: 至誠，至意，至交，至友 -*cherng*, -*yih*, -*jiau*, -*yoou*↓.

Adv. Most: 至爲無聊 most boring; 至大至公 most high and most just (God, sovereign); 至當 (-*dahng*) most proper, appropriate; 至忠，至孝 most loyal, most filial; 至仁，至剛 most kind, most strong; 至矣盡矣 (praise) that is the highest limit of perfection; 至德 most perfect virtue; 仁至義盡 most perfectly fulfilled both in love and duty.

Prep. To, till: 自東至西 from east to west; 自冬至夏 from summer to winter; 至於 -*yu*↓.

至寶 *jyhbaau*, n., extremely valued treasure.
至誠 *jyhcherng*, (1) n., utmost sincerity; (2) adj., most sincere.
至親 *jyhchin*, n., closest of kin.
至情 *jyhchirng*, n., most genuine feeling (of friendship, kinship).
至德 *jyhder*, n., perfect virtue.
至交 *jyhjiau*, n., best friend.
至竟 *jyhjihng*, adv. phr., (MC) after all.
至今 *jyhjin*, phr., (from sometime past) to the present; at present (notice difference in use from Eng. "until now"): 至今不廢 persist up to the present.
至樂 *jyhleh*, n., as in 至樂世界 paradise; imagined blessed state.
至理 *jyhlii*, n., God's own truth: 至理名言 most true sayings.
至人 *jyhrern*, n., (Taoism) a perfect man.
至若 *jyhruoh*, prep. phr., as to, as regards.
至如 *jyhrur*, prep. phr., ditto.
至日 *jyhryh*, n., winter or summer solstice.
至少 *jyhshaau*, adv. phr., at least (ten days, etc.).
至善 *jyhshahn*, adj., perfect; n., acme of perfection.
至上 *jyhshahng*, (1) adj., most high, most revered; (2) v. i., come first: 國家至上 the country comes first.
至聖 *jyhshehng*, adj., Most Sage Master (Confu.); 至聖先師.
至性 *jyhshihng*, n., man's deepest instinct (love of parents and child).
至行 *jyhshihng*, n., most perfect character.
至尊 *jyhtzun*, adj., the most high sovereign, emperor.
至言 *jyhyarn*, n., a profound saying.
至要 *jyh yauh*, phr., most important, admonition not to forget.
至意 *jyhyih*, n., most sincere sentiment or thought.
至友 *jyhyoou*, n., best friend, see -*jiau*↑.

至於 *jyhyur* (-*'yu*), phr., (1) as to, as regards (another item); (2) (-*'yu*) to the extent: 雖然虧空, 不至於破產 suffer a severe loss, but not to the extent of bankruptcy.

型 31.11

shirng.

N. (1) A mold, frame for molding contents: 字型 matrix; 紙型 (printing) a mat, *papier maché*. (2) Pattern, model: 模型 model for manufacture, building or exhibit; gen. form; model as ideal (mother, etc.); 典型, 型範 standard, norm, model; 外型 contour, outward appearance or features; 大型, 小型汽車 large-sized, small-sized car; 新型 new model.

垩 31.11

eh.

N. & v. t. Whitewash.

垩粉 *ehfeen*, n., whitewash powder.
垩帚 *ehjoou*, n., brush for whitewashing.

聖 31.11

shehng.

N. A sage, a saint, the perfect one: 至聖先師 "The Sage Master" (official title of Confucius); 聖人, 聖賢 -*rern*, -*shiarn*↓; 超凡入聖 (Budd.) become a saint; laudatory epithet for the perfect ideal; 詩聖 Sage of Poetry (杜甫); 草聖 Sage of Calligraphy (王羲之).

Adj. The divine, highest, supreme (used of emperor, God): 聖命 imperial order; 聖諭, 聖旨 -*yuh*, -*jyy*↓; 聖誕 -*dahn*↓; 聖德 divine character; 聖功 divine work (AC, of education); 聖恩 divine or imperial favor.

聖誕 *shehngdahn*, n., Christmas (also 耶穌聖誕); birthday of sages (Buddha, Confucius); 聖誕節 Christmas festival; 聖誕老人 Santa Claus.
聖地 *shehng-dih*, n., the Holy Land.
聖公會 *sheng-guanghueh*, n., Anglican Church.
聖躬 *shehnggung*, n., imperial body or health.
聖蹟 *shehng-ji*, n., saint's or sage's relics; God's divine work or activities.
聖經 *shehngjing*, n., the Holy Scripture, Holy Bible; Confu. sacred classics.
聖主 *Shehngjuu*, n., the Lord Savior; Your (His) Enlightened Majesty.
聖旨 *shehng-jyy*, n., imperial decree.
聖靈 *Shehnglirng*, n., the Holy Ghost.
聖廟 *shehngmiauh*, n., Confu. temple.
聖明 *shehngmirng*, (1) adj., (of ruler) of divine intelligence: 聖明之主 an extraordinary, enlightened ruler; (2) (-*'ming*) v. i., (coll.) understand: 沒有你不聖明的 nothing that you cannot understand.
聖母 *Shehngmuu*, n., (1) the Holy Mother, Madonna; (2) emperor's mother.
聖人 *shehngrern*, n., a sage, usu. confined to Confucius and 周公, 文王; a great Buddhist master; (history) inventors of script, sericulture, agriculture, etc.
聖善 *shehngshahn*, adj., (AC) perfect (mother).
聖上 *shehngshahng*, n., Your Majesty.
聖賢 *shehng-shiarn*, n., the great of the past (聖 sage, and 賢 the wise men).
聖手 *shehng-shoou*, n., (praise of) a divine physician.
聖水 *shehng-shueei*, n., holy water; water at some temple, credited with performing cures.
聖餐 *shehngtsan*, n., (Christian) the Lord's Supper, Holy Communion.
聖童 *shehngturng*, n., (AC) a child prodigy (usu. 神童).
聖諭 *shehngyuh*, n., imperial decree.

璽 31.11

shii.

N. Official seal, restricted to imperial seals since Chirn 秦 Dyn.: 國璽 seal of the state or emperor; 玉璽 jade seal; 璽綬 seal and tassels; 璽節 (AC) official seal; 璽書 (AC) document with official seal.

§ 31.20 (丅/廾)

弄 31.20

luhng (also *nuhng*, *nehng*).

N. (1) A ditty. (2) An alley, alleyway (also wr. 衖).

V. i. & t. (1) To play with, exercise skill as at a game: 戲弄, 侮弄 to play with, make fun of; 賣弄 to show off; 弄刀, 弄槍 play with knife, spear; 弄筆 (love to) write as hobby; 舞文弄墨 (of lawyers, shysters) play with the letter of the law—unscrupulous or pedantic writing; 玩弄 play with toy, ball; 玩弄女人 dally with women; 吟風弄月 to enjoy the air and moon; 弄法 find loopholes in the law; 弄權 play politics, play for power; 弄兵 seek war, prepare for war; 弄假成眞 playful (love, friendship) becomes serious; 弄巧反拙 suffer from being too smart. (2) To play a musical instrument or do for amusement: 弄笛, 弄簫 play the flute, flageolet; 弄把戲 play tricks, sleight of hand, etc.; 弄戲法 play magic tricks; 弄潮 to frolick in the waves; 弄潮兒 swimmers. (3) To try to obtain, fish or wangle for: 弄錢, 弄飯 get money, cook food; 弄點吃的來 get s. t. to eat. (4) To cause to: 弄得頭昏腦脹 it makes one dizzy; 弄得大家不好意思 so that (with the result that) everybody was embarrassed; 弄壞了 play with and break (watch, etc.).

弄臣 *lungchern*, n., (LL, contempt.) court favorite.

弄璋 *luhngjang*(*nuhng-*), v.i., (AC) "play with jade"—formula for birth of a boy; see *-waa*↓.

弄堂 *nuhngtarng*, n., (Shanghai dial.) alleyway.

弄瓦 *luhngwaa*(*nuhng-*), v.i., (AC) "play with a tile"—formula for birth of girl, see *-jang*↑.

§ 31.21 (丅/乚)

函 31.21

harn.

N. (1) (AC) protective armorplate, breastplate. (2) A case, shield: 劍函 scabbard, 鏡函 dressing case containing mirror. (3) Letter of correspondence: 來函 your ("incoming") letter; 公函 official letter; 函請, 函邀 invite by letter; 函授 *-shouh*↓.

V. i. Var. of 涵 63A.21 and 含 81.40.

函洞 *harnduhng*, n., railway tunnel.

函丈 *harnjahng*, n., (court. salutation in letter to) teacher.

函件 *harnjiahn*, n., correspondence, mail, letters.

函授 *harnshouh*, n., as in 函授學校 correspondence school.

函數 *harnshuh*, n., (math.) function.

画 31.21

huah.

[Pop. of 畫 22.30]

§ 31.22 (丅/丨)

不 31.22

Re. pr. *bu* (sp. pr. *buh*, except *bur* before 4th tone: thus 不是 *burshyh*, 不怕 *burpah*).

Adv. Not: see many common combinations in list; typical of special uses are: (1) In elliptical sentences: "你去不去?" "我不" "Are you going?" "I am not." (2) With another negative to form double negative: 不無 not without; 不無可取 not without merit; 無不, 莫不 all, without exception; 莫不感激 (we) all are grateful; 不免 "cannot help," (common MC) must, have to: 不免回去一趟 have to go home and see; 不免心中不樂 could not help feeling disappointed. (3) In comb. 不 . . . 不 neither this nor that: 不大不小 not too big nor too small—just right; 不清不楚, 不明不白 not clear; 不三不四 cannot make head or tail; irregular, shapeless; 不知不覺 unconsciously; 不男不女 effeminate man, manly woman; 不倫不類 nondescript; neither fowl nor fish; 不偏不黨 fair to all; 不卑不亢 neither obsequious nor arrogant—cordial but independent; 不即不離 neither accepting nor rejecting (proposal), maintaining discreet distance; 不多不少 just the right amount. (4) In comb. 不 . . . 而 without: 不問而知 one knows without asking; 不學而能 do a thing easily, naturally; 不寒而慄 makes one shudder (at sight); 不勞而獲 gain results without working for them; 不脛而走 "runs without legs"—disappear; 不翼而飛 "fly without wings," ditto; 不約而同, 不謀而合 agree, fit without previous consultation, be a coincident. (5) Placed before auxiliary verbs: 不能, 不克 cannot, unable; 不會 will not, cannot; 不必 it's not necessary; 不合, 不宜, 不該, 不應 should not; 不是 is not; 不肯 not willing; 不可, 不可以 may not, must not; 不得 *-der*↓. (6) With common vbb.: 不知 do not know; 不識 ditto; 不料 did not expect; 不想 never thought; 不見得 *-jiahn'de*↓; 不妨 *-farng*↓; 不禁 *-jihn*↓; 不外, 不過 *-waih, -guoh*↓; 不如 *-rur*↓. (7) Sometimes, rarely, combined with nn.: 不衫不履 without shirt or shoes; 不毛之地 barren land. (8) With other advv.: 不但 not only, more than; 不寧 not only. (9) Freely with adjj.: 不行 *-shirng*↓; 不同 different, unlike; 不多 not much; 不好 *-haau*↓; 不便 *-biahn*↓; 不舒服 unwell, uncomfortable; 不滿意 dissatisfied; 不安 *-an*, 不快 *-kuaih*↓.

不礙 *bur-aih*, phr., (不礙事) does not matter; no harm (trying, etc.), see *-farng*↓.

不安 *buh-an*, adj., uneasy; unwell; unsatisfied.

不備 *burbeih*, phr., (1) (at end of letter) there is more than I can tell you in this letter; (2) adj., unprepared: 乘其不備 take advantage of s.o.'s unpreparedness.

不必 *buhbi*, adv., not necessary, need not: 不必客氣 need not stand on ceremony; 不必說 that goes without saying; 不必等 do not wait.

不便 *burbiahn*, adj., inconvenient: 不便告訴你 inconvenient to in-

亅	小	⺊	十	土	ナ	卄	乚卜	丨	一	丅	フ	口	区	冈	ㄱ	厂	尸	亠	广	宀	丶	乚	弋	心	八	人	乂	一	ノ	丿	ㄥ	く
00	01	02	10	11	12	20	21	22	30	31	32	40	41	42	50	51	52	60	61	62	63	70	71	72	80	81	82	83	90	91	92	93

A

不 form you.

不辰 *buh-chern*, phr., 我生不辰 I was born under unlucky star.

不成 *buh-cherng*, phr., (1) will not do (=不行 *-shirng*↓); (2) 難道不成 you don't mean (s.t. quite uncalled-for).

不成話 *buh-cherng-huah*, phr., (s.t.) is ridiculous.

不器 *buh-chih*, phr., 君子不器 (AC) "a gentleman's ability is not confined to any one thing" (versatile).

不起 *buh-chii*, (1) adj., in 不起之症 incurable sickness; (2) vb. complement: 看不起 despise; 買不起 cannot afford to buy; 想不起來 cannot recall, or call up to mind; cannot lift up, etc.

不求人 *buh-chiour-rern*, n., bamboo or wooden back-scratcher with long handle.

不情 *buh-chirng*, adj., as in 不情之請 unreasonable demand; also (court.) my presumptuous demand.

不揣 *buh-chuaai*, phr., (court.) am presumptuous.

不啻 *buh-chyh*, phr., same as, as if: 不啻天地 same as the difference between heaven and earth.

不羣 *buh-chyurn*, phr., stand out among the group.

不齒 *buh-chyy*, phr., be ashamed to be regarded in same group.

不倒翁 *buh-daau-weng*, n., a doll which always rights itself up; (fig.) a politician surviving all upheavals.

不大離兒 *bur-dah-lir(-lier'l)*, adv., almost (=差不多).

不但 *bur-dahn*, adv., not only.

不到 *bur-dauh*[1], phr., not quite: 不到三十 under thirty.

不道 *bur-dauh*[2], (1) phr., contrary to expectations (see *-liauh*↓); (2) adj., unreasonable, wicked.

不得 *buh-der*, phr., cannot, unable: 不得而知 cannot know (results; answer); 不得勁(兒) (s.t., s.o.) does not work properly; in awkward position; 不得不 cannot but, cannot help (doing); 不得已 could not help (doing), have no choice but to; 不得了 be in a bad way, disastrous, impending; 了不得 wonderful.

不弔 *bur-diauh*, adj., (AC) fall under bad times, unlucky.

B

不第 *bur-dih*, phr., (1) fail in examinations for degrees; (2) not only.

不定 *bur-dihng*, adv., not necessarily (bad, etc.), (also 不一定).

不對 *bur-dueih*, adj., (1) (of answers) wrong, not so; (2) do not get along (with person): 不對勁(兒) not right, do not fit in or agree, do not get along well.

不動產 *bur-duhng-chaan*, n., immovable (real property).

不獨 *buh-dur*, phr., (LL) not only, see *-dahn*↓.

不爾 *bur-eel*, phr., not so, see *-rarn*↓.

不貳 *bur-ehl*, adj., loyal (to one master only).

不法 *buh-faa*, adj., illegal (acts).

不凡 *buh-farn*, adj., extraordinary, unusual.

不妨 *buh-farng*, phr., no harm (trying, speaking directly to person, etc.).

不服 *buh-fur*, phr., (1) unwilling (to admit, recognize, accept decision); (2) 不服水土 body does not agree with climate.

不敢 *burgaan*, vb. aux., dare not; 不敢當 *--dang*, phr., (formula for thanking) I am unworthy.

不甘 *buh-gan*, phr., dissatisfied, chagrined, will not take it lying down.

不根 *buh-gen*, adj., baseless (talk).

不更事 *buh-geng-shyh*, phr., 少不更事 inexperienced in life.

不辜 *buh-gu*, n., an innocent person.

不管 *buhguaan*, adj. & conj., regardless (of what happens): 不管什麽人 regardless of persons.

不軌 *buh-gueei*, adj., irregular (activities).

不規則 *buh-guei-tzer*, adj., irregular, not regular.

不顧 *bur-guh*, phr., disregarding (obligations, "face", requests, taboos).

不過 *bur-guoh*, (1) adv., only, merely: 不過如此 it's only so-so; 不過看一看 merely take a look; (2) conj., but, on the other hand; 不過意 phr., feel embarrassed (by hospitality etc.).

不國 *buh-guor*, phr., already does not function as a country.

不古 *buh-guu*[1], phr., 世風不古 customs nowadays are no longer what they were.

C

不穀 *buh-guu*[2], phr., (AC, said by ruler court.) I (" not competent one").

不好 *buhhaau*, adj., not good, will not do; 不好意思 embarrassed; 不好了 (a thing) has been spoiled, turned worse.

不合 *buh-her*, (1) vb. aux., should not have (done); (2) conflict with (opinion, rules, etc.), does not meet with (s.o.'s wishes).

不遑 *buh-huarng*, phr., (LL) have no time to, too busy to.

不會 *bur-hueih*, vb. aux., cannot, (conjecture) could not.

不諱 *bur-hueih*, (1) v.i., (of person) pass away; (2) phr., 直言不諱 speak without fear or favour.

不惑 *buh-huoh*, n., (allu.) aged forty: 不惑之年, 年已不惑.

不羈 *buh-ji*, adj., (person, conduct) untrammeled, free, nonconformist ("not bridled").

不見得 *bur-jiahn'de*, phr., don't appear to be: 不見得兩樣 does not appear to be different; as a phr., "I don't think so," "does not seem so to me."

不見了 *bur-jiahn'le*, v.i. disappear, vanish.

不結盟國家 *buhjiemerng guorjia*, n., non-aligned countries.

不濟 *bur-jih*, phr., (1) does not help; (2) will not succeed: 不濟事 useless, will fail, will die.

不記名 *bur jihmirng*, phr., anonymous (votes), unregistered (stocks).

不禁 *bur-jihn*, vb. aux., cannot help (laughing out loud, crying, etc.).

不給 *buh-jii*, adj., insufficient, inadequate (funds).

不景氣 *buh-jiing-chih*, n., (economic) depression.

不經 *buh-jing*, adj., absurd; 不經濟 uneconomical; 不經事 inexperienced; 不經意 paying no attention; inattentive.

不久 *buh-jioou*, n., soon, soon later.

不及 *buh-jir*, (1) phr., (this) cannot compare with (that); (2) vb. complement, as in 來不及 it's too late (to do).

不住 *bur-juh*, (1) vb. complement, "not firmly," "not securely": 站

A

不住 cannot stand one's ground; 抓不住 cannot catch hold of; (2) ceaselessly: 不住口 talk continuously.

不中聽 *bur-jung-ting*, phr., (words) displease person.

不中用 *bur-jung-yuhng*, adj., useless (person); (euphem.) (person) is dead.

不准 *buh-juun*, phr., do not permit, it is forbidden to (do).

不支 *buh-jy*, phr., cannot stand up under strain.

不知情 *buh-jy-chirng*, phr., (1) do not know what happened (used in affidavit); (2) do not feel grateful.

不置 *bur-jyh*[1], adv., (LL) continuously: 稱賞不置 praise ceaselessly.

不治 *burjyh*[2], adj., incurable.

不至於 *bur-jyh-yur*, phr., not to the extent of: 他雖不喜歡你,但也不至於恨你 he may not like you, but surely does not hate you.

不職 *buhjyr*, adj., derelect in duty.

不拘 *buh-jyu*, adv., regardless (of person, class, kind); any, whatever.

不龜手 *buh-jyuu-shoou*, adj., (AC, of washing agent) does not disfigure the skin.

不刊 *buh-kan*[1], adj., (of work) immortal.

不堪 *buh-kan*[2], (1) adv., (used after vb. or adj.,) as in 窮之不堪 extremely or unbearably poor; (2) phr., cannot stand (noise, bother, etc.): 不堪入耳的話 unspeakable words (of abuse).

不可 *buhkee*, vb. aux., may not, must not; (also 不可以); oft. in double negative: 不可(以)不聽 must not ignore (s.o.'s) advice; 不可不愼 must be careful, 不可告人 private and confidential; secret or shameful (act, disease, etc.); 不可抗力 beyond human control; act of God; 不可一世 (phr.) hoity-toity; haughty airs.

不克 *buh-keh*, vb. aux., (LL) cannot (=不能).

不快 *buh-kuaih*, adj., (1) displeased; (2) slightly unwell.

不匱 *buh-kueih*, phr., (AC) endlessly: 孝思不匱 forever filial.

B

不了 *buh-liaau*, (1) vb. complement, expressing "cannot accomplish": 算不了 countless; (2) phr., 以不了了之 leave in *status quo*, like "agree to disagree"; 不了情 unfulfilled but eternal love.

不料 *buh-liauh*, phr., never thought.

不列顛國協 *buhliehdian guorshier*, n,, The British Commonwealth of Nations.

不利 *bur-lih*, (1) adj., disadvantageous; (2) v.i., do harm to: 不利於你 means to kill you, or harm you.

不吝 *bur-lihn*, n., (court. and rather formal) I (in self-reference).

不理 *buh-lii*, (1) v.t., ignore; (2) 不理於人口 will be criticized by people; 不理會 inattentive.

不離(兒) *buhlir(-lier'l)*, adv., pretty good; 差不離(兒) almost.

不靈 *buh-lirng*, adj., (1) (of medicine, machine) does not work well; (2) 不靈了 (=不行, 不成) (s.t.) is spoiled.

不論 *bur-luhn*, adv., regardless (of persons, etc.).

不律 *bur-lyuh*, n., (AC dial.) a pen (筆).

不滿 *buh-maan*, adj., dissatisfied.

不毛 *buh-maur*, adj., as in 不毛之地 barren land.

不美 *buh-meei*, adj., "does not look pretty."

不免 *buh-miaan*, vb. aux., have to (esp. in MC dramas).

不眠症 *buhmiarnjehng*, n., insomnia.

不敏 *buh-miin*, n., (LL, in self-reference) I (the first person).

不耐煩 *bur-naih farn*, adj., impatient.

不能 *buh-nerng*, vb. aux., cannot.

不佞 *bur-nihng*, n., (rather formal, in writing and speech) I, yours truly.

不怕 *bur-pah*, v.i., don't care, am sure: 不怕他不答應 I am sure, I don't doult, he will agree.

不配 *buh-peih*, adj., unworthy, not qualified (to criticize).

不平 *buh-pirng*, adj., (1) unfair; (2) uneven; (3) phr., 抱不平 feel injustice done to s.o.

C

不讓於 *bur-rahng-yur*, phr., quite equal to, can match (s.o.).

不然 *buh-rarn*, (1) conj., otherwise, if not: 不然的話 ditto; (2) phr., 不以爲然 (s.o.) thinks it is not so, (s.o.) disagrees.

不忍 *buh-reen*, phr., cannot bear to: 不忍人之心 a heart of mercy.

不仁 *buh-rern*, adj., (1) unkind, malevolent; (2) (hands, feet) benumbed.

不姙症 *burrern-jehng* n., infertility, sterility.

不如 *buh-rur*, phr., would rather (go home, etc.).

不容 *buh-rurng*, phr., (1) (condition) does not permit; (2) 爲人所不容 is unwelcome by people.

不日 *bur-ryh*, phr., in a few days.

不勝 *buh-sheng*, adv., (before or after vb.) overwhelmed: 不勝感愧 or 感愧不勝 feel overwhelmed.

不想 *buh-shiaang*, phr., never thought, do not want.

不下 *bur-shiah*, phr., not less (than thirty, etc.).

不像話 *bur-shiahng-huah*, adj., too ridiculous.

不像樣(兒) *buh-shiahng-yahng('l)*, adj., disreputable (conduct).

不相稱 *buh-shiang-chehng*, adj., incompatible.

不相干 *buh-shiang-gan*, phr., (affair) does not concern (person).

不相能 *buh-shiang-nerng*, phr., do not get along well together.

不相下 *buh-shiang-shiah*, phr., will not yield to each other; 不相上下 more or less equal in strength, value.

不祥 *buh-shiarng*[1], adj., unlucky.

不詳 *buh-shiarng*[2], phr., not given not known, not stated: 名不詳 anonymous.

不消 *buh-shiau*, phr., do not need: 不消說 needless to say; 不消半小時 do not need more than half an hour.

不孝 *bur-shiauh*[1], n., person recently bereaved of his parent (used in obituary notice) "I, the unfilial son."

不

不 下

不肖 ***bur-shiauh***[2], adj., (1) unfilial; (2) foolish (opp. to 賢): 賢不肖 the wise and the foolish.

不屑 ***bur-shieh***, phr., to despise (doing), will not condescend to: 不屑與辯 will not condescend to argue with person.

不興 ***buh-shing***, adj., not fashionable or seasonable; not decent (to do).

不行 ***buh-shirng***, phr., (1) (this) will not do, not up to standard; (2) should not be done.

不朽 ***buh-shioou***, adj., immortal (work, deeds).

不殊 ***buh-shu***, phr., same as.

不舒服 ***buh-shu'fu***, adj., (1) unwell, under the weather; (2) uncomfortable.

不爽 ***buh-shuaang***, phr., (1) (God's justice) never fails; (2) do not feel well.

不淑 ***buh-shur***, phr., 遇人不淑 ill-matched in marriage.

不是 ***bur-shyh***[1], (1) adv., be not, is not; oft. used to mean "if not": 不是你提起, 倒忘記了 if you did not remind me, I would have forgotten it; (2) (*-'shy*) n. & adj., wrong: 這就是你的不是了 this is your mistake.

不適 ***bur-shyh***[2], adj., (LL) not well.

不時 ***buh-shyr***, adv., (1) not in proper time; (2) always, daily: 不時之需 (medicine) may be needed any time.

不須 ***buh-shyu***[1], vb. aux., need not (+vb.).

不需 ***buh-shyu***[2], phr., do not need (+n.).

不宣 ***buh-shyuan***, phr., 心照不宣 (end of letter) will stop here, without further occupying your attention.

不許 ***buh-shyuu***, phr., do not permit.

不腆 ***buhtiaan***, adj., (AC) my humble (gift).

不倸 ***buh-tsaai***, v.t., ignore (person).

不才 ***buh-tsair***, n., (in formal correspondence) I, the worthless person.

不測 ***buh-tseh***, n. & adj., any untoward event.

不錯 ***bur-tsuoh***, phr., pretty good, not bad, very good indeed.

不次 ***buh-tsyh***, phr., not in normal sequence.

不通 ***buh-tung***, adj., (1) (writing) ungrammatical, unidiomatic; (2) (person) stupid, bigoted, educated but mind still closed; (3) (road) closed to traffic; (4) (statement) illogical.

不圖 ***buh-tur***, phr., (LL) see *-liauh* ↑.

不在 ***bur-tzaih***, phr., (1) (importance) does not lie in; (2) not at home; 不在乎 immaterial, nonchalant, could not care less; 他不在乎 he does not mind, is not important to him.

不做美 ***bur-tzuo-meei***, phr., do not, or will not, help (happy occasion, marriage), such as rain on wedding day.

不足 ***buh-tzur***, phr., not enough, not sufficient, not qualified (to be teacher).

不貲 ***buhtzy***, phr., 所費不貲 went to a lot of expenses.

不自在 ***bur-tzy-tzaih***, adj., unwell, do not feel fit or comfortable.

不外 ***bur-waih***, prep., only, nothing more than.

不韙 ***bur-weei***, n., (usu. 大不韙) a great error, a heinous crime.

不穩 ***buh-ween***, adj., unsteady, unstable (market, position).

不謂 ***bur-weih***, phr., never thought that.

不惟 ***buh-weir***, phr., not only.

不無 ***buh-wur***, phr., not without: 不無少補 not without some benefit.

不揚 ***buh-yarng***, adj., (LL) ugly-looking: 其貌不揚.

不要 ***bur-yauh***, vb. aux., (1) will not, do not want (to, or a thing); (2) (optative) do not (do s.t.): 不要動 do not move; (photography) hold it; 不要臉 shameless.

不一 ***buh-yi***, phr., (1) (also 不一一) and so forth; innumerable; (2) not uniform (opinion).

不意 ***buh-yih***, phr., (LL) never thought that.

不已 ***buh-yii***, adv., without stop.

不由 ***buh-your***, phr., (1) see *-jihn* ↑; (2) 不由分說 without giving one the opportunity to explain.

不由得 ***buhyour'de***, phr., see *-jihn* ↑.

不遇 ***buh-yuh***[1], phr., had no chance to meet or recognized by person who might help.

不豫 ***bur-yuh***[2], adj., (1) (LL) not well; (2) displeased.

不用 ***bur-yuhng***, vb. aux., (1) need not (tell you, etc.); (2) (optative) you need not (go, doubt, etc.); 不用說 needless to say, let alone.

不渝 ***buh-yur***[1], adj., (love, etc.) unchangeable.

不虞 ***buh-yur***[2], adj. & n., an untoward event.

下 31.22

shiah.

N. (1) Underneath, the position under, position below: 樓下 downstairs; 山下 foothills; 桌下 beneath the table; 燈下 in the light; indicating relative position of person being addressed in letters or spoken to: 閣下 esteemed sir (at the tower); 膝下 my dear parents (at your knees); 麾下 addressed to a general (at your flag of command); 殿下 to a prince (at the palace); 陛下 to His Majesty (at the steps of royal palace); 足下 gen. use (at your feet), 足下 and 閣下 also used as "sir": 閣下 (足下) 以爲如何 what do you think. (2) Indicating time or situation: 這下子 at present; 比較之下 (loses) in comparison; 想了一下 after due thinking; 等一下子 wait a while; 一下子就完了 will soon be finished; 目下 at present discourse—will not go into it now; 不在話下 not in context of present discussion. (3) Place: 兩下相思 longing for each other in different places; 四下亂找 look for in all directions; 八下張羅 try to get (money) in all directions; 都下 at the capital; 鄉下 in the village; 鄉下人 villagers, peasants. (4) Person in inferior position: 在下 people under; 底下人 people under s. o.; 上下, 上上下下 those above and below; 愚下 (court.) my stupid self. (5) A number of times: 打三下手心 give three strikes on the palm; 鐘打一下 the clock strikes one.

31.22 (ㄒ/ㄧ)

V. i. & t. (1) To descend, dismount, unload, disembark: 下樓 come downstairs; 下船 go on board; 下飛機 disembark; 下貨 unload; 下馬 dismount; 下山, 下坡 go down the slope; 下臺 get off the stage, political or theatrical; 下不了臺 cannot find a way out of embarrassing situation; 臉上下得去 will not look too bad. (2) To fall, to drop: 下雨, 下雪, 下雹 it rains, it snows, hails; to drop; 下炸彈 drop bombs; 下雞蛋 lay eggs; 下淚 tear falls. (3) To set down, put down, pull down: 下旗 hoist flag down; 下筆 to set down with pen on paper; 下箸 to take food with chopsticks; 下鍋 to put raw food into cooking pan; 下帷 to let down curtains. (4) To issue (edicts, orders, appointments): 下令 issue orders; 下詔 issue imperial edict; 下定義 lay down, give a definition; 下帖 send out invitation card; 下聘書 send letter of appointment. (5) To take, make a move: 下決心 take a firm resolve; 下功夫 to put forth effort; 下壓力 put pressure on; 下棋 play chess; 下棋子 make a move in chess; 這一只下得不錯 it is a good move; 下酒 take (canapé) to go with wine; 下飯 to take s.t. to go with rice. (6) To put up money: 下本錢 put up capital; 下定錢 put down deposit; 下一注 put up stakes. (7) Go into: 下店 put up at an inn; 下獄, 下監牢 go into gaol; 下地獄 go into hell; 下海 put out to sea; 下鄉 to go to the country. (8) To come off from (school, duty): 下學 come off from school; 下班, 下課 come off from class; 下班, 下伍 off from duty. (9) (LL) to be courteous toward: 禮賢下士 courteous. (10) (LL) to take a city: 連下三城 took three cities.

Adj. (1) Inferior: 下等貨 inferior goods; 下流 lower-grade; also (person) ungentlemanly, unprincipled. (2) Following next, below: 下文 the following; 下一天 following day; 下午 afternoon; 上卷, 下卷 first, second volume; 上半, 下半 first half, second half; 下禮拜一 next Monday; 下一次, 下回 next time; 下下星期 week after next.

Adv. Down: 投下, 扔下 throw down; 攻下 capture (a city); 坐下 sit down; 打下基礎 lay the foundation; 訂下合同 sign a treaty; 拋下妻子 abandon family; 賸下一個 be left alone.

Prep. Under, beneath (as postposition in Chin. used after the nn. it governs: 桌下, 山下 under the table, below the hills (nominal sense under N. 1–5 ↑).

下巴頦(兒) *shiah'bake('l)*, n., the chin.

下把 *shiah-baa*, phr., stretch hand: 下把去抓 stretch hand to grab s. t.

下襬 *shiahbaai*, n., hem of long gown.

下半晌(兒) *shiah-bahn-shaang('l)*, n., afternoon.

下半天(兒) *shiahbahntian(-tia'l)*, n., ditto.

下半夜(兒) *shiah-bahnyieih (-yeh'l)*, n., later half of the night.

下拜 *shiahbaih*, v. i., to bow low (to person).

下班 *shih-ban*, v. i., to come off from class; off from duty.

下輩(兒)(子) *shiah-beih(-beh'l) (tz)*, n., the lower generation.

下邊(兒) *shiahbian(-bia'l)*, n., the underneath.

下筆 *shiah-bii*, v. i., to set down on paper, to write.

下膊 *shiahbor*, n., the lower arm.

下不去 *shiah'bu-chyuh*, v. i., will not go down.

下不來 *shiah'bulair*, v. i., as in 臉下不來 feel embarrassed.

下部 *shiahbuh*, n., the lower part of body.

下茶 *shiah-char*, v. i., to make a gift of tea as token of betrothal.

下場 *shiahcharng*, n., the sequel of event; 下場頭 the end of person's career.

下車 *shiah-che*, v. i., formerly, to arrive at post of appointment.

下欠 *shiahchiahn*, v. i., to owe (a sum).

下妾 *shiahchieh*, n., formerly, (wife's self-reference) your wife.

下氣 *shiah-chih*, v. i., feel pacified.

下情 *shiah-chirng*, n., feelings of common people.

下處 *shiah'chu*, n., a lodging for the night.

下去 *shiah'chyuh*, adv., down: 吞下去 swallow (s.t.) down; 讀下去 read on and on (usu. away from speaker, opp. 下來 down toward speaker); 拖下去 take it away; 拖下來 take it down.

下的 *shiah'de*, v.t., (MC) bear to (also wr. 下得).

下得去 *shiah'dechyuh*, adj., tolerable, passable.

下等 *shiahdeeng*, adj., of inferior grade.

下第 *shiah-dih*, v. i., to fail at examinations.

下定 *shiah-dihng*[1], v.i., to make gift in token of formal betrothal.

下椗 *shiah-dihng*[2], v. i., to cast anchor.

下(個)底 *shiah('ge)dii*, v. i., to map out course of action.

下放 *shiah fahng*, v.i. & t., reassign from urban to rural areas.

下凡 *shiah-farn*, v. i., (of fairy) to come down to earth.

下風 *shiahfeng*, n., leeway; in inferior position.

下疳 *shiahgan*, n., a chancre.

下脘 *shiahguaan*, n., (Chin. med.) exit of stomach, duodenum.

下國 *shiahguor*, n., (LL court.) speaker's own country.

下海 *shiahhaai*, v. i., to put out to sea.

下懷 *shiahhuair*, n., (LL court.) my concern, feelings.

下嫁 *shiah-jiah*, v. i., formerly, (of a princess) to marry commoner, or people of lower rank.

下賤 *shiahjiahn*, adj., cheap, low (person) undignified (work).

下焦 *shiahjiau*, n., exit of bladder.

下界 *shiahjieh*, n., the human world, opp. fairyland.

下注 *shiahjuh*, v. i., put up stakes, capital.

下款(兒) *shiahkuaan(-kuaa'l)*, n., signature on the side of a scroll.

下來 *shiah'lai*, adv., down (usu.

toward speaker), see *-chyuh* ↑.

下里 *shiahlii*, n., the country side; 下里巴人 a popular song.

下流 *shiahliour*, n. & adj., lower part of stream; low class (people).

下落 *shiahluoh*, n., whereabouts.

下面(兒) *shiah'mian(-mia'l)*, n., below, see *-bian* ↑.

下女 *shiahnyuu*, n., (Jap.) maid servant.

下品 *shiahpiin*, n., lower grade.

下身(兒) *shiahshen(-she'l)*, n., (1) lower part of body; (2) pants.

下弦 *shiahshiarn*, n., third quarter of the moon.

下手 *shiahshoou*[1], v.i., to start (doing).

下首 *shiahshoou*[2], n., the place next below.

下水禮 *shiahshueeilii*, n., ceremony of launching a ship.

下世 *shiah-shyh*[1], n., future generation.

下室 *shiahshyh*[2], n., (AC) bedroom.

下旬 *shiahshyurn*, n., the next ten days; the last ten days of a month.

下死的 *shiahsyy'de*, adv., with all one's energy.

下台 *shiahtair*, v. i., to be relieved of office.

下堂 *shiah-tarng*, v. i., to be divorced.

下體 *shiahtii*, n., lower part of body, see *-shen* ↑.

下頭 *shiah'tou*, n., (1) underneath; (2) the servants in gen.

下策 *shiahtseh*, n., inadvisable plan.

下土 *shiah-tuu*, n., the earth, the countryside.

下作 *shiah'tzou*, adj., low, contemptible (work, person).

下浣 *shiahwaan*, n., the third ten days of a month.

下問 *shiahwehn*, v. i., to ask of one less learned than oneself.

下帷 *shiahweir*, v. i., to pull the curtains and teach, or study.

下文 *shiahwern*, n., the continuation; what follows an event: 不見下文 sequel unknown.

下意識 *shiah-yihshy*, n., the subconscious.

下游 *shiah-your*, n., lower stretch of river, estuary.

下元 *shiahyuarn*, n., formerly, 15th day of 10th lunar month.

下愚 *shiah-yur*[1], n., very stupid person.

下餘 *shiah-yur*[2], n., remnant.

冡 31.22

auh.

N. Name of anc. person.

Adj. U.f. 傲 91A.82.

---

§ 31.30 (ㄒ/ㄧ)

工 31.30

gung.

N. (1) A manual worker: 工人 *-rern*, 工匠 *-jiahng*, 工役 *-yih*[1] ↓; 技工 a skilled worker; 勞工 labor, the working class. (2) Manual labor, craftsmanship: 工事 *-shyh*, 工程 *-cherng* ↓; 工價 labor cost; 工錢, 工資, 工銀 wages; 工料 labor and materials; 手工 handicraft; 精工 skilled labor; 人工 human labor, manpower: 人工授精 artificial insemination; 木工 carpentry; 鐵工 ironwork(er)s; 工商 industry and trade; 農工 agriculture and industry; 半工半讀 working one's way through college; 工讀生 a part-time student worker, work scholarship student; 包工 contractual labor; 散工 odd jobs, piece labor; 長工 day labor; 開工 to start work; 收工 to cease work; 完工 completion of work. (3) Man-days.

Adj. (1) Skilled, skillful, dexterous: 工細 *-shih*, 工巧 *-chiaau*, 工筆 *-bii* ↓. (2) Good at, expert: 工於此道 good at this kind of work; 工書 (be) expert at calligraphy.

工本 *gungbeen*, n., cost of production.

工筆 *gungbii*, n., (painting) works done with fine, delicate strokes.

工兵 *gungbing*, n., (mil.) engineer corps.

工部 *gungbuh*, n., formerly, one of the six boards of the central government in charge of public works: 工部局 formerly, the Municipal Council of foreign concessions.

工廠 *gungchaang*[1], n., a factory, plant.

工場 *gungchaang*[2], n., an industrial plant or working area, a workshop.

工潮 *gung-chaur*, n., labor strike.

工程 *gungcherng*, n., engineering, construction work: 工程師 an engineer; 土木工程, 電氣工程, 化學工程 civil, electrical, chemical (etc.) engineering; 機械工程, 建築工程 mechanical, construction engineering.

工巧 *gungchiaau*, adj., skillful, dexterous.

工錢 *gungchiarn*, n., wages.

工尺 *gungchyy*, n., the Chin. musical scale.

工黨 *gungdaang*, n., the labor party.

工夫 *gungfu*, n., (1) work, labor; (2) (*-'fu*) time, leisure, labor spent on a piece of work, degree of perfection attained in any line of work; (3) (*-'fu'l*) a point of time: 正在説話的工夫兒, 他就來了 he came as I was talking; a spare moment: 你有工夫兒麼 do you have a moment to spare?

工會 *gung-hueih*, n., trade or labor union.

工整 *gungjeeng*, adj., (callig.) neat and orderly.

工匠 *gungjiahng*, n., an artisan, a mechanic.

工緻 *gungjyh*, adj., neat and refined.

工具 *gungjyuh*, n., a tool, an instrument: 工具書 reference books.

工科 *gung-ke*, n., (school of) engineering.

工課 *gungkeh*, n., lessons, studies (also 功課).

工力 *gunglih*, n., labor force; (callig.) force and skill.

工碼兒 *gungmaa'l*, n., chips representing wages.

工人 *gungrern*, n., a laborer, a manual worker.

工細 *gungshih*, adj., (of material products or artistic works) fine, skillful, refined, meticulously finished, see *-jyh*↑.

工事 *gungshyh*, n., engineering works.

工頭 *gungtour*, n., a foreman.

工徒 *gungtur*, n., an apprentice.

工作 *gungtzuoh*, (1) n., work, job; (2) v.i., to work: 不能工作 cannot work.

工資 *gungtzy*, n., wages.

工穩 *gungween*, adj., (of artistic or litr. works) elegant and in good taste.

工業 *gungyeh*, n., industry (opp. 農業 agriculture); 工業革命 industrial revolution.

工役 *gungyih*¹, n., manual service or work.

工藝 *gungyih*², n., craftsmanship, technical skill.

工友 *gung-yoou*, n., an office boy; (modn. & polite) any worker.

五 31.30

wuu.

Adj. The number five: 五尺之童 (AC) a young boy of five anc. feet; 五體投地 complete prostration; 五斗米 (allu.) five bushels of rice—petty salary; 五世 for five generations; also see many compp.↓; 五角大厦 Pentagon; 五旬節 Pentacost; 五日京兆 (allu.) governor of capital frequently changed—said of constant shift of office; 五里霧中 lost in impenetrable fog or mystery; used in sense of multifarious: 五方雜處 (city where) peoples from all regions congregrate; 五零四散 all dispersed; 五花綳裂 crackled; 五光十色 all kinds (of people, things); 五花八門 all kinds of skill; 五胡 five tribes of Mongols (匈奴, 鮮卑, 氐, 羌, 羯), northern barbarians, 五湖四海 all the seas and lakes everywhere; 五行 *-shirng*¹↓; 五行 (*-harng*) 八作, various small tradesmen; 五月 May; 五四運動 May Fourth Movement (1919).

五霸 *wuu bah*, n., the five successive leaders of alliances of states in 春秋 period: 齊桓公, 宋襄公, 晉文公, 秦穆公, 楚莊王.

五倍子 *wuubeihtzyy*, n., galls or knobs formed on leaves by insects or bacteria, rich in tannic acid and used in medicine.

五釵松 *wuu-chai-sung*, n.,(bot.) a variety of pine, *Pinus parviflora* var. *pentaphylla*.

五常 *wuu-charng*, n., (1) the five cardinal human relationships, see *-lurn*↓; (2) the five basic virtues: 仁 kindness, 義 justice, 禮 good manners, 智 wisdom and 信 honesty.

五七 *wuu-chi*, n., (1) the 35th day after death of person (of fifth multiple of seven) when mass is said; (2) five to seven, like saying "five or six."

五權憲法 *wuu-chyuarn shiahn-faa*, n., the five branches of government in mod n. Chin. constitution: legislative, executive, judicial, censorate and civil service.

五代 *wuu-daih*, n., the "Five Dynasties" (907–960 A.D.): 後梁, 後唐, 後晉, 後漢 and 後周 see Appendix D.

五帝 *wuu dih*, n., the five legendary emperors in prehistoric China 太昊, 炎帝, 黃帝, 少昊, 顓頊 see Appendix D.

五短 *wur duaan*, n. & adj., person short in head, arms and legs.

五毒 *wuu dur*, n., the five poisonous animals in Chin. med.: the snake, the lizard, the scorpion, the toad and the centipede, used to "fight poison with poison."

五方 *wuu-fang*, n., all directions: 五方人士 people from all regions.

五分 *wuu-fen*, adj., fifty percent: 五分明兒 early dawn.

五服 *wuu-fur*¹, n., the five degrees of mourning: (a) 斬衰 with cut and unhemmed hempen cloth, worn for parents and husbands for 27 months; (b) 齊衰 with cut and hemmed hempen cloth, worn for grandparents, etc. for one year; (c) 大功 for brothers, sisters, etc., worn for 9 months; (d) 小功 for uncles, aunts, etc., for 5 months; (e) 緦麻 for distant relatives for 3 months.

五福 *wuu-fur*², n., the five blessings, according to AC explanation: long life, wealth, good health, good relations with others, and natural death (壽, 富, 康寧, 攸好德, 考終命).

五更 *wuugeng* (sp. pr. *-jing*), n., (1) the fifth watch of the night, near dawn; (2) 三老五更 (AC) venerable elders of the country, treated with special honors (更 explained as experience in various affairs).

五官 *wuu-guan*, n., the five sense organs: the ear, the eye, the mouth, the nose and the heart.

五鼓 *wur-guu*¹, n., the fifth watch, see *-geng*↑.

五穀 *wur-guu*², n., the different grains of harvest.

五虎棍 *wur-huu-guhn*, n., an acrobatic fight with clubs, played by five or six persons.

五加 *wuujia*, n., a spicy plant, *Acanthopanax spinosum*; 五加皮 liquor soaked in bark of this plant.

五金 *wuu-jin*, n., the five metals: gold, silver, copper, iron, pewter; 五金行 dealers in metals in gen.

五經 *wuu-jing*, n., the Five Classics: 詩, 書, 易, 禮, 春秋 the *Book of Poetry*, *Book of History*, *Book of Changes*, *Book of Li* (social forms and ceremonies) and the *Annals*.

五魁 *wuu-kueir*, n., first five top candidates in second degree examinations, also interpreted as No. 2–6, excluding No. 1.

五勞 *wuu-laur*, n., (Chin. med.)

the ailments of the heart, liver, spleen, lungs and kidneys.

五斂子 *wuuliahntzyy*, n., (bot.) *Averrhoa carambola*, a tropical tree; its fruit made into jelly.

五靈脂 *wuulirngjy*, n., a Chin. med. made from droppings of certain insects.

五倫 *wuu-lurn*, n., (Confu.) the five cardinal relationships: between ruler and subject, father and son, husband and wife, between brothers and between friends.

五律 *wuu-lyuh*, n., a prescribed verse form of eight lines of five characters each.

五內 *wuu-neih*, n., the viscerals: 五內俱焚 feelings extremely upset with sorrow, etc.

五色 *wuuseh* (sp. pr. *-shaai*), the five colors: blue, yellow, red, white and black.

五聲 *wuu-sheng*, n., the five notes of the pentatonic scale: 宮, 商, 角, 徵 (pr. *jy*) 羽 *do, re, mi, sol, la*.

五線譜 *wuushiahnpuu*, n., the musical score (with five lines).

五項運動 *wuu shiahng yuhn-duhng*, n., pentathlon.

五香 *wuu-shiang*, n., a mixture of various spices.

五星 *wuu-shing*, n., the five planets: 金, 木, 水, 火, 土 Venus, Jupiter, Mercury, Mars, Saturn.

五刑 *wuu-shirng*[1], n., the five anc. punishments: tattoo, cutting off nose, feet, castration and death, 墨, 劓, 剕, 宮, 大辟.

五行 *wuu-shirng*[2], n., the Five Elements, representing five states of forces of expansion or condensation (the plus energy, or *yarng*, expansion; the minus energy, or *yin*, condensation); 木 wood (Lesser Yarng)＋; 火 fire (Greater Yarng)＋＋; 土 earth (Equilibrium)＋－ or 0; 金 metal (Lesser Yin) －; 水 water (Greater Yin) －－.

五鬚松 *wuushyu-sung*, n., see *-chai-sung*↑.

五彩 *wur-tsaai*, adj., multicolored.

五臟 *wuu-tzahng*, n., the five internal organs: the heart, liver, spleen, lungs and kidneys.

五族 *wuu tzur*, n., the Five Races: 漢, 滿, 蒙, 回, 藏 Chinese, Manchus, Mongolians, Mohammedans and Tibetans.

五味 *wuu weih*, n., the five flavors: 甜, 酸, 苦, 辣, 鹹 sweet, sour, bitter, hot and salty.

五味子 *wuuweihtzzy*, n., (bot.) of two kinds: 北五味子 *Schizandra chinensis*, and 南五味子 *Kadsura japonica*.

五言詩 *wuuyarn-shy*, n., poem of five-character lines.

五音 *wuu-yin*, n., see *-sheng*↑.

五嶽 *wuu yueh*, n., the five sacred mountains: 泰山 Taihshan in Shantung, 衡山 Herngshan in Hunan, 華山 Huarshan in Shensi, 恆山 Herngshan in Hopei, 嵩山 Sungshan in Honan.

五月節 *wuuyueh-jier*, n., the fifth day of the fifth lunar month, called the festival of 端陽 *duanyarng* or 端午 *duanwuu*.

互 31.30

huh.

Adj. & adv. Mutual, -ly, each other: 互相 *-shiang*↓; 互愛 love one another; 互忌, 互妒 jealous of each other; 互選 mutually elect; 互不侵犯 (條約) (mutual) non-aggression (treaty); 互不干涉 mutual non-interferenee.

互保 *huhbaau*, v. i. & n., (give) guarantee for each other.

互惠 *huh-hueih*, adj., (of agreements) of mutual benefit.

互助 *huh-juh*, (1) adj., cooperative; (2) n., mutual aid or help.

互相 *huhshiang*, adv., mutually, each other: 互相敬愛 mutually respect and love; 互相干涉 interfere with each other; 互相牽連 involve each other, be interrelated, etc.

亙 31.30

gehn (also *gehng*).

[Var. 亘]

N. A surname.

V.i. Extend across, from one end to another: 亙以淥水 the river Lu runs right through it; 橫亙 lie across; 綿亙 extend in an unbroken line; 聯亙 be interconnected.

Prep. From: 亙古 from ancient times; 亙古以來 from of old; 亙古一人 the one and only man from of old, referring to Confucius; 亙古通 (至) 今 from the earliest times down to the present.

丕 31.30

pi.

V. t. (AC) receive, inherit in comb. 丕承.

Adj. (LL) Great, grand: 丕功, 丕績 grand achievement; 丕基, 丕業 the great heritage, usu. referring to founding of royal house.

Adv. (LL) Greatly, gloriously: 丕烈, 丕顯 splendid, glorious.

正 31.30

jehng (**jeng*).

N. (1) Chief: 里正, 村正 formerly, chief of precinct, of village. (2) Wife in 令正 your wife (from 正室, dist. 副室 concubine); 扶正 make the concubine wife after wife is dead; cf. 明媒正娶 legally married. (3) Orthodoxy: 去邪歸正 return to orthodox path; 正誤表 errata. (4) (**jeng*) First month: 正月 January; 新正 New Year; 來正 coming New Year.

V. t. To rectify, make correct, adjust properly, follow the law: 正其衣冠 adjust dress and hat properly: 正襟危坐 sit properly (with dress buttoned) and sit gin-

A

gerly; 正名 *-mirng* ↓; 改正 to correct; 正誤 to correct misprints; 修正 revise (laws, text); 訂正 establish correct text; 指正 act as correct guide; 就正有道 ask for guidance or correction from those who know; 尚請教正 please advise and correct; 正法 *-faa* ↓.

Adj. (1) Right (side, doctrine), proper, correct: 正面 *-miahn* ↓; 正道, 正路, 正途, 正軌 *-dauh*, *-luh*, *-tur*, *-gueei* ↓; not oblique: 端正 (face) properly proportioned, proper (conduct). (2) Main, center opp. 偏 *pian*, side: 正廳 main hall; 正殿 main temple or palace; 正室 legal wife; 正門 main or center door; principal, opp. 副 secondary or subsidiary: 正科 major course, opp. 副科 minor course; 正業 main occupation (opp. 副業); 正號 correct, formal title. (3) Exact, due: 正東, 正南 exact due east, due south; 正中 exact center. (4) Orthodox: 正統 *-tuung* ↓; 正枝正葉 or 嫡正子孫 the linear descendants. (5) Upright, just: 正直 *-jyr*[1]; 正氣, 正義 *-chih*, *-yih* ↓. (6) Positive (electricity): 正電, 負電 positive and negative electricity. (7) Pure, unmixed: 正味 pure flavors; 正色 *-seh* ↓.

Adv. (1) Just, exactly: 正合我的意思 that is exactly my idea; 正是那個人 exactly that person; 正巧 *-chiaau* ↓; 正應該 just what should be done; 正十二時 exactly tweleve o'clock; (put behind numbers in checks to prevent alteration): 三千元正 three thousand dollars exact. (2) Just in the process of doing: 正在 or 正吃飯 was just having dinner; 正想 I was just thinking (of calling you up, etc.); 正要 was just going to.

正本 *jehng-been*, (1) n., the orthodox copy (of book); ribbon copy (of letter, document) (opp. 副本 carbon copy); (2) v.i., as in 正本清源 (王陽明) reform from the bottom, or from the heart.

B

正比例 *jehng biilih*, n., as in 成正比例 is in direct proportion.

正常 *jehngcharng*, adj., normal (opp. 反常 abnormal).

正巧 *jehngchiaau*, adv., by a happy chance (he walked in when I needed him).

正氣 *jehngchih*, n., the sense of honor, sense of right, the moral sense.

正寢 *jehngchiin*, v. i., esp. in 壽終正寢 die peacefully in bed.

正確 *jehngchyueh*, adj., correct (figures, understanding): 思想不正確 questionable thinking or ideas.

正取 *jehngchyuu*, adj., regularly passed candidate, dist. 備取 those on reserve list.

正大 *jehngdah*, adj., as in 正大光明 (signboard for the throne room) impartial, just and open.

正旦 *jehngdahn*, n., (1) main female role in opera; (2) (*jeng-) New Year's Day.

正當 *jehngdahng*, (1) adj., proper (opportunity, work, relations); (2) (*-dang*) adv., just as (I was leaving, etc.).

正道 *jehngdauh*, n., orthodox doctrine or teachings.

正電 *jehngdiahn*, n., positive electricity.

正對點 *jehngduehdiaan*, n., (astron.) antipode.

正法 *jehngfaa*, v. t., to execute (prisoner) ("according to law"): 就地正法 execute(d) on the spot.

正犯 *jehngfahn*, n., main culprit.

正方 *jehngfang*, (1) adj., exactly square; 正方形 exact square; (2) phr., just as (one was doing s. t.).

正該 *jehng gai*, phr., should exactly: 正該如此 exactly as it should be.

正軌 *jehnggueei*, n., the right track, the correct path (of conduct).

正規 *jehngguei*, adj., regular: 正規軍 *--jyun*, n., units of the regular army.

正宮 *jehnggung*, n., the rightful queen or empress (opp. imperial concubines).

正果 *jehngguoo*, n., (Budd.) spiritual progress through right path.

C

正好 *jehnghaau*, (1) adv., at the right (apposite) moment; (2) phr., just right.

正號 *jehnghauh*, n., correct title.

正張兒 *jehngjang'l*, n., regular pages of newspaper, opp. 副張兒 supplement.

正轍 *jehngjer*, n., right track, path.

正角 *jehngjiaau*, n., (math.) right angle.

正經 *jehng'jing*, adj., serious, not frivolous: 正經人 a man with serious occupation; 正經話 serious words, not said in fun; 正經貨 the real article, not imitation.

正中 *jehngjung*, adj., squarely in the middle.

正支 *jehngjy*, n., (1) legitimate expense; (2) branch of eldest son.

正直 *jehngjyr*[1], adj., morally upright.

正値 *jehng jyr*[2], phr., just happen (to be a Sunday).

正覺 *jehngjyueir*, n., (Budd.) real awakening to truth.

正理 *jehnglii*, n., (1) justice; (2) proper manner or way: 這樣做是正理 this is the right way to do it.

正路 *jehngluh*, n., the right path.

正論 *jehngluhn*, n., correct, impartial opinion.

正面 *jehngmiahn*, n., the right side, opp. 反面 the reverse side.

正命 *jehngmihng*, n., (AC) natural death.

正名 *jehngmirng*, n., as in 正名主義 (Confu.) the doctrine of calling a thing by its right name.

正派 *jehngpaih*, adj. & n., (1) (people) of the serious, gentlemanly type; (2) the orthodox school.

正牌兒 *jehngpar'l*, n., original brand (of goods).

正人 *jehngrern*, n., gentleman: 正人君子 gentleman; (also derog.) hypocrite, quasi-gentleman.

正三角形 *jehng sanjiaaushirng*, n., (math.) right triangle.

正色 *jehngseh*, n., (1) severe countenance: 正色厲聲 with a severe countenance and a harsh voice; (2) solid, pure colors.

正身 *jehng-shen*, v. i., as in 先正其

正

亅	小	⺊	十	土	ナ	廾	ㄴト	丨	一	丅	フ	口	図	冈	ㄱ	厂	尸	亠	广	宀	丶	乚	七	心	八	人	乂	⌒	一	丿丿	𠂉	く
00	01	02	10	11	12	20	21	22	30	31	32	40	41	42	50	51	52	60	61	62	63	70	71	72	80	81	82	83	90	91	92	93

正 歪 巫 亞

身 (Confucian) start by right personal conduct as an example.

正生 *jehngsheng*, n., main male role in opera.

正獻 *jehngshiahn*, n., chief officer at sacrifices.

正項 *jehngshiahng*, n., (math.) positive term.

正心 *jehng-shin*, v. i., (Confu.) to set the heart in the right place, one of the steps of self-cultivation.

正書 *jehngshu*, n., the formal style of script (＝楷書).

正數 *jehngshuh*, n., (math.) a plus quantity, dist. 負數 minus quantity.

正朔 **jengshuoh*, n., (1) the New Year's Day; (2) official calendar: 改正朔 change the calendar.

正式 *jehngshyh*[1], adj. & adv., formal, -ly (adoption, marriage, resign, -nation, negotiate, -tion, etc.).

正事 *jehngshyh*[2], n., what is one's proper duty; proper avocation.

正室 *jehngshyh*[3], n., wife.

正是 *jehng shyh*[4], phr., be exactly: 正是心所願 exactly what I wish.

正學 *jehngshyuer*, n., (Confu.) orthodox school or opinions, opp. 曲學, 異端 heresy, heterodoxy, not orthodox opinions.

正兇 *jehngshyung*, n., main culprit.

正史 *jehngshyy*, n., standard, authorized history, dist. 野史 privately compiled history.

正堂 *jehngtarng*, n., formerly, chief magistrate.

正體 *jehngtii*, n., standard way of writing (characters).

正途 *jehngtur*, n., proper avocation; the moral path.

正統 *jehngtuung*, n., (1) orthodox tradition of thought or ideas; (2) (Chin. history) standard line of succession, or universal sovereignty, dist. rulers of parts of China only.

正在 *jehng-tzaih*, phr., 正在 or 正在 . . . 中 in the process of (writing a letters, planning, etc.).

正則 *jehngtzer*, n., correct procedure.

正宗 *jehngtzung*, n., main school of thought; main line of succession; the right and conventional, accepted tradition.

正文 *jehngweern*, n., the text, dist. running commentary.

正午 *jehngwuu*, n., midnoon.

正顏 *jehng-yarn*, severe countenance.

正業 *jehngyeh*, n., main occupation.

正義 *jehngyih*, n., (1) justice, the cause of justice; 正義感 sense of righteousness; (2) often name of book of commentary on classic, chiefly exegetical.

正音 *jehngyin*, n., correct pronunciation.

正月 **jengyueh*, n., January.

歪 31.30

wai (**waai*).

V. i. & t. (1) To incline to one side: 歪著頭 turn head sideaways. (2) To take a nap or rest by lying down on one side: 歪一下 take a short rest on couch. (3) To shift the blame: 竟把這事歪到我身上來 shift the blame on me. (4) To twist: 歪了腳 (**waai*) to twist the ankle, to trip one's foot; 歪七扭八 (*wai*) to twist around, to jiggle body.

Adj. (1) Not straight, not balanced, inclined to one side: 歪歪 *-wai* ↓. (2) Devious, crooked (words, thoughts): 歪念頭, 歪主意 crooked ideas. (3) Immoral, indecent: 歪剌, 歪貨 *-lah*, *-huoh* ↓.

歪憋 *waibie*, v. i., make disorderly conduct, make mischief.

歪纏 *waicharn*, v. t., to bother persistently.

歪曲 *waichyu*, v. t., to falsify: 歪曲事實 to distort story or facts.

歪貨 *waihuoh*, n., (sl.) woman of loose morals.

歪著 *wai'je*, v. i., to incline on couch for short rest.

歪盔子 *waikueitz*, n., (sl.) false pretext for starting trouble.

歪剌 *wailah*, adj., indecent, undesirable: 歪剌骨, 歪剌貨 (abuse) a louse, blackguard.

歪毛兒 *waimaur'l*, n., a child's hair done on one side, also such child: 歪毛兒, (淘氣兒) (1) mischievous child; (2) a loafer, ne'er-do-well.

歪派 *wai'pai*, v. t., to shift blame on s. o.

歪斜 *waishier*, adj., inclined on one side, slanting (hat, etc.).

歪詩 *waishy*, n., rotten verse; not serious poetry.

歪詞兒 *waitser'l*, n., indecent defamatory talk.

歪歪 *waiwai*, adj., slanting, crooked: 歪歪扭扭, 歪歪擰擰 twisting, ed.

巫 31.30

wur (also *wu*, *sp. pr*).

N. (1) A witch, sorcerer, -ress. (2) A surname.

巫蠱 *wuguu*, n., sorcery.

巫咒 *wujouh*, n., sorcerer's incantation.

巫婆 *wupor*, n., a sorceress.

巫覡 *wushir*, n., sorcerer (覡) and sorceress (巫).

巫術 *wushuh*, n., sorcery, witchcraft.

巫師 *wushy*, n., sorcerer.

巫醫 *wuyi*, n., (AC) one who practised magic and medicine.

亞 31.30

yah (also *yaa*).

N. (*yah* or *yaa*) Asia, short for 亞細亞洲; 東南亞 Southeast Asia; 歐亞 Europe and Asia; 亞美 Asia and America.

Adj. Second: 亞子, 亞軍 *-tzyy*, *-jyun* ↓; 不亞於人 second to none; 亞飯 second meal; 亞獻 second in series of three sacrificial offerings.

亞鉛 *yahchian*, n., zinc (＝鋅).
亞喬木 *yah-chiaurmuh*, n., medium-sized trees, like peach, pear, fig.
亞膠 *yahjiau*, n., gelatine.
亞洲 *Yahjou*, n., Asia.
亞軍 *yahjyun*, n., winner of second prize in contests.
亞麻 *yahmar*, n., (bot.) flax, a flowering plant, *Linum usitatissimum*, whose bark fiber is woven like hemp.
亞賽 **yaasaih*, v.t., to match in value, skill, etc.
亞細亞 *Yahshiyah*, n., Asia.
亞似 **yaasyh*, v.t., see *-saih*↑.
亞子 *yahtzyy*, n., (LL) second son.

盂 31.30

yur.

N. A receptacle: 痰盂 a spittoon; 盂鉢眞傳 inherited teachings of a Budd. master (see 鉢 92S.10).

盃 31.30

bei.
[Anc. var. of 杯 10B.01]

噩 31.30

eh.

Adj. (1) Shocking (news). (2) (AC) solemn.

噩噩 *eh-eh*, adj., (AC) solemn in countenance.
噩耗 *eh-hauh*, n., shocking news, usu. of s.o.'s death.
噩夢 *eh-mehng*, n., evil-foreboding dream.

§ 31.32 (ㄒ/フ)

歹 31.32

daai.

N. Bad deed: 爲非作歹 do misdeeds; 不知好歹 do not appreciate what is good, do not distinguish good and bad, friend and foe.

Adj. Bad, wicked: 歹人, 歹徒 wicked people; 歹意 bad intention; 歹念 immoral thoughts.

歹毒 *daaidur*, adj., vicious (also 歹鬬 *-douh*).

琴 31.32

chirn.

N. (1) A gen. term for various stringed instruments: 鋼琴 piano; 風琴 organ: 手風琴 accordion; 口琴 harmonica; 小提琴 violin; 中提琴 viola; 大提琴 cello; 豎琴 harp; 月琴 lute; 胡琴 regular two-stringed instrument accompanying Peking opera; 琴劍 the lute and the sword, imagined to be hobbies of an elegant scholar; 琴心 music which communicates the player's personal sentiment (love). (2) A surname.

琴牀 *chirnchuarng*, n., a flat support of stringed instrument.
琴鍵 *chirnjiahn*, n., the stops of stringed instrument.
琴鳥 *chirnniaau*, n., (zoo.) the lyrebird.
琴譜 *chirnpuu*, n., music sheets or album; musical score.
琴瑟 *chirn-seh*, n., the *chirn* and *seh* 瑟 (31.72), base stringed instrument—fig., of matrimonial harmony: 琴瑟不調 marital discord.
琴手 *chirnshoou*, n., professional musician (at night clubs, etc.).
琴師 *chirnshy*, n., music master.
琴操 *chirntsau*, n., songs for 琴.

§ 31.40 (ㄒ/口)

否 31.40

foou (**pii*).

Fin. Part. (LL) fin. part. at end of questions＝or not?—汝知之否 do you know it or not? 汝知之乎 ditto (＝modn. 麽).

Adj. (**pii*) Evil, bad: 否極泰來 after extreme bad luck, comes good luck; 臧否人物 (used as v. t.) criticize people.

Adv. Or not (LL, also common in vern.) usu. used closely with auxiliaries: 可否 may . . . or may not (＝可以, 不可以); 是否 is it . . . or not (＝是不是); 能否 can . . . or not; 肯否 willing or not; 唯唯否否 answering "yes" and "no."

否定 *fooudihng*, v. i., decide in the negative.
否決 *foouj yuer*, v. i. & t., vote against, in the negative; 否決權 veto power.
否認 *foourehn*, v. i. & t., to deny: 否認有罪 plead not guilty; 否認借錢 deny having borrowed money.
否則 *foou'tze*, adv. conj., or else, if not: 你陪我們來, 否則大家不去 come with us or else let's not go at all.

亞 盂 盃 噩 歹 琴 否

亅	小	⺊	十	土	ナ	卄	ㅏ	丨	一	丁	フ	口	区	冈	ㄱ	厂	尸	亠	广	宀	丶	乚	七	心	八	人	乂	乛	㇀	リ	𠂉	く
00	01	02	10	11	12	20	21	22	30	31	32	40	41	42	50	51	52	60	61	62	63	70	71	72	80	81	82	83	90	91	92	93

A

吾 啓 石

吾 31.40

wur.

Pron. (AC, LL and dial.) I, the first person, my, me: 吾弟, 吾友 my brother, my friend; 不吾欺 did not deceive me; 吾人, 吾儕 *-rern, -chair* ↓.

吾儕 *wurchair*, pron., (LL) we.
吾人 *wurrern*, pron., (LL and modn.) we.
吾兄 *wurshyung*, pron., "my elder brother"; (court. among friends) you: 吾兄以爲然否 do you think so?
吾曹 *wurtsaur*, pron., (LL) we.
吾子 *wurtzyy*, pron., (1) (LL) you; (2) my son.

啓 31.40

chii.

[Pop. of 啟 63S.82]

石 31.40

shyr.

N. (1) (*-tz*) Stone, rock: 石頭 *-'tou* ↓; 石塊 piece of stone; 石堆 a heap of rocks; 石穴, 石洞, 石窟 stone cave; 石室, 石柱, 石橋 stone house, pillar, bridge; 海枯石爛 (lovers' pledge) till the seas dry up and rocks melt away; 石破天驚 devastating (opinion, event); 鐵石心腸 heartless ("heart of iron or stone"); 泉石之樂 the pleasures of living among rocks and springs; 浮石 pumice; 鵝卵石 round pebbles; 碎石 crushed stones; 磁石, 吸鐵石 loadstone; 滑石 soapstone; 青石 granite; 崖石 rocky cliff. (2) A dry measure for grain, a picul (of 100 catties, varying between 132 and 140 lbs.). (3) Stone inscriptions: 金石, 金石文 inscriptions on bronze and stone. (4) Mineral elements in medicine: 藥石 medicine in gen. (5) A surname.

B

Adj. (1) Made of stone. (2) Unproductive: 石田 *-tiarn* ↓; 石女, 石胎 *-nyuu, -tai* ↓.

石板 *shyrbaan*[1], n., see *-baan*[2] ↓.
石版 *shyrbaan*[2], n., (1) a slab of stone; (2) slate: 石版石 *--shyr*, n., lithographic stone.
石斑魚 *shyrbanyur*, n., garoupa.
石鼈 *shyrbie*, n., (zoo.) *Liolophura japonica*.
石壁 *shyrbih*, n., stone wall, precipice, cliffside.
石筆 *shyrbii*, n., slate pencil; 石筆石 *--shyr*, n., slate.
石菖蒲 *shyrchangpur*, n., (bot.) Japanese sweet flag, *Acorus gramineus*.
石長生 *shyrcharngsheng*, n., maidenhair fern, *Adiantum monochlamys*.
石器 *shyrchih*, n., stone implements: 石器時代 the stone age.
石青 *shyrching*, adj., dark green; mineral color much used in Chin. painting.
石牀 *shyrchuarng*, n., stalagmite.
石蓴 *shyrchurn*, n., (bot.) the common sea lettuce, *Ulva lactuca*.
石膽 *shyrdaan*, n., (min.) chalcanthite (also called 胆礬).
石黛 *shyrdaih*, n., black lead, graphite, anciently used as eye pencil.
石刁柏 *shyrdiau-baai*, n., (bot.) garden asparagus, *Asparagus officinalis*.
石耳 *shyr-eel*, n., an edible mushroom grown on rocks, *Gyrophora rellea*.
石髮 *shyrfaa*, n., (bot.) lichens, hair-like growth on rocks (also called 髮菜).
石帆 *shyrfarn*, n., (zoo.) a fan-shaped deposit of insects like coral, *Rhipidogorgia*.
石敢當 *shyr-gaan-dang*, n., a piece of stone tablet, inscribed with these words and placed facing street corners, to ward off evil spirits.
石膏 *shyrgau*, n., gypsum, plaster of Paris.

C

石工 *shyrgung*, n., stone mason.
石鼓 *shyr-guu*, n., set of ten ancient stone drums containing inscriptions (石鼓文) variously ascribed to between 8th and 3rd cen. B.C.
石畫 *shyr-huah*[1], n., mosaic.
石化 *shyr-huah*[2], v. t., petrify, -fied.
石黃 *shyrhuarng*[1], n., (min.) orpiment (also called 雄黃).
石磺 *shyrhuarng*[2], n., (zoo.) a sea animal, *Onchidium verruculatum*.
石花菜 *shyrhuatsaih*, n., (bot.) a seaweed, agar-agar, *Gelidium cartilagineum*.
石灰 *shyrhuei*, n., lime; 石灰燈 limelight; 石灰水 *Aqua calcariae*, 石灰石 *--shyr*, limestone; 石灰酸 carbolic acid, phenol; 石灰岩 limestone.
石火 *shyr-huoo*, n., a flash of flint sparks, symbolic of shortness of human life.
石斛 *shyrhur*, n., (bot.) *Dendrobium moniliforme*.
石胡荽 *shyrhursuei*, n., (bot.) the pennywort.
石基 *shyrji*, n., (geol.) groundmass.
石鹼 *shyrjiaan*, n., Chin. lye concoction, used like soap.
石匠 *shyrjiahng*, n., stone mason.
石經 *shyrjing*, n., inscriptions of classics on stone.
石櫧 *shyrju*, n., (bot.) a variety of oak.
石鐘乳 *shyrjungruu*, n., stalactite.
石竹 *shyrjur*, n., (bot.) pinks; carnations, *Dianthus chinensis*.
石決明 *shyrjyuermirng*, n., (zoo.) a kind of abalone.
石拒 *shyrjyuh*, n., the octopus (also called 章魚).
石刻 *shyrkeh*, n., sculpture, stone carvings.
石坑 *shyrkeng*, n., stone pit.
石蠟 *shyrlah*, n., (chem.) paraffin; 石蠟容電器 paraffin condenser.
石理 *shyrlii*, n., rock structure.
石榴 *shyuliour*, n., the pomegranate: 石榴裙下 infatuated with a woman ("prostrate before pomegranate skirt"); 石榴石 *--shyr*, n., (min.) garnet.
石硫黃 *shyr-liourhuarng*, n., crude sulphur.
石淋 *shyrlirn*, n., stone in the bladder.

石聾 *shyrlurng*, adj., stone-deaf.

石龍芻 *shyrlurngchur*, n., (bot.) the Baltic rush, *Juncus balticus*, whose stems can be woven into mats.

石龍子 *shyrlurngtz*, n., a lizard.

石綠 *shyrlyuh*, n., (min.) malachite.

石綿 *shyr-miarn*, n., (also 石絨 *-rurng* ↓) (1) asbestos; (2) chrysotile.

石脈 *shyr-moh*[1], n., (geol.) veins of minerals.

石墨 *shyr-moh*[2], n., (min.) graphite.

石腦油 *shyrnaau-your*, n., naphtha: 石腦油精 naphthalene.

石南 *shyrnarn*, n., (bot.) *Rhododendron metternichii*.

石女 *shyrnyuu*, n., woman organically incapable of sexual intercourse.

石蕊 *shyrrueei*, n., (bot.) *Cladonia rangiferina*, a plant whose leaves are used like tea, called 雲茶; (chem.) litmus: 石蕊試紙 litmus paper.

石絨 *shyrrurng*, n., see *-miarn* ↑.

石乳 *shyrruu*, n., see *-jungruu* ↑.

石像 *shyr-shiahng*, n., stone statue.

石首魚 *shyrshoou-yur*, n., croaker, a fish, *Seiaena schlegeli*, also called 黃花魚 or 黃魚.

石室 *shyrshyh*, n., a stone house, sometimes used as vault for document, library, or mausoleum.

石蒜 *shyrsuahn*, n., (bot.) *Lycoris radiata*.

石髓 *shyrsueei*, n., stalactite (also *-jungruu* ↑).

石松 *shyrsung*, n., (bot.) *Lycopodium clavatum*: 石松類 *Lycopodiales*.

石筍 *shyrsuun*, n., stalagmite.

石炭 *shyrtahn*, n., coal: 石炭系 carbonaceous system; 石炭紀 (geol.) Carboniferous period; 石炭酸 carbolic acid.

石胎 *shyr-tai*, n., a dead embryo or other growth.

石田 *shyr-tiarn*, n., barren, unproductive soil.

石頭 *shyr'tou*, n., a rock: 石頭子兒 pebble.

石蠶 *shyrtsarn*, n., (zoo.) (1) *Rhyacophila*; (2) coral-like growth, *madrepora*.

石蓯蓉 *shyrtsungrurng*, n., (bot.) *Statice arbuscula*.

石子 *shyrtz*, n., pebble: 石子路 pebble walk.

石韋 *shyrweei*, n., (bot.) a fern, *Polypodium lingua*.

石巖 *shyryarn*[1], n., (1) stone cliff or cliffside; (2) (bot.) *Rhododendron obtusum*.

石鹽 *shyryarn*[2], n., rock salt.

石衣 *shyryi*, n., a water plant (also called 烏韭, 石苔).

石印 *shyryihn*, n., lithograph, -y.

石英 *shyrying*, n., (min.) quartz.

石油 *shyryour*, n., petroleum; 石油苯 (*--been*) benzine; 石油氣 (*--chih*) liquidized petroleum gas, also known as 瓦斯.

石尤風 *shyryour-feng*, n., (LL) windstorm (also 石郵風).

碧 31.40

bih.

N. Jade, a precious stone usu. of greenish color: 碧玉 white jade with green tints.

Adj. (Poet.) blue, azure, greenish blue: 碧海 blue sea; 碧雲 bluish clouds; 碧空, 碧落, 碧漢, 碧霄, 碧虛 the blue sky.

碧蘭 *bih-larn*, n., (bot.) greenish orchid.

碧蘿春 *bihluorchun*, n., a special brand of tea.

碧綠 *bihlyuh*, adj., beautifully green (lawn, sea, etc.).

碧紗廚 *bihsha-chur*, n., a bed-like compartment, covered with gauze to keep out mosquitoes.

碧血 *bih-shyueh*, n., blood of those who died in war or love: 碧血丹心 (praise of) loyalty until death.

碧桃 *bih-taur*, n., (bot.) a kind of peach＝千葉桃.

碧瓦 *bih-waa*, n., glazed tiles＝琉璃瓦.

碧梧 *bih-wur*, n., (bot.) the plane tree.

碧眼 *bihyaan*, adj., blue-eyed.

碧玉 *bihyuh*, n., (min.) jasper; 小家碧玉 pretty daughter of simple family, buxom lass.

磊 31.40

leei.

磊塊 *leeikuaih*, n., grievances: 胸中磊塊 (also 壘塊).

磊磊 *leirleei*, adj., (1) descriptive of a pile of rocks; (2) numerous; (3) frank, candid, openhearted: 磊磊落落, 光明磊落 done in the open, without secretiveness.

磊落 *leeiluoh*, adj., confused, numerous, see *-leei* ↑.

---

§31.41 (丅/図)

百 31.41

baai (re. pr. **bor*). (Re. pr. preferred in certain literary phrr.; otherwise *baai* general; ***baai*, ***bor* indicate alternate pr. permissible.)

N. 百里 *Borlii*, a surname.

N. & adj. Hundred: 幾百 several hundreds; 百萬 million; 百萬噸 megaton; 百千萬 hundreds and and thousands, vast number; 百兒八十 round about a hundred; 百十來個 about a hundred; 百倍 a hundredfold; 百分之三 three per cent; 百分 100%, see 百分法 *-fen-faa* ↓; 百度(表) *-duh* ↓; 百裏挑一 one in a hundred; 百中無一 not one in a hundred; 百聞不

百 晉 西

如一見 (*bor) seeing for oneself is better than all hearsays; 百尺竿頭, 更進一步 (Complim. phr.), make further progress; 百歲後, 百年後 (euphem.) after person's death.

Adj. (*bor) All, all kinds, classes, multifarious, numerous: 百業 all professions; 百僚 (LL) all officials; 百工 all artisans; 百獸, 百穀, 百花, 百艸 all kinds of animals, grains, flowers, plants; 百感交集 a multitude of feelings surges up; 百弊叢生 all kinds of corruption creep in; 百廢待擧 a thousand things wait to be done, restored; 百般 -ban↓; 千方百計 by all manners or methods, planned or tried; 百孔千瘡 full of ills and troubles, in disastrous state.

Adv. Very, always: 百伶百俐 very smart; 百依百順 obedient in all things; 百發百中 the shots hit every time; 百無 (a frequent comb.) totally without (not even one in a hundred): 百無一長, without a single talent or skill; 百無禁忌 without restraint, stop at nothing; 百無一失 you cannot possibly go wrong; 百無可爲 absolutely nothing can be done; 百無聊賴 thoroughly bored.

百拜 *borbaih, v. i., (LL) a hundred courtsies, greetings, now rare, at end of letters.

百般 **bor-ban, adv., using all sorts of ways; all manners of; infinitely (considerate, etc.): 百般無賴 using all rascally means; 百般温柔 infinitely affectionate.

百部 *borbuh, n., (bot.) *Stemona sessilifolia*.

百度表 *baaiduh-biaau*, n., centigrade.

百分法 *baaifen-faa*, n., (1) percentage system; (2) centesimal method of dividing into hundredths; 百分之三, 之十, 3%, 10%; 百分率 --*lyuh*, n., percentage system; 百分數 --*shuh*, n., per cent, as 3%.

百合 *baaiher*, n., artichoke.

百花生日 **bor-hua shengryh*, n., birthday of all flowers, 12th day of second lunar month; also called 花朝.

百貨公司 ***baaihuoh gungsy*, n., department store.

百家 **borjia*, n., the different schools of philosophy in AC; 百家言 philosophies of the different schools; 百家姓 (*baai*--) a book of Chin. clan names; 百家衣 (***baai*--) child's dress made of rags from different friends' families, worn for long life.

百襉裙 **borjiaan-chyurn*, n., fine-pleated skirt.

百結衣 **borjier yi*, n., ragged clothing.

百科全書 ***baaike chyuarnshu*, n., encyclopaedia.

百揆 **borkueei*, n., (AC) chief minister of state.

百鍊剛 **borliahn-gang*, (剛 wr. for 鋼), n., extremely fine steel.

百里侯 *bor-lii-hour*, n., (LL) county magistrate, now rare; 百里才 --*tsair*, small talent, good only for county magistracy.

百六 ***bor-liouh*, n., the *Chingmirng* festival, 106 days after winter solstice.

百靈 **borlirng*, n., the Mongolian lark.

百米賽跑 *bairmii saihpaau*, n., hundred yards race.

百衲本 **bornahbeen*, n., edition of anc. works made up of collated passages, or of best existing editions of parts, cf. -*nahyi*.

百衲衣 **bornahyi*, n., monk's ragged robe, made of patches.

百年紀念 *baainiarn jiiniahn*, n., centenary.

百辟 **borpih*, n., (AC) the princes and dukes.

百忍 **bor-reen*, n. & v.i., "a hundred times patience", formula given for keeping large family in harmony (meant seriously, not sarcastically).

百日 *baairyh*, n., hundred days after person's death, a form of sacrifice; 百日咳 --*keh*, n., whooping cough; 百日紅 --*hurng*, n., =紫薇 (bot.) a flowering tree, *Lagerstroemia indica*.

百舌 ***borsher*, n., the Chin. blackbird.

百姓 ***borshihng*, n., the common people of a country.

百壽圖 **borshouh-tur*, n., scroll consisting of hundred forms of the character for "*shou*" (longevity).

百事通 ***bor-shyh-tung*, adj. & n., (person who) knows everything.

百索 **bor-suoo*, n., child's first anniversary, named after varicolored braid worn on neck.

百斯篤 ***baaisyduh*, n., bubonic plague, early transliteration for "pest".

百晬 **bortsueih*, n., party given on child's hundred days.

百足 **bortzur*, n., centipede.

百子 **bortzyy*, n., the ancient philosophers (also 百家 -*jia*↑).

百葉 ***bor-yeh*, n., (1) (AC) calendar; (2) (AC) a hundred generations; (3) a cake of many thin layers, made of bean curd; (4) cow's or sheep's tripe; (5) flowers with many compound petals; 百葉窗 --*chuang*, n., Venetian blinds.

晉 31.41

jihn.

[Pop. 晋]

N. (1) A surname. (2) Short for Shansi Province. (3) The Jihn Dyn. 265–420 A.D.

V.t. (1) (AC, LL) related 進 91.83. (2) Raise in rank, promote.

晉封 *jihnfeng*, v. t., confer further honors on ancestor or wife.

晉京 *jihn-jing*, v. i., (LL) go to the capital.

晉爵 *jihn-jyuer*, v. t., raise to a higher rank of the nobility.

晉授 *jihnshouh*, v. t., see -*feng*↑.

晉贈 *jihntzehng*, v. t., confer a posthumous title.

晉謁 *jihnyieh*, v. t., have an audience with (a high official, superior).

西 31.41

shi.

A

N. (1) West: 自東徂西 from east to west. (2) Spain (short for 西班牙): 駐西大使 Chin. ambassador to Spain.

Adj. & adv. (1) West: 南京西路 Nanking Road West; 西半球 Western Hemisphere; 西部 western region; 西岸 west coast. (2) Western, pertaining to the Western or gen. foreign world: 西人, 西婦, 西服, 西裝, etc., *-rern*, *-fuh*, *-fur*, *-juang*↓; see esp. 西洋 *-yarng*↓; 西餐 Western meal; 西式 Western fashion; for Western music, medicine, see 西樂, 西醫, *-yueh*, *-yi*↓. (3) To the west, westwards: 西去 go west. (4) A surname.

西班 *shiban*, n., (Tarng Dyn.) the military officers on the west in court ceremony, opp. civilian officers on the east; 西班牙 n., Spain.

西北 *shibeei*, adj., northwest.

西賓 *shi-bin*, n., family tutor, see *-shir*↓, cf. 東家 the host.

西伯利亞 *Shiborlihyaa*, n., Siberia.

西部 *shibuh*, n., (1) western region; (2) (movies) a western.

西成 *shi-cherng*, n., (MC) harvest.

西垂 *shi-chueir*, n., (AC) west side.

西法 *shi-faa*, adj., Western method (dry cleaning, etc.).

西番蓮 *shifanliarn*, n., (bot.) *Passiflora caerulea*.

西方 *shifang*, n. & adj., the western world, also (Budd.) referring to after world.

西婦 *shifuh*, n., Western woman.

西服 *shi-fur*, n., Western dress.

西瓜 *shigua*, n., watermelon.

西貢 *Shiguhng*, n., Saigon.

西宮 *shi-gung*, n., "western palace" where ladies-in-waiting lived.

西穀米 *shigur-mii*, n., sago; 西穀椰子 the sago palm, *Sagus rumphii*.

西紅柿 *shihurng-shyh*, n., tomato.

西淨 *shi-jihng*, n., (Budd.) western lavatory (as eastern lavatory is called 東淨); see *-shyuh*↓.

B

西裝 *shi-juang*, n., Western or European dress.

西曆 *shi-lih*, n., the Western or Gregorian Calendar (now generally called 公曆).

西米 *shi-mii*, n., sago, see *-gur-mii*↑.

西南 *shinarn*, adj., southwest.

西皮 *shipir*, n., name of song from 黃陂縣 in Hupei, current in Peking opera (see 皮^黃 22.82).

西人 *shirern*, n., Westerner.

西廂記 *shishiang-jih*, n., *The Western Chamber*, a famous Chin. classical novel.

西夕 *shi-shih*, n., (AC) old age.

西席 *shi-shir*, n., see *-bin*↑.

西施舌 *shishy-sher*, n., a small edible shellfish with elongated "tongue" or valve.

西序 *shi-shyuh*, n., the western wing of Buddhist monastery.

西臺 *shi-tair*, n., Suhng Dyn. name for the Censorate (御史臺).

西天 *shi-tian*, n., Buddhist paradise, believed to be in the west of China.

西崽 *shitzaai*, n., a houseboy or "boy" in the employment of foreigners in China.

西字臉 *shitzyh liaan*, n., broad-shaped face, like the character 西.

西洋 *shiyarng*, n., "Western ocean," i. e., Western or from the West (of. shortened to 洋 or to 西): 西洋音樂, 畫 Western music, painting; 西洋歷史 history of the Western world; 西洋景 peep show (also called 西洋鏡); 西洋參 *ginseng* grown in the United States.

西藥 *shi-yauh*, n., Western medicine.

西醫 *shi-yi*, n., Western doctor.

西元 *shiyuarn*, n., A.D. of Christian calendar (now gen. called 公元).

西樂 *shi-yueh*, n., Western music.

西域 *Shiyuh*, n., Turkestan, in region now called 新疆 "Hsinkiang."

C

酉 31.41

yoou.

N. (1) No. ten of the duodecimal cycle (see Appendix A). (2) 酉時 5–7 p. m. (3) A radical (as in 酌, 醉); index No. "31C."

面 31.41

miahn.

N. adjunct. 一面鏡子 a mirror; 一面國旗 a national flag.

N. (1) Face: 人面桃花相映紅 the girl's face and the peach flowers reflect each other's glow; 臉面 the face; 面孔, 面部, 面相 *-kuung*, *-buh*, *-shiahng*↓; 面團團 a fat, plump face; 面對現實 to face the realities; 面無人色 ghastly, pale-faced; 面對面 face to face, see esp. 面子 *-tz*↓ honor, social standing. (2) The surface: 表面 surface; 場面, setup, *milieu*, occasion. (3) Side, dimension, aspect: 上面, 下面 top, underneath; 前面, 後面 front, behind; 對面, 側面 opposite, on the side; 正面 front; 背面, 反面 the back; 四面 on all sides; 面面週到 in every way very attentive, every detail thought of; 面面相覷, see 面面 *-miahn*↓. (4) On one side: 一面之辭 onesided story; 一面吃, 一面談 talk while eating; 見過一面, 一面之交 have met once.

V. t. To face: 面朝裏 face inside; 面東, 面西 (of houses) face east, west; 面壁 face the wall, do nothing, (Budd.) face the wall and meditate; 面牆 face to the wall, see nothing.

Adj. Superficial: 面友, 面朋 superficial friend.

Adv. Personally (freely attached to vbb.): 當面 personally; 面談, 面

面 靣 而

敍 personal interview, talk; 面洽, 面商, 面議 discuss personally; 面謝 thank personally; 面陳 explain personally; 面折人過 point out person's mistake to his face; 面試 personal interview in examinations; 面論 order personally; 面交 deliver personally, etc.

面般 *miahnban*, n., (MC) facial contour=modn. 臉盤兒.

面部 *miahnbuh*, n., the facial region, the face.

面前 *miahnchiarn*, n., (1) bodily presence: 當人面前 in person's presence; (2) front area, near a person.

面縛 *miahnfur*, v. i., (AC) gesture of surrender, hands at back, face outstretched.

面見 *miahnjiahn*, n. & v. t., personal interview, meet personally.

面巾 *miahnjin*, n., face towel.

面積 *miahnjir*, n., area.

面具 *miahnjyuh*, n., mask: 假面具 mask, false front or appearance.

面寬 *miahnkuan*, n., width of surface.

面孔 *miahnkuung*, n., a person's face; facial expression.

面兒 *miah'l*, n., see *-tz*↓.

面貌 *miahnmauh*, n., facial looks, features: 面貌一新 take on a new look.

面門 *miahnmern*, n., face, front view.

面面 *miahnmiahn*, adv., in every aspect: 面面相覷 look at each other in astonishment.

面目 *miahnmuh*, n., (1) facial expression, demeanor: 面目清秀 have delicate looks; 面目可憎 repulsive looks; (2) looks of things in gen.; 面目全非 all looks wrong, or differently; (3) honor=面子 see *-tz*↓: 有何面目見人 how can I face the world?

面嫩 *miahn-nehn*, adj., shy.

面軟 *miahn-nuaan*, adj., soft-hearted, easily soften.

面龐(兒) *miahnparng('l)*, n., facial contour.

面皰 *miahnapuh*, n., pimples.

面皮 *miahnpir*, n., esp. 面皮厚 thick-skinned, unashamed; 面皮軟, 薄 thin-skinned, easily ashamed.

面容 *miahnrurng*, n., demeanor, expression; features.

面色 *miahnseh*, n., complexion (good, bad); momentary expression (angered, offended, etc.).

面紗 *miahn-sha*, n., veil covering the face.

面善 *miahnshahn*, adj., looking familiar: 這人很面善 his face seems familiar.

面上 *miahshahng*, n., on the face: (在情) 面上過不去 cannot do it because of our friendship; 表面上 on the face of it.

面相 *miahn-shiahng*, n., a person's features, physiognomy.

面熟 *miahnshur*, adj., looking familiar.

面子 *miahntz*, n., "Chinese face," a man's self-respect, standing among fellowmen: 很有面子, 面子很大 has high social standing; 沒有面子 lose face (=丟臉); 給面子, 賞面子 do one the honor (of coming to his party); 他不給我面子 won't do me the honor; 賣面子 do s. t. as a personal favor or in friendship; 不要面子 be shameless; also appearance of clothing: 這件衣服面子已舊了 this garment is getting shabby.

靣 31.41

liour.

[Var. of 留 90.41]

§31.42 (丅/冈)

而 31.42

erl.

Fin. part. (AC) 已而已而 this is the end ("finished, all finished"), also 乎而.

Pron. (AC, rare) you, your (related 汝, 女).

Conj. (1) And: 聞善而不善 (AC) heard of anything good and bad; connecting oft. two vbb.: 學而時習之 to learn and review it from time to time; or two adjj.: 恭而有禮 modest and courteous; connecting an adv. with vb.: 呱呱而泣 wail and cry; and yet, oft. reinforcing advv. like 況, 竟, 乃: 而況 how much more then; 而竟, 而乃 and contrary to reason or expectations; coupled with negative 不, meaning "and yet," "but": 富而不驕 rich and yet not conceited; 羣而不黨 is sociable, but not clannish. (2) 而且 Furthermore, besides. (3) Having the force of 之 "of": 君子恥其言而過其行 a gentleman is ashamed of his words being more pretentious than his conduct.

Prep. From . . . on, up, down, etc.: 三十而上 (=以上) from thirty up; 三十而下 below thirty; 而今而後 from now on.

而且 *erlchiee*, adv., besides, furthermore.

而何 *erlher*, adv., (AC)=如何 how.

而後 *erlhouh*, adv. conj., (1) and then: 言而後退 speak and then retire; (2) hence forth, thenceforth.

而竟 *erljihng*, adv., contrary to rule or expectations (left without saying good-bye); actually, so indeed, at last.

而今 *erljin*, adv., now, now then.

而況 *erlkuahng*, adv., besides, furthermore.

而來 *erllair*, adv., (AC) since: 由孔子而來 (=以來), 至今百有餘歲 it is now over hundred years since Confucius.

而立 *erllih*, adj., (LL) 而立之年 thirty years of age (allu. Confucius learned to stand firm at thirty).

而上 *erlshahng*, adv., upwards (=以上).

而下 *erlshiah*, adv., from . . . down (=以下).

而已 *erlyii*, adv., only (after modified wd. or phr.): 三十而已 only thirty; 而已矣 emphatic form of 而已.

再 31.42

tzaih.

Adv. Again, once more: 再接再厲 make unremitting efforts; 再三, 再四, 再三再四, 一再 repeatedly; 再議, 再審 be discussed over again; 再說 *-shuo*↓; 再次 once more; 再演一次 encore; 再行改期 postpone, reschedule; 再過幾天 in a few more days; 再運心思 reconsider; 東山再起 (usu. of a politician) stage a comeback; 再生 *-sheng*↓; 再造 *-tzauh*↓; 再談 let's discuss it later; 再見 see you again, good-bye! 不再說了, 相見 never mention it, never see each other again.

再版 *tzaih-baan*, v. i. & n., (of a book) (have) a second edition.
再拜 *tzaih-baih*, phr., (in letter) a polite complimentary close ("yours cordially" or "respectfully").
再不 *tzaih'bu*, adv., never again.
再乘 *tzaih-cherng*, n., (math.) the cube, the third power.
再發 *tzaihfa*, v. i. & adj., recur, -rent.
再犯 *tzaih-fahn*, v. i. & n., (commit) a second offense, a person committing it.
再會 *tzaihhueih*, phr., good-bye! see you again!
再婚 *tzaihhun*, v. i., re-marry.
再者 *tzaihjee*, adv., furthermore, in addition, by way of a postscript, ("p.s.").
再醮 *tzaih-jiauh*, v. i., (of a woman) re-marry.
再來 *tzaih lair*, phr., (1) come back: 時乎時乎不再來 time (lost) will never come again; (2) do (s.t.) over again: 再來一盤棋 let's have another game of chess; (3) have another help of (s.t.): 再來點兒水 give me some more water, please.
再生 *tzaih-sheng*, n. & v.i. & adj., rebirth, (be) born anew, reborn.
再現 *tzaih-shiahn*, v. i., (1) reappear; (2) (a former experience) reappears in one's mind.
再說 *tzaihshuo*, v. t., (1) talk about it later; (2) speak again, repeat; (3) adv., moreover, furthermore.
再再 *tzaihtzaih*, adv., again and again, repeatedly.
再造 *tzaih-tzauh*, v. i., be born anew, given a new lease of life.

雨 31.42

yuu (**yuh*).

N. Rain: 雨水 *-shueei*↓; 下雨, 降雨 it rains; 風雨 wind and rain; 雷雨 thunder and rain; 暴雨 rainstorm; 大雨 heavy rain; 陣雨 a spell of rain; 密雨 heavy downpour; 細雨 light drizzle; 毛毛雨 drizzle; 櫛風沐雨 brave the winds and the rain; 雨淋淋 descriptive of dripping rain; 雨星星 light drizzle; 雨後春筍 to spring like bamboo shoots after a spring rain.

V. i. (**yuh*) To rain: 雨雪 snow falls.

雨布 *yuubuh*, n., oilcloth, waterproof.
雨前 *yuuchiarn*, n., name of a superior tea, plucked before solar season of 穀雨 April 20.
雨泣 *yuu-chih*, v. i., weep profusely.
雨點兒子 *yurdiaan'ltz*, n., raindrops.
雨虎 *yurhuu*, n., (zoo.) *Aplysia* a small sea animal (also called 海兔, 海鹿).
雨腳 *yurjiaau*, n., splash of rain on the ground.
雨季兒 *yuu-jih(-jieh'l)*, n., the raining season.
雨巾 *yuu-jin*, n., formerly, rain hat.
雨久花 *yurjioou-hua*, (bot.) *Monocharia vaginalis*, a flowering water plant.
雨集 *yuu-jir*, phr., (LL) swarm together.
雨珠兒 *yuuju'l*, n., raindrops.
雨具 *yuujyuh*, n., things providing against rain (umbrella, boots, etc.).
雨量 *yuu-liahng*, n., volume of rain; 雨量計 *--jih* n., rain gauge.
雨漏 *yuu-louh*, v. i., leak in the roof.
雨露 *yuu-luh*, n., rain and dew—timely help in time of need; the blessings of peace from God or ruler.
雨帽 *yuumauh*, n., rain cap.
雨棚 *yuuperng*, n., rain shetter.
雨傘 *yursaan*, n., umbrella.
雨鞋 *yuushier*, n., rain boots.
雨星兒 *yuushing'l*, n., light drizzle.
雨水 *yurshueei* (coll. -'*shuei*), n., (1) rain water; (2) volume of rain (of locality); (3) a solar season (Feb. 19-Mar. 4).
雨靴 *yuu-shyue*, n., rain boots.
雨絲 *yuusy*, n., light falling rain.
雨天 *yuu-tian*, n., a rainy day.
雨字頭兒 *yuu'tztour'l* n., the radical 雨, index No. "31D."
雨蛙 *yuuwa*, n., (zoo.) *Hyla arborea*, a tree animal whose croaking noise presages coming rain.
雨燕 *ynuyahn*, n., (zoo.) *micropus pacificus*, a small bird.
雨衣 *yuuyi*, n., raincoat.
雨意 *yuu-yih*, n., as in 有雨意 (the sky) has the look of going to rain.
雨纓 *yuu-ying*, *n.*, (Manchu Dyn.) tassels of yak hair on mandarin official hat in summer.

丙 31.42

biing.

N. The third in the decimal cycle,

而 再 雨 丙

丙 兩 甭 鬲 爾 覇

see App. A; 甲乙丙丁 used like A, B, C, D; the third grade, third category, etc.; 付丙 burn (letter) after perusal.

丙丁 *biingding*, n., days in 干支 *ganjy* cycle, of "fire" element; used sometimes in LL for "fire."

丙舍 *biingsheh*, n., house for storing coffins pending arrangement for transshipment for burial in home district.

丙夜 *biingyeh*, n., midnight.

兩 31.42

liaang.

[Pop. 㒳 in sense of "ounce"]

N. & adj. Two, in gen. use as adj. in speaking of two pieces, things, sides, parties, dist. 二, used only in counting: 兩百元 two hundred dollars (in counting, 二百元 would be more common); 兩個人 two persons; 兩夫妻 man and wife; 母子兩口兒 the two of them, mother and son; 兩姓婚姻 marriage between two families; 兩頭兒跑 be kept busy between two offices; 兩頭兒大 a marriage where wife and concubine are treated as equal; 兩下子就好了 will finish it in a few moments; 兩邊, 兩邊廂, 兩面 both sides; 兩造 both parties to contract or litigation; 三心兩意; 猶疑兩可 undecided; 兩訖, 兩清 accounts cleared between two parties; 兩不找 goods and payments match; 兩面光 try to please both sides; 兩端 the two extremities; 兩小無猜 two innocent ones, boy and girl, grew up together; 兩相情願 both parties agree of free will, mutual consent; 兩相好 two lovers; 兩虎相鬪 fight between the two biggest (powers, warlords); 兩極 the Arctic and the Antarctic, the North and South Poles; two extremities.

兩棲類 *liaangchi leih*, n., (zoo.) amphibious animals.

兩腳規 *liarngjiaauguei*, n., compasses.

兩性花 *liaangshihng hua*, n., bisexual flower.

兩造 *liaangtzauh*, n., both plaintiff and defendant; both parties to contract, lawsuit.

兩樣 *liaangyahng*, adj. & n., (1) different, -ce: 有什麽兩樣 is where the difference? opp. 一樣 same; 情形兩樣 the situation is different; (2) two pieces or 兩三樣 two or three.

兩儀 *liaangyir*, n., the *yin* and the *yang*, the two polarities.

兩院制 *liaangyuahnjyh*, n., bicameral system (House of Commons and House of Lords.).

甭 31.42

berng.

Vb. aux. Contraction of 不用 *buryuhng*, need not: 你甭客氣 don't stand on ceremony; 你甭想 don't think that.

鬲 31.42

lih.

[Var. of 鬲 30.42]

爾 31.42

eel.

Part. (1) (AC) a final particle as alternative of 耳 (＝而已), meaning "merely": 唯謹爾 be only careful, (see 耳 31.10). (2) Adv. particle, like Eng. "like," "-ly" in stupid-like, stupidly (from its meaning "like" ＝如此) see Adj. ↓: 率爾而對 answer thoughtlessly; 卓爾 distinguished-like, eminent, -ly; 偶爾 occasionally; see Adv. ↓.

Pron. (AC, LL) you, your (related closely 汝; 汝 is more familiar); see 爾汝 *-ruu* ↓; 爾 oft. used as possessive: 爾父 your father, 爾妻 your wife; or as accusative: 爾詐我虞 you cheat and I deceive—mutually deceive; 爾 used as plural (like Eng. "you"): 爾等, 爾曹 *-deeng, -tsaur* ↓.

Adj. (1) (LL) that: 爾時, 爾日 that time, that day. (2) (LL) thus, like this (＝如此): 不得不爾 has to be this way; 所說乃爾 what (he) said was, this is what he said; 云爾 thus, so; 不過爾爾 it was only so-so. (3) U. f. 邇 near; 爾來 *-lair* ↓.

Adv. suffix. (AC, LL) 莞爾 smilingly; 嘑爾 shouting-like, unceremoniously; 僕僕爾 in a busy and restless manner, repeatedly; 故爾 therefore.

爾等 *erldeeng*, n., you (plural).

爾爾 *erleel*, adj., so-so.

爾來 *eellair*, adv., recently, in recent months or years.

爾汝 *erlruu*, pron. & v. t., (AC) to use the familiar you (like Fr. "tu"): 或爾汝之 (AC) treat him familiarly; 無受爾汝之實 (孟子) not to be influenced by personal (familiar) considerations, 爾汝交 (AC) friends who use familiar address to each other, (爾 *eel*, 汝 *ruu*, were originally very close in pronunciation, as still in many dialects).

爾日 *eelryh*, phr., (LL) that day.

爾馨 *eelshin*, adj., (dial.) thus, like this (see 寧[A]馨 62.01).

爾時 *eelshyr*, phr., (LL) at that time.

爾許 *erlshyuu*, adj., (LL) so many.

爾曹 *eeltsaur*, n., you (plural).

覇 31.42

bah.

[Corrupt form of 霸]

§ 31.50 (丅/ㄱ)

万 31.50

wahn.
[Var. of 萬 20A.42]

丐 31.50

gaih.
[Var. 匄, 匃]

N. Beggar: 乞丐 a beggar; 老丐 an old beggar; 丐頭 the leader of a group of beggars.

V. t. Beg for: 丐飯 beg for food.

焉 31.50

yan.

Fin. part. Descriptive of a situation similar to Eng. "in it" or "there" at end of sentence: 心不在焉 one's mind is not in it; 有人焉 there is a man there; 其心休休焉 his mind was contented; sometimes gives a sense of completion: 名不稱焉 one's name is not known; 芻蕘者往焉 the woodcutters went (there or to him, etc.); 衆好之必察焉 if many like it, one should look into it. (Usu. unaccented as fin. part.)

Adv. (1) (LL) how? (similar to 安): 焉能, 焉可 how can? 焉得 how could? 焉用 what is the need to use? 焉知 how does one know? (2) (AC) then (=modn. 然後, 乃): 焉能治之 (=乃能) and then could set it in order; 焉始乘舟 and then take the boat.

𠌶 31.50

huar.
[Arch. var. of 華 20A.10]

羈 31.50

ji.
[Pop. of 羈 41D.50]

§ 31.63 (丅/丶)

烈 31.63

lieh.

N. A surname.

Adj. & adv. (1) Violent, hot, extreme, -ly: 烈火 very hot fire; 烈日當空 scorching sun overhead; 烈風 violent wind, storm; 烈焰 raging flames; 烈暑 hot summer; 暴烈 (of temper) violent; 猛烈, 劇烈 (of poison) deadly, (slaughter, contest) violent; 慘烈 horrifying (massacre, etc.); 壯烈 brave, high-spirited. (2) Shining, brilliant: 烈名 brilliant fame. (3) Having sharp sense of honor: 節烈, 貞烈, see 烈士, 烈女 *-shyh*, *-nyuu*↓. (4) (Of medicine) strong, potent: 藥性很烈 causing sharp reaction.

烈婦 *liehfuh*, n., *-nyuu*↓.
烈烈 *liehlieh*, adj., (1) glorious, inspiring: 轟轟烈烈 (of career, campaign, achievement) astounding, glorious, heroic; (2) 憂心烈烈 (AC) burning with sorrow.
烈女 *liehnyuu*, n., "heroic women," women who died in defense of their honor or committed suicide after husband's death rather than re-marry (烈婦), much encouraged by Neo-Confucianists.
烈性 *liehshihng*, n. & adj., violent temper; (of medicine) violent.
烈士 *liehshyh*, n., hero who died for the country; martyr.

§ 31.70 (丅/乚)

无 31.70

wur.

Adv. No, not (AC var. of 無): 无妄之災 an undeserved catastrophe; 无咎 (AC) no fault or mistake, not to blame.

瓦 31.70

waa (**wah*).

N. (1) A roof tile: 寧作玉碎，不爲瓦全 rather be a broken jade than a whole piece of tile—prefer death or ruin to dishonor; 他人瓦上霜 the frost on neighbor's roof—none of one's business; 弄瓦 (AC) allu.) when a girl baby is born, let her play with tiles—hence give birth to baby girl (see 瓦窰 *-yaur*↓). (2) An earthenware: 瓦器, 瓦罐 *-chih*, *-guahn*↓: 黄鐘毀棄，瓦釜雷鳴 (LL, allu.) earthen pots making a lot of noise instead of the classical bells—said of bombastic politicians in power while god men are out.

V.t. 瓦瓦 (**wah-waa*) put tiles on roof; 瓦刀 *-dau*↓.

瓦卜 *war-buu*, n., (MC) to break up a tile and read the line of

万 丐 焉 𠌶 羈 烈 无 瓦

丨 00 小 01 𣥂 02 十 10 土 11 ナ 12 廾 20 ㄴ 21 卜 22 一 30 丅 31 フ 32 口 40 区 41 冈 42 丌 50 尸 51 亠 52 广 60 宀 61 丶 62 乚 63 七 70 心 71 八 72 人 80 乂 81 ～ 82 ⼀ 83 丿 90 ノ 91 ⺈ 92 く 93

cleavage for divination.
瓦碴兒 *waachar'l*, n., broken tiles.
瓦器 *waa-chih*, n., crude earthenware.
瓦刀 **wah-dau*, n., a trowel for laying tiles on roof.
瓦房 *waa-farng*, n., house with brick roof.
瓦溝 *waagou*, n., roof sill.
瓦罐 *waa-guahn*, n., earthen jar.
瓦合 *waaher*, adj., as in 瓦合之衆 rabble troops.
瓦灰 *waa-huei*, adj., deep grey.
瓦匠 *waa-jiahng*, n., a mason for laying roof.
瓦解 *warjiee*, v. i., to break up (like defeated army); disintegrate.
瓦塊(兒) *waakuaih* (*-kuah'l*), n., broken tiles.
瓦楞帽 *waalerng-mauh*, n., formerly, common man's hat with depression in middle, dist. 方巾 gentlemen's hat.
瓦裂 *waalieh*, v.i., see *-jiee*↑.
瓦木作 *waa-muh-tzuoh*, n., shop combining carpentry and bricklaying.
瓦舍 *waa-sheh*, n., (1) a brick house; (2) (Suhng Dyn.) a brothel, orig. brothel for barracks.
瓦斯 *waasy*, n., (translit.) gas.
瓦特 *waateh*, n., (translit.) watt.
瓦作 *waatzuoh*, n., bricklaying profession.
瓦子 *wartzyy*, n., see *-sheh*↑.
瓦窰 *waayaur*, n., (1) brick kiln; (2) (facet.) a woman who gives birth only to girls (see 弄瓦 under 瓦 N. 1↑).

琵 31.70

pir.

琵琶 *pirpar* (sp. pr. *pir'pa, pir'ba*), n., pipa, a musical instrument like guitar: 琵琶別抱 phr., said of woman who remarries.
琵琶蟲 *pirparchurng*, n., a louse (shaped like guitar).
琵琶骨 *pirpar-guu*, n., collar bone.
琵琶記 *Pirpar-jih*, n., name of well-known drama.
琵琶襟 *pirpar jin*, a former woman's costume, where the front bottoms come down not from armpit, but near the right chest.

琶 31.70

par.

N. See 琵▵琶 31.70.

兀 31.70

wuh.

N. (AC) one whose feet had been amputated as punishment.

Adj. (1) Erect; proud: 兀傲 *-auh*↓. (2) Upright: 兀坐 sitting upright. (3) Bald, bare: 兀鷹 *-ying*↓ (cf. 杌木 bare trees).

Adv. (MC) abruptly, immovably, alone: 兀自在櫃身坐地 was sitting immovably at cashier's deck; 兀自一人 a person alone.

兀傲 *wuhauh*, adj., proud, upright.
兀的 *wuhdih*, (MC) (1) adj., this: 兀的賤囚 this thief; (2) adv., how: 兀的不羞殺人也 how shameless.
兀剌 *wuhlah*, (MC) an adv. suffix, like Eng. "like": 軟兀剌 soft-like; 奔兀剌 abrupt-like.
兀臬 *wuhnieh*, adj., (LL) uneasy (also wr. 兀𨹃, 杌隉).
兀然 *wuhrarn*, adj., adv., immovable, -bly: 兀然不動.
兀兀 *wuhwuh*, adj. & adv., (1) in a distressed manner (probably related 鬱 *yuh*); (2) drunk: 醉兀兀 very drunk; 兀兀禿禿 adv., (MC) (contempt.) nondescript, cheap (wine).
兀鷹 *wuhying*, n., a kind of bald-headed vulture, *Gyps fulvus*.

虺 31.70

hueei.

N. A large, poisonous snake; a lizard, see 虺蜴 *-yih*↓.

虺蝮 *hueeifuh*, n., poisonous snake: 虺蝮之行 (derog.) sneaky, contemptible ways, like snakes.
虺虺 *hueirhueei*, adj., (AC) rumbling (of thunder).
虺蛇 *hueeisher*, n., a large poisonous snake; a viper.
虺蜴 *hueeiyih*, n., a lizard.

死 31.70

syy.

N. (1) Death: 生死關頭 critical point between life and death; 生死有命 life and death lie in the lap of the gods; 生死不忘 will never forget as long as I live. (2) Dead people: 死而有知 if the dead knew.

V. i. (1) To die: 死亡, 死活 *-warng, -huor*↓; 九死一生 extreme danger, a ten percent chance of survival; 半生不死 (不活) dead-alive; 病死 老死, 暴死 die of illness, old age, from violence. (2) Die for (cause): 死難 *-nahn*↓; 死節 (man, woman) die for integrity, honor or in loyalty to dead husband.

Adj. (1) Dead, condemned to die: 死囚, 死罪, 死刑 *-chiour, -tzueih, -shirng*↓; 死鬼, 死人 (abusive) *-gueei, -rern*↓; 該死 (excl. or abusive) damnation! simply awful; 眞該死 really awful (of a bad mistake); 死馬當作活馬醫 make a last try to save an impossible situation, as a last resort; 死不瞑目 die with injustice unredressed ("refuse to close eyes in death"); 死文字 a dead language; 死灰 *-huei*↓; 死水兒 stagnant water; 死火山 dead volcano; 死路 dead end; 死胡同兒 dead alley; 死信 dead, undeliverable letter; 死肌 dead muscle; 死結, 死扣兒 a fast knot; 死契 irrevocable deed; 死門兒 agreement never to see again child sold or given away; 釘死了 nailed fast; 睡得眞死 dead asleep; 耳朵發死 hearing is blocked; 面部表情發死 show a dead or dead-pan expression; 死挺挺 dead and stiff or lie stiffly. (2) Inflexible: 死規矩, 死套子 inflexible rule and regulations; 死法子 time-worn but useless method; 死板 *-baan*↓; 死頭腦 blockhead; 死工夫 by sheer work; 死心眼兒 single-minded, bent on one purpose; 死心塌地 completely, abjectly (in love), give one's heart. (3) Solid, not empty: 這管子是死的 it is a solid tube; 死瞠兒鐵柱 a solid iron pillar. (4) Dead set: 死仇 *-chour*↓; 死敵 irreconcilable enemy; 死對頭 deadly foe.

Adv. (1) Extremely, (as in Eng. "dead tired" or "die of waiting"): 好看死了 wonderfully pretty; 壞死了 frightfully bad, wicked; 死辣, 死鹹 (food) frightfully hot, salty; 甜死了 much too sweet; 冷死了 bitterly cold; 這人死不要臉 this person is devoid of shame; 死不 not for one's life; 死不承認 will never admit; 死要面子 dead determined to save face; 死要錢 dead set on getting money; 死不改 die hard; 死賣氣力 give all one's worth (to do s. t.); 哭(打)得死去活來 cried (beaten) half dead. (2) (Defend, etc.) to the death: 死打, 死戰, 死鬪 (殊死戰) fight to the death; 死守 defend to the death; 敢死隊 (mil.) suicide squad; 死黨, 死士 *-daang*, *-shyh*↓; 死皮賴臉 shamelessly (beg, pester); 死乞白賴 lie shamelessly. (3) In a stupid, mechanical way: 死記 memorize mechanically; without doing any thing: 死丕丕閒坐 sit about the house without moving; 死等 wait forever; 死吃 eat without earning one's bread.

死板 *syrbaan* (*-'ban*), adj., mechanical (singing), rigmarole (repeating); inflexible, solely guided by rules.

死別 *syy-bier*, v. i., part never to see each other again.

死併 *syybihng*, v. i., fight to the death.

死契 *syychih*, n., irrevocable deed.

死囚 *syychiour*, n., one condemned to death; 死囚牢 death house.

死仇 *syychour*, n., eternal enemy.

死黨 *syrdaang*, n., partisans sworn to the death.

死鬼 *syrgueei* (*-'guei*), n., (abuse) the devil.

死灰 *syhuei*, phr., 死灰復燃 old fire ("dead ashes") is kindled again—said of repeated flare-ups of rebellion; 枯木死灰 (of a person) dead-alive, lifeless, a living corpse.

死活 *syy-huor*, phr., (不管) 死活拉他來 bring him in regardless; 不知死活 have no news of person, dead or alive; (coll.) have no idea of death or danger.

死者 *syrjee*, n., (respectful reference) the dead, a dead person.

死角 *syrjiaau*, n., dead angle, corner sheltered from fire.

死紀兒 *syy-jieh'l*, n., souvenir left by the dead.

死忌 *syy-jih*, n., anniversary of a person's death.

死絕 *syy-jyuer*, v.i., be completely annihilated, die out.

死啃 *syrkeen*, v.i., (1) eat without work; (2) persist unduly in request or work; (3) read (book) without thinking.

死摳兒 *syykou'l*, (1) n., stubbornness; (2) adj., miserly, niggardly; studious, industrious.

死力 *syy-lih*, n., brute force, utmost exertion: 盡死力 with all one's might.

死路(兒) *syyluh('l)*, n., dead end; also fatal route.

死麵(兒) *syy-miahn*(*-miah'l*), n., unfermented flour.

死命 *syy-mihng*, (1) n., destiny of death; 制其死命 get a stranglehold on s.o.; (2) adv., 死命抵抗 resist with all one has got, fight to the last man.

死難 *syy-nahn*, v.i , (1) to die in tragic accidents such as shipwreck, flood, fire or airplane crash; (2) die a martyr's death.

死牌子 *syypairtz*, n., fixed, unchangeable rule.

死人 *syyrern*, n., (1) a dead person; (2) (abuse) dunderhead,

死傷 *syyshang*, n., war casualties; killed and wounded.

死生 *syy-sheng*, n., question of life or death; life and death: 死生有命 a person's life and death are matters of fate.

死相 *syyshiahng*, excl., a teasing remark in disgust (girl to boy).

死性 *syyshihng*, n., obstinacy, inflexible character.

死心 *syyshin*, v. i., (1) give up hope (of romance, etc.); (2) (do s.t.) with all one's heart and soul: 死心不息 persistently pleading, would not give up.

死刑 *syy-shirng*, n., death penalty.

死屍 *syyshy*, n., a corpse.

死士 *syy-shyh*, n., (LL) dare-to-die soldier.

死胎 *syytai*, n., stillborn baby.

死催的 *syytsuei'de*, n., (abuse) one bent for hell.

死鑿兒 *syytzaur'l*, n., person unable to accommodate anybody.

死罪 *syytzueih*, phr., (1) sentence to death; (2) (court. at end of letter) 死罪, 死罪! pardon for what I have said; (in speaking to emperor) risk life to give straight advice.

死亡 *syywarng*, (1) v.i., to die; fall victim to famine, war, etc.; (2) n., those that have died: 死亡約會 rendezvous with death; 死亡證 death certificate.

死樣 *syyyahng*, n., dead pattern without change.

死硬 *syyihng*, adj., intransigent, irreconcilable, stiff and unbending: 死硬派 *--paih*, die-hard.

死友 *syryoou*, n., (LL) friends sworn to the death.

覓 31.70

mih.

死
覓

亅	小	⺊	十	土	ナ	卄	⺊	丨	一	丁	フ	口	区	冈	冂	厂	尸	亠	广	宀	丶	乚	弋	心	八	人	乂	乛	一	丿	𠂉	く
00	01	02	10	11	12	20	21	22	30	31	32	40	41	42	50	51	52	60	61	62	63	70	71	72	80	81	82	83	90	91	92	93

[Pop. of 覓 90.70]

§31.71 (丅/弋)

戛 31.71-1

jiar.

[Pop. 戛]

N. An anc. weapon, a lance.

V. t. To strike: 戛擊 to tap lightly.

Adj. & adv. 戛戛 extraordinary, (-ily), extreme(-ly): 戛戛乎其難哉 how formidable or impossible the task is! 戛戛獨造 (of literary or artistic works) creative, original, out of the common run.

§31.72 (丅/心)

忑 31.72

teh.

Adj. See 忐忑 21A.72.

恧 31.72

nyuh.

恧縮 *nyuhsuo,* adj., bashful.

恐 31.72

kuung.

V. i. & t. Fear: (esp. vern.) 恐怕 *-pah,* see other compp. ↓; 驚恐, 惶恐 fear, trepidation.

Adv. (LL) 恐, (vern.) 恐怕 perhaps, I am afraid: 恐不容易 I am afraid it is not easy; 恐非原意 I am afraid (perhaps) it was not the original intent; 惟恐, 惑恐 perhaps, lest; 惟恐得罪 afraid it should offend (s. o.); 或恐有失 perhaps it may not be done properly (mail miscarried, etc.); 恐其有誤 (LL) perhaps there was a mistake.

恐怖 *kuungbuh,* v. i. & n., (be in) terror; 恐怖政策 (主義) policy of terror; 恐怖時代 reign of terror.

恐喝 *kuungheh*[1], v. t., to threaten with force.

恐嚇 *kuungheh*[2], v. t., see *-heh*[1] ↑.

恐慌 *kuunghuang,* v. i. & n., be in terror, desperately afraid, take alarm: 恐慌起來 take fright; 經濟恐慌 economic depression.

恐懼 *kuungjyuh,* n., (LL) fear, awe.

恐龍 *kuunglurng,* n., (zoo.) dinosaur.

恐怕 *kuungpah,* (1) v. i., fear: 不要恐怕 don't be afraid; (2) adv., perhaps: 恐怕不能來 I'm afraid (s. o.) cannot come; 恐怕不成 I am afraid it won't do.

恐水病 *kurngshueei-bihng,* n., (med.) hydrophobia.

惡 31.72

eh (**wuh, *wu, *ee*).

[Abbr. 悪]

N. (1) Evil, vice, wickedness: 善惡 good and evil; 惡有惡報 vice is punished. (2) Poison: 中惡 contract sudden ailment from various causes.

V. i. & t. (1) (**wuh*) To hate loathe, dislike heartily: 厭惡 to loathe; 可惡 damnable (person, behavior); 羞惡之心 feeling of shame, moral sense. (2) (**wuh*) (MC) to offend (person).

Adj. (1) Bad in gen., evil, poor: 惡劣 *-lieh* ↓; 惡衣惡食 poor food and dress; 惡少年 young hooligan; 惡環境 bad surroundings; 惡俗 bad customs; 惡疾 disgusting disease, euphemism for venereal disease; 惡札 (court.) my poor writing; 惡心 *-shin* ↓; 惡聲 *-sheng* ↓; 惡耗 bad news, usu. of s.o.'s death. (2) Fierce, ferocious: 惡狠狠, 惡拉拉, 惡惡實實的 very fierce, -ly; 惡戰 terrific fight; 惡婦 ferocious wife; 惡辣, 惡賴, 惡鬼 *-lah, -laih, -gueei* ↓. (3) Malignant (sore): 惡瘡 *-chuang* ↓.

Adv. (1) (**wu*) (LL) how: 惡可, 惡能 how can (it be?); 惡在 how can it be said that. (2) (*eh*) (MC) very: 惡靈利 very able; 惡憐人 (poet.) so charming.

惡霸 *ehbah,* n., a village hooligan.

惡報 *ehbauh,* n., proper retribution for sin.

惡氣 *ehchih,* n., evil smell; unpleasant manner or atmosphere.

惡臭 *ehchouh,* adj., evil-smelling, smelly.

惡瘡 *ehchuang,* n., malignant sores, ulcer.

惡德 *ehder,* n., wicked conduct, a vice, a sin.

惡惡 **wuh-eh,* v. i., to hate evil.

惡煩 *ehfarn,* adj., tedious; nauseating, -ted.

惡感 *ehgaan,* n., bad impression, adverse reaction: 引起惡感 arouse bad feelings.

惡鬼 *ehgueei,* n., (abuse) devil; (Budd.) evil spirit.

惡棍 *ehguhn,* n., a roughneck, rascal, scoundrel.

惡果 *ehguoo,* n., bad results; (Budd.) evil results of evil-doing.

惡漢 *ehhahn,* n., a rascal.

惡寒 **wuhharn,* n., (med.) a chilling spasm.

惡化 *ehhuah,* v. i., (1) to deteriorate, be vitiated; (2) (of beggars, monks) solicit money by disgusting tactics.

惡口 *eh-koou,* n., bad language: 惡口傷人 use bad language to insult people.

惡辣 *ehlah,* adj., ruthless.

惡賴 *ehlaih,* adj., rotten, vulgar.

惡劣 *ehlieh,* adj., bad in gen., esp.

in quality, morals.
惡名 *eh-mirng*, n., a bad reputation.
惡魔 *ehmor*, n., (1) (Budd.) devil; (2) evil person or force.
惡癖 *eh-pii*, n., evil habit.
惡人 *eh-rern*, n., bad person.
惡訕 *ehshahn*, v. t., to taunt, deride.
惡少 *eh-shauh*, n., young culprit, hoodlum, scallawag: 惡少年 juvenile delinquent.
惡聲 *eh-sheng*, n., (1) (AC) immoral music or song; (2) verbal abuse; (3) bad reputation.
惡限 *eh-shiahn*, n., (MC) a spell of bad luck.
惡相 *eh-shiahng*, n., evil or angry countenance.
惡嫌 **wuhshiarn*, v. t., to loathe.
惡戲 *ehshih*, v. t., see *-tzuohjyuh* ↓.
惡行 *eh-shihng*, n., immoral conduct.
惡性的 *ehshihng'de*, adj., malignant: 惡性瘤 (贅瘤) malignant tumor.
惡心 *ehshin*, (1) n., wicked thought; (2) v. i., (**eeshin*) nauseate.
惡識 *ehshyh*, v. t., (MC) mistake (person) for what he is not.
惡歲 *eh-sueih*, n., year of bad crops.
惡徒 *eh-tur*, n., "bad guys," hoodlums.
惡作劇 *ehtzuohjyuh*, v. i., to make fun (of person).
惡阻 *ehtzuu*, v. i., (1) lose appetite; (2) show morning sickness and change of appetite during pregnancy.
惡子 *ehtzyy*, n., (AC) young hooligan.
惡言 *eh-yarn*, n., words of abuse or vituperation.
惡業 *ehyeh*, n., (Budd.) evil thought, speech or conduct.
惡意 *ehyih*, n., malice: 沒有惡意 was not malicious, (said or done) without malice.
惡因 *ehyin*, n., (Budd.) cause or antecedent of evil results, see *-guoo* ↑.

憨 31.72

han.

N. A surname.

Adj. & adv. (1) Pleasant and silly, rapt in love, see compp. ↓. (2) Coarse: 憨繩子 a coarse rope or string.

憨癡 *hanchy*, adj., coquettish, gayly provocative.
憨厚 *han'houh*, adj., (of scholar) poised, not flighty.
憨直 *hanjyr*, adj., straightforward (character).
憨笑 *hanshiauh*, v.i. smile coquettishly.
憨子 *hantz*, n., a ninny, nincompoop, idiot.

瑟 31.72

seh.

N. A long, base stringed instrument, anciently with 5 or 10 strings, later with 25 strings: 琴瑟 (high and base stringed instruments) symbolizing marital harmony.

Adj. (1) Rustling sound: 瑟縮, 瑟瑟 ditto. (2) U.f. 索 10.01 in 蕭瑟 dreary.

§31.80 (丅/八)

頁 31.80

yeh.

N. (1) A page. (2) A leaf or double folded page in wood-block editions where half a leaf equals one Eng. page: 頁數 number of pages; 第一頁 page 1. (3) 冊頁 album of sheets of painting or calligraphy.

貢 31.80

guhng.

N. (1) A surname. (2) Tribute paid by a vassal state.

V. t. (1) To pay tribute to: 進貢 to pay tribute; 貢獻 *-shiahn*, 貢奉 *-fehng* ↓; 貢品 also local goods selected for His Majesty. (2) Recommend, select: 貢生 *-sheng* ↓.

貢奉 *guhngfehng*, v. t., (of vassal states) give (s. t.) as tribute.
貢生 *guhngsheng*, n., formerly, a senior licentiate.
貢獻 *guhngshiahn*, v. t. & n., contribute, -tions.

賈 31.80

jiaa (**guu*).

N. (1) A surname. (2) (**guu*) A merchant: 商賈 a trader, businessman.

V. t. (**guu*) (1) (LL) sell in commerce. (2) (LL) to invite: 賈禍 invite disaster; 賈怨 invite hatred.

§31.81 (丅/人)

天 31.81

tian.

天 **N.** (1) The sky, heaven: 天空 the sky, aerial space; 天下 *-shiah*↓; 天上 in the sky above; 天底下 all under heaven, the world over; 天大的事情 a tremendous event; 天無二日 only one supreme ruler, as "there is only one sun in heaven"; 天字第一號 "A-l," the very best; oft. coupled with 地 (the earth) in phrr.: 天地 *-dih*[1]↓; 天長地久 as long as the heaven and earth endure; 天公地道 the most natural and fair arrangement; 天翻地覆 turned completely upside down (of disasters, confusion); 天南地北, 天懸地隔 (of friends) separated far apart; 不識天高地厚 (of child) do not know what is what; 天崩地裂 natural disasters like giant earthquakes and landslides; 天網恢恢 God's justice is inescapable; 天羅地網 (of Taoist demons' magic) an invisible net preventing all escape; 天聾地啞 completely unmindful of anything, like one deaf and dumb. (2) Nature, what is given by nature, esp. 天然 see *-rarn*↓: 天資, 天賦, 天成, 天性 *-tzy*[2], *-fuh*[2], *-cherng*, *-shihng*[2]↓; 天年 man's natural span of life; 天造地設 (of natural scenery) made by nature; 天作之合 (marriage) made in heaven; 天衣無縫 (of art, master piece in fiction) completely natural, without artifice; 天經地義 what is most appropriate, ordained in nature (moral obligations, eternal principles, etc.); 聽天由命 resign to one's fate or God's will, be fatalistic; 靠天吃飯 have no regular income, live by what one can find. (3) God, the supreme ruler, the celestial spirits: 天老爺 Father Heaven; 皇天后土 (prayer to) Ye Gods! heavenly father and mother earth; 天堂, 天國 *-tarng*, *-guor*↓; 天怒人怨 the gods are angry and the people resentful; 怨天尤人 blame everybody but oneself; 無法無天 completely lawless and Godless, licentious; 天不怕, 地不怕 fear neither God nor men; 天之驕子 "the chosen of God," an unusually blessed or lucky person, God's favored one, (a tint of sarcasm in Chin. usage.); used coll. like Eng. "God": 天啊, 天哪 O God! good heavens! 我的天 oh, my God! 老天爺 oh, God! 天曉得 God knows (nobody knows); 天可憐見 how pitiful! 天誅地滅 may the gods strike (him) down! (4) A day: 今天, 明天, 昨天 today, tomorrow, yesterday; 過兩天 in two or three days; 前幾天 a few days ago; 每天 everyday; 成天, 一天到晚 all day; 大白天 in broad daylight. (5) Season, weather: 春天, 夏天, 秋天, 冬天 spring, summer, autumn, winter; 三伏天 hottest summer days; 黃梅天 rainy season in spring; 晴天 clear day, 天晴了 it is clear now; 天朗氣清 it is clear and dry; 雨天, 陰天 rainy, cloudy day; 熱天, 大熱天 hot, very hot, day; 天熱了 it has become hot; 天冷了 it has become cold; 天變了, 變天了 the weather has changed; 天亮了 it is dawn; 五更天 at early dawn; 天明 early dawn, daybreak; 天黑 at dusk, twilight; 天昏地暗 it is dark, overcast, like night. (6) N. & adj., emperor, imperial, of the emperor: 天子 the Son of Heaven, Emperor; 天朝 the Celestial Court (fomerly, used in communication with foreign countries); 天恩 the emperor's grace; 天顏 His Imperial presence; 天闕 imperial court. (7) The most important thing in life: 民以食爲天 food is next to God for the people; 王者以民爲天 a king's life depends upon the people. (8) Husband: 失其所天 lost her husband.

天表 *tianbiaau*, n., beyond heaven, beyond the skies.

天變 *tian-biahn*, n., natural calamities; change of weather: 天變了 it's going to rain.

天邊(兒) *tianbian('l)*, n., beyond the horizon: 天邊海角 far beyond, in distant places.

天稟 *tianbiing*, n., native endowments.

天兵 *tianbing*, n., (1) (Taoist) celestial troops; (2) formerly, imperial troops.

天產 *tianchaan*, n., local product, land product.

天朝 *tianchaau*, n., imperial court.

天成 *tiancherng*, adj., natural, springing from nature: 天成佳偶 a good match as if made in heaven; 文章本天成 good writing is completely like nature.

天譴 *tianchiaan*, adj., God's punishment.

天塹 *tianchiahn*, n., natural barrier for defense (such as wide river).

天橋 *tianchiaur*, n., (1) overpass at railways; (2) anc. scaffolding for attacking city walls.

天氣 *tianchih*, n., the day's weather.

天青 *tianching*, n., (of brocades, etc.) dark wine color.

天窗 *tianchuang*, n., skylight: 打開天窗說亮話 to be quite frank.

天趣 *tianchyuh*, n., beauty of natural objects or phenomena.

天衢 *tianchyur*, n., formerly, busy thoroughfares of the capital.

天道 *tiandauh*, n., God's way, divine order of things, spiritual principles: 天道好還 God's way goes in a cycle; (dial.) the weather.

天地 *tiandih*[1], n., (1) heaven and earth, the universe, the world: 天地間 in the whole world; 小天地 a little world in itself; 兒童天地 the child's world; 別有天地 a different world, a utopia; (2) the upper and lower margins of a scroll.

天帝 *tiandih*[2], n., Celestial Ruler (appellation of Taoist gods).

天定 *tiandihng*, adj., predetermined, predestined.

天底下 *tian-diishiah*, phr., under the sun; in the world.

天鵝 *tian-er*, n., the swan.

天方夜譚 *Tienfang Yehtarn*, n., *Arabian Nights*.

天分 *tianfehn* (*-'fen*), n., born gifts, talent: 天分甚高 has high intelligence.

天父 *Tianfuh*[1], n., (Christ.) God the Father.

天賦 *tianfuh*[2], n., natural gifts.

天府 *tianfuu*, n., self-sufficient region, with natural defense against invaders: 天府之國 a country with rich natural resources—a name given to 四川.

天干 *tiangan*, n., the decimal cycle, 甲, 乙, 丙, 丁, 戊, 己, 庚, 辛, 壬, 癸, used as serial number like A, B, C, D—see Appendix A.

天光 *tianguang*, n., daylight.

天癸 *tiangueei*, n., menstruation.

天工 *tiangung*[1], n., nature's work, said in praise of great art: 巧奪天工 it rivals nature.

天宮 *tiangung*[2], n., heavenly abode of the gods.

天國 *tianguor*, n., (Christ.) the Kingdom of Heaven.

天鼓 *tianguu*, n., (rare, LL) thunder.

天河 *tianher*, n., the Milky Way (also called 銀河, 天漢).

天花 *tianhua*, n., (1) smallpox; (2) (Budd.) flowers dropped from the sky; 天花亂墜 said of extravagant talk; 天花板 ceiling.

天潢 *tianhuarng*, n., (LL) royal descendants.

天火 *tian-huoo*, n., fire from heaven, said of houses struck by lightning.

天眞 *tianjen*, adj., innocent, naïve, frank, gen. showing traits of children: 你太天眞了 you are too naïve, believe too much in people's words.

天機 *tianji*, n., hidden plans of providence: 不可洩漏天機 (a seer) may not reveal what is coming or decree of God; the secret springs of nature, such as divine inspiration.

天戒 *tianjieh*, n., born teetotaler.

天井 *tianjiing*, n., courtyard, a small yard; air shaft.

天津 *Tianjin*, n., Tientsin, a port city.

天九 *tianjioou*, n., game of dominoes.

天竺 *Tianjur*, n., anc. term for India.

天竺桂 *tianjurgueih*, n., a kind of cinnamon, *Cinnamonum pedunculatum*.

天主 *tianjuu*, n., Catholic term for God: 天主教 Catholicism, Roman Catholic Church; 天主(教)堂 cathedral.

天職 *tianjyr*, n., man's natural duty: 國民的天職 a citizen's natural duty.

天空 *tiankung*, n., the sky, outer space.

天籟 *tianlaih*, n., sounds of nature (whistling of winds, etc.).

天藍 *tianlarn*, n., pale blue, skyblue.

天良 *tianliarng*, n., conscience.

天理 *tianlii*, n., Nature's law: 天理昭彰 God's law is manifest, i.e., evil is punished; 天理不容 intolerable injustice; 沒有天理 unscrupulous, lawless, a law to oneself, unreasonable.

天靈蓋 *tianlirnggaih*, n., the crown of the head.

天祿 *tianluh*, n., (1) a fabulous creature in anc. sculptures; (2) anc. idea of official rank in heaven.

天倫 *tianlurn*, n., the natural bonds and relationships of men, esp. the bonds of family: 天倫之樂 the happiness of family reunion, happy home.

天門冬 *tianmerndung*, n., (bot.) *Asparagus lucidus*.

天命 *tianmihng*, n., fate, destiny, God's will: 受天之命 divine mandate, a king rules by the grace of God.

天幕 *tianmuh*, n., awning over open space; painted backdrop of stage, indicating open space.

天南星 *tiannarnshing*, n., (bot.) jack-in-the-pulpit, *Arisaema serratum*.

天牛 *tianniour*, n., a class of beetles with very long feelers, *Apriona rugicollis*.

天疱瘡 *tianpauh-chuang*, n., (med.) pemphigus, an infection with blisters on skin.

天棚 *tianperng*, n., awning of cloth or bamboo.

天平 *tian(')pirng*, n., weighing scales.

天壤 *tian-raang*, n., as in 天壤之別 wide difference (as distance between the sky and the earth).

天然 *tianrarn*, adj. & adv., natural, not artificial; naturally, of course.

天人 *tianrern*, n., (1) nature and man: 天人合一 theory that man is integral part of nature; (2) a celestial being, an extraordinary beauty.

天日 *tianryh*, n., daylight; 重見天日 release after imprisonment or great injustice; 不見天日 living in darkness or dark oppression.

天色 *tianseh*, n., time of the day, as judged by color of sky: 天色已晚 it is getting dark.

天生 *tiansheng*, adj., born: 天生才子 born great artist, a genius.

天神 *tianshern*, n., celestial spirit.

天險 *tianshiaan*, n., natural defense, such as high mountains, cliffs, etc.

天下 *tianshiah*, n., the world: 今日的天下 the world today; 天下的人 all people in the world; anciently used to denote China.

天線 *tianshiahn*, n., antenna.

天象 *tianshiahng*, n., natural phenomena, esp. in the skies; the heavenly bodies.

天仙 *tianshian*, n., fairy: 美若天仙 beautiful like a fairy; 天仙果 --*guoo*, n., (bot.) a kind of fig, *Ficus erecta*.

天香 *tianshiang*, n., as in 國色天香 woman of great beauty; 天香百合 --*bairher*, n., (bot.) gold band lily, *Lilium auratum*.

天幸 *tianshihng*[1], n., rare luck.

天性 *tianshihng*[2], n., human nature, disposition (of wolves, foxes, villains, heroes, etc.).

天書 *tianshu*, n., (1) Taoist writings; (2) imperial edict.

天數 *tianshuh*, n., predestination.

天師 *tianshy*, n., Taoist master.

天時 *tianshyr*, n., weather.

天使 *tianshyy*, n., angel.

天算 *tian-suahn*, n., short for 天文算術 astronomy and mathematics.

天堂 *tiantarng*, n., heaven in religious sense.

天條 *tiantiaur*, n., the laws of God in heaven.

天體 *tiantii*, n., (1) heavenly body; (2) the nude: 天體運動 nudist movement; 天體營 nudist colony.

天庭 *tiantirng*, n., (1) the forehead: 天庭飽滿 a full forehead; (2) anc. the imperial court.

天才 *tiantsair*, n., (1) natural talent, aptitude; (2) genius, very brilliant person.

天蠶 *tiantsarn*, n., a wild species of silkworm.

天曹 *tiantsaur*, n., celestial officials.

天災 *tiantzai*, n., natural calamity; act of God..

天擇 *tiantzer*, n., natural selection in evolution: 物競天擇 survival of the fittest in natural selection.

天縦 *tian-tzuhng*, adj., as in 天縦之才 heroes, sages, especially gifted leaders of men.

天尊 *tiantzun*, n., (Taoism) god, spirit.

天足 *tiantzur*, n., unbound, "natural" feet.

天姿 *tiantzy*[1], n., beauty of looks.

天資 *tiantzy*[2], n., person's natural endowment or intelligence (high, low).

天子 *tiantzyy*, n., "the Son of Heaven," designation of emperor.

天王星 *tianwarngshing*, n., (astron.) Uranus.

天文 *tianwern*, n., science of astronomy; 天文鏡 *--jihng*, n., telescope; 天文臺 *--tair*, n., astronomical observatory.

天演 *tianyaan*, n., theory of evolution.

天閹 *tianyan*, n., naturally impotent person.

天涯 *tianyar*, n., the limits of the earth: 天涯海角 the four corners of the earth.

天意 *tianyih*, n., God's will.

天淵 *tianyuan*, n., as in 天淵之別 great difference, as the sky is separated from ocean depths, see *-raang*↑.

天元 *tianyuarn*[1], n., anc. Chin. algebra.

天緣 *tianyuarn*[2], n., predestined friendship or marriage; predestination.

天宇 *tianyuu*, n., the sky; the whole world; the capital of country.

耎 31.81

ruaan.

[Cogn. 輭 10D.81]

燹 31.81

shiaan.

N. Wild fires: 兵燹之禍 the ravages of war.

---

§31.82 (ㄒ/ㄨ)

更 31.82

geng (**gehng* as adv.; **jing*).

N. (1) A surname. (2) (Also **jing*) one of the five watches in a night: 三更半夜 about midnight; 更深夜漏 in the dead of night; 鷄鳴五更 day break, dawn (lit., "when the cock crows at the last night watch"); 五更雞 chicken simmered for a whole night.

V. t. (1) To change, alter, modify: 更改, 更動, 更換 *-gaai, -duhng, -'huahn*↓; 變更 make changes in; 改弦更張 introduce reforms. (2) Rotate, take turns at: 更番 *-fan*, 更代 *-daih*↓. (3) Revise, correct, amend: 更正 *-jehng*, 更訂 *-dihng*↓. (4) To experience: 更事 *-shyh*↓.

Adv. (1) (**gehng*) Once more, over again, still further: 更上一層樓 go up a storey still higher. (2) To a higher degree: vern. oft. 更加 *-jia*↓; 更多 more; 更好 much better; 更難 more difficult; 更苦 more bitter or harder; 更使我爲難 embarrass me so much the more; 更叫人不知如何是好 place one in an impossible fix.

更代 *gengdaih*, v. t., replace (s. o.) with another, take turns.

更迭 *gengdier*, adv., in succession.

更訂 *gengdihng*, v. t., revise (books, etc.).

更端 *gengduan*, n., new beginning.

更動 *gengduhng*, v. t., modify, change (personnel, post, texts, etc.).

更番 *gengfan*, v. i., be assigned to duties by rotation.

更夫 *gengfu*, n., a night watchman.

更改 *genggaai*, v. t., alter, change (dress, plans, etc.).

更鼓 *gengguu*, n., a night watchman's drum or clapper.

更換 *geng'huahn*, v. t., replace, substitute, change (dress, position, regulations, etc.).

更張 *gengjang*, v. t., as in 改絃更張 to reform (lit., re-string musical instrument).

更正 *gengjehng*, v. t., make corrections: 來函更正 letter to a newspaper editor to correct an inaccurate report.

更加 **gehngjia*, adv., as in 更加厲害 still worse; 更加可憐 still more pitiful.

更漏 *genglouh*, n., hourglass, a device for measuring time of the night watches.

更樓 *genglour*, n., a watch tower.

更名 *geng-mirng*, phr., to change one's name.

更深 *gengshen*, adv., late at night: 更深人靜 all is quiet in the dead of night.

更生 *gengsheng*, v. t., as in 自力更生 put forth new life by one's efforts.

更新 *gengshin*, v. t. & n., renew, -al, renovate, -tion: 一元復始, 萬象更新 with the beginning of another year, everything is fresh again; 更新設備 (of industrial plants) renovate equipment and facilities.

更戍 *geng-shuh*, v. t., transfer garrison forces.

更事 *gengshyh*, v. i., have experience of, be experienced: 少不更事 too young and inexperienced; 更事未多 with little experience in practical affairs.

更始 *genshyy*, v. i., begin a new page: 與民更始 (pledge to) give the people a new deal.

更替 *gengtih*, v. i. & t., to substitute, to change.

更頭 *gengtour*, n., the time of a night watch; 五更頭 at the fifth watch.

更次 *gengtsyh*, n., as in 一個更次 a night watch (=*tour*↑).

更卒 *gengtzur*, n., troops assigned

to garrison duties by turns.

更衣 *geng-yi*, phr., to change dress.

更易 *gengyih*, v. t., alter, change (plans, etc.).

夏 31.82

shiah (**jiah*).

N. (1) Summer: 夏季, 夏天, 夏日 *-jih, -tian, -ryh* ↓; 初夏 early summer; 夏收 summer harvest; 炎夏 hot summer; 夏日可畏 of official superior who is a severe disciplinarian, compared to the summer sun, contrasted with 冬日可愛 the gentle superior like the pleasant sun of winter; "夏五," "郭公" (LL) missing passages, from those in 左傳; 夏蟲語冰 as a summer insect discusses ice—of one who talks what he knows nothing about. (2) The Shiah Dyn. (usu. wr. Hsia, 2205–1766 B.C.): 夏后 *-houh* ↓; 夏朝, 夏代, 夏室 the Shiah Dyn.; 夏禮 the rituals and institutions of Shiah Dyn. (3) 華夏 China; Chinese. (4) 夏國 anc. name of Bactria (also 大夏). (5) A surname.

夏布 *shiahbuh*, n., fine linen.

夏楚 **jiarchuu*, n., a rod, a ferule for punishing pupils.

夏后 *Shiahhouh*, n., usu. 夏后氏 name of royal house of Emperor Yuu (禹), founder of Shiah Dyn.

夏正 *shiahjehng*, n., the first month of the lunar year.

夏節 *shiahjier*, n., (1) the fifth day of fifth lunar month—the Dragon Boat Festival; (2) summer solstice.

夏季 *shiahjih*, n., the summer season; see *-lihng* ↓.

夏至 *shiahjyh*, n., summer solstice.

夏曆 *shiahlih*, n., the lunar calendar.

夏令 *shiahlihng*, n., summer season; 夏令會 summer conference; 夏令營 summer camp.

夏眠 *shiah-miarn*, n., (of certain tropical insects) summer hibernation.

夏日 *shiah-ryh*, n., summer day; summer sun.

夏天 *shiahtian*, n., summer, summer days.

憂 31.82

you.

N. (1) Sorrow, anxiety, concern: 消憂, 解憂 to dissipate sorrow; 忘憂 forget one's sorrow; 隱憂 secret worry; 憂苦 affliction. (2) Parents' funeral: 丁憂 compulsory retirement from public life during parents' mourning.

V. t. To be concerned for: 憂國, 憂民 be concerned, worried, for the country, for the people.

Adj. Sorrowful, anxious, concerned: 憂愁, 憂慮 *-'chour, -'lyuh* ↓.

憂愁 *you'chour*, n. & adj., sorrow, -ful, sad, -ness.

憂憤 *youfehn*, adj. & n., angry, anger, exasperated, -tion.

憂患 *youhuahn*, n., disaster.

憂懼 *youjyuh*, n. & adj., fear and worry.

憂慮 *you'lyuh*, n., concern, worry.

憂悶 *youmehn*, adj., depressed, sad, grieved.

憂傷 *youshang*, adj. & n., grief,

憂心 *youshin*, n., sad heart.

憂思 *yousy*, n., worry, anxiety.

憂悒 *youyih*, adj., sad, disappointed.

憂鬱 *youyuh*, adj., vexed.

覆 31.82

fuh.

V. i. & t. (1) To overturn: 傾覆 to overthrow (government); 顚覆 totter, about to fall, also v.t., to overthrow (government); 舟覆 ship overturns; see 覆沒, 覆轍 *-moh, -cheh* ↓; 覆車之戒, 前車覆, 後車戒 (anc. proverb) overturned cart in front is warning for those behind; 覆盆之冤 dark injustice (like being under a overturned tub). (2) Cover: 覆蓋 cover; 天之所覆, 地之所載 what is under heaven and borne by the earth; 覆(醬)瓿 (modest) my worthless writing ("useful for covering condiment jars"). (3) Pour out: 覆水難收 water poured on the ground cannot be recovered, said by husband unwilling to take back separated wife. (4) To reply (unnecessary var. of 復): 答覆, 覆信, 回覆; 覆命 report on termination of assignment.

Adv. Used like "re-" as prefix & vb., denoting "double check": 覆查 re-examine; 覆校 re-proof; 覆核 double check on figures for budget, expenses; 覆選 second election; 覆審 re-examine case at court; 覆考, 覆試 re-examination, double tests.

覆敗 *fuhbaih*, v. i., be defeated.

覆車 *fuhche*, n., a bird trap; an overturned cart.

覆轍 *fuhcheh*, n., route of overturned cart. 「see *-moh* ↓.

覆滅 *fuhmieh*, v. i., be defeated;

覆沒 *fuhmoh*, v. i., (of ship) overturn: 全軍覆沒 whole army is drowned.

覆盆子 *fuhperntz*, n., (bot.) plant of rose family, *Rubus tokkura*.

覈 31.82

her.

V. i. & t. See var. 核 10B.81 vb.

Adj. Severe, penetrating: 深覈.

§ 31.83 (T/∼)

迂 31.83

yu.

Adj. (1) Doctrinaire, dogmatic, abstruse, impractical: 迂闊, 迂腐 *-kuoh*, *-fuu*↓. (2) Roundabout, remote (interch. 紆 93B.00), intricate: 迂曲, 迂迴 *-chyu*, *-hueir*↓.

迂氣 *yu'chi*, adj., stubborn, unrealistic.
迂曲 *yuchyu*, adj., twisted, with many turns.
迂誕 *yudahn*, adj., perverse, absurd and pretentious, bombastic.
迂道 *yu-dauh*, adv., by roundabout path.
迂夫子 *yu-fu-tzyy*, n., (contempt.) a cranky professor; a person with encrusted opinions.
迂腐 *yufuu*, adj., antiquated, reactionary, dogmatic (person, ideas), senile-minded.
迂緩 *yuhuaan*, adj., slow, cumbersome (progress).
迂迴 *yuhueir*, adj., (road) twisting about.
迂見 *yu-jiahn*, phr., impractical, doctrinaire opinion.
迂久 *yujioou*, adj., a very long time.
迂拙 *yujuor*, adj., stupid and narrow-minded.
迂滯 *yujyh*, adj., sluggish.
迂直 *yujyr*, adj., stubborn and simple-minded (opinion).
迂拘 *yujyu*, adj., dogmatic, impractical.
迂闊 *yukuoh*, adj., abstruse, unrealistic.
迂陋 *yulouh*, adj., vulgar and uninformed.
迂路 *yu-luh*, n., see *-dauh*↑.
迂論 *yu-luhn*, n., bombastic talk or opinion.
迂儒 *yu-rur*, n., encrusted Confu. scholar.
迂遠 *yuyuaan*, adj., remote.

迺 31.83

naai.

[Pop. & anc. var. of 廼 80.83]

还 31.83

huarn.

[Pop. of 還 41D.83]

迒 31.83

yirng.

[Abbr. of 迎 90.83]

逕 31.83

jihng.

N. (Var. 徑) a footpath.

Adv. Directly, freely, impulsively, see 徑 91B.30: 逕啟者 (phr. used in business letters) "This is to advise you that. . . ."

逐 31.83

jur.

N. (1) To pursue: 追逐 pursue (fame, power, girl); 逐鹿 *-luh*↓. (2) To drive out, expel: 驅逐 drive out; 放逐 expel from country.

Adj. Each: 逐一 each one; 逐件 each piece; 逐條 each article (of treaty) or item.

Adv. Gradually, one by one: 逐漸 *-jiahn*↓.

逐北 *jurboh*, v. i., be defeated.
逐臭 *jurchouh*, v. i., run after "filth"—i. e., have strange hankerings or tastes, as flies like garbage.
逐電 *jurdiahn*, adv., quick as lightning flash.
逐漸 *jurjiahn*, adv., gradually (grow, diminish, etc.).
逐客令 *jur-keh-lihng*, n., as in 下逐客令 order guest unceremoniously to get out.
逐鹿 *jur-luh*, phr., (allu.) 逐鹿中原 fight for the throne (lit., to see who gets the deer 鹿死誰手 in a deer hunt).
逐末 *jur-moh*, n., as in 棄本逐末 run after the less important things, forgetting the important.
逐日 *jurryh*, (1) adv., everyday; (2) v. i., (LL) race with the sun (in speed).
逐勝 *jur-shehng*, v. i., chase defeated enemy.
逐勢 *jur-shyh*, v. i., to run after the rich and powerful.
逐次 *jurtsyh*, adv., (1) gradually; (2) each time.
逐一 *juryi*, adv., one by one.
逐疫 *jur-yih*, v. i., perform rite to exorcise evil spirits.

遷 31.83

chian.

V. i. (1) To move to another place: 遷移, 遷徙, 遷居 *-yir*, *-shii*, *-jyu*↓; 遷入 move into (a new house); 喬遷 celebration of moving to new house or official post; 遷怒 *-nuh*↓. (2) To change, esp. slowly, to shift: 苟不教, 性乃遷 a man's nature changes for the worse if not properly taught. (3) (LL) to be appointed to a certain post: 升遷, 遷調; also to be degraded or exiled: 遷謫, 遷戍 *-jer*, *-shuh*↓.

遷除 *chianchur*, v. i., be appointed (to post, rank).
遷調 *chiandiauh*, v. i., transfer to another post.
遷鼎 *chian-diing*, n., change dynasty (allu., "transport sacrificial tripod," symbol of royal

rule).

遷都 *chian-du*, v. i., to move capital.

遷祔 *chian-fuh*, v.i., move grave to ancestral graveyard.

遷化 *chianhuah*, v.i., (1) to change, deterioriate; (2) (Budd.) to die.

遷換 *chianhuahn*, v.i., to change (currency, location, etc.).

遷謫 *chianjer*, v.i., to go into exile.

遷就 *chianjiouh*, v.i., be accommodating, accept lower position or cheaper terms.

遷居 *chian-jyu*, phr., to move into another house.

遷怒 *chian-nuh*, phr., vent one's anger on a third party.

遷染 *chianraan*, v.i. & t., to change in character; be corrupted by (influence).

遷善 *chian-shahn*, v.i., (LL) to reform one's ways.

遷徙 *chianshii*, v.i. & t., cause (person, whole population) to, migrate, move away from original place of residence; to change residence.

遷戍 *chianshuh*, v.t., to exile (person), be exiled.

遷次 *chiantsyh*, n., (1) (LL) change of lodgings on journey; (2) promotion to higher post; (3) seasonal changes; (4) adv., hurriedly, disorderly.

遷葬 *chian-tzahng*, phr., move graveyard to another place.

遷延 *chianyarn*, v. i., to dillydally, delay, procrastinate.

遷移 *chianyir*, v. i., remove, shift (place of residence, post, responsibility).

邇 31.83

eel.

Adj. (LL) near: 親邇 go near; 邇近 near; 邇來 recently; 遐邇 far and near.

跫 31.83

chyurng.

Adj. (AC) descriptive of sound of footsteps: 跫跫, 跫然.

甦 31.83

su.

V. i. To wake up; to revive (also wr. 穌, 蘇): 復甦 revive.

甦醒 *sushiing*, v. i., wake up from coma, stupor: 甦醒過來 recover from coma on unconsciousness.

---

§ 31.93 (丅/く)

耍 31.93

shuaa.

V. i. To play for pastime: 玩耍 ditto; 作耍 make a joke or do s.t. for pastime; 好吃好耍 like to eat and to play; 不是耍的 it is dangerous, not a joke.

V. t. (1) To play (an act, a role, a trick), make (a gesture), show off: 耍把戲 *-baashih*↓; 耍手段, 耍花槍 play a trick, show skill to confuse; 耍花着的 ditto, also make a special flourish in painting or calligraphy; 耍光棍 play the scoundrel; 耍勢力 show off one's power, use power to impress. (2) To gamble: 耍錢 *-chiarn*↓; 把錢耍光了 gambled away all one's money; 耍家兒 *-jia'l*↓. (3) To give a professional show: 耍刀 exhibit swordplay; 耍拳腳 exhibit boxing; 耍獅子 give a lion dance; 耍猴子, 耍狗熊 give a monkey, bear show.

耍把戲 *shuar-baashih*, v. i., to play a trick; to give acrobatic or similar show.

耍叉 *shuaa-cha*, v. i., to create trouble for s.o.

耍錢 *shuaa-chiarn*, v. i., to gamble.

耍骨頭 *shuaa-gur'tou*, v. i., try to show off.

耍滑 *shuaahuar*, v. i., to play fast and loose.

耍貨(兒) *shuaa-huoh('l)*, n., children's toys.

耍家兒 *shuaa-jia'l*, n., a gambler (also 耍家子 *--tz*).

耍兒 *shuaa'l*, n., gambling.

耍臉子 *shuar-liaantz*, v. i., give an angry look.

耍弄 *shuaaluhng*, v. t., to make a fool of (s.o.).

耍脾氣 *shuaa-pir'chi*, v. i., indulge in fits of temper.

耍頻(貧)嘴 *shuaa-pirntzueei*, v. i., love to gossip.

耍人兒的 *shuaa-rer'l'de*, n., a labor hand.

耍像兒 *shuaa-shiahng'l*, v. i., to give a sign with a wink, nod, glance, etc.

耍笑 *shuaashiauh*, v. i., to occupy time with jokes, tomfoolery.

耍戲 *shuaa-shih*, v. t., to make a fool of.

耍手藝 *shuar-shoou'yi*, v. i., make a living by some skill.

耍子 *shuaatz*, (1) n., (MC) a display of skill, a pastime; (2) v. i., to play, while away time.

耍嘴皮子 *shuar-tzueeipirtz*, n., (coll.) professional clown or joker.

要 31.93

yauh (**yau*).

N. Necessity, need, urgency: 必要 necessity; 沒有必要 there is no need; 主要 prime importance; 需

要 要 need, necessity, also v.t., to need.

Vb. aux. (1) Want: 我要走 I want to go; 他不要 he does not want (to, it). (2) Going to: 將要 ditto: (將) 要下雨了 it is going to rain; 天快要黑了 it is going to be dark soon. (3) Should: 你要知道, 要小心 you should know, should be careful.

V.t. (1) To want (s. t.); to demand or request: 我要他來 I want him to come; 這本書我要了 I have already requested for this book; 他要了去 he has requested and taken it away; 要得, 要不得 *-der*, *-'bu'de* ↓. (2) (**yau*) (LL) to sum it up: 要之. (3) (**yau*) (a) Demand: 要求 *-chiour* ↓; (b) coerce: 要挾, 要盟 *-shier*, *-merng* ↓; (c) (AC) ambush and capture on the way: 將要而殺之 was going to ambush and kill him.

Adj. Important: 要緊 *-jiin* ↓; 重要 important; 急要 urgent; 主要 of prime importance; 最要 most important; 至要 most important and do not forget; 要言不煩 an important statement need not be prolix.

Conj. If (=若, related): 要是 *-'shy* ↓; 要不然 *-'buhrarn* ↓; 你要不來 if you don't come; 要不, 我們回去罷 if not, we'll go back.

要隘 *yauh-aih*, n., strategic pass.

要便 *yauhbiahn*, adv., (MC) often, usually.

要不的 *yauh'bu'de*, (1) adv., extremely: 窮得要不的 unbearably poor; (2) phr., extremely bad: 這肉壞了要不的 this meat is spoilt, to be rejected.

要不然 *yauh'burarn*, phr., if not, otherwise (I refuse to go, etc.).

要強 *yauh-chiarng*, v.i., to want to forge ahead, be a success.

要求 **yauchiour*, v.i. & t., to demand, request (s.t., that).

要衝 *yauh-chung*, n., place which bears the brunt of attack; strategic area.

要道 *yauh-dauh*, n., (1) main route, highway; (2) important teaching.

要得 *yauhder* (*-'de*), adj., (Szechuan dial.) desirable, good; 要不得(的) see *-'bu'de* ↑.

要點 *yauh-diaan*, n., important point.

要地 *yauh-dih*, n., important place, position.

要端 *yauh-duan*, n., important point.

要犯 *yauh-fahn*, n., chief culprit; important convict.

要飯(兒)的 *yauhfahn(-fah'l)'de*, n., a beggar.

要港 *yauh-gaang*, n., principal port.

要括 *yauhgua*, v.i. & t., to summarize.

要乖乖 *yauhguaiguai*, v.i., to kiss, see *-tzuee'l* ↓.

要故 *yauhguh*, n., serious business.

要公 *yauhgung*, n., important official business.

要好 *yauhhaau*, v.i., be good friends with: 兩個人很要好 the two are very good to each other.

要害 *yauhhaih*, n., (1) vital part of body; (2) vital area of defense.

要謊 *yauh-huaang*, v.i., (seller) asks fantastic price in preparation for haggling.

要賬 *yauh-jahng*, v.i., to ask for repayment.

要價兒 *yauhjiah'l*, n., the price offered for sale.

要件 *yauhjiahn*, n., important items, articles, documents.

要近 *yauhjihn*, n., (LL) those close to the ruling power.

要勁(兒) *yauhjihn(-jieh'l)*, n., strenuous effort.

要緊 *yauhjiin*, adj., important: 不要緊 unimportant, never mind.

要津 *yauh-jin*, n., (LL) important road or avenue, esp. to success or power.

要擊 **yaujir*, v. t., to waylay and attack.

要著 *yauhjuor*, n., an important move step; essential point (of book), prime aim.

要旨 *yauhjyy*, n., essential point (of book), prime aim.

要口 *yauhkoou*, n., important point of entry or exit.

要臉 *yauh-liaan*, v. i., to care for "face," also 要臉面; 不要臉 shameless.

要領 (1) *yauhliing*, n., main themes, main points of discussion: 不得要領 completely at sea; (2) (AC) also pr. (**yau-*), main point; 得全要領 (=腰領) keep head on shoulders, escape being dismembered.

要路 *yauh-luh*, n., vital route, esp. to power.

要略 *yaulyueh*, n., a summary.

要買 **yaumaai*, v.i., as in 要買人心 to win people's hearts.

要盟 **yaumerng*, v.i., to obtain treaty by threat of force.

要眇 **yaumiaau*, adj., (AC) enticing, engaging.

要妙 **yaumiauh* (*yauh-*), adj., (AC) engaging, attractive.

要命 *yauhmihng*, adv., desperately: 窮的要命 desperately poor; 疼的要命 ghastly painful; 要命鬼(兒) (said of one's child) a pest.

要目 *yauhmuh*, n., principal points.

要鬧 *yauhnauh*, adj., busy (thoroughfare).

要人 *yauhrern*, n., important person, V.I.P.

要塞 *yauhsaih*, n., vital area of defense, a fortress.

要項 *yauh-shiahng*, n., main items.

要挾 **yaushier*, v.t., to coerce (person) by threat of force.

要是 *yauh'shy*, conj., if (=若是).

要事 *yauhshyh*, n., important business.

要素 *yausuh*, n., main factor, essential element.

要菜 *yauhtsaih*, v.i., (1) (sl.) assume airs; (2) to order food in restaurant.

要圖 *yauh-tur*, n., important plan.

要在 *yauh tzaih*, phr., the important thing is.

要嘴兒 *yauhtzuee'l*, v.i., to make a kiss.

要嘴吃 *yauh-tzueei-chy*, phr., to ask for food like a glutton.

要聞 *yauhwern*, n., summary of important news, headline stories of the day.

要務 *yauh-wuh*, n., important affairs.

要樣兒 *yauh-yahng'l*, phr., care about putting on a good front.

要義 *yauh-yih*, n., essential points.

要因 *yauh-yin*, n., important cause.

娶 31.93

chyuu (re. pr. *chyuh*).

V. t. (Of man) to marry (wife), cf. 嫁 (of woman) to marry (husband): 娶妻，娶媳婦兒 to take a wife (for son); 婚娶，嫁娶 marriage; 明媒正娶 legally marry; 迎娶，娶過來，娶來了 marry a girl ("into the family"); 再娶，續娶 re-marry a second wife.

娶親 *chyuuchin*, v. i., hold a wedding, marry: 娶親了沒有 is he married?

蚕 31.93

tsarn.

[Pop. of 蠶 51.93]

蛩 31.93

chyurng.

N. (1) Locust. (2) Cricket.

Adj. 蛩蛩 (AC) worried, concerned.

SECTION 31A

§31A.00 (王/亅)

琦 31A.00-1

chir.

N. A fine jade.

Adj. Admirable: 琦行 admirable conduct; 琦瑋 admirable, distinguished.

玎 31A.00-3

ding.

玎璫 *ding-dang*, adj., descriptive sound of jingling jade.

珂 31A.00-3

ke.

N. (1) A white semi-precious stone. (2) A decoration on harness.

珂羅版 *keluorbaan*, n., (translit.) collotype.

珂雪 *keshyuee*, (LL) adj., snow-white.

瑜 31A.00-8

yur.

[Usu. printed 瑜]

N. Excellent jade or its luster: 瑕不掩瑜 the flaws do not detract from the jade's essential beauty—blemishes do not detract man's greatness; 瑕瑜俱見 see both its good and bad points.

瑜伽 *yurchier*, n., yoga.

琤 31A.00-9

cheng.

Adj. Descriptive of jangling (of jade), twanging (of string) gurgling (of flowing water).

珩 31A.00-9

herng.

N. A horizontal piece of jade in dress.

§31A.01 (王/小)

琳 31A.01-1

lirn.

琳琅 *lirnlarng*, (1) n., beautiful jade; sound of jade; (2) adj., resplendent: 琳琅滿目 (of multitude of beautiful things) dazzle the eye.

珠 31A.01-1

ju.

N. (1) (*-tz*) A pearl, a bead: 珍珠

pearl; 養珠 culture pearl; 珠寶 *-baau*↓; 珠簾 bead curtains; 珠履 bead shoes; 珠圓翠繞 surrounded by ladies decorated with pearls and jade; 念珠 to finger the beads of rosary in prayer; 珠圓玉潤 a round voice and jade-like skin; 珠喉 a round feminine voice; 魚目混珠 a fish eye passes as pearl. (2) A bead-like thing, eye pupil: 眼珠 eye pupil; 有目無珠 "eye without pupil"—(derog.) of stupid people who do not know a good thing when they see it; 淚珠 drops of tears; 妙語如珠 pearls of wisdom, sparkling sayings; 彈珠 playing marble.

珠寶 *jubaau*, n., jewelry: 珠寶店 jewelry shop; 珠寶商 jeweller.
珠蚌 *jubahng*, n., mother-of-pearl.
珠粉 *jufeen*, n., pearl powder, used as tonic.
珠花 *juhua*, n., hair decoration of pearl.
珠還 *ju-huarn*, phr., 珠還合浦 (allu.) restoration of pearl industry to place 合浦; (fig.) restoration of original condition; recovery of lost article.
珠戶 *juhuh*, n., pearl divers.
珠璣 *juji*[1], n., pearl and jade; 滿腹珠璣 (fig.) sparkling ideas in writing.
珠鷄 *juji*[2], n., quail (also called 珍珠鷄).
珠江 *jujiang*, n., The Pearl River, the third longest in China.
珠蘭 *jularn*, n., (bot.) tree with fragrant yellow bead-like seeds, *Chloranthus inconspicuus*, used for scenting tea.
珠母 *jumuu*, n., mother-of-pearl.
珠算 *jusuahn*, n., the abacus; art of using it, dist. 筆算 arithmetic with pen or pencil.
珠胎 *jutai*, n., human embryo in woman's body.
珠翠 *ju-tsueih*, n., pearls and jade decorations.

璨 31A.01-2

tsahn.

Adj. Bright, scintillating (also wr. 燦).

璪 31A.01-4

tzaau.

N. (AC) silk tassels threaded with jades hanging from a coronet.

璟 31A.01-4

jiing.

N. The luster of gems.

琛 31A.01-6

chen.

N. (LL) a treasure.

珎 31A.01-9

jen.

[Pop. of 珍 31A.91]

璵 31A.01-9

suoo.

[Var. of 瑣 31A.80]

§ 31A.02 (王/㐅)

球 31A.02-1

chiour.

N. (1) (-'*l*) A ball, a ball game: 足球 football; 籃球 basketball; 排球 volleyball; 網球 tennis; 羽毛球 badminton; 保齡球 bowling; 高爾夫球 golf; 棒球, 壘球 baseball; 鉛球 shot put; 打球 play ball; 拍球 hit ball with racket; 踢球 kick ball; 滾球 dribble; 曲棍球(短柄) hockey; (長柄) lacrosse. (2) A sphere: 地球 the globe, the earth: 球半徑 *-bahnjihng*, 球面 *-miahn*↓; 日球, 月球 the sun, the moon; 星球 a star; 花球, 綵球 a silk festoon; 繡球 an embroidered ball. (3) (AC) jade; jade-stone of a certain musical pitch (玉磬).

球半徑 *chiourbahnjihng*, n., (math.) radius.
球場 *chiourchaang*, n., football field; basketball, handball or tennis court, baseball diamond.
球隊 *chiourdueih*, n., a ball team.
球房 *chiourfarng*, n., a poolroom.
球竿 *chiourgan*, n., hockey stick, golf club.
球根 *chiourgen*, n., bulbous root of a plant.
球徑 *chiourjihng*, n., diameter.
球莖 *chiourjing*, n., bulbous underground stalk.
球面 *chiourmiahn*, n., (math.) surface of sphere.
球迷 *chiourmir*, n., a ball game (baseball, etc.) fan.
球拍 *chiourpai*, n., a racket.
球賽 *chioursaih*, n., a ball match.
球鞋 *chiourshier*, n., tennis shoes; other shoes or boots for games.
球心 *chiourshin*, n., (math.) center of sphere.
球形 *chiourshirng*, n.. spheroid; adj., spherical.
球衣 *chiouryi*, n., jacket for different games (as tennis, etc.).
球員 *diouryuarn*, n., player of a ball team.

璩 31A.02-2

chyur.

N. (1) (AC) an earring. (2) A surname.

琢 31A.02-3

juor.

V.t. To chisel, to grind, esp. jade; 琢玉 grind jade; 雕琢 to chisel and carve, also to embellish unnecessarily; 雕章琢句 write in ornate style.

琢磨 *juormor*, v.i., to polish by slow painful work; to mold and polish character; to study by hard grind.

環 31A.02-4

huarn.

N. (1) A bracelet: 玉環 jade bracelet. (2) A ring-shaped object of any material; 耳環 earring. (3) A surname.

Adv. Around: 環遊世界 tour around the world; 環拜 to make a circling movement and bow to all guests; 環列 stand around; 環視 look around gen. situation; 環堵 surrounding walls; 環堵蕭然 in a cold, bare room; 燕瘦環肥 of two anc. beauties, 趙飛燕 was thin, and 楊玉環(貴妃) was plump.

環球 *huarnchiour*, adj. & adv., around the world (also wr. 寰).
環海 *huarnhaai*, adv., (1) along the coast; (2) within the encircling seas.
環境 *huarnjihng*, n., environment, material background: 環境不同 one's background is different; 環境關係 factors of environment.
環佩 *huarupeih*, n., formerly, jade hangings on girdle.
環繞 *huarurauh*, adv., circle round: 環繞一週 circle round once.

瓌 31A.02-6

guei.
[Interch. 瑰]

N. A Precious stone: 瓌寶.

琅 31A.02-6

larng.
[Pop. 瑯]

N. A surname.

琅當(璫) *larngdang*, n., (1) (=鋃鐺) fetters, shackles: 琅璫入獄 be fettered and thrown into prison; (2) a tinkling sound.
琅玕 *larnggan*, n., a kind of white carnelian.
琅琅 *larnglarng*, n., a tinkling sound.

瓈 31A.02-9

lir.
[Var. of 璃 31A.42]

§ 31A.10 (王/十)

琫 31A.10-1

beeng.

N. (AC) decoration on knife carried on girdle.

瑋 31A.10-2

weei.

N. Valuable jade: 瑋玉 rare treasure.

璘 31A.10-2

lirn.

N. Luster of jade.

玕 31A.10-3

gan.

N. See 琅玕 31A.02

珥 31A.10-3

eel.

N. (1) Earring of jade, pearl or similar decorations. (2) (AC) writing brush, sable tail, etc. stuck on side of hat.

璋 31A.10-6

jang.

N. An anc. jade ornament; a jade plaything: 弄璋 (LL, from AC allu.) give birth to a boy (given jade to play with; if a girl, given tile to play with).

§ 31A.11 (王/土)

珪 31A.11-1

guei.

N. Anc. form of 圭.

瑾 31A.11–2

jiin (also *jihn*).

N. A beautiful gem.

璀 31A.11–2

tsueei.

璀璨 *tsueeitsahn*, adj., lustrous, gleaming (jade, pearls, etc.).
璀璀 *tsueirtsueei*, adj., ditto.

玨 31A.11–3

jyuer.
[Var. 珏]

N. Two joined pieces of jade.

理 31A.11–4

lii.

N. (1) Reason, what is right, reasonable, and proper: 道理 reason; 天理 divine law, law of nature; 公理 justice; 情理 justifiability, reasonableness; 不近情理 unreasonable; 合理 conforming to reason; 講理 reasonable in speech or action, to weigh the pros and cons; 入情入理 perfectly logical and reasonable; 無理取鬧 refuse to listen to reason; 理直氣壯 self-confident on the strength of one's being right; 理所當然, 理當如此 it's only right and proper; 不可理喻 will not listen to reason; 據理力爭 try to convince one's opponent with an argument; 理屈詞窮 have nothing more to say on realizing one's own shaky stand; 理虧 (of actions, arguments, etc.) indefensible; 理短 ditto; 於理不合 improper and unreasonable; 理應, 理合 duty-bound, as a matter of course, the proper course to take is . . .; 理由 *-your* ↓; 原理 basic principles; 定理 axioms. (2) Line, grain, vein, line of thought: 條理 logical arrangement; 條理分明 (writing) clearly arranged; 有條有理 properly and logically arranged, orderly; 分理 proper disposition; 肌理 skin texture; 腠理 ditto; 紋理 veins, wood grain, arrangement of lines and curves; 文理 literary style, diction; 文理清順 reads smoothly. (3) The rationale of things: 物理(學) physics; 事理 the wherefore and why of things; 學理 academic theories; 心理(學) a mental state; 心理學 psychology; 地理 geography; 論理 logic; 倫理 ethics; 理學 *-shyuer* ↓. (4) The natural sciences: 理科 *-ke*, 理工 *-gung* ↓. (5) (AC) prison official, a judicial officer. (6) A surname.

V.t. (1) Take notice of, pay attention to: 不理 ignore; 不要理他 take no notice of him; 要理不理 attend to (person, duty) half-heartedly; 理會 *-hueih* ↓. (2) To polish (gems), hence, to clean up, regulate, arrange, repair, put in proper order, manage: 修理 to mend; (sl.) (of police methods) to give s.o. the works; 清理 clear up (desk, drawer, room, books, etc.); 整理 readjust, rearrange; 料理 handle, manage; 自理 take care of (s.t.) oneself; 理髮 *-faa* ↓; 理頭髮 to comb hair; 梳理 (lit.) to comb hair, (fig.) straighten out or arrange (things, data) in proper order; 理東西 clean up things; 理書包 clean up the book bag (of a schoolchild); 理行李 pack up baggage; 理理屋子 to tidy up the rooms a bit; 理衣服 adjust clothing. (3) To manage: 理喪事 manage a funeral; 理財 *-tsair* ↓; 處理 deal or cope with; 治理 to rule or manage; 署理, 代理 act for (s.o.); 辦理 do, carry out; 掌理 be in control of; 管理 manage; 監理 supervise; (總)經理 (general) manage(r); 綜理 oversee; 總理 exercise general supervision over, a director general, premier; 助理 an assistant; 副理 a deputy manager; 襄理 an assistant manager; 協理 a deputy assistant manager; 理事 *-shyh* ↓. (4) To review, go over (lessons): 理書 review the lessons; 理一理功課 review the school work. (5) Realize, appreciate, understand: 理會, 理解 *-hueih*, *-jiee* ↓.

Adj. Orderly, well-regulated: 則天下理焉 (AC) then the country will be well-governed.

理兒 *liee'l*, n., reason: 說不出理兒來 cannot explain the reason why.
理髮 *lirfaa*, (1) v.i., to cut hair; (2) n., haircut: 理髮師, 理髮匠 a barber, hairdresser; 理髮店 a barbershop; beauty salon.
理工 *lii-gung*, n., (departments, schools of) science and engineering.
理化 *lii-huah*, (1) n., physics and chemistry; (2) v.i., (LL) to govern and educate the people.
理會 *liihueih*, v.t., (1) realize, appreciate, be clear about, understand (a situation, explanation); (2) pay attention to, receive (a visitor or friend): 不加理會 ignore (s.o. or s.t.); 別理會他 don't pay any attention to him; 他一點也不理會 he doesn't heed it at all; (3) take care of, deal with, arbitrate or mediate, take measures or steps to; (4) (AC) conform to.
理家 *lii-ja*, v.i., manage domestic affairs: 她很會理家 she is a very good housewife.
理障 *liijahng*, n., (Budd.) hindrances to truth.
理解 *lirjiee*, n. & v.t., apprehend, -sion, comprehend, -sion.
理智 *liijyh*[1], n. & adj., the rational (faculty) esp. as opp. 情感 emotions.
理致 *liijyh*[2], n., interesting point or development.
理科 *liike*, n., the physical sciences.
理亂 *lii-luahn*, (1) n., order or lack of it; (2) v.i., bring order out of chaos.
理路 *liiluh*, n., the logical se-

quence of things or events: 理路分明 clear line of reasoning.

理論 *liiluhn*, (1) n., theorizing, theories (opp. 實驗, 實行 experimentation, practical application): 理論上 theoretically; 空談理論 empty speculation; 理論與事實相左 conflict between theory and practice; 理論化學 theoretical chemistry; 理論科學 theoretical sciences; (2) v.i., argue, debate, discuss: 我要和他理論 I'll have to straighten out the matter with him.

理門(兒) *liimern(-mer'l)*, n., formerly, a sect against opium and drinking.

理想 *lirshiaang*, n. & adj., ideal: 理想與事實 ideal and reality; 理想主義 idealism; 理想家 an idealist; 理想化 to idealize; 理想上 in theory, ideally; 合乎理想 be ideal; 最理想的人物 most ideal choice for the job; 眞太理想了 really perfect, ideal.

理性 *liishihng*, n., (1) rational faculty; (2) reasonableness.

理事 *liishyh*; (1) n., a director (of firm, organization); 理事會 board of directors; 理事長 chairman of the board (of directors); (2) v.t., to direct (business operations, etc.).

理學 *liishyuer*, n., (1) the moral theories of the Suhng Neo-Confucian scholars; (2) 理學士 a bachelor of science.

理睬 *lirtsaai*, v.t., take notice of, pay attention to, heed the presence of (s.o.).

理財 *lii-tsair*, v.i., administer financial affairs: 理財家 a financier.

理由 *liiyour*, n., reasons, arguments for or against: 說不出理由 cannot give the reasons; 發展的理由 reason for the development.

斑 31A.11-6

ban.

[Dist. 班 ↓]

N. A spot (on leopard's skin); 窺見一斑 see segment of a whole.

Adj. Motley-colored, spotted: 斑色 variegated colored; 斑鬢 grey haired, grey-templed.

斑斑 *banban*, adj., spotted; of variegated design.

斑白, 斑駁 *banbor*, adj., motley, chopped in appearance.

斑點 *bandiaan*, n., spots, dots.

斑疹 *banjeen*, n., a kind of measles.

斑鳩 *banjiou*, n., turtledove.

斑竹 *banjur*, n., bamboo bearing black spots.

斑斕 *banlarn*, adj., of variegated colors; rich in hues.

斑馬 *banmaa*, n., zebra.

斑蝥 *banmaur*, (also wr. 盤蝥, 班貓) n., *Cicindela chinensis*, a poisonous striped fly, the Chinese cantharis.

斑銅礦 *banturng-kuahng*, n., (min.) bornite.

斑紋 *banwern*, n., striped pattern, wood grain.

班 31A.11-9

ban.

[Dist. 斑]

N. (1) Class in school, workers' team: 高班, 低班 upper class, lower class; 早班, 晚班, 夜班 morning, afternoon, night class. (2) Scheduled unit of work: 輪班 on duty by turn; 排班 arrange(d) team of work; 這班機 this flight (of airplane), 這班火車 this train; 下班 next flight, train; 班次 number of train or flight; 站班, 值班 on duty. (3) A surname: 班門弄斧 phr., (derog.) foolish display of wooden axe in front of famous carpenter's (魯班) home.

V.t. (1) To call back troops: 班師. (2) To spread about: 班荊道故 (AC allu.) spread on the grass and chat of old times.

班班 *banban*, (AC) adj., in good order; n., (AC) rumble of carts.

班駁 *banbor*, adj., grey (hair); motley-colored; chopped in appearance (paint, bark) (also 斑白, 頒白).

班輩 *banbeih*, n., rank, status seniority.

班禪 *Bancharn*, n., the Panchan Lama (of Tibet).

班底(兒) *bandii('l)*, n., the supporting cast in play; inner group of people to assist political leader.

班房 *banfarng*, n., employee's quarters in office of high officials (for transmission of messages, etc.).

班長 *banjaang*, n., leader of class; patrol leader.

班級 *banjir*, n., school class.

班子 *bantz*, n., actors of one troupe (戲班).

班位 *ban-weih*, n., scheduled or arranged order (of seating, etc.).

§ 31A.21 (王/ㄴ)

瑤 31A.21-9

yaur.

N. Fine jade: 瑤琴 jade-decorated stringed instrument.

Adj. (1) White like jade. (2) Much valued: 瑤函, 瑤箋 your esteemed letter. (3) Associated with fairyland or abode of immortals: 瑤臺, 瑤草, 瑤池 *-tair*, *-tsaau*, *-chyr* ↓.

瑤池 *Yaurchyr*, n., abode of immortals, associated with mythical 西王母 fairy mother goddess.

瑤華 *yaurhua*, (1) n., pure jade; (2) adj., (AC) pure, glistening like jade; esteemed.

瑤臺 *yaurtair*, n., jade terrace, esp. of immortals.

瑤草 *yaurtsaau*, n., a plant of fairyland.

§ 31A.22 (王/丨)

环 31A.22-3

huarn.

[Abbr. of 環 31A.02]

瑯 31A.22-6

larng.

[Pop. of. 琅]

N. 琺▵瑯 (pr. *larn*) 31A.93.

§ 31A.30 (王/一)

瑳 31A.30-8

tsuoo.

Adj. (AC) lustrous (jade); fresh, bright, smiling.

§ 31A.40 (王/口)

玷 31A.40-2

diahn.

N. A flaw in jade, in character.

V.i. To disgrace: 沾汚, 沾辱 *-wu*, *-ruu* ↓.

沾辱 *diahnruu* (*-ruh*), v.t., to besmear (person's reputation); to humiliate.

沾汚 *diahnwu*, v.t., to besmear, cast a stain upon character; humiliate (a virgin).

璐 31A.40-4

luh.

N. A kind of jade.

琀 31A.40-8

hahn.

N. Jade kept in mouth of a dead person when buried.

瑲 31A.40-8

chiang.

瑲瑲 *chiangchiang*, adj., descriptive of jingling sound of jade.

珞 31A.40-9

luoh.

N. See 瓔▵珞 31A.93.

§ 31A.41 (王/図)

璿 31A.41-2

shyuarn.

[Var. of 璇 31A.83]

璫 31A.41-2

dang.

N. (1) Jewelry, esp. earring: 耳璫. (2) Eunuch, from 貂璫 eunuchs' gold headdress.

瑠 31A.41-3

liour.

[Var. of 琉 31A.70]

瑁 31A.41-4

meih.

N. (1) (AC) ceremonial jade. (2) 玳瑁 *daih-*, tortoise shell.

珀 31A.41-9

poh.

N. See 琥▵珀 31A.70.

瑙 31A.41-9

naau.

N. 瑪▵瑙 See 31A.50.

§ 31A.42 (王/冈)

瑚 31A.42-1

hur.

N. See 珊△瑚 31A.42.

瑚 璉 *hurliarn*, n. (AC) vessels of grain at ancestral temple; hence 瑚璉之器 (AC) a person of high caliber.

瑞 31A.42-2

rueih.

N. (1) A jade tablet used as a token of authority and good faith in anc. times. (2) A good omen: 祥瑞 a happy omen; 吉瑞 signs of good luck; 人瑞 a venerable old man (woman), usu. a benefactor of mankind.

Adj. Auspicious: 瑞兆 auspicious portents; 瑞雪 *-shyuee* ↓; 瑞氣 celestial phenomena portending peace and prosperity.

瑞 典 *Rueihdiaan*, n., Sweden.
瑞 符 *rueih-fur*, n., (AC) a tally used for ordering troop movements.
瑞 禾 *rueih-her*, n., auspicious cluster of rice (also 嘉禾).
瑞 麥 *rueih-maih*, n., auspicious tassels of wheat.
瑞 腦 *rueihnaau*, n., (med.) Borneo camphor (also 冰片, 瑞龍腦).
瑞 相 *rueih-shiahng*, n., (1) (Phrenology) facial signs portending good luck or luck in gen.; (2) (Budd.) auspicious signs.
瑞 仙 桃 *rueihshian-taur*, n., (bot.) the peach, *Prunus persica*.
瑞 香 *rueihshiang*, n., (bot.) the winter daphne, *Daphne odora*.
瑞 士 *Rueihshyh*, n., Switzerland.
瑞 雪 *rueih-shyuee*, n., (1) (euphem.) winter snow; (2) (Chin. med.) roots of *Tricho-santhes japonica*.
瑞 草 *rueih-tsaau*, n., a grass which, owing to its rarity, is regarded as a lucky portent.

珊 31A.42-4

shan.

珊 篤 寧 *shanduhnirng*, n., (translit.) santonin.
珊 瑚 *shanhur*, n., coral; 珊瑚島 coral island; 珊瑚礁 coral reef.

琱 31A.42-4

diau.

V.i. & t. To carve (jade), (AC var. of 雕).

璃 31A.42-6

lir.
[Var. 瓈]

N. See 琉△璃 31A.70; 玻△璃 31A.82.

§ 31A.50 (王/⺄)

璹 31A.50-1

daih.
[Var. of 玳 31A.71]

瑪 31A.50-5

maa.

瑪 瑙 *marnaau*, n., (min.) agate, cornelian.

琇 31A.50-9

shiouh.

N. A jade-like stone.

§ 31A.63 (王/丶)

玲 31A.63-8

lirng.
[Usu. printed as 玲]

Adj. Sound of jade, see comp. ↓.

玲 瓏 *lirnglurng*, adj., (1) (also 玲玲 *-lirng*, 玲玎 *-ding*, 玲琅 *-larng*) all descriptive of jangling of jade; (2) (of art objects) 玲瓏可愛, 小巧玲瓏 lovely, cleverly carved; (of persons) small and pretty; 心竅玲瓏 very bright-minded.

§ 31A.70 (王/乚)

珧 31A.70-2

yaur.

N. See 江△珧 63A.30.

琥 31A.70-2

huu.

琥 珀 *huupoh*, n., amber.

玩 31A.70-3

wahn (**warn.*).

N. (1) Curios: 古玩 ditto; 珍玩 valuable curios. (2) (**warn*) A game: 玩兒 *-war'l* ↓.

V.i. (**warn*) To play, have fun with, fondle, enjoy oneself: 玩笑, 玩賞 *-shiauh*, *-shaang* ↓; 玩月 enjoy the moon; 玩雪 enjoy the snow.

V.t. To fool with, dicker with (law), take lightly: 玩忽 *-hu*, 玩法 *-faa*, 玩世 *-shyh*[1] ↓.

玩 法 *wahn-faa*, v.i., to juggle with the law.

玩 好 *wahn-hauh*, n., favorite pastime, hobby.

玩 忽 *wahnhu* (*warn-*), v.t., to ignore.

玩 話 **warnhuah*, n., a joke, an empty promise.

玩 具 **warnjyuh*, n., a toy.

玩 兒 **war'l*, n., a trick, a pastime, a joke, an amusement: 不是玩兒的 not to be fooled with—i.e., will have grave consequences.

玩 弄 *wahnluhng* (*warn-*), v.t., to play with (person), to fondle (art object).

玩 偶 **warn-oou*, n., a toy figurine.

玩(兒)票 *warn*(*war'l*)*piauh*, v.i., (1) to sing Chin. opera as amateur or as hobby; (2) to sing without pay.

玩 賞 **warnshaang*, v.t., to enjoy (moon, flowers, etc.).

玩 笑 **warnshiauh*, (1) n., s.t. done for fun; (2) v.i., 開玩笑 play jokes upon (person); to play and relax.

玩 習 *wahnshir*, v.t., to study and slowly appreciate (history, etc.).

玩 耍 **warnshuaa*, n. & v.i., to play, to relax; relaxation, pastime.

玩 世 *wahn-shyh*[1], phr., 玩世不恭 to live dangerously or in defiance of conventions.

玩 視 *wahnshyh*[2] (or **warn-*), v.t., to take lightly, ignore (laws, statutes).

玩 味 *wahnweih* (**warn-*), v.t., to appreciate slowly (a profound saying).

玩 物 (1) **warnwuh*, n., a toy; (2) (*wahn-*) phr., 玩物喪志 to play through life and have no serious ambition.

玩 意 兒 **warnyeh'l*, n., (1) a toy; (2) s.t. interesting; (3) a trifle, a little thing: 小玩意兒 just a little trifle.

玩 泄 *wahnyih*, v.i., (AC) to spend life in pleasures.

琨 31A.70-4

kun.

N. Beautiful jade.

現 31A.70-4

shiahn.

N. Cash: 現金 *-jin*[2] ↓; 兌現 pay cash on check, (fig.) redeem promise; 貼現 discount on rate of exchange; 付現 pay cash.

V.i. & t. To show, become visible, be revealed: 現了原形 reveal original shape (snake-spirit, etc.); 現出來 appear, be visible, (slip) shows; 出現 (comet, anything) appear; 呈現, 顯現 present (flaws, symptoms, etc.); 表現 to express, -ion.

Adj. (1) Now, present, current: 現在 *-tzaih*; 現代 *-daih* ↓; 現務 current duty; 現役 (soldiers) in active service; 現狀 *-juahng* ↓; 現場 on the spot; 現職 present post, office; 現值, 現價 current value, price. (2) Available in goods or money: 現貨 stock on hand; 現錢 *-chiarn*[2] ↓.

Adv. Immediately: 現賣 cash sale; 現買現賣 straight cash deal; 現吃現做 (food) freshly prepared as ordered; 現用現買 buy as one needs for the day; 現官現管 in the grip of bureaucracy; 現存 amount in current account; 現有 there is (are) now.

現 報 *shiahn-bauh*, n., see *-shyh*[1] ↓.

現成(兒) *shiahncherng'l*, adj., ready-made (answer), immediately available without trouble: 吃現成飯 have a living without any work; 說現成話 answer with stock phrases.

現 前 *shiahnchiarn*[1], adv., at present, before one's eyes.

現 錢 *shiahnchiarn*[2], n., cash (payment): 現錢交易 cash deal.

現 期 *shiahnchir*, adv., for the time being; during that time.

現 出 *shiahn-chu*, v.i. & t., show, reveal, grow: 現出毛病 (machines) show trouble of operation.

現 代 *shiahndaih*, (1) n., contemporary era, modern age; (2) adj., contemporary.

現 今 *shiahnjin*[1], adv., now, nowadays, at the present juncture.

現 金 *shiahn-jin*[2], n., cash reserve.

現 狀 *shiahn-juahng*, n., present conditions (of city, education, justice, etc.).

現 款 *shiahn-kuaan*, n., cash.

現 露 *shiahn-luh*, v.i. & t., to show, reveal.

現 弄 *shiahn'nung*, v.i., to show off.

現 批 *shiahn-pi*, n. & v.i., wholesale purchase on cash.

現 任 *shiahnrehn*, adj. & adv., current office; currently.

現 身 *shiahn-shen*, n., (1) (Budd.) the present body of flesh; (2) different manifestations of Buddha, representing his different capacities: 現身說法 Buddha bodily appeared and taught; (fig.) personally appear (at meetings, etc.).

現 生 *shiahn-sheng*, n., (Budd.) the present incarnation.

現下 *shiahnshiah*, adv., see *-tzaih* ↓.

現象 *shiahnshiahng.*, n., (1) phenomenon; (2) see *-juahng* ↑.

現行 *shiahnshirng*[1], adj., current (prices, statutes, customs, etc.).

現形 *shiahn-shirng*[2], (1) v.i., to manifest in material body; (2) n., see *-juahng* ↑.

現世 *shiahn-shyh*[1], n., present generation or incarnation; 現世報 retribution in present life, not in future life.

現勢 *shiahn-shyh*[2], n., present situation.

現時 *shiahnshyr*[1], (1) n., the present time; (2) adv., at present.

現實 *shiahnshyr*[2], (1) n., present reality; (2) adj., practical, realistic: 這個人眞現實 this man is very realistic; 現實主義 realism; 現實主義者 n., a realist.

現在 *shiahntzaih*, (1) n., the present time; (2) adv., at present now: 現在怎麽樣了 how is (person, thing) now?

現眼 *shiahn-yaan*, adj., shameful (affair, condition).

現銀 *shiahn-yirn*, n., cash (silver).

珮 31A.70-4

peih.

N. A jade ornament worn on girdle.

玘 31A.70-5

chii.

N. (AC) a jade pendant.

琉 31A.70-6

liour.

[Var. 瑠, 璢]

琉球 *liourchiour*, n., the Ryukyu Islands.

琉璃 *liour'lir*, n., (1) glass; (2) glazed color tile: 琉璃瓦; (3) coll. for dragonfly; 琉璃球兒 *--chiour'l*, chandelier, also a very smart person, a slippery fellow; 琉璃廠 section in Peking, formerly, famous for book shops.

瓏 31A.70-6

lurng.

瓏璁 *lurngtsung*, adj., (1) jangling sound of jade or metal; (2) (of hair) fluffy; (3) (of wood) luxuriant and green (also wr. 蘢葱); (4) hazy (light of dawn).

琬 31A.70-6

waan.

琬圭 *waanguei*, n., jade with soft luster.

琬琰 *warnyaan*, n., ditto; (AC fig.) the soft mature character of a gentleman.

瑰 31A.70-9

*guei (*gueih).*

N. (1) A kind of jasper. (2) (-**gueih*) 玫瑰 a rose.

Adj. Extraordinary, admirable: 瑰麗 *-lih*, 瑰異 *-yih*, 瑰岸 *-ahn* ↓.

瑰岸 *guei-ahn*, adj., (of a person's appearance) stately, imposing, stalwart.

瑰麗 *gueilih*, adj., elegant.

瑰異 *gueiyih*, adj., preeminent.

§ 31A.71 (王/尢)

珉 31A.71-5

mirn.

N. Name of a jade-like stone.

琖 31A.71-7

jaan.

N. A carved jade cup.

琙 31A.71-7

jen.

N. Semi-precious stone.

玳 31A.71-9

daih.

玳瑁 *daihmeih*, n., tortoise shell.

璣 31A.71-9

ji.

N. (1) A pearl not perfectly round in shape: 字字珠璣 (of litr. works) every phrase a gem. (2) 璇璣, 璿璣 an anc. astronomical instrument, armillary sphere.

§ 31A.72 (王/心)

璁 31A.72-9

tsung.

N. A precious stone.

§ 31A.80 (王/八)

瑱 31A.80-1

tiahn (also *jehn*).

N. Jade earring.

瓚 31A.80-1

tzahn.

N. (AC) a ceremonial ladle, used in libation.

琪 31A.80-2

chir.

N. A kind of jade: 琪花瑤草 jade flowers of fairy land; 琪樹 jade tree, also described as a tree whose branches hang down like willows and bear berries.

璜 31A.80-2

huarng.

N. A jade pendant of semi-circular shape.

瑣 31A.80-2

suoo.

[Dist. 鎖 81A.80]

N. A chain of jade: 瑣連環.

Adj. (1) Petty, trivial, insignificant: 瑣碎, 瑣細 *-sueih, -shih* ↓; 繁瑣 tedious, annoying. (2) Interlocked, of chain design: 瑣窗 *-chuang* ↓.

瑣窗 *suoochuang,* n., a form of lattice window with interlocked design.

瑣屑 *suooshieh,* n. & adj., petty trifles.

瑣細 *suooshih,* (1) n., trifles, details; (2) adj., small and tedious (work, things).

瑣事 *suooshyh,* n., trifles, sundry work to do.

瑣碎 *suoosueih,* adj., fragmentary, tedious, multitudinous (items, work); annoying, as a child is prone to small illnesses.

瑣瑣 *suorsuoo,* adj., trivial, piffling.

瑣聞 *suoowern,* n., sundry news or anecdotes, fragmentary records.

頊 31A.80-3

shyuh.

N. Personal name: 顓[A]頊 21S.80.

璵 31A.80-5

yur.

N. (AC) beautiful jade.

§ 31A.81 (王/人)

瑛 31A.81-2

ying.

N. Gem luster; translucent jade.

璞 31A.81-2

pur.

N. Uncarved jade; (fig.) original nature of man in Taoist philosophy (cf. 樸 10B.81)); 歸眞返璞 return to nature, preserve man's natural simplicity of character; 璞玉渾金 jade and gold in natural state, symbolic of beautiful untutored talent.

玦 31A.81-9

jyuer.

N. A semi-circular piece of jade.

玖 31A.81-9

jioou.

N. (1) A jade-like dark-hued stone. (2) Capital form of 九 (nine) in writing checks.

§ 31A.82 (王/乂)

玻 31A.82-2

bo.

玻璃 *bolir*, n., glass; used also to denote a variety of transparent material (nylon, cellophane, etc.); 玻璃版 *--baan*; n., photogravure; 玻璃窗 *--chuang*, n. glass window. 玻璃墊 *--diahn*, glass top for tables; 玻璃粉, *--feen*, jello; 玻璃磚 *--juan*, glass bricks; 玻璃紙 *--jyy*, cellophane; 玻璃杯 *--bei*, tumbler, a glass.

瑕 31A.82-5

shiar.

N. A flaw in jade: 瑕疵 *-tsy* ↓; 瑕瑜俱見 see what is perfect and what is not—(瑜 flawless jade).

瑕謫 *shiarjer*, n., (AC) flaws: 無瑕可謫 flawless.
瑕釁 *shiarshihn*, n., flaws, imperfections, cracks.
瑕疵 *shiartsy*, n., imperfections, minor faults.

玫 31A.82-9

meir.

玫瑰 *meir'guei* (*-gueih*), n., rose: 玫瑰紫 rose purple; 玫瑰露 rose wine; 玫瑰油 attar of rose petals.

瓊 31A.82-9

chyurng.
[Abbr. 琼]

N. Poetic synonym for "jade"; rare jade; symbolic of luxury: 瓊筵, 瓊宴 a luxurious dinner; 瓊樓玉宇 "towers of jade"—a fabulously rich residence.

瓊花 *chyurnghua*, n., a very rare flower now extinct.
瓊華 *chyurnghuar*, n., beautiful jade, symbolic of poetic talent.
瓊漿 *chyurngjiang*, n., (LL) excellent wine.
瓊玖 *chyurngjioou*, n., beautiful 「jade.
瓊林 *chyurnglirn*, n., collection of selected phrr. or sentences; 瓊林宴 formerly, dinner in honor of successful 進士 graduates.
瓊瑤 *chyurngyaur*, n., beautiful jade.

§ 31A.83 (王/〜)

璇 31A.83-6

shyuarn.

N. Fine jade: 璇室, 璇閨 a room, boudoir, decorated with jade; 璇宮 jade-decorated hall.

璇璣 *shyuarnji*, n., (astron.) armillary sphere; 璇璣圖 see 廻^Δ紋詩 41.83.

瑽 31A.83-9

tsung.

N. See 錚^Δ瑽 81A.00, tinkling of jade or metal.

§ 31A.91 (王/ノ)

璆 31A.91-5

chiour.

N. Beautiful jade: 璆然 jangling of jade.

珍 31A.91-8

jen.

N. (1) Rare valuables, treasure, what is highly prized, see Adj. ↓. (2) A delicacy in food: 山珍海味 delicacies from land and sea.

Adj. Rare, highly prized, valuable: 珍貴, 珍品 *-gueih*, *-piin* ↓; 珍本 rare edition; 珍禽異獸 rare birds and animals; attached to vbb. indicating esteem: 珍愛, 珍賞, 珍藏 *-aih*, *-shaang*, *-tsarng* ↓; 珍視 prize, cherish.

珍愛 *jen-aih*, v.t., love dearly, cherish.
珍寶 *jenbaau*, n., jewelery; rare treasures.
珍奇 *jenchir*, n., rare objects.
珍怪 *jenguaih*, n., ditto.
珍貴 *jengueih*(*-'guei*), adj., valuable, precious, priceless, of great value.
珍珠 *jenju*, n., pearl; 珍珠蘭 see 珠^Δ蘭 31A.01; 珍珠毛(兒) *--maur(e'l)*, skin of lamb embryo; 珍珠米 corn; 珍珠菜 a vegetable, *Lysimachia clethroides*.
珍重 *jenjuhng*, v.i. & t., to take good care (of health): 千萬珍重 please take good care of yourself.
珍品 *jenpiin*, n., a highly valued art object.
珍賞 *jenshaang*, v.t., to appreciate highly.
珍攝 *jensheh*, v.i., as in 善自珍攝, see *-juhng* ↑.
珍羞(饈) *jenshiou*, n., delicacy of food.
珍惜 *jenshir*, v.t., to cherish, love dearly.
珍藏 *jentsarng*, v.t., to keep (rare editions, art works) as of great value.

珍物 *jenwuh*, n., rare objects, also rare food.
珍聞 *jenwern.*, n., strange and interesting news.
珍異 *jenyih*, adj., rare, highly esteemed.

§ 31A.93 (王/く)

琺 31A.93-1

fah.
[Interch. 珐]

珐(琺)瑯 *fanhlarg*, n., cloisonné; enamel.

瓔 31A.93-4

ying.

瓔珞 *yingluoh*, n., jade necklace.

瑜 31A.93-8

yur.
[Printed form of 瑜 31A.00]

SECTION 31B

§ 31B.00 (石/丨)

磚 31B.00-1

juan.
[Pop. of 甎 10S.70]

硎 31B.00-3

shirng.

N. Whetstone.

碍 31B.00-4

aih.
[Pop. of 礙 31B.83]

砑 31B.00-5

yah.

V. t. To press (cloth, silks) in a mangle, to give a shining surface: 砑綾, 砑羅 silks pressed even between rollers.

砑光 *yahguang*, v. t. to roll even and give a shine; 砑光機 a calender, a mangling machine for pressing paper, silks.

§ 31B.01 (石/小)

硃 31B.01-1

ju.

N. Cinnabar, used as red pigment and medicine; hence red ink; 硃砂 *-sha* ↓.

硃筆 *jubii*, n., writing brush used for writing with red ink.
硃卷 *jujyuahn*, n., script or scroll in red ink; (Manchu Dyn.) red-ink copy of examination papers, made from black-ink copy written by candidates, to prevent favoritism by the judges.
硃批 *jupi*, n., documents containing the emperor's comments in red ink.
硃砂 *jusha*, n., cinnabar.
硃諭 *juyuh*, n., imperial decree.

碟 31B.01-2

dier.

N. (*-tz*, *'l*) Dinner plate, dish: 一碟蔬菜 a dish of vegetable.

磉 31B.01-3

saang.

N. Pedestal, base of pillar.

磔 31B.01-9

jer.

N. (Callig.) the right-hand slanting stroke.

V. t. (AC) to dismember criminal

for extreme crime: 磔於市.

礫 31B.01-9

lih.

N. Gravel, shingle: 瓦礫 broken tiles, rubble.

§ 31B.02 (石/ㇵ)

碾 31B.02-5

niaan.

N. Roller for grinding, crushing or husking, see 碾子 *-tz*↓; 藥碾子 a mortar and pestle.

V. t. To grind, crush, pound, polish or husk: 碾米 husk or polish rice; 碾碎 crush, grind or pound to small particles.

碾房 *niaanfarng*, n., a mill for milling or husking grain.
碾子 *niaantz*, n., a mill for husking grain or rice.

硠 31B.02-6

larng.

Adj. (LL) resounding: 磅硠 reverberating sounds of falling rocks; 磅硠 descriptive of the sounds of drum-beating or of falling stones bang.

碌 31B.02-9

luh.

Adj. (1) Rocky. (2) Busy: 忙碌 busily occupied; 勞碌 working without respite, very busy. (3) Mediocre, common: 庸碌 common: 碌碌庸才 very mediocre person. (4) Var. of 轆 10D.70.

碌碡 *luhdur*, n., stone roller for husking rice, crushing oats, etc.

§ 31B.10 (石/十)

磷 31B.10-2

lirn.

N. (Chem.) phosphorus (var. 燐).

磷氫 *lirnching*, n., (chem.) phosphines.
磷酐 *lirn-gan*, n., (chem.) phosphoric anhydride.
磷化氫 *lirnhuahching*, n., (chem.) hydrogen phosphide.
磷灰石 *lirnhueishyr*, n., (min.) apatite.
磷磷 *lirnlirn*, adj., (AC) rocks in water.
磷酸 *lirnsuan*, n., (chem.) phosphoric acid; 磷酸質 phosphate; chemical fertilizer; 磷酸鈣 *--gaih*, calcium phosphate; 磷酸亞鐵 *--yahtiee*, ferrous phosphorate.

砰 31B.10-3

peng.

N. "Bing, bang!" big noise such as roar of waves, rumble of thunder, crash of water, crackle of rifles, boom of guns.

砰宕 *pengdahng*, n., (LL) sound of water lapping against ships.
砰轟 *penghung*, n., (LL) rumble of thunder.
砰磕 *pengke*, n., (LL) crackle of thunder.
砰磅 *pengpang*, n., crash of water against rocks.
砰砰 *pengpeng*, n., sound of drums, crackle of rifles.

碎 31B.10-6

sueih.

N. Broken bits.

V.t. To break to pieces.

Adj. (1) Broken: 碎玻璃 broken glass: 碎金 gold crumbs; 寧爲玉△碎 see 31.11; 碎屑, 碎塊 *-shieh, -kuaih*↓. (2) Piecemeal, tedious, paltry: 瑣碎 disconnected, trifling (affairs), multifarious. (3) (AC of writing) too elaborate and dull.

碎步兒 *sueihbuh'l*, v.i., to hurry on in small steps.
碎塊 *sueihkuaih*, n., broken bits.
碎片 *sueihpiahn*, n., fragments, shrapnels.
碎小 *sueihshiaau*, n., (MC) family dependents.
碎屑 *sueihshieh*, n., broken bits.
碎修兒 *sueih-shiou'l*, v.i., make small repairs.
碎嘴子 *sueihtzueeitz*, n., a tedious talker.

碑 31B.10-9

bei.

N. A stone tablet: 墓碑 tombstone.

碑 版 *bei-baan*, n., see *-jih* ↓.
碑 額 *bei-er*, n., inscription at top of tablet.
碑 碣 *bei-jier*, n., stone inscription.
碑 記 *bei-jih*, n., inscriptions on a tablet, recording an event.
碑 誌 *bei-jyh*, n., ditto.
碑 林 *bei-lirn*, n., collection of anc. tablets housed in Si-an, Shensi.
碑 銘 *bei-mirng*, n., inscriptions on tablet.
碑 帖 *bei-tieh*, n., rubbings from ancient tablets, used as models of calligraphy.
碑 亭 *bei-tirng*, n., a pavilion housing a tablet.
碑 文 *bei-wern*, n., inscribed text on tablet.
碑 陰 *bei-yin*, n., the back face of a tablet.

§ 31B.11 (石/土)

硅 31B.11-1

guei.

N. (Chem.) silicon.

碓 31B.11-9

dueih.

N. Pestle for hulling rice; 碓臼 pestle and mortar; 水碓 water mill for hulling rice.

碓 頭 *dueihtour*, n., pestle.

確 31B.11-9

chyueh.

Adj. (1) Sure, definite, true: 確定 *-dihng* ↓; 的確 truly, really; 確耗, 確訊 definite news; 確證, 確據 definite evidence. (2) Accurate: 準確 accurate (news, etc.); 確論 an accurate and just opinion.

Adv. Definitely: 確實 *-shyr* ↓; 確信, 確認, 確知 definitely believe, recognize, know.

確 切 *chyueh-chieh*, adv., in earnest, factually (carry out, live up to, etc.).
確 定 *chyueh-dihng*, adj., definite and sure.
確 乎 *chyueh'hu*, adv., really: 確乎不錯 really not bad: 確乎不成問題 really is not a problem.
確 實 *chyueh-shyr*, adj. & adv., (1) definite, -ly; (2) really: 確實不錯 really not bad (very good).
確 鑿 *chyueh-tzuoh*, adj., definite, well-established (evidence).

§ 31B.20 (石/廿)

研 31B.20-3

yarn (**yahn*).

N. (**yahn*) Var. of 硯 ink slab.

V.i. & t. (1) To grind: 研究 grind into powder; 研碎 grind up; 研墨 grind ink. (2) To study: 研究, 研討 *-jiouh*, *-taau* ↓.

研 求 *yarnchiour*, v.t., to study, search for (truth).
研 覈 *yarnher*, v.t., (LL) to examine: 研覈是非 to weigh the *pros* and *cons*.
研 究 *yarnjiouh*, v.t., to study, do research; 研究院 institute for research; 研究所 department in a graduate school.
研 討 *yarntaau*, v.t., to study and discuss (problems); 研討會 seminar.

§ 31B.21 (石/乚)

磌 31B.21-2

kahn (**jen*).

N. (**jen*) (As var. of 砧) stone slab for beating laundry.

Adj. 磌碍 (AC) high, rugged (rocks).

砸 31B.21-5

tzar.

V. i. & t. (1) To smash, break, crush: 砸開 to force open; 砸開門 to burst open the door; 砸破 smash to pieces; 砸碎 pulverize, decimates; 砸壞 break and make unusable; 砸扁 crush flat; 砸爛 wreck, demolish; 砸死 batter to death. (2) To pound: 砸蒜(薑) to crush garlic (ginger). (3) Cause to accumulate: 錯過時機, 貨就砸到手裏了 if we miss the opportunity, the goods would become a part of the dead stock. (4) V.i., to foul up, usu. as vb. complement, meaning "fouled up": 説砸了 say s.t. wrong; 辦砸了 have fouled up s.t.; 唱砸了 sing badly; 砸鍋 *-guo* ↓.

砸 兌 *tzar'duei*, v. i., make sure: 你到底來不來, 要砸兌準了 please be sure whether you will be coming or not.
砸 鍋 *tzarguo*, v. i., fail in a task (work, assignment); 砸鍋槌兒 one who makes a mess of things.
砸 了 *tzar'le*, v.t., (p.p.) broken up: 這件事砸了 this matter has been broken up; 把碟子砸了 have dropped the plate and broken it.
砸 字 兒 *tzartzeh'l*, n., a defaced coin.

§ 31B.22 (石/丨)

砷 31B.22-2

shen.

N. (Chem.) arsenic.

碲 31B.22-6

dih.

N. (Chem.) tellurium.

斫 31B.22-9

juor.

V. t. To heck, chip (var. of 斵).

砟 31B.22-9

jah.

N. (*-tz, 'l*) 煤砟子 or 砟兒 coal cinders (usu. wr. 煤渣子 or 兒).

§ 31B.30 (石/一)

碴 31B.30-1

char.

N. (*-'l*) (1) Broken bits (of bone, glass): 鬍子碴兒 bits of beard which show after shaving. (2) (Coll.) thing: 提起那個碴兒 in regard to that thing. (3) Quarrel, dispute: 找碴兒 looking for faults to pick up quarrel; 我和他有個碴兒 we two have an old grudge to settle.

磕 31B.30-1

ke.

V. i. & t. To knock, bump: 磕破 knock to pieces; 磕著了 bump into (stone); see 磕頭 *-tour* ↓; 磕烟灰 knock the ashes from a pipe.

Adj. Descriptive of sound of hitting stone, drum beat: see 磕磕巴巴 *-kebaba* ↓.

磕磕巴巴 ***kekebaba***, v. i. & adj., to stutter; 磕磕絆絆 *--bahnbahn*, adj., (of road) uneven, difficult to walk on.

磕碰 ***kepehng***, n. & v. t., crack (in cups, etc.) caused by knocking; knock against.

磕膝蓋(兒) ***keshigaih(-gah'l)***, n., kneecap.

磕頭 ***ketour***, v. i., to kowtow (interch. 叩頭 *kouhtour*), i.e., knock head on the ground in kneeling position as a form of ceremonial greeting; to perform such ceremony to establish master-disciple relationship: 你給誰磕的頭 who is your master? or as sworn brother: 他們是磕過頭的; as a phrase, meaning "thanks": 先給你磕頭了 first let me thank you; 磕頭, 磕頭 thanks a lot! 磕頭蟲 (兒) (a) *Melanotus legatus*, an insect (=叩頭蟲); (b) a subservient fellow (ready to kowtow on every occasion).

磕牙 ***keyar***, v. i., to jabber, palaver, chat idly: 閒磕牙 or 磕打牙兒 indulge in gossiping at leisure; 別拿他磕打牙兒了 don't sit there prating and making fun of him (cf. 嗑 40A.30).

硜 31B.30-3

keng.

硜硜 ***kengkeng***, adj., hard and intractable like pebbles: 硜硜乎小人哉 (AC) such petty, small people!

磴 31B.30-3

dehng.

N. Stone steps on hill path.

碰 31B.30-8

pehng.
[Pop. form of 掽]

V. i. & t. (1) To run into, encounter, chance upon: 碰見老朋友 run into an old friend; 碰不着 didn't meet him. (2) Knock against, cause damage by collision: 碰破, 碰壞, 碰傷 knock and break (bowl, etc.); 碰撞 collide with another car or boat; 碰釘子, 碰一鼻子灰 knock against a nail with a bare hand, knock one's nose into ashes, i. e., receive serious rebuff in speaking to high personage; 碰鼻轉彎, to change after getting one's finger burned; 碰壁 run into a blind alley. (3) To have a try at it: 碰一碰, 碰運氣 try one's luck. (4) Run into bad luck: 碰了=碰釘子, see 2↑; make a mistake in opera singing or acting: 她碰了.

碰場 ***pehng-charng***, v. i., combine two meetings in one.

碰巧 ***pehngchiaau***, v. i., happen to, it happens that: 碰巧他不在家 he happened to be away.

碰面 ***pehng mihan***, v.i., meet

headlong.

碰頭 *pehngtour*, v. i., (dial.) meet (of friends); 碰頭好兒 enthusiastic applause of audience on actor's, actress's entrance to stage; enthusiastic reception of first novel, etc.

碰瓷兒 *pehngtsyr'l*, n., racketeer who claims damage by carrying broken porcelain and dropping it on encounter; one who tries to create an accident.

磋 31B.30-8

tsuo.

V. i. & t. (1) To grind, polish (jade, etc.): 磋磨 *-mor* ↓. (2) To examine, study or discuss carefully: 磋商 *-shang* ↓; 切磋 education as a gradual polishing process; 切磋琢磨 ditto.

磋磨 *tsuomor*, v. i., see V. i. & t. 2 ↑.

磋商 *tsuoshang*, v. i., to discuss together (negotiated matter, etc.).

§ 31B.32 (石/フ)

碜 31B.32-2

cheen.

Adj. (MC) indecent: 碜短命 (term of scolding) a wretch, scoundrel; 碜兒 (MC) indecencies.

矽 31B.32-9

shih.

N. (Chem.) silicon.

矽化氫 *shihhuah-ching*, n., (chem.) hydrogen silicide.

矽灰石 *shihhuei-shyr*, n., (min.) wollastonite, native calcium silicate.

矽鋅鑛 *shihshin-kuahng*, n., (min.) willemite, native silicate of zinc.

矽石 *shihshyr*, n., (min.) silica or silex.

矽酸 *shihsuan*, n., (chem.) acids of silicon: 矽酸鉀 potassium silicate; 矽酸鋁 aluminum silicate; 矽酸鈣 calcium silicate; 矽酸鈉 sodium silicate.

矽藻 *shihtzaau*, n., (bot.) a tiny water plant, *Diatomaceae* (also called 硅藻).

矽岩 *shihyarn*, n., (min.) quartz.

§ 31B.40 (石/口)

砧 31B.40-2

jen.

N. (1) A stone slab for laundry by beating with wooden club (杵): 砧板 slab and laundry club. (2) A chopping block: execution on chopping block with an axe (鑕).

砧板 *jenbaan*, n., kitchen chopping board (also wr. 椹板).

硌 31B.40-9

geh.

V. t. Cause pain through pressure exerted by bulging object: 這硬板牀，躺着好硌人 it's so painful to lie on this bed made of hard boards; 硌窩兒 eggs damaged through pressure.

§ 31B.41 (石/囚)

硇 31B.41-2

luu.

硇砂 *luusha*, n., (鹵砂, 硇砂) (min.) *Sal ammoniac.*

礌 31B.41-3

leih (**leir*).
[Var. 礧]

V. t. Push stones down from a height: 礌石相擊 throw stones on enemy.

礌石 *leihshyr* (**leir-*), n., stone missiles used by defenders of a besieged city.

磻 31B.41-9

parn.

N. Name of a river in Shensi.

硇 31B.41-9

naur.

硇砂 *naursha*, n., (min.) ammonia salt.

§ 31B.42 (石/冈)

硝 31B.42-2

shiau.

N. Saltpeter; niter (nitre); potassium nitrate used as a preservative: 硝皮子 leather treated with nitre.

硝鏹水 *shiauchiarng-shueei*, n., (chem.) nitric acid (=硝酸).
硝化甘油 *shiauhuah-ganyour*, n., nitroglycerine, an explosive.
硝基 *shiauji*, n., (chem.) nitro radical (e.g., 硝基苯 nitrobenzene).
硝石 *shiaushyr*, n., saltpeter or niter (potassium or sodium nitrate).
硝酸 *shiausuan*, n., nitric acid; 硝酸鈉 sodium nitrate; 硝酸鉀 potassium nitrate; 硝酸銀 silver nitrate, etc.

碉 31B.42-4

diau.

N. Fortified watch tower.

碉堡 *diaubaau*, n., military watch tower for outpost.
碉樓 *diaulour*, n., formerly, military watch tower.

硼 31B.42-4

perng.

N. (Chem.) boron, an element.

硼磕 *perngke*, n., sound of crashing water (var. of 砰△磕 31B.10).
硼砂 *perngsha*, n., (min.) borax.
硼酸 *perngsuan*, n., boric acid.

礪 31B.42-5

lih.

N. A whetstone.

V. t. (Of knives, etc.) sharpen: 砥礪 (lit.) sharpen any instrument with a cutting edge, (fig.) harden oneself by self-discipline: 砥礪德行.

确 31B.42-9

chyueh.

Adj. Rocky (soil, ground): 确犖, 磽确, 确瘠 ditto.

§ 31B.50 (石/冂)

砌 31B.50-1

chih (**chieh*).

N. (1) Brickwork. (2) Inlays: 雕欄玉砌 carved railings and jade inlays.

V. t. To build up in layers (as bricks): 砌牆 to build brick wall; 砌高 build up; 砌階 lay stone or brick steps; 堆砌字句 to pile up words and phrases in writing.

砌末(子) **chiehmoh('tz)*, n., (Chin. opera) stage equipment (also wr. 切).

碡 31B.50-1

dur.

N. See 碌△碡 31B.02.

碭 31B.50-4

dahng.

N. 碭山 place name in Kiangsu.

碣 31B.50-4

jier.

N. A commemorative stone tablet.

Adj. (Of mountain) towering, lofty.

碼 31B.50-5

maa.

N. (1) Number: 門牌號碼 house number; 數碼不對 the number is wrong. (2) Yard (length measure): 三碼 three yards.

碼頭 *maatour*, n., wharf, jetty.
碼子 *maatz*, n., (1) number, also 碼兒 *maa'l*; (2) (comm.) cash at bank.

磅 31B.50-6

bahng (**pang*).

N. (1) Pound, a measure of weight: 英磅 English pound (money); 磅量 weight in pounds. (2) *(*pang*) (AC) sound of rocks.

V. t. To weigh: 磅一磅 weigh it.

磅秤 *bahngchehng*, n., weighing scales in pounds.

§ 31B.63 (石/丶)

礁 31B.63-9

jiau.

N. (Half-) submerged rocks: 明礁 rocks rising above water; 暗礁 a reef, completely submerged rocks; 觸礁 (of ship) run aground, strike on a rock.

礁石 *jiau-shyr*, n., reef, sandbar.

§ 31B.70 (石/乚)

磽 31B.70-1

chiau.
[Var. 墝]

Adj. (Of land) barren, unproductive: 磽薄, 磽角 ditto.

砒 31B.70-2

pi.
[Var. 礔]

N. Arsenic, see 砒霜 *-shuang*↓.

砒霜 *pishuang*, n., arsenic.
砒石 *pishyr*, n., (min.) arsenopyrite.

硯 31B.70-4

yahn.

N. Ink slab, ink stone, the grinding of which seems to occupy writer's labors, hence 硯耕, 硯田 *-geng*, *-tiarn*↓; as symbol of study at school: 同硯 classmate "having shared the same ink slab"; 硯友, 硯兄, 硯弟 *-yoou*, *-shyung*, *-dih*↓.

硯池 *yahn-chyr*, n., depression in ink slab for collecting water.
硯滴 *yahndi*, n., a small container for dripping water on ink slab.
硯弟 *yahn-dih*, n., junior classmate.
硯耕 *yahn-geng*, v.t., (LL) to make a living by writing.
硯室 *yahn-shyh*, n., case for ink stone.
硯兄 *yahn-shyung*, n., senior classmate.
硯臺 (commonly 台) *yahn'tai*, n., an ink stone.
硯田 *yahn-tiarn*, n., (LL) writer's way of making a living, see *-geng*↓.
硯瓦 *yahnwaa*, n., ink stone.
硯友 *yahn-yoou*, n., classmate.

砈 31B.70-5

eh.
[Translit. of 鋨 81A.83]

硫 31B.70-6

liour.

N. Short for 硫磺 sulphur, *-huarng*↓.

硫化 *liourhuah*, n., (chem.) sulphide: 硫化氫 hydrogen sulphide; 硫化銀 silver sulphide; 硫化銅 copper sulphide; 硫化銨 ammonium sulphide; 硫化鋅 zinc sulphide; 硫化錫 stannic sulphide; 硫化鎘 cadmiun sulphide.
硫黃 *liourhuarng*, n., (chem.) sulphur (also wr. 硫磺); 硫磺酸 thionic acids.
硫酸 *liorsuan*, n., (chem.) sulphuric acid, sulphate; 硫酸鈉 sodium sulphate (Glauber's salt); 硫酸鈣 calcium sulphate; 硫酸鉀 potassium sulphate; 硫酸鉛 lead sulphate; 硫酸鉻 chromic sulphate; 硫酸銅 cupric sulphate; 硫酸銨 ammonium sulphate; 硫酸鋁 aluminum sulphate; 硫酸鋇 barium sulphate; 硫酸鋅 zinc sulphate; 硫酸鎂 magnesium sulphate; 硫酸鎳 nickel sulphate; 硫酸鐵 ferric sulphate; 硫酸治瘧鹼 quinine sulphate.

碗 31B.70-6

waan.
[Pop. of 椀, 盌]

N. A bowl (for rice, tea, soup, etc.).

矻 31B.70-9

kuh.

矻矻 *kuhkuh*, adj. & adv., busy, -ily: 終日矻矻 busily occupied all day.

砲 31B.70-9

pauh.
[Var. 礟, 礮]

N. (1) Cannon, gun, ballista: 開砲 open gunfire, (coll.) attack; 放砲 fire a gun; 大砲 big guns, artillery; 槍砲 arms and supplies in gen. (2) A chessman in Chin. chess.

砲兵 *pauhbing*, n., artillery man, unit.
砲車 *pauhche*, n., gun carriage.
砲彈 *pauhdahn*, n., shell.
砲轟 *pauh-hung*, v. t., to bombard with artillery.
砲火 *pauh-huoo*, n., cannon fire.
砲仗 *pauhjahng*, n., firecrackers.
砲戰 *pauh-jann*, n., artillery duel.
砲竹 *pauhjur*, n., firecrackers.
砲艦 *pauhjiahn*, n., gunboat; cruiser.
砲手 *pauhshoou*, n., gunner.
砲臺 *pauhtair*, n., fort.

§ 31B.71 (石/乜)

碱 31B.71-7

jiaan.
[Pop. of 鹼 21S.81]

砥 31B.71-9

dii (also *jyy*).

N. A grinding stone of fine quality.

V.i. 砥礪 To polish character by continuous association with friends, to urge each other in moral cultivation.

磯 31B.71-9

ji.

N. A submerged rock.

V. t. (AC) to obstruct (current).

§ 31B.80 (石/八)

磧 31B.80-1

chih.

N. Sand and gravel: 磧礫 piles of gravel; 磧壓 sediments of gravel.

磺 31B.80-2

huarng.

N. See 硫^A磺 31B.70↑.

碘 31B.80-2

diaan.

N. (Chem.) iodine.

碘酊 *diaanding*, n., tincture of iodine.
碘酒 *diarnjioou*, n., ditto.

碩 31B.80-3

shyr (re. pr. *shuoh*).

Adj. (1) Big, large, great: 碩大, 碩量, 碩果 *-dah, -liahng, -guoo*↓; 豐碩 (feast) rich; 壯碩, 肥碩 (person) bodily big, stout, corpulent, obese, robust, sturdy. (2) Great, scholarly: 碩儒, 碩士 *-rur, -shyh*↓; 碩畫 great plan; 碩交 (LL) a great friend.

碩大 *shyrdah*, n., large: 碩大無朋 exceptionally large.
碩輔 *shyr-fuu*, n., (LL) a great minister.
碩果 *shyr-guoo*, n., as in 碩果僅存 one of the few still left.
碩老 *shyr-laau*, n., an old venerable scholar.
碩量 *shyr-liahng*, n., great capacity.
碩人 *shyrrern*, n., (AC) (1) a beauty; (2) a hermit scholar.
碩儒 *shyrrur*, n., a great Confu. scholar.
碩士 *shyrshyh*, n., (1) a Master of Arts (M.A.); (2) (AC) great scholar.
碩學 *shyrshyuer*, n. & adj., scholar, -ly: 碩學通儒, 碩學鴻儒 a profound scholar.
碩望 *shyr-wahng*, n., (LL) great reputation.
碩言 *shyr-yarn*, n., (LL) a boast, exaggeration.

礦 31B.80-6

kuahng.
[Var. 鑛]

N. (1) A mine, ore pit: 金礦, 煤礦 gold mine, coal mine; 礦區 mining area; 開礦, 採礦 to open mines. (2) Ore, mineral.

礦產 *kuahngchaan*, n., mineral, mining products.
礦牀 *kuahngchuarng*, n., (geol.) ore bed.
礦泉 *kuahngchyuarn*, n., (geol.) mineral spring.
礦毒 *kuahngdur*, n., poisonous material or gas in mines.
礦工 *kuahnggung*, n., a miner.
礦坑 *kuahng-keng*, n., mining pit.
礦苗 *kuahngmiaur*, n., outcroppings of ore.
礦脈 *kuahngmoh*, n., a mineral vein, a lode.
礦山 *kuahngshan*, n., mining area, ore-producing hill.
礦石 *kuahngshyr*, n., an ore.
礦藏 *kuahngtsarng*, n., ore deposits.
礦層 *kuahngtserng*, n., strata of ores.

礦物 *kuahngwuh*, n., a mineral.
礦業 *kuahngyeh*, n., mining industry.

§ 31B.81 (石/人)

硤 31B.81–1

shiar.

N. 硤石 place name in Chekiang.

碳 31B.81–2

tahn.
[Anc. var. 炭]

N. (Chem.) carbon, a chemical element.

碳化 *tahnhuah*, n. & v. i., (chem.) carbonize, -zation; 碳化氫 hydrocarbons; 碳化水 carbonic water; 碳水化合物 carbohydrate; 碳化鈣 calcium carbide.
碳酸 *tahnsuan*, n., (chem.) carbonic acid; 碳酸氣 carbonic acid gas; 碳酸鈣 calcium carbonate; 碳酸鈉 sodium carbonate or soda; 碳酸鹽 carbonate.

砍 31B.81–9

kaan.

V. t. (1) To chop down, off: 砍下來 chop down; 砍成兩半 chop into two halves; 砍斷 cut down; 砍腦袋 chop off one's head. (2) Hit with brick, rock: 拿磚頭砍人 hit s. o. with bricks.

砍伐 *kaanfar*, v. t., to chop down (trees).
砍頭 *kaantour*, v. t., to behead (person); 砍頭癰 (*-yung*) a kind of malignant boil on the neck.

§ 31B.82 (石/乂)

破 31B.82–2

poh.

V.i. & t. (1) To break: 破例, 戒, 約 break rules, vows, treaty or agreement; 破臉 quarrel openly; 破口(罵人) break into abuse, use abusive language; 破膽 frightened out of one's wits; 破顏, 破涕爲笑 melt into smiles (of face); 破土 break ground (of construction). (2) To crush (enemy ranks): 破陣, 勢如破竹 smash enemy easily (like splitting bamboo); 攻破南京 capture Nanking; 破賊 crush rebels. (3) To show, reveal: 説破 reveal (secret); 一語破的 hit the nail on the head ("hit target with one remark"); 破露 betray (conspiracy, plan), (plan) is exposed; 破盤 leak out plan; 破着沒臉 disregard modesty by appearing in public (of women); 破綻 *-'jan*↓; 破斧沉舟 no-retreat policy ("burning the bridges"). (4) To analyze, explain, define: 破題 *-tir*↓. (5) To spend: 破鈔, 破財, 破費 spend money; 破工夫 spend a lot of time. (6) To brave: 破浪 ride the waves. (7) To break out: 破空而下, appear, burst out of the blue.

Vb. complement. Through: 看破 (*kahn-*) see through (世情 pomp, the material world); 打破 break (a cup); 打破難關 break through a difficult situation; 撕破 tear up; 攻破 capture a city; 讀破 read character with different pronunciation, representing different word.

Adj. Broken down: 破屋子, 衣服, 皮鞋 broken-down house, tattered clothing, shoes; 破罐子 *-guahntz*↓; 破鏡重圓 reunion of couple after separation, divorce; 家破人亡 family ruined; 破家子弟 spendthrift son of family; penniless person; 國破 country destroyed.

破敗 *pohbaih*, v.t., destroy (property, plan).
破產 *pohchaan*, n. & adj., bankrupt, -cy.
破除 *pohchur*, v.t., overcome prejudices, obstacles, superstition.
破格 *pohger*, adv., as an exceptional favor.
破瓜 *poh-gua*, v.i., lose virginity; 破瓜之年 age sixteen, (AC) also age sixty-four (of women).
破罐子 *pohguahntz*. n., (contemp.) unchaste woman; a physical wreck.
破壞 *pohhuaih*, v. t., break (neutrality, marriage), violate (agreement), damage (reputation).
破綻 *poh'jan*, n., flaw (in clothing, secret, argument).
破折號 *pohjerhauh*, n., printer's dash mark ("—").
(打)破紀錄 (*daa*) *pohjih-luh*, v. i., break the record.
破爛 *pohlahn*, adj., torn-down, ragged (furniture, dress).
破裂 *pohlieh*, v.i. & adj., split, break, broken (friendship, marriage).
破落戶 *pohluoh-huh*, n., penniless person, family; fallen into decline.
破嗓子 *poh-saang-tz*, n., broken voice, lost voice.
破傷風 *pohshangfeng*, n., tetanus infection.
破身 *pohshen*, v.i., lose virginity.
破曉 *pohshiaau*, n., daybreak.
破碎 *pohsueih*, adj., piecemeal, broken up, out of line; n., broken bits.
破天荒 *pohtianhuang*, adj. & adv., unprecedented, breaking all precedents.
破體字 *pohtiitzyh*, n., corrupt or abbreviated form of a character.
破題(兒) *pohtir'l*, n., the opening sentence of essay in civil examinations defining the theme; (fig.) the first thing.

破字 *pohtzyh*, n., special pronunciation of a character different from normal, and used with different meaning.

破五兒 *pohwuue'l*, n., fifth of January in old calendar.

破音 *pohyin*, n., special pr. of character used with different meaning.

硬 31B.82-3

yihng.

Adj. (1) Hard: 硬繃繃, 硬邦邦 very hard. (2) Stubborn, firm, adamant (attitude): 骨頭硬, 脾氣硬 stubborn in temperament. (3) Hard-hearted: 心腸硬 opp. 軟 soft-hearted. (4) Raw, stiff, not fluent: 舌頭硬 tongue is stiff in learning language; 生硬 not well learned, forced, not skillful or smooth. (5) Solid, well-equipped: 陣容很硬 staffed with the best personnel; 戲碼兒硬 theater has solid program.

Adv. By force, doggedly, without flinching: 硬拉 pull by force; 硬掙, 硬撐 hold up by force; esp. 硬著頭皮, 硬著臉子 braving all rebuff; 硬著心腸 with hardened heart, i.e., unwillingly (do s.t. cruel); 硬把他的名掛上 put his name on the list against his will.

硬幣 *yihng-bih*, n., hard currency.

硬氣 *yihngchih*, n. & adj., firm, -ness: 兒子偏不硬氣 unfortunately the son is weak in character.

硬度 *yihngduh*, n., (jewels, steel) degree of hardness.

硬幹 *yihnggahn*, v.i., to do recklessly.

硬膏 *yihnggau*, n., (med.) plasters.

硬漢 *yihng-hahn*, n., a strong-willed person, one who never yields.

硬化 *yihnghuah*, v.i., to harden, stiffen: 動脈血管硬化 sclerosis;

硬化症 --*jehng*, n., cirrhosis.

硬黃紙 *yihnghuarng-jyy*, n., sized paper.

硬貨 *yihnghuoh*, n., metallic coins.

硬脂 *yihngjy*, n., (chem.) stearin, suet, tallow.

硬朗 *yihng'lang*, adj., robust (health).

硬臉 *yihng-liaan*, phr., accept no compromise.

硬裏子 *yihngliitz*, n., important supporting actors in troupe.

硬領(兒)(子) *yihng-liing ('l) (tz)*, n., stiff collar.

硬煤 *yihngmeir*, n., anthracite coal.

硬麵(兒) *yihng-miahn(-miah'l)*, n., hard noodles, made with less water.

硬木 *yihng-muh*, n., hardwood.

硬橡皮 *yihng-shiahngpir*, n., ebonite.

硬性 *yihngshihng*, n., hardness, rigidity.

硬手(兒) *yihng-shoou('l)*, n., an able hand or assistant.

硬水 *yihng-shueei*, n., hard water.

硬頭貨 *yihng'touhuoh*, n., (1) money; (2) indigestible stuff.

硬彩 *yihng-tsaai*, n., deep-colored enamel on porcelain.

硬玉 *yihngyuh*, n., jadeite.

礟 31B.82-5

pauh.

[Var. of 礮 31B.82]

礮 31B.82-5

pauh.

[Var. of 砲 31B.70 ↑]

礉 31B.82-9

chiau (**her*).

Adj. (1) Jagged (var. of 磽 31B.70 ↑). (2) (**her*) To check officially (var. of 核10B.81 and 覈 31.82).

§ 31B.83 (石/〜)

礎 31B.83-1

chuu.

N. Foundation stone: 礎石 ditto; 基礎 foundation, (lit. and fig.) (of strength, wisdom, etc.); 礎潤知雨 certain stones show changes of weather by their wet color.

礙 31B.83-2

aih.

N. Obstacle, hindrance, detriment: 障礙 ditto; 有礙, 無礙 (於) is hindrance, is no hindrance, to (plan, progress): 有礙衛生 is deleterious to health.

V. t. (1) To hinder, stand in the way: 阻礙 hinder (progress, cooperation, etc.); 礙眼, 礙口 *-yaan, -koou* ↓; 礙事 *-shyh* ↓. (2) Difficult, embarrassing: 礙難 *-narn* ↓; 礙于情面 one cannot do s.t. (refuse, etc.) for fear of hurting another's feelings.

礙口 *aih-koou*, phr., too embarrassing to speak out.

礙目 *aih-muh*, phr., an eyesore.

礙難 *aihnarn*, adj., (official language) inconvenient for certain reasons, i.e., cannot: 礙難照准 cannot or do not approve.

礙手 *aih-shoou*, phr., (affair) difficult to handle: 礙手礙腳 in the way.

礙事 *aihshyh*, adj., detrimental,

highly inconvenient; usu. in negative form: 不礙事 does not matter, is quite all right (to do s.t.).

礙眼 *aih-yaan*, phr., be an eyesore, see *-muh* ↑.

碇 31B.83-6

dihng.

N. Anchor of a ship: 啟碇 to weigh anchor.

砭 31B.83-9

bian.

N. (AC) fine-pointed stone for puncturing skin.

V.t. Anciently to probe with stone point, now with metal point in acupuncture; 針^Δ砭 81A.10 n., acupuncture, also v.t. to probe and criticize (faults) severely.

砭骨 *bianguu*, adj., very cold, stinging (of cutting wind); very severe (of criticism).

砭灸 *bianjioou*, n., (med.) anc. method of acupuncture, puncture (砭 to puncture and 灸 to cauterize).

§ 31B.91 (石/ノ)

砂 31B.91-2

sha.

N. (1) Sand (usu. interch. 沙). (2) Gritty marks in measles.

砂布 *shabuh*, n., emery cloth.

砂金 *shajin*, n., placer gold; 砂金石 *--shyr*, (min.) corundum, varieties of quartz.

砂紙 *shajyy*, n., see *-buh* ↑.

砂礫 *shalih*, n., gravel.

砂輪 *shalurn*, n., emery wheel.

砂漠 *shamoh*, n., desert (usu. 沙).

砂囊 *shanarng*, n., the gizzard of a fowl.

砂皮 *shapir*, n., emery cloth or paper.

砂糖 *shatarng*, n., unrefined sugar.

砂鐵 *shatiee*, n., magnetic sand.

砂土 *shatuu*, n., sandy soil.

砂眼 *sha-yaan*, n., trachoma.

砂岩 *shayarn*, n., sandstone.

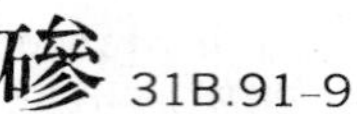

磣 31B.91-9

cheen.

[Var. 碜]

Adj. (1) Gritty (food mixed with sand). (2) Ugly, unsightly: 磣可可, 磣得慌 very ugly, pitiful-looking (related 慘 22A.91).

§ 31B.93 (石/く)

砝 31B.93-1

far.

砝碼 *farmaa*, n., brass or lead weights, used in old-style scales.

磁 31B.93-8

tsyr.

N. (1) Magnetism: 磁氣 *-chih*¹ ↓; 磁性, 磁石, 磁針 *-shihng, -shyr, -jen* ↓. (2) U.f. 甆 porcelain, 80.70: 磁器 *-chih*² ↓.

磁場 *tsyrchaang*, n., (phys.) magnetic field.

磁氣 *tsyrchih*¹, n., (phys.) magnetic force: 地磁氣 terrestrial magnetism; 磁氣感應 magnetic induction; 磁氣赤道 magnetic equator.

磁器 *tsyrchih*², n., porcelain, chinaware.

磁電 *tsyrdiahn*, n., (phys.) electromagnetism.

磁針 *tsyrjen*, n., magnetic needle.

磁極 *tsyrjir*, n., (phys.) magnetic pole.

磁軸 *tsyrjour*, n., (phys.) magnetic axis.

磁力 *tsyrlih*, n., (phys.) magnetic force: 磁力線 line of magnetic force.

磁性 *tsyrshihng*, n., magnetism, magnetic properties.

磁實 *tsyr'shy*, adj., (coll.) substantial, well-built, solid (house).

磁石 *tsyrshyr*, n., loadstone; 磁石棍 or 磁條 bar magnet.

磁條 *tsyrtiaur*, n., bar magnet.

磁鐵 *tsyrtiee*, n., magnetic iron, magnet: 馬蹄磁鐵 horseshoe magnet; 圓條磁鐵 cylindrical magnet.

SECTION 31C

§ 31C.00 (酉/亅)

酎 31C.00-1

jouh.

N. (AC) double-fermented wine.

酵 31C.00-1

shiauh (also *jiauh*).

N. Yeast, leaven: 發酵 to ferment.

酵母 *shiauhmuu*, n., leaven, yeast.
酵素 *shiauhsuh*, n., (biol.) enzymes.

酊 31C.00-3

diing.

Adj. See 酩▵酊 31C.40.

酧 31C.00-6

chour.
[Pop. of 酬 31C.22]

醇 31C.00-6

churn.
[Var. of 醕]

N. (1) Mellow wine: 醇酒婦人 indulgence with wine and women. (2) 乙醇 ether.

Adj. (1) U.f. 淳 simple, unsophisticated: 醇厚, 醇樸 *-houh, -pur* ↓. (2) U.f. 純 pure: 醇備, 醇謹, 醇粹 *-beih, -jiin, -tsueih* ↓.

醇備 *churnbeih*, adj. (AC) perfect (also 純備), without flaws of character.
醇醇 *churnchurn*, adj., (AC) primitively simple-hearted.
醇厚 *churnhouh*, adj., careful and honest (also wr. 純, 淳).
醇化 *churnhuah*, adj., mellowed, well blended (customs, callig., also 淳化).
醇謹 *churnjiin*, adj., see *-houh* ↑.
醇精 *churn-jing*, n., (chem.) ether.
醇醪 *churn-laur*, n., exceptionally strong wine.
醇醨 *churn-lir*, n., good (醇) and bad (醨) wine, (fig.) tough and refined customs, manners.
醇美 *churnmeir*, adj., mellow, superb (also 純, 淳).
醇醲 *churn-nurng*, adj., wine of old vintage; (fig.) mellow character of a people.
醇樸 (朴) *churnpur*, adj., simple, unsophisticated (also 淳, 純).
醇粹 *churntsueih*, adj., unadulterated, pure (also 純, 淳).

酹 31C.00-9

leih.

V.t. Perform libation.

釂 31C.00-9

jiauh.

V. i. (AC) empty a cup of wine at one gulp.

§ 31C.01 (酉/小)

醥 31C.01-3

piaau.

N. (MC) light wine.

醾 31C.01-6

mir.
[Var. of 醿 31C.01]

N. See 酴▵醾 31C.01 ↓.

酴 31C.01-8

tur.

N. (AC) yeast.

酴醾 *turmir*, n., see 荼▵䕷 20A.01.
酴酥 *tursu*, n., see 屠▵蘇 52A.41.

酥 31C.01-9

su.

N. Light, fluffy or crisp edible (cakes, etc.): 桃酥 crisp preserved peach; 酥糖 crisp sweetmeat.

Adj. (1) Crisp, light and fluffy (cookie). (2) Soft like butter: 酥胸 woman's soft breasts; 酥髮 soft, silky hair. (3) Luxuriously relaxed: 酥麻, 酥輭 *-mar, -ruaan* ↓.

酥酪 *sulauh*, n., yogurt.

酥麻 *sumar*, adj., (limbs) numb and weak, sensually soothed.
酥輭 *sunuaan*, adj., (legs) gone soft, weak from excitement.
酥油 *suyour*, n., butter from cow's or mare's milk.

§ 31C.02 (酉/ㄎ)

醵 31C.02-2

jyuh.

V. i. Contribute money for a common purpose, esp. to buy drinks: 醵金 to chip in; 醵資 ditto.

醲 31C.02-2

nurng.

N. Rich wine.

Adj. Rich: (of wine, tea, etc.) rich-flavored (cf. 濃 63A.02).

釀 31C.02-6

niahng.

N. Wine or its by-product: 佳釀 vintage wine; 酒釀 sweet fermented rice; see 釀母 *-muu* ↓.

V. t. (1) To brew wine: 釀酒, 釀造, 釀製 make wine. (2) Cause (s. t.) to mature gradually: 釀蜜 (of bees) make honey; 釀成 (of bad habits, evil tendencies, etc.) suffer to grow or develop; 釀禍 ferment trouble; 醞釀 (lit.) brew wine, etc.; (fig.) (of mischiefs, trouble, rebellion, etc.) brew, ferment.

釀母 *niahngmuu*, n., (=酵母) yeast.
釀造 *niahngtzauh*, v. t., make (wine, etc.) by fermentation.

醁 31C.02-9

luh.

N. 醽醁 *lirngluh*, name of wine.

§ 31C.10 (酉/十)

醰 31C.10-3

tarn.

Adj. (Of wine) good and rich-flavored: 醰醰 full-flavored.

醉 31C.10-6

tzueih.

Adj. Drunk: 醉漢 *-hahn* ↓; 醉鬼 *-gueei* ↓; 醉客 a drunken man; 醉貓兒 a person walking and acting unsteadily under the influence of alcohol; 醉薰薰 drunk, tipsy; 醉貌咕咚 sottish; 醉眼惺忪 sleepy-eyed from drink; 醉咧咧兒 habbling (faltering) from too much drink; 醉了 got drunk, intoxicated; 醉倒 lying paralyzed by drink; 醉死 dead drunk, drink oneself to death; 醉酒 drunk with wine; 喝醉了酒 have had a cup too many; 酒醉飯飽 dined and wined to satiety; 醉酒飽德 (litr.) expression of thanks for host's hospitality ("have partaken of your vintage wine and basked in your kindness"); 醉生夢死 lead a happy-go-lucky life; 酒不醉人人自醉 it's not the wine that intoxicates but the drinker who gets himself drunk; 醉意 unusually talkative or high-spirited after a drinking bout, half-tipsy; 醉翁之意不在酒 some ulterior motive.

V.t. (1) Be addicted to: 醉心 *-shin* ↓. (2) Steep (crab, shrimps) in wine.

醉鬼 *tzueihgueei*, n., a drunken sot, a tippler, an alcoholic.
醉漢 *tzueihhahn*, n., a drunkard, a drunken person.
醉雷公 *tzueih leirgung*, phr., a busybody fond of making superficial comments on men and events ("a drunken thunderer").
醉墨 *tzueih-moh*, n., painting or calligraphy done under the influence of wine.
醉鄉 *tzueih-shiang*, n., the state of ecstasy in which a drinker finds himself.
醉心 *tzueih-shin*, v. t., be infatuated with (honor, fame, music, poetry, art).
醉魚草 *tzueihyur-tsaau*, n., (bot.) *Buddlea japonica*.

§ 31C.11 (酉/土)

醛 31C.11-2

chyuarn.

N. (Chem.) aldehyde.

醒 31C.11-4

shiing (*shing*).

V. i. (1) To wake up, be awake: 他醒了 he is awake; 昏迷又醒過來 come out of coma; 甦醒, 夢醒 wake up from sleep, dream; 喚醒他 wake him up; 醒獅 awaken lion (oft. used to describe awakened China). (2) Sober up: 酒醒了 become sober; v. t., 醒酒

help to wake up from drink. (3) To realize one's mistake: 醒悟 *-wuh* ↓.

醒腔 *shiingchiang*, v. i., (coll.) come to realize: 他總是不醒腔 (coll.) he would never come to realize his mistake, see *-wuh* ↓.
醒豁 *shiinghuoh*, adj., striking, bright in appearance.
醒覺 *shiingjyuer*, adj., wake up from (error, sleep).
醒木 *shiingmuh*[1], n., a gavel used by teahouse storyteller to call attention.
醒目 *shiing-muh*[2], adj., refreshing to the eye, attractive-looking (billboard, etc.).
醒脾 *shiingpir*, (1) v. i., 醒人脾胃 to refresh one's mind; to make fun of: 你別拿我們醒脾 don't make fun of us; (2) adj., amusing, refreshing, appetizing (anecdote, etc.).
醒世 *shiing-shyh*, adj., (moral tract, story) moralizing, calculated to make one reform.
醒悟 *shiingwuh*, v. i., to come to realize (truth, error); to reform.
醒眼 *shirng-yaan*, adj., see *-muh*[2] ↑.

§ 31C.21 (酉/ㄴ)

酗 31C.21-2

shyuh.

V. i. To become drunk and violent: 酗酒 ditto; 酗訟 get into a drunken brawl.

§ 31C.22 (酉/丨)

酬 31C.22-2

chour.
[Pop. 酧]

N. Reward, remuneration: 卻酬 decline any remuneration; 酬金, 酬勞 *-jin*, *-laur* ↓.

V.i. (1) To pledge a cup of wine, to toast and return toast: 應酬 v.i. & n., have a round of social events, parties, invitations and return invitations; repartees at parties: 酬答, 酬對 *-dar*, *-dueih* ↓; 酬應, 酬酢 *-yihng*, *-tzuoh* ↓; write poems and reply in poems: 酬和, 酬唱 *-heh*, *chahng* ↓. (2) To reward, give thanks: 酬報 *-bauh* ↓; 酬謝 *-shieh* ↓.

酬報 *chourbauh*, n., remuneration for service; (theology) retribution.
酬唱 *chourchahng*, v.i., to write back and forth, esp. poems, between friends.
酬答 *chourdar*, v. i., (1) express appreciation; (2) give remuneration; (3) see *-chahng* ↑.
酬對 *chourdueih*, (1) v.i., to hold conversation; (2) the art of conversation.
酬和 *chourheh*, v.i., see *-chahng* ↑.
酬金 *chourjin*, n., service fees.
酬直 *chourjyr*, v.i., to repay for service (properly 值).
酬勞 *chourlaur*, n. & v.t., remunerate, -tion.
酬賽 *choursaih*, n. & v.i., thanksgiving to gods, a religious festival with parades.
酬謝 *chourshieh*, v.t., to repay with thanks; n., remuneration.
酬酢 *chourtzuoh*, n. & v.i., (1) invitations back and forth; (2) drink toasts to each other.
酬應 *chouryihng*, v.i., ditto.
酬庸 *chouryung*, n., (LL) remuneration, reward for past services.

醡 31C.22-6

jah.

N. Wine press.

醾 31C.22-6

mir.
[Var. of 醿 31C.01 ↑]

酢 31C.22-9

tzuoh.

V.t. To toast the host: 酬酢 mutual toasting between host and guests, dining and wining.

§ 31C.30 (酉/一)

醢 31C.30-1

haai.

N. Minced meat sauce; pickled meat.

V. t. (AC) to cut slices of flesh as a form of torture.

醴 31C.30-2

lii.

醴 醞 醯 醓 酤 酷 醽 醅 酩 酪 酣 醋

N. (1) 醴泉 A sweet spring. (2) 醴酒 sweet wine.

醞 31C.30-4

yuhn.

V. i. To ferment.

醞 藉 *yuhnjieh*, adj., poised (character); rich but restrained (style of writing), also wr. 蘊.
醞 釀 *yuhnniahng*, v. i., to ferment; (fig.) (of troubles, revolutionary movement) are brewing.

醯 31C.30-6

shi.

N. (AC) vinegar; pickles.

醯 鷄 *shiji*, n., gnat-like insect found on pickles.
醯 醬 *shijiahng*, n., pickled condiment.

醓 31C.30-8

shi.
[Var. of 醯 31C.30↑]

§ 31C.40 (酉/口)

酤 31C.40-1

gu.

V. t. Sell or buy: 酤酒 sell or buy wine (cf. 沽 63A.40).

酷 31C.40-1

kuh.

Adj. & adv. (1) Strong (bouquet of wine). (2) Brutal: 殘酷, 酷烈 brutal; 酷吏 merciless judge or prison warden; 酷虐 tyrannical cruel; 冷酷 cold, severe, without human warmth; 酷刑 *-shirng*↓. (3) Severe, extreme, -ly: 酷熱, 酷寒 extremely hot, severely cold (weather); 酷似 very much resembling.

酷 烈 *kuhlieh*, adj., (1) severe, cruel; (2) strong (smell).
酷 刑 *kuhshirng*, n., torture.

醽 31C.40-3

lirng.

醽 醁 *lirngluh*, n., (MC) name of fine wine.

醅 31C.40-6

pei.

N. Unstrained spirits.

酩 31C.40-9

mirng (*miing*).

酩 酊 (大 醉) *mirngdiing* (*dah tzueih*), adj., dead drunk.

酪 31C.40-9

luoh (*lauh* in coll.).

N. (1) Kinds of cheese: 奶酪, 乳酪 cream cheese. (2) (AC) fruit jelly, jam.

§ 31C.41 (酉/図)

酣 31C.41-2

han.

Adj. & adv. Rapturous, -ly, soundly and comfortably: 酣飲 rapturously drunk, drink to one's heart's content; 酒意半酣 half drunk, comfortably drunk; 酣睡 sleep soundly; 酣歌, 酣舞 to sing, dance rapturously; 酣樂 enjoy with rapture.

醋 31C.41-2

tsuh.

N. (1) Vinegar. (2) Jealousy (from adj. 酸 sour): 醋意 *-yih*↓; 吃醋 feel jealous; 醋海生波 a storm of jealousy.

醋 大 *tsuhdah*, n., penniless fellow, oft. 窮醋大 (also wr. 措大); formerly, sour and haughty scholars.
醋 罐 子 *tsuhguahntz*, n., "a bottle of vinegar"—extremely jealous wife or husband.
醋 勁 (兒) *tsuhjihn(-jieh'l)*, n., jealousy, see *-yih*↓.
醋 心 *tsuh'shin*, n., belching of acid from stomach.
醋 酸 *tsuhsuan*, n., (chem.) acetic acid; 醋酸鈉 sodium acetate; 醋酸鈣 calcium acetate; 醋酸鉀 potassium acetate; 醋酸鉛 lead acetate; 醋酸銅 cupric acetate; 醋酸鉻, 鋁, 鐵 chromium, aluminum, ferric acetate.
醋 意 *tsuhyih*, n., feeling of jealousy.

A

醕 31C.41-6

churn.

[Var. of 醇 31C.00↑]

§31C.42 (酉/冈)

酺 31C.42-1

pur.

N. & v.i. A drink fest.

醐 31C.42-1

hur.

N. See 醍ᐞ醐 31C.83↓.

§31C.50 (酉/㇆)

酌 31C.50-9

juor.

N. (1) A feast, banquet: 喜酌 wedding banquet. (2) Small, informal dinner with a little wine: 清酌, 便酌, 隨意小酌 ditto; 對酌 have a drink together.

V.i. (1) To drink: 獨酌 drink without company; 小酌, 對酌 see N. 2↑; 淺酌 have a little drink. (2) To pour wine (for guest, etc.). (3) To deliberate (as to measure wine by jigger): 斟酌 to deliberate (together), consider before decision; 酌定, 酌奪, 酌量 *-dihng*, *-duor*, *-liarng*↓.

B

Adv. (As vb. prefix) at discretion, according to needs or circumstances: 酌付, 酌改 pay, correct, at your discretion; 酌復 reply as you think fit; 酌減 decrease according to circumstances; 酌取 take as much as you consider desirable, etc.

酌辦 *juorbahn*, v.i. & t., proceed at your discretion.
酌定 *jourdihng*, v.t., please kindly decide.
酌奪 *juorduor*, v.t., ditto.
酌量 *juorliarng* (*-liahng*), adv., according to circumstances: 酌量辦理, see *-bahn*↑.
酌獻 *juorshiahn*, v.i., to offer sacrifices with libation.
酌裁 *juortsair*, v.t., (await) your decision.

§31C.63 (酉/丶)

醺 31C.63-9

shyun.

Adj. Drunk: 醉醺醺 very drunk, tipsy.

醮 31C.63-9

jiauh.

N. A Taoist or Buddhist sacrifice: 打醮 hold sacrifice to appease the gods or exorcise the demons.

V.i. (Of women) marry: 再醮 remarry after husband's death.

C

§31C.70 (酉/乚)

醃 31C.70-1

yan.

V.t. To pickle, marinate, salt; p.p., salted, marinated: 醃菜 salted vegetable.

配 31C.70-5

peih.

V.t. (1) To match, be worthy of: 配不上 be unworthy of post or match; 他配說這種話嗎 is he the person qualified to say such things? 配對 to make a pair, to mate. (2) To compose, blend, make up: 配藥 make up a prescription; 配戲 cast a play; 配貨 buy, replenish supplies for stores; 配製 make, compose from different elements, such as medicine. (3) To send (person) to exile.

Adj. Side (wing, construction): 配殿, 配房 *-diahn*, *-farng*↓.

配備 *peihbeih*, n., (mil.) arms; and equipment things, decorations that go with (a thing); v.t., to furnish with arms.
配搭(兒) *peihda* (*'l*), v.t., arrange (accessories, equipment, subsidiary roles).
配殿 *peih-diahn*, n., side temple.
配房 *peih-farng*, n., side room.
配合 *peihher*, v.t. & adj., match (things together); well-matched, appropriate.
配件兒 *peihjiah'l*, n., accessories.
配給 *peihjii*, n. & v.i., ration, supply, usu. free.
配角(兒) *peihjyuer* (*-jyuer'l*), n., minor roles in play.
配軍 *peihjyun*, n., troops of exiled persons.

配 酡 酖 醜 醎 醭 醱 醱 釅 酘

配偶 (耦) *paih-oou*, n., spouse, matrimonial match.
配流 *peihliour*, v.t. send to exile.
配享 *peihshiaang*, v.i., to be worshipped by side of (main spirit, ancestor), to share sacrifices with.
配售 *peihshouh*, n., rationed purchase.
配所 *peihsuuo*, n., place of exile.
配音 *peihyin*, n., sound track in films.

酡 31C.70–6

tuor.

Adj. Face flushed with drink: 酡顏, 酡醉.

酖 31C.70–9

dan (**jehn*).

N. (**jehn*) Poisoned wine: 酖毒 wine poison.

V.i. Be infatuated with, addicted to: 酖迷酒色 addicted to wine and women, also wr. 耽.

醜 31C.70–9

choou.

N. (1) (Abusive) blackguard, scoundrel: 小醜 underling, scoundrel; 跳梁小醜 little rascal, scamp; 羣醜 the rascals; 醜虜 a term of abuse of enemy. (2) Disgrace: 出醜 expose oneself to ridicule for clumsiness (awkwardness, incompetence, etc.), be exposed for s.t. immoral; 獻醜 (self-deprecating of performance) show my immature skill.

Adj. (1) Ugly, loathsome, unsightly: 醜婦 ugly woman; 醜臉 ugly face; 醜極了 frightfully bad-looking. (2) Disgraceful, shameless: 醜話, 醜事 *-huah, -shyh*↓; 醜行 *-shihng*↓; 醜史 story of s.o.'s shameless doings; 醜樣子 grisly appearance; 醜名 *-mirng*↓; 醜聲四溢 notorious; 醜態百出 behave in a revolting manner (show flattery, etc.). (3) (AC) matching: 天下地醜德齊 (AC) the countries are equally strong in territory and power.

Adv. Frightfully, horribly; 醜罵, 醜詆 give a merciless scolding; 一頓醜打 beat up (person) mercilessly.

醜巴怪 *chooubaguaih*, n. & adj., disfigured, monstrous-looking (person).
醜惡 *choou-eh*, adj., loathsome, despicable (conduct).
醜話 *choou-huah*, n., scandal, scandalous gossip.
醜類 *choou-leih*, (1) n., (LL, abusive) gang of scoundrels; (2) 比物醜類 (AC) to classify according to categories.
醜陋 *chooulouh*, adj., ugly, loathsome, unsightly.
醜名 *choou-mirng*, n., bad reputation.
醜行 *choou-shihng*, n., notorious conduct, indecencies.
醜事 *choou-shyh*, n., a scandal.
醜態 *choou-taih*, n., disgusting manner.

§ 31C.71 (酉/弋)

醎 31C.71–7

shiarn.

[Var. of 鹹]

§ 31C.81 (酉/人)

醭 31C.81–2

bur (also *pur* or *mur* in Peking).

N. White spots on surface of vinegar, soy sauce, usu. 醭兒 *bur'l.*

§ 31C.82 (酉/乂)

醱 31C.82–3

chuoh.

V.t. (LL) to drink, sip.

醱 31C.82–3

poh.

N. & vb. Secondary fermentation.

醱酵 *pohshiauh*, v.i., cause fermentation by yeast.

釅 31C.82–4

yahn.

Adj. Strong (liquor, tea).

酘 31C.82–4

tour.

V.i. (MC) to have a small drink

(酘一酘) after heavy drinking the previous day, believed to be a good way of working it off.

酸 31C.82-9

suan.

N. An acid: 碳酸 carbonic acid; 鹽酸 hydrochloric acid; 硫酸 sulphuric acid; 醋酸 acetic acid; 磷酸 phosphoric acid; 硝酸 nitric acid.

Adj. (1) Sour in taste: 酸溜溜, 酸不唧(兒)的, 酸不唧溜兒的 all meaning very sour. (2) Jealous: also 酸溜溜 very jealous (cf. 醋 31C.41). (3) Putrid, rancid: 酸咕嚷的 very rancid in smell. (4) Feeling deeply touched in pity: 心酸 ditto; 酸鼻 *-bir* ↓. (5) U.f. 痠 61A.82, muscular ache. (6) Puritanical, pettily critical of others, narrow-minded: 寒酸, 窮酸 poor and jealous of others; 酸文假醋 one who poses as a cultured gentleman, hypocrite, -ical.

酸敗 *suanbaih*, adj., turned sour.
酸鼻 *suan-bir*, v.i., cause one's heart to ache: 令人酸鼻 makes one want to cry out of pity (describing a feeling in sinus).
酸慳 *suanchian*, adj., miserly.
酸切 *suanchieh*, adj., touching (words).
酸楚 *suanchuu*, adj., mournful, heart breaking.
酸丁 *suanding*, n., (contempt.) an unsuccesful and morose or crabbed person.
酸度 *suanduh*, n., acidity.
酸腐 *suanfuu*, adj., puritanical, doctrinaire.
酸根 *suangen*, n., (chem.) acid radicals.
酸寒 *suanharn*, adj., poor and unhappy (person) (=寒酸).
酸懷 *suanhuair*, adj., sorrowful.
酸漿 *suanjiang*, n., (bot.) "Chinese lantern" or winter cherry, *Physalis alkekengi* (also called 燈籠草).
酸款 *suankuaan*, adj., sour and aloof, conceited (person).
酸懶 *suanlaan*, adj., (legs, body) limp and aching.
酸辣湯 *suanlah-tang*, n., a sour-and-hot soup (of slices of bean-curd and blood).
酸類 *suanleih*, n., (chem.) acids.
酸溜溜(兒) *suanliou'liou('l)*, adj., very jealous; very puritanical; (muscles) aching.
酸梅湯 *suanmeir-tang*, n., wild-plum juice, a cold drink.
酸軟 *suanruaan*, adj., (limbs) limp.
酸性 *suanshihng*, n., acidity: 酸性岩 acid rocks; 酸性鹽 acid salts; 酸性反應 acid reaction.
酸心 *suanshin*[1], (1) n., acidity in stomach; (2) adj., touching (=心酸).
酸辛 *suanshin*[2], adj., sad, hard-pressed, in hard circumstances.
酸疼 *suanterng*, adj., (muscles) aching.
酸甜兒 *suan-tiar'l*, adj., sweet and sour (dishes); 酸甜苦辣 all the sweet and bitter experiences of life.
酸頭兒 *suantour'l*, n., slightly sour flavor.
酸菜 *suantsaih*, n., sour pickled cabbage.
酸痛 *suantuhng*, adj., see *-terng* ↑.
酸棗 *suantzaau*, n., a wild date, *Zizyphus vulgaris*.

§ 31C.83 (酉/〜)

醍 31C.83-4

tir.

醍醐 *tirhur*, n., essential oil of butter; (Budd.) Buddha nature in man; 醍醐灌頂 phr., pleasure of understanding or receiving wisdom (like "pouring rich liquor over one's head").

§ 31C.91 (酉/ノ)

醪 31C.91-5

laur.

N. Wine with dregs: 醪糟 the sediment of wine or spirits.

SECTION 31D

§ 31D.00 (雨/丿)

 31D.00-3

merng.
[Anc. var. of 霧 31D.50↓]

N. Heavy fog.

雺淞 *merngsung* (*mehngsuhng*), n., thick fog.

§ 31D.01 (雨/小)

霖 31D.01-1

lirn.

N. Rain, esp. long rain: 霖雨 heavy rain; 甘霖 sweet rain, good for the crops.

§ 31D.02 (雨/𠂆)

霢 31D.02-4

moh.

N. (AC) drizzle.

震 31D.02-5

jehn.
[Related 顫]

N. (1) One of the eight diagrams, see 八卦 80.80. (2) (AC) thunder; earthquake: 地震.

V.i. & t. (1) To shock, strike by thunder: 雷震 struck by thunder; 震死了 struck dead by lightning; to shock by brilliance: 震古鑠今 galvanize the world. (2) To quake, crash: 震撼 *-hahn*↓; 震動 *duhng*↓; 震天駭地 shake the universe; 震耳(欲聾) deafening (noise). (3) To frighten, be frightened (oft. prefixed to adj. or p.p.): 震懼, 震驚, 震恐, 震慴 *-jyuh*, *-jing*, *-kuung*, *-jer*↓, etc., meaning greatly frightened; 震怒 *-nuh*↓, greatly angry. (4) (AC) pregnant (related modn. 娠).

震顫 *jehnchahn*, n., tremor.
震旦 *Jehndahn*, n., ancient Hindu name for China.
震怛 *jehndar*, adj., frightened.
震悼 *jehndauh*, adj., shocked by s.o.'s death.
震動 *jehnduhng*, (1) v.i., to quake, tremble; (2) v.t. & p.p., be greatly moved, restless: 人心震動.
震耳 *jehn-eel*, adj., earsplitting, deafening (noise).
震撼 *jehnhahn*, v.t., shake, -en agitate, -ed; shatter, -ing, -ed.
震駭 *jehnhaih*, v.i. & t., shock, -ed. 「-ed.
震慴 *jehnjer*, v.i. & t., frighten,
震悸 *jehnjih*, v.i., to quiver, quake with fear.
震驚 *jehnjing*, v.i., greatly frightened, afraid.
震懼 *jehnjyuh*, v.i., tremble with fear. 「ed.
震恐 *jehnkuung*, adj., (p.p.) shock-
震慄 *jehnlih*, v.i., see *-jyuh*↑.
震怒 *jehnnuh*, adj., furious.

§ 31D.10 (雨/十)

霹 31D.10-5

pi.

霹靂 *pilih*, adj. & n., descriptive of crashing thunder, lightning flash: 霹靂一聲雷 a thunderbolt; 霹靂火 quicktempered person; 霹靂手 a fast mover, one quick at decisions.

§ 31D.11 (雨/土)

霪 31D.11-6

yirn.

N. Excessive rain.

霾 31D.11-9

mair.

V.i. Blow sandstorm.

霾晦 *mairhueih*, adj., (of sky) overcast by sandstorm.

霍 31D.11-9

huoh.

N. A surname.

Adv. 霍地, 霍然 *-dih*, *-rarn*↓.

霍地 *huohdih*, adv., quickly, in a flash.
霍霍 *huohhuoh*, adv., as in 光霍霍 shining bright; 磨刀霍霍向豬羊 sharpen knife to kill lamb and pig.
霍亂 *huohluahn*, n., (translit.) cholera.
霍然 *huohrarn*, adv., see *-dih*↑.
霍閃 *huohshaan*, v.i., flash (of lightning).

§ 31D.22 (雨/丨)

霏 31D.22-2

fei.

Adj. Descriptive of snowfall: 雨雪霏霏 snow flying about.

霽 31D.22-6

jih.

V. i. (1) Cease raining: 雨霽 the rain is over; 晴霽 (of weather) fair and clear; 霽色 *-seh*↓. (2) Calm down after a fit of anger: see compp.↓.

霽色 *jihseh*, n., sky blue, a blue sky.
霽威 *jih-wei*, v. i., to calm down, stop raging.
霽顏 *jih-yarn*, v. i., ditto.
霽月 *jih-yueh*, (1) n., a bright moon after rainfall; (2) adj., (of persons) openhearted, open-minded ("like an unclouded moon").

霈 31D.22-6

peih.

N. Plentiful rain; (fig.) gracious kindness, favour.

Adj. (Of rain) pouring, torrential.

§ 31D.30 (雨/一)

靈 31D.30-4

lirng.
[Arch. 霛; pop. 灵]

N. (1) Spirit, soul: 神靈 spirit, the gods; 精靈, 幽靈 soul of departed; 靈魂 *-hurn*↓. (2) Spiritual world, power: 顯靈 (of gods, idol) show supernatural power; 通靈 in touch with spiritual world; 靈感 inspiration; 靈修 attending to spiritual things. (3) Coffin; spirit tablet: 停靈 deposit coffin pending burial; 扶靈 carry the hearse; 靈骨 collected bones of deceased relative; 靈牌, 靈位, 靈柩 *-pair*, *-weih*, *-jiouh*↓. (4) The people: 生^靈 10.11. (5) A surname.

Adj. (1) (Of persons) intelligent, bright, clever, 靈巧, 靈敏 *-chiaau*, *-miin*↓. (2) (Of things) alert, responsive, alive: 靈通, 靈便, 靈活 *-tung*, *-biahn*, *-huor*↓. (3) Spiritual, pertaining to the spirits: 靈魂, 靈氣 *-hurn*, *-chih*↓. (4) (Of med.) efficacious: 靈驗 *-yahn*↓; (of things) work well; 這把鎖靈不靈 does this lock work? 不靈 do not work properly.

靈便 *lirngbiahn*, adj., light and convenient.
靈車 *lirngche*, n., the hearse carriage.
靈櫬 *lirngchehn*, n., the hearse.
靈巧 *lirngchiaau*, adj., clever, (of devices) well made.
靈竅 *lirngchiauh*, adj. & n., wit, intelligence.
靈氣 *lirngchih*, n., (of beautiful mountains) spiritual influence or atmosphere: 靈氣所鍾 such influence on persons born in certain place.
靈床 *lirngchuarng*, n., deathbed; person's bed and room furniture kept as when he was living.
靈感 *lirnggaan*, n., inspiration (in writing).
靈慧 *lirnghueih*, adj., (of person, child) very intelligent.
靈活 *lirnghuor*, adj., quick in response, alert; (style of writing, descriptive passage) alive, interesting.
靈魂 *lirnghurn*, n., soul; departed spirit.
靈機 *lirngji*, n., (sudden) inspiration: 靈機一動 a bright idea occurs.
靈柩 *lirngjiouh*, n., coffin and scaffold support.
靈芝 *lirngjy*, n., a mythic plant of long life.
靈貓 *lirngmau*, n., (zoo.) the civet cat (also called 香貓, 香狸).
靈敏 *lirngmiin*, adj., intelligent, quick to respond.
靈牌 *lirngpair*, n., spirit tablet.
靈山 *lirngshan*, certain fairies' abode (Buddhist, Taoist).
靈效 *lirngshiauh*, n. & adj., efficacy, -cious.
靈性 *lirngshihng*, n., man's spiritual nature.
靈修 *lirngshiou*, v.i., to retreat for spiritual contemplation.
靈秀 *lirngshiouh*, adj., delicately beautiful (person, landscape).
靈透 *lirngtouh*, adj., very clever.
靈通 *lirngtung*, n., as in 消息靈通 quick, efficient report of news.
靈座 *lirngtzuoh*, n., seat of spirit tablet.
靈位 *lirngweih*, n., ditto.
靈驗 *lirngyahn*, n. & adj., efficacy, -cious (of prayer, medicine).

雪 31D.30-5

shyuee (**shyueh* as an exception; cf. 血 *shyueh* or *shiee*).

N. (1) Snow: 下雪了 it snows; 大雪 heavy snow; 大風雪 snow blizzard; 冰天雪地 snow and ice-bound, all covered in ice and snow; 冰雪聰明 extreme crystal-like intelligence; 雪中送炭 phr.,

霏 霽 霈 靈 雪

亅	小	卜	十	土	ナ	卄	ㅏ	丨	一	丅	フ	口	区	冈	ㄱ	厂	尸	亠	广	宀	丶	乚	弋	心	八	人	乂	一	㇀	リ	㇗	く
00	01	02	10	11	12	20	21	22	30	31	32	40	41	42	50	51	52	60	61	62	63	70	71	72	80	81	82	83	90	91	92	93

real friend in need—"send coal during snow"; 雪泥鴻爪 (fig.) human life likened to the life of birds of passage, uncertain or passing travels; 雪兆豐年 snow as an omen of a bumper harvest; 雪上加霜 disasters pile up on one another; 雪肌, 雪膚 white smooth skin like snow; 雪白 *-bair* ↓. (2) A surname.

V. i. To wipe away shame, restitute a wrong, rehabilitate a good name: see 雪冤, 雪仇, 雪恥 *-yuan*, *-chour*, *-chyy* ↓; 雪涕, 雪淚 wipe away a tear; 雪汚 cleanse stains on good name.

雪白 **shyuehbair*, adj., snow-white.
雪車 *shyuee-che*, n., sledge, toboggan.
雪青 *shyueeching*, adj., pale mauve color.
雪蛆 *shyueechyu*, n., an edible insect found in 峨嵋 Omei mountains in Szechuan.
雪恥 *shyuer-chyy*, v. i., to wipe out shame, avenge a former insult or humiliation.
雪膚 *shyueefu*, n., a lady's snow-white skin.
雪恨 *shyuee-hehn*, v. i., to get even with hated enemy.
雪花(兒) *shyuee hua('l)*, n., snowflakes; 雪花膏 cold cream, face cream; 雪花石膏 alabaster.
雪肌 *shyueeji*, n., see *-fu* ↑.
雪茄 *shyueejia*, n., (translit.) cigar.
雪景 *shyuer-jiing* (*shueih-*), n., snow landscape.
雪裏蕻 *shyuerliihuhng*, n., a kind of leaf mustard, *Brassica cernua*.
雪柳 *shyuer-lioou*, n., a wand or staff, wrapped with white paper, held by employed people preceding a funeral procession.
雪梨 *shyueelir*, n., (1) a kind of pear; (2) a place name, Sydney, Australia.
雪片 *shyuee-piahn*, n., snowflakes: 函電雪片而來 mail and telegrams pour in like snowflakes.
雪人 *shyuee-rern*, n., a snow man.
雪線 *shyuee-shiahn*, n., (geog.) the snow line.
雪鞋 *shyuee-shier*, n., snowshoes.
雪橇 *shyuee-tsueih*, n., a sledge.
雪刺 *shyuee-tsyh*, phr., (LL) white, stubby hair (of old man).
雪衣娘 *shuee-yi-niarng*, n., poetic name for a white parrot or cockatoo.
雪冤 *shyuee-yuan*, v. i., to avenge a wrong.

霳 31D.30-5

lih.

N. & adj. See 霹^A^霳 31D.10.

§ 31D.40 (雨/口)

霝 31D.40-4

lirng.

V. i. (AC) (rain) fall.

Adj. Related to 靈 in 空靈 spaced.

露 31D.40-4

luh.

N. (1) Dew: 雨露之恩 (poet.) gracious favors; 甘露 sweet dew which nourishes plants. (2) Essence, fruit juice: 花露水 *eau de cologne*; 玫瑰露 rose essence, rose wine; 杏仁露 essence of almond, etc. (3) A surname.

V. t. To leak out, expose, to bare to view: 露臉, 露面, 露頭兒 show one's face: 永不露臉 never show one's face (in public); 露相(兒) ditto; 露骨 *-guu* ↓; 露苗 sprout shows; 露餡(兒) secret (lit. "stuffing") is exposed; 露馬腳 (a flaw, a lie) unintentionally shows, is exposed; 露齒而笑 laugh openly, grin.

Adj. & adv. Bare, open, in open air: 露天 *-tian* ↓; 露宿 pass night in the open: 風餐露宿 exposed to cold and wet (wind and dew) on a journey; 露立 stand in the open; 露臺 *-tair* ↓.

露白 *louh-bair*, phr., (of traveller) reveal silver in pocket or luggage.
露布 *luhbuh*, n., (1) an unsealed letter; (2) announcement of victory.
露點 *luhdiaan*, n., (phys.) dew-point temperature.
露兜樹 *luhdoushuh*, n., a kind of palm, *Pandanus odoratissimus*.
露骨 *luhguu*, (1) phr., to have corpse exposed; (2) adj., (of criticism, etc.) blunt, overt, make no bones about s.t.
露珠 *luhju*, n., dewdrops.
露水 *luhshueei*, n., dew: 露水夫妻 phr., man and woman not married, meeting secretly (at night in the open).
露臺 *luhtair*, n., open terrace.
露天 *luhtian*, adj. & adv., open-air, outdoor, in the open, unsheltered (theater, movie, concert).
露營 *luhyirng*, n., camp in the open.

霑 31D.40-6

jan.

V. i. & t. (1) To soak with rain (interch. 沾 as in 霑衣, 霑濕 see 沾 63A.40 V.i. & t.); 霑醉 drunk like a fish. (2) Receive benefit, favors: 霑恩, 霑惠.

§ 31D.41 (雨/図)

霜 31D.41-1

shuang.

N. Frost: 結霜, 落霜, 降霜 form frost; 霜雪 frost and snow; 霜露 frost and dew benefiting vegetation; 霜天 the cold "frosted" sky; 霜草 frosted grass; 傲霜 "defy frost," said of chrysanthemum; (-'*l*) white powdery coat (as on some persimmons); symbolic of severity in countenance: 冷若冰霜 (cf. 孀 for widow); 秋霜, 霜威 coldness of demeanor.

Adj. White like frost: 霜鬢 frosted or grey temples; 霜鋒 gleaming sword.

霜降 *shuangjiahng*, n., a solar term, Oct. 23rd or 24th.

雷 31D.41-4

leir.

N. (1) Thunder: 雷雨 *-yuu*↓; 打雷 a thunderclap; 雷聲大, 雨點小 full of sound and fury but with little action. (2) Mine: 地雷 a land mine; 水雷 a sea mine; 魚雷 a torpedo. (3) A surname.

雷鞭 *leirbian*, n., a flash of lightning.

雷池 *leirchyr*, n., orig., the name of a lake in Anhuei Province: 不能越雷池一步 the utmost limit one can go.

雷打 *leirdaa*, phr., be struck by lightning (also 雷擊).

雷達 *leirdar*, n., radar.

雷電 *leirdiahn*, n., thunder and lightning.

雷動 *leirduhng*, adj., loud-sounding like thunder: 邊境雷動 tumults in border regions; 歡聲雷動 a thundering applause.

雷公 *leir'gung*, n., god of thunder, equiv. Thor in Norse mythology.

雷鼓 *leirguu*, n., (1) a drum used in anc. times in sacrificing to the celestial god; (2) drum taps.

雷汞 *leirguung*, n., (chem.) fulminating powder (same as 雷酸汞).

雷轟 *leirhung*, v. i., to sound like thunder.

雷震 *leirjehn*, n., the roll of thunder (also 雷鳴).

雷擊 *leirjir*[1], v. t. & n., see *-daa*↑.

雷殛 *leirjir*[2], v. t., killed by lightning.

雷厲 *leirlih*, adj. & adv., fierce(ly), violent(ly): 雷厲風行 strictest enforcement (of an order, law and regulations).

雷鳴 *leirmirng*, n., (1) the roll of thunder; (2) any loud sound.

雷墨 *leirmoh*, n., (Chin. med.) a mineral believed to be good for infant cramps.

雷鳥 *leirniaau*, n., (zoo.) *Lagopus mutus*.

雷劈 *leirpi*, n., a thunderclap.

雷射 *leirsheh*, n., laser: 雷射光線 laser beams.

雷師 *leirshy*, n., the god of thunder.

雷霆 *leirtirng*, n., thunder: 大發雷霆 break into a furious rage; 雷霆之怒 a thunderous rage.

雷同 *leirturng*, v. t., (oft. in plagiarism) identical with another.

雷音 *leiryin*, n., (Budd.) the Buddha's sayings (lit., "the voice of thunder").

雷雨 *leiryuu*, n., a thunderstorm.

§ 31D.42 (雨/冈)

霸 31D.42-2

bah.

[Pop. 覇]

N. Dictator, tyrant; chief of feudal princes.

V. t. Rule, occupy, by force: 霸天下 rule world by force; 霸諸侯 be overlord of the dukes; 霸奪 *-duor*, 霸據 *-jyuh*, 霸佔 *-jahn*↓; 霸市, dominate, corner the market; 獨霸 dominate (political, literary, commercial world); 爭霸 compete for hegemony; 稱霸 be acknowledged the master or overlord among states.

Adj. Arrogant, tyrannical, belonging to tyrants, see compp.↓.

霸氣 *bahchih*, adj. & n., arrogant, -nce.

霸道 *bahdauh*, n., rule by force of dictators, contrasted with 王[4]道 31.11 (Mencius); adj., overbearing; violent in action (of med.).

霸奪 *bahduor*, v.t., take possession arbitrarily.

霸功 *bahgung*, n., accomplishments of dictator, i.e., conquests.

霸佔 *bahjahn*, v. t., usurp, occupy illegally (property, inheritance).

霸者 *bahjee*, n., a dictator.

霸據 *bahjyuh*, v. t., occupy, take possession by force.

霸略 *bahlyueih*, n., see *-shuh*↓.

霸術 *bahshuh*, n., the strategies of national expansion of dictators.

霸王 *bahwarng*, n., (AC) chief of feudal princes, self-proclaimed king in time of Warring Kingdoms; 西楚霸王 assumed title of 項羽 (died 202 B.C.); 坐霸王車 ride bus without ticket.

霸業 *bahyeh*, n., = 霸功 *-gung*↑.

霄 31D.42-2

shiau.

N. (1) The sky: 凌霄 soar to the skies; 雲霄 the cloudy regions, high up; 霄壤之別 a great difference, as that between heaven and earth. (2) Var. of 宵 night.

霄漢 *shiauhahn*, n., the sky, skies, firmament.

需 31D.42-3

shyu.

[Dist. 須 91S.80 must]

N. Need(s): 軍需 army supplies; 需要 *-yauh*↓.

V. t. Need: 所需 what one needs; 需要 *-yauh*↓; 必需 must needs have; 急需 need urgently; 需款甚殷 need funds badly.

Prep. (LL) according to: 需次陞用 will be promoted according to qualifications, status.

需求 *shyuchiour*, v.i., beg for need; be in need of; n., need, demand.

需索 *shyusuoo*, v. i., look for urgently.

需要 *shyuyauh*, (1) v. i. & t., have need of; (2) n., a need; necessity: 沒有這個需要 no need or necessity for this.

§ 31D.50 (雨/冖)

雩 31D.50-3

yur (**yuu*).

N. (**yuu*) (AC) the rainbow.

V.i. To offer sacrifices and pray for rain.

霧 31D.50-3

wuh.

N. Mist: 大霧, 濃霧 heavy mist; 雲霧 cloud and mist; 霧裏看花 have blurred vision; 霧鬢 a lady's fluffy hair; 墜入五里霧中 completely lost at sea, enveloped in clouded, ill-understood ideas, problems.

霧氣 *wuh'chi*, n., mist, haze.

霧縠 *wuhhur*, n., formerly, thin, transparent gauze.

霧淞 *wuhsung*, n., (MC) icycles formed on trees (modn. coll. 樹掛).

霝 31D.50-5

lirng.

[Var. of 靈 31D.30]

雱 31D.50-6

parng.

[Var. 霶]

Adj. Immense (of clouds).

靄 31D.50-6

aai.

N. Haze: 暮靄 evening haze; 靄氣 haze over the country.

Adj. Hazy, with diffused light.

霶 31D.50-6

parng.

Adj. Immense (cloud); pouring (rain).

霶霈 *parngpeih*, adj., torrential (rain); cf. 澎^湃 rushing water, 63A.91.

雰 31D.50-8

fen.

N. (LL) mist; atmosphere.

雰雰 *fenfen*, adj., misty.

雰圍氣 *fenweir-chih*, n., surrounding atmosphere (of fear, suspicion, etc.); atmosphere surrounding earth.

霉 31D.50-9

meir.

N. Mold, mildew.

Adj. Mildewed, damp, moldy: 發霉 become mildewed.

霉氣 *meir-chih*, n., damp.

霉乾菜 *meirgan-tsaih*, n., stem of cabbage processed by molding and sun-dried.

霉爛 *meir-lahn*, adj., spoiled by mildew.

霉天, 霉雨 *meir-tian*, *meir-yuu*, n., see 梅^天, 梅^雨 10B.50.

§ 31D.63 (雨/丶)

零 31D.63-8

lirng.

[Usu. printed 零]

N. The number zero: 一百零五 105; 一千零一十, 1010; 點零零零三 .0003; 一點三 1.3; 零點零二五 0.025.

Adj. (1) Withered: 凋零; 飄零 floating about. (2) Retail trade: 零賣, 零售 *-maih*, *-shouh*↓. (3) Odd: 零頭 (兒) odd lots; 零件, 零用 *-jiahn*, *-yuhng*↓; 找零兒 give customer small change.

零丁 *lirngding*, adj., alone without relatives (also wr. 伶仃).

零度 *lirngduh*, n., zero degree: 零下三度 three degrees below zero.

零活(兒) *lirnghuor('l)*, n., odd jobs (dist. 靈活 31D.30).

零件 *lirngjiahn*, n., (1) odds and ends, accessories; (2) spare parts.

零亂 *lirngluahn*, adj., confused, piled together.

零落 *lirngluoh*, adj., (of plants) withered, bare without leaves; (2) (family, etc.) in bad circumstances; (3) incomplete in a set.

零賣 *lirngmaih*, v. i. & t., sell by retail.

零售 *lirngshouh*, v.i. & t., ditto.

零數 *lirngshuh*, n., (1) the number zero; (2) remainder.

零碎(兒) *lirngsueih('l)*, n., odd pieces, leftover: 零零碎碎 (adj.) too detailed, not welded together; (n.) such odd details.

零頭(兒) *lirngtour'l*, n., remainder; (cloth) odd lots.

零用 *lirngyuhng*, n., sundry expenses; pocket money.

§ 31D.70 (雨/乚)

電 31D.70-4

diahn.

N. & adj. (1) Electric, -ity: usu. 電氣 electricity; 電力 electric power, or force; 發電, 生電 generate electricity; forming many compp. connected with electricity and some merely imagined to be so: see 電瓶 *-pirng*, 電棒 *-bahng*, 電驢子 *-lyurtz* ↓; 動電, 靜電 dynamic, static electricity; 正電, 負電 positive, negative electricity; 無線電 wireless, radio; 電子 *-tzyy* ↓. (2) Telegram, short for 電報: 急電 urgent telegram; 賀電 telegram of congratulations; by telegram: 電賀 wire congratulations; 電匯 (business) telegraphic transfer (abbr. T.T.); 電覆 reply by wire. (3) Lightning: 雷電 thunder and lightning; 風馳電掣 lightning fast. (4) (Court.) 電察, 電照 (sometimes used in correspondence) for your bright consideration.

V.i. & t. To wire, communicate by wire: 電示, 電復 wire reply; 電知 inform by wire; 電某人 wire to s.o; 電殛 electrocuted by lightning.

電版 *diahnbaan*, n., electroplate.

電棒 *diahnbahng*, n., portable flashlight.

電報 *diaanbauh*, n., telegram, -graph: 發電報 send telegram; 電報局 telegraph office; 電報重發器 telegraph repeater; 電報符號 telegraphic code, or indicator, such as Morse.

電表 *diahnbiaau*, n., electric meter.

電波 *diahnbo*, n., electric waves.

電唱機 *fiahnchahngji*, n., electric phonograph, a record player.

電場 *diahncharng*, n., electric field.

電插頭 *diahnchatour*, n., socket for electric light or power.

電車 *diahnche*, n., tramcar, streetcar, trolley car.

電氣 *diahnchih*[1], n., electricity.

電器 *diahnchih*[2], n., electric appliances.

電池 *diahnchyr*, n., battery: 乾電池 dry battery.

電傳照相 *diahnchyuarn jauhshiahng*, n., radiophoto, telephoto; 電傳打字機 *--daatzyhji*, n., teletype.

電導 *diahndauh*, n., electric circuit.

電燈 *diahndeng*, n., electric light; 電燈泡 *--pauh*, n., light bulb, globe; also unwanted third party accompanying lovers.

電鍍 *diahnduh*, n., electroplate.

電動機 *diahnduhng-ji*, n., electric motor; 電動力學 electrodynamics; 電動勢 electromotive force.

電杆 *diahngan*, n., telegraph pole, also 電線杆.

電光 *diahnguang*, n., light of electricity, lightning.

電荷 *diahnheh*, n., electric charge; 電荷密度 charge density.

電花 *diahnhua*, n., electric spark.

電話 *diahnhuah*, n., telephone: 打電話 to telephone; 電話簿 telephone directory; 電話號碼 telephone number; 電話亭 telephone booth.

電弧燈 *diahnhur-deng*, n., arc lamp.

電解 *diahnjiee*, n., electrolysis; 電解液 (or 質) n., electrolyte; 電解分離 n., electrolytic dissociation.

電擊 *diahn-jir*[1], n., electric shock; lightning stroke.

電極 *diahnjir*[2], n., electrode.

電纜 *diahnlaan*, n., electric cable.

電量計 *diahnliahng-jih*, n., voltameter.

電療 *diahnliaur*, n., electrotherapy.

電力 *diahnlih*, n., electric force; electric power; 電力線 line of electric force.

電流 *diahnliour*, n., electric current; 電流計 galvanometer; 電流密度 electric current density; 直電流 direct current; 交電流 alternate current.

電鈴 *diahnlirng*, n., electric bell.

電路 *diahnluh*, n., electric circuit.

電爐 *diahnlur*, n., electric stove, furnace.

電驢子 *diahnlyurtz*, n., (sl.) motorcycle.

電碼 *diahnmaa*, n., telegraphic code.

電門 *diahnmern*, n., electric switch.

電木 *diahnmuh*, n., bakelite.

電腦 *diahnnaau*, n., storage system in computer, (oft. loosely used of washing machine, etc.).

電鈕 *diahnnioou*, n., electric button.

電瓶 *diahnpirng*, n., electric cell, storage battery, accumulator; also (pop.) thermos bottle.

電容 *diahnrurng*, n., electric capacity.

電扇 *diahnshahn*, n., electric fan.

電線 *diahnshiahn*, n., electric wire.
電視 *diahnshyh*, n., television.
電石燈 *diahnshyr-deng*, n., acetylene lamp.
電學 *diahnshyuer*, n., the science of electricity.
電燙 *diahntahng*, n., (of woman's hair-do) permanent wave.
電臺 *diahntair*, n., radio or television station; such broadcast.
電梯 *diahnti*, n., elevator.
電筒 *diahntuung*, n., flashlight, also called 電棒 *-bahng*↑.
電阻 *diahntzuu*, n., electric resistance: 電阻箱 resistance box; 電阻係數 specific resistance.
電磁 *diahntzy*, n., electromagnetism; 電磁鐵 *--tiee*, n., electromagnet; 電磁説 *--shuo*, n., theory of electromagnetism; 電磁波 *--bo*, n., electromagnetic wave.
電子 *diahntzyy*, n., electron; 電子學 *--shyuer*, n., electronics; 電子顯微鏡 *--shiaanweir-jihng*, n., electronic microscope; 電子音樂 electronic music.
電網 *diahnwaang*, n., charged barbed wire fence.
電位 *diahnweih*, n., electric potential.
電壓 *diahnya*, n., electric pressure, voltage.
電眼 *diahnyaan*, n. magic eye.
電椅 *diahnyii*, n., electric chair.
電影(兒) *diahnying('l)*, n., movie; 有聲電影 talkie; 電影明星 movie star.

霓 31D.70–9

nir.

N. A rainbow (also wr. 蜺).

霓虹燈 *nirhurng-deng*, n., neon lamp.
霓旌 *nirjing*, n., a banner of multicolored feathers.

雹 31D.70–9

baur (re. pr. **bor*).

N. Hail: 下雹了 it hails; oft. 冰雹.

§ 31D.81 (雨/人)

霙 31D.81–2

ying.

N. (AC) (1) sleet. (2) snowflakes.

§ 31D.82 (雨/乂)

霰 31D.82–2

shiahn.

N. Sleet.

霞 31D.82–5

shiar.

N. Rosy cloud: 晚霞 rosy sunset; 朝霞 morning glow; 彩霞 roseate clouds.

霞帔 *shiarpeih*[1], n., scarf over jacket for bride or lady on formal occasions.
霞珮 *shiarpeih*[2], n., ladies' pendants.

雯 31D.82–6

wern.

N. Cloud patterns.

§ 31D.83 (雨/一)

霆 31D.83–9

tirng.

N. Thunderbolt: 雷霆 crash of thunder, symbolic of anger: 雷霆之怒 (之威).

§ 31D.93 (雨/〈)

雲 31D.93–3

yurn.

N. (1) Cloud(s): 浮雲 floating clouds; 彩雲 clouds of many colors; 雲彩 *-tsaai*↓; 祥雲 clouds that are lucky omens; 雲霧 *-wuh*, 雲雨 *-yuu*↓; 雲消霧散 sky has cleared up, oft. (fig.) (of fears, worries) clear up, disappear; 雲山霧罩 extravagant and baseless talk; 雲起龍驤 the rise of great heroes; 雲譎波詭 sudden and perplexing changes, also changing kaleidoscopically; symbol of multitudes: 雲集 swarm about; 僕從如雲 myriads of servants, retinue. (2) Short for 雲南 Yunnan Province: 雲腿 Yunnan ham; 雲貴 Yunnan and Kweichow. (3) A surname.

雲鬢 *yurn-bihn*, n., lady's hair.
雲車 *yurn-che*, n., (AC) a high carriage.
雲梯 *yurn-chiaur*, n., ladder with scaffolding (for storming city).
雲氣 *yurnchih*, n., cloud mists.
雲衢 *yurn-chyur*, n., formerly, main highway in capital city.
雲(稨)豆 *yurn(biaan)douh*, n., a kind of bean.
雲端 *yurn-duan*, phr., high in the clouds.
雲海 *yurn-haai*, n., a sea of clouds.

雲漢 *yurnhahn*, n., the Milky Way.

雲鬟 *yurnhuarn*, n., a lady's hair.

雲章 *yurn-jang*, n., (LL) an emperor's handwriting.

雲際 *yurn-jih*[1], phr., high in the clouds.

雲髻 *yurn-jih*[2], n., a lady's hair-coil.

雲集 *yurn-jir*, v.i., swarm about together.

雲羅 *yurn-lour*[1], n., sheets of clouds.

雲鑼 *yurnluor*[2], n., a set of small gongs.

雲履 *yurn-lyuu*, n., shoes with wavy cloud patterns.

雲母 *yurnmuu*, n., (geol.) mica.

雲泥 *yurn-nir*[1], phr., great difference in status (clouds and mud).

雲霓 *yurn-nir*[2], n., (AC) clouds presaging rainstorm.

雲片糕 *yurnpiahn-gau*, n., a kind of Chin. wafers.

雲擾 *yurn-raau*, v.t., to disturb.

雲仍 *yurn-rerng*, n., distant great-grandchildren (cf. 孫 32S.01).

雲霞 *yurnshiar*, n., beautiful clouds; 雲霞之交 (LL) high-minded friendship.

雲霄 *yurnshiau*, n., the sky, the region of clouds.

雲實 *yurnshyr*, n., (bot.) the Mysore thorn, *Caesalpinia sepiaria*.

雲梯 *yurnti*, n., see *-chiaur*↑.

雲天 *yurn-tian*, n., high regions of the clouds.

雲頭 *yurn-tour*, phr., the clouds; 雲頭兒 wavy cloud pattern.

雲彩 *yurn'tsai*, n., clouds, beautiful clouds.

雲霧 *yurnwuh*, n., cloudy mist, haze.

雲吞 *yurntun*, n., Chin. ravioli, wonton, (also 餛吞).

雲煙 *yurnyan*, n., cloud and mist; s.t. which vanishes quickly.

雲液 *yurnyeh*[1], n., (LL) wine.

雲葉 *yurnyeh*[2], n., (bot.) *Euptelea polyandra*.

雲遊 *yurn-your*, v.i., to travel about or abroad in freedom.

雲雨 *yurn-yuu*, n., (1) favors, blessings from on high; (2) (euphem.) sexual intercourse (from allu., a fairy maiden in the Szechuan Gorges who commanded the clouds and rains).

霎 31D.93–6

shah.

N. (1) Light drizzle. (2) A wink, blink.

霎霎 *shahshah*, adj., descriptive of sound of drizzling rain.

霎時 *shahshyr*, adv., a short moment (time of batting an eye).

SECTION 31S

§ 31S.00 (Tˢ/亅)

耐 31S.00–1

naih.

V.t. Bear, endure: 耐勞 can endure hardships; 耐煩 *-farn*↓; 耐時 wait patiently for an opportune moment; 耐心煩(兒) bear annoyance patiently; 耐不住 cannot bear it.

Adj. (1) (Adj. & n.) patient, -nce, tolerant, -ce, having resistance: 忍耐 patient or tolerant; 不耐 impatient or intolerant; 耐寒 resistant (-ce) to cold; 能耐 n., ability, staying power. (2) Enduring: 耐用, 耐久 capable of standing wear and tear; 耐人尋味 stand careful reading or pondering about; 耐嚼 (of food) tasty and savory.

耐煩 *naihfarn*, v.i., have patience.

耐火磚 *naihhuoojuan*, n., fire-brick made to resist heat, as in chimneys, fireplaces, etc.

耐性 *naihshihng*, n., patience.

耐心 *naihshin*, n., ditto.

列 31S.00–2

lieh.

N. (1) Row: 行列 row or column; 第三列 the third row (＝排). (2) A surname.

V. i. To arrange in order, form line, to enter in list: 列名 to enter or appear on a list of persons; 列單 make out list (of goods, in-

亅	小	卜	十	土	ナ	卄	𠃊卜	丨	一	丁	フ	口	区	冈	㇆	厂	尸	亠	广	宀	丶	乚	弋	心	八	人	乂	乛	㇀	ノ	𠂉	く
00	01	02	10	11	12	20	21	22	30	31	32	40	41	42	50	51	52	60	61	62	63	70	71	72	80	81	82	83	90	91	92	93

vited guests, candidates, etc.); 列坐 be seated in a row with others; 列成隊伍 (mil.) to fall in, form company; 列於 be named, appear on (list); 左列 as appears below.

Adj. Prefaced to nn., signifying a group: 列星 the stars; 列宿 the constellations; 列強, 列島 *-chiarng*, *-daau* ↓; 列肆 group of shops together; 列位 (used in public address): "ladies and gentlemen," those of you here.

Adv. Instance after instance: 列舉人名, 罪狀 give list of names, counts of crimes.

列車 *liehche*, n., railroad train, a train of wagons.

列強 *liehchiarng*, n., the Great Powers.

列島 *liehdaau*, n., archipelago.

列鼎 *liehdiing*, n., (LL, rare) great feast.

列國 *liehguor*, n., the different countries: 春秋列國 the city states of time of Confucius.

列傳 *liehjuahn*, n., biographies, esp. section on biographies in different dynastic histories.

列列 *liehlieh*, adj., clearly shown in order; big in stature; sound of wind.

列女 *liehnyuu*, n., famous women in history (see 烈[a]女 31.63).

列席 *liehshir*, v. i., (1) be present at meeting; (2) be observer at conference.

列士 *liehshyh*, n., (1) (AC) the gentry, a class below 大夫; (2) u.f. 烈[a]士 31.63.

列氏表 *Liehshyh-biaau*, n., Réaumur's thermometer.

列土 *lieh-tuu*, v.i., (AC) to divide into fiefdoms, given to royal princes.

刑 31S.00-2

shirng.

[Var. 刑]

N. Punishment: 刑罰, 刑事, 刑法 *-far*, *-shyh*, *-faa* ↓; 刑訊 *-shyuhn* ↓; 處刑 mete out, submit to punishment; 徒刑, 死刑 sentence to hard labor, to death; 笞刑 punishment by whipping; 絞刑 punishment by strangling; 酷刑 torture, third degree; 上刑 "put on the works" (shackles, whipping, etc.); 緩刑 suspend execution of sentence, delay punishment; 受刑不過 could not stand the torture (and confessed).

刑場 *shirng-chaang*, n., execution ground.

刑臣 *shirng-chern*, n., (AC) eunuch (lit., "castrated officer").

刑典 *shirngdiaan*, n., criminal code.

刑法 *shirng-faa*, n., criminal law.

刑罰 *shirngfar*, v. t. & n., to punish, -ment.

刑房 *shirng-farng*, n., formerly, department of criminal prosecution.

刑杖 *shirngjahng*, n., staff used for thrashing.

刑章 *shirngjang*, n., see *-diaan* ↑.

刑具 *shirng-jyuh*, n., instruments of torture.

刑戮 *shirngluh*, v. t., to kill as punishment.

刑律 *shirnglyuh*, n., see *-faa* ↑.

刑名 *shirngmirng*, n., (1) (AC) law, esp. criminal laws; 刑名之學 (philosophy of legalist school, e. g., 韓非); (2) 刑名師爺 formerly, government secretary, who is specialist in law, known for skillful use of a judicious word to incriminate people (深文, 周納).

刑人 *shirng-rern*, n., (AC) a person permanently crippled or disfigured by punishment.

刑賞 *shirng-shaang*, n., the administration of justice ("punishment and award").

刑書 *shirng-shu*, n., (AC) book of criminal laws.

刑事 *shirngshyh*, adj. & n., pertaining to crimes, criminal (act, case); 刑事訴訟法 code of criminal procedure.

刑訊 *shirngshyuhn*, v. i. & n., cross-examination with application of torture.

刑庭 *shirng-tirng*, n., criminal court.

刑網 *shirng-waang*, phr., the long arm of the law.

刑問 *shirngwehn*, v. i. & n., see *-shyuhn* ↑.

刑餘 *shirngyur*, n., (1) (AC) eunuch, see *-chern* ↑; (2) (AC) ex-convict.

刵 31S.00-2

ehl.

V. t. To lop off the ear, an anc. punishment.

到 31S.00-2

dauh.

V. i. & t. (1) Arrive: 到家 arrive at home, also see *-jia* ↓; 已經到了 have arrived; 時間到了 the (appointed) time has come. (2) Go to (destination): 到日本去 go to Japan; 到那裏去 where are you going? (3) 到過 been to; 沒到過 have never been to.

Vb. complement. Showing completed action: 看到, 聽到 see, hear (as dist. look, listen); 收到 have received, 找到 have found; 來到 come to; 拿到 got hold of; 做不到 cannot do it; 想得到, 做得到 what he wanted to do, he accomplished; 想不到 never thought or imagined that; 夢想不到 never dreamed (that).

Prep. At, up to, upon: 到次日 upon the next day; 到今天 up to today; 到此 (地) 爲止 stop here; 到處 *-chuh* ↓.

到案 *dauh-ahn*, v.i., appear at court.

到岸價格 *dauh-ahn jiahger*, n., cost, insurance and freight (c.i.f.)

到差 *dauh-chai*, v.i., arrive at post, appear for duty.

到場 *dauh-charng*, v.i., be present (at party, meeting).

到期 *dauhchir*, phr., when time is

due; 到期日 date of maturity.

到處 *dauh-chuh*, adv., everywhere: 到處去找 look for it everywhere.

到達 *dauhdar*, v.t., reach: 到達某地 reach certain place; 到達目的 reach goal.

到得 *dauh-der*, conj., until, as soon as: 到得那個時候 when that time arrives.

到底 *dauhdii*, adv., (1) after all: 到底不是壞 after all this is not a bad thing; 到底沒錯 after all there was nothing wrong; (2) to the end: 抗戰到底 fight to the bitter end.

到家 *dauhjia*, (1) adj., (of art, artist) accomplished, skilled, proficient; (2) v.i., come home.

到了 *dauhliaau*, v.i., (1) *dauh'le*, arrive: 到了那個時候 when the time comes; (2) 到了兒 *dauhliau'l*, adv. phr., in the end.

到任 *dauh-rehn*, v.i., assume post.

到手 *dauh-shoou*, phr., succeed in getting: 錢拿到手 have money in hand; 弄不到手 fail in getting.

到頭來 *dauh-tour-lair*, adv. phr., in the end (lose everything, etc.).

刵 31S.00-2

huah.

[Pop. of 劃 22S.00]

剄 31S.00-2

jiing.

V. i. To cut the throat: 自剄 commit suicide by slashing the throat.

剽 31S.00-2

piauh.

V. t. (1) To rob, take what is not one's own. (2) (AC) slice off (property).

Adj. (AC, of animals) fast, agile.

剽剝 *piauhbo*, v. t., (AC) attack (doctrine, etc.).

剽竊 *piauhchieh*, v. t. & n., plagiarize, -ism.

剽輕 *piauhching*, adj., blusterirg, combative (youth).

剽悍 *piauhhaan*, adj., warlike.

剽劫 *piauhjier*, v. t., roam and rob.

剽疾 *piauhjir*, adj., fast (fighter, etc.).

剽掠 *piauhlyueh*, v. t., loot the country.

肵 31S.00-2

suoo.

[Abbr. of 所 90S.22]

殍 31S.00-9

piaau.

[Var. 莩]

N. Exposed bodies of those who died from starvation.

§31S.01 (T^s/小)

殊 31S.01-1

shu.

Adj. (1) Different: 殊異, 殊別 *-yih, -bier* ↓; 特殊 special (circumstances, etc.); 殊途同歸 different roads lead to the same goal ("all roads lead to Rome"). (2) Excellent, distinguished, unusual: 殊色 outstanding beauty; 殊功, 殊勳, 殊績 outstanding, notable service; 殊能 unusual ability; 殊恩, 殊遇 uncommon royal or imperial favors.

Adv. (1) Indeed: oft. 殊屬, 殊爲, 殊非, 殊難, etc.; 殊爲不該 (s.t.) is indeed wrong, improper; 殊屬非是 ditto; 殊非原意 that was not (my) original intention; 殊難解決 indeed difficult to settle or decide. (2) Very: 殊久 (LL) very long; 殊念 deeply miss (s.o.).

殊別 *shubier*, adj., different.

殊等 *shu-deeng*, n., special class.

殊方 *shu-fang*, phr., different places, distant places.

殊功 *shu-gung*, n., distinguished service.

殊技 *shu-jih*, n., excellent skill.

殊絕 *shujyuer*, adj., rare, distinguished (art, talent).

殊科 *shu-ke*, n., different category.

殊類 *shu-leih*, n., different tribe, type.

殊力 *shu-lih*, n., special effort, see *-syy* ↓.

殊禮 *shu-lii*, n., special, privileged treatment.

殊能 *shu-nerng*, n., special skill.

殊派 *shu-paih*, n., different school, clan or party.

殊榮 *shu-rurng*, n., unusual honor.

殊勝 *shushehng*, adj., (LL) unusual, meritorious.

殊效 *shu-shiauh*, n., marked efficacy.

殊行 *shu-shirng*, n., admirable, distinctive conduct or character.

殊選 *shu-shyuaan*, adj., select, out of common run (of men).

殊俗 *shu-sur*, (1) n., different custom; (2) adj., unconventional (character).

殊死 *shusyy*, adj., as in 殊死力 utmost effort; 殊死戰 heroic fight, fight to the death.

殊態 *shu-taih*, n., distinctive manner.

殊異 *shyuyih*, adj., distinctive.

殊尤 *shuyour*, adj., ditto.

殊域 *shu-yuh*[1], n., distant regions.

殊遇 *shu-yuh*[2], n., unusual honor

or recognition.

臻 31S.01–1

jen.

V. t. (LL) to attain (a height), to realize (a high ideal): 已臻上乘 arrive at excellent or superior condition; 曷克臻此 how could this be otherwise attained (without s.o.'s help)?

§ 31S.02 (Tˢ/k)

殨 31S.02–8

sun.
[Pop. of 飧 92S.02]

§ 31S.10 (Tˢ/十)

殫 31S.10–4

dan.

V. t. (LL) give all one has got (=vern. 盡): 殫心, 殫力 (=盡心, 盡力) give all one knows, all of one's strength; 殫竭其力 ditto; 殫精(思)竭慮 think of everything one can (to do).

§ 31S.11 (Tˢ/土)

殣 31S.11–2

jiin (also *jihn*).

V. i. & t. (AC) (1) V. i., die of hunger, starve to death. (2) V. t., bury, inter, entomb.

§ 31S.22 (Tˢ/丨)

殢 31S.22–2

tih.

Adj. Tired, fatigued.

邛 31S.22–3

chyurng.

N. (AC) a hillock; labor.

邛杖 *chyurngjahng*, n., a bamboo cane.

邦 31S.22–3

harn.

N. (1) Name of a river. (2) A surname.

邢 31S.22–3

shirng.

N. A surname.

邳 31S.22–3

peir.

N. (1) 邳縣 *Peirshiahn*, name of district. (2) A surname.

郅 31S.22–3

jyh.

N. A surname.

Adj. (AC) var. of 至 very, ultimate: 郅治 (=至治) complete peace; 郅盛 (=至盛) great prosperity.

耶 31S.22–3

yer (*ye).

Fin. part. (LL) used in interrogation: 是耶, 非耶 is it true or is it not? (also wr. 邪).

耶和華 *Yeherhuar*, n., Jehovah.
耶路撒冷 *Yeluhsaleeng*, n., Jerusalem.
耶魯 *Yeluu*, n., Yale.
耶穌 *Yesu*, Jesus; n., 耶穌教 Christianity, the Christian religion or church.

鄢 31S.22–3

yan.

N. A surname.

豨 31S.22–8

shi.

N. (AC) hog.

聊 31S.22–9

liaur.

V. i. (1) To chat idly: 請多聊一會 please stay and chat a while yet;

聊天, 聊聊 *-tian, -liau*↓. (2) To endure: 聊賴 *-laih*↓; 民不聊生 the people find it hard to live on; 無聊 adj., bored, oppressed, find time idle, also boring, (play, performance) most uninteresting: 無聊的很 (of meeting, play) boring; beneath concern: 這個人太無聊 this person is not worth keeping company with, is a bore.

Adv. Rather, just, just a little: 聊勝於無 better than nothing; 聊陳愚見 just express my opinion; 聊勝一等 just a little better; 聊以助興 just for entertainment; 聊以自慰 comfort oneself with thought.

聊且 *liaurchiee*, adv., just, see Adv.↑.
聊浪 *liaurlahng*, adj., (AC) unrestrained, wandering freely.
聊賴 *liaurlaih*, v. i., to endure (boredom): 百無聊賴 be completely bored, despondent.
聊聊 *liaur'liau*, v. i., have a chat.
聊天(兒) *liaurtian(-tia'l)*, v. i., chat idly (＝談天).

聯 31S.22-9

liarn.
[Abbr. 联, 聨; pop. 聫; dist. 連 10.83 with same pr., "combine," "continue"; 聯 "unite"]

N. Couplet, written or inscribed, oft. hung up as decoration: 對聯 couplet; 輓聯 scroll of condolence; 門聯 couplet on door panels; 楹聯 couplet on posts; 春聯 New Year couplet.

V.i. To unite; hence oft. in p.p. form, "United" (name of company, etc.).

聯保 *liarnbaau*, v.i., system of making two or more persons responsible for one another's action.
聯邦 *liarnbang*, adj. & n., federal, confederate, -acy, federation: 聯邦政府 federal government.
聯璧 *liarnbih*, n., see 連^{A}璧 10.83.
聯大 *liarndah*, n., short for 聯合國大會 United Nations General Assembly.
聯單 *liarndan*, n., duplicate or joint forms for receipt, etc.
聯貫 *liarnguahn*, v.i. & n., continue, -uity: 不相聯貫 disjointed.
聯合 *liarnher*, v.i., unite(d); 聯合國 United Nations (UN); 聯合國大會 General Assembly of the UN (GA); 聯合國安全理事會 Security Council of the UN (SC); 聯合國憲章 Charter of the UN: 聯合國教科文組織 United Nations Educational, Scientific, and Cultural Organization (UNESCO); 聯合國糧農組織 Food and Agriculture Organization of the UN (FAO); 聯合政府 coalition government.
聯歡 *liarnhuan*, n., social get-together: 聯歡會 get-together party.
聯軍 *liarnjyun*, n., the allied troops.
聯絡 *liarnluoh*, v.i., to get in touch with each other, keep in contact, (also wr. 連絡); 聯絡官(員) liaison officer.
聯袂 *liarn-meih*, adv., as in 聯袂而來 arrive together as a group (lit., "joining sleeves").
聯盟 *liarnmerng*, v.i., ally oneself with; n., alliance; 國際聯盟 League of Nations.
聯緜 *liarnmiarn*, adv., (come) in close succession, in continuous stream.
聯名 *liarn-mirng*, phr., with joint signatures.
聯翩 *liarnpian*, adv., see *-miarn*↑.
聯票 *liarn-piauh*, n., coupon with connection tickets for journey.
聯想 *liarnshiaang*, v.i. & n., by association of thought, mental association: 我聯想到 remind one of s.t.
聯繫 *liarnshih*, n. & v.i., connection; make connection (with person) for some business.
聯席 *liarn-shir*, phr., at the same table; 聯席會議 joint session or conference.
聯手 *liarn-shoou*, v.i., join hands (with person).
聯屬 *liarnshuu*^{1}, v.i., belong together.
聯署 *liarnshuu*^{2}, v.i., give joint signatures.
聯宗 *liarntzung*, v.i., combined branches of clan.
聯誼 *liarnyih*, n., fellowship; 聯誼會 social, fellowship party.
聯姻 *liarnyin*, v.i., be related by marriage.
聯營 *liarnyirng*, n., joint management; 聯營事業 enterprise by joint investment (government and private); 聯營公司 affiliated company.

§ 31S.30 (ㄒˢ/一)

殖 31S.30-1

jyr.
[Usu. printed 殖]

N. Plantation: 種殖, 種殖園.

V. t. (1) To cultivate crops, to plant: 移殖 transplant (trees, heart, kidney). (2) To trade, "grow" in business: 貨殖 commerce; 殖財, 殖利 trade for profit; 增殖 expand business; 殖產 business property. (3) 生殖, 蕃殖 (of plants and animals) to grow and multiply; 生殖器 sexual organs. (4) To settle population: 殖民 *-mirn*↓.

殖民 *jyrmirn*, n., colonization (policy); 殖民地 n. & adj., colony, colonial (government, policy, people).

聊 聯 殖

亅	小	⺊	十	土	ナ	卄	ㄴ	丨	一	丁	フ	口	区	冈	ㄱ	厂	尸	亠	广	宀	丶	乚	弋	心	八	人	乂	⌒	一	ノ	㇀	く
00	01	02	10	11	12	20	21	22	30	31	32	40	41	42	50	51	52	60	61	62	63	70	71	72	80	81	82	83	90	91	92	93

殪 31S.30-1

yih.

V. i. & t. (AC) to die; to kill.

耻 31S.30-2

chyy.

[Pop. of 恥 31S.72]

殭 31S.30-3

jiang.

Adj. Dead but not yet putrefied: 殭巴 dry and shriveled; 殭斃 *-bih,* 殭屍 *-shy,* 殭蠶 *-tsarn*↓; 死而不殭 dead but showing no signs of rigor mortis.

殭 斃 *jiangbih,* adj., dead and stiff.
殭 屍 *jiangshy,* n., a vampire, a reanimated corpse.
殭 蠶 *jiang-tsarn,* n., silkworms that die before spinning.

殛 31S.30-3

jir.

V. t. (AC) to kill: 殛鯀於禹山 executed Guun at Yushan; 遭雷殛 (LL) struck by lightning.

殂 31S.30-4

tsur.

V. i. To die: 殂落 (AC, of ruler) pass away.

§ 31S.40 (T^{s}/口)

聒 31S.40-9

gua.

Adj. (Of noise) loud and confusing: 聒耳 deafening to the ear.

聒 聒 叫 *guaguajiauh,* adj., (Shanghai) (of things, persons) the best there is.
聒 絮 *guashyuh,* v. i., babble endlessly.
聒 噪 *guatzauh,* v. i. & adj., make disturbing noises (as birds); boisterous and clamorous.

殆 31S.40-9

daih.

Adj. (1) Dangerous: 殆哉 (exclam.) dangerous indeed; 思而不學則殆 (Confu.) thinking without reading makes one flighty (學而不思則罔 reading without thinking makes one muddled). (2) Tired, exhausted: 力殆 strength exhausted.

Adv. (LL) almost, it is feared: 存款殆盡 cash is almost exhausted; 殆存 (s.t.) barely exists; 其愚殆不可及 the foolishness, I am afraid is unmatched.

§ 31S.41 (T^{s}/図)

豬 31S.41-1

ju.

[Pop. 猪]

N. Pig, hog: 公豬, 母豬 male, female pig; 豬毛 pig's bristle; 豬肉 pork; 豬油 pork fat, used in cooking; 豬肝 liver of pig, etc.; 野豬 boar; 豬仔 *-tzaai*↓; 豬玀 *-luor*↓; swine (a term of abuse), symbol of stupidity, but not of gluttony or filth as in Eng.: 蠢豬 pig-headed person; 豬狗不如 worse than pigs or dogs, like a swine.

豬 公 *jugung,* n., male pig.
豬 貛 *juhuan,* n., (zoo.) the badger.
豬 圈 *jujyuahn,* n., a pigpen.
豬 欄 *jularn,* n., a pigpen.
豬 苓 *julirng,* n., a kind of "China root."
豬 玀 *juluor,* n., (abusive) swine.
豬 籠 草 *julurngtsaau,* n., the pitcher plant, *Nepenthes Rafflesiana.*
豬 婆 龍 *juporlurng,* n., a giant sea turtle, giant tortoise.
豬 頭 三 *jutoursan,* n., (Shanghai coll.) fool, "pig head."
豬 仔 *jutzaai,* n., (1) (Cantonese) a piglet; (2) victim of slave trade, sold and shipped abroad as cheap labor.
豬 鬃 *ju-tzung,* n., pig's bristles.

§ 31S.42 (T^{s}/図)

聃 31S.42-2

dan.

[Var. 聸]

N. Personal name of Laotse: 老聃.

§ 31S.50 (T^{s}/ㄱ)

聘 31S.50-2

pihn (**pihng*).

N. & v.t. (1) Appoint: 聘爲 invite

as; 聘為顧問, 教授 appoint as advisor, professor; 延聘, 邀聘, 徵聘 invite, appoint (teacher, etc.); 應聘 accept appointment; 聘請, 聘任, 聘用 *-chiing*, *-rehn*, *-yuhng* ↓. (2) (**pihng*) Betroth, -thal: 定聘 formally betroth; (also *pihn*) (AC) be married to; 出聘 (於) be married to; 聘禮, 聘金 *-lii*, *-jin* ↓. (3) (LL) diplomatic mission between countries.

聘 妻 *pihnchi*, n., fiancée.
聘 請 *pinchiing*, v.t., appoint (person) as: 聘請教授, 專家 appoint professor, specialist.
聘 姑 娘 *pihn* or **pihng gu'niang*, v.t., marry a girl off.
聘 金 *pihnjin*, n., gift of groom's family to family of betrothed.
聘 禮 *pihnlii*, ditto.
聘 任 *pihnrehn*, v.t., appoint to post, used as *-chiing* ↑.
聘 書 *pihnshu*, n., letter of appointment.
聘 使 *pihnshyy*, n., (AC) diplomatic missions.
聘 用 *pihnyuhng*, v.t., see *-chiing*, *-rehn* ↑.

巧 31S.50–3

chiaau.

N. (1) Small skills: 技巧 skillful, also skills; 巧奪天工 divine skill. (2) Seventh day of seventh lunar month: 巧夕 *-shih* ↓.

Adj. (1) Intelligent, clever, skillful: 靈巧 clever (handicraft, mind); 巧思 a clever thought; 巧言 clever words; 巧語 a clever saying; 巧計 clever strategy: 巧工 clever art work; 巧匠 clever carpenter or artisan; 巧手 a skillful hand, artisan; 巧婦難為無米之炊 even a clever woman cannot cook a meal without rice; 巧發奇中 a clever, penetrating remark. (2) Artful, deceiving: 巧詐 *-jah* ↓; 巧辯 specious argument; 花言巧語 a lot of artful talk, pretty words; 奸巧 deceitful (person); 巧言令色鮮矣仁 (Confu.) artful speech and flashy manners seldom indicate a real man; 取巧 do things by irregular ways; 巧吏, 巧宦 clever politician.

Adv. (1) Cleverly: 巧詆 criticize or attack artfully. (2) Fortuitously, by a happy chance: 巧遇 extraordinary meeting (of a person); 巧合 strangely fits (prophecy, etc.); 恰巧 ditto; see 巧當兒 *-dang'l* ↓; 湊巧 it happens by luck; 趕巧兒 at the most opportune moment (s. o. arrives, etc.); 巧極了, 巧得很 what a coincidence! 這可巧了 this is indeed an extraordinary (meeting, etc.); 不巧 unfortunately.

巧 當 兒 *chiaaudang'l*, adv. & n., by a good chance, a chance opportunity.
巧 故 *chiaauguh*, n., (AC) artful deceit.
巧 詐 *chiaaujah*, adj., deceitful.
巧 勁 兒 *chiaaujieh'l*, n., (1) great skill (usu. manual); (2) unexpected meeting, event.
巧 捷 *chiaaujier*, adj., skillful, fast.
巧 計 *chiaaujih*, n., clever stratagem, trick.
巧 妙 *chiaaumiauh*, adj., wonderful (turn of events, art work).
巧 舌 *chiaau-sher*, n., clever words.
巧 夕 *chiaaushih*, see the seventh day of the seventh lunar month, see 七$^{\Delta}$夕 70.70.
巧 宗 兒 *chiaautzung'l*, n., a piece of good luck: 是巧宗兒, 你們都得了 if good luck comes, you all will share it.

功 31S.50–9

gung.

N. (1) Achievements, accomplishments: 功名 *-mirng*, 功德 *-der*, 功勞 *-'laur*, 功勳 *-shyun*, 功利 *-lih*[1], 功績 *-jir*, 功業 *-yeh* ↓; 功虧一簣 just one step short of success or completion; 功不補過 demerits outweigh merits; 徒勞無功 make futile efforts; 功成身退 retire after having made one's mark; 成功 success; 有功 deserving of recognition for services rendered; 立功 accomplish a great service or achievement. (2) Efficacy, good results: 功效 *-shiauh*, 功用 *-yuhng*, 功能 *-nerng*, 功力 *-lih*[2] ↓. (3) Action deserving reward, merit (opp. 過 demerit): 記功, give mark of credit; 紀功碑 memorial tablet. (4) (Phys.) work. (5) A mourning garment: 功服 *-fur* ↓.

功 臣 *gungchern*, n., formerly, loyal ministers with a record of distinguished service, (fig.) anyone who has rendered great service.
功 德 *gungder*, n., (1) an achievement or contribution to general welfare: 功德無量 a great service to mankind; (2) (Budd.) meritorious works.
功 夫 *gung'fu*, n., (1) (interch. 工夫) time and energy expended on work; (2) degree of perfection attained in any line of work: 功夫甚深 knowledge of subject is profound.
功 服 *gungfur*, n., formerly, a mourning garment worn for nine months in case of 大功 and for five months in that of 小功.
功 架 *gungjiah*, n., (1) a person's conduct and carriage; (2) an actor's movements and gestures on stage.
功 績 *gungjir*, n., merits, contributions.
功 課 *gungkeh*, n., lessons, studies (also 工課).
功 勞 *gung'laur*, n., meritorious services, contribution (great, small) to work, nation, etc.
功 利 *gunglih*[1], n., utility, material gain: 功利主義 utilitarianism.
功 力 *gunglih*[2], n., (1) merits, efficacy; (2) (coll.) force and skill, esp. in regard to training.

功率 *gunglyuh*, n., (phys.) power, degree of power.

功名 *gungmirng*, n., formerly, official honor or rank, esp. academic degrees in civil examinations.

功能 *gungnerng*, n., function, skill, ability.

功效 *gungshiauh*, n., effect (-iveness), efficacy (of medicine, etc.).

功勳 *gungshyun*, n., services to the nation.

功業 *gungyeh*, n., outstanding accomplishments to nation or society.

功用 *gungyuhng*, n., purpose, function; efficacy.

勁 31S.50–9

jihng (sp. pr. *jihn*).

N. Physical strength, force: 勁頭 *-tour*, 勁兒 *jieh'l* ↓.

Adj. (1) Strong, tough, powerful: 強勁 sturdy, stout, hardy: 勁敵 *-dir*, 勁旅 *-lyuu*, 勁卒 *-tzur* ↓. (2) Violent: 勁風 furious wind.

勁敵 *jihng-dir*, n., a redoutable enemy.

勁兒 *jieh'l*, n., (1) muscular strength: 這股勁兒 this force or spirit of action; 他很有勁兒 he is very strongly built; 傻勁兒 brute force; (2) vigor: 帶勁兒 vigorous, spirited (writing, performance); (3) interest: 起勁兒 arousing, exciting, be interested in; (4) deep affection, attachment: 上勁兒 (of lovers) be deeply attached to each other; (5) a person's bearing, manner, or appearance: 蹩扭勁兒 lackadaisical manner.

勁旅 *jihng-lyuu*, n., crack troops.

勁頭(兒) *jihntour('l)*, n., (1) muscular strength; (2) a person's general bearing, manner, or appearance.

勁卒 *jihng-tzur*, n., see *-lyuu* ↑.

勔 31S.50–9

miaan.

[Var. of 勉 92.70]

殉 31S.50–9

shyuhn.

V. i. & t. (1) In very early days, before paper men and horses were invented, a custom of burying servants and maids in royal tomb: 殉葬. (2) Be martyr for, to die for: see compp. ↓.

殉情 *shyuhn-chirng*, phr., die (commit suicide) for love.

殉道 *shyuhn-dauh*, phr., be martyr for religion.

殉國 *shyuhn-guor*, phr., die for country.

殉教 *shyuhn-jiauh*, phr., die for religion.

殉節 *shyuhn-jier*, phr., die for honor in loyalty to regime or deceased husband.

殉利 *shyuhn-lih*, phr., perish from love of wealth.

殉名 *shyuhn-mirng*, phr., kill oneself to gain name.

殉難 *shyuhn-nahn*, phr., be killed during some disaster (defeat, etc.).

殉身 *shyuhn-shen*, phr., sacrifice one's life.

殉財 *shyuhn-tsair*, phr., see *-lih* ↑.

殤 31S.50–9

shang.

V. i. To die young or prematurely.

§ 31S.63 (T^s/ˋ)

聆 31S.63–8

lirng.

[Usu. printed 聆]

V. t. (LL court.) to hear: 聆教, 面聆教益 to benefit by your advice; 聆悉 have learned (from letter) that.

聯 31S.63–9

liarn.

[Abbr. of 聯 31S.22]

§ 31S.70 (T^s/ㄴ)

甄 31S.70–3

jen.

N. (1) 甄者 (AC) potter. (2) A surname.

V. t. (LL) to select, discriminate, see compp. ↓.

甄拔 *jenbar*, v. t., select and promote (talents).

甄別 *jenbier*, v. t., to pick, discriminate different grades of quality, to screen; 甄別試 test of the unfit. and evaluate.

甄審 *jensheen*, v. t., to examine and evaluate.

甄選 *jenshyuaan*, v. t., to pick, select (talents, commercial products).

甄汰 *jentaih*, v. t., to eliminate (the unqualified).

甄陶 *jentaur*, v. t., to mold character as potter molds clay.

甄用 *jenyuhng*, v. t., select for appointment.

覡 31S.70-4

shir.

N. (AC) sorcerer (dist. 巫 sorceress).

覥 31S.70-4

tiaan (**miaan*).

Adj. (LL) unashamed, shameless.

覥臉 *tiarnliaan*, adj., unashamed.
覥然 *tiaanrarn*, adj. & adv., unashamed, shamelessly.
覥䩄 **miarntiaan*, adj., thick-skinned, unashamed.
覥顏 *tiaanyarn*, adj., thick-skinned: 覥顏事仇 shamelessly collaborate with enemy.

覼 31S.70-4

luor.

覼縷 *luorlyuu*, v. t., (LL) tell, narrate in detail.

飄 31S.70-4

piau.

[Var. 飃]

N. Hurricane, gale.

V. i. (1) To blow about: 隨風飄舞 whirl about in the wind; 風飄葉落 the wind blows and the leaves fall to the ground. (2) Drift about (in this sense used like 漂, as 飄泊, 飄流, 飄海, 飄泛, see 漂$^{\Delta}$ 63A.01).

Adj. See 飄飄, 飄然 *-piau*, *-rarn* ↓.

飄布 *piau-buh*, n., cotton badge of membership in former secret societies.
飄帶(兒) *piau-daih*(*-dah'l*), n., streamers.
飄高 *piaugau*, v. i., fall from a height (of workman).
飄忽 *piauhu*, adj., passing like a wind (of time, events).
飄疾 *piaujir*, adj., swift (wind), also (fig.) of s.t. passing swiftly (飄疾而逝).
飄擧 *piaujuu*, v. i., soar aloft.
飄零 *piaulirng*, adj., lonely and adrift (of person): 飄零無依 friendless, also 飄落, 飄蓬.
飄眇 *piaumiaau*, adj., lingering softly (of music); elusive, difficult to discern.
飄飄 *piaupiau*, adj., (of person's character, ambition) lofty.
飄然 *piau-rarn*, adj., ditto: 飄然欲仙 walking on clouds almost like a fairy.
飄蕭 *piaushiau*, adj., (MC) adrift.
飄字(兒) *piautzyh*(*-tzeh'l*), v.t., (of opera singer) unprecise in enunciation.
飄揚 *piauyarng*, v. i., flutter in the wind (of flag).
飄搖 *piauyaur*, v.i., drift about.

豝 31S.70-5

ba.

N. (AC) female hog, also u. f. 豝 80S.70.

耽 31S.70-9

dan.

[Dist. 躭, 眈]

V.i. (1) Tarry, in 耽擱, 耽誤 *-'ge*, *-wuh* ↓. (2) Indulge, lose oneself in (pleasure, wine, etc.). (3) Bear (burden, sorrow): 耽憂, 耽心 *-you*, *-shin* ↓.

耽擱 *dan'ge*, v.i. & t., delay; stop over (at) place: 別把這事耽擱了 don't delay this matter; 耽擱時間 waste time or holdup of other things.
耽惑 *danhuoh*, v.t., be infatuated with (wine, women).
耽湎 *danmiahn*, v.t., ditto.
耽心 *danshin*, v.i., be worried: 這件事耽心 be worried about this, also wr. 擔心.
耽誤 *danwuh*, v.t., hold up, interfere with (other things) by neglect, also wr. 躭.
耽憂 *danyou*, v.i., worry.

§ 31S.71 (丅^{s}/七)

職 31S.71-6

jyr.

[Pop. 耺]

N. (1) Office, post, position: 職位, 職銜, 職員 *-weih*, *-shiarn*, *-yuarn* ↓; 就職 assume office; 在職 active in office; 任職 is serving certain office; 退職 retire from office; 辭職 resign; 離職 no longer at post; 免職 dismiss (-ed) from post. (2) Duty, work, profession: 職務, 職業 *-wuh*, *-yeh* ↓; 職責 *-tzeh* ↓; 職守 *-shoou* ↓; 本職 person's regular or full-time job; 兼職 concurrent job; 盡職 carry out one's duties faithfully; 稱職 (*chehng-*) competent at the job.

Prep. For: 職是故, 職此之故 for this reason: 職此而已 it is only for this reason.

職稱 *jyrcheng*, n., title of post.
職權 *jyrchyuarn*, n., official powers.

覡 覥 覼 飄 豝 耽 職

亅	小	⺊	十	土	ナ	卄	⺊	丨	一	丅	フ	口	区	冈	乛	厂	尸	亠	广	宀	丶	乚	七	心	八	人	乂	一	乛	丿	乀	く
00	01	02	10	11	12	20	21	22	30	31	32	40	41	42	50	51	52	60	61	62	63	70	71	72	80	81	82	83	90	91	92	93

A

職等 *jyrdeeng*, n., rank of office.

職分 *jyrfehn*, n., duty natural to an office.

職蜂 *jyrfeng*, n., worker bees (also called 工蜂).

職掌 *jyrjaang*, v. t., to be in charge of (affairs).

職志 *jyrjyh*¹, n., a person's life-work or life profession (e. g., education).

職秩 *jyrjyh*², n., see *-deeng*↑.

職任 *jyr-rehn*, n., duty and responsibility.

職銜 *jyrshiarn*, n., rank of office.

職守 *jyrshoou*, n., official responsibility.

職事 *jyrshyh*, n., duties, terms of reference.

職責 *jyrtzer*, n., ditto.

職位 *jyrweih(-'wei)*, n., official position.

職務 *jyrwuh (-'wu)*, n., affairs of office.

職業 *jyryeh(-'ye)*, n., profession, employment, also self-imposed life-work; 職業學校 vocational school; 職業病 professional disease.

職員 *jyryuarn*, n., staff, staff member.

殘 31S.71–7

tsarn.

V.t. To injure, destroy: 摧殘 to destroy (life, talent); 殘傷 to injure; 殘害, see Adv.↓.

Adj. (1) Cruel, ruthless: 殘忍, 殘暴, 殘酷 *-reen, -bauh, -kuh*↓. (2) Broken (house, utensil), crippled (army, person), wilted (flower): 殘破, 殘缺 *-poh, -chyue*↓; 殘廢, 殘疾 *-feih, -jir*↓. (3) Remnant, last: 殘餘 *-yur*↓; 殘存 survive, shabbily survive; 殘年, 殘歲 remaining years of life; 殘冬 the end of winter; 殘春 fast departing spring, end of spring; 殘夏 late summer; 殘陽, 殘紅 sunset, sunset glow; 殘月 remnant moon; 殘花 destroyed flowers after storm; 殘兵 remnant soldiers after defeat; 殘花敗柳 women, esp. prostitutes, after their prime; 殘杯冷炙 dinner leftovers.

B

Adv. (Forming v.t. with vbb.) cruelly, brutally: 殘害, 殘賊, 殘毀, 殘殺 *-haih, -tzer, -hueei, -sha*↓.

殘暴 *tsarnbauh*, adj., cruel, brutish, merciless, tyrannical.

殘喘 *tsarn-chuaan*, n., lingering breath of life.

殘缺 *tsarnchyuei*, adj., broken (series), incomplete (set).

殘廢 *tsarnfeih*, adj. & n., crippled, physically disabled.

殘害 *tsarnhaih*, v.t., to injure (life), to oppress, persecute (people), to kill ruthlessly.

殘骸 *tsarn-hair*, n., (LL) "remaining bones"—frail body ready for retirement.

殘疾 *tsarnjir (-'ji)*, adj. & n., see *-feih*↑.

殘局 *tsarnjyur*, n., a lost situation, last act of a drama (army after defeat, etc.): 收拾殘局 pacify country after war or period of anarchy, salvage a hopeless situation.

殘酷 *tsarnkuh (-'ku)*, adj., merciless, brutal, relentless.

殘留 *tsarnliour*, v.i., to linger on in life.

殘年 *tsarnniarn*, n., (1) (of self) old age; (2) end of the year.

殘破 *tsarnpoh*, adj., decrepit (house, furniture).

殘忍 *tsarnreen*, adj., cruel, brutal.

殘殺 *tsarnsha*, v. t., kill brutally.

殘生 *tsarnsheng*, n., remaining years of life, see *-niarn*↑.

殘歲 *tsarnsueih*, n., see *-niarn*↑.

殘賊 *tsarntzer*, v. t., see *-haih*↑.

殘餘 *tsarnyur*, adj., remaining (years, time).

殲 31S.71–8

jian.

V. t. Kill off: 殲滅 exterminate; 殲敵 annihilate the enemy; 盡殲 wipe out by killing; 圍殲 surround (encircle) and destroy; 就殲 be exterminated.

C

§ 31S.72 (丅ˢ/心)

聽 31S.72–1

ting (**tihng*). [Abbr. 听]

V.i. & t. (1) To hear, listen: 聽見 *-jiahn*, 聽說 *-shuo*↓; 聽得見, 聽不見 can, cannot hear (voice, speaker); 聽不明白 cannot bear clearly; 聽而不聞 to listen but not hear, to hear but pay no attention. (2) To listen and obey: 聽話 *-huah*↓; 聽從 to listen to, be obedient to. (3) (**tihng*) To let go, to let s.t. happen of its own accord: 聽其自然 let things take their natural course; 聽天由命 resign to fate, be fatalistic; 聽憑, 聽便 *-pirng, -biahn*↓. (4) (**tihng*) To supervise: 聽政 supervise government; 聽訟 *-suhng*↓.

聽便 **tihngbiahn*, phr., let s.o. have option, at s.o.'s option.

聽差 *tingchai*, n., a servant attendant.

聽取 *tingchyuu*, v.t., listen to, hear (opinion).

聽斷 **tihngduahn*, v.i. & t., (of judge) decide at court.

聽官 *tingguan*, n., the sense of hearing.

聽候 *tinghouh*, v.i., to wait (for arrival, decision, etc.).

聽話 *ting-huah*, v.i., to obey, listen to s.o.'s advice: 小孩不聽話 child will not obey what he is told to do.

聽診器 *ting-jeen-chih*, n., stethoscope.

聽政 **tihngjehng*, v.i., to supervise administration.

聽講 *tingjiaang*, v.i., to hear it said, to attend lectures.

聽見 *ting-jiahn*, v.i., to hear: 聽得見, 聽不見 able, unable to hear.

聽覺 *tingjyuer*, n., sense of hearing, see *-guan*↑.

聽命 **tihngmihng*, v.i., (1) to obey orders, instructions; (2) to let fate take its course.

聽能 *tingnerng*, n., the power or

function of hearing.

聽憑 *tihngpirng*, v.t., to let come what may, to offer no obstruction: 聽憑你裁決 do what you decide (on case, with person).

聽任 *tihngrehn*, v.t., to let go: 聽任自然 let it take its own course.

聽審 *ting-sheen*, phr., (of judge) to sit at session.

聽寫 *tingshiee*, v.i. & n., dictate, dictation.

聽戲 *ting-shih*, v.i., go to opera.

聽信 *tingshihn*, v.t., (1) to listen to and believe (rumors); (2) await news.

聽書 *ting-shu*, v.i., to attend a recitation by storytellers.

聽說 *tingshuo*, v.i., hear; it is said that.

聽訟 **tihng-suhng*, v.i., to preside at law court.

聽提 *tingtir*, v.t., pay attention: 滿不聽提 pay no attention.

聽頭 *ting'tou'l*, n., s.t. worth listening to: 沒甚麽聽頭兒 nothing worth listening.

聽蹭兒 *tingtsehng('l)*, v.t., to see ("hear") a play at Chin. theater without pay.

聽筒 *tingturng*, n., earphone.

聽聞 *tingwern*, v.t., to hear (story, news, etc.).

恥 31S.72-6

chyy.

[Pop. 耻]

N. A shame, sense of shame: 無恥 shameless; 不知恥 have no sense of shame; 羞恥 a shame; 羞恥之心 sense of shame or honor; 廉恥 honesty and honor.

V. t. To be ashamed, to regard as shameful: 恥之 (LL) regard it as a shame; 恥爲人師 ashamed to be called a teacher; 恥辱, 恥笑 *-ruh, -shiauh*↓.

恥辱 *chyyruh*, v. t. & n., to humiliate (person); a humiliation.

恥笑 *chyyshiauh*, v. t., to scoff at, sneer at (person).

聰 31S.72-9

tsung.

Adj. (1) Sharp of hearing. (2) Bright (mentally).

聰慧 *tsunghueih*, adj., see *-mirng*↓.

聰敏 *tsungmiin*, adj., see *-mirng*↓.

聰明 *tsungmirng* (*-'ming*), adj., (person) mentally bright, clever, quick of understanding.

§ 31S.80 (Tˢ/八)

殰 31S.80-1

dur.

V.i. Die in embryo, be stillborn.

聵 31S.80-2

kueih.

[Dist. 瞶]

Adj. Deaf, hard of hearing: 聵聵無知 dense, like a deaf person.

頂 31S.80-3

diing.

N. adjunct. A top: 一頂帽子 a hat; 一頂轎 a sedan chair; 一頂蚊帳 a mosquito net.

N. (1) Summit, top, crown: 腦頂, 頭頂 crown of head; 滅頂 head submerged, i. e., drowned; 屋頂 roof; 山頂 summit of hill; 自頂至踵 from head to foot. (2) (*-tz, 'l*) Official cap in Manchu Dyn. with distinguishing precious stone on top indicative of rank.

V. i. & t. (1) To carry on head: 頭上頂着一包東西 carry a parcel on one's head; 頂戴 *-daih*↓; 頂天立地 a man dependent on self without fear or shame, has place in the sun. (2) To prop up, to set against: 把門頂住 prop up the door; 頂不住 cannot hold against (weight, pressure, censure, enemy); 頂水, 頂流 hold against the current; 頂風 against the wind; 頂賬 set against account. (3) To take over, substitute: 頂房屋 to sublease, take over lease; 承頂 take over shop, business; 頂名 take over s. o.'s name (assume false name); 頂上 take over (responsibility, etc.); 一個頂一個 take over by turns in relay; 頂人受過 take the blame for others, 頂當, 頂充, 頂替, etc. *-dang, -chung, -tih*↓.

Adv. Most: 頂好 best; 頂聰明 most intelligent; 頂壞 worst; 頂瓜瓜 (dial.) very best.

頂拜 *diingbaih*, v. i., bow in worship.

頂包 *diingbau*, v. i., to substitute packages—a swindling trick.

頂承 *diingcherng*, v. t., take over (duty, property).

頂充 *diingchung*, v. t., assume (false identity).

頂戴 *diingdaih*, n., (Manchu Dyn.) official cap showing various ranks by button of precious stone on top.

頂當 *diingdang*, v. i. & t., bear (blame, responsibility).

頂點 *dirngdiaan*, n., top, apex, (geom.) vertex.

頂缸 *diing-gang*, v. i., take blame for others.

頂槅 *diingger*, n., see *-perng*↓.

頂 項 頏 頸 殞 殯 殮 联

頂骨 *diinggur*, n., (biol.) parietal bones.

頂換 *diinghuahn*, v. i. & t., to exchange, substitute.

頂針兒 *diingje'l*, n., thimble.

頂眞 *diingjen*, v. i. & adj., take seriously: 不要太頂眞 don't take too seriously or calculate too finely.

頂角 *dirngjiaau*, n., (geom.) vertical angle.

頂尖 *diingjian*, n., the peak, highest point.

頂珠 *diingju*, n., (Manchu) official cap button.

頂撞 *diingjuahng*, v. t., charge, knock, against (person, object); offend by rude remarks.

頂兒 *diing'l*, n., (Manchu) official cap.

頂禮 *dirnglii*, v. i., worship: 頂禮膜拜 prostrate in worship.

頂門 *diingmern*, (1) n., crown of head; (2) v.i., take blame for others.

頂牛兒 *diingniour'l*, v.t., knock head against head; lock horns in Chin. bullfight.

頂盤 *diing-parn*, v.i., take over shop, business, by agreement.

頂棚 *diingperng*, n., Chin. ceiling, usu. of paper, to keep off dirt from girders.

頂批 *diingpi*, n., critical comment on top of page.

頂上 *diingshahng*, (1) n., top; (2) *dieng'shang*, v.t., take over (duty, etc.).

頂心 *diingshin*, n., top center of crown of head.

頂手 *dirng-shoou*, v.i., take over.

頂兇 *diing-shyung*, v.i., to take over guilt by s.o. hired by culprit.

頂替 *diingtih*, v.t., to substitute (for person, object).

頂頭 *diingtour*, (1) n., top; superior officer; (2) adj., opposite.

頂子 *diingtz*, n., (Manchu) official cap.

頂嘴 *dirng-tzueei*, v.t., bicker, to talk back to.

頂窩兒 *diing-wo'l*, v.i., adopt son for line of deceased son.

項 31S.80–3

shiahng.

N. adjunct. One thing, item, clause: 這項事情, 爭辯, 戰爭 this affair, this controversy, this war; 第三項 clause three; 八項條件 eight conditions; 三項贈品 three gifts; 這項買賣 this business deal, etc.

N. (1) The neck: 頸項 ditto; 強項 stiff-necked (policy); 項背相望 a huge jostling crowd ("neck to back"). (2) A sum, an item (in account): 款項 an amount of money; 進項 income; 欠項 debit; 用項 expenditure; 官項 government fund. (3) (Algebra) a term: 初項 first term; 末項 last term; 同類項 like term; 外項 external term. (4) A surname.

項圈 *shiahngchyuan*, n., necklace; choker.

項練 *shiahngliahn*, n., ditto.

項領 *shiahngliing*, n., the neck, (fig.) vital point.

項目 *shiahngmuh*, n., an article or clause; an item (of expenditure); a sum.

項下 *shiahng-shiah*, phr., in certain account: 在本人項下 in my account; 收入項下 under the column of receipts.

頏 31S.80–3

han.

Adj. & adv. See 顢頏 20S.80.

頸 31S.80–3

jiing.

N. The neck: 頸項, 頸子 the neck, the throat; 吊頸 commit suicide by hanging; 長頸鹿 the giraffe; 刎頸之交 bosom friends who are willing to die for one another.

殞 31S.80–4

yuun.

V. i. To die; vanish.

殞滅 *yuunmieh*, v. i., be destroyed, vanish.

殞命 *yuun-mihng*, v. i., to lose life, die.

殞沒 *yuunmoh*, v. i., see *-mieh* ↑.

殯 31S.80–6

bihn.

V. t. & n. Funeral, esp. that part between laying-in in coffin (殮) and burial (葬): 出殯 funeral ceremony and procession.

殯車 *bihnche*, n., hearse.

殯殮 *bihnliaan*, n., laying-in and funeral ceremony.

殯葬 *bihntzahng*, n., funeral and burial.

殯儀館 *bihnyirguaan*, n., funeral parlor.

§ 31S.81 (丅^{s}/人)

殮 31S.81–8

liahn.

N. & v.t. Laying-in in coffin: 大殮 the ceremony of laying-in; 入殮 to lay in coffin; 收殮 have corpse buried.

联 31S.81–8

liarn.

[Abbr. of 聯 ↑]

殀 31S.81-9

yaau.

V.i. To die young (interch. 夭).

殃 31S.81-9

yang.

N. (1) A disaster: 災殃 ditto; 遭殃 encounter a disaster. (2) Death, see 殃榜 *-baang*↓.

V.t. To bring disaster to: 殃禍 to bring on disaster; 禍國殃民 ruin a country and bring sorrow to its people; 殃及池魚 (a fire on city wall) brings disaster to the fish in the moat; 殃及無辜 trouble involves the innocent people.

殃 榜 *yangbaang*, n., an astrologer's certificate of horoscope of the deceased, etc., serving as death certificate at court.

耿 31S.81-9

geeng.

N. A surname.

Adj. (1) Bright, shining, glorious, see 耿耿 *-geeng*↓. (2) Having moral integrity: 耿介 *-jieh*, 耿直 *-jyr*↓.

耿 餅 *gerngbiing*, n., dried and pressed persimmons.

耿 耿 *gernggeeng*, adj., (1) bright and shining; (2) uneasy: 耿耿不寐 disquieted and unable to sleep; 耿耿於懷 deeply concerned at heart.

耿 介 *geengjieh*, adj., (1) great and glorious; (2) governed by strict moral principles.

耿 直 *geengjyr*, adj., fair and just, loyal and honest.

歌 31S.81-9

ge.

N. (1) A song, the words of a song: 歌曲 *-chyuu*↓; 國歌 national anthem; 校歌 school or college song; 民歌 folk song; 戀歌 love song; 聖誕頌歌 Christmas carols; 讚美歌 hymn; 藝術歌 art songs; 輓歌 an elegy; 歌譜 *-puu*↓; 歌詞 the lyrics of a song; 歌兒 a little song; 唱歌 to sing songs; 歌星 *-shing*, 歌女 *-nyuu*↓. (2) A poem that can be set to music and sung.

V.i. & t. (1) To sing, chant: 歌唱 *-chahng*↓; 高歌一曲 to chant a melody; 能歌善舞 good at both singing and dancing. (2) To praise: 歌功頌德 sing praises of; 可歌可泣 (of heroic actions) touching and deserving a song; 歌詠, 歌誦 *-yuhng*, *-suhng*[2]↓.

歌 板 *gebaan*, n., a musical clapping board for keeping time in singing.

歌 唱 *gechahng*, v.i. & t., to sing.

歌 曲 *gechyuu*, n., songs: 流行歌曲 pop music, pop songs.

歌 妓 *geji*, n., a singsong girl.

歌 劇 *gejyuh*, n., an opera; 歌劇院 opera house; 小歌劇 operette; 喜歌劇 comic opera, or musical comedy.

歌 女 *genyuu*, n., a female professional singer.

歌 譜 *gepuu*, n., a music score for songs.

歌 星 *ge-shing*, n., a star singer of either sex.

歌 行 *geshirng*, n., (litr.) a poem that can be set to music and sung.

歌 手 *geshou*, n., professional singer of either sex.

歌 頌 *gesuhng*[1], v. t., to praise, eulogize: 歌頌聖賢 eulogize the sages.

歌 誦 *gesuhng*[2], v. i., & t., to sing or chant, to celebrate by song, to praise.

歌 詞 *getsyr*, n., the lyrics of a song.

歌 舞 *gewuu*, v.i. & t. & n., sing and dance; 歌舞劇 opera; 歌舞表演 exhibitions of song and dance; 歌舞昇平 to celebrate peace.

歌 謠 *geyaur*, n., folk songs, ballads.

歌 詠 *geyuhng*, v. i., *-suhng*[2]↑.

聯 31S.81-9

liarn.

[Pop. of 聯 31S.22]

§ 31S.82 (T^s/乂)

取 31S.82-3

chyuu.

V. t. (1) To take, get, obtain: 取得同意 get s. o.'s consent; 取得學位 get an academic degree; 不取分文 will not take a cent—gratis; 非分 (*fehn*) 不取 will not take what is improper; 予取予求 phr., rapacious, demand everything. (2) Oft. preceded by another vb. to indicate various forms of obtaining (by seizure, seeking, picking, etc.): 獵取 hunt (game); 追取 to pursue; 尋取, 覓取 look for; 攻取, 奪取 attack (territory), rob; 獲取 obtain in gen.; 採取 adopt (policy). (3) Aim for, select for specific reason: 取其便 choose it for its convenience; 從中取利 make a profit for oneself in some deal; 取涼, 取快, 取樂, 取巧 *-liarng*, *-kuaih*, *-leh*, *-chiaau*↓; 取

便 for convenience; 取其外貌 select a person by his looks; 取友 select friends; 取人之善 take a person's good points. (4) To pass in examinations: 選取 select talents as by examinations; 錄取, 考取了, 被取 pass in examinations; 正取, 備取 pass on regular, on reserve list. (5) Approve: 可取 commendable; 一無可取 nothing to recommend (person, course of action). (6) (AC) used as var. of 娶, to marry.

Vb. complement. Esp. in poetry: 記取 remember (=記得); 聽取意見 hear different opinions; 看取 to see.

取保 *chyur-baau*, v. i., ask s. o. to act as guarantor.

取便 *chyuubiahn*, (1) v. i., do as one pleases without restraint; (2) phr., so as to facilitate: 取便宣傳 to facilitate propaganda: 取便 (=以便) 推銷 in order to facilitate distribution (of goods).

取償 *chyuu-charng*, v. i., to be reimbursed for cost or labor.

取巧 *chyurchiaau*, v. i., to take short cut, choose the easy way, not the orthodox way.

取齊 *chyuuchir*, v. i., (1) to fall in line; (2) to take as measure: 衣服長短, 照舊樣取齊 take the old dress as sample; 東西多少, 要拿錢取齊兒 how much one will buy depends on how much one is willing to spend.

取道 *chyuu-dauh*, adv., by way of (Shanghai, Nanking, etc.).

取燈兒 *chyuu-deng'l*, n., (Peking dial.) matches (also 洋取燈兒).

取得 *chyuu-der*, v. t., obtain (consent, sympathy, doctor's degree, wealth and position, etc.).

取締 *chyuudih*, v. t., to ban (publications, etc.); deprive (person) of certain rights.

取法 *chyur-faa*, v. t., copy s. o. as example.

取告 *chyuu-gauh*, v.i., (AC) take leave (=告假).

取和兒 *chyuu-her'l*, v. i., go for peaceful settlement.

取回權 *chyuu-hueir-chyuarn*, n., right of recovery.

取給 *chyurjii*, v. i., to lean for support of living: 取給於人 depend on s. o. for support.

取決 *chyuujyuer*, v. i., to make decision: 由他取決 let him make the final decision.

取快 *chyuukuaih*, adv., for pleasure, for the fun of it.

取樂(兒) *chyuu-leh('l)*, v. i., (do s. t.) to have fun: 罵人取樂 criticize others as a pastime.

取涼 *chyuu-liarng*, v. i., to enjoy the cool shade.

取錄 *chyuuluh*, v. t., to pass (person) at examinations; to admit after test.

取名 *chyuu-mirng*, v. i., to be given a name, be called (Paul, James, etc.).

取譬 *chyuu-pih*, v. i., to give example, cite analogies: 能近取譬 can explain by simple analogy.

取擾 *chyur-raau*, v. t., (court.) to bother s. o. (=打擾).

取容 *chyuu-rurng*, v. i., to aim at pleasing s. o.

取舍(捨) *chyur-shee*, n., the power of judgment, of taking or rejecting.

取勝 *chyuu-shehng*, v. i., (1) desire to excel; (2) to win victory.

取消 *chyuushiau*, v. t., to cancel (promise, reservation, treaty, etc.).

取笑(兒) *chyuu-shiauh('l)*, v. i. & t., to make fun, make fun of person.

取士 *chyuu-shyh*, v. i., select scholars for government service.

取材 *chyuu-tsair*, v. i., to get material (for writing) from.

取次 *chyuutsyh*, adv., (1) (MC) in order, one by one; (2) (MC) casually (=造次).

取問 *chyuuwehn*, v. t., to cross-examine (accused, witness).

取義 *chyuu-yih*, phr., to prefer right to might: 捨生取義 to die for principle.

取盈 *chyuuyirng*, phr., (1) to strive for satisfaction; (2) (AC) to require that tax assessments be paid in full.

取友 *chyur-yoou*, v. i., to select friends by certain standards.

取悅 *chyuu-yueh*, v. t., to please (person), to curry popularity: 取悅於人.

豭 31S.82-9

jia.

N. (AC) a male pig, a boar.

歿 31S.82-9

moh.

[Dist. 沒 63A.82]

V. i. Die: 病歿 die of illness.

攻 31S.82-9

gung.

V. t. (1) To attack, assault: 進攻 take the offensive; 攻擊 -*'jir* ↓; 攻伐 invade; 攻打 strike against; 猛攻 to storm (a city, fortification, etc.); 攻守同盟 military alliance for mutual defense; 攻下 take (a city) by assault; 久攻不下 fail to take (a city) after a long siege; 攻剽 to pillage; 攻城 lay siege to a city; 攻堅 attack a strong point of enemy; 攻佔 attack and occupy; 攻克 overrun, conquer; 圍攻 lay siege to; 反攻 to counterattack. (2) Find fault with (s. o.), criticize, rebuke: 攻訐 -*jier* ↓; 鳴鼓而攻之 attack s.o. publicly and severely by concerted action; 攻人之過 pick on s.o. (3) To study, specialize in: 攻讀 -*dur*, 攻書 -*shu* ↓; 專攻醫學 to major in medicine.

攻讀 *gungdur*, v. t., to study, learn: 攻讀博士學位 to work for a doctorate.

攻訐 *gungjier*, v. t., to censure, flay (s. o.)

攻擊 *gung'jir*, v. t., (1) mount an attack, assault; (2) to criticise, reprove, reprach, attack verbally.

攻書 *gung-shu*, v. i., devote oneself to reading.

攻勢 *gung-shyh*, n., military offensive (opp. 守勢 defensive): 採取攻勢 to mount an offensive.

攻錯 *gung-tsuoh*, v. i., learn by other's mistakes.

政 31S.82-9

jehng.

N. (1) The government of a state, administration: 政府 *fuu*↓; 行[A]政 administration, 91B.00; 地方行政 the local administration; 國政 national affairs; 爲政之道 the proper governance of a state; 從政 to join the government; 民政 department or administration of domestic affairs; 財政部 the finance ministry; 財政 finance in gen. (e. g., of firm, etc.); 軍政 army administration. (2) Rules: 觴政 rules of wine games at dinner; 家政 home economics, family rules, also family finance. (3) Chief: 學政 formerly, minister of education or educational commissioner; 鹽政司 chief of salt monopoly, director general of salt gabelle.

V. t. (LL) u. f. 正: 呈政, 教政, 指政, 量政 (court. request for) advice, correction.

政變 *jehngbiahn*, n., *coup d'état*, sudden overthrow of government.

政柄 *jehngbihng* (*-biing*), n., the control ("helm") of government.

政潮 *jehng-chaur*, n., political upheaval or crisis.

政權 *jehngchyuarn*, n., political power; political rights of the people.

政黨 *jehngdaang*, n., political party.

政敵 *jehng-dir*, n., political enemy.

政府 *jehngfuu*, n., government (federal, central, provincial, local, etc.).

政綱 *jehnggang*, n., party platform, main principles of government; proper functioning of government: 政綱大振 the government begins to function properly, esp. regarding law and order, promotion and punishment.

政躬 *jehnggung*, n., (LL & court.) the health of a very important official or ruler.

政化 *jehnghuah*, n., political and cultural aspects of country.

政績 *jehng-ji*, n., records of official career.

政見 *jehng-jiahn*, n., political views.

政教 *jehngjiauh*, n., see *-huah*↑, also political and religious affairs.

政界 *jehngjieh*, n., officialdom, official circles.

政治 *jehngjyh*[1], n., politics; 政治犯 political prisoner; 政治家 politician, also statesman; 大政治家 a great statesman.

政制 *jehngjyh*[2], n., system of government, governmental hierarchy.

政局 *jehngjyur*, n., political situation.

政客 *jehngkeh*, n., (derog.) politician: 小政客 petty politician.

政況 *jehngkuahng*, n., gen. conditions of the government.

政令 *jehnglihng*, n., a governmental order: 政令不行 government's orders are not obeyed.

政論 *jehng-luhn*, n., political essay; views on current politics.

政略 *jehng-lyueh*, n., main policies of government.

政聲 *jehng-sheng*, n., gen. reputation of an official.

政事 *jehngshyh*, n., government affairs; state of government (good, bad, etc.).

政體 *jehngtii*, n., form of government (democracy, autocracy, etc.).

政策 *jehngtseh*, n., administrative policy (of government, school, institution).

政務 *jenngwuh*, n., governmental affairs; 政務次長 political vice-minister, opp. 事務次長 administrative vice-minister.

政要 *jehngyauh*, n., high-ranking government officials; main structure and policy of government.

致 31S.82-9

jyh.

N. (1) Charm, winsome or interesting quality: 雅致 elegance, also adj.; 幽致 charm of seclusion; 極致 extreme achievement. (2) Poetic sentiment, fascination felt for hobbies: 興致 fascination (for games, chess, wine); 雅人深致 poetic love of beauty (in landscape, poetry, etc.).

V. t. (1) To deliver (gift), send (letter, congratulations, thanks, etc.): 致送 send, deliver; 致書 send letter to (person); 致賀, 致謝, 致敬 *-heh*, *-shieh*, *-jihng*↓; 致疑, 致意 *-yir*, *yih*↓. (2) To invite, collect: 招致 invite (scholars, experts) for post; 羅致 to look for and assemble (experts, etc.). (3) To cause, cause to become, cultivate: 致富, 致死 *-fuh*, *-syy*↓; 致知 *-jy*↓; 以致 so that, with the result that: 以致身亡 with the result that he died. (4) To lay down: 致仕, 致政 *-shyh*, *-jehng*↓.

Adv. 大致 mostly, generally; 一致 unanimously (approve, etc.).

致富 *jyh-fuh*, v. i., amass a fortune.

致賀 *jyh-heh*, v.i., to send congratulations.

致政 *jyh-jehng*, v. i., to lay down office, resign from government.

致祭 *jyh-jih*, v. i., to offer sacrifices.

致敬 *jyh-jihng*, v. i., pay respects by sending gifts, scroll, etc.

致知 *jyhjy*, v.i., attend knowledge.

致 攷 敢 靉 瓢 殄 形

致力 *jyh-lih*, v. i., concentrate on (work).

致命 *jyh-mihng*, v. i., (LL) to sacrifice one's life; 致命處 vital parts of body, fatal if injured; 致命傷 fatal injury, also fig.

致謝 *jyh-shieh*, v. i., to send thanks, to thank.

致書 *jyh-shu*, v. i., send letter (to s. o.).

致仕 *jyh-shyh*, v. i., to resign from government.

致送 *jyhsuhng*, v. t., to send (gift).

致死 *jyh-syy*, v. i., cause death: 致死的原因 cause of death.

致辭 *jyh-tsyr*, v. i., give or recite an introductory remark or welcome on solemn occasions.

致意 *jyhyih*, v. t., to devote attention (to studies), send best regards: 代我致意 give s. o. my best regards.

致疑 *jyh-yir*, v.i., raise doubt.

致用 *jyh-yuhng*, v.i., as in 學以致用 education with a view to service to country or application to society.

攷 31S.82–9

kaau.

[Var. of 考 11.50]

敢 31S.82–9

gaan.

V. i. & t. (1) Dare, venture, presume: 我不敢 I dare not; 豈敢 how dare I? 不敢當 (court.) I don't deserve it (e. g., compliments, etc.); 他不敢那樣做 he dare not do such a thing; 敢死 *-syy*↓; 用敢申請 I venture to request; may I venture to inquire? (2) Be bold enough to: 他居然敢反抗我 he has the audacity to oppose me. (3) To challenge to do s. t.: 你敢再說一次 I challenge you to say it again.

Adj. & adv. (1) Perhaps, probably: 敢是他 perhaps it is he: 敢怕, 敢是 *-pah, -shyh*↓. (2) Bold (ly), brave(ly), courageous(ly): 勇敢 be brave enough; 敢作敢爲 act with courage and determination; 敢作敢當 be bold enough to do s. t. and accept responsibility for it.

敢情 *gaanchirng*, adv., (MC) (1) perhaps indeed: 敢情他是個騙子 perhaps he was in fact a cheat; (2) naturally, of course: 敢情他會, 他學了三年了 of course he can do it after having studied it for three years; 那敢情好 it's naturally good.

敢待 *gaandaih*, v. t., (MC) be on the point of doing (s. t.).

敢當 *gaandang*, v. t. & adj., (be) deserving (of): 那怎敢當 how can I possibly deserve it? 不敢當 thank you, but really I don't deserve it, a phr. for replying to praise, "I am unworthy"; 泰山石敢當 a stone tablet inscribed with these characters and erected on the roadside supposedly as a charm to ward off evil influences.

敢怕 *gaanpah*, adv., perhaps, probably.

敢是 *gaanshyh*, adv., maybe, possibly: 敢是你不願意 maybe you are not willing.

敢死 *garnsyy*, v. i., dare to die; 敢死隊 a suicide squad, dare-to-die corps.

敢則 *gaantzer*, adv., (MC) see *chirng*↑.

敢自 *gaantzyh*, adv., (MC) see *-chirng*↑.

靉 31S.82–9

aih.

靉靉 *aih-aih*, adj., luxuriant (forest), brilliant (clouds).

靉靆 *aihdaih*, (1) adj., ditto; (2) n., (MC) interpreted as eyeglasses.

§ 31S.83 (Tˢ/乛)

瓢 31S.83–9

piaur.

N. Dried gourd serving as dipper: 一瓢飲 a gourdful of liquid (allu. to Confucius' disciple 顏回) happy in frugal living.

瓢蟲 *piauchurng*, n., ladybird, ladybug, a winged insect.

瓢兒 *piau'l*, n., a gourd dipper; also (facet.) 開了瓢兒 break one's skull.

§ 31S.91 (Tˢ/ノ)

殄 31S.91–8

tiaan.

V. t. (AC) to cut off, extirpate, destroy: 殄絕, 殄滅 destroy utterly, exterminate; 殄戮, 殄殲 destroy, kill enemy; 暴殄天物 wantonly destroy or waste products of nature, like grain.

形 31S.91–9

shirng.

N. (1) Material form, shape: 形像 *-shiahng*, 形體 *-tii*↓; 四方形 square shape; 三角形 triangular shape; 球形 globe shape; 形形色色 the myriad shapes, all kinds of things; 有形 having material form; 無形 invisible, not material; 形而上 *-ershahng*↓. (2) Appearance, look: 形態, 形狀, 形貌 *-taih, -juahng, -mauh*↓; 情形 condition (of people, things), situation; 形跡 *-ji*↓; 形銷骨立 thinned to the bone; 自慚形穢 (court.) ashamed of my own appearance. (3) Personal body or presence: 形骸 skeleton; 形影相隨 (of couple, lovers, close friends) never leave each other's side (like "form and shadow"); 形單影隻 lonely, -liness.

V. t. (1) To appear in visible form, to express itself: 喜形於色 happiness written on one's face; 難以形於筆墨 difficult to put in words; 形諸言論 (thoughts and feelings) are expressed in words. (2) To compare: in 相形見絀 show to disadvantage by comparison.

形成 *shirng-cherng*, v. t., to become, crystallize (into form, movement): 形成仇敵 become enemies; 形成僵局 an impasse; deadlock.

形而上 *shirngershahng*, n. & adj., metaphysics, -sical.

形骸 *shirnghair*, n., person's physical body; 放浪形骸 given to sensual pleasures.

形迹 (跡) *shirngji*, n., (1) person's movements: 形跡可疑 (person's) movements are suspicious; (2) external formalities: 不拘形跡 do not stick to formalities.

形景 *shirngjiing*, n., gen. outlook, condition: 形景可憐 in a pitiable condition.

形狀 *shirngjuahng*, n., (1) shape, form: 形狀似某人 (one's) appearance resembles a certain person; (2) see *-jiing*↑.

形質 *shirngjyr*, n., material body.

形貌 *shirngmauh*, n., facial look (like one's father, in distress, etc.).

形容 *shirngrurng*, (1) n., personal expression: 形容憔悴 a sorrowful look; (2) (*-'rung*) v. t., to describe, express by words: 非筆墨所能形容 cannot be described by words; 形容詞 (gram.) an adjective.

形勝 *shirngshehng*, n., scenic spot; the outlay of the land and waters.

形聲 *shirngsheng*, n., one of six principles of formation of Chin. characters, (see 六ᐞ書 60.80) by use of a component for phonetic value—the most prolific principle, e. g., the use of 青 in 淸, 情, 請, etc. (also called 諧聲).

形象 *shirngshiahng*[1], n., (1) form, appearance; (2) statue, portrait.

形相 *shirngshiahng*[2], n., build and appearance of person, as indicating character, condition or luck: 嬉皮的怪形相 the outlandish appearance of the Hippies.

形式 *shirngshyh*[1], n., form (versus substance), formalities: 新形式 new form(s); 形式主義 formalism, -listic, coldly conventional.

形勢 *shirngshyh*[2], n., (1) geographical outlay (山川形勢); (2) gen. trend, outlook, prospect: 形勢不穩 the situation of the army is quite vulnerable; 形勢不佳, 甚佳, it looks very bad, very good.

形似 *shirngsyh*, n., likeness, similarity.

形態 *shirngtaih*, n., (1) posture, bodily carriage, esp. of woman; (2) gen. appearance or condition or expression.

形體 *shirngtii*, n., material body of a certain shape (as of earth, a comet).

影 31S.91-9

piau.

影帶 *piau-daih*, n., streamer (also 飄帶).

SECTION 32

§ 32.00 (フ/亅)

了 32.00

liaau (*'le* see vb. complement).

V. t. (1) To understand: 了解, 了悟, 了事, 了然 *-jiee, -wuh, -shyh, -rarn*.↓ (2) To finish, complete, settle, dispose of, fulfill: 完了 to finish; 了畢, 了卻, 了結, 了淸, 了事 *-bih, -chyueh, -jier, -ching, -shyh*↓; 了案 settle case; 了債, 了賬 settle debt, accounts; 未了之事 unfinished business; 以不了了之 leave it unsettled, conclude without conclusion; 不了情 unrequited but eternal love; 不得了 disastrous; 了不得 see *-buhder*↓; 得了此願, 了此心願 able to fulfill this wish; 了此宿緣 fulfill this love regarded as working out of destiny. (3) (Coll.) to put in, take away: 誰把一塊石頭了到井裏了 who threw a rock into the well? 皮襖也讓他了去了 consider the fur jacket as also taken away; forget about it.

Vb. complement. (1) (*liaau*) 得了 and 不了 after vbb. are idiomatic complements for "can" and "cannot" or "able" and "unable": 此事辦不了 unable to finish this business; 不容易辦得了 not easy to finish; 他來不了 he is unable to come (prevented by business); 去不了 cannot go (on account of rain, etc.); 死不了 there will never be an end to these rascals. (2) (*'le*) Unaccented, complement with the sense of conclusion (Eng. perfect tense); (*liaau*) if accented: 他走了 he has gone; 畢業了 has graduated; 飯熟了 rice is cooked; 病好了 illness is recovered; 債還了 debt has been paid; with the sense that s.t. has

形 影 了

亅	小	⺊	十	土	ナ	廾	㇗	丨	一	丅	フ	口	区	冈	㇆	厂	尸	亠	广	宀	丶	乚	七	心	八	人	乂	㇖	㇒	丿	㇀	く
00	01	02	10	11	12	20	21	22	30	31	32	40	41	42	50	51	52	60	61	62	63	70	71	72	80	81	82	83	90	91	92	93

started moving: 來了, 來了 (he) has come or is coming! (I) am coming!

Fin. Part. In imperative sentence: 好了, 好了, 不要多講了 well, well, don't talk any more! 大家回房去睡了 go back to your rooms and get in bed!

了畢 *liaaubih*, v.i., to finish.

了不得 *liaaubuhder*, adj., oft. in excl., marvellous (praise of person); 好的了不得 very, very good; 他的本領眞了不得 his skill is truly marvellous; extremely: 痛的了不得 extremely painful; note: 不得了 has opposite meaning of "disastrous."

了清 *liaauching*, v.t., settle (accounts).

了卻 *liaauchyueh*, v.t., as in 了卻一樁心事 finish s.t. I have always wanted to do; 了卻這些糾紛 settle all this dispute.

了當 *liaaudahng*, adj., as in 直截了當 simple and direct, uncomplicated; (MC) settled.

了得 *liaauder*, (1) v.t., settle, complete, also understand: 可以了得, 了得了 can understand or able to settle (business); 這還了得 how horrible! (s.t. has got out of control); (2) adj., very good, useful, serviceable: 十分了得 very good, commendable indeed; 着實了得 really excellent; see difference between 了不得 and 不得了 *-buhder* ↑.

了鳥 *liaurdiaau* (*-niauh*), (1) adj., hanging and swinging; (2) n., brass or iron knocker ring on gate; device to hold window in position.

了斷 *liaauduahn*, v.i., settle (case): 自尋了斷 find short way out, commit suicide.

了賬 *liaau-jahng*, v.i., settle account; (coll.) pass away.

了解 *liaarjiee*, v.t., to understand: 你不了解我 you do not understand me.

了結 *liaaujier*, v.t., conclude (affair).

了局 *liaaujyur*, n., end, settlement: 也不是個了局 this will not be the end—is no settlement.

了兒 *liaau'l*, n., the end: 到了兒還是落空 in the end get nothing; 這事未了兒之前 before this affair has ended.

了了 *liaurliaau*, adj., understanding at heart: 心中了了 understand (without saying much); 不甚了了 do not quite understand; (MC) intelligent: 小時了了 was intelligent as a child.

了亮 *liaauliahng*, adj., simple, direct (in conduct, negotiations, etc.).

了然 *liaaurarn*, v.i., understand: 心中了然 understand in one's mind; 一目了然 understand at one glance.

了事 *liaau-shyh*, (1) v.t., to settle disputes, dispose of (matter): 敷衍了事 to do s.t. in a perfunctory manner; (2) adj., 了事的, 了事之人 experienced, competent person; 了事人 arbitrator, settler of disputes.

了悟 *liaauwuh*, v.i. & t., to comprehend, understand (truth, teaching), wake up to, realize (one's mistakes): 了悟前緣 understand fate caused by previous incarnation.

孑 32.00

jier.

Adj. (1) Alone, solitary: 孑立 standing alone; 孑然 *-rarn* ↓; 孑身 single, all by oneself. (2) Left over, surviving, remaining: 孑遺 *-yir* ↓.

孑孑 *jierjier*, adj., (1) conspicuous, prominent; (2) tiny.

孑孓 *jierjyuer*, n., the larvae of mosquitoes.

孑然 *jierrarn*, adj., solitary, lonely: 孑然一身 with no relatives, friendless.

孑遺 *jieryir*, n., that which remains: 靡有孑遺 all have died off, no survivor.

孓 32.00

jyuer.

孑孓 *jierjyuer*, n., larvae of insects.

予 32.00

yur (**yuu*).

Pron. (AC) I, me: 予取予求 (LL) demand everything of me.

V.t. (**yuu*) (AC, LL=與): 予之 give him; 不予 will not give; 賜予 (court.) to give; 給予 give; 施予 to dispense (help, favor); 予奪 (the power) to give and take away.

矛 32.00

maur.

N. Spear.

矛盾 *mauhduhn* (re. pr. *-duun*), n. & adj., self-contradiction, -tory, inconsistent, -cy: 自相矛盾 to contradict oneself; 矛盾政策 contradictory policies; 矛盾律 principle of contradiction.

子 32.00

tzyy(**tz* unaccented as particle).

Part. (**tz*) Attached to nn. for phonetic effect and for forming a bisyllablic n. to help distinguish it from a monosyllablic homonym; the use of *tz*, or of *'l* is determined entirely by usage: 桌子 (table, desk), 椅子 (chair), 筷子 (chopsticks), 金子 (gold), 銀子 (silver), 驢子 (donkey), 猴子 (monkey).

N. (1) The fruit or seeds of plants: 種子 seeds; 花子 flower seeds; 桃子 peaches; 梨子 pears. (2) Eggs of animals: 魚子 the roe of fish; 鳥魚子 caviar. (3) Offspring: 子嗣 *-syh*, 子孫 *-sun*, 子姪 *-jyr*[1], 子女 *-nyuu*, 子媳 *-shir*↓; 太子 the crown prince; 王子 prince; 世子 the son of a feudal lord; 宗子 the eldest son born of the first wife; 長子, 次子, 少子 eldest, second, youngest son; 義子 adopted son, godson; 遺腹子 posthumous son; 獨生子 one's only son. (4) The first character in the duodecimal cycle, see Appendix A: 子時 *-shyr*↓. (5) Title of respect for men of distinction: 孔子 Confucius; 孟子 Mencius; 先秦諸子 the pre-Chirn philosophers; 諸子百家 the various schools of thought; 天子 the Emperor ("the son of heaven"). (6) Pupil, disciple: 子弟 *-dih*↓. (7) One's spouse: 內子 my better half, wife; 外子 my husband; 妻子 wife, family: 他的妻子 his wife and children. (8) A person: 舟子 boatman; 士子 scholar; 男子 men; 女子 women, girls; 孩子 boy; 小子 child; 赤子 baby, young boy, an innocent child: 赤子之心 innocent heart; 童子 boy: 童子軍 Boy Scouts; 孺子 boy; 稚子 child. (9) A nobleman, viscount ranking next below an earl or count (伯) and above a baron (男): 子爵 *-jyuer*↓. (10) Anything standing in relation to another like mother and child: 分子 (math.) the numerator (opp. 分母 the denominator): 子金 *-jin*↓. (11) Anything small in size: 銅子兒 copper coin; 彈子 bullet, billiard balls; 丸子 a meat ball, a pill (pellet) of medicine.

子本 *tzyr-been*, n., capital and interest.

子部 *tzyybuh*, n., "philosophy," the third main division of traditional classification of Chin. books, as distinct from "Confucian classics" (經), "history" (史), and "belles-lettres" (集).

子城 *tzyycherng*, n., minor division of a metropolitan city, an extension of the old city.

子錢 *tzyychiarn*, n., (1) money put out at interest; (2) interest from money lent.

子彈 *tzyydahn*, n., bullet.

子道 *tzyy-dauh*, n., filial duties.

子弟 *tzyydih*, n., (1) children in relation to elders; sons and younger brothers of a family (opp. 父兄 father and elder brother); able-bodied men (opp. 父老 elders); (2) patron of prostitutes; 子弟書 *--shu*, n., songs sung to the accompaniment of a drum, as originated by Manchu boys.

子房 *tzyyfarng*, n., (bot.) the ovary.

子婦 *tzyyfuh*, n., (1) formerly, son and daughter-in-law; (2) daughter-in-law.

子規 *tzyyguei*, n., (zoo.) the cuckoo.

子宮 *tzyygung*, n., the womb, the uterus; 子宮頸部 cervix.

子薑 *tzyyjiang*, n., young ginger.

子金 *tzyyjin*, n., interest from capital (母金).

子注 *tzyyjuh*, n., small-type explanatory notes in books.

子姪 *tzyyjyr*[1], n., sons and nephews.

子職 *tzyyjyr*[2], n., filial duties.

子爵 *tzyyjyuer*, n., viscount(cy).

子句 *tzyyjyuh*, n., (grammar) a clause.

子口 *tzyrkoou*, n., formerly, an inland customs station: 子口稅 transit dues.

子兒 *tzee'l*, n. (1) plant seeds; (2) a bundle (of noodles, etc.); number of anything long and slender lumped together; (3) anything small and hard: 石頭子兒 pebbles; 子兒表 *--biaau* n., small pocket watch; 子兒繩 *--sherng*, n., a kind of thin string made of flax fiber.

子粒 *tzyylih*, n., tiny particles.

子門 *tzyymern*, n., (Chin. med.) the cervix of the womb.

子民 *tzyymirn*, n., the people.

子目 *tzyymuh*, n., detailed list of contents.

子母 *tzyrmuu*, n., (1) mother and child; (2) capital and interest; (3) two things, one heavy and the other light, as contrasted with one another; 子母彈 (mil.) shrapnel; 子母環 two links, one big and the other small, joined together; 子母扣兒 a button, of which one half is male and the other female, a snap-button.

子囊 *tzyynarng*, n., (bot.) a spore case.

子女 *tzyr-nyuu*, n., son and daughter.

子平 *tzyypirng*, n., horoscopy, after the name of person (徐子平) who was well versed in the art.

子絃 *tzyyshiarn*[1], n., very fine silk strings of musical instrument.

子癇 *tzyyshiarn*[2], n., (med.) cramps during pregnancy.

子系 *tzyyshih*[1], n., posterity, offspring.

子細 *tzyyshih*[2], adj. & adv., (1) meticulous, paying attention to every detail; (2) careful, attentive (usu. wr. 仔細).

子姓 *tzyyshihng*, n., (AC) descendants, offspring (=子孫).

子息 *tzyyshir*, n., (1) one's children; (2) profits from capital investment.

子書 *tzyyshu*[1], n., works of anc. philosophers other than those of Confucius.

子數 *tzyyshu*[2], n., (math.) the first term in a ratio (opp. 母數 the second term); the numerator of a fraction.

子時 *tzyyshyr*, n., period from 11 p.m. to 1 a.m.

子實體 *tzyyshyr-tii*, n., (bot.) mycelium.

子虛 *tzyyshyu*, n., unreal, nonexistent things: 子虛烏有 pure imagination.

子婿 *tzyyshyuh*, n., son-in-law, daughter's husband.

子孫 *tzyysun* (-'*sun*), n., children and grandchildren, descendants, offspring; 子孫桶 (euphem.) commode forming part of the bridal dowry.

子嗣 *tzyysyh*, n., one's children, descendants, offspring.

子午蓮 *tzyrwuuliarn*, n., (bot.) a kind of lotus which blossoms between midday and midnight;

子午痧 (Chin. med.) an acute disease accompanied by stomach-ache, vomiting, chills, perspiration, and thirst, usu. fatal within a few hours; 子午線 (astron.) the meridians; 子午儀 a transit instrument.

子藥 *tzyy-yauh*, n., bullets and gunpowder.

子夜 *tzyyeh*[1], n., midnight; 子夜歌 an anc. ballad or its later imitations.

子葉 *tzyyeh*[2], n., (bot.) a cotyledon.

子胤 *tzyyyihn*, n., sons and daughters.

子音 *tzyyyin*, n., (anc. phonetics) consonants (opp. 母音 vowels).

孕 32.00

yuhn.

N. Pregnancy: 懷孕, 有孕 pregnant; 受孕 conceive (a child); 避孕 birth control; 不孕 barren.

孕婦 *yuhn-fuh*, n., a pregnant woman.

孕育 *yuhnyuh*, v.t., to give birth to and raise (child); (fig.) to conceive, to nurse (an idea, conception).

承 32.00

cherng.

V.t. (1) (Court.) to receive from above (instructions, mandate, appointment, letter, gift): 承受, 承賜, 承命, 承奉 *-shouh -tsyh*, *-mihng*, *-fehng*, etc.↓. (2) To take over (in vb. compp., 承＋vb.—having the connotation of "taking over" "on the receiving end"): 承繼, 承租, 承包 *-jih*, *-tzu*, *-bau*↓; 承擔 *-dan*↓. (3) To continue: 承上起下 (a conjunction like "however" which) carries forward in a new paragraph; 承先啟後 carry on the past heritage and open up the future. (4) To serve: 承歡, 承顏 *-huan*, *-yarn*↓; 奉承 to please or flatter another. (5) To admit, promise: 承認, 承諾 *-rehn*, *-nuoh*↓; 應承 to promise.

承保 *cherngbaau*, v.i. & t., to act as guarantor.

承辦 *cherngbahn*, v.i. & t., to contract for job.

承包 *cherngbau*, v.i. & t., ditto.

承差 *cherngchai*, n., (MC) servant (＝modn. 聽差).

承塵 *cherng-chern*, n., (1) formerly, parasol held over emperor during journey; (2) the ceiling (lit., "catch dust" from roof).

承情 *cherng-chirng*, v.i., to receive s.o.'s gift or favor.

承寵 *cherng-chuung*., vi., to receive royal favor.

承擔 *cherngdan*, v.t., undertake (task, job), accept (risks), be responsible (for success, mistakes).

承當 *cherngdang*, v.t., ditto.

承兌 *cherngdueih*, v.t., accept or honor (check); 承兌交單 documents against acceptance.

承恩 *cherng-en*, v.i., to receive royal favor.

承乏 *cherngfar*, v. i., (court.) unworthily fill a post.

承奉 *cherngfehng*, v.t., to receive (order, instructions, letter).

承購 *cherngeouh*, v.t., to act as purchasing agent.

承管 *cherngguaan*, v.t., to have charge (of property, affairs).

承歡 *chernghuan*, v.i., (1) to do everything to please (parents); (2) to cater to (superiors).

承教 *cherng-jiauh*, phr., to receive your advice, (court.) meet personally.

承睫 *cherng-jier*, v.i., (LL) (1) (tears) brim over ("lashes"); (2) look on the ground ("lower eyelashes").

承繼 *cherngjih*, v.t., to inherit (also 繼承); 承繼權 right of inheritance.

承重孫 *cherngjuhng-sun*, n., eldest son of eldest branch during grandfather's funeral, when one's father is dead (thus acting in "doubly heavy" responsibility).

承攬 *chernglaan*, v.t., to take over or take entire control (of duties, responsibilities).

承霤 *chernglíouh*, n., receptacle for catching rain water from the eaves.

承露盤 *chernglúh-parn*, n., basin for catching dew water.

承蒙 *cherngmerng*, v.i., (LL, court.) to be favored with (letter, etc.): 承蒙不棄 to meet with (your gracious consent, etc.).

承命 *cherngmihng*, v.t., (court.) receive (instructions).

承諾 *cherngnuoh*, v.i., to answer "yes" to request, to promise.

承平 *cherngpirng*, adj., peaceful (era).

承認 *cherngrehn*, v.i. & t., to admit (mistakes, blame, etc.); to recognize (a government, a cousin, illegitimate son); 法律承認 de jure recognition; 事實承認 de facto recognition.

承襲 *cherngshir*, v.t., to inherit (rank).

承受 *cherngshouh*, v.i. & t., to receive (responsibility, gift, order, etc.).

承祧 *cherngtiau*, v.i., (a son of one branch) is legally adopted as heir of another branch without progeny; 承祧子 now also refers to the proper heir (嗣子).

承賜 *cherngtsyh*, v.t., (court.) receive (gift).

承租 *cherngtzu*, v.i., to rent (a house).

承望 *cherngwahng*, v.i., to hope, expect: 不承望 or 誰承望 didn't expect, or who would have thought.

承顏 *cherngyarn*, v.i., (1) see *-huan*↑; (2) to meet personally.

承運 *cherng-yuhn*, v.i., receive "heaven's mandate" or call to rule as emperor.

§ 32.01 (フ/小)

朶 32.01

duoo.

N. adjunct. 一朶花 a flower; 一朶雲 a cluster of cloud.

N. Petal-like form: 花朶 flower 耳朶 ear lobe.

朶頤 *duooyir*, v.i., (LL) "move cheeks"—(of food) inviting, attractive.

柔 32.01

rour.

Adj. (1) Weak, flexible, pliant (opp. 剛 strong, rigid): 柔弱 *-ruoh*↓; 柔軟 *-ruaan*↓; 柔韌 flexible, pliable; 柔懦 weak, timid; 柔茹 ditto; 好柔 very weak (soft); 柔得很 extremely soft (supple, flexible). (2) Soft, mild, gentle: 柔和 *-'he*↓; 柔順 meek, submissive; 溫柔 gentle, meek; 柔媚 effeminate, ingratiating; 柔柔的 soft to the touch; 柔婉 gentle and genial; 柔嫩 soft and tender; 柔然 an anc. Tartar tribe; 輕柔 light and soft; 柔惠 gentle and kind; 柔風 a gentle breeze; 柔光 a soft light.

柔腸 *rourcharng*, n., a woman's (wife's) pining for her lover (husband): 柔腸寸斷 the heart breaks to think of one's love.

柔情 *rourchirng*, n., the tender feelings of a lover: 柔情萬種 the indescribable feelings of one desperately in love.

柔道 *rourdauh*, n., (1) the soft approach (opp. 霸道 the way of the bully); (2) judo.

柔汗 *rourhahn*[1], n., (Chin. med.) cold sweat.

柔翰 *rourhahn*[2], n., the writing brush.

柔和 *rour'he*, adj., soft, gentle.

柔化 *rourhuah*, (1) v.i., soft down, weaken; (2) n., softening (weakening) of attitude.

柔曼 *rourmahn*, adj., (AC, LL) (of woman's flesh) soft and supple.

柔麻 *rourmar*, n., mulberry and hemp (material or occupation of sericulture and weaving).

柔軟 *rourruaan(-'ruan)*, adj., soft, flexible, easily bent: 柔軟體操 calisthenics.

柔弱 *rourruoh*, adj., weak, soft, meek.

柔日 *rourryh*, n., even days designated by 乙, 丁, 己, 辛 and 癸 in the 天干 system of reckoning time (opp. 剛日 odd days designated by 甲, 丙, 戊, 庚 and 壬), see Appendix A.

柔色 *rourseh*, n., a smiling face put on by the son in the presence of his father.

柔性 *rourshihng*, n., flexibility (opp. 剛性 rigidity).

柔術 *rourshuh*, n., judo, jujitsu.

柔荑 *rourtir*, n., a woman's lovely hands ("as soft and white as young reeds").

柔握 *rourwoh*, n., a woman's tender hands.

柔遠 *rour-yuaan*, phr., show kindness to people from distant lands.

柔魚 *rouryur*, n., (zoo.) the cuttlefish, *Ommastrephus pacificus* (also 魷魚).

桑 32.01

sang.

N. (1) The mulberry: 桑樹 ditto; 桑間濮上 mulberry orchard on river Puu—(allu.) place of illicit love-making; 桑中之會 (AC allu.) lovers' rendezvous (in mulberry field). (2) A surname.

桑果 *sangguoo*, n., the berry of mulberry.

桑蠖 *sanghuh*[1], n., the looper caterpillar.

桑扈 *sanghuh*[2], n., the hawfinch.

桑牛 *sangniour*, n., a beetle oft. found on mulberries, *Apriona rugicollis*.

桑皮 *sangpir*, n., mulberry bark; 桑皮紙 durable paper made from this.

桑葚(兒) *sangshehn (-sheh'l)*, n., the mulberry fruit (also 桑子 *-tzyy*).

桑田 *sang-tiarn*, n., mulberry orchard.

桑土 *sangtuu*, n., (1) mulberry field; (2) (*-duh*) (AC) mulberry root.

桑梓 *sang-tzyy*, n., childhood home town ("the mulberry home, and the catalpa"): 關心桑梓 concern for one's home town.

桑榆 *sang-yur*, n., time of old age (from AC allu. where the sun sets on "the mulberry and the elm"): 桑榆晚景 in the evening of one's life.

檃 32.01

yiin.

N. See 檃栝 *-gua*↓.

V.t. To rectify.

檃栝 *yiingua*, n., a mason's device for straightening surface or line.

§ 32.02 (フ/⺊)

隳 32.02

huei.

V.i. & t. (Of walls) to crumble; to raze (city wall).

§ 32.11 (フ/土)

圣 32.11

shehng.

[Pop. of 聖 31.11]

墮 32.11

duoh (**huei*).

[Cogn. 墜]

V.i. (1) To fall down, off, into: 墮下 fall down; 墮馬 fall off horse; 夕陽西墮 the sun is setting west; 墮其術中 fall into his trap; 墮入五里霧中 be completely at a loss (as in a fog). (2) (**huei*) Be destroyed (var. of 隳).

Adj. Var. of 惰 lazy.

墮落 *duohluoh*, v.i., go to pieces morally, sink into bad habits; be in bad days, decay.

墮胎 *duohtai*, v.i., have miscarriage or abortion.

墜 32.11

jueih.

N. (*-tz*, *'l*) Pendant type of earring, see 墜子 *-'tz* ↓.

V.i. To fall, fall down: 墜馬 fall off horseback; 墜樓 fall down from top floor; 墜地 *-dih* ↓.

Adj. Fallen: 墜胎, 墜典 *-tai*, *-diaan* ↓.

墜典 *jueihdiaan*, n., (LL) customs or institutions of olden times.

墜地 *jueih-dih*, v.i., (1) as in 呱呱墜地 child is born with a cry; (2) 文武之道, 未墜於地 when the tradition of Kings Wern and Wuu had not yet fallen apart.

墜肚 *jueih-duh*, v.i., to have loose bowels.

墜歡 *jueih-huan*, phr., (1) the pleasures of bygone days; (2) lost favor of lover: 墜歡重拾 revive old romance.

墜緒 *jueih-shyuh*, n., lost tradition.

墜胎 *jueih-tai*, v.i. & n., (have) miscarriage or abortion.

墜體 *juei-tii*, n., (phy.) a falling body.

墜子 *jueih'tz*, n., (1) pendant earrings; (2) a form of folk entertainment, song and narrative recitation, with drum accompaniment.

§ 32.22 (フ/丨)

鼐 32.22

naih.

N. (AC) a large tripod used as sacrificial vessel.

§ 32.30 (フ/一)

丞 32.30

cherng.

N. (1) A magistrate: 府丞, 縣丞 magistrate of district, county. (2) Premier, minister: 輔丞 high minister; 丞相 *-shiahng* ↓.

丞相 *cherngshiahng*, n., prime minister.

亟 32.30

jir (**chih*).

Adv. (1) Anxiously, urgently: 亟欲 want to have or do (s.t.) right away; 亟須 must be done without delay. (2) (**chih*) Repeatedly, again and again: 亟請 insistently request; 亟問 repeatedly ask questions of (s.o).

孟 32.30

mehng.

N. A surname: 孟子 Mencius.

Adj. (LL) First in series 孟, 仲, 季, oft. in brothers' names, esp. in seasons' names: 孟春, 孟夏, 孟秋, 孟冬 first month of spring, summer, autumn, winter.

孟晉 *mehngjihn*, v.i., (AC) press forward＝猛進.

孟浪 *mehnglahng*, adj., reckless: 孟浪之言 reckless, improper talk.

孟祿主義 *Mehngluh juuyih*, n., Monroe Doctrine.

孟陬 *mehngtzou*, n., (LL) first month of the year.

盈 32.30

yirng.

N. Surplus (also wr. 贏): 盈餘 *-yur* ↓.

Adj. (1) Full: 豐盈 in abundance; 惡貫滿盈 sunk in sin, having a full record of crimes and misdeeds; 盈千累萬 in hundreds and thousands. (2) Light and supple: 輕盈 supple (body).

盈虧 *yirng-kuei*, n., (1) profit and loss; (2) waxing and waning of the moon.

盈滿 *yirngmaan*, adj., full to overflow.

盈盈 *yirngyirng*, adj., (1) supple (figure, gait); (2) clear, lucid (light, water).

盈餘 *yirngyur*, n., surplus profit.

登 32.30

deng.

V.i. & t. (1) To climb, go aboard (boat, airplane, car), enter, mount: 登山 climb mountain; 登高, 登天 climb high, ascend to heaven; 登峯造極 reach the peak (of art); 一登龍門 enter the dragon gate, i.e., the hall of honor; 登梯, 樓 climb stairs, go up to upper floor; 登殿 go into temple or palace; 登門拜謝 go to friend's to thank him; 登臺 go on the stage (to speak, perform); 登基, 登極 mount the throne; 登位 begin reign as ruler. (2) To register: 登賬 enter in the accounts; 登記, 登載, 登錄 *-jih*, *-tzaih*, *-luh* ↓. (3) To publish in papers: 消息報上已登出來了 news has been published in the papers; (article) has been published. (4) (LL) harvest: 五穀豐登, 不登 produce good, bad, harvests.

登第 *deng-dih*, v.i., formerly, pass civil examinations, receive government degrees.

登東 *deng-dung*, v.i., (MC) go to toilet.

登記 *dengjih*, v.i., to enrol, register name in official record; register mail; 登記商標 registered trademark.

登科 *deng-ke*, v.i., see *-dih* ↑.

登臨 *denglirn*, v.i., visit famous mountains, historic sites.

登錄 *dengluh*, v.i., to register.

登陸艇 *dengluh-tiing*, n., landing barge, LST.

登龍 *denglurng*, v.i., esp. 登龍術 secret of success (oft. derog.).

登仙 *dengshian*, v.i., become an immortal; (euphem.) die, pass away.

登時 *dengshyr*, adv., at once.

登徒子 *dengturtzyy*, n., playboy.

登載 *dengtzaih*, v.i., be carried in the papers.

登聞鼓 *dengwernguu*, n., drum at court, beaten by one who lodges complaint against some injustice.

登月艙 *dengyuhtsang*, n., Lunar Module or 登月艇 *--tiing.*

登庸 *dengyurng*, v.i., select and promote talent for post.

鍪 32.30

mour.

N. (1) A kind of axe. (2) See 兜[Δ] 鍪 90.70.

叠 32.30

dier.

[Pop. of 疊 41.30]

§ 32.41 (フ/囚)

瞀 32.41

mauh, or *mouh*.

Adj. (AC) Obscure, blind, confused: 瞀視, 瞀病 purblind; 瞀儒 ignorant Confucianists; 瞀亂 confused.

瞀瞀(然) *mauhmauh(rarn)*, adv., blindly; not daring to look straight.

函 32.41

harn.

[Anc. var. of 函 31.21]

§ 32.42 (フ/冈)

胥 32.42

shyu.

Fin. part. (AC) 君子樂胥 the gentlemen are enjoying themselves.

N. (AC) officer; secretary: 胥吏, 胥徒 *-lih*, *-tur* ↓.

V.i. (1) To assist: 與人相胥 (AC) to assist others. (2) (AC) to wait: 胥後命 to wait for further order. (3) (AC) to observe: 于胥斯原 to observe these plains.

Adv. (LL) all: 胥賴 depend all on; 胥是君力 all is due to your efforts.

胥吏 *shyulih*, n., (LL) government clerks in gen., also officers.

胥徒 *shyutur*, n., ditto.

甬 32.42

yuung.

N. (AC) (1) A drum stick. (2) A dry measure.

甬道 *yuungdauh*, n., (1) a tunnel; (2) covered corridor or passage way.

甬路 *yuungluh*, n., ditto.

矞 乃 勇 騖 鶩 騭 烝

矞 32.42

yuh.

矞 皇 *yuhhuarng*, adj., (LL) splendid, magnificent.

§ 32.50 (フ/㇆)

乃 32.50

naai.
[Anc. var. 廼, 迺]

Pron. (AC) (1) You, your, his: 乃祖乃父 your (his) grandfather and father; 乃兄乃弟 your (his) elder and younger brothers; 乃夫 your husband; 各修乃職, 考乃法, 待乃事 (AC) let each one of you do his duties conscientiously, study his rules and regulations carefully, and be ready to answer all calls for his service. (2) Your, followed by a n., has the force of a reflexive pron. referring to the person speaking, consequently, 乃父 I, your father; 乃翁 I, your old man or grandfather.

V.i. Be (in definite assertion), be really, be indeed: 他乃我兄 he is (really) my elder brother; 此乃我國所產 this is a native product.

Adv. (LL) (1) Then, only then, after that, afterwards: 太陽出來,我乃起床 I get up only after sunrise; 乃克成行 then it will be possible for (s.o.) to go; 乃可 then it will be all right; 無乃太簡乎 is it not too simple then? (2) Even: 乃至如此 it even came to such a pass. (3) (AC) so, such: 子無乃稱 don't so call yourself; 乃爾 *-eel*↓. (4) Actually, really, such, formerly: 乃是 *-shyh*↓; 乃如 *-rur*↓; 乃者 *-jee*↓.

乃 爾 *naai-eel*, adv., to such an extent, degree.
乃 者 *naaijee*, adv., (AC) formerly, the other day, not long ago, yesteryear.
乃 如 *naairur*, adv., such as, for example.
乃 是 *naaishyh*, v.i., really is, are.
乃 因 *naaiyin*, conj., it is because.

勇 32.50

yuung.

N. (1) Soldier, conscript: 兵勇 ditto. (2) Bravery, courage: 匹夫之勇 animal courage.

Adj. (1) Brave: 勇敢 *-gaan*↓; 勇士 *-shyh*↓; 勇者 the brave; 義勇隊 volunteers; 忠勇 loyal and brave; 勇德 fortitude. (2) Forward, ready: 勇於私鬭, 怯於公憤 ever ready for private fights, but leaning backwards in public cause; 勇往 proceed courageously. (3) Fierce: 勇猛, 勇悍 *-meeng*, *-hahn*↓.

勇 氣 *yuungchih*, n., courage.
勇 敢 *yurnggaan*, adj., brave, daring.
勇 悍 *yuunghahn*, adj., fearless, ferocious (fighter).
勇 決 *yuungjyuer*, adj., decisive, determined (person).
勇 猛 *yurngmeeng*, adj. & adv., brave, -ly, fearless, -ly.
勇 士 *yuungshyh*, n., warrior, fighter.
勇 退 *yuung-tueih*, phr., 急流勇退 "retreat bravely"—i.e., draw back wisely in face of overwhelming odds.
勇 往 *yurng-waang*, phr., 勇往直前 go forward courageously.
勇 武 *yurngwuu*, adj., martial (spirit).

騖 32.50

wuh.

V.i. (1) To gallop. (2) To run after, strive after: 貪高騖遠 run after high position or far-off things; 騖外, 旁騖 be derelict in duty and run about irrelevant business.

鶩 32.50

wuh (also *muh*).

N. (AC) wild duck.

騭 32.50

jyh.

N. (1) (AC) a stallion. (2) 陰騭 (=陰功) good works done in secret which will be rewarded by heaven.

V.t. (AC) to promote (var. of 陟 32A.91); to bless: 上天陰騭下民 (AC) Heaven secretly blesses the people.

§ 32.63 (フ/丶)

烝 32.63

jeng.

N. (AC) winter sacrifice.

V.t. (AC) to have incest with father's mistress (probably from 蒸 heat goes up).

Adj. (AC) many: 烝民, 烝黎 the (many) common people.

§ 32.70 (フ/ㄴ)

乙 32.70

yii.

N. (1) Number 2 in decimal cycle, see Appendix A. (2) Second: 乙等, 乙級 second grade. (3) A suppositional person: 某甲, 某乙 a certain Mr. X, and a certain Mr. Y. (4) Second watch in the night: 乙夜. (5) U.f. 一: 乙乙 or 一一 (munition) one by one.

虱 32.70

shy.

[Var. of 蝨 32.93]

飛 32.70

fei.

V.i. & t. (1) To fly, send flying, as birds, insects, snowflakes: 飛上, 下, 來, 去 ditto; 飛來之禍 unexpected trouble; 天外飛來 out of nowhere; 飛進 fly into; 飛落 drop (of flower petals); 飛行 *-shirng* ↓; 飛書 send letter at once (for help, etc.); 飛報 report quickly; 飛簷走壁 (of great thief) climb walls and leap onto roofs; 眉飛色舞 (of face) open up in smiles of exultation. (2) Dart: 飛眼兒 make a darting glance.

Adj. (1) Flying: 飛吻 a flying kiss; 飛石, 飛矢, 飛劍 flying rocks, arrows, sword; 飛閣 tower connected by flying corridor; 飛禽, 飛鳥 birds; 飛禽走獸 birds and beasts; 飛砂走石 flying sands (sandstorm in desert); 飛騎 fast cavalry; 飛(蜚)語流長 flying rumors; 飛鷹 flying eagle; 飛鷹走狗 hawks and hounds (underlings); 飛腿, 飛踢 flying kick. (2) 飛仔 (Cantonese) a juvenile delinquent.

飛瀑 *feibauh*, n., (flying) waterfalls.

飛奔 *feiben*, v.i., dash (away).

飛白 *feibor*, n., style of cursive calligraphy with dry brush, showing hollow lines.

飛橋 *feichiaur*, n., flying or very high bridge.

飛券 *feichyuahn*, n., kind of anc. paper-money.

飛彈 *feidahn*, n., (1) stray bullet; (2) missile, rocket: 反飛彈 antimissile; 彈道飛彈 ballistic missiles; 洲際彈道飛彈 intercontinental ballistic missiles (ICBM).

飛碟 *fei dier*, n., flying saucer, unidentified flying object (UFO).

飛蛾 *fei-er*, n., moth.

飛歸 *feiguei*, v.i., a way of reckoning division with abacus.

飛蝗 *feihuarng*, n., (flying) locust pest.

飛黃騰達 *feihuarng-terngdar*, phr., get rapid promotion or series of successes in polities or business.

飛漲 *feijahng*, n. & v.i., sudden (-ly) or rapid (-ly) increase (of prices).

飛機 *feiji*, n., airplane; 飛機場 airport; 直昇飛機 helicopter.

飛腳 *feijiaau*, n., flying kick.

飛撾 *feijua*, n., a metallic weapon thrown at enemy, shaped like eagle's claw.

飛樓 *feilour*, n., anc. scaffolding for laying siege and attacking city wall.

飛輪 *feilurn*, n., (phys.) flying wheel.

飛毛腿 *feimaurtueei*, n., a fast walker.

飛跑 *feipaau*, v.i., run very fast.

飛蓬 *feiperng*, n., see 蓬 20A.83 N.

飛昇 *feisheng*, v.i., fly up (to heaven).

飛錫 *feishir*, phr., of monk's travel, see 錫^杖 81A.50.

飛行 *feishirng*, v.i., to fly (around the earth, etc.), to go by plane; 飛行員 air pilot.

飛騰 *feiterng*, v.i., to go up (to the sky).

飛梯 *feiti*, n., anc. weapon for scaling enemy city wall.

飛艇 *feitiing*, n., dirigible airship (lighter-than-air type).

飛子 *fektzyy* (-'*tz*), formerly, narrow slip of paper, used like chips for drawing pay.

飛揚(颺) *feiyarng*, v.i., float in the sky; grow in strength: 飛揚跋扈 to become powerful and intransigent.

飛魚 *feiyur*, n., flying fish.

沓 32.70

jiin.

N. The nuptial wine cup: 合沓, 交沓 drink the nuptial wine cup as part of the wedding ceremony.

凳 32.70

dehng.

N. (-*tz*) Stool, bench: oft. 板凳.

§ 32.72 (フ/心)

恿 32.72

yuung.

[Pop. var. of 慂 63.72; anc. var. of 勇 32.50]

乙 虱 飛 沓 凳 恿

§ 32.80 (フ/八)

𧴪 32.80

shiarn.
[Abbr. of 賢 51.80]

§ 32.81 (フ/人)

癸 32.81

gueei.

N. (1) The last character of 天干 (the decimal cycle), see Appendix A. (2) A surname.

癸水 *gueirshueei*, n., menstruation.

§ 32.82 (フ/㐅)

又 32.82

youh.
[Usu. printed 又]

Adv. (1) Again: 你又來了 you again! 又過了一天 another day passed again; in many combinations expressing the idea "again": 又復, 又再, 更又 again; 且又 besides; 又加, 又兼 in addition (besides). (2) Oft. containing a rebuke, disapproval: 又是他 it's he, the same person, again! 又來官樣文章 again the bombastic talk of bureaucracy; 你又不是一個小孩 besides, you are not a child (and should not listen to him).

Conj. And: 一又三分之二 one and two-thirds; oft. 又 . . . 又 . . . : 又高又大 big and tall; 又聾又啞 both deaf and mute; 又冷又下雨 it's cold and raining; 又餓又渴 both hungry and thirsty.

叉 32.82

cha (**char*, **chaa*).

N. (*-tz*) A fork, a prong: 刀叉 knife and fork; 叉竿, 木叉 (also wr. 杈) a pronged stick; 鐵叉 an iron prong or poker; 火叉子 fire tongs; 魚叉子 a fish spear.

V.t. (1) To cross: 叉手 *-shoou*↓; 叉指 to interlace fingers; 交叉 to cross (lines, roads); 交叉點 crossroads, point of intersection. (2) To pick up with a fork, hold at bay or push as with a fork; 用叉叉魚 spear a fish; 叉起一塊肉 pick up meat with fork; 叉出門外 push (person) out of the gate with both hands. (3) To play mahjong: 叉麻雀 or 麻匠. (4) (**char*) To stick in the throat: 叉在嗓子裏 (bone) sticks in the throat. (5) (**char*) To hook up a railway car: 叉車 cars stack up and block the road. (6) (**chaa*) To fork out, branch out in different directions: 叉開 *-kai*↓; 叉牙 *-yar*↓; 褲叉 (in tailoring) where the legs of trousers meet; 叉門 to stand at door and block entrance with arms spread out.

叉股子話 *chaguutz huah*, n., (coll.) contradictory statements.

叉灰泥 **chaa-hueinir*, n., mixed cement.

叉開 **chaa-kai*, v.i., fork out, push aside with both hands.

叉劈 *chaa'pi*, adj. & adv., divergent: 走叉劈了 (our) ways diverge in different directions.

叉手 *cha-shoou*, v.i., to fold hands in salute.

叉牙 *cha-yar*, (1) v.i., to fork; (2) adj., (branches) forking out (also wr. 杈枒).

及 32.82

jir.

V.t. (1) Come up to, reach, attain: 及冠 *-guahn*, 及笄 *-ji*, 及格 *-ger*, 及第 *-dih*, 及門 *-mern*, 及肩 *-jian*↓; 罪不及妻孥 a wife and children are not punished for crimes of the husband and father; 今恩足以及禽獸 (AC) now that even birds and animals can bask in your favor; 趕得及, 來得及 be in time for; 力所難及 beyond one's power or physical strength. (2) Compare with: 及不上他 be no match for him.

Prep. In, on, to: 及時 in or on time; 由東及西 from east to west; 由近及遠 from the near to the distant; 由親及疏 from close relations to mere acquaintances.

Conj. (1) When: 及期 when the time comes; 及其長也 when he grew up to manhood; 及其覺也 when he woke up; 及至 when the point is reached. (2) And: 孔子及其門徒 Confucius and his disciples.

及第 *jir-dih*, v.i., formerly, be successful in government examinations.

及格 *jir-ger*, v.i., pass in an examination, to qualify: 不及格 disqualified.

及冠 *jir-guahn*, v.i., (of men) formerly, come of age, usu. at 20.

及笄 *jir-ji*, v.i., (of women) formerly, come of age, usu. at 15.

及肩 *jir-jian*, adj., come up to the shoulder.

及門 *jir-mern*, adj., 及門弟子 pupils, disciples directly taught by master.

及時 *jir-shyr*, adj. & adv., timely, in or on time: 及時努力 make timely efforts; 及時採取行動 take timely action; 及時趕上 be just in time for; 及時到達 arrive in time.

及早 *jir-tzaau*, adv., early, while there's yet plenty of time.

發 32.82

fa.

V.i. & t. (1) Send out, give out, dispatch: oft. 發出去,下; 發給某人 give out to person; 發電, 發信, 發出通告 send telegram, letter, send out general notice; 發號施令 give out orders; 發兵 send out troops; 發薪, 發餉 pay out salary, army rations; 發矢 shoot arrow; 發誓, 發言 *-shyh*[1], *-yarn* ↓; 發愿 take religious pledge; 發聲, 發光 give out sound, light; 發稿, 發排 send out script to printer; see 發遣, 送, 交, 付, 回, 還, 落 *-chiaan*, *-suhng*, *-jiau*, *-fuh*, *-hueir*, *-huarn*, *-luoh* ↓; 分發, 頒發 give out, distribute (handbills, prizes, pay). (2) Open up, discover, expose: 發明, 發覺, 發現 *-mirng*, *-jyuer*, *-shiahn* ↓; 發冢, 發姦 open tomb, expose adultery; 發掘 *-jyur*, excavate ↓; 開發 open up (industry, mines, new country, etc.). (3) Start, put forth, grow+n.: 發芽, 發苗, 發苞 put forth sprouts, shoots, buds; 發起, 發生 *-chii*, *-sheng* ↓; 發汗 perspire, also induce perspiration; 發疹子, 紅點 have measles, a rash; 發痧 have attack of cholera, colic; 發瘧子 have attack of malaria; 發火, 發怒, 發脾氣 become angry; 發顫, 發抖 tremble, shiver; 發財 *-tsair* ↓. (4) Develop, become, grow+adj.: 發冷, 發熱 feel chill, have fever; 發紅, 白, 黑, 黃 grow red, white, black, yellow; 發亮 become bright, shiny; 發麻, 發木 become numb; 發硬, 乾, 潮, 霉 become hard, dry, damp, mildewed; 發癢, 煩 become itchy, irritable; 發懶 feel lazy; 發狂, 瘋, 憤 *-kuarng*, *-feng*, *-fehn*[2] and many compp. ↓.

發呆 *fa-air*, adj., stunned, nonplussed.

發報機 *fabauh-ji*, n., machine for sending out telegram.

發表 *fabiaau*, v.t., publish, give out to public (statement, opinion, new rules, results of contests).

發標 *fabiau*, n., (MC) take it out on s.o.

發布 *fabuh*, v.t., publish (laws, etc.).

發遣 *fachiaan*, v.t., send away; send to exile; send (troops, etc.).

發起 *fachii*, v.i. & t., to start (a new society, etc.); 發起人 *--rern*, sponsor(s); cause to happen: 發起辯論 cause controversy; 甚麽時候發起 when did it start?

發愁 *fa-chour*, v.i., be, become sad, sullen, worried.

發出 *fa-chu*, v.t., send out, produce, give rise to: 發出毛病 give rise to troubles; 發出宣言 publish official statement (of position, program, policy); 發出聲音 produce a sound; send out (telegram, warning, mail, salary, etc.).

發喘 *fachuaan*, v.i., pant, feel short of breath.

發獃 *fadai*, v.i., be dazed.

發達 *fadar*, v.i. & adj., prosper, (be) prosperous.

發抖 *fadoou*, v.i., shiver.

發動 *faduhng*, v.i. & t., to start and push (movement, campaign, an engine), take the initiative; 發動機 *--ji*, n., dynamo, electric motor.

發發 *fafa*, adj., (AC, of wind) fast.

發放 *fa-fahng*, v.t., send away (to the country, prisoners).

發凡 *fa-farn*, n., introduction.

發奮 *fa-fehn*[1], v.i., make firm resolve: 發奮圖強 resolve to make the country strong; 發奮用功 resolve to study hard.

發憤 *fa-fehn*[2], v.i., ditto.

發瘋 *fa-feng*, v,i., grow crazy.

發付 *fa-fuh*, v.t., pay out (sum, to person).

發福 *fa-fur*, v.i., grow fat.

發個兒 *fa-geh'l*, v.i., grow bodily taller.

發行 (1) *faharng*, v.i. & t. & n., sell wholesale; such firm; (2) *-shirng*, v.t., publish; 發行人 publisher.

發狠 *faheen*, v.i. & adv., with angry determination; diligently, with force.

發橫 *fahehng*, adj., become obstinate, violent.

發話 *fa-huah*, v.i., (MC) speak angrily.

發慌 *fa-huang*, v.i., to panic.

發還 *fa-huarn*, v.t., send back.

發皇 *fa-huarng*, v.i., grow or prosper beautifully.

發揮 *fahuei*, v.t., develop, expand on (idea, talent).

發回 *fa-hueir*, v.t., send back.

發昏 *fa-hun*, v.i., faint; grow dizzy; (derog.) go crazy.

發火 *fa-huoo*, v.i., become angry.

發展 *fajaan*, v.i. & t., develop, expand (business); show, give expression (to natural talent).

發顫 *fa-jahn*, v.i., tremble.

發怔 *fa-jehng*, v.i., be stunned.

發迹 *fa-ji*, v.i., make good, be a success.

發見 *fajiahn* (*-shiahn*), v.t. & n., discover, find out; discovery;

發交 *fajiau*, v.t., deliver (to person).

發解 *fajieh*, v.i., (MC) receive M. A. degree (舉人).

發急 *fa-jir*, v.i., get nervous, worried.

發咒 *fa-jouh*, v.i., swear an oath; swear.

發莊 *fa-juang*, v.i. & n., sell wholesale; wholesale merchant.

發覺 *fajyuer*, v.t., discover.

發噱 *fa-jyuh*, v.i., laugh out loudly.

發掘 *fajyur*, v.t. & n., excavate, -tion.

發刊 *fa-kan*, v.t., publish; 發刊詞 *--tsyr*, n., inaugural statement on first issue of periodical.

發客 *fa-keh*, v.i., sell to customers (goods).

發狂 *fa-kuarng*, v.i., grow crazy, become mad.

發楞 *fa-lehng*, v.i., be stunned.

發落 *faluoh*, v.t., dispose of, dismiss with term of punishment.

發賣 *famaih*, v.i. & t., put out for sale: 發賣房屋 sell house.

發毛 *fa-maur*, v.i., be afraid (to sleep alone, etc.), be covered with goose flesh.

發麪 *famiahn*, v.i. & n., to leaven dough; leavened dough.

亅	小	⺊	十	土	ナ	廾	丬	丨	一	丅	フ	口	区	冈	㇕	厂	尸	亠	广	宀	丶	乚	弋	心	八	人	乂	㇀	丆	丿	𠂉	𡿨
00	01	02	10	11	12	20	21	22	30	31	32	40	41	42	50	51	52	60	61	62	63	70	71	72	80	81	82	83	90	91	92	93

發明 famirng, v.i. & t., n., invent; invention: 發明家 inventor.
發難 fa-nahn, v.i., be the first to start revolt.
發怒 fa-nuh, v.i., become angry.
發票 fa-piauh, n., invoice.
發熱 fa-reh, v.i., run a fever; feel hot.
發軔 fa-rehn, v.i., start on journey.
發散 fa-sahn (-'san) v.i., to diffuse (of gas); (Chin. med.) to let out perspiration, otherwise loosen up bodily humors.
發喪 fa-sang, v.i., send out obituary, cf. 出殯△ 31S.80.
發燒 fa-shau, v.i., run a fever.
發射 fa-sheh, v.i. & n., shoot (arrow, bullet, missile); 洲際發射機 international ballistic missile.
發身 fa-shen, v.i., reach puberty.
發生 fa-sheng, v.i. & t., (1) arise, cause to happen: 發生事件, 問題 cause events, problems to arise; 事件, 問題發生 events, problems arise; 發生誤會, 爭執 cause misunderstanding, dispute (also difficulties, suspicion, obstruction, doubt, etc.); (2) pr. fah'sheng, (Peking coll.) prosper.
發下 fa-shiah, v.t., send down (order, instructions, etc.).
發現 fashiahn, v.t. & n., discover, -ry (new facts, comet, etc.); to appear, arise: 不會發現 will not find, appear; also wr. 發見 pr. -shiahn.
發祥 fashiarng, v.i., prosper; 發祥地 place of origin of a new dynasty or of wealth.
發酵 fa-shiauh[1], v.i., (of dough) ferment, leaven.
發笑 fa-shiauh[2], v.i., to laugh out.
發洩(泄) fashieh, v.t. & i., blow off steam, anger; dissipate.
發行 fashirng, v.i., see -harng, (2) ↑.
發售 fashouh, v.i., be for sale; sell.
發誓 fa-shyh[1], v.i., take an oath; swear.
發市 fa-shyh[2], v.i., open for customers.
發送 fa'suhng (-'sung), v.i., (1) to send out (invitations, etc.); (2) transport body to grave in procession, see 出殯△ 31S.80.
發條 fatiaur, n., spring in clockwork.
發財 fa-tsair, v.i., get rich.
發燥 fa-tzauh, v.i., become nervous, irritable.
發作 fatzuoh, v.i., have an attack of anger, disease.
發往 fa-waang, v.t., send to.
發問 fa-wehn, v.i., ask question, to question.
發芽 fa-yar, v.i., sprout.
發言 fa-yarn, v.i., to state opinion in assembly; 發言人 spokesman.
發揚 fayarng, v.i., develop, expand (truth, tradition): 發揚光大 bring to greater height of development.
發瘧子 fa-yauhtz, v.i., (vern.) have attack of malaria.
發引 fa-yiin, v.i., make funeral procession with coffin leading.
發音 fa-yin, v.i. & n., pronounce, pronunciation.

---

§ 32.83 (ㄅ/～)

疋 32.83

pii.

N. adjunct. 一疋布 a length, or factory roll of clothing material (also wr. 匹).

疋頭 pii'tou, n., piece goods.

迅 32.83

shyuhn.

Adj. & adv. Fast: 迅走 walk fast; 迅即啟程 start immediately; 迅流 a fast current; 迅雷不及掩耳 (of actions) lightning flash, blitz, before precautions can be taken (lit., "thunderclap gives no time for covering ears").

迅捷 shyuhnjier, adj. & adv., fast (mail, traffic, etc.).
迅疾 shyuhnjir, adj. & adv., ditto.
迅速 shyuhnsuh, adj. & adv., ditto.

通 32.83

tung.

N. adjunct. 一通信 one piece of correspondence; 一通文書 an official document, communication; 打一通鼓 one stretch of drumbeating.

V.i. & t. (1) To communicate, connect with, transmit: (互)通消息 communicate news; 通信, 通報, 通知 -shihn, -bauh, -jy ↓; 通電話 talk by telephone; 通風報信 send news, esp. secretly; (of roads, etc.) lead toward; 四通八達 (open square) leads in all directions; 錢能通神 money talks ("even to spirits"); 通情 send messages of love; 通情達理 show common sense, be reasonable; 暗通款曲 send secret message, usu. of love; 通敵 secretly communicate with enemy; 通關節 bribe people in power; 通竅△ see 62A.82. (2) Have intercourse with: 通商, 通好 -shang, -haau ↓; have sexual intercourse: (AC) 通, (mod.) 私通; 和某人私通 have illicit relations with a certain person. (3) To understand thoroughly, to master (the classics): 博古通今 to master ancient and modern learning; 萬事通 a master of everything; 中國通 an old China hand, a China expert; 精通國語 master the national language; 無師自通 self-taught, learned without teacher; 通權達變 adaptable to changing circumstances, not bound by old rules; 通宵, 通達 -shiau, -dar ↓. (4) Join, share: 通財 share wealth or possessions (between friends); 通家, 通譜 -jia, -puu ↓.

Adj. (1) As vb. complement, through: 打通了電話 put (telephone) line through; 說通了 have come to an understanding with s.o., have persuaded or informed (person) duly; 講不通 (of argument) unconvincing, unreasonable, stretched, also could not get (person) to understand or agree; 交通 communicate, -ions; 變通 change method to suit circumstances; 溝通 connect up and exchange (cultures); 疏通 privately speak to (influential people); 打通 break up barriers; 串通, 勾通 bribe, conspire with. (2) Bribe, conspire with. (3) Thoroughly conversant with subject, competent in writing: 書念通了 be really well educated; 不通 (of person, or his writings) ill educated, half baked; 通順 good, clear writing; 通暢 -chahng↓. (4) General, all, entire: 通國 the whole country; 通身酸痛 the whole body aches; 通夜, 通宿(兒) all night; 通宵 see -shiau↓; 通盤 -parn↓; 通力合作 phr., everybody pitching in for common work. (5) Common, general: 普通 general, -ly; 通常 -charng↓; 通病 -bihng↓; 通俗, 通例, 通論 -shur, -lih, -luhn↓.

Adv. All: see 通通, 通統, 通共 -tung, -tuung, -guhng↓.

通寶 *tungbaau*, n., anc. Chin. coin.

通報 *tuungbauh*, n., news despatch, intelligence report, a circular notice.

通便劑 *tungbiahnji*, n., laxative.

通病 *tungbihng*, n., common failing.

通暢 *tungchahng*, adj., (writing) pleasantly expressive.

通常 *tungcharng*, adj. & adv., usual, -ly, ordinary, -ily.

通車 *tungche*, (1) n., through express (train); (2) v.i., be open to traffic.

通徹 *tungcheh*, adj., thorough (statement).

通稱 *tungcheng*, n., general or common name for things.

通緝 *tungchih*[1], v.t., wanted by police; 通緝令 general public notice for the arrest of a criminal at large.

通氣(兒) *tungchih*[2]*('l)*, adj. & v.i., (1) in touch with each other; (2) ventilate, -ed.

通衢 *tungchyur*, n., main thoroughfare.

通達 *tungdar*, adj., well versed, experienced and understanding: 通達事理 understand things.

通道 *tungdauh*, n., a through street; thoroughfare.

通典 *tungdiaan*, n., see -kaau↓.

通電 *tungdiahn*, v.i. & n., make electric connection; (send) public statement (in the press) in the form of a cabled message.

通牒 *tungdier*, n., diplomatic note; 最後通牒 ultimatum.

通都 *tungdu*, n., a great metropolis: 通都大邑 metropolitan cities.

通粉 *tungfeen*, n., unrefined flour.

通分 *tungfen*, n., reduction of fractions to a common denominator.

通風 *tungfeng*, (1) adj., well ventilated, let air get through; (2) v.i., send secret message: 通風報信.

通告 *tunggauh*, v.t. & n., (give) public notice.

通關 *tungguan*, v.i. & n., (1) 通關節 bribe those in power; (2) (Chin. med.) open up blocked circulation; (3) (coll.) person with high nose bridge; (4) palmistry) long, extended horizontal lines on palm.

通共 *tungguhng*, adv., altogether: 通共四十六人 altogether 46 persons.

通過 *tung-guoh*, (1) v.t., pass through; (2) pass (a resolution); (3) adv., by way of, via: 通過雙方同意 after agreement by both parties.

通古斯族 *Tungguusy Tzur*, n., Tungus, race in east Siberia.

通好 *tunghaau*, v.i., establish friendly relations as between nations, tribes.

通滙銀行 *tunghueih yirnharng*, n., correspondent bank.

通貨 *tunghuoh*, phr., country's currency: 通貨膨脹 inflation; 通貨收縮 deflation.

通紅 *tunghurng* (also pr. *tuhng-*), adj., 滿面通紅 phr., flush red all over.

通家 *tungjia*, n., family related, or friends for generations.

通假 *tungjiaa*, n., (of Chin. characters) interchangeable with other characters.

通姦 *tungjian*, n. & v.i., (commit) adultery.

通經兒 *tungjing'l*, v.i., know the classics.

通知 *tungjy*, v.t. & n., notify, -fication; 接到通知 receive notice; 通知書 a formal notification.

通考 *tungkaau*, n., a comprehensive historical compendium of social, economic, and political institutions.

通款 *tungkuaan*, v.i., make approaches to enemy for terms of settlement.

通例 *tunglih*, n., generally accepted rules.

通令 *tunglihng*, v.t. & n., general order to whole country: 通令全國.

通禮 *tunglii*, n., commonly accepted practice or ritual.

通靈 *tunglirng*, adj., (of objects) supernatural, having magical power.

通論 *tungluhn*, n., (1) general introduction (to subject); (2) convincing arguments; (3) theory of general application.

通眉 *tung-meir*, adj., having joined eyebrows.

通名 *tung-mirng*, v.i., exchange name cards or announce one's name.

通謀 *tung-mour*, v.i., conspire (with person).

通盤 *tungparn*, adv., as a whole: 通盤計劃, 籌算 to plan, calculate expenses as a whole.

通票 *tungpiauh*, n., through ticket.

通品 *tungpiin*, n., see -rern↓.

通譜 *tung-puu*, adj., be sworn brothers; regarded as same clan.

通人 *tungrern*, n., (high praise) profound scholar.

通融 *tungrurng*, v.i., relax or circumvent regulations to accommodate; accommodation; to allow temporary credit: 通融一下 to ask person to make an accommodation.

通儒 *tung-rur*, n., profound Confucian scholar.

通日 *tungryh*, adv., all day.

通塞 *tung-seh*, phr., (of circumstances) smooth-going or otherwise.

通商 *tungshang*, v.i., open to international trade and commerce; 通商條約 commercial treaty; 通商口岸 treaty ports.

通曉 *tungshiaau*, v.i., understand thoroughly.

通宵 *tungshiau*, adv., all night: 跳(舞)通宵 dance all night; 通宵達旦 all night till dawn.

通信 *tungshihn*, v.i. & n., correspond by letter, (keep up) correspondence; 通信處 mailing address.

通性 *tungshihng*, n., (1) character shared by all mankind; (2) (grammar) common gender.

通心 *tungshin*, adj., hollow in center; 通心粉 macaroni.

通宿(兒) *tungshioou('l)*, adv., all night.

通行 *tungshirng*, adj. & v.i., current (language, customs); go through, open to traffic: 可以通行, 通行無阻 open thoroughfare, accessible to public; 通行證 pass for entering area.

通書 *tungshu*, n., (1) formerly, farmer's almanac; (2) formerly, notice by groom's family to bride's on date set for wedding.

通順 *tungshuhn*, adj., (of writing) simple, clear, idiomatic.

通事 *tungshy*, n., formerly, translator or interpreter in government office.

通學 *tungshyuer*, v.i., study in day school: 通學生 day student.

通訊 *tungshyuhn*, n., news despatch; 通訊社 news agency.

通史 *tungshyy*, n., general history.

通俗 *tungsur*, adj., popular, current (usage); (writing) for mass consumption; 通俗文體 popular style; 通俗文學 popular literature.

通套 *tungtauh*, n., hackneyed formula.

通天 *tungtian*, adj., all-powerful, "sky-reaching," i.e., very great: 通天的本事 very special skill or ability.

通體 *tungtii*, adv., the entire body, the whole.

通透 *tungtouh*, adj., penetrating (insight, etc.).

通草 *tungtsaau*, n., the five-leaf akibia, *Akebia quinata*.

通才 *tungtsair*, n., gifted person; one who has received a liberal education: 通才教育 liberal education.

通通 *tungtung*, adv., all, altogether, entirely: 通通丟了 entirely lost; 通通走開 get away, all of you!

通脫 *tungtuo*, adj., unconventional, romantic: 通脫自喜, 通脫之才 person who is not too concerned about social approval; 通脫木 (bot.) the rice-paper plant, *Aralia papyrifera*.

通同 *tungturng*, adv., together (work, share): esp. 通同作弊 work together in illegal transactions.

通統 *tungtuung*, adv., all, entirely: 通統拿走 take away all of it (also 通通).

通則 *tungtzer*, n., common regulations, general rules.

通問 *tungwehn*, v.i. & n., exchange news, keep up correspondence.

通夜 *tungyeh*, adv., all night.

通義 *tungyih*[1], n., the general acceptance of the term.

通譯 *tungyih*[2], v.i. & n., (now rare) translate, -tor, interpret, -ter.

通姻(婚) *tungyin (-hun)*, v.i., be related by marriage.

通韻 *tungyuhn*, n., (of rhymebooks) anc. rhyme categories which are now interchangeable.

通用 *tungyuhng*, adj., current (terms, paper money, etc.).

遜 32.83

shyuhn (also *suhn*).

V.i. & t. (1) To give way, give up: 遜位, 遜國 *-weih, -guor* ↓. (2) To lose by comparison: 遜色 *-seh* ↓; 彼遜於此 (LL) that is inferior to this.

Adj. Humble, modest: 謙遜 ditto.

Adv. Modestly: 遜謝 modestly decline; 遜順 modestly obey.

遜遁 *shyuhnduhn*, v.i., (1) (LL) to draw back out of modesty; (2) to get out of the picture, disappear.

遜國 *shyuhn-guor*, v.i., abdicate the throne.

遜色 *shyuhn-seh*, v.i., to lose in comparison, compare unfavorably.

遜遜 *shyuhnshyuhn*, adj., modest, retiring in manner (cf. 恂恂).

遜位 *shyuhn-weih*, v.i., to abdicate in favor of son or conqueror.

§ 32.93 (フ/く)

婺 32.93

wuh.

Adj. (AC) beautiful.

蚤 32.93

tzaau.

N. The flea: 跳蚤.

Adj. & adv. (Interch. 早) early: 蚤起 get up early in the morning.

蛋 32.93

dahn.

N. (1) Egg: 雞蛋, 鴨蛋 hen's eggs, duck eggs; 蛋殼 eggshell. (2) Word of abuse: 混蛋, 壞蛋 bad egg; 傻蛋, 笨蛋 idiot, imbecile.

蛋白 *dahnbair*, n., egg white; 蛋白質 *--jy*, n., albumin; 蛋白石 *--shyr*, n., opal.
蛋黃 *dahnhuarng*, n., yolk.
蛋戶 *dahnhuh*, 蛋家 *dahnjia*, n., boat population in southern China.

蝥 32.93

maur.

N. (1) Var. of 蟊 32.93. (2) 斑蝥 name of a beetle, *Cicindela chinensis*, which destroys grain-eating insects.

蟊 32.93

maur.

N. A grain-destroying insect.

蟊賊 *maurtzer*, n., destroying agent: 國家, 社會之蟊賊 vermin of a country, of society.

蝨 32.93

shy.
[Var. 虱]

N. (*-tz*) A bug, bedbug, louse: 蝨處褌中 a bedbug in trousers—sarcasm against Confucian doctrinaires who follow a "straight path" as bugs follow trousers' seams.

蝨蠅 *shy-yirng*, n., a gadfly.

SECTION 32A

§ 32A.00 (阝/亅)

阿 32A.00-3

e (**a*, **aa*, **ah*).

Fin. part. See 啊 40A.00.

N. (1) (AC) Hillock. (2) (AC) Swamp, recess corner. (3) A surname. (4) (**ah*) Used in translit. of foreign names: as 阿剌伯 Arabia, 阿根廷 Argentina, etc., (see Appendix E, Geographical Names); in translit. of Buddhist terms, 阿 represents Sanskr. "a" sound, although commonly read in Peking as *e* (Wade: *eh*), as 阿彌陀佛, 阿難 *Amita*, Ananda.

Pron. (**ah*) (Also in varying accents) prefix to familiar address (to father, mother, sister, etc.) in gen., a mother oft. employs term of address used by her child, as addressing husband's father as 阿翁 grandfather (from point of view of family), see compp. ↓.

V.t. (1) To flatter, gain favor, side with: 阿諂, 阿諛, 阿私, 阿附 *-chaan*, *-yur*, *-sy*, *-fuh* ↓. (2) U.f. 屙 52A.00, in 阿尿 to urinate.

Excl. (1) (**ah*) U.f. 啊 40A.00. (2) (**aa*) Excl. of unpleasant surprise: 阿, 他死了嗎 oh, is he dead?

阿阿 **a-a*, adj., as in 阿阿大笑 laugh out loud, guffaw, "aha!"
阿保 *e-baau*, (1) v.t., (AC) to nurse (a child); (2) n., (AC) a nurse.
阿鼻 **a-bir*, n., (Budd.) the hell of uninterrupted torture, last and deepest of eight hot hells (from Sanskr. *avici*).
阿伯 **ahbor*, n., uncle (familiar address and self-reference).
阿諂 *e-chaan*, v.t., (LL) to flatter.
阿黨 *e-daang*, v.i., (AC) to be partial.
阿爹 **ahdie*, n., daddy (familiar address and self-reference).
阿弟 **ahdih*, n., younger brother (familiar address).
阿堵物 **ahduuwuh*, n., (1) (anc. coll., contempt.) that thing; (2) (LL allu.) money.
阿父 **ahfuh*, n., (anc. coll.) father, also (AC) uncle (=伯父, 叔父).
阿附 *e-fuh*, v.t., to attach oneself to (some authority): 阿附權貴 to curry favor with those in power.
阿芙蓉 *e-furrurng*, n., (LL) opium.
阿哥 **ahge*, n., (1) elder brother (familiar address and self-reference); (2) Manchu word for crown prince: 大阿哥.
阿閣 *e-ger*, n., (AC) a pavilion surrounded with courtyards.
阿姑 **ahgu*[1], n., (1) auntie; (2) (AC, MC) husband's mother.
阿家 **ahgu*[2], n., (MC) see *-gu*[1] ↑; 阿家翁 husband's parents; 阿家阿翁 husband's father and mother: 不癡不聾, 不作阿家(阿)翁 unless one pretends to know nothing and hear nothing, don't be a father-in-law or mother-in-law.
阿公 **ahgung*, n., (1) husband's father; (2) grandfather; (3) gen. address of an elderly person, see *-weng* ↓.
阿嗄 **a-har*, excl., aha! I see! You don't say! (exc. of surprise).
阿好 *e-hauh*, v.i., to curry favor, to assent to one party: 阿好之言 statement to please one side.
阿訇 **ahhung*, n., Moslem mullah.
阿監 **ahjiahn*, n., (MC) eunuch officer.
阿膠 *e-jiau*, n., glue made from cowhide, produced in 阿縣 (*E*

亅	小	⺊	十	土	𠂇	廾	𠂉	丨	一	丁	フ	口	囗	冂	𠃌	厂	尸	亠	广	宀	丶	乚	弋	心	八	人	乂	乛	ノ	刂	𠂉	く
00	01	02	10	11	12	20	21	22	30	31	32	40	41	42	50	51	52	60	61	62	63	70	71	72	80	81	82	83	90	91	92	93

county) in Shantung.

阿姐 *ahjiee*, n., elder sister (familiar address and self-reference).

阿舅 **ahjiouh*, n., mother's brother.

阿拉 (1) **Ahla*, n., (Mohammedan) Allah; (2) **ala*, (Ningpo dial., self-reference) me, I.

阿拉伯 *Ahlabor*, n., Arabia; 阿拉伯數字 Arabic numerals: 1, 2, 3, 4, 5, 6, 7, 8, 9, 0; 阿拉伯文 Arabic language.

阿蘭若 *elarnree*, n., a Buddhist retreat, quiet abode (from Sanskr. *aranya*).

阿羅漢 *eluorhahn*, n., *arhan*, arhat or *lohan* (羅漢) (from Sanskr. *arhat*).

阿媽 **ahma*, n., (1) mamma; (2) (MC) also grandma.

阿嘛 **ah'ma*, n., (Manchu) papa.

阿妹 **ahmeih*, n., little sister.

阿門 **ah'men*, n., (Christian) amen.

阿米巴 **ahmirba*, n., amoeba.

阿彌陀佛 *emirtour'fo*, n., *Amitabha*, Buddha of boundless light, or eternal life (from Sanskr. *amitabha*); 南無阿彌陀佛 Namo— Blessed be, glory to *Amitabha*!

阿摩尼亞 **ahmorniryah*, n., (chem.) ammonia.

阿木林 **ahmuhlirn*, n., (Shanghai, contempt.) a nitwit, dullard.

阿母 **ahmuu*, n., (1) mamma; (2) (AC) also wet nurse.

阿嬭(奶) **ahnaai*, n., (term of respect for elderly woman) mother, grandmother or wet nurse.

阿難 *E-narn*, n., (Budd.) Ananda, the most learned disciple of Buddha.

阿娘 **ahniarn*, n., mother, much used in MC literature.

阿尼林 **ahnirlirn*, n., aniline dye.

阿奴 **ahnur*, n., (MC) term of endearment for little child or younger brother, like "little rascal" (lit. "little slave").

阿儂 **ahnurng*, n., (Shanghai) I, myself.

阿旁 *eparng*, n., (Budd.) ox-head torturers in Hades.

阿片 **ahpiahn*, n., opium (usu. wr. 鴉片).

阿婆 **ahpor*, n., term of respect for elderly woman.

阿闍梨 *esherlir*, n., spiritual teacher, master, perceptor (from Sanskr. *acarya*).

阿香 **Ahshiang*, n., (myth.) girl driver of the chariot of God of Thunder: 阿香車 such chariot.

阿咸 *ahshiarn*, n., (LL) nephew (allu. to 阮咸, nephew of 阮籍).

阿修羅 *eshiouluor*, n., (Budd.) a frightful demon (from Sanskr. *asura*).

阿誰 **ahshueir*, pron., (LL & modn.) who: 阿誰之過 whose fault is it?

阿叔 **ahshur*, n., uncle (familiar address and self-reference).

阿兄 **ahshyung*, n., elder brother (familiar address and self-reference).

阿私 *e-sy*, v.i., to be partial to one's own.

阿司匹靈 **ahsypilirn*, n., (translit.) aspirin.

阿嚏 **a-tih*, n., (sound of) a sneeze: 打阿嚏 to sneeze.

阿姊 **ahtzyy*, n., elder sister (familiar address and self-reference), (also pr. *-jiee*, and wr. 阿姐).

阿魏 *e-weih*, n., (bot.) *Ferula scorodosma*.

阿翁 **ahweng*, n., see *-gung*↑.

阿物兒 **ahwuh'l*, n., (familiar, facet.) "this thing," meaning a person.

阿呀 **a-ya*, excl., oh! oh! (cry of pain or surprise).

阿耶(爺) **ahyer*, n., (AC, coll.) papa, also grandpa.

阿姨 **ahyir*, n., (familiar address or self-reference) mother's sister, wife's sister, auntie or nursemaid.

阿喲 **a-yo*, excl., oh! oh!—a groan.

阿諛 *e-yur*, v.i., to flatter, toady.

隃 32A.00–8

yur.

[Var. of 踰 40B.00]

附 32A.00–9

fuh.

V.i. & t. (1) Adhere to, attach to; oft. as adj. attached, appended: 附着身上 attached to body; 附勢, 依附權貴 rely on the powerful: 趨炎附勢 be follower of the rich and powerful; 魂不附體 frightened out of one's wits; 鬼附在身 be possessed of the devil; see 附屬, 附隸, 附庸 *-shuu*, *-lih*^{2}, *-yurng*↓. (2) Enclose, -ed, send enclosed: 附上 enclosing herewith; 附鈔, 附呈, 附錄 send as enclosure.

Adj. (1) Supplementary: 附件, 附張 supplement; 附卷, 附篇 supplementary volume, chapter; 附筆 additional note; 附筆致意 s.o. sends regards; 附錄, 附則 *-luh*, *-tzeh*↓. (2) Adjacent, near to: see 附近, 附鄰 *-jihn*, *-lirn*↓; 附耳而言 whisper to one's ear.

附帶 *fuhdaih*, adj., supplementary: 附帶聲明, 條件 supplementary note, conditions attached; 附帶問題 incidental problem.

附地菜 *fuhdihtssaih*, n., (bot.) wolfsbane, *Trigonotis peduncularis*.

附和 *fuhher*, v.i., follow another's lead in voicing opinion: 隨聲附和.

附會 *fuhhueih*, n. & v.i., see connection where none exists, false assumption without true basis: 附會穿鑿 make far-fetched, unwarranted conclusions.

附張 *fuhjang*, n., attached paper or sheet.

附加 *fuhjia*, v.t. & adj., additional, supplementary (tax, fee): 附加刑 additional sentence on another count.

附件 *fuhjiahn*, n., enclosure(s).

附驥(尾) *fuhjih(weei)*, v.i. (court. & LL) have the honor to follow your lead.

附近 *fuhjihn*, n., neighborhood.

附藉 *fuhjir*, n., taking clan name by adoption.

附著力 *fuhjuor-lih*, n., (phys.) adhesive strength.

附賴 *fuhlaih*, v.t., lean on (person).

附麗 *fuhlih*^{1}, v.i., be attached to (object), belong to (category).

附隸 *fuhlih*^{2}, v.t., to attach, be-

A

long to s.t. bigger, as stars in space.

附 鄰 *fuhlirn*, n., close neighbor.

附 錄 *fuhluh*, n., appendix.

附 順 *fuhshuhn*, v.i., obey, submit to greater force.

附 屬 *fuhshuu*, v.i., as in 附屬於 belong to (category); owe allegiance to; 附屬品 accessories; 附屬權利 additional, incidental rights.

附 則 *fuhtzeh*, n., bylaws.

附 益 *fuhyih*[1], v.i., add, increase.

附 議 *fuhyih*[2], v.i., to second motion.

附 庸 *fuhyurng*, n., political satellite, small state attached by big neighbor.

§ 32A.01 (阝/小)

陳 32A.01-1

chern.

N. (1) Name of anc. city-state. (2) Name of a dynasty (557–588 A.D.). (3) U.f. 陣 32A.10 (**jehn*). (4) A surname.

V.t. (1) To lay out (for exhibit, etc.): 陳列, 陳設 *-lieh, -sheh* ↓; 陳兵 line up soldiers in battle array, review troops; 陳屍 (of corpse) to lie exposed in the open; 陳詩 (AC) show collection of poems. (2) To narrate and explain (plan, purpose, innermost feelings, etc.): 陳說, 陳述 *-shuo, -shuh* ↓. (3) To plead, make a plea, request: 陳訴, 陳情, 陳詞 *-suh, -chirng, -tsyr* ↓.

Adj. Old: 陳舊, 陳腐 *-jiouh, -fuu* ↓; 陳迹 *-ji* ↓; 陳病兒 old sickness; 陳人 old staff, servants; 陳陳相因 keep on doing the same thing over and over again; 陳腔爛調 *cliché*.

B

陳 啟 *chernchii*, v.i., to write (a letter), to explain or report.

陳 請 *chernchiing*, v.i. & t., to request.

陳 情 *chernchirng*, v.i., to plea, explain (reason of request, esp. of resignation).

陳 椽 *chernchuarn*, v.i., (AC) to go about with a group (=modn. 夤緣).

陳 腐 *chernfuu*, adj., antiquated, stale, outworn (views, opinions).

陳 張 *chernjang*, v.i., (AC) to lay out (for show).

陳 迹 *chernji*, n., old traces, path that has been trodden before; historic sites.

陳 久 *chernjioou*, adj., old, time-worn.

陳 舊 *chernjiouh*, adj., very old (clothing).

陳 鍊 *chern'lian*, v.i., train, be trained, practised (in art).

陳 列 *chernlieh*, v.t., to arrange; to exhibit; 陳列室 exhibit room (for curios, samples, etc.).

陳 年 *chern-niarn*, adj., (wine, etc.) of many years' standing.

陳 皮 *chernpir*, n., dried orange peel, used in Chin. med.; 陳皮梅 preserved dry plums.

陳 紹 *chern-shauh*, n., vintage Shauhshing (紹興) wine.

陳 設 *chernsheh*, (1) v.i. & t., to exhibit; (2) (*-'she*) n., things on exhibit.

陳 述 *chernshuh*, v.i. & t., to explain (as in letter), to recount (past events, conditions).

陳 說 *chernshuo*, v.i. & t., to explain (purpose, situation) to superior.

陳 事(兒) *chernshyh(-sheh'l)*, n., past affairs.

陳 訴 *chernsuh*, n. & v.i., make a plea; to plead.

陳 詞 *cherntsyr*, v.i. & t., see *-shuo* ↑.

陳 言 *chern-yarn*, n., outworn phrases.

陳 已 *chernyii*, adv., (coll.) formerly: 他陳已在這兒住過 he lived here once.

C

隙 32A.01-2

shih.

[Pop. 隟]

N. (1) A fissure, a crack (in wall, etc.). (2) A period for rest: 農隙 farmers' free season when not busy with the farms. (3) A quarrel, dispute: 與人有隙 has a quarrel with s.o.; 尋隙 look for a chance to fight (s.o.); 隙嫌 an old grudge. (4) An opening or pretext for attack: 乘隙 take advantage of an opening or lax moment; 有隙可乘 a flaw or chance for attack.

Adj. (1) Vacant: 隙地 *-dih* ↓. (2) (AC) neighboring (land).

隙 地 *shihdih*, n., vacant space.

隙 罅 *shihshiah*, n., a crack, fissure.

除 32A.01-8

chur.

N. (1) (LL) steps leading to palace, temple: 階除 ditto; 庭除 steps of the court. (2) (Math.) division: 除法, 除數 *-faa, -shuh* ↓. (3) End: 歲除 the year-end.

V.t. (1) To exterminate, remove, destroy: 除蟲 exterminate insects; 除害 destroy the evils; 除暴安良 drive out the rascals and protect the people; 除去 *-chyuh* ↓; 免除 to prevent; 解除 to remove (restrictions, obstacles); 消除, 化除 dissolve (differences of opinion); 減除 to diminish; 廢除, 破除 to abolish. (2) To dismiss: 開除 to dismiss (from school), expel (from party, etc.); 被除 be expelled: 除名, 除籍 *-mirng, -jir* ↓. (3) To invest in office: 除授, 除拜 *-shouh, -baih* ↓; 除某官 be appointed to certain office. (4)

附
陳
隙
除

亅	小	⺊	十	土	ナ	卄	㇄	丨	一	丁	フ	口	区	冈	㇆	厂	尸	亠	广	宀	丶	乚	弋	心	八	人	乂	⺈	ノ	リ	𠂉	く
00	01	02	10	11	12	20	21	22	30	31	32	40	41	42	50	51	52	60	61	62	63	70	71	72	80	81	82	83	90	91	92	93

除 際 隈 限

(Math.) to divide: 以甲除乙 divide B by A; see 除法 -*faa* ↓.

Conj. Unless: 除非 -*fei* ↓; (in MC and poetry) 除 u.f. 除非 unless, except: 除 (＝除非) 你心似鐵 unless your heart is made of iron—without pity; 除是＝除非是 unless, see 除外 -*waih* ↓.

Prep. 除了 besides: 除了這件還有別的緣故 there are other reasons besides this; 除了 . . . 以外 besides this; (in official documents) 除 (insert a long clause) 外 besides (having already reported to authority concerned, etc.) I now communicate, etc.

除拜 *churbaih*, v.t., to invest (person) as official: 除拜郎中, 太子太傅 appoint as minister, as imperial tutor to crown prince, etc.

除臭劑 *churchouhjih*, n., deodorants.

除蟲菊 *churchurng-jyur*, n., (bot.) a variety of chrysanthemum used for insecticide, *Chrysanthemum roseum* or *cinerarüfolium*.

除卻 *chur-chyueh*, (1) conj., unless, except; (2) v.t., to remove (cause of trouble, etc.).

除去 *chur-chyuh*, v.t., to remove (obstacles), extirpate, weed out (cause).

除掉 *chur-diauh*, v.t., to remove (prejudices, obstacles, etc.).

除法 *churfaa*, n., (math.) division, see -*shuh* ↓.

除非 *churfei*, conj., unless, except: 除非 . . . 不行 it will not do unless; 除非 . . . 方可 or 才可 only when . . . then it may.

除服 *chur-fur*, v.i., cease mourning when period is over.

除根 *chur-gen*, v.t., as in 斬草除根 to uproot (evil).

除官 *chur-guan*, v.i., to be appointed official.

除號 *churhauh*, n., (math.) sign of division: "÷".

除召 *churjauh*, v.t., appoint as official and summon to imperial audience.

除籍 *chur-jir*, v.t., to expel, remove from list of members.

除開 *chur'kai*, v.t., to take away, remove.

除了 *chur'le*, prep., besides: 除了你沒有別人 there are no others besides you.

除靈 *chur-lirng*, v.i., to burn the spirit tablet after completing the mass for the deceased.

除名 *chur-mirng*, v.i., to dismiss, expel ("remove from list of names").

除禳 *churrarng*, v.i., pray to remove influence of evil spirits.

除日 *churryh*, n., the day before New Year, see -*shir* ↓.

除喪 *chur-sang*, v.i., to cease mourning when period is over.

除身 *chur-shen*, v.i., (LL) to retire from office.

除夕 *churshih*, n., New Year's Eve, see -*ryh* ↑.

除授 *churshouh*, v.t., to invest as official or military officer.

除數 *churshuh*, n., (math.) the divisor; 被除數 the dividend.

除是 *churshyh*, (poet.)＝除非是, see -*fei* ↑.

除汰 *churtaih*, v.t., to sift out, eliminate.

除罪 *chur-tzueih*, phr., pardon.

除外 *churwaih*, prep., (placed after n.) not counting, excluding, excepted: 星期日除外 Sundays excepted, see Prep. ↑.

除夜 *churyeh*, n., see -*shih* ↑.

際 32A.01–9

jih.

N. (1) Crevice between walls. (2) A border, boundary, limit: 邊際 a margin: 邊際效用 (econ.) marginal utility; 水際 water front; 天際 the horizon; 際畔 -*pahn* ↓; 耳際 near at hand, within hearing distance; 無際 boundless, limitless; 涯際 shores, limit; 實際 reality; 實際上 in reality, as a matter of fact: 不切實際 out of touch with reality, impractical. (3) A duration of time: 唐虞之際 during the reigns of Yaur and Shuhn; 春秋之際 in the era of Spring and Autumn; 臨別之際 at the time of taking leave; 死生之際 the moment between life and death.

V.i. (1) Have relations, be related: 交際 (have) social functions; entertain friends. (2) Happen, occur unexpectedly: 際會 -*hueih*, 際遇 -*yuh* ↓; 遭際 one's lot in life ("what one comes upon"); 幸際承平 fortunately, it was a time of peace. (3) Reach: 高不可際 height cannot be reached.

Prep. Among, between: 國際 between nations, international; 洲際 intercontinental; 星際 interstellar, interplanetary; 校際 intercollegiate; 級際, 班際 interclass.

際會 *jihhueih*, n., a chance meeting: 際會風雲 (of political figures) emergence into prominence in times of crisis, riding on the crest of success.

際畔 *jihpahn*, n., a margin, brink, edge.

際遇 *jihyuh*, n., a chance (to meet with or be of service).

§ 32A.02 (阝/k)

隈 32A.02–4

wei.

N. A recess; a bay, cove, inlet.

限 32A.02–5

shiahn.

N. Limit: 界限 boundary; 門限爲穿 the threshold is worn smooth (with many visitors); 限期 -*chir* ↓; 限量 -*liahng*, 限度 -*duh* ↓; 極限 extreme limits (of patience, insolence, etc.).

V.t. To limit: 限制 *-jyh*↓; 限定 *-dihng*↓.

Adj. Limited: 無限 limitless, unlimited; 有限 limited (supplies, etc.); 有限公司 limited company; 限價 officially limited price.

限期 *shiahn-chir*, adv., within a set time.
限定 *shiahn-dihng*, v.t., to limit, set limit to; (passive) limited (persons admitted, time, expenditure).
限度 *shiahn-duh*, n., the limit, extent.
限額 *shiahn-eh*, n., quota.
限制 *shiahnjyh*, (1) n., control; (2) v.t., to control, set limit to (time, quota, etc.).
限量 *shiahn-liahng*, n., capacity.

隊 32A.02–8

dueih.

N. (1) A group, team, corps: 一隊人 a group of people; 音樂隊 music band; 工程隊 engineering corps; 衛生大隊 sanitation corps; 救護隊 ambulance corps; 足球隊 football team; 脂粉隊 (facet.) group or team of ladies. (2) Army unit: 軍隊, 部隊 troops; 步隊 infantry; 騎兵隊 cavalry; 縱隊 column of troops; 支隊 detachment; 後隊 rear guard; 排隊 (of troops) fall in; 列隊 in formation, in file.

隊球 *dueihchiour*, n., volleyball, also called 排球.
隊長 *dueihjaang*, n., captain of a ball team, company leader.
隊伍 *dueihwuu*, n., troops, rank and file.
隊員 *dueihyuarn*, n., member of company, or corps, or of ball team.

§ 32A.10 (阝/十)

陣 32A.10–1

jehn.

N. (1) Battle formation: 陣容, 陣線, 陣勢 *-rurng, -shiahn, -shyh*↓; 雁陣 a flock of wild geese flying in formation; 布陣 deploy soldiers; 排陣 fall in line; in line; 方陣 square formation; 嚴陣以待 stand ready in battle formation; 擺龍[Δ]門陣 60S.70. (2) (*-tz, 'l*) A spell, a passing phase: 一陣風, 一陣雨 alternate spells of wind and rain; a spell (of laughter, anger, etc.). (3) Battle: 上陣, 出陣 go to battle; 陣地 battlefield; 陣亡, 陣歿 fall in action, die in battle; 敗陣 be defeated; 臨陣逃脱 run away when battle begins.

Adv. Spasmodically: 陣雨, 陣痛 or 陣陣雨, 陣陣痛 spells of rain, pain.

陣地 *jehndih*, n., battlefield.
陣法 *jehnfaa*, n., art of military formations.
陣仗兒 *jehn'jang'l*, n., a battle combat: 沒見過大陣仗兒 never saw combat; (fig.) never went through some august ceremony.
陣陣 *jehnjehn*, adv., in successive spells.
陣容 *jehn-rurng*, n., battle array; gen. appearance or make-up (of delegation, etc.).
陣線 *jehnshiahn*, n., line of battle; line of moving troops.
陣勢 *jehn-shyh*, n., gen. appearance of battling army (strong, crumbling, etc.).

隣 32A.10–2

lirn.

[Pop. of 鄰 22S.22]

障 32A.10–6

jahng.

N. An obstruction, obstacle, barrier, cover for defense or protection: 屏障 natural cover for defense (e.g., high mountain range); 保障 (n. & v.t.) protection, guarantee (of life, human rights, etc.), 孽[Δ]障 see 20A.00.

障礙 *jahng-aih*, n., obstacle to progress; 障礙競走 obstacle race.
障蔽 *jahngbih*, n., an obstruction, what hinders (view, understanding).
障泥 *jahngnir*, n., mudguard in saddle.
障扇 *jangshahn*, n., ceremonial fan-shaped insignia in parade (also wr. 掌扇).
障翳 *jangyih*, n., an obstruction to clear vision or understanding.

阡 32A.10–9

chian.

N. (1) A path in fields, leading north and south, see 阡陌 *-moh*↓. (2) A path by a grave, see 阡表 *-biaau*↓.

阡表 *chianbiaau*, n., a stone inscription by a grave.
阡陌 *chianmoh*, n., a crisscross of paths separating farms (阡 leading north and south, 陌 east and west).

陴 32A.10–9

pir.

N. Parapets: 陴牆.

降 陸 陛 陻 陞 陲 隍 隆

降 32A.10-9

jiahng (**shiarng*).

V.i. & t. (1) Descend, fall, drop, come down: 降落 *-luoh*, 降生 *-sheng*, 降凡 *-farn* ↓; 降旨 issue a royal decree; 降旗 *-chir* ↓; 升降 ascend and descend; 升降機 an elevator, a lift; 下降 come down, drop; 空降 to parachute; 降福 to shower blessings on; 降禍 send down calamity; 降臨 condescend to come; 降雨, 降雪 it rains, snows (rain, snow is falling). (2) Lower, reduce, curtail, cut down: 降格 *-ger* ↓; 降職 demote; 降價 reduce price; 降革 (of officials) degrade and dismiss; 降調 (of officials) transfer to a lower position. (3) (**shiarng*) Submit, surrender: 投降 (of troops) surrender to the enemy; 降服 *-fur* ↓; 歸降 return to allegiance; 降將 a general who has surrendered; 降敵 go over to the side of the enemy (4) (**shiarng*) Subdue, put under control: 降伏 *-fur* ↓; 降龍伏虎 (Buddhism and Taoism) ability to subdue wild animals, (Taoism) ability to control one's passions, physical prowess; 降得住 can be subdued, able to resist the enemy.

降表 **shiarngbiaau*, n., a declaration of surrender.

降旗 *jiahngchir*, (1) (**shiarng-*) n., flag of surrender; (2) v.i., lower the flag, as at sunset.

降凡 *jiahngfarn*, v.i., (of divine beings) be born incarnate.

降附 **shiarngfuh*, v.i., go over to, come over from, the enemy.

降伏 **shiarngfur*, v.t., subdue (enemy).

降服 *jiahngfur*, (1) n., mourning garment one grade lower than the ordinary; (2) (**shiarng-*) v.i., lay down arms and surrender to the enemy.

降格 *jiahngger*, v.i., (1) (LL) (of gods) to grace with presence; (2) condescend: 降格以求 to set one's aim lower than usual, look for (person, thing) without insisting on the best.

降號 *jiahnghauh*, n., (mus.) flat ("b").

降落 *jiahngluoh*, v.i., descend, come down, (of airplanes) to land: 降落傘 *--saan*, a parachute.

降生 *jiahngsheng*, v.i., be born, see the light of day; 耶穌降生 A.D.; the Incarnation.

降神 *jiahng-shern*, v.i., offer sacrifices to the gods and pray for their presence.

降香 *jiahngshiang*, (1) n., a famous perfume, lignaloes; (2) v.i., (of kings) to offer prayer for rain.

降世 *jiahng-shyh*, v.i., be born into the world.

§ 32A.11 (阝/土)

陸 32A.11-1

luh.

[Abbr. 陆]

N. (1) Land: 大陸 continent, mainland; 歐洲大陸 the European Continent; 水陸 by land and water; by land: 陸棲 (of animals) live on land; 陸運 land transportation; 陸沉 country sunk in chaos, (AC) stuck with the past (知古而不知今). (2) Land forces: 陸軍, 陸戰隊 *-jyun*, *-jahndueih* ↓. (3) Capital writing in checks for "six" (六) pr. (*liouh*). (4) A surname.

陸半球 *luhbahnchiour*, n., continental hemisphere (opp. 水半球 oceanic hemisphere).

陸圈 *luhchyuan*, n., (geog.) continental sphere.

陸稻 *luhdauh*, n., upland rice.

陸戰隊 *luhjahndueih*, n., (mil.) Marine corps.

陸軍 *luhjyun*, n., the army (cf. 空^Δ軍 air force, 62A.30, 海^Δ軍 navy 63A.50).

陸離 *luhlir*, adj., weirdly beautiful.

陸續 *luhshyuh*, adv., continuously, from time to time (send money, etc.).

陸田 *luhtiarn*, n., dry farm (opp. paddy).

陛 32A.11-2

bih.

N. The flight of steps leading to the throne hall.

陛陛 *bihbih*, (AC) everywhere (var. for 比比).

陛下 *bihshiah*, n., Your Majesty (term of address).

陻 32A.11-3

yin.

[Interch. 堙 11A.11]

陞 32A.11-9

sheng.

[Var. of 升 90.20]

陲 32A.11-9

chueir.

N. Frontier: 邊陲 frontier region: 西陲 western frontier.

隍 32A.11-9

huarng.

N. Dry city moat, chiefly in phr.; 城^Δ隍 god of the city, 11A.71.

隆 32A.11-9

lurng.

N. A surname.

Adj. (1) High, solemn and great: 隆恩 (court.) high, great favor; 隆情盛意 (court. of gifts, courtesies) your great favors; 隆儀 your great gifts; 隆厚, 隆貴, 隆重 *-houh*, *-gueih*, *-juhng* ↓. (2) Physically high: 隆準, 隆鼻 high nose (bridge); 隆乳 prominent, pointed breasts; 隆起 high, swollen, prominent. (3) At the peak: 隆冬, 隆夏 deep winter, high summer; 隆寒 severely cold; 隆替 rise and fall of power, influence. (4) 豐隆 prosperous, plentiful; 隆多 plentiful.

V.i. To swell up: 隆起 swell or be swollen up (of mound, breast, wound).

隆貴 *lurnggueih*, adj., very high (prices).

隆厚 *lurnghouh*, adj., (of friendship, sentiment) deep, generous.

隆重 *lurngjuhng*, adj., solemn (ceremony, gathering).

隆隆 *lurnglurng*, adj., booming (sound), rumbling.

隆盛 *lurngshehng*, adj., sumptuous, rich (feast); prosperous (country, commerce).

§ 32A.20 (阝/廿)

阱 32A.20-2

jiing.

N. 陷阱 A trap, a snare for catching wild animals, a pitfall.

§ 32A.21 (阝/乚)

陋 32A.21-3

louh.

Adj. (1) Narrow: 陋巷 a narrow land; 陋室 a humble room. (2) Lowly, unsightly: 卑陋 lowly, plain (house); 醜陋 ugly. (3) Vulgar, coarse, unrefined: 陋見 *-jiahn*, 陋習 *-shir* ↓, 鄙陋 vulgar, lacking in refinement; 殘陋 superficial. (4) Vile, rude, corrupt: 陋規, 陋俗 *-guei*, *-sur* ↓.

陋規 *louh-guei*, n., a corrupt practice, such as bribery.

陋見 *louh-jiahn*, n., (self-disparagement) my humble views.

陋劣 *louhlieh*, adj., vile, detestable, sordid.

陋儒 *louh-rur*, n., a doctrinaire or superficial Confucianist.

陋習 *louh-shir*, n., common, vulgar practice.

陋識 *louh-shyh*, n., superficial views.

陋俗 *louh-sur*, n., common, stupid customs.

陷 32A.21-9

shiahn.

N. A trap: 陷阱, 陷坑 *-jiing*, *-keng* ↓.

V.i. (1) To sink down, fall into (river, trap, well, sin and error). (2) (City) falls, (enemy) collapses, (wall) crumbles.

V.t. (1) To trap, entrap (s.o.), to lead (s.o. into sin, crime): 陷于死地 lead (s.o.) to his doom. (2) To capture (city) break (enemy force): 陷敵 to defeat enemy, also fall into enemy hands; 陷堅挫銳 break the force of enemy strength. (3) To injure, possibly to kill: 陷害 *-haih* ↓.

陷害 *shiahnhaih*, v.t., to design to kill: 陷害性命 kill (s.o.'s) life.

陷陣 *shiahn-jehn*, v.i., break enemy ranks: 衝鋒陷陣.

陷阱 *shiahn-jiing*, n., (lit. & fig.) a trap.

陷坑 *shiahn-keng*, n., ditto.

陷落 *shiahn-luoh*, v.i., to sink into iniquity; sink down (into well, quagmire): 陷落計中 fall into enemy's trap or plan; (city) falls.

陷沒 *shiahnmoh*, v.i., to drown.

陷溺 *shiahnnih*, v.i., to sink into (snake pit, sin).

§ 32A.22 (阝/丨)

隮 32A.22-6

ji.

N. (AC) a rainbow: 朝隮于西 (AC) there was a rainbow in the west in the morning.

V.i. (1) (Anc. var. 躋) to ascend: 由賓階隮 go up by the stairs reserved for guests. (2) To fall, to trip, stumble: 我乃顛隮 (AC) thus I faltered.

阼 32A.22-9

tzuoh.

N. (1) (AC) a flight of steps on the eastern side of the hall where the host stood to welcome the guests. (2) (AC) the throne on which the emperor sat at his

亅	小	⺊	十	土	ナ	廾	乚	丨	一	丅	フ	口	区	冈	乛	厂	尸	亠	广	宀	丶	乚	弋	心	八	人	乂	一	乛	丿	𠂉	く
00	01	02	10	11	12	20	21	22	30	31	32	40	41	42	50	51	52	60	61	62	63	70	71	72	80	81	82	83	90	91	92	93

coronation: 踐阼 ascend the throne.

§ 32A.30 (阝/一)

阯 32A.30-2

jyy.

N. (1) Var. 址 11A.30. (2) Var. of 沚 63A.30. (3) Interch. 趾 40B.30 in 交趾(支那) Indochina.

陘 32A.30-3

shirng.

N. (AC) a defile, a mountain pass; edge of kitchen stove.

阻 32A.30-4

tzuu.

N. A mountain pass: 險阻 a dangerous pass.

V.t. (1) To stop, prevent, block: 阻止 *-jyy* ↓; 攔阻 to bar, block (the way). (2) To rely on: 阻兵 rely on military might. (3) Separate, isolate: 阻隔 *-ger* ↓.

阻礙 *tzuu-aih*, v.t., hinder, impede, obstruct.
阻擋 *tzurdaang*, v.t., impede, block, hamper.
阻遏 *tzuu-eh*, v.t., to deter (aggression), check (flood water).
阻隔 *tzuuger*, v.t., to separate, isolate, stand in the way of: 山川阻隔 separated by mountains and rivers.
阻滯 *tzuujyh*, v.t., impede, hinder, obstruct.
阻止 *tzurjyy*, v.t., stop, prevent, hinder, obstruct.
阻攔 *tzuularn*, v.t., hinder, obstruct, bar (the way).
阻力 *tzuulih*, n., resistance.
阻難 *tzuunahn*, v.t., thwart, baffle, embarrass.
阻撓 *tzuunaur*, v.t., hamper, hinder, foil.
阻塞 *tzuuseh*, v.t., obstruct, block.
阻深 *tzuushen*, v.t., see *-ger* ↑.
阻修 *tzuu-shiou*, adj., (LL) separated by a long distance.

隘 32A.30-8

aih.

N. A narrow pass, a defile: 要隘, 險隘 strategic pass; 關隘 a fort, or fortified pass.

Adj. (1) Narrow (alley), confined, crowded and small (house): 狹隘 crowded, confined; 湫隘 damp and low (place). (2) (**eh*) U.f. 阨 32A.70.

隘口 *aihkoou*, n., a mountain pass.

§ 32A.40 (阝/口)

阽 32A.40-2

diahn.

N. & adj. Danger, -ous: 阽危 in state of danger.

陪 32A.40-6

peir.

V.t. (1) Accompany, keep company with: 陪他坐談(玩兒, 看戲) keep person's company in talks, (play, seeing a play); 奉陪 v.i. & t., (court.) keep company. (2) To own, confess, pacify: 陪不是 to own blame, apologize to (person); 陪小心 pacify (person) by being respectful. (3) As prefix, meaning "assisting at," "be company for," "assistant," see compp. ↓.

N. Company at party: 作陪 be among the invited.

陪綁 *peir-baang*, n., person taken along with one kidnapped.
陪伴 *peirbahn*, v.t., keep company with (person).
陪拜 *peir-baih*, v.i., to assist and kowtow in ceremony.
陪襯 *peirchehn*, n. & v.t., (as, be, for) contrast, add for contrast.
陪乘 *peir-cherng*, v.i., be in the same carriage.
陪持 *peirchyr*, v.i., apologize.
陪都 *peir-du*, n., secondary capital of country.
陪房 *peir-farng*, n., maid of bride accompanying bride to new home and serving wifely duties to groom.
陪嫁 *peir-jiah*, n., dowry; v.i., (of bride's personal maid) go into new home with bride (see *-farng* ↑).
陪酒 *peir-jioou*, v.i., (of singsong girls) assist at wine parties.
陪客 *peir-keh*, n. & v.i., be among guests at party to honor s.o.; such guest(s).
陪禮 *peirlii*, n., gift as token of apology, cf. 賠 41C.40.
陪審 *peir-sheen*, v.i. & n., (be) an assessor at court.
陪笑(臉) *peir-shiauh* (*liaan*), v.i., make smiles to pacify.
陪侍 *peirshyh*, v.i., assist in attendance.
陪罪 *peirtzueih*, v.i., to apologize.

§ 32A.41 (阝/図)

階 32A.41-2

jie.

N. (1) Stairs, a flight of steps: 階梯 *-ti*↓; 臺階 an outdoor flight of steps; 石階 stone stairs; 階前萬里 distance is no barrier (to understanding or friendship); 初階 a primer, ("first steps"). (2) Official hierarchy: 官階 official ranks; 階級 *-jir*↓.

階段 *jieduahn*, n., phase, stage: 現階段 the present stage (of development).

階級 *jiejir* (-'*ji*), n., (1) social classes: 上層, 下層階級 upper, lower, classes of society; 階級鬪爭 class struggle; (2) official ranking.

階梯 *jieti*, n., stairs, a flight of steps, a ladder; introduction (to subject).

階層 *jietserng*, n., stratum.

陌 32A.41–3

moh.

N. Footpath among fields, see 阡△陌 32A.10; (AC) street.

陌路 *mohluh*, n., casually-met acquaintance, stranger: 陌路相逢 casually met.

陌生 *mohsheng*, adj., not acquainted: 陌生人 stranger; 陌生面目 have not seen that face before.

陌頭 *mohtour*, n., (1) roadside; (2) (AC) scarf for binding hair = 帕頭.

§ 32A.42 (阝/冈)

隋 32A.42–1

sueir.

N. (1) Sueir Dyn. 隋朝 (581–618 A.D.). (2) A surname.

隔 32A.42–3

ger (**jie*, **jier*).

V.t. (1) Separate, divide, partition, isolate: 隔離 separate (s.o., s.t.) from another; 隔開, 間隔 to partition (rooms, etc.); 隔絕 isolate, be separated from; 阻隔 to bar; 隔別 take leave of; 隔膜 *-mor*, 隔閡 *-her*, 隔斷 *-duahn*↓; 遠隔 be far removed from; 隔行 (*harng*) 如隔山 the barrier separating one occupation from another is as forbidding as a mountain pass. (2) Bear, endure: 隔不住 (opp. 隔得住) cannot stand: 桌子隔不住壓 the table cannot stand a heavy weight; 老人隔不住生氣 an old man cannot stand fits of anger.

Adj. Past, gone by, immediately preceding, next-door: 隔夜, 隔宿 overnight; 隔日 the following day; 隔年 following year; 隔了這麼多天 after an interval of so many days; 隔手 through a third person; 隔三跳四 proceeding by irregular steps, skipping over; 隔壁 *-bih*↓; 隔鄰 next-door neighbor; 隔代遺傳 atavism; 隔房同輩 male cousins.

Prep. Across, on or from the other side of: 隔着籬笆, 一條小河, 一道牆 across a fence, a small stream, a wall; 隔岸觀火 show utter unconcern (lit., "to watch a fire on the other side of the river"); 隔牆有耳 warning not to talk too loudly (lit., "s.o. may be listening on the other side of the wall"); 隔靴搔癢 fail to lay one's finger on the right spot (lit., "to scratch an itch from outside the boot").

隔壁(兒) *gerbih* (also **jiehbieh'l*), (1) n., next-door neighbor; (2) adj., neighboring, adjacent.

隔斷 *gerduahn* (**jieh-*), (1) n., partitions of rooms; (2) v.t., to obstruct, to isolate.

隔閡 *gerher*, n. & adj., losing contact, out of touch, failure to understand completely, see *-mor*↓.

隔肢 *ger'jy*, v.t., to tickle (s.o.).

隔離 *gerlir*, n. & v.i. & t., isolation, guarantine; to isolate; 隔離病房 isolation ward.

隔膜 *germor*, n., (1) (-'*mo*) misunderstanding: 由於語言不通, 造成這種隔膜 the misunderstanding between them was due to linguistic difficulties; (2) (also '*mo*) disagreement, enmity: 他一直和我這樣隔膜 there has been disagreement (enmity) between him and me all this time; (3) (*-mor*) (physiol.) (= 膈膜) the diaphragm; (4) adj., (also -'*mo*) ignorant, not in touch: 我於此事, 實在隔膜 I don't really understand this affair.

隔山 *gershan* (**jier-*), n., the relationship between siblings of different mothers.

隔扇 *ger'shan* (**jier'-*), n., the paper or wooden partition between two rooms: 隔扇心兒 the empty space in such partition, usu. decorated with calligraphy or painting.

隔子 *gertz*, n., (1) a bookcase, a cupboard: 書隔子 simple bookcase; (2) (**jier-*) a latticed door.

隅 32A.42–4

yur.

N. Corner, remote part: 海隅 remote parts of the sea; side, aspect: 擧一隅, 不以三隅反 (AC) (the teacher) mentions one side (and the student) fails to think out the other three sides for himself; sometimes shortened to 隅反 (think for oneself) or 擧一反

三；隅目 (AC, rare) give angry look out of corners of one's eyes.

§ 32A.50 (阝/⺄)

陽 32A.50–4

yarng.

N. (1) The *yarng* principle in *yin-yarng* philosophy, the positive, active, the male, opp. 陰 *yin*, the negative, passive, the female. (2) The sun: 太陽 ditto; 斜陽 the setting sun; 當陽, 正陽 facing the south (the sun). (3) North side of a mountain. (4) The virile member: 壯陽 (med.) to use aphrodisiacs, to increase virility.

Adj. (1) Male, positive, strong, bright, sunny: 陽性 *-shihng*↓; 陽電 *-diahn*↓; 陽光, 陽面兒 *-guang*, *-miah'l*↓. (2) The positive in inscriptions: 陽識, 陽文 *-jyh*, *-wern*↓; 陽螺絲 male thread in screw. (3) Sexual: 陽物, 陽道 *-wuh*, *-dauh*↓.

Adv. Openly: 陽奉陰違 outwardly obey orders but secretly ignore them—passive resistance.

陽起石 *yarngchii-shyr*, n., (min.) actinolite.

陽秋 *yarngchiou*, n., (rare) var. of 春秋 annals, on account a temporary taboo on 春.

陽春 *yarngchun*, n., the springtime; 陽春白雪 (allu.) name of an anc. melody (opp. popular songs)—s.t. selected and among the best; 陽春麵 plain noodles.

陽道 *yarngdauh*, n., (LL) the male genitals.

陽電 *yarngdiahn*, n., positive electricity.

陽剛 *yarnggang*, adj., strong, positive, stern in character.

陽溝 *yarnggou*, n., open sewerage.

陽關 *yarng guan*, n., a place name in anc. China, (fig.) place of departure; 陽關曲 *--chyu*, n., a parting song.

陽光 *yarngguang*, n., sunlight.

陽和 *yarngher*, adj., mild (weather), pleasantly warm.

陽宅 *yarngjair*, n., human habitation, house, opp. 陰宅 grave.

陽間 *yarngjian*, n., the present world of living beings, opp. 陰間 hell.

陽九 *yarngjiour*, n., (AC) a critical period, period of disaster (with varying interpretations).

陽極 *yarngjir*, n., (phys.) anode.

陽識 *yarngjyh*, n., characters cut in relief, opp. 陰識 characters cut below surface.

陽具 *yarngjyuh*, n., male sexual organ.

陽曆 *yarnglih*, n., Gregorian calendar.

陽面兒 *yarngmiah'l*, adj., open, candid (character), not secretive.

陽平 *yarngpirng*, n., the second tone of words symbolized by "r" here, as 明 *mirng*, 來 *lair*.

陽性 *yarngshihng*, (1) adj., male, positive, assertive; (2) n., the male sex, masculinity.

陽壽 *yarng-shouh*, n., person's life in present world, opp. 陰壽 celebrations of birthday of departed.

陽世 *yarngshyh*, n., this present world, see *-jian*↑.

陽燧 *yarngsueih*, n., (AC) a speculum, brass mirror placed in the sun and generating enough heat to ignite dry grass.

陽遂足 *yarngsueihtzur*, n., (zoo.) a sea animal, *Ophioplocus*.

陽臺 *yarngtair*, n., terrace.

陽萎 *yarngweei*, n., sexual impotence.

陽文 *yarngwern*, n., see *-jyh*↑.

陽烏 *yarngwu*, n., (LL) the sun (with supposed image of a three-legged crow).

陽物 *yarngwuh*, n., penis.

陽陽 *yarngyarng*, adj., (AC) happy, gay, floating about (cf. 洋洋 63A.10).

防 32A.50–6

farng.

[Dist. 妨 93A.50: as 妨礙 obstruct, 不妨事 does not matter; but 防 guard against: 防禦, 防範]

N. (1) Dam, embankment: 隄防. (2) A surname.

V.i. & t. Defend against, provide against: 防不勝防 no way to prevent or guard against absolutely; 防患 guard against disaster; 防患於未然 make provisions before troubles occur; 防微杜漸 destroy evils before they become apparent; 防疫, 防毒 immunize, take measures against, epidemic, poisoning; 防火隊, 消防隊 fire brigade; 防水災 check flood; 防水紙, 布 waterproof paper, cloth; 防空 *-kung*↓; 防洪 flood control; 防颱 against typhoon; 養兒防老 raise children to provide against old age; 防諜 watch against spies.

防備 *farngbeih*, n. & v.i., defend, defense measures, precautions.

防範 *farngfahn*, n. & v.i., guard against (misconduct); rules and measures of precaution.

防風 *farngfeng*, n., (Chin. med.) an herb, *Siler divaricatum*.

防腐劑 *farngfuh-jih*, n., preservative.

防己 *farngjii*, n., (Chin. med.) an herb, *Cocculus thunbergii*.

防空 *farngkung*, n., various devices against air raids; 防空洞 air-raid shelters.

防閑 *farngshiarn*, v.t., stop and prevent loiterers or transgressors.

防臭劑 *farngshiouh-jih*, n., deodorizer.

防守 *farngshoou*, v.t., stand guard over, defend (posts, fort).

防水劑 *farng shueeijih*, n., chemical for waterproofing.

防蝕劑 *farngshyr-jih*, n., anticorrosive.

防頭 *farngtour*, v.i., careful, esp. 不防頭: 假如說話不防頭 if one should make a careless slip of the tongue.

防禦 *farngyuh*, n. & v.t., guard against (thieves); defense or defense works.

陶 32A.50–6

taur.

N. (1) A surname. (2) Earthenware, pottery.

V.t. To mold (character) as with clay, 陶冶 *-yee* ↓.

Adj. Happy, contented; 陶陶, 陶情 *-taur*, *-chirng* ↓.

陶塲 *taurchaang*, n., potter's workshop or factory.
陶器 *taurchih*, n., pottery, earthenware.
陶情 *taurchirng*, v.i., enjoy oneself: 陶情於山水 relax one's mind in nature.
陶匠 *taurjiahng*, n., potter.
陶鑄 *taurjuh*, v.t., educate and train talents (as potters and blacksmiths mold and form utensils).
陶鈞 *taurjyun*, n. & v.t., (AC) potter's wheel; to mold character as potter molds clay.
陶煉(鍊) *taurliahn*, v.t., to train through hardships and discipline.
陶染 *taurraan*, v.t., influence (character) by association or contact.
陶然 *taurrarn*, adj., carefree, happy, contented.
陶鎔 *taurrurng*, v.t., see *-juh* ↑.
陶陶 *taurtaur*, adj., happy; drunk.
陶土 *taurtuu*, n., potter's clay.
陶醉 *taurtzueih*, v.t., be infatuated with (women, Western culture).
陶瓦 *taurwaa*, n., bricks and tiles.
陶硯 *tauryahn*, n., earthen ink slab.
陶冶 *tauryee*, v.t., to mold, influence through contact: 陶冶性情 to shape or cleanse one's spirit (as with poetry).

隝 32A.50–9

wuh.

[Var. of 塢 11A.50]

§ 32A.63 (阝/丶)

隰 32A.63–4

shir.

N. (LL) (1) Swamps. (2) Newly cultivated farm.

隰皐 *shir-gau*, n., swamps, low pasture grounds.
隰草 *shir-tsaau*, n., grass on swampy land.

§ 32A.70 (阝/乚)

阮 32A.70–3

ruaan.

N. (1) An anc. musical instrument. (2) A surname.

阮囊 *Ruaan-narng*, n., a purse: 阮囊羞澀 short of funds, in straitened circumstances, allu. to the story of 阮孚 of the Jihn Dyn.
阮咸 *Ruaanshiarn*, n., a kind of guitar, named after its supposed inventor of the Jihn Dyn.

阨 32A.70–5

eh.

N. Strategic point: 阨塞 *-saih* ↓.

Adj. Adverse (circumstances): 阨窮 *-chyurng* ↓.

阨窮 *ehchyurng*, adv., poverty-stricken.
阨塞 *ehsaih*, n., strategic fort or pass.

隴 32A.70–6

luung.

N. Alternate name for Shensi Province; 得隴望蜀 having control of Shensi, one hopes to control Szechuen—allu. insatiable ambition.

隴畝 *lurngmoou*, n., (AC) countryside: 起於隴畝之間 (of person) rise from a farm boy.

陀 32A.70–6

tuor.

N. Sharp bank: 坡陀 uneven slope.

陀螺 *tuorluor*, n., a top.
陀羅經被 *tuorluorjing-beih*, n., *dharani* quilt, formerly, quilt embroidered with Buddhist charms or *dharani*.

阬 32A.70–6

keng.

[Var. 坑 11A.70]

院 32A.70–6

yuahn.

N. (1) A court, courtyard: 庭院 ditto; 宮院 palace court; 院子, 院落 *-tz*, *-luoh* ↓. (2) An institute, institution of learning, college: 學院 a college: 文學院 college of arts; 理學院 college of science; 書院 anc. type of college; 研究院 research institute; 博物院 museum; 寺院, 僧院 monastery; 戲院 theater; 妓院 brothel; 病院 hospital; 療養院 sanatorium; 養老院 old people's home; 育幼院 orphanage, etc. (3) A department, branch of government: 行政院 Executive *Yuan*; 立法院 Legislative *Yuan*; 司法院 Judicial *Yuan*; 監察院 Censorial *Yuan*; 考試院 Civil Service *Yuan*; (衆) 議院 congress; 參議院 senate; 國務院 state department; 法院 court of justice.

院本 *yuahn-been*, n., (MC) opera or theater as played in singsong houses.
院公 *yuahngung*, n., (MC) old servant.
院長 *yuahnjaang*, n., (1) director of hospital, museum, institute, etc.; (2) head of branch of government, see N. 2 & 3 ↑.
院宅 *yuahnjair*, n., living house.
院君 *yuahnjyun*, n., (MC) a lady of rank.
院兒 *yuah'l*, n., see *-luoh* ↓.
院落 *yuahnluoh*, n., court or open ground around house.
院子 *yuahntz*, n., ditto.
院宇 *yuahnyuu*, n., house buildings.

隗 32A.70-9

weei.

N. A surname.

Adj. High, lofty (related 嵬巍).

阬 32A.70-9

yih.
[Var. of 屹 21A.70]

§ 32A.72 (阝/心)

隱 32A.72-9

yiin.
[Dist. 穩 *ween*, 90A.72]

N. A secret: 難言之隱 a secret which could not be told.

V.i. & t. (1) To conceal, hide: 隱藏, 隱匿, 隱瞞, *-tsarng*, *-nih*, *-marn* ↓; 隱身, 隱形 *-shen*, *-shirng* ↓; 隱姓埋名 to conceal one's name and surname; 隱惡揚善 to conceal faults of others and praise their good points. (2) To live as recluse: 隱居, 隱士 *-jyu*, *-shyh* ↓. (3) (AC) to take pity: 隱其無罪而就死地 take pity on its being innocently killed; 惻隱之心 the heart of mercy.

Adj. (1) Hidden, secret: 隱患, 隱憂, 隱疾 *-huahn*, *-you*, *-jir* ↓. (2) Latent: 隱力 *-lih* ↓. (3) Small, invisible, nuclear: 隱微, 隱約 *-weir*, *-yue* ↓. (4) (AC) poor: 隱民多取食焉 many poor people lived on it.

隱蔽 *yiinbih*, v.t., to conceal (s.t.), (s.t.) be concealed.
隱親 *yiin-chin*, v.i., (AC) to attend or comfort personally, thoughtfully.
隱情 *yiin-chirng*, n., hidden, unspoken thoughts or feelings, see *-jung* ↓.
隱遁 *yiinduhn*, v.i., to escape, live in hiding.
隱伏 *yiinfur*, v.i., to lie low; (of troubles, disease) lie dormant.
隱宮 *yiingung*, n., (AC) secret house for castration.
隱患 *yiinhuahn*, n., latent trouble or cause for worry.
隱諱 *yiinhueih*, n. & v.t., taboo (on parent's or emperor's personal name); to conceal as secret.
隱者 *yirnjee*, n., a recluse.
隱疾 *yiin-jir*, n., a secret or ugly disease, euphem. for venereal disease or impotence.
隱衷 *yiinjung*, n., hidden, unspoken thoughts or feelings.
隱居 *yiinjyu*, v.i., to live as recluse or in retirement.
隱君子 *yiinjyuntz*, n., (1) a recluse scholar; (2) (facet.) an opium smoker (pun on 癮 *yiin*, addict.).
隱力 *yiinlih*, n., latent force.
隱瞞 *yiinmarn*, v.t., to conceal (s.t. or from person).
隱祕 (密) *yiinmih*, adj., hidden, secret.
隱沒 *yiinmoh*, v.i., to pass unnoticed by public.
隱囊 *yiinnarng*, n., (MC) a cushion.
隱匿 *yiinnih*, v.i. & t., to hide, conceal, from view.
隱忍 *yirnreen*, v.t., to bear or suffer (injustice, distress) patiently without protest.
隱身 *yiinshen*, v.i., (Taoist) to make oneself invisible; 隱身法 *-faa*, n., such magic; 隱身草兒 *-tsaau'l*, (fig.) a person acting as cover.
隱姓 *yiin-shihng*, phr., to conceal one's surname: 隱姓埋名 incognito ("to disguise name and personal name").
隱形 *yiin-shirng*, v.i., to render oneself invisible; 隱形眼鏡 contact lens.
隱士 *yiinshyh*, n., a recluse scholar.
隱慝 *yiinteh*, n., (AC) hidden, past or evil deeds.
隱藏 *yiintsarng*, v.i. & t., to conceal (s.t., s.o.); be concealed.
隱惻 *yiintseh*, v.i., (AC) to feel sorrow, pity.
隱痛 *yiintuhng*, n., secret pain; regret.
隱微 *yiinweir*, adj., latent, invisible, deep (meaning); minute (particle).
隱逸 *yiinyih*, n. & adj., recluse; scholar who keeps away from politics esp. in times of national trouble.
隱隱 *yirnyiin*, adj., unclear, barely visible: 隱隱可見 may be seen indistinctly, see *-yue* ↓.
隱憂 *yiinyou*, n., deep grief (= 殷憂), also secret worry.
隱約 *yiinyue*, adj., (1) indistinctly visible; (2) implicit (meaning).

隱語 *yirnyuu*, n., a riddle; an enigma, an elliptical line.

§ 32A.80 (阝/八)

隤 32A.80–2

tueir.

[Var. of 頹 90S.80]

隕 32A.80–4

yuun (**yurn*).

V.i. & t. (1) To fall down, to make a slip: 隕越 *-yueh*↓. (2) To let fall (tears): 隕淚, 隕涕 shed tears. (3) To die (interch. 殞 31S.80): 隕命 *-mihng*↓.

隕墜 *yuunjueih*, v.i., to decline and fall (said of tradition, a ruling power).
隕落 *yuun-luoh*, v.i., to fall down.
隕命 *yuun-mihng*, v.i., to lose life, to die (also wr. 殞命).
隕星 *yuunshing*, n., a meteor.
隕石 *yuunshyr*, n., meteorite.
隕鐵 *yurntiee*, n., meteoric iron.
隕越 *yuunyueh*, v.i., to fall down; to make a slip, commit dereliction of duty.

§ 32A.81 (阝/人)

陜 32A.81–1

shaan (**shiar*).

N. 陜西 Shensi Province.

Adj. (**shiar*) U.f. 狹 narrow.

險 32A.81–8

shiaan.

N. (1) A strategic position: 天險 natural defense, barriers (as mountain range, rivers); 無險可守 untenable defensive position; 憑險固守 hold natural advantage of defense position. (2) Risky adventure: 冒險 to risk danger; 探險 explore (dangerous peaks, North Pole, etc.); 行險以僥倖 choose foolish, risky means to gain end; 歷險 go through hardships and difficulties; 保[4]險 insurance, see 91A.01. (3) Accident: 遇險 meet with car or other accident and die or be assassinated.

Adj. (1) Dangerous, risky, unsafe: 艱險 (road) difficult to pass; 危險 dangerous; 險症 *-jehng*↓. (2) Difficult, startling: 險句, 險語 startling sentence, esp. in prose or poetry; 險韻 a rhyme class of words, with few words in it, and therefore a difficult rhyme class. (3) Tricky, dishonest: 險詐 *-jah*↓; 奸險 treacherous (person).

Adv. Nearly, almost: 險遭毒手 was nearly killed; 險遭不測 barely escaped accident; 險些 *-shie*↓.

險隘 *shiaan-aih*, n., a strategic pass.
險詖 *shiaanbih*, adj., (LL) crooked (conduct).
險道神 *shiaan-dauh-shern*, n., (1) (coll.) a paper image opening the way for a funeral procession; (2) (fig.) a very tall person.
險惡 *shiaan-eh*, adj., wicked, crafty (heart); treacherous, ominous (aspect).
險固 *shiaanguh*, adj., strong defensively.
險詐 *shiaanjah*, adj., crafty, deceitful.
險症 *shiaanjehng*, n., dangerous disease.
險棘 *shiaanjir*, adj., (road) treacherous and overgrown with underbrush.
險譎 *shiaanjyuer*, adj., see *-jah*↑.
險峻 *shiaanjyuhn*, adj., (cliff) steep.
險澀 *shiaanseh*, adj., difficult (road, terrain).
險些(兒) *shiaanshie(-shie'l)* adv. phr., almost, nearly: 險些掉下去 nearly fell into (chasm, river, etc.); 險些死了 almost died; 險些釣上來 almost caught the fish.
險戲 *shiaanshih*, adj., (LL) see *-seh*↑ (also wr. 巇).
險阻 *shiarntzuu*, adj., (terrain) difficult to cross.
險要 *shiaanyauh*, n., a strong natural defense position.
險易 *shiaan-yih*, n., degree of safety or risk.

隩 32A.81–9

yuh (**auh*).

N. A cove, a bend in river.

Adj. (1) U.f. 燠 warm. (2) (**auh*) U.f. 奧 profound.

§ 32A.82 (阝/乂)

陵 32A.82–1

lirng.

N. (1) Hill, mound: 丘陵, 岡陵 mound, hillock; 陵谷易處 "hill and valley change places"—great changes between periods. (2) Mausoleum, imperial tomb: 明陵 the Ming Tombs; 中山陵 Chungshan Mausoleum. (2) A surname.

V.t. Var. of 凌 63A. 82, humiliate, soar aloft, etc.

陵寢 *lirngchiin*, n., king's or ruler's resting place.
陵廟 *lirngmiauh*, n., mausoleum temple.
陵墓 *lirngmuh*, n., usu. tomb of distinguished person.
陵苕 *lirngtiaur*, n., (bot.) *Tecoma grandiflora* (＝紫葳).
陵替 *lirngtih*, n. & v.i., decline (of dynasty).
陵夷 *lirngyir*, v.i., gradual decay (of power).
陵園 *lirngyuarn*, n., tomb garden.

陂 32A.82–2

po (AC also **pir*).

N. (1) Slope, see 坡 11A.82. (2) (AC) reservoir.

Adj. (**pir*) sloping, biassed in 偏陂.

陂陀 *potor*, adj., winding, with ups and downs (of embankments, hill lines).
陂塘 *potarng* (**pir*-), n., small pond.

陬 32A.82–3

tzou.

N. (1) A secluded place: 邊陬 (LL) the border regions. (2) A corner: 四陬 (LL) the four corners (of a city, town, country).

V.i. Live together in a group: 陬落 (LL) a village settlement.

阪 32A.82–9

baan.

[Var. of 坂, 岅, current in Japan]

N. Slope: 阪上走丸 phr., ride the crest of fortune, do s.t. most easily; 阪田 (AC) rugged area.

§ 32A.83 (阝/〜)

陡 32A.83–1

doou.

Adj. Steep.

Adv. Suddenly, abruptly: 夜來陡覺霜風急 suddenly felt the chilly frost at night; 陡起歹念 suddenly a wicked idea came to mind.

隨 32A.83–1

sueir.

[Abbr. 随]

N. A surname.

V.t. (1) To follow: 隨從, 隨順 *-tsurng*, *-shuhn* ↓; 追隨 to follow a leader about; 隨波逐浪 follow the winds and waves (i.e., the fashions, trends); 入鄉隨俗 when in Rome, do as the Romans do; 隨娘改嫁 (of children of remarried women) follow the mother into new home. (2) To adjust, to change, to take what comes: 隨機應變 do as the circumstances dictate; 隨風轉舵, 隨風兒倒 cut the rudder to the wind (change course for convenience); 隨高就低, 隨方就圓 be adjustable to circumstances; 隨聲附和 to follow the majority blindly; 隨遇而安 take what comes (and be contented); 各隨所好 let each do what he wants. (3) To let: 隨便 *-biahn* ↓; 隨他去, 隨他怎麽的 let him do what he likes. (4) To do naturally without extra effort: 隨口答應 promise at once without hesitation; 隨手關門 shut the door as you pass by. (5) To favor (a parent): 他長得隨他父親, 説話的神氣隨他母親 he looks like his father, and talks like his mother.

Adj. Any: 隨時 any time, *-shyr* ↓; 隨處, 隨地 anywhere, *-chuh*, *-dih* ↓; 隨叫隨到 to be available on hand, at one's back and call.

Adv. & conj. As, as soon as: 隨來隨吃 guests are served as they arrive; 隨學隨忘 no sooner learned than it is forgotten; 隨即 *-jir* ↓.

隨便(兒) *sueirbiahn* (*-bia'l*), adj. & adv., (1) as one wishes, freely, not restricted: 隨便走 go wherever and whenever you like; esp. invitation to take off gown or coat at party: 隨便寬衣; 不可隨便吐痰 do not spit freely; (2) carelessly, cursorily: 做事不可隨便 don't do slipshod work.
隨筆 *sueirbii*, n., a form of informal or familiar essay, casual literary notes.
隨常 *sueircharng*, adv., usually.
隨趁 *sueirchehn*, v.t., to keep company with (person).
隨牆門(兒) *sueirchiarng-mern* (*--mer'l*), n., "hole in the wall" used as entrances.
隨處(兒) *sueirchuh* (*'l*), adv., everywhere, anywhere.
隨羣(兒) *sueirchyurn*(*'l*), adv., following others, conforming to fashion.
隨帶 *sueirdaih*, v.t., to bring along (luggage, children, staff).
隨地(兒) *sueirdih*(*-dieh'l*), adv., anywhere, everywhere: 隨地吐痰 spit everywhere.
隨分 *sueirfehn*, adv., (1) according to one's status or ability (to drink, etc.); (2) joining as part of group action (in presenting gifts, etc.).
隨和 (1) *sueir-ho*, (allu.) 隨和之寶 (AC) two owners of priceless treasures; (2) (*-heh*) v.i., follow others blindly; (3) (*-'he*) adj.,

friendly, not contentious.

隨後 *sueirhouh*, adv., later on, soon after: 你先去，我隨後就到 you go first, I'll be there soon.

隨機 *sueir-ji*, adv., as the situation allows or demands: 隨機應變 act according to circumstances.

隨即 *sueirjir*, adv., immediately: 説完隨即出去 went out immediately after saying s.t.

隨口(兒) *sueirkoou('l)*, adv., (promise) freely.

隨溜(兒) *sueirliouh('l)*, adv., conforming to current style (in dress, action).

隨身 *sueir-shen*, v.i., carry s.t. (stick, pipe) always on body; 隨身燈 *--deng*, n., lamp lighted before a coffin during vigil.

隨喜 *sueirshii*, n. & v.i., (1) (Budd.) visit temples, join in celebrations; (2) join in the fun in gen.

隨心 *sueir-shin*, phr., (do) as one pleases: 隨心所欲 as the heart desires; 隨心草兒 choice or fashion, each one according to his taste.

隨手(兒) *sueir-shoou('l)* adv., (1) quickly (forget, etc.); (2) while convenient, without trouble: 隨手關門 shut the door as you come in or go out.

隨順 *sueirshuhn*, v.t., to obey (another).

隨事 *sueir-shyh*[1], adv., in everything (be careful, etc.).

隨侍 *sueirshyh*[2], v.i. & t., to attend upon (s.o.).

隨時 *sueirshyr*, adv., (available) any time, any time one likes.

隨俗 *sueir-sur*, v.i., follow local custom.

隨從 *sueirtsurng*, (1) (*-tsuhng*) n., a member of the retinue; (2) v.t., to accompany (a superior).

隨同 *sueirturng*, adv. & prep., together; together with.

隨意 *sueiryih*, adv., as one pleases (drink, pluck flowers, leave place); 隨意肌 *--ji*, n., voluntary muscle.

隨宜 *sueiryir*, adv., as one likes or chooses.

隨員 *sueiryuarn*[1], n., assistant, secretary, member of staff, esp. on a mission.

隨緣 *sueiryuarn*[2], adv., (Budd. & gen.) (donate) according to situation.

隄 32A.83–4

tir (**di*).

[Var. 堤]

N. 隄防 dike, embankment.

V.t. (**di'fang*) Guard against (= 提防).

隧 32A.83–8

sueih.

N. (1) A tunnel; a tunnel gate, underground pass. (2) (AC) bonfire as war signal; torch, (u.f. 燧 91D.83).

隧道 *sueihdauh*, n., tunnel, underground passage.

§ 32A.91 (阝/ノ)

陟 32A.91–2

jyh.

V.i. & t. To climb (mountain, staircase); to promote: 陟級 promote, be promoted in rank; 陟用 promote to higher position.

陟黜 *jyh-chuh*, n., promotion and downgrading of officials.

陟方 *jyh-fang*, phr., (AC) an emperor travels for visits; an emperor dies ("goes up to great distance"; cf. 升遐).

陟罰 *jyh-far*, n., promotion and punishment.

陟降 *jyhjiahng*, n., see *-chuh*↑.

§ 32A.93 (阝/く)

陰 32A.93–8

yin (**an*, **yihn*).

[Var. 陰]

N. (1) The principle of *yin* in 陰陽 *yin-yarng* philosophy, the principle of the female, the quiescent, the passive, opp. 陽 *yarng*, the male, the active, the expansive: 太陰 the moon, opp. 太陽 the sun. (2) The genitals of man or woman: 男陰, 女陰; 陰戶 *-huh*, 陰莖 *-jing*↓. (3) (AC) the north side of mountain; south side of river. (4) The back side of monuments: 碑陰. (5) The nether world 陰魂, 陰司, 陰府 *-hurn*, *-sy*[1], *-fuu*↓; 陰宅, 陰狀, 陰壽 *-jer*, *-juahng*, *-shouh*↓. (6) The shady side: 向陰 facing the shade; the moving shadow of the sundial, hence 光陰 time. (7) (**an*) (AC) hut near grave for mourner. (8) (**yihn*) (AC) u.f. 蔭 tree shade. (9) A surname.

Adj. (1) Minus, negative (electricity): 陰電, 陰極 *-diahn*, *-jir*↓. (2) Female, quiescent, see N. 1↑. (3) Negative in seal, photography: 陰文 *-wern*↓; 陰畫 *-huah*↓. (4) Rainy: 陰天 *-tian*↓; 陰晴 rain and shine. (5) Crafty, sinister: 陰謀, 陰險, 陰詐 *-mour*, *-shiaan*, *-jah*↓.

陰暗 *yinahn*, adj., dark, gloomy.

陰兵 *yinbing*, n., (MC) women soldiers (cf. Amazons).

A

陰 險

陰部 *yinbuh*, n., private parts (of man, woman).

陰辰 *yinchern*^{1}, n., (Chin. astrology) the even numbers in duodecimal cycle: 丑, 卯, 巳, 未, 酉, 亥, see Appendex A (cf. *-gan*^{1} ↓).

陰沈 *yinchern*^{2}, n., not open, crafty, secretive (person); deadpan (face); dark, gloomy (sky); 陰沈木 a kind of hard, fine-grained wood.

陰譴 *yinchiaan*, n., God's retribution (punishment for sin).

陰慶 *yinchihng*, n., see *-shouh* ↓.

陰脣 *yinchurn*, n., (physiol.) labia majora; labia minora.

陰道 *yindauh*, n., (physiol.) the vagina.

陰德 *yin-der*, n., good deeds done in secret.

陰電 *yin-diahn*, n., negative electricity.

陰地蕨 *yindihjyuer*, n., (bot.) *Botrychium ternatum*.

陰毒 *yindur*, adj., (person) vicious with a friendly exterior.

陰惡 *yin-eh*, adj., evil deeds unknown to other men.

陰阜 *yinfuh*, n., (physiol.) *Mons veneris*.

陰府 *yinfuu*, n., the nether world, Hades.

陰干 *yingan*^{1}, n., (Chin. astrology) the five even numbers in decimal cycle: 乙, 丁, 己, 辛, 癸, cf. *-chern*^{1} ↑.

陰乾 *yingan*^{2} (*-'gan*), v.t., to let (pickles, meat) dry gradually in the shade.

陰溝 *yingou*, n., sewerage, covered drain.

陰功 *yin-gung*, n., see *-der* ↑.

陰寒 *yinharn*, adj., cold and damp.

陰狠 *yinheen*, adj., see *-dur* ↑.

陰核 *yinher*, n., (physiol.) clitoris.

陰畫 *yinhuah*, n., formerly, photographic negative.

陰晦 *yinhueei*, adj., overcast, cloudy.

陰戶 *yinhuh*, n., the vagina.

陰魂 *yinhurn*, n., ghost.

陰詐 *yinjah*, adj., crafty, deceitful.

陰著兒 *yinjau'l*, n., a dastardly act.

陰宅 *yinjer*, n., graveyard (opp. 陽宅 residence of the living).

陰間 *yinjian*, n., the Hades.

B

陰莖 *yinjing*, n., the penis.

陰極 *yinjir*, n., (phys.) the cathode.

陰狀 *yinjuahng*, n., letter left by one who committed suicide ("a complaint in hell").

陰重 *yin-juhng*, adj., (AC, rare) not given to many words, secretive.

陰識 *yinjyh*^{1}, n., inscription in intaglio, with characters below surface.

陰騭 *yinjyh*^{2}, n., see *-der* ↑.

陰涼 *yinliarng*, adj., cool: 陰涼兒 cool shade.

陰曆 *yinlih*, n., the lunar calendar.

陰靈兒 *yinlirng'l*, n., departed soul of person.

陰毛 *yinmaur*, n., pubic hair.

陰門 *yinmern*, n., see *-huh* ↑.

陰面子 *yinmiahntz*, n., dastardly person; friendly attitude with concealed viciousness.

陰謀 *yinmour*, n., secret conspiracy.

陰囊 *yinnarng*, n., (physiol.) the scrotum.

陰平 *yinpirng*, n., the first tone in Chin. language (陽平=second tone).

陰人 *yinrern*, n., (sl.) a woman.

陰森 *yinsen*, adj., dark, gloomy place; crooked (person).

陰險 *yinshiaan*, adj., sly and crafty, dastardly.

陰性 *yinshihng*, n., feminine character, gender; the *yin* nature.

陰行草 *yinshirng-tsaau*, n., (bot.) *Siphonostegia chinensis*.

陰壽 *yinshouh*, n., anniversary of a parent's death.

陰事 *yinshyh*, n., secret doings not known to others.

陰桫 *yinsuo*, n., (bot.) a hard wood.

陰損 *yinsuun*, n., secret evil deed which detracts from man's lot of happiness.

陰司 *yinsy*^{1}, n., the judges in hell; the hell.

陰私 *yinsy*^{2}, n., a man's personal secrets not known to others.

陰天 *yintian*, n., a cloudy day.

陰曹 *yintsaur*, n., see *-sy*^{1} ↑.

陰萎 *yinweei*, n., (physiol.) impotence (=陽萎).

陰文 *yinwern*, n., inscription in intaglio, with characters below surface.

C

陰陽 *yinyarng*, n., *yin* and *yarng*, (see N. 1 ↑); 陰陽家 an astrologer; 陰陽生 (AC) astrologer; 陰陽人 *--rern*, n., a bisexual person; sex-intergrade (biol.).

陰影 *yinyiing*, n., shadow.

陰陰 *yinyin*, adj., cloudy: 陰陰沉沉 cloudy and gooomy.

險 32A.93–8

yur.

[Var. of 踰 40B.00]

SECTION 32S

§ 32S.00 (フ^s/亅)

对 32S.00-1

dueih.

[Abbr. of 對 22S.00]

剁 32S.00-2

duoh.

V. To chop, mince, pare: 剁肉 to mince meat; 剁碎 to chop fine.

剟 32S.00-2

duor.

V.t. To cut, chop (meat, etc.), to prick; (AC) to cut wood block: 剟刊 to publish (rare).

孖 32S.00-3

tzy.

N. Twins.

§ 32S.01 (フ^s/小)

疎 32S.01-1

shu (also *su*).

N. A surname.

Adj. (Interch. 疏 32S.70) negligent; distant; thin, scattered apart; 疎懶, 疎失, 疎散, etc., see 疏 32S.70.

疎隔 *shuger*, adj., silent in correspondence, having not corresponded (=疏△濶 32S.70).
疎慌 *shuhuang*, adj., out of practice.
疎交 *shu-jiau*, n., distant, not close friend.
疎快 *shukuaih*, adj., (MC) carefree.
疎剌剌 *su-lah-lah*, adj., (MC) forlorn, wind-blown.
疎頑 *shuwarn*, adj., (AC) carefree, insouciant, see 疏△慢, 疏△放 32S.70.

孫 32S.01-9

sun (**suhn*).

N. (1) A surname. (2) (*-tz*, *'l*) A grandchild: 孫子, 孫女 *-tz*, *-nyuu* ↓; 男孫, 女孫 grandson, granddaughter. (2) A relative of grandchild's generation or lower: 曾孫 great-grandson; 玄孫, 元孫 great-great-grandson; 來孫, 昆孫, 仍孫, 雲孫, 耳孫 (counting from 孫 as the 3rd generation) the 5th, 6th, 7th, 8th, 9th generation grandson in that order; 外孫 grandson on daughter's side; 姪孫 nephew of 3rd generation; 長孫 eldest grandson; 重孫 eldest grandson by eldest son; 承重孫 eldest grandson in absence of eldest son during funeral.

V.i. & adj. (AC) u.f. 遜 32.83.

孫兒 *sun-erl*, n., grandchild.
孫婦 *sunfuh*, n., grandson's wife.
孫竹 *sunjur*, n., bamboo shoot grown from the main root.
孫女(兒) *sunnyuu* (*-'nyue'l*), n., granddaughter.
孫媳 *sunshir*, n., grandson's wife.
孫婿 *sunshyuh*, n., granddaughter's husband.
孫子 *suntz*, n., grandson.

§ 32S.02 (フ^s/⺊)

艰 32S.02-5

jian.

[Abbr. of 艱 20S.02]

豫 32S.02-9

yuh.

N. (1) A surname. (2) Name for Honan Province: 豫劇 Honan opera.

V.i. To take part in (see 預 32S.80).

Adj. (LL) happy, contented: 逸豫 carefree; 不豫 displeased.

Adv. Interch. 預; in advance, beforehand, see 預 32S.80 compp.

§ 32S.11 (フ^s/土)

难 32S.11-9

narn (*nahn*).

[Abbr. of 難 20S.11]

鄧 矜 孺 務 鷸 劝 鳮

§ 32S.22 (フ^s/丨)

鄧 32S.22–3

dehng.

N. A surname.

§ 32S.32 (フ^s/フ)

矜 32S.32–8

jin (**guan*).

V.t. To pity: 矜恤 *-shyuh*, 矜惜 *-shir*, 矜全 *-chyuarn* ↓.

N. & adj. (**guan*) (Interch. 鰥 92B.02) a widower, widowed: 矜寡 widows and widowers; 矜夫 a widower.

V.i. & adj. (1) Taking pride in oneself, proud: 驕矜 show pride, proud and boastful; 自矜其能 boast of oneself; 矜誇 *-kua* ↓; 矜貴 think much of (oneself, others); 矜功 be puffed up with one's own services to the country. (2) Showing self-respect, acting with dignity: 矜持 *-chyr*, 矜矜 *-jin*, 矜重 *-juhng*, 矜式 *-shyh* ↓.

矜持 *jinchyr*, v.i., (1) to affect, put on airs; (2) show embarrassment, behave awkwardly.

矜全 *jinchyuarn*, v.t., commiserate and help.

矜矜 *jinjin*, adj., (AC) longing.

矜重 *jinjuhng*, v.i., act with dignity, show self-respect.

矜誇 *jinkua*, v.i., brag, bluster, show off.

矜惜 *jinshir*, v.t., feel pity for, take pity on.

矜式 *jinshyh*, n., model: 足爲矜式 worthy of emulation; v.t., to look up to: 有所矜式 have s.o. to serve as a model.

矜恤 *jinshyuh*, v.t., sympathize with, take pity on (orphan).

§ 32S.42 (フ^s/冈)

孺 32S.42–3

rur (also *ruh*).

N. (1) A child: 孺子 *-tzyy* ↓; 孺齒 milk (baby) teeth; 婦孺 women and children. (2) A blood relation: 孺人 *-rern* ↓.

Adj. Affectionate, loving: 和樂且孺 (AC) happy and innocent; 孺慕 have an affectionate attachment for s.o.; 孺愛 filial love.

孺人 *rurrern*, n., (LL) wife; a scholar's wife.

孺子 *rurtzyy*, n., (1) children in gen.: 孺子可教也 that's a good boy! (paternalistic praise for a promising young man); (2) (AC) concubines of the nobility; (3) (AC) the eldest heir.

§ 32S.50 (フ^s/コ)

務 32S.50–9

wuh.

N. (1) Affairs, business: 事務 affairs in gen.; 職務 duties; 公務 office business, opp. 私務 private business; 校務 school affairs; 政務 political business, administrative duties; 服務 n. & v.i., service; 債務 debts; 業務 business affairs, professional business; 庶務 business (department); 總務 gen. management. (2) (Suhng Dyn.) tax bureau: 市易務.

Vb. aux. Must, should: 務必, 務須 *-bih*, *-shyu* ↓; 務得 so that (+vb. or adj.): 務得妥當 so that it will be in order; 務使 so as to make it (attractive, neat), or so that.

V.t. (1) To lay emphasis on, to be concerned with, to concentrate on: 務正, 務本 *-jehng*, *-been* ↓; 不務正業 does not attend to own main profession. (2) To take as profession: 務農 be a farmer; 務醫 be a doctor. (3) To try to be (+adj.): 務新奇 strive for novelty; 務實 try to be practical; 務全 to seek after perfection, completeness.

務本 *wuh-been*, v.i., concentrate on the essentials, on the foundation.

務必 *wuh-bih*, v.b. aux., must, should (return on time, etc.).

務求 *wuh-chiour*, v.i., strive to or for.

務正 *wuh-jehng*, v.i., attend to proper business; attend to moral conduct.

務須 *wuh-shyu*, vb. aux., must, should, see *-bih* ↑.

鷸 32S.50–9

yuh.

N. The crane: 鷸蚌相爭 fable of the crane and the mother-of-pearl in a fight to death, to the benefit of the fisherman.

劝 32S.50–9

chyuahn.

[Abbr. of 勸 20S.50]

鳮 32S.50–9

ji.

[Abbr. of 雞 90S.11]

§ 32S.70 (フ^{s}/乚)

孔 32S.70-2

kuung.

N. (1) A hole, an opening: 耳孔, 鼻孔 the ear, the nose or nostril; 穿孔 drill or thread through a hole; 孔竅, 孔穴 *-chiauh*, *-shyueh* ↓. (2) A surname.

Adv. (AC) very: 孔多 very many; 孔碩 very big (stature), huge, immense; 孔急, 孔殷 most urgent.

孔竅 *kuungchiauh*, n., a crevice, an opening (in wall, organ, etc.).
孔雀 *kuungchyueh*, n., the peacock; 孔雀石 (geol.) malachite.
孔道 *kuungdauh*, n., (1) teachings of Confucius; (2) thoroughfare.
孔方兄 *kuungfang-shyung*, n., (sl.) money (from anc. coin with a square hole).
孔懷 *kuunghuair*, n., (AC) 兄弟孔懷 the brothers think very much of each other, hence (LL) n., brothers.
孔教 *Kuungjiauh*, n., Confucianism.
孔孟 *Kuung-Mehng*, phr., Confucius and Mencius, oft. used as a phr. denoting Confucianism.
孔廟 *Kuungmiauh*, n., Confucian temple.
孔目 *kuungmuh*, n., (MC) secretary in charge of official documents.
孔穴 *kuungshyueh*, n., opening, hole; the openings in the human bodily system.
孔子 *Kurngtzyy*, n., Confucius (from 孔夫子, Master Kung).

疏 32S.70-6

shu (also *su*; **shuh*).

N. (1) (**shuh*) Memorandum to emperor: 上疏 send memorandum. (2) (**shuh* or *shu*) Commentary on earlier commentary: 注疏 commentary and further commentary by later scholar. (3) A surname.

V.i. & t. (1) To clear, dredge (river bed): 疏導, 疏通, 疏濬 *-dauh*, *-tung*, *-jyuhn* ↓. (2) To disperse: 疏散 *-sahn* ↓; 疏財仗義 disburse money in public cause.

Adj. (Interch. 疎 32S.01) (1) Scattered, far apart, distant: 疏星 scattered (few) stars; 疏網 a loose net; 疏髮 thin hair; 親疏 close and distant relatives; 久疏音問 have been negligent in correspondence; 疏遠 *-yuaan* ↓. (2) Raw, crude: 疏食, 疏糲 (also 蔬) coarse food, *-shyr*, *-lih* ↓; 才疏學淺 (self-deprecation) I am crude and unlearned. (3) Negligent, careless, inadequate (in plan, duty, attention): 疏忽, 疏略, 疏慢 *-hu*, *-lyueh*, *-mahn* ↓; 疏虞, 疏失 *-yur*, *-shy* ↓.

疏宕 *shudahng*, adj., untrammeled, unconventional (character, spirit).
疏導 *shudauh*, v.t., to dredge (river), to channel water into course.
疏放 *shufahng*, adj., see *-dahng* ↑.
疏忽 *shuhu*, (1) adj., careless, negligent; (2) n., an oversight, small mistake; (3) v.t., to neglect (person, duty).
疏濬 *shujyuhn*, v.t., to dredge (river).
疏狂 *shukuarng*, adj., see *-dahng*, *-fahng* ↑.
疏濶 *shukuoh*, adj., (1) cool (relationship), negligent in correspondence, long separated; (2) not cogent (reasoning).
疏懶 *shulaan*, adj., negligent, indolent (in duty).
疏朗 *shulahng*, adj., bright (weather, room).
疏糲 *shu-lih*, n., crude repast.
疏理 *shulii*, v.t., put to order, disentangle (confused situation).
疏落 *shuluoh*, adj., thin, scattered (population, leaves).
疏略 *shulyueh*, adj., inadequate, sketchy (report).
疏慢 *shumahn*, adj., see *-hu* ↑.
疏散 *shusahn*, v.i. & t., (1) to disperse (population, crowded area), relieve (congestion); (2) relax by taking stroll.
疏神 *shushern*, v.i., to relax the mind.
疏懈 *shushieh*, adj., see *-laan* ↑.
疏率 *shushuaih*, adj., careless, untrammeled, incautious.
疏失 *shushy*, n., slight mistake, oversight.
疏食 *shu-shyr*, n., a coarse meal.
疏鬆 *shusung*, adj., puffy (hair, cake).
疏頭 **shuhtour*, n., (AC) a sacrificial prayer to the dead.
疏材 *shu-tsair*, n., (self-deprecative) my unworthy ability.
疏辭 **shuhtsyr*, n., see *-tour* ↑.
疏通 *shutung*, (1) v.t., (a) to dredge (water course), (b) to remove misunderstandings, spec. to speak for s.o.: 向他疏通一下 please speak for me to s.o.; (2) adj., 疏通知遠 (AC) showing deep penetration and foresight.
疏宗 *shu-tzung*, n., a distantly related clan.
疏鑿 *shutzuoh*, v.t., to cut through (tunnel).
疏外 *shuwaih*, v.t., (LL) see *-yuaan* ↓.
疏野 *shuyee*, adj., raw, crude (person).
疏遠 *shuyuaan* (-'*yuan*), (1) adj., distant, not in close touch; (2) v.t., to neglect (person), keep at distance.
疏虞 *shuyur*, n., see *-shy* ↑.

舔 32S.70-9

ruung.

毧 戏 戤 預 頟 孩 欢 敠 双

N. Down, fine hair: 毧毛兒 fine soft hair; 毧刺 fine fish bones.

Adj. Fine, soft: 頭髮發毧 the hair is fine and soft.

§ 32S.71 (フ^{S}/乇)

戏 32S.71–7

shih.

[Abbr. of 戲 21S.71]

戤 32S.71–7

gaih.

V.t. (1) (Commerce) counterfeit: 戤牌 a counterfeit trademark. (2) To pawn.

§ 32S.80 (フ^{S}/八)

預 32S.80–3

yuh.

V.i. & t. To take part in: 參預 take part in planning (celebration, revolt); 干預 interfere in or with affair.

Adv. Oft. used as prefix meaning "previously" or "beforehand," like Eng. "pre-": 預備, 預算, 預約 *-beih, -suahn, -yue* ↓.

預報 *yuhbauh*, n. & v.t., warning, report of coming events; 天氣預報 weather forecast.
預備 *yuhbeih* (*-'bei*), v.i. & n., prepare, -ration.
預卜 *yuhbuu*, v.i., to foretell.
預期 *yuhchir*, v.t., to expect, see *-liauh* ↓.
預定 *yuhdihng*, v.i., to reserve (seats, date for party); prepare beforehand.
預防 *yuhfarng*, v.i. & t., to prevent, provide against (accident, forgery).
預付 *yuhfuh*, v.t., to prepay, pay in advance.
預告 *yuhgauh*, n., notice of coming events; legal notice, advance notice.
預兆 *yuhjauh*, n., an omen.
預計 *yuhjih*, v.t. & n., reckon in advance.
預支 *yuhjy*[1], n. & v.i., advance payment.
預知 *yuhjy*[2], v.i. & t., predict (the future), foretell.
預科 *yuhke*, n., preparatory school.
預料 *yuhliauh*, v.t. & n., predict, -ion, expect, -ation: 出了預料 unexpected.
預謀 *yuh-mour*, phr., take part in plan or conspiracy.
預賽 *yuhsaih*, n., preliminary contest.
預先 *yuhshian*, adv., (tell, warn, prepare) beforehand.
預習 *yuhshir*, n., preparatory training.
預選 *yuhshyuaan*, n., preliminary or primary election.
預算 *yuhsuahn*, n., budget.
預測 *yuhtseh*, v.i. & t., to calculate the future, to predict.
預演 *yuhyaan*, n., rehearsal.
預言 *yuhyarn*, n., a prophecy; v.i., to prophesize; 預言家 *--jia*, n., a prophet, one who foretells.
預約 *yuhyue*, n. & v.i., (1) (make) previous engagement; (2) advance subscription or sale.

頟 32S.80–3

saang.

N. (AC) the forehead, the brow: 稽頟 to kowtow.

§ 32S.81 (フ^{S}/人)

孩 32S.81–6

hair.

N. (*-'l, -tz*) A child: 男孩 a boy; 女孩 a girl; 小孩 children in gen.; 嬰孩 a baby; see 孩兒 *-er'l* ↓.

孩抱 *hairbauh*, n., stage of infancy yet unable to walk.
孩氣 *hairchih*, n., as in 孩子氣 childishness, childish fun.
孩兒 *hair-er'l*, n., my child (spoken by parents); your child (sons' and daughters' self-reference speaking to parents).
孩提 *hairtir*, n., stage of infancy, toddling stage.
孩童 *hairturng*, n., children.

欢 32S.81–9

huan.

[Abbr. of 歡 20S.81]

§ 32S.82 (フ^{S}/乂)

敠 32S.82–2

duor.

V.i., See 战敠 21S.82.

双 32S.82–3

shuang.

[Abbr. of 雙 91.82]

A

孜 32S.82-9

tzy.

Adj. & adv. Diligent(ly): 孜孜 *-tzy* ↓.

孜 煎 *tzyjian*, v.i., to worry, fret, grieve: 無事孜煎 to pine away for nothing.

孜 孜 *tzytzy*, adj., (1) diligent, industrious: 孜孜不倦 persevering, indefatigable, hard-working; 惟日孜孜 working hard day in and day out; (2) (=吱吱 *tztz*) imitation of hissing sounds.

§32S.83 (フ^{s}/〜)

乂 32S.83-9

bo.

Adj. See 卡$^{\triangle}$乂 21A.22.

孤 32S.83-9

gu.

N. (1) An orphan: 孤兒 *-er'l* ↓; 孤哀子 *-aitzyy* ↓; 撫孤 bring up the child of a deceased friend; 託孤 entrust child to a friend on deathbed. (2) (AC) a high-ranking official: 三孤 the three deputies to the tutors of the crown prince.

Pron. (AC) (court.) my humble self, a term generally used by anc. prince or king: 孤王 I, your humble prince (cf. Eng. "we"); 孤家寡人 ditto, (facet.) an elderly bachelor; 稱孤道寡 address oneself as king (see 寡$^{\triangle}$人 62.50).

B

V.t. Show ingratitude to: 孤恩, 孤負 *-en*, *-'fuh* ↓.

Adj. (1) Lonely, solitary: 孤獨 *-dur*, 孤單 *-dan*, 孤另 *-lihng*, 孤立 *-lih*, 孤本 *-been* ↓; 孤陋 *-louh* ↓; 孤零零的 lonely and helpless; 孤苦 *-kuu* ↓; 孤掌難鳴 helpless and without friendly support ("cannot clap with one hand"); 孤臣孽子 (AC) a son born of a concubine and out of imperial favor, also (LL) a supporter of a lost dynasty or cause; 孤城 a deserted or isolated city; 孤墳 a lone grave; 孤山 a lone hill; 小孤山 name of a hill in the middle of the Yangtze near Kiukiang. (2) (Of persons or things) aloof, detached: 孤僻 *-pih*, 孤憤 *-fehn*, 孤芳 *-fang*, 孤峭, *-chiauh* ↓; 孤雲野鶴 descriptive of the life of a carefree hermit (lit., "like a lone cloud or a wild crane").

孤 哀 子 *gu-aitzyy*, n., a newly bereaved son (of both parents), a term generally used in funeral notices.

孤 本 *gu-been*, n., as in 海內孤本 only extant copy of a rare book.

孤 標 *gubiau*, adj., (1) (of persons) preeminent, distinguished, in looks or conduct; (2) (of mountains) steep, rising high into the sky.

孤 峭 *guchiauh*, adj., (of persons) independent, aloof in temperament and character.

孤 單 *gudan*, adj., solitary, living alone.

孤 丁 *gu'ding*, n., (1) a protuberance; (2) an unexpected development or impediment; (3) (gambling) the entire stake, see *-juh* ↓; (4) (*guding*) a person all by himself.

孤 獨 *gudur*, adj., solitary, standing alone.

孤 恩 *gu-en*, v.i., to forget former favors, turn against benefactor.

孤 兒 *gu-er'l*, n., an orphan: 孤兒寡婦 orphans and widows; 孤兒院 an orphanage.

孤 芳 *gu-fang*, adj., as in 孤芳自賞 narcissistic; spurning publicity.

C

孤 憤 *gu-fehn*, adj., disillusioned with the world, championing an unpopular cause.

孤 負 *gu'fuh*, v.i., be ungrateful to others; fail (a friend, one's parents) (also wr. 辜$^{\triangle}$負 10.10).

孤 寡 *guguaa*, n., widows and orphans.

孤 拐 (兒) *gu'guai* (*-gua'l*), n., (1) the cheekbone; (2) the ball of the foot.

孤 鬼 兒 *guguee'l*, n., (humorous) one who lives alone without family or companions (lit., "lonely ghost").

孤 魂 *gu-hurn*, n., (1) a wandering soul; (2) one without family or friends.

孤 寂 *gujir*, adj., lonely.

孤 注 *gu-juh*, n., usu. in 孤注一擲 stake the whole amount, (fig.) make a last-ditch stand against the opponent with all one has.

孤 苦 *gukuu*, adj., alone and helpless; 孤苦零丁.

孤 老 *gulaau*, n., (1) an old man without children; (2) a woman's paramour; a singsong artist's protector.

孤 立 *gulih*, adj., isolated; 孤立主義(者) isolationism (-ist).

孤 另 *gulihng*, adj., see *-dan* ↑.

孤 陋 *gulouh*, adj., uncultured: 孤陋寡聞 poorly read and ignorant (usu. self-deprecatory).

孤 鸞 *guluarn*, n., widower.

孤 露 *guluh*, n., (LL) an infant orphan.

孤 僻 *gupih*, adj., (1) holding oneself aloof, disinclined to associate with others; (2) (of localities) remote and not easily accessible.

孤 孀 *gushuang*, n., (1) a widow and her orphaned child; (2) a widow.

SECTION 40

§ 40.01 (口/小)

呆 40.01

air (also *dai*).
[Var. 獃 21S.81]

Adj. Stupid, dull: 痴呆 ditto; 呆瞪瞪 standing still without any expression; 呆若木雞 standing like a log; 呆裏撒奸 of a calculating type behind a feigned appearance of docility; 呆笑 imbecile smile.

呆板 *airbaan* (*dai-*), adj., stupidly mechanical (interpretation, etc.), doing things by the book.
呆笨 *airbehn* (*dai-*), adj., stupid, awkward, slothful.
呆帳 *air-jahng*, n., a bad debt (payment doubtful).
呆僗 *airlaur*, n., (MC) stupid fellow.

§ 40.02 (口/k)

饕 40.02

tau.

Adj. Covetous, greedy.

饕餮 *tautieh*, n., a mythical figure, oft. found on anc. bronze vessels, representing greed, looking like gargoyle: 饕餮之徒 gluttons, greedy persons; name of anc. savage tribes.

§ 40.10 (口/十)

單 40.10

dan (**shahn*, **charn*).

N. (1) List, bill (*-tz*, *-'l*): 名單 list of names; 菜單 menu; 清單 bill, invoice; 貨單 bill of lading; 提貨單, 提單 packing list; 借單 I.O.U. (2) Bed sheet: 牀單, 被單. (3) Brochure, handbill given out to publicity: 傳單. (4) Monk's sojourn at temple: 落單, 掛單 register at certain temple. (5) (**shahn*) A surname.

Adj. (1) Single, simple (opp. complex): 簡單 ditto; odd: 單數 odd number; 單日 on odd days; 單人獨(匹)馬 (go) single-handed; 單刀直入 speak up without beating about the bush, make simple, direct attack on subject; 單桅 single-masted; 單跪 kneel on one knee; 單擺 (phys.) simple pendulum. (2) Thin (of clothing): 你的衣服太單了 your dress is too little for the weather; 單衫, 襖 unlined jacket, opp. 夾 lined. (3) Lone, lonely: 孤單 alone.

Adv. 單單 only: 單單你一個人 only you alone; 不單 not only.

單幫 *danbang*, phr., esp. in 跑單幫 (of petty businessman who) makes business trip on his own account.
單本位制 *dan-beenweih-jyh*, n., single standard system of currency (gold or silver).
單比例 *dan biilih*, n., simple equation, proportion.
單薄 *danbor*, adj., meager, weak: 身子很單薄 body is weak (from illness).
單純 *danchurn*, adj., pure, simple, unmixed.
單單 *dandan*, adv., only.
單掉兒 *dandiau'l*, adj., (of one who) plays a lone hand.
單調 *dandiauh*, adj., monotonous.
單丁 *danding*, n., one without brothers, only son.
單獨 *dandur*, adj. & adv., alone: 單獨一個人 a man alone.
單方 *danfang*, n. & adj., one side (-sided).
單軌 *dangueei*, n. & adj., single track: 單軌鐵路 monorail.
單果 *danguoo*, n., (bot.) simple fruit.
單靜 *danjihng*, adj., (of family) simple and quiet (not too many in-laws).
單據 *danjyuh*, n., voucher, supporting document, bill.
單兒 *da'l*, n., any bill, list, also *-tz*.
單戀 *danliahn*, n., one-sided, unrequited love.
單利 *dan-lih*, n., simple interest.
單身(漢) *danshen*(*hahn*), n., bachelor.
單相電流 *dan-shiahng diahnliour*, n., single-phase current.
單相思 *dan-shiangsy*, phr., one-sided love.
單細胞 *dan-shihbau*, adj., unicellular.
單行本 *danshirng-been*, n., a volume sold by itself, not by set.
單行法 *dan-shirng-faa*, n., law or regulation applying to only one province or area.
單行道 *dan-shirng-tauh*, n., (street sign) one-way traffic.
單式 *danshyh*, n., blank form.
單子 *dantz*, n., any printed sheet; prescription; bed sheet.
單字 *dantzyh*, n., whole character, individual characters; new words to be learned.
單位 *danweih*, n., unit (of organization, measurement).
單葉 *dan-yeh*, n., (bot.) single leaf.
單一 *danyi*, adj., one, only one; 單一神教 n., monotheism.
單音節 *danyinjier*, adj., monosyllabic.
單元 *danyuarn*, adj., of one origin; 單元論 monism, monistic (universe).
單于 **charnyur*, n., a Mongolian chieftain, Khan.

斝 40.10

jiaa.

N. An anc. wine cup.

§ 40.11 (口/土)

呈 40.11

cherng.

N. (*-tz, 'l*) A petition, a letter to superior: 呈文 *-wern*↓; 辭呈 a letter of resignation; 簽呈 a signed petition.

V.i. & t. (1) To appear: 呈現 *-shiahn*[1]↓. (2) V.t., to show: 呈露 *-luh*↓; 呈出笑容 show a smiling face; 呈祥, 呈瑞 to show lucky omens. (3) To petition, present or communicate to superior: 呈報, 呈明 *-bauh, -mirng*↓; 呈請 *-chiing*↓; 呈閱 to present for perusal; 呈獻 *-shiahn*[2]↓; 呈堂 s.t. presented at court hearing; 呈堂證物 court exhibit (law).

呈報 *cherngbauh*, v.i., to report to superior.

呈請 *cherngchiing*, v.i., to request officially.

呈遞 *cherngdih*, v.t., to present to: 呈遞國書 (foreign envoy) presents credentials (to the chief of state).

呈露 *chernglush*, v.i. & t., to reveal, show (flaws, uncertainty, etc.).

呈明 *cherng-mirng*, v.i., to explain officially.

呈現 *cherngshiahn*[1], v.i. & t., see *-luh*↑.

呈獻 *cherngshiahn*[2], v.i. & t., to present offering.

呈文 *cherngwern*, n., an official petition, a memorandum to superior.

§ 40.21 (口/ㄴ)

喦 40.21

yarn.

[Var. of 巖 21.82]

§ 40.22 (口/丨)

吊 40.22

diauh (*dih).

[Pop. of 弔 50.22]

§ 40.40 (口/口)

口 40.40

koou.

N. adjunct. 一口刀, 劍, 水缸 one knife, sword, water jar; mouthful: 扒幾口飯 take a few mouthfuls ("bites") of rice; 喝一口水 have one drink of water; 一口氣 one breath; 一家三口 see N. 2↓.

N. (1) The mouth: 開口 open mouth, break silence; 不敢開口 dare not say anything; 開口得罪人 offend people every time one speaks; 閉口 (無言) shut up, refrain from speaking; 口口聲聲 repeatedly (declare, etc.); 口說無憑 verbal promise is not enough; 利口, 口若懸河 a great talker, make a torrent of words; 口拙 not good at expressing oneself; 口蜜腹劍 honey words and a dastardly heart; 口是心非 false words, pretense; 口誅筆伐 denounce by spoken word and writing; 口授 teach by word of mouth, dictate; 口講指畫 gesticulate; 口渴, 口乾 thirsty; 出口成章 talk beautifully, a good impromptu talker; 衝口而出 say without thinking, blurt out; 破口大罵 denounce openly; 可口, 爽口 good to eat; 口腔, 口味 *-chiang, -weih*↓. (2) (Also as n. adjunct) number of persons: 人口, 戶口 population; 五口之家 a family of five ("with five mouths" to feed); 大小口 the young and old counted together; 倆口子 husband and wife, the two in the family; 老倆口兒 the old couple; 計口授田 allot land according to number of persons in the family; 牲口 domestic animals, cattle, etc. (3) Open end: 刀口 edge of knife; 槍口, 砲口 gun muzzle; 碗口 rim of bowl. (4) Entrance, gate, opening: 出口, 入口 exit, entrance; 關口, 卡口 customs station; 隘口 entrance to gully; 河口 river mouth; 海口 seaport; 窗口, 門口 outside of window, doorway; 傷口 opening of wound; 缺口 crack (in utensil); 口子 a crack. (5) A surname.

口岸 *koou-ahn*, n., seaport, river port.

口碑 *koou-bei*, n., as in 有口皆碑 (of official) enjoy great popularity among the people, also popular impression, opinion or assessment.

口磣 *kourcheen*, adj., (MC) vulgar of speech.

口沉 *kouchern*, adj., liking food salty: 這個人真口沉 this man eats his food highly salty.

口腔 *kouchiang*, n., (1) mouth cavity; (2) dialect accent.

口強 *kouchiarng*, adj., argumentative.

口器 *kouchih*[1], n., (zoo.) mouth organ.

口氣(兒) *kouchih*[2]*(-chieh'l)*, n., the tone of voice (angry, boding evil, timid, etc.)

口輕 *kouching*, adj., (1) eating

food without too much seasoning; (2) (of cattle) young.

口琴 *koouchirn*, n., harmonica.

口臭 *koouchouh*, n., halitosis.

口傳 *koouchuarn*, (1) n., hearsay; (2) v.t., transmit teaching by word of mouth.

口齒 *kourchyy*, n., ability to talk: 口齒伶俐 fluent of speech, a good talker; 口齒不清 enunciation not clear.

口袋(兒) *koou'dai* (*-dah'l*), n., pocket in coat; a bag.

口德 *koou-der*, n., virtue of not speaking evil of others.

口笛 *kooudir*, n., whistle.

口腹 *koou-fuh*, n., as in 口腹之慾 desire for creature comforts, bodily desires (eating, drinking).

口福 *koou-fur*, n., joy of eating, luck of having good food.

口供 *koouguhng*, n., affidavit.

口過 *koouguoh*, n., slip of the tongue, errors of speech.

口號 *koouhauh*, n., slogan; password, also see *-lihng*↓; (MC) song of eulogy at court ceremony.

口惠 *koouhueih*, n., empty promise without substance.

口紅 *koouhurng*, n., lipstick.

口罩(兒) *kooujauh('l)*, n., antiseptic gauze worn over mouth and nose.

口角 *kourjiaau*, v.i. & n., (1) bickering, quarrel: 兩人口角 two persons quarrel; (2) corner of mouth; 口角春風 praise by word of mouth.

口技 *kooujih*, n., forms of entertainment by voice (ventriloquist, etc.).

口徑 *kooujihng*, n., diameter of opening.

口吃 *kooujir*, v.i. & adj., stutter, stuttering.

口訣 *kooujyuer*, n., formula for incantation; instructions in rhyme.

口快 *kooukuaih*, adj., careless of speech: 心直口快 saying what one thinks without much deliberation.

口糧 *koouliarng*, n., ration (for soldiers, groups).

口令 *kooulihng(-'ling)*, n., (mil.) password; shouted order.

口蘑 *kooumor*, n., a kind of mushroom grown outside the Great Wall (口外).

口哨 *kooushauh*, n., a whistle (吹口哨).

口舌 *koousher*, n., argument; (-'*sheh*) dispute: 這事讓他知道了，又是一場口舌 if he knows it, it will cause another dispute.

口香糖 *kooushiang-tarng*, n., mint gum, chewing gum.

口涎 *kooushiarn*, n., saliva.

口信(兒) *kooushihn(-shieh'l)*, n., message or word left or orally transmitted.

口水 *kourshueei*, n., saliva.

口試 *koou-shyh*, n., oral examination.

口實 *koushyr*, n., as in 授人以口實 give people basis for gossip.

口條 *kooutiaur*, n., (coll.) pig's tongue, used as food.

口頭 *kooutour*, adj. & n., (1) oral communication, as opp. to written: 口頭的話 s. t. said orally; 口頭交(兒) nominal friend; 口頭禪 (*--charn*), n., cliché, shibboleth; 口頭語 common idiom or phr.; (2) (-'*tou*), flavor, taste (of fruit, etc.).

口才 *kooutsair*, n., eloquence: 很有口才 is very eloquent.

口外 *koou-waih*, n., outside the Great Wall.

口吻 *kourween*, n., tone of speech (rather than the words actually said) revealing state of thinking.

口味(兒) *koouweih(-weh'l)*, n., (1) flavor of food; (2) person's inclinations in taste: 合他口味 just what he likes to eat; (fig.) what agrees with one's taste (novel, political views, etc.).

口音 *koouyin*, n., pronunciation, (clear, unclear; foreign or dialect) accent: 湖北口音 Hupei accent.

口語 *koouyuu*, n., (1) vernacular speech: 文章口語化 to write as one speaks; (2) gossip.

口 40.40

weir.

[Anc. var. of 圍 41.41]

凸 40.40

tur (**guu*, **dier*).

V. i. (**guu*) To bulge, protrude: 凸出來 (of eye, belly, forehead) bulge, protrude; 凸嘴凹鼻 protruding lips and snub nose.

Adj. (*tur*) Convex, opp. of 凹 concave: 凸凹不平 rough, uneven in surface; 凸凹的 ditto; 凸紋, 凸花 raised carving or design.

凸版 *turbaan*, n., positive plate engraving.

凸出 *guuchu*, adj., bulging out.

凸鏡 *turjihng*, n., convex mirror.

凸透鏡 *turtouh-jihng*, n. convex lens.

凹 40.40

au (also **wah*, **yau*).

Adj. Concave (surface), hollow, depressed: 凸凹 convex and concave; 凹地, 凹處 *-dih*, *-chuh*↓ (related 窪 62C.11).

凹版 *aubaan*, n., a die cut with designs or characters in intaglio.

凹處 *au-chuh*, n., hollow place, depression.

凹地 *au-dih*, n., hollow ground.

凹鏡 *au-jihng*, n., a concave mirror.

凹心臉兒 **wahshinliaa'l*, n., a face hollow below the cheekbones.

凹透鏡 *autouh-jihng*, n., concave lens.

凹窰兒 **wahyaur'l*, n., a depression on a plane or surface.

呂 40.40

lyuu.

N. (1) A surname. (2) Name of a

music pitch: 律呂 the musical scale, see 律△呂 91B.10.

呂宋 *Lyuusuhng*, n., the Philippines, Manila; 呂宋烟 Manila cigar or tobacco; 呂宋草帽 Manila straw hat.

品 40.40

piin.

N. (1) Rank, grade; one of nine ranks (九品) of officials in empire days, 一品 being highest and 九品 lowest; grading of painters, writers in anc. books (詩品, 畫品). (2) Common term for article, product, quality: 物品 different products; 佳品, 劣品 good, inferior products; 產品 products; 贈品 gifts; 食品 eatables; 化粧品 cosmetics, etc. (3) Moral character: 人品 personal character; 品性, 品貌, 品學 *-shihng*[2], *-mauh*, *-shyuer* ↓.

V. t. (1) To criticize, judge, grade: 品鑑, 品評 *-jiahn*, *-pirng* ↓; 日子一長, 可以品出他的性格來 after living with a person, you find out his character. (2) To sample, taste: 品茶 (茗) drink tea critically; 品嘗 *-charng* ↓; 你品品這塊肉 try to taste this meat. (3) To play the flute: 品簫.

品嘗 *piincharng*, v.i. & t., to taste (flavor) critically.

品第 *piindih*, v.t., to judge and grade; n., grade.

品服 *piinfur*, n., formerly, official costume (marking rank).

品格 *piinger*, n., character of person: 品格高雅, 不高 high, low character (of person, painting).

品官 *piinguan*, n., formerly, official of rank.

品紅 *piinhurng*, n., a dyestuff, rosaniline chloride.

品鑑 *piinjiahn*, v.t., enjoy, examine critically (art works).

品節 *piinjier*, n., sense of honor; (AC) etiquette pertaining to rank.

品級 (秩) *piinjir* (*-jyr*), n., official rank.

品質 *piinjy*, n., quality (of product).

品藍 *piinlarn*, n. & adj., bluish purple.

品類 *piinleih*, n., variety of things; category.

品綠 *piinlyuh*, n. & adj., light green.

品貌 *piinmauh*, n., personal appearance; character and looks.

品評 *piinpirng*, v.t., criticize, evaluate: 品評人物 criticize people (not in a good sense).

品行 *piinshihng*[1], n., personal conduct: 品行端正 upright conduct.

品性 *piinshihng*[2], n., temper, individual character (peaceable, irascible, etc.).

品學 *piinshyuer*, n., personal character and scholarship: 品學兼優 good both in character and scholarship.

品胎 *piin-tai*, n., triplet babies.

品題 *piintir*, n. & v.t., comments usu. wr. on paintings, volumes; to write such comments, usu. favorable.

品脫 *piintuo*, n., (translit.) pint, a liquid measure.

品藻 *piintzaau*, v.t., evaluate art works, persons.

品味 *piinweih*[1], v.t., taste flavor; n., tasty, well-prepared food.

品位 *piinweih*[2], n., personal status.

品月 *piinyueh*, n. & adj., moonstone color, pale blue.

喦 40.40

yarn.

[Cogn. 巖]

器 40.40

chih.

[Pop. 噐]

N. (1) Vessel, utensil, ware: 器具, 器皿 *-jyuh*, *-miin* ↓; 器物, 用器 utensils, appliance; 武器, 兵器 arms, weapons; 陶器 earthenware, pottery; 瓷器 chinaware; 樂器 musical instrument; 電器 electrical appliances; 儀器 scientific apparatus. (2) Measure of a man's usefulness, talent, capability or stature: 器量, 器宇 *-liahng*, *-yuu* ↓ (oft. interch. 氣 92.70); 大器晚成 a great talent takes time to mature; 各以其器使之 (AC) use each one according to his talent; 不能成大器 cannot amount too much in life; 玉不琢, 不成器 jade requires chiselling—as man needs training and discipline.

V. t. To employ or respect (s. o.) for his talent, ability: 器重 *-juhng* ↓; 器使, 器任 to employ according to talent.

器官 *chihguan*, n., (physiol.) organ.

器重 *chihjuhng*, v. t., to regard highly, depend on (one) for his ability (for special work).

器質 *chihjyr*, n., quality and talent

器具 *chihjyuh*, n., appliances, furniture; apparatus.

器局 *chihjyur*, n., gen. ability (as manager, etc.).

器類 *chihleih*, n., quality (good, bad).

器量 *chihliahng*, n., a man's heart (big, mean).

器皿 *chihmiin*, n., kitchenware (bowls and trays, etc.), utensils.

器械 *chihshieh*, n., apparatus; military weapons; 器械體操 physical exercise with dumbbells, etc.

器識 *chihshyh*, n., a man's breath of mind and judgment.

器樂 *chihyueh*, n., instrumental music.

器宇 *chihyuu*, n., a man's stature and gen. impression (of high order.).

嚚 40.40

yirn.

Adj. (AC) (1) Argumentative, talkative: 嚚訟 ditto (related 斷 21S.22). (2) U.f. 瘖, 喑 mute, inarticulate.

囂 40.40

shiau.

Adj. Noisy, loud: 甚囂塵上 (news, rumor) makes a great noise, sensational; 囂謗 uproar or protest or criticism; 囂風 strident, contentious criticism.

囂塵 *shiauchern*, adj., tumultuous, in a turmoil; din.
囂浮 *shiaufur*, adj., blatant, superficial.
囂張 *shiaujang*, adj., blatant.
囂競 *shiaujihng*, adj., making fanfare, clamor of contention.
囂然 *shiaurarn*, adj., hungry.
囂囂 *shiaushiau*, adj., (1) (AC) like a babel of confusion; (2) (AC) detached and self-contented.

§ 40.41 (口/図)

啚 40.41

bii.

[Anc. var. of 鄙; var. of 圖]

§ 40.50 (口/ㄱ)

另 40.50

lihng.

Adj. & adv. Another, other, some other (denoting s.t. besides what is already known or discussed): 那是另一回事 that is another matter; 另日 another day; 另有他故 there must be some other reasons; 另做打算, 另打主意 make some other plans, seek some other ways; 另起爐竈 start all over again, make new plans; 另請高明 find some better person than myself (refusal); 另函 in separate letter, write separately; 另眼看待 look upon (person) with special respect, fondness.

另外 *lihngwaih*, adj. & adv., separate, separately, some other: 另有一件事 there is another matter (to be done, discussed); 另外有個愛人 have another sweetheart; 另外有事 be otherwise occupied.

号 40.50

hauh.

[Var. of 號]

罵 40.50

mah.

[Pop. form of 罵 41D.50]

鷺 40.50

luh.

鷺鷥 *luhsy*, n., (zoo.) the egret.

§ 40.63 (口/丶)

呴 40.63

shyuu.

[Var. of 煦 41.63]

§ 40.70 (口/乚)

兄 40.70

shyung.

N. (1) Elder brother. (2) Used socially somewhat like "friend," irrespective of age: 老兄 (familiar) my old friend, you: 老兄到那兒去呢 where are you going, old fellow? attached to personal name, a court. address among friends: 文德兄 (文德 being personal name); 仁兄 (LL) address in letter opening to a man like "dear so-and-so"; 學兄 court. address among fellow students; 道兄 address in letters to a scholar or person of high position; 宗兄 address to one of same clan name; 尊兄 somewhat equiv. "my esteemed friend"; 世兄 court. address to one of lower generation in friend's family (賢弟, 仁弟 usu. reserved for one's student).

兄弟 *shyungdih*, n., (1) brothers: 兄弟之國 allied states, usu. related by royal marriage; (2) (-'*di*) (a) my younger brother; (b) a younger person of same generation; (c) a usu. polite term "I (myself)": 兄弟不敢推辭 your younger brother (i.e., I) dare not decline; used also in public address meaning "I."
兄長 *shyungjaang*, n., address to older person; a senior person.
兄臺 (usu. 兄台) *shyungtair*, n., (in letters to a man, court.) you: 兄台何時來臺 when are you coming to Taiwan?

邑 40.70

yih.

N. (1) (AC) city-state. (2) Town, township: 城邑 city (esp. with regard to walls and defense).

邑人 *yihrern*, n., (LL) townspeople.
邑宰 *yihtzaai*, n., (LL) town chief or city magistrate.
邑尊 *yihtzun*, n., ditto.
邑子 *yihtzyy*, n., (AC) townspeople, see *-rern*↑.

邑 40.70

miin.

[Abbr. of 黽 42.70]

兕 40.70

syh.

N. Male rhinoceros: 兕觥 wine cup made from rhinoceros horn.

咒 40.70

jouh.

N. (1) Incantations; magic formula for exorcizing demons: 畫符念咒 (of Taoists) draw magic characters and make incantations; 咒水 magic water, i. e., plain water with Taoist-scribbled paper, served to cure stomach-ache, etc. (2) A curse, an oath.

V. i. & t. To curse: 咒人 curse a person; 咒他死 to damn a person, to curse him to death.

咒罵 *jouhmah*, v. i. & t., curse and swear (at person).
咒詛 *jouhtzuu*, v. i. & t., see *-mah* ↑.
咒願 *jouhyuahn*, n. & v. i. & t., (take) an oath, pledge.
咒語 *jouhyuu*, n., magic formula; a curse.

鼉 40.70

tuor.

N. A large reptile, also called 鼉龍.

鼉鼓 *tuorguu*, n., drum made with *tuor* hide.

§ 40.80 (口/八)

只 40.80

jyy.

Fin. part. (AC) 母也天只, 不諒人只 oh, mother! God! How is it he would not understand!

N. adjunct. (*jy) U.f. 隻 91.82, a piece: 一只戒指 a ring, etc.

Adv. An extremely commonly adv. forming many idioms: (1) Only: 只須, 只要, 只消 you only need to; 只該, 只當, 只合, 只宜 should only (the only proper way to do is); 只有 there is only; 只能, 只可 can only (let it go, etc.); 只得, 只好 the only way is (to let it go); 只因 only because; 只不過 it's only (a dog barking, etc.); 只此一次 only this once. (2) Just, simply: 只管, 只顧 go ahead without hesitation, be unconcerned with other things; 有話只管說 if you have anything to say, just say it; 只管念下去 kept reading on (although told to stop); 只想 just thinking. (3) Used like "and," without particular adverbial meaning: 他進來, 只見一人站住 he came in and saw a man standing; 只聽一聲炮響 (and) heard a gunshot.

Conj. Except, but, however: 只是 except that, but (he would not consent, etc.); 只怕 only I am afraid, I suspect; 只恐 ditto; 只怕不在家 I suspect he is not at home.

只得 *jyy'de*, adv., see Adv. 1↑.
只管 *jyrguaan*, adv., see above, Adv. 2.
只顧 *jyyguh*, adv., ditto.
只好 *jyrhaau*, phr., see Adv. 1↑.
只今 *jyyjin*, adv., now, at present.
只怕 *jyypah*, conj., see Conj.↑.
只是 *jyyshy*(-*'shy*), conj., see Conj.↑.
只有 *jyryoou*, adv., only, there is only: 只有一人在家 there is only one person at home; 只有熟客 only familiar friends; see Adv. 1↑.

員 40.80

yuarn.

[貟 in *lih* callig.]

N. Person with definite duties, member of staff (oft. complim. as 生員 for 學生, 傭員 for 傭人): 教員 teacher; 職員 staff member; 駕駛員 pilot; 海員, 船員 seaman; 打字員 typist; 委員 member of committee; 議員, 衆議員 member of parliament, congressman; 參議員 senator; 會員, 社員 society member; 團員 member of delegation; 運動員 athlete; 球員 ballplayer; 機員 mechanic; 辦事員 man in charge, clerk, etc.

員外 *yuarnwaih*, n., (1) formerly, ministry councillor; (2) formerly, address of a rich landowner, etc., somewhat like "esquire."

§ 40.81 (口/人)

吳 40.81

wur.

[Pop. 呉]

N. (1) Name of anc. *Wur* Kingdom in lower Yangtze area; esp. of *Wur* (222–277 A.D.) in the Three Kingdoms period; gen. name for *Wur* dial. in Shanghai region; 吳鹽 salt of fine quality produced in 淮 *Huair* valley; 吳牛喘月 a *Wur* cow shivering before the moon—undue fear before s.t. rarely seen. (2) A surname.

吳鉤 *wurgou*, n., a decorative hook-shaped hanging.
吳茱萸 *wurjuyur*, n., a spice plant, *Evodia rutaecarpa*.
吳儂 *wurnurng*, n., as in 吳儂軟語 the Shanghai soft dial. (esp. Soochow), known for using 儂 in place of 你 "you."
吳語 *Wur-yuu*, n., Shanghai or Soochow dial.

哭 40.81

ku.

V. i. Wail, weep aloud, cry (opp. 泣 cry silently): 大哭, 放聲大哭 weep aloud; 哭哭啼啼 weep and sniffle; 抱頭大哭 fall upon one another's shoulders and weep; 痛哭流涕 (LL) bewail; crying bitterly: 哭爹哭娘 yell inordinately; 哭鬧 cry and scream; 哭求 beg with tears; 哭笑不得 one can neither cry nor laugh, in distress or impossible situation.

哭主 *ku-juu*, n., relative of victim in a murder case.
哭喪 *kusang*, v. i., wail at funeral; 哭喪棒 stick held for support by son in funeral procession; 苦喪臉 (facet., derog.) extremely sad, unpleasant face, a mournful face.

§ 40.82 (口/乂)

嚴 40.82

yarn.

N. (1) One's own father: 家嚴 my father; 先嚴 my deceased father. (2) A surname.

Adj. (1) Strict, stern, rigid (discipline), opp. 寬 loose, lax: 嚴格, 嚴密 *-ger, -mih*↓; 戒嚴 impose curfew, martial law; 解嚴 lift curfew, martial law; 嚴師 a stern teacher. (2) Solemn: 威嚴 dignity; 嚴肅 *-suh*↓. (3) Harsh, oppressive, severe (administration): 嚴冬 harsh winter; 嚴寒 *-harn*↓; 嚴霜, 嚴刑 *-shuang, -shirng*↓.

嚴親 *yarnchin*, n., (LL) father.
嚴惡 *yarn-eh* (-'*e*), adj., harsh, severe (teacher, etc.).
嚴父 *yarnfuh*, n., (LL) father: 嚴父慈母 stern father, indulgent mother—pattern of parental love.
嚴格 *yarnger*, adj., strict (examination, etc.): 嚴格的講 strictly speaking.
嚴寒 *yarnharn*, adj., severely cold.
嚴整 *yarnjeeng*, adj., orderly, neat, well-disciplined (troops).
嚴正 *yarnjehng*, adj., impartial, unyielding.
嚴緊 *yarnjiin*, adj., rigid, carefully guarded.
嚴妝 *yarn-juang*, n., in formal attire.
嚴重 *yarnjuhng*, adj., (1) serious, grave (situation); (2) (AC) inflexible, rigid, stern.
嚴君 *yarnjyun*, n., (LL) father.
嚴苛 *yarnke*, adj., harsh (administration of law).
嚴刻 *yarnkeh*, adj., harsh, exacting.
嚴酷 *yarnkuh*, adj., cruel, unrelenting.
嚴冷 *yarnleeng*, adj., severely cold; cold in temperament.
嚴厲 *yarnlih*, adj., harsh, exacting, stern.
嚴令 *yarn-lihng*, n., strict order; v.t., strictly order.
嚴密 *yarnmih* (-'*mi*), adj., stiff (rules); carefully guarded (secret).
嚴命 *yarn-mihng*, n., (1) a stern order; (2) father's command.
嚴明 *yarnmirng*, adj., stern and impartial (administration of law).
嚴刑 *yarn-shirng*, n., harsh punishments; tortures; inflexible administration of justice.
嚴霜 *yarn-shuang*, n., severe frost, symbolic of cold temperament: 冷若嚴霜.
嚴師 *yarn-shy*, n., stern teacher, disciplinarian (traditionally in complim. sense).
嚴肅 *yarnsuh*, adj., solemn (appearance).
嚴慈 *yarn-tsyr*, n., father (嚴) and mother (慈).

§ 40.83 (口/⌒)

足 40.83

tzur (**jyuh*).

N. (1) The lower limbs, the feet: 足跟 *-gen*↓; 足迹 *-ji*↓; 足不出戶 never leave one's home (go abroad); 天足 women's feet in their natural shape (not having been bound); 失足 a *faux pas*, a serious blunder, a moral transgression, a sin; 自首至足 from head to foot; 赤足 barefooted, feet without shoes. (2) The legs

A

(of chairs, tables, etc.): 鼎足 (lit.) the legs of a tripod, (fig.) division into three parts; 三足鼎 a tripod (a vessel with three legs).

Adj. & adv. (1) Enough, full(y), sufficient(ly), ample(ly): 足夠 *-gouh* ↓; 足能 fully (cap)able; 充足 ample, sufficient; 滿足 (be) satisfied, contented; 知足 ditto; 酒足飯飽 wined and dined to satiety; 豐足 abundant, plentiful; 心滿意足 (be) fully satisfied; 足吃足喝 have enough to eat and drink; 豐衣足食 well-clad and well-fed; 足食足兵 (of a country) well-provided with food and well-protected (from external attack); 足智多謀 clever and resourceful; 足有一年 fully one year; 不一而足 too many to enumerate; 無足掛齒 not worth mentioning, don't mention it; 不足以當大事 unworthy of great responsibilities; 不足稱, 不足道 not worthy, not worth mentioning; 何足怪 no wonder that . . . why wonder? (2) (**jyuh*) (AC) excessively: 足恭 **jyuhgung* ↓.

足球 *tzurchiour*, n., football (as a game).

足赤 *tzurchyh*, n., pure gold.

足敷 *tzurfu*, v. i. & adj., be ample (enough, sufficient).

足跟 *tzurgen*, n., the heels.

足夠 *tzurgouh*, v. i. & adj., (be) sufficient, enough.

足恭 **jyuhgung*, adj., (AC) excessively polite, unnecessarily obsequious.

足迹 *tzurji*, n., (1) footprints (also 腳印兒); (2) places where one has been.

足繭 *tzurjiaan*, n., callus on feet.

足見 *tzur jiahn*, phr., it suffices to show; thus it is seen that, it is evident.

足金 *tzurjin*, n., =足赤 *-chyh* ↑.

足壯 *tzurjuahng* (-'*juang*), adj., physically strong, robust, sturdy.

足色 *tzur-seh*, adj., (of gold, silver) up to the standard purity.

足下 *tzurshiah*, pron., (LL) "you,

B

sir," term of respect oft. used in letters to friends or respected person: 足下意見如何 what is your opinion?

足心 *tzur-shin*, n., the sole of the foot.

足足 *tzur'tzu*, adv., fully (one year, a hundred ounces).

足紋 *tzur-wern*, n., =足銀 *-yirn* ↓.

足以 *tzur-yii*, adj., good enough to: 他的擧動足以做學生們的模範 his conduct is good enough to serve as a model for the students; 足以自豪 enough to make oneself proud.

足銀 *tzur-yirn*, n., silver of standard purity.

逞 40.83

cheeng.

V. t. (1) To rely upon, show overweening confidence in (force, violence, cleverness): 逞凶, 逞強, 逞蠻 *-shyung*, *-chiarng*, *-marn* ↓. (2) To brag, show off, give free play to (ability, skill, courage): 逞能, 逞才 *-nerng*, *-tsair* ↓. (3) To follow (desires, wishes) without restraint: 逞願 *-yuahn* ↓; 志不得逞 have one's wish or ambition frustrated; 逞性 *-shihng* ↓; 不逞之徒 the frustrated, unemployed people. (4) To put up a false front: 逞著面子.

逞強 *cheeng-chiarng*, v. i., to strut about; rely on superior brute force.

逞志 *cheeng-jyh*, v. i., succeed in having one's way.

逞蠻 *cheeng-marn*, v. i., see *-chiarng* ↑.

逞能 *cherng-nerng*, v. i., rely on one's cleverness.

逞性 *cheeng-shihng*, v. i., act recklessly.

逞心 *cheeng-shin*, v. i., do as one wishes and incautiously.

逞凶 *cheeng-shyung*, v. i., see

C

-chiarng ↑.

逞才 *cheeng-tsair*, v.i., to act in undue confidence of one's own ability.

逞願 *cheeng-yuahn*, v. i., to have one's wish fulfilled.

逞勇 *cheeng-yuung*, v. i., be reckless.

§ 40.93 (口/く)

虽 40.93

suei.

[Pop. of 雖 40S.11]

SECTION 40A

§ 40A.00 (口/丿)

叮 40A.00-1

'da.

Excl. *(dah-dy-rrr)* Sound made to urge donkey forward.

喇 40A.00-1

laa.

Adv. A term used in describing sounds: 嘩喇 (-*'la*) descriptive of thumping or crashing noise.

喇叭 *laa'ba*, n., a trumpet; 喇叭管 n., (physiol.) oviduct, Fallopian tube (also 輸卵管); 伸縮喇叭 trombone; 喇叭蟲 --*churng*, n., (zoo.) stentor; 喇叭花 --*hua*, n., (bot.) morning-glory (also 牽牛花); 喇叭口 --*koou*, n., mouth-piece of a trumpet; anything with a wide opening at its end: 喇叭袖, 喇叭褲 sleeves, trousers, broad at the end; bell-shaped pants.

喇喇 *lar'la*, v. i., drip; adj., dripping.

喇嘛 *laa'ma*, n., (Tibetan Budd.) Lama; 喇嘛教 Lamaism.

囀 40A.00-1

juaan.

N. & v. i. Bird song, its trilling melody; (fig.) 囀喉 trilling; to trill.

哮 40A.00-1

shiau.

V. i. (1) (Of lion) to roar; to yell: 咆哮 to roar (as lions), to scream (as scolding woman); 哮吼 yell and scream. (2) To cough: see 哮喘 -*chuaan* ↓.

哮喘 *shiauchuaan*, n. & v. i., (med.) asthma, to cough and gasp for breath.

嚇 40A.00-1

heh (sp. pr. **shiah*).

V. t. (1) To frighten, scare (s. o.): 嚇殺, 嚇死 frighten to death. (2) (**shiah*) Be frightened: 嚇了一跳 get a fright. (3) To threaten, intimidate.

嚇嚇 *hehheh*, adj., ha! ha! (descriptive of laughter).

嚇唬 **shiah'hu*, v. t., to give (person) a scare, intimidate.

嚇殺 *heh-sha*, v. t., frighten to death.

嚇阻 *hehtzuu*, v. t., to stop (s. o.) by threat, to shout (at s. o.) to stop.

嘑 40A.00-2

huh.

嘑爾 *huh-eel*, adv., with a shout: 嘑爾而與之 (AC) give s.t. to s.o. with a yell of contempt.

叮 40A.00-3

ding.

V.t. (1) Bite by insect: 被蚊子叮了一下 get a bite by a mosquito. (2) To question or instruct repeatedly: 叮問 see compp. ↓.

叮噹 *ding-dang*, adj., tinkling.

叮囑 *dingjuu*, v. i., give repeated advice on departure.

叮嚀 *dinglirng*, v. i. & adv., give advice repeatedly: 叮嚀吩咐.

吁 40A.00-3

shyu.

Excl. Ah! (a sigh): 吁! 是何言歟 (AC) my, what kind of talk is this?

V. i. To sigh: 長吁短歎 sigh and groan.

Adv. 喘吁吁 pant for breath.

呵 40A.00-3

he (**o*).

V. i. & t. (1) To scold, shout: 呵責 -*tzer* ↓; 呵禁 to forbid, to cry "stop" as by guards. (2) To warm (benumbed hands, etc.) by blowing breath: 呵手 to blow on hand; 呵凍 blow off the chill. (3) 呵呵大笑 to roar with laughter (LL) for vern. 哈哈大笑 40A.40.

Excl. (**oh*) Ah! oh!: 呵, 我忘記了 oh, I forgot! (cf. wr. 啊 pr. *ah*).

呵欠 *hechiahn*, v.i., as in 打呵欠 to yawn.

呵叱 *hechyh*[1], v. i., to shout (at servants) angrily.

呵斥 *hechyh*[2], v. t., to reprimand

呵導 *he-dauh*, v. i., (formerly, of escorts, guards) to shout at passengers to open way for coming official, hence 呵殿 (呵 lead in front and 殿 bring up the rear).

呵喝 *he-heh*, v. i. & t., to shout, yell at (servants, etc.).

A

呵護 *hehuh*, v. t., see 訶^Δ護 60A.00.
呵責 *hetzer*, v. t., see *-chyh*² ↑.

咧 40A.00-3

lie (**liee*, **lier*).

V. i. (**liee*) To crack open at one end: 咧嘴 open mouth slyly and barely; 咧開 crack from one side.

咧咧 (1) *lie'lie*, v. i., (of children) blubber; (2) **lier'lie* or *lie-* 罵罵咧咧 chatter.
咧子 *lietz*, (1) n. & v.t., as in 罵咧子, 拽咧子 to criticise s. o. behind his back; (2) v.t., to criticize: 咧子他兩句 said a word or two unfavorable about him.

啊 40A.00-3

a (also *wo*).

Fin. part. Used at end of phrase or sentence, addressing s.o.: 兒啊, 我的兒啊 son, O my son! calling s. o. to do s.t.: 來啊 come! 走啊 let's go! 上車啊 (get) on board! or merely prolonging an assertion: 是啊 it's right, I say; 很不錯啊 it's not half bad, you know; (sometimes wr. 阿).

Excl. Used in exclamations with varying, indeterminate accent, like Eng. "Oh!" "ah!" "aha!" cf. similar excl. under 阿 *a*, *ar*, *aa*, *ah*; 喔 *o*; 哦 *or*; 噢 *oo*; 欸 *ei*; 欸 *eei*; 誒 *eih*; 哎, 嗳 *ai*, *aai*, *aih*! 恩 *en*!

啊哈 *aha*, excl., aha!
啊呀 *aya*, excl., alas oh, my!
啊唷 *ayo*, excl., oh, my!—a groan of pain; an excl. expressing surprise, admiration, oft. mixed

B

with irony.

呀 40A.00-5

ya (**shia*).

Fin. part. Used in emphasis: 是呀 it is true!

Adj. (1) Descriptive of creaking sounds: 咿呀 *yiya*; 嘔呀 *ouya* to make inarticulate noises; also of children's baby talk; of sudden noise: 呀的一聲門開了 the door squeaks open. (2) (**shia*) (MC) descriptive of open mouth, gate.

Excl. Ah! (surprise, alarm); 哎呀 or 嗳呀 *aih'ya*, (where *y* slips in on account of preceding final *i*) oh, my!

嚂 40A.00-5

larn.

嚂哰 *larnlaur*, adj., (of speech) rambling and incoherent, unintelligible.

哼 40A.00-6

heng (also *hm*!).

V. i. (1) To hum: 哼幾句 hum a few lines (of song). (2) 哼哼哈哈的 "Yes, sir" type of person. (3) 哼哼唧唧 to mumble, whisper, make inaudible sounds.

Excl. Indicating exasperation, a grunt or a growl: 哼! 你也配嗎 Tut! do you think you are qualified?

C

啍 40A.00-6

tun.

啍啍 *tuntun*, adj. & adv., repeatedly, sincerely (giving advice); (AC) rumble (of big carts, 大車啍啍).

嚀 40A.00-6

nirng.

V. i. & adv. See 叮^Δ嚀 40A.00↑.

喻 40A.00-8

yuh.

[Usu. printed 喩 40A.93]

N. (1) A surname. (2) Example, analogy: 譬喻, 比喻 for example, also a parable.

V. i. & t. (1) To explain, expound, persuade: 曉喻民衆 explain to the public; 喻以利害 explain the consequences of action; 勸喻 to explain and allay fear or anger; 不可以理喻 (s. t.) cannot be explained by reason, (person) not open to reason. (2) To understand: 不言而喻 it goes without saying.

呼 40A.00-9

hu.

N. A surname.

V. i. & t. (1) To exhale: 呼吸 *-shi* ↓; 呼出一口氣 exhale a breath. (2) To call (person): 呼名 call one by name or one is called; 稱呼 proper address to a person; 呼喚 *-huahn*

亅	小	⺊	十	土	ナ	卄	𠃊	丨	一	丅	㇇	口	図	冈	㇆	厂	尸	亠	广	宀	丶	乚	七	心	八	人	乂	乛	一	丿	𠂉	く
00	01	02	10	11	12	20	21	22	30	31	32	40	41	42	50	51	52	60	61	62	63	70	71	72	80	81	82	83	90	91	92	93

↓; 呼醫生 call for a doctor; 呼天叫地 call to heaven and earth, to scream; 呼風喚雨 (Taoist magic) call for wind or rain; 呼牛呼馬 if a person calls me a cow, then I am a cow; if he calls me a horse, then let me be a horse, let people call me what they will ("a cow" or "a horse")—disregard hostile opinion; 呼鈴 ring the bell to call servants or attendants; see 招^A^呼 10A.40. (3) To yell, scream, cry out: 呼喊, 呼叫, 呼號 *-haan, -jiauh, -haur* ↓; 登高一呼 (a leader) makes a public appeal, calls for the people to do s. t.; 呼口號 give password or shout slogans; 歡呼 shout for joy; 三呼萬歲 call "*Banzai*" (Long live. . . .) thrice; 呼求 cry for help; 呼救, 呼苦 "Help! help!", cry "pain"; 呼爺喊娘 cry in pain "for papa, mamma"; 呼門 call for opening the door; 呼天搶地 cry to heaven; 呼盧喝雉 (at dice) shout for top number to come up; 呼么喝六 ditto, also to shout at people right and left; 呼喝 *-heh* ↓.

呼 叱 *huchah*, v. i. & t., to shout at (people).

呼 喊 *huhaan*, v. i., to cry in distress, to shout, to howl.

呼 號 *huhaur*, (1) v.i., to wail aloud; (2) n., (*-hauh*) a call signal (as at aloud; broadcast).

呼 喝 *huheh*, v. t., to bawl at, shout at.

呼 呼 *huhu*, v. i., make sound of respiration in sleep; (of winds) whistle.

呼 喚 *huhuahn*, v. t., to call (servants).

呼 叫 *hujiauh*, v. i., cry out (for help).

呼 救 *hujiouh*, v. i., to cry for help: 呼救無門 nowhere to turn for help.

呼 搧 *hu'shan*, v. i. & t., (1) to stir and make loose, as tucked-in blanket in winter; (2) shake (like creaking floor).

呼 聲 *hu-sheng*, n., (1) noise of shouting; (2) 呼聲甚高 (during election) great popular demand for a person to be elected, be favored to win.

呼 吸 *hushi*, n. & v. i., respiration; inhale and exhale; 呼吸器 organs of respiration.

呼 嘯 *hushiauh*, v. i., (crowd) roar and shout, (wind, storm) whistle.

呼 圖 克 圖 *Huturkehtur*, n., the Mongolian Living Buddha.

呼 延 *Huyarn*, n., a double surname.

呼 應 *huhyihng*, v. i. & t., to act in cooperation, to respond as echo to sound: 此呼彼應, 互相呼應 take concerted action.

呼 冤 *huyuan*, v. i., to cry one has been wronged, to call for justice.

呼 籲 *huyuh*, v. i. & t., to appeal for, plead for (unity, etc.).

嚼 40A.00-9

jyuer (sp. pr. *jiaur*; **jiauh*).

V.i. & t. (1) Chew: 嚼啐 masticate; 細嚼慢嚥 take one's time in eating; 咀嚼 (of food) chew carefully, (fig.) ponder over what one is reading; 味同嚼蠟 tasteless like chewing a candle. (2) Erode: 水嚼沙洲樹出根 (LL) the soil being eroded by water, tree roots lay exposed. (3) (**jiaur*) V.i., prattle, prate, talk tediously: 嚼蛆 *-chyu*, 嚼舌 *-sher*, 嚼舌根 *-shergen* ↓. (5) (**jiauh*) V.i., 反嚼 (of certain animals) chew the cud.

嚼 蛆 **jiaurchyu*, v.i., (abuse) to talk nonsense, talk rot.

嚼 裹 兒 **jiaur'guo'l*, n., (coll.) food and clothing.

嚼 舌 **jiaursher*, v.i., to gossip: 嚼舌根 *--gen*; (a) to gossip; (b) tell lies, spread rumors.

嚼 子 **jiaurtz*, n., a horse's bit.

嚼 用 **jiauryuhng*, n., (coll.) a family's daily expenses.

咐 40A.00-9

fuh.

V.t. Instruct: 吩^A^咐 40A.50, command, order; 囑咐 give instructions (to do s.t.).

嘚 40A.00-9

de.

嘚 啵 *de'bo*, v.i., (MC) bicker, jabber.

§ 40A.01 (口/小)

味 40A.01-1

weih.

N. adjunct. 一味藥 one medicine or prescription.

N. (1) Flavor, taste, smell: 香味, 臭味 good, bad smell; 五味 sweet, sour, bitter, hot and salty; 滋味, 美味 good taste in food; 味同嚼蠟 tastes like chewing candle—completely flat; 知味 a gourmet's sense; 意味 *yih-*, n. & v. i., meaning; to imply, to give the feeling (of disapproval, etc.). (2) Food, delicacy: 美味 delicacy; 海味 sea food; 臘味 sausages, preserved meat. (3) Interest: 趣味 interest; 有趣味 interesting; 興味 mood for enjoyment; 無味 tasteless, flat, dull. (4) Tone, mood: 情味 tone of love; 韻味 poetic tone; 禪味 meditative state of mind.

V.t. To sample flavor: 玩味 slowly appreciate (poetic thought, meaning of a line); 體味 to appreciate, comprehend.

味 氣 *weih-chi*, n., smell (also 氣味).

味 道 *weihdauh*, n., taste of food; fun, interest, excitement (in reading, drama, conversation, etc.): 有味道 is interesting.

味官 *weih-guan*, n., sense of smell.

味精 *weihjing*, n., sodium glutamate.

味覺 *weihjyuer*, n., see *-guan* ↑.

味兒 *weh'l*, n., ditto; 味兒事 something trivial.

嗦 40A.01-1

suo.

V.t. (1) To suck (thumb, etc.). (2) See 囉ᐞ嗦 40A.11.

嗉 40A.01-1

suh.

N. (1) (*-tz*) The crop of a bird: 嗉囊 ditto. (2) (Sl.) a wine pot.

噤 40A.01-1

jihn.

V.i. Remain silent, be speechless: 噤口 shut one's mouth; 噤聲 silence! 噤若寒蟬 maintain a discreet silence.

嘹 40A.01-1

liaur.

Adj. (Sound of bird cries, singing) clear and round, sonorous.

嘹喨 *liaurliahng*, adj., (person's voice) clear, resonant.

嚇 40A.01-2

su.

V.i. See 嚕ᐞ嚇 40A.41.

喋 40A.01-2

dier.

V.i. & t. Twitter, chatter, see compp. ↓ ; to bleed 喋血.

喋喋 *dierdier*, v.i., chirp, chatter: 喋喋不休 chatter without stop.

喋囁 *diernieh*, v.i., twitter, chirrup.

咪 40A.01-2

mi.

V.i. Cat's call, meow.

Adv. 笑咪咪 with a big, full smile; 小咪咪 teeny-weeny.

嘌 40A.01-3

piau.

Adj. (AC) passing swiftly.

嘌唱 *piauchahng*, n., (MC) popular ditties.

嘌嘌 *piaupiau*, adj., (AC) rolling along swiftly (of carriage).

嗓 40A.01-3

saang.

N. The throat, the larynx: 嗓子 *-tz*; 嗓門兒 *-mer'l*; 嗓兒 *-'l* ↓.

嗓兒 *saang'l*, n., (1) the throat; (2) voice, quality of voice in singer: 調嗓兒 (Chin. opera) voice practice, usu. in open spaces in the early morning; see *-tz* ↓.

嗓門兒 *saangmer'l*, n., the larynx; one's voice.

嗓子 *saangtz*, n., condition of throat, quality of voice in singer.

嗓音 *saangyin*, n., the human voice.

噪 40A.01-4

tzauh.

V.i. (1) Make noise: 噪聒 *-gua* ↓ ; 鼓噪 make a row, uproar, clamor. (2) (Of birds) to chirp noisily: 鵲噪, 蟬噪 chirping of birds, cicadas.

噪聒 *tzauhgua*, (1) v.i., make loud, confused noise; (2) adj., irritatingly noisy.

噪音 *tzauhyin*, n., disturbing noise, din (as of car horns).

嘛 40A.01-6

mar ('ma).

N. See 喇ᐞ嘛 40A.00, lama.

咻 40A.01-9

shiou.

N. & adj. Sound of respiration, hushing.

咻 囔 噱 噥 啄 喂 哏 嚎 嚷 咏 喙 叶 吽

V. t. (1) To hush (a baby), "hushaby"; to comfort s.o. in pain. (2) To brawl, make a disturbing noise: 咻咻 ditto.

§40A.02 (口/ㄎ)

囔 40A.02-1

'nang.

V.i. 嘟囔 *du'nang*, mumble to oneself.

噱 40A.02-2

jyuer (**shyue*).

V.i. Laugh aloud: 發噱 break into a loud laugh; 噱 (**shyue*) 頭 (Shanghai dial.) trickery, deception, gimmick: 耍噱頭 play tricks; 擺噱頭 put on false pretenses; 沒啥噱頭 (shanghai) be at the end of one's tether.

噥 40A.02-2

nurng.

Adj. Garrulous: 噥噥, 咕噥 talking in a low tone.

啄 40A.02-3

juor.

[Dist. 喙↓]

V.i. & t. (Of birds, fowl) to peck: 啄食 peck at food; 啄毛 preen feathers; 剝啄 to rap at door, make pecking, chopping sound.

啄啄 *juorjuor*, n., pecking sound; rap-tap.

啄木鳥 *juormuh-niaau*, n., the woodpecker.

喂 40A.02-4

weih.

V.t. To feed (interch. 餵 81B.02).

Excl. Hey! (used to call attention).

哏 40A.02-5

gern.

N. Jokes, joking: 逗哏, 抓哏 make fun with jokes.

Adj. Cute (of children): 孩子長得眞哏 or 哏氣.

嚎 40A.02-6

haur.

V.i. To yell, scream.

嚎啕 *haurtaur*, v.i., to wail aloud (also wr. 嚎咷, 嗥咷, 號啕).

嚷 40A.02-6

raang (also *rang*).

V.i. To shout, yell: 喧嚷 to clamor, make a row; 嚷鬧 to quarrel; 嚷罵 to scold, upbraid, rail at; 吵嚷 to shout at the top of one's voice; 嚷叫 to bellow, howl; 高聲嚷 to roar, yell out; 嚷嚷 to bawl; 別嚷 don't make such a noise, quiet please!

咏 40A.02-6

yuung.

[Anc. var. 詠]

V.i. & t. To sing, hum, chant: 吟咏, 歌咏 to sing, hum (a tune), sing praises of; 咏懷 to express heart feelings by verse or song; 咏史 versify on historic events; 咏歎 hum a regret.

喙 40A.02-9

hueih.

N. (LL) mouth, esp., a bird's beak: 百喙莫辯 even a hundred mouths cannot absolve guilt.

§40A.10 (口/十)

叶 40A.10-1

shier.

[Anc. var. of 協 10S.50]

V.i. 叶韻 formerly, a way of changing pronunciation of words in classic poetry which no longer rhyme in order that they could rhyme.

吽 40A.10-1

hung.

Sanskr. "hum," a word used in Buddhist mystic spell; (cf. 唵 "om," 40A.70).

唪 40A.10–1

feeng.

V. i. (Budd.) to incant text: 唪經, 唪誦經文 read or incant Buddhist text.

叫 40A.10–2

jiauh.

V.i. & t. (1) V.i., (of persons, animals, birds) to cry: 叫喚, 叫喊, 呼叫 to shout, yell, cry; 哭叫 weep and cry; 叫救命 call for help; 大叫三聲 utter shrill cries; 鳥叫 chirp, chirrup, twitter, warble; 鷄叫 the crowing of a cock; 狗叫 to bark. (2) V.t., hail, greet, call, address: 叫他老師 call him teacher; 叫聲老伯 greet person as uncle. (3) To summon, send for, order, hire: 叫局 *-jyur*, 叫條子 *-tiaurtz*↓; 叫車 hire a car; 叫菜 to order food.

叫吃 *jiauhchy*, phr., (chess) call to indicate a checkmate.

叫屈 *jiauhchyu*, v.i., complain of unfair treatment, discrimination or undeserved punishment.

叫哥哥 *jiauhge'ge*, n., a singing grasshopper.

叫聒 *jiauhgua*, adj., (of noise) loud and confused.

叫好 *jiauh-haau*, v.i., (Peking opera) applaud an actor's acting or singing ("shout 'bravo!").

叫號 *jiauhhauh*, v.i., to call out the numbers (of waiting cars, winning tickets, etc.).

叫橫 *jiauhhehng*, v.i., to use strong words, speak tough language.

叫喚 *jiauh'huan*, v.i., to yell, shout, call out.

叫花子 *jiauhhuatz*, n., a beggar (also wr. 化子).

叫陣 *jiauhjehn*, v.i., to challenge an opponent to a fight.

叫街的 *jiauhjie'de*, n., a beggar roving the streets and crying for pity.

叫局 *jiauhjyur*, v.i., formerly, send for a singsong girl to come and wait on table.

叫渴 *jiauh-kee*, v.i., be thirsty, to thirst for water.

叫苦 *jiauhkuu*, v.i., complain of hard lot, grunt, grumble: 叫苦連天 incessant grumbling (of one's hard lot).

叫驢 *jiauhlyur*, n., a male donkey.

叫賣 *jiauhmaih*, v.i., to cry goods for sale.

叫囂 *jiauhshiau*, v.i. & adj., raise a hue and cry; clamor, -ous.

叫水 *jiauh-shueei*, v.i., be thirsty, to thirst for water.

叫條子 *jiauhtiaurtz*, v.i., see *-jyur*↑.

叫子 *jiauhtz*, n., a whistle of wood or brass.

叫做 *jiauh-tzuoh*[1], v.t., (p.p.) called: 孔子叫做至聖先師 Confucius is called the greatest sage and teacher.

叫座(兒) *jiauh-tzuoh*[2]*('l)*, v.i., (of actors or actresses) draw capacity audiences, have good box office.

叫字號 *jiauh-tzyh'hau*, phr., (1) (of business firms) winning goodwill through superior quality of goods; (2) (of persons) earning popular respect for one's exemplary conduct.

嘩 40A.10–2

huar.

V.i. Create a lot of noise (also wr. 譁).

嘩喇 *huar'la*, (1) v.i., as in 嘩喇了 has crashed down; (2) adj., descriptive of crashing sound; also 嘩喇喇.

囁 40A.10–3

nieh.

V. i. Move the lips in speaking.

囁嚅 *niehrur*, v. i., hem and haw.

嗶 40A.10–4

bih.

嗶嘰 *bihji*, n., transliteration of English "beige," soft wool fabric.

啐 40A.10–6

tsueih.

V. i. & t. To spit; to spit upon (person): 啐他一口 spat upon him; to make a sound of disapproval, like "tut! tut!"

啤 40A.10–9

pir.

N. Beer: 啤酒.

嗥 40A.10–9

haur.

V. i. To cry, esp. of dogs, wolves: 嗥陶大哭 to bawl, wail aloud.

亅	小	卜	十	土	ナ	卄	㇄ト	丨	一	丅	フ	口	囗	冂	㇕	厂	尸	亠	广	宀	丶	乚	弋	心	八	人	乂	一	㇀	刂	𠂉	く
00	01	02	10	11	12	20	21	22	30	31	32	40	41	42	50	51	52	60	61	62	63	70	71	72	80	81	82	83	90	91	92	93

§ 40A.11 (口/土)

吐 40A.11–1

tuu (**tuh*).

V.i. & t. (1) To spit out: 把他的唾沫吐在他臉上 spit in his face; 吐口水 spit; 吐舌頭 stick out tongue, gesture of surprise; 吐氣 *-chih*↓; 蠶吐絲 silkworm spins out silk; 吐剛茹柔 (AC) avoid the strong and bully the weak; 吐哺握髮 (AC allu. to 周公) stopped a mouthful in the middle of eating and bound up his hair in the midst of a bath in order to see visitors. (2) Speak out from the heart, esp. 吐露 *-luh*↓: 吐實 confess the truth; 不吐不快 have to get it out of one's chest. (3) Adopt a style of conversation: 談吐; 談吐高雅 have a refined style of conversation, see also 吐屬 *-shuu*↓. (4) (**tuh*) Throw up, vomit: 嘔吐 ditto; 他吐了, 吐出來 vomit s.t.; 吐血, 吐瀉 *-shiee*, *-shieh*↓. (5) (**tuh*) Cough up illegal gains: 他贏的錢全部吐還 cough up all his profits.

吐氣 *tuu-chih*, v.i., heave a sigh of satisfaction: 揚眉吐氣 appear very proud and self-satisfied.
吐蕃 *Tuhfan* n., place name in Tibet (also wr. 番 pr. *tuhbo*).
吐谷渾 *Tuhguuhurn*, n., tribe in Chinese Turkestan.
吐劑 **tuh-jih*, n., (med.) emetic.
吐露 **tuh-luh*, v.t., reveal from the heart: 吐露實情 (心腹) reveal one's true feelings.
吐沫 **tuh'mo*, v.i., spit out saliva (also wr. 唾沫).
吐納 **tuhnah*, v.i., from 吐故納新 Taoist art of controlled breathing and swallowing of saliva toward achieving long life.
吐血 **tuhshiee*, v.i., throw up blood.
吐瀉 **tuhshieh*, n. & v.i., suffer from vomiting and diarrhoea; cholera.
吐綬鷄 *tuushouh-ji*, n., rare litr. name for turkey (=火鷄).
吐屬 *turshuu*, n., style and manner of conversation.
吐痰 *tuu-tarn*, v.i., spit (saliva or phlegm).

哇 40A.11–1

wa.

V. t. To throw up, vomit.

Adj. Descriptive of baby cries: 哇哇 *-wa*↓; 哇的一聲 cry aloud; 淫哇之聲 sentimental crooning.

Excl. (Excl. of surprise) wow: 哇呀, 這麽多 wow, so much!

哇哇 *wawa*, v.i., to bellow, make a crying noise.

咥 40A.11–3

shih (**dier*).

V.i. & t. (1) To roar in laughter. (2) (**dier*) To bite.

囉 40A.11–4

luor (*'*luo*).

Fin. part. (**luo*) A slightly argumentative final particle: 你不聽我的話, 聽他的囉 you do not listen to me, but to him; 有的看囉 wait and see, something is coming up.

N. See 嘍^Δ^囉 40A.93.

囉唆 *luo'suo*, adj., (1) garrulous, talkative; (2) bothersome (also wr. 囉嗦, same word as 嚕囌): 囉哩囉唆 *luorliiluo'suo*; 囉囉唆唆 *luorluor'suosuo*, ditto.
囉唣 *luortzauh*, v.i., twaddle, noisy useless talk.

哩 40A.11–4

li.

Fin. part. Emphasizing assertion: 那哩! 那哩! no, no, not at all! 謝謝您, 我手裏還有哩 thank you, sir, I *still* have some with me; 他還沒有來哩 he *hasn't* come yet.

N. A mile (dist. 公里 kilometer).

哩嚕 *lilu*, v. i., to mumble; also 哩哩囉囉 *lililolo*, v. i., to mumble away, talk endlessly.

嘿 40A.11–4

moh (**me*, unaccented).

Adv. 嘿嘿 silently=默默.

Fin. part. (*'*me*) (MC) particle reinforcing statement (weak form of 麽): 我是爛熟的嘿 I am quite acquainted with it indeed.

喔 40A.11–5

woh (**wu*, **o*).

Adv. (Also **wu*) descriptive of crying, esp. 喔喔 *-wu*↓.

Excl. (Excl. of disgust) ough!

喔嚄 **o-huoh*, excl., o-ho! (seeing a mishap).
喔喔 **wuwu*, adv., descriptive of crying, esp. cock-a-doodle-do.
喔呀 **o-ya*, excl., oh, my! (excl. seeing mishap, disaster).
喔唷 **o-yo*, excl., cry of pain or disapproval, mockery.

唾 40A.11-9

tuoh.

N. Saliva, spittle, see compp. ↓.

V.i. & t. To spit: 唾人 spit on person; 唾面自乾 to be spat on the face and let dry without wiping—extreme obsequiousness.

唾棄 *tuohchih*, v.t., to spurn with contempt.
唾壺 *tuohhur*, n., spittoon.
唾罵 *tuohmah*, v.t., excoriate, abuse, rebuke coarsely (person).
唾沫 *tuoh'mo* (*tuh'mo*), n., spittle.
唾腺 *tuohshiahn*, n., salivary gland.
唾手 *tuoh-shoou*, adj., as in 唾手可得 (accomplish) with extreme ease.
唾液 *tuohyeh*, n., saliva.

唯 40A.11-9

weir (**weei*).

V. i. (**weei*) To say "yes": 唯唯 yes, yes; 唯唯否否 say "yes" or "no"—change answer unpredictably; 唯諾 to promise; 唯唯諾諾 to say "yes, yes" repeatedly.

Adv. & prep. Only (interch. 惟 22A.11); 唯一 *-yi*, ditto; see 惟△一 and other compp. under 惟 22A.11.

喤 40A.11-9

huarng.

N. (AC) sound of child booing; resounding sound of music.

§ 40A.20 (口/廿)

呺 40A.20-3

luhng (**'nou*).

V. i. (Birds) sing.

Fin. part. (**'nou*) Used like 哪 at the end of a soft, intimate sentence: 令小弟佩服得很呺 I am utterly charmed, overwhelmed.

唵 40A.20-8

arn.

V.i. To mumble.

唵默 *arnmoh*, v.i., as in (LL) 唵默唯唯 mumble "yes, yes."
唵囈 *arnyih*, v.i., mumble incoherently, as in sleep.

§ 40A.21 (口/乚)

囓 40A.21-1

nieh.
[Var. of 齧 10.21]

咄 40A.21-2

duoh.

Excl. Tut! tut!

咄咄 *duohduoh*, excl., tut! tut! 咄咄怪事 phr., what a strange situation!
咄嗟 *duohjie*, adv., in a short moment (quick as blowing a breath): 咄嗟立辦 can be done at once.

咂 40A.21-2

tza.

V. t. (1) To lick up with the tongue (as cat licks up milk). (2) Suck: 咂乾 suck dry.

咂兒 *tza'l*, n., pop. name for the teat.
咂模 *tza'mo*, v. t., meditate on, ponder, think over.
咂嘴(兒) *tza tzueei*(*-tzue'l*), v. i., to click one's teeth in admiration.

嘔 40A.21-2

oou (**ou*, **ouh*).
[Abbr. 呕]

V. i. & t. (1) (Also **ou*) to vomit; (fig.) to strain, give of one's blood: 嘔血, 嘔心 *-shyueh*, *-shin* ↓. (2) (**ouh*) To enrage, rouse one's spleen: 嘔氣 *-chih* ↓.

嘔氣 *oouchih*, v.i., to feel enraged, to carry on a fight with s.o. out of spite or vanity: 和人嘔氣.
嘔泄 *ooushieh*, n., (Chin. med.) vomiting and diarrhoea.
嘔心 *oou-shin*, v. i., strain one's heart and mind (to write poems).
嘔血 *oou-shyueh*, v.i., to throw up blood.
嘔吐 **outuh*, v. i., to vomit.
嘔啞(鴉) **ouya*, n., (sound of) creaking, swishing of oars, twitter of birds, and similar sounds.
嘔軋 **ouyah*, n., see *-ya* ↑.

唔 哈 嘟 嘶 呻 嘯 啡 吓 呷 叩 哪 啼

唔 40A.21-9

shah.

[Interch. 歃 90S.81]

哈 40A.21-9

dahn.

[Var. of 啖 40A.81]

§ 40A.22 (口/丨)

嘟 40A.22-1

du.

嘟勒兒 *du'le'l*, v.i., to trill the tongue: 打嘟勒兒.

嘟嚕 *du'lu*, (1) n., 一嘟嚕葡萄 a cluster of grapes; (2) v. i., see *-'nang* ↓.

嘟囔 *du'nang*, v. i., mumble in whispers, mutter to oneself; also 嘟囔嘟囔 *du'nang du'nang*, or 嘟嘟囔囔 *du'du nang'nang*.

嘟噥 *du'nung*, v.i., see *-'nang* ↑.

嘶 40A.22-2

sy.

V. i. (Horses) neigh.

Adj. & adv. Split (voice): 聲嘶 hoarse, split voice.

呻 40A.22-2

shen.

V. i. (1) To groan. (2) To recite (poetry) with intonation.

呻呼 *shenhu*, v. i., to groan for pain.

呻喚 *shenhuahn*, v. i., to yell for s.o.

呻吟 *shenyirn*, v. i., (1) to recite (writing); (2) to groan in pain; to moan.

嘯 40A.22-2

shiauh.

V. i. To whistle, make a birdcall or signal call, make a shrill cry: 呼嘯, 嘯聚 (of gangsters, rebels) call each other and form a gang; 仰天長嘯 make a long wheezing noise in open air; 虎嘯 to roar like tigers; 海嘯 tidal waves; 怒嘯 shriek; 嘯詠, 歌嘯 sing aloud; 嘯諾 to hem and haw in office.

啡 40A.22-2

fei.

N. See 咖△啡 40A.40; 嗎△啡 40A.-50.

吓 40A.22-3

shiah.

[Var. of 嚇 40A.00]

呷 40A.22-4

shiar.

V. i. To quaff, swallow (liquid): 呷了一口酒 take a swallow of wine.

叩 40A.22-5

kouh.

V.i. & t. (1) To knock: 叩門 knock at door; 叩閽 formerly, to knock at palace gate and lodge complaint; see also 扣 10A.40. (2) To ask: 叩其姓名 ask his name; 叩安(＝問安) send greetings. (3) To kotow, knock head on floor as ceremony (often fig., not lit.): 叩頭 *-tour* ↓; 叩首 kotow; 叩拜, 叩稟 (in letters to superiors) I bow in salute; 叩謁, 叩見 pay respects, pay visit; 叩求 to request humbly; 叩辭 to decline politely; 叩謝 to thank or decline politely.

叩頭 *kouhtour*, v. i., to kotow, ceremoniously knock head on floor; (fig.) to request, to thank: 我給你叩頭 I thank you; 叩頭蟲 an insect, *Melanotus legatus*.

叩問 *kouh-wehn*, v. t., to ask, to question politely.

哪 40A.22-5

naa.

Adj. Which: 哪一箇 which one? 哪箇人 which man? (oft. wr. simply as 那); 哪裏＝那裏.

啼 40A.22-6

tir.

[Anc. var. 嗁]

V. i. (1) Whimper, blubber, make weak crying sounds: 啼哭 *-ku* ↓; 啼笑 tears and laughter. (2) Crow, twitter: 鳥啼 birds twitter; 雞啼 cocks crow.

啼泣 *tirchih*, v. i., cry weakly, wail or sob.

啼叫 *tirjiauh*, v. i., scream, screech, wail.

啼哭 *tirku*, v. i., cry: 啼啼哭哭 weep and wail.

啷 40A.22-6

lang.

Adj. 啷噹 a jingling sound.

啷噹(兒) *langdang('l)*, n., an assortment of odds and ends; 吊兒啷噹 utterly carefree (suggesting "the hell with it").

嗛 40A.22-8

*chian (*chiaan, *chiahn, *shiarn).*

N. (**chiaan*) See 頰ᐞ嗛 12S.81.

V. t. (**shiarn*) (1) Dislike (var. of 嫌). (2) To keep in cheek (var. of 銜, 含).

Adj. (1) (*chian*) Humble, modest (var. of 謙). (2) (**chiaan*) 嗛嗛 small, unsatisfying. (3) (**chiahn*) Guilty, ashamed (var. of 歉).

唏 40A.22-8

shi.

V. i. To sob; to sigh: 唏噓, 唏吁 (*-shyu*) to draw a long sigh.

唧 40A.22-9

*jir (*ji).*

N. Chirping of insects, noise made by persons (also **ji*).

唧咕 *ji'gu*, v. i., (1) to murmur: 這兩人唧咕了半天 the two have been whispering to one another for a long while; 唧唧咕咕 to babble on and on; (2) mutter to oneself; (3) (of liquids) to drip.

唧唧 *jirjir*, n., (1) the humming of insects; (2) sighing of persons; (3) whispering.

唧拉 *ji'la*, v.i., make a confused noise: 唧拉喳拉 *ji'lajala*, ditto.

唧溜 *jiliou*, adj., clever, intelligent, keen, quick-witted.

唧噥 *ji'nung*, v.i., as in 唧唧噥噥 *ji'jinungnung*, to whisper, see -*'gu*↑.

唧筒 *jituung (-'tung)*, n., a pump.

唧嘖 *jirtzer*, n., chirping of insects.

咋 40A.22-9

*tzer (*jah).*

V. i. To click one's tongue: 咋舌 -*sher*↓.

Adv. (AC) (**jah*) loudly; abruptly (=乍 92.22).

咋舌 *tzersher*, v. i., to click one's tongue in regret or fear, or surprise.

啣 40A.22-9

shiarn.

V. t. To hold in the mouth, see 銜 91B.00.

§ 40A.30 (口/一)

啦 40A.30-1

la.

Fin. part. Particle of assertion, usu. drawn out, like *laaaaa*! more emphatic than the unaccented 了: 自然啦 of course, it's only natural; 不必啦 no more fuss about it; 不見得啦 not necessarily so; 得啦 don't bother about it any more; 好啦 let it be so, that will do; 何必啦 why bother about it? 算啦 forget about it; 未必啦 it may not be so.

Adj. Descriptive of certain sounds, such as yelling, gabbling, chattering: 啦啦隊 -*ladueih*↓; 哇啦哇啦 *walawala*, a hubbub of voices.

啦啦隊 *laladueih*, n., cheering squad, rooters: 啦啦隊長 n., a cheer leader.

喳 40A.30-1

cha.

Adj. Descriptive of whispering, twittering, jabbering sounds: 喳喳的, 嘰嘰喳喳, 唧啦喳啦.

嘒 40A.30-1

hueih.

Adj. (AC) small: 嘒嘒 (AC) small voice.

啷 嗛 唏 唧 咋 啣 啦 喳 嘒

亅	小	⺊	十	土	ナ	廾	凵	丨	一	丁	フ	口	囟	冈	ㄱ	厂	尸	亠	广	宀	丶	乚	弋	心	八	人	乂	〜	一	ノ	𠂉	く
00	01	02	10	11	12	20	21	22	30	31	32	40	41	42	50	51	52	60	61	62	63	70	71	72	80	81	82	83	90	91	92	93

嗑 40A.30-1

keh.

V. t. To break with teeth: 嗑瓜子兒 break dried melon seeds between teeth, a pastime; 嗑牙 to indulge in idle talk (also wr. 磕).

嗑睡 *kehshueih*, v.i., to doze off, to take a nap.

噎 40A.30-1

ye.

V. i. To hiccup, choke: 因噎廢食 stop eating altogether just because of a hiccup.

嘘 40A.30-2

shyu (*shy).

V. i. (1) To breathe out: 嘘一口氣 blow a breath, blow on s. t. to cool or warm it; (fig.) 吹嘘 "blow s. o.'s horn," to praise a third party before s. o. (2) To boo: 嘘他下去 boo him off the stage; 嘘聲四起 a wave of hisses all around.

Excl. (1) Ah! (2) (*shy) Ugh! (excl. of distaste).

咺 40A.30-3

shyuaan.

Adj. (AC) manifest, impressive (appearance), cf. 烜 91D.30.

呃 40A.30-3

nh.

Excl. (Exclamation of curt consent or hidden anger, contempt) Hm! Hm!

呸 40A.30-3

pei.

Excl. Pfui!

啞 40A.30-3

yaa (*ya, *eh).
[Pop. 哑]

Adj. (1) Dumb, mute: 啞吧, 啞子 -*'ba, -tz*↓; 啞劇 -*jyuh*↓; 喝啞酒 drink without playing finger game or other games. (2) (Throat, voice) hoarse: 啞嗓 -*saang*↓; 沙啞 (voice) hoarse; 嗓子啞了 throat is hoarse.

Adv. (*ya) Sound of creaking, crackling: 啞然, 啞啞 -*rarn, -ya*↓.

啞巴 *yaa'ba*, adj. & n., dumb; a dumb person; 啞巴虧 or 啞巴苦子 suffering which cannot be told others.
啞咤 **yajah*, n., bird cry or any inarticulate sound.
啞劇 *yaajyuh*, n., pantomime.
啞鈴 *yaa-lirng*, n., dumbbell.
啞謎(兒) *yaamir(-mie'l)*, n., a riddle, an enigma.
啞嘔 **ya-ou*, adj., lisping like a child; creaking of oars.
啞然 *yaararn* (**ehrarn*), adj., a sudden laugh, guffaw.
啞嗓(兒)(子) *yarsaang('l)(tz)*, n., a hoarse or feeble voice.
啞子 *yaatz*, n., a dumb person.
啞啞 (1) **yaya*, adj., descriptive of bird cry, creaking or crackling sound; (2) **eh-eh*, n., (AC) a chuckling sound.

嗢 40A.30-4

wah.

V.t. To swallow.

嗢噱 *wahjyuer*, v.i., to chuckle.
嗢咽 *wahyirn*, v.t., to swallow.
嗢噦 *wahyue*, v.i., (AC) to clear the throat.

咀 40A.30-4

jyuu.

V.t. Suck, chew.

咀嚼 *jyuujyuer*, v.t., chew, masticate; (fig.) chew the meaning of words.

嚦 40A.30-5

lih.

Adj. 嚦嚦 chirping sound.

喧 40A.30-6

shyuan.

V. i. To clamor, wrangle noisily, raise a hubbub; to shout, yell.

喧嘩 *shyuanhuar*, adj., noisy, tumultuous (crowd).
喧鬧 *shyuannauh*, v. i. & adj., creating a din, uproar.
喧擾 *shyuanraau*, v. i., to cause a disturbance.
喧囂 *shyuanshiau*, adj., given to outcries, unpleasantly demanding; disturbingly noisy.
喧天 *shyuan-tian*, phr., 鑼鼓喧天 a stifling din of gongs and drums.
喧闐 *shyuantiarn*, adj., see -*nauh*↑.

嗟 40A.30-8

jie (also **jyue*).

V. i. & t. To sigh, deplore, lament: 嗟憤 to sigh in anger; 嗟愍 take pity on (s.o.); 不食嗟來之食 won't eat anything rudely offered.

Interjection. Expressing regret or sorrow: 嗟乎, 嗟夫 alas! 嗟嗟 how lamentable or wonderful!

嗟悼 *jiedauh*, v. i. & t., to lament (s. o.'s) death.
嗟歎 *jietahn*, v. i. & t., to lament, regret, to sigh in sorrow.

嗌 40A.30-8

yih.

N. (AC) the throat.

唫 40A.30-8

yirn.

V. t. (AC) to close the mouth: 口呿而不唫 mouth was open, not closed.

噬 40A.30-9

shyh.

V. t. To bite: 噬狗 a biting dog; 噬臍莫及 one cannot bite one's own navel—too late to repent.

§ 40A.32 (口/フ)

啰 40A.32-4

luor.

[Pop. of 囉 40A.11]

吟 40A.32-8

yirn.

N. (LL) a song, used in name of certain melodies.

V. i. & t. (1) To sing: 吟咏, 吟哦 *-yuung, -er* ↓; 吟詩 to sing a song; 行吟河畔 sing while strolling on lake front. (2) To hum (a tune), to con (a text), to incant as a form of reading: 吟誦 *-suhng* ↓; coupled with 弄: 吟風弄月 to write pastoral poetry. (3) To make animal cries, also n., such cries: 蟬吟 cicada's song; 猿吟 monkey's cry; 龍吟虎嘯 cries of dragons and tigers. (4) To groan, make a sighing sound: 呻吟 to groan or mutter in pain; 沈吟 to make no sound while thinking. (5) U. f. 唫, to close the mouth.

吟哦 *yirn-er*, v. i., to sing or hum; to incant.
吟嘯 *yirnshiauh*, v. i., (1) to sing or whistle or shout in freedom: 吟嘯自若 ditto; (2) to make cries of pain or despair: 吟嘯扼腕 wring one's hands and sigh.
吟誦 *yirnsuhng*, v.i., to read aloud rhythmically.
吟壇 *yirntarn*, n., the poets' circle.
吟味 *yirnweih*, v. i., to hum and appreciate (a line).
吟詠 *yirnyuung*, v. i., to sing, incant (a poem); v. t., to celebrate (sentiment) by verse: 吟詠情性.

哆 40A.32-9

duo (**chee*, see vb.).

V. i. (**chee, chaa, chih*) (AC) to open mouth.

哆囉哆嗦(的) *duo'luo-duo'suo'de*, adj. & adv., cringing.
哆嗦 *duo'suo*, v. i. & adj., cringe, tremble.

§ 40A.40 (口/口)

咕 40A.40-1

gu.

V. i. & t. To mumble, mutter, chatter, whisper, murmur, rumble.

咕嘟 *gudu*, (1) v.i., (of flowing water) murmur, bubble; (2) v.i., to pout one's lips or mouth in displeasure or anger: 咕嘟著嘴; (3) v.t., (*gu'du*) bring to a boil: 把這鍋湯再咕嘟一會兒 please bring this pot of soup to a boil for a little longer.
咕咚 *gudung*, (1) v.i., (make) a thumping sound; (2) v.t., (*gu'dung*) attack with guns: 拿砲把城門咕咚開了 force open the city gate with artillery fire.
咕唧 *gu'ji*, v. i., murmur or mumble to oneself or each other: 他倆咕唧了半天 the couple were whispering to each other for quite a while; 他自己一個咕唧了好一會兒 he was mumbling to himself for a long time.
咕嚕 *gu'lu*, v. i., (1) (of speech) mumble, talk tiresomely and indistinctly; (2) (of the stomach) make a rumbling sound: 餓得肚子裏咕嚕地響 be so hungry that the stomach is beginning to gurgle; (3) (of carts) to rumble.
咕噥 *gu'nung*, v. i., to whisper, chatter.
咕容 *gu'rung*, v. i., to walk with a sidle.

咭 40A.40–1

ji.

Adj. Descriptive of whispering or giggling sounds: 咭吱咯吱 (*jijygejy*) 的響 crackling as of dry branches.

咭噔 *jideng* n., sounds of passing carts, footsteps, etc. (also 咭噔咯噔 *jidenggedeng*).

咭咭 *jiji*, n., sound of giggling, crackling laughter: 咭咭嘎嘎 *jiji-gaga*, ditto.

嘻 40A.40–1

shi.

Adj. Mirthful, merry: 嘻皮笑臉 comically cheerful, a face beaming with laughter; 嘻嘻哈哈 laughing, -ly; 笑嘻嘻 very happy-looking.

Excl. 噫嘻 alas!

嘻和(兒) *shi'he('l)*, n., (coll.) as in 遞嘻和兒 do s. t. to make everybody happy.

嘻笑 *shishiauh*, v. i., to laugh merrily.

喏 40A.40–2

ree.

N. Polite expression used in saluting others: 唱喏 to salute by using such an expression.

Adv. (U.f. 諾 *nuoh*) yes: 連聲喏喏 quickly answered, "Yes, sir!"

嗒 40A.40–2

tah.

Adj. Frustrated, lost.

嗒然 *tahrarn*, adj., looking lost, dejected: 嗒然若喪 or 嗒喪 *-sahng*, ditto.

咕 40A.40–2

cheh (**jan*).

V. i. (1) To whisper: 咕囁, 咕嚅 *-jer*, *-rur* ↓. (2) (**jan*) To read with intonation: 咕嗶 *-bih* ↓.

咕嗶 **janbih*, v. i., read text without truly understanding meaning.

咕囁 *chehjer*, v. i., to whisper.

咕嚅 *chehrur*, v. i., ditto.

唔 40A.40–3

wur (also *m*).

Pron. (Shanghai dial.) I, first person (dial. form of 我 *woo*).

V. i. See 咿唔 40A.91.

Adv. (Cantonese dial.) equiv. Mandarin 不: 唔得=不得.

唁 40A.40–6

yahn.

V.i. (LL) to offer condolences: 唁電 telegram of condolence.

喀 40A.40–6

kah (**ka*, **keh*).

Adj. A sound-descriptive word: 喀吧 word in rendering foreign names (as 喀土木 Kahtumuh for Khartum).

喀吧 **kaba*, adj., descriptive of cracking sound.

喀喀 **kehkeh*, adj., (AC) 喀喀然 sound of coughing.

嗐 40A.40–6

haih.

Excl. An exclamation of regret (also wr. 咳).

哈 40A.40–8

ha (**haa*).

N. A surname.

V. i. & t. (1) To blow one's breath: 哈氣 ditto: 在窗玻璃上哈一口氣 to blow breath on a windowpane. (2) (AC) to sip.

Adv. See 哈哈 *-ha* ↓.

哈巴狗 **haa'bagoou*, n., a Pekingese dog; 哈巴腿(兒) *haa'batueei* (*--tuee'l*), adj., bowlegged.

哈達 *ha'da*, n., a Tibetan silk scarf, often given as present or votive offering: 獻哈達 to present such offering.

哈哈 *haha*, adv., as in (1) 哈哈大笑 roar with laughter; (2) 哈哈兒 something funny: 打哈哈兒 make fun; 你別打哈哈了 don't make fun; 讓人家看哈哈兒 become a laughingstock; (3) n., sound of threat: 哈哈，你竟敢罵我 hah! hah! you dare insult me!

哈喇 *ha'la*, (1) n., a Tibetan woolen cloth, (also pr. *ka'la*); (2) 哈喇味 adj., smell of food decay; (3) v.t., (MC) to kill: 不如一刀哈喇了他.

哈喇叭 **haa'laba*, n., shoulder blade (also wr. 哈叻巴).

哈密瓜 *hamih-gua*, n., Turkestan melon (from Hami).

哈士蟆 *hashyh-mar*, n., a kind of frog found in Kirin, Manchuria and used as a valuable tonic.

哈 40A.40-8

han.

V.t. To keep (olive, pill, etc.) in the mouth without chewing.

啥 40A.40-8

shar.

Adj. (Soochow dial.) what＝甚麽.

嗆 40A.40-8

chiang (**chiahng*).

V. i. & t. (1) To choke while drinking. (2) (Birds) peck at. (3) (**chiahng*) Choke by smoke: 嗆鼻子 (smoke) irritates the nose; 嗆了嗓子 choke the throat; 塵土嗆人 dust chokes; 嗆死人 suffocate.

嗆哼 *chiangheng*, adj., (MC) stupid.

咖 40A.40-9

ka.

咖啡 *kafei*, n., coffee: 咖啡壺 coffee pot; 咖啡館, 廳, 室 coffee shop (or parlor, or house).

咯 40A.40-9

ger (**ge*, **kaa*, *'lo*).

Fin. part. (**'lo*) Used in announcing s. t.: 他來咯 he is coming! also as more emphatic form of 了: 是咯 that's right (indeed); 好咯 well, well! 你怎麽咯 what's the matter with you!

V. t. (**kaa*) To spit out: 咯痰 cough up phlegm; 咯血 spit blood (also wr. 喀).

咯噠 **ge'da*, n., (coll.) (bot.) mustard (＝芥菜): 咯噠頭, 咯噠纓兒 mustard head, leaves.

咯噔 *ger'deng*, adj., (1) descriptive of creaking sounds (on stairs, swinging windows, etc.); (2) uneven, rough.

咯吱 *ger'jy*, adj., descriptive of creaking sound (of dry branches, etc.).

咯菜 **getsaih*, n., coll. for mustard.

咍 40A.40-9

hai.

Excl. Excl. of regret, usu. wr. 咳.

§ 40A.41 (口/囗)

嗜 40A.41-1

shyh.

N. A hobby, special love of certain things (smoke, food): 嗜好 *-hauh* ↓.

V. t. To love, be fond of: 嗜賭, 嗜酒 love to gamble, drink; 嗜口腹 love food and drink; 嗜色 love women; 嗜殺人 love to kill.

嗜好 *shyhhauh*, n., a hobby, special liking for drink, food, distractions.

嗜痂 *shyh-jia*, phr., (LL) 嗜痂成癖 have an addiction for (stamps and the like), (allu. from one who likes to lick his scabs).

嗜癖 *shyhpii*, n., see *-hauh* ↑.

嗜慾 *shyhyuh*, n., carnal desires, longing.

喈 40A.41-2

jie.

N. Sound of chirping, laughing.

嚐 40A.41-2

charng.

V. i. To taste (var. of 嘗 22.41, in V.i. 1).

嘈 40A.41-2

tsaur.

Adj. Noisy, booming (noise).

嘈鬧 *tsaurnauh*, adj., tumultuous, turbulent. (crowd).

嘈雜 *tsaurtzar*, adj., noisy

喵 40A.41-2

miau.

N. & v. i. Mewing of cat.

咁 40A.41–2

gaam.

Adj. (Cantonese) this: 咁樣 this way or manner.

噹 40A.41–2

dang.

Adj. Descriptive of clanging or tinkling sound: 噹噹 *dangdang*, 叮叮噹噹 *dingdingdangdang*.

哂 40A.41–3

sheen.

V. i. To smile, oft. smilingly, see compp.↓.

哂納 *sheen-nah*, v. i., (court.) please accept (my gift, opinion) with a smile.
哂笑 *sheen-shiauh*, v. i., laugh at (with contempt).
哂收 *sheen-shou*, v. i., see *-nah*↑.

咽 40A.41–4

yan (**yahn*, **yeh*).

V. t. (1) (**yahn*) To swallow (also wr. 嚥). (2) (**yeih*): 哽咽 to sob.

咽喉 *yanhour*, n., the throat; (fig.) vital defense area, strategic point.

唱 40A.41–4

chahng.

N. Ditty, song: 小唱 a ditty.

V.i. & t. (1) To sing: 唱歌 *-ge*↓; 唱戲 *-shih*↓; 賣唱 to sing as minstrel at restaurants and streets; 歌唱 sing; 合唱 (sing) chorus; 混聲合唱 mixed chorus; 獨唱 (sing) solo; 獨唱會 vocal recital; 演唱, 齊唱 sing on stage; sing in unison; 唱不入調 sing out of key; 清唱 to sing or rehearse without accompaniment or stage make-up; 唱唱咧咧 (coll.) descriptive of singing freely. (2) To shout out loud: 唱名 call out names in roll call; 唱好 *-haau*↓; 唱諾 *-nuoh*↓.

唱本(兒) *chahngbeen(-be'l)*, n., song text.
唱唱兒 *chahngchahng'l*, v. i., to sing in streets as profession: 唱唱兒的 street singer.
唱酬 *chahngchour*, v. i., see *-heh*↓.
唱導 *chahngdauh*, v. i. & t., to lead (movement).
唱的 *chahng'de*, n., (MC) a street or restaurant singer. ⌈songs.
唱歌 *chahng-ge*, v. i., to sing
唱好 *chahnghaau*, v. i., (MC) to give cheers as audience.
唱和 *chahngheh*, v. i., to write and reply in poems between friends, usu. on some occasion.
唱機 *chahngji*, n., gramophone (usu. called 留聲機).
唱叫 *chahngjiauh*, v. i., to yell and scream.
唱兒 *chahng'l*, n., a song, ditty: 唱個唱兒 sing a ditty.
唱禮 *chahng-lii*, n., (Budd.) prayer at end of mass with "five forgiveness" and "five wishes."
唱名 *chahng-mirng*, v. i., make roll call.
唱喏 *chahng-nuoh*, v. i., (servants, retinue) make a vocal response, similar to answer "here" in roll call, but more like "Yes, sir!"
唱片(兒) *chahngpian(-pia'l)*, n., gramophone record.
唱戲 *chahngshih*, v. i., to hold, have or sing an opera; to play in theater.
唱書 *chahngshu*, v. t. & n., to give monologue recital of story to the accompaniment of drum or string.

啯 40A.41–4

guo.

N. A gurgling sound; cricket's chirp.

喑 40A.41–6

yin.

Adj. (1) Hoarse (voice). (2) Mute (interch. 瘖 61A.41).

喑嗚 *yinwuh*, v. i., (AC) to yell, shout.
喑啞 *yinyaa*, adj., mute (person).

噌 40A.41–8

cheng (**tseeng*, **tseng*).

V.i. (**tseng*) To shout at: 噌人 shout at person.

Adj. (**tseeng*) Split: 他們倆人說噌了 they two have broken relationships.

噌吰 *chenghurng*, adj., booming (noise).

噲 40A.41–8

kuaih.

V. t. (AC) to swallow; 噲噲 (AC) clear and fair-minded.

噆 40A.41–9

tzaan.

V.t. (1) Carry (food) in mouth, like

birds. (2) To bite: 蚊虻噆膚 bitten by mosquitos and gnats.

啪 40A.41-9

pa.

[Dist. 咱 40A.41 ↓]

Adj. With a flap, rapping sound 啪的一下打落 flap down.

啪啦 *pa'la*, adj., (of bad coins) having a dull sound.

咱 40A.41-9

tzarn (also *tzar*).

Pron. I (Peking dial.): 咱們 *-'men* ↓; 咱們倆, 咱兩個 we two, the two of us; 咱兩兒 *-liaa'l* ↓.

咱家 *tzarjia*, pron., I myself.

咱兩兒 *tzarnliaa'l*, pron., the two of us.

咱們 *tzarn'men*, pron., we.

喒 40A.41-9

tzarn.

[Var. 咱 40A.41 ↑]

嚕 40A.41-9

lu.

嚕囌 *lusu*, 嚕哩嚕囌 *lulilusu*, v.i., talk unnecessarily or annoyingly; cf. 哩嚕 *lilu*, 哩哩囉囉 *liliiluoluo* 40A.11.

§ 40A.42 (口/冈)

哺 40A.42-1

buu.

V. t. (1) Chew. (2) Feed (infant) after chewing, like birds, or from breast: 反哺 (of crows reputed) to feed parents.

哺乳類 *bur-ruu-leih*, n., (zoo.) mammalia.

喃 40A.42-1

narn.

Adj. Chattering, mumbling: 喃喃 *-narn* ↓; 呢喃 muttering, chattering, (birds) twittering.

喃喃 *narnnarn*, adj., (1) mumbling: 喃喃自語 mumbling to oneself; (2) (of voice in reading) low and indistinct.

嘲 40A.42-1

jau (**chaur*).

V. i. & t. (1) To sneer at, jeer, scoff: 嘲笑, 嘲弄 *-shiauh, -luhng* ↓; 譏嘲 to ridicule (person); 解嘲 to explain or defend oneself against ridicule; 冷嘲熱諷, 連嘲帶罵 alternately taunt and jeer (at person). (2) (**chaur*) To provoke, annoy by taunting: 嘲惹, 嘲撥 *-ree, -bor* ↓. (3) (Birds) twitter: 嘲啾 *-jiou* ↓.

嘲撥 **chaurbor*, v. t., to tease (a decorous lady), to try to flirt with. 「heartily.

嘲歌 **chaurge*, v. i., (MC) to sing

嘲哳 *jaujar*, v. i., to make vexing or confusing noise, as birds' twitter, make a hubbub.

嘲啾 *jaujiou*, n. & v. i., birds' twitter or similar light, confusing noise, murmur.

嘲弄 *jauluhng*, v. t. & n., make fun of, twit, sneer.

嘲罵 *jaumah*, n. & v. t., scold, taunt, twit, jeer.

嘲惹 **chaurree*, v. t., to provoke by words.

嘲訕 *jaushahn*, v. t., to sneer at, scoff, ridicule (person).

嘲笑 *jaushiauh*, v. t., to ridicule (person).

啃 40A.42-2

keen (**kehn*).

V.t. (1) To bite, chew: 啃骨頭 chew bones; 死啃書本 try to memorize books without thinking. (2) (**kehn*) (Coll.) to eat, nibble.

哨 40A.42-2

shauh.

N. (1) A patrol, sentinel: 放哨 set up sentinels along road for security; 哨兵, 哨馬, 哨船 *-bing, -maa, -chuarn* ↓. (2) (*-tz, 'l*) A whistle: 吹哨 blow whistle; 吹口哨 blow whistle with bare mouth.

V. i. & t. To whistle; (of birds) to twitter or sing.

Adj. whistling: 哨箭 a whistling arrow.

哨棒 *shauhbahng*, n., a wooden truncheon, club.

哨兵 *shauhbing*, n., a sentinel.
哨船 *shauhchuarn*, n., a patrol boat.
哨馬 *shauhmaa*, n., cavalry guard.
哨探 *shauhtahn*, n., army scout.

嘴 40A.42-2

tzueei.

N. (1) The bill (beak) of a bird. (2) The snout of an animal. (3) The mouth of a human being: 嘴甜心苦(辣) a cruel heart under the cover of sugar-coated words; 嘴嘴舌舌 garrulous, loquacious; 七嘴八舌 conflicting views, divided counsel; 回嘴 to answer back, retort; 多嘴 talkative, gossipy; 插嘴 interrupt (conversation); 撇嘴 a disdainful look, to pout (as a child about to cry); 歪嘴 wry-mouthed; 努嘴 make a signal with one's mouth or closed lips; 抿嘴 to purse up one's lips; 親嘴 to kiss; 張嘴 open mouth; 閉嘴 close mouth, also (tell s.o.) to shut up; 油嘴 glib-tongued; 利嘴 sharp-tongued; 掌嘴 a slap on the face, a box on the ear. (4) Anything that sticks out: 山嘴 the spur of a hill; 瓶嘴 the mouth of a bottle; 煙袋嘴 the mouthpiece of a tobacco pipe; 茶壺嘴 the spout of a teapot.

嘴巴 *tzueei'ba*, n., the mouth: 打嘴巴 give s.o. a box on the ear (a slap across the mouth); 打自己嘴巴 contradict oneself; 嘴巴子 a box on the ear, a slap on the face; 嘴巴骨 the jawbone, (also wr. 吧).
嘴把式 *tzueirbaa'shy*, n., a person given to empty talk.
嘴把子 *tzueirbaatz*, n., the cheeks as part of mouth.
嘴笨 *tzueei-behn*, adj., clumsy of speech.
嘴鼻 *tzueeibir*, n., facial appearance ("mouth and nose").
嘴不穩 *tzueei-buhween*, adj., talkative and unable to keep a secret.
嘴敞 *tzueirchaang*, adj., talkative, gossipy, long-tongued.
嘴岔兒 *tzueeichah'l* n., corners of the mouth; 嘴岔子 (*--tz*), ditto.
嘴饞 *tzueei-charn*, adj., greedy, gluttonous.
嘴嗛 *tzueei-chiarn*, v.i., apt to offend people with words.
嘴強 *tzueei-chiarng*, adj., unyielding, obstinate in argument, argumentative.
嘴勤 *tzueei-chirn*, adj., fond of talking, ready of speech.
嘴唇(兒) *tzueeichurn(-chuer'l)* n., the lips.
嘴吃屎 *tzueei chyshyy*, phr., to fall prostrate.
嘴打人 *tzueir daarern*, v. i., to abuse, slander or ridicule people.
嘴乖 *tzueei-guai*, adj., clever in speech, clever-tongued.
嘴尖 *tzueei-jian*, adj., sharp-tongued: 嘴尖舌巧 gifted with a quick and sharp tongue.
嘴急 *tzueei-jir*, adj., impatient to eat.
嘴直 *tzueei-jyr*, adj., honest (straightforward) in speech, outspoken.
嘴啃地 *tzueir-keen-dih*, phr., to fall prostrate ("bite the dust").
嘴快 *tzueeikuaih*, adj., given to making crude or unthinking remarks.
嘴兒 *tzueei'l*, n., (1) eloquence; (2) a pointed mouth (of bottle, jug, kettle).
嘴懶 *tzueir-laan*, adj., reticent, not disposed to talk.
嘴冷 *tzueir-leeng*, adj., blunt, rash in speech.
嘴臉(兒) *tzueirliaan(-liaa'l)*, n., (contemptuous) hideous (ugly) looks.
嘴抹兒 *tzueei'mo'l*, n., (contempt.) wasteful words ("spittle").
嘴末子 *tzueei'motz*, n., ditto.
嘴皮子 *tzueeipirtz*, n., (coll.) a ready tongue.
嘴貧 *tzueei-pirn*, adj., given to nasty talk (also 嘴頻).
嘴碎 *tzueei-sueih*, adj., see *-pirn*↑.
嘴損 *tzueirsuun*, adj., sharp-tongued, cutting in speech.
嘴頭兒 *tzueei'tour'l*, n., see *-tourtz*↓.
嘴頭子 *tzueeitourtz*, n., (1) ability to talk: 嘴頭子厲害 cutting in speech, sharp-tongued; (2) the lips.
嘴嚴 *tzueei-yarn*, adj., close-mouthed, tight-lipped.
嘴硬 *tzueei-yihng*, adj., see *-chiarng*↑.

喘 40A.42-2

chuaan.

N. Lingering breath: 殘喘 ditto; 哮喘 asthma.

V.i. To pant: 喘一口氣 draw a long breath; 喘嘘 to pant, be short of breath; 喘喘氣 pause for breath.

喘氣 *chuaan-chih*, v.i., to pant, short of breath.
喘息 *chuaan-shir*, v.i., pause for breath: 喘息初定 just as one recovers one's breath (s.t. happens), recover from fear and confusion.

嗃 40A.42-2

hau.

嗃矢 *haushyy* n., (LL) forerunner, beginning (of events).

嗝 40A.42-3

ger.

V. i. To belch: 嗝噎, 打嗝兒 hiccup; 嗝症 hiccup.

嚅 40A.42-3

rur.

嚅哯 *rur-erl*, v.i., make a forced smile.
嚅囁 *rurnieh*, v.i., to mumble in low voice (as if out of fear).

喟 40A.42-4

kueih.

V.t. To sigh, draw a long breath.

喟然 *kueihrarn*, adv., as in 喟然興嘆 (LL) draw a long breath and sigh.
喟嘆 *kueihtahn*, v.i., to sigh.

喁 40A.42-4

yurng (also *yur*).

Adj. 喁喁 waiting anxiously; 喁喁待哺 waiting with open mouth to be fed.

啁 40A.42-4

jou.

V. i. (Of birds) to twitter: 啁啁, 啁哳, 啁啾 make cries like the peet-weet.

啁噍 *joujiou*, n., a very small bird like the wren (=鷦鷯).

喎 40A.42-4

kuai.
[Var. of 咼 42.42]

嘱 40A.42-5

juu.
[Abbr. of 囑 40A.50↓]

唷 40A.42-6

yo.

Excl. 啊唷, 喔唷 *a-yoh*, *o-yoh*, excl. of regret, disapproval.

噙 40A.42-8

chirn (also *hern*).

V. t. To keep in mouth; to bite (related 含 81.40).

呐 40A.42-8

nah.

Adv. (Of speech) hesitating, slow: 呐呐 *-nah*↓.

呐喊 *nahhaan*, n. & v. i., (utter) loud shouts in support: 搖旗呐喊 flag-waving and slogan-shouting as a sign of support at a mass rally or (fig.) in a political or social movement.
呐呐 *nahnah*, adj., slow of speech.

响 40A.42-9

shiaang.
[Pop. of 響 93.41]

§ 40A.50 (口/ㄱ)

哼 40A.50-1

kuaa.

Adj. (North China coll.) (of person's speech) foreign in accent.

嘠 40A.50-2

gar (also pr. *ger* in transliterating foreign names).

V. i. To bet, wager.

嘠點兒 *gardiaa'l*, v. i., (northern dial.) to bet: 咱們嘠個點兒吧 I'll bet you!
嘠東兒 *gardung'l*, v. i., (northern dial.) to wager: 咱們嘠個東兒吧 let's wager something!

嘞 40A.50-2

'le.

Fin. part. Used in such expressions as 那才怪嘞! that would be strange, indeed! 何必嘞 why so much fuss? 去就去嘞 let's go and not hesitate, (same as unacented 了).

喝 40A.50-4

he (*heh).

V. i. & t. (1) To drink (water, tea, liquid): 喝醉 get drunk; 喝風 esp. 喝西北風 to suffer from cold and hunger, having nothing to eat; 喝

亅	小	⺊	十	土	ナ	廿	Ŀ	丨	一	丅	フ	口	区	冈	ㄱ	厂	尸	亠	广	宀	丶	乚	弋	心	八	人	乂	㇀	一	丿丿	⺧	く
00	01	02	10	11	12	20	21	22	30	31	32	40	41	42	50	51	52	60	61	62	63	70	71	72	80	81	82	83	90	91	92	93

啞吧酒 to drink silently at feast without conversation; 喝冬瓜湯 be matchmaker; 喝過墨水 (person) has read a great deal ("has drunk ink"); 喝過洋墨水 has studied foreign books or abroad; 喝邊兒 to visit singsong house in company and without pay. (2) (_he_ or *_heh_) To shout, to command by shouting: 吆喝 to threaten; 喝令 to shout command (to do s. t.); 喝止 yell at s. o. to stop; 喝六呼么 to gamble at dice game ("shout for 6 or 1 to turn up").

Excl. Ah! oh!

喝 道 *_heh-dauh_, v. i., to act as escort to open the way for approaching official (also wr. 呵導).

喝 (兒) 呼 _he'hu_ (_he'l'hu_), v. i., to shout and yell, threaten.

喝 采 _he-tsaai_ (_heh'_-), v.i. & t., to applaud (performer) (also wr. 喝彩).

噣 40A.50-4

jiouh (*_jour_).

N. A bird's bill.

V. i. & t. (*_juor_) To peck at (usu. wr. 啄).

噚 40A.50-4

_eh_.

[Var. of 腭 42A.50]

叼 40A.50-5

diau.

[Dist. 叨]

V. i. & t. To hold in the mouth: 叼着香煙, 煙斗 have a cigarette, pipe, hanging in mouth; 狗叼骨頭 dog holding bone in mouth.

叨 40A.50-5

tau (*_dau_).

V.t. (1) To receive: 叨蒙 (LL) receive (gifts, visit, etc.); see 叨教, 叨光 -_jiauh_, -_guang_↓. (2) (*_dau_) Chatter.

Adj. Unworthy: 叨在知己 (court.) unworthily (i.e., have the honor to) be reckoned among your friends.

叨 叨 *_daudau_, v.i., chatter 叨叨念念 muttering, grumbling, see also -_lau_, -'_deng_↓.

叨 登 (叨 蹬) *_dau'deng_, v.i., chatter, jabber: 又來叨蹬這件事 again came to talk about this thing; turn things upside down.

叨 光 _tauguang_, v.i., have the honor—(LL, court.) formula for thanking person for gifts or favors or for request.

叨 教 _taujiauh_, v.i., have the benefit of your advice.

叨 嘮 *_dau'lau_, v. i., grumble, mutter.

叨 念 *_dauniahn_, v.i., ditto.

叨 擾 _tauraau_, v.i., (court.) apologize for the trouble one has caused to one's host; 叨擾了 "thank you ever so much!"

叨 沓 _tautah_, adj., greedy.

呣 40A.50-5

_m_ (varying tone).

Excl. Denoting the sound "m," sometimes rendered in English as "hmm," but used to express variously disapproval, surprise reaction, grim consideration; cf. 唔 40A.40, and 嘸 40A.63.

嗎 40A.50-5

_ma_ (indeterminate questioning tone and *_maa_).

Fin. part. Final particle used at end of questions: 是你嗎 is it you? 你來嗎 are you coming? 她要嗎 does she want it, want to? 這不是很不合理嗎 isn't this very unreasonable? (also wr. 麽).

嗎 啡 *_maafei_ n. morphine: 打嗎啡, 嗎啡針 injection of morphine.

嗎 呼 *_maa'hu_, adj., lousy, slipshod (see 麻△呼 61.01).

囑 40A.50-5

juu.

N. Will: 遺囑 person's will or dying instructions.

V. i. & t. To leave word for s. t. to be done; to ask (a friend) to do s. t.; to entrust (s. o.): 叮囑 to repeat order or instructions of parting (as mother on son going away from home).

囑 咐 _juufuh_, v. t., ask (s. o.) to do s. t.

囑 託 _juutuo_, v. t., to entrust (friend) with a message or mission.

嗙 40A.50-6

paang.

V. i. To boast esp. 胡吹亂嗙.

嗨 40A.50-6

hai.

A

Excl. Hai! an exclamation, bespeaking regret (usu. wr. 咳 40.81).

吩 40A.50-8

fen.

吩咐 *fenfuh*, v. i. & t., give order, order (person), often used in courtesy, "just command me": 聽你吩咐 will do what you say.

嗡 40A.50-8

weng.

Adj. 嗡嗡 descriptive of humming (flies, distant geese).

噏 40A.50-8

shi.

V. i. & t. (1) To suck in (=吸). (2) (AC) to compress, opp. to 張 expand.

嗚 40A.50-9

wu.

Adj. Descriptive of sound of train whistle, distant horns, etc.

Excl. 嗚呼 Ough! Oo! see 嗚呼-*hu*↓.

嗚呼 *wuhu*, (1) adj., Ough! alas; (2) v.i., to die: 一命嗚呼 alas, he died! (also wr. 嗚虖).

嗚嗚 *wuwu*, adj., see Adj.↑.

B

嗚咽 *wuyeh*, v. i., to sob.

鳴 40A.50-9

mirng.

V. i. & t. (1) To cry, utter a cry (of horse, cow, birds, insects): 雞鳴 the cock crows; 鳴嘶 to neigh; to make a booming sound: 雷鳴 thunder rumbles. (2) To beat (drum, gong) and make a sound: 鳴鼓 beat drum; 鳴鼓而攻之 (Confucius said of a disciple), "Beat a drum and drive him out"; 鳴鞭 crack a whip; 鳴鑼 strike a gong; 鳴金 war signal for retreat; 鳴砲 fire a gun salute; 鳴琴 to strike a stringed instrument. (3) To cry aloud: 鳴謝 cry thanks; 鳴冤 cry for redress of wrong; 自鳴得意 crow over one's success; 不平之鳴 voice of protest.

鳴禽類 *mirngchirn-leih*, n., (zoo.) *Passeriformes*, small birds (including swallows, sparrows).

鳴鏑 *mirng-dir*, n., (AC) singing arrow as war signal.

鳴鳳 *mirng-fehng*, n., crying phoenix, (fig.) very rare, distinguished individual, a voice from the wilderness.

鳴管 *mirng-guaan*, n., (zoo.) the syrinx, vocal organ of songbirds.

鳴鐘 *mirng jung*, n., clock strikes (half-past-two, etc.).

鳴榔(根) *mirnglarng*, n., wooden clapper used by fishermen to frighten and chase fish into net.

鳴鑾 *mirng-luarn*, n., (AC) emperor's procession on a trip.

鳴蜩 *mirngtiaur*, n., a form of cicada.

嘮 40A.50-9

laur.

C

V. i. To chatter.

嘮叨 *laur'dau*, adj., loquacious, garrulous.

嘮嘮 *laurlaur*, adj., noisy.

嘮呶 *laurnaur*, adj., ditto.

吻 40A.50-9

ween.

N. A kiss: 親吻, 接吻 ditto.

V.t. To kiss.

吻合 *weenher*, v.t., (joints) fit together well; (several reports or report and actual happenings) agree, fit together well.

啕 40A.50-9

taur.

V.i. See 嚎[A]啕 40A.02↑.

呦 40A.50-9

you.

Adj. 呦呦 (AC) sound of flowing water, deer crying.

Excl. Excl. of surprise, disapproval.

喲 40A.50-9

yau.

[Var. of 唷 excl. 40A.42↑]

嚥 嗻 噍 咚 嘸 嘵 唵 呲 唬 叱 咷 吭 吼 呪

§ 40A.63 (口/丶)

嚥 40A.63-2

yahn.

V.t. To swallow: 嚥下去 swallow (it); 嚥氣 to draw last breath.

嗻 40A.63-6

jeh.

Adv. Gabby, talkative; 嗻嗻 (MC) yes, yes!

噍 40A.63-9

*jiauh (*jiau, *jiou).*

V. t. Chew, munch, nibble: 噍類 -*leih*↓.

Adj. (1) (**jiau*) Strident: 噍殺 -*sha*↓. (2) (**jiou*) (Of birds) chirping twittering.

噍類 *jiauhleih*, n., living beings: 無噍類 (AC, LL) all exterminated, not a living soul remains.

噍殺 **jiausha*, adj., (of voice) strident.

咚 40A.63-9

dung.

Adj. 咕咚 *gudung*, descriptive of rumbling sounds or cart rattle.

嘸 40A.63-9

mr.

Adv. (Soochow dial.) in comp. 嘸不 have not; 嘸啥 quite good, fair.

§ 40A.70 (口/乚)

嘵 40A.70-1

shiau.

嘵嘵 *shiaushiau*, adv., (1) disturbed, restless; (2) garrulous, arguing endlessly.

唵 40A.70-1

aan.

Excl. (Budd.) rendering of Sanskr. *Om*, opening syllable in charms.

呲 40A.70-2

tsy.

V. t. To chide: 挨呲 be chided (also wr. 雌).

唬 40A.70-2

huu.

N. Tiger's roar.

V. t. To frighten: 嚇唬 to scare (by trick); 唬人 to scare person by trick; 唬事 ditto.

叱 40A.70-2

chyh.

V. i. & t. To scold, shout at, bawl out (person), to bellow: 大叱一聲 shouted out loud; 叱令 shouted an order.

叱叱 *chyhchyh*, v. i., to make shouting noise, like "Tut! tut!"

叱咄 *chyhduoh*, v. i., shouting and yelling.

叱喝 *chyhheh*, v. i. & t., to yell, yell at s. o.

叱咤 *chyhjah*, v. i., see -*duoh*↑.

叱嗟 *chyhjie*, v. i., see -*duoh*↑.

叱罵 *chyhmah*, v. t., to scold, rebuke harshly.

叱責 *chyhtzer*, v. t., ditto.

咷 40A.70-2

taur.

V.i. See 號[Δ]咷 40S.70.

吭 40A.70-3

eei.

Excl. (Disapproval): 吭, 你怎麽這様 Oh, how can you do this?

吼 40A.70-3

hoou.

N. & v. i. A roar of lions, tigers, etc.: 吼聲 a roaring or shrill cry; 大吼, 怒吼 a great cry.

呪 40A.70-4

jouh.

[Pop. of 咒 40.70]

呃 40A.70–5

eh.

V.i. To belch: 呃逆 ditto.

呢 40A.70–5

nir (**ne*).

Fin. part. (sp. pr. **'ne*) Used in asking questions for purposes of emphasis: 這怎麽行呢 how can this do? 你爲什麽不來呢 why didn't you come? 多麽美呢 how pretty it is! 他還沒來呢 he hasn't come yet; having the sense of "how about the other?" 你去看戲, 我呢 you are going to the movie, how about me?

N. Woolen cloth: 呢子 woolen goods; 毛呢 coarse woolens; 花呢 checkered woolens; 呢絨 woolens and flannels.

Adj. Murmuring: 呢喃 (of swallows) twittering; (of persons) whispering.

吧 40A.70–5

ba (usu. *'ba*).

Fin. part. (Usu. unaccented), as var. of 罷. (1) Showing command, request, termination of discussion: 來吧來吧 come, come! 去吧去吧 go! do not stand around! 算了吧! have done with it! (2) Showing doubt, hesitation, questioning mood: 不會吧 I don't think it could be that; 不是吧 I doubt it; 沒有來過吧 you have never been here, have you? (3) Marking an alternative supposition: 不去吧, 他要怪我們 on the other hand, if we don't go, he will blame us; cf. 罷 41.70.

Adj. 啞▵吧 40A.30, dumb.

吧吧 *baba*, adj., loquacious.
吧嗒嘴(兒) *badatzueei('l)* v. i., make clicking noise with tongue, as in eating; adj., greedy, envious of others.
吧噠棍 *badarguhn*, n., a six-foot stick, used in fighting (also 巴棍子 *baguhntz*).
吧唧 *ba'ji*, v. i., move jaw up and down as in eating.
吧兒吧兒 *ba'l-ba'l*, adj., clear, flowing-voiced.
吧呀吧呀 *ba'ya-ba'ya*, n., big-mouthed (child); v. i., quarrel (among children).

吭 40A.70–6

harng.

N. The throat: 引吭高歌 to sing or shout with outstretched neck; 絕吭自盡 cut one's throat in suicide.

喨 40A.70–6

liahng.

Adj. See 嘹▵喨, 40A.01.

嚨 40A.70–6

lurng.

N. See 喉▵嚨 40A.81.

吒 40A.70–6

jah.

V. i. (1) To roar, bellow: 叱▵吒 ditto, see 40A.70. (2) (AC) 毋吒食 do not chew noisily.

吒 40A.70–9

jah.

[Var. 吒 40A.70 ↑]

唣 40A.70–9

tzauh.

Adj. 囉唣 noisy, vociferous.

嘅 40A.70–9

kaai (also *kaih*).

V. i. Sigh, regret (also wr. 慨).

吪 40A.70–9

er.

[Anc. var. 訛 60A.70]

吃 40A.70–9

chy (**jir*).

[Interch. 喫]

V. i. & t. (1) To eat (lit.), sometimes also drink, smoke: 吃了 have already taken (food); 吃得 eatable; 吃不得 (person) must not eat, not eatable; 吃不了 (person) cannot finish food portion, (thing) insupportable; 好吃的 good to eat; 好難吃 very unpalatable; 吃不下 (person) cannot take food, (food) unpalatable; 窮得吃不上了 so poor that one has nothing to eat; 吃飯 take a meal; 吃飯了沒有 have you already eaten? also see 2↓; 吃酒 drink wine; 吃花酒 attend dinner with singsong girls; 吃喜酒 go to wedding feast; 吃烟 smoke; 吃大烟 smoke opium; 有吃有喝 have plenty to eat and drink; 吃喝不盡 enough to live on for life; 吃犒勞 (shop employees, etc.) eat special dinner on holidays; 吃豆腐 to enjoy s. t. at s. o.'s expense, also flirt with girl; 吃獨食 will not share (gain, profit) with others; 吃瓦片 live off rentals; 吃西北風 feeding on cold wind—having nothing to eat. (2) To depend (on job, person) for a living, to eat off (s. o.): 一家子吃他一個人 the whole family depend on him alone for living; 這個飯不容易吃 this is a hard way to earn a living; 吃大戶 eat off a rich person in times of famine; 吃喝不分 fare and share all together; 吃現成 (兒) 飯 live off s. t. without work; 吃你的, 吃我的 board provided by you, by myself. (3) To bear, receive, take (in many senses, as insults, bullets, etc.): 吃不消 cannot bear any longer (job, way of living); 吃槍彈, 吃一刀 receive a shot, a knife cut; 吃黑棗兒 be shot as punishment; 吃罪 *-tzueih*↓; 吃驚 *-jing*, 吃力 *-lih*, 吃苦 *-kuu*↓; 吃便宜 take advantage of others; 吃官司 be involved in lawsuit; 吃掛絡兒 get into lawsuit by being involved with others; 吃墨紙 *-moh-jyy*↓. (4) To take advantage of, to overcome, absorb, cover up, displace: 吃棋子 to take off opponent's piece at chess; 吃軟不吃硬 bully the weak but yield to one who can fight back; 這船吃多深水 what is the displacement of this ship; 屋簷被那堵牆吃住了 the roof is blocked from view by that wall; 淺黃色被深紅吃住 light yellow loses its color when placed next to crimson; 我的錢被小偷吃去了 my money was pilfered by pickpocket; 吃那厮騙了 was swindled by that fellow.

吃本 *chy-been*, v. i., run business at a loss.

吃錢 *chy-chiarn*, phr., to take bribe.

吃的 *chy'de*, n., things to eat: 吃的穿的都有 have enough food and clothing.

吃館子 *chy-guaantz*, v. i., to dine out at restaurant.

吃喝兒 *chy'he'l*, n., foodstuffs: 吃喝兒太貴 foodstuffs are too expensive.

吃齋 *chy-jai*, v. i., take vegetarian food (a Budd. vow).

吃勁 *chyjihn*, adj., (work) takes a lot of strength to do.

吃緊 *chyjiin*, v. i., (turn of events) becomes critical, (hear bad news from the war, etc.).

吃驚 *chy-jing*, v. i., get a fright: 吃一大驚 get a shock.

吃重 *chyjuhng*, v. i., bear the brunt of burden.

吃虧 *chy-kuei*, (1) v. i., to take a loss, not receive what is due: 吃個大虧 take a bad loss (in deal); 好漢不吃眼前虧 a wise man does not fight when the odds are against him—beautiful term for collaboration; (2) conj., unfortunately: 吃虧他不在此 unfortunately he is not here (and so misses a good opportunity).

吃苦 *chy-kuu*, v. i., (1) to suffer: 他要吃苦了 he is going to pay for it; (2) have the capacity for enduring hardships.

吃兒 *che'l*, n., things to eat: 今天有什麽好吃兒 what food have we got for today?

吃糧 *chy-liarng*, v. i., (coll.) to get government rations, i. e., serve as soldier.

吃力 *chy-lih*, v. i., (things) take a lot of doing: 吃力不討好 a thankless task.

吃墨紙 *chymoh-jyy*, n., blotting paper.

吃香 *chyshiang*, v. i., be popular, in current demand or fashion: 現在理科很吃香 now the study of science is very popular.

吃心 *chyshin*, v. i., (1) (=吃心力) take a lot of thinking; (2) to worry one.

吃水 *chy-shueei*, v. i., (1) (ship) have a displacement of water; (2) (person) drink water; (3) (soil) retain water.

吃食 *chyshyr*, n., snacks, tidbits.

吃素 *chy-suh*, v. i., take only vegetarian food.

吃私 *chy-sy*, v. i., mishandle public funds.

吃醋 *chy-tsuh*, v. i., (of man or woman) be jealous.

吃罪 *chytzueih*, v. i., suffer or suffer blame: 吃罪不起 responsibility for the blame will be too great for me.

咆 40A.70–9

paur.

N. & v.i. Roar.

咆哮 *paurshiau*, v. i., rage and roar, like a lion (var. 咆咻 *-shiou*, 咆烋 *-shiau*).

吮 40A.70–9

shuun.

V. t. To suck: 吮乳 suck at breast; 含毫吮墨 moisten tip of writing brush with lips (pause to think while writing); 吮癰舐痔 suck the ulcers and piles of another person—play the lickboot.

嗁 40A.70–9

tir.

[Anc. var. of 啼 40A.22]

§ 40A.71 (口/弋)

嚱 40A.71–2

shi.

Excl. Ah, oh! 嘘嚱 ditto.

嘎 40A.71-3

ga (also *gar*).

Adj. Descriptive of sounds, see compp.↓, also used to translate foreign names with *ga-*, *ca-* sounds.

嘎叭 *gaba*, adj., cracking, splitting sound.

嘎巴 *ga'ba*, (1) n., a solidified mass: 糊嘎巴 the burnt rice or other food that adheres to the bottom of the cooking pot; 鼻涕嘎巴 solidified mucus from the nose; 嘎巴兒 anything solidified into a mass; (2) v. i., solidify, become solidified: 他的鼻涕都嘎巴上了 the mucus from his nose has caked; 嘎巴流星 the same solidified into a dirty mass; 嘎裡嘎巴 dirty and disgusting; untidy.

嘎迸脆 *gabihng-tsueih*, adj., crisp (cake).

嘎調 *gardiauh*, n., (Chin. opera) staccato.

嘎嘎 *gaga*, (1) adj., sound of laughter: 嘎嘎的笑; (2) 嘎嘎兒 *gar'ga'l*, of a long, slender shape with a bulging middle: 嘎嘎棗兒 olive-like dates; 嘎嘎兒 any olive-like thing, (facet.) a naughty fellow; 嘎嘎兒天 days cool in the morning and evening and hot at noontime; (3) 嘎嘎渣渣 *gagajaja*, n., dregs.

嘎吱 *gajy*, adj., crackling, laughing sound.

嘎啦 *gala*, adj., rumbling sound.

喊 40A.71-7

haan.

V.i. To shout, yell, howl: 大喊, 喊叫 yell (as for help); 吶喊 shout as a crowd; oft. ＋adj. or vb.: 喊好兒 to yell applause; 喊冤枉 to call attention by shouting a grievance; 喊救命 cry "Help! Help!" 喊痛 shriek with pain; 喊苦 bawl out pain or suffering; 喊殺連天 the air is filled with shouts of "Kill! Kill!"

喊 40A.71-7

chi.

Adj. (A low sibilant sound) whispering, hissing: 大家都喊喊喳喳 there was a lot of tittle-tattle (in the room).

哦 40A.71-9

or (also *er*).

V.i. 吟哦 to recite (poem) with intonation.

Excl. (Surprise) oh? is that so? really?

哦呵 *or'ho* (also *er-*), excl., (surprise, satisfaction, admiration) aha!: 哦呵, 來了這麽多的人 aha! so many people have come!

哦呀 *or'ya* (also *er-*), excl., (surprise) oh, my! (again another murder, etc.).

哦唷(喲) *or'yo* (also *er-*), excl., (surprise, sometimes mocking) oh, my! (so much! etc.).

嘰 40A.71-9

ji.

V.i. & t. (1) V.i., to sigh in disapproval. (2) V.t., take a small bite of.

Adj. & adv. Imitating a variety of sounds, see compp.↓.

嘰咕 *ji'gu*, v.i., (1) to grumble, mumble, murmur, complain; (2) to set one person against another, sow seeds of discord.

嘰嘰嘎嘎 *jiji-gaga*, v.i., cackle in laughter, giggle (also 咕咕呱呱 --*guagua*).

嘰嘰咕咕 *jiji-gugu*, v.i., to whisper together.

嘰哩咕嚕 *jili-gulu*, v.i., to talk in low whispers; 嘰哩旮旯兒 --*galar'l*, (look for s.t.) everywhere, every nook and corner.

§ 40A.72 (口/心)

噫 40A.72-6

yi (also *yih*).

Excl. Alas!

唸 40A.72-8

niahn.

V. t. To read, chant: 唸書 read a book; 唸經 chant Buddhist scriptures (oft. wr. 念).

唿 40A.72-9

hu.

唿哨 *hushauh*, n. & v. i., (give) a whistle call.

§ 40A.80 (口/八)

嘖 40A.80-1

tzer.

V. i. (1) To grumble: 嘖有煩言 (LL) there are complaints all around. (2) 嘖嘖 (Of birds) to chirp; (of persons) sing the praises of s.o.: 嘖嘖稱善 praise with clicking of tongue.

噴 40A.80-1

pen (also *pehn*, **fehn*).

V. i. & t. To spray, sprinkle, spit out, gush out as in spring 噴水: ditto; 噴氣 blow out, send out steam, gas; to sneeze in 噴嚏 *-tih* ↓; 噴鼻而(兒)香 feel sharp aroma, extremely fragrant; pungent; 噴蛆口 (derog.) foul-mouthed person ("spit out worms"); 噴雲吐霧 (of opium smokers) filling room with a cloud of smoke.

噴勃 *penbor*[1], adj., (AC) filling room (of music).

噴薄 *penbor*[2], v. i., (AC) gush forth.

噴泉 *penchyuarn*, n., fountain, geyser.

噴飯 *pen-fahn*, v. i., choke with laughter.

噴火山 *penhuuo-shan* n., =火山, volcano.

噴口 *penkoou*, n., crater.

噴噴 *penpen*, adj., (AC) fast in talking.

噴射 *pensheh*, n., jet; 噴射機 *--ji*, n., jet airplane.

噴水池 *penshueei-chyr*, n., fountain.

噴嚏 *pentih* (also **fehn-*), v. i., sneeze.

噴桶 *pentung*, n., can for sprinkling flowers.

噴霧器 *penwuh-chih*, n., spray can, atomizer.

噸 40A.80-1

duhn.

N. A ton, measure of weight or cubic measure: 噸位 tonnage (of ship).

囋 40A.80-1

tzahn.

[Var. of 讚 60A.80]

V.i. & t. (AC) give more information than asked for.

哄 40A.80-2

hung (**huung*).

V. i. (Of a crowd) to roar, make an uproar: 哄堂大笑 the audience roared in laughter, an uproar of laughter in the audience; 哄傳 (of news) circulate abroad.

V. t. (**huung*) (1) To scare (person) by a false story: 你不要哄人 you are trying to throw a scare, I won't believe what you say. (2) To coax (a child).

哄動 *hungduhng*, v.i., as in 哄動一時 to cause a sensation.

哄鬧 *hungnauh*, v. i., to make a lot of noise.

哄騙 **huungpiahn*, v. t., to cheat by a hoax.

嗔 40A.80-2

chen.

N. Angry expression: 含嗔 to pout, i. e., show contained anger.

V. i. & t. (1) To show anger: 嬌嗔 (of woman) to pout prettily; 嗔笑 pouting smile. (2) To taunt, chide (person): 嗔着他 taunting him.

嗔詬 *chengouh*, v.t., (LL) to vilify, berate (person).

嗔怪 *chenguaih*, v.t., to upbraid (person).

嗔喝 *chenheh*, v.t., to yell at, rail at.

嗔狂 *chengkwarng*, adj., crazy, deranged.

嗔睨 *chennih*, v.t., to glance at (person) with anger.

嗔怒 *chennuh*, v.i., to become angry.

嗩 40A.80-2

suoo.

嗩納 *suoo'na*, n., a flute-like instrument of Turkish origin.

唄 40A.80-4

baih.

N. 唄讚 intonation of Buddhist litany; such singing; c.f. 貝△文 41.80.

叭 40A.80-8

ba.

N. See 喇△叭 40A.00.

叭叭=巴△巴 52.70.

§ 40A.81 (口/人)

嗽 40A.81-1

souh.

V.i. & t. (1) To cough: 咳嗽. (2) To gargle: 嗽口 (also wr. 漱口).

喫 40A.81-1

chy.
[Interch. of 吃 40A.70]

吠 40A.81-1

feih.

V.i. (Dogs) bark: 吠影吠聲 from 一犬吠形, 百犬吠聲 one dog barks at a shadow and the pack barks at the noise, (contempt.) servile echoes; 蜀犬吠日 (allu.) a dog barking at the sun where sun is rarely seen as in the mountains of Szechuan, i.e., excitement over nothing; 桀犬吠堯 a pack of hounds barking at a good man.

咦 40A.81-1

yir.

Excl. An excl. of surprise, of peevish disapproval; also modn. excl. of surprise, pr. *yee.*

噗 40A.81-2

pu.

噗嗤(兒) *puchy* (-*che'l*), adv., making sound of breaking into laughter (onomatopoetic word): 噗嗤笑了起來, oft. wr. 撲⁴哧 10A.81.

嘆 40A.81-2

tahn.
[Var. of 歎 20S.81]

噘 40A.81-5

jyue.

V.i. Protrude lips, as a sign of displeasure: 噘嘴 pout.

咳 40A.81-6

ker (**kaa, *hai, *haih*).

V.i. (1) To cough: 咳嗽 -*'sou*↓. (2) (**kaa*), To cough up: see 咳痰, 咳血 -*tarn*, -*shyueh*↓; 咳出來 cough it out.

Adj. Descriptive of child's laughter.

Excl. (**hai* or **hai*!) An audible sign: 咳！我怎麽忘了 ah! how I forgot! (**haih*) an emphatic expression of regret: 咳！這眞是意料不到的事 alas! who would ever think this would happen?

咳血 **kaashyueh*, v.i., to cough blood.
咳嗽 *ker'sou*, v.i., to cough.
咳痰 **kaatarn*, v.i., to spit out phlegm.
咳唾 *kertuoh*, n. & v.i., spittle; to make spitting sound.

嗾 40A.81-6

tzur (*soou*).
[Cogn. 唆 *suo*, 40A.82]

V.t. To instigate, orig. whistle to dog to attack.

嗾使 *sourshyy* (also *tzur.*), v.t., to instigate s.o. (to do s.t.).

噷 40A.81-6

hm.

Excl. H'm!

唳 40A.81-6

lih.

V.i. (Of birds) to cry: 風聲鶴唳 be scared at "the whistling of winds and the crying of cranes"—nervous atmosphere of war and turmoil.

咲 40A.81-8

shiauh.
[Anc. var. of 笑 92A.81]

叺 40A.81-8

yii.
[Abbr. of 以 21.81]

嗅 40A.81-9

shiouh.

V.t. To smell: 嗅覺 the sense of smell; 嗅嗅看 try to smell it; 嗅到香味 smell s.t. sweet, fragrant.

嗽 喫 吠 咦 噗 嘆 噘 咳 嗾 噷 唳 咲 叺 嗅

亅	小	[illegible]	十	土	ナ	卄	[illegible]	丨	一	丅	フ	口	区	[illegible]	[illegible]	厂	戸	亠	广	[illegible]	丶	乚	弋	心	八	人	乂	一	ノ	儿	[illegible]	く
00	01	02	10	11	12	20	21	22	30	31	32	40	41	42	50	51	52	60	61	62	63	70	71	72	80	81	82	83	90	91	92	93

喉 40A.81-9

hour.

N. The throat, the larynx: 咽喉 "throat," (fig.) strategic area; 喉科 (med.) laryngology, specialty on throat diseases.

喉急 *hourjir*, adj., desperately anxious.
喉嚨 *hourlurng* (-'*lung*), n., (phys.) the throat: 喉嚨疼 a sore throat.
喉痧 *hoursha*, n., (med.) diphtheria (also called 白喉).
喉舌 *hoursher*, n., "throat and tongue"—mouthpiece: 爲民喉舌 person who speaks for the people.
喉頭 *hourtour*, n., the larynx.
喉痛 *hourtuhng*, n., sore throat.
喉音 *hour-yin*, n., glottal sound.

啾 40A.81-9

dir.

啾咕 *dirgu*, v.i., jabber or whisper: 他們啾咕了半天 they have been jabbering together a long while; feel restless: 心裏一直在啾咕 feeling restless, palpitating, also 啾啾咕咕 *dirdir-gugu*.

啖 40A.81-9

dahn.
[Var. 啗]

V.i. & t. (1) To feed or bait. (2) To bite and chew (food); cf. 噉 40A.82.

吹 40A.81-9

chuei (**chueih*).

V.i. & t. (1) To blow: 風吹雨打 the wind blows and the rain beats down; 吹簫, 吹笛 play the fife, the flute; 吹氣 blow breath; 吹拂, 吹嘘 -*fur*, -*shyu*↓; 吹口哨 or 吹哨 -*shauh*↓; 吹糖人兒 blow sugar dolls; 吹毛求疵 pick fault unfairly (like "see the mote in your brother's eye"); 吹鬍子瞪眼睛 snort ("blow whiskers") and stare in anger; 吹皺一池春水, 干卿底事 what has that to do with you? (from allu.—a king disapproves of a poet's line about the breeze rippling the water in the pond); 不費吹灰之力 with minimum effort (less than "blowing dust" off table). (2) To blow one's own horn, to brag: 吹牛, 吹嗙 -*niour*, -*paang*↓; 吹法螺 to brag, also to blow the conch shell in Budd. ceremony. (3) V.i., fizzle out: 這件婚事吹了 the romance has gone to pieces; 這對青年男女已經吹了 the boy and girl have broken off; 買賣吹了 the deal is off. (4) (**chueih*) In 鼓吹 to boost up s.t.

吹鞭 *chueibian*, n., anciently, a singing whip, described as attached to a whistle.
吹腔 *chueichiang*, n., a type of local opera (弋腔) with flute accompaniment, any such accompaniment.
吹脣 *chueichurn*, v.i., to whistle, see -*shauh*↓.
吹打 *chueidaa* (-'*da*), v.i., play flutes, horns or trumpets and beat drums.
吹風(兒) *chueifeng*('*l*), v.i., to start people talking: 這幾天他吹風兒説大話 he has been bragging and letting it be known.
吹拂 *chueifur*, v.i. & t., (1) see -*shyu*↓; (2) to flap about in wind (as flag).
吹鼓手 *chei'gushoou*, n., formerly, the fife and drum players at wedding, funeral.
吹管 *chueiguaan*, n., blowpipe.
吹呼 *chuei'hu*, v.t., to bawl at (person): 把他吹呼了一頓 gave him a scolding.
吹指 *chueijyy*, v.i., to whistle with fingers in mouth.
吹牛 *chueiniour*, v.i., to brag (also 吹牛皮): 自己吹牛 brag of oneself; 吹牛拍馬 phr., to boast and flatter.
吹嗙 *chueipaang*, v.i., ditto; 胡吹亂嗙 ballyhoo.
吹哨 *chueishauh*, v.i., to whistle.
吹簫 *chuei-shiau*, v.i., (1) to play the fife; (2) (LL allu.) to be a beggar, from story of 伍子胥.
吹手 *chueishoou*, n., see -'*gushoou*↑.
吹嘘 *chueishyu*, v.t., to praise, speak in favor of s.o., esp. to influential person.
吹臺 *chuei-tair*, v.i., to fizzle out.
吹彈 *chueitarn*, n. & v.i., music for occasions (with horns and string).
吹筒 *chueituung*, n., formerly, hunter's horn.
吹網 *chuei-waang*, v.i., (Budd.) to inflate a fish net by blowing—obviously futile.
吹雲 *chuei yurn*, phr., to paint clouds by blowing white spots of powder over wet silk.

喚 40A.81-9

huahn.

V.t. (1) To call (person): 呼喚 call for a person; 呼兄喚弟 address each other as brothers; 叫喚 to cry out (for help) or bid servant to do things; 喚他過來 ask him to come; 呼風喚雨 (Taoist magic) bid wind and rain to come. (2) To be called: 你喚什麽名字 what are you called; 我喚着狗兒 I am called Doggie.

唉 40A.81-9

ai.

Excl. Ai! (cry of pain or extreme misery, identical with vocalized sigh); also wr. 哎 40A.82, 嗳 40A.82.

§ 40A.82 (口/乂)

吱 40A.82-1

tzy.

Adj. Imitation of hissing sounds: 吱嘍嘍 (of doors) grating, (of leaves, branches of trees) rustling, sighing; 吱吱喳喳 (of birds) chirping together, (of women, children) talking in confusion; 吱吱(叫) chirping, (of children) crying, shrieking.

吱歪 *tzzwai*, v.i., to slouch.

嗷 40A.82-1

aur.
[Var. 嗸]

Adj. Noisy, making a hubbub.

嗷嗷 *aur-aur*, adj., as in 嗷嗷待哺 (young of birds, children) clamoring for food.
嗷嘈 *aurtsaur*, adj., making a din, hubbub.

哎 40A.82-2

ai (also *aih*, indeterminate tone).

Excl. Excl. of pain; extreme misery: oft. 哎呀 *ai-yah*! or 哎喲 *ai-yoh*! (identical with a vocalized sigh of pain, extreme distress), also wr. 唉, 嗳.

嚄 40A.82-2

huoh (*uh).

Excl. (**uh*) Oh!: 嚄, 我錯了, oh, it's my mistake, see 嚄唷 -'*yu*↓; 嚄, 這是什麽意思 what do you mean, hey?

嚄唶 *huohtzeh*, n., (AC) sound of laughter.
嚄嘖 *huohtzer*, v.i., (AC) babble, talk too much.
嚄唷 *huoh'yu*, excl., (AC) a-ha! exclamation of surprise (modn. version also *ohyoh*↓): 嚄唷, 你的寶寶這麽胖 oh, how plump your darling baby!

哽 40A.82-3

geeng.

V. i. To choke from grief or anger: 哽咽 -*ye*↓.

哽塞 *geengseh*, v. i., be choked and unable to speak.
哽咽 *geengye*, v. i., to choke with sobs.

嗄 40A.82-3

shah (**ar*).

Adj. Hoarse (voice, also 唦).

Excl. (**ar*) Expressing surprise, disbelief.

噉 40A.82-3

dahn.
[Var. of 啖]

V. t. To bite and chew: 噉蔗 chew sugar cane; to enjoy quietly and slowly, as in chewing.

吸 40A.82-3

shi.

V. t. (1) To draw in, attract, absorb: 吸收, 吸引 -*shou*, -*yiin*↓; 吸入 draw in (new members); 吸出 drain or suck out; 呼吸 to breathe (exhale and inhale); 吸氣 draw in the air; 吸水 to draw water from well; 吸去靈魂 (of ghost) suck away s. o.'s soul; 吸了一點文明空氣 breathe the air of the modn. world. (2) To drink: 吸飲 to drink (wine, etc.); 一吸而盡 drink up in one swallow.

吸根 *shi-gen*, n., (bot.) sucking roots of parasitic plants.
吸管 *shi-guaan*, n., respiratory tract; bronchi; a sucking tube.
吸力 *shilih*, n., magnetic force; force of attraction.
吸墨紙 *shimoh-jyy*, n., blotting paper.
吸盤 *shi-parn*, n., (zoo.) sucker (as in octopus).
吸收 *shishou*, v. t., to absorb, take in (moisture, liquid, gas, shares, followers, new subscribers, new ideas, etc.); 吸收口 (zoo.) sucking organ, proboscis (in mosquitoes, etc.).
吸濕性 *shishy-shihng*, n., (phys.) hygroscopic power.
吸鐵石 *shitiee-shyr*, n., a magnet (also called 磁石).
吸烟 *shiyan*, v. i., to smoke (cigarette, pipe).
吸引 *shiyiin*, v. t., to attract (followers, etc.).

啜 40A.82-3

chuoh.

V. t. (LL) to sip (tea, liquid).

啜泣 *chuohchih*, v. i., to sob.

嘬 唚 咬 啵 嗳 嗷 呶 唆 唓 嚏 咮

嘬 40A.82–4

chuaih (re. pr. **tzuo*).

V. t. (1) (AC) to gobble up. (2) (Of gnats) to bite and suck.

唚 40A.82–5

chihn.

[Related 吣, 吢]

V. i. & t. (Of animals like dogs) to vomit, (fig.) (derog.) to spit out nonsense, hogwash; 混唚, 胡唚 to rail, yelp, talk hogwash; 唚不出好話 (derog.) spit out only dirty language.

咬 40A.82–6

yaau.

V.t. (1) To bite: 咬一口 give a bite; 咬斷了 to bite off; 咬不動 (food) too tough to bite; 蟲咬 bitten by insect; 咬菜根 to live on bare subsistence. (2) To persist in accusing person at court: 咬定是他 accused him definitely; 賊咬一口 the thief accuses s.o. as accomplice; 一口咬定 to accuse definitely. (3) To bark: 聽見狗直咬 heard dog barking incessantly. (4) To gnash teeth: 咬牙 *-yar* ↓; 咬緊牙根 keep a stiff upper lip.

咬扯 *yaurchee*, v.i., to chafe, give vent by angry talking.
咬春 *yaau-chun*, v.i., (Peiking dial.) formerly, a custom of eating turnip raw on 立春 (arrival of Spring); 立春 see Appendix B.
咬羣(兒) *yaau-chyurn*(*-chyuer'l*), v.i., "bite the herd"—create trouble inside group.
咬耳朶 *yaur-eel'duo*, v.i., "bite the ear"—whisper.
咬筋 *yaau-jin*, n., maxillary muscle.
咬破 *yaau-poh*, v.i., bite open, bite to pieces.
咬舌兒 *yaau-sher'l*, v.i., to lisp, talk with unclear consonants, also 咬舌子.
咬手 *yaur-shoou*, v.i., to have chilblains.
咬字兒 *yaau-tzeh'l*, v.i., (Chin. opera) training in enunciation, particularly difference between *ch* and *ts*.
咬文 *yaauwern*, phr., 咬文嚼字 or 咂字, to "chew words"—overfastidious and oft. too literal interpretation of words.
咬牙 *yaauyar*, v.i., (1) pay too much attention to details, too dogmatic or insistent; (2) to grind one's teeth in sleep: 咬牙切齒 to gnash teeth in hatred.

啵 40A.82–6

bo (unaccented).

Fin. part. (MC) denoting request, command, etc.=modn. 吧 40A.70 ↑.

嗳 40A.82–9

aai (also *aih*, indeterminate tone).

Excl. 嗳呀 *aih'ya*, 嗳唷 *aih'yo*, exclamations of pain, painful surprise, disappointment, also wr. 哎.

嗷 40A.82–9

jiauh.

V. i. (1) To call, yell, cry. (2) Weep, mourn.

呶 40A.82–9

naur.

[Var. 譊]

呶呶 *naurnaur*, adj., noisily complaining, murmuring.

唆 40A.82–9

suo.

V. t. To incite, instigate: 教唆 ditto; 調唆 to make fun of, tease (person).

唆使 *suoshyy*, v. t., to incite (to mischief).

§ 40A.83 (口/〜)

唓 40A.83–1

shah (**shier*).

唓嗻 var. of 唼[Δ]喋 40A.93 ↓.

嚏 40A.83–1

tih.

V. i. & n. To sneeze, a sneeze: 打嚏, 噴嚏 (*fehntih*), 打噴嚏 to sneeze.

咮 40A.83–1

dou.

Excl. Excl. of angry dismissal, "beat it!"

呱 40A.83-9

gu (sp. pr. **wa*).

V.i. To utter a child's shrill cry: 呱呱墜地 a baby is born with a cry; 呱呱叫 (*wawa-jiauh*) keep on wailing (see 聒聒叫 31S.40).

§ 40A.91 (口/ノ)

吵 40A.91-2

chaau.
[Dist. 炒]

V. i. & t. To create a disturbance, a brawl, row or noisy dispute: 吵架 *-jiah*↓; 吵鬧 *-nauh*↓; 爭吵 to fight noisily, quarrel; 別吵了 stop the noise, keep quiet; 吵散 *-saan*↓.

Adj. Noisy: 吵得慌 terribly noisy.

吵架 *chaaujiah*, v.i., as in 跟人吵架 fight, quarrel with s. o.
吵鬧 *chaaunauh*, adj., noisily quarrelsome: 吵吵鬧鬧, 大吵大鬧 create noisy disturbance.
吵擾 *chaauraau*, v.t., disturb.
吵散 *chaur-saan*, v. t., to break up (celebrations, etc.) by disturbance.
吵喜 *chaur-shii*, v. i., (coll.) to announce big good news (such as passing of degrees, official promotion) at the house door.
吵嘴 *chaurtzueei*, v.i., to quarrel: 兩人吵嘴 the two are having a quarrel.

嘐 40A.91-5

shiau.

嘐嘐 *shiaushiau*, adj., as in (AC) 其志嘐嘐然 his will was free and unhampered—vain and self-pleased.

唦 40A.91-6

sha.

Fin. part. (MC) final particle, similar to 啊, indicating assertion (related AC 些, MC 者).

喭 40A.91-6

yahn.

Adj. (AC) stubborn, rude.

咿 40A.91-9

yi.

Adj. Used in compp. only, descriptive of creaking sound.

咿喔 *yiwoh*, adj., descriptive of cackling (hens).
咿唔 *yiwur*, v. i., to recite or intone in reading.
咿啞 *yiyaa*, v. i., to make a creaking sound (as of oars); to make baby sounds.
咿咿 *yiyi*, adj., any creaking, inarticulate sound (as of insects, pigs).
咿呦 (嚘) *yiyou*, adj., descriptive of inarticulate animal sounds (such as given by deer).

§ 40A.93 (口/く)

呿 40A.93-1

chyu.

Adj. (AC) open-mouthed.

囈 40A.93-2

yih.

N. Somniloquy: 夢囈 ditto; (fig.) crazy or incoherent talk.

囈怔 *yih'jeng*, n., talk or action in sleep: 撒囈怔 to talk or act in sleep.
囈語 *yihyuu*, n., incoherent or crazy talk.

嗤 40A.93-2

chy.

V.i. & t. (1) To sneer at, laugh at: 嗤之以鼻 give a snicker; 自嗤 laugh at oneself. (2) To snort, chortle: 嗤的一笑.

嗤鄙 *chybii*, v.t., sneer at with contempt.
嗤詆 *chydii*, v.i., to deride.
嗤笑 *chyshiauh*, v.i., chuckle, sneer.

嘍 40A.93-2

lour (*'*lou*).

Fin. part. ('*lou*): 好嘍 it's ready;

得嘍 that will do; 來嘍 I'm coming; see 咯, 啦, 嘞 similar final particles.

嘍 囉 *lourlour*, n., (also 僂儸) (contempt.) followers of any leader.

嚶 40A.93-4

ying.

V. i. (Of birds) to chirp: 嚶鳴 (LL) to seek friendships.

唼 40A.93-6

shah (**tza*).

V.t. (1) (**tza*) Eat noisily. (2) Gnaw, suck: 這棵死樹根被螞蟻唼了 the root of this dead tree has been gnawed away by ants; 唼眼 -*yaan* ↓. (3) Sift, as with a sieve; spit out (small grains of sand, etc. in food).

唼 氣 *shah-chih*, v. i., (of cars, rickshaws) have a flat tire.
唼 喋 *shahdier*, n., sound made by waterfowls when eating in a group.
唼 臘 蟲 *shahlah-churng*, n., a worm feeding on corpses.
唼 唼 *shahshah*, n., imitation of sound made in eating, as by fish.
唼 血 *shahshyueh*, v. i., (1) suck the blood of the sacrificial animal to cement a pledge (an alliance) among participating princes; (2) redden the ground with the blood of persons killed in war.
唼 眼 *shahyaan*, n., small holes bored by worms in furniture or other things.

喩 40A.93-8

yuh.

[Printed form of 喻 40A.00]

吆 40A.93-9

yau.

吆 喝 *yau'he*, v. i. & t., to yell, esp. at servants.

SECTION 40B

§ 40B.00 (足/亅)

躊 40B.00-1

chour.

躊 躇 *chourchur*, v. i., (1) to hesitate, dillydally; (2) 躊躇滿志 be self-satisfied, puffed up with pride.

踦 40B.00-1

jii (**yii*).

N. (1) The shin bone, the tibia. (2) Misfortune, mishap.

V. t. (**yii*) Lean on: 相與踦閭而語 (AC) they talked while leaning against the gateway; press, squeeze (as with legs).

躪 40B.00-2

lihn.

V. t. To trample down, upon: 蹂躪 trample upon (people); 躪轢 to ride roughshod over.

蹡 40B.00-2

chiang.

蹡 蹡 *chiangchiang*, adv., (walking) in a hurry (also wr. 蹌).

蹰 40B.00-6

chur.

V.i. See 踟[A]蹰 40B.40, hesitate.

跡 40B.00-6

ji.

[Var. of 迹 60.83]

蹲 40B.00-8

dun (re. pr. **tsurn*).

V.i. (1) Squat: 蹲在地上 squat on the ground. (2) (**tsurn*) (AC) stamp in savage dance.

蹲膘兒 *dunbiau'l*, v.i., become obese with overeating and no exercise.

踰 40B.00-8

yur.

V. t. (1) To transgress. (2) (Interch. 逾 81.83) to exceed, go beyond, climb over.

踰侈 *yurchyy*, adj., (AC) too extravagant.
踰封 *yur-feng*, phr., (AC) cross state boundary.
踰矩 *yur-jyuu*, phr., (AC) to transgress what is right.
踰閑 *yur-shiarn*, phr., break moral conventions.
踰越 *yuryueh*, v. t., to exceed, go beyond (rules, powers).

跗 40B.00-9

fu.

N. Instep, metatarsus.

§ 40B.01 (足/小)

蹀 40B.01-2

dier.

V. i. Walk in small steps, pace.

蹀蹀 *dierdier*, v.i., walk in mincing gait.
蹀躞 *diershieh*, v. i., to pace about.

跺 40B.01-3

duoh.

跺脚 *duohjiaau*, v. i., stamp one's feet (as in anger, regret).

蹂 40B.01-3

rour.

V. t. Trample, tread on: 蹂躪 -*lihn*↓; 蹂踐 trample down, crush under the feet, stamp on; 蹂若 trample, grind underfoot.

蹂躪 *rourlihn*, v. t., (1) grind underfoot; (2) destroy, annihilate, devastate.

躁 40B.01-4

tzauh.

V. i. Be excited (uneasy, vexed): 輕躁 be frivolous; 躁擾 to trouble, annoy; 躁鬧 cause disturbance, raise a row.

Adj. Impatient, quick-tempered, restive, jittery: 躁進 anxious to push ahead; 躁競 eager for riches and honors; 發躁 annoyed, vexed; 煩躁 wrought-up, fidgety.

躁狂 *tzauhkuarng*, n., mania (also 瘋狂).
躁鬱的 *tzauhyuh'de*, adj., manic-depressive.

踝 40B.01-4

huair (re. pr. **huah*).

N. The ankle: 足踝; 踝骨 ankle-bone.

踪 40B.01-6

tzung.

[Var. of 蹤 40B.83]

躒 40B.01-9

luoh.

V. i. (AC) move: 一躒 in one step.

蹰 跡 蹲 踰 跗 蹀 跺 蹂 躁 踝 踪 躒

亅	小	⺊	十	土	ナ	卄	卜	丨	一	丅	フ	口	区	冈	乛	厂	尸	亠	广	宀	丶	乚	弋	心	八	人	乂	⌒	丿	刂	𠂉	く
00	01	02	10	11	12	20	21	22	30	31	32	40	41	42	50	51	52	60	61	62	63	70	71	72	80	81	82	83	90	91	92	93

A

§ 40B.02 (足/k)

跟 40B.02-5

gen.

N. The heel: 腳跟, 腳後跟, 後跟 the heel; 高跟鞋 high-heeled shoes; 鞋跟兒 the back part of a shoe.

V. t. (1) Follow, accompany, attend on: 跟在後面 follow from behind; 跟著他 accompany or attend on him, be a member of his entourage; 跟蹤 to shadow (s. o.); 跟牌 (of card game) follow suit. (2) Catch up with: 跟不上功課 cannot catch up with one's lessons.

Prep. To, from, with: 他要跟你談一談 he wants to talk to you; 她跟我借了一支鉛筆 she has borrowed a pencil from me; 這小孩跟李太太學琴 the boy is taking piano lessons with Mrs. Lee; 請你跟他去 please go with him.

Conj. And: 他跟她是同班 he and she are classmates; 她跟她的丈夫 she and her husband.

跟班(兒)(的) *genban(-ba'l) ('de)*, n., see *-bau* ↓.

跟包(的) *genbau('de)*, n., (coll.) a footman, servant of an official, attendant, entourage.

跟前 *genchiarn*, n., (1) the front of s. t. (also 跟前兒): 走到講臺跟前 come to the front of the platform; (2) (*-'chian*) presence: 在他跟前別亂說 don't talk too freely in his presence; (3) (*-'chian*) children in relation to their parents: 你跟前有幾位少爺 how many sons do you have with you (now)? (4) (coll.) 跟前人 a concubine.

跟著 *gen'je*, adv., (1) in the wake of; (2) immediately, at once, right away.

跟腳(兒) *gen-jiaau('l)*, adj., (of shoes) fitting perfectly and comfortable to wear.

B

跟勁 *genjihn*, adj. & n., get a purchase or grip, be capable, competent or serviceable.

跟主兒 *gen-juu'l*, phr., (coll.) be s. o.'s servant.

跟媽(兒) *genma('l)*, n., personal maid of a prostitute.

跟人 *genrern*, n., an attendant, a follower.

跟手(兒) *genshoou('l)*, adj. & adv., (1) immediate(ly); (2) smooth(ly), successful(ly), without a hitch.

跟隨 *gensueir*, (1) v. t., follow (s. o.) from behind; (2) n., follower.

跟頭 *gen'tou*, (1) n., a fall, somersault: 栽跟頭 get a fall; 翻跟頭 turn a somersault; 他摔了一個跟頭 he had a fall; (2) adj., (coll.) frustrated: 咱們跟頭啦 we are faced with failure.

跟蹤 *gen-tzung*, v. t., follow in the track of, to shadow (s. o.).

跟尾兒 *gen-yee'l*, adv., right away, at once: 他跟尾兒就出來了 he'll come out right away; see *-'je* ↑.

蹍 40B.02-5

jaan.

V. t. (AC) step on (toes).

踉 40B.02-6

liahng (also *larng*).

踉蹌 *liahngchiahng*, adj. & adv., hurried(ly) and unstead(-ily) (also wr. 踉蹡).

C

§ 40B.10 (足/十)

踔 40B.10-2

juor.

V. i. & t. (AC) to surpass.

Adj. (AC) outstanding, lofty: 踔絕 lofty; 踔遠 far distant; 踔厲風發 be an incisive and interesting talker.

躡 40B.10-3

nieh.

V. i. & t. (1) Follow: 追躡 follow from behind. (2) 躡足 *-tzur* ↓.

躡機 *niehji*, n., silk loom with foot paddle.

躡足 *niehtzur*, v. i., (1) step on s. o.'s foot; (2) walk on tiptoe; (3) (AC) take one's position in: 躡足行伍之間 served in the army.

蹕 40B.10-4

bih.

V. i. (1) (AC) emperor's visit or stopping place: 蹕臨 visit, arrive (of emperor); 駐蹕 place of emperor's stop or temporary residence. (2) (AC) (temple, palace grounds) to clear traffic, close to passengers.

躃 40B.10-5

bih.

[Var. of 躄]

Adj. Lame in both legs.

§ 40B.11 (足/土)

跬 40B.11-1

kueei.

N. Half a step, short step: 跬步難行 difficult to move even a short step; 跬譽 (LL) a temporary popularity.

蹚 40B.11-2

tang.

V. i. (1) To tread, step on mud or water: 蹚土 kick up dust on dusty road; 蹚渾水 (兒) go about with bad characters; 胡蹚 go about as playboy, go about quite recklessly. (2) Try: 蹚一蹚, 蹚一次 have a try, try once.

躍 40B.11-5

yueh.

V.i. (1) (LL) to jump: 跳躍 jump up or about; 躍馬 jump on a horse, mount; 踴躍 (support cause, contribute) with great enthusiasm; 躍進 progress by leaps and bounds; 雀躍 happy about s.t., esp. used by younger generation in speaking to elders, parents; 躍躍欲試 anxious to try one's chance. (2) (AC) to stir (s.t.).

躔 40B.11-6

charn.

V. i. (AC) tread on.

躔度 *charnduh*, n., degree of the zodiac; course of the stars.

踵 40B.11-9

juung.

N. The heel: 踵接 *-jie* ↓; 不旋踵 in a short while, before you turn your back (it perishes, etc.).

V. i. (1) To follow, follow in footsteps: 踵至 follow closely upon heels, successively; 踵其後塵 follow in one's "trail," i.e., footsteps; 踵武 follow in footsteps of illustrious forefather; 踵事增華 embellish a story, add flourishes for effect. (2) To arrive: 踵門拜別 personally pay a farewell call.

Adv. In close succession on foot: 踵見仲尼 (AC) saw Confucius repeatedly; 踵踵 *-juung* ↓.

踵接 *juungjie*, adv., closely upon heels.

踵踵 *juungjuung*, adv., back and forth, many times.

踵謝 *juungshieh*, v. i., a formula (from 踵門拜謝) pay personal visit to say thanks for attendance at wedding, funeral, etc.

§ 40B.20 (足/廿)

趼 40B.20-3

jiaan.

[Usu. wr. 趼]

N. Blisters, callus.

§ 40B.21 (足/ㄴ)

距 40B.21-5

jyuh.

N. (1) A bird's claws. (2) A cock's spur. (3) Distance between two points: 距離 *-lir* ↓.

V. i. & t. (1) V.i., be distant: 相距不遠 not far from one another. (2) V.t., (=拒) oppose, resist.

Adj. Great, huge, immense, gigantic.

距離 *jyuhlir*, n., distance separating one point (place) from another; gap, difference (between opinions); 近距離 close quarter, at short range.

蹈 40B.21-9

dauh.

V. i. & t. Stamp with feet as in dance, step into, step over: 手舞足蹈 phr., dance and stamp, descriptive of dancing with joy; 舞蹈 gen. term for dance; 赴湯蹈火 go through fire and water; 蹈虎尾 step on tiger's tail ("twist lion's tail"); 蹈海而死 jump into the sea and die; 躬蹈 (LL) set personal example (follow the line yourself); 蹈常襲故 shortened as 蹈襲 get into a rut, be a slave to old methods of doing things.

§ 40B.22 (足/丨)

蹄 40B.22-6

tir.

[Var. of 蹏]

N. (1) Hoof: 豬蹄 pork knuckles; 馬蹄 horse's hoofs; 馬不停蹄 make a hurried journey without stop; 蹄聲答答 clatter of horse's hoofs; 失蹄 (horse) stumble. (2) (AC) hare trap.

蹄膀 *tir'pang*, n., shoulder of pork.

蹄子 *tir'tz*, n., (1) hoofs; (2) 小蹄子 (abusive) little wench (chiefly used in scolding maids).

躋 40B.22-6

ji.

V. i. Ascend, go up, climb: 躋列 be ranked among, take one's position among one's equals; 躋入, 躋進 enter; 躋升 go up, mount; 躋攀 clamber up.

躑 40B.22-8

jyr.

躑躅 *jyrjuh*, v. i., to loiter, linger round.

§ 40B.30 (足/一)

踷 40B.30-1

chaa.

V. i. & t. To splash or drag one's foot in mud; (fig.) meddle, muck: 這事你不要踷在裏頭 don't dirty yourself with this muck.

趾 40B.30-2

jyy.

N. Toe: 趾骨 toe bones; indicating a person's steps: 擧趾 standing or walking gait; 趾高氣揚 proud manner of one with head in the clouds; 請移芳趾 or 玉趾 (LL) "please move your gracious steps"—please come.

蹬 40B.30-3

dehng.

V.i. Stamp on ground; 蹭$^{\Delta}$蹬 40B.41.

踁 40B.30-3

jihng.

[Var. of 脛 42A.30]

蹉 40B.30-8

tsuo.

V. i. To err, slip, see compp. ↓.

蹉跌 *tsuodier*, v. i., to fall down, slip down.

蹉跎 *tsuotuor*, v. i., (AC) to make faltering steps: 歲月蹉跎 the years roll by—spend one's life in fruitless efforts.

§ 40B.40 (足/口)

跖 40B.40-3

jyr (also *jeh*).

N. Paw; name of famous robber: 盜跖 (AC) robber.

踞 40B.40-5

jyuh.

V.i. & t. (1) V.i., squat: 龍蟠虎踞 a terrain of strategic importance. (2) V.t., sit on: 盤踞 occupy (a seat, city, territory), cf. 據 10A.02.

踣 40B.40-6

bor.

[Dist. 掊 10A.40]

V. i. (AC) drop down dead.

蹌 40B.40-8

chiang (**chiahng*).

Adv. (Running) fast: see compp. ↓; 踉蹌 (pr. *chiahng*) run away in embarrassment, higgledy-piggledy.

蹌蹌 *chiangchiang*, adj. & adv., (AC) as in (1) 濟濟蹌蹌 parade in dignity; (2) (birds) dancing; (3) 啾啾蹌蹌 (walk) suavely.

蹌捍 *chianghahn*, adv., (AC) (horses) galloping fast.

跏 40B.40-9

jia.

跏趺 *jiafur*, v. i., (Budd.) sit cross-legged.

路 40B.40-9

luh.

N. (*'l*) (1) Road, street, avenue, path: 馬路 road, usu. well-surfaced, avenue, boulevard; 公路 highway; 鐵路 railroad; 大路 boulevard, highway; 山路 hill path; 小路 path; 路途, 路徑, 路程, *-tur*, *-jihng*, *-cherng*↓; 死路 dead end, blind alley, road to perdition; 無路可走 helpless, nowhere to turn; what happens on the road: 路斃 die on the road; 路劫 highway robbery; 路祭 sacrifices offered on the route of funeral procession; 路上 *en route*, on the road; 路經 pass (place) on the way; 路不拾遺 (of good gen. custom) lost articles are always returned. (2) Way: 思路 way of thinking (不清 confused); 生路, 活路 way of escape (to life); 財路 source of income, wealth (very prosperous, etc.); 門路 way of approach, access (to persons); 路線 a lead (to mystery), approach, access through friends (to important person); route; 此路不通, 路不通行 (road) closed to vehicle or pedestrian. (3) (*'l*) Class, kind: 這路人 this kind of person; 他們都是一路人 they are of the same gang, group; 一路貨 same kind, class, of goods. (4) A surname.

路程 *luhcherng*, n., journey (long, short, smooth, arduous, etc.).
路費 *luhfeih*, n., travel expenses.
路政 *luhjehng*, n., maintenance, control, development of public roads.
路基 *luhji*, n., roadbed.
路徑 *luhjihng*, n., road, path, pass, route.
路客 *luhkeh*, n., formerly, highwayman.
路兒 *luh'l*, n., (1) road, way; (2) kind, see N. 3↑.
路人 *luhrern*, n., strangers, casual onlookers.
路線 *luhshiahn*, n., see N. 2↑.
路條 *luhtiaur*, n., travel permit, pass for going through.
路透社 *Luhtouhsheh*, n., Reuter's News Agency.
路途 *luhtur*, n., road; journey.
路子 *luhtz*, n., see N. 1↑: 沒路子可走 nowhere to turn.

踟 40B.40-9

chyr.

踟躕(躇) *chyrchur*, v. i., (1) to hesitate; (2) to pace to and fro: 踟躕不進 tarry and not go forward.

§ 40B.41 (足/図)

躇 40B.41-2

chur.

V.i. See 躊躇 40B.00↑, to hesitate, deliberate.

蹧 40B.41-2

tzau.

蹧蹋 *tzauta*, v.t., (1) to waste (good food), trample upon, spoil by rough usage; (2) to insult (person) by words.

踏 40B.41-2

tah.

V.i. & t. (1) To step on, stamp on: 腳踏實地 stand on solid ground, practical, always have regard for facts; 踏歌 song accompanied by stamping on the ground; 踏繩 walk on tightrope; 踐踏 trample upon; 踏破了 crush under foot; 踏扁了 crush flat under foot; 踏破鐵鞋無覓處, 得來全不費工夫 find s.t. accidentally after tracking miles ("wearing out iron shoes") in vain for it; 腳踏兩條船 divided loyalties. (2) (Poet.) to tread: 踏青 have an outing in spring ("tread on green"); 踏雪尋梅 look for plum flowers treading on snow.

踏板(兒) *tahbaan(-baa'l)*, n., plank for crossing, loading; footstool near bed; pedal.
踏步 *tah-buh*, v.i., (mil.) mark time.
踏蹺 *tahchiau*, v.i., walk on stilts.
踏碓 *tahdueih*, v.i. & n., pestle for husking rice worked by foot.
踏踐 *tahjiahn*, v. t., trample upon.

跴 40B.41-3

tsaai.

V. t. (1) To step on: 跴扁了 flatten under foot; 跴蹺 *-chiau*↓. (2) To search for wanted criminal: 跴案 *-ahn*↓.

跴案 *tsaai-ahn*, v. i., to make police investigation of crime.
跴蹺 *tsaai-chiau*, v. i. & n., (walk on) stilts.

跴 蹭 蹯 蹣 踹 蹦 踊 跚 蹁 踽 蹻 跨

跴緝 *tsaaichih*, v. i. & t., see *-ahn* ↑.

跴蛋兒 *tsaai-dah'l*, v. i., (of poultry) copulate.

跴訪 *tsairfaang*, v. i. & t., see *-ahn* ↑.

蹭 40B.41-8

tsehng.

V. i. (1) To stroll leisurely: 剛蹭到這裏來 just strolled into this place. (2) Dillydally: 蹭稜子 *-lerngtz* ↓. (3) To strip: 蹭蹬 *-dehng* ↓.

蹭蹬 *tsehngdehng* (*-'deng*), adj., frustrated in career, running into mishaps.

蹭兒(戲) *tsehng'l*(*shih*), n., as in 拿蹭兒, 聽蹭兒 formerly, walk into theater, linger and walk out again without pay.

蹭稜子 *tsehnglerngtz*, v. i., to dillydally.

蹯 40B.41-9

farn.

N. Paw: 熊蹯 (LL) bear's paw—a delicacy.

§ 40B.42 (足/冈)

蹣 40B.42-2

marn.

V. t. (AC) trespass.

蹣跚 *marn'shan* (*parnshan*), adv., to walk with waddle or limp.

踹 40B.42-2

shuahn (**shuaih*, **chuaih*).

N. The heel.

V. i. & t. (1) To stamp: 踹足而怒 stamped his foot in anger. (2) (**chuaih*) To kick, trample on: 踹他一腳 to step on one's foot. (3) (**shuaih*) To spoil: 一樁買賣被人給踹了 somebody spoiled a business deal.

蹦 40B.42-2

behng.

N. Hopping, usu. 蹦兒: 他急得打蹦兒 jumped about in excitement.

V. i. To hop, hop about.

Adv. (Coll.) brightly: 蹦兒亮 shining bright.

蹦蹦(兒)戲 *behngbeh('l) shih*, n., a form of dramatic show.

踊 40B.42-3

yuung.

V. i. (1) To jump, leap: 舞踊 stamp on ground in savage dance. (2) U. f. 踴; see 踴ᐞ躍 40B.50.

跚 40B.42-4

shan.

[See 蹣ᐞ跚 40B.42]

蹁 40B.42-6

piarn.

蹁躚 *piarnchian*, adv., (walk, dance) with a swing or in a sidling manner: 蹁躚而來.

踽 40B.42-9

jyuu.

Adv. Alone, all by oneself: 踽踽獨行 walk alone.

蹻 40B.42-9

chiau (**jyuer*, **jiaau*).

N. (1) (AC) wooden clogs. (2) 高蹻 stilts; see 趫 11.83.

V. t. To lift up one's leg (also wr. 蹺): 蹻起腳來 ditto; 蹻足 *-tzur* ↓.

Adj. (1) (**jiaau*) 蹻勇 mighty (fighter); cf. 驍勇 51B.70; see 蹻蹻 *-jiaau* ↓. (2) (**jyuer*) (AC) 蹻然不固 fluid, unstable.

蹻工(兒) *chiaugung('l)*, n., art of walking in high-soled boots (of actress in Chin. opera), also called 跐工, 跴工.

蹻蹻 **jiaurjiaau* adj., mighty, haughty-looking, (also wr. 赳).

蹻足 *chiau-tzur*, v. i., to curl up one's leg: 蹻足以待 curl up one's leg and wait at ease.

§ 40B.50 (足/ㄱ)

跨 40B.50-1

kuah.

V.i. & t. (1) To bestride, straddle, pass over: 跨上去 step up (a platform) with big stride; 跨馬, 跨在車上 to mount astride horse, cart; 跨過 pass over (stile, threshold); 跨界 sit astride boundary; 跨馬桶 sit over stool (in toilet). (2) To carry (s. t.) hanging on arm or finger: 跨筐兒, 跨菜籃 carry basket on arm; 跨孝 wear arm band in mourning. (3) To carry on the side: 又跨了一件差事 hold a concurrent job, carry a job on the side; 旁邊又跨上一行小字兒 carry an insertion beside the line, insert a line of small-type characters.

跨刀 *kuahdau*, v. i., (1) carry a knife on the belt; (2) (formerly, Chin. opera) to play supporting role.

跨名兒 *kuahmirng'l*, v. i., (=掛名兒) hold an empty title, put in person's name for form's sake.

跨年 *kuahniarn*, adv., from year-end to the beginning of next year, over the year-end.

跨子 *kuahtz*, n., a long narrow boat for negotiating the Yangtze Gorges; 跨子車 (coll.) motorbike with sidecar.

跨竈 *kuah-tzauh*, phr., (of son) excel the father.

跨院(兒) *kuahyuahn(-yuah'l)*, n., a sidecourt in Chin. house.

踴 40B.50-3

yuung.

[Var. 踊]

V. i. To jump for joy or in dance.

踴躍 *yuungyueh*, (1) v. i., to jump and dance; (2) adv., gladly, energetically (contribute, take part in).

踼 40B.50-4

ti.

V. i. & t. To kick: 踼開 kick away, off; 踼足球 play football; 踼中了, 踼進了 score goal in football; 踼毽子 kick shuttlecocks; 踼死人 kick a person to death; 連踼帶打 both kick and beat; 踼飛腳 give a flying kick.

蹋 40B.50-4

tah.

V. i. (1) To step on, tread (var. of 踏). (2) To slip while walking: 蹋倒; see 蹋攞 -'*la* ↓.

蹋伏 *tahfur*, v. i., crawl on ground.

蹋鞠 *tahjyur*, n., ancient game of football.

蹋攞 *ta'la*, v. i., to shuffle; 蹋攞鞋 cloth shoes worn with heels folded down.

躅 40B.50-4

jur.

N. (LL) footprint: 芳躅 (court.) your whereabouts; see 躑[△]躅 40B.22.

跼 40B.50-5

jyur.

Adj. (1) Bent down, crouching, stooping: 跼天蹐地 (LL) be cramped for room. (2) Hobbling, limping: 跼躅 -*jur* ↓.

跼蹐 *jyurjir*, adj., confined, cooped up in a narrow space.

跼躅 *jyurjur*, adj., walking hesitatingly.

跼促 *jyurtsuh*, adj., (1) narrow-minded; (2) uneasy, cramped for action.

趵 40B.50-9

bauh.

V.i. To spring forth (associated with names of famous springs).

§ 40B.63 (足/丶)

蹠 40B.63-6

jyr.

N. (AC) animal's paw.

V. t. (AC) to tread (distances).

蹠骨 *jyrguu*, n., (physiol.) metatarsus.

§ 40B.70 (足/乚)

跣 40B.70-1

shiaan.

Adj. (LL) barefooted: 跣足.

蹺 40B.70-1

chiau.

V. i. To put leg up (cf. 翹 11.70 lift up wings, head).

跨 踴 踼 蹋 躅 跼 趵 蹠 跣 蹺

亅	小	⺊	十	土	ナ	卄	⺊	丨	一	丁	フ	口	区	冈	ㄱ	厂	尸	亠	广	宀	丶	乚	弋	心	八	人	乂	一	𠂉	ノ	⺈	く
00	01	02	10	11	12	20	21	22	30	31	32	40	41	42	50	51	52	60	61	62	63	70	71	72	80	81	82	83	90	91	92	93

蹺敧 *chiauchi*, adj., (of roads) bumptious.
蹺蹺板 *chiauchiau-baan*, n., a seesaw.
蹺捷 *chiaujier*, adj., quick-footed.
蹺蹊 *chiaushi*, (sp. pr. -'*shi*), adj., shady (conduct), not straightforward or open (also 蹊蹺).

跧 40B.70-1

chyuarn.

跧跼 *chyuanjyur*, adj., frustrated, cut off (also wr. 蜷).

跐 40B.70-2

tsy (**tsyy*, **tsaai*).

V. i. (1) To slip down: 腳一跐落下水去了 with a slip (he) fell into the water. (2) (*tsyy*) To step on: 跐著門檻子 step on the railing; sometimes pr. **tsaai*, see 跴 40B.41.

跳 40B.70-2

tiauh.

V. i. (1) To jump: 跳上, 下, 出, 進 jump up, down, out, into; 跳高 high jump; 跳遠 broad jump; 連跑帶跳 skip and run; 蹦蹦跳跳 skip and jump about; 跳過 jump over (creek); skip (a chapter); to jump off, down: 跳 (下) 樓 jump off a building; 跳井, 河, 海, 水 jump into well, river, sea, water; 狗急跳牆 (fig.) take desperate measures if pushed to the wall; 跳出火炕 (fig.) escape from hell, esp., (prostitute) effects escape from profession. (2) To twitch, palpitate: 心跳 heart palpitates; 眼皮跳 eyelids twitch; 心驚肉跳 jumpy with fear; 嚇了一跳 give one a start (from fright); 急得跳腳兒 make one jump up with nervousness. (3) 跳牛, 跳馬 (coll.) to cover a cow, a mare.

跳板(兒) *tiauhbaan(-baa'l)*, n., gangplank.
跳布札 *tiauh-buhjar*, v. i., (Tibetan Lamaism) dance to exorcise demons on New Year's holidays.
跳蟲 *tiauhchurng*, n., flea.
跳動 *tiauhduhng*, v. i., jump about, move about restlessly.
跳高 *tiauh-gau*, v. i., do high jump.
跳行 *tiauh-harng*, v. i., (1) skip a line in reading; (2) begin a new line above margin (on coming across emperor's or superior's name, as sign of respect); (3) change profession, see -*tsaur* ↓.
跳加官 *tiauh jiaguan*, v. i., scene opening opera performance, invoking blessings (esp. official promotion) for audience.
跳欄 *tiauhlarn*, v. i., jump hurdles.
跳踉 *tiauhlarng*, v. i., hustle about in confusion.
跳梁 *tiauhliarng*, v. i., "jump across the beams" like a burglar, esp. 跳梁小醜 petty burglar, contemptible rebel.
跳龍門 *tiauh lurngmern*, v.i., formerly, pass civil examinations successfully, get a degree.
跳傘 *tiauh-saan*, v.i. & n., parachute.
跳神(兒) *tiauh-shern(-sher'l)*, v.i. to dance before the gods to exorcise evil spirits.
跳繩 *tiauh-sherng*, v.i., skip rope.
跳蝨 *tiauhshy*, n., flea (also wr. 虱, also called 跳蚤 -*tzaau*).
跳蹋 *tiauhtah*, v.i., fling oneself about in anger.
跳槽 *tiauhtsaur*, v.i., change employment; (of professional girls) discard one lover for another.
跳蚤 *tiauhtzaau*, n., flea.
跳丸 *tiauhwarn*, v.i., juggle balls; the quick passing of time.
跳舞 *tiauhwuu*, v.i. & n., dance: 跳舞音樂 dance music.
跳遠 *tiauhyuaan*, v.i., do broad jump.
跳月 *tiauhyueh*[1], v.i., Miao (aborigines) custom of communal dance, followed by selection of girls and boys for mates.
跳躍 *tiauhyueh*[2], v.i., to jump, hop for joy.

蹮 40B.70-3

shian.

[Var. of 躚 40B.83]

蹴 40B.70-6

tsuh.

V. t. (1) To kick (ball, etc.). (2) To leap: 一蹴即至 reach goal in a shot—very quickly.

Adj. See 蹴然 -*rarn* ↓.

蹴踘 *tsuh-jyur*, v. i., anc. game of kicking ball (football).
蹴然 *tsuhrarn*, adj., (AC) solemn (manner), polite, reverential.

跎 40B.70-6

tuor.

V.i. See 蹉[A]跎 40B.30.

躥 40B.70-6

tsuan.

V. i. (1) To leap up: 躥房越脊 (of thief) jump to, run on the roof and descend into rooms; (fig.) be promoted quickly: 他這兩年躥得好快 he got promoted very fast in the last two years. (2) To have diarrhoea: 躥稀 have loose, watery bowels; 躥鞭桿子 (sl.) have diarrhoea. (3) To scold severely, to berate (person), see also under 村 10B.00.

跑 40B.70-9

paau (**paur*).

V. i. (1) Run, escape: 跑來跑去 run about; 跑出來 rush out; 他跑了 he has escaped; 跑開了 has left; 跑細了腿 rush about for nothing (wear one's legs out); 跑跑顛顛的 rush about like mad. (2) Walk, move: 跑不動 cannot walk any more. (3) (Also *paur*) to make a dash or sprint.

V. t. Used in specific phrr. like "running errands": 跑外的 or 跑街的 (*paau* or *paur*) employee for running errands, one for field work, itinerant salesman, pedlar; 跑海 travelling salesman; 跑單幫 commercial traveller who makes trips for special purpose; 跑堂(兒)的 restaurant waiter (Peking dial.); 跑廳的 servant in brothels (Peking dial); 跑途子貨 (contempt.) woman of loose morals, streetwalker; 跑上房 (maid or servant) serve in inner court; 跑警報 run for air raid shelter; 跑賬的 collector of debts; 跑旱船 a kind of vaudeville act; 足跑地 (**paur*), dig ground with foot or hoof.

跑冰 *paau-bing*, v. i., ice skate.
跑道 *paau-dauh*, n., athletic track; 跑道兒 v. i., run around.
跑肚子 *paau-duhtz*, v. i., have loose bowels (make constant trips to toilet).
跑狗 *paur-goou*, v.i. & n., dog race; 跑狗場 dog race stadium.
跑馬 *paur-maa*, v.i. & n., horse race; 跑馬場(廳) n., race course.
跑腿 *paur-tueei*, n. & v. i., footman, courier, messenger; run on errand.

跪 40B.70-9

gueih.

V.i. Kneel: 下跪 kneel down before s.o.; 跪拜 to kowtow to s.o.: 謹辭跪拜 (in funeral services) polite notice to mourners not to kowtow to the deceased; 跪倒, 跪下 (command s.o.) to kneel down; 跪倒爬起 to kowtow and then get up; 跪門 kneel before s.o.'s gate to ask for forgiveness; 跪鎖(子), 跪鏈子 to kneel on an iron chain, formerly, a third degree method, 三跪九叩 three times kneel down, each time performing three kowtows, extreme form of reverence close to prostration.

躐 40B.70-9

lieh.

V. t. (1) Pass over: 躐等而進 to get into higher class (by-passing intermediate steps); 學不躐等 learning should proceed step by step; 躐山越嶺 crossing hills and mountains. (2) Trample upon.

踬 40B.70-9

tir.
[Var. of 蹄 40B.22]

§ 40B.71 (足/乇)

跩 40B.71-7

juaai.

V. i. & t. To waddle, walk with a swagger (of duck, fat person): 一跩一跩的走.

踐 40B.71-7

jiahn.

V. t. (1) To tread upon, step on: 踐踏 trample under foot; 自相踐踏 trample on each other; 踐冰 pick one's steps carefully for fear of imminent danger ("walk on thin ice"); 作踐 crush, grind underfoot. (2) Carry out, implement, put to practice: 踐言 *-yarn*, 踐約 *-yue*, 踐諾 *-nuoh*, 踐履 *-lyuu* ↓; 實踐 practical action, opp. 空言 mere talk. (3) Follow, observe.

踐極 *jiahn-jir*, v. i., ascend the throne.
踐履 *jiahnlyuu*, (1) v. i., put a plan into action; (2) n., action thus taken.
踐諾 *jiahn-nuoh*, v. i., fulfill an agreement.
踐石 *jiahn-shyr*, n., a stepping-stone for mounting on horses.
踐祚 *jiahn-tzuoh*, v. i., ascend the throne.
踐言 *jiahn-yarn*, v. i., keep one's word.
踐約 *jiahn-yue*, v. i., keep one's promise, go to an appointment.

§ 40B.72 (足/心)

跽 40B.72-5

jih.
[Related 跪 40B.70]

V. i. Kneel for a long time, go down on all fours, prostrate.

§ 40B.80 (足/八)

躦 40B.80-1

tzuan.

V. i. & t. (1) Make a forward or upward movement: 跳跳躦躦 gamboling, jumping and skipping about; 燕子躦天兒 dash past swiftly like a swallow. (2) (＝鑽) Delve into (subject, books): 躦研 make an intensive study of. (3) (＝鑽) Pierce, make a hole in, go through: 躦洞 go into (hide in) a hole (cf. 鑽 81A.80).

蹟 40B.80-1

ji.

[Var. of 迹 60.83, also wr. 跡 40B.00]

趴 40B.80-8

pa.

[Var. 爬, 扒]

V.i. & t. Crouch down: 趴坑 flop down out of exhaustion, for rest; 趴下 crouch down or flop down.

躓 40B.80-9

jyh.

V. i. To totter: 困躓 (LL) fallen upon bad days.

躓頓 *jyhduhn*, v.i., (LL) to totter, about to collapse.
躓蹶 *jyhjyuer*, v.i., (LL) to falter.

§ 40B.81 (足/人)

跌 40B.81-1

dier.

V. i. Fall down: 跌倒, 跌一交 to trip over, fall down; 跌落水裏 fall into the water; (of prices) fall.

跌蕩 (宕) *dierdahng*, adj., (of writing, art) having free or surprising turns, untrammeled.
跌價 *dier-jiah*, v. i., fall in price.
跌落 *dier-luoh*, v.i., drop (into well, trap).

趺 40B.81-1

fu.

趺坐 *fu-tzuoh*, v. i., to sit cross-legged, as Buddhist priests do.

蹼 40B.81-2

pur.

N. Web on birds' feet.

蹶 40B.81-5

jyuer (**jyuee*).

V. i. & t. (1) Tread on, trample, grind underfoot. (2) To fall down, to trip over: 一蹶不振 (lit.) unable to get up after a fall, (fig.) fail utterly, be roundly defeated. (3) (Of horse) to kick: 蹶子 **jyueetz*↓.

蹶然 *jyuerrarn*, adj., jumping up in surprise.
蹶子 **jyueetz*, n., the hind legs of animals: 尥蹶子 kick with hind legs.
蹶窩 **jyuee'uo*, adj., emaciated.

蹊 40B.81-9

shi.

N. A footpath, a hill path.

V. t. (AC) to trample (on a field).

蹊蹺 *shichiau*, adj., as in 蹊蹺古怪 strange, devious: 此事有點蹊蹺 there's a hitch or s. t. devious in this affair.
蹊徑 *shijihng*, n., footpath; path to (success, etc.).
蹊要 *shiyauh*, n., strategic point on path.

趹 40B.81-9

jyuer.

Adv. (Of horse) running fast.

§ 40B.82 (足/乂)

跂 40B.82-1

chir (**chih*).

Adj. (1) (AC) having extra toes. (2) Crawling: 跂行, 跂跂 ditto. (3) Standing on tiptoe: 跂足以待, 跂踵而望 to wait, to look forward to on tiptoe.

跂蹻 *chirchiau*, n., (AC) a kind of sandals.
跂想 **chihshiaang*, v.i., to look forward to on tiptoe.
跂坐 *chirtzuoh*, v.i., to sit with crossed legs.

跂訾 *chitzyy*, adj., (AC) self-opinionated.
跂望 *chirwuahng*, v.i., see *-shiaang* ↑.

跋 40B.82-1

bar.

N. Postscript, colophon, used for comments on book, painting scroll (also 題^A^跋 41.83).

V. i. & t. Cross on foot (also 跋履山川 across hills and rivers); 跋前疐後 (MC) phr. meeting hindrances; 跋涉 *-sheh* ↓.

跋扈 *barhuh*, adj., (of local rulers, commanders) recalcitrant.
跋剌 *barlah*, n., make splashing noise (of flapping wings, fins).
跋涉 *barsheh*, v. i. & t., cross land and water (difficult travel).

踧 40B.82-2

tsuh.

踧踖 *tsuhjir*, adj., (AC) in mincing steps or manner as show of respect.

蹩 40B.82-2

bier.
[Var. of 蹩 22.83]

跛 40B.82-2

boo (**bih*).

Adj. Lame: see 跛腳, 跛足 *-jiaau*, *-tzur* ↓; 跛鼈千里 a lame turtle can go a thousand *li*, i.e., by perseverance.

跛躃 *boobih*, adj., (AC) lame.
跛蹇 *borjiaan*, adj., (AC) lame.
跛腳 *borjiaau*, adj., lame; (dial.) (of goods) poor quality.
跛躓 *boojyh*, v.i., (LL) to stumble.
跛蹶 *boojyuer*, v.i., ditto.
跛腿 *bortueei*, adj. & n., lame, a lame person.
跛子 *bootz*, n., a lame person.
跛足 *bootzur*, adj., lame.
跛依 **bihyii*, adj., (AC) slanting, unbalanced.

趿 40B.82-3

sah (**ta*).

V.i. (1) To slip foot into a slipper. (2) (**ta*) 趿拉 *tala*, ditto: 趿拉著鞋 walk in slippers.

跤 40B.82-6

jiau.

V.i. To trip, to fall down: 摔跤 (a) stumble and fall; (b) wrestling.

踱 40B.82-6

duoh.

V. t. To pace the floor: 踱來踱去 pace about.

踱步 *duoh buh*, v. i., to pace.

躞 40B.82-6

shieh.

N. (LL) tip of roller in mounting for scrolls.

躞蹀 *shiehdier*, v. i., to sidle along in mincing steps.

§ 40B.83 (足/⌒)

躂 40B.83-1

tah.

V.i. To kick, stamp on foot: 躂倒 (also 蹋倒) slip and fall.

踶 40B.83-4

dih.

V. i. (AC) kick.

蹤 40B.83-9

tzung.
[Var. of 踪]

N. Footprints: 蹤跡 *-jih*, 蹤影 *-yiing* ↓; 追蹤 to shadow a person, pursue, follow from behind; 失蹤 (man, dog) get lost.

V. t. (1) To follow, catch up with. (2) Alight on: 被蒼蠅蹤過的東西不要吃 don't eat any food touched by flies.

蹤跡 *tzungjih*, n., footprints (traces) of person.
蹤影 *tzungyiing*, n., traces and shadows: 蹤影毫無 not the least trace was found.

蹝
踥
踰
别
別
槑

蹝 40B.83–9

shii.
[Var. of 屣 52A.83]

§ 40B.93 (足/く)

踥 40B.93–6

chieh.

踥踥 *chiehchieh*, adv., (AC) to and fro.
踥蹀 *chiehdier*, adv., (AC) in sidling manner.

踰 40B.93–8

yur.
[Printed form of 踰 40B.00]

SECTION 40S

§ 40S.00 (口ˢ/亅)

别 40S.00–2

bier.
[Usu. wr. 別]

N. & v. i. (1) Distinguish, distinction; separate (-ation): 男女有別 separation, distinction between sexes; 區別 distinction between things; 分別 separation of two similar things, also difference; 識別, 辨別 know, make the distinction. (2) (To) leave, (take) departure, esp. from friends, (during) absence: oft. 離別, 別來, 別後, 離別以來 since departure; 別後念念 have been thinking of you since departure, in your absence; 別來無恙 hope that you are well (since departure); 別了 here I go! (on departure) so it is good-bye! 告別 (court.) take leave (with your permission); 辭別, 拜別, 道別, 話別 visit to say good-bye; 小別, 短別 temporary separation, absence; 生離死別 separation between loved ones in life or death; 別緒 feeling of absence.

V. t. (1) To pin up: 別起來, 別上, 別住 pin it up, fix with pin, 別針 *-jen*↓. (2) Turn: 別起一條腿來 lift up a leg; 別過頭, 臉, 來 turn head, face.

Vb. aux. Contraction of 不要 *buryauh*: 你別走 don't go away; 別這樣想 don't look at it this way; 別提了 let's not talk about it.

Adj. Other, another, some other: 別的 other; 別人, 別的人 others; 別處 elsewhere; 別本 another edition, other editions; 別途 some other routes, lines (profession); 別解 another explanation; 特別 especial(ly), unusual: 特別招待 special welcome arrangements.

Adv. In another way: 別有用心, 看法 have another motive, another way of looking at it; 別有高見 have a brighter idea; 別有所指 implies another thing; 別有天地 like another world; 別有所本, 依據 is based on another source; 別有所聞 have heard of another (detail, aspect of) story; 別無所有, 依靠 have no other possession, friends or relatives for help; 別無出路 have no other way out; 別具隻眼, 慧心 have a special insight, understanding; 別開生面 open up a fresh outlook, new ideas, fresh style.

別號 *bierhauh*, n., a man's poetic name, apart from 字 courtesy name.
別針 *bierjen*, n., pin.
別集 *bierjir*, n., an author's collected works, as dist. from 總集 collection or anthology by period or genre of writing.
別致 *bierjyh*, n. & adj., interesting and novel (of art works, decoration).
別名(兒) *biermirng(-mir'l)*, n., see *-hauh*↑, also nickname.
別墅 *biershuh*, n., villa, country villa.
別史 *biershyr*, n., privately compiled history, as dist. from official history.
別樣 *bieryahng*, adj., another, other: 別樣東西 another thing, article.
別業 *bieryieh*, n., (1) villa; (2) another piece of property.

別 40S.00–2

bier.
[Wr. form of 别]

§ 40S.01 (口ˢ/小)

槑 40S.01–4

meir.

[Rare var. of 梅 10B.50]

§ 40S.02 (口^{s}/卜)

䍐 40S.02–5

chaan.

Adv. 䍐然而笑 (LL) to give a sweet smile.

§ 40S.11 (口^{s}/土)

雖 40S.11–9

suei (also **sueir*).
[Pop. 虽]

Conj. Although: 雖然 *-rarn*↓; 雖故, 雖則 MC equivalents of 雖是 *-shyh*↓.

雖然 *sueirarn* (**sueir-*) conj., (common form in vern. for LL 雖) though, although.
雖說 *suei shuo*, conj., although it is said.
雖是 *sueishyh* (**sueir-*), conj., though, although, see *-rarn*↑.
雖則 *sueitzer*, conj., another var. of 雖是 *-shyh*↑.

§ 40S.22 (口^{s}/丨)

郢 40S.22–3

yiing.

N. Name of anc. city.

鄂 40S.22–3

eh.

N. (1) Name for 湖北 Hupeh Province. (2) A surname. (3) (AC) border.

鄂博 *ehbor*, n., Mongolian cairn (*obo*) for marking boundary.

鄙 40S.22–3

bii (also *bih*).

N. Frontier town; small town: 北鄙 (AC) northern border.

Adj. (1) Vulgar, rustic, unpolished, insignificant; 卑$^{\Delta}$鄙 91.10. (2) Courtesy reference to oneself in 鄙人 I; 鄙意 my humble opinion; 鄙國 my humble country; 鄙親 my relative.

V. t. (LL) disdain, look with contempt: 鄙其人, 鄙之 despise the person, him.

鄙薄 *biibor*, v. t., to slight, despise (person); adj., mean, petty, vulgar.
鄙夫 *biifu*, n., a rustic person, bumpkin.
鄙見 *biijiahn*, n., (court.) my humble opinion.
鄙劣 *biilieh*, adj., mean, low-class, inferior (goods).
鄙吝 *biilihn*, n., vulgarity; adj., miserly; vulgar.
鄙俚 *birlii*, adj., vulgar (expressions).
鄙陋 *biilouh*, adj., (of views) superficial; worthless, also used in courtesy phrr. of oneself.
鄙笑 *biishiauh*, v. t., scoff at.
鄙事 *biishyh*^{1}, n., menial work, humble tasks; small matters.
鄙視 *biishyh*^{2}, v. t., to despise, look with contempt.
鄙夷 *biiyir*, v. t., disdain.

§ 40S.50 (口^{s}/乛)

嗣 40S.50–5

syh.

N. Progeny: 後嗣, 子嗣 ditto; 絕嗣 die without issue, heirless.

V. i. & t. To continue (ancestral line), succeed (office).

Adv. Later: 嗣後 *-houh*↓.

嗣承 *syhcherng*, n. & v. t., line of succession; succeed in line.
嗣後 *syhhouh*, adv., later on.
嗣繼 *syhjih*, v. i. & t., to inherit, succeed: 嗣繼問題 question of succession.
嗣立 *syhlih*, v. t., to appoint, be appointed, as heir.
嗣響 *syh-shiaang*, n., response or continuing influence, like an echo to voice.
嗣續 *syhshyuh*, v. i., inherit, succeed.
嗣子 *syhtzyy*, n., heir, natural or adopted.
嗣位 *syh-weih*, v. i., to succeed to the throne.
嗣業 *syh-yeh*, v. i., inherit the family estate, continue to carry on father's work.
嗣音 *syhyin*, n., (AC) echo, response.

鴞 40S.50–9

shiau.

N. (1) An owl, also a bird reputed to eat its own mother: 鴟$^{\Delta}$鴞 90S.50. (2) Var. of 梟 in 梟$^{\Delta}$首 91.01.

鵑 40S.50-9

jyuan.

N. 杜鵑 the cuckoo: 杜鵑花 the azalea.

鶚 40S.50-9

eh.

N. (Zoo.) the osprey, fish hawk.

勛 40S.50-9

shyun.
[Anc. var. of 勳 90S.50]

§40S.70 (ㄏˢ/ㄥ)

號 40S.70-2

hauh (**haur*).
[Var. 号]

N. (1) A name, esp. poetic name for person: 國號 dynastic title; 別號 person's extra name (oft. poetic and chosen by person himself); 道號 Taoist monastic name; 法號 Buddhist monastic name (in last two cases, clan or surname is dropped). (2) A mark, an arithmetic figure: 符號 a punctuation mark; 記號 a mark; 句號 full stop, period; 分號 semicolon; 冒號 colon; 引號 quotation marks; 感歎號 exclamation mark; 問號 question mark; 連號 (連字號) hyphen; 破折號 dash. (3) 號 or 號碼 number in series: 第幾號 what number (of house, post box); 門牌號碼 house number; serial number referring to persons: 病號 patient's number in hospital. (4) Name of shop or firm: 商號, 店號 ditto; 寶號 (court.) your shop or firm. (5) An order, esp. military: 號令 -*lihng* ↓; 信號 prearranged signal; 暗號 secret password; 口號 password, also slogan.

V.t. (1) To entitle, to claim: 號稱三萬兵, claim or allege to be 30,000 strong; 號爲酒中八仙 were called the "Eight Immortals of Wine." (2) (**haur*) To cry aloud: 號爽, 號咷 -*sang*, -*taur* ↓.

號兵 *hauhbing*, n., (mil.) bugler.
號單 *hauhdan*, n., ticket with serial number.
號燈 *hauhdeng*, n., (mil.) flash signal.
號房 *hauhfarng*, n., (1) formerly, the reception clerk in office or house, similar to *concierge*; (2) serially numbered room (as in civil examinations); reception or registration room in house or office.
號召 *hauhjauh*, v.t., to call for supporters, to attract (followers) through prestige or political platform.
號角 *hauhjiaau*, n., a bugle, a horn.
號哭 **haurku*, v.i., to cry aloud, wail.
號令 *hauhlihng*, n. & v.i. & t., (1) an order, to issue an order; (2) (-*'ling*) formerly, a public execution.
號碼 *hauhmaa*, n., mark; serial number; 號碼機 a numbering machine.
號脈 *hauhmoh*, v.i., (Northern dial. of physicians) to examine patients by feeling pulse.
號礮 *hauhpauh*, n., gun signal.
號爽 **haursang*, v.i., to cry at funeral; (derog.) to yell (as if at funeral).
號數(兒) *hauhshuh('l)*, n., serial number; number (of persons, things).
號咷 **haurtaur*, v.i., to scream, yell.
號頭(兒) *hauhtour('l)*, n., (1) a mark or number; (2) a foreman.
號筒 *hauhturng*, n., a bugle.
號外 *hauhwaih*, n., extra edition of papers.
號衣 *hauhyi*, n., formerly, uniform.

§40S.71 (ㄏˢ/ㄤ)

戢 40S.71-7

jir.

N. A surname.

V.t. (1) Put aside or away, hide: 戢兵 renounce war, disarm voluntarily; 戢翼 retire from office (lit., "fold up wings"); 事戢 the furor has died down; 戢影 to retire; 戢斂 lighten taxes; to make oneself scarce. (2) Prohibit, forbid: 嚴戢吏弊 put a stop to official abuses; 戢暴鋤強 run down the people's oppressors.

戰 40S.71-7

jahn.
[Pop. 战 21S.71]

N. (1) A surname. (2) War, battle: 交戰 ditto; 二次大戰 Second World War; 英法之戰 war between England and France; 海戰, 陸戰 naval, land battle; 空戰 air battle, air fight; 游擊戰 guerrila war; 內戰 civil war; 炮戰 artillery duel; 作戰 do battle; 開戰 open hostilities; 停戰 armistice; 宣戰 declare war; 挑戰 challenge to fight; 血戰 bloody battle; 戰雲 war atmosphere; 百戰百勝 ever-victorious; 戰時 wartime, during the war; 戰事, 戰爭, 戰鬬 -*shyh*², -*jeng*, -*douh* ↓; 細菌戰 bacteriological warfare; 化學戰 chemical warfare; 生物戰 biological warfare.

V. i. & t. (1) To fight (person, country), engage in war: 戰勝, 戰敗 to win, lose war, battle; 戰死 die in battle; 戰無不勝, 戰無不克 never lose a battle. (2) 打戰, 寒戰 (var. of 顫) to shiver, shudder with cold.

Adj. 戰戰兢兢 to be extremely mindful of one's steps, fearful of making mistakes, meticulous.

戰表 *jahnbiaau*, n., (MC) letter declaring war.
戰筆 *jahnbii*, n., wavy line (as in painting of dress).
戰塲 *jahnchaang*, n., battlefield.
戰車 *jahnche*, n., chariot, armored tank.
戰船 *jahnchuarn*, n., warship of various types.
戰地 *jahndih*, n., the battle front, where war takes place.
戰抖 *jahndoou*, v. i., to shudder with fear or cold.
戰鬪 *jahndouh*, n. & v. i., to fight, a fight: 戰鬪力 fighting strength; 戰鬪機 a fighter plane.
戰犯 *jahn-fahn*, n., war criminal.
戰俘 *jahn-fur*, n., prisoner of war.
戰功 *jahn-gung*, n., merits in military exploits.
戰果 *jahn-guoo*, n., accomplishments, results in battle.
戰國 *Jahnguor*, n., period in history, called Warring Kingdoms (403–221 B.C.).
戰骨 *jahn-guu*[1], n., skeletons on battlefield.
戰鼓 *jahn-guu*[2], n., war drums.
戰壕 *jahn-haur*, n., war trench.
戰爭 *jahnjeng*, n., war, warfare: 戰爭與和平 war and peace (also name of a novel by Leo Tolstoy).
戰艦 *jahnjiakn*, n., battleship, also used of cruisers, destroyers, etc.
戰局 *jahn-jyur*, n., the war situation.
戰況 *jahn-kuahng*, n., conditions of war area, also war situation.
戰慄 *jahnlih*, v. i., to shudder.
戰利品 *jahnlih-piin*, n., war booty.
戰略 *jahnlyueh*, n., military strategy.
戰袍 *jahnpaur*, n., formerly, knee-length jacket of officers.
戰線 *jahnshiahn*, n., battle line.
戰守 *jahn-shoou*, n., attack and defence.
戰書 *jahnshu*, n., declaration of war.
戰術 *jahn-shuh*, n., military tactics, art of conducting warfare.
戰士 *jahnshyh*[1], n., a warrior.
戰事 *jahnshyh*[2], n., warfare, war.
戰史 *jahn-shyy*, n., history of a war.
戰役 *jahnyih*, n., a military campaign.
戰友 *jahn-yoou*, n., comrade in arms, war ally.

§40S.80 (口S/八)

顎 40S.80–3

eh.

N. Jaw.

§40S.81 (口S/人)

獸 40S.81–1

shouh.

N. Beast: oft. coupled with 禽 birds: 禽△獸 81.42, the animals; 野獸 wild beasts; 猛獸 ditto; 獸性, 獸慾 *-shihng*[1], *-yuh* ↓.

獸環 *shouhhuarn*, n., brass ring on gate, with head of a beast.
獸圈 *shouhjyuahn*, n., corral, stockade.
獸爐 *shouhlur*, n., an incense tray, shaped like a beast.
獸香 *shouhshiang*, n., incense contained in 獸爐 *-lur* ↑.
獸性 *shouhshihng*[1], n., beastly nature; bestiality.
獸行 *shouh-shihng*[2], phr., beastly conduct.
獸心 *shouh-shin*, phr., heart of a beast.
獸炭 *shouhtahn*, n., animal charcoal, bone black (also 骨炭).
獸臟粉 *shouhtzahngfeen*, n., (chem.) glycogen or animal starch.
獸醫 *shouhyi*, n., a veterinary, veterinarian.
獸慾 *shouhyuh*, n., animal desire; sexual passion.

SECTION 41

§ 41.01 (囗/小)

果 41.01

guoo.
[Pop. 菓 fruit]

N. (1) (Bot.) the fruit of any plant: 果實, 果子 *-shyr*, *-tz* ↓; 水果 fruit; 開花結果 to blossom and bear fruit; 果盤 a fruit bowl; 果盒 a fruit box; 果類 fruits as a class; 果品 different kinds of fruit; 果木(樹), 果樹 fruit trees; 果瓤 the flesh of fruits; 果子藥兒 sugar-coated pills; 果脯 dried fruits; 果核, 果仁 kernels; 果局子 a shop selling fresh fruits; 果園 an orchard. (2) Result: 因果 (報應) cause and effect, retribution; 成果 result, achievement; 效果 result, effect (of medicine, advice, etc.); 結果 consequences, results; 自食其果 suffer the consequences of one's action; 善果, 惡果 good, bad consequences. (3) A surname.

V.t. To fill: 果腹 to fill, satisfy, the stomach.

Adj. Resolute, determined: 言必信, 行必果 be truthful in speech and firm in action; 果決, 果斷, 果敢 *-jyuer*, *-duahn*, *-gaan* ↓.

Adv. Ultimately, actually: 果伏劍而死 he actually killed himself with a sword; 不果來 actually did not come; 果然, 果眞 *-rarn*, *-jen* ↓.

Conj. If, if actually: 如果 if it should come to pass; 若果 in case; 果若 *-ruoh* ↓.

果報 *guoo-bauh*, n., retribution.
果碟(兒)(子) *guoo-dier* (*-dier'l*) (*tz*), n., a dish of fruits served as dessert.
果斷 *guooduahn*, adj., resolute, unwavering.
果餌 *guoreel*, n., candies, fruit and cookies.
果敢 *guorgaan*, adj., resolute and daring.
果眞 *guoojen*, adv., true to promise, indeed as expected.
果醬 *guoojiahng*, n., jam, marmalade.
果汁 *guoo-jy*, n., fruit juice.
果決 *guoojyuer*, adj., firm and resolute.
果料兒 *guooliauh'l*, n., nuts in candies.
果皮 *guoo-pir*, n., fruit peel.
果然 *guoorarn*, (1) adv., indeed as expected; (2) n., (zoo.) a long-tailed black monkey with a white face.
果若 *guooruoh*, adv. phr., in case that (also 果如 *-rur*).
果實 *guooshyr*, n., fruit of trees.
果酸 *guoosuan*, n., (chem.) tartaric acid.
果糖 *guootarng*, n., (chem.) fructose.
果子 *guootz*, n., fruits of any kind.
果子露 *guootzluh*, n., fruit juice.
果毅 *guooyih*, adj., resolute and daring.

累 41.01

leei (in sense of 'accumulation'); **leih* (in sense of 'cause trouble,' 'implicate,' 'fatigue'); **leir.*

N. (**leih*) Burden, responsibility: 室家之累 family burden; 重累 heavy responsibility.

N. & v.t. (1) (**leih*) Implicate, involve, -ment: 連累, 帶累, 受累, 拖累 be implicated, get (s.o.) involved; 累及 *-jir* ↓; 受累, 受人之累 be involved in (s.t., usu. unpleasant) by others. (2) (**leih*) Run into debt, indebtedness: 虧累 suffer financial losses; 私累 owe personal debts; 賠累 lose money in business. (3) V.t. & p.p., to tire out: 累死人 tires one out completely; 累病了 sick from overwork. (4) (**leir*) U.f. 縲, (AC) fasten, bind, put in chains: 係累其子弟 (AC) seize his children and throw them into prison. (5) Accumulate, lay (s.t.) on top of another: 勢如累卵 hazardous, precarious like a pile of eggs; 累積 *-ji* ↓; 累牆 lay bricks to build a wall; 累黍 *-shuu* ↓.

Adj. (1) Tired, tiring, wearisome, exhausted (**leih*): 勞累, 累乏 tired out with too much exertion; 累極了, 累死了 dead tired; 累的慌 tired and nervous. (2) Tiring, wearisome: 累活兒 *-huor'l*, 累人 *-rern* ↓. (3) (**leir*) Troublesome: 累贅 *-'juei* ↓; 累牘連篇 long and tedious writings.

Adj. & adv. (1) One on top of another, progressively: 累進 *-jihn* ↓; 累月 *-yueh* ↓; 累日 *-ryh* ↓; 累歲 *-sueih* ↓; 累年 *-niarn* ↓. (2) Repeated(ly), again and again: 累次 *-tsyh* ↓; 累累 *-leei* ↓; 累遷 *-chian* ↓; 累戰皆捷 one victory after another; 累著大功 score signal successes again and again; 累徵不起 repeatedly refuse to be drafted for official service; 累試不第 fail to pass the government examination year after year.

累遷 *leeichian*, n., (1) (of residence) repeated removal; (2) (of officials) repeated promotions; (3) v.i., be repeatedly promoted.
累代 *leeidaih*, adv., one generation after another, for generations.
累堆 **leirduei*, adj., burdensome, troublesome, see *-'juei* ↓.
累犯 *leeifahn*, v.i., (1) run foul of the law more than once; (2) commit repeated offenses.
累活(兒) **leihhuor('l)*, n., tiresome or laborious chores.
累積 *leeiji*, v.t., gradually accumulate.
累計 *leeijih*, n., total amount, sum total.
累進 *leeijihn*, adj., progressive: 累進法 mathematical progression; 累進稅 progressive taxation.
累及 **leih-jir*, v.t., involve (others) in trouble: 累及無辜 make the

innocent suffer.
累贅 *leir'juei[1], adj., tedious, repetitious (esp. speech).
累墜 *leir'juei[2], adj., ditto.
累懇 *leihkeen, v.i., (coll.) please be so glad as to (also 累肯).
累掯 *leih'ken, v.t., (coll.) force (s.o.) to do (s.t.); restrain (s.o.) from doing (s.t.).
累累 *leirleei*, adv., (1) oftentimes; (2) one after another.
累利 *leei-lih*, n., compound interest (also 複利).
累年 *leeiniarn*, adv., year after year, for years.
累人 *leihrern, adj., tiring: 抱這孩子眞累人 holding the child in one's arms is so tiring.
累日 *leeiryh*, adv., day after day, for days.
累心 *leih-shin, adj., suffering from too much mental strain.
累黍 *lei shuu*, n., a very small quantity: 不差累黍 (LL) no whit different, not an iota of difference.
累世 *leeishyh*, adv., for generations.
累事 *leihshyh, adj., overworked.
累時 *leeishyr*, adj., standing the test of time, lasting.
累歲 *leeisueih*, adv., year after year.
累次 *leeitsyh*, adv., repeatedly: 累次三番 again and again.
累月 *leeiyueh*, adv., month after month: 累月經年 month after month and year after year.

景 41.01

jiing (**yiing*).

N. (1) A view, sight, prospect: 風景 scenery; 景色 *-seh*, 景物 *-wuh*, 景象 *-shiahng*, 景狀 *-juahng* ↓; 美景 a lovely view; 見景生情 memories revive at the sight of familiar places. (2) Condition, circumstance: 景況 *-kuahng* ↓; 順景, 佳景 good fortune, prosperity; 逆景 bad fortune, adversity; 晚景悽涼 lonely and poor in old age. (3) A surname. (4) (**yiing*) (U.f. 影) shadows: 日景 shadows cast by the sun: 景印本 photostatic edition.

V.t. Admire, look up to: 景慕 *-muh*, 景仰 *-yaang* ↓.

Adj. Great: 景福 great blessing; 景行 *-shirng* ↓.

景氣 *jiingchih*, n., economic prosperity: 不景氣 economic depression.
景風 *jiingfeng*, n., (LL) (1) a lucky wind; (2) the southern wind.
景光 *jiingguang*, n., (1) light that brings good fortune; (2) condition, appearance, circumstance (=光景).
景教 *Jiingjiauh*, n., Nestorianism; 景教碑 the Nestorian Tablet.
景狀 *jiingjuahng*, n., 景象 see *-shiahng* ↓.
景致(兒) *jiingjyh* (*-jeh'l*), n., an especially beautiful scenery (also wr. 景緻).
景況 *jiingkuahng*, n., (1) state of affairs, condition of things, circumstances; (2) a person's fortune, good or bad.
景慕 *jiingmuh*, v.t., esteem, adore, venerate.
景色 *jiingseh*, n., panoramic view, scenery.
景象 *jiingshiahng*, n., prospects, condition, appearance, outlook (of things).
景星 *jiingshing*, n., a lucky star.
景行 *jiing-shirng*, n., noble character.
景泰藍 *jiingtaihlarn*, n., cloisonné enamel.
景天 *jiingtian*, n., (bot.) the stone crop, *Sedum purpureum*.
景物 *jiingwuh*, n., the world of nature before one's eyes.
景仰 *jirngyaang*, v.t., admire, esteem, hold in high respect.
景雲 *jiing-yurn*, n., bright colored clouds regarded as harbingers of good fortune.

県 41.01

shiahn.

[Abbr. of 縣 41S.01]

纍 41.01

leir.

N. (AC) a big strong rope.

V.t. (1) To link together. (2) Fasten, bind. (3) Put in chains: 纍囚 a bound prisoner; 纍臣 a minister thrown into prison.

纍纍 *leirleir*, adj., (1) emaciated and weak; (2) clusters: 結實纍纍 fruits growing in clusters; (3) dejected, despondent: 纍纍若喪家之犬 looking dejected like a lost dog; (4) innumerable, scattered all over: 傷痕纍纍 with cuts and bruises all over.

§41.02 (囗/⺊)

暴 41.02

bauh, (re. pr. **puh* in some LL phrr. in sense of "expose").

N. (1) A surname. (2) Violence: 以暴易暴 change one tyranny for another tyranny.

V.t. (*bauh* or **puh*) Expose, broadcast: 暴骨疆場 expose skeletons on battlefield; 暴露, 暴揚 *-luh*, *-yarng* ↓.

Adj. & adv. (1) Violent (event, temper), harsh and tyrannical (regime): 暴君, 暴主 tyrant; 暴脾氣, 暴性子 violent, irascible temper; 暴跳如雷 in a thundering rage. (2) Sudden, abrupt: 暴發 sudden attack (of illness) or rise in fortune, see 暴發戶 *-fa-huh*↓; 暴病 fall ill suddenly; 暴卒, 暴亡 die suddenly, sudden death by violence; 暴富, 暴貴 sudden wealth, rise in power; 暴漲 sudden rise in flood or stock prices; 暴殄天物 phr., waste natural products (grain, etc.); 粗暴 coarse, unruly; 強暴 violent (conduct), tyrannical (regime).

暴斃 *bauhbih*, v.i., meet sudden death.

暴棄 *bauhchih*, v.i., abandon, be abandoned (in conduct): 自暴自棄 live in self-abandon, without ambition in life.

暴動 *bauhduhng*, n., street violence, riot.

暴發戶(兒) *bauhfa-huh('l)*, n., upstart, *nouveau riche*.

暴風雨 *bauh-fengyuu*, n., tempest.

暴橫 *bauh-herng* (=橫暴), adj., arrogant, defying law and order.

暴虎馮河 *bauh-huu-pirng-her*, phr., (AC) brash physical courage (kill tiger with bare hands and swim across river).

暴著 **puhjuh*, adj., (LL) manifest, well-known.

暴客 *bauh-keh*, n., see *-tur*↓.

暴烈 *bauhlieh*, adj., violent.

暴戾 *bauhlih*[1], adj., violent tempered, cross-grained (暴戾恣睢).

暴力 *bauhlih*[2], n. & adj., violence, (-t), use of force.

暴露 **puhluh* (sp. pr. *bauhluh*), v. i. & t., to expose, be exposed in public (of crime, etc.): 連年暴露 (*puh-*) (LL) exposed to the sun and rain; 這女明星太暴露了 (*bauh-*) this film star strips or exposes her body too much.

暴虐 *bauhnyueh*, adj., cruel, tyrannical (ruler, regime).

暴行 *bauh-shihng*, n., unruly conduct, act of violence.

暴徒 *bauh-tur*, n., roughneck, hoodlum.

暴躁 *bauhtzauh*, adj., irascible, unruly; (coll.) feverish.

暴揚 **puhyarng*, v.t., (LL) broadcast, publish (one's deeds).

畏 41.02

weih.

N. Fear, reverence: 無畏 fearlessness.

V.t. (1) To fear: 畏懼, 畏恐 *-jyuh, -kuung*↓; 畏首畏尾 timid. (2) To respect: 敬畏 fear, reverence (God); p.p., respected: 畏友 respected friend.

Adj. Afraid: 畏怯 *-chyueh*↓.

畏避 *weihbih*, v.t., avoid meeting (person).

畏怯 *weihchyueh*, adj., timid.

畏服 *weihfur*, v.t., obey or submit in fear; regard with great respect.

畏忌 *weihjih*, (1) v.i. & t., have aversion to; (2) n., aversion, fear as restraint: 無所畏忌 stop at nothing.

畏懼 *weihjyuh*, v.i. & t. & n., fear.

畏恐 *weihkuung*, v.i. & t. & n., ditto.

畏難 *weih-narn*, phr., 畏難而退 awed by the difficulty and stop.

畏葸 *weihshii*, adj., timid, timorous.

畏縮 *weihsuor*, adj., ditto.

畏途 *weih-tur*, n., as in 視爲畏途 to regard as dangerous, to keep away from s.t.

畏罪 *weih-tzueih*, phr., 畏罪而逃 flee to escape punishment.

晨 41.02

chern.

N. The morning: 清晨, 早晨 ditto; 凌晨 dawn; 晨起 wake up in the morning; 寥如晨星 rare as morning stars—very few; 晨昏定省 (*shiing*) (AC) attend upon parents personally (seeing them to bed and upon waking up).

晨操 *chern-chau*, n., morning exercise.

晨熹 *chernshi*, n., light at dawn.

晨運 *chern-yuhn*, n., morning exercise.

曩 41.02

naang.

Adv. Formerly, (LL) erstwhile: 曩昔, 曩者, 曩時 in former days, in times gone by; the other day.

§ 41.10 (囗/十)

早 41.10

tzaau.

N. Morning: 早晨 *-chern*↓; 早晌, 早上, 早間 *-'shang*[1], *-shang*[2], *-jian*↓; 早清(兒), 清早, 一早 early in the morning; 早出晚歸 go out in the morning and return in the evening; 早晚 *-waan*↓; 早安 good morning! 早起 *-chii*↓; 早飯 *-fahn*, 早點 *-diaan*↓; 早尖 (of traveler) have a light meal in the morning; 早茶 morning tea; 早朝 (*-chaur*) (of a monarch) hold a morning audience; 早會 morning briefing (discussion); 早操 morning exercise; 早經 matins.

Adj. & adv. (1) Former(ly), previous(ly): 早年 former years; 早歲 ditto; 早先 *-shian*, 早時 *-shyr*↓; 早婚 marry before reaching maturity; 早夭 die prematurely; 早世 ditto; 早已 *-yii*↓; 早就 *-jiouh*↓; 早則 already; 老早 some time previously, a long while ago; 早知如此 if I knew it beforehand; 提早(交貨) (goods delivered) in advance; 早了三天 three days ahead of time. (2) Early: 早早的 as early as possible; 儘早, 趁早, 趕早, 及早 ditto; 太早 too early; 尚早, 還早 it's yet early; 天不早了 it's getting late; 早些兒, 早些箇 be early; 早點兒(來) do come early; 早到, 早退 attend, leave office early; 早日 *-ryh* ↓; 早熟 *-shour* ↓; 早產 *-chaan* ↓; 早期 *-chir* ↓.

早半天(兒) *tzaau'bantian(--tia'l)*, adv., in the morning, before noon (also 早半晌兒).
早產 *tzaurchaan*, n., (med.) premature birth.
早晨 *tzaauchern(-'chen)*, adv., early in the morning.
早起 *tzaurchii(-'chi)*, v.i. & adv., (get up) early in the morning.
早期 *tzaauchir*, n., earlier period (stage, batch).
早春 *tzaau-chun*, n., early spring.
早稻 *tzaau-dauh*, n., early-maturing varieties of rice (opp. 晚稻 late-maturing varieties).
早點 *tzaurdiaan*, n., a light breakfast.
早飯 *tzaaufahn*, n., breakfast.
早慧 *tzaau-hueih*, adj., precocious (also 早惠).
早間 *tzaaujian*, n., the morning.
早經 *tzaau-jing*, adv., already.
早就 *tzaau-jiouh*, adv., since sometime ago.
早年 *tzaauniarn*, (1) n., early years; (2) adv., some years ago.
早日 *tzaauryh*, adv., earlier than planned or scheduled.
早晌 *tzaau'shang*[1], n., morning.
早上 *tzaau'shang*[2], n., morning; adj., earlier: 早上五六年 five or six years earlier.
早先 *tzaaushian*, adv., in former times, formerly.
早熟 *tzau-shour*, adj., (1) (of plants) early-maturing; (2) (of persons) reaching maturity earlier than others.
早是 *tzaau-shyh*, adv., (1) happily, luckily, fortunately; (2) already.
早時 *tzaaushyr*, n., former times.
早晚 *tzaauwaan*, (1) n., morning and evening; time; (2) adv., sooner or later; early or late: 這早晚才來 come late, came at this late hour; 多早晚回來 when are you coming back?
早已 *tzaur-yii*, adv., (1) already, for quite some time; (2) formerly, previously, earlier.

旱 41.10

hahn.

N. & adj. (1) A drought: 旱災 *-tzai* ↓; 連年大旱 a great drought for successive years. (2) Land (transportation in contract to 水 water): 趕旱路 go by land. (3) Dry, without water: 旱筆 (callig.) comparatively dry brush; 旱稻, 旱芹 rice, celery which grows on dry land; 旱雷 thunder without rain; 旱煙 *-yan* ↓.

旱魃 *hahnbar*, n., the demon causing drought.
旱蓮(子) *hahnliarn(-tzyy)*, n., (bot.) forsythia, *Hypericum erectum* (also called 小連翹).
旱傘 *hahnsaan*, n., parasol.
旱獺 *hahntah*, n., (zoo.) the Russian marmot, *Arctomys bobac.*
旱災 *hahntzai*, n., drought famine.
旱煙 *hahnyan*, n., old-fashioned tobacco pipe with long stem (opp. 水[4]煙 22.02, the pipe filled with water).

畢 41.10

bih.

N. A surname.

V.i. & t. (LL) To finish, complete: 誦畢, 念畢 after reading; 事已完畢 business is completed.

Adj. & adv. (LL) Complete, whole, all, entire: 畢生, 畢世 the whole life, for life; 畢肖 very alike; 畢至, 畢集 all (guests, birds) arrive, flock to a place; 原形畢露 to show one's true colors.

畢眞 *bihjen*, adj., very true to life, (usu. wr. 逼眞).
畢竟 *bihjihng*, adv., after all: 畢竟打不過他 after all (one) is defeated by him; 畢竟歸空 after all, nothing is gained.
畢命 *bih-mihng*, v.i., (LL) end life.
畢肖 *bihshiauh*, adj., see *-jen* ↑.
畢業 *bihyeh*, v.i., graduate; 畢業生 a graduate (of certain school); 畢業典禮 graduation ceremony; 畢業獻辭 valedictory.

暈 41.10

*yun (*yuhn, *yihn).*

N. (1) (**yuhn*) Sun's, moon's halo. (2) (**yihn*) 血暈 state of coma, unconsciousness.

V.i. To faint: 暈過去 faint off.

Adj. Dizzy: 頭暈 dizzy; 暈眩 dizzy spell; 暈頭 *-tour* ↓.

暈車 **yuhn-che*, adj., car-sick.
暈船 **yuhn-chuarn*, adj., seasick.
暈倒 *yun-daau*, v.t., to faint off.
暈頭 *yuntour*, adj., muddle-headed; 暈頭巴腦 ditto.

§ 41.11 (図/土)

里 41.11

lii.

N. (1) A place of residence: 里居 *-jyu* ↓. (2) A neighborhood: 鄉里, 鄰里 village neighborhood, one's native district; 里門 *-mern*, 里落 *-luoh* ↓; 故里 one's old home or native district. (3) A precinct. (4) 一里 one Chin. *lii*;

早 旱 畢 暈 里

亅	小	⺊	十	土	ナ	卄	𠃊	丨	一	丅	𠃌	口	図	冈	𠃍	厂	尸	亠	广	宀	丶	乚	弋	心	八	人	乂	乛	丆	丿	𠂉	く
00	01	02	10	11	12	20	21	22	30	31	32	40	41	42	50	51	52	60	61	62	63	70	71	72	80	81	82	83	90	91	92	93

英里 (wr. 哩) one mile; 公里 one kilometer. (5) 這里 this place, here; 那里 that place, there (var. of 這裏, 那裏). (6) A surname.

里程碑 *liicherngbei*, n., a milestone, a landmark.

里長 *lirjaang*, n., (current) precinct chief.

里正 *liijehng*, n., (AC) official village chief, chief of precinct.

里居 *liijyu*, n., (1) life in the countryside; (2) one's home address.

里落 *liiluoh*, n., a village.

里閭 *lir-lyuu*, n., formerly, a precinct division (*-mern* ↓).

里門 *liimern*, n., (1) the village entrance; (2) a village neighborhood, one's native district.

里巷 *liishiahng*, n., streets and lanes.

里胥 *liishyu*, n., formerly, (1) a village officer; (2) a local constable.

星 41.11

shing.

N. (1) A star, a heavenly body, a planet: 恆星 a fixed star; 行星 planet; 衞星 satellite; 彗星 comet; 流星, 賊星 meteor; 水星 Mercury; 金星 Venus; 火星 Mars; 土星 Saturn; 海王星 Neptune; 天王星 the planet Uranus; 福星 lucky star; 壽星 person whose birthday is being celebrated, also god of longevity; 救星 savior (in any crisis); 星宿 *-shiouh* ↓; comb. with 斗 (=北斗 North Pole Star); 星移斗轉 passing of night; 斗換星移 passing of hours of the night, or of months; 物換星移 (LL) things change with the passing of years; 星廻 the stars come back to original position in one year; 寥如晨星 rare, scarce ("like stars in morning"); 披星戴月 make a starlight journey, work very late or start before dawn. (2) Prominent artist, actor or actress: 影星 movie star; 紅星, 明星 popular actor or actress; 舞星, 歌星 popular dancer, singer. (3) Sparks: 火星兒. (4) Marks on silver scales or steelyard indicating fractions of an ounce. (5) Tiny amount: 一星半點 ditto; 零星, 零零星星 n. & adv., piecemeal, odd pieces; 零星交付 give out by small amounts, not by whole amount.

Adv. (1) Spread, scattered: 星散 scattered; 星羅棋布, 星敷 spread out ("like stars and chess pieces"). (2) Under the starlight: 星夜奔喪 run home under starlight for funeral in "great haste"; 星發, 星行 make a starlight journey; hence in great haste; 星速 immediately; 星馳 hurry off on journey.

星辰 *shingchern*, n., stars collectively: 日月星辰 the sun, moon and the stars.

星球 *shingchiour*, n., a star or planet (considered as globe).

星期 *shingchir*, n., (1) a week: 星期日, 一, 二, 三, 四, 五, 六 Sunday, Monday, Tuesday, Wednesday, Thursday, Friday, Saturday; (2) Sunday: 今天是星期 or 星期日 today is Sunday.

星島 *Shingdaau*, n., another name for Singapore 星加坡.

星斗 *shingdoou*, n., stars and constellations with reference to their course in sky.

星漢 *shinghahn*, n., the Milky Way.

星河 *shingher*, n., ditto.

星火 *shing-huoo*, n., a spark: 星火燎原 a spark causes a prairie fire—(fig.) spark of social or political revolution.

星加坡 *Shingjiapo*, n., Singapore; see *-daau* ↑, *-jou* ↓.

星鮫 *shing-jiau*, n., (zoo.) a giant octopus, *Mustellus manazo* (also called 白沙).

星洲 *Shingjou*, n., name for Singapore.

星主 *shing-juu*, n., (MC coll.) upright prime minister or head of political group to pull country out of chaos.

星曆 *shing-lih*, n., map of stars in different seasons.

星綠藻 *shingluh-tzaau*, n., a tiny water plant, *Zygnemaceae*.

星芒 *shingmarng*, n., pointed rays of star.

星命 *shing-mihng*, n., the star under which person is born.

星散 *shingsahn*, v.i., (of relatives, bandits, etc.) to scatter.

星象 *shingshiahng*, n., astrology; 星象導航 navigation by stars.

星星 *shingshing*, (1) adj., tiny (white hair, etc.); (2) n., (-'*shing*) the stars.

星宿 *shingshiouh*, n., (1) constellations: 十二星宿 the twelve constellations; (2) (-'*su*) a man's star controlling his luck.

星形 *shing-shirng*, n., (math.) star polygon.

星霜 *shing-shuang*, n., the passing of years.

星使 *shing-shyy*, n., formerly, an emissary.

星速 *shing-suh*, adv., hurriedly, without delay.

星彩 *shing-tsaai*, n., (min.) asterism (as in star sappire).

星團 *shing-tuarn*, n., (astron.) star clusters.

星座 *shing-tzuoh*, n., constellation.

星子 *shingtzyy*('*tz*), n., little bits; 油星子 spots of oil stain; 火星子 sparks; 唾沫星子 sprays from coughs.

星眼 *shing-yaan*, n., woman's clear eyes.

星夜 *shingyeh*, adv., see Adv. 2 ↑.

星翳 *shingyih*, n., (med.) small opaque dots on the cornea, nebula.

星魚 *shing-yur*, n., a starfish.

星雲 *shing-yurn*, n., (astron.) nebula, -ae.

量 41.11

liarng (vb. mostly); *liahng* (n.).

N. (1) Measure: 度量衡 weights and measures, measures of length, capacity and weight; 量制 system of measures. (2) (*liahng) Measure or capacity: 飯量, 酒量 capacity for rice, wine; 量大 have great capacity; 容量 capacity of container; 重量 weight. (3) (*liahng) Generosity, capacity for toleration: 器量大, 小 capacity, incapacity, for tolerating and forgiving small things; 度量, 氣量 generous character or lack of it.

V.i. & t. (1) To measure length, weight, distance: 量布, 米, 身材, 地 measure cloth, rice, human figure, land; 量尺寸 take measures of length, size; 丈量 to measure land; 稱量, 衡量 measure weight. (2) As in 衡量文章 to grade writings; 衡量局勢 to consider and judge a situation; 測量 (geometry and geol.) to survey; 計量 to calculate, reckon; 估量 to estimate value. (3) (*liahng) To limit: 量力而行 do what one's strength allows; 不量力 (contempt.) overestimate one's own ability; 量入爲出 limit expenditures in accordance with income.

量杯 *liarngbei*, n., graduated cup.
量度 *liarng-duoh*, v.t. to measure, survey.
量角器 *liarngjiaau-chih*, n., protractor.
量子 *liahngtzyy*, n., (phys.) quantum; 量子論 quantum theory.

墅 41.11

shuh.

N. A country villa: 別墅 ditto.

墨 41.11

moh.

N. (1) Ink, ink cake: 繩墨 guideline; 中繩墨 following guidelines (of conduct). (2) Writing: 筆墨 a writer's art, style or skill; 筆墨有力 forceful writing. (3) A surname: 墨翟, 墨子 Moh Dir, Mocius, or Motse, anc. philosopher of universal love; 墨家, 墨子之徒 Mocian (-ist).

Adj. (1) Done in ink: 墨竹, 墨蘭 bamboo, orchid painted in black and white. (2) Black, dark: 墨鏡 dark glasses, sunglasses; 墨晶 dark crystal; 墨絰 (AC) black linen mourning cloth; 墨詔 edict in black ink.

墨版 *mohbaan*, n., wood block for printing.
墨寶 *mohbaau*, n., as in 敬求墨寶 request callig. scroll or handwriting for preservation.
墨七 *mohchi*, n., (dial.) a burglar.
墨牀 *mohchuarng*, n., case for ink sticks.
墨斗 *mohdoou*, n., carpenter's ink box and line for printing guidelines.
墨海 *mohhaai*, n., ink slab or bowl for grinding ink.
墨盒 *mohher* (*-tz*, *-'l*), n., ink box, usu. made of copper containing ink pad.
墨壺 *mohhur*, n., ink bottle.
墨跡 (迹, 蹟) *mohji*, n., writer's handscript.
墨家 *Mohjia*, n., Mocian (-ists), see N. 3↑.
墨汁 *mohjy*, n., prepared liquid ink (sold in bottles).
墨客 *mohkeh*, n., usu. in 騷人墨客 writer, poet.
墨吏 *moh-lih*, n., (LL) corrupt official (from 貪墨=貪冒).
墨綠 *mohluh*, adj., dark yellowish green.
墨瀋 *mohsheen*, n., luster of ink on paper: 墨瀋未乾 the ink is hardly dry (before the treaty is broken).
墨戲 *mohshih*, n., painting in a few strokes, of *wernrern* school (文人畫).
墨刑 *mohshirng*, n., branding on forehead as punishment.
墨守 *mohshoou*, v.t., guard (tradition) vigilantly, resist change: 墨守成規 follow stereotype routine.
墨水 *mohshueei*, n., fluid ink: 肚子裏喝了不少墨水 (fig.) have read a great many books.
墨硯 *mohyahn*, n., ink slab.
墨油 *mohyour*, n., printing ink.
墨魚 *mohyur*, n., cuttlefish, (also called 烏賊 "black thief").

壘 41.11

leei.

N. (1) A rampart, a wall or partition: 堡壘 a fort, fortification; 壁壘分明 with sides clearly drawn, issues clearly stated; 雙方對壘 with both sides entrenched, ready to fight. (2) (Baseball) base: 一壘, 二壘 first, second base; 全壘打 home run.

壘球 *leeichiour*, n., baseball (commonly called 棒球).
壘塊 *leeikuaih*, n., grievances: 胸中壘塊 grievances in one's heart (also 磊塊 31. 40).

瞿 41.11

chyu (also *chyur*, *jyuh*).

N. A surname.

Adj. Agog, staring: 瞿視 staring blankly (also 瞿瞿, 瞿然).

瞿麥 *chyumaih*, n., a variety of wheat.

§41.20 (区/廾)

昇 41.20

sheng.

昇 罌 罍 甲 畀 昂 界

[Cogn. 升, 陞]

V.i. To rise: 旭日東昇 the morning sun rises in the east; to go up, be promoted (＝升).

昇汞 *shengguung*, n., (chem.) corrosive sublimate, mercuric chloride.
昇華 *shenghuar*, n. & v.i., (1) sublimate, -ion; (2) upsurge of spirit: 昇華氣象 (era, world).
昇平 *shengpirng*, adj., peaceful

§ 41.21 (図/乚)

罌 41.21

ying.
[Var. 甖]

N. A round jar with a small opening.

罌粟 *yingsuh*, n., poppy.
罌子桐 *yingtzyy-turng*, n., (bot.) Chin. wood oil tree, *Aleurites cordata*.

罍 41.21

leir.
[Anc. var. 櫑]

N. (AC) a wooden drinking vessel.

§ 41.22 (図/丨)

甲 41.22

jiaa (*jiah).

N. (1) (Also *jiah*) the first of the ten characters in 天干 decimal cycle, see Appendix A; 甲子 -*tzyy*↓; 花甲 sixty years of age. (2) A suit of armor: 鎧甲 (AC) battle armor; 盔甲 helmet; 甲冑 -*jour*↓. (3) Nails: 指甲 fingernails. (4) A natural or artificial shell: 甲蟲 -*churng*↓; 龜甲 tortoise shell; 鐵甲船 an ironclad; 鐵甲車 an armored car, tank; 裝甲兵 an armored force or units. (5) A unit of land measure in Taiwan equal to 0.96992 hectare. (6) A unit of civil administration: 保甲 the basic unit of local self-government; 保甲制度 such a system. (7) A substitute word for an indefinite person or thing: 某甲 Mr. "X"; 甲校 "X" school.

Adj. First: 甲組, 甲班 the first section, class; 甲等 of the best quality.

V.t. Be better than, excel: 甲天下 number one in the world.

甲板 *jiarbaan*, n., the deck of a ship.
甲榜 *jiarbaang*, n., formerly, Grade A in the highest government examination.
甲兵 *jiaabing*, n., (1) a fully armed soldier; (2) military force in gen.
甲蟲 *jiaachurng*, n., crustaceans.
甲第 *jiaadih*, n., (1) an influential family; (2) rankings in government examinations.
甲骨文 *jiarguu-wern*, n., anc. script on tortoise shells or bones.
甲長 *jiarjaang*, n., a neighborhood chief.
甲冑 *jiaajour*, n., armor.
甲狀腺 *jiaajuahng-shiahn*, n., (physiol.) the thyroid gland: 甲狀腺腫大 goiter.
甲馬 *jiarmaa*, n., (1) armor and horses; (2) painted images of Buddha on paper.
甲士 *jiaashyh*, n., armored soldiers.
甲子 *jiartzyy*, n., (1) a person's age; (2) a cycle of sixty years.
甲魚 **jiahyur*, n., the turtle.

畀 41.22

bih.
[Cogn. of 俾 91A.10]

V.t. Confer, give: 畀以重任 give (person) a responsible post.

昂 41.22

arng.

V.t. To raise: 昂首 raise one's head; 昂首濶步 to strut about.

Adj. (1) Soaring (price), expensive. (2) Proud in bearing, standing straight: 氣貌軒昂 straight and impressive looking.

昂昂 *arng-arng*, adj., towering, proud in appearance.
昂貴 *arnggueih*, adj., (prices) high.
昂然 *arngrarn*, adj., see -*arng*↑.
昂藏 *arngtsarng*, adj., see -*arng*↑.

界 41.22

jieh.

N. (1) Boundary: 分界 ditto; 界限 -*shiahn*[1]↓. (2) World: 仙界 fairyland; 外界 the outside world, people outside; 世界 the world. (3) Circles: 教育界, 新聞界, 商界 educational, journalistic, commercial circles; 男界 (toilet for) gentlemen; 女界 the ladies; 各界人士 (addressed to) all people of different walks of life. (4) Poetic level: 境界 elevation of spirit.

V.t. To be bound by: 東界黃海 bound by the Yellow Sea on the east.

界碑 *jieh-bei*, n., boundary stone.
界尺 *jiehchyy*, n., a foot rule.
界址 *jiehjyy*, n., boundary.
界限 *jiehshiahn*[1], n., the limit.

界線 *jiehshiahn²*, n., boundary line.
界說 *jiehshuo*, n., definition (of word).
界約 *jieh-yue*, n., treaty defining boundary between two countries.

鼎 41.22

diing.

N. (1) Tripod, a sacrificial or commemorative vessel: 鼎足 on three legs; 鼎足而三, 鼎足之勢 a situation dominated by three powerful rivals; 鼎立, 鼎峙 ditto. (2) As symbol of dynasty: 鼎祚, 鼎運 the destiny of a state; 鼎革 change of dynasty; hence 鼎新 change, presenting new aspect; see 鼎沸, 鼎鼐 *-fuh, -naih* ↓.

Adj. Weighty, carrying weight, important: 鼎力, 鼎言 *-lih, -yarn* ↓; prosperous: 鼎盛 *-shehng* ↓.

鼎鼎 *dirngdiing*, adj., very important in 鼎鼎大名 great reputation.
鼎沸 *diingfuh*, adj., boiling (turmoil).
鼎輔 *dirngfuu*, n., high minister of state.
鼎革 *diingger*, n. & v.i., change of dynasty.
鼎鑊 *diinghuh*, n., cauldron (without legs); ancient punishment by boiling.
鼎甲 *dirngjiaa*, n., first three names in national civil examination.
鼎力 *diinglih*, v.i., (court.) use one's great strength to support: 鼎力扶持.
鼎鼐 *diingnaih*, n., (1) cooking vessels; (2) office of prime minister.
鼎盛 *diingshehng*, adj., strong, in the prime of life: 春秋鼎盛.
鼎新 *diingshin*, v.i., make gen. reform, gen. change.
鼎言 *diingyarn*, n., (LL) weighty advice, from 言重九鼎 one's word carries weight of nine tripods.

§ 41.30 (囟/一)

旦 41.30

dahn.

N. (1) Dawn, morning: 坐以待旦 sit waiting for the dawn; 明旦 tomorrow morning; 元旦 New Year's Day; 一旦 (adv.) if, once; 一旦不幸 if in some future day s.t. untoward happens. (2) (*-tz*) Actress or female impersonator: 小旦, 花旦 one who plays role of young woman; 老旦 impersonator of old woman; 刀馬旦 actress versed in sword play, etc.

旦旦 *dahndahn*, adv., (AC) everyday; adj., (AC) 信誓旦旦 clear, definite pledge.
旦角 *dahnjyuer*, n., role of female 「actress.
旦暮 *dahmuh*, n., see *-shih* ↓.
旦夕 *dahnshih*, adv., a short moment, any moment: 旦夕之間 in a short moment; 危在旦夕 danger may come any day, any time.

昱 41.30

yuh.

N. The sunlight.

Adj. 昱昱 bright.

盟 41.30

merng.

N. Alliance; (AC) sworn oath of alliance among countries: 結盟, 聯盟 form alliance; 國際聯盟 League of Nations; 背盟 break treaty; 同盟 allies; 生死盟 sworn friends for life or death; 鴛盟 lovers' pledge, see 鴛^△鴦 92.50.

盟邦 *merngbang*, n., allies.
盟國 *mernqguor*, n., ditto.
盟主 *merngjuu*, n., (AC) person who administers oath of alliance; acknowledged leader of alliance.
盟軍 *merng-jyun*, n., the allied forces.
盟首 *merngshoou*, n., (AC) leader of alliance.
盟誓 *merngshyh*, n., oath of alliance.
盟約 *merngyue*, n., treaty of alliance, covenant.

疊 41.30

dier (**dar*).
[Pop. 叠]

N. (**dar*) (*-tz*) A pile: 一疊子紙片, 鈔票 a pile (pack) of cards, a wad of bank notes.

V.t. (1) To pile up: 疊起來 pile up, fold up; 疊羅漢 make a human pyramid, 層巒疊嶂 layer upon layer of mountains; 疊牀架屋 senseless piling up of phrases. (2) (AC) 震疊 be frightened. (3) (AC) 疊鼓 rattle drum.

Adj. & adv. Repetitious: 重疊, 重重疊疊 layer after layer, repeatedly.

疊句 *dierjyuh*, n., reiterative phr. or sentence, like "凄凄, 慘慘," also called 疊字.
疊次 *diertsyh*, adv., again and again, repeatedly (give warning, etc.).
疊韻 *dieryuhn*, n., two words

having same vowel formation, e.g., *danglang* (噹啷), cf. two words having same consonant, e.g., *dingdang* (叮噹), called 雙聲.

§ 41.40 (図/口)

罯 41.40

lyueh.

[Var. of 略 41S.40]

晷 41.40

gueei.

N. (1) The sun's shadow. (2) A sundial. (3) A duration of time: 日無暇晷 (LL) with no time to spare, busy from morning to night; 焚膏繼晷 (LL) burn candles till daybreak (in studies).

§ 41.41 (図/図)

日 41.41

ryh.

N. (1) The sun: 日光 sunshine, sunlight; 日光浴 sun bath; 日光節約 (時間) daylight-saving (time); 日華 the glory of the sun; 日球 *-chiour* ↓; 日系 *-shih*[2] ↓; 日薄西山 (fig.) in the evening of life; 日出 sunrise; 日沒 sunset; 日暮途窮 destitute, poor and homeless; 日蝕 *-shyr*[2] ↓; 日上三竿 late in the morning ("the sun is high up in the sky"); 日升月恆 in the ascendant ("the sun is rising and the moon waxing"); 日色 sunlight; 日影 shadows cast by the sun. (2) Daytime: 白日 daytime, broad daylight; 日裏 *-lii* ↓; 日間 *-jian* ↓; 日夕 *-shih*[1] ↓; 日場 *-chaang* ↓; 日夜 day and night. (3) One full day: 三日不見 haven't seen s.o. for three days; 每日 every day; 日日 day by day; 日又一日 day in and day out; 逐日 from day to day; 終日 all day long; 日利 *-lih*[1] ↓; 日課 *-keh* ↓; 日刊 *-kan* ↓; 日積月累 by slow accumulation; 日誌 *-jyh* ↓; 日程 *-cherng* ↓; 日給 *-jii* ↓; 日計 *-jih*[1] ↓; 日記 *-jih*[2] ↓; 日就月將 with steady progress from day to day and from month to month; 日新月異 never-ending changes and improvements; 日省月試 subject to constant supervision and testing; 日支 *-jy* ↓. (4) Time in gen.: 往日 in the past; 昔日 formerly; 吉日 lucky day; 佳日 a fine day; 來日 coming days; 異日 another day; 他日 some day in the future; 日不暇給 fully occupied from morning to night, have no time to spare; 日子 *-tz* ↓; 日期 -(')*chir* ↓; 日內 *-neih* ↓; 日來 *-lair* ↓; 近日 recently, in recent days; 日後 *-houh* ↓; 日久天長 for many, many years to come, for a long, long time; 日前 *-chiarn* ↓; 日昨 *-tzuor* ↓; 不日 in a few days; 今日 today, now, at present; 平日 usually (in the past); 明日 tomorrow; 永日 the whole day; 無日無之 not a day passes without it; 連日 day after day, for days on end. (5) Short for 日本 Nippon, Japan: 日人 Japanese; 日文 Japanese language.

日斑 *ryh-ban*, n., sunspots.

日報 *ryhbauh*, n., (1) a daily newspaper; (2) daily reports or accounts rendered.

日本 *Ryhbeen*, n., Japan, Nippon.

日表 *ryh-biaau*, n., (1) utmost reaches of the universe; (2) a sundial.

日晡 *ryhbu*, n., twilight, dusk, nightfall.

日差 *ryh cha*, n., daily difference in the length of shadows cast by the sun.

日場 *ryh-chaang*, n., a matinée.

日常 *ryhcharng*, adj. & adv., usual(ly), ordinar(il)y, daily.

日程 *ryh-cherng*, n., a daily schedule, agenda.

日前 *ryh-chiarn*, adv., a few days ago, only the other day, recently.

日球 *ryhchiour*, n., the sun regarded as a planet.

日期 *ryhchir* (-'*chi*), n., a date.

日珥 *ryh-eel*, n., (astron.) solar prominences.

日耳曼 *Ryh-eelmahn*, n., Germany.

日光燈 *ryhguang-deng*, n., a fluorescent lamp.

日晷 *ryh-gueei*, n., (1) shadows cast by the sun; (2) a sundial.

日圭 *ryh-guei*[1], n., a sundial.

日規 *ryh-guei*[2], n., ditto.

日後 *ryh-houh*, adv., later on, in the future.

日照 *ryh-jauh*, n., sunshine.

日者 *rhy-jee*, (1) n., a diviner, a soothsayer; (2) adv., (LL) the other day, a few days ago.

日間 *ryh-jian*, n., daytime.

日計 *ryh-jih*[1], adj., calculated on a daily basis.

日記 *ryh-jih*[2], n., a daily written record; 日記本 a diary; 日記帳 (bookkeeping) daily ledger.

日給 *ryh-jii*, n., daily allowance or pay.

日中 *ryh-jung*, n., (1) high noon, midday; (2) the vernal equinox.

日支 *ryh-jy*, n., daily expenses (expenditures).

日誌 *ryh-jyh*, n., a daily record: 航海日誌 a logbook.

日腳 *ryh-jyuer*, n., (1) the light of a setting sun; (2) (Shanghai dial.) (=日子 *-tz* ↓).

日刊 *ryh-kan*, n., a daily publication.

日課 *ryh-keh*, n., daily lessons (studies).

日來 *ryh-lair*, adv., recently, in recent days.

日利 *ryh-lih*[1], n., (banking) daily interest.

日曆 *ryh-lih*[2], n., a calendar.

日裏 *ryh-lii*, n., (=日間 *-jian* ↑).

日錄 *ryh-luh*, n., (1) a daily record of events; (2) a diary.

日輪 *ryh-lurn*, n., the sun ("solar disk").

日冕 *ryh-miaan*, n., corona of the sun.

日內 *ryh-neih*, adv., in a day or two.
日內瓦 *Ryhneihwaa*, n., Geneva.
日射病 *ryhsheh-bihng*, n., sunstroke, heatstroke, heat exhaustion.
日下 *ryh-shiah*, n., (1) the present time; (2) formerly, the national capital.
日夕 *ryh-shih*¹, n., day and night.
日系 *ryh-shih*², n., the solar system.
日食 *ryh-shyr*¹, n., (1) (＝日蝕 *-shyr*² ↓); (2) way of living: 日食艱難 live a hard life.
日蝕 *ryh-shyr*², n., an eclipse of the sun.
日天 *ryh-tian*, n., (Shanghai dial.) one full day: 走了幾日天 took several days on the way.
日頭 *ryh'tou*, n., (1) the sun; (2) daytime as opp. to nighttime; (3) some particular day.
日子 *ryhtz*, n., (1) one full day; (2) some particular day: 今天是他結婚的日子 today is his wedding day; (3) a date: 你有日子走沒有 have you a date for your departure? (4) a period of time: 他要請假，我只給他三天的日子 he wants to have a leave of absence and I have given him only three days; (5) way of living: 他半生過的都是愁苦的日子 he has led a sad and miserable existence almost all his life; livelihood: 那時他家的日子很不好過 his family was then having a hard time of it.
日昨 *ryh-tzuor*, adv., (LL) yesterday.
日曜日 *ryhyauh-ryh*, n., Sunday.
日月 *ryh-yueh*, n., (1) the sun and the moon.
日暈 *ryh-yuhn*, n., halo around the sun.
日用 *ryh-yuhng*, n., daily expenses; 日用品 daily necessities.

曰 41.41

yue.

V.i. (LL) say: 子曰 Confucius said; 子曰詩云 fond of quoting the classics.

昌 41.41

chang.

V.i. & adj. (1) To prosper, -ing; thrive, -ving: 昌大, 昌盛 *-dah, -shehng* ↓; 昌時, 昌期 (LL) age of prosperity, peak; 五世其昌 (AC) may the family prosper five generations running. (2) Bright: 昌明 *-mirng* ↓; 東方昌矣 (AC) it is bright on the eastern horizon. (3) (AC) good: 昌言 good words. (4) (AC) u.f. 猖 violent, unruly.

昌大 *changdah*, v.i. & adj., grow, become great; prosperous (period).
昌歜 *changjur*, n., (Chin. med.) ground roots of calamus (菖蒲 20A.41).
昌明 *changmirng*, adj., bright, peak (period).
昌盛 *changshehng*, adj., prosperous.
昌言 *changyarn*, v.i., announce openly.

晶 41.41

jing.

N. Crystal: 結晶 crystallization; 水晶 quartz; 紫水晶 amethyst; 紅晶 garnet; 電晶體 (收音機) transistor (radio).

Adj. Bright, clear: 晶晶 clear and bright; 晶熒 glittering, 晶瑩 radiant, resplendent; 亮晶晶 sparkling.

晶體 *jing-tii*, n., crystal (form).

暑 41.41

shuu.

N. Summer; summer heat: 暑天 *-tian* ↓; 暑期, 暑假 *-chir, -jiah* ↓; 避暑 go to summer resort; 中暑, 受暑 suffer sunstroke.

暑氣 *shuu(')chih*, n., summer heat.
暑期 *shuuchir*, n., summer season; holidays; 暑期班 summer school or class.
暑伏 *shuufur*, n., generally thirty days after summer solstice, the hottest days of summer.
暑假 *shuu-jiah*, n., summer holidays.
暑熱 *shuu-reh*, n., heat of summer.
暑溽 *shuuruh*, n., summer damp.
暑天 *shuutian*, n., summer days.
暑暍 *shuu-yeh*, n., sunstroke, heat prostration.

冒 41.41

mauh.

N. A surname.

V.i. (1) To risk, brave (danger): 冒生命的危險 risk one's life; 冒風雨 brave winds and rain; 冒死進言 to appeal (to emperor) at the risk of death; 冒嫌疑 risk people's suspicion; 冒大不韙 go in the face of public opinion or statutes. (2) To act under false pretences: 冒名頂替 substitute for another, assuming latter's name; 冒籍考試 assume false district of origin and take civil examinations; 冒領 get pay under another's name; 冒餉 pad payroll of army; 冒認 assume false identity; 冒姓 take false surname. (3) To cover, cap: 下土是冒 (AC) cover this lower earth. (4) To send up, burst: 冒烟 belch smoke; 瞧的我的兩眼冒金星兒 stares at me until stars dance before my eyes; 冒熱氣 do things by spurts and darts.

Adj. Rash, thoughtless, see 冒失 -'*shy*↓.

冒瀆 *mauhdur*, v.t., bother: 冒瀆清神 (court.) bother your attention.

冒犯 *mauhfahn*, v.t., violate openly (statutes, etc.).

冒壞 *mauh-huaih*, v.t., spoil by bad advice (also 冒壞水兒 -*huaishueei'l*).

冒火 *mauh-huoo*, v.i., get very angry; shoot up flame.

冒兒咕冬 *mauh'lgudung*, adj. & adv., rashly (break into room).

冒冒失失 *mauh'mau-shyshy*, adj. & adv., absent-minded, disorderly, reckless, -ly.

冒猛(子) *mauhmeeng*(*tz*), adv., suddenly.

冒昧 *mauhmeih*, adj., (court.) presumptuous, rash: 冒昧的很 it is very presumptuous of me to.

冒名 *mauh-mirng*, v.i., take another's name (under false pretense).

冒牌(兒) *mauh-pair* (-*par'l*), n. & adj., infringe trademark; 冒牌貨 --*huoh*, imitation or pirated goods under false name; 冒牌醫生 unlicensed doctor.

冒險 *mauh-shiaan*, v.i. & adj., take risks, adventure; adventurous: 冒險精神 adventurous spirit.

冒失 *mauh'shy*, adj., rash, thoughtless, scatterbrained: 冒失鬼 (derog.) a madcap.

冒充 *mauhtsung*, v.t., pretend to be: 冒充某人 pretend to be Mr. X.

冒嘴兒 *mauh-tzuee'l*, v.i., (of the sun) begin to show up on the horizon.

目 41.41

muh.

N. (1) The eye: 怒目 with angry look; 觸目 meets the eye; 觸目皆是 (distress, wounded soldiers) meet the eye everywhere; 注目, 矚目 focus eye or attention (on person, thing); 醒目 adj., easy on the eye, neat and clear; 奪目 ravishing, conspicuous; 不堪入目 disgusting; 夫妻反目 husband and wife quarrel; 目不見睫 cannot see the beam (lit. lashes) in one's own eye; 目不交睫 never sleep a wink ("close lashes"); 目不窺園, 目不斜視 absolute concentration on studies; 目瞪口呆 stunned speechless; 目眦欲裂 (AC) eyes bursting with anger; 目不轉睛 stare continuously; 過目成誦 can repeat after seeing once; 一目十行 read ten lines at one glance; 不曾寓目 never set eyes on; 目中無人, 目空一切, expressions of pride and haughtiness; 目無法紀, 目無尊長 have no regard for laws or superiors; 目指氣使, 目使頤令 giving order by look or glance; 目往神受 see (idea, thought) with real concentration; 目語 language of the eyes; 目無全牛 (allu.) a master butcher sees through parts and joints (of cow without cutting; 耳濡目染 colored by what one sees and hears constantly; 目送手揮 hands and eyes acting in coordination of painting); 目不識丁 completely illiterate. (2) Article, list, category, number: 數目 number; 價目 price; 項目, 條目 article, item on list; 科目 category, branch of study; 題目 title (of essay, lecture); 名目 title, name; 標目 label, tag; 書目 catalogue; 編目 catalogue, prepare catalogue. (3) Head, officer: 頭目 leader of group, gang; 盜目 chief of bandit; 吏目 petty officer. (4) A surname.

V.i. & t. Look: 目之 (LL) look at it; 目爲 (LL) regard as (unimportant, follower, etc.).

目標 *muhbiau*, n., target, aim.

目前 *muhchiarn*, adv., at present.

目的 *muhdih*, n., aim, object: 甚麼目的 what is the object? 目的地 destination.

目覩 *muhduu*, v.t., to witness.

目光 *muhguang*, n., a man's vision, ability to size up person or scheme: 目光遠大 have farsight; 目光銳利 have sharp eye; 目光如豆 extremely shortsighted, myopic view of things; 目光無神 dull-looking.

目今 *muhjin*, adv., now (in surveying present situation).

目擊 *muhjir*, v.t., to witness.

目眶 *muhkuang*, n., eye socket.

目力 *muhlih*, n., sight, vision; power of judgment.

目錄 *muhluh*, n., catalogue, contents (of book).

目下 *muhshiah*, adv., at present.

目笑 *muhshiauh*, v.i., (LL) give a smiling glance.

目神 *muhshern*, n., a person's look (bright, dull, suspicious, etc.).

目眩 *muhshyuarn*, adj., giddy.

目送 *muh-suhng*, v.t., to gaze while bidding farewell.

目逃 *muh-taur*, v.i., (LL) having nervous look, dare not look straight.

目次 *muhtsyh*, n., contents (of book).

田 41.41-1 丅

tiarn.

N. (1) A surname. (2) Farm: 良田 good farm; 稻田, 水田 paddy field; 旱田 dry land, farm for wheat, cotton, etc. other than rice; 桑田 mulberry field; 公田 public farm, see 井ᐞ田 20.20; 心田 the mind considered as ground for cultivation.

V.i. & t. (1) (AC) to farm. (2) To hunt: 田獵.

田產 *tiarnchaan*, n., landed property; farm product.

田疇 *tiarnchour*, n., (AC) farm land.

田盪 *tiarndahng*, n., a kind of implement for levelling field.

田地 *tiarndih*, n., farm land; situation (usu. bad): 弄到這個田地 got into such a situation.

田賦 *tiarnfuh*, n., tax on farm land.

田黃 *tiarnhuarng*, n., honey-colored stone, prized as seal stone.
田雞 *tiarnji*, n., frog: 四眼田雞 (facet.) bespectacled person, esp. schoolchild.
田家 *tiarnjia*, n., farmer: 田家翁 (poet.) old farmer; 田家子 farmer's child.
田假 *tiarn-jiah*, n., school holidays in country when children are needed for the farm, such as during harvest.
田徑賽 *tiarnjihng-saih*, n., (athletics) track and field events.
田莊 *tiarnjuang*, n., farmstead.
田獵 *tiarnlieh*, v.i. & n., hunt(ing).
田螺 *tiarnluor*, n., edible snail.
田廬 *tiarnlur*, n., farmer's hut, house at the farm.
田賽 *tiarnsaih*, n., (athletics) field events.
田舍 *tiarnsheh*, n., farmhouse; 田舍翁, 田舍郎 (poet.) country squire, see *-jia* ↑.
田鼠 *tiarnshuu*, n., field mouse, mole.
田田 *tiarntiarn*, n., (AC) healthy, beautifully green (of ponds, fields).
田頭 *tiarntour*, n., formerly, minor officer in charge of land properties; field path.
田土 *tiarn-tuu*, n. field, farm land.
田租 *tiarntzu*, n., farm rent.
田字面 *tiarntzyh miahn*, n., (MC) person with square face.
田野 *tiarnyee*, n., the countryside, open country.
田園 *tiarnyuarn*, n., farm garden, rustic home.

毌 41.41-1

guahn.

[Anc. var. of 貫 41.80]

因 41.41-1

yin.

N. Cause, reason: 因由, 因緣 *-your*, *-yuarn* ↓; 因果 *-guoo* ↓; 主因 main cause; 要因 important cause or reason; 前因 (a) reason to be found in previous incarnation; (b) antecedent; 遠因 distant cause; 近因 immediate cause; 種因 to saw the seeds of (future trouble, war, etc.); 有因 there's a reason; 無因 for no reason at all; 何因 why? what cause?

V.i. & t. To carry on: 因仍, 因襲 *-rerng*, *-shir*² ↓.

Prep. (1) On the basis of, by the support of: 因人成事 do s.t. by the help of s.o.; 因陋就簡 to economize because of lack of funds. (2) According to, in accord with: 因病下藥 apply medicine according to indications; 因時制宜 do what is appropriate according to the circumstances; 因勢利導 guide or channel action according to circumstances; 因材施敎 teach a person according to what he is good for. (3) (Prep. & conj.) for, on account of, because of: 因爲 *-weih* ↓; 因此 *-tsyy* ↓; 因而 (because of s.t.) therefore; 因禍得福 luck grows out of adversity; 因小失大 lose the main goal because of small gains; 因噎廢食 stop eating altogether on account of a hiccup—unjustified giving up of a good cause.

因革 *yinger*, n., historical development (=沿革).
因故 *yin-guh*, phr., for this reason.
因公 *yin-gung*, phr., on account of official duty.
因果 *yin-guoo*, n., (Budd.) retribution, chain of cause and effect: 前因後果 antecedents and consequences; 因果報應 retribution for sin; 因果律 principle of efficient casuality.
因何 *yin-her*, phr., for what reason?
因著 *yin-je*, phr., because of, on account of.
因之 *yin-jy*, phr., (LL) because of that.
因明 *yinmirng*, n., (Hindu) the science of logic.
因仍 *yinrerng*, v.i. & t., to persist without change: 因仍舊慣 follow old routine.
因習 *yinshir*¹, v.i. & t., ditto.
因襲 *yinshir*², v.i. & t., ditto.
因數 *yinshuh*, n., (math.) factor.
因是 *yin-shyh*, phr., because of this.
因循 *yinshyurn*, v.i., to follow old routine.
因此 *yin-tsyy*, phr., because of this (=therefore).
因子 *yintzyy*, n., cause; factor; 因子分析 factorization (math.).
因爲 *yinweih* (*-'wei*), conj., because.
因應 *yinyihng*, v.i., (AC) to adjust, react: 因應變化 change according to changing circumstances.
因由(兒) *yinyour('l)* (*-'you*), n., reason, cause.
因緣 *yinyuarn*, n., (1) a chance, opportunity (cf. 姻^A緣 93A.41); (2) (Budd.) the chain of cause and effect; 因緣生法 the law of mutual causation of all actions.

困 41.41-1

kuhn.

V.t. To surround: 被困 be surrounded (by enemy); 困於酒色 addicted to drink and sex, steeped in wine and surrouned by women; 坐困愁城 wallow in slough of despond; 困擾 perplex.

Adj. & adv. (1) Hard pressed, hard up, in straits: 窮困 hard up; see many compp. ↓. (2) Tired, exhausted: 他困了 (vern.) he is tired. (3) Sleepy (also wr. 睏): 困了就去睡 go to bed when you are tired; 困倦 *-jyuahn*. ↓.

困窮 *kuhnchyurng*, adj., impoverished, in difficult circumstances.

困頓 *kuhnduhn*, adj., tired, exhausted; frustrated.

困阨 *kuhn-eh*, adj., in difficult straits.

困乏 *kuhnfar*, adj., tired, exhausted; in difficult position.

困惑 *kuhnhuoh*, n., difficulty, difficult problem, situation; perplexity.

困覺 *kuhnjiauh*, v.i., go to sleep.

困倦 *kuhnjyuahn*, adj., tired, weary, fatigued.

困窘 *kuhnjyuung*, adj., in distress.

困苦 *kuhnkuu*, adj. & n., difficult, -y, hardship, suffering: 困苦難堪 suffering unbearable hardships.

困惱 *kuhnnaau*, adj. & n., vexed, -xation, confused, -sion.

困難 *kuhnnarn*, adj. & n., difficulty: 有甚麼困難 what the difficulty? 事情很困難 the thing is very difficult.

囤 41.41-1

duhn (**turn*).

N. Grain basket.

V.t. (**turn* or *duhn*) To store up: 囤糧 store up food for army; 囤貨 store up goods, hoard.

囤積 **turnji*, v.t., hoard up: 囤積居奇 to corner goods; hoarding and speculation.

固 41.41-1

guh.

N. A surname.

V.i. & t. (1) V.i., become solid: 凝固 solidify, 固結 *-jier* ↓. (2) V.t., strengthen, defend: 鞏固 consolidate, strengthen; 固國不以山谿之險 it's not high mountains and deep valleys that best serve to defend a country.

Adj. (1) Solid, firm: 堅固 strong; 牢固 secure; 固體 *-tii* ↓. (2) Stable: 固定 *-dihng* ↓; 國可以固 (LL) then the country can have peace and stability. (3) Obstinate, stubborn, insistent, resolute, steadfast: 固執 *-'jyr* ↓; 固請 an insistent request or invitation; 固辭 resolute refusal; 固留 insist on s.o. to stay; 固持己見 self-opinionated; 頑固 die-hard, stubborn, unyielding. (4) Base, mean, ignorant: 君子謂之固 (LL) a superior man would call it mean; 固陋 *-louh* ↓. (5) Chronic: 固疾 *-jir* ↓.

Adv. (1) Originally, certainly, assuredly: 固有 *-yoou*, 固然 *-'rarn*, 固守 *-shoou* ↓. (2) Indeed, once upon a time: 臣固聞之 your humble servant heard it said once upon a time that . . .; 固有之矣 yes, it did happen indeed; 仁人固如是乎 is that the way of a worthy man?

固定 *guhdihng*, adj., fixed, stationary, unshakable: 固定資本 fixed capital (opp. 流動資本 circulating or floating capital).

固結 *guhjier*, v.i. & adj., (become) solidified, tied up.

固疾 *guhjir*, n., a chronic disease (=痼疾).

固執 *guh'jyr*, adj. & adv., (1) stubborn(ly), obstinate(ly), unyielding(ly); (2) (*-jyr*) steadfast(ly): 擇善固執 choose what is good and hold to it fast; (3) v.i. & t., to stick to (one's opinion), obstinate.

固陋 *guhlouh*, adj., ignorant, vulgar, rustic, provincial.

固然 *guh'rarn*, adj. & adv., (1) assured(ly), certain(ly), doubtless: 事有必至, 理有固然 it is bound to happen—is logical and natural; (2) adv. & conj., though, it is true that. . . : 你這樣做, 固然不錯 granted that (it is true that) the way you do it is right, still. . . .

固守 *guhshoou*, (1) v.i. & t., keep without change, to stand one's ground 固守成規 stick to old rules; (2) adj., conservative.

固實 *guhshyr*, n., (=故實) past precedents.

固體 *guhtii*, n., (phys.) a solid (body) (opp. 液體, 氣體 a liquid, gas).

固有 *guhyoou*, adj. & adv., proper(ly), original(ly): 固有名詞 (gram.) proper nouns (opp. 普通名詞 common nouns); 固有權 inherent or original rights; 固有此說 originally there was such a theory or assumption, it was originally so stated; 固有道德 traditional ethics.

囿 41.41-1

youh.

N. (LL) garden: 園囿, 苑囿 a pleasure garden; an enclosure for animals (deer, etc.): 鹿囿.

V.i. To be hampered, limited in vision: 囿於一隅 be restricted to a narrow confine; 囿於俗見 blinded by current prejudices.

圃 41.41-1

puu.

N. (1) Orchard, garden: 菜圃 vegetable garden; 菓圃 fruit orchard; 花圃 flower nursery. (2) (AC) gardener. (3) A patch of ground: 場圃.

圉 41.41-1

yuu.

N. (1) A stable, corral, enclosure. (2) (AC) border territory.

圊 41.41–1

ching.

N. Lavatory: 圊桶 night pot; 圊溷 manure pit in countryside.

圈 41.41–1

chyuan (**jyuan, *juahn*).

N. (1) A circle: 圓圈 a circle drawn on paper or any circle; 畫圈 draw a circle; 跑了一圈 run a distance back to starting point. (2) Any circular object: 花圈 a wreath; 橡皮圈 rubber band; 救生圈 life belt; 游泳圈 swimming belt for beginners. (3) Group: 文化圈, 教育圈 literary, educational circle(s); 商業圈 commercial circle(s); 大氣圈 ionosphere. (4) (**jyuahn*) A corral: 牛圈 enclosure for cows; 豬圈 pigpen.

V.t. (1) To encircle, to fence in: 圈上, 圈住, 圈起來 to fence in. (2) To draw a circle over or by a word: 圈點 *-diaan*↓. (3) (**jyuan*) To shut up: 圈住, 圈起來 to shut up (person, animals, etc.).

圈閉 *chyuanbih*, v.t., to shut up (person, animal).

圈圈(兒) *chyuan-chyuan* (*-chyua-'l*), phr., (1) v.i., to draw circles on paper (first *chyuan* used as vb.); (2) n., a drawn circle: 這麼一個小圈圈兒 such a small circle; (3) n., a group: 搞小圈圈 form small cliques: 別加入這類圈圈裏去 don't join such circles of friends.

圈點 *chyuandiaan*, v.t. & n., to punctuate, -tion; mark a good (passage) with circles.

圈禁 *chyuanjihn*, v.t., to keep within enclosure; to detain.

圈口(兒) *chyuoukoou'*(*l*), n., diameter (of bracelet, ring, etc.).

圈兒 *chyua'l*, n., (1) see N.↑; (2) esp. enclosure or permissible grounds: 鬧得都出了圈兒 has got beyond all bounds; (3) a trap, see *-tauh*↓.

圈弄 *chyuannuhng*, v.t., to frame up (person), to entrap.

圈套(兒) *chyuantauh*('*l*), n., a trap to frame up (person) or keep him under control: 上了他的圈套 fall into his trap.

圈子 *chyuantz*, n., see 圈 N.↑ esp. 圈套 *-tauh*↑; an inner circle: e.g., 難以打進這個圈子 difficult to be admitted into the clique.

園 41.41–1

yuarn.

[Var. in callig. 囩]

N. (1) A garden: 花園 ditto; 菓園 orchard; 菜園 vegetable patch. (2) A park, place of public amusement: 公園 ditto; 動物園 zoological garden; 植物園 botanical garden; 戲園 theater; 茶園 tea garden; 梨園 theatrical school or troupe.

園地 *yuarndih*, n., park area, garden area.

園丁 *yuarnding*, n., gardener.

園林 *yuarnlirng*[1], n., tree garden.

園陵 *yuarnlirng*[2], n., mausoleum.

園廬 *yuarnlur*, n., garden home.

園圃 *yuarnpuu*, n., garden.

園子 *yuarntz*, n., (1) garden; (2) theater.

園藝 *yuarnyih*, n., horticulture, art of gardening.

園囿 *yuarnyuh*, n., (LL) garden.

團 41.41–1

tuarn.

N. (1) A roundish mass, a circle, a lump of indefinite shape: 一團麵 a lump of noodles; 一團和氣 a prevailing mood of harmony; 一團糟 a complete mess; 團成一團 form a circle; 一團線, 亂髮 a mass of thread, loose hair; 粉團 dumpling. (2) A body, group of people: 團體 *-tii*↓: 集團 group (of delegates, visitors, etc.); 社團 a group, a society; 訪問團 group of visitors; 使節團 diplomatic corps; 義和團 Boxers (band) of 1900; 財團 body of financiers, investors; 主席團 presidium. (3) (Mil.) regiment: see 團長, 團副 *-jaang, -fuh*↓.

V.i. To unite: 團結, 團聚 *-jier, -jyuh*↓.

Adj. & adv. (1) Round: 團形 round-shaped; 團臉 round face; 面團團 a roundish, fleshy face. (2) As a body, collective: 團拜 pay respects as a group, mutual congratulations at a group meeting on New Year's Day.

團契 *tuarnchih*, v.i., unite in friendly spirit.

團臍 *tuarnchir*, n., roundish shell of female crab.

團丁 *tuarnding*, n., member of volunteer group.

團粉 *tuarnfeen*, n., noodles made of bean flour.

團匪 *tuarnfeei*, n., name for the Boxers of 1900 (義和團).

團副 *tuarnfuh*, n., second in command of regiment.

團長 *tuarnjaang*, n., regiment commander.

團結 *tuarnjier*, v.i., to unite, esp. in spirit.

團聚 *tuarnjyuh*, v.i. & n., have a reunion (of friends, relatives).

團練 *tuarnliahn*, v.t. & n., training of militiamen.

團欒 *tuarnluarn*, (1) n., have reunion; (2) adj., round, also wr. 團圞.

團龍 *tuarnlurng*, n., circle of embroidered dragon on ceremonial robes.

團牌 *tuarnpair*, n., round rattan shield used by soldiers.

團扇 *tuarnshahn*, n., silk round fan.

圊 圈 園 團

亅	小	卜	十	土	ナ	卄	㇄	丨	一	丁	フ	口	区	冈	㇆	厂	尸	亠	广	宀	丶	乚	弋	心	八	人	乂	乛	ノ	儿	⺊	く
00	01	02	10	11	12	20	21	22	30	31	32	40	41	42	50	51	52	60	61	62	63	70	71	72	80	81	82	83	90	91	92	93

團體 *tuarntii*, n., body, group (of students, strikers, etc.).

團團 *tuarntuarn*, adj. & adv., round and round: 團團轉 turn round and round; 團團圍住 completely surround(-ed).

團圓 *tuarnyuarn*, v.i. & n., esp. family reunited: 大團圓 grand union; (fig.) happy ending; 一家團圓, 團圓節 Mid-Autumn Festival (of family reunion); 團圓媳婦 formerly, used of daughter-in-law raised from childhood in the family.

團魚 *tuarnyur*, n., var. name for turtle (鱉).

圍 41.41-2

weir.

N. (1) (AC) distance between two stretched arms, esp. in measuring circumference of trees. (2) Circumference, enclosure, limits: 周圍 circumference; 範圍 the limits of action or movement, orig., corral, stockade; 圍子 *-tz*↓. (3) Cover: 轎圍 cover for sedan chair; 車圍 cover for wagons; 牀圍 cover or skirt for area below mattress; 圍巾 *-jin*↓.

V.t. (1) To surround, corral: 圍繞 surround; 圍住, 圍上 have s.t. surrounded; 包圍 to encircle, surround. (2) To corral, round up: 圍攻 attack from all sides; 打圍 to round up game in hunting.

圍標 *weir-biau*, v.i., to agree among bidders by collusion.

圍脖兒 *weirbor'l*, n., muffler.

圍場 *weirchaang*, n., hunting grounds.

圍牆 *weirchiarng*, n., surrounding walls; 柏林圍牆 Berlin Wall.

圍棋 *weir-chir*, v.i., to play chess; a Chin. chess game using black and white chips, *go* in Japanese.

圍裙 *weirchyurn* (-'*chyun*), n., apron.

圍尺 *weir-chyy*, n., bamboo strip for measuring curving distance.

圍堵 *weirduu*, v.t., to contain; 圍堵政策 containment policy.

圍攻 *weir-gung*, v.t., attack from all sides.

圍巾 *weirjin*, n., muffler.

圍桌 *weirjuo*, n., dinner table with cover which hangs over the sides.

圍困 *weirkuhn*, v.t., to besiege (city); p.p., besieged.

圍獵 *weirlieh*, v.i., to round up game from different directions.

圍爐 *weirlur*, n., New Year's Eve dinner.

圍屏 *weirpirng* (-'*ping*), n., a portable screen.

圍繞 *weirrauh*, v.t., to surround, encircle.

圍隨 *weirsueir* (-'*suei*), v.t., to hang around (important official).

圍子 *weirtz*, n., an earthen stockade.

圍腰兒 *weiryau'l*, n., formerly, lady's girdle.

囝 41.41-3

nan (also **tzaai*).

N. (Soochow dial.) a baby, infant, pr. **tzaai*. in Cantonese.

圄 41.41-3

yuu.

N. See 囹圄 prison, 41.41.

圂 41.41-3

huhn.

N. (LL) lavatory.

回 41.41-4

hueir.

[Anc. var. 囘; pop. 囬]

N. (1) A chapter in story, an incident: 甚麽一回事, 怎麽回事 what has happened? (2) Number of times: 上回對他說 the last time I spoke to him; 好幾回 a good many times. (3) 等一回兒 (＝會兒) in a short while. (4) Moslem: 回族, 回人, 回民 Moslem people, short for 回回, see 回回, 回教 *-hueir*, *-jiauh*↓. (5) A surname.

V.i. (1) To return, turn round or back: 回來, 回復, 回頭, 回顧, 回去, *-'lai*, *-fuh*, *-tour*, *-guh*, *-'chyuh*, ↓; 回暖 (the weather) has turned warm; 回黃轉綠 from autumn yellow to the green of spring. (2) To reply: 回覆 or 回復 to reply by letter; 回稟 to report back; 回電 reply telegram; 回示 *-shyh*↓; 已經回了 have already reported (to superior); 請你替我回一下 please send message in for me; 回嘴, 回罵 *-tzueei*, *-mah*↓; 回命 return with message.

Adj. & adv. (1) Going round, curving: 回廊 (＝廻廊) curving corridor; 回翔 (＝廻轉) (of birds) circling in the air. (2) Reflected: 回光返照 the sun's reflected light at evening, also return to consciousness before death; 回味, 回響 *-weih*, *-shiaang*²↓.

Adv. (After vb.) back: 收回, 取回 take back; 送回 send back; 贖回 claim pawned article; 折回 turn back on the road; 回敬 *-jihng*↓.

回報 *hueirbauh*, (1) n., revenge, retribution; (2) v.i., to report back.

回避 *hueirbih*, v.t., see 廻避 41.83.

回程 *hueircherng*, n., return journey.

回青 *hueirching*, n., a mineral green for painting.

回春 *hueir-chun*, v.i., return to spring; (of doctors) bring back life to patient.

回去 *hueir'chyuh*, v.i., to go home.

回答 *hueirdar*, v.i., & n., answer by word or letter.

回復 *hueirfuh*, v.i., (1) to recover (health) or (health) recovers; (2) to reply by word of mouth or letter.

回歸熱 *hueirgueireh*, n., recurrent or relapsing fever.

回歸線 *hueirguei shiahn*, n., (astron.) the tropics: 北回歸線 Tropic of Cancer; 南回歸線 Tropic of Capricorn.

回顧 *hueirguh*, v.t., to look back (on road, past).

回鍋肉 *hueirguo rouh*, n., a Szechuan dish of pork (first boiled, next cut into slices, and finally fried with rich seasoning).

回話 *hueirhuah*, n., message of reply usu. carried by servant.

回惶 *hueirhuarng*, adj., afraid.

回回 *Hueirhueir*, adj. & n., Moslem, the Moslems.

回護 *hueirhuh*, v.t., to take s.o.'s side, to side with (person).

回見 *hueir'jiahn*, phr., see you again (abbr. from 回頭見).

回教 *Hueirjiauh*, n., the Moslem religion, see *-hueir* ↑.

回敬 *hueirjihng*, v.t. & n., to send present in return or propose toast in return: 回敬一杯.

回轉 *hueirjuaan*, v.i., to turn round, see *-shin* ↓.

回扣 *hueirkouh*, n., discount; commission for agent.

回來 *hueir'lai*, (1) v.i., to come back; (2) adv., afterwards: 回來他不答應 he might disapprove afterwards.

回力球 *hueirlih chiour*, n., hai alai, a game of Spanish origin.

回禮 *hueirlii*, v.i. & n., (to, a) reply in salute, toast, see *-jihng* ↑.

回鑾 *hueir-luarn*, phr., emperor's return to capital.

回祿 *hueirluh*, n., god of fire: 回祿之災 a fire disaster.

回籠 *hueir-lurng*, v.i., (econ.) cause bank notes to return to the bank of issue.

回罵 *hueirmah*, v.i. & t., to answer back and scold in return.

回門 *hueir-mern*, v.i. & n., the return of bride to her mother's home on third day of wedding.

回眸 *hueir-mour*, v.i., (of woman) glance back.

回片兒 *hueirpiah'l*, n., a receiver's name card as sign of receipt.

回煞 *hueirshah*, n., (Taoist) return of soul of deceased to visit own home a few days after death.

回生 *hueir-sheng*[1], v.i., usu. in 起死回生 (praise of doctors) make the dead come back to life.

回聲 *hueirsheng*[2], n., echo.

回想 *hueirshiaang*[1], v.i., to think back, recollect.

回響 *hueirshiaang*[2], n., (1) an echo; (2) a response (to appeal).

回信 *hueirshihn*, n., letter of reply.

回心 *hueir-shin*, v.i., to soften determination: 回心轉意 to change one's mind and come back (to former relation).

回手(兒) *hueir-shoou*[1]*('l)*, v.i., to return (blow); to do s.t. with a turn of the hand.

回首 *hueir-shoou*[2], v.i., (LL) to look back or think back: 不堪回首 cannot bear to think of the past.

回示 *hueirshyh*, n., (court.) your reply, instruction.

回旋 *hueirshyuarn*, v.i. & adv., (to go) round and round.

回條(兒) *hueirtiaur('l)*, n., a note of reply.

回頭 *hueirtour*, (1) adv., by and by: 我回頭就來 I will come in a moment; (2) v.i., turn back: 回頭一看 turn back to look; 回頭是岸 (Budd.) just repent and salvation is at hand.

回嘴 *hueirtzueei*, v.i., to answer back; also 應嘴 to retort.

回味 *hueirweih*, n., aftertaste (of good tea, olives, etc.).

回文 *hueirwern*, n., (1) Moslem language; (2) official reply; see 廻[Δ]文詩 41.83.

回憶 *hueiryih*, v.i., to think back, recall: 回憶錄 book of reminiscences, memoirs.

回音 *hueiryin*, n., a letter of reply; echo.

回郵 *hueiryour*, n., & v.t., return mail.

回佣 *hueiryuhng*, n., commission (discount) for servant.

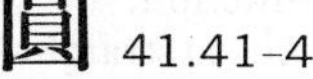

圓 41.41-4 *yuarn.*

N. (1) A circle: 圓圈 *-chyuan* ↓. (2) A dollar: 三圓 three dollars (usu. wr. 元); 美圓 American dollar; 銀圓 money, dollars.

V.t. (1) To complete (a circle), round out (a lie): 自圓其說 to fill up gaps in person's theory; 圓謊 *-huaang*; 圓成 *-cherng* ↓. (2) To interpret (dream): 圓夢 *-mehng* ↓.

Adj. (1) Round: 圓球 round ball; 圓桌 *-juo* ↓; 圓裏嚕嘟 very round; 圓顱方趾 "round skull and square toes"—all human beings are alike; 圓徑 *-jihng* ↓, etc.; 橢圓 oval-shaped; 扁圓形 disc-shaped. (2) Satisfactory, complete: 圓滿, 圓全 *-maan*, *-chyuarn* ↓. (3) Smooth, not rough: 圓活, 圓通 *-huor*, *-tung* ↓.

圓成 *yuarncherng*, v.t., to complete (undertaking), also wr. 完成.

圓蟲類 *yuarnchurngleih*, n., (zoo.) *Nemathelminthes.*

圓圈(兒)(子) *yuarnchyuan (-chyua'l) (tz)*, n., a circle.

圓全 *yuarn'chyuarn*, (1) adj., complete, satisfactory; (2) v.t., to help bring off successfully.

圓飯 *yuarnfahn*, n., formal dinner on second day of wedding when bride and groom eat together.

圓房(兒) *yuarn-farng('l)*, v.i., to consummate marriage.

圓墳(兒) *yuarn-fern(-fer'l)*, v.i., visit the grave on third day of burial.

圓光 *yuarnguang*, n., (1) halo of idol; (2) a form of gazing at mirror or blank white paper to perceive image, similar to crystal gazing: 圓光兒 a circular shape; 剪個圓光兒 cut a round piece of paper.

圓規 *yuarnguei*, n., compasses.

圓函數 *yuarnharnshuh*, n.,

圓
圖
圜
國

(math.) circular function.
圓謊 *yuarnhuaang*, v.i., to straighten out contradictions in a lie and make it plausible.
圓滑 *yuarnhuar*, adj., tactful, smooth (person, methods).
圓活 *yuarnhuor*, adj., (1) flexible; (2) (-'*huo*) rich, round (voice).
圓弧 *yuarnhur*, n., (math.) an arc.
圓渾 *yuarnhurn*, adj., round and smooth.
圓徑 *yuarnjihng*, n., (math.) diameter; 半圓徑 radius.
圓寂 *yuarnjir*, v.i., (of Budd. priests) pass away.
圓周 *yuarnjou*, n., circumference; 圓周率 --*lyuh*, the ratio of circumference to diameter—3.1416.
圓錐 *yuarnjuei*, n., (math.) cone; 圓錐根 (bot.) conical root; 圓錐面 conic surface.
圓柱 *yuarnjuh*, n., cylinder; 圓柱根 (bot.) cylindrical root.
圓桌 *yuarn-juo*, n., round table: 圓桌會議 round-table conference.
圓臉 *yuarn-liaan*, (1) v.i., to save face; (2) n., a round face.
圓滿 *yuarnmaan*, adj., satisfactory (results, etc.).
圓夢 *yuarn-mehng*, v.i., to interpret dreams.
圓面積 *yuarn-miahnji*, n., spherical surface.
圓心 *yuarnshin*, n., (math.) center of a circle.
圓形 *yuarnshirng*, adj. & n., circular (shape).
圓通 *yuarntung*, adj., flexible (temperament, method).
圓子 *yuarntz*, n., dumpling.
圓圓 *yuarnyuarn*, n., pop. term for 龍^Δ^眼 fruit, 60S.70.
圓月 *yuarn-yueh*, phr., to have dinner in moonlight on 中秋 Mid-Autumn Festival.

圖 41.41-4

tur.

[Var. of 啚]

N. (1) A picture, map, illustration, any kind of drawing: 地圖 map; 插圖 illustrations for book, article; 畫圖 drawing; 統計圖 (圖表) statistical chart; 藍圖 blueprint; 剖面圖 a cross section, sectional plan; 圖窮而匕首見 (allu.) the dagger is out after pretended friendship. (2) Script of prophecy: see 河^Δ^圖 63A.00; 圖讖, 圖籙 -*chehn*, -*luh* ↓. (3) Plan: 圖謀 -*mour* ↓; 企圖 plan for some enterprise; 遠圖 long plans, ambitions.

V.i. & t. To plan, to try to; to hope for: 希圖 hope to (of ambitious plans); 希圖倖免 hope for lucky escape from s.t. undesirable; strive for: 圖名, 圖利 strive for fame, wealth; 有利可圖 there's profit to be made, worth striving for; 圖財害命 phr., murder for money; 別有所圖 have other aims, plans; 貪圖 crave for s.t. beyond one's deserves; 圖飽私囊 try to enrich oneself (from public services); 圖呑公款 try to embezzle; 發奮圖強 determine to make country strong; 圖報 hope to repay kindnesses.

圖案 *tur-ahn*, n., a sketch, design, plan (of construction, etc.); blueprint.
圖板 *turbaan*, n., printing plates, also wr. 圖版.
圖表 *turbiaau*, n., illustrations and charts.
圖讖 *turchehn*, n., book of prophecy, esp. regarding dynastic fortunes.
圖釘 *turding*, n., thumbtacks.
圖畫 *turhuah*, n. & v.t., painting, drawing; to draw, to paint (picture).
圖章 *turjang*(-'*jang*), n., stamp, personal seal.
圖解 *turjiee*, n., illustrated manual, analytical table or chart.
圖記 *turjih*, n., seal, stamp, an official chop.
圖籍 *turjir*, n., maps of territory and population, land charts and census registers.
圖賴 *turlaih*, v.i. & t., try to dishonor obligations, disown responsibility or to cheat or libel.
圖利 *turlih*, v.i., try to make profits, gains.
圖籙 *turluh*, n., see -*chehn* ↑.
圖謀 *turmour*, v.i. & t., to plan (usu. s.t. sinister), to conspire: 圖謀不軌 plan rebellion or lawless acts.
圖形 *tur-shirng*, n., portrait work; geometric contour.
圖書 *turshu*, n., books in gen.; 圖書館 library; (*tur'shu*) personal seal.
圖說 *turshuo*, n., illustrated manual or primer, charts with explanatory notes.
圖騰 *turterng*, n., (translit.) totem.
圖樣 *turyahng*, n., a sketch, design of construction; drawings in gen.

圜 41.41-4

huarn (**yuarn*).

N. & adj. (**yuarn*) (AC) circular body, heaven: 圜丘 the altar to heaven; var. of 圓.

V.i. & t. (*huarn*) To surround.

國 41.41-7

guor.

N. & adj. (1) A country, nation, -nal: 國內 inside the country; 國內航線 domestic lines; 國外 abroad; 各國, 列國 the nations of the world; 國難, 國恥, 國力, 國富 national crisis, humiliation, strength, wealth; 國光, 國運, 國華, 國威 national glory, fortune, prosperity, prestige; 國讎, 國賊 national enmity, traitor; 國立 (of educational or other institutions) national, supported by the central government; 國產 national product; 國有 government-owned; 國定 (of textbooks, rituals, etc.) approved by the government; 國營 (of business enterprises) government-operated. (2) A surname.

國寶 *guorbaau*, n., (1) national

treasures such as anc. objects of art, imperial seals, etc.; (2) a nation's best talents; (3) the national coin.

國本 *guor-been*, n., (1) the foundation of a nation; (2) (LL) the crown prince.

國幣 *guorbih*, n., the national currency.

國柄 *guor-bihng*, n., the political power of a nation.

國步 *guor-buh*, n., the national fortune: 國步方艱 the nation is being faced with a difficult crisis or crises.

國朝 *guor-chaur*, n., the reigning dynasty.

國慶 *guorchihng*, n., the National Day.

國旗 *guor-chir*, n., the national emblem, flag.

國情 *guor-chirng*, n., the current condition or situation of a country and its people.

國初 *guor-chu*, n., the first years of a new dynasty.

國都 *guordu*, n., the national capital.

國度 *guorduh*, n., (1) a country, nation; (2) national expenditures.

國法 *guorfaa*, n., (1) national laws; (2) the constitution and administrative laws of a country.

國防 *guorfarng*, n., national defense; 國防部 Ministry of National Defence.

國父 *guorfuh*, n., the Father of a Nation (Dr. Sun Yat-sen).

國府 *guorfuu*, n., the National Government of the Republic of China (short for 國民政府).

國歌 *guor-ge*, n., the national anthem.

國故 *guorguh*, n., (1) the national cultural, esp. literary, heritage; (2) (AC) a national mourning.

國號 *guor-hauh*, n., the title of a reigning dynasty.

國花 *guor-hua*, n., the national flower.

國畫 *guor-huah*, n., Chin. painting (opp. 西畫 Western painting).

國徽 *guor-huei*, n., the national insignia.

國會 *guorhueih*, n., the national legislature or assembly.

國貨 *guor-huoh*, n., native products.

國魂 *guor-hurn*, n., the soul of a nation, the national genius.

國丈 *guor-jahng*, n., the prince's father-in-law.

國債 *guor-jaih*, n., national debts.

國家 *guorjia*, n., the state or nation: 國家主義 nationalism; 先進國家 advanced countries; 未發展國家 underdeveloped countries; 落後國家 backward countries.

國交 *guor-jiau*, n., diplomatic relations between countries.

國界 *guor-jieh*, n., the national boundary.

國計 *guor-jih*[1], n., (1) the national economy; (2) national policies.

國際 *guorjih*[2], (1) n., the International: 第一, 第二, 第三國際 First, Second, Third International; (2) adj., international: 國際公法 international law; 國際私法 international private law, conflict of laws; 國際組織, 關係 international organization, relations; 國際音標 the International Phonetic Alphabet; 國際法 law of nations, international law; 國際聯盟 the League of Nations; 國際法院 International Court of Justice (ICJ) (UN); 國際軍事法庭 International Military Tribunal; 國際勞工局 International Labor Office; 國際勞工組織 International Labor Organization (ILO); 國際貨幣基金 International Monetary Fund (IMF); 國際扶輪社 Rotary Club International; 國際獅子會 International Association of Lions' Club; also see *-liarn* ↓.

國境 *guor-jihng*, n., national territorial limits.

國紀 *guor-jii*, n., laws and social conventions of a country.

國舅 *guor-jiouh*, n., the prince's maternal uncle.

國籍 *guorjir*, n., the nationality of an individual: 入某國籍 become citizen of a cetrain country, see 籍 92A.41; 國籍之衝突 conflict of nationality; 國籍法 law of nationality.

國軍 *guor-jyun*, n., the national armed forces.

國庫 *guor-kuh*, n., the national treasury.

國聯 *guorliarn*, n., the defunct League of Nations (short for 國際聯盟 dist. 聯合國 the United Nations); 國聯理事會 Council of the League; 國聯大會 Assembly of the League; 國聯盟約 Covenant of the League of Nations.

國命 *guor-mihng*, n., (1) (AC) governmental authority; (2) a nation's life line or fortunes.

國民 *guormirn*, n., (1) (collectively) all the people of a nation; (2) an individual citizen: 國民學校 national schools (primary, secondary); 國民大會 the national assembly.

國母 *guormuu*, n., (AC) the queen mother.

國人 *guorrern*, n., the general mass of people: 中國人 Chinese; 外國人 foreigners; 美國人 Americans.

國喪 *guor-sang*, n., a state funeral.

國色 *guorseh*, n., a national beauty: 國色天香 celestial beauty, also the peony.

國殤 *guor-shang*, n., a national martyr.

國憲 *guor-shiahn*, n., (1) the national constitution, the fundamental law of the land; (2) (AC) a gen. term for all the laws of a country.

國璽 *guor-shii*, n., the national seal.

國手 *gour-shoou*, n., the national champion in any line of activity, esp. sports and games.

國書 *guor-shu*, n., (1) (diplomacy) a letter of credence: 呈遞國書 to present credentials; (2) (diplomacy) notes exchanged between governments; (3) formerly, the national characters used by the Tartars, Mongols, and Manchus.

國術 *guor-shuh*, n., Chinese boxing.

國是 *guor-shyh*[1], n., important affairs of state.

國事 *guor-shyh*[2], n., national affairs.

國勢 *guor-shyh*[3], n., (1) national power; (2) the national situation at a given moment.

國學 *guorshyuer*, n., the Chinese national literature, Chinese studies.

國史 *guor-shyy*, n., the history of a nation: 國史館 the *Academia Historica*, the Bureau of National History.

國帑 *guor-taang (nur)*, n., public funds.

國太 *guortaih*, n., (MC) the queen mother.

國體 *guor-tii*, n., (1) the form of state such as monarchy or republic; (2) a country's governmental structure or prestige.

國策 *guor-tseh*, n., national policies.

國粹 *guor-tsueih*, n., a nation's cultural heritage, national legacy.

國土 *guor-tuu*, n., national territory.

國葬 *guor-tzahng*, n., a state burial.

國祚 *guor-tzuoh*, n., the duration of a reigning dynasty.

國王 *guorwarng*, n., (1) the king; (2) the prince of a country; (3) title conferred on the chiefs of state of countries paying tribute to China.

國文 *guorwern*, n., Chinese as the national language.

國務 *guorwuh*, n., national affairs, affairs of state; 國務卿 (U.S.) the Secretary of State; 國務院 (U.S.)the Department of State.

國音 *guoryin*, n., the gen. received pronunciation as adopted by the government and used by the people at large: 國音字母 the Chin. national phonetic alphabet better known as 注音字母.

國樂 *guor-yueh*, n., (1) music officially approved by the government to be played on great ceremonial occasions; (2) the traditional Chin. music (opp. 西樂 Western music).

國用 *guor-yuhng*, n., national expenditures.

國語 *guoryuu*, n., (1) the national language, written or spoken (opp. 方言 local dialects); 國語文學 literature written in the vernacular; (2) the language used by the reigning dynasty.

囚 41.41-8

chiour.

N. Prisoner, criminal, convict: 囚犯, 囚徒 *-fahn, -tur* ↓; 要囚 important prisoner; 階下囚 prisoner of war ("lined up below the steps"); 死囚 criminal sentenced to death; 囚衣, 囚服 prisoner's garb; 囚髻 a woman's hairdo fashion in Tarng Dyn. (in imitation of convict's coil on head); 囚糧 prisoner's fare; 囚首垢(喪)面 untidy appearance with prisoner's unkempt hair and unwashed face (or mourner's face).

囚犯 *chiourfahn*, n., a prisoner.

囚禁 *chiourjihn*, v.t., to imprison.

囚牢 *chiourlaur*, n., prison.

囚籠 *chiourlurng*, n., convict's cage, on cart or ground.

囚牛 *chiourniour*, n., (myth.) the convict cow, son of the Dragon King, fond of music.

囚徒 *chiourtur*, n., prisoners, convicts in gen.

囹 41.41-8

lirng.

囹圄 *lirngyuu*, n., prison: 身陷囹圄 (LL) be thrown into prison (also 囹圉).

圇 41.41-8

lurn.

Adj. See 囫圇 41.41.

四 41.41-8

syh.

Adj. Four: 第四 number four; 4 and 5, oft. connote the sense of dispersal: 四分五裂 all split up; 四分五落 from all sides (things appear); 四捨五入 (in accounting) omitting decimal fractions smaller than 0.5 and counting all others, including 0.5, as 1; 4 and 8,usu. indicating foursquare,well-balanced: 四停八當, 四平八穩 (affair) very well disposed indeed; 4 and 6: 四六夾開 clearly presented; 四六(句子) *-liouh* ↓; four sides, all around: 四面, 四方, 四邊, 四圍 *-miahn, -fang, -bian, -weir*[1] ↓, 四下, 四起 *-shiah, -chii* ↓; 四處 *-chuh* ↓; 四脖子流汗 sweating all the neck round; 四面落地 all four walls covered with paper; 四海 *-haai* ↓; 四至 *-jyh* ↓; 四腳兒朝天 falling backwards with hands and legs in the air.

四拜 *syh baih*, phr.,(AC) deep bow four times.

四表 *syh biaau*, phr., in all directions, beyond confines of visible world.

四邊(兒) *syh bian(-bia'l)*, phr., in all four directions: east, west, north, south; all around; 四邊形 *--shirng*, a square.

四壁 *syh bih*, phr., on all the walls of a room: 家徒四壁 a house empty of all furniture; also all around, on all sides.

四部 *syh-buh*, phr., standard library classification into four categories: (a) 經 classics, (b) 史 history, including geography, (c) 子 philosophy and the arts and sciences, and (d) 集 collected works (subject or author); see 四庫 *-kuh* ↓.

四不像 *syh-buh-shiahng*, (1) adj., nondescript; (2) n., a fly swatter.

四稱 *syh-chehn*, adj., (face) well-balanced, well-proportioned.

四起 *syh-chii*, adv., all around (uprising).

四垂 *syh-chueir*, adv., (AC) on all frontiers (垂 u.f. 陲).

四處(兒) *shychuh('l)*, adv., (look for s.t.) everywhere.

四大 *syh dah*, phr., (1) (Budd.) the four elements of earth, water, fire, air; (2) 四大金剛 the statues of four guardian spirits at entrance to temple; (3) 四大門兒 the fox, the skunk, the porcupine and the snake, superstitiously considered as spirits to influence human life.

四德 *syh der*, n., the traditional four fundamentals in girl's education: 婦德 behavior, 婦言 speech, 婦容 appearance, and 婦功 needlework and cookery.

四地 *syh-dih*[1], (1) adv., see *-chuh*↑; (2) adj., neat: 這個人好四地 (coll.) this person is very neat and tidy.

四諦 *syh dih*[2], n., (Budd.) the four "truths" of life: 苦 misery and pain, 集 acquisition, 滅 extinction, and 道 salvation by the right path.

四方 *syh-fang*, adj. & adv., (1) everywhere, in (from) all directions; (2) foursquare, square; 四方步兒 solemn measured steps; 四方塊兒 a square piece, also (facet.) a short, stumpy person; 四方臉兒 a square face, square-jawed.

四海 *syh-haai*, (1) adv., "the four seas"—the whole world: 四海一家 the whole world is one family; 四海之內, 皆兄弟也 (子夏) all the people of the world are brothers; (2) (*-'hai*) adj., (coll.) generous: 爲人很四海 is very generous to people.

四合 *syh-her*, (1) adv., (dust) closing all around; (2) 四合房(兒) or 四合兒 Chin. house with courtyard in center and rooms on four sides (三合兒 rooms on three sides).

四呼 *syh hu*, n., (MC Chin. phonetics) the four classes of syllabic forms: 開口 regular or open; 齊齒 beginning with "i" (*yi*) sound; 合口 beginning with "u" (*wu*) sound, 撮口 beginning with ü (*yu*) sound: thus *an, ian, wan, yuan.*

四胡 *syh-hur*, n., a junior *hu* stringed instrument, with four strings.

四郊 *syh-jiau*, n., the suburbs.

四季(兒) *syh-jih(-jieh'l)*, n., the four seasons; 四季花兒 the representative flowers of the four seasons: peony (spring), pomegranate (summer), chrysanthemum (autumn), and plum (winter).

四極 *shy-jir*, n., the ends of the universe.

四周 *shy-jou*, adj., on all sides: 四周遭兒, 四周圍 ditto.

四柱冊 *shy-juh-tseh*, phr., formerly, (in official accounting) the four "columns" of "carried over," "income," "expenses" and "balance."

四知 *syh jy*[1], phr., the "four knows"—"heaven knows; god knows, I know and you know"—there is no absolutely secret dealing.

四肢 *syh-jy*[2], n., the four limbs—arms and legs.

四至 *syh-jyh*, n., the exact boundaries on four sides of land, specified in deeds; 四至兒 ditto, also 定四至兒 set limits to undertaking; 辦事有四至兒 be precise in one's affairs.

四塊瓦兒 *syh-kuaih waa'l*, n., a hat (in cold countries) with reversible flabs on four sides.

四框闌兒 *syh-kuang-lar'l*, n., the radical "囗"; index No. 41.

四庫 *shy-kuh*, n., usu. 四庫全書 the imperial library of Chienlung named after the "four vaults" of classics, history, philosophy and collected works of literature, see *-buh*↑.

四稜(兒)(子) *syh-lerng('l)(tz)*, n., a utensil with four-cornered shape; 四稜子 *--tz*, (a) n., a vulgar, coarse fellow; (b) adj., rude in speech.

四令 *syh-lihng*, n., see *-jih*↑.

四六 *shy-liouh*, n., a euphuistic style of parallel constructions, known esp. for pairs of sentences of four and six characters.

四鄰 *syh-lirn*, n., next-door neighbors.

四靈 *shy lirng*, n., (AC) the four spirits in AC mythology: the unicorn, the phoenix, the turtle and the dragon.

四面(兒) *shy-miahn(-miah'l)*, adv., on all sides: 四面受敵 surrounded by enemy on all sides; 四面楚歌 (allu.) ditto—hear the *Chuu* songs (of enemy) on all sides; 四面體 (math.) a tetrahedron.

四民 *syh-mirn*, n., the four classes of people in order of importance: 士 scholars, 農 farmers, 工 artisans, and 商 merchants.

四明兒 *syh-mirng'l*, adv., (coll.) all around: 四明兒都是籬笆 hedges all around.

四旁 *syh parng*, adv., all around.

四平調 *syhpirng-diauh*, n., (Chin. opera) the songs of 二黃 *ehlhuarng* (also called 平調).

四散 *shysahn*, adj., dispersed, scattered about.

四聲 *shy sheng*, n., the four tones: (1) 陰平 (*a*), (2) 陽平 (*ar*), (3) 上 (pr. *shaang*) (*aa*), and (4) 去 (*ah*) in standard national tongue, without 入聲 the "entering tone"; in other classifications, (1) and (2) are regarded together as 平, while 入聲 is added.

四下(裏) *shy-shiah(lii)*, adv., everywhere.

四向 *syh-shiahng*, adv., toward all directions.

四鄉 *syh-shiang*[1], n., suburbs (on all sides).

四廂 *syh-shiang*[2], n., the suburbs in four directions, esp. Peking.

四絃琴 *syh-shiarn-chirn*, n., the violin (usu. called 小提琴).

四星 *syh-shing*, n., the end part, lower part (orig., end of steelyard, marked by four asterisks).

四書 *syh-shu*, n., *The Four Books*: (1) 大學 *The Great Learning,* (2) 中庸 *The Doctrine of the Mean,* (3) 論語 *Confucian Analects,* and (4) 孟子 *The Works of Mencius*—formerly, required reading in all elementary grades.

四時 *syh-shyr*, n., see *-jih*↑.

A

四序 *syh-shyuh*, n., (LL) the four seasons (序=時序).
四體 *syh-tii*, n., see *-jy*² ↑.
四則 *syh-tzer*, n., (arithmetic) addition, subtraction, multiplication and division.
四坐 *syh-tzuoh*, n., the audience around, the company at a dinner.
四圍 *syh-weir*¹, adv., all around.
四維 *syh weir*², phr., the four basic virtues of 禮, 義, 廉, 恥 (管子) manners, justice, integrity and honor, regarded as the "hawsers" (or anchors) of the ship of state.
四五子 *syh-wuu-tz*, n., wine (a pun, from 4+5=9, "nine" 九 *jiou*, being homonym for "wine."
四眼人 *syh-yaan-rern*, n., (vulgar) a pregnant woman (counting two eyes for the embryo).
四言詩 *syh-yarn-shy*, n., a poem with lines of four characters each esp. in 詩經 *Book of Poetry*.
四野 *syh-yee*, n., the open countryside.
四裔 *syh-yih*, n., (AC) distant regions.
四夷 *syh yir*, n., the barbarians on borders of China.
四元 *syh-yuarn*, n., (anc. Chin. polynomial algebra) 天地人物 standing for A, B, C, D.
四月 *syhyueh*, n., (1) the fourth lunar month; (2) April.
四運 *syh-yuhn*, n., see *-shyr*, *-shyuh* ↑.

囮 41.41-9

er.

N. (sp. pr. *your*): 鳥兒囮子 bird decoy.

V.t. U.f. 訛 60A.70, to cheat.

囫 41.41-9

hur.

B

囫圇 *hurlurn*, adj., entire, whole: 囫圇吞棗 to swallow a date without chewing—to read hastily and without thinking.

囡 41.41-9

nan.

N. (Soochow dial.) a girl, daughter.

图 41.41-9

tur.

[Abbr. of 圖 41.41]

圝 41.41-9

luarn.

[Pop. 圞]

N. & adj. See 團^圞 41.41.

§ 41.42 (図/冈)

昺 41.42

biing.

[Anc. var. for 炳]

胃 41.42

weih.

N. The stomach: 胃病 stomach illness; 胃疼, 胃痛 pains in the stomach, stomach-ache; 胃酸 stomach acid; 胃汁 stomach juice, gastric juice; 胃癰, 胃潰瘍 stomach ulcer; 胃癌 stomach cancer; 胃炎 stomach inflammation, gastritis; 胃穿孔 stomach perforation; 胃下垂 gastroptosis; 胃擴張 dilated stomach.

C

胃腸 *weih-charng*, n., stomach and intestines; 胃腸炎 enterogastritis.
胃火 *weih-huoo*, n., (Chin. med.) overactivity of the stomach.
胃口 *weihkoou*, n., appetite: 胃口不好 bad appetite.
胃腺 *weihshiahn*, n., gastric gland.
胃痛 *weihtuhng*, n., stomach-ache.

禺 41.42

yur.

N. (AC, rare) a district.

§ 41.50 (図/ㄱ)

毋 41.50

wur.

[Related 無]

N. A surname.

Adv. (1) (LL) do not (imperative): 毋自欺 do not deceive yourself; 毋誇 do not boast; 毋違此示 do not disobey this order; 毋誤前途 do not hurt your career; 毋貽後悔 do not do s.t. that you'll regret. (2) (LL) not, no, nothing (Interch. 無 92.63): 毋友不如己 have no friend who is worse than yourself; 毋乃 is it not: 毋乃太簡乎 is it not too simple? 毋寧 would it not be better to, would rather: 毋須 *-shyu*¹ ↓; 毋庸 *-yurng* ↓.

毋須 *wur-shyu*¹, vb. aux., need not (+vb.).
毋需 *wur-shyu*², v.t., do not need

(to) or need＋noun.

毋庸 *wur-yurng*, vb. aux., need not: 應毋庸議 this need not be considered; 毋庸詳述 need not go into the details.

母 41.50

muu.

N. (1) Mother, usu. 母親: 親生母, 親母 real mother; 母道 maternity (dignity of mother), motherhood; 母子之情 mother and child love; 家母 my mother; 繼母 stepmother; 義母, 契母 adopted mother; 慈母 (slightly litr.) mother. (2) Part of term for aunts and elderly female relatives: 伯母, 叔母 (嬸母) wife of father's elder, younger brother; 姑母 father's sister; 姨母 maternal aunt; 舅母, 妗母 wife of mother's brother; 祖母 grandmother. (3) Part of term for elderly woman: 乳母 wet nurse. (4) Alphabet, sound element: 字母 letter of alphabet; 聲母 consonant; 韻母 vowel, syllabary. (5) A surname.

Adj. Female of species: 這是母的 this is a female; 母雞, 母鴨, 母牛 hen, duck, cow, cf. 牝 10C.70, 牡 10C. 11.

母愛 *muu-aih*, n., maternal love.
母錢 *muuchiarn*, n., capital, investment capital, opp. 利錢, 子息 interest.
母親 *muuchin*, n., gen. term for mother; 母親節 *--jier*, Mother's Day.
母權 *muu-chyuarn*, n., maternal authority; matriarchy.
母範 *muu-fahn*, n., model mother.
母國 *muu-guor*, n., mother country.
母后 *muu-houh*, n., queen-mother.
母猴 *muuhour*, n., see 獼猴 91C.42.
母艦 *muu-jiahn*, n., aircraft carrier (also) 航空母艦.
母教 *muujiauh*, n., mother's upbringing of child.
母舅 *muujiouh*, n., mother's brother.
母校 *muushiauh*, n., mother school, *alma mater*.
母系 (社會) *muu-shih* (*shehhueih*), n., matriarchal society.
母性 *muu-shihng*, n., maternal instinct.
母數 *muushuh*, n., (math.) denominator of a fraction.
母胎 *muutai*, n., mother's womb.
母音 *muuyin*, n., vowel (more commonly 元音).
母儀 *muuyir*, n., model mother.

男 41.50

narn.

N. & adj. (1) (Belonging to) the male sex: 男子漢, 大丈夫 a he-man or a man of honor; 男兒, 男丁 an able-bodied man; 男人 *-rern* ↓; 男性 a male, the male sex; 男方 the bridegroom; 男家 the bridegroom's family; 男系 paternal descent; 男媒 a go-between representing the bridegroom; 男孩(子)(兒) a boy; 男僕 a manservant; 男花兒 (MC) a boy (possibly a contraction of *hair'l* 孩兒); 男生 a boy student; 男朋友 a boy friend; 男裝 man's dress; 男耕女織 division of labor between men and women in a family with the former working in the fields and the latter sitting at the loom; 男扮女裝 a man dressed like a woman; 男大當婚 a man should get married on coming of age; 男盜女娼 (a curse phrase) a thief if a man, and a whore if woman (shop announcement against imitator or infringer of trademark). (2) A baronet, a baron. (3) A male child: 長男 the eldest son; 生有一男二女 have a son and two daughters. (4) A surname.

Pron. (Oft. in letters, a son in relation to his parents) I, your son.

男低音 *narn dijin*, n., bass.
男兒 *narn-erl*, n., (1) a son; (2) a member of the male sex: 男兒當自強 a man should be self-reliant.
男風 *narn-feng*, n., homosexual relation between males.
男高音 *narn gauyin*, n., tenor.
男中音 *narn jungyin*, n., baritone.
男女 *marn-nyuu*, n., (1) son and daughter; (2) men and women: 男女平等 equality between men and women, equal rights for both sexes.
男人 *narnrern*, n., (1) a member of the male sex; (1) husband (opp. 女人).
男色 *narn-seh*, n., (＝男風↑).
男性 *narn-shihng*, n. & adj., male, masculine gender or sex.

勗 41.50

shyuh.

[Err. var. of 勖 41S.50]

易 41.50

yih.

N. (1) A surname. (2) 易經 the *Book of Changes* ("Yi King"). (3) Ease: 居易 (AC) live in peace and contentment.

V.i. & t. (1) To change (policy, tools, habits, etc.); also (policy, etc.) changes: 更易, 變易 ditto; 數易寒暑 go through many changes of seasons, i.e., years; 易地則皆然 one would do the same thing if put in the other's place; 易手 change hands; 易俗 change

易 曷 昜 黑

custom. (2) To exchange: 貿易 trade; 互易 exchange (goods) with each other, esp. in trade; 易貨制度 barter system. (3) (LL) to regard as easy or unimportant: 易之. (4) (AC) cultivate: 易其田疇 cultivate one's fields; 易墓 (AC) to weed grass on grave.

Adj. & adv. Easy, -sily: 容易 dit-to; 易知, 易學 easy to understand, to learn; 易於 easy to (get mouldy, etc.); 淺易 elementary; 簡易 simple; 平易近人 (person) democratic and easy to approach.

易轍 *yih-cheh*, phr., to change one's course or plans (lit., "tracks").
易名 *yih-mirng*, phr., (1) to change names; (2) (AC) to give posthumous name.
易姓 *yih-shihng*, phr., to change name of royal house, i.e., change dynasty.
易簀 *yih-tzer*, ph., (AC) change mat for dying person.
易位 *yih-weih*, phr., (1) see *-shihng*↑; (2) change places.
易易 *yihyih*, adj., very easy.
易與 *yih-yuu*, adj., (person) easy to get along with.

曷 41.50

her.

Adv. (1) (AC & LL) why: 曷故 (=何故) for what reason; 曷極 (=何極) to what extremity; 曷若 (=何若) it would be better to. (2) 曷勝 (*-shehng*) (LL) very, extremely: 曷勝詫異 was extremely surprised.

昜 41.50

mahn.

[Pop. of 曼 41.82]

§ 41.63 (図/、)

黑 41.63

hei (re. pr. *heh*; **heei*).

N. A surname.

V.t. To hide: 他把錢都黑起來了 he has hidden away all the money; to blacken: 黑了良心 have blackened conscience.

Adj. (1) Black: 黑白花兒 black-and-white pattern; 黑白 right and wrong: 黑白不分 do not distinguish between right and wrong; 黑裏俏 black beauty; 黑不溜偢, 黑糝糝 (*-tsantsan*), 黑蒼蒼 *-tsang-tsang*) very black in appearance; 黑眉烏嘴 dark in complexion; 黑乾枯瘦 dark and emaciated. (2) Dark: 天黑了 it is getting dark; 黑夜 dark night; 黑更半夜 midnight; 黑燈下火怎麽走 how can one go in this dark night? 黑家白日 every day, all the days (gambling, drinking, etc.); 黑騰騰 (*-terngterng*), 黑沉沉 (*-chernchern*), 黑洞洞 (*-duhngduhng*) 黑漆漆 (*-chichi*) 黑碌碌 (*-luhluh*) descriptive of darkness; 黑咕隴咚 (*-gulungdung*), 黑忽忽 (*-huhu*), 黑壓壓 (*-yaya*) so dark it is difficult to make out anything; 黑股影, 黑影兒 a dark shadow; 摸黑兒 grope in the dark; 黑甜鄉 "dark, sweet land" of sleep. (3) Secret, underground: 黑話, 黑店, 黑幕, 黑市 *-huah*, *-diahn*, *-muh*, *-shyh*↓; 心黑手辣 blackened conscience and unscrupulous methods.

黑暗 *hei-ahn*, adj. & n., dark (-ness): 黑暗時代 the Dark Ages.
黑板 *heibaan*, n., blackboard.
黑白 *heibair*, n., black and white, right and wrong.
黑鉛 *heichian*, n., fibrous lead (in lead pencil).
黑錢 *heichiarn*, n., (sl.) night burglar; also underhand payment, bribery.
黑道日 (子) *heidauh-ryh('tz)*, n., unlucky day.
黑店 *hei-diahn*, n., an inn which is a trap for unwary travelers.
黑豆 **heeidouh*, n., the black bean.
黑稿 *hei-gaau*, n., a pencil sketch, a sketch for making cuts.
黑鍋 *hei-guo*, n., (lit.) a blackened pot; 背黑鍋 to take the blame for others.
黑海 *Heihaai*, n., the Black Sea.
黑話 *heihuah*, n., professional slang; thieves' argot.
黑貨 *hei-huoh*, n., (1) opium; (2) contraband goods.
黑醬 *hei-jiahng*, n., black soya sauce.
黑籍 *hei-jir*, n., (1) narcotic addicts; (2) a black list.
黑種 *hei-juung*, n., the black race.
黑龍江 *Heilurng-jiang*, n., Heilung-kiang, a province in Manchuria (usu. spelled "Heilung-kiang"); also name of river in that province.
黑麥 *heimaih*, n., buckwheat.
黑煤 *heimeir*[1], n., soft coal, bituminous coal, opp. 白煤 anthracite.
黑黴 *heimeir*[2], n., lichens.
黑門坎兒 *heimernkaa'l*, n., formerly, sheriff's deputy.
黑名單 *hei-mirngdan*, n., a blacklist.
黑眸 *hei-mour*, n., the eye pupil.
黑幕 *hei-muh*, n., secret and usu. unprintable goings-on behind the scenes; scandalous story.
黑奴 *hei-nur*, n., the Negro slave.
黑熱病 *heirehbihng*, n., (med.) kala-azar, dumdum fever.
黑人 *heirern*, n., (1) the Negro; (2) (coll.) one who lives in hiding: 作了三年黑人 lived in hiding for three years.
黑上 *hei'shang*, v.t., (Peking coll.) to love and want: 黑上這所房子 want very much this house.
黑下 *hei-shiah*, adv., at night.
黑猩猩 *heishing'shing*, n., (zoo.) the orangutan.
黑市 *hei-shyh*, n., the black market.
黑松 *heisung*, n., (bot.) the pine, *Pinus thunbergii*.
黑死病 *heisyy-bihng*, n., the Black Death.
黑炭 *hei-tahn*, n., black coal or soft coal.

黑 頭 *heitour*, n., (theater slang), "black head" (＝淨角), the role of a man (from the mask of 大花面).

黑 菜 *hei-tsaih*, n., (1) black seaweed; (2) various pickled vegetables.

黑 土 *hei-tuu*, n., opium; black soil.

黑 早 (兒) *hei-tzaau('l)*, adv., early at dawn, pre-dawn.

黑 子 *heitzyy*, n., (1) a birthmark, a mole; (2) a black piece in chess (*tzyy* or *tzee'l*).

黑 業 *hei-yieh*, n., (Budd.) black deeds.

黑 油 *heiyour*, n., coal tar.

黑 魚 *hei-yur*, n., (zoo.) *Onychodactylus japonicus*.

煦 41.63

shyuu.

V.i. & t. To radiate warmth: 煦沫 (fish, crabs) ooze moisture from mouth; 煦育萬物 make all things grow by action of heat; cf. 煦伏 *-fur* ↓.

Adj. Warm, warm and gentle: 煦日 comfortably warm sun.

煦 伏 *shyuufur*, v.i., (hens) sit on eggs.

煦 仁 *shyuu-rern*, n., petty kindness: 煦仁孑義.

煦 煦 *shyurshyuu*, adj., see *-rern* ↑.

煦 嫗 *shyuuyuh*, v.t., to comfort (baby) with gentleness and warmth.

照 41.63

jauh.

N. (1) Photograph (short for 照相 *-shiahng*): 玉照 your portrait; 拍照 take a photograph; 寫照 a portrait or accurate portrayal in writing. (2) A certificate, permit: 護照 passport; 執照 license (for driver, trade); 無照行車 drive without license. (3) Illumination, glow: 夕照 glow of sunset; 廻光反照 temporary clearing up of mind before death, compared to sunset glow.

V.i. & t. (1) To shine, cast or reflect light: 照射 *-sheh* ↓; 照亮 to illuminate by light; 探照燈 searchlight; 映照 to brighten atmosphere with luminaries; 照影子 cast a shade or reflection. (2) To look after: 照顧, 照料, 照管, 照拂 *-guh, -liauh, -guaan, -fur* ↓; 關▲照 52B.00. (3) Look at reflection: 照鏡子 see oneself in mirror; 照鏡自憐 admire oneself in the mirror. (4) Used in communications: 台照 for your perusal; 知照 to inform, be informed; 查照 for your information (at end of official communication), and 知照 used esp. to inferior; 照得 *-der* ↓.

Prep. According to: 照你說 according to what you say; 照理講 theoretically speaking; 照事實講 according to the facts; 照本分, 照禮 according to duty, ceremony; 照規矩 according to custom; 照價收購 buy up (land) in accordance with published rates; 照方兒抓, 照章辦理 proceed according to regulations; 按照, 依照 according to (regulations, agreement, etc.); 遵照 to do as one is told; 照辦, 照例, 照樣 *-bahn, -lih, -yahng* ↓.

照 辦 *jauhbahn*, v.i., do accordingly.

照 壁 *jauhbih*, n., a short wall facing gate of mansion.

照 常 *jauhcharng*, adv., as usual: 照常辦公 office open as usual; 照常進行 proceed as usual.

照 牆 *jauhchiarng*, n., see *-bih* ↑.

照 得 *jauhder*, phr., opening formula in official communication to subordinate: in regard to your letter saying that . . .

照 拂 *jauhfur*, v.t., see *-liauh* ↓.

照 管 *jauh'guaan*, v.t., look after (house, property, children, etc.).

照 顧 *jauhguh*, v.t., (1) look after another's welfare; attend to (patient, child, etc.); (2) (*-'gu*), attend to customers.

照 會 *jauhhueih*, n., official communication, an aide-memoire, a diplomatic note; more modn. see 通▲牒 31.83.

照 舊 *jauhjiouh*, adj., unchanged, as usual: 照舊有效 be valid as usual.

照 准 *jauhjuun*, v.t., (official communication to subordinate) request granted.

照 看 *jauhkahn*, v.t., see *-guh* ↑.

照 料 *jauhliauh*, v.i. & t., to look after another's welfare, comforts.

照 例 *jauhlih*, adv., according to the rules: 照例免費 fees exempted according to regulations.

照 面 (兒) *jauhmiahn(-miah'l)*, v.i., (meet) face to face; (see person) personally.

照 明 *jauhmirng*, v.i. & t., to illuminate; n., lighting (stage); 照明彈 (mil.) a flare.

照 片 *jauhpiahn*, n., a photograph.

照 射 *jauhsheh*, v.t., to project light upon; to illumine.

照 相 *jauhshiahng*, v.i. & n., to photograph, a photograph; 照相機 camera.

照 樣 (兒) *jauhyahng('l)*, adv., (1) accordingly; in the same manner (as previous one): 照樣剪裁 cut according to pattern; (2) in a routine manner, as others do.

照 妖 鏡 *jauhyau-jihng*, n., (myth.) a mirror which reveals disguise of monster or demon.

照 耀 *jauhyauh*, v.t., to illuminate, shine in glory.

照 應 *jauh'yihng*, v.i. & t., (1) to look after, see *-liauh* ↑; (2) to fit with (prophecy, original).

旯
見

§ 41.70 (図/乚)

旯 41.70

lar.

N. See 旮▵旯 91.41.

見 41.70

jiahn (**shiahn*).

N. Notion, idea, opinion, view, judgement: 見解 *-jiee*, 見識 *-shy* ↓; 意見 views, opinions; 高見, 卓見 (court.) your (esteemed) views; 成見 a preconceived notion, prejudice; 淺見 shallow view; 見地 *-dih* ↓; 遠見 farseeing, farsighted; 婦人之見 worthless (shortsighted) views not to be taken seriously (cf. "she's only a woman"); 偏見 one-sided views, prejudice; 定見 fixed idea; 少見多怪 (contempt.) shocked through lack of experience; having seen little, get excited easily; 顯而易見 crystal-clear, self-evident; 管見 shortsighted view, also (self-deprecation) my views.

V.i. & t. (1) V.t., see, look at, behold: 見到 catch, (get) sight (a glimpse) of, actually see; 親眼看見 see with one's own eyes; 見世面 get to know the world; 見聞 *-wern* ↓; 見個高低 (of two opponents) fight it out; 見高低 (gambling) win or lose; 能見度 visibility; (活)見鬼 nonsense! you're (he's) day-dreaming! 一見鍾情 love at first sight; 見票即付 (of checks) payable at sight; 先見之明 foresight; 相見恨晚 wish that we had met earlier! 我見猶憐 phr. for expressing love of one indeed beautiful; 瑕瑜互見 there are both good and bad qualities (strong points and weaknesses); 名不見經傳 (of person) obscure, little known; 見分曉 to clear up (matter, doubts), arrive at final results; 見縫兒就鑽 behave like a social climber (a go-getter); 見天日 (of rooms) sunny and airy; (fig.) injustice redressed; 見兔顧犬 (AC allu.) take instant advantage of an opportunity that comes only once in a long while; 百聞不如一見 hearing is no substitute for seeing ("seeing is believing"); 見利忘義 forget honor at sight of money; 見獵心喜 reminds one of former sport of hunting, interest reawakened; 見怪不怪 become inured to the unusual (weird, uncanny); 見景生情 recall old memories at familiar sights; 瞎子見錢眼開 even the blind man will open his eyes if you give him money; 見仁見智 each according to his lights; 見財起意 be moved to commit crimes by sight of money; 見異思遷 changeful, fickle, capricious; 見賢思齊 emulate those better than oneself; 見風使船 (fig.) sail with the wind; 見義勇爲 never hesitate to do what is right; 見危授命 (of statesman) be ready to die for one's country in times of national crisis; 見機而作 take the cue and act accordingly; 見得 *-der* ↓; 見得到 may be seen (is visible), be wise (intelligent) enough to see a subtle point. (2) V.t., call on, visit with: 見面 *-miahn* ↓; 覲見, 朝見 have an audience with (a monarch); 拜見 pay a courtesy call on; 進見 have an interview with; 請見 ask for an interview; 想見 wish to meet; 見不著 fail to see s.o. one wishes to interview; 相見 meet one another; 見不得人 unpresentable; 見不起人 dare not show one's face; 見人 *-rern* ↓; 見閻王 (sl.) to kick the bucket. (3) V.t., receive (callers): 見客 *-keh* ↓; 接見 extend welcome to (visitor). (4) (Passive) be+p.p. 見怪 *-guaih*, 見惠 *-hueih*, 見教 *-jiauh*, 見笑 *-shiauh*, 見責 *-tzer*, 見罪 *-tzueih*, 見外 *-waih*, 見輕 *-ching* ↓; 見諒 be forgiven; 見棄 be forsaken, abandoned, deserted; 見復 receive a reply; 見賜 be presented with; 見疑 be subject to suspicion, be doubted; 見用 be taken into service, be assigned work to do; 見稱 be spoken well of, praised. (5) V.i., appear, look, become: 見好 *-haau*, 見背 *-beih* ↓; 見瘦, 見老 get thinner, older (be aging); 見氣 get angry. (6) V.i., (**shiahn*) (=現) appear, manifest.

Adj. Every: 見天 *-tian* ↓.

Adv. complement. Sense of completed sensation: 看見, 聽見 have seen, have heard; 聞見 have heard or smelled; 夢見 have dreamed; 遇見, 碰見 happened to meet.

見報 *jiahn-bauh*, v.i., appear (be published) in newspaper.

見背 *jiahnbeih*, v.i., be orphaned: 生孩六月, 慈父見背 my father passed away when I was only six months old.

見輕 *miahnching*, v.i., (1) (of illness) get better; (2) (of person) be slighted, looked down upon, treated with contempt.

見道 *jiahn-dauh*, v.i., come to know the truth, used in a philosophical or religious sense.

見得 *jiahnder*, v.i., to know, perceive: 怎見得, 何由見得 how do you know? 不見得 I don't see it, not necessarily so.

見地 *jiahndih*, n., perception, viewpoint: 甚有見地 the point is well taken; 見地甚高 farsighted, clear-sighted.

見方 *jiahnfang*, adj., square: 一尺見方 one foot square.

見怪 *jiahnguaih*, v.i., be blamed, taken to task; v.t., take offense at: 別見怪我 do not blame me.

見光 *jiahnguang*, v.i., polish; adj., translucent.

見好 *jiahnhaau*, (1) v.i., (of illness) get better; (2) v.t., go out of one's way to please (person).

見惠 *jiahnhueih*, v.i., be presented with (a gift).

見證 *jiahnjehng*, n., (1) evidence, clear proof; (2) a witness.

見幾 *jiahnji*[1], v.i., foresee s.t. before it happens, have foresight.

見機 *jiahnji*[2], v.i., as in 見機而作 decide on the spot.

見教 *jiahnjiauh*, v.i., give, be given, advice.

見解 *jiahnjiee*, n., understanding,

judgement, personal opinions, views.

見客 *jiahnkeh*, v.i., receive callers.

見禮 *jiahnlii*, n., (1) salute of welcome; (2) gift given at first meeting, see *-miahnlii* ↓.

見面 *jiahnmiahn*, v.t., (1) meet face to face, see, talk with; (2) (of estranged persons) meet for the first time to be reconciled; 見面禮 *--lii*, n., a present given to s.o. whom one sees for the first time.

見人 *jiahnrern*, v.i., appear in public: 你做下這樣事，將來怎麽見人呢 if you do such a thing, how can you ever show your face again?

見小 *jiahnshiaau*, v.i., (1) be more discerning than others; (2) be narrow-minded, petty, mean.

見效 *jiahn-shiauh*[1], v.i., (medicine, advice) show results.

見笑 *jiahnshiauh*[2], v.i., be laughed at, ridiculed: 見笑大方 be a laughingstock, expose oneself to ridicule.

見習 *jiahnshir*, v.i., get practical experience by actual work, serve as an apprentice; n. & v.i., learn (-ing) from demonstration.

見説 *jiahnshuo*, phr., it's said that.

見識 *jiahnshy*, n., insight, judgement.

見天 *jiahntian*, adj., everyday: 見天日 see the light of day.

見責 *jiahntzer*, v.i., be blamed, punished, taken to task.

見罪 *jiahntzueih*, v.i., be blamed.

見字 *jiahntzyh*, phr., used in letters from elders to children or subordinates as part of the salutation, roughly equiv. "This note is for . . ." preceded by the name of the recipient.

見外 *jiahnwaih*, v.i., be considered as an outsider: 不要見外 phr. used to urge one to accept gift.

見聞 *jiahnwern*, n., what one sees and hears, general knowledge: 見聞不廣 have only limited knowledge.

昆 41.70

kun.

N. (1) Elder brother: 昆仲, 昆季 *-juhng*, *-jih* ↓. (2) Progeny, 昆裔 *-yih* ↓. (3) Insect: 昆蟲 *-churng* ↓.

昆布 *kunbuh*, n., (bot.) *Laminaria japonica*, an edible giant seaweed (also called 海帶).

昆蟲 *kunchurng*, n., insects in gen.

昆季 *kunjih*, n., brothers.

昆仲 *kunjuhng*, n., ditto.

昆明 *Kunmirng*, n., name of city and lake in Yunnan.

昆裔 *kunyih*, n., progeny.

晃 41.70

huaang.

V.i. (1) To flash: 拿銀子向他一晃 flash a piece of silver in his face; 有個人一晃過去 a man flashed past the door. (2) To dazzle: 晃得人眼都睜不開 (lightning) blinds one's eyes. (3) To float about: 晃來晃去, 晃了(裏)晃蕩 (flag) flap about, swing, rock; 搖晃, 晃搖 to swing and sway.

Adj. & adv. Shining, dazzling: 晃朗, 晃耀 dazzling bright; 明晃晃, 亮晃晃, 白晃晃 dazzlingly clear, bright, white.

晁 41.70

chaur.

N. A surname.

冕 41.70

miaan.

[Top part strictly 日, a hat, and not 日; ignored in common writing]

N. Official cap; ruler's cap: 加冕, 冠冕 coronation; 冕服 official costume.

冕旒 *miaanliour*, n., king's crown (with tassels in front ＝旒).

鼂 41.70

chaur.

[Anc. var. of 晁 ↑]

罌 41.70

ying.

[Var. 罌 41.21]

毘 41.70

pir.

[Var. of 毗 40S.70]

§ 41.71 (図/弋)

晟 41.71

shehng.

[Cogn. 盛 71.30]

見 昆 晃 晁 冕 鼂 罌 毘 晟

亅	小	⺊	十	土	ナ	廾	㇄	丨	一	丅	フ	口	図	冈	㇕	厂	尸	亠	广	宀	丶	乚	弋	心	八	人	乂	乛	一	丿	𠂉	く
00	01	02	10	11	12	20	21	22	30	31	32	40	41	42	50	51	52	60	61	62	63	70	71	72	80	81	82	83	90	91	92	93

§ 41.72 (囗/心)

思 41.72

sy (**syh*, **sai*).

Fin. part. (Unaccented) a vague sentence ending: (AC) 不可求思, 不可泳思 cannot be solicited, cannot be swum across; 神之格思 when spirit descends; (related AC fin. part. 斯 22S.22, 者 11.41 and 些 22.30).

N. (1) Thought(s): 鄉思 thoughts of home; 愁思 sad thoughts or remembrance; 文思 the flow of thoughts in writing. (2) (**syh*) In 意思 meaning, interest: 很有意思 is very interesting.

V.i. & t. (1) (LL) to think, ponder, deliberate (vern. 想): 思想 *-shiaang*; 思考, 思惟 to consider, *-kaau*, *-weir* ↓; 思前想後 to think of the past and future; 再思, 三 (pr. *sahn*) 思 think twice, thrice; 深思 think deeply; 不思之甚 how thoughtless; 思過半矣 can largely comprehend the rest. (2) (LL) to remember, think of, admire: 思念, 思慕 *-niahn*, *-muh* ↓; 追思 think back; 相思 long for (lover); 思凡 *-farn* ↓; 思鄉 think of home; 思故, 思舊 think of old times or the past. (3) (LL) to try to, want to: 思歸, 思退 want to go home, to resign; 思往他鄉 is thinking of going abroad; 見異思遷 be fickle, look for a change for s.t. better; 思有以救之 is thinking how to save a situation; 見賢思齊 when one sees another better than oneself, try to equal him.

Adj. (**sai*) 于思 having a thick beard.

思辨 *sybiahn*, v.i., to analyze mentally, make intellectual enquiries.

思潮 *sychaur*, n., popular trend of ideas, current of thought.

思凡 *sy-farn*, phr., (of immortals in heaven, nuns) have worldly thoughts (凡間 the secular world).

思過 *sy-guoh*, v.i., feel remorse.

思舊 *sy-jiouh*, v.i., think of old friends, times.

思致 *syjyh*, n., interesting thoughts.

思考 *sykaau*, v.i., to ponder, consider, deliberate.

思戀 *syliahn*, v.i. & t., to long for lover.

思量 *syliarng*, v.i., to deliberate, to consider in the mind.

思路 *syluh* (-'*lu*), n., line of thought (clear, twisted).

思慮 *sylyuh*, v.i. & n., think, -ing.

思慕 *symuh*, v.t., to admire or love (person).

思念 *syniahn*, v.t., to remember fondly.

思想 *syshiaang* (-'*shiang*), v.i. & n., think, a man's thinking, ideas (clear, unclear, new, crazy); a nation's philosophy; 思想史 history of thought (in period, country); 思想家 a thinker.

思省 *syshiing*, v.i., see *-liarng* ↑.

思緒 *syshyuh*, n., thoughts and feelings; mood or line of thinking.

思索 *sysuoo*, v.i., try to understand by thinking: 不待思索 phr., without stopping to think—self-evident.

思存 *sytsurn*, v.i. & t., (AC, LL) to remember (friend).

思忖 *sytsuun*, v.i., to wonder, imagine (unknown situation).

思(維)惟 *syweir*, v.i., to philosophize, think deeply; to deliberate; n., thinking as a process.

思議 *syyih*, v.i., to comprehend: 不可思議 incomprehensible, mysterious, incredible.

恩 41.72

en.

N. (1) A bounty, blessing, a favor or kindness from above: 施恩 grant a favor, a blessing; 承恩, 受恩 receive a favor; 求恩, 謝恩 to beg, thank for, favor; 開恩 grant special favor, esp. grant pardon; a past favor: 報恩 do s.t. in return for some past favor; 忘恩負義 being ungrateful; 將仇報恩, 恩將仇報 return kindness with hatred. (2) Love as between husband and wife; or between parent and child: 恩愛夫妻.

Adj. (1) Pertaining to imperial favor, by imperial favor: 恩詔, 恩科 *-jauh*, *-ke* ↓; 恩准, 恩赦 approved, pardoned by His Majesty. (2) Kind; pertaining to a gift, a favor: 恩惠, 恩禮, 恩典 *-hueih*, *-lii*, *-diaan* ↓.

恩愛 *en-aih*, n., love, esp. between husband and wife.

恩勤 *enchirn*, n., (AC) (the debt of gratitude one owes to) parents' love and care.

恩情 *enchirng*, n., love, sentiment of friendship; some past kindness.

恩仇 *en-chour*, n., debt of gratitude and of revenge.

恩寵 *en-chuung*, n., special kindness of a ruler.

恩德 *en-der*, n., kindness shown to another, the debt of gratitude owed to s.o.

恩典 *endiaan*, n., (1) royal favor, special gift, award or grant; (2) a friend's kindness.

恩公 *en-gung*, n., benefactor.

恩惠 *en(')hueih*, n., special gift or kindness.

恩詔 *en-jauh*, n., imperial decree of award or pardon.

恩眷 *en-jyuahn*, n., see *-chuung* ↑.

恩科 *en-ke*, n., civil examinations specially decreed; degrees given at such examinations.

恩禮 *enlii*, n., gifts and kindness.

恩念 *enniahn*, n., s.o.'s kindness, kind thoughtfulness.

恩人 *enrern*, n., benefactor.

恩潤 *enruhn*, n., bounty, benefice from above.

恩榮 *enrurng*, n., royal honor.

恩賞 *enshaang*, n., gift by ruler.

恩赦 *ensheh*, v.t., pardon by ruler; amnesty.

恩幸 *enshihng*[1], n., royal favor.

恩倖 *enshihng*[2], n., a court favorite.

恩澤 *entzer*, n., bounty, benefit received from above.

恩意 *enyih*[1], n., kind consideration by ruler.

恩義 *enyih*[2], n., gratitude owed on account of past relations, as between husband and wife, father and son.

恩怨 *en-yuahn*, n., past kindness and old grudge.

恩遇 *enyuh*, n., special recognition by ruler.

慁 41.72

huhn.

V.t. (AC) to upset, disturb.

愚 41.72

yur.

Pron. (Court. oft. in letters) I, yours humbly: 愚以爲不然 I do not agree; see 愚兄, 愚弟 *-shyung, -dih*↓.

V.t. To deceive: 愚民 *-mirn*↓; 被人所愚 was deceived by others; 愚弄 *-luhng*↓.

Adj. Foolish, stupid, ignorant: 愚夫愚婦 the uneducated public; 愚鈍, 愚笨 *-duhn, -behn*↓.

愚騃 *yur-air*[1], adj., (LL) stupid, childish.

愚呆 *yur-air*[2], adj., blockheaded, dull, slow to learn.

愚獃 *yur-air*[3], adj., moronic, idiotic.

愚笨 *yurbehn*, adj., stupid, silly.

愚氣 *yurchih*, n., (1) futile anger: 何必賭生愚氣 why get mad which serves no purpose? (2) (-'*chi*) foolish, silly-looking.

愚蠢 *yurchuun*, adj., stupid, thick-witted, foolish (opinion).

愚弟 *yurdih*, n., (formal self reference) your stupid younger brother, used among friends regardless of age.

愚鈍 *yurduhn*, adj., slow-witted, dull, unrefined.

愚公 *yurgung*, n., a foolish old man.

愚者 *yurjee*, n., (1) ignorant or unthinking people; (2) (court.) I.

愚見 *yur-jiahn*, n., (court.) my humble opinion.

愚忠 *yurjung*, adj., stupid but honest.

愚拙 *yurjuor*, n., stupid; also used court. of oneself.

愚直 *yurjyr*, adj., blunt but honest.

愚陋 *yurlouh*, adj., (oft. court.) vulgar, unrefined.

愚弄 *yurluhng* (*-nuhng*), v.t., to fool, deceive (person).

愚魯 *yurluu*, adj., simple, uninformed.

愚昧 *yurmeih*, adj., ignorant, unenlightened.

愚蒙 *yurmerng*, adj., ditto.

愚民 *yur-mirn*, phr., 愚民政策 policy of keeping people ignorant; policy to misguide, deceive people.

愚懦 *yurnuoh*, adj., ignorant and timid.

愚人 *yurrern*, n., a fool.

愚下 *yurshiah*, pron., (court. self-reference) I, me.

愚孝 *yurshiauh*, adj., stupid but filial.

愚兄 *yurshyung*, n., (court. self-reference) your stupid elder brother, used by one of senior age among friends.

愚晚 *yurwaan*, n., (court. self-reference) your stupid pupil, used by one of younger generation.

愚頑 *yurwarn*, adj., imbecile, insensitive, slow-witted.

愚意 *yur-yih*, phr., my humble opinion.

恖 41.72

jyuh.

[Anc. var. of 懼 22A.11]

懸 41.72

shyuarn.

V.i. & t. (1) To hang, to suspend in midair, to hoist up, hang up: 懸在空中 suspend in midair; 懸牌 hang up a shop sign; 懸燈(結綵) hang up lantern; 懸旗 hoist up flag; 懸空 -'*kung*↓. (2) To occupy the mind, be on the mind: 懸念 *-niahn*↓; 懸腸掛肚 cause extreme worry and distress (腸肚 the viscera considered as the seat of emotions), see 腸 and 肚 42A.50, 42A.11).

Adj. (1) Overhanging, unsupported, dangerous: 懸崖 overhanging cliff; 懸崖勒馬 draw up short at overhanging cliff—withdraw sharply from imminent disaster; 懸谷 valley with steep sides. (2) (Pop.) steep: 懸得很 very steep. (3) Longstanding, unresolved: 懸案 *-ahn*↓; 懸缺 *-chyue*↓. (4) Different: 懸殊, 懸絕, 懸異 *-shu, -jyuer, -yih*↓.

Adv. Based purely on conjecture, imaginary: 懸想, 懸斷, 懸擬 *-shiaang, -duahn, -nii*↓.

懸案 *shyuarn-ahn*, n., a longstanding, unresolved case at court; unsettled question.

懸欠 *shyuarnchiahn*, v.i., to owe in account unpaid.

懸磬 *shyuarn-chihng*, n., a suspended music stone (see 磬 11.40); symbolic of bareness: 室如懸磬 house is quite bare—living in poverty.

懸揣 *shyuarnchuaai*, v.i., to surmise, conjecture.

懸鶉 *shyuarn-churn*, phr., 衣若懸鶉 (AC) bedraggled dress like a beggar's (like a "quail hung upside down").

懸泉 *shyuarn-chyuarn*, n., a falling cataract.

懸缺 *shyuarn-chyue*, n., unfilled vacancy.

懸膽 *shyuarndaan*, n., a long,

恩 慁 愚 恖 懸

亅	小	丬	十	土	𠂇	廾	卜	丨	一	丁	乛	口	囟	冈	冂	厂	尸	亠	广	宀	丶	乚	弋	心	八	人	乂	乛	一	丿	𠂉	乂
00	01	02	10	11	12	20	21	22	30	31	32	40	41	42	50	51	52	60	61	62	63	70	71	72	80	81	82	83	90	91	92	93

dropping nose ("like suspended gall").

懸斷 *shyuarnduahn*, v.i., to judge, surmise without sufficient basis.

懸法 *shyuarn-faa*, phr., (AC) statutes or regulations, pasted over gates, which served as public notices.

懸峯 *shyuarn-feng*, n., overhanging cliff, perpendicular peak.

懸隔 *shyuarnger*, v.i., to be separated at a distance.

懸掛 *shyuarnguah*, v.i., to remember always, be concerned (over s.t.).

懸果 *shyuarnguoo*, n., (bot.) a plant, *Cremocarp*, with split kernels.

懸河 *shyuarn-her*, phr., 口若懸河 a torrent of words—symbolic of eloquence.

懸衡 *shyuarn-herng*, phr., (AC) (1) to show (laws, etc.) as a public standard; (2) 不能與齊懸衡 would not be considered equal in power to 齊.

懸乎 *shyuarn'hu*, v.i., depend on.

懸弧 *shyuarn-hur*[1], phr., (AC) to give birth to a son ("hang a bow" on the door).

懸壺 *shyuarn-hur*[2], v.i., to practise medicine (hang a gourd or bottle as shop sign).

懸記 *shyarnjih*, v.t., to have constantly in mind.

懸旌 *shyuarn-jing*, phr., 心如懸旌 (LL) my heart flutters like a pennant in the wind.

懸肘 *shyuarn-joou*, adv., "with raised elbow" (not resting on table)—for writing characters over a foot big.

懸車 *shyuarn-jyu*, phr., put carriage in storage—resign from government.

懸絕 *shyuarnjyuer*, adj., completely different, wide apart.

懸軍 *shyuarn-jyun*, phr., (LL) isolated column of soldiers.

懸曠 *shyuarnkuahng*, adj., (Budd.) abstruse, difficult to follow.

懸空 *shyuarn'kung*, (1) adv., out of the blue, without basis: 懸空虛構 invent a story (by imagination); (2) v.i., to dangle: 兩腳懸空着 leave one's feet dangling without support.

懸梁 *shyuarnliarng*, v.i., "suspend from a beam"—hang oneself.

懸門 *shyuarnmern*, n., (AC) a portcullis, suspended gate which could be dropped.

懸念 *shyuarnniahn*, v.i. & t., to think of (person in absence).

懸擬 *shyuarnnii*, v.i. & t., to conjecture (a plan), to imagine, surmise.

懸瀑 *shyuarn-puh*, n., a cataract, waterfalls.

懸賞 *shyuarn-shaang*, v.i., to announce award (for wanted criminal, etc.).

懸想 *shyuarnshiaang*, v.i., to imagine.

懸象 *shyuarnshiahng*, n., (AC) astronomical phenomena.

懸心 *shyuarn-shin*, v.i., be worried, concerned.

懸首 *shyuarn-shoou*, v.i., to display chopped-off head (of criminal, rebel) usu. over city gate.

懸殊 *shyuarnshu*, adj., different (in situation, circumstances, etc.).

懸虛 *shyuarnshyu*, adj., abstruse, incredible (talk); unfounded.

懸榻 *shyuarn tah*, phr., (allu.) to extend great welcome ("letting down a bunk" reserved for special friend).

懸談 *shyuarntarn*, v.i., make a rambling, discursive talk.

懸望 *shyuarnwahng*, v.i., to wish, to long for, think of longingly, hope in the distance.

懸異 *shyuarnyih*, adj., see *-shu* ↑.

§ 41.80 (図/八)

具 41.80

jyuh.

N. A tool, an implement: 器具 tools, instruments; 家具 furniture; 文具 stationery, writing utensils; 餐具 dinner-service, -set; 茶具 tea-service, -set; 用具 tools and implements; 工具 equipment, tools; 刑具 instruments of punishment (torture); 農具 agricultural implements; 賭具 cards, dice, etc. used in gambling. (2) Talent, ability: 才具 ability, talents, parts; 將相之具 a person of good ministerial timber. (3) A unit of things: 屍首一具 one corpse.

V.t. Provide, furnish, supply: 具呈 submit a memorial to a superior; 具文 *-wern*, 具備 *-beih*, 具結 *-jier*, 具保 *-baau* ↓; 具報 make a written report; 開具 give an itemized list of; 謹具 "respectfully submitted by"; 檢具 enclose and submit; 具名 *-mirng* ↓.

Adj. Concrete: 具體 *-tii* ↓.

Adv. (Interch. 俱) all, completely, fully.

具保 *jyuh-baau*, v.i., sign a guarantee.

具備 *jyuhbeih*, adj., fully supplied (furnished, equipped) with.

具慶 *jyuhchihng*, phr., be fortunate enough to have both parents still living.

具結 *jyuhjier*, v.i., sign a written promise or agreement.

具名 *jyuh-mirng*, v.i., put one's own signature (on a document).

具體 *jyuhtii*, adj., (1) concrete (opp. 抽象 abstract); (2) complete: 具體而微 having everything in miniature.

具草 *jyuh-tsaau*, v.i., make a rough draft of a document.

具足 *jyuhtzur*, adj., (=具備 *-beih* ↑).

具文 *jyuh-wern*, (1) v.i., prepare a document for submission to a superior; (2) n., a dead letter.

具有 *jyuhyoou*, v.t., be provided (supplied, equipped) with.

異 41.80

yih.

V.i. & t. (1) To separate: 離異

separate, be alienated from. (2) To feel surprise: 驚異, 詫異 be greatly surprised or shocked; 異之 to regard (s.o. or s.t.) as strange or unusual. (3) To look with special favor: 寵異.

Adj. (1) Different: 異口同聲 unanimous (praise, etc.); 異途同歸 all roads lead to same goal; 異曲同工 different approaches contribute to same end; 異類 different class or species, see 異類 *-leih*, 性 *-shihng*[1]↓. (2) Strange, unusual, remarkable, extraordinary: 奇異 strange; 異人, 異相 *-rern*, *-shiahng*[1]↓; 異才 *-tsair*↓; 奇裝異服 singular dress; 異形 abnormal shape; 異狀 abnormal strange appearance; 異香 exotic fragrance; 異彩 strange burst of color; 異聞 *-wern*↓; 異書 a rare and little-known book. (3) Another: 異日, 異時 *-ryh*, *-shyr*↓. (4) Foreign (place) 異域, 異鄉 *-yuh*, *-shiang*↓. (5) Disloyal, changing mind: 異志, 異心 *-jyh*, *-shin*↓.

異邦 *yih-bang*, n., foreign land.

異稟 *yih-biing*, n., unusual talent.

異常 *yihcharng*, adj. & adv., unusual, -ly; abnormal, extraordinary.

異趣 *yih-chyuh*, n., difference of tastes and interests.

異代 *yih-daih*, n., a different or past age.

異道 *yih-dauh*, n., (1) different route or path; (2) different faith.

異等 *yih-deeng*, adj., unusual, remarkable (talent); special grade.

異地 *yih-dih*, n., foreign land.

異端 *yihduan*, n., heterodox teaching, heresy.

異國 *yih-guor*, n., foreign country.

異乎 *yih-hu*, phr., different from (the usual, etc.).

異兆 *yih-jauh*, n., strange omen.

異教 *yih-jiauh*, n., a religion not one's own, pagan religion; 異教人 pagan.

異己 *yih-jii*, n., a person not of one's own party.

異志 *yih-jyh*, n., a disloyal heart.

異類 *yih-leih*, n., (1) (contempt.) person not of one's own culture; foreign tribe; (2) different beasts or demons.

異母 *yih-muu*, adj., not of same mother: 異母弟 brother born of a different mother.

異能 *yih-nerng*, n., remarkable talent, ability.

異人 *yih-rern*, n., (1) (in Chin. novels, stories) a Taoist immortal, a saint in disguise, any rare person, sometimes with magical powers; (2) (AC) another person.

異日 *yih-ryh*, adv., (LL) on another day; some future day.

異想 *yih-shiaang*, n., phantasy, whimsy: 異想天開 (person) comes out with most fantastic ideas.

異相 *yih-shiahng*[1], n., (person's) remarkable physiognomy.

異象 *yih-shiahng*[2], n., strange heavenly phenomena.

異鄉 *yihshiang*, n., foreign land.

異性 *yih-shihng*[1], n., opposite sex.

異姓 *yihshihng*[2], n., different clan or clan name; also different tribe.

異心 *yih-shin*, n., disloyalty of heart.

異數 *yih-shuh*, n., unusual or extra favor or courtesy.

異說 *yih-shuo*, n., (1) different version or theory; (2) strange doctrines.

異事 *yih-shyh*, n., strange happening.

異時 *yih-shyr*, adv., see *-ryh*↑.

異俗 *yih-sur*, n., foreign, strange customs.

異才 *yih-tsair*, n., remarkable talent.

異爨 *yih-tsuahn*, phr., (of brothers, close relations) live separately ("separate kitchens").

異同 *yih-turng*, n., differences and similarities.

異族 *yih-tzur*, n., (1) foreign tribe (contempt); (2) different race.

異味 *yih-weih*, n., rare delicacy (food).

異聞 *yih-wern*, n., strange news, story.

異物 *yih-wuh*, n., a strange, unknown object or animal.

異樣 *yih-yahng*, adj. & adv., different, -ly.

異言 *yih-yarn*, n., dissent of opinion.

異議 *yih-yih*, n., dissent; objection; 執行異議 (law) objection to execution.

異域 *yih-yuh*, n., far-distant land.

貝 41.80

beih.

N. (1) Cowry, a small sea shell. (2) Money (cowry used as money in early stages of civilization); hence (3) as radical in characters referring to money or property (as 財 wealth, 寶 treasure, 賦 tax, 貨 goods, etc.): 寶貝 treasure. (4) Translation of Sanskr. *pattra*, see 貝葉, 貝文, 貝多 *-yeh*, *-wern*, *-duo*↓. (5) A surname.

貝多 *beihduo*, n., translation of Sanskr. *pattra*, palm leaves from *Borassus flabellifor*, used as paper in writing Buddhist sutras.

貝貨 *beih-huoh*, n., commercial goods.

貝錦 *beihjiin*, n., silks with wavy, shell-like patterns.

貝柱 *beihjuh*, n., edible ligaments which control closing and opening of clam shells, as in 江珧柱.

貝殼 *beihker*, n., shell of shell animals, like mother-of-pearl (蚌殼).

貝勒 *beihleh*, n., (Manchu) a Manchu prince.

貝母 *beihmuu*, n., (bot.) *Fritillaria verticillata*, a medicinal herb.

貝子 (1) *beihtzyy*, n., cowries, anciently used as currency; (2) *-'tz*, n., a Manchu rank, son of *-leh*↑.

貝文 *beihwern*, n., Buddhist script written on palm leaves,

see *-duo*↑.

貝葉 *beihyeh*, n., leaves of *-duo* ↑.

貫 41.80

guahn.

[Arch. 毌]

N. (1) A string for holding cash in place. (2) Place of one's ancestral home: 鄉貫 one's native district; 籍貫 one's native province. (3) Formerly, a string of 1,000 cash. (4) A surname.

V.t. (1) To thread, pass through: 貫穿 *-chuan*, 貫串 *-chuahn*, 貫通 *-tung*↓; 聯貫 be connected; 直貫到底 go straight to the bottom or the farthest end. (2) To hit (the bull's eye).

貫徹 *guahncheh*, v.t., carry (s.t.) through: 貫澈(徹)始終 stick to (a task) to the bitter end; 貫澈到底 do a thorough job of.

貫穿 *guohnchuan*, v.t., (1) pierce through; (2) know (s.t.) thoroughly.

貫串 *guahnchuahn*, v.t., to piece together, interconnect, interrelate.

貫耳 *guahneel*, v.i., as in 如雷貫耳 like a thunderclap piercing through the ear—sharp advice which wakens one.

貫跤 *guahnjiau*, v.i., to trip and fall, (see 摜 10A.80).

貫珠 *guahnju*, (1) n., a string of beads; (2) adj., (of sounds) pleasing to the ear.

貫注 *guahnjuh*, adj., attentive: 精神貫注 concentrate attention.

貫通 *guahntung*, v.t., to master (a subject): 融會貫通 know (a subject) from A to Z.

貫盈 *guahnyirng*, adj., full to the brim: 惡貫滿盈 guilty of the worst crimes.

贔 41.80

bih.

贔屓 *bihshih*, (1) n., giant land turtle, seen sometimes in carved stone base of tablets; (2) adj., straining (muscles).

§41.81 (図/人)

昃 41.81

tzeh.

N. & adj. (LL) post meridiem.

昊 41.81

hauh.

N. 昊天 (AC) term for heaven; (AC) (fig.) parents' great, good kindness.

§41.82 (図/乂)

旻 41.82

mirn.

N. Autumn: 旻天 (AC) the sky in autumn.

曼 41.82

mahn.

Adj. (1) Graceful, soft and beautiful: 曼麗 *-lih*↓; 曼辭 (AC) sophisticated words; 曼澤 (AC, of hair) smooth and shining. (2) Trailing (of voice, vine): 曼延 *-yarn*↓.

曼波 *mahbuo* n., mambo.

曼麗 *mahn-lih*, adj., beautiful.

曼妙 *mahnmiauh*, adj., soft and charming.

曼靡 *mahnmii*, adj., (of music) softly appealing.

曼陀羅 *mahntuorluor*, n., (bot.) a plant, *Datura alba*.

曼衍 *mahnyaan*, v.i., grow and spread; adj., continuous.

曼延 *mahnyarn*, v.i. & adj., ditto (also wr. 蔓[Δ]延 20A.82).

最 41.82

tzueih.

Adj. & adv. Best, most, least, to the highest (lowest) degree: 最好 *-haau*↓; 最好的 the best one; 最佳 best, finest; 最便宜 cheapest; 最美 most beautiful; 最初 *-chu*↓; 最先 earliest; 以此爲最 this one is the best; 最難 the hardest, most difficult; 最終的 the last one; 最後 *-houh*↓; 最要緊 most important; 最爲至要 of the utmost importantce; 最關緊要 of the utmost urgency and importance; 最新式 most stylish, chic, *à la mode*; 最時髦 most fashionable; 最不要臉 most shameless, brazen, thick-skinned; 最高 tallest, highest, supreme; 最低 lowest; 最大 maximum, maximal; 最小 minimum, minimal; 最細 infinitesimal; 最多(少) most (least) numerous.

最初 *tzueih-chu*, adj. & adv., (at) first, initial(ly).

最殿 *tzueih-diahn*, n., the first and the last successful contestants.

最凡 *tzueih-farn*, n., see *-muh*↓.

最高法院 *tzueihgau-faryuaan*, n., supreme court.

最好 *tzueih-haau*, adj., best of all.

最後 *tzueih-houh*, adj., final, ultimate: 最後關頭 final reckoning, the moment of truth; 最後通牒 an ultimatum; 最後一次 the last round (turn, time); 最後一分鐘 at the last minute.

最惠國 *tzueih-hueih-guor*, n., (international law) the most-favored nation: 最惠國條款 the most-favored-nation clause.

最目 *tzueihmuh*, n., a summary table of contents.

矍 41.82

jyuer.

Adj. (1) Sound and healthy, physically vigorous: 矍鑠 *-shuoh*↓. (2) Looking askance: 矍矍 *-jyuer*↓.

矍矍 *jyuerjyuer*, adj., (1) staring in surprise; (2) eager, anxious, spoiling for.

矍然 *jyuerrarn*, adj. & adv., with a surprised look.

矍鑠 *jyuershuoh*, adj., (of old people) hale and hearty.

§41.83 (図/〜)

迴 41.83

hueir.

[Var. 廻]

V.i. & t. (1) To go round or backwards: 迴旋, 迴轉 *-shyuarn, -juaan*↓; 巡迴 to patrol, make circuit tour; 迴天乏術 cannot make the universe turn back on its course—impossible. (2) To return (var. of 回).

Adj. & adv. Curving: 迂迴曲折 going in a roundabout way (as in argument, explanation); 迴誦 to read (letter) again and again.

迴避 *hueirbih*, v.i. & t., (1) to make way for high official coming one's way; (2) to avoid confrontation with (person) for some valid reason.

迴腸 *hueircharng*, n., (physiol.) the ileum, part of intestines; (fig.) disturbed thoughts, feelings, longings.

迴環 *hueirhuarn*, adv., round and round, back and forth.

迴轉 *hueirjuaan*, v.i., to turn around.

迴廊 *hueirlarng*, n., a circling or curving corridor.

迴翔 *hueirshiarng*, v.i., to fly back and forth, to circle in the sky.

迴旋 *hueirshyuarn*, adv., in a circular manner, back and forth; 迴旋風 tornado.

迴文 *hueirwern*, n., as in 迴文詩 a poem which can be read backward or forward and still make sense.

迴斡 *hueirwoh*, v.i. & t., to turn.

遇 41.83

yuh.

N. (1) A surname. (2) Circumstances, situation: 境遇 ditto; 機遇, 際遇 opportunity, chance. (3) Treatment, remuneration: 待遇甚厚(甚薄) good (bad) salary; 隆遇, 殊遇 special, extra reception, courtesy, etc.

V.t. (1) To meet: 遇見 *-jiahn*↓; 路上相遇 meet on the way; 巧遇 meet by chance; 遇便 *-biahn*↓. (2) To find, meet (a lover, s.o. who understands): 外遇 n., a lover outside marriage; 所遇 what one meets, also lover: 別有所遇 has a lover outside; 遇人不淑 phr., married a bad husband; 尋遇 find and meet.

遇便 *yuh-biahn*, phr., whenever convenient.

遇害 *yuh-haih*, v.i., was murdered.

遇合 *yuhher*, v.t. & n., to meet together, get along together; coming together.

遇見 *yuh-jiahn*, v.t., meet, meet with (person, event).

遇難 *yuh-nahn*, phr., was killed.

遇險 *yuh-shiaan*, phr., meet an accident.

遏 41.83

eh.

V.t. To suppress, keep down, stop: 遏慾 suppress desires; 遏亂 suppress rebellion; 遏絕, 遏止 *-jyuer, -jyy*↓; 遏惡揚善 overlook other people's weaknesses and extol their virtues.

遏折 *ehjer*, v.i., to stop.

遏制 *ehjyh*, v.t., to suppress.

遏絕 *ehjyuer*, v.t., to suppress entirely.

遏止 *ehjyy*, v.t., to stop (what is wrong).

遏密 *ehmih*, v.t., as in (AC) 遏密八音 stopped music during imperial funeral.

遏捺 *ehnah*, v.t., to suppress, keep down by force.

遏阻 *ehtzuu*, v.t., to stop, prevent, deter.

遏抑 *eh-yih*, v.t., ditto.

遏雲 *ehyurn*, phr., (singer's voice) pierce the clouds.

遢 41.83

tah.

V.i. & adj. See 遢拉 *ta'la*, see 蹋△撒 40B.50; 邋△遢 93.83.

暹 41.83

shian.

V.i. (AC) (1) (sun) rises. (2) Go forward.

暹羅 *Shianluor*, n., Siam (Thailand).

逷 41.83

tih.

[Var. of 逖 91.83]

是 41.83

shyh.

N. In 國是 the affairs of the country.

Pon. This: 如是 like this.

V.i. (1) To be: 這是, 你是 this is, you are, etc.; oft. stands for "it is," as though "it" is understood: 是我的錯 it is my mistake; 是你的不幸 it is your bad luck; 是我說的 it is I who said it; 該 (應) 是時候了 it should be time (to go now); 是下雨了 it is raining; 是必有故 there must be a reason; oft. like "if it is": 是你做的, 就該承認 if you (it is you who) did it, you should admit it; 是 (or vb. to be) idiomatically not required before a predicative adj.: 他大我小 he (is) big, and I (am) small; 他病了 he (is) ill; 這個容易 this (is) easy; 是...的 used in assertion, where phrase ending in 的 is felt as "one which," "one who": 這塊布白 or 很白 this cloth (is) white, but 這塊布是白的 this cloth is a white one; 他不是我生的 he was not one born by me; 不是我說的 (the words) are not said by me; 是不是, 是否 is it or is it not, used in beginning questions: 是不是你說的 did you say it or didn't you? 是不是你要走了 are you going away? 可不是 is it not indeed, it is indeed (his own fault); 莫不是 (in sense of conjecture) could it be that, might it not be that: 莫不是他病了 it might be that he is sick. (2) Used in answering "Yes": 是 or 是的 Yes; 不是 No; 是了 that's it; 口是心非 he says "Yes" but means "No." (3) To justify: 自是其所是 to justify what one holds or believes; 是其所爲 justify his action.

Adj. (1) That: 是日, 是時 that day, that time. (2) Right, true, opp. 非 *fei*, wrong, untrue: 自以爲是 assumes he is right; 是耶, 非耶 is it true or is it not? 各行其(所)是 each does what he think is right; 是非 *-fei* ↓.

是必 *shyh bih*, phr., it must be, there must be (a reason, etc.).

是非 *shyh-fei*, n., (1) right and wrong, dispute, quarrel: 不管他人的是非 do not meddle in others' disputes; 是是非非 questions as to who is right and who is wrong; (2) sense of right and wrong: 是非之心, 人皆有之 (孟子) every man has a sense of right and wrong.

是否 *shyhfoou*, phr., is it true or isn't it? a phr. beginning a question, like Eng. "It is . . . , isn't it?" "You have . . . , haven't you?" 是否要我幫忙 do you need my help?

是故 *shyhguh*, adv. & conj., therefore, in consequence (oft. rhetorical, leading to another aspect rather than consequence).

是荷 *shyh-her*, phr., (at the end of request in letters) much obliged.

是正 *shyhjehng*, v.t., to correct (an error), to put right (oft. court., used in submission of writing); 請求是正 please point out any errors.

是日 *shyhryh*, adv., that day.

是幸 *shyhshihng*, phr., (at end of request) much obliged.

是所 *shyh suoo*, phr., this is what: 是所至盼 (the above) is what I am anxiously waiting for.

是則 *shyh tzer*, phr., it is then.

是味兒 *shyhweh'l*, adj., having the right flavor: 菜做得是味兒 the dish is cooked just right.

是爲 *shyh weir*, phr., it is, this is, that is, which is, all that in the preceding sentence is.

是樣兒 *shyhyahng'l*, adj., of correct form or shape.

是以 *shyhyii*, conj., therefore, see *-guh* ↑.

匙 41.83

chyr (*-'sh*).

N. (1) (*-tz*, *-'l*) Spoon: 湯匙 soup spoon; 茶匙 teaspoon. (2) (*-'sh*) 鑰匙 (*yauh'sh*) key.

尟 41.83

shiaau.

Adj. Few, little (cogn. 少 22.91).

韙 41.83

weei.

N. Used only in phr. 大不韙 a great crime, crime against the state.

題 41.83

tir.

N. Subject, theme of essay: usu. 題目 *-muh* ↓; 出題 to set subject for composition or questions for examination; 標題 give title to, entitle(d); 破題 opening sentence stating theme of essay; 承題 explanation, enlargement of above after first sentence (in 八股 *baguu* essay); 題外文章 digression from subject of paper; 文不對題 composition irrelevant to subject; 離題太遠 (discussion) digress too far afield; 小題大做 make too much fuss over trifle, make a mountain out of a molehill.

V.i. & t. & n., (1) Inscribe, -cription, write beautiful calligraphy: 題簽, 題署, 題款 *-chian, -shuh, -kuaan* ↓; 題字 autograph, write inscription or a few words; 題匾, 題額 inscription fronting shop or hall; 題壁 write line or poem on wall; 題詩 write poem on occasion; 題評 critical comments on book, scroll; 題贈 inscribe to (person). (2) (MC) u.f. 提: 休題舊事 do not mention bygones.

題跋 *tirbar*, n., remarks on scrolls of calligraphy or painting; postscript to essays, books.
題簽 *tirchian*, n. & v.i., book title written on book cover, to write such a title.
題額 *tir-er*, n., inscription on top of tablet.
題主 *tirjuu*, n., person selected to write name of deceased on ancestral tablet.
題款 *tirkuaan*, n., (on a scroll) name of writer and the person it is dedicated to.
題目 *tirmuh*, n., subject of essay, speech.
題署 *tirshuh*, n. & v.i., sign(ature) on scroll, tablet, etc.
題材 *tirtsair*, n., subject matter.
題辭 *tirtsyr*, n., complimentary remarks in front matter of book.

鶗 41.83

tir.

N. 鶗鴂 *tirjyuer*, n., the cuckoo (=子規).

§ 41.93 (図/く)

晏 41.93

yahn.

N. A surname.

Adj. (1) Late: 晏起 get up late; 晏駕 *-jiah* ↓. (2) Peaceful: 海內晏如 the country is in peace; 晏安酖毒 (of ruler) to indulge in pleasures and ruin the country; 天清日晏 a peaceful, sunny day.

晏駕 *yahn-jiah*, v.i., (of ruler) to pass away.
晏然 *yahnrarn*, adj., contented, relaxed.
晏晏 *yahnyahn*, adj., friendly, genial.

嬰 41.93

ying.

N. An new-born babe, an infant: 嬰兒, 嬰孩 *-'l, -hair* ↓; 育嬰院 orphanage, nursery.

V.t. (1) (AC, u.f.) 攖 to ruffle, rub the wrong way: 嬰鱗 *-lirn* ↓. (2) (AC) to surround, to bother: 世網嬰我身 I am enmeshed in worldly concerns; 嬰城而守 patrol around city in defense.

嬰兒 *yingerl*, n., an infant.
嬰孩 *yinghair*, n., ditto.
嬰疾 *ying-jir*, phr., to catch sickness, fall ill.
嬰鱗 *ying-lirn*, phr., (AC allu.) to ruffle the dragon's neck scales—to offend the ruler by frank criticism (see 攖 10A.93).

曇 41.93

tarn.

N. 曇花 *tarnhua*, n., (bot.) night-blooming cereus, the *Ficus carica*, (優曇鉢) tree whose flower blooms once a year, and lasts only one night; hence 曇花一現 rare and brief appearance.

县 41.93

shiahn.

[Abbr. of 縣 41S.01]

時

SECTION 41A

§ 41A.00 (日/丿)

時 41A.00-1

shyr.
[Abbr. 时]

N. (1) Time: 時間, 時候(兒), 時光 *-jian*[2], *-'hou('l)*, *-guang* ↓; 長時, 短時 long time, short time; 暫時 temporary; 此時, 彼時 at this time, at that time; 此時此日 this day and hour; 那時 at that time; 何時何地 when and where; 一時 (impulse of) a moment; 當時 at that time; 同時 at the same time; 即時 immediately; 及時 timely, before it is too late; 臨時 (a) temporary (government), (b) just at the moment, on the spot (propose a resolution, back out, etc.); 隨時 at any time; 不時之需 thing which may be needed any time, money for exigencies; 時不我與 time is running out. (2) Date, hour: 一小時 an hour; 時辰 *-'chern*, 時刻 *-keh*, 時期 *-chir* ↓; 定時 appointed hour; 準時, 依時 punctually; 過時, 逾時 belated (for appointment, etc.), after appointed time; 限時 set time limit. (3) O'clock: 三時 three o'clock; 三時半 or 三時三十分 half past three or three thirty. (4) Ancient system of dividing 24 hours into 12 two-hour periods, named by duodecimal cycle 子丑寅卯辰巳午未申酉戌亥, beginning with 子時 11:00 p.m.–1:00 a.m.; 子時正 12:00 midnight; 午時正 12:00 midnoon; 卯時 around 8:00 a.m.; see Appendix A. (5) Period, times, days, season: 少時 youth; 老時 old age; 舊時 old times; 古時 ancient times; 時代 *-daih*, 時運 *-yuhn*, 時世 *-shyh*[1] ↓; 入時 fashionable (dress); 逆時 against the times or prevailing customs.

Adj. (1) Current (affairs, fashion, etc.): 時事 *-shyh*[3], 時裝 *-juang*, 時尚 *-shahng*, 時髦 *-maur* ↓. (2) Timely: 時雨, 時雪 timely rain, snow.

Adv. Often, continuously: 時時 *-shyr* ↓; 學而時習之 learn and review it from time to time.

時輩 *shyrbeih*, n., people (usu. scholars) of the times.

時變 *shyrbiahn*, n., (1) political changes; (2) the change of seasons.

時病 *shyr-bihng*, n., (1) the ills of the times; (2) (Chin. med.) epidemic.

時不常兒 *shyr'bucharng'l*, adv., oftentimes (=時常).

時差 *shyrcha*, n., (1) difference in hours between different longitudes; (2) seasonal changes in length of day.

時常 *shyrcharng*, adv., often.

時辰 *shyr'chern*, n., (1) hour, time in gen. sense (=時候 *-houh*): 在這個時辰 at this (late, etc.) hour; 時辰不早了 it is late; (2) see N. 4 ↑ (see Appendix A).

時氣 *shyrchih*, n., (1) epidemic; (2) (*-'chi*) adj., lucky: 他眞是時氣 he is really lucky.

時期 *shyrchir*, n., (1) time limit; (2) period: 在這個時期 during this period; 乾隆時期 Chiarnlurng (Chienlung) period.

時代 *shyrdaih*, n., epoch, era, period: 時代不同 the times are different; 那個時代 in those days; 時代偶像 idol of the times.

時調 *shyrdiauh*, n., popular song.

時分 *shyrfehn*, n., season; time (early, late).

時光 *shyrguang*, n., time (early, late); passing hours: 時光流逝 the days (years) pass.

時好 *shyrhauh*, n., popular fashion.

時候(兒) *shyr'hou('l)*, n., time: 這個時候 at this time; 甚麼時候兒 what time, when?

時會 *shyrhueih*, n., luck, right time (as person comes "at the right time" and succeeds).

時貨 *shyr-huoh*, n., goods of the season.

時政 *shyr-jehng*[1], n., current politics.

時症 *shyr-jehng*[2], n., (Chin. med.) seasonal illness.

時機 *shyrji*, n., an opportune moment.

時價 *shyr-jiah*, n., current price.

時艱 *shyr-jian*[1], n., (LL) problems and difficulties of the country.

時間 *shyrjian*[2], n., (common term) time, duration; time as a philosophic notion: 空間與時間 space and time; 開會的時間太長 the meeting lasts too long; 時間不早了 it is late; 有時間性 limited to a period only, temporary, (news) of temporary interest, (offers, business quotations) valid for a limited time; 時間表 n., timetable.

時節 *shyrjier*, n., (1) festival; (2) (AC) seasonal changes; (3) (*-'jie*) see *-hou('l)* ↑.

時忌 *shyr-jih*[1], n., taboo of the times.

時計 *shyr-jih*[2], n., chronometer, clock, watch.

時禁 *shyr-jihn*, n., current taboo, ban.

時景 *shyr-jiing*, n., the times (good, bad); gen. conditions of a time.

時裝 *shyr-juang*, n., current fashion in dress.

時中 *shyrjung*[1], adj., (AC) moderate, appropriate, not extreme.

時鐘 *shyrjung*[2], n., a clock.

時値 *shyrjyr*, n., current price or value.

時局 *shyrjyur*, n., gen. situation (of country).

時刻 *shyrkeh*, (1) n., time, hour; (2) adv., every moment: 時刻不忘, 不離 not forget, not separate, for a single moment.

時曆 *shyrlih*, n., (AC) calendar.

時令 *shyrlihng*, n., (1) (AC) seasonal regulation; (2) seasonal changes; (3) (*-'ling*) epidemic (also 時令病 *--bihng*).

時流 *shyrliour*, n., scholars of the times, contemporaries.

時論 *shyr-luhn*, n., (1) current criticism, essays on current topics; (2) public opinion.

時髦 *shyrmaur*, (1) adj., fashionable; (2) n., vogue: 新時髦 new vogue.

時鳥 *shyr-niaau*, n., seasonal bird.

時派(兒) *shyrpaih(-pah'l)*, n. & adj., fashion, -able.

A

時牌 *shyr-pair*, n., (MC) tablet indicating hour of the day, hung at office.

時評 *shyr-pirng*, n., (1) newspaper editorial, criticism on current topics; (2) prevailing criticism.

時人 *shyrrern*, n., people of the period, contemporaries.

時日 *shyrryh*, n., date, time limit.

時尚 *shyr-shahng*, n., fashion.

時下 *shyr-shiah*, adj. & adv., present: 時下的情形 the present condition.

時限 *shyr-shiahn*, n., time limit.

時鮮 *shyr-shian*, adj., fresh (fish, fruit, etc.).

時賢 *shyr-shiarn*, n., the great scholars of the period, social leaders of the time.

時效 *shyr-shiauh*, n., time limited efficacy.

時新 *shyrshin*, adj., novel, new-fangled.

時興 *shyrshing*, adj., fashionable, novel at the time.

時行 *shyrshirng*, adj., current (vogue, disease); popular, enjoying popularity.

時世 *shyrshyh*[1], n., the generation.

時式 *shyrshyh*[2], adj., fashionable.

時事 *shyrshyh*[3], n., current affairs.

時勢 *shyrshyh*[4], n., current trend of events.

時時 *shyrshyr*, adv., always, at every moment.

時序 *shyrshyuh*, n., the course of the seasons.

時望 *shyr-wahng*, n., a person's popularity: 時望所歸 the object of public esteem.

時文 *shyrwern*, n., formerly, essay in the eight paragraphs prescribed for civil examinations (八股 80.80), as opp. to other non-prescribed forms.

時務 *shyr-wuh*, n., current public affairs: 識時務 familiar with the current situation; (AC) farmer's activities of the season.

時彥 *shyr-yahn*[1], n., see *-shiarn*↑.

時諺 *shyr-yahn*[2], n., local proverb.

時樣(兒) *shyryahng('l)*, n. & adj., fashion, -able.

時醫 *shyr-yi*, n., a popular physician.

B

時疫 *shyr-yih*, n., epidemic, plague.

時宜 *shyryir*, adj., appropriate, proper (dress, opinion): 不合時宜 unpopular (opinion).

時遇 *shyr-yuh*[1], n., luck in popular reception or in timely recognition by superior.

時譽 *shyr-yuh*[2], n., popularity, gen. esteem.

時運 *shyr-yuhn*, n., luck, times: 時運不濟 run into bad luck or times.

時雨 *shyr-yuu*, n., timely rain; (fig.) a teacher's good influence.

时 41A.00–1

shyr.

[Abbr. of 時 41A.00↑]

§ 41A.01 (日/小)

昧 41A.01–1

meih.

V. t. (1) Hide away: 把東西昧了起來 keep hidden s. t. secretly. (2) Darken: 昧了良心 or 昧心 darken (or ignore) one's conscience. (3) 昧死 risk life (in presenting frank letter to emperor), from 冒昧 Adj. 2↓.

Adj. (1) Stupid, dull: 愚昧, opp. 明 or 明察 intelligent, discerning. (2) Being rash, adv., rashly: 冒昧陳詞, 陳情 (court.) make bold to inform, request, etc.

昧旦 *meihdahn*, n., (AC) the dim dawn.

昧昧 *meihmeih*, adj., (1) dark; (2) slow of understanding; (3) (AC) dark and mysterious: 昧昧芒芒.

C

昧爽 *meihshuaang*, n., (LL) early dawn.

晾 41A.01–6

liahng.

V. i. & t. (1) To air (clothing, etc.): 晾衣服, 晾一晾 give it an airing; 晾乾 to dry in the air; 晾開 spread out for airing. (2) To sun (laundry).

§ 41A.02 (日/⺊)

曚 41A.02–2

merng.

[Cf. 朦, 艨]

曚曨 *mernglurng*, adj., in twilight, predawn condition: also hazy moonlight (usu. wr. 朦朧).

曝 41A.02–4

puh.

V. t. To sun (clothing): 一曝十寒 sun one day and rain ten days (of futile, frequently interrupted, effort).

曝露 *puhluh*, v.t., expose (corpses, evil), also wr. 暴露.

曝獻 *puh-shiahn*, n., (court.) my humble present (allu. to 野人獻曝 a countryman who thought of presenting good country sunshine to ruler).

亅	小	⺊	十	土	ナ	卄	⊢卜	丨	一	丅	フ	口	区	冈	㇆	厂	尸	亠	广	宀	丶	乚	弋	心	八	人	乂	𠂊	㇀	丿丿	⺈	く
00	01	02	10	11	12	20	21	22	30	31	32	40	41	42	50	51	52	60	61	62	63	70	71	72	80	81	82	83	90	91	92	93

§41A.10 (日/十)

曄 41A.10-2

yeh.

Adj. Bright, prosperous (also wr. 燁).

晬 41A.10-6

tzueih.

N. One full year after a child's birth: 晬盤 an assortment of articles placed on the table for a child to choose from on its first birthday anniversary, as a test of its inclinations and capabilities in later life.

暉 41A.10-6

huei.

N. (LL) light: 落日餘暉 light of the setting sun; 斜暉 the slanting sunlight; 暉映成趣 cast beautiful reflections, also intricate play of contrasting or matching thoughts.

§41A.11 (日/土)

旺 41A.11-3

wahng.

Adj. (1) Prosperous: 興旺 ditto; 旺盛 *-shehng* ↓. (2) Lucky: 旺運 *-yuhn*, 旺地 *-dih* ↓; 旺月 month doing much business. (3) Hot, bright: 火勢很旺 fire is burning intensely.

旺地 *wahng-dih*, n., productive land; land bringing prosperity.

旺盛 *wahngshehng*, adj., (business, family) prosperous.

旺運 *wahng-yuhn*, n., spell of good luck.

曜 41A.11-5

yauh

N. (1) Sunlight. (2) Names of days of the week assigned to sun, moon and the planets: 日曜日, 月曜日 Sunday, Monday; 火曜日, 水曜日, 木曜日, 金曜日, 土曜日 Tuesday to Saturday in that order (not in gen. use).

曈 41A.11-6

turng.

曈曨 n., twilight of daybreak.

§41A.21 (日/乚)

暱 41A.21-5

nih.

[Var. 昵]

V. i. Be close to or intimate with: 親暱 be on intimate terms with; 狎暱, 私暱 live secretly and intimately, or be on intimate terms, with (opposite sex, disreputable character).

暱愛 *nih-aih*, v. t., have a passionate love for (s. o.).

暱就 *nih-jiouh*, v. t., draw near to.

暱嫌 *nih-shiarn*, n., personal grudge.

§41A.22 (日/丨)

晰 41A.22-1

shi.

Adj. Clear: 明晰 clear in meaning.

晞 41A.22-8

shi.

V. i. (1) To dawn: 東方未晞 sun has not yet come up on the east. (2) To sun dry: (AC) 晞髮 to dry hair in the sun.

Adj. (AC) dry, dried in the sun.

昕 41A.22-9

shin.

N. Sunrise, day, dawn: 昕夕 morning and night.

昨 41A.22-9

tzuor.

N. & adv. Yesterday, (in) the recent past: 昨日 *-ryh*, 昨天 *-tian* ↓; 昨夜, 昨宵 last night; 日昨 the other day; 昨死今生 reform one's ways and be reborn; 今是昨非 realize how one has been wrong (in the past).

昨非 *tzuorfei*, n., (LL) past mistakes.

昨兒 *tzuor'l*, n. & adv., yesterday: 昨兒個 ditto.
昨日 *tzuorryh*, n. & adv., yesterday.
昨天 *tzuortian*, n. & adv., ditto.

§ 41A.30 (日/一)

曀 41A.30–1

yih.

N. & adj. (AC) cloudy, -diness, misty, -tiness.

暄 41A.30–6

shyuan.
[Var. 煊]

Adj. (AC & LL) warm: 暄風 warm wind.

暄寒 *shyuanharn*, v. i., (AC) talk, enjoy a chat (＝寒暄).
暄暖 *shyuannuaan*, adj., warm, cozy.

§ 41A.40 (日/口)

晤 41A.40–3

wuh.

V. t. To meet face to face, personally: 晤面, 面晤, 會晤, 相晤 ditto; 晤別以來 since meeting you last.

昭 41A.40–5

jau.

V. i. & t. (LL) to show: 昭雪, 昭示 *-shyuee, -shyh*↓; 以昭畫一 to show uniform treatment; 昭信中外 to show good faith to the nation and abroad.

Adj. (1) Clear, manifest: 昭昭, 昭明, 昭彰 *-jau, -mirng, -jang*↓. (2) Illustrious (dynasty): 昭代 *-daih*↓.

昭代 *jaudaih*, n., a glorious epoch.
昭彰 *jaujang*, adj., clear, unmistakable: 天理昭彰 God's justice is manifest; 罪惡昭彰 one's sins are known to all.
昭昭 *jaujau*, adj., as in 以其昏昏, 使人昭昭 (AC) with one's own darkness and confusion, expect to make others see the light; 斯昭昭之多 so many bright illuminating (stars).
昭著 *jaujuh*, adj., see *-jang*↑.
昭明 *jaumirng*, adj., brilliant (period, dynasty).
昭穆 *jau-muh*, adj., (pertaining to anc. royal ancestral temples) the first founder of dynasty in the center; those ancestors of 2nd, 4th and 6th generations on the left, called 昭 *jau*, and those of the 3rd, 5th and 7th generations on the left, called 穆 *muh*.
昭然 *jau'rarn*, adj. & adv., clear, -ly, manifest, -ly: 昭然若揭 clearly exposed, laid before the public (said of sinister motive, etc.).
昭示 *jaushyh*, v. t., (1) (of official superior) to instruct the people; (2) to lay before the public.
昭雪 *jaushyuee*, v. t., to wipe out (a shame, injustice).
昭蘇 *jausu*, v. i., to revive after hibernation.

§ 41A.41 (日/囚)

晒 41A.41–3

shaih.
[Var. of 曬 41A.70]

曙 41A.41–4

shuh.

N. Daybreak: 曙光, 曙色 the first light of day, daybreak.

V.i. Day breaks: 方曙 day was breaking.

暗 41A.41–6

ahn.

Adj. (1) Dark: 黑暗 dark; 昏暗 dusk, twilight, heavily shadowed or overcast; (fig.) dark ways, opp. the right path: 棄暗投明 (of rebel) return to government or orthodox church; 暗無天日 gross lack of justice under misgovernment. (2) Secret, covert (code, plan, etc.): 暗號 *-hauh*↓; 暗殺 *-sha*↓; 暗度陳倉 secret relations with sweetheart (allu. secret crossing of river at 陳倉).

Adv. Secretly: 暗想 secretly think or wonder: 暗猜 guess at riddle; 暗笑 laugh at person's back; 暗泣 weep secretly; 暗襲 attack in the dark; 暗藏 hide, conceal; 暗射 *-sheh*↓.

暗暗 *ahn-ahn*, adv., secretly, clandestinely.
暗場 *ahn-chaang*, n., (Chin. theater) a scene in plot which is

merely suggested and not acted out.
暗娼 *ahn-chang*, n., private prostitute.
暗潮 *ahn-chaur*, n., (lit. & fig.) undercurrent.
暗器 *ahn-chih*, n., concealed weapons, such as hidden arrows, darts.
暗處(兒) *ahn-chuh('l)*, n., a dark place, a secret place.
暗澹 *ahndahn*, adj., obscure, pale, not fresh (color) (also wr. 暗淡, dim, dismal).
暗地(裡) *ahndih('li)*, adv., secretly, behind one's back.
暗房 *ahn-farng*, n., (photography) darkroom.
暗溝 *ahn-gou*, n., covered sewerage.
暗害 *ahnhaih*, v.t., to plot murder or injury secretly.
暗含著 *ahnharn'je*, adj. & adv., containing covert, indirect (hint, criticism).
暗號(兒) *ahn-hauh('l)*, n., secret signal.
暗合 *ahn-her*, v.i., coincide naturally and without effort with (another's wish).
暗花兒 *ahn-hua'l*, n., veiled design or pattern.
暗間兒 *ahn-jia'l*, n., (Peking coll.) comparatively darker rooms in house, opp. 明間兒 bright or front rooms.
暗箭 *ahn-jiahn*, n., arrow shot from concealed source; anonymous attack.
暗礁 *ahnjiau*, n., hidden or submerged rocks in current.
暗計 *ahnjih*[1], n., see *-suahn* ↓.
暗記 *ahnjih*[2], n., (1) secret marking; (2) make a mental note of s.t.: 暗記兒 --*'l*, n., silent signal.
暗九 *ahnjioou*, n., multiple of nine (such as 18, 27) days or years.
暗疾 *ahn-jir*, n., secret ugly disease—euphemism for venereal disease.
暗轉 *ahn-juaan*, v.i., (theater) change scene with lights out.
暗樁 *ahn-juang*, n., hidden piles in stream for blocking boats.
暗中 *ahn-jung*, adv., secretly, furtively.
暗裡 *ahn-lii*, adv., secretly.
暗流 *ahn-liour*, n., undercurrent, see *-chaur* ↑.
暗樓子 *ahn-lourtz*, n., an attic.
暗碼(兒)(子) *ahnmaa('l)('tz)*, n., secret code; any secret marking.
暗昧 *ahnmeih*, adj., underhand, stealthy; disgraceful (affair); also wr. 闇昧.
暗門子 *ahnmerntz*, n., secret house of prostitution.
暗色 *ahnseh*, n., dark color.
暗殺 *ahnsha*, v.t., to assassinate.
暗射 *ahnsheh*, v.t., to hint at; to make concealed reference to person under disguise or by fictitious name. 「scura.
暗箱 *ahnshiang*[1], n., camera obscura.
暗香 *ahnshiang*[2], n., as in 暗香疏影 (illu.) reference to the plum flower ("darkly sweet scent and sparse branch lines").
暗笑 *ahn-shiauh*, v.i. & t., sneer at.
暗示 *ahnshyh*[1], v.i. & t., to suggest, hint; n., a hint.
暗事 *ahn-shyh*[2], n., shady affair.
暗室 *ahn-shyh*[3], n., a dark room; (photography) darkroom.
暗算 *ahnsuahn*, v.t., to plot secretly against s.o.
暗探 *ahntahn*, n., secret agent.
暗喻 *ahnyuu*, n., a concealed analogy, a metaphor.

§41A.42 (日/冈)

晡 41A.42-1

bu.

N. Late afternoon.

晴 41A.42-1

chirng.

Adj. Clear (sky), fair, not rainy (weather): 天晴了 sky has cleared, rain has stopped; 放晴了 ditto; 晴空萬里 a big, clear open sky; 晴雨無阻 rain or shine; 晴空 cloudless sky; 晴天霹靂 bolt from the blue.
晴和 *chirngher*, adj., clear and mild (weather).
晴朗 *chirnglaang*, adj., bright and clear (weather).
晴爽 *chirngshuaang*, adj., dry and pleasant (weather).
晴天 *chirngtian*, n., a clear day.
晴雨表 *chirngyur-biaau*, n., barometer.

明 41A.42-4

mirng.

N. (1) Name of dynasty: 明朝, 明代 (1368–1643). (2) Clearness, brightness, derived from adjj. (3) The present life dist. from after life: 幽明異路 the living and the dead live in different worlds.

V. i. & t. To understand: 明白 *-'bair* ↓; 能明大義 understanding the principles of right and wrong; 明恥 understand a sense of honor; 明禮 understand the rules of propriety; 明心見性 (Confucianism, Budd.) "find thy true self."

Adj. & adv. (1) Open, -ly, not hidden or underhand: 明人不做暗事 an honest man does not deal underhand; 明媒正娶 legally married; 明局 open gambling place; 明溝 open sewerage; 明碼 open code (opp. 密碼 secret code) (telegraph, in plain code, price in plain figures, price); 明槍, 明火打劫 open robbery; 明目張膽 openly defiant or openly commit acts; 明顯 evident; often coupled with 暗, openly . . . but (and) secretly: 明去暗來 secret goings-on; 明查暗訪 investigate openly and secretly; 明爭暗鬬 fight both with open and secret means; 明棄暗取 profess to spurn, but secretly take; 明知故犯 knowingly and wilfully break the law. (2) Clear, -ly, bright, -ly: 明窗淨几 a neat desk before a bright window (comfortable place for study); 明眸皓齒 bright eyes and white teeth; 春光明媚 beautiful, bright spring days; 明文 clear statement (of law, will); 古有明訓 the clear teachings of the ancients; 明鏡, 明鑑 clear example of history; 明德 the original, untarnished human heart. (3) Clear-sighted, discerning, understanding, wise: 明察, 明辨是非 clearly distinguish right and wrong; 明察秋毫 "able to see the fine down of birds in autumn": very perspicacious; 明斷 bright, wise judgment; 明主, 明王 the wise ruler; 明公 (address to eminent people) your illustrious self; 聰明 clever; 光明 bright and open, glorious, bright (future).

明版 *mingbaan*, n., Mirng Dyn. edition.

明白 *ming'bair*, (1) v. t., understand: 我明白你的意思 I understand what you mean; 明白嗎 do you understand? (2) adj., clear: 明白得很 it is very clear; 明白人, 你是明白人 (complim.) you understand (I don't need to explain more).

明蟾 *mirng-charn*, n., (LL) the moon.

明前 *mirng-chiarn*, n., name of tea (picked before 清明 festival).

明器 *mirngchih*, n., things buried with and for the dead; also 冥器.

明確 *mirngchyueh*, adj., clear and definite (advice, instructions, explanation).

明代 *Mirngdaih*, n., Mirng Dyn.

明礬 *mirngfarn*, n., (chem.) alum.

明河 *Mirngher*, n., the Milky Way.

明哲 *mirngjer*, adj., wise: 明哲保身 phr., wise for personal survival, i. e., cautious during bad government.

明間兒 *mirngjia'l*, n., the brighter room in northern houses: 兩暗一明 one bright room and two darker rooms on the sides.

明鑑 *mirngjiahn*, n., history held up as example.

明膠 *mirngjiau*, n., glue made from ox hide or animal bones and tendons.

明珠 *mirngju*, n., bright pearl: 夜明寶珠 pearl luminescent at night.

明兒 *mir'l*, n., common short for 明日, 明天 tomorrow; some future time, in the near future: 明兒丢了, 别怪我 if you should lose it, don't blame me; 明兒見 see you tomorrow.

明朗 *mirnglahng*, adj., bright (day, room); 明朗化 *--huah*, v.i., become clear (attitude).

明了(瞭) *mirngliaau*, v.t. & adj., understand; clear.

明亮 *mirngliahng*, adj., clear (sky, room, print); honest, generous.

明理 *mirnglii*, adj., reasonable, understanding: 你這個人不明理 you are being unreasonable; 讀書明理 education and understanding (as one concept), be an educated person.

明碼 *mirngmaa*, n., open code (telegraph, figures in code), in plain figures, price.

明媚 *mirngmeih*, adj., bright and beautiful (day).

明明 *mirngmirng*, adv., clearly: 明明是他 clearly it is he.

明日 *mirngryh*, n. & adv., tomorrow, see *-'l* ↑.

明信片 *mirngshihnpiahn*, n., postcard.

明星 *mirngshing*, n., movie star; star.

明天 *mirngtian*, n. & adv., tomorrow, see *-'l* ↑.

明駝 *mirngtuor*, n., (LL) the camel.

明瓦 *mirngwaa*, n., thin, ground pieces of mother-of-pearl, used in windows in place of glass.

明眼人 *mirngyaan-rern*, n., person who is not easily deceived by appearances.

明衣 *mirngyi*, n., (1) (AC) costume used before ceremonial offerings; (2) dress of mourning.

晌 41A.42-9

shaang.

N. (1) A moment: 一晌, 半晌 (coll.) a short moment, a stretch of time; 半晌不語 was silent for a moment. (2) Noon: 晌午 ditto; 吃晌飯 have noon meal; 睡晌覺 take afternoon nap. (3) (Dial. in Manchuria) a land measure, said to be an area of farm land a farmer can sow in a day.

§ 41A.50 (日/ㄱ)

暘 41A.50-4

yarng.

V.i. & adj. The sun coming out.

昉 41A.50-6

faang.

N. (AC) dawn.

V. i. (AC) start, begin.

晦 41A.50-9

hueih.

N. (1) Last day of the lunar month: 晦朔 the last and first days of the month. (2) A dark night: 風雨如晦 (AC) it blows and rains like a dark night; 晦明 the alternate night and day.

Adj. (1) Dark, unclear in meaning; 晦澀 *-seh* ↓. (2) Unlucky: 晦氣 *-chih* ↓.

晦氣 *hueihchih*, (1) n., unlucky star, hard luck; (2) adj., un-

晦 曛 曉 晻 曬 昵 曨 晚

lucky: 眞是晦氣 (damned) unlucky.

晦澀 *hueihseh*, n., (of style) unclear in meaning, hard to understand, obscure.

§ 41A.63 (日/丶)

曛 41A.63–9

shyun.

N. (1) Reflected light of sunset. (2) Dusk, twilight.

曛黑 *shyunheh*, adj., dim, dark.
曛黃 *shyunhuarng*, n., twilight.

§ 41A.70 (日/乚)

曉 41A.70–1

shiaau.

N. Daybreak: 天將曉 toward daybreak; 破曉, 拂曉 dawn, daybreak; 曉行夜宿 (of traveller) get up early and stop for the night; 春眠不覺曉 in spring, one sleeps and wakes up to find it is already day.

V. i. & t. To know, understand: 曉得 -*'de*↓; 洞曉, 通曉 (LL) understand thoroughly (a subject).

Adj. & adv. Clear, -ly, explicit, -ly: 曉諭, 曉示 -*yuh*, -*shyh*^{1}↓; 曉暢 -*chahng*↓.

曉暢 *shiaauchahng*, adj., (of writing) lucid, clear and expressive.

曉得 *shiaau'de*, v. i., to know: 曉得了 (I) know already, (in answer to instructions) I understand; 不曉得 do not know.

曉會 *shiaauhueih*, v. i., realize.

曉了 *shiaauliaau*, v. i., to understand.

曉譬 *shiaau-pih*, n., to make clear by analogy, parable.

曉人 *shiaaurern*, n., one who understands, knowledgeable person.

曉示 *shiaaushyh*^{1}, v. t., to explain explicitly: 曉示民衆 to announce to the people or instruct the public.

曉事 *shiaaushyh*^{2}, adj., understanding, experienced (person): 他很曉事 he is very understanding and experienced.

曉悟 *shiaauwuh*, v. i., to realize (truth, mistake).

曉諭 *shiaauyuh*, v. t., to instruct and explain (to the public).

晻 41A.70–1

aan (ahn).

晻昧 *aanmeih* (*ahn*-), adj., (1) disgraceful (affair) (related 曖昧); (2) (AC) murky, dusky (light).

曬 41A.70–3

shaih.
[Var. 晒]

V. t. (1) To sun (clothing, etc.), expose to the sun: 曬乾了, 曬黑了 has been dried, darkened in the sun; 曬台 -*tair*↓; 曬太陽 to sun oneself, take a sunbath; 曬暖兒 to get warm in the sun; 曬車板兒 without customers ("sun the cart planks"). (2) To print a photograph by light: 曬相片 ditto; 曬藍圖 make a blueprint.

曬台 *shaihtair*, (1) n., sun terrace; (2) v. i., (coll.) to drop out on a project.

昵 41A.70–5

nih.

V.i. Be close to or intimate with: 親昵 be on intimate terms with; 昵比 -*bii*↓.

Adv. Intimately, closely, passionately: 昵愛 -*aih*↓.

昵愛 *nihaih*, v.t., to love passionately (a woman) (usu. wr. 溺愛; cf. 暱愛).

昵比 *nihbii*, v.i., associate with: 昵比罪人 (AC) associate with criminals.

昵交 *nihjiau*, n., an intimate friend.

曨 41A.70–6

lurng.

N. & adj. See 曈▵曨 41A.11; 矇▵曨 41A.02.

晚 41A.70–9

waan.

N. (1) Evening: 晚上 -*'shang*^{1}↓; 今晚 this evening; 昨晚 last evening, last night; 晚安 good evening; 傍晚 late afternoon; 早晚 every morning and evening, also sooner or later; 晚半天兒, 晚半晌兒 toward dusk. (2) (In letters) the writer himself, younger than addressee and acknowledging himself as "pupil," short for 晚生 -*sheng*↓; 鄉晚 "pupil" of the same village; 晚輩 -*beih*↓.

Adj. (1) Late, latter part of: 歲晚 toward end of the year; 晚唐 late Tarng Dyn.; 晚清 latter part of Manchu Dyn.; 太晚了 it's too late; 未晚 it's not too late; 悔之晚矣 it's too late to repent; 晚稻, 晚莊稼 late harvests; 晚秋 late autumn. (2) Late in life: 晚年 -*niarn*↓.

Adv. Coming late: 晚達, 大器晚成 a great man becomes famous late in life; 晚歸 come home late.

晚班 *waan-ban*, n., evening class.
晚報 *waanbauh*, n., evening paper.
晚輩 *waanbeih*, n., the younger generation, oft. court. self-reference, said in humility.
晚車 *waan-che*, n., evening train.
晚弟 *waandih*, n., (in letters, self-reference) your humble younger brother.
晚飯 *waanfahn*, n., evening meal, supper.
晚會 *waan-hueih*, n., evening gathering, meeting, party.
晚婚 *waan-hun*, phr., marry late; 晚婚兒 *--'l*, n., a remarried woman.
晚照 *waan-jauh*, n., sunset glow.
晚間 *waanjian*, n., evening.
晚節 *waan-jier*, n., (1) man's integrity in his old age; (2) (LL, rare) the latter part of dyn.
晚近 *waanjihn*[1], adv., lately.
晚進 *waanjihn*[2], n., one of new generation that has come up.
晚景 *warn-jiing*, n., a man's circumstances in old age.
晚兒 *waa'l*, n., (1) evening: 昨晚兒 last night; (2) time: 這晚兒 now; 那晚兒 at that time.
晚禮服 *warn-lii-fur*, n., evening dress.
晚年 *waan-niarn*, n., the latter part of man's life, (in) old age.
晚娘 *waan-niarng*, n., stepmother.
晚上 *waan'shang*[1], n., evening.
晚晌 *waan'shang*[2], n., ditto.
晚生 *waansheng*, n., see N. 2↑; formerly, pupil, oft. self-reference in writing or speaking to teacher.
晚霞 *waan-shiar*, n., sunset clouds.
晚世 *waanshyh*, n., latter days, nowadays.
晚學 *waan-shyuer*, n., see N. 2↑.
晚歲 *waan-sueih*, n., (in) latter years, old age.
晚餐 *waantsan*, n., evening meal, supper or dinner.
晚走 *warn-tzoou*, v.i., (coll. of woman) to remarry.
晚宴 *waan-yahn*, n., evening dinner.
晚運 *waan-yuhn*, n., a man's circumstances in old age.

§ 41A.71 (日/乜)

曦 41A.71–8

shi.

N. Early dawn: 晨曦.

§ 41A.80 (日/八)

曠 41A.80–6

kuahng.

V.i. & t. (1) To skip: 曠工 skip work, walk out on work; 曠課 skip school work, play hooky; 曠職 neglect duties. (2) To waste: 曠日持久 extend over days, maintain for a long time, be time-consuming.

Adj. (1) Far-ranging, understanding, emancipated: 心曠神怡 free of mind and happy of heart; 曠達 *-dar*↓. (2) Open, covering whole area: 空曠 open (spaces). (3) Unexcelled, unrivalled, unprecedented: 曠世無雙 stand without peer in one's generation; 曠代佳人 unrivalled national beauty; 曠古以來 since ancient days; 曠典 unprecedented great ceremony or one not seen for a long time. (4) Bachelor see 曠夫 *-fu*↓; 久曠 life without a woman for a long time. (5) Far, long: see 曠久, 曠遠 *-jioou*, *-yuaan*↓.

曠達 *kuahngdar*, adj., showing deep understanding or breadth of mind: 曠達之士 a profound scholar, one with an open mind, not bigoted.
曠費 *kuahngfeih*[1], v.t., to waste: 曠費時間, 學業 waste time, neglect studies.
曠廢 *kuahngfeih*[2], v.t., to neglect (school work, etc.).
曠夫 *kuahngfu*, n., a bachelor.
曠古 *kuahngguu*, adj. & adv., since ancient days: 曠古未有 never seen in past history; 曠古奇聞 unprecedented story.
曠久 *kuahngjioou*, adv., for a long time: 曠久未見 has not been seen for a long time.
曠曠 *kuahngkuahng*, adj., (AC) big, open, bright.
曠野 *kuahngyee*, n., open spaces, open country, prairie.
曠遠 *kuahngyuaan*, adj., very far away (in time or space).

暝 41A.80–6

mirng (**mihng*).

N. (**mihng*) Night.

Adj. Dark, obscure; cf. 冥 62.80.

§ 41A.81 (日/人)

暵 41A.81–2

hahn.

V.t. (AC) to dry by exposing to the sun.

亅	小	⺊	十	土	𠂇	廾	㔾	丨	一	丅	𠃌	口	囗	冂	𠃍	厂	尸	亠	广	宀	丶	乚	乜	心	八	人	乂	乛	丿	𠃋	𠂉	𡿨
00	01	02	10	11	12	20	21	22	30	31	32	40	41	42	50	51	52	60	61	62	63	70	71	72	80	81	82	83	90	91	92	93

暌 41A.81-3

kueir.
[Dist. 睽 41B.81]

V. i. (Of friends) to be apart.

暌合 *kueirher*, v. i., (LL) separation and reunion.
暌索 *kueirsuoo*, v. i., (LL) to be dispersed.
暌違 *kueirweir*, v. i., (LL) to be separated.

㬉 41A.81-3

nuaan.
[Var. of 暖 41A.82]

映 41A.81-9

yihng.

V. i. & t. (1) To reflect light: 互相輝映 add to each other's splendor. (2) To project a movie: 首映 first showing of movie, première, 重映 repeat showing.

映帶 *yihngdaih*, v. i., increase beauty or brilliance by mutual reflection.
映照 *yihngjauh*, v. i., to cast light upon.
映雪 *yihng-shyuee*, phr., (allu.) to study by light of snow (without lamp), to work hard as student.
映月 *yihng-yueh*, phr., to study by moonlight, see *-shyuee* ↑.

§41A.82 (日/乂)

暇 41A.82-5

shiah (*shiar*).

N. & adj. Leisure, -ly: 餘暇, 閒暇, 空暇 free time; 無暇 have no time for; 無暇及此 have no time for this; 自顧不暇 have enough to do to look after myself; 應接不暇 too busy with seeing guests.

暇晷 *shiahgueei* (*shiar-*), n., unoccupied time.
暇刻 *shiahkeh* (*shiar-*), n., a free moment.
暇日 *shiahryh* (*shiar-*), n., days of leisure.
暇時 *shiahshyr* (*shiar-*), n., leisure time.

暾 41A.82-6

tun.

Adj. (AC) bright (of morning sun, fire).

暖 41A.82-9

nuaan.
[Var. of 煗]

V. t. To warm: 暖手, 暖牀 warm one's hands, bed; 取暖 keep oneself warm (as to sit by fire).

Adj. Warm, genial: 暖和 *-'her* ↓; 暖風 genial breezes; 暖烘烘, 暖融融 comfortably warm; 温暖 kind and genial; 飽暖 well-fed and well-clothed, hence, warm and comfortable; 飽暖思淫慾 material comforts lead to sexual desire.

暖廠 *nuarnchaang*, n., public building for the poor in winter.
暖氣 *nuaanchih*, n., warm air; 暖氣管 steam radiator.
暖耳 *nuarn-eel*, n., earflaps.
暖房 *nuaanfarng*, v.i. & n., (to give) a house-warming party.
暖閣 *nuaanger*, n., heated room; (in North China) private rooms in gen.; formerly, heated rooms for entertainment.
暖鍋 *nuaanguo*, n., chafing dish (＝火鍋).
暖和 *nuaan'her*, adj., warm (room, air, climate), also wr. 暖活.
暖壺 *nuaanhur*, n., tea cozy.
暖轎 *nuaanjiauh*, n., curtained sedan chair.
暖炕 *nuaankahng*, n., built-in earthen bed, called *kahng*, heated from outside.
暖簾 *nuaanliarn*, n., quilted-cotton door screen.
暖爐 *nuaanlur*, n., a stove for heating room.
暖壽 *nuaanshouh*, n., party given in honor of s. o. on the eve of his birthday.
暖水瓶 *nuarnshueei-pirng*, n., a hot water bottle (also 暖水壺).
暖室 *nuaanshyh*, n., a greenhouse.
暖翠 *nuaantsueih*, adj., soft green (of spring meadows).

曖 41A.82-9

aih.

曖昧 *aihmeih*, adj., shady (affair), secret (romance).

§41A.91 (日/ノ)

旷 41A.91-6

kuahng.
[Abbr. of 曠 41A.80]

SECTION 41B

§ 41B.00 (目/亅)

盱 41B.00–3

shyu.

V.i. To stare.

Adj. (AC) big.

盱衡 *shyuherng*, v.i., (1) (AC) stare, glare, glower; (2) survey: 盱衡天下大勢 make a gen. survey of the world situation.

盱睨 *shyushih*, v.i., (AC) knit one's brow in disapproval.

盱盱 *shyushyu*, adj., glowering.

瞯 41B.00–5

jiahn.

[Var. of 覸 52B.70]

矙 41B.00–5

kahn.

V.i. & t. See 瞰 41B.82.

睜 41B.00–9

jeng.

V. i. & t. To open (eyes), to stare: 睜開眼睛, 睜眼 open one's eyes; 眼睛睜不開 cannot open one's eyes; 睜一眼, 閉一眼 pretend not to see—purposely overlook (irregularities); 睜著眼睛說瞎話 tell a tall tale, talk barefaced nonsense.

§ 41B.01 (目/小)

眛 41B.01–1

meih.

[Dist. 昧]

Adj. (1) Obscure. (2) Color-blind; blind, esp. 眛於 blind to (事實 the facts, 國情 the conditions of the country); cf. 昧 41A.01.

睞 41B.01–1

laih.

V. t. (AC) look at, squint, glance sideways: 明眸善睞 clear-eyed with a winning look; 青睞 (court.) your favor or patronage.

瞭 41B.01–1

liaau (*liauh).

V. i. (*liauh) Survey at distance: 瞭望, 瞭高 -*wahng*, -*gau*↓.

Adj. (1) Clearly visible: 瞭如指掌 clear, easy to see. (2) Clear-sighted, see 瞭亮 -*liahng*↓.

瞭高(兒) *liauhgau('l), v.i., to act as thief's lookout man; to arrange everything and then watch at a distance.

瞭亮 *liaauliahng*, adj., (of voice, eyesight) clear, resonant, resounding.

瞭然 *liaaurarn*, adj., clear, easy to see.

瞭望 *liauhwahng, v. i., watch at a distance; 瞭望台 watchtower.

眯 41B.01–2

mii.

V. t. 眯著眼 close eyes into narrow slits; have dust in the eye: 眯了眼兒.

眎 41B.01–3

shyh.

[Var. of 視 63B.70]

瞟 41B.01–3

piaau.

V. t. Look out of corner of eye: 瞟了一眼 give a contemptuous look, glance quickly at.

瞟眇 *piaurmiaau*, adj., see (be seen) indistinctly (also 縹緲 93B.01).

睬 41B.01–9

tsaai.

[Var. 倸]

V. t. (1) To look carefully. (2) Pay attention, esp. with negative adv., to ignore: 不要睬他, 不睬 ignore person, leave him alone, (refuse to look at).

盱 瞯 矙 睜 眛 睞 瞭 眯 眎 瞟 睬

亅	小	⺌	十	土	ナ	卄	乚	丨	一	丁	フ	口	区	冈	冂	厂	尸	亠	广	宀	丶	乚	弋	心	八	人	乂	一	丿	𠂉	く
00	01	02	10	11	12	20	21	22	30	31	32	40	41	42	50	51	52	60	61	62	63	70	71	72	80	81	82	83	90	91	92

§ 41B.02 (目/ㄎ)

矇 41B.02–2

merng (**meng*).
[Cogn. of 曚, 朦, 蒙, 懵]

V. t. (**meng*) To hoodwink and deceive: 我真把他矇住了 I have really made him believe (what is not true); 一時倒矇住了 was really misled for a while; 矇着鍋兒 hide the truth ("cover the pot").

Adj. Blurred in vision: 矇朧, 矇昧 *-lurng, -meih* ↓.

矇混 *merng'huhn*, v. i., deceive by assuming similar appearance (=蒙混).
矇朧 *mernglurng*, adj., (eyes) drowsy.
矇昧 *merngmeih*, adj., ignorant, unknowing (=蒙昧).
矇矇 *merngmerng*, adj., blurred, unclear: 矇矇亮兒 pre-dawn twilight.
矇騙 **mengpiahn*, v. i. & t., deceive, swindle, cheat (person).
矇瞍 *merngsuoo*, adj., blurred in vision.

眼 41B.02–5

yaan.

N. (1) The eye: 眼睛 *-'jing* ↑; 開眼, 張眼 open one's eyes; 合眼 close eyes; 瞎眼blind; 眼跳 eyes twitch (said to be omen of bad news); 瞥眼 (see) in a flash; 眼裏不揉沙子 refuse to be hoodwinked; 眼不見爲淨 (food) is regarded as clean so long as you do not see how it is prepared; 眼絲兒不見就走了 in a wink he was gone; 眼看著 see with one's own eyes; 另眼看待 treat, welcome, with special regard; 打馬虎眼 pretend not to see, to overlook; 礙眼 it hurts to see (s. t.); 偷眼 give a furtive glance; 笑眼 a smiling glance; 虎眼 angry look; 鼠眼 narrow slits of eyes; 獨眼龍 (facet.) one-eyed person (cf. the Cyclops); 四眼田雞 (facet.) person wearing short-sighted spectacles; 青眼 look with favor (with black of eye); 白眼 look with disfavor (with white of eye). (2) Insight, vision, power of vision, angle or level of judgment: 眼界, 眼光, 眼力 *-jieh, -guang, -lih* ↓; 眼高 highly critical; 眼高手低 high in aim but low-rate in execution, have high ambition but no real ability; 眼拙 (court.) not to recognize a distinguished person; 眼岔 vision blurred; 眼離 *-lir* ↓; 望眼欲穿 expect to see s. o. who never comes; shade in eyes as showing certain emotions: 眼紅 jealous; 眼藍 (正爲這件事急得眼藍) desperately anxious; 眼黑愛鈔 greedy, with a black conscience; 眼白 *-bair* ↓; 眼饞, 眼熱 greedy to possess a thing after seeing it; 眼尖 sharp-eyed. (3) A hole: 針眼 needle hole; 洞眼 opening to cave; 錢眼 hole in coin; 井眼 hole in the well; 雙眼井 well with double holes; 屁股眼兒 anus; 心眼 the mind's eye; 點眼 fill a space in chess. (4) Salient or weighted point: 字眼 meaning of a phrase; 字眼兒 choice of words, special phrases; 板眼 the beat in operatic song, stress in musical bar.

眼巴巴 *yaan-baba*, adv., (waiting) anxiously.
眼白 *yaanbair*, n., (physiol.) the white of the eye (also called 鞏膜, 白膜).
眼波 *yaanbo*, n., a fluid glance (of woman).
眼前 *yaanchiarn*, adv., in the present moment, in immediate presence: 吃眼前虧 accept a present loss; 眼前歡 a momentary pleasure; 眼前花(兒) children at home regarded as flowers to please the eye; 眼前報 immediate retribution.
眼球 *yaanchiour*, n., eyeball; see *-ju'l* ↓.
眼圈兒 *yaanchua'l*, n., the region of eye socket: 眼圈兒一紅 about to cry (also 眼圈子).
眼毒 *yaan-dur*, n., as in 招人的眼毒 meet with hostile looks.
眼福 *yaan-fur*, n., a chance to enjoy seeing s. t. unusual or delightful.
眼光(兒) *yaanguang('l)*, n., (1) judgment, discrimination (good, bad, superficial); (2) state of attention (focussed, distracted, listless, etc.); (3) taste: 這件怕不對他的眼光兒 this I'm afraid will not suit his taste.
眼花 *yaanhua*, adj., dim in vision: 眼花撩亂 see things in a blur; 眼花兒 darling, the apple of one's eye: 看他的兒女好像眼花兒似的 his children are his darlings.
眼睜睜 *yaan-jengjeng*, adv., seeing with open eyes (an act committed).
眼瞼 *yarnjiaan*, n., the eyelid.
眼見得 *yaan-jiahn'de*, adv., before one's eyes (s. t. happens).
眼界 *yaanjieh*, n., range of experience: 眼界廣 has a wide range of experience; 開眼界 open up a new vista, see s. t. novel.
眼睫毛 *yaan-jiermaur*, n., eyelashes.
眼結膜 *yaanjier mor*, n., conjunctiva.
眼犄角兒 *yaan'jijiaau'l*, n., corners of one's eyes.
眼鏡 *yaanjihng* n., spectacles; 眼鏡蛇 *--sher*, (zoo.) the cobra.
眼睛 *yaan'jing*, n., the eye; also (fig.) 做他的眼睛 be spy for him, see *-muh* ↓.
眼珠兒 *yaanju'l*, n., pupil of the eye; (fig.) power of discrimination: 眞沒眼珠兒 fail to recognize thing for what it is; 眼珠子 (a) eyeball; (b) darling in one's eyes.
眼中釘 *yaanjungding*, n., an eyesore, a hated person that one wishes removed: 眼中刺 ditto; 眼中人 sweetheart.
眼科 *yaanke*, n., ophthalmology, study dealing with diseases of the eye: 眼科專家 oculist, ophthalmologist.
眼眶(子) *yaankuahng(tz)*, n., the eye socket.
眼庫 *yaan-kuh*, n., eye bank.
眼孔 *yarnkuung*, n., (1) the eye; (2) see *-jieh* ↑; 眼孔大 wide range of experience.

眼淚 *yaanleih*, n., tears.
眼簾 *yaanliarn*, n., iris (of the eye).
眼力 *yaanlih* (-'*li*), n., power of discrimination; 眼力見兒 --*jiah'l*, tact.
眼離 *yaan-lir*, n., hallucination.
眼面前(兒) *yaan'mianchiarn* (--*chiar'l*), phr., 眼面前的事 things of common daily occurrence.
眼目 *yaanmuh*, n., (1) the eye; (2) spy who reports to s. o. what he sees.
眼皮(兒) *yaanpir*(-*pier'l*), n., the eyelid: 眼皮子底下 under one's eyes, at present; 眼皮子淺 shortsighted; 眼皮兒雜 has many social contacts.
眼色 *yaanseh*, n., (1) a look, glance of the eye as signal: 遞箇眼色與他 gave him a meaningful glance; (2) facial expression, countenance: 看人的眼色 watch s. o.'s look or mood, esp. superior's.
眼生 *yaan-sheng*, adj., looking unfamiliar; cf. -*shur* ↓.
眼神(兒) *yaanshern* (-*sher'l*), n., look, expression in one's eyes.
眼下 *yaan-shiah*, adv., at present (also 目下); within survey.
眼線 *yaanshiahn* (-'*shian*), police informer leading to culprit's hide-out.
眼系兒 *yaanshieh'l*, n., the structure of nerves, muscles, etc. which constitute the eye (also 眼系子).
眼熟 *yaan-shur*, adj., familiar-looking.
眼同 *yaan-turng*, prep., together with: 眼同證人 (=會同) together with the witness(es).
眼子 *yaantz*, n., a hole in flute, tube, etc.
眼網膜 *yarnwaang-moh*, n., retina.
眼窩(兒)(子) *yaanwo*('*l*)(*tz*), n., the eye socket.
眼暈 *yaanyuhn*, adj., dizzy, giddy.

脈 41B.02-9

moh.

[Cogn. 脈 42A.02]

V. i. (AC) stare with eyes wide open.

睩 41B.02-9

luh.

V. t. (AC) to look, glance.

§ 41B.10 (目/十)

瞵 41B.10-1

lirn.

V. t. (AC) see, descry (of eagles).

睟 41B.10-6

sueih.

Adj. (AC) clear-eyed, shining: 睟然 (AC) shining (face).

瞬 41B.10-9

shuhn.

N. A wink, a flash: 轉瞬之間 in a wink (of time).

V. t. To wink, glance: 瞬目, 瞬盼 to flash a glance.

瞬華 *shuhn-huar*, n., (LL) the rapid passing of time.
瞬間 *shuhn-jian*, adv., in a twinkling.
瞬息 *shuhn-shir*, adv., in a very short moment, like a flash.

睥 41B.10-9

bih.

睥睨 *bihnih*, v. t., look askance at: 睥睨一世 wear a proud, arrogant look, feeling on top of the world.

眸 41B.10-9

mour.

N. (LL) pupil of the eye, the eye in gen.: 明眸皓齒 clear eyes and white teeth.

眸子 *mour-tzyy*, n., (AC) pupil of the eye.

§ 41B.11 (目/土)

睦 41B.11-1

muh.

N. A surname.

Adj. Peaceful, living in peace and friendliness: 和睦 in peace and harmony; 親睦 in friendly relations.

瞠 41B.11-2

cheng.

V.i. To stare, look stunned: 瞠乎

其後 to be left ("staring") far behind.

矐 41B.11-3

huoh.

V. t. (AC) to blind one's eyes in punishment.

睚 41B.11-5

yair.

睚 眦 *yairtzyh*, n., hostile or angry look: 睚眦必報 would seek revenge for even an angry look; 睚眦殺人 kill for trifles.

瞳 41B.11-6

turng.

N. The eye pupil: 瞳孔, 重瞳 double pupils (alleged of great personalities, as 舜, 項羽, etc.).

Adj. (AC) innocent.

瞳 矇 *turngmerng*, adj., (AC) ignorant.
瞳 人(兒) *turngrern(-rern'l)*, n., the pupil of the eye (which reflects the onlooker's image).

睡 41B.11-9

shueih.

V. i. To sleep: 睡覺, 睡眠 *-jiauh, -miarn* ↓; 小睡 nap; 瞌睡 to doze off; 熟睡 sleep soundly; 昏昏欲睡 drowsy; 想睡 feel sleepy.

睡 虎 子 *shueih-huutz*, n., a sleepyhead.
睡 著 *shueih-jaur*, v. i., to go into sleep: 睡著了 is sleeping; 睡不著 cannot sleep.
睡 覺 *shueihjiauh*, v. i., go to bed; go to sleep: 在那兒睡覺 where (are you, am I) going to sleep?
睡 蓮 *shueihliarn*, n., (bot.) a kind of lotus which closes its petals after noon, *Nymphaea tetragona* var. *angustata*.
睡 眠 *sueihmiarn*, v. i. & n., sleep; 睡眠病 *--bihng*, n., sleeping sickness.
睡 魔 *shueih-mor*, n., compulsive desire to sleep.
睡 袍 *shueih-paur*, n., sleeping gown.
睡 晌 覺 *shueihshaangjiauh*, v. i., take afternoon nap.
睡 鄉 *shueih-shiang*, n., (fig.) dreamland.
睡 醒 *shueih-shiing*, v. i., to wake up from sleep.
睡 衣 *shueih-yi*, n., sleeping jacket or gown, pajamas.
睡 遊 病 *shueihyour-bihng*, n., sleepwalking, somnambulism.

睢 41B.11-9

suei.

V. i. (1) (LL) to stare at: 萬衆睢睢 all eyes staring (in hope, wonder). (2) 恣睢 to do what one likes.

§ 41B.21 (目/ㄴ)

眶 41B.21-5

kuahng.

N. Eye socket: 奪眶而出 brim over (with tears).

瞘 41B.21-5

kou.

Adj. With sunken eyes, see 摳ᐞ摟 10A.21.

§ 41B.22 (目/丨)

睇 41B.22-8

dih.

V. i. & t. Glance quickly: 睇視 glance; 斜睇 glance out of corner of eye.

§ 41B.30 (目/一)

瞌 41B.30-1

ke.

瞌 睡 *keshueih*, v. i., take nap, doze off: 打瞌睡, 瞌睡了 is having a nap.

瞪 41B.30-3

dehng.

V.i. & t. Stare: 瞪眼, 瞪著眼 stare wide open; 目瞪口呆 stunned speechless; v.t., 瞪了他一眼 stare, glower, at person.

瞪 視 *dehng-shyh*, v.t., stare one in the face.

§ 41B.32 (目/フ)

眵 41B.32-9

chy.

N. (AC) (med.) eye cataract.

§ 41B.40 (目/口)

瞎 41B.40–6

shia.

Adj. Blind: 盲人騎瞎馬 a blind person riding a blind horse; 瞎了眼睛 oft. a rebuke, you don't seem to know who you are talking to, bump into; 瞎字不識 phr., illiterate.

Adv. Recklessly, blindly, without heed or caution, disorderly: 瞎忙 hustle without plan or purpose; 瞎聊, 瞎談 chat aimlessly, see 瞎說 *-shuo*↓; 瞎猜 a mere conjecture, guess blindly; 瞎找 look for things without plan; 瞎賴 to deny responsibility by talking nonsense; 瞎碰 hope to find s. t. by luck; 瞎貓拖死耗子 a blind cat catching a dead mouse; 瞎摸合眼 to grope in the dark.

瞎 掰 *shiabai*, v. i., to waste effort to no purpose.
瞎 扯 *shiachee*, v. i., to ramble aimlessly; to lie or invent stories.
瞎 道 兒 *shiadauh'l*, n., (1) a futile action; (2) harmful pursuits (=邪道兒).
瞎 話 *shiahuah*, n., a lie.
瞎 抓 *shiajua*, v. i., see *-bai*↑.
瞎 鬧 *shianauh*, v. i., do foolish things; be unruly, boisterous.
瞎 說 *shiashuo*, v.i. & n., (to talk) nonsense: 別瞎說 don't talk nonsense.
瞎 子 *shiatz*, n., a blind person.
瞎 眼 *shia-yaan*, adj., blind, also 瞎了眼.

眙 41B.40–9

chyh.

N. 盱眙 a county in Anhwei.

V.t. To stare at.

瞻 41B.40–9

jan.

[Dist. 贍 *shahn*, 41C.40]

V. i. To look afar, be on the lookout, to hope: 瞻望 *-wahng*↓; 瞻前顧後 to weigh one's steps by thinking of consequences; look about.

瞻 顧 *janguh*, v. i., to look ahead (at the future).
瞻 視 *janshyh*, v. i., to watch attentively.
瞻 徇 *janshyuhn*, v. i., be moved by personal reasons (=徇情).
瞻 望 *janwahng*, v. i., to survey, look ahead (at the future).
瞻 仰 *janyaang*, v. t., (1) to admire (person's character, reputation) from the distance; (2) to look up (at, to).
瞻 依 *janyi*, v. i., to respect and depend upon one's parents, from allu. 靡瞻匪父, 靡依匪母(詩).

§ 41B.41 (目/図)

睹 41B.41–1

duu.

[Var. of 覩 11S.70; dist. 賭 gamble]

瞄 41B.41–2

miaur.

V. i. & t. (1) Glance: 瞄他一眼 throw a quick glance at him. (2) To aim.

瞄 準(兒) *miaurjuun(-juee'l)*, v. i. & t., take aim at (in shooting).
瞄 頭 *miaurtour*, n., (coll.) sign: 我看不出有甚麽瞄頭 I can't see anything special.

睏 41B.41–4

kuhn.

V.i. Sleep: 睏覺 *-jiauh*↓.

Adj. Sleepy.

睏 覺 *kuhnjiauh*, v.i. & adj., go to sleep: 睏覺了 has fallen asleep.

§ 41B.42 (目/冈)

睛 41B.42–1

jing.

N. The pupil of the eye: 眼睛 eyes; 目不轉睛 look at s.t. (s.o.) intently ("without winking"); 睛球 *-chiour*, 睛珠 *-ju*↓.

睛 球 *jingchiour*, n., (physiol.) the eyeball.
睛 珠 *jingju*, n., ditto.

眵 瞎 眙 瞻 睹 瞄 睏 睛

亅	小	⺊	十	土	ナ	廾	𠃊	丨	一	丅	フ	口	図	冈	冂	厂	尸	亠	广	宀	丶	乚	弋	心	八	人	乂	𠂉	一	丿	㇀	く
00	01	02	10	11	12	20	21	22	30	31	32	40	41	42	50	51	52	60	61	62	63	70	71	72	80	81	82	83	90	91	92	93

瞞 41B.42–2

marn.

V. i. & t. Deceive, hide from: 隱瞞 hide secret (from person); 我不瞞你 I am telling you the truth; 實不相瞞 to tell you honestly; 瞞心昧己 blot out one's conscience, deceive oneself; 瞞上欺下 to hoodwink those above and bully those below.

明 41B.42–4

mirng.

[Var. of 明 41A.42]

§ 41B.50 (目/㇕)

眄 41B.50–3

miaan.

V. i. Glance sideways.

眄睞 *miaanlaih,* v. i., (AC) cast loving glance.
眄眄 *miarnmiaan,* adj., (LL) (1) glancing; (2) dull-looking.
眄睨 *miaannih,* adj., (LL) glancing sideways.

矚 41B.50–5

juu.

V. i. To focus eyes on: 高瞻遠矚 having great foresight or plan for the future.

矚目 *juumuh,* v. i., to focus attention (on person, thing).
矚視 *juushyh,* v. t., to eye s. t. with purpose.

盼 41B.50–8

pahn.

V. i. To hope: 切盼 to look forward to anxiously; look kindly at; 盼睞 *-laih* ↓.

Adj. (AC) beautiful (of eyes), clear-eyed.

盼倩 *pahnchiahn,* adj., attractive in looks and smiles.
盼禱 *pahn-daau,* v. i. & n., (court.) my sincere hope, request.
盼睞 *pahnlaih,* v. i., (court.) your favors, consideration.
盼慕 *pahnmuh,* v. t. admire (person) from distance.
盼念 *pahnniahn,* v. i., think of (person), remember from a distance.
盼想 *pahnshiaang,* v. i., to hope.
盼頭 *pahntour,* n., (coll.) hope: 這可有了盼頭 there is hope then.
盼望 *pahnwahng,* v.i. & t., to hope, to yearn for.

肹 41B.50–8

shih.

[Dist. 盼↑]

Adj. (AC) looking on with tired or uneasy look.

§ 41B.63 (目/丶)

瞧 41B.63–9

chiaur.

V. t. To see (in vern. only): 瞧著 *-'je* ↓; 瞧瞧 (看), 瞧一瞧 take a look; 瞧你這樣胡搞 (in scolding) look at what you have done, are doing; 瞧你的 now it's your turn, see what you can do; 瞧熱鬧 go and look at the crowd on holidays; 瞧病 see the doctor; 瞧哈哈(笑)兒 to sit on the side and laugh at (another's discomfort); 甭瞧了 not worth seeing—let's go away; oft. used with 得 and 不: 瞧得起, 瞧不起 have (or have no) regard for (person); 瞧不起他 look down upon him; 瞧得過兒 passable; 瞧不過兒 intolerable; 瞧得透, 瞧不透 see through, fail to do so; 瞧得慣, 瞧不慣 used or not used to the sight of (such injustice, rowdiness, hippies, etc.).

瞧著 *chiaur'je,* phr., that depends, depending on circumstances; 瞧著辦 act on your discretion; 瞧著給 you decide how much to give (to each).
瞧見 *chiaurjiahn,* v. t., to see: 他瞧見了 he saw it; 瞧不見 cannot see.
瞧上 *chiaur'shang,* v. t., to admire and wish to have: 瞧上一個金表 (a thief) sets his eye on a gold watch.

§ 41B.70 (目/乚)

盹 41B.70–1

duun (also *duhn*).

N. & v.t. (Take) a nap: 打盹, 打了一個盹兒; 盹睡 take a nap.

眦 41B.70–2

tzyh.

[Var. 眥 21A.41]

A

眺 41B.70–2

tiauh.

V.i. To scan, survey the distance: 遠眺, 憑眺.

眺望 *tiauhwahng*, v.i., survey or see at a distance.

睍 41B.70–4

shiahn.

Adj. (LL) overcautious: 伈伈睍睍 timorous (manner).

矓 41B.70–6

lurng.

Adj. See 矇^矓 41B.02.

眊 41B.70–9

mauh.

Adj. (1) (AC) blurred in eyesight: 眊聵 weak in eyesight and heavy of hearing. (2) Var. of 耄 11.70.

眊 眊 *mauhmauh*, adj., dim in vision.

睨 41B.70–9

nih.

V. i. To squint: 斜睨 to look askance.

B

眈 41B.70–9

dan.

Adv. With a covetous look, in 虎視眈眈 (of tiger) casting a greedy eye on its prey.

§ 41B.71 (目/弋)

眠 41B.71–5

miarn.

N. & v. i. (LL) sleep: 睡眠 sleep; 眠在地下 sleep on the floor; 長眠 die; 冬眠 hibernate; 蠶眠 silkworm's dormancy; 醉眠 drunk asleep; 眠花宿柳 sleep in brothels; 眠思夢想 think of lover; 眠雲 live like hermits, "sleep on clouds"; 眠輿 sedan chair good for taking a nap.

§ 41B.80 (目/八)

瞋 41B.80–2

chen.

V.i. & t. To glower, glance at (person) with anger (interch. 嗔).

聵 41B.80–2

gueih (kueih).
[Dist. 瞶]

Adj. Dim-sighted, blind: 振聾啟聵 (LL) open the ears of the deaf and the eyes of the blind—said of a great teacher.

C

矉 41B.80–6

pirn.
[Rare var. of 顰 22.10]

V. t. (AC) stare with hatred.

瞑 41B.80–6

*mirng (*miing, *miahn).*
[Cogn. 冥]

V.i. To close the eyes: 瞑目而逝 closed one's eyes and passed away; 死不瞑目 die without closing eyes, i.e., with regret, with grudge unsatisfied.

瞑 瞑 *mirngmirng*, adj., hazy, dim-sighted.

瞑 眩 **miahnshyuarn*, (AC) upset, giddy: 若藥不瞑眩, 厥疾不瘳 a potent medicine does not cure disease without a spell of dizziness.

§ 41B.81 (目/人)

睽 41B.81–3

kueir.

V. i. (1) (Interch. 暌 LL) to be separated (among friends). (2) (LL) to avoid seeing, to look askance.

Adj. (LL) singular, queer, odd, incompatible.

瞡瞡 *kueirkueir*, v.i. & adj., as in 衆目瞡瞡 all eyes are directed toward (person, object).

瞅 41B.81–9

choou.

V. t. (1) To see (related 瞧 *chyaur*): 瞅不見 cannot see or find (object); 瞅不得 is not to be seen. (2) To pry, watch for opportunity: 瞅空兒 *-kuhng'l* ↓ (3) To cast a look: 瞅著他 fix a look on him; 不瞅不理 completely ignore (person); 瞅睬 *-tsaai* ↓.

瞅空兒 *chourkuhng'l*, v. i., wait for an opportunity.

瞅睬 *chourtsaai*, v. t., to cast a look at, hence to pay attention: 全不瞅睬 won't pay any attention (to person's words).

§ 41B.82 (目/乂)

瞰 41B.82–3

kahn.

V. i. & t. To overlook (distant view): 俯瞰城中 overlook the town (from high position); 鳥瞰(圖) bird's-eye view.

§ 41B.83 (目/乛)

睫 41B.83–1

jier.

N. The eyelash: 迫在眉睫 of the utmost urgency; 近在眉睫 close at hand; 交睫 close the eyelids: 目不交睫 have not had any sleep at all; 眉睫之間 in close proximity.

瞇 41B.83–2

mi.

[Also wr. 眯]

V. i. Barely close the eyelids: 瞇一瞇眼兒 have a cat nap, doze uncomfortably; 瞇縫眼兒 eyes close into a narrow slit.

眨 41B.83–9

jaa.

[Dist. 貶 41C.83]

V. i. To wink.

眨眼 *jar-yaan*, phr., to make a wink: 眨眼會意 give a wink (as silent signal); 眨眼工夫 in the winking of an eye—a short moment; 眨眼就過去了 will pass away in a very short while; 殺人不眨眼 kill man without batting an eye, coldly, brutally (also 眨眼, 眨巴).

§ 41B.91 (目/丿)

眇 41B.91–2

miaau.

[Cogn. 渺, 藐, 杳]

V. i. & t. (U. f. 瞄) to aim at: 眇準.

Adj. (1) Blind in one eye: 眇一目. (2) Very small, minute: 眇乎小哉 (AC) how small it is!

眇眇 *miaurmiaau*, adj., very small, distant: 眇眇忽忽 *--hu'hu*, elusive, hardly discernible (shape), also wr. 渺渺.

眇小 *miaaushiaau*, adj., very small (=渺小).

§ 41B.93 (目/𡿨)

瞜 41B.93–2

lou.

V. t. (Coll.) glance, look at: 瞜他一眼 give him a glance.

眩 41B.93–6

shyuahn.

Adj. Dizzy, giddy: 目眩 eyes dizzy; 頭眩 giddy.

眩晃 *shyuahn-huahng*, adj., (eyes) dazzled.

眩疾 *shyuahnjir*, n., (LL) fainting fits.

眩人 *shyuahnrern*, n., (AC) magician.

眩眩 *shyuahnshyuahn*, adj., giddy, dizzy.

眩暈 *shyuahnyuhn*, v. t. & n., to faint, swoon off; a fainting fit.

A B C

SECTION 41C

§ 41C.00 (貝/亅)

財 41C.00-1

tsair.

N. (1) Wealth, money and goods: 財貨, 財物, 財產 *-huoh*, *-wuh*, *-chaan* ↓; 財富 *-fuh*[1] ↓; 財政 *-jehng* ↓; 發財 make money, get rich; 理財 manage finance; 生財 produce wealth, make money; 不義之財 ill-gotten gains; 財不露眼 let not your wealth be exposed. (2) (AC) u. f. 才 talent: 有達財者 some great talents. (3) (AC) u. f. 裁 decision: 財察＝裁察 your discerning judgment; 財取 select and take.

財 寶 *tsairbaau*, n., goods, properties.

財 帛 *tsairbor*, n., money and silks (often used as presents).

財 產 *tsairchaan*, n., properties (of person, firm); 財產權 property right.

財 氣(兒) *tsair'chih* (-*'chieh'l*), n., luck or good fortune in making money.

財 權 *tsairchyuarn*, n., (law) right of ownership.

財 東 *tsair-dung*, n., formerly, financial backer.

財 閥 *tsairfar*, n., financial magnate.

財 富 *tsairfuh*[1], n., wealth (of nations, etc.).

財 賦 *tsairfuh*[2], n., wealth and taxes, government income.

財 賄 *tsairhueih*, n., (AC) tax on grains and goods.

財 貨 *tsairhuoh*, n., goods; wealth.

財 政 *tsairjehng*, n., public finance: 財政部長 minister of finance.

財 主 *tsairjuu*, n., (1) owner of properties; (2) (-*'ju*) formerly, a wealthy person.

財 力 *tsairlih*, n., financial power.

財 禮 *tsairlii*, n., gift in money to family of betrothed girl.

財 命(兒) *tsair'ming('l)*, n., see *-yuhn* ↓.

財 迷 *tsair-mir*, adj., money-mad.

財 神 *tsairshern* (-*'shen*), n., god of wealth; an extremely wealthy person.

財 團 *tsairtuarn*, n., a banking group which finances a business; a financial syndicate.

財 物 *tsairwuh*, n., wealth and properties.

財 緣 兒 *tsairyuar'l*, n., see *-yuhn* ↓.

財 源 *tsairyuarn*, n., source of money, financial resources.

財 運 *tsairyuhn*, n., luck in making money.

財 用 *tsairyuhng*, n., finance, financial management.

賻 41C.00-1

fuh.

N. Gift of money at funeral: 賻贈, see 賻儀 *-yir* ↓.

賻 儀 *fuhyir*, n., funeral gift of money.

則 41C.00-2

tzer.

N. (1) Rule, law, regulation: 法則 a pattern, rule or law; 規則 regulation; 準則 standard, criterion; 以身作則 set oneself up as an example; 則例 *-lih* ↓; 例則 an example; 則度 *-duh* ↓; 有物有則 there are things and laws to govern them; 稅則 tariffs, customs duties. (2) Grades: 等則 classes and grades. (3) An item: 笑話一則 a joke; 新聞一則 a news story.

V. t. (1) Make, do: 則聲 make a noise; 不則聲 keep silent. (2) Copy, imitate: 唯天爲大, 唯堯則之 (AC) great is Heaven and only Yao would imitate its ways; 則天 to imitate Heaven.

Adv. (1) Only: 多則一年, 少則半載 between six months and a year; 則是 only that (＝只是): 則是年紀小, 性氣剛 only that he is too young and self-willed. (2) Then: 不進則退 either one goes forward or he will be left behind; 君子不重則不威 if a superior man doesn't behave with dignity, he will command no respect (cf. 卽 *jir*, to be; immediately).

Conj. (MC) but, however: 人皆好名, 我則不然 others may be fond of titles and honors, but I am not.

Prep. For: 則甚 why? what for? 則恁 ditto (corruption of 做甚).

則 刀 兒 *tzerdau'l*, n., the character "刀" used as a radical and written "刂," as in "列," "則," "利," "別," etc.

則 度 *tzerduh*, n., regulations, rules.

則 個 *tzergeh*, phr., (MC) used as a final particle in a sentence for purposes of emphasis.

則 例 *tzerlih*, n., a set example to be followed, a precedent.

貯 41C.00-6

juu.

[Related 儲 *chuu*, 91A.41]

V. i. & t. To store up.

貯 備 *juubeih*, v. t., to save, hoard for future needs.

貯 蓄 *juushyuh*, v. i. & t., to save, have savings (also 儲[Δ]蓄 91A.41).

貯藏 *juutsarng*, v. i. & t., to keep in vault or storehouse.

§ 41C.01 (貝/小)

賒 41C.01–8

she.

V. i. To buy on credit: 賒欠, 賒賬 *-chiahn, -jahng*↓.

Adj. (MC, poet.) long, distant (journey).

賒欠 *shechiahn*, v. i., to owe account, to buy on credit.
賒賬 *shejahng*, v. i., ditto.

§ 41C.02 (貝/ㄎ)

賕 41C.02–1

chiour.

N. & v. t. (LL) bribe, -ery.

賑 41C.02–5

jehn.

N. Relief, as in 施賑 give relief to (the poor, famine victims).

V. t. To relieve (the poor, famine victims, etc.).

Adj. (AC) rich: 鄉邑殷賑 the countryside is prosperous.

賑濟 *jehnjih*, v. t., to relieve, help with food, necessities or money.
賑款 *jehn-kuaan*, n., relief fund.
賑贍 *jehnshahn*, v. t., see *-jih*↑.
賑災 *jehn-tzai*, v. i., to work for relief of victims of natural disaster.

賬 41C.02–5

jahng.

[Pop. of 帳; var. of 帳 in sense of "accounts," 22B.02]

§ 41C.11 (貝/土)

賍 41C.11–6

tzang.

[Pop. for 贓 41C.71]

§ 41C.22 (貝/丨)

賺 41C.22–8

*juahn (*tzuahn).*

V. t. (1) To gain, profit: 賺錢 *-chiarn*↓: 賺得 to gain; 賺得不少 earn a great deal of profit; 賺利息 earn interest; 賺夠本 get capital back, break even; (fig.) gain: 賺吃 get meals free; 賺便宜 gain advantage; 賺好處 gain profit; 賺好名 earn a good name. (2) (**tzuahn*) To cheat, play tricks: 賺騙 *-piahn*↓; 賺弄 to fool s. o.: 受人賺弄 was fooled by others.

賺錢 *juahn-chiarn*, v. i., to make money: 不賺錢 sell at cost.
賺騙 **tzuahnpiahn*, v. t., to fool, cheat (s. o.).
賺頭兒 *juahn'tou'l*, n., profit: 沒多大賺頭兒 not much profit (in this).

§ 41C.30 (貝/一)

贐 41C.30–2

jihn.

N. Parting gifts: 贐儀 farewell presents; 餽贐 delicacies as gifts to parting friends.

賉 41C.30–9

shyuh.

[Var. of 卹 91S.22]

§ 41C.40 (貝/口)

貼 41C.40–2

tie.

V.i. (1) To paste up or on: 貼郵票 stick stamps on a letter; 貼在一齊 paste together; 貼膏藥 stick on medicated ointment plaster; 貼在牆上 stick (poster) on wall. (2) To make up a deficiency: 貼錢 to lose in bargain; 倒貼 to sell at a loss; to support a gigolo (e.g., 倒貼小白臉); 津貼, 幫貼 to subsidize, a subsidy; 貼匯水 discount on exchange, see 貼水 *-shueei*↓. (3) To come close, snuggle close: 貼近 come close; 貼着席子睡 sleep on a mat; 貼着臉 face rubbing against face; 貼耳 lend ear closely to listen; 他們兩個人貼着 they snuggle in each other's arms; 體貼 v.t., be considerate of (person).

Adj. Cozy, well settled: 妥貼 (affair) well arranged, settled; 熨貼 cozy, warmly attached to.

貼本 *tiebeen*, adj., below cost: 貼本生意 a losing business.
貼補 *tiebuu*, v.t., subsidize: 貼補家用 help out with expenses.
貼切 *tieicheh*, adj., very much to the point (instructions).
貼旦 *tiedahn*, n., (MC) formerly, secondary female actress.
貼梗海棠 *tiegerng haaitarng*, n., (bot.) a kind of wild pear, *Pirus spectabilis* (also called 海棠梨).
貼近 *tiejihn*, adj., close (neighbor, servants).
貼己 *tiejii*, adj., intimate, close (talk).
貼金 *tiejin*, adj., gilt, gold-plated (ring, etc.): 別往臉上貼金 (fig.) don't blow your own trumpet.
貼身(兒) *tieshen (-she'l)*, adj., personal (maid): 貼身丫頭 personal maid, (underclothes) worn next to body; (dress) fitting.
貼現 *tieshiahn*, v.i., discount on checks.
貼書 *tieshu*, n., formerly, copyist-clerk.
貼水 *tieshueei*, n., discount due to inferior intrinsic value of coins.

賠 41C.40-6

peir.

V. i. (1) To lose money, make up deficit, indemnify, compensate: 賠他多少錢 compensate (person) for his loss; 賠不起 cannot afford to repay for loss or damage. (2) U.f. 陪 apologize (for mistake), see 陪△不是, 陪△罪 32A.40.

賠本(兒) *peirbeen(-bee'l)*, v. i., to lose money in investment.
賠補 *peirbuu*, v. i. & t., make up for loss: 賠補損失.
賠錢貨 *peirchiarn-huoh*, n., (facet.) (the raising of) daughter as a losing proposition on account of dowry.
賠償 *peircharng*, v. t. pay indemnity to (person) for (loss); repay (debt).
賠墊 *peir-diahn*, v. i., to put money in to keep business going.
賠還 *peirhuarn*, v. t., repay (person) for loss, repay (debt).
賠款 *peirkuaan*, n., indemnity.
賠累 *peirleih*, v. i. & n., to lose money steadily.
賠釋 *peirshyh*, v. i., apologize (var. 陪△侍 32A.40).
賠贈 *peirtzehng*, n., dowry, gift from bride's family.

賂 41C.40-9

luh.

N. Gift in kind; goods.

V. t. To bribe with money or gifts: 賄賂.

贍 41C.40-9

shahn.
[Dist. 瞻]

V. t. To support financially (parents, widows): 贍恤, 贍養 *-shyuh*, *-yaang* ↓.

Adj. (1) (LL) adequate: 力不贍也 beyond one's strength. (2) Rich (in style): 典贍 rich and elegant.

贍恤 *shahnshyuh*, v. t., to give subsidy to (those in distress).
贍養 *shahnyaang*, v. t., to support (parents, widows) financially; 贍養費 allowance for maintenance, alimony.

貽 41C.40-9

yir.
[Related 遺 22.83]

V. i. & t. (1) To give as present. (2) To bequeath.

貽害 *yirhaih*, v. t., to cause trouble to future or future generations.
貽禍 *yirhuoh*, v. t., to bring about disaster, disadvantage or harm to future.
貽厥 *yirjyuer*, n., (pedantic allu.) descendants (from 貽厥孫謀).
貽累 *yirleei*, v. t., to involve others in trouble.
貽謀 *yirmour*, n., policy or plan handed down to descendants, see *-jyuer* ↑.
貽笑 *yirshiauh*, v. t., to invite ridicule: 貽笑大方 be laughed at by experts.
貽羞 *yirshiou*, v. t., to bring shame to oneself.
貽訓 *yirshyuhn*, n., ancestral advice, instructions (=遺訓).
貽送 *yirsuhng*, v. t., to give as gift (to person).
貽贈 *yirtzehng*, v. t., ditto.
貽誤 *yirwuh*, v. t., to spoil, cause disruption (of plan, traffic): 貽誤大局 disrupt the gen. plan.
貽遺 *yiryir*, v. t., to hand down (to posterity).

§ 41C.41 (貝/図)

賭 41C.41-1

duu.

V.i. & t. (1) To gamble, wager, bet: 賭輸贏 bet with money; 賭東兒 bet with a dinner as forfeit; 賭麻將, 撲克 play mahjong, poker; 賭運氣 play for luck, try luck; see compp.↓. (2) To contest: 賭賽 contest (in athletics); 賭力氣 contest in strength; 賭眼力 bet who has better judgment.

賭博 *duubor*, v.i. & n., to gamble, gambling.
賭場 *duucharng*, n., gambling place.
賭錢 *duuchiarn*, v.i., bet money, gamble.
賭氣 *duuchih*, adv., for spite, out of rage: 賭氣走了 went away in a rage (against calmer judgment).
賭犯 *duufahn*, n., arrested gambler.
賭鬼 *durgueei*, n., confirmed gambler.
賭棍 *duuguhn*, n., (derog.) professional gambler, cardsharper.
賭債 *duujaih*, n., gambling debts.
賭咒 *duujouh*, v.i. & n., swear; an oath (to do, or not do, s.t.).
賭具 *duujyuh*, n., things used in gambling (dice, etc.).
賭局 *duujyur*, n., gambling party.
賭賽 *duusaih*, v.i. & n., contest.
賭誓 *duushyh*, v.i., to swear.
賭徒 *duutur*, n., habitual gambler.

賵 41C.41-4

fehng.

N. (AC) funeral gifts.

贈 41C.41-8

tzehng.

V. t. (1) To present (s.o.) with a gift: 贈品 *-piin*↓; 贈送 *-suhng*↓; 贈給 give a present to (friend); 贈遺 send a gift to s.o.; 贈與 *-yuu*↓; 互贈 give presents to each other; 餽贈 make a present of; 敬贈 "cordially (respectfully) presented by"; 遺贈 to leave as gift; 捐贈 donate, make financial or other contribution (for charity or other purpose). (2) Confer honorary titles on deserving government officials: 追贈 confer posthumous honors; 封贈 (of ancestors of officials) ditto; 誥贈 (of ancestors of high-ranking officials) ditto by royal mandate.

贈別 *tzehng-bier*, v. t., bid good-bye to (departing friend), see (s.o.) off.
贈賻 *tzehngfuh*, v. i., send money gift to a family in mourning.
贈品 *tzehngpiin(-'pin)*, n., a present, gift.
贈序 *tzehngshyuh*, n., a form of literary composition conveying the writer's best wishes to a departing friend.
贈送 *tzehngsuhng*, v. t., give a present to (s.o.).
贈言 *tzehng-yarn*, n., words of advice sent to a departing friend.
贈與 *tzehng-yuu*, v. t. & n., donate, -tion; (make) a grant-in-aid (opp. 貸款 loans).

§41C.42 (貝/冈)

賄 41C.42-1

hueih (also *hueei*).

N. (1) Bribery: 行賄 commit bribery: 受賄 receive bribes. (2) Goods (related 貨).

V. t. To bribe: 賄賂 *-luh*↓; 賄選 buy votes for election; 賄買 buy votes or office appointment with money; 賄託 ask s. o. to do s. t. for a consideration.

賄賂 *hueihluh*, n. & v. t., bribery; to bribe (s. o.).

購 41C.42-2

gouh.

V.t. Buy, purchase: 購備 buy for future use; 採購 purchase supplies, goods (for business); 收購 buy up; 求購 offer to buy; 購入 buy in; 購買 *-maai*↓.

購辦 *gouhbahn*, v.t., (business house) buy goods.
購買 *gouhmaai*, v.t., to purchase.
購買力 *gouhmaailih*, n., the purchasing power.

賙 41C.42-4

jou.

V. t. To help in charity: 賙濟, 賙恤 (usu. wr. 周).

§41C.50 (貝/冂)

賜 41C.50-4

syh (sp. pr. *tsyh*).

N. A favor, a grant from a superior, a gift.

V. t. To grant (favor, award): 賞賜, 惠賜, 賜給 (court.) to give.

賜帛 *syh-bor*, phr., (of emperor) to grant a white silk for committing suicide by hanging.
賜復 *syh-fuh*, phr., be so kind as to grant a reply.
賜福 *syh-fur*, v. i., (of god) to bless.
賜光 *syh-guang*, v. i., to give "face," to honor one with presence.
賜顧 *syhguh*, v. i., (court.) to honor one by visiting or buying from a shop.
賜環 *syh-huarn*, phr., (AC) grant a jade ring as a symbol to call back to office.
賜教 *syh-jiauh*, phr., (court.)

please advise, please let me know.

賜姓 *syh-shihng*, phr., an extraordinary honor of granting person the same surname as the emperor's.

賜示 *syhshyh*, (1) n., (court.) your kind letter or reply; (2) v. i., be so kind as to reply.

賜死 *syh-syy*, phr., formerly, (of emperor) grant a person the privilege of suicide.

賜宴 *syh-yahn*, phr., (court.) to give graciously a dinner (to a friend).

賜予(與) *syh-yuu*, v. t., (AC) to give to (person).

§41C.63 (貝/丶)

貺 41C.63–5

jihn.

[Abbr. of 贐 41C.30]

§41C.70 (貝/乚)

貺 41C.70–4

kuahng.

N. (1) A surname. (2) (LL) a gift, present.

§41C.71 (貝/弋)

賊 41C.71–7

tzeir (sometimes AC re. pr. **tzer*).

N. A thief, robber, traitor, rebel, enemy: 盜賊 robbers, bandits; 賊子 a young rascal: 亂臣賊子 rebels and traitors; 賣國賊 a traitor, a quisling; 民賊 an enemy of the people; 家賊(難防) a thief from within (is hard to guard against); 毛賊 a term of abuse for thieves, a burglar; 賊黨 band of rebels, gang of thieves (robbers); 賊兵 enemy forces, rebel troops; 賊類 robbers, rebels, brigands; 賊首 a rebel chief, the leader of a gang of thieves (robbers); 賊頭兒 ditto; 賊性難改 the habitual criminal is incorrigible; 賊出關門 lock the barn after the horse is stolen; 作賊心虛 uneasy lies the head of one with a guilty conscience; 賊巢 thieves' (robbers') den; 賊窠子 ditto; 賊店 an inn run by a member of the underworld; 賊贓 booty, spoils, plunder; 賊相 criminal looks; 賊骨頭 a petty thief; 賊囚根(子) (abusive) a bad egg; 賊禿 (abusive) (of a monk) a shining pate.

V. t. Kill: 賊害 *-haih*↓; 賊虐 terrorize, ill-treat.

Adj. Wily, treacherous, deceitful: 眼睛發賊 with a villainous look in the eye; 賊眉賊眼 roguish looks; 賊頭賊腦 treacherous looks; 賊鬼溜滑 dishonest, deceitful, tricky.

Adv. Extraordinarily, unusually: 賊亮 *-liahng*↓.

賊冰 *tzeir-bing*, n., treacherous icy spots or road.

賊風 *tzeir-feng* (*tzer-*), n., a draft which, unnoticed, may cause a cold.

賊鬼 *tzeir'guei*, adj., sensitive and wily, treacherous.

賊害 *tzeirhaih* (1) n., source of trouble, what is injurious; (2) v. t., to murder, kill (person).

賊話兒 *tzeir-huah'l*, n., as in 聽賊話兒 to eavesdrop.

賊亮 *tzeirliahng*, adj., uncomfortably bright, glaring, dazzling.

賊肉 *tzeir-rouh*, n., (contempt.) fatty tissue: 長一身賊肉 (of a person) overgrown with fat.

賊性 *tzeir-shihng*, n., (1) wiles, trickery; (2) wickedness, viciousness, villainy.

賊心 *tzeir-shin*, n., a wicked heart.

賊星 *tzeir-shing*, n., (1) a meteor; (2) an evil star: 賊星發旺 (sarcastic) (of a mean fellow) have a streak of good luck.

賊眼 *tzeir-yaan*, n., a knavish look.

賦 41C.71–7

fuh.

N. (1) Tax, levy: 賦役 levy of labor; 田賦, 賦課 tax, levies on crops, merchandise. (2) Natural endowment: 天賦, 稟賦 born gift (for music, poetry, etc.). (3) A special form of rhapsodic poem, chiefly in parallel constructions, often wr. for celebration of event.

V.t. (1) To give, endow: 賦與(予) give to; 天賦之才 God-given talent; 賦有 be endowed (with some gift). (2) To levy or pay tax: 賦稅. (3) To compose poetry: 賦詩 compose poem on occasion; 賦事陳詞 write poem descriptive of occasion. (4) (AC) spread (= 布).

賦稟 *fuhbiing*, n., natural endowment.

賦額 *fuh-er*, n., tax rate.

賦貢 *fuhguhng*, v.t. & n., (pay) tribute to emperor.

賦斂 *fuhliahn*, v.t. & n., levy taxes.

賦閑 *fuhshiarn*, v.i., (euphem.) be unemployed ("compose poem on idleness").

賦性 *fuhshihng*, n., natural temperament.

賦役 *fuhyih*, v.t. & n., gen. term for farm tax and labor levy (combined in Manchu Dyn.).

賤 41C.71–7

jiahn.

V. t. Despise, look down upon: 賤之 regard as worthless; 賤視 to disdain, scorn; 輕賤 treat with indifference.

Adj. (1) Cheap, inexpensive, worthless: 賤價 *-jiah*, 賤物 *-wuh* ↓; 賤賣 sell cheap; 賤售 ditto. (2) Lowly, humble: 低賤 lowly; 卑賤 humble. (3) (Self-deprecatory) my, my humble: 賤內 *-neih*, 賤軀 *-chyu*, 賤室 *-shyh*, 賤恙 *-yahng* ↓; 賤姓 my name. (4) Despicable: 賤人 *-rern*, 賤骨頭 *-gur'tou* ↓; 下賤 low, mean, base, low-down; 賤女人 a shameless woman, a cheap woman.

賤妾 *jiahn-chieh*, n., (1) a concubine of inferior rank; (2) (of a woman referring to herself in speaking to her husband) "I, your unworthy wife." 「self.
賤軀 *jiahn-chyu*, n., my worthless
賤骨頭 *jiahn-gur'tou*, n., a worthless scamp.
賤貨 *jiahn-huoh*, n., (1) cheap goods; (2) a contemptible fellow, a mean person, (abuse) "hussy."
賤價 *jiahn-jiah*, adj., low-priced.
賤丈夫 *jiahn-jiahngfu*, n., a shameless and avaricious person.
賤內 *jiahn-neih*, n., my (worthless) wife (cf. "my better half").
賤年 *jiahn-niarn*, n., a year of drought.
賤人 *jiahn-rern*, n., a term of reprobation for women.
賤息 *jiahnshir*, n., (rare) my unworthy son.
賤室 *jiahnshyh*, n., my wife.
賤物 *jiahn-wuh*, n., a thing of little or no value, trash.
賤恙 *jiahn-yahng*, n., my illness.
賤業 *jiahn-yieh*, n., a dishonorable business, a lowly occupation.

臟 41C.71–7

tzang.

N. Booty: 臟物 *-wuh*[2] ↓; 賊臟 stolen goods; 分臟 divide booty among (between) thieves.

Adj. Corrupt: 臟官 *-guan* ↓.

臟官 *tzang-guan*, n., a corrupt official.
臟埋 *tzangmair*, v. t., (MC) malign, slander, accuse falsely.
臟誣 *tzangwuh*[1], v. t., ditto.
臟物 *tzangwuh*[2], n., booty, stolen goods.

§ 41C.80 (貝/八)

贖 41C.80–1

shur.

[Abbr. 赎]

V. t. (1) To ransom, redeem: 贖回, 贖出 redeem (pawned article), buy back (sold children), pay ransom (for kidnapped person); 贖身 *-shen* ↓; 贖命 *-mihng* ↓; 取贖 to ransom; 百死莫贖 irredeemable mistake. (2) To atone for: 贖罪 *-tzueih* ↓. (3) To pay for (a prescription).

贖當 *shur-dahng*, n., redeem pawns.
贖回 *shurhueir*, v. t., to redeem (pawn, life, sold child).
贖命 *shur-mihng*, v. i., to pay price for pardon of criminal.
贖身 *shur-shen*, v. i., to buy back freedom (for slaves, prostitutes). 「for sin.
贖罪 *shur-tzueih*, v. i., to atone

§ 41C.81 (貝/人)

賅 41C.81–6

gai.

Adj. Comprehensive, all-inclusive: 意簡言賅 a few simple ideas succinctly expressed; 簡賅 simple and concise.

§ 41C.82 (貝/乂)

販 41C.82–9

fahn.

N. Pedlar, hawker, itinerant salesman, keeper of small booth (*-tz*): 小販 small pedlar; 攤販 booth keeper; 奴販子 slave dealer; 人肉販子 white slave traffic dealer; 販夫走卒 small tradesmen and porters.

V. t. To peddle, vend, sell: 販菜, 販魚, 販食物 sell vegetable, fish, foodstuff; esp. ship and sell, see 販賣 *-maih* ↓.

販賣 *fahnmaih*, v. t., deal in some traffic: 販賣鴉片 deal in opium traffic; 販賣人口 dealer in white slave traffic.
販運 *fahnyuhn*, v. t., transport for trade.

敗 41C.82–9

baih.

V. i. & t. (1) To fail, usu. 失敗: 事情, 計劃失敗了. (2) (AC) to defeat: 敗秦師 defeated the *Chirn* army; (modn.) 把敵打敗 defeat the enemy, also 擊敗. (3) To break (alliance, treaty 敗盟, 敗約). (4) To spoil (good name of family 敗家風).

Adj. (1) Defeated: 敗兵, 敗軍 defeated troops; 打敗仗 defeated in battle; 敗不成軍 army is completely routed. (2) Spoiled, broken-down: 敗家子弟 children of broken-down family or children who ruin the family; 敗葉, 草 withered leaves, grass; 敗絮 old cotton wool as stuffing for quilts; 敗柳殘花 prostitutes no longer young, hags or women no longer pure; 敗肉 bad flesh, like gangrene; 敗血病 *-shyueh-bihng*↓.

敗北 *baihbeei*, v. i., be defeated.
敗筆 *baih-bii*, n., a bad stroke in callig., a flaw in writing.
敗羣(之馬) *baihchyurn*, (=害羣) n., one whose conduct hurts the whole group (like "scab" in labor union).
敗道 *baih-dauh*, adj., one who fails in discipline to become Taoist immortal.
敗德 *baih-der*, n., atrocious behavior, licentious character.
敗壞 *baih-huaih*, v. i. & t., to spoil, destroy, corrupt; p.p., corrupt, spoiled: 敗壞門楣 to shame the name of the house (門楣 lintel).
敗火 *baih-huoo*, adj., (of medicine which) brings down fever.
敗績 *baihji*, v. i., (LL) suffers defeat.
敗家子(兒) *baih-jia tzyy(-tzel)*, n., black sheep of the family.
敗醬 *baihjiahng*, n., (bot.) *Patrinia scabiosaefolia*, with edible stem, so named because it smells like spoiled sauce, also called 苦菜 ("bitter vegetable").
敗類 *baih-leih*, n., the bad elements of a class or group; a shameless lout.
敗露 *baih-luh*, v. i., (of secret plan) leak out.
敗落 *baih-luoh*, v. i., fail, become poor, (of flower) wither.
敗衄 *baihnyuh*, v. i., (LL) be defeated in war.
敗興 *baih-shihng*, v. i., feel disappointed, frustrated; crestfallen.
敗訴 *baihshuh*, n. & v. i., lose, loss in lawsuit.
敗血病 *baih-shyueh-bihng*, n., (med.) blood infection (*septicemia*).
敗歲 *baih-sueh*, n., year of bad crops.
敗財 *baih-tsair*, phr., (foretunetelling) destined to lose money.
敗挫 *baih-tsuoh*, p.p., routed.
敗退 *baih-tueih*, v. i., be defeated and flee.
敗子 *baih-tzyy*, n., prodigal son: 敗子悔改 prodigal son's repentance; 敗子回頭 return of prodigal son.

§ 41C.83 (貝/乛)

貶 41C.83-9

biaan.

N. Criticism, reduction in price, degrading in rank: 貶詞, 貶評 words of criticism; 褒貶 praise or blame, also v. t., criticize (person, work).

V. t. Reduce: 貶價 reduce in price; degrade in rank, post; 貶黜, 貶抑 *-chuh, -yih*↓.

貶黜 *biaanchuh*, v. t., demote.
貶謫 *biaanjer*, v. t., degrade in rank, send to lower post (often in remote provinces).
貶損 *biarnsuun*, v. t. criticize (person), damage (reputation).
貶抑 *biaanyih*, v. t., put (person) in his place.

SECTION 41D

§ 41D.00 (皿/亅)

羈 41D.00-2

ji.

[Pop. 覊 31.00; dist. 羈 41D.50]

N. An inn, a lodging house.

V. i. To sojourn, be away from home: 羈旅 *-lyuu*↓.

羈愁 *jichour*, adj. & n., homesick (-ness).
羈滯 *jijyh*, v. i., (be) forced to remain at a place longer than one has expected.
羈客 *jikeh*, n., a traveller.
羈旅 *jilyuu*, n., one who is away from home: 羈旅之臣 a government official living in exile.

罽 41D.00-5

jih.

N. Rug, carpet.

罰 41D.00-6

far.

[Pop. 罸]

N. & v. t. Punish, -ment, penalty, fine: 受罰 be punished; 處罰, 刑罰, 懲罰 punish; sentence to: 罰跪, 罰立 make person kneel, stand (in corner) as punishment; 罰做苦工 sentence to hard labor; 罰酒 drink (so many cups of) wine as forfeit; 罰球 penalty kick (foot-

亅	小	⺊	十	土	ナ	廾	⺊	丨	一	丅	フ	口	区	冈	㇕	厂	尸	亠	广	宀	丶	乚	乁	心	八	人	乂	乛	乛	丿丿	⺈	く
00	01	02	10	11	12	20	21	22	30	31	32	40	41	42	50	51	52	60	61	62	63	70	71	72	80	81	82	83	90	91	92	93

ball); 罰錢, 金, 款, 鍰 fine, be fined money.

罰金 *far-jin*, n., fine money.

罦 41D.00-9

fur.

N. A bird trap.

§41D.02 (罒/k)

眾 41D.02-9

juhng.

[Var. of 91.02 衆; pop. 眾]

§41D.10 (罒/十)

睪 41D.10-1

gau.

N. 睪丸 the testicles.

罩 41D.10-2

jauh.

N. (1) A bamboo basket for catching fish. (2) (*-tz*, *-'l*) Cover: 燈罩 lampshade; 罩衫, 罩袍 outer jacket, garment.

V. t. To cover from on top; (fig.) to darken one's heart like a shadow.

§41D.11 (罒/土)

罣 41D.11-1

guah.

V. t. Hinder: 罣礙 obstruct, impede; 罣誤 be delayed by some hindrance.

罣礙 *guah-aih*, v. t., obstruct, impede (also wr. 掛礙).

罣誤 *guahwuh*, n. & v. i., delay; missing word or error in print.

罹 41D.11-2

lir.

N. Sorrow, grief, troubles.

V. t. Be caught in: 罹難 die a tragic death, fall victim to a disaster; 罹禍 be killed in an accident, implicated in a political crime.

羅 41D.11-9

luor.

N. (1) A net for catching birds: 門可羅雀 can set up bird trap at house door—complete absence of callers; 羅掘 to spread net for sparrows and dig for rats in times of starvation—forced to borrow, beg, mortgage; 羅掘俱窮 exhaust all sources of getting money; 天羅地網 (Taoist magic) invisible net in air and on land to prevent escape. (2) A kind of gauze, muslim: 綾羅 different kinds of silks; 羅裳, 襪, 襦 muslim skirts, stockings, underwear. (3) A bag for sifting (flour, powder, liquid). (4) A surname. (5) A gross, twelve dozen: 大羅 twelve gross.

V.i. & t. (1) To spread out, arrange: 羅列, 羅布 *-lieh*, *-buh* ↓. (2) To gather, wind up: 羅致 *-jyh*[1] ↓; 搜羅 to search out (talents, hidden goods); 羅拜 form a line around a person to pay homage.

羅布 *luorbuh*, v.i., spread out (as stars in the sky).

羅捕 *luorbuu*, v.t., search for criminal.

羅刹 *luorchah*, n., (Sanskr.) raksha, demon.

羅圈兒 *luorchyuan* (*-chyua'l*), adv., as in 羅圈兒架 round after round of fights, quarrels; 羅圈兒揖 make a general bow to all sides; 羅圈腿兒 walk bowlegged.

羅敷 *Luorfu*, n., (allu.) a married woman: 羅敷有夫.

羅鍋(兒)(子) *luorguo*('*l*)(*tz*), n., a humpback.

羅漢 *luorhahn*, n., (Budd.) lohan, arahat, Buddhist saint: 十八羅漢 the eighteen disciples of Buddha; 羅漢松 the Chinese yew; 羅漢柏 a kind of cypress; 羅漢果 mangosteen; 羅漢椅子 a wooden easy chair; 羅漢牀 a divan; 羅漢齋 special vegetarian dish; 叠羅漢 pyramiding (gymnastics).

羅致 *luorjyh*[1], v.t., to round up: 羅致人才 look out for talents and engage their services.

羅織 *luorjyh*[2], v.i., to frame up (lit., to "weave"), build up case by unscrupulous methods: 羅織成獄 frame up a case.

羅列 *luorlieh*, v.i., to spread out, arrange for show.

羅馬 *Luormaa*, adj., Roman; 國語羅馬字 *Guoryuu Romatzyh*, National Romanization; 羅馬字母 Roman alphabet; 羅馬帝國 the Roman Empire; 羅馬教宗 the Pope in Rome.

羅曼蒂克 *luormahndihke*, adj., (translit.) romantic.

羅曼史 *luormahnshyy*, n., romance (曼 also wr. 漫).

羅盤 *luorparn*, n., the compass.

羅宋 *Luorsuhng*, n., older translation for "Russian": 羅宋湯 Russian beef soup, borsch.

羅網 *luorwaang*, n., a trap, snare: 自投羅網 playing into the trap.

羅紋 *luorwern*, n., (1) wood grain; (2) fingerprint (usu. wr. 螺紋).

§ 41D.22 (皿/丨)

罪 41D.22–2

tzueih.

N. (1) A criminal act: 犯罪 commit crime; 有罪 guilty; 無罪 innocent; 死罪 a capital crime; 罪上加罪 doubly guilty; 罪有應得 serve you right; 罪該萬死 hideous crime deserving the harshest punishment; 罪犯 *-fahn*, 罪人 *-rern*↓; 罪名 *-mirng*, 罪狀 *-juahng*↓; 罪魁 *-kueir*↓. (2) Wrongdoing, misconduct, a sin, moral transgression: 罪過 *-guoh*, 罪孽 *-nieh*↓; 罪過兒 a wicked act, (retribution for) wrongdoing; 罪惡 *-eh*↓; 罪戾 *-lih*[1]↓; 罪愆 *-chian*↓; 得罪 give offense to (s.o.); 問罪 denounce and punish: 興問罪之師 make a punitive expedition; 告罪 (LL) publicly announce criminal charges against person: (modn.) "excuse me, please," "pardon me," "I am sorry"; 請罪 ask person for pardon, acknowledge one's guilt (fault, mistake). (3) Hardships, sufferings, painful experience: 受罪 suffer mental agony (physical pain).

罪案 *tzueih-ahn*, n., (law) a criminal case.

罪愆 *tzueihchian*, n., a guilty conscience, wicked acts.

罪惡 *tzueih-eh*, n., a deadly crime.

罪犯 *tzueihfahn*, n., a criminal, a condemned prisoner.

罪過 *tzueihguoh*, n., a guilty conscience: "罪過, 罪過" (court.) "you give me a guilty conscience" (by extending courtesies).

罪己 *tzueih-jii*, v.i., to blame oneself for wrongdoing: 下罪己詔 (of a ruler) acknowledge by royal decree one's responsibility for misgovernment or national calamity.

罪狀 *tzueihjuahng*, n., an indictment against person for crime committed.

罪魁 *tzueihkueir*, n., chief culprit.

罪戾 *tzueihlih*[1], n., criminal responsibility.

罪隸 *tzueihlih*[2], n., dependents of criminals forced into slavery.

罪名 *tzueihmirng* (-'*ming*), n., criminal charges leveled against a person.

罪孽 *tzueihnieh* (-'*nie*), n., (1) wrongdoing, sin; a (2) retribution for wrong done.

罪人 *tzueihrern*, (1) n., a convict; (2) v.i., to blame s.o. for misconduct.

罪行 *tzueihshihng*, n., a criminal act.

罪責 *tzueihtzer*, n., responsibility for misconduct.

罘 41D.22–3

fur (also *four*).

N. Net for catching hares.

罘罳 *fursyh*, n., (AC) screen or latticed partition which one could see through.

§ 41D.30 (皿/一)

置 41D.30–1

jyh.

[Usu. printed 置]

V.t. (1) To place (s.t. in position), to put down, lay down: 設置, 安置 to set s.t. in place (e.g., a bed, a table); 裝置, 配置 to arrange, set up (things) in place (e.g., a frigidaire); 佈置 or 布置 to spread out, to arrange (furniture), to deploy (troops); 位置 a given place for s.t., a position; 在那個位置 in that position; 置於死地 expose (s.o.) to mortal danger, doom a person to death 置身局外 to keep aloof from, refrain from getting involved. (2) To set aside, to leave unattended: 置之不理 to ignore it, put it on the shelf; 置若罔聞 ignore completely; 置疑 doubt, suspect (the feasibility, truthfulness, etc.); 不置一辭 did not utter a comment; 擱置 to put aside; 棄置 to abandon (wife, lover). (3) To purchase provisions: 置產業 or 購置產業 buy up property; 置酒 prepare wine for dinner; 置辦, 置備 -'*bahn*, -'*beih*↓.

置辦 *jyh'bahn*, v.t., to buy (provisions, wedding dresses, etc.), prepare (dinner).

置備 *jyh'beih*, v.t., to make preparations for things needed.

置辯 *jyhbiahn*, v.t., to give reply in argument.

罡 41D.30–3

gang.

N. (1) (Astron.) short for 天罡, the Great Dipper. (2) (Taoism) wind in upper space. (3) Also for the heroes of *All Men are Brothers* (水滸傳).

§ 41D.32 (皿/フ)

罗 41D.32–9

luor.

[Abbr. of 羅 41D.11]

亅	小	卜	十	土	ナ	卄	𠃊	丨	一	丅	フ	口	囗	冂	冖	厂	尸	亠	广	宀	丶	乚	弋	心	八	人	乂	乛	丆	丿	𠂉	く
00	01	02	10	11	12	20	21	22	30	31	32	40	41	42	50	51	52	60	61	62	63	70	71	72	80	81	82	83	90	91	92	93

§41D.40 (罒/口)

罟 41D.40-1

guu.

N. A net for catching birds or fish: 網罟 a fishing net.

詈 41D.40-6

lih.

V.t. To scold, using severe language, curse: 詈罵, 惡詈.

§41D.41 (罒/㐫)

署 41D.41-1

shuu (as n.; **shuh*, vb.).

N. An official bureau: 官署, 公署 ditto; 警署 police station.

V.i. & t. (**shuh*) (1) To sign one's name: 署名 *-mirng*↓; 署押 *-ya*↓; 簽署 to sign signature. (2) To deputize, carry on as acting officer: 署理, 署辦 *-lii, -bahn*↓. (3) Arrange, put in order 布署: 布署一切 make arrangements (as for journey).

署辦 **shuhbahn*, n., deputy.
署理 **shuhlii*, n., acting officer, also v.i., to act thus.
署名 **shuh-mirng*, v.t., sign signature.
署任 **shuh-rehn*, v.i., see *-lii*↑.
署事 **shuh-shyh*, v.i., see *-lii*↑.
署押 **shuhya*, v.i., to sign signature.

罾 41D.41-8

tzeng (**tzehng*).

N. A fishing net.

Adj. (**tzehng*) 巴巴罾兒 knotty or pitted (face, surface).

罶 41D.41-9

lioou.

N. Fishing trap.

§41D.50 (罒/⺄)

羈 41D.50-2

ji.
[Pop. 覊]

N. (1) A halter: 羈紲 *-shieh*↓. (2) A temporary lodging. (3) (Hairdressing) a bun.

V.i. & t. (1) V.t., to tie, fasten, restrain, control: 不羈 unfettered, free from restraint; 羈絆 *-bahn*↓. (2) V.t., to capture and put in chains: 羈紲 *-shieh*↓. (3) V.i., to put up at a temporary lodging.

羈絆 *jibahn*, (1) n., a hindrance to action; (2) v.t., serve as restraint, hinder; p.p., hindered.
羈泊 *jibor*, v.i., be away from one's native district.
羈棲 *jichi*, v.i., (LL) to live temporarily abroad.
羈牽 *jichian*, v.t., see *-bahn*↑.
羈滯 *jijyh*, v.i. & adj., (be) forced to remain at a place longer than one has expected (also wr. 覊).
羈居 *jijyu*, v.i., sojourn abroad.
羈勒 *jileh*, n., restraint, control, bondage (also 覊).
羈留 *jiliour*, v.t., (law) detain (a suspect); be detained on business abroad.
羈旅 *jilyuu*, v.i., to live abroad (also wr. 覊).
羈縻 *jimir*, v.t., to tie up, be tied up, by business or emotional ties; stay on (in post), continue.
羈紲 *jishieh*, (1) v.i., be fettered; (2) n., fetters.
羈束 *jishuh*, v.t. & n., restrain(t), control.
羈押 *jiya*, n., detention.

罵 41D.50-5

mah.

N. & v.t. To scold, abuse, curse: 打罵 beat and scold (s.o.); 罵人 scold person; 罵不絕口 let off a string of invectives, abuse; 罵他一頓 give him a good scolding; 咒罵 curse; 挨罵 receive scolding; 罵爹打娘 abuse and beat parents (unfilial); 罵人不帶髒字兒 fine art of insulting people, difficult to reply to.

罵擋子 *mah-dahngtz*, n., butt, target, of scolding.
罵街 *mah-jie*, v.i., abuse people in public, esp. 潑婦罵街 woman hysterically shouting and cursing in public.
罵題 *mah-tir*, v.i., (1) stray off from subject of composition; (2) conduct oneself in manner improper to one's station; (3) fail to live up to what one preaches.
罵座 *mah-tzuoh*, v.i., scold at a party, with all present.

蜀 41D.50-9

shuu.

N. Ancient name for Szechuan Province: 蜀道難 celebrated difficult mountain paths of Szechuan; 蜀犬吠日 phr., a Szechuan dog barks when sun comes out (being so rare)—referring to astonishment at unfamiliar sights; 巴蜀 (AC) Szechuan region.

蜀漢 *Shuuhahn*, n., one of the Three Kingdoms (222–265 A.D.) in modn. Szechuan.

蜀椒 *shuujiau*, n., wild pepper of Szechuan.

蜀葵 *shuukueir*, n., the mallow, *Althaea rosea*.

蜀黍 *shurshuu*, n., Szechuan sorghum.

§ 41D.63 (皿/丶)

羆 41D.63–9

pir.

N. (Zoo.) the brown bear, also called 人熊 because of its ability to stand on hind legs.

§ 41D.70 (皿/㇄)

罨 41D.70–1

yaan.

N. (1) (Med.) a compress: 冷罨 cold compress; 熱罨 hot compress. (2) (AC) a net, snare.

罷 41D.70–9

bah.

[Pop. 罢; var. of 疲 *pir* 61B.82]

Fin. part. (Unaccented=吧) expressing mood of casual invitation, forced concurrence: 你來罷 come, if you wish; or in simple command: 去罷 well, go! or simple informal invitation: 坐罷 please sit down; or termination of rambling or useless discussion: 你說罷 say what you want to say, I am listening; 就這樣辦罷 all right ("we'll do it"), do so (what we have been discussing so long); expressing doubt: 這樣不行罷 I doubt it will do.

N. In 作罷(論) *tzuo bah*, forget about it, 罷論 *-luhn* ↓.

V.i. & t. Finish, dismiss, terminate, close, stop: 罷! 罷! order to stop ceremonial forms (kowtowing); 罷事 terminate official duties; 罷工 *-gung* ↓; see other compp. ↓.

Excl. Usu. 罷了! 罷了! (also wr. 罷咧) "have done with it," "it's all over," "I give up," signifying admission of defeat, and of struggle or disappointment: 也罷 all right, then (after tiresome discussion).

罷黜 *bahchuh*, v.t., dismiss (from office).

罷官 *bah-guan*, v.i., suspend, be relieved of, official duties.

罷工 *bah-gung*, n. & v.i., labor strike.

罷職 *bahjyr*, v.i., retire from office.

罷課 *bah-keh*, n. & v.i., school strike.

罷論 *bahluhn*, n., as in 此事已作罷論 the case is already dropped.

罷免 *bahmiaan*, v.t., dismiss (person from office); 罷免權 (law) recall by popular vote.

罷閒 *bahshiarn*, v.i., (MC) be dismissed and enjoying leisure, (euphem.) out of job.

罷休 *bahshiou*, v.i., let go of (lawsuit, fight): 不肯罷休 will not settle out of court, etc.

罷手 *bah-shoou*, v.i., stop: 不肯罷手 cannot, will not stop.

罷市 *bah-shyh*, n. & v.i., general strike of shopkeepers.

罷演 *bah-yaan*, v.i., walk out from performance.

§ 41D.80 (皿/八)

買 41D.80–4

maai.

V. t. (1) To buy: 買雜物 buy sundries; 買地, 房產 buy land, property; 買不起 cannot afford to buy; 買不了, 不着, 不到, 不來 cannot buy; 買進 buy in (goods), opp. 賣出 sell out; 買方 the buying party in a contract; 買櫝還珠 buy casket without the jewels; 買菜求益 (LL) always want some more for the price; 買路錢 pay for protection on journey from robber gangs. (2) Pay bribe for: 買官, 爵 pay bribe to obtain official post; 買上告下 bribe all the way through bureaucracy; 買關節 bribe the authorities concerned, see 買通 *-tung* ↓; 買囑 bribe official to order (s. t.). (3) Cater to: 買名, 買譽 cater to publicity by sordid methods. (4) Pay for certain objects: 買笑 visit prostitutes ("pay for smiles"); 買春, 買醉 get a drinking spree; 買樂 pay for pleasures; 買人心 get people's support by money or political chicanery; 買臉 spend money to gain "face" (show-off); 買鄰 choose neighbors in buying land. (5) Hire: 買舟, 櫂 hire a boat.

買辦 *maaibahn*, n., compradore, local chief for all local trade of foreign firms; formerly, supply master in coastal ships.

買骨 *mairguu*, v. t., make fervent quest for talent (allu.—if one could not find a thoroughbred, would be contented to buy its skeleton).

買好 *mairhaau*, v. t., try to secure good will, friendship, etc. of (person); try to please (person).

買主 *mairjuu*, n., customer, buying party.

買客 *maaikeh*, n., customer at shops.

買空賣空 *maaikung-maihkung*, n. & v. i., speculate (-tion) on stock market, buy on margin.

買賣 *maaimaih*, n. & v. i., trade, buying and selling; 做買賣的 a merchant; 買賣道兒(地兒) the trade profession; 買賣人口 slave traffic, also white slave traffic.

買山 *maaishan*, v. i., (1)buy rural property; (2) live in retirement.

買通 *maaitung*, v. t., pay bribe to (s. o.).

§41D.83 (皿/〜)

逻 41D.83–1

tah.

Adj. 雜逻＝沓^雜, see 22.41.

還 41D.83–3

huarn (**hair*).

[Abbr. 还]

N. A surname.

V. i. & t. (1) To return: 還鄉 return to one's village; 還都 (of ruler) return to the capital (after absence or flight); 往還 to go back and forth; 和人往還 to have frequent contacts as between friends; 生還 return alive; 班師還朝 recall the army and return to court. (2) To return (borrowed object), to repay: 還賬, 還債 repay loan: 還清兒 fully repay; 還人情, 還禮 make gift in return; 還禮 also to bow in return; 還請 give a dinner in return for one given; 還繃子 (*-bengtz*) a tit for tat.

Adv. (**hair*) (1) Still, yet: 他還不來 he still has not appeared yet; 還有 still have some more; 還嫌不足 still regard it as not enough; 還是不行 still won't do. (2) After all: 還是他對 after all, he is right; 還是你自己走一趟 after all, you'd better go yourself. (3) Besides, in addition: 他還説 he says besides; 他還要一雙鞋子 he wants, besides, a pair of shoes; 還得謝謝他 in addition, you have to thank him.

Conj. 以還 (＝以來) since: 庚子之亂以還 (LL) since the Boxer Uprising.

還報 *huarnbauh*, n. & v. t., a retribution.

還本 *huarnbeen*, v. i., to recover capital invested: 夠還本 come out even.

還魂 *huarnhurn*, v. i., (fiction) "soul returns," i. e., dead person revives after return of lover.

還價 *huarnjiah*, v. i., to haggle.

還敬 *huarnjihng*, v. i., to return bow or courtesy.

還口 *huarn-koou*, v. i., to talk back.

還禮 *huarn-lii*, v. i., (1) to return courtesy; (2) to bow in return as host.

還席 *huarn-shir*, v. i., (1) to give a return dinner; (2) (facet.) to throw up everything when drunk at dinner.

還手 *huarn-shoou*, v. i., to strike back after receiving blow.

還俗 *huarn-sur*, v. i., (of monks) to leave the order, return to secular life.

還嘴 *huarn-tzueei*, v. i., to answer back in abuse or self-defense.

還陽 *huarn-yarng*, v. i., (patient) to return to consciousness.

還願 *huarn-yuahn*, v. i., to redeem a vow pledged before Buddha.

還原 *huarnyuarn*, (1) v. i., to be restored to original shape or position; (2) n., (chem.) reduction; (3) v.i., (math.) to return to original equation.

邏 41D.83–9

luor.

N. & v. i. A patrol, to patrol: 巡邏, 邏卒 soldiers on patrol.

邏輯 *luorjir*, n., (translit.) logic: 不合邏輯 illogical.

§41D.93 (皿/く)

罢 41D.93–1

bah.

[Abbr. of 罷 41D.70↑]

SECTION 41S

§ 41S.00 (図^{S}/丿)

畸 41S.00–1

ji.

N. Small irregular pieces of land.

Adj. (1) (Of numbers) not round, odd: 畸零 *-lirng*↓. (2) One-sided: 畸重畸輕 lopsided, unevenly balanced; 畸角 *-jiaau*↓. (3) (Interch. 奇) strange, unique, extraordinary, unusual, abnormal: 畸人 *-rern*, 畸態 *-taih*, 畸形 *-shirng*↓.

畸 角 (兒) (子) *jijiaau('l)(tz)*, n., a corner, coign, edge.

畸 零 *jilirng*, n., (1) (of numbers) a remainder after taking off a round sum; (2) odds and ends; (3) a solitary person.

畸 人 *jirern*, n., (1) a person out of tune with the times; (2) an extraordinary person.

畸 形 *jishirng*, n., (1) deformity; (2) abnormality.

畸 態 *jitaih*, n., an abnormal growth or development.

疇 41S.00–1

chour.

N. (1) (AC) farm, farmland. (2) (AC) farm boundary. (3) (AC var. of 儔) rival, equal: 疇類, 疇輩 *-leih, beih*↓.

Adj. Ancient: see 疇昔, 疇日 *-shir, -ryh*↓.

疇 輩 *chourbeih*, n., (LL) equals, people of same class.

疇 類 *chourleih*, n., (LL) ditto.

疇 曩 *chournarng*, adv., (LL) in ancient, early days.

疇 人 *chourrern*, n., (LL) astronomers, mathematicians; 疇人傳 book about ancient astronomers.

疇 日 *chourryh*, adv., (LL) in early days.

疇 昔 *chourshir*, adv., (LL) formerly.

剔 41S.00–2

ti.

V. t. (1) To scrape meat off bone: 剔肉, 剔骨頭. (2) To pick out, scrape off: 剔出 pick out and throw away; 剔除 *-chur*↓; 挑剔 pick fault with; pick and select (goods, fruit, etc.); 剔牙 pick teeth; (剔) 牙籤 toothpick; 剔翎 preen feather.

剔 除 *ti-chur*, v. t., pick and get rid of (undesirable parts).

剔 紅 *tihurng*, n., carved lacquerware.

剔 莊 *tijuang*, n., odd lots (goods, clothing) put out for cheap sale: also 剔莊貨.

剔 騰 *titerng*, v. t., (MC) expose maliciously (secrets).

剔 透 *titouh*, adj., beautifully clear and well-expressed (writing), extremely keen, perceptive (person) (also 玲瓏剔透).

剔 團 圞 *tituarnluarn*, adj., (MC) beautifully round and clear (moon).

町 41S.00–3

tiing.

N. (1) Raised path between farm fields. (2) A Japanese measure of length=119 yards; 町村 a land division.

町 畦 *tiingshi*, n., a bank between fields.

町 疃 *tirngtuaan*, n., (AC) a waste land, a paddock.

野 41S.00–3

yee.

N. (1) The open country, countryside: 田野 rural district. (2) (People, party) outside government, not in power: 朝野 both the rulers and the people: 在野 (of party) not in power, opp. 在朝 party in government. (3) Field, district: 分野 different fields; 分野綫 boundary line.

Adj. (1) Wild, not domesticated: 野馬, 野牛, 野犬, etc. *-maa, -niour, -chyuaan*↓; 野雞, 野豬 *-ji, -ju*↓. (2) Savage: 野蠻 *-marn*↓; 野人 *-rern*↓. (3) Rustic, simple, primitive (manners): 村野 ditto; 野小子, 野孩子 (abuse) ragamuffin; 野丫頭 (abuse) flibbertigibbet, (sl.) cheap skirt; 野頭野腦 silly blockhead.

Adv. (Coll.) extremely: 風大野了 storm is mounting fast; 天冷野了 it's getting bitterly cold.

野 百 合 *yer-baaiher*, n., (bot.) *Crotalaria sessiliflora.*

野 薔 薇 *yee-chiarngweir*, n., (bot.) rambler rose, *Rosa multiflora.*

野 犬 *yer-chyuaan*, n., wild dog.

野 地 *yee-dih*, n., open country.

野 服 *yee-fur*, n., rustic dress; simple dress, opp. formal.

野 葛 *yee-ger*, n., (bot.) *Rhus toxicodendron.*

野 狗 *yer-goou*, n., wild dog.

野 菰 *yee-gu*, n., (bot.) *Aeginetia indica.*

野 漢 子 *yee-hahntz*, n., (abuse) a woman's lover.

野 鶴 *yee-heh*, phr., 閒雲野鶴 a

丿	小	⺊	十	土	ナ	卄	凵	丨	一	丅	フ	口	区	冈	冂	厂	尸	亠	广	宀	丶	乚	七	心	八	人	乂	𠂉	一	丿	ㄥ	く
00	01	02	10	11	12	20	21	22	30	31	32	40	41	42	50	51	52	60	61	62	63	70	71	72	80	81	82	83	90	91	92	93

free and happy recluse.

野合 *yee-her*, phr., to have illicit sexual union.

野花(兒) *yee-huah(-hua'l)*, n., wild flower; (fig.) girl or woman not one's wife: 家花不如野花香 wild flowers smell sweeter—ex-marital relationships more pleasurable.

野火 *yer-huoo*, n., (1) prairie fire; (2) will-o'-the-wisp.

野狐禪 *yee-hur-charn*, n., not orthodox teaching.

野戰 *yee-jahn*, n., (1) field battle; (2) irregular guerrilla warfare: 野戰砲 field artillery; 野戰病院 field hospital.

野雞 *yeeji*, n., (1) pheasant; (2) streetwalker, a low-class prostitute; (3) any fly-by-night operation, as 野雞店, 野雞船 such shop, boat.

野祭 *yeejih*, n., sacrifices in the open during 清明 festival.

野豬 *yeeju*, n., boar.

野種 *yerjuung*, n., (abuse) hybrid, bastard.

野菊 *yeejyur*, n., (bot.) *Chrysanthemum indicum*.

野馬 *yer-maa*, n., (1) a mustang; (fig.) uncontrollable person; (2) (AC) mirage (images in clouds).

野蠻 *yeemarn*, adj. & n., (1) savage: 野蠻民族 savage tribe; (2) (person) unruly, violent, discourteous.

野貓 *yee-mau* n., (1) mountain cat; (2) (sl.) hare; (3) (abuse) ragamuffin.

野牡丹 *yer-muudan*, n., (bot.) *Melastoma candidum*.

野牛 *yeeniour*, n., wild ox; bison.

野砲 *yeepauh*, n., field gun, fieldpiece.

野人 *yeerern*, n., a savage.

野食兒 *yee-sher'l*, n., food picked from the fields (cf. *-tsan*↓); (fig.) extra irregular income.

野性 *yeeshihng*, n., violent, untamed nature.

野心 *yeeshin*, n., greed; illegitimate ambition, wild hope; 野心家 adventurist.

野獸 *yeeshouh*, n., beasts.

野史 *yer-shyy*, n., romance; unofficial historical record.

野臺子戲 *yee-tairtz-shih*, n., temporary theater put up in country places.

野草 *yer-tsaau*, n., wild vegetation: 野草閑花 (fig.) loose women picked up by men.

野菜 *yeetsaih*, n., vegetable grown in nature.

野餐 *yeetsan*, n., picnic.

野蠶 *yeetsarn*, n., wild silkworms.

野兔 *yeetuh*, n., hare.

野外 *yeewaih*, n., open air, suburbs.

野味 *yeeweih*, n., game (food).

野鴨(子) *yeeya(tz)*, n., mallard.

野宴 *yeeyahn*, n., picnic, open-air dinner.

野意兒 *yeeyieh'l*, n., rustic flavor (on an outing).

野鴛鴦 *yee-yuanyang*, n., illicit lovers.

§ 41S.01 (図s/小)

黥 41S.01-6

chirng.

V. t. To brand (criminal): 黥刑 such punishment; 黥面, 黥首 brand the face, the head.

縣 41S.01-9

shiahn.

N. A county, subdivision of 府 (*fuu*) prefecture, district: 縣官, 縣長 *-guan, -jaang*↓; 知縣 formerly, county magistrate; 縣太爺 formerly, address of county magistrate; 首縣 the capital or first county of a 府; 縣議會 county assembly.

縣分 *shiahnfehn*, n., county area.

縣官(兒) *shiahnguan(-gua'l)*, n., county magistrate.

縣長 *shiahnjaang*, n., administrative head of county.

縣治 *shiahnjyh*, n., county jurisdiction.

縣令 *shiahnlihng*, n., see *-guan*↑.

縣宰 *shiahntzaai*, n., formerly, county magistrate.

縣尊 *shiahntzun*, n., ditto.

§ 41S.10 (図s/十)

畔 41S.10-2

pahn.

N. (1) Boundary, esp. field boundary; lake or river bank: 河畔, 湖畔 river front, lake front. (2) (AC) var. of 叛 to rebel, a rebellion.

V. (AC) to deviate from, to rebel against: 離經畔道 deviate from orthodox truth; 畔約 (AC) break agreement (=叛約).

畔援 *pahnyuaan*, adj., (AC) recalcitrant.

§ 41S.11 (図s/土)

畦 41S.11-1

*shi (*chir).*

N. (1) An area of 50 *mou* 畝. (2) A division of farm land (sp. pr. **chir*).

畦丁 *shi-ding*, n., gardener.

畦畛 *shi-jeen*, n., (LL) (1) field boundary; (2) difference of opinion, dispute.

畦徑 *shi-jihng*, n., a bypath.

雎 41S.11-9

jyu.
[Dist. 睢 41B.11]

N. A kind of fish hawk: 雎鳩 the male and female fish hawk, symbols of conjugal felicity.

V. i. Interch. 趄 11.83.

§ 41S.21 (図^S/乚)

黜 41S.21-2

chuh.

V. i. (1) To demote, downgrade. (2) To dismiss from office: 黜免 *-miaan*↓; 罷黜 to dismiss from office. (3) To rebuke: 黜斥 *-chyh*↓; 黜退 *-tueih*↓.

黜斥 *chuhchyh*, v. t., to rebuke (person).
黜陟 *chuh-jyh*, v. t. & n., to promote and downgrade; promotion and demotion.
黜免 *chuhmiaan*, v. t., to dismiss from office.
黜升 *chuh-sheng*, v. t. & n., see *-jyh*↑.
黜退 *chuhtueih*, v. t., to bawl out (person).

黮 41S.21-2

taan.

Adj. Dark, unclear: 黮闇 (LL) dark, blurred.

§ 41S.32 (図^S/フ)

黔 41S.32-8

chiarn.

N. Short name for Kweichow (貴州) Province: 黔驢技窮 show feet of clay (from allu. a donkey, newly imported into Kweichow, got on very well and was feared by the tiger until he tried to kick the tiger).

Adj. (AC) black, see 黔首 *-shoou*↓.

黔黎 *chiarnlir*, n., (AC) the common people ("black-haired").
黔首 *chiarnshoou*, n., (AC) "black-haired tribe," curiously used by Chirn 秦 ruler to refer to the local people.

夥 41S.32-9

huoo.

N. (1) Companion, co-worker: 店夥 shop employees; 夥伴, 夥友 *-bahn*, *-yoou*↓. (2) Partner, -ship: 合夥, 入夥 join partnership; 拆夥, 散夥 dissolve partnership. (3) A crowd: 一大夥 a great number of people or things; 一小夥 a small group; 同夥 in partnership, together.

Adj. (LL) many: 甚夥 (of crowd, products, etc.) very many.

夥伴(兒) *huoobahn(-bah'l)*, n., co-worker in shop (also wr. 火, 伙).
夥計 *huoo'jih*, n., employee in shop, waiter (also wr. 伙, 火).
夥頤 *huooyir*, adj., very many.
夥友 *huoryoou*, n., (a more polite form of *-'jih*↑) fellow employees.

§ 41S.40 (図^S/口)

黠 41S.40-1

shiar.

Adj. (1) Cunning, resourceful: 狡黠 crafty; 黠吏 crafty officials; 黠鼠 alert and resourceful rat. (2) Intelligent.

黠慧 *shiarhueih*, adj., intelligent, smart.
黠智 *shiarjyh*, adj., ditto.

點 41S.40-2

diaan.
[Pop. 点, 奌]

N. (1) A drop (of liquid): 雨點 raindrops; a tiny amount; esp. 一點兒 *yidiaa'l*, a little bit, a little; 一點兒不怕 not the least bit frightened, also 一點點 ditto; 一點點零錢 a small amount of change or spare money; 一點(兒)小意思 (modest of gift) just a small token; 不能有一點錯 do not allow the slightest mistake; 差一點兒 a little off, by a small margin, almost; 大一點 slightly bigger; 點滴歸公 every cent goes into the public account. (2) A dot in callig.: 污點 a dirty mark, a blot (on paper, upon character). (3) A point: 交叉點 (in geometry) point of intersection; 起點, 終點 point of departure, terminal point; 重點, 要點 important point; 焦點 focal point; 第一點 firstly, the first point; the decimal point: 零點一 (0.1); 零點十二 (0.12). (4) An hour: 兩點半 half past two; 一點鐘 one hour, one o'clock. (5) Light refreshment: 早點 breakfast; 點心 *-shin*↓.

雎 黜 黮 黔 夥 點 點

亅	小	⺊	十	土	ナ	卄	㇗	丨	一	丅	フ	口	図	冈	㇆	厂	尸	亠	广	宀	丶	乚	乁	心	八	人	乂	乛	㇀	刂	𠂉	く
00	01	02	10	11	12	20	21	22	30	31	32	40	41	42	50	51	52	60	61	62	63	70	71	72	80	81	82	83	90	91	92	93

V.i. & t. (1) Touch lightly, as with finger, brush or rod, make slight movement: 點首 (示意) make a slight nod; 點手 beckon with hand; 點頭哈腰兒 make a nod and bend slightly in greeting; 蜻蜓點水 use a light touch in writing as dragonfly skims water surface; 點鐵 (or 石) 成金 the golden touch in writing by dextrous use of a word; 點金成鐵 disastrous correction; 畫龍點睛 put life into, like dotting the eyeball in painting a dragon; 點破, 點穿 expose (lie, falsehood), point out the secret; 點醒 remind gently (of a mistake), make a timely reminder, help understanding by a clue. (2) Mark off, tick off, punctuate, underline: 點去錯字 cross out wrong word; 圈點句子 mark off sentence by punctuation or making circles and dots along line (for good or important sentences); 點句讀 (*-jyuhdouh*) mark by commas and periods; 點定 in editing, decide on correct word among variant texts; 點竄 delete and interpolate. (3) Check, tick off on inventory: 點交, 點收 thus deliver, receive; 點勘, 點檢 inspect, check item by item; 請你點一點 please check if all is there; 點名, 點卯 make roll call; 點齊 see that all is in, all accounted for; select by marking off: 點將 (select and) appoint commander for war; 點菜 select dishes from menu, *à la carte*; 點戲 select play from repertoire offered. (4) Light, kindle: 點香烟, 燈, 火 light a cigarette, lamp, fire.

點兵 *diaan-bing*, v.i., muster soldiers.

點滴 *diaandir*,n., droplet: 點滴在心頭 much left unsaid.

點饑 *diaanji*, v.i., have slight snack to relieve hunger.

點脚(兒) *diarnjiaau('l)*, v.i., walk lamely, with one foot barely touching the ground.

點綴 *diaanjueh*, v.t. & n., add a lively detail on painting or writing or furniture in a room, such details serving for contrast or ornament: 點綴一下 give a touch of color, embellish a little.

點鐘 *diaanjung*, n., hour, o'clock: 兩點鐘 two hours or two o'clock.

點主 *diarnjuu*, v.i., formerly, to officiate at a funeral ceremony, to consecrate spirit tablet (神主) by putting dot on the character 主.

點名 *diaan-mirng*[1], v.i. & n., (make) roll call.

點明 *diaanmirng*[2], v.t., point out (importance, meaning).

點染 *diarnraan*, v.t. & n., add little details in writing, painting.

點心 *diaanshin*, n., snack; pastry.

點穴 *diaanshyuer*, v.i. & n., part of Chin. karate, hitting at selected points, capable of causing internal bleeding and death.

點頭 *diaantour*, v.t., give a nod: 點頭示意 do so as a signal.

點子 *diaantz*, n., a drop, a dot, point (as in price index).

點字 *diaantzyh*, n., braille.

點眼 *diarn-yaan*, v.i., secure a point of anchorage in Chin. chess or *go*.

略 41S.40-9

lyueh (also *liauh*).
[Var. 畧]

N. (1) Essentials, main points, resumé: 大略 main points, also adv., mostly, about; 約略 about (1,000 people); 史略 outline history. (2) Strategy: 謀略, 策略 strategy; 戰略 military strategy.

V. i. & t. (1) To supervise, plan: 經略. (2) To ignore: 忽略 to neglect. (3) To invade (interch. 掠): 攻城略地 capture territory; 侵略 commit aggression, invade; 劫略 rob, loot.

Adv. About, cursorily, not intensely: 略如從前 about like what it was; 略看一看 take a cursory glance; 略知一二 know just a little; 略言梗概 just tell the main points; 大致略同 mostly similar; 略微 just a little (show gratitude, dissatisfaction, remonstrate, etc.).

§41S.41 (図ˢ/図)

黯 41S.41-6

ahn.

Adj. Dark, dismal, dreary.

黯黯 *ahn-ahn*, adj., dark, gloomy.

黯淡 *ahndahn*, adj., dull, lacking in life, dreary (situation, prospect).

黯然 *ahnrarn*, adj. & adv., gloomy, -mily, sad, -ly.

§41S.50 (図ˢ/㇕)

助 41S.50-9

juh.

N. (1) Help: 借助, 求助 ask for help (from s. o.); 無助於 of no help to; 補助 subsidy. (2) 內助 a good wife; 賢內助 your excellent wife.

V. t. & n. Help, assist, aid: 相助 help each other; 助我一臂之力 lend me a hand; 助人 help others; 贊助 to assist by action, to give moral support; 襄助 (其成) to help accomplish s. t.; 輔助 to help on the side, to lend support to; 天助我也 thanks be to God; 助紂爲虐 give support to a tyrant; 天助自助者 heaven help those who help themselves.

助動詞 *juhduhng-tsyr*, n., (gram.) auxiliary verb.

助長 *juhjaang*, v. t., to accelerate

growth artificially, to force growth: 勿長勿助 let the good in man grow naturally (without too much conscious cultivation)—Mencius.

助賑 *juh-jehn*, v. i., to give aid in famine relief.

助教 *juhjiauh*, n., an assistant at college.

助裝 *juh-juang*, n., money given friends on departure (to help buy 行裝 or things needed on journey).

助力 *juh-lih*, n., help, a helping hand.

助理 *juhlii*, v. t. & n., to assist; an assistant.

助手 *juhshoou*, n., an assistant (in surgery, etc.).

助勢 *juhshyh*, v. i., give oral or moral support.

助學金 *juhshyuer-jin*, n., scholarship for needy students.

助產士 *juhtsaanshyh*, n., midwife.

助詞 *juhtsyr*, n., (gram.) an auxiliary, also used of grammatical particles.

助威 *juh-wei*, v. i., see *-shyh*↑.

勖 41S.50-9

shyuh.

[Err. var. 勗]

V. t. To enjoin, advise, preach to (persons).

V. i. To endeavor.

勖勉 *shyuhmiaan*, 勖勵 *shyuhlih*, v.i. & t., to admonish, preach; to endeavor, encourage.

昀 41S.50-9

yurn.

Adj. 昀昀 (AC) well-cultivated (farms).

黝 41S.50-9

yoou.

Adj. Jet black: 黝黑 dark, overcast mirky (sky): 黝黝 swarthy, dark-skinned.

嬲 41S.50-9

niaau.

V. t. To tease, to flirt with.

鴨 41S.50-9

ya.

N. (*-tz*, *'l*) Duck, wild duck, mallard: 烤鴨, 臘鴨 roast, preserved duck; 板鴨 flattened prepared duck, preserved in oil; 野鴨 wild duck, mallard; 番鴨 imported duck.

鴨蛋 *ya-dahn*, n., duck's egg; 鴨蛋臉兒 oval face; 鴨蛋圓兒 oval shape.

鴨黃 *ya-huarng*, n., a duckling.

鴨掌 *ya-jaang*, n., duck's webbed feet—a delicacy.

鴨跖草 *yajyr-tsaau*, n., (bot.) *Commelina communis*, a herb whose juice is used as blue pigment.

鴨兒芹 *ya'l-chirn*, n., (bot.) *Cryptotaenia japonica* (also called 野蜀葵).

鴨兒梨 *ya'l-lir*, n., a kind of juicy pear (also called 廣梨).

鴨爐 *ya-lur*, n., a duck-shaped incense container.

鴨舌帽 *ya-sher-mauh*, n., a cap.

鴨舌草 *ya-sher-tsaau*, n., (bot.) pickerelweed, *Monocharia vaginalis*, a flowering plant; broom plant.

鴨條 *ya-tiaur*, n., fine sliced duck.

鴨子 *yatz*, n., (1) duck; (2) (coll.) the foot (also called 腳丫子).

鴨子兒 *yatzee'l*, n., duck's egg.

鴨嘴筆 *ya-tzueei-bii*, n., compasses for drafting; 鴨嘴帽 a cap.

鴨嘴獸 *ya-tzueei-shouh*, n., (zoo.) a duckbill, platypus.

鴨圓兒 *ya-yuar'l*, n., an oval shape.

鸚 41S.50-9

ying.

鸚哥(兒) *yingge('l)*, n., the parrot.

鸚鵡 *yingwuu*, n., ditto; 鸚鵡螺 the pearly nautilus, *Nautilus pompilius*.

鸜 41S.50-9

chyur.

[Var. 鴝 92S.50.]

鷃 41S.50-9

yahn.

N. The quail (also called 鵪ᐞ鶉 12S.50).

§41S.70 (図ˢ/乚)

毗 41S.70-2

pir.

V. t. Connect; assist; see 毗輔 *-fuh*↓.

毗 晼 氍 黷 顆 顋 顒 顥 顯

Adj. Connecting, adjacent to.

毗輔 *pirfuh*, v. t., be support for (ruler).

毗連 *pirliarn*, adj., adjacent to (of territory).

毗倚 *piryii*, v. t., lean for support.

晼 41S.70-6

waan.

N. (AC) land measure of 20 or 30 畝 *moou*, 60S.81.

氍 41S.70-9

chyur.

氍毹 *chyurshu*, n., wool carpet, rug.

§41S.80 (囟S/八)

黷 41S.80-1

dur.

V.t. To besoil, besmirch (var. of 瀆).

Adj. Dirty, soiled: 黷黑 black and dirty.

黷武 *durwuu*, v.i., be bellicose: 窮兵黷武 (of ruler) love wars and military exploits.

顆 41S.80-3

ke (**kee*).

N. adjunct. 一顆珍珠 a pearl; 幾顆星 a few stars; 一顆心 one's heart (feelings); 顆粒 a round piece, grains (of sand, etc.) (cf. 棵 10B.01).

N. (**kee*) (AC) a clod of earth.

顋 41S.80-3

sai.

[Common var. 腮]

顒 41S.80-3

yurng.

Adj. (1) Grand, majestic. (2) Hoping: 顒望 hoping anxiously (cf. 喁 40A.42).

顥 41S.80-3

hauh.

Adj. (AC) white (related 皓).

顯 41S.80-3

shiaan.

V. i. & t. (1) V. i., to show, appear: 顯示 *-shyh*, 顯露 *-luh*, 顯明 *-mirng* ↓; to appear (+adj.): 顯得好看, 亮 appear good-looking, bright; 顯得小氣 would appear niggardly (too small present). (2) V. t., show (s. t.): 顯出真意 show real intentions, see 顯出 *-chu* ↓; 顯手段, 顯本領, 顯本事 or 顯出本事 show one's skill; 顯不出她的美來 does not show her at her best. (3) V.t., (of gods) to reveal oneself: 顯形(兒), 顯靈, 顯聖 *-shirng('l)*, *-lirng*, *-shehng* ↓.

Adj. (1) Manifest, clear, distinct: 顯明 *-mirng* ↓; 顯而易見 obvious, easy to see. (2) Illustrious, in honored position: 顯官, 顯宦 high officials; 顯士 (MC) well-known scholar; 顯要 *-yauh* ↓. (3)(Specifically on tombstones) illustrious: 顯考, 顯妣, 顯祖 the late illustrious father, mother, grandfather.

Adv. Clearly: 顯有關係 clearly there is a connection; 顯見 it clearly shows; 顯違法令 clearly violates the law; 顯戮 openly executed by law; 顯然 *-rarn* ↓.

顯擺 *shiaan'bai*, v. t., reveal, show (s. t.).

顯比 *shiarn-bii*, n., a simile.

顯白 *shiaan'bo*, (1) v. t., reveal, show (one's intentions, loyalty, etc.); (2) adj., clear, obvious.

顯出 *shiaan-chu*, v. t., to show out, make (s. t.) stand out; show (one's prowess, skill, etc.): 顯出原形 (of spirit) show its original shape (a snake, etc.).

顯達 *shiaandar*, adj. & n., successful, occupying high position; the successful politicians, very important people.

顯赫 *shiaanheh*, adj., impressive, powerful, resplendent.

顯懷 *shiaan-huair*, v.i., (of woman) pregnancy already shows.

顯晦 *shiaan-hueih*, n., the ups and downs of political career or man's reputation.

顯豁 *shiaanhuoh*, adj., bright and clear (space); clear and good (reputation).

顯章 *shiaanjang*, v. t., to be distinguished.

顯着 *shiaan'je*, v. i., become (+adj.): 市面上更顯着熱鬧 the market becomes still more crowded; 顯着不方便 one feels it is inconvenient.

顯者 *shiarnjee*, n., the very important people.

顯見 *shiaan-jiahn*, phr., (s.t.) clearly shows.

顯著 *shiaanjuh*, adj., distinct (results, difference), prominent: 刊登於顯著地位 published prominently in the papers.

顯考 *shiarnkaau*, n., one's own deceased father.

顯靈 *shiaanlirng*, v.i., (of idols, spirits) to show bodily presence, to show supernatural power.

顯露 *shiaan-luh*, (1) v. t., reveal, (weakness), uncover (past misdeeds); (2) adj., revealed, exposed.

顯明 *shiaanmirng*, (1) v. t., show, show off; (2) adj., obvious, plain.

顯弄 *shiaannuhng*, v. i., to show off (skill, etc.).

顯然 *shiaanrarn*, adv., clearly, evidently.

顯聖 *shiaan-shehng*, v. i., (1) (of gods, spirits) show supernatural power; (2) n., epiphany.

顯顯 *shiarnshiaan*, adj., as in 顯顯令德 (AC) how illustrious the virtue.

顯現 *shiaanshiahn*, v. i., (ghosts, spirits) materialize; 顯現日 epiphany.

顯像 *shiaanshiahng*, v. i., (photography) develop; 顯像液 developer.

顯形(兒) *shiaanshirng('l)*, v.i., *-shiahn*↑.

顯示 *shiaanshyh*, v. i. & t., to show, reveal (power, weakness); (spirits) show themselves to believers.

顯微 *shiaan weir*, phr., to show the minute points; 顯微鏡 microscope; 顯微軟片 microfilm.

顯眼兒 *shiarn-yaa'l*, adj., (1) plainly visible (cause of trouble); (2) attracting attention, attractive (dress).

顯揚 *shiaanyarng*, v. t., to glorify, make widely known.

顯要 *shiaanyauh*, n., the very important people.

§41S.81 (図ˢ/人)

畎 41S.81-1

chyuaan.

N. A field ditch: 畎畝 the fields; 舜生於畎畝 (AC) Emperor Shun was born a farmer's son.

默 41S.81-1

moh.

N. & v.i. Recitation from memory; recite.

Adj. & adv. Silent, -ly: 沉默 silent; 默坐 sit silently; 默禱 silent prayer, pray silently; 默記, 默識 *-jih, -jyh*↓; 默佑 silently protect (of God).

默契 *moh-chih*, n., tacit understanding (between parties, governments).

默讀 *mohdur*, v.i., mental reading.

默稿 *moh-gaau*, n., mental notes for speech, composition, not written down.

默記 *moh-jih*, v.i. & t., silently remember.

默識 *moh-jyh*, v.i. & t., ditto.

默劇 *moh-jyuh*, n., pantomime.

默默 *mohmoh*, adj., (1) silent, without saying anything; (2) unnoticed: 默默無聞 (of person) not known to public.

默念 *moh-niahn*, n. & v.i., recite, -tation; to teach with book closed; silently think of.

默片 *moh-piahn*, n., silent movie.

默然 *mohrarn*, adj. & adv., silently, speechless.

默認 *moh-rehn*, n. & v.t., tacit recognition, permission; recognize tacitly.

默想 *mohshiang*, v.i. & t., meditate, contemplate.

默示 *moh-shyh*, v.t. & n., reveal, revelation (by God).

默許 *moh-shyuu*, n. & v.t., tacit approval; approve tacitly: 芳心默許 give a woman's heart to one without some open admission.

默誦 *moh-suhng*, v.t., (at school) recite a passage with book closed.

歇 41S.81-9

shie.

V. i. & t. To rest, to stop (work).

Adj. (AC) finished, over: 憂未歇也 still had not got over his grief.

歇泊 *shiebor*, v. i., to lie at anchor.

歇處 *shiechuu*, n., a place to stop over for the night.

歇頂 *shie-diing*, adj., bald-headed.

歇乏 *shiefar*, v. i., to rest when fatigued.

歇伏 *shie-fur*, v. i., to stop work during the hottest summer days (三伏).

歇工 *shie-gung*, v. i., to stop work for holiday.

歇後語 *shie-houh-yuu*, n., (a custom, esp. in Peking dial.) have the last word of a well-known phrase understood and not spoken; 禮義廉＝禮義廉恥 with 恥 omitted, which means without shame (無恥).

歇腳(兒) *shie-jiaau('l)*, v. i., "rest one's foot"—stop a while during a walk.

歇枝(兒) *shie-jy (-je'l)*, phr., (of fruit trees) bear less fruit the year after a big crop.

歇馬 *shie-maa*, v. i., (1) stop work in gen.; (2) dismount for rest.

歇拍 *shie-pai*, n., the last beat, or last bar (of *tzyr* 詞 a verse form, 60A.50).

歇晌(兒) *shie-shaang('l)*, v. i., to rest or take a nap after lunch.

歇息 *shie'shi*, v. i., to stop for rest; to stop over for night.

歇歇兒 *shie'shie'l*, v. i., take a little rest.

歇心 *shie-shin*, v. i., to dismiss thoughts from one's mind, to relax, stop worrying.

歇手 *shie-shoou*, v. i., stop, give up (doing work, fighting): 不肯歇手 keep on (beating, pushing, etc.).

歇宿 *shiesuh*, v. i., to stop for the night, to sleep (at some place).

歔 畋 畯 斁 畛 影 黲

歔斯底里 *shiesydiilii*, n., & adj., (translit.) hysteria; hysterical.

歔腿(兒) *shie-tueei* (*-tuee'l*), v. i., see *-jiaau*↑.

歔業 *shieyeh*, v. i., close up business.

§41S.82 (図^{s}/乂)

畋 41S.82–9

tiarn.

V. i. (AC) to till the farm: 畋獵 to hunt.

畯 41S.82–9

jyuhn.

N. (1) An anc. agricultural officer: 田畯 (AC) a bailiff. (2) Poor, rugged grassland: 寒畯 a poor scholar.

斁 41S.82–9

yih (**duh*).

V.i. (1) (AC) be weary of: 無斁 without tiring. (2) (**duh*) To spoil, waste: 耗斁.

§41S.91 (図^{s}/ノ)

畛 41S.91–8

jeen.

N. Boundary.

V. t. (AC) to inform the spirits.

畛域 *jeenyuh*, n., proper area or field, limits: 不分畛域 draws no line between.

影 41S.91–9

yiing.

N. (1) (*-tz, 'l*) Shadow cast by object: 投影 cast shadow; 日影 shadow in the sun; 陰影, 暗影 penumbra, a blurred shadow; 形影相隨 two persons inseparable, like object and its shadow. (2) Trace: 沒影兒 no trace (of person); 終日不見影兒 never saw person the whole day; 沒聲沒影兒 without any trace. (3) Image, photograph, portrait, reflection: 小影 portrait, 攝影 (to, a) photograph; 留影 a memento; to take photograph as souvenir; 定影 to fix photographic film; 水影, 倒影 reflection in water; 影響 *-shiaang*↓. (4) Short for 電影 movie: 影星, 影迷, 影片 *-shing*, *-mir*, *-piahn*↓.

V. i. To project a shadow: 只有松林裏影著一個人 saw a human figure flit across the pine forest; 影射 *-sheh*↓.

Adj. Shadowy, see 影影 *-yiing*↓.

影壁 *yiingbih* (*-'bi*), n., a screen wall opposite gate or inside gate.

影鈔 *yiingchau*, v. i. & n., (to make) an exact replica by hand of some old editions; to reproduce thus.

影燈 *yiingdeng*, n., a lantern with rotating or moving shadows.

影戤 *yiinggaih*, n., imitation, forgery of trademark goods.

影格(兒) *yiingger'l*, n., exercise book with model calligraphy under a sheet for copying.

影展 *yirng-jaan*, n., photographic exhibition, film festival: 國際影展 International Film Festival, International Exhibition of Photography.

影劇 *yiingjyuh*, n., see *-shih*↓.

影迷 *yiing-mir*, n., a movie fan.

影片(兒) *yiingpiahn*(*-piah'l*), n., movie film.

影評 *yiing-pirng*, n., movie review.

影射 *yiingsheh*, v. t., to describe a figure in novel or to imitate on stage, in order to suggest a certain person.

影響 *yirngshiaang* (*-'shiang*), n., (1) influence: 受人影響 was influenced by certain person; 壞的影響 bad influence; (2) hearsay and not direct testimony: 影響之談.

影像 *yiingshiahng*, n., a portrait.

影戲 *yiingshih*, n., (1) movie; (2) an anc. form of projecting cut-out and manipulated paper shadows on screen, somewhat similar in effect to marionette.

影星 *yiingshing*, n., a movie star.

影子 *yiingtz*, n., shadow: 影子內閣 shadow cabinet.

影影 *yirngyiing*, adj., as in 影影綽綽 *--chocho* indistinct, shadowy.

影院 *yiingyuahn*, n., movie theater (also 影戲院).

黲 41S.91–9

tsaan.

Adj. & adv. Dark, darkly: 黑黲黲的 dismally dark.

SECTION 42

§ 42.30 (冈/一)

皿 42.30

miin (also *miing*).

N. (1) A vessel, utensil: 器皿 utensil. (2) A radical, category for vessels, such as 盂, 盤, 盒, 盆.

且 42.30

chiee (**jyu*).

Fin. part. (**jyu*) (AC) 士曰既且 the man said, "I have been already"; 曰父母且 I call you our parent; cf. (MC) 者 and modn. 着, possibly related.

Adv. (1) Expressing a temporary request or order: 且住 please stop (for a while); 且慢 slowly please, let's stop and discuss; 且別管他 let's forget about him for the present; 且請稍坐 please take a seat (and wait); 這衣服且穿哪 keep the dress, don't throw it away; 暫且, 姑且 for the time being; 姑且置之勿論 let's not discuss it for the present. (2) Expressing impending event: 城且拔矣 the city will soon be taken. (3) Even (＝尚且): 犬且有忠義 even a dog has a sense of loyalty. (4) At random: 苟且偷安 seek peace at any price, without ambition or at sacrifice of principles.

Conj. (1) Now (introducing a new thought): 且夫 now (introducing a gen. statement); 且說 formula for opening or continuing a story. (2) Furthermore, besides: 且爾言過矣 and further you are wrong in your statement; 且如 and besides for example; 而且 moreover; 抑且, 況且 moreover, besides; 或且 perhaps. (3) And, while: 且戰且走 fight a retreat back, fight while falling back; 君子有酒, 多且旨 (AC) the gentleman has wine, good and plenty of it.

§ 42.42 (冈/冈)

月 42.42

yueh.

N. (1) The moon: 月亮, 月球 *-liahng, -chiour* ↓; 月裏嫦娥 fabled lady who ran to the moon to escape from her husband; 月下老人 (allu.) the old man found in moonlight night in charge of tying a red silk of new-born boys and girls destined to be married; 月下花前 under the moon and flowers, evoking love or longing; 滿月, 新月, 月牙, 半月, 上弦月, 下弦月: full, new, crescent, half, first quarter, last quarter moon. (2) A month: 月月, 每月, 逐月 every month; 上月, 下月 last month, next month; 按月 (pay, etc.) by the month; 月初, 月杪, 月底 *-chu, -miaau, -dii* ↓; 滿月, 彌月 baby's completed first month (a celebration); 二月 February; 七月 July; 十一月 November; 十二月 December. (3) A surname.

月半 *yueh-bahn*, n., about the 15th day of the month.

月白 *yueh-bair*, adj., pale bluish-white.

月報 *yueh-bauh*, n., a monthly, monthly bulletin, see *-kan* ↓.

月餅 *yueh'biing*, n., "moon cake" eaten during Mid-Autumn Festival.

月布 *yueh-buh*, n., sanitary belt.

月城 *yueh-cherng*, n., semi-circular enclosure between outer and inner city gates.

月錢 *yueh-chiarn*, n., monthly payment.

月牆兒 *yueh-chiarng'l*, n., see *-cherng* ↑.

月球 *yuehchiour*, n., the moon as a heavenly body.

月琴 *yuehchirn*, n., a moon-shaped guitar.

月初(兒) *yueh-chu('l)*, n., the beginning of the month.

月旦 *yueh-dahn*, n., usu. 月旦評 (litr. allu.) criticism.

月底 *yueh-dii*, n., the end of the month.

月分(兒) *yueh-fehn(-feh'l)*, n., month as a period of time: 多月分兒 many months long; 月分牌(兒) a monthly calendar hung on the wall.

月費 *yueh-feih*, n., monthly expense.

月桂 *yuehgueih*, n., the laurel; 月桂冠 laurel wreath.

月宮 *yueh-gung*, n., (alleged) the palace of the moon.

月黑天 *yueh hei tian*, n., a moonless night.

月華 *yueh-huar*, n., corona of the moon.

月賬 *yueh-jahng*, n., monthly account.

月季 *yueh jih*, n., the monthly rose.

月經 *yuehjing (-'jing)*, n., menstruation, the menses; 月經帶 sanitary belt.

月終 *yueh-jung*, n., end of the month.

月刊 *yuehkan*, n., a monthly.

月窠兒 *yueh-ke'l*, n., the period of the baby's first month.

月老 *yueh-laau*, n., see 月下老人 under N. 1 ↑.

月闌 *yueh-larn*, n., halo of the moon.

月亮 *yuehliahng*, n., (1) usu. vern. term for the moon; (2) moonlight.

月利 *yueh-lih*[1], n., see *-shir* ↓.

月曆 *yueh-lih*[2], n., calendar by the month.

月例 *yuehlih*[3], n., (MC) monthly allowance.

月輪 *yueh-lurn*, n., (LL) the moon.

月杪 *yueh-miaau*, n., the end of the month.

月末 *yueh-moh*, n., ditto.

月色 *yueh-seh*, n., moonlight.

月下香 *yuehshiahshiang*, n., the tuberose.

月信 *yueh-shihn*, n., see *-jing*↑.

月薪 *yueh-shin*, n., monthly salary.

月息 *yueh-shir*, n., monthly interest.

月形 *yueh-shirng*, n., (math.) lune, a crescent-shaped figure.

月事 *yueh-shyh*, n., see *-jing*↑.

月食 *yueh-shyr*, n., (月蝕) eclipse of the moon.

月臺 *yuehtair*, n., car or railway platform.

月頭 *yueh-tour*, n., beginning of the month; 月頭兒 monthly account which begins on the first of the month.

月子 *yueh'tz*, n., as in 坐月子 woman's special care during first month after childbirth.

月總 *yueh-tzuung*, n., monthly reckoning of accounts.

月尾 *yueh-weei*, n., end of the month.

月牙兒 *yueh-yar'l*, n., the new moon; things resembling it.

月曜日 *yuehyauh-ryh*, n., (LL) Monday.

月月紅 *yuehyuehhurng*, n., the monthly rose, see *-jih*↑.

月暈 *yueh-yuhn*, n., halo of the moon.

骨 42.42

guu (gur).

N. (1) A bone: 骨架, 骨子, 骨頭, 骨骼, 骨肉 *-jiah, -'tz, -'tou, -ger, -rouh*↓; 排骨 the ribs, spareribs, (sl.) a skinny person; 骨瘦如柴 emaciated like a stick; 皮包骨 skinny; 骨立 *-lih*[2]↓. (2) Bone structure, type of personality, moral character: 風骨 a person's temperament and character; 傲骨 a proud character; 骨氣 *-'chih*↓. (3) A corpse, skeleton: 下無怨骨, 上無怨人 no one, whether dead or living, will have any cause to complain; 朱門酒肉臭, 路有凍死骨 while the rich dine and wine, the poor die of cold by the roadside.

骨棒 *guu'bang*, adj., very hard in character.

骨氣 *guu'chih*, n., (1) independence of character: 這人很有骨氣 the man is noted for his backbone, i.e., for his sterling character; (2) (callig.) firm and steady strokes.

骨董 *guu'dung (-duung)*, n., curios, antiques (also wr. 古董).

骨朶兒 *gur'duo'l*, n., an unopened flower bud.

骨法 *gurfaa*, n., (Chin. painting) building of the structure of a picture.

骨粉 *gurfeen*, n., fertilizer made from bones.

骨肥 *guufeir*, n., fertilizer made from animal bones.

骨幹 *guugahn*, n., (1) leading spirit in group, leading staff; (2) practical ability.

骨鯁 *gur-geeng*, adj., upright, fair and just (also wr. 骨骾).

骨骼 *guuger*, n., a skeleton, structural pattern (also wr. 骨格).

骨折 *guu-je*, n., fracture of bones.

骨架 *guujiah*, n., a framework, skeleton structure.

骨節 *guujier*, n., (physiol.) joints.

骨質 *guu-jyr*, n., bone substance or structure.

骨科 *guu-ke*, n., orthopedics: 骨科醫生 an orthopedist, a bone specialist.

骨力 *guulih*[1], (1) n., (callig.) strength or force of strokes; (2) *(gur'li)* adj., strong; (3) *(gur'li)* adj., of strong texture: 這張紙很有骨力 this piece of paper has a very strong texture.

骨立 *guulih*[2], adj., bony, with bones sticking out.

骨碌 *gur'lu*, adj., rolling, spinning, turning round and round.

骨膜 *guu-mor*, n., (physiol.) periosteum.

骨牌 *guupair*, n., dominoes.

骨盤 *guuparn*, n., (physiol.) the pelvis (also 骨盆).

骨肉 *guurouh*, n., blood relationships, kith and kin: 骨肉至親 of one's own flesh and blood.

骨相 *guushiahng*, n., a person's bone structure as indicating type of personality: 賤骨相 lazybones; s.o. not worthy of help; 骨相學 the study of bone structure as indicating character (as in phrenology).

骨血 *guushyueh*, n., one's flesh and blood, see *-rouh*↑.

骨髓 *gur-sueei*, n., (physiol.) marrow.

骨炭 *guutahn*, n., bone black.

骨頭 *gur'tou*, n., (1) a piece of bone: 骨頭兒筷子 chopsticks made of bone; (2) (abusive) a person with ugly looks: 瞧你這塊骨頭 just see what a figure you are cutting! (3) one's moral character: 硬骨頭 a person of moral integrity; 有骨頭 has backbone; 沒骨頭 weak-kneed; 輕骨頭 flippant; 賤骨頭 (abusive) you cheap skate, louse.

骨子 *guu'tz*, n., (1) ribs of umbrella, fan: 傘骨子, 扇骨子; (2) innermost part: 這是他骨子裏頭的事 that's his most personal affair; 這人骨子裏很厲害 this man is really very shrewd inside.

骨癌 *guu-yarn*[1] (*-air* preferred), n., cancer in the bones.

骨炎 *guryarn*[2], n., osteitis; 骨髓炎 osteomyelitis.

骨瘍 *guuyarng*, n., (med.) bone ulcer.

丹 42.42

dan.

N. (1) Pill: 膏丹丸散 medical pill, ointment and powder, esp. the pill of immortality sought by alchemists: 金丹, 仙丹 elixir of life, the philosopher's stone; 煉丹 the practice to form this pill. (2) Cinnabar: 丹砂 *-sha*↓.

Adj. Red: 丹楓 red maple; 丹桂 cinnamon; 丹書, 丹詔 imperial edict written in red.

丹忱 *danchern*, n., pure loyalty

of heart.

丹誠 *dancherng*, n., ditto.

丹鉛 *danchian*, n., the business of proofreading or revision, from practice of using red ink (丹 vermilion and 鉛 white lead powder).

丹青 *danching*, n., painting (red and green).

丹墀 *danchy*, n., terrace area in imperial palace.

丹第 *Dandih*, n., (translit.) Dante (usu. 但丁).

丹鼎 *dandiing*, n., furnace of alchemists for concoction of pill of immortality.

丹毒 *dandur*, n., (med.) erysipelas, a streptococcus disease of the skin.

丹方 *danfang*, n., medical prescription; prescription for making pill of immortality.

丹黃 *danhuarng*, n., red and yellow ink used in proofreading and revising.

丹魄 *danpoh*, n., amber.

丹砂 *dansha*, n., cinnabar, material for red color.

丹參 *danshen*, n., (bot.) salvia, *Scutellaria indica*.

丹心 *danshin*, n., heart of pure loyalty: 留取丹心照汗青 that my loyalty may leave a page in the annals.

丹田 *dantiarn*, n., the pubic region (seat of prostate and ovary) considered as region for forming internal pill of immortality; 丹田氣 n., breath control by the exercise of diaphragm.

冊 42.42

tseh (**chaai*).

[Var. 册; cogn. 策]

N. (1) Anc. form of book consisting of series of bamboo strips strung together. (2) A volume: 第一冊 volume one; 共十冊 in ten volumes; 冊子, 冊頁 *-tz*, *-yeh*↓. (3) A formal writ, conferring honors, praising service: 封冊, 玉冊 etc., see 冊書 *-shu*↓. (4) (Rarely u. f.) 策 strategy, 92A.01. (5) (**chaai*) 樣冊兒 pattern book.

V. t. (1) To confer title of prince (親王): imperial concubine (妃). (2) To adopt, set up formally, invest with office: 冊命, 冊封, 冊立 *-mihng*, *-feng*, *-lih*↓.

冊封 *tsehfeng*, v. t., to invest with rank, title.

冊府 *tsehfuu*, n., (LL) library, hall of books.

冊正 *tseh-jehng*, v. t., to set up formally as legal wife.

冊立 *tsehlih*, v. t., to crown (empress).

冊命 *tseh-mihng*, v. t. & n., formal order, esp. in conferring honors.

冊書 *tsehshu*, n., (AC) a formal writ conferring honors, ranks, etc.

冊子 *tsehtz*, n., a small volume, pamphlet, oft. 小冊子 small pamphlet.

冊頁 *tsehyeh*, n., an album of unbound sheets, paintings, calligraphy (also wr. 冊葉).

用 42.42

yuhng.

N. (1) Use, function: 用處 *-chuh*↓; 功用 function (of medicine, etc.); 所學非所用 a person's education does not fit him for a certain job; 實用 practical use; 適用, 合用 convenient for use. (2) Expenses: 費用 ditto; 國用 national expenditures; 家用 domestic expenses; 日用 daily expenses.

V.t. (1) To use, employ (person): 用人 *-rern*↓; 任用 appoint to post; 用賢 to use able men; 聘用 to appoint (teacher, musician, etc.); 僱用 to employ (servants, etc.); 用人不當 use wrong or incompetent men for jobs; 試用 use on probation; 重用 to commission s. o. and rely on him heavily. (2) To spend: 挪用 to use certain funds temporarily; 借用 to borrow; 用不了 do not need so much (money); 濫用公款 irregularities in use of public funds; 用錢無度 extravagant with money. (3) To apply, operate (tool, instrument), to make use: 運用 to apply (brains, learning, common sense, etc.); 應用 to serve a purpose; 利用 to utilize, make use (of person for certain end), take advantage (of wind for sail, of certain regulations, loopholes, etc.); 善用 know how to handle (men, money, time). (4) To serve as, in order to: 用以增加知識 in order to increase one's knowledge. (5) As more elegant substitute for "eat," "drink": 用茶 drink tea; 用飯 eat rice; 請用 please help yourself to food.

Prep. With: 用刀殺人 kill with a knife; 用目阻止 stop (s.o.) with a look; 用心, 用力 *-shin*, *-lih*↓.

用兵 *yuhng-bing*, phr., skill in military command.

用不著 *yuhng'bujaur*, phr., there is no need to (do); useless.

用塲 *yuhngcharng*, n., use, application: 沒有用塲 is of no use.

用錢 *yuhngchiarn*, (1) to spend money; (2) (*-'chian*) commission fee.

用情 *yuhng-chirng*, n., quality in directing one's affections: 用情不專 liable to change lovers.

用處 *yuhngchuh*, n., use, practical application.

用度 *yuhng-duh*, n., habit of spending money.

用法 *yuhng-faa*, n., handling of justice.

用費 *yuhng-feih*, n., fees, expenses.

用功 *yuhnggung*, v.i., to work hard, esp. at studies.

用工夫 *yuhng-gung'fu*, v.i., to study hard, practice hard.

用戶 *yuhng-huh*, n., subscriber to electric power, telephone, etc.

用間 *yuhng-jiahn*, phr., see 離^間 60S.11.

亅	小	⺊	十	土	ナ	廾	乚	丨	一	丅	フ	口	囚	冈	乛	厂	尸	亠	广	宀	丶	乚	弋	心	八	人	乂	乛	丿	丿	𠂉	𡿨
00	01	02	10	11	12	20	21	22	30	31	32	40	41	42	50	51	52	60	61	62	63	70	71	72	80	81	82	83	90	91	92	93

用計 *yuhng-jih*, phr., by strategy, plan, trick.

用盡 *yuhng-jihn*, v.t., to exhaust (efforts, etc.).

用具 *yuhng-jyuh*, n., appliance(s).

用來 *yuhng-lair*, v.i., for use (convenient, etc.).

用力 *yuhng-lih*, adv., (work) hard, with concentrated effort.

用命 *yuhng-mihng*, phr., (LL) obey orders.

用品 *yuhngpiin*, n., appliance(s), material or articles for use (as cosmetics).

用人 *yuhng-rern*, n., (1) employee; (2) skill or tact in handling personnel.

用項 *yuhng'shiang*, n., expenditures.

用心 *yuhngshin*, adv., with concentrated effort.

用世 *yuhngshyh*[1], phr., to serve in society.

用事 *yuhng-shyh*[2], v.i., (1) to be in power; (2) (litr.) literary allusions.

用頭 *yuhng'tou*, n., (coll.) some specific use.

用途 *yuhngtur*, n., purpose of expenditure.

用武 *yuhng-wuu*, phr., to choose the warpath.

用意 *yuhngyih*, n., intention, careful thought or hidden purpose: 用意甚善 (law, etc.) serves a very good purpose.

网 42.42

waang.

[Arch. var. of 網 93B.42]

同 42.42

turng.

N. (1) Commonwealth: 大同世界 the world commonwealth; 世界大同 the world is a commonwealth, Confucius' ideal of human society. (2) A surname.

Adj. & adv. (1) Same, similar: 同一 *-yi*↓; 相同 are alike; 如同 as if; 如同身受 would consider it as a personal favor to me; 如同刀割 like cutting of one's own flesh; 不同 be different; 同樣的 similar(ly), in the same manner; 同年, 同月生 born in same year and month; 同音字 homonym; 同義字 synonym; 同時 same time; 同路人 *-luhrern*↓; 同類 same kind, class or species; 同類相殘 kill one's own kind; 同列 same rank; opp. 異: 大同小異 are alike with minor differences; 同異 similarities and differences; 同工異曲 or 異曲同工 s. t. which achieves same goal with different means; 同父異母 same father, different mothers; 同胞 *-bau*↓; 同袍 *-paur*↓; 同室操戈 internecine warfare; 同病相憐 fellow sufferers (of same illness) understand one another; 聖人先得吾心所同然 the sage discovered what was common in the human heart. (2) Together, in common: 共同, 一同 (work, proceed, leave) together; 會同, 協同 in conjunction or cooperation with one another; 同來同去 come and go together; 同坐同食 sit together, eat together; 同遊 take pleasure trip together; 同甘苦 fare and share alike, for better, for worse; 同住, 同宿 live together; 同居 *-jyu*↓; 同舟共濟, 風雨同舟 people "in the same boat" help each other in distress; 同衾共枕 (of husband and wife) share same quilt and pillow; 同牀異夢 strange bedfellows, persons thrown together but each having a different problem or ambition; 同聲讚許 give praise in unison; 異口同聲 all agree; 同一鼻孔出氣 talk exactly one like the other; 同流合污 associate oneself with undesirable elements or trend; 同歸於盡 all perish together; 殊途同歸 reach same goal by different means (cf. "all roads lead to Rome"); 同穴 husband and wife buried in same grave.

Prep. With (used like vern. 和, LL 與): 他同你在一起 he is together with you; 我同你去 I'll go with you; 同他說話 talking with him.

同案 *turng-ahn*, n., formerly, one who was admitted to school in the same year in the civil service system.

同伴 *turngbahn*, n., companion (in travel, etc.).

同班 *turngban*, n., fellow classmate.

同胞 *turngbau*, n., brothers of the same mother; term for compatriot.

同輩 *turngbeih*, n., person of the same generation.

同步 *turngbuh*, v. i. & adj., synchronize, synchronous.

同儕 *turngchair*, n., (LL) fellow, colleague.

同情 *turngchirng*, v. i. & t., to sympathize: 同情你 or 於你 sympathize with you; 同情心 n., sympathy.

同窗 *turngchuang*, n., schoolmate, classmate ("same window").

同道 *turngdauh*, n., person of same belief or convictions.

同等 *turngdeen*, adj. & n., equal, -ity; same in status, energy, remuneration, etc.

同調 *turngdiauh*, n., person with same common purpose or taste: 引爲同調 draw person into the same political group.

同房 *turngfarng*, v. i., cohabit; share the same room.

同行(兒) *turngharng('l)*, n., fellow craftsman, person of same profession; (2) (*-shirng*) v. i., go together.

同好 *turng-hauh*, n., same tastes or hobby.

同化 *turnghuah*, v. t., (1) assimilate, be assimilated; (2) (of foreign tribes) adopt Chin. dress, language and customs.

同夥 *turnghuoo*, n., fellow worker in same shop; member of group or gang.

同種 *turngjuung*, adj. & n., (person) of same race.

同志 *turngjyh*, n., comrade; member of same party.

同居 *turngjyu*, v. i., live together, esp. live as husband and wife without marriage, cohabit: 同居分爨 live in the same house, but eat separately (of relatives).

同僚 *turngliaur*, n., colleague in office.

同路人 *turngluhrern*, n., (communist) fellow traveller.

同門 *turngmern*, n., (1) pupils of same master; (2) husbands whose wives are sisters; 同門異戶 holding the same views with minor differences.

同盟 *turngmerng*, n., allies; 同盟國 allied nations; 同盟會 *Tungmenghui*, China's revolutionary party which later became the *Kuomintang*.

同謀 *turngmour*, v. i., conspire together: 同謀者 conspirator.

同年 *turng niarn*, phr., (1) in or of the same year; 不可同年而語 should not be mentioned in the same breath—far inferior, now usu. 同日 (see *-ryh*↓); (2) graduates of the same class in the civil examinations.

同袍 *turngpaur*, n., comrades in the same army: 同袍同澤 ditto.

同人 *turngrern*[1], n., (fellow-) member of a group (such as cosponsors of meeting, audience being addressed in meeting).

同仁 *turngrern*[2], n., ditto.

同日 *turng ryh*, phr., in the same day: 不可同日而語, see *-niarn* ↑.

同鄉 *turngshiang*, n. & adj., person of the same village, country or province.

同姓 *turngshihng*[1], member of the same clan.

同性 *turngshihng*[2], n., same sex; 同性愛, 同性戀 homosexual, -lity.

同心 *turngshin*, adj., united at heart or in common purpose; 同心同德 with one heart and one mind; 同心圓 (math.) concurrent circle; 同心結 a "lovers' knot," also used on Buddhist cassocks.

同事 *turngshyh*, n., common term for "colleague."

同時 *turngshyr*, adv., at the same time, simultaneously, in the meantime.

同學 *turngshyuer*, n., fellow student; 同學會 alumni association.

同堂 *turngtarng*, n., cousin (＝堂兄弟) of same family name.

同宗 *turngtzung*, adj., of the same clan branch.

同族 *turngtzur*, adj., of the same tribe.

同位素 *turngweihsuh*, n., (chem.) isotope.

同溫層 *turngwentserng*, n., stratosphere.

同文 *turngwern*, adj., of the same language and culture.

同硯 *turngyahn*, n., fellow student (＝同學).

同樣 *turngyahng*, adv., equal, -ly: 同樣美麗, 報酬 equally beautiful, equally paid.

同業 *turngyeh*, n., member of the same profession; 同業公會 a trade union.

同一 *turngyi*, n., same: 同一方向, 步伐 same direction, steps.

同意 *turngyih*, v. i. & n., agree, consent: 我不同意 I disagree; 得你同意 have your consent; 同意書 letter of agreement.

周 42.42

jou.

N. (1) Name of dynasty (Wade: Chou Dyn.). (2) A surname. (3) Circumference: 周徑, 周圍 *-jihng*, *-weir*↓. (4) A week (interch. 週); anniversary: 周年 *-niarn*↓. (5) (Phys.) cycle: 千週 kilocycle; 兆周 megacycle; 周率, 周波 *-lyuh*, *-bo*↓.

V. t. To help tide over (crisis): 周急 ditto; 周全, 周濟 *-chyuarn*, *-jih*[2]↓.

Adj. & adv. Complete, thorough: 周到, 周至 *-dauh*, *-jyh*↓; 周密, 周詳 *-mih*, *-shiarng*↓, cf. 週 42.83↓.

周遍 *joubiahn*, adj. & adv., (interch. 週) all around, all over a place, also prep., 周遍全球 all over the world.

周邊 *joubian*, n., (math.) perimeter.

周髀 *Joubih*, n., an anc. work on astronomy and trigonometry, based on conception of the sky as a vault.

周波 *joubo*, n., (phys.) cycle.

周親 *jouchin*, (AC) closest relatives.

周全 *jouchyuarn*, v. t., to help others, esp. with money: 周全人家.

周到 *jou'dauh*, adj., thorough and satisfactory (in service, hospitality).

周回 *jouhueir*, adv., around, back and forth.

周章 *joujang*, adj., (1) around; (2) flurried (also wr. 輈張); (3) full of difficulties, see *-jer*↓.

周正 *jou'jeng*, adj., properly in place: 帽子戴周正了 put hat on properly.

周折 *joujer*, adj., (affair) difficult to deal with: 此事頗費周折 this matter is quite complex.

周角 *joujiaau*, n., (math.) perigon.

周浹 *joujiar*, (1) adj., very attentive (to guests); (2) adv., ＝周匝 *-tza*↓.

周忌 *joujih*[1], n., first anniversary of person's death.

周濟 *joujih*[2], v. t., to help (person) in charity.

周徑 *joujihng*, n., diameter.

周轉 *jou'juaan*, v. i., to have cash available: 周轉不靈 not enough cash to answer needs.

周桌 *jou-juo*, v. i., to turn over table in anger.

周至 *joujyh*, adj., very attentive (to guests), providing for all needs.

周流 *jouliour*, v. i., to circulate; to travel around.

周率 *joulyuh*, n., radio frequency.

周密 *joumih*, adj., see *-jyh*↑.

周內 *jounah*, v. i., (AC) to weave a legalistic trap to condemn person (now commonly 深文周納).

周年 *jou-niarn*, n., anniversary: 五周年紀念 fifth anniversary (usu. wr. 週年).

周身 *joushen*, adv., all over the body (ache, bruise).

周詳 *joushiarng*, adj., detailed and complete (report, etc.).

周旋 *joushyuarn*, v. i., (1) to go back and forth; (2) make the social round of dinners; (3) (AC) to meet on battlefield ("chase back and forth"); (4) deal with person in complex or changing situation.

周歲 *jou-sueih*, n., first anniversary of child (also wr. 週).

周天 *joutian*, n., (astron.) a complete circle of 360 degrees.

周匝 *joutza*, adv., in one round.

周遭 *joutzau*, adj. & adv., (LL) around.

周圍 *jouweir*, n., (1) surroundings; (2) circumference. ⌈round.

周延 *jouyarn*, adj., the complete

周易 *Jouyih*, n., *Book of Changes*, one of the "Six Confucian Classics," (also called 易經 *Yihjing*).

岡 42.42

gang (also *gaang*).

N. The crest of a hill: 山岡 a mountain ridge.

岡陵 *ganglirng*, n., a high mound.

岡桐 *gangturng*, n., (bot.) *Aleurites cordata*, the wood oil tree (also 罌子桐, 油桐).

罔 42.42

waang.

[Dist. 岡↑]

N. U.f. 網 a net, 93B.42.

V.t. (1) To deceive: 欺罔 to cheat, deceive; 欺天罔人 deceive God and man. (2) U.f. 網 to net: 罔利 (AC) to net profits.

Adj. U.f. 惘: 罔然 *-rarn*↓.

Adv. (LL) no, not (related 無): 罔不 all, without exception (=無不); 罔極 *-jir*↓; 罔見 fail to see (=不見); 罔效 without results (=無效); 罔顧 disregard (=不顧); 罔有 have not (=無有).

罔極 *waangjir*, adv., (AC) boundless, extremely, beyond all bounds.

罔兩 *warngliaang*, n., (1) spirits, demons of the wilds (also wr. 魍魎); (2) (AC) the penumbra, fringe shadow.

罔然 *waangrarn*, adj., feeling lost, disconcerted.

罔養 *warngyaang*, v. i., (AC) hesitate, without decision.

咼 42.42

kuai.

咼斜 *kuaishier*, adj., twisted (mouth), squint-eyed.

---

§ 42.50 (冈/乛)

囘 42.50

hueir.

[Anc. var. of 回 41.41]

---

§ 42.70 (冈/乚)

几 42.70

jii (sp. pr. **ji*).

N. A small or low table: 几案 *-ahn*↓; 茶几 a teapoy, a small side table.

几案 *jii-ahn*, n., (1) an office desk; (2) a small table.

几閣 *jiiger*, n., (MC) a shelf (for books, etc.).

几席 *jiishir*, n., a desk.

几筵 *jiiyarn*, n., (AC) ceremonial dinner.

凡 42.70

farn.

N. The secular world, life of the senses: 塵凡, 凡世 (Budd. & LL) the material world, life of the senses; 神仙下凡 fairy becomes incarnate; 尼姑思凡 a nun desires normal human life; 超凡入聖 phr., overcome all worldly thoughts and enter sainthood.

Adj. (1) Common, ordinary: 平凡 ordinary (writing, person); 凡人 ordinary mortal; 凡夫, 凡民 ordinary people; 庸夫凡卒 common laborer and private; 不凡 distinguished, uncommon (talent, person); 不同凡響 phr., not of the common sort; 非凡人物 extraordinary person. (2) Any, all: 凡人 all people; 凡事 all things; 凡事小心 be careful in all things.

Pron. & adv. Any, all, anybody, anytime, everytime: 凡有 whenever there is; 凡見 everytime you meet or see, also all who see; 凡要 all who wish, everytime you wish; 凡百 all and sundry.

凡間 *farnjian*, n., the material life subject to the senses.

凡例 *farnlih*, n., part of foreword setting out principles of editing, selection, etc.; guiding formation of book.

凡目 *farnmuh*, n., main idea and contents of book.

凡世 *farnshyh*, n., see *-jian*↑.

凡士林 *farnshyhlirn*, n., (translit.) vaseline.

甩 42.70

shuaai.

[Var. of 摔 *shuai*, 10A.10]

V. i. & t. (1) To cast away, abandon (friend, lover): 把朋友甩了 abandon friend; 被女朋友甩了 thrown overboard by a girl friend; 甩外衣 throw down overcoat. (2) To wag tail: 甩尾巴.

甩車 *shuaai-che*, v. i., to detach coaches from locomotive, free car being trailed by unhooking it.
甩大鞋 *shuaai-dahshier*, v. i., to strut about, carry a haughty, overbearing manner.
甩髮 *shuairfaa* (-'*fa*), n., (Chin. opera) long, hanging wig; v.i., to swing such hair.
甩臉子 *shuair-liaantz*, v. i., pull a long face, turn hostile look.
甩咧子 *shuair-lietz*, v. i., grumble.
甩賣 *shuaaimaih*, v. t., to dump, sell at cheap price.
甩閑話 *shuaai-shiarnhuah*, v. i., to grumble.
甩手(兒) *shuair-shoou('l)*, v. i., wash one's hands of the matter.
甩子 *shuair-tzyy*, v. i., (of insects) lay eggs.

夙 42.70

suh.
[Related 素 11.01, 宿 62.41]

Adj. (1) Early: 夙夜 *-yeh*↓; 夙興夜寐 (LL) get up early and go to bed late. (2) (Interch. 宿) old: 夙仇, 夙怨, 夙昔, 夙緣 *-chiour, -yuahn, -shir, -yuarn*↓. (3) (Interch. 宿) (Budd.) inborn, inherited: see 宿ᐞ緣, 宿ᐞ業 62.41.

夙仇 *suh-chiour*, n., old enemy.
夙慧 *suh-hueih*, n., (Budd.) inborn intelligence.
夙駕 *suh-jiah*, phr., (LL) come early ("early carriage").
夙昔 *suhshir*, adv., of old, in olden times.
夙素 *suh-suh*, n., old, deep wish.
夙夜 *suhyeh*, adv., morning and night: 夙夜匪懈 (LL) never relax morning and night.
夙怨 *suh-yuahn*, n., old grudge (also wr. 宿).
夙緣 *suhyuarn*, n., (Budd.) fate inherited from previous incarnations (also wr. 宿).

凬 42.70

feng.
[Abbr. of 風 42.70]

凤 42.70

fehng.
[Abbr. of 鳳 42.70]

凰 42.70

huarng.

N. See 鳳ᐞ凰 42.70↓.

鳳 42.70

fehng.

N. (1) A mythic bird, the phoenix: 鳳皇 (also 凰) female (凰) and male (鳳), symbol of married couple; 鳳凰于飛 the pair fly together happily; a wedding compliment; 鳳凰來儀 phoenix appears at court, an auspicious omen; 鳳求凰 the male chasing after the female; 鳳凰 (fig.) the elite scholars; oft. coupled with 龍: 龍翻鳳舞 dance in swirling motion; see also 鸞 93.50; 鳳冠 bride's headdress; 鳳毛麟角 s.t. rare, unique (talent, etc.); 鳳鳴朝陽 phoenix singing in morning sun, unusually good omen for country. (2) A surname.

鳳翹 *fehngchiaur*, n., (1) a ladies' hair ornament; (2) ladies' turn-up shoes.
鳳雛 *fehngchur*, n., child prodigy, promising young man (oft. of friend's son).
鳳蝶 *fehngdier*, n., common white butterfly, *Papilio xuthus*.
鳳詔 *fehngjauh*, n., imperial edict.
鳳舉 *fehngjyuu*, v. i., soar aloft, achieve heights (of fame); (MC) be sent on mission abroad.
鳳梨 *fehnglir*, n., pineapple.
鳳仙花 *fehngshianhua*, n., balsam flower, *Balsaminaceae*.
鳳簫 *fehngshiau*, n., flute.
鳳子 *fehngtz*, n., a variety of big butterfly.
鳳藻 *fehngtzaau*, n., flowery passage in writing.
鳳尾蕉 *fehngweeijiau* or 鳳尾松 *--sung*, n., (bot.) a graceful palm, *Cycas revoluta*; 鳳尾草 *--tsaau*, ferns.

黽 42.70

miin.

黽勉 *mirmiaan*, v. i., work hard, try hard.

風 42.70

feng.

N. (1) Wind, breeze, storm: 清風(徐來), 涼風 pleasant breeze; 颱風, 大風 typhoon; 旋風, 羊角風 whirlwind, tornado; 季候風 monsoon; 狂風暴雨, 風暴, 颱風, 風災 storm; 風吹草動 grass bends as wind blows—influence, also state of restlessness, sensitive to slight upsets; 風聲鶴唳 wind whistles and wild geese cry—state of fear and turmoil; 樹欲靜而風不止, 子欲養而親不待 (AC allu.) a son's regret at not being able to serve parents in their old age, shortened as 風樹 or 風木; 風前燭 can-

A

風 dle before a draft, short time left for aged people, also 風燭殘年. (2) A prolific term, associated with clouds, rain, moon, frost, water: 風雲, 風雨, 風月, 風霜, 風水 *-yurn*, *-yuu*, *-yueh*, *-shuang*, *-'shueei* ↓; with waves, stream, tide: 風浪, 風流, 風潮 *-lahng*, *-liour*, *-chaur* ↓; with light, landscape: 風光, 風景 *-guang*, *-jiing* ↓; 風花雪月 wind, flower, snow and moon—romantic themes. (3) Of utensils having to do with wind: 風扇, 風帽 *-shahn*, *-mauh*[2], etc. ↓. (4) Of customs, atmosphere: usu. 風氣 *-chih* ↓; 風俗, 風土 *-sur*, *-tuu*, etc. ↓; 民風 people's customs; 文風 literary atmosphere; 門風, 家風 traditional atmosphere, culture of family; 妖風, 刁風 immoral atmosphere; 歪風 eccentric or corrupt atmosphere; 男風 sodomy; 國風 collection of folk songs in classical *Book of Poetry*. (5) Charm, tone, style: 風韻 charm; 風趣, 風度, 風味, 風格, 風致 *-chyuh*, *-duh*, *-weih*, *-ger*, *-jyh* ↓; character: 高風亮節 (in praise of a person's) high and upright character; 聞風而起 (AC) heard of the reputation and came; 風骨, 風節, *-guu*, *-jier* ↓; appearance, demeanor: 風姿, 風儀, 風範, 風采 *-tzy*, *-yir*, *-fahn*, *-tsaai* ↓. (6) Various ailments: 傷風 common cold; 頭風疼 headache, migraine: 風濕, 風痛 *-shy*[1], *-tuhng* ↓. (7) A surname.

V.i. (1) Spread rumor: 風聞, 風傳 *-wern*, *-chuarn* ↓; var. of 諷 to criticize: 風示, 風議 show opinion, criticize by innuendo; 可風 (=可爲風範) (LL) may be a model for others. (2) To move, spread out, like air: 風行一時 be popular; 風發, 意氣風發 angers rise; 風馳電掣 come like a storm, flash like lightning; 風起雲湧 erupt like a storm.

Adj. (1) Handsome, romantic, talented, elegant: 風雅 *-yaa* ↓. (2) (MC) u.f. 瘋: 他風了 he has gone crazy. (3) In heat, see 風馬牛 *-maa-niour* ↓.

風暴 *fengbauh*, n., storm.
風痺 *fengbih*, n., paralysis.

B

風伯 *fengbor*, n., god of wind.
風潮 *fengchaur*, n., crisis, school or labor strike: 鬧風潮 create a crisis.
風車 *fengche*, n., windmill; propeller-like toy.
風塵 *fengchern*, n., hardships of journey, dust of journey: 風塵僕僕 hard journey; secular world of trials and temptations: 墮落風塵 (of woman) become prostitute; 風塵女子 such professional women.
風氣 *fengchih*, n., current customs, fashion: 不良風氣 bad moral atmosphere; style of character: 豪邁風氣 a heroic air or style.
風琴 *fengchirn*, n., reed or pipe organ.
風情 *fengchirng*, n., romantic feeling (of friendship, love): 一段風情 a romantic episode; 風情萬種 exceedingly fascinating and charming (woman).
風傳 *fengchuarn*, v.i., it is rumored.
風圈 *fengchyuan*, n., halo around moon on windy night.
風趣 *fengchyuh*, n., charm of personality: 此人甚有風趣 this man has an exceedingly charming personality.
風燈 *fengdeng*, n., storm lantern.
風調 *fengdiauh*, n., tone or style (of personality, writing).
風度 *fengduh*, n., suavity of style.
風洞 *fengduhng*, n., wind tunnel.
風範 *fengfahn*, n., ideal or ideal personality.
風帆 *fengfarn*, n., sail of boat.
風概 *fenggaih*, n., inspiring personality.
風乾 *fenggan*, adj., sun-dried or dried by hanging (duck, sausage, etc.).
風格 *fengger*, n., style of person, writing; mode of a generation.
風光 *fengguang*, n., landscape; special atmosphere; beautiful impression.
風骨 *fengguu*, n., (exotic, strong) character; personality.
風寒 *fengharn*, n., cold: 受了 or 感冒風寒 catch cold.
風花菜 *fenghua-tsaih*, n., (bot.) nasturtium.
風化 *fenghuah*, n., (1) moral atmosphere: 有傷風化 corrupting atmosphere; hence 風化區 district of loose women; (2) (geol.) weathering of rocks; (3) (chem.) efflorescence.

C

風懷 *fenghuair*, (1) n., poetic or romantic sentiment; (2) v.t., worship (the anc. great).
風華 *fenghuar*, n., beauty, elegance: 絕代風華 unsurpassed beauty (woman) of a generation.
風疹 *fengjeen*, n., a kind of measles; German measles (urticaria).
風箏 *fengjeng*, n., kite.
風鑑 *fengjiahn*, n., (1) (LL) knowledge of human character; (2) physiognomist: 風鑑家.
風敎 *fengjiauh*, n., moral culture, moral customs.
風節 *fengjier*, n., integrity of character.
風紀 *fengjih*, n., moral standards: 風紀蕩然 moral standards have disappeared.
風鏡 *fengjihng*, n., glasses worn as protection against sandstorm.
風景 *fengjiing*, n., scenery; 風景區 scenic spots.
風致 *fengjyh*, n., charm (of painting, person).
風口 *fengkoou*, n., draft: 站在風口 stand in a draft.
風兒 *feng'l*, n., breath of rumor: 有點風兒 there is a kind of rumor.
風浪 *fenglahng*, n., storm during voyage; crisis: 經過多少風浪 went through many crises; 興風作浪 create nuisance, stir up trouble; 風平浪靜 the storm abates, all is calm.
風蘭 *fenglarn*, n., a kind of orchid, *Angraecum falcatum*.
風涼 *fengliarng*, adj., cool: 風涼地方 a cool corner; 說風涼話 make cool, sly criticism.
風流 *fengliour*, adj., (1) romantic: 風流人物 a romantic person; (2) distinguished, handsome, lovable: 風流可愛, 風流蘊藉, 倜儻 ditto; (AC)=流風餘韻 surviving influence of poets, high characters.
風馬牛 *feng-maa-niour*, adj., when a horse and a cow are in heat, they have nothing to do with each other (不相及)—gen. term for "totally unconnected" affair.

風 貌 *fengmauh*[1], n., handsome appearance.

風 帽 *fengmauh*[2], n., a cowl, storm cap, covering jowl and neck.

風 靡 *fengmii*, v.i., be popular, fashionable: 風靡一時 (LL) be popular for a time.

風 魔 *fengmor*, n., as in 中風魔 become crazy; (v.t.) 風魔了他 made him head over heels in love.

風 木 *fengmuh*, phr., see N. 1 ↑.

風 鳥 *fengniaau*, n., bird of paradise.

風 波 *fengpo*, n., upsets, trials during progress, crisis: 渡了這一場風波 pass over this crisis; 平地起風波 a crisis out of nowhere.

風 人 *fengrern*, n., poet.

風 騷 *fengsau*, adj., (1) (of woman) men-crazy, amorous; (2) poetically sentimental.

風 色 *fengseh*, n., force of wind; changing weather; changing countenance: 看風色 watch a person's countenance or moods.

風 痧 *fengsha*, n., see *-jeen* ↑.

風 扇 *fengshahn*, n., rotating fan; electric fan.

風 尚 *fengshahng*, n., fashion of the times.

風 聲 *fengsheng*, n., rumor, news: 風聲不對 bad news.

風 神 *fengshern*, n., handsome looks or expression.

風 向 *fengshiahng*, n., direction: 失了風向 lost bearings.

風 箱 *fengshiang*, n., bellows.

風 癇 *fengshiarn*, n., epilepsy.

風 邪 *fengshier*, n., ailment said due to cold or exposure.

風 信 *fengshihn*, n., seasonal wind; 風信子 *--tzyy*, n., (bot.) hyacinth; 風信子石 (geol.) hyacinth, a semi-precious stone.

風 行 *fengshirng*, v.i., be fashionable, popular: 風行全世界 popular all over the world; 風行草偃 phr., where the wind passes, the grass bends—influence of gentlemen.

風 霜 *fengshuang*, n., wind and frost; climatic hardships: 受盡風霜之苦 endure all the hardships of exposure; severity of countenance.

風 水 *feng'shuеei*, n., Chin. science of geomancy or the influence of landscape (hills, river, layout of land) on people and their fortunes, esp. concerning gravesites, orig. esthetic: 這地風水好 the *fengshueei* is good or propitious; 風水先生 geomancer; 看風水 examine site of building, grave from geomantic point of view.

風 樹 *fengshuh*, n., an allu., see N. 1 ↑.

風 濕 *fengshy*[1], n., arthritis, rheumatism.

風 師 *fengshy*[2], n., see *-bor* ↑.

風 俗 *fengsur*, n., social customs (good or bad).

風 頭 *fengtour*, n., person's prestige, pomp: 風頭十足 very pompous; 出風頭 in the limelight, given to publicity; to show off.

風 采 *fengtsaai*, n., (court.) your elegant appearance; person's attractive looks.

風 從 *fengtsurng*, v.i., (LL) follow the lead: 四海風從 the world follows.

風 痛 *fengtuhng*, n., arthritic pain.

風 土 *fengtuu*, n., locality: 風土人情 local customs, practices.

風 災 *fengtzai*, n., disaster of storm.

風 姿 *fengtzy*, n., looks: 風姿綽約 (of lady) charming appearance and personality.

風 味 *fengweih*, n., flavor (of prose, personality, regional cooking).

風 聞 *fengwern*, v.i. & t., hear by rumor or current talks, get wind of.

風 物 *fengwuh*, n., local customs and products.

風 雅 *fengyaa*, adj. & n., elegant, -ce, cultured, sometimes affected: 附庸風雅 do the culture bit, join the art or literary cult; 風流儒雅 cultured.

風 謠 *fengyaur*, n., =民風歌謠 folk rhymes, folk songs, oft. a criticism of current affairs.

風 義 *fengyih*, high conduct, high principles; deep respect among friends: 風義人情 deep respect and friendship.

風 儀 *fengyir*, n., (court.) your noble appearance.

風 月 *fengyueh*, n., wind and moon, romance, romantic (talk, affairs).

風 韻 *fengyuhn*, n., charm and tone of person's style, appearance, character or poetry: 徐娘半老, 風韻猶存 the woman in her thirty-forties still retains a great deal of charm.

風 雲 *fengyurn*, n., winds and clouds; high position; austere heights: 風雲際會 riding the crest of fortune; 叱咤風雲 (of great spirit) can command the sea and waves; 風雲不測 sudden change of fortune; disaster; 風雲人物 men in the news, headlines.

風 雨 *fengyuu*, n., stormy weather: 風風雨雨 disturbances, rumor.

颷 42.70

biau.

[Var. 飆]

N. Storm, hurricane.

颭 42.70

jaan.

Adj. (AC) 颭颭 floating in wind.

颼 42.70

sou.

V.t. (Of wind) blow: 被風颼乾了 has been dried in the wind.

Adj. Descriptive of sousing sound: 颼颼.

亅	小	卜	十	土	ナ	卄	⺊	丨	一	丅	フ	口	図	冈	乛	厂	尸	亠	广	宀	丶	乚	七	心	八	人	乂	㇀	一	刂	㇗	く
00	01	02	10	11	12	20	21	22	30	31	32	40	41	42	50	51	52	60	61	62	63	70	71	72	80	81	82	83	90	91	92	93

飃 42.70

piau.
[Var. of 飄 31S.70]

颶 42.70

jyuh.

N. 颶風 a hurricane.

颺 42.70

yarng.

V.i. To float, to flutter, to soar aloft, see 揚 10A.50.

颳 42.70

gua.

V.i. (Of wind) to blow: 颳風 a storm is blowing; 今天颳風 it is windy today.

颱 42.70

tair.

N. Typhoon: 颱風, 風颱.

§ 42.82 (冈/乂)

殳 42.82

shu.

N. (AC) a long pole, an anc. weapon.

§ 42.83 (冈/乛)

迥 42.83

jyuung.
[Pop. 逈]

Adj. & adv. Far, vast(ly): 迥迥 *-jyuung*↓; 迥遠 *-yuaan*↓.

迥别 *jyuungbier*, adj., entirely different.
迥迥 *jyurngjyuung*, adj., faraway, distant.
迥空 *jyuungkung*, n., the sky as a boundless open space.
迥然 *jyuungrarn*, adv., utterly, entirely: 迥然不同 definitely different.
迥殊 *jyuungshu*, adj., see *-bier*↑.
迥異 *jyuungyih*, adj., ditto.
迥遠 *jyurngyuaan*, adj., far, faraway.

週 42.83

jou.

N. (1) A week: 週末 *-moh*↓; 週刊, 週報 *-kan*, *-bauh*↓. (2) One year: 週歲 one full year, first anniversary; 週年 *-niarn*↓. (3) One round: 繞場一週 walk one round; 環遊世界一週 make a trip round the world.

Adv. All around: 週知 it is known to all; 週而復始 round and round.

週半兒 *jou-bah'l*, n., a child is full eighteen months.
週報 *joubauh*, n., a weekly.
週期 *jouchir*, n., a period, time for one full circle of movement; 週期性 periodic, cyclical; 週期表 periodic table (chem.); 週期律 periodic law.
週轉 *joujuan* n. & v.i., turnover (finance).
週刊 *joukan*, n., a weekly.
週率 *joulyuh*, n., (phys.) frequency.
週末 *jou-moh*, n., weekend.
週年 *jou-niarn*, n., anniversary.

過 42.83

*guoh (*guo).*

N. (1) Error, mistake, fault, anything wrong: 過錯, 過失 *-tsuoh -'shy*↓; 知過必改 if a mistake is found, then correct it; 聞過則喜 thankful for being told of one's errors; 記過 give s.o. a demerit for misconduct; 大過 a serious offense; 過處 *-chuh*↓. (2) (*guo) A surname. (3) Number of times: 多少過兒 how many times?

V.i. & t. (1) Pass over or through, go across: 過不去 cannot pass through, also feel embarrassed: 他老和我過不去 he is ever trying to pick on me; 過路兒的 a pedestrian; 過河折橋 burn the bridge after crossing it; 過日子 to while away time, eke out a living; 時過境遷 times have passed and circumstances have changed; 過不來 cannot come over, be unaccustomed to; 難過 feel uneasy, vexed or embarrassed. (2) Surpass, exceed, be in excess of: 過半(數) more than one half, a majority; 精力過人 strength surpasses others; 過量, 過分, 過當, 過度 *-liahng*, *-fehn*, *-dahng*, *-duh*[1]↓; 過猶不及 too much is as bad as too little. (3) Indulge oneself in: see 過過 *-'guo*↓; 過過風兒 enjoy a little breeze; 過癮 *-yiin*↓. (4) To strain, sift, cause to go through: 過籮, 過秤 *-luor*, *-chehng*↓; 過水 dunk hot noodles in cool water before serving them; 過油 skim off the fat. (5) To present as gift: 過嫁粧 send dowries to the bridegroom's family before wedding; 過禮 *-lii*↓; 過錢 make money payment. (6) Celebrate: 過年, 過節 *-niarn*, *-jier*↓; 過生日, 過壽 hold a birthday party. (7) Be chummy with: 過不着 (of relations between friends) be incompatible with; 過

得多 be on most intimate terms with; 過財 be generous in lending money between friends; 過頑笑 play jokes at one another's expense without taking offense.

Adj. (1) Past: 過去 *-chyuh* ↓. (2) Later on: 過幾天, 過兩天(兒) in a few, a couple of days; 過後 *-houh* ↓; 過一會 in a moment or a few minutes.

Adv. Too much, to an excessive extent or degree: 過剩, 過激, 過多 *-shehng*, *-ji*, *-duo* ↓; 過忙 too busy; 操之過急 to act precipitately or impulsively.

Vb. suffix. Used to express a completed action (pr. *'guo*): 讀過 have read about it; 聽説過 have heard of it; 看見過 have seen it; 吃過了 have had one's meal; 打過招呼 have said hello to s. o.; 遞過暗號 have given s. o. a secret signal.

過板(兒) *guohbaan(-baa'l)*, n., (mus.) interval between singing when string accompaniment plays alone (also 過門兒↓).

過飽和 *guoh-baauher*, n., (chem.) supersaturation.

過磅 *guohbahng*, v. t., to weigh (luggage, etc.) (also pr. *guoh-behng*).

過班 *guohban*, v. t., formerly, get an official promotion.

過秤 *guohchehng*, v. t., to weigh.

過稱 *guohcheng*, n., discrepancy between praise and real worth.

過程 *guohcherng*, n., a process.

過謙 *guohchian*, adj., overmodest.

過橋麵 *guohchiaurmiahn*, n., (Yunnanese cuisine) a special form of preparing noodles.

過期 *guohchir*, adj., overdue, after the expiration of a set time limit.

過處 *guohchuh*, n., misdeed, error.

過去 *guoh-chyuh*, (1) adj., past; (2) v. i., pass through; be gone; go over; die.

過當 *guohdahng*, adj., excessive (praise, punishment): 失之過當 (praise, judgement) excessive, unfair.

過道兒 *guohdauh'l*, n., (Peking sp. pr. *-daau'l*) a passageway, corridor.

過得去 *guoh-der-chyuh*, adj., (1) (of road, etc.) passable; (2) (things, performance) fairly good; (3) 給他過得去 do not embarrass him; (4) 心裏過得去 feel at ease (not guilty).

過電 *guohdiahn*, v. t., to conduct or transmit electricity; short-circuit.

過度 *guohduh*[1], (1) adv., excessively: 酒色過度 too much wine and women; 過度浪費 too extravagant; (2) v.i., to while away time, eke out a living.

過渡 *guohduh*[2], n. & adj., (1) transition(al): 過渡狀態, 過渡時代, 過渡措施 transitional condition, period, measure; (2) a ford, ferry.

過冬 *guoh-dung*, phr., pass the winter.

過多 *guoh-duo*, adj., too much, too many, excessive.

過訪 *guohfaang*, v. t., to visit (s. o.): 昨承過訪 thank you for your visit yesterday.

過飯 *guohfahn*, v. i., have meat and vegetables to go with rice.

過房 *guohfarng*, v. t., adopt a brother's son as one's heir.

過分 *guohfehn*, adj. & adv., excessive, -ly: 你做得太過分了 (of action) you have gone too far; 這人過分糊塗 the man is far too muddle-headed.

過風兒 *guohfeng'l*, adj., with good ventilation.

過付 *guohfuh*, v. t., pay through an intermediary in a business deal.

過福 **guofur*, v. i., (of well-to-do persons) be dissatisfied with what one has in terms of creature comforts.

過關 *guoh-guan*, v. i., go through a mountain pass or (fig.) a critical period.

過過 *guoh'guo*, v. t., satisfy (one's desires, etc.): 過過煙癮 enjoy a smoke.

過後(兒) *guohhouh('l)*, adv., later on, some time later: 過後方知 learned only after the event.

過話 *guoh-huah*, v. t., (1) to talk with; (2) transmit a verbal message through an intermediary.

過戶 *guoh-huh*, v. t., (law) to transfer the ownership of (s. t.) to another person.

過火(兒) *guohhuoo('l)*, adj., intemperate.

過活 *guoh-huor*, v. i., make a living.

過賬 *guoh-jahng*, v. t., (banking) to transfer accounts.

過激 *guohji*, adj., too much excited, emotional, precipitate or radical (opinion or action).

過獎 *guoh-jiaang*, v. t., (court.) as in 承蒙過獎 thank you for the undeserved compliments.

過街樓(兒) *guohjielour('l)*, n., an overhead pass across the street.

過節 *guoh-jier*, n., (1) a festival; (2) festivities: 過節兒 celebrate festivities; after the festivities; (3) grudge: 他們有過節兒 they bear grudges against each other; (4) 小過節兒 trivialities, trifles.

過繼 *guohjih*, v. t., adopt a brother's or close relative's son as one's heir.

過境 *guoh-jihng*, (1) adj., in transit: 過境旅客 a transient passenger; (2) v. i., to pass in transit.

過景 *guoh-jiing*, adj., unseasonable, past the season.

過重 *guoh-juhng*, adj., overweight.

過客 *guohkeh*, n., a traveller, passenger, in transit.

過來 *guoh'lai*, v. i., come over: 請過來談一談 come over and have a chat; 過來人 an experienced hand.

過量 *guoh-liahng*, adv., exceed one's capacity, said esp. of wine.

過禮 *guoh-lii*, v. t., to present gifts to the bride's family before marriage.

過籮 *guoh-luor*, v. t., cause (s. t.) to pass through a sieve.

過慮 *guoh-lyuh*[1], (1) n., needless worries; (2) v. i., to worry needlessly.

過濾 *guohlyuh*², v.t., filter; 過濾性病毒 virus infection.

過門 *guoh-mern*, v. i., (of woman) get married (lit. "to go across the threshold"); 過門兒 see *--baan*↑.

過敏 *guohmiin*, adj., allergic; 過敏反應 allergy; 光線過敏症 photosensitivity (of skin).

過目 *guohmuh*, v. t., read over: 請你過目 please read it over; 過目不忘 gifted with an extraordinarily retentive memory.

過年 *guoh-niarn*, (1) v. i. & n., (hold) a party on New Year's Eve, celebrations on New Year's Day; (2) adv., the next year, also (-'*l*).

過排 *guohpair*, v. t., (dramatics) rehearse.

過山龍 *guohshanlurng*, n., (sl.) a siphon.

過山砲 *guohshanpauh*, n., a light artillery piece.

過甚 *guohshehn*, adv., excessively, too much.

過剩 *guohshehng*, n. & v. i., (have) a surplus.

過手 *guohshoou*, v. i., pass through s. o.'s hands; change ownership.

過數(兒) *guohshuh('l)*, v. t., to count.

過失 *guoh'shy*, n., a mistake, an error, a fault.

過世 *guoh-shyh*, v. i., (1) die, pass away; (2) rise superior to all others.

過時 *guohshyr*, adj., (1) late, past a set time limit: 過時不候 we'll not wait for you if you come late; (2) (style) out-of-date.

過堂 *guoh-tarng*, v. i., appear before a law court; 過堂風兒 wind gusts coming through a narrow passageway.

過天 *guoh'tian*, adv., a few days later.

過頭(兒) *guohtour('l)*, adj. & adv., (1) beyond a given point: 你跑過頭兒了 you've overshot yourself; (2) excessive(ly): 他吹得過頭兒了 he has bragged too much.

過錯 *guohtsuoh*, n., a wrong doing, fault, mistake, error.

過從 *guohtsurng*, v. i., have friendly intercourse with s. o.: 過從甚密 be on very intimate terms with one another.

過往 *guohwaang*, v. i., (1) come and go; (2) see *-tsurng*,↑.

過望 *guohwahng*, adj. & adv., beyong one's expectations: 大喜過望 delighted with unexpectedly good results.

過問 *guohwehn*, v. t., have a hand in, interfere with: 概不過問 won't have anything to do with it.

過五關(兒) *guoh-wuugua('l)*, n., a kind of Chin. solitaire.

過眼 *guoh-yaan*, adj., (1) (of anything wr.) that is read over; (2) passing: 過眼煙雲 (lit.) like floating smoke and passing clouds, (fig.) fleeting, ephemeral, transient; (3) pleasant to the sight: 過不得眼 unsightly.

過夜 *guoh-yeh*, v. i., to stay overnight.

過意 *guoh-yih*, adj., (1) feeling offended: 不怕你過意 I do not care if you are over-sensitive; (2) comfortable, at ease: 過意不去 feel sorry; 不過意 ill at ease.

過癮 *guoh-yiin*, v. t., satisfy one's craving for (gambling, wine, tobacco, etc.).

過於 *guoh-yuh*¹, adv., too much: 過於小心 too careful; 過於嚴酷 too strict and ruthless.

過譽 *guoh-yuh*², v. t., over praise.

遁 42.83

duhn.

V.i. (1) To flee, escape, hide away, (var. of 遁 see 90.83). (2) (AC) deceive.

§ 42.93 (ㄈㄨ/ㄑ)

蜚 42.93

feir.

N. 蜚蟲 *feirchurng* bedbug.

SECTION 42A

§ 42A.00 (月/亅)

肘 42A.00-1

joou.

N. (*-tz, 'l*) The elbow: 掣肘 have no elbowroom, i. e., be controlled by others; 捉襟見肘 describing a jacket which is too small, pulled from the front, it shows at the elbow—hard up for cash; 肘腋 elbow and armpit; 肘腋之患 trouble coming from those closest.

肘子 *joou'tz*, n., (1) shoulder of pork; (2) the elbow.

膊 42A.00-1

bor.

N. Arm: 臂膊 upper arm; 胳[Δ]膊 the arm, 42A.70; 赤膊 barechested and barebacked; completely naked; 轉膊 change shoulders when carrying a load.

V.i. (AC) dismember criminal's corpse.

膊膊 *borbor*, n., (AC) sound of crowing cocks.

膊風 *borfeng*, n. var., of 搏[Δ]風 10A.00.

膊甲 *borjiah*, n., shoulder blade.

脖 42A.00-1

bor.

N. (*-tz, 'l*) Neck: 打脖兒拐 to twist the neck; 抹脖子 to commit suicide by slashing one's neck.

脖頸子 *borjihngtz,* n., (also *-jihng'l*) the neck.
脖領兒 *borliing'l,* n., collar.

膞 42A.00-1

juan.

N. Crop or maw of a bird.

刖 42A.00-2

yueh.

V. t. & n. Cutting off the feet as an ancient punishment.

腑 42A.00-6

fuu.

N. The chest; internal organs usu. in combb.: 胸腑 the breast: 肺腑之言 talk from the heart; 臟腑 gen. term for internal organs, comprising the stomach, liver, intestines, spleen and bladder.

脬 42A.00-9

pau.

N. 尿脬 (*niauhpau*) urine bladder.

胕 42A.00-9

fu.

N. (AC) var. of 膚 skin.

§ 42A.01 (月/小)

膆 42A.01 -1

suh.
[Var. of 嗉 40A.01]

縢 42A.01-1

terng.

N. (1) (AC) cord binding: 行縢 leggings.

V. t. (AC) to bind as with cord.

臊 42A.01-4

sauh (**sau*).

N. (MC) (*-tz*) minced meat.

Adj. (1) Ashamed: 害臊 feel ashamed; 不害臊 how shameless; 臊不搭, 臊眉搭眼的 looking ashamed; 臊得滿臉通紅 blush to the ears. (2) (**sau*) Having body odor: 臊氣 *-chih*↓.

臊氣 **sauchih,* adj., having body odor.
臊根 **saugen,* n., (MC sl.) male genitals.
臊皮 *sauhpir,* adj., ashamed, "lose face."

§ 42A.02 (月/⺦)

膝 42A.02-1

shi.

N. The knee: 雙膝跪下 kneel down ("on both knees"); 屈膝而談 bend one's leg, have a talk together "on bent legs," i. e., freely and informally; 膝行, 膝步 to move forward on one's knees, i.e., in kneeling position.

膝蓋 *shigaih,* n., kneecap.
膝下 *shishiah,* n., (1) address in letter beginning to one's parents; (2) children conceived as surrounding parents' knees: 膝下兒女.

滕 42A.02-1

terng.

N. (1) A surname. (2) (AC) name of a country.

朦 42A.02-2

merng.
[Cf. 曚, 矇, 懵 all cogn. words]

朦朧 *mernglurng,* adj., hazy, drowsy: 醉眼朦朧 eyes drowsy from drink; hazy (moonlight).

膿 42A.02-2

nurng (re. pr. *nerng*).

N. Pus.

膿包 *nerngbau,* n., (derog.) a worthless scoundrel.
膿瘡 *nerngchuang,* n., an abscess.
膿腫 *nurngjuung,* n., abscess.
膿水 *nerngshueei,* n., pus.
膿血 *nerngshyueh* (*-shiee*), n., bloody pus.

脖 膞 刖 腑 脬 胕 膆 縢 臊 膝 滕 朦 膿

亅	小	⺦	十	土	𠂇	卄	乚⺊	丨	一	丁	㇇	口	区	冈	㇕	厂	尸	亠	广	宀	丶	乚	弋	心	八	人	乂	乛	㇀	刂	𠂉	𡿨
00	01	02	10	11	12	20	21	22	30	31	32	40	41	42	50	51	52	60	61	62	63	70	71	72	80	81	82	83	90	91	92	93

豚 42A.02-3

turn.

N. A suckling pig: 豚兒, 豚犬 (court.) formerly, reference to one's own children; 豚魚 (lit.) "suckling pigs and fish," (AC) 信及豚魚 one's sincerity can move even the lowest creatures.

豚鼠 *turnshuu*, n., (zoo.) the guinea pig, *Cavia cobaya.*

脹 42A.02-5

jahng.

V. i. (1) To swell up (balloon, stomach): 澎 (膨) 脹 ditto; 脹破了 burst open (from swelling); 腹脹 the stomach is swollen. (2) To swell up from inflammation: 腫脹 ditto; 水脹 dropsy; 脹氣 flatulence, gas in the belly.

脹率 *jahnglyuh*, n., (phys.) degree of expansion caused by heat.

脉 42A.02-6

moh.
[Pop. of 脈 42A.02↓]

脈 42A.02-9

moh (also *maih*).
[Pop. 脉]

N. (1) Pulse, pulse beat: 動脈 artery; 靜脈 vein; 血脈 blood, blood circulation; blood kinship. (2) Vein, vein pattern: 山脈 mountain range; 地脈 geological pattern; 礦脈 veins of minerals; 葉脈 veins on leaves; 脈絡 *-luoh*↓; 一脈相傳 master-disciple tutorship in certain arts or crafts.

脈搏 *moh-bor*, n., pulse beat.
脈錢 *moh-chiarn*, n., doctor's fee for visit.
脈翅類 *mohchyh-leih*, n., (zoo.) *Neuroptera*, family of four-winged insects (dragonfly, etc.).
脈管 *mohguaan*, n., blood vessel.
脈理 *moh-lii*[1], n., (wood) grain; (Chin. med.) condition of pulse (good, bad, etc.).
脈禮 *moh-lii*[2], n., present to physician.
脈絡 *mohluoh*, n., (wood) grain, vein; (fig.) thread of thought, argument: 脈胳分明 clear line of thought; 脈胳膜 *--mor*, n., choroid coat in eye.
脈門 *moh-mern*, n., location near wrist for feeling pulse.
脈脈 *mohmoh*, adj., loving (look): 脈脈含情, 情脈脈, 意綿綿 very much enamored.
脈息 *moh-shir*, n., pulse beat.
脈石 *moh-shyr*, n., (min.) gangue, veinstone.
脈岩 *moh-yarn*, n., vein rock.

腺 42A.02-9

shiahn.

N. Ductless gland: 甲狀腺 thyroid; 淋巴腺 lymphatic gland; 唾腺 salivary gland; 腎上腺 adrenal glands; 蝶鞍腺 pituitary gland (also called 垂體); 前列腺, 攝護腺 prostatic gland; 腺腫 swelling of gland (adenoma).

§ 42A.10 (月/十)

膵 42A.10-2

tsueih.

N. The pancreas: 膵臟 ditto; 膵液 (*-yih* or *-yieh*) pancreatic juice; 膵液素 pancreatin.

胖 42A.10-2

pahng (**parng*).

Adj. (1) Fat (of person), of wide girth: 肥胖 fat; 胖嘟嘟兒 said of a plump, handsome baby; 胖胖大大兒 very fat, paunchy. (2) (**parng*) (AC) 心廣體胖 of wide girth and ample heart.

胖襖 *pahng-aau*, n., padded jacket worn under gown by opera actors to simulate chest of military heroes.
胖病 *pahngbihng*, n., obesity.
胖子 *pahngtz*, n., (coll.) fatty, a fat person, also 大胖子: 打腫臉充胖子 stretch one's means to put up a big front (lit., "beat up face and pretend being plump").

肝 42A.10-3

gan.

N. (Physiol.) the liver: 肝臟 *-tzahng*, 肝膽 *-daan*, 肝腸 *-charng*↓; 心肝 beloved person: 我的心肝 my darling, sweetheart; 沒有心肝 heartless; 披肝露膽 lay bare one's heart; 肝腦塗地 scene of a bloody battle (disemboweled bodies are strewn over the ground); (to emperor) willing to repay a favor with extreme sacrifice.

肝腸 *gancharng*, n., (1) the liver and the intestines; (2) feelings, emotions: 肝腸寸斷 emotionally upset; 哭斷肝腸 cry one's heart out.
肝氣 *gan-chih*, n., (1) (Chin. med.) a pain or congested feeling in the chest and the gen. region below; (2) nervous symptoms with tendencies to anger, melancholy, and depression.

肝膽 *gandaan*, (1) n., liver and gall, courage: 英雄肝膽 heroic spirit; (2) adj., 肝膽相照 open-heartedness between intimate friends.

肝火 *ganhuoo*, n., (1) an inflammatory condition of the liver; (2) anger: 動肝火 get angry; 肝火旺, 肝火盛 easily given to anger (cf. Eng. "bilious temperament.")

肝精 *ganjing*, n., (med.) liver extract.

肝蛭 *ganjyh*, n., (zoo.) liver flukes, *Distoma*.

肝臟 *gantzahng*, n., (physiol.) the liver.

肝炎 *gan-yarn*[1], n., (med.) hepatitis; 血清肝炎 serum hepatitis.

肝癌 *gan-yarn*[2] (*-air*), n., (med.) cancer in the liver.

肝硬化 *gan-yihnghuah*, n., (med.) cirrhosis.

肝油 *gan-your*, n., cod-liver oil (also 魚肝油).

胕 42A.10-8

shih.

V. i. & Adj. (To) spread about; boisterous.

脾 42A.10-9

pir.

N. (Biol.) the pancreas, sweetbread, the spleen.

脾氣 *pirchih*, n., temperament: 脾氣好, 壞 good, bad temperament; anger: 發脾氣 vent one's spleen, burst of anger; 脾氣大 violent-tempered.

脾疳 *pir-gan*, n., (med.) swelling of pancreas.

脾寒 *pir-harn*, n., (med.) inflammation of pancreas.

脾泄 *pirshieh*, n., (med.) diarrhoea.

脾臟 *pirtzahng*, n., the pancreas.

脾胃 *pirweih*, n., appetite, also (fig.) tastes: 脾胃相投 have similar tastes, like the same things.

§ 42A.11 (月/土)

肚 42A.11-1

duh (**duu*).

N. (1) The belly (*-tz*, *-'l*): 大肚子 be pregnant, big belly; the belly as seat of feeling or learning: 一肚子火 (氣) a bellyful of anger; 一肚子學問 a bellyful of learning; 肚裏明白, 肚裏有數 know in one's heart (without saying anything). (2) (**duu*) The stomach, tripe: 肚子 usu. pig's tripe; 炒肚尖 fried ridge of pig's tripe; 牛肚, 羊肚 cow's, sheep's tripe. (3) (*duh*) Bowel movement: 拉肚子, 瀉肚子 have loose bowels.

肚臍眼(兒)(子) *duhchiryaan* (*-yaa'l*)(*-tz*), n., the navel.

肚兒 *duh'l*, n., as in 有了肚兒了 be pregnant.

肚量 *duhliahng*, n., generosity, capacity for tolerating others or offence: 肚量大, 肚量小 generous or narrow-minded.

肚皮 *duhpir*, n., belly=肚, see N. 1↑.

塍 42A.11-1

cherng.

[Var. of 堘]

N. Boundary path of rice field.

膗 42A.11-2

chuair.

Adj. (Coll.) fat, fatty: 他身子很膗 he is very fat; 膗肉 very fat pork.

脞 42A.11-2

tsuoo.

N. (AC) minced meat.

膛 42A.11-2

tarng.

N. (*-'l*, *-tz*) (1) The chest: 拍拍胸膛 beat one's chest, a gesture indicating self-confidence; 挺起胸膛 stick out one's chest (in defiance, to show one is not afraid); 膛兒裏頭舒服 feel good at heart; 膛嗓兒 big chest voice; 膛子大 big chest. (2) Inside cavity: 槍膛 bore, barrel of gun or rifle; 膛口 muzzle of gun.

腥 42A.11-4

shing.

N. Raw meat.

Adj. Rank, smelling like stale rancid meat, gamy; (fig.) ill-smelling: 腥德 notorious reputation; 腥賭 gambling with loaded dice; 腥聞 ill repute.

腥氣 *shingchih*, n., gamy or provoking smell (of goats, fish, etc.).

腥臭 *shingchouh*, adj., rank-smelling.

腥臊 *shingsau*, adj., raw, rancid smelling, fishy.
腥羶 *shingshan*, adj., goaty smell.
腥味 *shing-weih*, n., fishy or gamy smell.

臞 42A.11-4

chyur.

Adj. Thin, emaciated (also wr. 癯).

臃 42A.11-6

yuung (also *yung*).

Adj. Swollen.

臃肥 *yuungfeir*, adj., staunchy, stodgy.
臃腫 *yurngjuung*, adj., swollen (with inflammation).

膣 42A.11-6

jyh.

N. The vagina: 膣炎 vaginal inflammation.

腫 42A.11-9

juung.

V. i. & adj. To swell up with inflammation: 腫起來 swell up; (as p.p.) swollen; 紅腫 swollen and inflamed; 腫疼 swollen and painful; 臃腫 swollen big; 打腫臉充胖子, see 胖子 *pahngtz* ↑.

腫皰 *juungbauh*, n., pimples (also wr. 疱).
腫大 *juungdah*, adj., swollen up.
腫脹 *juungjahng*, adj., ditto.
腫噲 *juungkuaih*, adj., (AC) coarse and freckled.
腫瘍 *juungyarng*, n., (AC) an ulcer, benign or malignant.

§ 42A.20 (月/廾)

胼 42A.20-8

piarn.

胼胝 *pianjy*, n., calluses.

§ 42A.21 (月/乚)

朏 42A.21-2

feei.

Adj. (LL) descriptive of translucent light of nascent noon.

§ 42A.22 (月/丨)

胏 42A.22-2

tzyy.

N. Dried meat with bones.

腓 42A.22-2

feir.

N. (AC) calf muscle.

V. t. (AC) avoid; (AC) wither.

胛 42A.22-4

jiaa.

N. The shoulder blade, (fig.) backbone: 有肩胛, 沒肩胛 (Shanghai dial. pr. *-gah*) have, have no guts; stouthearted, weak-kneed; have, have no sense of responsibility.

肺 42A.22-6

feih.

N. Lungs: 肺肝; 如見其肺肝然 as if one could see into his inner thoughts ("lungs and liver"): 狼心狗肺 the heart of a beast; 肺葉 the lobes of lungs; 肺活量 lung capacity, vital capacity.

肺病 *feihbihng*, n., tuberculosis.
肺腸 *feihcharng*, n., heart feelings: 不知是何肺腸 how beastly! how cruel-hearted!
肺腑 *feihfuu*, n., a man's heart: 肺腑之言 hearty talk, heart-to-heart talk; 肺腑之交 bosom friend; cf. *-charng* ↑; 動人肺腑, 感人肺腑 touch one's heart.
肺脹 *feihjahng*, n., emphysema.
肺結核 *feihjieher*, n., tuberculosis.
肺癆 *feihlaur*, n., tuberculosis; also 癆病 *laurbihng*.
肺水腫 *feihshueirjuung*, n., pulmonary edema.
肺癌 *feihyarn*[1] (*-air*), n., lung cancer.
肺炎 *feiyarn*[2], n., pneumonia.
肺魚類 *feihyur-leih*, n., lung-breathing fish.

臍 42A.22-6

chir.

N. (1) The navel: 肚臍 ditto. (2) The belly flap in crabs (round in females, pointed in males).

(3) Ligament at base of pearl in mother-of-pearl. (4) Base of melon where it joins the stem.

臍帶(兒) *chirdaih(-dah'l)*, n., placenta cord ending in the navel.
臍屎 *chirshyy*, n., first bowels in new-born babe.

腳 42A.22-8

jiaau (sp. pr.); **jyuer* (re. pr. rare).
[Pop. 脚]

N. (1) The foot: 光腳, 赤腳 barefooted; 小腳, 纏腳 bound feet; 大腳, 天腳 unbound feet; 托大腳 (Cantonese) to flatter; 腳底下 the sole of the foot, near one's feet: 腳底下人 (Szechuan dial.) people from the lower reaches of the Yangtse ("down under"); 腳踩 to tread on; 腳踢 to kick; 腳踏實地 stand on solid ground; 腳踏兩條船 to sit on the fence. (2) The leg or base on which a thing stands or rests: 桌腳, 椅腳 the legs of a table, chair; 山腳 foot of a mountain; 杯腳 the base of a drinking vessel; 高腳杯 a goblet.

腳本 **jyuerbeen*, n., the libretto of a play or song.
腳脖(子) *jiaaubor(tz)*, n., the ankle.
腳步 *jiaaubuh*, n., (1) manner of walking, gait; (2) (fig.) footsteps: 踏着前人的腳步兒 follow in the footsteps of one's predecessor.
腳步鴨(兒)(子) *jiaaubuhya('l)(tz)*, n., (coll.) the foot.
腳錢 *jiaauchiarn*, n., (1) delivery fee; (2) formerly, transportation cost.
腳氣 *jiaauchih*, n., (med.) beriberi.
腳登子 *jiaaudengtz*, n., (1) a footstool; (2) a pedal.
腳底板兒 *jiaaudirbaa'l*, n., the sole of a foot.
腳夫 *jiaaufu*, n., a coolie, a porter.
腳(後)跟 *jiaau(houh)gen*, n., the heel.
腳行 *jiaauharng*, n., an agent or firm rendering carrier service.
腳鐐 *jiaauliauh*, n., shackles.
腳力 *jiaaulih*, n., (1) a messenger or carrier; (2) see *-chiarn*↑.
腳爐 *jiaaulur*, n., a foot warmer.
腳面 *jiaaumiahn*, n., the instep.
腳色 **jyuerseh*, n., (=角色) a dramatic actor, a person of outstanding ability.
腳下 *jiaaushiah*, n., (1) the place where one stands; (2) the foot; (3) the present moment.
腳心 *jiaaushin*, n., the sole of the foot.
腳踏板 *jiaautahbaan*, n., a pedal.
腳踏車 *jiaautahche*, n., a bicycle.
腳腕(子) *jiaauwahn(tz)*, n., the ankle.
腳鴨(子)(兒) *jiaauya(tz)('l)*, n., (coll.) the foot.
腳丫縫兒 *jiaauyafehng'l*, n., the space between toes.
腳印(子) *jiaauyihn(tz)*, n., footprints.

胙 42A.22-9

tzuoh.

N. (AC) sacrificial meat.

V. t. (1) To bless: 天地所胙 (AC) blessed by the gods. (2) Confer on: 胙之土 (AC) grant him a fief.

§ 42A.30 (月/一)

臚 42A.30-2

lur.

V.t. To arrange in a row: 臚列 show item by item; 臚列如左 as enumerated below; 傳ᐞ臚 91A.00.

肛 42A.30-3

gang.

N. (Physiol.) the anus: 肛門.

胚 42A.30-3

pei.
[Anc. var. 肧]

N. Early form of embryo; developing form of sprout in plant seeds.

胚軸 *peijour*, n., (bot.) hypocotyl.
胚珠 *peiju*, n., (biol.) ovule.
胚囊 *peinarng*, n., (biol.) gastrula.
胚盤 *peiparn*, n., (biol.) blastoderm.
胚乳 *peiruu*, n., (biol.) albumen.
胚胎 *peitai*, (1) n., embryo, (fig.) young beginnings; (2) v. i., to form beginnings, to conceive.
胚子 *pei'tz*, n., biological strain or type: 好胚子, 壞胚子 person with good, bad traits (cf. 坯ᐞ子 11A.30).

脛 42A.30-3

jihng.

N. The shank: 脛骨 the shinbone.

胆 42A.30-4

daan.
[Pop. of 膽 42A.40]

膃 42A.30-4

wah.

膃 肭 *wahnah*, n., the otter; 膃肭劑 dried genital organs of male otter, used for promoting virility.

膻 42A.30-6

shan.

[Var. of 羶 80S.30]

腔 42A.30-6

chiang.

N. (1) (*-tz*) A cavity: 胸腔, 腹腔 chest, belly cavity; 口腔 mouth cavity, also speech accent. (2) (*-'l*) The belly or chest as seat of emotions (=Eng. "breast"): 一腔熱誠 (血) great (chestful of) enthusiasm; 滿腔怨氣 a chestful of hate. (3) (*-'l*) Speech accent, tone, melody of local music: 腔調 *-diauh* ↓; 南腔北調 mixed accent of north and south—hybrid, nondescript; 土腔 local accent; 改腔 change accent; 花腔 (music) coloratura, (Chin. opera) a long drawn-out aria; 賊腔 (Shanghai dial.), 娘娘腔 (disgusting), having the air of a sissy; 裝腔作勢 make pretense of dignity, assume airs; 陳腔濫調 hackneyed phrases, clichés, platitudes.

腔 調 兒 *chiangdiauh('l)*, n., (1) tone of speech; (2) melody or tune.

腔 窠 *chiangke*, n., as in 落腔窠 get into a rut, follow old routine (cf. 窠ᐞ臼 62A.01).

§ 42A.40 (月/口)

謄 42A.40-1

terng.

V. t. To make clean copy: 謄過, 謄一謄, 謄一遍, 謄正 make a clear copy; 謄文公 a copycat writer.

謄 清 *terngching*, v. i., make a clean copy.

謄 錄 *terngluh*, v.t., copy clearly.

謄 寫 *terngshiee*, v. t., ditto.

膪 42A.40-6

chuaih.

N. The fatty part of belly pork; see 囊ᐞ膪 10.02 (cf. 膗 42A.11).

膳 42A.40-8

shahn.

[Interch. 饍]

N. Board, meals: 早膳, 午膳, 晚膳 breakfast, lunch, supper; 用膳 take meal; 膳費 boarding fees; 膳宿, 膳食 *-suh, -shyr* ↓.

膳 房 *shahnfarng*, n., (short for 御膳房) royal dining room.

膳 食 *shahnshyr*, n., the meals; 膳食費 boarding fees.

膳 宿 *shahnsuh*, n., board and lodging.

膳 堂 *shahntarng*, n., mess hall.

胳 42A.40-9

ge.

[Var. of 肐, 骼, see 肐 42A.70]

脗 42A.40-9

ween.

脗 合 *weenher*, see 吻ᐞ合 40A.50.

膽 42A.40-9

daan.

[Pop. 胆]

N. (*-tz, 'l*) (1) Gall bladder. (2) Courage, "guts": 沒有膽子 timid; 放開膽子 stop being afraid; 仗着膽子 summon up enough courage; 膽大 brave; 膽小 timid; 膽大心細 brave but not reckless; 膽戰 tremble with fear; 膽破 frightened to death; 膽寒, 膽虛, 膽怯 afraid, disheartened, nervous; 喪膽 lose heart (for battle); 色膽包天 phr., driven by passion, risk sex adventures; 膽小如鼠 cowardly as a mouse; 卧薪嘗膽 (allu.) sleep on firewood and taste gall—in determination for revenge. (3) Inner tube of thermos bottle or football.

膽 氣 *daanchih*, n., courage.

膽 石 症 *daanchyrjehng*, n., gallstone.

膽 礬 *daanfarn*, n., sulphate of copper.

膽 敢 *darngaan*, v.i., dare to; to have the gall to.

膽 汁 *daanjy*, n., gall, bile.

膽 量 *daanliahng*, n., courage ("big" or "small").

膽 力 *daanlih*, n., strength of purpose.

膽 略 *daanlyueh*, n., daring plan: 這人很有膽略 this man has daring.

膽 囊 *daannarng*, n., gall bladder.

膽 瓶 *daanpirng*, n., big-bellied vase.

膽 識 *daanshyh*, n., daring, superior judgment.

胎 42A.40-9

tai.

N. (1) Pregnancy, embryo: 有胎, 懷胎, 胞孕 pregnant; 胞胎, 胎兒 embryo in the womb; 打胎, 墮胎 abortion; 胎死腹中 a plot (scheme, idea) died abortively; 投胎 (of spirit) be conceived of woman; 安胎 (medicine to) prevent miscarriage; birth: 一胎三子 triplet birth; 頭胎,第二胎 first, second baby; 胎前產後 pre- and postnatal period; 私胎 illegitimate birth; 懷鬼胎 (fig.) entertain fear from sense of guilt conceiving a plot or fear of suspicion; 胎裏紅 born in rich family; 胎裏壞 born wicked; (fig.) of embryonic growth: 胚胎 (v. i.) form rudiments; 脫胎換骨 imitation of litr. model keeping form but changing substance; 禍胎 roots of trouble. (2) (Translit.) tyre: 車胎, 輪胎.

胎胞 *taibau*, n., the placenta.
胎氣 *taichih*, n., sense of life in the womb: 動了胎氣.
胎毒 *taidur*, n., congenital disease.
胎兒 *tai-erl*, n., embryo: 頭胎兒 first-born.
胎教 *taijiauh*, n., prenatal influence.
胎記 *taijih*, n., birthmark.
胎盤 *taiparn*, n., placenta.
胎生 *taisheng*, adj., viviparous, life-born (not by eggs) as some fish and all mammals; 胎生學 embryology.
胎息 *taishir*, n., (Taoist) art of controlling and swallowing breath from mouth.
胎座 *taitzuoh*, n., (bot.) placenta of a flower, bearing ovules.
胎衣 *taiyi*, n., placenta.

§ 42A.41 (月/囟)

腊 42A.41-2

shir (**lah*).

N. (1) Abbr. for 臘 (**lah*): 腊肉 (=臘肉) preserved meat (sausage, etc.). (2) (AC) (pr. *shir*) preserved meat, esp. used in sacrifices.

脂 42A.41-2

jy.

N. (1) Fat, fatty tissue: 油脂 ointment; 樹脂 resin; 民脂民膏 (fig.) the fat of the land and its people, i.e., taxes which could be squeezed out of the people; 脂肪素 cholesterol. (2) Short for 胭脂 rouge, lipstick: 脂粉 *-feen*↓.

脂肪 *jyfarng*, n., fat of beef, pork, etc.; adipose tissue; 脂肪酸 see *-suan*↓.
脂粉 *jy-feen*, n., rouge and powder: 脂粉塲中, 隊中 among pretty ladies; 脂粉氣 (of man) sissy.
脂膏 *jygau*, n., (1) ointment; (2) fat, see N. 1↑.
脂酸 *jysuan*, n., (chem.) fatty acids.
脂澤 *jytzer*, n., luster of skin.
脂油 *jyyour*, n., pork fat.

腷 42A.41-3

bih.

腷腷膊膊 *bihbih-borbor*, n., flip-flap sound (of wings); crackle of breaking ice.

腼 42A.41-3

miaan.

腼腆 *miaan'tian*, adj., embarrassed; blushing.

胭 42A.41-4

yan.

[Var. 臙]

胭粉 *yanfeen*, n., rouge and powder.
胭脂 *yanjy* (-'*jy*), n., rouge, lipstick; 胭脂虎 a ferocious woman, a shrew.

腤 42A.41-6

an.

腤臢 *antzan*, adj., dirty, filthy (place), disgraceful (affair).
腤臢 *antzang*, adj., ditto.

膾 42A.41-8

kuaih.

N. Minced meat; 膾炙人口 phr., (of food, good story) popular and much relished, pleasant to eat (hear).

膰 42A.41-9

farn.

N. Sacrificial meat.

腦 42A.41-9

naau.

N. (1) (Physiol.) the brain: 大腦 the cerebrum; 小腦 the cerebellum; 腦震盪 concussion of the brain; 電腦 computer; 腦滿腸肥 (derog.) a person with a fair round belly and a swelled head. (2) Head: 主腦 the mastermind; 首腦人物 leading personages; 首腦 head, leader. (3) Brains: 此人很有頭腦 this man has brains: 用頭腦 use your head; 沒頭沒腦 listless, absent-minded, without any clues.

腦出血 *naauchushyueh* (*-shiee*), n., (med.) apoplexy, a stroke; brain hemorrhage.

腦充血 *naauchungshyueh* (*-shiee*) n., (med.) *Hyperemia cerebri*, cerebral blood obstruction.

腦袋 *naaudaih*, n., (physiol.) the cranium: 腦袋瓜子, 腦袋瓜兒 (sl.) s.o.'s block.

腦蓋(兒) *naaugaih* (*-gah'l*), n., the top of the skull, cranium.

腦瓜(子)(兒) *naaugua*(*tz*)(*'l*), n., the head: 腦瓜頂兒 the crown of the head.

腦海 *naurhai*, n., the brain, the mind.

腦漿 *naaujiang*, n., the substance of the brain.

腦積水 *naaujishueei*, n., hydrophalus.

腦筋 *naaujin*, n., (1) the cranial nerves; (2) brains, intelligence, mental ability: 用腦筋 do a lot of thinking; 傷腦筋 (s.t.) requires a lot of careful thinking, vexations.

腦汁 *naaujy*, n., (1) (=腦漿) the substance of the brain; (2) the cranial nerves: 絞腦汁 doing feverish mental work, engaged in mental drudgery.

腦殼 *naauker*, n., the skull.

腦兒 *naau'l*, n., (1) the brain of an animal; (2) any semi-liquid substance: 豆腐腦兒 semi-congealed bean curd.

腦力 *naaulih*, n., mental power, intelligence.

腦門(子)(兒) *naaumern*(*tz*) (*-mer'l*), n., the forehead.

腦膜 *naaumor*, n., (phys.) the three membranes that envelop the brain and the spinal cord; 腦膜炎 *--yarn*, n., (med.) meningitis.

腦瓢兒 *naaupiaur'l*, n., the pate: 亮腦瓢兒 a shining pate; 禿腦瓢兒 a baldhead.

腦貧血 *naaupirnshyueh* (*-shiee*), n., (med.) *Anaemia cerebri*, anemia in the brain.

腦勺(子)(兒) *naaushaur*(*tz*)(*'l*), n., the hind part of the head.

腦下垂體 *naaushiahchueitii*, n., pituitary gland.

腦血管血栓症 *naaushyuehguaan shyuehchyuarnjehng*, n., cerebral artery thrombosis.

腦髓 *naursueir*, n., the substance of the brain.

腦子 *naautz*, n., (1) the brain; (2) mental power, intelligence: 沒腦子 no brains.

腦炎 *naauyarn*, n., (med.) encephalitis.

腦溢血 *naauyihshyueh* (*--shiee*), n., (med.) apoplexy, a stroke.

§ 42A.42 (月/冈)

脯 42A.42–1

fuu (**pur*).

N. (1) Preserved meat or fruit: 肉脯, 牛脯, 鹿脯 preserved pork, beef, venison; 桃脯, 杏脯 preserved peach, plum; 脩脯 teacher's salary, anciently consisting of preserved meat. (2) (**pur*) (*-tz*) The breast: 胸脯.

脯醢 *fuuhaai*, n., anciently, making minced meat of enemy prisoner—the extreme punishment.

腩 42A.42–1

naan.

N. Dried meat: 牛腩 fillet, sirloin, tenderloin; 肉腩 dried pork.

膈 42A.42–3

ger.

膈膜 *germor*, n., (physiol.) the diaphragm, midriff (also 横膈膜).

朋 42A.42–4

perng.

N. (1) Friend, esp. 朋友 *-yoou*↓; 良朋 good, worthy friends; 高朋滿座 a party of many distinguished friends. (2) Political clique: 朋黨, 朋比 *-daang*, *-bih*↓. (3) (AC) comparison, equal: 碩大無朋 huge without compare. (4) (AC) an ancient coin.

Adv. Together, as a group: 朋分 (AC) share together; 朋劫 (AC) group robbery, referring to corrupt officials.

朋比 *perngbih*, adv., in 朋比爲奸 phr., conspire for illegal or selfish ends.

朋儔 *perngchour*, n., (LL) friends and associates.

朋黨 *perngdaang*, n., political clique.

朋附 *perngfuh*, v.t., join hands, team up with (person in power).

朋僚 *pernglíaur*, n., friends and colleagues.

朋朋 *perngperng*, n., sound of winds.

朋從 *perngtzuhng*, n., friends and companions.

朋友 *perngyoou*, n., friend: 好, 壞朋友 good, bad friends; 患難朋友 friends in need or during crisis; 酒肉朋友 playboy friends.

胴 42A.42–4

duhng.

N. Large intestine.

胴體 *duhngtii*, n., the trunk of human body.

腡 42A.42–4

luor.

N. Fingerprint (=螺△旋 22D.01): 腡肌 fingerprint part of finger.

肭 42A.42-8

nah.

N. See 膃△肭 42A.30.

§ 42A.50 (月/ㄱ)

胯 42A.50-1

kuah.

N. Pelvis: 胯下 between the thighs; 胯下之辱 the grossest insult.

胯骨 *kuah'gu*, n., the pelvic bones; 胯骨軸兒 the hip joint; (coll.) 胯骨軸兒上的親戚 a remote relative.

勝 42A.50-1

shehng (**sheng*).

N. (1) Victory: 勝利 *-lih*, 勝負, 勝敗 *-fuh*, *-baih*↓; 戰勝, 得勝 win victory, to triumph; 大勝 a great victory; 制勝 to hold superiority or advantage; 勝利沖昏頭腦 to be dizzy with success. (2) Scenic view: 尋幽覽勝 visit places of scenic beauty. (3) A woman's hairdress: 方勝, 春勝 formerly, slanting hair decorations.

V.t. & adj. (1) To excel, be better than: 勝過, 勝似 *-guoh*, *-shyh*↓; 勝於 *-'yu*↓. (2) (**sheng*) To be competent, able to bear: 勝任 *-rehn*↓; esp. 不勝 extremely, unbearably: 不勝感激, 悲痛 extremely grateful, grieved; 不勝其煩 extremely difficult or troublesome; 不可勝數 innumerable; 指不勝屈 more than one can count on one's hand; 小別勝新婚 a brief parting is as sweet as honeymoon.

Adj. (1) Triumphant. (2) Excellent, distinctive: 勝地 *-dih*↓; 勝會 *-hueih*↓; 勝友 distinguished friends; 勝遊 a glorious outing or trip.

勝敗 *shehng-baih*, n., victory and defeat.

勝朝 *shehng-chaur*, n., the defunct dynasty.

勝地 *shehng-dih*, n., a divine spot; a place of glorious views.

勝負 *shehng-fuh*, n., victory or defeat: 決勝負 decide victory; 勝負未卜 cannot predict winner.

勝概 *shehng-gaih*, n., an overwhelming emotion.

勝冠 **sheng-guan*, phr., (AC of children) to reach puberty.

勝過 *shehng-guoh*, v.i., to excel, be better than (person, thing).

勝國 *shehngguor*, n., the conquered nation or (defunct) dynasty.

勝會 *shehng-hueih*, n., a great, festive occasion.

勝迹 *shehng-ji*, n., (LL) places of historic interest.

勝家(兒) *shehngjia('l)*, n., (gambling) the winner; Singer (sewing machine).

勝利 *shehnglih*, n., victory, triumph.

勝任 **shengrehn*, adj., competent: 勝任愉快 very competent at a job.

勝如 *shehng-rur*, adj., see *-shyh*↓.

勝似 *shehng-shyh*, adj., (esp. MC or poetic) better than, also as good as (seeing you in person, etc.).

勝算 *shehng-suahn*, n., a good plan, sure of success: 可操勝算 can be sure of success.

勝訴 *shehngsuh*, v.i., to win a lawsuit; n., favorable decision at court trial.

勝衣 **shengyi*, v.i., (AC of child) be big enough to wear a formal dress: 弱不勝衣 (gen. of a woman) very delicate.

勝義 *shehng-yih*, n., (Budd.) higher understanding of truth.

勝於 *shehng'yu*, adj., better than: 聊勝於無 better than nothing; 勝於常人 better than average person.

騰 42A.50-1

terng (**teng*).

V.i. (1) To mount, ascend: 騰上馬 mount a horse; 騰起 soar up; 騰雲駕霧 fly up to the cloudy regions; 騰蛟起鳳 (complim.) a rapidly rising talent; 騰降 (of prices) go up and down; 騰空, 騰貴 *-kung*, *-gueih*↓. (2) Gallop, prance, fly swiftly: 奔騰 dash about (萬馬奔騰); 騰逐 dash after; 飛騰 fly about; 騰驤 prance. (3) Signifying commotion: 沸騰 (public opinion) seethes in protest; 騰歡 in a wave of joy, hilarity; 薄海騰歡, 萬衆歡騰 universal rejoicing. (4) V.t., move aside, make space: 騰出一間房間 make available one room; 騰出來 set aside for some purpose; 騰挪 *-nuor*↓.

Adv. 騰地 (**teng-*) abruptly.

騰達 *terngdar*, v.i., (of career) soar aloft: 飛黃騰達.

騰歡 *ternghuan*, v.i., be joyous, roar with joy.

騰貴 *ternggueih*, v.i., (of prices) soar.

騰空 *terngkung*, v.i., soar to the skies.

騰挪 *terngnuor*, v.t., set aside, make available (a sum).

騰笑 *terngshiauh*, invite laughter: 騰笑海內 be laughed at in the whole country.

騰騰 *terngterng*, adv., as in 慢騰

騰 very slowly; (MC) in great prosperity; descriptive of flying, 醉騰騰 torpid, drunk.

腭 42A.50-4

eh.
[Var. of 齶 21S.50]

N. Palate.

腸 42A.50-4

charng.

N. (1) Intestines: 直腸 rectum; 大腸 lower intestines; 小腸 intestines; 十二指腸 duodenum; 肥腸 fatty and stuffed intestines. (2) Sausage: 香腸, 臘腸 ditto. (3) (Intestines as seat of emotions like "heart" in Eng.) deep emotions, esp. of longing: 心腸 heart; 好心腸 a good heart, "bowels of mercy"; 壞腸子 a wicked heart; 斷腸 broken heart ("broken intestines"); 斷腸人 one broken-hearted; 肝腸寸斷 sorrow-stricken ("gall and intestines broken to bits"); 盪氣廻腸 agitated ("in the intestines"); 肝腸 esp. courage ("liver and intestines," see 肝 42A.10); 腸肚 *-duh*↓.

腸出血 *charng-chushiee*, n., (med.) intestinal bleeding, enterorrhagia.
腸穿孔 *charng-chuankuung*, n., perforated intestines, enterobrosia.
腸肚 *charngduh*, n., similar to Eng. "heart"; also 肚腸: 好肚腸 a good heart; 牽腸掛肚 infinite longing; 直肚腸 straight-forward.
腸結核 *charng-jieher*, n., (med.) *Phthisis abdominalis.*
腸胃 *charngweih*, n., appetite; digestive system: 腸胃不好 lose appetite.
腸炎 *charngyarn*, n., (med.) enteritis, bowel catarrh.

鵬 42A.50-4

perng.

N. The roc, a mythical bird of giant size and terrific flying power: 鵬鯤 the giant bird and giant fish, symbol of hugeness; 鵬鷃 the giant bird and the tiny bird in the bush—contrast of size; a symbol of person soaring to the cloudy heights, esp. said of young man of great promise in court: 鵬飛 soaring flight; 鵬舉, 鵬搏 great start; 鵬程萬里 rise to unknown heights; 鵬圖 any great (esp. commercial) plan for expansion.

肪 42A.50-6

farng (also *fang*).

脂肪 *jyfarng* (*-fang*), n., animal fat, fatty tissue.

膀 42A.50-6

baang (**bahng*, **pang*, **parng*).

N. (1) (*baang*) The arm: 臂膀 upper arm, (fig.) right-hand man; 肩膀 shoulder; 翅膀 wing of birds; 膀子 *-tz*↓. (2) (**parng*) Bladder in 膀胱 *-guang*↓. (3) (**pang*) Breast in 奶膀子 woman's breast.

Adj. (**pang*) Swollen (of muscles).

膀胱 *parng-guang*, n., urine bladder; 膀胱炎 inflammation of the bladder; 膀胱結石 *--jie-shyr*, stone in the bladder.
膀子 *baangtz*, n., arm; 吊膀子 pr. *diauhbahngtz*, go out with a girl (arm in arm) in the street, to seek company of member of an opposite sex.

胎 42A.50-8

shih.
[Err. var. of 胏 42A.10]

V.i. To spread about.

肋 42A.50-9

leh (**leih*).

N. A rib.

肋骨 *lehguu*, n., ribs (also 肋巴骨, 肋條).
肋膜 *lehmor*, n., (physiol.) the pleura; 肋膜炎 *--yarn*, n., (med.) pleuritis, pleurisy.
肋軟骨 *lehruaan-guu*, n., (physiol.) intercostal muscles (also 肋間骨).
肋窩 **leihwo*, n., the armpit.

脇 42A.50-9

shier.
[Var. 脅 91.42]

N. Armpit; ribs.

朐 42A.50-9

chyur.

N. (AC) dried flank meat: 朐肉, 朐脯 ditto.

胸 42A.50-9

shyung.

N. (1) The chest, the thorax: 胸部, 胸腔 *-buh*, *-chiang*↓; 撫胸 beat the breast (chest); 雞胸 pigeon breast, a rickety disease. (2) Woman's breast: 露胸, 坦胸露

乳 go topless, bare breast; 隆胸 full bosom; 平胸 flat-chest (-ed). (3) Degree of generosity, capacity for greatness, tolerance, largeness of view: 心胸, see 胸襟, 胸懷 *-jin*[2], *-huair* ↓; 胸有成竹 phr., allu., having ready plans to meet a situation; 胸無點墨 completely illiterate; 胸無大志 with no ambition at all; 胸懷狹窄 narrow-minded; 胸中一塊石頭落地 as if a great burden had been taken off one's mind; 胸中甲兵 said of armchair strategist; 胸中鱗甲 vicious ("chest of scales and armor," like a reptile's); 胸中丘壑 what is seen by the mind and imagination; 胸呼吸 costal respiration, breathing by rib motion.

胸部 *shyungbuh*, n., the chest.
胸腔 *shyungchiang*, n., the chest cavity, see *-kuoh* ↓.
胸牆 *shyung-chiarng*, n., (mil.) breastwork.
胸鰭 *shyung-chir*, n., pectorial fin.
胸腹 *shyungfuh*, n., "chest and belly," (fig.) like Eng. "belly," the vulnerable spot of enemy territory.
胸管 *shyung-guaan*, n., (physiol.) the thorax.
胸骨 *shyung-guu*, n., breastbone.
胸花 *shyung-hua*, n., corsage.
胸懷 *shyunghuair*, n., a man's breadth of mind, capacity for rising above trivialities: 胸懷豁達 open-minded, having a large view or breadth of mind (also 胸襟).
胸針 *shyungjen*, n., brooch.
胸肌 *shyungji*, n., (physiol.) (1) chest muscles; (2) transversal muscles of the thorax which help breathing.
胸甲類 *shyungjiaa-leih*, n., (zoo.) *Thoracostraca*, certain crustacean animals (like crabs, shrimp) with chest formations of various shapes.
胸筋 *shyungjin*[1], n., see *-ji* ↑.
胸襟 *shyungjin*[2], n., see *-huair* ↑.
胸椎 *shyungjuei*, n., thoracic vertebrae.
胸口 *shyungkoou*, n., the center of chest.
胸廓 *shyungkuoh*, n., (physiol.) the thorax.
胸肋膜 *shyungleih-mor*, n., (physiol.) pleura of chest.
胸毛 *shyung-maur*, n., chest hair.
胸膜炎 *shyungmohyarn*, n., pleuritis.
胸脯 *shyungpuu*, n., chest: 挺起胸脯 throw out one's chest, (fig.) show courage in the face of danger.
胸腺 *shyungshiahn*, n., (physiol.) the thymus gland.
胸像 *shyungshiahng*, n., sculpture or portrait of bust.
胸膛 *shyungtarng*, n., see *-puu* ↑.
胸次 *shyungtsyh*, n., see *-huair* ↑.
胸圍 *shyungweir*, n., chest circumference.
胸衣 *shyungyi*, n., brassiere (usu. called 奶罩).
胸臆 *shyungyih*, n., one's feelings, heart; see *-huair* ↑.
胸宇 *shyungyuu*, n., (LL) see *-huair* ↑.

§ 42A.63 (月/丶)

臙 42A.63-2

yan.
[Var. 胭 42A.41]

臕 42A.63-6

biau.

Adj. (AC) well-bred, fat (of horses).

§ 42A.70 (月/乚)

肫 42A.70-1

jun.

N. Gizzard: 雞肫 chicken gizzard; 肫肝 gizzard and liver.

Adj. (AC) sincere: 肫肫, 肫篤, 肫誠 sincere, -ly.

腌 42A.70-1

ang.
[Related 醃 *yan*, 31C.70, 骯 42B.70]

腌臢 (骯髒) *angtzang* (*atza*), adj., dirty, filthy, also wr. 腌臢.

胱 42A.70-2

guang.

N. (Physiol.) 膀胱 the bladder.

肊 42A.70-3

yih.
[Var. of 臆 42A.72]

肌 42A.70-4

ji.

N. Muscles or flesh, meat on the bones: see compp. ↓; 香肌, 玉肌 a woman's lovely flesh or skin.

肌膚 *jifu*, n., the skin: 肌膚之親 blood relations, intimate relations between man and woman.
肌骨 *jiguu*, n., muscles and bones, the body as a whole.
肌理 *jilii*, n., skin texture: 肌理細膩 a fine-textured skin; (litr. criticism) texture theory of po-

亅	小	卜	十	土	𠂇	廾	𠃊	丨	一	丅	㇇	口	囗	冂	⺄	厂	尸	亠	广	宀	丶	乚	乁	心	八	人	乂	㇀	㇀	丿	㇗	く
00	01	02	10	11	12	20	21	22	30	31	32	40	41	42	50	51	52	60	61	62	63	70	71	72	80	81	82	83	90	91	92	93

etry of 翁方綱.

肌肉 *jirouh*, n., muscles, flesh.

肌體 *jitii*, n., the body.

肥 42A.70-5

feir.

N. (1) Fertilizer: 糞肥 natural fertilizer; 氮肥 nitrogen fertilizer, etc, see 肥料 *-liauh* ↓. (2) Spoils: 分肥 divide the spoils or illegal gain.

V. t. To enrich in 肥己 "fatten oneself" by illegal transactions; cf. 中飽△ 81B.70.

Adj. (1) Fat, greasy, well-bred, see compp. ↓. (2) Fertile (of soil): 肥田, 肥地. (3) Fat (jobs): 肥差, 肥缺 official post with good (usu. illegal) revenue; 肥年 a prosperous year.

肥蠢 *feichuun*, adj., fat and stupid; awkwardly fat.

肥大 *feirdah*, adj., plump; 肥大症 hypertrophy.

肥遯 *feirduhn*, v. i., (LL) retire in comfort.

肥甘 *feirgan*, adj. & n., things good to eat, delicacies.

肥料 *feirliauh*, n., fertilizer; 化學肥料 chemical fertilizer.

肥美 *feirmeei*, n., plump; well-fed (of horses, etc.); rich (soil).

肥膩 *feirnih*, n., rich, greasy (food).

肥胖 *feirpahng*, n., fat, plump (of person); 肥胖症 obesity.

肥饒 *feirraur*, adj., rich (soil).

肥潤 *feirruhn*, n., sleek, smooth and glossy.

肥瘦(兒) *feirsoou('l)*, n., width of gown, girth: 肥瘦得中 good figure (not too slender or plump); half lean pork.

肥田粉 *feirtiarn-feen*, n., chemical fertilizer, potassium sulphate.

肥皂 *feirtzauh*, n., soap; 肥皂粉 soap powder; detergent.

肥沃 *feirwo*, adj., (LL) rich (soil).

脃 42A.70-5

tsueih.

[Common var. 脆 42A.70]

朧 42A.70-6

lurng.

Adj. 朦△朧 42A.02.

脘 42A.70-6

guaan (waan).

N. The internal cavity of the stomach.

腕 42A.70-6

wahn.

N. The wrist: 手腕 ditto; 腳腕 ankle; 扼腕 wring hands in regret.

腕釧 *wahn-chuahn*, n., (MC) bracelet.

腕法 *wahn-faa*, n., (callig.) method of holding wrist: (a) 枕腕 resting wrist on table, (b) 提腕 lifting wrist, (c) 懸腕 keeping wrist and elbow suspended in air—in writing characters of progressively bigger sizes.

腕鐲 *wahn-juor*, n., bracelet.

腕力 *wahn-lih*, n., wrist power.

脱 42A.70-8

tuo.

V. i. & t. (1) To cast off, take off: 脱去, 脱下來 take off, strip off; 脱卸, 脱掉 *-shieh, -diauh* ↓; 脱衣 to strip; 脱衣舞 strip tease; 脱衣舞女 stripteaser; 脱膊, 脱光 strip naked; 脱帽 take off one's hat; 脱毛(髮) lose hair; 脱殼 hatch (as chicken), come out of egg. (2) To escape (danger): 脱出 escape; 脱險, 脱難 escape from crisis or accident; 脱網 escape from encirclement, physical or legal; 金蟬脱殼 (phr.) cicada leaving behind its cast-off part in molting, a disappearance act from an entangled situation; 脱口而出 words escape from one's lips, speak by impulse or without forethought; 脱口成章 speak beautifully (worthy to be written down); 脱手 *-shoou* ↓. (3) To drop out, drop out by mistake: 脱漏, 脱誤 *-louh, -wuh* ↓; 脱韁野馬 uncontrollable as wild horse without bridle.

Vb. suffix. Off: 失脱, 遺脱 lose, drop (line, words, in printing); 虛脱 so weak as to be prostrate; 卸脱 cast off (responsibility); 逃脱 effect an escape.

Adv. (MC) perhaps: 脱使可行 perhaps it can be done.

脱班 *tuo-ban*, v. i., miss schedule (of train, etc.).

脱腸 *tuo-charng*, n., prolapsus of the rectum, hernia.

脱黨 *tuo-daang*, v. i., renounce party membership.

脱掉 *tuo-diauh*, v.t., discard, take off (dress).

脱幅 *tuo-fur*, v. i., (AC) dispute between husband and wife.

脱稿 *tuo-gaau*, v. i., finish manuscript, ready for printing.

脱肛 *tuogang*, n., see *-charng* ↑.

脱滑(兒) *tuohuar('l)*, adj., slippery (character).

脱節 *tuojier*, v. i., lose continuity or proper contact, become disjointed.

脱臼 *tuojiouh*, v. i., (med.) (be) dislocate (-ed.)

脱籍 *tuojir*, v. i., drop party membership (黨籍) or nationality (國籍); formerly, (of women sold or sentenced to become singsong girls) be officially released from profession (妓藉).

脱 開 *tuoo'kai*, v.i., to get away, be separated from.

脱 空 *tuokung*, v.i., come out a loser or without results; (of plan, promise) fail.

脱 懶(兒) *tuolaan(-laa'l)*, v.i., play hooky, escape from duty, also *tuor-*.

脱 離 *tuolir*, v.i., to escape from, sever connections, leave, separate from: 脱離關係 break off relations; 脱離現實 divorced from reality.

脱 漏 *tuolouh*, v.i. & t., be dropped by mistake (of words, letters in printing).

脱 落 *tuoluoh*, v.i. & t., drop, fall off (as hair, leaves).

脱 略 *tuolyueh*, adj., unrestrained.

脱 卯 *tuo-maau*, v.i., miss roll call.

脱 毛 的 *tuomaur'de*, n. & adj., depilatory.

脱 然 *tuorarn*, adj. & adv., free, untrammeled.

脱 灑 *tuosaa*, adj., easy and unrestrained; handsome in manner.

脱 身 *tuo-shen*, v.i., get away: 不得脱身, 脱不開身 cannot get away (from business).

脱 險 *tuo-shiaan*, v.i., escape from crisis, danger, accident.

脱 孝 *tuoshiauh*, v. i., pass the period of mourning.

脱 卸 *tuoshieh*, v. t., shake off (duty, etc.).

脱 屣 *tuoshii*, n., cast off slippers—s. t. of no consequence.

脱 手 *tuo-shoou*, v. i., get rid of, sell (property, stocks).

脱 水 *tuoshueei*, v.i. & n., dehydrate, -tion.

脱 粟 *tuosuh*, n., hulled but not yet polished rice.

脱 俗 *tuo-sur*, v. i., shake off, not be bound by conventions (of person's character).

脱 胎(兒) *tuotai(-ta'l)*, v. i., (lit.) "come from a certain placenta," to compose by borrowing the form of some anc. model but changing the subject—curiously approved in art of composition from emphasis on copying ancients; also 脱胎換骨.

脱 套 *tuo-tauh*, v. i., do not observe formalities.

脱 逃 *tuotaur*, v. i., to escape.

脱 體 *tuotii*, v. i., (1) shake off disease and get well; (2) (of Chin. characters) be written out of shape.

脱 兔 *tuo-tuh*, phr., (fast as) an escaped hare.

脱 網 *tuo-waang*, v.i., escape net or encirclement.

脱 誤 *tuowuh*, v.t., drop out (word or letter) by mistake.

脱 穎 *tuoyiing*, v.i., (allu.) you cannot keep a good man down (as the "awl-point finds its way out of pocket").

肐 42A.70-9

ge.

[Var. of 胳, 骮]

肐 膀 *gebaang*, n., the upper arm.

肐 臂 *gebih*, n., the arm.

肐 膊 *ge'bo*, n., the arm: 大肐膊 the upper arm; 小肐膊 the lower arm; 肐膊肘 *--joou*, the elbow (=肘子); 肐膊腕 *--waan*, the wrist.

肐 肢 窩 *gejywo*, n., the armpit.

肐 臊 *ge-sau*, n., armpit odor.

胞 42A.70-9

bau.

N. (1) The womb. (2) The placenta of a child: 胞衣. (3) (Biol.) the cell: 細胞. (4) Abbr. for 同胞 (lit.) "same womb," term emphasizing consanguinity: 胞兄, 胞弟 brothers of the same mother; 胞伯, 胞叔 father's brothers of the same mother; 同胞 fellow countryman, common term for compatriots; 僑胞 overseas compatriots (=華僑); 難胞 compatriot refugees; 山胞 aboriginal compatriots (in Taiwan).

脆 42A.70-9

tsueih.

[Pop. of 脃 42A.70↑]

Adj. (1) Crisp in flavor, voice or style (not drawn-out). (2) Brittle, frail, fragile. (3) Clear-cut, simple: 乾脆 simply (do s.t.), without hemming and hawing.

脆 薄 *tsueihbor*, adj., brittle (friendship), thin (wafer).

脆 怯 *tsueihchieh*, adj., timid.

脆 骨 *tsueih'gu*, n., cartilage.

脆 快 *tsueihkuaih*, adj., simple and direct (in doing things).

脆 弱 *tsueihruoh*, adj., weak, fragile.

脆 性 *tsueihshihng*, n., brittleness (of glass, ice).

臘 42A.70-9

lah.

[Pop. 腊]

N. (1) Year-end sacrifice to the gods, hence the 12th lunar month: 臘月 *-yueh*, 臘日 *-ryh*↓; 臘盡冬殘 end of the year. (2) Dried or preserved meat or fish made in winter: 臘肉 *-rouh*, 臘味 *-weih*↓; 燒臘 collective name for all dried and preserved meat and fish; 臘魚, 臘鴨 dried or salted fish, duck. (3) (LL) the age of a Buddhist monk.

臘 八 *lahba*, n., the 8th day of the 12th lunar month; 臘八粥 *--juo*, gruel with nuts and dates eaten on that day.

臘 腸 *lahcharng*, n., sausage; 臘腸狗 *--goou*, n., dachshund, so called presumably for its physical likeness to a sausage.

臘 鼓 *lahguu*, n., drum beaten on the 8th day of the 12th lunar month, hence the approaching year-end.

臘梅 *lahmeir*, n., (bot.) the winter-sweet, *Calycanthus praecox* (same as 蠟梅).

臘肉 *lahrouh*, n., dried or preserved meat.

臘日 *lahryh*, n., the 8th day of the 12th lunar month (same as 臘八).

臘味 *lahweih*, n., (1) collective name for all dried and salted meat and fish; (2) wine brewed in winter.

臘月 *lahyueh*, n., the 12th lunar month.

§ 42A.71 (月/弋)

臟 42A.71-2

tzahng.

N. The internal organs: 五臟六腑 the viscera, the entrails; 心臟 the heart; 肝臟 the liver; 肺臟 the lungs.

臟腑 *tzahngfuu*, n., (1) the internal organs of the body; (2) one's mental attitude, disposition, frame of mind.

膩 42A.71-7

nih.

N. (1) Grease, fat. (2) Dirt, grime: 塵膩 dust and dirt; 滿身油膩 covered with grime.

V.i. (1) Feel dull and listless or depressed: 膩得慌 feel extremely dull and bored; 煩膩 be disgusted or depressed. (2) Be boring, annoying, annoyed: 膩煩 *-farn* ↓; 膩人 *-rern* ↓; 膩畏 *-'weih* ↓.

V.t. (1) (Of food) be disagreeable to: 膩胃 *-weih*[2] ↓; 好膩人 too greasy; 膩死了 too greasy, exhausted by tedious work; 膩味 *-weih*[1] ↓. (2) Fill small cracks with putty: 用膩子膩上去 apply some putty to keep it in place.

Adj. (1) Oily: 肥膩 (of food) rich, greasy; 油膩 ditto. (2) Smooth, glossy: 膩理 *-lii* ↓. (3) Tired or sick of, satiated with; 玩膩了 tired of playing or loafing; 吃膩了 satiated with eating.

膩煩 *nihfarn*, v.i. & adj., (be) boring, annoying, annoyed: 他好膩煩人 he is so tiresome or boring; 我一看見這東西, 心裏就膩煩 I am disgusted at seeing this (loathsome person or thing).

膩粉 *nihfeen*, n., cosmetics, (LL) rouge and powder.

膩糊 *nih'hu*, adj., (of liquids) well diluted and mixed.

膩理 *nihlii*, adj., smooth and glossy.

膩抹 *nihmo*, (1) n., a trowel for plaster (*-moo'l*); (2) v.t., make dirty, to soil; to smear.

膩人 *nihrern*, adj., (1) (be) boring, tiresome; (2) too greasy: 這肉太膩人了 this meat is too greasy for me.

膩子 *nihtz*, n., (1) putty for fixing small cracks; (2) a customer who lingers in a place of business unnecessarily long: 茶膩子, 酒膩子, 澡膩子 such customer in a teahouse, a restaurant, a bathhouse.

膩味 *nihweih*[1], adj., (of food) be too rich and greasy.

膩胃 *nihweih*[2], adj., (of food) too rich and greasy: 這菜眞膩胃 this dish is too rich to be agreeable to the stomach.

膩畏 *nih'weih*, v.i., invite dislike by forcing one's attentions on another: 他太讓人膩畏了 he is tiresome with his attentions.

膩友 *nihyoou*, n., a very close friend: 閨中膩友 a woman's paramour.

胝 42A.71-9

jy.

N. Callus, -es: usu. 胼胝 calluses.

§ 42A.72 (月/心)

腮 42A.72-4

sai.

[Common var. of 顋 41S.80]

N. The cheek: 落腮鬍 whiskers.

腮幫子 *saibangtz*, n., (coll.) the cheek.

腮骨 *saiguu*, n., cheekbone.

腮頰 *saijiar*, n., the cheek.

腮腺 *saishiahn*, n., parotid; also 胙腮; 腮腺炎 mumps (parotitis).

臆 42A.72-6

yih.

N. The chest: 胸臆 breadth of view, tolerance, generosity.

V.i. To conjecture: see compp. ↓.

臆斷 *yihduahn*, v. i., (1) to make arbitrary decision; (2) to guess.

臆度 *yihduh*, v. i., to conjecture.

臆說 *yihshuo*, n., guesswork, what is pure imagination.

臆測 *yihtseh*, v. i. & n., (to, a) conjecture.

§ 42A.80 (月/八)

臢 42A.80-1

tzang.

Adj. See 腌[A]臢 *angtzang*, filthy, 42A.70.

A

賸 42A.80-1

shehng.

V. t. To leave over, be left over (usu. wr. 剩 90S.00).

腆 42A.80-2

tiaan.

Adj. (1) (AC) proper, decent: 辭無不腆 all words were proper; 不腆之儀 (AC) my unworthy present. (2) To throw forward or expose: 腆胸, 腆肚子, 腆背 to expose chest, belly, back. (3) Unashamed, see 靦腆 42A.41.

臏 42A.80-6

bihn.
[Var. of 髕]

N. Kneecap; anc. punishment of removing kneecap.

§ 42A.81 (月/人)

胰 42A.81-1

yir.

N. (1) Pancreas: 胰臟. (2) Soap.

胰子 *yirtz*, n., soap (also called 肥皂).
胰臟 *yirtzahng*, n., pancreas (also called 胰腺).

B

腠 42A.81-1

tsouh.

N. 腠理 the natural fibre line of meat; (fig.) the thread of thought in writing.

膜 42A.81-2

moh (**mor*).

N. (1) Membrane in plants or animals, such as diaphragm, peritoneum, mucous membrane. (2) See 膜拜 *-baih* ↓.

膜拜 **morbaih*, n. & v. i., religious prostrations, adore, worship: 焚香膜拜 worship at temples.
膜外 *moh waih*, phr., not one's concern (seat of feeling being considered in abdominal organs).

朕 42A.81-8

jehn.

Pron. The first person, I, since 秦 Chirn Dyn., restricted to imperial use.

N. An omen, foreboding: 朕兆 ditto.

臉 42A.81-8

liaan.

N. (-'l, *-tz*) (1) Face: 鴨(鵝)蛋臉兒 oval-faced; 臉孔, 臉面 *-kuung*, *-'miahn* ↓. (2) Facial expression of anger, embarrassment, shame, etc.: 臉容, 臉色 facial expression; 臉上無光 a dull

C

face; 臉紅 face red with anger, shame; 滿臉通紅 face reddens all over; 笑臉 smiling face; 醜臉 ugly face, angry look; 鬼臉 grimace; 轉臉, 變臉, 翻臉 face changes, become angry; 臉上下不來 embarrassed; 臉急 *-jir* ↓; 臉紅脖子粗 hot-tempered. (3) Oriental "face," the ability to face fellowmen with self-respect, akin to "honor": 丟臉 "lose face" (to be known to do s.t. improper); 沒臉見人 cannot face fellowmen; 賞臉 give "face," honor one by accepting invitation, etc.; 不要臉 shameless; 臉子大 used to being treated with respect. (4) Sensitivity: 臉軟, 臉硬 easily, not easily persuaded to give in; 臉嫩 easily ashamed, a sensitive face; 臉熱 easily excited; 臉軟 easily persuaded; 臉皮 *-pir* ↓.

臉蛋(兒)(子) *liaandahn(-dah'l)(tz)*, n., face (pretty, reddens, etc.).
臉紅 *liaanhurng*, v. i., & adj., blush, feel ashamed or angered.
臉頰 *liaanjiar*, n., cheeks.
臉急 *liaan-jir*, phr., hot-tempered, excitable.
臉孔 *liarnkuung*, n., face, (fig.) "face," see N. 3 ↑.
臉面 *liaan'miahn*, n., face: 我有甚麽臉面見人 how can I face people? 看在他老人家臉面上 or 臉上 out of respect for the old man (do what he desires).
臉盤(子)(兒) *liaanparn(tz)(-par'l)*, n., facial contour (long, square, etc.).
臉皮(兒) *liaanpir(-pier'l)*, n., sensitivity to shame: 臉皮厚 thick-skinned, "thick-skinned," unashamed; 臉皮薄 thin-skinned, timid, sensitive to shame; 沒臉皮 without shame.
臉譜(兒) *liarnpuu('l)*, n., theatrical mask, make-up; (fig.) facial sketch.
臉容 *liaanrurng*, n., facial expression.
臉色 *liaanseh*, n., facial expression: 看人臉色 watch another's expression, also to have to please s. o.

賸 腆 臏 胰 腠 膜 朕 臉

亅	小	卜	十	土	ナ	廾	ㄴト	丨	一	丁	フ	口	区	冈	㇕	厂	尸	亠	广	宀	丶	乚	乁	心	八	人	乂	乛	㇀	刂	⺧	く
00	01	02	10	11	12	20	21	22	30	31	32	40	41	42	50	51	52	60	61	62	63	70	71	72	80	81	82	83	90	91	92	93

臉水 *liarnshueei*, n., basin of water for washing face.

臉膛兒 *liaantarng'l*, n., facial contour (long, square, etc.).

臉子 *liaantz*, n., (1) facial expression, usu. unpleasant: 臉子不好看 ugly expression on face; (2) oft. a pretty face.

腴 42A.81–9

yur.

N. Fat part of belly pork.

Adj. Fat, rich, fertile (land): 膏腴之地 rich soil.

§ 42A.82 (月/乂)

肢 42A.82–1

jy.

N. The legs of animals, wings and feet of birds, arms and legs of man: 四肢 arms and legs; 上肢 arms; 下肢 legs; 頭腦簡單, 四肢發達 well-developed limbs but head of a moron; 肢骨 bones of arms or legs.

肢解 *jyjiee*, v. i., ancient practice of dismembering a criminal.

肢體 *jytii*, n., person's physique.

臟 42A.82–1

guu.

臟脹 *guujahng*, (1) n., an abnormal swelling of any part of the body: 氣臟 swollen with gas; 水臟 dropsy; (2) v. i., to swell, protuberate, bulge; (3) adj., bloated, swollen.

胈 42A.82–1

bar.

N. (AC) Hair on calves, arms.

股 42A.82–4

guu.

N. adjunct. 一股香氣, 一股新鮮空氣 a whiff of fragrance, fresh air; 一股頭髮 a strand of hair; 一股熱氣 a blast of hot air; 一股熱情 a spell of enthusiasm; 一股土匪 a band of robbers.

N. (1) The thigh, the haunches, the rump: 屁股 the buttocks; 屁股眼 the anus. (2) A share of capital stock: 合股生意 joint partnership; 計股分利 distribute dividends by shares; 股市 *-shyh*, 股本 *-been*, 股金 *-jin*, 股票 *-piauh*, 股息 *-shir*, 股東 *-dung*↓; 入股 buy shares; 退股 sell shares. (3) A section of a government office: 第一股, 第二股 first, second section. (4) (AC) (math.) the longer side of a right triangle.

股本 *gurbeen*, n., shares of capital investment.

股東 *guudung*, n., a shareholder: 股東大會 a shareholders' (stockholders') meeting.

股份 *guufehn*, n., shares of capital stock (also 股分): 股份公司 joint-stock company.

股肱 *guugung*, n., one's right-hand man: 股肱之臣 (AC) the most trustworthy ministers or advisers.

股掌 *gurjaang*[1], n., (1) (LL) the palm of a man's hand: 玩之於股掌之上 have s. o. under one's complete control; (2) (AC) *-gung*↑.

股長 *gurjaang*[2], n., a section chief of a government office.

股金 *guu-jin*, n., cash payment for shares.

股兒 *guu'l*, n., (1) a stock share; (2) a strand, band, bundle (of hair, thread).

股利 *guu-lih*, n., interest on shares.

股票 *guupiauh*, n., stock shares: 股票市場 the stock market (abbr. 股市); 股票交易所 the stock exchange.

股息 *guu-shir*, n., annual dividends per share.

股市 *guu-shyh*, n., the stock market.

股子 *guutz*, n., (1) see *-fehn*↑; (2) a strand, band, bundle.

服 42A.82–5

fur.

N. (1) A surname. (2) Dose: 一服藥 a dose of medicine. (3) Dress, garment, clothes: 便服 informal, daily wear; 禮服 formal dress; 洋服, 中服 Western, Chinese dress; 軍服, 制服 uniform; 朝服 court costume; 華服, 美服 beautiful dress, attire; 素服 white mourning garment; 服飾, 服裝, 服色 *-shyh*[1], *-juang*, *-seh*↓. (4) (AC) subjugated territory; 五服, 六服. (5) Mourning, period of mourning: 喪服 mourning dress; 有服 in mourning; 服滿, 除服, 服除, 脱服 mourning over; 國服 national mourning; 期服 one-year mourning, see 服制 *-jyh*↓; 服內 during mourning; 服內納妾 take concubine during mourning, an offense; 服內生子 have son after 10 months of parents' death and before end of 27th month—a sin and disgrace.

V. i. & t. (1) To dress: 服單衣 put on unlined gown; 服裝 *-juang*↓. (2) Take, swallow: 服藥, 服毒 take medicine, poison: 服餌 take Taoist concoctions to become immortal; 內服, 口服 take (medicine) orally: 服法 directions for taking medicine. (3) Take well: 不服水土 do not agree with climate of place; 這藥吃不服 do not take well this medicine, it does not agree. (4) To serve: 服務, 服役, 服侍 *-wuh*, *-yih*, *-shyh*[2]↓; 服刑 receive meted-out punishment; be executed. (5) Obey:

服(從)命令, 法律 obey orders, law. (6) Surrender, obey, submit, respect: 佩服 respect (person); 欽服, 敬服 respect and admire, -tion; 降服 surrender, also compel to surrender; 心悦誠服, 悦服 gladly surrender, admire, accept leadership; 順服 obey; 歸服 come under control (of neighboring country); 屈服 accept defeat; force (person) to accept defeat; 不服, 心裏不服 be not convinced; 不服議論 cannot accept statement; 不服輸 defeated but not convinced. (7) V. t., compel submission, convince: 以德服人 compel submission by kindness or generosity; 服人之心 make people accept at heart; 説服他 convince him by argument.

服氣 *furchih*, v.i., accept inwardly, esp. 不服氣 be not convinced.

服裝 *furjuang*, n., dress, attire: 服裝設計 costume design.

服制 *fur-jyh*, n., (1) dress regulations; (2) elaborate system of prescribed mourning dress and periods; 斬衰 27 months for parents (3 times period of pregnancy); 齊衰, 期服 1 year for grandparents and certain others; 大功 9 months for brothers, sisters, etc; 小功 5 months for uncles, aunts, etc.; 緦麻 3 months for distant relatives.

服勞 *furlaur*, v.i., serve; work as employee.

服輭 *fur-nuaan*, v.i., admit mistake.

服喪 *fursang*, n., mourning.

服色 *furseh*, n., color of dress.

服輸 *fur-shu*, v.i., admit defeat.

服飾 *furshyh*[1], n., gen. attire.

服侍(事) *furshyh*[2], v.t., serve (person, parents, etc.).

服貼 *furtie*, adj., willing to follow or obey wish: 他對你很服貼 he always does what you want; also 服服貼貼 very loving and obedient; 穿起來很服貼 fit well.

服從 *furtsurng*, v.t., obey (person, orders, discipline).

服罪 *furtzueih*, v.i., be executed.

服務 *furwuh*, v.i. & n., serve, service; 服務中心 service center; 社會服務 social service; 服務社會 serve society; 服務員 attendant, steward.

服役 *furyih*, n. & v. i., labor service, to serve (corps, etc.) military service.

服膺 *furying*, v.t., admire, render homage; remember (advice) at heart.

服用 *furyuhng*, n., articles for personal use.

腹 42A.82-9

fuh.

N. (1) Belly, abdomen, specifically the stomach: 肚腹 the stomach; 胸腹 chest and belly; 腹部 belly; 大腹 big belly; 口腹之欲 the bodily wants of food and drink; 專爲口腹 just for animal sustenance; 果腹 to fill the belly; 捧腹 hold the sides in laughter; 口蜜腹劍 honeyed words and a dagger at heart; 心腹之交 bosom friend; 心腹之患 enemy within, danger of betrayal or revolt from those closest; 剖腹明心 slit belly (i.e., lay all open, conceal nothing) to show loyalty; 腹背受敵 surrounded by enemy at the front and rear; 腹背相親 very intimate; 腹背之毛 (LL) insignificant trifle. (2) In the mind only: 腹稿 "belly manuscript," i.e., mental notes before lecture or writing; 腹議, 腹誹 criticism or opposition in the heart, not expressed; 腹笥 "belly as satchel," store of learning in the mind; 腹笥甚寛, 甚儉 well-read, scope of knowledge limited.

V.t. (AC) carry: 出入腹我 (of mother) nursed me.

腹腔 *fuhchiang*, n., abdominal cavity.

腹地 *fuhdih*, n., central region, opp. frontier, 邊地.

腹脹 *fuhjahng*, n., swelling of the belly, dropsy.

腹結 *fuhjier*, n., constipation.

腹毛類 *fuhmaur-leih*, n., (zoo) *Gastrotricha*.

腹膜 *fuhmor*, n., peritoneum; 腹膜炎 --*yarn*, n., peritonitis.

腹瀉 *fuhshieh*, n., diarrhoea.

腹心 *fuhshin*, n., as in 敢布腹心 make frank statement without reservations; 腹心人, 腹心之交 bosom friend.

腹痛 *fuhtuhng*, n., bellyache.

腹足類 *fuhtzur-leih*, n., (zoo) *Gastropoda*.

腹語 *fuhyuu*, n., ventriloquism.

腠 42A.82-9

jyuan (*tzuei).

N. (*tzuei) (Coll.) a child's penis.

V. t. Exploit, deprive of.

§ 42A.83 (月/乛)

腱 42A.83-2

jiahn.

N. (Beef) shank.

腿 42A.83-5

tueei.

N. (1) Leg, thigh: 腿子, 大腿 thigh; 小腿 calf; 玉腿 beautiful legs (of women); 長腿 long-legged person, 粗腿 big legs; 光腿 bare legs; 鐵腿 good hiker whose legs are never tired; 飛毛腿 a fast runner. (2)

Capacity for walking, running, leg action: 腿快, 腿勤 one who is on his toes all the time; 跑腿 to run about on errands; 跑腿的 one assigned to run errands, etc.; 狗腿子 (contempt.) "running dog"; 大腿舞 burlesque, leg show; 腿上工夫 beautiful leg work. (3) Condition of legs: 腿酸 leg sore, have stiff legs; 腳腿不便 have difficulty in walking; 邁不開腿 too weak to stand or walk or have no room for action. (4) Ham, leg of pork, mutton, etc.: 豬腿 leg of pork; 火腿 ham; 雲腿, 南腿 ham of Yunnan; 金華火腿 Kinhua ham; 雞腿 chicken leg.

腿肚(子) *tueeiduh(tz)*, n., the calf (of leg).
腿跟 *tueeigen*, n., the heel.
腿骨 *tueirguu*, n. leg bone.
腿腳(兒) *tueirjiaau('l)*, n., steps (firm, weak, etc.).
腿毛 *tueeimaur*, n., hair on legs.
腿腕(兒) *tueirwaan(-waa'l)*, n., ankle.

腋 42A.83-6

yih (sp. pr. *yeh*).

N. (1) Armpit. (2) The fur on the legs of a fox: 集腋成裘 make fur coat from many pieces of felt —get the benefit of many opinions.

腋氣 *yeh-chih*, n., armpit odor.
腋臭 *yeh-chouh* n., ditto.
腋下 *yeh-shiah*, n., under the armpit.

腚 42A.83-6

dihng.

N. Hips (pop. cogn. of 臀 52.42): 光腚 bare buttocks.

§ 42A.91 (月/ノ)

膨 42A.91-1

perng.

V. i. & adj. Swell, swollen, inflated (prices, belly).

膨脹 *perngjahng*, v. i. & adj. & n., inflate (-ed, -tion); 通貨膨脹 gen. inflation; inflated.

膠 42A.91-5

jiau.

N. (1) Glue, gum, rubber or similar substance: 膠水 *-shueei* ↓; 樹膠 resin, gum; 橡膠 rubber; 皮膠 common glue; 魚膠 fish glue; 塑膠 plastics; 乳膠 foam rubber; 香口膠 chewing gum. (2) (AC) an imperial academy: 東膠 the East Academy. (3) A surname.

V. i. & t. (1) V. t., to glue: 膠住了 stuck together; 膠附 *-fuh* ↓; 膠上 glue together. (2) V. i., (AC) run aground: 置杯焉則膠 (AC) a cup placed in a cupful of spilled water will be stranded.

Adj. (1) Sticky, gluey: 膠泥 *-nir* ↓. (2) Stubborn, obstinate: 膠固 *-guh* ↓; 膠執成見 bigoted, prejudiced, diehard; 膠柱鼓瑟 acting with a one-track mind, unadaptable to changing circumstances.

膠版 *jiau-baan*, n., a manifolding apparatus.
膠漆 *jiauchi*, n., (of friends or couple) mutual attachment: 如膠似漆 inseparable, closely bound together ("like glue and varnish") between lovers.
膠帶 *jiaudaih*, n., insulating tape.
膠附 *jiaufuh*, v. t., to stick together (as) with glue.
膠葛 *jiauger*, n., complications, confusion, dispute.
膠管 *jiauguaan*, n., a rubber tube.
膠固 *jiauguh*, adj., (1) firm, solid, immovable; (2) pigheaded, dogged, unyielding.
膠捲(兒) *jiaujuaan(-jyuaa'l)*, n., (a roll of) photographic film.
膠質 *jiaujyr*, n., glue, gum, any gelatinous substance.
膠囊 *jiaunarng*, n., gelatine capsules.
膠泥 *jiaunir*, (1) n., clay, cement; 膠泥巴兒 caked mud; (2) adj., sticky.
膠片 *jiaupiahn*, n., photographic film.
膠皮 *jiaupir*, n., (1) India rubber; (2) (northern dial.) rickshaw with rubber tires (opp. 鐵皮(車) rickshaw with iron tires).
膠水 *jiaushueei*, n., glue.
膠續 *jiaushyuh*, v. i., remarry after wife's death.
膠衣 *jiauyi*, n., (1) rubber coat; (2) gelatine capsules.

胗 42A.91-8

jen.

N. (1) Gizzard of birds, fowl: 胗肝兒 gizzard and liver. (2) U.f. 疹 (pr. *jeen*) 61A.91.

§ 42A.93 (月/く)

胠 42A.93-1

chyu.

V. t. (AC) to pry open: 胠篋 open a trunk to steal.

肱 42A.93-1

gung.

N. The forearm: 股肱 right-hand man, able and reliable assistant, loyal ministers.

媵 42A.93-1

yihng.

N. (1) A personal maid who goes with bride to new home. (2) A concubine: 媵妾.

V.t. To escort (bride).

螣 42A.93-1

teh.

N. A small insect destroying rice seedlings or young sprouts.

腰 42A.93-3

yau.

N. (1) (-'*l*) The waist: 彎腰 bend from the waist; 折腰 (LL) bow in courtesy; 柳腰, 細腰 slender waist; 熊腰虎背 thick powerful back (and shoulders); 蜂腰 "bee's waist"—(fig.) an error in versification or slender middle part of writing; 撐腰, 抱腰 to back and support s. o. (2) (-*tz*) The kidney: 豬腰 pork kidneys. (3) Middle part or kidney-shaped object: 土腰 an isthmus; 海腰 strait(s); 棍子半腰 middle part of stick; 故事中腰 middle part of story.

腰板兒 *yaubaa'l*, n., waist, back: 挺着腰板兒 stand up straight.
腰包 *yaubau*, n., wallet carried on girdle, hence 腰纏 money carried on body.
腰帶 *yau-daih*, n., belt, girdle.
腰刀 *yau-dau*, n., knife on girdle.
腰房 *yau-farng*, n., side rooms connected with main court by corridor.
腰櫃 *yau-gueih*, n., cash box.
腰花(兒) *yauhua('l)*, n., kidney finely slit: 炒腰花 fried kidney.
腰斬 *yau-jaan*, v.t., to cut things in half; formerly, to execute criminal by cutting body in half at the waist.
腰站兒 *yau-jah'l*, n., a wayfarer's station.
腰肢 *yaujy*, n., waistline.
腰胯 *yaukuah*, n., hip, hip joint.
腰裏硬 *yau'liyihng*, n., broad trousers belt or hard braid girdle, oft. used for carrying things.
腰領 *yauliing*, n., see 要[△]領 31.93.
腰門(兒) *yaumern(-mer'l)*, n., a side door.
腰身 *yau(')shen*, n., (tailor) waistline.
腰腿(兒) *yautueei(-tuee'l)*, n., strength or weakness of one's steps.
腰圍 *yauweir*, n., (1) girth (of body, tree); (2) girdle; (3) waist measure.
腰窩兒 *yauwo'l*, n., lamb flank.
腰眼(兒)(子) *yauyaan(-yaa'l)(tz)*, n., hip spine.
腰圓(兒) *yauyuarn(-yuar'l)*, adj., oval-shaped, kidney-shaped.

脍 42A.93-8

kuaih.

[Abbr. of 膾 42A.41]

SECTION 42B

§ 42B.00 (骨/丿)

髆 42B.00-1

bor.

N. Shoulder blade (cf. 膊 42A.00).

§ 42B.01 (骨/小)

髁 42B.01-4

ke.

N. Thigh bone; kneecap.

§ 42B.10 (骨/十)

髀 42B.10-9

bih.

N. The thigh; thigh bone: 拊髀 (LL) slap the thigh; 髀肉復生 phr., getting stout again (allu. to regret of 劉備 for not riding on horseback for a long time.)

髀骶 *bihdii*, n., the red, exposed buttocks of monkey.
髀骨 *bih-guu*, n., thigh bone; pelvic bones.

肱 媵 螣 腰 脍 髆 髁 髀

亅	小	⺊	十	土	ナ	卄	ㄣ	丨	一	丅	フ	口	区	冈	冂	厂	尸	亠	广	宀	丶	乚	乀	心	八	人	乂	⌒	冖	刂	⺈	く
00	01	02	10	11	12	20	21	22	30	31	32	40	41	42	50	51	52	60	61	62	63	70	71	72	80	81	82	83	90	91	92	93

§ 42B.20 (骨/卄)

髒 42B.20-2

tzang.

Adj. Dirty: 髒東西 foul stuff; 髒死了 abominably dirty; 髒兮兮 disgustingly dirty; 髒相 unkempt (unwashed), dirty looks; 骯髒 unclean, dirty; 髒了 soiled, smudged.

髒 瘡 *tzang-chuang*, n., pop. term for syphilis.
髒 房 *tzang-farng*, n., a house in which s.o. has died a violent death.
髒 症 *tzang'jeng*, n., syphilis ("the dirty disease").
髒 心 *tzang-shin*, adj., evil-minded.
髒 字 (眼) 兒 *tzang-tzeh(ya)'l*, n., four-letter words.

§ 42B.30 (骨/一)

體 42B.30-2

tii.

[Common abbr. 体]

N. (1) The body: 身體, 身體健康 physical health; 三位一體 Trinity. (2) Style, structure, form: 文體 style of writing, literary style of a period; 政體 form of government (monarchy, republic, oligarchy, etc.). (3) Physical state: 物體 material body; 液體 fluid; 氣體 gas, gaseous state; 固體 solid state. (4) 體系 (思想體系) systems of thought; 本體 essence; 本體論 ontology; 體大思精 broad in conception and meticulous in details.

V.t. To place oneself mentally in another, to realize, understand: 體察, 體會, 體諒 *-char*, *-hueih*, *-'liahng* ↓; 體味 to savor s.t. carefully.

體 察 *tiichar*, v.t., to understand (another's situation).
體 沉 *tiichern*, adj., heavy.
體 氣 *tiichih*, n., style and character (of writing), character (of person, vigor (of body).
體 罰 *tiifar*, n., corporeal punishment.
體 格 *tiiger*, n., person's physical stature or health.
體 會 *tiihueih* (-'*huei*), v.t., to try to realize (another's situation).
體 積 *tiiji*, n., physical volume.
體 己 *tii'ji*, (1) adj., intimate, confidential: 説體己話 confidential talks; (2) a confidant(e); personal possessions.
體 制 *tiijyh*, n., form and structure, system (of government, etc.).
體 質 *tiijyr*, n., one's physical endowments; born constitution (person's).
體 諒 *tii'liahng*, v.t., to understand and forgive.
體 例 *tiilih*, n., form and arrangement of a book.
體 面 *tiimiahn*, adj. & n., outward show of honor: 很體面 given honor, be honored, it's an honor.
體 魄 *tiipoh*, n., a person's physique.
體 認 *tiirehn*, v.t., to examine what is not obvious, to understand motives.
體 系 *tiishih*, n., a system; 太陽體系 the solar system.
體 行 *tiishirng*[1], v.i., to do, perform, behave personally.
體 型 *tiishirng*[2], n., body (of car), bodily form, model.
體 式 *tiishyh*, n., form (of ceremony, etc.).
體 恤 *tiishyuh*, v.t., to show consideration to.
體 態 *tiitaih*, n., form, body contour and gesture: 體態輕盈 a supple body.
體 貼 *tii'tie*, v.t., to show consideration to (one in distress, etc.): 體貼入微 to be extremely considerate, thoughtful.
體 裁 *tiitsair*, n., form of writing.
體 操 *tiitsau*, n., physical exercise.
體 統 *tiituung*, n., social form and behavior: 不成體統 behave very badly.
體 溫 *tiiwen*, n., bodily temperature; 體溫表 clinical thermometer.
體 驗 *tiiyahn*, v.t., to examine and understand, to place oneself in another's position.
體 育 *tiiyuh*, n., physical education; 體育館 gynasium.
體 用 *tii-yuhng*, n., substance and function.

§ 42B.40 (骨/口)

骷 42B.40-1

ku.

骷 髏 *kulour*, n., dry skeleton, dugup skull.

髂 42B.40-6

kah.

N. Pelvic bones.

骼 42B.40-9

ger.

N. (1) The bone: 骨骼 bones, the skeleton, the gen. physical build of a man. (2) Dead man's bones. (3) Var. of 胳 42A.40.

§ 42B.50 (骨/ㄱ)

骻 42B.50-1

kuah.

N. (1) Hipjoint. (2) Space between the thighs (var. 胯).

髑 42B.50-4

dur.

髑髏 *durlur*, n., dead man's skull.

髈 42B.50-6

baang.
[Var. of 膀 42A.50]

§ 42B.70 (骨/乚)

髐 42B.70-1

shiau.

Adj. 髐然有形 (AC) (of a skull) with well-defined features.

骯 42B.70-6

ang (**kang*).

骯髒 *angtzang*, adj., (1) dirty, filthy (also wr. 腌臢). (2) (**kang-*) (AC) fat, upright.

骩 42B.70-9

weei.
[Err. var. 骫]

骩髀 *weeibih*, adj., (AC) complicated.

骩法 *weir-faa*, phr., (AC) to violate the law.

骲 42B.70-9

bor.

N. Bone arrowhead: 骲頭 ditto.

§ 42B.71 (骨/乁)

骶 42B.71-9

dii.

N. Pelvis, pelvic bones.

§ 42B.80 (骨/八)

髕 42B.80-6

bihn.
[Var. of 臏 42A.80]

§ 42B.81 (骨/人)

骸 42B.81-6

hair.

骸骨 *hairguu*, n., (1) the tibia bone; (2) a human skeleton: 乞骸骨 formerly, asking for one's remains to be buried at home town, phr. in requesting permission to resign from office.

§ 42B.82 (骨/乂)

骳 42B.82-2

bih.

Adj. See 骩髀 42B.70.

骾 42B.82-3

geeng.
[Interch. 鯁]

N. S.t. that sticks in the throat.

V.i. To stick in the throat: 骨骾在喉，一吐爲快 feel suffocated (lit. choked) if I do not speak out.

骰 42B.82-4

shaai.

N. (-*tz*, -'*l*) Dice: 擲骰兒, 打骰兒 throw dice; 骰花兒 dots indicating number on side of a dice; 骰子塊兒 shapes like dice, as diced chicken.

§ 42B.83 (骨/〜)

髓 42B.83-1

sueei.
[Abbr. 髓]

N. (1) Bone marrow: (fig.) 骨髓, 精髓, 神髓 essence, vital part (of writing, thinking): 恨入骨髓 hate (s. o., s. t.) to the bones. (2) 芝髓 resinous formation; 石髓 stalactite, chalcedony, crystalline vein in rocks.

§ 42B.93 (骨/ㄑ)

髏 42B.93-2

lour.

N. The skull or skeleton of a dead person: 髑髏 a skull; 骷髏 a skeleton.

SECTION 42S

§ 42S.00 (冈S/亅)

刪 42S.00-2

shan.

V. t. To delete, eliminate: 刪去 (刪了) 兩行 deleted two lines; 刪掉 strike off (words, sentences); see compp. ↓.

刪 除 *shan-chur*, v. t., to eliminate (undesirable elements).

刪 訂 *shan-dihng*, v. t., revise (edition).

刪 改 *shan-gaai*, v. t., to revise, including cutting out lines.

刪 潤 *shan-ruhn*, v. t., to revise and polish (manuscript).

剛 42S.00-2

gang.

Adj. Hard, unyielding, rigid (opp. 柔 soft, pliant, flexible): 剛強 -*'chiarng*, 剛直 -*jyr* ↓; 血氣方剛 (of young men) impetuous and ready to pick quarrels; 柔能克剛 gentleness can overcome strength; 剛柔相濟 to temper force with mercy; 剛毛 tough bristles; 剛板硬正 upright and outspoken.

Adv. (1) Just, a very short time ago: 剛才, 剛纔 -*tsair* ↓; 剛剛 -*gang* ↓; 剛走了不到一分鐘 went out less than a minute ago; 剛拿到手 have just come to hand; 剛到 have just arrived; 剛吃 be just eating; 剛開始 just beginning to do s.t. (2) Only, barely, at an opportune moment: 剛巧 -*chiaau*, 剛好 -*haau* ↓; 剛剩一口 just a mouthful is left over; 剛夠買車票 just enough money to buy a ticket.

剛 愎 *gangbih*, adj., obstinate, stubborn: 剛愎自用 obstinate and self-willed.

剛 巧 *gangchiaau*, adv., (1) by a happy coincidence; (2) at a most opportune moment.

剛 強 *gang'chiarng*, adj., firm and uncompromising.

剛 剛 (兒) *ganggang('l)*, adv., (1) just now, a short while ago; (2) by chance or coincidence.

剛 好 *ganghaau*, adv., at the right moment: 剛好他來 just at the right moment he turned up.

剛 正 *gangjehng*, adj., upright, impartial: 剛正不阿 standing on principles and not yielding to pressure.

剛 直 *gangjyr*, adj., upright, firm in principle.

剛 性 *gangshihng* (-*'shing*), n. & adj., rigid, (-ity), inflexible, (-bility).

剛 纔 *gangtsair*, adv., (usu. 剛才) just a moment ago, just now.

剛 毅 *gangyih*, adj., resolute and firm; fortitude.

剮 42S.00-2

guaa.

V. i. (1) Cut off the flesh from the bones. (2) (AC) punish a criminal by cutting pieces of his flesh—a form of slow death as extreme punishment. (3) Get cut by anything sharp: 剮了一個口子 have got a cut on the body.

§ 42S.11 (冈S/土)

雕 42S.11-9

diau.

N. Var. of 鵰 a hawk, bird of prey.

V.i. & t. & adj. To carve, carved

(wood, figurine, stone, pillars): 雕蟲小技 (contempt. of writing) ornate writing, occupied with embellishments.

雕板 *diaubaan*, n., wood block for printing.
雕漆 *diauchi*, n., carved and lacquered objects.
雕花 *diau-hua*, n. & v. i. & t., carving, to carve.
雕琢 *diaujuor*, v. i., chisel and embellish (prose, jade, art objects).
雕刻 *diaukeh*, v. i. & t., to carve; n., carving, sculpture.
雕龍 *diaulurng*, adj., masterly in rhetoric.
雕塑 *diausuh*, v. i. & t., carve (wood) and mold (plaster) figures.

§ 42S.42 (冈^S/冈)

朙 42S.42-4

mirng.
[Rare var. of 明 41A.42]

§ 42S.50 (冈^S/⺄)

鵰 42S.50-9

diau.

N. Eagle, falcon, vulture (=鷲): 鵰扇 fan of eagle feathers; 鵰翎 an arrow with eagle feathers.

鵰鶚 *diau-eh*, n., hawk, person of extraordinary strength.
鵰悍 *diauhahn*, adj., fierce (=刁悍).

§ 42S.82 (冈^S/乂)

雘 42S.82-2

huoh.

N. A red mineral dye.

§ 42S.91 (冈^S/丿)

彤 42S.91-9

turng.

Adj. (1) (AC) red, vermilion: 彤弓 red painted bow; 彤管 red pipe. (2) (MC) 彤雲 dark clouds.

彫 42S.91-9

diau.

V. t. (1) To carve, carved (var. of 雕): 彫弓 engraved bow. (2) Wither, -ed (var. of 凋): 彫謝 withered; 彫殘, 彫喪 (AC) derelict, dissipated, exhausted.

SECTION 50

§ 50.00 (⺄/亅)

尋 50.00

shyurn (**shyuer*).

N. Ancient measure of eight ancient feet, approximately a fathom.

V.t. (1) To search, look for: 尋覓 *-mih*↓; 尋究, 尋求, 尋找 *-jiouh*, *-chiour*, *-jaau*↓; 尋不著, 尋不見, 尋不到 cannot find (person, object); 尋人 look for lost relative (esp. in newspaper advertisements); 尋屋 look for house for rent; 尋用人 look for household help; 尋字 look for word in dictionary; 尋詩 look for inspiration for a poem; 尋幽, 尋勝 seek some quiet, beautiful spot; 自尋煩惱 to torture oneself with unpleasant thoughts, give oneself unnecessary trouble; 尋根究底 investigate, probe to the bottom; 尋章摘句 look for quotes in order to criticize or to embellish one's writing; 尋花問柳 visit the brothels. (2) (**shyuer*) To grope for: 尋摸 *-'mo*↓; 尋摟, 尋溜 *-'lou*, *-'liou*↓. (3) To resort to: 尋死, 尋短見 try to commit suicide. (4) To ask for: 尋盟, 尋和 ask for alliance, for peaceful settlement.

尋查 *shyurnchar*, v.t., to search for (evidence, cause, etc.).
尋常 *shyurncharng*, adj. & adv., usual, -ly.
尋趁 *shyurnchehn*, v.i. & t., (coll.) (1) to run about, hustle for trade or profit; (2) to quarrel; (3) to pick fault and scold.
尋求 *shyurnchiour*, v.t., to seek (friends, lost relative, truth, origin, etc.).

尋芳 *shyurn-fang*, v.i., to go about in the hope of finding girls or flowers.
尋找 *shyurnjaau*, v.i., to look for (s.t. lost).
尋究 *shyurnjiouh*, v.i. & t., to investigate, find out (cause, origin).
尋樂 *shyurnleh*, v.i., look for distractions, seek pleasures.
尋溜 **shyuer'liou*, v.t., (coll.) to run hands over body.
尋摟 **shyuer'lou*, v.t., ditto; (hands) ramble over body and hug.
尋盟 *shyurn-merng*, phr., seek alliance.
尋覓 *shyurnmih*, v.t., to look for.
尋摸 (1) **shyuer'mou*, v.i., grope for (object, truth); (2) **shyuer'mo*, v.i., to touch and fondle (body).
尋釁 *shyurn-shihn*, v.i., pick a quarrel, find pretext for war.
尋休兒 *shirn-shiou'l*, phr., (coll.) look for lodging (also wr. 尋宿兒).
尋事 *shyurn-shyh*, v.i., try to pick a quarrel.
尋誦 *shyurnsuhng*, v.t., (LL) peruse repeatedly.
尋俗 *shyurnsur*, adj., (MC) ordinary: 這人不尋俗 this man is not an ordinary person.
尋思 *shyurnsy*, v.i., to meditate, ponder.
尋繹 *shyurnyih*, v.i., look for meaning of certain lines.

§ 50.01 (ㄱ/小)

彙 50.01

hueih.
[Var. of 彙 92.01]

§ 50.10 (ㄱ/十)

翠 50.10

tsueih.

N. (1) 翡翠 jadeite, malachite. (2) 翡翠鳥 the kingfisher whose blue feathers are used in decorations.

Adj. Kingfisher-blue.

翠翹 *tsueihchiaur*, n., (AC, MC) woman's hair decoration, studded with kingfisher feathers.
翠黛 *tsueihdaih*, n., formerly, eyebrow pencil; painted eyebrows.
翠華 *tsueihhuar*, n., (AC) imperial colors framed with kingfisher feathers.
翠鬟 *tsueihhuarn*, n., a woman's hair-do.
翠菊 *tsueihjyur*, n., (bot.) a Chin. variety of chrysanthemum, *Callistephus chinensis*.
翠綠 *tsueihlyuh*, adj., jade-green (vegetation).
翠鳥 *tsueihniaau*, n., a kind of kingfisher (also 翠碧鳥).
翠蕤 *tsueihrueir*, n., (MC) a flowery colored flag.
翠微 *tsueihweir*, n., (1) the bluish-green soft tints of hillside; (2) hill slope.
翠月 *tsueihyueh*, adj., aquamarine color.
翠玉 *tsueihyuh*, n., chrysoprase (cf. 綠寶石 emerald).
翠羽 *tsueihyuu*, n., kingfisher feathers.

翬 50.10

huei.

N. (AC) a pheasant, known for beautiful plumes, associated with queen's carriage.

Adj. Of variegated colors like pheasant.

§ 50.11 (ㄱ/土)

翟 50.11

jair (re. pr. *jer*, **dir*).

N. (1) (AC) (**dir*) a long-tailed pheasant. (2) A surname.

§ 50.20 (ㄱ/廾)

羿 50.20

yih.

N. Name of legendary famous archer (also called 后羿).

§ 50.21 (ㄱ/ㄴ)

卍 50.21

wahn.
[Symbolic sign for 萬 in 萬福 good luck.]

§ 50.22 (ㄱ/丨)

弔 50.22

diauh (**dih*).
[Pop. 吊, esp. in V.i. & t. 2↓]

N. Formerly, a string of 100 cash, (=one dollar).

V.i. & t. (1) To console with the

bereaved, to lament, esp. *-sang*↓; 弔祭, 弔文, 弔喪 *-jih*, *-wern*, *-sang* ↓; 弔客 guests at funeral ceremony; 開弔 hold a funeral ceremony; (AC) to console and comfort: 弔民伐罪 punish the tyrant and comfort the people; 弔古戰場 think of the dead on ancient battlefields; 憑弔 think of the dead and gone on historic sites. (2) To hang up: 弔起來 hang it up; 弔水 haul water from well; objects that can be opened and suspended: 弔窗, 弔牀, 弔橋 *-chuang*, *-chuarng*, *-chiaur*↓; hang to death: 弔死, 上弔. (3) (Peking coll.) 弔皮襖 fix cover on fur coat. (4) Identical with 調: 弔案, 弔卷＝調案, 調卷; see 調 60A.42. (*dih) (AC) be present (of deities); 神之弔矣.

弔膀子 *diauh-bahngtz*, v.i., (Shanghai coll.) to accost a passing girl one doesn't know, go out with girl "arm in arm."
弔橋 *diauhchiaur*, n., suspension bridge.
弔窗 *diauhchuang*, n., window which can be propped up, hinged on top.
弔牀 *diauhchuarng*, n., hammock.
弔蛋 *diauhdahn*, n., (sl.) term of abuse to inferiors.
弔詭 *diauhgueei*, adj., bizarre: 弔詭矜奇 try to be novel for effect.
弔祭 *diauhjih*, v.i., participate in worship ceremony for the dead.
弔鐘花 *diauhjung-hua*, n., (bot.) flowers like inverted cups or bells, Chinese New Year flower: *Enkyanthus quinque florus*.
弔毛兒 *diauh-maur'l*, v.i., make a kind of somersault in stage plays.
弔喪 *diauhsang*, v.i., offer condolences at funeral.
弔銷 *diauhshiau*, v.t., suspend (license).
弔孝 *diaushiauh*, v.i., condole with bereaved son.
弔死鬼 *diauhsyr-gueei*, n., ghost of person who hanged himself.
弔桶 (弔水桶) *diauhtuung*, n., well bucket.
弔文 *diauhwern*, n., prayer for the dead, written out and burned.
弔唁 *diauhyahn*, v.i., offer condolences.
弔影 *diauhyiing*, v.i., be lonely, from 形影相弔 body has only its shadow for company.

帚 50.22

joou.

N. A broomstick: 掃帚.

帚星 *journshing*, n., a comet.

§ 50.30 (ㄱ/一)

丑 50.30

choou.

N. (1) (-'l) A clown. (2) Number two of the duodecimal cycle (Appendix A); 丑時 1–3 a.m. period. (3) A surname.

丑旦 *chooudahn*, n., a woman clown on stage.
丑角(兒) *chourjiaau('l)* (*-jyuer'l*), n., the role of a clown; one who plays such role.
丑婆子 *chooupортz*, n., (coll.) a hag on stage, see *-dahn*↑.

翌 50.30

yih.

Adj. (LL) The next in time: 翌日, 翌年 (LL) the next day, year.

§ 50.40 (ㄱ/口)

召 50.40

jauh (*shauh).

N. (1) An imperial decree (interch. 詔 61A.40). (2) A surname (*shauh).

V.t. (Except in sense "1," interch. 招). (1) (Of emperor) to summon: 召見 to command an audience with ruler or emperor; 召對 have interview with emperor; 宣召 have the imperial decree read publicly; 徵召 (government) call for possible talents to join government. (2) To give notice of "want ads" (house to let, tenant, business apportunities, etc.): 召盤, 召租 *-parn*, *-tzu*↓. (3) To solicit (recruits, etc.): 召募, 召集 *-muh*, *-jir*↓. (4) To cause, engender: 召禍 *-huoh*↓.

召禍 *jauh-huoh*, v.i., to invite disaster.
召集 *jauhjir*, v.t., to assemble (people) for some purpose.
召募 *jauhmuh*, v.t., to recruit (soldiers, volunteers).
召盤 *jauh-parn*, v.i., offer to sell out business.
召租 *jauhtzu*, v.i., (give notice of) house to let.

§ 50.41 (ㄱ/図)

習 50.41

shir.

N. (1) A surname. (2) Habit, customs: 惡習 bad habits; 陋習

bad customs; 積習 old habits; 習慣, 習氣, 習性 *-guahn*, *-'chih*, *-shihng* ↓; 習慣成自然 what is habitually done becomes natural; 習與性成 (AC) habit becomes second nature; 性相近, 習相遠 men are born about the same, but habits make them differ.

V.i. & t. (1) To learn, practise, exercise: 學習 learn (writing, medicine, technique, etc.); 練習 to exercise, an exercise; 温習, 複習 review (lessons); 講習 teach (history, etc.); 演習 (n. & v.i.) exercise, military drill, practice. (2) Be used to, accustomed to, form habit: 習非成是 what becomes customary is accepted as right; 習惰 (LL) become habitually lazy; 習以爲常 get accustomed to s.t.

Adj. Familiar: 習俗 *-sur* ↓; 狎習 become intimate with (person).

Adv. Often: 習見 see oftentimes; 習 be familiar with (a fact); 習聞 have often heard.

習兵 *shir-bing*, (1) v.i., to be trained as soldier; (2) adj., versed in military matters.
習氣 *shir'chih*, n., habits (good, bad), habitual temperament.
習得性 *shir-der-shihng*, phr., acquired habit, response.
習定 *shirdihng*, v.i., (Budd. & Neo-Confucian) mental discipline to free mind of thoughts and desires.
習慣 *shirguahn*, n., habits; customs: 惡習慣 bad customs or habits (cf. *-sur* ↓); 習慣法 common law based on actual practice; 習慣性 habitual nature.
習流 *shirliour*, n., (AC) soldiers trained in swimming.
習滅 *shir-mieh*, phr., from 習善滅惡 (Budd.) learn good and forsake evil.
習染 *shirraan*, n., habit (from "contagion").
習性 *shirshihng*, n., temperament, habitual nature.
習習 *shirshir*, adj., (AC) rustling of wind or wings; (AC) gaily gathered together.
習熟 *shirshur*, adj., familiar.
習俗 *shisur*, n., local customs.
習題 *shir-tir*, n., exercises provided in textbooks.
習字 *shir-tzyh*, v.i., to learn calligraphy; learn new words.

§ 50.42 (ㄱ/冈)

鬻 50.42

yuh.

N. (1) 鬻子 (AC) a child. (2) A surname.

v.t. (LL)to sell: 鬻文 make a living by writing, selling articles; 鬻妻, 鬻女, 鬻子 sell one's wife, daughter, son.

§ 50.50 (ㄱ/ㄱ)

刁 50.50

diau.

N. A surname.

Adj. Artful, knavish, rascally, see compp.↓: 刁棍 rascal; 刁婦 shrew: 刁筆 rabid, wretched writing; 放刁 act rascally, play the bully.

刁刁 *diaudiau*, (AC) adj., flickering in the wind.
刁斗 *diaudoou*, n., army cooking pot, formerly used as alarm gong at night, hence 刁斗森嚴 strict army discipline.
刁惡 *diau-eh*, adj., rascally brutal, wicked.
刁悍 *diauhahn*, adj., strong and arrogant, fierce.
刁猾 *diauhuar*, adj., artful, deceitful.
刁賴 *diaulaih*, v.i., repudiate (loans), make groundless accusations.
刁蠻 *diaumarn*, adj., obstinate, unruly.
刁難 *diaunarn*, v.i. & t., purposely make difficulties for (person), also 挑難.
刁脾(皮) *diaupir*, adj., knavish, (of children) naughty.
刁鑽 *diautzuan*, adj., wily.
刁頑 *diauwaan*, adj., stubborn, obstinate.

刀 50.50

dau.

N. (1) The radical 刀, appearing on right as 刂. (2) Various kinds of knives: 一把刀 a knife; 菜刀 kitchen chopper; 鐮刀 sickle; 剃刀, 刮鬍刀 razor; 剪刀 scissors; 大刀 long-handled sword; 單刀 broad sword; 刺刀 bayonet; 刀背 dull side of knife; 刀口 knife edge; 這刀沒有口 knife is dull; 刀靶 knife handle; (fig.) 叫人拿刀靶兒 let opponent hold the power. (2) (AC) ancient coin in form of knife.

刀筆 *daubii*, n., in 刀筆吏, 刀筆先生 man versed in law or in charge of legal documents (who uses the pen like a knife).
刀兵 *daubing*, n., war, battle.
刀創藥 *dauchuang-yauh*, n., herb for treating wounds.
刀尺 *dauchyy*, n., (1) scissors and tapeline; (2) standards for judging the fitness of people for jobs.
刀豆 *daudouh*, n., bean, *Canavallia ensiformis*.
刀斧手 *daufur-shoou*, n., executioner.
刀圭 *dauguei*, n., ancient small measure of Chin. medicine; the practice of medicine.
刀錐(之利) *daujuei*, n., small amount (of profit).
刀螂 *daularng*, n., (zoo.) mantis (=螳螂).

刀馬旦 *daumaa-dahn*, n., actress versed in swordplay.

刀牌手 *daupair-shoou*, n., soldier equipped with knife and shield.

刀片兒 *daupiah'l*, n., razor blade.

刀俎 *dautzuu*, n., chopping board: 人爲刀俎，我爲魚肉 at people's mercy (like fish or meat on chopping board).

刀魚 *dauyur*, n., the long-tailed anchovy, *Coilia nasus*.

刃 50.50

rehn.

N. The cutting edge of a knife or sword: 刃兒, 刀刃 ditto; 開刃 sharpen a knife or sword; 兵刃 arms, weapons.

V.t. Kill: 自刃 commit suicide; 刃牛 to slaughter cattle; 迎刃而解 solve problems (difficulties) with the greatest ease; 刃傷事主 cut and injured the victim; 手刃其子 killed his son with his own hand.

弓 50.50

gung.

N. (1) A bow: 弓箭 bow and arrow; 弓弩 a cross bow; 強弓 a heavy bow; 張弓搭箭 with bows drawn and arrows set; 弓弦 a bow string; 弓袋 a bow case; 弓手 an archer; 弓人 a bow maker. (2) A land measure equal to five Chinese feet. (3) A surname. (4) A radical, "50A" in this index.

Adj. Bent, crooked: 弓腰駝背 hunch backed.

弓背兒 *gungbeih (-beh'l)*, (1) n., the back of a bow; (2) adj., hunchbacked, arched.

弓鞋 *gungshier*, n., shoes worn by women with bound feet.

弓子 *gungtz*, n., a bow-shaped article.

弓足 *gungtzur*, n., formerly, bound feet of Chin. women.

司 50.50

sy.

N. (1) An administrative department, an independent bureau: 司長 *-jaang*↓; 都司, 土司, 藩司 bureau in charge of frontier regions; 稅務司 Commissioner of Customs. (2) Official: 有司 (AC, LL) officials; 上司 superior in government office 打官司 go to court; 筆墨官司 controversy in articles; 職司 official duties. (3) Part of compound surnames: 司馬, 司徒, 司空 *-maa*, *-tur*, *-kung*↓.

V.t. To take charge of: 司其事 be in charge of certain tasks; 各有所司 each has his duties; forms compounds designating offices in many words, like 司閽 *-hun*, doorkeeper; 司賬, 司儀 *-jahng*, *-yir*↓; 司法 *-faa*↓; 司機 *-ji*↓; 牝雞司晨 a hen cries cock-a-doodle-doo—domineering wife.

司鐸 *syduor*, n., Roman Catholic priest.

司法 *syfaa*, n., the judiciary; 司法院 the Judicial Yuan; 司法官 a judge; 司法界 judicial circles.

司長 *syjaang*, n., department or section chief.

司賬 *syjahng*, n., treasurer, cashier.

司機 *syji*, n., driver; private chauffeur.

司寇 *sykouh*, n., (AC) minister of justice.

司庫 *sykuh*, n., official treasurer; keeper of treasury vaults.

司空 *sykung*, n., (1) a compound surname; (2) (AC) minister of public works.

司令 *sylihng*, n., commander: 總司令 commander in chief; 司令部 commander's headquarters; 司令塔 conning tower; 司令臺 reviewing stand.

司理 *sylii*, n., officer in charge.

司馬 *symaa*, n., (1) (AC) minister of war; (2) a compound surname.

司命 *symihng*, n., an arbiter of human destiny; (coll.) kitchen god.

司牧 *symuh*, n., (AC) the ruler (lit., "shepherd").

司書 *syshu*, n., formerly, official copyist.

司事 *syshyh*, n., person in gen. charge.

司徒 *sytur*, n., (AC) minister of culture; 大司徒 cabinet minister or premier in various dynasties; (Manchu Dyn.) minister of finance; a compound surname.

司務 *sywuh*, n., gen. reference to workman in charge; esp. 大司務, 廚司務 the *chef*.

司儀 *syyir*, n., master of ceremony.

§50.70 (ㄱ/ㄴ)

兎 50.70

miaan.

[Var. 免 92.70]

V.i. & t. (1) Be free from, absolved, excused, relieved from (work), used oft. as vb. aux.: 兎去, 兎得去 excused from going, do not have to go; 可兎則兎去 don't go unless you have to; 兎得, 以兎 so that one need not, to save (embarrassment, offending, etc.); oft. negative 兎不了, 兎不得 cannot help; 兎不了試一試 cannot help trying; esp. 難兎, 未兎: 未兎傷情 cannot help feeling sad; (in depreciation) 未兎無聊 really boring; 未能免俗 (slightly apologetic) have to follow the conventions. (2) (Imperative) do not: 免開尊口 you had better shut up; 請免介意 please do not worry; 免勞駕 please do not bother. (3) V. t., dismiss: 免職 dismiss from office; 免官, 免黜 *-guan*², *-chuh* ↓.

免黜 *miaanchuh*, v. t., dismiss, degrade.

免除 *miaanchur*, v. t., dismiss, excuse; to clear up, remove, save from (worries).

免費 *miaan-feih*, adv., free of charge.

免冠 *miaan-guan*¹, v. i., take off the hat.

免官 *miaan-guan*², v. t., dismiss from office.

免戰牌 *miaanjahn-pair*, n., formerly, signal for truce, (like white flag).

免職 *miaanjy*, v. t., dismiss: 給他免職 dismiss him from post.

免禮 *miarn-lii*, v. i., be excused from usual courtesy gestures.

免票 *miaan-piauh*, adv., free admission.

免喪 *miaan-sang*, v. i., terminate mourning when period is over.

免身 *miaan-shen*, v. i., (AC) deliver baby.

免席 *miaan-shir*, v. i., excuse oneself from table.

免稅 *miaan-shueih*, adv., tax-free, tax-exempt.

免試 *miaan-shyh*, v. i., be excused from examination.

免役 *miaanyih*, v. i., be excused from conscription.

免疫性 *miaanyih-shihng*, n., (biol.) immunity; 免疫作用 immunization.

兎 50.70

tuh.

[Var. 兔]

N. (*-tz*, *'l*) Rabbit, hare: 家兎 rabbit; 野兎 hare; 玉兎 the rabbit in the moon, (poet.) the moon; 兎兒爺 *-'lyer* ↓; 兎死狐悲 the fox is sad at death of hare—sympathy for one of its kind; 兎死狗烹 cook the hound (as no longer needed) when the hares have been run down—allu. when country was unified, the king killed off his underlings; 兎起鶻落 the moment a hare is flushed out, the falcon swoops down—said of quick flow of writer's thoughts and imagination; 脱兎 (fig.) swift-footed hare, which has escaped a chase.

兎脣 *tuhchurn*, adj., hare-lipped.

兎缺 *tuhchyuei*, adj., ditto.

兎毫 *tuhhaur*, n., writing brush made of rabbit's hair.

兎葵 *tuhkueir*, n., (1) (zoo.) the sea anemone; (2) (bot.) the winter aconite (also wr. 菟葵).

兎兒爺 *tuh'lyer*, n., (1) clay rabbit at Mid-Autumn Festival; (2) (coll.) a pederast.

兎絲 *tuhsy*, n., the dodder (also wr. 菟絲).

兎脱 *tuhtuo*, v.i., make good one's escape.

兎子 *tuh'tz*, n., rabbit.

兎園策 *tuhyuarntseh*, n., popular books for villagers; chapbooks (also wr. 兎園冊).

§ 50.72 (ㄱ/心)

忌 50.72

jih.

N. Anniversary of the death of one's father or mother: 忌辰 *-chern* ↓.

V.t. (1) To envy, to hate: 忌恨 *-hehn* ↓; 忌刻 *-keh* ↓; 猜忌 be suspicious and jealous of; 疑忌 ditto; 妬忌 be envious of. (2) To dread, to fear: 忌憚 *-dahn* ↓; 畏忌 be afraid of. (3) Shun, avoid: 忌賭, 忌酒, 忌烟 abstain from gambling, wine, tobacco; 忌嘴 *-tzueei*, 忌口 *-koou* ↓; 忌諱 *-(')hueih* ↓; 禁忌 taboos: 百無禁忌 nothing is taboo; 童言無忌 children say what they like.

忌辰 *jihchern*, n., date of the death of one's father or mother.

忌憚 *jihdahn*, v.i., have scruples: 肆無忌憚 utterly unscrupulous.

忌恨 *jihhehn*, v.t., be jealous of and hate.

忌諱 *jih hueih* (*-'huei*), n., (1) taboos; (2) (northern coll.) another name for vinegar.

忌刻 *jihkeh*, adj., mean and cruel.

忌口 *jihkoou*, v.i., avoid certain foods.

忌門 *jihmern*, n., formerly, taboo for women from other clans to visit family during New Year.

忌日 *jihryh*, n., see *-chern* ↑.

忌嘴 *jihtzueei*, v.i., see *-koou* ↑.

忍 50.72

reen.

V.i. & t. (1) V.t., endure, suffer, tolerate, bear: 容忍 be tolerant of; 忍耐 *-naih* ↓; 忍氣吞聲 suffer indignities without a protest; 忍涕 refrain from crying; 忍痛 endure pains silently; 忍尤含垢 passively accept insults and humiliations; 忍住這口氣 suppress one's anger, control oneself without blowing up; 忍受 *-shouh* ↓; 忍辱 *-ruh* ↓; 忍字心頭一把刀 even the most forbearing, if provoked too far, may become desperate; 忍無可忍 come to the end of one's patience, to tax one's patience to the limit; 忍饑, 忍餓 suffer hunger (starvation); 百姓弗能忍 the people can no longer tolerate (such excesses). (2) Would not, short for 豈忍 ("how could"): 忍更思量 how could I think of it again? 宗族忍相遺 you wouldn't leave your family and clan, would you? (3) V.i., (coll.) live in seclusion, cut oneself off from the outside world. (4) (Coll.) take a nap.

Adj. Cruel, merciless: 殘忍 ruthless.

忍冬 *reendung*, n., (bot.) the honeysuckle (also 金銀花).
忍垢 *reen-gouh*, v.i., meekly submit to insults: 忍垢貪生 allow oneself to be insulted to remain alive.
忍教 *reenjiauh*, phr., how could one bear to: 忍教兒啼饑號寒 how could I bear to let my child cry from hunger and cold?
忍俊 *reenjyuhn*, v.i., to smile gently: 忍俊不住 (禁) cannot help smiling.
忍耐 *reennaih*, v.t., endure patiently.
忍辱 *reen-ruh*, v.i., meekly accept abuses, insults: 忍辱負重 discharge one's duties conscientiously in spite of slanders.
忍性 *reenshihng*, v.i., restrain oneself, try to be patient.
忍心 *reenshin*, adj., hardhearted, unfeeling, pitiless: 忍心害理 ruthless and devoid of human feelings.
忍受 *reenshouh*, v.t., endure, suffer (cold, hunger, privations, physical pain, mental anguish).
忍事 *reen-shyh*, v.i., put up with adversities.
忍死 *rern-syy*, v.i., hold on to life and save it for some worthy cause.

§ 50.80 (ㄱ/八)

翼 50.80

yih.

N. (1) (LL) a wing: 拍翼 flap wings; 折翼 "broken wing"—(lit.) with clipped wings, (fig.) the death of a brother; 機翼 plane wing; (rare, poet.) boat sails. (2) Front fins of fish. (3) A surname.

V.t. To shelter as with wings: 翼護 *-huh*↓; to support as with wings: 翼戴 *-daih*↓.

翼翅 *yihchyh*, n., wings; fins.
翼戴 *yihdaih*, v.t., (LL) to support (ruler).
翼護 *yihhuh*, v.t., (LL) to shelter and protect.
翼翼 *yihyih*, adj., (LL) as in 小心翼翼 very, very careful.

負 50.80

fuh.

[var. 負]

N. (1) Burden: 如釋重負 as if relieved of a heavy burden. (2) Loss: 虧負 deficit, debt. (3) Defeat: 勝負 (未卜) victory or defeat (not yet decided).

V.i. & t. (1) To carry, to shoulder, to carry on back: 負(起)責任 to shoulder responsibility; 負擔, 戴, 累, see *-dan*, *-daih*, *-leih*↓; 負劍, 芻 carry sword, firewood; 負米 carry bags of rice (to feed parents); 負笈求師 "carry suitcase" (go abroad) as student to seek teacher; 負荆請罪 carry rod to ask for punishment, i.e., to apologize; 負謗 bear the blame, see 負屈 *-chyu*↓. (2) To back against as defense: 如虎負嵎 like a tiger at bay; 負嵎依險 to fight from high position, back to cliffside. (3) To rely on: 負固死戰 fight hard, relying on strategic strength; 自負 rely on one's own ability, think too highly of oneself. (4) To owe, to bear debt: 負債 *-jaih*↓; 負租 owe rent. (5) To show loss, deficit, therefore to owe debt of gratitude; 虧負 show deficit, fail to square one's debt; 辜負朋友 to fail a friend; 欠負債務 owe debts. (6) To run out on debt, to fail to meet obligations: 負約 fail in treaty obligations, break one's promise; 負命 fail in mission, act contrary to one's mission; 負德, 忘恩負義 be ungrateful; 有負衆望, 厚望 to disappoint those who had hopes or confidence in person. (7) V.i., be defeated in battle: 負敗而逃 be defeated and run away.

Adj. Negative, opp. of 正 positive: 負電, 負號, 負數 *-diahn*, *-hauh*, *-shuh*↓.

負氣 *fuhchih*, v.i., be in fit of resentment and self-reliance: 負氣不服 rely on oneself to fight again.
負屈 *fuh-chyu*, v.i., suffer a wrong or injustice.
負戴 *fuhdaih*, v.i., carry on the head.
負擔 *fuh-dan*, n. & v.t., (bear) burden of responsibilities; 負擔太重 the responsibilities, expenses, are too great; 負擔不起 cannot bear the expenses or take the responsibility.
負電 *fuh-diahn*, n., negative electricity.
負負 *fuhfuh*, n., sound of panting: 徒呼負負 only blow one's breath, admitting defeat.
負號 *fuhhauh*, n., the minus sign.
負債 *fuh-jaih*, v.i. & n., to owe debts; debit; (finance) liability: 負債累累 owe lots of debts.
負疚(咎) *fuh-jiouh*, v.i., feel guilty, feel the blame.
負勞 *fuh-laur*, n., (zoo.) a species of dragonfly, also known as 蜻蛉.
負累 *fuh-leih*, n. & v.t., burdens of debt or expenses.
負數 *fuh-shuh*, n., (algebra) negative quantity.
負責 *fuh-tzer*, adj., responsible: 這個人不負責 the man is irresponsible.

§ 50.81 (ㄱ/人)

灵 50.81

lirng.

[Pop. for 靈]

§ 50.83 (ㄱ/～)

迢 50.83

tiaur.

Adj. Distant.

迢遞 *tiaurdih*, adj., (LL) faraway.
迢迢 *tiaurtiaur*, adj., (LL) far, faraway: 迢迢千里.
迢遙 *tiauryaur*, adj., far, faraway.

逯 50.83

guei.
[Var. of 歸 91S.22]

§ 50.93 (ㄱ/ㄑ)

翣 50.93

shah.

N. (1) (AC) a decorative covering for coffin. (2) (AC) a large flag.

翣舌 *shahsher*, n., a disease of swollen tongue which could be fatal; 翣舌風 a disease in which the patient lolls his tongue continuously.

SECTION 50A

§ 50A.01 (弓/小)

弥 50A.01-9

mir.
[Abbr. of 彌 50A.42]

§ 50A.02 (弓/k)

張 50A.02-5

jang (**jahng*).

N. adjunct. (1) A flat piece, a leaf: 一張紙 a piece of paper; 一張告白 a public notice; 一張牌 a playing card; 一張桌 a table. (2) A piece which can be stretched or opened: 一張弓 a bow; 一張嘴 a mouth.

N. (1) A surname: 張 and 李 are commonly taken to mean "this ... and that": 張三李四 Tom, Dick or Harry, this or that person, i.e., any common person; 張家長, 李家短 gossip about this or that person; 張冠李戴 fasten one person's story upon another person. (2) 主張 one's decision, position one has taken, see 主 63.11.

V.t. (1) To stretch a bow or string: 張弓搭箭 stretch bow and fix arrow; 改弦更張 refix bowstring—change business or policy; 外張內弛 empty bombastic talk. (2) To open wide: 張口便咬 (dog) opens mouth and bites; 張口便説 talk carelessly or out of place; 張口結舌 tongue-tied; 張牙舞爪 show one's fangs and claws—ready to fight; 張手 or 張開手 open one's hand; 張眼 open one's eyes; 張望 *-wahng*↓. (3) To set up: 開張 open new shop, firm, etc.; 張樂 (*-yueh*) 設飲 set up orchestra and drinks; 供張 (**-jahng*) the setup for occasions; 張燈結綵 hang up lanterns and silk festoons. (4) To open up, expand: 擴張, 伸張 (v.i. & t.) expand (market, power). (5) To boast, exaggerate: 誇張 to boast; 鋪張 to embellish for show, deceive by putting up front; 囂張 make a boisterous show or demand, (adj.) unruly.

Adj. Nervous: 慌張 flurried; 緊張 tense, nervous; 張皇 *-huarng*↓.

張本 *jangbeen*, n., a copy as model; a ground plan or outline for future reference.
張大 *jangdah*, v.t., to exaggerate: 張大其詞 exaggerate situation, paint picture as darker than the reality.
張皇 *janghuarng*, (1) adj., flurried, nervous: 張皇失措 nervous, lose mental control; (2) v.t., (AC) 張皇六師 to expand or increase effect of the army.
張致 *jangjyh*, v.i., (MC) make pretense, show false modesty.
張開 *jang-kai*, v.i. & t., to open up or wide: 張開眼睛 open eyes wide; 張不開 cannot open.
張狂 *jangkuarng*, v.i., to be unruly, insolent.
張羅 *jangluor*, (1) v.i., to set bird snares; (2) (*-'luo*) (a) to attend to person's needs: 張羅鳳姐吃菓酒 have wine and fruit served to Fehngjiee; (b) to try by various ways to get: 張羅銀子 try to find money for certain needs.
張設 *jangsheh*, v.i. & t., to set up (curtains, tables, decorations) for occasions.
張心 *jang-shin*, v.i., to trouble oneself or person with request (=勞神).
張貼 *jangtie*, v.t., to post (bills).
張嘴 *jangtzueei*, v.i., bring up matter which is embarrassing or out of place; speak out of turn (cf. opp. 閉嘴 "shut up").
張望 *jangwahng*, v.i., to look about or watch for (signs of enemy, etc.).

張揚 *jangyarng*, v.i. & t., to make open, publicize: 此事不可張揚起來 must hush up the matter.

§ 50A.10 (弓/十)

弭 50A.10–3

mii.

N. A surname.

V.t. To quell, stop, prevent: 弭兵 stop warfare; 弭亂 suppress rebellion; 弭患 prevent troubles, revolts; 弭謗 quell rumors.

彈 50A.10–4

dahn (**tarn*).

N. Bullet: 槍彈, 子彈 rifle bullet; 砲彈 artillery shell; 原子彈 atomic bomb; 炸彈 bomb; 手榴彈 grenade; 飛彈 rocket; 氫彈 hydrogen bomb; 烟幕彈 smoke-screen bomb; 催淚彈 tear-gas bomb.

V.t. (**tarn*) (1) To shoot (pellet). (2) To play on string instrument: 彈鋼琴, 彈琵琶 play piano, pipa. (3) To impeach: 彈劾 *-her* ↓. (4) To twang the bow: 彈弓; 彈棉花 to flick cotton with a bow and make it fluffy; 彈跳 to bounce. (5) To flick (dust) with a finger: 彈灰; 彈冠 flick cap—expression of joy; 彈指之間 in a short moment, quickas snapping a finger.

彈棋 **tarn-chir*, v.i., play chess or chess-like game.
彈道 *dahndauh*, n., ballistic curve; 彈道引導 ballistic guidance; 彈道學 ballistics; 反彈道飛彈系統 anti-ballistic missile system (ABM).
彈劾 **tarnher*, v.t., to impeach.
彈簧 **tarnhuarng*, n., mechanical spring, spring coil; 彈簧性 elasticity.
彈殼 *dahnker*, n., cartridge or shell.
彈力 **tarnlih*, n., elasticity.
彈性 **tarnshihng*, n., (lit. & fig.) elasticity, flexibility.
彈頭 *dahntour*, n., bullet.
彈子 *dahntz*, n., (1) bullet; (2) billiard.
彈詞 **tarntzyr*, n., a form of recital of story or its text, told partly with accompaniment of string and drum.
彈丸 *dahnwarn*, n., a bullet; more commonly 彈丸之地 a tiny place.
彈壓 **tarnya*, v.t., to quell (a riot, rebellion).

§ 50A.21 (弓/乚)

彄 50A.21–5

kou.

N. (1) (AC) a ring. (2) (AC) notch for bowstring on the bow.

§ 50A.22 (弓/丨)

引 50A.22–2

yiin.

N. (1) Introduction, foreword to a book: 小引 a brief foreword; 引論 gen. introduction to subject of a book. (2) A medical infusion or concoction in which medicine is suspended: 引子 *-tz* ↓. (3) A short song, a prelude. (4) A fuse, a conductor, a guiding rope: 引火, 引帶, 引布 *-huoo, -daih, -buh* ↓; 引線, 引導體 *-shiahn, -dauhtii* ↓. (5) Formerly, 鹽引, 茶引 government license for sale of salt, tea: 引地 *-dih* ↓; 錢引 a kind of paper money in the Suhng Dyn. (6) Formerly, a measure of distance = 100 feet or 10 丈 *jahng*. (7) Formerly, a measure of weight, of varying value, usu. of several catties; 水引 50 bags of salt of 100 catties each, term used in water transportation.

V.t. (1) To introduce, to quote, to present (person), to induce (evidence): 引見, 引用, 引號 *-jiahn, -yuhng, -hauh* ↓; 引證 *-jehng* ↓; 引進 to usher in; help (younger generation); 薦引 to recommend one for post. (2) To draw out, to stretch out (one's neck): 引弓 draw a bow full; 引頸, 引領 *-jihng, -liing* ↓; 引吭 to stretch neck and sing. (3) To seduce: 引誘 *-youh* ↓; 逗引, 勾引 to seduce. (4) To lead, induce, guide gently: 引人入勝 open up a new view, vista; 引人爲善 lead one to right conduct; 引起 to cause, lead to, *-chii* ↓.

引岸 *yiin-ahn*, n., see *-dih* ↓.
引避 *yiinbih*, v.i., (1) to withdraw to avoid meeting person, (of lady) to avoid meeting men; (2) to retire and give room to better men: 引避賢路.
引布 *yiin-buh*, n., two parallel strips of outstretched white cloth within which the closest relatives of deceased march behind the coffin.
引柴 *yiin-chair*, n., kindling wood.
引磬 *yiin-chihng*, n., a brass hand bowl, struck like a bell by Budd. priest during service.
引起 *yirn-chii*, v.t., to cause (dispute, dissatisfaction, war, lawsuit, etc.); to attract (attention).
引擎 *yiinchirng*, n., (translit.) engine.

引帶 *yiindaih*, n., (mech.) conductor belt.

引導 *yiindauh*, v.i. & t., to lead, to conduct; 引導體 *--tii*, (electricity) conductor.

引得 *yiinder*, n., (translit.) the index of a book (also called 索引).

引地 *yiin-dih*, n., formerly, licensed area for sale of government salt; see *-shueih*↓.

引對 *yiindueih*, v.i., introduce (scholar) to emperor, ruler for personal interview.

引渡 *yiinduh*, v.t., (law) to extradite (criminal).

引服 *yiinfur*, v.i., to plead guilty under torture.

引港 *yirn-gaang*, n., harbor pilot.

引號 *yiinhauh*, n., quotation marks.

引河 *yiinher*, n., a man-made canal outlet to reduce force of river current.

引火 *yirn-huoo*, v.i., to kindle fire; 引火點 *--diaan*, n., (phys.) flash point.

引證 *yiin-jehng*, v.i., to cite (past events, facts) as evidence.

引見 *yiin(')jiahn*, v.t., to present s.o. to ruler.

引接 *yiinjie*, v.t., to welcome and introduce visitor.

引頸 *yirnjihng*, v.i., to crane one's neck to look forward.

引經 *yiin-jing*, phr., 引經據典 to give quotations from classics or ancient works.

引咎 *yiin-jiouh*, v.i., to take the blame on oneself (and resign).

引疾 *yiin-jir*, v.i., to take illness as reason for resignation.

引重 *yiinjuhng*, v.t., (1) to speak highly of (person); (2) to place trust and responsibility on (person).

引決(訣) *yiinjyuer*, v.i., (LL) to commit suicide.

引力 *yiinlih*, n., (phys.) gravitation, attraction: 萬有引力 universal gravitation; 地心引力 gravitation pull of the earth.

引領 *yirn-liing*, v.i., to crane one's neck in hope.

引年 *yiin-niarn*, phr., (1) (AC) to resign from age; (2) (LL, rare) to extend life span (＝延年).

引伸 *yiinshen*, v.t., to extend meaning of word in a new context; to mean figuratively.

引線 *yiinshiahn*, n., (1) a fuse; (2) a contact man.

引嫌 *yiin-shiarn*, phr., 引嫌辭退 to withdraw from post to avoid suspicion.

引信 *yiinshihn*, n., gun fuse.

引水人 *yirn-shueei-rern*, n., harbor pilot, see *-gaang*↑.

引稅 *yiinshueih*, n., formerly, salt tax.

引退 *yiintueih*, v.i., to resign.

引子 *yiintz*, n., (1) (Chin. drama) an opening song of four sentences; (2) an infusion in which medicine is suspended.

引誘 *yiinyouh*, v.i., to seduce (person); (MC, rare) to induce to do good.

引用 *yiin yuhng*, v.t. & n., to quote, a quotation; 引用號 a quotation mark.

§ 50A.30 (弓/一)

彊 50A.30–3

chiarng.

[Dist. 疆 50A.30]

N. A surname. In all other senses, interch. 強 50A.93, strong, etc.

§ 50A.42 (弓/冈)

彌 50A.42–3

mir.

[Abbr. 弥]

N. A surname.

V.t. & adj. (1) (LL＝modn. 滿) to fill, filling, be filled: 彌缺 fill vacancy; 彌天大罪 one's sins fill the sky; 彌縫, 彌補 *-'feng*[1], *-buu*↓. (2) Full, whole: 彌年, 彌日 whole year, whole day, 彌月 *-yueh*↓.

Adv. (LL) the more (＝愈): 老而彌堅 become more firm as one grows old; 仰之彌高 the higher it seems; 彌多 all the more numerous.

彌補 *mirbuu*, v.t., make amends for past mistakes; fill (a crack); fulfill (a wish).

彌縫 *mir'feng*, v.i. & t., to join a seam or crack; to forestall discovery by covering up.

彌封 *mirfeng*, v.t., to seal completely examination papers.

彌敬 *mir-jihng*, n., gift for child's full month (*-yueh*↓).

彌勒(佛) *mir'le(for)*, n., Buddha Maitreya, the "Laughing Buddha" (with big belly), the friendly Buddhist Messiah.

彌留 *mirliour*, v.i., be in a critical period, dying but not dead: 彌留之際 while life was still lingering.

彌綸 *mirlurn*, v.i., restore deficiencies.

彌滿 *mirmaan*, adj., vigorous, full of energy: 精力彌滿.

彌漫 *mirmahn*, adj., widespread, filling the sky, boundless.

彌撒 *mirsah*, n., Catholic mass.

彌賽亞 *Mirsaihyah*, n., Messiah.

彌陀 *Mirtuor*, n., (Budd.) Amitabha, the perfect one.

彌望 *mirwahng*, adj., covering the horizon, filling the landscape: 沃野彌望, 彌望無際 boundless horizon.

彌月 *miryueh*, n., a child's first full month.

弸 50A.42–4

beng.

Adj. Tensely drawn, drawn to the full (of bow); 弸中彪外 (LL) smooth, beautiful appearance resulting from solid worth.

弸弓(子)(兒) *beng-gung(tz)(-'l)*, n., automatic spring device for closing door.

§ 50A.50 (弓/㇆)

粥 50A.50–2

juh (sp. pr. *jou*).

N. Gruel, congee: 小米粥 millet congee; 甜粥 sweetened congee.

粥會 *juhhueih*, n., a luncheon meeting where congee with simple fare is served.
粥粥 *juhjuh*, adj., (1) chuck-chuck sound: 羣雌粥粥 gathering of women with cackling or gurgling voices; (2) 粥粥無能 weak and incompetent.
粥餳 *juhshirng*, n., (MC) sweetened congee.

弼 50A.50–3

bih.

N. (AC) Device for keeping proper form of bows.

V.t. (LL) To assist, esp. assist king in government: 弼臣 minister assisting the king.

§ 50A.70 (弓/乚)

弛 50A.70–2

shyy (also *chyr*).

V.i. & t. (1) To relax, loosen: 鬆弛 to relax, go slow. (2) To fall off, fall out of use: 廢弛 (laws, regulations) be forgotten, ignored, fall into desuetude.
弛緩 *shyrhyaan*, adj. & adv., slow, -ly; loosely held (statutes).
弛張 *shyy-jang*, phr., degree of tension; tension and relaxation.
弛禁 *shyy-jihn*, v.i., to lift a ban or restrictions.

弝 50A.70–5

bah.

N. (AC) handle of sword; center of bow where it is held in position.

§ 50A.80 (弓/八)

彍 50A.80–6

kuoh.

V.t. (AC) 彍弩 to bend bow for shooting.

§ 50A.82 (弓/乂)

弢 50A.82–2

tau.
[Var. of 韜 22S.21]

§ 50A.83 (弓/⌒)

弧 50A.83–9

hur.

N. (1) A bow. (2) An arc: 弧形 arc-shaped.
弧度 *hurduh*, n., (math.) radian.
弧光 *hurguang*, n., arc light; 弧光燈 an arc lamp.

§ 50A.93 (弓/く)

弦 50A.93–6

shiarn.

N. (1) String on musical instrument (also wr. 絃) or on a bow: 弓弦 bowstring; 箭在弦上 the arrow is on the bow—poised to strike; 弦琴 *-chirn* ↓; 弦子 *-tz* ↓; 心弦 heartstring; 動人心弦 tuck at one's heartstrings. (2) (Math.) a chord, hypotenuse; 正弦 sine; 餘弦 cosine. (3) Jumpy pulse: 弦脈. (4) The crescent moon: 上弦 the new moon; 下弦 the crescent after full moon. (5) Fig. of wife: 斷弦 wife dies (string of musical instrument snaps); 續弦 to remarry or n., second wife (lit., "restring" instrument).

V.i. (AC) to play on stringed instrument.

弦琴 *shiarnchirn*, n., a stringed instrument with a number of strings: 三弦 a popular three-stringed instrument, used for telling stories; 四弦, 六弦, 十三弦 of 4, 6, 13 strings.
弦歌 *shiarnge*, v.t., to sing with stringed accompaniment, sign of calm in crisis, and (allu.) good government.
弦紐 *shiarn-nioou*, n., peg on stringed instrument.
弦線 *shiarnshiahn*, n., cord, thread, line.

弦誦 *shiarnsuhng*, v.i., sing aloud a text, read with intonation.

弦索 *shiarnsuoo*, n., stringed instruments collectively.

弦子 *shiarntz*, n., a stringed instrument, esp. 三弦.

弦韋 *shiarnweei*, n., girdle hangings (with 弦 silk strings, and 韋 leather strips).

弘 50A.93–9

hurng.

N. A surname.

V.t. To promote, expand (interch. 宏 62.93): 弘道 to promote, expand the teachings; 弘揚 *-yarng* ↓.

Adj. (LL) great (interch. 宏): 弘願 (LL) great wish; 弘志 (LL) great ambition.

弘揚 *hurngyarng*, v.t., to develop and expand: 弘揚文化 to promote and develop the culture (also 宏).

強 50A.93–9

chiarng (**chiaang*, **jiahng*). [Err. var. 強]

N. (1) A surname. (2) Short for 強國 big country: 列強 the powerful nations; 五強 The Big Five in United Nations.

V.t. (**chiaang*) To insist, to accomplish by force or against person's will: 強逼, 強迫 *-bi*, *-poh* ↓; 強買強賣 to buy or sell by force; 強詞奪理 to exaggerate by rhetoric, to quibble; 強記 to memorize; 勉強 to do s.t. against one's will, also to strive one's best; 不必勉強 don't do it if you do not wish.

Adj. (1) Strong, powerful: 強國 a powerful nation; 強有力 *-yoolih* ↓; 強暴 *-bauh* ↓; 強弩之末 on the decline, no longer what it was. (2) Better: 強似一個人在此 or 強乎 better than be here alone. (3) Over: 三十強 thirty plus. (4) (**jiahng*) Stubborn: 木強 stiff; 倔強 stubborn.

強半 *chiarngbahn*, n., over half, the great half.

強暴 *chiarngbauh*, adj., violent, brutal; v.t., to violate (girl).

強逼 **chiaangbi*, v.t., coerce (person).

強辯 *chiarngbiahn*, v.i., to argue forcefully; (**chiaang-*) to call white black, refuse to admit one's mistake.

強求 **chiaangchiour*, v.t., to insist on getting s.t.

強權 *chiarngchyuarn*, n., force, autocracy; 強權政策 policy of force.

強盜 *chiarngdauh*(*-'dau*), n., a robber.

強調 *chiarngdiauh*, v.t. & n., to emphasize, -sis: 強調他不能參加 emphasized he could not take part.

強度 *chiarngduh*, n., degree of strength; adv., (interfere, etc.) with force.

強幹 *chiarnggahn*, v.i. & t., to rely on force or persistence (to do s.t.).

強梗 *chiarnggeeng*, adj., stubborn.

強悍 *chiarnghahn*, adj., powerful, brutal.

強橫 *chiarngherng*, adj., arrogant, brutal.

強健 *chiarngjiahn*, adj., physically strong.

強姦 *chiarngjian*, v.t., to rape (woman).

強記 *chiaangjih*, adj., good in memory: (**chiaangjih*) to memorize by rote.

強壯 *chiaangjuahng*, adj., powerful, strong.

強制 **chiaangjyh*, (1) v.t., to force, enforce, restrain by law; (2) adj. & adv., compulsory: 強制執行 compulsory execution.

強梁 *chiarngliarng*, adj., unruly, defiant.

強迫 **chiaangpoh*, v.t., to force, coerce s.o. to do s.t.

強韌 *chiarngrehn*, adj., durable.

強人 *chiarngrern*, n., robber.

強如 *chiarng-rur*, phr., better than, see *-syh* ↓.

強盛 *chiarngshehng*, adj., strong, prosperous (nation).

強襲 *chiarngshi*, v.t., lay down artillery barrage, spring mass attack.

強項 *chiarngshiahng*, adj., resolute, inflexible.

強水 *chiarngshueei*, n., popular term for strong acids (like sulphuric acid).

強似 *chiarng-syh*, phr., better than.

強死 *chiarngsyy*, v.i., (AC) meet violent death.

強挺 *chiarngtiing*, adj., obdurate, inflexible.

強宗 *chiarng-tzuung*, n., powerful clan.

強顏 **chiahngyiarn*, v.i., (1) to force a smiling face; (2) (**jiahng-*) shamelessly.

強硬 *chiarngyihng*, adj., unyielding.

強有力 *chiarng-yoolih*, adj., powerful (person, country).

SECTION 50S

§ 50S.10 (ㄱ^{s}/十)

群 50S.10–8

chyurn.
[Pop. of 羣 52.10]

§ 50S.22 (ㄱ^{s}/丨)

那 50S.22–3

nah (oft. unaccented *neh*; in questions **naa*, "which one?"; *nah* in sense "that one"; **neih* =那一; in AC re. pr. **nuor*, unacented *'nuo*; as surname **na*).

Fin. part. **neh* (=哪 **'na*): 還多著那 (哪) there are a lot more, don't worry! 問足下願那不願 would you rather like it or not?

N. (**na*) A surname.

Pron. That, what (when used as object, usu. precedes vb.): 那我不知道 that I do not know; 那我不管 I don't bother with that; 那不是你幹的好事 isn't that mess made by you? 那有什麽可説 what is there to say about such a thing; (as subject) 那不行 that won't do; 那就完了 then it is all over.

Adj. (1) That (opp. 這 *jeh*, this; pl. 那些 those; opp. 這些 these): (pr. *nah*, also **neih* when it is contracted from *nah-yi* 那一) 那裏 *-lii* ↓; 那兒 *-'l* ↓; 那處, 那邊, 那壁廂, 那廂 (*nah-*) that place, there or (**naa-*) what place, where? 那個 *-'ge* ↓; 那塊 that piece or place; 那位 (court.) that one, referring to person; 那廝 (contempt.) that fellow; 那般, 那麽樣 in that manner; 那樣(兒)(子) *-yahng('l)(tz)* ↓; 那麽 *-'mo* ↓; 那話兒 that story, that thing (where speaker wishes not to be explicit); 那其間 during the interval; 那時 at that time; 那種 that kind of; 那類 ditto; 那宗 that bunch of, that batch of; 那天, 那年, 那會兒 that day, year, moment; 那當兒 that juncture; 那陣兒 that moment; 那回 that time; 那步田地 in that condition, plight. (2) In questions, (*naa* or *neei*) which one, in what manner, how: 那裏 *narlii* ↓; 那搭兒 which place? 那廂, 那處 ditto; 那兒 *-'l* ↓; 那一門子 what kind of? 那不是 that's the one, isn't it? 那得 how can? 那知 how can anyone know? 那能 how can it possibly be? 那堪 how can one stand such a (thing)? 那更堪 how can anyone stand any more of such (a thing)?

那 個 *nah'ge*, adj., (1) that one; (2) (sarcastic, humorous) 他這人作事, 眞有點那個 he is a bit what-do-you-call-it; 他眞太那個 he is really too much (I refuse to say "too much what").

那 兒 **naa'l*, adv., where: 你在那兒 where are you? 那兒聽見 where did you hear (this)?

那 裏 **narlii*, adv., (1) where: 書在那裏 where is the book? (2) how could: 那裏有 (=沒有) 這樣事 how could such a thing be? 那裏會 (=那不會) could not be; 説那裏話 how could you say so? 那裏, 那裏, 你太客氣了 don't mention it, you are too kind (formula in reply to "thank you"); 那裏的話 ditto; (3) (*nahlii*) over there.

那 麽 *nah'mo*, adv., (also 那麽着, 那們) (1) so, to such a degree: 你何必那麽緊張呢 why should you be so wrought-up? (2) then: 他旣不來, 那麽我也不走罷 since he doesn't come, then I won't go, either.

那 怕 *nahpah*, (1) conj., even if: 那怕爲你赴湯蹈火, 我也情願 I would be willing to die for you even; (2) phr., nothing to fear: 那怕什麽 what are you afraid of?

那 咱 喒 *nah'tzan*, n., (coll.) at that time.

那 樣 (兒) (子) *nahyahng('l)(tz)*, adv., so, in such a manner, to such a degree.

邵 50S.22–3

shauh.

N. A surname.

§ 50S.30 (ㄱ^{s}/一)

疆 50S.30–3

jiang.

N. A border, boundary, frontier: 疆土 *-tuu* ↓, 疆域 *-yuh* ↓; 邊疆 the border region, frontier area; 疆界 boundaries; 新疆 Sinkiang; 封疆大吏 civil or military governors of provinces; 無疆 limitless: 萬壽無疆 many happy returns of the day to eternity! (formerly, restricted only to rulers.)

疆 埸 *jiangchaang*, n., battlefield.

疆 徼 *jiang-jiauh*, n., border area, frontier districts.

疆 土 *jiangtuu*, n., the territory of a country.

疆 域 *jiangyuh*, n., national territorial limits.

§50S.50 (ㄱ^{S}/ㄱ)

羽 50S.50–5

yuu.

[Usu. wr. 羽]

N. (1) A surname. (2) Feather: 羽類, 羽毛 *-leih*, *-maur* ↓. (3) Wing: 羽翼 *-yih* ↓. (4) A light cloth, camlet: 羽紗, 羽皺 *-sha*, *-jouh* ↓. (5) Fifth note of pentatonic scale, *la*, see 五△音 31.30.

Adj. Made of feather: 羽蓋, 羽旗 *-gaih*, *-chir* ↓.

羽葆 *yur-baau*, n., see *-yir* ↓.
羽旗 *yuu-chir*, n., feather flag or pennant.
羽緞 *yuuduahn*, n., camlet, a silk and wool fabric.
羽蓋 *yuu-gaih*, n., a feathered parasol in parade.
羽化 *yuu-huah*, v.i., (Taoist) to fly away as disembodied spirit and become a fairy immortal.
羽皺 *yuu-jouh*, n., a kind of crepe.
羽軸 *yuujour*, n., (zoo.) feather quill.
羽狀脈 *yuu-juahng-moh*, n., (bot.) feather-like veins on leaves.
羽類 *yuuleih*, n., feathery tribe.
羽獵 *yuulieh*, v.i., (AC) to hunt.
羽流 *yuu-liour*, n., Taoist (cf. *-shyh* ↓, *-huah* ↑).
羽林 *yuu-lirn*, n., formerly, imperial palace guards.
羽綾 *yuulirng*, n., a silk and wool fabric; 羽綾緞 see *-duahn* ↑.
羽毛 *yuumaur*, n., feather; 羽毛紗 a light cloth; 羽毛書 urgent military despatch, marked with a feather, see *-shir* ↓.
羽旆 *yuu-peih*, n., a flag decorated with feathers.
羽紗 *yuu-sha*, n., a light cloth, camlet, lastings.
羽扇 *yuu-shahn*, n., a feather fan.
羽觴 *yuu-shang*, n., (AC) wine vessel which was in shape of a sparrow.
羽檄 *yuu-shir*, n., an urgent military despatch marked with a feather.
羽士 *yuu-shyh*, n., a Taoist, cf. *-huah* ↑.
羽藻 *yur-tzaau*, n., plants whose leaves are arranged on stalk like wings.
羽族 *yuu-tzur*, n., the feathered tribe—fowls.
羽衣 *yuu-yi*, n., a garment made of feather.
羽翼 *yuu-yih*, n., a wing, (fig.) an assistant, right-hand man; camp followers.
羽儀 *yuu-yir*, n., parade of insignias and parasols in procession.

弱 50S.50–5

rouh.

[Usu. wr. 弱]

Adj. (1) Weak (opp. 強 strong): 弱者 *-jee* ↓; 弱點 *-diaan* ↓; 強弱 strong or weak; 弱小民族 small and weak nations; 弱不勝強 the weak are no match for the strong; 弱肉強食 the weak at the mercy of the strong; 弱不禁風 (of a person) too frail to stand a gust of wind; 弱不勝衣 (rhet.) tender and frail; 孱弱 frail, weak; 虛弱 delicate, feeble; 衰弱 weak, sickly; 柔弱 flabby, flaccid; 疲弱 tired out and weak; 軟弱 weak-kneed, fickle, irresolute; 脆弱 brittle, easily broken; 體弱 physically weak; 老弱 old and infirm: 老弱殘兵 motley troops unfit for combat duty, (fig.) incompetent persons for a given job. (2) Young: 弱冠 *-guahn* ↓; 弱歲 childhood; 弱齡 youthful; 弱女 a young girl; 弱不好弄 not fond of childish pranks, though young.

V.i. Die off, pass away: 又弱一個 another one has passed away.

弱點 *ruoh-diaan*, n., weaknesses, weak points.
弱風 *ruoh-feng*, n., southeast wind.
弱冠 *ruohguahn*, n., (1) formerly, the coming of age at 20; (2) youth.
弱翰 *ruohhahn*, n., the writing brush.
弱者 *ruohjee*, n., the weaker of two parties, the weak, the underdog, the weaker sex.
弱植 *ruoh-jyr*[1], adj., (of a person's character) weak and unable to stand up firmly.
弱質 *ruoh-jyr*[2], n., tender body (gen. of women).
弱累 *ruoh-leih*, n., the burden of rearing one's children.
弱息 *ruoh-shir*, n., one's children.
弱行 *ruoh-shirng*, v.i., (AC, of a crippled person) be unable to walk properly.
弱顏 *ruoh-yarn*, v.i., (LL) be ashamed to face others.
弱音器 *ruohyinchih*, n., (mus.) a damper.

劭 50S.50–9

shauh.

Adj. (AC) beautiful (character): 年高德劭 of venerable age and respected character.

鶴 50S.50–9

juor.

鶴雉 *juorjyh*, n., a kind of pheasant, *Phasianus scintillaus* (also called 山雞).

§50S.70 (ㄱ^{S}/ㄴ)

翫 50S.70–3

warn (also *wahn*).

[Var. of 玩 31A.70]

§50S.71 (ㄱ^{s}/弋)

戮 50S.71–7

luh.

V.t. (1) To kill: 戮屍 to chop up corpse (as revenge). (2) 戮力同心 to pull together and work hard as a team.

戳 50S.71–7

chuo.

N. (*-tz, 'l*) A business stamp: 郵戳 post office stamp to cancel postage; 橡皮戳 rubber stamp; 戳記 *-jih* ↓.

V.i. & t. (1) To stab, poke, pierce: 戳他一指 poke him with a finger; 戳穿 pierce through, also leak a secret; 戳死 stab to death; 你這話他眞戳肺管子 your words hurt him badly; 戳脊梁骨 backbite ("poke on spine"). (2) To stand up, as a bag packed solid, not collapse (like Eng., "the law still *stands*," "the charge won't *stand up*"): 戳得住 will stand up, (fig.) will hold one's ground or enjoy public confidence; 戳不住 fail to hold public confidence.

戳個兒 *chuoge'l,* n., bodily height, stature.

戳活兒 *chuo-huor'l,* v.i., to select number for monologuist (大鼓書) to sing.

戳記 *chuojih,* n., a business or shop stamp.

戳紗 *chuosha,* n., needle-point lace.

戳舌 *chuosher,* v.i., to talk too much: 兩頭戳舌 carry gossip.

戳事 *chuo-shyh,* v.i., (of swindler) look for chance to poke one's hand into.

戳印 *chuoyihn,* v.i. & n., to stamp; a stamp.

SECTION 51

§51.00 (ㄏ/亅)

牙 51.00

yar.

N. (1) A tooth: 牙齒 -(')*chyy* ↓; 奶牙 milk tooth; 大牙, 板牙, 槽牙 molar; 門牙 incisor; 鑲牙 have tooth filled; 蛀牙, 爛牙 decayed tooth; 暴牙 projecting tooth; 缺牙 missing tooth; 恨的牙癢癢 gnash one's teeth with hatred; 咬牙切齒 ditto; 張牙舞爪 let out the fangs and claws; 伶牙利齒 sharp-tongued; 牙白口清 pronounce words very distinctly. (2) Ivory: 象牙 ditto; 牙章 ivory seal; 牙筋 ivory chopsticks; 牙籌 ivory chips for gambling; 牙牌 ivory mahjong set. (3) A broker: 牙行, 牙子, 牙婆 *-harng, -tz, -por* ↓; 牙儈, 牙人 *-kuaih, -rern* ↓.

Adj. (Sl.) smart: 這孩子眞牙 this child is very smart.

牙幫兒(子) *yarbang'l* (*-tz*) n., (satir.) a smart aleck; a too calculating fellow.

牙碜 *yar'chen,* phr., (food) gritty, grates the teeth; (words) offensive to good taste; (sound) grating (to the ear).

牙城 *yarcherng,* n., formerly, commander's headquarters or fort.

牙籤 *yarchian,* n., (1) ivory pin on de luxe book cover; (2) (*-chia'l*) a toothpick.

牙牀 *yarchuarng,* n., (1) (*-tz*) jawbone; (2) (phonetics) alveolus, -lar; (3) ivory-inlaid bed.

牙蟲 *yarchurng,* n., "toothworm," formerly, believed to be the cause of tooth decay.

牙齒 *yar(')chyy,* n., tooth.

牙粉 *yarfeen,* n., tooth powder.

牙縫兒 *yarfehng'l,* n., crevice between teeth.

牙風 *yarfeng,* n., tooth decay; toothache.

牙疳 *yargan,* n., pyorrhea, alveolus.

牙膏 *yargau,* n., tooth paste.

牙關 *yarguan,* n., maxillary joint.

牙行 *yarharng,* n., a broker house, house of commission agents.

牙花子 *yarhautz,* n., (coll.) dirt accumulated on teeth.

牙慧 *yarhueih,* n., trite expression: 拾人牙慧 (contempt.) words (pickings) copied from another source.

牙將 *yarjiahng,* n., formerly, a loose term denoting an officer subordinate to general, an *aide-de-camp.*

牙祭 *yarjih,* n., usu. in 打牙祭 have a great "feed," a special dinner (esp. for shop employees on first and fifteenth of month).

牙質 *yarjy,* n., dentine.

牙科 *yarke,* n., dentistry; 牙科醫生 dentist.

牙儈 *yarkuaih,* n., a broker.

牙郎 *yarlarng,* n., ditto.

牙門 *yarmern,* n., (1) (AC) yamen, magistrate's or other officials' office (now currently wr. 衙門), orig. wr. 牙門 from following usage; (2) general's camp where the general's flag stood.

牙牌 *yarpair,* n., ivory blocks used in mahjong; any ivory chips.

牙婆 *yarpor,* n., procuress; woman trading in girls as slaves, concubines, etc.

牙人 *yarrern,* n., a broker, middleman.

牙色 *yarseh,* n., ivory color.

牙刷(子) *yarshua(tz),* n., toothbrush.

牙疼咒(兒) *yarterngjouh('l),* n., (coll.) a worthless oath, swearing only a toothache as punishment.

牙磁 *yartsyr,* n., tooth enamel.

牙痛 *yartuhng,* n., toothache.

牙子 *yartz,* n., (1) a broker; (2) an expert (on curios, etc.); (3) inlaid part of furniture.

牙牙 *yar-yar*, n., inarticulate sound of infant.

牙醫 *yaryi*, n., a dentist.

牙印子 *yar-yihntz*, n., tooth mark.

鬁 51.00

lih.

N. See 鬎鬁 51.00↓.

鬇 51.00

jeng.

鬇鬡 *jengnirng*, adj., shaggy-haired.

鬎 51.00

lah.

鬎鬁 *lahlih*, n., (usu. wr. 瘌痢) in 鬎鬁頭 head bald from scabies.

鬋 51.00

jian.

N. (Women's) bangs.

V.t. To shave (var. of 剪).

鬡 51.00

nirng.

Adj. 鬇鬡 (Of hair) dishevelled.

擥 51.00

laan.

[Var. of 攬 10A.70]

---

§51.01 (ㄏ/小)

緊 51.01

jiin.

Adj. (1) Tight, tense (opp. 鬆 loose): 緊繃 *-beng*↓; 抓緊 hold firmly in hand; 拉緊 pull tight; 綁緊 fasten tight; 緊握 grip, keep strong grasp, firm hold. (2) Urgent, pressing: 緊急 *-jir*, 緊迫 *-poh*↓; 緊慢遲急兒 in case of emergency (a crisis); 緊要關頭 a turning point, a crisis; 要緊 most urgent, pressing, important; 加緊辦理 expedite, do with dispatch; 趕緊 make redoubled efforts; 緊張 *-jang*↓; 戰爭吃緊 fighting has become critical. (3) Close at hand, near, hard by: 緊密 *-mih*↓; 緊防 take precautionary measures against; 加緊看守 keep a close watch over; 緊跟 follow close behind; 緊隨 close on the heels of.

緊繃 *jiinbeng*, v.t., draw tight (as drum surface).

緊襯 *jiinchehn*, v.t., (1) fit to a T; (2) fasten, make secure.

緊張 *jiinjang*, adj., (of situation) critical; (of person) nervous, tense.

緊急 *jiinjir*, adj., dangerously critical, calling for immediate action: 緊急避難 avert imminent danger; 緊急狀態 state of emergency.

緊密 *jiinmih*, adj., close fitting: 緊密注意 pay close attention to.

緊迫 *jiinpoh*, adj., pressing hard, allowing of no respite.

緊身兒 *jiinshe'l*, n., a close fitting undergarment.

緊縮 *jiinsuo*, v.t., cut down (expenses, personnel, budget); 緊縮政策 policy of retrenchment.

緊湊 *jiintsouh*, adj., (1) (of writing) concise and to the point (opp. 鬆懈 rambling, disconnected); (2) (successive events) tightly packed or arranged.

緊促 *jiintsuh*, adj., urgently pressing.

緊自 *jiin'tz*, adv., often, repeatedly, over and over: 緊自一説就可厭了 to repeat oneself again and again would be boring.

緊要 *jiinyauh*, adj., important, essential, vital, crucial.

繄 51.01

yi.

Fin. part. (AC) used like 矣 93.81.

V.i. (AC) to be.

鬃 51.01

tzung.

[Var. of 騣, 鬉, 騌]

N. Animal hair growing on the neck: 馬鬃 a horse's mane; 豬鬃 pig's bristles; 鬃毛 bristles in gen.

髹 51.01

shiou.

N. (AC) light brown lacquer.

V.t. (AC) to coat with lacquer; 髹漆 ditto.

§51.02 (厂/k)

長 51.02

charng (**jaang*, **jahng*).

N. (1) Specialty, what one excels in: 特長, 擅長, 專長, 所長 ditto; 長處 -'*chuh* ↓. (2) (**jaang*) Head, chief (of bureau, department, etc.): 部長 minister of government; 首長 the ministers and chiefs of special bureaus; 校長 president, principal of school; 師長 division commander; 團長 regiment commander; 董事長 chairman of the board; 家長 head of family, parents of students.

V.i. (**jaang*) (1) To grow up, grow in years: 長大, 長成 -*dah*, -*cherng* ↓; 長了一歲 become one year older; grow up to be: 長得太難看了, 很漂亮 grow up to look awful, to look pretty. (2) To grow, increase (in wisdom, price, etc.): 長見識 open mental horizon; 長價 -*jiah* ↓; 長行市 increase in price; 長脾氣 grow proud; 長調門子 grow in (assumed) stature, airs; 長他人志氣, 滅自己威風 to puff up the enemy and lower our morale.

V.t. (**jaang*) To grow s.t.; 長鬍子 grow a beard; 長疙瘩, 長瘡 grow pimples, sore; 長牙 put forth teeth; 長芽, 長霉 put forth sprouts, get moldy.

Adj. (1) Long, opp. short 短: 長途 long journey; 長城 -*cherng* ↓; 長風 swift wind; 長嘆 long sigh; 長吁短嘆 sigh incessantly; 長號 throw up a long yell; 長嘯 to give a long whistle; 長短 -*duaan* ↓; 長話短說 to make a long story short; 長袖善舞 long sleeves help in dancing (as 長財善賈) ample capital makes it easy to trade. (2) (**jaang*) Elder, senior, opp. 幼 junior: 長者, 長老, 長輩 -*jee*, -*laau*, -*beih* ↓. (3) (**jaang*) The eldest: 長子, 長孫 eldest son, grandson; 長房 branch of the eldest son; 他居長 he is the eldest; 長兄, 長姊 eldest brother, sister. (4) (**jahng*) Extraneous: 身無長物 (LL phr.) have only bare necessities at home (no savings); 冗長 long drawn-out, wordy.

長安 *Charng-an*, n., capital of Tarng Dyn. (=modn. 西安), famed in Tarng poetry; 長安路, 長安道上 route to Charng-an, associated with route to officialdom and civil examinations.

長輩 **jaangbeih*, n., the elder generation, an elder.

長臂猿 *charngbeihyuarn*, n., type of long-armed ape in India and Malaysia, *Hylobates lar*.

長編 *charngbian*, n., book of full data and detailed stories, from which a particular history is compiled—full version of chronicles.

長波 *charng-bo*, n., (electronics) long wave.

長成 **jaangcherng*, v.i., (1) to grow up (in certain city), become adult; (2) grow into (an ulcer, etc.).

長城 *Charngcherng*, n., the Great Wall, symbol of eternal strength; (fig.) a great warrior.

長期 *charngchir*, adj., long-term (deposit, etc.).

長川 *charngchuan*, adj. & adv., continually, normally (write each other, etc.).

長處 *charng'chuh*, n., one's strong points.

長蟲 *charng'chung*, n., (coll.) snake.

長驅 *charng-chyu*, phr., 長驅直入 drive straight in (into enemy city).

長大 **jaangdah*, v.i., grow up.

長短 *charng-duaan*, n., (1) length: 三尺長短 three-foot long (also -'*l*); (2) criticism, discussion as to who is right (long) and who is wrong (short): 說人長短 criticize people; (3) s.t. untoward: 萬一有什麽長短 if s.t. untoward should happen; 長短句=宋詞 the *tsyr* form of verse, with varying sentence lengths; 長短詩 verse in which some sentence lengths vary.

長度 *charngduh*, n., length.

長法兒 *charngfaa'l*, n., a regular way: 不是個長法兒 shouldn't be a regular way, but occassionally allowable.

長方 *charngfang*, n., rectangle: 長方形 rectangular.

長房 **jaangfarng*, n., the eldest branch of family.

長庚 *charnggeng*, n., the planet Venus (金星).

長官 **jaangguan*, n., superiors in office; officers.

長跪 *charnggueih*, v.i., to prostrate on the ground.

長工 *charnggung*, n., formerly, hired farm hand on permanent or yearly basis.

長公主 **jaanggungjuu*, n., the emperor's sisters.

長活 *charnghuor*, n., see -*gung* ↑.

長齋 *charngjai*, v.i., to fast from meat for a long period.

長者 **jarngjee*, n., elders, aldermen; village gentry.

長征 *charngjeng*, v.i., to go on a long journey or campaign.

長角 *charngjiaau*, n., (bot.) elongated pod of seeds.

長假 *charngjiah*, n., (take) long leave, i.e., resign.

長價 **jaangjiah*, v.i., rise in price.

長江 *Charngjiang*, n., the Yangtze River.

長技 *charngjih*, n., special skill.

長進 **jaang'jihn*, v.i., to improve (in character, studies): 永不長進 be a sluggard.

長徑 *charngjihng*, n., (math.) major axis.

長頸鹿 *charngjiing-luh*, n., giraffe.

長鯨 *charngjing*, n., the big whale as symbolic of great drinking capacity.

長久 *charngjioou*, adj. & adv., for long, lasting: 長久之計 a permanent arrangement.

長支 *charngjy*, v.i., formerly, for shop employees to draw money

亅	小	k	十	土	ナ	廾	ㄴト	丨	一	丁	フ	口	囗	冂	ㄱ	厂	尸	亠	广	宀	丶	乚	七	心	八	人	乂	乛	乛	丿丨	𠂉	く
00	01	02	10	11	12	20	21	22	30	31	32	40	41	42	50	51	52	60	61	62	63	70	71	72	80	81	82	83	90	91	92	93

on credit, the accounts to be reckoned at year's end.

長至 *charngjyh*, n., (AC) winter solstice ("longest day"), also (AC) summer solstice.

長局 *charngjyur*, n., permanent arrangement, see *-faa'l*↑.

長空 *charngkung*, n., the sky.

長兒 *charng'l*, n., (1) length; (2) a long time: 這東西不耐長兒 this article will not last long.

長老 **jarnglaau*, n., (1) elder, alderman; (2) elder in Presbyterian Church; (3) senior monk; 長老會 Presbyterian Church.

長吏 **jaanglih*, n., superior officer.

長曆 *charnglih*, n., (lunar) calendar which reckons the dates of seasons for centuries.

長毛 (1) **jaang-maur*, v.t., to mildew; (2) (*charng-*) n., long hair.

長眠 *charngmiarn*, n. & v.i., death ("the long sleep").

長命 *charngmihng*, n., long life: 長命富貴 longevity with wealth and honor, a long life of abundance and respectability.

長明燈 *charngmirngdeng*, n., altar lamp which burns day and night.

長年 *charngniarn*, adv., regularly: 長年在這裏住 stay here regularly; for a long time.

長跑 *charngpaau*, n., (track and field) long-distance run.

長篇 *charngpian*, (1) phr., 長篇大論 discourse eloquently on subject; (2) 長篇小說 a novel.

長衫(兒) *charngshan(-sha'l)*, n., long gown.

長生 *charngsheng*, n., long life, longevity: 長生不老 perpetual rejuvenation; 長生祿位 a tablet and altar in honor of great benefactor, for whom prayer is said.

長生果 *charngsheng-guoo*, n., peanut (=落花生).

長舌 *charngsher*[1], adj., as in 長舌婦 a loquacious woman.

長蛇 *charngsher*[2], n., as in 封豕長蛇 (fig.) a greedy monster; 長蛇陣 snake formation (as in snake dance).

長相兒 **jaangshiahng'l*, n., usual appearance or condition.

長辛螺 *charngshin-luor*, n., (zoo.) long shellfish, *Fusus perplexus*.

長壽 *charngshouh*, n. & adj., longevity.

長逝 *charngshyh*, v.i., to pass away.

長石 *charngshyr*, n., (geol.) feldspar.

長天 *charngtian*, adv., as in 長天大日, 長天老日 in broad daylight, all day (doing nothing, etc.).

長挑 *charng'tiau*, adj., (person) tall and slender.

長條兒 *charngtiaur'l*, n., a long slip.

長亭 *charngtirng*, n., formerly, rest pavilion on highway: 十里一長亭, 五里一短亭 a big station every ten *lii*, a small station every five *lii*.

長途 *charngtur*, (1) n., long journey; (2) adj., long distance: 長途電話 long-distance telephone call; 長途汽車 bus system between cities.

長尾雞 *charngweeiji*, n., (zoo.) a special variety of fowl with a long tail, *Gallus domesticus*, cultivated in Japan.

長尾猿 *charngweeiyuarn*, n., (zoo.) an African ape with long tail, *Cercopithecus aethiops*.

長物 **jahngwuh*, n., surplus: 生平無長物 have no savings—have just the necessities of living.

長夜 *charngyeh*, adv., all night long.

長揖 *charngyi*, v.i., to make a long bow, the clasped hands reaching to the knees.

長音程 *charngyin-cherng*, n., (mus.) major interval.

長音階 *charngyin-jie*, n., (mus.) major scale.

長幼 **jaangyouh*, n., the young and old.

長遠 *charngyuaan*, adj., long, distant: 長遠之計 a long plan for the future.

長圓 *charngyuarn*, adj., oval in shape.

鬢 51.02

huarn.

N. A coil of hair: 鬢髻 a woman's hairdo; 丫鬢, 小丫鬢 formerly, young maidservant.

§51.11 (厂/土)

堅 51.11

jian.

N. (1) Armor: 披堅執銳 be fully armed and ready for combat ("put on armor and hold weapons"). (2) A stronghold, citadel, fortress: 攻堅, 陷堅 to assault the enemy's stronghold, take it by storm; 中堅 the main body of an army: 中堅分子, 中堅人物 key personnel. (3) A surname.

Adj. (1) Solid, firm, durable, strong: 堅牢 *-laur*↓; 堅固 *-guh*, 堅實 *-shyr*, 堅硬 *-yihng*↓; 堅壁清野 (of army) clear the deck for action: 堅甲利兵 equipped with strong armor and sharp weapons. (2) Resolute, steadfast, staunch: 堅定 *-dihng*, 堅苦 *-kuu*, 堅決 *-jyuer*, 堅貞 *-jen*, 堅忍 *-reen*, 堅毅 *-yih*↓. (3) (Of prices) strong, rapidly rising, (of business conditions) booming (opp. 疲 weak): 堅挺 *-tiing*↓; 轉堅 (of market conditions) turning strong, (of prices) becoming higher.

Adv. Firmly, resolutely, steadfastly: 堅執 *-jyr*↓; 堅信 firmly believe; 堅守 guard securely, hold fast, keep (promises); 堅拒 flatly refuse; 堅稱 declare categorically, positively assert; 堅不吐實 (of criminal suspects) obstinately refuse to speak up.

堅白(同異) *jianbor*, n., sophistry, a school of sophists during the Warring Kingdoms.

堅巧 *jianchiaau*, adj., of good quality and fine workmanship.

堅持 *jianchyr*, v.t. & adj., insist (ent).

堅定 *jiandihng*, adj., resolute,

firm, determined.

堅固 *jianguh*, adj., strong, firm, unshakable.

堅貞 *jianjen*, adj., faithful (loyal) to the bitter end.

堅緻 *jianjyh*, adj., of strong make and finely finished.

堅執 *jianjyr*, v.t., insist strongly, declare emphatically.

堅決 *jianjyuer*, adj. & adv., decided, -ly, determined, -ly.

堅苦 *jiankuu*, adj., staunch: 堅苦卓絕 staunch through trials and tribulations.

堅牢 *jianlaur*, adj., (of articles) strong and durable, strongly built.

堅凝 *jiannirng*, adj., (of things) congealed, solidified, hardened, (of persons) firm, resolute, unwavering.

堅忍 *jianreen*, adj., persevering, unrelenting, indefatigable: 堅忍不拔 firm and unyielding.

堅韌 *jianrehn*, adj., flexible, elastic, pliant, malleable.

堅實 *jianshyr*, adj., solid, strong, durable (fabric).

堅挺 *jiantiing*, adj., (of business condition) booming, flourishing, (of prices) strong, rising, (stock exchange) bullish.

堅毅 *jianyih*, adj., resolute, with firm determination.

堅硬 *jianyihng*, adj., strong and tough, hard and solid.

§51.21 (厂/乚)

匭 51.21-1

gueei.

N. A casket, small box (as ballot box).

匵 51.21-1

dur.

N. Cabinet, casket (var. of 櫝), (AC) animal cage.

匱 51.21-2

kueih (**gueih*).

N. (**gueih*) A desk counter, a cabinet, abbr. for 櫃 10B.21.

Adj. Exhausted: 力匱.

匱乏 *kueihfar*, adj., lacking, short (of money): 不虞匱乏 freedom from want, one of Franklin D. Roosevelt's "Four Freedoms."

匿 51.21-2

nih.

V.i. Hide: 逃匿 escape and hide oneself; 匿避 *-bih*↓; 藏匿 be hidden; 匿伏 *-fur*↓; 隱匿 be concealed; 匿迹銷聲 abscond quietly, cease all public activities.

匿避 *nibbih*, v.i., run away to escape notice or capture.

匿情 *nih-chirng*, v.i., conceal fact before the law.

匿伏 *nihfur*, v.i., hide oneself to escape capture.

匿名 *nihmirng*, adj., anonymous: 匿名信 an anonymous letter; 匿名投書 write an anonymous letter.

匿喪 *nih-sang*, v.t., conceal the fact of the death of s.o., esp. one's parents.

匿怨 *nih-yuahn*, v.t., entertain secret grudge.

匝 51.21-2

tza.

N. A full circle: 一匝 make a full circle: 匝月 one full month: 匝地 here, there, and everywhere.

匜 51.21-2

yir.

N. (AC) a wash basin; a wine vessel with a spout.

臣 51.21-2

chern.

N. (1) A minister *vis-à-vis* 君 the ruler; a public servant: 忠臣, 奸臣 a loyal, disloyal minister; 人臣 a minister at court; 大臣 minister of state, high minister. (2) Subject or servant owing allegiance to the ruler: 臣民, 臣僕, 臣下 *-mirn*, *-pur*, *-shiah*↓; used by minister in self-reference when speaking to emperor, like Eng. "Your servant."

V.t. (1) (LL) to subjugate or be subjugated: 臣服 *-fur*↓; 以力臣天下 to subjugate world by force. (2) (LL) to regard as subject: 王臣公, 公臣大夫 (AC) the king is lord to the duke, and the duke is lord to the barons.

臣妾 *chern-chieh*, n., (AC) male and female servants.

臣服 *chernfur*, v.i., to swear allegiance to another.

臣工 *cherngung*, n., (AC) the ministers and officials (under a king).

臣僚 *chernliaur*, n., the officials at court.

亅	小	⺊	十	土	ナ	卄	ㅏ	丨	一	丁	フ	口	区	区	冂	厂	尸	亠	广	宀	丶	乚	弋	心	八	人	乂	⌒	一	リ	𠂉	く
00	01	02	10	11	12	20	21	22	30	31	32	40	41	42	50	51	52	60	61	62	63	70	71	72	80	81	82	83	90	91	92	93

臣民 *chernmirn*, n., the subjects of a ruler.
臣僕 *chernpur*, n., officials as servants to the king.
臣下 *chernshiah*, n., self-reference of minister to king.
臣庶 *chernshuh*, n., all the king's subjects.
臣事 *chernshyh*, v.t., to owe allegiance as subject or vassal.
臣子 *cherntzyy*, n., official as subject to the king.

匪 51.21-2

feei.

N. (1) Bandit: 土匪, 盜匪; 匪巢 bandits' lair; 匪首, 匪酋 bandit chief. (2) Criminal class, criminals: 奸匪; 匪人, 匪類 *-rern, -leih* ↓. (3) Rebel: 匪黨, 軍 rebel gang, army; 匪禍 evil brought about by rebels; 匪諜 *-dier* ↓.

Adv. (AC, LL) not (=modn. 非): 匪夷所思 phr., fantastic, what one could never imagine; 夙夜匪懈 phr., never slacken morning or night; 匪遙 not far; 匪特 not only (=modn. 非特).

匪諜 *feei-dier*, n., enemy spy.
匪話 *feei-huah*, n., thief's slang.
匪類 *feei-leih*, n., banditry; criminals, ex-convicts.
匪人 *feei-rern*, n., bandit; bad character.
匪徒 *feei-tur*, n., bandits; scamps, vagrants, rascals.

匡 51.21-3

kuang.

V.t. (1) To restore, recover, revise (mistakes): 匡復, 匡正 *-fuh, -jehng* ↓. (2) To help: 匡救 *-jiouh* ↓.

匡復 *kuangfuh*, v.t., to restore (lost territory).
匡正 *kuangjehng*, v.i., to correct (errors).
匡濟 *kuangjih*, v.t., to relieve distress, help over (crisis).
匡救 *kuangjiouh*, v.t., to rescue (from disaster, errors).
匡助 *kuangjuh*, v.t., to help, lend a helping hand.
匡時 *kuang-shyr*, v.i. & adj., guide country over crisis, do things for the good of society.

叵 51.21-4

poo.

[Cogn. of 否, contraction of 不可; dist. 巨]

Vb. Cannot: 叵信=不可信 (MC) cannot believe.

Adv. (AC) forthwith.

叵羅 *pooluor*, n., (AC) anc. goblet.
叵奈 *poonaih*, phr., MC equiv. modn. 無奈 despite everything, but unfortunately: 叵奈一行書也無 alas! despite everything, (he) did not write a single letter, also 叵耐.
叵測 *pootseh*, adj., unfathomable, unpredictable (of human heart).

匣 51.21-4

shiar.

N. (*-tz*, *'l*) A box (for jewels, antiques, pastry, etc.).

區 51.21-4

chyu (**ou*).

N. (1) Region, area: 分區 subdistrict, subdivision of an area; 地區 area; 區域 *-yuh* ↓; 住宅區 residential area; 風景區 park area, one noted for scenic beauty; 商業區 downtown district of city. (2) Precinct, a subdivision of district. (3) (**ou*) A surname.

V.t. To classify, subdivide: 區分, 區別 *-fen, -bier* ↓.

區別 *chyubier*, v.t., to distinguish between (sexes, classes, sizes); 區別詞 (gram.) modifier.
區處 *chyuchuu*, v.t., to handle or dispose of.
區區 *chyuchyu*, (1) adj., tiny, very small (used also of one's own contributions, etc.); (2) pron., my humble self.
區分 *chyufen*, v.t., to separate into classes or categories.
區理 *chyulii*, v.t., to deal with separately.
區域 *chyuyuh*, n., area, region in gen.; 區域安全 regional security.
區宇 *chyuyuu*, n., (AC) territory.

巨 51.21-5

jyuh.

N. A surname.

Adj. Great, huge, immense (opp. 細 tiny, small, little): 巨富 (loosely) a millionaire, a very wealthy person; 巨盜 a notorious robber (bandit); 巨奸 a very treacherous person; 巨額 a huge sum of money, (of bank notes) large denominations; 巨擘 *-boh*, 巨細 *-shih* ↓.

Adv. Interch. 詎.

巨擘 *jyuhboh*, n., (1) the thumb; (2) the most outstanding of all.
巨蠹 *jyuh-duh*, n., a gangster leader.
巨靈 *jyuh-lirng*, n., a monster spirit.
巨人 *jyuhrern*, n., giant.
巨細 *jyuh-shih*, n. & adj., (the) big and (the) small: 事無巨細 all matters whether important or trivial.

巨型 *jyuh-shirng*, n., large model (of cars, etc.).

巨室 *jyuh-shyh*, n., (1) a mansion; (2) (AC) a family wielding great social and political influence.

巨頭 *jyuh-tour*, n., a great leader; 三巨頭 a triumvirate; 四巨頭 the Big Four.

巨子 *jyuh-tzyy*, n., (1) a leading expert; (2) a leader of 墨子 Motse school.

巨萬 *jyuhwahn*, n. & adj., a hundred million, myriads.

匟 51.21-6

kahng.

N. A divan for two.

匾 51.21-6

biaan.

N. (1) (Dial.) flat, round split-bamboo container. (2) See 匾額 *-er*↓.

匾額 *biaan-er*, n., horizontal tablet over door; shop sign; inscribed hall name, (also wr. 扁額).

滙 51.21-6

hueih.
[Common var. 滙]

N. Concourse (of rivers, people): 總匯 a great clearinghouse (of knowledge), a compendium, gen. depository or gathering up (of many streams, currents of thought, etc.).

V.i. (1) To flow into, gather together: 匯集 gather together; 匯注 flow into (common stream). (2) Transmit, remit money: 郵匯 postal money order; 電匯 telegraphic transfer; 信匯 mail transfer; 匯票, 匯兌, 匯費 *-piauh*, *-dueih*, *-feih*↓; 外匯 foreign exchange; 結匯 money transfer; 套匯 (foreign exchange) arbitrage.

匯撥 *hueihbo*, v.t., transfer (sum), give a draft on.

匯單 *hueihdan*, n., see *-piauh*↓.

匯兌 *hueihdueih*, n., transfer of funds.

匯費 *hueihfeih*, n., bank charge for transmitting money.

匯付 *hueihfuh*, v.t., pay to.

匯款 *hueihkuaan*, n., a remittance, sum transferred.

匯率 *hueihlyuh*, n., rate of exchange; 收盤匯率 closing rate; 法定匯率, 浮動匯率, 開盤匯率 fixed rate, floating rate, opening rate of exchange.

匯票 *hueihpiauh*, n., a money order, draft; bill of exchange; 即付匯票 sight draft; 銀行匯票 bank draft; 商業匯票 commercial draft; 銀單匯票 documentary draft.

匯水 *hueihshueei*, n., see *-feih*↑.

匳 51.21-8

liarn.

N. Mirror box; casket; 香匳 container for incense; 粧匳 dowry; 匳敬 gifts to bride.

医 51.21-9

yi.
[Pop. abbr. of 醫 51.41]

匠 51.21-9

jiahng.

N. A workman, a mechanic: 木匠 a carpenter; 瓦匠 a bricklayer; 石匠 a mason; 鐵匠 a blacksmith; 匠人 *-rern*↓; 匠氣 *-chih*↓.

Adj. Skillful: 匠心 *-shin*↓; 匠意 *-yih*↓.

匠氣 *jiahngchih*, adj., tone, style of commercial artist, lacking in creative imagination.

匠人 *jiahngrern*, n., an artisan, a craftsman.

匠心 *jiahngshin*, n., mental strategy, a master craftsman's conception: 匠心經營 original thought in any creation.

匠意 *jiahngyih*, adj. & n., ditto.

匹 51.21-9

pii.

N. adjunct. 一匹馬 a horse; 匹馬 lone rider; 三匹馬 three horses: 匹馬單槍 phr., go to battle single-handed; 一匹布 a length of clothing material; a roll of clothing material (also wr. 疋).

N. Mate, match, equal: 無有其匹 without equal; 勇敢無匹 brave without equal; 匹偶 *-oou*↓.

V.t. To match: 匹敵 *-dir*↓.

Adj. Equal; lone: 匹夫 *-fu*↓.

匹儔 *piichour*, n., equal, a worthy match.

匹敵 *piidir*, n., worthy opponent, good match (in strength).

匹夫 *piifu*, n., an ordinary person, a lone person, everyman: 匹夫匹婦 everyman, common people, person without rank; 天下興

亡, 匹夫有責 everyman is responsible for his country; 匹夫之勇 (derog.) mere physical courage; 匹夫不可奪志 even an ordinary person has his unchangeable ambitions; 匹夫無罪懷璧其罪 (AC) a man's wealth is his own ruin (by causing others' greed).

匹練 *piiliahn*, n., (LL) waterfalls (similar to a stretch of shining silk).

匹鳥 *pir-niauu*, n., (LL) mandarin ducks who always go in pairs.

匹偶 *pir-oou*, n., mate, life mate.

匹配 *piipeih*, n., life mate; equal match.

匹庶 *piishuh*, n., common people.

匹亞 *piiyah*, n. & adj., match, equal.

§51.22 (ㄏ/丨)

髴 51.22

fur.

髣髴 *faangfur*, v.i., it seems to, seems like: 髣髴聽見 seem to hear a voice (var. of 彷ᐞ佛 91B.50).

鬀 51.22

tih.

[Var. 剃 80S.00]

§51.30 (ㄏ/—)

竪 51.30

shuh.

[Pop. for 豎 ↓]

豎 51.30

shuh.

[Pop. 竪↑]

N. (1) (AC) a boy before puberty: 豎子 *-tzyy*↓; 童豎 children under age; boy servant. (2) Eunuch: 豎臣, 豎宦 *-chern*, *-huahn*↓; 內豎 palace eunuch. (3) (-'*l*) The vertical stroke in calligraphy.

Adj. Vertical: 豎立 standing vertically; 橫ᐞ豎 "horizontal or vertical" —either way, see 橫 10B.80.

V.i. & t. To stand up: 毛髮豎起來 (髮豎) one's hair stands up; 豎旗竿 plant flagstaff; 豎碑 set up monument; 豎起脊梁 straighten one's back, i.e., show backbone, self-reliance.

豎臣 *shuhchern*, n., small palace attendants.

豎琴 *shuh-chirn*, n., a harp.

豎褐 *shuh-her*, n., (AC) a servant's coarse jacket (also wr. 短褐).

豎宦 *shuhhuahn*, n., eunuch(s).

豎柱 *shuh-juh*, n., a vertical post.

豎直立 *shuhjyrlih*, v.i., to stand on one's head.

豎立 *shuhlih*, v.i. & t., to stand up; to set up, to plant.

豎儒 *shuhrur*, n., (Hahn Dyn.) contempt. term for petty Confucians.

豎心兒 *shuhshie'l*, n., The 心 radical, wr. "小."

豎子 *shuhtzyy*, n., (LL) children in gen.; also an AC term of abuse, like "young rascal."

豎眼 *shuhyaan*, n., an angry look.

毉 51.30

yi.

[Anc. var. of 醫 51.41]

鑒 51.30

jiahn.

V.t. (1) To discern; (in letter) for s.o.'s perusal: as in 鈞鑒, 台鑒. (2) Var. of 鑑 81A.30.

監 51.30

jian (**jiahn*).

N. (1) A jail, prison: 監獄 *-yuh*, 監牢 *-laur*, 監犯 *-fahn*↓; 收監 throw into prison; 坐監 serve a prison term. (2) (**jiahn*) 太監 a eunuch. (3) (**jiahn*) Formerly, certain government offices: 國子監 the Imperial Academy; 欽天監 the Imperial Observatory. (4) Inspector supervisor: 總監 director general; 學監 a school proctor; 監督 *-du*, 監察 *-char*↓.

V.t. Supervise, 監考, 監試 serve as an examiner; 監票 supervise (-visor) at ballot; 監工 *-gung*↓; 監守自盜 custodian turned thief.

監場 *lianchaang*, v.i. & n., supervise, supervisor at, examination.

監察 *jianchar*, (1) v.t., supervise; (2) n., a supervisor; 監察人 controllers.

監查人 *jiancharrern*, n., inspector.

監察院 *jiancharyuahn*, n., the Control *Yuan*.

監督 *jiandu*, (1) v.t., inspect, supervise; (2) n., an inspector, a supervisor: 海關監督 Superintendent of Customs.

監犯 *jianfahn*, n., a prison convict.

監管 *jianguaan*, v.t., to take charge of.

監工 *jiangung*, v. i. & n., oversee workers, such an overseer.

監國 *jianguor*, n., (1) (AC) the crown prince acting for the king; (2) the Lord Protector during an interregnum; (3) the regent.

監候 *jianhouh*, v. i. & n., formerly, a death sentence not immediately carried out, pending imperial review.

監護 *jianhuh*, v.t., serve as a guardian for (a minor): 監護人 a guardian.

監禁 *jianjihn*, v.t., incarcerate, throw into prison.
監牢 *jianlaur*, n., a cell, a prison, a detention house.
監理 *jianlii*, v.t., to supervise; n., supervisor.
監修 *jianshiou*, v.i., supervise construction; n., such supervisor.
監事 *jianshyh*[1], n., a member of the board of supervisors.
監視 *jianshyh*[2], v.t., keep a close watch over (s.o.), keep an eye on, to shadow (a suspicious character); 監視犯 prisoner under surveillance.
監造 *jiantzauh*, v.t., made under supervision (of bureau, etc.).
監印 *jianyihn*, n., a keeper of the seal.
監獄 *jianyuh*, n., a prison, a jail: 監獄官 a jail warden.

盬 51.30

guu.

[Dist. 鹽]

N. (1) (AC) salt pond. (2) Leisure: 王事靡盬 there was no let-up in the king's affairs.

V.t. (AC) to suck.

鹽 51.30

yarn (**yahn*).

[Abbr. 塩, 圤]

N. Salt: 食鹽, 白鹽 table salt; 瀉鹽 Epsom salt; 官鹽 legal salt which has paid salt duty; 私鹽 smuggled salt; 鹽課, 鹽稅 salt tax.

V.t. (**yahn*) to treat with salt.

鹽池 *yarnchyr*, n., natural deposits of salt.
鹽泉 *yarnchyuarn*, n., brine-spring.
鹽花(兒) *yarnhua('l)*, n., fine grains of salt.
鹽井 *yarnjiing*, n., salt well in Szechuan, worked with derricks.
鹽滷 *yarnluu*, n., salt sediments.
鹽酸 *yarnsuan*, n., (chem.) hydrochloric acid.
鹽灘 *yarn-tan*, n., salt pans.

§51.40 (厂/口)

髫 51.40

tiaur.

[Cogn. 齠]

N. Tufts of hair at front of child's head.

髫齔 *tiaurchehn*, v.i, see 齠[A]齔 21S.40.
髫年 *tiaurniarn*, n., young age.

髻 51.40

jih.

N. A woman's dressed hair, a bun or coil.

§51.41 (厂/区)

瞖 51.41

yih.

[Var. 翳]

N. Cataract (of the eye).

醫 51.41

yi.

[Abbr. 医]

N. A physician: 獸醫 a veterinary, -rian; 醫卜星相 doctors, fortune-tellers and astrologers or their arts.

V.t. To cure (patient, illness): 醫治 *-jyh*↓; 醫好 get cured; 頭痛醫頭, 腳痛醫腳 take stop-gap measures.

醫道 *yidauh*, n., a doctor's knowledge or skill, see *-shuh*↓.
醫方 *yifang*, n., doctor's prescription.
醫館 *yiguaan*, n., hospital; see *-yuahn*↓.
醫家 *yijia*, n., a physician.
醫治 *yijyh*, v.t., to cure (illness, patient).
醫療 *yiliaur*, v.t., ditto.
醫理 *yi-lii*, n., principles or person's understanding of medicine.
醫生 *yisheng*, n., a doctor.
醫術 *yi-shuh*, n., a doctor's art.
醫師 *yi-shy*, n., (court.) a doctor.
醫學 *yishyuer*, n., science of medicine.
醫藥 *yi-yauh*, n., medicine.
醫院 *yiyuahn*, n., hospital.

§51.42 (厂/冈)

腎 51.42

shehn.

N. (1) The kidney (also 內腎); urinary functions or system. (2) The testes (also 外腎): see 腎子 *-tzyy*↓; sexual functions: 腎虧 *-kuei*↓; 補腎 (of med.) restore virility. (3) Gizzard (also wr. 肫): 鴨腎 duck gizzard.

腎 髯 髼 鬍 馬

腎虧 *shehn-kuei*, phr., (1) sexual debility; (2) incontinence of urine (also 腎子虧).
腎門 *shehnmern*, n., (physiol.) hilum of kidney.
腎囊 *shehnnarng*, n., the scrotum.
腎上腺 *shehnshahng-shiahn*, n., suprarenal or adrenal glands.
腎臟 *shehntzahng*, n., the kidney; 腎臟炎 *--yarn*, n., nephritis.
腎子 *shehntzyy*, n., the testicles.
腎盂 *shehnyur*, n., the pelvis.

髯 51.42

rarn.
[Pop. 髥]

N. (1) The whiskers, the beard. (2) A person with bushy whiskers or a long beard: 美髯公 a whiskered (bearded) gentleman; 髯翁 an old man with whiskers (beard).

髯口 *rarn'kou*, n., (Peking opera) an artificial beard worn by an actor.
髯蛇 *rarnsher*, n., a boa constrictor (also 蚺蛇, 蚦蛇).

髼 51.42

perng.

髼鬙 *perngseng*, adj., see *-sung*↓.
髼鬆 *perngsung*, adj., fluffy, (hair); more commonly wr. 蓬鬆.

鬍 51.42

hur.

N. Beard; whiskers.

鬍匪 *hurfeei*, n., (Manchurian) bandits, see *-tz*↓.
鬍鬚 *hurshyu*, n., beard, moustache.
鬍子 *hurtz*, n., (1) (*hur*) (Manchurian) bandits: 大鬍子 ditto; (2) beard, moustache, whiskers: 大鬍子 bushy beard; 八字鬍, 兩撇鬍 moustache extending both sides; 絡腮鬍 whiskers; 連鬢鬍 side whiskers extending to temples; 鬍子拉碴 face covered with beard and whiskers.

§ 51.50 (ㄏ/ㄇ)

馬 51.50

maa.

N. Horse, things that have to do with riding and carriage: 馬鞭 horsewhip; 馬棒 short stick for urging horse; 馬童 stable boy; 馬販 horse dealer; 馬衣 cover for horse; 馬醫 horse doctor, veterinary; 馬棚 shed for horses; 馬兵, 馬隊 cavalry; pertaining to battle: 人仰馬翻 confused fighting on battlefield; 馬革裹屍 terrible battle ("corpses wrapped in horses' hides"); 千軍萬馬 hordes of troops and horses; pertaining to racing: 賽馬, 跑馬; pertaining to journey: 人馬已齊 all vehicles and servants are ready; 車馬 traffic; 車[a]水馬龍 10.10; 馬上 *-shahng*↓; 馬前數 a form of quick divination "while you wait"; 馬到功成 immediate success (upon arrival); 倚馬可待 (of fast talented writer) dash off a piece in no time—("leaning on a horse"); 馬後砲 parting shot, a belated effort; 馬首是瞻 follow one's lead; 馬不停蹄 hurried journey without stop; 馬鬃(鬣) horse's mane; 牛頭馬面 devils in animal forms; 馬生角 an impossibility ("horse grows horn"); 馬齒已長 (fig.) advanced in age; 馬腳, 露出馬腳 show feet of clay, betrayed by a slip (in lies, etc.); 馬耳東風 hear s.t. through one ear and out the other.

馬鞍(子) *maa-an(tz)*, n., saddle.
馬寶 *maabaau*, n., (Chin. med.) a hard growth found inside horses, said to cure epilepsy.
馬棒 *maa-bahng*, n., short stick for urging horse.
馬表(錶) *maa-biaau*, n., a large watch.
馬鞭 *maa-bian*, n., horsewhip.
馬鱉 *maabie*, n., horseleech, see *-jyh*↓.
馬兵 *maabing*, n., cavalry.
馬勃 *maabor*, n., (bot.) a kind of mushroom, *Lycoperdon boviste*, used as medicine.
馬伯六 *maaborliouh*, n., (MC) one who arranges rendezvous for men and women.
馬車 *maache*, n., horse carriage, buggy.
馬前 *maachiarn*[1], adv., posthaste; 馬前卒 foot soldier attendant going before officer.
馬錢 *maa-chiarn*[2], n., formerly, fee for doctor's visit.
馬球 *maa chiour*, n., polo.
馬齒莧 *maachyy-shiahn*, n., (bot.) *Portulaca oleracea*.
馬道 *maa-dauh*, n., bridle path or ground for training horses.
馬吊 *maadiauh*, n., a 16th cen. card game, possibly forerunner of mahjong.
馬兜鈴 *maadoulirng*, n., (bot.) *Aristlochia debilis*.
馬房 *maa-farng*, n., stables.
馬糞紙 *maafehn-jyy*, n., strawboard.
馬蜂 *maafeng*, n., (zoo.) hornet.
馬夫 *maafu*, n., horse buggy driver; stable boy.
馬杆(兒) *maa-gan(-ga'l)*, n., blind man's staff.
馬褂 *maaguah*, n., jacket put on top of gown, sometimes as part of formal dress (長袍馬褂).
馬號 *maahauh*, n., (1) formerly, parking area for horses; (2) cavalry signals.
馬蟥 *maahuarng*, n., horseleech (see *-bie*↑).
馬虎子 *marhuutz*, n., tiger (馬虎子來了) a term used to frighten children (also 麻虎子).
馬掌 *mar-jaang*, n., horse hoof; horseshoe.
馬甲 *marjiaa*, n., (1) armor on horse; (2) (Soochow dial.) vest.
馬蛭 *maajyh*, n., horseleech.

馬克 *maakeh*, n., German currency, mark.
馬克斯 *Maakehsy*, n., Karl Marx; 馬克斯主義 n., Marxism.
馬口鐵 *maakour-tiee*, n., tin.
馬快 *maakuaih*, n., formerly, sheriff's help for catching thieves.
馬拉松 *maalasung*, n., Marathon race.
馬蘭 *maalarn*, n., (bot.) *Aster trinervius*, of aster family.
馬牢子 *maalaurtz*, n., (coll.) stable boy.
馬列主義 *Maa-Lieh Juuyih*, n., Marxism-Leninism.
馬力 *maalih*, n., horsepower (of engines).
馬鈴瓜 *maalirng-gua*, n., (bot.) a long-shaped melon.
馬鈴薯 *maalirng-shuu*, n., potato, also called 洋山芋.
馬陸 *maaluh*[1], n., name of a worm, millipede, *Julus*.
馬路 *maaluh*[2], n., modn. surfaced street in city, avenue.
馬門 *maamern*, n., door in Chin. houseboat, connecting compartment.
馬匹 *maapi*, n., horse.
馬屁精 *maapih-jing*, n., (sl.) lickspittle, toady.
馬上 *maashahng*, adv., (1) at once: 我馬上來 I will come at once; (2) on horseback; (3) phr., (fig.) military rule: 馬上治天下 rule the world by force.
馬哨 *maashauh*, n., formerly, security officer charged with security duties.
馬勺 *maashaur*, n., dipper for serving rice.
馬戲 *maashih*, n., circus.
馬術 *maashuh*, n., circus acts.
馬靴 *maashyuer*, n., riding boots.
馬蹄 *maatir*, n., horse's hoof, things resembling it: 馬蹄表 desk clock; 馬蹄金 *--jin*, n., (1) gold ingot; (2) a kind of lichee tree; 馬蹄兒 *-tier'l*, n., horse-hoof shaped pastry; 馬蹄袖(兒) *--shiouh('l)*, n., a form of sleeve in Manchu Dyn. costume; 馬蹄銀 *--yirn*, n., silver ingot (in form of a horse hoof).
馬桶 *maatuung*, n., night stool.
馬子 *maatz*, n., (1) chips in gambling; (2) *-tuung* ↑.
馬尾蜂 *marweei-feng*, n., (zoo.) a long tailed wasp, *Bracon penetrans*.
馬尾藻 *marweei-tzaau*, n., (bot.) a water weed growing on sea rocks, *Halochloa macrantha*.
馬蠅 *maayirng*, n., (zoo.) a large fly, whose eggs hatch in horses' intestines, *Gastrophilus equina*.

髣 51.50

faang.

髣髴 *faangfur*, it seems like, var. of 彷[A]彿 91B.50.

髩 51.50

bihn.

[Pop. of 鬢 51.80]

翳 51.50

yih.

N. (1) Cataract (in the eye). (2) Pheasant tail fan in anc. dance.

V.i. (AC) wither and die.

翳障 *yihjahn*, n., cataract in eye, any obstruction to vision or understanding.
翳翳 *yihyih*, adv., (AC) darkly.

鬄 51.50

tih.

[Var. of 髢 51.70 wig, cf. 剃 80S.00 to shave]

§51.63 (厂/丶)

熙 51.63

shi.

Adj. (1) Prosperous; bright; broad: 熙朝 prosperous and peaceful reign. (2) Happy: 熙熙笑, 樂熙, 怡 happy, joyful; 熙春 joyful spring. (3) Noisy, restless: 熙熙 *-shi*↓.

熙壤 *shiraang*, adj., restless, see *-shi*↓, also 熙攘.
熙熙 *shishi*, adj., (1) happy, contented; (2) 熙熙壤壤 (攘攘) restless, hustle and bustle about.

黳 51.63

yi.

N. A birthmark.

Adj. Dark, black.

§51.70 (厂/乚)

髢 51.70

tih.

N. (AC) wig, tress of false hair.

髦 51.70

maur.

N. (1) Horse's mane. (2) Children's bangs. (3) Var. of 旄 60S.70.

Adj. Young and talented, fashionable: 髦俊之士 talented scholars; 時髦 fashionable (clothes, etc.).

髦兒戲 *maur'l-shih*, n., formerly, drama played by women.

髭 51.70

tzy.

N. The moustache: 髭鬚 *-shyu* ↓.

Adj. (Of hair) bristling: 髭毛兒 *-maur'l* ↓; 髭髭着 (of hair) unkempt, ruffled.

髭毛兒 *tzymaur'l*, adj., furious with anger: 他聽了這句話, 當時就髭毛兒 on hearing the remark, he got furious ("bristled up").
髭鬚 *tzyshyu*, n., moustache and beard.

鬈 51.70

chyuarn.

N. & adj. Curling hair, a curl of hair; curling.

鬣 51.70

lieh.

N. Horse's mane; fish's fin; pine burr; bird's crest; snake's scales; tuft of broomstick; (AC) human beard.

鬣狗 *liehgoou*, n., the hyena.

髡 51.70

kun.

[Pop. 髨]

V.t. To shave off hair; lop off tree leaves: 留髡 (allu.) singsong girl asks guest to stay for the night (allu. 髡 a personal name).

覽 51.70

laan.

[Pop. 覧]

V.t. Take a look at, watch, inspect, read, display: 觀覽 watch with interest; 遊覽 sight-seeing; 覽勝 *-shehng* ↓; 覽古 visit historic places; 展覽 exhibit (of fashions, art, etc.); 閱覽(室) read, a reading room in a public library; 一覽無餘 take in everything at one glance; 博覽(羣書) widely read; 覽視 inspect; 覽悉 (of letters, documents, etc.) read and learn.

覽揆 *laankueir*, n. & v.i., (AC) birthday, be born.
覽勝 *laan-shehng*, v.t., visit scenic spots.

§ 51.72 (ㄏ/心)

慝 51.72

teh.

N. & adj. Wicked, -ness: 邪慝 wickedness; 讒慝 sycophant, -cy; flatterer, also wicked person.

§ 51.80 (ㄏ/八)

賢 51.80

shiarn.

N. A sage, a wise man: 聖賢, 往聖先賢 the sages of the past; 大賢 a great man, usu. referring to the past; 見賢思齊 see a wise, good man and try to emulate him; 讓賢, 讓賢路 give way to the good men in government administration: 選賢與能 (AC) appoint the good men and able men to office.

Adj. (1) Good and wise (as a concept like Eng. "wise" combining moral and intellectual qualities, as in 賢惠(慧) *-hueih* ↓): 賢不肖 the good and bad (sons, persons); 賢人, 賢良, 賢德 *-rern, -liarng, -der* ↓. (2) (Court.) your, your good (husband, etc.), also vocatively, my good (husband, etc.): 賢兄 your elder brother, also used like "my good friend"; 賢弟 your younger brother, also used by teacher or elder in addressing pupil or one younger; 賢甥 your nephew, my good nephew; same with 姊, 妹, 婿, 妻 elder sister, younger sister, son-in-law, wife; 賢荆 (court.) your or my dear wife; 賢昆仲 your brothers; 賢內助 your good wife; 賢妻良母 understanding wife and loving mother; 賢郎 (vocative) younger person, son-in-law; 賢阮 nephew (allu. 阮咸, 阮籍 uncle and nephew both distinguished).

賢倩 *shiarnchiahn*, n., (vocative) son-in-law.
賢契 *shiarnchih*, n., (vocative) pupil, also nephew.
賢達 *shiarndar*, adj. & n., wise and honored; such person.
賢德 *shiarnder*, adj. & n., virtuous; virtue.
賢惠 *shiarn'hueih*, adj., (also wr. 賢慧) (of wife) good and wise: 他的媳婦很賢惠 his wife is

capable and good.

賢者 *shiarnjee*, n., see *-rern*↓; as in 賢者多勞 (court.) a good man is always wanted for every thing.

賢哲 *shiarnjer*, n., good and wise teachers of the past.

賢良 *shiarnliarng*, n. & adj, good men; good and virtuous: 賢良方正 good and able men promoted by selection and recommendation in Hahn Dyn.

賢明 *shiarnmirng*, adj., wise (administrator), enlightened (ruler).

賢能 *shiarnnerng*, adj., able and good.

賢人 *shiarnrern*, n., good and wise man.

賢淑 *shiarnshur*, adj., (of woman) good and refined.

賢士 *shiarn-shyh*, n., distinguished men; (Budd.) a teacher living at home.

賢才 *shiarn-tsair*, n., bright talent of a nation.

賢彥 *shiarn-yahn*, n., the distinguished men.

鬒 51.80

jeen.

Adj. (AC) black and beautiful (hair).

鬚 51.80

shyu.

N. (1) Beard, moustache: 鬍鬚 beard; 鬚髯如戟 prickly moustache; 留鬚 grow a beard; 撚鬚 stroke one's own beard in peace and satisfaction. (2) Feelers (of lobster, crab, rat, etc). (3) Pistil of flowers: spike of certain plants (wheat, etc.).

鬚兒 *shyue'l*, n., tassel-like formations; frayed ends.

鬚根 *shyugen*, n., fibrous roots.

鬚眉 *shyumeir*, n., as in 鬚眉男子 manly man ("bearded").

鬚生 *shyusheng*, n., (Chin. opera) actor wearing beard.

鬚子 *shyutz*, n., see *-e'l*↑.

鬢 51.80

bihn.

[Pop. 鬂]

N. (1) Temples, hair on temples: 銀鬢 silver-grey temples; 白鬢 white hair on the temples. (2) Generally of hair: 雲鬢 woman's hair-do: 鬢亂釵橫 phr., of woman's intimate appearance after sleep and before make-up.

鬢角 *bihnjiaau* (*-jyuer*), n., hair just below the temple; this region, also wr. 鬢腳.

§51.82 (厂/乂)

髮 51.82

faa.

N. (1) Hair on head (cf. 毛 90.70): usu. 頭髮; 毛髮 hair in gen.; 假髮 wig, false hair; 石髮, 苔髮 mosses; 金髮碧眼 blonde; 落髮爲尼, 削髮爲僧 shave one's head and be a nun, monk; 披髮佯狂 wear shaggy hair and feign madness; 束髮 tie hair up on top of head, formerly, on boy reaching puberty; 髮短心長 (AC) old in age but vigorous in mind, spec. still planning things. (2) One thousandth part of one Chin. inch.

髮妻 *faachi*, n., first wife, from 結髮夫妻 betrothed and married when both were young.

髮匪 *farfeei*, n., rebel army of Taiping Rebellion (1850–1864), so named because the rebels wore long hair, instead of Manchu imposed queue.

髮膏 *faagau*, n., hair cream.

髮針 *faajen*, n., hairpin.

髮夾 *faajiar*, n., hairpin.

髮晶 *faajing*, n., hair-like crystals of quartz.

髮指 *far-jyu*, phr., 令人髮指 make one's hair stand up in great anger.

髮小兒 *farshiaau'l*, n., childhood friend.

髮型 *faashing*, n., hair style.

髮菜 *faatsaih*, n., an edible moss of long thin threads.

髮網 *farwaang*, n., hair net.

鬘 51.82

marn.

Adj. Beautiful, long (hair); 鬘華 Budd. term for jasmin.

§51.83 (厂/〜)

迓 51.83

yah.

V.t. (LL) to welcome formally (bride, etc.): 迎迓 ditto.

§51.93 (厂/く)

鬆 51.93

sung.

賢 鬒 鬚 鬢 髮 鬘 迓 鬆

亅	小	卜	十	土	ナ	廾	ㅏ	丨	一	丁	フ	口	区	冈	冂	厂	尸	亠	广	宀	丶	乚	七	心	八	人	乂	〜	一	ノ	𠂉	く
00	01	02	10	11	12	20	21	22	30	31	32	40	41	42	50	51	52	60	61	62	63	70	71	72	80	81	82	83	90	91	92	93

鬆 蠶 厨 辱 厨

N. Shredded dried meat: 肉鬆, 魚鬆, 鷄鬆 dried shredded pork, fish, chicken.

V.t. To relax: 放鬆 go easy on rules, restrictions, debt payments, etc.; 鬆口, 鬆手 *-koou*, *-shoou* ↓; 鬆一口氣 draw a deep breath in relief; 鬆綁 untie (a bound person).

Adj. (1) Loose, fluffy: 蓬鬆 fluffy (hair); 鞋帶鬆了 shoelace gets loose; 鬆脆 *-tsueih* ↓. (2) Lax, relaxed: 輕鬆 relaxed (spirit, style of writing); 鬆懈, 鬆勁 *-shieh*, *-jihn* ↓; 管理太鬆 regulations are lax, too easy-going.

鬆動 *sungduhng*, adj., ample, not tight (in money), allowing some movement.
鬆泛 *sung'fan*, adj., (MC) lax, easy-going.
鬆勁(兒) *sungjihn(-jieh'l)*, v.i., of relax hold on s.t.
鬆緊 *sung-jiin*, n., degree of tightness, flexibility, elasticity; 鬆緊帶 elastic band.
鬆口 *sung-koou*, v.i., to relax a bite; also to show degree of flexibility in negotiations, lessen hardness.
鬆快 *sungkuaih*, adj., relaxed and refreshing.
鬆軟 *sungruaan*, adj., soft and fluffy.
鬆散 *sungsaan (-'san)*, adj., loose, not compact.
鬆懈 *sungshieh*, v.i., to take things easy, to idle on job.
鬆心 *sung-shin*, adj., feeling relaxed, opp. 揪心 tense.
鬆手 *sung-shoou*, v.i., to let go, to ease off on hold.
鬆脆 *sungtsueih*, adj., light, crisp (pastry).
鬆通 *sung'tung*, adj., see *-duhng* ↑.
鬆嘴 *sung-tzueei*, v.i., see *-koou* ↑.

蠶 51.93

tsarn.

[Pop. 蚕; var. 蠺]

N. Silkworm: 養蠶 sericulture.

蠶箔 *tsarnbor*, n., reed mat for silkworm culture (also 蠶薄).
蠶蛆 *tsarnchyu*, n., an insect which destroys mulberry leaves.
蠶豆 *tsarndouh*, n., broad beans.
蠶蛾 *tsarner*, n., silkworm moth.
蠶工 *tsarngung*, n., the culture of silkworms.
蠶繭(兒) *tsarnjiaan (-jiaa'l)*, n., cocoon.
蠶忌 *tsarn-jih*, n., things to avoid in raising silkworms.
蠶連 *tsarnliarn*, n., paper on which silkworm lays its eggs.
蠶眠 *tsarnmiarn*, v.i., (of silkworms) to hibernate.
蠶蓐 *tsarnruh*, n., grass mats for raising silkworms.
蠶桑 *tsarnsang*, n., the sericulture industry.
蠶沙 *tsarnsha*, n., dung of silkworms.
蠶山 *tearn-shan*, n., frame for silkworms to weave cocoons on.
蠶事 *tsarn-shyh*[1], n., sericulture industry.
蠶室 *tsarn-shyh*[2], n., (1) house where silkworms are kept; (2) formerly, locked basement where castration was performed and where those operated upon remained during recuperation.
蠶食 *tsarnshyr*, v.t., to nibble at neighbor's territory.
蠶蔟 *tsarntsuh*, n., see *-shan* ↑.
蠶子 *tsarntzyy*, n., silkworms' eggs.
蠶蟻 *tsarnyii*, n., newly hatched silkworms.
蠶月 *tsarnyueh*, n., the 4th lunar month, the silkworm season.
蠶蛹 *tsarnyuung*, n., chrysalis of silkworm.

SECTION 51A

§ 51A.00 (ㄏ/ㄐ)

厨 51A.00–1

chur.

[Pop. of 廚 61.00]

辱 51A.00–3

ruh (also *ruu*).

V. t. To abuse, insult, humiliate: 侮辱 to insult, vilify; 欺辱 humiliate, put to shame, snub; 辱罵 *-mah* ↓.

Adj. Shameful, disgraceful: 恥辱 dishonorable, infamous, shameful; 羞辱 ditto.

Adv. (Court.) condescendingly: 辱承 *-cherng* ↓; 辱臨 *-lirn* ↓.

辱承 *ruhcherng*, phr., you are (have been) so good as to . . . .
辱荷 *ruhheh*, phr., (=辱承 *-cherng* ↑).
辱臨 *ruhlirn*, phr., you are (have been) so kind as to come.
辱罵 *ruh-mah*, v. t., scold and humiliate.
辱命 *ruh-mihng*, v. i., (1) fail in one's mission; (2) be honored by a royal order.
辱沒 *ruhmoh*, v. t., humiliate, disgrace, put to shame.
辱游 *ruhyour*, v. i., (MC) be so kind as to befriend me.

厨 51A.00–3

chur.

[Pop. of 廚 61.00]

厚 擘 厠 原

厚 51A.00-4

houh.

Adj. & adv. (1) Thick (board, volume): 厚薄 *-bor* ↓; 臉皮厚 thick-skinned, unashamed. (2) Kind, great, generous, cordial: 民風淳厚 the people are honest and warmhearted; 忠厚 simple and honest; 厚德, 厚恩 great kindness, kind favors; 隆情厚誼, 厚意 (court. of friend's hospitality) your great cordiality, hospitality; 厚酬, 厚報, 厚賞 liberal recompense; 厚待 *-daih* ↓.

Adv. Greatly: 厚望 greatly hope; a great hope; 厚誣 a great slander.

厚薄(兒) *houhbor('l)* (sp. pr. *-baur*), n., thickness, degree of closeness of relations.

厚待 *houhdaih*, v.t., to treat royally, courteously.

厚道 *houh'dau*, adj., honest and kind, generous, kindhearted.

厚度 *houhduh*, n., (degree of) thickness.

厚敦兒 *houhduu'l*, n., a material thickness.

厚重 *houhjuhng*, adj., (of comportment) decorous, goodmannered.

厚臉 *houhliaan*, adj., brazen-faced, shameless.

厚皮香 *houhpirshiang*, n., see *-poh* ↓.

厚朴 *houhpoh*, n., (Chin. med.) bark of magnolia.

厚生 *houh-sheng*, phr., (AC, LL) that all living things may multiply and live in comfort.

厚實 *houhshyr*, adj., thick and solid.

厚顔 *houh-yarn*, adj., see *-liaan* ↑.

擘 51A.00-4

yeh.

[Var. 擫]

V. t. To press down with a finger.

厠 51A.00-4

tsyh (also *tseh*).

[Pop. of 廁 61.00]

§51A.01 (厂/小)

原 51A.01-9

yuarn.

N. (1) A plain, plateau: 平原 flat stretch of land; 高原 plateau; 原野, 原隰 *-yee*, *-shir* ↓; 中原; main part of China; 九原 cemetery, Hades. (2) Origin, source, beginnings (related 源 63A.01), cause: 原本, 原因 *-been*, *-yin*[1] ↓; 本原 origin; 推原 trace the cause; 溯本追原(源) trace to the beginnings. (3) A surname.

V.i. & t. (1) To have its beginning or cause: 原於 start from (s.t.). (2) To pardon: 原諒, 原宥 *-liahng*, *-youh* ↓; 情有可原 it is understandable, excusable.

Adj. Original: 原裝, 原封 original package; 原封不動 keep intact, untouched; 原形, 原狀 original shape; 原本 original copy; 原處 original place; 原任, 原職 original post before transfer; 原址 original address, etc.

Adv. (1) In fact, as a matter of fact, in the first place: 原來 *-lair* ↓; 原不該 as a matter of fact, one should not (in the first place); 原不曾 one never did or had. (2) Originally: 原是, 原係 originally was; 原訂 originally set date at.

原本 *yuarnbeen*, (1) n., origin, cause; (2) adv., originally.

原起 *yuarnchii*, (1) n., origin (of events); (2) originally: 原起由他辦 it was originally his task.

原權 *yuarn-chyuarn*, n., (law) primary or antecedent right.

原點 *yuarndiaan*, n., (math.) origin, point of origin.

原底(子) *yuarndii(tz)*, n., original draft.

原動機 *yuarnduhn-ji*, n., (mechanics) prime mover, original generator of force.

原動力 *yuarnduhng-lih*, n., (1) original force or power; (2) source of power (as water, heat, etc.).

原稿(兒) *yuarngaau('l)*, n., (original) draft of manuscript.

原告(兒) *yuarngauh('l)*, n., the plaintiff.

原根兒 *yuarnge('l)*, n., original intention.

原故 *yuarnguh*, n., cause, reason (also 緣故).

原價 *yuarn-jiah*, n., (1) (commercial) cost, costing price; (2) original price.

原舊(兒) *yuarnjiouh('l)*, adj. & adv., as usual.

原籍 *yuarn-jir*, n., original nativity of person.

原主(兒) *yuarn-juu('l)*, n., original owner.

原質 *yuarnjyr*, n., (chem.) element, see *-suh* ↓.

原來 *yuarnlair*, adv., (1) as a matter of fact, in the first place: 原來如此 so it is; (2) originally, see Adv. ↑; 原來頭 *--tour*, n., article or goods which have not altered, as from factory.

原諒 *yuarnliahng*, v.t., understand and pardon: 不可原諒 unpardonable.

原料 *yuarnliauh*, n., raw material.

原理 *yuarnlii*, n., principle (of change, motion, light, etc.).

原煤 *yuarn-meir*, n., mixture of bits of coal (also called 混煤).

原棉 *yuarn-miarn*, n., raw cotton.

原配 *yuarnpeih*, n., first wife (also wr. 元配).

原人 *yuarn-rern*, n., primitive man.

原色 *yuarn-seh*, n., basic color.

原先 *yuarnshian*, adv., originally, at first.

原隰 *yuarn-shir*, n., (AC) plateau and low grounds.

原形 *yuarn-shirng*[1], n., original

亅	小	⺊	十	土	ナ	卄	ㄴ	丨	一	丁	㇇	口	囗	冂	㇆	厂	尸	亠	广	宀	丶	乚	弋	心	八	人	乂	一	㇀	丿	㇐	く
00	01	02	10	11	12	20	21	22	30	31	32	40	41	42	50	51	52	60	61	62	63	70	71	72	80	81	82	83	90	91	92	93

shape; 原形質 --*jyr*, n., protoplasm; 原形體 --*tii*, n., (bot.) plasmodium.

原 型 *yuarnshirng²*, n., model; prototype.

原始 *yuarnshyy*, n., origin (of things), the primitive beginnings; 原始人 primitive man, prehistoric man. 「ment.

原素 *yuarnsuh*, n., (chem.) ele-

原則 *yuarntzer*, n., principle(s) of (management, organization, politics, etc.): 原則上 in principle (agree, etc.).

原子 *yuarntzyy*, n., (chem.) atom; 原子能 atomic power; 原子筆 ball pen; 原子彈 atomic bomb; 原子核 atomic nucleus; 原子論 atomic theory; 原子價 valence of atoms; 原子量 atomic weight; 原子輻射 atomic radiation; 原子武器 atomic weapons; 原子塵 nuclear fallout; 原子爐 nuclear reactor; 原子粒 (dial.) transistor.

原委 *yuarnweei*, n., origin and development; complex reasons: 説明原委 explain why and how.

原文(兒) *yuarnwern(-wer'l)*, n., original text. 「cle.

原物 *yuarn-wuh*, n., original arti-

原野 *yuarnyee*, n., the prairie, primitive valley. 「tion.

原意 *yuarn-yih*, n., original inten-

原因 *yuarnyin¹*, n., cause.

原音 *yuarnyin²*, n., high fidelity (Hi Fi).

原宥 *yuarnyouh*, v.t., to pardon.

原由 *yuarnyour*, n., reason(s) for things.

原韻 *yuarn-yuhn*, n., rhyme-class of friend's poem, which is applied in poem in reply (see 和 *heh*, 90A.40).

§ 51A.02 (厂/ k)

辰 51A.02–3

chern.

N. (1) A unit of the duodecimal cycle, see Appendix A. (2) 星辰 the stars: 日月星辰 the sun, the moon and the stars. (3) Time: 時辰 the hour or two-hour period; 辰時 the period 7–9 a.m.; 良辰 (佳日) a beautiful day; 生辰 day and hour of birth; 誕辰, 壽辰 birthday; 我生不辰, 生不逢辰 (AC) I was born unlucky (i.e., at wrong hour).

辰告 *chern-gauh*, v.t., (AC) to make a public admonition.

辰勾 *chern-gou*, n., the planet Mercury: 似等辰勾 like watching for Mercury—s.t. difficult to see. 「dial.) time.

辰光 *chernguang*, n., (Shanghai

辰旒 *chern-liour*, n., a flag with painting of the sun, moon and planets on it.

辰砂 *chern-sha*, n., a mineral red pigment produced at 辰州.

饜 51A.02–4

yahn.

Adj. Satiated: 饜足 more than satisfy; overabundant: 貪求無饜 greedy without stop, never satisfied.

§ 51A.10 (厂/十)

解 51A.10–9

jieh.

[Pop. of 廨 61.10]

§ 51A.11 (厂/土)

厓 51A.11–1

yair.

N. (AC) (1) U. f. 崖 cliff. (2) U. f. 涯 river bank. (3) U. f. 睚 41B.11.

厘 51A.11–2

jiin.

[Pop. of 廑 61.11]

壓 51A.11–4

ya.

[Abbr. 压]

N. Pressure: 氣壓 air pressure; 血壓 blood pressure; 水壓 water pressure, cf. 壓力 -*lih* ↓.

V. t. (1) To press down, (fig.) suppress by force: 壓下去 press down; 壓倒 -*daau* ↓; 壓住 -*juh* ↓; 壓得住, 壓不住 -*'der-juh*, -*'bur-juh* ↓; 壓驚 -*jing* ↓; 壓迫, 壓伏 (壓服) -*poh*, -*'fur* ↓; 高壓政策 highhanded policy, policy of force; 鎮壓, 彈壓 to squelch riot, rebellion; 壓氣兒 -*chieh'l* ↓. (2) To crush, flatten: 壓扁, 壓平 to flatten; 壓破, 壓碎 crush to pieces; 壓實 press solid; 壓緊 compress tightly; 壓塌 collapse under pressure. (3) To pile up, come near: 壓肩疊背 of a huge crowd standing shoulder to shoulder; 壓山兒 (the sun) is setting near the horizon; 壓境 (of army) threaten the border. (4) To rank first, to supervise from behind: 壓倒一切 excel all the rest in examinations; 壓卷 -*jyuahn* ↓; 壓隊 -*dueih* ↓; 壓寨夫人 see -*jaih* ↓; 壓陣 to stabilize battle formation; 壓後 to act as rear guard. (5) To shelve, delay answering: 這件案子先壓幾天 shelve this case for a few days. (6) (Callig.) press brush from the right with index finger.

壓寶 *ya-baau*, n., a gambling or guessing game; orig. with a coin (寶) under a bowl, now played with dice.

壓不住 *ya'bur-juh*, v.i., (1) cannot keep under control; (2) unworthy to bear the honor or responsibility; see *-'der-juh*↓.

壓車 *ya-che*, v. i., to go with cart personally as a supervisor during transportation (also wr. 押).

壓氣兒 *ya-chieh'l*, v. i., to calm down anger.

壓倒 *ya-daau*, v. t., to excel (competitors) in literature and contests; v. i., be crushed down, overwhelming victory.

壓得住 *ya'der-juh*, v.i., be able to undertake task or responsibility; can keep down (anger, etc.).

壓隊 *ya-dueih*, v. i., to bring up the rear and supervise.

壓伏(服) *ya'fur*, v. t., to vanquish, to subdue by force.

壓根兒 *ya-ge'l*, adv., (Peking coll. also *yah-*) in the first place, to start with (did not like study, etc.).

壓搾 *yajah*, v. t., to crush by weight: 壓搾機 n., compressor.

壓寨 *ya-jaih*, phr., 壓寨夫人 bandit chief's wife.

壓鎮 *yajehn*, v. t., to suppress (also 鎮壓).

壓驚 *yajing*, v. i., (med.) to becalm nerves after a shock.

壓冑子 *ya-jouhtz*, n., (Chin. theater) next to last play on program (also wr. 壓軸子): 壓軸好戲 (lit. & fig.) best show.

壓住 *yajuh*, v.t., to suppress, keep down by force.

壓桌 *ya-juo*, n., (1) *hors d'oeuvres*; (2) (facet.) person last to leave table.

壓制 *yajyh*, v. t., to suppress.

壓卷 *ya-jyuahn*, n., the top-ranking examination paper.

壓力 *yalih*, n., force of pressure; 壓力衣 pressure suit (astron.); 壓力表 manometor, pressure gauge.

壓派 *ya'pai*, v. t., (coll.) to blame (others).

壓迫 *yapoh*, v. t., to oppress (workers, weak country, etc.).

壓綫 *ya-shiahn*, v. i., (LL allu.) be kept busy on other's account, (like a seamstress making gold braids for other's wedding dress).

壓碎 *ya-sueih*[1], v. t., to crush to pieces.

壓歲 *ya-sueih*[2], v. i., to give New Year gift to children as token wish for a good year: 壓歲錢.

壓縮性 *yasuo-shihng*, n., (phys.) compressibility.

壓子息 *ya-tzshir*, phr., to adopt child from another clan in the hope that it may lead to birth of one's own child.

壓載 *ya-tzaih*, n., ship's ballast.

壓尾 *ya-weei*, v. i., to stand last (also wr. 押).

壓抑 *yayih*, v. t., to suppress, keep down.

壓韻 *ya-yuhn*, v. i., see 押^Δ韻 10A.22.

雁 51A.11-9

yahn.

[Interch. 鴈]

N. Wild geese, crane, stork: 秋雁 geese in autumn; 雁陣 geese flying in formation; 雁行, 雁序 *-harng*, *-shyuh*↓; 雁字 line of flying geese resembling the characters 人 and 一.

雁齒 *yahn-chyy*, phr., a neat formation like flying geese.

雁行 *yahnharng*, n., geese flying in formation: used as symbol of orderly life of brothers: 雁行折翼 death of a brother.

雁戶 *yahnhuh*, n., (AC) homeless, wandering person, persons without a settled home.

雁來紅 *yahnlairhurng*, n., (bot.) *Amaranthus gangeticus*.

雁皮 *yahnpir*, n., (bot.) *Wikstraemia sikokianum*, a plant whose fiber can be made into paper.

雁序 *yahnshyuh*, n., see *-harng*↑.

雁堂 *yahntarng*, n., ancient term for Buddhist hall.

雁足 *yahntzur*, phr., (LL) messenger of letter (similar to carrier pigeon).

§ 51A.22 (厂/丨)

厮 51A.22-2

sy.

[Var. of 廝 61.22]

厅 51A.22-4

ting.

[Abbr. of 廳 61.72]

§ 51A.30 (厂/一)

歷 51A.30-9

lih.

N. What has taken place: 閱歷 experience; 經歷 what one has passed through; 履歷 biographical data; 來歷 background history, origins: 來歷不明 (of persons) of dubious origins, (of things) of questionable background.

V. i. & t. (1) To pass through (periods, place), to experience: 歷盡辛苦 gone through many hardships; 遍歷各地 passed through different places; 遊歷各國 travel through many countries. (2) Overstep: 不歷位而相與言 (AC) do not step beyond one's assigned position to speak to another; 歷任 served successively as.

Adj. Past, successive: 歷年, 歷屆 in the past successive years, sessions; 歷朝, 歷代 in the past dynasties, generations.

Adv. All through, all over, one by

歷 唇 厝 靨 曆 厲

one, in detail: 歷覩 cast a glance all over; 歷經 to witness or experience successively; 歷覽名山大川 visit all the renowned mountains and great rivers; 歷述 describe in detail; 歷陳 give an account of (s. t.) in detail.

歷朝 *lih-chaur*, n., successive dynasties.

歷程 *lihcherng*, n., a process a thing passes through.

歷代 *lih-daih*, adj. & n., (in the) past generations.

歷屆 *lih-jieh*, n., successive batches: 歷屆畢業生 successive batches of graduates; 歷屆大會 conferences of succesive years.

歷劫 *lihjier*, v. t., pass through one crisis after another; through eons of time.

歷久 *lihjiour*, (1) v.i., to last long; (2) adv., through or for many years: 歷久不衰 no slackening of effort with the passage of time.

歷來 *lihlair*, adv., in times gone by; since the earliest days.

歷練 *lih'lian*, n., experience and training.

歷歷 *lihlih*, adj. & adv., clear(ly), distinct(ly).

歷亂 *lihluahn*, adj., confused, mixed up, untidy, slovenly.

歷落 *lihluoh*, adj., (1) frank, candid; (2) arranged in no particular order, fouled up; (3) (of sounds) ceaseless.

歷年 *lihn-niarn*, adv., in the past years.

歷史 *lihshyy*, n., history; 歷史性 adj., historic.

§51A.40 (厂/口)

唇 51A.40-3

churn.

[Pop. 脣 51A.42]

N. Lips: 嘴唇 ditto: 唇亡齒寒 phr., teeth are exposed when lips are gone—interdependence of neighboring states (see also 脣 51A.42); 反唇相稽 bicker with each other.

§51A.41 (厂/図)

厝 51A.41-2

tsuoh.

V. t. To put under shelter: 厝身 to find a shelter for oneself; 厝棺 to put away coffin in some place, hut, temple, pending removal to homeland for burial.

靨 51A.41-4

yeh.

N. A dimple.

靨鈿 *yehdiahn*, n., (AC) woman's decoration on cheek.

靨輔 *yehfuu*, n., (AC) dimpled cheek.

靨子 *yehtz*, n., birthmark on cheek.

靨靨 *yeh-yeh*, adj., (MC) twinkling (stars).

曆 51A.41-9

lih.

[Dist. 歷 51A.30]

N. The calendar: 曆法 *-faa*↓; 日曆 the solar or Gregorian calendar; 月曆, 農曆 the lunar calendar; 曆書 *-shu*↓; 推曆觀象 observe the stars and calculate calendar.

曆本 *lihbeen*, n., see *-shu*↓.

曆法 *lihfaa*, n., system of determining the beginning, length, and divisions of a year.

曆書 *lihshu*, n., an old-fashioned calendar with full horoscopic details, an almanac.

曆數 *lihshuh*, n., (1) predestined length of dynasty; (2) time of the year.

曆頭 *lihtour*, n., (1) the beginning of the almanac, the new year; (2) the almanac.

曆尾 *lihweei*, n., the end of the almanac, year-end.

§51A.42 (厂/冈)

厲 51A.42-2

lih.

N. (1) (Var. of 礪) a whetstone. (2) Pestilence, an epidemic disease. (3) Malicious ghost: 爲厲 or 厲鬼 ghost which haunts or harasses human beings. (4) A surname.

V. t. (1) Sharpen, grind, whet: 秣馬厲兵 make army combat-ready. (2) Oppress: 厲民 oppress the people. (3) Encourage: 以厲賢材 (AC var. of 勵) in order to encourage real talent.

Adj. & adv. (1) Stern(ly), grim(ly), strict(ly): 嚴厲 severe (rules, etc.); 厲聲 harsh voice; 厲色 harsh countenance; 厲禁 severe restrictions; 厲行禁令 carry out law strictly; 變本加厲 getting more and more objectionable. (2) Wicked(ly), fierce(ly), terribl(e)y: 厲鬼 malicious ghost.

厲害 *lih'hai*, (1) adj., severe, terrible, efficient and cruel: 這人厲害極了 the man is merciless; 好厲害 how terrible, how cruel! (2) adv., very, intensely: 餓得厲害 unbearably hungry; 痛得厲害 terribly painful.

厲階 *lihjie*, n., (AC) the source of future trouble.

脣 51A.42-3

churn.
[Pop. var. 唇]

N. The lip(s): 脣亡齒寒 (AC) with bared lips, the teeth feel cold—interdependence of neighboring states; 脣齒, 脣舌 *-chyy, -sher* ↓: 酒不沾脣 never touch wine ("wet lips" with wine); 脣乾口燥 (talk until) lips are dry and mouth is parched; 缺脣 harelipped.

脣齒 *churn-chyy,* n., 脣齒相依 close interdependence.
脣脂 *churnjy,* n., (LL) lipstick, rouge (modn. 口紅).
脣舌 *churn-sher,* n., (1) dispute; (2) prattle: 大費脣舌 takes a lot of talking (to convince).

§ 51A.50 (厂/ㄱ)

厉 51A.50-3

lih.
[Abbr. 厲 51A.42]

鴈 51A.50-9

yahn.
[Var. of 雁 51A.11]

§ 51A.63 (厂/丶)

黶 51A.63-4

yaan.

N. (LL) a blackhead.

§ 51A.70 (厂/乚)

厐 51A.70-1

parng (marng).
[Var. of 龐, 尨]

Adj. Deep, extensive.

魘 51A.70-4

yaan.

N. A nightmare: 夢魘 ditto.

魘魅 *yaanmeih,* n., phantoms, apparitions conjured up by sorcerer to unnerve victim.

厄 51A.70-5

eh.

Adj. Adversity: 困厄 distress; 危厄 crisis.

厄難 *ehnahn,* n., adversity, disaster.
厄閏 *ehruhn,* n., (AC) bad times.
厄運 *ehyuhn,* n., bad luck.

龎 51A.70-6

parng.
[Pop. of 龐 61.70]

§ 51A.72 (厂/心)

廰 51A.72-3

ting.
[Pop. of 廳 61.72]

愿 51A.72-9

yuahn.

Adj. Cautious in conduct: 謹愿 ditto; 鄉愿 (AC) hypocrite.

§ 51A.80 (厂/八)

贋 51A.80-9

yahn.

Adj. Fake, imitation, not genuine: 贋本 a forged copy or version; 贋品 imitation articles; 贋鼎 (AC allu.) an imitation article; 贋幣 counterfeit money.

§ 51A.81 (厂/人)

厭 51A.81-4

*yahn (*yan).*

V.i. & t. (1) To loathe, be tired of: 厭惡, 厭煩, 厭棄 *-wuh*[1], *-'fan, -chih* ↓; 可厭 detestable; 討厭, 惹厭 disgusting; 喜新厭舊 tired of the old and fascinated by the new (lover, etc.). (2) (AC) u.f. 饜 satiated. (3) (*yan) See 厭厭 -yan↓.

厭氣 *yahn'chi*, adj., disgusting.
厭棄 *yahnchih*, v.t., to abandon (lover), spurn (old doctrines).
厭煩 *yahn'fan*, (1) v.i. & t., to feel annoyed; (2) adj., annoying.
厭恨 *yahnhehn*, v.t., to loathe, hate, dislike heartily.
厭倦 *yahnjyuahn*, (1) adj., tired, fatigued; (2) v. i., grow tired of.
厭世 *yahn-shyh*, adj., cynical, tired of living; 厭世主義 cynicism.
厭食 *yahnshyr*, n., (anorexia) lack of appetite.
厭惡 *yahnwuh*[1] (-'*wu*), v.t., to loathe.
厭物 *yahnwuh*[2], n., (LL) a disgusting, abominable thing.
厭厭 **yanyan*, adj., (AC) (a) relaxed; (b) thriving (vegetation).

厥 51A.81-8

jyuer.

Pron. (AC) its, his (her), their: 厥後 thereafter, later on; 厥初 at first; 厥終 finally, in the end; 厥等 things of that sort; 厥功甚偉 great are his services to the country; 厥疾不瘳 his disease is incurable.

V. i. To faint off: 昏厥.

厥角 *jyuerjyuer*, v. i., (AC) to kowtow.

仄 51A.81-8

tzeh.

N. 仄聲 The second, third, and fourth tones of a character (opp. 平聲 the first tone): 仄韻 poems rhyming with such characters; 平仄 versification with the use of characters of different tones according to certain generally recognized rules (serving as verse rhythm as "accent" in Eng. verse)—uneven tone.

Adj. (1) (Interch. 側) slanting, leaning: 仄日 the setting sun; 傾仄 leaning to one side; 仄聞 learn by hearsay. (2) Narrow: 仄徑 a bypath, side-path; 狹仄 (of space) narrow and small, (of person) narrow-minded, bigoted.

灰 51A.81-9

huei.

[Pop. of 灰 12.81]

§ 51A.82 (厂/乂)

廠 51A.82-2

chaang.

[Pop. of 廠 61.82]

厦 51A.82-3

shiah.

[Pop. of 廈 61.82]

§ 51A.91 (厂/丿)

厂 51A.91-5

an.

[Abbr. of 庵; index No. 51A]

§ 51A.93 (厂/く)

蜃 51A.93-3

shehn.

N. A big clam; clams in gen.

蜃氣 *shehnchih*, n., mirage.
蜃樓 *shehnlour*, n., ditto: 海市蜃樓 image of towns and markets in mirage.
蜃市 *shehnshyh*, n., ditto.

SECTION 51B

§ 51B.00 (馬/亅)

騎 51B.00–1

chir (**jih*).

N. (1) Horse, esp. cavalry horse. (2) (**jih*) Cavalry: 鐵騎 a brave war horse; 飛騎 flying cavalry, air-borne cavalry; 善騎 a good rider.

V.i. & t. To ride, esp. on horseback; to straddle: 騎馬 ride on horseback; 騎馬兒找馬兒 looking for another job while holding on to present one: 騎兩頭馬 headed for both directions; 騎自行車 ride a bicycle; 騎着掃帚 ride on a broomstick; 騎射, 能騎善射 expert at horseback riding and shooting arrow; 騎驢覓驢 looking for donkey on donkey back—absent-minded, see 騎驢 *-lyur* ↓; 勢成騎虎, 騎虎難下 "riding on a tiger"—afraid to go on and unable to get down; 騎鶴上揚州 want material comfort and immortality at the same time—an impossible dream; 騎牆 *-chiarng* ↓; 騎劫 to highjack.

騎兵 *chirbing* (**jih-*), n., cavalry soldier.
騎牆 *chirchiarng*, phr., sitting on the fence; 騎牆主義, 騎牆派 one betting on both parties or sides, timeserver, opportunist.
騎縫(兒) *chirfehng('l)*, line of junction of two edges, a seam; 騎縫印 seal placed across detachable check or contract and copy or stud.
騎箕 *chirji*, v.i., (AC) "riding on a star"—pass away.
騎軍 **jihjyun*, n., cavalry.
騎路 *chirluh*, v.i., (facet.) "riding on the road"—walk on foot.
騎驢 *chirlyur*, v.i., (1) to ride on donkey; (2) to make an illegal cut on dealing.
騎馬布 *chirmaabuh*, n., (coll.) woman's sanitary tissue.
騎士 **jihshyh*, n., a cavalryman.
騎從 **jihtzuhng*, n., cavalry retinue.
騎月雨 *chiryueh-yuu*, n., a rain extending over end of month.

駙 51B.00–9

fuh.

N. (AC) assistant carriage driver.

V. i. To drive fast.

駙馬 *fuhmaa*, n., husband of princess; (AC) anc. title for chief of palace guards: 駙馬都尉 *--duweih*.

§ 51B.01 (馬/小)

驃 51B.01–3

piauh.

N. (1) Buff and white horse. (2) Name of anc. country (now eastern Burma).

Adj. Brave, fast (of horse).

驃騎將軍 *piauhchir jiangjyun*, n., anc. title of a high military general.
驃勇 *piauhyuung*, adj., brave (fighters).

騾 51B.01–4

luor.

[Anc. var. 嬴]

N. (*-tz*) Mule.

騾車 *luorche*, n., mule cart.
騾馱子 *luorduohtz*, n., a mule load; 騾馱轎 sedan chair carried by mules.
騾夫 *luorfu*, n., muleteer.

§ 51B.02 (馬/⺊)

驟 51B.02–3

tzouh.

V. i. (Of a horse) to trot: 馳驟 dash around, as in a race (lit. & fig.).

Adv. Suddenly, unexpectedly: see compp. ↓.

驟然 *tzouhrarn*, adv., suddenly, unexpectedly, all at once.
驟雨 *tzouh-yuu*, n., a (summer) shower, a sudden downpour.

驤 51B.02–6

shiang.

V. i. (Fine horse, dragon) dash with rearing head: 騰驤 (fig.) forge ahead; 虎奮龍驤 prancing ahead.

驤騰 *shiangterng*, v. i., (LL) prance ahead, forge ahead.

§51B.10 (馬/十)

驊 51B.10-2

huar.

驊騮 *huarliour*, n., (AC) name of a famous horse; characters now used chiefly in personal names.

驛 51B.10-4

yih.

N. Courier; horse-relay system, government post; 驛馬 courier horse.

驛傳 *yihchuarn*, v. t., send by anc. courier system.
驛道 *yihdauh*, n., courier route.
驛館 *yihguaan*, n., courier station.
驛站 *yihjahn*, n., ditto.
驛舍 *yihsheh*, n., ditto; a post house.
驛使 *yihshyy*, n., official courier.
驛亭 *yihtirng*, n., resting pavilion for couriers.
驛卒 *yihtzur*, n., courier.

騂 51B.10-6

shing.

Adj. (Of horse) bay color.

§51B.11 (馬/土)

驩 51B.11-2

huan.

[AC var. of 歡 20S.81]

駐 51B.11-6

juh.

V. t. (1) Orig., to draw up a horse to a stop. (2) To encamp, to be stationed at, (of embassies) to be accredited (to country): 駐美, 駐英大使 ambassador to Washington, London; 駐軍, 駐紮 *-jyun*, *-jar* ↓; 駐節 *-jier* ↓; 派駐 appoint (diplomat) to (certain country); 駐泊之地 port for anchoring ships.

駐蹕 *juhbih*, n., emperor's stop-over place during journey.
駐防 *juhfarng*, n. & v. i., military station, camp or fort.
駐紮 *juhjar*, v. i., to encamp.
駐節 *juhjier*, n., embassies accredited to a country, or governors stationed in area: 各國駐節 the different embassies.
駐軍 *juh-jyun*, v. i., to encamp, station soldiers at place.
駐守 *juhshoou*, v. t., defend (city, area) with stationed troops.
駐顏 *juhyarn*, v. i., (LL) (method or medicine for) retaining youthful looks: 駐顏無術 no recipe for eternal youth.

騅 51B.11-9

juei.

N. (AC) a piebald horse.

§51B.20 (馬/廾)

駢 51B.20-9

piarn.

N. A pair of horses, as in driving a carriage.

Adj. (1) Joint, coupled (of things paired together): see esp. 駢體文 *-tiiwern* ↓. (2) Superfluous: 駢拇, 駢枝 *-muu*, *-jy* ↓.

駢比 *piarnbii*, adj., connected in a stretch (of land, houses).
駢肩 *piarn-jian*, adj., packed shoulder to shoulder.
駢枝 *piarn-jy*, n., see *-muu* ↓.
駢拇 *piarn-muu*, n., an extra thumb, sixth finger, superflous growth: 駢拇枝指.
駢脅 *piarn-shier*, adj., (AC) with joined or invisible ribs (of fat person).
駢四儷六 *piarn-syh-lih-liouh*, n., a euphuistic style consisting of antithetical or parallel constructions of four and six characters, also known usu. as 駢體文 *-tiiwern*.
駢闐 *piarntiarn*, adj., (AC) connected in a row or stretch (also wr. 駢田).
駢體(文) *piarntii(wern)*, n., see *-syh-lih-liouh* ↑.

§51B.21 (馬/乚)

驅 51B.21-5

chyu.

N. 先驅, 前驅 vanguard.

V. t. (1) To drive a horse: 驅馬 ditto; 驅策 *-tseh* ↓; 並駕齊驅 (fig.) to rival in strength or progress. (2) To drive away, to send one about: 驅逐 *-jur*, 驅遣 *-chiaan*, 驅使 *-shyy* ↓; 驅出去 drive out; 驅魔, 驅神, 驅鬼, 驅邪 to exorcise, drive out evil spirits.

驅遣 *chyuchiaan*, v. t., to order (person) about, dictate (another to do things).

驅除 *chyuchur*, v. t., to banish, exterminate (pests, etc.).

驅馳 *chyuchyr*, v. i., to run errands or labor hard for another.

驅逐 *chyujur*, v. t., expel (from country): 驅逐機 a fighter plane; 驅逐艦 (navy) a destroyer.

驅口 *chyukoou*, n., Mongolian word for "slave."

驅迫 *chyupoh*, v. t., to force; p. p. forced: 饑寒所驅迫 driven by hunger and cold to do s. t.

驅使 *chyushyy*, v. t., to dictate, to order about.

驅策 *chyutseh*, (1) v. t., to drive and urge (person) forward hard; (2) v. i., to bend all one's energies (to do s. t.).

駆 51B.21–5

chyu.

[Abbr. for 驅 ↑]

§ 51B.22 (馬/丨)

驌 51B.22–2

suh.

驌驦 *suhshuang*, n., (AC) name of famous horse (AC also wr. 肅爽).

馴 51B.22–2

shyurn.

Adj. (1) Tame, tamed (horse, elephant, etc.): 馴獸師 animal tamer. (2) Obedient, peaceful: 馴行 (LL) good moral conduct; 馴良, 馴和, 馴善 *-liarng, -her, -shahn* ↓. (3) Polished (writing): 文不雅馴 the writing is not polished.

Adv. (Related 旋) gradually (become): 馴至公開反抗 gradually become open revolt.

馴服 *shyurnfur*, adj., tame; tamed, subdued.

馴和 *shyurnher*, adj., peaceful-tempered.

馴良 *shyurnliarng*, adj., peaceful and kind (people); law-abiding; affable, quiet (temperament).

馴鹿 *shyurnluh*, n., the reindeer.

馴善 *shyurnshahn*, adj., peaceful and kind.

馴順 *shyurnshuhn*, adj., obedient, law-abiding.

馴養 *shyurnyaang*, v. t., to raise and train (horse, dog).

騑 51B.22–2

fei.

N. (AC) horse of a team.

騑騑 *feifei*, adj., (AC) descriptive of horse running.

駵 51B.22–3

liour.

[Var. of 騮 51B.41]

骄 51B.22–9

jiau.

[Pop. of 驕 51B.42]

§ 51B.30 (馬/一)

驢 51B.30–2

lyur.

N. (*-tz, -e'l*) Donkey, ass: 毛驢 young donkey; 驢駒子 young donkey; 驢臉 long face (like donkey's); 驢性子 stubborn like a donkey; 驢年馬月 impossible date, since there is no "mule year"; 驢脣不對馬嘴 irrelevant answer or reasoning.

駔 51B.30–4

tzaang (*tsaang, *tzuh).

N. (1) A broker: 駔儈 *-kuaih* ↓. (2) (**tzuh*) A fine horse, a noble steed. (3) (**tsaang*) A villain, rascal, scoundrel: 駔子 *-'tz* ↓.

駔儈 *tzaangkuaih*, n., a (clever, sharp) broker.

駔子 **tsaang'tz*, n., a scoundrel, ruffian, mean person.

§ 51B.40 (馬/口)

騞 51B.40–1

huoh.

Adj. (AC) sound of crashing (var. of 砉).

駱 51B.40–9

luoh.

N. (1) White horse with black mane (cf. 雒 92S.11). (2) A surname.

駱駝 *luohtuor*, n., camel, dromedary; 駱駝絨 camel's hair (coat), or similar fabric.

駘 51B.40–9

tair.

N. Inferior horse: 駑駘.

Adj. Stupid, slow witted.

駘藉 *tairjir*, (1) adj., (AC) overlapping, fouled up; (2) v.t., trample, crush under the feet: 兵相駘藉 soldiers trampling on one another.

§ 51B.41 (馬/図)

馹 51B.41–4

ryh.
[Cogn. 驛 *yih*]

N. Formerly, horses for courier service.

駟 51B.41–4

syh.

N. A team of four horses: 駟馬高車 (AC) high carriage and four—symbol of wealth and nobility; 駟不及舌 and 一言既出, 駟馬難追 a word (lightly) spoken goes faster than a team of four horses.

騮 51B.41–9

liour.

N. See 驊▵騮 51B.10.

§ 51B.42 (馬/冈)

駉 51B.42–4

jyung.

N. (AC) (horse) stable.

騙 51B.42–6

piahn.

V. i. & t. (1) Cheat, swindle, trick (person) into: 騙不了 (人), 騙我不過 or 騙不過我 cannot deceive (me, person); 你別胡說騙人 I don't believe you, you cannot fool people; 受騙 be fooled, cheated; obtain by cheating: 騙錢, 騙走財物 get money, jewels, etc. by cheating; 騙吃, 騙酒, 騙嘴 eat and drink without pay by some trick. (2) (Rare) jump on horseback.

騙案 *piahn-ahn*, n., a case of swindling.
騙局 *piahn-jyur*, n., plot of swindling, confidence game.
騙馬 *piahnmaa*, n., (MC) circus horse.
騙術 *piahn-shuh*, n., trickery.
騙腿(兒) *piahntueei('l)*, v.i. mount horse, carriage with one leg first: 一騙腿上了車.
騙子(手) *piahntz(shoou)*, n., a cheat, swindler.

驕 51B.42–9

jiau.

V. i. & t. (1) V. i., be proud of oneself: 驕傲 *-auh*, 驕盈 *-yirng*, 驕誇 *-kua*↓; 驕兵 proud or self-conceited troops. (2) V. t., look down upon, scorn, hold in contempt: 驕人 to show off (wealth, etc.) to people; 驕敵 to disdain, underestimate enemy.

Adj. (1) Supercilious, conceited, unruly, rebellious: 驕態 arrogant manner; 驕縱 *-tzuhng*, 驕恣 *-tzyh*↓. (2) Strong, fierce (sunlight): 驕陽 *-yarng*↓.

驕傲 *jiauauh*, adj., (be) proud, arrogant, haughty, overbearing; also in sense of Eng. "proud": 叫我為你驕傲 make me proud of you.
驕橫 *jiauhehng*, adj., overbearingly rude.
驕蹇 *jiaujiaan*, adj., arrogant, supercilious.
驕矜 *jiaujin*, adj., puffed up, self-conceited.
驕誇 *jiaukua*, v. t. & adj., boast(ful), brag(ging).
驕慢 *jiaumahn*, adj., arrogant, supercilious.
驕色 *jiauseh*, n., self-conceited or overbearing manner.
驕奢 *jiaushe*, adj., vain and extravagant.
驕狎 *jiaushiar*, adj., contemptuous.
驕縱 *jiautzuhng*, adj., unruly, unmanageable.
驕恣 *jiautzyh*, adj., ditto.
驕子 *jiautzyy*, n., (1) a dearly beloved son, a father's (mother's) pride; (2) 天之驕子 a specially privileged person, God's chosen one.
驕陽 *jiauyarng*, n., a hot, scorching sun.
驕盈 *jiauyirng*, v. i. & adj., (be) self-conceited, vainglorious.

§51B.50 (馬/ㄱ)

騁 51B.50-2

cheeng.

V. i. (1) (LL) to dash, prance about: 馳騁 to rove about, dash about in battlefield; (fig.) to be busy about political or other activities. (2) (LL) to roam, rove about in joy and freedom: 游目騁懷 let the eye travel over the great scene and let fancy free; 騁目 let the eye wander over; 騁詞 to scatter phrases about as one wishes. (3) To show off, give free play to (interch. 逞 40.83, V.t. 1, 2): 騁能 show off one's skill or ability.

騸 51B.50-6

shahn.

V. t. To geld (animals), castrate (chicken): 騸馬 a gelding; 騸羊 a wether; 騸雞 a capon.

駒 51B.50-9

jyu.

N. (1) A colt: 白駒過隙 in a split second; 駒光 a passing shadow; 千里駒 a swift-footed thoroughbred of rare breed; (fig.) a promising boy. (2) A surname.

騶 51B.50-9

tzou.

N. (1) A surname. (2) (AC) An officer in charge of the royal carriage. (3) Mounted guards: 騶卒 attendants; 騶從 footmen accompanying a nobleman or official; 騶唱 (LL) cries of mounted escorts to clear the way.

§51B.52 (馬/尸)

馿 51B.52-6

lyur.

[Abbr. of 驢 51B.30]

§51B.70 (馬/乚)

驍 51B.70-1

shiau.

N. A powerful horse.

Adj. Stalwart, strong: 驍將 valiant general; 驍騎 a well-trained cavalry.

驍驍 *shiaushiau*, adj., valiant (soldier).
驍勇 *shiauyuung*, adj., ditto.

馳 51B.70-2

chyr.

V. i. (1) To run fast: 疾馳 ditto; 馳馬 gallop; 奔馳 run around on errands, see compp.↓. (2) To spread afar: 馳名 *-mirng*↓; 名馳天下 is known all over the world.

Adv. Forming compp. with vbb. of thinking, remembering, indicating "far off": 馳思, 馳念 *-sy*, *-niahn*↓.

馳辯 *chyrbiahn*, v. i., make eloquent, impassioned defense.
馳騁 *chyrcheeng*, v. i., (1) to gallop about as in hunt or race; (2) (fig.) make oneself seen and heard: 馳騁文壇 make a noise in the literary world.
馳驅 *chyrchyu*, v. i., to dash about, esp. in contest; bustle about business.
馳道 *chyrdauh*, n., formerly, highway for the emperor.
馳名 *chyrmirng*, v. i., become famous.
馳念 *chyrniahn*, v. t., to think afar of s. o. absent.
馳系 *chyrshih*, v. t., ditto.
馳檄 *chyr-shir*, v. t., to send military despatch immediately.
馳思 *chyrsy*, v. t., see *-niahn*↑.
馳驟 *chyrtzouh*, v. i., see *-chyu*↑.
馳騖 *chyrwuh*, v. t., to run after (empty fame, power, money).
馳驛 *chyryih*, n., imperial courier system, such stations.

驪 51B.70-3

lir.

N. (1) A black horse. (2) Name of a hill.

驪歌 *lir-ge*, n., a parting song.
驪珠 *lir-ju*, n., (Chin. folklore) a pearl supposed to grow under the chin of a black dragon: 探驪得珠 (fig.) (of a piece of writing) to the point, bring out the best.

駝 51B.70-6

tuor.

N. Camel: 駱駝 camel; 駝鳥 (var. 鴕鳥) see *-niaau*↓.

Adj. Hunchbacked.

V.t. To carry burden on back: 駝負 (cf. 馱 51B.81).

駝背 *tuorbeih*, adj., hunchbacked, humpbacked.
駝峯 *tuorfeng*, n., hump of camel.
駝鳥 *tuorniaau*, n., the ostrich; sometimes used for the emu.
駝絨 *tuorrurng*, n., camel-hair, textile so made of.
駝子 *tuor'tz*, n., humpback.

§ 51B.72 (馬/心)

騐 51B.72–8

yahn.

[Pop. of 驗 51B.81]

驄 51B.72–9

tsung.

N. A piebald horse.

§ 51B.80 (馬/八)

騏 51B.80–2

chir.

N. (AC) a thoroughbred; a piebald horse with irregular patches of black and white.

驥 51B.80–2

jih.

N. (1) A thoroughbred horse. (2) A cultured, well-bred person.

驥足 *jihtzur*, n., a person capable of shouldering heavy responsibilities ("the hoofs of a thoroughbred").
驥尾 *jihweei*, n., a person reflecting glory on those near him: 附驥尾 ride on s.o.'s coattail to success, shine by reflected glory.

§ 51B.81 (馬/人)

馱 51B.81–1

tuor (**duoh*).

N. (**duoh*) A load carried on muleback, etc.

V.t. Carry on back by beast of burden: 馱不動, 不住 too heavy for the beast; 馱上, 馱上山去 carry, carry up the hill; 背馱 carry on back.

馱轎 *tuorjiauh*, n., litter; mule litter.
馱子 **duoh'tz*, n., load carried by beast of burden.

駭 51B.81–6

haih (also *shieh*).

V. i. & t. & adj. Shock(ing), shocked, surprised: 駭異 *-yih*↓. 駭人聽聞 shocking (news); 驚濤駭浪 terrifying waves.

駭怪 *haihguaih*, v. i. & t., be shocked.
駭然 *haihrarn*, adv., shockingly.
駭異 *haihyih*, v. i., be surprised: 不勝駭異 was greatly surprised.

驗 51B.81–8

yahn.

[Pop. 騐↑]

N. (1) Efficacy (of medicine, prayer): 效驗 ditto; 靈驗 great efficacy; 應驗 fulfill a prophecy. (2) 經驗 experience.

V.t. To inspect, examine: 實驗, 試驗 experiment; 考驗 examine (results, capacity, etc.); 檢驗, 查驗 to inspect (goods as at Customs), examine (blood, urine); check up (general health); 測驗 test by experiment.

Adj. Efficacious, true to claim: 屢試屢驗 every time it works (of prayer, medicine).

驗光 *yahn-guang*, v.t., examine eyesight (at optician's).
驗看 *yahnkahn*, v.t., to inspect (goods).
驗明 *yahn-mirng*, v.i., to verify by examination.
驗傷 *yahn-shang*, v.i., to examine wounds.
驗屍 *yahn-shy*, v.i., to examine corpse; perform autopsy.
驗血 *yahn-shyueh*, v.i., to conduct blood test.
驗疫 *yahn-yih*, v.i., to inspect for epidemic disease, to quarantine.

騃 51B.81–9

air (also *dai*).

Adj. Dull, stupid (interch. 獃 21S.81, 呆 40.01): 童騃 childishly stupid.

§ 51B.82 (馬/乂)

馭 51B.82–3

yuh.

[Var. of 御 91B.00 to ride, drive a horse]

駸 51B.82–5

chin.

駸駸 *chinchin*, adv., (AC) (horses go) at a gallop, (advancing) fast.

駁 51B.82–8

bor.

V.i. & t. (1) To argue (oft. 辯駁); rebut, contradict (person): 駁倒他, 駁不倒他 can, cannot overcome (person) by argument; to argue back, disprove, correct; 駁正 *-jehng*↓; to reject, reverse: 駁勘, 駁回 *-kahn, -hueir*↓. (2) To unload from ship.

Adj. (1) Mixed, esp., in colors, motley (斑駁); 駁馬 piebald horse. (2) Confused: 駁雜 *-tzar*↓.

駁船 *borchuarn*, n., a lighter, tugboat.

駁斥 *borchyh*, v.t., reject (petition, etc.) or reject with comment.

駁還 *bor-huarn*, v.t., reject (petition, communication).

駁回 *bor-hueir*, v.t., ditto.

駁正 *borjehng*, v.t., correct (opinions, statements).

駁價(兒) *bor-jiah('l)*, v.i., haggle (at prices).

駁詰 *borjier*, v.t., contradict, point out errors.

駁勘 *borkahn*, v.t., annul, reject (decision) by higher court.

駁犖 *bor-luoh*, adj., motley-colored; n., such cow.

駁辭 *bor-tsyr*, n., (LL) quibble, long-winded but confused argument.

駁雜 *bortzar*, adj., disorderly, mixed (opinions, ideas); complicated (affairs).

駁議 *bor-yih*, v.t. & n., criticise, (-ism) and reply.

駛 51B.82–9

shyy.

V.i. To sail or fly: 疾駛, 飛駛 sail or fly fast; 駛往 sail or drive to (place).

V.t. To sail (boat), drive (car), pilot (airplane).

駿 51B.82–9

jyuhn.

N. A spirited horse: 八駿 eight legendary horses of an anc. emperor (周穆王); 駿馬 *-maa*↓; 駿足 *-tzur*↓.

Adj. (1) Great, lofty: 駿業 *-yeh*, 駿惠 *-hueih*↓. (2) Swift, fleet: 駿發 *-fa*↓.

駿發 *jyuhnfa*, v. i., quickly make a name for oneself or become rich and prosperous.

駿惠 *jyuhnhueih*, n., great kindness, unbounded generosity.

駿馬 *jyuhnmaa*, n., a fine horse, a noble steed.

駿命 *jyuhnmihng*, n., the divine mandate.

駿足 *jyuhntzur*, n., see *-maa*↑.

駿業 *jyuhnyeh*, n., a great enterprise, a flourishing business.

§ 51B.91 (馬/ノ)

驂 51B.91–9

tsan.

N. (AC) the outside two of a team of horses; (AC) three horses: 驂乘 to sit on the right side of carriage.

§ 51B.93 (馬/く)

騷 51B.93–3

sau.

N. (LL) sorrows, sadness: 離騷 name of long poem by 屈原, describing his sorrows and disappointments.

V. t. To annoy, upset (place, people); p. p., upset, despoiled: 騷動, 騷擾 *-duhng, -raau*↓.

Adj. (1) Nymphomaniac, (of woman) lewd, lascivious: 風騷 ditto; 騷女人 lascivious woman; 騷婊子 slut, strumpet. (2) Sentimental, poetic: 騷人, 騷客 *-rern, -keh*↓.

騷動 *sauduhng*, v. i., be, become restless, ready for revolt.

騷攪 *saujiaau*, v. t., to trouble: (court.) 騷攪你 trouble you, take so much of your time, see *-raau*↓.

騷客 *saukeh*, n., see *-rern*↓.

騷亂 *sauluahn*, adj., (land) disrupted (by riots, etc.).

騷擾 *sauraau*, (1) adj., see *-luahn* ↑; (2) to trouble person by taking so much of his time, see *-jiaau* ↑.

騷然 *saurarn*, adj., in mood for revolt, disaffected.

騷人 *saurern*, n., (LL) poet: 騷人墨客 poets and writers.

SECTION 51S

§ 51S.00 (ㄏˢ/丨)

劂 51S.00–2

jyuer.

V.t. 剞劂 To engrave (wood blocks).

§ 51S.10 (ㄏˢ/十)

肆 51S.10–2

syh.

[Dist. 肄 22S.10]

N. A shop: 酒肆, 茶肆 wine shop, teahouse; 市肆 (LL) shopping district.

V.i. & t. (1) To let go, exert utmost: 肆其所欲 do what one wishes without restraint; 肆力 exert all one's strength (to study, etc.); 肆目 strain one's eyes to look at distance; 肆赦 (AC) to pardon; 肆筆直書 let go the pen and write as one thinks; 肆行 act without restraint; 肆口 talk without restraint (in scolding). (2) To display, to set out: 肆陳貨物 display goods for sale; 肆筵設席 set out table for guests.

Adj. (1) U.f. 四 four, in writing checks to avoid mistakes. (2) Dissolute, reckless: 放肆, 恣肆 ditto; 肆無忌憚 reckless and without inhibition.

Conj. (AC) (1) Thereupon, then: 肆類於上帝 thereupon offered sacrifices to God; 肆可行否 is this then practicable? (2) Although.

肆志 *syh-jyh*, v.i., to make a determined effort (to study, etc.).

肆力 *syhlih*, v.i., to exert one's best.

肆行 *syhshirng*, v.i., to indulge oneself, to act defiantly: 肆行劫掠 indulge in looting.

肆意 *syhyih*, adv., without restraint, defiantly.

肆虐 *syhnyueh*, v.i., (of man or natural forces) play havoc, cause widespread destruction.

§ 51S.11 (ㄏˢ/土)

雅 51S.11–9

yaa.

N. (1) (LL) pleasure, honor: 一日之雅 the pleasure of a day together; 同寅之雅 the pleasure of being colleagues in office. (2) 大雅, 小雅 name of sections in *Book of Poetry* (詩經), consisting of ceremonial songs of early Jou Period.

Adj. (1) Elegant, refined, cultivated: 雅俗 *-sur* ↓; 高雅 distinguished and elegant; 文雅 high-class, refined; 風雅 poetic (person); 素雅, 淡雅 simple and refined; 幽雅 (place) quiet and beautiful; 不雅 (language, dress) coarse, vulgar; 無傷大雅 quite acceptable in high-class society, no breach of acceptable code of conduct. (2) (Court.) your, your gracious: 雅量, 雅教, 雅正, 雅愛 *-liahng*, *-jiauh*, *-jehng*, *-aih* ↓. (3) (AC) often: 子所雅言 (AC) what Confucius often talked about.

Adv. (LL) indeed, esp. in 雅不願, 雅不欲 indeed reluctant (to do).

雅愛 *yaa-aih*, n., (court.) your kindness.

雅步 *yaa-buh*[1], n., leisurely steps.

雅部 *yaa-buh*[2], n., section of 崑曲 *kunchyuu* opera in 乾隆 Chienlung's regime, opp. 花部 all the other forms of opera.

雅趣 *yaa'chyu*, n., elegant taste, refined pleasure.

雅歌 *Yaage*, n., Song of Solomon in the Old Testament.

雅觀 *yaaguan*, n. & adj., nice appearance: 不雅觀 hideous or not refined to look at.

雅故 *yaaguh*, n., (LL) (1) ancient literary works; (2) old friends.

雅號 *yaahauh*, n., your gracious 號 or poetic name, other than legal name.

雅懷 *yaa-huair*, n., refined or poetic mind.

雅正 *yaajehng*, v.t., (court.) your correction, formula in presenting author's calligraphy, painting or book.

雅教 *yaajiauh*, n., (court.) your honored advice, message, or reply.

雅集 *yaa-jir*, v.i. & n., (hold) meeting of scholars or poets.

雅致 *yaajyh*, (1) n., beauty, refined enjoyment (of travel, drink); (2) (-'*jy*) adj., interesting to look at (home, decoration), refined.

雅量 *yaa-liahng* n., (1) generosity; (2) great drinking capacity.

雅人 *yaarern*, n., a person of poetic temperament: 雅人深致 refined pleasure of poetic minds.

雅士 *yaa-shyh* n., a refined scholar.

雅馴 *yaashyurn*, n., (language, prose) elegant, smooth.

雅素 *yaasuh*, (1) adj., (dress, habits) simple, of refined taste, not ostentatious; (2) n., (AC) old friends.

雅俗 *yaa-sur*, phr., the refined and the vulgar (people): 雅俗共賞 (writing, art) admired by scholars and laymen alike.

雅座(兒) *yaa-tzuoh('l)*, n., comfortable seats (advertisement of restaurants).

雅玩 *yaa-wahn*, n., (court.) for your amusement, formula in presenting art works.

雅望 *yaa-wahng*, n., nice reputation.

雅言 *yaa-yarn*, n., (AC) (1) refined discourse; (2) phr., often talked about.

雅意 *yaa-yih*, n., (court.) your thoughtfulness in giving presents; your hospitality.

雅樂 *yaayueh*, n., (AC) ceremonial classical music.

§ 51S.22 (厂s/丨)

臥 51S.22-2

woh.

V. i. (1) To lie down: 臥軌 lie down on railway tracks; 橫臥 lie across; 高臥 (of great men) to stay away from politics; 臥薪嘗膽 to "sleep on woodpile and taste gall"—(allu.) endure hardships to accomplish some ambition. (2) To sleep: 一夜不臥 go without sleep the whole night; 臥病 *-bihng* ↓; 臥榻 *-tah*, etc.↓.

臥病 *wohbihng*, v. i., to be confined in bed.

臥車 *wohche*, n., sleeping car.

臥起 *woh-chii*, v. i., (LL) go to bed and get up as part of daily routine.

臥底 *woh-dii*, v. i., (of thieves, etc.) to act from inside, do inside job.

臥房 *wohfarng*, n., bedroom.

臥具 *wohjyuh*, n., beddings, pillows, etc.

臥龍 *woh-lurng*, n., a great man compared to a "sleeping dragon."

臥內 *woh-neih*, n., (AC) bedroom.

臥舖 *wohpuh*, n., sleeping berth.

臥人兒 *wohrer'l*, n., the character 人, index No. 81; dist. the upright 亻 radical, index No. 91 A.

臥室 *wohshyh*, n., bedroom.

臥榻 *wohtah*, n., (LL) bed.

臥蠶眉 *woh-tsarn-meir*, n., a slender arched eyebrow.

臥游 *woh-your*, v. i., to dream of travelling in bed.

臥魚兒 *wohyuer'l*, n., (Chin. opera) a posture of sleep.

邪 51S.22-3

shier (**yer*).

Fin. part. (**yer*, as var. of 耶) (AC & LL) interrogative particle at end of sentence (=modn. 嗎): 豈其然邪 is that so indeed? also expressing doubtful attitude: 我以女爲聖人邪 (AC) I thought you were a sage.

N. (1) (Chin. med.) miasma, infected air of swamps, but more commonly malign or harmful air as cause of various disorders: 邪氣 *-chih* ↓; 中邪 (*juhng-*) infected by tainted air; 去邪 remove such effects. (2) Monsters, evil spirits: 妖邪 ditto; 邪魔 *-mor* ↓.

Adj. (1) Evil, wrong, corrupt, opp. 正 *jehng*, orthodox or right: 心邪, lewd, have an evil mind; 邪念, 邪道, 邪術, 邪說 *-niahn*, *-dauh*, *-shuh*, *-shuo* ↓; 走邪路 walk in evil. (2) Underground, covered, unfair (tactics): 邪謀, 邪計 immoral or underhand scheme.

邪氣 *shierchih*, n., (1) noxious or infectious air affecting health; (2) depraved, evil ways, atmosphere or influence in gen.

邪曲 *shierchyu*, adj., base, vile, corrupt (ways, teachings).

邪蕩 *shierdahng*, adj., lewd, licentious (conduct).

邪道 *shierdauh*, (1) n., heterodox doctrines; impious, corrupt teachings; 邪道兒 immoral or illegal doings (gambling, smuggling, etc.); (2) (*shier'dau*) adj., suspicious, devious: 都說這人來得邪道 they all say there is s.t. suspicious about this person.

雅 臥 邪

亅	小	𠄌	十	土	𠂇	卄	𠃊	丨	一	丁	𠃍	口	区	冈	冂	厂	尸	亠	广	宀	丶	乚	弋	心	八	人	乂	一	㇒	丿	𠂉	𡿨
00	01	02	10	11	12	20	21	22	30	31	32	40	41	42	50	51	52	60	61	62	63	70	71	72	80	81	82	83	90	91	92	93

邪法 *shierfaa*, n., black magic; witchcraft.

邪蒿 *shierhau*, n., (bot.) a grass, *Seseli libanotsis*, var. *daucifolia*.

邪譎 *shierjyuer*, adj., crafty.

邪媚 *shiermeih*[1], adj., seductive.

邪魅 *shiermeih*[2], n., demons.

邪門兒 *shiermer'l*, n., s. t. unorthodox or unexpected.

邪謬 *shiermiouh*, adj., absurd (opinion); depraved, corrupt (conduct).

邪魔 *shiermor*, (1) n., demons: 邪魔外道 heterodox doctrines; (2) adj., (person) devilish, quite a devil.

邪念 *shierniahn* n. lewd or indecent thoughts.

邪佞 *shiernihng*, n. & adj., flatterer, scheming or sycophant (person).

邪僻 *shierpih*, adj., unorthodox, depraved, queer (person, conduct).

邪行 (1) *shiershihng*, n., immoral conduct; (2) *shier'shing*, (a) adv., (coll.) very, terribly: 天氣冷得邪行 the weather is horribly cold; 脾氣壞的邪行 has a very bad temper; (b) adj., odd: 這話問的有點邪行 it's a rather odd question (what a strange question!).

邪術 *shiershuh*, n., sorcery, black magic.

邪説 *shiershuo*, n., heterodox or immoral doctrines: 異端邪説 ditto; teachings that lead one astray.

邪僞 *shierweih*, adj., false, deceitful (teaching, conduct).

邪淫 *shieryirn*, adj., lewd, immodest, debauched.

郾 51S.22-3

yaan.

N. Name of county in Honan.

§ 51S.40 (ㄏS/口)

臨 51S.40-1

lirn.

V. i. & t. (1) As vb. participle, oft. equiv. Eng. "at -ing," "upon coming to": 臨去, 臨行, 臨別, 臨走 (said s.t.) at parting; 臨產 at time of child delivery; 臨睡 just before sleep; 臨死 at time of dying; 臨危 in time of danger; 臨難 at critical moment; 臨刑 at time of execution; 臨陣逃脱 flee before battle begins; 臨渴掘井 begin to dig well when feeling thirsty —lack of forethought; 如臨深淵 feel like standing upon edge of abyss. (2) (Of ruler) supervise, be present at, descend upon: 臨民 rule the people; 臨朝 hold court audience; 臨幸 (of king) visit (a place); 臨凡 (of god) descend upon earth. (3) (Court.) confer honor of a visit: 敬請光臨 may I have the honor of your presence (at . . .); 涖臨 (court.) ditto; 親臨 personally attend. (4) (Events) come upon: 五福臨門 the five blessings descend upon the house; 大禍臨頭 disaster strikes ("one's head"). (5) To copy (models of script, painting): 臨一臨漢碑 try to copy a Hahn inscription, see 臨摹 *-mor* ↓.

Prep. At, facing: 臨街 (of house) facing the street; see V. t. 1↑.

臨期 *lirn-chir*, adv. phr., when the date arrives.

臨牀 *lirn-chuarng*, adj., clinical: 臨牀經驗 clinical experience.

臨池 *lirn-chyr*, n., (LL, allu.) to practise calligraphy.

臨到 *lirn-dauh*, v. t., come to: 臨到考期 come to time for examination.

臨症 *lirn-jehng*, v. i., (med.) examine, visit patient.

臨機 *lirn-ji*, adv., in an emergency: 臨機應變 decide on the spot, decide as situation demands.

臨界點 *lirnjieh-diaan*, n., (phys.) critical point.

臨近 *lirnjihn*, adj., close by.

臨終 *lirnjung*, adv., at time of death, on one's deathbed.

臨了(兒) *lirnliaau('l)*, adv., in the end, after all: 臨了兒落空 lost out, failed in the end.

臨摹 *lirnmor*, v. i. & t., to copy calligraphy (臨 by having model on desk, 摹 by tracing paper).

臨盆 *lirn-pern*, v. i., about to deliver child (盆 basin).

臨蓐 *lirn-ruh*, v. i., ditto (蓐 mattress for receiving child).

臨時 *lirnshyr*, (1) adv., at the time: 臨時想出來 thought of idea at last moment; 平時不燒香, 臨時抱佛脚 to neglect saying prayers when there is no need and then hug the Buddha's feet during a crisis; (2) adj., temporary, provisional: 臨時政府 provisional government.

臨帖 *lirn-tieh*, v. i., practise calligraphy after a master sheet.

臨月 *lirn-yüeh*, n., month when childbirth is due.

§ 51S.50 (ㄏS/ㄱ)

劻 51S.50-9

kuang.

劻勷 *kuangrarng*, adj., (LL) critical, hard pressed.

勵 51S.50-9

lih.

V. i. & t. (1) Encourage: 獎勵 foster, promote; 鼓勵 actively support, encourage s. o. to do; 勉勵 endeavor, persuade (s. o.) to greater effort. (2) Exert oneself: 奮勵 make great effort; 勵精圖治 (of governments) make great efforts to make a strong country; 勵志 to aim high, be determined to make good.

勵行 *lihshirng*, v. i., (1) (*-shirng*) act vigorously; (2) (*-shihng*) show self-discipline; conduct oneself properly.

鴉 51S.50-9

ya.

N. A crow: 烏鴉, 老鴉 ditto, known for its croaking cry and its blackness: 寒鴉 jackdaw; 鴉雀無聲 dead silent; 鴉巢生鳳 ugly mother gives birth to a pretty daughter; 鴉鬢 *-bihn* ↓.

鴉鬢 *yabihn*, n., a lady's black coiffure.
鴉青 *yaching*, adj., dark purple.
鴉鬟 *yahuarn* (sp. pr. *-'huan*), n., a slave girl (see 丫ᐞ鬟 80.00).
鴉髻 *yajih*, n., see *-bihn* ↑.
鴉片 *yapiahn*, n., opium: 鴉片煙 opium (smoke); 鴉片戰爭 Opium War (1840–42).
鴉色 *yaseh*, adj., dark purple.
鴉頭襪 *yatour-wah*, n., stocking with forked toes (in Tarng Dyn.).
鴉嘴 *yatzueei*, n., crow's bill; 鴉嘴鋤 a sharp hoe; 鴉嘴帽 a cap.

鷗 51S.50-9

ou.
[Pop. 鸥]

N. The sea gull: 鷗波 to float along in life as sea gulls on water; 鷗盟 (LL, of recluse poet) swear friendship with sea gulls.

§51S.70 (ㄏˢ/ㄴ)

甌 51S.70-3

ou.
[Pop. 瓯]

N. (*-tz*) A small cup (for wine or tea): 茶甌, 酒甌.

甌摳 *oukou*, adj., (MC) concave (face).
甌脫 *outuo*, n., (AC) entrenchment on border of desert; no man's land.
甌臾 *ouyur*, n., (AC) a hollow in ground.

§51S.80 (ㄏˢ/八)

賾 51S.80-1

tzer.

Adj. Deep, profound: 探賾索隱 delve into the profundities of the unknown.

頤 51S.80-3

yir.

N. Cheek: 支頤 resting cheek on hand; 朵頤 pleasing to the palate; 頤指 *-jyy* ↓.

Adj. Well-nourished.

頤和園 *Yirheryuarn*, n., the Summer Palace outside Peking.

頤指 *yir-jyy*, phr., 頤指氣使 to order people with only a tilt of the chin and without speaking—arrogant airs.
頤神 *yir-shern*, phr., pleasing, calming to the spirit.
頤養 *yiryaang*, v.i., to recuperate, live easy life in old age or for health reasons.

願 51S.80-3

yuahn.

N. A wish, pledge: 心願, 志願 heart's wish; 許願 make a pledge before God for a wish; 還願 redeem a pledge; 如願, 償願, 如願以償, 了願 fulfill a wish; 天從人願 God be willing; 願望 *-wahng* ↓; 志願 v.i. & n., personal choice.

V. i. & t. To wish, hope, pray: 但願, 惟願 only wish; 願你快樂 wish you happiness.

Adj. Willing: 甘願, 情願 ditto; 願意 *-yih* ↓; 自願 to volunteer to.

願心兒 *yuahn'shie'l*, adj. & adv., willing, -ly.
願望 *yuahnwahng*, n., one's hope, wish.
願意 *yuahnyih*, adj. & adv., willing, -ly; willing to (do).

§51S.81 (ㄏˢ/人)

臥 51S.81-8

woh.
[Printed form of 卧 51S.22]

歐 歐 毆 擘 檗 糪 艮 襞 羣

歐 51S.81-9

ou.

[Abbr. 欧]

N. (1) A surname. (2) Short for 歐洲 Europe; 歐美 Europe and America; 西歐 Western Europe; 東歐 Eastern Europe; 歐西 *-shi* ↓.

V.i. & t. (1) U.f. 嘔 (AC) to vomit: 歐泄 (AC, rare) vomiting and diarrhoea. (2) U.f. 毆 (AC) to strike. (3) U.f. 謳 (AC) to sing.

歐刀 *oudau*, n., (AC, rare) executioner's knife.
歐化 *ou-huah*, v.t., to Europeanize, Westernize in gen.
歐戰 *Oujiahn*, n., European War =World War I.
歐洲 *Oujou*, n., Europe.
歐羅巴 *Ouluorba*, n., Europe, see *-jou* ↑.
歐姆 *oumuu*, n., (electricity) ohm.
歐西 *Ou-shi*, n., Europe and the West: 歐西各國 the Western countries; cf. 西歐 West Europe.
歐陽 *Ouyarng*, n., a compound surname.

§51S.82 (ㄏˢ/乂)

敺 51S.82-2

ou.

[Arch. of 驅 51B.21]

毆 51S.82-4

ou (**oou*).

[Pop. 殴]

V.i. & t. (also **oou*) To beat up, fight with fists: 毆打 ditto; 毆殺, 毆傷 kill, wound, with fists.

SECTION 52

§52.00 (ㄕ/丿)

擘 52.00

boh.

N. (LL) thumb, esp. 巨擘 leader, (fig.) giant among equals, as 東方之巨擘 giant among oriental nations, also 擘指 the thumb.

V.t. (1) To break, separate: 擘開 break open, break off; 擘餅 break bread; 擘紙 tear paper. (2) To analyse: 擘肌分理 (LL) phr., make fine analysis.

擘畫 *bohhuah*, v.t., to outline plans for, as in blueprint: 擘畫經營 to create and execute plans for project, institution.
擘裂 *bohlieh*, v.i., to break open.

§52.01 (ㄕ/小)

檗 52.01

boh.

[Interch. 蘗 20A.01; dist. 擘]

糪 52.01

bor.

N. (AC) half-cooked rice.

§52.02 (ㄕ/ㄎ)

艮 52.02

gehn (**gen*).

N. (1) One of the eight diagrams for divination, see *baguah* 八卦 80.80. (2) A surname.

Adj. (**geen*) (1) Hard, tough: 艮蘿蔔 crisp turnips. (2) (Of character) straightforward, obstinate, upright. (3) (Of dress) plain, simple, (of speech) pointed, unadorned.

襞 52.02

bih.

V.t. Fold (clothing).

襞褶 *bihjer*, n., crease or crinkle lines from folding.
襞積 *bihji*, v.t., to fold (clothing) (coll. 打褶兒).

§52.10 (ㄕ/十)

羣 52.10

chyurn.

[Pop. 群]

N. (1) Group, community, herd: 一羣人 a crowd, a group of people; 這一羣 this group; 人羣 human society, crowd; 人羣生活 social life of men and women; 馬羣, 牛羣 herd of horses, cattle; 狐羣狗黨 (contempt.) a bunch of rascals or petty politicians; 害羣之馬 the black sheep of the family; 鶴立雞羣 (fig.) distinguished, outstanding man in a common crowd; 超羣 preeminent, outstanding. (2) Used in sense of "group of," "many": 羣芳, 羣花 group of flowers, also of women; 羣書, 羣籍 books of all kinds; 羣小 group of petty people; 羣雄 a group of independent warlords; 羣龍無首 (AC) "dragons without a leader"—a group of men in a common cause without a leader.

Adj. Communal: 羣體 *-tii* ↓.

Adv. As a group, together: 羣居 live together; 羣起攻之 rise together and expel him; 羣策羣力 work and pull together.

羣青 *chyurnching*, adj. & n., ultramarine color.
羣情 *chyurn-chirng*, n., public sentiment (enraged, bitter, etc.).
羣島 *chyurndaau*, n., an archipelago.
羣化 *chyurn-huah*, v.t., (of tribes) to be assimilated into the community.
羣衆 *chyurnjuhng*, n., the public, a crowd, the common masses: 羣衆路線 mass line.
羣性 *chyurn-shihng*, n., gregarious instinct.
羣體 *chyurntii*, n., the community (of insects, animals).
羣從 *chyurntzuhng*, n., young friends or followers.
羣英 *chyurnying*, n., a group of selected beauties, stars, etc.

§ 52.11 (尸/土)

壁 52.11

bih.
[Dist. 璧↓]

N. (1) Wall (of house, temple): 牆壁 any wall-like structure; 隔壁壁兒 neighbor, next house; 影△壁 41S.91. (2) Perpendicular cliffside: 絕壁 unscalable cliff. (3) Section of territory in 半壁江山, 東南半壁 an independent section of country, section on southeast.

壁報 *bih-bauh*, n., handwritten wall posters of news.
壁錢 *bihchiarn*, n., (zoo.) *Uroctea compactilis*, an insect of spider family.
壁櫥 *bihchur*, n., built-in wardrobe.
壁燈 *bihdeng*, n., bracket lamps.
壁畫 *bih-huah*, n., fresco.
壁虎 *bih-huu*, n., (zoo.) common house lizard found on walls, *Gecko japonicus*.
壁壘 *bih-leei*, n., (mil.) breastwork: 壁壘森嚴 strong defense preparations.
壁立 *bih-lih*, v.i., stand up perpendicularly.
壁爐 *bihlur*, n., fireplace.
壁上觀 *bih-shahng-guan*, phr., detached view, uninvolved (AC allu. to armies standing by watching others' battles from walls).
壁廂 *bihshiang*, n., (MC) side: 這壁廂 over here=這邊兒.
壁蝨 *bihshy*, n., bedbug=牀蝨.
壁衣 *bih-yi*, n., cloth covering wall.
壁魚 *bihyur*, n., cloth-eating moth (also called 蠹△魚 10.93).

璧 52.11

bih.
[Dist. 壁↑]

N. A piece of carved jade, (AC) usually round with hole in center: 白璧無瑕 flawless jade, of man's flawless character or girl's virginity; 原璧歸趙 (AC) allu. referring to successful mission in obtaining return of jade to 趙 Kingdom, hence 璧還, 璧謝 *-huarn, -shieh* ↓.

璧璫 *bihdang*, n., cornice.
璧還 *bih-huarn*, v.t. (court.) am returning (article to you).
璧翣 *bih-shah*, n., frame for bells and musical stones.
璧謝 *bih-shieh*, v.t. (LL) return (gift) with thanks.

§ 52.20 (尸/廾)

异 52.20

yih.
[Interch. of 異 41.80]

§ 52.40 (尸/口)

㠯 52.40

yii.
[Anc. var. of 以 21.81]

君 52.40

jyun.

N. (1) A monarch: 君王 *-warng*, 君主 *-juu*, 君上 *-shahng* ↓; 國君 the king; 君權 monarchical power; 君權神授(說) (theory of) the divine right of kings; 君命 royal mandate; 君無戲言 the king's words are to be taken seriously; 明君 an enlightened monarch; 昏君 a do-nothing king, also a tyrant king; 君臣 the king and his ministers; 君臣佐使 (Chin. med.) four categories of drugs of varying importance in a prescription. (2) A feudal title: 孟嘗君, 信陵君, 平原君, 春申君 four of the most powerful merchant-princes of the Warring Kingdoms. (3) One's father, mother or husband: 先君 my late father; 夫君 my husband; 府君 my late father (grandfather); 太君 your or his mother. (4) (Vocative.) sir: 祝君早安 good morning, sir! 請君光臨 please honor us with your company; 君知否 do you know it? (5) Mister as a title: 王君, 李君 Mr. Wang, Li; 諸君 (in public address) my good friends. (6) A person of a certain description: 少君 your son("the young man"); 細君 my (little) wife. (7) A surname.

君侯 *jyunhour*, n., a title of respect for feudal princes or high officials.

君主 *jyunjuu*, n., the monarch: 君主國 monarchy; 君主政治 monarchical form of government; 君主立憲 constitutional monarchy.

君上 *jyunshahng*, n., His Majesty the King.

君子 *jyuntzyy*, n., (1) a superior man, a gentleman; (2) the ruler of a country.

君王 *jyunwarng*, n., the king, the emperor.

譬 52.40

pih.

N. Parable, example, illustration: 設譬, 取譬 illustrate by parable or analogy; 罕譬而喻 make a striking, yet easily understood analogy; 譬如, 譬方 for example, take for example (=比方); 譬若, 譬如 it is as if (cf. 比如).

譬喻 *pihyuh*, n., parable, illustration.

§ 52.41 (尸/冈)

眉 52.41

meir.

N. (1) A surname. (2) Top margin of page: 眉批 *-pi*↓. (3) Edge of well. (4) The eyebrows, oft. used as denoting facial expression, esp. coupled with 眼: 愁眉不展, 愁眉苦臉 knitted eyebrows, preoccupied or sad look; 眉來眼去, 眉眼傳情 flirting glance between sexes; 做眉眼 make eyes at; 擠眉弄眼 wink and glance as signal; 直眉瞪眼 stare in anger; 柳眉倒豎 raise eyebrows in anger; 濃眉大眼 with big eyes and thick eyebrows; 眉開眼笑 face melts in smiles; 眉飛色舞 look of exultation; 眉目 *-muh*↓.

眉筆 *meirbii*, n., eyebrow pencil.

眉黛 *meirdaih*, n., black for painting eyebrows.

眉睫 *meirjier*, n., eyelashes: 禍在眉睫 disaster close by, like fire already "singeing eyelashes."

眉急 *meirjir*, adj. & n., urgent, -ncy; short for 燃眉之急, see *-jier*↓.

眉毛 *meirmaur*, n., eyebrow hair; eyebrow.

眉目 *meirmuh*, n., (1) looks: 眉目傳情 cast glances of love; 眉目清秀 have beautiful, delicate eyes; (2) order and sequence: 有了眉目 have established sequence, have got the main lines (of tangled affair).

眉批 *meirpi*, n., comment on top margin (oft. in printed editions).

眉梢(兒) *meirshau('l)*, n., tip of brow or eye, showing nuances of expression.

眉心 *meir-shin*, n., the place where the two brows meet.

眉壽 *meirshouh*, n., long life (old people oft. having long eyebrows): 以介眉壽 best wishes for long life.

眉頭 *meirtour*, n., the eyebrow region: 眉頭不展 with knitted brows.

眉語 *meiryuu*[1], n., the language of eyes between lovers.

眉宇 *meiryuu*[2], the forehead.

昬 52.41

hun.

[Var. of 昏 90.41]

暋 52.41

miin.

Adj. (AC) 暋不畏死 (of people) tough and are good fighters.

§ 52.42 (尸/冈)

臂 52.42

bih (also *beih*).

N. The arm: 肩臂 shoulder and arms; 手臂, 胳臂 (vern.) the arm; 一臂之助 lend a hand, (usu.) help; 獨臂將軍 one-armed general; 攘臂 raise hand to fight.

臂膀 *bihbaang*, n., the upper arm.

臂膊 *bihbor*, n., shoulder region near arm.

臂肘 *bih'jou*, n., the elbow.

臂助 *bihjuh*, n. & v. t., help; to help.

臀 52.42

turn.

N. Buttocks: 臀鰭 hind fins of fish.

臀部 *turnbuh*, n., the buttocks.
臀疣 *turnyour*, n., the hardened behind of apes.

§52.50 (尸/ㄱ)

劈 52.50

pi (**pii*).

V. t. To split (wood), slice, chop into pieces: 劈斷 cut in half; 劈碎 chop into pieces; 劈下來 cut down; 劈柴 *-chair*↓; 劈水 (LL) cut the water (of moving boat).

劈柴 **piichair*, n., kindling, firewood.
劈開 *pi-kai*, v. t., slice open. 劈開面 cross section (in microscope slides, etc.).
劈空 *pikung*, adv., out of the blue, suddenly (of pure inventions).
劈臉 *pi-liaan*, adv. phr., (scold) to one's face; (blow) direct in the face.
劈歷 *pilih*, adj., descriptive sound of crashing thunder; (fig.) sudden catastrope (also wr. 霹靂, 辟歷, 礔礰).
劈面 *pi-miahn*, adv., see *-liaan*↑.
劈手 *pi-shoou*, adv., in a flash of hand: 劈手搶來 grab s. t. in a flash.
劈頭 *pi-tour*, adv., right at the beginning, open up with.

鷿 52.50

pih.

鷿鷉 *pihdir*, n., (zoo.) a small waterfowl.

§52.70 (尸/乚)

己 52.70

jii.

[Dist. 已, 巳↓]

N. The sixth of the decimal cycle, see Appendix A.

Pron. Oneself: 我自己, 你自己, 他自己 I myself, yourself, he himself; 己身 one's self; 據爲己有 appropriate to oneself; 己饑己溺 be filled with compassion for s.o. else's sufferings ("as if one were starving or drowning oneself"); 引爲己任 take as one's own responsibility; 己所不欲, 勿施於人 do not do unto others what you would not like others to do unto you; 克己 self-denial, self-restraint; 捨己 self-sacrifice; 知己 a bosom friend; 反求諸己 self-examination, introspection.

已 52.70

yii.

[Dist. 巳, 己 52.70]

Fin. part. 也已 (LL) already, enough, expressing s.t. already done (=也矣); 而已 only.

V. i. Stop: 不已 without stop, on and on; 無已 phr., since there is no other way; 不得已 be forced to; 死而後已 no release until death.

Adv. (1) Already: 已經 *-jing*↓; 已去, 已來 already gone, come; 會已散 meeting already closed; 已久 already a long time; 已亡 already dead; 已冠 over twenty years of age ("already capped"). (2) Too, too much: 已甚 *-shehn*↓.

Excl. Well! Enough! 已而 *-erl*↓ "nothing more to say!"

已而 *yii-erl*, (1) excl., (AC) alas! "nothing more to say!" (2) adv. phr., later on (regretted it, etc.).
已後 *yiihouh*, adv., later on (=以後).
已經 *yiijing*, adv., already (done, etc.).
已來 *yiilair*, adv., since (=以來).
已然 *yiirarn*, adj., already so, already.
已甚 *yiishehn*, phr., (1) too much, extreme: 不爲已甚 do not overdo, push person too far; (2) already very, already much.
已事 *yii-shyh*, n., past event.
已往 *yirwaang*, adj. & adv., in the past: 已往的事 s.t. bygone.
已已 *yiryii*[1], phr., refrain: 不能已已 (AC) could not refrain or stop (thinking, etc.).
已矣 *yiryii*[2], excl., of despair.

巳 52.70

syh.

[Dist. 己, 已↑]

N. One of the duodecimal cycle, see Appendix A; 巳時 from nine to eleven a.m.

巴 52.70

ba (**par*, **baa*).

N. (1) Crust, crust-like formation: 鍋巴 *guo'ba*, rice crust sticking to pot; 膠泥巴兒 *jiaunirba'l*, cake of mud on foot; cf. 瘡巴 61A.40, scar on wound. (2) Part of compounds denoting tip, end, tail: 下巴 chin; 嘴巴 mouth; 尾巴 tail (of anything); 巴子 *-tz*↓. (3) Ancient name of East Szechuan; 巴縣=重慶 in Szechuan; 巴山夜

巴 霹 民

雨 phr., (allu.) hope of reunion among friends. (4) A surname. (5) U.f. 芭, 芭△蕉 20A.70 and 笆, 笆△籬 92A.70.

V. i. & t. (1) To form crust: 巴了鍋兒 crust sticks to pot. (2) Be close to: 前不巴村, 後不着店 phr., a desolate place, not close to anything. (3) To wish, hope, wait anxiously for, strain one's eyes in waiting: 巴想他能來 live in hope he will come; 巴望 *-wahng* ↓; 巴得＝巴不得 *-der*, *-'bu-'de* ↓, also 巴不能夠兒 to wish anxiously; 巴不到天亮 wait patiently for the dawn; 巴得箇(到長安) (MC) waiting anxiously to (arrive at Charngan); 巴瞪眼兒 wink or stare in blank disappointment; hence 巴頭探腦 to peep furtively from behind; see 巴巴 *-ba* ↓. (4) To climb, physically and socially: 巴高望上 have ambition to rise in society; 巴高枝兒 (fig.) marry above one's station; cf. cogn. 攀 10.00; also **par*＝爬 in 巴山度嶺. (5) (**baa*) U. f. 把 in 把△攬, 把△鼻 10A.70.

巴巴 *baba*, adv., (1) reiterative adv. in 焦巴巴 scorched hard; 乾巴巴 very dry; (2) in vain: 巴巴的等着 wait in vain; 巴巴的從家裏送來 take all the trouble to send for it from home (quite without need); 眼巴巴望着關山遠 longing in vain for the distant home country; 巴巴睜兒 *--tzehng'l*, badly wrought, knotty net; 巴巴睜兒似的 said of people's twisted face or of unnecessary fuss: 巴巴睜兒去湊熱鬧; a wobbly pot; (also wr. 八不甑兒).

巴壁虎 *babihuu*, n., var. for 扒△山虎 10A.80.

巴不得 *ba'bu'de*, v. i., wish anxiously, perhaps in vain; only too anxious to.

巴答一聲 *bada yih sheng*, phr., make a slap or flopping noise.

巴旦杏 *badahn shihng*, n., (bot.) a Thibetan plum (also 八擔杏, 叭噠杏).

巴到 *badauh*, phr., see *ba-der* ↓.

巴得 *ba-der*, phr., (MC) wish anxiously,＝巴不得 *-'bu'de* ↑.

巴豆 *badouh*, n., croton oil bean.

巴棍子 *baguhntz*, (also 巴噠棍 *badarguhn*), n., cudgel, truncheon.

巴掌 *bajaang*, n., palm of hand; 打一個巴掌 give a slap with the palm.

巴結 *ba'jie*, v. t., to flatter and win approval (of people, esp. the rich and important: 巴結某人); 巴結一筆錢到手 to manage to come by certain sum of money.

巴戟天 *bajiitian*, n., (bot.) a medicinal herb.

巴兒狗 *ba'lgoou*, n., Pekinese dog.

巴謾 *bamahn*, n., (MC), an ancient head-or-tail game; v. i., (MC) to contrive a living dishonestly.

巴山虎 *bashanhuu*, n., (also **par--*) var. for 扒△山虎 10A.80.

巴蛇 *basher*, n., python, reputed to swallow elephants in mythological work 山海經; hence 巴蛇呑象 inordinately greedy.

巴縣 *Bashiahn*, n., (geog.) Chungking.

巴蜀 *Bashur*, n., (geog.) two ancient states covering modern Szechuan.

巴士 *bashyh*, n., (translit.) bus.

巴圖魯 *Baturluu*, n., *Baturu*, Manchu term for bravery, an honor for military service.

巴子 *ba'tz*, n., woman's genitals; (joc.) of a person's greedy mouth; male genitals in southern children's talk; *see* also 雞巴 90S.50.

巴望 *bawahng*, v. i., hope: 巴望你能來 I hope you can come.

霹 52.70

pih.

N. Brick.

§ 52.71 (尸/ㄤ)

民 52.71

mirn.

N. (1) The people: 人民 the people; 平民 common citizen; 公民 citizen; 國民 the people of the country, see 國 41.41. (2) In many LL phrr.: 民爲邦本 the people are the foundation of the country; 民胞物與 from "民吾同胞, 物吾與焉" of 張載 the people are my brothers, the creation is part of me; 民以食爲天 food is (No. 1 need) god for the people; 民不堪命, 民不聊生 the people are hard pressed, living in misery; 民脂民膏 the "people's fat" (to be squeezed by taxes). (3) Freely used in LL in place of coll. 百姓: 民害 evils to the common people; 民賊, 民蠹 thieves, parasites of the people (bad ruling class); 民聲 the people's voice; 民隱 hidden grievances of the people; 民主, 民有, 民享 by the people, of the people, for the people; 民時 (AC) the times for planting and harvest of the people; see 三△民主義 Sanmin Doctrine, 30.30.

民權 *mirnchyuarn*, n., the people's rights; 民權主義 *--juuyih*, Doctrine of People's Rights, one of Three People's (Sanmin) Doctrines, see *-sheng*, *-tzur* ↓.

民法 *mirnfaa*, n., civil law.

民房 *mirn-farng*, n., common people's houses.

民風 *mirn-feng*, n., the customs and morals of the people.

民夫 *mirnfu*, n., formerly, conscripted labor.

民歌 *mirn-ge*, n., folk songs.

民國 *mirnguor*, n., republic; 中華民國 *Junghuar--* the Republic of China; 民國以來, 以前 since the founding of the Republic, before the Republic; as year of reckoning from 1912, subtract eleven: 1944＝M. G. 33, 1960＝M. G. 49.

民政 *mirnjehng*, n., domestic affairs; 民政廳 Department of Civil Affairs; 民政機關 civil administration.

民間 *mirnjian*, adj., of the folks: 民間故事 *--guhshyh*, n., folk tales.

民衆 *mirnjuhng*, n., the masses; the populace.

民主 *mirnjuu*, n., democracy; adj., 民主的 democratic; 不民主(的) not democratic; 民主黨 the Democratic Party in U.S.A. versus 共和黨 the Republican Party.

民治 *mirnjyh*, n., government by the people, now usu. called 民主 *-juu* ↑.

民牧 *mirn-muh*, n., magistrate, regarded as "the shepherd of the people."

民生 *mirnsheng*, n., the people's livelihood; 民生主義 *--juuyih*, one of the Sanmin Doctrines; see *-chyuarn* ↑, *-tzur* ↑.

民心 *mirnshin*, n., the loyalty of the people: 得民心, 失民心 win, lose, the loyalty of the people.

民事 *mirnshyh*, adj., civil (offence, law): 民事訴訟 civil case in court.

民選 *mirnshyuaan*, n., adj. & v.i., popular election, elected by people; 民選機關 elected body.

民俗 *mirnsur*, n., people's customs (good, bad); 民俗學 *--shyuer*, ethnology; 民俗文學 folk literature.

民團 *mirntuarn*, n., formerly, militia.

民族 *mirntzur*, n., race, tribe: 新興的民族 newly risen races; 民族主義 *--juuyih*, nationalism, one of Sanmin Doctrines; 民族自決 national self-determination; 民族自治 national autonomy; 民族解放陣線 National Liberation Front.

民望 *mirnwahng*, n., a person's command of loyalty of the people; prestige.

民謠 *mirn-yaur*, n., folk songs, folk rhymes often bearing political satire or forecast.

民意 *mirnyih*, n., the people's consensus of opinion: 以民意爲指歸 follow, reflect the public sentiment; 民意所歸 the public sentiment favors (a leader); 民意測驗 popular opinion survey, poll.

§ 52.72 (尸/心)

愍 52.72

miin.

V. i. (AC var. of modn. 憫) take pity: 愍恤 have pity, show kindness (toward people).

Adj. (1) (AC) sad. (2) Var. of 晵 52.41.

慰 52.72

weih.

V. t. To comfort, to console (person, soldier, patient): 慰問, 慰安 *-wehn, -an* ↓; 慰情勝無 a little gift for comfort is better than nothing; 慰留 *-liour* ↓; 勸慰 to calm down one in distress or anger; 安慰, 撫慰 to show kindness and consideration, to allay fear or distress; 自慰 to comfort oneself (by thinking, remembering, etc.); 聊堪告慰 this may be a comfort for you to know.

Adj. Comforted (p.p.); happy (oft. in letters): 喜慰 happy; 得來札甚慰 very happy to get your letter.

慰安 *weih-an*, v. t., to comfort, console the distressed.

慰解 *weihjiee*, v. t., to console by making one see that.

慰藉 *weihjieh*, v. t. & n., to render comfort, to console; p.p. to feel relieved.

慰勞 *weihlauh*, v. t., to comfort soldiers by gifts, entertainment, etc.

慰留 *weihliour*, v. t., to beg (person) not to quit.

慰問 *weihwehn*, v. t., to visit (the sick, distressed).

慰唁 *weihyahn*, v. t., to console (the bereaved).

§ 52.80 (尸/八)

巽 52.80

shyuhn (also *suhn*).

N. One of the eight diagrams of *baguah*, 八卦 80.80.

Adj. Modest, obedient (=遜 32.83).

§ 52.81 (尸/人)

熨 52.81

yuhn.

V.i. To press (clothes).

熨斗 *yuhndoou*, n., pressing iron.

熨貼 *yuhntie*, adj., (1) very affectionate; (2) (matter) very smoothly arranged.

亅	小	卜	十	土	ナ	廾	𠃊卜	丨	一	丁	フ	口	区	冈	冂	厂	尸	亠	广	宀	丶	乚	弋	心	八	人	乂	乛	一	丿	𠂉	く
00	01	02	10	11	12	20	21	22	30	31	32	40	41	42	50	51	52	60	61	62	63	70	71	72	80	81	82	83	90	91	92	93

A B C

§ 52.83 (尸/乀)

退 52.83

tueih.

V. i. & t. (1) To retreat, set back: 退出去 get out! 退後 move back; 向後退 (of troops) retreat; 進退兩難 difficult to proceed or draw back; 進退應對 one's behavior in company of superiors; 不知進退 do not know when to act and when not; 退出 withdraw, come out from audience or important meeting; 退不得, 退不了 may not, cannot retreat or go back, also cannot get out of it; 退避三舍 retreat about thirty miles as condition for peace, now generally, keep person at a pole's length, will not come near person; 退一步想 on second thought (it was not all bad, etc.); 退身步兒 a measure for safe retreat in case of failure. (2) To retire: 退休 retire from office or active life; 退歸 retire to the country; 退隱 *-yiin*↓; 引退 to retire from active public life; 功成身退 retire from public life after great work is done. (3) (V.t.) to dismiss, reject, return: 退卻, 退還 reject, send back; 退敵 to drive back enemy; 退貨 reject goods; 退票 ask for refund of admission fee or reject check; 退錢 (ask for) refund for purchase; 退不得 no refund allowed; 退換 *-huahn*↓; 退庭 n. & v. i. to adjourn court session (law). (4) To resign, step back: 退兩步 step back two paces; 退位 step down from the throne; 退職 resign from office; 退出黨籍 resign from party; 謙退 to step back as a courtesy. (5) To decline, ebb: 衰退 decline in health; 退熱, 熱退 reduce fever, fever comes down; 退汗 arrest perspiration; 水退 water recedes; 潮退, 退潮 to ebb, at low ebb. (6) (Interch. 褪) lose skin, hair, fade in color (退皮, 退毛, 退色).

退保 *tueihbaau*, v. i., cease being guarantor.
退避 *tueihbih*, v. i. & t., avoid (person), avoid meeting.
退筆 *tueih-bii*, n., a worn-out writing brush.
退兵 *tueih-bing*, v.t. & n., (1) to cause troops to draw back; (2) defeated troops; (3) 退敵兵 to cause enemy to retreat.
退步 *tueih-buh*, (1) n., a step backwards; (2) v. i., to slow down, fall behind in work; (3) v.i., to give place to s.o. in courtesy: 退讓一步; (4) n., a back room.
退潮 *tueih-chaur*, n., ebb tide.
退親 *tueih-chin*, phr., break engagement for marriage.
退出 *tueih-chu*, v. i. & t., to resign membership; to leave house, meeting; to waive right of election; withdraw from contest.
退卻 *tueih-chyueh*, v. i., (1) to step back; (2) to send back, return (gift, privilege); (3) (of troops) to retreat.
退股 *tueih-guu*, phr., to withdraw share from a stock company.
退後 *tueih-houh*, v. i. & adj., fall (-en) behind.
退化 *tueih-huah*, v. i., fall behind in development, become decadent; (biol.) atrophy.
退換 *tueihhuahn*, v. t., to exchange goods after purchase.
退還 *tueih-huarn*, v. t., send back: 退還原主 return to owner; reject (diplomatic letter of protest).
退回 *tueih-hueir*, v. i. & t., return to starting point; send back (gift, etc.).
退婚 *tueih-hun*, phr., annul engagement for marriage.
退職 *tueih-jyr*, v. i. & t., resign or dismiss; 退職金 pension.
退路 *tueih-luh*, n., a way out.
退讓 *tueihrahng*, v. i., step back in favor of s. o. else: 退讓賢路 to let abler men take my place (phr. much used upon resignation).
退然 *tueihrarn*, adj., (AC) physically weak.
退熱 *tueih-reh*, phr., reduce fever.
退燒 *tueih-shau*, phr., reduce fever.
退閒 *tueihshiarn*, adj., out of office, free from office duties, retired.
退省 *tueihshiing*, v. i., examine oneself for faults.
退休 *tueihshiou*, v. i., retire at age limit; 退休金 pension fund.
退席 *tueih-shir*, v. i., leave meeting or dinner party.
退稅 *tueihshueih*, n., tax refund.
退食 *tueih-shyr*, v. i., formerly, have breakfast after imperial audience; formerly, have reduced fare at meals as a gesture of sorrow.
退學 *tueih-shyuer*, v. i. & t., stop schooling, give up school.
退縮 *tueihsuo*, (1) v. i., to shrink back; (2) adj., cowering back, quiet and timid; unobtrusive, soft-spoken.
退堂 *tueih-tarng*, phr., court adjourned: 打退堂鼓 drum announcing such adjournment, (euphem.) beating a graceful retreat.
退位 *tueih-weih*, v. i., abdicate.
退伍 *tueih-wuu*, v. i., leave army service: 退伍軍人 ex-service men; veterans.
退役 *tueih-yih*, v. i., ditto.
退隱 *tueihyiin*, v. i., to leave office and live in retirement.

遐 52.83

shiar.

Adj. & adv. (1) (LL) far away, long lasting or stretching: 遐布 (reputation) spreads far and wide; 遐福 long-lasting luck; 遐眺 look into the distance. (2) (AC, rare) 遐不＝何不 why not.

遐棄 *shiarchih*, v. t., to abandon: 不我遐棄 (AC) do not disdain or abandon me.
遐邇 *shiar-eel*, adv. phr., (LL) far and near, on all sides.
遐方 *shiarfang*, n., (LL) distant lands.
遐軌 *shiargueei*, n., (LL) the long-established models of conduct.
遐荒 *shiarhuang*, n., distant lands.
遐迹 *shiar-ji*, n., the stories left behind by the ancient ones.

遐 擧 *shiar-jyuu*, v. i., to travel to some far land, also soar high.
遐 齡 *shiarlirng*, n., long life, venerable age.
遐 年 *shiarniarn*, n., see *-lirng* ↑.
遐 想 *shiarshiaang*, v. i., to fancy, think or wish faraway things.
遐 心 *shiar-shin*, n., (AC) cooling off or getting tired of old friend, lover.
遐 脩 *shiarshiou*, adj., (LL) long and far away.
遐 思 *shiarsy*, v. i., see *-shiaang* ↑.

選 52.83

shyuaan.

N. (LL) the choice part: 人才之選 the pick of the men, see V.t.↓.

V. t. (1) To choose, select: 選好的 pick the best; 選定了 have made the selection; 選日子 choose a day; 選來選去 after a careful selection; 選擇 *-tzer*↓; 挑選, 揀選 to pick, select. (2) To select for office post: 選用 *-yuhng*↓; 推選 recommend for post, also elect (officer); 遴選 select (good men); 考選 select by examinations; 入選 be selected; 圈選 select men by marking name with a circle; p.p., selected, chosen: 選手 *-shoou*↓; 選民 *-mirn*↓. (3) To elect: 選擧 *-jyuu*↓; 被選 be elected; 競選 run for election to office; 候選 n., candidate for election; 票選 elect by vote; 落選 fail in election.

Adj. Elective: 選科, 選修 *-ke*, *-shiou*↓.

選 拔 *shyuaanbar*, v. t., to select (men) for promotion.
選 塲 *shyuarnchaang*, n., formerly, hall for civil examinations (usu. 考場).
選 出 *shyuaan-chu*, v. t., to select, pick out, elect.
選 鋒 *shyuaanfeng*, phr., a picked combat force.
選 佛 塲 *shyuaan-for-chaang*, n., (Budd.) ground where monks are ordained.
選 購 *shyuaangouh*, v. i., to purchase after careful selection; oft. p. p.
選 官 *shyuaanguan*, n., formerly, selected officials; also officials in department of appointments.
選 家 *shyuaanjia*, n., formerly, successful candidates whose examination essays were collected and published as models for study.
選 間 *shyuaanjian*, adv., (LL) in a short while.
選 中 *shyuaan-juhng*, v. i. & t., to pick out (man) by choice or competitive examinations; to succeed in such examinations.
選 種 *shyuarn-juung*, n., selection of crop seeds, selected breeds; select quality (of tea, etc.).
選 擧 *shyuarnjyuu*, n. & v. t., (1) formerly, selection of talents by national examinations; (2) election by vote; to vote: 選擧權 the right to vote; 選擧人 the voter.
選 科 *shyuaanke*, n., elective subject of study.
選 美 *shyuarn-meei*, n., beauty contest; 選美會 ditto.
選 民 *sbyuaanmirn*, n., (1) (Christian) God's chosen people; (2) (politics) the electorate.
選 募 *shyuaanmuh*, v. t., to enlist men for the army by selection.
選 派 *shyuaanpaih*, v. t., to select and appoint.
選 票 *shyuaanpiauh*, n., the vote, ballot.
選 修 *shyuaanshiou*, (1) v. t., to take an elective subject: 選修英文, 歷史 choose courses of English and history; (2) n., elective subject or course.
選 習 *shyuaanshir*, v. t., take a course of instruction: 選習工程 study engineering.
選 手 *shyuarn-shoou*, n., champion; chosen men (athletes, etc.) to represent a college or locality.
選 士 *shyuaan-shyh*[1], n., picked scholars of a district.
選 侍 *shyuaanshyh*[2], n., (Mirng Dyn.) palace maid.
選 事 *shyuaanshyh*[3], v. i., (1) (AC) love to meddle in affairs; (2) formerly, department of appointments: 選事之官.
選 曹 *shyuaan-tsaur*, n., formerly, official in charge of appointments.
選 擇 *shyuaantzer*, v. t., to choose, pick out.
選 閱 *shyuaan-yueh*, v. t., to review and select (persons).
選 用 *shyuaanyuhng*, v. t., to select and appoint to post.

避 52.83

bih (also *beih*).

V.i. & t. Avoid, seek shelter, disappear from view, seek safety: 暫避一避 lie low for a moment until furor blows over; 避風雨 seek shelter from wind, rain; 避嫌疑, 避閑談 (forbear from doing s.t. to) avoid suspicion, talk; 避罪 flee from justice; 避債 dodge creditors; 避難就易, 避重就輕 choose the easier, lighter task or way; 避繁就簡 take the simple, less complicated way; 避實就虛 (of army) strike where the enemy is weakest; 避之若浼 phr., avoid person like a plague (浼＝contamination); 避坑落井 phr., avoid a trap to fall into a well; 逃△避 91.83 to flee; 躲△避 91S.01 to avoid meeting or being seen.

避 彈 衣 *bihdahn-yi*, n., bullet-proof garments.
避 諱 *bih-hueih*, n., taboo (esp. character in emperor's or father's name); (see 諱 60A.10).
避 火 梯 *bih-huooti*, n., fire escape.
避 靜 *bih-jihng*, n., (rel.) retreat.
避 就 *bih-jiouh*, v.i., avoid difficult task (short for 避難就易).
避 雷 針 *bihleir-jen*, n., lightning rod.
避 免 *bihmiaan*, v. t., avoid, save from (trouble, blame, war, etc.).
避 面 *bih-miahn*, v. i., avoid seeing (person).

亅	小	⺊	十	土	ナ	卄	ㄴ	丨	一	丅	フ	口	区	冈	㇆	厂	尸	亠	广	宀	丶	乚	弋	心	八	人	乂	㇀	㇀	丿	㇐	く
00	01	02	10	11	12	20	21	22	30	31	32	40	41	42	50	51	52	60	61	62	63	70	71	72	80	81	82	83	90	91	92	93

避難 *bih-nahn*, v. i., seek refuge; 避難所 n., refuge shelter.
避匿 *bihnih*, v. i., hide away.
避席 *bih-shir*, v. i., (AC) rise from tablet (mat).
避壽 *bih-shouh*, v. i., stay away from one's own birthday celebrations (by personages, to avoid calls, gifts).
避暑 *bih-shuu*, v. i., go to summer resort.
避世 *bih-shyh*, v. i., retire from the world (esp. to avoid politics).
避役 *bih-yih*, n., (zoo.) chameleon.
避孕 *bih-yuhn*, v. i. & n., (practise) birth control.

躄 52.83

bih.

[Var. of 躃 40B.10]

§52.91 (尸/ノ)

尸 52.91

shy.

[As radical in 52A]

N. (1) Corpse (interch. 屍): 死尸 dead body; 鞭尸 to dig up corpse and whip it as post-mortem revenge or punishment; 尸居餘氣 dead-alive, as good as dead. (2) Formerly, person representing spirit of the dead person during sacrifices, usu. a child. (3) A radical (as in 尼, 尿, 尾); index No. 52A.

V. t. (1) (AC) to act in charge: 誰其尸之 who was the man directing it? 尸盟 (AC) to act as chief in alliance of states. (2) To hold a job without doing anything (like a "corpse"): 尸位, 尸祿, 尸利 *-weih, -luh, -lih* ↓.

尸諫 *shy-jiahn*, v. t., to remonstrate with the emperor by sending letter and committing suicide.
尸解 *shy-jiee*, v. i., (of Taoist immortals) to dissolve bodily into a spirit.
尸利 *shylih*, v. i., (AC) as in 近而不諫, 則尸利也 to fail to speak up (to ruler) when there is opportunity to do so is to hang on to job for profit.
尸祿 *shy-luh*, v. i., hold sinecure job and act like a "corpse."
尸身 *shyshen*, n., a dead body.
尸首(兒) *shyshoou('l)*, n., ditto.
尸體 *shytii*, n., ditto.
尸位 *shy-weih*, v. i., to hold a sinecure job: 尸位素餐 hold a sinecure job and eat white rice.

尹 52.91

yiin.

N. (1) A surname. (2) A magistrate: 令尹 ditto; 府尹, 道尹 chief magistrate of *fuu* (district), of *dauh* (subdivision of a province).

V. t. (AC) to rule: 以尹天下 to rule the country.

§52.93 (尸/く)

嬖 52.93

bih.

V. t. To show favors to woman, take as favorite.

Adj. Favorite mistress.

嬖妾 *bihchieh*, n., favorite concubine.
嬖人 *bih-rern*, n., (LL) ditto.
嬖倖 *bihshihng*, v. t., favorite, take as favorite.

SECTION 52A

§52A.00 (尸/丨)

屙 52A.00-3

e.

V.t. Go to toilet: 屙屎 ease bowels; 屙尿 urinate.

孱 52A.00-3

*charn (*tsahn).*

Adj. Weak, small, feeble: 孱軀 (LL) feeble body; 孱夫 (LL) a weakling.

孱羸 *charnleir*, adj., (LL) weak and feeble in health.
孱弱 *charnruoh*, adj., ditto.
孱瑣 *charnsuoo*, adj., (LL) unworthy.
孱頭 *chahn'tou*, n., (coll.) a coward.
孱微 *charnweir*, adj., (LL) small, insignificant.

§52A.01 (尸/小)

屎 52A.01-2

shyy.

N. (1) Animal or human excrement, animal or bird droppings, ordure: 拉屎 go to stool; 屎尿 stool and urine; 驗屎 stool examination; (fig.) filth; 眼屎 secretions of the eyes. (2) As term of abuse, meaning "execrable": 屎詩, 屎棋 execrable poem, chess; 屎蛋 *-dahn* ↓.

屎 屪 屧 展 尿 犀 羼

屎蛋 *shyydahn*, n., term of abuse, dog sh-t.
屎蚵蜋 *shyykeh'lang*, n., dung beetle.
屎坑 *shyykeng*, n., country-style public toilet, dung pit.
屎盆子 *shyy-perntz*, n., commode.
屎桶 *shyr-tuung*, n., ditto.

屪 52A.01-6

liaur.

N. (Coll.) male genital organ.

屧 52A.01-9

shieh.

N. Wooden clogs.

§ 52A.02 (尸/卜)

展 52A.02-2

jaan.

N. A surname.

V. i. (1) To open up, expand, develop: 展開 open up (situation, field); 舒展, 開展 expand, develop (powers, ability); 展卷 to open a book (lit. a "roll"); 展誦 open (letter, book) and read; 展翅 (birds) open wings; 大展身手 show one's capabilities; 施展鴻才 put one's talents to use; 發展 develop (industries, etc.), or (industries) develop; 進展 make progress: 沒有什麽進展 no new developments. (2) To extend (time limit): 展緩, 展期, 展限 *-huaan*, *-chir*, *-shiahn*↓. (3) To visit: 展墓 *-muh*↓. (4) To show, exhibit: 展技 show one's skill; 展覽 *-laan*↓; 展驥 to show what a thoroughbred can do if given opportunity, (fig.) of capable persons.

展拜 *jaanbaih*, v. i., to kotow (kowtow).
展布 *jaanbuh*, v. t., (AC) to expound; to put (one's talents) to good use.
展期 *jaan-chir*, v. i., to extend time limit.
展緩 *jarnhuaan*, v. i. & t., to postpone.
展轉 *jarnjuaan*, v. i., to proceed amidst setbacks or by circuitous route; wander aimlessly or restlessly (also 輾轉).
展覽 *jarnlaan*, v. t. & n., (make) exhibit, -tion (of art, etc.).
展墓 *jaan-muh*, v. i., (AC) visit the grave.
展限 *jaanshiahn*, v. i., to extend time limit.
展縮 *jaansuor*, v. i., be flexible ("expand and shrink").
展望 *jaanwahng*, n. & v. t., a survey, to survey (world situation, future) prospect, hope.
展樣 *jaanyahng*, adj., stately: 又展樣, 又大方 stately and dignified.

尿 52A.02-2

niauh.

N. Urine: 尿液, 溺尿, 撒尿 pass urine.

V. i. To urinate (var. 溺): 尿炕, 尿床 (babies) wet the bed; 尿褲子 wet the pants; 尿尿 pass urine.

尿布 *niauhbuh*, n., diaper.
尿道 *niauhdauh*, n., the urethra.
尿毒症 *niauhdurjehng*, n., uremia.
尿缸 *niauhgang*, n., a receptacle for urine.
尿管 *niauhguaan*, n., the urethra.
尿壺 *niauhhur*, n., chamber pot.
尿盆(兒) *niauhpern(-per'l)*, n., chamber pot.
尿酸 *niauh-suan*, n., uric acid.
尿素 *niauh-suh*, n., urea.
尿桶 *niauhtuung*, n., wooden pail for urine.

§ 52A.10 (尸/十)

犀 52A.10-2

shi.

N. Rhinoceros: 犀牛.

Adj. Sharp, see 犀利 *-lih*↓; 犀兵 well-trained, dashing army.

犀錢 *shi-chiarn*, n., coin made of rhinoceros horn.
犀帶 *shi-daih*, n., belt with rhinoceros horn.
犀函 *shi-harn*, n., shield of rhinoceros hide.
犀照 *shii-jauh*, phr., (allu.) orig. oil torch from rhinoceros horn which penetrated into a dark pool—now complim. of person's penetrating insight into right and wrong.
犀甲 *shi-jiaa*, n., shield of rhinoceros hide.
犀角 *shi-jiaau*, n., rhinoceros horn.
犀利 *shi-lih*, adj., sharp (weapon), penetrating (remark, judgment).

羼 52A.10-8

chahn.

V. i. To interpolate: 羼入 adulterate (text) by insertions.

羼雜 *chahntzar*, adj., (1) adulterated (text); (2) mixed, disorderly (crowd, gathering).

§ 52A.11 (尸/土)

屋 52A.11–3

wu.

N. (*-tz, 'l*) (1) A house: 房屋, 住屋 house, home; 茅屋 a hut; 書屋 a studio, a bookshop; 愛屋及烏 love the house and extend love to crow on its roof ("love me, love my dog"). (2) A shelter.

屋頂 *wudiing*, n., roof.
屋脊 *wujii*, n., ridge of roof.
屋主 *wu-juu*, n., house owner.
屋裏人 *wu'liirern*, n., (coll.) concubine.
屋漏 *wu-louh*, n., (AC) dark corners of house.
屋廬 *wu-lur*, n., (LL) a house to live in.
屋社 *wu-sheh*, phr., (AC) a building stays where a temple to the god of the land stood—a country destroyed.
屋簷 *wuyarn*, n., eaves.

§ 52A.20 (尸/廾)

屏 52A.20–9

pirng (**bing*, **biing*).

N. Screen wall against gate to block off view from outside: 圍屏 standing screen, usu. portable or collapsible; 屏風 *-feng* ↓; scroll with writing or painting; 屏條 *-tiaur* ↓.

V.t. (**biing*) (Cogn. of 摒 *bihng*, 10A.20 and 擯 *bihn*, 10A.80) to remove, send away, cast aside: 屏棄 *-chih* ↓; hold back: 屏氣 hold back breath; 屏氣凝神 deep concentration.

V.i. (**biing*) Retire, stop: 屏居 retire and live in seclusion; 屏絕交際 isolate oneself from social activities.

Adj. (**bing*) Trembling: 屏營待命 awaiting order with fear and trepidation (to emperor).

屏蔽 *pirngbih*, n., buffer state or frontier provinces.
屏棄 **biingchih*, v. t., abandon, cast aside (business affairs 俗務), see also 摒 *bihng* 10A.20.
屏除 **biingchur*, v. t., remove, (obstacles 障礙).
屏斥 **biingchyh*, v. t., dismiss (with scolding).
屏藩 *pirngfan*, n., powerful governors or generals in border regions.
屏風 *pirngfeng*, n., screen (usu. portable).
屏障 *pirngjahng*, n., (1) screen or screen wall at gate; (2) frontier defense, outpost; (3) (fig.) mountain range: 峯巒屏障 surrounding ranges of hills.
屏門 *pirng-mern*, n., door separating outer and inner courts in Chin. house.
屏條 *pirngtiaur*, n., hanging scroll.

§ 52A.21 (尸/乚)

屆 52A.21–1

jieh.

[Pop. 届 52A.41]

N. An item in a series, session: 第一屆畢業生 the first batch of graduates; 第十屆校友會 tenth alumni meeting; 上屆, 下屆 the last, next batch, session, conference, etc.; 歷屆 the different sessions (of conference, etc.); 屆滿 term expires.

V. i. Become due: 屆時 when the time comes, at an appointed time; 屆期 when the day arrives, at an appointed date.

屈 52A.21–2

chyu.

N. (1) A surname. (2) A grievance, thwarting of justice: 枉屈 (suffer) a wrong.

V. i. & t. (1) To bend (a stick, leg, etc.): 屈膝 *-shi* ↓; 屈指 bend one's fingers in counting; 屈指已三月 it's already three months (on counting); 指不勝屈 innumerable. (2) To bend in submission: 屈伏 *-fur* ↓; 屈辱 *-ruh* ↓; 威武不能屈 will not submit to force; 忠勇不屈, 不屈不撓 indomitable heart of loyalty; 志不可屈 indomitable will or ambition; 屈節 change loyalty; 大丈夫能屈能伸 a great man knows when to yield and when not. (3) To crouch, be in an inferior or uncomfortable position: 屈居人下 to occupy an inferior position; used courteously in asking a person to "condescend": 屈尊, 屈駕, 屈就 *-tzun, -jiah, -jiouh* ↓; 屈座 host's apology to guest for giving a lower seat at dinner table. (4) To suffer wrong, injustice: 冤屈, 受屈, 委屈 be accused falsely; 屈打成招 obtain confession under torture; 屈死 die under false accusation.

Adj. (1) Crooked. (2) Wrong: 理屈 shown to be unreasonable, worsted in argument. (3) U. f. 倔 *jyuer*, 91A.21 stubborn.

屈曲 *chyuchyu*, adj., crooked, twisted (branch, etc.).
屈伏 *chyufur*, (1) v. i., to submit to external force; (2) admit defeat in contest (also wr. 屈服).
屈折 *chyujer*, (1) adj., crooked,

twisted; (2) n. & v. i., (phys.) refraction of light.

屈駕 *chyu-jiah*, v. i., (court.) please condescend to come.

屈就 *chyujiouh*, v. t., (court.) condescend to take up (unworthy) position.

屈滯 *chyujyh*, v. i., remain in obscure position, unpromoted.

屈指 *chuy-jyy*, see V.i. & t. 1↑.

屈量(兒) *chyuliahng('l)*, v. i., fail to drink to one's capacity.

屈蟠 *chyuparn*, adj., twisted, entwining (tree trunks, branches).

屈辱 *chyuruh*, v. t., to humiliate; (p. p.) humiliated.

屈膝 *chyu-shi*, v. i., (1) "to double knees," sit with crossed knees: 屈膝談心 have heart-to-heart talk with knees together; (2) to kneel.

屈心 *chyu-shin*, adj., unconscionable (=虧心), against conscience.

屈戌(兒) *chyu'shyu(-shyue'l)*, n., a fastening for window.

屈尊 *chyu-tzun*, v. i., (court.) please "condescend" to come.

屈枉 *chyu'wang*, v. t., falsely accuse: 不可屈枉好人 must not falsely accuse an innocent man.

屜 52A.21–9

tih.

[Var. 屉]

N. (*-tz, 'l*) A desk drawer: 抽屜(子) drawer; 鞋屜 shoe pad; 籠屜 steamer with sectional trays for food.

§ 52A.22 (尸/丨)

屌 52A.22–4

diaau.

N. (Coll.) male genital organ.

§ 52A.30 (尸/一)

昼 52A.30–4

jouh.

[Pop. of 晝 22.30]

§ 52A.40 (尸/口)

居 52A.40–1

jyu (**ji*).

Fin. particle. (**ji*) (AC) used to express surprise: 何居? 我未之聞也 how so? I never heard of it before.

N. (1) Dwelling place: 居所 a dwelling place; 蝸居 (self-deprecatory) my humble home; 遷居 change residence; 別居 a villa. (2) As a part of the name of a restaurant or teahouse: 六朝居, 金陵居 names of two restaurants in Nanking. (3) A surname.

V.i. & t. (1) V.i., live, reside, dwell: 居住 *-juh*, 居留 *-liour* ↓; 僑居 live abroad; 客居, 旅居 live away from home; 居家人等 all members of a family who live together; 居處 *-chuh* ↓; 寄居 live temporarily, have lodgings; 起居 one's daily activities: 起居注 a court official in charge of recording the emperor's daily activities, such a record; 閒居 live at home, not in office. (2) V.t., gather together, keep in hand: 居積 *-ji*, 居奇 *-chir* ↓; 奇貨可居 make a profit by cornering, take advantage of a rare opportunity that comes one's way. (3) V.t., serve in certain position: 居官 *-guan*, 居攝 *-sheh*, 居中 *-jung*, 居間 *-jian*, 居首 *-shoou* ↓; 居安思危 vigilance in peace (time); 居仁由義 to walk in the path of virtue; 居之不疑 have no hesitation in assuming a high office; 屈居人下 accept an inferior status; 居身 one's way of life; 居高臨下 vantage point.

居哀 *jyu-ai*, v.i., be in bereavement.

居奇 *jyuchir*, v.t., (comm.) to corner (a commodity), buy up (s.t.) in order to sell it at a profit later on.

居處 *jyuchuh*, (1) n., residence, dwelling place; (2) v.i., live (at place), occupy (position).

居多 *jyu-duo*, phr., mostly, for the most part.

居官 *jyuguan*, v.i., serve as an official: 居官守法 be a law-abiding official.

居功 *jyugung*, v.i., claim the credit for oneself.

居長 *jyu-jaang*, v.i., be the first born or the eldest.

居積 *jyuji*, v.t., amass (riches), stow away, hoard, accumulate.

居家 *jyujia*, (1) v.i., be at home; (2) n., one's daily life at home.

居間 *jyujian*, (1) v.i., serve as a go-between, or intermediary: 居間人 middleman; (2) phr., in the center.

居住 *jyujuh*, v.i., live, reside, dwell.

居中 *jyujung*, v.i., remain in the middle: 居中調停 mediate between two parties to a dispute.

居止 *jyujyy*, v.i., (LL) live, dwell, reside: 頗堪居止 it's a nice place to live in.

居留 *jyuliour*, v.i., sojourn, stay, reside: 居留地 place of (temporary) residence.

居民 *jyumirn*, n., a resident, an inhabitant.

居然 *jyurarn*, adv., (1) unexpectedly, surprisingly; (2) offhand, easily, imperturbably.

居喪 *jyusang*, v.i., be in bereavement.

屈 屜 屌 昼 居

亅	小	⺊	十	土	ナ	卄	𠃊	丨	一	丁	フ	口	囗	冂	㇆	厂	尸	亠	广	厶	丶	乚	弋	心	八	人	乂	㇀	ノ	丿	㇏	く
00	01	02	10	11	12	20	21	22	30	31	32	40	41	42	50	51	52	60	61	62	63	70	71	72	80	81	82	83	90	91	92	93

居攝 *jyusheh*, v.i., to act as the regent.

居心 *jyu-shin*, (1) v.t., have (good, bad) intentions; (2) n., intentions: 居心不良 with bad intentions; 居心何在 what is (his) motive? 居心叵測 with concealed intentions.

居首 *jyushoou*, v.i., to head a group, come or rank first, take precedence over others.

居孀 *jyushuang*, adj., live as a widow.

居士 *jyushyh*[1], n., (1) a recluse, a hermit; (2) a person practising Budd. at home.

居室 *jyushyh*[2], n., (1) living quarters; (2) 男女居室 (AC) live as man and wife; (3) (AC) name of a prison.

居停 *jyutirng*, n., as in 居停主人 (1) one's landlord; (2) a person employing a private tutor to teach his children.

居易 *jyuyih*, v.i., live a plain, simple life.

§ 52A.41 (尸/区)

屠 52A.41-1

tur.

N. (1) A surname. (2) A butcher; 屠沽 (contempt.) butchers and wine sellers—lower class of people; 屠狗 one who deals in dog meat—a contemptible profession; 過屠門而大嚼 to feast oneself in imagination at butcher's door—of vain ambition; 放下屠刀, 立地成佛 lay down the butcher's knife and immediately become a buddha—admonition for repentance. (3) Butchery: 禁屠 ban butchery, a temporary measure to pacify the gods.

V. t. To butcher (animals, population): 屠城 to kill all residents of a conquered town.

屠場 *turchaang*, n., slaughterhouse, abattoir, also called 屠宰場.

屠夫 *turfu*, n., see *-huh* ↓.

屠戶 *turhuh*(-'*hu*), n., a butcher.

屠戮 *turluh*, v.t., to massacre (people).

屠殺 *tursha*, v. t., to kill, massacre (innocent people).

屠蘇 *tursu*, n., a plant; name of a wine, in some places drunk at New Year's Day as preventive against illness.

屠宰 *turtzaai*, v. t., to butcher (animals) for food.

届 52A.41-2

jieh.

[Pop. of 屆 52A.21]

層 52A.41-8

tserng.

N. (1) ('*l*) Layer: 上層, 下層 top, bottom layer (of cake, etc.). (2) Floor, storey: 三層樓 a three-storeyed building; 第二層 second floor (also 二樓).

Adj. & adv. Layer upon layer, multiple: 層巒疊嶂 layer upon layer of peaks and knolls; 層出不窮 (tricks, troubles) pile up one after another; 層瀾 rolling wave piled up one on another; 層臺, 層樓 multiple-storeyed terraces, towers; 層雲 multiple layers of clouds.

層累 *tsernglei*, adj., multiple, successive (misfortunes).

層次 *tserngtsyh* (-'*tsy*), n., series, orderly arrangement.

§ 52A.42 (尸/冈)

屑 52A.42-2

shieh.

N. Bits, scraps, filings: 紙屑 scraps of paper; 碎屑 little bits; 木屑 filings, odd small pieces of wood; 鋸屑 sawdust; 煤屑 coal scraps.

Vb. aux. To mind, used only negatively in 不屑 disdain to, unwilling to: 不屑爲 disdain to do; 不屑傾家蕩產爲之 is not worth spending a whole fortune on it.

屑屑 *shiehshieh*, adj., trivial.

屑窣 *shiehsuh*, adj., descriptive of tiny squeak.

屑意 *shiehyih*, v. i., to mind, be concerned.

属 52A.42-9

shuu.

[Pop. of 屬 52A.50]

§ 52A.50 (尸/ㄱ)

屬 52A.50-2

shuu (**juu*).

[Pop. 属]

N. (1) Category, class: 金屬 metals. (2) Blood or other relations: 家屬, 親屬 relatives; 戚屬 wife's relatives; 部屬 soldiers, units under command; 屬員, 屬僚 *-yuarn*, *-liaur* ↓. (3) Cycle of twelve years named after animals: 屬相 *-shiahng* ↓; 屬牛的, 屬豬的 was born in year of cow, of pig, etc.

V. t. (1) 屬 or 屬於, 屬乎 belong to, under, be one of a category: 屬於他, 於我 belong to him, to me; 屬誰管 who is in charge of this? 屬陰, 屬陽 belong to *yin, yarng* category; 屬在相好 I am counted among your friends; 屬靈, 屬肉 spiritual, carnal. (2) Owe allegiance to: 屬於吳 (a town) belongs to Wur Kingdom; 歸屬 come under suzerainty of (another power); 屬地, 屬國 *-dih, -guor* ↓. (3) (*juu) To give instructions (u.f. 囑): 屬託 *-tuo* ↓; 屬令 *-lihng* ↓. (4) (*juu) To compose piece of writing: 屬文 *-wern* ↓; 屬對 *-dueih* ↓; 屬辭 to give proper wording to text; 屬辭比事 (AC) write prose narrative; 屬草, 屬稿 to draft (document, etc.). (5) (*juu) To concentrate, center upon: 屬目, 屬意, 屬望 *-muh, -yih, -wahng* ↓. (6) (AC) to assemble, gather together: 相屬於道 gather on the road.

屬邦 *shuubang*, n., see *-guor* ↓.
屬地 *shuudih*, n., annexed territory, imperialist colony, territorial possession.
屬對 *juu-dueih, v. i., to make or complete a literary couplet.
屬國 *shuuguor*, n., subjugated and annexed country, a vassal state.
屬和 *juuheh, v. i., to write poems to each other, usu. on prescribed rhyme-class.
屬乎 *shuu'hu*, v. i., belong to, be of certain class or type.
屬者 *jurjiee, adv., (AC) lately.
屬纊 *juukuahng, v. i., (AC) place cotton near nostrils and mouth to determine if dying person has stopped breathing.
屬僚 *shuuliaur*, n., colleagues under an official.
屬吏 *shuulih*, n., secretary, clerk, assistant under an official, subordinates.
屬令 *juulihng, v. i., give instructions, instruct that s.t. be done.
屬目 *juumuh, v. i., center attention upon (person, subject); look carefully.
屬下 *shushiah*, n., see *-lih* ↑.
屬相 *shuushiahng* (*-'shiang*), n., 十二屬相 (also called 生相) the twelve animals assigned to the duodecimal cycle of years, see Appendix A.
屬性 *shuushihng*, n., basic character; characteristics, material character.
屬實 *shuushyr*, adj., (story) is true.
屬草 *jurtsaau, v. t., to draft (telegram, etc.).
屬託 *juutuo, v. t., to request, instruct s.o. to do s.t.
屬望 *shuuwahng* (*juu-), v. i., as in 屬望於 center hope on (person), favor (s.o. to be elected).
屬文 *juuwern, v. i., to compose (prose).
屬意 *juuyih, v. i., as in 屬意於 pay attention to (person): 屬意於她 set one's heart on her; favor (a candidate).
屬員 *shuuyuarn*, n., see *-liaur* ↑.
屬於 *shuu-yur* (*-'yu*), v. t., belong to, be of a certain class; also *-'hu* ↑.

局 52A.50-5

jyur.

N. adjunct. 一局戲 a theatrical performance; 一局棋 a game of chess.

N. (1) A bureau, institution, office: 教育局 Bureau of Education; 警察局 the police office, station; 郵政局 the post office; 書局 a bookstore; 藥局 a drugstore, pharmacy; 印書局 a publishing company; 局子 *-'tz*, 局所 *-suoo* ↓; 當局 the authorities; 分局 a substation. (2) A part of s.t.: 局部 *-buh* ↓. (3) A chessboard: 棋局 a game of chess: 這局棋 this game of chess. (4) A party: 飯局 a dinner party; 賭局 gambling house or party; 不成局 failure to make up a party for pleasure; 散局 break up a social gathering. (5) Gen. condition or situation: 殘局 a devastated aftermath; 局勢 *-shyh* ↓; 大局 the gen. situation; 時局 current developments; 戰局 the war situation; 世局 the world situation; 政局 the political situation; 危局 a crisis; 局面 *-miahn* ↓. (6) Pattern: 格局 framework, pattern of events; 佈局 general pattern, layout, arrangement; 騙局 a fraud, deception, swindle; 和局 a contest ending in a draw; 了局 put an end to s.t. (7) Moral character: 局度, 局量 *-duh, -liahng* ↓.

Adj. (U.f. 跼) stooping, bent down: 局蹐 treading carefully, crouching.

局部 *jyurbuh*, n., parts of a whole: 局部 or 局部的 adj. & adv., partial, -ly (surrender, change, etc.).
局氣 *jyur'chi*, n., fair-minded(ness).
局度 *jyurduh*, n., a person's capacity for rising to great heights of magnanimity, charity or kindness.
局方 *jyur-fang*, n., formerly, an official recipe.
局長 *jyurjaang*, n., director of a bureau (department).
局詐 *jyurjah*, n., a swindle.
局量 *jyurliahng*, n., see *-duh* ↑.
局面 *jyurmiahn*, n., (1) gen. conditions of place, country or the world; (2) the pattern (of things, a game play, a chess game, etc.); (3) (*-'mian*) a show-off.
局內 *jyurneih*, n., as in 局內人 a person in the know, an insider.
局騙 *jyurpiahn*, n., a swindle.
局限 *jyurshiahn*, n., limitations, restrictions, constraint.
局束 *jyurshuh*, v. i. & n., (be subject to) restraint, (have) no freedom of action, (be under) compulsion.
局勢 *jyurshyh*, n., (1) the march of events; (2) circumstances, conditions, state of affairs.
局所 *jyursuoo*, n., an office.
局促 *jyurtsuh*, adj., (1) narrow-minded; (2) nervous, per-

屬 局

亅	小	⺊	十	土	ナ	廾	乚	丨	一	丁	フ	口	区	冈	ㄱ	厂	尸	亠	广	宀	丶	乚	弋	心	八	人	乂	乛	丆	丿丨	𠂉	く
00	01	02	10	11	12	20	21	22	30	31	32	40	41	42	50	51	52	60	61	62	63	70	71	72	80	81	82	83	90	91	92	93

turbed, disquieted, discomfited.

局子 *jyur'tz*, n., (1) an office; (2) a place without shop front for the sale or manufacture of goods.

局外 *jyur-waih*, n., as in 局外人 an outsider.

局員 *jyuryuarn*, n., staff members of a bureau.

§ 52A.63 (尸/丶)

尽 52A.63–6

jihn.

[Pop. of 盡 22.30]

§ 52A.70 (尸/乚)

屁 52A.70–2

pih.

N. Wind (from bowels): 放屁 break wind, (fig.) talk rot; 放狗屁 (abusive) talk rot, bosh; 狗屁不通 (abusive) rotten (of writing); 拍馬屁 (derog.) to flatter; 馬屁精 flatterer; 屁大的事弄得有聲有色 make a fuss about nothing; 嚇得屁滾尿流 frightened to death.

屁股 *pih'gu*, n., the buttocks: 屁股眼 the anus.

尼 52A.70–2

nir.

N. A nun: 尼僧 a nun; 尼庵 nunnery; 尼寺 ditto; 女尼 a nun; 老尼 an old nun; 尼姑 *-gu*↓.

尼姑 *nirgu*, n., a nun.

尼古丁 *nirguuding*, n., (translit.) nicotine (also 菸鹼).

尼龍 *nirlurng*, n., (translit.) nylon.

屍 52A.70–3

shy.

[Interch. 尸]

N. A corpse: 死屍 a dead body; 驗屍 autopsy; 借屍還魂 (of ghost) enter a fresh and unburied corpse and be reincarnated; 屍變 the mysterious rising of a corpse; 屍單, 屍格 coroner's certificate of death.

屍骨 *shy-guu*, n., skeleton of a corpse.

屍首 *shyshoou*, n., dead body (in an accident, or after execution).

屍體 *shytii*, n., dead body: 屍體解剖 autopsy.

尾 52A.70–9

weei (**yii*).

N. adjunct. 一尾魚 one fish.

N. (-'*l*) Tail, end: 尾巴 *-'ba*↓; 搖尾 wag its tails; 夾尾 (like a dog) slink away, tail between legs; 尾大不掉 the tail wagging the dog; subordinate growing too powerful; 馬尾(兒) horse's tail; 狗尾(兒) dog's tail; 巷尾 end of alley; 船尾 the stern; 首尾, 頭尾 beginning and end; 無頭無尾 without beginning or end; (murder case) without clues; 後尾, 末尾 the end.

V.t. To tail after: 尾其後 ditto; 尾之 (LL) tail after him.

Adj. The rear, the last: 尾位 the last seat; 尾數 *-shuh*↓.

尾巴(兒) **yii'ba('l)*, n., tail, end part, also remnant followers.

尾鰭 *weei-chir*, n., tail fin.

尾擊 *weei-jir*, v.i., to attack from the rear.

尾閭 *weir-lyuu*, n., an alleged hole in ocean where all water sinks down.

尾聲 *weei-sheng*, n., the last echo, last act of some disappearing movement, (mus.) coda.

尾數 *weeishuh*, n., the decimal points.

尾隨 *weeisueir*, v.t., to follow after, tail after.

尾子 *weeitz*, n., (1) decimal points; (2) the end of story.

尻 52A.70–9

kau.

N. End of spine; the rump, the pelvic region.

§ 52A.80 (尸/八)

屭 52A.80–4

shih.

屭屭 *shihshih*, n., a giant turtle, oft. a stone base of tablet.

屄 52A.80–6

bi.

N. Vagina.

§ 52A.82 (尸/乂)

屐 52A.82–9

ji.

N. Wooden shoes, clogs: 木屐 ditto; 草屐 straw sandals; 錦屐 (MC) silk slippers; 屐齒 spikes of wooden shoes; 屐痕 (poet.) traces of clog prints in travel.

履 52A.82–9

lyuu.

N. (1) (LL) shoes: 西裝革履 in Western dress and leather shoes; 布履 cloth shoes; 草履 sandals. (2) (AC) 福履 blessings. (3) (AC) territory. (4) A surname.

V. i. (1) To step on, tread, to fulfill (promise), follow (teachings): 履冰 to tread on ice—caution; 履諾 fulfill promise; 履虎尾 to step on tiger's tail—place oneself in a dangerous position. (2) To assume office: 履新, 履任 *-shin, -rehn*↓.

履歷 *lyuulih*, n., biographical data (age, school, experience, career).
履任 *lyuurehn*, v. i., assume office.
履新 *lyuushin*, v. i., take up new post.
履行 *lyuushirng*, v. t., to fulfill (promise, treaty obligation, etc.).

§ 52A.83 (ㄕ/～)

遲 52A.83–2

chyr (**jyh*).

N. A surname.

V. i. (**jyh*) (AC only) to wait, hope: 遲帝還 wait for emperor to return.

Adj. & adv. (1) Late, slow, -ly: 來遲了 arrive late; 我來遲了 sorry, I'm late; 悔之已遲 too late to repent. (2) Later: 遲些時 a few minutes later; 遲一日 one day later; 遲幾天 late a few days, or a few days later: 遲早 *-tzaau*↓. (3) (Also **jyh*) toward (time): 遲旦, 遲明 *-dahn, -mirng*↓. (4) Slow of understanding: 遲鈍, 遲疑 *-duhn, -'yir*↓.

遲遲 *chyrchyr*, adj. & adv., (1) slow, -ly: 遲遲其行 slow to get started, go slowly; (2) leisurely, poised: 春日遲遲 the spring days pass leisurely; 威儀遲遲 (AC) poised, leisurely in manner.
遲旦 *chyrdahn* (**jyh-*), adv., (LL) toward dawn, daybreak.
遲鈍 *chyrduhn*, adj., dull, slow-witted.
遲緩 *chyr'huaan*, adj. & adv., slow, -ly, sluggish, -ly, tardy, -ily.
遲回 *chyrhueir*, v. i., to loiter, tarry, hesitate.
遲滯 *chyrjyh*, adj., slow (in progress, business); at crawling pace.
遲留 *chyrliour*, v. i., to loiter around; to stop over at place.
遲慢 *chyr'mahn*, adj., slow in progress. 「see *-dahn*↑.
遲明 *chyrmirng* (**jyh-*), adv., (LL)
遲暮 *chyrmuh*, adv., late in the day, toward sunset; toward year's end.
遲早 *chyrtzaau*, adv., sooner or later: 只是遲早問題 only a question of time.
遲誤 *chyrwuh*, v.i., to procrastinate, cause missing of schedule.
遲延 *chyr'yarn*, v.i. & adj., postpone, drag on, slacken.
遲疑 *chyr'yir*, adj., unable to decide.

咫 52A.83–4

jyy.

N. Eight inches in Jou Dyn.: 咫聞 (AC) within hearing distance.

咫尺 *jyrchyy*, n., a very short distance: 咫尺之間 only a short distance; 咫尺天涯, 咫尺山河 physically very near but separated as if by long distances.

尺 52A.83–5

chyy.

N. (1) A foot (measurement= 10寸 and 1/10 丈): 市尺 standard foot; 公尺 meter; 英尺 English foot; 丁字尺 T-square; 平行尺 parallel ruler; 比例尺 scale; 深淺尺 depth gauge; 垂線尺 plumb rule; 水平尺 spirit level; 計算尺, 滑尺 slide rule; 卷尺 tape measure; 摺尺 folding ruler; 尺有所短, 寸有所長 every man is useful according to his ability. (2) A letter: 尺牘, 尺翰, 尺簡 *-dur, -hahn, -jiaan*↓; 尺書, 尺素 *-shu, -suh*↓. (3) (**chee*) The note *sol* in pentatonic scale, see 工ᐞ尺 31.30.

尺八 *chyyba*, n., an anc. flute-like instrument.
尺版 *chyrbaan*, n., tablet held in hand during imperial audience (=手版). 「land.
尺地 *chyydih*, n., a tiny piece of
尺度 *chyyduh*, n., dimensions.
尺牘 *chyydur*, n., (LL) letters; oft. models of letter writing used in schools.
尺幅 *chyyfur*, n., dimensions; canvas (of novel, project).
尺翰 *chyyhahn*, n., (LL, court.) letter, correspondence.
尺蠖 *chyyhuh*, n., looper caterpillar; symbolic of yielding before advance.
尺簡 *chyrjiaan*, n., letter, short note, *-hahn*↑. 「ing.
尺錦 *chyyjiin*, n., a gem of writ-
尺籍 *chyyjir*, n., (AC) military reg-

屐 履 遲 咫 尺

亅	小	⺊	十	土	ナ	廾	㔾	丨	一	丁	フ	口	囗	冂	乛	厂	尸	亠	广	宀	丶	乚	弋	心	八	人	乂	乛	丿	丿	㇄	ㄑ
00	01	02	10	11	12	20	21	22	30	31	32	40	41	42	50	51	52	60	61	62	63	70	71	72	80	81	82	83	90	91	92	93

尺 屣 㞞 尸 屢 屨 閉

ister.

尺碼 *chyrmaa*, n., dimensions.

尺書 *chyyshu*, n., letter, correspondence.

尺素 *chyysuh*, n., ditto.

尺頭 *chyy'tou*, n., piece goods; 尺頭兒 a bolt of cloth, standard dimensions.

尺寸 *chyytsuhn* (-'*tsun*), n., small quantities, area; dimensions.

尺土 *chyrtuu*, n., tiny area.

屣 52A.83–9

shii.

N. Slippers: 視如敝屣 to regard as of no importance ("old slippers"); 倒屣而迎 to slip on slippers hurriedly to extend welcome; 屣履 to wear cloth shoes with the heel back folded down.

㞞 52A.83–9

surng.

N. (Coll.) semen.

§ 52A.91 (尸/丿)

尸 52A.91–5

shy.
[Cf. 52.91]

§ 52A.93 (尸/〈)

屢 52A.93–2

lyuu.

Adv. Oftentimes: 屢經挫折 repeatedly met with setbacks; 屢年 year after year, in many succesive years; 屢試 tried many times: 屢試不售 fail in civil examination again and again; 屢戰屢敗 repeatedly fought and lost; 屢告不聽 would not listen to repeated advice.

屢屢 *lyurlyuu*, adv., repeatedly.
屢次 *lyuutsyh*, adv., many times.

屨 52A.93–9

jyuh.

N. Straw sandals.

V. t. Tread, step on, tramp over.

SECTION 52B

§ 52B.00 (門/亅)

閉 52B.00–1 閇, 閍

bih.

V.i. & t. To close: 關閉 to close; 閉目, 閉眼, 閉目養神 close the eyes for rest; 閉口, 閉嘴, 閉上你的嘴 shut up; 閉會 close meeting; 閉歇營業 close up shop and stop business; 幽閉 keep under detention; 閉門 *-mern*↓; 閉塞 *-seh*↓; 閉月羞花 woman's beauty puts the flowers to shame and outshines the moon.

閉氣 *bih-chih*, v.i., stop breathing voluntarily; draw last breath.

閉糴 *bih-dir*, v.i., ban buying of rice (stop hoarding).

閉戹 *bih-eh*, adj., in difficult circumstances.

閉關 *bih-guan*, v.i., close the border, i.e., stop foreign trade; 閉關自守 stop international intercourse for defence; also live in isolation, stop seeing friends; 閉關主義 n., isolationism.

閉經 *bih-jing*, v.i. & n., menopause.

閉蟄 *bihjyr*, v.i., hibernate.

閉靈 *bih-lirng*, v.i., stop receiving condolences at funeral after a certain period.

閉路 *bih-luh*, n., closed circuit (television, broadcast), also called 閉合電路.

閉門 *bih-mern*, v.i., close door: 閉門謝客 stop receiving visits from friends; 閉門不納 be not received (of visitor); 嘗閉門羹 "drink the soup of closed door," be denied entrance; 享以閉門羹 to give such "soup," deny (person) entrance; 閉門造車 phr., (a) (AC allu.) to be able to build a carriage at home and fit the car body, i.e., with standardization; (b) indulge in fantasy, build air castles.

閉幕 *bihmuh*, v.i., curtain down at plays, close conference, meeting; 閉幕典禮 ceremony at closing of conference.

閉塞 *bihseh*, v.t., stop(ped) up (nose, sewer, avenue of expression).

閗 52B.00–1

douh.

[Var. of 鬭 52B.00]

閑 52B.00–1

shiarn.

N. (AC) a stable: 防閑 to prevent disorderly conduct; 踰閑 overstep the bounds.

Adj. (1) Leisurely, quiet, having free time (in this sense freely interch. 閒). (2) Practised, familiar (interch. 嫻): 閑習 *-shir*↓.

閑習 *shiarnshir*, v. i., to practise until (subject, art) is familiar; (also wr. 嫻).

闌 52B.00–1

larn.

N. (1) A door screen. (2) (Interch. 欄): 闌干 *-gan*↓.

V.t. To bar, separate (interch. 攔): 遮闌 to screen; 闌截 *-jier*↓.

Adj. (1) (Of time) late: 夜闌人靜 all is quiet in the dead of night; 歲闌 late in the year; 酒闌 wine has flowed freely at end of dinner. (2) Flagging; declining: 闌珊 *-shan*↓.

Adv. Without permission: 闌出 leave forbidden grounds without permission; 闌入 *-ruh*↓.

闌風 *larn-feng*, n., unceasing winds.

闌干 *larngan*, (1) n., (=欄杆) a wooden railing, banister; (2) n., crisscross pattern; (3) adj., tearful.

闌檻 *larnjiahn*, n., a wooden railing (闌干 *-gan*↑).

闌截 *larnjier*, v.t., (=攔截) intercept, hinder, cut off.

闌入 *larnruh*, v.t., (1) enter (forbidden grounds) without authorization; (2) interpolate.

闌珊 *larnshan*, adj., decayed, worn-out: 意興闌珊 with flagging interest, satiated; 春意闌珊 the declining days of spring.

闌尾炎 *larnweeiyarn*, n., (=盲腸炎) appendicitis.

闌遺 *larnyir*, v.t. & n., (leave) articles left unclaimed.

閨 52B.00–1

guei.

N. (1) A small gate. (2) Women's quarters, boudoir: 深閨 a lady's private rooms; 春閨 a lady's chamber where she pines for her lover; 待字閨中 a girl not yet betrothed; 閨閣, 閨房 *-ger*, *-farng*↓; 閨秀 *-shiouh*↓; 蘭閨, 香閨 a boudoir.

閨器 *gueichih*, n., (LL, rare) a chamber pot for women.

閨範 *gueifahn*, n., (a model of) feminine virtue.

閨房 *gueifarng*, n., a lady's bedroom.

閨閣 *gueiger*, n., (1) a lady's chamber; women in gen.; (2) a side gate in palace.

閨門 *gueimern*, n., (1) a door to the women's apartments; (2) a side gate in palace or city walls.

閨秀 *gueishiouh*, n., (1) young ladies: 大家閨秀 girls from respectable families; (2) a woman with literary talents.

閨女 *gueinyuu*, n., (1) a virgin; (2) one's daughter.

闔 52B.00–1

her.

[Related 合 81.40]

V. i. & t. To close: 闔上門 close the door; 闔扇 door panel; 闔眼 close eyes.

Adj. Whole: 闔第光臨 your whole family is invited; 闔府平安 hope your whole family is doing well.

Adv. (AC) var. of 何 why, why not, where, see 盍 11.30.

闥 52B.00–1

tah.

N. (1) Gate. (2) Side gate in palace: 排闥而入 push door open unceremoniously and enter.

閎 52B.00–1

hurng.

N. A surname.

Adj. Big, vast, broad (cf. 宏, 弘, 鴻, 洪 same sound and meaning, slightly different usage).

閹 52B.00–1

yan.

閹 闚 閧 閧 闓 闐 閩 闈 闠 閂 鬪 閈 閏 開

V.t. To castrate; p.p., castrated: 閹割 to castrate; 閹人 a eunuch; 閹寺 a palace eunuch.

闚 52B.00-1

kuei.

[Var. of 窺 62A.70]

閧 52B.00-2

huhng.

[Var. 鬨]

V. i. To make a lot of noise: 閧堂大笑 an uproar of laughter in the audience (also wr. 哄堂); 起閧 create a big noise.

Adj. Boisterous, noisy.

閧動 *hungduhng*, v. t., to stir up a sensation in (city, area) (usu. 哄動).

閧 52B.00-2

huhng.

[Err. var. of 閧 52B.00↑]

闓 52B.00-2

kaai.

V. t. To open wide.

Adj. (Interch. 愷 22A.30) kind, gentle; (interch. 凱 21S.70) triumphant.

闐 52B.00-2

tiarn.

Adj. Full of people: 賓客闐門 (LL) the house is full of guests.

闐闐 *tiarntiarn*, adj., (AC) descriptive of rumbling, rolling sound.

閩 52B.00-2

mirn (also *miin*).

N. Fukien Province.

閩侯 *Mirnhour*, n., Foochow.
閩南 *mirnnarn* (*miin-*), n., South Fukien; 閩南話 South Fukien dialect.

闈 52B.00-2

weir.

N. (1) Palace side gate. (2) Living quarters: 庭闈 parents' living quarters. (3) Examination hall in palace examinations: 入闈 join the palace examinations.

闠 52B.00-2

hueih.

N. See 闤^闠 52B.00.

閂 52B.00-3

shuan.

N. Door bolt.

鬪 52B.00-3

douh.

[Pop. of 鬭 52B.00↓]

閈 52B.00-3

hahn.

N. (1) (AC) entrance gate to a block of houses (里門). (2) (AC) walls.

閏 52B.00-3

ruhn.

Adj. (1) Intercalary: 閏年 *-niarn*, 閏月 *-yueh*, 閏日 *-ryh*↓. (2) (Politics) without the benefit of legitimacy: 閏位 *-weih*↓; 閏統 illegitimate rule.

閏年 *ruhn-niarn*, n., a leap year.
閏日 *ruhn-ryh*, n., February 29 in a leap year.
閏位 *ruhn-weih*, n., illegitimate political power.
閏月 *ruhn-yueh*, n., the intercalary month in a lunar leap year.

開 52B.00-3

kai.

N. (1) A term indicating size of page: 四開 quarto; 八開 octavo. (2) Carat: 十八開 "18k" gold. (3) A surname.

V. t. (1) To open: 開門 open door; 開門見山 "door facing mountain," (of speech, conversation) come straight to the point; 開門七件事 seven daily needs of household: fuel, rice, oil, salt, soya sauce, vinegar, and tea; 開門揖盜 open the door to invite thief, a politician's mistake in alliance; 開房間 rent hotel room for a few hours for illicit love; 開天窗 suffer ravages of venereal diseases on face; leave blank space in newspapers on account of censorship; 開燈 put on the light; 開卷 open a book: 開卷有益 (of useful books) reading enriches the mind; 開眼界 see s.t. new from travel, open mental horizon; 開雲見日 (of people suffering wrongs) see justice again; 開誠佈公 have a frank and straight talk. (2) To begin, open (shop, school, class, exhibition, performance, hospital), start (fighting, negotiations, meeting): 開首, 開頭, 開手, 開始 begin, at the beginning, see *-shoou*^{1}, *-tour*, *shoou*^{2}, *-shyy*^{1}↓; 開創, 開設 to found, establish, *-chuahng*, *-sheh*↓; 開國 found a dynasty or nation; 開飯 (order to) have meal served; 開筆 (student) first begin to write composition, (columnist) write first article in a new year; 開標 open public bids; 開彩 *-tsaai*↓; 開市 open for business, open market; 開工 *-gung*↓; 開例 *-lih*↓; 開八大慶 begin age of seventy-one in expectation of celebrating eightieth birthday; 開歲, 開春 begin a new year; 開宗明義 purpose, goal or theme stated in opening chapter or sentences. (3) To open up: 開路 open a new road, lead the way; 開路先鋒 pioneer, trail blazer; 開山 cultivate mountain district for habitation; 開山祖師 founder of religious sect; 開河 open up a waterway, (of ice in river) to thaw; 開河道 open up river route; 開濬 dredge and deepen river; 開鑿, 開礦, open mines; 開採礦物 mine minerals; 開荒, 開墾 *-huang*, *-keen*↓; 開源節流 earn more income and cut down expenses; 開花, 花開了 to flower, blossom, flower blossoms; 開顏, 笑逐顏開, 眉開眼笑 to beam, to smile happily; 開凍 thaw. (4) To remove restrictions, to let: 開禁 lift ban (on fishing, etc.); 開葷 break vegetarian fast; 開戒 break, terminate vows (not to drink, smoke, etc.); 開脫 *-duo*, 開除 *-chur*↓. (5) To set going: 開車, 開船 start car, boat; 開倒車 to turn the clock back; 開夜車 burn the midnight oil, 開船了 boat sails; 開步走 (mil.) forward march! 開行 *-shirng*↓; 開出 has started out; 開到 (boat, train) arrive; 開往 going to (destination); 開炮, 開槍, 開火 open fire in battle. (6) To set, set out in detail, itemize: 開單 give itemized bill; 開賬 render bill, account: 開花賬 render false account; 開名單 give list of names; 開列 set out details (expenses, names); 開計 total sum. (7) Do, make, in many phrr.: 開玩笑 make fun of (person); 開荒腔 tell a tall tale, talk about things one doesn't know; 開店, 開舖子 run or keep a shop.

Adj. (1) 開水 boiled, -ing, water; 水開了 water is boiling. (2) 開年, 開春 next year, next spring. (3) Liberal, open, modern: 開朗, 開明, 開通 *-laang*, *-mirng*, *-tung*↓.

Adv. Away, off, out: 走開 go away; 打開 open (package), settle (confusion); 解開 untie (knot); 分開 separate; 分不開 cannot be separated; 剖開, 劈開 split open; 張開 open (umbrella, mouth, etc.); 離開 separate, leave; 滾開 scram; 躲開 hide away, get away from fight, dodge blow.

開辦 *kaibahn*, v. t., start (business, school, hospital, etc.).

開拔 *kaibar*, v. i., (of troops) set out to (place).

開苞 *kaibau*, v. t., deflower (a virgin).

開本 *kaibeen*, n., the size of sheet (in printing), see N.↑.

開衩 *kai-chah*, v. t. & adj., (ladies' skirt) open slit; also 開隙(兒), 開氣(兒), see *-chih*↓.

開差 *kai-chai*, v. i., (1) be removed from office; (2) (mil.) despatch on mission.

開場 *kaicharng*, v. i. & n., opening of theatrical play or other public activity; 開場白 n., opening statement (usu. in Chin. plays).

開腔 *kaichiang*, v. i., "open one's mouth" and say s. t.: 他一直不開腔 he would never say a word; 開謊腔 invent tall tales.

開竅兒 *kaichiauh'l*, v. i., (1) (of teenage person) begin to have interest in opposite sex; (2) to see more and understand more; 這下子, 他可開竅兒了 now he begins to understand.

開氣(兒) *kai-chih('l)*, see *-chah*↑, (also wr. 開隙).

開創 *kaichuahng*, v. t., start, found (school, hospital).

開除 *kaichur*, v. t., dismiss (from school, party).

開缺 *kai-chyue*, v. i., formerly, (official) quit office, thus leaving a post vacant.

開單(兒)(子) *kai-dan(-da'l)(tz)*, phr., send bill for payment.

開襠褲 *kaidang-kuh*, n., children's pants with seat cut open.

開刀 *kai-dau*, v. i., to operate in surgery; (fig.) 拿他開刀 the first (student) to be punished.

開導 *kaidauh*, v. t., to explain and convince (person).

開弔 *kaidiauh*, v. i., hold memorial service for deceased.

開端 *kaiduan*, v. i. & n., the beginning (of affairs, relations).

開動 *kaiduhng*, v. t., start (machine, course of action).

開恩 *kai-en*, v. i., show forgiveness, lenient treatment.

開發 *kaifa*, v. t., (1) educate (minds); open up (source of income); ('*fa*), pay off (laborer for service); (2) (AC) open and read government communications; (3) colonize (land); open up (natural resources); n., development.

開放 *kaifahng*, v. t., to set free, to open (park, garden) to public; to open (port) to trade with foreign nations.

開方 *kaifang*, v. i., (1) (math.) to find square or cube; (2) (*fang* or *fangtz*) write prescription for patient.

開封 *Kaifeng*, n., capital of Northern Suhng Dyn., in Honan.

開復 *kaifuh*, v. t., (1) to recover lost territory; (2) to restore (official) to former post.

開割 *kaige*, v. t. & n., to operate in surgery.

亅	小	卜	十	土	ナ	廾	卜	丨	一	丁	フ	口	囗	冈	冂	厂	尸	亠	广	宀	丶	乚	七	心	八	人	乂	乛	一	刂	𠂉	く
00	01	02	10	11	12	20	21	22	30	31	32	40	41	42	50	51	52	60	61	62	63	70	71	72	80	81	82	83	90	91	92	93

開

開關 *kai-guan*, (1) n., electric switch, any mechanical control button, water faucet; (2) v. t., to open city gate or sentry post.

開光 *kai-guang*, phr., (1) Buddhist ceremony of consecrating newly completed idol; (2) at laying-in ceremony (大殮) the children of deceased wipe latter's eyes with wet cotton.

開工 *kaigung*, v. i., begin construction: 已經開工了 construction has begun.

開花彈 *kaihua-dahn*, n., shrapnel.

開花兒 *kaihua'l*, v. i., to blossom; (of shoes, etc.) show cracks.

開化 *kaihuah*, v. i. & adj., civilized (country): 未開化國家 uncivilized country; 半開化 semicivilized; 開化(兒) thaw; (coll. of plants, *'hua*), thrive.

開荒 *kaihuang*, open up, colonize wild country.

開懷兒 *kaihuar'l*, v. i., (1) to enjoy oneself, relax: 開懷痛飲 have a hearty drink; (2) 沒開過懷兒 (of woman) has never given birth to baby.

開會 *kai-hueih*, phr., hold a meeting.

開豁 *kaihuoh*, adj., generous, openhearted.

開火(兒) *kai-huoo('l)*, v. i., open fire.

開齋 *kaijai*, v. i., break vegetarian fast.

開張 *kaijang*, v. i., (of shops) open for business.

開獎 *kai-jiaang*, phr., draw lottery in public and announce winner.

開價 *kaijiah*, v. i. & n., asking price at beginning of haggle.

開交 *kaijiau*, v. i., settle dispute: 鬧得不可開交 get into a hot dispute.

開戒 *kai-jieh*, v. i., break vow (to refrain from meat, wine, etc.).

開支 *kaijy*, v. i. & n., expenses: 開支浩大 heavy expenses.

開開 *kaikai*, v. i., (reiterative) as in 開開門 please open the door; 開開玩笑 have a little fun at s.o.'s expense; 開開心 to relax and enjoy oneself.

開墾 *kaikeen*, v. t., to colonize; to open up wild country; to till (land).

開口 *kai-koou*, v. i., (1) to speak up or out: 開口 to smile broadly, laugh out loudly; (2) to sharpen knife; (3) to break dam, (dam) breaks; 開口兒 baby's first sucking at breast.

開闊 *kaikuoh*, adj., openhanded, generous (heart); open, broad (country).

開朗 *kailaang*, adj., discerning, clear-minded; clear (weather), bright open (view).

開臉 *kai-liaan*, phr., formerly, screw off facial hair and tidy up hairline at temples of bride before wedding.

開例 *kailih*, v.i., set a precedent.

開列 *kailieh*, v. i., show in itemized list, make list of names, books, etc.

開鑼 *kai-luor*[1], phr., "open gong," i. e., begin theatrical performance.

開羅 *Kailuor*[2], n., Cairo; 開羅會議 Cairo Conference (1943).

開蒙 *kai-merng*, v. i., educate very young mind (as at kindergarten).

開廟 *kai-miauh*, phr., hold village fair at temple grounds on set dates.

開明 *kaimirng*, adj., liberal, enlightened, progressive (times, policy, attitude).

開幕 *kai-muh*, v. i., (1) (of plays, cinemas) give first public performance; (2) open inaugural (ceremony for conference, new building).

開年 *kainiarn*, n., beginning of year; (Shanghai) next year.

開嗙 *kaipaang*, v. i., to brag.

開盤(兒) *kaiparn(-par'l)*, v. i., (of stock market) opening quotation for the day (cf. 收盤兒 closing quotation); 開盤子 formerly, pay the bill at singsong houses.

開票 *kai-piauh*, phr., count votes at poll.

開闢 *kaipih*, v. i. & t., (1) open up country; (2) 開天闢地 creation of the world ("separate heaven and earth").

開設 *kaisheh*, v. t., to found or start (shop, hospital, etc.).

開綫 *kai-shiahn*, phr., show seams in dress.

開消 *kaishiau*, v. i. & n., (1) pay out; expenses: 開消很大 the running expenses are heavy; (2) to dismiss (worker), see *-chur* ↑.

開心 *kaishin*, (1) adj., happy, enjoying happy moment: 玩得眞開心 had lots of fun; (2) v. t. & n., to make fun of (person): 別拿我開心, 尋開心 don't make fun of me; happiness; (3) v.t., (AC, rare) edify, stimulate thinking; (4) v. i., open one's heart: 開心見誠 talk from the heart, with nothing concealed; (5) phr., (*kai shin*) open the heart surgically.

開行 *kaishirng*, v.i., (of boat, train) start going.

開首 *kaishoou*[1], v. i. & n., to begin, the beginning.

開手 *kaishoou*[2], v.i., ditto.

開水 *kaishueei*, n., boiled, boiling water.

開釋 *kaishyh*, v. i. & t., (1) explain to (person): 向他開釋 explain to him; (2) pardon (criminal).

開學 *kai shyueir*, phr., school opens, commence school work.

開始 *kaishyy*[1], v. i. & n., begin, -ning: 剛開始 has just begun; 開始工作 begin to work; 工作的開始 beginning of work.

開駛 *kaishyy*[2], v. i., (of boat, car) start.

開泰 *kaitaih*, v. i., in full form: 三陽開泰 the spring comes in full form; ("auspicious beginning of a new year").

開堂 *kai-tarng*, v. i., to declare court in session.

開庭 *kai-tirng*, v. t., (law) court in session.

開頭 *kaitour*, v. i. & n., begin, -ning: 凡事開頭最難 the beginning is always the most difficult part; 從開頭到現在 from the beginning to the present.

開彩 *kai-tsaai*, phr., draw lottery.

開通 *kaitung*, (1) v. t., break through obstructions; (2) (-*'tung*) adj., liberal, modern-minded: 這個人很開通 this man is very modern-minded.

開脫 *kaituo*, v. t., pardon (crime), free (criminal).

開拓 *kaituoh*, v. t., expand (territory, business market).

開罪 *kaitzueih*, v. i., to offend: 開罪於他 offend him.

開外 *kaiwaih*, prep. & adv., beyond, over: 五十開外 over fifty in years.

開胃 *kai-weih*, (1) adj., appetizing; (2) v.t., tease: 別拿我開胃 don't make fun of me.

開業 *kai-yeh*, v. i., open for business.

開印 *kai-yihn*, v. i., formerly, (in bureaucracy) take out seal again after its being locked up during New Year holidays.

聞 52B.00-3

wern (**wehn*).

N. (1) A surname. (2) News, story: 新聞 news; 舊聞 old stories, hearsay tradition

V.i. & t. (1) (LL) to hear, but (vern.) to smell; thus 聞聲 hear a noise, but 聞味 smell s.t.: 風聞 hear from gossip; 如是我聞 (Budd.) thus I have heard from Buddha; 傳聞 it is said that; 百聞不如一見 better see for oneself once than hear s.t. a hundred times; 未之前聞 (LL) never heard of such a thing before; 置之罔聞 (LL) paid it no attention. (2) (AC) to report: 弗敢以聞 dared not report. (3) To smell: 聞到甚麼味 smell a certain smell.

Adj. (**wehn*) Famous: 聞人, 聞達 *-rern, -dar* ↓; 博聞 well informed, widely read.

聞達 **wehndar*, adj., well-known: 不求聞達 (AC) did not seek fame.

聞見 *wern-jiahn*, (1) n., (所聞所見) what one sees and hears—gen. knowledge: 聞見有限 one's knowledge is limited; (2) (*-'jian*) v.t., (vern.) to smell s.t.

聞名 *wernmirng*, (1) adj., famous, well-known; (2) v.i., to hear of person's name.

聞人 **wehnrern*, n., (LL) a celebrity.

聞聽 *wernting*, v.i., to hear.

聞望 **wehnwahng*, n., fame.

闞 52B.00-3

kahn (also *haan*).

N. A surname.

V. i. & t. To peep at: 闞其動靜 watch secretly his activities.

闞闞 *kahnkahn* (*harnhaan*), adj., (1) sound of tiger's cry; (2) fierce.

闋 52B.00-3

chyueh.

N. A division in a song: 歌一闋 sang one song or verse.

V. i. (AC) (1) To close the door. (2) To stop. (3) To cease mourning: 服闋 end of mourning period.

問 52B.00-4

wehn.

N. (1) A question: 問答 question and answer. (2) Communication: 音問 news, correspondence.

V. i. & t. (1) To ask, inquire: 問一問 try and ask; 問明 *-mirng*[1] ↓; 問他 ask him; 詢問 ask, also interview for news; 訪問 to interview (person), study (country) while travelling; 問道於盲 ask the way from a blind man; 問長問短, 問東問西 ask all sorts of questions; 不聞不問 neither care to inquire nor to hear; 不問好歹 without first asking about what happened; 不恥下問 (Confucius) was not ashamed to ask from common people. (2) To examine, cross-examine, question: 訊問, 審問, 究問 examine at court; 責問 to hold responsible; 查問 inquire into facts; 追問 ask about the past. (3) To consult: 顧問 v.t., ask for advice, n., advisor; 問卜, 問卦 *-buu -guah* ↓; 問醫 consult a doctor. (4) To hold responsible: 唯子是問 (LL) hold you responsible.

問案 *wehn-ahn*, phr., to hold court.

問安 *wehn-an*, v. i. & t., to give greeting, ask about health.

問卜 *wehn-buu*, phr., to consult fortunetellers.

問寢 *wehn-chiin*, phr., (AC) to say "good night" to parents in bed.

問取 *wehn-chyuu*, v. t., (MC) to ask (cf. 聽取意見 listen to opinions).

問倒 *wehn-daau*, v. t., as in 給他問倒 to be stymied in questions, unable to answer.

問答 *wehn-dar*, n., dialogue: 一問一答 answer to each question successively.

問鼎 *wehn-diing*, phr., (AC, allu.) "inquire about the tripod"-symbol of royal power—entertain ambition to be king.

問短 *wehn-duaan*, v. t., see *-juh* ↓.

問卦 *wehnguah*, phr., consult oracles.

問官 *wehn-guan* (*-'guan*), n., the examining judge.

問供 *wehngung*, v. i., examine and take affidavit.

問好 *wehnhaau*, v. i., to give greeting.

問號(兒) *wehnhauh('l)*, n., the question mark.

問候 *wehnhouh* (*-'hou*), v. t., to greet (person), ask about his health.

問話 *wehn-huah*, v. i., to ask questions; n., a question.

問斬 *wehn-jaan*, v. t., sentence to execution.

問禁 *wehn-jihn*, phr., 入境問禁 ask about taboos and bans upon arrival in foreign country.

問津 *wehn-jin*, phr., (AC, allu.) to ask for directions (lit., "about ferry").

問疾 *wehn-jir*, phr., visit a patient.

開 聞 闞 闋 問

問住 *wehn'jur*, v. i., 問住了 to be unable to answer a difficult question.

問明 *wehn-mirng*[1], v. t., ask for explicit answers, find out: 問明原委 find out origin of affair.

問名 *wehn-mirng*[2], phr., formerly, to ask for name and horoscope of one about to be formally betrothed.

問難 *wehnnahn*, v. i. & t., to test with difficult questions.

問心 *wehn-shin*, phr., 問心無愧 feel one has done one's best upon self-examination.

問世 *wehn-shyh*[1], v. i., to present, be presented, to the public by publication of book, or setting up to be physician.

問事 *wehnshyh*[2], v. i., to attend to work.

問事處 *wehnshyh-chuh*, n., information desk.

問訊 *wehn-shyuhn* (*-'shyun*), v. i. & n., to inquire, -ry; 問訊處 information desk.

問題 *wehntir*, n., problem to be solved; questions in examinations.

問罪 *wehntzueih*, v. i., (1) to sentence as guilty; (2) 興師問罪 send a punitive expedition.

問業 *wehnyeh*, v. i., ask advice from master on learning or professional subjects.

閭 52B.00-4

lyur.

N. (1) (AC) the main gate to a village (*li* 里) of twenty-five families; now generally a village: 倚門倚閭 (of a mother) waiting at house door and village gate (for return of her son). (2) See 尾△閭 52A.70. (3) A surname.

閭里 *lyurlii*, n., village.

閭巷 *lyurshiahng*, n., ditto.

閭閻 *lyuryarn*, n., gen. term for the local inhabitants.

閶 52B.00-4

baan.

N. 老閶 *-laur*, (coll.) shop owner, boss; 老閶娘 boss's wife.

闡 52B.00-4

chaan.

V. t. To expound; propagate.

闡究 *chaanjiouh*, v. t., to study and clarify.

闡明 *chaanmirng*, v. t., to explain, expound (teaching, doctrine).

闡述 *chaanshuh*, v. t., to explain, expound (doctrine, history of events, etc.).

闡揚 *chaanyarng*, v. t., to promote, propagate, extol (teaching, truth); to praise, glorify.

鬭 52B.00-4

douh.

[Var. 鬥, 鬦, 鬪, 鬬]

V. i. & t. (1) To fight: 相鬭 fight each other; 鬭不過他 cannot match him; 戰鬭 fight; 奮鬭 struggle; 決鬭 to duel, fight to decide; 搏鬭 hand-to-hand fight; 械鬭 fight among clans or villagers. (2) To contest, match: 鬭智, 鬭心思 match wits; 鬭力 match strength; 鬭口齒 engage in battle of words; 賭鬭 to bet (against s.o.). (3) Have fights or games: 鬭牌, 鬭棋 play cards, chess; 鬭草 match grass (a girls' game); 鬭雞, 鬭牛, 鬭鵪鶉, 蟋蟀 cockfight, bullfight, quail fight, cricket fight. (4) To fit into one another: 鬭榫 fit mortise and tenon.

鬭巧 *douhchiaau*, v. i., be a coincidence (=湊巧); match cleverness.

鬭氣 *douhchih*, v. i. quarrel or compete just for emotional reasons.

鬭法 *douhnfaa*, v. i., to match magical powers.

鬭很 *douhheen*, v.i., inclined to violence: 好勇鬭狠(很).

鬭話 *douhhuah*, v.i., dispute, quarrel.

鬭爭 *douhjeng*, v.i. & t., to struggle; (in Communist China, v.t.) to hold public meetings to disgrace s.o.

鬭雞眼(兒) *douh-jiyaan*(*-yaa'l*), adj., cross-eyed, cockeyed.

鬭腳 *douhjiaau*, v.i., have bowlegs or toes turned inwards.

鬭勁 *douhjihn* n., contest of strength.

鬭經紀 *douhjing'ji*, v.i. & t., to provoke.

鬭志 *douhjyh* n., fighting morale.

鬭力 *douh-lih*, n. & v.i., wrestle.

鬭悶子 *douhmehntz*, v.i., fight (each other) in the dark, under cover.

鬭牛 *douhniour*, n., bullfight.

鬭蟋蟀 *douh-shishuaih*, n., cricket fight.

鬭閑氣 *douh-shiarnchih*, v.i., keep up fight for vain reasons.

鬭嘴 *douhtzueei*, v.i., quarrel, bicker.

間 52B.00-4

jian (**jiahn*).

N. adjunct. A unit (of rooms): 一間臥室 a bedroom; 一間茅屋 a hut; 安得廣廈千萬間 O, that I could have ten thousand houses (to house the homeless!).

N. (1) A place or locality: 田間 the fields; 人間 among the living: 尚在人間 is still living; 世間 the world; 置之案間 put on the desk; 陽間 the world of the living; 陰間 the world of the dead. (2) Midpoint: 中間(人) in the middle, middleman; 居間(調停) act as a go-between, as an intermediary. (3) (**jiahn*) Space, opening: 間隙 *-shih*↓; 間不容髮 by a hair's breadth; 乘間 take advantage of an opening. (4) A duration of time: 時間 a period of time; 其間 in the interval; 夜間 during nighttime; 日間 during daytime; 晚間 in the evening or night; 晨間 in the morning; 少間 in a little while; 忽然之間 all of a sudden; 百年之間 in a person's lifetime, a century; 瞬間 in the twinkling of an eye.

V. t. (1) (*jiahn) To separate, divide: 間隔 *-ger*, 間斷 *-duahn* ↓; 離間, 反間 to alienate one person from another; 間諜 *-dier* ↓. (2) Find fault with: 禹吾無間然矣 I can't find any fault with Yu.

Adj. (*jiahn) Mixed, commingled: 間色 *-seh* ↓; 相間 alternate, -ly: 紅白相間 red and white intermingled.

Adv. (*jiahn) Occasionally, sometimes: 間或 *-huoh* ↓; 間有 every now and then; 間然 by accident, infrequently, by chance.

間壁 **jiahnbih*, n. & adj., next-door (neighbor).
間步 **jiahnbuh*, v. i., go leisurely on foot (usu. 閒步 pr. *shiarn*).
間出 **jiahnchu*, v. i., go out furtively.
間道 **jiahndauh*, n. & adv., (by) short cuts.
間諜 **jiahndier*, n., a spy, a secret agent.
間斷 **jiahnduahn*, v. t. & adj., disconnect(ed), detach(ed), turn(ed) off.
間隔 **jiahnger*, (1) v. t., set apart, partition, divide into compartments; (2) n., an interval of space or time.
間或 **jiahnhuoh*, adv., occasionally, now and then, sometimes.
間接 **jiahnjie*, adj. & adv., indirect(ly).
間濶 **jiahnkuoh*, adj., (of friends) separated for a long time.
間色 **jiahnseh*, adj., many-colored, variegated.
間歇 **jiahnshie*, adj., intermittent: 間歇熱 intermittent fever; 間歇性 by fits and starts.
間隙 **jiahnshih*, n., a cleft, a slit; a misunderstanding.

閶 52B.00-4

chang.

閶闔 *changher*, n., front gate of palace.
閶門 *Changmern*, n., famous street of Soochow.

闒 52B.00-4

tah.

N. (1) (AC) door, window on upper story. (2) (AC) sound of drums and bells.

闒茸 *tahrurng*, (1) adj., mean, worthless, contemptible; (2) n., (AC) trifles, insignificant details.

闤 52B.00-4

huarn.

闤闠 *huarnhueih*, n., (LL) the market, business district; 闤闠中人 (derog.) (LL) shopkeepers.

閘 52B.00-4

jar.

N. (1) A sluice gate, a lock in canal. (2) A brake in motorcar. (3) A control station on river for domestic revenue: 關閘.

閘板 *jarbaan*, n., (1) sluice board for controlling water in lock gate; (2) a wooden panel protecting window.
閘盒 *jarher*, n., a fuse box controlling electric current.
閘口 *jarkoou*, n., place near lock gate in canal.

閫 52B.00-4

kuun.

N. (1) Threshold. (2) Women's quarters: 閫內 inside domestic affairs, hence what pertains to women or the home; 閫闈 boudoir; see 閫令, 閫闈 *-lihng*, *-wei* ↓. (3) City gate; 閫外 the field command ("outside the city") where the general has full powers, see 閫寄 *-jih* ↓.

閫奧 *kuun-auh*, n., sanctum, private rooms; (fig.) the inner sanctum, mysteries or depths of ideas.
閫寄 *kuun-jih*, v. i., (LL from 寄以閫外之事) confer full discretionary power to commanding general.
閫令 *kuunlihng*, n., (facet.) wife's commands.
閫威 *kuunwei*, n., (facet.) (submit to) wife's power.
閫闈 *kuunweir*, n., women's apartments.

閒 52B.00-4

shiarn (**jian*, **jiahn*).

N. (1) (AC) var. of 間 (pr. *jian*). (2) Leisure time: 不得閒 have no time.

Adj. (1) (Interch. 閑 52B.00) lei-

閒 門

surely, free, quiet, having not much to do: 閒坐, 閒談 *-tzuoh*, *-tarn* and many compp.↓; 閒適, 閒逸 *-shy*, *-yih*↓; 閒磕牙兒 or 閒磕打牙兒 to indulge in idle chats; 野草閒花 women of loose morals, prostitutes; 閒雲野鶴 a recluse with no fixed abode or occupation; 閒是閒非 (take no interest in) irrelevant disputes about affairs. (2) Unoccupied (land or time), vacant: 閒時, 閒空 *-shyr*, *-kuhng*↓; 閒屋,閒地 vacant house, land; 閒不住 be never unoccupied or unemployed. (3) Adj. & adv., (**jiahn* also wr. 間) separate: 閒斷的 off and on; 閒隔 be separated in time or space.

閒步 *shiarnbuh*, v. i., take a stroll.
閒常 *shiarncharng*, adv., usually.
閒錢 *shiarnchian*, n., spare dime.
閒氣 *shiarnchih*, n., quarrel: 與人爭閒氣 quarrel with s. o. on trivial matters.
閒的兒 *shiarn'de'l*, n., a person out of job, poor and unemployed.
閒地 *shiarn-dih*, n., vacant land (not interch. 閑).
閒房 *shiarn-farng*, n., room to rent (not interch. 閑).
閒官 *shiarn-guan*, n., an official post with very little to do.
閒漢 *shiarn-hahn*, n., a loafer, unemployed person.
閒話 *shiarnhuah*, n., (1) gossip: 鬧了很多閒話 cause a lot of gossip; (2) chat in leisure.
閒章兒 *shiarnjang'l*, n., an unofficial personal seal, usu. containing poetic thoughts.
閒靜 *shiarnjihng*, adj. & v. t., quiet, undisturbed: 閒靜一會 enjoy a little quiet.
閒居 *shiarn-jyu*, v. i., to have no official duty; to live freely at home.
閒空(兒) *shiarnkuhng('l)*, n., spare time: 沒閒空兒 have no time.
閒民 *shiarn-mirn*, n., (LL) unemployed people.
閒盤兒 *shiarnpar'l*, n., (1) unimportant affairs: 沒工夫管閒盤兒 no time to bother such; (2) malicious gossip: 放閒盤兒 spread idle gossip.
閒篇兒 *shiarnpia'l*, n., an idle, rambling talk.
閒人 *shiarnrern*, n., loiterer, person with nothing to do: 閒人免進 (a sign) loiterers keep away.
閒散 *shiarnsaan*, adj., (of office) with nothing much to do; (person, time) free, at leisure.
閒暇 *shiarnshiar*, n., leisure time.
閒笑 *shiarn-shiauh*, n., pleasant chatter.
閒心 *shiarn-shin*, n., a free, unburdened mind (to tackle s. t.).
閒書 *shiarn-shu*, n., idle reading.
閒適 *shiarnshyh*[1], adj., leisurely and contented (life), esp. free and easy (style of writing or poems); of leisure and contentment.
閒事 *shiarn-shyh*[2], n., as in 莫管閒事 do not meddle in others' business.
閒時 *shiarnshyr*, adv., when time allows.
閒談 *shiarntarn*, n. & v.i., gossip, talk at random.
閒田 *shiarn-tiarn*, n., (1) land lying fallow; (2) (AC) public land.
閒雜兒 *shiarntzar'l*, n., trivialities (in talk).
閒坐 *shiarntzuoh*, v.i., sit around in idleness.
閒雅 *shiarnyaa*, adj., carefree, elegant.
閒燕 *shiarnyahn*, adj., (AC) free and quiet.
閒言 *shiarn-yarn*, n., (1) gossip; (2) balderdash.
閒逸 *shiarnyih*, adj., leisurely, carefree, fanciful (style, mood).
閒月(兒) *shiarn-yueh(-yueh'l)*, phr., off season on farm, months when farmers are less occupied.
閒語 *shiarn-yuu*, n., see *-yarn*↑.

門 52B.00–5

mern.

Index. Words in this section are classified according to "top of remainder", i.e., character minus 門.

N. adjunct. 三門大砲 three cannons; 這一門親事 this marriage, or marriage proposal; 這門學問 this branch of study.

N. (1) Door, gate, (see 門兒, 門子 *-'l*, *-tz*↓): 大門 gate; 房門 door; 城門 city gate; 便門, 腰門 side door; 太平門 fire exit; 門鈴 door bell; 門環子 gate knocker; 入門 enter door, introductory course; 上門 to visit, also to close door; 敲門 knock at door; 門可羅雀 no callers or customers; 門庭若市 thriving business, many callers. (2) Opening: 耳門 the ear; 糞門, 肛門 anus. (3) School (of thought), sect, branch of study: 孔門弟子 Confucian disciples; 佛門中人 Buddists; 門徒 disciples; 及門弟子 first-generation disciples. (4) Class, branch of study: 分門別類 classify according to subjects; 專門 a special art or line of study; 門門精通 knows every subject or profession. (5) (Fig.) house, family: 門當戶對 (of two related families united by marriage) of equal status or prestige; 門第, 門風, 門楣, *-dih*, *-feng*, *-meih*↓. (6) A surname.

V. t. (AC) defend the gate; attack the gate.

門包(兒) *mern-bau('l)*, n., formerly, gift to gatekeeper of official residences for passing message.
門牆 *mern-chiarng*, n., (LL) symbol of admission to teacher-disciple relationship: 忝列門牆 honored to be counted among the disciples.
門齒 *mern-chyy*, n., (physiol.) incisor (teeth).
門道 *mern-dauh*, n., covered passage leading to house.
門第 *mern-dih*, n., family status: 門第相稱 (of families related by marriage) equal in social status.
門丁 *mern-ding*, n., gatekeeper.
門斗 *mern-doou*, n., door hinge; lintel; formerly, servants of examiner at civil examinations.
門對 *mern-dueih*, n., couplets on doorposts.
門洞(兒) *mern-duhng('l)*, n., see *-dauh*↑.
門房 *mernfarng'l* n., gatekeeper, concierge.

門風 *mernfeng*, n., family reputation, esp. of old families.

門館 *mernguaan*, n., private tutorship; house of 門客 *-keh* ↓; 門館先生 resident private tutor.

門公 *merngung*, n., eunuch.

門戶 *mernhuh*, n., (1) house status, esp. of the rich or high officials: 權貴門戶; (2) strategic area commanding communications; (3) sect: 門戶之見, 之爭 sectarian views, controversies; 自立門戶 establish own school of thought or clique; 門戶人家 formerly, term for brothels; 門戶開放政策 open door policy.

門診 *mernjeen*, n., section for outpatients; visit at doctor's office.

門禁 *mernjihn*, n., control at entrances for passing and exit.

門徑 *mernjihng*, n., proper channel of approach, initiation into subject: 得窺門徑 just learned the approaches to the subject.

門檻 *mernkaan*, n., threshold, the ways, esp. of doing business: 門檻甚精 sharp in business ways and methods.

門客 *mernkeh*, n., usu. scholars acting as friends and advisors to important persons and treated as house guests.

門口 *mernkoou*, n., doorway.

門框 *mern-kuang*, n., door frame on all sides of door.

門兒 *mer'l*, n., door; see *-luh* ↓; branch of study: 你學那一門兒 what is your line?

門臉兒 *mernliaa'l*, n., shop front; neighborhood of city gate.

門聯(兒) *mernliarn*¹*(-liar'l)*, n., poetic couplets on sides of gate.

門簾(兒, 子) *mernliarn*²*(-liar'l, -tz)*, n., door screen.

門吏 *mern-lih*, n., petty officer in charge of gate entrance.

門樓 *merlour*, n., gate tower.

門路 *mernluh*, n., (1) openings or connections for securing jobs; (2) tricks of the trade: 摸到門路 have learned the ways of the trade.

門羅主義 *Mernluor juuyih*, n., Monroe Doctrine (1823).

門脈 *mernmaih*, n., (1) (Chin. med.) portal vein; (2) visit as outpatient.

門楣 *mernmeih*, n., lintel, as symbol of family reputation or status.

門面 *mernmiahn*, n., (1) shop front; (2) public appearance; 不過壯壯門面而已 just for creating a good public impression; 門面話 routine courteous expressions without sincerity.

門牌 *mernpair*, n., house number: 門牌號碼.

門票 *mernpiauh*, n., admission ticket.

門人 *mernrern*, n., disciple; gatekeeper; *-keh* ↑.

門扇 *mern-shahn*, n., door panel.

門生 *mernsheng*, n., pupil; 收門生 take in pupils: 門生故吏 (LL) disciples and old followers or minor officials; 拜門生 formerly, a graduate who had passed civil examination performed ceremony as pupil of chief examiner.

門神 *mernshern* (*mern'shen*), n., spirit guarding entrance to house or temple.

門下 *mernshiah*, n., see *-keh* ↑; acknowledged disciple, see *-sheng* ↑; 拜他門下 be accepted as his disciple; 門下士 scholar friends of official, see *-keh* ↑.

門限 *mern-shiahn*, n., threshold.

門閂 *mern-shuan*, n., door bolt.

門塾 *mern-shur*, n., classes at home given by private tutor.

門市 *mernshyh*, n., sales, retail sales: 門市部 *--buh*, n., sales department; 門市生意 sales at shop.

門婿 *mern-shyuh*, n., son-in-law.

門帖 *merntiee*, n., poster on door (for rent, etc.); couplet pasted on doorposts.

門子 *merntz*, n., (1) gatekeeper; (2) 串門子 phr., (usu. of women who) pass from house to house (to spread gossip); (3) 鑽門子, 托門子 phr., seek, ask s. o., to get a job through connections, ＝門路 *-luh* ↑; (4) house: 濶門子, 大門子 rich house.

門祚 *mern-tzuoh*, n., family tradition.

門外漢 *mern-waih-hahn*, n., layman, opp. 專家 specialist.

門衛 *mern-weih*, n., gatekeeper, esp. in football. 「cisor.

門牙 *mern-yar*, n., front teeth; in-

門業 *mern-yeih*, n., traditional profession of family.

閂 52B.00-5

douh

[Var. of 鬭 52B.00 ↑]

闖 52B.00-5

chuaang (AC also *chehn*).

V.i. & t. (1) To rush in by force or improperly, to roam about: 闖進去 break into room against rules; 闖大運 take great risks for some fortune; 闖婚作 formerly, rush into marriage without consulting astrologers; 闖光棍 a ne'er-do-well; 闖江湖 to make a living from town to town (as boxers, like Western circuses). (2) To collide: 闖禍 *-huoh* ↓ (related 撞 10A.11). (3) To learn by some hard knocks: 闖出膽兒來了 gain courage by experience; 闖鍊 *-liahn* ↓.

闖禍 *chuahng-huoh*, (sp. pr. *-chuaang*), v. i., to get into a serious accident (in driving, by political mistake).

闖鍊 *chuaangliahn*, v. i., gain experience from real life.

闖喪 *chuahngsang*, v. i., (sl. abusive) to roam about, ("run into s. o.'s funeral").

闖子 *chuaangtz*, n., (coll.) a ruffian.

闢 52B.00-5

pih.

亅	小	卜	十	土	ナ	卄	𠃊	丨	一	丁	フ	口	囗	冂	丁	厂	尸	亠	广	宀	丶	乚	弋	心	八	人	乂	一	丿	丿	𠂉	く
00	01	02	10	11	12	20	21	22	30	31	32	40	41	42	50	51	52	60	61	62	63	70	71	72	80	81	82	83	90	91	92	93

闢 鬧 閔 閡 誾 闇

V. t. (1) To open: 闢戶, 闢牖 (LL) open door, window. (2) To break path, open up country: 開闢 open up; 開天闢地 created the universe; 闢荒, 闢田 open up wild country. (3) To correct: 闢謠 correct, deny rumors; 闢邪歸正 attack heresy and restore orthodox religion; 闢佛, 闢墨 argue against Buddhism, Motse's teachings.

鬧 52B.00-6

nauh.

V.i. & t. (1) To quarrel, dispute hotly, create confusion, cause disturbance, stir up trouble, make a loud noise, do anything disorderly: 吵鬧 quarrel noisily; 擾鬧 cause disturbance; 胡鬧 talk nonsense, play antics; 別胡鬧 don't make a fool of yourself! 別鬧 be quiet, please! 鬧風潮 stir up unrest (among students, workers, etc.), call a strike; 鬧房 *-farng* ↓; 鬧亂子 cause trouble, start a riot, commit a serious blunder; 鬧鬨 cause an uproar; 鬧家務 have domestic trouble; 鬧酒 become quarrelsome as result of too much drinking; 鬧着玩兒 do(s.t.)silly for the fun of it; 鬧吵子 to squabble; 鬧事 *-shyh* ↓; 鬧脾氣 show ill temper, get into a passion; 鬧氣 *-chih* ↓; 鬧意見 have difference of opinion; 鬧擰兒, 鬧擰了 have misunderstanding; 鬧性子 fly into a rage; 鬧心眼兒 be suspicious, reticent, uncommunicative; 鬧彆扭 be at odds: 兩口子又在鬧彆扭 the couple are bickering again. (2) Suffer from, be troubled by, undergo, experience: 鬧病 *-bihng* ↓; 鬧肚子, 鬧嗓子, 鬧脚氣, 鬧眼睛 suffer from or have diarrhoea, a sore throat, beriberi, eye trouble; 鬧天氣 (of climate) be "under the weather"; 鬧水災 have floods, be inundated; 鬧鬼 *-gueei* ↓; 鬧饑荒 suffer famines; 鬧賊 be visited by burglars; 鬧窮 *-chyurng* ↓. (3) Cause (s.t.) to happen: 鬧了滿身的水 get soaked all over; 鬧出一身大汗 perspire all over; 鬧得一團糟, 一場糊塗 create havoc, make a mess of it; 鬧得天翻地覆 turn the whole world upside down; 鬧得滿城風雨 cause a big scandal; 鬧得雞犬不寧, 鬧得頭昏腦脹 cause such utter confusion as to make everybody nervous, to drive one crazy. (4) Make a clear distinction, distinguish: 鬧不清 cannot distinguish one thing from another; 鬧不清誰是誰 cannot tell who is who; 鬧不清誰是誰非 cannot tell who is right and who is wrong.

Adj. Noisy: 鬧得慌 noisy and irritating; (MC) 鬧騰, 鬧火火, 鬧轟轟, 鬧鑊鐸, 鬧荒荒 tumultuous; 鬧炒炒, 鬧吵吵 clamorous; 鬧市 *-shyh* ↓; 鬧熱, 熱鬧 (of festival, party) noisy and lots of fun.

N. Spree, boisterousness: 看熱鬧 to watch a big crowd at celebrations; 鬧中取靜 keep quiet in a noisy neighborhood.

鬧病 *nauh-bihng*, v.i., be ill.

鬧氣 *nauh-chih*, v.i., look for trouble in a fit of anger.

鬧窮 *nauh-chyurng*, v.i., be poor, lack money or funds.

鬧房 *nauh-farng*, v.i. & n., (also 鬧新房) "tease the bride," esp. to make the bride laugh.

鬧鬼 *nauh-gueei*, v.i., (1) (of houses) be haunted; (2) play antics.

鬧鐘 *nauh-jung*, n., an alarm clock.

鬧喪鼓(兒)(子) *nauhsang-guu* (*'l*) (*tz*), n., a kind of musical instrument used at funerals.

鬧事 *nauh-shyh*[1], v.i., to cause trouble.

鬧市 *nauh-shyh*[2], n., busy streets.

鬧虛 *nauhshyu*, v. i., affect politeness (also 客氣).

鬧羊花 *nauhyarnghua*, n., (bot.) rhododendron, *Rhododendron sinense* (also 羊躑躅).

鬧油 *nauh-your*, adj., uneasy, disturbed.

閔 52B.00-6

miin.

N. (1) A surname. (2) (AC) disastrous news: 閔凶 (parents' death).

V. i. & t. (1) (AC) to endeavor. (2) (AC) take pity on, ＝憫 22A.00.

閡 52B.00-6

her.

N. & v.t. To obstruct; an obstruction: 隔閡 lose contact, not familiar; 阻閡 an obstruction.

誾 52B.00-6

yirn.

Adj. (AC) friendly: 誾誾如也.

闇 52B.00-6

ahn.

N. (AC) dusk, nighttime.

V.t. (AC) to close (gate).

Adj. (1) Dark, gloomy, dismal (interch. 黯 41S.41). (2) Stupid: 闇弱, 闇懦 *-ruoh, -nuoh* ↓.

闇闇 *ahn-ahn*, adj., gloomy, shady.

闇淺 *ahnchiaan*, adj., (LL) superficial in knowledge, not well informed.

闇劣 *ahnlieh*, adj., stupid (person).

闇懦 *ahnnuoh*, adj., stupid, weak in character.

闇然 *ahnrarn*, adj., obscure: 闇然而日章 (of truth) though obscure for a time, yet will daily become more accepted.

闇弱 *ahnruoh*, adj., see *-nuoh* ↑.

闇誦 *ahnsuhng*, v.i., recite fluently (also wr. 諳).

閼 52B.00-6

eh.
[Var. 遏 41.83]

V. t. To block up: 閼塞.

閬 52B.00-6

laang (also **lahng*).

N. A high door or gate: 閬苑 fairyland, Elysium.

Adj. Lofty, spacious: 閬閬 exalted.

闊 52B.00-6

kuoh.
[Pop. 濶]

V. i. (1) (Of friends) be separated, live apart: 闊別 *-bier* ↓; 久闊音候 have not heard from (friend) for a long time. (2) (AC) to ease off: 闊其租賦 ease their tax burdens.

Adj. (1) Broad, wide: 闊四尺 four feet wide; 寬闊, 廣闊 wide (room, space, circle); 闊步 (take) long steps; 高談闊論 talk high-sounding phrases, highfalutin. (2) Showily rich: 闊老, 闊少, 闊人 such people; 這家闊極了 this family is very rich; 闊氣, 闊綽 *-chih, -chuoh* ↓.

闊別 *kuohbier*, v. i., (of friends) live apart, have not seen each other for sometime.
闊氣 *kuohchih*, adj., (1) showily rich; (2) generous with money.
闊綽 *kuohchuoh*, adj., luxurious, free with money.
闊大 *kuohdah*, adj., broad (in space or viewpoint).

悶 52B.00-6

mehn (**men*).

N. Boredom, state of mental depression: 解悶 to distract the mind, relieve boredom.

V.i. & t. (**men*) (1) To be tongue-tied, stop speaking: 悶了口, 悶住了. (2) To cover (bank) fire with ashes: 悶火, 悶著火. (3) To simmer, let simmer: 把沏好的茶再悶一會兒 let the tea stand a while to draw flavor.

Adj. (1) Sad and silent, depressed: 心中惡悶 sad and heavy-laden; 煩悶 worried; 悶悶不樂 depressed and not talking much; 悶坐 sit sullently. (2) Depressing, -sive: 悶沉沉 depressive (of atmosphere); 屋子裏眞悶 the room is stuffy; 悶的慌 very stuffy. (3) (**men'le*) 悶了 cynical about everything. (4) (**men*) dull in sound (such as bad coins), see 悶板 *-baan* ↓.

悶板 **menbaan*, n., bad silver coins.
悶表 *mehnbiaau*, n., a watch with opaque cover.
悶腔兒 **menchiang'l*, n., a habitually reticent person.
悶氣 (1) **menchih*, n., stuffy air; (2) *mehnchih*, n., sad, depressed mental state.
悶弓兒 **mengung'l*, (1) adj., sullen, in beat-up situation; (2) 打悶弓兒 (chess) immobilize the King.
悶葫蘆 *mehn-hur'lu*, n., complete mystery; 悶葫蘆罐(兒) *---guahn* (*---guah'l*), n., coin bank.
悶香 *mehnshiang*, n., narcotic incense to put one to sleep.
悶頭兒 **mentour'l*, n., (1) person who is holed up, unable to exercise his talent or wealth; (2) person who works silently without publicity.
悶子車 *mehntz-che*, n., (dial.) covered wagon.

閟 52B.00-6

bih.

V.i. (AC) to hide.

Adj. (AC) secret.

閾 52B.00-7

yuh.

N. A threshold.

Adj. In 隔閾 separated, not in touch, not informed.

関 52B.00-8

guan.
[Pop. of 關 52B.00]

閲 52B.00-8

yueh.

V.i. & t. (1) To see, read, peruse, go over (letter, document): 閲書, 閲報 read a book, a newspaper; 閲覽 *-laan* ↓; 閲悉 have read your letter and learn that; 閲卷 go over examination papers; 評閲 to go over critically; 核閲 to examine (report, account). (2) To come across in experience: 閲歷, 閲世 *-lih, -shyh* ↓; 閲人多矣 have known many men, spec. of woman. (3) To review (troops): 巡閲, 檢閲, 校閲 inspect troops; 閲兵, 閲操 *-bing, -tsau* ↓.

閲兵 *yueh-bing*, v.i. & n., to review troops, a military review.
閲讀 *yuehdur*, v.t., to read.
閲覽 *yuehlaan*, v.t., to read

亅	小	⺊	十	土	ナ	卄	𠃊	丨	一	丅	フ	口	区	冈	ㄱ	厂	尸	亠	广	宀	丶	乚	乀	心	八	人	乂	㇀	一	丿	ㄥ	く
00	01	02	10	11	12	20	21	22	30	31	32	40	41	42	50	51	52	60	61	62	63	70	71	72	80	81	82	83	90	91	92	93

(books, newspapers); 閱覽室 reading room in library.
閱歷 *yuehlih*, n., experience (long, hard, etc.).
閱世 *yuehshyh*, n., experience in society.
閱操 *yuehtsau*, v.i. & n., see *-bing*↑.

闕 52B.00-8

chyue (**chyueh*).

N. (**chyueh*) (1) Watch tower on rampart of palace. (2) Symbol of where emperor lived: 闕下 *-shiah*↓; 宮闕 palaces; 闕門 palace gate; 望闕行禮, 朝天闕 to face the palace and make obeisance (in all other senses, pr. *chyue*). (2) Mistake, error: 闕失 *-shy*↓.

Adj. Missing, wanting (=缺): 闕字 missing words.

闕翦 *chyuejiaan*, v.t., (AC) destroy: 又欲闕翦我公室 wanted to destroy our royal house.
闕如 *chyuerur*, adj., wanting, missing: 尚付闕如 phr., still wanting (not yet done).
闕下 *chyuehshiah*, n., (AC) Your or His Majesty: 上書闕下 wrote to Your or His Majesty.
闕失 *chyueshy*, n., mistake, error.
闕文 *chyuewern*, n., a missing sentence or passage (in anc. scripts).
闕疑 *chyueyir*, n., uncertain point yet to be explored.

閃 52B.00-8

shaan.

V. i. & t. (1) To make way for, evade, shun, dodge: 躲閃, 逃閃 hide out; 閃路, 閃道, 閃開 move out of the way, clear the way! 閃避 *-bih*↓. (2) To flash (as lightning): 電閃 lightning flashes: 閃電, 閃鑠 *-diahn*, *-shuoh*↓. (3) To have a mishap: 閃失 *-'shy*↓; 閃得, 閃下 *-'de*, *-shiah*↓. (4) To strain, sprain, injure: 閃了腰 strain one's waist; 才閃了手 sprain one's arm; 閃了風 catch cold.

閃避 *shaanbih*, v. i. & t., to hide out, evade confrontation with (person), give the slip to.
閃得 *shaan'de*, v. i., (MC) end up in (poverty, etc.).
閃電 *shaandiahn*, n., a lightning flash: 閃電戰 blitzkrieg.
閃緞 *shaanduahn*, n., name of a scintillating silk.
閃光 *shaan guang*, v. i. & n., light flashes; 閃光燈 *--deng*, flash light (photography).
閃開 *shaan-kai* (*-'kai*), v.i., move away; get out of way or sight of another person.
閃亮兒 *shaanliahng'l*, (1) v. i., to scintillate; (2) adv., at day-break.
閃閃 *sharnshaan*, adj., flickering; scintillating.
閃下 *shaanshiah*, v. i., (coll.) to end up with, leave behind.
閃鑠 *shaanshuoh*, v. i., to flicker, flash, scintillate.
閃失 *shaanshy* (*-'shy*), n., mishap: 恐路上有閃失 lest s.t. should happen on the way.

閤 52B.00-8

ger (**her*).

N. (1) A small side door. (2) (U.f. 閣↓).

Adj. (**her*) (Interch. 闔) 閤府 your whole family; 閤第 ditto.

閲 52B.00-9

shih.
[Pop. 閲]

V. i. Fight: see 閲牆 *-chiarng*↓.

閲牆 *shih-chiarng*, phr., from 兄弟閲於牆 brothers fight among themselves—internal strife.

闇 52B.00-9

hun.

N. A gate; a palace gate; 司闇 gate keeper, janitor.

闃 52B.00-9

chyuh.

Adj. (LL) silent, still: 闃寂, 闃然 still; 闃無人聲 silent without a human voice.

閥 52B.00-9

far.

N. Established house or power group: 門閥 powerful family; 軍閥 war lord; 學閥 power group among professors.

閣 52B.00-9

ger.

N. (1) A chamber, a storied building: 亭臺樓閣 pavilions, terraces, and towers; 閣子 *-tz*↓; 出閣 (of a girl) get married (lit., "leave the boudoir"); 置之高閣 have (s. t.) shelved and forgotten. (2) The cabinet: 內閣 cabinet of government; 組閣 form a cabinet; 入閣 be appointed to a ministerial office; 閣揆 (LL) the premier or prime minister; 閣議 a cabinet meeting; 閣員 a minister of State; 閣老 the prime minister.

閣道 *gerdauh*, n., (1) palace corridors; (2) a pathway along a cliff or a precipice.
閣下 *gershiah*, n., (1) Your Honor, Your Excellency, the Honorable . . . ; (2) used in letters generally, like "Dear Sir"; (3) in court. discourse＝先生; 閣下以爲何如 what do you think?
閣子 *gertz*, n., a small room, an attic.

閻 52B.00-9

yarn.

N. A surname.

閻君 *Yarnjyun*, n., see *-warng*↓.
閻羅 *Yarnluor*, n., (Budd.) King of Hades (short from 閻魔羅社 Sanskr. *Yama Raja*).
閻(羅)王 *Yarn(luor)warng*, n., King of Hades, Pluto: 見閻羅, die; 閻王賬 usury. 閻王爺 n., King of Hades.

鬮 52B.00-9

jiou.
[Pop. 鬮 52B.00]

N. A lot, a ticket: 拈鬮, 抓鬮 draw lots; 鬮兒 a lot or ticket; 紙鬮 a paper lot.

關 52B.00-9

guan.
[Pop. 関]

N. (1) A frontier pass or gate, customs barrier, check point: 關口 *-koou*, 關隘 *-aih*²↓; 海關 maritime customs; 守關, 把關 to guard the passes; 出關 go to the other side of a mountain pass, esp. the Great Wall. (2) A mechanism: 機關 a public or private organization; 關鍵 *-jiahn*↓. (3) Important parts of the human body: 關脈 *-moh*↓; 關門 *-mern*↓; 關元 *-yuarn*↓. (4) A wooden bolt for the door. (5) A surname.

V. t. (1) Shut, close: 關門 close the door; 關上 shut up (door, window, etc.); 開關 a device for opening and closing, a switch; 關不住 (of doors, windows, boxes, etc.) cannot be closed, (of things or persons) cannot be shut out: 春色關不住 the beauties of spring cannot be shut out. (2) To pick up or make (money payments): 關俸 to pick up one's salary; 關餉 (of soldiers) get paid; 關支 receive money payments. (3) Connect, implicate, involve: 關聯 *-liarn*, 關係 *-shih*↓. (4) To concern or be concerned: 關照 *-jauh*, 關心 *-shin*, 關切 *-chieh*↓.

關愛 *guan-aih*¹, v. t., express solicitude for the well-being of (s.o.).
關隘 *guan-aih*², n., a frontier pass.
關板兒 *guan-baa'l*, v. i., (of business concerns) suspend business, shut down.
關卡 *guanchiaa*, n., a check point, customs barrier.
關竅 *guanchiauh*, n., orifices on the human body.
關切 *guanchieh*, (1) v. i. & t., be concerned about (s. o.); (2) adj., intimately related, connected.
關刀 *guan-dau*, n., a halberd, a sword with a long hilt, so called because it was once wielded by Kuan Yu (關羽).
關防 *guan'farng*, n., (1) a frontier pass; (2) an oblong official seal; (3) measures taken to forestall the leaking of secrets.
關關 *guanguan*, n., (AC) imitation of the sound made by birds.
關懷 *guanhuair*, (1) v. i. & t., be concerned about, for, show interest in; (2) n., solicitude.
關棧費 *guan-jahn-feih*, n., bonding fee.
關張 *guan-jang*, n., suspension of business by shops (opp. 開張 open business).
關照 *guanjauh*, v. t., (1) notify, inform: 請關照一聲 please let me know; (2) take care of.
關鍵 *guanjiahn*, n., (1) catch for a lock; (2) pivot of a door; (3) key to a situation, crux of the matter.
關節 *guanjier*, n., (1) (physiol.) the joints; (2) secret request for official assistance (暗通關節), oft. involving bribery; 關節炎 (med.) arthritis.
關津 *guanjin*, n., key communication points on land or river.
關注 *guanjuh*, v. i. & t., pay close attention to, be intensely concerned about, for.
關口 *guankoou*, n., (1) a strategic pass, customs station; (2) a critical point in a given situation.
關聯 *guanliarn*, v. t., be related or interconnected with; n., relations, connections (of problems, consequences).
關捩(子) *guanlieh(tz)*, n., (mechanics) an axle; crux of problem.
關門 *guan-mern*, (1) v.i., close the door; (2) n., (Chin. med.) the kidneys.
關脈 *guanmoh*, n., (herb med.) the pulse on wrist.
關目 *guanmuh*, n., major incidents in a play.
關內 *guanneih*, n., this side of a mountain pass, esp. the Shanhaikuan (opp. 關外 Manchuria lying to the north of Shanhaikuan).
關平 *guanpirng*, n., the Chinese Customs silver scale (1 oz.＝10.13 庫平 Treasury Scale).
關涉 *guansheh*, (1) n., relations, connections, effects on other aspects; (2) v. t., have effects on s. t. else: 關涉跟人私事 have to do with s. o.'s private affairs.
關係 *guanshih*, (1) v. t., be related to one another; (2) n., relationship: 跟你甚麼關係 what relation is he to you? (3) n., consequences: 沒有關係 of no conse-

亅	小	⺊	十	土	ナ	廾	ㄴ	丨	一	丁	フ	口	区	冈	冂	厂	尸	亠	广	宀	丶	乚	弋	心	八	人	乂	一	乛	丿	𠂉	く
00	01	02	10	11	12	20	21	22	30	31	32	40	41	42	50	51	52	60	61	62	63	70	71	72	80	81	82	83	90	91	92	93

quence, never mind.

關心 *guanshin*, v. t., (1) be concerned about (s. o.) or for (s. t.); (2) take care of, pay attention to, show interest in.

關書 *guanshu*, n., formerly, a contract or written appointment.

關説 *guanshuo*, v. i., ask favor of s. o. for a friend: 替我關説 speak for me.

關税 *guan-sueih*, n., customs duties, tariffs.

關頭 *guantour*, n., a critical point or period: 到了緊要關頭 at a critical juncture.

關託 *guantuo*, v. t., to request (s. o.) to intercede on one's behalf.

關子 *guantz*, n., (1) (MC) paper money of the Southern Sung Dyn.; (2) (MC) a blank pass or order; (3) (of novels or dramas) climax.

關外 *guanwaih*, n., opp. 關內 *-neih* ↑.

關亡 *guan-warng*, n., sorcery by which the souls of the dead can be summoned.

關文 *guanwern*, n., formerly, a form of official communications between officials of equal rank.

關眼兒 *guanyaa'l*, n., a hole in any article for fastening.

關元 *guanyuarn*, n., (1) (Chin. med.) a point on the human body just below the 17th vertebra; (2) (Taoist physiol.) the pubic region, said to be the fountain of life; the solar plexus.

關於 *guan-yur*, prep., regarding, concerning, about: 關於此事, 我全不知 I know nothing about this matter; 關於哲學的智識 concerning philosophical knowledge.

闔 52B.00-9

jiou.

[Pop. of 鬮 52B.00]

SECTION 52S

§ 52S.00 (尸S/亅)

尉 52S.00-1

weih (**yuh*).

N. (1) (AC) an officer: 廷尉 court officer. (2) A military rank, lower than 校 10B.82: 上尉 captain; 中尉 first lieutenant; 少尉 second lieutenant; 准尉 warrant officer. (3) 尉遲 (**yuhchyr*) a compound surname.

刷 52S.00-2

shua (**shuah*).

N. (*-tz*) A brush: 牙刷 toothbrush; 鞋刷 shoe brush.

V. t. (1) To brush (teeth, clothing, shoes, horse), polish (floor); 洗刷 clean, clean up generally; 刷清 to brush clean. (2) To apply color, whitewash: 刷色 *-shaai* ↓; 刷油漆 ink, apply varnish; 印刷, 刷印 *-yihn* ↓. (3) (**shuah*) (MC) 刷選 *-shyuaan* ↓.

Adj. Descriptive of sound: 刷刷的響 arousing, crackling sound; 刷拉 *-la* ↓.

刷扮 *shuabahn*, v. i., (MC) brush up personal appearance.

刷白 **shuahbair*, adj., pale (face).

刷括 *shuagua*, v. t., (dial.) scrape together (journey expenses).

刷拉 *shuala*, adj., descriptive of rustle (of falling leaves, etc.), also 刷拉拉.

刷色 *shuashaai*, v. t., to paint (walls).

刷洗 *shuashii*, v. i., (1) to perform morning ablutions; (2) to scour country for money from the people; (3) clear (s.o.'s name).

刷新 *shuashin*, v. t., to renovate, put on new look on (politics, education, etc.).

刷選 **shuahshyuaan*, v. t., (MC) to pick, select.

刷印 *shuayihn*, v. t., to print (usu. 印[Δ]刷 91S.22).

§ 52S.10 (尸S/十)

辟 52S.10-6

bih (**pih*).

[AC var. for 闢, 避, 僻]

N. (1) (AC) the law; the ruler (in compound 復[Δ]辟 91B.82). (2) (**pih*) (AC) punishment: 大辟 capital punishment; 宮辟 castration.

V.t. (1) Call to office: 辟召 king's order to serve government; 辟舉 confer post on (person): 徵辟 select and raise to office. (2) To fight off (evil spirit, doctrine): 辟邪 (var. of 闢邪). (3) To escape, avoid: 辟世, 辟易 to retire from world (var. of 避); 辟邪 counteract evil force. (4) (**pih*) (AC) to cultivate (land): 辟草萊, 辟土地 cultivate wild land (var. of 闢). (5) (**pih*) (AC) to spin: 辟纑 spin hemp.

辟聑 **pih-ehl*, v.i., (AC) incline ear to listen.

辟惡 *bih-eh*, n., (bot.) musk.

辟穀 **pihguu*, stop even vegetarian food, as a way of becoming Taoist immortal.

辟易 *bihyih*, n., (AC) retreat.

辟雍 *bihyung*, n., (AC) Royal Academy, in Chou Dyn.

辟踊 *bihyuung*, v.i., see 擗[Δ]踊 10A.10.

§ 52S.22 (尸^{s}/丨)

郡 52S.22-3

jyuhn.

N. An anc. administrative district: 郡縣 *-shiahn* ↓.

郡主 *jyuhnjuu*, n., (AC) a princess.
郡馬 *jyuhnmaa*, n., (AC) the husband of a princess.
郡縣 *jyuhnshiahn*, n., the system of administrative districts (prefectures and countries) introduced after the abolition of feudalism by 秦始皇.
郡庠 *jyuhnshiarng*, n., formerly, a prefectural academy.
郡守 *jyuhnshoou*, n., (Hahn Dyn.) a prefect.
郡望 *jyuhnwahng*, n., (AC) influential families of a prefecture.

即 52S.22-5

jir.

[Wr. form of 卽 91S.22]

§ 52S.50 (尸^{s}/ㄱ)

鳲 52S.50-9

shy.

鳲鳩 *shyjiou*, n., the turtledove; wood pigeon.

鷴 52S.50-9

shiarn.

N. A fowl of pheasant family, *Phasianus nycthemerus.*

§ 52S.70 (尸^{s}/乚)

覸 52S.70-4

jiahn.

[Interch. 瞯 41B.00]

V. t. See, keep an eye on, peep at, watch.

既 52S.70-5

jih.

[Wr. form of 旣 91S.70]

§ 52S.82 (尸^{s}/乂)

殿 52S.82-4

diahn.

N. Hall, temple, palace: 神殿 temple to gods; 宮殿 palace; 登殿 emperor goes up to throne hall.

V.i. & adj. Rear, bring up the rear; the last: 殿最 the last (殿) and the first (最) in former examinations; 殿後 to bring up the rear.

殿軍 *diahnjyun*, n., (mil.) rear guard: 冠軍, 亞軍, 季軍, 殿軍 1st, 2nd, and 3rd and the 4th winners in a contest.
殿下 *diahnshiah*, n., term of address to princes.
殿堂 *diahntarng*, n., temple or palace hall.
殿宇 *diahnyuu*, n., hall buildings.

改 52S.82-9

gaai.

N. A surname.

V. t. To change, reform, remodel, transform, correct: 改變 *-biahn*, 改革 *-ger*, 改換 *-huahn*, 改進 *-jihn* ↓; 改了脾氣 (of an ill-tempered person) become good-tempered; 改了念頭 change one's mind; 改頭換面 make only superficial changes: 改弦更張 cut loose from the past and make a new start; 改弦易轍 (of conduct, politics, etc.) strike out a new path; 改邪歸正 give up an evil way of life and reform; 痛改前非 repent of one's former sins; 改土歸流 (of aboriginal chieftains) come under Chin. jurisdiction; 批改 (of students' papers, etc.) comment on and correct; 刪改 (of manuscripts, compositions) amend and correct; 改作業 read students' homework; 改文章 correct a literary essay; 改河道 change river course.

Adj. Other than the current one: 改日 (天), 改歲, 改次 another day, year, time; 改頓再吃 reserve (s. t.) for another meal.

改變 *gaaibiahn*, v. i. & t., to change, (rules, schedule, fashion, voice, attitude, etc.): 改變過來 change over.
改編 *gaaibian*, v. t., (1) reorganize: 改編軍隊 regroup troops into new units; (2) (of literary works) revise and rewrite.

改 期 *gaaichir*, v. t., postpone to a later date.

改 革 *gaaiger*, n. & v. t., (to institute) reforms.

改 觀 *gaaiguan*, v. i., to present a new look.

改 過 *gaai-guoh*, v. i., repent: 改過自新 repent and reform; 改過遷善 repent and be good.

改 行 *gaai-harng*, v. i., change to new occupation.

改 換 *gaaihuahn*, v. t., to exchange or substitute one for another, make changes in (words, titles, fashions, etc.).

改 正 *gaai-jehng*, v. t., correct (errors).

改 轍 *gaai-jer*, v. i., to change one's course of action.

改 嫁 *gaaijiah*, v. i., (of widow) remarry.

改 醮 *gaaijiauh*, v. i., (of widow) remarry.

改 節 *gaai-jier*, v. i., to change one's course of conduct, switch loyalty (to new ruler).

改 進 *gaaijihn*, v. t., to improve (upon), make improvements in.

改 裝 *gaai-juang*, v. i., (1) change into another kind of dress, disguise; (2) (of building) remodel; (of industrial product) put in new containers.

改 口 *gairkoou*, v. i., (改口供) give a different story or affidavit.

改 良 *gaailiarng*, v. t., improve, reform.

改 日 *gaairyh*, adv., another (later) day.

改 善 *gaaishahn*, v. t., improve (method, treatment).

改 選 *gairshyuaan*, n. & v. i., (hold) a new election of elected officers.

改 削 *gaaishyueh*, v. t., expunge and correct.

改 天 *gaaitian*, adv., some other day, later: 改天來 come later.

改 竄 *gaaitsuahn*, v. t., (secretly) change wording (of text).

改 塗 *gaaitur*[1], v. i., change one's course of action (also wr. 途).

改 圖 *gaaitur*[2], v. i., change plans.

改 造 *gaaitzauh*, v. t., (1) (of building, etc.) remodel; (2) to reform.

改 嘴 *gairtzueei*, v. i., (=改口↑).

改 組 *gairtzuu*, v. t., (of a cabinet, group, etc.) reshuffle, reorganize.

改 樣 *gaai-yahng*, v. i. & t., (1) refashion, remold; (2) (person) change manner.

改 易 *gaaiyih*, v. t., to change, transform.

改 元 *gaai-yuarn*, v. i., adopt a new year-title of an emperor's reign.

SECTION 60

§ 60.00 (亠/亅)

亦 60.00

yih.

Adv. (LL=vern. 也) also: 亦係 is also; 亦好 also good; 亦可 also will do, may also; 不亦 is it not (also); 不亦善乎 is it not good? 不亦危乎 is it not dangerous? 亦 . . . 亦 both . . . and; 亦步亦趨 follow (leader) walking or running, i. e., completely; 亦哭亦笑 both cry and laugh.

亦 且 *yihchiee*, adv. & conj., and also, as well: 亦且省錢 save money as well.

亦 發 *yihfa*, adv., (MC) all the more; simply.

亦 復 *yihfuh*, adv. & conj., see *-chiee* ↑.

亦 然 *yihrarn*, adv., also, too, similarly.

亨 60.00

heng (also *herng*).

Adj. Prosperous, going smoothly.

亨 通 *hengtung*, adj., (of business) prosperous, doing well.

享 60.00

shiaang.

V. t. (1) To enjoy (peace, happiness, long life, good health): 享受, 享用 *-shouh, -yuhng* ↓; 享國, 享位 (king) enjoys reign of so many years; 以享天年 to live out the remaining years in peace; 享年八十八 died at eighty-eight; 安享富貴 enjoy wealth and honor. (2) (Of gods, spirits) to enjoy or taste of the sacrifices (=饗): 享殿 temple for sacrifices.

享福 *shiaang-fur*, v. i., to live a good, happy life; live in luxury.
享樂 *shiaangleh*, v. i., to enjoy oneself; 享樂主義 hedonism.
享受 *shiaangshouh*, v. t., to enjoy (the good things of life, good luck).
享有 *shiaangyoou*, v. t., to possess, have in possession.
享用 *shiaangyuhng*, v. t., to have at one's disposal.

亭 60.00

tirng.

N. (*-tz*) A pavilion, arbor; wayfarer's station; booth: 茶亭 tea kiosk; 電話亭 telephone booth; 驛亭, 郵亭 formerly, courier station; 亭臺 pavilions and terraces in garden.

Adj. Erect, esp. of ladies' figure, see 亭亭 *-tirng*↓.

V. t. (AC) 亭之毒之 to nurture and develop it.

亭長 *tirngjaang*, n., anc. sheriff.
亭障 *tirngjahng*, n., (AC) defense works at military pass.
亭侯 *tirnghouh*, n., (AC) military station, outpost.
亭亭 *tirng-tirng*, adj., graceful: 亭亭玉立 standing gracefully (of young lady).
亭子間 *tirng'tzjian*, n., (Shanghai dial.) small back room facing landing.
亭午 *tirngwuu*, n., midnoon.

孪 60.00

lyuarn.

[Abbr. of 攣 93.00]

斈 60.00

shyuer.

[Pop. of 學 90.00]

§ 60.01 (亠/小)

京 60.01

jing.

N. (1) A metropolitan city: 京都 *-du*, 京師 *-shy*↓; 南京 Nanking; 東京 Tokyo, Tonkin; 北京 Peking, Peiping. (2) Ten million. (3) A surname.

Adj. Equal: 莫之與京 without an equal, nothing is comparable.

京報 *jingbauh*, n., the official gazette of the capital.
京城 *jingcherng*, n., the capital city.
京腔 *jingchiang*, n., (1) =京調 *-diauh*↓; (2) the Mandarin or Peking dial.
京調 *jingdiauh*, n., Peking opera or other songs popular there.
京都 *jingdu*, n., the national capital; (Japan) Kyoto.
京官 *jingguan*, n., formerly, officials in the capital.
京華 *jinghuar*, n., the national capital.
京畿 *jingji*, n., the national capital and its suburbs.
京京 *jingjing*, adj., (AC) sad, sorrowful: 憂心京京 disconsolate is my sad heart.
京劇 *jingjyuh*, n., the Peking opera.
京派 *jingpaih*, n., the Peking style of singing (opp. 海派 the Shanghai style).
京平 *jingpirng*, n., formerly, a unit of weight for measuring silver, which was slightly smaller than 庫平, the Treasury Scale.
京師 *jingshy*, n., the national capital.
京室 *jing-shyh*, n., the imperial household.
京曹 *jingtsaur*, n., see *-guan*↑.

禀 60.01

biing.

[Pop. of 稟↓]

稟 60.01

biing.

[Pop. 禀; interch. 廩 and 懍]

V. i. (1) (Court.) receive (order): 稟命 report to superior for instructions; act according to received order. (2) (Court. to superior, prefaced to almost any verb, esp. in correspondence) pray to, beg to: 稟報, 稟告, 稟陳, 稟奏, 稟呈 ="beg to report"; to ask, request: 稟請, 稟祈, 稟懇, 稟假 request for leave of absence; 敬稟者 (formula for opening of letter) I beg to inform you or communicate with you in regard to following matter; 專此敬稟, 叩稟, 拜稟 formula for closing letter; 稟覆, 回稟 I beg to answer, report.

Adj. Born (of natural talent, temperament): 稟賦, 稟性 *-fuh*, *-shihng*↓.

稟賦 *biingfuh*, n., born talent.

享 亭 孪 斈 京 禀 稟

A　　B　　C

稟 紊 栾 棄 杂 稾 襲 豪

稟性 *biingshihng*, n., born character, temperament.

紊 60.01

wehn.

Adj. Disorderly, confused: 紊亂 ditto; 有條不紊 all in good order.

栾 60.01

luarn.
[Pop. of 欒 93.01]

棄 60.01

chih.

V. t. To abandon, forsake: 放棄, 捨棄 to abandon (rights, friends, duties, etc.); 棄官 to resign from political post and retire; 自暴自棄 be self-abandoned, waste one's talent or capabilities; 棄暗投明, 棄邪歸正 return to lawful living, also quit illegal associations and activities; 棄舊換新 change new (lovers, etc.) for the old; 拋棄, 丟棄 desert (friends, family, lover); 背棄 forsake (old friends), violate (treaty, agreement); 遺棄 desert, forsake, leave uncared for (family, children); 棄婦, 棄妻 deserted wife; 棄兒 waifs and strays, abandoned orphan; 棄物 abandoned articles or not in use; 捐棄 forget (old grudges); 棄短取長 forget s.o.'s shortcomings and make use of his strong points; 摒棄 renounce, discard, shut off (prejudices, evil thoughts, etc.); 廢棄 abolish (reign, institution, custom); 棄置 lay aside; 棄甲曳兵 (of troops) drag weapons and abandon armor in a rout.

棄背 *chihbeih*, v.t., (1) to desert, turn one's back on; (2) to suffer loss of parents: 父母棄背 our parents have passed away, left us.

棄權 *chih-chyuarn*, v.i., (law) to waive rights, abstain from voting.

棄觚 *chih-gu*, phr., (LL) throw down the pen, stop writing (觚 anc. bamboo slip for writing).

棄井 *chih-jiing*, n., (AC allu.) abandoned well, (fig.) task left unfinished.

棄捐 *chihjyuan*, v.t., (of wife) abandon, be abandoned; (of) scholars) be neglected and not promoted to jobs.

棄世 *chih-shyh*[1], v.i., (1) to pass away, die; (2) (AC) abandon worldly life.

棄市 *chih-shyh*[2], v. i., be executed in public square.

棄養 *chihyahng*, v. i., (rhet., of parents) die, pass away.

杂 60.01

tzar.
[Abbr. of 雜 60S.11]

稾 60.01

gaau.
[Interch. 稿 90A.42]

---

§ 60.02 (亠/ㄎ)

襲 60.02

shir.

N. A set: 一襲衣服 a set of dress.

V.i. (1) To carry on without change: 因襲, 沿襲 carry on (old custom, etc.); 承襲 to inherit (rank, property); 世襲 hereditary; to inherit. (2) Receive hereditary rank: 襲封, 襲爵 *-feng*, *-jyuer* ↓. (3) To make a raid, give surprise attack: 偷襲 attack surreptitiously; 空襲 air raid; 襲擊 *-jir* ↓; 侵襲 to invade. (4) To plagiarize: 抄襲 ditto. (5) (Of gas, smell) to steal, assail silently: 邪氣襲余形體 (AC) swampy air assails my body; 花氣襲人 fragrance of flowers steals into the room.

襲蹈 *shirdauh*, v.i., see *-ji* ↓.

襲奪 *shirduor*, v.t., to attack and take an unprepared city.

襲封 *shir-feng*, v.i., receive hereditary rank.

襲迹 *shir-ji*, v.i., follow in the footprints of the past.

襲擊 *shirjir*, v.t., to spring an attack on (city, etc.).

襲爵 *shir-jyuer*, v.i., receive hereditary rank.

豪 60.02

haur.

N. (1) A hero, champion: 英豪 a hero: 文豪, 大文豪 a great writer; 豪傑, 豪俠 *-jier*, *-shiar* ↓. (2) The socially prominent: 富豪 a rich man; 土豪 (contempt.) local rich bourgeois.

Adj. (1) Heroic, romantic, extravagant, chivalrous: 豪飲 drink freely with great capacity; see compp. ↓. (2) Adj. & adv., strong, relying on force: 豪奪 take away by force; 豪橫 *-hehng* ↓.

豪強 *haurchiarng*, adj. & n., the powerful and strong or rich.

豪氣 *haur-chih*, adj. & n., chivalry, -rous, generous, -rosity.

豪放 *haurfahng*, adj., (of litr. style) romantic, given to emotions, expansive, of heroic manner.

豪富 *haurfuh*, n., the rich.

豪橫 *haurhehng*, adj., (1) overbearing, arrogant; (2) (-'*heng*)

stubborn.
豪華 *haurhuar*, adj., gorgeous, sumptuous (party, mansion).
豪家 *haur-jia*, n., a well-known powerful family.
豪傑 *haurjier*, n., hero.
豪豬 *haurju*, n., a porcupine.
豪壯 *haurjuahng*, adj., heroic, daring, valiant.
豪舉 *haurjyuu*, n., an heroic act.
豪客 *haurkeh*, n., as in 綠林豪客 swordsmen of the Robin Hood type.
豪邁 *haurmaih*, adj., magnanimous, energetic, determined.
豪門 *haur-mern*, n., see *-jia*↑.
豪奴 *haur-nur*, n., formerly, servants of powerful family who bullied the people.
豪俠 *haurshiar*, n., man of honor and courage.
豪興 *haur-shihng*, n., exhilarating mood for a drink or writing poetry.
豪爽 *haurshuaang*, adv., generous, offering freely money or service.
豪士 *haurshyh*, n., man of honor and courage.
豪恣 *haurtzyh*, adj., abandoned, unrestrained.

饔 60.02

yung.

N. (1) (AC) gift of cooked meat, opp. 餼 raw foodstuff. (2) (AC) breakfast, opp. 飧 (*sun*) supper.

衣 60.02

yi (**yih*).

N. (1) Dress, coat, clothing, garment: 衣服, 衣裳 *-'fu, -charng*↓; 衣冠 *-guan*↓; 衣帽間 cloak room, check room; 單衣, 夾衣 unlined, lined dress (jacket); 毛衣 sweater, woolen knitwear; 皮衣 fur coat; 大衣 topcoat, overcoat; 雨衣 raincoat; 內衣 undergarment; 號衣 uniform; 衣食住行 clothing, food, shelter and transportation—the four basic needs of everybody; 衣香鬢影 perfumed clothes and gorgeous hair—descriptive of ladies in high society. (2) Coating: 糖衣 sugar-coating, -ed; 花生衣 membrane of peanuts.

V. i. & t. (**yih*) To dress: 以衣 (*yi*) 衣 (*yih*) 人 to clothe the poor with clothing; 衣錦還鄉 return home in glory ("clothed in silks," of home-town boy who makes good): 衣錦夜行 to parade beautifully dressed in the dark, go without due appreciation.

衣包 *yi-bau*[1], n., clothing bag, used for travel.
衣胞 (兒) *yi-bau*[2]*('l)*, n., placenta.
衣被 *yihbeih*, (1) n., clothing and bedding; (2) (**yih-*) v. t., 衣被蒼生 (fig.) to spread all-round benefit to people (to clothe and shelter the poor).
衣鉢 (缽) *yi-bo*, n., (lit.) the cassock and alms bowl of a Buddhist master, passed on to disciple as symbol of apostolic succession: 衣鉢眞傳 received or is keeper of true teachings.
衣補兒 *yibuu'l*, n., the radical "ネ"; index No. 63C.
衣裳 *yicharng*, n., (1) jacket and petticoat; (2) (*-'shang*) dress, clothing in gen.
衣衾 *yichin*, n., burial dress and coverlet: 衣衾棺槨 burial gown, coverlet, coffin and coffin case.
衣廚 *yichur*, n., wardrobe, clothing cabinet.
衣服 *yi'fu*, n., dress in gen. (for man and woman).
衣冠 *yi-guan*, n., hat and gown: 衣冠禽獸 (abuse) a beast in human dress; 衣冠冢 a grave containing the hat and gown of deceased in the absence of missing corpse.
衣櫃 *yigueih*, n., wardrobe, chest of drawers for clothing.
衣架 (兒) *yijiah('l)*, n., clothing stand, clothes tree, clothes horse (also 衣裳架).
衣巾 *yijin*[1], n., hat and dress (巾＝帽).
衣襟 (兒) *yijin*[2]*(-jie'l)*, n., see 襟 63C.01.
衣裝 *yijuang*, n., traveller's clothing bag.
衣著 *yijuor*, n., what one wears, clothing.
衣料 (兒) *yiliauh('l)*, n., dress material.
衣馬 *yi-maa*, n., (LL) gowns and horses (of the rich).
衣帽年 (兒) *yi-mauh-niarn* (*--niar'l*), phr., times when people are judged by their dress.
衣衫 *yishan*, n., dress (and gen. appearance).
衣刷 *yi-shua*, n., clothes brush.
衣蝨 *yi-shy*, n., lice in underclothing.
衣魚 *yi-yur*, n., silverfish that eats into clothing.

褻 60.02

shieh.

V. t. (1) To be sacrilegious, disrespectful: 褻瀆 *-dur*↓. (2) To take liberties with woman: 褻玩 *-wahn*↓; 褻近, 褻狎 *-jihn, -shiar*↓.

Adj. (1) Indecent, immodest: 猥褻 indecent (story, language); 穢褻 dirty (story). (2) Intimate: 褻衣, 褻服 *-yi, -fur*↓.

褻器 *shieh-chih*, n., (LL) chamber pot.
褻瀆 *shiehdur*, v. i., (1) to be sacrilegious or disrespectful to (what is sacred or highly honored); (2) (self-deprecative) am presumptuous to: 褻瀆淸神 bother you with such trifle.
褻服 *shieh-fur*, n., (LL) underclothing.
褻近 *shiehjihn*, v. t., to be intimate with (woman).

褻慢 *shiehmahn*, v. i. & t., to show disrespect.
褻狎 *shiehshiar*, v. t., see *-jihn*↑.
褻尊 *shiehtzun*, v. i., (court.) am presumptuous.
褻玩 *shiehwahn*, v. t., to tease, dally with (woman).
褻衣 *shieh-yi*, n., (LL) underwear, underclothes.

衷 60.02

jung.

N. The heart, esp. bottom of the heart: 內衷, 私衷 innermost feelings; 隱衷 secret feelings, longings; 言不由衷 do not speak honestly; 由衷之言 words spoken from the heart; 無動於衷 not touched, apathetic.

Adj. (1) U. f. 忠 loyal: 衷款, 衷誠 loyal heart. (2) U. f. 中 middle: 折衷 compromise; 折衷辦法 a compromise.

衷腸 *jungcharng*, n., one's feelings, heart of sorrow, longing.
衷情 *jungchirng*, n., innermost feelings. [and longings.
衷曲 *jungchyu*, n., secret thoughts
衷懷 *junghuair*, n., see *-charng*↑.
衷心 *jungshin*, n., the heart: 衷心佩服 admire from the heart.

衺 60.02

mauh (mouh).

N. (AC) longitude, north-south direction: 廣衺數千里 several thousand *li* in length and breadth.

哀 60.02

ai.

N. (1) Sorrow: 哀樂 joys and sorrows. (2) Grief at funeral: 擧哀 mark ceremony by proper lamentation; 誌哀 to express one's grief; 節哀 please restrain your grief; 生榮死哀 lament at death of a famous man; hence 榮哀錄 collection of tributes by friends to one deceased.

V.i. & t. To lament, grieve, feel sorry for: 哀之 take pity on him; 哀憐 *-liarn*↓; 哀矜 *-jin*↓.

Adj. & adv. (1) Bewailing, doleful, dolorous, sad, tragic: 悲哀 ditto; 哀痛 *-tuhng*↓; 哀傷 *-shang*↓; 哀而不傷 (AC) deeply felt but not sentimental; 哀豔 *-yahn*↓. (2) Pertaining to funeral: 哀悼, 哀詞 *-dauh*, *-tsyr*, etc.↓; see 哀子 *-tzyy*↓. (3) Sorrowfully (oft. forming prefix to vv.): 哀求, 哀祈, 哀懇 beg pitifully or I beg humbly and urgently; 哀告 *-gauh*↓; 哀啓 (end of letter) sorrowfully yours; 哀號 cry pitifully; 哀泣 weep properly at funeral; 哀鳴 a cry of lament; 哀慟 lament bitterly.

哀哀 *ai-ai*, excl., as in 哀哀父母 (AC) ah! my parents!
哀戚 *aichi*, adj., sorrow-stricken.
哀悼 *aidauh*, v.t., to bemoan.
哀的美頓(敦)書 *aidihmeeiduhn-shu*, n., (translit.) an ultimatum.
哀告 *aigauh*, (1) v.i. & t., announce (death, etc.); (2) n., obituary notice.
哀歌 *ai-ge*, n., a dirge.
哀鴻 *ai-hurng*, phr., 哀鴻遍野 (LL) famine refugees swarm the countryside (possibly reference to encircling vultures).
哀詔 *ai-jauh*, n., announcement of emperor's death by his sucessor to the throne.
哀祭 *ai-jih*, v.i. & n., funeral sacrifice; sacrificial prayers.
哀矜 *aijin*, v.i., as in 哀矜而勿喜 to sympathize and not gloat over (s.o.'s mishap).
哀樂 *aileh*, n., (1) joys and sorrows of human life; (2) (*-yueh*) funeral music, dirge.
哀憐 *ailiarn*, v.t., to take pity (on child or one in distress).
哀厲 *ailih*, adj., (music, song) heartbreaking.
哀榮 *ai-rurng*, n., see N. 2↑.
哀傷 *aishang*, (1) v.i. & t., to feel grief; grieve over (s.o.'s death); (2) adj., sad, heart-rending.
哀冊 *ai-tseh*, n., formerly, official eulogy upon death of an empress.
哀詞 *ai-tsyr*, n., eulogy in rhyme of s.o.'s life at his funeral.
哀痛 *aituhng*, adj. & n., deep sorrow, profound grief.
哀哉 *ai-tzai*, excl., (AC, LL) alas!
哀子 *ai-tzyy*, n., son bereaved of mother with father living.
哀豔 *aiyahn*, adj., sadly touching, sad and beautiful, tragic (love story).

衰 60.02

shuai.

V.i. To decline (in age, strength, business); 盛衰 rise and decline (of nations, fortunes, etc.).

衰敗 *shuaibaih*, v. i., decline, degenerate; be defeated.
衰耗 *shuaihauh*, v. i., ditto.
衰倦 *shuaijyuahn*, adj., old and tired.
衰老 *shuailaau*, adj., become old, advanced in age.
衰陵 *shuailirng*, adj., (AC) see *-baih*↑.
衰落 *shuailuoh*, v. i., decline (in business, attendance, power, prestige).
衰邁 *shuaimaih*, adj., see *-laau*↑.
衰暮 *shuaimuh*, adj., advanced in years: 衰暮之年.
衰弱 *shuairuoh*, adj., old and weak, feeble (health).
衰謝 *shuaishieh*, adj., (of flowers, hair) past bloom, thinning out.
衰世 *shuai-shyh*, n., period of decline and chaos.
衰退 *shuaitueih*, v. i., to decrease (in strength, prestige); n., (econ.) recession.
衰頹 *shuaitueir*, adj., decrepit, deteriorated (condition, appearance).

衰微 *shuaiweir,* adj., (ruling house) weak, on the decline.

裛 60.02

yih.

V.t. (1) (AC) to cover up, wrap up. (2) Interch. 浥 63A.70.

裏 60.02

lii.

[Pop. 裡; dist. 裹↓]

N. (1) The inside, interior part of anything: 裏裏外外 inside and out; 表裏 outside and inside; 表裏如一 external appearance corresponds to inside; 表裏相應 coordinated attack or action from without and within; 裏外裏 either way: 反正裏外裏都是一樣浪費 either way it is expensive. (2) A place: 這裏, 那裏 this, that place (oft. wr. 里). (3) A duration of time: 日裏 daytime; 夜裏 nighttime (oft. wr. 里). (4) Lining (of dress, overcoat, etc.): 裏子 *-tz*↓.

Adj. Internal, interior, inside: 裏面, 裏邊, 裏頭 the inside, within, *-miahn, -bian, -tour*↓; 裏懷裏 inside or rear part (of table, etc.); 裏間兒 inside rooms; 裏勾兒外聯 to pull wires from both within and without; 裏出外進 (of things) uneven, with too many people coming in and going out.

裏邊 *liibian,* n., the inside.
裏海 *Lirhaai,* n., Caspian Sea.
裏脊肉 *lii'ji rouh,* n., the meat nearest spinal column of pig or sheep.
裏襟 *lii-jin,* n., inside lapel of dress.
裏面(兒) *liimiahn(-miah'l),* n., the inside.
裏頭(兒) *liitour('l),* n., ditto.
裏子 *liitz,* n., (1) the lining (of a coat, etc.); (2) (Chin. opera) a supporting cast.

裹 60.02

guoo.

[Dist. 裏]

N. An outer cover: 包裹 a package or parcel.

V.t. (1) To wrap up, bind together: 裹肚 a wrapper for the waist; see compp.↓; 裹創 to bandage wounds; 裹頭(巾) a wrapper for the head, a turban. (2) Encircle, confine: 裹脅 *-shier*↓.

裹腳 *guorjiaau,* n., (1) footbinding by women; (2) the cloth used for foot-binding.
裹亂 *guooluahn,* v.t., interrupt, disturb: 現在我們正忙, 你別在裏頭裹亂了 as we are busy, please don't disturb us.
裹抹 *guoo'mo,* v.t., (1) cover up: 才把她這句話給裹抹過去了 only in this way did we cover up the nonsense she had said; (2) mix up in: 沒留神把他的書給裹抹過來啦 inadvertently had his books mixed up in ours and took them away.
裹脅 *guooshier,* v.t., coerce, force to take part.
裹腿 *guootueei,* n., puttee putties.
裹足 *guootzur,* v.i., (1) hesitate for fear of danger: 行旅裹足 (LL) travellers hesitate to come; 裹足不前 hesitate to proceed; (2) (anc. custom) to bind the feet of women.

襄 60.02

shiang.

N. A surname.

V. i. & t. (1) To assist in management: 襄理 *-lii*↓; 襄助 *-juh*↓. (2) Mutually help: 共襄盛舉 help by united efforts to make an undertaking a success.

襄辦 *shiangbahn,* (1) v. t., to act as deputy or assistant; (2) n., deputy director or assistant manager.
襄助 *shiangjuh,* v. i. & t., to help, assist, support (person in some public undertaking).
襄理 *shianglii,* v.t. & n., see *-bahn*↑.
襄贊 *shiangtzahn,* v.i. & t., ditto.

褭 60.02

niaau.

[Interch. 裊 91.02]

衮 60.02

guun.

[Interch. 袞]

N. (1) (AC) robes worn by the emperor and feudal princes. (2) (AC) feudal princes.

衮衮 *gurnguun,* adj., a great many: 衮衮諸公 high-ranking government officials.

袠 60.02

jyh.

[Var. of 帙 22B.81; var. of 秩 a decade, 90A.81]

裒 60.02

pour.

衰 裛 裏 裹 襄 褭 衮 袠 裒

亅	小	⺊	十	土	ナ	廾	乚	丨	一	丅	フ	口	区	冈	冂	厂	尸	亠	广	宀	丶	乚	七	心	八	人	乂	乛	一	ノ	𠂉	く
00	01	02	10	11	12	20	21	22	30	31	32	40	41	42	50	51	52	60	61	62	63	70	71	72	80	81	82	83	90	91	92	93

裒 裦 褎 褒 辛 卒 夅 章

[Dist. 褒]

V. t. Gather; reduce.

裒輯 *pourjir*, v. i. & t., (LL) collect and edit.
裒斂 *pourliaan.*, v. i., (LL) lay heavy taxes.

裦 60.02

youh.
[Dist. 褎↓]

Adj. (AC) gorgeously dressed: 褎然.

褎 60.02

bau.
[Pop. of 褒↓]

褒 60.02

bau.
[Pop. 褎]

Adj. (AC) ample: 褒衣博帶 ample gown and loose girdle of Confucians.

V. t. To honor with praise, decoration or gift: 褒賜, 褒贈 *-syh*, *-tzehng*↓.

褒貶 *baubiaan*, n. & v. t., (praise and blame) criticize, -cism.
褒章 *baujang*, n., official decoration=徽章.
褒獎 *baujiaang*, n. & v. t., (give) official recognition; (court.) undeserved praise.
褒狀 *baujuahng*, n., certificate of decoration or other awards.
褒卹 *baushyuh*, n. & v. t., gift by government to family of deceased.
褒賜 *bausyh*, v.t., to confer (gift, honor).
褒贈 *bautzehng*, v.t., ditto.
褒揚 *bauyarng*, n. & v. t., (give) public tribute (to person's services).

§ 60.10 (亠/十)

辛 60.10

shin.

N. (1) Number eight of the 天干 31.81 decimal cycle, see Appendix A; 辛亥革命 the Revolution of 1911; 辛丑條約 Treaty of 1901. (2) A surname.

Adj. (1) Bitter in taste: 辛辣 *-lah*↓. (2) Bitter in experience: 辛酸 *-suan*↓. (3) Hard-working, laborious: 辛勤, 辛苦, 辛勞 *-chirn*, *-'kuu*, *-laur*↓.

辛勤 *shinchirn*, adj. & adv., laborious, -ly, working hard: 辛勤工作 work hard.
辛楚 *shinchuu*, adj., sad, saddening, see *-'kuu*↓.
辛狄開 *shindirkai*, n., (also 辛廸卡) (translit.) syndicate.
辛金 *shinjin*, n., (var. of 薪金) salary.
辛苦 *shin'kuu*, adj. & adv., hard, exhausting: 千辛萬苦 untold hardships, laboriously; 辛苦工作 work hard; (court.) take trouble, give trouble: 辛苦了你 thanks for the trouble; 你就辛苦一趟吧 please be so good as to do this.
辛辣 *shinlah*, adj., hot in flavor; biting in criticism.
辛勞 *shinlaur*, n., trouble: 不辭辛勞 took all the trouble (to do s. t.).
辛酸 *shinsuan*, adj., sad, tearful.
辛夷 *shinyir*, n., (bot.) the magnolia, *Magnolia kobus*.

卒 60.10

tzur (**tsuh*).

N. (1) A servant, an attendant: 販夫走卒 the lower classes of society ("pedlars and menial servants"). (2) A common soldier: 士卒 officers and men; 兵卒 troops; 卒子, 卒兒, 小卒 privates; 卒伍 the rank and file; 過河卒子 (chess) a soldier in opponent's territory which can advance, but not retreat.

V. i. (1) To end, finish: 卒業 *-yeh*↓. (2) Die: 暴卒 die all of a sudden.

Adv. (1) Finally, at last, in the end: 卒償素願 had one's wishes fulfilled at long last. (2) (**tsuh*) (=猝) All of a sudden: 卒倒 *-daau*, 卒中 *-juhng*↓; 卒乍 suddenly, unexpectedly; 卒卒 hurriedly; 倉卒 abruptly, suddenly.

卒倒 **tsuhdaau*, n., (med.) an apoplectic stroke.
卒中 **tsuhjuhng*, n., (herb med.) apoplexy.
卒哭 *tzurku*, n., the end of the period of mourning.
卒業 *tzuryeh*, v. i., to graduate (from school), to complete a course of study.

60.10

jyuu.
[Pop. of 舉 91.10]

章 60.10

jang.

N. (1) A piece of writing, a composition, structure or pattern: 文章 literary writing, see 文 60.82; 出口成章 ad-lib, make polished impromtu speech; 章法 composition, structural pattern; order: 雜亂無章 without order or logical connection; 章段 paragraph division; 章句 -*jyuh*↓. (2) A memorial to emperor: 章奏 or 奏章. (3) A chapter: 第一章 Chapter One; 章節 chapter and verse; 章回小說 a long novel (divided into chapters). (4) Regulations, constitution: 憲章 constitution (of society, institution): 大憲章 (Eng. history) the Magna Charta; 規章 regulations; 簡章 brief regulations; 章程 -*cherng*↓; 違章 or 違反警章 against police regulations. (5) Stamp, seal: 圖章, 印章 seal; 牙章 ivory seal. (6) Medal of award: 徽章 medal of honor; 校章 school medal. (7) A surname.

章程 *jangcherng*, n., (1) regulations (of school, etc.); (2) (-'*cheng*) order: 他連吃飯都沒個章程 act disorderly even at meal.

章服 *jang-fur*, n., formerly, regulation dress, costume.

章皇 *janghuarng*, adj., undecided, flurried.

章句 *jangjyuh*, n., a commentary or text with sentence division: 章句之學 a study of the classics confined to proper sentence division, pronunciation and meaning of words, without attention to system of thought.

章草 *jangtsaau*, n., a simplified form of cursive script (草書), made or approved by 漢章帝 (76–88 A.D.).

章奏 *jang-tzouh*, n., a memorial to emperor.

章魚 *jang-yur*, n., an octopus.

率 60.10

shuaih (re. pr. *shuoh*; **lyuh*).

N. (1) Model for others: 表率. (2) (**lyuh*) Rate (of speed, growth, progress): 速率 velocity; 變率 rate of change; 效率, 能率 efficiency; 比率 ratio; 利率 rate of interest; 出生率 birth rate; 死亡率 death rate; 稅率 tax rate; 生產率 productivity, rate of production. (3) (**lyuh*) (AC) law, statute.

V. t. (1) To lead (troops): 率領 -*liing*↓; 率師, 率兵 lead troops. (2) To follow a line: 率由舊章 (LL) to follow the established pattern; 率教 take advice; 率職 perform one's duties.

Adj. (1) Cursory, offhand: 輕率 rash (action), without due consideration; 草率 careless: 草率了事 dispose of matter carelessly. (2) Straightforward, forthright: 率直 -*jyr*↓; 直率, 坦率 candid, forthright. (3) Handsome: 打扮的眞率 dress handsomely (also wr. 帥).

Adv. Mostly: 大率 ditto; 率常 -*charng*↓.

率常 *shuaihcharng*, adv., usually: 率常不來 usually does not come (to office, meeting).

率爾 *shuaih-eel*, adv., abruptly; impetuously, hastily.

率懷 *shuaih-huair*, adv., (LL) follow heart's desire, bent.

率眞 *shuaihjen*, adj., naïve, forthright.

率直 *shuaihjyr*, adj., forthright, direct (character).

率角 *shuaihjyuer*, v. i., var. for 摔[A]跤 to wrestle, 10A.10.

率領 *shuaihliing*, v. t., to lead (troops, followers).

率然 *shuaihrarn*, adv., see -*eel*↑.

率任 *shuaihrehn*, adj., acting with abandon, without self-control.

率先 *shuaihshian*, adv., (go) in front (of others); in advance.

率性 *shuaihshihng*, (1) adj. & adv., impetuous, -ly, rash, -ly; (2) v.t., 率性之謂道 (AC) to follow nature is called 道 *dauh*.

率同 *shuaihturng*, adv. phr., together with (colleagues, etc.).

率土 *shuaih-tuu*, phr., 率土之濱 (AC) all this land, all within the boundaries.

率悟 *shuaihwuh*, adj., (LL) quick in understanding.

率易 *shuaihyih*[1], adj., (LL) simple and direct.

率意 *shuaihyih*[2], adj. & adv., impetuous(ly), following one's bent (=任意).

牽 60.10

chian.

V. t. (1) To lead by the hand, to pull: 牽牛, 羊 to lead a cow, lamb; 順手牽羊 to take s.t. that doesn't belong to oneself; 手牽手 hand in hand; 牽手 lead by hand; 牽繩子 to pull a rope; 牽挽 pull by rope. (2) To involve, draw in, drag out: 牽連, 牽涉, 牽累 -*liarn*, -*sheh*, -*leei*, etc.↓; 牽絲扳籐 dilly-dally, shilly-shally, drag out (affair, argument) interminably (like "drawing out treacle or spreading vine"). (3) (Coll.) to sew up (pieces, dress). (4) To remember, unable to forget: 牽腸掛肚 be deeply concerned, to cause deep personal concern; 牽掛, 牽念 -*guah*, -*niahn*↓.

牽扯 *chianchee*, v. t., to drag in (others, details) into topic of conversation; to involve (person) in allegations at court.

牽掣 *chiancheh*, v. t., (1) to control, see -*jyh*↓; (2) to lead through connections into other aspects: 互相牽掣 (the two problems) are tied up together.

牽強 *chianchiarng*, adj., arbitrary: 牽強附會 farfetched, irrelevant, fasten on an unwarranted conclusion.

牽動 *chianduhng*, v. t., involve, upset: 牽動大局 upset the gen. situation (as one move at chess).

牽掛 *chianguah*, v. t., to remember fondly, be concerned, worried, over (another's welfare).

牽合 *chianher*, v. t., force or manipulate (two separate units) into one; make unwarranted deductions.

牽制 *chianjyh*, v. i. & t., to tie up (actions, movements, etc.), impede; to involve and affect, restrict the freedom of (another, or each other).

牽累 *chianleei*, v. i., involve (person) in s. t. unpleasant (debts; lawsuit).

牽連 *chianliarn*, v. i., to link or be mutually linked together; n., 牽連犯 implicated offender.

牽念 *chianniahn*, v. t., to remember fondly (person), be concerned about (child).

牽牛花 *chianniour hua*, n., (bot.) the morning glory, *Pharbitis*.

牽紗 *chian-sha*, phr., to hold bride's veil.

牽涉 *chiansheh*, v. t., to involve (a third party); implicate or be implicated in crime; to be linked up with.

牽線 *chianshiahn*, v. i., be a matchmaker.

牽絲 *chiansy*, v. i., (1) (LL) to receive a government post (絲 the girdle sashes); (2) a game of drawing lots by choice of tapes leading to unseen objects; 牽絲戲 puppet show.

牽挺 *chiantiing*, n., formerly, the treadle in a loom, a pedal in weaving machine.

牽引 *chianyiin*, v. t., to involve, to link up with.

聾 60.10

lurng.

N. & adj. Deaf: 聾子 a deaf person; 又聾又啞 both deaf and dumb; 推聾裝啞 pretend to be deaf and dumb—ignore requests for attention; 你聾了嗎 are you deaf?—don't you hear? 把我耳朵震聾了 (noise) deafens, make a deafening noise; 聾啞學校 school for the deaf and dumb.

§ 60.11 (⼀/土)

主 60.11

juu.

N. (1) Master, chief owner, possessor: 主人, 主子 *-rern*, *-'tz*↓; 主奴 master and servants or slave; 作主 make final decison; 是誰作主 who makes the decisions? 由他作主 let him assume final responsibility; 一家之主 head of the family; 房主 house owner; 船主 the boatman (boat owner, oft. the captain); 車主 car owner; 債主 creditor; 財主 a wealthy man, the person who puts up the money. (2) Host: 主客 host and guest; guest of honor (opp. 陪客 all other guests). (3) Main aim, goal: 主旨 *-jyy*↓; 以清潔爲主 the principal thing is cleanliness. (4) Lord, sovereign: 救主 Lord Saviour; 天主 (Roman Catholic) God; 主上 *-shahng*↓; 一國之主 head of the state. (5) 公主 princess. (6) 神主, 木主 spirit tablet for worship: see 點^A主 41S.40.

V. t. (1) To direct, to head (group, activity): 主管 *-guaan*↓; 主持 *-chyr*↓; 君主, 民主 monarchy, democracy; 主其事 direct the whole business; 主婚 *-hun*, 主任 *-rehn*↓. (2) To control, determine: 心不由主 lose self-control; 六神無主, 沒有主心骨兒 a floating feeling of not knowing what one is doing; 自主 be independent (country); 主動, 主使 *-duhng*, *-shyy*↓. (3) (AC) to lodge at (s.o.'s house). (4) (Divination) indicate: 主吉, 主凶 indicates good, bad, luck. (5) To stand for, to sponsor, lead or hold (an opinion against others): 主戰, 主和 stand for war, for negotiation; 主張 *-jang*↓.

Adj. Main, principal: 主題, 主旨, 主要 *-tir*, *-jyy*, *-yauh*↓; 主流 main stream; 主峯 principal peak; 主犯, 從犯 main culprit, accomplice; 主食 staple food (rice, wheat, etc.).

主辦 *juubahn*, v. t. & n., (be) prime mover, director: 誰主辦的 who is the director (of paper, movement)?

主編 *juubian*, v. t. & n., (be) editor in chief.

主筆 *jurbii*, v. t. & n., (be) editor; editorial writer.

主持 *juuchyr*, v. t., (1) to manage, direct (household, organization); (2) to uphold (an opinion, theory): 主持正義 uphold justice.

主權 *juuchyuarn*, n., sovereignty (of a country); power of decision: 主權在我 I make the decisions; 主權國 a sovereign country; not dependent.

主動 *juuduhng*, v. i. & n., (to hold, retain) initiative; to initiate: 誰主動的 who is back of this (the prime mover)?

主犯 *juufahn*, n., main culprit.

主婦 *juufuh*, n., mistress of a house; 家主婦 housewife.

主稿 *juugaau*, v. i. & n., person elected or appointed to draft a statement.

主管 *jurguaan*, v. t. & n., to manage; manager.

主觀 *juuguan*, adj., subjective (opinion, criticism), opp. 客觀 objective; oft. 主觀的.

主顧 *juuguh*, n., customer.

主公 *juugung*, n., (MC) address to ruler, somewhat similar to "My Lord."

主婚 *juuhun*, v. i., to officiate at wedding; 主婚人 *--rern*, n., such person.

主張 *juujang*, (1) v. i. & t., to decide, to believe in: 主張去, 不去 (person) decides to go, not to go; 主張讓步 believe in making concessions; (2) n., opinion, decision: 是誰的主張 whose idea is this? 各有主張 each has his opinion; 主張不同 opinions differ; 主張公道 stand for justice.

主講 *jurjiaang*, v. i., make the main speech; speak on special subject.

主角 *jur-jiaau*, n., main actor or actress; main character in story.

主見 *juujiahn*, n., (1) subjective

view: 這人沒主見 this person has no opinions of his own; (2) preconceived opinion, cf. 成見 prejudice.

主將 *juujiahng*, n., commander in chief.

主教 *juujiauh*, n., bishop; 總主教 archbishop.

主計 *juujih*[1], n., formerly, treasurer.

主祭 *juujih*[2], v. i. & n., (be) the officer offering sacrifices.

主旨 *jurjyy*, n., aim, goal.

主客 *juu-keh*, n., (1) host and guest; (2) principal guest.

主兒 *juu-l*, n., master; anyone of master's family or class.

主力 *juu-lih*, n., principal strength, force; main body of army.

主謀 *juu-mour*, v. i. & n., (person who) hatches idea of a plan; the mastermind.

主母 *jurmuu*, n., mistress, the lady of the house.

主腦 *jurnaau*, n., (1) the essential point or aspect of matter; (2) leader in group action.

主僕 *juu-pur*, phr., master and servant.

主任 *juurehn*, n., chairman of committee, commission, group, department, bureau; chief, head (of publicity, promotion, etc.): 主任秘書 chief secretary; 主任委員 chairman of committee.

主人 *juurern*, n., (1) the owner (of house, shop, dog, umbrella, etc.); (2) master, boss: 主人翁, 主人公 *--weng*, *--gung*, n., (a) principal character in play, novel; (b) address of master.

主日 *juuryh*, n., (Christian) the Lord's Day, Sunday; 主日學 Sunday school.

主上 *jushahng*, n., Your Majesty.

主席 *jushir*, n., chairman of meeting; chairman of political party or committee: 主席團 presidium, board of chairmen in collective leadership system.

主刑 *juu-shirng*, n., punishment for the chief count or charge, dist. other counts.

主帥 *juushuaih*, n., address to commander in chief.

主使 *jurshyy*, (1) v. i. & t., to instigate; (2) n., instigator.

主體 *jurtii*, n., (1) main body, item; (2) principal aim, idea, purpose; (3) the active element.

主題 *juutir*, n., main theme (of speech, music composition, etc.), chief point of interest (in painting, photograph).

主子 *juu'tz*, n., (1) address to master; (2) Your Majesty.

主宰 *jurtzaai*, n., lord (of creation); master.

主位 *juu-weih*, n., (1) host's seat at table; (2) seat of the throne.

主文 *juuwern*, n., leading paragraph of judge's review, summing up the juristic position of case.

主物 *juuwuh*, n., (law) principal object of dispute (such as property rights).

主演 *jur-yaan*, v. i., to be the main speaker or performer; to have for subject (of speech, etc.).

主要 *juuyauh*, adj., principal, main, essential (point, aim, problem, agency, etc.).

主意 *juuyih*[1], n., see *-jang* ↑.

主義 *juuyih*[2], n., equivalent of "-ism" in "socialism," "pragmatism," "opportunism," "patriotism," etc.).

主因 *juu-yin*, n., principal factor or cause.

望 60.11

wahng.

N. (1) The day of full moon, the fifteenth day of the lunar month: 朔望 1st and 15th day of the lunar month; 既望 the 16th day. (2) Reputation, fame, prestige: 名望, 聲望 ditto; 人望, 威望 prestige. (3) Hope, expectation: 盼望, 希望, 冀望 hope; 願望 wish; 期望 expectation; 無望 hopeless; 絕望 despair; 喜出望外 happy beyond expectations.

V. i. & t. (1) To hope, expect, wish (see N. 3 ↑): 渴望 hope anxiously; 望巴巴 hope and wait anxiously; 所望 what one hopes for. (2) To look up (at moon), look over or gaze into distance, to glance at (valley, clouds, the sea) sentimentally: 仰望 look up in hope; 望遠鏡 *-yuan-jihng* ↓; 望而生畏 inspire awe even from distance; 望洋興歎 view with despair the vast ocean or vast work to be done; 望梅止渴 (allu.) look at plums to quench thirst, Barmecide's feast, imagined satisfaction; 望風 *-feng* ↓; 望雲 gaze at the clouds and think of distant friends; 望塵莫及 to fall so far behind in comparison as unable even to see the dust of the rider ahead. (3) To visit, inspect: 觀望 to observe, stand aside and not make up one's mind; 探望 to visit (friend, etc.). (4) To approach: 望七 (望八) 之年 approaching seventy (eighty).

Prep. Toward: 望前走 go forward; 望後退 retreat backward; see 往 91B.11, Prep.

望長 *wahng-charng*, phr., 望長久遠 to plan for permanent future.

望風 *wahng-feng*, phr., (1) stand facing the wind and feel (remembrance, etc.); (2) 望風而逃 to run away at rumor of approach; (3) to admire (great leader) and wish to follow.

望候 *wahnghouh*, v. t., to send greetings.

望看 *wahng'kan*, v. t., to pay respects.

望門(兒)寡 *wahngmern(-mer'l) guaa*, n., (coll.) widow who remains unmarried after fiancé dies; 望門兒妨 (coll.) man who remains unmarried after fiancée dies.

望日 *wahng-ryh*, n., the 15th day of lunar month.

望鄉臺 *wahng-shiang-tair*, n., terrace in hell where the deceased can see their homes in the distance.

主 望

亅	小	⺊	十	土	ナ	廾	乚	丨	一	丅	𠃌	口	囗	冂	𠃍	尸	亠	广	宀	丶	乚	七	心	八	人	乂	乛	𠂉	丿	𠂉	〈
00	01	02	10	11	12	20	21	22	30	31	32	40	41	42	50	51	52	60	61	62	63	70	71	72	80	81	82	83	90	91	92	93

望視 *wahngshyh*, v. i., (AC) to look upwards (of a hunchback).

望天兒 *wahngtia'l*, n., a kind of goldfish with protruding eyes.

望子 *wahngtz*, n., corruption of 幌[A]子 22B.70, a flagpole as sign of wine shop.

望族 *wahngtzur*, n., respected clan.

望望 *wahngwahng*, (1) adv., as in 望望然去之 depart with a look of disappointment or embarrassment; (2) (-'*wang*) v.i., to drop in at friend's place.

望遠鏡 *wahng-yuaan-jihng*, n., telescope, field glass, opera glass; 雙眼望遠鏡 binocular.

望雲 *wahng-yurn*, phr., (1) to gaze at clouds (and think of s. o.); (2) (allu.) to think of parents.

產 60.11

chaan.

N. (1) Property: 財產 property; 房產 realty; 治產 buy, own or manage property; 承產 inherit property; 共[A]產 Communism, -nist, 20.80; 私產 private property; 家產 family property; 破產 bankrupt, -cy; 遺產 inherited property; 不動產 real property. (2) Production, product, produce: 生產 production of goods; 產品, 產物 -*piin*, -*wuh* ↓; 產地 where goods are produced; 農產 farm produce; 水產 marine products; 土產 local products. (3) Industry: 產業 -*yeh* ↓. (4) Maternity, see V.t. 1 ↓.

V. t. (1) To give birth: 產科 -*ke* ↓; 產婆, 產婦 -*por*, -*fuh* ↓; 生產 give birth to children, (of animals) reproduce their kind. (2) To produce (goods, vegetables, etc.): 多產, 盛產 multiply fast, very reproductive.

產權 *chaanchyuarn*, n., property rights.

產額 *chaan-er*, n., rate or volume of production.

產房 *chaanfarng*, n., maternity ward.

產婦 *chaanfuh*, n., a lying-in mother (the mother during maternity).

產後 *chaanhouh*, adj., puerperal; 產後熱 puerperal fever.

產科 *chaanke*, n., obstetrics, maternity department.

產量 *chaanliahng*, n., capacity or volume of production.

產門 *chaan-mern*, n., (rare) woman's genitals.

產娩 *charnmiaan*, n., parturition.

產品 *charnpiin*, n., product(s).

產婆 *chaan(')por*, n., midwife.

產蓐 *chaanruh*, n., child delivery; 產蓐(褥)熱 puerperal fever, see -*houh* ↑.

產生 *chaansheng*, v. t., (1) to produce (fish, grapes, etc.); (2) to cause, give rise to (misunderstanding, riots, trouble, results, etc.).

產物 *chaanwuh*, n., products of land.

產業 *chaanyeh* (coll. -'*ye*), n., (1) property; (2) industry.

堃 60.11

kun.

[Var. of 坤 11A.22]

童 60.11

turng.

N. (1) A surname. (2) Child: 兒童 gen. term for children; 孩童 child; 童稚 the young; 返老還童 rejuvenation; 童叟無欺 (in shop advertisement) we are equally honest with aged and child customers; 童言無忌 take no offense at child's babble, a child says what he thinks; 神童 child prodigy; 頑童 mischievous or naughty child. (3) (Interch. 僮) house boy, page: 書童, 琴童 boy servant attending to library, music room. (4) (N. used as modifier) virgin: 童男女 young unmarried boys and girls; 童女 virgin; 童身 virginhood, maidenhood; 童貞 chaste, without sexual experience; 童顏皓髮 white hair and rosy complexion.

Adj. (1) Young, innocent: 童蒙 innocent childhood; 童騃 young and ignorant; 童昏 young and silly. (2) (Of cattle, sheep) yet without grown horns. (3) Bald: 童山濯濯 a bare hill without trees; 頭童齒豁 hoary-headed and toothless.

童便 *turngbiahn*, n., (Chin. med.) child's urine regarded as having medical property.

童兒 *turng-erl*, n., child (-ren); child servant.

童工 *turnggung*, n., child labor.

童話 *turnghuah*, n., fairy tales.

童貞 *turngjen*[1], adj. & n., chaste (maiden), chastity, virginity.

童眞 *turngjen*[2], n., naïveté, naïveness.

童男(子)(子兒) *turngnarn(tzyy)(tzee'l)*, n., boy without sexual experience.

童年 *turngniarn*, n., childhood: 童年時代 teen-age.

童女 *turngnyuu*, n., virgin.

童生 *turngsheng*, n., formerly, underage participant in civil examinations.

童心 *turngshin*, n., heart of innocence; innocence of youth: 童心未泯 (of grownups) still retain child's innocence.

童童 *turngturng*, adj., (LL) bare, bald; hidden.

童子 *turngtzyy*, n., boy: 童子軍 boy scout; 童子雞 cockerel.

童養媳 *turngyaang-shir*, n., child daughter-in-law, raised in family of future husband.

童謠 *turngyaur*, n., folk rhymes, generally of satirical nature.

塾 60.11

shur.

N. A private primary school: 私塾 ditto; 家塾 school at home with private tutor; 塾師 schoolteacher, schoolmaster.

壅 60.11

yuung (also *yung*).
[Var. of 㙲]

V.t. (1) To obstruct. (2) To apply fertilizer or pad soil around a growing plant.

壅閉 *yuungbih*, adj., blocked up (nose, sewerage).
壅疾 *yuung-jir*, n., morbid swollen feet.
壅滯 *yuungjyh*, v.i., to become stagnant or sluggish (of circulation, etc.).
壅門 *yuungmern*, n., enclosure between inner and outer city gates (usu. wr. 壅城).
壅塞 *yuungseh*, adj., blocked up.

壟 60.11

luung.
[Var. of 壠]

N. A rise in land, a mound.

壟斷 *luungduahn*, v. t., to corner the market, to monopolize: 壟斷市場, 壟斷一切.

雍 60.11

yung (also *yuhng*).

N. A surname.

V. i. & t. (1) U. f. 擁 to jostle. (2) U. f. 壅 to block up: 雍遏 *-eh*↓.

Adj. Majestic (music, personality).

雍遏 *yung-eh* (*yuhng-*), adj., blocked up.
雍和 *yungher*, adj., harmonious (music), friendly and at ease (manner).
雍穆 *yungmuh*[1], adj., majestic, poised and dignified.
雍睦 *yungmuh*[2], adj., friendly, peaceful.
雍容 *yungrurng*, adj., poised, at ease: 雍容自得 poised, in peace of mind.
雍雍 *yungyung*, adj., friendly, harmonious.

§60.20 (亠/廾)

弈 60.20

yih.
[Dist. 奕 60.81]

N. Game of chess.

弃 60.20

chih.
[Anc. var. of 棄 60.01]

§60.21 (亠/ㄴ)

亡 60.21

warng (**wur*).
[Anc. var. 亾]

V. i. & t. (1) To lose: 亡魂 lost one's soul, also (p.p.) soul of departed; 亡國 to lose a country, also (p.p.) a lost country; 亡羊補牢 mend the sheepfold after losing the sheep—not too late to take future precautions. (2) To die: 死亡 ditto; 亡者 *-jee*↓; 陣亡 die in battle; 滅亡 (country) be destroyed; 未亡人 widow (in self-reference), one who is unable to die yet. (3) To flee, escape: 逃亡, 出亡, 流亡 to flee, live in exile; 亡酒 (AC) escaped drinking, excused from drinking.

Adj. (1) (As p.p.) lost, deceased, destroyed, see Vb 1 & 2↑; 亡兄, 亡弟 my deceased elder, younger, brother; 亡父, 亡母, 亡妻 deceased father, mother, wife, etc. (2) (**wur*=無) no, not a: 亡何, 亡狀, 亡賴 *-her*, *-juahng*, *-laih*↓; see 無 92.63 for other compp.

亡故 *warngguh*, adj., deceased, past.
亡國 *warng-guor*, n., a destroyed country: 亡國奴 (abuse) "a slave without a country"; 亡國之音 effeminate, sentimental music, without manly strength.
亡何 **wurher*, adv., very soon, not long afterwards.
亡化 *warnghuah*, v. i., (MC) die, pass away.
亡者 *warngjee*, n., the dead, also the missing in battle.
亡狀 **wurjuahng*, adj., (court. of oneself) it was very rude or presumptuous of me.
亡賴 **wurlaih*, n., a ne'er-do-well.
亡慮 **wurlyuh*, adv., see 無^慮 92.63.
亡命 *warngmihng*, v. i., live in exile: 亡命之徒 refugees from justice.
亡奈 **wurnaih*, adv., unfortunately, against one's wish, see 無^奈 92.63.

峦 60.21

luarn.
[Pop. of 巒 93.21]

亅	小	⺊	十	土	ナ	廾	ㄴ⺊	丨	一	丁	フ	口	囚	冈	ㄱ	厂	尸	亠	广	宀	丶	ㄴ	七	心	八	人	乂	～	一	リ	ㄥ	く
00	01	02	10	11	12	20	21	22	30	31	32	40	41	42	50	51	52	60	61	62	63	70	71	72	80	81	82	83	90	91	92	93

甕
卞
市
帝
齊

甕 60.21

wehng.

[Var. of 甕 a jar, 60.70]

§ 60.22 (亠/丨)

卞 60.22

biahn.

N. A surname.

Adj. As in 卞急 nervous (cf. 褊[Δ]急 63C.42).

市 60.22

shyh.

N. (1) Market, trade: 市場 *-charng*↓; 菜市, 魚市 vegetable, fish market; 上市 (certain fish, fruit) is in season; 罷市 gen. strike with all shops closed; 夜市 night fair; 早市 trade in morning; 行市 market price, rate; 開市 shops open for business after holiday, trade market opens; 應市 to supply the market demands; 市面 *-miahn*↓. (2) City, town: 城市 town (versus country); 都市 city; 市聲 city noise; 市區, 市鎮, 市郊 *-chyu, -jehn, -jiau*↓.

V.t. (1) (LL) To buy, sell, deal in: 市馬 deal in horses; 市藥 buy medicine. (2) To fish for favors, profits, etc.: 市恩, 市惠 show special favor to s.o.; 市寵, 市歡 to curry s.o.'s favor; 市怨 invite enmity, sow seeds of discontent; 市利 try to make money, earn profits.

Adj. Part of term of metric system: 市里, 市尺, 市升 *-lii, -chyy, -sheng*↓, see Appendix C.

市塵 *shyhcharn*, n., (AC) business district, market place.
市場 *shyhcharng*, n., sales market: 國際市場 international market; 市場研究 market research; (2) (*-chaang*) local market for food, vegetables.
市朝 *shyhchaur*, n., (AC) public market place.
市區 *shyhchyu*, n., a business district; urban area.
市尺 *shyhchyy*, n., one-third of a meter.
市公所 *shyh-gungsuo*, n., city or town hall, municipal sub-office; county office.
市鎮 *shyhjehn*, n., a township; a city sub-division: 市鎮公所 township office, branch office of city government.
市政 *shyhjehng*, n., municipal administration: 市政府 municipal government.
市價 *shyhjiah*, n., market price, rate.
市郊 *shyhjiau*, n., suburb.
市井 *shyhjiing*, n., town: 市井之流 (之徒) the average man about town; 市井無賴 the ne'er-do-well, the riffraff.
市斤 *shyhjin*, n., half a kilogram.
市集 *shyhjir*, n., a town fair or country fair.
市口兒 *shyhkoou'l*, n., the busy streets, center of town.
市儈 *shyhkuaih*, n., (contempt.) shopkeeper, philistine.
市兒 *shyh'l*, n., a street or place where small traders congregate.
市立 *shyh-lih*, adj., (school, hospital) belonging to or supported by the city: 市立圖書館 municipal library.
市里 *shyhlii*, n., half a kilometer.
市樓 *shyhlour*, n., (MC) town restaurant, wineshop.
市面(兒) *shyhmiahn(-miah'l)*, n., the market (conditions of): 市面蕭條 business is slow.
市民 *shyhmirn*, n., townspeople.
市畝 *shyhmuu*, n., an area measure=6,000 sq. *-chyy*↑.
市人 *shyhrern*, n., townspeople.
市容 *shyh-rurng*, n., appearance or gen. condition of the streets.
市升 *shyhsheng*, n., a liter.
市刑 *shyhshirng*, n., formerly, light punishment such as flogging taking place in public square.
市肆 *shyhsyh*, n., (LL) shops.
市曹 *shyhtsaur*, n., (1) market place; (2) (MC) public square where punishment of criminals was carried out.
市隱 *shyhyiin*, n., a recluse who lives in city and enjoys quiet life.
市語 *shyhyuu*, n., traders' slang, business jargon.

帝 60.22

dih.

N. Supreme ruler: 皇帝 emperor; 上帝 regular term for Christian God; also various Taoist gods: 玉皇上(大)帝 Jade Emperor of Heaven; 天帝, 帝君 various gods.

帝國 *dihguor*, n., empire: 帝國主義 imperialism.
帝制 *dihjyh*, n., imperial system, monarchy.
帝君 *dihjyun*, n., a Taoist or Buddhist god, as 關帝君 (=關羽) God of Chivalry.
帝鄉 *dihshiang*, n., God's abode.
帝王 *dihwarng*, n., king and emperor.
帝業 *dihyeh*, n., the empire; imperial house, a person's successful exploits in founding a new dynasty: 卒成帝業 succeeded in founding an empire.

齊 60.22

chir (**jai, *tzy*).

N. (1) A surname. (2) Name of anc. kingdom, now in northern Shantung Province; 齊大非偶 phr., (allu.) declining marriage proposal from rich or influential family; 齊人之福 (AC) joy of man having two or more wives. (3) (**tzy*) (AC) skirt of robe: 攝齊升堂 gather the skirt on entering hall. (4) (**jih*) See 火[Δ]齊 91.81.

V.t. To arrange, put in order: 齊家 to have a good family (as basis of good society)—basic Confucian philosophy; 齊賬 to set accounts in order.

Adj. (1) Neat, tidy: 整齊, 整整齊齊 neat, even; 齊頭齊腦兒 in even row; 齊臻臻 very tidy; 齊截 -*'jie* ↓. (2) Complete: 齊備, 齊全 -*beih*, -*chuarn* ↓. (3) Equal: 齊年, 齊齒 of same age; 齊名 rival each other in reputation; adv., equally: 並駕齊驅 (lit. & fig.) run neck and neck, rank equally in power; 擧案齊眉 (allu.) wife brings lunch tray to the height of her eyebrow as polite form—used to refer to husband and wife keeping up politeness between each other (夫婦相敬如賓). (4) Adj. & adv., together: 一齊 ditto; 齊集一堂 assemble in one place; 齊聲 (applaud) in unison; 齊唱 -*chahng* ↓; 齊心合(協)力 pull together. (5) (**jai*) As var. of 齋: 齊肅 -*suh*[1] ↓.

齊備 *chirbeih*, adj., all ready, all complete (luggage, utensils, attendants).

齊唱 *chir-chahng*, phr., sing in unison.

齊盛 **tzycherng*, n., sacrificial offerings of millet (also wr. 粢盛).

齊全 *chirchuarn*, adj., complete (gathering, articles of a set).

齊楚 *chirchuu*, adj., (dress) neat, well arranged.

齊墩果 *chirdun-guoo*, n., (bot.) *Styrax japonica*.

齊整 *chirjeeng*, adj. & adv., neat, -ly, well arranged (also 整齊); (coll.) good-looking (cake, candlesticks, etc.).

齊家 *chir-jia*, phr., see V.t. ↑.

齊截 *chir'jie*, adj., neat: 字寫得很齊截 characters are well-formed; 東西都準備齊截了 all have been arranged.

齊給 *chirjii*, adj., (AC) well arranged, well provided.

齊理 *chirlii*, v. t., to arrange in order.

齊眉 *chirmeir*, phr., see Adj. 3 ↑; 齊眉棍 a boxer's staff which comes up to the eyebrows in height; 齊眉穗兒 bangs on forehead.

齊肅 *chirsuh*[1] (*chir*-), adj., neat, (army) in splendid form; (2) (**jai*-) decorous, august (manner).

齊宿 **jaisuh*[2], v. i., (AC) to observe fasting and sleep alone on night before sacrifices.

齊頭 *chirtour*, adj., (1) cut even; (2) (Shanghai dial.) by chance; 齊頭蒿 --*hau*, n., (bot.) wormwood (also 牡蒿).

齊衰 **tzytsuei*, n., a mourning dress of coarse hemp with hemmed borders—second degree of mourning for grandparents, etc.

齋 60.22

jai.

[Pop. 斎, var. of 斋]

N. (1) A studio: 書齋 studio, library (room) in private house; 齋舍, 齋屋 -*sheh*, -*wu* ↓; used oft. in name of art shops and restaurants. (2) Vegetarian food: 吃齋 eat vegetarian food on certain days or for period according to pledge; 小齋 (Catholic) abstinence; 開齋 end of period for vegetarian food; 長齋念佛 a pledge to eat vegetarian food and say prayers (Budd.); 齋戒 -*jieh* ↓; 齋期 days of fast.

齋飯 *jaifahn*, n., (Budd.) food obtained by begging by monks.

齋戒 *jaijieh*, v. i. & n., (Confucian) to observe "fast" day before sacrifices by refraining from wine and meat; fasting.

齋主 *jaijuu*, n., donor to temples; person who pays monks for prayer rites at home; (. . .)齋主人 owner of studio (as poetic name of scholar).

齋舍 *jaisheh*, n., (1) formerly, room for observing religious abstinence before worship; also 齋堂 -*tarng*; (2) private study; (3) formerly, school dormitory.

齋壇 *jaitarn*, n., altar set up for prayer rites.

齋屋 *jaiwu*, n., a study.

齋務 *jaiwuh*, n., formerly, management of school dormitory; 齋務主任 school proctor.

齎 60.22

ji.

[Pop. 賫, 賷 10.80]

N. (1) (AC) baggage, bags, traps. (2) (Interch. 資) (AC) equipment, tools, instruments: 齎用益饒 have more and more funds and supplies.

V.t. (1) To hold (in mind), to harbor: 齎恨 die without fulfilling one's ambitions; 齎志 ditto. (2) To give: 齎送 to send or forward (s.t.); 齎呈 to present (s.t.) to a superior.

齏 60.22

ji.

[Var. of 韲]

N. Minced condiments.

Adj. Cut or broken into pieces: 碎如齏粉 be dashed into pieces, ground into powder, killed off.

§ 60.30 (亠/一)

立 60.30

lih.

V. i. & t. (1) To stand, remain in an erect position: 直立 stand straight; 站立 remain standing; 起立 stand up, rise from seat; 肅立 stand up and remain silent; 立定 stand without moving; 立定主意 see 2↓; 立馬 (of rider) draw horse to a stop; 立正 *-jehng*↓; 立眉立眼 fly into a rage (lit., "with raised eyebrows and angry looks"); 立談之間 soon, in no time; 貧無立錐之地 so poor as to have "no place to stick an awl"; 立杆見影 to produce an immediate effect (lit., "a shadow is cast as soon as a pole is raised"); 立足, 立塲 *-tzur*, *-charng*↓. (2) Set up, establish, accomplish, achieve, have (s. t.) done: 建立 to set up; 成立 establish, inaugurate; 樹立 to found; 功成名立 achieve success and win recognition; 立法 *-faa*↓; 立國 to found a kingdom, or create a nation; 立家 marry and have a home; 己欲立而立人 being able to establish oneself, one should help others to do so; 立身 *-shen*↓; 立業 engage in some work or business; 立論 *-luhn*↓; 立德, 立功, 立言 do one of three things to be remembered by posterity, by one's character, by outward achievements or by ideas and sayings; 立志 *-jyh*↓; 立品 cultivate moral virtues; 立名 make a name; 立下規矩 draw up a set of rules; 標奇(新)立異 to attract attention by being eccentric, peculiar; 立定主意 be determined; 立意 make up one's mind to; 立誓 take an oath, pledge oneself to; 立嗣 appoint an heir; 立案 *-ahn*↓. (3) (LL) to ascend the throne. (4) To sign or conclude an agreement: 訂立合同 to sign a contract; 立約 make an agreement; 立單保證 give a written guaranty; 立契 sign a written contract; 立字據, 立字(兒) sign a note.

Adv. Immediately, at once: 立刻, 立即 right away; 立逼 compel (s. o.) to do (s. t.) at once; 立待, 立等, 立候 wait for (s.t.) right away; 立地 all at once; 立時 *-shyr*↓; 立下此城 take the city by storm immediately; 立效 (of med.) immediately effective.

立案 *lih-ahn*, v. i., be registered, to register.

立塲 *lihcharng*, n., standpoint, a position one takes on a given question.

立秋 *lihchiou*, n., (a solar term) beginning of autumn, about August 7–21, see Appendix B.

立春 *lihchun*, n., (a solar term) beginning of spring, about February 5–18, see Appendix B.

立冬 *lihdung*, n., (a solar term) beginning of winter, about November 7–21, see Appendix B.

立法 *lihfaa*, (1) v. t., to legislate; (2) n., legislation: 立法機關 the legislature, the legislative branch of government; 立法院 the Legislative *Yuan* of the Government of the Republic of China.

立方 *lihfang*, n., (math.) the cube: 立方體 (math.) a cube; 立方根 cube root.

立櫃 *lihgueih*, n., a closet, cupboard, cabinet.

立正 *lihjehng*, (1) n., (mil. command) "attention!" (2) v. i., stand at attention.

立志 *lihjyh*, v. i., make a determination (to accomplish certain objectives in life).

立決 *lihjyuer*, n., (anc. law) immediate execution of a prisoner.

立論 *lihluhn*, n. & v. t., (take a certain) basic standpoint on questions.

立身 *lihshen*, v. i., (1) behave oneself properly and correctly; (2) to place oneself in a certain situation or position: 立身處世 ways of conducting oneself in society.

立夏 *lihshiah*, n., (a solar term) beginning of summer, about May 5–18, see Appendix B.

立憲國 *lihshiahn-guor*, n., a country with a constitutional government.

立式 *lihshyh*, adj., upright: 立式鋼琴 n., upright piano.

立時 *lihshyr*, adv., immediately.

立體 *lihtii*, n., (math.) a solid.

立足 *lihtzur*, v. i., stand on one's own feet, (lit. & fig.) 立足點 n., standpoint.

亹 60.30

weei.

Adj. 亹亹 (AC) busy, untiring, progressing.

銮 60.30

luarn.

[Pop. of 鑾 93.30]

§ 60.40 (一/口)

言 60.40

yarn.

Pron. (AC) I, we (related MC 俺 *an*, and modn. Fukien 阮 *goan*): 言告言歸 I say I'll be going home; 駕言出遊 take me (us) for a drive.

N. (1) A radical (as in 説話, see 60A). (2) A surname. (3) Speech, talk, what one says or professes, opp. 行 what one does: 言行不符 one does not do what one preaches; 言論, 言談 *-luhn*, *-tarn* ↓; 言笑 pleasant chatter; 言語 *-yuu*↓; 言不由衷 does not say what one thinks in his mind; 言過其實 to exaggerate; 言聽計從 (of ruler) always take a person's advice; 言簡意賅 what one says is precise and to the point; 言近旨遠 some simple words carry a profound meaning; 言外之意 the meaning between the lines; 直言 a straight talk; 大言 a boast; 失言 to make a slip of the tongue; 食言 fail in one's promise, "eat one's word"; 發言 to speak during a conference. (4) Language, spoken language: 語言 spoken language (of a country); 外國語言 foreign language; 方言 dialect; 文言 literary language (LL). (5) A word, a sentence, a saying: 一言以蔽之 in one word, to sum up: 謊言 a lie; 流言 rumor; 格言 a popular saying, a proverb; 寓言 parable, fable; 片言 a word from s. o., a few words; 留言 leave word, message; 讒言 backbite; 忠言逆耳 straight advice is difficult to take; 巧言 clever talk.

V.i. Speak, say: 言之有理 it stands to reason, sensibly said.

言筌 *yarn-chuarn*, phr., 不落言筌 to grasp a passage without clinging to a too literal interpretation (also wr. 言詮).
言動 *yarnduhng*, n., what one says and does.
言官 *yarnguan*, n., formerly, imperial censor with duty of criticizing government policy.
言重了 *yarn juhng-le*, phr., (court.) am embarrassed by your words.
言路 *yarnluh*, n., avenue of expression, i. e., access (blocked or free) of public opinion to reach the rulers.
言論 *yarnluhn*, n., public opinion; 言論自由 freedom of speech.
言行 *yarnshihng*, n., one's words and deeds; 言行錄 --*luh*, n., life and sayings of a person, a form of biography.
言談 *yarntarn*, n., manner or ability in talking: 言談之間 during a converation.
言詞 *yarntsyr*, n., language used on some occasion (violent, etc.).
言責 *yarntzer*, n., (AC) duty of expressing criticism or opinion during tenure of office.
言語 *yarnyuu*, (1) n., spoken language, speech; (2) (-'*yu*) v.i., speak: (coll.) 怎麽不言語呢 why don't you say s. t.? 言語學 --*shyuer*, n., philology.

吝 60.40

lihn.

[Var. of 悋, 㤻]

V. i. & adj. Stint, -ing; 貪吝 miserly.

吝嗇 *lihnseh*, adj., miserly (person).
吝惜 *lihnshir* (-'*shi*), v. t., to stint: 吝惜財物 be sparing with money and goods, not willing to spend.

啻 60.40

chyh (also *tih*).

Adj. Like: chiefly in 不啻 same as, tantamount to: 不啻天壤之別 difference tantamount to that between heaven and earth; 何啻 what's the difference? as good as (killing with your own hand, etc.).

礱 60.40

lurng.

V. t. To grind, to hull grain: 礱糠 chaff; 礱利 to grind sharp.

§ 60.41 (亠/図)

盲 60.41

marng.

[Cogn. 茫 20A.21]

Adj. Blind: 盲人 blind person; 盲人騎瞎馬 the blind leading the blind; 盲眼 blind eyes; (fig.) 盲目不盲心 blind in the eyes, but not in the mind; 盲點 blind spot; 盲啞學校 school for the blind and dumb.

Adv. Blindly: 盲從 follow blindly.

盲腸 *marngcharng*, n., (physiol.) appendix; 盲腸炎 --*yaan*, n., appendicitis.
盲蜘蛛 *marng-jyju*, n., a kind of spider, *Phalangium*.
盲目 *marngmuh*, adj. & adv., blind, -ly; without clear understanding: 盲目崇拜 worship blindly.

音 60.41

yin.

N. (1) Sound, voice, pronunciation, tone, pitch: 聲音 person's voice; 樂音 musical sounds; 和音 harmony; 雜音 disturbing noise; 女高音 soprano; 女低音 alto or contralto, 男高音 tenor; 男低音 bass; 清音 voiceless consonant; 濁音 voiced consonant; 子音, 輔音 consonant; 母音, 元音 vowel; 正音 correct pronunciation; 土音, 鄉音 local accent; 發音 to pronounce, pronunciation; 拼音 spell, -ing; 知音 a true friend (from allu. an anc. musician and his only friend who appreciated his music). (2) News, tidings: 音信, 音訊, 音問 -*shihn*, -*shyuhn*, -*wehn* ↓; 德音, 玉音 or 音玉 (court.) news from you; 佳音 good news; 回音 reply to letter.

音標 *yinbiau*, n., phonetic symbol: 國際音標 International Phonetic Alphabet.
音波 *yinbo*, n., sound wave: 超音波 supersonic.
音叉 *yincha*, n., a tuning fork.
音塵 *yinchern*, n., news, tidings of one far away (news and traces).
音程 *yincherng*, n., (mus.) interval.
音調 *yindiauh*, n., (1) tone of reading or speech; (2) (mus.)

言 吝 嗇 礱 盲 音

pitch: 音調不諧 off key.

音符 *yinfur*, n., (1) phonetic notation; (2) (mus.) note.

音耗 *yinhauh*, n., news (from friends, etc.).

音簧 *yinhuarng*, n., a reed (as in flute).

音階 *yinjie*, n., mus. scale: 半音音階 chromatic scale; 五音階 pentatonic scale; 全音階 diatonic scale; 長音階 major scale; 短音階 minor scale.

音節 *yinjier*, n., (1) syllable: 單音節 monosyllable, -bic; 多音節 polysyllabic; (2) key or pitch in music.

音級 *yinjir*, n., (mus.) scale.

音質 *yinjy*, n., tonality.

音兒 *ye'l*, n., (1) sound; (2) tone of voice: 聽話要聽音兒 when you listen, listen to speaker's tone of voice.

音量 *yinliahng*, n., volume of sound.

音律 *yinlyuh*, n., the rise and fall of tone in a piece of writing.

音容 *yinrurng*, n., usu. in 音容猶在(已杳) voice and facial expression of the deceased are still vividly remembered, (are no longer there).

音色 *yinseh*, n., (mus.) timbre.

音響 *yinashiaang*, n., echo, resonance.

音信 *yinshihn*, n., news, letters.

音書 *yinshu*, n., ditto.

音學 *yinshyuer*, n., see *-yuhn*↓.

音訊 *yinshyuhn*, n., letters, news.

音吐 *yintuu*, n., (LL) a person's manner of talking.

音組 *yintzuu*, n., see *-jie*↑.

音問 *yinwehn*, n., news, tidings, correspondence.

音位 *yinweih*, n., a phoneme.

音義 *yinyih*[1], n., pronunciation and meaning of text.

音譯 *yinyih*[2], n., transliteration by sound rather than meaning (as 布爾喬亞 *buh-ee-chiaur-yaa* for "bourgeois").

音樂 *yinyueh*, n., music; 音樂會 a concert; 音樂家 a musician; 音樂廳 concert hall; 音樂院 music conservatory.

音韻 *yinyuhn*, n., (1) 音韻學 *--shyuer*, n., phonology; (2) sound and music of a piece of writing.

畜 60.41

chuh (**shyuh* as vb.).

N. A domesticated animal (pig, dog, etc.): 家畜 ditto; 六畜 (horse, cow, sheep, chicken, dog and pig); 畜生 *-sheng*↓.

V. t. (**shyuh*) (1) To pasture (sheep, etc.): 畜牧 *-muh*↓. (2) U. f. 蓄 20A.41, to store up.

畜類 *chuhleih*, n., the domesticated animals.

畜牧 **shyuhmuh*, (1) v. t., to pasture sheep, cattle and horse; (2) n., pasturing, animal husbandry.

畜生 *chuhsheng*, n., (severe abuse of person) dog, beast, vermin, contemptible cur.

畜養 **shyuhyaang*, v. t., to raise (dogs, rabbits, etc.).

§ 60.42 (ㄧ/ㄨ)

肓 60.42

huang.

[Dist. 盲 60.41]

N. The region between the heart and the diaphragm: occurs only in the phr. 病入膏肓 disease has spread to the vital organs—regarded as hopeless.

育 60.42

yuh.

N. Education, nurture: 教育 education; 德育, 智育, 體育, 靈育 moral, intellectual, physical and spiritual education; 育嬰院 nursery.

V.t. (1) To give birth: 生育 ditto. (2) To nurture, bring up (children): 養育, 憮育 raise to maturity; 育孤 bring up orphan; 作育人才 train up useful men; 育種 cultivate certain species; 育花, 育樹 cultivate flowers, trees; 育才 to cultivate educated men.

膂 60.42

lyuu.

[Pop. 膐]

N. Backbone.

膂力 *lyuulih*, n., muscular power.

膏 60.42

gau (**gauh*).

N. (1) Fat, grease: 膏粱 *-liarng*, 膏火 *-huoo*↓; 民脂民膏 "the people's fat and marrow"——pressed by excessive taxes, levies, etc. (lit., "the people's fat"). (2) The region below the heart: 膏肓 *-huang*↓. (3) Ointment, plaster: 枇杷膏 a cough mixture made with the loquat as the main ingredient; 糖膏 a syrup; 膏藥 *-yauh*↓; 藥膏 an ointment; 雪花膏 cold cream, facial cream.

V. t. (**gauh*) To moisten.

Adj. (1) (Of soil) fertile: 膏腴 *-yur*↓. (2) (Of rain) timely, good for the crops: 膏雨 timely rain.

膏肓 *gauhuang*, n., the region below the heart: 病入膏肓 be critically ill.

膏火 *gauhuoo*, n., formerly, tuition fee in private schools.

膏粱 *gauliarng*, n., rich fare; 膏粱子弟 children from well-fed families.

膏澤 *gautzer*, n., (AC) material benefits.

膏藥 *gauyauh*, n., a plaster.

膏腴 *gauyur*, adj., (of soil) fertile, productive: 膏腴之地 fertile land, district or region.

高 60.42

gau.

[Pop. 髙]

N. A surname.

Adj. (1) High, tall: 高低 *-di*↓; 高矮(兒) *-aai(-aa'l)*↓; 高度 *-duh*↓; 高大 *-dah*↓; 高箇子, 高箇兒 a tall fellow; 高敞 big and spacious (building); 高來高去 ability to scale walls and other heights, extraordinary physical ability; 高擡貴手, 高高手兒 formula for asking for forgiveness, or higher pay for goods or services rendered; 高架鐵路 elevated railway; 高揚臉兒 arrogant, turn away without heeding anyone; 高舉雙手 with both hands raised; 吉星高照 to experience a spell of good luck; 高山 high mountain; 高山流水 (allu.) understanding and appreciative friends; 高山仰止 to behold a high mountain (great man) with awe; 高屋建瓴 be strategically situated; 登高一呼 make a clarion call, make a public appeal; 高樓大廈 tall and big buildings; 高山景行 (LL) showing great admiration or respect for s. o.; 高不成, 低不就 (of people looking for life partners or jobs) too choosy to succeed; 眼高手低 one's ability does not match his wishes or high goal; 高枕無憂 retire or rest without worries; 高視闊步 strut about; 高瞻遠矚 transcendent views (complim.). (2) Respectable, noble: 高貴 *-gueih*↓; 崇高 exalted; 高尚 *-shahng*↓. (3) Expensive, dear, high-priced: 價錢太高 it's too costly; 高價收購 to buy up at high prices; 物價高漲 an inflation of prices. (4) Old, advanced in age: 年高德劭 (of elder people) venerable; see 高年, 高壽, 高齡 *-niarn, -shouh, -lirng*↓. (5) Supreme, sublime, exemplary: 高風亮節 exemplary conduct and nobility of character; 高誼 *-yih*, 高明 *-mirng*↓. (6) Higher, superior, better: 高級 *-jir*, 高等 *-deeng*, 高深 *-shen*↓; 技高一等 more skillful than others; 高手 *-shoou*↓; 才高八斗 endowed with extraordinary talents. (7) High-pitched, high-keyed: 高歌一曲 raise one's voice to sing a song; 高唱入雲 sing with a resounding voice; 高聲朗誦 read aloud; 大聲高呼 shout from the housetops.

高矮(兒) *gau-aai(-aa'l)*, n., height, tallness: 比一比高矮 let's see who is taller; 不高不矮 of medium height; 這般高矮 of this height, this high.

高昂 *gau-arng*, adj., rising, becoming higher: 物價高昂 rising commodity prices; 士氣高昂 the morale of troops is higher than ever.

高傲 *gau-auh*, adj., arrogant, haughty.

高把兒 *gaubah'l*, n., anything with a long handle: 高把兒苕帚 a long broomstick; 高把兒碟子 a long-handled cup.

高超 *gauchau*, adj., superb: 技藝高超, 手法高超, 文筆高超 superb skills, tricks, writing.

高潮 *gauchaur*, n., (1) a high tidal wave, a bore; (2) a climax: 劇情進入高潮 (of movies or stage play) the story is reaching its climax; 事態嚴重, 達於高潮 the situation has become serious and reached a critical point; 製造高潮 create mounting tension; (3) climax in sexual intercourse.

高強 *gauchiarng*, adj., of superior quality.

高蹺 *gau'chiau*, n., stilts (also 高橇, 高蹻): 踩高蹺 walk on stilts.

高峭 *gauchiauh*, adj., (of cliffs) steep and precipitous.

高情 *gau-chirng*, n., great kindness: 高情隆誼 (court.) your highly esteemed kindness and invaluable friendship.

高大 *gaudah*, adj., big and strong.

高蹈 *gau-dauh*, v. i., (1) (AC) go on a long journey; (2) live a retired life.

高等 *gaudeeng*, adj., (1) of a higher class: 高等中學 senior middle school; 高等動物 the more highly developed animals; (2) of a higher grade: 高等法院 high court (of justice); 高等考試 higher government examination (opp. 普通考試 general government examination).

高低 *gau-di*, adj., (1) high and low, better or worse: 不分高低 be equally matched; (2) high- or low-pitched; (3) adv., anyway, at any rate: 高低他也得來見我 he must come to see me anyway; 高低他打敗了 at any rate he has been beaten.

高第 *gaudih*, adj., (1) of a higher grade or class; (2) ranking high in government examinations.

高調(兒) *gaudiauh('l)*[1], n. & adj., high-sounding (phrases): 唱高調 make high-flown but impractical utterances.

高掉兒 *gau-diauh'l*[2], n., a heavy fall from on high.

高度 *gauduh*, (1) n., height; (2) n. & adj. & adv., (to or of) a high degree: 高度警惕 a high degree of alertness; 高度戒備 fully prepared for any eventualities: 高速度 high speed.

高爾夫(球) *gau-eelfu(chiour)*, n., (translit.) golf; 高爾夫球場 golf course.

高發 *gaufa*, v. i., formerly, pass a government examination.

高峯 *gaufeng*, n., (1) a mountain peak; (2) the apogee, the highest point (of fame, etc.); 高峯會議 summit conference, talk.

高跟(兒)鞋 *gaugen(-ge'l)-shier*, n., high-healed shoes.

高貴 *gaugueih*, adj., noble, refined, of superior quality, elegant.

高著兒 *gaujau'l*, n., an ingenious plan, a clever swordplay (also 高招兒).

高技兒 *gauje'l*, n., anyone in a higher position: 扒高技兒 to

curry favor with social superiors, to marry into higher family.

高價 *gau-jiah*, n., a high price: 高價收購 offer to buy at a handsome price.

高見 *gaujiahn*, n., (court. & lit.) farsighted or profound views: 有何高見 what are your views? 願聞高見 I'd like to hear your views.

高階層 *gau-jietserng*, n., high-rank, top rank: 高階層會議 a summit conference; 高階層人物 top personalities.

高就 *gau-jiouh*, n., a better job: 另有高就 have landed a better job.

高級 *gaujir*, adj., (1) high-grade: 高級品, 高級貨 high-quality articles, goods; (2) belonging to a higher class: 高級生 higher-class students; (3) of a higher grade: 高級中學 senior high school; 高級顧問 senior adviser; (4) superior, superb, excellent: 這辦法眞高級 the method is most ingenious; 高級手法 superior maneuver.

高樁兒 *gaujuang'l*, n., (coll.) anything of more than normal height: 高樁兒饅頭 a steamed bread of unusual thickness; 高樁兒柿子 such a persimmon.

高中 *gaujung*, (1) n., senior high school; (2) (pr. *-juhng*) v.i., pass an examination.

高峻 *gaujyuhn*, adj., (of mountain) high and steep.

高亢 *gaukahng*, adj., resounding, reverberating, ringing.

高空 *gaukung*, n., the upper space.

高麗 *Gau'li*, n., anc. name for Korea.

高粱 *gauliarng* (-*'liang*), n., (bot.) the sorghum, -*'liang*: 高粱酒 liquor made from sorghum.

高良薑 *gau-liarngjiang*, n., (bot.) the lesser galangal, a ginger, *Alpinia chinensis*.

高利貸(款) *gaulih daih* (*kuaan*), n., high-interest loans, usury.

高齡 *gau-lirng*, n., (court.) advanced age.

高論 *gau-luhn*, n., (court.) highly esteemed views.

高買 *gaumaai*, v.i., to shoplift while pretending to buy.

高帽(兒)(子) *gaumauh('l)(tz)*, n., flattery: 戴高帽子 make flattering remarks.

高門 *gau-mern*, n., a politically or socially influential family.

高棉 *Gaumiarn*, n., Cambodia, also called 柬埔寨.

高妙 *gaumiauh*, adj., ingenious, clever.

高明 *gaumirng*, adj., brilliant, discerning (views, etc.).

高末兒 *gaumoh'l*, n., better-quality tea from sprouts.

高年 *gau-niarn*, n. & adj., (persons of) advanced age.

高攀 *gauparn*, v. t., befriend or marry (s. o.) of higher social position: 高攀不上 cannot be friends or marry (s. o.) of a richer or more influential family.

高人 *gaurern*, n., (1) (also 高士) a scholar who spurns official preferment; (2) a lofty character.

高僧 *gauseng*, n., a Buddhist monk of great repute.

高尚 *gaushahng*, adj., respectable, refined, of good taste (reading, amusement, etc.).

高射炮 *gausheh-pauh*, n., an antiaircraft gun, an ack-ack.

高深 *gaushen*, adj., profound, advanced.

高升 *gausheng*, v. i., to advance in grade.

高小 *gaushiaau*, n., senior primary school.

高下 *gau-shiah*, adj., (1) high and low; (2) good and bad.

高行 *gaushihng*[1], n., upright conduct.

高興 *gaushihng*[2], v. i. & t. & adj., (be) interested, pleased, glad, happy: 他不高興別人打擾他 he doesn't like to be disturbed; 我高興打網球 I am interested in playing tennis; 他今天有點不高興 he seems to be unhappy today; 他們倆很高興 they two are in high spirits.

高手(兒) *gaushoou('l)*, n., an expert.

高壽 *gau-shouh*, n. & adj., (1) a long life, longevity, long-lived; (2) (court.) age of the person spoken to: 先生高壽幾何 how old are you, sir?

高軒 *gaushyuan*, n., (1) (LL) a big and spacious porch or pavilion; (2) (LL) (court.) your carriage or car.

高血壓 *gaushyuehya*, n., hypertension; high blood pressure.

高聳 *gausuung*, adj., lofty, high.

高堂 *gautarng*, n., (1) a hall with high ceiling: (2) (court.) one's parents.

高才生 *gautsair-sheng*, n., a gifted student (also wr. 高材生).

高徒 *gautur*, n., a favorite student.

高足 *gautzur*, n., (court.) your student, see *-tur* ↑.

高祖 *gautzuu*, n., (1) great-great-grandfather; (2) a remote ancestor; (3) founder of an imperial or royal dynasty.

高位 *gauweih*, n., a high-ranking position.

高臥 *gauwoh*, v. i., live a quiet and leisurely life.

高壓 *gauya*, adj., high-pressured (method): 高壓線 high-tension wire.

高眼 *gau-yaan*, adj., farsighted, keen-sighted.

高誼 *gauyih*, n., esteemed friendship.

高音 *gauyin*, n., (mus.) a high pitch or voice; 男高音 a tenor; 女高音 a soprano; 高音部記號 (mus.) G clef.

高原 *gauyuarn*, n., a plateau, highland.

商 60.42

shang.

N. (1) Commerce, trade, esp. as profession: 商人 *-rern* ↓; 商業, 商行, 商務 *-yeh*, *-harng*, *-wuh* ↓; 士農工商 the four classes of people, scholars, farmers, artisans and traders; 進口商, 出口商 importers, exporters; 批發商 wholesalers; 行商, 從商 go into business; 經商 carry on business. (2) The musical note *re*; see 五[a]音 31.30. (3) Shang Dyn. (1783–1123 B.C.). (4) A surname.

V. i. To discuss: 協商, 磋商 discuss together (terms, procedures); 相商 consult each other; oft. as prefix of vb., meaning "discuss and"; 商定 discuss and decide, *-dihng*↓; 商量, 商酌, 商榷, 商討 *-liarng*, *-juor*, *-chyueh*, *-taau*↓.

商標 *shangbiau*, n., trademark.
商埠 *shang-buh*, n., treaty port.
商場 *shang-chaang*, n., (1) a bazaar, an emporium; (2) the market, market conditions.
商情 *shang-chirng*, n., market conditions (good, bad).
商船 *shang-chuarn*, n., merchant ship, freighter, freight boat.
商榷 *shangchyueh*, v. i. & t., to discuss together (problems, affairs).
商店 *shang-diahn*, n., a shop.
商定 *shang-dihng*, v. t., decide after discussion.
商兌 *shangdueih*[1], v. i. & n., (litr.) discussion of problems.
商隊 *shang-dueih*[2], n., traders travelling as a unit.
商販 *shang-fahn*, n., trader, retail salesman.
商港 *shang-gaang*, n., seaport, trading port.
商股 *shang-guu*[1], n., shares subscribed to by private capital, opp. 官股 government-owned shares.
商賈 *shangguu*[2], n., shopkeepers, tradesmen, merchants.
商行 *shangharng*, n., commercial firm.
商號 *shanghauh*, n., a shop.
商會 *shanghueih*, n., chamber of commerce: 總商會 general chamber of commerce.
商戰 *shang-jahn*, n., trade war.
商家 *shang-jia*, n., businessman.
商界 *shang-jieh*, n., the commercial circles.
商酌 *shangjuor*, v. i. & t., to discuss (situation, etc.).
商量 *shangliarng*, v. i. & t., to discuss (prices, terms, problems, etc.): 和人, 跟人商量 discuss with people.
商陸 *shangluh*, n., (bot.) the poke root, *Phytolacca acinosa*.
商略 *shanglyueh*, v. i., see *-juor*↑.
商旅 *shang-lyuu*, n., tradesmen and travellers.
商民 *shang-mirn*, n., tradesmen as a class, shopkeepers.
商品 *shang-piin*, n., commercial products; things for sale.
商人 *shang-rern*, n., tradesman, businessman.
商數 *shangshuh*, n., (math.) quotient, number obtained by division.
商事 *shang-shyh*, n., commercial affairs.
商討 *shangtaau*, v. i. & t., discuss (problems, etc.).
商團 *shang-tuarn*, n., group or society of businessmen.
商務 *shangwuh*, n., trade and commerce.
商業 *shangyeh*, n., ditto.
商議 *shangyih*, v. i. & t., to discuss (problems, terms, etc.).
商約 *shangyue*, (1) v. i., decide together (to do s. t.); (2) n., (short for 通商條約) treaty of commerce between two countries.

裔 60.42

yih.

N. (1) Progeny; 四裔 (AC) descendants of the four tribes. (2) (AC) hem of garment.

斋 60.42

jai.

[Var. of 齋 60.22]

离 60.42

lir.

[Abbr. of 離 60S.11]

[illegible] 60.42

luarn.

[Pop. of 亂 93B.42]

§ 60.50 (亠/乛)

方 60.50

fang.

N. (1) A surname. (2) Direction: 東方 the East, Orient; 西方 the West, Occident; 東方學術, 西方文化 Oriental scholarship, Western culture; 左方, 右方, 四方 left, right side, all sides; 南方人, 北方話 southerner, northern dialect; 萬方 all the world; 天各一方 friends separated far away. (3) Locality, rarely country: 地方 local, -lity: 土方 local (dialect, product); 方土 territory; 方內 within the country, 方外 *-waih*↓. (4) Party, side: 單方的話 one-sided statement; 雙方和解 two sides are reconciled; 對方 the other party; 男方, 女方 groom's, bride's side; 校方, 店方 on the side or region of the school, shop; 美方, 日方 on the American, Japanese side; usu. 方面, see *-miahn*↓. (5) Method, oft. medical recipe: usu. 方法 *-faa*↓; 千方百計 by all kinds of methods; 管教無方 bring up children badly; 方略 *-lyueh*↓; 方術, 方技 *-shuh*, *-jih*↓; 方針 *-jen*↓; 藥方, 丹方, 醫方 medical recipes, prescriptions; 良方, 秘方 well-tried, secret, recipes. (6) (Math.) square: 平方 plane; (a) a square; (b) the product of a number multiplied by itself; 立方 cube, see 方根 *-gen*↓; 方程式 *-cherng-shyh*↓; 方尺, 寸, 哩 square foot, inch, mile; 方三寸 three inches square; 三方寸 three square inches.

V. t. (1) (AC) to disobey: 方命 disobey order. (2) Criticize and compare: 好方人 (AC) love to

A B C

方 旁

criticize and compare people; 不可方物 (AC) cannot discriminate or compare.

Adj. (1) Square: oft. 方的, 方形 *-'de, -shirng*↓; 正方 regular square; 長方 rectangular; 方格 *-ger*↓; 方頂, 方額, 方頰 square top, brow, jaw; 方面大耳 square face and big ears; 方磚, 方桌 square brick, table; 方枘圓鑿 put round peg in square hole; 方底圓蓋 square case and round cover—would not fit; 圓顱方趾 "round skull, square toes"—all humankind made of the same clay. (2) Upright, principled (of conduct, character): 外圓內方 smooth on the surface, firm at heart.

Adv. Just now, just then, just beginning to: usu. 方才 *-tsair*↓=剛才 *gangtsair* or 才 *tsair*; 天方曙 day was just breaking; 方知是你 only then did I realize it was you; 方開學 school was just opening; 方悔失言 then regretted having said s.t. wrong; 方興未艾 just starting to grow; see 方且, 方始, 方今 *-chiee, -shyy, -jin*↓; 方行 (AC) spread about (=橫行).

方案 *fang-ahn*, n., plan.

方便 *fang'biahn*, (1) adj., convenient: 不方便 inconvenient; (2) n., special consideration: 行方便, 與人方便, 大開方便之門 give special consideration, open special avenue for doing things, to facilitate; (3) euphem. for 大小便 toilet.

方伯 *fangbor*, n., (1) chief of district; (2) provincial high commissioner.

方步 *fangbuh*, (1) n., square area of one step in each direction; (2) 邁方步 make special walking gait swinging from sides, as seen on stage.

方程式 *fangcherng-shyh*, n., (math.) equation; 二次, 三次, 四次方程式 binomial, trinomial, quadrinomial equation; 方程根 *--gen*, root of equation.

方且 *fangchiee*, adv., and then, only then: 方且曉喻 and then began to understand.

方丘 *fangchiou*, n., square altar for worship of Earth (圜丘 round altar for Heaven).

方尺 *fangchyy*, n., square foot.

方的 *fang'de*, adj., square in shape.

方法 *fangfaa*, n., method, way, means: 用什麼方法 by what means? 方法論 methodology.

方沸石 *fangfeih-shyr*, n., (min.) analcite.

方根 *fanggen*, n., square root.

方格 *fangger*, n., checkered design; correct pattern: 方格紙 paper with squares for practice on calligraphy.

方皇 *fanghuarng*, v. i., (AC var. for 旁皇) hesitate.

方丈 *fangjahng*, n., (1) ten feet square; (2) *-'jang*, abbot of monastery.

方鎮 *fangjehn*, n., military governor.

方正 *fangjehng*, adj., upright (in character).

方針 *fangjen*, n., goal; principle.

方解石 *fangjiee-shyr*, n., (min.) calcite.

方技 *fangjih*, n., the professions, esp. necromancy, astrology, medicine, etc.

方濟會 *Fangjihhueih*, n., Franciscan Order.

方今 *fangjin*[1], adv., now, surveying the present time: 方今之時.

方巾 *fangjin*[2], n., a scholar's flat-top cap of Mirng period.

方竹 *fangjur*, n., special species of bamboo, squarish in shape.

方塊 *fangkuaih*, n., square block; 方塊字 Chin. characters; such cards for practice; 方塊新聞 news in box; 方塊舞 square dance; 方塊阿哥哥 square à gogo.

方兒 *fang'l*, n., medical prescription (藥方).

方里 *fanglii*, n., square *li*.

方領 *fangliing*, n., formerly, square collar worn by students.

方略 *fanglyueh*, n., plan, strategy.

方帽 *fangmauh*, n., square cap worn by graduates.

方面 *fangmiahn*, n., aspect; section or area; direction: 從另一方面看來 to look at it from another aspect.

方脈 *fangmoh*, n., the art of feeling pulse.

方勝 *fangshehng*, (Peking coll. *-'sheng*), n., a woman's headdress, with sides sliding up.

方向 *fang'shiang*, n., direction: 迷失方向 lost bearings; 看方向做事 see which way the wind blows.

方形 *fangshirng*, adj., square-shaped.

方術 *fangshuh*, n., see *-jih*↑.

方式 *fangshyh*[1], n., formula, way of presentation, method.

方士 *fangshyh*[2], n., necromancers.

方始 *fangshyy*, adv., only then (begin to).

方糖 *fang tarng*, n., cube sugar.

方才 (纔) *fangtsair*, adv., just (=剛才): 他方才到 he has just arrived; 方才明白 only then begin to understand.

方冊 (策) *fangtseh*, n., anc. records (pack of bamboo or wooden strips): 布在方策 is in the anc. records.

方寸 *fangtsuhn*, n., (1) square inch; (2) small quantity: 方寸之地 a small piece of land; (3) the heart: 方寸已亂 or 無主 heart is troubled or confused, cannot decide or think.

方字 *fangtzyh*, n., square cards for learning characters.

方外 *fangwaih*, n., territory beyond China; 方外人 Buddhist, Taoist monks.

方言 *fangyarn*, n., dialect; name of anc. treatise on dialect words.

方音 *fangyin*, n., dialect pronunciation: 北京方音 Peking dialect.

方圓 *fang-yuarn*, n., square and circles (woodcraft).

方隅 *fangyur*[1], n., corner, portion of territory.

方輿 *fangyur*[2], n., geography, map.

旁 60.50

parng.

Adj. (1) Side, at the side, close by: 旁舍 detached house on the side; 旁門 side door, informal and self-sought training (opp. 正途 formal training); 旁門左道 heretical branch, heresy; 旁路 sidewalk;

旁注, 旁批 running comments in book. (2) Collateral: 旁證 collateral evidence, side witness; 旁系 side branch of family, not direct line, 旁系親 cousins, nephews.

Adv. Elsewhere, all around: 旁求 look for all around or elsewhere; 旁插花 (coll.) make irrelevant remarks; 旁敲側擊 make innuendoes; 旁徵博引 well-provided with supporting material; 旁行 going sideways, crab-like; 旁行文字 alphabetic writing running horizontally like English.

N. Side: 路旁 roadside; 左旁, 右旁 the left, right side; 旁若無人 supercilious, completely informal; 旁邊 *-bian*↓.

旁白 *parngbair*, n., aside (drama).
旁邊 *parngbian*, n., side, close-by position.
旁礴 *parngbor*, adj., expansive, expanding, free (of air, manner), bold (art style) (also wr. 薄).
旁岔兒 *parngchah'l*, n., digression from subject under discussion.
旁妻 *parngchi*, n., "side wife," i.e., concubine.
旁觀 *parngguan*, v. i., observe at the side: 旁觀者清 an outsider sees more objectively; 旁觀者 an observer at conference.
旁皇 *parnghuarng*, adj., see 徬^Δ徨 91B.50.
旁孽 *parngnieh*, n., (LL) children born of concubines.
旁魄 *parngpoh*, adj., see *-bor*↑.
旁人 *parngrern*, n., others: 不顧旁人利益 disregard others; 不管旁人 do not care for others.
旁生 *parngsheng*, n., (bot.) plant which sprouts from side of trunks; (Budd.) animal kind.
旁聽 *parngting*, v. t., to be present at lecture; 旁聽生 student at university course, not enrolled; be observer at conference; cf. *-guan*↑.
旁坐 *parngtzuoh*, n., (anc. law) crime which makes criminal's family punishable, such as plot against emperor; cf. 連^Δ坐 10.83.

弯 60.50

wan.
[Pop. of 彎 93.50]

鵉 60.50

luarn.
[Pop. of 鸞 93.50]

鷲 60.50

jiouh.

N. A condor or vulture.

[illegible] 60.50

lyuu.
[Pop. of 膂 60.42]

§ 60.63 (亠/丶)

烹 60.63

peng.

V. t. (1) To quick-fry in hot oil: 烹蝦 shrimp so treated and served with sauce; 治大國若烹小鮮 rule a big country like frying small fish (*fritures*), i.e., avoid constant turing over—leave people alone (Laotse). (2) To pour boiling water over: 烹茶 make tea thus. (3) (Coll.) to frighten by a hoax: 把他烹走了 frightened him away; 烹勁兒 situation favorable for frightening people.

烹醢 *penghaai*, v. t., (AC) boil and make into mincemeat sauce, anc. form of punishment.
烹飪 *pengrehn*, n., art of cooking.
烹調 *pengtiaur*, n., ditto.

熟 60.63

shur (**shour*, ***shur* or *shour*, the latter in coll.).

Adj. (1) Cooked, opp. 生 raw: 煮熟 cooked, well done; 半生不熟 half-cooked, (fig.) "half-baked"; 熟食 *-shyr*↓. (2) Ripe (fruit, grain). (3) Of good crops: 熟年, 歲熟 a year of good crops. (4) Well learned, familiar in sight, recitation, etc.; expert, well-trained: 熟練 *-liahn*↓; 熟能生巧 practice makes perfect; 駕輕就熟 easy going ("light load on familiar route"); 面熟 a familiar face; 眼熟 familiar, often seen; 耳熟能詳 often heard and well remembered; 手熟 skillful, dexterous; 熟讀 well learned; 熟道, 熟路 familiar road; 熟字 familiar word; 熟人 *-rern*↓.

Adj. & adv. Deep, -ly, sound, -ly, mature, -ly: 熟睡, 熟眠, 熟寐 sound sleep; 熟視 look carefully, also 熟視無睹 one does not see what has become familiar sight; 熟思, 熟慮 ponder carefully, duly.

熟諳 *shur-an*, adj., well-learned, expert (also 諳熟).
熟地 ***shurdih*, n., (Chin. med.) short for 熟地黃 steamed root of *Rehmannia lutea*.
熟慣 ***shurguahn*, adj., familiar, well used to.
熟貨 ***shurhuoh*, n., prepared or

preserved goods, finished product, opp. 生貨 raw products.
熟勁 *shurjihn*, adj., expert, skillful.
熟客 ***shour-keh*, n., familiar guest.
熟臉兒 ***shourliaa'l*, n., a familiar person ("face").
熟練 *shurliahn*, adj., expert, adept.
熟料 ***shur-liauh*, n., partly finished or shaped timber material.
熟路 ***shur-luh*, n., familiar route.
熟皮 ***shurpir*, n., leather, dist. 生皮 hide.
熟人(兒) ***shour-rern(-rer'l)*, n., familiar person (acquaintance, friend).
熟肉 **shour-rouh*, n., cooked meat.
熟悉 *shurshi*, v. i., know well, be familiar with (situation, etc.).
熟習 ***shur(')shir*, adj., well-trained.
熟手(兒) ***shour-shoou('l)*, n., an old hand at s.t.
熟水 ***shourshueei*, n., boiled water, opp. 生水 unboiled.
熟識 ***shurshyh*, adj. & n., familiar; a familiar person or friend.
熟食 *shur-shyr*, n., cooked food.
熟炭 *shur-tahn*, n., charcoal.
熟鐵 *shur-tiee*, n., wrought iron.

§ 60.70 (ㄧ/ㄥ)

亳 60.70

boh.
[Dist. 毫 *haur* 60.70]

N. Name of AC district.

毫 60.70

haur.
[Dist. 亳]

N. (1) Fine, long hair: 毫毛, 毫髮 *-maur*, *-faa*↓; hair used for writing or painting brush, such as 羊毫, 狼毫, 雞毫 of goat, wolf, chicken, chosen for flexibility and stiffness, hence such brush; 濡毫 wet the brush with tip of tongue; 毫素 (LL) brush and paper. (2) (Weight) a centigram; (length) one-hundredth of a centimeter. (3) (Coll.) a dime. (4) One of the three strings on top of steelyard: 頭毫, 二毫, 三毫 serving as the fulcrum between the weight and the thing to be weighed. (5) A surname.

Adv. 毫無, 毫不 not the least bit: 毫無損失 not the least loss; 毫不留情 absolutely without consideration for others, see 毫髮 *-faa*↓; 毫無疑問 there is no doubt, hardly any doubt.

毫髮 *haurfaa*, adv., the least bit ("hair breadth"): 毫髮無差 exactly the same, without the least difference.
毫氂 *haurlii*, n., a modicum, tiniest bit: 毫氂不爽 not the least loss.
毫芒 *haurmarng*, n., tip of hair; spike; extremely fine point.
毫毛 *haurmaur*, n., hair of birds or animals.
毫末 *haurmoh*, n., tip of hair, extremely small amount.

甕 60.70

wehng.
[Var. of 罋 60.21]

N. (1) A big jar: 酒甕 wine jar; 甕中捉鼈 catch a turtle in the jar—inescapable situation; 甕聲甕氣 low sound or voice as in an enclosure. (2) A surname.

甕鼻 *wehngbir*, n., a blocked-up nose.
甕城 *wehngcherng*, n., enclosure (for defense) outside a city gate.
甕圈兒 *wehngchyuah'l*, n., ditto.
甕洞兒 *wehngduhng'l*, n., gate tunnel.
甕闊 *wehngkuoh*, adj., liberal with money.
甕門 *wehngmern*, n., gate of outer enclosure of city gate, see *-cherng*↑.
甕頭 *wehngtour*, n., first draw of new wine, also called 甕頭清, 甕頭春.
甕牖 *wehng-yoou*, n., usu. in 甕牖繩樞 mouth of a jar used for window and door fastened by a rope—descriptive of extreme poverty.

亢 60.70

kahng (**gang*).

N. (1) (**gang*) (AC) a person's neck. (2) Name of a constellation: 亢宿. (3) A surname.

Adj. Towering, high, upright, proud: 不卑不亢 (a man's behavior) with self-respect, neither fawning nor arrogant; 亢禮, 分庭亢禮 meet as equals.

Adv. Extreme: 亢旱 severe drought.

亢直 *kahngjyr*, n., very straightforward, not servile.
亢陽 *kahngyarng*, n., (1) (Chin. med.) exuberance of *yang* energy as a cause of illness; (2) drought.

充 60.70

chung.

V.i. & t. (1) To fill (box, post, etc.): 充滿, 充溢 *-maan*, *-yih*↓; 充塞 *-seh*, 充實 *-shyr*↓; 充任 *-rehn*↓; 充缺 fill a vacancy; 充其量 phr., at the worst, at most: 充其量給他罰款算了 at the worst, pay a penalty for it. (2) To pass for, pose as: 冒充 to assume name and pose as (another person); 充行家, 假充內行 pose as expert; (假) 充正經

pretend to be gentleman or serious person; 充能幹 pretend to ability.

Adj. Full, solid: 充滿, 充實, 充裕 *-maan*, *-shyr*, *-yuh*↓; 充足 *-tzur*↓.

充暢 *chungchahng*, adj., richly expressive.

充斥 *chungchyh*, v. i. & t., (bad things, thieves) abound.

充詘 *chungchyu*, v. i., (AC) as in 不充詘富貴 not elated with riches or success.

充當 *chungdang*, v. t., (1) to fill (a post, need), sometimes temporarily: 充當主席 act as chairman; (2) to pose as (relative, etc.).

充耳 *chung-eel*, (1) v. i., usu. in 充耳不聞 ignore what is said ("stuff one's ears"); (2) n., hat tassels (AC) that reach down to the ears.

充分 *chungfehn*, adj. & adv., completely, to full capacity: 充分練習 complete training.

充公 *chunggung*, v. t., to confiscate (property).

充饑 *chung-ji*, v. i., eat s. t. to stop hunger.

充軍 *chungjyun*, v. i. & t., to exile, be exiled.

充量 *chungliahng*, adj. & adv., to full capacity, see *-fehn*↑; 充其量 adv., at most, the most that may be expected.

充滿 *chungmaan*, v. t. & adj., to fill up, be filled up with, full: 庫藏充滿 the treasury or vault is full; 會場人滿 or 充滿 the hall is filled up.

充任 *chung-rehn*, v. t., to take, accept, a post, be appointed.

充塞 *chungseh*, v. i. & t., to fill up (the universe), be stocked up with: 盜賊充塞 thieves abound.

充羨 *chungshiahn*, adj., (LL) as in 不充羨於富貴 not self-satisfied with riches and honor.

充數 *chungshuh*, v. i., (court.) merely take a part, nominally "make up the number."

充實 *chungshyr*, (1) adj., solid, substantial, having real substance; (2) v. t., to give real substance to (speech), to strengthen from inside (financial, physical power): 充實府庫 strengthen national coffers.

充血 *chung-shyueh*, v. t., increase blood pressure; 腦充血 cerebral hemorrhage; 充血性 adj., congestive.

充足 *chungtzur*, adj., full, adequate (supplies, etc.).

充溢 *chungyih*, v. i., to fill to overflow.

充盈 *chungyirng*, adj., full, well provided with (harvest, etc.).

充裕 *chungyuh*, adj., ample (means).

兖 60.70

yaan.

N. 兖州 former name of a district in Shantung.

亮 60.70

liahng.

V. t. Give a quick show just for a glance: 亮一亮刀 to flash the blade once.

Adj. (1) Bright: 光亮, 明亮, 亮光 bright, shining; 天亮了 it is daybreak; 亮堂堂的, 亮晶晶 very shiny; 油亮亮的 oily, shining; 高風亮節 (laudatory) your esteemed and shining example or conduct; 說亮話 speak plainly; 清亮, 宏亮, 響亮 (of voice) clear, carries easily; 亮掝子 the fifth watch of daybreak. (2) Transparent, not opaque: 亮藍, 亮隔 *-larn*, *-ger*↓.

Adv. Brightly, with understanding: 亮察, 亮照 (in correspondence) your understanding, consideration; cf. 諒 60A.01, to understand and forgive.

亮度 *liahngduh*, n., (phys.) brightness, density of light.

亮隔 *liahngger*, n., semi-transparent partition (also wr. 槅).

亮張 *liahngjang*, v. i., (comm.) open for business before formal inauguration.

亮藍 *liahnglarn*, adj., bright, transparent blue.

亮盤兒 *liahngpar'l*, n., bare coffin without covering in simplest funeral.

亮像兒 *liahngshiahng'l*, v. i., (of actor, actress) appear on stage, make an actor's stance in particular pose for admiration (also wr. 亮相); to show off.

竟 60.70

jihng.

N. (1) (U.f. 境) territory. (2) The end: 歲竟 year's end.

V.t. (1) To finish: 竟書 finish writing; 以竟全功 to bring work to completion; (p.p.) finished, completed; 事竟 work completed. (2) (AC) to investigate (=究): 不竟 did not investigate.

Adv. (1) Ultimately, finally: 畢竟 after all, at last; 竟成 finally succeeded; 究竟 after all. (2) To one's surprise, with sense of "how one dares": 竟然 *-rarn*, 竟敢 *-gaan*, 竟自 *-tzyh*↓; 他竟說出這種話來 how could he say such a thing? (I didn't expect he would say it).

竟敢 *jihnggaan*, v. t., have the audacity to.

竟然 *jihngrarn*, phr. & adv., (it) actually (happened that . . .).

竟自 *jihngtzyh*, adv., without further ado, forthwith, without hesitation.

A B C

⿱亠鬼 ⿱亠見 嬴 羸 贏 忘 意

⿱亠鬼 60.70

hurn.
[Var. of 魂 30S.70]

⿱亠見 60.70

jiaur (*jyuer*).
[Pop. of 覺 90.70]

嬴 60.70

yirng.

N. (1) A surname. (2) (AC, u. f. 贏) surplus, profits: 嬴絀 profit and loss.

Adj. Weak, feeble.

羸 60.70

leir.
[Dist. 嬴, 贏]

V. t. (AC) entangle, bind: 羝羊觸藩，羸其角 a ram has its horns entangled in a hedge while butting it.

Adj. Emaciated, haggard: 羸憊 physically exhausted; 羸劣 thin and weak; 羸瘠 haggard and thin; 羸瘵 weak and consumptive; 羸瘦 emaciated; 羸弱 haggard and weak; 身病體羸 a physical wreck.

贏 60.70

yirng.

N. Profit, gain: 贏餘 *-yur* ↓.

V. i. & t. To gain, win: 贏得 gain (millions, hollow reputation, hatred, etc.); 贏錢 to gain money; 打贏了 to win in contest.

贏利 *yirng-lih*, v. i., to make profit.
贏縮 *yirng-suh*, (1) v. i., (LL) to stretch and shrink; (2) n., gain and loss.
贏餘 *yirngyur*, n., surplus, profit.

§ 60.72 (亠/心)

忘 60.72

wahng (re. pr. **warng*; marked **when both common and permissible).

V. i. & t. To forget: 難忘 difficult to forget; 永遠不忘 will never forget, 善忘, 健忘 absent-minded, habitually forgetful; 忘不了 (sp. pr.) cannot forget; 遺忘 v. t., to forget s. t., to lose, leave behind; 忘食, 忘餐 forget one's meals.

忘八 **warng'ba*, n., (severe, vulgar, abuse) son of a bitch (also wr. 王八).
忘本 ***wahngbeen*, v. i., be ungrateful ("forget where one comes from").
忘情 ***wahngchirng*, v. i., forget love and friendship: 不能忘情 always remember old sentiments.
忘筌 ***wang-chyuarn*, phr., see 筌 92A.11.
忘卻 *wahng-chyueh*, v. i. & t., to forget.
忘掉 *wahng-diauh*, v. t., ditto.
忘恩 *wahng-en*, phr., 忘恩負義 be ungrateful, turn on one's friend.
忘懷 ***wahng-huair*, v. i., see *-chirng* ↑.
忘機 ***wahng-ji*, phr., (litr.) lose oneself in nature, forget the "self" and merge with nature.
忘記 *wahngjih* (*-'ji*), v. i. & t., to forget.
忘舊 *wahng-jiouh*, phr., forget old friends and relatives.
忘年(交) ***wahngniarn*(*jiau*), n., (lit. phr.) friends despite difference of age.
忘性 *wahngshihng*, n., forgetfulness.
忘形 ***wahng-shirng*, phr., 得意忘形 lose all bearings in moment of pride and satisfaction; 忘形交, see 忘年(交) *-niarn*(*jiau*) ↑.
忘憂 ***wahng-you*, phr., drown all sorrows: 忘憂草 see 萱 20A.30.

意 60.72

yih.

N. (1) (Confucian) will, purpose: 意誠而後心正 make the will sincere in order to set the heart right. (2) Purpose, desire, intention, mind, idea: 意向, 意志 *-shiahng*[1], *-jyh* ↓; 意見 *-'jiahn* ↓; 意氣, 意趣 *-'chih*, *-chyuh* ↓; 意思, 意念 *-'sy*, *-niahn* ↓; 心意 wish, desire, intention; 善意, 好意 good intentions; 惡意, 壞意 malice; 主意 a mind set, mental decision; 鄙意 my humble opinion; 如意 as the heart desires; 萬事如意 may all your heart's wishes be fulfilled; 任意 as one pleases, without inhibition or restraint; 當意 pleases (one), suits one's fancy; 故意, 作意 on purpose; 失意 disappointed, -ment; 有意 have a mind to, entertain desire or wish; 立意 determine to; 意外 *-waih* ↓; 會意 81.41. (3) Regard, attention: 不以爲意 to disregard; 留意, 注意 notice, pay attention; 加意, 特意 pay special attention; 大意 adj., too sure of oneself, not careful enough; 著意 have mind set (on s. t. or to do). (4) Short for 意大利 Italy (commonly wr. 義): 意文 Italian language.

V. i. & t. To think, imagine, wonder: 意料 *-liauh*; 意想 *-shiaang* ↓.

意表 *yihbiaau*, n., as in 出乎意表 unexpected, see *-waih* ↓.
意錢 *yihchiarn*, n., (AC) anc. gambling game.

意氣 *yih'chih*, n., impulse; momentary emotion, anger: 意氣用事 act on impulse, be impulsive; 意氣之爭 a dispute due to personal feelings.

意趣 *yihchyuh*, n., interest (in project, subject); charm of suggestion in painting, writing.

意故 *yihguh*, n., (MC) reason (= 緣故).

意會 *yih-hueih*, v. i., understand by insight: 可以意會, 不可言傳 can be subtly appreciated, but not put into words.

意見 *yih'jiahn*, n., opinion, idea: 意見不同 different opinions.

意匠 *yihjiahng*, n., mental construction or composition, thought before painting or writing.

意中人 *yih-jung-rern*, n., lover, sweetheart.

意志 *yihjyh*, n., ambition, will (to succeed).

意旨 *yihjyy*, n., (1) wish: 遂你的意旨 obey your wish; (2) main idea (of essay, philosophy, etc.).

意料 *yihliauh*, v.i. & n., expect, conjecture: 出乎意料 (之外) totally unexpected.

意念 *yihniahn*, n., thought, idea in mind, a felt desire.

意色 *yihseh*, n., countenance.

意想 *yihshiaang*, v. i., think: 意想不到 never thought of it.

意下 *yihshiah*, n., opinion, meaning: 意下不大贊成 one seems not to be in favor of it (although not quite so expressed).

意向 *yihshiahng*[1], n., direction of one's thought, ambition, inclination.

意象 *yihshiahng*[2], n., idea, concept; (litr.) image.

意識 *yihshyh*, (1) n., consciousness; 意識流 stream of consciousness; 意識形態 ideology; (2) v. t., appreciate, be conscious of.

意緒 *yihshyuh*, n., mood, condition of mind.

意思 *yih'sy*, n., (1) (my, your) opinion; (2) meaning (of word, sentence); (3) fun: 有意思 interesting, having fun; 沒意思 uninteresting, dull; (4) 小意思 my humble gift (just a show of respect); (5) 不好意思 embarrassing (to accept, etc.).

意態 *yihtaih*, n., mental attitude.

意圖 *yih tur*, v. t., intend to do (s.t. improper).

意外 *yihwaih*, n., (1) an accident (of car, etc.); (2) 出乎意外 contrary to expectations.

意味 *yihweih*[1], (1) n., interest: 很有意味 very interesting; (2) v.i., to suggest or appreciate (a certain meaning).

意謂 *yih weih*[2], phr., seems to say.

意義 *yihyih*[1], n., meaning: 沒有意義 is without meaning.

意譯 *yih-yih*[2], v. i. & n., translate by idea of phrase or sentence, opp. 直譯 literal translation.

意淫 *yihyirn*, n., mental adultery, (psych.) Eros.

恋 60.72

liahn.

[Pop. of 戀 93.72]

憝 60.72

dueih.

[Var. 懟, 譈]

N. (1) (AC) 元惡大憝 chief sinister figure, man of iniquity. (2) (AC) hatred and resentment.

戇 60.72

juahng (or *gahng*).

Adj. Simple and honest.

戇直 *juahngjyr*, adj., simple and honest.

§ 60.80 (亠/八)

六 60.80

liouh.

N. The number six (wr. 陸 in checks as print).

六朝 *Liouh-chaur*, n., the Six Dyns. (3rd to 6th centuries inclusive) 吳, 東晉, 宋, 齊, 梁, 陳 all with Nanking as capital, known for culture of the South during northern occupation, beginning 420 A.D., see Appendix D.

六陳 *liouh-chern*, n., the six grains (rice, wheat, barley, soy bean, small bean, sesame) which are called 陳, "old," because imperishable; 六陳行 grain shop.

六親 *liouh-chin*, n., the six relations, brothers, wife and children, i.e., (a) 父, 母, 兄, 弟, 妻, 子; (b) 父, 子, 兄, 弟, 夫, 婦; 六親不認 not to recognize one's own closest relatives.

六畜 *liouh-chuh*, n., the six domestic animals: horse, cow, sheep, chicken, dog and pig.

六法 *liouh faa*, n., the six laws (criminal, civil, commercial, etc.).

六根 *liouh-gen*, n., (Budd.) the six senses: eye, ear, nose, tongue, body and mind: 六根不淨 the senses still in control; 六根不全 the senses are deficient.

六合 *liouh-her*, n., the six directions: east, west, north, south, heaven (up) and earth (down); the material universe: 六合之內 all within the universe.

六指兒 *liouh-jee'l*, n., "six fingers" i.e., one extra thumb or finger.

六角形 *liouhjiaau-shirng*, n. & adj., hexagon, -al.

六經 *liouh-jing*, n., the "Six Classics": *The Book of Poetry* (詩), *Book of History* (書), *Book of*

Changes (易), *Book of Rites* (禮), *Book of Music* (樂), *Spring and Autumn Annals* (春秋) (actually *Book of Music* is missing, so the term "Five Classics" is more common).

六禮 *liouh-lii*, n., (1) the six ceremonies of betrothal and marriage (納采, 問名, 納吉, 納徵, 請期, 親迎); (2) the anc. six ceremonies in classics: capping, wedding, funeral, sacrifice, communal festival, presentation (冠, 婚, 喪, 祭, 鄉飲酒, 相見).

六面體 *liouhmiahn-tii*, n. & adj., hexahedron, -dral.

六婆 *liouh-por*, n., the six classes of professional women: 牙婆, 媒婆, 師婆, 虔婆, 藥婆, 隱婆 slave trader, matchmaker, priestess, thief, herb woman and midwife.

六神 *lioul-shern*, n., source of energy controlling the 六臟 six organs (心, 肺, 肝, 腎, 脾, 膽 the heart, lungs, liver, kidneys, spleen, gall-bladder): 六神無主 the internal organs are out of order.

六書 *liouh-shu*, n., the six principles of formation of Chin. script: 象形 pictograph, 指事 picture of action, 會意 ideograph, 諧聲 phonetic symbol, 轉注 figurative extension of meaning, 假借 making one form stand for another word ("u.f." in this dictionary).

六言詩 *liouh-yarn shy*, n., Chin. verse form, with six syllables in each line.

六藝 *liouh-yih*, n., the classical six arts (禮, 樂, 射, 御, 書, 數 propriety, music, archery, riding, writing, arithmetic).

六月 *liouhyueh*, n., June.

龔 60.80

gung (also *guung*).

N. A surname.

§ 60.81 (ㄧ/人)

亥 60.81

haih.

N. (1) The last of the duodecimal cycle (十二支), see Appendix A. (2) 亥時 the period between 9 and 11 p.m. (3) A surname.

奕 60.81

yih.
[Dist. 弈 60.22]

Adj. (AC) (1) Orderly. (2) Big. (3) Beautiful. (4) 奕世 (also 奕葉) (LL) for generations.

§ 60.82 (ㄧ/乂)

文 60.82

wern (**wehn*).

N. (1) Writing, document, paper, text: 文字 *-tzyh*↓; 公文 official document; 文牘, 文書 *-dur*, *-shu* ↓; 條文 text of agreement; 具文 prepare a memorandum; 作文 compose, -sition; 原文, 本文 original text; 譯文 translated text; 上文, 下文 passage above, below; 文不加點 write well, fast and without need of revision; 文不對題 get off the subject, go off on a tangent. (2) Language, spoken or written: 日文, 英文, 法文, 中文 Japanese, English, French, Chinese. (3) Literary and artistic pursuits: 文學, 文藝 *-shyuer*, *-yih*[2]↓; culture, civilization: 文明, 文化 *-mirng*[2], *-huah*↓. (4) Lines, patterns (in cloth, pebbles). (5) A cash: 一文 one cash; 一文不名 penniless. (6) A surname.

V.t. (**wehn*) To cover up (mistake): 文過, 文飾 *-guoh*, *-shyh*↓.

Adj. (1) Literary, cultural: 斯文 cultured, civil in manner; 文縐縐 (also 謅謅) too literary in style, not simple; 文風 *-feng*↓. (2) Civilian, opp. 武 military: 文官 *-guan*↓; 文武全才 a man versed in both literature and military affairs. (3) Gentle: 文火 *-huoo*↓. (4) Containing patterns or lines: 文蛤, 文犀, 文石, 文竹 *-ger*, *-shi*, *-shyr*, *-jur*↓.

文案 *wern-ahn*, n., office of official documents; such documents.

文筆 *wernbii*, n., a person's literary style or skill.

文場 *werncharng* (*-chaang*), n., (1) hall of civil examinations; (2) formerly, orchestra of Chin. theater.

文契 *wernchih*[1], n., contract, deed.

文氣 *wern-chih*[2], n., force of writing.

文綺 *wernchii*, n., (LL) stylistic decorations.

文禽 *wern-chirn*, n., (AC) pheasant.

文情 *wern-chirng*, n., content and style of writing: 文情並茂 rich in both.

文丑(兒) *wern-choou('l)*, n., (Chin. theater) actors for civilian roles.

文旦 *werndahn*, n., the pomelo.

文定 *werndihng*, n., (AC allu.) betrothal for marriage.

文牘 *werndur*, n., correspondence, official communications; bureau in charge of this, secretariat.

文法 *wernfaa*, n., (1) grammar; (2) composition technique.

文房 *wernfarng*, n., a scholar's studio: 文房四寶 "four treasures of the studio"—writing brush, ink, ink slab, paper—stationery requisites.

文風 *wern-feng*, n., literary atmosphere or fashion.

文告 *werngauh*, n., government statement, public notice, proclamation.

文蛤 *wernger*, n., a clam, *Meretrix meretrix*.

A

文官 *wern-guan*, n., civilian official.

文過 **wehnguoh*, phr., 文過飾非 to cover up one's errors by excuses.

文翰 *wernhahn*, n., literary compositions.

文豪 *wernhaur*, n., a well-known writer.

文化 *wernhuah*, n., culture: 文化水準 cultural level; 文化復興 cultural renaissance; 文化機構 cultural organizations; (cf. 文明 *-mirng*↓, civilization); 文化界 cultural circles.

文火 *wernhuoo*, n., slow fire (for steaming), opp. 武火 hot fire.

文虎 *wernhuu*, n., literary riddles, esp. as program amusement.

文章 *wernjang*, n., (1) a literary composition, essay; (2) prose style; (3) (-'*jang*) exciting or unexpected development (based on idea that a literary composition is a legerdemain): 這話裏頭有文章 this statement contains some sly hints, innuendos; 底下有文章看 some exciting development (of strike, etc.) may follow.

文件 *wernjiahn*, n., documents.

文教 *wernjiauh*, n., culture and education: 聯合國科學文教組織 the UNESCO; 文教界 cultural and educational circles.

文靜 *wernjihng*, adj., quiet and refined.

文旌 *wernjing*, n., (court. to scholars) your travelling schedule.

文集 *wernjir*[1], n., a writer's works.

文籍 *wernjir*[2], n., books.

文竹 *wernjur*, n., a variety of fine, slender bamboo.

文治 *wern-jyh*[1], n., government by civilians rather than military men; government promotion of literature and the arts.

文致 *wernjyh*[2], (1) v.t., as in 文致成獄 to frame up a person by legal experts; (2) (-'*jy*) n., literary charm, artistic beauty.

文職 *wern-jyr*, n., civilian post.

文具 *wernjyuh*, n., stationery.

文科 *wernke*, n., college or department of arts.

文庫 *wernkuh*, n., (1) a library; (2) a publisher's collection or "library" of books.

B

文兒 *wern'l*, n., style of writing.

文理 *wern-lii*, n., order and organization of composition, line of thought in writing: 文理密察 (AC, LL) cogent, lucid piece of writing.

文林 *wern-lirn*, n., literary world or circle.

文馬 *wernmaa*, n., piebald or checkered horse.

文盲 *wern-marng*, n., an illiterate.

文貌 *wernmauh*, n., refined appearance.

文面 *wernmiahn*, n., tattoo.

文廟 *wern-miauh*, n., Confucian temple.

文名 *wern-mirng*[1], n., literary fame.

文明 *wernmirng*[2], (1) n., civilization; (2) adj., (a) civilized, opp. 野蠻 savage; (b) modern or modern-style: 文明結婚 modern wedding, also marriage by the young people's choice; 文明戲 modern play; 文明棍兒 a walking stick.

文莫 *wernmoh*[1], adj., (AC, according to one interpretation) hard-working, industrious (related 密勿, 黽勉).

文墨 *wern-moh*[2] (-'*mo*), n., (1) writing activities; (2) writing style.

文魔 *wern-mor*, n., bookworm; literary magic.

文鳥 *wernniaau*, n., (zoo.) a small bird, *Munia oryzivora*.

文旆 *wernpeih*, n., see *-sheng*↓.

文憑 *wernpirng* (-'*ping*), n., diploma.

文人 *wernrern*, n., (1) a writer; (2) a civilian, opp. 武人 military man.

文弱 *wern-ruoh*, adj., effeminate, physically weak: 文弱書生 a frail scholar.

文身 *wern-shen*, n., tattoo.

文生 *wern-sheng*, n., formerly, a student, one of the scholar class.

文犀 *wernshi*, n., lined rhinoceros horn.

文獻 *wernshiahn*, n., literary or historical data (of country, period); documents pertaining to period; a country's political and cultural systems, institutions.

C

文戲 *wern-shih*, n., a theater show without acrobatics.

文繡 *wernshiouh*, n., (AC) silk dress.

文書 *wernshu*, n., (1) official correspondence, despatch; (2) secretariat, secretary.

文士 *wernshyh*, n., a scholar, a literary man.

文飾 **wehnshyh*, v.t., to whitewash (faults), see *-guoh*↑.

文石 *wernshyr*, n., name for agate.

文選 *wernshyuaan*, n., selected works, esp. 昭明文選 a well-known selection noted for essays of florid style of early centuries A.D.

文軒 *wernshyuan*, n., (LL) your beautiful carriage, your movements.

文學 *wernshyuer*, n., literature; person's literary cultivation.

文孫 *wernsun*, n., (AC) your grandson.

文思 *wern-sy*, n., the flow of thoughts and ideas in a piece of writing.

文壇 *wern-tarn*, n., literary world or circles; literary forum.

文體 *wern-tii*, n., literary style; literary form.

文采 *werntsaai*, n., beauty of appearance (of person), beauty of style of writing.

文才 *werntsair* (-'*tsai*), n., literary talent.

文辭 *werntsyr*, n., vocabulary and style.

文藻 *werntzaau*, n., decorative embellishments of writing.

文宗 *werntzung*, n., acclaimed first writer (of period, place).

文字 *werntzyh*, n., (1) written language of a country; (2) choice of words in writing: 文字獄 prosecution of writers on account of literary offence to ruler.

文網 *wernwaang*, n., the long arm of the law.

文物 *wernwuh*, n., cultural objects and institutions (of period, country).

文

文武 *wern-wuu*, adj., both literary and military, see Adj. 2↑.

文雅 *wernyaa*, adj., refined, not coarse.

文言 *wernyarn*, n., the literary language (LL), i.e., language developed through classical patterns, not "sayable," and used exclusively in writing; opp. 白話 *bairhuah* or vernacular style of writing.

文鰩魚 *wernyaur-yur*, n., the flying fish (also called 飛魚).

文義 *wern-yih*[1], n., literary content; thought or ideas expressed in writing.

文藝 *wern-yih*[2], n., (1) literature and the arts; (2) the literary craft: 文藝界 literary and artistic circle.

文茵 *wern-yin*, n., (AC) tiger skins as cart mattress.

文苑 *wern-yuahn*, n., the literary field (lit., "garden").

文運 *wern-yuhn*, n., (1) success in literature or writing; (2) gen. literary movement or tendency.

文魚 *wernyur*, n., (various interpretations including): goldfish, carp, flying fish (*-yaur-*↑).

交 60.82

jiau.

N. (1) Friend: 故交, 知交 old friends; 生死交 friends for life. (2) Friendship: 訂交, 結交 become friends; friendly relationships: 國交, 邦交 international relations; 絕交 break up or sever relations; 復交 restore relations; 深交, 淺交 deep, shallow friendship; 外交 diplomatic relations; 交情, 交誼 *-chirng*, *-yih*[2]↓.

V. t. (1) Hand over, transfer: 交付 *-fuh*, 交割 *-ger*, 交卸 *-shieh*↓; 移交 hand over (duties of office, documents, real estate); 交出 render up; 交下 hand down; 交辦 assign (work, task to subordinate); 交到 deliver to; 交上 present (to superior); 送交 deliver by messenger boy; 遞交 give to s.o. in person; 點交 turn over item by item; 交白卷 fail to answer any of the questions in an examination, (fig.) fail to carry out an assignment; 交卷 turn in the examination paper; 交卷主義 a get-it-over-with and devil-may-care attitude; 交錢, 交款 make payments or pay bills; 交清 (of goods) all delivered; 交貨 deliver goods; 船上交貨價 F.O.B. (free on board); 交稿 submit manuscript; 交還 return, give back; 交回 ditto. (2) Be on good terms with, come into contact with: 交好 *-haau*, 交歡 *-huan*, 交際 *-jih*↓: 神交 (of two persons reciprocally) know a person by reading his works; 交結 *-jier*[1]↓; 交朋友 be friends, (of boy or girl) have girl friends, boy friends; 交友 *-yoou*, 交往 *-waang*↓. (3) Come close to, join, alternate, engage in: 交兵 *-bing*, 交鋒 *-feng*, 交戰 *-jahn*↓; 交頭接耳 whisper into each other's ears, talk confidentially; 交談 *-tarn*, 交換 *-huahn*↓; 成交 close a business deal. (4) Unite in sexual intercourse: 交媾 *-gouh*↓, 交合 *-her*↓; 交尾 *-weei*↓; 性交 sexual copulation. (5) (Of two straight lines) to cross: 交點 *-diaan*, 交叉 *-cha*↓.

Adj. & adv. (1) Simultaneous(ly): 交加 *-jia*↓. (2) Each other: 交互 *-huh*↓.

交保 *jiau-baau*, v. t., let (suspect) go on bail.

交拜 *jiaubaih*, v. i., (of bridegroom and bride) kowtow to each other to formalize the marriage.

交杯酒 *jiaubei-jioou*, n., formerly, mutual toasting by the bridegroom and the bride on their wedding day.

交臂 *jiau-beih*, n. & adj., (1) n., a chance meet: 交臂失之 fail to meet s.o. by a narrow chance; (2) adj., arm in arm; close together.

交兵 *jiau-bing*, v. i., to wage war, to fight (with weapons).

交叉 *jiaucha*, v. t. & n., intersect, -ion: 交叉點 point of intersection.

交差 *jiau-chai*, v. i., render a report of what one has done in line of duty.

交鈔 *jiau-chau*, n., (MC) the paper currency of the Yuarn and Mirng Dyns.

交契 *jiau-chih*, v. i., be on friendly terms (with person).

交情 *jiau-chirng*, n., friendship, mutual affection.

交代 *jiaudaih*, v. t., (1) (of two or more persons) succeed one another; (2) (-'*dai*) bid, order, give instructions: 交代他不要嚕囌 tell him not to pester me; 交代的清清楚楚 have given clear and precise orders; (3) transfer of duties: 交代差事, 辦交代 transfer duties; give an account of one's charge: 他沒有交代一聲就走了 he went away without leaving a word.

交道 *jiaudauh*, n., personal relations: 他很難打交道 he is hard to get along with.

交點 *jiau-diaan*, n., a point of intersection.

交耳 *jiau-eel*, v. i., to whisper into each other's ears.

交鋒 *jiau-feng*, v. i., engage in battle, fight with weapons.

交付 *jiaufuh*, v. t., hand over (things); pay (money, bills).

交感神經 *jiaugaan-shernjing*, n., (physiol.) the sympathetic nerve.

交給 *jiau-geei*, v. t., hand to (s.o.).

交割 *jiauger*, n., a business transaction.

交媾 *jiaugouh*, v. i. & n., (have) sexual intercourse, coitus.

交關 *jiauguan*, adv., (Shanghai dial.) very, extremely, exceedingly.

交好 *jiauhaau*, v. t., be friends with: 咱們交好有年 we have been friends for many years.

交合 *jiauher*, v. i. & n., (have) sexual intercource, see *-gouh*↑.

交換 *jiauhuahn*, v. t., to change, interchange.

交歡 *jiauhuan*, v. i., establish cordial relations with one another.

交互 *jiauhuh*, adv., mutually, reciprocally.

交鬨 *jiauhuhng*, v. i. & n., wrangle, squabble, brawl, feud.

交戰 *jiaujahn*, v. i., go to war, become a belligerent: 交戰國 a belligerent.

交加 *jiaujia*, adv., all at once: 貧病交加 dogged by poverty and illness at one and the same time; 拳足交加 give (s.o.) both punches and kicks.

交接 *jiaujie*, v. t., (1) come into contact with; (2) maintain friendly relations with.

交界 *jiaujieh*, n., boundary, frontier, borders.

交結 *jiaujier*[1], v. t., (1) (of persons) associate with; (2) (of things) interconnect, intertwine.

交睫 *jiaujier*[2], v. i., close one's eyes to sleep.

交節氣 *jiau-jierchih*, n., (1) a sudden seasonal change; (2) relapse of chronic illness with seasonal change.

交際 *jiaujih*, (1) n., friendly or social intercourse; (2) v. i., 善交際 be socially active; 交際花 a social butterfly; 交際費 allowance for entertainment, social contact, etc.

交頸 *jiaujiing*, v. i., "necking," make love.

交口 *jiaukoou*, v. i., speak in unison: 交口稱讚 praise by one and all.

交流 *jiauliour*, (1) v. i., (of air currents or water) to flow in opposite directions; (2) n., crosscurrents, (electricity) alternating current: 文化交流 cultural interchange.

交買賣 *jiau-maaimaih*, phr., maintain long-time patronage by clients.

交派 *jiaupaih*, v. t., assign as a duty.

交迫 *jiaupoh*, v. i., (of pressures) come from all sides: 饑寒交迫 suffer from both cold and hunger.

交涉 *jiausheh*, v. i. & n., negotiate, -ation, discuss, -ion.

交響曲 *jiaushiarng-chyuu*, n., (mus.) symphony; 交響樂 *-shiaangyueh*, n., ditto: 交響樂團 symphony orchestra.

交卸 *jiaushieh*, v. i., hand over the duties of office to one's successor.

交手 *jiau-shoou*, v. i. & t., (1) to salute with the hands folded and raised in front; (2) hold one hand with another; (3) fight with fists.

交綏 *jiausuei*, v. i., (of armies) to fight, be locked in battle.

交談 *jiautarn*, v. t., talk with, discuss, exchange views with.

交替 *jiautih*, v. i., come one after another.

交錯 *jiautsuoh*, adj., interlocked, intertwined, intermingled: 縱橫交錯 arranged in a crisscross pattern.

交通 *jiautung*, n., (1) communications and transportation: 交通車 office bus; (2) traffic: 交通警察, 交通規則, 交通事件, 交通法庭, 交通訊號 traffic police, rules, accidents, court, signals.

交子 *jiautzyy*, n., (MC) name of a paper note issued during the Suhng Dyn.

交往 *jiauwaang*, v. i., associate with, have dealings with.

交尾 *jiauweei*, v. i. & n., (of animals and insects) copulate, -tion.

交惡 *jiau-wuh*, v.i., become enemies.

交午 *jiauwuu*, n., noontime.

交易 *jiauyih*[1], v. i. & n., interchange, (engage in) trade, (do) business transactions: 交易所 stock market.

交誼 *jiauyih*[2], n., friendly relations, friendship.

交椅 *jiauyii*, n., an armchair.

交友 *jiau-yoou*, v. i., make friends.

交遊 *jiauyour*, n., a circle of friends; v.i., make friends.

交運 *jiau-yuhn*, v. i. & n., (have) a spell of good fortune.

変 60.82

biahn.

[Pop. of 變 93.82]

§ 60.83 (亠/〜)

夜 60.83

yeh.

N. Night: 日夜, 晝夜 day and night; 一夜 one night, also whole night; 整夜, 盡夜, 終夜 whole night; 夜半, 半夜 midnight; 巡夜, 守夜 keep night patrol; 熬夜 work or keep awake all night; 坐夜 sit up all night; 長夜 long night; 月夜 moonlight night; 黑夜 dark night; 夜長夢多 (fig.) prospect is dark and dreary; 夜深人靜 in the dead of night; 夜闌 the night is far spent; 夜未央 it is not dawn yet.

Adj. & adv. Nocturnal, in the night, by night: 夜行 travel or roam about by night; 夜航 sail, fly in the night; 夜景 night view; 夜飯 supper, midnight supper; 夜場 evening show (of cinema, etc.); 夜襲 night attack; 夜班 night duty, night class.

夜半 *yehbahn*, adv., midnight.

夜叉 *yeh'cha*, n., (Sanskr. *yaksha*) demons that fly by night, (fig.) a very ugly person (also 母夜叉 a shrew).

夜車 *yehche*, n., night train.

夜氣 *yeh-chih*, phr., (AC) the spirit of well-being after a good night's rest.

夜勤 *yeh-chirn*, n., night duty.

夜度娘 *yehduh-niarng*, n., (MC) prostitute; 夜度資 n., prostitute's fees for a night.

夜分 *yehfen*, adv., midnight.

夜光錶 *yehguang-biaau*, n., luminescent watch.

夜合 *yehher*, n., (bot.) (1) mimosa; (2) *Polygonum multiflorum* (also called 何首烏).

夜活 *yeh-huor*, n., night work.

夜壺 *yehhur*, n., chamber pot.

夜間 *yeh-jian*, adv., during the night.

夜禁 *yeh-jihn*, n., curfew.

夜淨兒 *yeh'jihng'l*, n., chamber pot.

夜中 *yeh-jung*, adv., in the night.

夜課 *yeh-keh*, n., evening class, homework.

夜來 *heh-lair*, adv., during the night.

夜來香 *yehlairshiang*, n., (bot.) tuberose.

夜郎 *Yehlarng*, n., (AC, LL) a small kingdom in southwest China: 夜郎自大 (allu.) *Yeihlarng* people think their country is bigger than China—ignorant boastfulness.

夜裏(頭) *yeh'li('tou)*, adv., in the night, at night.

夜裏個 *yeh-li'ge* (*yeh'l'ge*) n., last night.

夜漏 *yehlouh*, n., nighttime (漏 sand clock).

夜盲症 *yehmarng-jehng*, n., night blindness.

夜貓子 *yeh'mautz*, n., night owl, nighthawk.

夜明珠 *yehmirng-ju*, n., luminescent pearl.

夜尿症 *yehniauh-jehng*, n., enuresis, incontinence.

夜盆兒 *yehper'l*, n., night basin.

夜消兒 *yehshiau'l*, n., night snack (also wr. 宵; usu. called 宵夜).

夜戲 *yeh-shih*, n., evening performance, evening show.

夜行人 *yeh-shirng-rern*, n., night prowlers.

夜市 *yeh-shyh*, n., night fair.

夜學 *yeh-shyuer*, n., night school.

夜臺 *yeh-tair*, n., (LL) the grave, graveyard.

夜啼 *yeh-tir*, n., morbid crying at night of babies.

夜總會 *yeh-tzunghueih*, n., night club.

夜作 *yeh'tzuo*, n., night work.

夜晚 *yehwaan*, n., evening.

夜眼 *yeh-yaan*, n., some people's ability to see in the dark.

夜夜 *yeh-yeh*, adv., every night, nightly.

夜鷹 *yehying*[1], n., the nighthawk.

夜鶯 *yehying*[2], n., the nightingale, bulbul.

夜遊神 *yehyourshern*, n., one who turns night into day (also 夜遊子).

蹵 60.83

tsuh.

[Var. 蹴 40B.70]

迹 60.83

ji.

[Commonly interch. 跡, 蹟]

N. (1) Impressions left: 足迹 footprints; 迹印 imprints. (2) Outward manifestations of work done: 功迹 creditable accomplishments, achievements (also wr. 績); feats; 實迹 actual attainments; 劣迹 dishonorable records; 惡迹 wicked deeds. (3) Traces, marks, images: 事迹 occurrence, events; 痕迹 tracks, traces, scars; 遺迹 remains (of buildings), ruins; 形迹 (of persons) traces, movements; 古迹 (oft. 古跡, 古蹟) anc. relics or monuments; 心迹 inner feelings, sentiments; 奇迹, 神迹 (oft. 蹟, 跡) miracles; 異迹 strange phenomena; 陳迹 old marks of the past; 迹象 *-shiahng*↓.

V. i. & t. (1) V. t., search out, hunt or track down: 追迹 to look for (men, game, etc.); 迹盜 ferret out robbers; 迹捕 to shadow and arrest. (2) V. i., to follow: 不踐迹 not to follow the old rut. (3) V. i., make a study of, investigate: 迹漢功臣 study the history of great ministers of the Hahn Dyn.

迹象 *jishiahng*, n., outward appearance, evidences.

這 60.83

jeh (**jeih*).

[Pop. 这]

Pron. & adj. This: 這人, 這地 this man, this place; 這個那個 this and that; 這廝 (coll.) this fellow; 這回 this time; 這等, 這樣, 這麽 *-deeng*, *-yahng*, *-'mo*↓; 這還了得 how dare you (do this)? what a mess! 這可不行 this simply won't do; 這年, 月, 日 (這天) this year, month, day; 這咱, 這會子, 這一向 at this moment; (**jeih*) contraction of 這一 this one, or this: 這邊 this side; 這塊兒 *-kuah'l*↓; 這門生意 this business; 這個 this one; 這班人 this kind of people, these people (cf. contraction of 那一 into *neih*).

這般 *jehban*, adj. & adv., so, such: 這般模樣 such a figure or looks (of girls).

這邊(兒) *jeinbian(-bia'l)*, adv., here, over here.

這壁 *jehbih*, (also 這壁廂, 這廂) adv. phr., this side.

這其間 *jeh-chir-jian*, adv. phr., during this while, in all this.

這搭兒 *jehdah'l*, adv., this place: 來這搭兒 come here; 這搭兒是何處 what is this place?

這等 *jehdeeng*, (1) adj. & adv., so: 這等美麗 so beautiful; (2) pron., these, this kind (of people, goods, etc.).

這番 *jeh-fan*, phr., this time.

這個 *jeh'ge* (**jeih'ge*), pron., this, this one: 你這個人 (in rebuke) you fellow; when in objective case, oft. precedes vb. as usual: 這個我不要了 I don't want this.

這陣兒 **jeih-jeh'l*, adv. phr., at this time; 這陣子 (*-tz*) quite recently, during the last few days (he didn't come to see me, etc.).

這塊兒 **jeih-kuah'l*, (1) pron., this piece; (2) adv., here, hereabouts.

這裏 *jeh'lii*, adv., here: 不在這裏 is not here.

這溜兒 **jeihliouh'l*, adv., hereabouts.

這們 *jeh'men*, adj. & adv., (MC) corruption of 這麽 *-'mo*↓.

這麽 *jeh'mo*, adv., such, so: 這麽大的人 such a grown-up person like you.

這廂 *jeh-shiang*, adv., on this side.

這些 *jehshie*, adj. & pron., these (plural of 這 this).

這咱 *jeh'tzan*, adv., now.

這早晚兒 *jeh'tzaurwaa'l*, adv., so late: 你怎麽這早晚兒才來 why do you come so late?

這様(兒)(子) *jehyahng('l)(tz)*, adv., in this way, this manner.

遊 60.83

your.

[Pop. 遊; very largely interch, 游 63A.00]

V. i. & t. (1) To travel, roam, wander: 遊遍 travel all over; 遊行 *-shirng* ↓; 遨遊, 雲遊, 浪遊, 漫遊 roam about in freedom; 冶遊 visit singsong house; 嬉遊 relax and play; 閒遊 to take a stroll; 游説, 遊子, 遊客 *-shueih, -tzyy, -keh* ↓. (2) To follow a master: 從先生遊 studied under a teacher. (3) To associate intimately: 交遊 make friends with. (4) To have room for play: 遊刃, 遊目 *-rehn, -muh* ↓. (5) To play: see esp. compp. of 游 63A.00.

Adj. Floating, unattached: 遊魂, 遊絲 *-hurn, -sy* ↓.

遊憩 *yourchih*, v. i., to relax and play.

遊蕩 *yourdahng*, v. i., (1) to loaf, to indulge in pleasure; (2) 精遊神蕩 (of mind) to feel unreal.

遊惰 *yourduoh*, v. i., to loaf.

遊方 *your-fang*, v.i., (Budd. & Taoism) travel widely.

遊蜂 *yourfeng*, n., the male bee.

遊逛 *yourguahng*, v. i., to take a stroll, to visit (temples, fairs).

遊觀 *yourguan*, v. t., to visit (historic place, etc.).

遊魂 *yourhurn*, n., homeless spirits unattached to a body; (fig.) s. o. whose spirit is about to depart, a listless person.

遊街 *yourjie*, v. i., (1) to hold a street demonstration; (2) to parade a criminal about to be executed, or to disgrace person.

遊記 *yourjih*[1], n., a travel sketch.

遊騎 *yourjih*[2], n., cavalry unit to be despatched as needed.

遊軍 *yourjyun*, n., formerly, an army unit uncommitted and to be sent as desired.

遊客 *yourkeh*, n., tourist.

遊覽 *yourlaan*, v. t., to visit (historic places, etc.), to tour (a place): 遊覽車 tourist car or bus.

遊廊 *yourlarng*, n., covered corridor in Chin. garden.

遊樂 *yourleh*, v. i., to enjoy oneself; 遊樂場 amusement park.

遊獵 *yourlieh*, v. i., to hunt.

遊歷 *yourlih*, v. i., to visit (foreign countries, etc.).

遊目 *your-muh*[1], phr., 遊目騁懷 to let the eye take in the landscape and please the spirit.

遊幕 *yourmuh*[2], n., a scholar attached to governor's office as friend, advisor and as secretary to draft important reports.

遊刃 *your-rehn*, phr., 遊刃有餘 (AC allu.) have plenty of room for play of butcher's knife—fulfill a task easily.

遊戲 *yourshih*, (1) v. i., play, play games; (2) n., amusement, games, sports; 遊戲人間 fairies descending to earth and worldly pleasures; (fig.) world of fun and frolic.

遊興 *your-shihng*, n., excitement of travel, interest in sightseeing.

遊心 *your-shin*, phr., 遊心物外 to let the mind wander free beyond material things.

遊息 *yourshir*, v. i., see *-chih* ↑.

遊行 *yourshirng*, v. i., (1) to wander freely; (2) to hold a procession or street demonstration.

遊手 *yourshoou*, n., as in 遊手好閒之徒 loafers.

遊説 *yourshueih*, v. i., (AC of scholars) travel about different countries to sell certain ideas.

遊食 *yourshyr*, n., (LL) as in 遊食之徒 people without definite profession.

遊學 *yourshyuer*, v. i., to study abroad.

遊絲 *yoursy*, n., floating gossamer.

遊艇 *yourtiing*, n., pleasure boat for hire on lakes, etc., private yacht.

遊蹤 *yourtzung*, n., a person's travels, places one has covered in travel.

遊子 *yourtzyy*, n., a traveller away from home.

遊玩 *yourwarn*, v. i., to play for pastime.

遊冶 *youryee*, v. i., to visit singsong houses.

遊豫 *youryuh*, v. i., to indulge in pleasures.

適 60.83

*shyh (*dih)*.

V. i. & t. (1) (LL) to go: 何適 where are you going? 適秦, 適宋 go to Chirn, to Suhng. (2) (LL) (girl) to marry s.o.: 已適人 already married. (3) To suit (taste, use, body, pleasure): 適口, 適用, 適體, 適意 *-koou, -yuhng, -tii, -yih* ↓. (4) (**dih*) (AC) to insist: 無適也, 無莫也 (of Confu.) never insisted on doing or on not doing, also interpreted as without prejudice for or against person.

Adj. (1) Comfortable: 舒適, 安適 comfortable, free and easy, contented; 閒適 contented, leisurely. (2) Proper, fitting, convenient: 適齡 of age; 適合, 適宜, 適當 *-her, -yir, -dahng* ↓; 適者生存 survival of the fittest.

Adv. (1) Just: 適逢, 適值 just happens (to be Sunday, etc.); 適逢其會 came just at the right time (some occasion); 適來 *-lair* ↓; 適到 have just arrived; 適可而止 not overdo a thing. (2) Just now, just a moment ago: 適從何來 where did you just come from? 適間 *-jian* ↓; 適纔(才) *-tsair* ↓.

適當 *shyhdahng*, adj., fitting and proper (time, opportunity), just right (person for job), legally proper.

亅	小	⺊	十	土	ナ	廾	ㄴ卜	丨	一	丁	フ	口	区	冈	㇆	厂	尸	亠	广	宀	丶	乚	弋	心	八	人	乂	〜	㇀	ノ丨	𠂉	く
00	01	02	10	11	12	20	21	22	30	31	32	40	41	42	50	51	52	60	61	62	63	70	71	72	80	81	82	83	90	91	92	93

適合 *shyhher*, adj., just right (of dress, shoes), just fit: 適合用處 just what one needs.
適間 *shyhjian*, adv., just now, just a moment ago.
適中 *shyhjung*, adj., not extreme, moderate: 適中地點 central location.
適口 *shyh-koou*, adj., (of food, flavor) pleasing to the palate.
適來 *shyhlair*, adv., (MC) just now, see *-tsair* ↓.
適然 *shyhrarn*, adj. & adv., (1) (LL) occassionally; (2) (LL) proper, -ly.
適體 *shyhtii*, adj., appropriate (composition), in proper form.
適纔(才) *shyhtsair*, adv., just a moment ago: 適才走了 had just left.
適從 *shyhtsurng*, v. t., to follow, choose (line of action, etc.).
適意 *shyh-yih*, adj., enjoyable, comfortable (chair, position).
適應 *shyhying*, v. t. & n., to adapt, -ation (to need, situation, environment). 「arrangement).
適宜 *shyhyir*, adj., proper (match,
適用 *shyhyuhng*, adj., useful, practical, suitable for use (penknife, house jacket, etc.).

§ 60.91 (ㄧ/ㄋ)

彥 60.91

yahn.

N. (AC) a handsome man, excellent scholar: 彥士, 俊彥 ditto; 美彥 handsome.

§ 60.93 (ㄧ/ㄑ)

妄 60.93

wahng.

Adj. & adv. Absurd, -ly, preposterous, -ly, outrageous: 妄證 false witness; 妄斷 jump to a conclusion; 狂妄 reckless, rash; 妄口巴舌 blasphemous talk; 妄自尊大 self-conceited, with exaggerated opinion of oneself; 不可妄自菲薄 don't undervalue yourself.

妄人 *wahngrern*, n., (severe condemnation, yet quite litr.) preposterous or conceited person, self-opinionated imbecile.
妄想 *wahngshiaang*, v.i. & t., indulge in wild or unjustified hope, fancies.
妄作 *wahngtzuoh*, v.i., act wildly, foolishly or illegally.
妄爲 *wahngweir*, v.i., as in 膽大妄爲 act in foolhardy manner.
妄言 *wahng-yarn*, (1) n., foolish or baseless talk; (2) phr., 姑妄言之 just talk for talking's sake; 妄言妄聽 don't take it too seriously.
妄庸 *wahngyung*, adj., (person) very common and somewhat conceited.

妾 60.93

chieh.

N. (1) Concubine: 立妾, 置妾, 納妾 take a concubine. (2) 妾, 妾身 formerly, wife referring to herself.

妾婦 *chiehfuh*, n., (AC) (1) woman referring to herself; (2) (AC) (derog.) common woman.

孪 60.93

lyuarn.

[Pop. of 孿 93.93]

玄 60.93

shyuarn.

N. (1) A surname. (2) The (Taoist) mysteries: 談玄 discuss Taoist mysticism.

Adj. (1) Dark, black: 玄服 black gown; 玄圭, 玄玉 black jade; 玄狐 black fox. (2) (Taoist) mystic: see 玄學, 玄門, 玄根, 玄牝 *-shyuer, -mern, -gen, -pihn* ↓; (Budd.) 玄關 the path to right doctrine; 玄軌 (Budd.) the mysterious way. (3) Abstruse, mysterious, subtle, profound: 這話説的太玄了 this talk is getting too abstruse, mysterious; 玄奧, 玄妙 *-auh, -miauh* ↓; 玄理, 玄旨 mystic truth; 玄德 the concealed, profound virtues; 玄策, 玄略, 玄謀 subtle, profound strategy; 玄談 abstruse talk; 玄虛 *-shyu* ↓.

玄奧 *shyarn-auh*, (1) adj., abstruse, difficult to comprehend; (2) n., mystery, profundity.
玄裳 *shyuarn-charng*, n., (AC) black dress of mourning.
玄青 *shyuarnching*, adj., deep black color.
玄穹 *shyuarn-chyung*, n., (AC) the profound vastness beyond the skies.
玄根 *shyuarngen*, n., (1) (Taoist) the mysterious root of all things; (2) (Budd.) person's endowment at birth.
玄宮 *shyuarn-gung*, n., (1) (AC) (Taoist) the hall of profound meditations; (2) (AC) the inner palaces.
玄鶴 *shyuarnheh*, n., (zoo.) the black crane, *Grus cinerea*.
玄黃 *shyuarn-huarng*, n., (LL) heaven (玄 black) and earth (黃 yellow): 玄黃未判 before the heaven and earth were separated or before creation; 天地玄黃 first sentence in 千字文 sometimes used as index words (like A, B, C, D).
玄機 *shyuarn-ji*, n., (Taoist) the mysteries of the universe; in pop. Taoism, the mysterious workings of fate.
玄教 *shyuarn-jiauh*, n., Taoism.
玄津 *shyuarnjin*, n., (Budd.) the ferry to salvation.
玄籍 *shyuarnjir*, n., (Budd.) the sutras.

玄覽 *shyuarn laan*, phr., (Laotse) observe all universe with a quiet meditative mind.

玄理 *shyuarnlii*, n., the mystic truth.

玄流 *shyuarnliour*, n., (Budd.) the monks and nuns (in black, or grey robes).

玄門 *shyuarnmern*, n., (1) (Budd.) the Buddhist truth or doctrines; vestibule; (2) Taoism; Taoist church.

玄妙 *shyuarnmiauh*, adj., mysterious, subtle, profound: 玄妙莫測 difficult to guess or comprehend.

玄默 *shyuarnmoh*, adj., silent, reticent (associated with calm and meditation).

玄鳥 *shyuarn-niaau*, n., poetic name for the swallow.

玄女 *shyuarn-nyuu*, n., (Chin. mythology) a goddess who assisted the Yellow Emperor (黃帝) to subdue 蚩尤 (also styled 九天玄女).

玄牝 *shyuarnpihn*, n., (Laotse) the Mysterious Mother of things in universe.

玄圃 *Shyuarn-puu*, n., a mythical fairyland on 崑崙 Kunlun Mountain.

玄塞 *shyuarn-saih*, n., (LL) the Great Wall.

玄參 *shyuarnshen*, n., (bot.) a species of black jinseng, *Scrophularia oldhami* (also called 黑參).

玄象 *shyuarn-shiahng*, n., meteorological phenomena.

玄室 *shyuarn-shyh*, n., (1) (LL) mausoleum; (2) (LL) a dark room.

玄石 *shyuarn-shyr*, n., loadstone, magnetic stone.

玄虛 *shyuarnshyu*, (1) adj., abstruse, mystical; (2) n., 故弄玄虛 play tricks, make things look unnecessarily mysterious.

玄學 *shyuarnshyuer*, n., (1) metaphysics; (2) mysticism; (3) Taoism; (4) Buddhism.

玄孫 *shyuarnsun*, n., great-great-grandson, cf. 曾孫 great-grandson.

玄談 *shyuarntarn* n., abstruse, mystic talk; Buddhist or Taoist discussion.

玄堂 *shyuarntarng*, n., (1) (AC) a northern room; (2) (in Tang Dyn.) a mausoleum.

玄天 *shyuarn-tian*, n., the Northern Sky: 玄天上帝 (Taoist) God of Northern Heavens.

玄宗 *shyuarntzung*, n., a gen. term for Buddhist church.

玄悟 *shyuarnwuh*, v. t., have mystic insight.

玄武 *shyuarnwuu*, n., (1) the seven constellations of northern sky (斗, 牛, 女, 虛, 危, 室, 壁); (2) (Taoism) spirit of Northern Sky: 玄武大帝 (also 真武大帝) also interpreted as Spirit of Water.

玄武岩 *shyuarnwuu-yarn*, n., (min.) black basalt.

蛮 60.93

marn.

[Pop of 蠻 93.93]

蝱 60.93

marng.

[Abbr. of 虻 22D.21]

N. (Zoo.) gadfly: 牛蝱 horsefly.

螽 60.93

wern.

[Var. of 蚊 22D.82]

SECTION 60A

§ 60A.00 (言/亅)

討 60A.00-1

taau.

V. t. (1) To beg, dun, ask for payment: 討賬, 討債 ask for payment of debt; 討價還價 haggle over price; 討飯 *-fahn*↓; 討賞 ask for tips, gratuities; 討取 ask for s.t.; 討個明白答復 ask for definite reply; 討個公道 ask for justice; 討饒, 討人情兒 to beg for pardon, special considerations; 討人家喜歡, 討好 ingratiate oneself; ask for trouble, incur: 討麻煩, 討煩惱 ask (gratuitously) for trouble for oneself; 討野火 (MC) risk, incur anger; 討賤 invite contempt; 討人嫌 disgust, -ing: 討厭 *-yahn*↓; 討沒趣 do s.t. that will result only in a rebuke or embarrassment; 自討苦吃 walk into trouble; 討巧 try to get s. t. for nothing (討巧的辦法); 討便宜 get a cheap bargain, take advantage of s. t. (2) To marry: 討親, 討老婆, 討媳婦 get a wife. (3) To discuss, study: 討論, 討教 *-luhn*, *-jiauh*↓. (4) To invade with army: 討賊 fight enemy; see 討伐 *-fa*↓. (5) To seek: 討頭路, 討生活 seek a job, a living.

討親 *taau-chin*, v. i., to marry a wife.

討求 *taauchiour*, v. i., ask, beg, demand.

討情(兒) *taauchirng('l)*, v. i., ask for leniency.

討伐 *taaufa*, v. i., make war on (country, rebels) to vindicate authority.

討飯 *taaufahn*, v. i., be beggar: 討飯的 a beggar.

討好 *taurhaau*, v. t., to ingratiate

oneself with (person); to toady.

討教 *taaujiauh*, v. i., ask for advice.

討債鬼 *taaujzaihgueei*, n., oft. spoken of children who spend away family fortune or die young and give no recompense to parents for bringing up.

討論 *taauluhn*, v. i. & n., discuss, -ion.

討饒 *taauraur*, v. i., ask for pardon.

討厭 *taauyahn*, adj., annoying, objectionable, disgusting.

討要 *taauyauh*, v. t., demand.

詩 60A.00-1

shy.

N. Poem, verse; poetry: 律詩 Tarng poem of prescribed tonal pattern; 古詩 "ancient poem" not so prescribed; 七言詩, 五言詩 poems with seven, five words to each line; 新詩 *vers libre*, new poetry in contrast to classical; 自由詩 *vers libre*; 抒情詩 lyric poetry; 史詩 epic; 詩篇 Book of Psalms; 詩劇 drama in verse; 散文詩 poetic prose; 詩人 *-rern* ↓; 詩聖, 詩仙 sage poet (杜甫 "Tu Fu"), fairy poet (李白 "Li Po"); 詩集 collection of poems; 詩社 poetry club; 詩翁 (term of honor) a poet; 詩思 poetic thought; 詩意 *-yih* ↓; 作詩 compose poetry; 和詩 (*heh-*) to write poem with rhyme words used in friend's poem—a poetic game.

詩伯 *shy-bor*, n., (LL) term of respect for honored poet.

詩情 *shy-chirng*, n., poetic sentiment.

詩歌 *shyge*, n., song.

詩話 *shy-huah*, n., a form of literary notebook containing criticisms of and anecdotes about poems and circumstances of writing them.

詩虎 *shy-huu*, n., see *-mir* ↓.

詩家 *shyjia*, n., a poet.

詩鐘 *shy-jung*, n., a literary pastime in which poems are written on two distinctive subjects with unlikely associations.

詩禮 *shy-lii*, phr., poetry and good manners—the two together meaning culture: 詩禮傳家 cultured family.

詩律 *shy-lyuh*, n., restrictions of verse form, esp. in tones.

詩謎 *shy-mir*, n., a riddle in verse.

詩魔 *shy-mor*, n., (1) a craze to write poems; (2) verse in abstruse or eccentric style.

詩人 *shyrern*, n., a poet.

詩興 *shy-shihng*, n., inspiration for poetry; mood for writing it.

詩壇 *shy-tarn*, n., circle of poets.

詩眼 *shy-yaan*, n., (1) the telling word in a poetic line; (2) an eye for poetry.

詩意 *shy-yih*, n., poetic sentiment: 有詩意 (of scenes, prose) poetic.

詩韻 *shy-yuhn*, n., (1) rhyme; (2) rhyme dictionary.

詩餘 *shy-yur*, n., the Suhng *tsyr* (詞), with varied tonal patterns and sentence lengths.

譸 60A.00-1

jou.

譸張 *joujang*, v. i., to swagger, deceive.

訂 60A.00-3

dihng.

V.i. & t. (1) Make agreement, cement (friendship): 訂於 due to, scheduled to; 訂合同 sign a contract; 訂密約 make secret agreement; 訂約, 訂盟, 訂婚, 訂交 *-yue, -merng, -hun, -jiau* ↓. (2) Subscribe (to periodical): 訂報. (3) To revise, make up book: 修訂, 校訂 edit correct version, 訂正 *-jehng* ↓; 裝訂 bookbinding.

訂定 *dihngdihng*, v.t., make (contract, treaty): 訂定日期 set date (for party).

訂戶 *dihnghuh*, n., subscriber (to newspaper, periodical).

訂婚 *dihng-hun*, v.i. & n., betroth, -al.

訂正 *dihngjehng*, v.t., correct, revise: 訂正錯誤 correct errors of printing.

訂交 *dihng-jiau*, v.i., cement friendship, become friends.

訂立 *dihnglih*, v.t., set up, make (agreement, contract).

訂盟 *dihng-merng*, v.i., make alliance, make pledge (by lovers, etc.).

訂約 *dihng-yue*, v.i., make an agreement, treaty, sign a contract.

訏 60A.00-3

shyu.

V. i. (1) (AC) to sigh. (2) (AC) to boast, exaggerate.

Adj. Big, broad: 訏謨 (AC) statesmanlike counsel, great plan; 訏訏 big and broad.

訶 60A.00-3

he.

V. i. To shout at, to curse or abuse: 訶佛罵祖 to "curse at Buddha."

訶護 *he-huh*, v. t., (of gods) to protect.

訶子 *hetzyy*, n., (1) (MC) brassière; (2) (bot.) the myrobalan tree, a plant in Southern China, *Terminalia chebula* (also wr. 訶黎 (羅) (勒).

訶 60A.00-3

ge.

[Var. of 歌 31S.81]

訝 60A.00–5

yah.

V.i. (1) To be surprised, startled: 驚訝 ditto; 訝異 to be surprised at. (2) (AC) u.f. 迓 to welcome, 51.83.

讕 60A.00–5

larn.

V. i. Make false or irresponsible statements, spread rumors: 詆讕 make unfounded allegations.

Adj. False, unfounded: 讕言 baseless accusations, fabrications; 讕辭 ditto.

讇 60A.00–5

chaan.

[Var. of 諂 60A.21]

諄 60A.00–6

jun.

Adv. Repeatedly, warmly: 諄懇 sincerely request; 諄囑 repeatedly and warmly instruct s. o. to do.

諄 切 *junchieh*, adv., sincerely and warmly (advise).

諄 諄 *junjun*, (1) adv., untiringly: 諄諄善誘 teach and guide untiringly; (2) adj., cautious, sincere.

諭 60A.00–8

yuh.

[Usu. printed. 諭]

N. (1) A surname. (2) A decree: 上諭, 聖諭 imperial decree. (3) (Court.) your letter: 來諭, 手諭, 賜諭 your esteemed "instructions," i. e., letter.

V. i. To explain (by superior): 諭知 explain and inform; 面諭 give order personally (also wr. 喻).

諭 旨 *yuhjyy*, n., imperial decree, order.

諍 60A.00–9

jeng (also *jehng*).

V. i. (1) To give frank, straightforward advice, to admonish: 諫諍 to admonish ruler; 諍言 friendly admonition; 諍友 friend who will give frank advice. (2) U. f. 爭 90.00, dispute: 諍訟 lawsuit.

謝 60A.00–9

shieh.

N. A surname.

V. i. & t. (1) To thank, offer thanks: 感謝 to thank s. o.; 拜謝 to thank profoundly ("bow thanks"); 鳴謝, 致謝, 道謝 to express one's thanks; 領謝 to accept with thanks; 答謝 to return thanks (by visit or gift) or thank by letter; 謝謝你 thank you; 謝天謝地 thank heaven! (an exclamation). (2) To decline (invitation, etc.): 辭謝 to decline politely (offer); 謝卻 to politely refuse (gift); 謝絕應酬 decline all social parties; to resign for some reason; 謝老, 謝病 *-laau, -bihng* ↓. (3) To pay a call of thanks for certain purposes: 謝步, 謝親, 謝客, 謝孝 *-buh, -chin, -keh, -shiauh* ↓; 謝別 to say good-bye; 謝罪 *-tzueih*, 謝恩 *-en* ↓. (4) To wither, decline: 花謝 flower wilts; 凋謝 wilt and wither; 新陳代謝 metabolism; 謝世 *-shyh* ↓.

謝 表 *shieh-biaau*, n., letter of thanks to emperor for some appointment or other favor.

謝 病 *shieh-bihng*, v. i., to decline office on account of age.

謝 步 *shieh-buh*, v. i., to make return call to guests who attended weddings, funerals.

謝 忱 *shieh-cherng*, n., gratitude.

謝 親 *shieh-chin*, v. i., (of bridegroom) to visit and thank bride's family after wedding.

謝 恩 *shieh-en*, v. i., to thank s. o., esp. emperor or high official, for favor.

謝 候 *shieh'hou*, v. i., to express thanks.

謝 章 *shieh-jang*, n., see *-biaau* ↑.

謝 客 *shieh-keh*, v. i., (1) to visit and express thanks to friends for their presence at some party; (2) not at home for visitors.

謝 老 *shieh-laau*, v. i., to resign from office on account of age.

謝 禮 *shiehlii*, n., a gift of thanks.

謝 幕 *shieh-muh*, v. i., performers appear on stage to thank audience for curtain calls.

謝 神 *shieh-shern*, n. & v. i., a festival with offerings to god (eaten by offerers) in thanksgiving; a prayer of thanks for answering prayer (oft. to redeem a pledge).

謝 孝 *shieh-shiauh*, v.i., to visit and thank friends present at funeral.

謝 謝 *shiehshieh*, v. i., to thank: 謝謝你, 謝謝他 thank you, him.

謝 信 *shiehshihn*, n., an acknowledgement of thanks by letter; "thank you" letters.

謝 世 *shieh-shyh*, v. i., to pass away.

謝帖 *shiehtiee*, n., a card of thanks.
謝罪 *shiehtzueih*, v. i., to apologize.
謝儀 *shieh-yir*, n., a gift expressing gratitude.

§ 60A.01 (言/小)

諫 60A.01-1

jiahn.

V.t. (Of inferior in relation to superior or between equals) urge to do or not to do, plead with, entreat, remonstrate: 勸諫 persuade or dissuade; 直言勸諫 use blunt words to remonstrate; 苦諫 make earnest remonstrances; 忠諫 loyally entreat; 諫諍 make earnest appeal to, remonstrate and entreat; 諫官 an official censor at court; 諫言 earnest plea to ruler.

誄 60A.01-1

leei.

N. (1) Funeral prayer or eulogy of the dead. (2) A posthumous title.

誅 60A.01-1

ju.

V. t. (1) To kill as punishment for crime: 誅戮 *-luh*↓; 伏誅 was executed; 天誅地滅 (a curse) may (person) be destroyed by the gods. (2) To invade or fight (country, regime) for alleged transgressions, to "punish" by war. (3) To scourge with words: 誅心, 誅意 *-shin, -yih*↓. (4) (LL) to cut (grass): 誅茅.

誅求 *juchiour*, v.i., as in 誅求無厭 (*yan*) phr., to make incessant, exorbitant demands.
誅除 *ju-chur*, v. t., to eradicate (evils, bandits, etc.).
誅戮 *juluh*, v. t., to execute or kill (prisoners), usu. *en masse.*
誅論 *ju-luhn*, v. t., (LL) sentence to death.
誅滅 *jumieh*, v. t., utterly destroy (whole groups, families) by death penalty.
誅心 *ju-shin*, phr., 誅心之論 cutting criticism of personal motives rather than outward acts.
誅意 *ju-yih*, phr., see *-shin*↑: 赦事誅意 (AC) excuse the act, but not the motive.

謀 60A.01-2

mour.

N. Plan, strategy: 計謀 plan; 謀策 *-tseh*, 謀略 *-lyueh*↓; 陰謀 conspiracy; 足智多謀 phr., resourceful, masterly in planning and execution, see V.i & t.↓.

V.i. & t. To plan (s.t.), plan to: 謀事 make plans for future, also look for job; 謀事在人, 成事在天 phr., man proposes, God disposes; 謀反, 謀叛, 圖謀不軌 plan revolt; 謀財害命 murder for money; 謀殺, 謀害 *-sha, -haih*↓; 謀面 try to arrange for personal meeting with or introduction to (person).

謀害 *mourhaih*, v.t., plan to kill (person).
謀略 *mourlyueh*, n., plan, strategy.
謀慮 *mourlyuh*, v.i., plan and contrive.
謀殺 *moursha*, v.t., try to kill.
謀生 *mour-sheng*, v.i., make a living.
謀策 *mourtseh*, n., see *-lyueh*↑.

諜 60A.01-2

dier.

N. (1) Espionage: 間諜 spy. (2) Var. of 牒 91S.01.

V. i. (1) Spy on. (2) Var. of 喋 40A.01.

諜報 *dierbauh*, n., military intelligence, espionage report.

譟 60A.01-4

tzauh.

V. i. (Of a crowd) shout noisily: 魏人譟而返 (AC) the soldiers of Weih shouted and went away; 鼓譟 raise a hue and cry; 譟擾 make trouble, cause disturbance (also wr. 噪).

課 60A.01-4

keh.

N. (1) Lesson, class work: 課業 *-yeh*↓; 功課 school work: 做功課 do class work; 課餘, 課外 extracurricular (activities). (2) Class in school: 上課, 下課 class begins, dismissed; 日課, 夜課 day, night class; 罷課 school strike. (3) Tax: 國課, 鹽課 national, salt tax. (4) A session at divination: 卜課, 占課. (5) A sub-office or bureau: 事務課 business office or bureau.

V. t. (1) To levy tax: 課稅; 課以重稅 levy heavy tax. (2) To supervise: 課讀 to supervise pupil's studies.

課本(兒) *kehbeen(-bee'l)*, n., textbook.
課表 *kehbiaau*, n., (=功課表) class schedule.
課程 *kehcherng*, n., schedule of study.
課卷 *kehjyuahn*, n., examination papers.
課馬 *kehmaa*, n., (MC) mare, see

驟 51B.01.

課堂 *kehtarng*, n., classroom.

課題 *kehtir*, n., subject of study or tests; task set by oneself or others.

課文(兒) *kehwern(-wer'l)*, n., text of school book.

課業 *kehyeh*, n., class schedule or work.

諒 60A.01-6

liahng.

V.i. I think, I believe, conjecture: 諒必有故不來 I believe he must be detained by s.t.; 諒他不敢 believe he does not dare; 諒不會來 believe he will not come.

V.t. Forgive: 原諒, 曲諒, 宥諒, 見諒, 鑒諒 all court. phrr. asking for forgiveness; 請你原諒 please forgive me; 體諒 to understand and forgive; 諒解 *-jiee*↓.

Adj. (1) (AC) stubborn: 君子貞而不諒 a gentheman is firm, but not stubborn. (2) (AC) sincere: 友直友諒 make friends with those who are straightforward and those who are sincere.

諒陰 *liarng-an*, v.i. & n., (AC) imperial mourning; mourning shed (also wr. 諒闇).

諒解 *liahngjiee*, v.t., to be reconciled: 諒解我的苦衷 understand why I had to do it; 彼此諒解 reconciled with each other.

§ 60A.02 (言/⺊)

諑 60A.02-3

juor.

N. Gossip, slander: 謠ᴬ諑 60A.21.

讓 60A.02-6

rahng.

V. t. (1) To blame, rebuke, scold: 責讓 reproach, chide, upbraid, censure. (2) Yield to, give in to: 讓位 *-weih*↓; 遜讓 give way to (s.o.) out of respect for him; 哥哥要讓弟弟一些 an elder brother should give in a little to his younger brother; 讓步 *-buh*↓; 相讓 yield (give way) to. (3) Usher in, welcome: 讓他上坐 seat him in the seat of honor; 把他讓進門來 (please) usher him in. (4) Make a polite gesture: 讓讓就是, 不來也算了 we have invited him, but if he doesn't come, why bother? 讓讓也就是了, 不必眞磕頭 a polite gesture will do, don't kowtow; 讓烟, 讓茶, 讓酒 offer s.o. cigarettes, tea, wine. (5) Give (s.o.) an advantage over oneself: 下棋讓他一步 give him a handicap when you play chess with him; 打拳讓他一手兒 don't punch him too hard (pull your punches). (6) Cede, transfer: 割讓 cede (territory) to another country; 轉讓 transfer the ownership of; 出讓 offer to sell; 讓渡 *-duh*↓; 讓與 *-yuu*↓. (7) Reduce, cut, lower (prices): 讓價 *-jiah*↓; 讓分量 *-fehn'liang*↓; 讓五元, 實收九十 give the buyer a five-dollar discount and charge him 90 dollars. (8) Dodge, duck, avoid: 一閃身, 把這一刀讓過去 I dodged the slash of his knife by ducking. (9) Let, permit: 讓他走 allow him to go; 讓他去辦 let him do it. (10) To order: 他讓我到這裏來的 it's he who has asked me to come.

Prep. By: 讓他打破了 it has been broken by him; 讓老虎吃了 it has been devoured by a tiger.

讓步 *rahng-buh*, v. i., make concessions.

讓渡 *rahngduh*, v. t., transfer (property or other rights) to another person.

讓分量 *rahng-fehn'liang*, v. i., (of business) give the customer an extra measure of the article bought.

讓過(兒) *rahng-guoh('l)*, v. i., yield, give in: 兩人吵起來, 誰也不讓過兒 the two men started to quarrel and neither would give in to the other.

讓賬 *rahng-jahng*, v. i., pay a bill for another.

讓着 *rahng-je*, v. t., give (s.o.) the better of an argument.

讓價(兒) *rahng-jiah('l)*, v. i., reduce the sales price.

讓開 *rahng-kai*, v. i., make way for s.o.

讓梨 *rahng-lir*, v. i., show fraternal affection among brothers ("let one's elder brother have the bigger pear," allu. to the story of 孔融).

讓路 *rahng-luh*, v. i., step aside to let s.o. else pass.

讓賢 *rahng-shiarn*, v. i., give up one's position in favor of a better qualified person.

讓座 *rahng-tzuoh*, v. i., give up one's seat to a lady (elder person).

讓位 *rahng-weih*, v. i., (1) (of monarchs) abdicate throne in favor of s.o. else; (2) give up one's seat to another.

讓與 *rahng-yuu*, v. t., to cede (one's rights) to s.o. else.

詠 60A.02-6

yuung.

[Var. of 咏 40A.02]

§ 60A.10 (言/十)

計 60A.10-1

jih.

N. (1) A plan, device, strategem: 計策 *-tseh*, 計謀 *-mour*, 計略 *-lyueh* ↓; 妙計 a clever device or strategem; 錦囊妙計 a master stroke, stratagem up one's sleeve; 奸計 treachery; 詭計 trickery; 中計 fall into a trap; 計窮 at one's wit's end; 無計可施 at a loss as to what to do. (2) A surname.

V. t. (1) Calculate, reckon: 計算 *-suahn* ↓; 核計 examine the accounts carefully; 會 (*kuaih*) 計 accounting, an accountant; 會計師 an accountant; 審計 to audit, an auditor; 統計 statistics; 計程 *-cherng*, 計時 *-shyr* ↓; 合計 sum total; 共計 grand total. (2) To plan, to plot: 計畫 *-huah*[1], 計議 *-yih* ↓; 工於心計 be calculating, tricky, scheming; 計分 to score; 計分員 scorer.

計 程 *jihcherng*, adj., calculated according to mileage; 計程 (汽) 車 a taxi charging by meter; 計程表 taximeter.

計 畫 *jihhuah*[1] (*-'hua*), v. t., to plan, arrange, map out, sketch, devise: 計畫經濟 planned economy.

計 劃 *jihhuah*[2] (*-'hua*), v. t., ditto.

計 較 *jihjiauh* (*-'jiouh*), v. t., (1) to dispute; (2) discuss in minute detail, go over thoroughly; (3) plan (to do).

計 開 *jihkai*, adv., (preceding list) as follows.

計 量 *jihliarng*, v. t., to measure, to estimate.

計 略 *jihlyueh*, n., strategy.

計 謀 *jihmour*, n., a secret plot, a strategem.

計 時 *jih-shyr*, adj., (of labor) paid by the hour or the day: 計時工資 hourly or daily wages.

計 算 *jihsuahn*, v. t., compute, calculate: 計算一遍 make calculations, go over the accounts; 計算尺 a slide rule; 計算機 a calculating machine; 電子計算機 a computer.

計 策 *jihtseh*, n., a plan of action, a carefully worked-out scheme.

計 最 *jih-tzueih*, v. t. & n., (AC) (make) periodic ratings of official performance.

計 議 *jihyih*, v. t., consider, discuss, weigh carefully: 從長計議 need further consideration.

譁 60A.10-2

huar.

V.i. Create a tumult: 喧譁 (of crowd) vociferous, tumultuous; 譁衆取寵 phr., seek popularity by shocking statement.

譁 變 *huarbiahn*, v.i., refuse to obey orders: 軍士譁變 army mutiny.

譁 然 *huarrarn*, adj., rising up in an uproar of protest.

諱 60A.10-2

hueih.

N. Personal name of respected person (father, emperor): 先考諱叔平 my deceased father, personal name *Shuhpirng*; 犯諱 to write or use word contained in respected name (esp. of emperor), thus, to violate a taboo, (such words are carefully avoided, or if unavoidable, written with a missing stroke or with substitute character).

V. t. To regard as taboo, to conceal: 避諱, 忌諱 to regard as taboo (see N. ↑); 諱疾忌醫 hesitate to see a doctor, though ill, conceal illness rather than tell the doctor; 諱莫如深 carefully conceal or avoid mentioning (scandal); 諱言 to cover up; 有所隱諱 there are things concealed and unspoken of.

訐 60A.10-3

jier.

V. t. Speak ill of, flay, attack: 攻訐 defame, malign (person).

訐 直 *jierjyr*, v. t., rebuke (s.o.) in his face.

訐 揚 *jieryarng*, v. t., expose the weaknesses or failings of (s.o.).

評 60A.10-3

pirng.

N. & v.t. (1) Criticise, -ism, evaluate, -tion, comment, usu. 批評, 公評 open discussion; 評點, 評註 edition with comments; 書評 book review; 文評 literary criticism; 影評, 戲評 review on movie, play; 短評, 小評 brief comment; 定評 agreed, accepted opinion; 的評 just criticism; 評論, 評閱 *-luhn*, *-yueh*, etc. ↓. (2) To judge: 評定高下 judge the performance; 評定分數 give marks to papers, performance; 評劇 dramatic criticism; a school of drama in Chin. northern provinces.

評 定 *pirngdihng*, v.t., see N. & V.t. 2 ↑.

評 斷 *pirngduahn*, n. & v.t., to judge; 評斷員 judge (of contests).

評 話 *pirnghuah*, n., storyteller's copy of Suhng Dyn., usu. wr. 平話.

評 價 *pirng-jiah*, n. & v. t., evaluation (articles, writings, philosophy); estimate.

評 傳 *pirng-juahn*, n., critical biography.

評 量 *pirngliarng*, v. t., weigh, evaluate.

評 論 *pirngluhn*, n. & v. t., discuss;

評論是非得失 discuss the rights and wrongs; 時事評論 comment on current events; 評論家 critic.

評脈 *pirngmoh*, v. i., (Chin. med.) feel the pulse.

評判 *pirngpahn*, n. & v.t., judgement, to judge contest: 評判員 *--yuarn*, n., judge of contests.

評書 *pirngshu*, v. i., (MC) storytelling at teahouses, ＝說[Δ]書 60A.70.

評議 *pirngyih*, n. & v.t., discuss (-ion), esp. on merits of case; 評議會 *--hueih*, n., advisory council; 評議員 *--yuarn*, n., member of advisory council.

評閱 *pirngyueh*, v. t., grade (examination papers); edit (books) with comments.

評語 *pirngyuu*, n., critical comment, remarks.

譚 60A.10-3

tarn.

N. A surname, also used as var. of 談 60A.81.

譯 60A.10-4

yih.

V. t. & n. To translate, -tion: 譯出 translate (a language); 譯成, 譯入 translate into (another language); 音譯 translate by sound; 直譯 literal translation, opp. 意譯 a translation giving equivalent in meaning without being literal; 節譯 abridged translation; 轉譯 retranslation; 即譯 instantaneous translation.

譯本 *yih-been*, n., translated version, a translation.

譯電 *yih-diahn*, v. t., translate telegraphic code into regular characters.

譯者 *yihjee*, n., translator.

譯名 *yih-mirng*, n., foreign words translated into another language.

譯述 *yihshuh*, v. t., to translate orally.

譯文 *yih-wern*, n., translated text.

譯音 *yih-yin*, n., translation by approximately similar sounds (as 羅馬 *Luormaa* for Rome).

誶 60A.10-6

sueih.

V. i. & t. To scold, to berate; (AC) to counsel against.

諢 60A.10-6

huhn.

N. & adj. Jokes, joking: 打諢 to make fun, to joke, indulge in raillery.

諢名 *huhnmirng*, n., nickname.

諢詞 *huhntsyr*, n., (Suhng Dyn.) a form of light entertainment by storytelling, also 諢詞小說 storyteller's copy or chapbook.

詳 60A.10-8

shiarng.

V.i. (1) (LL) tell, explain, know in detail: 不詳, 未詳 do not know the details or is not indicated; 內詳 (written on envelope) for contents please see inside, 名內詳 sender's name—see inside; 另詳 is explained separately elsewhere. (2) To write or report to an official superior: 詳了上司才定 must be decided after the matter has been reported to superior; 詳咨 to communicate and ask for opinion; 詳請 respectfully request; 勘詳 to check over carefully, officially go over. (3) To interpret dreams: 詳夢.

Adj. & adv. (1) In detail, detailed: 詳細 *-shih*↓; 詳密, 詳盡 *-mih*, *-jihn*↓; 詳說, 詳述, 詳陳 tell, narrate in full detail; 詳問 question minutely; 詳究 carefully examine. (2) Calm, poised in 安[Δ]詳 62.93.

詳情 *shiarng-chirng*, n., detailed or exact or true condition.

詳盡 *shiarngjihn*, adj., with complete detail, complete (exposition).

詳略 *shiarng-lyueh*, n., degree of completeness.

詳密 *shiarngmih*, adj., thorough, detailed.

詳明 *shiarngmirng*, (1) adj., clear and explicit (instructions, explanation); (2) v.t., to report to superior.

詳細 *shiarngshih*, adj. & adv., careful, -ly, complete, -ly; in good and clear detail: 詳細研究, 詳細解釋 examine, explain, carefully.

詳文 *shiarngwern*, n., report to official superior.

許 60A.10-9

shyuu.

N. (1) (LL) place: 不知何許人 do not know what place (he) comes from; 吾將惡許 (＝何處) 用之 (AC) where can I use him? (2) A surname.

V.i. & t. (1) To allow, to give consent: 不許, 弗許 do not permit: 不許他再來 I forbid him to come again; 你許不許 will you permit it or not? 許可, 許諾 *-kee*, *-nuoh*↓; 默許 give silent consent. (2) To pledge s.t., to promise: 許嫁, 許聘, 許字 pledge daughter in marriage, see *-jiah*, *-pihng*, *-tzyh*↓; 許了人家 already engaged to s.o.; 心許 (of girl) give her heart to s.o.; 許下一個願 give a pledge before God; 許下一頓飯 I promised a dinner (last month). (3) To dedicate oneself: 許身報國, 以身許國 dedicate oneself to country's cause. (4) To promise to do, to aim at: 期許 aim at a goal; 期許學成回國 expect s.o. to finish his studies and come home; 自許 make a promise to oneself to become somebody. (5) Give praise: 讚許, 嘉許 (from a superior) to praise, show appreciation.

Adj. & adv. (1) A little, more: 三十許 (LL) over thirty (years); 少許, 些許 a little, a few (drops, etc.); 幾許 how many, how much; 埋沒幾許好漢 how many worthy men have passed unnoticed. (2) So, very: 許多 very many; 許久 very long time; 許大 so big; 如許大桃 such big peaches. (2) Perhaps (from "it is allowed that"): 也許, 或許 perhaps; 他許 (or 也許) 不來了 perhaps he isn't coming.

許婚 *shyu-hun*, v.i., pledge daughter's hand in marriage.
許嫁 *shyuu-jiah*, v.i., ditto.
許可 *shyurkee*, (1) v.i. & t., to consent, approve, permit; (2) n., permission; 許可證 license.
許諾 *shyuunuoh*, n., a promise.
許配 *shyuu-peih*, v.i., see *-hun*↑.
許聘 *shyuu-pihng*, v.i., see *-hun*↑.
許字 *shyuu-tzyh*, v.i., see *-hun*↑.
許願 *shyuu-yuahn*, v.i., give a pledge before God.

§ 60A.11 (言/土)

讙 60A.11-2

huan.

V.i. To cheer: 萬衆讙呼 the crowd cheered vociferously.

謹 60A.11-2

jiin.

Adj. & adv. (1) Careful(ly) conscientious(ly): 謹愼 *-shehn*↓; 謹防 to guard against (thief, pickpocket, fire, accident); 謹記 keep in mind, commit to memory; 謹嚴 *-yarn*↓; 嚴謹 meticulously careful; 謹戒 *-jieh*↓; 謹守 carefully keep (promises), obey (rules, injunctions). (2) Respectful(ly): 敬謹 reverent(ly); 恭謹 polite(ly): 謹領 receipt is hereby acknowledged of . . .; 謹具 (of letter, invitation, receipt) signed by, (of gift) presented by; 謹稟, 謹啟, 謹呈 (of letters to parents, elders, superiors) "yours respectfully" used as complimentary close; 謹書 "respectfully hand written by"; 謹祈 I beg respectfully.

謹戒 *jiinjieh*, v.t., guard against with the utmost care.
謹愼 *jiinshehn*, adj., careful, cautious, discreet.
謹嚴 *jiinyarn*, adj., (1) meticulous, painstaking, conscientious; (2) strict, cogent (reasoning).

註 60A.11-6

juh.

[Var. of 注 63A.11]

N. Exegesis: (var. 注) 註解, 註疏 *-jiee*, *-shu*↓; 註兒 the exegetical part, dist. main text; 加註 add notes and comments; 附註 footnote, reference note.

V.t. (1) To give exegesis, see N.↑. (2) To register, clarify: 註冊, 註銷, 註明 *-tseh*, *-shiau*, *-mirng*↓.

註定 *juhdihng*, v.t., destine(d): 生前註定 predestined in previous incarnation; 命裏註定 destined by fate (also wr. 注).
註解 *juhjiee*, explanation and pronunciation of text (also 注).
註明 *juhmirng*, v.i., to add note of explanation.
註銷 *juhshiau*, v.i., to register loss (of check), to invalidate.
註疏 *juhshu*, n., exegesis and commentary (疏 commentary on earlier commentary, also 注).
註失 *juhshy*, v.i., to register loss (of check, etc.).
註冊 *juhtseh*, v.t., to register (for enrollment, etc.): 註冊商標 registered trademark.

詮 60A.11-8

chyuarn.

N. True meaning: 眞詮 ditto; 詮釋 *-shyh*↓.

V.t. To comment on text, to explain: 詮釋 *-shyh*↓; 詮解, 詮註 give exegesis of text.

詮證 *chyuarnjehng*, v.t., to explain correct meaning of text point by point.
詮釋 *chyuarnshyh*, v.t., to give exegesis or explanation of text.
詮次 *chyuarntshy*, v.t., arrange text in proper order.

誰 60A.11-9

shueir.

Pron. (1) Who: 誰說 who says? 誰謂 (LL) who says? 誰知道, 誰料到 who would have thought, also to one's surprise: 誰知道一個人也不來 to one's surprise, not a single person showed up; 誰想 who would have thought; 誰指望, 誰承望 who (i.e., no one) expects. (2) Anyone: 誰也會 anyone can do it; 誰也不敢 no one dares. (3) What: 姓甚名誰 what is his name?

誰差 *shueircha*, v.i., (AC) 誰差天下, 求索賢人 to scour the country for able and good men, inquire and seek (for able men).
誰分 *shueirfehn*, phr., (MC) who would have thought (＝誰料).
誰何 *shueirher*, pron., who: 誰何人 what person, any person; 不管誰何人 no matter who.
誰家 *shueirjia*, pron., who: 問是誰家 ask "who is it?"
誰某 *shueirmoou*, pron., some (unspecified) person.
誰人 *shueirrern*, pron., who, what person.

誑 60A.11-9

kuarng.

V.i. & t. To lie, deceive: 你別誑我 don't try to deceive me.

誑騙 *kuarngpiahn*, v.t., to cheat.
誑言 *kuarngyarn*, n., a lie, wild talk.
誑語 *kuarngyuu*, n., ditto.

§ 60A.21 (言/L)

諶 60A.21-2

chern.

N. A surname.

Adj. (AC) sincere, honest.

訕 60A.21-2

shahn.

V.t. (1) To slander, revile, vilify. (2) To ridicule: 訕笑 *-shiauh*↓.

Adj. Embarrassed: 訕訕的 feeling or looking embarrassed; 搭訕的 embarrassed; 訕臉 *-liaan*↓.

訕謗 *shahnbahng*, v.i. & t., to vilify, defame, spread vicious gossip.
訕不搭的 *shahnbuhda'de*, adj. & adv., in embarrassed manner.
訕臉 *shahnliaan*, adv., putting on a brave look, rather shamelessly (also 訕著臉).
訕笑 *shahnshiauh*, v.t., to ridicule (person) (also 姍笑 pr. *shan-*).

詘 60A.21-2

chyu (**chuh*).

(1) Var. of 屈 52A.21. (2) (**chuh*) Var. of 黜 41S.21.

謔 60A.21-2

nyueh.

V.t. 諧謔, 戲謔, 謔浪 to ridicule, mock; 謔弄 play tricks on (s.o.), make fun of.

詎 60A.21-5

jyuh.

Adv. (LL) how: 詎料 unexpectedly ("how could it be expected?"); 詎知 who would have thought? 詎能 how could it have been possible?

誆 60A.21-5

kuang.

V.t. To cheat, lie: 誆人 to cheat people by lie or threat (interch. 誑↑).

誆哄 *kuanghuung*, v.t., to coax (person, child).
誆騙 *kuangpiahn*, v.t., to cheat.
誆言 *kuangyarn*, n., a lie, false words (also 誆話).

謳 60A.21-5

ou.
[Abbr. 讴]

V.i. (AC) to sing.

謳歌 *ouge*, v.i., to sing, sing in praise.
謳鴉 *ouya*, v.i., make swishing, creaking sound (also wr. 嘔鴉, 嘔啞).

謟 60A.21-9

tau.
[Dist. 諂↓]

Adj. (AC) Uncertain: 天道不謟 heaven's way is not uncertain.

諂 60A.21-9

chaan.

V.t. To flatter.

諂媚 *chaanmeih*, v.t., to flatter (s.o.).

亅	小	⺊	十	土	𠂇	卄	⺃⺊	丨	一	丁	フ	口	㐅	冈	冂	厂	尸	亠	广	宀	丶	乚	弋	心	八	人	乂	乛	乛	丿丿	⺈	く
00	01	02	10	11	12	20	21	22	30	31	32	40	41	42	50	51	52	60	61	62	63	70	71	72	80	81	82	83	90	91	92	93

諂笑 *chaanshiauh*, v.i., to give an ingratiating smile.
諂諛 *chaanyur*, v.t., to flatter.

謠 60A.21-9

yaur.

N. (1) Rumor, gossip: 謠言, 謠傳 *-yarn*, *-chuarn*↓; 造謠 create rumors; 闢謠 deny rumors. (2) A folk song: 民謠, 童謠 ditto, oft. containing political satire.

謠傳 *yaurchuarn*, n., rumor, hearsay.
謠諑 *yaurjuor*, n., smear, smearing campaign; many rumors.
謠俗 *yaursur*, n., popular custom.
謠言 *yauryarn*, n., (1) rumor; (2) (-'*yan*) baseless talk.

§60A.22 (言/丨)

訃 60A.22-2

fuh.

N. & v.i. (Give) obituary notice.

訃聞 *fuhwern*, n., obituary notice, sometimes a chance for publicizing ranks and honors of all relatives, also 訃告 *-gauh*.

訓 60A.22-2

shyuhn.

N. (1) Moral teachings: 教訓 v.t., to teach, to scold; n., teaching, training; 古訓 anc. teachings; 家訓 family teachings, family training, oft. name of book containing teachings for one's own family. (2) Exegesis, explanation of meaning of words and sentences: 訓詁 *-guu*↓.

V.t. (1) To teach, to train, instruct: 教訓 to teach, to scold: 被他教訓了一番 received a scolding from him; 軍訓 military training; 受訓 undergo (military) training. (2) (LL, a word) means: 亟訓急 character 亟 means 急 (hurriedly).

訓斥 *shyuhnchyh*[1], v.t., to reprimand, rebuke sharply (an inferior).
訓飭 *shyuhnchyh*[2], v.t., give sharp advice to (inferiors).
訓導 *shyuhndauh*, (1) v.t., to monitor (children, schoolchildren), to guide and assist (new development); (2) n., student counsellor.
訓廸 *shyuhndir*, v.t., to teach (the young), open student's mind.
訓詁 *shyuhnguu*, n., one branch of study of classics, concerned with anc. meanings of words.
訓話 *shyuhnhuah*, (1) v.i., sermonize; (2) n., a homily, moral sermon (be good, obey the law, be punctual, etc.).
訓誨 *shyuhnhueih*, v.t. & n., (to give) advice, chiefly moral.
訓誡 *shyuhnjieh*, v.t. & n., warn (inferior) against evil.
訓練 *shyuhnliahn*, v.t. & n., to train (special skill, body, etc.); training.
訓令 *shyuhnlihng*, v.t. & n., a mil. or govenmental order to subordinates; to issue such order.
訓蒙 *shyuhn-merng*, phr., to teach very young children (as in kindergarten).
訓勉 *shyuhnmiaan*, v.t. & n., to give a homily; to urge to be good, brave, honest, etc.
訓名 *shyuhn-mirng*, n., formerly, name given by parents.
訓示 *shyuhnshyh*, v.t. & n., to instruct (subordinate); instructions.
訓辭 *shyuhntsyr*, n., a public talk consisting of homilies (strive for ever, love your country, etc.).
訓誘 *shyuhnyouh*, v.t., to guide by education, to instruct (the youth).
訓育 *shyuhnyuh*, n., part of school education, concerned with development of character.

誹 60A.22-2

feei.

N. & v.t. Slander: 怨誹 people's grievances, baseless or not.

誹謗 *feeibahng*, n. & v.t., slander.

諦 60A.22-6

dih.

N. True meaning, esp. religious: 眞諦, 妙諦 true meaning (of Budd., etc.).

Adv. Carefully, attentively: 諦聽, 諦視 listen, look, carefully.

謙 60A.22-8

chian.

[Usu. printed 謙]

Adj. Modest, humble: 謙虛 *-shyu*↓; 過謙 too modest; 自謙 modest about oneself.

謙謙 *chianchian*, adj., as in (LL) 謙謙君子 a modest, cautious gentleman.
謙沖 *chianchung*, adj., see *-shyu*↓.
謙恭 *chian'gung*, adj., polite and modest.
謙和 *chianher*, adj., modest and gentle.
謙克 *chiankeh*, adj., (LL) self-restrained.
謙讓 *chianrahng*, adj., modest, unobtrusive, self-effacing.
謙虛 *chianshyu*, adj., modest, courteous.

謙遜 *chianshyuhn*, adj., humble, modest.
謙辭 *chiantsyr*, (1) v.i., to express in court. terms; (2) v.t., to decline politely.
謙退 *chiantueih*, adj., retiring, unobtrusive.

訴 60A.22-9

suh.

V.t. (1) To tell, narrate, esp. to complain of s.t.: 告訴 tell; 我告訴你 I tell you; 訴說 *-shuo*↓; 訴衷情 to express heart feelings; 訴苦, 訴冤 *-kuu*, *-yuan*↓; 訴委屈 complain of being wronged. (2) To go to court: 訴訟, 訴狀 *-suhng*, *-juahng*↓; 訴之變更 alteration of action; 訴之追加 subjoining of action; 訴之撤回 withdrawal of an action.

訴告 *suhgauh*, v.i. & t., to lodge complaint.
訴狀 *suhjuahng*, n., a plaint filed at court.
訴苦 *suh-kuu*, v.i., to complain.
訴說 *suhshuo*, v.t., to narrate (some event), state (wish, feelings).
訴訟 *suhsuhng*, n., a lawsuit.
訴願 *suh-yuahn*, v.i. & n., (to lodge) an administrative complaint.
訴冤 *suh-yuan*, v.i., to complain of injustice.

詐 60A.22-9

jah (*jaa).

V.t. (1) To obtain by fraud, deceit, cheating, to swindle: 詐騙 *-piahn*↓; 欺詐 to deceive, also adj., deceitful; 詐欺破產罪 crime of frandulent bankruptcy; 敲詐 to blackmail; 詐取 obtain by fraud. (2)(*jaa) To trick into: 拿話來詐我 try to trick me with words into betraying secrets. (3) To pretend, feint (death, illness, defeat): 詐爲不知 pretend not to know; 詐窮 feign to be poor.

詐騙 *jahpiahn*, v.i. & t. & n., deceive, commit fraud.
詐屍 *jah-shy*, phr., feigned corpse which can suddenly stand up to frighten people.
詐僞 *jahweei*, adj., deceitful, dishonest (conduct).
詐語 *jah-yuu*, n., a fraudulent story.

§ 60A.30 (言/一)

訌 60A.30-3

hurng.

N. 內訌 internal strife.

証 60A.30-3

jehng.
[See var. 證 60A.30↓]

誣 60A.30-3

wur (sp. pr. *wu*).

V.t. (1) To lie, to deceive with intent to injure: 誣罔, 誣衊 *-waang*, *-mieh*↓; 誣害, 誣賴 *-haih*, *-laih*↓. (2) To vilify, defame, make false accusation, commit libel against: 誣告 *-gauh*↓; 誣良爲盜 accuse an innocent person of theft.

誣告 *wurgauh*, v.t., to accuse (person) falsely.
誣害 *wurhaih*, v.t., to make false charges against (person).
誣賴 *wurlaih*, v.t., ditto.
誣衊 *wurmieh*, v.t., to besmear, make unjustified defamation of character.
誣染 *wurraan*, v.t., to involve s.o. in criminal proceedings.
誣陷 *wurshiahn*, v.t., to injure by false accusation.
誣罔 *wurwaang*, v.t., ditto.

證 60A.30-3

jehng.
[Common var. 証]

N. (1) Evidence, proof: 憑證 proof (of theft, indebtedness, etc.); 物證 material evidence, proof(s); 明證 clear proof or evidence. (2) Witness: 干證, 見證, 人證 witness (of crime, etc.). (3) A certificate: 出入證 permit for admission; 身分證 I.D. card, card of identity.

V.t. To prove, verify: 考證 scholarly research (to verify authorship, age, different editions, etc.); 證明 *-mirng*↓.

證券 *jehngchyuahn*, n., stocks and bonds, stock certificate, securities: 證券交易所 stock exchange; 有價證券 negotiable instrument.
證果 *jehngguoo*, n., (Budd.) consummation of religious enlightenment or cultivation.
證候 *jehnghouh*, n., disease symptoms (u. f., 症候).
證件 *jehngjiahn*[1], n., credentials, certificates.
證見 *jehngjiahn*[2], n., evidence.
證據 *jehngjyuh*, n., proof(s), evidence, (receipt, etc.): 證據調查 investigation of evidence.
證明 *jehngmirng*, v.t., to prove, establish truth of.
證人 *jehngrern*, n., personal wit-

ness; 證人臺 witness box.
證書 *jehngshu*, n., certificate, diploma, credentials.
證實 *jehngshyr*, v.t., to verify.
證物 *jehngwuh*, n., exhibits presented at court as evidence.
證言 *jehngyarn*. n., testimony of witness.

詛 60A.30-4

tzuu.

V.i. & t. (1) To curse: 詛咒 *-jouh*↓; 詛祝 *-juh*↓. (2) Swear, make a vow, take an oath: 詛盟 *-merng*↓.

詛咒 *tzuujouh*, v.t., to curse and swear.
詛祝 *tzuujuh*, n., (1) (AC) an anc. official in charge of administering oaths; (2) (AC) to curse and swear.
詛盟 *tzuu-merng*, n., agreement sealed by an oath.

誼 60A.30-6

shyuan.

[Var. of 諼 (AC) to forget; var. of 喧 noisy]

誼 60A.30-6

yih (also *yir*).

N. (1) Duties, obligations and feelings arising out of certain relations (friends, relatives, etc.): 情誼 ditto; 友誼, 交誼 friendship; 世誼 longstanding friendly relationships of two families; 親誼, 戚誼 of father's, mother's relatives; 鄉誼 of people of the same town; 誼同手足 feeling like owns brother; 雅誼, 高誼, 盛誼 (court.) your great kindness. (2) (AC) u.f. 義 justice, 80.71 and 議 discussion, 60A.71.

謐 60A.30-6

mih.

Adj. Quiet, esp. 安謐 quiet and peaceful.

謚 60A.30-8

shyh.

[Var. of 諡]

N. Posthumous title (of emperor, distinguished minister): 謚法 code by which such titles are conferred.

§ 60A.40 (言/口)

詁 60A.40-1

guu.

N. & v.t. Exegesis of meaning of words, esp. anc. meanings, usu. 訓詁; explain, to interpret in such a way.

誥 60A.40-1

gauh.

N. A written admonition: 誥命 (AC) a royal edict.

V.t. (AC) (of superiors) to admonish, enjoin, issue orders.

詰 60A.40-1

jier.

N. The morrow: 詰旦, 詰朝 *-dahn*, *-jau*↓.

V.t. Inquire into, investigate, probe: 詰責 *-tzer*, 詰問 *-wehn*↓; 反詰 (give) counter-question; 盤詰 interrogate, cross-examine.

詰屈 *jierchyu*[1], adj., twisted, bent: 詰屈聱牙 (of writings) difficult to pronounce or comprehend.
詰詘 *jierchyu*[2], adj., ditto.
詰旦 *jierdahn*, n., (LL) the next morning.
詰朝 *jierjau*, n., ditto.
詰責 *jiertzer*, v.t., rebuke, reprimand, censure.
詰問 *jierwehn*, v.t., to question (a suspect), interrogate, ask for an explanation.

諾 60A.40-2

nuoh.

N. Approval: 畫諾 put "okay" on a document; 諾言 *-yarn*↓.

V.t. To promise: 諾言, 允諾, 許諾, 承諾 make a promise.

Adv. The particle "yes": 連聲諾諾 "Yes, sir! yes, sir!"

諾貝爾獎 *Nuobeiherl jiaang*, n., Nobel prizes (in literature, for peace, etc.).
諾言 *nuohyarn*, n., a verbal promise.

語 60A.40-3

yuu (**yuh*).

N. (1) A word, phrase: 語辭 word; 成語 a common or accepted phrase; 連語 a compound word (bisyllabic); 外來語 imported word or phrase. (2) A saying, proverb: 俗語 proverb, popular saying; 妙語 a clever line; 警語 a striking saying; 謎語 a riddle;

雙關語 a pun. (3) Language: 言語 language, words spoken; 口語 colloquial speech; 土語 local patois; 國語 national spoken language; 英語, 日語 English, Japanese. (4) Means of communication: 手語 language of hand signals; 目語 signal by wink or glance; 鳥語 bird's twitter.

V.i. To speak: 自言自語 talk to oneself; 不言不語 keep silent.

V.t. (*_yuh_) (LL) to tell (s.o.), to speak of (s.t.): 吾語汝 let me tell you; 語其友 tells his friend; 不可以語人 must not tell others; 語道 speak of and discuss the truth.

語病 _yuu-bihng_, n., mistake in use of words, a rhetorical error.

語冰 _yuu-bing_, phr., 夏蟲不可以語冰 (AC) do not speak of ice to insects that live only one summer.

語氣 _yuuchih_ (-'_chi_), n., tone of one's words.

語調(兒) _yuudiauh('l)_, n., sentence intonation.

語法 _yurfaa_, n., grammar (usu. 文法).

語彙 _yuuhueih_, n., vocabulary.

語助詞 _yuujuhtsyr_, n., a particle which serves only to relate words, an auxiliary.

語句 _yuujyuh_, n., sentence, line.

語錄 _yuuluh_, n., transcripts of master's sayings by disciples (Budd. or Suhng Confucianists), largely in vernacular style.

語聲兒 _yuu'sheng'l_, n., sound of voice.

語系 _yuu-shih_, n., linguistic family.

語勢 _yuushyh_, n., tone or force of one's words, apart from the words themselves.

語體文 _yurtiiwern_, n., vernacular style of writing (also called 白話文 _bairhuahwern_).

語次 _yuu-tsyh_, phr., while one was speaking.

語詞 _yuutsyr_, n., a word, as dist. 字 _tzyh_; a particle, see _-juh-tsyr_ ↑; language used by s.o. (coarse, etc.).

語族 _yuu-tzur_, n., linguistic family.

語言 _yuuyarn_, n., (1) language; (2) one's use of language (refined, vulgar, etc.); 語言學 philology, science of language, linguistics.

語意 _yuu-yih_, n., meaning suggested by the words; 語意學 semantics.

語音 _yuu-yin_, n., accent; pronunciation; voice; 語音學 phonetics.

語源學 _yuu-yuarn-shyuer_, n., etymology.

詔 60A.40–5

jauh.

N. An imperial decree: 詔書 _-shu_ ↓; 敕詔, 下詔, 降詔 issue decree.

V.i. To decree: 詔令 _-lihng_ ↓; 詔用 appoint by decree; 詔告 instruct by decree.

詔令 _jauhlihng_, v.t. & n., (to, an) order by imperial decree.

詔書 _jauhshu_, n., imperial decree.

諮 60A.40–9

tzy.

V.t. (Interch. 咨) consult, confer.

諮詢 _tzyshyurn_, v.t., seek official opinion, counsel.

諮議 _tzyyih_, (1) v.i., to counsel, advise; (2) n., a counsellor, an adviser to the government.

話 60A.40–9

huah.

N. (1) Speech, talk, saying: 白話 vernacular; 閒話 gossip; 談話 to talk, (make) conversation; 問話 a question; 會話 conversation; 説你壞話 said things against you; 別聽他的話 don't listen to him; 土話 local patois; 官話 mandarin language, also bureaucratic gibberish; 俗話 colloquial speech, also popular saying: 笑話 a joke; 瞎話 rubbish; 謊話 a lie; 廢話 nonsense, rubbish; 黑話 thieves' argot; 話中有刺 hidden barbs in his words; 話裏有話 s.t. hinted at, s.t. one means but never says; 話裏無話 a talk leading to other topics or to unintentional disclosure. (2) A statement, word, message: 這話怎麽講 how do you explain this statement? 這是什麽話 what kind of a statement is this? 那裏的話 no such thing, I never said it, also a formula for reply to "thank you"; 留話 leave word or message; 留個話兒 leave a word; 傳話, 傳個話 bring a message, speak to person for another. (3) A story, a discussion: 話分兩頭 to tell story from two angles; 不在話下 that is not under discussion for the present; 話説 the story says (oft. in beginning of story); 舊話重提 to go over the matter discussed before; 説來話長 it is a long story. (4) A supposition: 不然的話 if not; 要是他不肯的話 if he does not consent.

V.i. (LL & MC) to reminisce, narrate: 話別, 話別離 to say farewell or to talk of the time during absence; 話當初, 話當年, 話舊 talk of old times; 話天寶 talk about the years of 天寶 reign.

話靶 _huahbaa_, n., target, topic of gossip.

話把兒 _huahbah'l_, n., see _-bihng_ ↓.

話 詬 譫 詒 諸 詣 諧

話本 *huahbeen*, n., chapbook, storyteller's copy of stories told at teahouses, esp. in Shung Dyn.: 宋人話本.

話柄 *huahbihng*, n., target or material for gossip.

話碴兒 *huahchar'l*, n., meaning of what one has in mind or not quite says.

話劇 *huahjyuh*, n., a play in modern vernacular.

話癆 *huahlaur*, n., (sarcas.) a chatterbox.

話料兒 *huahliauh'l*, n., material for gossip.

話匣子 *huahshiartz*, n., (1) gramophone; 話匣子片兒 gramophone record (=唱片); (2) a chatterbox: 打開話匣子 start to chatter along.

話頭兒 *huahtour'l*, n., a thing to talk about: 沒什麽話頭兒 nothing to talk about.

話筒 *huahtuung*, n., microphone, telephone transmitter.

話音兒 *huahye'l*, n., tone of one's voice: 你聽他話音兒, 準是不願意去 from his tone of voice, you know he is reluctant to go.

詬 60A.40-9

gouh.

V.t. To scold, rail at.

詬病 *gouhbihng*, v.t., take to task, criticize severely: 人所詬病 this is what people generally disapprove of.

詬罵 *gouhmah*, v.t., to curse aloud, berate.

譫 60A.40-9

jan.

譫語 *janyuu*, n., words said in delirium.

詒 60A.40-9

yir.

V.t. (AC) to bequeath, send, see 貽 41C.40.

§ 60A.41 (言/図)

諸 60A.41-1

ju.

Fin. part. (AC) contraction of 之乎: 有諸 is it true? is there?

N. A surname.

Adj. (1) Plural of "the," similar to "these" but oft. meaning a class or group: 諸事如意 all goes as you wish; 諸如此類 like this kind of things, *et cetera*; 諸般武藝 the different kinds of acrobatic show or skill with spear, sword, etc; 諸同學 the schoolmates; 諸姑姊妹 the different aunts and sisters. (2) Used vocatively in address to a group: 諸公 sirs, gentlemen; 諸位, 諸君 *-weih, -jyun* ↓.

Prep. At, from, to, etc. (=於): 聞諸夫子 (AC) I heard from the Master; 求諸己 seek it within oneself (for failure), rely on oneself (for success); 加諸我也 put (blame) on me; 失諸正鵠 miss the target; 譬諸草木 may be compared to the plants.

諸多 *juduo*, adj. & adv., the different, the many: 諸多事情 the many different matters; 諸多不便 in many ways inconvenient.

諸葛 *Juger*, n., a surname; 諸葛菜 broccoli, a plant of the mustard family, *Brassica campestris*.

諸侯 *juhour*, n., the feudal princes of Jou Dyn., actually chiefs of different states.

諸柘 *jujeh*, n., (AC) sugar cane (also wr. 諸蔗, 藷蔗).

諸君 *ju jyun*, n., (used in public address) equiv. of "ladies and gentlemen," "sirs."

諸色 *ju-seh*, phr., the different kinds of people: 諸色人等.

諸生 *ju-sheng*, n., (1) the different students as a group; (2) formerly, the scholars of the first degree (秀才 *shiouhtsair*).

諸夏 *Jushiah*, n., (AC) the Chinese, as a body of different states and dist. from foreign tribes.

諸子 *jutzyy*, n., "the philosophers," referring to the philosophers or their works, outside the Confucianists (such as 老子, 莊子, 墨子, etc.); 諸子百家 the different philosophers and authors, esp. in time of the Warring Kingdoms.

諸位 *ju-weih*, n., see *-jyun* ↑.

詣 60A.41-2

yih.

N. Scholastic achievement: 造詣甚深 profound scholarship.

V.i. To pay visit to superior (person, place): 詣闕 visit the imperial court (闕=palace gate).

諧 60A.41-2

shier.

N. A surname.

V.i. To get along well: 事諧 negotiations come through; 不諧 fail to come through.

Adj. (1) Facetious, humorous: 詼^諧 60A.81; 諧戲, 諧謔 *-shih, -nyueh* ↓; 諧語 humorous remark; 諧笑 to laugh. (2) (Of sounds, music) harmonious: 諧和 ditto; 諧音, 諧聲 *-yin, -sheng* ↓; 諧偶 a harmonious couple.

諧比 *shier-bih*, n., (LL) close friends.

諧臣 *shier-chern*, n., a court clown.

諧趣 *shierchyuh*, n., fun, pleasantry.

諧附 *shierfuh*, v.t., (AC) to curry favor of (s.o.).

諧和 *shierher*, adj., friendly, cordial together.

諧價 *shier-jiah*, phr., negotiate on prices, haggle.

諧謔 *shiernyueh*, (1) v.i., to banter words about, to twit each other, to mock; (2) adj., satirical, joking for fun.

諧聲 *shiersheng*, n., one of the six principles of formation of characters, by having one part serve as " phonetic " and the other as " radical " (thus: 可 is " phonetic " in 河, 何, 柯)—the most prolific principle, see 六▵書 60.80.

諧戲 *shiershih*, (1) v.i., to indulge in mocking and light raillery; (2) n., tomfoolery.

諧星 *shier-shing*, n., a comedian star.

諧易 *shieryih*, (LL) simple and easy to get along with.

諧音 *shier-yin*, n., (mus.) harmonics.

諳 60A.41-6

an.

Adj. Familiar, knowing thoroughly: 諳熟 quite familiar (in recitation, recital, certain operation, etc.); 不諳 not familiar, not well learned.

Adv. Familiarly, thoroughly: 諳識 know (friend, foreign language) thoroughly; 諳誦 repeat fluently.

諳練 *anliahn*, adj., skillful, experienced (hand).

譇 60A.41-6

sheen.

V.i. (LL, chiefly in correspondence) to learn from your letter: 譇知, 譇悉.

譜 60A.41-8

puu.

N. (1) Table, chart, giving relations (oft. *-tz*, *'l*): 家譜 (record containing) family tree; 宗譜, 族譜 genealogy of clan. (2) Book, album, esp. music album or sheets: 食譜 book of recipes; 歌譜 song book; 琴譜 piano score, music notations for the *chin*; 樂譜 music score notations; 五線譜 music score sheet; 棋譜 book on chess, with illustrations of moves; 離譜 (兒) (fig.) departing from standard: 這件事做得眞離譜兒 this has been handled in most irregular way.

V.t. (1) To write melody for (song): 譜曲. (2) (AC) to put in proper relations (譜錄).

譜表 *pur-biaau*, n., musical notation.

譜號 *puu-hauh*, n., musical signs.

譜系 *puu-shih*, n., (chart of) clan relations.

譖 60A.41-9

tzehn.

V.t. Malign, calumniate, slander: 夫人譖公於齊侯 (AC) she maligned him before the marquis of Chir; 譖人 *-rern*↓.

譖人 *tzehnrern*, n., a slanderer.

譖言 *tzehnyarn*, n., calumny, slander, wilful misrepresentation of s.o.'s character.

§ 60A.42 (言/冈)

諵 60A.42-1

narn.

[Dist. 喃]

諵諵 *narnnarn*, adj., loquacious, talkative.

請 60A.42-1

chiing.

V.i. & t. (1) Used like Eng. " please " + vb. to express polite request: 請進 please come in; 請坐 please sit down; 請入席 please be seated at table; 請, 請 "please, please" (offering a drink); 請歇一會 please stop a moment for rest; 請告訴我 please tell me; 請問 may I ask; 請教 please to advise me. (2) To request: 請求 *-chiour*, 請託 *-tuo*↓; 申請 to make an application, request for permission; 請見, 請謁 request for an interview; 敬請指敎 humbly request your advice; 敬請光臨 request your company (at a reception, etc.); 懇請 earnestly beg; used as n. 不情之請 (court.) my bold request; 不允所請 request has been turned down; 請君入甕 (allu.) a hated judge known for torturing prisoners was to be tried himself, without knowing it. On being asked by another judge the best way of extracting confession, he suggested putting prisoner in jar heated by hot coals. When jar was ready, he was told, "Now, please step into the jar." (3) To invite: 邀請, 約請 invite s.o.; 請客

諧 諳 譇 譜 譖 諵 請

亅	小	⺊	十	土	ナ	廾	⺊	丨	一	丅	フ	口	㓁	冈	冂	厂	尸	亠	广	宀	丶	乚	弋	心	八	人	乂	乛	一	丿	𠂉	く
00	01	02	10	11	12	20	21	22	30	31	32	40	41	42	50	51	52	60	61	62	63	70	71	72	80	81	82	83	90	91	92	93

-*keh*↓; 請茶 invite to tea; 是請來的 come by invitation; 聘請 to invite to post; 聘請教授, 專家, 家庭教師 appoint professor, specialist, home tutor; 請醫生, 請大夫 ask a doctor; 敦請 (court.) invite; 請不到 was not able to secure services or company at dinner; 請不起 cannot afford to give a dinner. (4) In religious ceremony, to call upon the spirit to descend: 請財神 call upon the god of wealth; 把神主請出來 ceremoniously take ancestral tablet out for worship; 請香蠟 call for bringing the incense-sticks and candles; 請雨 to pray for rain.

請安 *chiing-an*, v.i., (1) to inquire after s.o.'s health, or to wish the best of health; (2) (in north China) to make a curtsy by bending one knee and lowering body (also called 打千).

請便 *chiing-biahn*, v.i., please make yourself at home, do as you please.

請求 *chiingchiour*, v.i. & t., to beg, request (another for help), also to demand (freeing of prisoners, etc.); 請求權 right of demanding.

請期 *chiingchir*, v.i., agreement between bride's and groom's families on date of wedding.

請柬 *chirng-jiaan*, n., invitation card.

請假 *chiing-jiah*, v.i., ask for leave.

請見 *chiing-jiahn*, v.i., request an interview.

請教 *chiing-jiauh*, v.i. & t., to ask for advice, ask s.o.'s opinion.

請客 *chiing-keh*, v.i., to give a dinner.

請兒 *chiing'l*, n., (coll.) dinner, party given by s.o.: 吃飯聽戲都是我的請兒 the dinner and theater party will all be on me.

請命 *chiing-mihng*, v.i., (1) to ask for instructions; (2) to beg for s.o.'s life.

請脈 *chiing-moh*, v.i., (court.) to ask a doctor (to examine pulse).

請閒 *chiing-shiarn*, v.i., (AC) ask s.o. for an interview at his convenience.

請示 *chiing-shyh*, v.i., beg for instructions.

請訓 *chiing-shyuhn*, v.i., (in Manchu Dyn.) to ask the emperor for instructions before departing on duty.

請帖 *chirng-tiee*, n., invitation card.

請託 *chiingtuo*, v.t., to request another's help: 請託人做一件事 ask s.o. to do s.t.

請罪 *chiing-tzueih*, v.i., (1) to confess guilt and ask for punishment; (2) to ask for lenient consideration.

請問 *chiingwehn*, v.i., may I ask (where did you hear this? etc.).

請業 *chiing-yeh*[1], v.i., to ask questions concerning lessons.

請謁 *chiing-yeh*[2], v.i., (1) to ask for interview; more oft. (2) to ask s.o. to use his influence.

請益 *chiing-yih*, v.i., (LL) to ask for more instruction from teacher.

請纓 *chiing-ying*, v.i., (LL) to volunteer for the army.

請願 *chiingyuahn*, (1) v.i., to demand (usu. at popular demonstration): 市民請願 the people of the city presented a petition; (2) n., a demand or petition.

講 60A.42-2

jiaang.

N. A discourse, a lecture: 第一講, 第二講 the first, second lecture; 人生十講 Ten Discourses on the Life of Man.

V.i. & t. (1) Speak, talk: 講講 speak of, talk about; 演講 to address an audience; 講演 *jiarng-yaan*↓; 講話 -*huah*↓; 講不出口 too embarrassed to mention s.t. (2) Discuss, negotiate, bargain: 講和 -*her*, 講價 -*jiah*, 講理 **jiarnglii*↓; 講好, 講妥 get s.t. agreed upon, settled; 講定 -*dihng*↓. (3) Take into consideration, pay special attention to: 講面子 (see below↓); 講交情 do s.t. for the sake of friendship; 講道理 appeal to reason, be reasonable; 講人情 intercede for s.o., do s.t. as a special favor, generally contrary to regulations; 講面子 phr., be particular about appearances, save s.o.'s face. (4) Have recourse to: 咱們講文的, 還是講武的 shall we argue it out or fight it out?

講求 *jiaangchiour*, v.t., (1) to study carefully, delve into; (2) be fond of: 講求外表 pay special attention to appearances, cf. -*jiouh*↓.

講情 *jiaangchirng*, v.i., ask for special favor, intercede for another: 講情理 phr., be amenable to reason.

講道 *jiaangdauh*, v.i., preach, sermonize, moralize.

講定 *jiaang-dihng*, (1) v.i., settle s.t. by verbal agreement; (2) adj., settled, agreed.

講古 *jiarng-guu*, v.i., recount anc. tales, tell stories of the past.

講和 *jiaang-her*, v.i., hold peace talks, negotiate peace, settle differences (disputes) amicably.

講話 *jiaang-huah*, v.i., talk informally between friends, carry on conversation.

講價(兒) *jiaang-jiah('l)*, v.i., to bargain over prices.

講交情 *jiaang jiau'ching*, phr., do s.t. for the sake of friendship.

講解 *jiarngjiee*, v.t., explain, as a teacher to students.

講究 *jiaangjiouh*, (1) v.t., analyze, make a careful study of; (2) adv., (**jiaang-'jiou*) (be) particular about: 他穿衣裳可講究了 he's particular about what he wears; (3) v.t., speak ill of (s.o.) in his absence: 你們不用講究我, 我早知道了 don't you talk behind my back, I know all about it; (4) n., matter to be taken into account: 難道這裏面還有甚麽講究麽 could there have been any trick here?

講兒 *jiaang'l*, n., meaning, sense, import: 這句書會念, 就是不知道講兒 I can read this sentence, but don't know what it means; 這是甚麽個講兒 what's the matter with this, anyway?

講理 *jiarnglii*, v.i., (1) be amenable to reason, be reasonable; (2) settle disputes by appealing

講 誚 誦 諝 譎 謂 詗 調

to reason and arguing it out in public: 咱們找地方講理去 let's go somewhere to thresh it out between ourselves.

講明 *jiaangmirng*, v.t., explain clearly, put in unambiguous terms: 講明白 phr., state clearly and fully and leave nothing in doubt.

講席 *jiaangshir*[1], n., a seat from which a tutor lectures to his pupils.

講習 *jiaangshir*[2], v.i., hold discussion meetings, conduct training classes.

講授 *jiaangshouh*, v.t., teach, lecture, offer (academic courses).

講書 *jiaang-shu*, v.i., explain passages in textbook.

講師 *jiaangshy*, n., an instructor or lecturer in college or university.

講學 *jiaang-shyuer*, v.i., to lecture on academic subjects.

講臺 *jiaangtair*, n., (1) a lecture platform; (2) a lectern.

講壇 *jiaangtarn*, n., a rostrum, a forum, a pulpit.

講堂 *jiaangtarng*, n., a classroom, lecture hall.

講題 *jiaangtir*, n., topic of discussion, the subject of a speaker.

講座 *jiaangtzuoh*, n., a professorship, a chair: 哲學講座 the Chair of Philosophy.

講武 *jiarng-wuu*, phr., learn, practise military arts.

講演 *jiarngyaan*, v.i., (of a teacher) lecture to students, give a public lecture; n., a lecture, address.

講義 *jiaangyih*, n., (1) commentary on Confucian classics; (2) lecture notes, usu. given by professor to students.

誚 60A.42-2

chiauh.

V.i. To jeer at: 譏誚 *jichiauh*, v. t., to satirize (person, conduct).

誦 60A.42-3

suhng.

V.t. (1) To read aloud, to chant, incant (classics, poems, sutras); (LL) to read another's letter: 得誦來函 I have read your letter. (2) To repeat by heart (classics, Buddhist chants, litany). (3) (AC) u.f. 訟, lawsuit.

誦讀 *suhngdur*, v.i., (LL) to read or read aloud (incoming letter, etc.).

誦習 *suhngshir*, v.i. & t., to study (lessons), to study.

誦說 *suhngshuo*, v.t., to read and explain (classics).

諝 60A.42-3

shyuu.

N. (AC) (1) Cleverness, intelligence. (2) Strategy.

譎 60A.42-3

jyuer.

Adj. & adv. Cunning, artful, see compp.↓.

譎觚 *jyuergu*, adj., (LL) wily, crafty, tricky, artful.

譎詭 *jyuergueei*, adj., perfidious, deceitful.

譎詐 *jyuerjah*, adj., dishonest, deceitful, tricky, cheating.

譎諫 *jyuerjiahn*, v.t., remonstrate with (s.o.) by indirect means.

謂 60A.42-4

weih.

N. Meaning: 何謂 what is the meaning? 無謂 no meaning, meaningless; 是此之謂 this is the meaning.

V.i. & t. (1) (LL) to tell: 謂之 tell him; 謂我 tell me. (2) To say (that), to regard as: 謂曰(he) says that; 或謂 some people say; 勿謂 don't say that (I didn't warn you); 大不謂然 definitely regard it as wrong, greatly oppose it; 可謂 it may be said that; 無所謂 phr., (person) do not regard s.t. as vital, can take it or leave it. (3) To mean: 何謂 what does it mean? 不謂 never thought, never expected. (4) To call, to name: 謂之不孝 is called lack of filial piety; 謂之不忠 is called disloyalty.

詗 60A.42-4

shyuhng.

V. t. To detect: 詗伺, 詗邏, 詗察 v. t. & n., (LL) a spy, detective; to detect, spy on.

調 60A.42-4

tiaur (**diauh*).

N. (1) (**diauh*) A melody, tune: 曲調 a song; 聲調 tone of voice; 腔調 accent of speech; 調子, 調兒 a song, melody; 小調 a short song, a short Yuarn play. (2) (**diauh*) 才調 ability, talent.

V.t. (1) To blend, harmonize (flavors, opinions): 琴瑟不調 the stringed instruments clash, (fig.) marital troubles; 調和, 調劑, 調製 *-her, -jih, -jyh*[2]↓; to readjust: 調整 *-jeeng*↓. (2) To mediate: 調停, 調解 *-tirng, -jiee*↓; 調人 *-rern*↓. (3) To tease, make fun of: 調戲, 調情, 調笑 *-shih, -chirng,*

亅	小	⺊	十	土	ナ	廾	㇄ト	丨	一	丅	フ	口	区	冈	冂	厂	尸	亠	广	宀	丶	乚	弋	心	八	人	乂	⌒	㇀	ノ丿	⺈	く
00	01	02	10	11	12	20	21	22	30	31	32	40	41	42	50	51	52	60	61	62	63	70	71	72	80	81	82	83	90	91	92	93

-*shiauh*↓. (4) To recuperate: 調養, 調理 -*yaang*, -*lii*↓. (5) (**diauh*) To transfer (troops, officials): 調兵 transfer troops; 徵調 call up, enlist soldiers; appoint officials to new post; 調補, 調充, 調升, 調用 -*buu*, -*chung*, -*sheng*, -*yuhng*↓. (6)(**diauh*) To change direction, to interchange: 調過來 change to this direction; 調換, 調一調 to interchange; 調頭 turn one's head; 調虎離山 to lure tiger out of mountain. (7)(**diauh*) To investigate: 調查 -*char*↓.

調撥 **diauhbo*, v.t., to sow dissension, to alienate.

調補 **diauhbuu*, v.t., appoint to (post).

調查 **diauhchar*, v. t., to investigate; 調查表 a chart for reference.

調遣 **diauhchiaan*, v.t., to send to different places.

調情 *tiaurchirng*, v. i., to court (a lady), to flirt with.

調充 **diauhchung*, v.t., see -*buu*↑.

調調兒 **diauh'diauh'l*, n., (1) air of importance; (2) trickery, devious developments.

調度 **diauhduh*, v.t., to regulate; reorganize.

調動 **diauhduhng*, v. t., to transfer (troops, officials).

調羹 *tiaurgeng*, n., a spoon.

調和 *tiaurher*, v. t., (1) to blend (flavors); (2) to mediate; (3) to readjust.

調貨 *tiaur'huo*, n., food ingredients, like rice,meat, vegetable.

調整 *tiaurjeeng*, v. t., to readjust, reorganize.

調解 *tiaurjiee*, v. t. & n., to mediate, -tion; reconcile, -ciliation.

調節 *tiaurjier*, v. t., (1) to tune up musical instrument; (2) to make readjustments, to set right proportions.

調劑 *tiaurjih*, v. t., (1) make up in proportions as a medical prescription; to set right proportions; (2) to make adjustments.

調治 *tiaurjyh*[1], v. t., to receive medical treatment.

調製 *tiaurjyh*[2] (**diauh*-), v. t., manufacture, esp. by a formula (as sauce, flavoring).

調侃 *tiaurkaan*, v. t., to ridicule (person).

調理 *tiaurlii*(-'*li*), v. t., (1) to recuperate; (2) to train up, to discipline.

調弄 *tiaurluhng*, v.t., (1) to make fun of; (2) to play (musical instrument).

調門(兒) **diauhmern*(-*mer'l*), n., (Chin. opera) a singer's voice with regard to pitch.

調皮 **diauhpir* (*tiaur*-), adj., (1) (of child) naughty (also called 調猴兒 a "monkey"); (2) tricky.

調任 **diauhrehn*, v.t., transfer (s. o.) to new post.

調人 *tiaurrern*, n., mediator.

調攝 *tiaursheh*, v.i., see -*yaang*↓.

調升 **diauhsheng*, v. t., be promoted.

調笑 *tiaurshiauh*, v. t., to ridicule, tease.

調協 *tiaurshier*, v.t. & adj., harmonious; to mediate (disputes).

調戲 *tiaurshih*, v. t., to flirt with (girl).

調息 *tiaur-shir*, v. i., sit down for a while, regain breath.

調停 *tiaurtirng*, v. t., to settle dispute amicably.

調歪 **diauhwai*, v. i., purposely make difficulties.

調味 *tiaur-weih*, v. i., to blend flavors; 調味品 seasoning.

調養 *tiauryaang*(-'*yang*), v. i., to recuperate.

調驗 **diauhyahn*, v.t., to subject to examination, to investigate.

調用 **diauhyuhng*, v. t., to transfer (official) to another post.

調勻 *tiauryurn*, v. t., to stir even.

謫 60A.42-6

jer.

V. t. To demote, downgrade, exile to distant province.

謫降 *jerjiahng*, v. i. & t., (1) to downgrade, be downgraded, as official; (2) (of fairies) sent down to earth for transgressions in heaven.

謫居 *jer-jyu*, v. i., to live in exile.

謫戍 *jershuh*, v. t., to exile to post in outlying district.

諞 60A.42-6

piarn (**piaan*).

[Dist. 騙 51B.42]

N. (1) Clever talk. (2) (**piaan*) Brag.

論 60A.42-8

luhn (also **lurn* in Tarng poetry).

N. (1) An essay, discussion: 議論 discuss, -ion; 辯論 argue, -gument; 言論 (person's) published statements on various topics; 論著 (person's) published works; 通論 general treatise (on subject); 緒論, 總論 general introduction; 社論 newspaper editorial; 輿論 public opinion; 論說, 論文, 論調 -*shuo*, -*wern*, -*diauh*↓; 作爲罷論 regard (matter) as closed, given up, need not discuss further; 以作廢論 consider as null and void, see also V.i. & t. 1↓. (2) Old women's tales or opinions: 媽媽論兒(on taboos, herb cures, etc.). (3) A surname.

V. i. & t. (1) (Also as n.) to discuss, criticize, argue: 爭論 dispute; 評論 comment, review (magazines), critical opinion; 論難 to argue, debate on controversial points; 議論 opinion, discussion, person's view on things, or ability for expressing comments; 討論 discuss, -ion; 莫論他何以如此 without going into the reason for his doing like this. (2) To decide on price, merit, order: 論罪 decide on (s.o.'s) guilt; 論功行賞 decide on awards on basis of merit; 論價 discuss price; 論列, 論次 advance reason for and against, to discuss in order.

Prep. By, on basis of, regarding: 論年, 論月, 論日 by year, by month, day (pay rent, etc.); 論斤買賣 buy, sell by weight; 論理你不該 according to reason, you should not, see 論理 -*lii*↓; 論交情 on basis of friendship (be generous, etc.); 無論你怎樣 regardless of what you do; 不論你來與不來 regardless of whether you come or not.

論點 *luhndiaan*, n., point of view taken in discussion.
論調 *luhndiauh*, n., tenor of argument, thinking.
論斷 *luhnduahn*, n., judgment, opinion.
論戰 *luhnjahn*, n., controversy in papers, magazines.
論證 *luhnjehng*, n., (logic) demonstration, proof; 論證法 dialectic.
論據 *luhnjyuh*, n., basis of opinion.
論理 *luhnlii*, phr., according to reason; 論理學 logic.
論説 *luhnshuo*, n., a treatise, exposition; essay.
論文 *luhnwern*, n., essay, treatise, school papers: 博士論文 doctoral thesis.
論語 *Luhnyuu*, n., the Confucian Analects.

訥 60A.42-8

nah (also pr. *neh*).

Adj. Slow of speech: 訥口少言 tight-lipped, not communicative; 訥澀 have difficulty in expressing oneself; 木訥 dull and reticent.

§ 60A.50 (言/ㄱ)

誇 60A.50-1

kua.

V. i. (1) To boast, brag: 自誇 boast of oneself. (2) To praise, see 誇獎 -*'jiaang* ↓.

誇大 *kuadah*, v. t., to boast, exaggerate.
誇官 *kua-guan*, n., formerly, the No. 1 in national examinations (狀元) parading in the capital for three days.
誇張 *kua'jang*, v. i., to exaggerate: 誇張過甚 exaggerate too much.
誇獎 *kua'jiaang*, v. t., (from a superior) to praise a younger man.
誇口 *kuakoou*, v. i., to boast, brag.
誇示 *kuashyh*[1], v. t., to show off (to people).
誇飾 *kuashyh*[2], v. t., exaggerate and embellish (the good points).
誇讚 *kua'tzahn*, v. i. & t., to praise before others.
誇嘴 *kuatzueei*, v. i., see -*koou* ↑.
誇耀 *kuayauh*, v. i., to show off (to people).

諤 60A.50-4

eh.

Adj. Straightforward (speaking, advice).

謁 60A.50-4

yeh.

V. t. To pay respects to an official: 謁見 -*jiahn* ↓; 進謁, 晉謁, 拜謁 ditto; 謁請 to request by personal visit; 謁告 tell personally on formal visit.

謁見 *yehjiahn*, v. i., to pay respects to official.
謁刺 *yehtsyh*, n., visiting card.

訒 60A.50-5

rehn.

Adj. (Of speech) deliberately hesitating, reluctant to speak out: 仁者其言也訒 a true man is slow to talk.

詞 60A.50-5

tsyr.

N. (1) (Interch. 辭) literary phraseology, the language of writing: 詞翰, 詞華, 詞藻 -*hahn*, -*huar*, -*tzaau* ↓; 文詞 language of writing with respect to style; 詞章 -*jang* ↓; 詞不達意 language fails to express the meaning; 詞窮 (理屈) to shut up when defeated in argument; 淫詞, etc., see 辭 90S.10. (2) (Interch. 辭) words, phrases, spoken language: 言詞 the way a person talks; 言詞不雅 use slang or low-class talk; 詞頭, 詞尾 -*tour*, -*weei* ↓; 詞典, 詞彙 -*diaan*, -*hueih* ↓. (3) Part of speech: 詞性, 詞類 ditto; 名詞 noun; 代(名)詞 pronoun; 動詞 verb; 形容詞 adjective; 副詞 adverb; 前置詞 or 介詞 preposition; 連接詞 conjunction; 感嘆詞 exclamation; 冠詞 article. (4) A special poetic form, usu. associated with Suhng Dyn., using sentence patterns based on song melodies (as words to music): 塡詞 to write *tsyr* poems (lit. to fill in words according to tone patterns); 豔詞 sentimental love poems; 詞牌, 詞譜, 詞韻 -*pair*, -*puu*, -*yuhn* ↓. (5) A lawsuit: 詞訟 -*suhng* ↓.

詞典 *tsyrdiaan*, n., a dictionary of words and phrases (also wr. 辭).
詞鋒 *tsyrfeng*, n., eloquent, forceful language.
詞翰 *tsyrhahn*, n., (1) see -*jang* ↓; (2) u.f. 書翰 letter of correspondence.
詞話 *tsyrhuah*, n., (1) critical comments or talks about *tsyr* poems; (2) (MC) a novel.
詞華 *tsyrhuar*, n., see -*tzaau* ↓.

詞彙 *tsyrhueih*, n., (1) (also 辭) vocabulary (rich, inadequate); (2) a phrase dictionary.

詞章 *tsyrjang*, n., literature; prose, the art of writing as special study.

詞句 *tsyrjyuh*, n., sentence structure; how a piece of writing reads (fluently, etc.).

詞類 *tsyrleih*, n., part of speech, see N. 3↑.

詞林 *tsyrlirn*, n., literary circles.

詞律 *tsyrlyuh*, n., laws or style of writing.

詞牌(子) *tsyrpair(tz)*, n., name of song to be sung at dinner, etc.; name of *tsyr* poem, which is mentioned by its melody.

詞譜 *tsyrpuu*, n., book containing melody patterns of *tsyr*.

詞人 *tsyrrern*, n., a poet, spec. *tsyr* poet.

詞性 *tsyrshihng*, n., part of speech, see N. 3↑.

詞訟 *tsyrsuhng*, n., lawsuit.

詞頭 *tsyrtour*, n., prefix, as 阿 in 阿姨, 老 in 老王.

詞藻 *tsyrtzaau*, n., ornate phraseology in pedantic writing (also 辭).

詞宗 *tsyr-tzung*, n., leading poet of a time.

詞尾 *tsyrweei*, n., suffix, as 兒 in 孩兒, 子 in 傻子, 頭 in 木頭.

詞韻 *tsyryuhn*, n., a rhyme dictionary.

詡 60A.50–5

shyuu.

V. i. To boast, brag: 詡言 ditto.

訪 60A.50–6

faang.

N. & v.i. & t. (1) Personal call, visit, interview: 訪親, 友 visit with relatives, friends; 拜訪 pay visit, pay respects to; 探訪, 相訪, 過訪 drop in for a visit. (2) Visit to find out: 訪查 find out by visiting on the location; 探訪消息 find out news; 訪問 interview (person), have an interview with; 訪古 visit archaeological sites.

訪問 *faangwehn*, v.t. & n., interview; to visit foreign country: 訪問法國 visit France (euphem. for travelling of official).

訪員 *faangyuarn*, n., newspaper reporter; inspector appointed to look over place.

謗 60A.50–6

bahng.

N. & v. t. Smear, make malicious attack: 誹謗, 毀謗 make such rumors, esp. about personages, God; 謗僧罵道 abuse Buddhist and Taoist priests.

謗聞 *bahngwern*, n., (LL) malicious gossip.

謗言 *bahngyarn*, n. malicious rumors.

譾 60A.50–8

jiaan.

[Var. of 淺 *chiaan*, 63A.71]

Adj. Shallow, superficial: 譾陋 lacking in intellectual depth.

誘 60A.50–9

youh.

V. i. & t. (1) To guide gently into course of action: 誘導, 誘掖 *-daau, -yih*↓. (2) To persuade, induce: 勸誘 to persuade (to good path); 誘供 induce to talk at court. (3) To seduce, to cheat: 誘姦, 誘拐, 誘騙 *-jian, -guaai, -piahn*↓.

誘導 *youhdaau*, (1) v. t., to guide and instruct; (2) v. t, & n., (electricity) induce, induction: 誘導反應 induced reaction.

誘拐 *youhguaai*, v. t., kidnap (young childen) for sale; seduce (girls, women) in white slave traffic.

誘惑 *youhhuoh*, v. t., to tempt, lead astray (youth), to seduce.

誘姦 *youhjian*, v. t., seduce and rape.

誘騙 *youhpiahn*, v. t., to cheat, deceive by false promises.

誘掖 *youhyih*, v. t., to help: 誘掖後進 to help and encourage the younger generation.

誘引 *youhyiin*, v. t., to attract (younger generation) toward good or evil.

譌 60A.50–9

er.

[Var. of 訛 60A.70]

詢 60A.50–9

shyurn.

V. i. & t. To inquire, gather information: 詢問 *-wehn*↓; 詢商 to inquire and discuss: 詢明 ask and make certain, verify; 相詢 to inquire from a friend; 詢及 ask about (certain point); 諮詢 ask for advice, to transmit official matter for opinion.

詢察 *shyurnchar*, v. t., to investigate on the spot.

詢訪 *shyurnfaang*, v. t., to interview personage, or visit a country.

詢問 *shyurnwehn*, v. t., to inquire about (facts, situation), to ask for (opinion).

A

詾 60A.50-9

shyung.
[Var. of 訩]

詾詾 *shyungshyung,* adj., uproarious, turbulent.

誨 60A.50-9

hueih (also *hueei*).

N. & v. t. (1) Teaching, to teach: 教誨, 訓誨 lecture on (students') conduct, morals; 誨人不倦 "was never tired of teaching people"—Confucius. (2) To invite: 冶容誨淫, 慢藏誨盜 to dress prettily invites adultery and to let jewels lie about invites burglary.

謅 60A.50-9

tzou.

V. i. Talk nonsense: 胡謅 make absurd (wild, incoherent) utterances.

§60A.63 (言/丶)

讌 60A.63-2

yahn.

N. & v.i. (To hold) feast (interch. 宴).

B

讜 60A.63-2

daang.

Adj. Straightforward: 讜言高論 honest and wise counsel.

譙 60A.63-9

chiaur (*chiauh).

N. (1) A surname. (2) A tower, see compp. ↓.

V. t. (**chiauh*) (LL) to scold, remonstrate: 譙呵, 譙責 ditto.

譙樓 *chiaurlour,* n., (LL) the drum tower; watchtower.
譙櫓 *chiaurluu,* n., (LL) see *-lour* ↑.
譙門 *chiaurmern,* n., see *-lour* ↑.

§60A.70 (言/乚)

譊 60A.70-1

naur.

V.i. Wrangle, contend, dispute.

Adj. 譊譊 (of disputants) wrangling.

詵 60A.70-1

shen.

Adj. Swarming, numerous.

C

謊 60A.70-2

huaang.

N. A lie: 不許說謊 (說謊話) do not lie; 耍謊 (of shopkeeper) ask unfair prices.

謊話 *huaanghuah,* n., a lie.

諕 60A.70-2

shiah.
[Var. of 嚇 40A.01]

訑 60A.70-2

yir.

Adj. 訑訑 (AC) arrogant.

訊 60A.70-3

shyuhn.

N. News transmission, news, letter, intelligence: 通訊 correspondence; 通訊社 news agency; 來訊 your letter; 佳訊, 喜訊 good news, happy news; 音訊 news from friends; 電訊 telegram, telegraphic report, cable (cabled news); 航訊 airmail (story); 專訊 special correspondence (from city).

V.t. To try at court, see compp. ↓.

訊辦 *shyuhnbahn,* v. i., to try at court and pass sentence (on case).
訊斷 *shyuhnduahn,* v. i. & t., to judge (guilty or not guilty).
訊供 *shyuhngung,* v. i. & t., to give affidavit.

亅	小	丬	十	土	𠂇	廾	𠃊	丨	一	丁	フ	口	⊠	冈	𠃌	厂	尸	亠	广	宀	丶	乚	弋	心	八	人	乂	乛	㇒	刂	𠂉	く
00	01	02	10	11	12	20	21	22	30	31	32	40	41	42	50	51	52	60	61	62	63	70	71	72	80	81	82	83	90	91	92	93

訊檢 *shyuhnjiaan*, v. i. & t., to investigate (case) and prosecute.

訊究 *shyuhnjiouh*, v. i. & t., ditto.

訊鞫 *shyuhnjyur*, v. t., to try at court.

訊息 *shyuhnshir*, n., news (from friends, etc.).

訊聽 *shyuhnting*, v. t., to inquire about news (＝打聽).

訊問 *shyuhnwehn*, v. i. & t., (1) to try at court; (2) to inquire after information.

諷 60A.70-4

fehng.

V.i. & t. (1) Incant, read with intonation. (2) Satirize, ridicule, persuade or make a person see a point by clever analogy.

諷諫 *fehngjiahn*, v. t. & n., remonstrate(-tion) with (ruler) by clever analogy.

諷誦 *fehngsuhng*, v.t., read (poem, etc.) aloud with intonation; (court.) read (your letter) as if to memorize.

諷刺 *fehngtsyh*, v. t., satirize (person); 諷刺畫 cartoon.

記 60A.70-5

jih.

N. (1) Classical works, written accounts of events, essays: 禮記 the *Book of Rites*; 史記 "The Historical Records" by Ssŭma Chien; 日記 diary; 遊記 accounts of travels, record of a journey; 週記 weekly reports; 大事記 table of major events; 奏記 (AC) a memorandum. (2) A seal: 圖記 a chop; 鈐記 a signet. (3) A mark, sign, mole: 標記 distinguishing marks, signpost, guidepost; 記號(兒) -*'hauh*('l)↓; 表記 a marking, also a keepsake.

V. t. (1) Keep in mind: 記仇(兒) to bear a grudge; 記取 -*chyuu*, 記住 -*juh*↓. (2) To record: 記過 -*guoh*, 記功 -*gung*, 記帳 -*jahng*, 記錄 -*luh*↓; 記下來 put down in writing; 筆記(take) notes; 速記 shorthand; 簿記 bookkeeping.

記取 *jihchyuu*, v. t., to recall, remember: 記取教訓 learn a lesson.

記得 *jih'de*, v. t., remember, keep in mind.

記掛 *jihguah*, v. t., bear in mind, be concerned about.

記功 *jih-gung*, v. t., give credit for meritorious work.

記過 *jih-guoh*, v. t., give a demerit.

記號(兒) *jih'hau*('l), n., a sign, a mark.

記帳 *jihjahng*, v. t., charge to an account.

記者 *jihjee*, n., a newspaper reporter, correspondent, journalist.

記住 *jih*(')*juh*, v. t., bear in mind, never forget.

記臉子 *jihliaantz*, n., a person with moles on face.

記錄 *jihluh*, (1) v. t., to record; (2) n., minutes of meetings; (3) an athletic record (also wr. 紀錄).

記名 *jih-mirng*, adj., (of papers, documents) bearing the name of the holder: 記名股票 (business) untransferable shares; 不記名投票 secret ballot.

記事兒 *jihsheh'l*, n., the first beginnings of a child's intelligence and memories: 那時我才記事兒 I was then only beginning to remember things.

記性(兒) *jih'shing*('l), n., the memory power.

記事 *jihshyh*[1], (1) v. i., to record events; (2) n., written records, chronicles.

記室 *jihshyh*[2], n., (AC) a clerk, secretary.

記誦 *jihsuhng*, v. t., repeat from memory.

記載 *jihtzaaih*, (1) v.t., put down in writing; (2) n., written records.

記憶 *jihyih*, v.i. & t. & n., to remember; memories: 記憶力 memory power; 記憶喪失症 amnesia.

詫 60A.70-6

chah.

V. i. (1) To be shocked by surprise: 詫異 -*yih*↓; 驚詫 greatly surprised. (2) To exaggerate: 以自誇詫 to brag.

詫異 *chahyih*, v. i., be greatly surprised, be struck with surprise.

說 60A.70-8

shuo (**shueih*, **yueh*).

N. Theory: 學說 ditto; 又一說 another theory (explanation): doctrine: 異說, 邪說 heresy, strange, evil doctrine.

V. i. & t. (1) To speak, say, talk, mention: 說話 -*huah*↓; 說好話, 說壞話 speak well, ill, of person; 說他好, 不好 praise him, disapprove of him; 說大話, 謊話 boast, lie; 說鬼話, see 說話 -*huah*↓; oft. with vb. complements 來, 去, 上, 下, 出, 開, 得, esp. with 得 (positive) and 不 (negative), see 說得, 說來, 說不上, 說不得, 說不清, -*der*, -*lair*, -*buh-shahng*, -*buh-der*, -*buh-ching*, etc.↓; 說不出 cannot say; 說得過去, 說不過去 makes sense, does not make sense; 說來說去 after all is said and done, no matter how you put it; oft. coupled with 道, chat freely, without order: 說東道西, 說天道地, 說三道四, 說長道短 just talk, gossip, random talk; 說著玩兒 talk for talking's sake, do not take one seriously; 說了不算 words do not count, just talk; 胡說, 瞎說, 亂說 talk nonsense; 說溜了嘴 make a slip of the tongue; 說叉了 get into a dispute by using strong words. (2) To rebuke, scold: 說了他一頓 gave him a scolding; 數說 to reprove (s.o. for his mistakes). (3) To explain: 解說 ditto; 說明 -*mirng*↓. (4) (**shueih*) 游說 (AC, scholars who went from country to country) to see rulers and "sell an idea"; 説客 *-keh* ↓. (5) (**yueh*) U.f. 悅 v.t. & p.p., to like, be pleased with (person, teaching).

説白 *shuobair*, n., (Chin. opera) passages which are spoken, not sung.
説不清 *shuo-buh-ching*, phr., see *-ching* ↓.
説不齊 *shuo-buh-chir*, phr., cannot say for sure.
説不得 *shuo-buh-der*, phr., see *-der* ↓.
説不來 *shuo-buh-lair*, phr., (1) cannot say it; (2) 彼此説不來 they cannot get along with each other.
説不上 *shuo-buh-shahng*, phr., unqualified to be mentioned as such: 你這些話都説不上 all that you say is irrelevant.
説不定 *shuo-bur-dihng*, phr., perhaps; it is hard to say.
説不過來 *shuo-bur-guoh-lair*, phr., contrary to common sense or common decency (not to include person on list, etc.).
説起 *shuo-chii*, v.i. & t., to mention: 説起這件事 to mention this affair; 説起來我們還是同學 now that it is mentioned, we were in the same school; 説起來 to discuss (subject); in regard to.
説親 *shuo-chin*, v. i., to speak for a girl's hand in marriage.
説清 *shuo-ching*, v. t., to make clear: 説不清 (affair) difficult to explain.
説情(兒) *shuo-chirng('l)*, v. i., to plead for leniency for friendship's sake.
説穿 *shuo-chuan*, v. t., to expose (a secret).
説處 *shuo-chuh*, n., as in 有説處 (MC) have s.t. to say.
説道 *shuo-dauh*, v. i., (s.o.) says.
説得 *shuo-der*, phr., possible to mention; with complement: 説得好, 説得妙 well said; 説不得 (a) unmentionable, unspeakable: 他人品壞得説不得 his character is unspeakably bad; (b) perhaps: 説不得要你親自對他説 there is perhaps no way except to speak to him yourself; 説得着 *-'dejaur*, phr., (a) permissible or necessary to say: 這些話都是説得着的; (b) qualified to speak to s.o.; (c) can get along together: 説得來 (cf. *-buh-lair* ↑).
説法 *shuo-faa*, v. i., (Budd.) to expound teachings: 另外一種説法 another way of looking at it; 現身説法 personally appear to teach or explain; 憑你的説法 according to what you say.
説方便 *shuo fangbiahn*, phr., (MC)=説好話 to speak in favor of s.t. or s.o.
説服 *shuo-fur*, v. t., to convince (another).
説古 *shuo-guu*, v. i., (coll.) tell old tales, of anc. custom, etc.
説好 *shuo-haau*, v. t., agree upon, settle after discussion: 説好説歹 use all means of persuasion.
説和 *shuo'he*, v. i., to mediate.
説合 *shuo-her*, v. i., to bring the two parties together, bring about meeting, union or marriage.
説謊 *shuo-huaang*, v. i., to tell a lie (also 説謊話).
説話 *shuo-huah*, v. i. & n., (1) talk: 説什麽話 what are you talking about? 説大話 boast; 説鬼話 talk nonsense; 説閒話 to gossip; 説冷話 make sly remarks, etc.; 説話不當話 one's words do not count—unreliable; 不好説話 difficult to talk with, also inconvenient (for me) to say anything; 説話之間 while talking; also in a short while; 説話就來 I'll come in a moment; (2) gossip: 要防旁人説話 beware of gossip; (3) (Suhng Dyn.) tell stories as a professional in teahouse: 説話的, 説話人 the storyteller.
説章兒 *shuo-jang'l*, n., (1) talk; (2) (dial.) terms of negotiation.
説教 *shuo-jiauh*, v. i., to preach.
説知 *shuo-jy*, v. t., to inform, let s.o. know: 向他説知 let him know.
説開 *shuo-kai*, v. i. & t., (1) to explain, explain away, allay fears; (2) (phrase, term) has become current.
説客 *shuo(')keh*, (1) n., one who undertakes to "sell an idea": 疑我做説客 suspects I am a hired agent (to speak for s.o.); (2) (**shueihkeh*) n., (AC) professional politicians who travelled from country to country to convince ruler of some scheme.
説口 *shuo-koou*, v. i., (MC) boast: 不是我説口 I am not boasting.
説兒 *shuo'l*, n., (1) s.t. to say: 沒什麽説兒 nothing to say; (2) terms, esp. reference to bribery.
説來 *shuo-lair*, phr., to mention (a subject): 説來話長 it's a long story to tell; 説來都是朋友 come to speak of it, we are all friends.
説理 *shuo-lii*, v.i., to talk reason, be reasonable.
説夢 *shuo-mehng*, phr., talk nonsense: 癡人説夢 tell some fantastic tale or idea.
説媒 *shuo-meir*, v. i., to act as go-between for betrothal: 請人説媒 ask s.o. to act as go-between.
説明 *shuo-mirng*, v.t. & n., to explain, an explanation; 説明書 a booklet of a (movie) synopsis, instructions.
説票兒 *shuo-piauh'l*, phr., discuss terms of ransom for kidnapped person (cf. 票 31.01).
説破 *shuo-poh*, v. t., expose (secret); 説破嘴 talk oneself hoarse (in futile long persuasion).
説下 *shuo-shiah*, v. i., say definitely; phr., it's a deal.
説項 *shuoshiahng*, v. t., try to persuade; to ask leniency or special consideration: 爲人説項 speak for s.o.
説笑 *shuoshiauh*, v.i., engage in gay banter: 説説笑笑 just have a pleasant talk together; 有説有笑 (of friends) talking and joking at informal gathering.
説戲 *shuo-shih*, v. i., to teach opera singing and acting.
説媳婦(兒) *shuo shir'fu('l)*, phr., see *-chin* ↑.
説書 *shuoshu*, v. i., (1) to explain the classics; (2) to give monologue, a form of storytelling

with a small drum and gestures—a special literary form.

說耍 *shuoshuaa*, v. i., to joke.

說士 **shueihshyh*, see *-keh*↑.

說事 *shuo-shyh*, v. i., (1) to negotiate: 說事過錢 negotiate and conclude transaction; (2) to talk big, or trying to "sell an idea."

說死 *shuo syy*, phr., 說死也不去 I won't go whatever you say.

說帖 *shuotiee*, n., a memorandum containing subject matter of discussion.

說頭兒 *shuo'tou'l*, n., things to discuss: 沒什麼大說頭兒 there is nothing much to discuss.

說辭 *shuo-tsyr*, v. i. & n., a plea.

說嘴 *shuo-tzueei*, v. i., to boast.

說文 *shuowern*, n., name of the famous anc. dictionary by 許愼—a study of principles of composition of Chin. characters.

託 60A.70–9

tuo.

V. i. & t. (1) To entrust s. t. to s. o., to ask s. o. to do s. t.: 委託 commission (s. o.), ask s. o. to be responsible for s. t.; 託人 ask another person to do s.t.; 寄託, 託寄 v. i., entrust; give (idea, sentiment) an expression; 信託 banker's trust; 託孤 entrust orphan to s. o.'s care; 拜託, 請託 to request; 託你一件事 ask you to do one thing for me; 受人之託 I am entrusted with (s. t. by s. o.). (2) To give pretext, excuse: 託病不來 fail to come with sickness as excuse; 託以他辭 evade by making excuses.

託庇 *tuobih*, phr., 託庇平安 am very well, thanks to your protecting influence.

託情(兒) *tuochirng('l)*, v. i., ask s. o. to put in a nice word for oneself.

託大 *tuodah*, v. i., have exaggerated idea of one's importance, be overconfident.

託兒所 *tuo-erlsuoo*, n., day nursery, where working mothers deposit their children for the day.

託諷 *tuofeng* (*-fehng*), n., use gentle hint or indirect reference to change s. o.'s mind.

託付 *tuo(')fuh*, v. t., to entrust (s. t.) to (s. o.).

託福 *tuofur*, phr., see *-bih*↑.

託管 *tuoguann*, n., trusteeship; 託管委員會 Trusteeship Council; 託管領土 trust territories; 國際託管制度 international trusteeship.

託故 *tuo-guh*, v. i., use some pretexts.

託迹 *tuo-jih*, phr., take abode in (place), find resting place in (some faith).

託夢 *tuo-mehng*, v. i., (spirit of deceased) appear in a dream to give a message.

託名 *tuo-mirng*, v. i., to do (s. t.) in s. o.'s name; to assume false name.

託身 *tuo-shen*, n., to take abode in some place, or job (life being a sojourn).

託生 *tuo'sheng*, v. i., be reincarnated (in some animal form).

託心 *tuo-shin*, v. i., (rare) give one's heart in friendship.

託食 *tuo-shyr*, v. i., find boarding (with s. o.).

託宿 *tuo-suh*, v. i., find lodging (in some place, with s. o.).

託辭 *tuo-tsyr*, v. i., give some excuses.

託足 *tuotzur*, v. i., see *-shen*↑.

託運人 *tuoyuhn rern*, n., consignor.

訛 60A.70–9

er.

V.i. & t. (1) To cheat, extort: 訛詐, 訛賴 *-jah, -laih*↓. (2) To nag, persist in asking: 訛著茶點 constantly asking for tea and things. (3) (AC) to move about, stir.

Adj. Erroneous, incorrect (report, etc.): 訛言訛語 erroneous and irresponsible talk; 訛傳, 訛舛 *-chuarn, -chuaan*↓; 以訛傳訛 circulate erroneous reports, pass on erroneous version; 訛音 incorrect pronunciation.

訛舛 *erchuaan*, adj., (LL) erroneous, absurd.

訛傳 *erchuarn*, n., false report.

訛奪 *erduor*, n., missing characters in text.

訛火 *erhuoo*, n., prairie fire.

訛詐 *erjah*, v.i. & t., to extort money by false pretences.

訛賴 *erlaih*, v.i., to deny, or to involve s.o., by lying.

訛詞兒 *ertser'l*, v.i., find pretexts: 真會訛詞兒 is good at finding pretexts and excuses.

訛言 *er-yarn*, n., rumor.

訖 60A.70–9

chih.

Adv. (Used after vb.) finished: 訖了; (MC official) time is over, will not receive; 查訖, 驗訖 passed (customs, etc.) after examination: 收訖 (official and commercial) duly received; 付訖 paid; 清訖 (account) has been cleared.

詭 60A.70–9

gueei

Adj. (1) Sly, cunning, crafty, deceitful: 詭詐 crafty, treacherous; 詭辯 (學派) sophistry, the sophists; 詭計多端 foxy, wily; 詭辭 an ill-concealed lie, specious arguments. (2) Unique, unusual, remarkable, extraordinary: 詭譎 *-jyuer*, 詭特 *-teh*, 詭異 *-yih*↓; 詭色 false appearance.

詭病 *gueei'bihng*, n., underhanded maneuvers or dealings, irregularities.

詭道 *gueei-dauh*, n., (1) (mil.

tactics) deception; (2) a short cut.

詭譎 *gueeijyuer*, adj., (1) shifting, unpredictable; (2) unique, strange.

詭戾 *gueeilih*, adj., treacherous and perverse.

詭秘 *gueeimih*, (1) n., a hidden secret; (2) adj., (of secrets) carefully concealed.

詭隨 *gueeisueir*, v. t., follow blindly.

詭特 *gueeiteh*, adj., marvellous, remarkable.

詭異 *gueeiyih*, adj., strange (tactics).

讒 60A.70-9

charn (**tsair*).

N. Malicious talk.

Adv. (**tsair*) Frequently wr. 才, meaning just: 剛纔 (=剛才) just a moment ago; 纔晴又雨 the sky has just cleared up, and starts to rain again.

讒謗 *charnbahng*, v. t., to slander, smear (a person).

讒害 *charnhaih*, v. t., to vilify (person), attack by malicious talk.

讒言 *charnyarn*, n., malicious, slanderous talk.

§60A.71 (言/弋)

識 60A.71-6

shyh (**jyh*).

N. (1) Recognition (of truth), real understanding, power of discrimination: 知識 knowledge; 常識 common sense; 見識 insight, intellectual discrimination; 膽識 courage of one's convictions; 學識 learning plus insight or definite convictions or views gained from knowledge; 才識 ability and power of discrimination; 識者 *-jee*↓; 意△識 60.72. (2) (**jyh*) Record, inscriptions: 款識 inscriptions on scrolls, bronze; 標識 a marking sign, stick or flag.

V. t. To know (a character, person): 相識 v.i. & n., know each other, acquaintance; 識得某人 know a certain person; 熟識 know (person) well; 識字 can read; 目不識丁 completely illiterate ("do not know even character 丁"); 賞△識 22.80; 認△識 60A.72.

識拔 *shyhbar*, v. t., to recognize a person's ability and promote him.

識別 *shyhbier*, v. t., to distinguish, tell the difference: 識別力 *--lih*, n., power of discrimination.

識竅 *shyh-chiauh*, adj., tactful.

識趣(兒) *shyh-chyuh* (*-chyueh'l*), adj., understanding subtleties, also tactful.

識貨 *shyh-huoh*, phr., expert judge (of goods).

識者 *shyhjee*, n., experts: 爲識者所笑 be laughed at by the experts.

識見 *shyhjiahn*, n., definite views gained from superior knowledge.

識荆 *shyh-jing*, v. i., (court.) to make your esteemed acquaintance (from allu.).

識相 *shyh-shiahng*, adj., tactful, knowing when to go forward and when to withdraw: 不識相 tactless.

識野 *shyh-yee*, n., (psych.) field of awareness.

識域 *shyh-yuh*, n., ditto.

試 60A.71-7

shyh.

N. A trial, a test: 考試 a test, examination; 面試, 口試 oral test; 筆試 written test; 應試 go to take an examination; 監試 supervise examination, also a supervisor; 嘗試 an attempt, a trial.

V. i. & t. To try out, test (strength, etc.): 試一試 have a try; 試試 *-shyh*↓; 試説 try and tell us; 試工, 試用 *-gung*, *-yuhng* ↓; 試驗 *-yahn*↓; 試步兒 tentatively; 試步兒辦 try and see; 試兩天再説 try a few days and see.

試燈 *shyh-deng*, v. i., hold the lantern contest on 15th day of first lunar month.

試兒 *shyh-erl*, v. i., test baby's future inclinations on its first anniversary by having different objects (pen, money, tool, etc.) displayed within its reach and see what it grabs (also *-jou*, *-tzueih* ↓).

試工(兒) *shyh-gung('l)*, v. i., try out a workman or employee.

試婚 *shyh-hun*, phr., trial marriage.

試金石 *shyh-jin-shyr*, n., touchstone.

試周 *shyhjou*, v. i., see *-erl*↑.

試卷 *shyhjyuahn*, n., examination paper.

試紙 *shyhjyy*, n., see *-yahnjyy*↓.

試試 *shyhshyh*, v. i., have a try.

試算表 *shyhsuahnbiaau*, n., work sheet in accounting receipts and expenditures.

試探 *shyh'tahn*, v. t., to explore (the moon, etc.).

試帖 *shyhtieh*, n., (Tarng Dyn.) civil examinations in writing poetry, also in classics.

試晬 *shyhtzueih*, v. i., see *-erl*↑.

試問 *shyh-wehn*, phr., (1) may I ask; (2) formula in asking questions, esp. classroom exercises.

試演 *shyhyaan*, v. i. & n., to rehearse, a rehearsal.

試驗 *shyhyahn*, v. i. & n., to (or an) experiment; 試驗管 test tube; 試驗紙 *--jyy*, litmus paper.

試用 *shyhyuhng*, v.t. try out (person, utensil); be on probation.

誠 誡 讖 議 詆 譏

誠 60A.71-7

cherng.

Adj. (1) Honest, sincere: 誠實, 誠懇, 誠意 *-'shyr, -keen, -yih* ↓. (2) True: 誠然 *-rarn* ↓.

Adv. Truly, indeed: 誠不能免 indeed it cannot be helped.

Conj. (Subjunctive) if it is true: 誠如所說 if as you say (if what you say is true).

誠 懇 *cherngkeen*, adj., sincere (request).
誠 然 *cherngrarn*, (1) adj., is true: 所言誠然 what you say is true; (2) adv., indeed: 誠然不錯 good indeed.
誠 心 *cherngshin*, adj. & adv., sincere, -ly.
誠 實 *cherng'shyr*, adj., honest (person, confession).
誠 壹 *cherngyi*, adj., devoted.
誠 意 *cherngyih*, n., sincerity (in negotiations): 沒有誠意 lack sincerity.

誡 60A.71-7

jieh.

N. A precept, injunction, exhortation, admonishment: 摩西十誡 the Ten Commandments given by God to Moses.

V. t. Warn, exhort, admonish: 告誡 forewarn, put on guard, give fair warning; 嚴誡 issue strict orders, forbid; 屢誡不改 incorrigible; 訓誡 advise, counsel, admonish.

讖 60A.71-7

chehn.

N. A prophetic saying, prophecy; foreboding.

讖 兆 *chehnjauh*, n., a foreboding.
讖 緯 *chehnweei*, n., Taoist science of prophecy through study of *yin-yarng* 陰陽 and 五行 *wushirng* (31.30) or by common divination, esp. in Hahn Dyn.; such books.
讖 語 *chehn'yuu*, n., a prophecy: 完成讖語 a saying turns out to be a prophecy.

議 60A.71-8

yih.

N. (1) A form of composition like editorial on current affairs. (2) 會議 conference; see v.i. & t.↓. (3) Legislative assembly: 議會, 議員, 議長 *-hueih, -yuarn, -jaang* ↓; 參議院 Senate; 衆議院 House of Representatives.

V. i. & t. Discuss, -ion, propose, -al: 議論 discuss, -ion; 商議 discuss, negotiate; 計議 discuss a plan; 評議 criticize, evaluate, judge; 議價 discuss price; 議和 *-her*[2] ↓; 議案 *-ahn* ↓; 提議 propose a resolution; 動議 propose a motion; 附議 to second a motion; 異議 dissent, difference of opinion.

議 案 *yih-ahn*, n., a resolution (in congress, etc.).
議 處 *yihchuu*, v. t., formerly, to consider punishment for offending official.
議 定 *yihdihng*, v. i. & t., to conclude agreement; 議定書 draft for treaty.
議 合 *yihher*[1], v.i., (coll.) to discuss together: 等我們議合議合再說 wait till we have a chance to discuss it together.
議 和 *yihher*[2], v. i., negotiate for peace.
議 會 *yihhueih*, n., national assembly, congress, assembly of representatives; 省議會 provincial assembly; 市議會 municipal assembly.
議 長 *yihjaang*, n., speaker of assembly (national, provincial or municipal).
議 決 *yihjyuer*, v. t. & n., (pass) a resolution; 議決案 *--ahn*, n., a resolution.
議 論 *yihluhn*, v. i. & t. & n., discuss, -ion; criticize, -cism.
議 事 *yih-shyh*, v. i. & t. & n., discuss business; 議事所 room for board meeting.
議 題 *yih-tir*, n., agenda of discussion.
議 院 *yihyuahn*, n., legislative assembly, see N. 3 ↑.
議 員 *yihyuarn*, n., member of parliament, congress, or assembly, congressman.

詆 60A.71-9

dii.

V. t. Deprecate, condemn.

詆 毀 *dirhueei*, v. t., spread rumor against, discredit (person).

譏 60A.71-9

ji.

V. t. (1) To ridicule, mock, deride: 譏諷 *-'feng*, 譏笑 *-shiauh* ↓. (2) To inspect, examine critically: 譏察 *-char* ↓.

譏 察 *jichar*, v. t., inspect; 譏察使 (MC) an inspector who ferreted out criminal elements.
譏 誚 *jichiauh*, v. t., to ridicule, to jeer at.
譏 諷 *ji'feng*, v. t., satirize.
譏 笑 *jishiauh*, v. t., to laugh at, make fun of.
譏 彈 *jitarn*, v. t., to censure severely, impeach.
譏 刺 *jitsyh*, v. t., to satirize, deride.

§ 60A.72 (言/心)

誌 60A.72–1

jyh.

N. (1) A record (of events, interch. 志). (2) A monument: 碑誌 memorial monument; 墓誌銘 tombstone inscription giving life record of deceased. (3) Sign, signpost: 標誌 trademark; insignia, special marking card or tablet.

V. t. (1) To record, inscribe for posterity: 永誌不忘 inscribe for ever in memory. (2) To register (a sentiment): 誌哀, 誌賀, 誌喜, etc. *-ai, -heh, -shii* ↓.

誌 哀 *jyh-ai,* v. i., to register sorrow (at friend's funeral, etc.).

誌 慶 *jyh-chihng,* v. i., to celebrate by scroll, gift).

誌 悼 *jyh-dauh,* v. i., to register sorrow.

誌 賀 *jyh-heh,* v.i., to send s.t. as mark of congratulation.

誌 念 *jyh-niahn,* v.i., to send as souvenir.

誌 喜 *jyh-shii,* v.i., to send congratulations (on happy occasion).

讔 60A.72–3

yiin.

N. A riddle, an elliptical line (讔語 also wr. 隱語).

認 60A.72–5

rehn.

V. t. (1) Recognize, take cognizance of, be aware of: 認一認 take a close look at; 認認看 see if one can recognize; 認得 *-'de* ↓; 認定 affirm, put one's finger on; 認明 look carefully and know clearly; 認清 recognize clearly; 認識 *-shyh* ↓; 認領 *-liing* ↓; 認字 be able to read, literate; 認票不認人 (of checks) payable to the bearer; 認不清 unable to recognize for sure; 認左了 mistook s.o. (s.t.) for another; 認狼爲犬 take a wicked person for a good one; 認賊作父 take a rascal (thief) as one's benefactor; 認賊作子 (Budd.) take the seeming as real; 冒認 claim (s.t.) as one's own under false pretenses; 錯認 mistake one thing (person) for another. (2) Admit, acknowledge, concede: 認罪 confess one's guilt, plead guilty; 認罰 submit to punishment; 認賠 be prepared to pay compensation; 認賬 agree to pay what one owes, (fig.) acknowledge one's fault (mistake); 認輸 admit defeat; 認錯 *-tsuoh* ↓; 六親不認 be unfeeling towards everybody, utterly devoid of human feelings; 認不是 admit one is in the wrong; 直認 make a straight confession; 自認 willingly admit (concede); 認不得 be a total stranger to, cannot admit (agree, concede); 招認口供 (of criminal suspects) make a deposition in court; 承認 confess, admit, concede, recognize; 認了 *-'le* ↓; 認背 silently accept any ill luck (misfortune) that has befallen one; 認頭 *-tour* ↓; 認命 *-mihng* ↓. (3) Consent, agree: 認可 *-kee* ↓; 認股 subscribe to corporate shares; 認保 serve as guarantor; 認准 approve, allow, let it be done. (4) Take into one's family as a member: 認親 first meeting on the wedding day between members of the families of the bridegroom and the bride; 認乾爹, 認乾媽 be formally adopted by a man (woman) as his (her) child.

認 得 *rehn'de,* v. i., be able to recognize: 認得這個字 know the meaning of this character; 認得這個人 know who this man is.

認 眞 *rehnjen,* v. i., make earnest efforts to do one's best.

認 可 *rehnkee,* v. t., (1) approve, endorse, assent to; (2) give legal force to, authorize, sanction.

認 了 *rehn'le,* v. t., accept without a protest: 吃多大的虧, 我都認了 I won't say a word about it even if I didn't get a square deal.

認 領 *rehnliing,* v. t., (1) (law) adopt (a child); (2) go to claim (s.t.) one has lost and found by others.

認 命 *rehnmihng,* v. i., take one's lot in life philosophically.

認 生 *rehnsheng,* v. i., be shy, said esp. of children.

認 識 *rehnshyh,* (1) n., (psych.) cognition; 認識論 (phil.) epistemology; (2) v. t., be familiar with; (3) (**rehn'shy*) (=認得 *rehn'de* ↑).

認 許 *rehnshyuu,* v.i. & t., acknowledge; approve.

認 死 扣(兒)(子) *rehn syykouh('l) ('tz),* phr., be stubborn (obstinate, unyielding).

認 頭 *rehntour,* v. t., (1) to consent with much reluctance; (2) passively endure (suffer).

認 錯 *rehn-tsuoh,* (1) v.i., admit one's fault or mistake (also 認錯兒); (2) v. t., mistake (s.o., s.t.) for another.

認 爲 *rehnweir,* v. t., take for, regard as, consider to be.

訫 60A.72–8

sheen.

V. i. & t. (AC) (1) Remember. (2) Speak out frankly.

§ 60A.80 (言/八)

讚 60A.80–1

tzahn.

[Interch. 贊 10.80]

N. A literary eulogy.

V. t. (1) Endorse, approve. (2) Praise, acclaim, applaud.

讚美 *tzahnmeei*, n., to praise hymn.
讚賞 *tzahn shaang*, v.t., to praise.
讚頌 *tzahnsuhng*, n. & v. t., eulogy; to eulogize.

讀 60A.80–1

dur (**douh*).

N. (**douh*) Pause in middle of sentence, caesura: 句讀 punctuation marking sentence (句) by a period, and pause (讀) by "、", corresponding usu., but not always, to comma; text so punctuated.

V. t. (1) To read (newspapers, books, letters): 默讀 silent reading; 朗讀 read aloud; 讀經 scripture reading. (2) To pronounce: 讀法 way of pronouncing; 讀音 *-yin*↓. (3) To go to school: 讀大學, 夜校 study at university, night school; 寄讀 be boarding student; 走讀 attend school living at home; 讀不起書 cannot afford to go to school.

讀本 *durbeen*, n., reader, school text.
讀者 *durjee*, n., reader (of book, article).
讀書 *dur-shu*, v. i., read (a book): 讀這本書 read this book; to have ability to read, be literate; 讀過書沒有 can one read? 讀書人 a scholar, or a literate person.
讀物 *durwuh*, n., reading material.
讀音 *duryin*, n., pronunciation.

諜 60A.80–5

juahn.

[Interch. 撰 10A.80]

§ 60A.81 (言/人)

詼 60A.81–1

huei.

Adj. Facetious, sarcastic.

詼詭 *hueigueei*, adj., surprising, novel (ideas, style) (cf. 恢[Δ]奇 22A.81).
詼諧 *hueishier*, adj. & n., humorous, laughter-provoking.

謨 60A.81–2

mor.

N. & v. i. (AC & LL) plan: 大禹謨, 皋陶謨 chapters in Shujing, *Book of History*; 鴻謨 (LL) great plan (for expansion, etc.); 謨罕默德 Mohammed the Prophet, also wr. 穆.

讞 60A.81–2

yahn.

N. Verdict: 成讞 verdict is passed; 定讞 final verdict.

誤 60A.81–4

wuh.

N. A mistake, error: 誤謬 *-miouh*↓; 失誤, 差誤 error.

V. i. & t. (1) To miss (hour, appointment): 誤時, 誤點 *-shyr*, *-diaan*↓; 誤了時機 miss an opportunity. (2) To cause injury or disadvantage to (person, country): 誤人 to cause person to lose s.t., lead s.o. astray; 誤國 to betray country; 誤人子弟 mislead and cause harm to the young men; 誤盡蒼生 mislead the whole world.

Adv. By mistake, by accident: 誤會 *-hueih*↓; 誤傷, 誤殺 to wound, kill, accidentally; 誤傳, 誤報 report s. t. through a mistake; 誤入岐途 misled into wrong path.

誤點 *wuh-diaan*, v. i., to be late (as train; 點=點鐘 the hour).
誤會 *wuhhueih*, v. i. & n., a misunderstanding: 彼此誤會 to misunderstand each other.
誤解 *wuh-jiee*, v. i. & n., a misinterpretation, to misinterpret.
誤卯 *wuh-maau*, v. i., see *-diaan*↑.
誤謬 *wuhmiouh*, n. & adj., error, erroneous.
誤事 *wuh-shyh*, v.i., spoil s.t. (by oversight, arbitrary decision, being late, etc.).
誤時 *wuh-shyr*, v.i., see *-diaan*↑.

該 60A.81–6

gai.

Aux. vb. Should, ought to: 該當, 合該, 應該 should, ought to; 不該 ought not to: 他不該如此 or simply 他眞不該 he is wrong, he should not do this; 你該走了 you should go now; 該死 *-syy*↓; 該打 deserve a spanking; 該罰 should be punished.

V. i. & t. (Vern.) to owe money:

該賬 owe debts; 該着, 該下 owe (so much money); 你該他多少錢 how much do you owe him? 我又不該你的情 I don't see what I owe you by way of gratitude.

Adj. (1) The said . . . , a term used in official documents in referring to a subordinate: 該員, 該局, 該校 the said individual, bureau, school. (2) That: 該處, 該地, 該案, 該項 that place, locality, case, item. (3) (Var. of 賅) comprehensive, all-inclusive.

該 班 (兒) *gaiban(-ba'l)*, v. i. & adj., (be one's turn to be) on duty.
該 博 *gaibor*, adj., learned, well-read, erudite.
該 當 *gaidang*, v. i., (1) ought to: 該當如此 should be so; 該當何罪 what should be the punishment? (2) be predestined: 命裏該當 destined to be so.
該 管 *gaiguaan*, adj., proper (authority): 該管機關 the competent authorities.
該 着 *gai'je*, v. i., (1) (of debt) remain unpaid for the time being: 該筆錢暫時該着 I'll pay you the money later on; (2) be one's turn: 這次該着你說了 now it's your turn to speak; (3) (*-jaur*) be predestined: 命裏該着 fate would have it so; 該着是你輸錢 (in gamble) you are fated to be the loser.
該 死 *gai syy*, phr., be damned (lit., "ought to die").

訣 60A.81-9

jyuer.

N. A formula: 訣竅 *-chiauh*↓; 口訣 a magic formula, a set of practical methods put in words for easy memory; 妙訣 a clever expedient; 秘訣 a secret formula; 訣要 *-yauh*↓.

V. t. Bid farewell to, take leave of: 訣別 *-bier*↓; 永訣 to part (with s.o.) for ever.

訣 別 *jyuerbier*, v.i., say farewell to (s.o.).
訣 竅 *jyuerchiauh*, n., the secret (of doing s.t.).
訣 要 *jyueryauh*, n., ditto.

諛 60A.81-9

yur.

V. t. To flatter, truckle to: 阿諛 ditto; 面諛 flatter to one's face; 諛言, 諛詞 flattering, unctuous words; 諛色 unctuous manner; 諛墓 "flatter the grave" said of dishonest eulogy of the dead.

談 60A.81-9

tarn.

N. (1) A surname. (2) Talk, conversation: 閒談 conversation as relaxation, small talk; 座談(會) meeting for discussion of topics; 清談 idle talk; spec. fashion in East Jihn period (4th cen.) for cultured, esp. Taoist conversation; 鄉談 local patois; 老生常談 moral platitudes; 街談巷議 street gossip; 筆談 gossip on paper, lit. notes; 言談 person's style or ability of conversation.

V. i. & t. To talk : 談什麽 talk about what? 談(到)他 talk about him; 談他作什麽 why talk about it? 談得來 can make conversation with (person); 談不到 (不上) 朋友 not qualified to be called friend; 談何容易 it's so easy to talk and criticize; 談正經的 let's talk seriously; 談公事, 談政治 talk business, politics; 談天說地 talk of anything under the sun; 談空說有 talk speculative philosophy; 談玄 talk mysticism; 談心說性 Neo-Confucian speculation on mind and nature; 談情說愛 talk love; 談虎色變 turn pale at the mere mention of tiger—easily scared; 談笑風生 a fascinating, lively talk at party; 健談 a good, interesting talker; 談笑自若 be completely at ease; 談言微中 (*-juhng*) talk not much, but always to the point; 談判, 談論 *-pahn*, *-luhn*↓.

談 柄 *tarnbihng*, n., butt of jokes.
談 鋒 *tarnfeng*, n., ability to talk: 談鋒甚健 a very good talker.
談 話 *tarnhuah*, n., conversation.
談 助 *tarnjuh*, n., material for gossip.
談 論 *tarnluhn*, v.t. & n., discuss, -ion.
談 判 *tarnpahn*, v.i., & n., negotiate, -ion, with a view to settling disputes.
談 心 *tarnshin*, v.i., have a heart-to-heart talk among very good friends.
談 天 *tarntian(-tia'l)*, v.i., have idle gossip, to chat, chew the rag.
談 吐 (兒) *tarntuu('l)*, v. i. & n., style of conversation (風雅 cultured, 粗鄙 coarse, etc.).

誒 60A.81-9

eh.

Excl. (1) Ay, yea! yes! (2) Exclamation of sorrow, disappointment.

§ 60A.82 (言/乂)

護 60A.82-2

huh.

N. A surname.

丨	小	𠂇	十	土	𠂇	廾	㆑	丨	一	丅	冂	口	囚	冈	冂	厂	尸	亠	广	宀	丶	乚	弋	心	八	人	乂	乛	一	丿	𠂉	𡿨
00	01	02	10	11	12	20	21	22	30	31	32	40	41	42	50	51	52	60	61	62	63	70	71	72	80	81	82	83	90	91	92	93

護 詖 諏 謾 謖 設

V. t. (1) To protect, maintain, defend: 庇護 protect (by influence); 保護 take good care of; 維護 maintain (level, status), support (party, etc.); 看護 keep watch over, nurse (patient); 守護 watch, defend (city, gate) from attack; 掩護 cover (exposed troops) from the side, defend (attacked unit); 辯護 defend by argument. (2) Take sides, cover: 護短 cover one's mistakes; 護己 defend oneself, one's own; 袒護 take s. o. 's side.

護 兵 *huhbing*, n., military guards.
護 符 *huhfur*, n., (1) charm for protecting against demons; (2) any person acting as protector (usu. 護身符).
護 照 *huhjauh*, n., passport.
護 脛 *huhjihng*, n., shin guard.
護 理 *huhlii*, n., (1) nursing: 護理學校, 護理科 nursing school, department; 護理工作 work of nursing; (2) a nurse; (3) formerly, deputy or *chargé d'affaires*.
護 喪 *huhsang*, n., head responsible for funeral affairs, usu. eldest member of family.
護 身 符 *huhshenfur*, n., see *-fur* ↑.
護 膝 *huhshi*, n., kneecap.
護 書 *huhshu*, n., folder (for documents).
護 士 *huhshyh*, n., a nurse (male or female).
護 胸 *huhshyung*, n., chest plate.
護 送 *huhsuhng*, v. t., to escort.
護 腿 *huhtueei*, n., leggings.
護 衛 *huhweih*, n., bodyguard; v. t., to act as escort.

詖 60A.82-2

bih.

V. i. To argue: (AC) 詖辯.

Adj. (AC) Biassed and argumentative: 詖辭 argumentative talk, special pleading.

諏 60A.82-3

tzou.

V. t. (1) To plan, consult: 諏訪 (LL) ask for advice. (2) Choose, select: 諏吉 (LL) pick an auspicious day.

謾 60A.82-4

mahn (*marn).

V. i. & t. (1) To slight: 輕謾 slight (person); 謾罵 abuse (person). (2) (**marn*) Deceive (=瞞): 謾天謾地 try to deceive everybody; 謾語 deceitful words.

謖 60A.82-4

suh.

Adj. (AC) standing straight up.

設 60A.82-4

sheh.

V. t. (1) To set up (school, trap, dinner, defense, plan, etc.): 設立, 設置 *-lih, -jyh* ↓; 設局, 設防, 設計 *-jyur, -farng, -jih* ↓; 設座 give dinner at; 設館 give private tutoring. (2) Arrange for occasion: 陳設 arrange, set up (exhibit); 擺設 lay out (table 酒席); 席設 dinner to be given at (place). (3) Plan, provide: 設備, 設施 *-beih, -shy* ↓; 設法 *-faa* ↓.

Conj. If: 設使, 設若, 設如, 設或 *-shyy, -ruoh, -rur, -huoh* ↓; 設有不幸 if s.t. should happen.

設 擺 *sheh'bai*, v.t., lay out for occasion (altar, dinner, etc.).
設 備 *shehbeih* (*-'bei*), (1) n., provisions, facilities, equipment, etc.: 設備很好 with good equipment or facilities; (2) v. t., to provide facilities.
設 奠 *sheh-diahn*, v. i., to set up libation ceremony.
設 定 *sheh-dihng*, v. t., to define (certain rights), to set up (laws and regulations).
設 法 *shehfaa*, v. i., try to, think of ways to (save s.o. in distress, provide money, escape, etc.).
設 防 *sheh-farng*, v. i., set up patrol or defense: 不設防城市 (international law) an open city.
設 伏 *shehfur*, v. i., to lay ambush.
設 或 *shehhuoh*, conj., if.
設 弧 *sheh-hur*, phr., (AC) hang a bow on left door as sign of birth of a boy.
設 帳 *sheh-jahng*, v. i., (AC, allu.) to set up place for teaching.
設 教 *sheh-jiauh*, v. i., (1) to found a religion, establish a church; (2) to set up as teacher (at a place).
設 計 *sheh-jih*, v. i., (1) to contrive (to destroy s.o., etc.); (2) draw up blueprint for building, plan for project, sketch or composition in painting.
設 穽 *sheh-jiing*, v. i., lay a trap.
設 置 *shehjyh*, v.i. & n., arrange, -ment, facilities, equipment.
設 局 *sheh-jyur*, v. i., ditto: 設騙局 lay a plan for swindle.
設 立 *shehlih*, v. t., (1) to establish (school, free dispensary, temporary headquarters; etc.); (2) to ordain (priest, king).
設 論 *sheh-luhn*, n., (AC) a literary dialogue form.
設 若 *shehruoh*, conj., if.
設 如 *shehrur*, conj., if.
設 色 *sheh-seh*, v. i., to apply colors (to painting).
設 想 *shehshiaang*, v. i., to conjecture; to consider for (s.o).
設 施 *shehshy*, v. i. & n., arrange, -ments; management (of hospital); provisions, facilities (for flood control, against epidemics, etc.).
設 使 *shehshyy*, conj., if.
設 辭 *sheh-tsyr*, (1) v. i., find some excuses (for delay, etc.); (2) n., a pretext.

A

譈 60A.82-6

dueih.

[Var. of 懟, 憝]

N. (AC) resentment and hatred.

議 60A.82-8

yih.

[Abbr. of 議 60A.71]

諼 60A.82-9

shyuan (**shuahn*).

N. Var. of 萱 20A.30.

V. i. & t. (1) (AC) to forget: 永矢弗諼 I swear never to forget. (2) (AC) to cheat. (3) (**shuahn*) To fail in promise or appointment: 把人諼 (or 涮) 了.

譊 60A.82-9

naur.

[Var. of 呶 40A.82]

§60A.83 (言/⌒)

謎 60A.83-2

mir (**mih, *meih*).

N. Puzzle, riddle (謎兒 pr. *meh'l*): 猜謎 guess at riddle; 謎樣人物 mysterious person; 燈謎 a riddle pasted on lamps at parties.

B

謎底 *mirdii*, n., answer to the riddle.
謎面 *mirmiahn*, n., the riddle as given or stated.
謎語 *miryuu*, n., a puzzle, puzzling statement.

譴 60A.83-2

chiaan.

V. t. (1) To punish: 天譴 God's punishment. (2) To scold, reprimand severely.

譴訶 *chiaanhe*, v. t., (LL) to reprimand, rebuke harshly.
譴怒 *chiaannuh*, v. i., (of God, ruler) to be wrath and punish (s. o.).
譴責 *chiaantzer*, v. t., to rebuke.

諟 60A.83-4

shyh.

V.t. 諟正 (somewhat arch., pompous) to examine for approval, see 是^Δ正 41.83.

讁 60A.83-6

jer.

[Var. of 謫]

誕 60A.83-9

dahn.

N. Birth, birthday: 華誕, 壽誕 birthday celebration for elderly people; 聖誕, 耶誕 Christmas; 誕辰, 誕日 *-chern, -ryh* ↓.

C

V. i. Give birth to, be born: 誕生 be born: 誕子 give birth to son.

Adj. Deceitful, extravagant (talk); odd, absurd: 怪誕不經 crazy, fantastic (talk); 荒誕 absurd; 妄誕 false, deceitful.

誕辰 *dahnchern*, n., birthday.
誕日 *dahnryh*, n., birthday.
誕生 *dahnsheng*, v. i., be born, give birth to.

§60A.91 (言/ノ)

謬 60A.91-5

miouh (*also *niouh*).

Adj. (1) Wrong, false, absurd: 荒謬 absurd; 謬論, 謬見 *-luhn, -jiahn* ↓. (2) (Court.) 謬愛＝錯愛 undeserved kindness, favors; also adv., 謬承 unworthily receive (your praise, etc.).

謬見 *miouh-jiahn*, n., false, erroneous views; my humble views.
謬種 *miouh-juung*, n., (derog.) bastard, heretic: 謬種流傳 phr., school of bastard thought.
謬戾 *miouhlih*, n., absurd, false.
謬論 *miouh-luhn*, n., false, erroneous opinions.
謬耄 *miouhmauh*, adj., senile.
謬妄 *miouhwahng*, adj., false, absurd (conduct, opinions, etc.).
謬誤 *miouhwuh*, adj., mistaken.

諺 60A.91-6

yahn.

譈 議 諼 譊 謎 譴 諟 讁 誕 謬 諺

亅	小	卜	十	土	ナ	卄	上	丨	一	丅	7	口	区	冈	丁	厂	尸	亠	广	宀	丶	乚	弋	心	八	人	乂	⌒	ノ	リ	𠂉	く
00	01	02	10	11	12	20	21	22	30	31	32	40	41	42	50	51	52	60	61	62	63	70	71	72	80	81	82	83	90	91	92	93

N. A proverb: 俗諺 popular saying.

諺語 *yahnyuu*, n., a proverb, popular saying.

診 60A.91-8

jeen (also *jen*).

V. t. (Of physician) to examine (patient, pulse, etc.): 診斷, 診治 *-duahn, -jyh* ↓; 診病 examine illness; 出診 visit homes of patients; 應診 answer calls for home visits; 就診 see a doctor; 急診 emergency treatment.

診察 *jeenchar*, v. t., examine (patient, illness).
診切 *jeenchieh*, v. i., to examine pulse.
診斷 *jeenduahn*, v. t. & n., to diagnose, a diagnosis.
診候 *jeenhouh*, v. t., to diagnose.
診治 *jeenjyh*, v. t., to give medical treatment.
診療 *jeenliaur*, v. t., ditto.
診夢 *jeen-mehng*, v. i., to interpret dreams.
診脈 *jeenmoh*, v. i., examine the pulse.
診視 *jeenshyh*, v. t., (of doctor) examine (patient, illness).
診所 *jernsuoo*, n., clinic, doctor's office.

§ 60A.93 (言/く)

訟 60A.93-8

suhng.

N. Lawsuit: 訴訟 ditto; 涉訟 (公庭), 構訟 involve in lawsuit, go to court; 息訟 settle dispute.

V.i. & t. (1) To argue: 爭訟 to argue; 聚訟紛紜 in a great controversy. (2) (AC) blame: 吾未見能見其過而內自訟者也 (AC) I have never seen anyone who can see his own mistake and put the blame squarely on himself. (3) (AC, rare) u.f. 頌, to praise.

訟案 *suhng-ahn*, n., a case in court.
訟棍 *suhngguhn*, n., a shyster.
訟狀 *suhngjuahng*, n., a legal plaint.
訟師 *suhngshy*, n., law practitioner, attorney at law.
訟事 *suhngshyh*, n., a legal case.
訟言 *suhngyarn*, n., (AC) public criticism.

諭 60A.93-8

yuh.

[Usu. wr. 論 60A.00]

諉 60A.93-9

weei.

V.t. (1) To shift blame: 推諉 evade, pass (task) to others; 諉過 shift blame. (2) (AC) entrust.

SECTION 60S

§ 60S.00 (亠^{S}/刂)

刘 60S.00-2

liour.

[Pop. of 劉 90S.00]

刻 60S.00-2

keh (*ke).

N. (1) A quarter of an hour (lit. a "notch") 一刻鐘; 此時此刻 this hour and moment; 時時刻刻 all the time, every minute; 一刻工夫 quarter of an hour, soon, a moment; 一刻千金 value every minute (for study); 立刻, 卽刻 at once; 刻下 right now; 刻不容緩 must not lose a minute. (2) Edition: 宋刻, 元刻 Suhng, Yuarn edition of wood-block printing.

V. t. (also *ke) To carve, inscribe, inscribe in memory: 雕刻 carve, carving; 刻花 carved design; 刻字, 刻圖章, 刻石 carve words, carve seal, inscribe on stone; 刻印 carve wood blocks for printing; 刻圖章 to carve a seal; 刻書 (loosely) to publish book; 刻骨銘心 inscribe (debt of gratitude) on one's mind, in one's heart; 刻舟求劍 carve a mark on gunwale in moving boat where a sword was lost—ridiculous stupidity.

Adj. (1) Petty, fault-finding, exacting, mean: 苛刻 petty (criticism); 刻毒, 刻薄, 刻苦 *-dur, -bor, -kuu* ↓; 深刻 deep, penetrating (criticism, understanding). (2) (As var. of 剋) 刻日 this very date; 刻期 punctually on set date.

Adv. Harshly: 刻待 treat harshly; 刻己待人 self-sacrificing, self-denial in service to fellowmen.

刻剅剖剷劑爛竚旖竦

刻板 *kehbaan*, (1) n., wood block for printing; (2) adj., adhering to rules and regulations without human considerations, going by the book: 這個人好刻板 this man is very stiff, inflexible.

刻本 *kehbeen*, n., edition of wood-block printing.

刻薄 *kehbor*(*keh'bo*), adj., mean, ungenerous, carping (criticism): 他待人很刻薄 he is very mean toward people (servants, etc.); 這件事做得太刻薄了 this affair has been settled too harshly.

刻刀 *kehdau*, n., knife used in carving, inscribing.

刻毒 *kehdur*, adj., petty, cruel, venomous (of a man's heart, dealings).

刻畫 *kehhuah*, adj., (1) as in 刻畫入微 realistic portrayal of character; (2) see *-baan* ↑.

刻苦 *kehkuu*, adj., hard-working, self-sacrificing: 刻苦用工 work hard at studies; 刻苦耐勞 willing to go through hardships; 刻苦成家 build up a family by hard work and thrift.

刻漏 *kehlouh*, n., an ancient waterclock with hour markings.

刻書 *keh-shu*, v. i., to publish book, formerly, by carving wood blocks.

刻絲 *kehsy*, n., formerly, silk tapestry with cut designs.

刻意 *kehyih*, adv., with studious or intent effort: 刻意求工 do one's very best to achieve perfection.

剅 60S.00–2

chirng (**lyueh*).

V. t. (1) U. f. 黥 41S.01, tattoo, brand (a criminal). (2) (**lyueh*) U. f. 掠 10A.01.

剖 60S.00–2

poou (vern. also *pou*).

V. t. (1) To cut open, slice, split in two: 剖分 cut in two; 剖開 cut open; 剖腹 cut open belly; 剖腹藏珠 allu. to story of one who cut his belly to hide a pearl, i. e., sacrifice life to gain; 剖心 bare one's heart in all sincerity; 剖肝泣血 ditto. (2) To dissect, analyze, and thus reveal: 剖解, 剖析 *-jiee*, *-shi* ↓; 剖白 *-bair* ↓; 剖斷如流 phr., said of a judge quick in deciding lawsuits; 剖斗折衡 phr., (AC) destroy weights and measures (in return-to-nature philosophy).

剖白 *poou-bair*, v. t., reveal completely.

剖腹生產 *poufuh-shengchaan*, n., Caesarean section or operation.

剖解 *pourjiee*, v. t., to explain, dissect (meaning of text).

剖面 *pooumiahn*, n., cross section, sectional view.

剖析 *pooushi*, v. t., see *-jiee* ↑.

剖字 *pooutzyh*, n., (=拆字) art of taking a character apart and revealing hidden meaning or oracle.

剖驗 *poouyahn*, v. t., hold inquest.

剷 60S.00–2

chaan.

[Interch. 鏟 81A.11; anc. var. 剗 71S.00]

V.t. To level off, pare down, raze to the ground: 剷平 to quash (rebellion).

剷除 *chaan-chur*, v.t., to abolish, exterminate (vice, obstructions).

劑 60S.00–2

jih.

N. (1) A medicinal preparation: 藥劑 drugs; 強心劑 cardiac stimulant; 毒劑 poison; 催化劑 a catalyst; 混合劑 a mixture. (2) A dose of medicine: 一劑藥 one dose. (3) (AC) a bond closing a business deal: 質劑 (AC) a form of business contract.

V. t. Adjust, arrange, put in order: 調劑 (of food) to season, (fig.) alternate work (hardships) with rest or play (lighter jobs).

爛 60S.00–5

larn.

Adj. See 斑$^{\Delta}$爛 31A.11.

竚 60S.00–6

juh.

[Var. of 佇 91A.01]

旖 60S.00–9

yii.

旖旎 *yirnii*, adj., charming, graceful (female figure); charming, enticing, glorious (landscape).

§ 60S.01 (亠^{s}/小)

竦 60S.01–1

suung.

Adj. & adv. (1) Var. of 悚 22A.01,

亅	小	卜	十	土	ナ	卄	山	丨	一	丁	フ	口	区	冈	ㄱ	厂	尸	亠	广	宀	丶	乚	七	心	八	人	乂	乛	一	丿	𠂉	く
00	01	02	10	11	12	20	21	22	30	31	32	40	41	42	50	51	52	60	61	62	63	70	71	72	80	81	82	83	90	91	92	93

shivering in fright. (2) Solemn, -ly.

辣 60S.01–1

lah.

Adj. (1) (Of food) pungent, hot (flavor): 味辣 pungent, peppery taste; 辣餗餗(兒)的 somewhat but not too pungent in taste; 辛辣 pungent, peppery. (2) Cruel, harsh, ruthless: 心黑手辣 black-hearted and cruel; 毒辣 ruthless.

辣瓣兒醬 *lahbah'ljiahng*, n., soy sauce with a pungent taste.
辣醬 *lahjiahng*, n., (Chin.) hot sauce.
辣椒 *lahjiau*, n., hot pepper.
辣浪 *lahlahng*, adj., (MC) gallant, dashing.
辣蓼 *lahliaau*, n., (bot.) *Palygonum flaccidum.*
辣手 *lahshoou*, n. & adj., cruel or sinister.
辣實 *lahshyr*, adj. & adv., bitter (ly), violent(ly), sinister(ly): 冷的辣實 bitterly cold; 手段辣實 sinister tactics.
辣撻 *lah'ta*, adj., untidy, slovenly (=邋遢, also wr. 辣闒).
辣子 *lahtz*, n., (1) hot pepper; (2) an impetuous and overbearing person.
辣燥 *lahtzauh*, adj., hot-tempered and cruel.

§60S.02 (ㄧ^{S}/ㄎ)

旅 60S.02–9

lyuu.

N. (1) Formerly a body of 500 troops, now gen. a brigade: 混成旅 mixed brigade; 軍旅 troops in gen. (2) Travel: 逆旅 journey abroad, see V.i ↓. (3) A surname.

V.i. (1) To travel: 旅費 travelling expenses; 旅次 during travel; 旅居 away from home, to stay abroad.

旅店 *lyuudiahn*, n., inn, hotel.
旅館 *lyurguaan*, n., hotel.
旅長 *lyurjaang*, n., commander of brigade.
旅客 *lyuukeh*, n., traveller, tourist.
旅社 *lyuusheh*[1], n., hotel: 大旅社 "grand" hotel.
旅舍 *lyuusheh*[2], n., hostel, hotel.
旅行 *lyuushirng*, v. i., to travel; n., a journey, trip: 旅行社 tourist agency; 旅行團 group of tourists; 春季旅行 spring trip.
旅順 *Lyuushuhn*, n., Port Arthur.

§60S.10 (ㄧ^{S}/十)

辯 60S.10–6 .

biahn.
[Dist. 辨, 瓣, 辮 ↓]

N. & v.i. Argue, discuss, dispute: 爭辯 argue (gument); 好辯 love to argue; 善辯 eloquent, have controversial skill; 巧辯 v.i. & n., clever argument; 狡辯, v.i. & n., 詭辯 quibble; 強辯 v.i. & n., stubborn argument by distortion of facts or subterfuges; 把人辯倒 defeat person in argument.

辯白 *biahnbair*, v.t., clear up case, present one party's point of view.
辯駁 *biahnbor*, v.i., argue: 與人辯駁 argue with person.
辯護 *biahnhuh*, v.t. & n., defend person at court or elsewhere: 爲人辯護; n., 辯護人 defender, advocate.
辯證法 *biahnjehng-faa*, n., dialectic.
證給 *biahnjir*, n., (LL) talent for eloquence.
辯論 *biahnluhn*, n. & v.i., carry on controversy, argument, debate in court or parliament.
辯難 *biahn-nahn*, n. & v. i., (to, a) dispute on points.
辯士 *biahn-shyh*, n., sophist, person good at argument.
辯才 *biahn-tsair*, n., natural eloquence, forensic skill.

瓣 60S.10–9

bahn.

N. Petal (of flower), segment (of fruit, beans).

瓣兒 *bahn'l*, n., a segment (of fruit or flower).
瓣香 *bahnshiang*, n., (LL allu.) symbol of respect, worship.

辨 60S.10–9

biahn.
[Dist. 辯, 辮, 瓣]

V.t. (1) Distinguish: 辨別 *-bier* ↓; 辨是非, 黑白, 眞假 establish the right and wrong, distinguish black from white, true from false; 分辨 distinguish, discern difference. (2) Recognize: 辨味 recognize taste; 辨色 recognize colors; 察顏辨色 subtly react by noticing superior's countenance; 辨認, 辨識 *-rehn, -shy* ↓. (3) Make known: 辨志 (LL) make clear one's intentions, motives, ambition.

辨白 *biahnbair*, v.t., clear up (doubts, suspicions).
辨別 *biahnbier*, v.t., distinguish, sort out.
辨惑 *biahn-huoh*, v.t., (LL) clear up unbelief, false notions.
辨明 *biahn-mirng*, v.t., =*-bair* ↑.
辨認 *biahnrehn*, v.t., recognize, know by difference (true parent, precious stone, handwriting).
辨析 *biahnshi*, v. t., analyze.

辨識 *biahnshy*, v. t., recognize.

辨異 *biahn-yih*, v. i., compare difference esp. in texts.

辦 60S.10-9

bahn.

[Abbr. 办; dist. 辨, 辯, 辮, 瓣]

V.i. & t. (1) To do, manage, handle, prepare, take charge of (affairs): usually 辦理 *-lii* ↓; 辦事 execute, attend to business; often with vb. complements: 辦得到, 辦得來, 辦得了 (pr. *liaau*) can do it; 辦不到, 辦不來, 辦不了 cannot do it; 辦不完 cannot finish; 辦得好 do it well; 辦酒席 prepare a banquet; 辦壽, 辦生日 make preparations to celebrate birthday; 辦喪事, 辦(理)後事 make preparations for funeral; 辦賑務 take charge of famine or flood relief; 辦稿 prepare a draft, draft statement. (2) To punish: 重辦 punish heavily; 辦賊 punish criminal; 辦罪 punish crime. (3) To purchase supplies: 辦貨. (4) As second part of many compp.: 幫辦 *bang-*, n., official assistant; 備辦 *beih-*, v.i. & t., prepare; 查辦 *char-*, v. t., investigate (charges); 創辦 *chuahng-*, v. t., establish (schools, hospitals), initiate; 代辦 *daih-*, n., deputy, *chargé d'affaires*; 督辦 *du-*, n., commissioner, high commissioner; 照辦 *jauh-*, v.i., do accordingly (usu. official language); 開辦 *kai-*, v. t., open, establish, to found; 買辦 *maai-*, n., compradore.

辦案 *bahn-ahn*, v. i., (of judge, official) take charge of a case.

辦差 *bahn-chai*, v. i., take charge of missions.

辦法 *bahnfaa*, n., way, means: 你有什麽辦法 what can you do? 另有辦法 there is another way of dealing with it; 沒辦法 be helpless, without means or resources.

辦理 *bahnlii*, v. t., to take charge of, manage, handle (affairs).

辦事 *bahnshyh*, v.i., to handle administrative affairs, business.

辮 60S.10-9

biahn.

N. Pigtail, queue, usu. 辮子 *biahn-*; 辮繩, 辮線 braid for queue; a long braid.

V. t. (AC) Make hair braid.

§60S.11 (⊥ˢ/土)

旌 60S.11-9

jing.

N. A banner made of feathers: 旌旗 *-chir* ↓.

V. t. To honor officially: 旌表 *-biaau*, 旌卹 *-shyuh*, 旌節 *-jier* ↓; 請旌 formal request for posthumous honors; 旌德 to honor the virtuous.

旌表 *jingbiaau*, n., an official testimonial conferred on women for chastity or on men for loyalty or filial piety.

旌旗 *jingchir*, n., banners and flags.

旌節 *jingjier*, n., (1) formerly, insignia heralding the approach of a high official; (2) formerly, an envoy's credentials.

旌卹 *jingshyuh*, v. t., confer posthumous honors on (deceased) and pension his family for meritorious services to the country.

雜 60S.11-9

tzar.

[Anc. var. 襍]

V. i. & t. Mix, blend, mingle: 夾雜 mix together; 攙雜 blend; 雜在其中 mingled with; 雜入 mix in with other things.

Adj. (1) Mixed: 複雜 complex, complicated; 閒雜 not wanted, unnecessary, unessential: 閒雜人等 loafers, idlers, intruders; 雜牌 nondescript, of inferior quality; 人多嘴雜 divided counsel, too many people, too many ideas; 嘈雜 noisy; 雜種 crossbred, a hybrid, a mongrel, (vulg.) children of a mixed marriage; 雜交 cross-breed, cross fertilization; promiscuous friends. (2) Additional, extra: 雜稅 irregular levies (taxes); 雜費 sundry expenses; 雜項 *-shiahng* ↓. (3) Composite, manifold, many and varied: 雜質 of unequal quality; 雜八湊兒 an assemblage of disparate things; 雜湊兒 put dissimilar things together; 雜貨(店) groceries (ry); 雜拌兒 *-bah'l* ↓; 雜様兒 an assortment of different things; 雜糧 *-liarng* ↓; 雜合麵兒 flour made from a mixture of corns, peas and beans; 雜合菜, 雜會菜 a dish made of leftover foods; 雜碎, 雜燴 chop suey, mixed stew; 雜劇 *-jyuh*, 雜技 *-jih²*, 雜耍 *-shuaa* ↓; 雜卉 plants of various kinds; 雜草 wild grass; 雜居 (of people of different social or racial origins) live together without discrimination; 雜處 ditto: 五方雜處 inhabited by people from all walks of life; 雜院兒 one house with many families; 大雜院 ditto. (4) Trivial, petty, trifling: 雜務 minor duties, small tasks; 雜事 sundry work; 雜物 sundry items, odds and ends; 打雜(的) (serve as) a handy man.

雜拌兒 *tzarbah'l*, n., (1) an assortment of dried fruits, eata-

雜 離 郊

bles; (2) a mixture of different kinds of tobacco.

雜布 *tzar-buh*, n., coarse cloth.

雜婚制 *tzarhunjyh*, n., (sociology) primitive promiscuity.

雜記 *tzarjih*¹, n., random notes.

雜技 *tzarjih*², n., sundry theatrical shows, such as acrobatics.

雜誌 *tzarjyh*, n., a magazine, a periodical.

雜職 *tzar-jyr*, n., formerly, an official with minor duties.

雜劇 *tzarjyuh*, n., Yuarn comedy; also 北曲 dramas of "Northern" type.

雜勞 *tzarlaur*, n., a chronic disease of elderly people.

雜糧 *tzarliarng*, n., miscellaneous cereals, any crop other than rice and wheat.

雜流 *tzarliour*, n., people of different low professions.

雜亂 *tzarluahn*, adj., disorderly, untidy, in a state of confusion.

雜麵 *tzarmiahn*, n., noodles made of mixed flour, as that of wheat and millet.

雜評 *tzarpirng*, n., (journalism) editorial paragraphs, shorter comments.

雜然 *tzarrarn*, adv., (AC) one and all, without exception.

雜糅 *tzar-roou*, v. i. & t., intermix, intermingle.

雜項 *tzarshiahng*, (1) n., miscellaneous items; (2) (-'*shiang*) adj., of various sorts: 這院子裏住的人很雜項 the people who live in this compound come from different walks of life.

雜耍 *tzarshuaa*, n., variety show.

雜學 *tzar-shyuer*, n., unsystematic knowledge, bits of odd information.

雜史 *tzar-shyy*, n., unofficial histories (opp. 正史 official histories).

雜碎 *tzar'suei*, (1) adj., minor, petty, trivial; (2) n., entrails of animals used as food; (3) n., chop suey: 他沒安著好雜碎 (sl.) he has got a bad "noodle."

雜沓 *tzartah*, adj., in a state of confusion.

雜錯 *tzartsuoh*, adj., intertwined, intermingled. ⌈confused.

雜厠 *tzartsyh*, adj., disorderly,

雜纂 *tzartzuaan*, n., a compilation of miscellaneous accounts, a miscellany.

雜字 *tzar-tzyh*, n., rhymed phrases of individual characters for easy memory.

離 60S.11–9

lir.

[Var. 离; used sometimes as var. for 鸝; sometimes interch. with 籬, 縭, 蘺, 螭, 璃, 褵]

N. (1) Separation, departure. (2) One of the eight diagrams in 易經, see *baguah* 八⁴卦 80.80.

V.t. (1) Separate, leave, go away from: 離別 *-bier*↓; 別離 be separated; 離散 *-sahn*, 離合 *-her*, 離開 *-kai*↓; 離不開 cannot be separated from; 離得開 can be separated from; 離不開手兒 too busy to get away from what one is doing; 離不開身兒 cannot afford to get away for a moment; 離不開眼兒 must always keep an eye on; 離不開人兒 always need s.o. to care for; 離得了, 離不了 can, cannot separate from (person); 離鄉背井 leave one's native district; 遠離 gone far away; 離羣索居 live the life of a recluse; 分崩離析 (of a country's political or social order) disintegrating and torn by dissension; 離愁別恨(緒) grief of parting; 離婚 *-hun*↓; 離間 *-jiahn*↓. (2) Dispense with, go without: 他離不得手杖 he cannot go without a walking stick. (3) Go against or counter to: 叛離 to rebel; 離經叛道 be guilty of heterodoxy; 離叛 to desert and rebel. (4) Shift from, deviate from: 離格兒 deviate from standard, stray off; 離譜兒 ditto; 說話別離格兒 talk within limits; 離股兒 (of the joints of furniture, etc.) loose, not closely knit.

離岸價格 *lir-ahn jiahger*, n., free on board (f. o. b.) (shipping).

離別 *lirbier*, v. t., take leave of.

離塵 *lirchern*, n., (LL) synonym for cassock.

離奇 *lirchir*, adj., unbelievably strange, extraordinary.

離貳 *lirehl*, v. i., to defect, be disloyal at heart, alienated.

離宮 *lirgung*, n., (LL) summer or winter palace; temporary imperial headquarters away from the capital.

離合 *lir-her*, n., separation and reunion: 悲歡離合 joys and sorrows, separation and reunion.

離婚 *lirhun*, v. i. & t., to divorce, be divorced.

離間 *lirjiahn*, v. t., to sow dissension between or among.

離開 *lir-kai*, (1) v. t., depart from (place), part from (person); (2) n., departure.

離離 *lirlir*, adj., (1) separated, isolated; (2) hanging down; (3) arranged in rows; (4) few and scattered; (5) loose and showing cleavage.

離樓 *lirlour*, adj., (1) intricate, (of trees) intertwining; (2) carved, engraved (also wr. 麗廔, 蠡廔).

離娘飯 *lir-niarng-fahn*, n., a dinner paid as gift to the bride's family by the groom's family on their wedding day (lit., "a dinner at which the bride bids good-bye to her mother").

離譜(兒) *lirpuu('l)*, adj. & adv., off or below the standard.

離散 *lirsahn*, v. i., be scattered about, be separated from one another.

離騷 *Lirsau*, n., one of the works by Chyuh Yuarn (屈原).

離心 *lirshin*, adj., centrifugal; 離心力 (phys.) centrifugal force; 離心離德 divided loyalty.

§ 60S.22 (亠^{S}/丨)

郊 60S.22–3

jiau.

N. (1) Suburb: 郊野 *-yee*, 郊外 *-waih*↓; 郊區 suburban districts; 郊原 *-yuarn*↓; 郊遊 *-your*↓; 城郊, 市郊 city limits; 郊迎 *-yirng*↓; 四郊 the surrounding districts of a city. (2) Sacrifices to Heaven and Earth.

郊甸 *jiaudiahn*, n., suburbs and the surrounding region.

郊外 *jiauwaih*, n., outskirts, suburbs.

郊野 *jiauyee*, n., the countryside.

郊迎 *jiauyirng*, (1) v. i., go outside the city gates to welcome distinguished guests; (2) n., such welcome.

郊遊 *jiauyour*, n., a picnic, an outing, an excursion.

郊原 *jiauyuarn*, n., an open country.

部 60S.22-3

buh.

N. adjunct. 一部書 a volume; 這部書 this volume.

N. (1) Part, region, division, section: 上部, 下部 upper part, lower part, section; 外部, 內部 exterior, inner part; 頭部, 頸部 the head, the neck, neck region; 前部, 後部 (of body) the front, the back; 局部 part, partially. (2) Section or division of any organization; (of a government) ministry: 外交部, 教育部 Foreign Ministry, Ministry of Education, etc.; (of department store) section (for shoes, ladies' wear, etc.): 售賣部 sales division: 購買部 purchase division, etc.; 部分 *-fehn*, 部門 *-mern*↓. (3) One of four divisions in traditional library classification (四部), consisting of the Classics (經部), History (史部), Philosophy (子部), Collected Works (集部), see 四⁴部 41.41. (4) Short for 部首 radical, see 部首 *-shoou*↓. (5) Army units: 部屬, 部下, 部陣 *-shuu*, *-shiah*, *-jehn*↓.

V.t. (LL) command (troops): 所部甚衆 command many troops.

部隊 *buhdueih*, n., troops of a given unit.

部分 *buhfehn*, n., part, in part.

部會 *buh-hueih*, n., term referring to the ministries and commissions or administrative units.

部長 *buhjaang*, n., (cabinet) minister; head at a department in organizations.

部陣 *buhjehn*, n., troops of a given unit in their appearance, discipline: 部陣整齊.

部帙 *buhjyh*, n., collection or set of books with reference to their quantity, condition: 部帙浩繁; see N. 3↑.

部列 *buhlieh*, v. t. & n., arrange, arrangement, formation (of books, troops).

部落 *buhluoh*, n., tribe, tribal region.

部門 *buhmern*, n., section, class; classification.

部下 *buhshiah*, n., troops or officers under a commander.

部首 *buhshoou*, n., the radical, one of the 214 divisions in the Kangshi Dictionary, such as 宀, 木, 火.

部屬 *buhshuu*, n., troops under a certain commander.

部署 *buhshyuh*, v. t., put in order: 部署一切 prepare everything, as packing before departure.

部位 *buhweih*, n., part (of body, ship, etc.).

部伍 *buhwuu*, n., troops of a certain unit.

部院 *buhyuahn*, n., the ministries and the five *yuan* (五院) of the government.

部員 *buhyuarn*, n., member of staff of ministry, or military staff.

郭 60S.22-3

guo.

N. (1) The outer city or city wall (opp. 內城 the inner city): 城郭 city and outer city; the suburbs. (2) The outer rim, contour: 輪郭 the outer rim of a wheel, general outline; contour sketch. (3) A surname.

旂 60S.22-9

chir.

N. Formerly, a dragon flag with bells on tassels, now a flag in gen. as var. of 旗 60S.80.

旆 60S.22-9

peih.

[Pop. 旆]

N. (LL) a flag, pennant in gen.; esp. one with colored borders.

新 60S.22-9

shin.

V. t. To make new, renew: 自新 reform oneself; 一新耳目 to present a new appearance.

Adj. (1) New, opp. old (舊): 新舊兒 *-jiouh'l*↓; 新生 new student; rebirth; new (dress, house, law, regulations, invention, etc.); 新臺幣 (NT) new Taiwan currency; 新幣 new coin; 新幣制 new currency; 新紀錄 new record; 新世界 the New World; 新大陸 the New Continent (the Americas); 新氣象 a new atmosphere; 革新, 維新 to reform, modernize, modernization; 推陳出新 put forth new ideas; 新陳代謝 metabolism. (2) Beginning: 新年 *-niarn*, 新正 *-jeng*↓; 新春, 新歲 the New

新 竝 旜 站

Year; 新秋 beginning of autumn. (3) Modern: 新女性 the modern woman; 新名詞 modern terms; 新文藝 modern literature and arts; 新文學 modern literature; 新時代 the modern age; 新世紀 the new century; 新家庭 the modern home. (4) Novel: 新奇, 新穎 *-chir*, *-yiing* ↓; 日新月異 incessant changes (in fashion, ideas, improved products). (5) Pertaining to wedding: 新郎 *-larng*, 新娘 *-niarng*, 新房 *-farng*, 新婚 *-hun*, etc. ↓. (6) Recent, fresh, see Adv. ↓.

Adv. & adj. Recent, -ly, newly: 新出版 newly published; 新出品 recent products, publications; 新朋友, 新交 new friends; 新開張 (shop) newly opened; 新晴 the sky has just cleared; 新綠 the fresh green vegetation; 新涼 fresh cool of autumn; 舊恨新愁 all the old and recent sorrows; 新下樹兒 (fruit) freshly plucked from the trees; 新鮮 fresh (fruit, sea food).

新潮 *shin-chaur*, n., new wave, trend.

新奇 *shinchir*, adj., novel, interesting (event, fashion).

新房 *shin-farng*, n., bridal chamber: 鬧新房 custom of teasing the bride on wedding night to provoke the correctly solemn bride to laugh.

新婦 *shinfuh*, n., the bride; (MC) used in reference to wife, daughter-in-law or by the wife to herself.

新姑娘 *shin-gu'niang*, n., bride.

新姑爺 *shin-gu'ye*, n., term for the bridegroom from the point of view of the family.

新貴 *shin-gueih*, n., person newly appointed to high post.

新歡 *shin-huan*, n., new sweetheart.

新婚 *shinhun*, n., wedding.

新正 *shinjeng*, n., the New Year.

新疆 *Shinjiang*, n., Chinese Turkestan (usu. spelt "Sinkiang").

新教 *shin-jiauh*, n., Protestantism.

新近 *shinjihn*[1], adj. & adv., recent, -ly.

新進 *shinjihn*[2], n., the upcoming generation of scholars.

新舊兒 *shin-jiouh'l*, n., the degree of oldness: 衣裳的新舊兒 degree of oldness of dress.

新裝 *shin-juang*, n., new fashion, new style.

新居 *shin-jyu*, n., new house.

新劇 *shin-jyuh*, n., the modern drama.

新來 *shinlair*, adv., (MC) recently.

新郎 *shinlarng*, n., the bridegroom: 新郎官 term of formal address of bridegroom.

新曆 *shin-lih*, n., the solar calendar.

新年 *shinniarn*, n., the New Year.

新娘 *shinniarng*, n., the bride; also 新娘子 (*-tz*).

新派兒 *shin-pah'l*, adj., of new style.

新任 *shin-rehn*, adj., newly-appointed.

新人 *shinrern*, n., (1) the bride; (2) new person: 新人新事 new people and new happenings.

新聲 *shin-sheng*, n., newly introduced song.

新生代 *Shin-sheng-daih*, n., (geol.) Cenozoic era.

新禧 *shinshi*, n., Happy New Year.

新鮮 *shin'shian*, n., (1) fresh (air, fruit, vegetable, meat); (2) new (atmosphere).

新興 *shin-shing*, adj., new (dynasty, industry).

新媳婦兒 *shin-shir'fu'l*, n., (coll.) the bride.

新手 *shin-shoou*, n., newcomer, novice.

新式 *shin-shyh*, adj., new or modern style.

新學 *shin-shyuer*, n., the new learning; modern learning.

新特 *shin-teh*, n., (AC) new mate.

新屜兒 *shin-tieh'l*, phr., fresh from the oven.

新聞 *shinwern*, n., news; 新聞記者 newspaper correspondent, news reporter; 新聞事業 journalism; 新聞紙 newspaper.

新藝綜合體 *Shinyi-tzuhngher-tii*, n., CinemaScope.

新藝拉瑪 *Shinyihlamaa*, n., Cinerama.

新穎 *shinyiing*, adj., novel, refreshingly different.

新約 *Shinyue*, n., the New Testament.

新月 *shin-yueh*, n., the crescent moon.

§60S.30 (⊥^{s}/一)

竝 60S.30-6

bihng.

[Anc. var. of 並]

旜 60S.30-6

jan.

[Var. of 旃 60S.42]

§60S.40 (⊥^{s}/口)

站 60S.40-2

jahn.

N. A station: 車站 railway or bus station; 起站, 終站 terminal stations, start and destination of line; 加油站 filling station; 供應站 supply station.

V. i. (1) To stand up: 站起來 ditto; 站開 stand back. (2) To stand one's ground: 站得住 hold one's ground; 站不住(腳) lose ground or position, also unable to bear (noise, etc.).

站班 *jahnban*, v. i., stand in line at attention.

站崗 *jahngaang*, v. i., to stand guard at a post.

站長 *jahnjaang*, n., stationmaster.

站住 *jahn-juh*, v. i., (1) to stop, (a call) stop! (2) hold one's ground: 站得住腳 to be able to stand on one's feet, tenable, convincing; 站不住 cannot hold position or cannot bear.

站立 *jahnlih*, v. i., to stand up.

站籠 *jahnlurng*, v. i., (of criminal) be put in a cage and shown in public.

站排 *jahnpair*, v. i., to stand in line.

站臺 *jahntair*, n., railway platform.

韶 60S.40-5

shaur.

N. Name of music of Emperor Shun, 2255-2206 B.C.

Adj. (AC) beautiful: 韶光, 韶華 *-guang*, *-huar* ↓.

韶刀 *shaur'dau*, adj., (coll. of speaker) garrulous; flippant.

韶光 *shaurguang*, n., beautiful springtime, the prime of life or youth; a passing moment: 韶光易逝 time passes quickly.

韶華 *shaurhuar*, n., ditto.

韶景 *shaurjiing*, n., beauties of spring.

韶秀 *shaurshiouh*, adj., young and handsome.

韶子 *shaurtz*, n., a subtropical fruit akin to the lichee.

§60S.41 (一^{S}/囟)

旛 60S.41-9

fan.

[Var. 幡]

N. Banner, pennant.

§60S.42 (一^{S}/冈)

靖 60S.42-1

jihng.

N. A surname.

V. t. Pacify, appease, placate: 靖難, 靖亂 suppress a disturbance, revolt; 綏靖 make peaceful, give peace to; 靖國, 靖邊 pacify the country, the border regions; 靖逆 quell a rebellion.

Adj. Peaceful: 安靖 quiet and peaceful (related 靜 10S.00).

端 60S.42-2

duan.

N. adjunct. An event: 這端事件 this incident, occurrence, business; 這端道理 this piece of teaching, this principle; 兩端案件 two cases; 布一端 a piece of cloth.

N. (1) Head, beginning: 這端 this end (of pole, cloth, etc.); 開端 starting point; 首鼠兩端 cannot decide which to follow, undecided; 更端 have a new beginning; 端的, 端底 *-dih*, *-dii* ↓. (2) Cause, origin: 無端 without cause (offend people, etc.); 借端 use as pretext; 造端 originate, have origin in. (3) An affair: 事端 affair; 萬端 all things, all kinds; 異端 heresy.

V. t. To hold in the hand, esp. with both hands: 端茶, 端菜 bring tea, a dish of food; 端桌子, 端燈 bring or carry a table, a lamp; 端上來 bring up.

Adj. & adv. (1) Upright, proper, careful (in posture, dress, character): 端坐, 端立 sit, stand, properly; 端視 look decorously; 端正, 端莊 *-jehng*, *-juang* ↓. (2) Chiefly: 端賴 chiefly depend on.

端的 *duandih*, (1) adv., really: 端的好看 really pretty; (2) n., the bottom of things, see *-dii* ↓.

端底 *duandii*, n., (get at the) bottom of things.

端整 *duanjeeng*, adj., very proper-looking; not broken.

端正 *duanjehng*, adj., upright, right: 品行端正 upright character; 品貌端正 well-shaped figure and decorous appearance.

端莊 *duanjuang*, adj., severely correct (in countenance), (of conduct) upright and correct.

端木 *Duanmuh*, n., a compound surname.

端倪 *duannir*, n., the beginnings, chief points, clues (to mystery, etc.).

端日 *duanryh*, n., New Year's Day.

端相 *duanshiahng*, v. t., (MC) var. of 端詳 ↓.

端詳 *duanshiarng*, (1) v. t., scrutinize, examine esp. s. t. in hand; (2) n., the whole story of how it happens: 細聽端詳.

端緒 *duanshyuh*, n., main points or threads.

端委 *duanweei*, n., the whole story from the beginning.

端午 *duanwuu*, n., the fifth day of fifth lunar month, Dragon Boat Festival.

端硯 *duanyahn*, n., ink stone from 端縣 of Kwangtung.

端陽 *duanyarng*, n., see *-wuu* ↑.

媥 60S.42-6

ban.

[Cogn. 斑 31A.11]

旃 60S.42-9

jan.

亅	小	⺊	十	土	ナ	廾	𠃊	丨	一	丅	フ	口	囟	冈	ㄱ	厂	尸	亠	广	宀	丶	乚	七	心	八	人	乂	一	一	ノ	𠂉	く
00	01	02	10	11	12	20	21	22	30	31	32	40	41	42	50	51	52	60	61	62	63	70	71	72	80	81	82	83	90	91	92	93

旃 竭 翊 劾 効 勍 勷 韵 鶉 鸇 於

Fin. part. Used in exclamation or command: 尚愼旃哉 (AC) explained as contraction of 之 and 焉.

N. (1) (AC) flag with bent pole. (2) U. f. 栴 10B.42.

§60S.50 (一^{S}/ㄱ)

竭 60S.50-4

jier.

V. i. & t. Make utmost efforts, try one's best, exhaust: 竭力 *-lih*, 竭誠 *-cherng* ↓; 竭澤而漁 kill the goose that lays the golden eggs ("drain the pond to catch all the fish to be found there"); 力盡氣竭 utterly exhausted; 竭慮 *-lyuh* ↓; 枯竭 completely dried up.

竭誠 *jiercherng*, phr., do one's best, wholehearted, -ly.
竭盡 *jierjihn*, v. i., spare no effort.
竭力 *jierlih*, v. i., do one's best, make greatest efforts.
竭慮 *jierlyuh*, v. t., give thorough consideration to.

翊 60S.50-5

yih.

V.t. (LL) to help, assist: 翊贊 to assist (ruler); 翊戴 to assist and support (ruler).

劾 60S.50-9

her.
[Dist. 核]

V.t. To impeach: 彈劾, 劾奏 to impeach in memorandum to emperor; 劾問, 劾究 to investigate person or matter of impeachment.

効 60S.50-9

shiauh.
[Cf. 效 60S.82]

V.i. To serve.

効勞 *shiauhlaur*, v.i. to serve.
効力 *shiauhli*, v.i., to serve, to exert oneself.

勍 60S.50-9

chirng.

Adj. (AC) powerful (enemy).

勷 60S.50-9

rarng (**shiang*).

V.t. (1) 劻勷 *kuangrarng*, adv., hurriedly. (2) (**shiang*) (Interch. 襄) to help, assist.

韵 60S.50-9

yuhn.
[Var. 韻 60S.80]

鶉 60S.50-9

churn.

N. Quail, short for 鵪鶉 12S.50.

鶉服 *churn-fur*, n., ragged and patched clothing (as a beggar's).
鶉居 *churn-jyu*, n., uncertain lodging.
鶉衣 *churn-yi*, n., see *-fur* ↑.

鸇 60S.50-9

jan.

N. A sparrow hawk.

§60S.63 (一^{S}/丶)

於 60S.63-8

yur (**wu*).
[Var. of 于, see 31.00]

N. A surname.

Prep. (1) To, at, in, from, with, than, by, varying with context: 死於海 drown at sea; 生於美國 born in the United States; 置於某處 put at certain place; 施於 apply to; 及於 spread to; 於心何忍 how can one have the heart to do it? 始於 began from; 振民於水火 save people from deep misery; 出於偶然 comes from (by) accident; 莫要於此 nothing more important than this; 有求於我 has s.t. to beg of me. (2) Forms part of certain phrr.: 關於 concerning; 對於這個問題 regarding this problem; 對於我, 對於他 to me, to him (advantageous, etc.); 等於 same as; 長於, 善於 good at s.t.; 勇於 brave at (private quarrels); 怯於 shy away from (public causes); 明於是非 clear in sense of right and wrong; 於此, 於是, 於是乎, 於焉 from this, therefore; 於此可見 thus from this one can see that; 由於, 緣於, 基於 because of, etc.

於戲 **wuhu*, excl., (AC) alas!
於今 *yurjin*, adv., now, at, to the present; nowadays.
於是 *yurshyh*, adv., therefore,

from this, hence; also 於是乎.

於菟 *wutuh*, n., (AC dial.) tiger.

於焉 *yur'yan*, adv., see *-shyh*↑.

於邑 *yuryih*, adj., u.f. 紆 sad, distressed, oppressed (in feeling) (＝紆鬱).

---

§60S.70 (ㄧS/ㄥ)

就 60S.70-1

jiouh.

V. i. & t. (1) V. t., accomplish, achieve, realize: 成就 get s.t. done. (2) Approach, draw near, come close to: 就木 *-muh*, 就位 *-weih*, 就職 *-jyr*, 就教 *-jiauh*, 就義 *-yih*↓; 就逮 get arrested; 就學 *-shyuer*↓. (3) Yield oneself to: 俯就 condescend to; 半推半就 (of friendly offers) half refusing, half accepting, (of amorous advances) half rejecting, half yielding; 將就 to compromise, make the best of a bad bargain. (4) Take advantage of, turn to profit: 就近 *-jihn*, 就時 *-shyr*, 就勢 *-shyh*[4], 就手 *-shoou*↓. (5) Take (one thing) to go with (another): 就飯 *-fahn*, 就酒 *-jioou*↓; 吃兩口飯就一口菜 alternately take mouthfuls of meat (vegetables) and rice; 就菜 *-tsaih*↓. (6) V. i., will do: 這個就可, 那樣就行 this, that will do.

Adj. Very, no other: 就此 *-tsyy*↓.

Adv. (1) Soon, at once, immediately: 他就來 he will come right away; 馬上就送過去 send this over immediately; 就要 want it at once. (2) In a certain way: 就這樣辦吧 let it be so. (3) Then: 他不來就算了 if he doesn't come, then leave him out.

Prep. According to: 就眼前情勢判斷 judged by present circumstances; 就事論事 take the matter on its merits.

Conj. (1) Supposing: 就令 *-lihng*, 就使 *-shyy*↓. (2) Either . . . or: 不是你, 就是他 it's either you or he; 不殺就放 either kill him or let him go; 不戰就降 either fight or surrender.

就寢 *jiouhchiin*, v. i., go to bed, retire for the night.

就親 *jiouh-chin*, v. i., hold marriage ceremony at a place convenient to both bride and bridegroom.

就道 *jiouh-dauh*, v. i., set off on a journey.

就得 *jiouh-der*, v. i., must act in a certain way, have to: 你要病好, 就得吃藥 if you want to get well, you've got to take drugs.

就地 *jiouh-dih*, adv., right on the spot: 就地正法 carry out death sentence on the spot, summary execution.

就飯 *jiouh-fahn*, v. t., have (meat, fish, vegetables) to go with rice.

就館 *jiouh-guaan*, v. t., formerly, serve as private tutor or secretary to an official.

就和 *jiouh'he*, v. i., draw near, strike a compromise.

就枕 *jiouh-jeen*, v. i., go to bed ("put one's head to the pillow," cf. "hit the hay").

就正 *jiouhjehng*, v. i., submit writings to s.o. for comment.

就教 *jiouh-jiauh*, v. i., go to take lessons from teacher, ask for advice.

就近 *jiouhjihn*, v. i., take advantage of geographical propinquity, choose the nearer one; phr., close at hand.

就酒 *jiouh-jioou*, v. t., have (food) to go with wine.

就職 *jiouh-jyr*, v. i., take up post, assume duty.

就令 *jiouh-lihng*, conj., even if.

就木 *jiouh-muh*, v. i., die ("be put in coffin").

就手(兒) *jiouh-shoou('l)*, v. i., do s.t. that doesn't require any extra effort.

就衰 *jiouh-shuai*, v. i., become weak, frail, decline in physical strength.

就世 *jiouh-shyh*[1], v. i., pass away ("pass from the world").

就事 *jiouh-shyh*[2], v. i., (1) take up responsibility; (2) take matter into account.

就是 *jiouh-shyh*[3], (1) v. i., be, as a copula: 這就是王先生 this is Mr. Wang; (2) phr., that's it; 我盡我的力量去辦就是 I shall make every effort to do it—that's it or that's all to be done; (3) conj., either . . . or: 不是他, 就是你 it's either he or you; not only, but also: 不但我生氣, 就是他也很不高興 not only was I angry, but also he was very much displeased; (4) conj., even if: 就是打我也不怕 I shan't be afraid even if you beat me up.

就勢 *jiouh-shyh*[4], v. i., (1) take advantage of an opportunity; (2) do s.t. that involves no extra effort.

就時 *jiouh-shyr*, v. i., take advantage of an opportune moment.

就學 *jiouh-shyuer*, v. i., formerly, (of pupils) go to study with a private tutor.

就緒 *jiouh-shyuh*, v. i., be put in proper order, be near completion.

就使 *jiouhshyy*, conj., even though.

就菜 *jiouh-tsaih*, v. t., have meat (fish, vegetables) to go with (rice).

就此 *jiouh-tsyy*, n., this very one, none other; adv., thenceforth.

就位 *jiouh-weih*, v. i., take seat.

就養 *jiouhyaang*, v. i., (1) take care of the needs of one's parents; (2) (of parents) go to live with one's son.

就業 *jiouh-yeh*, v. i., to take up employment; 就業輔導 placement or appointments service.

就醫 *jiouh-yi*, v. i., see or consult a doctor.

就義 *jiouh-yih*, v. i., die for a just cause, pay the supreme sacrifice.

龍 60S.70-2

lurng.

N. (1) Dragon: 龍王 (myth.) Dragon King (of the seas and lakes); 龍宮 crystal palace of Dragon King: 走筆龍蛇 swift curling style of calligraphy; 龍驤(行)虎步 martial gait; 龍潭虎穴 dragon's pond and tiger's cave—dangerous places; 龍肝鳳髓 great delicacies; 龍鳳 the dragon and the phoenix, generally, symbolic of male and female; 龍飛鳳舞 of swift movement of dancing or calligraphy. (2) Dragon as symbol of emperor: 龍袍 imperial robe; 龍顏 His Majesty's face, countenance; 龍廷 imperial court; 龍心大悅 His Majesty was greatly pleased. (3) As litr. substitute for horse: 龍駒 a spirited horse, a precocious child; 龍驤 thoroughbred. (4) As symbolic of great men: 龍章鳳姿 great handsome appearance; 人中龍 the "dragon among men"; 龍馬 the great and distinguished among men; 龍生龍, 鳳生鳳 compliment to having unusual sons and daughters. (5) A surname.

龍船 *lurngchuarn*, n., dragon boat, racing boat with raised prow: 賽龍船 such boat race on Dragon Boat Festival, 5th day of 5th lunar month.

龍泉 *lurngchyuarn*, n., (1) name of sword; (2) (name of site producing) pale green monochrome porcelain.

龍膽 *lurngdaan*, n., (bot.) ("dragon's bile") the gentian, *Gentiana scabra*, whose root is used for medicine.

龍燈 *lurngdeng*, n., as in 耍龍燈 the dragon dance, lighted from within at night.

龍鳳餅 *lurngfehng-biing*, n., betrothal cake gift distributed to friends as announcement (also called 餅子).

龍骨 *lurngguu*, n., (1) teeth and bones of anc. animals used as medicine; (2) main beam, prow to stern, of boat; (3) 龍骨車 system of water wheels for hauling up water.

龍介 *lurngjieh*, n., a shellfish, *Serpula contortuplicata*.

龍井 *lurngjiing*, n., name of famous tea.

龍舟 *lurngjou*, n., see *-chuarn* ↑.

龍鍾 *lurngjung*, adj., as in 老態龍鍾 old appearance with bent back and unsteady steps.

龍卷 *lurngjyuahn*, n., (1) dragon robe of emperor; (2) (*-jyuaan*) 龍卷風 cyclone, twister, tornado.

龍門 *lurngmern*, n., "dragon gate" (myth.) where a carp becomes transformed into a dragon: 一登龍門, 身價百倍 phr., prestige increases a hundred fold once a person is admitted to s. o.'s friendship; place famous for anc. sculptures on cliffside.

龍腦 *lurngnaau*, n., "dragon's brain"—Borneo camphor (also called 片腦, 冰片), valued as incense.

龍蝦 *lurngshia*, n., lobster.

龍涎 *lurngshiarn*, n., ambergris, found in sperm whales, used in perfumes.

龍蝨 *lurngshy*, n., (zoo.) an edible beetle in Canton, *Cybister chinensis*.

龍鬚 *lurngshyu*, n., a kind of edible seaweed, grown on rocks; 龍鬚菜 asparagus.

龍套 *lurngtauh*, n., actors' robes with dragon design, generally worn by court attendants or soldiers; such actors: 跑龍套 to play such roles.

龍頭 *lurngtour*, n., (1) water faucet (usu. 水龍頭); (2) (coll.) head of any group, esp. of gangsters.

龍圖 *lurngtur*, n., (myth.) stone tablet carried by dragons and horses from river, as omen of Huangti's reign.

龍眼 *lurngyaan*, n., the longan, *Nephelium longana* ("dragon's eyes"); 龍眼茶 (=桂圓茶) tea made from this dried fruit.

龍芽 *lurngyar*, n., (bot.) the vervain (also 龍芽草), *Verbena officinalis*.

龍陽 *lurngyarng*, n., 龍陽癖 (allu.) homosexuality.

瓿 60S.70-3

poou.

N. A small jar: 以供覆瓿 (contempt. of writing) good enough to serve as cover wrapping for a jar.

親 60S.70-4

chin (**chihng*).

N. (1) Relative, blood kin: 親戚 *-'chi* ↓; 親族, 親屬 relatives, clan; 六親不認 a man who (after success) disdains to recognize his kinsmen; often coupled with friends, 親故, 親朋, 親舊 *-guh*, *-perng*, *-jiouh* ↓; 探親 visit relatives; 親誼 sentiment of relationship; 內親 wife's relatives; 姻親 kin by marriage; 遠親, 近親 distant, close relatives; 血親 blood kin. (2) Parents: 父親, 母親 father, mother; 親長 parents and uncles; 省親 visit one's parents; 親情深似海 a parent's love is infinite. (3) (**chihng*) Family or its members related by marriage: 親家, 親家太太, 親家娘 *-'jia*, *-jiataihtaih*, *-jianiarng* ↓. (4) Marriage: 定親 betroth, -al; 親事 *-shyh* ↓; 娶親, 成親 be married; 迎親 bridegroom goes to bride's family to welcome her to ceremony, see 親迎 *-yihng* ↓; 提親 bespeak a boy or girl for marriage; 求親 seek girl's hand in marriage; 攀親 seek marriage with a higher-class family; 悔親, 退親 annul betrothal.

V.t. (1) To love, to be close to: 親愛, 親暱, 親近, 親切 *-aih*, *-nih*, *-jihn*, *-chieh* ↓; 相親相愛 very loving, deeply attached to each other; 親女色 have relationships with women; 親男色 to have homosexual relations. (2) To kiss: 親她一下 kiss her; 親嘴, 親吻 *-tzueei*, *-ween* ↓.

Adj. (1) Loving, close, intimate: 親愛, 親熱, 親暱, 親近 *-aih*, *-'reh*,

-*nih*, -*jihn*↓. (2) Related by blood: 親生 -*sheng*↓; 親兄弟, 親姊妹 brothers, sisters of same mother; 親兒子 one's own child; 親爹, 親母, 親娘 -*die*, -*muu*, -*niarng*↓ (pr. *chin* and **chihng* with different meanings); 親的已的 one's very own kin; 親的熱的 very close relative.

Adv. Personally: 親自, 親手, 親口, 親筆, 親身 -*tzyh*, -*shoou*, -*koou*, -*bii*, -*shen*↓; 親率, 親兵, 親征 personally lead the army in battle; 親展, 親啟 (letter) to be personally opened; 親眼看見 see with one's own eyes; 親臨 personally attend (meeting).

親愛 *chin-aih*, adj., dear, affectionate, esp. 親愛的 darling, beloved: 親愛的母親, 朋友 my dear mother, friend.
親傍 *chinbahng*, n., (MC) close relative.
親筆 *chin-bii*, phr., written by person's own hand.
親戚 *chin'chi*, n., relatives in gen. (外親 maternal relatives; cf. 戚, 外戚 queen's or mother's relatives).
親切 *chinchieh*, adj., warm (friends); moving: 親切動人 (writing, advice) warm, from the heart, touching.
親爹 *chindie*, n., (1) one's own father, as dist. stepfather; (2) (**chihng*-) see -'*jia*↓.
親丁 *chin-ding*, n., blood kin.
親耕 *chin-geng*, phr., the emperor personally and symbolically ploughs the land.
親貴 *chingueih*, n., princesses, the royal kin.
親故 *chinguh*, n., old friends and relatives.
親供 *chingung*, n. & v. i., personal testimony before court, affidavit.
親長 *chinjaang*, n., elderly relatives.
親政 *chin-jehng*, v. i., emperor assumes government duties after coming of age.
親家 **chihng'jia*, n., (1) relatives by marriage; (2) families related by marriage, also used as address to each other; (3) added to term of relation, in mutual address (used more broadly than Eng. "in-law," extending to whole related family): 親家哥哥, 親家兒子, 親家女兒 brother, son, daughter of the r. f. (related family); 親爹, 親家老兒 father, uncle of r. f.; 親爺爺 grandfather and granduncle of r. f.; 親奶奶, 親娘 mother, aunt of r. f.; 親家娘 --*niarng*, bride's or groom's mother; 親家太太 --*taihtaih*, grandmother, grandaunt of r.f.; 親家老爺 master of r. f.; (4) 親家兒 (Peip. coll.) mistress, lover: 靠親家兒 taken as mistress.
親近 *chinjihn* (1) v. t. & adj., close, intimate; be close to; (2) n., close friends or relatives.
親舊 *chinjiouh*, n., see -*guh*↑.
親知 *chin-jy*, n., relatives and close friends (知友).
親炙 *chin-jyh*, v. t., (LL) be personally tutored, study under (person).
親眷 *chinjyuahn*, n., family relatives, womenfolk of one's family.
親口 *chinkoou*, adv., (told) by person himself: 親口答應 personally promise.
親密 *chinmih*, adj., very intimate (friend, lover, relative).
親母 *chinmuu*, n., one's own mother, as dist. stepmother; child of concubine referring to her own mother as dist. the mother of the family.
親娘 *chinniarng*, n., (1) one's own mother; (2) (**chihng*-) see -'*jia*↑.
親暱 *chinnih*, v. t., develop intimate, esp. illicit relations with person; regard as favorite.
親朋 *chinperng*, n., relatives and friends.
親熱 *chin'reh*, adj., warm and affectionate (with person); very close (relative), bosom (friend).
親人 *chinrern*, n., a relative.
親善 *chinshahn*, (1) v. t., to befriend; (2) adj., friendly.
親身 *chinshen*, adv., personally.
親生 *chinsheng*, adj., (of parents, children) first kin, one's own.
親信 *chinshihn*, n., confidant, right-hand man; v. t. & adj., trusted (friend, associate).
親手 *chinshoou*, adv., with one's own hand: 親手交付 deliver personally.
親疎 *chin-shu*, adj. & n., both close and distant relatives.
親事 *chin-shyh*, n., the matter of marriage of a boy or girl: 親事已定 the boy or girl is already engaged.
親隨 *chinsueir*, n., personal attendant.
親嘴 *chintzueei*, v. t., to kiss: 給他親嘴 kiss him.
親族 *chintzur*, n., kinsmen.
親自 *chintzyh*, adv., personally: 親自到場 personally attend.
親王 *chinwarng*, n., a prince.
親吻 *chinween*, v. t., to kiss.
親眼 *chinyaan*, adv., (see) with one's own eyes.
親迎 *chinyihng*, v. i., (the bridegroom) goes to bride's home to escort her to the wedding.
親友 *chin-yoou*, n., friends and relatives.

颯 60S.70-4

sah.

Adj. (1) Rustling (sound, wind). (2) Bleak, dreary.

颯然 *sahrarn*, adj., descriptive of sound made by wind or falling leaves, rustling.
颯颯 *sahsah*, adj., sound of whistling wind, rustling leaves.
颯爽 *sahshuaang*, adj., direct and simple, unconventional (character).
颯沓 *sahtah*, adj. & adv., descriptive of flying motion, soaring.

競 60S.70–6

jihng.

[Dist. 競 *jing*, 10S.70]

V. t. Compete, contest, contend: 競爭 *-jeng*, 競賽 *-saih*, 競技 *-jih*, 競走 *-tzoou*↓; 龍舟競渡 dragon boat race; 競存, 競勝 struggle for survival, victory; 競相讚美 vie in singing the praises of (s.o.); 競賣 sales campaign.

競爭 *jihngjeng*, v.t., compete, contend, struggle, contest.

競技 *jihngjih*, n. & v.i., games, sports, athletics.

競進 *jihngjihn*, v. i., advance shoulder to shoulder, run neck and neck.

競賽 *jihngsaih*, v. t. & n., compete, -tition, contest.

競選 *jihngshyuaan*, v. i., run for office, be a candidate for election.

競走 *jihngtzoou*, n., foot race.

施 60S.70–9

shy.

N. A surname.

V. i. & t. (1) To execute, carry out, put to practice: 施行 *-shirng*↓; 實施 put into practice; 措施 measures for carrying out policy, etc.; 施展雄才 (an opportunity) to put one's great ability to use. (2) To give, distribute: 施恩, 施惠 to give favors or blessings; 施與某人 give to certain person; 施捨 *-shee*↓; 己所不欲, 勿施諸人 do not do unto others what you do not want done to yourself; 樂善好施 always glad to give to charities; 施粥 give gruel to the poor; 佈施 (monks) beg for alms, also give to poor, temple; 施齋 *-tzai*, 施賑 *-jehn*, 施肥 *-feir*, 施放 *-fahng*↓. (3) To apply: 施手術 to make a surgical operation; 施刑 mete out punishment to criminal, apply torture; 施工 *-gung*, 施禮 *-lii*, 施醫 *-yi*↓.

施逞 *shycheeng*, v. t., to put to good use (one's talent, ability).

施恩 *shy-en*, v.t., (God) to bless; to grant favors; (judge) to show leniency.

施放 *shyfahng*, v. t., (1) to spread, to apply widely (belief, policy, insecticide); (2) to give (food, drink) to beggars, the poor.

施肥 *shy-feir*, v. t., apply fertilizer in farm fields.

施工 *shygung*, v. i., (1) to work on, revise, etc.; (2) to process (raw material) in industry.

施展 *shyjaan*, v. t., *-cheeng*↑.

施賑 *shyjehn*, v.i., give relief to famine, etc.

施政 *shy-jehng*, v. i., administer government affairs; carry out policies.

施教 *shy-jiauh*, v. i., (1) to do missionary work; to spread religion; (2) to teach knowledge and behavior.

施救 *shyjiouh*, v. t., to rescue and resuscitate (drowned man), help (destitute).

施主 *shyjuu*, n., benefactor (in charity).

施勞 *shylaur*, v. i., (AC) to boast of one's efforts.

施禮 *shy-lii*, v. t., to apply certain rites, esp. baptism, see *-shii*↓.

施散 *shysaan*, v. i., to scatter.

施捨 *shyshee*, v. i., to give alms, to give to charity (also wr. 舍).

施設 *shysheh*, v. t. & n., decorate, -tions; apportion, -ment.

施洗 *shyshii*, v. t., to baptize.

施行 *shyshirng*, v. t., to put into effect, to execute (orders): 施行細則 detailed regulations, rules of procedure.

施齋 *shy-tzai*, v. i., give food to monastery.

施威 *shy-wei*, v. i., use force; impress with force; (of gods) show anger or power.

施爲 *shyweir*, n., what one does.

施醫 *shy-yi*, v. i., (1) to practise medicine; (2) to give medical help free.

旄 60S.70–9

maur.

N. Ancient flag with yak's tail.

Adj. Rare var. of 耄 pr. *mauh* 11.70.

旎 60S.70–9

nii.

Adj. (1) Pliant, easily bent: 旖旎從風 fluttering with the wind. (2) Beautiful, lovely: 旖旎風光 an exquisite scenery, lovely scenes.

孰 60S.70–9

shur.

Pron. (LL) (1) Who: 孰謂 who says? 孰能當之 who is worthy of (such responsibility)? (2) What, which, which one: 孰是孰非 which is right and which is wrong? 是可忍也, 孰不可忍也 if one stands for this, what else will one not stand for? 孰若 what better than, it would be better to; 孰若准其所請 it would be better to comply with his request.

Adj. Arch. var. of 熟 cooked, ripe, 60.63.

旐 60S.70–9

jauh.

N. (AC) a long, square flag, with design of tortoise or snake.

旒 60S.70-9

liour.

N. Tassels (on spears, ancient crowns, etc.); see 冕$^{\triangle}$旒 41.70.

氈 60S.70-9

jan.

[Var. 氊; pop. 毡]

N. (1) Rug, carpet: 氈毯 ditto; 氈裘 light rug used for body cover. (2) Felt: 氈帽 felt hat.

§60S.71 (ㄧ^{S}/弋)

氓 60S.71-5

marng (*merng*).

N. (1) *marng* in 流氓 city loafers. (2) **merng*: (AC) the common people: 氓隸 *-lih.*

斌 60S.71-7

bin.

[Var. of 彬 10B.91]

§60S.80 (ㄧ^{S}/八)

頏 60S.80-3

harng.

V. i. & t. See 頡$^{\triangle}$頏 11S.80.

頦 60S.80-3

hair (also *ker*).

N. The chin: 下巴頦兒 (*--ker'l*) the chin.

顏 60S.80-3

yarn.

N. (1) A surname. (2) Facial appearance, countenance: 容顏 ditto; 朱顏 usu. refers to painted ladies; 紅顏薄命 tragic end of beauties; 童顏鶴髮 (old man) with white hair and ruddy complexion; 和顏悅色 cheerful, amiable manners. (3) "Face" as signifying "honor": 顏面 *-miahn* ↓; 顏厚 shameless, thick-skinned. (4) Color: 顏色, 顏料 *-'shai, -liauh* ↓; 駐顏有術 skilled in making oneself look youthful.

V.t. (LL) to give name to hall or residence by writing it on a tablet: 顏其室.

顏料 *yarnliauh*, n., dye, dyestuff, pigment, coloring material.

顏面 *yarnmiahn*, n., "face" as honor: 顏面攸關 has to do with one's face or social status.

顏色(兒) *yarn'shai('l)* (re. pr. *(-seh)*, n., (1) color, coloring material; (2) countenance, facial expression: 看人的顏色 watch for s.o.'s countenance (pleasure or displeasure).

顫 60S.80-3

jahn (also *chahn*).

V. i. (1) To shiver, quake, tremble: 顫聲 a quivering voice; 顫悠悠, 顫巍巍 trembling, quivering, shaking all over. (2) To vibrate: see 顫動 *-duhng* ↓.

顫筆 *jahnbii*, n., a quivering line (in painting of floating objects).

顫抖 *jahndoou*, v. i., shiver with cold or fear.

顫動 *jahnduhng*, v. i. & n., to vibrate, vibration; quake (of earthquake).

韻 60S.80-4

yuhn.

[Var. 韵]

N. (1) Charm, enticing tone or manner: 風韻 personal charm; 韻致 *-jyh* ↓. (2) Tone, agreeable sound of writing: 音韻 musical flow of language: 音韻學 phonology, science of classification and development of (Chin.) sounds. (3) Rhyme, rhyme-class: 韻腳 *-jiaau*, 韻書 *-shu* ↓; 聲韻學 phonology, see 2 ↑. (4) Vowel: 韻母 *-muu* ↓.

韻腳 *yuhnjiaau*, n., the rhyming word at end of a line.

韻致 *yuhnjyh*, n., charm (of woman, music, etc.).

韻目 *yuhnmuh*, n., rhyme-class in Chin. rhyme dictionary, see *-shu* ↓.

韻母 *yuhnmuu*, n., vowel-class, syllabary.

韻書 *yuhnshu*, n., a Chinese dictionary in which characters are arranged by syllabary minus initial consonant (thus *pian* under *ian*), as in 切韻, 廣韻, 集韻.

韻事 *yuhnshyh*, n., romantic affair.

韻味 *yuhnweih*, n., tone and flavor (of conversation, writing).

韻文 *yuhnwern*, n., rhymed prose or poetry.

旗 60S.80-9

chir.

N. (1) (*-tz*) A flag: 國旗 national flag; 軍旗 military, flag; 升旗 hoist up flag; 降旗 (pr. *jiahng-*) to lower flag or (pr. *shiarng-*) flag of surrender; 白旗 white flag of surrender; 旗竿 flagpole; 旗章 flag insignia. (2) Manchus, of the Manchus: 八旗子弟 the "bannermen," descendants of Manchu soldiers who conquered China in 1644, designated by their army colors and on permanent pensions until end of Manchu Dyn.; 旗籍, 旗下, 旗人 *-jir, -'shiah, -rern* ↓.

旗槍 *chirchiang*, n., tea leaves from stalks which bear only one leaf (like a flag).

旗鼓 *chir-guu*, n., banners and drums: 旗鼓相當 (fig.) equal in match or contest strength.

旗號 *chirhauh(-'hau)*, n., army signal, flag; title, rallying point, etc.

旗艦 *chirjiahn*, n., the flagship.

旗籍 *chirjir*, n., member(ship) among the Manchu "bannermen," see N. 2↑.

旗裝 *chirjuang(-'juang)*, n., Manchu dress; also with reference to unbound feet.

旗幟 *chirjyh*, n., flag, insignia, rallying point.

旗塊 *chir kuaih*, phr., pennant-shaped.

旗牌 *chirpair*, n., formerly, tablet bearing a mil. order; officer in charge of such tablets.

旗袍(兒) *chirpaur('l)*, n., women's long gown, formerly, a Manchu women's dress.

旗人 *chirrern*, n., a Manchu.

旗下 *chir'shiah*, (1) n., a Manchu; (2) adj., having feet unbound.

旗頭 *chirtour*, n., (1) formerly, the flag officer; (2) a woman's (Manchu) high coiffure.

旗望 *chirwuahng*, n., formerly, flag of a wine shop.

旗魚 *chiryur*, n., (zoo.) the sailfish.

旗語 *chiryuu*, n., (mil.) flag signal.

贛 60S.80-9

gahn.

N. Name of district in Kiangsi, also used to denote Kiangsi Province: 贛省.

§60S.81 (亠^{S}/人)

欬 60S.81-9

ker (**kaih*).

V. i. Var. of 咳 in 咳嗽.

欬逆 **kaihnih*, n., (LL) asthma, difficult breathing.

畝 60S.81-9

muu (*mouu*).

N. (1) A Chinese land measure, 6.6 *muu* equal 1 acre, approximately 60×100 Chinese feet or 六十方丈. (2) Arable land: 田畝 cultivated fields; also (AC) 甽畝.

族 60S.81-9

tzur.

N. (1) Blood relations: 九族 nine generations of direct descent counting from great-great-grandfather down to great-great-grandson; 親族 close relatives. (2) Clan, tribe: 同族 the same clan; 宗族 clansmen; 部族 tribes. (3) A class of animals: 水族 aquatic animals.

V. i. Execute all family members of a criminal: 罪人以族 a criminal is punished by having the entire family executed.

族弟 *tzur-dih*, n., a younger clan cousin.

族父 *tzur-fuh*, n., an uncle of same clan.

族長 *tzur-jaang*, n., an elder of a clan.

族誅 *tzur-ju*, n., execution of the whole clan relatives of a criminal.

族類 *tzur-leih*, n., a tribe, a clan.

族母 *tzur-muu*, n., an aunt of same clan.

族女 *tzur-nyuu*, n., the daughter of the same clan.

族譜 *tzur-puu*, n., the genealogical table of a clan.

族人 *tzur-rern*, n., clansmen.

族姓 *tzurshihng*, n., (1) (AC) all people of the same and different surnames; (2) the social status of a clan.

族兄 *tzur-shyung*, n., an older clan cousin: 族兄弟 (1) brothers born of the great-great-grandfather; (2) clan cousins.

族子 *tzur-tzyy*, n., clan nephew.

族望 *tzurwahng*, n., family of high social standing.

歆 60S.81-9

shin.

V. t. (1) (AC) receive offering (=饗): 其香上升, 上帝居歆 (AC) the fragrance goes up and may God take this offering. (2) To like, admire.

Adv. Gladly.

歆慕 *shinmuh*, v. t., cherish, adore (=欣慕).

歆羨 *shinshiahn*, v. t., to envy (another's beauty, luck=欣羨).

歆豔 *shinyahn*, v. t., adore, admire a beauty.

竢 60S.81-9

syh.

[Anc. var. of 俟 91A.81]

§60S.82 (亠^{S}/乂)

敲 60S.82-2

chiau.

N. (AC) a truncheon: 捧敲朴以鞭笞天下 (fig.) lash the people with a truncheon.

V.t. (1) To knock, tap (at door), beat (drum, gong): 敲更 to sound night watch with a clapper; 敲木魚 to beat the wooden fish (about 6–10 ft. long) serving like bells at Budd. temples; 敲鑼鼓 beat drums and gongs (as at theatricals); 敲鑼邊兒, 敲邊鼓 to egg s.o. on by lending him moral support, to instigate crowds for political support; 敲門磚 any means to find favor with influential persons, (lit.) "stone for knocking at gate"—open sesame to success, esp. at civil examinations; 敲棋 (棊) 子, 敲枰 to tap a chessman noisily on the table; 敲金戛石 make metallic sounds, (of sonorous composition that) rings in the ears. (2) (Fig.) to tap to find out, to prod into: 推敲 make careful choice of words, conjecture, deduce (meaning of words, statements); 旁敲側擊 make oblique references to, to make innuendos, take shots at, instead of making frontal attack. (3) To swindle, blackmail: 敲詐 *-jah*↓; 敲他一筆 obtain money by foul means, blackmail or swindle; 敲竹槓 to sponge on person, to obtain money, free meal, gift, etc.; 你不能這樣敲法 you want (some money, free meal, help) but shouldn't do it this way; 敲人 to swindle a person; 敲鏝兒 (MC), see 敲竹槓↑.

敲打 *chiau'da*, v. i. & t., (1) to beat up, strike; (2) to beat drums and gongs during festivities; (3) (AC) to provoke by words.

敲點 *chiaudiaan*, v. t., as in (MC) 用言語敲點他 prod him with words.

敲詐 *chiaujah*, v. i. & t., to blackmail.

敲(兒)撩(兒) *chiau('l)-liau('l)*, adv., as in 敲(兒)撩(兒)罵人, criticise person by all sorts of innuendos, to needle person, to prod.

敲詩 *chiaushy*, n., a poetic riddle, as a literary game.

皽 60S.82-2

jaan.

N. (AC) dead skin cells (of wounds).

毅 60S.82-4

yih.

N. & adj. Tough, -ness; determination, physical and moral strength: 果毅, 剛毅, 堅毅 ditto.

毅志 *yihjyh*, n., determination, ambition.

毅力 *yihlih*, n., moral strength, stamina, perseverance.

毅然 *yihrarn*, adv., courageously.

毅勇 *yihyuung*, n. & adj., courage, -eous.

放 60S.82-9

*fahng (*faang).*

V. t. (1) To let go, release: 放出, 放出去 let out (gas, rumor, news, etc.); 放羊, 牛, 囚犯 let off sheep, cattle, to pasture, let free prisoners; 放虎歸山 phr., let tiger back to the mountain—cause future trouble; 放鷹 release hawk for prey: (fig.) a confidence trick—set up a woman to ensnare a man, then run away with money, jewels (also 放白鴿); 放砲, 爆竹, 風箏 fire guns, firecrackers, fly kite; 放電, 放水 turn on electricity, water; 放槍, 放箭 shoot gun, arrow; 放學, 放假, 放榜 *-shyuer*, *-jiah*, *-baang*↓; 釋放 set free; 解放 emancipate. (2) To ease restraint, let up, open up, break free: 放聲大哭 cry aloud; 放言高論 phr., highflown talk; 放心, 放手, 放懷, 放膽 *-shin*, *-shoou*, *-huair*, *-daan*↓; 放辟邪侈, 無所不爲 live immorally; see also 放肆, 放縱, 放蕩, 放誕 *-syh*, *-tsuhng*, *-dahng*, *-dahn*↓. (3) To let out: 放大 enlarge (photograph); 放寬 loosen; 放長 let down hem line, make longer; 放鬆 *-sung*, 放晴 *-chirng*↓. (4) To exile, send away, forsake: 放逐, 放黜, 放棄 *-jur*, *-chuh*, *-chih*↓. (5) To appoint or send on mission abroad: 放欽差大臣 send as envoy plenipotentiary; 下放 reassignment to countryside; 外放 appointment to post outside of the capital. (6) To float (loans), lend for interest; distribute (relief): see 放債, 放利, 放賬 *-jaih*, *-lih*, *-jahng*↓; 放盤, 放賑 *-parn*, *-jehn*↓. (7) To put down, to place: 放下 put down; 放下去 let go from hand; 放不下 cannot let go; 放下簾子 let down the curtain; 放在一邊 place on one side; 放下屠刀, 立地成佛 put down the butcher's knife and become a Buddha right on the spot; 安放 put (away) in safe place; 存放銀行 deposit in the bank. (8) (*faang) 放於利而行 (AC) unrestrained in quest of profits; as var. of 仿 in 放效 imitate.

放榜 *fahngbaang*, v. i., publish

results of examination.

放棄 *fahngchih*, v. t., let go, throw away (s. t. useful): 放棄權利 waive rights; 放棄妻兒 abandon wife and children; 放棄責任 neglect duty.

放晴(兒) *fahng-chirng*(*-chir'l*), v. i., (of sky) clear up, become sunny.

放出 *fahng-chu*, v. t., let out (of confinement, container); spread abroad (news, rumor, etc.).

放黜 *fahngchuh*, v. t., degrade (official) and send to remote province.

放春 *fahng-chun*, v. i., (of vegetation) grow buds in spring.

放膽 *fahngdaan*, v. i. & adv., wholeheartedly: 放膽做去 go ahead without hesitation.

放大 *fahngdah*, v. t., to enlarge, blow up (photograph); 放大器 enlarger.

放大鏡 *fahngdah-jihng*, n., magnifying glass.

放誕 *fahngdahn*, adj., bombastic: 放誕不經 fantastic, absurd (talk).

放蕩 *fahngdahng*, adj., dissolute.

放刁 *fahngdiau*, v. i., be haughty and violent; be bully.

放定 *fahng-dihng*, v. i., (of groom's family) present gift to girl's family as formal engagement.

放過 *fahng-guoh*, v. t., let pass (some offence): 不能放過 cannot allow (s. t.) to pass without action; 放過機會 pass up an opportunity.

放懷 *fahng-huair*, v. i., (drink, etc.) to heart's content.

放火 *fahng-huoo*, v. i., to commit arson.

放賬 *fahng-jahng*, v. i., lend money for interest; sell on credit.

放債 *fahng-jaih*, v. i., lend money for interest.

放賑 *fahng-jehn*, v. i., give famine, flood relief.

放假 *fahngjiah*, v. i., (school, office) have holiday.

放逐 *fahngjur*, v. t., exile (offender); drive (tribes) outside border.

放款 *fahngkuaan*, n., loan: 通知放款 call loan.

放寬 *fahngkuan*, v. i. & t., loosen (clothing, binding): 放寬胸懷 relax, be broad-minded.

放浪 *fahnglahng*, v. i. & adj., be dissolute: 放浪形骸 be completely informal as among friends.

放量 *fahngliahng*, v. i. & adv., (drink, etc.) to capacity.

放利 *fahng-lih*, v. i., lend money for interest, practice usury.

放溜 *fahngliou*, v. i., let (boat) drift; (rain water) flood (streets).

放牧 *fahngmuh*, v. i. & t., let off to pasture.

放盤 *fahng-parn*(*-par'l*), v.i., hold cheap sale: 大放盤 great cheap sale.

放砲 *fahng-pauh*[1], v. i., fire guns; (of tires) explode; make high-flown talk or criticism with a view to publicity.

放炮 *fahngpauh*[2], v. i., let off firecrackers.

放屁 *fahngpih*, v. i., break wind: (abusive) 別放屁 don't talk rot, stuff and nonsense! 他說話等於放屁 his words cannot be taken seriously; 放狗屁 (severely abusive) dog sh-t.

放任 *fahngrehn*, v. i., indulgent, permissive, *laissez faire*: 放任自然 ditto.

放哨 *fahngshauh*, v. i., set up patrol (as security measure).

放射 *fahngsheh*, v. i. & t., to shoot (bullet), project (picture), emit (rays); 放射性 n., radiation; 放射塵 radioactive fallout.

放生 *fahngsheng*, v. i., (Budd.) buy (caught birds, fish) to stop slaughter; 放生池 *--chyr*, n., fish pool in temple.

放下 *fahng-shiah*, v. t., let go (responsibility, duty): 放不下 cannot let go.

放心 *fahngshin*, v. i., cease worry, fear: 請你放心 don't worry; 放心不下 cannot help worrying; (AC) 求其放心 recover original goodness of heart.

放手 *fahng-shoou*, v. i., let go: 放手做去 go to it without hesitation; 放手不下, 放不下手 cannot let go (responsibility).

放學 *fahng-shyuer*, v. i., (of school) close after day's work or semester.

放鬆 *fahngsung*, v. i. & t., loosen up, relax, be relaxed.

放肆 *fahngsyh*, v. i. & adj., take too much liberties, unruly: 不可放肆 do not forget your manners.

放縱 *fahngtzuhng*, v. i. & t., to break rules of conduct; allow the young to do so.

放洋 *fahng-yarng*, v. i., (of ship, person) go abroad.

放映 *fahngyihng*, v.t., to project; 放映機 projector.

效 60S.82–9

shiauh.

[Cf. 効 60S.50]

N. (1) Result, effect, function: 功效 effect, efficacy (of medicine); 效能, 效用, 效驗 *-nerng, -yuhng, -yahn*↓; 生效, 不生效 produce, do not produce effect; 靈效 adj., efficacious, effective. (2) Validity: 有效 be valid; also effective; 無效 invalid, also ineffective.

V. t. (1) To imitate, learn from model: 仿效 make an imitation copy of (an old master), follow example of (person). (2) To render service, give one's best: 效力, 效忠, 效勞 *-lih, -jung, -laur*↓.

效誠 *shiauhcherng*, v. i., to render one's loyalty (to person, country).

效法 *shiauhfaa* (*-'fa*), v. t., to learn (from s. o.) as an example: 效法於他 learn from him as an example.

效果 *shiauhguoo*, n., effect, result (of work, effort, teaching, etc.): 生出效果 produce results; 不良的效果 bad results.

效忠 *shiauhjung*, v. i., see *-cherng* ↑.

效勞 *shiauhlaur*, v. i., render service (to country, person): 效勞國家 or 於國家 (also wr. 効).

效力 *shiauhlih*, (1) v. i., render service, put forth strength and energy; (2) n., result: 沒什麽效力 do not see any change, results (also wr. 効).

效率 *shiauhlyuh*, n., efficiency.

效命 *shiauhmihng*, v. i., to render service: 效命疆場 serve on the battlefield.

效能 *shiauhnerng*, n., efficacy; function; capacity.

效顰 *shiauhpirn*, v. i., to learn unworthily to ape what one is not good at (from allu. "ape the knitted brows" of a famous beauty 西施 by an ugly woman 東施).

效驗 *shiauhyahn*, n., efficacy.

效用 *shiauhyuhng*, n., effect, results, function.

敦 60S.82-9

dun.

N. (*dueih*) (AC) vessel for holding grain.

Adj. & adv. Sincere, -ly, friendly, respectfully: 敦請 respectfully invite, request; 敦促 sincerely urge.

敦倫 *dunlurn*, v.i., have sexual intercourse.

敦實 *dunshyh*, adj., honest; solid.

竣 60S.82-9

jyuhn.

V. t. Finish, complete, end: 竣工 finish construction; 竣事 complete a given task (work); 完竣 come to a close, conclude; 告竣 all finished, come to an end.

敵 60S.82-9

dir.

N. (1) Enemy, foe, rival: 仇敵 enemy; 政敵, 情敵 political enemy, rival in love; 敵寇, 敵探 enemy bandit or army, enemy spy; 敵勢 force of the enemy. (2) Match: 天下無敵 without equal in strength.

V. t. To match in strength, resist: 不敵他 cannot match him; 敵不住 cannot hold up against (enemy): see 匹^△^敵 51.21.

Adj. Rival: 敵手 *-shoou*↓; 敵禮 (AC) ceremony of meeting of equals.

敵對 *dirdueih*, v. t. & n., show hostile attitude, stand against.

敵國 *dirguor*, n., enemy country.

敵愾 *dir-kaih*, n., hatred, hostile feeling.

敵人 *dirrern*, n., enemy (person or group).

敵手 *dir-shoou*, n., rival: 不是他的敵手 is no match for him.

敵視 *dirshyh*, v. i., regard as enemy.

敵體 *dirtii*, n., s. t. of equal status.

敵意 *diryih*, n., hostile attitude, enmity.

§60S.83 (ㄧˢ/ㄟ)

旋 60S.83-9

shyuarn (**shyuahn*).

V. i. (1) To turn round (as a screw, clock hand): 旋轉 *-juaan*↓; 旋繞 *-rauh*↓; 旋乾轉坤, 旋轉乾坤 have Herculean strength; be able to turn the tide (of national or world events), make the heavens turn backwards; 盤旋 (of airplane, bird) to circle about, (of person) loiter around. (2) To deal with, encounter as in combat: 與某人週旋 to deal with (person), check (person) move by move (as in chess game or battlefield encounter); 斡 (*wo-*) 旋 to mediate, act between two parties. (3) To return: 旋鄉, 旋里 return home ("to village"); 回旋, 旋歸 to return; 凱旋 return in triumph.

Adv. (1) Soon: 旋得旋失 (of things) no sooner obtained than lost again; 旋出旋沒 appear and disappear in quick succession. (2) (LL) and then, soon after: 旋即回里 returned home soon after; 旋見 and then saw; 旋悔 regret it soon after.

旋風 *shyuarnfeng* (**shyuahn-*), n., a cyclone, whirlwind.

旋覆花 *shyuarnfuh-hua*, n., (bot.) the convolvulus.

旋花 *shyuarn-hua*, n., (bot.) bindweed, *Calystegia sepium*.

旋火輪 *shyuarnhuoo-lurn*, n., (Budd.) a "wheel of fire," expression showing the futile cycle of life and death.

旋璣 *shyuarnji*, n., see 璇^△^璣 31A.83.

旋轉 *shyuarnjuaan*, v. i. & n., to revolve (as a wheel); revolution; 旋轉軸 axis of revolution; 旋轉圓錐 cone of revolution.

旋踵 *shyuarn-juung*, adv., (1) (or 不旋踵) in a very short moment (an empire collapses, etc., lit., "before you turn upon your heels"); (2) 旋踵而至 arrive in close succession.

旋兒 *shyuar'l*, n., a circle: 打旋兒 make a circle (as birds in sky); a coil in woman's hair.

旋螺 *shyuarnluor*, n., (1) a spiral (also 螺旋); (2) a species of seashell.

旋律 *shyuarnlyuh*, n., melody, melodic form; rhythm (of life, etc.).

旋毛蟲 *shyuarnmaur churng*, n., (zoo.) trichina.

旋木雀 *shyuarnmuh-chyueh*, n., (zoo.) a small bird like woodpecker, *Certhia familiaris*.

旋盤 *shyuarnparn*, n., a lathe (also called 車牀).

旋繞 *shyuarnrauh*, v. i. & t., to

revolve around (as a satellite). 旋子 *shyuahntz, n., (1) a whirlpool; (2) a cyclone; (3) an acrobatic feat of turning a somersault sidewise with head in mid-air.

旋渦 *shyuarnwo*, n., a whirlpool, an eddy: 旋渦星雲 (astron.) spiral nebula (also wr. 漩渦).

旋淵 *shyuarnyuan*, n., a deep pond, deep whirlpool.

瓤 60S.83-9

rarng.

N. (1) The eatable part of fruits or nuts: 瓤子 the flesh of fruits; 瓤兒 the pulp; 瓜瓤 the pulp of a melon; 果瓤 the pulp of a fruit; 核桃瓤 the kernel of walnuts; 花生瓤 the kernel of peanuts. (2) The interior part of a thing: 表瓤 the operating mechanism of a watch; 信瓤 the written message enclosed in an envelope; 瓤裏的事誰曉得 who can tell what the inside situation really is?

§60S.91 (ㄧㄥ^s/ㄋ)

妙 60S.91-2

miauh.

[Var. of 妙 93A.91]

彰 60S.91-9

jang.

V. t. To show, reveal, display: 彰善癉惡 (AC) to display the good people and shun the wicked—as examples to others; 表彰 to pay tribute to (worthy character or conduct) by praise or award.

Adj. Manifest, evident: 彰彰 very clear.

彰明 *jangmirng*, (1) adj., clear, unmistakable: 彰明較著 (of guilt) quite evident; (2) v. t., to reveal before the public (s. o.'s good points).

§60S.93 (ㄧㄥ^s/ㄑ)

竑 60S.93-1

hurng.

Adj. (AC) broad, wide.

畆 60S.93-9

moou.

[Pop. of 畝 (arch. of 畝 60S.81)]

SECTION 61

§61.00 (广/丿)

摩 61.00-1

mor.

[Dist. 磨 61.40]

V. i. (1) Rub, fondle: 玩摩 fondle and study constantly (jade, art objects, meaning of text); 撫摩 touch or fondle lovingly (art objects, forehead, etc.); 摩拳擦掌 "rub hands," clench fists in preparation for fight or hard work; 摩頂放踵 (AC) wear oneself out from head to foot (to help others). (2) Grind (cf. 磨 61.40): 摩厲以須 (AC) sharpen weapon to be ready for fight. (3) Learn from long and constant study: 觀摩 watch and study, observe and learn; 揣摩 find out (s.o.'s thinking), see 10A.42.

Adv. (MC 10th cen. dial. word) not, =沒, 無: 歸摩歸, 來摩來 have returned or not, have come or not.

摩盪 *mordahng*, v. i. & adj., (of air, atmosphere) be agitated; (of painting, art work) agitating, -ed and alive.

摩登 *mordeng*, adj., (translit.) modern: 摩登女郎 n., modern (-styled) girl.

摩練 *morliahn*, v. i., learn, become strong, mature from experience (of skill, talent).

摩弄 *mornuhng*, v. i. & t., fondle, play with, acquire familiarity.

摩挲 *morsuo* (also pr. *ma'sa*), v. t., fondle (child).

摩天屋 *mortianwu*, n., skyscraper.

摩擦 *mortsa*, n. & v. i., (cause) friction (physical or mental); rub together; 摩擦力 (phys.) friction; 摩擦系數 (phys.) coefficient of friction; 摩擦音 (phonetics) fricatives.

摩托 *mortuo*, n., motor: 摩托車 motor car; now also motorcycle.

廚 61.00-1

chur.
[Pop. 厨]

N. (1) A kitchen: 廚房 ditto; 廚子, 廚夫 see *-tz*, *-fu*↓; 廚頭灶腦 household chores. (2) U. f. 櫥 a cabinet.

廚房 *churfarng*, n., (1) kitchen; (2) a cook.
廚夫 *churfu*, n., a cook.
廚下 *churshiah*, n., kitchen, pantry, etc.
廚師 *churshy*, n., a head cook, *chef*.
廚司務 *chursywuh*, n., (common and polite reference) cook, *chef*.
廚子 *churtz*, n., (common) cook.

麝 61.00-2

sheh.

N. The musk deer.

麝香 *shehshiang*, n., musk; 麝香貓 (zoo.) the civet; 麝香牛 (zoo.) the musk ox, *Ovibos moschatus*.

序 61.00-3

shyuh.

N. (1) (AC) public school of town or village: 庠序之敎 public education. (2) A preface to a book (also wr. 敍). (3) Order, sequence: 次序 ditto. (4) Orderliness: 長幼有序 respect for seniority; 秩序 order in assembly; 秩序大亂 (meeting) broke out in great disorder.

V. t. To arrange in order by certain standard: 序齒 to arrange seats at table by seniority (齒 here=age); 序次 to seat in order.

序跋 *shyuh-bar*, n., preface (序) and postscript (跋).
序曲 *shyuhchyuu*, n., (mus.) prelude.
序傳 *shyuhjuahn*, n., (AC) preface by author.
序論 *shyuhluhn*, n., introductory chapter (of a book), introduction.
序幕 *shyuhmuh*, n., (1) opening scene in play; (2) prelude to social or political events.
序數 *shyuhshuh*, n., a cardinal number.
序文 *shyuhwern*, n., a preface, foreword.
序言 *shyuhyarn*, n., ditto.

厠 61.00-4

tsyh (also **tseh*; **syh*).
[Pop. 厕]

N. Toilet: 厠所 *-suoo*↓; 如厠 (LL) go to toilet; (pr. **syh*) in 茅厠 toilet; 厠紙 toilet paper.

V. t. To occupy a humble place, see compp.↓.

厠身 *tsyh-shen*, v. i., to occupy a humble place among others.
厠所 *tsyhsuoo*, n., toilet.
厠足 **tseh-tzur*, v.i., see *-shen*↑.

府 61.00-9

fuu.

N. (1) Prefecture, a division of a province 省, containing several 縣 *shiahn*; the prefect: 知府 the prefectural magistrate; 首府 the prefect where the capital is located. (2) Government office: 官府 the authorities, officials; 政府 the government; short for 政府 in 市(政)府, 省(政)府, 國(民政)府 city, provincial, national government. (3) Seat of learning: 學府 such as universities. (4) Treasury, storehouse, see 府庫 *-kuh*↓. (5) (Court.) your house, family, or district: 貴府是那裏 what district do you come from? 尊府 your residence; 府第, 府君 *-dih*, *-jyun*↓.

府城 *fucherng*, n., prefectural city.
府綢 *fuuchour*, n., Shantung silk.
府第 *fuudih*, n., official's residence, mansion.
府宅 *fuujair*, n., personal residence.
府治 *fuujyh*, n., the prefecture as a jurisdictional area.
府君 *fuujyun*, n., my deceased father, esp. in tomb inscriptions (even without official rank); (AC) prefecture magistrate in Hahn Dyn.
府庫 *fuukuh*, n., the treasury (e. g.—is empty); archives, government storehouse.
府上 *fuushahng*, n., (court.) your family: 府上好嗎 how is your family? your house: 到你府上 come to your house.
府學 *fuushyuer*, n., formerly, government prefect school.
府尹 *furyiin*, n., formerly, prefect magistrate.

§61.01 (广/小)

床 61.01-1

chuarng.
[Pop. of 牀 21S.01]

麻 糜 縻 麋 廩 庥

麻 61.01-1

mar.

N. (1) Hemp, flax, of various kinds (oft. wr. as 蔴): 芝麻 sesame; 胡麻 linseed; 麻袋 hempen sack; 麻繩 *-sherng*↓; 快刀斬亂麻 cut the Gordian knot. (2) Pockmarks: 麻子 *-'tz*↓. (3) A surname.

Adj. (1) Benumbed, having tingling feeling: 發麻 feel tingling sensation; 肉麻 disgusting, revolting ("give one goose flesh," but not in Eng. sense of frightening). (2) Pock-marked: 麻臉 pock-marked face.

麻痺 *marbih*, n., paralysis.
麻布 *mar-buh*, n., linen; hempen cloth.
麻雀 *marchyueh*, n., (1) sparrow; (2) mahjong (also wr. 麻將 *-jiahng*↓).
麻刀 *mar'dau*[1], n., (1) loose hemp chopped up to strengthen mortar; (2) bother: 這件事我倒鬧了一脖子麻刀 "hemp all over my neck," like "sand in one's hair."
麻擣 (擣) *mar'dau*[2], n., 麻刀 (2)↑.
麻豆蠅 *mar'dou-yirng*, n., a species of big fly; see *-yirng*↓.
麻煩 *mar'fan*, v. t. & n. & adj., annoy, to trouble, troublesome, a trouble: (adj.) 這事眞麻煩 this thing is troublesome, difficult to deal with; 太麻煩了 too troublesome; (v.t.) to trouble (person): 這事麻煩你了 I have to trouble you with this; 別麻煩我 don't bother me; (n.) 別來找麻煩 don't look for trouble.
麻呼 *marhu* (*ma'hu*), adj., as in slipshod (work), also wr. 麻糊 *mar'hu*, 麻麻呼呼 *-ma-hu'hu*↓.
麻花兒 *mar-hua'l*, (1) n., strands of hemp twisted together; (2) n., an eatable, twisted dough fried in oil; (3) adj., 都麻花了 (of dress, pants) worn smooth and shining.
麻黄 *marhuarng*, n., (med.) ephedrine; (bot.) the plant *Ephedra vulgaris*.
麻胡 *marhur*, adj., (1) (of face) full of beards and pockmarks; (2) see *-huutz*↓.
麻虎子 *marhuutz*, n., "spotted tiger" used to frighten children with.
麻疹 *marjeen*, n., measles.
麻將 *marjiahng*, n., mahjong (also called 麻雀 *-chyueh*↑).
麻雷子 *marleirtz*, n., large firecrackers.
麻俐 *mar'li*, adj., quick-witted, smart, agile, expert.
麻麻呼呼 *mar'ma-hu'hu*, adj., also wr. 麻麻糊糊, see *-hu*↑.
麻麻俐俐 *mar'malih'li*, adj., see *-'li*↑.
麻木 *marmuh* (*mar'mu*), adj., numbed (hand, arm, etc.); insensitive, benumbed (feelings): 麻木不仁 numbed, benumbed.
麻繩 *marsherng*, n., hempen cord.
麻團 *mar-tuarn*, n., fried dumpling of glutinous rice, covered with sesame seeds (also wr. 麻糰).
麻子 *mar'tz*, n., (1) pockmarks; (2) pock-marked person; (3) hemp seed; 麻子油 hemp seed oil.
麻醉 *martzueih*, v. i. & t., (1) anestheticize(d), narcotize(d), doped; (2) become crazy, hypnotized (by women, pleasures); drunk with (Western civilization, etc.): 麻醉自己 hypnotize oneself, give oneself over to (pleasures); 麻醉劑 *--jih*, n., drug, opiate, narcotic.
麻藥 *mar-yauh*, n., anesthetic.
麻衣 *mar-yi*, n., hemp mourning garment.
麻蠅 *maryirng*, n., a kind of common housefly, *Sarcophaga carinaria*.
麻油 *maryour*, n., sesame oil (=芝蔴油).

糜 61.01-1

mir.

N. Rice gruel, congee.

Adj. Like paste, pasty: 糜爛 *-lahn*↓.

糜費 *mirfeih*[1], v.i., spend extravagantly, waste money.
糜沸 *mirfeih*[2], adj., in a turmoil.
糜粥 *mirjou*, n., rice gruel.
糜爛 *mirlahn*, adj., become like paste or gruel; (fig.) downtrodden; (AC) v. t., 糜爛其民 trample upon the people.

縻 61.01-1

mir.

N. Halter for ox.

V. t. To harness: 羈縻 (fig.) be tied up (with business).

麋 61.01-2

mir.

N. (1) Reindeer, *Alces machlis*. (2) A surname.

麋沸 *mirfeih*, n., (AC) 麋沸之亂 social or political turmoil.

廩 61.01-6

liin.

[Arch. var. 㐭]

N. Granary: 倉廩 public granary; 廩膳 formerly, food ration free for students, see 廩生 *-sheng*↓.

廩生 *liinsheng*, n., formerly, student in district or county school in training for civil examinations, with free board given by government, also called 廩生員.

庥 61.01-9

shiou.

A

V. i. (1) Extend protection: 蔭庥 (LL) enjoy the "umbrage" or shelter of s. o.'s protection. (2) (LL) to retire from office.

§ 61.02 (广/⺊)

康 61.02-2

kang.

N. (1) A surname. (2) 小康 period of peace and social order, contrasted with 大[4]同 12.81.

Adj. (1) Peaceful, happy, healthy: 康樂, 康健 *-leh, -jiahn*↓; 康寧 *-nirng*↓; 健康 good health; 安康 enjoying peace and health; 康阜 peaceful and prosperous; 康年 year of good crops; 小康之家 a well-to-do family. (2) Broad, smooth (highway): 康莊 *-juang* ↓; 康衢 a broad street. (3) Empty: 康瓠 (LL) empty gourd; 康爵 (LL) empty wine cup (cogn. 空).

康白度 *kangborduh*, n., (translit.) comprador.
康強(彊) *kangchiarng*, adj., (of nation, person's health) prosperous, healthy, strong.
康健 *kangjiahn*, adj., healthy, enjoying good health.
康莊 *kangjuang*, n., (usu. 康莊大道) broad avenue, highway.
康樂 *kangleh*, adj., enjoying good health and happiness (oft. in letters); n., welfare, well-being: 康樂(大)隊 troupe of singers and dancers for the entertainment of the armed forces.
康寧 *kangnirng*, adj. & n., peace, -ful.
康泰 *kangtaih*, adj., ditto; in good health.

B

§ 61.10 (广/十)

庫 61.10-1

kuh.

N. (1) A treasury, storehouse, depot, vault: 公庫 government treasury; 保險庫 safe-deposit vault; 軍庫 armoury; 油庫 oil tank or depot; 火藥庫 ammunition depot; 倉庫 warehouse, godown, granary; 書庫 library; 寶庫 treasury (of jewels), (fig.) collection of poetry, etc. (2) A surname.

庫平 *kuhpirng*, n., as in 庫平兩 formerly, ounce of silver by Treasury Scale.
庫藏 *kuhtsarng*, n., collection (of silver, books, silks, etc.).
庫銀 *kuhyirn*, n., silver according to Treasury Scale.

麞 61.10-2

jang.

N. (*-tz*) (Zoo.) the roebuck; hornless river deer: 麞頭鼠目 (derog.) contemptible ugly fellow ("rat-eyed and buckheaded").

庠 61.10-8

shiarng.

N. Anc. term for county school of various grades, generally equiv. high school: 庠生 (LL) high school graduate; 縣庠 county school; 庠序 (LL) school in gen.; 庠序之教 (classical) public education.

C

庳 61.10-9

bih (also *bei, beih*).
[Related 卑 90.10]

N. Part of AC place name 有庳.

Adj. (AC) low (building, grounds); short (person).

廨 61.10-9

shieh (also *jieh*).
[Pop. 廨]

N. Public functionaries' office; 公廨 court hall.

§ 61.11 (广/土)

庄 61.11-1

juang.
[Pop. of 莊 20A.11]

廑 61.11-2

jiin (also *jihn*).
[Pop. 廑]

N. A hut.

Adj. (AC) diligent, careful, attentive: 其廑至矣 he was so industrious.

Adv. (Var. 僅) only.

廑注 *jiinjuh*, phr., (letter writing) "your kind solicitude for my welfare."
廑念 *jiinniahn*, phr., (letter writ-

ing) "your best wishes (constant concern)."

座 61.11-2

tzuoh.

N. adjunct. A separate unit: 一座城 a city; 幾座小山 several hills; 兩座塔 two pagodas.

N. (1) A seat: 座兒 *-'l* ↓; 客座 guest seats; 入座 be seated, take seats; 寶座 the most honored seat such as that occupied by the Buddha, the king's throne; 滿座 a packed house ("all seats occupied"); 座無虛席 no empty seat. (2) A rack, a stand: 盆座 a pot stand; 瓶座 a vase stand.

座前 *tzuoh-chiarn*, n., title of respect roughly equiv. "Your Honor," used in letters to elders and superiors.
座兒 *tzuo'l*, n., a seat.
座傘 *tzuohsaan*, n., formerly, ceremonial umbrella.
座談 *tzuohtarn*, n., group discussion; 座談會 symposium, discussion meeting.
座頭 *tzuoh'tou*, n., a seat.
座子 *tzuoh'tz*, n., a rack, a stand.
座位 *tzouhweih*, n., seat, seating place.
座右銘 *tzuohyouhmirng*, n., motto for one's personal guidance ("placed at desk").

塵 61.11-2

chern.

N. (1) Dust, ashes, cinders, dirt: 塵土, 塵埃 *-tuu, -ai* ↓; 灰塵 dust: 塵沙 dust and sand; 洗塵 dinner given on s. o.'s return from journey; 拂塵 to wipe off the dust (from table, etc.), a duster made of mane; 蒙塵 to "bite the dust" —fall in battle, or (emperor) run into mishap, be forced to seek shelter away from capital. (2) Traces: 塵跡 ditto; 絕塵 (of fast runner) leave no track; 塵封 (LL) covered with dust. (3) Turmoil, worldly occupations: 風塵碌碌 busy with worldly affairs; 塵囂, 塵世, 塵俗 *-shiau, -shyh, -sur* ↓. (4) (Budd., Taoist) incarnation: 前塵 previous incarnation; 尚隔兩塵 it will be another two incarnations yet.

Adj. Worldly, pertaining to present mortal life: 塵凡 *-farn* ↓; 塵念 worldly thoughts; 塵儀 my humble presents.

塵埃 *chern-ai*, n., dust in the air; (AC) (fig.) dirt.
塵表 *chernbiaau*, n., world beyond the material things.
塵凡 *chernfarn*, n., the present mortal life, this earthly life of the senses.
塵垢 *cherngouh*, n., dirt, smear, smudge.
塵寰 *chernhuarn*, n., this life of the senses; this mortal world.
塵界 *chernjieh*, n., the mortal world, as opp. world of saved spirits or Taoist fairies (仙).
塵襟 *chernjin*, n., (modest) my lowly comprehension.
塵勞 *chernlaur*, n., (Budd.) worldly occupations.
塵累 *chernleei*, n., duties and obligations of the material life.
塵慮 *chernlyuh*, n., worldly thoughts and occupations.
塵囂 *chernshiau*, adj. & v.i., sensational, noisy (events).
塵心 *chernshin*, n., worldly thoughts or mind.
塵世 *chernshyh*, n., see *-jieh* ↑.
塵俗 *chernsur*, adj. & n., vulgar (world).
塵土 *cherntuu*, n., dust; soil.
塵網 *chernwaang*, n., the "trap" of material concerns, "rat race."
塵妄 *chernwahng*, adj., (Budd.) unclean and untrue (thoughts, beliefs).
塵外 *chernwaih*, n., see *-biaau* ↑.
塵務 *chernwuh*, n., worldly affairs or occupations.
塵緣 *chernyuarn*, n., emotional involvements; love affair.

麈 61.11-2

juu.

N. A species of deer, described as having head like deer, neck like camel, and hoofs like ox, possibly a yak, since a deer is not likely to have much of a tail, for which it is valued: 麈尾 *juu*-tail, a whisk or fly-swat; used in leisurely conversation, called 麈談 fashionable in 3rd and 4th cen.

廛 61.11-4

charn.

[Usu. 㢆]

N. (1) (AC) ground-rent tax paid by occupant: 廛而不征 tax on trader's shop land, but not on his goods. (2) Market place: 市廛.

§ 61.22 (广/丨)

靡 61.22-1

mii.

V. t. To waste: 虛靡光陰, 金錢 waste time, money.

Adj. (1) Extravagant. (2) Beautiful: 靡曼 *-mahn* ↓. (3) Drooping, flagging: 望風披靡 (of army) flee at sight.

Adv. (AC) not: 國難靡止 there is no end to nation's troubles; 靡定 not secure.

靡費 *mii-feih*, v. i., waste money, spend unnecessarily, also wr. 糜[△]費 61.01.
靡爛 *miilahn*, adj., see 糜[△]爛 61.01.

靡曼 *miimahn*, adj., beautiful, charming.

靡靡 *mirmii*, adj., soft, effeminate (mus.): 靡靡之音.

席 61.22-2

shir.

N. (1) A mat (var. 蓆) 草席 straw mat. (2) Anciently, mat as place for sitting, now usu. referring to dinner table, conference table, a seat: 席次 order or seating, also during dinner; 就席 be seated at table; 主席 chairman, presiding officer; 離席 leave the table or conference; 出席, 列席 attend conference; 缺席 absent at conference; 首席 first seat of honor; 記者席 seats for the press. (3) A banquet: 酒席, 筵席 ditto; 席設 (on invitation card) dinner at (name of restaurant or residence); 一席 one table of guests at dinner; 全席 a full-course dinner; 全席的人 all the people at the table; 還席 a return dinner. (4) Formerly, an office: 刑席 criminal office; 錢席 tax office. (5) A surname.

V. t. (1) To be seated: 席地而坐 be seated on the floor. (2) (AC) to take advantage of: 席勝 take advantage of the victory.

席箕 *shirji*, n., hay as feed for horse (also wr. 息鷄, 塞蘆).

席卷 *shir-jyuaan*, v. i., to roll up, carpet-bagging: 席卷 (also 捲) 天下 conquer the whole world, "roll up" all the treasures of the world, also to absorb all conquered countries.

席帽 *shirmauh*, n., (Tarng, Suhng Dyns.) straw hat.

席夢思 *Shirmehngsy*, n., as in 席夢思床 (translit.) Simmons bed.

席面 *shirmiahn*, n., (1) the seat opposite the host; (2) (-'*mian*) the food presented at dinner.

席票 *shir-piauh*, n., formerly, food ticket, as a gift.

厮 61.22-2

sy.

[Var. 廝]

N. (1) Servant: 厮役, 厮皁 *-yih*, *-tzauh*↓; 女厮 woman servant. (2) 這厮, 那厮 (contempt.) this fellow, that fellow.

Adv. As prefix in some vbb., denoting "together" or "about," "round and round": 厮見, 厮打, etc. *-jiahn*, *-daa*↓; 厮混 *-huhn*↓.

厮併 *sybihng*, v. i., fight terribly.

厮吵 *sychaau*, v. i., make fuss together, make a row (over s. t.).

厮打 *sydaa*, v.i., fight each other with fists.

厮趕著 *sygaan'je*, v.i., going after at fast pace.

厮混 *syhuhn*, v.i., to idle away one's time to no purpose, to flirt together, mix in company, esp. with opposite sex.

厮見 *syjiahn*, adv., see, meet each other familiarly.

厮認 *syrehn*, v.i., recognize each other.

厮殺 *sysha*, v. i. & t., fight, combat esp. with weapons.

厮下 *syshiah*, n., low-class people.

厮守 *syshoou*, v. i., wait patiently for s.o. to come back or for s.t. to happen, keep remaining in a place, guard. [ants.

厮臺 *sytair*, n., (AC) menial serv-

厮徒 *sytur*, n., (AC) ditto.

厮皁 *sytzauh*, n., (LL) ditto.

厮養 *syyaang*, n., (LL) ditto.

厮役 *syyih*, n., ditto.

廓 61.22-6

kuoh.

[Related 闊 52B.00]

N. 輪廓 contour.

V.t. To expand, broaden: see 廓大 *-dah*↓; 廓清 clean up (obstructions, evils).

Adj. (1) Broad, spacious: 廓大 *-dah*↓. (2) Empty: 空廓, 廓廓 empty and spacious.

廓大 *kuohdah*, (1) adj., broad and spacious; (2) v. t., to broaden (sphere, etc.); 廓大鏡 another name for microscope (顯微鏡).

廓落 *kuohluoh*, adj., big, spacious, empty.

廊 61.22-6

larng.

N. A veranda, a porch, a corridor: 走廊 a passageway; 廻廊 a winding corridor; 遊廊 ditto; 廊簷 eaves of veranda; 廊子 a porch; 廊腰 the corner of a passageway or of a winding corridor.

廊廟 *larngmiauh*, n., (LL) the imperial court: 廊廟文學 court poetry, compositions of mandarindom.

廉 61.22-8

liarn.

[Var. 亷, wr. form 㢘]

N. (1) (AC) side. (2) A surname. (3) Official honesty; 廉恥 *-chyy*↓.

V.t. To investigate: 廉察, 廉訪 *-chaa*, *-faang*↓.

Adj. (1) Clean, honest 清廉 honest (official); 廉潔 *-jer*↓. (2) Low-priced: 價廉物美 (of shops) goods of good quality and low-priced; 廉價出售 cheap sale.

廉察 *liarnchaa*, v.t., secretly investigate: 廉察其情 carefully consider one's situation.

廉恥 *liarnchyy*, n., sense of honor: 禮義廉恥 sense of propriety, justice, honesty and honor; 不知廉恥, 沒有廉恥 shameless, no sense of shame.

廉訪 *liarnfaang*, v.t., investigate privately.

廉價 *liarnjiah*, n. & adj., low price, low-priced.

廉節 *liarnjie*, n. & adj., sharp sense of integrity.

廉潔 *liarnjier*, adj., clean (morally).

廉隅 *liarnyur*, adj., upright, uncompromising.

§ 61.30 (广/一)

盧 61.30–2

lur.

N. (1) A hut, mud hut or shack: 茅盧 thatched hut; 初出茅盧 completely inexperienced in society. (2) Name of famous mountain in Kiangsi, Lushan.

盧帳 *lurjahng*, n., Mongolian tent.

盧舍 *lursheh*, n., a humble house, or hut.

鏖 61.30–2

aur.

Adj. Tumultuous; fierce (fighting): 鏖兵, 鏖戰 bloody battle.

鏖槽 *aurtsaur*, adj., dirty (related 腌臢 *angtzang*).

鏖糟 *aurtzau*, adj., (1) dirty; (2) worried.

应 61.30–6

ying.

[Pop. of 應 61.72]

§ 61.40 (广/口)

磨 61.40–1

mor (**moh*).

N. (1) Difficulties on the way: 好事多磨 phr., love's course seldom runs smooth, also said of other worthy projects; 磨折, 磨難 *-jer*, *-nahn* ↓. (2) (**moh*) Mill, millstone: 水磨 water mill; 磨石 millstone; 磨床 grinding machine, grinder; 石磨 stone mill; 推磨 n., hand mill.

V.i. & t. (1) Grind, polish: 磨刀 sharpen knife; 磨穿鐵硯 grind through an inkstone—long years of study; 磨杵成針 grind mortar into a needle—show extraordinary persistence; 磨拳擦掌 to roll up one's sleeves for action; 磨(成)粉 grind into powder; 磨鏡 polish bronze mirror, also Lesbian practice; 磨光 polish; 如琢如磨 (of slow process of education and scholarship) like grinding stone and polishing jade; 脚磨了泡 foot blisters from friction (tight shoes, etc.); 磨墨 grind Chin. inkcake on slab. (2) To wear out (s.t.) slowly, to annoy constantly: 磨著媽媽帶他出去玩 (child) begs mother without stop to be taken out; 磨人功夫 require one's constant attention, constant effort at digging or plugging s.o.; 你別老磨人 don't keep on bothering me; 磨折 *-jer* ↓; 百世不磨, 不可磨滅 will endure for centuries; 磨滅 *-mieh* ↓. (3) (**moh*) To put through the grind, repeat annoyingly, bother: 磨豆腐 make bean curd by grinding, (fig.) repeat annoyingly; 磨煩 *-farn* ↓; 磨不開臉 feel embarrassed (also wr. 抹 10A.01). (4) Guide through: 不能磨車 (of narrow alley) cannot take car through.

磨煩 **mohfarn*, v.t., bother constantly (as child).

磨坊 **mohfarng*[1], n., flour mill.

磨房 **mohfarng*[2], n., mill house.

磨蝎 *morher*, n., (astrology) constellation of scorpion, destined for hard knocks.

磨折 *morjer* (also 折磨 *jermor*), v.i. & t. & n., (put through) privations, hardships, persecutions: 磨折死了 persecuted, or persecute (s.o.) slowly to death; 受磨折 be subject to daily small persecutions.

磨勁兒 *morjieh'l*, n., (1) power of persistent begging until one accedes; (2) dragging out work to kill time.

磨勘 *morkahn*, n., term for check and re-check of official records or examination papers (in sense of "putting through the mill"); results of such examinations.

磨鍊 *morliahn*, n. & v.t., (undergo) trials and hardships for strengthening character.

磨礪 *morlih*, n. & v.t., ditto.

磨滅 *mormieh*, v. t., obliterate: 其功不可磨滅 his work will always be remembered.

磨難 *mornahn*, n., hardships, trials, such as on pilgrimage.

磨跎 *mortuor*, v. i., to idle about: 磨跎子 *--tz*, (1) n., annoying person; (2) v. i., drag along: 等我和他磨跎子, 磨到那兒是那兒 I will drag along with him and see what happens (until he backs out).

磨蹭 *mor'tzehng*, v. i., dawdle, idle at work.

磨牙 *moryar*, v. i., be too talkative, indulge in arguments.

店 61.40-2

diahn.

N. (1) A shop, store: 店舖 *-puh*↓; 布店 textile store; 書店 bookstore; 酒店 a bar; 開店 set up shop; 關店 close up (shop). (2) An inn, hotel, esp. countryside inn: 客店 ditto.

店底 *diahn-dii*, n., the goods in store for sale, cf. *-miahn*↓.
店東 *diahndung*, n., hotel manager or shop owner.
店夥 *diahn-huoo*, n., shop employee.
店家 *diahnjia*, n., shop owner.
店客 *diahn-keh*, n., hotel guest.
店面 *diahn-miahn*, n., the shop front where the sales are conducted.
店舖 *diahnpuh*, n., shop.
店小二 *diahn-shiaau-eh*, n., formerly, hotel page boy, boy servant.
店員 *diahnyuarn*, n., salesman, salesgirl.

唐 61.40-2

tarng.

N. (1) A surname. (2) Name of Dyn. (618–906); 唐虞之世 time of 唐(堯) (2357–2258 B.C.) and 虞(舜) (2255–2208 B.C.). (3) Name of a kind of plum, see 唐棣 *-dih*↓.

Adj. Chinese (used among overseas people): 唐裝 Chinese costumes; 唐人 Chinese people; 唐人街 Chinatown; 唐話 Chinese language, used by Cantonese overseas referring to Cantonese.

唐棣 *tarngdih*, n., (AC) sparrow plum, or aspen plum, *Amelanchier asiatica.*
唐古忒 *Tarng-guu-teh*, n., the Tangut tribe.
唐花 *tarnghua*, n., flower forced to blossom early by heat (also wr. 堂花).
唐捐 *tarngjyuan*, v. t., & adj. abandon; wasted.
唐塞 *tarngseh*, v. t., do things perfunctorily, do s.t. to fulfill duty nominally (塞責); stop questions by evasive answer (also wr. 搪).
唐突 *tarngtur*, v.t., do s.t. out of turn or rude; offend (person) by rudeness.

麐 61.40-2

lirn.
[Interch. 麟]

§61.41 (广/囗)

廂 61.41-1

shiang.

N. (1) A room: 廂房 *-farng*↓; (east, west) wing of a house: 西廂 the western wing or set of rooms. (2) (MC) side, area: 這廂, 那廂 (=這邊) this side, that side; 城廂 area under city wall. (3) A box in theater: 包廂 a reserved box; 樓廂 box on balcony. (4) A compartment: 車廂 car compartment or covered cart; 船廂 room in boat; 機廂 engine room; 太空船廂 astronaut's compartment, module.

廂房 *shiangfarng*, n., room; set of rooms or apartment in old-style house.
廂屋 *shiangwu*, n., house wing.

麏 61.41-2

jyuhn.

N. The roebuck; the hornless river deer (cf. 麞 61.10).

庙 61.41-2

miauh.
[Pop. of 廟 61.42]

§61.42 (广/冈)

廟 61.42-1

miauh.
[Pop. 庙]

N. (1) Temple: 寺廟 temples in gen.; 宗廟, 廟寢 ancestral temple; 家廟 family temple; 太廟 emperor's ancestral temple; cf. 寺 11.00, 觀 20S.70. (2) Imperial court, in 廟庭, 廟堂, 廊廟; 廊廟文學 court poetry, court essays, largely having to do with praising ruler; 廟議, 廟謀 court conference, plans; 廟略, 廟算 plans of the court.

廟號 *miauhhauh*, n., posthumous title of deceased ruler, usu. with word 祖, 宗 (e. g., 康熙=聖祖, 乾隆=高宗).
廟會 *miauh-hueih*, n., temple fair on fixed days of the month.
廟見 *miauh-jiahn*, n., bride's visit to family temple ("meet ancestors' spirits").
廟季兒 *miauh-jih'l*, n., period of *-hueih*↑.
廟祝 *miauh-jur*, n., temple attendant in charge of incense and religious service.

亅	小	⺊	十	土	ナ	卄	𠃊	丨	一	丅	㇇	口	囗	冈	㇕	厂	尸	亠	广	宀	丶	乚	弋	心	八	人	乂	乛	ノ	丿	㇀	く
00	01	02	10	11	12	20	21	22	30	31	32	40	41	42	50	51	52	60	61	62	63	70	71	72	80	81	82	83	90	91	92	93

廟 庸 庽 腐 膺 廌 鷹

廟主 *miauh-juu*, n., abbot.

廟廊 *miauhlarng*, n., the court.

廟食 *miauh-shyr*, n. & v. i., to be given place among the spirits and receive offerings.

廟堂 *miauhtarng*, n., the court.

廟宇 *miauhyuu*, n., temple building.

庸 61.42-2

yung (also *yurng*).

Vb. aux. With negative to form 無庸 there's no need to, esp. in documentary style: 應無庸議 (the matter) need not be considered; 無庸 need not; 安庸 where's the need to?

Adj. (1) Common, mediocre: 平庸, 凡庸 common, trite, middling: 庸才, 庸俗 *-tsair*, *-sur* ↓; 庸人自擾 all unnecessary fuss made by the simple-minded; 庸中佼佼 distinguished from the common run. (2) Moderate, not extreme, not too much of anything: 中ᐞ庸 22.22; 庸言, 庸行 *-yarn*, *-shihng* ↓.

Adv. (LL) how, used in 庸可 how could; 庸詎 (also 庸遽, LL, rare) how could it be, could it be that? 庸詎不知乎 could it be that he didn't know about it? 庸何傷 what is the harm, what harm could it be?

庸闇 *yurng-ahn*, adj., dull and muddle-headed, insipid (person).

庸碌 *yurngluh*, adj., very ordinary, mediocre.

庸人 *yurngrern*, n., a common, unenlightened man.

庸行 *yurngshihng*, n., (AC) the conventional conduct (with implied common sense).

庸虛 *yurngshyu*, adj., (court. self-reference) so common and having no special ability.

庸俗 *yurngsur*, adj., vulgar, conventional.

庸才 *yurngtsair*, n., a mediocre man: 碌碌庸才 ditto.

庸言 *yurngyarn*, n., (AC) common saying (with implied common sense).

庸醫 *yurng-yi*, n., incompetent physician.

庸庸 *yurngyung*, adj., (1) common, undistinguished; 庸庸碌碌 *-luh* ↑. (2) (AC) bustling about.

庽 61.42-4

yuh.

[Var. of 寓 62.42]

腐 61.42-9

fuu.

N. & v.i. (To) decay, spoil, ferment: 腐朽 (of woodwork) decay, see 腐朽 *-shioou* ↓; curd in 豆腐 bean curd.

Adj. Rotten, decaying, spoiled: usu. 腐爛 *-lahn* ↓; 陳腐 very old, decadent (thinking, ideas), 腐化, 腐舊, 腐氣 *-huah*, *-jiouh*, *-chih* ↓.

腐敗 *fuubaih*, adj., (of government) corrupt.

腐氣 *fuuchih*, n., spirit of decay.

腐化 *fuehuah*, adj., corrupted, decadent: 腐化分子 corrupt elements.

腐舊 *fuujiouh*, adj., very old, decrepit.

腐爛 *fuulahn*, v. i. & adj., decayed, (of woodwork) musty, spoiled (of fish, etc.).

腐儒 *fuu-rur*, n., stale and pedantic scholar.

腐乳 *furruu*, n., fermented bean curd, treated with wine and vinegar.

腐心 *fuu-shin*, v. i., (AC rare) exhaust one's energy to.

腐刑 *fuushirng*, n., castration (also called 宮刑).

腐朽 *furshioou*, v. i. & adj., decay, decadent, putrid; 腐朽人物 worthless person.

腐蝕 *fuushy*, v. i., chip off with decay; slowly worn out.

膺 61.42-9

ying.

N. (LL) the chest: 義憤塡膺 (=塡胸) be filled with righteous indignation; 服膺 to cherish (s.o.) with admiration or respect.

V.t. (1) (LL) to receive: 膺選 be elected; 膺命 to receive governmental appointment; 膺懲 to punish or be punished. (2) (AC) to attack: 戎狄是膺 to punish the barbarian tribes.

§61.50 (广/㇆)

廌 61.50-2

jyh.

N. A beast, see 豸 91.00.

鷹 61.50-9

ying.

N. The eagle, hawk: 鷹鼻 hawk-nosed; 鷹視 to glare at, to covet; 鷹犬 *-chyuaan* ↓; 放鷹 fly falcon; 貓頭鷹 the owl; 鷹派 (politics) the militant hawks, opp. 鴿派 the doves.

鷹犬 *yingchyuaan*, n., the falcons and hounds; underlings at the bidding of their master.

鷹爪兒 *yingjaau'l*, n., "eagle's claws"—a type of curly sheep's wool.

鷹鸇 *yingjan*, n., hawks and falcons; (fig.) killers.

鷹架 *yingjiah*, n., scaffolding for construction.

鷹揚 *yingyarng*[1], v. i., to show military prowess.

鷹洋 *yingyarng*[2], n., the Mexican silver dollar.

§61.63 (广/丶)

庶 61.63-2

shuh.

[Anc. var. 庶]

N. The common people, the masses: 衆庶; 庶民, 庶人 *-mirn, -rern* ↓.

V. t. (LL) to hope: 庶其成功 hope for its success; oft. as vb. aux. 庶可, 庶能 hope (it) may; 庶能(可)完成 hope it may be completed; 其庶矣乎 it looks hopeful, there is hope; 庶幾 *-ji* ↓.

Adj. (1) The (plural), the many, numerous: 庶官 the many (these, those) officials; 庶衆, 庶類 *-juhng, -leih* ↓. (2) Various, multifarious: 庶物, 庶務 *-wuh*[1,2] ↓. (3) Born of concubine, pertaining to concubine: 庶母, 庶出, 庶子 *-muu, -chu, -tzyy* ↓.

庶出 *shuh-chu*, adj., born of concubine (but bearing father's name).

庶乎 *shuh'hu*, phr., it is hoped, hopefully: 庶乎得之 it is hoped that this is it; 庶乎無過 hopefully it may be free of mistakes, see *-ji* ↓.

庶政 *shuh-jehng*, n., the (multifarious) affairs of the government.

庶幾 *shuh-ji*, phr., (1) identical with 庶乎 *-'hu* ↑; (2) (LL) good enough, near enough: 庶幾之流 those good enough.

庶吉士 *shuhjirshyh*, n., (Mirng, Manchu Dyns.) an official rank.

庶衆 *shuhjuhng*, n., the common people, the multitudes.

庶類 *shuhleih*, n., the various things of life; the animal kingdom.

庶黎 *shuhlir*, n., see *-mirn* ↓.

庶民 *shuhmirn*, n., the common people.

庶母 *shuhmuu*, n., concubine-mother.

庶孽 *shuh-nieh*, n., (AC) son born of concubine.

庶人 *shuhrern*, n., the common people, those without rank.

庶姓 *shuh-shihng*, n., (AC) those tribes or chiefs not related to the royal house.

庶事 *shuh-shyh*[1], n., the various affairs.

庶室 *shuh-shyh*[2], n., (LL) a concubine (vern. 姨太太).

庶孫 *shuh-sun*, n., grandchildren born of concubines.

庶子 *shuh-tzyy*, n., concubine's son.

庶物 *shuh-wuh*[1], n., the things of the universe.

庶務 *shuhwuh*[2], n., business manager's work: 庶務科 business department.

麃 61.63-2

paur.

[Var. of 麾 61.70]

廉 61.63-8

liarn.

[Wr. form of 廉 61.22]

廡 61.63-9

wuu.

N. (1) Corridors around a terrace. (2) (LL) 屋廡 buildings and covered walks.

§61.70 (广/乚)

麾 61.70-1

huei.

N. A pennant, a flag: 麾下 (LL) address to a military general; 麾蓋 flags and parasols; 麾節 general's flag.

V. t. To direct: 指麾 to signal to troops with a flag.

魔 61.70-1

mor.

N. (1) Devil: 妖魔, 邪魔 demon. (2) Overpowering hold on person, charm, witchery: 走火入魔 phr., "possessed by the Devil"; 睡魔未退 phr., under the deep spell of sleep; 病魔纏身 phr., suffering from constant illness. (3) Magic power: 魔力 *-lih* ↓; black magic: 魔法, 魔術 *-faa, -shuh* ↓.

魔道 *mordauh*, n., heresy, black magic.

魔法 *morfaa*, n., black magic.

魔鬼 *morgueei*, n., devil(s).

魔障 *morjahng*, n., (Budd.) temptations, evil influence.

魔力 *morlih*, n., magic hold, spell-binding power (of attractive woman, great orator).

魔難 *mornahn*, n., trials and (devil's) temptations on the way, also wr. 磨難.

魔術 *morshuh*, n., magic, sleight

魔 彪 庵 庇 庀 鹿 麤 麀 麂 麑 麅 龐 庖

of hand, legerdemain: 變魔術 make such tricks.

魔王 *morwarng*, n., King Devil: 混世魔王 devil incarnate, person upsetting everything and everybody.

庬 61.70-1

parng.

[Pop. of 厖 51A.70]

庵 61.70-1

an.

[Abbr. 厂, 广; anc. var. 菴, 盦]

N. (1) A small hut: 庵廬, 庵舍 ditto (usu. 菴). (2) A small Buddhist temple; 尼姑庵 a nunnery.

庇 61.70-2

bih.

V. t. Give shelter, protection to (person).

庇短 *bihduaan*, (=護短) v. i., be partial and willing to overlook shortcomings.

庇護 *bih-huh*, v. t., to shelter, protect (person); 政治庇護 political asylum.

庇蔭 *bihyihn*, v. t. & n., protect, -tion, by providing riches, property, influence (to posterity).

庇佑 *bihyouh*, v. t. & n., protect, -tion, and bless, -ing (of God).

庀 61.70-2

pii.

V.t. (AC) arrange; provide.

鹿 61.70-2

luh.

N. (1) A deer, stag: 牝鹿 female deer; 牡鹿 stag; see 鹿茸 *-rurng*, 鹿角 *-jiaau*↓; 不知鹿死誰手 (allu.) cannot tell who will be the victor; 逐鹿中原 (same allu.) fight for the throne, ascendency of power among warring parties. (2) A surname.

鹿頂(兒) *luhdiing('l)*, n., open terraces on sides of main hall.

鹿藿 *luhhuoh*, n., a bean plant, *Rhynchosia volubilis*.

鹿角 *luhjiaau*, n., (1) antler, deer horn; (2) timber projecting outwards for defense in a stockade; 鹿角菜 *--tsaih*, a water plant growing on beaches, *Chondrus ocellatus*.

鹿巾 *luhjin*, n., formerly, a deerskin hat.

鹿梨 *luhlir*, n., (bot.) callery pear, a small wild pear, *Pirus calleryana*.

鹿盧 *luhlur*, n., pulley (=轆轤).

鹿鳴宴 *luhmirng-yahn*, n., formerly, dinner of successful candidates at provincial civil examinations (allu. to poem 鹿鳴 in *Book of Poetry*).

鹿茸 *luhrurng*, n., cartilagenous part of root of antler, much prized as tonic.

鹿葱 *luhtsung*, n., (bot.) autumn licorice, *Lycoris squamigera*.

麤 61.70-2

tsu.

[Interch. 粗; Pop. 麁, 麄]

麀 61.70-2

you.

N. Female deer: 聚麀 commit incest.

麂 61.70-2

jii.

N. (Zoo.) a deer-like animal, *Moschus chinensis*.

麑 61.70-2

nir.

N. A fawn.

麅 61.70-2

paur.

N. Small spotted deer; roe.

龐 61.70-6

parng (**lurng*).

[Pop. 龎; interch. 厖]

N. (1) (MC) face, esp. 龐兒 *parng'l*. (2) A surname.

Adj. Big, see 龐大 *-dah*↓; mixed, see 龐雜 *-tzar*↓; 龐眉皓髮 white hair and long eyebrows (of old person).

龐大 *parngdah*, adj., physically big, immense, tall (of building, stature, etc.).

龐龐 **lurnglurng*, adj., (AC) sleek and tall (of horse).

龐雜 *parngtzar*, adj., disorderly (of affairs).

庖 61.70-9

paur.

N. Kitchen, cooking.

A

庖廚 *paurchur*, n., kitchen.

庖代 *paurdaih*, v.i., (AC) or more usu. 代庖 *daihpaur*, to act in another's place.

庖鼎 *paurdiing*, n., (arch.) able minister.

庖丁 *paurding*, n., cook.

庖人 *paur-rern*, n., (AC) head of cuisine department in the book 周官; cook.

廐 61.70-9

jiouh.

[Var. of 廄]

§61.71 (广/弋)

底 61.71-9

dii.

N. (*-tz*) (1) Bottom, what is underneath: 筆底 style or power of writing, what flows from one's pen; 筐底, 箱底 bottom of the basket, trunk; 鞋底 shoe sole; 釜底 bottom of cauldron; 河底 bottom of river; 根底 roots, foundation; 底細 *-shih*↓; 到ˋ底 after all, 31S.00; 底子 *-tz*↓. (2) End of period: 月底, 年底 end of month, year. (3) Original of manuscript: 底稿; negative of photograph: 底片.

Adj. (MC oft. in Tarng, Suhng poetry) what: 底事 what thing; 干卿底事 what has that to do with you; 底時 what time; 底處 what place (=何).

Part. Used in place of 的 as particle sign of adj., affected by some modn. writers to imitate European languages: 金屬底 metallic, 亞細亞底 Asiatic; dist. from possessive part. 的 (我的, 你的) and from 地 as adv. part. corresponding to Eng. "-ly" (快快地 quickly) —usage among these imitators not established and not uniform, the three 的, 底, 地 being pr. alike as unaccented *'de*.

B

底本 *dirbeen*, n., cost (in cost accounting); original manuscript copy.

底邊 *diibian*, n., (math.) the base line, base side of a plane figure.

底定 *diidihng*, v. t., have rebellion suppressed and order restored.

底根兒 *diige'l*, adv., (also Peking dial. *dihge'l*) originally, at heart: 底根兒就不願意來 at heart he never wanted to come anyway.

底理 *dirlii*[1], n., the basic reason or situation: 剖析底理 analyze the true reason, see *-lii*[2]↓.

底裏 *dirlii*[2], n., the inside, true situation.

底面 *diimiahn*, n., underneath surface; (math.) base.

底片 *diipiahn*, n., photographic negative.

底下人 *diishiahrern*, n., servants in gen.

底細 *diishih*, n., the inside situation or details: 不知底細 do not know the inside details.

底薪 *diishin*, n., basic salary.

底冊 *diitseh*, n., office copy of records.

底子 *dii'tz*, n., (1) background, foundation of schooling: 學問有底子 (s. o.) has good grounding in knowledge; (2) draft of manuscript; 打底子 make a draft; (3) base coating of paint, etc; (4) commissions: 底子錢 established percentage received by domestics in purchase of goods.

底蘊 *diiyuhn*, n., inner secret.

C

§61.72 (广/心)

廳 61.72-3

ting.

[Abbr. 所; var. 聽]

N. (1) Hall, any fairly large room, such as sitting room, contrasted with 房 *farng*, bedroom: 客廳 sitting or reception room; 飯廳, 餐廳 dining hall; 舞廳 dance hall. (2) A department of provincial government, a government bureau: 教育廳 Department of Education; 官廳 government agencies, the authorities; 審判廳 court of law.

廳長 *tingjaang*, n., head of department.

廳堂 *tingtarng*, n., hall.

應 61.72-9

yihng (**ying*).

[Pop. 应]

N. A surname.

Vb. aux. (Conveying sense of conjecture or of duty) should: 應當, 應該 *-dang*, *-gai*↓; 應是不錯 or 應該不錯 should be all right; 應否 should or should not; 應毋庸議 (matter) need not be discussed or taken up (an official phr.); 相應函達 it is proper that I should inform you of the above (official style).

V.i. & t. (1) To promise: 答應 to promise; 應允, 應許, 應諾 *-yuun*, *-shyuu*, *-nuoh*↓. (2) To respond to situation, to answer (a need, a call, a prayer): 應戰 meet challenge to battle; 應征 respond to call for military service; 有求必應

庖 廐 底 廳 應

亅	小	⺊	十	土	ナ	廾	㇄	丨	一	丁	フ	口	区	冈	㇆	厂	尸	亠	广	宀	丶	乚	弋	心	八	人	乂	㇖	㇖	ノ	㇀	く
00	01	02	10	11	12	20	21	22	30	31	32	40	41	42	50	51	52	60	61	62	63	70	71	72	80	81	82	83	90	91	92	93

always grants requests; 應付, 應變 *-fuh*, *-biahn* ↓; 應急 *-jir* ↓; 應接, 應考, 應試 *-jie*, *-kaau*, *-shyh*² ↓; 反應 react, -tion; 響應 in response to, to respond to (call, etc.); 照應 look after (person). (3) To act in accordance with: 應時而動 act according to circumstances; 應機立斷 make quick decision as situation demands; 一應俱全 supply or provide everything.

應變 *yihngbiahn*, v. i., (1) to respond to changing situation; (2) (phys.) to react to outside influence.

應承 *yihngcherng* (**ying-*), v. i. & t., to promise.

應酬 *yihngchour* (*-'chou*), v. i. & n., (engage in) social parties, do according to due form, give parties: 太多應酬 too many parties.

應當 **yingdang*, vb. aux., should (as conjecture: should be here now, be enough); should as duty (should start at once).

應典 *yihngdiaan*, v.i., to do as promised: (coll.) 說話不應典 fail to carry out promise.

應對 *yihngdueih*, v.i. & n., proper manner of conversation (MC also wr. 應副).

應付 *yihngfuh*, v.t., to meet (a situation), to deal with: 應付局面 ditto; 難於應付 (person, situation) difficult to deal with; 應付不來 cannot deal with.

應該 **yinggai*, (1) vb. aux., should: 應該怎樣 what should I do? (2) adj., proper: 這是應該的 this is proper according to good form.

應詔 *yihng-jauh*, phr., to answer emperor's call.

應召女郎 *yihngjauh nyuularng*, n., a call girl.

應接 *yihngjie*, v.i., (1) to deal with, to meet and welcome (newcomers, etc.): 應接不暇 too many (affairs, visitors) to attend to; (2) to cooperate in separate moves: 彼此應接 coordinate actions with one another.

應景兒 *yihngjiing'l*, n., s.t. which is done for an occasion or as routine form.

應急 *yihng-jir*, phr., to meet an emergency.

應制 *yihng-jyh*, phr., 應制詩文 formerly, essays or poems written usu. in examinations, or by imperial order.

應舉 *yihng-jyuu*, phr., formerly, to take part in civil examinations.

應考 *yihngkaau*, v. i., to register for or take part in examinations.

應龍 *yihnglurng*, n., (AC) a winged dragon.

應卯 *yihngmaau*, v.i., (lit.) to answer roll call or sign arrival in office (卯=5–7 a.m.); (fig.) put in a routine appearance.

應募 *yihng-muh*, phr., to answer call for military service.

應諾 *yihngnuoh*, v.i., to answer "yes," to consent.

應聲 *yihngsheng*, n., echo: 應聲蟲 a yes man.

應世 *yihng-shyh*¹, v.i., to deal with business or social affairs; to know how to deal with people.

應試 *yihngshyh*², v.i., see *-kaau* ↑.

應時 *yihngshyr*, adj., (1) proper to season or fashion; (2) (**ying-*) 應時當令, 應時對景 fashionable, seasonable (dress, food).

應須 **yingshyu*, vb. aux., see *-gai* ↑.

應許 *yihngshyuu* (or **ying-*), v.i. & t., to promise, approve.

應物 *yihngwuh*, v.i., see *-shyh*¹ ↑.

應援 *yihngyuarn*, v.i., (chiefly mil.) to make move to help ally.

應運 *yihng yuhn* (or *-*ying*), phr., in response to needs of the times.

應用 *yihngyuhng* (or **ying-*), v.t., to apply; adj., applied (science, art).

應允 *yihngyuun*, v.i. & t., to consent, promise.

§ 61.80 (广/八)

廣 61.80-2

guaang.

N. (1) Width, breadth. (2) A surname. (3) Part of place name: 廣東, 廣西 Kwangtung, Kwangsi; 兩廣 the above two provinces.

V.t. Expand: 推廣 extend: 推廣銷路 promote sales; 廣募 canvass.

Adj. Extensive, wide, broad: 廣闊 *-kuoh*, 廣大 *-dah* ↓; 廣廈 a huge mansion; 廣庭 a spacious courtyard; 廣嗣 numerous progeny.

Adv. Extensively, widely: 廣被 spread far and wide; 廣濟 render assistance liberally, give freely.

廣播 *guaangboh*, n. & v.t., (1) broadcast: 無線電廣播, 電視廣播 radio, television broadcast; 廣播電臺 broadcasting station; 廣播網 broadcasting network; (2) spread (information, rumors, etc.): 他們早把這些話廣播出去了 they have long spread such gossip far and wide.

廣博 *guaangbor*, adj., erudite; extensive (reading, experience, etc.).

廣場 *guarngchaang*, n., a public square, a plaza.

廣大 *guaangdah*, adj., large, vast, spacious.

廣東 *Guaangdung*, n., Kwangtung.

廣泛 *guaangfahn*, adj. & adv., in general, general(ly), broad, not confined (to subject, area).

廣告 *guaanggauh*, n., advertisement.

廣角鏡 *guarngjiaau-jihng*, n., (photography) wide-angle lens.

廣州 *Guaangjou*, n., Canton, capital of Kwangtung Province (廣東省).

廣衆 *guaangjuhng*, n., a huge crowd: 大庭廣衆 in the open, before the public; adj., 廣衆讀者 wide reading public.

廣闊 *guaangkuoh*, adj., vast, broad, extensive: 門庭廣闊 huge gates and spacious courtyards; 交遊廣闊 with a large circle of friends and acquaintances.

廣袤 *guaangmauh*, n., the surface area of land, length and breadth.

廣漠 *guaangmoh*, adj., (of stretches of land) huge, vast, extensive.

廣西 *Guaangshi*, n., Kwangsi.

廣衍 *guarngyaan*, adj., (1) vast, extensive; (2) prolific, extending far and wide.

廣義 *guaang-yih*, n., what a word or phrase means in its broad(est) sense (opp. 狹義): 廣義地説 taking a word or phrase in its broad(est) sense, broadly speaking.

廎 61.80-2

chiing.

N. (LL) a small hall.

賡 61.80-9

geng.

V.t. Continue, go on doing (s.t.), see compp.↓.

賡酬 *gengchour*, n. & v.i., exchange poems among friends, usu. on same subject.

賡續 *gengshyuh*, v.t., to continue (+vb.).

§61.81 (广/人)

庻 61.81-2

shuh.

[Anc. var. of 庶 61.63]

庚 61.81-9

geng.

N. (1) The seventh character in the 天干 series of ten characters used for numbering years or itemizing persons or things, see Appendix A. (2) Age or year in which one is born: 貴庚 (court.) may I know your age, or the year in which you were born? 庚帖 *-tiee*↓; 同庚 born in the same year; 年庚八字 the hour, date, month, and year of one's birth. (3) A surname.

庚癸 *genggueei*, n., (AC) a secret military message asking for supplies of food and water: 呼庚呼癸 request for financial help.

庚信 *gengshihn*, n., (physiol.) the menses.

庚帖 *gengtiee*, n., a written marriage proposal on which are stated the hour, day, month, and year of one's birth: 交換庚帖 mutual exchange of such a document by both parties concerned, constituting a formal betrothal.

庾 61.81-9

yuu.

N. (1) An open granary. (2) A surname.

§61.82 (广/乂)

庋 61.82-1

jii.

N. A cupboard or pantry.

V.t. In 庋藏 put away for safekeeping.

废 61.82-1

feih.

[Abbr. of 廢 61.82]

度 61.82-2

duh (**duoh*).

N. (1) Measure of length, degree of arc or circle: 度量衡 measurements of distance, area and weight; 長度 length; 尺度 dimensions, breadth (of subject); 深度 depth (of thought); 溫度 temperature; 熱度 heat; 角度 degree of angle; 限度 limit; 沒有限度 without limit. (2) Proper system, limit or measure: 過度 excessive; 失度, 無度 unrestrained, improper (conduct); 法度 customary rules; 制度 institution, system. (3) Stature, style of conduct: 風度 charm or style of personality; 器度不凡 uncommon personality; 大度 generosity of character; 態度 attitude (toward subject, person). (4) Time in sequence: 初度 the first time; 再度 a second time; 三度 three times (of visit, etc.).

V.t. (1) To pass (time, day, etc.): 度日如年 the days are long (with waiting), have miserable life; 度日 *-ryh*↓; 度年關 pass the New Year by paying all the debts; 年華虛度 youth passes away (esp. for young woman). (2) (**duoh*) To conjecture: 忖度, 揣度 conjecture, imagine (another's attitude, thinking); 揣情度理 make an intelligent appraisal of the situation or question; 以己度人 place oneself in another's place; 置之度外 disregard entirely. (3) See 度曲 *-chyuu*↓.

度曲 *duh-chyuu*, v.i., write words for popular song.

度牒 *duhdier*, n., official permit

廣 廎 賡 庻 庚 庾 庋 废 度

亅	小	⺊	十	土	ナ	卄	乚	丨	一	丁	フ	口	囗	冂	冂	厂	尸	亠	广	宀	丶	乚	弋	心	八	人	乂	𠂉	丿	丿	㇐	く
00	01	02	10	11	12	20	21	22	30	31	32	40	41	42	50	51	52	60	61	62	63	70	71	72	80	81	82	83	90	91	92	93

to become a monk or nun and join monastery.

度支(部) *duhjy(buh)*, n., formerly, Ministry of Finance.

度量 *duhliahng*, n., man's generosity or (度量小) the lack of it.

度命 *duh-mihng*, n., (LL) make a living.

度日 *duh-ryh*, v.i., to live, pass the day (in easy, hard circumstances).

廠 61.82–2

chaang.

[Pop. 厰]

N. (1) A factory, workshop, shop: 工廠 factory; 木廠 timber shop; 花廠 flower nursery; 粥廠 public mess hall where rice gruel is given free to the poor; 造幣廠 government mint; 兵工廠 arsenal; 印刷廠 printing press. (2) A mat-shed.

廠房 *chaang farng*, n., factory premises.

慶 61.82–2

chihng.

N. (1) A surname. (2) Occasion for celebration, congratulations or such rites: 慶典 *-diaan* ↓; 壽慶 birthday celebration; 國慶 national day; 喜慶, 大慶, 吉慶 celebration on some happy occasion; 慶弔 occasions for celebration (wedding, etc.) and condolences (funeral). (3) Blessings: 餘慶 many blessings.

V.t. Congratulate (person, upon occasion): 慶賀, 慶祝 *-heh, -juh* ↓; 慶壽 to celebrate birthday; 慶功宴 dinner celebrating completion of campaign, etc.; 普天同慶 day for universal or national celebration; 慶賞 to celebrate (compaign) by giving awards.

慶典 *chihngdiaan*, n., rites of celebration.

慶賀 *chihngheh*, v.t., to congratulate (person); celebrate (occasion).

慶會 *chihnghueih*, n., meeting for celebration.

慶祝 *chihngjuh*, v.t., to congratulate; pray for blessings.

慶幸 *chihngshihng*, v.i., to rejoice: 不勝慶幸 have great cause for rejoicing.

慶慰 *chihngweih*, v. i., feel happy on occasion.

慶雲 *chihng-yurn*, n., auspicious clouds.

廋 61.82–2

sou.

V. i. (1) To hide: 廋辭 *-tsyr* ↓. (2) To seek (interch. 搜): 廋索 *-suoo* ↓.

廋索 *sousuoo*, v. t., ransack; look for s. t. hidden.

廋辭 *sou-tsyr*, n., (AC) evasive words.

廋語 *sou-yuu*, n., riddle, phrase with hidden meaning.

廈 61.82–3

shiah.

[Pop. 厦 51A.82]

N. (1) A big house, a mansion: 高樓大廈 a many-storied building; 摩天大廈 a skyscraper. (2) (AC) covered corridor area of a big house. (3) 廈門 Amoy.

廢 61.82–3

feih.

[Cf. 癈 61A.82]

V. i. & t. (1) Abandon, discard after use: 廢了, 被廢了 is discarded, no longer useful; oft. 廢去, 廢除 *-chyuh, -chur* ↑; 廢而不用 stop using; 半途而廢 stop midway; 廢學 drop out in school; 廢業 abandon profession; 廢帝 to depose (an emperor), opp. 立爲帝; 廢寢忘餐 forget meals and sleep, absorbed in work or study; 廢書而歎 close book and sigh, i. e., touched by historical passage. (2) Opp. 興 to start to develop; 國家興廢 the rise and fall of a regime.

Adj. (1) Abandoned, neglected: 廢址 abandoned site; 廢帝 deposed emperor. (2) Afflicted with incurable disease: 殘廢 crippled. (3) Invalid: 作廢 declare(d) invalid; 廢票 invalidated ballot or check; 廢紙 wastepaper.

廢棄 *feihchih*, v. t., abandon, discard, neglect (studies, etc.).

廢除 *feihchur*, v. t., cancel (treaties, agreement), stop (old customs), remove (obstacles).

廢去 *feih-chyuh*, v. t., throw away.

廢錮 *feihguh*, v. t., (LL) deprive for life the right to take part in civil examinations or government office.

廢話 *feih-huah*, n., nonsense, persiflage.

廢疾 *feih-jir*, n., crippling disease.

廢止 *feihjyy*, v. t., stop (customs), cancel (old regulations, etc.).

廢料 *feihliauh*, n., industrial waste.

廢票 *feih-piauh*, n., invalid ballot, or check.

廢人 *feihrern*, n., cripple, useless person.

廢弛 *feihshyy*, v. i. & adj., to neglect (duties, etc.); neglected, neglectful.

廢物 *feihwuh*, n., discards, useless article: 廢物利用 make good use of waste products (e. g., rags into paper).

廢業 *feih-yeh*, v.i., (AC) loaf.

廄 61.82–9

jiouh.

[Pop. 廐]

N. A stable.

§ 61.83 (广/乀)

遮 61.83-2

je (**jee*).

V. t. (1) To block off (progress of s. o.): 遮路, 遮止 *-luh, -jyy* ↓; 遮車 stop the car from proceeding. (2) To block enemy in fight: 遮擊, 遮架, 遮截 *-jir, -jiah, -jier* ↓. (3) To cover from view, to conceal: 遮蓋, 遮掩 *-gaih, -yaan* ↓; 遮太陽 to cover from the sun; 遮蔭 to cast a shade, or enjoy a shade; 遮蔽, 遮瞞 *-bih, -marn* ↓. (4) (**jee*) To cover up for shame, to evade by words, to maintain a false front: 遮羞兒, 遮醜 *-shiou'l, -choou* ↓; 遮場面 do s. t. (bring a small gift) as proper form; 遮説 *-shuo* ↓.

遮蔽 *jebih*, v. t., to conceal (fault), prevent (person) from knowing, block off (sunlight).

遮醜 **jer-choou*, v. t., to conceal shame or unpleasant sight; (usu. self-deprecatory) bring an unworthy gift so as not to let it look too bad.

遮斷 *je-duahn*, v. t., cut off (enemy retreat).

遮蓋 *jegaih*, v. t., to cover up; to prevent knowledge: 遮蓋起來.

遮扞 *jehahn*, v. i., to blunt enemy blow.

遮架 *je-jiah*, v. i., to parry off blow.

遮截 *jejier*, v. t., to cut off (retreat).

遮擊 *jejir*, v. t., to ambush.

遮止 *jejyy*, v. t., to stop s. o.'s progress.

遮闌 *jelarn*, v. i. & t., (or 遮欄) to cover from view, to block off: 用話遮欄 evade by words.

遮溜子 **jeelioutz*, v. i. & t., as in 拿別的話來遮溜子 evade issue by words.

遮路 *je-luh*, v. i., block the road.

遮瞞 *jemarn*, v. i., to conceal from s. o.'s knowledge.

遮羞兒 **jee-shiou'l*, v. i., see *-choou* ↑, also 遮羞臉 (兒).

遮説 **jeeshuo*, v. i., to defend by making excuses: 你不必替他遮説 you don't have to make excuses for him.

遮掩 *jeyaan*, v. t., see *-marn* ↑.

遮陽 *je-yarng*, v.i. & n., (s. t. that) acts as sunshade.

庭 61.83-9

tirng (**tihng*).
[Cf. 廷 91.83]

N. (1) The courtyard, court as symbol of house, home: 家庭 home; 庭訓, 過庭之訓 parental instruction; 庭園, 庭院 *-yuarn, -yuahn* ↓. (2) Big public space as in open court: 大庭廣衆之前 in open space, before a crowd; 庭爭 argument in the open; 庭辱 humiliate in public; 庭燎 (AC) public square lighted by torch at night. (3) The court of law: 法庭 law court; 出庭 appear at court; 開庭 to open court session. (4) (**tihng*) See 逕[Δ]庭 30.83.

庭長 *tirngjaang*, n., president of law court.

庭闈 *tirngweir*, n., parents' quarters; (LL) parents.

庭午 *tirngwuu*, n., (＝亭午) noon, also (rare, poet.) when moon is at zenith.

庭院 *tirngyuahn*, n., courtyard.

庭園 *tirngyuarn*, n., home garden.

§ 61.91 (广/ノ)

廖 61.91-5

liauh.

N. A surname.

§ 61.93 (广/く)

麽 61.93-1

ma (**mar*, *'me*).
[Common var. of 麼]

Fin. part. (*'ma* or *'me* indeterminate or questioning tone) final particle at end of questions: 你來麽 are you coming? 你不相信我麽 don't you believe me? (also wr. 嗎); 也麽哥 (MC) final particle as form of reinforced exclamation: 則被他閃殺人也麽哥.

Adj. & adv. 幹麽 *gahnmar*, adv., what for, why, do what: 幹麽不見我? why doesn't he (don't you) want to see me? 你在幹麽 what are you doing? 甚麽, 什麽 *shern'me, shyr'me*, adj., what: 甚麽事情 what is the matter? 甚麽消息 what news? 甚麽人, 地方, 時候 what person (who), what place (where), what time (when)?

廕 61.93-3

yihn.

N. Shade, shelter: (fig.) 庇廕 protection, inheritance or material benefit given by ancestor.

広 61.93-9

ma, me.
[Abbr. of 麽 61.93]

SECTION 61A

§ 61A.00 (疒/亅)

瘌 61A.00-1

lah.

N. 疤瘌 (-'*la*) a scar.

瘌痢 *lahlih*, n. & adj., scabby, head suffering from scabies (also 鬎鬁).

痔 61A.00-1

jyh.

N. (Med.) piles, hemorrhoids: 內痔, 外痔 internal, external piles.

痔瘡 *jyh'chuang*, n., bleeding piles.
痔核 *jyhher*, n., blind piles.
痔漏 *jyhlouh*, n., fistula.

疔 61A.00-3

ding.

N. Any of various boils, ulcers, some malignant; carbuncle.

疔瘡 *dingchuang*, n., boil, usu. the malignant kind.

疴 61A.00-3

e (also *ke*).

N. Long-standing illness: 沈疴 a chronic illness; 養疴 to recuperate.

痾 61A.00-3

e.

[Var. of 疴↑]

𤵸 61A.00-3

lih.

N. (AC) pestilence, an epidemic disease.

癇 61A.00-5

shiarn.

N. Epilepsy: 癲癇, 羊癇, 癇風 ditto.

瘉 61A.00-8

yuh.

[Usu. printed 癒; var. 瘉]

V. i. Recover from illness.

痢 61A.00-9

lih.

N. (Med.) dysentery, diarrhea.

痢疾 *lih'ji*, n., (med.) dysentery.

§ 61A.01 (疒/小)

痳 61A.01-1

lirn.

[Var. 淋 gonorrhea, 63A.01]

痲 61A.01-1

mar.

N. & adj. Pockmark(ed), (var. of 麻 61.01).

痲痺 *marbih*, n., paralysis.
痲瘋 *marfeng*, n., leprosy.
痲疹 *marjeen*, n., measles (also called 痧[A]子 61A.91).

療 61A.01-1

liaur (also *liauh*).

V. t. To cure, recuperate: 治療 or 療治 to treat illness; 診療 see a doctor for diagnosis and treatment; 電療 electrotherapy.

療治 *liaurjyh*, n. & v. t., medical treatment; to cure or treat disease.
療養 *liauryaang*, v. i., to recuperate; 療養院 sanatorium.

瘰 61A.01-4

luoo.

瘰癧 *luoolih*, n., disease with swelling of lymphatic gland in neck.

瘵 61A.01-9

jaih.

N. An illness: 癆瘵 tuberculosis.

§61A.02 (疒/⺊)

瘃 61A.02–3

jur.

N. Chilblains (=modn. 凍瘡).

瘝 61A.02–4

guan.

N. Physical pain, illness: (LL) 恫瘝在抱 be ill, suffer from physical pains.

V. t. To neglect: 瘝厥官 (AC) neglect one's duties as an official.

痕 61A.02–5

hern.

N. (1) A scar, a mark left: 刀痕, 傷痕, 創痕 scar from a wound; 疤痕, 瘢痕 a scar formation; 淚痕 tear stains. (2) A trace, a shadow: 春夢了無痕 vanish like a spring dream without a trace; 月影花痕 the shadow of the moon and flowers.

痕跡 *hern'ji*, n., a mark left (such as footprint, fingerprint); a trace (of dispute, correction, etc).

癢 61A.02–8

yaang.

N. & v.i. An itch; to itch.

§61A.10 (疒/十)

癉 61A.10–4

dahn.

V. t. (AC) shun: 彰善癉惡 praise what is good and shun evil.

癖 61A.10–5

pii.

N. (1) Personal, confirmed or exaggerated habit, weakness, personal vice, a habit, addicted habit: 煙癖 habit for smoking; 衣癖 weakness for fine dress; 酒癖, 賭癖 confirmed habit of drinking, gambling. (2) Personal idiosyncrasy. (3) U.f. 痞 61A.40.

癖好 *piihauh*, n., special or favorite hobby (like philately).
癖性 *piishihng*, n., highly personal character; pet tastes and hatreds.
癖嗜 *piishyuh*, n., favorite hobby, special liking (for s.t.).

瘁 61A.10–6

tsueih.

Adj. Worn out: 勞瘁 worn out with work; 鞠躬盡瘁 to tire oneself out, spare no energy at one's duty.

瘴 61A.10–6

jahng.

N. Miasma, swamp gas.

瘴氣 *jahngchih*, n., miasma, swamp vapours: 烏煙瘴氣 a turgid atmosphere of ignorance and confusion.
瘴癘 *jahnglih*, n., poisonous vapours; malaria.

痒 61A.10–8

yaang.
[Var. of 癢 61A.02]

痺 61A.10–9

bih.
[Err. var. of 痹 61A.22]

癬 61A.10–9

shiaan (sp. pr. *shyuaan*).

N. Ringworm; various skin diseases.

癬疥 *shiaanjieh*, n., skin disease.

§61A.11 (疒/土)

瘞 61A.11–1

yih.

V. t. (LL) to bury.

癱 瘢 癃 癯 痊 癰 瘧 疝 癌 疿 痱 痹 疥

癱 61A.11-2

tan.

N. Palsy, paralysis.

Adj. Paralytic: 他癱了 become paralyzed; 偏癱 semi-paralyzed, partially paralyzed.

癱瘓 *tanhuahn* (-*'huan*), (1) adj., paralytic; (2) n., paralysis.
癱子 *tantz*, n., a paralytic.

瘢 61A.11-3

ban.

N. Rash on skin, pimple (cf. 癍).

癃 61A.11-3

lurng.

N. (1) (AC) hunchback. (2) 癃閟 (AC) difficulty in urination.

癯 61A.11-4

chyur.

Adj. (LL) thin, emaciated: 清癯, 癯瘦 thin.

痊 61A.11-8

chyuarn.

Adj. Recovered from illness.

痊癒 *chyuarnyuh*, adj., recovered from illness.

癰 61A.11-9

yung.

N. An ulcer, abscess, a carbuncle.

癰瘡 *yungchuang*, n., an abscess.
癰腫 *yungjuung*, adj., abscess with swelling.
癰疽 *yungjyu*, n., an ulcer, carbuncle.
癰瘍 *yuungyarng*, n., a large carbuncle.

§61A.21 (疒/乚)

瘧 61A.21-2

nyueh (**yauh*).

N. Malaria.

瘧疾 *nyuehjir*, n., (med.) malaria.
瘧子 **yauhtz*, n., (coll. for) malaria: 發瘧子 have an attack of malaria.
瘧蚊 *nyuehwern*, n., (med.) malaria-carrying mosquito, *Anopheles sinensis*.

疝 61A.21-2

shahn.

疝氣 *shahnchih*, n., (Chin. med.) hernia; acute pain in groins.

癌 61A.21-4

yarn (some prefer *air* to distinguish it from homonym 炎 which is merely "inflammation").

N. Cancer: 肝癌 cancer of the liver; 乳癌 breast cancer; 子宮癌 cancer of the womb; 血癌 cancer in the blood, leukemia, etc.

§61A.22 (疒/丨)

疿 61A.22-2

feih.

N. (-*tz*) Prickly heat: 熱疿 prickly heat.

痱 61A.22-2

feih.
[U.f. 疿]

痹 61A.22-4

bih.

N. Paralysis (痲痹).

疥 61A.22-8

jieh.

N. A skin disease marked by itching: 疥瘡 -*chuang*, 疥癬 -*shyuaan*↓; 癬疥之疾 skin disease, also a negligible ill; 疥壁 meaningless scribbles on walls.

疥瘡 *jiehchuang*, n., sores from itch.
疥癬 *jiehshyuaan*, n., ringworm and similar skin diseases.
疥癬蟲 *jiehshyuaan-churng*, n., the acarus.

痄 61A.22-9

jah.

痄腮 *jahsai* (-'*sai*), n., (med.) glandular swelling below the ears, the mumps.

癤 61A.22-9

jier (also *jie*).

N. A small sore: 癤子 a boil; 木癤 abnormal swelling on tree stem.

§ 61A.30 (疒/一)

痘 61A.30-3

douh.

N. Smallpox, also called 天花: 種牛痘, 種痘 vaccination.

痘瘢 *douhban*, n., pockmark.
痘漿 *douhjiang*, n., vaccine.
痘苗 *douhmiaur*, n., vaccine virus.

疘 61A.30-3

gang.

N. 脫疘 rectocele, proctocele.

症 61A.30-3

jehng.

N. An illness, disease: 病症 disease, kind of disease; 絕症 incurable disease: 急症 acute disease; 癌症 cancer; 內症, 外症 internal, external disease.

症候 *jehnghouh*, n., symptoms of disease.

症狀 *jehngjuahng*, n., condition of illness.

痙 61A.30-3

jihng.

痙攣 *jihnglyuarn*, n., convulsions, convulsive contractions.

疸 61A.30-4

daan.

N. 黃疸 jaundice.

瘟 61A.30-4

wen.
[Usu. wr. 瘟]

N. Epidemic, plague: 牛瘟, 雞瘟 cattle, chicken plague.

瘟疫 *wenyih*, n., epidemic.

疽 61A.30-4

jyu.

N. An abscess, an ulcer: 癰疽 (*yung*-) a carbuncle.

癧 61A.30-5

lih.

N. See 瘰[Δ]癧 61A.01.

瘥 61A.30-8

chaih (also *chuor*).

V. i. (LL) recover from illness: 告瘥, 瘥愈 ditto.

§ 61A.40 (疒/口)

瘩 61A.40-2

dar ('*da*).

N. See 疙[Δ]瘩 61A.70.

瘩背 *darbeih*, n., tumor around shoulder blades; accomplice in swindle, gambling, etc. (also 搭[Δ]手 10A.40).

痁 61A.40-2

diahn.

N. (LL) malarial fever.

痞 61A.40-3

pii.

N. Chronic hardening of the spleen, cf. compp. ↓; (fig.) 地痞 local ruffian.

痄 癤 痘 疘 症 痙 疸 瘟 疽 癧 瘥 瘩 痁 痞

亅	小	⺊	十	土	ナ	卄	⺃	丨	一	丁	フ	口	区	冈	⺆	厂	尸	亠	广	宀	丶	乚	七	心	八	人	乂	一	ノ	ノ	⺊	く
00	01	02	10	11	12	20	21	22	30	31	32	40	41	42	50	51	52	60	61	62	63	70	71	72	80	81	82	83	90	91	92	93

痞積 *piiji*, n., hardened spot in the spleen.
痞塊 *piikuaih*, n., ditto.

瘡 61A.40-8

chuang.

N. (1) A wound: 刀瘡 a knife cut; 瘡痕, 瘡傷 *-hern, -shang* ↓. (2) Gen. name for sores, boil, ulcer: 生瘡, 長瘡 grow a boil, an ulcer; 惡瘡 malignant boil; 痔瘡 piles; 凍瘡 chilblains; 禿瘡 scabby, scabies, (esp. domestic animals) mange.

瘡疤 *chuangba*, n., a scab, wound scars.
瘡痕 *chuang-hern*, n., a wound scar.
瘡口 *chuang-koou*, n., knife cut, opening of sore.
瘡傷 *chuang-shang*, n., a knife cut.
瘡瘍 *chuangyarng*, n., a sore in gen.
瘡痍 *chuang-yir*, n., sores which disfigure; (fig.) 瘡痍滿目 a sight of war-torn area.

痂 61A.40-9

jia.

N. A scab over a sore.

痴 61A.40-9

chy.
[Pop. of 癡 61A.83]

§ 61A.41 (疒/図)

瘏 61A.41-1

tur.

Adj. (AC) sick.

疳 61A.41-2

gan.

N. A disease of children, see 疳積 *-ji* ↓.

疳瘡 *ganchuang*, n., (med.) chancre (also 下疳).
疳黃 *ganhuarng*, n., (med.) a form of anemia (also 黃胖).
疳積 *ganji*, n., a children's disease characterized by swelling of the belly and limbs, caused by malnutrition or parasitic worms.

痼 61A.41-4

guh.

N. A chronic disease.

Adj. Chronic, inveterate, deep-rooted: 痼疾 a chronic ailment; 痼癖 an inveterate weakness for s. t.; 痼習 a deep-rooted habit.

瘖 61A.41-6

yin.

Adj. Mute, dumb.

瘤 61A.41-9

liour.

N. Goiter.

§ 61A.42 (疒/冈)

痡 61A.42-1

pu.

Adj. (AC) sick.

癘 61A.42-2

lih.

N. (1) A sore, an ulcer. (2) Pestilence.

病 61A.42-3

bihng.

N. (1) Illness, sickness, disease: 生病, 患病 fall sick; 染病 contract disease, cold, etc.; 老病, 急病, 小病 chronic, critical, small illness; 托病, 稱病 on pretext of illness; 病魔纏身 prone to all kinds of sickness, bedridden; 病入膏肓 (*huang*) (fig.) deep-seated disease, hopeless case; 病假 sick leave; 語病 contradiction in terms. (2) Trouble, weakness: 毛病 imperfection, trouble (in engine, system); 弊病 abuse, corrupt practice, cause of trouble; 通病 common trouble, abuse in practice.

V. i. & t. (1) Be or fall sick: 病倒 fall sick. (2) To harm, injure: 病民 cause harm, trouble to people, injure the people's interests. (3) To worry, regard as imperfection: 君子病無能焉 a gentleman worries about his own lack of ability.

Adj. Sick: 他病了 he is sick; 病臥在床 lie sick in bed; 病亡, 病死, 病故 die of illness.

病包兒 *bihng-bau'l*, n. (coll.) a man always ill.

病病歪歪 *bihngbihng waiwai*, 病病殃殃 *--yangyang*, adj., (coll.) weak with old sickness, sickly in appearance.

病牀 *bihng-chuarng*, n., sickbed.

病毒 *bihngdur*, n., virus.

病房 *bihng-farng*, n., sickroom.

病根 *bihng-gen*, n., cause of disease.

病症 *bihngjehng*, n., disease, illness; symptoms.

病家 *bihng-jia*, n., patient.

病假 *bihng-jiaa*, n., sick leave.

病狀 *bihng-juahng*, n., condition of patient.

病況 *bihng-kuahng*, n., condition of patient.

病理(學) *bihnglii*, n., pathology.

病象 *bihng-shiahng*, n., symptoms.

病室 *bihng-shy*, n., hospital ward.

病勢 *bihng-shyh*, n., symptoms (improving or worsening); condition of patient.

病忘 *bihngwahng*, adj., absent-minded, suffering loss of memory.

病院 *bihngyuahn*, n. hospital.

病容 *bihng-yurng*, n., sickly appearance.

痛 61A.42-3

tuhng (vern. oft. **terng*).

[Cogn. 疼 *terng* 61A.63 in both senses of "pain" and "love"]

N. (1) Pain (oft. **terng*): 頭痛, 牙痛, 心痛 headache, toothache, heartache; 一陣陣痛 spells of pain; 痛癢 *-yaang*↓. (2) Anguish, sorrow, grief: 忍痛 "endure the pain," i.e., cut the loss or sell at a sacrifice, suffer s.t. to pass; 沉痛, 悲痛 deep pain or grief; 痛哉 (excl.) alas! ah, me! 痛定思痛 take one's painful experience to heart.

V.i. & adj. (1) Painful; used as vb. in the sense "it hurts": 痛不痛 does it hurt? 酸痛 (of muscles, bones) sore, stiff; 痛入骨髓 hurts to the bones; 痛得厲害, 好痛, 痛殺殺 very painful; 痛不可忍 unbearably painful. (2) To love, care (oft. **terng*): 痛惜 love (a child, girl); 憐痛 care for (person, esp. tender or helpless); 痛愛 love deeply (person), oft. 疼愛.

Adv. Deeply, bitterly: 痛打, 痛毆 beat mercilessly; 痛罵一頓 give a sound scolding; 痛惡, 痛恨 hate bitterly; 痛飲 drink to heart's content; 痛哭流涕 cry bitterly; 痛悔, 痛改前非 contrition, repent greatly, turn a new leaf; 痛快 *-kuaih*↓.

痛切 *tuhngchieh*, adj. & adv., deeply, earnestly, sincerely: 痛切陳詞 make a deeply felt plea.

痛楚 *tuhngchuu*, adj. & n., painful; sufferings.

痛風 *tuhngfeng*, n., gout; rheumatic pain.

痛快 *tuhngkuaih*, adj. & adv., also 痛痛快快 (1) to heart's content, without mincing matters: 痛痛快快喝一杯 drink or gulp it straight down; 痛快淋漓 (of writing, esp. virulous attack) with great eloquence, stirring, moving; (2) direct in dealings: 這人很痛快 this man is forthright and simple; 做事很痛快 get things done simply, quickly; 說話很痛快 does not mince words, or talks directly and simply; 你痛快點好嗎 will you please be more explicit?

痛苦 *tuhngkuu*, n. & adj., pain and sufferings: 痛苦的事 a painful affair.

痛心 *tuhng-shin*, phr., to hurt: 這事叫人痛心 this matter hurts deeply, is deplorable; 痛心疾首 resent or hate deeply; 痛心切齒 make one burn with anger.

痛癢 *tuhngyaang*, n., "pain and itch": 痛癢相關 care for one another's comfort and happiness; 不關痛癢 be completely indifferent to (another's welfare).

痌 61A.42-4

tung.

[Var. of 恫]

痌瘝 *tungguan*, n., sickness, miseries.

痭 61A.42-4

beng.

N. (Chin. med.) profuse bleeding (gynecological).

瘺 61A.42-5

louh.

N. (Med.) anal fistula: 痔瘺.

瘠 61A.42-9

jir.

Adj. (1) Lean, lank: 瘠瘦 skinny, lanky; 瘠弱 sickly. (2) Barren, poor: 貧瘠 poor and unproductive; 瘠土 land with low productivity, poor soil.

瘸 61A.42-9

chyuer.

N. & adj. Lame; a lame person: 瘸子 a cripple; 腿瘸, 瘸腿的, 瘸精瞎怪 the lame and the blind often are remarkably observant or clever, responsive.

癟 61A.42-9

biee.

[Var. 癟]

V. i. (Coll.) to dry up, to become hollow or sunk down: 癟下去了 to shrink down (as of deflated balloon); 癟着肚子 with an empty, shrunken stomach; 癟嘴子 a sunken, toothless mouth.

癟殼 *bieeker*, adj., helpless, with no way out.

癟螺痧 *bieeluorsha*, n., (coll.) cholera.

癟三 *bieesan*, n., esp. 小癟三 (Shanghai dial.) city bum.

癟子 *bieetz*, n., frustration; hardships.

§61A.50 (疒/冖)

瘍 61A.50-4

yarng.

N. Sores, ulcer: 潰瘍 a burst ulcer.

癆 61A.50-9

laur.

N. (Med.) tuberculosis, also any wasting disease: 肺癆 tuberculosis of the lungs; 腸癆 tuberculosis of the intestines; 癆病腔子 a consumptive, an extremely weak person; 癆病鬼 (abusive) a consumptive.

癆病 *laurbihng*, n., tuberculosis.

癆蟲 *laurchurng*, n., tubercle bacillus.

痀 61A.50-9

jyu.

痀僂 *jyulour*, adj., hunchbacked.

痀瘻 *jyulyur*, adj., ditto.

痗 61A.50-9

meih.

Adj. (AC) sick; 使我心痗 makes my heart ache (with anxiety).

§61A.63 (疒/丶)

瘀 61A.63-6

yu.

N. Decayed flesh with clogged-up blood.

瘀膿 *yu-nurng*, n., pus.

瘀肉 *yu-rouh*, n., decayed flesh (in wounds); gangrenous flesh.

瘀傷 *yu-shang*, n., a contusion, wound with blood clots.

瘀血 *yu-shyueh (-shiee)*, n., extravasated blood, blood clot.

疼 61A.63-9

terng.

[Cogn. 痛 *tuhng* 61A.42]

V. i. & t. (1) Love dearly: 好疼她 loves her dearly; twitch in the heart (love and pain are oft. felt as indistinguishable in Chin.)=這枚鑽石丟了，好心疼 the loss of the diamond hurts a great deal; 心疼小孩 love the child very dearly, see 疼痛 *-tuhng*↓. (2) Feel painful: 心疼, 頭疼 heartache, headache.

Adj. Painful, functions as Eng. v. i., hurt: 疼不疼 does it hurt? 好疼, 疼得厲害 hurts a great deal.

疼愛 *terng-aih*, v. t., love dearly.

疼熱 *terngreh*, adj., (MC) madly in love.

疼惜 *terngshih*, v. t., love tenderly (baby, etc.).

疼痛 *terngtuhng*, v. i. & t., ache: 骨頭疼痛 the bones ache.

§61A.70 (疒/乚)

疣 61A.70-1

your.

N. Goiter: 贅疣 s. t. redundant and not needed.

疵 61A.70-2

tsy (also *tsyr*).

N. (1) Fault: 疵議 *-yih*↓; 吹毛求疵 to find fault intentionally, criticize unfairly. (2) Disease: 疵癘 *-lih*↓.

疵癘 *tsylih*, n., (AC) epidemic.

疵瑕 *tsyshiar*, n., a flaw in jade, character.

疵議 *tsyyih*, v. t., to criticize, object, find fault with: 無可疵議 nothing to object to.

瘋 61A.70-4

feng.

N. & adj. (1) Mad, -ness, insane,

-nity; 發瘋 become crazy (lit. & fig.): 你瘋了 you are crazy; 瘋人説瘋話 crazy man's crazy talk; 別説 瘋話 do not talk nonsense. (2) monomania: 桃花瘋 (＝桃花狂) nymphomania, sex crazy.

瘋 癲 *fengdian*, adj., crazy, insane, demented: 瘋瘋癲癲 acting like crazy; 瘋瘋失失 acting like crazy, looking lost.

瘋 狗 病 *fenggoou bihng*, n., rabies.

瘋 狂 *fengkuarng*, adj. & n., insane, -nity; crazy about s.t.

瘋 癱 *fengtan*, n. & adj., paralysis, -lytic.

瘋 子 *feng'tz*, n., madman, half-crazy person, a "nut."

疤 61A.70-5

ba.

N. Scar, esp. 瘡疤 scar from wounds or disease.

疤 瘌 *ba'la*, adj., full of pock-marks or scars: 疤瘌臉 scarred face, eyelid; 疤瘌餅 cake with pitted surface; 疤瘌流星的 with pitted surface.

疕 61A.70-5

nieh.

N. (MC) a sore, abscess, skin ulcer: 瘕疕.

V. i. (MC) (sores, wounds) ache.

疙 61A.70-9

ge.

疙 瘩 *ge'da*, n., a pimple, a boil; any small round object: 皮膚上起疙瘩 have goose flesh; 土疙瘩, 冰疙瘩, 麪疙瘩 small lumps of earth, ice, dough; 疙瘩兒湯 soup made with small pieces of dough. 「sore.

疙 渣 兒 *ge'ja'l*, n., a scab over a

疙 裏 疙 瘩 *gelige'daa*, adj., troublesome, difficult to cope or get along with.

疱 61A.70-9

pauh.

N. Pimple; blister.

§61A.71 (疒/弋)

疷 61A.71-9

jy.

Adj. (AC) sick.

§61A.72 (疒/心)

痣 61A.72-1

jyh.

N. A mole, birthmark: 黑痣, 紅痣 black, red birthmark; 美人痣 beauty spot.

癮 61A.72-3

yiin.

N. A formed habit (as taking narcotics), addiction: 烟癮, 酒癮 smoking, drinking habit; 上癮 become addict; 過癮 have urge satisfied; 戒癮 to stop habit (as smoking); 發癮 feel strong need for (drugs, etc.); 癮大了 dose increases; 癮君子 (facet.) opium addict.

瘉 61A.72-8

yuh.

V. i. To recover from illness (usu. wr. 愈).

§61A.80 (疒/八)

癩 61A.80-1

laih.

N. (1) (Med.) leprosy. (2) Scabies (also wr. 瘌): 癩頭 *-tour* ↓; 癩瘡 *-chuang* ↓; 長癩 have leprosy.

Adj. Bad (opp. of 好): 東西有好有癩 some things are good, some are bad.

癩 瘡 *laihchuang*, n., scabs caused by scabies.

癩 狗 *laih-goou*, n., a mangy dog (also 癩皮狗).

癩 瓜 (子) *laih'gua(tz)*, n., (bot.) the bitter melon (also 苦瓜).

癩 蝦 蟆 *laihhar'ma*, n., the toad (also 蟾蜍): 癩蝦蟆想吃天鵝肉 aspire after the impossible (lit., "a toad dreaming of eating the swan's meat").

癩 葡 萄 *laihpur'tauo*, n., (bot.) the bitter melon (＝苦瓜).

癩 癬 *laihshyuaan*, n., (med.) scabies; a scaly skin disease.

瘢頭 *laihtour*, n., (med.) a scabby head (also 白癬); 瘢頭瘡 --*chuang*, scabby head.

瘢頭黿 *laihtouryuarn*, n., (zoo.) the sea turtle (also 黿).

瘢子 *laihtz*, n., a person suffering from scabby head.

癲 61A.80–2

dian.

[顛 as var. permissible and common]

Adj. Insane, crazy: 瘋癲 crazy; 瘋瘋癲癲 like crazy; 癲迷酒色 be crazy about wine and women.

癲狂 *diankuarng*, adj., crazy, demented: 癲狂酒色 be crazy about wine and women.

癲癇 *dianshiarn*, n., epilepsy.

§ 61A.81 (疒/人)

痍 61A.81–1

yir.

N. Wounds, usu. 瘡痍滿目 (fig.) pitiful sight of war-torn area.

瘼 61A.81–2

moh.

N. Illness, trouble, confined to phr. 民瘼: 關心民瘼 concerned with people's hardships, distress.

瘓 61A.81–9

huahn.

N. & adj. See 癱^瘓 61A.11.

瘊 61A.81–9

hour.

N. Common warts, verruca.

痰 61A.81–9

tarn.

N. Phlegm: 吐痰 expectorate; 化痰生津 act as expectorant; 痰迷心竅 blinded judgment ("phlegm blocks the heart").

痰氣 *tarn'chi*, n., (Chin. med.) asthma; various mental symptoms (including cerebral hemorrhage) ascribed to phlegm blocking of respiration.

痰喘 *tarnchuaan*, n., asthma.

痰盒(兒) *tarnher('l)*, n., spittoon, see -*yur* ↓.

痰厥 *tarnjyuer*, n., (Chin. med.) shortness of breath.

痰盂(兒) *tarnyur(-yur'l)*, n., spittoon.

瘐 61A.81–9

yuu.

V. i. To die of illness or malnutrition in prison: 瘐死.

疚 61A.81–9

jiouh.

N. (1) Chronic illness. (2) Sorrow, grief, anguish: 疚心 filled with remorse; 愧疚 be sorry and ashamed of oneself; 歉疚 grievously sorry; 負疚 have cause for shame; 內疚 feel the prick of conscience, be conscience-stricken.

疾 61A.81–9

jir.

N. Sickness, illness, ailment: 疾病 -*bihng* ↓; 力疾從公 attend to one's duties as usual in spite of illness; 無疾而終 die in one's sleep; 隱疾, 暗疾 venereal disease.

V. t. Hate: 疾惡如仇 abhor evils or evildoers as if they were personal enemies; 痛心疾首 detest thoroughly; distressed and disgusted.

Adj. & adv. (1) Ill: 疾苦 -*kuu* ↓. (2) Fast: 疾雷 -*leir* ↓; 疾風知勁草 adversity is the best testing ground for moral stamina ("only the toughest grass can stand strong winds"); 疾言厲色 sudden outpourings and fierce looks; 疾言遽色 nervous agitation accompanied by hasty speech and angry looks; 疾快 -*kuaih* ↓; 疾馳 gallop away at full speed; 疾走 go or run away as fast as one can.

疾病 *jirbihng*, n., sickness, illness, indisposition.

疾快 *jirkuaih*, adj., swift, fleet, flying.

疾苦 *jirkuu*, adj., suffering from heavy taxes and other forms of oppression.

疾雷 *jirleir*, n., a sudden thunderclap; (fig.) any swift, sudden action that catches others unawares (cf. Ger. *blitzkrieg*).

疾首 *jirshoou*, v. t., hate (s.o., s.t.) so much as to cause a headache.

疾視 *jir-shyh*, v. t., stare angrily.

§ 61A.82 (疒/乂)

疲 61A.82–2

pir.

Adj. (1) Tired, fatigued: 人疲馬

乏, 人困馬疲 (of troops) tired and exhausted; oft. 疲倦 *-jyuahn*↓; 疲於奔命 tired and exhausted from running about on missions. (2) Showing weakness in trading, see 疲弱 *-rouh*↓.

疲憊 *pirbeih*, adj., exhausted.
疲弊 *pirbih*, adj., exhausted.
疲鈍 *pirduhn*, adj., tired and slow in movement, trading (also wr. 疲頓).
疲倦 *pirjyuahn*, adj., tired.
疲勞 *pirlaur*, adj., exhausted, exhausting (of work): 疲勞轟炸 n., air raids aimed at exhausting patience; 疲勞審問 n., persistent cross-examination aimed at blunting prisoner's senses and mind.
疲癃 *pirlurng*, adj., decrepit.
疲軟 *pir-nuaan*, adj., (1) limp, having no energy (of body, limbs); (2) weak in trading (of stock prices).
疲弱 *pir-rouh*, adj., ditto.

瘦 61A.82-2

shouh.

Adj. (1) Thin, emaciated, opp. 肥 *feir*, fat: 瘦巴巴, 瘦溜溜, 瘦括括 very thin; 瘦筋巴骨 thin and bony; 消瘦 emaciated; 肥瘦得中 (body) round without being plump, slender without being bony. (2) Lean (meat): 瘦肉. (3) Tight (clothing). (4) Barren, unproductive (land). (5) Beautifully bony: 瘦硬 *-yihng*↓.

瘦弱 *shouhruoh*, adj., thin and feeble.
瘦削 *shouhshyueh*, adj., thin and slender.
瘦子 *shouhtz*, n., a thin person.
瘦硬 *shouhyihng*, adj., (callig.) slender and yet strong (in lines).

癈 61A.82-3

feih.

N. Crippling or incurable disease.

疫 61A.82-4

yih.

N. Epidemic: 瘟疫 ditto; 鼠疫 bubonic plague; 虎疫 cholera epidemic.

疫症 *yihjehng*, n., epidemic disease.
疫癘 *yihlih*, n., plague.
疫苗 *yihmiaur*, n., vaccine; 蘇克氏疫苗 Salk vaccine; 謝敏氏疫苗 Sabin vaccine; 沙門氏疫苗 Salmonella.

瘕 61A.82-5

jiaa.

N. An abnormal growth or hardening in the stomach.

癜 61A.82-5

diahn.

N. Name of skin disease: 癜風 pityriasis, scabies.

瘢 61A.82-9

ban.

N. Scar on skin; mole, see 瘢點 *-diaan*↓.

瘢點 *bandiaan*, n., freckles.
瘢風 *banfeng*, n., a kind of skin disease.
瘢痕 *banhern*, n., scars on skin.
瘢痣 *banjyh*, n., birthmark, mole.

癥 61A.82-9

jeng.

癥結 *jengjier*, n., hard formations in the bowels; (fig.) the crux of the problem: 癥結所在 where the problem lies.

痠 61A.82-9

suan.

V.i. & adj. To ache, aching, stiff (of muscles): 腿痠 aching or stiff leg or leg aches; 手痠 arm aches; 痠痛, 痠疼 *-tuhng*, *-terng*↓; 骨頭痠 bones ache (also usu. wr. 酸).

痠懶 *suanlaan*, adj., aching, limp.
痠軟 *suanruaan*, adj., ditto.
痠疼 *suanterng*, adj., aching, smarting, (muscles) painful.
痠痛 *suantuhng*, adj., ditto.

§ 61A.83 (疒/〜)

癡 61A.83-2

chy (*chyr*).
[Pop. 痴]

Adj. (1) Silly, stupid: 癡鈍 *-duhn*↓; 癡漢 *-hahn*↓. (2) Mad, insane, mentally deranged or arrested: 癡獃 (or 呆) *-dai*↓; 癡人說夢 talk fantastic nonsense. (3) Infatuated; faddish, having some form of inordinate fad: 書癡 a bookworm; esp. crazy with love; 情癡 infatuation (with a woman); 癡情, 癡心 *-chirng*, *-shin*↓.

Adv. With infatuation, in a silly manner: 癡想, 癡念 *-shiaang*, *-niahn*↓.

癡騃 *chy-air*, adj., childishly silly (also wr. 癡獃).
癡情 *chychirng*, n., infatuation (for person) mad love.
癡呆 *chydai*, adj., (1) crazed, addleheaded; (2) dull, stupid.
癡鈍 *chyduhn*, adj., dull (as a student).
癡肥 *chyfeir*, adj., unpleasantly fat, lumpy.
癡漢 *chyhahn*, n., a fool, a madman, dunderhead.
癡長 *chyjaang*, adj., (court. in self-reference to age) am stupidly aged so many years.
癡迷 *chymir*, adj., addicted, obsessed with some passion; v.t., madly in love with (person).
癡念 *chyniahn*, v. i. & t., remember always with affection, cannot put out of one's mind.
癡想 *chyshiaang*, v. i., be obsessed with (an idea, hope).
癡笑 *chyshiauh*, v. i., grin or make a silly smile.
癡心 *chyshin*, v. t., (1) love deeply (girl, learning); (2) as in 癡心妄想 hope madly.
癡子 *chytz*, n., a silly person; a mentally deranged person.
癡物 *chywuh*, n., (LL, contempt.) stupid thing, dullard.

§61A.91 (疒/ノ)

瘳 61A.91–5

chou.

V. i. (AC) to recover from illness.

痧 61A.91–6

sha.

N. (1) Cholera. (2) Colic. (3) 痧子 measles.

疹 61A.91–8

jeen.

N. Rash on skin, various illnesses with skin eruptions: 出疹子 get measles, also scarlet fever.

§61A.93 (疒/く)

瘻 61A.93–2

louh.

N. (1) (Med.) scrofula. (2) (=痛) hemorrhoids.

癭 61A.93–4

yiing.

N. (1) A burr. (2) A goiter.

痃 61A.93–6

shiarn.

N. (Chin. med.) a growth in stomach, causing discomfort, dyspepsia: 橫痃 buboes.

瘉 61A.93–8

yuh.

[Usu. wr. 愈 61A.00, var. of 癒]

痿 61A.93–9

weei.

N. (1) Paralysis. (2) 陽痿: sexual impotence (male).

Adj. Wilted: 痿靡不振 dejected, downcast in spirit.

SECTION 61S

§ 61S.00 (广ˢ/亅)

劘 61S.00-2

mor.

V. t. (Rare) make into mince.

§ 61S.10 (广ˢ/十)

麟 61S.10-2

lirn.

N. See 麒ᴬ麟 61S.80, the unicorn.

麟兒 *lirn-erl*, n., (complim.) a good son.
麟鳳 *lirnfehng*, n., the unicorn and the phoenix, auspicious animals, rarely seen; see *-jiaau* ↓.
麟角 *lirnjiaau*, adj., as in 鳳毛麟角 rare and precious things or persons.
麟經 *lirnjing*, n., the *Spring and Autumn Annals* 春秋 of Confucius (allu.).
麟趾 *lirnjyy*, n., "unicorn's toes," (allu.) blessing of many children.
麟麟 *lirnlirn*, adj., (AC) bright.

§ 61S.22 (广ˢ/丨)

鄺 61S.22-3

kuahng (also *guaang*).

N. A surname.

鄘 61S.22-3

yung (also *yurng*).

N. (AC) a small town (interch. 墉).

鄜 61S.22-3

fu.

N. Name of county in Shensi.

§ 61S.50 (广ˢ/乛)

鶊 61S.50-9

geng.

N. 鶬鶊 the oriole.

鷓 61S.50-9

jeh.

鷓鴣 *jehgu*, n., the partridge.

§ 61S.80 (广ˢ/八)

麒 61S.80-2

chir.

麒麟 *chirlirn*, n., the unicorn, a mythic animal of deer type; of good omen of appearing of a sage (Confucius); now used of the giraffe in Japanese; 麒麟兒 a bright young boy.

SECTION 62

§ 62.00 (宀/亅)

守 62.00-1

shoou (**shouh*).

N. (1) Magistrate: 太守, 郡守 district magistrate; 郡守, 邑令 or 守令 different magistrates. (2) Integrity: 操守 integrity: 有操守 has integrity; 有爲有守 can act and maintain certain principles. (3) Defense: 失守, 不守 (city) is taken, occupied by the enemy.

V. i. & t. (1) To keep, guard: 保守 conserve, -vative; 看守 watch (prisoner, house); 守門人 doorkeeper; 守更, 守望 *-geng, -wahng*↓. (2) To wait, keep close to: 守候 *-houh*↓; 守株待兔 phr. allu., stay by a tree hoping to catch a hare just because once a hare accidentally died there—stupid, lack of innovation; 守着老爺身邊 hang on to father's or master's side, never leave him. (3) To garrison (place): 守衞 *-weih*↓; 守城 defend city against attack; 守土 have charge of district or territory; 防守, 駐守, 留守, 戍守 v. t. & n., to garrison; garrison commander. (4) To maintain (integrity, honor, etc.): 守分 *-fehn*↓; 守本分, 守己安分 be law-abiding, act proper to one's status; 守信, 守義 *-shihn, -yih*↓; 守約 keep one's promise; 守舊 *-jiouh*↓; 守節 *-jier*↓; 守齋 observe fast or abstinence; 守經達權 maintain principles with flexibility (權 expediency). (5) (**shouh*) U.f. 狩 (AC) to hunt.

守常 *shooucharng*, v. i., maintain tradition: 守常不變 conservative and opposed to change.
守臣 *shoou-chern*, n., (AC) minister responsible for peace and order in the country.
守成 *shooucherng*, v. i., to carry on: 足以守成 (person) good enough to carry on, but 不足以創業 not good enough to found a dynasty or commercial house.
守錢虜 *shoouchiarnluu*, n., miser.
守法 *shour-faa*, v.i., obey the law; adj., law-abiding.
守分 *shoou-fehn*, v.i., behave properly and correctly, be content with one's lot in life.
守更 *shoou-geng*, v.i., to keep watches of the night.
守寡 *shourguaa*, v.i., to remain a widow.
守候 *shoouhouh*, v.i., to stay and wait.
守護 *shoouhuh*, v. t., to guard (city, place), look after (the sick or wounded).
守着 *shoou'je*, v. i., (1) to stay by the side (of person), keep up (hope); (2) (vern.) widow.
守眞 *shoou-jen*, v. i., keep one's original character (soul, purity, simplicity).
守節 *shoou-jier*, v. i., remain loyal; keep one's integrity against conquerors or keep widowhood despite pressure.
守舊 *shooujiouh*, adj., conservative, diehard, adverse to change.
守拙 *shoou-juor*, v. i., keep to one's primitive simplicity.
守制 *shoou-jyh*, v. i., formerly, to withdraw from government examinations or resign post during mourning for a parent for 27 months.
守吏 *shoou-lih*, n., magistrate or officer in charge.
守舍 *shoou-sheh*, phr., 魂不守舍 "spirit has left the body"—in a state of shock, result of fright.
守身 *shoou-shen*, v. i., conduct oneself correctly: 守身如玉 keep one's integrity or chastity.
守孝 *shoou-shiauh*, v. i., observe mourning for parent.
守信 *shoou-shihn*, v. i., keep promise, stick by contract.
守歲 *shoou-sueih*, v. i., stay awake all night on New Year's Eve.
守財奴 *shooutsairnur*, n., miser ("a slave to money").
守望 *shoouwahng*, v.i., be on guard: 守望相助 (neighbors) keep watch together in mutual defence, mutual help among neighbors.
守衞 *shoouweih*, n. & v.t., a guard, to guard.
守義 *shoou-yih*, v.i., maintain one's integrity or honor.

寄 62.00-1

jih.

V. t. (1) Entrust to: 寄賣, 寄售 consign for sale; 寄託 *-tuo*↓; 寄存 hand over for safekeeping. (2) Send, deliver, transmit: 寄信 mail letters; 郵寄 send by mail; 寄聖誕卡 mail Christmas cards; 寄郵包 send by parcel post; 寄錢 remit money; 寄意 convey thought, best wishes; 寄語 send message by word of mouth. (3) Lodge at: 寄居 put up at; 寄人籬下 depend on another person for support; 寄宿 have lodgings; 寄宿生 a student lodger; 寄宿舍 dormitory; 寄寓 (be in) temporary residence.

寄情 *jih-chirng*, v. i., give expression to one's feelings through writing.
寄碇 *jih-dihng*, v. i., (of boat) to anchor temporarily.
寄頓 *jihduhn*, v. t., to place in safekeeping.
寄放 *jihfahng*, v. t., temporarily keep at some place, deposit.
寄費 *jih-feih*, n., (1) postage, for mailing; (2) storage.
寄父 *jihfuh*, n., foster father.
寄懷 *jih-huair*, v. i., express one's feelings, usu. by literary means.
寄迹 *jih-ji*, v. i., sojourn temporarily.
寄籍 *jih-jir*, v. i. & n., (law) domicile.
寄居蟲 *jihjyu-churng*, n., (zoo.) a pagurian (as hermit crab, etc.).
寄名 *jih-mirng*, v. i., (1) become another person's foster child; (2) become apprenticed to a monk or nun but without taking vows.
寄母 *jihmuu*, n., foster mother.
寄女 *jihnyuu*, n., foster daughter.
寄身 *jih-shen*, v. i., live (abroad,

etc.) for the time being.

寄生 *jihsheng*, v. i., (of plants or animals) live on or within another organism; (of persons) depend on another for a living: 寄生蟲 n., (zoo.) parasites, a parasitic person; 寄生動物 a parasitic animal.

寄興 *jih-shihng*, v. i., give expression to one's momentary feelings, usu. in a verse.

寄售 *jihshouh*, v.i., sell on consignment.

寄食 *jihshyr*, v. i., to sponge upon another person, depend on s.o. for support.

寄託 *jihtuo*, (1) v. t., entrust to the care of s.o.; (2) v.i., (of poetry or prose) to record (personal feelings, belief).

寄子 *jihtzyy*, n., foster son.

搴 62.00-2

chian.

V. t. To wrest away by hand: 搴旗 to capture a flag.

宇 62.00-3

yuu.

N. (1) Building: 屋宇 house; 廟宇 temple building. (2) Shape and structure: 器宇 a man's stature, physical and spiritual; 眉宇 the look of one's forehead and brows as showing intelligence, brilliance; 德宇, 仁宇 (lit. & complim.) your gracious generosity. (3) Time-space universe, universal space: 宇宙 *-jouh* ↓; 寰宇 the whole world.

宇宙 *yuujouh*, n., the cosmos, the universe (as existing in time and space—宇 as time and 宙 as space); 宇宙論 cosmology; 宇宙線 cosmic ray.

宇量 *yuuliahng*, n., generosity.

宇內 *yuu-neih*, phr., within the universe, all the world.

宇下 *yuu-shiah*, n., under the roof; (fig.) s. o.'s protection.

字 62.00-3

tzyh.

N. (1) Characters, words: 字兒 *-'l* ↓; 字彙 one's vocabulary, a glossary of words; 字母 *-muu* ↓; 字音 the sound or pronunciation of a character; 字韻 its rhyme-class; 字句 words and phrases; 字例 principles governing the formation and derivation of characters; 字形 the form of a written character; 字部 the radicals of Chinese characters; 字義 the meaning of a word; 字裏行間 reading between the lines; 字面(兒) phraseology, wording, literal (meaning); 字跡 handwriting; 字條 a written note; 字帖 *-tieh* ↓; 字典 *-diaan* ↓; 寫字 write with a brush (pen, pencil): 寫字間 (Shanghai dial.) a business office; 用字 choice of words, diction; 別字 a wrongly written character; 錯字 ditto; 草字 the running style of Chinese writing; 篆字 an ancient form of Chinese writing, seal script; 鉛字 lead types used in printing; 字模 type forms, (matrix); 認字 learn the written characters; 識字 know the characters; 簡體字 simplified form of a character; 俗字 popular form of character. (2) A courtesy name by which a person is addressed by his friends (cf. 名 and 號).

V. t. Betroth: 字人 (of a girl) be engaged to marry; 待字閨中 (of a girl) not yet engaged.

字典 *tzyhdiaan*, n., a dictionary, thesaurus, lexicon.

字號 *tzyhhauh*, n., (1) characters used to designate particular groups of persons or things: 各有字號 each group (division, class, compartment) designated by a special character; (2) (-*'hau*) shop sign, a signboard; (3) (-*'hau*) good name, reputation, prestige: 字號人物 personages and their reputation; 字號舖兒 reputable firms.

字畫 *tzyh-huah*, n., (1) calligraphy and painting; (2) the strokes of a character.

字蹟 *tzyhji*, n., handwriting, record of writing.

字據 *tzyhjyuh('jyu)*, n., a written receipt.

字紙 *tzyh-jyy*, n., a piece of paper written on with characters: 字紙簍兒 a wastepaper basket.

字塊(兒) *tzyhkuaih(-kuah'l)*, n., characters separately printed on small pieces of square paper for use in teaching pupils.

字兒 *tzyh'l*, n., (1) a character; (2) a signed document, a receipt.

字謎 *tzyh-mir*, n., a riddle standing for one or more characters.

字幕 *tzyh-muh*, n., motion picture captions.

字母(兒) *tzyh-muu('l)*, n., letters of the alphabet.

字盤 *tzyh-parn*, n., a case for holding types.

字牝 *tzyhpihn*, n., (AC) a mare.

字書 *tzyhshu*, n., a dictionary, lexicon.

字條 *tzyhtiaur*, n., a simple note, an office memo.

字帖 *tzyhtieh*, n., (1) a copybook for pupils; (2) reproductions of the works of master calligraphers, usu. in the form of rubbings from stone tablets.

字體 *tzyh-tii*, n., (printing) types: style of calligraphy.

字眼 *tzyhyaan*, n., diction, choice of words: 字眼兒 (a) phraseology, literary expressions; (b) minor erroneous uses of words: 挑字眼兒 to quibble.

字樣 *tzyh-yahng*, n., (1) the form of a written character; (2) words and phrases used in a certain context: 並無此等字樣

there are no such words and phrases (in the document in question).

寧 62.00-6

nirng.

[Pop. 寧; interch. 甯, 寗]

N. A surname (also wr. 寗); (LL) Nanking.

V. i. (1) 歸寧 (of married daughter) to visit one's own parents. (2) To remain serene and unruffled: 寧心 to calm one's mind and spirit; 寧家 (of one's family) settle down, put domestic affairs in order; 寧息 *-shir* ↓.

Adj. Calm, peaceful, tranquil, quiet, healthy: 安寧 quiet and peaceful; 康寧 healthy and happy; 寧靖, 寧謐 *-jihng²*, *-mih* ↓.

Adv. (1) Rather: would rather, oft. 寧可, 寧願 *-kee*, *-yuahn* ↓: 寧可吃點小虧 rather cut the loss, suffer temporary loss; 寧折不彎, 寧死不辱 (屈) would rather die than submit or be humiliated; 寧缺毋濫 would rather go without (s. t.) than be contented with anything less satisfactory, sacrifice completeness in favor of discrimination; 寧爲玉碎, 不爲瓦全 rather stand on principles than accept humiliation (in national or personal affairs), (lit. "better be a piece of broken jade than an unbroken tile"); 寧可信其有, 不可信其無 rather believe it to be true than not. (2) In questions, suggesting "how could it be?" 寧有當乎 could it be right and proper? 寧有是理 how could it be? 不寧惟是 not only that.

寧綢 *nirngchour*, n., brocade, silk from Nanking.

寧家 *nirngjia*, v. i., (1) settle a home; (2) (MC) go home.

寧靜 *nirngjihng¹*, adj., tranquil: 寧靜以致遠 accomplish s. t. lasting by leading a quiet life.

寧靖 *nirngjihng²*, adj., (of political and social order) orderly and tranquil.

寧可 *nirngkee*, adv., rather, see Adv. 1 ↑.

寧肯 *nirngkeen*, adv., would rather, see *-kee* ↑, *-yuahn* ↓.

寧謐 *nirngmih*, adj., tranquil.

寧耐 *nirngnaih*, v. t., endure patiently.

寧波 *Nirngpo*, n., Ningpo, a port city in Chekiang Province.

寧夏 *Nirngshiah*, n., Ninghsia, a province in northwest China; also its capital.

寧馨 *nirngshing*, adj., such a: 寧馨兒 such a pretty and lovely child.

寧息 *nirngshir*, v. i., enjoy quiet and rest.

寧帖 *nirngtie*, adj., tranquil, unperturbed, (also wr. 貼).

寧願 *nirngyuahn*, adv., would rather, see Adv. 1 ↑.

§ 62.01 (宀/小)

宋 62.01-1

suhng.

N. (1) A surname. (2) Name of dynasty, 960–1276 A.D.; 宋版 a Suhng edition; 宋瓷 Suhng porcelain; 仿宋 style of character type face, "imitation Suhng."

寮 62.01-1

liaur.

N. A small house, shack, hut: 草寮 hut; 僧寮 monk's dwelling; 茶寮 tea booth; 妓寮 brothel (also u.f. 僚 91A.01).

寨 62.01-2

jaih.

N. (*-tz*) A brigands' stronghold; a stockade or fort with walled defense: 寨主 chief of brigands.

寐 62.01-2

meih.

N. & v. i. Sleep, be asleep: 睡不成寐 unable to sleep; 假寐 take a nap; 失寐 insomnia; 寤寐不忘 never forget, awake or asleep; 寢寐不安 lie awake with s. t. on mind, and worried.

宗 62.01-3

tzung.

N. (1) Lineage, ancestry: 祖宗 ancestor; 列祖列宗 forbears, forefathers; 大(小)宗 offspring by direct (lateral) descent. (2) A posthumous title for a king or emperor. (3) A clan: 同宗 a member of the same clan; 同姓不同宗 a person of the same surname but belonging to a different clan. (4) School of thought: 宗派 *-paih* ↓; 宗徒 apostle; 禪宗 the Zen sect (of Buddhism). (5) An item, a batch: 一宗 one item; 大宗郵件 a batch of mail; 宗宗件件, 宗宗樣樣 all kinds (sorts), things of every description; 卷宗 files, archives. (6) A surname.

V. t. (1) Venerate, revere: 宗仰 *-yaang* ↓. (2) Pay court to: 朝宗 pay homage to the ruler: 江漢朝宗於海 the Yangtse and the Hahn empty themselves into the sea.

宗臣 *tzungchern*, n., (1) (AC) a clan officer; (2) a respected minister of state.

宗器 *tzung-chih*, n., ceremonial vessels in the royal ancestral shrine.

宗親 *tzung-chin*, n., clan relatives.

宗弟 *tzung-dih*, n., (1) a younger

clan brother; (2) (AC) a younger brother born of the wife in relation to an elder one born of a concubine.

宗法 *tzung-faa*, n., ancient clan system: 宗法社會 ancient society based upon the family system.

宗藩 *tzung-farn*, n., (AC) members of the royal clan holding feudal benefices.

宗風 *tzung-feng*, n., (Budd.) the characteristic features of a sect.

宗婦 *tzung-fuh*, n., (AC) wife of the eldest son by direct descent.

宗工 *tzung-gung*, n., see *-jiahng* ↓.

宗國 *tzung-guor*, n., fatherland.

宗匠 *tzung-jiahng*, n., a great respected master.

宗教 *tzungjiauh*, n., religion.

宗主 *tzungjuu*, n., (1) a memorial ancestral tablet in ancestral shrine; (2) the eldest son born of one's wife (cf. 庶子 a son born of one's concubine); 宗主權 sovereignty, sovereign rights.

宗枝 *tzung-jy*, n., a lateral branch of the clan.

宗旨 *tzungjyy*, n., (1) aims and purposes (of association, club); (2) essential ideas, main points (of lecture, sermon).

宗老 *tzung-laau*, n., the elders of a clan.

宗類 *tzung-leih*, n., see *-tzur* ↓.

宗門 *tzung-mern*, n., (1) clan relatives; (2) a Buddhist sect.

宗廟 *tzung-miauh*, n., the royal ancestral shrine.

宗女 *tzung-nyuu*, n., (AC) a girl of royal descent.

宗派 *tzungpaih*, n., religious sects, schools of thought.

宗人 *tzung-rern*, n., royal clan members: 宗人府 an office in charge of the affairs of royal members.

宗社 *tzung-sheh*, n., the state as symbolized by the royal ancestral shrine and the temples.

宗師 *tzung-shy*, n., a great respected teacher and master.

宗室 *tzungshyh*, n., members of the royal clan.

宗學 *tzung-shyuer*, n., a school for members of the royal household.

宗兄 *tzung-shyung*, n., (1) an elder clan brother; (2) (AC) an elder brother born of the wife in relation to one born of the concubine.

宗祀 *tzung-syh*, n., clan ancestral temple.

宗祧 *tzung-tiau*, n., the ancestral shrine.

宗祠 *tzung-tsyr*, n., the ancestral temple of a clan.

宗族 *tzungtzur*, n., the paternal clan.

宗子 *tzung-tzyy*, n., the eldest son born of one's wife (opp. 庶子 a son born of one's concubine).

宗仰 *tzungyaang*, v. t., look up to with awe, admire at a distance (cf. 崇^A仰 21.01).

宗彝 *tzungyir*, n., ceremonial vessels of the royal ancestral shrine.

宷 62.01-9

tsaai.

N. (AC) feudal estate.

察 62.01-9

char.

V. i. & t. (1) Observe, notice, see: 審察, 觀察 observe, notice (conditions, facts, trend); 觀察人 n., observer (at conference); 察見, 察出 notice that, find out that; 不察, 未察 fail to notice; 未察 (LL) also do not know: 未察尊意如何 do not know what you think; 失察 careless, commit mistakes of omission; 細察 notice, observe, find out in detail; 細察來意 judge the motive of his coming. (2) (Interch. 查) officially look over, inspect, examine, detect: 察勘, 察核 *-kahn*[2], *-her* ↓; 監察, 督察 supervise, watch over; 警察 n., police: 糾察 investigate (case).

察察 *charchar*, adj. & adv., (1) (AC) discerning; (2) (AC) clean (physically).

察奪 *charduor*, v. t., (official letter) please use your discerning judgment.

察訪 *charfaang*, v. t., to go about finding out (conditions, suspects).

察核 *charher*, v. t., see *-duor* ↑.

察看 *charkahn*[1], v. t., to look over.

察勘 *charkahn*[2], v. t., to examine (place of robbery, landmarks, etc.) on the spot.

案 62.01-9

ahn.

N. (1) A table: 香案 altar; 書案 studio table or desk; 几案 a table; a low table with short props for serving food and drinks: 舉案齊眉 a husband and wife love and respect each other for life (a form of extreme humility) (from allu., the wife served lunch to her farmer husband, "raising the tray to eye level."). (2) Official documents, records: 案牘, 案卷 *-dur*, *-jyuahn* ↓; 檔案 official files, archives; 立案 to register for the record or for protection; 備案 prepare documents or communications, register for the record; 在案 in the official records. (3) A legal case: 案件 *-jiahn* ↓; 盜案 a case of robbery, 竊案 a burglary; 慘案 a tragic incident; 殺案, 命案 a murder case; 姦案 a case of rape; 凶案 a case of assault, violence or murder; 懸案 pending or unsettled case; 陳案, 舊案 long-standing case; 翻案 reopen case; 定案 a settled case or to hand down court decision; 公案 a Zen problem, a public issue, a *cause célèbre*.

案 褰 家

V.i. (Var. 按 10A.93) to investigate, to comment.

案板 *ahnbaan*, n., kitchen chopping board.

案比 *ahnbii*, v.t., (AC) make annual inspection of troops.

案情 *ahn-chirng*, n., the facts of a legal case.

案牘 *ahndur*, n., office correspondence.

案件 *ahnjiahn*, n., a case at court.

案酒 *ahnjioou*, n., (MC) snacks to go with drink.

案桌 *ahnjuo*, n., a long high table.

案卷 *ahnjyuahn*, n., files of documents.

案兒上的 *ah'lshahng'de*, n., pastry cook in restaurant.

案目 *ahnmuh*, n., (Shanghai dial.) usher at theater.

案事 *ahn-shyh*, v.i., (AC) to investigate case at court.

案頭 *ahntour*, phr., on the table.

案子 *ahntz*, n., (1) a big board table; (2) a case at court.

案杌 *ahnwahn*, v.i., (AC) give massage.

案問 *ahnwehn*, v.t., to cross-examine.

案驗 *ahnyahn*, v.t., to investigate (case).

案由 *ahnyour*, n., story of a case at court; title of an official document.

案語 *ahnyuu*, n., (editor's, author's) comment, remarks.

§ 62.02 (宀/k)

褰 62.02-2

chian.

V. t. To lift up: 褰裳 (AC) lift up skirt (as in wading river).

家 62.02-3

jia.

N. adjunct. (1) To make plural nn.: 孩子家 children; 婦道人家 women in gen.; 女孩兒家 girls as a class. (2) To form reflexive pronn.: 自家 oneself; 咱家 ourselves.

Adv. part. To form advv.: 鎮日家 all day long.

N. (1) Home, family, residence: 家庭 *-tirng*↓; 家徒壁立 (of families) utterly destitute ("with only bare walls"); 家給 (*-jii*) 人足 well-to-do, with ample means of support; 家喻戶曉 known by one and all, widely known, become a household word; 家破人亡 with the family broken up and decimated; 合家 the whole family: 合家歡 a happy reunion; 本家 a member of the same clan; 想家 homesick(ness); 回家 homecoming; 離家 going away from home. (2) An expert, specialist: 文學家 an author, writer, a man of letters; 藝術家 an artist; 科學家 a scientist; 哲學家 a philosopher; 畫家 a painter; 小說家 a novelist. (3) A school of thought: 儒家 the Confucianists; 法家 the Legalists; 道家 the Taoists; 佛家 the Buddhists; 道學家 a moralist, a stickler to strict rules of conduct, a Puritan. (4) Person engaged in some particular field of activity: 慈善家 a philanthropist; 探險家 an explorer; 外交家 a diplomat; 政治家 a politician, statesman; 運動家 an athlete; 考古家 an archeologist; 評論家 a critic; 鑒賞家 a connoisseur; 演說家 an orator; 革命家 a revolutionist; 冤家 a deadly enemy, an irreconcilable foe, also a lover; 仇家 one's enemy; 頭家 (gambling) the banker, keeper of a gambling house; 買家 the buyer; 輸家, 贏家 (gambling) the loser, winner; 方家 an expert, person with some special skill; 練家子 a person skilled in boxing, swordsmanship, etc. (5) A surname.

Adj. (1) Designating a member of speaker's family: 家父, 家兄 my father, brother; 家嚴 *-yarn*, 家慈 *-tsyr*[2]↓; 家祖 my grandfather. (2) Domesticated (opp. 野 wild): 家畜 *-chuh*↓; 家禽 domestic fowls; 家兔 domestic rabbits; 家雞野鶩 (雉) (a man given to) extramarital relations in one's family and outside; 家雀兒 pop. name for sparrows. (3) Belonging to the home or family: 家僕 family servant; 家丁 *-ding*↓; 家僮 formerly a boy servant; 家姑兒老 an old maid, spinster; 家賊 a pilferer working from within: 家賊難防 it's most difficult to forestall a thief within the house.

家產 *jiachaan*, n., patrimony, family estate.

家常 *jiacharng*, (1) n., domestic affairs: (話) 家常 (話) (engage in) small talk; (2) adj., common place, ordinary: 家常便飯 simple meal, potluck.

家慶 *jia-chihng*, n., family celebrations, e.g., those on parent's birthdays.

家醜 *jia-choou*, n., a family scandal: 家醜不可外揚 don't wash dirty linen in public.

家傳 *jiachuarn*, (1) n., family records, history of one's forefathers; (2) adj., handed down from generation to generation.

家畜 *jiachuh*, n., domestic animals or fowls.

家當(兒) *jia'dang('l)*, n., family possessions.

家道 *jiadauh*, n., economic condition of the family (rich, poor).

家的 *jia'de*, n., (MC coll.) wife.

家底兒 *jiadiee'l*, n., family heirloom.

家丁 *jiading*, n., formerly, a family servant.

家法 *jiafaa*, n., (1) tradition and discipline peculiar to certain schools; (2) domestic discipline; (3) the rod for punishing children.

家風 *jiafeng*, n., family tradition.

家規 *jiaguei*, n., family rules.

家公 *jiagung*, n., (1) (AC) father; (2) the head of a family, *paterfamilias*.

家火 *jiahuo*, n., (also wr. 家伙, 傢伙) (1) furniture, tools, utensils; (2) (contempt.) a man or boy, fellow, guy.

家長 *jiajaang*, n., the head of a family, *paterfamilias*.

家宅 *jiajair*, n., family dwelling place.
家政 *jiajehng*, n., home economics, "household management."
家家 *jiajia*, n., (1) every family: 家家兒, 家家戶戶 all families without exception; (2) (-'*jia'l*) the family.
家教 *jiajiauh*, n., family training, domestic discipline.
家祭 *jiajih*[1], n., sacrifice to ancestors.
家計 *jiajih*[2], n., family livelihood.
家境 *jiajihng*, n., economic condition of the family.
家主 *jiajuu*, n., head of the family: 家主公 (Soochow dial.) husband ("the old man of the family"); 家主婆 (Soochow dial.) wife ("mistress of the family"); 家主翁 the highest-ranking member of the family.
家眷 *jiajyuahn* (-'*juan*), n., family (wife and children).
家具 *jiajyuh*, n., furniture (also wr. 傢俱).
家君 *jiajyun*, n., (LL) my father.
家口 *jiakoou*, n., size of a family ("number of mouths to be fed").
家累 *jialeei*, n., family burden.
家裏 *jia-lii*, n., (1) one's home; (2) wife.
家門 *jiamern*, n., (1) family clan; (2) (AC) the family of a high-ranking official.
家廟 *jia-miauh*, n., ancestral shrine or temple.
家釀 *jia-niahng*, n., home-brew.
家奴 *jia-nur*, n., domestic servant ("family slave").
家譜 *jiapuu*, n., family genealogy.
家人 *jiarern*, n., (1) members of a family; (2) male servant: 一家人 all of the same family.
家聲 *jia-sheng*, n., family reputation.
家小 *jiashiaau*, n., wife and children collectively.
家下 *jiashiah*, adv., at home.
家鄉 *jiashiang*, n., one's native district.
家信 *jia-shihn*, n., letters from home.
家書 *jia-shu*, n., family letters.
家數 *jiashuh*, n., a school (of boxing, etc.).
家塾 *jiashur*, n., family school.
家屬 *jiashuu*, n., one's dependents.
家世 *jiashyh*[1], n., family background.
家室 *jiashyh*[2], n., (1) wife and children; (2) husband and wife.
家事 *jiashyh*[3], n., (1) family affairs; (2) home economics.
家什 *jiashyr* (-'*shy*), n., furniture, tools, utensils.
家學 *jia-shyuer*, n., knowledge transmitted from father to son: 家學淵源 (of persons) erudite through paternal teaching and influence.
家訓 *jia-shyuhn*, n., parental precepts.
家私 *jiasy* (-'*sy*), n., (1) family affairs; (2) family possessions.
家庭 *jiatirng*, n., family, home: 家庭教師 children's private tutor; 家庭教育 home education; 家庭醫師 family doctor; 家庭計劃 family planning; 家庭生活 home life; 甜蜜家庭 a sweet home; 家庭温暖 family love.
家財 *jiatsair*, n., family riches, patrimony.
家祠 *jiatsyr*[1], n., ancestral temple or shrine.
家慈 *jiatsyr*[2], n., my mother, a term used in speaking to a person from a different family; cf. -*yarn* ↓.
家族 *jiatzur*, n., (1) relatives of the same family; (2) family clan.
家務 *jia-wuh*, n., family affairs.
家宴 *jia-yahn*, n., family reunion or dinner.
家嚴 *jiayarn*., n., my father.
家業 *jiayeh*, n., family possessions, family status.
家園 *jiayuarn*, n., home garden; native district.
家用 *jia-yuhng*, n., domestic expenses.

冢 62.02-3

juung.

N. (1) A burial mound: 古冢 ancient grave. (2) (AC) top of hill.

Adj. The eldest: 冢子, 冢息 or 冢嗣 eldest son; 冢婦 eldest daughter-in-law.

冢宰 *jurngtzaai*, n., (AC) the chief steward; minister of state.

寰 62.02-4

huarn.

[In compp. only; cf. 環 31A.02]

寰球 *huarnchiour*, adj. & adv., all over the world: 寰球印刷公司 world publishing company.
寰區 *huarnchyu*, n., all within the country.
寰內 *huarn-neih*, adj. & adv., in all the world.
寰宇 *huarnyuu*, adj. & adv., see -*chiour* ↑.

宸 62.02-5

chern.

N. (1) A great mansion. (2) Imperial palace, the court.

Adj. Imperial: see compp. ↓.

宸斷 *chernduahn*, n., imperial decision.
宸翰 *chernhahn*, n., imperial pen or writing.
宸極 *chernjir*, n., celestial abode of emperor; also the North Star.
宸衷 *chernjung*, n., imperial heart.
宸慮 *chernlyuh*, n., imperial consideration.
宸算 *chernsuahn*, n., imperial judgment.
宸聰 *cherntsung*, n., imperial wisdom.

宸 垣 *chernyuarn*, n., (LL) national capital.

§ 62.10 (宀/十)

牢 62.10-1

laur.

N. (1) Stables. (2) (LL) cattle and sheep: 太牢 sacrificial ox; 少牢 sacrificial sheep and pigs. (3) Prison: 牢城 *-cherng* ↓; 監牢 a prison; 坐牢 be thrown into jail. (4) A surname.

V. i. Sad: 牢愁 *-chour*; 牢騷 *-sau* ↓.

Adj. Strong, firm, stable: 牢固 *-guh* ↓; 牢靠 *-'kauh* ↓; 牢不可破 stubborn; 記牢 keep in mind, be mindful; 立志要牢 make firm resolutions; 這椅子不牢 the chair is rickety.

牢 城 *laurcherng*, n., (MC) a prison.

牢 愁 *laurchour*, adj., sorrowful.

牢 固 *laurguh*, adj., firm (faith), secure (city walls, prison).

牢 棧 *laurjahn*, n., stockade for animals.

牢 記 *laurjih*, v. t., keep (s. t.) always at heart.

牢 靠 *laur'kauh*, adj., firm and reliable.

牢 落 *laurluoh*, adj., (1) thin, sparse; (2) silent, quiet; (3) keeping oneself aloof, being a bad mixer: 牢落不羣.

牢 籠 *laurlurng(-'lung)*, v.t., (1) include, comprehend: 牢籠天地 include everything (lit., "heaven and earth"); (2) entrap, get control over: 牢籠計 stratagem for gaining support; 牢籠人心 try to win popular support.

牢 騷 *laursau('sau)*, n., pent-up discontent: 發牢騷 grumble; 滿腹牢騷 given to grumbling.

牢 什 子 *laurshyrtz*, n., (coll.) an eyesore, anything disagreeable or abominable.

牢 頭 *laurtour*, n., (coll.) prison warden, jailer (=牢頭禁子).

牢 穩 *laur'ween*, adj., firm and reliable.

牢 獄 *lauryuh*, n., a prison.

軍 62.10-1

jyun.

N. (1) Soldiers: 軍士 *-shyh*[1] ↓; 軍人 *-rern* ↓. (2) Troops, armed forces: 三軍 a nation's armed forces; 陸軍 the army; 海軍 the navy; 空軍 the air force; 軍事 *-shyh*[2] ↓; 軍團 *-tuarn* ↓; 隨軍記者 a war correspondent; 隨軍牧師 an army chaplain; 青年軍 the youth corps; 禁衛軍 palace guards; 駐軍 garrison forces; 從軍 be in active military service; 行軍 (of an army) to march, advance; 救世軍 the Salvation Army; 娘子軍 (facet.) a group of women banded together for a specific purpose; 童子軍 Boy Scouts; 女童子軍 Girl Scouts; 軍管區 *-guaanchyu* ↓; 裁軍 (會議) disarmament (conference); 潰不成軍 (of an army) be completely routed. (3) Banishment, exile: 充軍 exile as a form of punishment.

軍 備 *jyunbeih*, n., armaments.

軍 便 服 *jyun-biahnfur*, n., a soldier's fatigue clothes..

軍 壁 *jyunbih*, n., the walls of barracks.

軍 器 *jyunchih*, n., arms, weapons.

軍 旗 *jyunchir*, n., a military flag.

軍 情 *jyunchirng*, n., (1) military situation at the front; (2) military intelligence.

軍 區 *jyunchyu*, n., a military district, a corps area.

軍 刀 *jyundau*, n., an officer's sword.

軍 隊 *jyundueih*, n., troops.

軍 法 *jyunfaa*, n., military law.

軍 閥 *jyunfar*, n., warlords, militarists.

軍 費 *jyunfeih*, n., military expenses.

軍 服 *jyunfur*, n., military uniform.

軍 港 *jyungaang*, n., a naval base.

軍 歌 *jyunge*, n., a military song.

軍 管 區 *jyunguaanchyu*, n., an army district.

軍 官 *jyunguan*, n., a military officer.

軍 規 *jyunguei*, n., military rules (regulations).

軍 棍 *jyunguhn*, n., a cane for corporal punishment in the army.

軍 功 *jyungung*, n., outstanding services rendered by soldiers in line of duty.

軍 國 主 義 *jyunguor juuyih*, n. militarism.

軍 漢 *jyunhahn*, n., formerly, privates.

軍 號 *jyunhauh*, n., a military bugle.

軍 火 *jyunhuoo*, n., munitions.

軍 長 *jyunjaang*, n., the commander of an army.

軍 政 *jyunjehng*, n., military administration.

軍 機 *jyunji*, n., classified military information: 軍機處 the Privy Council of the Manchu Court.

軍 健 *jyunjiahn*[1], n., formerly, privates.

軍 艦 *jyunjiahn*[2], n., a warship, a man-of-war.

軍 階 *jyunjie*, n., military ranks.

軍 紀 *jyunjih*[1], n., military discipline, morale.

軍 妓 *jyunjih*[2], n., corps of prostitutes in the army.

軍 籍 *jyunjir*, n., a name list of military personnel.

軍 裝 *jyunjuang*, n., (1) military uniform; (2) arms and ammunition.

軍 制 *jyunjyh*, n., military organization.

軍 職 *jyunjyr*, n., a military post.

軍 眷 *jyunjyuahn*, n., military dependents.

軍 壘 *jyunleei*, n., the walls of a barrack.

軍 糧 *jyunliarng*, n., provisions for the army.

軍 令 *jyunlihng*, n., military orders: 軍令狀 a written pledge placing oneself liable to punishment by military law in case of infraction.

軍禮 *jyunlii*, n., military salute.

軍律 *jyunlyuh*, n., military rules and regulations.

軍旅 *jyunlyuu*, n., troops: 軍旅之事 military matters.

軍帽 *jyunmauh*, n., military cap.

軍門 *jyunmern*, n., (1) the main gate of a barracks; (2) formerly, honorific title of a Provincial Commander in Chief.

軍人 *jyunrern*, n., soldiers, the military.

軍容 *jyun-rurng*, n., the impression an army makes of its morale and capabilities.

軍餉 *jyunshiaang*, n., funds for the payment of soldiers.

軍械 *jyunshieh*, n., arms, weapons.

軍興 *jyun-shing*, phr., an outbreak of war (hostilities).

軍書 *jyunshu*, n., military memos.

軍師 *jyunshy*, n., (1) formerly, an inspector-general of the army; (2) an adviser; (3) (of chess or card games) a kibitzer.

軍士 *jyunshyh*[1], n., soldiers.

軍事 *jyunshyh*[2], n., military affairs.

軍實 *jyunshyr*, n., military supplies.

軍需 *jyunshyu*, n., ditto.

軍臺 *jyuntair*, n., formerly, an officer responsible for the transmission of military intelligence and messages.

軍帖 *jyun-tiee*, n., an army bulletin.

軍團 *jyuntuarn*, n., an army corps.

軍務 *jyun-wuh*, n., military affairs.

軍衣 *jyunyi*[1], n., military uniform.

軍醫 *jyun-yi*[2], n., a military surgeon.

軍營 *jyunyirng*, n., barracks.

軍樂 *jyun-yueh*, n., military marches: 軍樂隊 a military band.

軍用 *jyun-yuhng*, adj., for use by the military: 軍用品 military supplies.

宰 62.10-6

tzaai.

N. An anc. official title: 冢宰 the chief minister of state; 太宰 ditto; 小宰 deputy prime minister; 宰相 *-shiahng*, 宰輔 *-fuu*, 宰執 *-jyr* ↓.

V. t. (1) Govern, rule: 宰制(萬物) to lord it over (all things); 宰物 take charge of matters; 主宰 be the master of, a ruler, the Supreme Being; 眞宰 the Creator, God. (2) Kill, slaughter, cut up: 宰割 *-ge* ↓; 宰殺 *-sha* ↓; 宰肉 cut up meat; 宰牛, 宰羊 slaughter cattle, sheep; 宰了他 give him the works (his quietus).

宰輔 *tzairfuu*, n., (LL) premier.

宰割 *tzaaige*, v. t., cut into pieces, divide up.

宰執 *tzaaijyr*, n., (LL) premier.

宰殺 *tzaaisha*, v. t., slaughter (animals).

宰相 *tzaaishiahng*, n., formerly, the prime minister, premier.

罕 62.10-8

haan.

N. (1) A surname. (2) (AC) a bird net.

Adj. & adv. Seldom, rare: 罕物 a rare thing; 罕事 rare event; 罕見 seldom seen; 罕聞 rarely heard; 罕有, 希罕 rare.

搴 62.10-9

an.

[Var. of 鞍 22S.93]

§ 62.11 (宀/土)

塞 62.11-2

seh (**saih*, **sai*).

N. (1) (**saih*) A frontier pass, a fort: 要塞 fortress; 關塞 mountain pass; 塞外 *-waih* ↓. (2) (**sai*) (*-tz, 'l*) A stopper.

V.i. (1) To fill up, stuff up: 塞耳不聞 turn a deaf ear to; 塞責 *-tzer* ↓. (2) (sp. pr. **sai*) To stuff up: 塞住 plug up (a hole, leak); 塞滿 stuff place full of things; 塞牙 (food morsels) stick between teeth; 塞狗洞 (sl.) give bribe ("fill dog kennel").

塞門 *sehmern*, n., (1) (AC) gate screen to prevent passengers from seeing house; (2) (**saih-*) fort gate; (3) (**sai-*) (water) faucet.

塞子 **saitz*, n., (bottle) stopper.

塞責 *seh-tzer*, v.i., do s.t. for form's sake or just enough to exculpate oneself ("to stop blame").

塞外 **saihwaih*, n., beyond the northern (Mongolian) frontier.

塞藥 **saiyauh*, n., (med.) suppository.

塞垣 **saihyuarn*, n., (LL) part of the Great Wall built during the Hahn Dyn.

宝 62.11-3

baau.

[Pop. for 寶 62.80]

室 62.11-3

shyh.

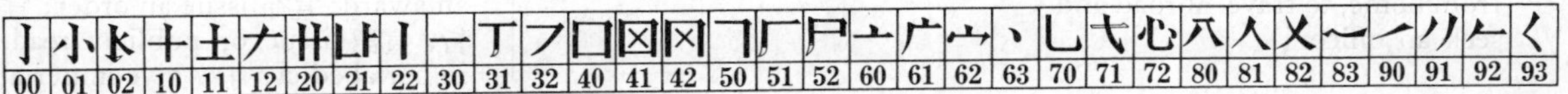

00 01 02 10 11 12 20 21 22 30 31 32 40 41 42 50 51 52 60 61 62 63 70 71 72 80 81 82 83 90 91 92 93

N. (1) House, home: 房室 house; 室外, 室內 outdoors, indoors; 室邇人遠 (LL) her house is near, but her person is difficult to approach. (2) Room: 浴室 bathroom; 教室 classroom; 臥室, 寢室 bedroom; 辦公室 office; 暗室 dark room. (3) Wife: 妻室 a wife; 未有妻室 not yet married; 正室, 側室 wife, concubine; 外室 mistress living outside; 繼室 second wife taken after first wife's death.

室女 *shyh-nyuu*, n., (LL) unmarried girl.
室人 *shyhrern*, n., (AC) (1) wife; (2) people in the family.
室樂 *shyh-yueh*, n., chamber music.

§62.21 (宀/ㄴ)

窤 62.21-3

baau.
[AC var. of 寶 62.80]

宦 62.21-5

huahn.

N. (1) Officialdom: 宦途 official career; 官宦, 仕宦 officials as a class; 宦海浮沉 the vicissitudes of official life; 宦囊 private savings of an official. (2) Eunuch: 宦官 *-guan* ↓. (3) A surname.

宦官 *huahnguan*, n., eunuch.
宦寺 *huahnsyh*, n., eunuchs as a class.
宦遊 *huahnyour*, v. i., formerly, be in government service away from home, to travel abroad and seek an office.

密 62.21-6

mih.
[Dist. 蜜 honey, 62.93]

Adj. & adv. (Quite freely used before nn. & vbb.) (1) secret, -ly: 密謀, 密議, 談, 訪, 函 secretly plan, discuss, talk, visit, write, etc., or secret plan, discussion, etc.; 密約, 密契 *-yue, -chih* ↓; 密令 secret, -ly, order; 密保 secret, -ly, recommend, -dation, etc. (2) Intimate: 密友, 親密的朋友 intimate friend; 很親密, 密切 very intimate (relations). (3) Close: 密不通風 stuffy (room without ventilation); 密布 spread closely; 密雲不雨 heavily overcast sky without rain; (fig.) sound and fury without action or weeping without tears.

密報 *mih-bauh*, n. & v. t., (send) secret message, report.
密契 *mih-chih*, n., a secret understanding.
密電 *mih-diahn*, n., secret telegram.
密度 *mihduh*, n., (phys.) density.
密教 *mih-jiauh*, n., (Budd.) esoteric sect, opp. 顯教 exoteric.
密集隊形 *mihjir dueihshirng*, n., (mil.) close formation: 密集數 most frequent number, mode (in statistics).
密碼 *mihmaa*, n., secret code.
密宗 *mihtzung*, n., (Budd.) esoteric doctrine; 眞言宗 Jenyarn (Shingon) Sect.
密網 *mihwaang*, n., "fine net," i. e., numerous laws, statutes and regulations.
密勿 *mihwuh*, adj., as in (AC) 密勿大臣 minister of privy council; adv., (AC) diligently: 密勿從事.
密約 *mih-yue*, n., secret agreement.

§62.22 (宀/丨)

冪 62.22-2

mih.
[Var. of 冪 62.22]

冪 62.22-4

mih.

N. (AC) cover for tripod.

冪 62.22-4

mih.
[Var. 冪, 冪, 幎]

N. Cloth cover (for food, etc.).

V. t. To cover with cloth.

§62.30 (宀/一)

宣 62.30-3

shyuan.

N. A surname.

V. i. & t. (1) To announce, declare: 宣告 make a public declaration or announcement (of bankruptcy, armistice, divorce, etc.); 宣誓 *-shyh*[2] ↓; 宣戰 *-jahn* ↓; 宣判 *-pahn* ↓; 宣赦 pardon (criminal) publicly; 宣揚 *-yarng* ↓; 秘而不宣 keep secret (important facts, such as emperor's death). (2) To issue (an order): 宣賞 issue an award; 宣命 issue an order; 宣旨, 宣詔 issue or publicly read, imperial edict; 宣赦 give imperial order; 宣付史館 order that it be communicated to the Government Archives (for record). (3) To preach, broadcast, propagate doctrine: 宣講, 宣科 *-jiaang*, *-ke*↓; 宣傳 *-chuarn*↓. (4) To exert, commit: 宣淫, 宣勞 *-yirn*, *-laur*↓. (5) To channel an outlet: 宣導, 宣泄 *-dauh*, *-shieh*↓.

Adj. (1) (Coll.) fluffy: 這饅頭眞宣 this bread is quite fluffy and light; 宣土地兒 where the ground is soft (not solid); 宣土窩兒 a soft, hollow spot on ground. (2) Swollen: 他的臉都胖得宣了 his face is swollen from fat, flabby.

宣布 *shyuanbuh*, v. t., to announce, declare (innocence, sentence, divorce, bankruptcy, etc.): 宣布獨立 declare independence; 宣布和約 announce a peace treaty; see *-jahn*↓.

宣傳 *shyuanchuarn*, (1) v. t., to do propaganda, publicize (sales): 廣為宣傳 give a great deal of publicity; (2) propaganda (work, bureau, etc.): 宣傳品 propaganda literature; 宣傳網 propaganda network.

宣導 *shyuandauh*, v. t., to channel an outlet; (Chin. med.) bring about better circulation of body fluids.

宣讀 *shyuandur*, v.t., to read out (pronouncement, sentence, etc.).

宣撫 *shyuanfuu*, v. t., to pacify (conquered people), to win over by generous policy.

宣告 *shyuangauh*, v. t., to declare, publicly announce, see *-buh*↑.

宣戰 *shyuan-jahn*, v. i., to declare war: 向 or 對某國宣戰 declare war against a certain country.

宣召 *shyuanjauh*, v. t., to summon to imperial audience or to capital.

宣講 *shyuanjiaang*, v. i. & t., to preach (Christian or Budd.).

宣紙 *shyuanjyy*, n., good paper for painting or calligraphy from 宣城 in Anhwei.

宣科 *shyuanke*, v.i., (MC) incant.

宣勞 *shyuanlaur*, (1) v. i., to do one's best: 為國宣勞 to labor for the country; (2) v. t., (*-lauh*) to comfort soldiers with gifts, recognize service with awards.

宣令 *shyuan-lihng*, v. i., issue order, usu. imperial order.

宣募 *shyuanmuh*, v. t., to seek (recruits), collect (funds for public purpose).

宣判 *shyuanpahn*, v. t., to sentence (person to imprisonment, death, etc.).

宣赦 *shyuan-sheh*, v. i., to announce amnesty.

宣泄 *shyuanshieh*, v. t., (1) to drain (a river course); (2) to leak out (secret).

宣示 *shyuanshyh*[1], v. i., (1) to publicize, make known; (2) to announce a court decision.

宣誓 *shyuanshyh*[2], v. i., to take public oath, to pledge, to declare solemnly.

宣言 *shyuanyarn*, n., a declaration (of policy), a public statement.

宣揚 *shyuanyarng*, v. t., to spread (culture, sect, teachings, etc.).

宣淫 *shyuanyirn*, v. i., to commit adultery openly.

宣猷 *shyuan-your*, phr., (AC) show distinguished services.

宜 62.30-4

yir.

N. (1) Propriety, appropriateness (of arrangement, remark). (2) 事宜 affairs in gen.; 機宜 measures for coping with a given situation: 請示機宜 ask for instructions from superior.

Vb. aux. (LL) Should: 宜速歸 should return home immediately; 不宜如此 should not be like this.

V.t. To suit, to fit in properly: 宜室宜家 (of bride) be a good wife, live harmoniously in new home; 不宜 do not fit in well.

Adj. Proper, suitable: 合宜 ditto; 便 (*piarn*) 宜 inexpensive; 不宜 not proper; 宜於 is suitable for; 宜乎 (LL) it is natural (that s.t. happens).

宜昌 *Yirchan*, n., a port in Hupeh Province (湖北省).

宜男 *yirnan*, adj., (of women) prone to have male children.

宜人 *yirrern*, n., (of woman) agreeable person; formerly, a lady of the 5th rank.

宜興 *Yirshing*, n., a city in Kiangsu Province (江蘇省); 宜興陶器 famous pottery of Yirshing.

§ 62.40 (宀/口)

害 62.40-1

haih (*her).

N. An evil, cause of trouble: 為民除害 remove the evils (such as banditry) from the people; 災害, 禍害 a disaster; 傷害 damage, injury; 有害 harmful, 無害 harmless.

Pron. (AC) (*her) (interch. 曷) why not: 時日害喪 (also wr. 曷喪) why does not the day blot out? (complaint of bitterly oppressed people); (AC cogn. 何) which: 害澣害否 which shall be washed and which not?

V. t. (1) To injure, to harm, be harmful to, do an ill turn: 這個辦法害人不淺 this procedure causes infinite harm to people; 害了我不能回去 prevented me from being able to go home; 他想害我 he wants to do me some harm; 傷害

to harm (reputation, crops, etc.); 害羣之馬 the "black sheep," individual who gives the group a bad name; 害國殃民 harm the nation and the country. (2) To kill: 謀財害命 to kill for money; 把他害死 to murder him; 謀害 attempt to murder; 殺害 to kill (person); 殘害 to kill or cripple. (3) To contract illness or disease: 害病 become ill; 害心臟病 have heart trouble; 害痧眼, 瘧疾 contract trachoma, malaria. (4) To feel: 害怕,害羞, 害臊 *-pah*, *-shiou*, *-sauh*↓.

Adj. Harmful: 害蟲 destructive insects; 害事 harmful affair; 害鳥 destructive, crop-eating birds.

害處 *haih'chu*, n., harm: 沒有什麽害處 there is no harm (in it).

害口 *haih-koou*, v. i., (of pregnant woman) show appetite for certain foods.

害怕 *haihpah*, v. i. & t., fear, be afraid: 我不害怕 I am not afraid; 害怕他 fear him.

害臊 *haihsauh*, v. i., to blush, feel ashamed.

害喜 *haihshii*, v. i., feel morning sickness of pregnant woman.

害羞 *haihshiou*, v. i., feel ashamed, see *-sauh*↑.

謇 62.40-2

jiaan.

Adj. (1) Stuttering. (2) Outspoken. (3) Faithful, loyal.

謇諤 *jiaan-eh*, adj., (LL) outspoken, frank, candid.

謇謇 *jiarnjiaan*, adj., (1) loyal, faithful; (2) honest, outspoken; (3) (=蹇蹇) beset with dangers ahead, in straits.

寤 62.40-2

wuh.

V. i. To waken up: 寤寐 awake or asleep—continuously.

宕 62.40-3

dahng.

N. Stone quarry, cave dwelling.

V.i. & t. Dally, defer: 延宕, 拖宕 procrastinate; 懸宕 keep unsettled; 宕賬 delay payment of accounts, bad debts; cf. 蕩 20A.50.

Adj. Unregulated, unrestrained: 放宕 (=蕩) dissolute; 流宕 moving freely; 跌宕 (of good writing) free, unrestrained, with surprising turns.

宕戶 *dahnghuh*, n., (1) stone mason; (2) one who runs out on debts.

官 62.40-4

guan.

N. (1) A public servant, an official: 官吏 *-lih*[1], 官員 *-yuarn*↓; 百官 the official hierarchy; 官府 *-fuu*↓; 清官 an upright and incorruptible official; 貪官 a corrupt official; 當官, 做官 become an official, hold an official post; 罷官 resign or be dismissed from office; 辭官 resign from office; 官迷 a form of obsession to be official. (2) (Physiol.) the sense organs: 器官 bodily organs; 五官 (physiol.) the five senses of sight, hearing, smell, taste, and touch, also the eyes, ears, nose, mouth, and hands: 五官端正 well-formed features; 官能 *-nerng*↓; 感官 sensory organs. (3) A surname.

V. i. & t. (LL) be posted at: 官貴陽 was official at 貴陽; 官至 (in biographies) he reached the rank of.

Adj. & adv. Belonging to the public or government: 官方 *-fang*↓; 官辦 government-operated; 官派 appointed by the government; 官面兒 *-miah'l*↓; 官立, 官准 established, authorized by the government; 官房 government offices or buildings; 官俸 official emoluments; 官地 public land; 官款 public funds; 官街 public streets and roads; 官產 public property; 官舍 official residence.

官罷 *guanbah*, n., (MC) settlement of dispute by official mediation.

官報 *guanbauh*, n., official bulletin or gazette.

官兵 *guanbing*, n., government troops.

官場 *guanchaang*, n., (1) officialdom; (2) public-operated markets.

官差 *guanchai*, n., (1) official business; (2) government messengers or servants.

官腔 *guanchiang*, n., official jargon: 打官腔 (of officials) to talk official jargon, assume official airs in speech and action, summarily turn down even reasonable requests.

官契 *guan-chih*, n., deeds or other documents officially registered with the authorities.

官親 *guan-chin*, n., relatives of officials.

官邸 *guandii*, n., an official residence.

官方 *guanfang*, (1) n., a code of official conduct; on the official side; (2) adj., belonging to the government; 官方子 (Chin. med.) a drug for pregnant women to prevent miscarriage.

官費 *guan-feih*, n., funds from public coffers: 官費生 government scholarship students.

官府 *guanfuu*, n., (1) government officers; (2) a high government official.

官桂 *guangueih*, n., best-quality cinnamon.

官話 *guanhuah*, n., (1) (of officialdom) high-sounding but insincere words; (2) formerly, the mandarin language.

官宦 *guanhuahn*, n., official service.

官長 *guanjaang*, n., a gen. term for officials in charge.

官箴 *guan-jen*, n., rules of official conduct: 有玷官箴 official misconduct.

官家 *guanjia*, n., (1) (MC) the king; (2) (MC) the government.

官價 *guan-jiah*, n., (1) official prices of commodities as fixed by the government; (2) formerly, special rate of prices paid for purchases made by the government.

官架子 *guanjiah'tz*, n., superior airs assumed by officials: 他的官架子十足! how he likes to assume superior airs!

官階 *guanjie*, n., official ranking.

官界 *guanjieh*, n., officialdom.

官妓 *guanjih*[1], n., formerly, state-owned prostitutes (generally from confiscated families of the condemned).

官計 *guan-jih*[2], n., rating of official performances at annual or other intervals.

官制 *guan-jyh*, n., (1) rules and regulations governing the organization, duties, and functions of government offices; (2) system of governmental organization.

官職 *guanjyr*, n., (1) duties and responsibilities of officials; (2) official ranking.

官爵 *guanjyuer*, n., official ranking and titular honors.

官客 *guankeh*[1], n., a male guest at parties (as dist. from 堂客 female guests).

官課 *guankeh*[2], n., formerly, government levies.

官僚 *guanliaur*, n., (1) (contempt.) a politician, a bureaucrat: 官僚政治, 官僚主義 bureaucracy; (2) a professinal politician.

官吏 *guanlih*[1], n., government official, functionaries.

官利 *guan-lih*[2], n., (business) fixed profits payable to shareholders, similar to preferred stocks.

官裏 *guanlii*, n., (MC) (1) the king; (2) a government office: 捉將官裏去 take into custody.

官賣 *guan-maih*, n., government monopoly sale.

官面兒 *guanmiah'l*, (1) n., the government; (2) adj., of the official class: 官面兒上的朋友 friends among the officials.

官名 *guan-mirng* n., an official title.

官能 *guannerng* n., organic functions.

官人 *guanrern* n., (1) (AC) appointment of officials; (2) (MC) sir, a squire with or without an official title (similar to Eng. sl. "governor"); (3) (MC) husband in relation to his wife, used in the second or third person; (4) (MC) government messenger or agent: 官人把他拿去了 he was arrested by a government agent.

官身 *guan-shen* n., (1) employment in government service: 官身不自由 restraints of official service; (2) (MC, of actors or prostitutes) formerly, command performance or service.

官聲 *guan-sheng*, n., reputation enjoyed by an official (honest, corrupt).

官銜 *guan'shiarn* n., an official rank.

官書 *guanshu* n., (MC) (1) official documents; (2) government publications or archives; (3) formerly, a collection of laws and regulations promulgated by the government.

官署 *guanshuu*[1], n., government offices.

官屬 *guanshuu*[2], n., bureaucrats.

官事 *guan-shyh*, n., (1) public affairs; (2) a lawsuit.

官所兒 *guansuoo'l*, n., (coll.) government offices.

官司 *guansy*, n., (1) (*guansy*) official duties and responsibilities; (2) (*guan'sy*) a lawsuit.

官堂 *guantarng*, n., better furnished rooms in a public bath.

官體 *guantii*, n., official dignity.

官廳 *guanting*, n., (1) government offices; (2) formerly, living quarters of garrison forces.

官艙 *guantsang*, n., second-class cabins on board a steamer.

官燕 *guan-yahn*, n., (Chin. cuisine) swallow's nests of the best quality.

官樣 *guanyahng*, adj., (1) dignified, elegant; (2) bureaucratic: 官樣文章 high-sounding verbiage, red tape.

官衙 *guanyar*, n., government office.

官鹽 *guan-yarn*, n., salt authorized by the government for sale on the open market.

官窰 *guan-yaur*, n., government porcelain works.

官醫 *guan-yi*, n., medical officer for prisons.

官印 *guan-yihn* n., (1) an official seal; (2) (formerly court.) a person's given name.

官員 *guanyuarn*, n., a government official.

官運 *guan-yuhn*, n., (1) (fortune-telling) a person's chances of official promotion: 官運亨通 a politician's spell of good fortune; (2) government freight or cargo.

宮 62.40-4

gung.

N. (1) A palace, a temple or shrine: 宮殿 *-diahn*↓; 行宮 imperial headquarters away from the capital; 天宮 paradise ("heavenly palace"); 月宮 the moon ("lunar palace"); 魔宮 the devil's den; 東宮 the heir apparent, the crown prince or his residence; 宮禁 forbidden grounds where the emperor lives; 宮闕 the palace gate; 宮闈 *-weir*↓. (2) A dwelling, an enclosure: 宮室 *-shyh*↓; 子宮 the womb; 迷宮 a labyrinth; 守宮 the gecko (lit., "the guardian of virginity"). (3) A note in the Chinese musical scale. (4) Punishment for adultery: 宮刑 *-shirng*↓. (5) (Astron.) a constellation. (6) A surname.

宮燈 *gungdeng*, n., "palace lantern," a decorative ceiling lamp.

宮殿 *gungdiahn*, n., a palace, a hall where the king or emperor holds court.

宮娥 *gung-er*, n., female court attendants.

宮女 *gungnyuu*, n., palace maid.

宮人 *gungrern*, n., female attendants at court.

宮扇 *gungshan*, n., a circular fan, originally used by court ladies.

宮刑 *gungshirng*, n., (AC) castration for men, isolated detention for women.

宮室 *gungshyh*, n., (1) a dwelling house, a mansion; (2) (AC) wife and family.

宮闈 *gungweir*, n., ladies' apartment in the palace.

宭 62.40-5

chyurn.

V. i. To herd together.

容 62.40-8

rurng.

N. A person's looks, appearance: 容表 one's outward appearance; 容貌 *-mauh* ↓; 容顏 facial appearance and expression; 容華 features and complexion; 容長臉兒 an oval face; 容態, 容觀, 儀容 deportment, bearing; 容儀 facial features, countenance; 容質 appearance and character; 容止 carriage, manners; 笑容 a smiling face: 笑容可掬 beaming with smiles; 正容 assume a serious look; 花容失色 (of a woman's face) turn pale, as from fear; 女爲悅己者容 a girl will doll herself up for him who loves her; 整容 tidy up one's appearance, visit the barber; 美容 ditto; 美容院 a beauty parlor; 修容 improve one's appearance, make up the face.

V. t. (1) Tolerate, allow, permit: 容受 *-shouh* ↓; 容忍 *-reen* ↓; 容恕 *-shuh* ↓; 容讓 give in, yield; 容諒 pardon, forgive and forget; 容不下 cannot endure, cannot accommodate; 容事 have the capacity for work; 容人之過 be tolerant of (forgive) other people's mistakes (wrongdoing, weaknesses); 容我幾天 please give me a few days' grace; 容留 give shelter to, allow to stay; 容身 *-shen* ↓; 容膝 *-shi* ↓; 容足地 a temporary shelter, a place to put up in; 難容 cannot get along with (endure, accommodate), also intolerable (misdemeanor); 無以自容 be ashamed of oneself ("nowhere to hide one's face"). (2) Let, permit: 容他過去 let him go; 容日再來 permit me to come another day; 容待 let's wait until; 容俟 ditto.

容乞 *rurngchii*, v. t., ask permission for, request.

容情 *rurng-chirng*, v. t., be lenient to, make special allowance for.

容電器 *rurngdiahn-chih*, n., (phys.) a condenser, a capacitor.

容光 *rurng-guang*, n., (1) one's facial expression, general appearance; (2) a slit, a fissure, a crevice.

容或 *rurnghuoh*, adv., perhaps, maybe, possibly.

容積 *rurngji*, n., volume as measured in cubic units.

容接 *rurngjie*, v. t., to welcome, receive (guests).

容裝科 *rurngjuang-ke*, n., (Peking opera) make-up men.

容車 *rurngjyu*, n., (1) formerly, a curtained carriage for women; (2) formerly, a funeral car intended for use by the soul of the deceased.

容量 *rurngliahng*, n., capacity to contain or hold, also 容額 *-er*.

容貌 *rurngmauh*, n., a person's facial appearance and expression.

容納 *rurngnah*, v. t., (1) be magnanimous enough to tolerate; (2) accept (ideas, views, suggestions).

容忍 *rurngreen*, v. t. & adj. & n., tolerate, -ant, -tion.

容熱量 *rurngreh-liahng*, n., (phys.) heat capacity.

容容 *rurngrurng*, adj., (1) (AC) negligent of one's duties, taking things lightly, lacking seriousness of purpose; (2) (AC) flying, fluttering, floating in the air.

容色 *rurngseh*, n., countenance.

容身 *rurng-shen*, v. i., have somewhere to stay: 無地容身 nowhere to live, ashamed to show one's face.

容膝 *rurng-shi*, n., a tiny spot, a small nook ("just big enough for the knees").

容限 *rurngshiahn*, n., limitation, limit of capacity.

容臭 *rurng-shiouh*, n., (AC) a bag of spices or perfume carried on body.

容受 *rurngshouh*, v. t., (1) be able to contain or hold; (2) endure, put up with.

容恕 *rurngshuh*, v. t., forgive, pardon.

容許 *rurngshyuu*, (1) v. t., permit; (2) adj., permissible; (3) adv., perhaps, maybe.

容易 *rurngyih*[1](-'*yi*), adj., (of things) easy to do or understand, simple, requiring not much skill or effort.

容裔 *rurngyih*[2], adj., (AC) (1) fluttering in the wind; (2) free from care or worry; (3) (of currents) undulating.

容隱 *rurngyiin*, v. t., try to cover up, not to reveal.

容悅 *rurngyueh*, v. t., flatter, toady to, try to please, curry the favor of.

容與 *rurngyuu*, (LL) (1) adj., carefree, at ease with oneself; (2) v. t., give free rein to, put under no constraint.

 62.40-9

keh.

N. (1) Guest, visitor, customer: 賓客 guest: 客人 *-rern* ↓; 來客 customer, visitor; 貴客 honored guest; 主客 host and guest; 生客, 熟客 new, old customer or visitor; 拜客, 送客 receive, send off visitor; 請客 give a dinner for friend; 待客 manner of receiving visitor; 旅客 traveller; 客官 formerly, address of visitor at hotel; 客滿 full house. (2) Term used for persons of certain professions: 政客 (contempt.) politician; 劍客, 俠客 professional swordsman; 刺客 assassin; 食客 (AC) professional scholars kept by wealthy families; 説 (*shuaih*) 客 (AC) professional diplomats who tried to sell their ideas to rulers. (3) A surname. (4) N. used as modifier (like "guest house," "guest professor"): 客卿 (AC) alien serving at court; 客座(教授) *-tzuoh*↓; 客館, 客店, 客棧 *-guaan*, *-diahn*, *-jahn*↓; 客舍 *-sheh*↓; 客廳, 客堂 *-ting*, *-tarng*↓; 客房 *-farng*↓; 客居 live abroad; 客旅 travel abroad; 客商, 客幫 *-shang*, *-bang*↓; 客死他鄉 die abroad.

客幫 *kehbang*, n., association of merchants working abroad; such group.

客車 *kehche*, n., passenger car, railway coach.

客氣 *keh'chih*, adj., (1) "manner of guest," polite, formal, showing restraint: 不要客氣 please feel at home; 你太客氣了 you are "too polite," i. e., very kind, hospitable, generous in gifts, etc. (2) (AC) impulse of a moment.

客卿 *kehching*, n., (AC) alien serving at court.

客串(兒) *kehchuahn(-chuah'l)*, adj. & n., "guest actor", often amateur participating in opera.

客船 *kehchuarn*, n., passenger boat.

客店 *kehdiahn*, n., hotel, inn.

客飯 *kehfahn*, n., a meal of set menu for customer, *prix fixe*.

客房 *kehfarng*, n., guest room.

客館 *kehguaan*, n., hotel, inn.

客觀 *kehguan*, adj. & n., objective, -vity: 客觀的批評 objective criticism.

客棧 *kehjahn*, n., lower-class hotel inn.

客家 *kehjia*, n., "Hakka" people and their dialect—in eastern Kwangtung.

客籍 *kehjir*, n., status of foreign resident.

客居 *kehjyu*, v. i., to live abroad.

客票 *kehpiauh*, n., seats for invited guests at a theatrical performance.

客人 *kehrern*, n., visitor at house or hotel.

客商 *kehshang*, n., merchant abroad.

客舍 *kehsheh*, n., guest house, hotel.

客歲 *kehsueih*, n., last year.

客堂 *kehtarng*, n., parlor.

客套 *kehtauh*, n., banal formalities.

客體 *kehtii*, n., foreign body in organization.

客廳 *kehting*, n., parlor, sitting room.

客次 *kehtsyh*, n., residence abroad, place stopped at.

客座 *kehtzuoh*, n., as in 客座教授 exchange or visiting professor.

§ 62.41 (宀/図)

宙 62.41-2

jouh.

N. Time as a concept: 宇宙 the universe ("space and time").

富 62.41-3

fuh.

N. (1) A surname. (2) Wealth: 財富, 富有; 國家之財富 wealth of nations; 求富 seek wealth; 富而可求 if wealth could be got by trying; 致富 build up a fortune; 驟富 sudden wealth; 富源 source of wealth; 富貴 *-gueih*↓.

Adj. Wealthy, rich, abundant: 富人 rich man; 富豪; 富戶, 富家 *-haur*, *-huh*, *-jia*↓; 富而無驕 rich but not smug; 富而好禮 rich but good-mannered; 富歲 year of good crops; 學富(五車) rich in learning; 富於春秋 in prime of life (rich in years); 年富力強 in prime of life; 富國強兵 to make country rich and strong; 貧富不均 wealth not well distributed.

富強 *fuhchiarng*, adj. & n., rich and strong (of nation).

富貴 *fuhgueih*, n. & adj., rich, rich and honored, having easy life: 富貴榮華 wealth and worldly glory; 富貴逼人 snobbish, ostentatious; 富貴花 peony; used to avoid the word beggar: 富貴雞 beggar's chicken, roasted whole, unfeathered and coated with mud; 富貴衣 beggar's rags.

富豪 *fuhhaur*, n., rich and powerful person or family.

富厚 *fuhhouh*, adj., rich, well-to-do: 資力富厚 solid financial strength.

富戶 *fuhhuh*, n., rich person or family.

富家 *fuhjia*, n., rich family: 富家子弟 sons of rich families; 富家翁 see *-weng*↓.

富給 *fuhjii*, adj., wealthy, abundant.

富麗 *fuhlih*, adj., sumptuous (building): 富麗堂皇 sumptuous, impressive-looking.

富饒 *fuhraur*, n., rich (of country, family, plantation).

富庶 *fuhshuh*, adj., rich and populous (country).

富翁 *fuhweng*, n., rich old man, rich man: 百萬富翁 millionaire.

富有 *fuhyoou*, n., wealth.

富裕 *fuhyuh*, adj., wealthy, having abundance (of nation, family).

富餘 *fuh'yur*, adj., (1) having enough and to spare; (2) surplus: 這些都是富餘下來的 all these are surplus.

宿 62.41-9

suh (**shiouh*, **shioou*).

N. (1) A surname. (2) (**shiouh*) A star constellation: 十二星宿 the twelve constellations. (3) (**shioou*) A night: 一宿 one night; 整宿 whole night; 宿夕 *-shih*↓.

V. i. To stop, rest, stay overnight: 宿一夜 stop (somewhere) for a night; 宿某家 stop at Mr. X's home; 宿旅館 stop at a hotel; 膳宿費 board and lodging fees for students.

Adj. (1) Old: 宿將, 宿好 *-jiahng*, *-haau*↓; 宿疾 old disease; 宿逋 (LL) old unpaid taxes; 宿賊 (LL) old experienced thief. (2) (Of scholar) learned: 宿儒 old scholar; 宿學 *-shyuer*↓; 宿志, 宿願 *-jyh*, *-yuahn*²↓. (3) Past, overnight, of past year(s): 宿諾 a promise made in previous night; 宿料 stored-up animal feed; 宿醉, 宿酲 hangover (from drink); 宿飽 (rare) feeling of being overfed from last night; 宿草, 宿莽 grass grown over the year(s); 宿麥 (AC) wheat planted the year before; 宿雨 (LL) rain of night before. (4) (Budd.) inherited, inborn, carried over from previous incarnation: 宿慧, 宿根, 宿緣, 宿業 *-hueih*, *-gen*, *-yuarn*, *-yeh*²↓.

宿根 *suhgen*, n., (Budd.) inborn gift for wisdom.

宿好 *suhhaau*, n., (1) old friend; (2) (*-hauh*) old hobby.

宿慧 *suhhueih*, n., (Budd.) inborn gift for understanding.

宿債 *suhjaih*, n., a long overdue debt.

宿將 *suh-jiahng*, n., veteran general.

宿主 *suhjuu*, n., host tree or animal (in reference to parasite).

宿志 *suh-jyh*, n., long-cherished ambition.

宿老 *suhlaau*, n., a respected old man.

宿留 *suhliour*, v.i., to stay overnight.

宿命 *suhmihng*, n., predestination.

宿舍 *suhsheh*, n., dormitory.

宿生 *suhsheng*, n., previous incarnation.

宿夕 *suhshih*, adv., (things expected) overnight: 不出宿夕 may come same night.

宿心 *suhshin*, n., see *-jyh*↑.

宿昔 *suhshir*, adv., of old, in olden times (also wr. 夙昔).

宿世 *suhshyh*, n., see *-sheng*↑.

宿學 *suhshyuer*, adj., well-read, erudite: 宿學之士 scholar of profound learning.

宿素 *suhsuh*, (1) adv., (LL) usually, heretofore; (2) adj., (LL) old and experienced.

宿頭 *suhtour* (-'*tou*), n., (MC) an inn, a place to stop over for the night.

宿望 *suhwahng*, n., old, solid reputation (also wr. 夙望).

宿衛 *suhweih*, n., palace guards.

宿夜 *suhyeh*¹, adv., morning and night (also wr. 夙夜).

宿業 *suhyeh*², n., (Budd.) karma, accumulated past, good and bad.

宿因 *suhyin*, n., (Budd.) cause going back to previous incarnation.

宿營 *suhyirng*, n., soldiers' camp.

宿怨 *suhyuahn*¹, n., old grudge.

宿願 *suhyuahn*², n., long-cherished wish (also 夙願).

宿緣 *suhyuarn*, n., see *-yin*↑.

審 62.41-9

sheen.

V. i. & t. (1) To examine carefully: 審查, 審察 *-char*¹,²↓; examine and approve: 審計, 審核 *-jih*, *-her*↓. (2) To hold court trial: 審問, 審訊 *-wehn*, *-shyuhn*↓; 審斷, 審決 *-duahn*, *-jyuer*↓; 提審 bring prisoner to court for trial; 會審 trial at joint session; 公審 public trial; 陪審 assist or take part as one of the judges; 陪審官 assessor. (3) (LL) know: 未審 do not know (＝未知); cf. 譜 60A.41.

Adv. Indeed: 審如是也 if it is so indeed.

審案 *sheen-ahn*, v. i., to hold court trial.

審查 *sheenchar*¹, v. t., to investigate; examine officially for approval.

審察 *sheenchar*², v. i. & t., to study carefully (circumstances, text, documents).

審諦 *sheendih*, v. i., to try to comprehend.

審定 *sheendihng*, v. t., to approve officially (textbook, form and wording).

審斷 *sheenduahn*, v. i., (1) to judge in gen.; (2) to give sentence at court, see *-pahn*↓.

審度 *sheenduoh*, v. i., to study and weigh: 審度情勢 to study and weigh conditions, situation; 審度情理 weigh the circumstances (including psychological factors).

審核 *sheenher*, v. i. & t., to examine and pass on (budget, expenses, plans, proposals, etc.), to audit (accounts).

審計 *sheenjih*, v. i., to audit, to examine accounts; 審計部 *--buh*, audit department.

審決 *sheenjyuer*, v. i. & t., (1) to judge in gen.; (2) to pass sentence at court.

審理 *shernlii*, v. t., (of court) to take up (case).

審美 *sheen-meei*, adj., esthetic: 審美觀念 esthetic sense or notions.

審判 *sheenpahn*, v. i. & t., to hold court trial; to pass sentence.

審視 *sheen-shyh*, v. i., to look at carefully.

審訊 *sheenshyuhn*, v. i., to try (defendant), also n., trial.

審問 *sheenwehn*, v. i., (1) to cross-examine; (2) to ponder deeply in studies.

審議 *sheenyih*, v. t. & n., to examine critically; title of a civil post.

§ 62.42 (宀/冈)

宥 62.42-1

youh.

宥 宵 寓 寗 寯 鶱 寡 寫

N. A surname.

V. t. (1) To pardon: 原宥, 寬宥 pardon, forgive for causing trouble; 宥諒 please understand and forgive; 宥貸, 宥免, 宥罪 to pardon a crime or offence. (2) (AC) to assist: 宥弼 to assist (ruler).

Adj. (LL) 宥密 profound.

宵 62.42-2

shiau.

[Cf. 霄 31D.42]

N. Night: 元宵 festival on 15th day of first lunar month, also dumplings eaten at this festival; 宵禁 *-jihn*↓; 宵衣旰食 get up before dawn and eat late—busy with state affairs; 宵旰之勞 labor incessantly on duties; 通宵 all night; 通宵不寐 could not sleep all night; 深宵 deep night; 中宵 midnight; 宵程, 宵征 night journey.

宵分 *shiau-fen*, n., midnight.
宵旰 *shiau-gahn*, phr., see N.↑.
宵禁 *shiau-jihn*, n., curfew.
宵中 *shiau-jung*, n., midnight.
宵類 *shiau-leih*, n., thieves and rascals.
宵魄 *shiau-poh*, n., (rare, LL) the moon.
宵人 *shiau-rern*, n., gangster, burglar and the like.
宵小 *shiaushiaau*, n., see *-rern*↑.
宵夜 *shiauyeh*, (1) n., night snack (also wr. 消夜); (2) v.t., to pass the time at night.

寓 62.42-4

yuh.

[Var. 庽]

N. Residence: 寓所, 寓公 *-suoo*, *-gung*↓; 公寓 an apartment house.

V. i. (1) To dwell in some house. (2) To imply, suggest (a meaning): 寓意, 寓託, 寓言 *-yih*, *-tuo*, *-yarn*↓. (3) To take in: 寓目 *-muh*↓.

寓公 *yuhgung*, n., a retired gentleman, esquire.
寓居 *yuhjyu*, v. i., to live (at 「place).
寓目 *yuh-muh*, v. i., to look over (a prepared statement, etc.); to take in, browse through.
寓所 *yuhsuoo*, n., place of residence.
寓次 *yuh-tsyh*, n., place during 「sojourn.
寓託 *yuhtuo*, v.t., imply (meaning), show by parable or indirect means.
寓言 *yuhyarn*, n., a parable, fable.
寓意 *yuh-yih*, n., implied or suggested meaning.

寗 62.42-6

nirng (**nihng*).

N. (**nihng*) A surname, see also 寧 62.00.

寯 62.42-9

jyuhn.

Adj. Talented, capable, gifted, smart.

§ 62.50 (宀/⺄)

鶱 62.50-2

chian (**jiaan*).

N. (AC **jiaan*) an inferior or worthless horse.

V. t. (1) To hold high up: 鶱旗 hold up flag, also to capture a flag, see 搴 62.00. (2) To fly up. (3) (AC) to fail: 鶱汚 (LL) be sullied in reputation.

鶱鶱 *chianchian*, adj., (AC) (1) descriptive of flying, flapping; (2) impetuous, impulsive.
鶱舉 *chianjyuu*, v. i., to fly up.
鶱騰 *chianterng*, v. i., to soar aloft (oft. of official promotion).

寡 62.50-3

guaa.

Adj. (1) Little, few: 寡斷 lacking in decision; 寡廉鮮恥 shameless, brazenfaced; 寡情 unfeeling, cold, devoid of human warmth; 寡恩 merciless, cruel; 寡二少雙 matchless, without peer; 寡欲 with few desires; 寡過, 寡尤 try to have few mistakes, misdemeanors; 寡聞 ignorant, not well read, uninformed. (2) Widowed: see 寡婦 *-'fu*↓; 寡居 widowhood.

寡婦 *guaa'fu*, n., a widow.
寡合 *guaaher*, adj., aloof from people, having few friends.
寡陋 *guaalouh*, adj., ignorant, uninformed.
寡人 *guaarern*, pron., (AC) (polite) I, your unworthy king, equiv. "royal we."

寫 62.50-9

shiee.

[Abbr. 冩, 寫]

V. i. & t. (1) To write: 寫字 *-tzyh*↓; 書寫, 手寫, 筆寫 to write

亅	小	⺊	十	土	ナ	廾	乚	丨	一	丁	フ	口	区	冈	⺄	厂	尸	亠	广	宀	丶	乚	七	心	八	人	乂	乛	一	丿	⺊	く
00	01	02	10	11	12	20	21	22	30	31	32	40	41	42	50	51	52	60	61	62	63	70	71	72	80	81	82	83	90	91	92	93

by hand; 抄寫, 謄寫 to copy by hand; 寫下來 write it down; 寫信, 寫日記 write a letter, a diary; 寫字據 make a written note; 寫口供 take down affidavit. (2) To compose: 寫文章, 寫小説 write or compose an essay, a novel; 撰寫 to compose; 寫稿 compose a draft. (3) To make portrait or draw plants and animals: 寫照, 寫生, 寫眞 *-jauh*, *-sheng*, *-jen*↓. (4) To write out (moods, sentiments) as an esthetic relief: 寫懷 pour out one's feelings; 寫憂 write out one's sorrows; 寫意 *-yih*↓.

寫本 *shier-been*, n., a hand copy.

寫白 *shiee-bor*, phr., (1) (MC) to make a clean copy; (2) (AC) to clean one's name of guilt.

寫賬 *shiee-jahng*, (1) n., treasurer; (2) v. i., to keep accounts.

寫照 *shieejauh*, v. i. & n., to portray (person, character); a portrayal (of conditions); a portrait.

寫眞 *shieejen*, v. i. & n., see *-jauh* ↑.

寫生 *shieesheng*, n. & v. i., a branch of painting, portraying living things; still life.

寫形 *shieeshirng*, v. i., to make portrait: 圖貌寫形 the art of making portraits; (AC) describe a patient's looks.

寫實 *shieeshyr*, v. i., write realistically, make actual portrayal of conditions; 寫實主義 realism.

寫字 *shiee-tzyh*, v. i. & n., learn to write characters; calligraphy; 寫字兒 (coll.) make a contract in writing.

寫意 *shieeyih*, (1) n. & v. i., a school or type of Chin. painting, emphasizing a few, rapid, rhythmic strokes (chiefly rocks, bamboo, flowers) rather than careful delineation; (2) adj., (person) pleased in spirit, relaxed, contented.

§ 62.63 (宀/丶)

寒 62.63-2

harn.

N. (1) A surname. (2) Cold, cold season: 三易寒署 three winters and summers; see Adj. ↓.

V. i. & t. (1) To tremble: 心寒 to tremble at heart. (2) Put in cold storage: 寒盟 to ignore treaty.

Adj. (1) Cold: 寒冷 *-leeng*↓; 天寒 the weather is cold; 嚴寒 severely cold; 一曝十寒 warm for one day and cold for ten days—inconstancy of purpose, esp. in studies, study haphazardly, with many interruptions; 寒灰 cold ashes; 寒林 wintry forest; 寒地 cold region; 寒衣 winter clothing; 噤若寒蟬 silent as the cicada in winter. (2) Poor: 貧寒 poor; 貧寒 (清寒) 子弟 students from poor families; 寒窗苦讀 phr., persevere in one's studies in spite of hardships; 寒士 a poor scholar. (3) Polite term: 寒門, 寒舍 my humble home; 寒門 also poor family; 寒荊 my wife.

寒磣 *harn'chen*, (1) adj., ugly, unseemly; (2) v.t., 被人寒磣了 was snubbed or made fun of.

寒帶 *harndaih*, n., (geog.) the Arctic Circle.

寒號蟲 *harnhauhchurng*, n., (zoo.) a large species of bat.

寒顫 *harnjahn*[1], v.t., to tremble with cold or fear.

寒戰 *harnjahn*[2], v.i., to tremble with fear.

寒假 *harnjiah*, n., winter holidays.

寒賤 *harnjiahn*, adj., poor and lowly: 出身寒賤 of humble origins.

寒劑 *harn-jih*, n., freezing mixture.

寒噤 *harnjihn*, v. i., shudder with cold: 打了一個寒噤 give a shudder.

寒極 *harnjir*, n., (geog.) the cold pole.

寒苦 *harn'ku*, adj., poor, from poor family.

寒冷 *harnleeng*, adj., cold (weather).

寒流 *harn-liour*, n., a cold current, cold snap.

寒露 *harnluh*, n., a solar term (October 8th or 9th).

寒毛 *harnmaur*, n., fine hair on human skin.

寒門 *harnmern*, n., (1) poor or humble family; (2) my humble home.

寒熱 *harn-reh*, n., fever: 發寒熱 have chills and fever; 寒熱病 malaria.

寒舍 *harnsheh*, n., my humble home.

寒心 *harnshin*, v. i., tremble with fear: 令人寒心 (of unscrupulous practice, betrayal of friendships, etc.) give people a chill, cause people to stop going forward.

寒暑表 *harnshur-biaau*, n., thermometer.

寒食 *harnshyr*, n., day before spring festival, when only cold food is served.

寒暄 *harnshyuan*, v. i., talk about the weather ("cold and warm") or usual formalities on visits (also 寒溫).

寒酸 *harnsuan*, adj., (1) (contempt.) full of jealousy, mean in criticism; (2) unseemly, poor (gifts).

寒微 *harnwei*, adj., (LL) in humble circumstances.

§ 62.70 (宀/ㄴ)

寬 62.70-2

kuan.

V. i. (1) To be lenient, to extend limits: 寬限 extend date (of delivery, etc.); 寬免, 寬宥, 寬恕, 寬假, 寬容 *-miaan*, *-youh*, *-shuh*, *-jiaa*, *-rurng*↓. (2) To relax: 寬衣 to take off coat or gown—invitation to do so on hot day; 寬

心 to relax, see *-shin*↓.

Adj. (1) Broad, wide (of room, clothing): 寬大, 寬濶 *-dah*, *-kuoh* ↓. (2) Broad-minded, liberal: 寬宏大量 generous. (3) Lenient, kind: 寬政 liberal policies.

寬敞 *kuanchaang*, adj., (of building, clothing) broad, spacious.
寬綽 *kuanchuo*, adj., (1) spacious; (2) liberal, generous; (3) well-to-do, generous with money.
寬大 *kuandah*, adj., generous, big-hearted.
寬貸 *kuandaih*, v. t., to allow delay of payment of debt, pardon, forgive. 「generous, kind.
寬厚 *kuanhouh*, adj., (of person)
寬窄 *kusan-jaai*, n., width (of room, clothing, etc.).
寬假 *kuanjiaa*, (1) phr., to allow extension of leave; (2) v.t., to forgive, see *-miaan*↓.
寬闊 *kuankuoh*, adj., spacious.
寬免 *kuanmiaan*, v.t., to forgive (taxes), to pardon (offense).
寬容 *kuanrurng*, (1) adj., tolerant, charitable: 寬容政策 a tolerant policy; (2) v.t., to pardon (offenses, person).
寬限 *kuanshiahn*, v.i., defer time limit; 寬限日 n., days of grace.
寬心 *kuanshin*, adj., relaxed, not worried: 寬心丸兒 a joke, a story told to make people relax.
寬恕 *kuanshuh*, (1) v.t., to pardon (person, misdemeanor); (2) adj., tolerant, indulgent (policy).
寬慰 *kuanweih*, v.i. & t., to comfort (person); to feel less worried.
寬宥 *kuanyouh*, v.t., see *-miaan* ↑.
寬裕 *kuanyuh*, adj., well-to-do: 手頭寬裕 with plenty of money to spend.

它 62.70-2

tuo (*ta; *'te when unaccented).

[Var. 他 91A.70]

Pron. (1) Modern invented pron. to represent English "it" as dist. from "he," "she." Theoretical pr. *tuo*, actually spoken as *ta*. (2) (AC) other, different: 或敢有它志 may perhaps entertain other, different, motives.

完 62.70-3

warn.

V.i. (1) To finish, complete: 完畢, 完工 *-bih*[1], *-gung*↓; 完了 *-liaau*; 完成 *-cherng*↓: 未完 unfinished; 完蛋 (vulg.) done for. (2) To pay tax: 完稅 ditto; 完錢糧 pay farm tax. (3) (AC) to keep (a country) intact: 完吳 preserve the state of Wur.

Adj. & adv. Complete, -ly, whole, tidy: 完全, 完好, 完美 *-chyuarn*, *-haau*, *-meei*↓.

完案 *warn-ahn*, phr., close a case at court.
完備 *warnbeih*, adj., complete, well provided.
完畢 *warnbih*[1], v.i. & t., (ceremonies) close; (work) comes to an end; to end (work).
完璧 *warn-bih*[2], phr., 完璧歸趙 (AC allu.) to return thing to owner intact.
完成 *warn-cherng*, v.t., to complete (project, building, etc.); p.p., is completed.
完清 *warn-ching*, v.t., to clear off (accounts).
完全 *warnchyuarn* (-'*chyan*), adj. & adv., complete, -ly.
完工 *warn-gung*, v.i., to complete work, (work) is completed.
完好 *warnhaau*, adj., intact, not cracked.
完婚 *warnhun*, v.i., to marry, be married: 已經完婚 already married; wedding.
完整 *warnjeeng* (-'*jeng*), adj., intact, not broken; complete, tidy, orderly (procession, etc.).
完結 *warnjier*, v.i. & t., to close accounts; closed.
完卷 *warn-jyuahn*, v.i., to finish an examination paper.
完聚 *warn-jyuh*, v.i., to gather together, be reunited.
完竣 *warnjyuhn*, v.i., see *-gung*↑.
完了 *warnliaau*, v.t., to complete (work); (-'*le*) it's finished; also one is broke; n., finis in movie.
完滿 *warnmaan*, adj., satisfactory (meeting, negotiations), happy (marriage).
完美 *warnmeei*, adj., happy (marriage), beautiful (work of art).
完納 *warnnah*, v.t., to pay tax.
完篇 *warn-pian*, v.i., to complete a written piece.
完品 *warnpiin*, n., a perfect piece; a perfect character.
完人 *warnrern*, n., a perfect man.
完善 *warnshahn*, adj., perfect, excellent (work).
完刑 *warn-shirng*, n., (AC) light punishment of shaving beard only.
完事(兒) *warnshyh*(-*sheh'l*), adj., finished, completed (business).
完稅 *warn-sueih*, v.i., to pay tax.
完姻 *warn-yin*, v.i., see *-hun*↑.

冠 62.70-3

guan (*guahn).

N. (1) Headgear: 衣冠 full dress worn by the gentry, the gentry as a class: 衣冠禽獸 (abusive) a beast in human form; 冠蓋 *-gaih*, 冠帶 *-daih*, 冠冕 *-'miaan*↓; 免冠 take off one's hat in the presence of a superior; 道冠, 黃冠 a Taoist cap; 王冠, 皇冠 royal crown, coronet; 張冠李戴 Chang's hat worn by Li, mixed-up identity. (2) A bird's comb or crest: 雞冠, 鵝冠, 鶴冠 cock's goose's, crane's comb. (3) A surname.

V.t. (1) (*guahn) To put a cap on:

冠禮 (AC) ceremony marking a man's coming of age at 20; hence 未冠 not yet of adult age, teenagers. (2) (*guahn) To excel, to top the rest: 冠軍 -jyun↓; 冠於儕輩 be head over shoulders above others.

冠弁 guanbiahn, n., a kind of ancient cap.

冠帶 guandaih, n., (1) cap and sash worn by the literati: 冠帶齊全 in full dress; (2) the literati as a class.

冠蓋 guangaih, n., high-ranking officials: 冠蓋雲集 a gathering of dignitaries.

冠狀的 guaanjuahng'de, adj., coronary: 冠狀動脈阻塞 coronary artery occlusion.

冠軍 *guahnjyun, n., the champion in any contest.

冠兒 gua'l, n., formerly, an article for tying up hair on top of the head.

冠毛 guanmaur, n., (bot.) pappus, -pi, down or hair on fruit, etc.

冠冕 guan'miaan, n., (1) government officials; (2) (of literary or artistic works) the best of its kind; (3) elegant, -ce: 冠冕堂皇 (of speech or action) having official elegance, (contempt.) dignified in form but insincere in substance.

冠詞 *guahntsyr, n., (gram.) the article: 肯定冠詞, 不肯定冠詞 the definite, indefinite article.

冠子 guantz, n., (1) a bird's comb or crest; (2) ancient headdress for women; (3) formerly, a kind of women's ornamental hairpin.

冠玉 guanyuh, n., (1) (orig.) a stuffed shirt (lit., "a cap studded with jade"); (2) (LL) masculine good looks.

寇 62.70–3

kouh.

N. (1) Bandit: 寇盜, 寇匪, 匪寇 robber, bandit; 流寇 roaming bandits. (2) Term for enemy; 敵寇, 寇賊 enemy, rebel. (3) A surname.

V.i. & t. To harass (border), to invade: 寇掠, 寇略, 寇奪 to loot.

寇讎 kouhchour, n., (AC) enemy.

冤 62.70–5

yuan.

[Pop. 寃]

N. (1) An injustice, a wrong done: 含冤 harbor a sense of being unjustly treated; 訴冤 complain of injustice; 伸冤 to right a wrong, redress an injustice; 不白之冤 a case of being wrongly accused. (2) Enmity: 結冤 become enemies; 報冤 revenge; 雪冤 avenge s.o.'s wrong; 冤冤相報 reprisal breeds reprisal; 冤家, 冤仇 -'jia, -chour↓.

V.t. To cheat, to wrong (s.o.): 冤枉 -waang↓; p.p., be wronged; 眞冤了 really cheated in purchase.

Adj. (AC) bent, crooked (=modn. 彎).

冤親 yuan-chin, n., the enemy and the relatives alike.

冤情 yuan-chirng, n., feeling of being wronged; injustice done.

冤仇 yuanchour, n., a sworn enemy.

冤屈 yuanchyu, (1) v.t., to wrong (s.o.) or be wronged: 受冤屈 be falsely accused; (2) n., false accusation.

冤大 yuan-dah, n., (sl.) person played for a big fool, a fathead: usu. 冤大頭, 冤大腦袋.

冤魂 yuanhurn, n., the ghost of one who had been wrongly accused.

冤家 yuan'jia, n., (1) an enemy, old antagonist, adversary; (2) a "predestined enemy," i.e., lover, sweetheart, whom one always comes back to despite quarrels.

冤孽 yuan'nie, n., a predestined enemy, a person's "stumbling block."

冤人 yuan-rern, phr., to deceive or wrongly accuse a person.

冤桶 yuantuung, n., a fathead, see -dah↑.

冤枉 yuanwaang, v.t., to wrongly accuse (person): 受冤枉 be wrongly accused.

冤抑 yuanyih, v.t., suffer a wrong.

冤獄 yuanyuh, n., a miscarriage of justice.

寵 62.70–6

chuung.

N. A favorite, mistress: 納寵 take a concubine.

V. t. To favor, be specially fond of (person): 寵愛, 寵信 -aih, -shihn↓; 受寵若驚 overwhelmed by special favor; 寵辱不驚 not moved by official honor or disgrace; 譁衆取寵 gain notoriety by shocking statement.

Adj. (1) Favorite: 寵姬 favorite mistress. (2) (Court.) 寵賜, 寵貺, 寵錫 your great (gift).

寵愛 chuungaih, v. t., to love especially (a child, mistress, courtier).

寵嬖 chuungbih, n., a court favorite (man or woman).

寵兒 chuungerl, n., favorite son: 天之寵兒 one especially blessed by Heaven.

寵信 chuungshihn, v. t., to trust especially, rely on (subordinate).

寵異 chuungyih, adv., extra special (treatment).

寵遇 chuungyuh, v. t., to look on (courtier, subordinate, mistress) with special favor.

宅 62.70–9

jeh (sp. pr. **jair*).

N. (1) Residence, home: 住宅, 私宅 private home; 張宅, 李宅 Mr. Jang's, Mr. Lii's home. (2) Grave: 宅兆, 宅憂 *-jauh*, *-you* ↓.

V. i. (1) (AC) 使宅百揆 make him occupy position of prime minister. (2) 宅心 (＝居心) 仁厚 (AC) is of a kindly disposition.

宅券 *jehchyuahn*, n., house deed.
宅第 *jehdih*, n., a mansion.
宅兆 *jehjauh*, n., graveyard, tomb site.
宅眷 *jehjyuahn*, n., a person's family.
宅裏 **jair'li*, n., formerly, a servant's self-reference vis-à-vis the master (cf. 家[Δ]的 62.02).
宅門(兒) **jairmern(-mer'l)*, n., home, usu. of a higher-class family.
宅子 **jairtz*, n., house, home.
宅憂 *jehyou*, v.i., as in 丁宅憂 (AC) be in mourning.

宂 62.70-9

ruung.
[Pop. 冗, 宂]

N. Business, busy occupations: 公宂 official business; 撥宂 (光臨) please spare a little time (to come).

Adj. (1) Superfluous, unnecessary, excessive, superabundant: 宂官 *-guan* ↓; 宂職, 宂員 supernumerary office, personnel; 宂兵 superfluous troops; 宂長 *-jahng* ↓; 宂散 (of jobs) entailing no work; 宂贅 *-jueih* ↓. (2) Busy, requiring much time and effort to do: 宂繁 occupied with many things, have no leisure; 煩宂 have no time to spare, busily engaged; 宂雜 *-tzar* ↓. (3) With no settled abode: 流宂道路 living the life of a tramp.

宂筆 *rurng-bii*, n., (1) superfluous words in writings; (2) unnecessary strokes in painting.
宂費 *ruung-feih*, n., unnecessary expenses, wasteful outlay.
宂官 *ruung-guan*, n., a sinecure official.
宂長 *ruungjahng*, adj., (1) loosely organized; (2) (*-charng*) (of writings, speeches) rambling and tediously long.
宂贅 *ruungjueih*, adj., (of writings) verbose.
宂宂 *rurngruung*, adj. & n., (1) adj., numerous, excessive; (2) n., (LL) hustle and bustle.
宂食 *ruungshyr*, n., (LL, of persons) wasteful consumption ("eating without working").
宂雜 *ruungtzar*, adj., (of things) multifarious, trivial.

宄 62.70-9

gueei.

N. Villains, treacherous persons: 姦宄 ditto.

宛 62.70-9

waan.

V.i. To seem: 音容宛在 the voice and expression (of the deceased) seem to be still there.

Adj. & adv. Seeming, -ly: 宛然, 宛若 *-rarn*, *-ruoh* ↓.

宛轉 *warnjuaan*, adv., (1) (persuade, explain) tactfully; (2) in roundabout way (deliver a letter).
宛妙 *waanmiauh*, adj., soft (music); charming (art work).
宛然 *waanrarn*, (1) adv., seemingly, appearing to be; (2) adj., true to life, vivid.
宛若 *waanruoh*, adj., just like.
宛宛 *warnwaan*, adv., (LL) clinging, twisting.

§ 62.72 (宀/心)

憲 62.72-1

shiahn.

N. (1) Constitution: short for 憲法 *-faa* ↓; 立憲 constitutional (government); 立憲君主制度 constitutional monarchy; 違憲 unconstitutional. (2) Laws of the land: see 憲章, 憲令, 憲綱 *-jang*, *-lihng*, *-gang* ↓. (3) Used in address to official superior: 憲裁 your excellency's decision; 憲恩 your excellency's favor.

憲兵 *shiahn-bing*, n., military police, gendarmerie.
憲典 *shiahndiaan*, n., national institutions, established tradition.
憲法 *shiahnfaa*, n., constitution (of country).
憲綱 *shiahngang*, n., constitutional law.
憲章 *shiahnjang*, n., charter of organization; sacred institutions.
憲令 *shiahnlihng*, n., laws.
憲書 *shiahnshu*, n., formerly, almanac.
憲臺 *shiahntair*, n., formerly, the censorate.
憲則 *shiahntzer*, n., laws and statutes.
憲網 *shiahn-waang*, n., laws of the land.

宓 62.72-6

mih.

N. A surname.

宅 宂 宄 宛 憲 宓

亅	小	卜	十	土	ナ	卄	㔾	丨	一	丅	フ	口	区	冈	冂	厂	尸	亠	广	宀	丶	乚	弋	心	八	人	乂	乛	丿	刂	𠂉	く
00	01	02	10	11	12	20	21	22	30	31	32	40	41	42	50	51	52	60	61	62	63	70	71	72	80	81	82	83	90	91	92	93

Adj. Quiet, silent: 安宓; (LL) in good health, condition.

窓 62.72-9

chyueh.

[Var. of 恪, 22A.40]

§ 62.80 (宀/八)

賽 62.80-2

saih.

N. (1) A surname. (2) A contest: 比賽 ditto; 球賽 a ball game; 田徑賽 track and field meet.

V. t. (1) To race (cars, horses): 賽跑, 賽車, 賽馬 -*paau*, -*che*, -*maa* ↓; 賽狗 dog race. (2) To give offerings of thanks to gods by a festival of parades: 賽神, 賽會 -*shern*, -*hueih* ↓. (3) To rival s. o. or s. t.: 賽真 (of copies of art work) be as good as or rival the original; 賽梨花 (beauty) rivals that of pear blossom or of girl named Pear Blossom; to excel: 賽過 excel (in skill, etc.); 姊妹長的一個賽過一個 the sisters grow up, each prettier than the last.

賽車 *saih-che*, v. i., to race cars.
賽球 *saih-chiour*, v. i., to play ball game.
賽船 *saih-chuarn*, v. i., to run boat race; 賽龍船 dragon boat race.
賽拳 *saihchyuarn*, n., boxing bout; v. i., to match fingers (drinking game).
賽取 *saihchyuu*, v. i., (MC) to give thanks offering.
賽過 *saih-guoh*, v. t., to excel.
賽會 *saihhueih*, n., (1) a religious festival with parades of idols, stilts, floats, etc.; (2) an exhibition of commercial goods, etc., an exposition.
賽璐珞 *saihluhluoh*, n., (translit.) celluloid.
賽馬 *saihmaa*, n. & v. i., (hold) a horse race.
賽跑 *saih-paau*, v. i., to hold a race.
賽社 *saih-sheh*, n., a village festival of offering of thanks to the gods, esp. after harvest.
賽神 *saihshern*, n., see -*hueih* (1)↑.
賽願 *saih-yuahn*, n., give offerings of thanks for wish granted.

寘 62.80-2

jyh.

[Cogn. 置]

寅 62.80

yirn.

N. (1) A unit in the duodecimal cycle: 寅吃卯糧 forced to borrow today's food against tomorrow's income (寅 being No. 3; 卯 No. 4); 同寅 colleagues in government service: 同寅之誼 or 寅誼 said of friends working as colleagues. (2) 3–5 a.m.

賓 62.80-3

bin.

[Abbr. 宾; Pop. 賔]

N. (1) A surname. (2) Guest: 賓主 guest and host; 喧賓奪主 minor taking precedence over a major issue; 上賓 guest of honor, distinguished guest; 國賓 guest of the government; 貴賓 distinguished guest(s); 外賓 foreign guest(s); 西賓 resident tutor, residing (west) versus host (east), cf. 東 10.01.; 禮賓司 protocol division; 賓至如歸 guests, customers, come in flocks; 賓朋滿座 the house is full of guests; 相敬如賓 (of married couple) never fail in mutual respect (and attentions); 佳賓 elegant guests.

V. i. 賓服 (AC) come as ally or vassal state.

賓白 *binbair*, n., (in Northern drama) dialogue (賓) and soliloquy (白).
賓格 *binger*, n., (gram.) objective case.
賓客 *binkeh*, n., guest.
賓禮 *binlii*, n., ceremony of reception of guest.
賓天 *bintian*, n., (AC) death of emperor.
賓鐵 *bintiee*, n., see 鑌 81A.80.
賓辭 *bintzyr*, n., (gram.) object.
賓位 *binweih*, n., (gram.) objective case.
賓語 *binyuu*, n., (gram.) object.

寶 62.80-3

baau.

[Pop. 寳, 宝]

N. (1) Currency, coin: 元寶, 通寶 ancient coin with square hole in center; 寶鈔 paper currency. (2) Treasure, treasured object: 無價之寶 priceless treasure; 國寶 national treasure.

Adj. (1) Antique, precious, treasured: 寶刀 especially valued or antique knife; 寶藏 treasured collection. (2) (Court.) your esteemed: 寶店, 寶號 your shop; 寶眷 your esteemed family; 寶山空回 phr., return empty-handed from treasure mountain, also (fig., court.) unable to benefit from seeing great master.

寶寶 *baurbaau*, n., darling child (also 小寶寶).
寶貝 *baaubeih*, n., treasure; (sl., contempt.) fellow, priceless creature: 寶貝兒 little darling (of child); 寶貝疙瘩 (facet.) parents' favorite child (lit., "pimple"), see -*huoh* ↓.

寶筏 *baaufar*, n., (Budd.) ferry for crossing over from confusion to the other shore (彼岸) of light; (fig.) way to understanding and clarity.

寶蓋(兒) *baaugaih(-gah'l)*, n., the top radical "宀".

寶貴 *baaugueih*, adj., valuable (thing, advice), precious: 寶貴光陰 valuable time not to be wasted.

寶盒 *baauher*, n., jewel box; box of treasures.

寶貨 *baauhuoh*, n., money; (facet.) fool, idiot (他這個寶貨 that incomparable idiot).

寶局 *baaujyur*, n., pawnshop for jewelry.

寶庫 *baaukuh*, n., treasury, treasury vault; any valuable collection.

寶藍 *baaularn*, adj., turquoise blue, azure, bluish green.

寶石 *baaushyr*, n., jewel, precious or semiprecious stone.

寶座 *baautzuoh*, n., throne.

冥 62.80-4

mirng.
[Interch. 溟, 暝]

N. (1) A surname. (2) Night, darkness.

Adj. (1) Dark, pertaining to the night; dull-witted; 冥頑 *-warn*↓. (2) Pertaining to the world of the dead or spirits, esp. 冥冥 *-mirng*↓.

冥報 *mirng-bauh*, n., retribution by the gods.

冥幣 *mirng-bih*, n., paper money burned for the dead.

冥鏹 *mirngchiaang*, n., see *-bih*↑.

冥契 *mirngchih*¹, n., unspoken agreement between persons.

冥器 *mirngchih*², n., paper furniture burned as offering for the dead.

冥府 *mirngfuu*, n., the underworld.

冥會 *mirng-hueih*, n., silent comprehension.

冥婚 *mirng-hun*, n., wedding ceremony for the dead.

冥冥 *mirngmirng*, n., (1) as in 冥冥之中 in the unseen world (forces governing our lives); (2) dark.

冥想 *mirngshiaang*, n. & v. i., daydream, contemplate, -tion.

冥頑 *mirngwarn*, adj., lacking in intelligence, stupid: 冥頑不靈 subhuman, inanimate, insensate (such as rock).

冥王星 *mirngwarng-shing*, n., (astron.) planet Pluto.

冥夜 *mirngyeh*, n., dark night.

冥衣 *mirngyi*, n., paper clothing burned for use of the dead.

冥佑 *mirng-youh*, n., unseen protection of the gods.

實 62.80-4

shyr.
[Abbr. 实]

N. (1) Fruit: 果實 ditto; 其實可食 its fruit is eatable; 結實 bear fruit, also adj., compact. (2) Fact, reality: 事實 fact: 事實如此 that is the fact; opp. 名: 名實 name and reality; 名實相符, 名不符實 reality corresponds, does not correspond, to its name; 實至名歸 reputation follows naturally real distinction; 言過其實 exaggerate; 失實 adj., untrue; 吐實 tell the truth; 據實招供 tell the facts in court.

V. t. To fill: 荷槍實彈 carry rifles with loaded bullets.

Adj. (1) True, honest: 誠實, 老實 honest; 樸實 simple, unadorned; 篤實 honest in character; 眞實 true (fact, situation, story); 實心, 實意 *-shin, -yih*↓; 實話 truthful story or statement. (2) Real: 現實 real, -ity; 實價, 實値 *-jiah, -jyr*↓; 實重 real weight; 實力 *-lih*¹↓; 實權 real power; 實情, 實境 real situation; 實數 real amount or number; 實際 *-jih*↓; 實現 *-shiahn*↓; 實體 *-tii*↓. (3) Practical: 實利, 實用 *-lih*², *-yuhng*↓; 實施, 實行 *-shy, -shirng*↓; 實踐 *-jiahn*↓; 實惠 practical benefit; 實效 *-shiauh*↓. (4) Actual, concrete, substantial: 實物 *-wuh*↓; 實據 *-jyuh*↓; 實體, 實質 *-tii, -jyr*¹↓; 實驗 *-yahn*↓; 實官, 實缺 actual official post, not rank only. (5) Solid, substantial, full: 充實, 實足 substantial, full, also v.t., to fill; 實學, 實字 *-shyuer, -tzyh*↓.

Adv. Really, actually, in fact, factually: 其實 in fact; 實爲, 實係, 實是, 實屬 is really; 實屬公便 (formula, official documents) it is fitting and proper; 實有其事 it really happened; 實所至望 (in letter) this is what I earnestly pray for or hope, beg; 實則 in reality (contrary to pretension); 實不相瞞 frankly, I admit; 着實 (*jaur-*) show by deeds, do one's best: 着實用功 work really hard.

實地 *shyrdih*, adj. & adv., on the spot, concrete, -ly: 實地試驗 put to concrete tests; 腳踏實地 practical, realistic, not flighty (have "foot solidly on the ground").

實頓位 *shyrdunweih*, n., dead weight.

實惠 *shyrhueih*, adj., substantial benefit.

實証 *shyrjehng*, n., concrete evidence; 實証論 positivism.

實價 *shyrjiah*, n., net price.

實踐 *shyrjiahn*, v. i., to put in practice (versus mere talk).

實際 *shyrjih*, adj., realistic, real (benefit, progress, etc.): 實際生活 real life; 實際主義 realism (in novel, in conduct of affairs); 實際上 --*'shang*, adv., in reality: 實際上沒有什麽用處 of no real use.

實質 *shyrjyr*¹, n., the inner substance or quality, essence (of teachings).

實値 *shyrjyr*², n., net value.

實據 *shyrjyuh*, n., solid evidence.

實牢 *shyr'lau*, adj., strong (joints, knots).

實力 *shyrlih*[1], n., real strength, military might.

實利 *shyrlih*[2], n., actual gains, net profit: 實利主義 utilitarianism.

實錄 *shyrluh*, n., (1) journal of an emperor's life and activities; (2) factual history; record (of meetings).

實落 *shyr'luo*, adj., (a strike or hit) to the point.

實拍拍 *shyrpaipai*, adv., really, actually (kicked him): 實拍拍一包米 there was a bag of rice, substantial and real.

實現 *shyrshiahn*, v. i. & t., to bring to pass, realize, be realized: 這事不容易實現 this plan is difficult to realize; adj., actual (property, etc.).

實像 *shyrshiahng*, n., (phys.) real image.

實效 *shyrshiauh*, n., real results, efficacy.

實心 *shyrshin*, adv., sincerely: 實心實意 ditto; 實心眼兒 --*yaa'l*, ditto.

實習 *shyrshir*, v. i. & n., to practise, learn (subject) with exercise or from life: 實習醫生 intern.

實行 *shyrshirng*, v. i. & t., (1) to do actually, put (theory) in practice; (2) to carry out (policy), be carried out.

實收 *shyrshou*, (1) n., actual or net receipt: 實收資本 paid-up capital; (2) v. i., to receive actually for sale.

實數 *shyrshuh*, n., (math.) (1) integral number; (2) number added to, subtracted from, multiplied or divided.

實施 *shyrshy*, v. i. & t., carry out (policy, program).

實事 *shyrshyh*, n., real fact: 實事求是 phr., objective method, be objective.

實實 *shyrshyr*, adv., really, in substantial fact.

實學 *shyrshyuer*, n., solid scholarship.

實體 *shyrtii*, n., material substance: 實體論 (phil.) ontology (also 本體論); 實體上 --'*shang*, adv., in reality, substantially (sustain a loss, etc.); 實體法 substantive law; 實體問題 substantive problem (not procedural).

實在 *shyrtzaih*, adj. & adv., (1) real, -ly: 實在不行 really will not do; 實在損失 real loss; 實在好 really good; (2) ('*tzai*) (a) honest, dependable; (b) solid, well constructed; 實在主義 realism, -istic, practical.

實足 *shyrtzur*, adj. & adv., fully (3 pounds, etc.).

實字 *shyrtzyh*, n., (Chin. gram.) a "substantive" word—all words except conjunctions, prepositions, exclamations and particles (which are called 虛△字 or functional words 21A.30).

實物 *shyrwuh*, n., real objects, specimens in instruction.

實驗 *shyryahn*, v. i. & n., (to, a) experiment: 實驗室 laboratory (also called 試驗室); 實驗心理學 experimental psychology; 實驗馬力 effective horsepower.

實業 *shyyeh*, n. & adj., industry, industrial: 實業發達 development of industry; 實業家 industrialist.

實意(兒) *shyryih(-yieh'l)*, adv., sincerely.

實用 *shyryuhng*, adj. & n., practical; practical use: 實用主義 pragmatism.

寘 62.80-4

mirng.

[Pop. of 冥 62.80]

穴 62.80-8

shyueh (**shyuer*).

N. (1) A cave, cavern, grotto: 洞穴 a cave; 孔穴, 穴隙 a hole (in wall, ground); 穴居, 穴處 live in caves. (2) A den: 巢穴 robbers' den; 鼠穴 a rat hole. (3) A grave: 墓穴. (4) Certain parts of human body containing vital arteries, such as armpit: 穴道, 點穴 vital points recognized in karate and acupuncture.

实 62.80-9

shyr.

[Pop. of 實 62.80]

§62.81 (宀/人)

寞 62.81-2

moh.

Adj. See 寂△寞 62.82.

灾 62.81-9

tzai.

[Var. of 災 93.81]

§62.82 (宀/乂)

寂 62.82-2

jir.

Adj. Still, silent: see compp. ↓.

寂靜 *jirjihng*, adj., silent, quiet.

寂寂 *jirjir*, adj. & adv., quiet(ly), silent(ly).

寂寥 *jirliaur*, adj., desolate, lonely.

寂滅 *jirmieh*, n., (Budd.) nirvana, relief from senses; death, true peace.

寂寞 *jirmoh*, adj., (1) cold and dreary; (2) lonesome, solitary, forlorn.

寂然 *jirrarn*, adj., (1) still, silent; (2) tranquil, composed.

寢 62.82-2

chiin.

N. (1) (LL) resting place, grave: 壽終正寢 die peacefully at home. (2) 陵寢 imperial mausoleum, see 寢廟 *-miauh*↓.

V. i. (1) (LL) to sleep: 入寢 go to sleep; 就寢 go to bed; 寢寐難安 restless sleep (from worries); 寢食不安 have no peace of mind day and night; 廢寢忘食 (or 餐) too busy to eat or sleep; 獨寢 sleep alone; 侍寢 attend to s. o.'s going to bed, esp. a parent's. (2) (LL) (of rumors, gossip) stop: 其事遂寢 the affair was no longer talked about; 寢兵 *-bing*↓.

Adj. (LL) ugly: 貌寢 ugly face; 寢陋 *-louh*↓.

寢兵 *chiin-bing*, v. i., to stop wars and preparations for wars.
寢處 *chiinchuu*, (1) v. i., "go to bed and get up"—daily activity; 寢處不安 restless; (2) (*-chuh*) n., a sleeping place.
寢疾 *chiinjir*, v. i., be confined to bed in illness.
寢陋 *chiinlouh*, adj., ugly.
寢寐 *chiinmeih*, v. i., (LL) to sleep.
寢門 *chiinmern*, n., back door to sleeping quarters.
寢廟 *chiinmiauh*, n., temple to deceased person (orig. of king, later on also of those who could afford it), the front hall (廟) containing spirit tablets for worship, the back hall (寢) containing articles and dress used by deceased.
寢室 *chiinshyh*, n., bedroom.
寢衣 *chiinyi*, n., bedclothes, sleeping gown.

冣 62.82-3

tzueih.

[Err. var. of 最 41.82]

寑 62.82-6

jihn.

[Var. of 浸]

叜 62.82-9

soou.

[Var. of 叟 22.82]

§ 62.83 (宀/乀)

寁 62.83-1

tzaan.

Adj. (AC) quick, fast.

運 62.83-1

yuhn.

N. (1) Luck, turn of events: 氣運, 運氣 *-chih*↓; 命運 person's fate; 國運 national fate, turn of national events (good, bad); 財運 luck in business; 時運 current trend of things; 壞運, 倒運 bad luck; 應運而生 rise in response to proper time and conditions. (2) Short for 運動 *-duhng*↓; 世運 Olympic Games; 亞運 Asian Games.

V.i. & t. (1) To revolve: 運轉 *-juaan*↓. (2) To transport (goods): 運輸, 運送 *-shu, -suhng*↓; 運糧, 運兵 transport food, troops; 貨運 freight; 運費 *-feih*↓; 承運 to contract for transportation; 空運 air freight; 海運, 陸運 sea, land transportation. (3) To exercise skill, ability, to control movement: 運用 *-yuhng*↓; 運筆 *-bii*↓; 運劍 to handle sword dexterously; 運籌 draw up plans, see 籌 92A.00.

運筆 *yuhn-bii*, v.i. & n., skill in handling brush.
運氣 *yuhn-chih*, (1) phr., to control breath as in Yoga; (2) (-'*chi*) n., luck, happiness.
運單 *yuhn-dan*, n., bill of lading.
運道 *yuhndauh*, n., fate.
運動 *yuhnduhng*, (1) n., sports, exercises; (2) n., movement (social, political, literary, etc.); (3) v.i. & t., to campaign for office through connexions, solicit votes; 運動場 athletic field; 運動會 track and field meet; 運動員 athlets.
運費 *yuhnfeih*, n., freight, fees for transportation.
運河 *yuhnher*, n., canal; the Grand Canal.
運會 *yuhnhueih*, n., trend of the times.
運貨 *yuhn-huoh*, n., freight shipment; v. i., to ship goods.
運腳 *yuhnjiaau*, n., freight, charges for loading and unloading.
運轉 *yuhnjuaan*, v.t. & n., (machine) to revolve, a revolution.
運命 *yuhnmihng*, n., person's fate.
運銷 *yuhnshiau*, v.t., to market, transport for sale.
運行 *yuhnshirng*, v.i., (heavenly bodies) to circulate, revolve.
運輸 *yuhnshu*, v.t. & n., transport, -ation.
運數 *yuhnshuh*, n., fate, destiny.
運送 *yuhnsuhng*, v.t., to send (cargo).
運祚 *yuhntzuoh*, n., destiny of ruling house.
運務 *yuhn-wuh*, n., transportation business.
運用 *yuhnyuhng*, v.t. & n., to use (pen, brain, intelligence, strength) with skill.

蹇 62.83-2

jiaan.

Adj. (1) Lame: 蹇跛 crippled, limping. (2) Dull, stupid, dumb: 蹇吃 *-jir*, 蹇澀 *-seh*↓. (3) Unlucky, fallen upon evil days: 蹇剝 *-bo*, 蹇滯 *-jyh*, 蹇運 *-yuhn*↓; 命蹇 have bad luck in life, be born under an evil star. (4) Proud, arrogant: 驕蹇 supercilious, puffed up, swollen with pride.

蹇剝 *jiaanbo*, adj., unlucky (times).
蹇步 *jiaan-buh*, n., slow and cumbersome, clumsy steps.
蹇蹇 *jiarnjiaan*, adj., (1) in great straits, faced with dangers ahead; (2) loyal, faithful, not given to flattery.
蹇吃 *jiaanjir*, v.i., stutter.
蹇滯 *jiaanjyh*, adj., (of situation) beset with difficulties, (of person) luckless, unfortunate.
蹇驢 *jiaan-lyur*, n., a skinny donkey.
蹇澀 *jiaanseh*, adj., (1) obtuse, half-witted, dull; (2) (of road) difficult of access.
蹇衞 *jiaanweih*, n., see *-lyur*↑.
蹇運 *jiaan-yuhn*, n., ill luck, misfortune.

定 62.83-3

dihng.

N. (1) (Budd.) state of complete cessation of thought: 入定. (2) (AC) forehead; a star in Pegasus.

V.i. & t. (1) To set, settle, fix: 定了主意 has made up one's mind; 定了案 (of lawsuit) case closed, (of official business) final decision made and publicly announced; 定都 choose site for capital; 定眼, 定睛 fix eyes (upon); 定眼看 look steadily; 定神 *-shern*↓; 定情 *-chirng*↓; 定心 fix or calm one's mind; 定天下, 安邦定國 bring peace and stability to country; 定於一 bring peace by unity. (2) Reserve, set, make deal for future, order ahead (oft. wr. 訂): 定座 to book seats; 定親 betroth to; 定貨 order goods for delivery; 定做 *-tzuoh*↓.

Adj. (1) Fixed, definite: 一定, 必定 certain, -ly; 不定 not certain; see many compp. (2) Peaceful: 安定, 平定, 穩定 stable, settled.

Adv. Definitely, certainly: 定可成功 certainly will succeed (vern. oft. 一定, 定然); 定難解決 certainly difficult to solve; oft. follows vb. as complement or as part of vb.: 注定 destined to; 抱定主義 hold firmly a belief; 抱定主意 hold firmly one's determination; 說定了 already verbally agreed; 商定 agree after negotiation; 保不定 cannot guarantee (definitely); 說不定 phr., perhaps indeed, it might be (there is a leakage, etc.); 必定 certainly.

定卜 *dihngbuu*, v.i., (court.) I am sure (you are enjoying good health, etc.).
定錢 *dihngchiarn*, n., deposit money, earnest (-money).
定期 *dihngchir*, adj., fixed term: 定期存款 time deposit; 定期交易 time bargain; 終身定期金 life interests.
定情 *dihng-chirng*, v.i., pledge love between lovers.
定當 *dihngdahng*, (1) adj., decided, settled, satisfactory; (2) (*-dang*) v. i., certainly must.
定單 *dihngdan*, n., order form for goods.
定等 *dihng-deeng*, v. i., to grade.
定鼎 *dihng-diing*, v. i., to unify country and set up dynasty.
定奪 *dihngduor*, v. i., decide: 由你定奪 you will please decide.
定分 *dihngfehn*, n., personal fate, destiny.
定歸 *dihngguei*, aux. vb., must eventually.
定滑輪 *dihng-huarlurn*, n., fixed pulley.
定戶 *dihnghuh*, n., subscriber.
定貨單 *dihnghuoh-dan*, n., order form.
定章 *dihngjang*, n., fixed regulations.
定價 *dihngjiah*, n., fixed price, list price.
定見 *dihngjiahn*, n., fixed opinion; prejudice: 我沒有定見 I am open-minded.
定計 *dihngjih*, n., fixed plan; v. i., to decide to.
定金 *dihngjin*, n., betrothal gift of money.
定準 *dihngjuun*, n., fixed standard; aux. vb., certainly will.
定製 *dihngjyh*, v.i. & t. make to order; adj., tailor-made.
定居 *dihngjyu*, v.i., to settle down (in a town).
定局 *dihngjyur*, n., a settled situation.
定力 *dihnglih*, n., (Budd.) strength of training in concentration.
定理 *dihnglii*, n., moral laws; law of physical universe; theorem, maxiom.
定論 *dihngluhn*, n., settled, accepted opinion.
定律 *dihnglyuh*[1], n., laws (moral, physical).
定率 *dihnglyuh*[2], n., a fixed rate, ratio or proportion.
定命論 *dihngmihngluhn*, n., determinism, fatalism.
定名 *dihng-mirng*, v.t., choose name for (person, thing).
定盤星 *dihngparnshing*, n., marks of weight on steelyard.
定聘 *dihngpihng*, v.i., betroth.
定然 *dihngrern*, adv., certainly.
定神(兒) *dihngshern(-shern'l)*, v.i., stop and think (after momentary flurry), remain serene and quiet.
定限 *dihngshiahn*, n., limit.
定向 *dihngshiahng*, n., direction of motion.
定像液 *dihngshiahngyeh*, n., (photography) fixer (also called 定影液).
定省 *dihngshiing*, v.i., fulfill filial duties: 晨昏定省 see parents to bed and greet them in morning.
定心丸 *dihngshin-warn*, n., tranquillizer, hence, anything that soothes the nerves.
定數 *dihngshuh*, n., (1) definite number; (2) fate, destiny.
定時炸彈 *dihngshyr jahdahn*, n., time bomb.
定弦(兒) *dihng-shyuarn('l)*, v. i., to tune string instrument.

定妥 *dihngtuoo*, (1) v. i., order (goods), agree (on deal); (2) adj., satisfactory.
定做 *dihngtzuoh*, v. i., make to order: 定做的 dtto.
定罪 *dihngtzueih*, v. t., to convict of crime, to sentence.
定義 *dihngyih*[1], n., definition (of term).
定議 *dihngyih*[2], n., closed decision; agreement on sale.
定音鼓 *dihnyinguu*, n., tympani.
定銀 *dihngyirn*, n., deposit money, earnest paid at time of order.

逭 62.83-4

huahn.

V. t. To evade, get away from: 逭暑 (LL) to go to summer resort; 罪無可逭 one cannot evade responsibity for guilt.

§62.91 (宀/ノ)

寥 62.91-5

liaur.

Adj. (1) Few, scarce: 寥若晨星 (talents, good plays) rare like morning stars. (2) Quiet: 寂寥 silent and lonely; n., solitude. (3) Abstruse, vague, broad and empty: 寥天 (LL) the broad sky; 寥闊 *-kuoh*[2]↓.

寥廓 *liaurkuoh*[1], adj., broad, apparently limitless; silent and serene.
寥闊 *liaurkuoh*[2], adj., ditto.
寥寥 *liaurliaur*, adj., empty, scarce: 寥寥無幾 only a few (left, etc.); lonely: 寥寥無伴.
寥唳 *liaurlih*, adj., (of sound, music) carrying far (嘹唳 preferred).
寥落 *liaurluoh*, adj., scarce, scanty, meager.

§62.93 (宀/く)

宏 62.93-1

hurng.

N. A surname.

Adj. Great, vast (more common form than 弘 50A.93, cf. also 鴻 63A.50, 洪 63A.80, same sound and meaning): 宏論 great essay or exposition of opinion; 宏富 great wealth; 宏辯 eloquent debate.

宏敞 *hurngchaang*, adj., great, spacious (building).
宏大 *hurngdah*, adj., great, vast, grand (plan, ambition).
宏放 *hurngfahng*, adj., free and untrammeled (style).
宏壯 *hurngjuahng*, adj., great and solid.
宏量 *hurngliah g*, n., great capacity (for win , etc.), great generosity.

宴 62.93-4

yahn.

N. A feast, public dinner: 喜宴 wedding dinner; 壽宴 birthday dinner; 餞別宴 farewell dinner; 接風宴 welcome dinner; 赴宴 attend dinner; 野宴 picnic.

V.t. To give a dinner: 宴請, 宴客, 宴集 *-chiing, -keh, -jir*↓.

Adj. Enjoyable: 宴安, 宴樂 *-an, -leh*↓.

宴安 *yahn-an*, v.i., feel happy, contented, relaxed.
宴請 *yahnchiing*, v.t., to invite (person) to dinner.
宴爾 *yahn-eel*, adj., as in (LL) 宴爾新婚 formula for wedding congratulations.
宴會 *yahnhueih*, n., a public dinner, a banquet.
宴集 *yahnjir* v.i., to gather together.
宴居 *yahnjyu*, (1) v.i., (AC) stay at home; (2) n., informal life at home (also wr. 燕居).
宴客 *yahn-keh*, v.i., be host at dinner.
宴樂 *yahnleh*, (1) v.i., to enjoy life, be given to pleasures; (2) adj., happy, contented, relaxed.
宴饗 *yahnshiaang*, v.i., (ruler) give a great dinner.
宴息 *yahnshir*, v.i., to relax.
宴飲 *yahnyiin*, v.i., to drink at a feast, dine and wine.

蜜 62.93-6

mih.

[Dist. 密 secret 62.21]

N. Honey: 蜜裏調油 very, very sweet to each other.

Adj. (1) Sweet: 蜜酒 sweet wine; 蜜柑, 蜜橘 *-gan, -jyur*↓. (2) Glazed, crystallized: 蜜餞, 蜜漬 *-jiahn, -tzyh*↓: 蜜棗 glazed date.

蜜房 *mih-farng*, n., honeycomb.
蜜蜂(兒) *mihfeng('l)*, n., honeybee.
蜜柑 *mihgan*, n., tangerine.
蜜供 *mih-guhng*, n., fried and honeyed noodles, oft. used in sacrifices.
蜜菓 *mihguoo*, n., sugar-treated fruit.
蜜餞 *mihjiahn*, n., sugar-coated

蜜安 fruit, fruit treated in syrup; confections; also wr. 蜜煎, 蜜餞 砒霜 sugar-coated arsenic, deceptive sweet words.

蜜橘 *mihjyur*, n., tangerine.

蜜蠟 *milah*, n., (1) beeswax; (2) (*mih'la*) a kind of semiprecious stone.

蜜嘴 *mih-tzueei*, adj., honey-tongued.

蜜漬 *mihtzyh*, n., sugar-treated preserves, fruits.

蜜語 *mih-yuu*, n., sweet, pleasant words: 甜言蜜語 ditto.

蜜月 *mihyueh*, n., honeymoon: 度蜜月 pass honeymoon; 蜜月旅行 honeymoon trip.

安 62.93-9

an.

N. (1) A surname. (2) Tranquillity, peace, security, opp. 危 chaotic conditions, danger: 安危 *-weir* ↓.

V.i. & t. (1) To install: 安放, 安置, 安裝 *-fahng*, *-jyh*, *-juang* ↓; to harbor, shelter (a thought): 不安好心, 安心不良 harbor thought of injuring s.o.; 安電燈 install electric lights; 茶壺安把兒 fix a handle on teapot. (2) To dwell in, settle down: 安於 feel contented in: 安於宴樂 feel happy in material pleasures: 不安於室 (AC of a woman) have extramarital relations; 安貧樂道 contented in poverty and devoted to things spiritual; 安土 *-tuu* ↓; 安居 *-jyu* ↓ 安常襲故 contented with old ways and loath to change; 安分, 安命 *-fehn*, *-mihng* ↓. (3) To pacify, to make happy: 保境安民 "maintain peace and security in the territory under one's control"—euphemism for armed neutrality in civil war; 安邦定國 bring peace and stability to the country.

Adj. Tranquil, peaceful, free from troubles: 安全 *-chyuarn* ↓; 平安 well and in good health; 問安, 請安, 叩安 to inquire after one's health, to give best regards; 安寧, 安靜, 安定 *-nirng*, *-jihng*², *-dihng* ↓; 安心 *-shin*, 安適 *-shyh* ↓.

Adv. (1) Leisurely, tranquilly: 安步 *-buh* ↓; 安居, 安坐 *-jyu*, *-tzuoh* ↓; 安詳, 安舒 *-shiarng*, *-shu* ↓. (2) How? where?: 安得 where can one find? 安能, 安可 how can? 安有 how can there be? 安知 how do you know; 安用 what use is there (for s.t.)?

安辦 *anbahn*, v.i. & t., to provide, make arrangements for.

安邊 *an-bian*, phr., to pacify the border area.

安泊 *an-bor*, v.i., (MC) to stop (at an inn).

安步 *an-buh*, phr., go slowly: 安步(以)當車 to stroll leisurely instead of taking a carriage—and enjoy it as much.

安插 *ancha*, v.t., to place (friend, etc.) in organization, find job for (s.o.).

安禪 *an-charn*, v.i., to reach peace and calm through meditation.

安車 *anche*, n., (AC) cart with seats in it.

安琪兒 *anchir'l*, n., (translit.) an angel.

安處 *an-chuu*, phr., see *-jyu* ↓.

安全 *anchyuarn*, adj. & n., safe, safety, security: 安全設備 provisions for security; 安全瓣 safety valve; 安全梯 fire exit (stairs); 安全火柴 safety match; 安全調查 security check; 安全人員 security personnel; 安全帶 safety belt; 安全第一 safety first; 安全保障條約 Security Pact; 安全區 safety zone.

安定 *andihng*, (1) adj., settled down, in peace; (2) v.t., stabilize: 安定金融 to stabilize the currency.

安頓 *anduhn*, (1) v.t., to place (person) in some secure position or place; place (object) in proper position: 無處安頓 nowhere to place (a bulky trunk, etc.); nowhere to settle; (2) v.i., to settle down: 安頓下來; (3) adj., comfortable (as patient after taking pill and a good nap): 安頓多了 feel much better now; 地方不安頓 this place or country is not very peaceful.

安放 *anfahng*, v.t., to put away (s.t.); to place (relative) in some organization.

安分 *anfehn*, adj., law-abiding: 守己安分 ditto.

安覆 *anfuh*, v.t., see *-fuu* ↓.

安伏 *anfur* (*-'fu*), v.t., (MC) to comfort one with words, to calm (person) down.

安撫 *anfuu*, v.t., to pacify people by abstention from force.

安根子 *an-gentz*, phr., to lay foundation (for future work).

安固 *anguh*, adj., secure.

安穀 *an-guu*, phr., (AC of patient) can take grain without throwing up.

安好 *anhaau*, adj., well, in good health.

安扎(札) *anjar*, v.t., to find a proper place for s.o. or s.t., see *-jyh* ↓.

安枕 *an-jeen*, phr., sleep peacefully: 夜不安枕 toss about in bed.

安宅 *an-jeh*, v.t., (AC) see *-jyu* ↓.

安家 *an-jia*, v.i., to settle down a family: 安家(居)樂業 (the people) are making a good living and contented each in his station; 安家費 allowance for family support, esp. when head is absent.

安靖 *anjihng*¹, adj., (district) peaceful, quiet.

安靜 *anjihng*² (*-'jing*), adj., (district, house) quiet, peaceful; (children) quiet; (person's character) serene, poised, not restless.

安輯 *anjir*, v.t., to let people settle down in peace.

安着(著) *anjour*, v.t., (MC) to keep (person in service).

安裝 *anjuang*, v.t., to install (telephone, etc.).

安置 *anjyh*, v.t., (1) to place (person) in certain post; (2) to install (telephone, etc.); (3) formerly, to exile official to remote district as punishment.

安居 *an-jyu*, phr., 安居樂業 see *-jia* ↑.

安康 *ankang*, adj., (LL usu. in letters) enjoying good health.

安老院 *anlaauyuahn*, n., home for the aged.

安瀾 *an-larn*, phr., (1) peaceful (world, compared to a calm

sea); (2) formerly, the Yellow River dykes stayed.

安樂 *anleh*, adj. & n., happy, -iness; 安樂窩 a happy retreat, a place for contented living; a love nest; 安樂國 n., a Utopia, (Budd.) Paradise.

安良 *anliarng*, phr., 除暴安良 weed out the wicked and let the law-abiding citizen live in peace.

安眠 *anmiarn*, v.i., to sleep well; 安眠藥 sleeping-pill.

安謐 *anmih*, adj., (LL) peaceful, free from disturbances (place, country, condition).

安命 *an-mihng*, adj., fatalistic; content with what one has.

安難 *an-nahn*, phr., (AC) not shrinking from hardships or crisis.

安寧 *annirng*, adj., peaceful.

安排 *anpair* (-'*pai*), v.t., (1) to arrange, put (chairs, etc.) in proper place; (2) to provide (meals, breakfast, etc.); (3) 隨人安排 to be shoved about by others.

安培 *anpeir*, n., (elect.) ampere.

安然 *anrarn*, adv., (1) calmly (see s.t. happen); (2) adj., well and in good shape.

安忍 *anreen*, (1) v.i., endure patiently; (2) adv., how can one endure or bear to do s.t. (see Adv. ↑).

安人 *anrern*, n., formerly, wife of a ranking official.

安設 *ansheh*, v.t., to install (telephone, etc.).

安身 *an-shen*, v.i., to find a secure job or settled place for life.

安聲 *an-sheng*, adj., silent, quiet: 這孩子整天沒一會兒安聲 this child is never still for a moment.

安神 *an-shern*, v.i., to calm down nerves; relax one's mind.

安下 *an-shiah*, v.i., to retire for rest or sleep.

安閒 *anshiarn*, adj., enjoying leisure: 安閒無事 have no work or duties.

安詳 *anshiarng* (-'*shiang*), adj., (manner of speech or behavior) leisurely, unhurried.

安歇 *anshie*, v.i., to rest, to sleep.

安心 *an-shin*, (1) adj., not worried, contented; (2) adv., setting one's mind to: 安心做去 do it without hesitation; 但要你安心留我 (from a maid) if you really want to keep me.

安息 *anshir*, (1) v.i., to rest and relax; 安息日 Sabbath; 安息年 sabbatical year; 安息日會 Seventh Day Adventist; (2) 安息香 gum benzoin.

安舒 *anshu*, adj. & adv., see *-shiarng* ↑.

安適 *anshyh*, adj., comfortable, comfortably set; leisurely (life).

安石榴 *anshyrliour*, n., pomegranate (usu. 石榴).

安泰 *antaih*, adj., (LL) peaceful; in good health.

安胎藥 *antaiyauh*, n., (Chin. med.) medicine to prevent miscarriage after mother went through some upsetting event.

安帖 *antie*, v.i., become subdued, calm down.

安厝 *an-tsuoh*, v.i., to store up coffin (with corpse) in some temporary place before burial.

安存 *antsurn*, v.i., see *-shen* ↑.

安托 *antuo*, v.t., to place (s.o.) in friend's home.

安妥 *antuoo*, adj., well placed, secure.

安童 *anturng*, n., formerly, boy servant.

安土 *an-tuu*, phr., to be content where one lives: 安土重遷 do not care to migrate from native land, to dislike transfer of population to new place.

安葬 *antzahng*, v.t., to bury in grave.

安坐 *an-tzuoh*, phr., 安坐而食 to be fed without work.

安足 *an-tzur*, phr., to "rest one's foot" a place to live.

安穩 *anween* (-'*wen*), adj., safe and secure.

安慰 *anweih*, v.t., to comfort (s.o.); 安慰劑 (med.) placebo.

安危 *an-weir*, n., peace or chaos, i.e., peace (depends on s.t. or s.o.).

安逸 *anyih*, adj., leisurely, enjoying leisure, unburdened.

安營 *an-yirng*, v.i., to encamp.

SECTION 62A

§ 62A.00 (穴/亅)

穿 62A.00-5

chuan.

V. t. (1) To wear (clothing): 穿上衣服 put on clothing; 穿不得 cannot wear, (clothing) does not fit; 穿不下 (clothing) too tight for wear; 穿不住 does not wear well, also (clothing) too warm or too cold; 穿長袍, 外套 wear long gown, overcoat; 穿孝, 穿素 *-shiauh, -suh* ↓. (2) To drill through, pierce through: 穿耳, 穿鼻 drill a hole in ear, nose; 穿井 drill a well; 箭穿胸 arrow pierces through chest; 百步穿楊 hit a willow branch at 100 yards by arrow. (3) To go through or by way of, lead or guide through: 穿街過巷 go through streets and alleys; 穿過山洞 go through a cave tunnel; 穿過後院 go in through the back court; 穿針 put thread through needle; 穿針引線 phr., try to make a match; 穿串兒 *-chuahn'l* ↓.

V. i. To have a hole, be worn through: 鞋底穿了 shoe sole is worn through; 船底穿了 boat bottom leaks.

Adv. Through (used after vb.): 看穿 see through (life, trick); 說穿 reveal (secret); 鑿穿 drill through; 打穿 break through (fence, wall).

穿插 *chuancha*, v.i. & t., to add or weave in details to give life to story.

穿串兒 *chuanchuahn'l*, v. i., to string up sections to make a string; weave a collection of stories together to make a novel.

穿戴 *chuandaih*, n., what one wears (hat, hair decorations and dress).

穿換 *chuanhuahn*, v. i., (MC) to exchange (wine cups).

穿章兒 *chuan'jang'l*, n., dress in gen.: 穿章兒打扮 a person's dress and gen. make-up.

穿廊 *chuanlarng*, n., a covered corridor (leading from one court to another).

穿山甲 *chuanshanjiaa*, n., ant-eater, armadillo.

穿孝 *chuanshiauh*, v. i., to wear mourning.

穿素 *chuansuh*, v. i., ditto.

穿堂 *chuantarng*, n., a hallway; room which opens on both sides serving as passage: 穿堂門兒 a through alley, alley gate.

穿鑿 *chuantzuoh*, adj., (argument, proof) forced, not natural; 穿鑿附會 ditto.

穿往 *chuanwang* (-'*wang*) v. i., keep up exchange of visits, presents.

穿衣鏡 *chuanyi-jihng*, n., dressing mirror.

穿越 *chuanyueh*, v. t., lead through or over (a hill, building blocks).

穿窬 *chuanyur*, n., as in 穿窬之盜 (AC) burglar who bores holes in wall.

窬 62A.00-8

yur.

[Usu. printed 窬]

N. A hole in the wall: 穿窬之盜 (AC) a petty burglar.

§62A.01 (穴/小)

窠 62A.01-4

ke.

N. A nest, a hole of burrow animals: 蜂窠 beehive.

窠臼 *kejiouh*, n., set pattern: 落了窠臼 fall into old ruts (of writing, thinking).

§62A.10 (穴/十)

窣 62A.10-6

suh.

V. i. (AC) to rush out.

Adj. & adv. (1) Abruptly: 窣地 -*dih*↓. (2) Rustling: 窣窣 -*suh*↓.

窣地 *suhdih*, adv., (1) abrupt, -ly; (2) with a rustling sound (of skirts).

窣窣 *suhsuh*, adj., descriptive of minute rustle (sound).

§62A.11 (穴/土)

窒 62A.11-3

jyh.

V. t. To obstruct: 窒息 -*shir*↓; 氣窒 be suffocated; 窒欲 to suppress desires.

窒礙 *jyh-aih*, n., obstruction(s), obstacle(s).

窒息 *jyhshir*, v. i., to be or feel suffocated.

窿 62A.11-3

lurng.

N. & adj. See 窟窿 62A.21, 穹窿 (隆) 62A.50.

窪 62A.11-6

wa.

N. A depression on ground.

Adj. Low, depressed (ground): 窪下, 窪地 low ground (cf. 凹 *wah* 42.21).

§62A.20 (穴/卄)

穽 62A.20-2

jiing.

[Anc. var. of 阱 32A.20]

§62A.21 (穴/乚)

窟 62A.21-5

ku.

N. (1) A cave, basement: 窟洞, 窟穴 -*duhng*, -*shyuer*↓; 地窟 basement, cellar; 窟藏 cellar containing precious goods, gold, etc.; 兔窟, 鼠窟 hare's hole, rat hole. (2) A slum, a hidden place: 賊窟 thieves' den; 淫窟 secret place for orgies; 貧民窟 city slums.

窟洞 *kuduhng*, n., a hole (in wall, etc.).

窟窿 *ku'lung*, n., (1) a hole (in wall, clothing, etc.); 窟窿洞, 窟窿眼兒 a hole; (2) a deficit: 掏窟窿 (coll.) borrow money.

窟穴 *kushyuer*, n., a cave.

窖 62A.21-9

yaur.

N. (1) A kiln: 瓦窰, 磚窰 a kiln for making tiles, bricks; 官窰 government-operated kiln for making porcelain; porcelain product of certain well-known kilns. (2) A mine pit: 煤窰 coal pit. (3) A loess cave dwelling in northwest China: 洞窰 ditto; 窰洞 *-duhng* ↓. (4) (Coll.) (*-tz*) a brothel: 逛窰子 visit brothel.

窰變 *yaurbiahn*, n., crackle, crackleware.
窰洞 *yaurduhng*, n., loess cave dwelling in northwest China.
窰姐兒 *yaurjiee'l*, n., (coll.) prostitute.
窰坑 *yaurkeng*, n., a pit.
窰痞 *yaurpii*, n., a rowdy who hangs around brothels.
窰桶子 *yaurtuungtz*, n., coal tunnel.
窰子 *yaurtz*, n., a brothel; formerly, a whore.
窰窰兒 *yaur'yau'l*, n., see *-duhng* ↑.

§ 62A.22 (穴/丨)

帘 62A.22-2

liarn.

N. (*-tz*, *'l*) (1) Flag on pole over wine house, esp. in countryside. (2) Interch. 簾 92A.22 curtain.

窄 62A.22-9

jaai (re. pr. *tzer*).

Adj. Narrow (path, room), tight (dress): 狹窄, 窄小 narrow and small; 窄巴巴的, 窄巃巃的 very narrow; 心窄 narrow-minded; 寃家路窄 enemies will meet in a narrow alley—confrontation inevitable.

§ 62A.30 (穴/一)

空 62A.30-3

kung (**kuhng*).

N. (1) The open air, the sky or skies, upper space: 空間, 空中 *-jian*, *-jung*[1] ↓; 天空 the sky, firmament; 晴空萬里 the vast clear sky; 碧空 (poet.) blue sky; 空際 in the sky; 航空 aviation, air navigation; 眞空 (phys.) vacuum; 太空 outer space. (2) (Budd.) emptiness, void of the world of senses: 空卽是色, 色卽是空 the void is the world of senses, (reality is unreal) and *vice versa*; 四大皆空 all space-directions are void. (3) (**kuhng*) A cleft, fissure, a blank, unoccupied space or time: 有空就來 will come when I find free time; 沒空 have no time; 空格, 空額 *-ger*, *-er* ↓; 空閒 leisure.

V. t. To leave empty, unfilled: 空一格 leave a blank space; 空着肚子 on an empty stomach; *(*kuhng*) 空着頭 hang upside down (with head hanging down).

Adj. (1) Empty, hollow, bare, unfurnished, unoccupied, deserted: 空虛, 空泛 *-shyu*, *-fahn* ↓; 空話, 空論 empty talk: 空落落的 quite empty, bare; 空空洞洞 having nothing substantial (in speech, letter), bare (room); 空口說 empty talk, just a verbal statement; 一場空夢 a vain dream; 空函 envelope without letter; 空架子 a hollow front, airs without substance; 空谷足音 sound of footsteps in a deserted valley—rare, welcome appearance; 空無所有 quite bare; 空手, 空頭, 空兒 *-shoou*, *-tour*, *-'l*; 一切落空 a complete failure; 一切成空 all is vanished like a dream. (2) (Budd.) void, unreal, see N. 2 ↑. (3) (**kuhng*) Deficient, vacant: 空房 vacant room; 空地 vacant ground; 空乏 short of (money, necessities); 虧空 financial loss.

Adv. To no purpose, vainly: 空走一趟 made a trip without results; 空等着 wait in vain; 空想 *-shiaang* ↓.

空白 **kuhngbair*, n. & adj., a blank: 留空白 leave a blank; 塡空白 fill the blank.
空腸 *kungcharng*, n., (physiol.) jejunum, part of the small intestine between the duodenum and the ileum.
空前 *kungchiarn*, adj., unprecedented.
空氣 *kungchih*, n., (1) the air; (2) atmosphere (social, artistic, political); 新空氣 new atmosphere; 新鮮空氣 fresh air; 放空氣 leak out information on purpose to test reaction, trial balloon.
空缺 **kuhngchyueh*, n., (1) vacancy; (2) scarcity (of food, water, etc.).
空羣 *kung-chyurn*, phr., 空羣之選 (LL) the pick of the best.
空檔 **kuhngdaang* (*-dahng*), n., (1) blank on schedule; (2) neutral gear; (3) a flaw for attack.
空肚兒 **kuhngduh'l* (*-duu'l*), adv., on an empty stomach.
空洞 *kungduhng*, adj., without real substance, see *-kung* ↓.
空額 **kuhng-er*, n., vacancy.
空泛 *kungfahn*, adj., (of speech, statement) containing only generalities, not specific.
空乏 **kuhngfar*, n. & adj., shortage, scarce, -ity.
空格 **kuhngger*, n., a blank space.
空幻 *kunghuahn*, adj. & n., insubstantial, unreal (dream), unrealistic, impractical, utopian (theory).

空戰 *kung-jahn*, n., air fight.

空間 *kungjian*, n., (1) empty space, space as a concept (cf. 時間 time); (2) the sky.

空集 *kung-jir*, n., (math.) empty, null set.

空中 *kungjung*[1], n., the sky: 空中小姐 air hostess; 空中堡壘 sky fortress; 空中樓閣 a mirage; castles in the air.

空鐘 *kungjung*[2], n., a wooden toy making a whirring noise when suspended and spun by a thread.

空竹 *kungjur*, n., see *-jung*[2] ↑.

空軍 *kungjyun*, n., the air force.

空曠 *kungkuahng*, adj., (of land) open, wide, spacious.

空匱 *kungkueih*, adj. & n., scarce, -ity, poor.

空空 *kungkung*, adj., all empty, void: 空空如也 (AC) all empty; 空空洞洞 with nothing in it; 空空兒的 empty-handed, (to visit) without bringing presents.

空闊 *kungkuoh*, adj., open and spacious.

空兒 **kuhng'l*, n., (1) free time: 得空兒就來 will come when I have time; opening, chance; (2) (*kung'l*) a name without substance, a hollow undertaking; 空兒事 s. t. good for show only.

空靈 *kunglirng*, adj., (of art, room decoration) not overstuffed, sparse, light and free, appealing by quiet restraint.

空門 *kungmern*, n., Buddhism: 遁入空門 take the monastic vow.

空濛 *kungmerng*, adj., in fine drizzle.

空明 *kungmirng*, adj., (LL) bright and effulgent (as in moonlight).

空盤 *kungparn*, n., buying or selling short: 做空盤 buy stocks on margin, see also *-tour* ↓.

空身(兒) *kungshen('l)*, adj., without luggage, unarmed; 空身人(兒) ditto, also bachelor without family.

空想 *kungshiaang*, v. i. & n., (1) hope in vain; (2) fantasy, idle dream.

空閒 **kuhngshiarn*, n., free hour, leisure: 沒空閒 have no time (for s. t.).

空隙 **kuhngshih*, n., (1) a crevice, crack; (2) an opening for attack.

空心(兒) *kungshin(-shie'l)*, adj., hollow, tubular: 空心(大)老倌 (Shanghai dial.) stuffed shirt; 空心菜 (=蕹) water convolvulus, *Ipomaea aquatica*.

空襲 *kungshir*, n., air raid.

空手兒 *kungshoou('l)*, adv., (1) with bare hands, empty-handed: 空手成家 build up one's fortune from scratch; 空手兒歸 come back empty-handed; 空手道 karate; (2) without copy or model: 空手兒畫 original, free sketch.

空疏 *kungshu*, adj., shallow, not profound.

空虛 *kungshyu*, adj., (1) hollow, empty; (2) 心空虛 scared (from being guilty), cf. 虛心 humble, open-minded.

空談 *kungtarn*, n., empty talk, idle talk, not followed by action.

空頭 *kungtour*, adj. & n., (1) (生意) buy or sell stock on margin (also 買空賣空); 空頭人情 empty (costless) show of sympathy; (2) (**kuhng-*) 空頭支票 bounced check.

空桶子 *kungtuungtz*, n., an empty barrel—(fig.) of hollow front.

空子 **kuhngtz*, n., (1) a free time for doing s. t.; (2) an opening, opportunity; (3) (coll.) deficit, debts.

空文 *kung-wern*, n., laws and statutes that exist on paper only: 一紙空文 a scrap of paper.

空運 *kung-yuhn*, n., air transportation.

§ 62A.32 (穴/フ)

穸 62A.32-9

shih.

N. See 窀^A穸 62A.70.

§ 62A.40 (穴/口)

窘 62A.40-5

jyuung (also *jyuun*).

Adj. Poor, embarrassed: 窘境 an embarrassing situation; 困窘 awkward, uncomfortable, distressing; 受窘 be embarrassed; 窘住 *-'ju* ↓; 發窘 confused by embarrassment; 窘迫 *-poh* ↓; 窘急 *-jir* ↓; 他很窘 he's hard up.

窘急 *jyuungjir*, adj., in distress or desperate straits.

窘住 *jyuung'ju*, v. i. & t., (1) be embarrassed; (2) to embarrass.

窘迫 *jyuungpoh*, adj., in straitened circumstances.

§ 62A.41 (穴/図)

窅 62A.41-4

yaau.

窅眇 *yaurmiaau*, adj., dark, fathomless.

窅然 *yaurarn*, adj., disappointed.

窅窱 *yaurtiaau*, adj., see *-miaau* ↑.

窨 62A.41-6

yihn.

N. Basement: 地窨子 ditto.

V.t. To keep in dark place, store away in cellar.

窗 62A.41-9

chuang.

[Var. of 窻, 窓, 牕]

N. (1) (*-tz*, *-'l*) Window: 窗戶 *-huh* ↓; 窗幔, 窗紗, 窗簾 window curtain; 百葉窗 Venetian blinds; 天窗 skylight; 打開天窗說亮話 have a frank, straight talk; 玻璃窗 glass window; 紙窗 papered window instead of glass; 落地窗 French window; 明窗淨几 a scholar's bright neat studio. (2) Associated with school studies: 同窗 schoolmate; 窗友 *-yoou* ↓; 窗下苦讀 hard studies ("before window").

窗戶 *chuang'huh*, n., window, also windows and doors: 窗戶小心 be careful to lock doors and windows at night; 窗戶簾兒 window curtain, or screen; 窗戶眼兒 a peephole through paper window; 窗戶紙 window paper (in place of glass): 臉上像窗戶紙 (frightened) one's face livid like paper; 隔一層窗戶紙 (fig.) very close together; 戳破這窗戶紙便一文不値 let out the secret and it is worthless.

窗課 *chuang-keh*, n., school lessons.

窗簾兒 *chuangliarn* (*-liar'l*), n., window curtains.

窗櫺 *chuang-lirng*, n., window grill made usu. of wood.

窗幔 *chuang-mahn*, n., window curtains.

窗紗 *chuang-sha*, n., ditto.

窗下 *chuang-shiah*, phr., in school.

窗臺(兒) *chuang-tair*(*-tar'l*), n., window sill.

窗屜 *chuang-tih*, n., props for window which opens from hinge above.

窗帷 *chuang-weir*, n., window curtains.

窗友 *chuang-yoou*, n., fellow students.

§ 62A.42 (穴/冈)

窩 62A.42-4

wo.

N. (1) A nest: 蜂窩 beehive; 鳥窩 bird's nest; 狗窩 kennel; 一窩蜂似的 like a swarm of bees; (fig.) 安樂窩 a love nest; a snug, cosy place. (2) A small construction: 窩棚, 窩鋪 *-'perng*, *-puh* ↓. (3) A hollow part of body: 心窩 heart, as seat of feeling; 胳肢窩 armpit; 酒窩 dimple. (4) A hiding place, esp. for booty: 窩家 *-jia* ↓; 窩藏 *-tsarng* ↓.

V.i. & t. (1) To turn about, to bend, to cramp, to depress: 窩擺, 窩憋 *-baai*, *-'bie* ↓; 窩心 *-shin*, 窩脖兒 *-bor'l* ↓ 窩風 *-feng* ↓. (2) To give shelter to: 窩娼 keep prostitute; 窩匪 shelter bandits; 窩藏 *-tsarng* ↓.

窩擺 *wobaai*, adj., giving hard work without appreciation, miserable (assignment).

窩憋 *wo'bie*, v.t. & adj., (1) cramped (room); (2) feeling frustrated, miserable, oppressed; see *-baai* ↑.

窩脖兒(子) *wobor'l*(*-'tz*), (1) n., wharf laborer, carrying heavy load on bent back and shoulders; (2) adj., oppressed, chafed and angry.

窩頓 *woduhn*, v.t., (MC) place in proper place (=modn. 安頓 62.93).

窩風 *wofeng*, (1) adj., (of courtyard) churning wind; (2) v.i., to prevent wind from passing through.

窩弓 *wogung*, n., a bow-and-arrow trap for wild animals.

窩家 *wojia*, n., person giving shelter to criminals or receiving deposits of booty.

窩集 *wojir*, n., (dial. in Manchuria) a jungle swampy area.

窩主 *wojuu*, n., owner of 窩家 see *-jia* ↑.

窩驅眼 *wo'kouyaan*, n., deep-sunken eyes.

窩兒 *wo'l*, n., a nook, corner, temporary shelter; 窩兒老 (contempt.) a person who keeps much to himself; 窩兒裏反 domestic conflict or dissension.

窩裏炮 *wo'li'pau*, v.i., (of domestic servants) fight among themselves.

窩囊 *wo'nang*, adj., timid, cowering, faint-hearted, good-for-nothing; 窩囊廢 (contempt.) a coward; imbecile.

窩膿 *wonurng*, v.i., to have pus formation.

窩盤 *woparn*, v.t., to comfort and bring around with words: 招呼他到後面窩盤他 take him alone and comfort him (to soothe his anger).

窩棚 *wo'perng*, n., a mat shed.

窩鋪 *wopuh*, n., ditto.

窩心 *woshin*, v.i., to feel irritated: 窩心氣 to feel irritated, mope around; 窩心腳 a kick in the chest.

窩逃 *wo-taur*, phr., to give shelter to a fugitive from justice.

窩頭 *wotour*, n., see *-'wo* ↓.

窩藏 *wotsarng*, v.t., to hide a booty or fugitive from justice.

窩子 *wotz*, n., (1) family in 窩子病 an illness which affects the whole family; (2) 賊窩子 thieves' lair; (3) a pool: 井窩子 bottom of well; 尿窩子 a pool of urine.

窩窩 *wo'wo*, n., Chin. corn muffin; 窩窩洞兒 a narrow opening, a burrow, dug-out; 窩窩頭 Chin. corn muffin.

窩腰 *wo-yau*, v.i., to do waist exercise.

竊 62A.42-9

chieh.

[Pop. 窃]

N. Thief, burglar, -ry: 盜竊 thieves and burglars; 鼠竊 petty burglar; 行竊 commit burglary.

V. t. (1) To steal: 竊取 *-chyuu* ↓; 被竊 be burglarized; 失竊 be stolen; 偷香竊玉 indulge in secret relations with women; 竊鉤者誅, 竊國者侯—莊子 (AC) who steals a hook is killed as a crook; who steals another's kingdom is made a duke. (2) To occupy territory, office illegally (from litr. tradition that a rebel or enemy contender for the throne is always called a "thief" 賊): 竊位 usurp office or throne; 竊職, 竊權 usurp office authority; 竊命 (AC) rule illegally.

Adv. (1) Secretly: 竊窺 peep at; 竊笑 laugh at secretly, sneer at; 竊查 investigate secretly. (2) Used court. like "my humble (opinion)": 竊思, 竊意 it is my humble opinion; 竊謂 I venture to think; 竊聞 I have heard (that); 竊念 I remember gratefully (s. o. past), I feel at heart (his mother is so old, etc.).

竊案 *chieh-ahn*, n., a case of theft.

竊竊 *chiehchieh*, adv., (1) (talk, whisper) in a low voice; (2) 竊竊然知之 (AC) was clearly aware of it (=察察).

竊取 *chiehchyuu*, v. t., to steal, obtain by stealing.

竊犯 *chiehfahn*, n., a caught burglar.

竊號 *chiehhauh*, v. t., usurp reign; call oneself "king," "emperor" illegally.

竊據 *chiehjyuh*, v. t., to occupy territory, throne, illegally.

竊賊 *chiehtzeir*, n., a burglar, thief.

竊衣 *chiehyi*, n., (bot.) a thistle-bearing plant, *Osmorhiza aristats.*

§ 62A.50 (穴/㇆)

窃 62A.50-1

chieh.

[Pop. of 竊 62A.42 ↑]

穹 62A.50-5

chyung (also *chyurng*).

N. Vault, see 穹蒼 *-tsang* ↓.

Adj. (1) Vault-shaped: 穹隆 *-lurng* ↓. (2) Cavernous: 穹谷 deep valley; 穹嵌 deep mountains.

穹窒 *chyung-jyh*, n., (AC) rathole.

穹廬 *chyung-lur*, n., a Mongolian tent.

穹隆 *chyunglurng*, adj., vault-shaped (also wr. 窿); long and bent.

穹冥 *chyungmirng*, n., the dark heavens, the void.

穹蒼 *chyungtsang*, n., the sky.

窮 62A.50-9

chyurng.

V. t. To pursue to the limit, to exhaust: 窮究 *-jiouh* ↓; 窮經 make thorough study of a classic; 窮理 to investigate to the bottom the laws of things; 窮兵黷武 exhaust all resources to build up military power, adopt a warlike policy; 窮年, 窮日, 窮年累日 spend years, days; 窮有生之日 devote all the remaining days of my life; 欲窮千里目, 更上一層樓 ascend another storey to see a thousand miles; 窮目 as far as the eye can see.

Adj. (1) Exhausted, hard pressed, frustrated, pushed to the limit: 窮運, 運窮 hard luck; 技窮 be at the end of one's tether, reach the end of one's power, ("exhaust all tricks"), hard up; 日暮途窮, 窮途, 山窮水盡 come to the end of one's rope; 窮冬 deep winter; 窮老 until old age; see 窮困, 窮愁 *-kuhn*, *-chour* ↓; 窮當益堅 the more hard-pressed, the more one must fight back; 窮寇勿追 don't push s.o. to the wall, do not press on a desperate thief; 詩窮而後工 in poetry one gains depth after suffering. (2) Poor, impoverished: see 窮苦, 窮乏 *-kuu*, *-far* ↓; 窮人 poor people; 窮親戚 poor relations; 窮鬼, 窮漢, 窮光蛋, 窮措大, 窮骨頭 (derog.) poor devil, miserable wretch; 窮滴滴, 窮拉拉, 窮巴巴的 very poor, destitute; 窮嫌富不要 (of goods) too costly for the poor and not good enough for those who can pay; 窮家富路 be thrifty at home and spend liberally while travelling; 窮鄉僻壤 a district shut off from the outside world.

Adv. (1) Despite poverty: 窮開心, 窮作樂 enjoy oneself despite poverty; 窮逛 play about without too much cash; 窮大手 spend extravagantly although poor. (2) Exhaustively: 窮追 pursue relentlessly; 窮治 to investigate thoroughly (a case); 窮究 *-jiouh* ↓.

窮愁 *chyurngchour*, adj., hard up and depressed.

窮髮 *chyurngfaa*, phr., 窮髮之北 (AC) up north where nothing grows.

窮乏 *chyurngfar*, adj., poor and needy.

窮盡 *chyurngjihn*, v. t., to exhaust (resources).

窮究 *chyurngjiouh*, v. t., pursue, investigate thoroughly (a case); study deeply (astronomy, etc.).

窮極 *chyurngjir*, (1) adv., extremely: 窮極奢麗 extremely extravagant; (2) phr., destitute.

窮困 *chyurngkuhn*, adj., needy, poverty-stricken, in straitened circumstances.

窮空 *chyurngkung*, adj., poverty-stricken.

窮苦 *chyurngkuu*, adj., hard-up.
窮忙 *chyurngmarng*, adj., kept busy making the ends meet.
窮民 *chyurng-mirn*, n., the poor and destitute.
窮人 *chyurngrern*, n., poor people.
窮生 *chyurngsheng*, n., (Chin. theater) the role of a poor scholar.
窮巷 *chyurng-shiahng*[1], n., a small alley.
窮相 *chyurng-shiahng*[2], n., abject look; unprepossessing appearance.
窮形 *chyurng-shirng*, n., in 窮形盡相 (1) see *-shiahng*[2] ↑; (2) (of lit. portrayal) give a penetrating description (of the wicked).
窮凶 *chyurngshyung*, phr., 窮凶極惡 villainous without any redeeming feature.
窮酸 *chyurngsuan*, adj., (of scholar) poor and envious, sharply critical of others.
窮措大 *chyurgtsuohdah*, n., a penniless person (orig. wr. 窮醋大 see *-suan* ↑).
窮通 *chyurng-tung*, n., fortune and misfortune, success and failure: 窮通有命 success and failure are predestined; 窮則變,變則通 (phr.) when all means are exhausted, changes become necessary; once changed, a solution emerges.
窮途 *chyurngtur*, n., (lit. & fig.) the end of the road, a rough time: 日暮途窮 poor and helpless.

窈 62A.50-9

yaau.

窈冥 *yaaumirng*, adj., dark, fathomless (also wr. 杳冥).
窈窕 *yaurtiaau*, adj., (1) (AC) poised and charming; (2) engaging, enticing; (3) (AC) deep hidden.

窵 62A.50-9

diauh.

Adj. Far, distant: 窵遠 ditto.

§ 62A.63 (穴/丶)

窯 62A.63-8

yaur.
[Var. 窰]

§ 62A.70 (穴/ㄴ)

窀 62A.70-1

jun.

窀穸 *junshih*, n., a grave.

竈 62A.70-1

tzauh.
[Pop. 灶]

N. A cooking stove: 竈火 a kitchen stove; 竈兒 ditto; 竈火炕 the empty space inside a kitchen stove where the fire burns; 竈窩 ditto; 竈突 the kitchen chimney; 倒竈 have bad luck, suffer loss (reverse), meet with failure (rebuff, disaster); 分竈 (of members of the same household) have separate kitchens; 祭竈 to sacrifice to the kitchen god; 辭竈 bid farewell to the kitchen god on the 23rd day of the 12th lunar month when he goes to make his annual report to the God of Heaven; 送竈 ditto; 封竈 stop cooking fresh meals on the Lunar New Year's Eve.

竈戶 *tzauhhuh*, n., formerly, a worker in saltworks.
竈君 *tzauhjyun*, n., god of the kitchen.
竈兒上的 *tzauh'l'shang'de*, n., (coll.) the cook in a restaurant.
竈馬 *tzauhmaa*, n., (1) (zoo.) a kind of cricket usu. found in the kitchen (also 竈雞); (2) a paper image of the kitchen god (竈王馬兒).
竈神 *tzauh-shern*, n., god of the kitchen.
竈下養 *tzauh-shiah-yaang*, n., (AC) a cook.
竈心土 *tzauhshintuu*, n., (Chin. med.) earth from the center of a earthen cooking stove.
竈頭 *tzauhtour*, n., kitchen place.

窺 62A.70-1

kuei.
[Var. 闚]

V. i. & t. (1) To peep, watch stealthily: 偷窺 ditto. (2) To watch with limited vision (as through a keyhole): 管窺蠡測 watch the sky from a tube, measure the sea with a shell—(fig.) (self-deprecatory) according to my (limited) view; 得窺一斑 able to see one ringed spot on a leopard, or 全豹 the whole leopard —(fig.) see a sample of s.t., or in its entirety.

窺伺 *kueisyh*, v.t., to watch secretly (a person's movements), or watch for an opening for attack.
窺探 *kueitahn*, v.i. & t., to spy on, to trail and discover (enemy situation, etc.).
窺測 *keuitseh*, v.t., to conjecture from what little is known.

窕 62A.70–2

tiaau.

Adj. See 窈[A]窕 62A.50.

竄 62A.70–9

tsuahn.

V. i. (1) To flee and hide: 逃竄 ditto: 抱頭鼠竄 run away frightened like a rat. (2) To interpolate text: 竄改 *-gaai*↓.

竄伏 *tsuahnfur*, v. i., to flee into hiding.
竄改 *tsuahngaai*, v. t., to alter, adulterate text.
竄匿 *tsuahnnih*, v. i., see *-fur*↑.

究 62A.70–9

jiouh (**jiou*).

V. t. To study, examine, investigate, probe, delve into: 究問 *-wehn*, 究辦 *-bahn*↓; 研究 to study, do research; 推究 analyze, probe, investigate; 考究 delve into, go thoroughly into (a case, question), also adj., fashionable, stylish; 深究 probe to the bottom; 根究 get to the root of a matter; 窮究 make a thorough investigation of; 追究 follow up a clue, probe: 追究責任 to fix responsibility (for misdeed, wrongdoing), allot blame; 既往不究 let bygones be bygones; 講究 stylish, fastidious, chic; 學究 a pedant; 老學究 an old-fashioned scholar.

Adv. After all, in the end, ultimately: 究竟 *-jihng*↓; 終究 finally, in the last analysis; 究欲如何 what do you want, anyway?

究辦 *jiouhbahn*, v. t., investigate and mete out due punishment to (person involved).
究斷 *jiouhduahn*, v. t., investigate and decide.
究詰 *jiouhjier*, v. t., ask for an explanation.
究竟 *jiouhjihng*, (1) adv., after all, in the end; (2) n., the whys and the wherefores: 探索究竟 try to find out the why and wherefore.
究細兒 *jiouhshieh'l* (**jiou-*), v. t., make a detailed investigation of.
究問 *jiouhwehn*, v. t., examine, question (a suspect, criminal), inquire into.

§ 62A.72 (穴/心)

窓 62A.72–9

chung.
[Pop. of 囱 62A.41]

窗 62A.72–9

chuang.
[Var. of 囱 62A.41]

§ 62A.80 (穴/八)

竇 62A.80–1

douh.

N. (1) A hole, kennel: 鼻竇, 耳竇 nostril, the ear; hiding place: 弊竇 breeding place for corrupt practices; 疑竇 suspicion, what breeds suspicion. (2) A surname.

§ 62A.81 (穴/人)

窾 62A.81–1

kuaan.

窾竅 *kuaanchiauh*, n., innermost recesses (of heart, matter).

突 62A.81–1

tur.

N. (AC) chimney: 曲突徙薪 "rectify blocked chimney and remove firewood"—advice to take precautions in time.

V.i. (1) Conflict: 衝突 conflict (with regulations, persons); 唐突 offend (person). (2) Shoot out, make abrupt sortie, break ranks: 突圍, 突破, 突擊 *-weir*, *-poh*, *-jir*↓.

Adj. Outstanding: 突出 *-chu*↓.

Adv. Abruptly, suddenly: 突如其來 phr., suddenly come, happen, appear; 突告失踪 suddenly disappear (of person); 突飛猛進 make a spurt of progress.

突變 *tur-biahn*, n., sudden change; (biol.) mutation.
突起 *tur-chii*, v.i., (of contour, event) suddenly arise; bulge.
突騎 *tur-chir*, n., cavalry for breaking up enemy rank.
突出 *tur-chu*, v.i., be outstanding.
突攻 *tur-gung*, v. i., to charge (in battle).
突擊 *tur-jir*, v.i. & t., make surprise attack.
突厥 *Turjyuer*, n., anc. Turks' kingdom; Turks, Turkic tribe.
突破 *tur-poh*, v.t., break through (enemy ranks).
突然 *turrarn*, adv., abruptly, unexpectedly.
突襲 *turshir*, v. i. & t., sudden raid.

突梯(滑稽) *turti(guuji)*, adj., humorous, jocular.
突突 *turtur*, v.i., (heart) palpitate.
突圍 *tur-weir*, v.i., break through siege, make sortie.
突兀 *turwuh*, adj., towering, distinguished, prominent (monument, stature).

§ 62A.82 (穴/乂)

竅 62A.82-9

chiauh.

N. (1) An aperture: 七竅 the seven apertures on person's head, see 七 10.70; 開竅兒 open up one's mind; 一竅不通 (lit.) "all apertures blocked up"—(of person) do not know a thing. (2) A key to understanding: 訣竅 a formula for remembering (instructions, etc.); 竅門, 竅兒 guide to secret or special techniques.

§ 62A.83 (穴/乛)

邃 62A.83-8

sueih.

Adj. Deep: 深邃, 精邃 deep, profound (scholarship).

窆 62A.83-9

biaan.

V. t. To lower coffin into grave; to bury.

窳 62A.83-9

yuu.

Adj. Bad, (goods) inferior in quality; deteriorated, decadent.

窳敗 *tuubaih*, v.i., deteriorate.
窳惰 *yuuduoh*, adj., (LL) weak and lazy.
窳陋 *yuulouh*, adj., degenerated, vulgar.
窳民 *yuu-mirn*, n., (LL) degenerated people.

§ 62A.93 (穴/く)

窶 62A.93-2

jyuh.

Adj. (LL) in poverty: 窶人子 children of a poor family: 貧窶 poor financially.

窬 62A.93-8

yur.
[Wr. form 窬 62A.00]

SECTION 62S

§ 62S.00 (宀S/亅)

剜 62S.00-2

wan.

V. t. To carve out (flesh): 剜肉醫(補)瘡 cut out good flesh to heal sore, sinking good money after bad; (related 刓 *waan* 30S.00).

割 62S.00-2

ge.

V. t. (1) Cut with a knife, cut off: 割破手 cut one's hand; 割股 cut off a piece of the flesh from the thigh to cure parents' illness—act of filial piety; 割肉 buy a cut of meat; 割席 *-shir* ↓; 割鬚 cut off one's beard; 割勢 castrate; 刀割 suffer a knife cut; 割靴子 *-shyuetz* ↓. (2) Divide, partition, cede, split, give away: 分割 divide, apportion; 割地 cede territory; 割裂 split into pieces; 割據 *-jyuh*, 割捨 *-shee*, 割讓 *-rahng*, 割愛 *-aih* ↓.

割愛 *ge-aih*, v. t., give away or part with what one loves.
割據 *gejyuh*, v. t., annex, occupy (a territory).
割讓 *gerahng*, v. t., cede (a territory) to a foreign country.
割捨 *geshee*, v. t., give or cast away.
割席 *ge-shir*, v. i., break up an old friendship.
割靴子 *ge-shyuetz*, v. i., (sl.) cut in on a friend in relation to a prostitute.

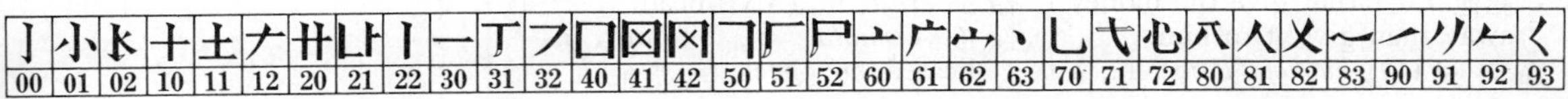

§ 62S.22 (宀S/丨)

鄆 62S.22-3

yuhn.

N. A surname.

§ 62S.40 (宀S/口)

豁 62S.40-8

huo (**huoh*, **huar*, **heh*).

N. A crack: 豁口兒, 豁嘴 *-koou'l*, *-tzueei* ↓.

V.t. (1) To risk life for, to fight for: 他和我豁上了 he and I started a fight; 豁命, 豁著 *-mihng*, *-'je* ↓. (2) 豁命 I'll risk everything. (3) (**huoh*) Exempt from tax payment: 豁免 *-miaan* ↓. (4) (**huar*) See 豁拳 *-chyuarn* ↓.

Adj. (1) Cracked (pot), split (lip): 豁脣 *-churn* ↓. (2) (**heh*) Clear, open: 豁亮, 豁達 *-liahng*, *-dar* ↓.

豁鼻子 *huo-birtz*, phr., to reveal s.o.'s secret.
豁脣(子) *huochurn(-tz)*, n., harelip, a harelipped person; adj., harelipped.
豁拳 **huarchyuarn*, v.i., to play the finger-guessing game at wine party.
豁達 **huohdar*, adj., (1) 豁達大度 generous; (2) open-minded, liberal-minded.
豁著 *huo'je*, v. t., (1) to stake all, to risk: 我豁著這條命 I'll fight with my life; 豁著這幾塊錢 I'll risk these few dollars; (2) would rather: 豁著把這筆錢送人, 也不給他 I'd rather give the money away than give it to him.
豁口兒(子) *huokoou'l(-tz)*, n., a crack (in pot, etc.).
豁亮 **hehliahng*, adj., open and well-lighted.
豁露 *huo'lu*, n., silk border of fur coat.
豁免 **huohmiaan*, v. t., to exempt from (taxes, fees).
豁命 *huo-mihng*, v. i., to risk life for s.t.
豁然 **huohrarn*, adv., open up with a flash of understanding: 豁然貫通 suddenly saw the light; 豁然開朗 the view suddenly cleared up.
豁子 *huotz*, n., a crack (in utensil, wall); a harelip.
豁嘴 *huo-tzueei*, n. & adj., harelip, harelipped.

§ 62S.80 (宀S/八)

額 62S.80-3

er.

N. (1) The forehead. (2) The front and top signboard of a shop or hall: 匾額. (3) Quota, amount (of money), total number of (soldiers in unit, men in group, etc.): 名額, 人額 the total or approximate number of people; 兵額 number of soldiers; 學額 quota of students, also a scholarship (subsidy); 款額 amount of money available; 缺額 deficiency, vacancy; 超額 excess (number); 額滿 all available posts, seats (in theater, etc.) taken; 額內 within the quota or fixed amount or number; 巨額 a big amount.

額駙 *erfuh* (sp. pr. *-'fu*) n., (Manchu) husband of princess.
額黃 *erhuarng*, n., yellow painted forehead of woman, current in 六朝, 3rd to 6th cen. and in Tarng Dyn.
額角 *erjyuer*, n., temples of head.
額顱 *erlur*, n., (MC) head.
額面 *ermiahn*, n., amount indicated on check (=票面).
額手 *ershoou*, v. i., as in 額手相慶 formerly, to place hands over forehead in greeting or congratulation.
額數(兒) *ershuh('l)* (*-'shu'l*), n., fixed number; number or amount.
額子 *ertz*, n., ditto.
額外 *erwaih*, n., extra, in addition to required or prescribed number.
額緣 *eryuarn*, n., the top frame (of window), border (of painting).

§ 62S.82 (宀S/乂)

皸 62S.82-2

jyun.

V. i. To chap: 皸烈 (of skin) be chapped.

SECTION 63

§ 63.00 (丶/亅)

挲 63.00

suo.

V.t. See 摩^A抄 61.00.

学 63.00

shyuer.
[Abbr. of 學 90.00]

§ 63.01 (丶/小)

柒 63.01

chi.

Adj. Seven, corresponding to "capital" for 七 (in writing checks).

染 63.01

raan.

V. t. (1) To dye: 染布, 染紙, 染衣服, 染指甲, 染頭髮 dye cloth, paper, dress, fingernails, hair; 染色 *-seh*↓; 染一染 have s.t. dyed; 染坊 a dyer's shop; 洗染店 a laundry and dyeing shop; 染缸 dyeing jars; 染工 a dyer; 臘染 batik. (2) To contract, catch, incur, become infected with: 染病 *-bihng*↓; 染患, 染上, 染着 be infected by; 染惡習 acquire a bad habit, (spec.) be addicted to opium smoking; 染毒 contract venereal disease; 染指 *-jyy*↓; 傳染 catch by infection: 傳染病 infectious, contagious disease; 習染 be accustomed (inured) to, acquire the habit of. (3) To soil, make dirty, contaminate: 染汚 *-wu*↓; 有染 have illicit sexual relations with a man (woman); 沾染 be tainted with, acquire (a bad habit); 汚染 pollute: 空氣 (飲水) 汚染 air (water) pollution. (4) Apply (ink, paint) to paper.

染病 *raan-bihng*, v. i., contract a disease, fall sick, be ill.
染逮 *raandaih*, v. i., (LL) be implicated (in crime).
染翰 *raan-hahn*, v. i., to wet writing brush with ink and be ready to write.
染化 *raanhuah*, v. i., come under the influence of a moral teacher.
染指 *rarn-jyy*, v. i., have a finger in the pie; 染指草 (bot.) the balsam.
染料 *raan-liauh*, n., dyestuffs.
染惹 *rarnree*, v. t., to soil, pollute, taint.
染色 *raanseh*, v. t., to dye, apply color to; 染色體 (biol.) chromosomes.
染習 *raanshir*, v. i., (Budd.) be contaminated by bad habit or customs.
染汚 *raanwu*, v. t., (1) to stain, pollute, contaminate; (2) be infected by (disease).

梁 63.01

liarng.

N. (1) (Unnecessary var. 樑) beam: 棟梁 beam and rafters; 社會棟梁 pillars of society; 梁上君子 "the gentleman on the beam" (allu.)—thief. (2) A bridge. (3) Ridge: 脊梁 spinal column; 鼻梁 nose bridge. (4) A surname.

渠 63.01

chyur.

N. Sewerage, drain, canal: 水到渠成 what happens without extra effort.

Pron. (LL) he: 渠稱 he says; 渠等, 渠輩 they, those people; 渠儂 (Shanghai dial.) he, the other person; 渠 (Cantonese dial.) he; 渠地 they.

Adj. Big, chief: 渠魁 *-kuei*↓.

渠衝 *chyurchung*, n., anc. heavy cart for ramming city gates.
渠渠 *chyurchyur*, adj., (1) (AC) (of mansion) deep and broad; (2) 其義則渠渠然 (AC) then the meaning (of law) is constrained.
渠答 *chyurdar*, n., ball-shaped spikes thrown on ground to obstruct cavalry.
渠魁 *chyurkueir*, n., rebel chief.
渠帥 *chyurshuaih*, n., rebel leader (also wr. 渠率).

粱 63.01

liarng.
[Dist. 梁]

N. Grain as food: 膏粱, 粱肉 grain and meat—signifying good living; 高粱 common sorghum; 高粱酒 spirits made from sorghum.

棨 63.01

chii.

N. Anc. military tally, in the shape

of a halbert, for transmitting messages: 棨戟 ditto; 棨信 message provided with tally.

桼 63.01

tzy.

N. (1) Sacrificial rice: 桼盛 (pr. *-cherng*) rice and other kinds of grain offered to gods in sacrificial vessels. (2) The various kinds of grain.

綮 63.01

chii (**chihng*).

N. (1) Interch. 棨 63.01. (2) (**chihng*) 肯^綮 21A.42.

---

§ 63.02 (丶/⺦)

永 63.02

yuung.

N. A surname.

Adj. & adv. (1) Ever, forever, permanent, -ly: 永遠 *-yuaan*↓; 永垂不朽 (fame) will go down to posterity; 永不分離 never will be separated again, always together; 永不敍用 (punishment for offending official) name to be struck out from civil service henceforth. (2) Eternal: 永生 *-sheng*↓. (3) (AC) long: 永晝, 永夜 *-jouh*, *-yeh*↓; 永日, 永年 *-ryh*, *-niarn*↓; 誰謂河永 (AC) who says that the river is too long?

永安 *yuung-an*, phr., eternal peace.

永輩子 *yuungbeeihtz*, adv., for life: 永輩子不得翻身 subjugated forever.

永別 *yuung-bier*, phr., parting forever.

永恆 *yuungherng*, adj., permanent, lasting, eternal.

永劫 *yuungjier*, adv., (Budd.) forever and ever.

永久 *yurngjioou*, adj. & adv., permanent, -ly, forever.

永晝 *yuung-jouh*, n., the livelong day.

永誌 *yuung-jyh*, v. i., to be remembered always: 永誌不忘 to remember forever.

永訣 *yuung-jyuer*, phr., see *-bier* ↑.

永命 *yuung-mihng*, n., (LL) long life.

永慕 *yuung-muh*, phr., to remember forever.

永年 *yuung-niarn*, n., (1) a long life; (2) a whole long year.

永日 *yuung-ryh*, n., the livelong day.

永生 *yuungsheng*, n., the eternal life.

永巷 *yuung-shiahng*, n., (AC) the "long alley" for imprisoning palace maids.

永壽 *yuungshouh*, n., longevity.

永世 *yuungshyh*[1], adv., forever, for life: 永世不忘 will never forget (kindness).

永逝 *yuung-shyh*[2], phr., to pass away forever.

永夜 *yuung-yeh*, n., the whole night.

永逸 *yuung-yih*, phr., 一勞永逸 to do s.t. well so that one never has to do it again (as a completely new installation instead of constant repairs).

永遠 *yurngyuaan*, adv., forever, always: 永遠記得 remember always.

良 63.02

liarng.

N. (1) Good people: 賢良 the good and able people, Hahn period system of selection for posts; 誣良爲盜 accuse good people as robbers; 迫良爲娼 force good family girls to be prostitutes; 從良 (of prostitutes) return to decent life; 良民, 良家 *-mirn*, *-jia*↓. (2) Conscience: 天良; 良心 *-shin*↓. (3) A surname.

Adj. (1) Good, law-abiding, decent: 良家 *-jia*↓. (2) Good, nice: 良機 nice opportunity; 良緣 good chance, good match for marriage; 良圖, 良策 good plan; the good and able in certain professions: 良師, 良醫 good teacher, doctor; 良將, 良相 good general, minister; 賢妻良母 good wife and loving mother as ideal of womanhood; 存心不良, see 良心 *-shin*↓; 不良於行 walk with difficulty; 不良少年 juvenile delinquent. (3) Good in quality: 良金 good quality gold; 良金美玉 (fig.) good advice, writing; 良田 fertile land, good quality farm; 良藥 good medicine. (4) Nice and pleasant: 良晤 pleasant meeting of friends; 良辰美景(奈何天) (what to do with) such a beautiful day in such pleasant surroundings? 如此良夜何 what to do with such a beautiful night? (5) Born, untaught: 良知, 良能 *-jy*, *-nerng*↓.

Adv. (1) (LL) very: 良久, 良多, 良深 very long, very many, very deep; 用心良苦 done out of deep-felt affection in roundabout way (help to friends, etc.). (2) (LL) indeed: 良有以也 (thus we see) indeed there was a good reason.

良導體 *liarngdauhtii*, n., (phys.) good conductor.

良方 *liarngfang*, n., good recipe.

良家 *liarngjia*, n. & adj., good decent family: 良家子, 婦人 son, women of good families; 良家女 good family girl, not a professional.

良知 *liarngjy*, n., conscience, instinctive moral sense.

良民 *liarngmirn*, n., law-abiding people.

良能 *larngnerng*, n., innate ability.

良善 *liarngshahn*, adj. & n., kind, humane (heart), good (breeding, family); meekness.

良心 *liarngshin*, n., conscience; 說良心話 to be quite fair; 良心發

現 stung by conscience.
良友 *liarng-yoou*, n., good companion.

裟 63.02

sha.

N. See 袈▵裟 91.02, cassock.

§ 63.10 (丶/十)

斗 63.10

doou.

N. (1) A peck, a dry measure, containing 10升: 升斗小民 poor people, peck and hamper people. (2) A liquid measure: 酒百斗 a hundred 斗 of wine; 市斗 10 catties of rice or 1.63 gallons; 水斗 a ladle, dipper. (3) The Constellation *Ursa Major*, the dipper, also called 北斗 the Northern Star; 南斗 constellation in Sagittarius; 滿天星斗 a starry night; (fig.) filled with puzzles and perplexities; 斗轉參橫 the dipper handle turns and the Constellation Orion is across, the daybreak. (4) The peck used as symbol of s.t. small: 斗城, 斗室, 斗帳 small city, room, tent.

斗膽 *dourdaan*, adj., presumptuous.
斗店 *dooudiahn*, n., grain shop.
斗方 *doufang*, n., sheets about one foot square with inscription for pasting on wall; 斗方名士 (contempt.) poetasters.
斗拱 *dourguung*, n., wooden square blocks supporting beams and girders.
斗箕 *doou-ji*, n., fingerprint, consisting of rounded (斗) and open (箕=dust bin) whorls.
斗記 *dooujih*, n., ditto.
斗笠 *dooulih*, n., large rain hat.
斗門 *doumern*, n., sluice gate.
斗篷 *doou'peng*, n., Chin. style overcoat, with hood covering head and neck.
斗筲 *dooushau*, n., rice basket: 斗筲之人 a rice-bag, Confucius' description of officials of his times.
斗宿 *dooushiouh*, n., the Constellation *Ursa Major*.
斗紋 *doouwern*, n., fingerprint containing spiral whorls.

準 63.10

juun.

[Err. var. 凖; dist. 准 63A.11]

N. (1) The nose: 鼻準 tip of the nose; 隆準 nose with a high bridge; 準頭 *-tour* ↓. (2) Target: 破準 (=破的) hit the target; 瞄準 take aim. (3) Standard, rule, guideline: 準則, 準繩 *-tzer*, *-sherng* ↓; 標準 standard; 以此爲準 take this as standard or model.

Adj. & adv. (1) According to: 準此 according to this (description, etc.); see 准▵此 63A.11. (2) Reliable, sharp, accurate, -ly: 準確 *-chyueh* ↓; 準落兒 *-lauh'l* ↓; 準脾氣 stable temperament; 沒準脾氣 unpredictable temperament; 準時 *-shyr* ↓; 準時候 punctually; 準八時入席 dinner served at 8 o'clock sharp; 準期 *-chir* ↓; 說話不準 one's words are not dependable. (3) Definite, -ly: 準定 *-dihng* ↓; 準來 will come definitely; 那準不對 that is definitely wrong; 沒準兒 see *-juun'l* ↓.

準備 *juunbeih*, v. i. & t. & n., prepare, -ation.
準成 *juuncherng*[1], adj., definite, reliable: 這件事不大準成 this matter is not very dependable.
準程 *juuncherng*[2], n., definite standard.
準期 *juun-chir*, adv., punctually: 準期發出 will send out punctually, according to set date.
準確 *juunchyueh*, adj. & adv., accurate, -ly; definite, -ly: 這話不大準確 that is not quite correct.
準的 *juundih*, n., goal, aim.
準定 *juundihng*, adv., definitely (=一定).
準話 *juun-huah*, n., honest words or statement.
準矱 *juunhuoh*, n., (AC) see *-sherng* ↓.
準斤 *juunjin*, n., (of sales) as in 那店賣的是準斤 that shop gives you honest weight.
準兒 *juun'l* (*-jun'l*), n., certainty; 沒準兒 adv., uncertain, one cannot be certain.
準落兒 *juunlauh'l*, n., a (coll.) dependable way of living: 他總算有準落兒了 at last he has a dependable job.
準擬 *jurnnii*, v. i., fully intend to.
準譜兒 *jurn-puu'l*, n., known and set rules, standard: 沒準譜兒 without any rules or standard.
準人 *juunrern*, n., (1) (AC) one who carries out the law; (2) (coll.) assigned person.
準舌頭 *juun-sher'tou*, phr., 沒準舌頭 (coll.) one's words are not dependable, trustworthy.
準繩 *juunsherng*, n., standard or guide of conduct.
準星 *jun-shing*, n., gun sight.
準式 *juunshyh*, n., see *-tzer* ↓.
準時 *juun-shyr*, adv., punctual, -ly.
準頭 (1) *juuntour*, n., (fortuneteller) tip of the nose; (2) (-'tou) (coll.) standard.
準則 *juuntzer*, n., standard, guideline.

肇 63.10

jauh.

V. i. (LL) to originate, to set a beginning and lead to later develop-

良裟斗準肇

亅	小	⺊	十	土	ナ	卄	⺊	丨	一	丁	フ	口	区	冈	冂	厂	尸	亠	广	宀	丶	乚	弋	心	八	人	乂	一	丿	丿	⺊	く
00	01	02	10	11	12	20	21	22	30	31	32	40	41	42	50	51	52	60	61	62	63	70	71	72	80	81	82	83	90	91	92	93

ments: 肇事 create an incident; 肇訟 cause a lawsuit; 肇國 found a country; 肇歲 begin a new year.

肇端 *jauhduan*, v. i., (1) to have beginning in; (2) to create an incident.
肇禍 *jauh-huoh*, v. i., to create or lead to disaster.
肇建 *jauhjiahn*, v. i. & t., to found (a large undertaking).
肇亂 *jauh-luahn*, v. i., to create disorder or rebellion.
肇釁 *jauhshihng*, v. i., to incite trouble, cause a break in relations; create an accident..
肇始 *jauh-shyy*, v. i., to begin, to assume form.
肇造 *jauhtzauh*, v. i., to create, found (a country, dynasty).

§ 63.11 (丶/土)

塗 63.11

tur.

N. (1) Mud: 塗炭 *-tahn*↓. (2) (Interch. 途 esp. LL roadside): 塗有餓殍 corpses of people who died of famine are seen by the roadside; 遇諸塗 met on the way; 道聽塗說 hearsay.

V. t. (1) To apply, smear: 塗上顏色 apply color; 塗一塗 smear it over; 塗不好 cannot paint or apply color well; 以粉塗面, 塗粉 apply powder on face; 塗膏 apply ointment; 塗脂抹粉 apply make-up. (2) Scribble badly, disfigure with marks and lines, cross out lines in composition: 別在牆上亂塗 don't scribble or draw on the wall; 塗消作廢 invalidate by crossing or blotting out; 塗改, 塗竄, 塗鴉 *-gaai, -tsuahn, -ya*↓; 一敗塗地 be completely routed in battle or venture ("bite the dust"); 肝腦塗地 entrails smear the ground (of defeated army). (3) (AC) to besmear (person's name).

塗附 *turfuh*, v. i., aggravate evil: 如塗塗附 (AC allu.) like piling up mud on mud.
塗改 *turgaai*, v. t., cross out lines in composition.
塗料 *turliauh*, n., color paint.
塗抹 *turmoo*, v. t., smear over; write in slipshod manner.
塗飾 *turshyh*, v. t., paint over (objects).
塗炭 *turtahn*, v. i. & t., trample people like mud and ashes: 塗炭生靈 or be so trampled; 生靈塗炭 i. e., treat people's lives with utter disregard.
塗竄 *turtsuahn*, v.t., to delete or interpolate passage.
塗鴉 *turya*, v. i., (derog. of) bad writing, esp. bad calligraphy.
塗乙 *turyii*, v. t., cross out and make a "reverse" mark (ᔕ) in composition.

§ 63.30 (丶/一)

盜 63.30

dauh.
[Err. var. 盜]

N. Thief, burglar, brigand: 強盜 robber; 海盜 pirate; 盜亦有道 (play on sound *dauh*) thieves have their code of honor.

V. t. To rob, steal: 盜掠, 盜劫 raid, ransack, rob; 被盜 be robbed; to cheat: 盜用公款 embezzle public funds; 盜賣 sell what is not one's own (property); 盜墓 rob a grave; 欺世盜名 (derog. of writers, artists) win notoriety or undeserved popular success by cheap means.

盜案 *dauh-ahn*, n., case of robbery, burglary.
盜版 *dauh-baan*, n., pirate edition.
盜竊 *dauchieh*, v. i., to steal.
盜匪 *dauhfeei*, n., bandit.
盜汗 *dauhhahn*, v. i., perspire during sleep.
盜寇 *dauhkouh*, n., bandit, robber.
盜藪 *dauh-soou*, n., thieves' lair.
盜賊 *dauhtzeir*, n., thieves and brigands.

盪 63.30

dahng.

V.i. & t. (1) U.f. 蕩 20A.50, to cleanse, drift, be agitated, etc. (2) Rarely used for 搪, 擋 to block off.

盪鞦韆 *dahng chiou-chian*, v. i., to sit on a swing.
盪滌 *dahngdir*, v. i. & t., to rinse, cleanse: 盪滌我心 (of scenery) refreshes my heart.
盪口 *dahng-koou*, v.i., rinse mouth.
盪漾 *dahngyahng*, v.i., adrift or afloat.

§ 63.40 (丶/口)

咨 63.40

tzy.

N. One form of official document, a memorandum: 咨文 *-wern*↓.

V. i. & t. (1) V. i., to sigh: 咨嗟 *-jie*↓; 咨咨 make a long sigh. (2) V. t., consult, discuss with: 咨謀 *-mour*↓; 咨詢 *-shyurn*↓; 咨訪 *-faang*↓.

咨請 *tzychiing*, v. t., to make official request, seek official opinion.
咨訪 *tzyfaang*, v. t., seek the opinion of, talk over (with official).

A　　B　　C

咨嗟 *tzyjie*, v. i., to sigh in regret or admiration.
咨謀 *tzymour*, v. i., take counsel with.
咨詢 *tzyshyurn*, v. t., to consult (person), esp. in official business.
咨文 *tzwern*, n., a memorandum between government offices of equal rank.

啓 63.40

chii
[see 啟 63S.82]

誉 63.40

yuh.
[Abbr. of 譽 90.40]

§ 63.41 (丶/図)

甾 63.41

liour.
[Abbr. of 留 90.41]

§ 63.50 (丶/㇕)

门 63.50

mern.
[Abbr. of 門 52B.00]

§ 63.63 (丶/丶)

鯊 63.63

sha.

N. (1) The shark. (2) A small fish which buries itself in the mud.

§ 63.70 (丶/乚)

瓷 63.70

tsyr.
[Pop. of 甆 80.70]

N. Porcelain.

瓷器 *tsyrchih*, n., porcelain ware.
瓷磚 *tsyrjuan*, n., enamel bricks.
瓷胎 *tsyrtai*, n., molded crockery before firing.
瓷土 *tsyrtuu*, n., kaolin.
瓷瓦兒 *tsyr-waa'l*, n., bits of broken china.
瓷窰 *tsyryaur*, n., kiln.

凴 63.70

pirng.
[Pop. of 凭 91.70]

V. t. To lean (on a low table, a railing).

覚 63.70

jiaau, jyuer.
[Abbr. of 覺 90.70]

§ 63.72 (丶/心)

恣 63.72

tzyh (also *tzy*).

V. i. Do as one pleases, indulge oneself: 恣情 give free rein to one's passions; 恣肆 throw off restraint, act with a high hand, (of writings) forceful; 恣意 indulge one's wishes, do as one likes; 恣縱 indulge in sensual pleasures; 恣行無忌 act recklessly.

慂 63.72

yuung.

V. t. See 慫慂 91.72.

憑 63.72

pirng.

N. Support, supporting evidence: warrant, certifying paper: 以此爲憑 this will serve as certification; 空口無憑 formula for certificate "as oral promise is not enough"; 憑據, 憑照, 憑證 *-jyuh*, *-jauh*, *-jehng*↓; 文憑 diploma.

V. t. (1) Lean on: 憑欄遠眺 or 憑眺 leaning on balcony and looking at the distance. (2) Base on, rely on, use as permit: 你憑甚麼說這話 what is your basis for saying so? 憑券入場 admission by ticket; 憑良心說 (say this on one's conscience) to be fair; 憑高臨下 advantage of commanding position overlooking below; 憑險 (of fort) based on natural strategic position (mountain pass, etc.).

憑 懣 懘 資 燙

(3) Let, with sense equiv. Eng. "come what may": 憑他怎麽説 let him say what he will; 憑他怎樣駡我 let him say what nasty things he wants; 憑你怎樣 do your damnedest (I will not yield).

憑弔 *pirngdiauh*, v. i., evoke sense of the past by looking at old historical places.
憑仗 *pirngjahng*, n. & v. t., basis for support; to rely on (s. t. or s. o.).
憑照 *pirngjauh*, n., certificate, permit.
憑證 *pirngjehng*, n., evidence.
憑摺 *pirngjer*, n., passbook, like savings passbook.
憑藉 *pirngjieh*, n. & v. t., reliance, support; rely on (connections, etc.).
憑準 *pirngjuun*, n., reliable standard.
憑據 *pirngjyuh*, n., (usu. wr.) evidence; basis for belief.
憑空 *pirngkung*, adv., without ground or basis: 憑空杜撰 create groundless rumors.
憑恃 *pirngshyh*, n. & v. t., see *-jieh*↑.
憑依 *pirngyi*, n. & v. t., see *-jieh*↑.

懣 63.72

mehn.

Adj. Sad: 憤懣 simmering with rage; 煩懣 depressed, mortified.

懘 63.72

chyh.

Adj. See 怗^{A}滯 22A.40.

§ 63.80 (丶/八)

資 63.80

tzy.

N. (1) Capital, wealth, resources: 資財 *-tsair*, 資本 *-been*, 資產 *-chaan*, 資源 *-yuarn*, 資金 *-jin*, 資業 *-yeh*↓; 家資 family (material) circumstances; 師資 the available supply or quality of teachers; 投資 to invest; 借資 borrow money; 郵資 postage; 筆資 writer's fees; 資遣 terminate s.o.'s service by paying him a lump sum of money; 資送回籍 give (s.o.) money and send him home. (2) Ability, natural endowment: 資賦 innate ability; 天資 native intelligence, aptitude; 資稟 natural endowments; 資質 *-jyr*↓; 資性 inborn character. (3) Qualifications: 資格 *-ger*, 資歷 *-lih*↓; 資履 qualifications and previous experience; 上資 a person of the highest caliber; 資望 *-wahng*↓.

V. t. (1) Furnish, supply, aid, assist: 資給 provide with funds, give monetary assistance; 資助 *-juh*↓; 資兵 aid with troops. (2) To help toward: 以資補助 to help as subsidy; 以資維持 help toward maintenance.

資本 *tzybeen*, n., (econ.) capital: 資本主義 capitalism; 資本家 (econ.) a capitalist; 資本性投資 capital investment.
資產 *tzychaan*, n., (1) wealth, property, riches; (2) (accounting) assets; 資產階級 propertied class, capitalists; 資產負債表 balance sheet of assets and liabilities.
資方 *tzyfang*, n., (econ.) the management (opp. 勞方 labor).
資斧 *tzyfuu*, n., travelling expenses.
資格 *tzyger*, n., one's qualifications or social standing.
資政 *tzyjehng*, n., a senior adviser to the president or, formerly, to ruler.
資金 *tzyjin*, n., capital (funds).
資助 *tzyjuh*, v.t., subsidize, assist financially.
資質 *tzyjyr*, n., inborn character.
資料 *tzyliauh*, n., data, materials for some specific use; 資料室 reference room.
資歷 *tzylih*, n., qualifications and previous experience.
資財 *tzytsair*, n., money, capital, wealth.
資望 *tzywahng*, n., a person's prestige, standing.
資業 *tzyyeh*, n., investment, enterprise, material property.
資源 *tzyyuarn*, n., resources: 天然(人力)資源 natural (manpower) resources.

§ 63.81 (丶/人)

燙 63.81

tahng.

V. t. (1) To scald and cause a burn: 燙傷 be scalded; 燙了泡兒 blister from a burn. (2) To heat up by placing in vessel containing hot water: 燙酒 heat up wine thus. (3) To iron: 燙衣服 to iron (press) clothes; 燙平了 press smooth; 燙得好平好亮 pressed beautifully; 燙焦了 burnt by ironing. (4) To treat (hair) by heat: 燙頭髮 wave by curling-irons or have permanent wave; 燙蠟 fill in with wax or wax a surface. (5) Have hot bath: 燙澡 hot bath; 用熱水燙燙腳 have a hot foot bath.

Adj. Hot to the touch: 很燙, 好燙, 滾燙 very hot; also 燙人: 這湯很燙人 this soup is scalding hot; 不燙了 no longer scalds.

燙斗 *tahngdoou*, n., pressing iron.
燙髮 *tahngfaa*, n., to have permanent wave.
燙手 *tahngshoou*, adj., hot to the touch: (fig.) 這個人很燙手 better not touch this man—keep away from him.
燙藥 *tahngyauh*, n., ointment or lotion for burns.

§ 63.82 (丶/乂)

隻 63.82

shuang.

[Pop. of 雙 91.82]

§ 63.83 (丶/乛)

之 63.83

jy (*'*jy*).

Fin. part. (*'*jy*) (LL) corresponding in meaning to "it": 總之, 總而言之 to sum it up; 要之 the important point is; 易地而居之, 則皆然 if they changed places, they would behave in the same way.

N. The character 之: 之字路 an S-shaped road; 不識之無 do not know even the simplest characters; 之乎者也 four words recognized as fin. part. of the literary language.

Pron. (*-'*jy*) (1) (a) (LL, used in objective case) it, him, her, them: 怒目視之 stare at it (him); 取而代之 take it over; 勸之不聽, 殺之可也 try to persuade him and if he won't listen, you can kill him; 妻之以女 marry one's daughter to him; 然之 (LL) approve of it; 諾之, 許之 (LL) promise him (her) or it; 獎之 (LL) reward him; 呼之 call him; (b) in AC, oft. precedes negative vb.: 未之知, 未之聞, 未之見 never knew it, heard it, or saw it (cf. 不我知 do not know me); 奈之何, 如之何 "why stand for it"—why, how. (2) LL used to indicate possessive case, see Prep.↓.

V. i. (AC & LL) to go: 君將何之 where are you going? 不知所之 do not know where (person) went; 將之楚 was going to 楚; 心之所之 where the mind longs to be.

Adj. (AC) this: 之子于歸 (AC) this girl is going to her new home; 之人也, 之德也 (AC) this type of man, this type of conduct.

Prep. (1) Possessive part., "of", like vern. 的: 汝之過也 this is your fault; 夫子之文章 the literary knowledge of the Master; used largely in mod. Chin. writing where there are several "of's", 之 may replace 的 for variation or dropped: thus "the development of rural education of Taiwan" may be 今日臺灣(的)鄉村教育之發展 or 的發展; 之謂 be the meaning of; 政者, 正之謂也 the meaning of 政 (government) is 正 (order). (2) A preposition of position placed after the n. it governs; thus "before the table" 桌之前; 桌之後, 之上, 之下 behind, on, under the table; 之中, 之間 the midst of; 普天之下 all under heaven; 談話之中, 之間 in (during) the talk; 之外 besides, outside; 月薪之外 beside the monthly salary. (3) (AC) until: 之死矢靡他 I will never marry another person until death. (4) To: 人之其 (=於其) 所親而愛焉 man loves those to whom he is related.

昶 63.83

chaang.

Adj. (1) (AC) a long day. (2) Relaxed and easy.

§ 63.91 (丶/丿)

戶 63.91

huh.

[Usu. wr. 户]

N. (1) Door, esp. one-panelled door: 門戶 door, gate; 窗戶 window. (2) The family: 幾百戶人家 several hundred families; 全戶人口 number of persons in entire family; 富戶 a rich family or person; 家家戶戶 in every home; 家喻戶曉 popularly understood, known to everybody; 戶稅 household tax. (3) A person of certain professions or status: 帳戶, 戶名 name in account book; 存戶 depositor in bank; 店戶 a shopkeeper; 漁戶, 獵戶 a fisherman, a hunter. (4) A surname.

戶部 *huhbuh*, n., formerly, Ministry of Interior.

戶長 *huhjaang*, n., head of family.

戶政 *huhjehng*, n., administration concerning residents and residency.

戶籍 *huhjir*, n., household record.

戶主 *huhjuu*, n., head of family.

戶口 *huhkoou*, n., population (statistics): 戶口檢查 census; 戶口冊 police record of residents.

戶限 *huhshiahn*, n., threshold: 戶限爲穿 many visitors.

戶庭 *huhtirng*, n., courtyard.

戶頭 *huhtour*, n., (1) a personal account in bank; (2) person of status: 大戶頭 a person of financial importance; 找個好戶頭嫁吧 find a rich man and marry him.

戶牖 *huhyoou*, n., doors and windows.

§ 63.93 (丶/く)

 63.93

tzy.

N. (1) Gesture, one's bearing or carriage: See compp.↓; 美姿 beautiful looks. (2) (U.f. 資 *tz*) innate capacity: 天姿 natural endowments.

姿貌 *tzymauh*, n., a woman's looks.
姿媚 *tzymeih*, adj., charming, enchanting.
姿容 *tzyrurng*, n., a woman's looks.
姿色 *tzyseh*, n., feminine beauty.
姿首 *tzyshoou*, n., (of women) a pretty face and beautiful hair.
姿勢 *tzyshyh*, n., gestures, bodily movements, posture.
姿態 *tzytaih*, n., one's bearing or carriage.

娑 63.93

suo.

Adj. 婆△娑 63.93.

娑羅 *suoluor*, n., (1) a tall tree of India, *Shorea robusta*; (2) cf. 桫△羅 10B.91.
娑娑 *suosuo*, adj. & adv., (AC) soft, -ly (like silk).

婆 63.93

por.

N. (1) Woman, dame, crone, (coll. or contempt. as in "that woman"), always in compp. (婆子 *por'tz*); 老婆 old woman, (coll.) wife; 家主婆 housewife, mistress of the home; 苦口婆心 with kind and compassionate persuasion. (2) Abbr. for 婆婆 -'*po*, husband's mother; 公婆 husband's father and mother; 婆家 or 婆婆家 husband's family; 有婆家了 is already betrothed; 婆媳 mother-in-law and daughter-in-law. (3) Woman of certain professions (媒婆 matchmaker, 師婆 medium, 牙婆 procuress, 穩婆 midwife, 藥婆 uneducated woman practitioner of medicine).

婆羅洲 *Porluorjou*, n., Borneo.
婆羅門 *Porluormern*, n., Brahman (-nical); 婆羅門教 Brahmanism; 婆羅門引, name of MC song.
婆娘 *por'niarng*, n., (dial.) lower-class woman.
婆婆 *por'po*, n., husband's mother (婆婆家, husband's family), also loosely, a woman of older generation, addressing one's maternal grandmother.
婆婆媽媽的 *porpormama'de*, adj., effeminate, sissy (of mother's boy); indecisive, hesitant.
婆娑 *porsuo*, adj., (lit.) whirling (of dance), loitering, lingering (of music).

SECTION 63A

§ 63A.00 (氵/亅)

浡 63A.00–1

bor.

Adv. 浡然 (＝勃然) (AC) pushing up, gushing, vigorously alive.

溥 63A.00–1

puu.

N. A surname.

Adj. & adv. Spread wide, covering much area: 溥被 covering wide area (cogn. of 普 80.41).

澍 63A.00–1

shuh.

N. Timely rain.

V. i. To give life like rain to fields.

濤 63A.00–1

taur (tau).

N. Big waves: 波濤, 海濤 sea waves; 松濤 motion and sound of wind through pine forest.

汀 63A.00–3

ting.

N. A sand bar, a shallow islet in a stream: 汀洲 sand shoal, also district name in Fukien.

汙 63A.00-3

wu.

[Var. of 汚 63A.50]

河 63A.00-3

her.

N. (1) A river, stream: 河邊, 河濱, 河畔, 河干 river bank; 河面 river surface; 河口 mouth of river; 河工 river conservancy work; 河牀 river bed; 河心 midstream; 河壩, 河隄 river embankment; 河閘 water gate, lock on river; 河魚 *-yur* ↓; 河鰻 fresh-water eel; 河魚腹疾 (LL) diarrhoea, intestinal troubles (as fish's decay begins from the entrails); 河漂子 one drowned; 吃個河落海乾 eat until a whole fortune disappears; 運河 canal. (2) The Yellow River (黃河) oft. without the modifier "Yellow": oft. appears in names of regions or provinces with reference to the Yellow River, like 河南, 河北, 河內, 河西 see *-narn*, *-beei*, *-neih*, *-shi* ↓; from the usu. muddy character of the Yellow River: 河清, 俟河之清 when the Yellow River is clear—once in a blue moon; 河清海晏 time of peace; 河伯 *-bor* ↓; 河東獅吼 (allu.) reference to hen-pecked husband married to a "roaring lioness." (3) A surname.

河北 *Herbeei*, n., the Hopei Province.
河伯 *herbor*, n., River God: 河伯娶婦 an anc. custom of sacrificing a young beautiful girl as the wife of the river god.
河渠 *herchyur*, n., canal.
河道 *herdauh*, n., course of river.
河防 *herfarng*, n., dam, embankment for preventing flood.
河漢 *herhahn*, n., the Milky Way: (fig.) 勿河漢斯言 do not regard it as empty high talk.
河洲 *her-jou*, n., a river islet.
河梁 *her-liarng*, phr., a river bridge.
河柳 *her-lioou*, phr., willows that grow on river bank.
河流 *herliour*, n., the river current.
河漏 *her'lou*, n., vermicelli made of buckwheat or other flour (forced through sieves).
河洛 *Her-Luoh*, n., The Yellow River and Luoh River (in Honan), see also *-tur* ↓.
河馬 *hermaa*, n., (zoo.) the hippopotamus.
河綿 *hermiarn*, n., fresh-water sponge found in lakes and rivers.
河南 *Hernarn*, n., the Honan Province.
河內 *Herneih*, n., (1) (AC) the land north of the Yellow River bend; (2) Hanoi.
河身 *her-shen*, n., the actual width of river water, not counting exposed river bed.
河西 *Hershi*, n., west of Yellow River (Shensi, Kansuh).
河系 *her-shih*, n., river system.
河灘 *hertan*, n., river rapids.
河圖 *hertur*, n., as in 河圖洛書 mythic diagram said to have s.t. to do with origin of Chin. script and the 八卦 the eight diagrams.
河豚 *herturn*, n., a fish (with delicious meat, but fatally poisonous if in the preparation the liver and roe are not taken out).
河右 *Heryouh*, n., see *-shi* ↑.
河運 *her-yuhn*, v., river transportation.
河魚 *her-yur*, n., fresh-water fish.

冽 63A.00-3

lieh.

[Interch. 洌]

Adj. Cold, chilling, icy: 冽泉 icy spring; 清冽 (of spring water) cold and crystal-clear; 凜冽 (of person's manner, wind) cold, chilly, forbidding.

洌 63A.00-3

lieh.

[Interch. 冽]

Adj. (Of water, wine) crystal-clear: 香洌 fragrant and icy clear.

測 63A.00-4

tseh.

V. t. (1) To conjecture, surmise: 揣測, 臆測 to guess, surmise (motives, intentions, cause, etc.); 推測 to guess, draw conclusions from certain facts; 測不透 cannot guess or penetrate (behind motives). (2) To survey (depth, height), trace (origins): 測量 *-liarng*, 測候 *-houh*, 測繪 *-hueih* ↓; 莫測高深 (of skill, knowledge) beyond one's depth, fathomless; 不測 s.t. untoward which may happen, unpredictable.

測度 *tsehduoh*, v.t., (1) to measure; (2) to surmise.
測桿 *tsehgaan*, n., (surveying) leveling staff (also 竿 *gan*).
測光表 *tsehguang-biaau*, n., exposure meter (photography).
測光器 *tsehguang-chih*, n., photometer.
測候 *tseh-houh*, n., make meteorological observations.
測繪 *tsehhueih*, v.i., to make drafts, blueprints, maps; 測繪員 draftsman, cartographer.
測量 *tsehliarng*, v.t., (math.) to survey; 測量局 survey office; 測

量員 surveyor.

測日鏡 *tsehryh-jihng*, n., heliometer.

測字 *tseh-tzyh*, v.i., practise the art of taking character apart and telling fortune by reading meaning into component parts.

測驗 *tsehyahn*, n. & v.t., (make) tests (in psychology, intelligence, gen. knowledge, physical fitness, etc.).

測音器 *tsehyin-chih*, n., acoustometer.

測遠鏡 *tseh-yuaan-jihng*, n., range finder.

測圓器 *tsehyuarn-chih*, n., cyclometer.

潯 63A.00-5

shyurn.

N. (AC) river bank.

溽 63A.00-5

ruh.

Adj. (1) Wet, damp: 溽暑 humid, sultry; 溽蒸 ditto; 溽熱 oppressively hot; 溽氣蒸騰 boiling hot, sweltering. (2) (AC) rich in flavor, greasy: 飲食不溽 eat a simple diet.

涮 63A.00-5

shuahn.

V. t. (1) To wash: 涮一涮 give it a wash. (2) 涮羊肉 To cook mutton by dipping very thin slices in boiling water, hence 涮鍋子, the usual special 鍋子 (pot) in which the mutton is dipped. (3) To cheat (person).

涮金作 *shuahn-jin-tzuoh*, n., station for washing gold.

潺 63A.00-5

charn.

Adj. Sound of flowing water: 潺潺河水.

潺湲 *charnyuarn*, adj., sound of gurgling or babbling (brook).

潤 63A.00-5

ruhn.

V. t. (1) Moisten, enrich, benefit: 滋潤 moisten, nourish, do good to; 濕潤 to moisten; 潤劑 a demulcent; 潤心養眼 (of things) be good to hear or see ("gladden the heart and please the eye"); 潤一潤 spray (sprinkle) a little water on. (2) Pay for services rendered: 潤筆 *-bii*, 潤毫 *-haur*, 潤資 *-tzy* ↓. (3) Decorate, embellish: 潤飾 *-shyh*, 潤色 *-seh* ↓.

Adj. Soft to the touch: 肥潤 fat, smooth to the touch: 光潤 lustrous (jade), supple (flesh).

潤筆 *ruhn-bii*, n., payment to a calligrapher (painter, writer) for services rendered.

潤腸 *ruhn-charng*, v. i., (Chin. med.) exert a restorative influence on the digestive organs.

潤肺 *ruhn-feih*, v. i., (herb med.) exert a restorative influence on the lungs.

潤格 *ruhn-ger*, n., scale of professional fees charged by painters, writers or calligraphers.

潤毫 *ruhn-haur*, n., ＝潤筆 *-bii* ↑.

潤色 *ruhnseh*, v.t., see *-shyh* ↓.

潤身 *ruhn-shen*, v.i., make life fuller and happier: 富潤屋, 德潤身 wealth enriches one materially, but virtue is its own reward.

潤飾 *ruhnshyh*, v.t., embellish, improve upon, make more beautiful.

潤澤 *ruhntser*, v.t., to polish (style); adj., polished, lustrous, supple.

潤資 *ruhntzy*, n., fee paid to artist or writer.

潤益 *ruhnyih*, n., profits, gains, returns, earnings.

濶 63A.00-5

kuoh.

[Pop. of 闊 52B.00]

澗 63A.00-5

jiahn.

[Usu. wr. 澗]

N. A brook: 山澗 a mountain brook; 澗水 a creek in a valley; 澗溪 a mountain brook.

瀾 63A.00-5

larn.

N. Waves, ripples; see 波[A]瀾 63A.82.

瀾瀾 *larnlarn*, adv., tearfully, weeping bitterly.

瀾漫 *lahnmarn*, adj., (1) (of ideas, thoughts) incoherent: 瀾漫不可收拾 profuse and breaking apart beyond remedy; (2) (of internal decoration) variegated; (3) (of music) formless.

淳 63A.00-6

churn.

Adj. (1) (With few exceptions in adv. usage, usu. interch. 純 93B.70) pure, unadulterated. (2) Simple, unsophisticated. (3) U.f.

醇 mellow (wine).

淳白 *churnbor*, adj., pure, clean.
淳風 *churnfeng*, adj., simple, unsophisticated (customs).
淳古 *churnguu*, adj., unsophisticated, with primitive simplicity.
淳和 *churnher*, adj., simple and kind.
淳厚 *churnhouh*, adj., ditto.
淳潔 *churnjier*, adj., pure, clean (also 純).
淳質 *churnjyr*, adj., primitive and simple.
淳良 *churnliarng*, adj., simple and kind.
淳魯 *churnluu*, adj., ditto.
淳樸 *churnpuu*, adj., ditto.
淳粹 *churntsueih*, adj., unadulterated.

游 63A.00-6

your.
[Var. of 㳺; see also 遊 60.83]

N. (1) Stream: 上游, 下游 upstream, downstream; upper, lower reaches of a river. (2) A surname.

V. i. (1) To swim: 游泳 *-yuung* ↓. (2) To play, play about (interch. 遊): 游於藝 (AC) find relaxation in art; 游戲 *-shih* ↓. (3) To travel (interch. 遊), float about, drift: 游牧, 游擊隊 *-muh*, *-jir-dueih* ↓.

Adj. Floating, drifting: 游民, 游資 *-mirn*, *-tzy* ↓.

游塵 *your-chern*, n., (LL) floating dust.
游宦 *yourhuahn*, v. i., to serve in government at different places.
游擊隊 *yourjir-dueih*, n., guerrillas; 游擊戰 guerrilla warfare.
游離 *yourlir*, adj., afloat, drifting, without a place for anchor: 游離分子 drifters, persons without political affiliation.
游龍 *your-lurng*, phr., a playing, dancing dragon.
游民 *yourmirn*, n., unemployed people, the homeless, vagabonds.
游牧 *yourmuh*, v. i., lead a nomad's life: 游牧民族 nomadic tribe.
游俠 *yourshiar*, n., (AC) champions of the underdog, free-lance fighter.
游戲 *yourshih*, n. & v. i., game, play (also wr. 遊): 游戲人間 fairies descending to earth and worldly pleasures, play through life, (fig.) world of fun and frolic.
游手 *yourshoou*, n., unemployed: 游手好閒之徒 loafers.
游說 *yourshuaih*, v. t., to sell an idea to interested parties.
游士 *your-shyh*, n., (AC) scholars who travelled abroad to find employers.
游辭 *yourtsyr*, n., (1) baseless talk; (2) light or playful remarks.
游資 *yourtzy*, n., idle capital.
游子 *yourtzyy*, n., (1) traveller away from home; (2) (phys.) freed electrons; ions.
游言 *youryarn*, n., (AC) rumor.
游揚 *youryarng*, v. t. (AC) to praise, extol.
游弋 *youryih*[1], v.t., to cruise (as a cruiser), also wr. 遊奕.
游藝 *youryih*[2], n., pastime, amusement; 游藝會 a social party with amusements.
游移 *your'yir*, adj., undecided: 游移兩可.
游泳 *youryuung*, v. i. & n., to swim, swimming; 游泳池 swimming pool; 游泳大會 n., aquacade.

濘 63A.00-6

nihng.

N. Mud: 泥濘 mud.

Adj. Stagnant, muddy: 濘淖 (of road) filled with mud; 濘滯 (of road) muddy.

湔 63A.00-8

jian.

V. t. Cleanse, purge, purify.

湔祓 *jianfur*, v. t., purge of impurities, moral blemishes, evil deeds.
湔濯 *jianjuor*, v. t., see *-fur* ↑.
湔洗 *jianshii*, v. t., to wash clean.
湔雪 *jianshyuee*, v. t., rehabilitate (a person's good name).

渝 63A.00-8

yur.
[Oft. printed 渝]

N. Name for 重慶 Chungking, capital of wartime China.

V. i. To change: 此志不渝 this determination will never change; 至死不渝 will never change until death; 渝盟 go back on one's promise.

浮 63A.00-9

fur (*four*, **fuh*).

V. i. (1) To float, drift, appear on surface: 浮出水面 float on surface; 浮在眼前 (of remembered scenes) appear in the mind; 浮現 appear (of images, mirage); opp. 沉 *chern*: 載浮載沉 now float up, now submerged—uncertain, insecure situation, see 浮沉 *-chern* ↓; 乘桴浮於海 float out to sea on a raft. (2) Exceed: 人浮於事

淳 游 濘 湔 渝 浮

丨	小	⺊	十	土	ナ	卄	⺊	丨	一	丅	フ	口	区	冈	丁	厂	尸	亠	广	宀	丶	乚	弋	心	八	人	乂	乛	冖	丿	𠂉	く
00	01	02	10	11	12	20	21	22	30	31	32	40	41	42	50	51	52	60	61	62	63	70	71	72	80	81	82	83	90	91	92	93

浮 淨 瀏

more personnel or candidates than work available; 罪浮於桀紂 crimes exceed those of well-known tyrants. (3) (*fuh) (Coll.) to swim: 浮水.

Adj. & adv. (1) Oft. prefixed to vbb., denoting excessive, irregular: 浮收 irregular levy; 浮報 false report of expenses; 浮借, 浮記 entry in accounts as temporary loan. (2) Excessive: 浮額 extra, surplus number, sum; 浮利 gross income before deductions; 浮名, 浮譽 empty reputation. (3) Flowery, ornate: 浮豔 purely ornamental; 浮詞, 浮文 puerile verbiage; 浮言 baseless talk. (4) Floating, insecure, transient: 浮生若夢 this floating life is like a dream; 浮厝 transient burial ground. (5) Floating: 浮屍 floating corpse; 浮島 floating, shifting island; 浮煙 floating mist or smoke. (6) Vagrant, superficial, fickle, inconstant: 輕浮 volatile, flighty (of temperament); 浮泛, 浮誇, 浮華 *-fahn*, *-kua*, *-huar* ↓.

浮標 *furbiau*, n., buoy.
浮薄 *furbor*¹, adj., superficial (of knowledge).
浮白 *fur-bor*², v.i., drink a forfeit, from 浮一大白 fine a cup (大白 possibly name of a cup).
浮沉 *fur-chern*, adj. & v.i. & n., uncertain (-ty): 宦海浮沉 uncertainty of official career; 與世浮沉 follow the crowd without personal principles; 付之浮沉 phr., of uncertain mail (may or may not reach addressee).
浮塵子 *furcherntz*, n., (bot.) a crop-destroying insect.
浮簽 *furchian*, n., a pasted marginal note which can be removed.
浮雕 *furdiau*, n., bas-relief.
浮動 *furduhng*, adj. & v.i., (be) restless; (small insects) wriggle about; 浮動率 floating rate of exchange.
浮泛 *furfahn*, adj., vague, superficial.
浮華 *furhuar*, adj., extravagant, showy, luxurious.
浮誇 *furkua*, v.i. & adj., boast, brag, vainglorious, ostentatious.
浮浪 *furlahng*, adj., vagrant, without fixed employment: 浮浪子弟 vagrant or unemployed persons.
浮力 *furlih*, n., buoyancy.
浮面(兒) *furmiahn*(*-miah'l*), n., what floats on top, flotsam.
浮沫 *furmoh*¹, n., scum.
浮沒 *furmoh*², v.i., see *-chern* ↑.
浮漚 *fur-ou*, n., bubbles on water surface.
浮皮(兒) *furpir*(*'l*), n., epidermis; cover (of brochures, etc.).
浮萍 *furpirng*, n., duckweed; symbol of uncertain life, chance meetings.
浮生 *fursheng*, n., ephemeral, floating life; 浮生若夢 life is but a dream; 浮生六記 *Six Chapters of a Floating Life*, a famous autobiography.
浮現 *furshiahn*, v.i., appear (of memory, image, submerged object).
浮水 **fuhshueei*, v.i., to swim.
浮世繪 *furshyhhueih*, n., (Japanese) woodcut cartoon.
浮石 *furshyr*, n., pumice.
浮臺 *furtair*, n., float (bathing beach).
浮頭 *furtour*, n., floating scum, flotsam.
浮屠 *furtur*, n., Buddha (also translated as 佛陀); pagoda; 浮屠道 Buddhism.
浮子 *furtz*, n., float on fishing line.
浮燥 *furtzauh*, adj., restless, violent-tempered, factious.
浮妄 *furwahng*, adj., false (of doctrine).
浮僞 *furweih*, adj., false, misleading.
浮餘 *furyur*, n., surplus.
浮雲 *furyurn*, n., passing clouds, symbol of insubstantial glory: 浮雲朝露 passing clouds and morning dew, not lasting.

淨 63A.00-9

jihng.

N. (Peking opera) an actor with a painted face.

V. t. Cleanse, wash: 淨手 *-shoou*, 淨面 *-miahn* ↓.

Adj. (1) Clean: 潔淨 clean, spotless, immaculate; 打掃得很乾淨 (of a house, room) dusted spotlessly clean; 收拾得乾乾淨淨 have (room, house) tidied up; 明窗淨几 (of a sitting room or study) tastefully furnished and kept spotlessly clean. (2) Pure, unalloyed: 純淨 pure, unmixed. (3) Empty, hollow, bare: 淨空 a cloudless sky; 輸個乾淨 lose every cent in gambling; 偷得乾乾淨淨 have everything stolen and nothing left. (4) Net: see 淨價, 淨重, 淨利 *-jiah*, *-juhng*, *-lih* ↓.

Adv. (1) Entirely: 這裏頭淨是水 there is nothing but water inside here. (2) Only: 屋裏淨剩下他一個人了 he alone is left in the room.

淨宅 *jihng-jair*, v. i., to exorcize evil spirits from a house.
淨價 *jihng-jiah*, n., the net price.
淨重 *jihng-juhng*, n., the net weight.
淨量 *jihng-liahng*, n., ditto.
淨利 *jihng-lih*, n., net profit (opp. 毛利 gross profit).
淨面 *jihng-miahn*, v. i., to wash face.
淨瓶 *jihng-pirng*, n., (Budd.) a washing pot.
淨身 *jihng-shen*, v. t., castrate.
淨手 *jihng-shoou*, v. i., to wash hands.
淨土 *jihngtuu*, n., (Budd.) the Pure Land or Paradise of the West.
淨桶 *jihng-tuung*, n., (Budd.) a urinal or stool.
淨院 *jihng-yuahn*, n., a Buddhist temple.

瀏 63A.00-9

liour.

Adj. (Of wind) whistling fast; (of water) clear.

瀏覽 *liourlaan*, v.i., to browse among books at leisure.

漪 63A.00-9

yi.

Adj. Swirling (water): 漪瀾 a swirl; ripples.

§63A.01 (氵/小)

凍 63A.01-1

duhng.

N. (*'l*) Jelly: 肉凍兒 meat jelly.

V.t. To freeze, congeal: 凍凝 freeze; 凍硬了 (coll.) freeze hard; 凍結 *-jier* ↓; 凍死, 凍斃 frozen to death; 凍殭 benumb, -ed, frozen unconscious.

Adj. Icy cold: 凍冷, 凍手凍腳 freezing cold; 冰凍 icy cold.

凍瘡 *duhngchuang*, n., chilblains, frostbite.
凍結 *duhngjier*, v.t., freeze (funds); freeze hard.
凍餒 *duhngnueei*, v.i., suffer from cold and hunger.
凍肉 *duhng-rouh*, n., frozen meat.
凍石 *duhngshyr*, n., (min.) steatite.
凍藏 *duhng tsarng*, v. i. & n., refrigerate, -tion.
凍原 *duhngyuarn*, n., tundra, arctic and antarctic regions permanently covered with ice.

沐 63A.01-1

muh.

N. A surname.

V.i. & t. Bathe: 沐髮 (LL) shampoo (=洗髮); 沐浴 *-yuh* ↓; 沐雨櫛風 work, travel in wind and rain; (fig.) 沐恩 bathe in superior's love, kindness; 沐猴而冠 (derog.) making a monkey show (stupid political figures).

沐日 *muhryh*, n., (AC) day of bath and rest.
沐浴 *muhyuh*, v.i., (LL) take a bath.

沬 63A.01-1

meih.
[Dist. 沫 ↓]

V. i. (AC) 沬血 bleeding on the face.

沫 63A.01-1

moh.

N. (1) Bubbles, foam on liquid surface, (oft. *-tz*, *'l*): 啤酒沫兒(子) foam of beer; 肥皂沫兒 soap bubbles, foam. (2) Saliva: 口沫, 吐沫.

V. i. (AC) stop.

沫沫丟丟 *moh'mo diu'diu*, n., scum, flotsam.

沭 63A.01-1

shuh.

N. Name of a river in Kiangsu.

淋 63A.01-1

lirn (**lihn*).

N. (Med.) gonorrhea: 淋病 *-bihng* ↓.

V. t. (1) To spray with water, sprinkle: 淋濕 sprinkled wet (as by rain); 淋雨 pouring rain; (Cantonese dial.) drenched in the rain. (2) (**lihn*) To filter.

淋巴 *lirnba*, n., lymph; 淋巴管 lymphatics; 淋巴腺 lymphatic glands.
淋病 *lirnbihng*, n., gonorrhea.
淋漓 *lirnlir*, adj., (of descriptive or oratorical passage) very moving, overwhelming, powerful.
淋淋 *lirnlirn*, adj., descriptive of pouring, dripping: 血淋淋 bloody in appearance; 雨淋淋 downpour or continuous rain; 濕淋淋 very wet.
淋浴 *lirnyuh*, n., shower bath.

洙 63A.01-1

ju.

N. Name of river in Shantung; 洙泗 the two rivers, area where Confucius taught.

潔 63A.01-1

jier.

V. t. To clean, cleanse, purify: 潔樽 *-tzun*, 潔己 *-jii* ↓.

Adj. Pure, clean, spotless: 潔白 *-bair*, 潔淨 *-jihng* ↓; 清潔 pure, clean; 整潔 tidy, neat and clean; 不潔 dirty, soiled, unhealthy.

潔白 *jierbair*, adj., spotlessly clean, pure and white.
潔淨 *jierjihng*, adj., clean, neat, tidy.
潔己 *jierjii*, v. i., lead a pure life.
潔癖 *jierpii*, n., morbid preoccupation with cleanliness.
潔身 *jiershen*, v.i., as in 潔身自愛 lead an honest and clean life.
潔樽 *jier-tzun*, v.i., as in 潔樽候教 (phr., used in formal invitations) look forward to have the pleasure of your company (lit., "clean the cups").

溱 63A.01-1

jen.

N. Name of river.

Adj. 溱溱 (AC) thriving (vegetation).

潦 63A.01-1

lauh (**laau, *liaur*).

N. (1) (**laau*) (AC) running pools of water on road: 行潦. (2) (*lauh*) To flood, inundate (interch. 澇).

Adj. (1) (**laau*) (Of rain) pouring: 潦雨. (2) 潦倒 *-'dau*↓; 潦草 *-tsaau*↓.

潦倒 *lauh'dau*, adj., (1) disappointed or unsuccessful in life; 潦倒梆子 (of persons) a failure; (2) **liaurdaau*, self-opinionated, difficult to get along with.
潦漿泡 **liaurjiangpauh*, n., blister caused by burn.
潦草 **liaurtsaau*, adj. & adv., (of work) careless, slovenly, also 潦潦草草.

凓 63A.01-3

lih.

Adj. Cold: 凓冽 chilly, bleak.

溧 63A.01-3

lih.

N. Name of river in Kiangsu.

漂 63A.01-3

piau (**piaau, *piauh*).

V. i. (1) Drift, esp. aimlessly, float about. (2) (AC) blow. (3) (**piauh*) Fail, end in failure: 這事情漂了 this thing has failed, is lost.

V. t. (1) (**piaau*) Bleach. (2) (**piauh*) Leave unattended: 漂賬 neglect to pay debt.

Adj. See 漂然 *-rarn*↓.

漂白 *piaaubair*, v. t., bleach; 漂白粉 *--feen.*, n., bleaching powder.
漂泊 *piaubor*, v. i., drift aimlessly.
漂泛 *piaufahn*, v. i., float about.
漂海 *piauhaai*, v.i., go overseas.
漂金 *piaujin*, n., gold vein on surface of mines.
漂兒 *piau'l*, n., float used by fishermen.
漂亮 **piauhliahng*, adj., handsome (of dress, person, generous gift); 不漂亮 stingy in tips.
漂流 *piauliour*, v. i., drift about.
漂落 *piauluoh*, v. i., ditto.
漂淪 *piaulurn*, v. i., drift unemployed or without aim in life.
漂沒 *piaumoh*, v. i., drift and sink.
漂鳥 *piau-niaau*, n., migratory bird.
漂染 *piaur-raarn*, v. i., dyeing and bleaching.
漂然 *piau-rarn*, adj. & adv., (soar) high and free.
漂孝兒 **piaaushiauh'l*, n., mourning cloak of finer fabric.
漂搖 *piauyaur*, v. i., drift about.

澡 63A.01-4

tzaau.

V. t. Wash, bathe: 洗澡 take a bath; 洗澡間 or 房 bathroom; 沖澡 have a shower (bath); 澡盆 *-pern*↓; 澡瓶 a water pot; 澡雪 *-shyuee*↓; 澡身浴德 (AC) develop one's moral being and lead a virtuous life.

澡盆 *tzaaupern*, n., bathtub.
澡雪 *tzaurshyuee*, v. t., (AC) cleanse: 澡雪而心 purify your heart.
澡堂(子) *tzaautarng('tz)*, n., public baths.

源 63A.01-5

yuarn.
[Var. of 原 51A.01]

N. (1) Spring, fountain, source: 泉源 spring; 水源 source (of river, etc.); 源流, 源本 *-liour, -been*↓: 同源 of the same origin; 起源 origin of events; 溯本求源 go back to the source or origins; 正本清源 (phil.) clear up the spring or source of moral character; 飲水思源 gratitude for source of benefit; 源遠流長 (a trend, an institution) of anc. origin and long development. (2) A surname.

源本 *yuarnbeen*, n., origin of events: 源源本本 (narrate) from the beginning (also wr. 原本).
源流 *yuarnliour*, n., origin and development.
源頭 *yuarntour*, n., source.
源委 *yuarnweei*, n., story of origin and development of event (usu. wr. 原委).
源源 *yuarnyuarn*, adv., continuously (like a stream): 源源而來.

涼 63A.01-6

liarng (**liahng*).

[Interch. 凉]

N. (1) A surname. (2) Cold, coolness: 着涼 catch cold; 乘涼 to enjoy the cool air (as under a shade), see Adj.↓.

V. t. (*liahng) To let cool by air: 涼一杯開水 (茶) let a cup of boiling water (tea) cool off; cf. 晾 41A.01.

Adj. (1) Cool, cold: 天氣變涼了 weather has turned cool; 冰涼 icy cold; 涼風 cool breeze; 涼氣 cool air; 清涼 (weather) clear and cool; the shade; 涼快, 涼爽 -kuaih, -shuaang↓; 涼水 cold water; 涼茶 cold tea, sometimes medicated; 涼飯 cold rice; 涼陰陰 or 蔭蔭 (兒) (yihn), 涼颼颼, 涼森森 very cold with sunlight shut out (as in cave). (2) Feel cold, disheartened: 他一看就涼了 he was greatly disheartened at one look; 涼了半截 heart chills with disappointment.

涼粉兒 *liarngfee'l*, n., cold jelly, agar-agar.
涼糕 *liarnggau*, n., pastry made of glutinous rice, served cold.
涼快 *liarngkuaih*, adj., nice and cool.
涼帽 *liarngmauh*, n., summer hat.
涼棚 *liarngperng*, n., mat shed.
涼蓆 *liarngshir*, n., fine mat for summer, woven of finely split bamboo.
涼爽 *liarngshuaang*, adj., refreshing.
涼血 *liarngshyueh*, adj., cold-blooded; 涼血動物 (zoo.) cold-blooded animals; also fig. of persons.
涼亭 *liarngtirng*, n., pavilion, wayfarer's sheltered station.
涼菜 *liarngtsaih*, n., cold dishes.

澟 63A.01-6

liin.

[Cogn. of 凜↓]

凜 63A.01-6

liin.

Adj. Fearful, severely cold, austere.

凜冽 *liinlieh*, adj., bitingly cold (wind).
凜凜 *lirnliin*, adj., severely cold, icy; (of manners) forbidding: 威風凜凜 forbidding appearance; 凜凜如生 (of portrait) seems alive.
凜然 *liinrarn*, adj., forbidding in appearance; arousing fear, reverence.

淙 63A.01-6

tsurng.

Adj. Gurgling, clanking sound: 淙淙泉水 the murmuring spring.

深 63A.01-6

shen.

Adj. (1) Deep: 深度 -duh↓; 深海, 深山 deep sea, mountains; 深林 deep forest; 深溝 deep ditch; 根深 deep roots. (2) Profound: 深遠, 深邃 -yuaan, -sueih↓; 深妙, 深奧 -miauh, -auh↓; 深恩 great favor; 深情 profound friendship, love; 深交 intimate friendship, close friend; 深趣 profound interest; 深謀遠慮 farsightedness, great forethought; 不識高深 do not comprehend (its) profundity. (3) Deep, dark in color: 深紅 dark red; 深夜 late in the night; 深更半夜 in the dead of night. (4) Hidden: 侯門深似海 a nobleman's mansion is deep like the sea—inaccessible; 深居簡出 live with few social contacts.

Adv. Deeply, greatly, very: 深深 -shen↓; 深感, 深覺 feel greatly; 深信 firmly believe; 深知, 深悉 truly know; 深思, 好學深思 of profound, thoughtful in, scholarship; 深念 remember fondly; 深疑 seriously doubt; 深惡 (痛絕) hate deeply; 深明大義 know clearly the right thing to do and the principles to follow; 深以爲非 firmly condemn; 深以爲恥, 爲憾 feel deeply ashamed, deeply regret.

深黯 *shen-ahn*, adj., dark (room, light).
深奧 *shen-auh*, adj., profound, difficult to understand.
深長 *shencharng*, adj., deep and profound (meaning).
深沈 *shenchern*, (1) adj., profound, not superficial, also severe, deliberate in speech, manner; (2) (-'chen) adj. & adv., serious, -ly, severe, -ly: 不好深沈責罰他 do not punish him too severely; 這個事情裏頗有深沈 this matter is quite serious.
深淺 *shen-chiaan*, n., degree of depth (of water); seriousness or depth (of meaning): 深淺兒 n., ditto.
深切 *shenchieh*, adj., earnest (appeal, explanation).
深度 *shenduh*, n., depth (of water, knowledge, etc.).
深分 *shenfen*, adv., seriously (discuss, etc.).
深更 *shen-geng*, n., the dead of night.
深閨 *shen-guei*, n., deep, hidden boudoir.
深痼 *shen-guh*, n., deep-rooted disease, habit, prejudice.
深宮 *shen-gung*, n., deep-hidden or inaccessible palace.
深厚 *shenhouh*, adj., profound (friendship).
深致 *shen-jyh*, n., profound interest, sentiment.
深刻 *shenkeh*, adj., penetrating (criticism, etc.), acute (observation); indelible (memory, impression, etc.).
深渺 *shenmiaau*, adj., see -yuaan↓.

深妙 *shenmiauh*, adj., enticing, deep-felt (thought), esoteric (doctrine).

深昧 *shenmeih*, adj., dark, obscure.

深入 *shenruh*, v. i. & t., (1) go beneath the surface, take root (in studies); (2) penetrate (foreign territory): 深入研究 make a deep study (of subject).

深深 *shenshen*, adv., deeply.

深宵 *shen-shiau*, n., deep night.

深心 *shenshin*, (1) n., deep mind or thought; (2) adv., (believe) firmly.

深邃 *shensueih*, adj., deep, impenetrable, obscure (past, origins).

深談 *shen-tarn*, v. i., hold serious discussion, deep conversation.

深造 *shen-tzauh*, n., deepened or higher studies: 以求深造 to pursue higher studies.

深微 *shenweir*, adj., close and fine (reasoning), precise (knowledge).

深文 *shen-wern*, n., (1) as in 深文周納 carefully framed-up argument or accusation; (2) difficult, obscure passage.

深夜 *shenyeh*, (1) n., deep night; (2) adv., deep at night.

深意 *shenyih*, n., very thoughtful purpose; very profound meaning.

深遠 *shenyuaan*, adv., showing great forethought; profound.

涂 63A.01-8

tur.

N. (1) A surname. (2) Interch. 塗 63.11, 途 81.83.

滌 63A.01-9

dir.

V. t. (LL) cleanse, wash away: 滌垢, 滌塵 cleanse off dirt, dust; 滌去 wash away.

滌除 *dirchur*, v. t., cleanse away, get rid of (bad practice, etc.),

滌蕩 *dirdahng*, v. t., wipe out, clean up (obstructions).

淙 63A.01-9

jih.

N. (1) Bank of river or sea. (2) Sea bottom.

瀠 63A.01-9

yirng.

V. i. (Water) to swirl around: 瀠洄.

§ 63A.02 (氵/亅k)

漆 63A.02-1

chi (**chyuh*).

N. (1) Paint; lacquer, varnish; 漆器 *-chih*, etc.↓. (2) A surname.

V.t. To paint, to coat with varnish: 漆上顏色 to cover with paint color; 漆一漆 give it a coat of paint; 漆房子 paint a house; 漆牆 to paint walls; 油漆 to paint or varnish.

Adj. (Also sp. pr. **chyuh*) 漆黑兒, 漆滿兒烏黑 pitch-dark.

漆布 *chi-buh*, n., lacquered cloth.

漆器 *chi-chih*, n., lacquer ware.

漆毒疹 *chidur-jeen*, n., skin rash owing to smell or contact with lacquer.

漆工 *chi-gung*, h., house painter; lacquer ware worker.

漆黑 *chihei*, adj., (sp. pr. **chyuh*-) pitch-dark.

漆畫 *chi-huah*, n., lacquer painting.

漆宅 *chijair*, n., term for coffin.

漆皮 *chipir*, n., lacquered leather; 漆皮兒 coat of paint.

漆書 *chishu*, n., writing with lacquer, before brush and ink were invented.

漆樹 *chi-shuh*, n., the lacquer-tree.

漆屎 *chi-shyy*, n., baby's first bowels after birth, dark in color, (also called 臍屎).

濃 63A.02-2

nurng.

Adj. Heavy, dense, thick (opp. of light, thin): 濃抹 (of women) heavy make-up; 濃妝 heavy make-up matched with bright-colored dress; 淡粧濃抹總相宜 (of a woman) always charming with either light or heavy make-up; 濃密 *-mih*↓; 顏色太濃 the color is too bright or loud; 味濃 (of food) heavy-flavored; 濃茶 strong tea; 濃雲密佈 (of sky) overcast with heavy clouds; 濃情蜜意 great tenderness among lovers.

濃度 *nurngduh*, n., (of liquids) density of concentration.

濃厚 *nurnghouh*, adj., (of material things) thick and heavy; (of feelings, interest) deep.

濃密 *nurngmih*, n., degree of density (of hair, tress), dense: 濃密相宜 proper distribution of trees, plants, etc., esp. in painting.

濃湯 *nurngtang*, n., thick soup, cream.

濃郁 *nurngyuh*, adj., (of wine, tea, etc.) rich and fragrant.

濛 63A.02-2

merng.

濛鴻 *mernghurng*, adj., (1) descriptive of the primeval world; (2) in drunken state.

濛濛 *merngmerng*, adj., drizzling: 濛濛細雨.

濛鬆雨(兒) *merng'sung yuu('l)*, n., drizzle.

冰 63A.02-2

bing.

[Pop. 氷; rarely as var. of 凝 pr. *nirng*]

N. (1) Ice: 結冰, 堅冰 (of water) freeze; 冰塊 pieces of ice, floes; 冰花 crystal patterns; 冰片 *-piahn* ↓; ice as symbol of purity of character: 冰清玉潔, 冰肌雪腸; of chasteness of soul: 一片冰心在玉壺, 冰壺秋月 as symbol of woman's delicate skin or beauty: 冰姿(肌)玉骨; of purity of soul: 冰姿雪魄; with 雪 snow, as symbol of brightness of mind: 冰雪聰明; with 霜 frost, as symbol of coldness of face or heart: 冷若冰霜, 冰霜氣貌; as the cool moon in 冰輪, 冰鏡, 冰盤 ("ice wheel, ice mirror, ice plate"); thin ice as symbol of danger: 如履薄冰; vanish like melting ice in 冰散, 冰泮, 冰消; dissolve: 冰消瓦解 dissolve like ice, 冰消霧散 dissolve like mist (of trouble, crisis); 渙然冰釋 (of misunderstandings) melt away: 冰蝕 (geol.) (of rocks) eroded by glaciers; with 炭 charcoal, 冰炭不相容 inimical, hostile to each other, like ice and hot charcoal. (2) In combb. of various utensils: 冰袋 ice bag; 冰窖, 冰庫, 冰室 basement for keeping ice, ice cabinet; 冰碗 ice bowl, 冰盞兒 clapping copper saucers used by cold drink pedlars in Peiping as trade signal; 冰桶 ice pail; 冰攛 *-tsuan*, 冰鑿 *-tzaur*; 冰橇 *-tsueih* ↓; 冰川 *-chuan* ↓.

V.t. To ice, put ice around: 把這瓶汽水冰一冰 put some ice in the soda water.

Adj. & adv. Ice-cold: 冷冰冰的; iced: 冰咖啡 iced coffee; 冰凍, 冰冷, 冰涼 *-duhng, -leeng, -liarng* ↓.

冰棒 *bingbahng*, n., ice sticks (of various flavors).

冰碴兒 *bingchar'l*, n., thin coating of ice on water surface.

冰川 *bingchuan*, n., glacier.

冰牀 *bingchuarng*, n., sled.

冰島 *bingdaau*, n., iceberg; Iceland.

冰刀 *bingdau*, n., the cutting edge of ice skates.

冰點 *bing-diaan*, n., freezing point.

冰度 *bing-duh*, n., freezing point, degree of ice.

冰凍 *bingduhng*, v. t. & adj., freeze, frozen, freezing cold.

冰斧 *bingfuu*, n. (LL) matchmaker.

冰棍 *bingguhn*, n., see *-bahng* ↑.

冰菓店 *bingguoo-diahn*, n., cold drink shop.

冰河 *bingher*, n., glacier, also 冰川; 冰河期 *--chir*, n., glacier epoch, ice age.

冰核(兒) *binghur('l)*, n., (dial.) clean part of natural ice (for eating or drinking).

冰淇琳 *bingjilirn*, n., ice cream.

冰敬 *bingjihng*, n., formerly, summer gift for Peking officials.

冰錐(兒) *bingjuei(-jue'l)*, n., see *-juh* ↓.

冰柱 *bingjuh*, n., icicles; (geol.) column formations in glaciers.

冰冷 *bingleeng*, adj., ice-cold, very cold.

冰楞 *binglerng*, n., see *-juh* ↑.

冰涼 *bingliarng*, adj., very cool, very cold.

冰排子 *bingpairtz*, n., (coll.) sled, sledge.

冰雹 *bingpaur*, n., hail.

冰片 *bingpiahn*, n., Baroos camphor from Borneo, also called 龍腦; pieces of ice.

冰人 *bingrern*, n., matchmaker (also called 冰斧 *-fuu* ↑, 冰下人).

冰山 *biangshan*, n., iceberg; (fig.) people temporarily in power, not to depend on; 冰山已倒 phr., power has collapsed.

冰箱 *bingshiang*, n., refrigerator, icebox, freezer.

冰鞋 *bingshier*, n., skates.

冰糖 *bingtarng*, n., crystal sugar; 冰糖胡蘆(兒) sweetmeat consisting of sugarcoated sour plums, pierced together on a stick.

冰攛 *bingtsuan*, n., sled, sledge.

冰橇 *bingtsueih*, n., ditto.

冰醋酸 *bingtsuhsuan*, n., (chem.) glacial acetic acid.

冰鑿 *bingtzaur*, n., see *-tsuan* ↑.

冰原 *bingyuarn*, n., (geol.) glacial plateau.

涿 63A.02-3

juo.

N. Name of a *shiahn*: 涿縣 in Hopei.

瀑 63A.02-4

puh (**bauh*).

Adj. (**bauh*) 瀑雨 torrential rain.

瀑布 *puhbuh*, n., waterfalls.

漲 63A.02-5

jahng.

[Related 脹 42A.02]

V. i. (1) To swell up: 漲起. (2) To rise in water, in prices; to inundate: 漲水, 漲大水 to flood; 漲潮 the rising tide; 漲價 rise in price; 漲落 *-lauh* ↓.

漲落 *jaanglauh*, n. & v. i., (the) rise and fall (of prices, tides).

滾 63A.02-6

guun.

[Pop. 滾]

V.i. (1) To turn round and round: 球在地上滾 the ball is rolling on the ground; 滾動 rotate, roll; 滾鐵環 roll a hoop; 車輪滾了, 螺旋槳滾了 the wheels, propellers are rotating; 打滾 turn a somersault; 滾來滾去 roll back and forth; 滿地亂滾 roll all over the ground; 雨滴沿着牆滾下來 raindrops are dripping from the wall; 滾兒 a somersault. (2) To boil: 水滾了 the water is boiling; 滾(開)水 boiling water. (3) (Banking) to compound interest: 利上滾利 with interest compounded (annually, etc.); 滾存 *-tsurn*↓. (4) (Command to) scram, go away: 滾蛋 be off! 滾出去 begone! 滾開 scram! 快滾 beat it! 滾, 滾, 滾 get out! get out!

Adj. (Of currents) rushing, torrential: 滾滾長江東逝水 eastward rush the torrential currents of the Yangtze; 滾滾而來 (of water) come in torrents; 財源滾滾 profits pouring in from all sides.

Adv. Very, to a high degree: 滾燙 red hot; 滾熱(兒的) (of human body) feverish, (of food) boiling hot; 滾圓 perfectly round; 滾亮 dazzlingly bright.

滾邊 *guunbian*, n., embroidered border (also 緄邊).

滾刀肉 *guundaurouh*, n., a desperado.

滾瓜 *guungua*, adj., (1) round and fat; (2) 滾瓜兒, 滾瓜爛熟 having s. t. at one's fingertips.

滾利 *guunlih*, v. i., (banking) deposit money at compound interest.

滾存 *guuntsurn*, adj., (accounting) accumulated, cumulative: 盈餘滾存 accumulated or cumulative surplus.

滾子 *guuntz*, n., a roller.

濠 63A.02-6

haur.

N. A moat (cf. 壕 11A.02).

瀼 63A.02-6

rarng.

Adj. Covered with dewdrops: 零露瀼瀼 (AC) heavily bedewed.

泳 63A.02-6

yuung.

V. i. To swim: 游泳 ditto; 游泳池 swimming pool; 游泳衣 swimming suit; 三點泳衣 bikini; 仰泳 back stroke; 爬泳 crawl stroke; 蛙泳 breast stroke; 蝶泳 butterfly stroke; 側泳 side stroke.

浪 63A.02-6

lahng.

N. A wave, swell of water: 波浪 waves; 海浪 ocean waves; 白浪滔天 white-crested waves surging and swelling sky-high; 浪潮 wave, tide; 大浪 rolling waves; 風浪 big waves, stormy sea, (fig.) esp. 冒風浪 take risk; 浪花 *-hua*, 浪頭 *-tour*↓; 光浪 light waves; 聲浪 sound waves; 熱浪 a heat wave.

Adj. (1) Profligate, reckless: 放浪 dissolute, lax, unrestrained; 浪放 *-fahng*, 浪莽 *-maang*, 浪蕩 *-dahng*, 浪職 *-jyr*↓; 孟浪 rough and rude; 浪女人 a licentious woman; 浪態 licentious manners or conduct. (2) Wasteful, extravagant, unfounded: 浪費 *-feih*↓; 浪得虛名 unearned reputation; 浪語, 浪傳 unfounded reports, rumors.

Adv. Freely, unwisely: 浪遊 travel freely, roam around; 浪信人言 unwisely believe in others' words.

浪橋 *lahngchiaur*, n., (gymnastics) a swinging bridge.

浪蕩 *lahngdahng*, adj., profligate, jobless and leading a life of dissipation.

浪放 *lahngfahng*, adj., without restraint (usu. 放浪).

浪費 *lahngfeih*, adj. & v. t., extravagant, wasteful (of money, time, energy); to waste.

浪花 *lahnghua*, n., (1) the foam of breaking waves; (2) flowers that do not bear fruit.

浪迹 *lahngji*, v. i., travelling footloose: 浪迹天涯 roaming freely all over the world.

浪職 *lahngjyr*, v. i., commit dereliction of duty.

浪莽 *lahngmaang*, adj., dissolute, lax in morals.

浪漫 *lahngmahn*, adj., (1) licentious, unrestrained; (2) (translit.) romantic; 浪漫主義 (litr.) romanticism; 浪漫史 n., (translit.) romance (also 羅曼斯).

浪木 *lahngmuh*, n., a seesaw, a swing log.

浪人 *lahngrern*, n., a hobo, vagabond; ruffian; (Japanese) *ronin*.

浪士 *lahngshyh*, n., (LL) a libertine.

浪頭 *lahngtour*, n., big waves; breaker, "white-caps": 浪頭很高 the waves are high.

浪子 *lahngtzyy*, n., a prodigal son: 浪子回頭 return of the prodigal son.

漾 63A.02-8

yahng.

V. i. & t. (1) (Water) swirl about: 動漾 drift and swirl, (fig.) agitated. (2) To overflow: 來晚了的人, 都往外漾 those who came late overflowed to the outside areas.

漾漾 *yahngyahng*, adj., agitated.

滄(滄) 63A.02-8

tsan.

[Var. of 餐 21A.02]

派 63A.02-9

paih.

N. School or current of thought, sect, groups of different beliefs: 流派 branch of thought; 學派, school of thought; 黨派 political party, wing; 新, 舊派 new, old elements in society; 左, 右派, leftists, rightists; 派別 *-bier* ↓; (AC) a branch of water current; 氣派 style (of dress, behavior).

V. t. To appoint (person) to post, mission; send (troops): 分派, to distribute, designate (work, gifts); allot blame (派他不是 put blame on him).

派別 *paihbier*, n., categories, schools of thought, belief.
派遣 *paihchiaan*, v.t., send s.o. on mission.
派出所 *paihchu suuo*, n., branch police station.
派發 *paihfa*, v. i., distribute.
派系 *paihshih*, n., affiliation with (school or party).
派頭 *paihtour*, n., style (of dress, behavior).

添 63A.02-9

tian.

V.t. (1) To add, increase, oft. 添上: 添本(兒) increase capital; 添錢, 添人 put in more money, more people on staff, 添貨 replenish store supplies; 添點兒, 添了一點 add a little; 添房 see 添箱 *-shiang* ↓; 添盆 throw coins of luck into baby's bath on third day; 添雙筷子 put on another pair of chopsticks (for unexpected guest); 添油加醋 garble story by adding details (to inflame hearer); 添枝帶葉 add or fabricate, details of story; 錦上添花 add to happy occasion or to glory, beauty; 添福添壽 "many happy returns of the day," to increase one's luck and long life. (2) Used as prefix to many vbb., meaning in addition: 添設, 添置 add annex or more furniture, etc.; 添購 buy in addition, buy more. (3) To give birth to: 又添了一個小孩兒 had another baby, see 添丁 *-ding* ↓.

添補 *tianbuu*, v.t., put in extra (capital, staff, etc.).
添丁 *tianding*, v.i., have another son.
添飯 *tian-fahn*, v. i., have another helping of rice.
添改 *tiangaai*, v.t., correct and insert words or phrases in manuscript.
添置 *tianjyh*, v.t., put in extra (furniture, etc.).
添設 *tiansheh*, v.t., add (to building, posts, etc.).
添箱 *tian-shiang*, v.i., give presents to bride (also 添房).

淥 63A.02-9

luh.

Adj. (Of water) clear: 濕淥淥 wet through.

V. i. (Var. of 漉) to filter.

---

§63A.10 (氵/十)

汁 63A.10-1

jy.

N. (-'*l*) Juice: 汁水 fluids; 果汁 fruit juice; 肉汁 meat juice; 墨汁 fluid ink; esp. for writing with brush.

澣 63A.10-1

huaan.

V. t. To wash (var. of 浣 63A.70).

淖 63A.10-2

nauh (*jauh*).

N. Mud: 泥淖 mire; 淖濘 full of mud and slush.

泮 63A.10-2

pahn.

V. i. (AC) melt (of ice).

泮宮 *pahngung*, n., (AC) name of banquet hall, now symbolic of academy of scholars, esp. in phr. 入泮 to pass degrees in civil examinations.
泮汗 *pahn-hahn*, adj., expansive (of flooding waters).
泮渙 *pahn-huah*, v. i., dissolve like floes.

津 63A.10-2

jin.

N. (1) A ferry: 津渡 *-duh*, 津梁 *-liarng* ↓; 問津 (lit.) ask the way to the ford, (fig.) to interest oneself in s.t.: 無人問津 no one shows any interest in (person, thing); 迷津 go astray, miss one's way: 指點迷津 show s.o. how to get to the right path. (2) An important communication center: 津要 *-yauh*, 津關 *-guan* ↓; 天津 Tientsin. (3) Saliva: 津液 *-yeh* ↓. (4) Money as fees or "lubricant": 津潤 *-ruhn* ↓; 津貼 *-tie* ↓.

津逮 *jindaih*, n., guide (to learning).
津渡 *jinduh*, n., a ferry crossing.
津筏 *jinfar*, n., (1) a bamboo raft for ferrying; (2) a path, a guide to doing things.
津關 *jinguan*, n., a customs barrier, a check point.
津津 *jinjin*, adj., (1) (of water) overflowing; (2) (of food) delicious, (of words) intensely interesting: 津津有味 appetizing, palatable.
津梁 *jinliarng*, n., guide or bridge (to learning).
津潤 *jinruhn*, (1) v. t., moisten; (2) n., money fees or subsidy.
津貼 *jintie*, n. & v. t., subsidy, -ize.
津要 *jinyauh*, n., a strategic point; a key position in government.
津液 *jinyeh*, n., saliva.

潾 63A.10–2

lirn.

Adj. (LL, of water) clear.

汗 63A.10–3

hahn.

N. Perspiration, sweat: 出汗, 流汗, 淌汗 to sweat; 多汗 sweaty; 一身臭汗 stink with perspiration; 滿頭大汗 head covered with big drops of perspiration; 汗流浹背 perspire all over with shame or gratitude; 汗下 perspire with shame; 一身冷汗 break out in cold sweat; 盜汗 (of sick people) night sweats; 發汗 to induce or give perspiration; 汗牛充棟 (of multitude of books) enough to fill the roof (to the beam) and cause cows to perspire in cart; 汗馬之勞 service in battle.

汗斑 *hahnban*, n., a skin disease, *Tinea versicolor* (also 汗癬).
汗青 *hahnching*, n., (LL) books, history ("sweat out the sap in bomboo"—anc. form of preparing bamboo strips for writing).
汗褂兒 *hahnguah'l*, n., see *-shan* ↓.
汗鹼 *hahnjiaan*, n., sweat deposits on shirts.
汗巾(兒) *hahnjin(-jie'l)*, n., formerly, a kerchief, handkerchief.
汗絡兒 *hahnlauh'l*, n., meshed shirt worn in summer.
汗漫 *hahnmahn*, adj., run riot, flooding over: 汗漫不可收拾 broken beyond all bounds; superficial, indiscriminate (stories, hearsays).
汗毛 *hahnmaur*, n., (physiol.) down.
汗衫 *hahnshan*, n., shirt; (lit., "sweat shirt") vest or T shirt.
汗腺 *hahn-shiahn*, n., sweat glands.
汗褟(兒) *hahnta('l)*, n., (dial.) shirt.
汗顏 *hahnyarn*, adj., ashamed ("sweat on face").

洱 63A.10–3

eel.

N. Name of lake in Yunnan, famous for its strong tea (普洱茶).

潭 63A.10–3

tarn.

N. Deep pool, pond, small lake: 水潭, 深潭 deep pond; 明潭 clear pond; 碧潭 blue lake.

潭第 *tarndih*, n., (court.) your house (lit. "deep mansion").
潭府 *tarnfuu*, n., ditto.

澤 63A.10–4

tzer.

N. (1) A marsh, swamp: 湖澤 lakes and swamps; 川澤 streams and marshes; 沼澤 swamps; 澤國 *-guor* ↓; 澤地 swampy ground, low land. (2) Kindness, beneficence: 恩澤 kindnesses done, favors shown; 澤民 to benefit the people: 上致君, 下澤民 give the prince wise counsel and let the people benefit thereby; 澤及 confer benefits on. (3) Ancestral handwriting: 手澤(猶存) ancestor's caligraphic works (are still extant). (4) Good influence: 君子之澤, 五世而斬 the good influence of men of virtue will not be lost for (at least) five generations. (5) Underwear: 與子同澤 (AC) I will share my shirts with you, hence 袍澤 comrades at arms.

Adj. Smooth, glossy: 光澤 radiant, lustrous; 潤澤 smooth and soft; 美澤可以鑑 such a bright surface that it can serve as a mirror.

澤漆 *tzerchi*, n., (bot.) the wart weed.
澤國 *tzerguor*, n., land flooded with water: 盡成澤國 all the land is inundated.
澤袍 *tzerpaur*, n., comrades at arms.
澤瀉 *tzershieh*, n., (bot.) the water plantain.

澼 63A.10–5

pih.

V. t. (AC) to bleach.

淬 63A.10-6

tsueih.

V. t. (1) To temper (iron, steel) by sudden plunge in water, (also wr. 焠); (fig.) to harden character: 淬礪. (2) To alter color, consistency: 以藥淬之 treat with certain chemical.

漳 63A.10-6

jang.

N. Name of place: 漳州 name of district in Fukien Province; 漳河 name of river; 漳絨 velvet of 漳州, 漳緞 brocade of 漳州 with velvet designs.

滸 63A.10-6

huu.

N. Marsh ground on lake side: 水滸傳 *Water Margins*, a popular picaresque novel.

滓 63A.10-6

tzyy.

N. Sediment, dregs: 滓穢 *-hueih* ↓; 塵滓 dust and dirt; 渣滓 (lit.) refuse, waste material, (fig.) the dregs of society.

滓穢 *tzyyhueih*, (1) n., dirt, filth, impurity; (2) v. t., make dirty, to soil, defile.

渾 63A.10-6

hurn (**huhn*, **huun*).

Adj. (1) Concealed, unrevealed: 渾涵 restrained, containing more than is expressed. (2) (**huhn*) Nebulous: see 渾沌 *-duhn*, 渾天 *-tian* ↓. (3) Muddy (interch. 混): 渾濁 *-juor* ↓. (4) (**huhn*) Stupid (interch. 混): 你這人好渾 how stupid you are; 渾人, 渾蛋 *-rern*, *-dahn* ↓. (5) Whole: 渾身 the whole body: 渾身解數 every means of solution, charm (of women).

Adv. (Chiefly MC and poet.) completely, almost: 渾然 *-rarn* ↓; 門前小灘渾欲平 the shallow rapids outside are almost submerged in water; 渾似 just like, almost like; 渾不似 *-buhsyh* ↓; 渾不比 completely unlike.

渾不似 *hurnbuhsyh*, n., an ancient four-stringed instrument (like 琵琶 and yet is not).

渾成 *hurncherng*, adj., (of composition, sentence) like nature itself, effortless—highest quality of art.

渾蛋 *hurndahn* (*huhn-*), n., (abusive) "rotten egg," rogue (also wr. 混蛋).

渾沌 **huhnduhn*, adj., in the nebulous state before the universe was formed: 渾沌初開 when the universe was taking shape.

渾噩 *hurn-eh*, adj., completely naïve, innocent: 渾渾噩噩 (universe) in nebulous state; (child's mind) yet undeveloped.

渾括 *hurngua*, v. t., include: 渾括一切 including all.

渾倌(兒) *hurnguan(-gua'l)*, n., adult prostitute, dist. 清倌 young girl in singsong house still a virgin.

渾涵 *hurnharn*, (1) v. t., to overlook (fault); (2) adj., restrained, not too explicit in language.

渾化 *hurnhuah*, adj., (of art work) completely transformed or merged.

渾渾 **huhnhuhn*, adj., unformed, nebulous, in original state.

渾家 *hurnjia*, n., (MC) wife.

渾金 *hurnjihn*, n., 渾金璞玉 phr., (of person's talent or art) "like unsmelted gold and unchiselled jade"—completely natural, a high praise.

渾濁 *hurnjuor*, adj., muddy, spoiled, filthy (also wr. 混濁).

渾亂 **huunluahn*, adj., mixed, disorderly (also wr. 混).

渾然 *hurnrarn*, adj., (1) completely natural, see *-cherng* ↑; (2) completely: 渾然不覺 do not feel at all.

渾人 *hurnrern*, n., (abusive) a lout, loafer, ruffian.

渾天 **huhntian*, n., an anc. theory that the sky was like an eggshell and the earth a yolk; 渾天儀 (astron.) an armillary sphere.

洋 63A.10-8

yarng.

N. (1) Ocean: 海洋 seas, oceans; 出洋, 放洋 go overseas; 印度洋 the Indian Ocean; 太平洋 the Pacific; 大西洋 the Atlantic; 北冰洋 the Arctic Ocean; 南冰洋 the Antarctic Ocean. (2) Dollars: 大洋 a dollar; 銀洋 silver dollar; 洋錢 money.

Adj. Foreign, Western, imported: 洋人 (西洋人), 洋貨 (西洋貨) *-rern*, *-huoh* ↓; 西洋東西 Western things; 洋畫, 洋餐, 洋裝 Western painting, food, dress, etc. (in this sense 西 or "Western" is just as common: 西畫, 西餐, 西裝); 東洋 Japan or Japanese.

洋白銅 *yarng-bairturng*, n., nickel or zinc alloy of copper, cf. *-tiee* ↓.

洋布 *yarngbuh*, n., calico, shirtings; 細洋布 muslin.

洋車 *yarngche*, n., jinricksha, rickshaw.

洋槍 *yarngchiang*, n., rifle.

洋錢 *yarngchiarn*, n., money in gen.: 沒有洋錢 have no money.

洋琴 *yarngchirn*, n., (1) piano; (2) harpsichord.

洋取燈兒 *yarng-chyuudeng'l*, n., (pop.) matches, see *-huoo* ↓.

洋燈 *yarng-deng*, n., kerosene lamp.

洋粉 *yarngfeen*, n., agar-agar, see *-tsaih* ↓.

洋服 *yarng-fur*, n., Western dress.

洋鬼子 *yarnggueeitz*, n., foreigner (not in polite intercourse).

洋行 *yarngharng*, n., a foreign firm.

洋槐 *yarng-huair*, n., (bot.) *Robinia pseudacacia*.

洋灰 *yarng-huei*, n., cement (also called 水門汀).

洋貨 *yarng-huoh*, n., imported goods.

洋火 *yarnghuoo*, n., matches (also called 自來火).

洋紅 *yarnghurng*, adj., carmine.

洋涇濱 *Yarngjingbang*, n., former International Settlement in Shanghai; 洋涇濱英語 pidgin English.

洋裝 *yarngjuang*, n., (1) Western dress; (2) Western bookbinding.

洋菊 *yarngjyur*, n., (bot.) the dahlia.

洋蠟 *yarnglah*, n., (Western) candle.

洋爐(子) *yarnglur(tz)*, n., Western stove.

洋面 *yarng-miahn*, n., sea surface.

洋奴 *yarngnur*, n., men servile to foreigners.

洋盤 *yarng-parn*, n., (Shanghai dial.) a raw hand, one not yet smart enough.

洋人 *yarngrern*, n., Westerner, foreigner.

洋傘 *yarngsaan*, n., (Western) umbrella.

洋紗 *yarngsha*, n., muslin.

洋繡球 *yarng-shiouhchiour*, n., (bot.) the hydrangea.

洋式 *yarng-shyh*, adj., Western-styled.

洋鐵 *yarngtiee*, n., galvanized iron; tinned iron.

洋菜 *yarngtsaih*, n., agar-agar.

洋葱 *yarngtsung*, n., Western (the common) onion.

洋磁 *yarngtsyr*, n., enamel (bathtub, etc.).

洋襪子 *yarngwahtz*, n., socks.

洋娃娃 *yarngwar'wa*, n., a foreign doll.

洋文 *yarng-wern*, n., foreign language.

洋務 *yarng-wuh*, n., formerly, foreign affairs.

洋烟 *yarng-yan*, n., cigarette.

洋洋 *yarngyarng*, adj., (1) vast, great, impressive; (2) overflowing, drifting; (3) leisurely.

洋藥 *yarng-yauh*, n., (1) formerly, opium; (2) Western medicine.

洋溢 *yarngyih*, v.i., (reputation) spread far and wide.

洋胰子 *yarng-yirtz*, n., modern soap.

洋銀 *yarngyirn*, n., a copper-nickel-zinc alloy.

洋油 *yarng-your*, n., kerosene.

湃 63A.10-9

paih.

Adj. See 澎ᐞ湃 63A.91.

浲 63A.10-9

jiahng.

N. (AC) a flood: 浲水 a deluge, inundation.

---

§ 63A.11 (氵/土)

灌 63A.11-2

guahn.

N. (1) A surname. (2) 灌縣 name of a country in Szechuan Province.

V. t. (1) To flood with water: 灌漑 *-gaih* ↓. (2) Pour in (liquid): 灌注 pour out or into; 灌水 pour in water, to flood; 灌酒 make (s. o.) drink wine against his will; 灌腸 *-charng* ↓; 灌迷湯 flatter, fawn; 灌漿 *-jiang* ↓; 灌輸 *-shu* ↓; 灌醉 make (s. o.) drunk; 灌入 pour into. (3) (Of sounds) to record: 灌片子, 灌唱片 to cut phonograph records.

Adj. (Of trees) growing in clusters: 灌木 *-muh* ↓; 灌莽 *-maang* ↓.

灌腸 *guahncharng*, n. & v. i., (1) (med.) (give) an enema; (2) (make) sausage.

灌漑 *guahnggaih*, n. & v. t., irrigate, -tion.

灌漿 *guahnjiang*, v. i., (archit.) to grout, pour liquid mortar to fill crevices: 灌漿兒 v. i., (med.) to form vaccinial vesicles.

灌莽 *guahnmaang*, n., coppice, underbrush.

灌木 *guahnmuh*, n., (bot.) shrubs, brushwood.

灌喪 *guahn'sang*, v.i., (abusive) dead drunk.

灌輸 *guahnshu*, v. t., pour into: 灌輸思想 indoctrinate, brainwash inject ideas into mind of people.

灘 63A.11-2

tan.

N. (1) Beach: 海灘 sea beach; 沙灘 sandy beach; 泥灘 mud beach; 灘頭陣地 beachhead of landing force. (2) Rapids.

灘船 *tanchuarn*, n., small boat of canoe size.

灘簧 *tanhuarng*, n., see 攤ᐞ簧 10A.11.

灘戶 *tanhuh*, n., makers of salt on the beach.

灘師 *tanshy*, n., pilot over rapids.

灘頭 *tantour*, n., beachhead; 灘頭小調 a kind of boatman's song.

灘子 *tantzyy*, n., (MC) worker on bank who pulls boat up through rapids or gorges by rope.

汪 63A.11-3

wang.

N. (1) A surname. (2) (LL) a stretch of water: 一汪河水.

V. i. To soak, wet: 連蓆子都汪著水 even the mat was soaked.

Adj. (Of water) vast; (LL) deep (favor).

汪然 *wangrarn*, adj. & adv., vast (stretch of water); profusely: 汪然出涕 weep profusely.
汪汪 *wangwang*, adj., (1) vast (water); profuse (tears: 眼淚汪汪); (2) bowwow, barking noise: 汪汪犬吠.
汪洋 *wangyarng*, n., a vast expanse of water; (fig.) big sweep of creative force, generosity of heart.

湮 63A.11-3

yin (also **yan*).
[Interch. 陻]

V.t. (1) To block up. (2) To sink down.

湮沉 *yinchern* (**yan-*), v.i., (1) to vanish and be forgotten; (2) to stay unknown and unrecognized.
湮蓋 *yingaih*, v. i., inundate.
湮滅 *yinmieh* (**yan-*), see *-chern* (1)↑.
湮沒 *yinmoh* (**yan-*), see *-chern*↑.

涇 63A.11-3

shy.
[Var. 濕 63A.63]

涅 63A.11-4

nieh.
[Pop. 湼; dist. 揑 10A.11]

N. (1) (Min.) alunite. (2) Black mud, slime.

V. t. (1) To blacken: 涅而不緇 be soaked in a dark liquid without becoming black. (2) (Of eggs) incubate. (3) To tattoo: 涅字 tattoo body with characters.

涅白 *niehbair*, n., an opaque white.
涅齒 *-niehchyy*, v.t., to blacken the teeth.
涅髮 *-niehfaa*, v.t., to dye the hair black.
涅面 *-niehmiahn*, v.t., to tattoo the face.
涅槃 *niehparn*, n., (Budd.) nirvana.

濯 63A.11-5

juor.

V. t. (LL) to wash (face, foot, hand): 洗濯 to wash, bathe; 濯纓濯足 (allu.) wash hat tassels if water is clean, and wash feet if water is turbid—win people's praise or contempt by one's own choice; 曲賜湔濯 (AC) wash away one's sins.

濯濯 *juorjuor*, adj., (AC) (1) bright; (2) (of fowl) sleek, well-fed; (3) (of hills) barren, without trees.

涯 63A.11-5

yar.

N. (1) River or lake bank, marsh area: 水涯 ditto; 涯涘 *-syh*↓. (2) Outer limit(s): 涯際, 涯岸 *-jih*, *-ahn*↓; 天涯地角 (海角) distant shores; 一望無涯 a vast expanse (of floods); 吾生也有涯 (AC) my life is finite. (3) Profession, livelihood: 生涯.

涯岸 *yarahn*, n., (LL) river bank, sea beach.
涯際 *yarjih*, n., (LL) limits, borders.
涯涘 *yarsyh*, n., (LL) the limits (of a river, a field of study or knowledge).

渥 63A.11-5

woh.

V. i. To soak wet.

Adj. & adv. Deep (in color, gratitude): 渥丹 deep red; 渥恩, 渥惠 generous favor; 渥赭 deep brown; 渥味 heavy flavor.

注 63A.11-6

juh.

N. adjunct. 一注買賣 one business deal.

N. (1) An entry in diary: 起居注 a diary. (2) U.f. 註 60A.11: 注兒 the commentary part, dist. text or 正文. (3) Stakes at gamble: 下注 put up stakes; 大注 big stakes; 孤一注擲 stake everything on one throw. (4) (MC) a pot: 一注子酒 a pot of wine.

V.t. (1) U.f. 註 to give exegesis or

explanation of text: 注解, 注釋, 注音 *-jiee*, *-shyh*[2], *-yin* ↓. (2) (Of streams) run into (river), pour: 灌注 to irrigate (fields); 傾注, 大雨如注 downpour, a pouring, torrential rain. (3) To concentrate: 注意, 注目, 注視 *-yih*, *-muh*, *-shyh*[1] ↓.

注定 *juhdihng*, v. i., destine(d): 前生注定 destined from previous incarnation.

注腳 *juhjiaau*, n., footnote: 六經皆我注腳 (陸象山) all the Six Classics are merely footnotes for my life experience.

注解 *juhjiee*, n., exegesis, giving explanation and usu. pronunciation of text.

注重 *juhjuhng*, v. t., to emphasize (technology, public sanitation, etc.).

注目 *juhmuh*, v. i., to focus attention: 四海注目 the whole world is watching carefully; 引人注目 (dress, behaviour) arouse or attract attention.

注射 *juhsheh*, (1) v. i., to inject; give injection of medicine; (2) n., an injection.

注心 *juh-shin*, v. i., (AC) concentrate.

注疏 *juhshu*, n., (var. 註疏) exegesis, see *-jiee* ↑; 注 commentary, and 疏 commentary on earlier authoritative commentary.

注視 *juhshyh*[1], v. i., watch attentively, regard as important, see *-muh* ↑.

注釋 *juhshyh*[2], n., exegesis, explanation of text.

注意 *juhyih*, v. i., pay attention, give heed, pay emphasis to (public sanitation, etc.): 請注意 please notice that.

注音 *juhyin*, n., sound notation: 注音字母 the official set of phonetic script system, written on right side of character as sound notation, also called 注音符號 phonetic symbols.

潼 63A.11-6

turng.

N. Name of strategic pass: 潼關.

Adj. 潼潼 (AC) rising very high.

淫 63A.11-9

yirn.

N. Adultery, fornication, debauchery: 行淫 have sexual intercourse, esp. in adultery; 縱淫 given to debauchery; 烝淫 incest.

V. i. & t. To commit adultery with (person): 姦淫 ditto; 淫人妻女 have illicit intercourse with married women and young girls.

Adj. (1) Immoral, licentious, wanton, lascivious, debauched: 淫夫, 淫婦 immoral man, woman; 淫鬼 demon of lust; 淫奔 *-ben* ↓; 淫行 *shihng* ↓; 淫風 immoral, wanton customs, laxity in morals; 淫談 obscene talks; 淫謔 obscene jesting; 淫書 pornograpy; 樂而不淫 joyous but not indecent. (2) Heterodox, impure (doctrine) opp. of 正 orthodox, correct, pure. (3) Extreme, excessive, unrestrained: 淫刑 *-shirng* ↓; 淫雨, 淫威 *-yuu*, *-wei* ↓; 淫水 (AC) floods.

淫奔 *yirnben*, v. i., to elope.

淫巧 *yirnchiaau*, adj., (AC) sophisticated, cunning (work of art).

淫蕩 *yirndahng*, adj., morally loose, promiscuous, lewd, sexually passionate.

淫亂 *yirnluahn*, adj., sexually promiscuous, immoral.

淫靡 *yirnmii*, adj., immoral, sexually loose (atmosphere).

淫念 *yirn-niahn*, n., immoral thoughts, lust.

淫辱 *yirnruh*, v. t., to violate (girls, women).

淫戲 *yirn-shih*, n., (1) obscene plays; (2) orgies.

淫行 *yirnshihng*, n., immoral conduct.

淫心 *yirn-shin*, n., immoral thoughts, sexual lust: 起淫心 is sexually aroused.

淫刑 *yirn-shirng*, n., illegal or extreme torture.

淫祀 *yirnsyh*, n., (AC) worship of popular but illegitimate gods.

淫祠 *yirntsyr*[1], n., (1) temple of popular, but illegitimate gods; (2) temple given to immoral practice.

淫辭 *yirn-tsyr*[2], n., (AC) unbridled talk.

淫哇 *yirnwa*, n., lewd songs.

淫娃 *yirnwar*, n., a depraved girl.

淫猥 *yirnweei*, adj., indecent, pornographic (novels, etc.).

淫威 *yirnwei*, n., tyrannical authority, despotic power.

淫羊藿 *yirnyarnghuoh*, n., (bot.) *Epimedium macranthum* var. *violaceum.*

淫液 *yirnyeh*[1], adj., (AC) depraved, debauched: 沈湎淫液 drunken.

淫業 *yirnyeh*[2], n., prostitution.

淫佚 *yirnyih*, adj., given to ease and luxury (also wr. 淫逸).

淫慾 *yirnyuh*, n., lust, sexual desire.

淫雨 *yirnyuu*, n., excessive rain (also wr. 霪).

准 63A.11-9

juun.

[Dist. 準]

V. i. & t. (1) To permit, allow: 批准, 照准 request approved; 不准 not approved, rejected; 准予 *-yuu* ↓; 准假 leave permitted. (2) Decide: 准于 (於), 准以 phr., setting date: 准于某月某日 date is set at; 准以十日爲限 date is set within ten days (to complete s. t.).

Adj. (1) According to, in accordance with: 准此 accordingly, according to the above (a common formula in official documents between equals for passing on matter without responsibility or recommendation) . . .; 等由, 准此, 相應函達 (after quotation of incoming letter) therefore I am writing to pass on the above information. (2) (Legal) quasi-, to be treated on equal basis as: 以准盜論, 以准強姦論 to be considered as equal to robbery, rape; 准共產黨 quasi-communist; 准佔有 quasi-possession.

准伏 *junfur*, v. i., (law) to sign affidavit.
准許 *jurnshyuu*, v. i. & t., to give permission to do: 准許回職 permit to resume office.
准予 *jurnyuu*, v. i., to give permission to do: 准予免試 give permission to be exempted from tests.

淮 63A.11-9

huair.

N. Name of a river in Anhuei Province.

瀅 63A.11-9

yirng.

Adj. (Water) pure, lucid.

§ 63A.20 (氵/卄)

漭 63A.20-2

maang.

Adj. Descriptive of flood water.

漭沆 *maangkahng*, adj., torrential (of flood water).
漭漭 *marngmaang*, adj., ditto.

洴 63A.20-8

pirng.

[Usu. wr. 泙]

洴澼 *pirngpih*, n., sound of water; 洴澼絖 --*kuahng*, v. i., (AC) to bleach cloth in water current.

濞 63A.20-9

pih.

N. (AC) sound of rushing water.

§ 63A.21 (氵/乚)

湛 63A.21-2

jahn (**dan*).

N. A surname.

Adj. (1) Deep, profound: 精湛 profound, deep (phil.). (2) Clear, tranquil: 清湛 clear (pond, lake). (3) (**dan*) U.f. 耽 31S.70.

湛恩 *jahn-en*, n., deep, profound favor or kindness.
湛露 *jahn-luh*, n., great imperial kindness (compared to "heavy dew" on grass).
湛然 *jahnrarn*, adj. & adv., tranquil, -ly, calm, -ly.

汕 63A.21-2

shahn.

N. (AC) a bamboo fish trap, a weir.

汕頭 *Shahntour*, n., Swatow, a port in Kwangtung.

泄 63A.21-2

shieh.

[Related 瀉 63A.50; var. of 洩 63A.71]

涵 63A.21-3

harn.

V. i. & t. To encompass; to tolerate and forgive: 海涵 to be generous like the sea and forgive; 包涵 to include (also wr. 包含), also to tolerate and forgive (errors).

涵容 *harnrurng*, v. t., to tolerate or pardon.
涵蓄 *harnshyuh*, adj., restrained; (in writing or speech) restrained but suggestive (also wr. 含蓄).
涵養 *harnyaang*, (1) n., culture, polite restraint: 有涵養, 涵養深, 涵養工夫 has deep culture, esp. shown in restraint, forbearance; (2) v. t., (of nature) 涵養萬物 to nourish and cherish all things.

滙 63A.21-5

shueih.

[Var. of 匯 51.21]

漚 63A.21-5

ouh (**ou*).

N. (**ou*) A bubble: 浮漚 bubbles on water surface.

V.t. To soak in water: 漚麻 to ret hemp.

滔 63A.21–9

tau.

Adj. Rampant, flooding, breaking restraint: see 滔滔, 滔天 *-tau*, *-tian*↓.

滔滔 *tautau*, adj., overflowing: 滔滔不絕 incessant (talk); 白浪滔滔 crashing waves; 滔滔者天下皆是也 the world is full of garrulous reformers.

滔天 *tautian*, adj., filling the heavens: 滔天大罪 iniquity stinks to heavens.

---

§ 63A.22 (氵/丨)

浙 63A.22–1

jeh.

N. Name of river and province: 浙江 Chekiang Province; 浙東 East Chekiang.

淅 63A.22–1

shi.

[Dist. 浙]

N. Water left after washing rice.

Adj. See compp.↓.

淅瀝 *shilih*, n., rustle of falling leaves, snow.

淅颯 *shisah*, adj., rustling, crackling sound.

淅淅 *shishi*, adj., whistling of wind.

漸 63A.22–1

jiahn (**jian*).

V. t. (**jian*) (1) (AC) flow into: 東漸於海 it empties into the sea in the east. (2) Moisten, soak: 漸漬 *-tzyh*↓; 漸潤 saturate with water. (3) Imbue, instil: 漸摩 *-mor*, 漸染 *-raan*[1]↓; 漸民以仁 (AC) inspire the people with love.

Adj. & adv. Gradual(ly): 漸漸 *-jiahn*↓; 漸入佳境 (of circumstances) becoming more enjoyable; 逐漸 step by step, little by little; 漸次 *-tsyh*↓; 漸進(主義) gradual(ism); 漸冉 *-raan*↓; 漸或 occasionally, rarely, now and then; 漸趨惡化 slowly deteriorate, go from bad to worse, degenerate.

漸漸 *jiahnjiahn*, adv., gradually, step by step, by degrees, little by little.

漸摩 **jianmor*, v. t., instil, inculcate, imbue.

漸染 **jianraan*[1], v. i. & t., accustom(ed) to bad habits.

漸冉 *jiahnraan*[2], adv., (LL) gradually, slowly, a little at a time.

漸次 *jiahntsyh*, adv., gradually, slowly.

漸漬 **jiantzyh*, v. i., (lit. & fig.) become imbued, soaked.

瀟 63A.22–2

shiau.

瀟灑 *shiausaa*, adj., (1) free, emancipated, unhampered by conventions; (2) (person, writing) spirited, wayward, forthright; (3) (character) pure, noble.

瀟瀟 *shiaushiau*, adj., windy, rainy.

澌 63A.22–2

sy.

V. i. (Of ice) break up into floes.

凘 63A.22–2

sy.

V.i. (Of water) to dry up, (of other things) vanish: 凘滅 (of fire) be extinguished, (of life) come to an end.

沖 63A.22–2

chung.

[Pop. 冲]

V. i. & t. (1) To soar: 沖天, 沖入雲霄, 沖霄 to soar to the skies, the clouds. (2) To pour boiling water over: 沖茶 make tea by pouring boiling water; 沖奶粉, 沖咖啡 similarly make milk from powdered milk, coffee; 沖開水 to prepare (drink) by adding boiling water: 沖服 *-fur*↓. (3) (Of flood) to wash away: 沖塌, 沖壞 destroy (bridge, building) by flood; 被水沖走了 is washed away by flood. (4) To violate (interch. 衝): 沖犯, 沖鋒 *-fahn*, *-feng*↓. (5) To counteract bad luck: 沖運氣 counter bad luck with s. t. good (as wedding); 沖喜 *-shii*↓.

Adj. (1) Modest, retired: 沖和, 沖退 *-her*, *-tueih*↓. (2) Mild: 沖淡 *-dahn*↓. (3) (LL) young, tender: 沖年, 沖齡, 沖弱 at a tender age; 沖昧 young and ignorant.

沖沖 *chungchung*, adv., angrily: 怒氣沖沖.

沖淡 *chungdahn*, (1) adj., mild (temperament), contented with few wants; (2) v. i. & t., dilute.

沖犯 *chungfahn*, v. t., to antagonize (person, superior), transgress (law).

沖鋒 *chungfeng*, v. i., (u. f. 衝) dash to the front of battle, bear the brunt.

沖服 *chungfur*, v. i., to take medical powder or herbs by pouring boiling water over them.

沖和 *chungher*, adj., mild (temperament), amiable.

沖積 *chungjir*, v. i., to be washed up and piled up by current; 沖積物 sedimentary, alluvial deposits.

沖撞 *chungjuahng*, v. t., to knock against, to collide (with another shop).

沖默 *chungmoh*, adj., quiet, reticent.

沖人 *chungrern*, n., (AC) self-reference by a young ruler ("our tender selves").

沖銷 *chung-shiau*, v. i., in business accounts, cancel out an error; also two accounts cancel out each other.

沖喜 *chung-shii*, v. i., to save patient's life by giving him a wedding to counteract bad luck.

沖虛 *chungshyu*, (1) adj., modest, open-minded, unburdened with material pursuits; (2) v. i., to soar aloft.

沖操 *chungtsau*, adj., (LL) keep one's integrity by being contented with simple life.

沖退 *chungtueih*, adj., retiring.

沖挹 *chungyih*, adj., ditto.

沛 63A.22-2

jii.

N. A kind of white wine.

沸 63A.22-2

feih (re. pr. **fuh*).

V. i. To boil, bubble: 沸湧 **fuhyuung*, gush.

Adj. Boiling, bubbling: 沸水 (=usu. 滾水, 開水) boiling water; 沸湯, 沸羹 boiling water, soup, also seething noise, criticism; (fig.) seething, tumultuous: 沸騰 *-terng*↓; 人聲鼎沸 noise and shouts in great commotion.

沸泉 *feihchyuarn*, n., bubbling spring.

沸點 *feih-diaan*, n., boiling point.

沸沸 **furfur*, adj., boiling.

沸石 *feihshyr*, n., (geol.) zeolite.

沸騰 *feihterng*, adv., boiling over, seething: 輿論沸騰 a great commotion in public criticism.

洲 63A.22-2

jou.

N. (1) A continent: 七大洲 the seven continents; 亞洲 Asia; 歐洲 Europe. (2) An islet, sandbar: 沙洲 sandy islet; 洲渚, 洲汀 ditto.

洲際 *joujih*, adj., intercontinental: 洲際彈道飛彈 Intercontinental Ballistic Missile.

淵 63A.22-2

yuan.

[Pop. 渊]

N. (1) A deep pond, abyss: 深淵 ditto; 天淵之別 difference between high heaven and deep sea—completely different, apart. (2) A surname.

Adj. Deep, profound: 淵博, 淵富, 淵遠 *-bor, -fuh, -yuaan*↓; 淵然而靜 (LL) profound and still.

淵博 *yuanbor*, adj., profound (scholar, scholarship); breadth and depth.

淵泉 *yuan-chyuarn*, n., deep springs.

淵富 *yuanfuh*, adj., rich and variegated.

淵廣 *yuanguaang*, adj., broad and dimensional (knowledge, experience).

淵海 *yuan-haai*, n., big sea.

淵默 *yuanmoh*, n., still and profound.

淵深 *yuanshen*, adj., deep (knowledge).

淵識 *yuan-shyh*, n., deep knowledge, insight.

淵藪 *yuansoou*, n., gathering ground of fish and beasts; the great sources of knowledge.

淵遠 *yuanyuaan*, adj., broad and deep.

淵淵 *yuanyuan*, adj., (1) deep and still; (2) (AC) sound of drums.

淵源 *yuanyuarn*, n., source and origin (of thought, philosoply).

滯 63A.22-2

jyh.

V. i. (1) To stagnate, be blocked up: 滯泥 *-nih*↓; 凝滯 freeze up, frozen, slow-moving; 滯阻 block up; 滯運 slow up luck; 滯訟, 滯獄 longstanding lawsuits. (2) To loiter, not move forward: 滯留 *-liour*↓.

Adj. & adv. Sluggish, slow-moving: 滯流 sluggish stream or current; 滯貨 slow-selling goods.

滯礙 *jyh-aih*, v. t., to obstruct (progress).

滯氣 *jyhchih*, n., apathy and inertia.

滯伏 *jyhfur*, v.i., (LL) be lacking in ambition, self-enclosed.

滯積 *jyhji*, v. i., pile up (back log.).

滯累 *jyhleei*, v. t., to be involved in material, sordid things.

滯留 *jyhliour*, v. i., to loiter (at a

place), not move forward.

滯泥 *jyhnih*, v. i., be a stickler, be obstructed or held up by trifles: 滯滯泥泥 sticky (manner of doing things).

滯下 *jyhshiah*, n., (AC) slow-moving bowels, a form of constipation.

滯銷 *jyh-shiau*, phr., slow-selling (goods).

滯胃 *jyh-weih*, phr., sluggish digestion.

滯淹 *jyhyan*, v. i., (LL) linger in life.

汓 63A.22-3

liour.

[Anc. var. of 流 63A.70]

汴 63A.22-6

biahn.

N. Ancient river and place name; 汴京=Kaifeng (開封), capital of Northern Suhng Dyn.

沛 63A.22-6

peih.

N. (1) Marsh grounds. (2) Name of district.

V. t. (1) To irrigate. (2) To falter, drift in 顛[4]沛 10S.80.

Adj. Handsome, full: 充沛 full, rich (in energy, etc.).

沛艾 *peih-aih*, adj., (AC) handsome and tall (of person).

沛沛 *peihpeih*, adj., (AC) swift (of current).

沛然 *peihrarn*, adj., (of rain) pouring with force, voluminous.

溓 63A.22-6

liarn.

N. Name of river in Hunan.

濟 63A.22-6

jih (**jii*).

V. t. (1) (Of rivers) go across, pass over: 濟河 cross a stream; 同舟共濟 be all in the same boat. (2) To help, aid, relieve: 濟急 *-jir* ↓; 濟貧, 濟困 help the poor, people in distress; 救濟 give relief; 濟弱扶傾 to champion the cause of the underdog; 請濟師於王 request the king for reinforcements. (3) Be helpful to, succeed in: 濟事 *-shyh*[2] ↓.

Adj. See 濟濟 *-jih* ↓.

濟度 *jihduh*, v. t., deliver from worldly miseries.

濟惡 *jih-eh*, v. t., aid and abet (s.o.) in wrongdoing.

濟濟 *jihjih*, (also **jirjii*) adj., numerous, a multitude of: 人才濟濟 a galaxy of talent; 濟濟多士 legions of men.

濟急 *jih-jir*, v. i., give urgent relief.

濟南 *Jihnarn*, n., capital of Shantung Province.

濟世 *jih-shyh*[1], v. i., be a benefactor to society.

濟事 *jih-shyh*[2], v. i. & adj., (be) of help: 不濟事 does not help at all; 無濟於事 of no help to the matter.

涕 63A.22-8

tih.

N. (1) (LL) tears: 涕淚 tears; 涕泗滂沱 phr., a flood of tears; 感激涕零 phr., shed tears of gratitude; 涕泣 to cry, sob; 痛哭流涕 phr., shed tears over some loss, feel loss bitterly or regret. (2) Mucus from the nose: 鼻涕.

沂 63A.22-9

yir.

N. A river in Confucius' home district.

§ 63A.30 (氵/一)

渣 63A.30-1

ja (**jaa*).

N. (1) (*-tz, 'l*) Dregs: 渣滓 *-tzyy* ↓; 糖渣 sugar dregs. (2) (**jaa*) Leftovers after burning or processing: 煤渣兒 (子) not completely burned-out coal bits; 甘蔗渣 sugar cane pulp.

渣兒 *ja'l*, n., (1) dregs, sucked out pulp; (2) (**jaa'l*) small bits (of coal).

渣子 *jatz*, n., see *-'l* ↑.

渣滓 *jatzyy*, n., dregs, sediment.

溘 63A.30-1

keh.

Adv. Abruptly (disappear, pass away), see 溘然 *-rarn* ↓; 溘逝 pass away suddenly.

溘溘 *kehkeh*, adj., (MC) descriptive of splash of waves against rocks; (MC) cold: 寒溘溘.

溘然 *kehrarn*, adv., as in 溘然長逝 (person) pass away all of a sudden.

A B C

沚 63A.30-2

jyy.

N. (AC) a small pond.

澥 63A.30-2

shieh.

Phr. See 沆△瀣 63A.70.

瀘 63A.30-2

lur.

N. Name of a river and district in Szechuan.

灃 63A.30-2

feng.

N. Name of river in Shensi.

灩 63A.30-2

yahn.

Adj. See 瀲△灩 63A.81.

灩 滪 堆 *Yahnyuhduei*, n., name of a gorge in Szechuan.

澧 63A.30-2

lii.

N. Name of river in Hunan.

江 63A.30-3

jiang.

N. (1) A river: 長江 the Yangtse River; 大江東去，江水東流 eastward flows the Yangtse; 江河行地 as immutable as the rivers; gravitate downwards 江河日下 fast deteriorating, going from bad to worse; 江口，江心，江邊 (江畔) the mouth, the middle, the bank, of a river. (2) A surname.

江 表 *jiangbiaau*, n., regions south of the Yangtse.
江 防 *jiang-farng*, n., flood control or defense works on the Yangtse.
江 干 *jianggan*, n., (LL) riverside.
江 皐 *jianggau*, n., (LL) river bank.
江 湖 *jianghur*, (1) n., 走江湖 or 江湖客 live life of adventurer, boxer, salesman, etc.; 江湖醫生 a quack; (2) (-'*hu*) adj., wise in the ways of the world, slippery, untrustworthy.
江 蘺 *jianglir*, n., (bot.) *Gracilaria confervoides*.
江 米 *jiangmii*, n., glutinous rice.
江 南 *Jiangnarn*, n., regions south of the Yangtse.
江 山 *jiangshan*, n., the national territory or authority over it: 得 (失) 江山 capture (lose) political power.
江 鄉 *jiangshiang*, n., a river or lake district.
江 瑤 *jiangyaur*[1], n., usu. 江瑤柱 edible ligament of a shellfish, *Pinna japonica*.
江 珧 *jiangyaur*[2], n., ditto.

沍 63A.30-3

huh.

Adj. (AC) blocked up.

洹 63A.30-3

huarn.

N. Name of river in Honan.

涇 63A.30-3

jing.

N. The name of a river, usu. referred to in conjunction with another river 渭 to form a contrast: 涇渭分明 make a clear distinction between purity and impurity; 不分涇渭 make no such distinction between good and evil, black and white.

澄 63A.30-3

cherng (**dehng*).

V.t. (Also **dehng*) to clarify water by letting it stand; to purify: 澄清 -*ching*↓; 澄心 purify the heart; 澄其思慮 purify one's thoughts.

Adj. Limpid, clear and quiet: 澄明, 澄澈 -*mirng*, -*cheh*↓; 澄空 a clear, cloudless sky.

澄 澈 *cherngcheh*, adj., transparently clear and limpid.
澄 清 *cherngching*, v.t., to purify: 澄清吏治 to cleanse out political corruption; 澄清天下 bring peace and order to the country.
澄 明 *cherngmirng*, adj., transparently clear.

溫 63A.30-4

wen.

[Usu. wr. 温]

沚 澥 瀘 灃 灩 澧 江 沍 洹 涇 澄 溫

亅	小	卜	十	土	ナ	卄	𠃊卜	丨	一	丅	フ	口	区	冈	㇆	厂	尸	亠	广	宀	丶	乚	弋	心	八	人	乂	㇀	㇀	丿丿	𠂉	く
00	01	02	10	11	12	20	21	22	30	31	32	40	41	42	50	51	52	60	61	62	63	70	71	72	80	81	82	83	90	91	92	93

N. (1) A surname. (2) Place name: 溫州 Wenchow in Chekiang.

V.t. (1) To review, go over what has been learned before: 溫習 *-shir*↓; 溫故知新 review what has been learned and learn s.t. new; 重溫舊夢 relive an old dream, oft. said of lovers' reunion; 溫舊情 renew old friendship. (2) To warm up, reheat (food, wine).

Adj. (1) Warm (water, tea, wine). (2) Hot: 溫泉, 溫牀 *-chyuarn, -chuarng*↓. (3) Gentle, mild in temperatment: 溫和, 溫柔, 溫順 *-her, -rour, -shuhn*, etc.↓. (4) (Coll.) over-cautious (person), dull, flat (play, writing).

溫飽 *wen-baau*, adj., warmly clothed and well-fed.
溫病 *wen-bihng*, n., (Chin. med.) fever without chills.
溫情 *wen-chirng*, n., warm feeling.
溫牀 *wenchuarng*, n., hotbed for forcing plants.
溫泉 *wen-chyuarn*, n., hot springs.
溫帶 *wen-daih*, n., (geog.) temperate zone.
溫度 *wen-duh*, n., degree of temperature; 溫度計 thermometer.
溫和 *wen-her* (-'*he*), adj., mild (weather), gentle (person).
溫厚 *wen-houh*, adj., kind (person): (AC) 居皆溫厚 luxurious (living).
溫凊 *wen-jihng*, phr., (AC) see that parents live in warm rooms in winter and cool rooms in summer.
溫居 *wen-jyu*, phr., to give house-warming party.
溫卷 *wen-jyuahn*, phr., (Tarng Dyn.) repeatedly send in one's writings to examiner together with names of well-known friends who know him.
溫炕 *wen-kahng*, n., warm or heated earthen bed.
溫克 *wenkeh*[1], adj., (MC dial.) gentle (disposition).
溫課 *wen-keh*[2], v.i., to review lesson.
溫良 *wenliarng*, adj., gentle and kind.
溫毛了 *wen-maur'le*, phr., to overheat wine until it bubbles over.
溫煖(暖) *wennuaan*, adj., warm (sun, bed, human fellowship).
溫朴 *wen'pu*, n., a kind of sugar-coated berry (cf. 榲[A]桲 10B.30).
溫柔 *wenrour*, adj., gentle, pleasingly affectionate, esp. toward lover; hence 溫柔鄉 *--shiang*, n., (AC allu.) love nest, bedroom pleasures.
溫潤 *wenruhn*, adj., (1) soft (lustre of jade); (2) (AC) kindly (disposition).
溫馨 *wenshing*, adj., softly fragrant.
溫習 *wen-shir* (-'*shi*), v.t., to review (lessons).
溫書 *wen-shu*, v.i., to review lessons.
溫順 *wenshuhn*, adj., filial, obedient.
溫室 *wenshyh*, n., hothouse.
溫煦 *wenshyuu*, adj., warm, gentle, mild.
溫存 *wentsurn* (-'*tsun*), (1) adj., gentle, kind; (2) v.i., to be kind and attentive to (person): 溫存話兒 comforting words.
溫暾 *wentun*, adj., (LL) warm, lukewarm (also wr. 燉).
溫婉 *wenwaan*, adj., filial, gentle, obedient.
溫溫 *wenwen*, adj., kindly, mild-mannered.
溫文 *wenwern*, adj., cultured in manners.
溫雅 *wenyaa*, adj., refined (person).

沮 63A.30-4

jyuh (**jyu*, **jyuu*).

N. (**jyu*) A surname.

V. i. & t. (**jyuu*) (1) Be dejected, lose heart: 沮喪 *-sahng*↓. (2) Stop, prevent: 沮止 to halt, stop, put an end to; 沮之以兵 stop him with armed force; 沮格 prevent; 沮駭 obstruct.

Adj. Marshy, boggy, swampy: 沮洳 *-ruh*↓; 沮澤 *-tzer*↓.

沮洳 *jyuhruh*, adj., marshy, damp.
沮喪 **jyuusahng*, v. i., be dispirited, downcast, gloomy.
沮澤 *jyuhtzer*, n., a swamp, marsh.

澀 63A.30-5

seh.

Adj. (1) Harsh, acrid, astringent in taste (like unripe fruit). (2) Rough, not smooth, not even (wooden surface); difficult, hard to read, abstruse (reading, style). (3) Slow of speech: 澀訥 *-neh*↓.

澀滯 *sehjyh*, adj., rough-going, not flowing easily (of writing).
澀吶 *sehnah*, adj., see *-neh*↓.
澀奈 *sehnaih*, adj., (MC) uneasy.
澀訥 *sehneh*, adj., slow of speech.
澀縮 *sehsuo*, adj., (MC) dilly-dallying, undecided, vacillating.

濫 63A.30-5

lahn.

V.t. (1) Overflow: 氾濫 to flood, inundate. (2) (AC) to covet.

Adj. & adv. Excessive(ly), immoderate(ly), indiscriminate(ly), illegal(ly), without restraint, without scruples: 小人窮斯濫矣 a mean man, when reduced to poverty, will do anything to gain his ends; 濫發 issue excessive numbers of (banknotes, invitations, etc.); 濫費 spend money immoderately; 濫取 accept illegal payments; 濫用 misuse, abuse: 濫用職權 abuse one's authority; 濫耗公帑 spend public funds too freely; 濫伐 illegal felling of trees; 濫殺 slaughter people without discrimination; 濫交 *-jiau*↓; 濫保 be guarantor for (s.o.) without due consideration; 濫支 lavish expenditure; 濫開數目 charge excessive amounts for services rendered; 濫惡 extremely bad, wicked or evil. (2) Stale, hackneyed, trite: 濫調 *-diauh*, 濫套 *-tauh* ↓.

濫調兒 *lahndiauh('l)*, n., hackneyed words and phrases: 陳腔濫調 hot air without substance, jargon, cliché.

濫交 *lahnjiau*, v. i., fall into bad company, make friends without discrimination.

濫觴 *lahnshang*, n. & v.i., (LL) origin; originate.

濫套(兒)(子) *lahntauh ('l)(tz)*, n., platitudes.

濫汚 *lahnwu*, adj., (Soochow dial.) dirty, tricky, unchaste: 拆濫汚 neglect one's duty; 濫汚貨 a woman of loose morals.

濫竽 *lahnyur*, adj., as in 濫竽充數 (of an untrained person) be included among a group of experts; just to fill up a vacancy.

瀝 63A.30–5

lih.

N. Sediment of wine, dregs.

V. i. & t. To drip, trickle, strain: 滴瀝 drip and trickle; 瀝血; 披肝瀝膽 lay bare my heart (lit., drip blood, bile).

瀝青 *lihching*, n., (1) pitch, asphalt; (2) resin: 瀝青炭 (min.) bituminous coal.

瀝瀝 *lihlih*, adj., (1) (of wind) whistling, rustling; (2) (of flowing water) babbling; (3) dripping: 瀝瀝拉拉弄了一桌子湯 the table is dripping with soup all over.

泣 63A.30–6

chih.

V.i. & t. (1) To sob, weep noiselessly: 涕泣, 悲泣 to weep silently; 哭泣 to weep; 飲泣 to swallow one's tears; 暗泣 to sob secretly. (2) Cause to weep: 動天地而泣鬼神 (rhet.) move the universe and cause the gods to weep—very moving. (3) To weep and (+vb.) (used like weepingly, adv.): 泣叩, 泣請, 泣訴 weepingly implore, request, complain; 泣罪 please pardon the offender (used by sentenced prisoner).

泣血 *chihshyueh*, phr., (rhet.) weep tears of blood: 泣血稽顙 "shed tears of blood and kotow on the ground"—formula used in obituary for loss of a parent.

泣涕 *chihtih*, v. i., to weep, shed tears.

澶 63A.30–6

charn.

澶漫 *charnmarn*, adj., (AC) usu. in 澶漫爲樂 have swing and rhythm in music.

涳 63A.30–6

kung.

涳濛 *kungmerng*, adj., descriptive of fine drizzle (also wr. 空濛).

渲 63A.30–6

shyuahn.

渲染 *shyuahnraan*, v. t., to add touches or color (to a story): 渲染事實 to distort facts by adding touches.

淦 63A.30–8

gahn.

N. Water in ship's hold.

溢 63A.30–8

yih.

V. i. To overflow: 外溢 (currency, money) flows out of country; 流溢 (of influence) spread; 四溢 spread in all directions.

Adj. & adv. Overflowing, -ly: 滿溢 full to overflow; exaggerated: 溢美, 溢惡 exaggerated praise, detraction; 溢譽 exaggerated reputation.

溢出 *yih-chu*, phr., flow outward, overflow.

溢滿 *yih-maan*, adj., full to overflow.

湓 63A.30–8

pern.

N. Name of place, also of river in Kiangse.

V. i. To gush forth (of water): 湓溢.

洫 63A.30–9

shyuh.

N. (AC) gutters: 溝洫 a field ditch; drain, gutters.

湼 涖 涔 汐 沽 浩 湱 沾

湼 63A.30-9

nieh.

[Pop. of 涅 63A.11]

涖 63A.30-9

lih.

N. Arrival, advent.

V. t. (Var. of 莅) come to, arrive at: 涖止, 涖臨 (court.) be present at; 涖任 assume office.

Adj. 涖涖 (AC) descriptive of rippling water.

---

§ 63A.32 (氵/フ)

涔 63A.32-2

tsern.

Adj. & adv. 涔涔 (1) Dripping (sweat, rain). (2) Murky sky (雪意涔涔). (3) Dizzy (headache); tearful, -ly (涔涔淚下).

汐 63A.32-9

shih.

N. The eventide ebb tide.

---

§ 63A.40 (氵/口)

沽 63A.40-1

gu.

V.t. (1) Sell: 市沽 sell in the market; 沽酒 sell wine. (2) Buy: 沽酒 buy wine or wine bought from the market; 沽物 make purchases; 沽名釣譽 to fish for fame and social recognition.

浩 63A.40-1

hauh.

N. Large, great, expansive: 浩劫, 浩大 *-jier, -dah*↓; 浩然 *-rarn*↓.

Adv. Greatly: 浩飲 drink inordinately; 浩歎 (a matter of) great regret, sigh deeply.

浩博 *hauhbor*, n., abundant, extensive (knowledge, thoughts and ideas).

浩氣 *hauh-chih*, n., (Mencius) man's expansive nature, idealistic impulse.

浩大 *hauhdah*, adj., very great (expenses, engineering works, achievements).

浩蕩 *hauhdahng*, adj., onrushing (flood), wide and expansive (waters, lakes): 浩浩蕩蕩 coming with great force, in formidable array.

浩繁 *hauhfarn*, n., bulky and multifarious, great and painstaking (work).

浩瀚 *hauhhahn*, adj., limitless, expansive.

浩浩 *hauhhauh*, adv., like rushing flood.

浩劫 *hauhjier*, n., a great crisis, physical suffering; period of trials and tribulations.

浩渺 *hauhmiaau*, adj., (of water) limitless.

浩然 *hauhrarn*, adj., usu. (Mencius) 浩然之氣 the idealistic impulse in man, great moral force.

湱 63A.40-1

huoh.

Adj. (AC) sound of crashing, (var. of 砉).

沾 63A.40-2

jan.

V. i. & t. (1) To wet, soak: 沾水 soak in water; 沾濕, 沾染 *-shy, -raan*↓; 沾脣 (of drinking) barely wet the lips; 酒不沾脣 never touch a drink; 沾泥 (of flowers) stained with mud; 禪心已作沾泥絮 my heart is like mud-coated catkins—no longer moved by passing winds; 淚沾襟 tears wet the jacket. (2) To touch, be touched with: 沾寒, 沾疾 be touched with a cold, illness; 沾花惹草 phr., to be promiscuous in sex relations. (3) To benefit or be influenced by touching: 沾便宜, 沾邊兒 to benefit on the sly, make secret or unnoticed gains; 沾潤, 沾光 *-ruhn, -guang*↓; 沾親帶故 to share (benefit) with relatives and friends.

Adj. 沾沾自喜 very pleased with oneself.

沾溉 *jangaih*, v. t., to irrigate (fields); (fig.) to spread benefit to people (as rain benefits the fields).

沾光 *jan-guang*, v. i., to share in reflected glory, to benefit by s. o.'s influence: 這回實在沾了你的光了 all thanks to you; it was all due to your influence.

沾染 *janraan*, v. i. & t., (1) to contract (bad habits) by association; (2) to take part in illegal benefit.

沾潤 *janruhn*, v. i., to make gains on the sly.

沾洽 *janshiar*, adj., (1) soaked; (fig.) soaked with learning; (2) (litr.) permeated, immersed extensively with royal favors.

沾手 *janshoou*, v. i. & t., (1) touch with hand: 這花一沾手就壞了 this flower is easily spoiled by touch; (2) to take part in: 這事你不必沾手 you need have no

part in this matter.
沾濕 *janshy*, v. t., to wet (clothing, etc. as by rain).

沿 63A.40–4

yarn (**yahn*).
[Related 緣 93B.02]

N. (1) (*-'l, -tz*) Border (of dress, quilts, territory). (2) (**yahn*) (Coll.) 河沿 river bank; 邊沿 edge, border of anything.

V. t. (1) To follow (street, river, customs, tradition): 沿街叫賣 to peddle s.t. in the streets; 沿河而上 follow the river up; 相沿成習 (a practice) has come down from the past and become customary; 沿襲, 沿革, 沿用 *-shir, -ger, -yuhng* ↓. (2) (Tailoring) to fringe, furnish with border: 沿條兒, 沿邊兒 *-tiaur'l, -bia'l* ↓.

Prep. Along (road, stream, shore): 沿道, 沿路, 沿途 *-dauh, -luh, -tur* ↓; 沿著河邊走 go along the river bank.

沿岸 *yarn-ahn*, adv., along the shore.
沿邊兒 *yarnbia'l*, n., braid (of dress); border piece of quilts.
沿道(兒) *yarn-dauh('l)*, adv., all along the road, see *-luh('l)* ↓.
沿革 *yarnger*, n., the history and development (of a district, customs, institutions).
沿例 *yarn-lih*, adv., according to precedents, old rules.
沿路(兒) *yarn-luh('l)*, adv., along the road, on the roadside.
沿門 *yarn-mern*, phr., 沿門托鉢 (of monks) beg for alms from house to house.
沿襲 *yarnshir*, v. t. & n., to follow (old customs).
沿條兒 *yarntiaur'l*, n., a braid or tape for joining parts of dress.
沿途 *yarn-tur*, adv., see *-luh('l)* ↑.
沿用 *yarnyuhng*, v. t., continue to use (old terms, etc.).

沼 63A.40–5

jaau.

N. (AC & LL) a pond: 池沼, 沼澤 ponds; 湖沼 lakes and ponds.

沼氣 *jaauchih*, n., marsh gas.

涪 63A.40–6

fur.

N. Name of river in Szechuan.

溏 63A.40–6

tarng.

N. Pool.

Adj. Not hardened: 溏心蛋 soft-boiled or soft-fried egg, fluid in center; 溏便 (Chin. med.) loose bowels.

溶 63A.40–6

rurng.

V.i. & t. Dissolve in water: 溶化 *-huah* ↓; 溶解 *-jiee* ↓; 溶入 dissolve into; 溶開 separate by dissolution; 溶合 make a solution of.

Adj. Overflowing with water: 溶溶 *-rurng* ↓.

溶化 *rurnghuah*, n., (chem.) solution, dissolution.
溶解 *rurngjiee*, n., ditto; 溶解度 (chem.) solubility, soluble point; 溶解熱 (chem.) melting point; heat of solution.
溶劑 *rurngjih*, n., (chem.) a solvent.
溶質 *rurng-jyr*, n., (chem.) the substance dissolved in a solution.
溶媒 *rurng-meir*, n., (chem.) a solvent (also 溶劑).
溶溶 *rurngrurng*, adj., (LL) (1) (of rivers) roaring, rushing; (2) vast, spacious, broad: 心溶溶其不可量兮 so immeasurably broad is his mind.
溶體 *rurngtii*, n., (chem.) a solution, a fluid.
溶液 *rurngyeh*, n., ditto.

浴 63A.40–8

yuh.

N. A bath: 海水浴場 bathing beach.

V.i. To bathe: 沐浴, 洗浴 take a bath; 浴盆, 浴池, 浴室 *-pern, -chyr, -shyh* ↓; 浴日 (water, lake) bathe in the sunlight; 浴血 a blood bath.

浴池 *yuhchyr*, n., swimming pool.
浴盆 *yuhpern*, n., bathtub.
浴室 *yuhshyh*, n., bathroom.
浴堂 *yuhtarng*, n., a public bath.

洽 63A.40–8

shiar (also *chiah*).

V. i. (1) To join or unite happily, to blend agreeably. (2) To meet and discuss: 商洽 or 洽商 *-shang*, 洽談 *-tarn* ↓; 洽請 discuss an invitation; 接洽 contact and discuss (with person): 和某人接洽 contact certain person.

Adj. Happy together, happily united: 歡洽 jolly (meeting), cordial, friendly; 融洽 (of feel-

洽 滄 活 洛

ings) very cordial.

Adv. Widely: 洽聞 widely read.

洽化 *shiarhuah*, v. i., (LL) (society) morally reformed.

洽驩 *shiarhuan*, adj., (LL) happy, cordial together.

洽商 *shiarshang*, v. i. & t., discuss (problems, terms of contract, etc.).

洽談 *shiartarn*, v. i., to discuss (problems) together.

洽議 *shiaryih*, v. i. & t., meet and discuss (with person), discuss (plans, etc.).

滄 63A.40–8

tsang.

Adj. (1) Blue (sea): 滄海, 滄桑 *-haai*, *-sang* ↓. (2) Cold: 滄滄 *-tsang* ↓.

滄海 *tsanghaai*, n., the wide, blue sea (related 蒼): 滄海桑田 what was the sea is now mulberry fields—(fig.) evanescence of worldly affairs, great changes in the course of time; 滄海一粟 a droplet in the vast ocean—(fig.) very small portion of s.t. vast.

滄江 *tsangjiang*, n., (poet.) the blue river.

滄浪 *tsanglarng*, adj., (of water) translucent.

滄溟 *tsangmirng*, n., (LL) the ocean, the briny deep.

滄桑 *tsangsang*, phr., see *-haai* ↑.

滄滄 *tsangtsang*, adj., usu. 滄滄涼涼 descriptive of coldness (of atmosphere).

活 63A.40–9

huor.

N. Work, livelihood: 做活 make a living: 這個活做得真好 this work is very neatly done; 找點活來做 find some work to do; oft. 生活 (a) life, (b) livelihood; 活計 (=生計) *-'jih* ↓.

V.i. & t. (1) To live: 活着五十歲 lived 50 years; 活不了 cannot live longer; 白活了一世 lived a life in vain (i.e., wasted). (2) Become alive, interested: 心活了 become interested (in plan, etc.). (3) To save lives: 活人無算 saved many lives.

Adj. (1) Live, alive, living: 活人 person still alive, opp. 死人 dead person; 活魚 live fish. (2) Moving, alive: 活水 fresh water, current (opp. stagnant); 生龍活虎, 活潑潑 (painting, descriptive) very much alive; 活生生打死 beat a person to death; 靈活 (style) alive, (skill) expert; 活潑, 活現 *-po*, *-shiahn* ↓; 活動 *-duhng* ↓. (3) Not fixed: 活期存款 demand deposit; 活頁 *-yeh* ↓.

Adv. 活像 *-shiahng* ↓; 生吞活剝 (lit.) skin alive, (fig.) force an interpretation of text without understanding.

活版 *huorbaan*, n., (also 活字版) printing from movable type.

活期 *huorchir*, n., as in 活期存款 deposit on demand.

活動 *huorduhng*, (1) n., activity (-ties): 各種活動 various activities; 體力, 政治活動 physical, political activities; (2) v.i. & t., to move, exercise: 活動筋骨 move muscles in exercise or work; 活動一官半職 run about to get an official post; come alive, show a change: 近來市面上有點活動 some sign of life in the market; 口氣有點活動 his tone has changed somewhat; become flexible, loose (chair legs, etc.); (3) active: 很活動 very active.

活佛 *huorfuor*, n., Living Buddha (in Tibet, Mongolia): 班禪活佛 Panchan Lama.

活該 *huorgai*, vb. aux., deservedly should: 活該如此 deservedly so.

活著(兒) *huorjau('l)*, n., a flexible move (in chess), a step that allows for flexibility.

活見鬼 *huor-jiahn-gueei*, excl., utter nonsense! impossible!

活計 *huor'jih*, n., needlework.

活劇 *huor-jyuh*, n., a drama in real life.

活局子 *huorjyurtz*, n., a trap.

活口 *huorkoou*, n., (1) person captured alive; (2) a living witness of a murder case; 活口米 rice for famine relief.

活扣兒 *huorkouh'l*, n., a knot that can be easily untied.

活兒 *huor'l*, n., a livelihood: 幹活兒, 做活兒 make a living, do what is one's profession.

活力 *huorlih*, n., vitality.

活路 *huorluh('l)*, n., a way out, a means of survival.

活埋 *huor-mair*, v. t., bury alive.

活門 *huormern*, n., (1) a piston; (2) a chance to live.

活命 *huormihng*, n., (save, spare) life.

活潑 *huorpo* (*-'po*), adj., lively, active, energetic.

活塞 *huorsai*, n., a piston.

活現 *huorshiahn*, (1) adj., arrogant, self-satisfied (air); coming alive (portrait); (2) v.t., reveal: 醜態活現 reveal one's weakness, shortcomings.

活像 *huorshiahng*, adj., remarkably like (the dead person, etc.); looking as if indeed.

活受 *huorshouh*, v.i., usu. in 活受罪 suffer terribly.

活水 *huor-shueei*, n., fresh current.

活死人 *huor-syy-rern*, n., a dead-alive person.

活頭兒 *huor'tou'l*, n., interest to live: 那還有甚麼活頭 then what does one want to live for?

活脫 *huortuo*, adj., (LL) remarkably like (spring).

活字版 *huor-tzy-baan*, see *-baan* ↑.

活頁 *huor-yeh*, n., loose-leaf (album).

活躍 *huoryueh*, adj., very lively, active.

活用 *huor-yuhng*, v.t., make flexible use of.

洛 63A.40–9

luoh.

N. Name of river and place: in Honan 洛陽 Loyang, capital of Northern Suhng Dyn.: 洛陽紙貴 (allu.) overwhelming popularity of a new work (causing shortage of printing paper).

澹 63A.40-9

dahn.

Adj. Calm, detached.

澹泊 *dahnbor*, adj. & v. t., usu. in 澹泊明志 live simple life, showing one's true goal in life; 澹泊名利 indifferent towards fame and wealth also wr. 淡泊.

洳 63A.40-9

ruh.

N. Name of a river in Hopei Province.

Adj. Damp: 沮洳 marshy, swampy.

冶 63A.40-9

yee.
[Dist. 治]

N. (AC) blacksmith: 良冶 a good blacksmith.

V.i. & t. (1) To forge (iron): 冶金 smelt metals; (fig.) to shape (character): 陶冶 to shape character by gradual influence. (2) To do make-up: 冶容 to touch up face; 冶容誨淫 to dress prettily is to arouse sex desires.

Adj. Well made-up: 妖冶 seductive-looking; 冶豔 *-yahn* ↓.

冶工 *yeegung*, n., blacksmith.
冶金 *yeejin*, v.i., to smelt metal; 冶金學 metallurgy.
冶豔 *yeeyahn*, adj., attractive-looking, gorgeous.
冶遊 *yeeyour*, v.i., to philander.

治 63A.40-9

jyh.

N. (1) Administration, government, jurisdiction: 省治 provincial capital; 縣治 county seat, jurisdiction. (2) A surname.

V. t. (1) To govern, administer, take charge of: 治理, 治國, 治家 *-lii, -guor, -jia* ↓; 統治 to rule (a country); 自治 self-governing, -ment. (2) To set up, manage, prepare: 治裝, 治喪 *-juang, -sang* ↓; 治酒 set up a wine dinner; 治宴 prepare a dinner; 大禹治水 The Great Yuu regulated the courses of rivers. (3) To treat (a disease): 治病, 治療 *-bihng, -liaur* ↓; 醫治 to treat (a disease); 治好了 has been cured; 不治之症 incurable disease. (4) To punish: 懲治 ditto; 治罪 *-tzueih* ↓; 治死 punish to death; 處治 to deal punishment to. (5) To study a special branch of learning: 治醫, 治史, 治經 study medicine, history, classics; 治學 *-shyuer* ↓.

治安 *jyh-an*, n., public security (from thefts, riots, etc.): 地方的治安如何 how is the public security of the place?
治辦 *jyhbahn*, v. t., to deal with officially, to administer s. t.
治本 *jyhbeen*, v. i. & n., (to effect) basic, fundamental reform; basic cure in medicine; cf. *-biau* ↓.
治標 *jyhbiau*, v. i. & n., alleviate symptoms of disease or social ills; temporary remedy; cf. *-been* ↑.
治病 *jyh-bihng*, v. i., to cure illness.
治兵 *jyh-bing*, v. i., to train, or command an army.
治產 *jyh-chaan*, v. i., to manage business or property.
治躬 *jyh-gung*, v. i., to take care of personal conduct.
治國 *jyh-guor*, v. i., to rule a country.
治化 *jyh-huah*, v. i., to rule and educate a people.
治迹 *jyhji*[1], n., results of a regime.
治績 *jyhji*[2], n., ditto.
治家 *jyh-jia*, v. i., to run a family properly.
治經 *jyh-jing*, v. i., to study the classics.
治裝 *jyh-juang*, v. i., to pack up for journey.
治具 *jyh-jyuh*, v. i., prepare a wine dinner.
治軍 *jyh-jyun*, v. i., train and command an army.
治療 *jyhliaur*, (1) n., therapy: 精神治療 psychotherapy, psychiatric treatment; (2) v. t., to cure.
治理 *jyhlii*, v. t., to rule, manage, put in order.
治平 *jyh-pirng*, v. i., from 治國平天下 rule the country and give peace to the world.
治戎 *jyh-rurng*, v. i., see *-bing* ↑.
治喪 *jyh-sang*, v. i., manage, set up a funeral.
治生 *jyh-sheng*, v. i., make a livelihood.
治下 *jyh-shiah*, phr., under a jurisdiction.
治行 *jyh-shirng*, (1) (AC) prepare for journey; (2) (*-shihng*) (AC) results of an administration.
治術 *jyh-shuh*, n., statecraft, the art of government.
治世 *jyh-shyh*, v. i., to rule the country.
治學 *jyh-shyuer*, v. i., to make a study of subjects.
治罪 *jyh-tzueih*, v. i., to punish.
治要 *jyh-yauh*, n., elements of art of government.

洛 澹 洳 冶 治

亅	小	⺊	十	土	ナ	卄	ㄴ	丨	一	丁	フ	口	区	冈	ㄱ	厂	尸	亠	广	宀	丶	乚	七	心	八	人	乂	一	ノ	丿	㇀	く
00	01	02	10	11	12	20	21	22	30	31	32	40	41	42	50	51	52	60	61	62	63	70	71	72	80	81	82	83	90	91	92	93

§ 63A.41 (氵/図)

湘 63A.41-1

shiang.

N. Name of river in Hunan; Hunan Province: 湘妃 fabulous queen of Emperor Shun 舜, see *-fei-jur* ↓; short for Hunan Province: 湘繡 Hunan embroidery.

湘妃竹 *shiangfei-jur*, n., spotted bamboo, said to grow from the tears of the queens of Emperor Shun 舜.

渚 63A.41-1

juu.

N. (LL) an islet in river.

泔 63A.41-2

gan.

泔水 *gan-shueei*, n., (1) water left after washing rice; (2) slop, kitchen waste water: 泔水桶 slop pail.

漕 63A.41-2

tsaur (also *tzauh*).

N. Canal, canal transport, esp. Grand Canal, used in transporting tribute grain to Peking from the south: 漕米, 漕糧, 漕運 *-mii*, *-liarng*, *-yuhn* ↓.

漕渠 *tsaurchyur*, n., canal.
漕耗 *tsaur-hauh*, n., wastage of grain through canal transport.
漕轉 *tsaurjuaan*, n., transport, by water 漕 and land 轉.
漕糧 *tsaur-liarng*, n., tribute grain, see N ↑.
漕米 *tsaur-mii*, n., tribute rice.
漕輓 *tsaur-waan*, n., see *-juaan* ↑.
漕運 *tsauryuhn*, n., canal transport, formerly, a bureau in charge of tribute grain.

滷 63A.41-2

luu.

N. (*-tz*) Thick gravy: 鹽滷 salted gravy.

V.t. & adj. (1) To treat by marinating, method of cooking, by boiling or simmering after treating with soya sauce and spices. (2) Marinated: 滷鴨, 滷蛋, 滷肉, 滷菜 marinated duck, egg, pork, vegetable.

滷湖 *luuhur*, n., salty lake.
滷麪 *luumiahn*, n., vermicelli coated with gluey sauce.
滷蝦油 *luushia-your*, n., shrimp sauce made from crushed shrimp.
滷鹽 *luuyarn*, n., natural salt.

濬 63A.41-2

jyuhn.
[Interch. 浚]

V. t. Dredge (a river).

Adj. Deep.

油 63A.41-2

your.

N. (1) Oil: 豬油 lard; 牛油 (黃牛) butter; 生油 peanut oil; 菜油 vegetable oil, rapeseed oil; 香油 (芝蔴油) sesame oil; 煤油, 石油 petroleum; 汽油 gasoline; 火油 kerosene; 豆油 soya sauce; 茶油 hair-oil made from camellia seeds; 桐油 wood oil. (2) Varnish: 油漆 *-chi* ↓.

V.t. To varnish: 油一油大門 varnish the gate; 油漆 *-chi* ↓.

Adj. (1) Greasy, oily: 衣服都油了 dress gets greasy; 油光 *-guang* ↓; 油晃晃的 very oily; 油汪汪 very shiny, -ing. (2) Glib, flippant: 油腔滑調, 油嘴滑舌 said of persuasive but not reliable talker; 這人油極了 this fellow is as slippery as an eel; 老油子 a crafty fellow.

Adv. Abundantly, spontaneously: 油然 *-rarn* ↓.

油碧幢 *yourbih-chuarng*, n., (1) cart with green oiled cloth cover; (2) painted cart cover.
油碧車 *yourbihjyu*, n., painted cart.
油餅 *yourbiing*, n., (1) oil cake used as fertilizer; (2) fried cake.
油布 *yourbuh*, n., waterproof cloth treated with wood oil.
油炒麪兒 *yourchaaumiah'l*, see *-char* ↓.
油茶 *yourchar*, n., a pasty drink made of butter, fried flour and sugar.
油漆 *yourchi*, v.t. & n., varnish, oil paints; 油漆匠 a (house) painter.
油綢子 *yourchourtz*, n., waterproof silks, used for packages.
油蟲 *yourchurng*, n., cockroach.
油裙 *yourchyurn*, n., cook's apron.
油點兒(子) *yourdiaa'l* (*-tz*), n., grease spots, stains.
油燈 *yourdeng*, n., oil lamp.
油坊 *yourfarng*, n., an oil store.
油倣紙 *yourfarng-jyy*, n., a semi-transparent paper used for tracing calligraphy.
油風 *yourfeng*, n., a disease characterized by falling hair, peeling and itchy skin.
油蓋 *yourgaih*, n., (MC) (1) painted top of carriage or cart; (2) oiled-paper umbrella.
油管 *yourguaan*, n., oil pipe.

油光(兒) *yourguang('l)*, adj., oily smooth.
油鍋 *yourguo*, n., cauldron of boiling oil—one of punishments of Buddhist hell.
油畫 *yourhuah*, n., oil painting.
油滑 *your(')huar*, adj., glib, flippant, not reliable.
油環 *yourhuarn*, n., (mech.) scraper ring.
油灰 *yourhuei*, n., putty.
油夥兒 *your(')huoo'l*, n., cook's assistant.
油葫蘆 *yourhurlur*, n., a kind of cricket, *Gryllodes mitratus.*
油炸鬼 *your'jagueei*, n., fritters.
油榨 *yourjar*, n., an oil press.
油炸果(兒) *yourjarguoo('l)*, n., see *-'jagueei* ↑, also called 油條.
油跡 *yourji*, n., grease spots, oil stains.
油煎 *yourjian*, v.t., to fry in oil.
油匠 *your'jiang*, n., house painter.
油井 *yourjiing*, n., an oil well.
油脂 *yourjy*, n., olein; fatty tissue.
油紙 *yourjyy*, n., oilpaper.
油庫 *your-kuh*, n., oil tank.
油兒 *your'l*, n., (1) oil, lard, fat; (2) see *-shueei* ↓.
油亮(兒) *yourliahng('l)*, adj., shining, shiny.
油簍 *your-loou*, n., oil hamper.
油綠 *yourlyuh*, adj., dark green.
油麻 *yourmar*, n., linseed.
油門 *yourmern*, n., (mech.) accelerator.
油墨 *yourmoh*, n., printing ink.
油膩 *yournih (-'ni)*, adj., greasy, too rich in oil.
油泥 *yournir*, n., oily dandruff, greasy dirt.
油盤 *yourparn*, n., lacquer tray.
油皮兒 *yourpier'l*, n., epidermis.
油然 *yourrarn*, adv., (of rain, cloud) fully, densely: 油然而生 arise spontaneously (a feeling).
油色 *yourseh*, n., oil color.
油杓兒 *yourshaur'l*, n., see *-tz* ↓.
油香 *your'shiang*, n., (a Moslem food) oil cake of flour, salt, fried in sesame oil.
油鞋 *yourshier*, n., waterproof shoes.
油星(兒)(子) *yourshing('l)(tz)*, n., small marks from cooking oil.
油水(兒) *yourshueei('l)*, n., that which is grease for the palm, illegitimate profit.
油飾 *yourshyh*, v.t., to paint over with wood oil.
油靴 *yourshyue*, n., waterproof boots.
油素 *yoursuh*, n., fine gauze for painting or calligraphy.
油絲絹 *yoursy-juahn*, n., ditto.
油田 *yourtiarn*, n., oilfield.
油條 *yourtiaur*, n., fritters of twisted dough (see *-jarguoo* ↑).
油菜 *yourtsaih*, n., rape.
油刺 *yourtsyh*, n., blackheads.
油桐 *yourturng*, n., (bot.) *Aleurites cordata.*
油子 *yourtz*, n., (coll.) old blackguard, an old fox.
油嘴 *yourtzueei*, adj., quick-tongued, flippant, argumentative.
油眼 *your-yaan*, n., (mech.) oil hole.
油煙(子) *youryan (-tz)*, n., soot, lamp-black.
油鹽店 *youryarn-diahn*, n., dry-goods store.
油衣 *youryi*, n., oilskins.
油印 *youryihn*, v.t. & n., mimeograph.
油油 *youryour*, adj., (AC) floating, billowing; unctuous.

洒 63A.41-3

saa.

Pron. (MC) 洒家 I (first person).

V.i. & t. Interch. 灑 63A.70.

酒 63A.41-3

jioou.

N. Wine, spirits, liquors, alcoholic beverages: 酒足(醉)飯飽 have dined and wined to satiety; 酒酣耳熱 in a state of drunken ecstasy; 酒氣噴噴 breathing alcohol; 酒氣熏人 ditto; 酒囊飯袋 a good-for-nothing person (a "rice bag, wine bag"); 酒肉朋友 friends only for wining and dining together, not in case of need; 酒色財氣 wine, women, avarice, and pride—the four cardinal vices; 酒言酒語 words uttered under the influence of liquor; 酒不醉人, 人自醉 if you get drunk, it's your own fault and not that of the wine; 戒酒 to swear off wine; 酗酒 intoxicating liquor; 敬酒 to toast s.o.; 把酒 serve wine, hold up wine cup; 嗜酒 be addicted to wine; 洋酒 imported wine; 私酒 bootleg liquor.

酒吧 *jiiouba*, n., (translit.) a bar saloon.
酒保(兒) *jiourbaau('l)*, n., a bartender, barkeeper.
酒杯 *jiioubei*, n., wine cup.
酒鼈 *jiioubiee*, n., formerly, a leather flask for wine.
酒錢(兒) *jiiouchiarn(-chia'l)*, n., tips, gratuities (cf. G. *Trinkgeld*, Fr. *pourboire*).
酒旗 *jiiou-chir*, n., a streamer hanging in front of a wine shop.
酒籌 *jiiou-chour*, n., wine counters.
酒德 *jiiouder*, n., (1) wine-drinking as a test of one's character and personality; (2) unwritten rules observed by gentlemen drinkers.
酒店 *jiioudiahn*, n., a wine shop.
酒瘋(兒) *jiioufeng('l)*, n., the silly behavior of a drunkard: 撒酒瘋兒 behave ridiculously, like a drunkard.
酒缸 *jiiougang*, n., a wine jar.
酒館 *jiourguaan*, n., an alehouse, a tavern, a bar.
酒鬼 *jiourgueei*, n., a drunkard.
酒荒 *jiiouhuang*, n., (1) excessive indulgence in wine; (2) shortage of wine.
酒會 *jiiouhueih*, n., cocktail party.
酒齇鼻 *jiioujabir*, n., red nose from excessive drinking.
酒家 *jiioujia*, n., (1) a wine shop, a tavern; (2) a girlie restaurant.
酒精 *jiioujing*, n., spirit of wine, alcohol: 酒精燈 *--deng*, n., a

酒 湎 瀦 汩 泪 泗 泅 洄 涸 溷 湄

spirit lamp.

酒盅(兒) *jioou-jung('l)*, a small wine cup. 「*jiooufeng*↑).

酒狂 *jioou-kuarng*, n., (=酒瘋

酒量(兒) *jioou-liahng('l)*, n., a person's capacity for liquor.

酒帘 *jioou-liarn*, n., see *-chir*↑.

酒力 *jiooulih*, n., (1) wine capacity; (2) tips, gratuities; (3) the strength of wine or spirits.

酒令 *jioou-lihng*, n., a wine drinking game with difficult questions (literary, opera titles, etc.) with wine as forfeit: 行酒令 to play such a game.

酒樓 *jiooulour*, n., a restaurant of the more sumptuous type.

酒母 *jiourmuu*, n., yeast for making wine. 「drunkard.

酒黏(兒) *jioouniar('l)*, n., a toper,

酒釀 *jioouniarng*, n., fermented rice for wine.

酒品 *jiourpiin*, n., (1) ability to remain sober and act normally in drinking; (2) conduct becoming a gentleman-connoisseur of wines. 「shop.

酒舖兒 *jiooupuh'l*, n., a wine

酒席 *jiooushir*, n., an elaborate feast, a formal banquet.

酒石酸 *jiooushyrsuan*, n., tartaric acid (also 果酸).

酒膆子 *jioousuhtz*, n., a wine jug, wine pot.

酒肆 *jioousyh*, n., a wine shop, tavern, alehouse.

酒罈子 *jiooutarntz*, n., wine jar.

酒菜 *jioou-tsaih*, n., dishes to go with wine.

酒刺 *jiooutsyh*, n., acnes, pimples.

酒徒 *jioou-tur*, n., a drunkard.

酒糟 *jiooutzau*, n., wine lees (also 酒渣): 酒糟鼻子 see *-jabir*↑.

酒醉 *jiooutzueih*, adj., drunk, overcome by liquor.

酒資 *jiooutzy*, n., see *-chiarn*↑.

酒滓 *jiourtzyy*, n., wine dregs.

酒窩兒 *jioouwo'l*, n., dimples.

酒肴 *jioouyaur*, n., wine and delicacies, a feast.

酒友 *jiour-yoou*, n., fellow lovers of the cup.

湎 63A.41-3

miaan.

V.i. See 沈△湎 63A.70.

瀦 63A.41-3

ju.

N. A cesspool; swamps.

汩 63A.41-4

*guu (*yuh).*

V. t. Sink: 汩沒 *-moh*↓.

Adj. (1) Confused, disorderly: 汩亂. (2) (Of water) rushing, precipitate. (3) (*yuh) (AC) hurry.

汩汩 *gurguu*, adj., descriptive of the rushing and dashing of waves; (fig.) quick flow of thoughts.

汩沒 *guumoh*, adj., (1) submerged, fallen into oblivion; (2) sound of rushing water.

泪 63A.41-4

leih.

[Var. of 淚 63A.81]

泗 63A.41-4

syh.

N. (1) Name of a river where Confucius taught: 洙泗. (2) (AC) nose mucus: 涕泗滂沱 shed streams of tears and mucus.

泅 63A.41-4

chiour.

V. i. To swim: 泅水 ditto; 泅水池 swimming pool (more commonly called 游泳池).

洄 63A.41-4

hueir.

V. i. & adj. (Of water) to whirl, churn about.

洄洑 *hueirfur*, (1) n., eddy, whirlpool; (2) v. i., to churn about.

洄瀾 *hueirlarn*, n., eddy.

涸 63A.41-4

her (sp. pr. *hauh*).

Adj. Dry, dried up: 乾涸, 涸乾了 (*hauh) (pond, river) have dried up; 涸轍鮒魚, 涸轍涸鮒 (allu. of poor people) hard up (like fish in dry pond).

溷 63A.41-4

huhn.

N. (1) Lavatory. (2) Pen for animals.

V. i. To mingle, muddle (interch. 混): 溷跡 to drift along, to live among people without special merit or purpose.

Adj. Muddy, addled: 溷濁 (=混△濁 63A.70).

湄 63A.41-5

meir.

N. (AC) river bank.

瀋 63A.41-6

sheen.

N. 墨瀋 ink fluid (esp. as shown on paper): 黑瀋未乾 before the ink is dry—soon after a document was signed, see 瀋陽 *-yarng*↓.

瀋陽 *Sheenyarng*, n., Mukden.

渲 63A.41-6

churn.
[Var. of 淳 63A.00]

澮 63A.41-8

kuaih.

N. (1) Name of a river in Shansi. (2) Ditch: 溝澮 ditch by roadside or in fields.

潛 63A.41-9

chiarn.
[Usu wr. 潜]

V. i. (1) To hide, go under. (2) To go underwater. (3) (AC) to wade across water.

Adj. & adv. Latent: secret, -ly, unnoticed: 潛蹤 to tail (a person); 潛師 (AC, of army) make a secret march; 潛行 go out in secret, travel incognito; 潛居 live quietly unknown to public; 潛德 a person's good deeds, unknown to the public; 潛移默化 a silent transforming influence (of culture, religion); 潛滋暗長 grow secretly and gradually (like underground movement); 潛龍勿用 (AC) the dragon hiding in deep waters—it's not time for action; (of a person) biding one's time; see 潛入 *-ruh*↓.

潛邸 *chiarndii*, n., house lived in by a future emperor.
潛伏 *chiarnfur*, v. i., to hibernate; live in hiding.
潛力 *chiarn-lih*, n., latent energy.
潛能 *chiarn-nerng*, n., latent force or capability.
潛熱 *chiarn-reh*, n., (phys.) latent heat.
潛入 *chiarn-ruh*, v. i., to infiltrate, enter secretly.
潛心 *chiarnshin*, v. i., to concentrate: 潛心研究 concentrate on studies.
潛水 *chiarnshueei*, adj., underwater, submarine: 潛水夫 frogman, diver; 潛水衣 diving suit; 潛水艇 submarine.
潛勢(力) *chiarn-shyh(lih)*, n., potentialities, latent force, a force in the making.
潛虛 *chiarnshyu*, v. i., to live in quiet retirement for religious attainment.
潛在 *chiarntzaih*, adj., latent, unexpressed, in abeyance.
潛望鏡 *chiarnwahngjihng*, n., periscope.
潛意識 *chiarn-yihshyh*, n., the subconscious.

溜 63A.41-9

liou (**liouh*).
[Interch. 霤]

N. (1) (**liouh*) Eaves: 屋溜 (also 霤) eaves. (2) (Coll.) lot, place: 這一溜房屋 this lot of houses; 這溜兒沒有賣水果的 there are no fruit-sellers round here.

V.i. (1) To slip, slip off, slip away: 溜走, 溜掉, 溜開 slip away; 溜號兒 fail to appear as one should, play hookie; 他溜了 he has gone away without attracting notice; 溜之乎也, 溜之大吉 let's abscond; 溜邊兒, 溜門子的 *-bia'l, -merntz'de*↓. (2) (Of stock prices) 下溜 slip down, take a dip. (3) To skate on ice: 溜冰. (4) Look, glance: 溜她一眼 give her a meaningful look; 溜一溜那女人 take a good look at that woman. (5) To quick-fry (food): 醋溜魚片 quick-fry fish slice with vinegar. (6) (**liouh*) Heat up (food): 溜冷飯 heat up rice already cooked.

Adj. & adv. (1) Fast-flowing: 順溜 flow easily. (2) As adv. adjunct: 光溜溜 (兒), 圓溜溜 (兒) very bare, very round; 酸溜溜 (兒) (flavor) very sour; 稀溜溜 (兒) very thin.

溜邊兒 *lioubia'l*, v.i., to slink away, slough off.
溜冰 *liou'bing*, v.i., to skate.
溜湫 *liou'chiou*, adj. & adv., (also 溜溜湫湫) secretive: 溜湫着眼 a secretive or falsely timid look; 溜溜湫湫往這裏來 slyly came over.
溜達 *liou'da* (**liouh'da*), v.i., take a stroll, go for a leisurely walk: 溜達溜達 have a short walk.
溜溝子 *liougoutz*, v.i., find secret connections to gain one's end (as in seeking official promotion).
溜光(兒) *liouguang('l)*, adj., (1) smooth and shining; (2) (people) have all gone away.
溜骨髓 *liou gur'sueei*, phr., to indulge in sex ("drain bone marrow").
溜號 *liouhauh*, v.i., (coll.) slink away when one should not.
溜滑 *liouhuar*, adj., (of road) slippery; (of person's eyes) shifty: 賊鬼溜滑的兩隻眼睛 two shifty eyes.
溜哄 *liou'hung*, v.t., flatter, please: 那孩子很會溜哄人兒 that child knows how to please people to get what he wants.
溜肩膀兒 *liou jianbaang'l*, phr., (1) with sloping shoulders; (2) irresponsible.
溜韁 *liou-jiang*, v.i., (of horses) slip the reins and run wild.

瀋 渲 澮 潛 溜

亅	小	⺊	十	土	𠂇	卄	⺊	丨	一	丅	𠃌	口	図	冂	冖	厂	尸	亠	广	宀	丶	乚	弋	心	八	人	乂	乛	一	丿	⺈	く
00	01	02	10	11	12	20	21	22	30	31	32	40	41	42	50	51	52	60	61	62	63	70	71	72	80	81	82	83	90	91	92	93

溜溜(兒) *lioulIou('l)*, adj. & adv., (1) (wind) softly stirring; (2) see Adj. & adv.↑; (3) slipping by silently: 等了溜溜兒的一年 waited a whole year as it slipped by.

溜門子的 *lioumerntz'de*, n., person who slips into house unnoticed to steal.

溜眼 *liouyaan*, v. i., cast a darting glance.

潘 63A.41-9

pan.

N. A surname; (obs. AC) liquid in which rice has been washed.

泊 63A.41-9

*bor (*poh).*

[Dist. 汨 63A.41↑]

N. (AC) a swamp, marshes.

V. i. & t. To lie at anchor: 泊停 moor at place; 泊岸 lie alongshore; 漂泊 to drift on water; (fig.) drift aimlessly.

Adj. (*poh) Mild, tranquil: 泊然 calm and at rest; 澹ᐞ泊 63A.40, serene with few desires.

洎 63A.41-9

jih.

N. (AC) meat juice, broth.

V. i. Pour water into a pot.

Prep. (LL) up to (a point or period of time): 洎乎近世 until recent times; 洎今 till now (=至今).

淄 63A.41-9

tzy.

N. & adj. (AC) black.

§63A.42 (氵/冈)

清 63A.42-1

ching.

N. Name of Manchu Dyn. (1644–1911): 朝清, 清代, 前清, 滿清 ditto; 清廷 the Manchu Court; 清宮 the Ching palaces; 清季, 清末 the latter part, the end, of the Manchu Dyn.

V. t. To clear up, to settle: 清賬, 清欠 clear up the accounts, debts; 清算 *-suahn*↓; clear up (room, table) 清理 *-lii*↓; 清堆兒 clear up rubble or heaps; 堅壁清野 clear the decks for action.

Vb. complement. Up, fully, clearly: 付清 paid in full; 還清前欠 clear up outstanding accounts; 算清 (accounts) have been settled or put in order; 數不清 innumerable; 說不清 cannot tell clearly (who was to blame, etc); 記不清 cannot remember clearly.

Adj. (1) Pure, clean: 清潔, 清淨 *-jier*[1], *-jihng*[2]↓; 清水 clear water; 清湯 *consommé*, clear soup; 清香 subtle fragrance; 兩袖清風 having not a cent; 清心寡欲 (Budd. & Taoism) a pure heart and few desires; 清課 (Budd.) daily lessons; 清規 *-guei*↓. (2) Morally elevated, incorrupt: 清廉 *-liarn*, 清操 *-tsau*↓, 清白, 清高, 清介, 清節 *-bor*, *-gau*, *-jieh*, *-jier*[1]↓; 清官 an honest official; 清耿耿 (LL) very upright and incorruptible. (3) Cool: 清風 cool air; 清曲 a sweet melody; 清涼 fresh and cool; 清秋 the fresh air of autumn. (4) Esteemed—oft. court. address="your": 清誨 your advice; (勞瀆) 清神 (take so much of) your valuable time or attention; 清聽 your ears, i.e., your attention; 清望 your great reputation; 清顏 your "face," i. e., presence; 清盼 your "look," i. e., attention (also wr. 青). (5) Peaceful, undisturbed, serene: 清時, 清世, 清平世界 peaceful times. (6) (Of photograph, print, account, etc.) sharp, well-defined: 清楚, 清晰 *-'chuu*, *-shi*↓. (7) Lonely, poor: 冷清清 lonely; 清鍋兒冷灶 living quite alone; 清寒, 清貧 poor; 清苦 hard up; see also 清白 *-bor*↓.

清拔 *chingbar*, adj., (of writing) distinguished.

清標 *chingbiau*, (1) adj., (AC) handsome (man); (2) n., (LL) the moon: 清標照人寒 the moon casts its cool light.

清蹕 *chingbih*, v. t., to clear the way for imperial carriage.

清白 *chingbor* (*-bair*), adj., pure, unsullied (reputation): 清白家世 come from a law-abiding family background.

清唱 *chingchahng*, v. i., (Chin. opera) to sing selections without stage make-up, as at parties, (cf. 清吟 *-yirn*↓).

清茶 *chingchar*, n., (1) green tea; (2) 清茶候教 inviting person to a tea without snacks or dinner.

清償 *chingcharng*, v. t., to pay back (debt).

清澈 *chingcheh*, adj., (of water) crystal clear; (of voice) clear, ringing.

清晨 *chingchern*[1], n., early morning.

清塵 *chingchern*[2], n., (LL, court.) your honorable presence: 自奉清塵, 於今五稔 it's five years since meeting you.

清切 *chingchieh*, adj., (1) sad, forlorn (music); (2) spotless, cozy (place).

清器 *chingchih*, n., (AC) night pot.

清綺 *chingchii*, adj., beautiful, elegant: 清綺絕世 of unexcelled elegance.

清清 *chingching*, adj., (in all senses of Adj.↑); (1) cool; (2) lonely

(冷冷清清); (3) clear; (4) pure.

清奇 *chingchir*, adj., (of callig., composition) novel and interesting.

清除 *chingchur*, v. t., (1) to clear out (debris, corrupt practice); (2) to clean up (room, street).

清楚 *ching'chuu*, adj., (1) clear: 説話不清楚, 不清不楚 never talk clearly; 看不, 聽不清楚 cannot see, hear clearly; (2) neat, well-arranged (dress, room).

清癯 *chingchyur*, adj., (LL, court.) thin-looking.

清淡 *chingdahn*, adj., (1) quiet and simple (life); (2) unexciting, placid (life); (3) mild (flavor).

清單(兒)(子) *chingdan(-da'l)(tz)*, n., detailed list or account.

清道 *chingdauh*, v. i., (1) to act as scavenger; (2) see *-bih* ↑.

清梵 *chingfahn*, n., (Budd.) sound of religious litany, chanting.

清芬 *chingfen*, adj. & n., pure, subtle fragrance, -ant.

清福 *chingfur*, n., blessing of quiet, peaceful life.

清高 *chinggau*, adj., (of scholar) self-contained, aloof from politics or material possessions, of simple living and high thinking.

清鯁 *chinggeeng*, adj., blunt, straightforward (advice, etc.).

清倌(兒) *chingguan(-gua'l)*, n., formerly, singsong girl who is still a virgin (also 清倌人).

清規 *chingguei*, n., (Budd.) monastic rules.

清貴 *chinggueih*, adj. & n., (1) eminent (persons); (2) *élite*, not vulgar (office, duty); 清貴衙門 (sl.) formerly, the Hanlin Academy (翰林院).

清寒 *chingharn*, adj., (1) cold and pure (moonlight); (2) a nice reference to the "poor": 清寒子弟(基金) (scholarships for) poor students.

清和 *chingher*, adj., (1) peaceful (times); (2) (coll.) lunar fourth month (about May).

清華 *chinghuar*, adj., (of landscape) lush green in vegetation; (of composition) beautiful and pleasing; (of person) eminent, refined.

清徽 *chinghuei*, adj., see *-tsau* ↓.

清丈 *chingjahng*, v. i. & n., (land) survey; official determination of land measurements.

清齋 *chingjai*, n., (1) (Budd.) vegetarian fast, abstinence from meat; (2) a clean studio.

清朝 *chingjau*, (1) n., early morning; (2) (*-chaur*) n., the Manchu Dyn.

清正 *chingjehng*, adj., upright (official).

清眞 *chingjen*, adj., of Moslems: 清眞教 Islam, Moslem religion; 清眞寺 a mosque.

清蒸 *chingjeng*, v. t., to steam, -ed (chicken, etc.).

清減 *chingjiaan*, adj., (MC) for *-shouh* ↓.

清醬 *chingjiahng*, n., soya sauce.

清介 *chingjieh*, adj., see *-gau* ↑.

清節 *chingjier*[1], adj., incorrupt (official), see *-tsau* ↓.

清潔 *chingjier*[2], adj., clean; n., cleanliness (of street, dress, etc.).

清淨 *chingjihng*[1], (1) adj., clean, not cluttered; (2) (Budd.) not bothered by material concerns.

清靜 *chingjihng*[2], adj., quiet, tranquil, serene: 清靜無爲 (Taoism) quiet and inaction.

清酌 *chingjuor*[1], n., (AC) another name for wine.

清濁 *ching-juor*[2], adj. & n., (1) the pure and the impure; the morally clean and the corrupt; (2) 清 voiceless and 濁 voiced consonants.

清客 *chingkeh*, n., literary friends of officials or rich men who help with conversation and advice; 清客串(兒) amateur opera singers.

清狂 *chingkuarng*, adj., (a type) romantic, abandoned and affecting disregard for common formalities.

清苦 *chingkuu*, adj., poor and hard up (euphemistically used): 他很清苦 he is rather hard up.

清朗 *ching'lang*, adj. (of weather) clear, bright.

清冷 *chingleeng*, adj., lonesome; (of business) dull.

清亮 *chingliahng*, adj., pure, shining.

清漣 *chingliarn*[1], adj., (of water) clear with light ripples.

清廉 *chingliarn*[2], adj., honest (as an official), not corrupt.

清涼 *chingliarng*, adj., fresh and cool.

清冽 *chinglieh*, adj., (of springs) clear and cool.

清麗 *chinglih*, adj., (of style) clear and lucid.

清理 *chinglii*, v. t., to clean up, put in order: 清理舊賬 clear up old accounts.

清流 *chingliour*, n., (1) a clear stream; (2) scholars who keep away from politics.

清明 *chingmirng*, (1) n., a spring festival corresponding to Easter, on April 5th or 6th—a festival for visiting family graveyards; (2) adj., (of patient's mind) clear: 神志清明; (3) adj., peaceful (times).

清貧 *chingpirn*, adj., "poor and unburdened"—a nice way of referring to s. o. being "poor."

清平 *chingpirng*, adj., pure and peaceful.

清尚 *chingshahng*, adj., see *-gau* ↑.

清聲 *chingsheng*, n., (1) a voiceless consonant; (2) a clean unsullied name, reputation for honesty.

清晰 *chingshi*, adj., clear and precise (mind, explanation).

清顯 *chingshiaan*, adj., esteemed, honored (official position).

清曉 *chingshiaau*, n., early morning.

清香 *chingshiang*, adj. & n., pure fragrance, -ant.

清閑 *chingshiarn*, adj., enjoying leisure, unburdened with work; euphem. for being "out of work."

清興 *chingshihng*, n., leisurely mood for enjoying wine, poetry, flowers, etc.

清醒 *chingshiing*, adj., wide awake: 清醒白醒 ditto.

清新 *chingshin*, adj., delightfully fresh (writing), free from clichés, etc.

清修 *chingshiou*, adj., (AC) leading a mild and simple life.

清秀 *chingshiouh*, adj., (of girl, callig.) delicate.

清瘦 *chingshouh*, adj., a nice reference to s. o. being "thin."

清爽 *chingshuaang*, adj., (weather) clear, dry; (mind, mood) feeling good and fit.

清水貨 *chingshueei-huoh*, n., unadulterated merchandise.

清虛 *chingshyu*, adj., (Taoism culture) having simple life and few worries.

清算 *chingsuahn*, v. t., (1) to liquidate (assets, undertaking); (2) to liquidate a person under Communist regime.

清泰 *chingtaih*, adj., (LL) enjoying good health: 政躬清泰 (to official) wish you good health.

清談 *chingtarn*, n., a trend in 3rd-5th cen. (魏晋清談) under Taoist influence for airy, philosophical discussions and dissociation from politics.

清恬 *chingtiarn*, adj., (LL) peaceful and quiet.

清頭 *chingtour*, n., (coll.) as in 弄個清頭 make things clear, clear up mess.

清操 *chingtsau* (*-tsauh*), adj., untarnished (conduct).

清脆 *chingtsueih*, adj., clear, well enunciated (voice).

清通 *chingtung*, adj., conversant with (branches of knowledge).

清早 *chingtzaau*, n., early morning; also 清早兒, 清早起, 大清早.

清玩 *chingwarn*, n., elegant, refined pastimes (curios, incense, poetry).

清雅 *chingyaa*, adj., elegant, refined.

清妍 *chingyarn*, adj., (face, writing) delicately beautiful.

清揚 *chingyarng*, adj., (1) (AC) bright-eyed, clear-featured; (2) widespread influence (of Budd.).

清要 *chingyauh*, adj. & n., much honored (position), such person.

清夜 *chingyeh*, n., quiet, still night.

清一色 *ching-yi-seh*, n., (1) flush (in card games and mahjong); (2) adj., without divergent colors, beliefs or partisans (in group).

清議 *chingyih*, n., political criticism by scholars, esp. in later Hahn Dyn.; public opinion.

清音 *chingyin*, n., (1) a kind of string orchestra used at funerals; (2) see *-chahng*↑.

清吟 *chingyirn*, n., usu. 清吟小班 formerly, first-class singsong house in Peking.

清幽 *chingyou*, adj., nice and secluded (place).

清越 *chingyueh*, adj., (of song, voice) clear and carrying far.

凊 63A.42-1

jihng.

Adj. Cool.

浦 63A.42-1

puu.

N. (1) River bank; river area. (2) A surname.

洧 63A.42-1

weei.

N. Name of river in Honan.

湖 63A.42-1

hur.

N. Lake: 西湖 West Lake; 湖濱 lake front; 五湖 Taihu (in Soochow) and its neighboring lakes; also various interpretations; 湖心亭 a pavilion in mid-lake, 湖田 farms in lake area; see 江[A]湖 63A.30.

Adj. Bluish-grey color: 湖色.

湖北 *Hurbeei*(*Hupei*), n., name of a province.

湖南 *Hurnarn*(*Hunan*), n., name of a province.

潸 63A.42-1

shan.

Adj. & adv. Tearful, -ly: 潸潸, 潸泣 ditto.

潮 63A.42-1

chaur.

N. (1) Tide: 潮水 *-shueei*↓; 漲潮, 高潮 flood tide, (fig.) crest of luck, fortune, peak of romance, success; 退潮 low tide, ebb; 低潮 ebb; (fig.) low point of fortune, romance; 潮汐 *-shih*↓. (2) Stream of events, current of thought: 潮流 *-liour*↓; 風潮 crisis in school, strike in factory; 思潮 current of thought; 新潮 new current of ideas; 狂潮, 怒潮 storm or flood of protests, violent radicalism; 心血來潮 a sudden inspiration.

Adj. (1) Moist, damp: 潮氣, 潮濕 *-chih, -shy*↓. (2) (Coll.) inferior: 銀子成色潮 low content of silver; 手藝潮 inferior skill.

潮白 *chaurbair*, n., a kind of sugar, produced in 潮州 Swatow.

潮氣 *chaurchih*, n., dampness.

潮解 *chaurjiee*, v. i. & n., (chem.) deliquesce, -cence, liquify.

潮州 *Chourjou*, n., Swatow.

潮流 *chaurliour*, n., (1) current (in sea, river); (2) trend or current of thought.

潮腦 *chaurnaau*, n., camphor of 潮州 (Swatow).

潮熱 *chaurreh*, n., (Chin. med.) intermittent fever (like "tides").

潮汐 *chaur-shih*, n., morning and evening tides.

潮信 *chaurshihn*, n., hours of flood tide.

潮水 *chaurshueei*, n., tide, flood water.

潮濕 *chaurshy*, adj., damp.

潮音 *chaur-yin*, n., (Budd.) swelling sound, litany.

滿 63A.42-2

maan.

N. Manchu, Manchus: 滿清 the Manchu or Ching Dyn.; 滿漢全席 a full, formal banquet, combining Manchurian and Chinese delicacies.

V. i. & t. Fill to full capacity, fill time, fill limit, usu. in participial use, filled: 水, 人滿屋 the room is filled with water, people; 滿假 leave of absence expires; 滿服 mourning period is over; 滿期, 滿限, 滿額 *-chir*, *-shiahn*, *-eh*↓.

Adj. (1) Full, satisfied, satisfactory; 飽滿 vigorous (see 飽 81B.70); 結果完滿, 圓滿 satisfactory results. (2) Everywhere, filled full: 滿街 all over the street; 滿處, 滿地 everywhere; 滿座 full house, all assembled; 滿處是人 people are everywhere; 滿坑滿谷 valley is full of; 滿門 the whole house is filled with; 滿城風雨 (news, rumor) spread all over city; 滿盤子滿碗 (results) completely satisfactory; 滿心歡喜 heart is full of joy; 滿腹牢騷 seem to have a grudge against everything; 滿腹經綸 full of ideas for state policy or programs; 滿面春風 face radiates happiness; 滿目瘡痍 see evidence of people's distress everywhere; 滿載而歸 come home loaded with (honors, money). (3) Proud, self-satisfied: 自滿, 志得意滿 ditto; 滿意 *-yih*↓.

Adv. (1) Completely, wholly: 滿不在乎 totally unconcerned, do not mind at all (losses); 滿沒聽見 completely ignore (what is said); 滿應滿許 promise anything and everything; 滿張羅 do everything to give a welcome. (2) Fully prepared: 滿打算, 滿打(着), 滿擬 was fully prepared to (do s.t. before meeting with obstruction).

滿期 *maan-chir*, phr., (time) limit expires.

滿處 *maanchuh*, adv., everywhere.

滿大人 *maan-dahrern*, n., supposed to be phr. of which "mandarin" (a Manchu official) is a transliteration.

滿額 *maan-eh*, phr., capacity filled, all taken.

滿貫 *maanguahn*, n., a full house, a flush (in cards, mahjong etc.).

滿江紅 *maanjianghurng*, n., name of melody for Suhng poem (詞).

滿州 *maanjou*, n., Manchuria; 滿州人 *--rern*, Manchus.

滿滿當當 *marnmaan-dangdang*, adj., descriptive of fullness, full capacity.

滿堂紅 *maantarnghurng*, n., red sashes, red scrolls and red candles on happy occasions.

滿限 *maan-shiahn*, phr., capacity filled up; time limit expires.

滿人 *maan-rern*, n., a Manchu; see *-jou*↑.

滿心 *maanshin*, adv., with full intention; see *-yih*↓.

滿天星 *maantianshing*, n., (bot.) a plant, *Serissa foetida*; *Enkianthus japonicus*; sky covered with stars.

滿足 *maantzur*, v.t. & adj., satisfy; be satisfied.

滿子 *marntzyy*, n., (coll.) youngest child.

滿意 *maanyih*, v.t. & adj., satisfy, be satisfied; satisfactory: 不滿意 not satisfied; 不能使人滿意 leave s.t. to be desired.

滿月 *maanyueh*, n., full month; celebration of baby's first full month.

溝 63A.42-2

gou.

N. (1) (*-tz*, *'l*) A narrow waterway: 溝渠 *-chyur*, 溝洫 *-shyuh*↓; 水溝 a gutter, ditch; 陰溝 a covered drain: 陰溝裏翻船 fail miserably in a very easy task; 陽溝 an open drain; 暗溝 a sewer; 溝耗子 a sewer rat. (2) A rut on road, a line cut on surface.

V.t. Connect, to bridge: 溝通 *-tung*↓.

溝幫 *goubang*, n., side embankment of a ditch.

溝渠 *gouchyur*, n., a ditch, an irrigation canal.

溝道 *goudauh*, n., a ditch.

溝瀆 *goudur*, n., see *-chyur*↑.

溝壑 *gouhuoh*, n., a gutter.

溝洫 *goushyuh*, n., a ditch in fields.

溝通 *goutung*, v.i., foster mutual understanding: 溝通感情 promote friendly relations; 溝通中西文化 to bridge the gulf between Chinese and Western cultures.

溝眼 *gouyaan*, n., opening of sewers.

溝沿(兒) *gouyahn(-yah'l)*, n., see *-bang*↑.

湍 63A.42-2

tuan.

N. Rapids: 急湍, 湍瀨, 湍水 rapids.

湍急 *tuanjir*, adj., (of river, fall) flowing rapidly.

湍流 *tuanliour*, n., a swift flow, stream, river, etc.

消 63A.42-2

shiau.

[Usu. printed 消]

消 淌 洏 濡

V. i. & t. (1) To diminish, vanish: 消滅, 消失, 消亡 *-mieh, -shy, warng* ↓; 消腫, 消炎 decrease swelling, inflammation. (2) To consume, spend, be used up: 消耗 *-hauh* ↓; 開消 expenditure. (3) To cancel in 取▵消 31S.82. (4) To melt, digest: 消化 *-huah* ↓; 消溶 *-rurng* ↓; 吃不消 (lit.) "cannot digest or hold in stomach," i. e., cannot stand, unbearable, intolerable (insult, expense); 吃得消 can take it. (5) usu. in 不消 does not need: 不消一個月已有回音 got a reply in less than a month; 不消說了 it's not necessary to say.

消遣 *shiau'chiaan*, n. & v. i., relaxation, distraction, pastime: 消遣消遣 have a little relaxation; 消遣一夜 have a night of fun; 今天如何消遣, 有甚麼消遣 what can we do today for a pastime? 消遣歲月 pass the years idly or in pleasure.

消除 *shiau-chur*, v. t., abolish, do away with (obstacles 障害), remove (prejudice, misunderstanding).

消卻 *shiau-chyueh*, v.t., to lessen, do away with, see *-chur* ↑.

消毒 *shiau-dur*, v. t., to sterilize, disinfect.

消防 *shiaufarng*, v. i., to fight fire: 消防隊 fire brigade.

消費 *shiaufeih*, v. i. & n., spend, consume; expenditure: 消費甚大 great deal of expenditure; 消費者 the consumer; 消費品 consumer goods; 消費人貸款 consumer credit.

消耗 *shiauhauh*, v. i. & n., (things) diminish in quality, quantity or value, or cost to maintain; (cars) consumption of gasoline; (persons) habit of expenditure; costs of maintenance; 消耗品 consumer goods, see *-feih* ↑.

消化 *shiauhuah*, v. i. & t. & n., digest, -tion; 消化液 digestive juice; 消化器官 digestive organs; 消化系統 digestive system, tract.

消火 *shiau-huoo*, v. t., to fight fire; 消火器 fire extinguisher (also 滅火器); 消火栓 hydrant.

消魂 *shiauhurn*, see 銷▵魂 81A.42.

消長 *shiau-jaang*, n., growth and decay; increase and decrease, wax and wane.

消減 *shiaujiaan*, v. i. & t., to decrease (expenditure, time, effort).

消極 *shiaujir*, adj., (1) negative, as opp. to 積極 positive: 消極作用 negative purpose; (2) inclined not to hope or struggle, passive, cynical: 他很消極 he is not interested, pessimistic; (3) the reverse: 消極方面 the reverse side.

消中 *shiau-jung*, n., anc. name for diabetes (also called 消渴 *-kee* ↓, modn. 糖尿病 "sugarurine disease").

消渴 *shiaukee*, n., ditto.

消滅 *shiaumieh*, v. t., to exterminate, destroy (enemy, danger, threat, groups, beliefs, future troubles, etc.).

消弭 *shiaumii*, v. t., to stop, to prevent (future trouble).

消磨 *shiaumor*, v. i. & t., to grow less and less, to wear off: 消磨歲月 to waste away the years; 歲月消磨 the years wear on, pass away.

消鎔(溶) *shiaururng*, v. i., (of substance) to melt.

消夏 *shiaushiah*, v. i., to take a summer holiday.

消閒 *shiaushiarn*, v. i., to kill time, pass time idly: 消閒兒 free leisure time.

消息 *shiaushir*, n., (1) (LL) growth and decay; (2) (*-shir* or *'shi*) news, news report (from battlefields, Paris, etc.); 消息兒 *--shie'l*, n., (coll.) a floor trap.

消受 *shiaushouh*[1], v. i. & t., (1) to take, bear (burden, hard days): 怎生消受 (MC) how can one bear this? also (2) to enjoy (great dinner, luck).

消瘦 *shiaushouh*[2], adj., emaciated.

消暑 *shiaushuu*, v. i., see *-shiah* ↓.

消失 *shiaushy*, v. i., to vanish, be forgotten.

消逝 *shiaushyh*[1], v. i., to pass away.

消釋 *shiaushyh*[2], v. i., (1) (Budd.) explain difficult text or passage; (2) remove (misunderstandings, worries); are removed.

消石 *shiaushyr*, n., saltpetre, niter (see correct 硝▵石 31B.42); 消石灰 calcium hydroxide, slaked lime.

消災 *shiau-tzai*, v. i., to remove (by magic, prayer, incantation) impending ill fortune.

消亡 *shiauwarng*, v. i., to perish.

消搖 *shiauyaur*, v. i., (AC) u.f. 逍▵遙 22.83.

消夜 *shiauyeh*, n., night snacks (also wr. 宵夜).

淌 63A.42-2

taang.

V. i. & t. To flow down, to drip: 淌眼淚 tears drop; 淌眼抹淚 crying and wiping tears; 淌汗 perspire; 淌出來了 (tears, sweat) come out, (water in cups) brim over.

洏 63A.42-3

erl.

Adj. 漣洏 with tears and mucus streaming.

濡 63A.42-3

rur.

V. t. Immerse, moisten: 濡染 *-raan* ↓; 濡潤, 濡濕 to wet; 沾濡 to taint, tinge or dye; 濡濡 dripping with water.

Adj. & adv. Late: 濡滯 to tarry or linger longer than necessary.

濡迹 *rur-ji*, v. i., (of persons) be delayed, linger for a long time.

濡染 *rurraan*, v. t., (1) immerse, imbue, permeate; (2) to wet, dip in liquid.

濡忍 *rurreen*, phr., be tolerant, forbearing, indulgent.

濡需 *rurshyu*, phr., (AC) muddle along.

A

灞 63A.42-3

bah.

N. Name of river near 長安, in Shensi, famed in poetry.

涌 63A.42-3

yuung.

[Var. 湧 63A.50]

涓 63A.42-4

jyuan.

N. (1) A small stream: 涓滴 *-dir* ↓; 涓涓 *-jyuan* ↓. (2) A surname.

V.t. To choose: 涓吉 *-jir* ↓.

涓埃 *jyuan-ai*, n., (lit.) tiny dust; (fig.) (LL) tiny bits, trivialities.
涓滴 *jyuandir*, n., small drops of water: 涓滴歸公 every cent goes to the public.
涓吉 *jyuanjir*, v. i., choose an auspicious day.
涓涓 *jyuanjyuan*, n., a streamlet: 涓涓不壅, 終爲江河 if small leaks are not plugged up in time, they will become streams.

泂 63A.42-4

jyuung.

Adj. (1) Deep: 泂泂 (of water) clear and deep. (2) (U.f. 迥) distant, vast.

B

洞 63A.42-4

duhng.

N. (1) Cave, cavern, grotto: 山洞 cave in mountains; 仙洞 fairy grotto; 洞穴, 洞窟 *-shyueh, -kuh* ↓. (2) A hole, leak: 洞孔, 孔洞 a hole; leakage (in argument, plan); 洞口 entrance to cave.

Adj. Open, clear, thorough: 空洞 empty; 洞明, 洞徹 clear, transparently clear; 洞若觀火 clear like looking at fire.

Adv. Clearly, through: 門戶洞開 gate is wide open; 洞見 see through; 洞燭其奸 see through his treachery; (in correspondence, court.) 洞悉, 洞察 see through; 洞鑒 please be kindly informed; 世事洞明皆學問 to understand practical affairs clearly is (also) knowledge (not only book knowledge).

洞徹 *duhngcheh*, adj. & adv., clear, -ly.
洞穿 *duhngchuan*, v.i. & t., penetrate, pierce through.
洞房 *duhngfarng*, n., nuptial chamber: 洞房花燭夜 wedding night.
洞府 *duhngfuu*, n., abode of fairies.
洞窟 *duhngkuh*, n., cave, cavern.
洞簫 *duhngshiau*, n., bamboo flageolet.
洞穴 *duhngshyueh*, n., cave.
洞天 *duhngtian*, n., cave as fairies' abode: 洞天福地 some scenically beautiful place (as near temple); 別有洞天 hidden but beautiful spot, a world all its own.
洞庭湖 *Duhngtirng Hur*, n., name of big lake in Hunan.

凋 63A.42-4

diau.

C

Adj. Withered, withering, see compp. ↓.

凋敝 *diaubih*, adj., (of living, business) on the decline, hard up.
凋零 *diaulirng*, adj., dwindling in numbers, quantity, volume (business, family, population, etc.).
凋落 *diauluoh*, adj., ditto.
凋謝 *diaushieh*, adj., withered, -ing (of flowers).
凋萎 *diauweei*, adj., ditto.

渦 63A.42-4

wo.

N. An eddy, whirlpool: 旋渦.

渦蟲 *wo-churng*, n., a tiny water insect, *Turbellaria.*
渦電流 *wo-diahn-liour*, n., (phys.) eddy current.
渦旋 *woshyuarn*, n., whirlpool.

滑 63A.42-4

huar.

N. A surname.

V. i. (1) To slip: 滑下去, 滑掉下去 to slip down; 滑倒 slip and fall down. (2) To glide as in skating, see 滑冰, 滑雪 *-bing, -shyuee* ↓.

Adj. (1) Slippery (floor, etc.): 光滑 shining smooth; 滑溜溜 very slippery. (2) Deceitful: 滑頭滑腦, see 滑頭 *-tour* ↓; 滑不嘰溜 (a) very slippery, (b) deceitful, oily, see 滑溜 *-liou* ↓. (3) Of sneaky, undependable character: 巧滑, 奸滑 deceitful; 刁滑, 狡滑 cunning; 油滑, 油腔滑調 flippant, cheaply popular; 油嘴滑舌 a flippant talker, see 滑稽 *-ji*↓.

滑冰 *huarbing*, v. i., to skate on ice.

滑車 *huarche*, n., a pulley.

滑竿 *huargan*, n., sedan chair, borne by two bamboo poles (Szechuan).

滑稽 *huarji*, (re. pr. *guuji*, now rare), adj., humorous, facetious.

滑跤 *huarjiau*, n., slip and fall down: 滑一跤.

滑劑 *huarjih*, n., grease for machines.

滑精 *huar-jing*, v. t., have nocturnal emission.

滑溜 *huarliou*, adj., very smooth and slippery.

滑輪 *huarlurn*, n., a pulley.

滑潤油 *huarruhn-your*, n., lubricant.

滑翔 *huarshiarng*, v. i., to glide and wheel round (as birds); 滑翔機 a glider.

滑水 *huarshueei*, v. i., & n., to water-ski; water-skiing.

滑石 *huarshyr*, n., talc.

滑雪 *huarshyuee*, v. i., to ski.

滑澾 *huartah*, adj., (of roads) slippery.

滑梯 *huarti*, n., a slide for children.

滑頭 *huartour*, adj., & n., cunning; a cunning person.

瀰 63A.42-5

mir.

V. i. Overflow.

瀰漫 *mirmahn*, v. t. & adj., to flood, overflow: 戰雲瀰漫 war clouds hang over the horizon, also wr. 彌^Δ漫 50A.42.

漏 63A.42-5

louh.

N. (1) An hourglass; a water clock or clepsydra: 漏刻 *-keh*, 漏鼓 *-guu*↓; 銅漏 a copper water clock; 漏盡更殘 the small hours of the dawn; 痔漏 piles, anal hemorrhoids. (2) (Budd.) depravity, defilement: 無漏, 有漏 free, not free, from defilement.

V. i. & t. (1) Leak (out), disclose, drip, evade: 洩漏 reveal secret, divulge; 透漏 make known; 走漏 unintentionally disclose; 漏風聲, 漏消息 leak out information; 漏洩 *-shieh*↓; 漏露 *-luh*↓; 說漏了(嘴) unintentionally divulge s. t. secret; 漏底 *-dii*↓; 漏了老底 leaked out one's personal secrets; 漏雨 (of roof, etc.) leaking; 漏水 (of cup, bottle, etc.) leaking; 漏孔 *-kuung*↓; 壺漏了, 雨衣漏水, 鋼筆漏水, the kettle, raincoat, fountain pen, is leaking; 漏出來 leaked out; 漏氣 not air-tight; 漏網 (of fish) escape from net. (2) Leave out, be missing, conceal from: 遺漏 drop out, be missing; 失漏 be lost, missing; 漏列 left out of a list or account; 漏報 fail to report or declare; 漏稅 evade tax, esp. by smuggling; 漏繳 fail to pay; 漏下 be left out; 漏掉 *-diauh*↓; 脫漏 be missing or omitted; 漏了一行, 漏去一字 a line, a word is missing; 漏唸一句 have skipped a sentence in reading; 紕漏 an error; 漏不了你 you'll never be left out; 甚麼事漏得了他? nothing can be concealed from him. (3) (Of bodily fluids) flow freely, exude, discharge, ooze (said of semen, tears, secretions or pus). (4) (In swordplay) to give (perhaps purposely) an opening as lure for attack.

漏瘡 *louhchuang*, n., (1) (med.) fistula; (2) (med.) vaccinia, cowpox.

漏掉 *louh-diauh*, v. i., be missing or left out.

漏底 *louh-dii*, n., (1) A leak in bottom of a vessel for liquids; (2) disclosure of confidential information(底=底細).

漏洞 *louhduhng*, n., (1) see *-dii* (1) ↑; (2) an inconsistency, a flaw in argument.

漏斗 *louhdoou*, n., a funnel for liquids.

漏兜 *louhdou*, v. i., reveal true nature.

漏縫 *louhfehng*, n., a crevice: 彌補漏縫 to mend a crack.

漏風 *louhfeng*, v.t. & adj. & n., (1) not air-tight; (2) (of secret) leak out; (3) (Chin. med.) apoplexy caused by alcoholism.

漏管 *louhguaan*, n., (1) (med.) anal fistula; (2) (med.) an ulcer that does not heal easily.

漏櫃 *louh-gueih*, n., theft of goods in a store by its own employee(s).

漏鼓 *louhguu*, n., drum beat to announce the watches at night.

漏壺 *louhhur*, n., a water clock, an anc. device for measuring time.

漏卮 *louhjy*, n., (1) a syphon; (2) an unfavorable balance of international payments.

漏刻 *louhkeh*, n., (1) hourglass or water clock; (2) a short interval of time.

漏孔 *louh-kuung*, n., see *-duhng*↑.

漏兒 *louh'l*, n., a flaw or weakness: 檢漏兒 pick fault with.

漏露 *louhluh*, v. t., reveal (a secret).

漏杓 *louhshaur*, n., a strainer, a colander.

漏現 *louhshiahn*, v. i., be exposed to public view.

漏洩 *louhshieh*, v. t., leak out (secret).

漏師 *louh-shy*, v. t., (AC) disclose military secret.

漏天(兒) *louhtian(-tia'l)*, n., a hole in the roof, through which light comes in (dist. in 露天 open air).

漏財 *louh-tsair*, (1) v. t., suffer financial loss; (2) adj., be incapable of becoming rich.

漏子 *louh'tz*, n., (1) a funnel for liquids (*-doou*↑); (2) a flaw or weakness.

漏夜 *louhyeh*, n., the dead of night.

漓 63A.42-6

lir.

V.i. To drip: see 淋^Δ漓 63A.01; 澆^Δ漓 63A.70.

滴 63A.42-6

di.

N. A drop, driplet (liquid, tear, rain, etc.).

V. i. & t. To drip one by one (tear, blood, sweat, oil, etc.): 滴血 anc. method of verifying blood affinity by dripping blood of son on deceased parent's bone to see if it is absorbed or not.

滴蟲 *dichurng*, n., (zoo.) infusoria.
滴答 *dida*, adj. & adv., descriptive of dripping sound, also 滴滴答答 *didi-dada*, 滴裏搭拉 *dili-dala*.
滴滴 *didi*, (1) adj., descriptive of dripping sound; (2) every drop; (3) adv., in phrr. 綠滴滴 dripping green, 嬌滴滴 very charming or pretty (of girls).
滴定管 *didihng-guaan*, n., (chem.) burette.
滴瀝 *dilih*, n., sound of dripping.
滴溜溜 *diliouliou*, n., sound of fluid dripping or flowing; 滴溜兒圓 *diliou'l yuarn*, very, very round (as of pearl).
滴瓶 *dipirng*, n., dripping bottle.

溯 63A.42-8

suh.

V.i. & t. Trace up (river); 溯流而上 going up river; (fig.) trace to origins: 溯本, 溯源 ditto; to reminisce: 追溯 think back (the past).

淪 63A.42-8

lurn.

N. Ripple.

V.i. To sink down, decline: 沈淪 to perish; be submerged, see 淪亡, 淪陷, 淪喪 *-warng*, *-shiahn*, *-sahng* ↓; 淪肌浹髓 (of person's gratitude) sink into the marrow—extreme gratitude.

淪落 *lurnluoh*, v.i., drift, decline or sink into (poverty, depravity, etc.).
淪滅 *lurnmieh*, v.i., see *-warng* ↓.
淪喪 *lurnsahng*, v.i., perish.
淪陷 *lurnshiahn*, v.i., be subjugated, be fallen.
淪胥 *lurnshyu*, v.i., sink together, one after another.
淪亡 *lurnwarng*, v.i., perish, sink into oblivion.

瀹 63A.42-8

yueh (also *yauh*).

V.t. To boil (tea).

淆 63A.42-8

yaur.

Adj. Confused, mingled: 混淆 ditto.

淆亂 *yaurluahn*, (1) adj., confused; (2) v.t., to upset (peace and order).

汭 63A.42-8

rueih.

N. (1) River bends. (2) The confluence of streams.

§ 63A.50 (氵/ㄱ)

渤 63A.50-1

bor.

N. 渤海 the Pohai, formerly, Gulf of Chihli.

瀚 63A.50-1

hahn.

Adj. Wide, extensive: 浩瀚 extensive, also 浩浩瀚瀚.

瀚海 *Hahnhaai*, n., the Mongolian desert, the Gobi.

沏 63A.50-1

chi (**chyu*).

V.i. & t. (1) 沏茶 to make tea (by pouring boiling water over it). (2) (**chyu*) 沏油 to pour hot oil over cooked meat or vegetable. (3) (**chyu*) To drench with water; 把香火兒沏了 to drench burning incense stick with water (and extinguish it).

汚 63A.50-3

wu (**wa*).

[Var. of 汙, 污]

N. (1) Stagnant pool: 同流合汚 (contempt.) "birds of a feather flock together." (2) Depressed state: 隆汚 rise and decline.

V.t. (1) To rape, violate (woman): 姦汙, 汙辱 *-ruh*↓. (2) To defile, smear, tarnish (name): 汙衊 *-mieh*↓. (3) (**wa*) To dig (=挖).

Adj. (1) Dirty, smudged, muddy, spattered, polluted: 汙濁, 汙垢 *-juor*, *-gouh*↓; 汙池 a muddy pool; 汙點 *-diaan*↓; 汙名 be smudged in name. (2) Base, corrupt (official): 貪汙, 汙吏 ditto.

汙點 *wudiaan*, n., a stain (on clothing, character).
汙瀆 *wu-dur*, n., a muddy pool.
汙垢 *wu-gouh*, n., dirt, filth; stain.
汙穢 *wuhueih*, (1) n., dirt, filth, garbage; (2) adj., disreputable (conduct), filthy (place).
汙濁 *wurjuor*, adj., dirty, filthy.
汙漫 *wumahn*, v. t. & adj., to smudge, besmirch; besmirched.
汙衊 *wumieh*, v. t., to smear (person's name); to humiliate (person); desecrate, calumniate (sacred name).
汙染 *wuraan*, v. t., to pollute, contaminate; befoul, corrupt; 汙染物 n., pollutant; 空氣汙染 pollution of the air; 汙染損毀 contamination. 「violate (woman).
汙辱 *wuruh*, v. t., to humiliate; to
汙臭 *wushiouh*, adj., foul smelling.
汙俗 *wusur*, adj., cheap and common.

污 63A.50–3

wu.

[Var. of 汙 63A.00]

沔 63A.50–3

miaan.

Adj. (AC) overflowing.

鴻 63A.50–3

hurng.

N. (1) The wild goose; wild swan: 輕如鴻毛 light as swan's-down; 鴻飛 to go away for some great undertaking; 鴻爪 footprints of birds—traces of past events; as carrier of letters, see 鴻雁 *-yahn*↓; hence 鴻便 when convenient to send a letter; 哀鴻遍野 phr., starving people fill the land. (2) A surname.

Adj. (LL) vast, grand (interch. 宏 62.93, 弘 50A.93 sometimes also 洪 63A.80): 鴻猷, 鴻圖 (LL) great plan or undertaking; 鴻恩 your great favor; 鴻文 (LL) your great piece of writing; 鴻儒 (LL) great scholar; 鴻福, 鴻禧 great luck or blessing; 鴻基 (LL) great foundation for undertaking.

鴻嗷 *hurng aur*, n., (AC, allu.) the cry of starving people.
鴻寶 *hurngbaau*, n., secret collection of books, usu. Taoist.
鴻博 *hurngbor*, adj., learned, widely read.
鴻溝 *hurnggou*, n., a gap or gulf separating two parties or units; a boundary line.
鴻鵠 *hurnghur*, n., a large swan; (fig.) 鴻鵠之志 great ambitions.
鴻爪 *hurngjaau*, n., "goose footprints," sundry traces.
鴻烈 *hurnglieh*, adj., great, meritorious.
鴻門宴 *hurngmern-yahn*, n., (AC, allu.) a dinner at 鴻門 where treachery (murder of invited guest) was planned.
鴻蒙 *hurngmerng*, n., (AC) primordial world, before the universe was formed (also wr. 濛).
鴻雁 *hurngyahn*, n., the wild goose, reputed in literary tradition as messenger carrying letters (see also 雁 51A.11); mail.

泐 63A.50–3

leh.

N. Marks, cracks or perforations on rocks made by action of waves.

V.i. & t. (1) (LL) v.t., carve, write, inscribe: 泐石 inscribe characters on a stone tablet; 手泐 written with one's own hand; 泐此奉覆 this is written in reply to yours; 泐布, 泐達 you are hereby informed. (2) V. i., (of rocks) split according to their natural veins.

湧 63A.50–3

yuung.

[Var. 涌]

V.i. (1) To gush forth (as spring): 湧出來 gush forth; 湧泉 a gushing spring; 潮湧 (crowd) push forward in waves. (2) (Prices) soar up.

渴 63A.50–4

kee.

N. & adj. Thirsty: 口渴, 嘴渴 thirsty; 饑渴 thirst and hunger; 好渴 very thirsty; 止渴 to slake thirst; 望梅止渴 to slake thirst by thinking of plums; 飲鴆止渴 stop thirst by drinking poison—senseless measure; 臨渴掘井 start to drill well when thirsty—too late; 渴筆 use of semi-dry brush in calligraphy.

Adv. Earnestly: 渴念 thinking of person greatly; 渴望 earnestly hope; 渴睡 very sleepy; 渴欲 wish very much; 渴仰, 渴慕 admire greatly from distance; 渴想 earnestly hope.

湯 63A.50–4

tang (**shang*).

N. (1) Hot water, hot springs: 湯沐 bath; 湯泉 *-chyuarn*↓. (2) Soup: 牛肉湯 beef broth; 雞湯

chicken soup; 湯麪 soup with noodles; 菜湯 vegetable soup; 高湯 simple plain soup, stock for cooking; 熬湯, 燉湯 soup in stew; 泡湯 diluted, spoiled: 這件事已泡湯了 this affair has been spoiled; 落湯雞 all wet, drenched through, like drowned chicken; 赴湯蹈火 willing to go through fire and water, take all risks; 金城湯池 golden city and boiling hot moat—(lit. & fig.) for strongly fortified city; 湯碟, 湯盤 *-parn*, 湯碗 *-waan* ↓; 湯羊 scalded or blanched lamb with skin on. (3) A surname.

湯包 *tangbau*, n., dumpling with juicy meat.
湯餅 *tangbiing*, n., as in 湯餅筵 celebration of third day of baby's birth, with noodles in soup, as a wish for long life.
湯匙 *tangchyr*[1], n., spoon: 大湯匙 ladle.
湯池 *tangchyr*[2], n., strength of city's defenses, see 金城湯池 under N. 2 ↑.
湯泉 *tangchyuarn*, n., hot springs, (more oft. called 温泉).
湯鍋 *tang'guo*, n., butcher's cauldron at slaughterhouse.
湯鑊 *tanghuoh*, n., anc., cauldron for boiling man alive.
湯兒 *tang'l*, n. & adj., soup; 湯兒事 s. t. insubstantial, empty show, pure talk.
湯盤 *tangparn*, n., soup plate.
湯婆子 *tangpor'tz*, n., bed-warmer, made of copper or pewter and filled with hot water for warming up bed.
湯湯 **shangshang*, adj., (AC) descriptive sound of water.
湯水(兒) *tangshueei(-shue'l)*, n., (1) drinks; light food like vegetable soup; (2) (MC) financial means: 戲子有多大湯水 an actor cannot afford much; (3) (coll.) n. & adj., trouble, -some: 這件事太湯水 this matter is too troublesome.
湯頭 *tang'tou*, n., medical recipes, decoctions.
湯糰 *tangtuarn*, n., dumplings.
湯碗 *tangwaan*, n., soup bowl.
湯藥 *tangyauh*, n., medical stews, concoctions.
湯液 *tangyeh*, n., medical potions.
湯引 *tangyiin*, n., liquid taken with medicine to help circulate in body.
湯圓 *tangyuarn*, n., see *-tuarn* ↑.

濁 63A.50-4

juor.

Adj. (1) Muddy, foul (water), turbid (stream): 汚濁 dirty, filthy; 混濁 turbid; 濁流 turbid stream; 濁醪 *-laur* ↓; 濁酒 inferior, unstrained wine; 濁世 an immoral world or times. (2) 濁母 voiced consonant, opp. 清母 voiceless consonant.

濁醪 *juorlaur*, n., (LL) unstrained wine.
濁人 *juorrern*, n., vulgar person.
濁物 *juorwuh*, n., (abusive) a lout, an oaf.
濁音 *juoryin*, n., voiced consonant.

溺 63A.50-5

nih (**niauh*).

N. (**niauh*) Urine: 便溺 to pass urine; 溺器 *-chih* ↓.

V.i. & t. (1) Be submerged in water: 溺死 be drowned; 溺鬼 ghost of one drowned. (2) Be addicted to: 沈溺 be fond of to excess; 耽溺 ditto; 溺於酒色 be addicted to wine and women; 溺愛 *-aih* ↓. (3) Urinate (**niauh*): 溺尿 (**niauhsuei*) pass water; 溺牀 to wet the bed; 溺炕 ditto; 溺褲子 to wet the pants.

溺愛 *nih-aih*, v. t., to love (s. o.) blindly.
溺器 *nihchih*, n., a urinal.
溺職 *nih-jyr*, v. i., fail to do one's duty.

馮 63A.50-5

ferng (**pirng*).

N. A surname: 馮婦 *Feng Fu*, personal name: one willing to take on risky, difficult job (AC allu., famous soldier and tiger killer who took up job of fighting a cornered tiger).

V.t. (**pirng*) 馮河 (AC) swim across river.

馮夷 **Pirngyir*, n., god of rivers, also called 河伯.

滂 63A.50-6

pang.

滂浡 *pangbor*, adj., (AC) convulsed, agitated (of air under pressure).
滂湃 *pangpaih*, 滂滂 *-parng*, 滂沛 *-peih*, 滂濞 *-pih*, adjj., describing voluminous, rushing water.
滂沱 *pangtuor*, adj., (of rain, tears) pouring.

瀉 63A.50-6

shieh.

[Closely related 泄 63A.21, 洩 63A.71]

V.i. (1) To flow down in a torrent; to pour down, out: 瀑布的水直瀉下來 the water pours down over the falls; 傾瀉下懷 pour out my thoughts (or troubles). (2) Suffer loose bowels: 上吐下瀉 vomit and have watery bowels; 吐瀉 cholera; 瀉肚(子) *-duh(tz)* ↓.

瀉肚(子) *shiehduh(tz)*, v.i. & n., have loose bowel movements, diarrhoea.
瀉痢 *shiehlih*, n., diarrhoea; 瀉痢鹽 Epsom salt, see *-yarn* ↓.
瀉鹵 *shiehluu*, adj., (soil) impregnated with lime or salt, therefore barren.
瀉土 *shiehtuu*, n., bare land which cannot retain moisture.
瀉鹽 *shiehyarn*, n., see *-lihyarn* ↑.
瀉藥 *shiehyauh*, n., a laxative.

汾 63A.50–8

fern.

N. Name of river and district in Shansi; 汾酒 wine produced in Shansi.

滃 63A.50–8

weeng.

Adj. (1) Flowing, rushing (flood). (2) Rising, dispersing (clouds).

潟 63A.50–9

shih.

N. Bad land containing deposits of salt.

澇 63A.50–9

lauh.

V.t. & n. Inundate, -ation: 旱澇無常 sometimes drought and sometimes floods.

洵 63A.50–9

shyurn.

Adv. (LL) indeed: 洵美且仁 (AC) indeed handsome and kind; 洵不誣也 (LL) indeed it is true and not hearsay.

洶 63A.50–9

shyung.

Adj. (Of sea) turbulent, tempestuous; roaring, uproarious.

洶動 *shyungduhng*, adj., restless.
洶洶 *shyungshyung*, adj., roaring.
洶湧 *shyungyuung*, adj., (of waves) dashing, crashing (also wr. 涌).

淘 63A.50–9

taur.
[Dist. 陶, 掏]

V.t. (1) To rinse, wash: 淘一淘 stir s.t. in water to cleanse; 淘乾淨 wash it clean; 淘米 wash and clean rice before cooking; 淘金, 淘砂揀金 wash gold. (2) Clean out (also wr. 掏): 淘井, 河, 陰溝 clean out well, dredge river, clean out sewer. (3) Eliminate in 淘汰 *-taih.* ↓ (4) Cleanse breast by writing: 淘寫, 淘瀉 *-shiee*, *-shieh*, ↓.

淘氣 *taurchih*, adj., naughty (child).
淘澄 *taurdehng*, v. t., stir (ointment, mixture).
淘淥 *taurluh*, v. i., become physically weakened through overindulgence in sexual pleasures.
淘神 *taur-shern*, adj., annoying (e. g., naughty child).
淘寫 *taurshiee*, v. t., to write of (emotions) as a form of catharsis.
淘瀉 *taurshieh*, v. t., pour out sentiments in writing.
淘汰 *taurtaih*, v. t., eliminate: 被淘汰 be eliminated.

海 63A.50–9

haai.

N. (1) The sea, also the ocean: 海外 overseas; 海洋 the ocean; 海上 at sea, also "at Shanghai"; 出海 go out to sea (as for fishing); 海船 sea-going ships; as a symbol of infinity: 海闊天空 in open sea and sky, also (of talk) at random, without reference to reality; 海角天涯 the corners of the world; 海枯石爛, 海誓山盟 lovers' pledge of eternal loyalty (until "the seas dry up and rocks decay"); 海市蜃樓 mirage, s. t. imaginary; 四海 the four seas, the universe around; 四海一家 all mankind is one family. (2) Fig. of a huge gathering: 人海 the sea of humanity (in a crowd): 人海戰術 human wave tactics; 學海, 文海 the ocean of learning, of literature; 孽海 the sea of sin and degradation; 苦海 (Budd. of the material or human life) a sea of troubles; 恨海無邊 a sea of eternal regets; 星海 the expanse of stars; 雲海 a sea of clouds.

Adj. & adv. Great, unlimited: 海量 great capacity: 海涵 *-harn* ↓; 海罵 (MC) random and unrestrained scolding; 海說 wild talk; 海碗 a very large bowl.

海岸 *haaiahn*, n., seacoast; 海岸線 coast line.
海百合 *hairbaaiher*, n., (zoo.) the sea lily, crinoid.
海拔 *haaibar*, n., sea level: 海拔一千尺 1000 ft. above sea level.
海豹 *haaibauh*[1], n., (zoo.) the seal.
海報 *haaibauh*[2], n., theater posters

on programs; any posters.

海表 *hair-biaau*, phr., beyond the seas.

海濱 *haaibin*, n., seacoast; sea beach.

海捕 *hair-buu*, v.t. warrant to find and arrest (criminal) on seas.

海產 *hairchaan*, n., marine products.

海潮 *haaichaur*, n., the tides.

海青 *haaiching*, n., (MC) dress with broad sleeves; also monk's robe.

海牀 *haai-chuarng*, n., the floor of the sea.

海膽 *hairdaan*, n., (zoo.) the sea-urchin.

海島 *hairdaau*, n., an island.

海帶 *haaidaih*, n., (bot.) an edible seaweed, *Laminaria angustata*.

海盜 *haaidauh*, n., pirate.

海燈 *haaideng*, n., (zoo.) a tiny phosphorescent animal at sea, *Doliolum tritomis*.

海底 *hair-dii*, adj., bottom of the sea; 海底電線 submarine cable.

海笛 *haaidir*, n., a small flute-like musical instrument.

海東青 *haaidungching*, n., a sea-bird on the China Sea, valued for its feather.

海法 *hair-faa*, n., maritime law.

海防 *haai-farng*, n., (1) coastal defense; (2) the port Hai-phong.

海風 *haai-feng*, n., sea breeze.

海港 *hairgaang*, n., harbor.

海狗 *hairgoou*, n., (zoo.) the seal.

海關 *haaiguan*, n., maritime customs.

海國 *haaiguor*, n., maritime country.

海股 *hairguu*, n., gulf.

海涵 *haaiharn*, (1) adj., with great generosity which forgives all; (2) v.t., (court.) to forgive or tolerate (errors).

海花石 *haaihua-shyr*, n., coral.

海貨 *haai-huoh*, n., marine products; overseas products.

海蜇 *haaijer*, n., (zoo.) jellyfish.

海鯽 *haaijih*, n., (zoo.) a life-bearing sea fish, *Ditrema temminckii*.

海禁 *haaijihn*, n., ban on foreign trade or intercourse: 海禁大開, 開放海禁 open country to foreign trade.

海鏡 *haaijihng*, n., (zoo.) a kind of flat shellfish, *Amusium japonicus*, whose shell is used in windows.

海軍 *haaijyun*, n., the navy.

海客 *haaikeh*, n., travellers or merchants from abroad.

海口 *hairkoou*, n., seaport.

海葵 *haaikueir*, n., (zoo.) sea anemone.

海浪 *haai-lahng*, n., sea waves.

海里 *hairlii*, n., nautical mile.

海流 *haai-liour*, n., sea or ocean current.

海狸 *haailir*, n., the beaver.

海洛因 *hairluohyin*, n., (translit.) heroin, also 海洛英.

海蘿 *haailuor*, n., (bot.) a kind of seaweed.

海龍王 *Haailurngwarng*, n., (myth.) Dragon King of the Seas.

海驢 *haailyur*, n., (zoo.) Steller's sea lion, a North Pacific sea animal.

海馬 *hairmaa*, n., (zoo.) the walrus, see *-shiahng* ↓.

海鰻 *haaimarn*, n., (zoo.) sea eel.

海面 *haai-miahn*, n., sea surface.

海綿 *haaimiarn*, n., sponge.

海難 *haai nahn*, phr., perils of the sea, shipwreck.

海內 *haai-neih*, n. & adv., in the country: 海內同胞 fellow citizens of China; 四海之內 "all within the Four Seas"—the world.

海牛 *haainiour*, n., (zoo.) the sea cow or manatee, *Manatus senegalensis*.

海漚 *haai-ou*[1], n., bubbles on sea, (Buddhist fig.) transient character of human life.

海鷗 *haaiou*[2], n., (zoo.) sea gull.

海派 *haaipaih*, n., "Shanghai style or school," orig., a school of Chin. opera, now generally (contempt.) of girls, magazines going after the fashion of the day: 海派女郎, 海派作風.

海盤車 *haaiparnche*, n., (zoo.) the starfish (also called 海星).

海螵蛸 *haai-piaushiau*, n., dried central part of cuttlefish.

海若 *haaireh*, n., (AC myth.) god of the sea.

海上 *haaishahng*, adj., maritime: 海上保險 maritime insurance.

海商法 *haai-shangfaa*, n., maritime law.

海參 *haaishen*, n., sea cucumber, *beche-de-mer*, a delicacy, *Stichopus japonicus*.

海蛇 *haaisher*, n., (zoo.) sea serpent.

海象 *haaishiahng*, n., (zoo.) the walrus (also called 海馬 *-maa* ↑).

海鮮 *haai-shian*, n., sea food (shrimps, oysters, fish, etc.).

海峽 *haaishiar*, n., (geog.) straits, channel.

海嘯 *haaishiauh*, n., tidal wave.

海星 *haaishing*, n., the star fish.

海螄 *haaisy*, n., (zoo.) a sea shell, *Scala lamellosa*.

海獺 *haaitah*, n., (zoo.) the seal, *Enhydra marina*.

海苔 *haaitair*, n., an edible seaweed.

海灘 *haaitan*, n., sea beach.

海棠 *haaitarng*[1] (-'*tang*), n., (bot.) the cherry apple tree or its fruit (the latter also called 海棠果 *Malus halliana*); begonia.

海塘 *haai-tarng*[2], n., sea wall, sea embankment.

海菜 *haaitsaih*, n., (bot.) agar-agar, an edible seaweed.

海錯 *haai-tsuoh*, n., sea delicacies: 山珍海錯 exotic food from mountains and seas.

海圖 *haai-tur*, n., maritime map.

海豚 *haaiturn*, n., (zoo.) the dolphin or porpoise (dist. 河[A]豚 63A.00).

海子 *haai'tz*, n., (North China) lakes, ponds.

海藻 *hairtzaau*, n., a large class of seaweeds.

海外 *haai-waih*, adj. & adv., overseas, abroad.

海灣 *haaiwan*, n., (geog.) gulf or bay.

海王星 *haaiwarngshing*, n., (astron.) the planet Neptune.

海味 *haai-weih*, n., sea food.

海燕 *haaiyahn*, n., (zoo.) the petrel, *Procellaria furcata*, making nest on sea cliffs—the origin of "birds' nest," a delicacy.

海灣濕淤泠冷

海牙 *Haiyar*, The Hague.
海鹽 *haaiyarn*, n., salt from the sea; also a county in Kiangsu.
海洋 *haaiyarng*, n., ocean.
海鷹 *haaiying*, n., (zoo.) sea eagle; osprey.
海員 *haaiyuarn*, n., sailor.
海芋 *haaiyuh*, n., (bot.) *Alocasia macrorhiza.*
海運 *haai-yuhn*, n., sea transportation.
海隅 *haai-yur*, n., a corner or small town by the sea.

灣 63A.50-9

wan.
[Pop. 湾]

N. A bay, cove, inlet: 港灣, 江灣 ditto; 海灣 gulf; 轉灣 to go around corner.

V.t. To anchor, tie up: 把船灣住; 灣泊港口 tie up at the harbor.

§63A.63 (氵/丶)

濕 63A.63-4

shy.
[Var. of 溼]

N. Moisture, damp, dampness: 濕氣 *-chih* ↓; 風濕 (Chin. med.) arthritis, rheumatism; 濕疹 *-jeen* ↓.

Adj. (1) Damp, moist, swampy: 潮濕 damp (climate); 濕地 swampy ground; 濕季 damp season; 濕答答, 濕淥淥, 濕津津 dripping wet. (2) Wet, soaked: 衣服濕了 clothing has got wet; 濕透了 soaked through.

濕氣 *shychih*, n., (Chin. med.) a term which includes rheumatism, arthritis, gout and some fungus disease.
濕度 *shyduh*, n., degree of humidity; 濕度表 *--biaau*, n., hygrometer.
濕疹 *shyjeen*, n., a kind of skin disease with boils.
濕熱 *shyreh*, adj. & n., (climate) hot and damp, sultry, damp heat.
濕窪 *shywa*, adj., swampy (region).

淤 63A.63-6

yu.

N. Silts, sediment: 淤泥 *-nir* ↓.

V.i. To silt, to block up: 淤塞 *-seh* ↓.

Adj. Clogged up, slimy, full of sediments.

淤溉 *yu-gaih*, v. t., to irrigate with muddy (and fertile) water.
淤積 *yuji*, v. i., to form sediment.
淤滯 *yujyh*, v. i., to become sluggish.
淤泥 *yunir*, n., mud sediment.
淤肉 *yu-rouh*, n., see 瘀^△^肉 61A.63.
淤塞 *yuseh*, v. t., to block up (river).
淤血 *yu-shyueh*, n., blood clot, see 瘀^△^血 61A.63.

泠 63A.63-8

lirng.
[Dist. 冷↓; usu. printed 泠]

Adj. Nice and cool; (of sounds, breeze) cooling.

冷 63A.63-8

leeng.
[Var. usu. printed 冷]

N. A surname.

V.i. & t. To cool, freeze, ignore: 這件事冷下來了 the matter has cooled down; 把他冷在一邊 let him cool his heels; 冷他一陣子 give him the cold shoulder, ignore him a while; 冷着臉 put on a stern face; 心冷了 have lost all interest, become indifferent; 心頭一冷 be suddenly seized by fear.

Adj. (1) Cold, cool, chilly: 寒冷 cold, wintry; 冰冷 icy cold; 冷極了 bitterly cold; 冷死了 dead cold; 冷峭 *-chiauh* ↓; 冷冰冰 cold like ice: 他對我冷冰冰地 he's so cold towards me; 冷森森, 冷呵呵 (of room, place, laugh, manner) dreadfully cold; 冷凍 *-duhng* ↓; 冷卻 *-chyueh* ↓; 冷藏 *-tsarng* ↓; 冷凝 congealed; 冷水(浴) cold water (a cold bath); 冷酒 unwarmed wine; 冷葷, 冷碟, 冷盤 *hors d'oeuvres, -hun, -dier, -parn* ↓; 冷飲 *-yiin*, 冷食 *-shyr* ↓; 冷風刺骨 the wind is piercingly cold; 冷汗 cold sweat; 冷血 cold blood; 冷面, 冷臉子 a cold face; 冷暖 *-nuaan* ↓. (2) Secluded, unfamiliar: 冷字 unfamiliar word; 冷巷 deserted lane; 冷僻 *-pih* ↓. (3) Disinterested, coolheaded: 冷眼 take a cool look, look at coolly. (4) Neglected, ignored, slighted, not in vogue: 坐冷板凳 be given a low job without much work, be kept waiting, slighted; 冷官 official with not much duty; 冷門, 冷宮, 冷貨 *-mern, -gung, -huoh* ↓; 冷清清, 冷冷清清, 冷湫湫 cold and dreary; 冷清, 冷淡, 冷落 *-'ching, -'dahn, -luoh* ↓. (5) Sarcastic, sneering, jeering, displeased: 冷笑 *-shiauh* ↓; 冷話 *-huah* ↓; 冷言冷語 shafts of ridicule, talking behind s. o.'s back; 冷冷地 in a sneering manner. (6) Done in secret: 冷箭 a covered barbed remark; 放冷槍 (lit. & fig.) to fire sniper shots; 打冷拳 hit (s. o.) from behind; 抽冷子給他一刀 to stab him unawares; 冷不防 be caught unawares; 冷酒兒後犯 wait for another chance to avenge oneself on an enemy.

冷布 *leeng-buh*, n., loose-textured

gauze for use as screen in summer.

冷腸 *leeng-charng*, adj., disinterested in human welfare or worldly affairs.

冷峭 *leengchiauh*, adj., (of speech) cuttingly cold, biting, sarcastic.

冷氣 *leeng-chih*, n., cold air; 冷氣機 air-conditioner.

冷清 *leeng'ching*, adj., solitary, quiet, desolate, also 冷清清的.

冷泉 *leeng-chyuarn*, n., (geol.) a cold spring.

冷卻 *leeng-chyueh*, v. i., to cool off, to slight; 冷卻器 cooling apparatus.

冷淡 *leeng'dahn*, (1) adj., indifferent, cool, apathetic; 態度冷淡 an indifferent attitude: (2) v. t., 冷淡着他 cool off toward him; (3) v. i., to cool down: 等這一陣狂熱勁冷淡下來 just wait for all this excitement to quiet down; (4) adj., plain, simple, homely: 白花冷淡無人愛 the white flowers are too plain and simple to be popular.

冷碟 *leeng-dier*, n., a cold dish, (also *-parn*↓).

冷凍 *leengduhng*, v. t., (1) to freeze; (2) leave in the cold: 把他冷凍起來 give him the cold shoulder, "freeze" person; 冷凍機 freezer.

冷宮 *leeng-gung*, n., palace where a queen or an imperial concubine fallen into disgrace lived: 打入冷宮 (fig.) fallen into disfavor.

冷話 *leenghuah*, n., cool, sacarstic remark.

冷葷 *leeng-hun*, n., cold meats, *hors d'oeuvres*.

冷貨 *leeng-huoh*, n., goods not much in demand.

冷戰 *leengjahn*, n., (1) the cold war; (2) a cold shudder.

冷劑 *leeng-jih*, n., (phys.) a freezing mixture.

冷靜 *leengjihng*, (1) adj., (of place) lonely, quiet; (2) v. i., 冷靜一下 keep cool, calm down, for a moment.

冷金 *leengjin*, n., (1) a kind of gold-sprinkled paper; (2) light-yellowish color.

冷酷 *leengkuh*, adj., cold-blooded, ruthless; lacking in human warmth.

冷落 *leengluoh*, (1) adj., (business, family) on the decline; (2) v. t., to slight or ignore (s. o.).

冷門(兒) *leeng-mern(-mer'l)*, n. & adj., s.t. not in popular demand, not in vogue: 走冷門 choose the less popular course; 爆出冷門 a "sleeper," a dark horse which has won; an unexpected success.

冷面 *leeng-miahn*, adj., displeased, stern-faced.

冷漠 *leeng-moh*, adj., (1) indifferent, apathetic; (2) unsentimental: 冷漠無情 sternly cool and unmoved.

冷暖 *lerng-nuaan*, adj., & n., (1) (of weather) degree of warmth: 天氣冷暖 the warmth of temperature; (2) 人情冷暖 fickleness of human nature, change of attitude among friends.

冷盤 *leengparn*, n., (Chin. cuisine) a dish of assorted cold meats (also *-dieih*↑).

冷僻 *leengpih*, lonely, deserted, obsolete, out-of-the-way; (of words, allusions) unusual.

冷笑 *leengshiauh*, v.i. & t., sneer at scoff, at, n., a sneer.

冷心 *leeng-shin*, adj., apathetic, unenthusiastic, discouraged.

冷食 *leeng-shyr*, n., a cold lunch, a cold meal, cold snacks.

冷血 *lerngshyueh*, adj., cold-blooded, hard-hearted: 冷血動物 cold-blooded animals.

冷藏 *leengtsarng*, v. t., keep in cold storage.

冷竈 *leeng-tzauh*, n., (1) a cold stove; (2) (fig.) a person out of office: 燒冷竈 befriend such a person so as to gain his favor in anticipation of his comeback.

冷眼 *lerng-yaan*, adj. & adv., detached: 冷眼旁觀 take a detached point of view.

冷罨法 *lerngyaan-faa*, n., (med.) the application of a cold compress to an affected part of the patient's body (also 冷敷).

冷飲 *lerng-yiin*, n., cold drinks.

漁 63A.63-9

yur.

N. A surname.

V.t. To fish: 漁獵, 漁翁 *-lieh, -weng*↓; (fig.) fish for profit: 漁利, 漁奪 *-lih, -duor*↓; 漁人得利 the third party benefits when two parties fight each other (from allu. 鷸蚌相爭, 漁人得利 fight between the crane and the mother-of-pearl).

漁唱 *yur-chahng*, n., fisherman's song.

漁奪 *yur-duor*, v. t., (officials) rob the people (as a fisherman catches fish).

漁夫 *yurfu*, n., fisherman.

漁父 *yurfuu*, n., (AC) ditto.

漁港 *yur-gaang*, n., fishing bay or harbor.

漁戶 *yurhuh*, n., a professional fisherman.

漁火 *yur-huoo*, n., lights from fishing boats.

漁具 *yur-jyuh*, n., fishing tackle (rod, net, etc.).

漁郎 *yurlarng*, n., (poet.) fisherman.

漁獵 *yur-lieh*, v. i., to fish and hunt.

漁利 *yur-lih*, v. i., to take illegitimate profit: 從中漁利 get personal profit from it.

漁婆(兒) *yur-por'l*, n., fisherman's wife.

漁人 *yurrern*, n., fisherman.

漁色 *yurseh*, v. i., to philander, go for women.

漁汛 *yur-shyuhn*, n., fishing seasons.

漁子 *yurtzyy*, n., (LL) fisherman.

漁翁 *yurweng*, n., (LL, poet.) old fisherman.

漁業 *yuryeh*, n., profession of fishing.

§ 63A.70 (氵/乚)

沌 63A.70-1

duhn.

Adj. See 混[A]沌 63A.70.

洗 63A.70-1

shii.

N. (1) A small vessel containing water for painting: 洗筆 or 筆洗. (2) A surname.

V.t. (1) To wash, to clean: 乾洗 dry clean; 洗臉 wash face; 洗不乾淨 cannot be washed clean; 洗頭, 洗髮, 洗手 *-tour*, *-faa*, *-shoou* ↓; 血洗全村 kill everybody (bloodbath) in the village. (2) To clear (s. o.) of suspicion, charges: 洗冤 *-yuan* ↓; 洗雪 *-shyuee* ↓.

洗兵 *shii-bing*, phr., clean military weapons—stop war.
洗塵 *shii-chern*, v. i., to give a dinner to friend on return from travel ("wash the dust").
洗城 *shii-cherng*, phr., have a bloodbath, killing all inhabitants of city.
洗盪 *shiidahng*, v. i., to wash clean (clothing).
洗滌 *shiidir*, v. t., to wash away dirt, to clean (dishes, clothing, bad habits, heart).
洗耳 *shii-eel*, v. i., (1) usu. in 洗耳恭聽 listen respectfully ("wash ears"); (2) (AC) to shut one's ears to turmoil of world affairs: 洗耳不聞.
洗兒 *shii-erl*, v. i., custom of giving bath to baby on its third day, see *-san* ↓.
洗髮 *shirfaa*, v.i., have hair washed, shampoo.
洗刮 *shiigua*, v. i., wash and polish.
洗甲 *shir-jiaa*, v. i., see *-bing* ↑.
洗濯 *shiijuor*, v. t., to wash (hands, feet); to bathe.
洗禮 *shirlii*, n., baptism: 行洗禮, 受洗禮 to give, receive baptism.
洗腦 *shir-naau*, n. & v. i., brainwash.
洗牌 *shii-pair*, v. i., to shuffle cards.
洗三 *shii-san*, v. i., see *-erl* ↑.
洗心 *shii-shin*, v. i., to change one's heart and reform: 洗心革面.
洗手 *shir-shoou*, v. i., (1) to "wash hands"—(of thieves) to leave the gang and reform; (2) go to lavatory; 洗手間 *--jian*, n., lavatory, toilet.
洗刷 *shii'shua*, v. t., (1) to wash and brush; (2) to clear person's name of guilt charges, see *-shyuee* ↓.
洗拭 *shiishyh*, v. t., wipe and wash (utensils).
洗雪 *shirshyuee*, v. t., to right a wrong, to clear charges.
洗削 *shiishyueh*, v. t., see *-shyuee* ↑.
洗頭 *shiitour*, v.i., have hair washed.
洗澡 *shirtzaau*, v. i., to take a bath.
洗眼 *shir-yaan*, phr., "wash eyes"—watch attentively.
洗衣 *shiiyi*, v. i., do laundry; n., 洗衣店 laundry shop.
洗冤 *shii-yuan*, v. i., to right a wrong.
洗浴 *shiiyuh*, v. i., to take a bath; 洗浴室 n., bathroom.

澆 63A.70-1

jiau.

V.t. To sprinkle with water, spray: 澆花 to water flowers; 澆水 to water (plants), sprinkle water on; 以酒澆愁 take to drinking to forget one's sorrows.

Adj. Degenerate, decadent: see compp. ↓.

澆薄 *jiaubor*, adj., (of customs, manners) bad, degenerate.
澆風 *jiau-feng*, n., degenerate ways, decadent manners.
澆浮 *jiaufur*, adj., see *-bor* ↑.
澆季 *jiau-jih*, n., decadent times, *fin de siècle*.
澆競 *jiau-jihng*, adj., pushing, grasping, greedy for influence and power.
澆漓 *jiaulih*, adj., see *-bor* ↑.
澆末 *jiaumoh*, n., see *-bor* ↑.

淹 63A.70-1

yan (**yahn*).

[Related 掩 10A.70]

V.i. & t. (1) To soak, to cover with liquid: 胰子水淹得眼睛疼 soap water gets into the eyes and hurts; 被汗淹得難受 (skin) is irritated by the sweat. (2) To flood over, to drown: 淹死了 drowned; 水淹 water floods (area); 淹沒 *-moh* ↓. (3) (**yahn*) (Coll.) to cover with water, to soak: 醃菜時,要讓水淹過菜來 immerse the vegetable (to be pickled) completely under water. (4) To stay, stop over: 淹留, 淹纏 *-liour*, *-'chan* ↓.

Adv. Widely read: 淹博, 淹貫 *-bor*, *-guahn* ↓.

淹博 *yanbor*, adj., widely read ("immersed" in learning).
淹纏 *yan'chan*, v. i., (1) (of illness) linger a long time; (2) to delay, (business) drag along.
淹沉 *yan'chen*, v. i., ditto.
淹貫 *yanguahn*, adj., see *-bor* ↑.
淹煎 *yanjian*, v. i., to "stew" in grief.
淹踐 *yan'jian*, v. i., to trample down, use roughly, abuse (a machine).
淹滯 *yanjyh*, v. i., to be bogged down in career.
淹留 *yanliour*, v. i., to linger in life; to stay over for a long period.
淹沒 *yan-moh*, v. t., (1) to drown in water; (2) to be overshadowed or forgotten; (3) to disregard

or abuse, see -'jian↑.

淹潤 *yanruhn*, adj., (MC, of girl) shy, coy.

淹識 *yanshyh*, adj., widely read.

淹恤 *yanshyuh*, v. i., (AC) as in 淹恤在外 to live in exile.

淹宿 *yansuh*, adv., (LL) overnight.

淹通 *yantung*, adj., conversant with many things, knowledgeable.

淹雅 *yanyaa*, adj., well-read and cultured.

淹月 *yan-yueh*, adv., (LL) for a whole month (without undressing).

港 63A.70-2

gaang.

N. (1) A small stream. (2) A harbor, port: 海港 a seaport; 漁港 a fishing port; 避風港 a bay, a harbor as a storm shelter; 港口 *-koou*, 港灣 *-wan*↓; 領港 a pilot licensed to steer ships into or out of a harbor; 領港船 a pilot-boat; 載貨港 port of loading; 卸貨港 port of discharge.

港警 *garng-jiing*, n., harbor police.

港口 *gaangkoou*, n., a port, harbor: 港口稅 port dues; 無稅港口 a free port.

港灣 *gaangwan*, n., a bay.

港務局 *gaangwuhjyur*, n., port authorities, harbor bureau.

泚 63A.70-2

tsyy.

N. (AC) moisture (sweat).

V.t. To wet: 泚筆 dip brush in ink.

Adj. (AC) clear, bright.

池 63A.70-2

chyr.

N. (1) A pond, a pool: 魚池 fish pond; 游泳池 swimming pool; 池堂 *-tarng*[2]↓; 噴水池 fountain; 池心 center of pool; 恐非池中物 (allu. fig.) of person of great abilities, not a common pool fish. (2) A city moat: 池魚遭殃 (when city burns) the fish in the moat suffer—victim of disaster of another's doing; 城池 city wall and moat—city defense. (3) A surname.

池沼 *chyrjaau*, n., pools, ponds in gen.

池榭 *chyrshieh*, n., pond and terrace in a rich mansion.

池塘 *chyrtarng*[1], n., ponds.

池堂 *chyrtarng*[2], n., pool path vs. 盆堂 tub bath in bathhouse.

池子 *chyrtz*, n., (1) pool; (2) formerly, pit in a theater.

洮 63A.70-2

taur.

N. Name of river, of lake in Kangsuh.

V.t. (AC) to clean away: 洮汰 var. of 淘Δ汰 63A.50.

灧 63A.70-2

yahn.

[Var. of 灩 63A.30]

沅 63A.70-3

yuarn.

N. Name of a river in Hunan.

灑 63A.70-3

saa.

[Var. of 洒 63A.41]

V. i. To splash (fluid on ground): 灑了一地 splashed all over the ground: 灑掃 *-saau*↓.

Adj. Big-hearted, genial: 灑落 *-luoh*↓; 灑脫 *-'tuo*↓; 瀟Δ灑 63A.22.

灑花 *saahua*, adj., (jacket, pants) embroidered (=綉花).

灑家 *saajia*, pron., (MC dial.) I (the speaker), usu. wr. 洒家.

灑淚 *saa-leih*, v.i., shed tears.

灑落 *saaluoh*, (1) adj., (a) generous, not inhibited; (b) dreary (scene); (2) v. t., to slight (person).

灑然 *saararn*, adj., (descriptive) alarmed (manner).

灑灑 *sarsaa*, adj., clear, lucid.

灑掃 *sar-saau*, v.i., to spray and sweep floor.

灑淅 *saashi*, adj., bleak, cold and dreary.

灑線 *saashiahn*, adj., embroidered, see *-hua*↑.

灑水車 *sarshueei-che*, n., cart for spraying water.

灑湯 *saatang*, v.i., to fail (like a drowned chicken): 那件事他辦的灑湯了 that affair entrusted to him is a complete fiasco.

灑脫 *saa'tuo*, adj., unconventional, taking it easy, free from sordid concerns.

汛 63A.70-3

shyuhn.

N. Flood tide: 潮汛 ditto; 春汛, 秋汛 swollen current of spring, of autumn.

汛地 *shyuhndih*, n., a check point;

also garrison area.

汎掃 *shyuhnsaau*, v. t., (AC) to sweep, wash away (former works).

況 63A.70-4

kuahng.

[see 况↓]

况 63A.70-4

kuahng.

[Pop. 況]

N. (1) Condition (of person, society): 景况, 情况, 狀况 gen. condition (of person, community, village, etc.); 近况 recent condition; 苦况 hard, impoverished condition; 概况 gen. condition, a gen. review. (2) A surname.

V.t. (1) (LL) to compare: 譬况 analogize; 以往况今 compare the present with the past. (2) (AC) var. of 訪, 貺 to visit, to give present.

Adv. (1) Furthermore, besides: 况且 *-chiee*, 况兼 *-jian*↓. (2) Not to speak of: 况 or 而况, 何况; 他連我都不聽, 何况是你 he would not even listen to me, not to speak of you.

况且 *kuahngchiee*, adv., besides, furthermore.

况兼 *kuahngjian*, adv., besides: 况兼她有兩個孤兒 besides, she has two orphans.

况味 *kuahngweih*, n., flavor (of poverty, etc.): 秋天的况味 the flavor of autumn; 鐵窗的况味 taste of prison life ("behind the bars").

浥 63A.70-4

yih.

V.t. To moisten.

浥潤 *yihruhn*, v.i., to moisten: (fig.) to provide with funds.

浥濕 *yihshy*, adj., damp.

浥浥 *yihyih*, adj., (LL of perfume) pervading.

混 63A.70-4

huhn (**hurn*, **huun*).

V. i. (1) To mix with or in: 混合 *-her*↓; 混入 to mix in with s.t. else. (2) To drift along, to muddle through, kill time: 混日子 to pass time or occupy job without real work; 混一時再說 willing to drift along for a time and then see; 胡混, 鬼混 do nominal work; 混飯吃, 混一頓 do s. t. for sake of the ricebowl; 混不下去 can no longer permit oneself to drift along; 混了一年 muddled or occupied job for one year.

Adj. & adv. (1) Without order, plan or purpose: 混雜 *-tzar*↓; 混跑 run foolishly about; 混鬧 make senseless fuss; 混戰 a free-for-all; 混說 talk without plan or purpose; 混世魔王 a devil to create chaos in life. (2) (**huun*) Mixed-up, see 混亂, 混淆, 混江龍 *-luahn*, *-yaur*, *-jianglurng*↓. (3) (**hurn*) Dirty, filthy: 混蛋, 混蟲 *-dahn*, *-churng*↓; 混人, 混水 *-rern*, *-shueei*↓.

混成 *huhncherng*, adj., mixed: 混成旅 a mixed brigade.

混充 *huhnchung*, v. t., to pass fictitiously for s. t. else.

混蟲 **hurnchurng*, n., (abusive) you silly goose, jackass (less severe than *-dahn*↓).

混蛋 **hurndahn*, n., (common abusive, esp. to inferiors) lout, poor devil, skunk (very offensive word).

混沌 *huhnduhn*, adj., (1) nebulous, before the universe took shape; (2) mentally dense or undeveloped.

混號 *huhnhauh*, n., nickname.

混合 *huhnher*, (1) v. t., to mix with; (2) adj., mixed; 混合法 (math.) combination; 混合物 (chem.) compound.

混混 *huhnhuhn*, (1) adj., dark, opaque; blackened, blurred; (2) v. i., to drift along or through: 混混罷了, see V.i. 2↑.

混帳 *huhnjahng*, excl., 混帳王八蛋 (also 混賬) (extreme abuse) "to mix curtains," i. e., get into wrong bed—completely immoral and shameless.

混跡 *huhn-ji*, v. i., to occupy place without being worthy of it.

混江龍 **huunjianglurng*, n., a dredging machine.

混濁 **hurnjuor*, adj., dirty, muddy (water), immoral (world).

混賴 *huhnlaih*, v. i., to lie fatuously.

混亂 **huunluahn*, adj., chaotic, disorderly.

混名 *huhnmirng*, n., nickname (also wr. 諢).

混凝土 *huhnnirng-tuu*, n., cement, concrete.

混然 *huhnrarn*, adj., without distinction.

混人* *hurnrern*, n., idiot (also 渾人).

混水 **hurnshueei*, n., muddy water: 混水摸魚 to fish in troubled waters.

混事 *huhn-shyh*, phr., to seek job without special skill or ability.

混血兒 *huhnshyueh'l*, n., "mixed blood," person born of parents of different races.

混子 *huhntz*, n., (contempt.) a nondescript member of profession without real qualification: 學混子, 報混子 one who makes a living by teaching, journalism, without merit.

混雜 *huhntzar*, adj., mixed, of mixed quality or elements, of different kinds: 遊客混雜 visitors of all kinds.

混淆 **huunyaur*, adj., all mixed up: 混淆視聽 to confuse the public opinion.

混一 *huhnyi*, adj., formed or blended into one.

混元 *huhnyuarn*, n., the primordial chaos.

汎 63A.70–4

fahn.

[Interch. 氾 63A.70 in sense of floating on water; var. of 泛 in sense of broadness]

V. i. (1) Float, flood: see 汎濫 *-lahn*↓. (2) Drift on boat: 汎舟.

Adj. & adv. General, -ly, broad, -ly: 汎愛衆 (AC) love all people; 汎稱 generally called; 汎論 (or 泛論) general discussion or survey; as translation of Eng. "pan": 汎美 Pan-American; 汎太平洋 Pan-Pacific; 汎非主義 Pan-Africanism; 汎拉丁主義 Pan-Latinism.

汎 汎 *fahnfahn*, adv., flowing freely.
汎 濫 *fahnlahn*, v. i., (of flood) spread over; (ideas, customs) spread like a flood.

淝 63A.70–4

feir.

N. Name of river in Anhwei.

澠 63A.70–4

miin.

N. Place name; name of river in Honan.

氾 63A.70–5

fahn.

[Interch. 汎 63A.70]

V. i. To flood.

Adj. Broad, unconfined: 氾論 general discussion.

氾 濫 *fahnlahn*, v. i., (of flood water) break dams and overflow (=汎濫).

汜 63A.70–5

syh.

[Dist. 氾]

N. Bank of river, lake: 涯汜 river banks, compared to limits of discussion; 無涯汜 limitless; also wr. 涯涘.

泥 63A.70–5

nir (**nih*).

N. (1) Mud, mire: 泥土 *-tuu*↓, 泥沙 *-sha*↓; 泥點(子)(兒) muddy stains, dirty or soiled spots; 爛泥 soft mud, quagmire; 淤泥 filthy mud; 泥巴 *-ba*↓; 泥濘 *-nihng*↓; 一身是泥 get muddy all over; 泥水 *-shueei*↓; 爛醉如泥 dead drunk; 和稀泥 do lousy work; 泥牛入海 like clay buffalo drowned at sea—disappear; 泥塑木雕 "an idol," a simpleton who does not move a finger to work. (2) Any paste-like matter: 棗泥, 蒜泥 (Chin. cuisine) mashed dates, garlic; 印泥 a stamp pad specially for use with seals; 肉泥 minced meat.

Adj. Muddy, soiled.

V.i. (1) (**nih*) be narrow-minded, limited in outlook: 拘泥 be bigoted, be a stickler for (forms, tradition); 泥古 *-guu*↓. (2) Linger, loiter: 她仍泥着不走 she still lingered around and wouldn't go.

V.t. Coax, cajole, wheedle: 泥他沽酒 coax him to buy some wine.

泥 巴 *nirba*, n., mud, earth.
泥 青 *nir'ching*, n., deep green.
泥 鰍 *nirchiou*, n., (zoo.) the loach.
泥 刀 *nirdau*, n., a trowel for plaster.
泥 封 *nirfeng*, v.t., to seal (a letter, etc.) with wax.
泥 溝 *nirgou*, n., a gutter or drain.
泥 古 **nihguu*, v.i., be ultra-conservative, be a slave to anc. authorities, customs, or traditions.
泥 火 山 *nir-huooshan*, n., a volcano of steaming lava.
泥 腳 *nir-jiaau*, n., (1) feet soiled with mud; (2) feet of clay.
泥 金 *nirjin*, n., gold dust used as surfacing material.
泥 酒 **nihjiou*, v.i., be addicted to liquor.
泥 滯 **nihjyh*, v.i., be bogged down, bigoted, old-fashioned.
泥 潦 *nirlauh*, n., a marsh, swamp, morass, bog.
泥 濘 *nirnihng*, n., deep mud, mire; adj., muddy.
泥 泥 pr. *nir-nii*, adj., 零露泥泥 (AC) with shining dew; 維葉泥泥 the shining, glistening leaves.
泥 坯 *nirpi*, n., moulded pottery not yet put in a kiln to bake.
泥 人(兒) *nirrern(-rer'l)*, n., earthen figurines—a kind of toy.
泥 沙 *nirsha*, n., (1) sediments, silt; (2) worthless things; (3) mud and sand.
泥 像 *nirshiahng*, n., (1) a Buddhist image; (2) any earthen image.
泥 首 *nir-shoou*, v.i., to kowtow by touching the ground with the forehead.
泥 水 *nirshueei*, n., (1) a mixture of earth and water; (2) sweat drips; (3) 泥水匠 bricklayer.
泥 炭 *nirtahn*, n., (min.) peat.
泥 胎(兒) *nirtai('l)*, n., (1) an earthen idol; (2) pottery not yet put in a kiln to bake, see *-pi*↑.
泥 塘 *nirtarng*, n., a mud pond.
泥 腿 *nirtueei*, n., (1) legs soiled with mud; (2) the rabble, riff-

raff: 泥腿光桿.

泥塗 *nirtur*, n., (1) muddy path; (2) (fig.) low social status or position; (3) v.t., (AC) to look down upon (honors, etc.) as dirt.

泥土 *nirtuu*, n., mud and soil.

泥澤 *nirtzer*, n., muddy pond, swamp; (fig.) where one flounders.

泥醉 *nir-tzueih*, v.i. & adj., (be) dead drunk, "plastered."

泥娃娃 *nirwar'wa*, n., (1) clay doll; (2) clay doll offering in temple of goddess of fertility.

泥丸 *nirwarn*, n., (Taoist) the upper pubic region.

泥飲 **nihyiin*, v.i., be insistent on inviting others to drink.

沅 63A.70–6

hahng (**harng*).

N. & v.i. (**harng*) A ferry; ferry across.

沅漭 *hahngmaang*, adj., (LL) see *-marng* ↓.

沅茫 *hahngmarng*, adj., (LL) (of flood) sweeping, rushing.

沅瀣 *hahngshieh*, phr., 沅瀣一氣 (orig.) like master and pupil (沅 and 瀣); (of people) of the same ilk.

流 63A.70–6

liour.

N. (1) (Of personal character, ability, composition, performance) class, grade, rate: 第一流人品 first-rate character; 第三流 third-rate; 一流人物 persons of the same type; 上流人士 (社會) higher-class people (society); 中流人物 (社會) middle-class persons, (society); 下流 low-brow, mean; 下流社會 lower-class society, esp. ruffians, racketeers; 未入流 "out of the run"—person not yet qualified in academic circles; 流品, 流亞 *-piin*, *-yah* ↓; 女流 ladies in gen.; … 之流 of a certain class; 社會名流 well-known persons, V.I.P.'s, fashionable society. (2) School of thought, current of ideas: 儒者之流 the Confucianists; 三教九流 the three religions and classical nine schools of thought, see 九[A]流 91.70; 流別 *-bier* ↓. (3) N. & v. t., (send to) exile. (4) Current, flow: 洋流, 海流 ocean current; 暖流, 寒流 warm, cold current of air, water; 赤道流 the tropical current; 河流 river, river current; 潛流 undercurrent, undertow; 主流 main current; 支流 subsidiary current, branch of river; 源流 current, trend, origin (of ideas, schools, institutions); 同流合汚 birds of a feather flock together, associate oneself with undesirable elements or group; 順流, 逆流 with, against the current; 輪流 take turns.

V.i. (1) To flow: 流汗 to perspire; 流血 bleed; 流淚 shed tears; 淚流滿面 tears cover one's face. (2) To drift, float, spread: 流傳, 流布 *-chuarn*, *-buh* ↓; 流芳 *-fang* ↓; to drift into: 流入俗套 drift into inanities; 流於形式 become formalistic. (3) V.t., (LL) to exile (s. o.).

Adj. (1) Floating about, without fixed place: 流娼, 流寇 *-chang*, *-kouh* ↓. (2) Without foundation: 流言 *-yarn* ↓.

流輩 *liourbeih*, n., class of persons (usu. contempt.).

流變 *liourbiahn*, n., change and historical development (of school).

流別 *liourbier*, n., a certain branch of thought, of belief; (=派別).

流弊 *liourbih*, n., malpractice; shortcoming, failure arising out of system.

流布 *liourbuh*, v. i., (of ideas, religion) spread abroad.

流產 *liourchaan*, v. i. & n., (have a) miscarriage; meeting for which quorum cannot be obtained; (of a plan) fail to materialize.

流娼 *liourchang*, n., streetwalker, floating prostitute.

流傳 *liourchuarn*, v. i., to spread in time or place: 謠言流傳 gossip spreads.

流彈 *liourdahn*, n., stray bullet.

流宕 *liourdahng*[1], (1) adj., (character, composition) undisciplined, ebullient; (2) v. i., spread or meander like river's course.

流蕩 *liourdahng*[2], adj., undisciplined, profligate; loaf about.

流動 *liourduhng*, adj. & v. i., drifting about, floating: 流動戶口 floating population; 空氣流動 air current, ventilation; 流動財產 liquid assets.

流毒 *liourdur*, v.t. & n., (have) evil effect (of teachings, opium): 流毒青年 poison young minds.

流放 *liourfahng*, v. t., send to exile.

流芳 *liourfang*, v. i., leave a good name: 萬世流芳, 流芳千古 leave a good name to posterity.

流風 *liourfeng*, n., as in 流風餘韻 remaining, lasting influence.

流光 *liourguang*, (1) n., the quickly passing time; (2) the floating moonlight on water; (3) (-'*guang*) to loaf about, unemployed.

流滑 *liour'hua*, adj., slippery, cunning (person).

流轉 *liourjuaan*, v. i., to float about, drift around; to move constantly from place to place.

流質 *liourjyr*, n., a liquid substance.

流寇 *liourkouh*, n., roving bandits.

流覽 *liourlaan*, v. i., to glance over (books) (commonly 溜覽), to survey a moving spectacle.

流浪 *liourlahng*, v. i., to travel freely, to work and drift from town to town: 流浪江湖 to move about the country without definite employment.

流連 *liourliarn*, v. i., to loiter, linger: 流連忘返 indulge in pleasures without stop.

流利 *liourlih*, adj. & n., fluent, -cy.

流離 *liourlir*, v. i., to live life of refugee: 流離失所 to wander about lost or homeless; n., corrupt form for 琉璃 glass.

流露 *liourluh*, v. i., show unintentionally (sentiment from writing, speech): 真情流露 reveal true sentiment.
流落 *liourluoh* (-'*luoh*), v. i., to drift about, homeless.
流氓 *liourmarng*, n., rascal, roughneck; ruffians as a group.
流民 *liourmirn*, n., refugee; poor people driven away from home.
流年 *liour-niarn*, n., (1) the passing years: 似水流年 years pass by quickly; (2) a fortune-teller's prediction of the year's course in person's life, also prediction year by year.
流盼 *liourpahn*, n., loving glance, lingering look: 美目流盼 bewitching glance of a beauty's eyes.
流派 *liourpaih*, n., branch or sect (of teachings); type (of persons), trend (of writing).
流配 *liourpeih*, v. t., send to distant exile.
流品 *liourpiin*, n., type, class of person (cultured, sophisticated, third-rate, etc.).
流人 *liourrern*, n., (MC) refugee; exiled person.
流冗 *liourruung*, n., (AC) refugees, unemployed.
流沙 *liourshα*, n., anc. term for desert; sandy loam, silt, bog.
流線型 *liourshiahng shirng*, adj., streamlined.
流星 *liourshing*, n., meteor, shooting star: 流星劍 very fast swordplay; 流星鎚 (anc. weapon) chain and hammers.
流行 *liourshirng*, (1) adj., fashionable, much in vogue (style, customs); epidemic: 流行性感冒 influenza; 流行病 epidemic; (2) v.i., circulate, become gen. accepted.
流水 *liourshueei*, phr., flowing water: 行雲流水 easy, freeflowing style of writing; 光陰如流水 time passes like flowing water; 流水賬, 流水簿 journal of accounts; 流水席 dinner served to guests as they arrive.
流矢 *liourshyy*, n., flying or stray arrow.
流蘇 *liourşu*, n., tassels (of flags).
流俗 *liourşur*, n., customary practice, common customs; gen. run of people.
流通 *liourtung*, v.i. & n., circulate (of air, currency); adj., current, common.
流亡 *liourwarng*, v.t., live as refugee abroad.
流亞 *liouryah*, n., (slightly derog.) class (of persons); degenerate or succeeding group.
流言 *liouryarn*, n., gossip, hearsay (esp. malicious).
流鶯 *liouryiŋg*, n., singing parakeet; oft. singsong girl.
流螢 *liouryirng*, n., firefly.
流域 *liouryuh*[1], n., river valley, river basin, area along a river.
流寓 *liouryuh*[2], v.i., to stay abroad: 流寓東京 live in Tokyo (for certain years).

瀧 63A.70–6

lurng.

N. (1) Name of a river. (2) Rapids: 瀧夫 good swimmer over rapids; 瀧瀧 sound of water or rain.

瀛 63A.70–6

yirng.

N. An occean: 東瀛 (=東洋) Japan.

瀛海 *yirnghaai*, n., sea, ocean.
瀛寰 *yirnghuarn*, n., the whole earth, the world.
瀛洲 *yirngjou*, n., (AC) a fairyland in Eastern Sea.

漉 63A.70–6

luh.

V.t. To drip through filter, to filter.

沱 63A.70–6

tuor.

N. Name of a river.

Adj. 滂沱 see 63A.50

浣 63A.70–6

huaan (also *waan*).

N. Ten days: 三月上浣, 中浣 first ten days, second ten days of the third month.

V.t. To wash (silk, laundry): 浣雪 to clean (one's name) of false accusations.

滬 63A.70–6

huh.

[Pop. 沪]

N. Another name for Shanghai: 滬杭鐵路 Shanghai-Hangchow Railroad.

沉 63A.70–6

chern.

[Pop. of 沈]

汍 63A.70–9

warn.

氿瀾 *warnlarn*, adj., (AC) weeping profusely.

沈 63A.70-9

chern (**sheen*).

[Pop. 沉, which is not used for surname]

N. (**sheen*) A surname.

V.i. (1) To sink (lit. & fig.): 沈下去 sink down; 沈落, 沈沒 *-luoh*, *-moh*[1]↓; 沈魚落雁之容 a beautiful face which "cause fish to sink out of sight and the flying crane to drop down" out of shame: 西沈 (the sun) sinks in the west; sink in sin, iniquity: 沈湎, 沈迷 *-miaan*, *-mir*↓. (2) (Coll.) to take a short nap, rest: 沈了一個盹兒 take a nap; 沈一沈再辦 rest a while, then take it up again.

V.t. To down, keep down: 沈下臉來 pull a long face; 沈住氣, 沈得住氣 contain anger.

Adj. & adv. (1) Deep, -ly, heavy, -ily, buried in (thought): 沈睡 soundly asleep; 沈痛 deep in sorrow, also deeply painful; 沈醉 heavily drunk; 自覺酒沈了 felt he had drunk too much already. (2) Dark, -ly, silent, -ly: 沈思, 沈慮, 沈憂 *-sy*, *-lyuh*, *-you*↓; 沈默, 沈寂 *-moh*[2], *-jih*↓. (3) Physically heavy: 這塊石頭太沈了 this rock is too heavy; 沈重 *-juhng*↓; 沈顛顛的, 沈甸甸的 very heavy. (4) Sluggish: 沈滯 *-jyh*↓.

沈沈 *chernchern*, adj. & adv., dark, -ly; deep, -ly: 醉沈沈 dead drunk; 夜沈沈 the night is dark and silent.

沈潛 *chernchiarn*, adj., pensive, meditative in character: 沈潛好學 quiet and studious.

沈達 *cherndar*, adj., thoughtful and clear-headed.

沈澱 *cherndiahn*, n. & v.i., (chem.) sedimentation; precipitation; precipitate.

沈底 *cherndii*, n., sediments.

沈頓 *chernduhn*, adj., delayed.

沈疴 *chern-e*, n., serious and protracted illness.

沈伏 *chernfur*[1], (1) v.i., stay under cover, (sorrow) keep contained; (2) adj., feeble (pulse).

沈浮 *chern-fur*[2], (1) v.i., to drift along ("sink and swim"); (2) n., the vicissitudes.

沈痼 *chernguh*, n., see *-e*↑; also inveterate bad habit.

沈酣 *chernhan*, (1) adj., comfortably drunk or soundly asleep; (2) v.i., 沈酣經史 be absorbed in studies of classics and history.

沈厚 *chernhouh*, adj., deliberate, considerate, thoughtful in conduct.

沈寂 *chernjih*, adj., (news) dead silent: 沈寂無聞 (person) unknown; (character, style) contemplative.

沈靜 *chern(')jihng*, adj., quiet, poised.

沈重 *chernjuhng*, adj., heavy physically; deliberate in character, action: 沈重兒 *--'l*, n., responsibility: 他作事不肯擔一點沈重兒 will not undertake responsible tasks.

沈著 *chernjuor*, adj., (words) carefully weighed, considered; (action) every step carries weight.

沈滯 *chernjyh*, adj., (1) bogged down; (2) long in a job without official promotion; (3) bored, depressed.

沈落 *chernluoh*, v.i., drop or sink down.

沈淪 *chernlurn*, v.i., be damned, sunk in sin.

沈慮 *chernlyuh*, v.i., think carefully: 沈思熟慮 plan carefully, deliberate thoroughly.

沈悶 *chernmehn*, adj., boring, dull (atmosphere); (feel) bored.

沈湎 *chernmiaan*, v.i., wallow in (pleasures of drink, women).

沈綿 *chernmiarn*, adj., (LL) long confined to bed.

沈迷 *chernmir*, adj., gone astray: 沈迷不悟 gone, lost in evil, stuck with wrong ideas.

沈沒 *chernmoh*[1], v.i., (1) sink in water, drown; (2) (LL) be unknown.

沈默 *chernmoh*[2], v.i. & adj., silent, be silent, reticent.

沈溺 *chernnih*, v.i., drown oneself (in pleasures, sex).

沈香 *chernshiang*, n., gharu-wood, ligumaloes.

沈心 *chernshin*, adj., (coll.) get angry, offended (＝嗔心).

沈邃 *chernsueih*, adj., deep.

沈思 *chernsy*, v.i., to contemplate, ponder.

沈毅 *chernyih*, adj., determined, having strength of character.

沈吟 *chernyirn*, v.i., to ponder.

沈憂 *chernyou*, n., deep, languishing sorrow or worry.

沈冤 *chernyuan*, v.i., suffer a grievous wrong, be falsely accused and condemned.

沈鬱 *chernyuh*, adj., deeply depressed, downcast.

沈勇 *chernyuung*, adj., silently determined.

漑 63A.70-9

gaih.

V.t. (1) To supply with water: 灌漑 irrigate; 漑田 to flood the fields. (2) Cleanse, wash.

汔 63A.70-9

chih.

Adj. (AC) dry, dried up.

Adv. (AC) almost: 汔可小康 is doing pretty well.

汽 63A.70-9

chih.

N. Steam, vapor.

汽表 *chihbiaau*, n., steam gauge.

汽車 *chihche*, n., automobile: 公共汽車 bus.

汽船 *chihchuarn*, n., steamboat, ⌈-ship, steamer.

汽笛 *chihdir*, n., steam whistle.
汽蓋 *chihgaih*, n., steam valve.
汽管(子) *chihguaan(tz)*, n., steam pipe.
汽鍋 *chihguo*, n., boiler of steam engine; a double boiler pot served on table (Yunnan Province).
汽化 *chihhuah*, v. i., to vaporize.
汽機 *chihji*, n., steam engine.
汽力 *chihlih*, n., steam power.
汽輾(子) *chihniaan('tz)*, n., steam roller.
汽水(兒) *chihshueei(-shuee'l)*, n., aerated water.
汽筒 *chihtuung*, n., steam cylinder (also called 汽缸 *-gang*).
汽油 *shihyour*, n., gasoline, kerosene; 汽油燈 kerosene lamp; 汽油機 internal combustion engine.

泡 63A.70-9

pauh.

N. Blister, foam, bubble: 起泡(兒) form a blister.

V.t. (1) To make by scalding: 泡茶 make tea; 泡飯 pour boiling water over cooked rice. (2) To marinate, soak (meat, vegetables) in water, sauce, as preparation for cooking. (3) (Sl.) (a) to court (girl); (b) get involved or mixed up in affairs: 他們泡上了 they have become lovers; they have got involved; 他已泡上了她 he has won her heart; 泡蘑菇 to chase a girl persistently.

泡幻 *pauhhuahn*, n., illusion.
泡沫 *pauhmoh*, n., foam, froth.
泡菜 *pauhtsaih*, n., a treated vegetable root from Szechuan.
泡影 *pauhyiing*, n., bubble; (fig.) an illusion, or short span of life.

浼 63A.70-9

meei.

V.t. Contaminate: 避之若浼 avoid person like a plague.

浼瀆 *meeidur*, v. t., (court.) 浼瀆清聽 bother (soil your ears) by request.
浼浼 *meirmeei*, adj., (AC) 河水浼浼 smooth-flowing river.
浼托 *meeituo*, v. t., (court.) entrust (person) to do s. t. ("soil your hands").
浼污 *meeiwu*, v.t., to soil, besmirch (good name, etc.).

§ 63A.71 (氵/乜)

濺 63A.71-4

jiahn.

V. i. & t. Splash: 濺了一身水 splashed with water all over; 濺泥 spatter with mud; 濺血 cover with drops of blood; 血濺 blood spurts.

濺濺 *jiahnjiahn*, adj., (of flowing water) murmuring, babbling, chattering, bickering.

泯 63A.71-5

miin.

V.i. Perish.

泯絕 *miin-jyuer*, v. i., be lost for ever; (race) extinguished.
泯滅 *miinmieh*, v. i., (of heritage, books, races) perish.
泯泯 *mirnmiin*, adj., confused, rushing; (AC) descriptive of clear flowing water.
泯沒 *miinmoh*, v. i., perish, be forgotten (of person's name).

洩 63A.71-7

shieh.

[Var. of 泄 63A.21; related 瀉 63A.50]

V.t. (1) To leak, let off (steam): 洩水 leak out water; 洩露 *-luh* ↓. (2) Give vent to: 洩怒, 洩憤 give vent to anger; 洩恨 to revenge; 洩慾 to release from sexual urge.

洩氣 *shiehchih*, v. i., (1) lose power or compression; (2) be frustrated, humiliated, deflated: 這麼輕的東西都拿不動, 太洩氣了 it's too humiliating to be unable to lift such a light object; 連這樣的女人都追不上, 眞太洩氣了 it's too humiliating to be rejected by such a plain-looking woman.
洩底 *shieh-dii*, v. i., to reveal one's past: 洩了他的老底 reveal his old past.
洩力 *shieh-lih*, v. i., to lose compression.
洩露 *shiehluh*, v. t., to leak out (a secret).

淺 63A.71-7

chiaan.

Adj. & adv. (1) Shallow (river, pool, plate): 不知深淺 unfathomable, do not know the depths or bottom of things; 擱淺 (of boat) run aground; 淺淺的盛一碗飯 give me just a small portion of rice; 淺斟低唱 sip (wine) slowly and hum a tune. (2) Superficial, not deep or profound: 淺薄, 淺陋 *-bor*, *-louh* ↓; 淺見, 淺識 superficial opinion, (also used court. of one's own opinion); 眼(光)淺

shortsighted; 浮淺, 粗淺 rough and superficial (knowledge); 才疏學淺 (court. phr.) an inexperienced and uninformed person like myself. (3) Elementary, easy to see and understand: 這書太淺了 this book is too elementary; 程度很淺 very elementary (grade); 淺近, 淺易 *-jihn*, *-yih* ↓. (4) Light, mild in color or flavor: 淺綠 light green; 淺紅 pale red, rose. (5) In a cursory manner: 淺笑 give a cursory smile; 淺嘗卽止 just have a tiny sip, (fig.) not going into subject in depth. (6) (Of animal furs) short.

淺薄 *chiaanbor*, adj., superficial, cursory (knowledge); uninformed.

淺近 *chiaanjihn*, adj., commonplace (facts); plain, simple (explanation), elementary.

淺陋 *chiaanlouh*, adj., untutored, uninformed, provincial (oft. court. of oneself), superficial.

淺明 *chiaanmirng*, adj., clear and easy to understand.

淺人 *chiaanrern*, n., (LL) an uncultured person.

淺鮮 *chiarnshiaan*[1], adj., little, flimsy (knowledge).

淺顯 *chiarnshiaan*[2], adj., plain, easy to understand (language, test).

淺說 *chiaan-shuo*, n., an introduction, or simple guide to subject (oft. title of a book): 相對論淺說 a simple introduction to the theory of relativity.

淺學 *chiaanshyuer*, adj., (LL) 淺學之士 a superficial scholar.

淺聞 *chiaanwern*, adj., not well-read, uninformed.

淺易 *chiaanyih*, adj., simple and easy, elementary.

淢 63A.71–7

shyuh.

[Var. of 洫 63A.30]

減 63A.71–7

jiaan.

V.t. Take away, deduct: 減法 *-faa* ↓; 減去 subtract; 加減 add and subtract; 減少 *-shaau* ↓; 增減 increase or decrease; 減價 slash prices; 減輕 *-ching* ↓; 減等 downgrade; 減俸 reduce salary (as a form of punishment); 減薪 cut down salary scale; 減刑 commute a sentence; 減衣縮食 practise austerity, be more economical; 減肥 reduce one's weight; 丰(風)采不減當年 (of person) as good-looking as ever; 減半 reduce by one half; 減罪 extenuate an offense or crime; 縮減 to cut (expenses, funds); 裁減 to cut (personnel, funds); 削減 ditto; 減色 *-seh* ↓; 減損 to waste, destroy.

減筆字 *jiarnbiitzyh*, n., characters written in a simplified form.

減輕 *jiaanching*, v. i. & t., become or make lighter, (fig.) extenuate, mitigate, lighten (burden, responsibility).

減法 *jiarnfaa*, n., subtraction.

減號 *jiaanhauh*, n., the minus sign (-).

減色 *jiaanseh*, v. i., lose color by fading, deteriorate, become less attractive.

減少 *jiarnshaau*, v. t., take away from a quantity (amount), make less.

減省 *jiarn(')sheeng*, adj. & v. i. & t., (be) economical, economize.

減刑 *jiaan-shirng*, n. & v. i., commute sentence.

減數 *jiaanshuh*, v. t., (math.) reduce the number of; n., a subtraction.

減速火箭 *jiaan-suh huoojiahn*, n., (astron.) retro-rocket.

滅 63A.71–7

mieh.

V.t. (1) Extinguish, blot out, obliterate: 滅火 extinguish fire, 滅火筒 fire-extinguisher; 滅水喉 fire hose; 滅燈 put out the light; 滅了良心 blot out conscience; 滅心, 滅性 dehumanize; 滅門, 滅戶 exterminate entire family; 滅族, 滅種 genocide, exterminate entire race; 毀屍滅跡 chop up corpse and obliterate traces; 滅口 silence witness of crime by killing him; 滅此朝食 (AC) (promise to) destroy enemy before breakfast. (2) Oft. used as vb. complement to form comp.: 撲滅 beat and put out fire; 剿滅匪寇 destroy completely bandits; 殲滅敵人 annihilate enemy.

滅掉 *mieh-diauh*, v. t., destroy, annihilate, obliterate.

滅頂 *mieh-diing*, v. i., be drowned ("head submerged").

滅絕 *mieh-jyuer*, v. t., destroy completely, annihilate.

滅沒 *mieh-moh*, v. i. & t., (make) disappear, be gone.

滅亡 *mieh-warng*, v. i., perish: 自取滅亡 seek one's own downfall; n., perdition.

§ 63A.72 (氵/心)

濾 63A.72–2

lyuh.

V.t. To filter, strain: 過濾 to filter; 濾紙 filter paper; 濾清 to filter clear; 濾器 a filter (apparatus); 濾波器 filter (electronics).

濾水池 *luhshueei-chyr*, n., filtered reservoir.

漶 63A.72–2

huahn.

Adj. See 漫漶 63A.82.

沁 63A.72-6

chihn.

N. Name of river.

V.i. To seep in: 沁人心脾 (of music, good writing) touch one's heart.

沁透 *chihntouh,* v.t., (of music, mood, atmosphere) penetrate; (of air, cold, fragrance) seep in; (of political enemies) infiltrate.

泌 63A.72-6

mih (also *bih*).

V.i. & n. To secrete: 分泌 secrete, -tion; 泌尿管, 泌尿器 urinary canal.

淰 63A.72-8

niaan.

N. (MC) a dredge.

Adj. 淰淰 (LL, of water) placid, calm.

§ 63A.80 (氵/八)

瀆 63A.80-1

dur.
[Var. of 瀆↓]

瀆 63A.80-1

dur.

N. Ditch, gutter: 溝瀆.

V.t. To disturb, bother: 冒瀆, 干瀆, 煩瀆 (court.) bother (with request, etc.); 褻瀆 besmirch, blaspheme (God); 自瀆 to masturbate.

瀆職 *durjyr,* v.i., be guilty of dereliction of duty.

滇 63A.80-1

tiarn (dian).
[Usu. printed 滇]

N. Another name for Yunnan Province.

瀨 63A.80-1

laih.

N. Rapids.

漬 63A.80-1

tzyh.

N. Stains: 油漬, 水漬, 墨漬 oil, water, ink stains.

V.t. Soak, steep: 浸漬 steep in water, ret.

洪 63A.80-2

hurng.

N. (1) Flood water: 山洪 mountain stream or current; 洪水 *-shueei* ↓. (2) A surname.

Adj. (LL) big, vast, grand: 洪濤 big waves; 洪流 big current; 洪鐘 big bell; 洪福 great luck; 洪恩 great favor; 洪才 great talent; 寬洪 generous, large-minded (interch. 鴻, 宏).

洪荒 *hurnghuang,* n., primordial times.
洪鈞 *hurngjyun,* n., (AC) nature or heaven as the source of life.
洪亮 *hurngliahng,* adj., (of voice) resonant.
洪水 *hurngshueei,* n., flood, flood water.

淇 63A.80-2

chir.

N. Name of river in Honan.

淟 63A.80-2

tiaan.

Adj. (AC) muddy, turbid; 淟汩 buried and lost.

潢 63A.80-2

huarng.

N. (1) A pool: 天潢 the cluster of stars near Auriga; 銀潢 the Milky Way. (2) A colored paper, now used chiefly in 裝[A]潢 mounting, 21.02.

滇 瀕 潰 灝 演 濱 溟 灨 汃

滇 63A.80–2

jen (also *jeng*).

N. Name of river in Kwangtung Province.

瀕 63A.80–2

bin (also *pirn*).

N. (Rare var. of 濱) river bank; sea beach.

Prep. About, near to: 瀕危, 瀕死 near death, about to die.

潰 63A.80–2

kueih (also *hueih*).

V.i. (Of dam, river) to break, overrun; (of troops) disperse, be routed; 潰兵 routed soldiers; 潰不成軍 army has collapsed; 潰敗 be defeated; (of boils, ulcers) break out, fester, see 潰爛 *-lahn* ↓; 潰盟 break alliance.

潰 決 *kueihjyuer*, v.i., (of dams) break.
潰 爛 *kueihlahn*, v.i., (of abscess, ulcer) fester, form pus.
潰 亂 *kueihluahn*, v.i., (of troops) disperse in confusion.
潰 散 *kueihsahn*, v.i., (of troops) be dispersed, collapse in disorder.
潰 圍 *kueihweir*, v.i., break through enemy blockade.
潰 瘍 *kueihyarng*, v.i., ulcerate; 胃潰瘍 n., stomach ulcer; 腸潰瘍 intestinal ulcer.

灝 63A.80–4

hauh.
[Interch. 浩 63A.40]

演 63A.80–6

yaan.

V.i. & t. (1) To perform (play, etc.): 演戲, 演員, 演出 *-shih*, *-yuarn*, *-chu* ↓; 扮演 to play (a certain role); 表演 to perform on stage; 上演 (play) be presented to public; 公演 public performance; 預演 preview; 導演 v.t. & n., to direct (movie, play), director; 演説, 演講 *-shuo*, *-jiaang* ↓. (2) To develop, evolve: 天演 natural evolution; 演化, 演變 *-huah*, *-biahn* ↓; 推演 to deduce, deduction; 敷演 explain in detail, expound (cf. 敷衍 to do in a perfunctory manner). (3) To do exercises: 演習, 演算 *-shir*, *-suahn* ↓; 操演 do military exercises.

演 變 *yaanbiahn*, v.i. & n., (history, events) evolve, develop.
演 唱 *yaanchahng*, v.i. & n., (give) singing performance.
演 出 *yaanchu*, v.i. & n., to present (a play, etc.), a presentation; 演出者 producer (of play, film).
演 化 *yaanhuah*, v.i., (situation, events) evolve, develop: 演化論 theory of evolution.
演 講 *yarnjiaang*, v.i. & n., to lecture, to deliver a speech, a lecture an address.
演 進 *yaanjihn*, v.i., make progress.
演 劇 *yaan-jyuh*, v.i., to give a stage performance, esp. 歌劇 opera.
演 戲 *yaan-shih*, v.i., ditto.
演 習 *yaanshir* (-'*shir*), v.i. & n., (1) (mil.) to carry out an exercise; (2) to learn to perform (boxing, fencing, etc.); (3) to rehearse.
演 説 *yaanshuo*, v.i., to give a talk, lecture, address; n., a lecture, an address.
演 算 *yaansuahn*, v.i., do exercise in mathematics.
演 奏 *yaantzouh*, v.i. & t., to perform on musical instrument.
演 義 *yaanyih*[1], n., a historical novel (as 三國志演義 *The Three Kingdoms*); (-'*yi*) adj., exaggerated, romanticized: 你説他的本領那麽大，未免有點演義了 you are exaggerating his physical prowess.
演 繹 *yaanyih*[2], v.i. & t., to deduce, make a deduction; 演繹法 deductive method (opp. 歸納法 inductive method).
演 員 *yaanyuarn*, n., actor, performer.

濱 63A.80–6

bin (also *pirn*).
[Pop. 浜]

N. Bank of river, sea: 海濱 sea beach; 溪濱 river bank.

Prep. Near, alongside: 濱海, 濱岸 alongside the sea, coast.

溟 63A.80–6

mirng.
[Interch. 冥 62.80]

N. (1) The dark ocean: 滄溟 the deep, blue sea. (2) (AC) drizzle.

溟 漭 *mirngmaang*, adj., boundless.
溟 濛 *mirngmerng*, (1) n., drizzle; (2) adj., heavily overcast.
溟 溟 *mirngmirng*, adj., drizzling.

灨 63A.80–6

gahn.

N. Name of river in Kiangsi.

汃 63A.80–8

pah.

Adj. 澎汃 *perngpah*, sound of

rushing water (var. 澎湃).

汃汃 *pah'pa*, adj., (LL) scintillating (of light ripples in water).

浜 63A.80-9

bang.

N. (1) Unnavigable stream, not leading to river: 洋涇浜 locality or dialect of suburbs of Shanghai. (2) (*bin) U. f. 濱 63A.80.

§ 63A.81 (氵/人)

漱 63A.81-1

souh (*shuh).

V.i. & t. To gargle; to wash: 枕流漱石 (poet.) to pillow oneself on a rock in stream and let water souse over the body; 盥漱 the morning ablutions.

漱口 *shuhkoou*, v. i., to rinse mouth.

汰 63A.81-1

taih.

V.t. Rinse, wash away: 淘汰 get rid of unnecessary or undesirable (personnel, posts, various growths); 天然(自然)淘汰 natural selection; 裁汰 reduce (personnel, etc.).

Adv. Too (=太): 汰侈 too extravagant.

洟 63A.81-i

yir.

N. Nasal mucus.

浹 63A.81-1

jiar.

V.i. & t. Saturate, soak, drench: 汗流浹背 perspire all over; 浹浹 *-jiar* ↓.

Adj. (1) Harmonious: 浹洽 *-shiar* ↓. (2) Forming a cycle: 浹辰 *-chern* ↓; 浹日 *-ryh* ↓.

浹辰 *jiarchern*, n., the duodecimal cycle of twelve days, see Appendix A.
浹浹 *jiarjiar*, adj., damp, moistened.
浹日 *jiar-ryh*, n., the decimal cycle of ten days, see Appendix A.
浹洽 *jiarshiar*, adj., agreeable, on friendly terms with.

湊 63A.81-1

tsouh.
[Pop. 凑]

V.i. & t. To assemble, fit into, fit together, make up number: 湊在一起 put together, 湊近 approach, press near (person, place); 湊過來 move over here; 湊合 *-'he* ↓; 湊分子 (*-fehntz*) join the pool; 湊熱鬧兒 join the fun.

湊巧 *tsouhchiaau*, adv., by chance, by luck.
湊趣兒 *tsouhchyueh'l*, v. i., to take part in and join the fun.
湊搭 *tsouh'da*, v. t., to patch together lines—as in bad writing.
湊膽子 *tsouh-daantz*, v. i., gather courage on the strength of numbers.
湊合 *tsouh'he*, v. i., (1) to pool together (a sum of money); (2) to do s. t. for form's sake.
湊集 *tsouhjir*, v. t., (people) come together, concentrate on place.
湊理 *tsouhlii*, adj., see 腠理 42A.81.
湊手 *tsouh-shoou*, adv., have (money) at hand.
湊數(兒) *tsouh-shuh('l)*, v. i., to make up a number without active work.
湊湊 *tsouh'tsou*, v. i., gather together among friends.

漠 63A.81-2

moh.

N. Desert in comb. 沙漠, desert, expanse, wasteland.

Adj. Aloof, cold: 漠不關心, totally unconcerned; 漠不相關 entirely unrelated; 冷漠 cold (attitude).

漠漠 *mohmoh*, adj., (AC) extended all over; silent, noiseless.
漠然 *mohrarn*, adj., cold, aloof.
漠視 *mohshyh*, v. t., look down upon, ignore, regard as unimportant.

漢 63A.81-2

hahn.

N. (1) The Chinese race: 漢人, 漢族, 漢文, 漢語 *-rern*, *-tzur*, *-wern*, *-yuu* ↓; (2) 漢室, 漢朝, 漢代 the Hahn Dynasty, 206 B.C.-220 A.D.: 漢家天子 a Hahn emperor; 漢磚, 漢瓦 brick, tile-brick of

漢 淚 渼 渙 沃 湫 溪 溴 澳 決

Hahn Dynasty; 漢碑 a Hahn monument or inscription; 漢儒 scholars of Hahn Dynasty; 漢學 -*shyuer* ↓. (3) The river Han (Hankow). (4) A man: 好漢 a good brave fellow; 男子漢 a manly man, a male with reference to brave manhood; 大漢 a great, big fellow; 壯漢, 猛漢 a husky man; 凶漢 ruffian; 瘋漢 a madman; 漢子 -*tz* ↓.

Adj. Chinese: 漢醫 Chinese medicine or physician; 漢席 Chinese feast, etc.

漢調 *Hahndiauh*, n., a Hupeh form of Chin. opera, forerunner of present Peking opera (see 皮簧 22.82).
漢奸 *Hahnjian*, n., a Chinese traitor.
漢人 *Hahnrern*, n., the Chinese people; 漢人言語 Chinese language.
漢姓 *Hahn-shihng*, n., Chinese surname adopted by people of foreign tribe.
漢書 *Hahnshu*, n., Chronicles of Hahn Dynasty.
漢學 *Hahnshyuer*, n., (1) Sinology; (2) the philology of Manchu Dyn., which aimed at restoring philology of Hahn period, opp. 宋學 or speculative school of Suhng Dyn.
漢子 *hahntz*, n., (1) A male, (coll.) a man with implied masculine qualities: 够得上是個漢子 a real masculine person; (2) (vulg.) husband: 偷漢子 (of woman) commit adultery.
漢族 *Hahntzur*, n., the Chinese race.
漢字 *Hahntzyh*, n., the Chinese characters or script.
漢文 *Hahnwern*, n., the Chinese language or literature.
漢語 *Hahnyuu*, n., Chinese language.

淚 63A.81-6

leih.
[Var. 泪]

N. A tear: 眼淚 tears; 流淚 to weep; 淚痕 tear stairs; 淚痕未乾 tears are not yet dry; 淚珠 tear drops; 淚人兒 person melting into tears; 淚汪汪 full of tears, tearful.

淚別 *leih-bier*, n., tearful farewell.
淚腺 *leih-shiahn*, n., (physiol.) the lachrymal glands.

渼 63A.81-8

meei.

N. Ripples.

渙 63A.81-9

huahn.

V.i. To thaw out: 渙然冰釋 to explain or understand clearly, like thawing of ice.

Adj. 渙渙 (of flood) overflowing.

沃 63A.81-9

woh (also *wuh*).

V.t. (1) To irrigate (field): 沃田. (2) To boil for a short moment: 沃雞蛋 to soft-boil shelled egg (also called 沃果兒 -*guo'l*).

Adj. Fertile (soil): 肥沃 ditto; 沃土, 沃壤 fertile fields; 沃野, 沃衍 (LL) fertile valley.

沃果兒 *wohguoo'l*, n., see V.t. 2↑.
沃饒 *wohraur*, adj., fertile (valley).
沃沃 *wohwoh*, adj., (AC) robust.

湫 63A.81-9

jiou.

N. (LL) a body of water.

Adj. Low, damp, narrow and small: 湫隘 damp and narrow.

溪 63A.81-9

shi (also *chi*).

N. A river: 小溪 a brook.

溪谷 *shi-guu*, n., river valley; river and valley.
溪澗 *shi-jiahn*, n., mountain brook.
溪流 *shi-liour*, n., river current, stream.

溴 63A.81-9

shiouh.

N. (Chem.) bromine.

澳 63A.81-9

auh (**yuh*).

N. (1) A sea inlet. (2) (**yuh*) (AC) a swampy ground. (3) Short for 澳大利亞 Australia: 澳洲 ditto (cf. 奧國 90.81 for Austria).

決 63A.81-9

jyuer.
[Pop. 决]

V.i. & t. (1) To dredge (rivers). (2) (Of dikes) burst open: 決口 -*koou* ↓. (3) Break off (friendly relations): 決裂 -*lieh*↓. (4) Decide, determine: 決定 -*dihng*, 決斷 -*duahn*, 決計 -*jih*↓; 民族自決 national self-determination; 否決 refuse, turn down (a request), veto (a resolution); 決戰 -*jahn*↓; 決死戰 a life-and-death struggle (war, battle); 決勝 -*shehng*↓; 決雌雄 wage a decisive fight (battle), challenge s.o. to fight it out; see who is the better one. (5) Put (prisoner) to death: 立決 summarily execute; 決其首 cut off his (their) head(s); 大決 formerly, annual execution of prisoners condemned to death; 自決 commit suicide. (6) (U.f. 訣) bid farewell to: 決別 take leave of (never to meet again).

Adj. Decided, firm: 堅決 resolute, firm.

Adv. Certainly: 決往 (LL) will certainly go; 決行 (LL) certainly carry out; 決不 certainly not.

決定 *jyuerdihng*, (1) v.i. & t., decide (to do); (2) adj. & adv., firmly decided, determined, resolved; (3) n., a decision.

決鬪 *jyuer-douh*, v.i. & n., (fight) a duel.

決斷 *jyueirduahn*, (1) v.i. make a firm decision; (2) n., decision.

決戰 *jyuer-jahn*, v.i. & n., (to fight) a decisive battle.

決計 *jyuerjih*, v.t. & adv., (1) v.t., decide: 我決計要走 I've decided to go; (2) adv., certainly: 決計是他來了 certainly it's he who has come.

決絕 *jyuerjyuer*, v.t., (1) break off with (lover, friend); (2) bid final farewell.

決口 *jyuer-koou*, v.i., (of floods) cause a breach in dikes, overflow.

決裂 *jyuerlieh*, v.i., (of persons) quarrel and break off friendly relations, (of situation) come to a breaking point.

決明 *jyuermirng*, n., (bot.) the foetid cassia, *Cassia tora*.

決然 *jyuerrarn*, adv., decidedly, resolutely, firmly.

決撒 *jyuersa*, v.t., cause (undertaking) to fail or flop.

決賽 *jyuersaih*, n., (athletic) finals.

決勝 *jyuershehng*, (1) adj., (of battle plans) capable of insuring victory; (2) v. i., make a final bid for victory.

決心 *jyuershin*, n., decision, resolution: 我下了決心 I've made a firm decision; v.i., decide: 我已經決心 I have decided.

決選 *jyuershyuaan*, n., a run-off ballot to choose between two top contenders.

決算 *jyuersuahn*, v.i. & n., (to make) final accounts, to close accounts at end of fiscal or calender year.

決擇 *jyuertzer*, v. i., make a final decision between possible alternatives.

決意 *jyueryih*[1], v. i., be determined, resolved, decided (to do).

決議 *jyueryih*[2], v.i. & n., (to have) a resolution adopted at a meeting or conference.

決疑 *jyuer-yir*, v. i., resolve doubts.

決獄 *jyuer-yuh*, v. i., pass judgement on legal case.

泱 63A.81-9

yang.

Adj. (1) (AC) broad and deep (flood): 泱泱 -*yang*↓. (2) (AC) massive (clouds).

泱漭 *yangmaang*, adj., (1) expansive, limitless (prairie, etc.); (2) misty (morning light).

泱泱 *yangyang*, adj., (AC) broad and deep; (AC) grand, impressive: 泱泱大風 orig. said in praise of 齊 Chir music, now used in praise of the impressive manner of a great country (泱泱大國).

洑 63A.81-9

fur (**fuh*).

N. Undercurrent.

V.t. (**fuh*) 洑水 to swim.

淡 63A.81-9

dahn.

Adj. Light, mild, (of color) pale: 淡紅, 淡綠 pale red (pink), pale green; (of food) simple, not flavored: 淡飯 plain rice; 淡茶, 淡酒 weak tea, diluted wine; (of water) fresh, not salty; (of soup) not salty enough; (of friendship, painting, dress, composition) simple, of refined simplicity: 淡掃蛾眉 unpainted eyebrows; 輕描淡寫 describe with a delicate touch; 君子之交淡如水 a gentleman's friendship is simple (but solid, not demonstrative); 清淡, 雅淡 of simple elegance (of writing); 平淡無奇 insipid, common; 冷淡 cool, indifferent; 淡季 slack season.

淡泊 *dahnbor*, adj. & v.t., as in 淡泊明志 live a simple life, showing one's goal in life; 淡泊名利 indifferent to fame and wealth; also wr. 淡薄, 澹泊.

淡氣 *dahnchih*, n., nitrogen, now generally wr. 氮.

淡淡 *dahndahn*, adj., mild-flavored.

淡竹 *dahnjur*, n., a special fine-quality bamboo.

淡漠 *dahnmoh*, adj., cool, indifferent.

淡然 *dahnrarn*, adj., cool, not too excited.

淡水 *dahnshueei*, n., (1) fresh water, opp. sea water; 淡水魚 fresh water fish; (2) town in Formosa, usu. spelled Tamsui.

淡菜 *dahntsaih*, n., a kind of shellfish.

淡濮次洟凌濩淑

淡雅 *dahnyaa*, adj., elegantly simple.

濮 63A.81-9

pur.

N. (1) Name of river. (2) A surname.

次 63A.81-9

tsyh.

N. (1) Order, sequence: 次序, 次第, 次比 *-shyuh*, *-dih*, *-bih* ↓; 依次 one by one in order; 位次 seating arrangement; 官次 official rank. (2) Number of times, time or instance: 次數 *-shuh* ↓; 多次 many times; 第一次 the first time; 再次 a second time; 歷次 many times in the past. (3) Location, stopping place during travel: 客次, 旅次 while sojourning abroad; 舟次 during voyage; 胸次 (lit.) the chest region, (fig.) mental attitude (broad- or narrow-mindedness). (4) Time: 正行之次 while walking.

V.t. (AC) to stop over (at some place).

Adj. (1) The second, the next: 次子, 次媳 second son, daughter-in-law; 次日, 次年 the next day, year; 居次 stand as number two; 次之 next to it; 其次 the next in order or importance; 次於 next to s. t. in order or importance; 次要 next in importance. (2) Second-rate: 次等, 次貨 *-deeng*, *-huoh* ↓; 求其次 look for the second best; 人頭太次 (coll.) has too few friends or social contacts.

次比 *tsyhbih*, (1) n., order of arrangement; (2) (AC) to rank with.

次等 *tsyhdeeng*, adj., second-class, grade.

次第 *tsyhdih*, (1) n., order, sequence; main threads; (2) adv., one after another.

次骨 *tsyh-guu*, phr., (AC)＝刺骨 cut to the bones (sharp wind, law).

次貨 *tsyhhuoh*, n., second-rate merchandise.

次長 *tsyhjaang*, n., vice-minister.

次纂 *tsyjuahn*, n., (LL) person's "second" or poetic name.

次席 *tsyhshir*, n., second highest seat.

次數 *tsyhshuh*, n., number of times.

次序 *tsyhshyuh* (-'*shyu*), n., order of sequence.

次印 *tsyhyihn*, n., see *-juahn* ↑.

次韻 *tsyh-yuhn*, v. i., to write poem with same rhyme words as those used in a previous poem by a friend, usu. about same occasion.

洟 63A.81-9

syh.

N. River bank: 涯洟 ditto, limits of expanse.

§ 63A.82 (氵/乂)

凌 63A.82-1

lirng.

[Err. var. 淩]

N. (1) Ice floes. (2) A surname.

V.t. (1) To provoke, invade, persecute, humiliate: 欺凌 bully, humiliate; 凌逼, 凌辱 *-bi*, *-ruh* ↓. (2) To soar aloft: 凌空, 凌虛, 凌霄, 凌雲 to soar to the skies, fly in the void; 凌波 (like fairies) walking over ripples.

凌暴 *lirngbauh*, v. t., persecute.

凌逼 *lirngbi*, v. t., persecute, force.

凌晨 *lirngcherng*, n., early dawn (cf. 侵晨).

凌遲 *lirngchyr*, v. t., anc. punishment for heinous crime by slow forture; (fig.) persecute.

凌駕 *lirngjiah*, v. t., to overtake.

凌藉 *lirngjir*, v. t., to bully.

凌厲 *lirnglih*, adj. & adv., (advance) fearlessly.

凌亂 *lirngluahn*, adj., in great disorder (also wr. 零亂).

凌虐 *lirngnyueh*, v. t., persecute.

凌辱 *lirngruh*, v. t., to persecute, publicly disgrace or humiliate.

凌霄 *lirngshiau*, phr., soaring to the skies (of person's career, ambition), also see V. t. 2 ↑.

濩 63A.82-2

huoh.

V.t. (1) (AC) to cook. (2) (Of water) to crash on.

淑 63A.82-2

shur.

Adj. (Of women) quiet, refined: 賢淑 good, understanding (wife); 淑德, 淑婉 *-der*, *-waan* ↓; 淑美, 淑女 *-meei*, *-nyuu* ↓; 淑心 good-natured, heart of refinement; 淑姿 ladylike demeanor.

淑德 *shurder*, n., refinement (of ladies).

淑範 *shurfahn*, n., model woman.

淑美 *shurmeei*, adj., refined and beautiful.

淑女 *shurnyuu*, n., beautiful girl, refined girl.

淑慎 *shurshehn*, adj., (of women) quiet and modest.

淑性 *shur-shihng*, n., the inborn refinement.

淑婉 *shurwaan*, adj., (of women) elegant, refined.

澂 63A.82-2

cherng.
[Var. of 澄 63A.30]

波 63A.82-2

bo (less commonly *po*).

Fin. part. MC var. of modn. 吧, "月兒, 你早些出來吧!" (probably pr. *ba*).

N. Wave: 水波 esp. in comp. 波浪 *-lahng* ↓; 風波 storm, crisis; 波動 *-duhng* ↓, wave motion; 波譎雲詭 (LL) phr., beautiful turns of thought, fast, unexpected, exciting changes.

V.i. To spread over: 波及, 波累 *-jir*, *-leih* ↓.

波昂 *Po-arng*, n., Bonn.
波波 *bobo*, v. i., run about＝奔波.
波長 *bocharng*, n., (phys.) wave length, frequency.
波臣 *bochern*, n., (LL) denizens of the sea.
波俏 *bochiauh*[1], adj., (MC) beautiful.
波峭 *bochiauh*[2], adj., (lit. & fig.) with ups and downs.
波蕩 *bodahng*[1], (1) v. i., surging and spreading; (2) adj., restless, agitated.
波盪 *bodahng*[2], v. i., (of ship) to rock and roll.
波動 *boduhng*, n. & v. i., wave motion; undulate; fluctuate.
波峯 *bo-feng*, n., wave crest.
波谷 *bo-guu*, n., trough of wave.
波折 *bojer*[1], n., frustrations on the way, unwelcome turns of events.
波磔 *bojer*[2], n., slanting strokes in calligraphy (＝modn. 撇捺).
波及 *bo-jir*, v. t., (of lawsuits, disasters) spread to involve (others), cause repercussion to.
波浪 *bolahng*, n., waves, breakers.
波浪鼓 *bolahng-guu*, n., child's toy drum, with beads striking drum by turning handle.
波蘭 *Bolarn*[1], n., Poland.
波瀾 *bolarn*[2], n., aftermath, sequel of events; interesting turns esp. in literature (文章波瀾), or minor developments in music.
波累 *boleih*, v. t., involve (others), like *-jir* ↑.
波稜 *bolerng* (*bor-*, also wr. 菠薐, or 菠菜 *bortsaih*), n., spinach; 波稜蓋 *--gaih*, n., kneecap.
波羅(蜜) *boluor*(*mih*), n., pineapple.
波羅門 *boluormern*, n., Brahmin; 波羅門教 Brahmanism.
波羅密多 *boluormihduo*, n., (Sanskr.) *paramita*, salvation, crossing from sensuous life to nirvana.
波士頓 *Boshydun*, n., Boston.
波斯 *Bosy*, n., Persia.
波濤 *botaur*, n., big waves.
波紋 *bowern*, n., ripples.

溲 63A.82-2

sou.

N. Urine.

溲便 *sou-biahn*, n., excrements; urine and feces.
溲溺 *souniauh*, n., urine, urination; urine and feces.

汊 63A.82-3

chah.

N. A branch of river or current: 汊流.

汲 63A.82-3

jir.

N. A surname.

V.t. Draw (liquid): 汲水 draw water from a well; 汲綆 a well-rope; 汲酒 draw wine from a jar; 汲水機 a chain pump.

汲道 *jir-dauh*, n., a conduit, a water channel.
汲汲 *jirjir*, adj. & adv., anxious (ly), restless(ly): 汲汲於名利 restlessly seeking for fame and riches.
汲引 *jiryiin*, v.t., (1) (of water) draw up and conduct from one place to another, as with a pipe; (2) 汲引後進 select and promote (younger men) to better positions.

潑 63A.82-3

po.

Vb. To splash, pour out (water) with a splash, sprinkle: 潑熄 extinguish by spraying water; 潑墨 *-moh* ↓; 潑冷水 (phr.) dampen enthusiasm of an occassion; throw a wet blanket.

Adj. Spiteful, coarse, esp. 潑婦 *-fuh*, n., loud-mouthed, sharp-tongued woman; 潑婦罵街 billingsgate; 潑辣 *-lah*[1] ↓.

潑辣 *polah*[1], adj., bad-tempered, violent (of persons), also aggressive; 潑辣貨 *--huoh*, n., (abuse) scoundrel.
潑剌 *polah*[2], adj., making splashing sound (of fish).
潑賴 *polaih*, adj., (Soochow dial.) rascally.
潑墨 *pomoh*, n. & v.i., splash-ink, technique of painting.
潑皮 *popir*, adj., mischievous (child).
潑潑 *popo*, adj., jumping about (of fish); 活潑潑的 adv. & adj., bouncing, lovely (of children,

spirit, descriptive passage).

潑婆娘 *poporniarng*, n., (MC) spiteful woman.

潑天 *potian*, adj., overwhelming: 潑天大禍 phr., overwhelming disaster; 潑天富貴 immensely rich.

漫 63A.82–4

mahn.

V.i. & t. (1) To flood, spread over (an area): 水漫金山寺 flood water reaches Jinshan Temple; 水漫過膝 flood water reaches the knees; 瀰漫 spread all over (of snow, atmosphere, etc.); 漫山遍野 (of flowers, etc.) all over the hills and valley. (2) Do not say, let alone: 漫説是他 (=休説) let alone it is he, even others will do the same.

Adj. & adv. Unconcerned(ly), (at) random, casual(ly): 漫遊 travel extensively, or without fixed schedule, destination; 漫談, 漫語 random, casual talks; 姑漫應之 (LL) just promise him casually (to save trouble); 漫不經心 phr., totally unconcerned or inattentive; 漫無止境 on and on, without limitation; 漫無限制 totally without restrictions.

漫筆 *mahnbii*, n., casual literary notes (=隨筆), also casual-style sketches.

漫畫 *mahnhuah*, n., cartoon, caricature.

漫漶 *mahnhuahn*, adj., flooded, illegible (of bad print); widespread (of disease): 漫漶不可收拾 situation is so far gone beyond control.

漫錄 *mahn-luh*, n., casual notes.

漫漫 *mahnmahn*, adj., descriptive of long stretch of (clouds, night); 漫漫長夜 all the long, dark night, also (fig.) long, dark period without hope or enlightenment; 漫漫地 adv., (pr. *mahnmande*) slowly.

漫射 *mahn-sheh*, n. & v. i., (phys.) diffusion.

漫談 *mahn-tarn*, v.i. & n., casual conversation.

漫天 *mahntian*, adj. & adv., as in 濃霧漫天 the air is covered with a heavy mist; 漫天討價 (of shopkeeper) quote sky-rocket prices, prepared for haggling.

漫衍 *mahnyaan*, v. i., grow and spread (=蔓^{A}衍 20A.82.).

浸 63A.82–5

jihn (also *jin*).

V.t. Immerse, soak: 浸透 *-touh*↓; 浸禮 *-lii*↓; 浸不透 waterproof; 浸濕 to wet, drench; 浸漬 *-jih*↓; 浸水 soak in water, drench; 油浸 soak in oil; 浸死 drown; 浸在水裏 immerse in water.

Adv. Gradually, step by step, little by little: 浸漸 *-jiahn*, 浸假 *-jiaa*, 浸染 *-raan*, 浸潤 *-ruhn*, 浸淫 *-yirn*↓.

浸假 *jihnjiaa*, adv., (LL) gradually, little by little.

浸漸 *jihnjiahn*, adv., slowly but surely, imperceptibly.

浸漬 *jihnjih*, adj., saturated.

浸禮 *jihnlii*, n., baptism: 浸禮會 the Baptist Church.

浸染 *jihnraan*, v. t., influence gradually, contaminate(d).

浸潤 *jihnruhn*, adv., gradually, imperceptibly.

浸信會 *Jihnshihnhueih*, n., the Baptist Church.

浸透 *jihntouh*, adj., soaked through and through.

浸淫 *jihnyirn*, adv., by degrees, through a long process.

澱 63A.82–5

diahn.

N. (1) Sediment: 沉澱 sedimentation; 沉澱物 n., precipitate. (2) Var. for 靛 indigo.

澱粉 *diahnfeen*, n., starch; glucose.

汶 63A.82–6

wern.

N. Name of river in Shantung.

澈 63A.82–6

cheh.

[Cf. 徹, 撤]

V.t. To penetrate, get to the bottom: 澈底 *-dii*↓; 洞澈 penetrate (truth, mystery); 大澈大悟 great awakening.

Adj. & adv. (1) Thorough (in gen., interch. 徹 91B.82, except in sense): 澈悟 completely understand or awaken to truth; 透澈 thorough, -ly; 貫澈 carry to the end; 貫澈主張 realize teaching, carry out principles. (2) (Water) pure, clean: 清澈.

澈底 *chehdii*, adj. & adv., thorough, -ly (also wr. 徹底).

渡 63A.82–6

duh.

N. Ferry, ferryboat.

V.t. To cross over: 渡河, 渡海 cross river, sea; 遠渡重洋 cross the big ocean; 過渡 transition; 過渡時代 transitional period; 引渡 (law) extradite, -tion; (Budd.) 超渡, 渡化, 渡過苦海 rescue from life of pains and misery and reach the other shore (彼岸) of salvation.

渡假 *duh-jiah*, v.i., spending a

holiday.

渡口 *duhkoou*, n., ferry station.

渡頭 *duhtour*, n., ditto.

渡子 *duhtz*, n., ferry boatman.

潋 63A.82-8

liahn.

N. Ripples.

潋灩 *liahnyahn*, adj., flooding; billowing.

湲 63A.82-9

yuarn.

Adj. Sound of gurgling water.

激 63A.82-9

ji.

V.t. (1) Incite, stir up, move emotionally: 激動 *-duhng*↓; 刺激 stimulate, excite; 感激 be grateful to; 激昂 *-arng*, 激發 *-fa*↓; 激於義憤 be moved to action by righteous indignation; 激勵 *-lih*², 激勸 *-chyuahn*, 激將 *-jiahng*↓. (2) (Of currents) to dam up and divert: 爲石隄激使東注 build a stone embankment to divert the currents eastward; 激濁揚清 cast out the wicked and cherish the virtuous ("eliminate the impure from the pure"). (3) Dunk: 冷水一激 soak(ed) in cold water; 驟雨一激 wetted by a sudden downpour.

Adj. & adv. (1) Rapid(ly), quick(ly), swift(ly): 激變 *-biahn*↓; 急激 hurriedly; 激浪, 激流 turbulent waves, currents. (2) Excessive(ly), extreme(ly): 激切 *-chieh*↓; 過激 immoderate(ly), extreme (opinion); 激論 extremist views; 激烈 *-(')lieh*↓.

激昂 *ji-arng*, adj. & v.i., (be) emotionally wrought up: 慷慨激昂 righteously indignant, aroused to action.

激變 *jibiahn*, v.i., (1) to burst out all of a sudden; (2) n., a violent change, mutiny.

激切 *jichieh*, adj., outspoken in expressing one's views: 言多激切 speak out without fear or favor.

激勸 *jichyuahn*, v.t., persuade, exhort, encourage, prevail upon.

激動 *jiduhng*, v.t., to excite (populace); p.p., get excited, be inflamed.

激發 *jifa*, v.t., arouse, incite, stir up.

激將 *ji-jiahng*, v.t., to goad into action, incite to greater efforts, by moving words.

激烈 *ji(')lieh*, adj., (1) vigorous, strenuous: 激烈運動 energetic physical exertions; (2) intemperate, unrestrained: 態度激烈 violent attitude; 言論激烈 extremist views.

激厲 *jilih*¹, v.i. & t., (1) v.t., encourage, stimulate (also 激勵↓); (2) see *-chieh*↑.

激勵 *jilih*², v.t., encourage, boost: 激勵士氣 give a boost to the morale (of the army or people).

激怒 *ji-nuh*, v.t., to anger, inflame, enrage.

激賞 *jishaang*, v.t., be moved to admiration, to appreciate greatly.

激刺 *jitsyh*, v.t., inflame, stimulate, goad.

激筒 *jituung*, n., a hose pipe.

激揚 *jiyarng*, (1) v.t., to inspire; p.p., be inspired; (2) adj., inspiring.

激越 *jiyueh*, adj., (of music) swelling with clear and shrill tones.

沒 63A.82-9

*meir (*moh).*

[Vor. 没]

V.i. & t. (*moh) (1) To drown, be buried: 沉沒, 淹沒 be drowned; 大水沒過屋頂 roof was submerged in the flood; (fig.) lie hidden; 隱沒 ditto; 埋沒英雄 let a hero or genius lie unknown; 沒沒無聞 be completely unknown or unrecognized. (2) To disappear: 泯沒 vanish; 沒落 *-luoh*↓. (3) To confiscate: 沒收, 沒入, 沒官 *-shou, -ruh, -guan*↓. (4) U.f. 歿 to die.

Adv. Not, have not, did not (gen. dist. 不 do not): 沒有 have not; 沒來 he has not come, did not come; 他沒說 he did not say; 沒料到 did not expect; 沒想到 never thought; 沒見過世面 has not known high society; in certain formations 沒敢 have not dared; 沒肯 was not willing; followed by n., meaning "have no" or "-less"; 沒有用, 沒用兒 useless, have no use for; 沒皮沒臉 shamelessly; 沒主意 without plan in mind; 沒法子 helpless; 沒意思 dull, insipid; further examples, alphabetically arranged: *(ch)* 沒出息 (person) without future or serious purpose in life; 沒尺寸 speak without measuring one's words; *(d)* 沒對兒 unequalled, peerless; *(f)* 沒份兒 is not lucky or entitled to a share; 沒福氣 have not the luck (to enjoy, etc.); 沒縫兒 without an opportunity; *(g)* 沒根基 without solid foundation; 沒骨頭 without backbone or determination; *(j)* 沒勁(兒) spiritless; 沒準兒 not certain (to come, etc.); 沒治兒 nothing can be done; 沒轍 no way to go about it; *(l)* 沒臉 be disgraced; 沒路兒 helpless; *(m)* 沒門兒 hopeless, blindly groping for; 沒命 recklessly (run, etc.), to die; 沒譜兒 without regular standard; *(r)* 沒日子 without any definite dates; 沒死活 recklessly; *(s)* 沒想兒

hopeless; 沒下梢 without further news; 沒興, 沒心腸 in no mood for; 沒心眼兒 mindless, unthinking; (*t*) 沒頭案 a mystery without clues; 沒頭帖 anonymous letter.

沒趣(兒) *meirchyuh(-chyueh'l)*, adj., receive a rebuff: 討沒趣兒.
沒齒 **mohchyy*, phr., 沒齒不忘 will never forget as long as I live.
沒的 *meir'de*, phr., nothing: 走吧, 我也沒的說了 let's go, I have nothing further to say; 沒的吃, 沒的穿 nothing to eat, nothing to wear.
沒地 **mohdih*, v.i., (LL) lie 「buried.
沒短(的) *meirduaan('de)*, adv., ceaselessly: 他沒短的來 he comes here continuously.
沒斷的 *meirduahn('de)*, adv., ditto.
沒官 **mohguan*, v.t., be confiscated by law.
沒來由 *meirlairyour*, adv., without any cause, for no reason.
沒落兒 *meirlauh'l*, adj., helpless, in a fix (also 沒落兒).
沒了 *meir'le*, v.i., to disappear, vanish; prep., without: 沒了他不成 we cannot do without him.
沒落 **mohluoh*, v.i., be on the decline.
沒奈何 **mohnaihher*, adv., cannot help (doing).
沒跑 *meirpaau*, phr., cannot get away,—certain of success.
沒入 **mohruh*, v.t., be confiscated.
沒甚麼(沒什麼) *meirsher'me*, phr., nothing important; not bad (quite good).
沒收 **mohshou*, v.t. & p.p., confiscate(d).
沒事 *meirshyh*, n., nothing important or exciting; phr., all right: 保你沒事 I guarantee you nothing will happen; 沒事人 a detached observer.
沒世 **mohshyh*, adv., for life: 沒世不忘 remember for life.

浚 63A.82-9

jyuhn.

V.t. (=濬) To dredge: 浚泥機 a dredger.

---

§ 63A.83 (氵/ㄧ)

漣 63A.83-1

liarn.

漣漪 *liarnyi*, adj. & n., (AC) rippling (water).
漣漣 *liarnliarn*, adj., as in 泣涕漣漣 weep profusely.

凝 63A.83-2

nirng.

V.i. & t. (1) (Of liquids) to congeal, freeze, solidify; (of vapor) turn into liquid; (of water) turn into ice: 凝成固體 (of liquids) become solid; 凝住 congeal; 凝固, 凝結, 凝凍 *-guh, -jier, -duhng* ↓. (2) To fix: 凝目, 凝眸 focus one's eyes upon (s. t or s. o.); 凝睇, 凝視 (of eyes) watch intently, see *-shyh* ↓. (3) To gather together; (of liquids) coagulate: 凝神, 凝集 *-shern, -jir* ↓.

凝凍 *nirngduhng*, v. i., coagulate, freeze.
凝固 *nirngguh*, v. i. & n., (of liquids) solidify, -fication; 凝固點 freezing point; 凝固劑 coagulant.
凝結 *nirngjier*, v. i. & n., condense, -ation.
凝集 *nirngjir*, v.i., to flock together.
凝妝 *nirngjuang*, adj., (of women) dolled up, prettily dressed.
凝佇 *nirngjuh*, v. i., stand transfixed; stand still waiting.
凝重 *nirngjuhng*, adj., (of manners) dignified.
凝脂 *nirngjy*, n., as in 膚若凝脂 skin smooth like lard or butter.
凝滯 *nirngjyh*, adj., (of speech or action) slow-moving, not flowing freely; involved, blocked up.
凝聚 *nirngjyuh*, v. i. & n., (1) (chem.) coagulate, -tion; (2) 凝聚精神 concentrate attention.
凝神 *nirngshern*, v. i., to concentrate.
凝想 *nirngshiaang*, v. i., meditate.
凝視 *nirngshyh*, v. t., to stare at, look intently.
凝思 *nirngsy*, v. i., meditate.

液 63A.83-6

yeh (re. pr. *yih*).

N. Fluid: 血液 blood (in circulation); 唾液, 涎液 saliva; 精液 semen.

液化 *yehhuah*, v.t., liquefy.
液汁 *yehjy*, n., juice.
液體 *yehtii*, n., fluid state.

漩 63A.83-6

shyuarn.

N. Whirlpool; eddy.

漩兒 *shyuar'l*, n., (1) whirlpool; (2) a whorl on fingerprint or in hair.
漩渦 *shyuarnwo*, n., whirlpool.

淀 63A.83-6

diahn.

N. Swamps, swampy region.

泛 63A.83-9

fahn.

[Var. of 汎 63A.70]

V.i. Drift: 泛舟 drift or go about in boat.

Adj. & adv. Broad, unconfined: 泛論 general discussion; 泛神論 pantheism; 泛觀 in a general survey; 泛問 ask in general; 泛覽 browse among books; 浮泛 vague, unspecified; 空泛 vague and devoid of content; 泛駕之馬 (AC) horse that throws rider.

泛常 *fahncharng*, adj. & adv., (1) superficial; (2) generally, frequently.
泛泛 *fahnfahn*, adj. & adv., vague, -ly, superficial, -ly, cursory.
泛溢 *fahnyih*, v. i., overflow (see 汎 63A.70).

涎 63A.83–9

shiarn.

N. Saliva: 口涎 ditto; 涎皮賴臉, 涎皮涎臉 disgusting, slobbering appearance.

§ 63A.91 (氵/ノ)

澎 63A.91–1

peng.

澎湖 *Pernghur*, n., the Pescadores Islands.
澎湃 *pengpaih*, adj., descriptive of crashing, booming sound of waves.
澎濞 *pengpih*, n., AC var. of *-paih* ↑.

涉 63A.91–2

sheh.

V.i. (1) To wade across water: 涉水 ditto; 跋涉 travel across land and water. (2) To run across, to experience: 涉險 explore places of difficult access (peaks, etc.); 涉世, 涉足 *-shyh*[1], *-tzur* ↓. (3) Be related to, connected with: 與我無涉 has nothing to do with me; 涉及 *-jir* ↓; 干涉 to interfere (rarely 關涉); 交涉 v. i. & n., to negotiate on diplomatic or legal matters; 辦交涉 start negotiations.

涉筆 *sheh-bii*, phr., (LL) "wet the pen"—to take pen and write when in mood: 涉筆成趣 make an interesting or sparkling line as it comes by itself.
涉及 *sheh-jir*, v. t., to involve, relate to incidentally: 涉及個人私事 involve a mention of a man's personal affairs (及 here is prep.).
涉覽 *shehlaan*, v. t., as in 涉覽羣書 read widely, esp. in cursory reading.
涉獵 *shehlieh*, v. i., ditto.
涉歷 *shehlih*, v. t., to go through, live through (periods, countries).
涉想 *shehshiaang*, v. i., to fancy, indulge in fanciful thinking; think of casually.
涉世 *sheh-shyh*[1], phr., to have experience (of life).
涉事 *sheh-shyh*[2], phr., to have experience or handle affairs.
涉訟 *sheh-suhng*, v. i., to be involved in lawsuit.
涉足 *sheh-tzur*, v. i., to go through tentatively, to have a taste of (gambling house, etc.).

沙 63A.91–2

sha.

N. (1) Sand: 細沙 fine sand; 風沙, 狂風沙 sandstorm; 一盤散沙 a tray of loose sand—a nation or group without cohesion, each individual for himself; 流沙 quick sands. (2) A surname.

Adj. (1) Hoarse (voice): 沙啞. (2) Gritty (taste): 沙瓤 sandy pulp (of pear, etc.). (3) Sandy in appearance: 沙板兒 *-baa'l* ↓.

沙板兒 *shabaa'l*, adj., as in 沙板兒錢 a coarse copper coin.
沙包 *shabau*, n., sandbag, also *-daih* ↓.
沙布 *shabuh*, n., emery cloth.
沙場 *shacharng*, n., battlefield.
沙淺兒 *shachiaa'l*, n., a shallow earthen basin.
沙錢 *shachiarn*, n., very thin bad ancient cash.
沙磧 *shachih*, n., (LL) desert dunes.
沙丘 *shachiou*, n., sand dunes.
沙船 *shachuarn*, n., sand junk, with flat bottom, esp. for avoiding getting stuck on river bed.
沙袋 *shadaih*, n., sandbag, also *-bau* ↑.
沙銚子 *shadiauhtz*, n., an earthen pot with wide cover on top and short spout.
沙丁魚 *shading-yur*, n., sardine.
沙發 *shafa*, n., (translit.) sofa.
沙方 *shafang*, n., a cheap coffin, consisting of a square (方) box of fir-wood (沙木) planks.
沙粉 *sha-feen*, n., emery powder.
沙阜 *shafuh*, n., sand dunes.
沙鍋 *shaguo*, n., an earthen pot, good esp. for stewing.
沙果 *shaguoo*, n., crab apple.
沙吒 *Shajah*, n., a Turkic surname.
沙雞 *shaji*, n., the sand grouse.
沙角 *shajiaau*, n., sand spit, also *-tzueei* ↓.
沙甲 *shajiah*, n., the dragonet fish.
沙洲 *shajou*, n., a sand bar; sand bank.
沙鐘 *sha-juung*, n., sand glass.
沙紙 *shajyy*, n., sandpaper.
沙坑 *sha-keng*, n., sand pit.

沙渺漻沪沴滲淒淞

沙拉 *shala*, n., also *-lyuh*, salad (also wr. 沙律).
沙稜 *sha'leng*, adj., gritty in taste.
沙礫 *shalih*, n., pebbles, gravel.
沙梨 *shalir*, n., a species of pear, with gritty pulp.
沙漏 *shalouh*, n., sand filter; such filter used for marking hours.
沙龍 *shalurng*, n., (translit.) salon (of art).
沙濾 *shalyuh*, n., sand filter.
沙猛 *shameeng*, n., the file fish.
沙門 *shamern*, n., Buddhist monk; a Shaman priest; 沙門教 Shamanism.
沙面 *shamiahn*, n., (1) sand bank; (2) (Shamiahn) Island of Shameen at Canton.
沙彌 *shamir*, n., (Budd.) an acolyte, novice; also 沙彌子 (*-tz*).
沙漠 *shamoh*, n., desert.
沙磨 *shamor*, v. t., to sandpaper, see *-jyy*↑; an emery wheel.
沙木 *shamuh*, n., a tree of fir family, *Cunninghamia sinensis*; c.f. 杉 10B.91.
沙勺 *shashaur*, n., an earthen ladle.
沙參 *shashen*, n., (bot.) the blue bell, *Adenophora verticillata*.
沙蟹 *shashieh*, n., "show hand", poker (also translit. as 梭哈).
沙石 *shashyr*, n., (1) gravel; (2) sandstone.
沙汰 *shataih*, v. t., to sift, eliminate (＝淘汰 63A.50).
沙灘 *shatan*, n., sandbank, also said of sandbar.
沙糖 *shatarng*, n., unrefined sugar.
沙田 *shatiarn*, n., tidal lands, sand flats.
沙隄 *shatir*, n., sand bar.
沙蠶 *shatsarn*, n., a sand bug, *Nereis diversicolor*.
沙土 *shatuu*, n., gravel; sandy soil.
沙子 *shatz*, n., grains of sand.
沙嘴 *shatzueei*, n., sand spit, a projection of sand bank into river or sea.
沙鵻 *shatzuei*, n., (zoo.) the sandpiper; the snipe.
沙啞 *shayaa*, adj., hoarse (voice).
沙雁兒 *shayah'l*[1], n., a paper kite with a long tail, appearing like a line of flying geese.
沙燕兒 *shayah'l*[2], n., the common kite, shaped like a swallow.
沙蠅 *sha-yirng*, n., sand fly.
沙魚 *shayur*, n., the shark (also wr. 鯊).

渺 63A.91-4

miaau.

[Cogn. 藐 20A.70, 秒 90A.91, 杳 10.41]

Adj. (1) Distant and difficult to see. (2) Descriptive of long stretch of water.

渺茫 *miaaumarng*, adj., elusive, indiscernible: 渺茫得很 completely at sea, uncertain.
渺渺 *miaurmiaau*, adj., very small and distant.

漻 63A.91-5

liaur.

Adj. (Of pool, current) deep and clear.

沪 63A.91-6

huh.

[Abbr. of 滬 63A.70]

沴 63A.91-8

lih.

Adj. Foul or poisonous: 沴孽 an evil genius; 沴氣 foul air, miasma.

滲 63A.91-9

shehn.

V.i. To seep through: 滲出 to leak out.

滲漏 *shehn-louh*, v. i., leak through (secret, liquid).
滲入 *shehn-ruh*, v. i., to infiltrate (of liquids, enemy agents): 滲入地下 seep through the ground.
滲透 *shehn-touh*, v. i., (1) to pass through filter; n., osmosis; (2) see *-ruh*, *-louh*↑.

§ 63A.93 (氵/く)

淒 63A.93-1

chi.

[Interch. 凄]

Adj. (1) Chilly, uncomfortably bleak: 淒淒 (AC) windy and rainy; 淒風苦雨 bleak wind and wretched rain. (2) Sad, mournful, disconsolate (var. 悽 22A.93): 淒切, 淒涼, 淒楚 *-chieh*, *-liarng* *-chuu*↓; 淒淚 forlorn tears; 淒咽 sad sobs.

淒切 *chichieh*, adj., (of weeping, song) mournful, disconsolate: 淒切動人 sadly moving.
淒愴 *chichuahng*, adj., sad and forlorn.
淒楚 *chichuu*, adj., see *-chieh*↑.
淒冷 *chileeng*, adj., cold, bleak.
淒涼 *chiliarng*, adj., sad; forlorn, lonely: 淒淒涼涼 ditto; 老景淒涼 lonely in old age.
淒厲 *chilih*, adj., (of wind) bitterly cold.
淒迷 *chimir*, adj., see *-liarng*↑.
淒心 *chishin*, adj., (coll.) discomfort in stomach.
淒慘 *chitsaan*, adj., sad, hard up, oppressed.
淒滄 *chitsang*, adj., var. of ⌈*-chuahng*↑.
淒豔 *chiyahn*, adj., (of love story) sad and beautiful.

淞 63A.93-1

sung.

N. Name of river in Kiangsu.

法 63A.93-1

faa (*fa, *far, *fah).

N. (1) (*-tz*, pr. *fartz*; *-'l*, pr. *fa'l*, *far'l* or *faa'l*) method, way, means: 法子, 法兒 way, method, means of doing: 用甚麼法子 in what way, by what means, can you do it? 沒法子 cannot do a thing, have no choice: 沒法子 (or 兒) 告訴他 there is no way to tell him; 想法, 設法 think of some way (to do); 無法勸他 there is no way to persuade him. (2) In art & literature, technique, method, principles of composition: 筆法 technique, style of writing; 章法 composition; 書法 calligraphy; 畫法 method of painting; 六法 six principles of art by 謝赫 c. A.D. 490. (3) The law: 法律 *-lyuh*↓; 民法 civil law; 刑法 criminal law; 司法 justice; 立法 legislature; 憲法 constitution; 法治 government by law; 法家 *-jia*↓; 守法, 犯法 obey, violate, the law; 執法 carry out the law, justice; 法學院 law college; 法學系 department of law; 法定 legal, fixed by law: 法定價格, 資格, 權利 legal price, qualifications, rights; 法定人數 quorum; 法定利率, 年齡, 代理人 legal interest, age, agent; 法令, 法規, 法則 *-lihng, -guei, -tzer*↓. (4) Tradition-honored institutions: 先王法典, 法章; 有王法, 沒有王法 respect, having no respect, for established code of behavior. (5) (Budd.) the Law, the church, the teachings of the church: 法師, 法座 term of address to abbot, master; 法鼓 temple drum; 法器, 法臺 music instruments, altar used in Buddhist mass; 法像 Buddhist portrait or statue; 法船普渡 paper boat burned on Buddhist All Souls' Day; 法輪常轉 the wheel of transmigration always goes on; 法海, 法力 great power of salvation; 法師, 法眼, 法緣 *-shy, -yaan, -yuarn*↓.

法案 *faa-ahn*, n., legal case.

法寶 *farbaau*, n., (1) the alms-bowl, walking stick of Budd. monks; (2) gen. term for magic weapon or formula, most precious secret: 隨身法寶 a stand-by (like a good dictionary).

法幣 *faabih*, n., legal tender.

法場 *faacharng*, n., execution ground.

法典 *fardiaan*, n., time-honored code, tradition, statutes.

法度 *faaduh*, n., (1) statutes, code; (2) method, means; correct pattern.

法官 *faaguan*, n., court judge; formerly, Taoist of rank.

法規 *faaguei*, n., regulations; statutes.

法國 *Faaguor*, n., France; 法國人 Frenchman; 法國號 French horn.

法繪 *faahueih*, n., (court.) your painting, see *-shu*↓.

法家 *faajia*, n., (1) The Legalist School of 4–2nd cen. B.C.; (2) (court.) professor (＝方家); (3) (AC) 法家拂士 learned men and advisors.

法駕 *faajiah*, n., (LL, rare) emperor's carriage.

法警 *farjiing*, n., the police.

法藍 *faalarn*, n., see 琺△瑯 31A.93.

法蘭絨 **fahlarnrurng*, n., flannel.

法郎 **fahlarng*, n., franc, a currency.

法蘭西 **Fahlarnshi* (*Faa--*), n., France.

法吏 *faalih*, n., officer of the law.

法令 *faalihng*, n., statutes, (mil.) law, order.

法理 *farlii*, n., legal theory, principle of law.

法螺 *faaluor*, n., conch shell used as trumpet in Buddhist and Taoist masses.

法律 *faalyuh*, n., the law, laws.

法碼(兒) *far'ma'l*, n., see 砝△碼 31B.93.

法門 *faamern*, n., initial approach to become Budd. believer; 不二法門 gen. term, the only correct approach to subject, success.

法人 *faarern*, n., legal person.

法書 *faashu*, n., (court.) your esteemed calligraphy.

法術 *faashuh*, n., magic trick; gen. effective means.

法師 *faashy*, n., (Budd., Taoist) master.

法式 *faashyh*^{1}, n., model, pattern (of conduct, composition).

法事 *faashyh*^{2}, n., Buddhist or Taoist mass.

法堂 *faatarng*, n., court of law.

法帖 *fartiee*, n., model of calligraphy for practice.

法庭 *faatirng*, n., law court.

法則 *faatzer*, n., model to be copied; rules.

法網 *far-waang*, n., the various laws and statutes regarded as elaborate net to catch violators.

法眼 *faryaan*, n., (court.) your esteemed judgment (of art); Buddha's eyes of magic power.

法言 *faayarn*, n., (AC) venerable, old teachings.

法衣 *faayi*, n., cassocks.

法院 *faayuahn*, n., court of law.

法緣 *faayuarn*, n., destined union with Budd. church.

泓 63A.93-5

hurng.

Adj. (Of water) deep and clear.

泫 63A.93-6

shyuahn.

泫然 *shyuahnrarn*, adv., tearfully: 泫然泣下, or 泫然流涕 shedding tears in profusion.

泫泫 *shyuahnshyuahn*, adj. & adv., gleaming (tears), glistening (dew).

灋 63A.93–6

faa (*fa, far, fah*).

[Anc. of 法 63A.93]

渝 63A.93–8

yur.

[Usu. wr. 渝 63A.00]

滋 63A.93–8

tzy.

N. Taste: 滋味 *-weih* ↓.

V.i. & t. (1) V. i., grow, thrive, flourish, develop: 蕃滋 (of plants) flourish, thrive; 滋長 wax, grow bigger; 滋殖 wax, multiply, procreate; 滋茂 (of plants) thrive, grow vigorously, luxuriate; 滋生 *-sheng*, 滋蔓 *-mahn* ↓. (2) (Of liquids) spurt out: 水管子向外滋水 water is bursting out from the hose. (3) V. t., nourish, foster, cultivate: 滋養 *-yaang*, 滋補 *-buu*, 滋潤 *-ruhn* ↓.

Adv. (LL) very, to a great degree: 其滋虐甚 he (it) is terribly cruel; 法令滋彰, 盜賊多有 the more laws and regulations, the more thieves and robbers there are.

滋補 *tzybuu*, (1) v. i., take nourishments; 滋陰補陽 nourishment for vitality. (2) adj., nourishing, nutritious.

滋蔓 *tzymahn*, v. i., (of grasses) spread in abundance.

滋膩 *tzy'ni*, adj., (of dough or the like) thoroughly mixed so as to appear smooth and shiny.

滋潤 *tzyruhn*, v. t. & adj., (1) v. t., (lit.) moisten, to water (plants), (fig.) to tone up, nourish (skin), moisten (throat), soften (skin); (2) adj., nourishing, kind to (the throat).

滋生 *tzysheng*, (1) v. i., wax, multiply, procreate; (2) v.t., stir up, incite: 滋生事端 to cause or make trouble.

滋息 *tzyshir*, v. i., (1) (interest) accrue; (2) (cattle) multiply.

滋事 *tzy-shyh*, v. i., cause trouble, create an incident, stir up disturbances.

滋嘴兒 *tzytzuee'l*, v. i., (1) beam with smiles; (2) (of flowers) burst open.

滋味 *tzyweih*, n., (1) the taste of food, flavor; (2) the sensation one feels: 讓你嘗嘗坐牢的滋味 let you have a taste of life in jail.

滋養 *tzyyaang*, v. t., nourish; 滋養品 nourishment; 滋養料 nutritious elements; 滋養分 ditto.

滋芽兒 *tzy yar'l*, v. i., to bud.

汝 63A.93–9

ruu.

N. A surname.

Pron. (AC, LL) you: 汝輩 *-beih* ↓; 汝曹, 汝等 (plural, familiar form) you.

汝輩 *ruubeih*, pron., (pl.) you, used by elders in speaking to children.

汝窯 *ruu-yaur*, n., a rare variety of chinaware of the Suhng Dyn., so called from the place 汝州 in Honan where it was made.

SECTION 63B

§ 63B.00 (礻/丨)

禱 63B.00–1

daau.

V.i. & t. To pray, beg: 禱祀 pray at temple; 禱祝 pray for blessing; 祈禱上帝 pray to God: 是所至禱, 是禱, 爲禱 (in letters, at the conclusion) this is what I beg of you.

禱告 *daaugauh*, v.i. & t., to pray (to God); n., a prayer: 做禱告 to pray.

禱文 *daauwern*, n., prayer.

祷 63B.00–1

daau.

[Abbr. of 禱 63B.00]

§ 63B.01 (礻/小)

禖 63B.01–2

meir.

N. & v.i. (AC) (make) prayer for progeny.

§ 63B.02 (礻/卜)

禳 63B.02–6

rarng.

N. A ritual to exorcise evils: 祈禳 such ritual.

V.t. Drive out by prayers or magic: 禳解 exorcise evil spirits; 禳災 make effort to avert calamity by sacrifices; 禳除 exorcise, drive away or out (demon, devil).

祿 63B.02-9

luh.

N. (1) A blessing: 福祿壽考 good luck and long life. (2) Salary: 俸祿. (3) Rank and post: 祿位, 祿秩 rank. (4) A surname.

§ 63B.10 (ネ/十)

禪 63B.10-4

charn (**shahn*). [Abbr. 禅]

N. (1) (Budd.) meditation, from Sanskr. *channa* (*zen* being Japanese spelling): 坐禪, 參禪 observe *charn* with crossed legs in quiet meditation for cleansing the mind of thoughts and for supreme realization of essence of reality, see 禪悟 *-wuh*↓. (2) (Generalized) Buddhism: 禪林, 禪杖 *-lirn*, *-jahng*↓. (3) (**shahn*) Special worship of the earth, or of sacred mountain in august ceremony.

V.i. (**shahn*) To abdicate in favor of another person: 禪讓, 禪位 *-rahng*, *-weih*↓; 受禪 accept rule abdicated by previous ruler.

禪牀 *charnchuarng*, n., bed or divan for meditation.

禪定 *charndihng*, n., the utter calm of mind attained by purging the mind of all thoughts.

禪房 *charnfarng*, n., a monastic room.

禪關 *charnguan*, n., ditto.

禪和子 *charnhertzyy*, n., (MC) one who practises meditation.

禪杖 *charnjahng*, n., Buddhist cane, orig. a cane with a padded head for knocking on head of one who falls asleep.

禪機 *charn-ji*, n., *charn* subtleties.

禪偈 *charnjier*, n., a *gatha* (short verse) containing a *charn* message.

禪經 *charnjing*, n., mass said for the deceased.

禪寂 *charnjir*, v.i., (Budd.) pass away (cf. 寂^A滅 62.82, Nirvana).

禪客 *charnkeh*, n., believer who practises *charn*.

禪林 *charnlirn*, n., the monasteries.

禪讓 **shahnrahng*, v.i., (in time of Emperors 堯 and 舜) to abdicate in favor of a chosen able man and not by heredity.

禪心 *charn-shin*, n., the meditative or purified mind.

禪師 *charn-shy*, n., the guru, *charn* master.

禪堂 *charntarng*, n., a monastic hall.

禪位 **shahn-weih*, v.i., to abdicate in favor of another (crown heir, etc.).

禪悟 *charnwuh*, v.i., to realize, a realization or awakening to truth.

禪椅 *charn-yii*, n., seat for meditation.

禪悅 *charnyueh*, n., the inner bliss and peace from meditation.

祥 63B.10-8

shiarng.

N. (1) Omens (orig. indicating good and bad, but generally limited to good augury). (2) Good luck, happy omens: 吉祥 common term for good luck (also wr. 吉羊); 不祥 bad omen, ill luck. (3) Sacrificial offering on the anniversary of the death of parents—小祥, 大祥 on the first, second such anniversary.

祥兆 *shiarng-jauh*, n., good omens.

祥金 *shiarng-jin*, n., term for ancient sacrificial bronzes.

祥瑞 *shiarngrueih*, n., good omens.

祥雲 *shiarng-yurn*, n., beautiful, auspicious clouds, used esp. in describing the skies accompanying appearances of Buddha.

§ 63B.11 (ネ/土)

社 63B.11-1

sheh.

N. (1) God of the land: 社祭, 社稷 *-jih*[1,2]↓. (2) A club, group, corporation, business agency: 會社 (esp. Japanese) corporation; 音樂社, 詩社 music club, poetry club; 旅行社 tourist agency; 通訊社 news agency; 服務社 service center or bureau; 報社, 雜誌社 newspaper, magazine corporation. (3) Day of sacrifice to the god of the land: 春社 spring sacrifice; 秋社 autumn sacrifice—occurring on the fifth 戊 day after 立春 and 立秋, see Appendix B.

社會 *shehhueih*, n., society: 上流社會 upper-class society; 社會心理, 教育 social psychology, education; 社會現象 social phenomena; 社會學 sociology; 社會主義 socialism; 社會福利 social welfare; 社會賢達 community leaders.

社火 *shehhuoo*, n., festival of

社 禋 神

"beginning of spring" (see 立^春 60.30).

社長 *shehjaang*, n., chief of agency, club, corporation, see N. 2↑.

社交 *shehjiau*, n., social intercourse, life: 社交界 men and women active in social life; 社交性 gregarious instinct, sociability.

社祭 *shehjih*[1], n., sacrifice to the god of land.

社稷 *shehjih*[2], n., (1) orig. the god of grains; (2) generally, the state, the nation: 社稷之前途 the future of the state; 社稷所賴 the mainstay of the country and the people; 社稷之臣 a pillar of the state; 社稷壇 altar to the god of grains and the soil.

社論 *shehluhn*, n., editorial comment.

社廟 *sheh-miauh*, n., temple to the god of the land.

社評 *shehpirng*, n., editorial comment.

社日 *shehryh*, n., see N. 3↑.

社鼠 *shehshuu*, n., "temple rats": 城狐社鼠 those who prey upon the people and fatten themselves.

社倉 *shehtsang*, n., formerly, public granary.

社團 *shehtuarn*, n., (1) a corporation, a corporate body; (2) any social group.

社土 *shehtuu*, n., (AC) feudal state given to a prince.

社友 *sheh-yoou*, n., a club member.

社員 *sheh-yuarn*, n., ditto.

禋 63B.11-3

yin.

V.i. To offer sacrifices: 禋祀.

§63B.22 (礻/丨)

神 63B.22-2

shern.

N. (1) Spirit, God, gen. term for the spirits, the gods, the deities, supernatural beings: 神仙, 神怪 *-shian, -guaih*↓; 神明, 神靈 *-mirng, -lirng*↓; 天神 celestial spirits; 山神 spirit of the mountains (cf. 妖 93A.81, 精 22C.42); oft. coupled with 鬼 demons: 神不知, 鬼不覺 without even the spirits knowing about it—mysteriously; 神出鬼沒 appear and disappear mysteriously; 神差鬼使 messengers of the gods and spirits; 神人共誅 abominated by both gods and men. (2) The mind, the soul, the man's spirit: 神完氣足 full of spirit and energy; 神不守舍 out of one's mind ("soul departed from its abode"); 神來之筆 an inspired passage; 心神 the mind, mental state; 安神 tranquilize the nerves; 養神 rest and restore energy; 用神, 費神, 勞神 to trouble oneself, hence a formula to thank people for taking the trouble; 凝神 focus attention; 出神 absent-minded, daydreaming; 失神 dejected; 留神 (please) be careful. (3) Demeanor, expression: 神色, 神容, 神態, 神志 *-seh, -rurng, -taih, -jyh*[1]↓; 傳神 (of painting) conveying the true spirit of the subject portrayed; to draw a portrait; 眼神 look, expression of eyes.

V.i. To appreciate, comprehend: 神而明之, 存乎其人 it is up to every individual to try to comprehend.

Adj. Divine, miraculous, superb: 神妙, 神奇 *-miauh, -chir*[2]↓; 神乎其神 marvellous! divine! 神效 magical effect (of medicine); 神醫 a great physician.

Adv. By, of the spirit: 神馳左右 my spirit is always with you; 無任神往 admire from the distance greatly; 神交 be spiritually attracted to a friend one has not met; 神解 to understand by the spirit, not the rational mind.

神氣 *shernchih*[1], (1) n., expression of face, atmosphere, painting or group; (2) (*-'chi*) adj., wearing a proud, self-satisfied look; 神氣活現 phr., looking self-satisfied.

神器 *shern-chih*[2], n., symbols of imperial power (throne, tripod, etc.).

神祇 *shern-chir*[1], n., celestial (神) and terrestial spirits (祇).

神奇 *shernchir*[2], adj., magical in effect, miraculous (event); extraordinary (art work).

神情(兒) *shernchirng('l)*, n., facial expression.

神廚 *shern-chur*, n., cabinet beneath a niche for idol.

神權 *shern-chyuarn*, n., (1) divine power; (2) 神權時代 period of theocracy.

神道 *sherndauh*, (1) n., (a) path leading to tomb; 神道碑 tablet on side of tomb giving biographical sketch (always laudatory) of deceased; (b) (MC) the deities in gen.; (2) (*-'dau*) adj., 眞神道 (child) unusually brilliant.

神父 *shernfuh*, n., Roman catholic father.

神福 *shernfur*, n., (MC) sacrifices for blessing of the gods.

神怪 *shernguaih*, n., spirits and demons: 神怪小說 supernatural tales.

神工 *shern-gung*, phr., 鬼斧神工 (of art masterpiece) extraordinary as if done by the spirits.

神話 *shernhuah*, n., mythology; a myth.

神魂 *shernhurn*, n., (1) soul (cf. 靈魂); (2) state of mind: 神魂不定 frightened or depressed, out of one's wits; 神魂顚倒 heart in torment, crazy with longing of loved one.

神迹 *shernji*[1], n., a miracle.

神機 *shernji*[2], n., (1) a sudden inspiration; (2) a divine plan: 不可洩露神機 God's secret may not be revealed (said by magicians, Taoists).

神姦 *shernjian*, (1) n., (AC) the deities and demons; (2) adj., hypocritical, deceitful (plotters).

神京 *shernjing*[1], n., (LL) euphemism for national capital.

神經 *shernjing*[2], (1) n., nerves; (2) adj., nervous; 神經系 the nervous systems; 神經細胞

nerve cells; 神經纖維 ganglions of nerves; 神經衰弱 nervous prostration, neurasthenia; 神經錯亂 mentally deranged, mental disorder; 交感神經 sympathetic nerves; 神經炎 neuritis; 神經病 mental derangement, in sanity; 神經痛 neuralgia; 神經質 neurotic; 神經過敏 oversensitive; 神經戰 war of nerves.

神 州 *Shenjou*, n., the Divine Continent—China.

神 主 *shernjuu*, n., a spirit tablet.

神 志 *shernjyh*[1], n., state of mind: 神志不清 (of patient) in confused state of mind; 神志清白 in a clear state of mind.

神 智 *shernjyh*[2], adj. & n., intelligent, -ce; mental agility.

神 君 *shernjyun*, n., laudatory epithet of sovereign, deity.

神 紙 *shern-jyy*, n., paper money burnt for use in nether world.

神 兒 *sher'l*, n., see *-chih*[1] ↑.

神 聊 *shernliaur*, v.i., to tell a tall tale.

神 力 *shern-lih*, n., God's power; magical power.

神 靈 *shernlirng*, n., the spirits, various deities: 神靈保祐 may God protect (us).

神 妙 *shernmiauh*, adj., astounding, subtle, utterly delightful (piece of writing): 神妙莫測 so subtle as to be difficult to guess what comes next.

神 秘 *shernmih*, adj., mystical, beyond one's comprehension, mysterious (movements).

神 明 *shernmirng*, n., (1) the deities, used also in address to God; (2) (AC) man's comprehending soul.

神 女 *sern-nyuu*, n., (1) a goddess; (2) a female enchanter: 神女生涯 prostitution.

神 品 *shern-piin*, n., (art criticism) one of the "divine class"—inimitable work of a genius.

神 人 *shernrern*, n., a person of extraordinary, God-like appearance.

神 容 *shernrurng*, n., facial expression.

神 色 *shernseh*, n., facial expression (downcast, etc.).

神 聖 *shernshehng*, adj., sacred, holy: 神聖不可侵犯 (regarded as) sacred, not to be touched or criticized.

神 像 *shernshiahng*, n., (1) an idol, an image; (2) portrait of an idol.

神 仙 *shernshian* (-'*shian*), n., a fairy, a Taoist immortal; 神仙故事 a fairy tale: 神仙中人 the happiest mortal alive; 神仙眷屬 most happily married.

神 行 太 保 *Shern-shirng taih-baau*, n., "Superman."

神 術 *shernshuh*, n., magic: (a) use of magical power by deities; (b) remarkable skill (of physicians).

神 學 *shernshyuer*, n., theology; 神學院 theological seminary.

神 算 *shern-suahn*, n., remarkable prediction of affairs.

神 速 *shernsuh*, adj. & adv., amazingly fast, with utmost speed.

神 思 *shernsy*, n., thinking of the distant ones; deep thinking.

神 似 *shernsyh*, (1) adj., looking like, resembling; (2) n., resemblance.

神 態 *sherntaih*, n., a man's look or expression.

神 彩 *sherntsaai*, n., glamour, spirit (in appearance), healthy look.

神 通 *sherntung*, n., magical power of the deities: 神通廣大 superior magic in battle of the spirits and demons; (fig.) a person's extraordinary power of getting what he wants: 大顯神通 show what one is capable of, (deity) shows his magic power.

神 童 *shernturng*, n., a child prodigy.

神 位 *shern-weih*, n., see *-juu* ↑.

神 物 *shern-wuh*[1], n., (1) a supernatural being; (2) an old tree, tortoise, etc., associated with myth or fable.

神 悟 *shernwuh*[2], v.i., to understand through the spirit.

神 武 *shernwuu*, adj., epithet of a great conquering general.

神 意 *shernyih*[1], n., God's will.

神 異 *shernyih*[2], adj., miraculous (tales, events).

神 穎 *shernyiing*, adj., remarkably intelligent.

神 韻 *shernyuhn*, n., flavor of poem or painting; (litr. criticism) flavor theory of poetry of 王漁洋.

神 勇 *shernyuung*, adj., see *-wuu* ↑.

祁 63B.22-3

chir.

N. A surname.

Adj. & adv. (AC) ample, very: 祁寒 (AC) severely cold.

祁 祁 *chirchir*, adj., (AC) slow; ample; numerous.

祈 63B.22-9

chir.

V.i. & t. (1) To pray (to s.o.) for (s.t.): 祈禱, 祈請 *-daau, -chiing* ↓; 祈年, 祈雨, 祈晴 to pray for New Year, for rain, for clear sky. (2) (Oft. in correspondence) I beg to ＋vb.: 祈請, 祈懇 I beg to request; 祈賜玉音 please reply; 祈望 I dare to hope; 尚祈原諒 I beg you to forgive.

祈 報 *chirbauh*, v.i., formerly, to offer sacrifices in spring (祈) and autumn harvest (報).

祈 請 *chirchiing*, v.i., to beg, request.

祈 祈 *chirchir*, adj., (AC) descriptive of drizzling rain: 甘雨祈祈.

祈 禱 *chirdaau*, v.i. & t. & n., to pray to God; a prayer; 祈禱會 a prayer service; 祈禱文 text of prayer.

祈 念 *chirniahn*, v.i., (Budd.) to pray to God.

祈 賽 *chirsaih*, n., a religious thanksgiving festival oft. with parades: from 祈神賽會.

祈嚮 *chirshiahng*, v.i., (AC) hope for some goal.

祚 63B.22–9

tzuoh.

N. (1) Throne: 卒踐帝祚 ascended the throne at last. (2) Year: 初歲元祚 (AC) in the first year of the reign.

V.t. To bless: 天祚明德 Heaven blesses the virtuous.

祚命 *tzouh-mihng*, n., (AC) divine blessing.

祚胤 *tzuoh-yihn*, n., (AC) posterity, descendants.

§ 63B.30 (ネ/一)

祉 63B.30–2

jyy.

N. (LL) good luck, blessing: 福祉, 嘉祉, 日祉 used in salutations in letters, like "wish you every happiness."

禮 63B.30–2

lii.

[Abbr. and anc. var. 礼]

N. (1) (Orig.) religious rituals, (later) ceremonial observances in general: 禮儀 *-yir*, 禮法 *-faa* ↓; 禮制 social institutions, set of etiquette; 禮體 forms and ceremonies; 禮俗 *-sur* ↓; 禮兒 ceremonial rules; 禮數 *-shuh*, 禮貌 *-mauh*, 禮節 *-jier*, 禮教 *-jiauh*, 禮路兒 *-luh'l* ↓; 典禮 a formal ceremony; 婚禮 wedding ceremony; 葬禮 burial rites; 喪禮 funeral services; 行禮 hold a ceremony, also to salute; 敬禮 to salute, a salutation; 禮下於人必有所求 when s.o. humbles himself before you, he must have some request to make of you; 禮多人不怪 you won't be blamed for being extra polite. (2) Gifts, presents: 送禮 give presents; 禮物 *-wuh*, 禮品 *-piin* ↓; 禮單 a list of gifts; 禮貨 items on sale in gift shops; 賀禮 wedding presents; 壽禮 birthday presents; 禮尚往來 etiquette requires reciprocity; 禮無不答 all courtesies must be returned; 禮輕意重 a small gift given with sincere wish. (3) Propriety, social customs, see 禮法, 禮俗 *-faa*, *-sur* ↓. (4) A body of social customs and cultural institutions as embodied in Confucianism, see 禮教 *-jiauh* ↓

V.t. Show respect to: 禮賢下士 (of kings, princes, etc.) go out of one's way to enlist the services of the talented and the learned; 禮遇 (以禮遇之) treat (s.o.) with high respect.

禮拜 *liibaih*, (1) v.i., (also 做禮拜) attend a religious service, go to church; (2) n., a week: 上禮拜 last week; 兩三禮拜 two or three weeks; 禮拜日, 禮拜天 Sunday, the day of worship; 禮拜寺 (Islam) mosque; 禮拜堂 a church or chapel.

禮部 *liibuh*, n., the Board of Rites under the monarchy (in charge of education and culture).

禮券 *liichyuahn*, n., gift coupon.

禮法 *lirfaa*, n., ceremonial rites and regulations.

禮服 *liifur*, n., ceremonial or formal dress.

禮教 *liijiauh*, n., Confucianism, the teaching of social order.

禮節 *liijier*, n., ceremonial rules, etiquette.

禮記 *Liijih*, n., *Book of Rites*, one of the Confucian classics (usu. spelled "Liki").

禮金 *liijin*, n., monetary gifts.

禮路兒 *liiluh'l*, n., politeness, etiquette.

禮貌 *liimauh*, n., politeness of manner.

禮砲 *lii-pauh*, n., gun salute.

禮品 *lirpiin*, n., gift.

禮讓 *liirahng*, n., courtesy of manners.

禮數 *liishuh*, n., etiquette, polite behavior.

禮俗 *liisur*, n., social customs and institutions.

禮堂 *liitarng*, n., an assembly hall, auditorium.

禮帖 *liitie*, n., formal invitation card.

禮物 *liiwuh*, n., presents.

禮儀 *liiyir*, n., ceremonials; gifts, etiquette.

祖 63B.30–4

tzuu.

N. (1) An ancestor: 祖父 *-fuh* ↓; 曾祖 great-grandfather; 高祖 great-great-grandfather; 鼻祖 one's earliest known ancestor; 太祖 posthumous title conferred on the founder of a dynasty. (2) A founder, an originator: 祖師 *-shy* ↓. (3) Sacrifice to god of travellers: 祖奠, 祖道, 祖餞 *-diahn*, *-dauh*, *-jiahn* ↓. (4) A surname.

祖輩(兒) *tzuubeih(-beh'l)*, n., ancestors, forefathers.

祖鞭 *tzuu-bian*, phr., vying to push ahead in friendly rivalry (allu. to the story of 劉琨 and 祖逖).

祖妣 *tzur-bii*, n., one's deceased grandmother.

祖產 *tzur-chaan*, n., ancestral estate.

祖傳 *tzuu-chuarn*, adj., handed down from generation to generation.

祖代 *tzuu-daih*, n., ancestors, forbears.

祖道 *tzuu-dauh*, v.i., bid good-bye to departing friend by offering sacrifice to the patron god of travellers.

祖奠 *tzuu-diahn*, n., a sacrifice to the deceased on the eve of his burial rites.

祖父 *tzuufuh*, n., grandfather.
祖國 *tzuuguor*, n., one's fatherland.
祖帳 *tzuujahng*, v.i., hold a sacrifice to the patron god of travellers to bid good-bye to a departing friend.
祖餞 *tzuujiahn*, v.t., give a party in honor of (a departing friend).
祖籍 *tzuujir*, n., the land of one's forefathers.
祖考 *tzurkaau*, n., one's deceased grandfather.
祖母 *tzurmuu*, n., grandmother; 祖母綠 (min.) pure emerald.
祖上 *tzuushahng*, n., remote ancestors.
祖神 *tzuushern*, n., the patron god of travellers.
祖先 *tzuushian*, n., ancestors, forbears, forefathers.
祖述 *tzuu-shuh*, v.t., follow in the ways of (sages, saints).
祖師 *tzuu-shy*, n., (1) founder of a religious sect; (2) the legendary founder of a craft or occupation.
祖送 *tzuu-suhng*, v.t., give a farewell party in honor of (s.o.).
祖宗 *tzuutzung*, n., remote ancestors, forbears.
祖武 *tzurwuu*, phr., be a worthy successor to ancestral greatness ("walking in the footsteps of one's ancestors").
祖業 *tzuuyeh*, n., (1) great achievements of one's ancestors; (2) ancestral estate.
祖遺 *tzuu-yir*, adj., (of property) bequeathed by ancestors.

§ 63B.40 (ネ/口)

祜 63B.40–1

huh.

N. (AC) blessing: 受天之祜 receive the blessings of heaven.

禧 63B.40–1

shi (shii).

N. & adj. Happiness (used in New Year greetings): 恭賀新禧 Happy New Year; 慶禧 to celebrate a happy occasion.

祐 63B.40–1

youh.

V.i. (Of God) to bless, protect (family, people).

§ 63B.41 (ネ/図)

褡 63B.41–2

jah.

[Interch. 蜡]

N. (AC) year-end sacrifice of thanksgiving for good crops.

福 63B.41–3

fur.

N. Blessing, happiness, good luck, prosperity, regarded as corresponding to one's character or destiny: usu. 福氣 *-chih*, 福分 *-fehn*↓; 有福(氣) under a good star; 享福 enjoy oneself or easy way of living; 福厚, 薄 destined, not destined, to enjoy life; 無福承受 do not have the luck to enjoy the good gifts of life; counted among the good things of life: 福祿壽考 prosperity, high position and long life; 福無雙至, 禍不單行 good fortune does not come in pairs, and disasters do not come alone; 福至心靈 when good luck comes, one has good ideas; 五福臨門 the five blessings come to this house; 發福 to grow plump.

V.t. (LL) to bless: 福善禍淫 God blesses the good and punishes the evil.

Adj. (1) Blessed, happy, lucky: 福人 lucky man; 洞天福地 blessed spot, usu. some scenic spot high on mountains or near temples. (2) Things connected with sacrifices: 福酒, 福物 sacrificial wine, offerings. (3) Used in letters in conveying good wishes: 福安, blessed with good health; 福體, 福躬 your bodily health; 福庇 enjoy the blessings of God.

福氣 *furchih*, n., good luck, one's alloted happiness: 沒有這福氣 haven't the good luck; 太太, 你眞福氣 madam, you are a blessed woman, implying that she deserves all the good luck, not just lucky.
福分 *furfehn*, n., one's allotted share of happiness, see *-chih*↑.
福利 *furlih*, n., welfare, fringe benefits: 福利基金 welfare fund; 社會福利 social welfare.
福色 *furseh*, n., deep liver color.
福星 *furshing*, n., lucky star.
福音 *furyin*, n., good news, the Christian Gospel: 福音堂 Christian church of some denominations.

§ 63B.42 (ネ/冈)

禰 63B.42–3

*nii (*mir).*

N. (1) One's deceased father whose tablet is preserved in the ancestral temple; such tablet carried in travel. (2) (**mir*) A surname.

禍 63B.42–4

huoh.

V. Disaster, misfortune, opp. of 福 good fortune: 禍不單行 misfortunes do not come singly; 禍福無門 God's even-handed justice; 旦夕禍福 sudden changes of fortune; (病從口入) 禍從口出 disaster emanates from careless talk; 禍起蕭牆 troubles start inside the house (such as fratricide); 惹禍, 闖禍 provoke or cause trouble; 黃禍 the Yellow Peril; 禍患, 禍害 *-huahn*, *-haih* ↓.

V.t. To bring disaster to: (LL) 禍民, 禍國殃民 bring disaster to the country and its people.

禍 根 *huohgen*, n., root of trouble; seed of future trouble.
禍 害 *huohhaih*, (1) n., disaster, evil; (2) (*-'hai*) v.t., to injure (people, country).
禍 患 *huohhuahn*, n., constant or continuing cause of trouble (flood, famine, banditry).
禍 首 *huohshoou*, n., chief culprit.
禍 水 *huohshueei*, n., (LL) woman compared to flood causing trouble to an individual or ruling dynasty.
禍 始 *huohshyy*, n., see *-gen* ↑.
禍 胎 *huohtai*, n., see *-gen* ↑.

§ 63B.50 (ネ/ㄱ)

祠 63B.50–5

tsyr.

N. (1) Ancestral temple, memorial temple: 宗祠 ditto; 祠堂 *-tarng* ↓; 生祠 memorial temple to a living person. (2) Sacrifices of worship.

V.i. & t. To offer sacrifices.

祠 祝 *tsyrjuh*, v.i. & n., (offer) sacrificial prayer.
祠 堂 *tsyrtarng* (*-'tang*), n., ancestral temple.
祠 尾 *tsyrweei*, n., owl's tail, decoration on roof ridge (usu. wr. 蚩尾, 鴟尾).

禡 63B.50–5

mah.

N. & v.t. Sacrifice to the place on hill where army stops: 禡牙 (MC) sacrifice to army colors before campaign.

§ 63B.70 (ネ/乚)

礼 63B.70–2

lii.

[Pop. and anc. var. of 禮 63B.30]

祧 63B.70–2

tiau.

N. Ancestral hall: 承祧 (in ancestor worship) nephew continues uncle's line if uncle has no son; 兼祧 the same nephew continues both his father's and uncle's lines.

祝 63B.70–4

juh.

N. (1) Officer administering the sacrifices: 廟祝 such officer at ancestral sacrifice. (2) A surname.

V.i. & t. (1) To pray for blessing, to bless: 祝福, 祝壽 *-fur*, *-shouh* ↓; (used in letters) to pray for s.o.'s health: 恭祝, 敬祝, 遙祝, 祝禱 I pray that; 祝辭 *-tsyr* ↓; 慶祝 to celebrate (occasion); 預祝 I pray in anticipation. (2) 祝髮而裸 (AC, of savage tribes) cut their hair and go naked.

祝 福 *juhfur*, v.t., to bless, to invoke blessing: 上帝祝福你們 may God bless you!
祝 嘏 *juhguu*, v.t., (LL, AC) pray for longevity.
祝 賀 *juhheh*, v.t., to congratulate.
祝 祝 *juhjuh*, v.t., make chuck-chuck sound to call chicken; chicken's sounds.
祝 融 *Juhrurng*, n., the god of fire: 祝融爲災 a conflagration.
祝 壽 *juhshouh*, v.i., offer birthday congratulations.
祝 辭 *juhtsyr*, n., the prayer for blessing; text of a felicitation on some occasion.
祝 文 *juhwern*, n., a prayer for blessing.

視 63B.70–4

shyh.

V.i. & t. (1) (LL) to look (modn. 看): 視而不見 look but do not see; 注視 look at closely; 凝視 look steadily, stare at; 正視 face (a fact); 斜視 look askance at; 偷視 peep at; 俯視 look down or over; 近視, 遠視 near-, far-sighted; 透視 see through, also 透視畫 painting in perspective. (2) To regard, consider, treat: 視爲, 視作 regard as (important, best man, a risk); 視 . . 而定 it all depends . . . ; 視如, 視同 treat like (one's own brother, etc.); 視作等閒 regard as light matter; 視財如命 worship money ("like his life"); 視死如歸 take death calmly ("like going home"); 重視, 輕視 regard seriously, despise; regard as important, not important; 鄙視, 藐視 despise; 善視 treat kindly; 仇視, 敵視 be hostile to (person, country). (3) To inspect: 巡視 patrol; 監視 keep (s.o. or his movements) under watch or surveillance; 檢視 inspect (goods, etc.); 視學 *-shyuer* ↓. (4) To take charge: 視事 *-shyh* ↓.

視差 *shyhcha*, n., (astron.) parallax.

視察 *shyhchar*, v.t., to inspect (school, etc.).

視朝 *shyh-chaur*, v.i., (of emperor) attend court, give audience.

視官 *shyhguan*, n., the sense of vision or sight.

視角 *shyhjiaau*, n., (phys.) visual angle.

視徑 *shyhjihng*, n., (視直徑) (astron.) apparent diameter.

視覺 *shyhjyuer*, n., sense of vision: 視覺器 sight organ.

視力 *shyhlih*, n., power of vision: 視力表 instrument for measuring vision.

視能 *shyhnerng*, n., (power or function of) eyesight.

視線 *shyhshiahn*, n., line of vision.

視事 *shyh-shyh*, v.i., to attend to duties (after leave or assuming post).

視學 *shyh-shyuer*, n., formerly, provincial inspector of schools.

視聽 *shyh-ting*, n., (1) what one sees and hears, personal observation; (2) 視聽教育 audio-visual method of education.

視野 *shyh-yee*, n., field of vision.

祀 63B·70-5

syh.

N. (1) (AC, in Shang Dyn.) a year. (2) V.t. & n., sacrifice to the gods or ancestor; 祀典 ceremony of sacrifices.

§ 63B.71 (礻/乚)

祇 63B.71-9

chir (**jy*).

N. (1) An earthly god, opp. 神 god in heaven: 上下神祇 (to) all the gods of heaven and earth. (2) (AC) peace and happiness; (in letter formula, interch. 祺) your peace and happiness.

Adv. (1) Greatly: 祇悔 greatly repent. (2) (**jy*) (LL) only, but, as var. of 只 *jyy*: 祇有 there is only; 祇是 is only, but, it's; 祇要 you need only to. (3) Respectfully: 祇遵, 祇仰 respectfully obey, request.

祗 63B.71-9

jy.

Adv. (LL) Respectfully (＝敬, used in letters): 祗奉, 祗承 respectfully received; 祗謝 respectfully thank; 祗遵 respectfully obey, etc.

禨 63B.71-9

ji.

N. Luck, good fortune.

禨祥 *jishiarng*, v.i. & n., pray (prayer) to the gods for blessing.

§ 63B.72 (礻/心)

祕 63B.72-6

mih (also *bih*).

[More common var. 秘; related 密]

N. A surname.

Adj. Secret, mysterious, abstruse: 祕密 *-mih* ↓; 祕而不宣 kept secret; 神祕莫測 mysterious; 祕籍 abstruse or esoteric treatises.

Adv. Secretly: 祕傳, 祕授 secretly handed down; 祕製 made from secret formulas.

祕方 *mih-fang*, n., secret formula (medicine).

祕訣 *mih-juer*, n., secret (of success, etc.).

祕密 *mihmih*, n., secret: 祕密文件 secret, classified documents; 祕密會議 secret conference; 祕密投票 secret ballot; adv., secretly; 祕密結社 secret society.

祕書 *mihshu*, n., secretary, private or official: 祕書長 *--jaang*, n., secretary-general; 私人祕書 personal secretary; 執行祕書 executive secretary; 機要祕書 confidential secretary; 祕書處 secretariat.

祕史 *mihshyy*, n., inside story.

祕聞 *mih-wern*, n., exclusively intimate news.

§ 63B.80 (礻/八)

禛 63B.80-1

jen.

Adj. (AC) blessed.

祺 禎 禊 祆 祅 祓 祛 襻 褥 襉 襴

祺 63B.80–2

chir.

N. Good luck, blessing: (used chiefly in greeting formula in letters) 文祺 greetings for literary men; 祺祥, 祺安, 祺福 generally, the best luck.

Adj. 祺然 (LL) serene, poised.

禎 63B.80–2

jen (also *jeng*).

Adj. Auspicious: 禎祥 a good omen.

§ 63B.81 (礻/人)

禊 63B.81–1

shih.

N. Anc. festival in spring and autumn held on water banks to drink (禊飲) and cleanse away the evil influences.

祆 63B.81–3

shian.

[Dist. 祅 (pr. *yau*) evil spirit]

祆教 *shianjiauh*, n., Zoroastrianism.

祅 63B.81–9

yau.

N. Evil spirit.

§ 63B.82 (礻/乂)

祓 63B.82–1

fur.

V.t. To cleanse away, to wash away evil influence.

祓除 *furchur*, v.t., to abolish, cleanse away.

祓禊 *furshih*, n., (AC) ceremony of washing away evil influence near river.

§ 63B.93 (礻/く)

祛 63B.93–1

chyu.

V.t. To drive off (cold), to exorcise (evil influence, etc.): 祛邪 exorcise evil spirits; 祛災 ward off disaster; 祛疑 to dispel doubts; 祛痰 (medicine to) relieve bronchial inflammation; 祛風去濕 (Chin. med.) relieve certain inflammations (arthritis, etc.); 祛退 reduce (fever); 祛散 disperse colds, congestions in patient's system.

祛祛 *chyuchyu*, adj., (AC) in great formation.

SECTION 63C

§ 63C.00 (礻/丨)

襻 63C.00–1

pahn.

N. Knot and loop in Chin. cloth button.

褥 63C.00–5

ruh.

N. A mattress, a cushion: 褥子 bedding; 牀褥 ditto; 被褥 quilt and blanket; 褥單(兒)(子) bed sheets; 褥套 quilt cover; 褥草 hay used as bedding (cf. "hit the hay").

襉 63C.00–5

jiaan (*jiahn*).

N. Pleats: 打襉 make pleats in (dress, skirt).

襴 63C.00–5

larn.

N. (AC) A gown, combination of blouse and skirt.

襴裙 *larnchyurn*, n., (AC) a supporter for the stomach.

襴衫 *larnshan*, n., (AC) a scholar's dress.

§ 63C.01 (衤/小)

袜 63C.01-1

wah (**moh*).
[Var. of 韈 63C.71]

袜肚 **mohduh*, n., formerly, woman's girdle, with pocket.
袜腹 **mohfuh*, n., see *-shyung*↓.
袜胸 **mohshyung*, n., formerly, woman's undervest, to keep breasts flat (also wr. 抹胸).

襟 63C.01-1

jin.

N. (1) Part of dress covering chest (interch. 衿 63C.32): 對襟 a coat that fastens down the front; 大襟, 小襟 (or 裏襟) the large, inner, lapel of a Chin. coat; 襟帶 a sash. (2) A brother-in-law: 連襟, 襟兄弟 brothers-in-law whose wives are sisters; 襟兄 *-shyung*, 襟弟 *-dih*↓. (3) Mental outlook: 襟懷 *-huair*, 襟期 *-chir*, 襟度 *-duh*↓; 胸襟 one's general attitude, temperament (lit., "chest") (broad-minded, etc.).

襟期 *jin-chir*, n., aspirations, life's ambition.
襟弟 *jindih*, n., brother-in-law who has married a younger sister of one's wife.
襟度 *jinduh*, n., attitude of person: 襟度寬宏 (狹小) broad-, narrow-minded.
襟懷 *jinhuair*, n., attitude of mind: 襟懷寬大(or 狹小) generous, magnanimous, charitable, tolerant (or miserly, narrow-minded, mean, revengeful, intolerant).
襟兄 *jinshyung*, n., brother-in-law who has married an elder sister of one's wife.

裸 63C.01-4

luoo.
[AC var. 倮, 躶, 臝]

Adj. Nude, bare, uncovered: 裸體 *-tii*↓; 裸跣 naked and barefooted; 赤裸裸的 completely naked; 裸裎 (AC) naked, undressed; 裸線 exposed wire; 裸子植物 plant with exposed seed, like pine, *gymnospermae*; 裸葬 naked burial.

裸花 *luoohua*, n., (bot.) flower without petals or calyx.
裸麥 *luoomaih*, n., a kind of barley (bearing seeds without spikes).
裸體 *luortii*, adj., naked: 裸體運動 nudist movement; 裸體營 nudist colony.

祼 63C.01-9

baau.
[Var. of 緥]

N. See 襁祼 63C.93.

襍 63C.01-9

tzar.
[Anc. var. of 雜 60S.11]

§ 63C.02 (衤/⺊)

裱 63C.02-1

biaau.

N. (AC) Neckerchief, neckcloth.

V.t. To mount (picture), see 裱褙 *-beih*↓.

裱褙 *biaaubeih*, v.t. & n., mount, mounting (for Chin. scrolls).
裱畫舖 *biaauhuapuh*, n., shop for mounting Chin. paintings.
裱糊 *biaauhur*, v.t., paste up (windows, wallpaper, etc.).

襛 63C.02-2

nurng.

Adj. (AC) (of dress) heavy; (of color) resplendent: 襛華 (AC) gorgeous.

襮 63C.02-4

bor.

V.t. Expose, bare; expose to the sun.

N. (Obs.) collar.

裉 63C.02-5

kehn.

N. Armpit (of clothing).

§ 63C.10 (衤/十)

褘 63C.10-2

huei.

N. (AC) ceremonial robe of empress.

褲 63C.10–6

kuh.

[Common var. of 袴 63C.50]

N. (*-tz*) Pants, trousers: 長褲 pants; 短褲 shorts; 三角褲 pantie, bikini; 卡其褲 khaki trousers; 褲袋 trouser pockets; 熱褲 hot pants.

褲叉兒 *kuhchaa'l*, n., underpants.
褲帶 *kuhdaih*, n., trousers belt.
褲襠 *kuhdang*, n., seat of trousers.
褲脚(兒)(子) *kuhjiaau('l)('tz)*, n., ends of trousers.
褲腿(兒)(子) *kuhtueei(-tuee'l)('tz)*, n., (1) the trouser-legs; (2) formerly, ankle cover for women with bound feet.
褲腰 *kahyau*, n., top of trousers; 褲腰帶 trousers belt or girdle.

褌 63C.10–6

kun.

N. (LL) trousers: 褌襠 (*-dang*) seat of pants.

裨 63C.10–9

bih (**pir*).

N. (1) Benefit: 有裨於學業, 公共秩序 is of help to school studies, to public order; see 裨益 *-yi* ↓. (2) (**pir*) An anc. surname.

Adj. Secondary, small, see 裨販, 裨將 *-fahn, -jiahng* ↓.

裨補 *bihbuu*, n., benefit, help.
裨販 *bihfahn*, n., small pedlar.
裨將 *bihjiahng*, n., (MC) minor or assistant commander.
裨益 *bihyi*, n., benefit: 有裨益於人類 is of service to mankind.

§ 63C.11 (衤/土)

裎 63C.11–4

cherng.

Adj. 裸裎 (AC) naked.

裡 63C.11–4

lii.

[Pop. of 裏 60.02]

衽 63C.11–9

rehn.

N. (1) The lapel of a coat next to and hidden beneath the row of buttons: 右衽 to button coat on the right-hand side; 左衽 button it on the left-hand side, as the barbarians do; 斂衽 (of a man or woman) formerly, salute by gathering up the folds of the coat before bowing. (2) The sleeves of a coat. (3) A sleeping mat: 衽席 a place where one sleeps.

V.t. To sleep: 衽金革 lie down to sleep fully armed.

§ 63C.22 (衤/丨)

褂 63C.22–1

guah.

[Var. 袿]

N. A long gown, a jacket worn over gown: 褂子 an outer garment; 藍布大褂 an indigo long gown; 馬褂 a jacket; 袍褂 the full dress with long gown and jacket.

褯 63C.22–6

jieh.

N. Swaddling clothes: 褯子 diapers.

§ 63C.30 (衤/一)

袒 63C.30–4

taan.

[Var. 襢]

V.t. To bare, leave naked: 袒裼裸裎 (AC) stand completely naked; 左袒 ancient custom of leaving left arm uncovered, hence 左袒, 偏袒 to be partial to one side, see 袒庇 *-bih* ↓.

袒庇 *taanbih*, v.t., be partial to.
袒護 *taanhuh*, v.t., ditto.
袒露 *taanluh*, v.t., to expose.
袒免 *taanwehn*, phr., (AC) anc. funeral custom of baring right shoulder and wrapping hair up inside turban.

襤 63C.30–5

larn.

N. Ragged garments.

襤褸 *larnlyuu*, adj., (of clothes) tattered, torn and ragged, shabby (also 襤縷, 藍縷).

§63C.32 (ネ/フ)

衿 63C.32–8

jin.

N. The lapel of coat: 青衿 (AC) scholar's robe with black collar.

§63C.40 (ネ/ロ)

褡 63C.40–2

da.

褡包 *da'bau*, n., waist band outside jacket, used to carry things.

褡連(兒) *da'lian(-lia'l)*, n., small band with pocket for holding things (money, etc.).

裙 63C.40–5

chyurn.

N. (1) (*-tz*, *-'l*) Skirt, petticoat: 襯裙 petticoat; 圍裙 apron; 迷你裙 miniskirt. (2) The fringe of turtle meat.

裙釵 *chyurnchai*, n., womenfolks: 裙釵政治 rule by petticoats.

裙帶 *chyurndaih*, n., (1) skirt and girdle; (2) having to do with wife's relations or influence: 裙帶關係 wife's relationships; 裙帶官 a man who owes his official position to wife's influence; 裙帶風 the rule of women.

裙帶菜 *chyurndaih tsaih*, n., (bot.) a plant of long leaves that grows on seaside, *Ulopteryx pinnatifida.*

裾 63C.40–5

jyu.

N. The large inner flap of Chin. dress; its lower border.

裕 63C.40–8

yuh.

Adj. (1) Ample, well-provided: 豐裕, 富裕 rich, wealthy; 充裕, 裕如 abundant, well stocked. (2) Lenient: 寬裕.

V.t. (LL) to enrich: 裕國裕民 "to enrich the state and the people" —slogan of tax collectors.

袷 63C.40–8

jiar.

N. (1) A lined garment. (2) (**jier*) (AC) a kind of collar.

襜 63C.40–9

chan.

N. (AC) the flap in Chin. jacket, covering the right chest.

§63C.41 (ネ/図)

褚 63C.41–1

chuu.

N. (1) (AC) a bag, satchel; 褚幕 pall, shroud. (2) A surname.

V.t. (AC) to pad with cotton wool.

袖 63C.41–2

shiouh.

N. (*-tz*, *'l*) Sleeves: 馬蹄袖 folded back sleeve, oft. seen on stage in military uniform; 長袖 long sleeves; 短袖, 半袖 short-sleeved, half sleeves; 無袖 sleeveless; 長袖善舞 long sleeves help in (Chin.) dancing; 多財善賈 plenty of capital makes it easy to trade.

V.t. To carry in sleeve: 袖刃 carry dagger concealed in sleeve; 袖手 *-shoou* ↓.

袖搭 *shiouhda*, n., section in cloth to be cut into sleeves.

袖章 *shiouhjang*, n., insignia worn on sleeve, chevron.

袖珍 *shiouhjen*, adj., pocket-sized, pocket (edition, dictionary): 袖珍戰艦 German pocket battleship built after Versailles.

袖箭 *shiouhjiahn*, n., formerly, arrow worked by spring concealed in sleeve.

袖口 *shiouhkoou*, n., cuff of sleeve; 袖口鈕 cuff links; 袖口兒裏頭説罷 let's talk in extreme privacy.

袖扣 *shiouhkouh*, n., sleeve button.

袖手 *shiouh-shoou*, phr., 袖手旁觀 look on with folded arms, hands in sleeves—not willing to help.

袖套 *shiouhtauh*, n., oversleeve, detachable cover for sleeve.

袖頭兒 *shiouhtour'l*, n., see *-koou*↑.

袖筒兒 *shiouhtuung'l*, n., the lower-arm part of sleeve.

襠 63C.41-2

dang.

N. Seat of pants: 褲襠 the hip part of trousers.

衵 63C.41-4

nih.

N. (AC) woman's undergarment: 衵服.

裀 63C.41-4

yin.

N. (1) (AC) undergarment. (2) U. f. 茵 coverlet, 20A.41.

褶 63C.41-5

jer.

N. A pleat in skirts: 百褶裙 pleated skirt; 褶曲 a geological fold.

§63C.42 (衤/図)

補 63C.42-1

buu.

V.t. (1) To repair, restore to good condition: oft. 補一補 have it repaired; 補衣, 襪, 鞋 repair or mend clothing, stockings, shoes; 補牙 fix up teeth by repairing cavities, etc.; 補鍋, 路 tinker pans, repair roads; 補漏 stop up holes in jars, also addenda in texts; 補天之力 (myth allu.) power to restore cracks in the sky (of 女媧), great strength; oft. 修補, 塡補, 打補 mend clothing. (2) Add, supplement, fill up deficiencies: often 補上, 補付, 賠補 pay or make up deficiencies in payment; 補假 take deferred holidays; 添補衣服 make more clothing; 吃補, 吃補藥 take tonic; 補肝, 心, 肺, 骨, 血 (of tonics) help nourish the liver, heart, lungs, bones, blood; 補元氣 help restore vitality. (3) Be of help to: 補助費用 help to defray expenses; 無補於事, 無補大局 be of no help, do not help matters; 不無小補 may be a little help. (4) Make amends, reparations, make up for, reform: 補課 make up for missed classes in school; 補過 make amends for mistakes; 將功補過(罪) lenient consideration for person's mistakes in view of past or future achievements; 補償, 抵補, 賠補 make reparations for damages or deficits in accounts; 勤能補拙 make up for lack of natural talent by hard work.

補白 *buubair*, n., material for filling up leftover space in magazines, etc., also (court.) of one's own humble contribution to journals.

補壁 *buu-bih*, v.i., (court.) serve to cover up a wall, (of one's own scrolls).

補償 *buncharng*, v.t. & n., compensate, -tion.

補情(兒) *buu-chirng* (*-chir'l*), v.i., show gratitude by gifts.

補充 *buuchung*, v.t. & n., add to (previous remarks, provision for expenses); supplement; 補充教材 supplementary text.

補缺 *buu-chyue*, v.t., to fill up vacant post.

補窮的 *buu-chyurng'de*, n., sewing woman who makes living by mending clothes.

補定語 *buudihng-yuu*, n., (gram.) complement.

補靪(釘) *buu'ding*, n., (coll.) as in 打補釘 mend shoes, clothes, etc.

補縫 *buuferng*, v.i. & t., (1) sew up; (2) *buufehng*, fill up cracks.

補缸的 *buu-gang'de*, n., mender of earthenware.

補骨脂 *bur-guu-jy*, n., (bot.) *Psoralea corylifolia*, medicinal herb for strengthening bones.

補角 *burjiaau*, n., (math.) supplement of an angle (to make up 180°).

補給 *burjii*, n., supplementary rations; 補給線 (mil.) supply route.

補景 *burjiing*, n., (of painting) background details.

補救 *buujiouh*, v.t., rescue from danger; rectify error.

補助 *buujuh*, n. & v.t., help, supply needs; give grants to.

補綴 *buujuoh*, v.t., mend, take up loose ends and make repair; edit or collect odd pieces to make a book.

補苴 *buujyu*, v.t., (LL) repair, restore.

補考 *burkaau*, n. & v.i., (take) examination after missing or failing.

補漏洞 *bur-louhdung*, v.i., to stop a leak, (fig.) to implement omission and errors.

補鞋的 *buu-shier'de*, n., shoe repair man or shop.

補習 *buushir*, v.i. & n., (take) supplementary classes: 惡性補習 extra coaching lessons to help pass examinations, which injure and upset students' health.

補足 *buutzur*, v.t., supply what is lacking (statement, expense).

補碗的 *bur-waan'de*, n., porcelain mender.

補藥 *buuyauh*, n., tonic.

補遺 *buuyir*, n., supplement oft. edited to supply missing material in collected works or main work; addendum.

裉 63C.42-2

kehn.

N. The armpit of clothing (var. of 裉).

褙 63C.42-2

beih.

N. & v.t. See 裱▵褙 63C.02.

襦 63C.42-3

rur.

N. (1) A jacket: 短襦 a short jacket; 襦褲 jacket and trousers. (2) Children's bib. (3) Fine silk.

褊 63C.42-6

biaan.

Adj. Small in area, narrow, crowded in: 褊小 small in territory.

褊淺 *biarnchiaan*, adj., narrow-minded, superficial.
褊急 *biaanjir*, adj., nervous, impatient.
褊狹 *biaanshiar*, adj., narrow-minded; narrow in area.

褵 63C.42-6

lir.

[Var. of 縭 93B.42]

衲 63C.42-8

nah.

N. (1) A Buddhist cassock. (2) A monk: 老衲 an old monk (usu. in self-reference).

V.t. (1) (Of clothes) mend, patch up: 百衲本 edition consisting of reprint of assorted anc. books. (2) Sew: 衲鞋底 to sew cloth soles of shoes.

§ 63C.50 (衤/冂)

袴 63C.50-1

kuh.

N. See common var. 褲 63C.10.

裼 63C.50-4

shir.

N. (AC) top jacket.

V.i. Go naked, see 袒▵裼 63C.30.

褐 63C.50-4

her.

N. (AC) coarse cloth: 衣褐 wear rough cloth; 褐夫 (AC) poor people.

Adj. Dark, dull brown: 茶褐色 "tea brown" color.

褐煤 *hermeir*, n., brown coal, lignite.
褐炭 *hertahn*, n., ditto.
褐鐵礦 *hertiee kuahng*, n., limonite.
褐藻 *hertzaau*, n., (bot.) a kind of seaweed.

褟 63C.50-4

ta.

N. (1) Lace hemming: 褟縧子 *tatautz*, such hemming. (2) 汗褟兒 undershirt.

初 63C.50-5

chu.

N. Beginning: 年初 (歲初), 月初 beginning of year, month; 起初, 最初 at the beginning; 太初 primordial beginnings of universe; 當初 in those days; 人之初 when man was first born.

Adj. (1) Added to first ten days of each month: 初一, 初二, 初三 the first, second, third day of lunar month; 初學, 初小, 初中 *-shyuer*, *-shiaau*, *-jung*↓. (2) First: 初稿 first draft; 初版 first edition or printing; 初步 first steps; 初期 first period; 初次 first time; 初試 first attempt, preliminary test; 初度 first experience.

Adv. First, just: 初出爐 just out of the oven; 初嘗新味 have a first taste of novelty; 初出茅廬 just having first experience in life after graduation; 初婚 newly married; 初生 just born, also first-born; 初晴 sky has just cleared.

初等 *chudeeng*, n., elementary grade: 初等小學 elementary school; 初等中學 junior high school (contracted 初中).
初犯 *chu-fahn*, n., first offender.
初伏 *chu-fur*[1], n., the first ten of the thirty days of hottest summer (三伏).

初服 *chu-fur*², n., simple dress (before person becomes official): 返初服 live life of common people, after being official.
初間 *chu-jian*, adv., (MC) at first.
初交 *chu-jiau*, n., new friend.
初階 *chu-jie*, n., first steps; first book of introduction (to subject).
初中 *chujung*, n., see *-deeng*↑.
初志 *chu-jyh*, n., original ambition (of youth).
初眠 *chu-miarn*, n., "first sleep" of new-born silkworm.
初民 *chu-mirn*, n., primitive people.
初日 *chu-ryh*, n., the morning sun.
初賽 *chu-saih*, n., preliminary contest.
初審 *chu-sheen*, n., first trial; first official review.
初小 *chushiaau*, n., see *-deeng*↑.
初獻 *chu-shiahn*, n., first offering of wine, the first libation in sacrifices.
初心 *chu-shin*, n., one's original intention.
初學 *chushyuer*, n., a beginning student; beginning studies; 初學者 beginner, novice.
初旬 *chu-shyurn*, n., the first ten days of month.
初頭 *chutour*, (1) n., beginning; (2) adv., at the beginning.
初祖 *chu-tzuu*, n., (Budd.) first founder of sect.
初夜 *chu-yeh*, n., (1) beginning of the night; (2) the wedding night; 初夜權 right of medieval feudal lord to sleep with vassal's bride on wedding night.
初願 *chu-yuahn*, n., one's original wish.
初月 *chu-yueh*, n., the new moon.

§ 63C.70 (衤/乚)

裩 63C.70-4

kun.
[Var. 褌 63C.10]

襬 63C.70-4

baai.

N. Hem of long grown: 下襬.

襯 63C.70-6

chehn.

N. (1) Underclothing: 襯衣, 襯衫 *-yi, -shan*↓. (2) ('*l*) Lining: 領襯兒, 袖襯兒 collar lining, sleeve lining.

V.t. (1) To set off contrast: 陪襯 to enhance honor, value, gaiety as guest at party, to serve as supporting character; 反襯 to serve for contrasting effect; 襯托 *-tuo*↓. (2) To help: 幫襯 (Cantonese dial.) (of buyer) patronize, help, assist in minor role: 襯鋪兒, 襯施 *-pu'l, -shy*↓.

襯布 *chehnbuh*, n., underlining.
襯錢 *chehn'chian*, n., (Budd.) gifts to the temple, see *-shy*↓.
襯裙 *chehnchyurn*, n., petticoat.
襯紙 *chehnjyy*, n., inserted paper (between pages); paper lining in clothing.
襯褲 *chehnkuh*, n., panties.
襯兒 *che'l*, n., ditto.
襯裏(兒) *chehnlii(-liee'l)*, n., lining.
襯綿 *chehnmiarn*, n., quilting, cotton padding.
襯鋪兒 *chehnpu'l*, n., padding for packing cases.
襯衫 *chehnshan*, n., shirt; undervest.
襯施 *chehnshy*, n., (Budd.) gifts to temple.
襯托 *chehntuo*, v.i., to serve for contrast (colors in painting, characters in novel).
襯字 *chehntzyh*, n., inserted words outside melodic form prescribed in a *tsyr* (宋詞) poem.
襯衣 *chehnyi*, n., underclothing.

褫 63C.70-9

chyy.

V.t. To strip off (clothing, rank, office).

褫奪 *chyyduor*, v.t., to deprive (person) of (s.t.): 褫奪公權 deprive (person) of citizen's rights.
褫革 *chyyger*, v.t., to dismiss, expel.
褫職 *chyy-jyr*, v.i., deprive of office.

袍 63C.70-9

paur.

N. Long gown, robe; military cloak: usu. 袍子 *-tz*; 長袍 full-length gown; 旗袍 modern woman's gown; 同袍 comrade in arms; 黃袍 emperor's yellow gown, sometimes symbolic.

袍哥 *paurge*, n., (dial.) member of secret society in Szechuan.
袍褂 *paurguah*, n., formal costume in Manchu court; 長衫馬褂 modn. Chin. gown and jacket.
袍笏 *paurhuh*, n., anc. costume at imperial audience (笏 memorial tablet): 袍笏登場 phr., (contempt. of officials) taking position of power, as in a dress rehearsal.
袍仗 *paurjahng*, n., military dress.
袍澤 *paurtzer*, n., comrade in arms (term of friendship).

褦 63C.70-9

naih (**le*).

褦襶 *naihdaih*, (1) n., a summer hat; (2) adj., stupid and dull; (of a person's appearance) unkempt, slovenly (also *le'de); 褦襶兵 *ledebing, n., a slovenly-dressed person.

§ 63C.71 (衤/弋)

襪 63C.71-2

wah.

[Var. 韈]

N. (*-tz*) Socks, stockings: 絲襪 silk stockings; 玻璃絲襪, 尼龍絲襪 nylon stockings; 毛襪 woolen socks; 布襪 formerly, cloth stockings; usu. 鞋襪 shoes and socks.

衹 63C.71-9

chir.

[Dist. 祇]

N. (1) A monk's cassock. (2) U. f. 衹 63B.71, but, only.

§ 63C.81 (衤/人)

裌 63C.81-1

jiar.

N. A lined garment (also 袷 63C.40).

襆 63C.81-2

pur.

N. Turban; a wrap: 襆被而出 (AC) come out in a wrap.

裣 63C.81-8

liahn.

N. 裣衽 var. of 斂⁴衽 81S.82.

袄 63C.81-9

aau.

[Pop. of 襖 63C.81↓]

袂 63C.81-9

meih.

N. (LL) sleeves: 分袂 to part among friends; 分袂以來 since friend's departure; 聯袂, 把袂 hold hands (lit., sleeves), reunite among friends.

袱 63C.81-9

fur.

N. 包袱 cloth scarf used as wrap.

襖 63C.81-9

aau.

[Pop. 袄]

N. A jacket: 夾襖 lined jacket; 棉襖 quilted jacket; 皮襖 fur jacket; 短襖 jacket.

§ 63C.82 (衤/乂)

被 63C.82-2

beih (in certain AC phrr. var. of 披 *pi*).

N. Quilted bedding, quilt: 棉被 cotton quilt, see 被服, 被蓋, 被單, 被套 -*'fu, -gaih, -dan, -tauh*↓.

V.t. To cover, spread: 澤被天下 benefits spread to all people; 被褐懷玉 phr., (AC) dress poorly and be rich spiritually (褐 poor man's dress); 被 (*pi*) 堅執銳 (=披堅) phr., well armed with armor and weapons.

Aux. vb. Equiv. "be" in passive voice: 被人聽見 be heard, overheard by others; 被選 be elected; 被人謀害, 侮辱, 推崇 be murdered, humiliated, worshipped by others; 被他拿走 was taken away by him; 權利被剝奪 was deprived of his rights, etc.; 被辱, 被害, 被累, 被欺, etc., be humiliated, murdered, implicated, cheated, etc.; except where clearly desirable to indicate recipient of action (elect, deprive, insult etc.), the passive voice does not require 被: 錢用完 (=錢被用完), 房子燒掉, 門關上 money is spent, house is burned down, door is closed (when n. is followed by v.t.).

被乘數 *beihcherng-shuh*, n., (math.) the factor to be multiplied, the multiplicand.

被除數 *beihchur-shuh*, n., (math.) the factor to be divided, dividend.

被搭子 *beihdatz*, n., bed sack.

被單 *beihdan*, n., bed sheet.

被動 *beihduhng*, adj., passive (contrast 主動 active, taking initiative).

被服 *beih'fu*, n., bedding: 被服

儒行 *-fur-rurshihng*, phr., (AC) keep Confucian conduct every moment (like personal clothing).

被覆線 *beihfuh-shiahn*, n., insulated wire.

被蓋 *beihgaih*, n., bedspread.

被告 *beihgauh*, n., the accused; defendant (opp. to 原告 plaintiff).

被酒 *beih-jioou*, adj., drunk.

被褥 *beihruh*, n., bedding and mattress, gen. term for beddings (一床被褥).

被選權 *beihshyuaan-chyuarn*, n., the right to be elected.

被套 *beihtauh*, n., bed sack.

被窩 *beihwo*, n., warm inside space of quilts: 在被窩裏 well wrapped up in bed.

衩 63C.82-3

chah.

N. (Tailoring) split on sides of gowns: 開衩 make a sidesplit.

裰 63C.82-3

duor.

V.t. To mend (clothing): 補裰; 直裰 cassock, gown of scholars or monks with girdle and low collar, also called 道袍.

襏 63C.82-3

bor.

襏襫 *borshyh*, n., (MC) farmer's raincoat; workman's jacket.

複 63C.82-9

fuh.

Adj. (1) Compound, complex, opp. simple: 複的衣服 dress with lining; 繁複 complicated; 複雜 *-tzar*↓. (2) Repeated, double: sometimes used for 覆 in 複選 second election; 複考, 複試 second examinations; 複審 appeal trial, a second examination for approval, see 覆 31.82; 複決 to cast a second vote.

複比 *fuhbii*, n., (algebra) compound proportion.

複分數 *fuh fenshuh*, n., (math.) compound fraction.

複合 *fuhher*, adj., compound; 複合物(品) *--wuh (piin)*, n., a compound; 複合詞 *--tsyr*, n., compound word.

複記法 *fuhjih faa*, n., double entry system.

複製品 *fuhjypiin*, n., duplicates, copy work.

複決權 *fuhjyuer*, n., right of referendum.

複利 *fuhlih*, n., compound interest.

複名數 *fuhmirngshuh*, n., (algebra) compound numbers.

複寫機 *fuhshieeiji*, n., duplicator, mineograph; 複寫紙 *--jyy*, n., carbon paper.

複姓 *fuhshihng*, n., compound (bisyllabic) surname.

複詞 *fuhtsyr*, n., compound word.

複雜 *fuhtzar*, adj., complicated, mixed (society, task, etc.).

複眼 *fuhyaan*, n., compound eyes (like those of flies).

複葉 *fuhyeh*, n., (bot.) compound leaf.

複印 *fuhyihn*, v.t., to make duplicate; 複印機 duplicator.

複元音 *fuh yuarnyin*, n., diphthong, also called 複韻 *-yuhn*.

§ 63C.83 (衤/一)

褳 63C.83-1

liarn.

N. See 褡△褳 63C.40.

褪 63C.83-5

tuhn.

V.i. & t. (1) To take off clothes. (2) To drop off (skin, hair): 花瓣褪了 the petals have fallen off. (3) To fade, see 褪色 *-seh*↓. (4) To shirk, fall behind: 褪頭縮腦 slink away; 褪後趨前 to rush forward and back to show anxiety to serve.

褪色 *tuhnseh*, v.i., fade in color.

褪手 *tuhnshoou*, v.i., to put hands inside sleeves.

褪套兒 *tuhntauh'l*, v.i., (of knots) loosen, slip; shirk off responsibility.

§ 63C.91 (衤/ノ)

袗 63C.91-8

jeen.

N. (AC) unlined jacket.

衫 63C.91-9

shan.

N. (*-tz*, *'l*) Jacket, gown, shirt: 長衫 long gown; 短衫 jacket, pajamas; 襯衫 shirt; 汗衫 inner vest; 運動衫 sport jacket; 毛線衫 knitted sweater; 衛生衫 knitted undervest; 衣衫 dress in gen.

衫子 *shantz*, n., (1) anc. woman's dress; (2) (Chin. opera) the role of a young woman (=青衣).

祛 褸 襁 扆 戽 雇 扉 啓 肩

§ 63C.93 (衤/く)

祛 63C.93-1

chyu.

N. (AC) end of sleeve.

V.t. (AC) hold up one's sleeves: 祛衣請受業 lift up one's arms in salutation and ask to be received as disciple.

褸 63C.93-2

lyuu.

Adj. See 襤△褸 63C.30.

襁 63C.93-5

chiaang.

N. & v.t. (To carry baby on back in) swaddling clothes: 襁負 to carry on back.

襁褓 *chiarngbaau*, n., swaddling clothes; 在襁褓中 during infancy.

襁抱 *chiaangbauh*, n., infancy.

SECTION 63D

§ 63D.02 (戶/⺊)

扆 63D.02-6

yii.

N. (1) (AC) the throne. (2) Door screen painted with a battle-axe.

§ 63D.10 (戶/十)

戽 63D.10-1

huh.

N. A bucket with rope for baling (bailing) water (for irrigation).

V.t. 戽水 to bale water (to irrigate).

§ 63D.11 (戶/土)

雇 63D.11-9

guh.

[Var. of 僱 91A.11]

雇員 *guhyuarn*, n., employee, clerk (usu. wr. 僱員).

雇傭 *guhyurng*, n. & v.i., hire of services.

§ 63D.22 (戶/丨)

扉 63D.22-2

fei.

N. Door panel: 打開你的心扉 open your heart.

§ 63D.40 (戶/口)

啓 63D.40-9

chii.

[Var. of 啟 63S.82, 啓]

§ 63D.42 (戶/冈)

肩 63D.42-4

jian.

N. The shoulder: 雙肩 the shoulders; 肩膀 *-baang*↓; 肩膀兒寬 have large circles of friends; 肩摩轂擊 overcrowded with people and traffic; 肩頭 *-tour*, 肩胛 *-jiaa*↓; 一肩擔載 assume full responsibility; 肩章 *-jang*, 肩帶 *-daih*↓; 並肩 shoulder to shoulder; 比肩 ditto; 鐵肩擔道義 be a champion of righteousness and justice.

V.t. (Lit. & fig.) to shoulder (responsibility), take on the shoulders: 肩負 *-fuh*, 肩荷 *-heh*↓; 肩挑 carry on the shoulder; 肩輿 *-yur*↓; 肩鎗 carry arms.

亅	小	⺊	十	土	ナ	廾	㇄	丨	一	丅	フ	口	囚	冈	㇕	厂	尸	亠	广	宀	丶	乚	七	心	八	人	乂	乛	丆	丿	𠂉	く
00	01	02	10	11	12	20	21	22	30	31	32	40	41	42	50	51	52	60	61	62	63	70	71	72	80	81	82	83	90	91	92	93

肩膀 *jianbaang*, n., the shoulders: 有肩膀 willing to shoulder responsibilities.
肩帶 *jian-daih*, n., a shoulder belt.
肩負 *jianfuh*, v.t., assume responsibility for, carry (a burden).
肩荷 *jianheh*, v.t., (lit. & fig.) carry on the shoulder.
肩章 *jianjang*, n., an epaulet.
肩胛 *jianjiaa*, n., the shoulder blade.
肩頭 *jiantour*, n., the shoulders.
肩輿 *jianyur*, n., a sedan chair, palanquin.

扁 63D.42–4

biaan (**pian*).

N. (1) Hall name or shop name over door, var. of 匾; 扁額 such inscription. (2) (**pian*) An anc. surname.

Adj. Flat: 壓扁了 crushed flat; 扁嘴, 扁鼻子 flat mouth (bill), snub nose.

扁柏 *biarnbaai*, n., (bot.) *Chamaecyparis obutosa*, a flat-leafed cypress.
扁擔 *biaandan*, n., carrying pole, with flat face resting on shoulders.
扁豆 *biaandouh*, n., a kind of large, flat bean, *Dolichos lablab*.
扁舟 **pianjou*, n., a skiff.
扁食 *biaan'sh*, n., a kind of Chin. ravioli or meat dumpling.
扁塌臉 *biaanta-liaan*, n., flat face.
扁桃 *biaantaur*, n., flat peach; 扁桃腺 --*shiahn*, tonsil; 扁桃腺炎 tonsillitis.
扁頭螺絲 *biaantour luor'sy*, n., thumbscrew.
扁蟲 *biaantsurng*, n., tapeworm; also an insect found near elms.
扁嘴鉗 *biarntzueei-chiarn*, n., flat-nosed pliers.

扃 63D.42–4

jyung (*jyuung*).

N. (1) A wooden bar for bolting door: 扃關 -*guan*↓. (2) A door.

V.t. To close, shut.

扃關 *jyungguan*, n., a door bolt.
扃鍵 *jyungjiahn*, n., lock, door bolt.
扃鐍 *jyungjyuer*, n., a hasp for locking.

§ 63D.50 (戶/ㄱ)

扇 63D.50–5

shahn (**shan* as vb.).

N. adjunct. 一扇門, 一扇窗 A door, a window.

N. (1) (-*tz*, *'l*) A fan: 一把扇子 a fan; 摺扇 folding fan; 團扇 round fan without folds; 羽扇 feather fan; 電扇, 電風扇 electric fan; 芭蕉扇 palm-leaf fan; 風扇 punkah; 打扇 to use a fan; 秋扇見捐 abandoned (lover) like fan in autumn. (2) A door panel: 單扇門 a single-panelled door.

V.i. & t. (**shan*) (1) To fan (fire, person). (2) To fan up (flame), instigate, (also wr. 搧, 煽): 扇起風潮 stir up crisis; 扇動 -*duhng*↓. (3) (**shahn*) (AC) to geld animals (also wr. 騸).

扇車(子) *shahn-che(tz)*, n., a winnowing machine.
扇蕩 **shandahng*, v.t., to stir up unrest.
扇動 **shanduhng*, v.t., to instigate (trouble, strike).
扇骨子 *shahn-guutz*, n., frame of fan.
扇惑 **shanhuoh*, v.t., to misguide (youth, etc.) by words.
扇墜兒 *shahnjuoh'l*, n., pendant attached to a fan.
扇面兒 *shahnmiah'l*, n., the "face" (covering) of a fan, oft. containing painting or calligraphy.
扇翣 *shahnshah*, n., (AC) parasol, a held-up shade during parade.
扇形 *shahnshirng*, adj., fan-shaped (window, etc.).
扇揚 **shanyarng*, v.t., (LL) (of fame) spread about.
扇誘 **shanyouh*, v.t., see -*huoh*↑.

房 63D.50–6

farng.

N. (1) A surname. (2) House (-*tz*) 房屋, 房舍 -*wu*, -*sheh*↓; 平房 one-storied house; 樓房 several-storied house; 房頂 house roof; 房脊 ridge of roof; 房錢, 房租 house rent; 房契 house lease; 房捐 house tax; 房客 tenant; 房帖(兒) poster of house for rent. (3) Room: 廂房 room; 上房, 下房 inner, outer rooms in house with courtyard, those living in these rooms; 客房 guest room; 套房 suite; (洗)澡房 bathroom. (4) Branch of family: 長房, 二房 eldest, second branch; 房長, 房頭(兒), 房老 (MC) head of branch. (5) Shop: 藥房 pharmacy. (6) Compartmentarized structure: 蜂房 beehive; 蓮房 lotus pod. (7) Name of office or service: 茶房 waiter; 門房 gatekeeper; 賬房 treasurer, cashier.

房產 *farngchaan*, n., house property, real estate.
房東 *farngdung*, n., landlord, landlady.
房分 *farngfehn*, n., order of family branch.
房中術 *farngjung-shuh*, n., art of love-making.
房老 *farnglaau*, n., (MC) head of maidservants; head of family branch.
房累 *farngleei*, n., (MC) family (of officials living abroad).

房櫳 *farnglurng*, n., house windows.
房舍 *farngsheh*, n., house.
房下 *farngshiah*, n., (MC coll.) wife.
房事 *farngshyh*, n., sexual intercourse.
房帖(兒) *farngtiee(-tie'l)*, n., poster of "house for rent."
房屋 *farngwu*, n., house, building.

§ 63D.70 (戶/乚)

扈 63D.70-4

huh.

N. (1) (AC) name of bird. (2) Retinue, see compp.↓; 跋$^{\Delta}$扈 40B.82. (3) A surname.

扈蹕 *huhbih*, n., emperor's retinue.
扈扈 *huhhuh*, adj., (AC) bright and broad.
扈駕 *huhjiah*, n., emperor's retinue.
扈從 *huhtzuhng*, n., see *-jiah*↑.
扈養 *huhyaang*, n., (AC) grooms and cooks.

§ 63D.81 (戶/人)

戾 63D.81-1

lih.

N. Offense, humiliations: 罪戾 sin, crime; 以自取戾 invite humiliations upon one's own head, commit offense.

V.t. (AC) come to: 戾止 reach; 鳶飛戾天 the hawk flies up to heaven (cf. 莅 20A.30).

Adj. Perverse, tyrannical: 乖戾 intractable, wicked; 戾氣 a foul or evil-foreboding atmosphere; 暴戾 ruthlessly oppressive.

§ 63D.83 (戶/乀)

遍 63D.83-4

biahn.
[Var. 徧 91B.42]

N. Time in repetition: 一遍 (say, sing) once; 許多遍 many times.

Adv. All around: 遍地 all over the place, see 徧 91B.42.

§ 63D.91 (戶/ノ)

戶 63D.91-6

huh.
[See 戶 63.91]

SECTION 63S

§ 63S.22 (丶S/丨)

郎 63S.22-3

larng.
[Usu. wr. 郎]

N. (1) A young man, a man: 少年郎 a youth; 兒郎 a young man or son; 新郎 a bridegroom; 伴郎 the best man; 令郎 (court.) your son; 郎才女貌 (matchmaking) a perfect match between a man and girl; 郎心如鐵 (a young girl complaining) you are so hardhearted; 情郎 a woman's lover; 賣油郎 a peddler of vegetable oils (unlikely but lucky lover); 牛郎 a cowherd (constellation); 大郎, 二郎, 三郎, the eldest, second, third son; 郎舅 *-jiouh*↓. (2) An official title under the monarchy: 侍郎 vice minister; 郎中 *-jung*↓; 員外郎 councillor, ranking next to 侍郎. (3) A surname.

郎罷 *larngbah*, n., (MC) (Fukien dial.) one's father (MC transcription of 娘父 *niourbeih*).
郎伯 *larngbor*, n., (1) (MC court.) my husband; (2) ＝郎罷↑.
郎當 *larngdang*, adj., (1) (of clothes) too ample; (2) (of manners) easy-going: 弔兒郎當 take things easy, take a devil-may-care attitude; (3) helpless: 不覺醉郎當了 soon become helplessly tipsy; (4) ＝鋃$^{\Delta}$鐺 81A.02.
郎將 *larngjiahng*, n., an official title under the monarchy (＝中郎將).
郎舅 *larngjiouh*, n., the husband of one's sister, the brother of one's wife.
郎中 *larngjung*, n., a pop. term for a doctor: 江湖郎中 a quack doctor; also a cheat in gambling.
郎君 *larngjyun*, n., (1) (court.) my

亅	小	⺊	十	土	ナ	卄	ㄴ	丨	一	丅	フ	口	区	冂	ㄱ	厂	尸	亠	广	宀	丶	乚	七	心	八	人	乂	乛	𠃌	ノ	𠂉	く
00	01	02	10	11	12	20	21	22	30	31	32	40	41	42	50	51	52	60	61	62	63	70	71	72	80	81	82	83	90	91	92	93

husband; (2) (LL) your son; (3) 新郎君 a newly successful candidate in a government examination under the monarchy.

§ 63S.42 (丶s/冈)

朗 63S.42-4

laang.

Adj. Clear, bright: 明朗 clear and distinct; 朗朗 brilliant; 天朗氣清 clear atmosphere under a blue sky; 清朗 clear and bright; 朗月 a bright moon; 朗讀 reading aloud; 朗誦 ditto, recitation; 朗聲 a clear voice.

§ 63S.50 (丶s/ㄱ)

翩 63S.50-5

pian.

Adj. Flying, fluttering in the wind (like butterfly wings): 翩若驚鴻 (of woman, dancer) elusive, gracefully moving or disappearing.

翩 躚 *pianchian,* adj., flying or dancing gracefully.
翩 翾 *pianhuarn,* adj., ditto.
翩 翩 *pianpian,* adj. & adv., (1) gracefully moving, flying, dancing; (2) happy and contented: 翩翩以自樂; (3) handsome and attractive: 翩翩佳公子 a handsome *beau*; 翩翩巍巍 impressive (of building).
翩 然 *pianrarn,* adv., gracefully: 翩然蒞止 graciously come, arrive.

§ 63S.80 (丶s/八)

顧 63S.80-3

guh.

N. A surname.

V.i. & t. (1) V.i., to look back: 回顧 cast a backward glance, make a retrospect; 義無反顧 proceed without hesitation. (2) V.t., to look at or around: 顧盼 *-pahn*↓; 不値一顧 not worth a glance; 顧影自憐 (a lonely girl) look at one's image in the mirror and fall in love with or pity oneself; 顧名思義 think what a title or name should imply; 四顧無人 look around to find nobody anywhere. (3) V.t., take care of, look after: 顧念 *-niahn*↓; 顧戀 be fondly attached to; 顧惜 *-shir,* 顧恤 *-shyuh*↓; 愛顧 care for out of love; 照顧 take good care of (children, kins, folk, etc. away from home), look after (house, etc.); 顧家 take care of one's family; 顧贍 *-'shan*↓. (4) V.t., take into account or consideration: 顧不得那許多 have to ignore those things; 顧不了 have to leave out of consideration; 顧不過來 have no time to consider; 顧及 *-jir*↓; 顧面子, 顧臉 for the sake of face; 顧慮 *-lyuh,* 顧忌 *-jih*↓; 顧此失彼 (of two persons or things) take one into consideration to the neglect of the other; 顧前不顧後 consider only the present and forget about the future.

Adv. (LL) however, thus, so, nevertheless, indeed, really: 顧乃 however; 顧而 nevertheless; 顧如是乎 how could it be so? is it so indeed? 顧忘之耶 have you really forgotten? (Cf. 固 41.41, Adv. 2).

顧 全 *guh'chyuarn,* v.i., show consideration for: 顧全大局 so to act in the interests of everybody concerned.
顧 曲 *guhchyuu,* v.i., listen to songs, be a patron of the singsong house.
顧 到 *guh-dauh,* v.t., take into consideration.
顧 忌 *guhjih,* v.t. & n., have scruples about: 肆無顧忌 have no scruples at all.
顧 及 *guh-jir,* v.t., have regard for, take into account.
顧 主 *guhjuu,* n., a client, customer.
顧 客 *guhkeh,* n., see *-juu*↑.
顧 慮 *guhlyuh,* v.t., be seriously concerned about or with: 顧慮周到 thoughtful about everything (said of hospitality).
顧 念 *guhniahn,* v.t., remember with love or concern (old friendship, etc.).
顧 盼 *guhpahn,* v.t., look around: 顧盼自雄 strut about pleased with oneself.
顧 贍 *guh'shan,* v.t., to look after, assist: 他肯顧贍人 he is always willing to look after others.
顧 惜 *guhshir,* v.t., to pity, love (children), take good care of (one's reputation, "face").
顧 恤 *guhshyuh,* v.t., have compassion on, to pity.
顧 問 *guhwehn,* n. & v.t., an adviser; 當顧問 be adviser.

§ 63S.82 (丶s/乂)

啟 63S.82-9

chii.

[Var. 啓, 㪣; pop. 启]

N. A letter: 書啟.

V.i. & t. (1) To open, open up: 開啟, 啟開 to open; 啟窗 open window; 啟顏 face opens up in smiles; to open letter: 親啟 "personal letter" marked "personal"; 大啟, 勛啟 (marking on envelope) addressed to very important person; to open up one's mind: 啟智, 啟知 ditto; 振聾啟瞶 phr., (fig.) to open mind ("make the deaf hear and the dim-sighted see"); 啟迪, 啟發 *-dir*, *-fa*↓. (2) To communicate by letter or notice: 敬啟者 (opening words of letter) wish to communicate; 啟上, 謹啟 (court. end of letter after signature) by so-and-so; 附啟 postscript; 稟啟 (to superior, parent) I wish to communicate; 啟奏 to send memorial to emperor; 啟告 to communicate (in public notice) 啟事 *-shyh*^{1}↓.

啟報 *chii-bauh*, v.i., to report (in official report).
啟閉 *chii-bih*, v.i., to open and close (as the seasons, doors, etc.).
啟處 *chiichuu*, n., (AC) a short rest.
啟齒 *chirchyy*, v.i., (1) to open up in smile; (2) to say s.t. difficult: 難於啟齒 difficult to say it (requesting unusual favor, asking for loan).
啟迪 *chiidir*, v.t., to open mind, esp. of the young, stimulate thinking.
啟發 *chiifa*, v.t., see *-dir*↑.
啟封 *chii-feng*, v.i., to break seal; open sealed envelope.
啟蟄 *chii-jyr*, v.i., to wake from hiberation in spring.
啟蒙 *chiimerng*, v.t., to instruct very young (as in kindergarten and primary school), enlighten: 啟蒙時期 beginning of thinking, age of enlightenment; 啟蒙老師 teacher who gave instruction at one's childhood.
啟行 *chiishirng*, v.i., to start on journey.
啟事 *chiishyh*^{1}, n., a public notice.
啟示 *chiishyh*^{2}, v.t. & n., reveal, revelation; 啟示錄 Revelation of New Testament.
啟沃 *chiiwoh*, v.t., (AC) to advise the king.

SECTION 70

§ 70.70 (乚/乚)

七 70.70

chi (*chir*).
[See 10.70]

匕 70.70

bii.
[See 21A.70]

SECTION 70S

§ 70S.22 (乚^s/丨)

邨 70S.22-3

tsun.
[See 10S.22]

§ 70S.50 (乚^s/㇕)

鸨 70S.50-9

baau.
[See 21S.50]

§ 70S.70 (乚^s/乚)

比 70S.70-2

bii (**bih*).
[See 21S.70]

SECTION 71

§ 71.30 (七/一)

盞 71.30

jaan.

N. adjunct. 一盞燈 a lamp (orig., oil-lamp stand with an oil cup).

N. (*-tz*) A small cup: 酒盞 wine cup.

盛 71.30

shehng (**cherng*).

N. (1) A surname. (2) (**cherng*) 粢盛 sacrificial offerings.

V.t. (**cherng*) To fill a bowl (with rice, etc.); 盛殮 *-'lian* ↓.

Adj. (1) Vast, stupendous, great: 豐盛 rich (harvest, business); 盛舉 *-jyuu* ↓; 年少氣盛 young and impetuous; 盛會 a grand occasion; 盛筵 a great banquet; 盛名 a great reputation; 盛怒 great anger. (2) Prosperous: 茂盛 thriving (garden, plants); 興盛 prosperous, thriving (commerce, industry, nation); 盛世 *-shyh* ↓; 盛衰 *-suai* ↓.

Adv. Greatly: 盛行 *-shirng* ↓.

盛氣 *shehng-chih*, n., explosive manner of person: 盛氣凌人 browbeat other people, carry an arrogant air.

盛情 *shehng-chirng*, n., (court.) your great hospitality or kindness.

盛服 *shehngfur*, n., (AC, LL) festive or formal dress.

盛舉 *shehng-jyuu*, n., a great undertaking: 共襄盛舉 cooperate with this great project.

盛殮 **cherng'lian*, n., proper laying-in of deceased.

盛年 *shehng-niarn*, n., a year of good crops.

盛夏 *shehng-shiah*, n., midsummer.

盛行 *shehng-shirng*, v.i., spread widely: 其道盛行 its teachings are very popular.

盛世 *shehng-shyh*, n., a great, prosperous era.

盛衰 *shehng-suai*, n., the rise and fall (of dynasties); prosperity and decline.

盛意 *shehng-yih*, n., see *-chirng* ↑.

§ 71.42 (七/冈)

觱 71.42

bih.

觱發 *bihfa*, adj., (AC) windy and cold.

觱篥(栗) *bihlih*, n., the Tartar pipe, piercing and mournful.

§ 71.50 (七/ㄱ)

鳶 71.50

yuan.

N. (1) A kite: 紙鳶 paper kite; 鳶飛魚躍 the kites fly in the air and fish jump in the water—(phil.) the pleasure of fulfilling nature or nature's functions. (2) A brown tea color.

鳶尾 *yuanweei*, n., (bot.) a kind of iris, *Iris tectorum* (＝紫羅蘭).

Section 71.71 (七/七)

弋 71.71

yih.

V.i. To shoot (birds), hunt with bow and arrow.

弋獲 *yih-huoh*, v.t., (1) to shoot down (game); (2) to capture (criminal).

弋人 *yihrern*, n., (AC) archer.

戈 71.71

ge.

N. (1) A spear, a lance: 干戈 weapons of war; 兵戈 weapons; 動兵戈 start open war; 戈矛 lances and spears. (2) A surname.

戈壁 *Gebih*, n., the Gobi desert (Mongol word for "desert").

弌 71.71

yi.

[Var. of "一"]

弍 71.71

ehl.

N. A "spelled out" form of 二, two (cf. 貳 71.71 ↓).

戎 71.71

rurng.

N. (1) Military affairs: 戎事 warfare, fighting; 戎機 military operations (secrets), strategy; 戎寄 a military assignment; 戎首 *-shoou* ↓; 戎行 *-harng* ↓; 軍戎 military matters; 戎伍 the rank and file, the army; 投筆從戎 give up civilian pursuits to join the army; 戎士 privates; 兵戎 troops; 戎馬 war-horses; 戎車 a war-chariot; 戎器 weapons; 戎裝, 戎服, 戎衣 military dress, uniform; 戎旃 military tent. (2) General name for barbarian tribes in the west: 西戎 the Western Barbarians; 犬戎 "the Canine Barbarians"; 戎蠻 an anc. barbarian tribe in the south; 戎狄 barbarian tribes to the west and the north. (3) A surname.

Adj. Great: 戎功 outstanding service to the country; 戎公 ditto.

戎行 ***rurng-harng***, n., troops.

戎葵 ***rurngkueir***, n., (bot.) the hollyhock, *Althaea rosea* (also 蜀葵).

戎路 ***rurngluh***, n., military chariots.

戎幕 ***rurng-muh***, n., military headquarters.

戎首 ***rurng-shoou***, n., (1) one who starts a war: 毋爲戎首 don't be the first to start a war; (2) the first to pick a fight.

戎菽 ***rurngshur***, n., the garden pea.

戎鹽 ***rurngyarn***, n., the rock salt.

戒 71.71

jieh.

N. A commandment; a vow or pledge to abstain from s.t.

V.t. (1) To warn, give warning: 警戒, 告戒 ditto. (2) (Mil.) 戒備 to be on the alert, take extra precautionary measures, declare curfew. (3) To put a stop to: 戒煙 stop smoking; 戒酒 refrain from drinking (alcohol). (4) To fast: 齋戒沐浴 to fast and take a bath before a religious observance.

戒備 ***jiehbeih***, v.i. & n., see V.t. 2↑.

戒除 ***jiehchur***, v.t., to cut out (bad habits).

戒尺 ***jiehchyy***, n., formerly, bamboo slat, or foot rule for spanking pupils.

戒旦 ***jieh-dahn***, n., "bugle" call to get up.

戒刀 ***jieh-dau***, n., a knife carried by a monk.

戒牒 ***jieh-dier***, n., a monk's or nun's document showing formal membership in monastic order.

戒方 ***jiehfang***, n., see *-chyy*↑.

戒指(兒) ***jiehjyy(-je'l)***, n., a (finger) ring.

戒律 ***jieh-lyuh***, n., monastic regulations.

戒心 ***jieh-shin***, n., restraint before danger, fear of making mistakes.

戒條 ***jiehtiaur***, n., commandments, see *-lyuh*↑.

戒嚴 ***jiehyarn***, n., martial law.

式 71.71

shyh.

N. (1) Model, standard. (2) Rituals, form of ceremony: 儀式 ditto; 結婚式 rituals of wedding; 畢業式 commencement exercises; 開幕式, 閉幕式 opening, closing ceremony. (2) Form, formula, style: 公式 formula; 樣式, 形式 shape, appearance (of pot, vase, ceremony, etc.); 方程式 (math.) an equation; 新式, 舊式 new, old style; 時式 fashionable, modern style; 正式 formal, -ly (announced, married, adopted, etc.). (3) (Gram.) tense: 現在式, 過去式 present, past tense; 未來式 future tense; 進行式 progressive tense, voice; cf. 態 93.72.

式子 ***shyhtz***, n., form, pattern (of dress, etc.).

式微 ***shyhweir***, v.i., (AC) fall in power, become weak, decay.

式樣 ***shyhyahng***, n., (1) form, shape of things; (2) sample.

或 71.71

huoh.

Pron. (1) A certain person: 或人 (＝某人); 或曰, 或問 some one may say, may ask. (2) (AC) who: 今此下民, 或敢侮予 who among the people would dare defy me?

Adv. & conj. Perhaps; or (LL for vern. 或者, 或許 *-jee*, *-shyuu*↓): 或有不是 if something should (perhaps) happen; 或改初志 perhaps should change one's mind; either . . . or: 或此或彼, 或東或西 either this or the other; either east or west.

或者 ***huohjee***, adv., perhaps: 或者是你 perhaps it is you; 或者認錯了人 may have mistaken one person for another; either... or 或者這個或者那個 either this or that.

或是 ***huohshyh***, adv., perhaps: 或是有甚麽過失 perhaps he may have done something wrong.

或許 ***huohshyuu***, adv., perhaps: 或許我不能來 perhaps I cannot come (＝或者 *-jee*↑).

戓 71.71

yuh.

Adj. Cultured (var. of 郁 12S.22).

忒 71.71

teh.

N. & v.i. (1) (AC) (make) a mistake: 差忒. (2) (AC) change: 不忒 do not change.

Adv. (MC, also modn.) too (in unfavorable sense): 忒甚 (＝太甚) too much; 忒小 too small; 忒厲害 too sharp in character.

忒兒的 *teh'l'de*, adv., as in 忒兒的飛 suddenly fly away; 忒兒摟麵條, 摟鼻涕 descriptive of sucking in noodles, dripping nose mucus.

忒楞楞 *teh'lengleng*, adv., (MC) descriptive of sound of wind or flight of birds.

忒煞 (殺) *teh'sha*, adv., too (esp. MC): 忒煞情多 too romantic, sentimental.

曳 71.71

yih (sp. pr. *yeh*).

V.t. (1) To trail (skirts) on the ground. (2) To trace: 曳光彈 *-guangdahn*↓.

曳白 *yihbair*, v.i., to hand in blank paper at examinations (also 曳白卷); formerly, in civil examinations, to skip a paper in copying.

曳光彈 *yihguangdahn*, n., tracing bullet.

曳引機 *yihyiinji*, n., a tractor.

武 71.71

wuu.

N. (1) A footstep: 步武 follow in the footsteps. (2) A surname.

Adj. (1) Military, opp. to 文 civilian or cultural: 武士, 武備 *-shyh, -beih*↓; 武力, 武人 *-lih, -rern*↓; 尚武 emphasis on military power; 用武 to resort to arms; 動武 start fisticuffs. (2) Martial, warlike, chivalrous. (3) Arbitrary in 武斷 *-duahn*↓.

武把子 *wurbaatz*, n., boxing postures.

武備 *wuubeih*, n., military preparedness.

武弁 *wuubiahn*, n., (1) petty officer; (2) (AC) military cap.

武器 *wuuchih*, n., weapon.

武丑(兒) *wur-choou('l)*, n., an acrobatic actor.

武旦 *wuu-dahn*, n., actress playing martial role.

武斷 *wuuduahn*, n., arbitrary (person, judgment).

武夫 *wuu-fu*, n., (1) a warrior; (2) (AC) a jade-like stone (also wr. 碔砆).

武官 *wuu-guan*, n., a military officer.

武工 *wuu-gung*[1], *n.*, acrobatic skill of actors.

武功 *wuu-gung*[2], n., (1) military achievements; (2) training in art of attack and defense.

武火 *wur-huoo*, n., intense fire in cooking, opp. 文火 slow fire for simmering.

武將 *wuu-jiahng*, n., military general (a loose term).

武裝 *wuu-juang*, n., military uniform; adj., equipped with weapons: 武裝部隊 armed forces.

武舉 *wur-jyuu*, n., formerly, a military officer of second degree (舉人) in examinations.

武庫 *wuu-kuh*, n., armory.

武力 *wuu-lih*, n., military power, force of arms; muscular power.

武林 *wuu-lirn*, n., the world or circle of boxers.

武廟 *wuu-miauh*, n., temple to military heroes.

武人 *wuu-rern*, n., (1) an army man, opp. 文人 scholar; (2) a war lord.

武生 *wuu-sheng*, n., (Chin. opera) man playing martial role; formerly, a cadet.

武俠 *wuushiar*, n., chivalry: 武俠小說 novel of swordsmen.

武術 *wuushuh*, n., art of personal attack and defense.

武師 *wuu-shy*, n., military teacher.

武士 *wuu-shyh*, n., a warrior; 武士道 *--dauh*, (Japanese) bushido, chivalry.

武藝 *wuu'yi*, n., acrobatic and boxing skills, art of using weapons.

戔 71.71

jian.

Adj. Small, tiny, fragmentary: 戔戔之數 an insignificant amount (of money).

貳 71.71

ehl.

V.i. To show disloyalty: 貳心 *-shin*↓.

Adj. (1) "Spelled out" form of "two" used in checks to avoid errors. (2) Disloyal.

貳臣 *ehlchern*, n., a disloyal minister who collaborates with conqueror.

貳心 *ehlshin*, n., disloyalty of heart.

貳言 *ehlyarn*, n., dissident talk or opinion.

戊 71.71

wuh.

N. The number 5 in the decimal cycle, see Appendix A.

戍 71.71

shuh.
[Dist. 戌, 戊 71.71]

N. (1) Garrison, frontier guard: 戍卒, 戍人, 戍役, *-tzur*, *-rern*, *-yih*↓. (2) No.

V.t. To guard frontier.

戍邊 *shuhbian*, v.i., to guard frontier regions.
戍鼓 *shuh-guu*, n., garrison drum.
戍樓 *shuh-lour*, n., watchtower.
戍人 *shuh-rern*, n., a frontier guard.
戍守 *shuhshoou*, v.i., to set up frontier garrison.
戍卒 *shuhtzur*, n., a frontier guard.
戍衞 *shuhweih*, v.i., see *-shoou*↑.
戍役 *shuhyih*, n., military service at border regions, oft. a punishment as exile.

戌 71.71

shyu.
[Dist. 戍, 戊]

N. (1) No. 11 of the duodecimal cycle (地支), see Appendix A. (2) The period between 7 and 9 p.m.

成 71.71

cherng.

N. (1) Result, achievement, accomplishment: 有成, 無成 has, has not results to show; 成功, 成績, 成果 *-gung*, *-ji*, *-guoo*↓. (2) One tenth, or ten per cent: 六成 60%. (3) (AC) 60 *li* of distance. (4) (AC) a storey: 九成宮 nine-storied hall. (4) A surname.

V.i. & t. (1) To complete: 成立 *lih*[1]↓; 成交 close a deal; 成婚 to be married; 事成之後 after the thing is over; 成事不足, 敗事有餘 (person) not good enough to accomplish anything, but more than enough to spoil things; 成人之美 to help completion of worthy goal, bring romance to happy ending. (2) To become: 成名, 成了名人 become famous; 成仙, 成佛 become an immortal, a Buddha; 成聖 to be sanctified; 成擒 become captive; 成爲無用 become useless; 成爲贅疣 become a redundancy; 成甚麽話 what will people say? (3) As vb. suffix, in the sense of "become" or "completed": 變成became; 形成 assume the shape, or appearance (of isolation, alliance, triangle, obstruction, etc.); 切成 cut into (slips, etc.); 製成, 做成 make (made) into s.t.; 寫成小說 make into a novel; 完成 complete (task), realize (goal), accomplish (mission); 贊成 to support, etc. (4) Used like Eng. "do": 那不成 that won't do; 成不成 will that do? esp. 不成 at sentence end or 難道...不成 you don't mean that (I should accept all your conditions, etc.), do you? (5) (MC) maybe: 不成只是等罷 maybe all we can do is just wait here.

Adj. (1) Full, a full measure, whole: 成雙, 成對 a pair; 成日, 成日家, 成天 whole day; 成桶 a whole barrelful; 成塊 the whole piece; 成年累月 for months and years; 成千成萬 thousands and tens of thousands. (2) Customary, established: 成例, 成規 *-lih*[2], *-guei*↓; 成語 *-yuu*↓; 成命 already announced order; 現成的 what is already there or available. (3) Enough: 成了 that's enough! not any more. (4) Capable, good: 那人很成 that man is very capable or useful. (5) Mature, complete: 成年, 成人 *-niarn*, *-rern*[1]↓; 成熟 *-shur*↓; 秋成 autumn harvest.

成案 *cherng-ahn*, n., (law) (1) a case on record; (2) case law.
成敗 *cherng-baih*, n., success or failure.
成本 *cherngbeen*, n., cost of production of merchandise, capital of investment.
成器 *cherngchih*, v.i., (1) (of child, person) amount to s.t., become independent in some way; (2) become a useful object.
成氣候 *cherng-chih'hou*, phr., (person's experience) come to maturity.
成親 *cherng-chin*, v.i., to be married: 已經成親 already married.
成仇 *cherng-chour*, v.i., become enemy.
成全 *cherngchyuarn*, v.t., to help others to succeed (in some undertaking).
成羣 *cherng-chyurn*, adv., in hordes, large groups.
成齒 *cherngchyy*, n., permanent teeth.
成典 *cherngdiaan*, n., promulgated laws.
成丁 *cherngding*, v.i., (of male persons) come of age.
成法 *cherngfaa*, n., established law or customs, usage, precedent.
成方兒 *cherngfang'l*, n., apothecary's formula, dist. physician's prescription.
成分 *cherngfehn*, n., percentages, ingredients.
成佛 *cherng-for*, v.i., become a Buddha (possible for every man).
成副兒 *cherngfuh'l*, n., complete(d) set (as in mahjong).
成服 *cherng-fur*, v.i., have gone into mourning dress after laying-in of deceased.
成個兒 *cherng-geh'l*, (1) v.i., have formed shapes: 果子已經成個兒了 the fruits are being formed; 他的字不成個兒 his characters still lack shape; (2) n., the whole piece.
成規 *chernggueí*, n., customary rules.
成功 *chernggung*, v.i. & n. & adj., succeed; success, -ful; 成功者 a successful man; 不成功 will,

do not succeed.

成果 *chengguoo*, n., results, achievements.

成歡 *chernghuan*, v.i., (LL) achieve sexual union.

成婚 *chernghun*, v.i. & adj., be married.

成長 *cherngjaang*, v.i., to grow up; n., growth.

成章 *cherng-jang*, phr., (1) 出口成章 talk with adroit phrases; (2) 順理成章 lucid and logical, follow as a matter of course.

成招 *cherng-jau*, phr., 屈打成招 (prisoner) confess after tortures.

成績 *cherngji*, n., scholastic records; result; military accomplishments.

成家 *cherng-jia*, v.t., become a family man, have a family.

成見 *cherngjiahn*, n., prejudice, stubborn ideas.

成姦 *cherngjian*, n., consummated rape.

成交 *cherng-jiau*, v.i., close a business deal.

成就 *cherngjiouh*, n., results to show for effort; achievements, progress made.

成竹 *cherng-jur*, phr., 胸有成竹 or 成竹在胸 definite ideas or plans to meet a situation (as concept of bamboo exists in painter's mind before painting).

成局 *cherngjyur*, (1) n., a settled situation or agreement; (2) v.i., form a (mahjong) party.

成兒 *cherng'l*, n., (1) 10%: 三成兒希望 thirty-percent chance; (2) success: 你看這事準有成兒 you see this thing will surely succeed.

成了 *cherng'le*, phr., (1) (this) will do, is enough; (2) come off, succeed.

成立 *chernglih*[1], v.i. & t., (1) to form (a society, church, faction, etc.); (2) (hope for child) to become adult and independent.

成例 *chernglih*[2], n., established rules, precedents.

成禮 *cherng-lii*, v.i., (1) ceremony is ended; (2) be married.

成命 *cherngmihng*, n., an issued order: 收回成命 withdraw an order.

成名 *cherng-mirng*, v.i., become famous.

成年 *cherng-niarn*, (1) n. & adj., adult: 成年人 an adult; (2) v.i., come of age; (3) adv., yearlong: 成年家 for a whole year.

成品 *cherngpiin*, n., a finished product.

成人 *cherngrern*[1], n., an adult: 成人教育 adult education.

成仁 *cherngrern*[2], phr., be a martyr for a cause: 成仁取義 die for a cause.

成日 *cherng-ryh*, adv., all day long (also 成日家, 成日價).

成色 *cherng'seh*, n., content of silver or gold in coins, jewelry.

成效 *cherngshiauh*, n., results to show.

成心 *cherngshin*, (1) adv., purposely: 成心作對 purposely antagonize person; (2) n., preconceived notion.

成數 *cherngshuh*, n., (1) round numbers; (2) percentage.

成訟 *cherng-shung*[1], v.i., take matters to court.

成誦 *cherng-shung*[2], phr., 過目成誦 can recite a passage after one perusal.

成說 *cherngshuo*, n., (1) an established theory; (2) an agreement.

成熟 *cherngshur*, adj., mature.

成事 *cherng-shyh*, (1) n., bygones: 成事不說 (AC) let bygones be bygones; (2) v.i., to succeed in doing s.t.: 不成事 will not accomplish anything.

成算 *cherngsuahn*, n., (1) preconceived idea of costs; (2) calculated plan.

成素 *cherngsuh*, n., elements in the making.

成俗 *cherngsur*, (1) n., established customs; (2) v.i., in 化民成俗 (AC) to influence the people and form moral customs.

成天 *cherngtian*, adv., all day long.

成材 *cherngtsair*, v.i., see *-chih* ↑.

成童 *cherngturng*, n., (AC) teenage child.

成總(兒) *cherngtzuung('l)*, n., (1) round numbers; (2) in quantity: 成總兒買比零碎便宜 cheaper to buy in quantities.

成文 *cherngwern*, (1) n., clear statement (letter) of the law; (2) n., (coll.) presentable: 沒有一件成文的東西 not one presentable thing; (3) adj., written in black and white: 成文法 written laws; 不成文法 customs and conventions.

成樣(兒) *cherngyahng('l)*, (1) adj., presentable: 不成樣兒 not presentable; (2) v.i., 成樣起來 to assemble into shape (from cut pieces).

成言 *cherngyarn*, n., a promised word.

成衣 *cherngyi*, n., as in 成衣兒 ready-made suits; 成衣匠 tailor, 成衣店 tailor shop.

成議 *cherng-yih*, phr., come to agreement.

成員 *cherng yarn*, n., standing member, constituent.

成語 *cheryngyuu*, n., a phrase; an idiom.

咸 71.71

shiarn.

N. A surname.

Adv. (LL) all: 咸集 all gathered together; 咸知, 咸聞 all have heard, all know; 咸因 all because; 咸稱, 咸謂 all (the people) say or think.

威 71.71

wei.

N. (1) Dignity. (2) Power, authority, might: 作威作福 assume great airs (of authority); 天威, 神威 the might of Heaven, of God; 示威 make a demonstration, esp. street demonstration of protest; 虎威 great military power.

V.t. To dominate by power.

Adj. & adv. (1) Powerful, mighty: 威信, 威望 *-shihn*, *-wahng* ↓. (2) By force: 威嚇, 威脅 *-heh*, *-shier* ↓.

威逼 *weibi*, v.t., to threaten by force, to coerce: 威逼利誘 coercion and bribery.

威權 *weichyuarn*, n., authority, prestige.

威風 *weifeng* (-'*feng*), n., air of importance; prestige, domineering influence.

威福 *weifur*, n., power (of punishment or leniency).

威嚇 *weiheh*, v.t., to threaten by force.

威重 *weijuhng*, n., (LL) weight and importance.

威力 *weilih*, n., political or military power.

威靈 *weilirng*, n., prestige, power of decision; 威靈仙 *Veronica virginica*, used as powerful medicine.

威猛 *weimeeng*, adj., domineering.

威名 *weimirng*, n., prestige.

威聲 *weisheng*, n., prestige, commanding voice.

威脅 *weishier*, v.t., to dominate by force, to threaten, coerce (person, country).

威信 *weishihn*, n., public prestige, public confidence.

威勢 *weishyh*, n., dominant power.

威士忌 *weishyhjih*, n., (translit.) whisky.

威望 *weiwahng*, n., public prestige.

威武 *weiwuu* (-'*wu*), adj., dominant (power).

威嚴 *weiyarn*, adj. & n., dignified, severe; dignity, severity.

威儀 *weiyir*[1], n., dignity, decorum, forbidding appearance.

威夷 *weiyir*[2], adj., (AC) leisurely (usu. wr. 逶迤).

戚 71.71

chi.

N. (1) A relative, esp. on wife's or mother's side: 親戚 relative in gen.; 皇親國戚 princes and princesses of the royal family; 戚畹 relatives of empress; 外戚, 戚屬, 戚族 wife's or mother's relatives. (2) An ancient weapon (ancient var. 鏚) see 戚揚 -*yarng* ↓. (3) Adversity: 休戚相關 share good and bad luck. (4) A surname.

Adj. Sad, uneasy: 悲戚, 憂戚, 哀戚 sorrow; 戚然 uneasy, see 戚戚 -*chi* ↓.

戚戚 *chichi*, adj., (1) troubled at heart, heavy-hearted; (2) (AC) brotherly: 戚戚兄弟.

戚施 *chishy*, adj., (AC) hunchbacked.

戚揚 *chiyarng*, n., (AC) battle-axe.

臧 71.71

tzang.

N. (1) A surname. (2) A slave: 臧獲 -*huoh* ↓. (3) (U.f. 贓) bribery: 貪污坐臧 guilty of corruption and accepting bribes.

Adj. (LL) good, right, correct (opp. 否 bad, wrong): 人謀不臧 (LL) ill-advised; 何用不臧 (AC) what does it not avail? how can it possibly go wrong?

臧獲 *tzanghuoh*, n., (AC) a male or female slave.

臧否 *tzang-pii*, (1) adj., good or bad: 未知臧否 don't know whether it's good or bad; (2) adv., yes or no; (3) v.t., criticize, speak well or ill of: 臧否人物 pass judgement on men and personalities.

感 71.71

gaan.

N. Feeling, sensation, emotion, one of the senses: 感覺 -*jyuer* ↓; 快感 a pleasurable sensation; 性感, 肉感 sex appeal; 惡感 enmity, sense of revulsion; 好感 good will; 感情 -*chirng*, 感念 -*niahn*, 感想 -*shiaang*, 感傷 -*shang* ↓; 百感交集 be moved by a mixture of feelings; 感慨 -*kaai* ↓; 有感而發 (of person) to explode not without reason; 敏感 sensitive, -ity, allergic, -gy; 非常敏感 be allergic to, be extremely sensitive; 頗有同感 I feel the same way as you do; 感觸 -*chuh* ↓; 第六感 the sixth sense, intuition; 靈感 inspiration.

V.i. & t. (1) V.i., to feel, to experience sensations, passions, etc. usu. 感覺, 感到: 感到不快 feel unhappy, or depressed; 感覺不安, 感覺難過, 感覺不舒服 feel uneasy, sad, unwell; 感覺出來 one can feel it; 多愁善感 always melancholy and moody. (2) V.i., feel grateful: 感謝, 感戴, 感激, 感恩 -*shieh*, -*daih*, -*ji*, -*en* ↓; 感同身受 shall feel grateful as a personal favor. (3) V.t., to move, touch emotionally: 感動 -*duhng* ↓; 感人至深 move people deeply, be deeply touched. (4) V.t., (of disease) to contract, be infected by: 感冒 -*mauh*, 感染 -*raan* ↓. (5) (AC, u.f. 撼 *hahn*) to shake.

感情 *gaanchirng*, n., (1) friendly feelings: 感情好 be on friendly terms; (2) passion, emotion: 感情用事 be swayed by emotions; 感情衝動 to act on momentary impulse; 發生感情 begin to be deeply attached to one another.

感觸 *gaanchuh*, n., emotional stirrings: 有所感觸 reaction on seeing, reading s.t.

感戴 *gaandaih*, v.i. be sincerely grateful.

感到 *gaan-dauh*, v.i. & t., to feel, to sense (+adj.).

感動 *gaanduhng*, v.t., to move, to touch the feelings of (person), to stir the emotions, passions, or sympathies of: 感動得使人流淚 move people to tears.

感恩 *gaan-en*, v.i., to feel grateful for some act; 感恩節 Thanksgiving Day.

感官 *gaanguan*, n., (physiol.) the sense organs.

感光 *gaanguang*, v.i. & adj., (be)

亅	小	⺊	十	土	ナ	廾	⺊	丨	一	丅	フ	口	囗	冂	乛	厂	尸	亠	广	宀	丶	乚	七	心	八	人	乂	乛	一	丿	𠂉	ㄑ
00	01	02	10	11	12	20	21	22	30	31	32	40	41	42	50	51	52	60	61	62	63	70	71	72	80	81	82	83	90	91	92	93

photosensitive: 感光紙, 感光片 photosensitive paper, films.

感荷 *gaanheh*, v.i., be sincerely grateful.

感化 *gaanhuah*, v.t., to move, influence, convert (criminals, etc.) to a better way of life; 感化所 reformatory.

感召 *gaanjauh*, v.t., inspire, rally (s.o.) to a worthy cause.

感激 *gaanji*, v.i. & t., be grateful to (s.o.) for (s.t.).

感覺 *gaanjyuer*, n. & v.t., feeling; to feel (uncomfortable, happy, etc.); see Vb. 1.

感慨 *garnkaai*, n., painful recollections, regrets: 感慨萬千 be filled with regrets or painful recollections.

感冒 *gaanmauh*, n. & v.i., (to catch) cold: 流行感冒 influenza.

感念 *gaanniahn*, v.t., remember (s.o.) in gratitude.

感染 *garnraan*, v.t., (1) be infected by (disease); (2) (of thoughts or ideas) be colored or influenced by: 她也感染上悲觀了 her thoughts have also been tinged with pessimism.

感傷 *gaanshang*, n., grief, sorrow; adj., sentimental (poetry, mood); 感傷主義 sentimentalism.

感想 *garnshiaang*, n., feeling, impression.

感謝 *gaanshieh*, (1) v.t., be thankful to (s.o.) for (s.t.); (2) adj., thankful.

感受 *gaanshouh*, v.i. & t., feel, be touched, react emotionally to (sermon, book, movie); 感受性 n., sensibility.

感歎 *gaantahn*, v.i. & n., to express deep regrets (for); 感歎詞 an exclamation; 感歎號 exclamation point.

感應 *gaanyihng*, n., reaction or response to some outer stimuli.

§ 71.72 (七/心)

慼 71.72

chi.

Adj. Sorrowful, heavy-hearted (also wr. 戚).

惑 71.72

huoh.

N. & v.t. (1) Entice, mislead, baffle: 妖言惑衆 evil doctrine misleads the public; 惑世 mislead the people; 惑弄 to delude; 迷惑 lead into false ways; 受迷惑 be led astray; 惑於婦言 (LL) listen to one's wife. (2) Doubt, suspicion, confuse, -sion: 疑惑 to doubt, a doubt; 智者不惑 a wise man is never confused; 惑志 causing doubts in faith.

§ 71.83 (七/乀)

蹙 71.83

tsuh.

[Cf. 促 91A.83]

V.t. To knit (brow).

Adj. Knitted (brow); cramped in space.

蹙頞 *tsuh-eh*, adv., with knitted brow (in worry).

蹙金 *tsuhjin*, n., a form of embroidery with gold thread ruffled.

蹙眉 *tsuhmeir*, v.i., knit eyebrows.

蹙蹙 *tsuhtsuh*, adj., (AC) restricted, constrained, not free.

SECTION 71S

§ 71S.00 (七^{s}/丿)

划 71S.00-2

huar.

V.t. (1) To paddle (a boat): 划船. (2) (Swimming) to paddle water.

划拳 *huarchyuarn*, v.i., to engage in finger-guessing game, each putting out one hand and guessing the total (0–10) of the two parties (also wr. 豁拳).

划水魚 *huarshueei yur*, n., a culinary dish containing the tail ends of fish.

划子 *huartz*, n., a small paddleboat.

剗 71S.00-2

chaan (*chahn).

V.t. (1) To pare off; raze to the ground. (2) (*chahn) To smash (rebellions).

§ 71S.50 (七^{s}/ㄱ)

鴮 71S.50-9

wuu.

N. See 鸆鴮 41S.50.

§ 71S.80 (七^s/八)

顣 71S.80-3

tsuh.

[Var. of 蹙 71.83]

SECTION 72

§ 72.72 (心/心)

心 72.72

shin.

N. (1) The heart: 心臟 *-tzahng*↓; 心悸, 心跳 palpitation of the heart; 心驚肉跳 tremble with fear; 心漏病 hole in heart. (2) The mind, intelligence: 心知, 心智 *-jy*, *-jyh*[1]↓; 勞心 do mental work (opp. 勞力 manual work); 心勞日拙 at wit's end; 身心舒服 body and mind at ease; 專心 concentrate one's mind; 決心 set one's mind to; 細心 carefully; 粗心 unthinkingly. (3) Feeling, thinking: 心中不安 do not feel at ease; 滿心 wish intensely; 平心而論 to be quite fair; 放心, 安心 to feel free to do s.t., not to worry; 稱心, 快心 feel happy; 醉心 be "crazy" about s.t.; 正心 set right one's purpose in life, set heart in the right place; 動心 aroused, tempted; 寬心 be relaxed; 耐心 persistent, -ce; 良心 conscience; 好心, 好心腸 a good heart; 壞心 malice; 出於本心 from one's heart; 誠心 sincere, -ly, -rity; 虧心 do s.t. against conscience; 齊心 with one mind all together; 存心 with the intention to; 忠心, 赤心, 丹心 loyal, -ty; 熱心 enthusiasm; 多心 oversensitive; 灰心 disappointed, give up hope; 死心 give up; 不在心上 not on one's mind; 心下不安 feel uneasy; 心裏頭 in one's mind or heart. (4) Affection, love: 你知道我的心 you know how I truly feel; 心愛的人 the one I love, sweetheart; 知心友 bosom friend; 心心相印 wholehearted response, their love is reciprocal; 心頭肉, 心肝 sweetheart; 我的心肝 my darling; 心尖子, 心上人 ditto. (5) 心+vb. or adj., describing different states of mind: 心愛 to love; 心安 feel at ease; 心契 bosom friend; 心動 be moved, aroused; 心蕩神馳 feel excited; distracted; 心煩意亂 confused and worried; 心服, 心折 admire from the heart; 心浮 flightly, not steady; 心甘 willing; 心不甘 unwilling; 心高 lofty-minded, aiming at big thing; 心寒 frightened, shudder at the thought; 心狠 cruel, brutal; 心慌 dismayed; 心灰 disappointed, disenchanted; 心活 moved to action; 心照不宣 no need to say how grateful I am; 心焦, 心急 tense, nervous with worry; 心淨 mind cleared of worries, at ease; 心肯 willing at heart; 心曠神怡 completely relaxed and happy; 心領 decline a gift while appreciate the thought, appreciate advice; 心熱 enthusiastic for some cause; 心輭 softhearted; 心散 distracted, unable to concentrate; 心賞 to appreciate; 心閒 relaxed, mind at ease; 心説 think in one's mind without expressing in words; 心虛 guilty, afraid of being found out; 心許 (usu. a girl) to love a man silently, willing to marry him; 心酸 feel pity, grieved; 心碎 heartbroken; 心疼 to love (child, woman), heart aches for; 心跳 heart palpitates; 心痛, 痛心疾首 regret, deplore greatly; 心醉 feel fascinated, "crazy"; 心癢 itch to do s.t., feel tickled mentally; 心儀其人 admire a person; 心猿意馬 prone to outside attractions, temptations, in a restless and jumpy mood. (6) Center: 圓心 center of circle; 核心 core, nucleus; 實心 solid; 空心 hollow; 向心力 centripetal force; 離心力 centrifugal force; 地心 center of earth; 地心吸力 gravity; 手心, 腳心 center of palm, sole; 湖心, 江心 center of lake, river.

心病 *shin-bihng*, n., some secret concern, longing, desire; a person's touchy or sensitive point.

心腸 *shin-charng*, n., (1) heart as

A B C

心 representing emotions of love, tenderness, hardness, concern; (2) (-'*chang*) mood, state of mind: 沒有甚麽心腸看戲 in no mood to enjoy a play.

心掣 *shincheh*, n., (Chin. med.) *angina pectoris.*

心竅 *shin-chiauh*, n., resourcefulness, intelligence, cunning: 有心竅 very resourceful (lit., "an opening of the heart" supposed to do the thinking).

心氣 *shin-chih*, n., (Chin. med.) a term used to indicate strength of heart beat; 心氣兒 person's mood or state of mind.

心情 *shinchirng*, n., state of mind, how one feels (happy, not so good, etc.).

心傳 *shin-chuarn*, n., personal teachings of master to pupil; also esoteric teachings.

心曲 *shin-chyu*, n., corner of one's heart, hidden feelings.

心膽 *shin-daan*, n., courage, gall, guts.

心得 *shinder*, n., personal insight, individual's understanding or discovery.

心電圖 *shindiahntur*, n., cardiogram.

心地 *shin-dih*, n., (1) disposition (kind, cruel, narrow, broad, etc.); (2) intentions (good, bad); (3) brains: 心地糊塗 muddle-headed.

心法 *shin-faa*, n., (Budd.) personal insight or understanding, aside from study of scriptures.

心房 *shin-farng*, n., ventricles and auricles of the heart.

心腹 *shin-fuh* (-'*fu*), n., (1) trusted aides, confidant: 心腹話 confidential talk, heart to heart talk; (2) 心腹地 central territory, strategic area; (3) one's inner feelings.

心肝 *shin-gan*, n., (1) courage, life ambition; (2) 我的心肝 my sweetheart; (3) conscience: 無心肝 without conscience.

心花 *shin-hua*, n., in 心花怒放 greatly elated, excited.

心火 *shin-huoo*, n., (1) tenseness, nervous excitement; (2) (Chin. med.) body's heat.

心齋 *shinjai*, n., (AC) "fasting of the heart," deep concentration.

心證 *shin-jehng*, n., (Budd.) realization of truth of teachings in scriptures by personal experience.

心迹 *shin'ji*[1] (-'*ji*), n., a person's motives as shown in actions.

心機 *shinji*[2] (-'*ji*), n., (1) mental cleverness, agility; (2) brooding.

心絞痛 *shinjiaau-tuhng*, n., *angina pectoris.*

心匠 *shin-jiahng*, n., mental planning or projection, mental creation behind art products.

心計 *shin-jih*[1], n., calculations, forethought, planning.

心悸 *shinjih*[2], n., palpitation.

心境 *shin-jihng*, n., state of mind (sorrowful, relaxed, etc.).

心筋阻塞 *shinjintzuuseh*, n., myocardial occlusion.

心旌 *shin-jing*[1], n., stirring of the mind.

心經 *shin-jing*[2], n., (1) a Budd. sutra; (2) 走心經 use the head (in meeting difficulties).

心疾 *shin-jir*, n., (1) a heart condition; (2) mental disorder.

心知 *shin-jy*, n., intelligence, the mind, consciousness.

心智 *shin-jyh*[1], n., intelligence, wisdom.

心志 *shinjyh*[2], n., ambition, purpose.

心坎(兒) *shin-kaan*(-*kaa'l*), n., (1) bosom, heartstrings, innermost feelings: 聽這話撞在心坎上 these words touched him to the quick; 姊妹兩人都是他心坎上的人 both the two sisters are his bosom friends; (2) the chest, the location of the heart.

心口 *shin-koou*, n., (1) the center of the chest; (2) 心口如一 what one says is indeed what one thinks.

心孔 *shinkuung*, n., the heart.

心裏 *shin'li*, n., (1) location of the heart; (2) in the mind: 把這事放在心裏 remember a warning, threat, insult, etc.; (3) feeling: 心裏不安 do not feel at ease; (4) love: 我心裏只有你 I love only you; 心裏份 (harbor) a grudge, etc.; 心裏勁兒 an unexpressed feeling (of hatred, hostility, etc.).

心力 *shin-lih*, n., mental exertion, will, energy.

心理 *shinlii*, n., what one feels or thinks about a situation; 心理學 psychology; 心理作用 psychological factor, imagination as opp. fact.

心靈 *shinlirng*, (1) n., the mind, the soul, the spirit; (2) adj., mentally quick, alert.

心路(兒) (-'*lu*) *shin-luh*('*l*), n., method of thinking; wit.

心盲 *shin-marng*, n., blindness due to psychic origin.

心苗 *shin-miaur*, n., budding of an idea; the mind as subject to growth, change.

心目 *shinmuh*, n., (in the) mind's eye, regard: 心目中只有他一人 set his (her) mind on one person.

心囊 *shin-narng*, n., (physiol.) pericardium.

心聲 *shin-sheng*, n., the voice of the heart.

心神 *shinshern*, n., state of mind: 心神不定 distracted, the mind wanders.

心想 *shinshiaang*, v.i., think: 我心想他準不來了 I think he will not come.

心象 *shinshiahng*, n., mental image.

心性 *shinshihng*, n., a person's disposition.

心行 *shinshirng*, n., a man's thoughts and conduct.

心術 *shinshuh*, n., (1) calculating mind, sincerity or lack of it.

心室 *shin-shyh*[1], n., ventricles, see -*farng* ↑.

心事 *shinshyh*[2], n., one's private, esp., personal affairs.

心血 *shinshyueh*, n., (labor which taxes) one's brains, heartfelt labor, labor of love.

心緒 *shinshyuh* (-'*shyu*), n., state of mind (disturbed, etc.).

心胸 *shinshyung*, n., (a broad, narrow) mind.

心算 *shinsuahn*, n., see -*ji*[2] ↑.

心思 *shinsy*, n., (1) thinking, cogitation; (2) a person's gen. habit of thinking; (3) motive: 誰知他甚麽心思 who knows what he is after? (4) mood: 沒心思聽戲 in no mind to see a play.

心田 *shintiarn*, n., heart domain.

心頭 *shintour*, n., see -*li* ↑.

心臟 *shintzahng*, n., the heart organ; 心臟病 a heart disease.

心窩(兒)(子) *shinwo*('*l*)(*tz*), n.,

bottom of the heart; where one feels.

心眼 *shinyaan*, n., point of view (short-sighted, etc.); 心眼兒 (a) disposition; (b) attention to details, focus of attention: 心眼兒太多 too much attention to details; heartstrings.

心藥 *shin-yauh*, n., psychological treatment.

心意 *shinyih*, n., intention, purpose.

心印 *shin-yihn*, n., (Budd.) appreciation of truth by meditation.

心影 *shin-yiing*, n., mental image.

心願 *shinyuahn*, adj. & n., willing, -ness.

必 72.72

bih.

V. aux. & adv. Must, be certain to; certainly: 必死 be certain to die; 必是 must be; 必能 must be able to; 必可 will certainly be able to; 未必 cannot be sure; 未必不成 cannot be certain it will fail; 未必如意 cannot be certain to turn out as you wish; 何必 is it necessary to...? why the need (for taking so much trouble, being angry, etc.); 敢必 I can be sure that; 必殺無赦 will be executed according to law; 必不可少 is a necessity; 雖未可必 although one cannot be certain; 必經之路 the only route or point on route which must be passed; 必傳之作 work destined to go down to posterity; 必定 *-dihng*, 必需, 必須 *-shyu*[1,2]↓.

必必剝剝 *bihbih-bohboh*, v.i., crackle (like burning logs).

必得 *bih-der*, v.i., must: 必得走一趟 simply have to make a trip; 必得如此 must do it this way.

必定 *bihdihng*, v.i. & aux., must: 必定失敗 certainly must fail.

必方 *bihfang*, n., mythical god of fire (also wr. 畢方).

必恭必敬 *bihgung-birjihng*, adj. & adv., phr., very polite(ly).

必然 *bihrarn*, adj. & n., (the) inevitable, the logically necessary: 必然之事 or 事有必然 the necessary and inevitable, what is bound to happen; 必然性 *--shihng*, n., inevitability.

必修科 *bihshiu-ke*, n., (in school) compulsory subject or course.

必需 *bihshyu*[1], v.t., need, vitally need (a thing, help, etc.): 必需品 a necessity (during travel, etc.); dist. from 必須 *-shyu*[2], an aux. vb. ↓.

必須 *bihshyu*[2], v.i. & aux., must: 必須看他 must see him.

必要 *bihyauh*, v.i. & t. & n., a need, need to, certainly want to: 我必要去 I am determined to go; 沒有必要 there is no need.

SECTION 80

§ 80.00 (八/丿)

前 80.00

chiarn.

V.i. (LL) to go forward: 勇往直前 march forward fearlessly; 不前 to hang back.

Adj. (1) In front, forward: 前面, 前邊 *-miahn*, *-bian*↓; 前排 the front row; 前鋒 *-feng*↓; 前呼後擁 (of important personage) with escorts in front and behind; 前仰後合 stagger forward and back; 前仆後繼 (in battle) as those in front fall, those behind take up their positions; 前車可鑒 where a car in front flounders serves as warning to those behind—learn from s.o.'s past mistakes; 前前後後 from front to rear, altogether; 向前 forward; 目前, 眼前 at present ("close before one's eyes"); 面前 in s.o.'s presence. (2) Preceding: 前夜 night before last; 前天, 前日, 前年 *-tian*, *-ryh*, *-niarn*↓; 前月 preceding month; 前夫, 前妻 former husband, wife; 前任總統 the former president; 前總統, 首相 ex-president, ex-premier; 前次 the last time; 前度劉郎 phr., former lover comes back; 前功盡棄 all previous work undone. (3) Past, of earlier times: 前王, 前朝 the past kings, dynasty, -ies; 前哲, 前賢, 前脩 the wise men of the past; 前愆 former mistakes; 盡捐前嫌 let bygones be bygones, forget the past animosity between two parties; 前無古人 unprecedented (character, event).

Adv. (1) Forward: 前來 come forward; 前往 go forward or to some definite place; 前往法國 go to France; 往前走 go forward. (2)

Ahead, beforehand: 前定 predestined, decided beforehand; 前知 have prescience, to know beforehand, prophesy.

前輩 *chiarnbeih*, n., the elder generation (uncles, older alumni).

前邊 *chiarnbian*, adv., in front.

前塵 *chiarnchern*, n., ("old track") the past: 回首前塵 to recall the past events.

前程 *chiarncherng*, n., prospect, future career: 前程保不住了 I am afraid (his) career is finished.

前妻 *chiarnchi*, n., former wife.

前情 *chiarnchirng*, n., (1) preceding circumstances; (2) the past (between lovers).

前驅 *chiarnchyu*, n., forerunner, vanguard.

前導 *chiarndaau*, n., pioneer, one who shows the way (also 先導).

前定 *chiarndihng*, adj., predestined.

前敵 *chiarndir*, n., battle front.

前番 *chiarnfan*, adj. & adv., the last time.

前方 *chiarnfang*, n., (1) the front of battle; (2) the place ahead.

前鋒 *chiarnfeng*, n., (mil.) vanguard (also 先鋒).

前夫 *chiarn-fu*, n., former husband.

前和 *chiarnher*, n., the front end of coffin.

前後 *chiarn-houh*, adv. phr., (1) in front and back; (2) before and after (usu. showing a difference): 他說的話前後不同 there's a difference between what he says now and what he said before; 前後腳兒 one following another.

前回 *chiarnhueir*, adv., the last time.

前兆 *chiarn-jauh*, n., an augury, an omen.

前者 *chiarnjee*, n., the former (opp. 後者 the latter).

前進 *chiarnjihn*, (1) adj., progressive (author, country, etc.); (2) v.i., go forward.

前景 *chiarnjiing*, n., the foreground of a painting.

前箸 *chiarnjuh*, n., see 箸 92A.41.

前知 *chiarnjy*[1], (1) v.i., foretell the future; (2) n., a seer; foreknowledge, prescience.

前肢 *chiarn-jy*[2], n., forelegs, fore limbs, of an animal.

前置詞 *chiarnjyh-tsyr*, n., (gram.) preposition (also called 介詞).

前科 *chiarn-ke*, n., record of previous crime; 前科犯 ex-convict (law).

前例 *chiarn-lih*, n., precedent.

前馬 *chiarnmaa*, n., (AC) a stable servant who leads the horse for his master.

前茅 *chiarnmaur*, n., see 茅 20A.00.

前面 *chiarnmiahn*, adv., (1) in front; (2) (what is said or mentioned) above, also n., the above.

前母 *chiarn-muu*, n., father's former wife (in relation to stepmother's child).

前年 *chiarn-niarn*, adv., year before last.

前任 *chiarnrehn*, n., predecessor in office.

前人 *chiarnrern*, n., (1) the people of the past; (2) person referred to above (esp. in anthology).

前日 *chiarnryh*, adv., day before yesterday.

前哨 *chiarnshauh*, n., the forward patrol, sentry.

前身 *chiarn-shen*, n., (1) the previous incarnation (also *-sheng*↓); (2) the precursor of an organization.

前生 *chiarn-sheng*, n., the previous incarnation.

前線 *chiarnshiahn*, n., the military front; the front line of battle.

前項 *chiarn-shiahng*, n., (1) (math.) antecedent; (2) the clause above; the matter referred to above.

前夕 *chiarnshih*, n., (1) the night before last; (2) the eve (of revolution).

前手 *chiarnshoou*, n., predecessor; (comm.) former owner.

前市 *chiarnshyh*[1], n., forenoon stock market.

前世 *chiarn-shyh*[2], n., (1) former generation(s); (2) (Budd.) previous incarnation(s).

前臺 *chiarn-tair*, n., the stage, opp. 後臺(台) backstage.

前天 *chiarntian*, adv., day before yesterday.

前提 *chiarntir*, n., (1) (logic) the premise; (2) the first concern (of the nation, undertaking, etc.).

前頭 *chiarn'tou*, adv., (1) in front, ahead; (2) before: 三年前頭 three years ago.

前此 *chiarntsyy*, adv., up to now, until now.

前途 *chiarntur*, (1) n., prospect, the road ahead; (2) pron., (in letters) indirect reference to a third party: 請轉告前途 please convey the message to Mr. So-and-so.

前奏 *chiarntzouh*, n., (mus.) prelude, overture; prelude to an event.

前晚 *chiarnwaan*, n., evening before last.

前衛 *chiarn-weih*, n., vanguard, *avant-garde*.

前言 *chiarnyarn*, n., (1) earlier promise or statement; (2) foreword to a book.

前因 *chiarnyin*, n., antecedents of course of events: 前因後果 causes and effects; the sequence of events in a story.

前緣 *chiarnyuarn*, n., predestination (for lovers, enemies).

尊 80.00

tzun.

N. (1) A title of respect: 尊長 *-jaang*↓; 令尊 (court.) your father; 尊大人 ditto; 府尊 a prefect; 邑尊 a city magistrate; 縣尊 a county magistrate. (2) (U.f. 樽) a bottle, a cup, a goblet. (3) An image or statue of a god or the Buddha.

V.t. To respect, revere, venerate: 尊重 *-juhng*, 尊敬 *-jihng*↓; 尊王攘夷 honor the king and drive off the barbarians; 尊師重道 honor the teacher and respect his teachings.

Adj. (1) Venerable, honorable, respectable: 尊貴 *-gueih*↓. (2) High (opp. 卑 low): 天尊地卑 the sky above and the earth below. (3) Your: 尊處 *-chuh*, 尊府 *-fuu*[2],

尊駕 *-jiah*, 尊命 *-mihng*, 尊祖 *-tzuu*[1]↓.

尊卑 *tzunbei*, (1) adj., high and low; (2) n., superiors and inferiors, elders and children.

尊稱 *tzungcheng*, n., your respectful name.

尊前 *tzun-chiarn*, phr., polite salutation used in letters to elders ("may I beg to lay this before you?"); (尊 u.f. 樽) (poet.) before wine cups, i.e., while drinking together.

尊親屬 *tzun-chinshuu*, n., (civil code) one's parents, grandparents, great-grandparents, and other relatives of similar ranks.

尊處 *tzun-chuh*, n., (court.) your home, the place where you live or work.

尊崇 *tzunchurng*, v.t., to honor, respect, hold in high regard.

尊大人 *tzun-dahrern*, n., your esteemed father.

尊夫人 *tzuu-furern*, n., (court.) your (charming) wife.

尊甫 *tzun-fuu*[1], n., your eminent father.

尊府 *tzun-fuu*[2], n., (1) your residence (home); (2) your eminent father.

尊貴 *tzungueih*, adj., (of persons) respectable, honorable.

尊公 *tzun-gung*, n., (AC) your esteemed father.

尊號 *tzun-hauh*, n., (1) titular honors conferred on the king, queen or other members of the royal family: 上尊號 to confer such honors; (2) your poetic name, see 號 40S.70.

尊侯 *tzun-hour*, n., (court.) (MC) your esteemed father.

尊長 *tzunjaang*, n., one's elders or superiors.

尊者 *tzunjee*, n., (1) one's elders; (2) (Budd.) a saint, a sage.

尊駕 *tzun-jiah*, n., your good self, esp. with reference to movements (駕=carriage).

尊紀 *tzunjih*, n., (LL, court.) your servant.

尊敬 *tzunjihng*, v.t., to honor, respect, venerate, revere.

尊重 *tzunjuhng*, v.t., esteem, value highly; respect (rights of privacy, etc.).

尊君 *tzun-jyun*, (1) n., (LL) your esteemed father; (2) phr., philosophy of elevating and upholding power of a monarch.

尊閫 *tzun-kuun*, n., (LL, court.) your (honored) wife.

尊老 *tzun-laau*, n., (1) to respect the aged people; (2) (LL) elderly parents.

尊門 *tzun-mern*, n., (LL, court.) your home, residence.

尊命 *tzun-mihng*, n., your wishes (request), instructions.

尊容 *tzun-rurng*[1], n., (1) your looks (appearance), generally used in complim. sense but also occasionally to show contempt: 看你那副尊容 see what a spectacle you are! (2) the dignified appearance of the Buddha.

尊榮 *tzun-rurng*[2], n., dignity and honor.

尊生 *tzun-sheng*, phr., to respect life.

尊顯 *tzunshiaan*, adj., enjoying high social position.

尊姓 *tzun-shihng*, phr., (court.) your name; may I know your name?

尊屬 *tzun-shuu*, n., (1) relatives of higher ranks than oneself; (2) your relatives.

尊師 *tzun-shy*, (1) n., a Taoist priests; (2) phr., to respect one's teacher: 尊師重道 (see V.t.↑).

尊兄 *tsun-shyung*, n., (1) your brother; (2) "my dear elder brother," used in letters between friends.

尊宿 *tzun-suh*, n., (Budd.) a venerable old monk.

尊堂 *tzun-tarng*, n., your venerable mother.

尊祖 *tzun-tzuu*[1], n., your grandfather.

尊俎 *tzun-tzuu*[2], n., plates and dishes (also wr. 樽): 折衝尊(樽)俎 be sent on a diplomatic mission, serve as a diplomat.

尊翁 *tzun-weng*, n., your eminent father.

尊嚴 *tzunyarn*, adj. & n., dignfied, -ity.

尊彝 *tzun-yir*, n., anc. ceremonial vessels.

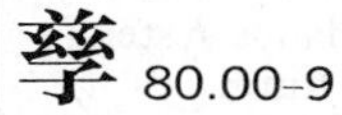

孳 80.00-9

tzy (**tzyh*).

V.i. To grow, multiply: 孳生, 孳息, 孳衍 *-sheng*, *-shir*, *-yaan*↓.

Adj. & adv. (1) Persistent, -ly: 孳孳 *-tzy*↓. (2) Thriving: 孳茂 *-mouh*↓.

孳茂 *tzymouh*, adj., luxuriant plant growth.

孳乳 *tzyruu*, v.i., (of cells) to grow, multiply; (of words, characters, meaning) grow or acquire new derived forms or meanings.

孳生 *tzysheng*, v.i., to multiply (as plants).

孳息 *tzyshir*, v.i., (cattle) multiply.

孳孳 *tzytzy*, adv., perseveringly (=孜孜): 孳孳爲利 work morning till night for money; 孳孳爲善 to persevere in doing good.

孳尾 **tzyhweei*, v.t., (AC) (of animals) copulate.

孳衍 *tzyyaan*, v.i., see *-shir*↑.

導 80.00

dauh (sp. pr. *daau*).

N. Guide: 先導, 前導, 嚮導 guide; 領導 leader.

V.t. (Oft. *daau*) to guide, instruct, show the way: 領導 to lead (any group); 指導 guide, instruct, show how; 誘導 induce or guide toward right conduct; 導致 to lead to, to result in, cause.

導播 *dauhbor*, v.i. & n., broadcast.

尊 孳 導

亅	小	⺊	十	土	ナ	卄	乚卜	丨	一	丅	フ	口	囗	冈	㇆	厂	尸	亠	广	宀	丶	乚	弋	心	八	人	乂	乛	一	丿	𠂉	く
00	01	02	10	11	12	20	21	22	30	31	32	40	41	42	50	51	52	60	61	62	63	70	71	72	80	81	82	83	90	91	92	93

導管 *dauhguaan*, n., pipe, duct.

導火線 *dauhhuooshiahn*, n., fuse, (lit. & fig.).

導論 *dauhluhn*, n., introduction (to book).

導線 *dauhshiahn*, n., guideline.

導向系統 *dauhshiahng shihtuung*, n., (astron.) guidance system.

導師 *dauhshy*, n., tutor.

導言 *dauhyarn*, n., foreword (to book).

導體 *dauhtii*, n., (phys.) conductor; 半導體 semiconductor.

導演 *dauhyaan*, v.t. & n., to direct, director (of play).

§ 80.01 (八/小)

槊 80.01

shuoh.

N. A long spear, lance.

§ 80.02 (八/丬)

養 80.02

yaang (**yahng*).
[Abbr. 养]

N. Nourishment: 營養 ditto; 營養不足 malnutrition.

V.t. (1) To keep (dogs, sheep, mistress, etc.), to raise (poultry, cabbage, etc.): 養漢 (of woman) keep a man-lover; 養小老婆 keep mistress; 養虎貽患 keep a tiger puppy and regret it afterwards. (2) To raise to maturity, to bring up (children), to care for: 養育 *-yuh* ↓; 撫養 bring up (children); 培養人材 to train men (for profession); 養護 to protect (the young); 收養 to adopt (children), take in (orphans); 扶養 to take care of (the aged, sick); 贍養 to support parents. (3) To feed, keep alive: 飼養 to feed (animals, babies); 養尊處優 to live a comfortable, well-fed life; 養寇 to be lenient towards bandits and let them grow; 養賊 to harbor s.o. who later will do one harm; 養癰, 養疽 to let an ulcer grow and fail to cut it in time. (4) To give birth: 養孩子 give birth to children. (5) To cure: 養病 convalesce, to recuperate from illness; 休養, 保養, 靜養 rest and recuperate. (6) To train, nourish, cultivate (character, ambition): 養成 *-cherng* ↓; 養心, 養性, 養生 *-shin, -shihng, -sheng* ↓; 養精蓄銳 to harness one's spiritual resources; 涵養 mental and moral culture, mental reserve; 養晦, 養拙 *-hueih, -juor* ↓.

Adj. Foster (parents, etc.): 養父, 養子 *-fuh, -tzyy*, etc. ↓.

養病 *yaang-bihng*, v.i., to recuperate after illness.

養兵 *yaang-bing*, phr., keep an army.

養成 *yaang-cherng*, v.i., to train, grow, raise (s.t.), to become: 養成習慣 develop a habit; 養成無賴 grow to become a ne'er-do-well.

養氣 *yaang-chih*, phr., nourish the spirit: 養吾浩然之氣 (孟子) nourish my vital spirit or spirit of fearlessness.

養親 *yahng-chin*, phr., to support and serve parents.

養分 *yaangfehn*, n., nutritive value of food.

養蜂 *yaang-feng*, phr., to keep bees.

養父 *yaang-fuh*, n., foster father.

養疴 *yaan-ge*, v.i., to recuperate from an illness.

養和 *yaang-her*, phr., to obey rules of physical and mental health, reason of health.

養晦 *yaang-hueih*, phr., (AC) to live in retirement to bide one's time, keep growing in spirit while keeping away from public life.

養護 *yaanghuh*, v.t., to look after (children).

養活 *yaang'huo*, v.i. & t., (1) to make a living; (2) to feed (a family).

養家 *yaang-jia*, phr., to support a family; 養家兒 (AC) madame of a brothel; 養家人 (MC) (1) a local resident with a family; (2) husband.

養濟 *yaangjih*, v.i. & t., (1) to convalesce; (2) to support (parents).

養靜 *yaang-jihng*, phr., to cultivate mental calm.

養珠 *yaangju*, n., cultured pearl.

養拙 *yaang-juor*, phr., (LL) to enjoy obscurity as a matter of culture.

養志 *yahng-jyh*, phr., (1) to nourish or keep alive one's ambition; (2) (**yahng*) (AC) to continue to do what one's parents wanted for life.

養口 *yarng-koou*, phr., to eat: 尋些野味養口 to find some wild game for food.

養老 *yarng-laau*, phr., (1) (AC) to honor and serve the aged; (2) to live on pension; 養老金 old age pension.

養廉 *yaang-liarn* (*-'lian*), phr., to encourage officials' honesty by paying sufficient salaries.

養料 *yaangliauh*, n., nutrition; feed for animals.

養路 *yaang-luh*, phr., to maintain roads in good repair; 養路費 tax for road maintenance.

養母 *yarng-muu*, n., foster mother.

養娘 *yaang-niarng*, n., (MC) maid; a wet nurse.

養女 *yarng-nyuu*, n., foster daughter.

養贍 *yaangshahn*, v.t., to support (parents, family).

養身 *yaang-shen*, phr., to nourish the body, to keep oneself physically fit.

養生 *yaang-sheng*, v.i. & n., to lead a life in sound health; hygiene: 養生之道 way of keeping good health; 養生送死 (AC) the basic filial duties of serving parents while living and giving proper burial.

養神 *yaang-shern*, phr., to refresh one's spirit by keeping quiet for a period.

養性 *yaang-shihng*, phr., to maintain one's original pure char-

acter, cultivate mental poise.
養心 *yaangshin*, v.i., cultivate mental calm.
養媳 *yaang-shir*, n., (for 童養媳) a daughter-in-law brought to husband's family while still a child.
養子 *yarng-tzyy*, (1) n., foster child; (2) (AC) phr., give birth to child.
養望 *yaang-wahng*, phr., (LL) to nourish, cultivate a reputation.
養養 *yarngyaang*, adj., (AC) uneasy.
養育 *yaangyuh*, v.i. & t., to bring up (child): 養育之恩 (gratitude for) the love and care from childhood.

§ 80.10 (八/十)

羊 80.10

yarng (**shiarng*).

N. (1) (-'*l*) Sheep, goat: 山羊 goat; 綿羊 sheep; 公羊, 牡羊 ram; 母羊, 牝羊 ewe; 羚羊 antelope; 羯羊 a castrated ram; 羊質虎皮 sheep in tiger's skin—a dressed-up weakling; 羊羣 a flock of sheep; 牧羊 a shepherd, to pasture sheep. (2) A surname. (3) U.f. 祥 (**shiarng*): 吉羊 (=吉祥) good luck.

羊白頭 *yarngbairtour*, n., a skin disease showing white specks.
羊腸 *yarngchang*, n., as in 羊腸小道 a small winding path.
羊齒 *yarngchyy*, n., (bot.) bracken, *Aspidium filix-mas*.
羊癲風 *yarngdian-feng*, n., epilepsy.
羊羔(兒) *yarnggau'l*, n., a lamb, a kid.
羊羹 *yarnggeng*, n., a kind of cake.
羊公鶴 *yarnggung-heh*, n., (allu.) Mr. Yang's crane, said to dance but unable to do so when called upon to do so—undeserved reputation.
羊毫 *yarnghaur*, n., writing brush made of wool.
羊角風 *yarng'jiau-feng*, n., epilepsy, see *-dian-feng*↑.
羊脂 *yarngjy*, n., suet; 羊脂玉 fine white tallow jade.
羊躑躅 *yarngjyrjur*, n., (bot.) the rhododendron (reputed to be "avoided by goats").
羊車 *yarngjyu*, n., a goat cart.
羊毛 *yarngmaur*, n., sheep's wool; 羊毛包 a woolpack.
羊膜 *yarngmor*, n., (zoo.) amnion, innermost membrane of sac enclosing embryo.
羊排骨 *yarng pairguu*, n., mutton chops.
羊皮 *yarngpir*, n., sheepskin; 羊皮紙 parchment.
羊肉床子 *yarng'rouh-chuarngtz*, n., (coll.) mutton shop.
羊絨 *yarngrurng*, n., fine wool.
羊乳 *yarngruu*, n., (bot.) *Codonopsis lanceolata*.
羊桃 *yarngtaur*, n., (bot.) *Averrhoa carambola* (also called 五斂子).
羊蹄草 *yarngtir-tsaau*, n., (bot.) the dock.
羊頭 *yarngtour*, n., as in 撞羊頭 to ram one's head against the opponent in a fight.
羊駝 *yarngtuor*, n., the alpaca.
羊棗 *yarngtzaau*, n., (bot.) a small variety of dates.

§ 80.11 (八/土)

坌 80.11

behn.

[Var. 坋]

N. (AC) dust.

V.i. (AC) to gather, together, to splash.

坌集 *behnjir*, v.i., (LL) gather at a place.
坌涌 *behnyuung*, v.i., (LL) gush up like gas.

塑 80.11

suh.

V.i. To sculpt: 泥塑 clay figure; 雕塑 sculpture; 塑像 v.i. & n., (make) plastic figure, statue.

塑膠 *suhjiau*, n., plastic (tubes, utensils, etc.), polyester.
塑像 *suhshiahng*, n., clay statue.

§ 80.20 (八/廾)

并 80.20

bihng.

[Pop. for 幷 90.20]

§ 80.21 (八/乚)

岔 80.21

chah.

[Related 叉 32.82; cogn. 差 80.30]

N. (1) A forked road: 分岔 (road) leads off in different directions: see 岔道, 岔路 *-dauh, -luh*↓; 岔批兒 *-pie'l*↓. (2) Unexpected or undesirable turn of events: 岔子, 岔兒 *-tz, -'l*↓. (3) Purposeful interruption of talk: 打岔 break off conversation by changing subject, see V.i. & t. 1↓.

V.i. & t. (1) To interrupt: 用話岔開 turn conversation into new direction. (2) To change in voice: 聲音岔了=his voice caught, became hoarse (and tears followed).

Adj. (1) Incorrect (statement): 這話岔了 what you say is incorrect (cf. 差 80.30). (2) Confused, uncomfortable: 岔眼 *-yaan* ↓; 岔氣 *-chih* ↓.

岔氣 *chahchih*, n., sudden pains in chest, angina pectoris.
岔曲 *chahchyuu*, n., a short song in certain type of Chin. opera (cf. 插△曲 10A.21).
岔道 *chahdauh*, n., a fork-shaped road crossing; a branch road.
岔換 *chahhuahn*, v.i. & t., to divert (mind): 把心中煩悶岔換岔換 to divert the mind from boredom.
岔口 *chahkoou*, n., where the road leads off in another direction.
岔兒 *chah'l*, n., (1) see *-tz* ↓; (2) broken bits: 缸岔兒, 瓦岔兒 broken jars, tiles.
岔路 *chahluh*, n., see *-dauh* ↑.
岔批兒 *chahpie'l*, v.i., as in 走岔批兒 go on different roads and miss each other.
岔子 *chahtz*, n., an untoward turn of events: 出了岔子 s.t. untoward has happened.
岔眼 *chah-yaan*, adj., (horse) takes fright from what it sees.

§ 80.22 (八/丨)

兹 80.22

tzy.
[Pop. of 茲 20A.93]

丫 80.22

ya.

N. A forked branch.

丫把兒 *ya'ba'l*, n., a forked junction: 樹丫把兒 ditto; 手丫把兒, 腳丫把兒 joint between fingers, toes.
丫叉 *yacha*, n., forked junction of branches, of hands.
丫鬟(兒) *ya'huan(-hua'l)*, n., a slave girl, so-called because girl's hairdo with double coils resembled character 丫 (also wr. 丫嬛; see *-'tou* ↓).
丫頭 *ya'tou*, n., a slave girl (see *-'huan* ↑); (contempt.) a girl; (formerly, used familiarly by elders) a girl: 這個丫頭 this girl; 丫頭片子 or 片兒 (facet.) little girl.

弟 80.22

dih (**tih*).

N. Younger brother: 舍弟 my brother; 令弟 your brother; 弟兄 brothers; 弟妹 younger brother and sister; 弟男子姪 nephews in gen.; 子弟 the younger generation; 弟 gen. term of reference to self in friendly letters, used in place of "I"; similarly 愚弟 in letters; 兄弟 in conversation, more rarely 小弟.

Adj. (**tih*) 孝弟 be good son and good brother, see 悌 22A.22; 豈△弟 21.30.

弟弟 *dihdih*, n., younger brother.
弟兄 *dihshiung*, n., brother (i.e., without specifying elder or younger), dist. 兄弟 (coll.) strictly younger brother; comrades in arms.
弟子 *dihtzyy*, n., disciple; pupil.

斧 80.22

fuu.

N. (*-tz*) Axe, hatchet.

V.t. (1) (LL) to hew with an axe: 斧木 chop wood, trees. (2) To trim, hew to the line: 斧削, 斧正, 斧政 (asking person to) trim, correct one's composition; 斧斤 (AC) hatchet for cutting down trees; 無斧鑿痕 (of masterpiece) without axe marks, i.e., completely without artificiality, showing consummate skill; 資斧 travelling expenses.

斧柄 *fuubihng*, n., (fig.) control of government ("axe-handle"); also 斧柯 *fuuke*.
斧鑊 *fuu-huoh*, n., punishment by axe and boiling cauldron.
斧頭 *fuutour*, n., axe.
斧鉞 *fuuyueh*, n., axe and hatchet, referring to execution of criminals: 斧鉞之誅.

养 80.22

yaang.
[Abbr. of 養 80.02]

兼 80.22

jian.

Pron. Both: 兼得 have both (of the things); 不可得兼 may not have both at one and the same time.

V.t. Bring together, unite in one: 兼幷 *-bihng* ↓; 兼弱攻昧 annex the weak and fall upon the stupid; 兼收並蓄 all-embracing; 兼容並包 all-inclusive, (of interest) catholic; 兼權熟計 give mature consideration to all aspects of a question; 兼營 concurrently operating.

Adj. (1) Both: 兼嗣兩房 be heir to two branches of a family. (2) Concurrent: 兼職 *-jyr* ↓; 兼業 concurrent business, enterprise.

Adv. (1) Double, twice: 兼人之量 be able to drink (eat, do) twice as much as another. (2) Also, as well: 兼司他職 also in charge of other duties; 兼辦, 兼管 have other functions as well. (3) Both…and: 品學兼優 (of a student) good both in character and at studies.

兼愛 *jian-aih*, n., the doctrine of universal love, as advocated by Motse 墨子.
兼幷 *jianbihng*, v.t., annex (territory).
兼差 *jianchai*, v.i. & n., (hold) concurrent posts.
兼程 *jiancherng*, adv., by forced march day and night.
兼顧 *jianguh*, v.t., look after (two things) at one and the same time; take into equal consideration.
兼毫 *jianhaur*, n., Chin. writing brush made with a mixture of wolf's and goat's hair.
兼金 *jianjin*, n., gold of the best quality ("twice the value").
兼職 *jianjyr*, v.i. & n., (hold) concurrent jobs.
兼理 *jianlii*, adv., concurrently.
兼任 *jian-rehn*, adv., concurrently, a concurrent posts.
兼旬 *jian-shyurn*, n., a period of twenty days.
兼祧 *jian-tiau*, v.i., be heir to two branches of family.

爺 80.22

yer.

N. (1) (Coll.) father: 爺娘 father and mother. (2) Gen. term of respect for older person, also for master: 老爺 master of house, also address of magistrate; 大爺, 二爺 address of master's oldest, second son; 少爺 young master, a gentleman's son, a rich young man: 少爺脾氣 air of a pampered young man. (3) Grandfather: 爺爺 *-'ye* ↓; 太爺 old master: 老太爺 master's father as dist. 老爺 master himself.

爺兒倆 *yer'l-liaa*, n., father and son, uncle and nephew, father and daughter, etc.
爺兒們 *yer'l'men*, n., the menfolks.
爺們兒 *yer'mel*, n., see *-'l'men* ↑.
爺們 *yer'men*, n., the men, opp. women; the menfolk.
爺娘 *yerniarng*, n., parents.
爺爺 *yer'ye*, n., (coll.) grandpa; also used of elderly person in clan or village.

§ 80.30 (八/一)

並 80.30

bihng.

[Err. var. 並; anc. var. 竝]

Adv. (1) Furthermore, and also, (LL 並, vern. 並 or 並且): 他來觀光, 並訪舊友 he came to visit the place, and also see some old friends; 他來送禮物, 並帶個信 he came to bring some gifts, and also pass a message. (2) (To reinforce a negative) really: 非如此 not so, but 並非如此 really not so; 我並不知道 I really do not know; 並未聞知, 並未見過 really have not heard, seen; 並不至此 not really so bad; 並非無因 not without cause; 並非得已 it is not because I wanted to. (3) Together, parallel with: 並坐, 並立 sit, stand together; 並肩作戰 fight shoulder to shoulder. (4) Both, equally: 兩樣並重 regard both as equally important; 並行 do both at the same time; 並行不悖 the two do not interfere with one another; 並存 keep both; 並駕齊驅 run neck to neck, share (progress) together, can well stand side by side with.

並且 *bihngchiee*, adv., furthermore, see Adv. 1↑.

並 80.30

bihng.

[Err. var. of 並↑]

差 80.30

cha (**chah*, **chai*, **tsy*, **tsuo*).

N. (1) Difference, mathematical difference: 差數, 差額 *-shuh*, *-er* ↓; 差別, 差異 *-bier*, *-yih* ↓; 日差, 年差 diurnal, annual variation; 週期變差 periodic variation. (2) (**chai*) A mission, an errand: 差事, 差役 *-'shy*, *-'yi* ↓; 郵差, 信差 mailman; 公差 official or business trip; 出差 be sent out on official business; 當差 on duty or serve as employee; 開小差 take French leave, absent without leave. (3) (re. pr. **tsy*) Grade: 等差 gradation (of kinship, status); 差等 *-deeng* ↓. (4) Mistake: 差錯, 差誤, 差跌 *-tsuoh*, *-wuh*, *-dier* ↓.

V.t. (1) (**chai*) To send (messenger, errand boy, etc.); to appoint on duty: 差使, 差派, 差遣 *-shyy*, *-paih*, *-chiaan* ↓. (2) (**chah*) Differ: 差好多, 差得遠 differ a great deal; 差不離(兒) almost right, not too much difference; 差不多 *-buh-duo* ↓; 差一點兒 (*-idiaa'l*) with a tiny difference, almost.

Adj. (1) (**chah*) Inferior, bad: 太差了, 差極了, 差多了 very bad, not up to the mark. (2) (**tsy*) Disorderly, jagged: 參差 mixed, not even; see 差池 *-chyr* (2) ↓.

Adv. Barely: 差可 will barely do,

serve the purpose; 差強人意 barely satisfactory, fair.

差別 *chabier*, n., difference.

差撥 **chaibo*, (1) v.t., to send (s.o.); (2) (MC) petty officer.

差不多(兒) **chah-buh-duo('l)*, adj. & adv., almost, good enough: almost (a thousand, finished, fell down, etc.).

差不離(兒)**chah-buh-lir(-lier'l)*, adv., almost the same, almost right.

差遣 **chaichiaan*, v.t., to send (servant, employee, etc.).

差池 *chachyr*, (1) n., (a) (also wr. 差遲) s.t. gone wrong, untoward accident; (b) mistake in commitment: 若有半點差池，我手裏不能放過你 shall not forgive you if there's the slightest mistake; (2) (**tsychyr*) adj., as in 差池其羽 (AC) its feathers are ruffled.

差遲 *cha'chyr*, n., see *-chyr*↑, (2) untoward accident.

差等 **tsydeeng*, n., (AC) gradations (in kinship, love).

差點兒 **chah-diaa'l*, (1) adv., almost (fell down, etc.); (2) adj., not quite as good.

差跌 **tsuodier*, n., mistake, slip-up (＝蹉跌).

差額 *cha-er*, n., difference in amount, quantity or number (of payment, enrolment, etc.); 借方差額 debit balance; 貸方差額 credit balance.

差號 *cha-hauh*, n., (math.) sign of difference "∼".

差勁 **chahjihn*, adv. & n., falling below standard.

差可 *chakee*, adj., barely can do.

差派 **chaipaih*, v.t., to send (s.o.); assign (work).

差配兒 **chahpeh'l*, v.i., be wrongly paired (as shoes, chopsticks).

差人 **chairern*, (1) n., the bearer (of letter); (2) v.t., to send s.o.

差數 *chashuh*, n., the difference in number.

差事 **chai'shy*, n., (1) a government post; (2) temporarily assigned duty; (3) formerly, a prisoner to be executed.

差使 **chaishyy*, v.t., to send (s.o.).

差忒 *chateh*, n., mistake in commitment.

差錯 *chatsuoh*, n., (1) mistake; (2) untoward accident.

差跎 **tsuotuor*, adj., (AC) drifting slowly (also wr. 蹉跎): 差跎歲月 the years drift by.

差子 **chahtz*, n., s.t. gone wrong.

差委 **chaiweei*, v.t., to appoint (s.o. to do).

差誤 *chawuh*, n., mistake, error.

差役 **chai'yi*, n., servant(s).

差異 *chayih*, n., difference.

羞 80.30

shiou.

N. (1) A shame: 羞恥, 羞辱 *-chyy*, *-ruh*↓; 貽羞 bring shame (to relatives, etc.); 含羞忍辱 suffer humiliations. (2) Flavory food: 珍羞 exotic dishes.

V.i. & t. Feel ashamed, shy: 害羞 ditto; 不羞 not ashamed; 羞與爲伍 ashamed to be his colleague (friend); 羞答答, 羞羞答答, 羞剌剌, 羞怯怯 very shy; 羞死人也, 羞殺人也 shames one to death, makes one die of shame; 羞得面紅耳赤 blush all over; 惱羞成怒 turn angry from embarrassment.

Adj. Shameful: 羞口難開 too embarrassed (or shy) to speak; 羞手羞腳 timid, dare not move; 羞刀難入鞘 a drawn sword cannot be put back into scabbard—must go through with a thing, once it is started.

羞怯 *shiouchieh*, adj., timid, timorous; shy.

羞恥 *shiouchyy*, n., sense of shame (or honor).

羞憤 *shioufehn*, adj., agitated for action from shame suffered.

羞花 *shiou-hua*, phr., (LL) "to shame the flowers"—of woman's resplendent beauty.

羞愧 *shioukueih*, adj. & v.i., feel ashamed: 羞愧難當 embarrassed beyond words.

羞明 *shioumirng*, n., (med.) photophobia.

羞惱 *shiounaau*, adj., humiliated and angry.

羞人 *shiou-rern*, phr., shames one: 羞人的事 s.t. which makes one shamed.

羞辱 *shiouruh*, v.t. & n., to humiliate (person); a shame, insult.

羞澀 *shiouseh*, adj., (1) awkward and shy; (2) as in 阮囊羞澀 phr., (allu.) embarrassingly short of money (阮 is person's surname.)

羞惡 *shiouwuh*, n., as in 羞惡之心 (AC & LL) a sense of shame.

釜 80.30

fuu.

N. (1) Pot, pan, cauldron: 釜底抽薪 withdraw fuel from boiling cauldron, i.e., a fundamental solution; 作釜中魚 like a fish in the pot, without hope of escape; 破釜沉舟 break cooking pots and sink boats, army's grim determination of no retreat, (like Eng. "burn one's boats"). (2) Anc. grain measure 6 斗 4 升.

盆 80.30

pern.

N. Basin, pot, tub, wooden or enamel or metal: 花盆 flower pot; 浴盆 bathtub; 臉盆 washing basin; 傾盆 (of rain) pouring; 臨盆 about to deliver a child (of expecting mother); 鼓盆而歌 allu. to Chuangtse who sang beating on a basin when his wife died; 戴盆望天 folly of trying to see the sky with basin over one's head.

V.t. To train (cricket) for fighting in a large bowl.

盆地 *perndih*, n., valley surrounded by mountains, river basin.

盆骨 *pernguu*, n., (biol.) pelvic bones.

盆景 *pernjiing*, n., miniature landscape or flower arrangement in a basin or bowl; such bowl with artificial flowers of precious stones.

盆堂 *perntarng*, n., public bath provided with tubs, dist. from 池堂.

盆栽 *perntzai*, n., a pot plant; drawf-tree culture.

益 80.30

yih (also *yir*).

N. Benefit, profit, advantage: 益處 *-chuh*↓; 有益, 無益 beneficial, profitless; 公益 public welfare; 權益 (law) right arising from ownership; 進益 progress in studies, increase in trade, etc.; 收益 income, receipts.

V.i. & t. (1) To benefit (the public, etc.). (2) (AC) to increase in money or population: 其家必日益 his family will grow in numbers.

Adv. Increasingly (cold, hot, poor, hectic, etc.): 益發 *-fa*↓; 益加 *-jia*↓; 益覺困難 feel it increasingly difficult.

益處 *yihchuh*, n., benefit, advantage.

益蟲 *yih-churng*, n., insect useful to man.

益多 *yih duo*, adv., more and more.

益發 *yihfa*, adv., all the more, increasingly (difficult, defiant, etc.).

益加 *yihjia*, adv., ditto.

益智 *yih-jyh*, adj., an intelligence (game)—which stimulates intelligence.

益母草 *yihmurtsaau*, n., (bot.) a grass, *Leonurus sibiricus*, said to help in maternity cases (also called 茺蔚).

益鳥 *yihniaau*, n., insectivorous birds (beneficial to man).

益足 *yih tzur*, phr., all the more serve to (cause harm, etc.).

益友 *yih-yoou*, n., good, helpful friends.

盖 80.30

gaih.

[Pop. of 蓋 20.30]

§ 80.32 (八/フ)

爹 80.32

die.

N. (1) Daddy (cf. 爸 *pa*, papa): 爹爹 daddy; 乾爹 adopted father; 爹媽 (coll.) father and mother. (2) Part of coll. word for uncle: 姨爹 uncle on mother's side; 姑爹 uncle on father's side.

§ 80.40 (八/口)

谷 80.40

guu.

N. (1) A valley, ravine: 幽谷 a secluded valley; 山谷 a ravine; 谷口 entrance to the valley; 谷風 winds coming through the valley. (2) A surname.

善 80.40

shahn.

N. (1) A surname. (2) The good: 善惡 good and evil; 眞善美 the true, the good and the beautiful; 爲善 (LL) do good; 善有善報 good is always rewarded.

Adj. (1) Good, opp. 惡 bad: 善人 good man; 善行 good conduct; 善類 *-leih*↓; 善效, 善歲 good results, good year of crops; 善價 a good price; 善哉 good, good! 這一頓打可不善也 he got a thorough beating. (2) Charitable, kind, (Budd.) devout: 慈善 kind (person); 慈善事業 philanthropic work; 樂善好施 philanthropic-minded; 善事 good deed; 善舉 *-jyuu*↓; 善菩薩, 善佛爺兒 (complim.) good, kind sir; 善男(子), 善男(信女) *-narn*↓. (3) Law-abiding, gentle: 善良 *-liarng*↓; 善柔 gentle; 善弱, 善懦 peace-loving, averse to fighting. (4) 善乎, 善於 good at, better than: 莫善乎(於)此 nothing better than this. (5) Familiar: 面善 (face) looks familiar.

V.i. & t. (LL) To consider as good: 帝善其言 the emperor approved of what he said; 善之 regard it as good; 親善, 友善, 相善 be good friends with.

Adv. Prone to, good at, well: 善舞 dance well; 善戰 fight well; 多財善賈 (*-guu*) it's easy to trade with much capital; 善哭 prone to weep; 多愁善感 oversensitive, sentimental; 善飯 (AC) has good appetite; 善爲我說辭 make a good excuse for me.

善敗 *shahn-baih*, n., (AC) success and failure.

善報 *shahn-bauh*, n., reward for good deeds.

善本 *shahn-been*, n., a rare edition.

善蟲子 *shahnchurngtz*, n., (sl.) a charity racketeer.

善根 *shahn-gen*, n., (Budd.) good endowment; capacity for spiritual development.

善棍 *shahnguhn*, n., charity racket-

善 荅 首

eer; see *-churngtz*↑.

善果 *shahn-guoo*, n., (Budd.) good rewards from good deeds.

善後 *shahn-houh*, (1) n., funeral arrangements: 善後事宜 rehabilitation measures (to be) taken after natural disaster; (2) v.t., 何以善其後 what to do to take care of the consequences.

善會 *shahn-hueih*, n., (Budd.) monks' dinner to thank donors.

善終 *shahn-jung*, v.i., die a natural death: 善始善終 see a thing through from beginning to end.

善擧 *shahn-jyuu*, n., a philanthropic act, project.

善類 *shahn-leih*, n., the good class of people, the nice type.

善良 *shahnliarng*, n., law-abiding, decent, also docile (people).

善門 *shahn-mern*, n., family of kind, philanthropic people.

善男(信女) *shahn-narn*, phr., 善男信女 (Budd.) the good believers, devout men and women; also 善男子, 善女子.

善善 *shahn-shahn*, phr., 善善惡惡 to love the good and shun evil.

善士 *shahn-shyh*, n., (1) (AC) the good scholars; (2) philanthropists.

善忘 *shahn-wahng*, adj., absent-minded, prone to forget.

善意 *shahn-yih*, n., good intentions, motives: 善意的批評 sincere criticism (not 惡意 malicious).

善緣 *shahn-yuarn*, n., (1) some special friendship, lucky meeting of good friends; (2) as in 結善緣 (Budd.) give donations to temple.

 80.40

da.

[Abbr. of 答 92A.40]

§ 80.41 (八/図)

首 80.41

shoou.

N. (1) Head: 點首 give a nod; 叩首, 稽首 knock one's head on the ground (oft. a formal salutation in letters); 斬首 beheaded; 絞首 strangle person as punishment. (2) Chief, leader: 首領, 領首 ditto; 元首 chief of state; 羣龍無首 group without a leader; 戎首 the aggressor in war; 匪首, 盜首, 魁首 head of gang of robbers; 酋首 tribal chief. (3) A verse division: 唐詩三百首 300 famous Tarng poems.

V.i. (1) To confess at court: 自首 (of a criminal) surrender oneself to police; 出首 ditto, inform against s.o. (2) To head a start: 首路; 首塗 *-tur*↓.

Adj. First in importance, time or place: 居首 stand first; first position in 首席, 首坐 *-shir*, *-tzuoh*↓; 首名 first on list; 首功 first in meritorious service; 首從 *-tzuhng*↓; 首妻 the first wife; 首惡 a cardinal sin, head culprit.

Adv. First, first to start: 首創, 首唱 *-chuahng*, *-chahng*↓; 首先 *-shian*↓; 首難 *-nahn*↓.

首唱 *shooucbahng*, v.t., be the first to lead (a movement, a revolution).

首七 *shoouchi*, n., the first seventh day in mourning.

首丘 *shoouchiou*, phr., (allu.) to be buried in home town.

首創 *shoouchuahng*, v.i., to start (fashion, institution).

首都 *shooudu*, n., national capital.

首服 *shooufur*, v.i., (LL) give oneself up to police.

首府 *shourfuu*, n., formerly, district where provincial capital is situated.

首告 *shoougauh*, v.i., to start court action by lodging complaint.

首長 *shour jaang*, n., chief (of tribe, bureau, department, ministry, etc.).

首級 *shooujir*, n., the cut-off head (of criminal, bandit, etc.).

首肯 *shourkeen*, v.i., to show approval by nodding.

首揆 *shooukueir*, n., (LL) premier.

首領 *shourliing*, n., leader, head.

首謀 *shooumour*, n., head of conspirators, prime mover.

首腦 *shournaau*, n., head, leading mind: 首腦人物 leading personages.

首難 *shoounahn*, v.i., first to start revolt.

首日封 *shoou-ryh-feng*, n., first day cover (philately).

首善 *shooushahn*, n., as in 首善之區 the national capital (which should be a "model" for others).

首縣 *shooushiahn*, n., formerly, county where district government is situated.

首相 *shooushiahng*, n., prime minister.

首先 *shooushian*, adv., first (to do s.t.).

首席 *shooushir*, n., seat of honor; chairman.

首鼠 *shourshuu*, adv., see *-shy*↓.

首施 *shooushy*, adv., as in 首施兩端 be undecided in course of action.

首事 *shooushyh*¹, v.i., (LL) start war, revolt.

首飾 *shooushyh*², n., personal ornaments, esp. on hair.

首選 *shourshyuaan*, n., first choice; first in list of winners.

首推 *shooutuei*, v.t., consider (person) as first.

首塗 *shooutur*, v.i., to start journey.

首從 *shooutzuhng*, n., chief culprit and associates in crime.

首座 *shooutzuoh*, n., (1) seat of honor; (2) abbot.

首尾 *shour-weei*, n., the story ("beginning and end") of an affair; also (coll.) s.o.'s business: 不是賈珍的首尾 has nothing to do with 賈珍.

首位 *shoouweih*, n., the first seat, first (delegate, etc.).

首要 *shoouyauh*, adj., of first importance.

首義 *shoouyih*, v.i., (LL) first to start revolt.

曾 80.41

tzeng (**tserng*).

N. A surname.

Adj. Great-grand, great-great-grand (used in comb. with nn.): 曾祖 *-tzuu*↓; 曾父, 曾大父 paternal great-grandfather; 曾祖父 ditto; 曾祖母 *-tzurmuu*, 曾孫 *-sun*, 曾玄 *-shyuarn*↓.

Adv. (**tserng*) Used before vbb. to indicate have yet, have not yet: 曾經 *-jing*↓; 未曾 never yet; 何曾 rhet. negative having the force of an affirmative: 何曾來過, 何曾看見 have never come, seen; 不曾到 never came; 不曾看(聽)見 never saw (heard); 吃了飯不曾 have you had lunch? 可曾看見 have you seen? did you ever see it? 曾有 there was (were)...once upon a time; 曾幾何時 not long since.

曾經 **tserngjing*, adv., yet, ever, already: 曾經有人看見 s.o. has seen it.

曾玄 *tzeng-shyuarn*, n., collective term for great-grandson and great-great-grandson.

曾孫 *tzengsun*, n., (1) great-grandson; (2) descendants of grandson in gen.

曾祖母 *tzengtzurmuu*, n., paternal great-grandmother.

曾祖 *tzengtzuu*, n., paternal great-grandfather.

曾益 *tzengyih*, v.t., to increase, add to, enhance: 曾益其所不能 (modn. 增益) broaden his knowledge, develop his capabilities.

普 80.41

puu.

N. (1) A surname. (2) Place name.

Adj. & adv. General, -ly, overall, reaching all: 普度 *-duh*↓; 陽光普照 the sunlight shines on the whole world; 普施濟衆 generous charity; 普天之下 in all the world; 普天同慶 (phr.) universal rejoicing; see esp. 普及 *-jir*↓.

普徧 *puubiahn*, adj. & adv., all around, everywhere: 普遍宣傳, 推廣 make publicity, push sales all around.

普度 *puuduh*, n. & v.t., (Budd.) festival similar to All Souls' Day in seventh lunar month, with prayers for those unburied and drowned at sea: 普度(渡)衆生 (of Buddha) save the masses of mankind.

普洱茶 *Puu-erl char*, n., special strong tea of Yunnan, taken as digestive.

普及 *puujir*, v.t. & adj., reaching all: 普及教育 popular education.

普通 *puutung*, adj. & adv., common, generally; 普通股 common stock.

着 80.41

juor (**jaur*, **jau*, **je*).

[Pop. of 著; see 著 20A.41]

酋 80.41

chiour.

N. Tribal chief: 匪酋 rebel chief.

酋長 *chiourjaang*, n., tribal chieftain.

§ 80.50 (八/ㄱ)

分 80.50

fen (**fehn*).

N. (1) Term of measure, time, and value: 1/10 of an inch, hundredth of an ounce; 10% interest: 兩分利 20% interest; a cent, a minute of time; 10% of *moou* 畝; 公分 centimeter; 分針 minute hand (time piece); 分鐘 minute. (2) Gen. expression of degree: 十分滿意 very, fully satisfied; 萬分, 十二萬分高興 extremely, enormously pleased; 七八分懂得 understand 70–80% (=七八成); 分毫 very small amount: 分毫不爽 not a tiny bit of difference; 分文 a penny: 分文不取 will not take a penny. (3) (**fehn*) Duty, status: 本分 duty; 分內 part of duty; 非分(越分) beyond what is proper (of request, etc.); 守己安分 law-abiding, dutiful; (看)情分(上) (in view of) friendly status, relations; 緣分 special, honored relationship, lover's luck; 身[Δ]分 personal status, see 91.00.

V.i. & t. (1) Separate: 分離, 分散, 分開 *-lir*, *-sahn*, *-kai*↓; 分途, 分道(揚鑣) part on journey, go separate ways; 分庭抗禮 (LL) be received as an equal; 分家, 分產 divide inheritance; 分爨 have separate kitchens, live separately among brothers; 分袂, 分襟 part (sleeves) among friends; 分心, 分身, 分神, 分手 *-shin*, *-shen*, *-shern*, *-shoou*↓; 分頭進行 (persons) proceed separately on common objective; 分門別類 sort out into categories; 分科 separate courses of study. (2) Distinguish: 分別, 分辨 *-bier*, *-biahn*[1]↓; 不分彼此 share together; 分不清 cannot distinguish; 不由分說 give no chance to explain; 分斤掰 (*bai*) 兩 count pennies, be stingy. (3) Divide, share: 分不到 fail to get share;

分我一杯羹 give me a share of the soup; 分利, 分潤 get share of profit; 分肥 share illegal gains; 分贓 share spoils, booty; 分甘共苦 fare and share alike; 分勞 help, relieve one of work; 分憂 share and lessen worry; 分謗 share the blame; 分心 divide attention to other affairs; 分工合作 division of labor; 分曹 formerly, divide official duties. (4) Distribute: 分給 give separately to persons; 分發 *-fa*↓; 分獎 give prizes; 分紅 *-hurng*↓; 分配, 分派 *-peih*, *-paih*↓. (5) Judge: 自分 (**fehn*) 必死 believe I shall die.

Adj. Branch: 分局, 分行, 分店 branch office.

Adv. Separately: 分送 send separately to persons; 分裝, 分運 load, ship separately; 分居 live separately.

分包 *fenbau*, n., two acts being played at the same time on the stage.

分辨 *fenbiahn*[1], v.t., compare and see the difference: 分辨是非黑白 distinguish right and wrong, black and white.

分辯 *fenbiahn*[2], v.i., explain, give explanation in defense.

分別 *fenbier*, (1) v.t., separate (two things); (2) adv., separately, respectively.

分布 *fenbuh*, v.i. & t., distribute, be distributed, spread, (races) scatter.

分歧 *fenchir*, v.i., grow apart, diverge: 意見分歧 opinions divide.

分度器 *fenduh-chih*, n., protractor.

分發 *fenfa*, v.t., give out, distribute.

分付 *fenfuh*, v.t., (1) pay, give out, separately; (2) order: 分付他回去 ask him to go home (usu. wr. 吩咐).

分割 *fenger*, v.t., cut up.

分號 *fenhauh*, n., semicolon (;).

分毫 *fenhaur*, n., a tiny amount: 分毫不肯讓人 will not give the slightest concession.

分化 *fenhuah*, v.i., disintegrate.

分紅 *fenhurng*, n. & v.i., bonus, to give bonus.

分爭 *fenjeng*, v.i., have disputes, fight for (thing).

分解 *fenjiee*, v.i., (1) break up into separate elements; (2) (*fen-'jie*) explain: 分解分解一下 please explain; 請聽下回分解 the story will be continued in next chapter.

分界 *fenjieh*, n., demarkation of boundary.

分開 *fen-kai*, v.t., set apart, separate: 他們兩人分不開 the two persons are inseparable.

分兒 **fehn'l*(*feh'l*), n., share: 沒有我的分兒 I do not expect to share it.

分量 **fehnliahng*, n., weight: 有分量的文字 solid writing.

分類 *fenleih*, v.t. & n., classify, -fication.

分裂 *fenlieh*, v.i. & t., split up, crack up (party, opinions).

分利 *fenlih*[1], v.i., to share in benefit; (Chin. med.) induce perspiration, bowel motion.

分力 *fenlih*[2], n., (phys.) component of force.

分離 *fenlir*, v.i. & t. & n., part (from friends, family); (chem.) dissociate, -tion.

分袂 *fen-meih*, v.t., part (among friends, "separate sleeves").

分娩 *fenmiaan*, v.i., give birth to child.

分泌 *fenmih*, v.t. & n., secrete, -tion (hormone, etc.).

分明 *fenmirng*, adj. & adv., clear, clearly.

分母 *fenmuu*, n., (math.) denominator of fraction.

分派 *fenpaih*, n. & v.i., branch, school (of thought); assign (work, etc.).

分配 *fenpeih*, v.t. & n., assign, -ment.

分散 *fensahn*, v.i. & n., dispel, disperse, -sal.

分身 *fen-shen*, v.i., to divide time or attention to another job.

分神 *gen-shern*, v.i., (court. to thank one for) giving attention.

分析 *fenshi*, v.t. & n., analyze, -lysis; 分析心理學 analytical psychology; 歷史的分析 historical analysis.

分曉 *fenshiaau*, (1) v.t. & n., understand, -ing: 這事沒分曉 do not know what is at the bottom of this; (2) adj., clear.

分銷 *fenshiau*, v.t. & n., sales distribution.

分心 *fen-shin*, v.i., divide attention (to another matter).

分手 *fenishoou*, v.i., to part company.

分書 *fenshu*, n., (1) divorce certificate; (2) 八分書 a style of script, see 80.80.

分水嶺 *fenshueir-liing*, n., (geog.) watershed; 分水線 *--shiahn*, line dividing river valley.

分數 *fenshuh*, n., (1) marks at examinations; (2) fraction.

分攤 *fentan*, v.t., to divide *pro rata*.

分寸 *fentsuhn*, n., (1) very small amount; (2) proper restraint: 說話有個分寸 talk with careful choice of words, do not overstep limits.

分子 *fentzyy*, n., (1) (math.) numerator of fraction; (2) **fehn-tzyy*, (phys.) molecule; 分子力 molecular force; 分子量 molecular weight; 分子式 molecular formula; (3) (**fehn'tz*) n., a part, member, element of society, group: 國民一分子 (also. wr. 份子) a member of the nation.

分野 *fenyee*, n., dividing line.

兮 80.50

shi.

Fin. part. Particle at end of sentence, esp. in verse, expressing admiration: 美目盼兮 (AC) how beautiful her eyes! 赫兮咺兮 (AC) how impressive and exciting! or celebrating a determination: 歸去來兮 Ah, let me go home! or marking a caesura or break in line of verse: 力拔山河兮氣蓋世 strength to move mountains, spirit unexcelled.

翁 80.50

weng.

N. (1) Respectful address or term for old man: 老翁 old man (of any station); 漁翁 an old fisherman; 醉翁 an old man drinking; 某翁 a certain old man; 東翁 the old landlord or host; 年翁 an old friend of the same age. (2) Father, father-in-law: 尊翁 (court.) your old father; 翁姑 father-in-law and mother-in-law; 翁婿 father-in-law and son-in-law. (3) A surname.

翁仲 *wengjuhng*, n., (LL) stone figure on grave.

剪 80.50

jiaan.

N. Scissors: 剪刀 ditto; 指甲剪 (finger) nail-clippers; 燭剪 candle snuffers.

V.i. & t. (1) V.i., to cut, divide, separate, lop off: 剪短 to trim; 剪髮 haircut; 剪開 cut open, sever; 剪綵 *-tsaai*, 剪影 *-yiing*↓; 剪接 splice films. (2) Annihilate, destroy completely: 剪除 *-chur*, 剪滅 *-mieh*↓; 剪草除根 (lit. & fig.) uproot, eradicate. (3) V.i., tie hands together.

剪報 *jiaanbauh*, n., newspaper clippings.
剪除 *jiaanchur*, v.t., wipe out, exterminate.
剪刀 *jiaandau*, n., scissors.
剪伐 *jiaanfar*, v.t., (AC) (of trees) to prune or cut, lop off (branches).
剪拂 *jiaanfur*, v.t., (1) to purge off, cleanse, wash away; (2) (MC underworld sl.) greet with a deep bow.
剪剪 *jiarnjiaan*, adj., (AC) (1) narrow-minded, bigoted, prejudiced; (2) (of wind) cutting, chilly, piercing.
剪徑 *jiaan-jihng*, v.i., (of robbers) hold up travellers.
剪絡 *jiarnlioou*, v.i., pick a person's pocket; n., a pickpocket.
剪滅 *jiaabmieh*, v.t., annihilate, exterminate.
剪綵 *jiarn-tsaai*, v.i. & n., ribbon-cutting ceremony.
剪裁 *jiaantsair*, v.i., (1) (tailoring) cut cloth to make dress or suit; (2) (of litr. works) polish, refine, cut out superfluous words and phrases.
剪子 *jiaantz*, n., scissors.
剪影 *jiarnyiing*, n., (1) silhouette; (2) a cross-section, a sketch.

翦 80.50

jiaan.
[Var. of 剪↑]

鶿 80.50

tsyr.

N. See 鸕^Δ鶿 21S.50.

§ 80.63 (八/丶)

羔 80.63

gau.

N. A lamb, a kid: 羔子 young of the sheep or other animal; 王八羔子 (abusive) son of a bitch; 羔羊 *-yarng*↓.

羔皮 *gaupir*, n., lambskin, leather or parchment made from it.
羔羊 *gauyarng*, n., (1) a young goat: 迷途羔羊 a stray lamb; (2) an innocent and helpless person; (3) a martyr or victim: 代罪羔羊 a scapegoat.

煎 80.63

jian.

V.t. (1) To fry in oil or boil in water: 油煎 fried; 水煎 boiled; 煎藥 make concoction of medicine; 煎魚 to fry fish, fried fish. (2) Make it hot for: 煎逼 *-bi*↓; 相煎何太急 (allu.) why press me so hard?

煎熬 *jian-aur*, v.i., endure long hardships and sufferings (heat, overwork, etc.).
煎逼 *jianbi*, v.t., press to the wall, make it hot for.
煎餅 *jianbiing*, n., fried cakes.
煎炒 *jianchaau*, v.t., to fry.
煎心 *jianshin*, adj., anxious, worried, in a stew.

⿱兼灬 80.63

jian.
[Abbr. of 兼 80.22]

鯗 80.63

shiaang.

N. Dried fish.

§ 80.70 (八/乚)

爸 80.70

bah (ba).

N. 爸爸 *bah'ba*, papa; used sometimes of friends of elder generation (vulg. var. 八八, 巴巴).

兌 80.70

dueih.

N. One of the eight trigrams of *baguah* (八卦 80.80).

V.i. & t. (1) To cash (check): 兌現 *-shiahn* ↓; 兌銀子 weigh silver, i.e., pay out; 兌交, 兌給 pay to (person); 兌支 ask for payment of a money order, to receive money. (2) To exchange, barter, make wholesale deal: 發兌 sell wholesale; 兌換 *-huahn* ↓. (3) To add water: 兌開水 add more boiling water to tea (also wr. 對).

兌換 *dueihhuahn*, v.t., exchange (goods, money): 兌換銀錢 change currency, as at money exchange shop.

兌現 *dueihshiahn*, v.t., to cash (checks); (fig.) fulfill election pledge, etc.

兌條(兒) *dueihtiaur('l)*, n., voucher in money exchange.

羌 80.70

chiang.

[Var. 羗, 羌]

Initial part. (AC dial.) initial part with indeterminate meaning, found esp. in 楚辭 (3rd. cen. B.C.): 羌無故實 (=了無故實) without basis in fact.

N. (1) A surname. (2) Name of a tribe in West Szechuan: 羌人, 羌胡 ditto.

羌笛 *chiangdir*, n., name of a short wind instrument, a flute of Chiang tribe.

羌活 *chianghuo*, n., (bot.) angelica, *Angelica sylvestris.*

羌鷲 *chiangjiouh*, n., a kind of vulture, *Haliaetus pelagicus.*

羌桃 *Chiangtaur*, n., the walnut (also called 核桃, 胡桃).

尩 80.70

wang.

[Var. 尪]

Adj. (1) Weak, feeble. (2) Bent-begged.

甆 80.70

tsyr.

[Pop. of 瓷 63.70]

§ 80.71 (八/七)

義 80.71

yih.

N. (1) Justice, righteousness, honor and right: 正義 the cause of right or honor; 道義 righteous (friends, companions), a moral principle; 信義 faith and righteousness, see 信 91A.40; 仗義疏財 give money to righteous cause; 恩義 love and duty; 情義 affectionate relationship between friends, husband and wife, benefactor and recipient of help; 就義 die a martyr; 大義滅親 punish own relations in the cause of justice. (2) Chivalry, sense of honor: 義形於色 one's face showed no compromise with evil; 義不容辭 one's sense of honor makes it impossible to refuse. (3) Meaning of words, exegesis: 義疏 *-shuh* ↓; 義理 *-lii* ↓. (4) A surname. (5) Short for Italy 義大利, now generally wr. 意大利.

Adj. (1) For charity, for public benefit: 義學 *-shyuer* ↓; 義田, 義莊 *-tiarn, -juang* ↓; 義舉 *-jyuu* ↓. (2) Righteous, pertaining to a righteous case: 義兵, 義師, 義軍 army on our (and therefore right) side. (3) Chivalrous, honorable: 義人, 義士 *-rern, -shyh* ↓; 義俠 *-shiar* ↓; 義胞 *-bau* ↓. (4) Volunteer: 義勇 *-yuung* ↓. (5) Adopted: 義父, 義母, 義子, etc., *-fuh, -muu, -tzyy* ↓. (6) Artificial: 義手, 義足, 義齒 artificial arm, leg, teeth; 義髻, 義甲 *-jih, -jiaa* ↓.

義胞 *yih-bau*, n., fellow citizen (同胞) who has fled opponent's territory.

義兵 *yih-bing*, n., (1) formerly, militia for self-defense; (2) volunteer army or soldier.

義氣 *yih'chi*, (1) n., sense of chivalry or honor; (2) adj., standing for the right, chivalrous.

義旗 *yih-chir*, n., flag of the righteous cause.

義齒 *yih-chyy*, n., artificial teeth.

義地 *yih-dih*[1], n., public cemetery.

義弟 *yih-dih*[2], n., sworn younger brother.

義帝 *yih-dih*[3], n., (history) an emperor set up in name.

義兒 *yih-erl*, n., adopted son.

義方 *yih-fang*, n., right kind of education.

義憤 *yihfehn*, n., righteous anger, indignation.

義風 *yihfeng*, n., prevailing sense of honor.

義父 *yih-fuh*, n., adopted father.

義戰 *yih-jahn*, n., a war for moral principles.

義甲 *yih-jiaa*, n., finger cap for plucking stringed instrument.

義髻 *yih-jih*, n., (LL) wig.

義莊 *yihjuang*, n., land publicly owned by a clan or village to maintain sacrifices or education of its children, a village foundation.

義冢 *yihjuung*, n., public cemetery.

義肢 *yih-jy*, n., artificial limb.

義軍 *yihjyun*, n., volunteer army,

army raised for a supposedly righteous cause.

義舉 *yih-jyuu*, n., an undertaking for some public good, a welfare project.

義例 *yihlih*, n., the rules which govern form and arrangement of a book.

義理 *yihlii*, n., (1) in Suhng philosophy, the study of reason; (2) reason, truth, principle.

義賣 *yih-maih*, n., a sale for public charity.

義母 *yih-muu*, n., adopted mother.

義女 *yih-nyuu*, n., adopted daughter.

義人 *yih-rern*, n., an honorable man, a just man.

義俠 *yih-shiar*, (1) n., chivalry, a chivalrous man: 義俠小說 picaresque novel; (2) adj., chivalrous.

義行 *yih-shihng*, phr., notable conduct.

義手 *yih-shoou*, n., artificial hand.

義疏 *hih-shuh*, n., commentary, elucidating a text; commentary of commentary, see 疏 32S.70.

義塾 *yih-shur*, n., formerly, private school charging no tuition.

義師 *yih-shy*, n., the loyal army versus the rebels; the rebels' army from rebels' own standpoint.

義士 *yih-shyh*, n., (1) a martyr, man who sacrifices life for justice; (2) a man of chivalry.

義學 *yih-shyuer*, n., public school charging no tuition.

義兄 *yih-shyung*, n., sworn elder brother.

義田 *yih-tiarn*, n., see *-juang* ↑.

義倉 *yih-tsang*, n., public granary for stabilizing farm prices.

義足 *yih-tzur*, n., artificial leg.

義子 *yih-tzyy*, n., adopted son.

義務 *yih'wuh*, n., (1) (law) obligation; (2) volunteer duty: 盡義務 service without pay; 義務兵 volunteer soldiers; 義務教育 free education.

義演 *yih-yaan*, n., a performance for some public charity.

義園 *yihyuarn*, n., see *-dih*[1] ↑.

義勇 *yihyuung*, n., volunteer for public service, esp. army; 義勇軍 *--jyun*, n., volunteer army.

羲 80.71

shi.

N. 伏羲 Furshi, one of the earliest legendary emperors, see under 伏 91A.81; 羲皇上人 people in earliest period of history believed to be free of all cares.

§80.72 (八/心)

忿 80.72

fehn.

[Var. 憤; cogn. 奮]

N. Anger, exasperation: 餘忿未平 anger not yet appeased; 忿氣, 忿火 wrath, fury, huff.

忿恨 *fehnhehn*, n., gall, bitterness.

忿懥 *fehnjyh*, n., (AC) anger, upset.

忿戾 *fehnlih*, adj., violent, irritable.

忿怒 *fehnnuh*, n., great anger.

恙 80.72

yahng.

N. Sickness; 無恙 well (in good health); 微恙 slightly unwell; 賤恙 (court.) my illness.

慈 80.72

tsyr.

N. (1) (Somewhat litr. reference to) mother (cf. 嚴 40.82 for father): 令慈 your mother; 家慈 my mother; 慈命 mother's command; 慈訓, 慈誨 maternal or parental instructions; 慈顏 kind face of parents. (2) U.f. 磁: 磁石 *-shyr* ↓.

Adj. Kind, gentle, compassionate, benevolent: 慈愛, 慈悲, 慈善, 慈祥 *-aih, -bei, -shahn, -shiarng* ↓; 父慈子孝 father is loving and son is filial.

慈愛 *tsyr-aih*, adj., kindly, gentle, compassionate.

慈悲 *tsyrbei*, (1) adj. & n., mercy, merciful; (2) (*-'bei*) v.i., be kind to: 請你慈悲慈悲罷 have pity (used in begging).

慈姑 *tsyrgu*, n., (bot.) *Sagittaria sagittifolia*, a water plant with edible bulbs.

慈航 *tsyr-harng*, n., (Budd.) the Merciful Ferry, way of salvation.

慈和 *tsyrher*, adj., amiable.

慈母 *tsyrmuu*, n., mother.

慈善 *tsyrshahn*, adj. & n., chartable: 慈善事業 work of charity.

慈祥 *tsyrshiarng*, adj., kindly, amiable.

慈石 *tsyrshyr*, n., var. of 磁石 magnet.

慈幃 *tsyrweir*, n., (LL polite address of) mother (also wr. 闈).

慈烏 *tsyr-wu*, n., a young crow reputed to feed its mother.

慾 80.72

yuh.

N. Passion, desire: 色慾, 性慾 sexual passion; 慾火 flame of sexual desire, hot desire; 私慾 mortal passions; 節慾 regulate sex; 禁慾, 戒慾 repress sex; 絕慾 suppress sex entirely; 利慾昏心 desire for money blinds one's mind; 慾壑難塡 desire is "bottomless"—insatiable.

慾海 *yuh-haai*, n., the sea of passions.

慾火 *yuh-huoo*, n., the fire of desire.

慾念 *yuh-niahn*, n., desire, craving.

慾望 *yuhwahng*, n., human desires.

愬 80.72

suh.

[AC var. of 訴 60A.22]

§ 80.80 (八/八)

八 80.80

ba.

[Var. 捌 used in checks for "spelling out" sum]

N. A surname (rare).

Adj. (1) (Number) eight: 八百年 ages (他早八百年來了 was here ages ago); 八九不離十 almost (你這個活兒做到八九不離十了 your work is almost done already); 八成兒 80%, greater part, most probably; 八成兒要下雨 most probably it will rain; 八八六十四 8×8=64, clearly, mechanically; 八字不見一撇 half of the character 八 is missing (of discussion too far away from the subject); 聖賢已是八字打開了 "the character 八 is quite open" (sages have made it quite clear); 八字鬍, 眉, 腳 moustache, eyebrows, feet shaped or turned like the character 八; 八開 *-kai*↓; 八節 the four equinoxes and solstices; 八寶 eight kinds of precious ingredients, see 八寶飯 *-baaufahn*↓; 八仙 the Eight (Taoist) Immortals; see 八仙桌 *-shianjuo*↓. (2) All around, all sides: 八面玲瓏 (of speech) cover all sides beautifully, (of character) manage to please everybody; 八面威風 make magnificent appearance; 八面週全 satisfactory to every detail; 八下裏去 all broken apart; 八方 eight points of the compass; 八表, 八荒, 八紘 all outlying areas (of China), on all sides.

八八兒 *baba'l*, n., mynah, see *-ge'l*↓.

八寶飯 *babaaufahn*, n., rice pudding with raisin and various nuts and seeds; 八寶 name given to things made of excellent ingredients, such as 八寶印Δ泥 90S.22, seal ink.

八拜(之)交 *babaih(jy) jiau*, n., sworn brother, sister.

八重奏 *bachurngtzouh*, n., octet.

八大山人 *Badah Shanrern*, n., painter of 17th cen.

八斗(才) *badoou (tsair)*, n., (praise) very gifted writer.

八度 *baduh*, n., octave.

八分(書) *bafen (shu)*, n., style of script, balanced right and left, of Hahn Dyn.; a form of 隸Δ書 10S.02.

八分音符 *bafenyinfur*, n., (mus.) quaver.

八分儀 *bafenyir*, n., (math.) octant.

八哥兒 *bage'l*, n., the mynah.

八卦 *baguah*, n., the eight diagrams, consisting of arrangement of continuous and broken lines in three lines each, symbolizing changing balance of forces and used in divination, as follows: 乾 (☰), 兌 (☱), 離 (☲), 震 (☳), 巽 (☴), 坎 (☵), 艮 (☶), 坤 (☷); cf. 五Δ行 31.30.

八股 *baguu*, n., prescribed form of essays in civil examinations, requiring strictly eight paragraphs, notorious for conformity; rigmarole writing surfeited with tiresome clichés (新八股, 黨八股).

八行書 *baharng-shu*, n., letter of recommendation for post; formal, brief letter of eight lines.

八角 *bajiaau*, adj., octagonal; 八角(茴香) n., star-aniseed; 八角楓 a kind of maple, *Marlea platanifolia*; 八角形 octagon, -al.

八進法 *gajihnfaa*, n., (math.) octonary scale.

八爪魚 *bajuaa-yur*, n., (pop.) octopus.

八開 *ba-kai*, n., (printing) octavo.

八面體 *bamiahn-tii*, n., (math.) octahedron.

八仙花 *bashian-hua*, n., (bot.) *Hydrangea hortensia.*

八仙桌(子) *bashianjuo(tz)*, n., a square dinner table seating eight.

八字 *batzyh*, n., the horoscope; eight cyclical characters giving year, month, day and hour of birth: 問八字 to consult horoscope; 八字帖兒 card of horoscope presented by candidate for betrothal; 八字不合 horoscopes (of proposed couple) do not agree.

八言 *ba-yarn*, n., poem of eight-character lines.

八佾 *ba-yih*, n., (AC) a dance with eight formations of dancers.

八音 *bayin*, n., eight categories of instrument in anc. orchestra (metal, stone, string, bamboo, gourd, clay, leather, wood).

八月 *bayueh*, n., August.

貧 80.80

pirn.

N. Poverty, the life of the poor: 安貧樂道 live contentedly as a poor scholar; 貧病交集 sick and in straits.

Adj. (1) Poor (usu. in more litr. phrr.=coll. 窮 62A.50): 赤貧 in stark poverty; 一貧如洗 penniless; 貧不擇妻 the poor can't choose wives; 貧寒, 貧苦, 貧困 *-harn, -kuu, -kuhn*↓. (2) needy, impoverished, of the poor class: 貧乏 *-far*↓; 貧家, 貧家子, 貧家婦女 poor family, poor family's son, women; 貧農 poor peasants; 貧富不均 too much difference between rich and poor;

A

貧賤 *-jiahn*↓. (3) Having qualities of those born to failure, bad luck, worthless, garrulous: 貧氣, 貧相 *-chih, -shiahng*↓; 貧骨頭 lazybones, garrulous person, miser; 貧嘴 (餓舌, 惡舌) disgustingly talkative, addicted to senseless talks; 貧婆 poor or gossip-mongering woman. (4) 貧僧, 貧道 (court., used by priests) I, your humble servant.

貧氣 *pirn-chih*, n., the physiognomy, manners of the poor; adj., shiftless, mean.

貧窮 *princhyurng*, adj., poor, needy.

貧乏 *pirnfar*, adj., needy.

貧寒 *pirnharn*, adj., needy: 貧寒子弟 children of poorer families (needing scholarships).

貧戶 *pirnhuh*, n., a poor family; the poor.

貧賤 *pirnjiahn*, adj., poor and humble: 貧賤之交 a friend in earlier poor days.

貧窶 *pirnjyuh*, adj., (LL) poor and needy.

貧困 *pirnkuhn*, adj., poor, hard up.

貧苦 *pirnkuu*, adj., living a poor, hard life.

貧民 *pirnmirn*, n., the poor people, the poorer classes; 貧民窟 *--ku*, slum.

貧相 *pirnshiahng*, n., see *-chih*↑.

貧血 *pirn-shyueh*, adj., anemic, suffering from anemia; 貧血症 anemia; 惡性貧血 pernicious anemia.

§ 80.81 (八/人)

关 80.81

shiauh.

[Abbr. of 笑 92A.81]

B

美 80.81

meei.

N. Beauty, perfection: 美不勝收 (landscape, etc.) rich in beauties, too beautiful to be absorbed all at once; 美中不足 some slight imperfection (a regret); 內在美 beauty of character, spiritual beauty.

V.t. (1) To regard it as beautiful, to praise: 美之 ditto; 讚美, 贊美 to praise, extol. (2) To use euphemism: 美其名曰 to call s.t. by euphemistic name (as 太平門, 太平梯 "peace door," "peace staircase" for fire exit, fire escape). (3) America, United States: 美國 ditto; 中美, 南美, 北美 Central America, South America, North America.

Adj. (1) Beautiful, pretty: 美麗 *-lih*↓; 美人, 美色 *-rern, -seh*↓; 美觀 *-guan*↓; 眞善美 the true, the good and the beautiful. (2) Pleasing, perfect, superior: 完美 perfect; 十全十美 perfect in every way; 優美 superior; 美妙 *-miauh*↓.

美備 *meeibeih*, adj., satisfactory, perfect (arrangement).

美缺 *meei-chyuer*, n., a desirable, well-paid job or post.

美德 *meei-der*, n., beautiful character.

美惡 *meei-eh*, n., beauty and deficiencies, things to admire and to detest.

美感 *meirgaan*, n., pleasant impression, esthetic sense.

美觀 *meeiguan*, n., beauty, esp. external beauty.

美好 *meirhaau*, adj., good and desirable.

美景 *meir-jiing*, n., a beautiful scene, sight.

美質 *meei-jyr*, n., beauty of character or quality.

美舉 *meir-jyuu*, n., an admirable enterprise.

美麗 *meeilih*, n. & adj., beauty, beautiful.

C

美滿 *meirmaan*, adj., happy (marriage, home).

美貌 *meeimauh*, n., beautiful face, looks.

美妙 *meeimiauh*, adj., wonderful (story), delicate.

美名 *meeimirng*, n., a good reputation.

美女 *meeinyuu*, n., a beautiful girl.

美盼 *meei-pahn*, n., a pretty glance.

美人(兒) *meirern(-rer'l)*, n., a beautiful woman: 美人計, 美人局 a plot with a woman as seducer.

美人蕉 *meirern-jiau*, n., (bot.) *Musa coccinea*.

美容 *meirurng*, n., the art of facial make-up: 美容院 beauty parlor, generally hairdresser; 美容術 art of make-up; plastic surgery; 美容技師 beautician.

美色 *meeiseh*, n., attractive woman, woman's beauty.

美秀 *meeishiouh*, adj., beautifully delicate.

美術 *meeishuh*, n., the fine arts; 美術家 an artist; 美術品 artistic products, creations, art works; 美術館 art gallery.

美談 *meei-tarn*, n., an anecdote concerning some well-known personality.

美味 *meei-weih*, n., things good to eat, a delicacy.

美豔 *meeiyahn*, adj., gorgeous.

美意 *meei-yih*, n., hospitality, desire to help.

美譽 *meei-yuh*[1], n., a good reputation.

美玉 *meei-yuh*[2], n., a beautiful jade.

羙 80.81

meei.

[Err. pop. var. of 美 80.81]

奠 80.81

diahn.

亅	小	卜	十	土	ナ	卄	ㄴ	丨	一	丁	ㄱ	口	区	冈	ㄱ	厂	尸	亠	广	宀	丶	乚	弋	心	八	人	乂	乛	一	丿	𠂉	く
00	01	02	10	11	12	20	21	22	30	31	32	40	41	42	50	51	52	60	61	62	63	70	71	72	80	81	82	83	90	91	92	93

N. & v.i. (1) Libation: 奠祭 pouring of wine on ground in sacrifice; 拜奠 perform libation. (2) To lay foundation stone: 奠基.

奠基禮 *diahnji-lii*, n., ceremony of laying foundation stone.
奠敬 *diahnjihng*, n., money gift for funeral.
奠儀 *diahnyir*, n., ditto.
奠鴈 *diahn yahn*, n., (AC) presentation of goose by bridegroom in wedding ceremony.

羨 80.81

shiahn.

V.t. (1) To admire, praise: 欣羨 admire (person), envy (his luck); 稱羨 praise. (2) Cherish, covet, envy: 羨慕 *-muh*↓; 傾羨 adore.

Adj. Full, surplus: 羨財 surplus money.

羨慕 *shiahnmuh*, v.t. & n., adore, -ration, admire, -ration, cherish (person, his talent, reputation); long for, crave, envy (luck, honor, wealth).
羨餘 *shiahnyur*, n., surplus, net gain.

羹 80.81

geng.

N. Soup: 羹湯 broth; 肉羹 meat soup.

羹匙 *gengchyr*, n., a spoon for soup, a ladle.

§ 80.82 (八/乂)

父 80.82

fuh.

[Cogn. 爸, 甫 10.42]

N. (1) Father: 家父 my father; 繼父 stepfather; 義父 adopted father; 養父 foster father; 父慈子孝 the father is kind, and the son obedient; 嚴父慈母 severe father and kind mother (regular concept); therefore 嚴父 father; 父令難違, 不敢不從 one should not disobey father's orders; 父債子還 it is the custom for a son to pay his (deceased) father's debts. (2) Part of address of relative of elder generation: 伯父, 叔父 uncles; 舅父 mother's brother; 姑父 father's sister's husband; 姨父 mother's sister's husband; 祖父 grandfather. (3) Elderly person, used like Eng. "uncle": 漁父 fisherman; 田父 farmer; 神父 Catholic father.

父輩 *fuhbeih*, n., elder generation.
父親 *fuhchin*, n., father, also used in direct address.
父黨 *fuh-daang*, n., relatives on father's side, of same clan name.
父執 *fuhjyr*, n., friends of father's generation, see *-beih*↑.
父老 *fuhlaau*, n., the elders (of a village).
父母 *fuhmuu*, n., parents; 父母官 local magistrate having direct jurisdiction over residents; 父母月兒(運兒) years when the parents are responsible for all expenses.
父兄 *fuhshyung*, n., the elders of a family.
父王 *fuhwarng*, n., my royal father, in direct or indirect address.

§ 80.83 (八/一)

送 80.83

suhng.

V.t. (1) To give (s.t.): 送給他 give him; 送禮物 send gifts; 送人情 give gifts or do favor to cement relationship; 送秋波 (woman) to flirt, give a parting glance. (2) To send off: 送人, 送客 to send person off; 送別 *-bier*↓; 歡送 give farewell party to (person); 送往迎來 meet and send off (visitors, etc.), also send gifts back and forth; 送故(舊)迎新 send off old (year, official) and welcome new (year, official); 送窮 *-chyurng*↓. (3) To deliver (message, newspaper, etc.): 送到 send to (person, place); 送貨 deliver goods; 送報 deliver newspaper; 送消息, 送信 send message; 送情報 make secret report; 送香火兒的 formerly, one who earned tips from wayfarers by trying to light cigarettes at public resorts. (4) To squander, waste (words, money, life): 送話, 送錢, 送命 *-huah*, *-chiarn*, *-mihng*↓.

送別 *suhngbier*, v.i. & t., to send off (friend, etc.).
送殯 *suhng-bihn*, v.i., attend funeral.
送錢 *suhng-chiarn*, v.i., (1) to waste money; (2) to send money.
送親 *suhng-chin*, v.i., accompany bride to groom's family on wedding day; 送親太太 woman selected by bride's family to accompany bride at wedding.
送情 *suhng-chirng*, v.i., as in 眉目送情 send speechless messages of love.
送窮 *suhng-chyurng*, v.i., formerly, a ceremony of farewell to poverty at end of first lunar month.
送寒衣 *suhng harnyi*, v.i., formerly, burn paper clothing for the dead for coming winter, at

end of 10th lunar month.

送話 *suhng-huah*, v.i., give opponent grounds for attack by using ill-advised statement: 向人嘴底下送話 say yourselves what your enemy wishes you to say.

送餞 *suhng-jiahn*, v.i., give farewell party.

送粧 *suhng-juang*, v.i., send bride's trousseau on display to groom's family.

送終 *suhng-jung*, v.i., to give proper burial ceremony to deceased parents.

送庫 *suhng-kuh*, v.i., signal end of Buddhist mass for the dead by burning paper towers or pavilions.

送老 *suhnglaau*, v.i., see *-jung*↑.

送力 *suhnglih*, n., tip given to messenger boy.

送禮 *suhng-lii*, v.i. & n., a gift; to give gift.

送路 *suhng-luh*, v.i., (1) to send s.o. off; (2) see *-san*↓.

送命 *suhng-mihng*, v.i., do s.t. foolish and pay with one's life.

送三 *suhng-san*, v.i., to send away ghost of deceased relative after "接三" welcoming him on the third day of his death.

送喪 *suhng-sang*, v.i., to attend funeral.

送聖 *suhngshehng*, v.i., see *-kuh*↑.

送神 *suhngshern*, v.i., to send spirits away after due sacrifice, and after ceremony of welcome (接神, 迎神).

送信 *suhng-shihn*, v.i., to send letter or message: 送信兒 send message through third party.

送行 *suhngshirng*, v.i., to send off (s.o.).

送死 *suhngsyy*, v.i., (1) to walk into a trap; (2) (AC) attend or give funeral.

送葬 *suhng-tzahng*, v.i., to attend burial.

送竈 *suhng-tzauh*, v.i., to send off kitchen god for New Year holiday, on the 23rd of 12th lunar month.

逆 80.83

nih.

N. A rebel, traitor.

V.t. (1) To rebel: 逆叛 *-pahn*↓; 叛逆 to betray. (2) Disobey, oppose: 拂逆 disobey the expressed will of a superior; 忤逆 openly oppose one's parents; 違逆 run counter to; 背逆 ditto; 逆著他的意思 go against his will; 逆天 *-tian*↓. (3) Be contrary to, go against: 逆耳 *-eel*↓; 逆流 *-liour*↓; 逆水行舟 sail against the current; 逆向 *-shiahng*↓; 逆風 *-feng*↓; 逆來順受 meekly accept humiliations, take insults philosophically; 逆取順守 (of founders of dynasties) retain political power by fair means after capturing it by foul; 倒行逆施 (of governments) carry out high-handed policies against sound principles, monstrously wicked. (4) Anticipate: 逆料 *-liauh*↓; 逆覩 *-duu*, 逆計 *-jih*↓; 逆知 *-jy*↓. (5) (AC) to welcome (＝迎).

Adj. (1) Traitorous: 逆產 property belonging to a traitor; 逆賊 *-tzeir*↓; 逆徒 a treacherous gang; 逆黨 a rebel party or group; 逆匪 bandits; 逆謀 a treasonable plot. (2) Unfilial: 逆子 *-tzyy*↓.

逆差 *nihcha*, n., unfavorable balance.

逆產 *nih-chaan*, n., (1) (med.) breech delivery; (2) property belonging to a traitor.

逆定理 *nih-dihnglii*, n., (math.) converse theorem.

逆覩 *nihduu*, v.t., know beforehand, forecast.

逆耳 *nih-eel*, adj., be unpleasant to hear: 忠言逆耳 good advice is unpleasant to hear.

逆風 *nih-feng*, v.i., go against the wind; (fig.) be at a disadvantage.

逆折 *nihjer*, v.i., turn back midway.

逆計 *nihjih*, v.t., conjecture, predict.

逆境 *nihjihng*, n., adverse circumstances, adversity.

逆知 *nihjy*, v.t., know beforehand, forecast.

逆料 *nihliauh*, v.t., conjecture, predict, expect: 不可逆料 cannot be foreseen or predicted.

逆理 *nih-lii*, v.i. & adj., (be) contrary to reason.

逆流 *nih-liour*, v.i., as in 逆流而上 go upstream; (fig.) run counter to the current of the times.

逆鱗 *nih-lirn*, v.t., as in 批逆鱗 rub one the wrong way, offend the powers that be.

逆倫 *nihlurn*, adj., incestuous; unfilial towards one's parents.

逆旅 *nihlyuu*, n., hotel, inn; travel: 逆旅途中 in one's journey.

逆叛 *nihpahn*, v.t., to rebel.

逆向 *nih-shiahng*, v.i., go in the opposite direction.

逆行 *nihshirng*, n., (1) movement in an opposite direction; (2) conduct contrary to normal rules; (3) treacherous acts or acts contrary to reason.

逆天 *nih-tian*, v.i., act against the laws of nature: 逆天行事 do godless things; 順天者存, 逆天者亡 he who obeys Heaven will survive and he who defies Heaven will perish.

逆賊 *nihtzeir*, n., traitor (lit., "a traitorous rebel").

逆子 *nihtzyy*, n., an unfilial son.

遡 80.83

suh.

[Cogn. 溯 63A.42]

迸 80.83

behng.

V.i. (1) To burst, gush forth: 迸出

來 burst out (of tears); 迸淚 tears gush forth; 迸流 gush forth (of spirings). (2) Dash: 亂迸 dash blindly (against s.t.).

迸裂 *behnglieh*, v.i., burst apart.
迸脆 *behngtsueih*, adj., crisp.

道 80.83

dauh.

N. adjunct. A stripe, streak, course, issue: 一道光, 氣 a streak of light, a jet of gas; 一道街, 河 a street, a stream; 一道煙 a stream or column of smoke; 一道菜, 點心 a course of food, dessert; 一道命令 an order.

N. (1) Doctrine, body of moral teachings, truth: 孔孟之道, 儒道 teachings of Confucius and Mencius; 邪道, 左道 heresy; the Tao of Taoism, the Way of Nature which cannot be given a name; 得道 (of person) have attained wisdom (Budd., Taoist or Confucian); 道不行 the right teachings do not prevail; 天下有道, 無道 moral order or chaos; 天道, 人道 the way of God (Heaven), the way of man, see 人[4]道 81.81; 王道, 霸道 enlightened, despotic rule, or the way of a king; 霸道 the way of a tyrant; 夫婦之道 the proper relations of husband and wife; 相處之道 the way to get along with people. (2) Path, route: 快車道 speedway on city road; 街道 street; 軌道 orbit, railroad track; 鐵道 railroad; 隧道 tunnel; 赤道 Equator; 道不拾遺 lost articles are always returned to owners—symbolic of good customs; 道聽塗說 hearsay, market gossip; 道路, 道途 *-luh*, *-tur* ↓. (3) A surname.

V.i. (1) To say: 說道 (s.o.) says, (followed by quotation); 笑道 say with a smile or laugh; 自古道, 常言道 as the saying goes; 道是無情卻有情 you might say (s.o.) is cold, but he isn't; 莫道, 難道 you do not mean to say, can it be . . . ? 道不出苦衷 cannot say clearly what is real trouble; 有些道不及的地方 there are things left unsaid, things that are hard to excuse; 不可勝道 too many to enumerate; 一語道破 hit the nail on the head; 道謝, 道喜, 道歉 *-shieh*, *-shii*, *-chiahn* ↓. (2) Guide (u.f. 導): 道之以德 (AC) guide them with morals.

Adj. Taoist: 道教, 道士 *-jiauh*, *-shyh* ↓.

道白 *dauhbair*, n., spoken part of dialogue in Chin. opera.
道場 *dauhcharng*, n., mass (Budd. or Taoist); place where it is held.
道歉 *dauhchiahn*, v.i., say sorry, apologize.
道情 *dauhchirng*, n., ballad or play with a moral or religious theme.
道德 *dauhder*, n., morals: 私人, 公共道德 private, public morals; a person's moral character; 道德重整 moral rearmament; 不道德 adj., immoral; 道德經 *Dauhder-jing* of Laotse.
道地 *dauhdih*, adj., genuine: 道地人參, 官話 genuine ginseng, Mandarin.
道姑 *dauhgu*, n., Taoist nun.
道冠兒 *dauhgua'l*, n., hair-fastener of a Taoist monk.
道觀 *dauhguan*, n., Taoist temple.
道故 *dauhguh*, v.i., reminisce on old days.
道號 *dauhhauh*, n., monastic name of person.
道教 *dauhjiauh*, n., the religion of Taoism.
道經 *dauhjing*, n., Taoist texts.
道具 *dauhjyuh*, n., prop for stage.
道兒 *dauh'l*, n., path, course, method.
道力 *dauhlih*, n., strength of religious training.
道理 *dauhlii*, n., the reason of things, phenomena: 你說得很有道理 you are right (corresponding to French *avoir raison*); 沒甚麼道理 there is nothing in it (e.g., a bad play); 說不出道理 cannot give the reason, cannot say way.
道林紙 *dauhlirnjyy*, n., good printing paper.
道路 *dauhluh*, n., road: 道路不通 road is blocked.
道貌 *dauh-mauh*, n., sanctimonious appearance.
道惱 *dauhnaau*, v.i., condole with.
道袍 *dauhpaur*, n., Taoist priest's robe.
道破 *dauhpoh*, v.t., reveal, expose by word of mouth.
道人 *dauhrern*, n., holy man, a Taoist priest.
道上 *dauh-shahng*, adv., on the road.
道山 *dauhshan*, n., place where the saints live: 歸道山 (euphem.) die.
道謝 *dauhshieh*, v.i., say thanks.
道行 *dauhshihng* (coll. *-'shing*, *-'hang*), n., moral conduct, spiritual character.
道喜 *dauhshii*, v.i., congratulate.
道士 *dauhshyh*, n., a Taoist priest.
道學 *dauhshyuer*, n. & adj., puritan, puritanical: 假道學, 道學先生 a hypocrite, holier-than-thou people.
道臺 *daugtair*, n., "taotai," formerly, Intendant of Circuit.
道途 *dauhtur*, n., road, see *-luh* ↑.
道統 *dauhtuung*, n., the body of transmitted orthodox teachings.
道義 *dauhyih*, n., moral relationships: 道義之交 friendship based on mutual respect, such friends; 道義上說不過去 not justified or excusable on moral grounds.
道友 *dauh-yoou*, n., friends of same church or belief, friends sharing same interest (oft. referred to drug addicts).
道院 *dauhyuahn*, n., Taoist monastery.

遂 80.83

sueih (also *sueir*).

V.t. (1) To complete (work), fulfill (wish), succeed: 得遂所願 have wish fulfilled; 遂初衷 succeed in what one has always wished—to retire; 遂心, 遂願, 遂意 *-shin*, *-yuahn*, *-yih* ↓; 未遂 (p.p.) uncompleted, failed; 遂過 *-guoh*↓. (2) (AC) to promote: 顯忠遂良 promote the loyal and good people. (3) (AC) to tolerate, refrain from inhibition.

Adj. Fulfilled, successful: 功成名遂 have work done and recognized.

Adv. (1) Then, and then, consequently: 遂破產 consequently became bankrupt; 遂不起 then died of illness; 遂和好如初 then became reconciled; proceeding to 遂至, 遂及 *-jyh, -jir*^{2}↓. (2) Immediately: 遂即, 遂則 *-jir*^{1}, *-tzer*↓.

遂過 *sueih-guoh*, v.i., (LL) to help consummate a mistake: 飾非遂過 cover up mistakes and complete the undoing.
遂即 *sueihjir*^{1} (*sueir-*), adv., immediatly (resign, etc.).
遂及 *sueih jir*^{2} (*sueir-*), *phr.*, and then proceed to: 遂及於亂 ended in adultery.
遂至 *sueih jyh* (*sueir-*), phr., end up in: 遂至不可收拾 ended up in a fiasco.
遂心 *sueih-shin* (*sueir-*), v.i., to fulfill one's desire.
遂事 *sueih-shyh*, n., (AC) bygones: 遂事不諫 let bygones be bygones.
遂則 *sueih tzer*, adv., and then, forthwith.
遂意 *sueih-yih*, adv., see *-shin*↑.
遂願 *sueih-yuahn*, v.i., have wish fulfilled, realized.

遒 80.83

chiour.

Adj. (1) Forceful, see compp.↓. (2) Near, close: 歲忽忽而遒盡 the year is drawing so fast to its close.

遒健 *chiourjiahn*, adj., (callig.) strong, powerful in strokes.
遒勁 *chiourjihng*, adj., (callig.) strong, rugged.
遒緊 *chiourjiin*, adj., (litr. or artistic composition) tightly composed, compact.
遒美 *chiourmeei*, adj., see *-jiahn*↑.
遒逸 *chiouryih*, adj., (callig.) forceful and free in movement.

遵 80.83

tzun.

V.t. Follow, obey: 遵命 *-mihng*↓; 遵教 comply with orders; 遵旨 obey imperial decree; 遵辦 do as instructed; 遵時養晦 abide one's time during period of ill luck.

遵奉 *tzunfehng*, v.t., faithfully obey (orders, instructions).
遵照 *tzunjauh*, v.t., do (act) according to (orders, instructions, laws, regulations).
遵陸 *tzun-luh*, v.i., go (travel) by land, take a land route.
遵命 *tzun-mihng*, v.i., follow instructions, act according to orders received.
遵行 *tzunshirng*, v.t., faithfully carry out (policy, directives, guidelines): 遵行方向 (road sign) "follow this direction," as indicated by an arrow.
遵守 *tzunshoou*, v.t., obey (rules, laws, orders).
遵循 *tzunshyurn*, v.t., follow (route, orders).
遵從 *tzuntsurng*, v.t., ditto.
遵依 *tzunyi*, v.t., *-jauh*↑.

§ 80.93 (八/く)

公 80.93

gung.

N. (1) Public affairs: 辦公 attend to official duties; 公務 *-wuh*, 公事 *-shyh*^{2}, 公家 *-jia*↓. (2) Office for the transaction of official business: 公門 *-mern*↓. (3) (AC) grand councillor or grand duke: 三公 the three offices of 太師, 太傅, 太保 or 大司馬, 大司徒, 大司空: 一國三公 divided counsel, a house divided against itself; 公卿 *-ching*↓. (4) (AC) a duke (-dom): 公侯 dukes and marquises; 公爵 rank of duke. (5) A male person of superior rank: 太公 great-grandfather, grandfather, father; 公公 *-'gung*↓; 叔公 father's uncle; 舅公 grandmother's brother; 外公 maternal grandfather; 公婆 husband's parents; 老公公 (court.) granddad, Santa Claus or any old man; (某)公 one Mr. (So and so); 明公 (LL) you illustrious Sir; 相公 (a) (MC) court. address to prime minister; (b) (MC, coll.) a common young scholar; (c) formerly, a pederast; 相公堂子 house of pederasts. (6) A surname.

V.t. To share with: 公天下 (of statesmanship) take one's position as a public trust (lit., "share the country with the people"); 公諸同好 let others with same taste share (artistic or creative work).

Adj. (1) Fair and just: 大公無私 fair-minded, unselfish; 公正 *-jehng*, 公平 *-pirng*↓; 不公 unfair, unjust; 公道 *-dauh*↓; 公公道道 fair and square. (2) Belonging to the male sex: 公雞 a cock; 公牛 a bull; 公母(倆) a male and a female, a couple; 公的 the male. (3) Belonging to the public, government-owned: 公園 *-yuarn*↓; 公物 public possessions; 公地 public land; 公款 public funds; 公產 public property; 公服 official dress; 公德 *-der*↓; 公假 official leave of absence; 公債 *-jaih*, 公賣 *-maih*, 公憤 *-fehn*, 公意 *-yih*^{2}↓. (4) Of a universal system, esp. metrical system: 公曆 *-lih*^{2}, 公里 *-lii*^{1}↓.

公 **Adv.** (1) Done or supported by the government: 公有 publicly owned; 公立 financed by the government, publicly established: 公立學校, 公立醫院 public schools, hospitals. (2) Done by general consensus: 公推 chosen by acclamation; 公舉 elected by popular vote; 公攤 (of expenses) shared equally by all.

公案 *gung-ahn*, n., (1) office desks; (2) official business; (3) a much discussed issue, a standing problem, esp. in Zen Budd.

公安 *gung-an*, n., public security; 公安局 police department.

公保 *gungbaau*, n., government insurance for public servants.

公報 *gungbauh*, n., government gazette.

公倍數 *gungbeih-shuh*, n., (math.) a common multiple.

公便 *gungbiahn*, adv. & n., (used in official documents) "for the benefit of all parties concerned": 實爲公便.

公比 *gungbii*, n., (math.) the common ratio.

公秉 *gungbiing*, n., a kiloliter, see Appendix C.

公布 *gungbuh*, adj., (also 公佈) (of laws or decrees) officially promulgated, publicly announced.

公差 *gungchai*, n., (1) a government messenger boy; public service; (2) (*-cha*) (math.) the common difference; (econ.) remedy, tolerance of the mint.

公娼 *gungchang*, n., licensed prostitution: 公娼制度 ditto.

公錢 *gungchiarn*, n., a decagram, see Appendix C.

公器 *gungchih*, n., (1) government property; (2) (LL) official titles and honors.

公啓 *gungchii*, n., (1) an open letter; (2) a joint statement signed by a number of persons.

公頃 *gungchiing*[1], n., (surface measure) a hectare, see Appendix C.

公請 *gungchiing*[2], v.i. & n., (give) a joint invitation or dinner in honor of s.o.

公卿 *gungching*, n., (AC) high ministers of rank.

公出 *gung-chu*, n., official leave of absence.

公權 *gungchyuarn*, n., political or civic rights.

公尺 *gungchyy*, n., (linear measure) a meter, see Appendix C.

公石 *gungdahn*, n., a hectoliter, see Appendix C.

公道 *gungdauh*, (1) n., justice, fairness; (2) (*-'dau*) adj., fair, just, reasonable.

公德 *gungder*, n., public behavior or morals, regard for public welfare.

公敵 *gung-dir*, n., public enemy.

公斗 *gungdoou*, n., a decaliter, see Appendix C.

公斷 *gungduahn*, n., arbitration, impartial judgement.

公牘 *gungdur*, n., official correspondence.

公法 *gungfaa*, n., (1) (jurisprudence) public laws: 國際公法 international law; (2) (math.) postulates (as the Euclidean postulates of geometry).

公份兒 *gungfeh'l*, n., a joint gift (also 公分兒).

公憤 *gung-fehn*, n., public indignation.

公費 *gungfeih*, n., (1) office expenses; (2) funds provided by the government or any organization for a specific purpose, such as scholarships or charity; (3) a lawyer's fee.

公分 *gungfen*, n., (1) (linear measure) a centimeter; (2) (measure of weight) a gram, see Appendix C.

公幹 *gungahn*, n., official business.

公告 *gunggauh*, (1) n., public announcement; (2) v.i. & t., make such an announcement.

公館 *gungguaan*, n., (1) formerly, residence provided by the government for officials; (2) private residence of a government official; (3) (court.) a private home.

公共 *gung'guhng*, adj., public, common, joint: 公共關係 public relations; 公共食堂 common mess hall.

公公 *gung'gung*, n., (1) grandfather; (2) the father of one's husband; (3) gen. term of respect for the aged; (4) a eunuch.

公海 *gunghaai*, n., the high seas.

公函 *gungharn*, n., (1) an official document; (2) a letter signed by a number of persons.

公毫 *gunghaur*, n., a centigram, see Appendix C.

公合 *gungher*, n., a deciliter, see Appendix C.

公衡 *gungherng*, n., ten kilograms, see Appendix C.

公會 *gunghueih*, n., a trade union, professional club.

公丈 *gungjahng*, n., a decameter, see Appendix C.

公債 *gungjaih*, n., bonds issued by the government or local self-governing bodies.

公正 *gungjehng*, adj., just, impartial, fair (person, judgment).

公證人 *gungjehngrern*, n., (1) a witness; (2) notary public.

公家 *gungjia*, n., the government; 公家的 adj., public, not private.

公價 *gungjiah*, n., official, controlled price.

公斤 *gungjin*, n., a kilogram, see Appendix C.

公積 *gungjir*, n., (business) reserve fund (also 公積金).

公轉 *gungjuaan*, n., (astron.) a revolution.

公衆 *gungjuhng*, n., the general public; 公衆假期 public holiday.

公主 *gungjuu*, n., a princess.

公決 *gung-jyuer*, v.t. & n., (pass) resolutions by the majority.

公開 *gungkai*, adj. & adv., (1) open(ly); (2) open to the public: 公開展覽 a public exhibition; 公開演講 a public lecture; 公開信 open letter.

公款 *gungkuaan*, n., public funds.

公空 *gungkung*, n., the outer space over which no country has jurisdiction.

公兩 *gungliaang*, n., a centigram, see Appendix C.

公例 *gunglih*[1], n., a conventional practice; a law of physics.

公曆 *gunglih*[2], n., reckoning by Christian era, A.D. or B.C. (also called 西曆).

公里 *gunglii*[1], n., a kilometer, see Appendix C.

公理 *gunglii*[2], n., (1) justice, universally accepted truths; (2) (math.) axioms.

公釐 *gunglir*, n., (1) a decigram;

(2) a millimeter; (3) a square meter, see Appendix C.

公路 *gungluh*, n., highway.

公論 *gungluhn*, n., public opinion, general consensus.

公賣 *gungmaih*, n., government monopoly (of tobacco, wine, etc.).

公門 *gungmern*, n., (1) a government office; (2) (AC) the palace gate.

公民 *gungmirn*, n., citizen of a country.

公民權 *gungmirn-chyuarn*, n., civic rights

公墓 *gung-muh*, n., a public cemetery.

公畝 *gungmuu*, n., an acre, equal to 100 sq. meters, see Appendix C.

公平 *gungpirng*, adj., just, fair, impartial.

公僕 *gungpur*, n., public servants.

公然 *gungrarn*, adv., openly.

公認 *gung-rehn*, adj., generally recognized or accepted.

公審 *gung-sheen*, n., public trial.

公社 *gungsheh*, n., a commune: 巴黎公社 the Paris Commune of 1871.

公升 *gungsheng*, n., a liter, see Appendix C.

公項 *gungshiahng*, n., (math.) a general term.

公廨 *gungshieh*, n., government office or building.

公勺 *gungshuoh*, n., a centiliter, see Appendix C.

公署 *gungshuu*, n., government office.

公式 *gungshyh*[1], n., a formula: 數學公式 mathematical formulas; 公式化 put in formulas, become a formula.

公事 *gungshyh*[2], n., (1) public affairs; (2) official business; (3) official documents; 公事包 attaché case, brief case.

公使 *gungshyy*, n., a minister accredited to a foreign country.

公訴 *gungsuh*, n., (law) public indictment.

公孫 *gungsun*, n., a surname.

公孫樹 *gungsun-shuh*, n., the ginkgo tree (usu. 銀杏).

公絲 *gungsy*[1], n., a milligram, see Appendix C.

公司 *gungsy*[2], n., a commercial company, a business firm; 公司法 corporation law; 公司債 corporation bonds.

公堂 *gungtarng*, n., formerly, a law court.

公庭 *gungtirng*, n., (1) a courtyard in front of the imperial ancestral shrine; (2) (=公堂) a law court: 對簿公庭 confront s.o. before a law court.

公撮 *gungtsuo*, n., a milliliter, see Appendix C.

公同 *gungturng*, adj. & adv., common(ly), joint(ly), in cooperation with one another.

公寸 *gungtzuhn*, n., a decimeter, see Appendix C.

公祖 *gungtzuu*, n., formerly, a term of respect for the local magistrate.

公子 *gungtzyy*, n., (1) (AC) the son of a feudal prince; (2) the son of a higher class family: 公子哥兒 rich man's sons, playboys.

公文 *gung-wern*, n., official document.

公務 *gungwuh*, n., public business, duties; 公務員 civil servant.

公益 *gungyih*[1], n., community benefit; 公益金 community chest.

公意 *gungyih*[2], n., opinion of majority.

公營 *gungyirng*, adj., government-, state-, operated enterprise; 公私合營 quasi-government enterprise.

公園 *gungyuarn*, n., park.

公寓 *gungyuh*, n., apartment house, apartment.

公用事業 *gungyuhng-shyhyeh*, n., public utilities.

姜 80.93

jiang.

N. A surname.

会 80.93

hueih.

[Abbr. of 會 81.41]

兹 80.93

tzy.

N. (1) Year, time: 今兹 this year, now, at present; 來兹 next year, in the future. (2) This, n. & adj.,: 念兹在兹 always remember this; now this: 兹事體大 now this matter is serious.

Adv. Now (usu. at beginning of sentence): 兹者 at this time, now, at present; 兹啓者 this is to advise that . . . ; 兹定於某月某日訂婚 this is to announce (our) engagement on a (certain) day of a (certain) month; 兹因 now because of . . . ; 兹有 (now) there is, here is . . . ; 兹查 (now) it has been found that . . . .

Adv. (U.f. 滋) very, extremely: 賦斂兹重 (LL) taxes and levies are inordinately heavy.

SECTION 80S

§ 80S.00 (八^S/亅)

剃 80S.00-2

tih.

V.t. Shave: 剃鬍子 shave beard; 剃汗毛 shave hair on armpit, legs, etc.; 剃得乾淨 shave clean; 剃髮修行(爲尼) cut off hair and be monk (nun).

剃 刀 *tihdau*, n., razor.
剃 度 *tihduh*, v.i., cut off hair and join monastery.
剃 頭 *tirtour*, v.i., have haircut: 剃光頭 shave head bald; 剃平頭 crew cut; 剃頭的, 剃頭匠 barber; 剃頭店, 舖 barbershop; 剃頭刀 razor.

§ 80S.22 (八^S/丨)

邠 80S.22-3

bin.
[Var. 豳]

N. Place name.

Adj. (AC) used as var. of 斌 60S.71, 彬 10B.91.

郤 80S.22-3

shih.
[Dist. 卻]

N. (1) An opening, a crack (interch. 隙). (2) A surname (also wr. 郄).

鄭 80S.22-3

jehng.

N. (1) A surname. (2) Name of anc. principality in classical times.

鄭 重 *jehngjuhng*, adj. & adv., with great care, formally, solemnly: 鄭重聲明 solemnly declare; 鄭重其事 act with due care and respect.

鄯 80S.22-3

shahn.

N. Name of place.

卻 80S.22-5

chyueh.
[Pop. 却]

V.i. & t. (1) V.t., to reject: 拒卻, 謝卻 to reject (invitation, offer); 卻情 decline a favor; 卻之不恭 "it would be disrespectful to decline"—formula for accepting; 推卻 to delay, shirk (responsibility); 卻死 (AC) afraid of death ("shun death"); 卻老 rejuvenation ("delay old age"); 卻病延年 banish illness and increase long life. (2) V.i., to step backward: 卻立, 卻步 -*lih, buh*↓.

Adv. (1) (Preceding vb.) yet: 他先提議的, 卻沒來 he was the first to propose it, yet does not come; often has the force of "but" "yet" combined, suggesting "on the other hand": 他卻反咬你一口 on the other hand he makes a countercharge ("bites back"); 你贊成, 我卻反對 you approve, but I don't; 卻不見回音 but yet there is no reply; 卻又來 not this again! (2) Emphasizing an affirmative or negative declaration like German *doch*: 原來卻是他 it is he after all; 事情卻不容易 the thing is really not so simple. (3) Opening a paragraph in storytelling, like English "now": 卻說 now the story goes. (4) As a vb. adjunct, meaning "off": 殺卻 kill off; 除卻 drive off. (5) Just: 卻夠 just enough.

Conj. However, but, on the other hand: 卻不料 however, to one's surprise; 卻不知 however, one does not know; 卻不提防 to one's surprise; 卻不道 to one's surprise, also is it not as the proverb says (you cannot put two saddles on one horse, etc.).

卻 步 *chyueh-buh*, v.i., to step backwards.
卻 待 *chyuehdaih*, v.i., is just waiting to (=正要): 接了銀子, 卻待分手 having received the money, they were just going to part, when....
卻 好 *chyuehhaau*, adv., fortunately, just at the right time.
卻 來 *chyuehlair*, adv. phr., (1) yet (same as 卻 Adv. 1↑): 他應該最知道, 卻來問 he should know best, yet comes to ask me about it; (2) in reality: 卻來 (=原來) 他們倆沒有什麽仇恨, in reality, they two had no ancient grudge.
卻 立 *chyuehlih*, v.i., to stand back.
卻 扇 *chyueh-shahn*, v.i., (allu.) become married.
卻 是 *chyuehshyh*, phr., emphatic form of 是: 卻是實的 but it is true (see 卻 Adv. 2↑).
卻 纔 *chyuehtsair*, adv. (MC) just now (=modn. 方才).
卻 走 *chyueh-tzoou*, v.i., run backward, turn away.
卻 又 *chyueh youh*, phr., (1) but again (emphatic "again"): 丢開不幹, 卻又不成 again it won't do to throw up the whole business; (2) (MC) then...later: 量輕發落, 卻又理會 give him a light sentence, then take it up later.

§ 80S.30 (八^{s}/一)

羶 80S.30-6

shan.
[Var. 膻]

N. Rank odor of raw lamb, mutton.

§ 80S.42 (八^{s}/冈)

朔 80S.42-4

shuoh.

N. (1) The first day of the lunar month: 朔日 ditto; 朔望 the first and fifteenth day of lunar month; 正朔 New Year's day, beginning of year. (2) The north: 朔方 *-fang*↓; 朔風 north wind; 朔野, 朔漠 northern prairies, desert; 朔氣 northern cold air.

朔方 *shuohfang*, n., the north.
朔望月 *shuohwahng-yueh*, n., the exact lunar month, 29.53 days.

§ 80S.50 (八^{s}/ㄱ)

羯 80S.50-4

jier.

N. (1) A castrated ram. (2) An anc. barbaric tribe.

蠲 80S.50-4

jyuan.

V.t. (1) (Interch. 捐) exempt, free from obligation: 蠲免 *-miaan*↓; 蠲賦 exempt from payment of the land tax. (2) Select: 蠲吉 choose an auspicious day. (3) Cleanse: 蠲滌 to clean with water, purify.

蠲除 *jyuan-chur*, v.t., relieve of excessive burden or oppressive measures (=捐除).
蠲減 *jyuanjiaan*, v.t., reduce tax burden.
蠲免 *jyuanmiaan*, v.t., exempt from tax payment.

刱 80S.50-5

chuahng.
[Anc. var. of 創 81S.00]

翔 80S.50-5

shiarng.

V.i. (1) To circle around, to wheel about (as birds): 飛翔, 翔空, 高翔 (of birds) wheel about, high in the air; 翔集 (AC) fly around and then settle down together; 翔泳 (birds and fish) fly and swim; 翔舞 (birds) fly and hop about. (2) Prices leap up: 翔貴; 翔踊 (LL, rare) spiral up.

Adj. & adv. (Var. of 詳) careful, -ly: 翔實 (=詳實) thoroughly; 和氣翔洽 (LL) a pervasive spirit of peace and harmony.

翔步 *shiang-buh*, v.i., (AC) pace about (in the room).
翔羊 *shiarngyarng*, n., loiter, pace about (also wr. 相羊, 襄羊).

鵜 80S.50-9

tir.

鵜鶘 *tirhur*, n., pelican.
鵜鴃 *tirjyuer*, n., cuckoo (=子規, also wr. 鶗鴂).

鵒 80S.50-9

yuh.

N. See 鸜$^{\Delta}$鵒 41S.50.

鷀 80S.50-9

tsyr.
[Var. of 鶿 80.50]

鶼 80S.50-9

jian.

N. A mythical bird supposed to have only one eye and one wing: 鶼鶼 a pair of such birds dependent on each other, inseparable, hence, husband and wife; 鶼鰈 birds and fish of this kind.

§ 80S.63 (八^{s}/丶)

羚 80S.63-8

lirng.

羶 朔 羯 蠲 刱 翔 鵜 鵒 鷀 鶼 羚

亅	小	⺊	十	土	ナ	廿	ㄴ	丨	一	丅	フ	口	凶	冈	ㄱ	厂	尸	亠	广	宀	丶	乚	七	心	八	人	乂	𠂉	一	丿	⺈	く
00	01	02	10	11	12	20	21	22	30	31	32	40	41	42	50	51	52	60	61	62	63	70	71	72	80	81	82	83	90	91	92	93

N. 羚羊 a kind of antelope: 羚羊掛角 (fig.) superlative poetic art, showing no traces of effort.

§ 80S.70 (八^{S}/乚)

瓶 80S.70-3

pirng.

N. Jar, bottle, jug, vase (often *-tz*, *'l*): 花瓶 flower vase, also girl in office useful only as a decoration; 酒瓶 wine bottle, jug; 藥瓶 bottle for medicine; 瓶花 cut flowers for vase, the art of arranging them; 守口如瓶 keep mouth tightly shut.

瓶 鉢 *pirngbo*, n., alms-bowl and pot of monks.
瓶 塞 兒 *pirngsaa'l*, n., bottle stopper.
瓶 笙 *pirngsheng*, n., a Suhng Dyn. whistling kettle.

甑 80S.70-3

tzehng.

N. A cooking pot: 甑中生塵 (LL) so poor that dust has collected in one's cooking pot; 甑兒糕 steamed pastry; 飯甑 a rice pot.

羓 80S.70-5

ba.

N. (AC) salted dried meat.

§ 80S.71 (八^{S}/七)

羢 80S.71-7

rurng.

N. (1) Wool of sheep. (2) Woollen goods (also 絨). (3) Down, felt (also 底羢).

馘 80S.71-7

guor.

N. A prisoner of war with the left ear cut off, the left ear thus cut off: 獻馘 to present the prisoners.

羝 80S.71-9

di.

N. Ram, he-goat: 羝羊觸藩 a ram bucking a hedge—unable to move forward or backward.

§ 80S.80 (八^{S}/八)

頒 80S.80-3

ban.

V.t. (1) To confer (prizes, medals, etc.): 頒獎, 頒賞, 頒贈. (2) To distribute: 頒給薪俸 distribute pay. (3) To publish officially, see 頒布 *-buh*↓.

頒 布 *banbuh*, v.t., promulgate (new laws, mandates).
頒 發 *banfa*, v.t., officially give out (order, bonus, etc.).
頒 行 *banshirng*, v.t., publish (order, statutes, etc.) for execution.
頒 贈 *bantzehng*, v.t., to confer (honors, degrees).

頌 80S.80-3

suhng (**rurng*).

V.t. & n. (1) Praise, chant: 稱頌 to praise; 頌揚, 頌讚 *-yarng*, *-tzahn*↓; 歌頌 to chant praise (of God, emperor); 歌功頌德 glorify a ruler's character and accomplishments; 頌聲載道 win popular praise ("in the streets"). (2) (**rurng*) To unfetter: 頌繫之 (AC) to take off the fetters from him.

頌 美 *suhngmeei*, v.t., (LL) to praise, speak well of (s.o.).
頌 詞 *suhngtsyr*, n., (1) a eulogy; (2) an ambassador's speech delivered at the presentation of his credentials.
頌 讚 *suhngtzahn*, v.t. & n., praise.
頌 揚 *suhngyarng*, v.t., sing the praises of.

§ 80S.81 (八^{S}/人)

猷 80S.81-1

your.

N. (LL) a grand plan: 嘉猷 a good plan; 鴻猷 a great plan.

V.t. (AC) to paint (images).

欲 80S.81-9

yuh.

N. Desire, human desire (also wr.

慾); wish, want: 大欲 great desire.

V.i. & t. To desire, want (LL for vern. 要): 從心所欲 follow what the heart desires; 非我所欲 is not what I want; 不欲 do not want to; 己所不欲, 勿施於人 do not do unto others what you do not want done unto you; 欲望, 欲願 *-wahng, -yuahn*↓; 欲求, 欲圖 try to, hope to, in order to; 欲速則不達 things done in a hurry cannot be done well.

欲心 *yuhshin*, n., wish, desire.
欲望 *yuhwahng*, n., wish, desire.
欲要 *yuhyauh*, v.i., want to.
欲願 *yuhyuahn*, n., wish, desire.

歉 80S.81-9

chiahn.

Adj. (1) Ill at ease, feel "guilty": 歉仄 *-tzeh*↓; 抱歉 (court.) feel "guilty" (for delay in answering letter, etc.); 道歉, 致歉 to extend apology, to apologize; 深以爲歉 (LL) I feel deeply apologetic. (2) Having bad crops: 歲歉 crop failure, a bad year in crops.

歉然 *chiahnrarn*, adj., apologetic.
歉收 *chiahnshou*, v.t. & n., bad crops, poor harvest.
歉仄 *chiahntzeh*, adj., (court.) ashamed of oneself.
歉意 *chiahnyih*, n., sense of being guilty or ill at ease.

§ 80S.82 (八s/乂)

羖 80S.82-4

guu.

N. (Zoo.) a black ram.

SECTION 81

§ 81.00 (人/亅)

俞 81.00

yur (*yuh*).
[Usu. printed 兪]

N. A surname.

V.i. (1) To consent, approve: 俞允 you approve; your approval. (2) U.f. 愈 recover from illness.

拿 81.00

nar.
[Pop. var. of 拏]

V.t. (1) Take (hold of), bring, keep, control, arrest: 拿開, 拿去, 拿走 take (s.t.) away; 拿定 take firm hold of, grasp: 拿定主意, 拿定方針 make up one's mind; 拿過來 bring (s.t.) over here; 拿穩 keep (s.t.) firmly in hand; 拿不穩 cannot be sure; 拿住(了) keep in hand, take hold of, have apprehended (s.o.); 拿得動, 不動 can, cannot move (s.t.); 拿不起來 (lit.) cannot lift (s.t.) heavy; (fig.) cannot control: 他雖當了主管, 但一切事都拿不起來 though he is the boss, he cannot get anything done; 拿不住 (lit.) cannot hold (s.t.) slippery; (fig.) cannot seize or arrest: 這麼多人, 拿不住一個小賊 so many men cannot seize even a petty thief; cannot keep in possession: 他拿不住錢, 一兩天就花光了 he can never save money but will spend every cent of it in a day or two; cannot control: 拿不住人, 當不了頭目 if you don't know how to keep men under control, you can never be boss; 捉拿, 拿捕 arrest or seize; 拿辦 arrest and punish; 拿獲 apprehend; 拿問 arrest and interrogate; 拿人 arrest people, coerce (s.o.) to yield to one's demands; 拿空子 take advantage of an opening for attack; 拿缺缺兒 find fault with; 拿三搬四 try to evade; 拿刀動杖 resort to force; 拿權, 拿事 get control of, have the power to do or dominate. (2) Pretend: assume (airs): 拿班做勢, 拿腔做事 put up a front, pretend to be busy; 拿把, 拿喬, 拿架子, 拿糖, 拿大, 拿揑 see *-baa, -chiaur, -jiahtz, -tarng, -dah, -'nieh*↓.

Prep. With: 拿話激他 to inflame or egg him on with words; (=把) introducing object of vb. and placing object before vb.: 拿他埋怨了一頓 grumble against him; 拿他開玩笑 make fun of him (=開他頑笑); 拿我當什麽人 regard me as what? 拿他摔了 throw it down and break it.

拿把 *nar-baa*, v.t., put on airs, strike a pose in order to enhance one's own importance.
拿拌 *narbahn*, v.i., purposely embarrass others.
拿喬 *nar-chiaur*, v.t., see *-baa*↑, *-jiahtz*↓.
拿情 *narchirng*, v.t., (MC) flirt with (=調情).
拿大 *nardah*, v.i., pretend to be superior; 拿大頂 see *-diing*↓.
拿(大)頂 *nar-(dah)diing*, v.i., stand on one's head.
拿滑 *narhuar*, v.i., hold fast: 這皮鞋底不拿滑 the soles of the pair of shoes do not catch well, i.e., slip easily.
拿架子 *nar-jiahtz*, v.i., put on airs.
拿毛 *narmaur*, v.i., look for trouble in: 拿毛打架 be rowdy and engage in fisticuffs.
拿揑 *nar'nieh*, v.i., (1) purposely put obstacles in the way of (s.o.); (2) pretend to conform to rules of propriety.
拿手 *narshoou(-'shou)*, adj., be good at, excel in: 拿手好戲

拿佘余汆食衾

what one most excels in, one's specialty.

拿糖 *nar-tarng*, v.i., see *-jiahtz*↑.

拿總(兒) *nar-tzuung('l)*, v.t., exercise general control or supervision.

§81.01 (人/小)

 81.01

she.

[Dist. 余]

N. A surname.

 81.01

yur.

N. A surname.

Pron. (AC, LL) I, my, me (=vern. 我).

§81.02 (人/𠂉)

 81.02

tsuan (*tuun*).

V.i. To boil with water (as different from stew and in shorter time): 汆湯 *-tang*↓.

汆兒 *tsua'l*, n., see *-tz*↓.

汆湯 *tsuantang*, n., soup (vegetable or meat); pop. also wr. 川.

汆子 *tsuantz*, n., (1) sauce made to go with noodles; (2) a small metal pot which can be lowered into earthen oven, causing water in it to boil almost instantly.

食 81.02

shyr (**syh*).

N. (1) Food: 酒食, 飲食 food and drink; 衣食 food and clothing; 食色 food and sex; 膳食, 伙食 board, the meals; 食用 *-yuhng*↓; 食堂 dining room; 食少事繁 lot of work and scanty meals; 食前方丈 (AC) have food spread out ten feet square—live in luxury. (2) (**syh*) 食不厭精 (AC) rice could never be white enough (of Confucius); 有酒食, 先生饌 when there's food and drink, it is served to the master. (3) A radical, 81B. (4) A surname.

V.t. (1) To eat: 食量 *-liahng*↓; 食其肉而寢其皮 want to eat his flesh and sleep on his hide—swear revenge; 食玉炊桂 (LL) food as expensive as jade and fuel as expensive as cassia—extremely high cost of living; oft. fig., to digest: 食古不化 read ancient teachings without digesting them—be slave to the ancients; 食言, *-yarn*¹↓. (2) To live on: 自食其力 live by one's own labor; 食租衣稅 (of officials) live on rents; hold a feudal benefice: 食祿, 食邑, 食土, 食地 *-luh, -yih, -tuu, -dih*↓. (3) Sometimes equivalent to drink: 食酒 (AC) drink wine. (4) (**syh*, =飼) To feed (dog, person).

V.i. To eclipse: 日食, 月食 eclipse of the sun, moon (also wr. 蝕).

食頃 *shyr-chiing*, phr., the time of a meal, a short moment.

食蟲類 *shyrchurng-leih*, n., Insectivora.

食單 *shyr-dan*, n., menu.

食道 *shyr-dauh*, n., (1) oesophagus, alimentary canal; (2) proper method of eating.

食地 *shyr-dih*, n., fief town, see *-yih*↓.

食俸 *shyr-fehng*, n., formerly, salary.

食復 *shyr-fur*, n., relapse of patient owing to wrong food.

食管 *shyrguaan*, n., (physiol.) the oesophagus.

食盒 *shyrher*, n., (1) food casket, usu. lacquered; (2) bridal caskets of food and clothing, etc. paraded on streets.

食貨 *shyrhuoh*, n., food and commerce, economic goods.

食火鷄 *shyrhuoo-ji*, n., (zoo.) the cassowary, *Casuaris*, an ostrich-like bird.

食積 *shyr-ji*, n., indigestion.

食忌 *shyr-jih*, n., taboos in food.

食茱萸 *shyrjuyur*, n., a tree whose fruit is edible, *Zanthoxylum ailanthoides*.

食具 *shyrjyuh*, n., table service (bowls, etc.).

食指 *shyrjyy*, n., (1) the index finger; (2) 食指浩繁 many mouths to feed.

食客 *shyrkeh*, n., (Warring Kingdoms) scholars and swordsmen retained by rich, powerful family.

食量 *shyr-liahng*, n., eating capacity.

食糧 *shyrliarng*, n., foodstuffs, army rations.

食料 *shyrliauh*, n., feed for horses, etc.

食祿 *shyr-luh*, n., formerly, official's salary.

食品 *shyr-piin*, n., eatables in gen.

食譜 *shyrpuu*, n., menu, recipe.

食肉 *shyr-rouh*, adj., carnivorous; 食肉獸 carnivorous animal.

食嗓 *shyr(')saang*, n., (coll.) the alimentary canal.

食土 *shyr-tuu*, n., fief town.

食物 *shyrwuh*, n., food in gen.

食言 *shyr-yarn*¹, v.i., to "eat one's words"—fail to live up to promise.

食鹽 *shyr-yarn*², n., table or kitchen salt.

食邑 *shyr-yih*, n., fief town.

食蟻獸 *shyryii-shouh*, n., (zoo.) the anteater.

食慾 *shyr yuh*, n., appetite.

食用 *shyryuhng*, n., livng expenses.

 81.02

chin.

N. Bed quilt: 衾枕 quilt and pillow; 被衾 bed quilt; 衾冷枕寒 phr., loneliness in bed; 衾衽 in privacy of bedroom; 衾影無慚 phr., a clear conscience in the still hours of the night; 衾裯 silk bedclothes.

§ 81.10 (人/十)

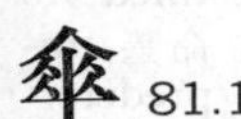 81.10

saan.

N. Umbrella, parasol, sunshade: 洋傘 modern umbrella; 雨傘 generally umbrella, orig. made of oiled paper and bamboo frame; 旱傘, 陽傘 parasol: 降落傘 parachute; 傘兵, 降傘兵 parachutist.

§ 81.11 (人/土)

全 81.11

chyuarn.

N. A surname.

V.t. To maintain, keep whole or intact: 保全 to keep well, maintain; 全節 (LL) to keep one's integrity (even sacrificing life); 全交 (LL) to keep friendship unchanged; 全性保真 (Taoist) to keep one's original nature; 兩全其美 satisfy both parties, have it both ways; keep the good points of both; 苟全性命 manage to stay alive with sacrifice of principles; 安全 security.

Adj. (1) Complete, perfect: 完全 complete, -ly; 全勝 a complete victory; 大全 "a compendium, alpha and omega"; 忠孝兩全 both loyalty and filial piety are attained; 才貌雙全 having both looks and real talent; 求全之心 the desire for perfection; 全始全終 perfect (in friendships, etc.) from beginning to end; 十全十美 perfect; 全受全歸 lived a perfect life ("return intact what one was born with"). (2) Whole: 全家, 全校 whole family, school; 全軍 the whole army (perished, etc.); 全世界 the whole world; 全部, 全盤 *-buh, -parn* ↓; 全局 the whole situation, whole stakes in gambling; 全數 entire; 全套 the complete set or full repertoire; 全年, 全月, 全日 the whole year, month, day; 全本(兒) the entire play, not a selection only; 全靠人兒 (coll.) a family intact with parents and children together; 全力, 全心 *-lih, -shin* ↓.

Adv. Completely, all: 全然 *-rarn* ↓; 全都 all, completely: 全都完了 all finished; 全來了 all have come; 全癒 completely recovered; 全無心肝 completely without scruples; 全無是處 absolutely without merit, totally wrong; 全無意思 totally uninterested, -ing; 全不管 totally ignore, will not bother.

全般 *chyuarnban*, adv., all, the entire amount.

全豹 *chyuarn-bauh*, phr., 得窺全豹 see the entire thing ("the whole leopard" as contrasted with 得窺一斑 see only one spot of leopard skin).

全部 *chyuarn-buh*, n., the complete works, the whole, all: 全部燒毀 all destroyed by fire.

全器 *chyuarnchih*, n., see *-tsair* ↓.

全權 *chyuarnchyuarn*, adj., with full powers; 全權大使 envoy plenipotentiary; 全權代表 delegate with full powers.

全等 *chyuarndeeng*, adj., (math.) identically equal or congruent.

全德 *chyuarn-der*, phr., perfect character.

全反射 *chyuarn faansheh*, n., (phys.) total reflection.

全分(兒) *chyuarnfehn(-feh'l)*, n., the whole, the entire part.

全副 *chyuarn-fuh*, n., the whole set.

全活 *chyuarn huor*, phr., the complete works (as in barbershop, haircut, shave, shampoo, massage—all).

全集 *chyuarn-jir*, n., complete works of author.

全力 *chyuarn-lih*, adj., with whole strength: 全力以赴 overcome (difficulty) with one's entire energy.

全能 *chyuarn-nerng*, adj., (1) omnipotent, almighty; (2) (sports) all-round (contests): 全能運動 decathlon, pentathlon.

全牛 *chyuarn-niour*, phr., 目無全牛 (allu.) a complete master (as a master butcher sees all the parts of a cow without cutting).

全盤 *chyuarn-parn*, n., the whole amount, the entire show; used as adv., completely: 全盤失敗 fail completely.

全然 *chyuarn-rarn*, adv., completely (unaware, etc.).

全人 *chyuarn-rern*, n., a sage, a perfect person.

全盛 *chyuarn-shehng*, adj., at the peak of development: 全盛時代 the golden age, period as when (Tarng poetry, etc.) was at its peak.

全身 *chyuarn-shen*, n., the whole body (covered with mud, etc.).

全心 *chyuarnshin*, adv., wholeheartedly.

全席 *chyuarn-shir*, n., a complete full-scale banquet.

全蝕 *chyuarn-shyr*, n., (astron.) total eclipse.

全體 *chyuarn-tii*, n., the whole body or group (of students, representatives); as adv., all: 全體贊成 all approved.

全才 *chyuarn-tsair*, n., a person versatile in all arts: 文武全才 one versed in literary and military arts.

全音 *chyuarn-yin*, n., (music) diatonic scale, diatonic tone: 全音音符 diatonic scale.

§ 81.21 (人/乚)

亾 81.21

warng.

[Anc. var. of 亡 60.21]

§ 81.22 (人/丨)

个 81.22

geh.

[Abbr. of 箇 92A.41]

介 81.22

jieh (**gah*).

N. (1) Armor, mail: 介夫 *-'fu*, 介冑 *-jour*↓. (2) (Zoo.) crustaceans: 介殼 *-ker*, 介蟲 *-churng*↓; 鱗介類 fish and crustaceans. (3) (Interch. 芥) a thing of little or no value, a trifle: 一介不取 will not take a cent. (4) Stage direction for certain movements: 飲酒介 drinking wine; 相見介 (of two persons) meeting; 張生笑介 Chang smiles or laughs. (5) (U. f. 价) a manservant. (6) A surname.

V.i. & t. (1) To lie between, interpose, serve as intermediary: 介紹 *-shauh*↓; 介於二者之間 situated between the two; 介紹 introduce one person to another; 媒介 a medium or go-between; 介詞 *-tsyr*↓. (2) Pray for blessing: 以介眉壽 to pray for blessing of long life; 介壽 *-shouh*↓. (3) Keep in mind, take seriously: 介意 *-yih*, 介懷 *-huair*, 介介 *-jieh*↓.

Adj. (1) Simple, plain: 一介書生 a mere scholar; 一介武夫 a plain soldier. (2) Huge, big: 介福 *-fur*↓. (3) (*gah*) Such a: 像煞有介事 (Shanghai dial.) make such a fuss about it, put on such airs. (4) Upright, straightforward, conscientious: 耿介 scrupulous, acting on principles; 介然 *-rarn*↓.

Adj. & adv. Alone: 介立 *-lih*, 介特 *-teh*↓.

介蟲 *jiehchurng*, n., (zoo.) crustaceans.

介弟 *jiehdih*, n., (court.) your brother.

介夫 *jieh'fu*, n., (AC) an armed soldier.

介福 *jiehfur*, n., great happiness, untold blessings; also v.i., pray for blessings.

介懷 *jiehhuair*, v.i., bear a grievance, take offense.

介介 *jiehjieh*, adj., uneasy, troubled, full of misgivings.

介冑 *jiehjour*, n., ancient military dress ("armor and helmet").

介殼 *jiehker*, n., shells of crabs, oysters, lobsters or snails.

介立 *jiehlih*, v.i., stand alone.

介然 *jiehrarn*, adj. & adv., steadfast(ly), uncompromising(ly).

介紹 *jiehshauh*, v.t., (1) introduce (one person) to another (also 紹介); (2) serve as an intermediary.

介壽 *jieh-shouh*, n., offer of birthday congratulations.

介特 *jiehteh*, n., (AC) one without family or friend: 養老疾, 收介特 (AC) take care of the aged and the sick and give shelter to the homeless.

介詞 *jiehtsyr*, n., (gram.) a preposition.

介子 *jiehtzyy*, n., (phys.) a mesotron.

介意 *jiehyih*, v.i., feel hurt: 請不要介意 please do not take it to heart, see *-huair*↑.

命 81.22

mihng.

N. (1) Order, command: 使命 mission abroad; 奉命 receive order; 違命 disobey order; 逆命, 抗命 defy order; 遵命 obey order. (2) Life: 生命 life; 長命, 短命 long, short, life; 壽命 life span; 救命 cry "help"; 喪命 to die; 拚命 risk life, work hard regardless; 命在旦夕 life hangs in the balance; 死於非命 die of violence or accident or unnatural death; 亡命 live in exile. (3) Luck, fate: 命運 luck, life course as predetermined (of person, nation); 命好, 命大 destined to good life; 命乖, 命薄, 命蹇 unlucky in life; 命中 predetermined, destined: 命中無子 destined not to have sons; 命也, 命矣乎 (LL) it's just hard luck, it is the will of God; 命也何如 what can I do against such luck?

V.t. (1) To order, command: 命令你去做 I order you to do it; 命駕 "order your carriage," do me the honor of your visit; 命筆直書 to write down as inspiration or feeling dictates. (2) To assign: 命名 assign name to (person, occasion, etc.); 命題 assign subject of essay.

命案 *mihng-an*, n., a case of murder.

命蔕 *mihngdih*, n., (1) (Chin. med.) placenta cord of newborn babe; (2) see *-mern*↓.

命婦 *mihng-fuh*, n., formerly, lady of rank, see *-guan*↓.

命服 *mihng-fur*, n., (AC) official costume.

命根 *mihng-gen*, n., the root of one's life, dearest (child, etc.)

命官 *mihng-guan*, n., ranking official.

命宮 *mihng-gung*, n., (1) constellation in which one is born; (2) (in fortunetelling) point where the eyebrows meet.

命令 *mihnglihng*, n. & v.t., order, command.

命門 *mihng-mern*, n., (fortunetelling) side temple; the region of the kidneys ("gate of life").

命脈 *mihngmoh*, n., the "life vein," "life pulse," (fig.) where life (of nation) depends.

命數 *mihngshuh*, n., one's luck.

命世(之才) *mihng-shyh(jy tsair)*, phr., dominant spirit (of generation); one destined to govern.

命途 *mihngtur*, n., course of events in one's life.

命運 *mihngyuhn*, n., one's luck; course of development.

令 81.22

lihng (**lirng*).

[See 令 81.63]

§81.30 (人/一)

仝 81.30

turng.

[Var. of 同]

N. A surname.

Adj. Same, same as (var. of 同): 仝上 (＝同上) same as above, ditto.

企 81.30

chih.

V.i. (1) To stand on tiptoe: see 企立, 企踵 *-lih, -juung*↓. (2) As adv. preceding vb. meaning "on tiptoe": 企望 to wait, await (as on tiptoe): 企望回音 awaiting your reply; 企禱 (court. in letters) I pray, see compp.↓.

企鵝 *chih-er*, n., the penguin.

企及 *chihjir*, v.t., as in 不可企及 cannot compare anywhere (with s.o.).

企踵 *chih-juung*, v.i., to stand on tiptoe.

企立 *chihlih*, v.i., stand on tiptoe.

企慕 *chihmuh*, v.t., to admire greatly; see *-yaang*↓.

企盼 *chihpahn*, v.i., see *-wahng*↓.

企圖 *chihtur*, v.i., attempt to (rescue, murder, etc.).

企望 *chihwahng*, v.i., to hope, look forward to.

企仰 *chihyaang*, v.t., see *-muh*↑.

企業 *chihyeh*, n., industry, enterprise: 企業公司 a commercial company for various enterprises (real estate, etc.).

金 81.30

jin.

N. (1) Gold: 黃金, 赤金 gold; 白金 platinum; 金子 *-tz*↓; 金幣 gold coins; 金鑛 *-kuahng*↓; 金銀 gold and silver money, riches, wealth; 包金 overlay with gold; 鍍金 gilt; 足金 pure gold; 飾金 gold, generally alloyed for making ornaments. (2) Metals: 五金 gold, silver, copper, iron, and tin; 金屬 *-shuu*↓; 合金 a metal alloy or compound. (3) Money, wealth, funds: 金融 *-rurng*↓; 金鈔 *-chau*↓; 金券 gold certificate; 美金 greenbacks; 金額 *-er*↓. (4) First of the five basic movements (金, 木, 水, 火, 土), see 五$^{\Delta}$行 31.30. (5) One of the eight kinds of musical instruments, see *bayin* 八$^{\Delta}$音 80.80. (6) Weapons: 金瘡 *-chuang*^{2}↓; 金革 *-ger*↓. (7) A surname.

Adj. (1) Firm, strong, secure, durable: 金湯 *-tang*, 金城 *-cherng*, 金甌 *-ou*↓; 金字招牌 A1, first-rate, first-class, (of person) most reliable, trustworthy; (of company) gilded sign, well established. (2) Grand, imposing, beautiful: 金碧輝煌 (of buildings) magnificent, splendid; 金迷紙醉 living an extravagent life, given to sensual pleasures; 金殿 royal palace; 金相(玉質) *-shiahng*, 金枝(玉葉) *-jy*^{2}↓. (3) Deserving of respect: 金口 *-koou*, 金言 *-yarn*↓.

金安 *jin-an*, phr., conventional expression used in complimentary close of letters to elders.

金榜 *jinbaang*, n., formerly, list of successful candidates in government examinations: 金榜題名 succeed in such an examination.

金鎊 *jinbahng*, n., the pound sterling.

金本位 *jin-beenweih*, n., the gold standard.

金箔 *jinbor*, n., gold foil, gold leaf.

金不換 *jinburhuahn*, n., (1) Chinese ink; (2) a rarity, anything highly valued for its scarcity ("not to be exchanged for gold"); (3) (herb medicine) *Gynura pinnatifida* (also called 三七).

金蟬 *jincharn*, n., an ancient headgear: 金蟬脫殼 escape unnoticed.

金鈔 *jinchau*, n., short for 黃金美鈔 gold and greenbacks.

金城 *jin-cherng*, n., an impregnable city.

金錢 *jinchiarn*, n., money, cash, wealth, riches.

金創 *jin-chuang*^{1}, n., wounds inflicted by sharp weapons.

金瘡 *jinchuang*^{2}, n., ditto.

金闕 *jinchyueh*, n., the imperial quarters.

金雀花 *jinchyueh-hua*, n., (bot.) the common broom, *Cytisus scoparius*.

金丹 *jindan*, n., (Taoist alchemy) the elixir of life, pill of immortality.

金店 *jindiahn*^{1}, n., a jeweler's.

金鈿 *jindiahn*^{2}, n., woman's golden hairpin.

金斗 *jindoou*, n., (1) an iron for pressing clothes; (2) (＝筋斗) somersault.

金額 *jin-er*, n., a sum of money.

金粉 *jin-feen*, n., (1) women's face powder, hence beautiful

A

金 women: 六朝金粉 the beauties of the Six Dynasties (420–589 A.D.); (2) yellow powder on male flower; (3) gold dust.

金風 *jin-feng*, n., autumn wind.

金剛 *jingang*, n., (1) a substance of immense hardness; (2) one of the four guardians (四大金剛) of Buddhist temples; (3) 金剛砂 grains of garnet; 金剛石 diamond; 金剛鑽 n., ditto.

金戈(鐵馬) *jin-ge*, n., wars, fighting.

金革 *jin-ger*, n., weapons of war, arms.

金龜婿 *jinguei-shyuh*, n., a son-in-law from a wealthy or politically influential family; 金龜子 (zoo.) a "golden beetle," *Mimela lucidula* (also 金蟲).

金匱 *jin-gueih*, n., (AC) metal trunk, a depository of state papers or other important documents.

金黃 *jinhuang*, adj., golden yellow.

金婚 *jin-hun*, n., a couple's golden wedding.

金壺 *jin-hur*, n., (1) an ancient clepsydra; (2) a wine jug.

金紅 *jin-hurng*, adj., golden-red.

金針菜 *jinjen-tsaih*, n., (bot.) the day lily, *Hemerocallis flava* (also 金鍼菜).

金雞 *jin-ji*, n., (1) (history) a cock put on top of a long pole on day of general amnesty; (2) a cock with golden feathers: 金雞獨立 (Chinese boxing) standing on one foot as the cock does; (3) 金雞納霜 quinine.

金甲 *jinjiaa*, n., armor.

金漿 *jin-jiang*, n., (1) wine of the best quality; (2) an elixir of life.

金裝 *jin-juang*, adj., overlaid with gold.

金鐘罩 *jinjung-jauh*, n., & v.i., (1) n., (boxing) ability to remain unscathed in fighting an opponent; (2) v.i., to scare off people by bragging or bluffing.

金汁 *jin-jy*¹, n., (1) molten gold; (2) human excrement used as fertilizer.

金枝(玉葉) *jin-jy*², n., descendants of royal families, the nobility, the aristocracy.

金橘 *jin-jyur*, n., (bot.) the cumquat, *Citrus nobilis* var. *microcarpa*.

B

金科 *jinke*, n., as in 金科玉律 (1) laws and regulations; (2) maxims, precepts.

金口 *jin-koou*, n., highly esteemed words: 金口玉言 oracular words.

金鑛 *jinkuahng*, n., a gold mine.

金庫 *jinkuh*, n., (1) government treasury; (2) a bank: 合作金庫 cooperative bank.

金蘭(之交) *jinlarn*, n., bosom friends, intimate friendship.

金蓮(兒) *jinliarn-(liar'l)*, n., formerly, women's bound feet.

金鈴子 *jinlirngtzyy*, n., (bot.) chinaberry (also 楝實).

金鑾殿 *jinluarn-diahn*, n., the main hall of the imperial palace.

金輪 *jinlurn*, n., a poetic term for the moon ("the golden wheel").

金馬 *jin-maa* n., (1) a horse cast in bronze; (2) the offshore islands of Kinmen (Quemoy) and Matsu.

金黴素 *jihnmeirsuh*, n., aureomycin.

金諾 *jin-nuoh*, n., a promise that can be relied upon.

金甌 *jin-ou*, n., national territory as compared to a golden goblet: 金甌無缺 unimpaired territorial integrity.

金牌 *jin-pair*, n., (1) a gold medal, the highest prize awarded to the winner in a contest; (2) an imperial decree sent by special delivery.

金瓶梅 *Jin-Pirng-Meir*, n., name of a Chinese satirical novel on sex.

金融 *jinrurng*, n., finance, currency, money and credit: 金融界 financial circles; 金融市場 the money market.

金身 *jin-shen*, n., the Buddha's image gilt with gold.

金線魚 *jinshiahn-yur*, n., (zoo.) *Euthyopteroma virgatum*.

金相 *jinshiahng*, n. as in 金相玉質 the sterling qualities, noted for nobility of character.

金仙 *jinshian*, n., (1) a fairy; (2) th Buddha.

金星 *jinshing*, n., planet Venus.

金屬 *jinshuu*, n., metals in gen.: 金屬品 metal products.

金石 *jin-shyr*, n., (1) ancient bronzes and stone tablets; (2) metals and precious stones: 心如金石堅 my heart is as constant as metals and stones are durable; 金石交 unbreakable friendship; (擲地)有金石聲 (fig. of writings) forceful and effective, pleasing to the ear; (3) bells and musical stones; (4) arms, weapons.

C

金絲雀 *jinsy-chyueh*, n., (zoo.) the canary bird; 金絲桃 (bot.) the Chinese St.-John's-wort, *Hypericum chinense*; 金絲燕 (zoo.) *Collocalia esculenta*.

金湯 *jin-tang*, phr., short for 金城湯池 a strongly fortified city.

金條 *jin-tiaur*, n., a gold bar.

金腿 *jin-tueei*, n., the best ham, a product of Chinhua (金華), Chekiang.

金童 *jin-turng*, n., esp. in 金童玉女 (Taoism) boy and girl attendants of fairies.

金子 *jintz*, n., gold.

金棗 *jintzaau*, n., a kind of date (fruit).

金字塔 *jintzyhtaa*, n., a pyramid.

金紫 *jintzyy*, n., insignia of high office.

金文 *jinwern*, n., inscriptions on ancient bronze vessels.

金屋 *jin-wu*¹, n., well-appointed living quarters for women: 金屋藏嬌 settle one's young wife or lover in a luxurious apartment.

金烏 *jin-wu*², n., a poetic term for the moon: 金烏西墜 the moon is sinking in the west; 金烏兔玉, two different terms for the moon.

金吾 *jinwur*, n., (AC) a rod carried by an official as a symbol of imperial authority: 執金吾 be such an official.

金言 *jin-yarn*, n., valuable advice, precious words.

金瘍 *jinyarng*, n., see *-chuang* ↑.

金曜日 *jinyauhryh*, n., (LL) Friday.

金葉(子) *jin-yieh(tz)*, n., gold foil.

金銀箔 *jinyirnbor*, n., gold and silver foils, gold and silver leaves; 金銀花 (bot.) the honeysuckle (also 忍冬).

金玉 *jin-yuh*, (1) n., gold and jade; (2) adj., precious like gems: 金玉其外 all that glitters is not gold.

金魚 *jinyur*, n., (1) the goldfish;

(2) (MC) an ornament worn by high officials; (3) another name for keys; 金魚草 (bot.) the common snapdragon.

 81.30

shin (*shing*).

V.i. To prosper, thrive in business (cf. 興 *shing* 90.80).

盒 81.30

her.

N. (*-tz*) A box, tin (of cigarettes, matches), casket (of jewels, etc.).

盒子 *hertz*, n., (1) a box; (2) a box-like display of fireworks; (3) (Peking dial.) a round box of roast meat, etc. (also called 盒子菜); 盒子砲 a Mauser pistol; 盒子錢 gratuities to servants who bring gifts; (4) 砌盒子 (sl.) to cheat at gambling.

 81.30

an.

N. (1) A hut, a small Buddhist temple (var. of 庵 61.70). (2) (AC) cover of vessel for food.

§ 81.32 (人/フ)

 81.32

jin.

N. The present time, here and now (opp. 古 ancient times): 博古通今 know all about ancient and modern times, erudite, learned; 今非昔比 times have changed; 如今, 當今, 方今 now(-a-days), at present; 至今 until now, up to the present; 迄今 ditto; 自今以後 from now on; 覺今是而昨非 now I have come to realize how wrong I have been all those years.

Adj. Present, this (opp. 昨 past, last): 今夜 *-yeh*, 今天 *-tian*, 今兒個 *-'l'ge*, 今晚 *-waan*, 今年 *-niarn* ↓; 今夕何夕 pray, what night is tonight? 今人 contemporaries; 今體 *-tii* ↓.

今番 *jinfan*, adv., this time, now.

今後 *jinhouh*, adv., from now on, in the future, hereafter.

今朝 *jinjau*, adv., today, this morning.

今兒(個) *jin'l('ge)*, n. & adv., today, (on) this day.

今年 *jinniarn*, n. & adv., this year, (in) the current year.

今日 *jinryh*, n., & adv., today, this (very) day.

今上 *jinshahng*, n., His Majesty the (present) King.

今生 *jinsheng*, n., this life (opp. 來生 the life to come).

今昔 *jinshir*, n., present and past, ancient and modern times: 今非昔比 no longer what it was before.

今世 *jinshyh*, n., this world, this age, this generation.

今天 *jintian*, n., & adv., today, this (very) day.

今體 *jintii*, n., the modern style (of poetry, prose, script) (opp. 古體 old style).

今茲 *jintz*, adv., now(-a-days), at the present time.

今晚 *jinwaan*, n., this evening.

今夜 *jinyeh*, n., tonight.

今雨 *jinyuu*, n., new friends (opp. 舊雨 old friends, from allu., 舊雨來, 今雨不來 (杜甫) old friends come even in rain, new friends do not).

§ 81.40 (人/口)

合 81.40

her (**gee*).

N. (1) A surname. (2) One round in fighting or tournament: 戰數合(回合) several close-in combats. (3) A matrimonial match: 天作之合 a match made in heaven. (4) (**gee*) One tenth of *sheng* (升), a rice measure.

V.i. & t. (1) To close, shut: 一夜不曾合眼 never closed one's eyes all night; 合口 (of wound) to heal, close up. (2) Combine, join, meet, unite: 兩條合爲一條 combine the two items; 聚合, 會合, 集合 to assemble, meet together; 合起來, 合在一起 put (several items) together; 分合 divide and combine; 聯合 unite, combine; 貌合神離 friends or allies apparently only. (3) To agree, suit (purpose), match: 合得來 (the two) can get along together; 落落寡合 have few friends; 合他意思 please him, suit his idea; 合他脾胃 suit his taste; 合理, 合意 *-lii*, *-yih*^{1}↓; 苟合 (a) to work together against principles; (b) to commit adultery. (4) Sexual intercourse: 交合 ditto; 野合 illegal intercourse.

Adj. & adv. (1) Fitting and proper, suitable: 合當, 合該 *-dang*, *-gai*↓; 不合 should not (have done), also not proper; 於理不合 improper, unreasonable; 合法, 合式 *-faa*, *-shyh*^{1}↓; 合則留, 不合則去 free to quit if conditions are not suitable; 合拍 in step. (2) Together, jointly: 合住, 合吃 live, eat together; 合請, 合送 jointly give a dinner, a present; 合唱 sing together, sing in chorus; 男女合唱 a mixed chorus. (3) The whole: 合葬 bury (couple, parents) in common grave; 合家, 合府 the whole family; 合族 the whole clan.

合辦 *herbahn*, v.i. & t., jointly manage or own (business); p.p., jointly managed.

合抱 *her-bauh*, phr., (of tree trunk) nearly a fathom in circumference (an "embrace" with outstretched arms).

合璧 *herbih*, n., (LL) a bilingual book in parallel paragraphs: 中英合璧 s.t. which is a combination of several pieces.

合幷 *herbihng*, v.t., combine into one (also wr. 合併); annex or absorb a country; 合併症 (med.) complication.

合唱 *herchahng*, v.i., (sing) in chorus; n., a chorus.

合成 *hercherng*, v.t., (1) combine into (s.t.); (2) (chem.) to form (by combining elements).

合氣 *her-chih*, v.i., (dial.) to quarrel: 與婆婆合氣 quarrel with mother-in-law; (cf. 和^{A}氣 90A.40 with same sound but opp. meaning).

合羣 *herchyurn*, (1) v.i., live together as a group; (2) adj., gregarious.

合當 *herdang*, vb. aux., should: 合當如此 should be so (=該當).

合度 *herduh*, adj., proper, of proper length or size.

合法 *herfaa*, adj., legal, conforming to law: 不合法 illegal.

合符字兒 *herfurtzeh'l*, n., (coll.) contract (=合同).

合該 *hergai*, vb. aux., conformably to (law, God's will): 合該釋放 should legally be freed; 合該不死 it's God's will he did not die.

合格 *herger*, adj., qualified (for examination, contest): 不合格 disqualified.

合股(兒)(子) *her-guu'('l)(tz)*, adj. & v.i., 合股 to form partnership: 合股公司 joint-stock company.

合乎 *herhu*, adj., in accordance with: 合乎道理 according to reason.

合歡 *herhuan*, (1) v.i., to meet and enjoy; (2) n., the mimosa, *Albizzia julibrissin*; 合家歡 family reunion.

合會 *herhueih*, n., a kind of temporary mutual loan club, in which each member subscribes to a monthly sum of money, the sum going to the bidder of highest interest for that month, until all members have had their turns: 合會儲蓄公司 mutual loan and savings company.

合昏 *herhun*^{1}, n., (1) see *-huan* 2↑; (2) (MC) toward dusk or twilight.

合婚 *herhun*^{2}, v.i., formerly, a custom of exchanging horoscopes of boy and girl before formal betrothal (cf. 結婚 wedding, 訂婚 betrothal).

合夥 *her-huoo*, n. & v.i., partnership; go into partnership (cf. *-guu*↑).

合掌 *her-jaang*, v.i., (Budd.) to close palms together in greeting or worship.

合轍兒 *her-jer'l*, v.i., (1) get into routine, take in its stride: 剛病好，還沒合轍兒哪 just got well and has not yet got into the routine; (2) (mus.) play in time and rhythm.

合尖 *her-jian*, v.i., put in the final touch, as completing the top of pagoda (塔尖).

合鏡 *her-jihng*, phr., 合鏡重圓 (of husband and wife) reunite after separation.

合卺 *her-jiin*, v.i., to drink the nuptial cup.

合金 *her-jin*, n., (chem.) alloy.

合衆 *herjuhng*, adj., united; 美利堅合衆國 the United States of America; 合衆社 United Press International (UPI).

合口 *herkoou*, adj., (1) agreeable in taste; (2) v.i., (MC) to quarrel; (of wounds) to heal.

合力 *her-lih*, (1) v.i., work together: 合力同心 work together in harmony; (2) n., (phys.) resultant force.

合理 *herlii*, adj., reasonable: 這事情不合理 this thing is unreasonable; 合理化 to rationalize, -ation.

合龍 *her-lurng*, phr., to complete work on river dam.

合下 *her-shiah*, adv., (MC) at that time (=modn. 當下).

合式 *hershyh*^{1}, adj., suitable, of standard quality or style: 不合式 wrong in style or quality.

合適 *hershyh*^{2}, adj., suitable.

合十 *hershyr*^{1}, v.i., (Budd.) to put palms together.

合時 *her-shyr*^{2}, adj., fashionable, in vogue.

合訊 *her-shyuhn*, v.i., to hold joint court trial.

合算 *hersuahn*, adj., reasonable in price: 不合算 not worth the cost.

合同 *her'tung*, n., a contract.

合奏 *hertzouh*^{1}, v.i., (music) to play together (as orchestra).

合作 *hertzuoh*^{2}, v.i., to cooperate at a common project: 生產(消費)合作社 producers' (consumers') cooperative.

合圍 *herweir*, (1) v.i., surround (enemy, hunted animal); (2) adj., (of tree trunk) large in circumference for one to embrace with outstretched arms.

合一 *heryi*, v.i., to unite, become one.

合意 *her-yih*^{1}, (1) adj., (of a proposal, draft, etc.) pleasing, acceptable; (2) 同心合意 with one heart and mind.

合議 *heryih*^{2}, n. & v.i., panel discussion; 合議庭 full court (law).

合宜 *heryir*, (1) adj., suitable, proper; (2) vb. aux., should.

含 81.40

harn (**hahn*).

V.t. (1) To keep in the mouth (sp. pr. *hern*): 含沙射影 "to spit sand on a shadow"—to make innuendos, spread groundless rumors; 含血噴人 make scurrilous attacks ("spit blood"); 含飴弄孫 to play with grandchildren with candy in mouth; 含英咀華 (of writing) containing the cream of the literary tradition; 含毫 wet the brush with tip of tongue. (2) To contain (a smile, anger), to hold back, to suffer without showing directly: 含怒, 含嗔 feel anger without showing; 含恨, 含怨 to nurse regret, hatred; 含冤 *-yuan*↓; 含羞 ashamed or shy; 含淚 restraining one's tears; 含苞未放 (of flowers) just budding, not yet opened, (of girls) yet a virgin; 含味 containing or sampling flavor. (3) To cover and protect: 包含 to cover and forgive. (4) (*hahn) Bury: 含玉, 含珠 bury with jade, pearls in mouth; 含殮 bury thus. (5) To bear (blemish): 含辱, 含垢忍辱 bear shame, humiliation.

含碜 *harn'chen*, adj., unseemly, ugly-looking (also wr. 寒碜).

含胡 *harn'hu*, adj. & adv., unclear, not explicit, careless, ambiguous (reply): 含胡了事 to settle case carelessly; 一點不含胡 make clear, definite commitment (also wr. 含糊).

含混 *harnhuun*, adj. & adv., see *-'hu* ↑.

含笑 *harnshiauh*, adj., (1) wearing a smile; (2) name of a flower in South China.

含羞 *harnshiou*, adj., feeling ashamed, timid; 含羞草 (bot.) *Mimosa pudica*, whose leaves are sensitive to touch.

含蓄 *harnshyuh*, adj., restrained but suggestive in speech or writing, not saying all on one's mind.

含桃 *harntaur*, n., (bot.) term for cherry apple.

含囈 *harnyih*, v.i., to talk during sleep.

含冤 *harnyuan*, v.i., suffer an injustice, nurse grievances.

舍 81.40

sheh.

N. (1) A dwelling house, a simple home: 房舍, 屋舍 house; 校舍 schoolhouse; 旅舍 an inn; 寒舍, 舍下, 舍間 my simple home; 茅舍 a thatched cottage; 精舍 small, elegant villa. (2) (AC) distance for one stopover for the night for army, said to be 30 *li* or about 10 miles.

V.i. & t. (1) To stop over, to stop for rest. (2) To abandon (interch. 捨): 舍身=捨身, see 捨 10A.40 and its compp.

Adj. (Court.) my: 舍妹, 舍弟, 舍妻, 舍姪 my sister, brother, wife, niece, etc.

舍間 *shehjian*[1], n., my humble home.

舍監 *shehjian*[2], n., proctor of school dormitory, house matron in school.

舍利 *shehlih*, n., a Buddhist relic; 舍利子 a luminous stone reputed to come out of the ashes of Buddha's cremated body; 舍利鹽 (min.) magnesium sulphate.

舍人 *shehrern*, n., (1) royal attendant, a rank such as 中書舍人, 起居舍人; (2) gen. personal attendant or close relative; (3) (in Suhng and Yuarn Dyns.) son of nobility.

舍下 *sheh-shiah*, n., my home.

舍次 *sheh-tsyh*, n., night stopping place of army.

舍營 *shehyirng*, n., barracks.

倉 81.40

tsang.

N. (1) Granary: 穀倉 ditto; 米倉 granary for rice, see compp. ↓. (2) U.f. 艙 91S.40, berth. (3) U.f. 滄 63A.40, sea. (4) U.f. 蒼 20A.40, blue sky.

倉場 *tsangchaang*, n., granary yard, farmyard.

倉房 *tsangfarng*, n., granary; storehouse.

倉庚 *tsanggeng*, n., the oriole.

倉皇 *tsanghuarng*, adj. & adv., hurried, -ly: 倉皇失措 startled and do not know what to do.

倉庫 *tsangkuh*, n., warehouse, godown; granary; treasury vault.

倉廩 *tsangliin*, n., (LL) granary; supply of grains (full, empty).

倉卒 (猝) *tsangtsuh*, adv., abruptly, in flurried manner, all of a sudden.

§81.41 (人/図)

畲 81.41

yur.

N. A cultivated field.

會 81.41

hueih (*hueei, *kuaih).

N. (1) Association, society, club, organization (including church, guild): 工會 labor union; 幫會 secret society; 會館 guild; 農會 farmers' association; 學會 learned society, academic association; 教會 church; 青年會 Y.M.C.A., 耶穌會 Society of Jesus (Cath.); 議會 congress; 社會 society in gen. (2) Committee, conference meeting: 委員會 committee; 董事會, 理事會 board of trustees, directors; 開會, 閉會 open, close meeting; 會議 *-yih*[2] ↓; 茶會 tea party, a reception; 酒會 cocktail; 晚會 dinner party; 宴會 dinner (esp. for some occasion); 博覽會, 展覽會 exposition; 廟會 temple fair. (3) Capital: 都會 metropolis; 省會 provincial capital. (4) Mutual loan and savings company: 合會 (合會儲蓄公司) a temporary group to raise money by monthly subscriptions, the money going to the highest bidder of interest for the month: 做會, 打會 form such association, hold association meeting; 標會 bid for the loan money; 抓會 draw lots for loan money; 投會 determine by dice; also instalment plan among merchants, in which one subscribes to amount of purchase wholesale, but pays by monthly installment plan: 上會, 塡會 pay the monthly installment. (5) A short moment: 這會兒 at present; 一會子工夫, 不多一會兒, 沒多大會(兒) in a short moment; 一會兒 (*huee'l) in a short while.

Vb. aux. (1) Can, will: 會做, 會吃 can work, can eat; 不會 cannot; 會不會 can it be? can (it, you, he)? see 會的 *-'de* ↓; 天不會晴 the sky will not clear up; 會下雨 it's going to rain; 會漲價 the prices will go up. (2) Could (subjunctive): 他會不會走錯路 could he have gone off in the wrong direction? 會不會是他偷的 could it be he who stole it?

V.i. & t. (1) Have the ability to, good at: 會彈會唱 can play the guitar and sing; 會水 good at swimming; 會說會道 good at talking; 樣樣都會, 無一不會 can do everything; 會天文星算 know astronomy and astrology. (2) Understand: 領會 appreciate, understand; 會悟, 會通, 會意, 會心 *-wuh*^{2}, *-tung*, *-yih*, *-shin* ↓; 理$^{\Delta}$會 31A.11. (3) To meet together: 聚會, 相會 (friends, etc.) meet together; 拜會 pay formal call; 會客 see visitors; 會親 visit relatives, meeting of prospective families before betrothal of marriage; 會同, 會合 *-turng*, *-her* ↓; 會齊, 會集, 會見 *-chir*, *-jir*, *-jiahn* ↓; 會商 put our heads together, discuss together. (4) To pay: 會賬, 會鈔 pay for accounts; 飯錢已經會過了 pay for friend's meal at chance meeting in restaurant. (5) To communicate officially: 照會 communicate to official of equal rank. (6) To come upon: 會日出 just as the day breaks; 會大風起 just as a wind storm comes up.

Adv. Jointly (forming words with *hueih* +vb.): 會餐 dine together; 會飮 come together for a drink; 會簽 sign jointly; 會呈 jointly sign petition; 會審 conduct trial jointly or formerly try by Mixed Court in foreign concessions; 會銜 official communication signed jointly.

會辦 **hueihbahn**, n., co-director.

會場 **hueihchaang**, n., place of meeting, assembly hall, auditorium.

會齊 **hueihchir**, v.i., to assemble to do s.t.

會得 **hueih'de**, v.i., (1) can; (2) understand.

會典 **hueihdiaan**, n., book on institutions and laws of a dynasty.

會董 **hueihduung**, n., board of trustees (short for 董事).

會費 **hueihfeih**, n., membership dues.

會館 **hueihguaan**, n., guild (of a clan, profession or native district).

會合 **hueihher**, v.i., to assemble; (of army units) join forces; 會合點 (math.) point of concurrence.

會話 **hueihhuah**, n., conversation; manual of conversation; dialogue.

會長 **hueihjaang**, n., president of club or association.

會戰 **hueihjahn**, v.i., (of two armies) meet for great battle.

會章 **hueihjang**, n., rules and regulations of association.

會見 **hueihjiahn**, v.t., meet, see visitor.

會計 ***kuaijih**, n., accountancy; treasurer; 會計師 accountant; 會計年度 Fiscal Year.

會集 **hueihjir**, v.i., to assemble.

會址 **hueihjyy**, n., address of association.

會考 **hueihkaau**, n., formerly, national examination for the third degree (進士) at the capital; nationally unified examination.

會盟 **hueihmerng**, n., (AC) conference of heads of states for signing treaties.

會面 **hueihmiahn**, v.i., meet face to face.

會社 **hueihsheh**, n., commercial firm, esp. in Japanese; association or society.

會心 **hueih-shin**, phr., silent appreciation: 會心的微笑 a smile of understanding.

會師 **hueih-shy**, v.i., (of army units) join forces for battle.

會事 **hueishyh**^{1}, adj., conversant, experienced (=懂事); 會事人 a man who knows how to handle a situation.

會試 **hueihshyh**^{2}, n. & v.i., see *-kaau* ↑.

會所 **hueihsuoo**, n., club building or office.

會萃 **hueihtsueih**, v.i., congregate (usu. of talents, scholars).

會通 **hueihtung**, v.t., to master, understand thoroughly, show unified comprehension.

會同 **hueihturng**, adv., jointly (manage, etc.).

會晤 **hueihwuh**^{1}, v.t., to meet or see personally (a friend).

會悟 **hueihwuh**^{2}, v.i., realize (a truth).

會務 **hueihwuh**^{3}, n., club or committee affairs.

會要 **hueihyauh**, n., a compendium of government and social institutions of a period or country.

會意 **hueihyih**^{1}, v.i., (1) silently appreciate, understand(ing); (2) a principle of Chinese character formation by two elements (as 信 honesty, belief, composed of 亻 "man" and 言 "words").

會議 **hueihyih**^{2}, n., conference: 和平會議 peace conference.

會陰 **hueihyin**, n., the perineum.

會友 **hueihyoou**, (1) n., member of association, see *-yuarn*^{2} ↓; (2) phr., 以文會友 form a literary circle.

會元 **hueihyuarn**^{1}, n., the first on list of candidates for the third degree 進士 (cf. 狀$^{\Delta}$元 21S.81)

會員 **hueihyuarn**^{2}, n., member of association; 會員大會 general assembly.

§ 81.42 (人/冈)

內 81.42

neih.

N. (1) The imperial court: 大內 the inner palace; 內廷 the grand hall where the emperor holds audience; 內庫 the imperial treasury; 內苑 the palace grounds. (2) (Court.) one's own wife or her relatives: 內人 *-rern*↓; 賤內 my (humble) wife; 內子 *-tzyy*↓; 內助 my better half (lit., "my internal assistant"); 懼內 henpecked; 內兄 wife's elder brother; 內嫂 wife's elder brother's wife; 內親 relatives of the family of one's wife; 內嬖 a concubine, a court favorite; 內寵 ditto. (3) The female sex: 內賓 female guests; 內眷 the female members of a family; 內掌櫃的 a shopowner's wife. (4) The heart: 內疚 prickings of conscience; 內視 Buddhist contemplation, introspection; 內觀 ditto; 內省 self-examination; 內秀 innate intelligence, wisdom or talent; 內慧 ditto; 內心 *-shin*↓; 五內 the viscera, the internal organs of the body as seats of feeling.

Adj. & adv. Internal(ly), interior(ly), inside, indoor(s), secret(ly): 內部 internal or interior parts, on the inside; 內裏 internal(ly); 內中 ditto, the imperial court; 分內 (of rights or duties) what is one's due; 在內 inside; 內幕 *-muh*↓; 內情 circumstances not known to the outsider, inside story; 內附 (of foreign countries) come to pay homage; 內屬 ditto; 內顧 look backwards; 內顧之憂 family troubles (financial or otherwise); 內擧 appoint one's close relations to office; 內才 capabilities, potentials, talent, knowledge (opp. 外才 outside appearance); 內容 *-rurng*↓; 內心 *-shin*↓; 內含 *-harn*↓; 內犯 foreign invasion, of the country; 內戰 civil war; 內爭 internal dissension; 內亂 internal rebellion; 內難 internal disturbances, civil commotion; 內訌 internal disputes; 內鬩 ditto; 內患 internal troubles; 內憂外患 internal revolt and foreign invasion; 內服 drugs for oral administration; 內地 *-dih*↓; 內開 (term formerly used in official documents) as stated in your memorandum, which says: "... etc."; 內奸 enemy's agent operating in any organization; 內賊 an enemy within, thief on inside job; 內綘 wirepuller; 內線 *-shiahn*↓; 內應 internal uprising in support of the enemy without; 內勤 person working inside an office (opp. 外勤 one working outside an office); 內調 transfer of an official from field service to capital, recall of official from a foreign post to an assignment at home; 內務 *-wuh*↓; 內政 internal or domestic affairs of a country, see 內政部 *-jehngbuh*↑; 內治 ditto, formerly, family affairs to be looked after by women; 內宅 women's quarters in a home; 內債 government bonds.

內圈 *neih-chyuan*, n., inner circle.

內地 *neihdih*, n., the inland.

內港 *neihgaang*, n., an inner harbor.

內閣 *neihger*, n., the Cabinet of a government.

內功 *neihgung*, n., (Chin. boxing) the art of building up one's strength through breathing and other exercises of the internal organs.

內海 *neihhaai*, n., (geog.) an inland sea.

內含 *neihharn*, n., contents, constituent elements.

內行 *neihharng*, adj., n., expert, an expert.

內河 *neihher*, n., a river with no outlet to the sea, inland river.

內政部 *neihjehngbuh*, n., Ministry of the Interior, the Home Office.

內角 *neihjiaau*, n., (math.) an interior angle.

內監 *neihjiahn*, n., a eunuch.

內景 *neihjiing*, n., an internal view, (motion pictures) scenes shot indoors.

內急 *neihjir*, adj., impatient to go to the toilet.

內痔 *neihjyh*, n., (med.) internal hemorrhoids.

內科 *neihke*, n., (med.) internal medicine.

內幕 *neihmuh*, n., inside story: 內幕消息 inside information.

內篇 *neihpian*, n., (1) (AC) that part of a book in which basic principles are enunciated (opp. 外篇 in which matters other than basic principles are treated); (2) (AC) works of a Taoist writer.

內人 *neihrern*, n., (court.) one's own wife, see *-tzyy*↓.

內容 *neihrurng*, n., contents (of a book, etc.)

內傷 *neihshang*, n., (med.) internal injury.

內線 *neihshiahn*, n., (1) the inside track of a racecourse (opp. 外線 the outside track); (2) an inside wirepuller: 走內線 to influence an official through his wife; (3) an informer: 做內線 serve as (s.o.'s) informer.

內心 *neihshin*, n. & adv., at heart.

內侍 *neihshyh*, (1) n., a eunuch; (2) v.i., serve as a eunuch at the court.

內臟 *neihtzahng*, n., (physiol.) internal organs of the body.

內在 *neihtzaih*, adj., inside, internal: 內在美 internal beauty, beauty of spirit; 內在因素 internal factors.

內子 *neihtzyy*, n., (court.) one's own wife (＝內人↑).

內務 *neihwuh*, n., (1) the domestic affairs of a country; (2) maintenance of cleanliness and orderliness in school dormitories or barracks; (3) family affairs.

肉 81.42

rouh (re. pr. **ruh*).

N. (1) Meat, flesh: 肉兒 *-'l*↓; 筋肉 flesh; 肌肉 muscles; 肉皮兒 the human skin; 肉體 *-tii*↓; 靈肉 body and soul; 肉慾 *-yuh*↓; 肉麻 *-mar*↓; 肉感 *-gaan*↓; 肉痛 *-tuhng*↓; 肉癢討打 (of children) so naughty as to invite parental discipline; 心驚肉跳 trembling with fear; 親骨肉 one's own flesh and blood; 肉泥爛醬 (of the human body) mutilated and bloody; 肉嘟嘟的 fleshy, fat; 肉球 so fat as to look like a ball of flesh; 肉勒咕咕 fat and clumsy, stout, corpulent, portly; 豬肉 pork; 羊肉 mutton; 牛肉 beef; 雞鴨魚肉 delicacies, meat and fish; 肥肉, 瘦肉 fat, lean meat; 肉核兒 the choicest portion of meat, fillet; 肉皮 pork skin; 皮肉生涯 the life of a prostitute; 碎肉 meat cut into small pieces; 肉頭兒 odd pieces of meat; 肉星兒 a tiny bit of meat; 肉釘兒 meat cut into small cubes; 肉片兒 meat cut into thin slices; 肉絲兒 meat cut into small threads; 肉醬 minced meat; 肉汁 meat broth; 肉乾 dried sliced meat; 肉脯兒 *-puu*↓; 臘肉 dried, salted meat; 烤肉 roast, barbecue; 肉鬆 *-sung*, 肉餅 *-biing*↓; 肉饅頭 steamed bread with meat stuffing; 肉包子(兒) ditto; 肉丸(子), 肉圓(子) *-warn(tz)*, *-yuarn(tz)*↓; 肉槓 meat stall; 肉案子 a counter where meat is sold; 肉店 a butcher shop. (2) The flesh of fruits or vegetables: 菓肉 fruit pulp.

Pron. My own (darling): 肉兒 darling child; 我的肉兒 my dear son, also used in love-making.

Adj. (1) Spongy: 這西瓜瓤兒太肉 (coll.) the pulp of this watermelon is too flabby. (2) Slow moving: 肉得慌 (coll.) so slow as to make you despair.

肉報子 *rouhbauhtz*, n., (sl.) one fond of passing gossip.

肉筆 **ruh-bii*, n., (LL) a hand-drawn picture or hand-written book as distinct from a printed one.

肉餅 *rouhbiing*, n., meat ball.

肉白骨 **ruh-borguu*, phr., (AC, rhet.) resuscitate, give life to the people once more.

肉丁 *rouhding*, n., (1) a boil, an ulcer (also 肉疔); (2) cubed pork or chicken.

肉豆蔻 *rouhdouhkouh*, n., (bot.) the common nutmeg.

肉粉 *rouh-feen*, n., fertilizer made of dried meat ground into powder.

肉感 *rouhgaan*, n., sensuality, sensual attraction, sex appeal.

肉冠 *rouh-guan*, n., the comb, the red fleshy crest of fowl.

肉桂 *roughgueih* (**ruh-*), n., cinnamon.

肉好 *rouhhauh* (**ruh-*), n., (sl.) a hole in the flesh, said of hole of anything in a circle.

肉紅 *rouhhurng* (**ruh-*) n., (1) pinkish color like that of the human flesh; (2) (Chin. med.) the bark of the Chinese redbud.

肉柱 *rouhjuh*, n., (physiol.) the adductor muscle.

肉芝 *rouhjy*, n., a kind of mushroom-like plant.

肉兒 *rouh'l*, n., (1) meat, flesh; (2) darling: 我的肉兒 "my own flesh."

肉麻 *rouhmar*, adj., (1) numb (feeling); (2) vulgar and coarse, giving one the creeps: 把肉麻當有趣 mistake coarseness for being funny.

肉票(兒) *rouhpiauh('l)*, n., a person held for ransom.

肉搏 *rouh-por* (**ruh-*), n., hand-to-hand combat.

肉脯 *rouhpuu*, n., dried meat in threads; 肉脯兒 said of portly, obese person.

肉色 *rouh-shaai*, n. & adj., flesh color, flesh-colored.

肉身 *rouh-shen*, n., (Budd.) the physical mortal body; the flesh.

肉聲 *rouh-sheng*, n., vocal singing.

肉刑 **ruh-shirng*, n., ancient punishment including physical mutilation.

肉食 **ruh-shyr*, adj., flesh-eating, carnivorous: 肉食獸 carnivorous animals; 肉食者 (AC) the well-fed officials.

肉蕈 *rouhshyuhn*, n., white mushrooms.

肉穗花 *rouhsuei-hua*, n., (bot.) a spadix.

肉鬆 *rouhsung*, n., dried fluffy meat.

肉袒 **ruh-taan*, v.i., (allu.) bare one's back to be threshed to show contrition.

肉胎 *rouh-tai*, n., (Budd.) mummy of a dead monk's body.

肉體 *rouhtii*, n., the human body.

肉頭 *rouh'tou*, adj., soft, fleshy.

肉蓯蓉 *rouhtsungrurng*, n., (bot.) *Boschniakia glabra.*

肉痛 *rouhtuhng* (**ruh-*), n., (1) physical pains, anxiety, apprehension; (2) (Shanghai dial.) unwillingness to part with s.t. one loves.

肉棗 *rouhtzaau*, n., (bot.) dog wood (also called 山茱萸); 肉棗兒 (a) a hardened formation in animals; (b) (coll.) a person who moves awkwardly and clumsily.

肉丸(子) *rouhwarn(tz)*, n., meat balls.

肉痿 *rouh-weei*, n., (Chin. med., AC) muscular insensitivity.

肉眼 *rouhyaan*, n., (1) the naked eye: 肉眼可見 can see s.t. (e.g., a distant star) without the aid of instruments; 肉眼泡兒 eyes with fleshy eyelids; (2) common or vulgar views: 肉眼凡胎 a shortsighted and good-for-nothing person; 肉眼無珠 dull, stupid ("having eyes, see not").

肉芽 *rouhyar*, n., (bot.) fleshy buds.

肉蠅 *rouhyirng*, n., (zoo.) a large blowfly, *Sarcophago carinaria.*

肉圓(子) *rouyuarn(tz)*, n., meat balls.

肉月兒 *rouhyueh'l*, n., the radical 月, representing 肉 meat, usu. not distinguishable from rad. 月.

肉慾 *rouhyuh*, n., carnal desires.

 81.42

tsauh.

V.t. (Obscene) to copulate with (woman).

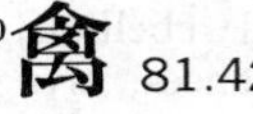 81.42

chirn.

N. (1) Gen. term for birds, contrasted with 獸 beasts: 禽獸 *-shouh*↓; 飛禽走獸 birds (that fly) and beasts (that run); 家禽 domestic fowl; 靈禽 auspicious birds. (2) A surname.

禽荒 *chirnhuang*, n., (AC) over-indulgence in hunting.
禽鳥 *chirnniaau*, n., bird.
禽獸 *chirnshouh*, n., (1) animal world; (2) subhuman world of beasts: 禽獸之行 beastly conduct, esp. incest and sodomy; 行同禽獸 act like beasts; 衣冠禽獸 beasts in human dress.

龠 81.42

yueh.

N. An ancient short flute (also wr. 籥).

§81.50 (人/乛)

翕 81.50

shih.

V.i. (1) (LL) to close up: 翕張 close and open; 翕翼 (LL) to contract wings. (2) (AC) to draw up (tongue).

Adj. & adv. Harmonious, -ly: 翕然, 翕如 *-rarn*, *-rur* ↓.

翕赫 *shih-heh*, adj., (AC) grand and harmonious.
翕合 *shih-her*, v.i., join together.
翕忽 *shih-hu*, adv., abruptly (also 倏忽).
翕然 *shih-rarn*, adj., united, harmonious.
翕如 *shih-rur*, adj., (mus.) harmonious, sounding together.

§81.63 (人/丶)

令 81.63

lihng (**lirng*).
[Var. 令; all compp. with 令, 令 are treated as 令 .63]

N. (1) Military or official order: 命令 order; 訓令 official instructions; 軍令 a military command, military discipline; 禁令 official ban; (oft. used in official documents) it is ordered, you are hereby ordered, instructed to: 申令 give order; 三令五申 we have repeatedly explained and ordered; 嚴令 it is strictly ordered; 令旗 formerly, flag of command; 令箭 formerly, mil. order given with an arrow; 令旨 emperor's wish. (2) The law: 法令, 律令 statutes; 令典 legal code. (3) Season: 時令, 月令 season of the year; 春令, 夏令 spring, summer season: 夏令大會 summer conference. (4) Formerly, magistrate: 令尹 district magistrate; 縣令 county magistrate; 尚書令 prime minister in Tarng Dynasty; cf. 尚^A書 22.42. (5) A surname. (6) A ream (500 sheets) of paper (translit.).

V.t. (Causative vb.) to make, (s.o.) to: (sometimes pr. **lirng*): 令即出京 order (s.o.) to leave capital at once; 令人滿意 make people satisfied—satisfactory; 令人懷疑 cause suspicion; 令人喜歡 be liked by people ("cause to like").

Adj. (1) (Court.) your (forming compp. as follows): 令尊 your father; 令堂, 令慈 your mother; 令正 your wife; 令兄, 令弟, 令姊, 令妹 your brother, sister (elder, younger); 令愛, 令嬡 your daughter; 令郎, 令嗣 your son; 令岳 your father-in-law; 令親 your parents; 令高足 your bright student. (2) Good, esteemed: 令名, 令聞, 令譽 good reputation; 令德 good character; 令節 fine festival or season; 令終 die a natural death, pass off peacefully; 巧言令色 pleasing words and smoothness of manner; suavity.

§81.70 (人/乚)

龕 81.70

kan.

N. A niche for idols.

瓮 81.70

wehng.
[Abbr. of 甕 60.70]

§81.72 (人/心)

念 81.72

niahn.

N. & adj. (1) Capital form of 廿: 念歲 twenty years old; 念五日 the twenty-fifth day. (2) A thought, an idea: esp. 念頭 *-'tour* ↓; 貪念 greedy thought; 邪念, 惡念 evil thought; 一念之差 (of mistakes) all arise from a wrong thought in the mind; 善念, 慈念 kind thoughts; 萬念俱灰 (俱消) all thoughts, ambitions are blasted (vanish). (3) Care, remembrance, see V.i. & t. 2↓.

V.i. & t. (1) Study, read: 念書 *-shu* ↓; 念經 *-jing* ↓; 你現在念幾

年級 which class are you in? 念小學 study in a primary school; 念甚麽系 which department are you studying in? (2) Remember, care, think of (all serve equally as nn.): 思念, 想念, 惦念, 掛念, 懸念 (of friends or relatives) be always thinking of one another; 追念, 悼念 grieve over (s.o.'s) death; 紀念 commemorate; 存念 think of, remember; 留念 keep as a momento; 回念 recall (the past); 懷念 keep ever in mind; 不復置念 forget all about it; 念舊 remember old friends or the good old days; 念茲在茲 be ever mindful of s.t. one is resolved to do; 不念舊惡 forget and forgive old grudges; 念交情 do s.t. for the sake of friendship; 念念不忘 never forget (s.t. or s.o.) for a moment; 口中念念有辭 be mumbling some words.

念白 *niahnbair*, n., (of Chin. opera) dialogue or monologue as distinct from singing.

念叨 *niahn'dau*, v.t., (1) remember (s.o.) in speaking to another: 她常常念叨着你 she often remembers you in our talks; (2) grumble: 他老是在那裡念念叨叨 he is always grumbling.

念法 *niahn-faa*, n., (1) pronunciation: 這個字怎麽念法 how is this word pronounced? (2) method of studying.

念佛 *niahnfor*, v.t., chant Buddhist scriptures or say prayers to Buddha.

念經 *niahnjing*, v.t., chant Buddhist scriptures (also wr. 唸).

念咒 *niahnjouh*, v.t., utter charms to exorcise demons (also wr. 唸).

念珠 *niahnju*, n. & v.t., (tell) beads.

念心兒 *niahn'shie'l*, n., souvenir, also called 念信, 念想.

念書 *niahnshu*, v.i. & t., (1) study or read; (2) study in school; (3) (in a gen. sense) receive an education: 念書有什麽用 what's the use of an education?

念誦 *niahnsuhng*, v.t., (1) remember (s.o.) in speaking to another: 老太太正念誦着你吶 the old lady is always mentioning you in our talks; (2) read (s.t.) aloud, also wr. 唸.

念頭 *niahn'tour*, n., idea, thought, what one is thinking of at any given moment, often evil thought: 不知他有什麽念頭 I don't know what are his intentions: 轉念頭 try to win the favors of s.o. (esp. of a woman).

念秧 *niahnyang*, n., (coll. north China) a fraud or deception.

念央兒 *niahnyang'l*, v.i., beat about the bush.

愈 81.72

yuh.

[Usu. printed 愈]

V.i. Recover from illness: 病愈 (also written 癒).

Adj. Better: 愈於 better than.

Adv. The more, more and more, increasingly (=vern. 越): 愈來愈多 more and more are coming; 愈不堪 getting worse and worse; 愈加 increasingly (difficult, etc.); 愈甚 more intensely; 愈益 all the more (complex, etc.); 愈讀愈愛 the more you read it, the more you love it.

忩 81.72

tsung.

[Var. of 悤 90.72]

§ 81.80 (人/八)

貪 81.80

tan.

V.t. To covet, be greedy for: 貪財 money-mad; wish improperly or beyond bounds: 貪爵位 covet or hang on to government position; 貪吃, 貪嘴 love food excessively; 貪飲, 貪酒 love wine; 貪女色 crazy about women; 貪圖富貴 desire wealth and honor greatly; 貪得無厭 have insatiable greed; 貪天之功 have inordinate ambitions; 貪生怕死 be a coward, prefer life to dishonor; 貪小失大 go for the small things and miss things that are worthwhile; 貪睡 love to sleep; 貪樂 love pleasures; 貪多嚼不爛 bite more than one can chew—greedy.

Adj. Greedy, avaricious: 貪官污吏 corrupt officials; 你這個人真貪 you are indeed greedy, you want too much; 貪念 covetous thoughts: 起了貪念 have immoral thoughts (about women or money).

貪婪 *tanlarn*, adj., greedy for wealth or women.

貪戀 *tanliahn*, v.t., love, cling to (women, government position, life of comfort).

貪吝 *tanlihn*, adj., miserly, avaricious; n., avarice.

貪心 *tanshin*, n. & adj., greed, -y.

貪饕 *tan-tau*, n., gluttony.

貪頭 *tantour*, n., bait, inducement.

貪圖(兒) *tan'tu('l)*, (1) v.t., desire excessively; (2) n., see *-tour* ↑.

貪嘴 *tantzueei*, adj., greedy for food.

貪污 *tanwu*, adj., corrupt (official).

§ 81.81 (人/人)

人 81.81

rern.

N. (1) Human beings: 人類 *-leih*, 人羣 *-chyurn* ↓; 人窮志短 poverty and ambition make strange bedfellows; 人面獸心 a brute under a human mask; 人模狗樣

pretending to be what one is not, also said of a pederast; 人頭畜鳴 an animal in human form; 人中騏驥 (compliment) a very clever child; 人不知，鬼不覺 done in complete secrecy; 人大心大 (usu. of a girl) become gradually more assertive as one grows older; 人小鬼大 a child daring to do great mischief, (facet.) a boy with a high ambition; 人敬人高 to be respected encourages one to be worthy of such respect; 人義水甜 perfect harmony between friends; 人有臉，樹有皮 "face" is as important to man as the bark is to tree; 人命關天 a case involving life and death; 人命案 a case of manslaughter; 人肉市場 a brothel; 人浮於食 too many workers with little to do; 人浮於事 ditto, more applicants than available jobs; 人定勝天 man is the master of his own fate; 人多嘴雜 a babel of voices, divided counsel, "too many cooks spoil the soup"; 人頭份兒 to share a thing equally among all ("to each a share"); 人傑地靈 a place propitious for giving birth to great men; 人間地獄 a veritable hell on earth; 人間天堂 heaven on earth; 人山人海 huge crowds ("a sea of human beings"); 人生於世 living in a time like this; to live this life; 人生朝露 the evanescence of life ("human life is like the morning dew"); 人微言輕 (self-derogatory) lowly placed as I am, my words can carry little or no weight; 人言可畏 advice to behave correctly for fear of incurring gossip; 人不可貌相 don't judge anyone by appearances; 做人 behave oneself properly; 爲人 to conduct oneself in a certain way; 大人 a superior man (opp. 小人 a mean fellow, a scoundrel), (lit.) a grown-up (opp. 小人 a child); 偉人 a great man. (2) Everybody: 人皆讚美 praised by one and all; 人人 all without exception; 人們 people in general; 人所共知 as everybody knows. (3) A grownup: 他的兒子業已成人了 his son has come of age. (4) A person of a certain character: 法人 a legal (juridical) person; 自然人 a natural person; 公證人 a notary public; 辯護人 (law) the defense counsel (attorney); 保護人 protector; 申請人 an applicant; 監護人 (law) the guardian of a minor.

Pron. Other: 人棄我取 I will take whatever others don't want; 人取我與 I will part with whatever others may want; 人一己百 if others succeed by making one ounce of effort, I will make a hundred times as much effort; 己所不欲，勿施於人 don't do to others what you would not have others do to you; 推己及人 do as you would be done by others, judge others as you would like to be judged by others.

人保 *rern-baau*, n., a personal guarantee (opp. 舖保 guarantee offered by a business firm).

人表 *rernbiaau*, n., a person of exemplary conduct, a paragon of virtue.

人稱 *rerncheng*, (1) n., (gram.) the first, second or third person; (2) a nickname by which a person is known.

人臣 *rernchern*, n., a minister of State.

人情 *rernchirng*, n., (1) what comes naturally to man, what is inherent in human nature; (2) a favor done to s.o.; (3) a present (gift); (4) a wedding or birthday party, a funeral service; (5) attendance at such a party or service; (6) affection, love, personal attachment; (7) a gesture of kindness or generosity: 人情貨 a person holding a job on the strength of a recommendation by an influential individual; 人情兒 a favor done to another; 人情味(兒) genuine human warmth.

人權 *rernchyuarn*, n., the rights of man, human rights: 人權宣言 (Fr. history) Declaration of the Rights of Man and the Citizen; 人權法案 (British history) the Bill of Rights of 1689.

人羣 *rernchyurn*, n., (1) a crowd of people; (2) mankind: 人羣兒 (*-chyuer'l*) a crowd.

人道 *rerndauh*, n., (1) kindness, humanity, mercy: 人道主義 humanitarianism; (2) sexual intercourse: 不能人道 impotency, -t; (3) (Budd.) the stage of human existence.

人燈 *rern-deng*, n., a person thin and frail ("like a lamppost").

人地 *rerndih*, n., the environment in which a person finds himself: 人地生疏 (be placed) in an unfamiliar environment; 人地不宜 finding oneself in an unsuitable environment.

人丁 *rernding*, n., (1) persons who have come of age; (2) people in general.

人堆兒 *rerndue'l*, n., a crowd of people.

人犯 *rernfahn*, n., a criminal (suspect).

人販子 *rern-fahntz*, n., one who traffics in human beings.

人夫 *rernfu*, n., coolies.

人根 *rerngen*, n., (Budd.) the human reproductive organ.

人格 *rernger*, n., (1) personal character, personality: 人格化 personify, -ication; (2) a legal entity.

人工 *rerngung*, (1) n., a man-day; (2) n., human effort; (3) adj., artificial, man-made (opp. 自然 natural); 人工呼吸 artificial respiration; 人工呼吸器 respirator; 人工授精 artificial insemination; 人工腎臟 artificial kidney.

人股(兒) *rernguu('l)*, n., formerly, annual bonus given to the manager of a business partnership.

人海 *rern-haai*, n., huge crowds: 人海浮沈 to experience all the vicissitudes of life; 人海戰術 human wave tactics of warfare.

人豪 *rern-haur*, n., the ablest and bravest of men, a man among men.

人和 *rernher*, n., group morale.

A

人

人話 *rern-huah*, n., seemly words, utterances becoming a decent man.

人寰 *rern-huarn*, n., the world of men.

人戶 *rernhuh*, n., the people.

人證 *rernjehng*, n., testimony given by a witness in a law court.

人家 *rernjia*, n., (1) a dwelling house; (2) s.o. else's home; (3) a high-class family: 清白人家 a decent family; 富貴人家 a rich and politically influential family; (4) a family engaged in a certain occupation: 務農人家 a farm family; 作工的人家 an artisan's (workingman's) family; (5) a wife: 娶個人家 get married; (6) (**rern'jia*) someone, one, used to denote (a) somebody else: 人家的事你不用管 don't meddle with somebody else's business; (b) used to denote others: 人家可不能像你那麼胡說 others, another, will not talk such nonsense as you do; (c) or to denote the speaker himself: 你成天拿人家開玩笑 you are making fun of me all the time; (d) to denote persons of a particular class: 男人家 the menfolk, 女人家 womenfolk; 婦道人家 ditto; 女孩人家 girls; (7) the husband's family before marriage: 給她找個人家 choose a prospective husband for her; 已經有人家兒了 she is already engaged.

人鑑 *rern-jiahn*, n., a loyal minister who can correct the prince's failings ("a human mirror in which one's true self is reflected"), (also 人鏡).

人間 *rernjian*, n., (1) this human world, this human life (with all that it may imply): 生於此人間 born into this world of ours; (2) social intercourse: 吾無宦情兼拙於人間 (LL) I don't care to be an official, nor am I a good mixer; 人間味 the flavor of human life; 人間苦 bitter human life.

人傑 *rernjier*, n., a hero among men.

人境 *rernjihng*[1], n., human habitations, a place where men make their homes.

B

人鏡 *rernjihng*[2], n., (=人鑑 *-jiahn* ↑).

人精 *rernjing*, n., a child with the ways of grownups; uncanny person.

人粥 *rernjou*, n., (fig.) a crowded mass of human beings.

人衆 *rernjuhng*, n., the masses, the people at large.

人中 *rernjung*, n., (physiol.) the middle line of upper lip; 人中白 (herb med.) urine sediments used as a drug; 人中黃 (herb med.) a drug to cure fever, made of powdered licorice root put in a bamboo tube and soaked in a cesspool for several months.

人主 *rernjuu*, n., the reigning monarch, ruler.

人種 *rernjuung*, n., the human species, a person's race.

人治 *rern-jyh*, n., (Confu.) government by men, the rule of men (opp. 法治 government by law, the rule of law).

人爵 *rernjyuer*, n., official titles (opp. 天爵 moral greatness).

人君 *rernjyun*, n., the monarch.

人客 *rernkeh*, n., guests (=客人, opp. 主人 the host).

人口 *rernkoou*, n., (1) population: 人口統計 census taking; (2) all the members of a family; (3) the mouth as an organ of speech: 膾炙人口 (of literary works) be spoken of with relish.

人兒 *rer'l*, n., (1) a person; (2) a concubine; (3) a human figure or picture; (4) a person's looks and conduct.

人籟 *rern-laih*, n., sounds of the human voice (opp. 天籟 the sounds of nature).

人來瘋 *rernlair-feng*, n., childish pranks in the presence of guests.

人類 *rernleih*, n., mankind, human beings, humanity at large, the human species.

人力 *rernlih*, n., manpower, manual labor, human force; 人力車 a rickshaw; 人力股(兒) =人股 *-guu* ↑.

人倫 *rernlurn*, n., (1) ethical relations; (2) personal character.

人馬 *rern-maa*, n., (1) coolies and beasts of burden; (2) people on the move as a group; (3) soldiers and horses.

C

人們 *rernmen*, n., people in gen., the indefinite "they."

人面 *rern-miahn*, n., the human face: 人面獸心 the brute of a man ("an animal under a human mask").

人命 *rernmihng*, n., human life: 人命官司 a case of murder or manslaughter; 人命攸關 a matter of life and death.

人民 *rernmirn*, n., the people: 人民陣線 popular front; 人民公社 Commune; 人民票(幣) currency of Communist China.

人謀 *rern-mour*, n., plans (schemes) made by men, opp. god's will.

人品 *rernpiin*, n., (1) personal character; (2) personal looks.

人人 *rernrern*, n., everybody: 人人爲我, 我爲人人 all for one and one for all.

人瑞 *rern-rueih*, n., a great benefactor of men, oft. a venerable highly respected character.

人日 *rernryh*, n., the 7th day of the first lunar month.

人勝 *rernshehng*, n., formerly, ornamental flowers (花勝) or figures cut from colored material and used as presents on the 7th day of the first lunar month.

人參 *rernshen*[1], n., the ginseng.

人身 *rernshen*[2], n., (1) the human body: 人身保護狀 a writ of habeas corpus; (2) man's physical frame: 投生人身 (Budd.) be reincarnated in human form; (3) personal character: 人身權 (law) personal rights.

人生 *rernsheng*, n., the life of man, human life: 人生如夢 life is but a dream: 人生觀 one's outlook on life, philosophy of life.

人相 *rernshiahng*[1], n., physiognomy.

人像 *rernshiahng*[2], n., a portrait.

人性 *rernshihng*, n., (1) human nature (opp. 獸性 animal nature; 神性 divine nature); (2) human feelings, emotions, and impulses; (3) (*-'shing*) a person's temperament and character: 他的人性不好 he is ill-tempered; (4) (-'shing) man's emotional and rational faculties: 這個人不通人性 this man knows nothing of human feelings, remains unmoved and unsympathetic.

人心 *rernshin*, n., (1) a person's disposition; (2) one's inclination: 人心不齊 people are of different minds; (3) human consience, one's better self: 他要有人心，才怪呢 it would be strange, indeed, if he had a conscience! (4) gratitude: 必有一份人心 I must express my human gratitude; 人心兒 *-shie'l*, n., the middle of a crowd: 在人心兒裏站著 stand in the midst of a crowd.

人行 *rernshirng*, n., human decency: 他簡直不是人行 he doesn't behave like a man at all; 人行道 a sidewalk.

人形兒 *rernshirng'l*, n., a human shape (form).

人手 *rern-shoou*, n., personnel engaged in a specific task, employees.

人壽 *rernshouh*, n., one's span of life; 人壽保險 life insurance.

人師 *rern-shy*, n., a person of exemplary conduct.

人士 *rernshyh*[1], n., men or scholars in gen.

人氏 *rernshyh*[2], n., persons born of a particular locality: 就是本地人氏 is a native son here.

人市 *rernshyh*[3], n., a densely populated place.

人世 *rernshyh*[4], n., this human world or life.

人事 *rernshyh*[5], n., (1) the conscious world: 昏迷過去，人事不知 fainted and lost all conciousness; (2) ways of the world: 不懂人事 ignorant of the ways of the world; (3) human efforts: 盡人事，聽天命 do one's human best and leave all else to God; (4) a present: 送黃金一百兩，權當人事 sent one hundred ounces of gold as a present; (5) sexual knowledge: 她已漸省人事 she is growing to be sex-conscious; (6) personnel affairs: 人事處(科) personnel department (section).

人熊 *rernshyurng*, n., (zoo.) the brown bear.

人體 *rerntii*, n., the human body: 人體美 beauty of the human figure, as exemplified in nudes.

人頭兒 *rerntour'l*, n., one's character, looks or ability.

人頭稅 *rerntour-shueih*, n., the poll tax.

人才 *rerntsair* (-'tsai), n., (1) a talented person; (2) good looks: 有幾分人才 pretty good-looking (also wr. 人材).

人造 *rerntzauh*, adj., artificial, man-made: 人造絲 artificial silk; 人造奶油(牛油) margarine.

人擇 *rern-tzer*, n., artificial selection.

人望 *rernwahng*, n., social prestige, good repute.

人味兒 *rernweh'l*, n., the joy of living, *joie de vivre*: 活着沒人味兒 there is no joy in continuing to live.

人位 *rernweih*, n., (1) personnel: 寶號人位一共多少 how many employees are there in your shop? (2) one's ability and the job he holds: 人位相宜 is the right man for the right job.

人爲 *rernweir*, adj., artificial, man-made: 人爲淘汰 artificial selection (opp. 天然淘汰 natural selection).

人文 *rernwern*, n., human culture: 人文主義 humanism; 人文地理 human (social, anthropo-) geography; 人文科學 the humanities.

人物 *rernwuh*, n., (1) an outstanding personage; (2) men and things.

人烟 *rernyan* (-'yan), n., (1) smoke from the kitchen chimney; (2) an inhabited area: 人烟稠密 a densely populated locality.

人樣 *rern'yang*, n., decent personal appearance or conduct: 把小孩子慣得一點人樣沒有 the child has been so spoiled that he doesn't know how to behave; 人樣兒 the human shape: 許多逃難的都不成人樣兒了 many refugees looked so wretched that they were hardly recognizable as human beings; 人樣子 a good, decent-looking person.

人牙子 *rernyartz*, n., formerly, one who traffics in human beings.

人言 *rern-yarn*, n., (1) human speech; (2) public opinion: 何恤於人言 pay no attention to what others say (of oneself); (3) a rumor: 人言不可信 don't believe rumors.

人妖 *rernyau*, n., (1) a devil in human form, an evil genius; (2) a freak, a person showing abnormal sex characteristics; (3) a person fond of fancy dress and excessive make-up.

人影兒 *rernyiing'l*, n., (1) the human form; (2) one's whereabouts.

人員 *rernyuarn*[1], n., staff members, personnel.

人猿 *rernyuarn*[2], n., the ape, anthropoid.

人緣(兒) *rernyuarn*[3](*-yuar'l*), n., ability to like people and be liked.

人欲 *rern-yuh*[1], n., human wants, pleasures of the flesh, esp. those of sex and food.

人慾 *rernyuh*[2], n., ditto.

人魚 *rernyur*, n., a mermaid, merman; 美人魚 a good woman swimmer.

入 81.81

ruh (*ruu, *ryh).

N. One of the four tones of a character: 入聲 *-sheng*↓.

V.i.& t. (1) Enter, come in or into, join, admit: 進入 make way into, enter; 插入 penetrate, intrude, meddle, interrupt; 潛入 sneak in, go in stealthily; 遷入 move in from one place to another; 入來 come in; 入去 go in; 請入 usher in; 入口 *-koou*↓; 出入(口) come and go, exit and entrance; 入場

00 01 02 10 11 12 20 21 22 30 31 32 40 41 42 50 51 52 60 61 62 63 70 71 72 80 81 82 83 90 91 92 93

A B C

入 (of a meeting place) go in; 入場券 admission ticket; 入室 *-shyh*↓; 入室操戈 turn s.o.'s argument against himself; 入幕之賓 serve as adviser (secretary) to s.o.; 入舍, 入婿 be married into wife's family; 入港 *-gaang*↓; 入闈 *-weir*[1]↓; 入圍 *-weir*[2]↓; 入學 formerly, pass the first-grade government examination, (modn. usage) matriculate in school; 入黨 join a political party; 入伍 *-wuu*↓; 入隊 join the ranks; 入會 become member of an association; 入局 take part in a game of chance; 加入 participate in, become a member of; 入夥 join in partnership; 入籍 *-jir*↓; 入教 be converted to a religion; 入境 *-jihng*[1]↓; 如入無人之境 (of troops) advance unopposed, meet with no enemy resistance ("as if entering no man's land"); 入國問俗 learn about customs and habits of the country one goes to; 入門問諱 learn about its taboos on going to a friend's; 入主出奴 (of schools of thought) think of oneself as having a monopoly of all truths and of others as heretics, take a sectarian attitude; 入木三分 (calligraphy) having forceful strokes, (of ideas, views, observations) penetrating, sharp, astute; 入席 take one's seat; 入座 ditto; 入殮 to coffin; 入肚 devour, swallow, gobble up; 入夜 at night, in the evening; 入手 *-shoou*↓. (2) Receive, take in, obtain: 入股 become a shareholder (partner); 歲入 annual revenue; 入款 funds received; 入錢 cash received; 收入 income, earnings, receipts; 入賬 enter in ledger; 入不敷出 live beyond one's means, income can't cover outlay; 量入爲出 spend no more than one's income; 出入相抵 income and expenses just balance. (3) Sink, go down, fall, descend: 日入 the sun is setting (has set), sunset; 沒入 confiscate; 沉入 sink into, go down. (4) Harmonize, agree with: 入時 keep up with the times, be modish, fashionable, *à la mode*; 入調 in tune, harmonize with; 入格 (be) fitting and proper; 入情入理 (be) fair and reasonable; 格格不入 inharmonious, discordant, cannot fit into; 不相入 be incompatible, incongruous. (5) (**ruu*) Misplace: 錢不知入那裏去了 I don't know where I've put the money. (6) (**ruu*) Hand over secretly: 暗中入給他手裏了 have secretly put it into his hands. (7) (**ruu*) Fall into, implicate: 一腳入到泥裏去 had one foot stuck in mud; 故入人罪 purposely implicate s.o. in crime. (8) (**ryh*) (MC) have sexual intercourse with (a woman).

入超 *ruh-chau*, v.i., (economics) have an unfavorable balance of trade.

入道 *ruh-dauh*, v.i., (Budd.) become a monk.

入地 *ruh-dih*, v.i., sink below the surface of the earth.

入定 *ruh-dihng*, v.i., (Budd.) sit quietly and meditate.

入耳 *ruh-eel*, (1) n., (zoo.) the house centipede, *Scutigera*, pop. name for 蚰蜒 (so called from its fondness for creeping into people's ears); (2) adj., audible, pleasant to hear.

入伏 *ruh-fur*, v.i., enter the period of hottest weather at end of summer.

入港 *ruh-gaang*, (1) v.i., (of ships) enter port; (2) adv., in full agreement, harmoniously: 他們兩人説得入港 the two of them got on swimmingly in their talks.

入告 *ruh-gauh*, v.t., to report to (a superior).

入彀 *ruh-gouh*, v.i., (1) come under s.o.'s control; (2) come within an arrow's shooting distance; (3) formerly, pass the examinations.

入官 *ruh-guan*, v.t., formerly, confiscate.

入貢 *ruh-guhng*, v.i., pay tributes to a suzerain state.

入骨 *ruh-guu*, v.i. & adv., (1) v.i., (Budd.) bury the bones of a devotee in a grave; (2) adv., deeply, strongly, vehemently: 恨之入骨 hate s.o. to the bones.

入號 *ruh-hauh*, v.t., (euphem.) to pawn.

入腳 *ruh-jiaau*, v.t., set afoot, start, begin.

入肩 *ruh-jian*, v.i., (MC) take part in an enterprise for some ulterior purpose.

入境 *ruh-jihng*[1], v.i., enter a country: 入境證 entry permit; 入境問禁 keep oneself informed of what things are forbidden in the country one is entering.

入靜 *ruh-jihng*[2], v.i., (Taoism) sit quietly in meditation.

入覲 *ruh-jiin*, v.t., have an audience with (the king, emperor).

入籍 *ruh-jir*, v.i., be naturalized.

入贅 *ruh-jueih*, v.i., marry into the wife's family, taking wife's surname.

入衆 *ruh-juhng*, v.i., (Budd.) live with the assembly of monks.

入直 *ruh-jyr*, v.i., (of ministers) wait on the king or emperor.

入龕 *ruh-kan*, v.i., (Budd.) put the body of a dead monk in monastic vault.

入口 *ruh-koou*, n., entrance, imports: 入口稅 import duties.

入寇 *ruh-kouh*, v.t., (of foreign troops) invade (another country).

入扣兒 *ruh-kouh'l*, adj., completely engrossed, fascinated: 他看這本小説看得入扣兒 he is entirely absorbed in reading this novel.

入庫 *ruh-kuh*, v.t., (1) (formerly, of stolen goods) confiscate; (2) (of newly arrived goods on board a ship) temporarily store(d) in warehouse.

入流 *ruh-liour*, v.i., (1) pass for fashionable; (2) (formerly, of the official hierarchy) belong to any one of the nine grades of officials: 未入流, 不入流 lower than the lowest grade; usu. out of the run, not qualified.

入馬 *ruh-maa*, v.i., make progress in courtship.

入梅 *ruh-meir*, n., coming of the rainy season in early summer (also 入霉).

入門(兒) *ruh-mern(-mer'l)*, v.i., be initiated into a subject, know the rudiments of s.t.

入迷 *ruh-mir*, v.i., become fascinated, enchanted, enraptured.

入魔 *ruh-mor*, v.i., (1) be completely bewitched; (2) go the way of the devil.

入泮 *ruh-pahn*, v.i., (LL) (formerly, of young boys) be admitted to study in a government school (泮宮).

入破 *ruh-poh*, n., (Chin. music) the finale.

入山 *ruh-shan*, v.i., become a hermit, live the life of a recluse (opp. 出山 join government service).

入射角 *ruhsheh-jiaau*, n., (physics) angle of incidence (also 投射角).

入聖 *ruh-shehng*, v.i., attain sainthood: 超凡入聖 ditto.

入聲 *ruh-sheng*, v., the fourth tone of a character; here indicated by "h" after vowel.

入神 *ruh-shern*, adj., (1) in mental concentration; (2) in ecstasy; (3) (of literary or artistic works) divine, supremely great.

入庠 *ruh-shiarng*, v.i., formerly, pass the first-grade (秀才) government examination.

入手 *ruh-shoou*, n. & v.i., (1) a start; (2) commence, get under way, start up; (3) receive.

入室 *ruh-shyh*, phr., be admitted to the sanctum sanctorum of learning; become real expert, specialist.

入選 *ruh-shyuaan*, v.i., be qualified in a contest, selected for a job, chosen for inclusion (in an anthology, on a team, etc.).

入塔 *ruh-taa*, v.i., (Budd.) bury a dead monk in a pagoda.

入頭 *ruh-tour*, n. & v.i., (1) n., (Chin. opera) point where the violin comes in; (2) ＝入門 *-mern* ↑.

入土 *ruh-tuu*, v.i., be buried: 入土爲安 (of a dead person) be laid to rest.

入味(兒) *ruh-weih(-weh'l)*, adj., (1) very interesting; (2) (of food) tasteful.

入闈 *ruh-weir*[1], phr., (modern usage) (of officials in charge of government examination) live incommunicado during period of examination; formerly, sit for a government examination; see 闈 52B.00.

入圍 *ruh-weir*[2], v.i., (of races, beauty contests, etc.) be qualified to take part in the finals; enter a circle, a trapped area.

入伍 *ruh-wuu*, v.i., become a cadet, be enlisted.

入眼 *ruh-yaan*, adj., pleasing to the eye, hence desirable.

入院 *ruh-yuahn*, v.i., (1) (of a sick person) be hospitalized; (2) (Budd.) be committed to a temple at birth.

入月 *ruh-yueh*, n., (1) the period of menstruation; (2) (LL) another name for the menses.

从 81.81

tsurng.

[Var. of 從 91B.83]

众 81.81

juhng.

[Abbr. of 衆 91.02]

僉 81.81

chian.

Adj. & adv. Unanimous, together (of a large group of persons): 僉謀 together plan to; 僉議 all discuss together; 僉同如一 it was unanimously agreed, there was not a dissenting voice.

僉壬 *chiarnrern*, n., (AC) a despicable (mean) person (opp. 君子 a gentleman, a man of culture).

僉事 *chianshyh*, n., formerly, title of lower-class secretary in government office.

§81.83 (人/〜)

途 81.83

tur.

N. Journey; road, path: 路途 journey; 途中, 途次 (meet, etc.) on the way; 沿途 along the road, during the journey; 旅途 travel (abroad); 歸途 return journey; 仕途, 宦途 official career; 前途 prospect; 前途遠大 (渺茫) great (dim) prospect, (of person) great career ahead; 老馬識途 knowledge of a vetean; 長途跋涉 long and arduous journey; 半途而廢 abandon (project) midway.

途徑 *turjihng*, n., path.

途路 *turluh*, n., (rare)＝路途 journey, path.

逾 81.83

yur.

[Usu. printed 逾]

V.t. To pass, exceed (time limit), pass over 逾垣, 逾牆 climb over wall; 逾矩, see 踰矩 40B.00.

Prep. Over: 逾月, 逾年 over a month, a year.

逾期 *yur-chir*, phr., past time limit, overdue.

逾額 *yur-eh*, phr., exceed allotted number.

逾分 *yur-fehn*, adj., beyond what is due: 逾分的要求 exorbitant demands.

逾過 *yur-guoh*, v.t., pass over, exceed.

逾恆 *yur-herng*, adv., more than usual (kindness, etc.).

逾限 *yur-shiahn*, phr., exceed the

limit or quota.

逾越 *yuryueh*, v.t., to exceed, go beyond: 逾越權限 exceed one's powers; 逾越尋常 go beyond the usual (courtesy, etc.)

§81.93 (人/く)

兪 81.93

yur.

[Printed form of 俞 81.00]

SECTION 81A

§81A.00 (金/亅)

鎛 81A.00–1

bor.

N. (1) (AC) large bell. (2) (AC) small hoe.

鑄 81A.00–1

juh.

V.t. To cast metals: 鑄造 cast (bell, statues); 鑄錢, 鑄幣 to mint coins; 鑄字模 to cast type; matrix from which lead type is cast; 陶鑄人才 to mold character; 鑄成, 鑄就 cast into; 鑄成大錯 make a permanent mistake, to make grave mistake; 鑄山煮海 mining and making salt by distilling sea water.

鑄模 *juhmor*, n., mold for casting, matrix.

鑄鐵 *juhtiee*, n., cast iron; pig iron.

錡 81A.00–1

chir.

N. (AC) (1) a kind of cooking pot. (2) A kind of drill or chisel.

鏄 81A.00–2

bor.

[Interch. 鎛]

鏘 81A.00–2

chiang.

Adj. Descriptive of jangling, jingling sound (of jade, etc.).

釗 81A.00–2

jau.

V.i. & t. (AC) (1) to cut out (flesh). (2) To strive.

釕 81A.00–3

liaau.

N. (Chem.) ruthenium.

釘 81A.00–3

ding (**dihng*).

N. (*-tz*) A nail: 鐵釘 iron nail; 圖畫釘 thumbtack; 螺絲釘 screw; 螺旋釘 bolt; 鍋釘 rivet; 大方釘 spike; 眼中釘 (fig.) thorn on one's side, person hated.

V.t. (1) Follow, trail, pursue closely and persistently: 死釘住他 follow person closely (like private detective); watch one particular opponent (as in basketball); question exhaustively: 釘問. (2) (**dihng*) To nail down, put nail in: 釘釘子 **dihng dingtz*, drive nail; 釘馬掌 nail horseshoe; 釘鈕子 sew button on; 釘死 nail fast; 釘劈了 **dihng-pi-'le*, cause a split while nailing, cross-question into silence.

釘疽 *dingjyu*, n., boil, see 疔ᴬ瘡 61A.00.

釘坑兒 *dingkeng'l*, adv., steadily: 你釘坑兒看我作什麼 why do

you stare at me?
釘鞋 *dingshier*, n., spiked shoes.
釘子 *dingtz*, n., nail; 碰釘子 get a rebuff, usu. at the hand of superior.

鈳 81A.00-3

ke.

N. (Chem.) niobium (also translit. 鈮) (formerly called columbium).

錒 81A.00-3

ah.

N. (Chem.) actinium.

鉶 81A.00-3

shirng.

N. (AC) an anc. bronze tripod with two ears for holding soup.

銍 81A.00-4

jar.

N. A sickle for cutting grass or hay.

鍀 81A.00-4

der.

N. (Chem.) technetium (also translit. 鎝).

鍆 81A.00-5

mern.

N. (Chem.) mendelevium.

鐦 81A.00-5

kai.

N. (Chem.) californium.

鐗 81A.00-5

jiaan (**jiahn*).

N. (1) A kind of anc. weapon. (2) (**jiahn*) Iron protection for wheel axle.

鑭 81A.00-5

larn.

N. (Chem.) lanthanum.

鐏 81A.00-8

tzun.

N. The cone-shaped bronze butt-end of a spear.

鎿 81A.00-8

nar.

N. (Chem.) neptunium (also translit. 錼).

鍮 81A.00-8

tou.
[Usu. printed 鍮]

N. (AC) copper (modn. 黃銅).

錚 81A.00-9

jeng.

Adj. Tinkling, ding-dong (metallic noise): 錚鏦, 錚鐄 (LL) ditto.

錚錚 *jengjeng*, n. & adj., fine timber; 錚錚響 make a clear metallic sound; 鐵中錚錚(庸中佼佼) outstanding person among mediocrity.

§81A.01 (金/小)

銖 81A.01-1

ju.

N. An anc. weight measure, now one-forty-eighth of an ounce; (fig.) a minuscule, diminutive amount: 錙銖必較 fight over the smallest trifles; 銖兩相稱 exactly equal; 銖積寸累 let small amounts accumulate.

鍊 81A.01-1

liahn.
[Cf. 練 usu. interch. in sense of "practice" and 煉 "harden by fire"]

N. Chain (var. 鏈 81A.83): 錶鍊

釘 鈳 錒 鉶 銍 鍀 鍆 鐦 鐗 鑭 鐏 鎿 鍮 錚 銖 鍊

亅	小	⺊	十	土	ナ	卄	ㄴ	丨	一	丁	フ	口	区	冈	乛	厂	尸	亠	广	宀	丶	乚	弋	心	八	人	乂	乛	一	丿	㇐	く
00	01	02	10	11	12	20	21	22	30	31	32	40	41	42	50	51	52	60	61	62	63	70	71	72	80	81	82	83	90	91	92	93

鍊 錸 鏭 鐐 鏢 錁 鑔 鎳 鑠 錶 鐻 鐶 銀

watch chain; 脖鍊 necklace; 鐵鍊 iron chain; 金鍊 gold chain; 拉鍊 zipper.

V.i. & t. To work metal by fire: 鍊鋼 make steel from iron; 鍊金術 (Taoist) alchemy, transmutation of gold; 鍛鍊, 磨鍊 build up character through hardships; 鍊石補天 (myth.) the goddess 女媧 melted a rock to mend sky after it was cracked during a battle, (fig.) have supernatural power to remedy situation.

Adj. Refined, matured, treated (see 煉 91D.01).

鍊句 *liahn-jyuh*, phr., shape a sentence with careful choice of words.

鍊字 *liahn-tzyh*, phr., to practice calligraphy.

錸 81A.01-1

lair.

N. (Chem.) rhenium.

鏭 81A.01-1

naih.

N. (Chem.) neptunium.

鐐 81A.01-1

liaur (*liauh*).

N. (1) Shackles: 手銬腳鐐 handcuffs and shackles. (2) Fine silver. (3) Oven with opening.

鏢 81A.01-3

biau.

N. (1) Spearhead, short piece of iron thrown at enemy by hand, also called 飛鏢. (2) In comb. 保鏢 bodyguard.

鏢鎗(槍) *biauchiang*, n., javelin, spear.

鏢局 *biaujyur*, n., professional firm furnishing armed escort.

鏢客 *biaukeh*, n., armed escort, bodyguard (professional), (also wr. 鑣).

錁 81A.01-4

keh.

N. (1) Silver or gold ingot. (2) 錁子 *-tz*, (Chin. opera) acrobatic jump landing on back.

鑔 81A.01-6

chaa.

N. Coll. name for cymbals.

鎳 81A.01-9

nieh.

N. (Chem.) nickel.

鑠 81A.01-9

shuoh.

V.t. (1) To melt: 鑠石流金 intense heat enough to melt stone and metals; to melt away, erode. (2) Interch. 爍 to shine, 91D.01.

§81A.02 (金/ㄎ)

錶 81A.02-1

biaau.

[Cf. 表 10.02]

N. (Pop. of 表) watch: 跑錶 stop watch; 手錶 wrist watch; 鐘錶 clock (oft. wr. 表).

鐻 81A.02-2

jyuh.

N. An anc. bell-shaped musical instrument.

鐶 81A.02-4

huarn.

N. A metal ring.

銀 81A.02-5

yirn.

N. (Chem.) silver; money: 銀子, 銀兩 *-tz*, *-liaang* ↓; 銀本位 silver standard of currency; 銀杯 silver cup.

Adj. Silver or powdery grey color: referring to the Milky Way: 銀河, 銀漢 *-her*, *-hahn* ↓; referring to the moon: 銀鉤, 銀兔 *-gou*, *-tuu* ↓; referring to color: 銀灰, 銀紅 *-huei*, *-hurng* ↓.

銀幣 *yirnbih*, n., silver coins or currency.

銀錢 *yirnchiarn*, n., money in gen.

銀鞘 *yirn-chiauh*, n., a wooden box for silver ingots.

銀錠(兒) *yirn-dihng('l)*, n., silver ingots.

銀耳 *yirn-eel*, n., "silver mushroom," a colorless tree fungus —a delicacy.

銀粉 *yirnfeen*, n., silver powder; adj., lightish grey.

銀釭 *yirn-gang*, n., (poet.) a lamp.

銀根 *yirn-gen*, n., the money market (is tight, etc.).

銀鉤 *yirn-gou*, phr., (LL) the crescent moon ("silver hook").

銀櫃 *yirn-gueih*, n., a safe (for money).

銀海 *yirn-haai*, n., the movie world (from 銀幕 *-muh*↓).

銀漢 *yirn-hahn*, n., the Milky Way.

銀行 *yirnharng*, n., a bank; 銀行結單 bank statement; 銀行提存準備 bank reserve.

銀號 *yirnhauh*, n., formerly, a money shop, exchange shop.

銀河 *yirn-her*, n., the Milky Way; see also *-hahn*↑.

銀花 *yirn-hua*, n., (1) icicles; (2) snow flakes; (3) the honeysuckle.

銀黃 *yirn-huarng*[1], phr., (1) (LL) silver and gold; (2) (AC) gold or silver official seal.

銀潢 *yirn-huarng*[2], n., (LL) the Milky Way.

銀灰 *yirnhuei*, adj., silver grey in color.

銀婚 *yirn-hun*, n., silver wedding anniversary.

銀紅 *yirnhurng*, adj., pale rose color.

銀甲 *yirn-jiaa*, n., silver finger cap worn for plucking stringed instrument.

銀角 *yirnjiaau*, n., silver dime.

銀價 *yirn-jiah*, n., price of silver.

銀匠 *yirn-jiahng* (-'*jiang*), n., a silversmith.

銀硃 *yirnju* (-'*ju*), n. & adj., cinnabar, mercuric sulfide, used as bright red pigment.

銀燭 *yirn-jur*, n., bright candle.

銀兩 *yirn-liaang*, n., silver as currency and counted by taels: 三十銀兩 thirty taels of silver.

銀樓 *yirn-lour*, n., a dealer in silverware.

銀幕 *yirnmuh*, n., the movie screen.

銀票 *yirnpiauh*, n., formerly, a money order, with amount stated in taels of silver.

銀色 *yirn-seh*, n., the grade of silver in coins; 銀色世界 screen world.

銀線草 *yirnshiahn-tsaau*, n., (bot.) *Chloranthus japonicus*.

銀杏 *yirn-shihng*, n., the gingko tree (also called 白果, esp. the edible fruit).

銀水 *yirn-shueei*, n., discount on account of difference of silver content in coins.

銀兔 *yirn-tuu*, phr., (poet.) the moon (with purported image of rabbit on it).

銀子 *yirntz*, n., money, amount (when it was customary to reckon in silver taels rather than dollars): 三千兩銀子 3000 taels of silver.

銀洋 *yirnyarng*, n., dollar, see also *-yuarn*↓.

銀元(圓) *yirnyuarn*, n., silver dollar.

銀魚 *yirnyur*, n., the silverfish; also formerly, a decoration of official rank.

鉉 81A.02-6

yii.

N. (Chem.) iridium.

鋏 81A.02-6

aih.

N. (Chem.) einsteinium (also translit. 鑀, 鎄).

鑲 81A.02-6

shiang.

V.t. (1) To inset with (gold, jade), inlay as decoration; (fig.) caught in predicament: 鑲住了 find oneself in situation difficult to extricate from. (2) To fill (tooth): 鑲牙. (3) To make a patch on: 鑲補 *-buu*↓. (4) To line with a border: 鑲旗 *-chir*↓.

鑲邊 *shiangbian*, v.t., (1) to rim with lace, border, tassels, etc.; (2) see 喝^邊兒 40A.50.

鑲補 *shiangbuu*, v.t., to make a decorative square patch on mandarin gown; n., such embroidered squares.

鑲嵌 *shiangchiahn*, v.t., to inset (with jade, pearl, etc.).

鑲旗 *shiangchir*, n., some of the eight Manchu armies, which had colored borders on their banners, as dist. those with solid colors.

鑲工 *shianggung*, n., artisan engaged in making insets on jewelry.

鑲牙 *shiang-yar*, n., refilled tooth; v.i., to have a tooth filled.

鋃 81A.02-6

larng.

鋃鐺 *larngdang*, n., (1) chains for prisoners: 鋃鐺下獄 be thrown into prison; (2) tinkling of bells.

鎵 81A.02-6

jia.

N. (Chem.) gallium.

錄 81A.02-9

luh.

N. (1) Record, selections: 筆錄, records (of speeches); 記錄, 紀錄 conference proceedings; 實錄 record of proceedings, journal of daily doings of emperor; factual records; 語錄 sayings of masters; 言行錄 sayings and personal stories of eminent men; 同學錄 register of alumni; 人名錄 biographical directory; list of persons; 嘉言錄 famous quotations or sayings. (2) A surname.

V.t. (1) To record, register: 紀(記)錄 record (proceedings, minutes of meeting, confessions at court, etc.); to make tape recording, see 錄音 *-yin*↓; 錄口供 to take a statement or testimony in writing. (2) To copy, make copy: 抄錄, 錄副張 make copy; 錄下來 put down in writing. (3) To select: 摘錄 make digest, make selections from (longer work); 錄取, 錄用 *-chyuu*, *-yuhng*↓.

錄取 *luhchyuu*, v.t., to select from candidates, pass examinee, admit student to college.
錄事 *luhshyh*, n., an office clerk.
錄影機 *luhyiingji*, n., video tape recorder.
錄音 *luhyin*, v.i., to record voice or sound; 錄音機 voice or tape recorder; 錄音帶 recording tape.
錄用 *luhyuhng*, v.t., to give post to (selected candidate).

§81A.10 (金/十)

針 81A.10-1

jen.

N. (1) Needle: 針線 *-shiahn*↓; 綉(花)針 fine needle for embroidery; 絨線針 darning or knitting needle; 心如針扎 feel greatly distressed ("like heart pricks"); 針鋒相對, see 針鋒 *-feng*↓. (2) A pin, tack, etc.: 別針 a pin; 大頭針 thumbtack; 錶針 hour and minute hands of watch; 時針, 分針, 秒針 hour, minute and second hands of clock or watch; 羅盤針 compass needle. (3) Injection: 打針 have an injection; 針劑 medicine for injection. (4) Acupuncture: 金針; 針砭, 針灸 *-bian*, *-jioou*↓; 針科 *-ke*↓.

V.t. To prick skin in injection or acupuncture.

針砭 *jenbian*, (1) n., acupuncture; (2) v.t., (fig.) give painful but much needed advice.
針鼻兒 *jenbier'l*, n., the eye of a needle.
針車 *jenche*, n., (sl.) sewing machine.
針對 *jendueh*, v.t., point exactly against (fact, argument).
針鋒 *jenfeng*, n., point of needle: 針鋒相對 two sides of argument match point by point.
針箍(兒) *jengu('l)*, n., thimble (also called 頂針兒).
針氈 *jenjan*, n., "cushion of needles": 如坐針氈 in uncomfortable position.
針尖兒 *jenjia'l*, n., fine or minute point.
針腳 *jen'jiau*, n., length between stitches, or alignment.
針芥 *jen-jieh*, n., magnet point and minute filings: 針芥相投 attracted to each other.
針灸 *jenjioou*, n., acupuncture.
針黹 *jenjyy*, n., fine needlework.
針科 *jenke*, n., acupuncture as a branch of medicine.
針路 *jenluh*, n., compass course in navigation.
針芒 *jenmarng*, n., fine or minute point.
針砂 *jensha*, n., iron dust from grinding of needle point, used in Chin. medicine (also called 鐵針砂).
針線 *jenshiahn*, n., (1) needle and thread; (fig.) clues or threads in detective work; (2) (*-'shian*) needlework in gen.: 針線活 needlewoman's work.
針形葉 *jenshirng-yeh*, n., (bot.) needle-shaped leaves (as in pine needle).
針眼 *jen-yaan*, n., (1) eye of a needle; (2) (*-'yan*) slight swelling of follicle in eyelid.

鉢 81A.10-1

bo.
[Pop. 缽]

N. (Budd.) monk's alms-bowl.

鉺 81A.10-3

eel.

N. (Chem.) erbium.

鑷 81A.10-3

nieh.

N. (1) (*-tz*) Tweezers, pincers, forceps. (2) A hairpin.

V.t. To extract (s.t.) or pick up with pincers, etc.

銲 81A.10-4

hahn.

V.i. & t. To solder, weld.

銲接 *hahnjie*, n., soldered joint.
銲藥 *hahnyauh*, n., solder, flux.

鐸 81A.10-4

duor.

N. Big bell: 木鐸 bell with wooden clapper, said of Confucius that he was like a clarion call to his times; hence 木鐸 refers to teacher's profession; 鐸安 (in correspondence, LL) greeting for "teacher's health."

鋅 81A.10-6

shin.

N. (Chem.) zinc: 鋅礦 zinc ores.

鋅 版 *shin-baan*, n., zinc plate.
鋅 白 *shin-bair*, n., (chem.) zinc white, zinc oxide used as white pigment.
鋅 華 *shin-huar*, n., (1) ditto; (2) hydrozincite.

鋒 81A.10-9

feng.

N. (1) Sharp point, blade: 刀鋒, 劍鋒 sharp point, edge of knife, sword; 筆鋒 point of pen; cutting power of one's pen; 針鋒相對 the two sides meet squarely on issue in argument. (2) (Fig.) weapons: 交鋒 "cross swords." (3) Troops in battle: 前鋒, 先鋒(隊) spearhead of army; 開路先鋒 pioneer (in art, etc.), trail blazer.

Adj. Sharp: 鋒銳, 鋒利 *-rueih*, *-lih*↓.

鋒 鏑 *fengdir*, n., (spearhead and arrowhead) weapons: 鋒鏑交加 in close combat.
鋒 利 *fenglih*, adj., sharp.
鋒 芒 (鋩) *fengmarng*, n., the fine edge of spear or lance: 鋒芒太露 too trenchant in style, (full of barbs), fail to show restraint; 鋒芒毫髮之事 trivial matters.
鋒 刃 *fengrehn*, n., tip of lance and bayonet, thick of battle.
鋒 銳 *fengrueih*, n. & adj., attacking power; sharp.

§ 81A.11 (金/土)

釷 81A.11-1

tur.

N. (Chem.) thorium.

鑵 81A.11-2

guahn.

N. A jar.

銼 81A.11-2

tsuoh.

N. A carpenter's file: 銼刀.

V.t. To file even (also u.f. 挫 10A.11).

鏜 81A.11-2

tang.

N. 鏜鏜 noise of drums, other loud noises.

鈺 81A.11-3

yuh.

N. Hard gold.

鑼 81A.11-4

luor.

N. A gong: 鑼鼓 gong and drum; 鳴鑼 strike the gong.

鋰 81A.11-4

lii.

N. (Chem.) lithium, the lightest known metal.

鏗 81A.11-5

keng.

鏗 鏘 *kengchang*, n. & adj., jangling of metal or jade instruments.

鏟 81A.11-6

chaan.

N. (-*tz*, -*'l*) A shovel, trowel.

V.t. (Interch. 剷 60S.00) to pare down.

鐘 81A.11-6

jung.
[Dist. 鍾]

N. (1) (-*'l*) A bell: 鐘樓 bell tower; 打鐘, 敲鐘 strike bell; 晨鐘暮鼓 matin bells and vesper drums. (2) A clock: 時鐘 clock; 自鳴鐘 formerly, clock; 電鐘 electric clock; 鐘表 clocks and watches; 鐘表行 clock shop; 鬧鐘 alarm clock; 掛鐘 wall clock.

鐘擺 *jungbaai*, n., clock pendulum.
鐘點(兒) *jungdiaan* (*-diaa'l*), n., hour, time of the day.
鐘鼎 *jungdiing*, n., (the study of) bronze inscriptions on early bells and tripods: 鐘鼎文 bronze script, roughly of Shang and Jou Dyns.
鐘乳 *jungruu*, n., (石鐘乳) stalactites and stalagmites.
鐘頭 *jung'tou*, n., hour: 幾個鐘頭 how many hours?

銓 81A.11-8

chyuarn.

V.t. (1) To weigh. (2) To select officials by certain standards: 銓擇, 銓取 select (officials) by qualifications; 考銓 to examine officials' work or knowledge.

銓衡 *chyuarnherng*, v.t., to measure, compare and select talents for government.
銓選 *chyuarnshyuaan*, v.t., to grade qualifications and select officials.
銓敍 *chyuarnshyuh*, v.t., ditto; qualification and appointment (placement); 銓敍部 ministry of personnel.

鍾 81A.11-9

jung.
[Dist. 鐘]

N. (1) (AC) u.f. 鐘 81A.11. (2) An anc. measure (of grain) defined as 64 斗 (*doou*). (3) A wine goblet. (4) A surname.

V.i. & t. (1) To love, cherish: 鍾愛, 鍾情 *-aih*, *-chirng*↓. (2) To impregnate with: 鍾天地靈氣 impregnated with the fine spirits of the universe—resulting in producing of talents or beauties. (3) (AC) to gather: 情之所鍾 when the love is concentrated on one person.

鍾愛 *jung-aih*, v.i., fall in love with (girl): 鍾愛於她.
鍾情 *jungchirng*, v.i., fall in love: 一見鍾情 love at first sight.
鍾馗 *Jungkueir*, n., (pop. myth.) person reputed for subjugating demons.

錘 81A.11-9

chueir.

N. (1) A metal ball with a chain, used as weapon: 銅錘, 鐵錘 copper, iron ball. (2) The weight on a steelyard.

V.t. To hammer into shape: 千錘百鍊(錘鍊) form (iron utensil, poem, human character) by persistent knocking into shape.

錐 81A.11-9

juei.

N. (*-tz*) An awl, a drill: 錐處囊中 (allu.) real talent will be discovered (like awl's point which must show through pocket); 錐刀, 錐尖 (AC) small trifles; 錐股 (allu.) scholar stabbed his own leg with an awl-point to keep himself from falling asleep while studying.

鍠 81A.11-9

huarng.

N. An anc. weapon.

Adj. 鍠鍠倉倉 (AC) sound of drums and bells.

§ 81A.20 (金/廾)

錛 81A.20-1

ben.

N. (*-tz*) Short axe.

錛得兒木 *bende'lmuh*, n., woodpecker=啄木鳥.

§ 81A.21 (金/乚)

鋩 81A.21-2

marng.

N. Edge of weapon (common form 芒).

鉅 81A.21-5

jyuh.

N. (1) Iron, steel. (2) A hook.

Adj. (Interch. 巨 51.21) great: 鉅公 *-gung*, 鉅子 *-tzyy*↓.

Adv. (U.f. 詎 60A.21) how.

鉅公 *jyuhgung*, n., (1) (AC) His Imperial Highness, the king; (2) a person of great authority, a leading personality.
鉅子 *jyuhtzyy*, n., (1) an expert, a specialist; (2) a leader of 墨子 Motse school.

鉕 81A.21-5

poo.

A

N. (Chem.) promethium.

鍤 81A.21-9

char.

N. (1) A shovel. (2) (Tailoring) a large pin for pinning border lines.

§ 81A.22 (金/丨)

鈽 81A.22-1

buh.

N. (Chem.) plutonium.

鈡 81A.22-2

jung.

[Abbr. of 鐘 81A.11]

釙 81A.22-2

pur.

N. (Chem.) polonium.

鉲 81A.22-2

kaa.

N. (Chem.) californium.

B

釧 81A.22-2

chuahn.

N. Bracelet: 金釧 gold bracelet.

鏽 81A.22-2

shiouh.

[Var. 銹]

N. Rust: 生鏽 to rust; 不鏽鋼 stainless steel.

鈈 81A.22-3

buh.

N. (Chem.) plutonium (also translit. 鈽).

鉀 81A.22-4

jiaa.

N. (Chem.) potassium.

鐮 81A.22-6

liarn.

N. Sickle: 鐮刀 ditto.

鍗(碲) 81A.22-6

dih.

N. (Chem.) tellurium.

C

鈰 81A.22-6

shyh.

N. (Chem.) cerium.

銻 81A.22-8

tih.

N. (Chem.) antimony.

釿 81A.22-9

yirn.

N. (AC) hollow or concave surface, opp. 鍔 a protrusion.

錦 81A.22-9

jiin.

N. Tapestry, embroidered work: 織錦 brocade; 錦緞 figured satin; 錦繡 *-shiouh*↓; 錦盒 gilded box (casket); 錦囊妙計 a secret master plan; 錦上添花 be blessed with a double portion of good fortune, winning honors (successes) one after another in quick succession; 錦袍, 錦衾(被) embroidered robe, coverlet; 錦帶 *-daih*↓.

Adj. Elegant, splendid, magnificent: 錦衣玉食 live an extravagant life ("elegantly dressed and feasting on delicacies"); 衣錦還鄉 glorious homecoming after having won high honors and social recognition; 錦心繡口 (of literary style) elegant and refined.

錦標 *jiinbiau*, n., championship, a trophy awarded a winner.

錦帶 *jiindaih*, n., an embroidered sash.
錦雞 *jiinji*, n., (zoo.) a species of pheasant, *Phasianus pictus*.
錦葵 *jiinkueir*, n., (bot.) the Chinese mallow, *Malva sylvestris*.
錦繡 *jiinshiouh*, n. & adj., (1) n., rich brocade; (2) adj., beautiful, colorful, elegant: 錦繡河山 beautiful landscape ("like brocade").

§ 81A.30 (金/一)

鑪 81A.30–2

lur.
[Var. 爐]

鎧 81A.30–2

kaai.

N. Armor: 首鎧 helmet; 鐵鎧 coat of mail.

鎧仗 *kaaijahng*, n., armor and weapons.
鎧甲 *kairjiaa*, n., armor in gen.

鉦 81A.30–3

jeng.

N. (AC) military gong used on march: 鉦鼓 gong and drum as signals for army's movement, forward or stop.

錳 81A.30–3

meeng.

N. (Chem.) manganese: 錳之游子 ions of manganese.

錳鋼 *meenggang*, n., manganese steel.
錳酸鉀 *meengsuanjiaa*, n., (chem.) potassium manganate; 錳酸游子 manganate ion.

鐙 81A.30–3

dehng.

N. Stirrup.

鉭 81A.30–4

dahn.

N. (Chem.) tantalum.

鉏 81A.30–4

chur.
[Interch. 鋤 81A.50]

鈕 81A.30–5

nioou.

N. (1) Button on a dress (interch. 紐 93B.30): 鈕扣 button and buttonhole; 鈕子 button. (2) A surname.

鈕扣 *niooukouh*, n., button.
鈕子 *niooutz*, n., ditto.

鑑 81A.30–5

jiahn.
[Var. 鑒 51.30]

N. (1) A looking glass, a mirror. (2) An example, a precept: 鑑戒 *-jieh*↓; 殷鑑(不遠) past examples serving as a warning to later generations (are not far to seek); 前車之鑑 take warning from s.o. else's failure. (3) History as a mirror of past events: "通鑑," "綱鑑" "A General History," "An Outline History"; 年鑑 a yearbook.

V.t. (1) To reflect or mirror: 光可鑑人 (of flat surface) so shining and bright that it can serve as a looking glass. (2) Scrutinize, examine, inspect: 鑑別 *-bier*, 鑑察 *-char*, 鑑賞 *-shaang*, 鑑核 *-her*, 鑑定 *-dihng*↓; (interch. 鑒) as in 臺鑒, 明鑒, 助鑒, 大鑒, 惠鑒 (in letters to friends) polite expressions used in the salutation.

鑑別 *jiahnbier*, v.t., appraise, evaluate, pass judgement on.
鑑察 *jiahnchar*, v.t., inspect, examine.
鑑定 *jiahndihng*, v.t., expertize, appraise by experts; authenticate.
鑑核 *jianher*, v.t., scrutinize, consider, look into.
鑑戒 *jiahnjieh*, n., a past example of failure serving as warning.
鑑賞 *jiahnshaang*, v.t., (of literary or artistic works) enjoy, appreciate as connoisseur.

鎰 81A.30–8

yih.

N. Anc. measure of gold, 20 or 24 ounces.

§ 81A.32 (金/フ)

鑼 81A.32–4

luor.

[Abbr. of 鑼 81A.11]

鈐 81A.32-8

chiarn.

N. & v.i. (AC) official seal, to stamp.

鈐章 *chiarnjang*, n., official stamp.
鈐鍵 *chiarnjiahn*, n., (＝關鍵) critical turning point.
鈐記 *chiarnjih*, n., official stamp; v.i., to stamp document with official seal.
鈐印 *chiarnyihn*, n., ditto.

§81A.40 (金/口)

鈷 81A.40-1

gu.

N. (Chem.) cobalt.

鋯 81A.40-1

gauh.

N. (Chem.) zirconium.

鎝 81A.40-2

taa.

N. (Chem.) technetium (also translit. 鎝).

鍩 81A.40-2

ruoh.

N. (Chem.) nobelium.

釦 81A.40-4

kouh.

N. (*-tz*, *-'l*) Button, knot, buckle; see 扣 10A.40.

鋁 81A.40-4

lyuu.

N. (Chem.) aluminium.

鉛 81A.40-4

chian.

N. (Chem.) lead: 鉛淚 a torrent of tears, tears flowing like molten lead; a more plausible explanation, tears mixed with make-up, see 鉛白 *-bor* (white) and 鉛黛 *-daih* (black) ↓.

鉛版(板) *chianbaan*, n., (1) lead sheet; (2) type plate used in printing.
鉛筆 *chianbii*, n., (1) pencil; (2) lead used for writing in anc. China, see *-huarng*, *-chiahn* ↓.
鉛玻璃 *chian bo'li*, n., flint glass.
鉛白 *chianbor*, n., (chem.) white lead.
鉛槧 *chianchiahn*, n., set-up for wood block printing (鉛 used in writing; 槧 a block to be cut).
鉛球 *chianchiour*, n., (athletics) the metal cast ball used in shot-put.
鉛垂線 *chianchueir-shiahn*, n., (nautical) lead line, a sounding line.
鉛黛 *chiandaih*, n., cosmetics in gen., facial make-up (like eye-pencil).
鉛丹 *chiandan*, n., (1) lead oxide as coloring material; (2) mercuric oxide used as pigment and in cosmetics.
鉛刀 *chian-dau*, n., a dull knife.
鉛鈍 *chianduhn*, adj., dull (like a blunted knife).
鉛粉 *chianfeen*, n., lead powder used in cosmetics.
鉛汞 *chian-guung*, n., lead and mercury (used in anc. alchemy).
鉛華 *chianhuar*, n., see *-feen* ↑.
鉛黃 *chianhuarng*, n., work of editing, correcting and blotting out passages (鉛 used in marking lines, and 雌黃 or yellow ochre used for blotting out).
鉛礦 *chiankuahng*, n., lead ores.
鉛駑 *chian-nur*, phr., (LL from 鉛刀駑馬) inferior talent, see *-dau* ↑.
鉛素 *chiansuh*, n., (LL) pen and paper (素＝white paper).
鉛絲 *chiansy*, n., zinc-covered wire.
鉛條 *chiantiaur*, n., (1) thin strip of graphite in pencils; (2) printer's lead or lead strips; (3) lead wire.
鉛鐵 *chiantiee*, n., (1) zinc-plated iron; (2) lead or lead alloy.
鉛子兒 *chiantzee'l*, n., bullets.
鉛字 *chiantzyh*, n., lead type, printing type.
鉛印 *chianyihn*, n., printing from lead type.

鋸 81A.40-5

*jyuh (*jyu).*

N. A saw: 刀鋸 anc. instruments of punishment for cutting and maiming; 鋼鋸 a steel saw; 鋼絲鋸 a coping saw; 拉鋸戰 a

鋸 鎔 錇 鉿 鎗 銛 銘 鉻 鉫 鍺

seesaw battle.

V.t. (1) To cut with a saw: 鋸斷 to saw asunder; 鋸開 to saw in two. (2) (**jyu*) Mend (crockery).

鋸扯 *jyuhchee*, (1) v.i., be irresolute, waver, vacillate; (2) v.t., to cut with a blunt knife.
鋸齒 *jyuh-chyy*, n., the teeth of a saw.
鋸子 **jyutz*, n., a saw.
鋸碗兒的 **jyu-waa'l'de*, n., a pedlar who mends crockery.

鎔 81A.40-6

rurng.
[Var. 熔]

N. A mold for casting: 上之化下，下之從上，猶金之在鎔 the relationship between the ruler and the ruled is like the shaping of molten ore in a mold.

V.t. Smelt, fuse (largely interch. 溶): 鎔冶 melt (ore); 鎔銷 ditto; 鎔化 *-huah* ↓; 鎔解 *-jiee* ↓.

鎔點 *rurngdiaan*, n., (phys.) the melting point (also 鎔融度).
鎔度 *rurngduh*, n., ditto.
鎔化 *rurnghuah*, v.i. & t., melt, fuse, (cause to) become liquid through heating.
鎔解 *rurngjiee*, v.i. & t., ditto.
鎔劑 *rurng-jih*, n., melting agent.
鎔金鍋 *rurngjin-guo*, n., a crucible, a melting pot (also 坩堝).
鎔融 *rurngrurng*, v.i. & t., ＝鎔解 *-jiee* ↑.
鎔岩 *rurngyarn*, n., (geol.) lava when solidified into rocks.

錇 81A.40-6

beei.

N. (Chem.) berkelium (also translit. 鉳).

鉿 81A.40-8

her.

N. (Chem.) hafnium.

鎗 81A.40-8

chiang.

N. Small arms, gun, pistol (interch. 槍): 手鎗 pistol; 毛瑟鎗 Mauser rifle or pistol; 機關鎗 machine gun; 鳥鎗 fowling piece, shotgun; 步鎗 rifle; 噴火鎗 flame thrower; 信號鎗 gun signal, signal gun.

鎗靶 *chiangbaa*[1], n., shooting range.
鎗把 *chiaugbaa*[2], n., stock of gun.
鎗彈 *chiangdahn*, n., bullet.
鎗桿(兒) *chianggaan(-gaa'l)*, n., (1) gun barrel; (2) gen. term for rifle (cf. 筆桿 writing brush, the pen).
鎗口 *chiangkoou*, n., gun muzzle.
鎗榴彈 *chiangliourdahn*, n., grenade fired from rifle.
鎗身 *chiangshen*, n., gun barrel.
鎗手 *chiangshoou*, n., gunman; substitute writer (exam.).
鎗膛 *chiangtarng*, n., gun barrel.
鎗刺 *chiangtsyh*, n., rifle and bayonet; bayonet.
鎗托 *chiangtuo*, n., gun stock.
鎗筒 *chiangtuung*, n., gun barrel.
鎗子(兒) *chiangtzyy(-tzee'l)*, n., bullet.
鎗眼 *chiangyaan*, n., (1) gun hole (for firing, or made by bullet); (2) gun muzzle.

銛 81A.40-9

shian.

N. (AC) (1) a shovel. (2) a harpoon, forked spear for hunting big fish or turtle.

Adj. Sharp, cutting: 銛利 ditto.

銘 81A.40-9

mirng.

N. (1) Inscription, usu. on stone. (2) A form of composition, a memorial piece: 墓誌銘 biographical sketch of the dead, on back of memorial tablet; 座右銘 inscribed or written maxim (as constant desk reminder).

V.t. To inscribe; to inscribe indelibly, keep in the heart: 銘感(不忘) remember with gratitude always; 刻骨銘心，銘肌鏤骨 (fig.) shall always remember in heart, as if inscribed on one's bones.

銘記 *mirngjih*, v.i. & t., to be engraved in one's heart, deeply impressed.
銘旌 *mirngjing*, n., banners displayed on funeral procession.

鉻 81A.40-9

geh.

N. (Chem.) chromium.

鉫 81A.40-9

rur.

N. (Chem.) rubidium.

§ 81A.41 (金/図)

鍺 81A.41-1

jee.

N. (Chem.) germanium.

錨 81A.41-2

maur.

N. Anchor: 下錨, 抛錨 cast anchor; also (fig.) break down on the way (of cars).

鉗 81A.41-2

chiarn.

[Anc. var. 箝 92A.21]

N. (1) (*-tz*) Pincers, pliers: 老虎鉗 wrench, wire cutters; 藥鉗 pincers for picking medical herbs; cf. 箝 92A.41. (2) An anc. iron collar used on prisoners; 鉗徒 such prisoner. (3) A surname.

V.t. To compress or hold closed by force; see compp.↓.

鉗忌 *chiarnjih*, v.t., (AC) be jealous and hostile.

鉗噤 *chiarnjihn*, v.i., to shut up (mouth).

鉗制 *chiarnjyh*, v.t., to suppress (movement, action).

鉗口 *chiarn-koou*, v.i., to shut up, refrain from airing opinions (also wr. 箝).

鉗子 *chiarn'tz*, n., (1) pincers; (2) (Peking coll.) earrings.

錯 81A.41-2

tsuoh.

N. (1) (AC) grinding stone. (2) A mistake: 是我的錯 the mistake is mine; 認錯 admit mistake; 改錯 correct mistake; 差錯 a mistake, error. (3) A delicacy: 珍錯, 山珍海錯 delicacies from land and sea.

V.t. (1) To miss opportunity: 錯過機會 ditto. (2) (AC) to tattoo (arm, etc.).

Adj. (1) Confused, complex: 錯亂, 錯雜, 錯綜 *-luahn*, *-tzar*, *-tzuhng*↓. (2) Mistaken, wrong, bad, esp. in 不錯 you are right, it is very good indeed (said of anything, food, performance, etc.); 大錯特錯 gravely mistaken; 錯計, 錯着 a wrong move, step; 說錯話 said s.t. which should not have been said.

錯愛 *tsuohaih*, v.i., (court.) as in 承你錯愛 have received undeserved kindness from you.

錯處 *tsuoh'chu*, n., mistake, error in commitment or conduct.

錯刀 *tsuohdau*, n., a file for polishing jade, etc. (properly wr. 銼刀).

錯愕 *tsuoh-eh*, adj., startled, taken by surprise, upset.

錯縫兒 *tsuohfehng'l*, n., flaw, mistake, see *-'chu*↑.

錯非 *tsuohfei*, conj., (dial.) for 除^A非 32A.01, except.

錯怪 *tsuohguaih*, v.i. & t., blame wrongly (on person).

錯過 *tsuoh-guoh*, (1) v.t., to miss (opportunity); (2) conj., (dial.)= 除非 except.

錯簡 *tsuoh-jiaan*, n., a mix-up in the arrangement of bamboo strips in anc. books—a textual error.

錯見 *tsuohjiahn*, n., misconception.

錯覺 *tsuohjyuer*, n., (psych.) an illusion.

錯兒 *tsuoh'l*, n., an error in conduct or calculations: 沒有錯兒 it's decidedly a good choice or decision.

錯亂 *tsuohluahn*, adj., confused: 神經錯亂 mentally deranged.

錯落 *tsuohluoh*, adj., mixed-up.

錯繆 *tsuohmiouh*, n. & adj., error, erroneous.

錯雜 *tsuohtzar*, adj., mixed-up, not assorted; complex (situation).

錯綜 *tsuohtzuhng*, adj., complicated: 錯綜變化 constantly vary.

錯誤 *tsuoh'wuh*, n., an error.

錯疑 *tsuohyir*, v.t., to suspect (person) wrongly.

鍩 81A.41-2

kaai.

N. Iron of fine quality.

鈾 81A.41-2

your.

N. (Chem.) uranium.

鐺 81A.41-2

dang.

N. (1) Flat frying pan, pan for making pancakes. (2) Vessel with legs for heating over charcoal fire: 茶鐺, 酒鐺.

Adj. Descriptive of jingling or clanging sound: 鐺鐺 *-dang*, 鋃鐺 *larng-*.

鐳 81A.41-3

leir.

N. (1) (Chem.) radium. (2) (AC) bottles and jars.

鈿 81A.41-4

diahn (also *tiarn*).

N. Woman's hair ornament of gold flowers: 花鈿, 鈿飾 such ornaments.

鉬 81A.41-4

muh.

N. (Chem.) molybdenum.

銦 81A.41-4

yin.

N. (Chem.) indium.

錮 81A.41-4

guh.

V.t. (1) Fill up cracks with melted metal. (2) Imprison, confine: 禁錮 throw into prison; 錮身 to shackle a prisoner.

Adj. Chronic: 錮疾 *-jir* ↓.

錮疾 *guhjir*, n., a chronic ailment (=痼^疾 61A.41, 固^疾 41.41).
錮送 *guhsuhng*, v.t., (of prisoners) put in fetters and send away under guard.

鋂 81A.41-5

meir.

N. (Chem.) americium (also translit 鎇).

鐠 81A.41-8

puu.

N. (Chem.) praseodymium.

鉑 81A.41-9

bor.

N. (1) Platinum. (2) U.f. 箔 92A.41: 金鉑, 錫鉑 gold leaf, tinfoil.

錙 81A.41-9

tzy.

N. An anc. measure of weight, weighing eight ounces: 錙銖 *-ju* ↓.

錙銖 *tzyju*, n., a very small amount: 錙銖計較 miserly, counting cents and pennies.

鎦 81A.41-9

liour.

N. (Chem.) lutecium.

§81A.42 (金/冈)

鋪 81A.42-1

pu.

[See also 舖 *puh*, of which 鋪 pr. *puh*, is common permissible var.]

N. Place for sleep: 牀鋪 bed; 打地鋪 sleep on the floor.

V.i. & t. (1) To spread (sand over snow). (2) To set in order: 鋪牀, 鋪炕 make the bed; 鋪路 pave road surface; 鋪滿了 has been properly covered. (3) Set for show: 鋪陳, 鋪張, 鋪設 *-chern*, *-jang*, *-sheh* ↓.

鋪陳 *puchern*, (1) n., beddings for travel; (2) (*pu'chen*) n., rags; (3) v.i., arrange for effect, make display.
鋪墊兒 *pudiahn(-diah'l)*, n., cushion.
鋪房 *pu-farng*, v.i., a ceremony, the bride's family sending furniture and beddings for bridal chamber to groom's family (in public display) on day before wedding.
鋪蓋 *pu-gaih*, n., gen. term for beddings: 鋪蓋捲兒 *--jyuaa'l*, n., roll of beddings.
鋪張 *pujang*, v.t., exaggerate (事實 facts): 鋪張揚厲 make things seem worse than they are; also just exaggerate (even in praise or blame).
鋪排 *pu'pai*, n., decorations; temple employee for setting up temporary altar in street or home.
鋪設 *pusheh*, n., furniture and decorations; setup.
鋪首 *pushoou*, n., brass knocker.
鋪敍 *pushyuh*, v.t. & n., portray (-al).
鋪位 *pu-weih*, n., bunk, berth, stall.

銪 81A.42-1

yoou.

N. (Chem.) europium.

銷 81A.42-2

shiau.

[Closely related 消 63A.42]

V.i. & t. (1) To melt (metals): 銷金 *-jin* ↓. (2) Distribute in sales: 銷售 *-shouh* ↓; 銷數不大 small sales; 暢銷, 滯銷 sell very well, not very well; 推銷 promote sales; 承銷 to act as sales agent. (3) To end or close (also 消): 銷假 *-jiah* ↓; 銷案 *-ahn* ↓. (4) To consume, spend (interch. 消): 銷耗 *-hauh* ↓.

銷案 *shiau-ahn*, v.i., close a legal case. ⌈mission.

銷差 *shiau-chai*, v.i., terminate

銷塲 *shiaucharng*, n., sales market, extent of sales (big, small).

銷耗 *shiauhauh*, (1) n., expenditure; (2) v.i. & t., spend, wear out, cost: 銷耗浩大 cost a great deal.

銷魂 *shiauhurn*, v.i., as in 黯然銷魂 "melt away soul"—be in love. ⌈leave.

銷假 *shiau-jiah*, v.i., terminate

銷金 *shiaujin*, (1) adj., gold-sprinkled (paper, curtain); (2) n., 銷金窟 also 銷金窩 "where gold melts away"—house of pleasure, an expensive mistress, gambling house.

銷路 *shiauluh*, n., sales: 銷路不好 the sales are small.

銷行 *shiaushirng*, n. & v.i., (commercial goods) sell well, badly.

銷售 *shiaushouh*, n. & v.i., sales; sell.

銷字 *shiau-tzyh*, n., characters which are cut and pasted on scrolls of congratulation or condolence.

鎘 81A.42-3

ger.

N. (Chem.) cadmium.

鐍 81A.42-3

jyuer.

N. (1) Links with a tongue as catch. (2) A hasp for locking: 扃鐍 ditto.

銅 81A.42-4

turng.

N. (Chem.) copper, brass, bronze: 紅銅, 赤銅 copper; 白銅 copper zinc alloy; 黃銅 brass; 古銅, 青銅 bronze; 銅礦 copper mine; 銅器 bronze utensils; 銅器時代 Bronze Age; 銅匠 coppersmith; 銅落,銅屑 copper shavings; 銅錢 copper coins; 銅人, 銅像 bronze statue; 銅鑼, 銅鉦 brass gong; 銅葉子 copper foil; 銅印, 銅瓦 copper seal, tile; 銅臭 (derog.) filthy rich in sense of "ostentatious" or placing too much value on money; copper as symbol of strength, in comb. with "iron": 銅筋鐵骨 a body of iron; 銅盔鐵甲 brass helmets and iron armor; 銅頭鐵額 head of iron—extremely courageous; 銅斗兒家私 (coll.) family of great means; 銅琵琶板 (of wartime manifestoes, etc.) extremely moving message; 銅駝荆棘 bronze camels buried in brambles—ruins of fallen royal house.

銅板 *turngbaan*[1], copper coin; (fig.) money: 這個人有幾個銅板, 就忘其所以 this man gets a swelled head the moment he has a little money.

銅版 *turngbaan*[2], n., copper plates for printing.

銅鈸 *turngbar*, n., brass cymbals.

銅幣 *turngbih*, n., copper coins.

銅器 *turngchih*, n., bronze utensils.

銅青 *turngching*, n., verdigris (also 銅綠).

銅管音樂 *turngguaanyinyueh*, n., brass instrument.

銅壺 *turnghur*, n., clepsydra, ancient water clock with markings of hours on copper bowl (also called 銅漏).

銅角 *turngjiaau*, n., Chin. brass trumpet.

銅龍 *turnglurng*, n., (1) anc. water clock with copper dragon's head; (2) a kind of faucet.

銅綠 *turnglyuh*, n., verdigris.

銅模 *turngmor*, n., copper matrix for Chin. lead type.

銅盆帽 *turngpernmauh*, n., formerly, the European felt hat, resembling inverted copper bowl.

銅子(兒) *turngtzyy(-tzee'l)*, n., a copper coin (=1 cent).

銅元 *turngyuarn*, n., a copper coin (also 銅圓).

鋼 81A.42-4

gang.

N. Steel: 純鋼 pure steel; 不銹鋼 stainless steel.

鋼版 *gang-baan*, n., (1) a stencil plate (also 鋼板); (2) steel engraving.

鋼筆 *gang-bii*, n., (1) a pen, fountain pen: 鋼筆尖, 鋼筆頭 a pen nib; 鋼筆套 a penholder; (2) a stylus (also 鐵筆).

鋼琴 *gangchirn*, n., a piano.

鋼戳子 *gang-chuotz*, n., see *-yihn* ↓.

鋼軌 *gang-gueei*, n., a steel rail.

鋼骨 *gang-guu*, n., (1) steel bars or mesh: 鋼骨水泥 reinforced concrete; (2) metal ribs of an umbrella.

鋼筋 *gang-jin*, n., structural steel, steel bars or mesh used as material for reinforced concrete.

鋼珠 *gang-ju*, n., (mech.) ball bearing.

鋼種 *gang-juung*, n., pop. term for aluminium.

鋼盔 *gang-kuei*, n., a steel helmet.

鋼條 *gang-tiaur*, n., steel bars.

鋼鐵 *gang-tiee*, n., steel and iron; 鋼鐵廠 a steel and iron works.

鋼印 *gang-yihn*, n., embossing stamp.

鍋 81A.42-4

guo.

N. A cooking-pot, saucepan: 鐵鍋, 銅鍋 iron, bronze pot; 飯鍋 a rice pot; 火鍋 a chafing dish; 鍋蓋 a pot cover.

鍋巴 *guo'ba*, n., rice crust on the bottom of the cooking pot.
鍋餅 *guobiing*, n., a thick, big wheat cake.
鍋圈(兒) *guochyua('l)*, n., (1) a bamboo ring on which a cooking pot can rest; (2) (of children's hair-dressing) a circular ring of hair on the lower part of the head after shaving off the center on the crown.
鍋伙(兒) *guo'huo('l)*, n., a common kitchen of small traders or workers.
鍋盔 *guokuei*, n., a small wheat cake.
鍋爐 *guolur*, n., a boiler, big or small.
鍋臺 *guotair*, n., a cooking range.
鍋貼(兒) *guotie(-tie'l)* n., (1) a baked patty with meat; (2) (sl.) a box on the ear, a slap on the face.
鍋子 *guotz*, n., a cooking pot.

鎬 81A.42-6

hauh (*gaau*).

N. (1) (AC) a stove. (2) (AC) 鎬京 anc. capital of King Wu (武王). (3) (**goou*) A shovel.

鏑 81A.42-6

dir.

N. Arrowhead.

鏞 81A.42-6

yurng (also *yung*).

N. (AC) a large bell.

鑰 81A.42-8

yueh (sp. pr. **yauh*).

N. (1) A key. (2) A lock: 鎖鑰 door lock.

鑰匙 **yauhshyr* (*yueh-*), n., a key.

鈉 81A.42-8

nah.

N. (Chem.) sodium, natrium.

鐫 81A.42-9

jyuan.

N. An instrument for carving wood; carvings.

V.t. (1) Carve, engrave: 鐫刻 engrave a printing block. (2) Demote: 鐫級 (of official) be demoted.

§81A.50 (金/ㄱ)

銬 81A.50-1

kauh.

N. Shackles: 手銬 handcuffs; 腳銬 shackles.

V.t. Put in handcuffs; 把他銬住.

鈣 81A.50-3

gaih.

N. (Chem.) calcium: 鈣化 calcify, -ied.

釢 81A.50-3

naai.

N. (Chem.) neodymium (also 釹).

鍔 81A.50-4

eh.

N. (AC) knife edge.

錫 81A.50-4

shir.

N. (1) Tin (mines, etc.), pewter: 錫壺, 錫罐 pewter pot. (2) Short for 錫杖, see *-jahng*↓, used of a monk's travel: 掛錫 stop at a temple; 飛錫 (錫飛) monk's travel, wanderings. (3) A surname.

V.t. (AC) (of king, God) to give, grant: 錫福 *-fur*↓; 錫命 give order, grant.

錫箔 *shirbor*, n., tin foil; paper coated with thin tin foil used as paper money for the dead.
錫器 *shirchih*, n., pewter ware.
錫福 *shir-fur*, v.t., to bless.
錫杖 *shir-jahng*, n., a monk's cane (錫 here explained as a rattling sound "錫錫" made by a metal ring).
錫紙 *shirjyy*, phr., zinc foil, aluminum foil.
錫鑞 *shirlah*, n., pewter.
錫賚 *shirlaih*, v.t., to award (by God, emperor), to bless.
錫奴 *shirnur*, n., pewter foot warmer containing hot water (also called 湯婆子).

鐲 81A.50-4

juor.

N. (*-tz*) Bracelet: 手鐲 ditto; 金鐲, 玉鐲 gold, jade bracelet.

鋤 81A.50-4

chur.

N. A hoe.

V.t. (1) To hoe (field, weeds). (2) 鋤滅 To extirpate, eradicate (evil).

鋦 81A.50-5

jyur.

N. (Chem.) curium.

鈁 81A.50-6

fang.

N. (Chem.) francium (also translit. 鍅).

鎊 81A.50-6

bahng.

N. (Rare var. of 磅) English pound (currency).

銹 81A.50-9

shiouh.

鎢 81A.50-9

wuh.

N. (Chem.) tungsten, also wolfram: 鎢鑛 tungsten ores; 鎢錳鐵鑛 wolframite.

鎢華 *wuhhuar*, n., (geol.) tungstite.

鎢酸 *wuhsuan*, n., (chem.) tungstic acid.

釣 81A.50-9

diauh.

V.i. & t. To fish, angle as sport: 釣魚翁(郎) angler (fisherman); 釣遊, 遊釣 to fish as a sport; 釣竿, 釣鉤 fishing pole, hook; 沽名釣譽 to fish for fame.

釣樟 *diauhjang* n., (bot.) silky spicebush, *Lindera sericea*.

鈞 81A.50-9

jyun.

N. (1) An anc. measure of weight equal to 30 catties: 千鈞一髮 in a most dangerous condition (very critical situation) ("thousands of catties hanging by a hair"); 雷霆萬鈞 a crushing blow, a devastating punch, an irresistible force. (2) A potter's wheel. (3) A surname.

Pron. (Court. to highly placed person) your: 鈞座 *-tzuoh*↓; 鈞安 *-an*, etc.↓.

Adj. (U.f. 均) equal, same: 鈞駟 *-syh*↓.

鈞安 *jyun-an*, phr., polite complimentary close used in letters to superiors or elders.

鈞啟 *jyuu-chii*, phr., (of letters to superiors) "to be opened by . . ."

鈞鑒 *jyuu-jiahn*, phr., polite salutation used in letters to superiors or elders ("please be graciously informed hereby").

鈞命 *jyuu-mihng*, n., (court.) your gracious commands.

鈞駟 *jyuusyh*, n., (AC) a team of four horses of the same color.

鈞座 *jyuu-tzuoh*, n., Your Excellency, Your Honor.

鈞諭 *jyuuyuh*, n., (court.) your kind letter.

鉤 81A.50-9

gou.

[Pop. 鈎]

N. (1) (*-tz*, *-'l*) A hook: 魚鉤 a fish-hook; 掛鉤 a hook on which anything can be hung; 衣鉤 a clothes rack, a coat hanger; 鉤形 hook-like; 秤鉤 the hook of a steelyard; 帳鉤 curtain hooks; 刈鉤 a sickle. (2) A barb: 倒鉤 inverted barbs; 鉤刺 barbs and thorns. (3) (AC) A hook-like sword. (4) (Callig.) a stroke with a hook. (5) A mark for checking off items in a list.

V.t. (1) To hook on: 鉤住 get hooked; 鉤出來 pull out (s.t.) with a hook; 鉤上了 be hooked up. (2) Sew with long stitches, baste; also crochet. (3) Make a searching study of: 鉤稽 *-ji*↓; 鉤索義理 search out the most essential principles; 鉤心鬬角 to maneuver for positions against rivals. (4) (Var. 勾) entice, seduce: see 勾⁴引, 勾⁴搭 92.50.

鉤黨 *gou-daang*, v.i., (AC) form cliques.

鉤爪 *goujaau*, n., talons.

鉤針 *goujen*, n., a crochet needle.
鉤稽 *gouji*, v.t., to audit (accounts); to make critical exegesis (of anc. history, etc.).
鉤扣 *goukouh*, n., a hook.
鉤兒 *gou'l*, n., a hook, a trap: 上鉤兒 be entrapped or ensnared; 鉤兒心 a crooked mind.
鉤藤 *gouterng*, n., (bot.) *Ouroupariá rhynchophylla*, a woody vine.
鉤子 *gou'tz*, n., a hook.

鈎 81A.50-9

gou.
[Pop. of 鉤↑]

鋂 81A.50-9

meei.

N. (Chem.) americium.

鐒 81A.50-9

laur.

N. (Chem.) lawrencium.

§81A.63 (金/丶)

鏜 81A.63-2

taang.

N. A military weapon, with long handle and crescent-shaped knife.

鑣 81A.63-6

biau.

N. (1) (AC) bridle, bit. (2) Currently used as var. of 鏢: 鑣客 killer, man of muscles (a swordsman, good shot, etc.); 保鑣 bodyguard, armed escort.

鈴 81A.63-8

lirng.
[Usu. printed 鈴]

N. Bell: 門鈴 doorbell; 警鈴 bell alarm; 馬鈴 bells on horses.

鈴鐺 *lirng'dang*, n., a hand bell, small rattling bells.
鈴鐸 *lirngduor*, n., bells on ends of temple roofs.
鈴鈴 *lirnglirng*, n., (AC) rumble (of earthquake, carts, etc.).

鐎 81A.63-9

jiau.

N. (AC) a cooking vessel with a handle.

§81A.70 (金/乚)

鈍 81A.70-1

duhn.

Adj. (1) Blunt (knife): 鈍刀慢剮 persecute slowly, like cutting skin with blunt knife. (2) Unsuccessful: 成敗利鈍 success or failure. (3) Mentally slow, stupid: 遲鈍, 愚鈍, 魯鈍, 頑鈍 slow to learn, dull-witted, thick-skulled.

鈍根 *duhngen*, n., (Budd. & LL) a dull spirit, incapabable of understanding, low intelligence.
鈍角 *duhnjiaau*, n., (geom.) obtuse angle.

銑 81A.70-1

shiaan.

N. 銑鐵 cast iron, wrought iron.

鐃 81A.70-1

naur.

N. A kind of musical instrument, hand bells: 鐃鈸 cymbals.

V.t. (Interch. 撓) (AC) disturb: 萬物無足以鐃心者 nothing can disturb the serenity of his mind.

鐃歌 *naurge*, n., an anc. military song.
鐃鼓 *naurgur*, n., a kind of military drum.

銠 81A.70-1

laau.

N. (Chem.) rhodium.

銧 81A.70-2

guang.

N. (Chem.) radium (now usu. called 鐳).

銚 81A.70-2

yaur (*diauh).

N. (1) (AC) a farm implement. (2) (**diauh*) A small cooking pan with handle and sprout: 銚子. (3) A surname.

釓 81A.70-2

gar.

N. (Chem.) gadolinium.

鈚 81A.70-2

beei.

N. (Chem.) berkelium.

釔 81A.70-3

yii.

N. (Chem.) yttrium.

釩 81A.70-4

farn.

N. (Chem.) vanadium.

鈀 81A.70-5

baa.

N. (Chem.) palladium.

鈮 81A.70-5

nir.

N. (Chem.) niobium (also translit. 鈳).

鈧 81A.70-6

keng.

N. (Chem.) scandium.

鉈 81A.70-6

ta.

N. (Chem.) thallium.

銃 81A.70-6

chuhng.

N. Anc. cannon.

鏡 81A.70-6

jihng.

N. (1) A looking glass, a mirror: 穿衣鏡 a dressing glass; 反射鏡 a reflector; 照照鏡子 look in the mirror; 面鏡 a face mirror; 鏡花水月 (fig.) a mirage, insubstantial objects ("flowers in a mirror and the moon's reflection in water"). (2) A piece of glass: 鏡片 *-piahn*↓; 眼鏡 eyeglasses, spectacles; 太陽鏡 sunglasses; 顯微鏡 a microscope; 望遠鏡 a telescope; 透鏡 a camera lens; 玻璃鏡 a glass mirror; 放大鏡 a magnifier, a magnifying glass; 潛望鏡 a periscope; 三稜鏡 a prism. (3) What serves as an example or warning: 鏡監 *-jiahn*↓; 鏡戒 *-jieh*↓.

鏡支兒 *jihngje'l*, n., a woman's dressing case with a propped-up mirror.

鏡監 *jihngjiahn*, n., an example to be followed or avoided.

鏡戒 *jihngjieh*, n., ditto.

鏡框 *jihngkuahng*, n., a picture frame.

鏡奩 *jihngliarn*, n., a woman's dressing case.

鏡面呢 *jihngmiahnnir*, n., treated, shining woolen.

鏡片 *jihngpiahn*, n., a piece of glass, a lens.

鏡箱 *jihngshiang*, n., see *-liarn*↑.

鏡匣 *jihngshiar*, n., ditto.

鏡臺 *jihngtair*, n., a dressing table.

鏡頭 *jihngtour*, n., (1) a camera lens; (2) a photographic shot, a sequence in motion-picture film.

鏡子 *jihngtz*, n., (1) a mirror; (2) a pair of spectacles.

鑹 81A.70-6

tsuahn (**tsuan*).

N. (1) (**tsuan*) Poker for breaking ice: 冰鑹. (2) (AC) a small spear.

銳 81A.70-8

rueih.

Adj. (1) Sharp, pointed, acute: 尖銳 keen-edged, razor-sharp; 銳利 sharp-edged, cutting; 銳眼 sharp-eyed, keen-sighted; 銳而不挫 so sharp that it cannot be blunted; 口銳 sharp-tongued; 失銳 disheartened, crestfallen; 銳敏 sharp-witted; 銳角 *-jiaau*↓. (2) Skilled, well-trained: 精銳 crack troops; 銳騎 fast moving cavalry; 銳師 hard-hitting troops; 銳兵 well-trained soldiers; 銳士 redoubtable warriors. (3) Tapering off at the top. (4) Quick, rapid, fast: 其進銳者其退速 a headlong start often ends in a

鋭 銫 鉋 鑱 鑞 鐵

hasty retreat.

鋭氣 *rueihchih(-'chi)*, n., dauntless courage, audacity, fortitude.

鋭髮 *rueih-faa*, n., tufts of hair hanging down from the temples.

鋭鼓 *rueihguu*, n., a musical instrument of the Yao (猺) tribe.

鋭角 *rueih-jiaau*, n., (math.) an acute angle.

鋭志 *rueih-jyh*, n., firm determination.

銫 81A.70–9

seh.

N. (Chem.) cesium.

鉋 81A.70–9

bauh.

[Var. 鑤; cf. 刨]

N. Carpenter's plane.

V.t. (1) To plane off: 鉋削 slice off and make smooth by planing; 鉋木頭 to slice wood. (2) Dig the ground, as with hoof: 鉋地.

鉋牀 *bauhchuarng*, n., lathe for planing.

鉋凳 *bauhdehng*, n., bench for planing.

鉋花 *bauh-hua*, n., shavings.

鑱 81A.70–9

charn.

N. A trowel, small shovel.

鑱斧 *charnfuu*, n., hoe for weeding.

鑱頭 *charn'tou*, n., a coulter for ploughing.

鑞 81A.70–9

lah.

N. Hard tin.

鑞箔 *lahbor*, n., tin foil for making paper money for the dead.

鑞鎗頭 *lahchiangtour*, n., a person putting on a bold front.

§ 81A.71 (金/弋)

鐵 81A.71–1

tiee.

[Pop. 鉄]

N. Iron: 鐵工廠 iron works; 鐵橋 steel bridge; 鐵搭 (*-ta*) a kind of farm rake; 鐵條 iron bar, rod iron; 鐵葉 sheet iron; 鐵管 iron-piping; 鐵釘 iron nail; 鐵索 iron chains; 鐵尺 iron staff, a weapon; 鐵器 ironware (see compp.); 鐵塔 iron pagoda; 巴黎鐵塔 Eiffel Tower; 鐵硯磨穿 (fig.) long years of persistence ("grind a hole in an iron slab"); 鐵杵磨針 ditto ("grind an iron pestle into a needle"); 鐵中錚錚 (allu.) true caliber, the distinguished among men; 鐵血主義 blood-and-iron policy; 白鐵, 洋鐵 tin-plates; 熟鐵 wrought iron; 生鐵 cast iron; 廢鐵 scrap iron.

Adj. (1) Iron grey: 鐵驄 black horse. (2) Strong, solid as iron: 鐵人, 鐵漢 *-rern, -hahn*↓; 鐵石人, 鐵石心腸 heart of steel, unmoved by feeling; 鐵面無私 unmoved by personal appeals, without fear or favor; 鐵口, 鐵嘴 (of arguer, fortuneteller) who is sure he is right; 鐵的事實 irrefutable fact, see 鐵證 *-jehng*↓; 鐵則 severe rules and regulations; 鐵主意 iron determination; 鐵門檻, 鐵門限 very rigid restrictions (of convent, prison, etc.).

鐵案 *tiee-ahn*, n., irrevocable, established case of fact.

鐵板 *tierbaan*, n., (1) sheet iron; (2) pair of metallic claps for marking rhythm; 鐵板快書, 鐵板大鼓 monologue storytelling with such claps; (3) 鐵板牛扒 broiled steak.

鐵餅 *tierbiing*, n., (sports) discus.

鐵布衫 *tieebuh-shan*, n., (Chin. boxing) a form of movement warding off all attacks.

鐵雀兒 *tierchiaau'l*, n., fried sparrow.

鐵器 *tieechih*, n., ironware; 鐵器店 hardware shop.

鐵青 *tieeching*, adj., metallic green, metal grey.

鐵球 *tiee-chiour*, n., (sports) shot for putting.

鐵窗 *tieechuang*, n., prison bars: 鐵窗風味 taste of prison life.

鐵泉 *tieechyuarn*, n., (geol.) a chalybeate spring.

鐵道 *tieedauh*, n., railroad (also 鐵路 *-luh*↓).

鐵定 *tieedihng*, adj., ironclad (evidence, etc.), fixed, irrevocable.

鐵笛 *tiee-dir*, n., iron flute.

鐵肺 *tiee-feih*, n., iron lungs.

鐵觀音 *tieeguanyin*, n., a species of Chin. tea.

鐵軌 *tiergueei*, n., the rails of railroad.

鐵公雞 *tieegungji*, n., (sl.) a man who will not lift a finger to help.

鐵漢 *tieerhahn*, n., a very powerfully built man.

鐵灰 *tieehuei*, adj., iron-grey color.

鐵證 *tieejehng*, n., ironclad evidence, irrefutable proof.

鐵甲 *tierjiaa*, n., armor; 鐵甲船 an ironclad ship; 鐵甲車 armored car, also tank.

鐵價 *tiee-jiah*, n., one-price system: 鐵價不二.

鐵匠 *tieejiahng*, n., blacksmith.

鐵蕉 *tiee-jiau*, n., (bot.) sago cycad, *Cycas revoluta* (also known as 鳳尾松).

鐵筋土 *tieejin-tuu*, n., reinforced concrete (now usu. called 鋼骨水泥).

鐵酒 *tier-jioou*, n., iron lotion, a tonic.

鐵券 *tiee-jyuahn*, n., anciently inscribed metal pledge of emperor conferring special privi-

leges on deserving ministers.
鐵軍 *tiee-jyun*, n., "iron army," invincible or tough army unit.
鐵礦 *tiee-kuahng*, n., iron mine: 鐵礦石 iron ores.
鐵鍊 *tiee-liahn*, n., iron chains.
鐵力 *tiee-lih*, n., strength of iron.
鐵路 *tieeluh*, n., railroad.
鐵馬 *tiee-maa*, n., (1) crack troops; (2) tinkling metal slips on end of temple roofs; (3) (sl.) railroad locomotive; (4) (sl.) bicycle.
鐵幕 *tiee-muh*, n., the iron curtain.
鐵皮 *tiee-pir*, n., iron hoops; iron-covered.
鐵人 *tiee-rern*, n., a man of great physical strength.
鐵掃帚 *tiee-sauhjoou*, n., (bot.) a kind of rush, *Lespedeza juncea.*
鐵砂 *tiee-sha*[1], n., iron filings.
鐵紗 *tiee-sha*[2], n., wire screen.
鐵線 *tiee-shiahn*, n., wire; 鐵線蓮 (bot.) cream clematis, *Clematis florida.*
鐵樹 *tiee-shuh*, n., see *-jiau*↑; 鐵樹生花 an impossibility.
鐵算盤 *tiee-suahnparn*, n., a trick for swindling money.
鐵絲 *tiee-sy*, n., wire; 鐵絲網 (barbed) wire entanglements.
鐵蹄 *tiee-tir*, n., rule of force.
鐵桶 *tier-tuung*, n., iron bucket; (fig.) impregnable city wall.

鉞 81A.71-7

yueh.

N. A halberd, battle-axe.

錢 81A.71-7

chiarn.

N. (1) Money, coins: 錢庫 bank vault; 錢櫃 cash counter or cabinet, also cashier; 錢市 the money market; 錢癖 miserly habit, love of money; 錢荒 shortage of supply of money; 金錢 coins or money in gen.; 現錢 cash; 付錢 pay cash; 銅錢 copper coins; 錢財 *-tsair*↓; 有錢 has money, rich; 沒錢 short of money, poor; 錢能通神, 錢可使鬼 (推磨) money talks (can bedevil the devil himself); 視錢如命 worship money ("like one's life"); 花大錢, 省小錢 penny-wise and pound-foolish. (2) One tenth of an ounce. (3) A surname.
錢板兒 *chiarnbaa'l*, n., (1) formerly, a wooden board with grooves for keeping cash; (2) a washing board.
錢包 *chiarnbau*, n., a wallet, a purse.
錢幣 *chiarnbih*, n., currency; money: 錢幣貶値 devaluation of currency (see 幣 22.22).
錢衩子 *chiarnchaatz*, n., see *-da-'lian, -datz*↓.
錢串(兒) *chiarnchuahn(-chuah'l)*, n., formerly, a string of cash (in units of 100, or 1000), the string running through the square holes in cash.
錢褡褳(兒) *chiarn-da-'lian(--lia'l)*, n., a cloth bag for coins; 錢褡子 *-datz*, ditto.
錢穀 *chiarnguu*, n., levies in kind and money; 錢穀師爺 formerly, magistrate's assistant in charge of taxes.
錢幌子 *chiarn huaangtz*, n., formerly, shop sign of money shop in the form of a string of big coins.
錢莊 *chiarnjuang*, n., money shop; old-style local bank.
錢兒癬 *chiarn'l-shyuaan*, n., ringworm.
錢糧 *chiarnliarng*, n., levies of grain crops, usu. paid in money.
錢龍 *chiarnlurng*, n., (1) a string of cash, see *-chuahn*↑; (2) (zoo.) a millepede.
錢盤兒 *chiarnpaa'l*, n., formerly, rate of exchange of silver dollars in terms of copper coins.
錢票兒 *chiarnpiauh'l*, n., formerly, paper money.
錢鋪 *chiarnpuh*, n., a money exchange shop.
錢樹子 *chiarn shuhtz*, n., a pop. singsong girl who brings in a lot of money to the madam.
錢財 *chiarntsair*, n., money, riches, wealth.
錢文 *chiarnween*, n., a piece of copper cash.
錢引 *chiarnyiin*, n., (MC) paper money in Suhng Dyn.

鋱 81A.71-7

teh.

N. (Chem.) terbium.

鍼 81A.71-7

jen.

[Var. 針 81A.10]

鍼言 *jenyarn*, n., (1) maxims; (2) Proverbs (a book of the Bible).

鏚 81A.71-7

chih.

N. (AC) battle-axe.

鋨 81A.71-9

er.

N. (Chem.) osmium.

鐵 鉞 錢 鋱 鍼 鏚 鋨

亅	小	⺊	十	土	ナ	卄	乚	丨	一	丁	フ	口	区	冈	ㄱ	厂	尸	亠	广	宀	丶	乚	弋	心	八	人	乂	乛	乛	丿	㇗	く
00	01	02	10	11	12	20	21	22	30	31	32	40	41	42	50	51	52	60	61	62	63	70	71	72	80	81	82	83	90	91	92	93

§81A.72 (金/心)

鑢 81A.72–2

lyuh.

N. A file, rasp.

V.t. To file even, to polish with rasp.

鍶 81A.72–4

sy.

N. (Chem.) strontium.

鐿 81A.72–6

yih.

N. (Chem.) ytterbium.

鉍 81A.72–6

bih.

N. (Chem.) bismuth.

§81A.80 (金/八)

鑽 81A.80–1

tzuan (**tzuahn*, **tzuaan*).

N. (**tzuahn*) (1) A drill, an awl: 鑽子 ditto; 鑽頭 *-'tou* ↓; 手鑽 a hand drill; 電鑽 an electric drill. (2) Diamond(s): 鑽石 *-shyr*, 鑽戒 *-jieh* ↓; 金鋼鑽 a diamond.

V.i. & t. (1) (Also **tzuaan*) to drill, bore: 鑽孔 drill (bore) a hole; 鑽木取火 bore wood to get fire; 鑽燧取火 to strike a flint to produce sparks. (2) Rely upon personal influence to get what one wants: 鑽營 *-'yirng* ↓; 鑽謀 *-mour* ↓; 鑽頭覓縫兒 leave no stone unturned to get a job through personal pulls; 鑽天入地 search for an opening (a job) for oneself by all possible means ("by going up to heaven or down to hell"). (3) Make a penetrating study of: 鑽研 *-yarn* ↓. (4) Penetrate, pierce, go through: 鑽山洞 (of a train) pass through a tunnel; 鑽過去 crawl (go) through; 鑽牛犄角 get oneself into a dead end; 鑽牛角尖 ditto; 鑽狗洞 do evil, lead a wicked life, (fig.) toady to the rich (powerful, influential). (5) (=躦) Make a forward or upward movement.

鑽機 *tzuan'ji*, v.i., (1) make use of personal pulls; (2) delve into a subject.

鑽戒 *tzuahnjieh*, n., a diamond ring.

鑽灼 *tzuanjuor*, (1) n., an ancient method of divination; (2) v.t., (=鑽研 *-yarn* ↓).

鑽門子 *tzuan-merntz*, v.i., to worm one's way into s.o.'s favor.

鑽謀 *tzuan-mour*, v.t., try hard to get (a job) through personal pulls.

鑽石 **tzuahnshyr*, n., diamond(s).

鑽頭 **tzuahn'tou*, n., an auger, a borer.

鑽仰 *tzuanyaang*, v.i., (LL) to search for the truth and hold fast to it.

鑽研 *tzuanyarn*, v.t., delve into (books, the past).

鑽營 *tzuan'yirng*, v.t., see *-mour* ↑.

鎮 81A.80–2

jehn.

N. (1) A town, a hamlet, a trading center: 市鎮 village or town, with marketing facilities; 鄉鎮 a village settlement or village in gen.; 鎮上人 townsfolk, village folk. (2) A commander (in Mirng and Ching Dyns.); a division (in army system of late 19th cen.).

V.t. (1) To suppress, keep down or keep in order: 鎮痛 *-tuhng* ↓; 鎮守 *-shoou* ↓; 鎮紙 *-jyy* ↓. (2); To suppress demons by magic: 鎮鬼 to shut up demon (as in pagoda basement); 鎮物 *-wuh* ↓. (3) To cool by ice: 冰鎮.

Adj. Calm, settled: 鎮定 *-dihng* ↓; 鎮日 (related 整) *-ryh* ↓.

鎮定 *jehndihng*, v.t. & adj., to calm (mind); be calm, settled.

鎮撫 *jehnfuu*, v.t., to pacify (rebellious district).

鎮公所 *jehngungsuoo*, n., township office, self-government office of a *jehn* (subdivision of city or village).

鎮長 *jehnjaang*, n., township chief, chief of *jehn* (see N. 1 ↑).

鎮靜 *jehnjihng*, adj., calm, unruffled despite crisis; 鎮靜劑 sedatives or tranquilizer.

鎮紙 *jehnjyy*, n., a paperweight; a brass frame for keeping paper flat during writing.

鎮日 *jehnryh*, adv., the whole day (also 整日).

鎮守 *jehnshoou*, v.t., to guard (city, region); 鎮守使 formerly, Defense Commissioner.

鎮痛 *jehn-tuhng*, v.i. to relieve pain; 鎮痛劑 sedative.

鎮物 *jehn-wuh*, n., (Taoist magic) object containing a curse for magical suppression of evil spirit.

鎮壓 *jehnya*, v.t., to suppress (riot, rebellion).

鎖 81A.80–2

suoo.

N. (1) (*-tz*) A lock: 鎖頭 *-'tour* ↓.

(2) Fetters, shackles, chain: 鍊鎖 *-liahn* ↓.

V.t. (1) To lock up: 鎖門 lock the door; 鎖上了 is already locked; 封鎖軍港 blockade enemy's naval base; 緘鎖 lock up (house) and place under seal. (2) To chain up (convict): 拘鎖 ditto; 鎖禁 to lock up (person). (3) To knit (eyebrows): 鎖眉(頭). (4) (Poet.) to envelop (in mist, cloud): 寒煙鎖隄 the mist envelops the bank.

鎖簧 *suoohuarng*, n., the wards (spring metals) of a lock.
鎖鍊(兒)(子) *suooliahn(-liah'l)(tz)*, n., iron chain (also wr. 鎖鏈).
鎖鐐 *suooliauh*, n., chain and shackles.
鎖吶 *suoo(')nah*, n., a Turkish flute (also wr. 哨吶).
鎖頭 *suoo'tour*, n., a lock.
鎖子 *suootz*, n., (1) a jade bracelet; (2) 鎖子花邊 chain pattern embroidery or braid; 鎖子甲 chain armor.
鎖陰 *suooyin*, n., an organic abnormality in woman preventing intercourse.
鎖鑰 *suooyueh*, n., a key; (fig.) strategic point of defense.

鐨 81A.80-2

feih.

N. (Chem.) fermium.

鋇 81A.80-4

beih.

N. (Chem.) barium.

鑌 81A.80-6

bin.

鑌鐵 *bintiee*, n., high quality iron.

鑛 81A.80-6

kuahng.

[Var. of 礦 31B.80]

鑕 81A.80-9

jyh.

N. (AC) case for executioner's axe.

§ 81A.81 (金/人)

鍥 81A.81-1

chieh.

N. A sickle.

V.t. To chisel, carve, cut: 鍥其軸 (AC) hack away the cart axle; 鍥而不舍 phr., (AC) to chisel incessantly—(fig.) to stick to s.t. with persistence.

鍥薄 *chiehbor*, adj., (AC var. of 刻薄) mean, vindictive.

銕 81A.81-1

tiee.

[Anc. var. of 鐵 81A.71]

鈦 81A.81-1

taih.

N. (Chem.) titanium.

鈇 81A.81-1

fu.

N. (AC) axe.

鈇鑕(質) *fujyh*, n., anc. instrument for cutting the body of the condemned in two at the waist.
鈇鉞 *fuyueih*, n., (AC) hatchet and axe; punishments by bodily mutilation.

鉄 81A.81-1

tiee.

[Pop. of 鐵 81A.71]

鋏 81A.81-1

jiar.

N. (1) Pincers, tongs. (2) A sword, dagger or its hilt.

鏷 81A.81-2

pur.

N. Wrought iron.

鏃 鍈 欽 鈥 鍬 鈸 釵 鑊 鈹 釵 鏝 鋟 鉸

鏃 81A.81–6

tzur (also *tsuh*).

N. An arrowhead: 矢鏃, 箭鏃 ditto.

Adj. (1) Fast-flying, swift (arrows). (2) 鏃新 brand-new.

鎂 81A.81–8

meei.

N. (Chem.) magnesium; 氯化鎂 magnesium chloride; 氧化鎂 magnesium oxide; 氫氧化鎂 magnesium hydroxide; 碳酸化鎂 magnesium carbonate; 硫酸鎂 magnesium sulphate.

欽 81A.81–9

chin.

V.t. To admire, respect: 欽佩, 欽敬, 欽仰 *-peih*, *-jihng*, *-yaang*↓.

Adj. & adv. (1) His Majesty's, imperial, by imperial order, command, etc.: 欽賜, 欽命, 欽定 granted, ordered, approved by His Majesty; 欽派, 欽頒 appointed, awarded by His Majesty; 欽差 *-chai*↓; 欽此 formula concluding edict. (2) (LL) respectfully: 欽佇, 欽望 respectfully waiting, hoping. (3) Respectfully to emperor: 欽遵 respectfully obey; 欽奉 respectfully receive.

欽差 *chinchai*, n., formerly, an imperial envoy, ambassador (also 欽差大臣).
欽崇 *chinchurng*, v.t. & n., adore (-ation).
欽敬 *chinjihng*, v.t., to admire, respect.
欽遲 *chinjyh*, v.t., (LL) admire.
欽佩 *chinpeih*, v.t., admire, esteem, value (s.o.'s accomplishment).
欽天監 *chintianjiahn*, n., formerly, Imperial Board of Astronomy; its director.
欽仰 *chinyaang*, v.t., admire (esp. from station below), honor, esteem (person, his reputation).

鈥 81A.81–9

huoo.

N. (Chem.) holmium.

鍬 81A.81–9

chiau.
[Var. of 鍫 90.30]

§81A.82 (金/乂)

鈸 81A.82–1

bar (*bor*).

N. Cymbals.

鈙 81A.82–2

aih.

N. (Chem.) astatine (also translit. 砈).

鑊 81A.82–2

huoh.

N. Caldron: 鼎鑊 (AC) punishment by boiling alive.

鈹 81A.82–2

pih.

N. (Chem.) beryllium.

釵 81A.82–3

chai.

N. Hair decorations, hairpin: 金釵, 玉釵 gold, jade hairpin; 釵光鬢影 glistening hair decorations.

鏝 81A.82–4

mahn.

N. Spade for applying plaster.

鋟 81A.82–5

chian (also *chiin*).

V.t. To carve on block: 鋟板 to carve wood block for printing.

鉸 81A.82–6

jiaau.

N. A pair of scissors.

V.t. (1) To cut with scissors. (2) Adorn with gold.

鉸刀 *jiaaudau*, n., (formerly, another name for) scissors.
鉸鍊 *jiaauliahn*, n., a hinge fixed on door, gate or lid.

鍍 81A.82-6

duh.

V.t. Electroplate: 鍍金 gilt, gold-plated; 鍍銀 silver-plated; 電鍍 electroplated.

鎩 81A.82-8

sha.

N. (AC) a long spear: 鎩羽 (LL) clipped wings, (fig.) downcast.

鍰 81A.82-9

huarn.

N. (1) Anc. measure of weight. (2) Money: 罰鍰 fine or be fined silver or cash.

鑀 81A.82-9

aih.

N. (Chem.) einsteinium.

鍛 81A.82-9

duahn.
[Var. 煅]

V.t. To forge (metal), see 鍛鍊 *-liahn*↓.

鍛鍊 *duahnliahn*, v.t., to forge (metal): 鍛鍊品行 to form and train character through experience (as blacksmith fires and shapes iron); 鍛鍊身體 train body.

鍛鐵 *duahntiee*, n., wrought iron.

§ 81A.83 (金/〜)

鏈 81A.83-1

liahn.
[Cf. 鍊]

N. (*-tz*, *'l*) (1) A chain of metal: 鐵鏈, 鎖鏈 iron chain; 金鏈 gold chain; 脖鏈兒 necklace; 鏈條 a chain. (2) (Geol.) lead ore.

V.t. To chain, enchain: 鏈上他 have him enchained; 鏈着, 鏈住 chained on.

鏈黴素 *liahnmeirsuh*, n., (med.) streptomycin.

鍵 81A.83-2

jiahn.

N. (1) A door bolt, the bolt of a Chin. lock: 下鍵 draw in the bolt; 鍵閉 to lock up; 管鍵 the catch of a lock; 啓鍵 to open the lock; 關鍵 key to a situation, a turning point, a crisis. (2) One of the keys on a piano keyboard: 鍵盤 piano or typewriter keyboard.

鏇 81A.83-6

shyuahn.
[Related 旋 60S.83]

N. (1) See 鏇子 *-tz*, 鏇鍋兒 *-guo'l* ↓. (2) A copper basin with upright sides.

V.t. (1) To cut wood by rotating it against a knife. (2) To warm wine with 鏇子 *-tz*↓. (3) To stir, see 鏇粉 *-feen*↓.

鏇粉 *shyuahnfeen*, n., noodle-like strips made of flour of green peas (菉豆) by stirring mixture in boiling water and cooling it (also 粉皮).

鏇鍋兒 *shyuahnguo'l*, n., vessel for warming wine by immersing pot in hot water.

鏇子 *shyuahntz*, n., ditto.

錠 81A.83-6

dihng.

N. adjunct. A cake: 一錠墨 an ink cake, ink slab.

N. (1) Ingot: 金錠, 銀錠 gold, silver ingot; 一錠銀子 a small ingot of silver, about 10 taels; 紙錠 tin foil or paper ingot burned for use of the dead. (2) Cake-shaped object: 錠硃 cake of vermilion ink; 粉錠 cake of face powder; cake of medicine to be rubbed, like 紫金錠. (3) An anc. food vessel with legs.

鋌 81A.83-9

tiing.

N. (1) Ingot: 黃金十鋌 ten bars of gold. (2) (AC) a big arrow; arrowhead.

V.i. Hurry forward: 鋌而走險 (oft. wr. 挺) become reckless in desperation, like animal at bay.

鎚 81A.83-9

chueir.
[Interch. 錘 81A.11]

§ 81A.91 (金/ノ)

鈔 81A.91-2

chau.

N. (Also *chauh*) paper money, money in gen.: 鈔票 *-piauh*↓; 美鈔 American dollar; 金鈔 gold and U.S. dollars; 破鈔 spend money.

V.t. (Interch. 抄) to copy.

鈔關 *chauguan*, n., formerly, tax bureau.
鈔票 *chaupiauh*, n., dollar bill; paper money of any kind.
鈔引 *chauyiin*, n., (Suhng Dyn.) paper money.

釤 81A.91-9

san.

N. (Chem.) samarium.

§ 81A.93 (金/く)

鎡 81A.93-2

tzy.

N. 鎡基 (AC) a farm implement, a plough.

鏤 81A.93-2

louh.

N. (1) Steel or iron plates used for engraving or carving. (2) A boiler. (3) A surname.

V.t. Engrave, carve, tattoo: 鏤版 to cut a block for printing; 鏤骨銘心 wholeheartedly grateful to (s.o.); 鏤金錯采 gilt and colored, elegant and refined; 鏤身 tattoo.

鏹 81A.93-5

chiaang.

N. A string of copper coins (also wr. 繈).

鏹水 *chiaangshueei*, n., sulphuric acid (short for 硝鏹水).

鍅 81A.93-6

faa.

N. (Chem.) francium (also translit. 鈁).

銩 81A.93-9

diou.

N. (Chem.) thulium.

釹 81A.93-9

nyuu.

N. (Chem.) neodymium.

SECTION 81B

§ 81B.00 (食/丿)

餑 81B.00-1

bo.

餑餑 *bo'bo*, n., a kind of small roll made of wheat or corn flour.

餺 81B.00-1

bor.

餺飥 *bortuo*, (MC) a kind of cake (also wr. 餢飥, 不托).

§ 81B.01 (食/小)

餗 81B.01-1

suh.

N. (AC) food in a tripod.

餜 81B.01-4

guoo.

N. A kind of cake, made with sesame seeds (麻花兒).

餘 81B.01-8

yur.

N. (1) A surname. (2) Surplus, leftover: 有餘 enough and to spare; 一百零餘 a hundred and over; 盈餘 surplus, net profit; 多餘 surplus; 其餘 the rest. (3) Leftover time: 研討之餘 the time left after studies; 業餘 after office hours, hobby, see *-shihng* ↓.

Adj. Remaining, leftover, spread-over, carried over: 餘音 lingering sound, tone, see compp. ↓.

餘波 *yur-bo*, n., the aftermath.
餘切 *yur-chie*, n., (math.) cotangent.
餘慶 *yur-chihng*, n., inherited ancestral blessing.
餘喘 *yur-chuaan*, n., dying breaths; panting after a scare.
餘齒 *yur-chyy*, n., see *-niarn* ↓.
餘黨 *yur-daang*, n., remnants of a political party or defeated bandits.
餘地 *yur-dih*, n., (1) spare lot or land; (2) 不留餘地 to push a person too far; 留餘地 spare some room for future contacts.
餘額 *yur-er*, n., available sum unused or vacancies not taken up.
餘風 *yur-feng*, n., influence left by person.
餘富 *yur-fuh* (*-fu*), adj., see *-yuh* ↓.
餘割 *yur-ger*, n., (math.) cosecant.
餘光 *yur-guang*, n., reflected glory, honor (from friend); bounty that costs the owner nothing.
餘暉 *yur-huei*, n., sunset light; reflected light.
餘弧 *yur-huu*, n., (math.) complement of an arc.
餘角 *yur-jiaau*, n., (math.) complement of an angle.
餘燼 *yur-jihn*, n., burnt ashes, (fig.) remnant troops.
餘款 *yur-kuaan*, n., leftover sum.
餘力 *yur-lih*[1], n., leftover strength or energy: 不留餘力 spare no effort or energy.
餘利 *yur-lih*[2], n., net profit; extra profit.
餘瀝 *yur-lih*[3], n., dregs in the cup; (fig.) friend's boon or kindness: 得霑餘瀝 share your boon.
餘論 *yur-luhn*, n., additional comments.
餘年 *yur-niarn*, n., the remaining years of one's life.
餘剩 *yur-shehng*, n., remainder.
餘生 *yur-sheng*, n., remaining years.
餘暇 *yur-shiar*, n., leisure time, free time.
餘興 *yur-shihng*, n., program for amusements after meeting; form of relaxation after work.
餘數 *yur-shuh*, n., (math.) remainder after subtraction; leftover number after division.
餘事 *yur-shyh*, n., (1) less important details of business: 猶其餘事; (2) unfinished business: 餘事未了.
餘弦 *yur-shyuarn*, n., (math.) cosine.
餘蓄 *yur-shyuh*, n., personal savings.
餘外 *yur-waih*, adj. & n., additional (items).
餘蔭 *yur-yihn*, n., inherited ancestral protection or benefit.
餘裕 *yur-yuh*, adj., ample (means).

§ 81B.02 (食/⺊)

餵 81B.02–4

weih.

[Var. of 餧]

V.t. To feed (chicken, dogs): 餵奶 to nurse (baby) with milk; 餵飽 be fed full.

餦 81B.02–5

jang.

N. (AC) dried sweetmeat: 餦餭 ditto.

§ 81B.10 (食/十)

餌 81B.10–3

eel.

N. (1) (Lit. & fig.) a bait for fish. (2) Pastry, food: 餅餌 cakes and sweets; 果餌 candies and cakes; 藥餌 tonics, drugs in gen.

V.t. (1) To bait (enemy), to entice (person). (2) (AC) to eat.

§ 81B.11 (食/土)

饉 81B.11

jiin (also *jihng*).

N. A year or season of dearth: 饑饉 crop failure, famine.

飪 81B.11–9

rehn.

V.i. Prepare food: 烹飪 to cook food, the art of cooking.

§ 81B.20 (食/卄)

餅 81B.20–8

biing.

N. (1) Cake, pastry, any of various

餅 餂 餡 餑 飦 飾 餖 饘 饈 饝 館

pastry made chiefly of flour, such as 油餅 fried wheat cake; 烙餅 baked wheat cake, etc. (2) Used of a round, flat object: 銀餅 (now rare) silver dollar; 壓成肉餅 crushed into a hamburger.

餅鐺 *biingcheng*, n., a large, flat pan used for roasting cakes.
餅餌 *birng-eel*, n., sweetmeats in general.
餅乾 *biinggan*, n., biscuits; also wr. 干.
餅金 *biingjin*, n., silver dollar; (MC) servants' tips.
餅子 *biingtz*, n., (1) pastry, esp. a kind of hard cake, made of flour and corn; (2) (dial.) a stubborn person.
餅銀 *biingyirn*, n., silver dollar (now rare).

§ 81B.21 (食/匕)

餂 81B.21-2

duoh.

N. 餶餂 former name for ravioli, dumpling.

餡 81B.21-9

shiahn.

N. (*-tz*) Stuffing (of a bun, ravioli, etc.).

§ 81B.22 (食/丨)

餑 81B.22-3

bor.

[Var. of 餺 81B.00]

飦 81B.22-6

fahn.

[Var. of 飯 81B.82]

飾 81B.22-9

shyh.

N. Decorations (on hair, body, carriage, style): 服飾 costume, style of dress; 外飾 external appearance.

V.t. (1) To decorate, polish, improve appearance: 修飾 to polish (writing, conduct), renovate (building), refurbish (furniture); 裝飾 to dress up, also pretend. (2) To cover up, hide (blemishes): 掩飾, 粉飾 cover up, whitewash (personal record); 文過飾非 cover up and whitewash mistakes; 飾詞, 飾説 *-tsyr*, *-shuo* ↓.

飾件兒 *shyhjiaa'l*, n., sundries, accessories (=什件兒).
飾終 *shyh-jung*, phr., to give proper burial ceremony.
飾説 *shyhshuo*, n., see *-tsyr* ↓.
飾詞 *shyhtsyr*, (1) n., purely decorative phrr.; (2) v. i., to invent story or excuse.
飾僞 *shyhweih*, v. i., to pretend.
飾物 *shyhwuh*, n., decorative items.

§ 81B.30 (食/一)

餖 81B.30-3

douh.

餖飣 *douhdihng*, n., various pastries arranged on altar; verbiage, piling up of phrr. for show.

饘 81B.30-6

jan.

N. Thick gruel: 饘粥 gruel in gen.

饈 81B.30-8

shiou.

N. Meals: 嘉饈 nice meals.

V.t. (AC) to offer.

§ 81B.40 (食/口)

饝 81B.40-6

mor.

饝饝 *mor'mo*, n., (Peking) Chinese bun (also wr. 饃).

館 81B.40-6

guaan.

[Interch. 舘]

N. (1) A public resort, private dwelling, establishment: 旅館 a hotel; 餐館, 飯館, 菜館 restaurant; 酒館 a bar, wine shop; 茶館 teahouse; 館子 *-'tz* ↓; 咖啡館 a coffee shop; 照相館 photography studio; 館兒 a place where food, tea, or wine is served; 館舍 *-sheh* ↓; 別館 a villa, country house; 公館 (court.) a private dwelling house; 館驛 *-yih* ↓; 會館 a guildhall, a club for members of a clan or district. (2) A public office or building: 國史館 the Bureau of National History; 資料館 archives; 博物館 museum; 圖書館 library; 科學館 science hall; 大使館 embassy; (總) 領事館 consulate (-general). (3) Formerly, a private school: 蒙館 formerly, a primary school; 家館 a family school; 就館 accept a teaching job in a private school; 館金 *-jin* ↓.

館地 *guaandih*, n., a tutor's post.
館金 *guaan-jin*, n., tutor's salary.
館舍 *guaansheh*, n., hostel.
館子 *guaan'tz*, n., a restaurant, an inn: 上館子, 下館子, 吃館子 dine in a restaurant.
館驛 *guaanyih*, n., (AC) a post house.

饍 81B.40–8

shahn.
[Var. of 膳 42A.40]

餂 81B.40–9

tiaan.

V.t. (AC) to lure or bait with sweet words.

飴 81B.40–9

yir.

N. Sweetmeats.

§ 81B.41 (食/因)

餾 81B.41–9

liouh.

V.t. To reheat, heat up (also wr. 溜): 把涼飯餾一餾 heat up the cold rice; 餾包子 heat up buns by steaming.

§ 81B.42 (食/冈)

餔 81B.42–1

bu (**buh*).

N. (LL) late afternoon, supper time: 餔時 (var. of 晡 40A.42).

V.t. & i. (1) (LL) to eat: 餔餟 eat and drink. (2) (**buh*) To feed (person), as var. of 哺 40A.42.

餬 81B.42–1

hur.

N. Gruel; paste.

餬口 *hurkoou*, v. i., make a living to feed the family.

餚 81B.42–8

yaur (*shiaur*).
[Var. of 肴 82.42]

餉 81B.42–9

shiaang.

N. Soldier's pay and rations: 糧餉 rations for army; now also salary in gen. (=薪): 發餉 give out pay; 領餉 receive pay; 扣餉 have pay deducted.

V.t. (LL) to give a gift, esp. food: 餉客 give dinner to guests; (fig.) 餉以老拳 give him a taste of one's blow.

餉錢 *shiaangchiarn*, n., soldier's pay and rations.
餉單 *shiaangdan*, n., bill of rations and food in the army.
餉饋 *shiaangkueih*, n., soldier's rations.
餉項 *shiaangshiahng*, n., army funds; soldier's pay.
餉銀 *shiaangyirn*, n., soldier's pay.

§ 81B.50 (食/㇆)

餳 81B.50–4

shirng.

N. Treacle made from malt.

Adj. (1) Sticky. (2) 餳澀 (eyes) drowsy, about to close.

餲 81B.50–4

aih.

Adj. (AC) spoiled, putrid, tainted (food).

飼 飭 餻 飩 饒 餛 飢 餽

飼 81B.50-5

syh.

V.t. To feed (cattle, baby, etc.).

飼料 *syhliauh*, n., animal feed.
飼養 *syhyaang*, v.t., to raise (cattle, silkworms, birds).

飭 81B.50-9

chyh.

V.i. & t. (1) (In official documents) order that s. t. be done: 嚴飭 order strictly; 申飭 order explicitly or repeatedly. (2) To readjust, put to order: 飭躬 order one's own conduct.

Adj. Neat, orderly: 謹飭 cautious in conduct; 整飭 neat, orderly.

飭知 *chyh jy*, phr., order to let it be known.
飭令 *chyhlihng*, v. t., order that . . . be done.
飭拿 *chyhnar*, v. t., issue order to arrest.
飭派 *chyhpaih*, v. t., to appoint for some duty.

§ 81B.63 (食/丶)

餻 81B.63-8

gau.

[Var. of 糕 22C.63]

§ 81B.70 (食/乚)

飩 81B.70-1

turn.

N. 餛飩 81B.70, wonton, a Chin. kind of ravioli.

饒 81B.70-1

raur.

N. A surname.

V.t. (1) Forgive, pardon: 饒恕 *-shuh*↓; 饒了他吧 let's forgive him; 饒人 *-rern*↓; 饒命 *-mihng*↓; 饒兒 pardon: 告個饒兒 ask for pardon; 討饒 ask for forgiveness; 求饒 ditto; 白饒 extra amount given free of charge, useless, vain, futile, easy to cope with. (2) Implicate, involve in: 我不告訴他吧，恐怕把他也饒在裏面 if I don't tell him, I'm afraid he may get involved. (3) Give as an extra: 饒給你一個 here's an extra one for you!

Adj. Abundant, plentiful: 富饒 rich, wealthy; 豐饒 plentiful, bountiful; 饒富 abundant, having plenty; 饒裕 well-to-do; 饒侈 lavish, extravagant; 饒衍 prolific, overflowing; 饒沃 (of soil) rich, fertile.

Adv. Even: 饒這麼著，還有人說閑話 even in such a case, some people would still be dissatisfied and grumble.

饒命 *raur-mihng*, v. t., spare (s.o.) his life.
饒讓 *raurrahng*, v. t., forgive and forget, condone.
饒人 *raur-rern*, v. i., (1) give s.o. an advantage over oneself; (2) forgive s.o.
饒舌 *raur-sher*, v. i., prattle, babble, gossip, be talkative.
饒恕 *raurshuh*, v. t., forgive, pardon, excuse, condone.
饒頭 *raur'tou*, n., anything extra.
饒益 *raur-yih*, adj., surplus, excess, extra.

餛 81B.70-4

hurn.

餛飩 *hurn'tun*, n., Chinese ravioli, with meat stuffing, usu. served in soup (also wr. as "wonton").

飢 81B.70-4

ji.

[Var. of 饑 81B.71]

N. Hunger: 飢荒 *-(')huang*↓; 飢寒交迫 suffering from cold and hunger; 飢困 afflicted by shortage of food; 飢火 *-huoo*, 飢渴 *-kee*↓.

Adj. Hungry: 飢餓 *-eh*↓; 飢民 starving masses; 飢不擇食 all food is delicious to the starving; 飢腸轆轆 rumblings of an empty stomach; 飢飽勞碌 to slave all day long with no assurance when the next meal will come; 飢名渴勢 greedy for honor and power; 肚飢 starving, famished; 飽漢不知餓漢飢 those with enough food to eat don't know how it feels to go without it.

飢餓 *ji-eh*, v.i. & adj., (feel) hungry, (be) without food to eat.
飢荒 *ji(')huang*, n., (1) famine, poverty: 鬧飢荒 reduced to destitution; (2) indebtedness: 拉飢荒 run into debt; (3) difficulties, hardships, adversity.
飢火 *jihuoo*, n., (1) a burning desire for food: 飢火中燒 acute hunger; (2) eager longing or intense desire for things other than food.
飢饉 *jijiin*, n., (=饑饉) starvation resulting from crop failure.
飢渴 *jikee*, n., (1) hunger and thirst; (2) an irresistible desire or longing: 性飢渴 sex-starved.

餽 81B.70-9

kueih.

N. A gift, friendly present.

餽贈 *kueihtzehng*, n., (LL) a gift.

飽 81B.70–9

baau.

V.t. (1) To give a full blow: 飽以老拳 hit one full in the face. (2) Fill: 飽我以德 (AC) imbue me with virtue.

Adj. Well-filled (with food), satisfied to the full, replete, saturated: 吃的飽飽的 eat one's full; 飽學之士 well-versed scholar.

Adv. Fully: 飽經世故 well-experienced in ways of the world; 飽嘗患難 fully taste all hardships; 飽看, 飽餐秀色 fully enjoy the beauty; 飽食終日, 無所用心 spend one's day in food (and drink) and have an empty head.

飽嗝兒 *baauger'l*, v.i., belch.
飽和點 *baauherdiaan*, n., (chem.) saturation point.
飽滿 *baurmaan*, adj., vigorous: 精神飽滿 full of energy.
飽暖 *baurnuaan*, adj., well-fed and well-covered, living a luxurious life: 飽暖思淫 luxury leads to sex.

餼 81B.70–9

shih.

N. (1) Live sacrifice: 餼羊 (AC) sacrificial lamb. (2) Grain for rations: 廩餼 (AC) horse-feed.

饞 81B.70–9

charn.

Adj. (1) Greedy, gluttonous: 嘴饞 loving to eat esp. outside meals; 手饞 have greedy hands. (2) Lewd, sex hungry: 眼饞 greedy looks at women; 饞眼孔 *-yarn-kuung* ↓. (3) (Of vegetables) take up a lot of oil to be palatable (such as spinach): 菠菜很饞.

饞癆 *charnlaur*, n., tuberculosis; hence (adj.) gluttonous for food or overindulgent in sex.
饞涎 *charnshiarn*, v. t., mouth watering at (the sight of food or women).
饞眼孔 *charn-yarn-kuung*, adj., lecherous looks at women.

§ 81B.71 (食/七)

餞 81B.71–7

jiahn.

N. Sweetmeats, preserves: 餞果 preserved fruits; 蜜餞 sweetmeats, glazed fruit.

V.i. See compp. ↓.

餞別 *jiahnbier*, v. i., give a farewell party.
餞行 *jiahnshirng*, v. i., ditto.

餓 81B.71–9

eh.

Adj. Hungry, starved: 飢餓 ditto; 餓死了 famished; 肚子餓 feeling hungry; 餓虎撲食 prey on victim like a famished tiger.

餓膈 *ehger*, adj., greedy, avaricious.
餓鬼 *ehgueei*, n., (1) (abuse) overgreedy person; (2) (Budd.) ghost condemned to be forever hungry in hell.
餓狼 *ehlarng*, n., a rapacious person (for sex, money).
餓莩 *eh-piaau*, n., (LL) corpses of those starved to death.
餓紋 *ehwern*, n., (fortunetelling) lines on both corners of the mouth, presaging death by starvation.

饑 81B.71–9

ji.

N. Hunger, dearth, scarcity, famine: 大饑 (AC) a great famine; 饑饉 *-jiin*, 饑歉 *-chiahn* ↓.

Adj. (Interch. 飢) hungry, starved, famished: 饑腸轆轆 rumblings of an empty stomach.

饑飽 *ji-baau*, n., the state of being hungry or satiated: 不知饑飽 too young to know when to eat.
饑歉 *jichiahn*, n., famine due to crop failure.
饑寒 *jiharn*, (1) adj., hungry and cold; (2) n., hunger and cold.
饑饉 *jijiin*, n., shortage of food, famine.
饑溺 *jinih*, n., (LL) sufferings of the masses.

§ 81B.72 (食/心)

馝 81B.72–6

bih.

N. (AC) flavor of food.

餽 飽 餼 饞 餞 餓 饑 馝

亅	小	⺊	十	土	ナ	廾	乚	丨	一	丅	フ	口	区	冈	㇆	厂	尸	亠	广	宀	丶	乚	七	心	八	人	乂	⺈	一	丿丨	⺊	く
00	01	02	10	11	12	20	21	22	30	31	32	40	41	42	50	51	52	60	61	62	63	70	71	72	80	81	82	83	90	91	92	93

§ 81B.80 (食/八)

饋 81B.80-2

kueih.

N. (1) (AC) food or lunch basket served to superiors. (2) A gift, see 餽 81B.70.

餵 81B.80-5

juahn.

N. (LL) food served at table: 肴饌 ditto; 盛饌 a rich dinner; 菜饌 simple meal; 設饌 prepare a dinner; 饌具 food vessels.

V.t. (AC) to eat: 有酒食 (*-syh*) 先生饌 (AC) when there is food and drink, it is served to the elders.

§ 81B.81 (食/人)

饃 81B.81-2

mor.

饃饃 *mor'mo*, n., (Peking) Chinese bun＝饅[A]頭 81B.82 (also wr. 饝).

飫 81B.81-9

yuh.

V.t. (AC) to fill full; p.p., well-filled, well-fed.

餱 81B.81-9

hour.

[Var. 糇 22C.81]

飲 81B.81-9

yiin (**yihn*).

N. A drink: 冷飲 cold drink; 熱飲 hot drink; 飲料 *-liauh* ↓.

V.i. & t. (1) To drink (water, tea, fluid): 飲食 *-shyr* ↓; 飲水思源 phr., "drink water and think of its source"—feel grateful; 飲鴆止渴 "drink poison to stop thirst"—remedy worse than what it is supposed to cure; 暢飲 drink to one's heart's content; 一飲而盡 quaff in one gulp; 飲醇自醉 said in praise of a fascinating character; 飲馬投錢 pay even for a horse's drink of water—extreme honesty. (2) (Fig.) to swallow: 飲彈而死 die of hit by bullet; 飲恨而終 die with a deep regret; 飲泣 "swallow tears"—to sob; 飲血 (from 泣血) swallow tears of blood; 矢乃飲羽 (AC) arrow sinks completely into object. (3) (**yihn*) To offer drink to (person): 飲之以水 give person water to drink.

飲冰 *yiin-bing*, phr., (AC) to cool oneself off by having some cold drinks.

飲茶 *yiinchar*, n. & v.i., (Cantonese) have tea and snacks.

飲泣 *yiinchih*[1], v.i., to sob.

飲器 *yiinchih*[2], n., (1) a drinking vessel; (2) (AC) use skull of enemy for a drinking vessel, interpreted also as use as chamber pot.

飲餞 *yiinjiahn*, v.i., (AC) give a farewell party to friend.

飲料 *yiinliauh*, n., liquid food, soup, any drink.

飲食 *yirnshyr*, n., food and drink; food in gen.

飲子 *yirntzyy*, n., (Chin. med.) medical potion or concoction (cf. 引[A]子 50S.22).

§ 81B.82 (食/乂)

餿 81B.82-2

sou.

Adj. (1) (Food) spoiled, putrid, bad (related 臊 42A.01). (2) Erroneous: 餿主意 wrong-headed idea.

餿臭 *souchouh*, adj., stinking, putrid, rancid.

饅 81B.82-4

marn.

饅頭 *marn'tou*, n., bread, bun; (Shanghai dial.)＝包子: 肉饅頭 a meat stuffed bun.

餃 81B.82-6

jiaau.

N. 餃子 Chin. ravioli: 水餃, 蒸餃, 煎餃, 肉餃, 魚餃, 蛋餃, 咖喱餃 boiled, steamed, fried, meat, fish, egg, curry ravioli.

飯 81B.82-9

fahn.

N. (1) Rice: 白米飯 white cooked rice; 乾飯 usu. rice, opp. 稀飯 gruel, congee; 炒飯 fried rice; 炒冷飯 (coll.) piping on an old theme, old talk; 蒸飯 steamed rice; 飯(米)粒兒, 飯巴粒兒, grains of rice. (2) Meal: 一天三餐飯 three meals a day; 飯後 after meal; 早飯, 午飯, 晚飯 breakfast, lunch, supper; 吃飯 eat; 沒飯吃 go without meals; 做飯 cook a meal; 開飯 dinner is served; 擺飯 lay table for dinner; 包飯 take board by the month; 討飯 be beggar; 飯店, 飯館, 飯廳, 飯車 *-diahn*, *-guaan*, *-ting*, *-che* ↓; 飯來開口 of those who eat and will not work. (3) Profession, means of living: 吃這口飯 to be in this profession; 這口飯不容易吃 it is difficult to make this kind of a living; 混飯吃 just to make a living somehow.

V.t. (LL) to feed: 飯牛 feed cattle; 飯僧 give food to monks.

飯車 *fahnche*, n., dining car.

飯袋 *fahndaih*, n., esp. 酒囊飯袋 useless person good only for feasting and drinking ("rice bag").

飯店 *fahndiahn*, n., food shop, restaurant; now also used for big hotels (大飯店).

飯館 *fahnguaan*, n., restaurant.

飯鍋 *fahngue*, n., pot for boiling rice.

飯盒(兒) *fahnher'l*, n., lunch basket.

飯莊 *fahnjuang*, n., (dial.) restaurant.

飯局 *fahnjyur*, n., dinner party.

飯量 *fahnliahng*, n., appetite, eating capacity.

飯粒 *fahnlih*, n., grains of rice.

飯落兒 *fahnluoh'l*, n., (coll.) means of living, where meals come from.

飯票 *fahn-piauh*, n., food ration: 這下子你可有長期飯票了 now you have a permanent job (means of living); (coll. usu. of girl) getting married as a means of security.

飯食 *fahnshyr*, n., (1) meals in general; (2) a rice meal.

飯廳 *fahnting*, n., dining room.

飯菜 *fahn-tsaih*, n., meal as a whole.

飯桶 *fahntuung*, n., (derog.) "rice bucket," good-for-nothing, a stupid person.

飯座兒 *fahntzuoh'l*, n., customer at restaurant.

飯碗(兒)(子) *fahnwaan(-waa'l, waantz)*, rice bowl, means of living: 打破飯碗 lose one's job.

餕 81B.82–9

jyuhn.

N. Leftovers in food.

§81B.93 (食/く)

蝕 81B.93–2

shyr.

V.i. (1) To eclipse: 日蝕, 月蝕 sun, moon eclipse. (2) Gradually decay, deteriorate in amount or value: 蝕本 *-been* ↓; 侵蝕 (a) (insects) eat into, erode, -sion, corrode; (b) 侵蝕公款 illegally appropriate public funds; (c) deteriorate; 剝蝕 (barks) fall off; v. t., to fleece (the people); 腐蝕 (of wood, dress) decay.

蝕本 *shyrbeen*, v. i., to lose in business: 生意蝕本 business loses; 蝕本生意 a losing business.

蝕損 *shyrsuun*, v. i., (of capital) deteriorate, lose in value.

餒 81B.93–9

neei.

Adj. (1) Hungry: 凍餒之苦 the sufferings of cold and hunger. (2) Deflated, downhearted: 氣餒 low-spirited, downcast. (3) (AC) (of fish) putrid, rotten.

餧 81B.93–9

weih.

[Var. of 餵 81B.02]

亅	小	⺊	十	土	ナ	卄	⺃	丨	一	丁	フ	口	区	冈	ㄱ	厂	尸	亠	广	宀	丶	乚	弋	心	八	人	乂	～	一	ノ	𠂉	く
00	01	02	10	11	12	20	21	22	30	31	32	40	41	42	50	51	52	60	61	62	63	70	71	72	80	81	82	83	90	91	92	93

SECTION 81S

§81S.00 (人^{S}/丿)

創 81S.00-2

chuahng (**chuang*).
[Anc. var. 刅]

N. (**chuang*) U. f. 瘡 a knife cut, wound: 身受重創 severely wounded; 創傷 wound (from spear, etc.); 創世記 Genesis.

V.t. (1) To found, establish: 創下 leave (record, example); 創立, 創辦, 創設 *-lih*, *-bahn*, *-sheh*↓; 創紀錄 make a record (athletics, etc.); 創事業 to found project, undertaking, firm, etc.; 開創 to found, open (school, hospital). (2) To create: 創造 ditto, *-tzauh*↓.

創辦 *chuahngbahn*, v. t., to found (an organization); 創辦人 founder.
創獲 *chuahnghuoh*, v. t., to discover, make (new results, theory).
創見 *chuahng-jiahn*, n., a new idea or viewpoint.
創制權 *chuuahngjyh-chyuarn*, n., (law) right of initiative.
創舉 *chuahngjyuu*, n., a new undertaking.
創立 *chuahnglih*, v. t., to found, open (school, institute, etc.), see *-bahn*↑; 創立會 inaugural meeting.
創設 *chuahngsheh*, v. t., ditto.
創始 *chuahngshyy*, v. i. & t. & n., to begin; beginning, new venture.
創造 *chuahngtzauh*, v. i. & t., to create (new theory, literature); 創造力 creative power; 創造文學 creative literature.
創作 *chuahngtzuoh*, n., a new creation in arts, literature; 創作者 creator (of new vogue), author.
創業 *chuahngyeh*, v. i., (1) to start an enterprise; (2) to found new royal house.
創艾 *chuahngyih*, v. t., to take as warning.

劊 81S.00-2

kuaih (also **gueih*).

劊子手 **gueihtz-shoou*, n., executioner.

劍 81S.00-2

jiahn.

N. A sword, dagger, saber: 劍術 swordsmanship; 寶劍 a treasured sword; 長劍 a lance; 鬪劍 fight a duel with swords; 比劍 sword fencing; 劍拔弩張 (of persons) ready to jump at each other's throat (of armies), all set for a showdown, (of situation) becoming dangerously explosive; 劍客 *-keh*, 劍俠 *-shiar*↓; 劍手 a swordsman, a fencer; 劍鋒, 劍柄, 劍鞘 the sharp edge, hilt, scabbard of a sword; 劍刃 the sharp edge of a sword; 舞劍 practise fencing; 撫劍 with sword in hand; 伏劍而死 die by the sword.

劍客 *jiahnkeh*, n., a swordsman.
劍仙 *jiahn-shian*, n., an expert swordsman known for his incredible exploits.
劍俠 *jiahnshiar*, n., a knight-errant, a swordsman who champions the cause of the downtrodden.

舒 81S.00-3

shu.
[Related 疏 32S.70, 踈 32S.01]

N. A surname.

V.i. To open up, hence to relax: 舒展 *-jaan*↓; 舒心, 舒懷 *-shin*, *-huair*↓; 舒眉 *-meir*↓; 舒散 *-saan*↓.

Adj. (1) Relaxed, comfortable: 舒服, 舒適 *-fur*, *-shyh*↓. (2) Lax, leisurely, slow: 舒步 in slow, leisurely steps; 舒遲, 舒緩 *-chyr*, *-huaan*↓.

舒暢 *shuchahng*, adj., relaxed, completely happy.
舒遲 *shuchyr*, adj., slow, leisurely.
舒服 *shufur*, adj., comfortable: 不舒服 uncomfortable; 身體不舒服 not well, slightly ill; 舒舒服服 leisurely, comfortably.
舒緩 *shuhuaan*, adj., slow, leisurely (steps).
舒懷 *shu-huair*, v. i., be relaxed.
舒展 *shujaan*, v. i. & t., to develop, open up (powers, plans), put (ability) to good use.
舒卷 *shu-jyuaan*, v. i., roll and unroll (as clouds).
舒眉 *shu-meir*, v. i., "unknit eyebrows"—feel happy at success.
舒散 *shusaan*, v. i., take a stroll, relax the mind (cf. 疏$^{\Delta}$散 32S.70).
舒心(兒) *shu-shin(-shie'l)*, v.i., feel happy.
舒適 *shushyh*, adj., comfortable (chair, feeling).
舒徐 *shushyur*, adj., leisurely.
舒坦 *shu'tan*, adj., at ease.

§81S.01 (人^{S}/小)

穌 81S.01-9

her.
[Interch. 和 90A.40]

§81S.10 (人^{S}/十)

斜 81S.10-1

shier (also *shiar*, rare).

N. A slant; slope.

Adj. Slanting, inclining, diagonal: 斜坡 a slope (land); 斜陽 the setting sun; 斜暉 ditto; 斜側 the side; 傾斜 to slant to one side; 斜半籤兒, 斜乜仟兒 diagonally across (of roads); 斜覷 *-shyh*↓; 斜眼 look out of corner of one's eye.

斜邊 *shierbian*, n., (math.) hypotenuse.
斜度 *shierduh*, (1) n., angle of inclination; (2) v. i., fly across.
斜高 *shiergau*, n., (math.) slant height.
斜角 *shierjiaau*, n., (math.) oblique angle.
斜綾 *shierlirng*, n., a light, thin twilled silk fabric.
斜面 *shiermiahn*, n., (math.) inclined plane.
斜線 *shiershiahn*, n., (math.) oblique line.
斜覷 *shiershyh*, (1) v. i., look askance; (2) n., a cross-eye, a squint.
斜紋布 *shierwernbuh*, n., twill, drill, denim.
斜玉兒 *shieryueh'l*, n., the radical 玉, appearing with a slant: 王.

§ 81S.11 (人ˢ/土)

糴 81S.11–5

dir.

N. Buy in rice or grain, opp. 糶 21S.11.

§ 81S.22 (人ˢ/丨)

鄶 81S.22–3

kuaih.

N. (AC) name of anc. city.

§ 81S.30 (人ˢ/一)

爼 81S.30–4

tzuu.

N. (1) An anc. sacrificial vessel: 爼豆 *-douh*↓; 越爼代庖 do on behalf of another s.t. not in one's own line of duty. (2) A chopping board: 刀爼 (lit.) chopper and the chopping board, (fig.) the oppressor (opp. 魚肉 "fish and meat," the oppressed); 爼上肉 meat on the chopping board, (fig.) a helpless victim.

爼豆 *tzuudouh*, n., two anc. sacrificial vessels.

§ 81S.40 (人ˢ/口)

舘 81S.40–6

guaan.
[Pop. of 館 81B.40]

§ 81S.42 (人ˢ/冈)

舖 81S.42–1

puh (*pu*).
[Pop. of 鋪]

N. (1) Shop: usu. 舖子; 店舖 shop; 小舖子 small shop; 開舖子 open shop; 米, 肉舖 rice, meat shop. (2) (MC) post station.

舖保 *puhbaau*, n., shop guarantee (by owner of a shop).
舖底 *puhdii*, n., (1) shop furniture; (2) deposit for shop rental.
舖夥 *puhhuuo*, n., shop employee (=夥計).
舖長 *puhjaang*, n., formerly, shop superintendent.
舖捐 *puhjyuan*, n., shop tax.
舖面 *puhmiahn*, n., shop front: 舖面房 *--farng*, shop building.
舖眼兒 *puhyaa'l*, n., (coll.) shop.

§ 81S.50 (人ˢ/ㄱ)

劒 81S.50–5

jiahn.
[Anc. var. of 劍 81S.00]

翎 81S.50–5

lirng.

N. Feather: 翎箭 feathered arrow; 花翎, 藍翎, 翎子 peacock feather on cap of mandarin officials in Manchu Dyn.

翎毛 *lirngmaur*, n., category of Chin. painting depicting birds and animals (lit., "feathers and furs").

鴒 81S.50–9

lirng.

亅	小	⺊	十	土	ナ	卄	𠃊⺊	丨	一	丅	㇇	口	図	冈	㇕	厂	尸	亠	广	宀	丶	乚	弋	心	八	人	乂	乛	㇀	刂	⺈	㇛
00	01	02	10	11	12	20	21	22	30	31	32	40	41	42	50	51	52	60	61	62	63	70	71	72	80	81	82	83	90	91	92	93

N. See 鶺鴒 91S.50.

鴿 81S.50–9

ge.

N. (Zoo.) (*-tz*) the dove, the pigeon; 鴿雛兒 a young dove; 乳鴿 a squab; 信鴿, 軍鴿 a carrier pigeon; 鴿派 the Pacifist Doves.

§ 81S.70 (人^{S}/乚)

瓴 81S.70–3

lirng.

N. (1) Upturned column of roof tiles, permitting flow of rain water. (2) A jar with ears.

覦 81S.70–4

yur.

V.t. See 覬覦 21S.70.

毹 81S.70–9

shu (also *yur*).

N. See 氍毹 41S.70.

§ 81S.71 (人^{S}/乜)

戧 81S.71–7

chiahng (**chiang*).

V.t. To sprinkle, see 戧金 *-jin* ↓.

Adj. (**chiang*) Broken off: 話説戧了 the talk was broken off, making further talk impossible.

Prep. (**chiang*) Against: 戧轍兒走 go in the opposite direction.

戧金 *chiahngjin*, v. t., to sprinkle gold (on furniture, etc.).

戧柱 *chiahngjuh*, n., buttress for strengthening support.

§ 81S.80 (人^{S}/八)

領 81S.80–3

liing.

N. adjunct. A piece of dress: 一領袍子, 襯衫 one gown, one shirt (lit., "one collar").

N. (1) The neck: 引領而望 crane one's neck to see, wait. (2) Collar (*-tz*): 衣領 collar of dress; 領扣 collar button. (3) Main thread: 綱領 outline; 提綱挈領 give outline, main points, like "gathering fish net by leading cord and lifting dress by collar"; hence also 領袖 "collar and sleeve"—leader.

V.t. (1) To lead, to head the list: 領兵, 領隊, 領帶人馬 lead troops; 率領 to lead (troops, mob, travelling group, etc.), see 領頭 *-tour* ↓; 領班 foreman; 領着頭兒 be the first in position; 領銜 to head the list of signers, sponsors; 領路 lead the way; to lead and guide, see 領帶 *-daih* ↓; to pilot, see 領港 *-gaang* ↓. (2) To receive: 領取, 領受 receive (gifts, ration, awards); 領教, 拜領教益 (LL court.) have the benefit of your wise counsel; 領情, 領謝 *-chirng*, *-shieh* ↓; 心領 (court.) express thanks for the thought while declining gift; 領罪 *-tzueih* ↓; 領賞 receive award or tip; 領洗 *-shii* ↓; 領命 to receive orders. (3) To take away s.t. as one's own or as owner: 這條狗沒人來領 no one has come forward to claim this lost dog; 招領 announcement for found property, 認領 to claim it; 冒領 to lay false claim on (money, etc.). (4) To adopt (a child): 領一個孩子來養 to adopt and raise a child not one's own; 這孩子是領的 (養的) this child is an adopted one. (5) To understand, to appreciate, to grasp: 領悟, 領會, 領略 *-wuh*, *-hueih*, *-lyueh* ↓.

Adj. Under jurisdiction of: 領土, 領空, 領海, 領事 see *-tuu*, *-kung*, *-haai*, *-shyh* ↓.

領情 *liingchirng*, v. i., to accept with thanks, or accept merely the sentiment, but not the gift: 領情就是了 thanks for the thought anyway.

領取 *lirngchyuu*, v. t., to receive as due.

領帶 *liingdaih*, (1) v.t., to lead (troops, etc.); (2) n., necktie.

領單 *liingdan*, n., receipt for delivery.

領地 *liingdih*, n., territory under jurisdiction.

領港 *lirnggaang*, (1) n., a harbor pilot; (2) v.i., to pilot.

領海 *lirnghaai*, n., territorial waters.

領航 *liingharng*, v.i., pilot (navigation, aviation, etc.).

領會 *linghueih*, v.t., to understand.

領章 *liingjang*, n., (mil.) collar insignia showing rank.

領教 *liingjiauh*, v.t., "to receive instructions," or merely to ask s.o.'s opinion, or pay visit: 不敢領教 (court.) disagree with what another person says.

領結 *liingjier*, n., (1) bow tie; (2) v.i., to sign receipt for goods.

領巾 *liingjin*, n., scarf.

領據 *liingjyuh*, n., receipt for goods.

領口 *liingkoou*, n., (width of) collar.

領扣 *liingkouh*, n., collar button.

領空 *liing-kung*, n., a country's

sovereign air space; 領空權 rights over air space.

領略 *liinglyueh*, v. t., to grasp, understand: 領略味道 to appreciate flavor; 領略風光 to see and appreciate scenery.

領銜 *liing-shiarn*, v. i., to head the list of sponsors: 領銜主演 (movies) featured actor, -tress.

領謝 *liingshieh*, v.t., to appreciate, show appreciation.

領洗 *lirngshii*, v. i., receive baptism.

領袖 *liingshiouh*, n., leader, chief (of group, nation, etc.).

領受 *liingshouh*, v. t., to receive formally (advice, baptism, etc.).

領水 *liingshueei*, n., see *-haai* ↑.

領事 *liingshyh*, n., consul: 領事館 consulate; 總領事 consular general; 領事裁制權 consul jurisdiction.

領條兒 *liingtiaur'l*, n., collar strip in Chin. dress.

領帖 *lirng-tiee*, n., receive condolence by bereaved family.

領頭 *liing-tour*, v.i., to lead the way.

領土 *liirng-tuu*, n., territory under jurisdiction.

領罪 *liing-tzueih*, v. i., to make apology.

領位 *liing-weih*, n., (gram.) possessive case.

領窩兒 *liingwo'l*, n., hole cut out for collar in Chin. dress.

領悟 *liingwuh*, v. t., comprehend (truth, doctrine).

領域 *liingyuh*, n., national territory.

頷 81S.80-3

hahn.

N. The chin and jowl.

V.i. To give a nod: 頷之而已 just gave him a nod; 頷首示意 give a nod as a signal.

顱 81S.80-3

yuh.

[Pop. 籲 92A.80]

§ 81S.81 (人S/人)

从 81S.81-8

tsurng.

[Anc. var. 從 91B.83]

歈 81S.81-9

yur.

N. (AC) folk song.

歙 81S.81-9

shih.

[Var. of 翕 81.50]

歙 81S.81-9

chuei.

[Var. of 吹 40A.81]

§ 81S.82 (人S/乂)

敍 81S.82-2

shyuh.

[Pop. 叙]

N. A preface (interch. 序 61.00).

V.t. (1) To recount, relate (past events), narrate, describe: 敍述 *-shuh* ↓; 敍別 *-bier* ↓; 敍濶 to recount things during time of separation; 敍舊 to go over the old days. (2) To meet for conversation: 敍談 *-tarn* ↓; 敍餐, 敍宴 a social dinner; 茶敍 an afternoon tea, meet over a cup of tea; 面敍 to go over (matter) in person; 請來一敍 please come over for a chat; 暢敍 enjoy a talk together. (3) To go over official record and decide on promotion, etc.: 敍功, 敍用 *-gung*, *-yuhng* ↓; 銓ᐞ敍 81A.11.

敍別 *shyuh-bier*, phr., talk of the happenings during absence after reunion of friends.

敍功 *shyuh-gung*, phr., 敍功行賞 go over the records and decide on awards.

敍記 *shyuhjih*, n., (LL) narrative prose, see *-shyh* ↓.

敍傳 *shyuhjuahn*, n., (LL) an author's preface.

敍述 *shyuhshuh*, v. t., to narrate, recount (events); state (one's attitude, feelings, etc.).

敍事 *shyuhshyh*, v. i., recount, narrate; 敍事詩 epic poetry; 敍事文 narrative prose.

敍勳 *shyuhshyun*, v. i., see *-gung* ↑.

敍談 *shyuhtarn*, v. i., hold a conversation.

敍言 *shyuhyarn*, n., a preface (＝序ᐞ言 61.00).

敍用 *shyuhyuhng*, v. t., make appointments to post according to qualifications (＝序用).

叙 81S.82-3

shyuh.

[Pop. of 敍]

頜 頷 顱 从 歈 歙 歙 敍 叙

亅 小 ⺊ 十 土 ナ 卄 ⺊ 丨 一 丅 フ 口 囗 冂 ㇆ 厂 尸 亠 广 亠 丶 乚 弋 心 八 人 乂 一 一 丿 ⺁ く
00 01 02 10 11 12 20 21 22 30 31 32 40 41 42 50 51 52 60 61 62 63 70 71 72 80 81 82 83 90 91 92 93

斂 希 肴 乂 乄

斂 81S.82–9

liahn (**liaan*).

V.i. & t. (1) (*liaan*) To gather, accumulate (wealth, etc.), see 斂財 *-tsair* ↓; to levy tax: 斂稅, 聚斂 (of official) levy tax and get rich; 收斂 to gather; to harvest. (2) (**liahn*) To keep back, hold back: 斂容 put on a sober face; 斂足, 斂步 to hold one's steps and not go forward, to go on tiptoe; 斂迹 to stop visiting places, to hide goings-on, stop illegal maneuvers; 斂衽 anciently a lady's greeting by holding lower corners of jacket. (3) (**liaan*) Var. of 殮 laying in coffin. (4) (**liaan*) Congeal, not disperse. (5) (AC) 斂三百里 less than 300 *li*.

斂財 *liahn-tsair*, phr., collect wealth.

SECTION 82

§82.22 (乂/丨)

希 82.22

shi.

V.i. To hope to: 希望, 希冀 *-wahng*, *-jih* ↓; 希能爲力 I hope it may help; 希可即復 hope to be favored with an early reply; 尚希笑納 hope you will graciously accept.

V.t. To strive for, aim at: 希求 *-chiour* ↓; 希寵 strive for superior's favor; 希榮 strive for high honors; 希聖, 希賢 strive for the ideal of a sage, a wise man; 希風 emulate s. o.'s example.

Adj. (1) Rare: 希有, 希奇, 希罕 *-yoou*, *-chir*, *-haan* ↓; 希世之寶 an extremely rare treasure; 古希 seventy years of age ("rare since old times"). (2) Indiscernible: 希聲 (AC) sound which can hardly be heard; 希微, 希夷 *-weir*, *-yir* ↓.

希企 *shi-chih*, v. i. & t., to hope for (to).

希求 *shichiour*, v. t., to hope for (to): 希求上進 hope to make progress.

希奇 *shichir*, (1) v. t., consider as rare: 不希奇 is quite common; (2) adj., rare (object); curious (story).

希罕 *shihaan*, (1) (*-'han* or *-haan*) v. i. & t., consider as valuable: 我不希罕他的好意殷勤 I don't appreciate (in fact I despise) his attentions; (2) adj., rare (object, event).

希冀 *shi-jih*, v. i. & t., (LL) to hope to (do s. t.); to strive for (progress, favor, etc.).

希旨 (指) *shijyy*, v. i., to cater to a superior's wishes.

希臘 *Shilah*, n., Greece.

希世 *shi-shyh*, (1) adj., extremely rare; (2) (AC) 希世而行 do things to win popularity.

希特勒 *Shitehleh*, n., Hitler.

希圖 *shi-tur*, v.i. & t., see *-jih* ↑.

希望 *shiwahng*, v. i. & t. & n., hope: 希望你早日回來 hope you will return soon; 他的希望不大 he does not expect too much.

希微 *shiweir*, adj., infinitesimal.

希夷 *shiyir*, (1) n., another name for 靈^{Δ}芝 31D.30, an auspicious plant; (2) phr., (AC) indiscernible by ear (希) and invisible (夷).

希有 *shiyoou*, adj., very rare.

§82.42 (乂/冈)

肴 82.42

yaur (also *shiaur*).

[Var. 餚]

N. Cooked or prepared meat in gen.: 酒肴 wine and meat at dinner; 佳肴 (court.) good dinner; 肴肉 freshly salted pork; 肴饌 delicate food.

§82.82 (乂/乂)

乂 82.82

yih (*aih*).

[Interch. 艾 20A.82; anc. var. of 刈 82S.00]

乄 82.82

yih.

[Pop. of 義 80.71]

爻 82.82

yaur (re.pr. *shiaur*).

N. (In *Book of Changes*) the basic continuous line (—) and broken line (— —); any combination of three lines from these makes a 卦 *guah*, or trigram, as ☰☱: see 八卦 *baguah*, 80.80; 上爻 highest line; 初爻 lowest line in *guah*.

Adj. Intertwined: 爻錯 intercrossing (branches); changing, replacing one another; 爻變, see 淆 63A.42.

SECTION 82S

§82S.00 (乂ˢ/亅)

乂刂 82S.00-2

yih.

N. A sickle.

V.t. To cut down (grass), (fig.) to weed out (undesirable elements).

刹 82S.00-2

chah.

N. Budd. temple: 古刹 ancient temple; 寶刹 sacred temple.

刹那 *chahnah*, n., (Budd. & current) (in) the twinkling of an eye: 刹那間 in a flash.

§82S.22 (乂ˢ/丨)

郄 82S.22-3

shih.

N. (1) A surname. (2) Var. of 郤 80S.22.

郗 82S.22-3

chy.

N. (1) A surname. (2) Interch. 郤.

§82S.71 (乂ˢ/七)

弑 82S.71-7

shyh.

V.t. To assassinate, to kill a superior (ruler, father, etc.), related 殺 82S.82.

§82S.81 (乂ˢ/人)

欷 82S.81-9

shi.

[Var. of 唏 40A.22]

§82S.82 (乂ˢ/乂)

殺 82S.82-4

sha (*shaih).

V.t. (1) To kill, slaughter: 殺人 kill a person; 殺人不眨眼 kill person without batting an eye, cold-blooded murder; 殺人不見血 destroy a person by smooth strategy; 殺身成仁 die martyr to a noble cause. (2) To exterminate, destroy: 殺菌, 殺蟲 *-jyuhn*, *-churng* ↓; 殺風景 do s.t. to spoil one's enthusiasm, dampen the spirit. (3) To engage in a fight: 二人殺在一處 the two were locked in combat. (4) To hurt:

殺 殺 教

這藥殺得慌 this medicine hurts terribly.

Adj. (**shaih*) Abated: 風稍殺 the winds have abated.

Adv. Extremely, like Eng. "die of": 樂殺, 恨殺, 痛殺 dying with joy, hatred, pain; 笑殺 could die with laughter.

殺氣 *sha-chih*, n., venom; desire or power or call to kill; (physiognomy) inclined to violence.
殺青 *shaching*, v.i., (of book manuscript, film production) completed; orig. preparation of bamboo strip for writing by heating process.
殺蟲 *sha-churng*, v.i., destroy insects; 殺蟲粉, 殺蟲劑 insecticide.
殺伐 *shafar*, v.i., as in 殺伐之聲 noise of slaughter.
殺害 *shahaih*, v.t., to destroy, to kill (person).
殺機 *sha-ji*, n., time, mood or plan to kill.
殺價 *sha-jiah*, phr., to sell at reduced price.
殺戒 *sha-jieh*, n., (Budd.) commandment against killing.
殺菌 *shajuhn*, v.t., disinfect; 殺菌藥 a disinfectant.
殺戮 *shaluh*, v.t., to slaughter and plunder.
殺坯 *sha-pi*, n., see *-tsair*↓.
殺生 *shasheng*, n., (Budd.) killing of living things.
殺熟兒 *shashour'l*, phr., (comm.) to ask unfair price of old customer (because he will not haggle).
殺頭 *sha-tour*, v.i., to behead.
殺材 *shatsair*, n., (abusive) wretch ("person deserving death").
殺尾 *shaweei*, n., the end (also wr. 煞尾).
殺威棒 *sha-wei-bahng*, n., (coll.) a torture to break prisoner's resistance.

殽 82S.82-4

yaur.

N. U.f. 肴 cooked meat, 82.42.

Adj. U.f. 淆 confused, 63A.42.

教 82S.82-9

jiauh (**jiau*).

N. (1) Short for 教育 *-yuh*↓. (2) An order, decree, edict: 教令 *-lihng*↓. (3) Religion: 佛教 Buddhism; 道教 Taoism; 基督教 Christianity; 回教 Islamism, Mohammedanism, Moslemism; 天主教 Catholicism; 教區 diocese; 教會 *-hueih*, 教士 *-shyh*[1], 教堂 *-tarng*, 教徒 *-tur*, 教友 *-yoou*, 教皇 *-huarng*, 教主 *-juu*↓; 三教九流 adherents of different religions and sects, people of varying social origins and backgrounds; 信教, 奉教 be follower of a religion; 傳教 be a missionary, preach, evangelize; 叛教 apostasy, be an apostate.

V. t. (1) Teach, instruct, educate, discipline: 教訓 *-shyuhn*, 教誨 *-hueei*↓; 領教 (court.) to benefit by s.o.'s advice; 候教 (court.) respectfully await your instructions; 受教 (court.) have the benefit of s.o.'s advice; 賜教 (court.) graciously advise me; 不教而誅 to deal out punishments without a period of instruction; 有教無類 proper education levels all social classes; 教導 *-dauh*, 教授 *-shouh*↓; 指教 offer opinions, make recommendations; 請教 ask for advice. (2) (**jiau*) To teach, train, drill: 教給 show s. o. how (to do s. t.); 教壞 teach wrong things (to children); 教書 *-shu*↓; 教他兩手 teach him a trick or two; 教歷史 teach history. (3) Cause to, ask to: 教他回來 tell him to come back; 教人傷心 make one sad; 教我如何不想他 how could I stop thinking of him?

教案 *jiauhahn*, n., (1) a teaching plan; (2) an incident involving foreign missionaries.
教本 *jiauhbeen*, n., a textbook.
教鞭 *jiauhbian*, n., a pointer for classroom use, teacher's rod.
教導 *jiauhdauh* (*-daau*), n. & v. t., teach, -ing, instruct, -tion; train,-ing.
教法 *jiauhfaa*, n., teaching methods, pedagogy.
教坊 *jiauhfang*, n., formerly, a school for court musicians.
教官 *jiauhguan*, n., (1) (AC) minister in charge of education and culture; (2) formerly, a teacher in a government school; (3) a military instructor.
教規 *jiauhguei*, n., church rules or canons.
教化 *jiauhhuah*, v. t., to educate, train in good manners, civilize; n.,culture, civilized intercourse.
教皇 *jiauhhuarng*, n., the Pope, see *-tzung*↓.
教誨 *jiauhhueei*, v. t., instruct, educate, train.
教會 *jiauhhueih*, n., the church.
教主 *jiauhjuu*, n., (1) the founder of a religion; (2) a religious leader.
教具 *jiauhjyuh*, n., teaching aids.
教科書 *jiauhkeshu*, n., a textbook.
教練 *jiauhliahn*, (1) n., a coach: 足球教練 football coach; (2) v. t., to teach, instruct.
教令 *jiauhlihng*, n., an religious decree or proclamation.
教門(兒) *jiauhmern*(*-mer'l*), n., (1) a Moslem; (2) the church.
教派 *jiauhpaih*, n., religious sects.
教習 *jiauhshi*, n., a school teacher.
教授 *jiauhshouh*, (1) n., a college professor; formerly, a teacher in a government school; (2) v.t., teach, instruct, coach, lecture;
教書 **jiaushu*, v. i., be a teacher, follow teaching as a career: 教書匠 (contempt.) a professional schoolteacher.
教師 *jiauhshy*, n., a teacher: 教師節 Teacher's Day.
教士 *jiauhshyh*[1], n., a priest, minister, pastor, preacher, clergyman.
教室 *jiauhshyh*[2], n., classroom.
教學 *jiauhshyuer* (**jiau-*), v. t., teach (a subject); 教學法 method of teaching.
教訓 *jiauhshyuhn*, v. t., (1) teach, instruct; (2) reproach, reprimand, rebuke: 教訓他一頓 give him a thorough scolding;

A

給他一個教訓 teach him a lesson.

教唆 *jiauhsuo*, v. t., instigate, incite: 教唆罪 n., guilt of instigation to crime.

教堂 *jiauhtarng*, n., (1) (Christianity) a church, chapel, cathedral; (2) (Islam) a mosque; (3) (Judaism) a tabernacle; (4) (Taoism) a temple; (5) (Shintoism) a shrine.

教廷 *jiauhtirng*, n., the Vatican, the Papacy; the Holy See.

教頭 *jiauhtour*, n., "chief trainer" roughly equivalent to "captain."

教材 *jiauhtsair*, n., teaching material, (textbooks, etc.).

教徒 *jiauhtur*, n., follower of a religion.

教澤 *jiauh-tzer*, n., the mellowing influence of education.

教宗 *Jiauhtzung*, n., Pope, the pontiff.

教務 *jiauhwuh*, n., school affairs; 教務長 dean of a school or college.

教養 *jiauhyaang*, (1) n., upbringing; (2) v.t., bring up (children).

教義 *jiauhyih*, n., church dogmas, beliefs.

教友 *jiauhyoou*, n., a fellow religious believer, member of a church.

教員 *jiauhyuarn*, n., a schoolteacher.

教育 *jiauhyuh*, n., education; 教育部 Ministry of Education; 教育電視 educational TV.

B

SECTION 90

§90.00 (ノ/亅)

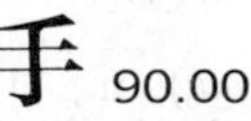

90.00

shoou.

N. (1) The hand: 一隻手 one hand; 手腳 hand and foot; 手足 *-tzur*↓; 手背, 手腕, 手指, 手心, 手紋 *-beih*, *-wahn*, *-jyy*[2], *-shin*, *-wern*↓; 手拉手兒 hand in hand; 雙手 with both hands; 手忙腳亂 very busy; 手不釋卷 never seen without a book in hand; 手急眼快 dexterous, adroit, -ly; 手舞足蹈 dance for joy. (2) The hand as symbolic of gesture, movement, maneuver: 手兒, 手下, 手底下 *-'l*, *-shiah*, *-dii'shiah*↓; 手段, 手面 *-duahn*, *-miahn*↓; 握手 shake hands; 揮手 lift a hand (as to give order or to write); 伸手 stretch hand; 舉手 raise hand; 縮手 shrink back; 垂手 hands hang down on sides; 順手 without special effort, while one is on it; 束手 fold one's hands—powerless or unable to act; 手快, 手慢 quick, slow of movement; 手軟 hand goes soft—pity toward intended victim; symbolic of grab of money: 手頭 *-tour*↓; 手滑 be used to doing s.t. and unable to control oneself; 手黏, 手不穩 has kleptomaniac tendency; 手緊, 手鬆 tight, loose with money; symbolic of work: 住手, 停手 stop (any work or movement); 入手 start work, also (work) comes to hand as one wishes, (girl victim) falls into clutch; 得手 successful, -ly; 動手, 著手 (person) begins to, (work) is begun; 放手做去 take matter in hand, go full steam ahead; 下手 to lay hands on, commit act of killing; 假手 have s.o. do s.t. (sinister) instead of oneself; symbolic of fight: 還手 strike back. (3) Quality or skill of player, contestant (like Eng. "a good hand at tennis"); a professional player: 好手, 能手, 高手 a good hand, expert (in game); 國手 national champion; 棋逢敵手 meet one's match in chess or any other contest; 熟手 an expert or experienced hand; 強手, 弱手 strong, inferior player; 鼓手 drummer; 箭手 archer; 拳擊手 boxer; 槍手 rifleman, sharp shooter; 打手 fighter, a person hired by another to fight for him; 手球 hai alai.

C

V.t. (LL) hold in hand: 人手一冊 everybody has a copy (in hand).

Adv. & adj. (1) Done by hand: 手稿 *-gaau*↓; 手鈔本 hand-written copy; 手書 hand-written (by s.o.); 手泐 ditto (at end of letter); 手植 (tree) personally planted (by s.o.); 手札, 手示, 手諭 *-jar*, *-shyh*, *-yuh*↓. (2) Portable: 手提包, 手提箱 *-tirbau*, *-tirshiang*↓; 手風琴 accordian; 手槍, 手榴彈 *-chiang*, *-liourdahn*, etc.↓.

手把子 *shourbaatz*, n., one's way of spending money, liberal or stingy: 手把子大 liberal with money.

手版 *shour-baan*, n., formerly, tablet held with both hands during imperial audience (also 手板) (=笏); 手板子 foot ruler, used for chastising schoolpupils.

手本 *shourbeen* (*-'ben*), n., (Manchu Dyn.) memo presented by successful candidate in formal call on examiner; memo submitted to superior.

手背 *shoubeih*, (1) n., back of the hand: 手背朝下 holding out hand with open palm—beg for money or help; (2) adj., (gambling) having bad luck.

手錶 *shourbiaau*, n., wrist watch.

手邊 *shoou-bian*, adj., books of reference, money on hand.

手筆 *shourbii* (*-'bi*), n., (1) personal handwriting; also personal style of writing; (2) style of squandering money: 自小手筆就濶 has been liberal with money since childhood.

手搏 *shoubor*, v. i. & t., strike in handfight.

手叉子 *shoouchatz*, n., a dagger.

手抄 *shoou-chau*, v. t. & n., (make) a hand copy.

手車 *shoou-che*, n., handcart.

手槍 *shoouchiang*, n., revolver, pistol.

手氣兒 *shoouchieh'l*, n., luck at gambling (esp. dice games): 手氣兒好, 不好 lucky, unlucky hand.

手輕 *shoou-ching*, adj., (person) light-handed.

手串兒 *shoouchuah'l*, n., string of beads.

手電燈 *shoou-diahn-deng*, n., hand flashlight (also called 手電, 手電筒, 手棒).

手底下 *shourdii'shia*, n., (1) a person in one's employ: 他在我手底下, 就得聽我使喚 he is employed by me, and must do my bidding; (2) see *-tour* ↓.

手段 *shoouduahn* (*-'duan*), n., (1) method of dealing, esp. vicious method; (2) skill of dealing with men or affairs: 看看我的手段 see how I deal with (him).

手法(兒) *shourfaa('l)* (*-'fa'l*), n., manual skill or dexterity (as at piano, basketball, etc.).

手乏 *shoou-far*, adj., short of money.

手風琴 *shoou-fengchirn*, n., hand organ.

手稿 *shoou-gaau*, n., draft (of composition).

手掌 *shour-jaang*, n., palm of hand.

手札 *shoou-jar*, n., personal note, letter.

手詔 *shoou-jauh*[1], n., order of ruler in personal writing.

手照(子) *shooujauh*[2]*(tz)*, n., (dial.) a lantern.

手摺 *shooujer*, n., (1) memo presented to superior; (2) a notebook recording commercial deliveries, orders, payments.

手迹 *shoouji*, n., original hand script (also 墨跡, 手蹟).

手簡 *shour-jiaan*, n., informal personal note to friend.

手技 *shooujih*, n., (1) handicraft; (2) acrobatic skills.

手巾 *shooujin*, n., handkerchief; also face and hand towels.

手鐲 *shoujuor*, n., bracelet; 手鐲腳銬 (rare) handcuffs and shackles.

手卷 *shourjyuaan*, n., a hand scroll.

手絹(兒) *shooujyuahn* (*-jyuah'l*), n., handkerchief.

手腳 *shooujyuer* (*-jiaau*), n., (1) movements (quick, slow); (2) 弄手腳 play tricks.

手紙 *shourjyy*[1], n., toilet paper.

手指 *shourjyy*[2], n., finger: 手指甲 fingernail.

手銬 *shooukauh*, n., handcuffs.

手工 *shooukung*, n., manual labor, handiwork, handicraft: 手工業 *--yeh*, n., handicraft industry; 手工藝 *--yih*, n., handicrafts.

手兒 *shoou'l*, n., (1) the hand, see N. 1 & 2↑; (2) see *-duahn*↑.

手榴彈 *shoouliourdahn*, n., hand grenade.

手爐 *shooulur*, n., hand warmer, usu. of brass.

手籠 *shooulurng*, n., hand warmer, shaped like basket.

手面 *shoomiahn*, n., see *shourbaatz* and *-duahn*↑.

手民 *shoomirn*, n., hand typesetter.

手模 *shooumor*, n., fingerprint, thumb print in lieu of signature for illiterate.

手帕 *shoou(')pah*, n., handkerchief (see *-jyuahn*↑).

手下 *shoou-shiah*, phr., (1) under one's employ or charge: 手下數百兵 has several hundred soldiers under him; (2) on hand: 手下沒錢 no money on hand; (3) 手下留情 (to judge) please be lenient.

手相術 *shoushiahng-shuh*, n., palmistry.

手心 *shoou-shin*, n., center of palm: 逃不出他的手心兒 cannot escape from his control.

手書 *shoou-shu*, n., (1) personal letter; (2) handwriting.

手術 *shooushuh* (*-'shu*), n., a surgical operation.

手勢 *shooushy*, n., hand gesture; force of strike.

手示 *shoou-shyh*, n., (court.) personal letter (示=advice).

手續 *shooushyuh*, n., procedure (in getting permit, etc.); 手續費 service charge.

手談 *shoou-tarn*, n., fancy term for playing chess or cards.

手套(兒) *shooutauh('l)*, n., gloves.

手提的 *shoou-tir'de*, adj., portable: 手提包 *--bau*, n., handbag; brief case; 手提箱 *--shiang*, n., suitcase; 手提式 *--shyh*, adj., portable (type).

手頭 *shooutour*, (1) adj., on hand: 不在手頭 not available for the moment; (2) n., financial condition (緊 tight or 寬 easy); (3) personal experience: 從手頭經歷過來 learned from personal experience; 手頭字 simplified forms of characters in current use.

手彩兒 *shourtsaa'l*, n., skill in sleight of hand; skill in cunning moves.

手冊 *shooutseh*[1], n., a handbook.

手策 *shooutseh*[2], n., (MC) see *-duahn*↑.

手字兒 *shoou-tzeh'l*, n., personal handwriting; written note.

手澤 *shoou-tzer*, n., heirloom; writing and personal articles of ancestor.

手足 *shoou-tzur*, n., (litr.) brothers.

手腕(兒) *shoouwahn*(*-wah'l*), n., (1) wrist; (2) *-duahn*↑.

手紋 *shoouwern*, n., lines on one's palm.

手藝 *shoouyih* (*-'yi*), n., handicraft; manual skill.

手印 *shoouyihn*, n., fingerprint; thumb print used in contracts in lieu of signature.

手淫 *shoou-yirn*, n., masturbation.

手諭 *shoou-yuh*, n., (court. to superior) your letter.

手語 *shour-yuu*, n., deaf-mute communication by fingers, dactylology.

舉 90.00

jyuu.

[Pop. 擧 90.10]

N. An act, action, move, deed: 舉動 *-duhng*, 舉止 *-jyy*, 舉措 *-tsuoh* ↓; 多此一舉 the action (measure, step) just taken was really unnecessary; 一舉兩得 kill two birds with one stone; 善舉 a good deed; 義舉 a philanthropic move a patriotic move; 此舉 this action (step, move).

V.t. (1) Lift, raise, hold up: 舉手 *-shoou*↓; 舉杯 raise the cup to drink to s.o.'s health; 舉槍 to present arms; 舉起 hold up, lift; 舉重 *-juhng*, 舉踵 *-juung*↓; 舉案齊眉 (allu.) not to forget courtesy between husband and wife; 舉棋不定 shilly-shally; 舉足輕重 to play a decisive role, carry weight; 舉頭 raise one's head; 舉目無親 be stranded in a foreign land, far away from one's kin. (2) Start, initiate, begin, undertake: 舉辦 *-bahn*, 舉行 *-shirng*, 舉兵 *-bing*, 舉事 *-shyh*, 舉義 *-yih*↓. (3) Nominate, recommend: 舉薦 *-jiahn*↓; 推舉 nominate; 選舉 select (person), elect, -tion. (4) Praise, laud: 稱舉 sing the praises of, speak highly of. (5) Give birth to: 舉子 *-tzyy*↓; 舉一女 give birth to a girl; 不舉 (of woman) barren, sterile, (of man) impotent. (6) Propose, suggest, offer, put forward: 舉發 *-fa*, 舉出 *-chu*↓; 舉一反三 learning by analogy, (student) think for himself; 舉例 *-lih*↓; 舉證 offer as proof (evidence); 檢舉 denounce, expose, indict.

Adj. All, every one of: 舉國 the whole country; 舉家 the entire family; 舉世 all the world; 舉座 every one of the audience.

舉哀 *jyuu-ai*, v.i. & n., wailing during funeral service.

舉辦 *jyuubahn*, v. t., initiate, undertake, found, sponsor.

舉兵 *jyuu-bing*, v. i., raise an army to fight.

舉步 *jyuu-buh*, (1) v. i., take a stride forward; (2) n., a person's gait.

舉出 *jyuu-chu*, v.t., enumerate, itemize, cite (as example).

舉動 *jyuuduhng*, n., an act, action, a move, activity: 一舉一動 every move; 舉動兒 *-'dung'l*, n., (euphem.) s.t. going on.

舉發 *jyuufa*, v.t., expose (the guilt, wrongdoing) of (s.o.); accuse publicly or at court.

舉凡 *jyuufarn*, adv., all without exception.

舉火 *jyur-huoo*, v. i., (make fire to) cook food.

舉證 *jyuujehng* n., give proof, evidence: 舉證責任 burden of proof.

舉架 *jyuujiah*, n., the altitude of a building.

舉薦 *jyuujiahn*, v. t., recommend (person) for service.

舉重 *jyuujuhng*, (1) v. i., to lift weights; (2) n., weightlifting.

舉踵 *jyur-juung*, v. i., to stand on tiptoe in an anticipatory mood.

舉止 *jyurjyy*, n., behavior, conduct.

舉例 *jyuu-lih*, (1) v.i., to give examples; (2) n., an example or illustration.

舉人 *jyuurern*, n., formerly, successful candidates of provincial examinations.

舉行 *jyuushirng*, v.t., hold (a meeting, discussion, ceremony), begin (to do).

舉手 *jyur-shoou*, v. i., raise hands, to vote by a show of hands.

舉事 *jyuu-shyh*, v. i., raise the standard of revolt, see *-yih*↓.

舉措 *jyuutsuoh*, n., an act, action, any measure taken.

舉子 *jyurtzyy*, (1) v. i., given birth to a son; (2) bring up a baby; (3) n., see *-rern*↑.

舉業 *jyuuyeh*, n., formerly, literary studies pursued by would-be candidates of government examinations.

舉義 *jyuu-yih*, v. i., raise the standard of revolt against a tyrant (an unpopular government).

乎 90.00

hu (usu. unaccented or *hur*).

Fin. part. (1) (LL) indicating a question (=vern. 嗎): 有所求乎 is there s.t. you (or they) want? 然乎否乎 yes or no? 如此可乎 would this do? (2) (LL) indicating an exclamation or calling a person: 知我者，其惟兄乎 perhaps only you understand me! 乎哉 in 危乎殆哉 how dangerous! 賜乎 Ah, Syh!

Prep. To, at (=於): 莫大乎此 nothing greater than this; 出乎不料 (=出於不料) came as a surprise; 合乎道理 is in accord with reason.

爭 90.00

jeng (*jehng).

V.i. & t. & n. (1) Compete, struggle, take part in contest: 相爭 compete with each other; 好爭 quarrelsome; 鬪爭 to struggle, a struggle (for supremacy), fight; 競爭 competition, contest, match; 爭權奪利 struggle for power and money; 爭功 fight to show results or for recognition of merit; 爭年 (AC) argue as to who is older; 爭閒氣 fight for vain or trivial reasons. (2) To argue, dispute: 爭辯, 爭論 *-biahn*, *-luhn*↓.

Adj. (*jehng) (Interch. 諍) straightforward, straight-speaking: 爭臣 (AC) honest-speaking minister; 爭友 (AC) friend who gives straight advice; 爭子 (AC) a son who gives candid advice to father.

Adj. & conj. (MC) how (=modn. 怎): 爭知 how does one know; 爭得, 爭可 how can; 爭忍 how can one bear to; 爭不 why not; 爭奈, 爭似 *-naih*, *-syh*↓.

爭霸 *jeng-bah*, v. i., (AC) compete for hegemony among states.

爭辯 *jengbiahn*, v. i. & n., argue,

dispute; a controversy: 不和他爭辯 will not argue with him.

爭吵 *jengchaau*, v. i. & n., squabble, brawl, altercation, fracas.

爭強 *jengchiarng*, v. i., to struggle in rivalry; compete for supremacy.

爭氣 *jengchih*, v. i., to fight for purely emotional reasons (for honor or rivalry).

爭持 *jengchyr*, (1) v. i., to wrangle, contend, to contest ground, not give in; (2) n., contention.

爭取 *jeng chyuu*, v.i. & t., to strive for, to fight for.

爭鬪 *jengdouh*, v. i. & n., (to) fight, wrangle.

爭端 *jengduan*, n., point of dispute, "bone of contention."

爭奪 *jengduor*, v. i. & n., to fight, a fight for possession (of land, power, position, beautiful woman).

爭風 *jeng-feng*[1], phr., 爭風吃醋 fight for a man's or woman's favors.

爭鋒 *jeng-feng*[2], v. i., to match on battlefield: 爭鋒對壘.

爭光 *jeng-guang*, v. i., vie for honor. ⌈rival.

爭衡 *jeng-herng*, v. i., contend, to

爭競 *jeng'jihng*, (1) v. i., to compete (also 競爭); (2) n., competition.

爭執 *jengjyr*, v. i. & n., see *-chyr* ↑.

爭論 *jengluhn*, v. i & n., (engage in) controversy.

爭奈 *jengnaih*, adv., (MC) however (=怎奈=無奈).

爭勝 *jengshehng*, v. i. & n., see *-chiarng* ↑.

爭先 *jeng-shian*, v. i., fight to be first: 爭先恐後 in a mad rush to be first.

爭些 *jengshie*, adv., (MC) almost (=modn. 差一點兒).

爭席 *jeng-shir*, v. i., indulge in argument on seating order at table.

爭雄 *jeng-shyurng*, v. i., fight for supremacy.

爭訟 *jengsuhng*, n., lawsuit.

爭似 *jengsyh*, adv., (MC) like: 多情爭似無情 true love conceals love ("ardent love appears like cold").

爭嘴 *jengtzueei*, v. i., to bicker, squabble.

豸 90.00

jyh.

[See 91.00]

孚 90.00

fur (*fu*).

V.i. (1) Inspire confidence: 名孚衆望, 不孚衆望 prestige commands, does not command, public confidence. (2) To trust: 孚信. (3) U.f. of 孵 90S.00 to hatch.

Adj. Sincere.

季 90.00

jih.

N. (1) A period of three months in a year: 四季 the four seasons; 春, 夏, 秋, 冬季 spring, summer, autumn, winter; 雨季 the rainy season; 季節 *-jier* ↓; 季刊, 季報 *-kan*, *-bauh* ↓. (2) A surname.

Adj. (1) Youngest: 季弟, 季子, 季女 the youngest brother, son, daughter; 季父 *-fuh* ↓. (2) Last month: 季春, 夏, 秋, 冬 the last month of spring, summer, autumn, winter; 季世 the declining years of a dynasty, a period of decadence.

季報 *jihbauh*, n., a quarterly.

季風 *jihfeng*, n., a seasonal wind, the monsoon.

季父 *jihfuh*, n., the youngest paternal uncle.

季節 *jihjier*, n., (1) one of the four seasons in a year; (2) one of the 24 periods of 15 days each into which a year is divided; see Appendix B.

季軍 *jihjyun*, n., second runner-up, the third winner in contest.

季刊 *jihkan*, n., a quarterly.

季兒 *jieh'l*, n., season (of fruit, etc.): 西瓜季兒, 螃蟹季兒 season for watermelons, crabs.

學 90.00

shyuer (**shiaur*).

[Abbr. 学, 斈]

N. (1) Learning, knowledge: 求學 go to school, pursue studies; 問學 (LL) to pursue knowledge, inquiry; 學問 *-wehn* ↓; 飽學之士 an erudite scholar ("full of learning"); 博學 widely read. (2) A branch of study: 數學, 天文學 mathematics, astronomy; 文學 literature; 科學 science; 自然科學 natural science; 醫學 medicine, etc. (3) School, college: 小學 elementary school; 中學 secondary or high school; 大學 college, university; 學院 *-yuahn* ↓; 學校 *-shiauh* ↓; 專科學校 schools of different special arts or sciences (polytechnic, commerce, accounting, etc.); 職業學校 professional or vocational school. (4) Course of education: 入學 entrance to school; 升學 be promoted to higher course of instruction; 留學 study abroad; 同學 fellow student, fellow alumnus, -ni; 休學, 輟學 drop out, stop schooling; 復學 return to school; 學業 *-yeh* ↓.

V.i. & t. (1) (Also **shiaur*) to learn from (person), to imitate: 學不上來 cannot learn (subject) or imitate (example); 學不會 cannot learn; 學嘴, 學舌 *-tzueei*, *-sher* ↓. (2) To learn and become: 學壞了 learn from bad example or habit; 學乖了 learn to be harmless, keep one's mouth shut, in gen., learn the ways of the world and be "a good boy." (3) To study (some subject); to learn (a skill): 學習 *-shir* ↓; 學如不及 study as if one could never learn enough; 學買賣 learn a trade, be an apprentice; 學禮貌 learn good manners; 學無老少 never too old to learn; 勤學, 苦學 study hard.

學案 *shyuer-ahn*, n., a work somewhat like national biography, limited to scholars and giving a résumé with important quotations from their philosophical thoughts: e. g., 明儒學案 devoted to scholars of Mirng period.
學伴兒 *shyuer-bah'l*, n., school companion.
學程 *shyuer-cherng*, n., (1) course of studies; (2) scholastic record.
學期 *shyuer-chir*, n., a semester.
學額 *shyuer-er*, n., (1) capacity for number of students; (2) a scholarship.
學費 *shyuer-feih*, n., tuition, school fees.
學分 *shyuer-fen*, n., school marks.
學風 *shyuer-feng*, n., gen. atmosphere of a school or of the scholarly world; tendency of scholars of a certain period or generation.
學府 *shyuer-fuu*, n., institution of higher learning; university or college circles.
學館 *shyuer-guaan*, n., a private school for tutoring at home.
學海 *shyuer-haai*, phr., the sea of learning.
學會 *shyuer-hueih*, n., a learned society.
學長 *shyuer-jaang*, n., (1) court. term of address among fellow students; (2) principal of a preparatory school.
學者 *shyuerjee*, n., a scholar, a learned man.
學政 *shyuer-jehng*, n., formerly, educational commissioner of a province.
學界 *shyuer-jieh*, n., the educational circles, the literati collectively.
學究 *shyuerjiouh*, n., (contempt.) a man of limited knowledge, a type bred by the civil examinations confined to rigmarole knowledge of the Confucian classics: 老學究, 村學究 a village schoolmaster.
學級 *shyuer-jir*[1], n., grade or year in school.
學籍 *shyuer-jir*[2], n., record of registration in certain school or college.
學制 *shyuer-jyh*, n., educational system.
學科 *shyuer-ke*, n., branch of study in school or college (physics, etc.).
學力 *shyuer-lih*[1], n., strength or depth of knowledge or lack of it.
學歷 *shyuer-lih*[2], n., *curriculum vitae*, a person's record of schooling.
學理 *shyuer-lii*, n., scientific truth or its explanation, theory.
學齡 *shyuer-lirng*, n., a child's school age: 學齡兒童 children of school age.
學名 *shyuer-mirng*, n., (1) scientific or Latin term; (2) formerly, a man's registered name in school, dist. 乳名 pet name at home.
學年 *shyuer-niarn*, n., an academic year.
學派 *shyuer-paih*, n., school of thought.
學人 *shyuerrern*, n., scholar; academic circles.
學舍 *shyuer-sheh*, n., school building.
學生 *shyuer'sheng*, n., (1) student, pupil; (2) sometimes used as self-reference vis-à-vis elder or scholar.
學舌 **shiaursher*, v. i., carry gossip.
學校 *shyuershiauh*, n., school, used generally. of many types, see N. 3↑.
學行 *shyuer-shihng*, n., scholarship and conduct (usu. of students at school).
學習 *shyuershir*, v. i. & t., (1) to learn (sciences, arts, technique, etc.); learn from (models); (2) (-'*shi*) to copy, learn (bad habits).
學術 *shyuershuh*, n., learning, scholarship in gen., but esp. with respect to thought: 學術界 academic circles; 學術論文 learned essays, scientific papers.
學說 (1) *shyuershuo*, n., theory of a school of thought; (2) *shiaur'shuo*, v. i., repeat what s. o. has said: 這一篇話是他學說給我聽了 I heard all this from him, as he repeated it.
學士 *shyuershyh*[1], n., (1) the learned class in gen.; (2) formerly, official title of high rank: 翰林學士 Hanlin academician; 某殿學士 councillor of certain high councils; (3) a modern college graduate, B. A.
學識 *shyuershyh*[2], n., insight, understanding: 有學無識 (a person) knows a great deal of books but lacks insight and discrimination.
學堂 *shyuertarng*, n., school (now more commonly called 學校 *-shiauh* ↑).
學徒 *shyuertur*, n., (1) student; (2) (oft. **shiaur-*) one learning a trade in shop, apprentice.
學童 *shyuerturng*, n., schoolchildren in gen.
學嘴 *shyuertzueei* (**shiaur-*), v.i., repeat gossip, see *-sher* ↓.
學子 *shyuertzyy*, n., (LL) a student, scholar.
學問 *shyuerwehn*, n., knowledge, learning, scholarship.
學位 *shyuerweih*, n., academic degree.
學務 *shyuerwuh*, n., as in 學務大臣 (19th cen.) minister of education.
學樣 *shyuer-yahng*, v.i., copy or imitate s.o.'s example.
學業 *shyueryeh*, n., a person's studies, esp. school or college studies.
學藝 *shyuer-yih*, n., gen. term for academic studies and the arts.
學友 *shyuer-yoou*, n., schoolmate, fellow alumni.
學院 *shyueryuahn*, n., an independent college, an institute of learning.
學員 *shyueryuarn*, n., member of an institution of learning; (court.) student.

爵 90.00

jyuer.

N. (1) A cup or goblet: 爵杯 a wine cup; 錫爵 give (s.o.) a goblet as present. (2) A feudal title, nobility: 爵祿 *-luh*, 爵位 *-weih*, 爵士 *-shyh*↓; 加官進爵 receive official promotion; 公爵 a duke; 侯爵 a marquis; 伯爵 a count.

爵祿 *jyuerluh*, n., a feudal title (a degree of nobility) and the emoluments that went with it.

爵士 *jyuershyh*, n., (1) the holder of a knighthood; (2) jazz: 爵士樂 jazz music; 爵士舞 jazz dance.

爵位 *jyuerweih*, n., any one of the five ranks of nobility: 公, 侯, 伯, 子, 男; official rank and honor.

§ 90.01 (丿/小)

禾 90.01

her.

N. (1) Grain in gen.: 禾苗 grain seedling; 禾稾 grain stalk; 禾菽 rice and beans; 禾木旁 the radical 禾, as in 秋, 租, 秧. (2) A surname.

采 90.01

tsaai (**tsaih*).

N. (1) Variegated color (interch. 彩 90S.91). (2) Color and facial expression: 神采 spiritual expression; 豐采 vital, attractive expression. (3) (**tsaih*) 采邑 fief town, feudal benefice.

V.t. To pluck, gather, select (vegetables, flowers) (interch. 採 10A.01).

Adj. Multi-colored (interch. 彩 90S.91).

采緝 *tsaaichih*, v.t., compile (also 採).

采芹 *tsaaichirn*, v.i., (LL) to get first degree in civil examinations.

采集 *tsaaijir*, v.t., to gather, collect (also 採).

采摭 *tsaaijyr*, v.t., to gather from various sources, esp. in patch-up work (also 採).

采色 *tsaaiseh*, n., variegated colors (also 彩).

采聲 *tsaaisheng*, n., applause (also 彩).

采戲 *tsaaishih*, n., game of dice (with different colors).

采采 *tsairtsaai*, adj., (AC) flowery, abundant.

采衣 *tsaai-yi*, n., colored dress (also 彩).

棃 90.01

lir.

[More common var. 梨]

N. (Bot.) the pear: 雪棃 a large white juicy pear; 鴨兒棃 a kind of sweet juicy pear; 涷棃 an old man's mottled skin like that of a pear.

V.t. (Interch. 剺) slash, cut with a knife: 棃面流血 with face cut and bleeding.

棃膏 *lir-gau*, n., (Chin. med.) a cough mixture made of mashed pears and honey.

棃花 *lirhua*, n., pear flower: 棃花槍 a set of fighting tactics with spears or lances; 棃花大鼓 a popular entertainment in which the singer sings folk songs to the accompaniment of a drum by herself (also 山東大鼓); 棃花簡 brass castanets used by *lirhua* singers.

棃棗 *lirtzaau*, n., wooden printing blocks (usu. made of pear and date wood).

棃渦 *lirwo*, n., a dimple (also called 酒渦).

棃園 *liryuarn*, n., (MC) a theater: 棃園子弟 actors; 棃園行 the profession of actors.

系 90.01

shih.

N. (1) A system: 系統 or 統系 a system, see *-tuung*↓; 體系 system of government, of institutions, of philosophy, of theology; 太陽系 the solar system; 神經系統 or 統系 nervous system, etc. (2) Lineage: 世系 family lineage; 帝系 ancestral lineage of royal house; 譜系 chart of family tree; 直系 direct descendant; 旁系 collateral branch of family. (3) Faction: 安福系, 直系 Anfu faction, Chihli faction. (4) Department in college: 政治系, 文學系 department of political science, of literature. (5) (Math.) corollary.

V.t. To involve, tie up with: 系絆 *-bahn*; 系念 *-niahn*↓.

系絆 *shihbahn*, n., to entangle, as with rope, to cause stumbling.

系列 *shihlieh*, n., a series (of events, successive theories, etc.).

系念 *shihniahn*, v. t., to be concerned, think always of (person).

系孫 *shihsun*, n., a grandson by lineage system, distantly related.

系統 *shihtuung*, n., a system (of thought, doctrines): 有系統的哲學 systematic philosophy.

系族 *shihtzur*, n., the clan, members of the clan.

秉 90.01

biing.

N. (1) Ancient unit of measure

=16 斛 *hur* or 160 斗 *doou*, bushels.

V.t. To hold: 秉燭, 秉筆 hold candle, pen; 秉燭夜遊 (LL) have night outings with candles in hand (a short but merry life); 秉筆直書 (of historian) write down the truth, even though unpalatable; 秉權, 秉鈞 to hold position of power; 秉鉞 (AC) hold axe, i.e., symbol of military power; 秉公辦理 decide case according to law.

秉持 *biingchyr*, n. & v.t., (esp. Budd.) self-discipline.
秉賦 *biingfuh*, n., born natural talent (=稟△賦 60.01).
秉正 *biingjehng*, adj., upright, just.
秉直 *biingjyr*, adj., ditto.
秉性 *biingshihng*, n., natural temperament (=稟△性 60.01).
秉彝 *biingyir*, n., (LL) the God-given laws, moral values.

乘 90.01

cherng (**shehng*).

N. adjunct. (Also **shehng*) 一乘車, 一乘轎 one carriage, one sedan chair.

N. (1) Multiplication: 乘方, 乘法, 乘號 *-fang*, *-faa*, *-hauh*↓. (2) (Also **shehng*) number of carriages: 車一乘 one carriage; 千乘之國 (AC) a (big) country with a thousand carriages of chariots. (3) (**shehng*) 史乘 historical works. (4) (**shehng*) A main division of Buddhist schools: 大乘 *mahayana*, the "greater vehicle"; 小乘 *hinayana*, the "lesser vehicle"; 三乘 the three orders of Buddha's disciples or saints: 菩薩乘 the *bodhisatva*; 辟支乘 the *pratyeka*; 聲聞乘 Buddha's personal disciples.

V.i. & t. (1) To multiply (as 3×8): 自乘 multiply a number by itself; 相乘 two numbers multiply each other. (2) To mount (horse, carriage, sedan chair), to go aboard (ship, airplane); 乘風破浪 to ride the wind and waves, smooth and swift sailing. (3) To take advantage of (chance, wind, current): 乘間, 乘隙, 乘虛 *-jiahn*, *-shih*, *-shyu*↓; 乘興 *-shihng*; 乘機會 take advantage of opportunity; 乘便宜 buy while it is cheap, see 乘便 *-biahn*↓; 乘人不備 take advantage of another's unpreparedness.

乘便 *cherng-biahn* phr., at one's convenience, without extra trouble.
乘槎 *cherng-char*, phr., (legend) to ride on a raft and reach the Milky Way.
乘除 *cherng-chur*, n., (1) multiplication and 除 division; (2) calculations.
乘法 *cherngfaa*, n., (method of) multiplication.
乘方 *cherngfang*, n., (math.) square, cube, power to nth degree.
乘號 *cherndhauh*, n., the multiplication sign (×).
乘積 *cherngji*[1], n., product of multiplication.
乘機 *cherng-ji*[2], v. t., take the chance and ....
乘間 *cherng-jiahn*, v. i., take the chance (of a good opportunity to speak, attack, etc.).
乘傳 *cherngjuahn*, n., (AC) courier system.
乘客 *cherngkeh*, n., passenger (on ship, plane).
乘空(兒) *cherng-kuhng('l)*, v. i., take advantage of free moment or unguarded situation.
乘涼 *cherng-liarng*, v. i., to enjoy cool air.
乘龍 *cherng-lurng*, v. i., as in 乘龍快婿 (allu.) a handsome or lucky son-in-law.
乘冪 *cherngmih*, n., (math.) power (nth power, etc.).
乘隙 *cherng-shih*, n., take advantage of opening for attack.
乘興 *cherngshihng*, phr., on an impulse to enjoy: 乘興而來 come on an impulse.
乘數 *cherngshuh*, n., a multiple.
乘勢 *cherng-shyh*, v. i., avail oneself of, to strike while the iron is hot.
乘時 *cherng-shyr*, v. i., take full advantage of opportunity.
乘虛 *cherng-shyu*, v. i., to attack where enemy is weak or unguarded.
乘凶 *cherng-shyung*, v. i., formerly, to hold wedding soon after parent's death.

§ 90.02 (丿/⺊)

忝 90.02

tiaan.

V.t. To disgrace: 無忝汝所生 (AC) not be a disgrace to your forefathers.

Adj. & adv. (LL, in self-deprecation) unworthy, -thily: 忝在知交 as your friend (although unworthily); 忝列門牆 have the honor to be counted among your disciples; 忝眷 as your unworthy relative in marriage; 忝居 unworthily (i.e., have the honor) to be (in certain position).

黍 90.02

shuu.

N. (1) (*-tz*) Glutinous millet: 黍酒, 黍醅 wine made from glutinous millet; 黍實, 黍米 millet grain. (2) Maize: 玉蜀黍 maize, Indian corn; 蜀黍 sorghum (also called 高粱).

黎 千 秊 秜

黎 90.02

lir.

N. (1) A surname. (2) An aboriginal tribe on Hainan island in South China Sea.

Adj. (1) Large in numbers, numerous: 黎民 the great masses of people; 黎首, 黎庶, 黎衆, 黎羣 the people at large. (2) Black: 黎黑 pitch-black, pitch-dark.

黎祁 *lirchir*, n., (MC) bean curd (豆腐).

黎豆 *lirdouh*, n., (bot.) cowhage, *Mucuna capitata.*

黎老 *lirlaau*, n., (AC) an aged person.

黎苗 *lirmiaur*, n., the *Li* aboriginal tribes of Hainan.

黎明 *lirmirng*, n., the dawn.

§90.10 (ノ/十)

千 90.10

chian.

N. & adj. (1) A thousand: 整千整萬 thousands; 以千計 count by the thousands; 千慮一得 even a fool may sometimes have a good idea; 千慮一失 even a wise man sometimes makes a mistake; 千鈞一髮 a thousand catties hang upon one hair—extremely delicate situation; 千載一時, 千載難逢 once in a lifetime, golden chance; myriad, innumerable, all sorts of, oft. in conjunction with 百 (hundred) or 萬 (ten thousand): 千方百計 use all sorts of wiles and methods; 千篇一律 (of speech, writing) stereotyped, all alike, monotonous; 千呼百喚 called a great many times (before lady will come out); 千廻百轉 innumerable twists and turns; 千奇百怪 all sorts of strange things; 千言萬語 innumerable words (to persuade); 千思萬想 think over and over again; 千頭萬緒 (of things) extremely complicated and difficult to unravel, a thousand things to attend to; 千千萬萬 tens of thousands. (2) A surname.

Adv. Very, a thousand times: 千祈 (LL) I pray a thousand times (for pardon, acceptance); 千祈勿怪 please do not take offence; see esp. 千萬 *-wahn* ↓; 千不該, 萬不該 deeply (a thousand times) regret; 千了百當 excellent to the nth degree; 千嬌百媚 a thousand charms; 千眞萬確 absolutely true, one can swear it is true.

千秋 *chianchiou*, n., (1) a thousand years; 各有千秋 each in his own way has made an important contribution; (2) a birthday congratulation.

千屈菜 *chianchyutsaih*, n., (bot.) the purple lythrum.

千伏特 *chian-furteh*, n., kilovolt.

千古 *chianguu*, adj., (1) historic, of the ages: 千古奇談 strange stories of the ages; (2) 某某千古 formula in condolences at funerals, "So-and-so has joint the ancients."

千金 *chianjin*, n., (1) (coll. & litr.) your daughter: 三千金 three daughters; (2) a thousand ounces of gold—a heavy price or extremely precious: 千金一笑 a million-dollar smile ("one smile is worth a thousand ounces of gold"); 千金之體 your precious health; 一擲千金 gamble at high stakes.

千週 *chian-jou*, n., kilocycle.

千兒 *chia'l*, n., see 打△千兒 10A.00.

千里 *chianlii*, n., (lit.) a thousand *li*, a long distance: 千里鏡 a telescope, a field glass; 千里馬 a good thoroughbred; 千里駒 a fine race pony, usu., (court.) your brilliant son; 千里眼 (myth.) one who can see several hundred miles away, sometimes (coll.) a field glass.

千門 *chianmern*, n., (LL) a palace gate.

千眠 *chianmiarn*, adj., arch. var. of 芊緜.

千年 *chian-niarn*, phr., a thousand years; 千年艾 (bot.) *Chrysanthemum decaisneanum*; 千年盫 (bot.) *Rhodea japonica* (usu. called 萬年青).

千日紅 *chianryhhurng*, n., (bot.) common globe amaranth, *Gomphrena globosa.*

千歲 *chian sueih*, phr., (1) a thousand years; (2) Your Highness (to a prince, dist. 萬歲 "*banzai*" for Your Majesty).

千層底 *chiantserngdii*, n., shoe sole made of many layers of cloth, firmly stitched together, hence 千底鞋 shoes with cloth soles.

千瓦 (瓩) *chian-waa*, n., kilowatt (kw.).

千萬 *chianwahn*, (1) adv., please do: 千萬小心 please do be careful: 千萬要記得 please do remember; esp. in emphatic negative: 千萬勿忘記 on no account fail to remember; (oft. at end of letter: 千萬千萬 or 千萬珍重 do take care of your health; (2) adj., numerous: 千千萬萬 myriads of.

千葉 *chianyeh*, n., (flowers) of multiple petals.

千億 *chianyih*, n., myriads; 一千億 (lit.) 100,000,000,000 (one hundred thousand million).

 90.10

niarn.

[Anc. var. of 年 92.10]

秜 90.10

lir.

[Var. of 犁]

N. A plough.

V.t. To plough (fields): 秜田 to till fields; 秜庭掃閭, 秜庭掃穴 to overthrow an independent country (lit., "to plough up its court and destroy its hide-outs").

犂牛 *lirniour*, n., black or mottled cow; a buffalo used in ploughing.

舜 90.10

shuhn.

N. Name of ruler (2255–2205 B.C.).

舜華 *Shuhnhuar*, n., (AC) name for hibiscus (also 舜英).

舉 90.10

jyuu.

[Pop. of 舉 90.00; abbr. 挙]

§90.11 (ノ/土)

壬 90.11

rern.

N. The ninth character in the decimal cycle, see Appendix A.

Adj. (1) Great, grand. (2) Artful, deceitful: 壬人 a crafty deceiver.

垂 90.11

chueir.

V.i. & t. (1) To let down (a line), hang down, suspend: 垂髮 let hair hang down; 垂淚 shed tears; 垂釣 *-diauh*↓; 垂直 hang down straight. (2) To leave s.t. for posterity: 垂名 *-mirng*↓; 名垂千古, 名垂竹帛 leave a name in history.

Adv. (1) Down, downward, forming court. compp. with the idea of "graciously," "condescend": 垂詢 you condescended to ask me; 垂愛, 垂青 *-aih*, *-ching*↓. (2) Almost, approaching: 垂老, 垂死 or 垂絕 approaching old age, death; 垂危 close upon death or a crisis; 功敗垂成 attempt fails when success is already in sight.

垂愛 *chueir-aih*, v.i., (court.) show gracious concern for me.

垂泣 *chueirchih*, v.i., to shed tears.

垂青 *chueirching*, v.t., see *-aih*↑; (see 青 10.42, representing a look with the black of the eye): 得蒙垂青 received your kind consideration.

垂垂 *chueirchueir*, adv., (MC poet.) gradually: 一樹垂垂發 a tree gradually grows.

垂釣 *chueir-diauh*, v.i., to angle for fish.

垂櫜 *chueir-gau*, phr., (AC) carry bow case downward, to show one is unarmed.

垂拱 *chueirguung*, v.i., to rule with folded hands—rule in peace.

垂教 *chueir-jiauh*, v.t., (court.) condescend to teach, give advice.

垂直線 *chueirjyr-shiahn*, n., perpendicular line, plumb line.

垂憐 *chueirliarn*[1], v.t., to take pity on.

垂簾 *chueir-liarn*[2], phr., (empress) rule in place of emperor ("behind screen").

垂柳 *chueir-lioou*, n., weeping willow.

垂名 *chueir-ming*, v.i., to leave name for posterity, to be remembered.

垂暮 *chueir-muh*, phr., about sunset or approaching old age.

垂念 *chueir-niahn*, v.i., (court.) so gracious as to remember me.

垂披 *chueirpi*, v.i., (shawl, hair) hang down in a spread.

垂線 *chueir-shiahn*, n., (math.) perpendicular line (cf. *-jyr-shiahn*↑; opp. 橫線 horizontal line).

垂涎 *chueir-shiarn*, v.i. & t., to hanker after, gloat upon (lit., "to slobber"): 垂涎欲滴 make one's mouth watery.

垂手 *chueir-shoou*, v.i., (1) as in 垂手而得 to get or win it with hands down (extreme ease); (2) to let the hands hang by the sides (form of respectful attention beginning Ming Dyn.).

垂髫 *chueir-tiaur*, phr., 垂髫之年 time of young childhood ("letting hair down," uncoiled).

垂涕 *chueir-tih*, v.i., to shed tears.

垂頭 *chueir-tour*, v.i., hang one's head down: 垂頭喪氣 be downcast in spirit.

垂統 *chueir-tuung*, n., (AC) a royal or cultural heritage: 創業垂統 to found a royal dynasty.

垂揚 *chueiryarng*, n., see *-lioou*↑.

重 90.11

juhng (*churng usu. as adv.).

N. (1) Weight, heaviness: 加重 increase weight. (2) (*churng) Layer: 重重 *-churng*↓; 九重天 (Budd.) the nine layers of heaven or the ninth layer.

V.t. To place value upon: 自重 self-respect; 君子自重 (in water-closet) leave the place clean; 珍重 take good care of (your) health; 重然諾 do not make promises lightly; 重友情 would do many things for a friend; 器重, 推重 regard highly (person).

Adj. (1) Heavy, thick: 味太重 flavor is too rich; 油太重, 色太重 oil, color is too heavy; 重心 *-shin*↓; 重利 usury; 重任 responsible post; 重工業 heavy industry; 重金屬 heavy metals; 重

犂 舜 舉 壬 垂 重

亅	小	⺊	十	土	𠂇	廾	⺊	丨	一	丁	フ	口	区	冈	冂	厂	尸	亠	广	宀	丶	乚	弋	心	八	人	乂	一	丿	𠂉	く
00	01	02	10	11	12	20	21	22	30	31	32	40	41	42	50	51	52	60	61	62	63	70	71	72	80	81	82	83	90	91	92	93

重 油 heavy oil; 重負 a heavy burden; 重酪 heavy cream. (2) Important, valuable: 重要, 重大 *-yauh*, *-dah* ↓; 重器, 重寶 valuable treasure; 重兵 a great army. (3) Serious, solemn: 加重 become more serious (of illness); 病重了 illness has become serious; 莊重 solemn (demeanor, ceremony); 莊重些 don't be frivolous; 死重於泰山 (AC) a person's death could be of the greatest significance (or 輕於鴻毛 of no importance at all); 爲人厚重 person is kind and generous. (4) (**churng*) Double, multiple: 重壁 double wall; 重關 series of fortified passes; 重譯 re-translation; 重圍 besieged in several depths; 遠涉重洋 across several oceans; 重瞳 (reputed to have) double eye pupils.

Adv. (1) Heavily, severely: 重打 flog heavily; 重責 rebuke harshly, also heavy responsibility; 重懲, 重罰, 重辦 punish severely; 重傷 severe wound; 重酬, 重賞 richly rewarded, rich reward. (2) (**churng*) Repeatedly, again, successively: 重複, 重疊 *-'fuh*, *-dier* ↓; 重寫 rewrite; 重來一遍 do it once again; 重張 re-open shop; 重整旗鼓 regrouped for battle (lit. or fig.); 重温舊夢 renew the old romance; 重修 *-shiou* ↓; 重婚 *-hun* ↓.

重遷 (1) *juhng-chian*, v. i., (AC) reluctant to move from native district; (2) (**churng-*) move again to new place.

重器 *juhngchih*, n., (AC) national treasure.

重親 **churngchin*, v. i., intermarry by several marriages between families.

重出 **churngchu*, v. i., (of a passage) appear twice in book (as in *Analects*).

重重 **churngchurng*, adj. & adv., layer after layer, multiple series (mountain ranges, roof tops): 重重疊疊 ditto.

重泉 **churng-chyuarn*, n., underground springs: 重泉之下 nether world.

重大 *juhngdah*, adj., weighty, important, serious (disaster, crime, undertaking, etc.).

重典 *juhngdiaan*[1], n., severe punishment, serious regulation.

重點 *juhngdiaan*[2], n., important point.

重疊 **churngdier*, adj. & adv., reduplicated, repeated, -ly, again and again: 重規疊矩 too numerous regulations; see *-churng* ↑.

重地 *juhngdih*, n., important precincts, place of strategic importance, not accessible without permission.

重噸 *juhngduhn*, n., gross ton, long ton.

重犯 *juhngfahn*, n., person convicted of grave crime.

重複 **churng'fuh*, adj., repetitious (writing), redundant.

重婚 **churnghun*, v.i., (of man or woman) be illegally married to two spouses.

重整 **churngjeeng*, v.t., readjust (debts, credit).

重鎭 *juhngjehn*, n., important military base; military governorship.

重繭 **churngjiaan*, adj., (AC) many calluses on feet.

重寄 *juhngjih*, n., (LL) post or appointment of heavy responsibility.

重九 **churngjioou*, n., the 9th day of 9th lunar month, a festival esp. for climbing mountains.

重重(的) *juhngjuhng('de)*, adv., (1) very heavily (punish, reward, etc.); (2) see *-churng* ↑.

重科 *juhngke*, n., a grave crime (felony, murder, etc.).

重量 *juhngliahng*, n., (1) weight; (2) substance: 有重量 (of writing) having real substance.

重力 *juhnglih*, n., gravitation.

重落 **churngluoh*, v. i., (of illness) relapse, take a turn for the worse.

重率 *juhnglyuh*, n., (phys.) specific gravity (also 比重).

重名 *juhng-mirng*, n., great reputation.

重明 **churngmirng*, n., (AC) the light of sun and moon.

重礮 *juhngpauh*, n., heavy artillery.

重申 **churngshen*, v.i. & t., to reiterate, recapitulate; adv., repeatedly.

重身子 *juhngshentz*, adj., pregnant.

重孝 *juhngshiauh*, n., deep mourning for parents.

重心 *juhngshin*, n., (phys.) center of gravity.

重新 **churngshin*, adv., again, anew.

重修 **churngshiou*, v. t., rebuild; (p. p.) rebuilt (temple, road, etc.); take (a given college course) again owing to failure to get passing marks the first time.

重水 *juhngshueei*, n., (phys.) heavy water.

重視 *juhngshyh*, v. t., to value (name, friendship, money, etc.).

重世 **churngshyh*, adj., (AC) generations of.

重侍下 **churngshyhshiah*, phr., the time when grandparents were alive.

重孫(子) **churngsun(tz)*, n., great-grandson.

重孫女 **churngsunnyuu*, n., great-granddaughter.

重聽 *juhngting*, adj., heavy of hearing.

重頭戲 *juhngtour shih*, n., an opera difficult to play or sing.

重罪 *juhngtzueih*, n., a grave crime.

重闈 **churngweir*, n., (1) inner palace; (2) address to grandparents.

重文 **churngwern*, n., repetitious passage; word that appears twice; an ancient variant in 說文 "Shuowern."

重午 **churngwuu*, n., the 5th day of 5th lunar month (also called 端午).

重壓 *juhngya*, n., heavy pressure.

重樣兒 **churngyahng'l*, adj., identical.

重陽 **churngyarng*, n., see *-jioou* ↑.

重要 *juhngyauh*, adj. & n., important (thing, person, task, etc.); ...的重要 the importance of....

重音 *juhngyin*, n., accented (syllable, vowel).

重茵 **churng-yin*, n., double-soft cushion.

重淵 **churng-yuan*, n., (LL) deep waters.

§ 90.20 (ノ/廾)

升 90.20

sheng.

N. A grain measure, a pint, one tenth of 斗 *doou.*

V.i. & t. To go up, to hoist, be promoted: 升旗 hoist a flag; 升高 go up, ascend; 升空 go up the sky, lift-off (astronautics, rocketry); 上升 to make progress upward; 升班, 升級 to be promoted to higher grade; 升階 go up the steps.

升班 *sheng-ban*, v. i., promote, be promoted to higher grade.
升沉 *sheng-chern*, phr., the ups and downs of official career.
升遷 *shengchian*, v. i. & t., to promote, be promoted.
升號 *sheng-hauh*, n., (musical notation) sharp (opp. 降號 flat).
升降 *sheng-jiahng*, phr., see *-chern* ↑; 升降機 *--ji*, n., elevator; crane.
升級 *sheng-jir*, v. i., promote to higher grade; 升級數 (math.) ascending series.
升麻 *shengmar*, n., (bot.) *Cimicifuga foetida.*
升冪 *shengmih*, n., (math.) ascending power: opp. 降冪 descending power.
升遐 *shengshiar*, v. i., (LL) pass away (of emperor).
升學 *sheng-shyuer*, v. i., enter higher class in school, enter higher school.
升堂 *sheng-tarng*, v. i., (1) formerly, (the judge) holds court trial; (2) to know the rudiments of study, contrasted with 入室 be accepted in the inner circle.
升騰 *shengterng*, v. i., (1) to fly up; (2) (*'teng*) to make good progress, flourish in business.
升天 *sheng-tian*, v. i., go up to heaven.

舁 90.20

yur.
[Pop. 舁]

V.t. To carry by two persons together (by pole or by hand): 舁屍 carry a corpse.

§ 90.21 (ノ/ㄴ)

臼 90.21

jiouh.

N. A mortar: 窠臼 (fig.) an old rut; 藥臼 a druggist's mortar; 石臼 a stone mortar; 臼杵 mortar and pestle; 脱臼 dislocation of joints.

臼齒 *jiouh-chyy*, n., the molar teeth, the molars.
臼砲 *jiouhpauh*, n., (ordnance) a mortar.

岳 90.21

yueh.

N. (1) A sacred or high mountain (interch. 嶽). (2) A man's father-in-law, mother-in-law: 岳父, 岳母 *-fuh, -muu* ↓; 家岳 my father-in-law. (3) A surname: 岳廟 temple to Yoh Fei 岳飛, a national hero.

岳伯 *yuehbor*, n., (LL) formerly, a governor in border province.
岳父 *yuehfuh*, n., man's father-in-law.
岳丈 *yuehjahng*, n., ditto.
岳母 *yuehmuu*, n., man's mother-in-law.

臿 90.21

cha.

N. A shovel.

舀 90.21

yaau (sp. pr. *waai, kuaai*).

N. (*-'l, -'tz*) A ladle.

V.t. To ladle up (liquid).

§ 90.22 (ノ/丨)

斤 90.22

jin.

N. (1) An axe, a chopper: 斧斤 axes, hatchets. (2) A measure of weight equal to 16 ounces: 臺斤 Taiwan catty (=600 grams); 公斤 a kilogram; 市斤 a standard catty (=500 grams).

Adj. & adv. (Acting) shrewdly, (seeing) clearly: 斤斤其明 (AC) paying close attention to every detail; 斤斤較量, 斤斤計較 be calculating and unwilling to make the smallest sacrifice, esp. in monetary matters.

斤兩 *jin-liaang*, n., weight of

things: 論斤兩 according to weight; (fig.) to quibble, pettifogging.

斥 90.22

chyh.

V.i. & t. (1) To scold, shout at, rebuke harshly: 駁斥 make a sharp reply in argument. (2) To dismiss sharply, expel (interch. 叱): 斥退 *-tueih*↓; 斥放 expel to distant land; 斥罵 *-mah*↓. (3) To open up land: 斥土, 斥地 ditto. (4) To set watch sentinel: 斥候 *-houh*↓; 斥騎 a cavalry on the watch. (5) To fill up: 充斥 fill up a place.

斥罷 *chyhbah*, v. i., (LL) to dismiss from office.
斥斥 *chyhchyh*, adj., (AC) broad, spacious.
斥革 *chyhger*, v. t., to dismiss from office.
斥候 *chyhhouh*, n., a sentinel.
斥逐 *chyhjur*, v. t., to dismiss angrily, to expel unceremoniously.
斥力 *chyhlih*, n., (phys.) power of repulsion.
斥鹵 *chyhluu*, n., land impregnated with salt, therefore barren.
斥罵 *chyhmah*, v. t., to bawl out s. o. (also wr. 叱罵).
斥賣 *chyhmaih*, v. t., (AC) sell out (horses).
斥退 *chyh-tueih*, v. t., to dismiss (person) from presence; expel (student) from school.
斥責 *chyhtzer*, v. t., to rebuke severely (also wr. 叱責).

乑 90.22

juhng.

[Cogn. 衆 91.02]

乖 90.22

guai.

Adj. (1) Preverse, obstreperous: 乖戾, 乖僻, 乖謬, 乖張 *-lih*, *-pih*, *-miouh*, *-jang*↓. (2) Quick-witted, shrewd: see 乖覺, 乖角 *-jyuer*[1], *-jyuer*[2]↓. (3) Well-behaved, lovely, good, usu., said of children: 乖乖兒的 be good and quiet! 乖兒子 (a doting father's) lovely son; 乖孩子, 乖小子 good little boy.

乖巧 *guaichiaau*, adj., clever, intellingent.
乖乖 *guaiguai*, n., (of children) (vocative) my darling: 小乖乖 my little darling.
乖張 *guaijang*, adj., perverse, intractable, refractory.
乖覺 *guaijyuer*[1], adj., quick-witted, intelligent, bright, clever.
乖角 *guaijyuer*[2], adj., ditto.
乖戾 *guailih*, adj., (1) disagreeable, unfriendly; (2) (of conduct) unreasonable, perverse.
乖謬 *guaimiouh*, adj., absurd, silly.
乖僻 *guaipih*, adj., odd, whimsical, peculiar.
乖違 *guaiweir*, adj., (1) contradictory, conflicting; (2) separate(d).
乖異 *guaiyih*, adj., odd, eccentric, unconventional.

帋 90.22

jyy.

[Var. of 紙 93B.71]

帮 90.22

bang.

[Pop. of 幫 11.22]

幚 90.22

bang.

[Var. of 幫 11.22]

乔 90.22

chiaur.

[Abbr. of 喬 90.42]

§ 90.30 (ノ/一)

丘 90.30

chiou.

[Pop. 坵 11A.30]

N. (1) A mound: 土丘, 小丘, 山丘; 丘陵 *-lirng*↓; 沙丘 sand dunes; specifically a grave: 丘木 tree planted on a grave; 丘墓, 丘墳, 丘壟 *-muh*, *-fern*, *-luung*↓. (2) Generally used to denote the open country, or wild country: 丘民 (AC) country people, the farmers; 丘野, 丘里, 丘墟 *-yee*, *-lii*, *-shyu*↓. (3) A surname.

Adj. (1) (AC) eldest: 丘嫂 eldest sister-in-law. (2) (MC) empty: 丘亭 an empty pavilion.

丘八 *chiouba*, n., (sl.) a soldier (from two components of the character 兵: 丘 and 八).
丘墳 *chioufern*, n., a grave in the form of an earthen mound; a graveyard.
丘壑 *chiouhuoh*, n., (lit.) "hills and ravines"—(1) a wooded country for retirement; (2) 胸中丘壑 a mind's intricate thoughts.
丘井 *chioujiing*, n., (Budd.) dried-up well, (fig.) of old, used-up person.
丘里 *chioulii*, n., native village.
丘陵 *chioulirng*, n., an earthen mound, knoll, hillock (oft. used for imperial mausoleum, see 陵 32A.82).
丘壟 *chiouluung*, n., an earthen mound.
丘墓 *chioumuh*, n., a grave.
丘山 *chioushan*, n., (1) a mound, a hill; (2) the wild country; (3) (AC) (fig.) a "mountain" of things.

丘墟 *chioushyu*, n., (1) wild country; (2) bare hills and devastated country.

丘野 *chiouyee*, n., the rural country.

丘園 *chiouyuarn*, n., a garden in the hills.

盥 90.30

guahn.

N. A washbowl.

V.i. & t. To clean with water: 盥濯, 盥洗 wash; 盥沐 bathe; 盥手 wash hands; 盥櫛 do washing and combing; 盥漱間 lavatory, washroom.

埀 90.30

chueir.

[Var. of 垂 90.11]

舋 90.30

shihn.

[Var. of 釁 90.50]

鍫 90.30

chiau.

N. A shovel.

§ 90.40 (ノ/口)

后 90.40

houh.

N. (1) A queen: 太后, 母后 queen mother; 后妃 the queen and maids of honor of different ranks; 皇后 empress; 皇太后 empress dowager. (2) (AC) sovereign, ruler.

Adv. Var. of 後.

后稷 *houhjir*, n., (1) the god of agriculture; (2) the minister of agriculture under Emperor Shun 舜 (2255–2205 B.C.).

后土 *houhtuu*, n., god of the earth: 皇天后土 Heaven and Earth personified or their spirits.

舌 90.40

sher.

N. (1) The tongue: 吐舌, 咋舌 put out the tongue; 結舌 tongue-tied; 口舌是非 disputes, wagging of tongues; 長舌 loquacious; 舌短, 舌鈍 slow of speech ("tongue is thick"); 饒舌 talk rot or unnecessarily, tittle-tattle; 嘴尖舌巧, 油嘴滑舌 flippant; 空口白舌 persiflage, pure bunk; 插舌 interrupt a talk; 舌劍脣槍 battle of wits, repartee; 舌戰 *-jahn* ↓; 喉$^{\Delta}$舌 40A.81. (2) The tongue of a bell (鐘舌); mouth of grain bin. (3) The flame of a fire (火舌); the inner flap of a shoe.

舌本 *sher-been*, n., the base of the tongue; see *-gen* ↓.

舌鋒 *sher-feng*, n., as in 舌鋒尖利 have a sharp tongue.

舌疳 *sher-gan*, n., (Chin. med.) tongue cancer.

舌根 *sher-gen*, n., the base of the tongue.

舌耕 *sher-geng*, v. i., to teach as a living ("plough with the tongue," cf. 筆$^{\Delta}$耕 92A.10).

舌骨 *sherguu*, n., (physiol.) the hyoid bone.

舌戰 *sherjahn*, n., a battle of wits, repartee.

舌尖 *sherjian*, n., the tip of the tongue.

舌門 *shermern*, n., valve.

舌衄 *shernyuh*, n., hemorrhage on the tongue.

舌下腺 *shershiah-shiahn*, n., (physiol.) sublingual gland.

舌苔 *shertair*, n., fur on the tongue, tongue-coating.

舌頭 *sher'tou*, n., (1) generally, front of the tongue; (2) ability to talk: 舌頭尖利 sharp-tongued; 舌頭精 (abusive) gossip-monger.

舌炎 *sheryarn*^{1}, n., tongue inflammation.

舌癌 *sheryarn*^{2}, n., tongue cancer.

舌葉 *sheryeh*, n., tongue blade.

舌音 *sheryin*, n., lingual sounds (plosives and liquids, like *d*, *t*, *l*, *n*).

舌癰 *sheryung*, n., tongue ulcer.

呑 90.40

tun.

V.t. (1) To swallow (lit. & fig.): 呑下去 swallow down; 呑不下咽 cannot swallow food (out of sorrow); 狼呑虎嚥 to eat voraciously; 呑雲吐霧 (fig.) to smoke opium or tobacco; 呑煙 to swallow opium as means of suicide; 呑金, 呑刀 swallow gold, knife as means of suicide; 忍氣呑聲 swallow insult and humiliation silently; 呑恨 to suffer grief, anger silently. (2) To absorb, annex another country: 呑併, 併呑鄰國 annex neighboring country; 呑併, 呑佔, 呑據 *-bihng*, *-jahn*, *-jyuh* ↓; 鯨呑 gobble up neighbor's

丘 盥 埀 舋 鍫 后 舌 呑

territory (蠶食 nibble at same).

呑併 *tunbihng*, v.t., to annex (territory) by force.
呑佔 *tunjahn*, v.t., take possession of land illegally.
呑據 *tunjyuh*, v.t., ditto.
呑滅 *tunmieh*, v.t., destroy (another country).
呑沒 *tunmoh*, v.t., (1) destroy (country); (2) embezzle (呑沒公款).
呑噬 *tunshyh*, v. t., to eat up in large mouthfuls, gobble up.
呑吐 *tuntuu*, v. i., not to speak out one's mind straightforwardly: 半呑半吐, 呑呑吐吐 "speak a word, swallow the next word"; 呑吐了半天 hem and haw for a long time.

嚳 90.40

kuh.

N. 帝嚳 name of legendary emperor.

礐 90.40

chyueh (**leh*).

Adj. (1) Rocky (mountain). (2) Descriptive of sound of falling rocks or (**leh*) rocks splashing the water.

譽 90.40

yuh (also *yur*).

N. A good name, fame: 名譽, 聲譽, 美譽 good reputation; 盛譽 a great reputation; 清譽 reputation for upright character.

V.t. To praise (person): 稱譽 ditto; 獎譽 give praise or encouragement by superior.

§ 90.41 (ノ/囗)

昏 90.41

hun.

N. (1) Twilight, dusk, evening: 黃昏 evening; 晨昏 early morning and late at night; 昏曉 (LL) ditto. (2) U.f. 婚 in 婚$^{\Delta}$姻 93A.41. (3) A surname.

V.i. To faint, swoon off: 他昏過去了 he has fainted.

Adj. (1) Muddled, confused, darkened: 昏天黑地 in total darkness, complete disregard of accepted ways of life (of character); 昏亂, 昏迷 *-luahn, -mir*↓. (2) Giddy, dimmed: 頭昏眼花 feel dizzy and dimmed in eyesight; 老眼昏花 cannot see clearly, eyesight is dimmed; 昏頭昏腦 muddle-headed, confused; 昏聵 *-kueih*↓. (3) Slow-witted, idiotic: 昏庸, 昏愚 *-yurng, -yur*↓.

昏憊 *hunbeih*, adj., extremely exhausted.
昏沈 *hunchern*, adj., (of person or his mind) muddled, beclouded, misguided.
昏黑 *hunhei*, adj., darkened (sky).
昏花 *hunhua*, adj., dim-sighted, dull-eyed.
昏黃 *hunhuarng*, adj., dusky, twilight (sky).
昏昏 *hunhun*, adj., murky, unclear; clouded (mind), in a semiconscious state.
昏厥 *hunjyuer*, adj., (LL) fainted off; in state of coma.
昏君 *hunjyun*, n., a licentious or lawless or idiotic sovereign.
昏聵 *hunkueih*, adj., dull in mind, capricious or lawless (ruler).
昏亂 *hunluahn*, adj., confusing, disorderly (affairs).
昏昧 *hunmeih*, adj., half-witted, stupid.
昏迷 *hunmir*, adj., (1) fainting, comatose; (2) sunk, depraved.
昏愚 *hunyur*, adj., stupid.
昏庸 *hunyurng*, adj., stupid (ruler) slow-witted.

 90.41

shiang.

N. (1) Spice, incense: 燒香拜佛 burn incense and pray; 進香 go on pilgrimage; 盤香 an incense coil; 香檀 sandalwood; 沉香 garuwood, lignaloes of East Indies; 蚊香 incense for driving away mosquitoes; 書香 family of scholar ancestors; 香袋, 香室 *-daih, -shyh*^{2}↓; 香爐 *-lur*↓. (2) Scent, aroma, fragrance: 鳥語花香 birds' twitter and fragrance of flowers; in comb. with 玉 (jade), refers to women: 憐香惜玉 tenderness toward woman; 香消玉殞 death of a pretty woman; 偷香竊玉 have illicit relations with women; 國色天香 a great beauty; 玉生香 scented flesh of woman. (3) Popularity, a good name: 留香百世 leave a good name for posterity; 吃香 (coll.) very popular. (4) A radical. (5) A surname.

V.t. To smell or sniff close to skin in lieu of kissing: 香香面孔 "kiss" the face (of child, woman); 香香嘴 to kiss.

Adj. (1) Nice-smelling, fragrant, aromatic: 香氣, 香味 *-chih, -weih*↓; 咖啡香濃 rich aroma of coffee; 香噴噴, 香馥馥 rich in fragrance; 香茶, 香片 *-char, -piahn*↓; 香酥鴨 crisp duck cooked in Szechuen style. (2) Richly satisfying (sleep, food): 這頓飯吃得很香 a very satisfying meal; 睡得很香 enjoyed a very sound sleep; 香睡 sweet slumber; 香甜 *-tiarn*↓. (3) (Coll.) fond: 他們原來很香 they were very fond of each other. (4) Popular: (coll.) 這種貨很吃香 these goods are very popular now. (5) Pertaining to woman: 香腮 feminine cheeks; 香閨 lady's chamber; 香柬 lady's letter; 香魂 a lady's departed spirit.

A

香案 *shiang-ahn*, n., incense table, the altar.

香賓 *shiangbin*[1], n., (translit.) champion.

香檳 *shiangbin*[2], n., (translit.) champagne.

香餑餑兒 *shiangbo'bo'l*, n., "fragrant dumpling"—sweetheart; matinee idol and the like.

香刹 *shiang-chah*, n., Buddhist temple.

香茶 *shiang-char*, n., scented tea, see *-piahn* ↓.

香腸 *shiangcharng*, n., sausage.

香橙 *shiangcherng*, n., orange.

香錢 *shiangchiarn*, n., gift of money to temples on visits.

香氣 *shiangchih*, n., aroma, scent, nice smell.

香臭 *shiang-chouh*, n., quality, good and bad: 不知香臭 do not know good from bad.

香椿 *shiangchun*, n., (bot.) the fragrant cedar, *Cedrala odorata*.

香袋 *shiang-daih*, n., perfume satchels.

香斗 *shiang-doou*, n., incense pot.

香墩兒 *shiang due'l*, n., wooden or clay base for sticking incense sticks.

香粉 *shiangfeeng*, n., cosmetics, face powder: 香粉之資 woman's pin money.

香分 *shiang-fehng*, n., see *-chiarn* ↑.

香楓 *shiangfeng*, n., sweet gum, balsam-producing tree.

香港 *Shianggaang*, n., Hong Kong; 香港腳 Hong Kong foot.

香瓜 *shianggua*, n., muskmelon; also different varieties of sweet melon.

香閨 *shiangguei*, n., lady's chamber.

香荷包 *shiang-her'bau*, n., see *-daih* ↑.

香灰 *shiang-huei*, n., incense ashes.

香會 *shianghueih*, n., (1) a pilgrimage; (2) a group of pilgrims, with acrobats, stilts-walkers, tailors, food vendors, etc.

香火 *shianghuoo*, n., (1) public worship at Buddhist temples: 香火盛 good attendance at temple ("many incense sticks and candles burning"); (2) the burning of candles and incense in an oath before spirits: 香火誓 such an oath; 香火弟兄 sworn brothers; 香火情 sworn love between man and woman.

B

香蕉 *shiangjiau*, n., banana.

香界 *shiangjieh*, n., Buddhist temples collectively.

香珠 *shiangju*, n., rosary (of sandalwood).

香饌 *shiang-juahn*, n., dinner with prayer served on anniversary, etc., of death of relative.

香燭 *shiang-jur*, n., incense and candle, joss sticks and candles, see *-huoo* ↑.

香菌 *shiangjyuhn*, n., champignon.

香客 *shiangkeh*, n., a pilgrim.

香蠟 *shiang-lah*, n., candle and incense.

香奩 *shiangliarn*, n., cosmetics: 香奩體 romantic verse praising woman.

香料 *shiangliauh*, n., condiments, spices.

香狸 *shianglir*, n., (zoo.) the civet.

香欒 *shiangluarn*, n., (bot.) pomelo (better known as 柚, 文旦), *Citrus decumana*.

香螺 *shiangluor*, n., conchshell fish; 香螺片 edible cartilage of conchshell.

香爐 *shianglur*, n., a censer, incense container.

香楠木 *shiang-narnmuh*, n., see 楠[a]木 10B.42.

香囊 *shiangnarng*, n., a perfume satchel.

香片 *shiangpiahn*, n., scented tea.

香蒲 *shiangpuu*, n., a kind of rush, *Typha latifolia*.

香肉 *shiang-rouh*, n., dog meat (Cantonese).

香水 *shiangshueei*, n., perfume, cologne water or *eau de cologne*.

香市 *shiang-shyh*[1], n., temporary fair or market associated with pilgrimage.

香室 *shiang-shyh*[2], n., a hall of Budd. temple.

香蕈 *shiangshyuhn*, n., champignon (also 香菌 *-jyuhn* ↑.).

香荽 *shiangsuei*, n., coriander, a favorite spice (also 芫荽).

C

香湯 *shiang-tang*, n., perfumed bath, practised in esoteric Budd. sects.

香甜 *shiangtiarn*, adj., sweet and nice-smelling (fruit); sweet (dream): 香甜的美夢 a sweet, beautiful dream.

香亭 *shiang-tirng*, a festooned rest pavilion for pilgrims or funeral procession when incense is burned.

香頭 *shiang-tour*, n., (1) head of organized group of pilgrims; (2) (-'*tou*) fragrance; 香頭兒 burnt incense.

香草 *shiangtsaau*, n., (1) vanilla; (2) (香蘭香) *Eupatorium chinensis*.

香菜 *shiangtsaih*, n., see *-suei* ↑.

香筒 *shiang-tuung*, n., incense holder.

香皂 *shiangtzauh*, n., soap.

香澤 *shiangtzer*, n., (1) (MC) hair ointment; (2) fragrance of woman's flesh.

香資 *shiangtzy*, n., see *-chiarn* ↑.

香味(兒) *shiangweih(-weh'l)*, n., fragrance, aroma (of flowers, coffee, cooked food).

香豔 *shiangyahn*, adj., romantic, sexy: 香豔故事 romantic story, novel of romantic love.

香烟 *shiangyan*, n., (1) cigarette; (2) altar incense, (fig.) of continuance of family line: 香烟絕了 the family line died out.

香嚴 *shiangyarn*, adj., (Budd.) austere, august.

香應 *shiang'ying*, n., profit: 他的生意很占香應 his business makes good profits.

香油 *shiangyour*, n., (1) scented ointment; (2) sesame oil; 香油蟲 the millepede or galleyworm.

香魚 *shiangyur*, n., a fresh-water fish, *Plecoglossus altivelis*.

香雲紗 *shiangyurnsha*, n., a kind of light silk.

90.41

kahn (**kan*).

香
看

亅	小	卜	十	土	ナ	卄	乚卜	丨	一	丁	フ	口	区	冈	㇆	厂	尸	亠	广	宀	丶	乚	七	心	八	人	乂	乛	丿	刂	𠂉	く
00	01	02	10	11	12	20	21	22	30	31	32	40	41	42	50	51	52	60	61	62	63	70	71	72	80	81	82	83	90	91	92	93

看 盾 留

看 **V.t.** (1) To look, see: 看一看, 看一下 have a look; 看了看 take a look, see again and again; see 看看 *-kahn*↓; 看呆了 watch intently, stare at with curious interest; 看書, 看報 read books, papers; 看不下去 not readable; 看電影, 看戲 see a movie, a play; 看熱鬧 join in the holiday crowd; 看風水 (geomancer) choose sites for houses or graves, (necromancer) see the layout of landscape from a particular spot; followed by 得 (positive) and 不 (negative) with complement: 看不出來, 看不清楚 cannot see clearly; 看得過眼兒 (thing) looks agreeable; 看不過眼兒 (person) get a revolting feeling (as seeing a bully); 看不順眼兒 (person) not used to the (disgusting) sight; 看見, 看不見 can, cannot see; 觀看 see and appreciate (exhibit, landscape); 查看 look into (accounts, etc.); 好看 good-looking; 不好看, 難看 ugly; 面子不好看 embarrassing. (2) To see a point, realize, appreciate: 依我看 as I see it; 看見, 看法 *-jiahn, -faa*↓; 看透了 see through (a trick); 看破 *-poh*↓; 看穿了 to realize futility or falsity, be more detached; 看中 (*juhng*) 了, 看上了 have a liking for (a girl, an object). (3) Watch: 看風頭, 看風使帆 trim the sail to the wind; 看機會 watch for opportunity; 看着辦 act as one sees fit; 看嘴臉, 看臉子, 看眉眼 watch (superior's) countenance; 看某人面上 to act to please s. o., for favor of s. o. (4) To visit: 看朋友, 病人 visit a friend, patient. (5) (**kan*) In specific words and phrr. denoting "in charge of" or "person in charge": 看酒, 看茶 (waiter) take charge of wine, tea; 看座, 看座兒的 waiter in charge of seating customers at restaurant or theater; 看門, 看家, 看守, 看護 *-mern, -jia, -shoou, -huh*, etc.↓; 看孩子 (maid) look after child; 看家狗 watchdog; 看財奴 miser; 看街的 formerly, sheriff's assistant in charge of law and order; 看車的 person keeping an eye on the cars, as in parking lot. (6) (**kan*) To detain: 看押 *-ya*↓; 看起來, 把他看住 detain (person) or keep under surveillance; 看死了 die in prison; (football) watch a particular opponent. (7) (**kan*) (Re. pr. in Tarng and MC poetry) to see, look.

Vb. complement. And see: 試試看, 做做看 try and see; 摸摸看 feel (in pocket) and see; 找找看 try to look for it; 稱稱看 weigh and see.

看病 *kahnbihng*, v. t., (patient) sees a doctor, (doctor) examines patient.
看輕 *kahnching*, v. t., to look down upon.
看齊 *kahnchir*, v. i., (mil.) "eyes right," etc.; (fig.) keep in line generally.
看穿 *kahnchuan*, v. t., see through, be disillusioned; see *-poh*↓.
看跌 *kahn-dier*, v.i., anticipate a lowering market.
看法 *kahnfaa*, n., way one looks at it: 依我看法 as I see it; 看法不同 another way of looking at it.
看管 **kanguaan*, v. t., (1) take care of, look after (house and garden); (2) put in prison.
看官 *kahnguan*, n., (in old-fashioned novels) an address to "my readers."
看顧 *kahnguh*, v. t., to look after, take care of (child, house, etc.).
看護 **kanhuh*, n., a nurse (now also called 護士).
看漲 *kahn-jahng*, v.i., anticipate a rising market.
看家 **kanjia*, v. i., to watch the house (while others go away): 看家的錢 money for household expenses; 看家的 formerly, guard for house and property.
看見 *kahnjiahn*, v. t., (actually) see: 看得見 can see; 看不見 cannot see; 看見光景不對 see that the situation is all wrong (and take departure).
看重 *kahnjuhng*, v. t., think greatly of, value (person) (cf. *-ching*↑).
看看 *kahnkahn*, v. t., take a look (at papers, museum, etc.); examine (eyes, intestines); wait and see: 看看情形如何 see how the situation develops; seeing that: 看看年終將到 seeing that the year-end is drawing near.
看來 *kahnlair*, phr., appear, look like.
看門 **kanmern*, v. i., to keep the gate: 看門的 gatekeeper.
看破 *kahnpoh*, n., see through (trick, falseness); decide to quit, after seeing through: 看破紅塵 (Budd.) see through the emptiness of the material world.
看小 *kahn-shiaau*, v.i., see *-dier*↑.
看相 *kahn-shiahng*, v. t., to read fortune (by face, palm lines).
看守 **kanshoou*, v. t., to keep (person) under detention; 看守所 detention house.
看押 **kanya*, v. t., as in 看押起來 arrest and detain.

盾 90.41

shuun (also *duhn*).

N. A shield: 盾牌 shield used in war for defense; 矛^△^盾 contradiction, 32.00.

留 90.41

liour.

[Classical form 畱; abbr. 畄]

N. A surname.

V.i. & t. (1) To stay, ask to stay, to remain: 留客 ask guest to stay; 留宿 stay overnight; 留飯 (asking guest to) stop for lunch or supper; 請留步 (court., asking host to) stop sending off to the gate; 留職停薪 on leave without pay; 留任 serve for a second term; 留級 fail to be promoted to higher class in school; 挽留 request (person) not to resign; 慰留 ditto; 久留 stay a long while (on visit, etc.); 停留 stop over (in place), to stop in progress; 彌留之時 time when person was still living, lying in a coma. (2) To leave behind: 留言, 留話 leave a message; 留下, 遺留 leave behind (children, property, gifts); 留待將來 leave s. t. to be done later; 留待後言 to be continued later (in story); to leave room: 留退步 leave room for retreat; 不留餘地 press (s.o.) too hard, not leave room for later compromise; 留點面子 leave "face" for s.o., not completely disgrace s.o.; 留後手兒 leave room for future maneuver. (3) To study abroad: 留英, 留美 study in England, U.S.; see 留學-*shyuer* ↓. (4) To grow, raise: 留鬍子 grow a beard; 留髮 let the hair grow long; 留辮子 keep a queue.

留别 *liourbier*, v.i., give souvenir on parting.

留情 *liourchirng*, v.i., show consideration: 處處留情 show kindness at every step; 筆下留情 forbear in critical remarks (not to hurt feelings).

留都 *liourdu*, n., old capital, after new one has been established.

留後 *liourhouh*, v.i., (1) be survived by children, leave posterity; (2) remain behind to take care of unfinished business.

留級 *liourjir*, v.i., fail and be kept in same grade at school.

留髠 *liourkun*, v. i., (allu., of prostitutes) show favor by asking patron to stay for the night.

留戀 *liourliahn*, v.i. & t., to keep thinking (of s.o., some place) in memory; sorry to leave.

留連 *liourliarn*, v.i., linger, unwilling to leave (place).

留難 *liournahn* (-'*nan*), v.t., to embarrass: 故意留難 make difficulties for (person).

留聲機 *liour sheng-ji*, n., gramophone.

留神 *liourshern*, v.i. & t., be careful (of hostile moves, speech, land mines).

留心 *liourshin*, v.i. & t., be careful: 留心世事 pay attention to world or national events.

留守 *liourshoou*, n. & v.t., commandant in charge of place, district: to be in such command.

留學 *liourshyuer*, v. i., to study abroad: 留日(本), 留法 study in Japan, France; 留學生 "returned student"; (Chinese) student abroad.

留意 *liouryih*, v.i. & t., keep in mind: 請你留意 please keep in mind (my desire for opening, etc.).

番 90.41

fan (**pan*).

N. adjunct. A course, a turn: 一番的好意, 盛情 such a show of hospitality; 那番事情不必提了 do not mention that course of events; in mahjong, a game: 和了一番牌 scored one game; see N. 2 ↓.

N. (1) Aborigines, such tribes: 土番 aborigines; 熟番, 生番 those influenced by Chin. customs, those who are not. (2) Turn or time: 今番, 這番 this time; 三番四次 so many times (give warning, etc.); 幾番 how many times; 連番 continuously.

V.i. & t. Take turns: 輪番, 更番 take turns; 番戍 period of garrison duty; 番代 take turns on duty.

Adj. Foreign, of foreign tribes: 番人, 番戶 foreigners, esp. those on border provinces, also Malay, Indonesia; 番地, 番國 foreign land(s); 番俗 foreign customs.

番茄 *fanchier*, n., tomato.

番番 *fanfan*, adj., (LL) grey or greyish (hair).

番鬼(子) *fangueei(tz)*, n., (sl.) foreigners; see 鬼 91.70.

番紅花 *fanhurnghua*, n., saffron, *Crocus sativus.*

番椒 *fanjiau*, n., pepper, *Capsicum.*

番薯 *fanshur*, n., potato.

番攤 *fantan*, n., a Cantonese form of gamble.

番禺 **Panyur*, n., name of district of Canton.

§ 90.42 (ノ/冈)

禹 90.42

yuu.

N. Name of emperor, (2205–2198 B.C.) founder of 夏 Shiah Dyn.

喬 90.42

chiaur.

N. A surname.

Adj. (1) False, assumed: 喬模喬樣 (=假模假樣) artificial manners; 喬裝 -*juang* ↓; 喬作衙 (MC) with assumed airs; 喬文假醋 assuming airs of a scholar. (2) High, tall (tree, mountain), stately: 喬木, 喬松 tall tree, pine; 二喬 (大喬, 小喬) two great beauties of Three Kingdoms.

喬扦 *chiaurchian*[1], n., a stack made of three bamboos tied together as support for drying stalks of grain.

喬遷 *chiaurchian*[2], v.i., move into a new house: 喬遷之喜 congratulations on such occasion.

喬裝(妝) *chiaurjuang*, v. t., to disguise one's dress.

喬麥 *chiaurmaih*, n., see 蕎^麥 20A.42.

喬才 *chiaurtsair*, adj., (MC dial.) crafty, tricky.

喬梓 *chiaurtzyy*, n., father and son, see 橋^梓 10B.42.

秀 舅 釁 舄 爲

§ 90.50 (ノ/ㄱ)

秀 90.50

shiouh.

V.i. To put forth flower: 秀而不實 (AC) put forth flower but bear no fruit.

Adj. Delicate, frail and beautiful, distinguished, refined: 優秀學生 students with excellent records; 清秀 beautiful and slender (girl), clean, pleasant (face), refined (talent); 秀外慧中 (of girl) clear-eyed and intelligent; 秀才, 秀女 *-tsair, -nyuu*↓.

秀拔 *shiouhbar*, adj., (callig.) graceful and distinguished.
秀氣 *shiouhchih*, n., (1) serene air of landscape; refined air of person; (2) (*-'chih*) adj., refined, delicate, well-made (article).
秀出 *shiouh-chu*, v. i., excel, be distinguished, see *-bar*↑.
秀發 *shiouhfa*, adj., distinguished-looking.
秀麗 *shiouhlih*, adj., delicate, graceful.
秀茂 *shiouhmauh*, adj., (of talent) rich, blooming.
秀美 *shiouhmeei*, adj., beautiful, pretty.
秀眉 *shiouh-meir*, n., (1) delicate eyebrows; (2) a few especially long pieces of hair in eyebrow in some elderly person.
秀女 *shiouhnyuu*, n., (1) formerly, girl working in the imperial court; (2) a young girl.
秀色 *shiouhseh*, n., prettiness: 秀色可餐 a beauty to feast one's eyes on.
秀士 *shiouhshyh*, n., (1) a bachelor of arts; (2) a well-cultivated young man.
秀才 *shiouhtsair*, n., formerly, a bachelor of arts or graduate of first degree: 秀才人情 gift by scholars, which are not expensive, but consist of some scroll of writing or painting; 窮秀才, 不通秀才 (contempt.) a poor scholar (usu. a village teacher who does not know much except a rigmarole knowledge of a few Confucian classics).
秀雅 *shiouhyaa*, adj., elegant, refined.

舅 90.50

jiouh.

N. (1) Mother's brother, maternal uncle: 舅父 *-fuh*, 舅舅 *-'jiou*, 舅媽 *-(')ma*, 舅母 *-muu*↓; 娘舅 (Shanghai dial.) maternal uncle; 母舅 ditto; 甥舅關係 the relationship between maternal uncle and nephew. (2) Husband's father: 舅姑 *-gu*↓. (3) Wife's brother: 舅子 *-tz*↓.

舅父 *jiouhfuh*, n., maternal uncle.
舅姑 *jiouhgu*, n., husband's parents.
舅公 *jiouhgung*, n., father's maternal uncle.
舅舅 *jiouh'jiou*, n., (=舅父 *-fuh*↑), a term generally used in speech.
舅老爺 *jiouhlaau'yie*, n., (1) father's or mother's maternal uncle; (2) s.o.'s wife's maternal uncle; (3) (court.) wife's brother, (coll.) ditto.
舅媽 *jiouh(')ma*, n., the wife of one's maternal uncle.
舅母 *jiouhmuu*, n., ditto.
舅奶奶 *jiouhnaai'nai*, n., (1) wife of father's maternal uncle; (2) formerly, wife of the master's maternal uncle, a term used by servants.
舅嫂 *jiouhsaau*, n., the wife of one's wife's brother.
舅氏 *jiouhshyh*, n., maternal uncle.
舅太太 *jiouhtaih'tai*, n., =舅奶奶, see *-naai'nai* (2)↑.
舅子 *jiouhtz*, n., wife's brother: 大舅子, 小舅子 wife's elder, younger brother.
舅祖 *jiouhtzuu*, n., father's or mother's maternal uncle.
舅爺 *jiouhyer*, n., (1) ditto; (2) (*-'ye*) wife's maternal uncle, (court.) wife's brother.

釁 90.50

shihn.

N. A feud, quarrel, dispute, oft. between warring nations: 釁端 cause of dispute; 尋釁 pick quarrel; 挑釁 challenge; 起釁 start war.

V.t. (1) (AC) to smear with blood (on bell, drum) as solemn oath. (2) (AC) to smear face to disguise: 釁面呑炭 disguise face and eat charcoal (to change voice); see 釁浴 *-yuh*↓.

釁鬯 *shihn-chahng*, n., (AC) wine for embalming corpse.
釁隙 *shihn-shih*, n., a feud, old dispute, cause of quarrel.
釁浴 *shihn-yuh*, n., perfumed bath with fragrant herbs.

舄 90.50

shih.

N. (1) Slippers; shoes. (2) Var. of 潟 salty soil.

爲 90.50

weir (**weih*).

[Common var. 為]

V.i. & t. (1) To do: 爲善, 爲惡, 爲人 *-shahn, -eh, -rern*↓; 爲學 to pursue studies; 爲非做歹 do wrong, break the law; 有爲 can accomplish things; 大有爲 accomplish great things; 無爲 (Taoist) *laissez faire*, let things take their natural course. (2) To be: 子爲誰 who are you? 十尺爲一丈 ten feet make a *jahng*; 有

詩爲證 there is a poem to prove the point; 爲主 is the principal aim; 到此爲止 stop here; 爲患 be a constant source of trouble; 爲難 *-narn* ↓; oft. with reference to the above passage: 爲禱 this (the above) is what I pray for; 爲祝, 爲頌 this is my wish or my prayer; 三日爲限 three days is the limit; 以字爲憑 this note serves as written proof. (3) To govern: 爲國 govern a country; 爲政 to govern.

Prep. (1) (**weih*) For, on account of: 爲何 for what reason? 爲甚麽 why, for what reason? 爲了 for the sake of; 因爲 because; 爲人辛勞 labor for others; 爲己 for oneself; 爲國, 爲家 for the country and home; 爲我 *-woo* ↓. (2) By (in form 爲...所+vb., with passive voice): 爲賊所盜 was stolen by a thief; 爲敵所敗 was defeated by the enemy.

爲惡 *weir-eh*, phr., do evil.
爲非 *weir-fei*, phr., ditto.
爲力 *weir-lih*, v. i., to be of help: 難以爲力 difficult to be of help.
爲難 *weirnarn*, (1) adj., difficult: 感到爲難 feel difficult; (2) v. t., to embarrass, be embarrassed: 爲難他, 使他爲難 embarrass him.
爲人 *weir-rern*, v. i., to behave as a human being: 太難爲人了 it's difficult to know how to behave or conduct oneself; 爲人很和氣 behaves kindly.
爲善 *weir-shahn*, phr., to do good.
爲生 *weir-sheng*, v. i., to manage a living: 無以爲生 have nothing to live on.
爲項 *weih'shiang*, n., (coll.) reason: 你們打架, 究竟有什麽爲項呢 what is the reason for your fighting?
爲首 *weir-shoou*, phr., be the leader (of some adventure).
爲頭(兒) *weirtour('l)*, phr., see *-shoou* ↑.
爲我 **weihwoo*, n., (phil.) self as the motive of all action (楊朱).
爲因 **weihyin*, conj., because (usu. 因爲).

鵞 90.50

er.
[Var. of 鵝 90S.50]

鶖 90.50

chiou.

N. 禿鶖 the bald crane, a water bird.

鷽 90.50

shyuer.

N. The bullfinch, *Pyrrhula griseiventris* (also called 山鵲).

§ 90.63 (ノ/丶)

乓 90.63

pang.

N. 乒乓 *ping-*, game of ping-pong, table tennis.

熏 90.63

shyun (**shyuhn*).
[Var. 薰; pop. 燻]

V.t. (1) To smoke, cure (fish, etc.) by smoking; p.p., smoked (fish, duck, etc.). (2) To scent, fumigate: 熏衣裳 fumigate clothing, also to scent over slow fire, see 熏爐 *-lur* ↓; 熏蚊子 drive out mosquitoes by special incense. (3) To assail the nostrils: 氣焰熏天 a person's power stinks to heaven; 臭氣熏人 its stink is irritating. (4) To poison by gas: 被煤氣熏着了 be suffocated by gas; 熏死了 suffocated to death. (5) (Coll.) to berate (person): 今天他熏了我一頓 he gave me a scolding today. (6) (**shyuhn*) To stain one's reputation: 這個人都熏了 this man has a bad reputation (therefore to be avoided), cf. 薰△染, 薰△陶 20A.63.

熏烘 *shyunhung*, v. t., to fumigate (also wr. 燻, 薰).
熏爐 *shyunlur*, n., a brazier with hot coal, covered by wire netting for smoking or scenting clothing (also 薰).
熏籠 *shyunlurng*, n., wire netting on brazier over which clothing may be dried or scented (also 薰).
熏香 *shyuhnshiang*, n., narcotic incense for putting victim to sleep.

勳 90.63

shyun.
[Var. of 勳 90S.50]

黧 90.63

lir.

Adj. Blackish-yellow: 黧黃 *-huarng* ↓; 黧雞 black hen: 兩眼像黧雞 jealous, watching eyes (like those of black hens).

黧黃 *lirhuarng*, n., (zoo.) the

Chinese oriole (also called 倉庚, 黃鶯, 黃鳥).

鵹鶯 *liryıng*, n., (zoo.) the Bonin bush warbler, *Cettia diphone*.

鱟 90.63

houh.

N. (Zoo.) horseshoe crab.

---

§ 90.70 (ノ/乚)

卮 90.70

jy.

[Var. 巵]

N. (AC) a goblet: 卮言日出 (AC) endless flow of words (as wine out of goblet).

甃 90.70

jouh.

N. (1) Well curb. (2) Any structure of bricks.

秃 90.70

tu.

Adj. Bald, devoid of hair, leaves or trees: 秃頭 baldhead, baldheaded; 秃山 barren hill; 秃筆 worn-out writing brush, also (self-deprecating) my awkward pen; 這棵樹秃了 this tree is leafless; 秃髮 or 髮秃 bald-headed.

秃鶖 *tuchiou*, n., bald-headed crane, (derisive of) a baldhead.

秃瘡 *tuchuang*, n., scabies.

秃頂 *tudiing*, adj., bald-headed.

秃髮症 *tufaa-jehng*, n., (med.) baldness.

秃鷲 *tujiouh*, n., (zoo.) the bald-headed vulture, *Aegypius monachus*.

秃嚕 *tu'lu*, adj., exhausted: 吃秃嚕了 all eaten up with nothing left; 問秃嚕了 stymied by a question.

秃驢 *tulyur*, n., a baldhead, "baldheaded donkey" (abusive of monks).

秃頭 *tutour*, n. & adj., baldhead, bald.

秃子 *tu'tz*, n., a baldhead.

兒 90.70

erl (when accented, but usu. nonsyllabic, spelled *-'l*; when thus used, it modifies certain syllabic forms: (1) final *n* and *i* are dropped: *an*>*a'l*, *ai* also>*a'l*; (2) *i* takes on an indistinct [ə]: *pir*>*pier'l*, *ti*>*tie'l*; (3) *y* becomes broadened into [ə]: *shyh*>*sheh'l*; the ㄦ sound in Chinese alphaet, *el*, *erl*, *eel*, *ehl* is characterized by curling of tongue, and is distinguished from ㄜ, *e*, *er*, *ee*, *eh*, spelled without "l," as in 惡, 俄).

Part. (1) A particle, oft. attached to n. or pron., adding coll. touch to LL form without it: 盤兒, 梨兒 (cf. LL 盤, 梨), 玩兒, 戲兒, 這兒, 那兒; the use of 兒 *-'l* or of 子 *-tz* is dictated by actual usage, no rule being possible. (2) A particle oft. attached to a n. in collective or plural sense: 花兒, 草兒, 米兒, 糖兒, 魚兒, 肉兒 flowers, grass, rice, sugar, fish, meat. (3) A particle oft. attached to adj. or adv.: 大模大樣兒 proudly; 壓根兒 basically.

N. (1) A child: 兒子 *-tzyy*↓; 孫兒, 小兒 child; 小兒科 pediatrics; 男兒 boy; 女兒 girl; 孫兒 grandchild; 孤兒 orphan; 吾兒 my child; used by child in self-reference, and by parent in addressing child; (MC) 兒夫 (used by woman) my husband; 兒童, 兒女 *-turng*, *-nyuu*↓. (2) (Familiar) fellow: 老兒 the old fellow.

Adj. Male, masculine: 兒馬, 兒花 *-maa*, *-hua*↓.

兒茶 *erlchar*, n., (Chin. med.) catechu, an astringent.

兒齒 *erlchyy*, n., new teeth grown in some old people.

兒夫 *erlfu*, n., (MC) my husband.

兒婦 *erlfuh*, n., daughter-in-law.

兒花(兒) *erlhua('l)*, n., (MC, corruption 男孩兒) male child; cf. 女[△]花 93.93.

兒(儿)化 *erlhuah*, v. i., change in syllabic form and pronunciation caused by adding *-'l* (*an*>*a'l*; *i*>*ie'l*; see 兒 pr.↑.

兒科 *erlke*, n., (med.) pediatrics.

兒郎 *erllarng*, n., a son.

兒馬 *erlmaa*, n., a stallion.

兒女 *erlnyuu*, n., (1) children (male and female); (2) sexual love: 兒女情多 or 情長 the power of sexual love (oft. overcoming political or professional considerations); 兒女債 the burden of raising children to maturity; 兒女態 childishness, sentimentality, lack of manliness; 兒女子 women and children (oft. contempt.).

兒嬉 *erlshi*, n., see *-shih*↓.

兒戲 *erlshih*, n., a child's play; v.t. to treat as child's play or cavalierly.

兒媳婦兒 *erlshirfuh'l*, n., daughter-in-law.

兒時 *erl shyr*, phr., childhood years.

兒孫 *erlsun*, n., grandchildren; children and grandchildren.

兒曹 *erltsaur*, n., (AC, LL) children (plural); you children.

兒童 *erlturng*, n., child, children: 兒童教育 children's education; 兒童讀物 children's reading material; 兒童歌隊 children's choir, etc.

兒子 *erltzyy* (-'tz), n., son; (AC) child; 兒子氣 childishness; adj., childish.

兒子花 *erltzyyhua*, n., see *-hua*↑.

覓 90.70

mih.
[Pop. 覔]

V.t. To look for: 尋覓 to look for; 覓得, 覓見 have sought and found; 遍覓不得 have looked for everywhere and could not find; 覓保 find a guarantor; 覓句 look for a suitable phrase; 覓求, 覓致人才 on the lookout for proper personnel; 覓訪 try to find and meet (person); 覓食 (animals) look for food.

覺 90.70

jyuer (*jiaau*, **jiauh*).
[Pop. 覚, 斍]

N. Feeling, sensation: 知覺 consciousness; 聽覺, 嗅覺, 視覺, 味覺, 觸覺 the senses of hearing, smell, vision, taste, touch; 感覺 feel (+adj.); feeling, sensation; 感覺得 feel that; 直覺 intuition; 幻覺 illusion.

V.i. & t. (1) Feel, be sensible of: 不覺如何 don't feel anything; 覺疼 feel pain; 先知先覺 a person whose ideas are far in advance of his age, a spiritual leader of men; 自覺 realize about oneself, aware of self; 覺今是而昨非 realize now that one has been wrong in the past. (2) Wake from sleep: 覺悟 *-wuh*, 覺醒 *-shiing*↓; 睡覺 (**jiauh*) go to sleep; 睡一大覺 had a long sleep; 夢覺 wake up from a dream. (3) Discover, find out: 覺察 *-char*, 覺得 *-'de*↓; 覺出 find out, to sense (s.t.). (4) Tell, inform, teach: 使先知覺後知 let those who know teach those who don't.

覺察 *jyuerchar*, v.t., discover, unearth, disclose, reveal.

覺得 *jyuer'de*, v.i., feel: 我覺得 I feel that (or+adj.); 他不覺得 he does not feel, is not aware.

覺乎 *jyuer'hu*, v.i., feel: 覺乎有一點兒痛 feel a little pain.

覺醒 *jyuershiing*, v.i., wake up from sleep.

覺悟 *jyuerwuh*, v.t., realize (one's mistake, etc.).

毛 90.70

maur.

N. (1) (*-'l*) Hair, fur, down: 毛髮 *-faa*↓, 細毛 down (=毫 60.70); 狗毛, 獸毛 hair or fur of dog, beasts; 羽毛 feather; 雞毛 chicken feather or down; 鵝毛被 goose-down quilt; 羊毛 wool; 腋毛 hair on armpit; 毛骨悚然 have goose flesh. (2) A ten-cent piece, ten cents: 一元三毛=$1.30 (also 角). (3) A surname: 毛遂自薦 phr., common allu. to 毛遂 who recommended himself to post—to recommend oneself.

Adj. (1) Hairy, furry: 毛竹, 毛筍, 毛桃 species of bamboo, bamboo shoot, peach with fine down on stem or fruit. (2) Woolen: 毛織品 woolen fabrics; 毛衣, 毛線 *-yi*, *-shiahn*↓. (3) Coarse: 毛手毛腳 flurried in movement, rough-handed, see 毛毛騰騰 *-'mau-'teng'teng*↓. (4) Flurried, nervous: 把他嚇毛了 made him nervous with fright; 心裏發毛 feel nervous, see 毛咕 *-'gu*↓. (5) Too detailed: 不勝毛舉 too numerous to mention one by one (cf. 枚$^\Delta$舉 10B.82). (6) Very young, not grown-up: 毛孩子 (coll.) little child; 毛丫頭 (coll.) young maid before puberty; 毛驢 young, small donkey. (7) Rough, approximate: 毛利, 毛息 approximate interest (income).

毛包 *maur-bau*, adj. & n., (person who is) bumptious.

毛邊紙 *maurbian-jyy*, n., common Chin. writing paper made from bamboo pulp.

毛筆 *maur-bii*, n., writing brush.

毛病 *maur'bing*, n., weakness, shortcoming, trouble: 機器常出毛病 engine often develops troubles; 毛病在那兒 what is the cause of the trouble? 胃的毛病 stomach trouble; 文章有小毛病 s. t. not quite right in an article.

毛玻璃 *maur-bo'li*, n., frosted glass.

毛蟲 *maurchurng*, n., caterpillar; also called 毛毛蟲.

毛翅類 *maurchyh-leih*, n., (zoo.) *Trichopteria*, family of winged insects.

毛豆 *maur-douh*, n., very young and tender soybean.

毛髮 *maurfaa*, n., hair on head, opp. 毛 or 汗毛 on rest of body.

毛茛 *maurgehn*, n., (bot.) *Ranunculus acris.*

毛咕 *maur'gu*, adj., frightened, flurried, see *-'lguji*↓.

毛氊 *maurjan*, n., felt.

毛腳雞 *maurjiaau-ji*, n., (derog.) rash, bumptious fellow.

毛薑 *maurjiang*, adj., (contempt.) rash, restless (of person).

毛巾 *maurjin*, n., hand towel, bath towel.

毛錐(子) *maurjuei(tz)*, n., (LL) writing brush.

毛重 *maur-juhng*, n., overall weight including packing.

毛孔 *maurkuung*, n., pore.

毛兒咕咕 *mau'lguji*, adj., see *-'lehguji*↓.

毛藍 *maurlarn*, adj., pale blue.

毛勒咕咕 *maur'lehguji*, adj., frightened.

毛毛騰騰 *maur'mau-'teng'teng*, adj., flurried and disorderly.

毛女(兒) *maur-nyuu('l)*, n., young virgin.

毛茸 *maurrurng*, adj., hairy, furry, also 毛茸茸.

毛衫兒 *maur'sha'l*, n., swaddling clothes.

毛瑟鎗 *maursheh-chiang*, n., Mauser rifle or pistol.

毛繩(兒) *maursherng'l*, n., woolen yarn.

毛線 *maurshiahn*, n., woolen yarn.

毛細管 *maurshih-guaan*, n., capillary: 毛細管現象 capillary action or phenomenon.

毛詩 *Maurshy*[1], n., the *Book of Poetry* (毛亨's version).

毛蝨 *maurshy*[2], n., a kind of louse which inhabits in hairy region of skin.

毛厠 *maur'sy*, n., privy, toilet (see 茅^厠 20A.00).

毛毯(子) *maurtaan(tz)*, n., woolen blanket.

毛桃(兒,子) *maurtaur('l, tz)*, n., a kind of small (furry) peach.

毛團 *maurtuarn*, n., (MC) the feathered tribe.

毛兎子 *maurtuhtz*, n., (abusive) "louse," "ass" (of person).

毛子 *maurtz*, n., (1) (coll. in times of Boxer Rebellion) foreigner, white man; 大毛子 white man; 二毛子 Chinese converts, employees of white men; (2) tuff of hair on child's head; (3) used in place of *maur'l*, in some cases, like fine hair on peach (桃毛子).

毛賊 *maurtzer*, n., burglar.

毛足類 *maurtzur-leih*, n., (zoo.) *Chaetopoda*, family of worms.

毛窩 *maurwo*, n., (Northern dial.) warm cloth shoes.

毛腰 *maur-yau*, phr., to bend down from the waist.

毛衣 *mauryi*, n., woolen sweater.

毛羽 *mauryuu*, n., feathers and furs.

毬 90.70

chiour.

N. Any ball-shaped thing (var. of 球).

毽 90.70

jiahn.

N. A shuttlecock: 雞毛毽 one made of chicken feathers; 踢毽子 to play the shuttlecock.

氊 90.70

jan.

[Var. of 氈 60S.70; pop. 毡]

毧 90.70

rurng.

N. (1) Fine hair or fur, down, felt. (2) (Interch. 羢, 絨) woolen goods.

氆 90.70

puu.

氆氌 *puu'lu*, n., Thibetan tapestry.

毺 90.70

yur (also **shu*).

[Var. of 毹 81S.70]

毯 90.70

taan.

N. (-*tz*) Carpet, rug: 毛毯 woolen blanket; 地毯 a carpet, rug.

氌 90.70

luu.

N. See 氆^氌 90.70↑.

毳 90.70

tsueih.

N. Fine hair of animals: 毳幕, 毳帳 felt tent.

Adj. (AC) u. f. 脆 42A.70, brittle.

兎 90.70

tuh.

[Pop. of 兔 50.70]

氂 90.70

maur, *lir*.

[Var. of 犛 10.70]

鼠 90.70

shuu.

N. ('*l*) A rat, mouse; class of rodents like squirrel, weasel, etc.: 老鼠 rat, mouse; known for stealing, hence 鼠輩 (abusive) the thieves; 鼠目, 鼠眼 thievish eyes, also shortsightedness; 鼠膽 chicken-hearted; 鼠技 contemptible trickery; 鼠肚雞腸 extreme pettiness of character; 鼠肝蟲臂 (AC) "rat's liver and insect legs"—infinitesimal parts of creation; 鼠牙雀角 litigation over trifles; 田鼠, 野鼠 field mouse; 黃鼠狼 weasel; 松鼠 squirrel; 銀鼠 ermine; 土撥鼠 marmot.

鼠竊 *shuu-chieh*, n., petty burglars.

鼠瘡 *shuu-chuang*, n., scrofula, scrofulous swelling (=瘰癧).

鼠麴草 *shuuchyur-tsaau*, n., (bot.) a grass, *Gnaphalium multiceps*.

鼠婦 *shuufuh*, n., an insect, the wood louse (also wr. 鼠負).

鼠狼 *shuu-larng*, n., (黃鼠狼) the weasel.

鼠瘻 *shuu-louh*, n., see -*chuang*↑.

鼠蹊 *shuu-shi*, n., (physiol.) the groin.

鼠竄 *shuu-tsuahn*, v. i., run away like rats: 抱頭鼠竄.
鼠子 *shurtzyy*[1], n., (abusive) a rat, skunk, scoundrel.
鼠梓 *shutzyy*[2], n., (bot.) *Ligustrum lucidum*.
鼠尾草 *shuweir-tsaau*, n., (bot.) *Salvia japonica*.
鼠疫 *shuu-yih*, n., the (bubonic) plague.

鼥 90.70

bar.

N. See 鼧[A]鼥 90.70.

鼬 90.70

youh.

N. (Zoo.) *Mustela itatis*, the Chinese weasel (also called 黃鼠狼).

鼫 90.70

shyr.

N. A squirrel; a marmot, ground hog.

鼯 90.70

wur.

N. (Zoo.) a kind of squirrel, *Petaurista leucogenys*.

鼴 90.70

yaan.

N. The mole (also wr. 偃鼠).

貂 90.70

diau.

[Var. of 貂 91S.40]

鼧 90.70

tuor.

N. The marmot: 鼧鼥.

鼢 90.70

fern.

N. Field mouse, a kind of mole.

鼷 90.70

shi.

N. A small mouse: 鼷穴 a mouse hole.

兜 90.70

dou.

N. (1) A wrap, pocket: 兜兜, 兜肚 *-'dou, -'duh*↓. (2) Covering for head: 兜風, 兜鍪 *-feng, -mour*↓. (3) (*-tz*) Mountain chair: 山兜子, 兜轎.

V.t. (1) To wrap up, surround: 兜着拿 wrap up in cloth and take; 兜捕 surround and arrest. (2) To dig up: 兜翻, 兜底子 *-'fan, -diitz*↓. (3) To hitch up: 兜搭, 兜攬 *-da, -laan*↓. (4) To go for a stroll: 兜圈子, 兜風逛逛 take the air, stroll around; 兜圈子 beat about the bush; 兜轉來 strol back.

兜搭 *douda*, v.i., hitch up as friends: 兜搭上了, 兜搭性子 (MC) wayward temperament.
兜的 *dou'de*, adv., (MC) suddenly.
兜底子 *dou-diitz*, v.t., dig up old personal stories to discredit s.o.
兜兜 *dou'dou*, n., stomacher, waistband worn next to skin serving as pocket; reverse brassiere formerly worn by young girls to depress breasts.
兜肚 *dou'duh*, n., ditto, also 肚兜.
兜翻 *dou'fan*, v. i., turn over: 兜翻老底 dig up old personal stories to discredit s. o.
兜風 *doufeng*, v. i., have a drive to enjoy countryside, take the air.
兜截 *doujier*, v. t., cut off retreat.
兜巾 *doujin*, n., bib worn by babies during feeding.
兜攬 *doulaan*, v. i. & t., (1) hitch up as friends; (2) find customers for trade: 兜攬生意 solicit business.
兜鍪 *doumour*, n., helmet.
兜率天 *doushuaih tian*, n., (Budd.) one of the highest abodes in heaven.
兜子 *doutz*, n., (1) mountain chair, also 山兜子; (2) a pocket, a wrap.

§ 90.71 (丿/乜)

氏 90.71

shyh (**jy*).

N. (1) (AC) surname on mother's line, as dist. 姓 on father's line and as means of differentiation in

鼠 鼥 鼬 鼫 鼯 鼴 貂 鼧 鼢 鼷 兜 氏

亅	小	卜	十	土	ナ	廾	𠂉	丨	一	丁	フ	口	囗	冂	㇆	厂	尸	亠	广	宀	丶	乚	乜	心	八	人	乂	㇀	ノ	刂	𠂉	く
00	01	02	10	11	12	20	21	22	30	31	32	40	41	42	50	51	52	60	61	62	63	70	71	72	80	81	82	83	90	91	92	93

氏 我 悉 愁 慇 憩 兵

lineage. (2) A surname denoting place of origin (like French "de" and German "von") or office, (as 太史氏, 職方氏). (3) (Esp. in common official documents) address of a woman: 張氏 the woman Jang; 夫人李氏 his wife *née* Lii; (LL) used also by woman in self-reference; rarely in reference to man. (4) School of thought: 釋氏 school of Sakyamuni—Buddhism; 老氏 school of Laotse—Taoism. (5) (*jy) Used in names of foreign tribes: 月氏, 閼氏.

氏族 *shyhtzur*, n., matriarchal tribe or system in anc. China.

我 90.71

woo (*ee in AC re. pr.).

Pron. (1) I (first person), my, me: 我見 my humble opinion; 自我作古 I'll be the first (to do s.t.). (2) (*ee) (AC) my, our, our country: 齊師伐我 the *Chir* attacked us; 我軍 our army. (3) (*ee) Self: 大公無我 great impartiality excludes consideration of self; 小我 the smaller material self, "me."

我輩 **eebeih*, n., we (slightly litr.).
我等 *wordeeng*, n., we.
我每 **ee'meei*, pron., MC equiv. 我們↓.
我們 *woomern* (-'*men*), pron., we, us (in extreme weak form, shortened to *woo'm*); 我們的 our. 「I, my.
我儂 **eenurng*, pron., (Shanghai)
我曹 **eetsaur*, pron., (litr.) we.

§ 90.72 (丿/心)

悉 90.72

shi.

V.i. (LL) to know (=知): 知悉 know; 聞悉 have heard or learned; 敬悉 (court., after reading your letter) "respectfully" learn.

Adj. & adv. (LL) all: 悉力, 悉心 *-lih*, *-shin*↓; 悉爲所有 was all taken by s. o.; 悉棄所學 abandon all one has learned before (after meeting a new master); 悉數 *-shuh*↓.

悉力 *shi-lih*, adv., with all one's strength.
悉心 *shi-shin*, adv., with concentrated effort.
悉數 *shi-shuh*, (1) adv., the entire amount: 悉數歸公 the entire amount was confiscated or contributed to the public; (2) (*-shuu*) v.t., tell or enumerate all.

愁 90.72

chour.

N. Sorrow: 憂愁 sorrow; 發愁 adj., to worry, sorrowful; 愁海 sea of sorrows.

V.i. & t. To worry, be concerned: 不用愁 don't worry; 愁他不回來 worry that he may not return.

Adj. Sorrowful, sad, disconsolate, distressed: 愁悶 *-mehn*↓; 發愁 feel distressed; 愁眉苦眼, 愁眉不展 a woebegone expression; 愁容 sad, forlorn look; 愁思 feeling of sadness; 愁雲, 愁霧 a cloud of sorrow; 愁城 valley of sorrow; 戴了一頂愁帽 wear a sad look.

愁腸 *chour-charng*, n., as in 愁腸百結 overwhelmed with sorrow and longing ("intestines tied into a hundred knots").
愁愁 *chourchour*, adj., (AC) sorrow-laden.
愁悶 *chourmehn*, n. & adj., distress, -ed.
愁緒 *chourshyuh*, n., a skein of sorrow.

愁思 *choursy*, n., deep longing, forlornness.

慇 90.72

yin.

慇懃 *yinchirn*, (1) adj., attentive (to duty, lady, office chief); (2) n., 獻慇懃 to pay attentions to (lady), do things to please (office chief); also wr. 殷懃.

憩 90.72

chih.

V.i. & n. To take a little rest.

憩息 *chihshih*, v. i., & n., a little rest, relax: 憩息一下 take a little rest.

§ 90.80 (丿/八)

兵 90.80

bing.

N. (1) Military weapons: 堅甲利兵 good armor and weapons; in combb. 兵器, 兵仗, 甲兵 such weapons; 短兵相接 in close combat. (2) Soldiers, troops: 士兵, 兵士 soldiers, privates; 練兵 train soldiers; 當兵 enlist; 徵兵 conscription; soldiers of various units, such as 砲兵 artillery unit; 步兵 infantry; 騎兵 cavalry; 工兵 labour corps; 精兵 crack troops; 敗兵, 散兵 defeated, stray troops; 亂兵 beaten, scattered soldiery; 伏兵 ambush. (3) War, things that have to do with war: 起兵, 興兵 raise troops in revolt or war; 進兵 advance, advancing troops;

用兵 launch troops, quality of war policy, (good, bad) command of troops; 交兵 meet in combat; 閱兵 review troops; 兵不厭詐 phr., all is fair in love and war; 兵荒馬亂 phr., troops in bad array; 兵連禍結 phr., continual wars.

兵變 *bingbiahn*, n., mutiny.
兵柄 *bingbihng*, n., military command.
兵部 *bingbuh*, n., anc. department of war.
兵差 *bingchai*, n., conscript labor: 當兵差 enlisted as soldier.
兵船 *bingchuarn*, n., gunboat.
兵丁 *bingding*, n., private soldier.
兵端 *bingduan*, n., as in 開兵端 start hostilities.
兵隊 *bingdueih*, n., troops.
兵房 *bingfarng*, n., barracks.
兵符 *bingfur*, n., commander's seal or tally.
兵戈 *bingge*, n., warfare, fighting.
兵革 *bingger*, n., military weapons.
兵工廠 *binggungchaang*, n., arsenal, ammunition works.
兵站 *bingjahn*, n., military supplies depot.
兵機 *bingji*, n., military strategy, plans.
兵家 *bingjia*, n., (AC) one of the nine schools of thinkers, specializing in military science.
兵艦 *bingjiahn*, n., gunboat.
兵略 *bing-liauh*, n., military strategy.
兵輪 *bing-lurn*, n., (obs.) gunboat.
兵馬 *bing-maa*, n., military affairs.
兵刃 *bing-rehn*, n., military weapons.
兵戎 *bing-rurng*, n., warfare: 兵戎相見 open hostilities.
兵燹 *bing-shiaan*, n., (LL) fire, havoc, turmoil caused by war.
兵餉 *bing-shiaang*, n., soldier's pay; costs of maintenance and supplies of army.
兵士 *bingshyh*[1], n., individual soldiers, privates.
兵勢 *bingshyh*[2], n., army power; shape, condition or position of army.
兵策 *bingtseh*, n., military strategy.
兵役 *bingyih*, n., military service.
兵營 *bingyirng*, n., barracks.

與 90.80

yuu (**yuh*).
[Abbr. 𠂔, 与]

V.i. & t. (1) To give: 與他, 與我 give him, me; 付與, 交與 give to; 與人方便 give help to others. (2) (LL) to wait: 歲不我與 time waits for no man. (3) (LL) to share: 民胞物與 the people are my brothers and I share the life of all creation. (4) To get along with: 易與 easy to get along with. (5) (**yuh*) To take part in: 與會 attend meeting; 與聞 take part in discussion (of plans); 參與 take part in, cooperate.

Prep. To, with, for (varying according to context): (a) to, in formula (vb.+與): 送與 give to (person); 加與 add to (it), apply to; (b) for (與+pron.): 與我想想 think for me; 與虎謀皮 "ask a tiger for its hide"—a doomed petition; (c) with: 與人相爭 compete with others; 與衆不同 different "with" (from) the others; 與世浮沉 sink or swim (tag along) with the trend of the times; together with: 同與, 共與; 與日俱增 to grow with each passing day.

Conj. (1) And: 你與我 you and I. (2) Rather: 與 or 與其 *-chir* ↓.

Excl. U.f. 歟 90S.81.

與其 *yuuchir*, conj., rather than: 與其...寧願...(寧可) or 與...其不如: 與其年年賠錢, 寧可(or 不如)停業 rather than suffer an annual deficit, it would be better to close up the business.
與黨 *yurdaang*, n., partner, partisan.
與奪 *yuu-duor*, phr., (the power) to give or take away.
與共 *yuuguhng*, adv., together with (s.o.).
與國 *yuu-guor*, n., (LL) friendly power.

㒷 90.80

shing.
[Pop. of 興]

興 90.80

shing (**shihng*).
[Abbr. 㒷]

N. (1) (**shihng*) Excitement, stimulation, joy, merriment: 興趣 *-chyuh* ↓; 高興 (adj. & n.) in high spirits, excited with joy; 敗興, 掃興 dampen the fun or gaiety; 盡興 fully enjoy before quitting; 興高采烈 in high spirits. (2) (**shihng*) A mood, impulse of the moment, keen desire to enjoy s.t.; 酒興正濃 keen excitement of and for wine; 詩興 impulse for writing poetry; 雅興 a mood to enjoy some quiet pleasure (chess, wine, poetry, etc.); spec, the impulse to write verse from some external experience; 興頭, 興味 *-'tour*, *-weih* ↓.

V.i. (1) To get up: 夙興夜寐 get up early and sleep late; 興居 *-jyu* ↓. (2) To rise, prosper: 興起, 興盛 rise in power; 興衰, 興替, 興亡 (as n.) the rise and fall (of nations). (3) To prevail, be popularly accepted: 興得開, 興不開 will, will not, sell well.

V.t. (1) To raise, cause to rise, grow: 興國, 興邦 to make a country strong; 興兵 raise an army, start war; 興干戈 start war; 興財 make money; 興利除弊, 興革 to start reforms; 大興土木 build many new buildings; 興波作浪 to

興 輿 貿 質

stir up trouble. (2) (Coll.) allow: 我不興你說話 I don't permit you to talk.

Adj. (1) Prosperous: 興盛, 興旺, 興隆 *-shehng, -'wahng, -lurng*↓; 新興 newly arisen: 新興國家 a new nation; 新興事業 a new industry. (2) Popular: 現在正興大沿草帽 broad-brimmed straw hats are now popular; 時興 fashionable.

興辦 *shingbahn*, v.t., to establish (a factory, school, hospital, etc.).
興兵 *shing-bing*, v.i., raise an army, send army to battle.
興起 *shing-chii*, v.i., (1) to spring up, rise in numbers: 學堂, 盜賊興起 schools, bandits, spring up; (2) to establish, found (institutions), start (reforms).
興趣 **shihngchyuh*, n., interest (in study, music, etc.): 有十分興趣 have great interest; 沒興趣 show no interest; 鼓起, 引起興趣 arouse interest.
興奮 *shingfehn*, adj., excited; showing great energy and interest (in studies, etc.): 興奮劑 a stimulant, (pep pills).
興革 *shingger*, phr., from 興利革弊 start reforms ("start the good and weed out the corrupt practices").
興工 *shing-gung*, v.i., to start construction.
興會 **shihnghueih*, n., proper mood (for painting, gaiety, etc.).
興建 *shingjiahn*, v.t., to build (schools, etc.).
興致 **shihngjyh*, n., mood to enjoy (flowers, hobbies, wine, etc.).
興居 *shingjyu*, n., a person's daily life (＝起居).
興隆 *shinglurng*, adj., (business) prosperous.
興戎 *shing-rurng*, v.i., see *-bing*↑.
興盛 *shingshehng*, adj., prosperous, strong.
興修 *shingshiou*, v.t., to renovate (building).
興衰 *shing-shuai*, phr., the rise and fall.
興師 *shing-shy*, v.i., see *-bing*↑.
興時 *shingshyr*, adj., popular at moment.
興許 *shingshyuu*, adv., (coll.) perhaps: 今天他興許 (＝也許) 不來了 perhaps he will not show up today.
興訟 *shing-suhng*, v.i., start lawsuit.
興替 *shing-tih*, phr., see *-shuai*↑.
興頭 **shihng'tour*, n., a fine mood to enjoy: 今天他興頭不淺 he is in a fine mood today; 興頭兒 the moment of impulse, a great mood.
興作 *shingtzuoh*, v.t., to start constructions.
興旺 *shing'wahng*, adj., (business, country) prosperous.
興亡 *shing-warng*, n., the rise and fall.
興味 **shihngweih*, n., keen interest (for game of cards, poetry, etc.).

輿 90.80

yur.

N. (1) A carriage: 輿馬 *-maa*↓. (2) A sedan chair: 肩輿 ditto; 輿夫 *-fu*↓. (3) The earth: 輿圖 *-tur*↓; 坤輿, 輿地 the earth, the land, also geography; 堪輿 geomancy.

V.i. & t. To ride or carry in cart (interch. 舁 90.20): 輿屍 carry corpse(s); 輿櫬 *-chehn*↓.

Adj. Public (opinion, etc.): 輿論, 輿情 *-luhn, -chirng*↓.

輿櫬 *yur-chehn*, phr., to go with one's coffin in cart to voice protest and show willingness to die for an opinion (like hunger strike).
輿情 *yur-chirng*, n., public sentiment.
輿地 *yurdih*, n., geography.
輿夫 *yurfu*, n., sedan chair carrier.
輿服 *yur-fur*, n., carriage and formal gowns.
輿論 *yurluhn*, n., public opinion or criticism.
輿馬 *yur-maa*, n., horse and carriage.
輿人 *yurrern*, n., (1) (AC) carpenter, cartwright; (2) (AC) foreman, noncommissioned officer; (3) (AC) the people in gen.
輿圖 *yurtur*, n., (LL) map (＝地圖).

貿 90.80

mauh (or *mouh*).

V.i. (1) Exchange, barter, see 貿易 *-yih*↓. (2) (AC) mix: 是非相貿 right and wrong are mixed up. (3) 貿首之讎 (AC) feud, sworn to get each other's "head" (life).

貿貿 *mauhmauh*, adj. & adv., as in. 貿貿然來 (AC) come foolishly, blindly.
貿名 *mauh-mirng*, phr., court publicity＝沽名.
貿然 *mauh-rarn*, adj. & adv., foolishly, recklessly (try s. t.).
貿易 *mauhyih*, n., trade: 貿易額 trade volume; 國際貿易 international trade; 自由貿易 free trade.

質 90.80

jyr (**jyh*).

N. (1) Substance, character, quality of material: 物質 matter; 物質主義 materialism; 品質 quality (of material), character (of person); 性質 character, nature (of iron, lead, poetry, irony, etc.); 實質 substance (as against title, reputation, etc.); 文質彬彬 balance of outward grace and solid worth. (2) Born character (of person): 資質, 素質 natural intelligence; 氣質 born capacity, personality (generous, mean, etc.). (3) (**jyh*) U. f. 贄 11.80, pledge, security. (4) (**jyh*) (AC) anc. battle-axe and case used for executing prisoners (also wr. 鑕).

V.t. (1) To question: 質問, 質詢, 質疑 *-wehn*, *-shyurn*, *-yir* ↓; 質之鬼神 address question to the spirits. (2) (**jyh*) To pawn: 典質淨盡 have pawned everything available; 交質 (AC) exchange of princes' relatives as hostages for pledge of alliance; 質押 *-ya* ↓.

Adj. Simple, unadorned: 質樸, 質直 *-pur*, *-jyr* ↓; 質言 (LL) truthful words.

質點 *jyrdiarn*, n., (phys.) particle (of matter).
質地 *jyrdih*[1], n., basic character (of person), basic material (of fabric, articles).
質的 *jyrdih*[2], n., (AC) target.
質正 *jyrjehng*, v. t., as in 質正有道 present to the scholars for advice and criticism.
質直 *jyrjyr*, adj., direct, straightforward.
質庫 **jyhkuh*, n., (LL) pawnshop.
質量 *jyrliahng*, n., (1) (phys.) mass; (2) gen. quality and quantity.
質料 *jyrliauh*, n., material of (furniture, clothing, etc.).
質明 *jyr-mirng*, phr., (AC) just before dawn.
質樸 *jyrpur*, adj., simple, not ostentatious.
質詢 *jyrshyurn*, v. t., ask for explanation (as congress asks of minister); to question; to ask opinion officially.
質責 *jyrtzer*, v. t., to entrust responsibility for certain course of action.
質子 *jyrtzyy*, (1) n., (phys.) proton; (2) (**jyh-*) v. i., to offer son as hostage.
質問 *jyrwehn*, v. i., see *-shyurn* ↑.
質押 **jyhya*, (1) v. t., to pawn s. t.; (2) n., collateral for mortgage (also 質押品).
質疑 *jyryir*, v. i., to present problems, doubts for enlightenment.

黌 90.80

hurng.

N. (AC) school, college: 黌門 college gate; 黌宇 college building.

§ 90.81 (ノ/人)

夭 90.81

yau (**aau*, **yaau*).

N. (**aau*) (AC) young animal or plant.

V.i. (1) (**yaau*) To die young: 夭折, 夭亡 *-jer*, *-warng* ↓. (2) (**yaau*) To stop, hinder: 夭遏 (閼) *-eh* ↓.

Adj. (AC, LL) young and luxuriant: 夭夭 *-yau* ↓; 夭桃穠李 (AC allu.) pretty girls.

夭遏 **yaau-eh*, v. t., (AC) stop, prevent (also wr. 夭閼).
夭昏 **yaauhun*, v. i., (AC) to die young, esp. from dissolute life.
夭札 **yaaujar*, v. i., (AC) to die young.
夭折 **yaaujer*, v. i., to die young.
夭矯 *yaujiaau*, adj., (LL) sprightly, alive, moving gracefully.
夭厲 *yaulih*, n., (AC) epidemic.
夭壽 **yaaushouh*, v. i., to die young.
夭亡 **yaauwarng*, v. i., ditto.
夭夭 *yauyau*, adj., (1) luxuriant, blossoming: 桃之夭夭 the peach tree is in full blossom—used in wedding felicitations; (2) (AC) pleasant or friendly in appearance.

奚 90.81

shi.

N. A slave: 奚童, 奚奴 *-turng*, *-nur* ↓. (2) A surname.

Adv. (AC & LL) how, what, why (=何): see 奚若 *-ruoh*, 奚如 *-rur*, 奚似 *-syh* ↓; 奚自 wherefrom? 奚堪 how can we bear? 奚可 how can? 子將奚先 which would you place first? 奚爲後我 why leave us to the last?

奚落 *shi'luoh*, v. t., to say things obliquely against (person): 奚落一陣 make sarcastic or oblique remarks against person.
奚奴 *shinur*, n., a slave.
奚若 *shiruoh*, adv. phr., why not (do s.t. else)? it would be better to.
奚如 *shirur*, adv. phr., see *-ruoh* ↑.
奚似 *shisyh*, adv. phr., see *-ruoh* ↑.
奚童 *shiturng*, n., (LL) a boy servant.

爨 90.81

tsuahn.

N. (1) An earthern kitchen stove: 分爨 (of brothers) have separate kitchens, live separately. (2) Name of an aboriginal tribe in Yunnan Province: 爨文 *Tsuahn* aboriginal script. (3) A surname.

V.t. To cook (food).

§ 90.82 (ノ/乂)

反 90.82

faan.

[Cogn. 返 90.83; 翻 90S.50]

N. (1) Opposite, reverse side: 正

亅	小	⺊	十	土	ナ	卄	凵	丨	一	丅	フ	口	区	冈	冂	厂	尸	亠	广	宀	丶	乚	七	心	八	人	乂	乛	一	ノ	𠂉	く
00	01	02	10	11	12	20	21	22	30	31	32	40	41	42	50	51	52	60	61	62	63	70	71	72	80	81	82	83	90	91	92	93

反 之反 (LL) opposite of right side; 適得其反 (LL) get just the opposite; see 平反 (pr. *-fan*) reverse court verdict. (2) Rebellion: 造反 raise rebellion; 謀反 attempt rebellion.

V.i. (1) Rebel: 反了, 反了 this is rebellion! (2) Return, come back (interch. 返): 反家 come home; 他不反回來 he does not come home; 反命 to report on mission after return; 反歸正道 return to orthodox church or to correct ways of life; 反(返)老還童 rejuvenate in old age; see 反古 *-guu*↓.

V.t. (1) To oppose, turn against, criticize: 反對 *-dueih*↓; 反孔, 反耶 oppose Confucianism, Christianity; 反復古, 反維新 be against traditionalism, against reform; 反邪歸正 return to orthodoxy. (2) To counter: 反問, 反詰 counter-question; 反駁 answer criticism; 反脣, 反目, 反臉 *-churn*, *-muh*, *-liaan*↓. (3) To turn over: 反過來 turn over; 反掌 *-jaang*↓, 反覆 *-fuh*↓; 舉一反三 (Confucius) teacher mentions one corner (aspect), student should reflect and think out the other three corners.

Adj. (1) Anti-: 相反的 contrary, opposite; 反教 anti-religion; 反帝國主義 anti-imperialism; 反面 *-miahn*↓; 反革命(的) counter-revolution(ary); 反作用 counter-effect. (2) Reversed: 反犬旁 the 犭 radical; 反文旁 the 攵 radical; 反片 the 片 in reverse position, 爿.

Adv. (1) On the contrary, instead, not as one might suppose, esp. 反而: 反(而)不如從前 on the contrary, it is worse than before; 反教他罵了我一頓 instead I was given a good scolding; 我送他錢, 反而得罪他 I gave him money and the result was I offended him; 反(而)把事情弄僵了 instead the matter got worse. (2) Back: 反觀 look back; 反顧 look back upon past or own mistake; 反求諸己 (Confucius) reflect and try to find fault in oneself; 反噬 bite back, accuse s. o. (who might be a friend); 反打瓦 accuse others while oneself is to blame; 反縛 hands tied on the back.

反本 *farnbeen*, v. i., go back to original basic teaching.

反辯 *faan-biahn*, v.t. & n., to refute, rebuttal.

反璧 *faanbih*, v. i., (LL) return (article).

反比(例) *farnbii(lih)*, n., inverse ratio.

反駁 *faanbor*, v. i. & t., reply to criticism.

反常 *faancharng*, adj., abnormal; (derog.) against all tradition.

反切 *faanchieh* (*fan-*), n., exact but cumbersome system of giving pronunciation of character by two other characters, first giving consonant, second giving vowel formations: thus 反 is indicated by 甫晚切 *fu* and *wan*, giving pronunciation *f-an*, *fan*.

反串 *faanchuahn*, v. i., (of actor) play not one's customary role.

反芻 *faanchur*, v. i., chew the cud.

反脣 *faanchurn*, v. i., quarrel.

反倒 *farndaau*, adv., on the contrary: 反倒不好.

反對 *faandueih*, v. t., to oppose (stand, policy, etc.): 他老是和你反對 he always opposes you; 反對派 the political opposition; 反對份子 recalcitrant elements.

反動 *faanduhng*, n., reaction, physical or political; adj., reactionary; 反動派 reactionaries.

反而 *faan-erl*, adv., see Adv. 1↑.

反覆(復) *faanfuh*, v. i., as in 反覆無常 change one's mind constantly; (adv.) again and again (explain), also 反反覆覆.

反感 *farngaan*, n., reaction; bad reaction.

反光 *faanguang*, n., reflected light, glare.

反顧 *faanguh*, v. i., look back; look back upon oneself: 無所反顧 never look back, set on determined course.

反共(主義) *faan-guhng*, adj. & n., anti-communist, -nism.

反攻 *faangung*[1], v. i., counter-attack.

反躬 *faan-gung*[2], v. i., examine oneself.

反古 *farnguu*, v.i., return to ancient ideas, customs.

反悔 *farnhueei*, v. i., to repent.

反掌 *farn-jaang*, v. i., in 易如反掌 (AC) as easy as turning over one's hand.

反照 *faanjauh*, v. i., reflect (light).

反證 *faanjehng*[1], n., counter-evidence.

反正 *faanjehng*[2], adv., anyway: 反正他是逃不了 anyway he cannot escape.

反真 *faanjen*, v. i., (Taoist) go back to original nature.

反間 *faanjiahn*, n., ruse, strategy to alienate allies.

反詰 *faanjie*, v. i., answer back, counter back.

反擊 *faanjir*, v. i., counter-attack.

反轉 *farnjuaan*, v. i., turn over, turn round.

反撞力 *faanjuahng-lih*, n., recoil (of rifles).

反抗 *faankahng*, v. t. & n., resist (enemy), -ance.

反臉 *farnliaan*, v. i., break up friendship, also 翻臉.

反亂 *faanluahn*, n., turmoil, revolts.

反面 *faan-miahn*, n., the opposite side, reverse.

反目 *faan-muh*, v. i., in 夫妻反目 quarrel between husband and wife.

反逆 *faannih*, n. & adj., (derog.) rebel, against established law and order.

反紐 *farn-nioou*, n., see 反切 *-chieh*↑.

反叛 *faanpahn*, n. & adj. & v.t., rebellion, -ious, to rebel.

反派 *faan-paih*, n., villain in a piece; person always against s.t.

反璞 *faan-pur*, v. i., go back to original, whole nature of man (Taoist).

反哺 *farn-puu*, v. i., (of black crow reputed to) feed its parents.

反射 *faansheh*, v. i. & n., reflect, -tion (of light).

反響 *farnshiaang*, n., echo; reaction (to speech, conduct).

反相 *faan-shiahng*, n., the looks or indications of planning rebellion.

反省 *farnshiing*, v. i., self-reflection, search oneself for mistakes.
反訴 *faan-suh*, v. i. & n., counter-accusation.
反側 *faantseh*, v. i., turn over restlessly; revolt in palace.
反坐 *faan-tzuoh*, v. t., make plaintiff pay penalty of accused.
反胃 *faanweih*, v. i., (Chin. med.) turn the stomach; also 翻胃.
反應 *faanyihng*[1], v. i. & n., react, -tion.
反映 *faanyihng*[2], v. i. & n., reflect, -tion (of light, character, period).

 90.82

shouh.

Vb. aux. Equiv. Eng. "be" in passive voice where the modn. 被 is more common: 受開除 (=被開除) be dismissed; 受打, 受罵 be beaten, scolded; 受枉屈 be wronged; 受選, 受任 elected, appointed; 受封 be appointed with title; (where passivity is not emphasized, the 受 or 被 is oft. dropped, as 學生 (受) 開除了 student is expelled; 門開了 door is opened; 行人擋住了 pedestrians are blocked; in this case, the v.t. is always a p.p.).

V.i. & t. (1) To accept: 接受, 收受 accept (gift, appointment); 受理 *-lii*[1] ↓; 受俘 (AC) receive prisoners of war; 受賄 accept bribe. (2) To bear, stand, suffer: 受不了, 受不起, 受不得, 受不住 cannot stand (noise, repeated begging, etc.); 受苦, 受難, 受氣 *-kuu*, *-nahn*, *-chih* ↓; 忍受 bear with patience, suffer (pain); 難受 adj., hard to bear, irritating, painful; 感受 to experience (pleasure, pain), feel (difficulty, cold, fright, etc.). (3) To be worthy of (look, hearing, eating): 受看, 受聽, 受吃 *-kahn*, *-ting*, *-chy* ↓; 受用 *-yuhng* ↓.

受癟 *shouh-biee*, v i., (coll.) be discomfited, get oneself into a bad fix.
受病 *shouh-bihng*, v. i., fall sick.
受茶 *shouh-char*, v. i., formerly, (girl's family) receives gifts of betrothal.
受潮 *shouh-chaur*, v. i., be affected by damp and cold.
受氣 *shouh-chih*, v. i., suffer petty annoyances: 受氣包兒 person subjected to daily persecutions.
受寵 *shouhchuung*, v. i., receive favor from superior: 受寵若驚 overwhelmed by superior's favor.
受吃 *shouhchy*, adj., good to eat, palatable, tasty.
受持 *shouhchyr*, v. i., (Budd.) to believe and hold on to the faith.
受屈 *shouh-chyu*, v. i., suffer an injustice.
受害 *shouh-haih*, v. i., (1) be murdered; (2) to suffer: 受害不淺 badly misguided or ill-advised.
受寒 *shouh-harn*, v. i., be affected by cold, catch cold.
受教 *shouh-jiauh*, v. i., be taught; receive instructions or guidance, be benefited by advice.
受戒 *shouh-jieh*, v. i., (Budd.) take oaths as monk.
受精 *shouh-jing*, v. i., (woman) conceives; be fertilized.
受知 *shouhjy*, v. i., to be recognized (for one's talent).
受看 *shouhkahn*, adj., good to look at.
受苦 *shouh-kuu*, v.i., to suffer.
受累 *shouhleei*, v. i., (1) to be involved on account of s. o. else; (2) (*-leih*) suffer hardships.
受理 *shouhlii*[1], v. i., (of court) accept a complaint.
受禮 *shouh-lii*[2], v. i., receive a gift, acknowledge salute.
受命 *shouh-mihng*, v. i., to be ordained or appointed to post; to benefit by friendly counsel: 受命於天 rule by the grace of God.
受難 *shouh-nahn*, v. i., to suffer hardships, die a martyr.
受騙 *shouh-piahn*, v. i., be cheated.
受辱 *shouh-ruh*, v. i., be humiliated.
受禪 *shouh-shahn*, v. i., (AC) accept transfer of government from previous ruler other than by inheritance.
受傷 *shouh-shang*, v. i., be injured.
受審 *shouh-sheen*, v. i., be tried at court.
受性 *shouh-shihng*, v. i., (LL) be born (clever, stubborn, etc.; modn. 生性).
受洗 *shouh-shii*, v.i., be baptized.
受刑 *shouh-shirng*, v.i., suffer torture.
受暑 *shouh-shuu*, v.i., be affected by heat, have sunstroke.
受胎 *shouh-tai*, v.i., become pregnant.
受聽 *shouhting*, adj., good to hear.
受托 *shouh-tuo*, v. i., be entrusted to do s. t. by friend (also wr. 託).
受罪 *shouhtzueih*, v. i., suffer (as from heat, exposure, crowded conditions): 我在受罪 I am suffering.
受業 *shouhyeh*, n., (oft. court. in self-reference) your pupil; a pupil.
受益人 *shouhyihrern*, n., beneficiary; 受益權 beneficial rights.
受孕 *shouh-yuhn*, v. i., see *-tai* ↑.
受用 *shouhyuhng*, adj., physically comfortable, enjoyable: 很受用 very enjoyable (a good concert, new fur coat).

爰 90.82

yuarn.

N. A surname.

Adv. & conj. (AC, LL) then, and then, therefore: 爰書數行 therefore have written a few words; 爰及其他 and then the others.

 90.82

aih.

亅	小	⺊	十	土	𠂇	廾	⺊	丨	一	丅	㇆	口	区	冈	冂	厂	尸	亠	广	宀	丶	乚	弋	心	八	人	乂	𠂉	一	丿	𠂉	く
00	01	02	10	11	12	20	21	22	30	31	32	40	41	42	50	51	52	60	61	62	63	70	71	72	80	81	82	83	90	91	92	93

N. Love: 仁愛 kindness to fellowmen; 博愛 universal love, broad love for mankind: 愛惡 or 愛憎 love and hatred; 戀愛 love affair.

V.i. & t. (1) To like, be pleased with, be fond of: 喜愛 to like (person, place, painting, etc.); 愛好 *-hauh* ↓. (2) To love (lover, parents, etc.): 戀愛 to be in love; 愛慕 *-muh* ↓; 可愛 lovable, lovely; 心愛 to love tenderly: 所心愛的人 the beloved; 溺愛 to be infatuated with (mistress, etc.) or to indulge and spoil children; 寵愛 to be fond of especially (one person); 愛莫能助 would be glad to help but cannot; 愛己及物 extend love of self to others. (3) To care for, to cherish: 愛惜, 愛護 *-shir*, *-huh* ↓. (4) Be prone to, liable to: 愛哭 (child) cries most of the time; 愛笑 always ready to smile or laugh; 天熱東西愛壞, 天冷花就愛死 things spoil easily in hot weather, and (many) flowers wither away in cold.

愛卿 *aih-ching*, phr., (1) dear wife; (2) formerly, (ruler to minister) dear minister, see 卿 90S.22.

愛情 *aihchirng*, n., love, esp. romantic love; affection in gen.

愛寵 *aihchuung*, v.t., to bestow special favor (on minister, mistress, child).

愛羣 *aih-chyurn*, n., the love of fellowmen; also gregariousness.

愛戴 *aihdaih*, v.t., to love (ruler, elder or superior).

愛服 *aihfur*, v.t., to admire from the heart.

愛撫 *aihfuu*, v.t., to love and protect (child, people), fondle, caress.

愛根 *aih-gen*, n., (Budd.) love and desire as the root of troubles.

愛顧 *aihguh*, v.t., (of superior) to bestow favor, to take interest in (one below).

愛國 *aihguor*, (1) v.t., to love one's country; (2) n. & adj., patriotism, -tic; 愛國心 patriotism.

愛好 *aihhauh*, v.t., (1) to take good care of (one's health, natural endowments); (2) to admire, be fond of (dress, gambling, joking); (3) (*-haau*) want to be good, to desire a good name: 愛好兒, 他們兩家是愛好兒做親 they are married for love.

愛護 *aihhuh*, v.t., to cherish, support and protect (country, church, etc.).

愛繼 *aih-jih*, phr., choice of heir by preference and not by seniority (應繼).

愛著 *aihjuor*, n., (Budd.) the entanglements of love and desire.

愛憐 *aihliarn*, v.t., to love (child, young girl), to show tenderness toward.

愛美 *aih-meei*, phr., love of beauty: 愛美的觀念 esthetic sense.

愛慕 *aihmuh*, v.t., to love, adore (lover, a great writer, etc.).

愛染 *aihraan*, n., (LL) see *-juor* ↑.

愛人 *aihrern*, n., (1) lover, sweetheart, one's beloved: 愛人兒 ditto; (2) adj., lovely: 這姑娘長得眞愛人兒 this girl has grown very lovely.

愛日 *aih-ryh*, phr., (1) (LL) the precious days left for serving old parents; (2) be economical of time; (3) lovable sunshine.

愛神 *aihshern*, n., goddess of love, Venus (Roman myth.), Aphrodite (Greek myth.).

愛小 *aih-shiaau*, adj., greedy for small gains or profits.

愛惜 *aihshir*, v.t., to love and cherish, see *-huh* ↑.

愛憎 *aih-tzeng*, phr., love and hatred, likes and dislikes.

---

§ 90.83 (ノ/～)

乏 90.83

far.

V.t. To lack, be lacking: 乏人照應 need people to look after; oft. 缺乏 lack, need; 乏味, 乏趣 dull, lacking in flavor, interest; 乏善可陳 phr., (LL) have nothing good or unusual to report (court.).

Adj. (1) Poor: 貧乏, 窮乏; 乏地 (LL) poor soil. (2) Tired: 我乏了; 走乏了, 玩乏了 tired from walking, playing. (3) (Derog. & coll.) useless: 乏桶, 乏貨, 乏人 useless person; 乏話 weak, ineffective talk.

爪 90.83

jaau (**juaa*).

N. (1) Fingernail. (2) (**juaa*) (*-tz*, *-'l*) Claw of animal.

爪牙 *jaauyar*, n., claws and fangs; (fig.) underlings of gangs, partisans or agents, esp. ruthless ones.

爪印 *jaauyihn*, n., footprints, traces, of past events.

爬 90.83

par.

V.i. & t. (1) To scratch: 爬癢 scratch an itch. (2) To crawl: 爬行 crawl along; 爬不起來 cannot get up from lying position. (3) To climb: 爬山, 爬牆 climb a mountain, a wall; 爬山過嶺 phr., over hills and crests.

爬蟲 *parchurng*, n., insect.

爬羅 *parluor*, v. t., haul, ransack (everything).

爬沙 *parsha*, adv., crawling like a crab.

爬梳 *parshu*, v. t., comb out and arrange (historical facts 史實).

瓜 90.83

gua.

N. (1) (Bot.) any kind of melon or gourd: 西瓜 the watermelon; 甜

瓜, 香瓜 the muskmelon; 冬瓜 the wax gourd; 絲瓜 the vegetable sponge, dish-cloth gourd; 南瓜 the pumpkin; 黃瓜, 胡瓜 the cucumber; 瓜果 melons and fruits; 瓜熟蒂落 (fig.) at the right time everything comes easy, (lit., "a melon falls when it is ripe"); 瓜田李[A]下 see 10.00; 瓜田不納履 don't bend to tie shoes on a melon patch—to avoid suspicion. (2) A stupid person: 傻瓜 a simpleton; 蠢瓜 a fool; 笨瓜 a stupid fellow; 破瓜 (of girl) sixteen yeas of age, lose virginity.

瓜期 *guachi*, n., a term of service.

瓜代 *guadaih*, n., (allu.) change of personnel between terms of service.

瓜瓞 *guadier*, n., (term of eulogy) 緜緜瓜瓞 may your family grow and prosper like spreading melon-vines!

瓜分 *guafen*, n. & v. t., to partition, divide (a country): 豆剖瓜分 divide up s. t. just as one separates pea-pods or cuts melons into slices.

瓜葛 *guager*, n., complications, involvement in dispute, interrelations, distant relatives.

瓜撓(兒)(子) *guanaur('l)* (*tz*), n., a peeler.

瓜皮 *guapir*, n., (1) melon skin; (2) anything that looks like melon skin: 瓜皮帽 a skull cap; 瓜皮艇 a small, light boat, canoe.

瓜瓤 *guararng*, n., the pulp of a melon.

瓜仁(兒) *guarern(-rer'l)*, n., the kernel of a melon seed.

瓜子 *guatzyy*, n., melon seeds.

廷 90.83

tirng.

[Cf. 庭 61.83; 廷 more spec. used for imperial court]

N. The court in royal government: 朝廷 formerly, the central government; 宮廷, 殿廷 the palaces; 天廷 imperial court; 廷對 imperial audience with questions by emperor; 廷議 court discussion; 廷爭 controversy at court; 廷寄 (in Manchu Dyn.) orders issued directly by the court without going through cabinet channels; 廷試 highest civil examinations held in the palace before the emperor (also called 殿試).

延 90.83

yarn.

N. A surname.

V.i. & t. (1) To spread about, to wind across or about (like vine): 蔓延 spread about, (vines, branches) ramify; 禍延子孫 retribution involves one's children and children's children; 延及 (fire) spreads to (neighbors); 延袤, 延蔓 *-mauh, -mahn*↓. (2) To stretch (neck): 延頸舉踵, 延頸企足 crane one's neck and stand on tiptoe (to welcome, pray for coming): 延性 *-shihng*↓. (3) To postpone, delay: 延會 postpone meeting; 延期 *-chir*↓; 推延, 拖延 to keep on postponing (payments, etc.); 延擱, 延遲, 延滯 *-ge, -chyr, -jyh*↓. (4) To invite: 延聘, 延請, 延納 *-pihn, -chiing, -nah*↓; 延師 invite teacher to school; 延祥納福 to induce good luck.

延長 *yarncharng*, v. t., to prolong (term, meeting); 延長記號 *--jihhauh*, n., (music) pause.

延企 *yarnchih*, v. i., as in 延頸企足 to stand on tiptoe to welcome, hope.

延請 *yarnchiing*, v. t., to invite, appoint (teacher), send for (doctor).

延期 *yarn-chir*, phr., to postpone, be postponed.

延遲 *yarnchyr*, adj., slow to arrive, delay.

延宕 *yarndahng*, adj., ditto.

延擱 *yarnge*, v. t., to delay, be delayed.

延會 *yarn-hueih*, phr., postpone meeting.

延胡索 *yarnhursuoo*, n., (bot.) *Corydalis ambigua.*

延接 *yarnjie*, v. t., to extend hand of welcome.

延佇 *yarnjuh*, v. i., see *-chih*↑.

延滯 *yarnjyh*, v. i., to be bogged down, keep on delaying.

延攬 *yarnlaan*, v. t., to search for and invite (good, able men).

延蔓 *yarnmahn*, v. i., spread about, ramify (as vines).

延袤 *yarnmauh*, v. i., (of Great Wall, mountain range) to spread about, stretch far and wide.

延命菊 *yarnmihng-jyur*, n., (bot.) *Belis perennis.*

延納 *yarnnah*, v. t., to invite (good, able men).

延年 *yarn-niarn*, phr., 延年益壽 (of tonic) calculated to prolong one's life.

延聘 *yarnpihn*, v. t., to invite, appoint (professors, etc.).

延釐 *yarn-shi*, phr., formula for inviting luck, oft. wr. on wall facing gate.

延性 *yarnshihng*, n., (phys.) ductility.

延壽 *yarn-shouh*, v. i., to prolong life.

延髓 *yarnsueei*, n., (physiol.) medulla oblongata.

延譽 *yarn-yuh*, v. i., (LL) to spread fame for s. o.; to cultivate publicity.

返 90.83

faan.

[Cogn. 反 90.82, interch. in sense of return]

V.i. To return (in AC wr. 反): 返國, 返里, 返家 return to country, village, home; 往者不返 (LL) those who go away do not return;

返程, 返棹 return journey; 返老還童 rejuvenate in old age; 廻光返照 brief glow of health before passing away; 返璞歸真 (Taoist) return to original nature; 返魂 *-hurn*↓.

返璧 *faanbih*, v. t., to return (article).

返潮 *faanchaur*, adj., very damp (place, house).

返魂 *faan-hurn*, v. i., to resuscitate those in coma or death.

返回 *faan-jueir*, v. i., to return.

返魂香 *faanhurn-shiang*, n., (AC) incense to resuscitate those in coma or under narcotic.

迁 90.83

chian.

[Pop. of 遷 31.83]

近 90.83

jihn.

V.t. (1) To approach, come close to: 接近 come near, approximate; 近朱者赤, 近墨者黑 moral influence by contact or close association; 迫近 (of time) drawing nearer and nearer; 切近 close at hand. (2) Be closely related to or on intimate terms with: 親近 become intimate with, befriend; 近親 a close relative; 近幸 a court favorite; 近侍 a personal attendant of the king; 近支 *-jy*↓.

Adj. (1) Nearby, close (opp. 遠 distant, far-off): 近便 *-'bian*, 近畿 *-ji*, 近郊 *-jiau*↓; 鄰近 neighboring; 近些 nearer; 靠近 adjacent, adjoining; 近水樓臺先得月 enjoy the benefits of a favorable position ("those on waterfront are the first to see the rising moon"); 近光 (photography) light in foreground, nearsighted; 近慮 immediate worries; 近地, 近處 vicinity, neighboring district; 近岸 near the shore, offshore; 近東 the Near East; 近海 inshore (opp. 遠洋 deep-sea); 近程, 近途 a short distance or journey; 臨近 nearby, adjoining, adjacent; 附近 near, close by, vicinity; 近路 a short cut. (2) Easy to understand: 淺近 can be readily understood. (3) Similar to, like: 近似 *-syh*↓; 相近 look like, approximate; 將近 about to, on the point of; 近理 *-lii*, 近情 *-chirng*↓. (4) Recent, current, present-day (opp. 久遠 old, past, bygone): 近代 *-daih*, 近年 *-niarn*, 近來 *-lair*, 近古 *-guu*, 近況 *-kuahng*, 近世 *-shyh*[1], 近日 *-ryh*, 近歲 *-sueih*↓; 近時 recent times, latter-day; 近因 *-yin*↓; 最近 (most) recently; 近事, 近聞, 近作 recent event, news, (literary or artistic) work; 近人 *-rern*↓; 近憂 current anxieties (worries, troubles); 近幾年 in the last few years; 近體 (詩) modern-style (poetry).

近便 *jihn'bian*, adj., not far away.

近情 *jihnchirng*, adj., human (personality, philosophy), consistent with human feelings.

近代 *jihndaih*, adj. & n., modern (times, age): 近代史 modern history; 近代人物 modern personages.

近古 *jihnguu*, n., the period relatively closer to classical period.

近乎 *jihn(')hu*, (1) adj., in close contact with, intimate; (2) adv., almost, approximately.

近畿 *jihnji*, n., surrounding districts of the national capital.

近郊 *jihnjiau*, n., suburbs of a city.

近支 *jihnjy*, n., a close branch of family.

近況 *jihnkuahng*, n., the current situation (condition).

近來 *jihnlair*, adv., recently, not long ago.

近理 *jihnlii*, adj., reasonable, fair, just, equitable.

近年 *jihnniarn*, n. & adv., recent years.

近人 *jihnrern*, n., a contemporary.

近日 *jihnryh*, n. & adv., (1) recent days; (2) recently.

近世 *jihnshyh*[1], n., modern times.

近視 *jihnshyh*[2], adj., nearsighted, myopia: 近視眼 *--yaan* adj. & n., nearsighted(ness), myopic; 近視鏡 *--jihng*, n., spectacles for near sight.

近歲 *jihnsueih*, n. & adv., (in recent years.

近似 *jihnsyh*, adj. & v. i., (to look) like, (be) similar to.

近因 *jihn-yin*, n., an immediate cause.

迎 90.83

yirng (**yihng*).

V.t. (1) To welcome, to meet, receive: 歡迎 ditto; 迎客 receive visitors; 迎賓 to usher at receptions; 迎接 *-jie*↓; 迎合 *-her*↓; 逢迎 to cater to person's wishes; 失迎 (court. apology) not being able to meet person during visit. (2) To meet face to face: 迎上來 went up to (person); 迎面, 迎頭 *-miahn*, *-tour*↓; 迎敵 meet the enemy; 迎擊 *-jir*↓; 迎刃而解 splits off as it meets the edge of knife without effort, (fig.) (question) easily solved. (3) (**yihng*) 迎親 bridegroom goes to bride's home to escort her to wedding.

迎晨 *yirngchern*, adv., toward dawn.

迎春 *yirngchurn*, n., (bot.) the jasmine, *Jasminum nudiflorum*.

迎娶 *yirngchyuu*, v. t., to marry (bride).

迎敵 *yirng-dir*, phr., to go out and challenge enemy, to meet face to face for battle.

迎阿 *yirng-e*, v. t., to toady.

迎合 *yirngher*, v. t., to cater to (another's wishes).

迎候 *yirnghouh*, v. t., to welcome (visitor).

迎見 *yirngjiahn*, v. t., to receive (callers).

迎將 *yirngjiang*, v. t., (AC) to welcome and send off.

迎接 *yirngjie*, v. t., to welcome in person.

迎擊 *yirngjir*, v. t., to make frontal attack, to meet enemy.

迎粧 *yirng-juang*, phr., (bridegroom's family) receives bride's trousseau before wedding.

迎面(兒) *yirngmiahn(-miah'l)*, adv., face to face.

迎年 *yirng-niarn*, phr., to welcome the arrival of the New Year.

迎頭(兒) *yirngtour('l)*, adv., meeting head on: 迎頭趕上 proceed with determination, to catch up forthwith.

迎迓 *yirngyah*, v. t., to welcome, receive (guest).

适 90.83

gua (also *kuoh*).

V.i. Hasten, hurry on.

逅 90.83

houh (also *gouh*).

V.i. See 邂逅 92.83.

透 90.83

touh.

V.i. & t. Pass through, penetrate, let out: 透消息 leak out news; 透露, 透漏 *-luh*, *-louh* ↓; 透了一口氣 breathe more easily after tension, give vent to some inmost feelings; 透過 pass through, penetrate, see *-guoh* ↓; 透汗 perspire; 涼風透骨 chilled to the bones.

Adj. Thorough: 透雨 thorough, adequate rain.

Adv. (1) Thorough, thoroughly: 糟透了, 壞透了 completely rotten; 煩透了 utterly vexed, annoyed, extremely troublesome; 恨透了 hate deeply; 涼透, 熟透, 濕透 thoroughly cool, cooked, soaked through; 透頂 *-diing* ↓. (2) As prefix, "over-," or "trans-": 透支, 透視, 透明 *-jy*, *-shyh*, *-mirng* ↓.

透澈(徹) *touhcheh*, adj. & adv., thorough, -ly: 講得透澈 give a thorough exposition.

透氣 *touh-chih*, (1) adj., well ventilated; (2) v. i., give vent to emotions: 透了這口氣 success in avenging wrongs or after suppression.

透頂 *touh-diing*, adv., thoroughly: 糟透頂了 absolutely rotten; 紅透頂了 at the top of popularity.

透風 *touh-feng*, (1) adj., (room) well ventilated: 不透風 no air goes through; (2) v. t., leak out news.

透過 *touh-guoh*, (1) prep., via, by way of: 透過某層關係 by way of certain connections; (2) v. t., penetrate, infiltrate: 透過機關 infiltrate organization.

透鏡 *touh-jihng*, n., lens.

透支 *touh-jy*, v. t., overdraw bank account.

透亮(兒) *touh'liang('l)*, adj., transparent, clear, through: 這話説得很透亮 this is stated very lucidly.

透漏 *touhlouh*, v.t., leak out.

透露 *touhluh*, adj., transparent, manifest.

透明 *touh-mirng*, adj., transparent; 透明體 transparent body.

透析 *touhshi*, n., (chem.) dialysis.

透心(兒)涼 *touh-shin(-shie'l) liarng*, adv., (1) chilled through (in disappointment); (2) immensely delighted, -ful.

透視 *touhshyh*, v.t., see through; 透視法 n., (drawing) perspective.

逶 90.83

wei.

逶隨 *weisueir*, adj. & adv., winding (road); leisurely (walking).

逶迤 *weiyir*, adj. & adv., winding (road); also wr. 逶移, 逶蛇 (*-yir*).

遁 90.83

duhn.

V.i. Evade, disappear, hide away: 遁逃, 逃遁 escape; 遁去 run away in hiding; 遁北 (of army) be routed, flee in defeat; 遁世, 遁跡 live in seclusion from society: 遁跡山林 live the life of a hermit in mountains.

遞 90.83

dih.

V.i. & t. Hand over, deliver by hand: 遞過來 pass me (the sugar, etc.); 遞給他 pass (it) to him; 遞個信 send a note; 遞名片 send in a visiting card; 傳遞消息 circulate the news; 遞送某人 deliver to s. o.; 遞和氣 or 遞嘻和兒 show a friendly face; 遞眼色 wink at, give message by a wink or look.

Adv. (1) In turn: 遞換, 更遞 replace from time to time. (2) Proportionately, in proportion: 遞加, 遞減 gradually increase, decrease, in proportion; 遞補 add gradually, replace, fill up (vacancy).

遞交 *dihjiau*, v. t., deliver to (place, person).

遞解 *dihjieh*, v. t., deport, send (criminal) under escort.

遞送 *dihsuhng*, v. t., send to, deliver by messenger.

遛 乒 丢 妥 委

遛 90.83

liour (**liouh*).

V.i. (1) Tarry: 逗遛 stay, stop over; 逗遛幾天 stop over for a few days. (2) (**liouh*) Take a stroll: 遛遛, 遛一遛, 遛一圈, 遛彎兒 go for a walk; 遛馬路, 遛街 walk around streets; 遛食兒 take a stroll after meal; 遛早兒 take morning walk for exercise; 遛馬 v.t., walk a horse.

遛達 **liouh'da*, (also wr. 溜), *liou'da* 63A.41) v.i., go for a walk.

§ 90.91 (ノ/ノ)

乒 90.91

ping.

乒乓 *pingpang*, n., ping-pong, table tennis: 打乒乓 to play ping-pong.

§ 90.93 (ノ/く)

丢 90.93

diou.

V.t. (1) To lose (s. t.): 丢東西, 東西丢了 lost s. t., s. t. is lost; 錢丢掉了 or 丢失了 money is lost; 丢臉 lose face; 這事眞丢臉 this thing is disgraceful; 丢體面, 丢面子 ditto; 丢人 ditto; 丢你的人 shame on you! you should be ashamed; 丢三落四, 丢頭落尾 miss this and that; 丢包術 a trick of substituting parcel for another =掉包. (2) To throw, cast, cast off: 丢石子 cast stone; 丢下, 丢開 throw down (object, responsibility, work); 丢不開 cannot shake off (work) or part with (family): 丢開不管 throw down job, duty; 丢眼色(兒) to wink at; 丢淚 drop a tear; 丢巧針 former custom among girls to cast needle into basin and look for it in moonlight on the seventh of seventh lunar month; 丢精 eject semen.

丢醜 *diouchoou*, v. i., be a disgrace, make a bad show.

丢臉 *diouliaan*, v. i., lose face; cause to lose face, disgrace.

丢人 *diourern*, v. i., ditto.

妥 90.93

tuoo.

Adj. (1) Satisfactory, well arranged, ready: 不妥 not satisfactory: 欠妥, 事未妥 ditto; 這件事辦妥了 this matter has been well arranged or concluded; 極妥, 妥極了 very good! well done! 妥當, 妥貼, 妥善 *-'dang*, *-tie*, *-shahn* ↓. (2) Finished, done: 事辦妥了沒有 has the matter been concluded?

Adv. Properly, competently, with due care: 妥商, 妥議 take time to discuss matter properly; 妥爲商量 ditto; 妥爲辦理 handle the matter with due care and consideration; 妥籌 make proper plans for.

妥當 *tuoo'dang*, adj., proper, satisfactory (arrangements, etc.).

妥靠 *tuookauh*, adj., reliable, dependable, trustworthy.

妥善 *tuooshahn*, adj., all in proper place, well arranged.

妥洽 *tuooshiah*, v. i., (1) discuss with a view to agreement; (2) appease, -ment.

妥協 *tuooshier*, v. i. & n., compromise.

妥貼 *tuootie*, adj., well settled, provided, everything in right place.

委 90.93

weei.

N. The end: 原委 the story (beginning and end), the origin of some event.

V.i. & t. (1) To appoint, send: 委派, 委任 *-paih*, *-rehn* ↓; 差委 to send (s. o.). (2) To entrust, shift: 委託 *-tuo* ↓; 委過 *-guoh* ↓. (3) To accumulate: 委積 *-ji* ↓. (4) To abandon: 委棄 *-chih* ↓.

Adj. (1) Withered, tired: 委靡, 委頓 *-mii*, *-duhn* ↓. (2) Winding, bent: 委蛇 *-yir* ↓; 委曲, 委屈 *-chyu*[1,2] ↓.

Adv. Really: 委實 *-shyr* ↓.

委棄 *weeichih*, v. t., to abandon, cast away on the ground.

委禽 *weei-chirn*, phr., (AC) send goose as betrothal present.

委曲 *weeichyu*[1], n., the twists and turns of events.

委屈 *weeichyu*[2], (1) adj., obstructed (in career), held back; (2) (-'*chyu*) v. t., usu. p.p., 受委屈 suffer from injustice, wrongly accused.

委的 *weei'de*, adv., see *-shyr* ↓.

委頓 *weeiduhn*, adj., (person) tired, exhausted, frustrated; (business) declined, slowed down.

委過 *weei-guoh*, phr., to shift blame.

委積 *weei-ji*, v. i. & t., to accumulate, pile up.

委質 *weei-jyh*, phr., (AC) to send or deliver present on first meeting (also wr. 委贄, 委摯).

委決 *weeijyuer*, v. i., as in 委決不下 delay decision.

委陵菜 *weeilirng-tsaih*, n., (bot.) *Potentilla chinensis*.

委命 *weei-mihng*, phr., entrust to fate, take fatalistic attitude.

委靡 *weirmii*, adj., effeminate, sentimental (music) (usu. wr. 萎).

委派 *weeipaih* (-'*pai*), v. t., to appoint (s. o.).

委任 *weeirehn*, v. t., to appoint an

official (of certain grade, see 任 91A.11); to appoint s. o. to task; mandate (United Nations); 委任統治國 mandatory power; 委任統治地 mandated territories.

委巷 *weei-shiahng*, n., (AC) a small alley.

委實 *weeishyr*, adv., (1) really (not bad, etc.); (2) 委實招供 confess truthfully.

委瑣 *weirsuoo*, adj., being a stickler for forms, details.

委託 *weeituo*, v. t., entrust (person, task).

委罪 *weei-tzueih*, phr., to shift blame.

委婉 *weirwaan*, adv., (explain) in a roundabout way or with soft words.

委窩子 *weeiwotz*, n., person fond of keeping to his bed.

委蛇 *weeiyir*, adv., leisurely, in roundabout way.

委員 *weeiyuarn*, n., committee member: 主任委員 chairman of committee; 委員會 committee.

SECTION 90A

§ 90A.00 (禾/刂)

利 90A.00-2

lih.

N. (1) Gains, advantage, profit, merit, what is good: 利益 *-yih* ↓; 有利可圖 there are profits to be made; 得利 make profits, gain advantage; 利弊得失 advantages and disadvantages, merits and demerits; 利病 good and bad, merits and demerits; 利害 *-haih*, 利權 *-chyuarn* ↓; 見利忘義 forget principles at the sight of profit; 利令智昏 money blinds, tends to make one do foolish things; 利慾 *-yuh* ↓; 利誘 lure by money offers; 從中取利 get a "cut" in transactions; 漁利 make profits by illegal means; 利之所趨 where profits are to be gained. (2) Income from capital: 利息 *-shir*, 利錢 *-chiarn*, 利潤 *-ruhn* ↓; 利兒 profits: 這項買賣很有利兒 this transaction is very profitable; 利上滾利 at compound interest; 餘利 surplus profits; 暴利 exorbitant profits. (3) Resources, public utility: 水利 water conservancy; 地利 land utilization; 利源 *-yuarn* ↓. (4) Wealth, riches: 利祿 *-luh* ↓; 名利雙收 gain both honor and money; 財利 material wealth; 功利（主義） utility, -tarianism. (5) A surname.

V.t. To profit, be of advantage to: 利他 benefit others, be altruistic; 利他主義 altruism; 利己 to benefit oneself, be selfish; 利己主義 egoism; 傷人而不利己 injure people without benefit to oneself; 利人 to benefit other people; 利國利民 to benefit the nation and the people; 利用 *-yuhng* ↓.

Adj. (1) Sharp, cutting, fluent, eloquent, quick: 利刃 a sharp knife; 利鈍 *-duhn* ↓; 銳利, 鋒利 (of knife, etc.) sharp; 快利 ditto; 流利 (of speech) fluent, eloquent; 利齒, 利口, 利嘴 quick of speech; 利器 *-chih* ↓. (2) Convenient, lucky, of good fortune: 便利, 利便 convenient, easy to do or obtain; 順利 without a hitch; 吉利 good fortune. (3) Smooth, orderly: 利落 *-luoh* ↓; 利颼 *-'sou* ↓.

利弊 *lih-bih*, n., advantages and disadvantages, merits and demerits.

利錢 *lihchiarn*, n., interest on bank deposits.

利器 *lihchih*, n., (1) sharp weapons; (2) military control (國之利器); (3) (AC) useful men at court.

利權 *lihchyuarn*, n., rights and privileges.

利得 *lihder*, n., (law) profits.

利鈍 *lih-duhn*, adj., (of the cutting edge of a knife, etc.) sharp or blunt: 成敗利鈍, 在所不計 irrespective of success or failure.

利害 *lihhaih*, (1) n., gains and losses: 利害關係 advantages and disadvantages; (2) adj., (correctly 厲害) severe, terrible, harsh (of person, plan), extremely capable (person).

利祿 *lihluh*, n., wealth and high honors: 功名利祿 high official positions and riches.

利落 *lihluoh*, adj., (＝俐落) smoothly done.

利率 *lihlyuh*, n., (banking) rate of interest.

利潤 *lihruhn*, n., (1) profits from business; (2) profits from capital investments.

利息 *lihshir*(-'*shi*), n., (banking) interest on deposits.

利市 *lihshyh*, (1) n., business profits: 利市三倍 threefold profits; (2) adj., lucky, of good fortune.

利颼 *lih'sou*, adj., orderly, tidy.

利益 *lihyih*, (1) n., gains, benefits; (2) v. t., to benefit (society, others).

亅	小	卜	十	土	ナ	卄	ㄴ卜	丨	一	丅	フ	口	区	冈	乛	厂	尸	亠	广	宀	丶	乚	弋	心	八	人	乂	㇇	ノ	刂	𠂉	く
00	01	02	10	11	12	20	21	22	30	31	32	40	41	42	50	51	52	60	61	62	63	70	71	72	80	81	82	83	90	91	92	93

利源 *lih-yuarn*, n., natural resources.

利慾 *lihyuh*, n., cupidity: 利慾薰心 lured by profits.

利用 *lihyuhng*, v. t., make use of, utilize, exploit: 廢物利用 utilize waste products; 被人利用 be utilized by others for their selfish ends; 利用時機 take advantage of opportunities.

§ 90A.01 (禾/小)

秫 90A.01-1

shur.

N. Glutinous rice.

秣 90A.01-1

moh.

V.t. To feed horse: 秣馬厲兵 keep army ready for combat.

稞 90A.01-4

ke.

N. (1) A species of wheat plant (see 青△稞子 10.42) produced in western China. (2) Gen. term for grains.

称 90A.01-9

cheng.

[Pop. of 稱 90A.42]

§ 90A.02 (禾/⺊)

穠 90A.02-2

nurng.

Adj. (Of flowers, trees) growing in clusters: 穠纖得中 right proportions; 穠豔 gorgeous, resplendent.

穰 90A.02-6

rarng (*raang).

N. (AC) stalks of grain.

Adj. (AC) (1) Abundant, luxuriant, bounteous. (2) (*raang) (AC) restless, uneasy, disturbed, crowded with people.

穰穰 *rarngrarng*, adj., (1) (AC) (of ears of grain) full; (2) (AC) abundant, confused, worried.

穅 90A.02-6

kang.

[Var. 糠]

稼 90A.02-6

jiah.

N. Sheaves of grain.

V.i. To sow grain: 稼穡 husbandry, farming ("sowing and reaping"); 莊稼 grain field; 莊稼人 farmer.

稂 90A.02-6

larng.

N. Weeds: 稂莠 tares, worthless, injurious things.

§ 90A.10 (禾/十)

科 90A.10-1

ke.

N. (1) Class, branch of study: 科目 *-muh*↓; 學科 department of study; 專科 special course of study; 選科 elective subject in school; 文科, 理科, 醫科 school of arts, science, medicine; 內科, 外科… internal medicine, surgery, etc.; 百科全書 encyclopedia. (2) The civil examinations in empire days: 科舉, 科甲, 科第, 科名 *-jyuu*, *-jiar*, *-dih*, *-mirng*↓; 登科 obtain degrees in civil examinations. (3) Administrative section in goverment; 總務科 business section; 文書科 section for documents (secretariat); 科長 section chief; 科員 member of section staff. (4) Criminal record: 犯有前科 record of former offense. (5) (Chin. opera) dialogue: 科白, 科諢 *-bair*, *-huhn*↓.

V.t. (1) To sentence punishment: 科罪, 科以刑責 punish by law, punish for criminal offense; 科罰 to set fine for offense. (2) To decree: 科斷 pass sentence; 科派 order payment or labor service.

科白 *kebair*, n. & v. i., (opera) dialogue part (not sung).

科班(兒) *keban(-ba'l)*, n., service in government: 科班出身 career official.

科第 *kerdih*, n., civil examinations.

科斗 *kedoou*, n., tadpole (also wr. 蝌蚪).

科段 *keduahn*, n., (MC) method of doing (＝手段).
科諢 *ke-huhn*, n. & v. i., see *-bair* ↑.
科甲 *kejiar*, see *-dih* ↑.
科擧 *kejyuu*, n., formerly, civil examinations for government degrees.
科名 *kemirng*, n., degrees in civil examinations.
科目 *kemuh*, n., (1) branch or subject of study; formerly, subject of civil examinations; (2) category, class of subjects or affairs.
科學 *keshyuer*, n., science: 自然科學 natural science; 人文科學 the humanities; 科學與技術 science and technology; adj., 不科學 not scientific; 科學家 *--jia*, scientist; 科學館 *--guaan*, science hall.
科條 *ketiaur*, n., statutes.

秤 90A.10-3

chehng (**pinng*).
[Anc. var. 稱 90A.42]

N. (1) Steelyard, both large and on miniature scale. (2) 天秤 (-**pirng*) scales.

秤錘 *chehngchueir*, n., metal weight suspended on steelyard.
秤桿(兒) *chehnggaan(-gaa'l)*, n., beam of steelyard.
秤鉤(兒) *chehnggou('l)*, n., hook of steelyard for hooking thing to be weighed.
秤星(兒) *chehngshing('l)*, n., brass markings on beam of steelyard.
秤坨 *chehngtuor*, n., see *-chueir* ↑.

稈 90A.10-4

gaan.

N. (*-tz*) Grain stalk.

稺 90A.10-5

jyh.
[Var. of 稚 10B.11]

稗 90A.10-9

baih.

N. Tares, weeds.

稗販 *baihfahn*, n., pedlar.
稗官 *baihguan*, n., stories and novels (with contemp. implication); 稗官野史 unofficial histories or records, as dist. official history (正史).
稗沙門 *baih shamern*, n., (Budd.) reprobate monk.
稗說 *baihshuo*, n., (rare) novel.
稗史 *baihshyy*, n., unofficial history, private records of political events.

§90A.11 (禾/土)

稑 90A.11-1

luh.

N. (AC) early-maturing variety of rice.

程 90A.11-4

cherng.

N. (1) Schedule, formula: 程式 *-shyh* ↓; 程序 *-shyuh* ↓; 課程 course of study, schedule of work; 工程 engineering; 程限 time limit. (2) Degree, measure: 程度 *-duh* ↓. (3) Journey: 途程, 路程 journey; 起程 start journey; 計程 reckon progress of s.o.'s journey; 計程車 meter taxi; 兼程 travel by day and night (on urgent trip); 遠程 a long journey; 前程 a person's career ahead, esp. official career. (4) A surname.

程度 *cherngduh*, n., degree (of hatred, love, knowledge of subject, etc.).
程限 *cherngshiahn*, n., time or place limit.
程式 *cherngshyh*, n., a formula, equation (chem., math., etc.).
程序 *cherngshyuh*, n., order, sequence (of program, etc.).
程儀 *cherngyir*, n., present for journey, voyage.

種 90A.11-9

juung (**juhng*).

N. (1) (*-tz*, *'l*) Seed: 種子 *-tzyy* ↓; 播種, 布種 sow seeds; 龍種 royal descendants, progeny; 傳種接代 that the family line may continue from generation to generation; 石種子 sterile seeds. (2) Race: 種族 *-tzur* ↓; 純種 pure breed, purebred; 雜種 (abuse) bastard, hybrid; 混血種 mixed blood; 白種, 黃種, 黑種, 紅種 the White, Yellow, Black, Brown (red Indian) Race; 同種, 異種 same, different, race. (3) Vaccine, graft: 種痘 ditto; 接種 to graft (trees). (4) Kind, sort, variety, species: 種別, 種類 *-bier*, *-leih* ↓; 各種人等, 各種禮物 different or all kinds of people, gifts; 特種 special kind; 種切 *-chieh* ↓. (5) Breed: 好種, 壞種 good, bad breed; 懦種 a weak breed; 遺種 progeny, descendants; 孽種 (abuse) "bad egg," "bastard."

V.t. (**juhng*) To plant, sow, cultivate: 種植, 種地, 種田 *-jyr*, *-dih*, *-tiarn* ↓; 種花 cultivate flowers;

科 秤 稈 稺 稗 稑 程 種

亅	小	⺊	十	土	ナ	廾	卜	丨	一	丁	フ	口	区	冈	冂	厂	尸	亠	广	宀	丶	乚	弋	心	八	人	乂	乛	𠂊	ノ	𠂉	く
00	01	02	10	11	12	20	21	22	30	31	32	40	41	42	50	51	52	60	61	62	63	70	71	72	80	81	82	83	90	91	92	93

種米 plant rice; 種莊稼 plant different grains; 種魚 raise fish (in nursery); 種瓜得瓜, 種麥得麥 reap as one has sown; (fig.) 種德 cultivate virtue which has its rewards; 種因 *-yin* ↓; 種下惡果, 種禍 sow seeds of future trouble.

種別 *juungbier*, n., variety, species, race.

種切 *juungchieh*, n., (LL, esp. in letters) different things: 聆悉種切 have learned different news; 種切情形 (report of) various aspects of things.

種地 **juhngdih*, v. i., to farm land.

種痘 **juhngdouh*, n. & v. t., to vaccinate, -tion.

種種 *jurngjuung*, adj., different kinds of (reasons, causes, results, etc.).

種植 **juhngjyr*, n. & v. i., planting; to plant; 種植園 plantation; flower nursery.

種類 *juungleih*, n., classes, kinds, varieties (of plants, fish, flowers, etc.).

種落 *juungluoh*, n., a settlement (of people), a tribe.

種田 **juhngtiarn*, v. i., see *-dih* ↑.

種族 *juungtzur*, n., race, tribe: 種族不同 of different race or tribe; 種族隔離 apartheid (in South Africa); 種族歧視 racial discrimination; 種族偏見 racial prejudice.

種子 *jurngtzyy*, n., seed, see N. 1 ↑.

種因 **juhngyin*, v. i., (Budd.) "sow the cause" and reap consequences.

種玉 **juhngyuh*, v. i., (LL) as in 藍田種玉 (allu.) to give birth to sons or (court.) give worthy son to worthy father.

稚 90A.11-9

jyh.

N. & adj. Childhood: 幼稚 very young, immature; 幼稚園 kindergarten; 稚年, 稚齒, 稚齡 childhood years.

稚氣 *jyhchih*, n. & adj., childish manner, spirit.

稚子 *jyhtzyy*, n., (AC) a child; (MC) bamboo shoots.

§ 90A.21 (禾/乚)

秸 90A.21-1

ji.

N. (1) (AC) place name. (2) A surname.

秈 90A.21-2

shian.

N. India rice, a variety of rice plant.

稻 90A.21-9

dauh.

N. (*-tz*) Rice plant, rice in the fields, cf. 米 rice served at table: 割稻 to harvest rice; 早稻 early-maturing rice variety; 水稻 paddy rice.

稻場 *dauhcharng*, n., drying ground for harvested rice.

稻田 *dauhtiarn*, n., paddy field.

稻草 *dauhtsaau*, n., hay from rice stalk: 稻草人 a scarecrow.

§ 90A.22 (禾/丨)

秭 90A.22-2

tzyy.

N. (AC) a billion.

稊 90A.22-8

tir.

N. (1) Tares: 稊米. (2) (AC) new shoot from old stem.

稀 90A.22-8

shi.

Adj. (1) Sparse (hair, trees). (2) Few, rare (interch. 希): 物以稀(or 希)爲貴 objects are valued because of their rarity; 月明星稀 with a clear moon and few stars; 稀少 *-shaau* ↓. (3) Diluted (liquids): 稀飯 *-fahn* ↓; 稀粥 thin gruel: 稀湯 clear light soup; 水泥和稀了 the cement is too much diluted. (4) Ragged, torn: 稀亂八糟 topsy-turvy.

稀薄 *shibor*, adj., thin and diluted.

稀奇 *shichir*, adj., rare (also wr. 希).

稀飯 *shifahn*, n., rice gruel; congee.

稀爛 *shilahn*, adj., ragged, rotten, torn, overcooked.

稀破 *shipoh*, n., adj., broken, tattered, ruptured, torn.

稀少 *shishaau*, adj., rare (also wr. 希).

稀疏 *shishu*, adj., thin, sparse (hair, trees).

稀鬆 *shisung*, adj., loose (plot, story); not compact; irrelevant.

§ 90A.30 (禾/一)

租 90A.30-4

tzu.

N. (1) The land tax. (2) Taxes in gen.: 租稅 *-shueih*↓. (3) Payment for the use of land or other things: 房租 house rent; 田租 farm rent; 租金 *-jin*↓; 租錢 rent paid in cash.

V.t. To lease, rent (house, land, etc.): 租賃 *-lihn*, 租借 *-jieh*[2]↓; 租用 to rent (car, office space) for use; 出租 to let, offer for rent; 租出去了 (house, room) leased out; 租來的 (of things) rented from another person; 租給, 租與 rent to; 轉租 sublease; 租房子 rent a house (room); 租田 to lease farm land; 召租 (room) to let; 納租 to pay rent; 交租 ditto; 催租 to press for payment of rent due; 加租 raise the rent; 收租 to collect rent.

租契 *tzu-chih*, n., a lease contract.
租戶 *tzu-huh*, n., the lessee.
租價 *tzu-jiah*, n., rent (in dollars and cents).
租界 *tzujieh*[1], n., formerly, a foreign concession in China, an international settlement in China's treaty ports.
租借 *tzujieh*[2], v. t., to lease, rent; 租借地 territory leased to another country; 租借法案 the Lend-Lease Act.
租金 *tzu-jin*, n., rent payable by lessee to lessor, usu. of land or building.
租賃 *tzulihn*, v. t., rent, lease (land, building, room).
租售 *tzushouh*, n., for rent or sale.
租稅 *tzu-shueih*, n., taxes and levies, taxation.
租子 *tzu'tz*, n., farm rent, usu. payable in kind.

§ 90A.32 (禾/フ)

移 90A.32-9

yir.

V.i. & t. (1) To move, to move round or about: 移動 *-duhng*↓; 遷移 move to another house; 移民, 移居 *-mirn, -jyu*↓; 移東就西 make up deficiency by funds elsewhere. (2) To change (course): 轉移 gradually change, also n., pivot; 移風易俗 gradually change the customs of people, to influence morals; 移天易日 change the course of heavens—s.t. audacious. (3) To send official communications: 移公文 ditto; 移書 *-shu*↓. (4) To transfer: 移交 *-jiau*↓.

移情 *yir-chirng*, v.i., (LL) change mind, esp., in love affairs: 移情別戀 turn the back on one lover and go with another.
移牒 *yir-dier*, phr., to send letter to official of same rank; send diplomatic note.
移鼎 *yir-diing*, v.i., (allu.) "move imperial tripods" (symbol of power)—change dynasty.
移動 *yirduhng*, v.t., to move, shift to another place: 不許移動 don't change emplacement; 花影移動 the flower shadows move.
移晷 *yir-gueei*, v.i., (sun's shadow) change the shadow on the dial.
移花 *yir-hua*, phr., 移花接木 (lit.) to graft and transplant; (fig.) to place a substitute by subterfuge.
移換 *yirhuahn*, v.t., to change (place of seats, etc.).
移禍 *yir-huoh*, phr., to put the blame (on another).
移交 *yirjiau*, v.i. & t., to effect transfer of office (to successor).
移節 *yir-jier*, v.i., to transfer authority (of governors, etc.).
移疾 *yirjir*, v.i., (AC) to write a letter asking for resignation on pretext of illness.
移轉 *yirjuaan*, v.i., (law) to change (ownership), transfer (rights).
移植 *yirjyh*, v.t., transplant (heart, kidneys, trees).
移居 *yir'jyu*, v.i., to change residence.
移民 *yir-mirn*, v.i. & n., to immigrate, -tion; 移民局 immigration office.
移山 *yir-shan*, phr., "to move mountains": 愚公移山 (allu.) do s. t. superhuman by sheer persistence.
移徙 *yirshii*, v.i. & t., to emigrate, change residence to another city or place; to move whole populations.
移書 *yir-shu*, v.i., to send letter, usu. official or business.
移時 *yirshyr*, adv., after a while, after lapse of time.
移樽 *yir-tzun*, phr., to take the cup and drink to person on another table: 移樽就教 to call personally on person.
移玉 *yir-yuh*, phr., (in letters) please come over.

§ 90A.40 (禾/口)

和 90A.40-4

her (**huoh*, *'*han*, **hur*, **heh*; re. pr. **huor*).
[Arch. 咊, interch. 龢]

N. (1) A sum (of 2 and 15): 總和 total, grand total. (2) Name for Japan, Japanese: 和文 Japanese language; 和裝 Japanese costume; 漢和字典 Chinese-Japanese dictionary. (3) Peace: 戰爭與和平 war and peace: 講和, 媾和 negotiate for peace; 和約 peace treaty; 和談, 和議 peace negotiations. (4) (AC) a small reed organ. (5) (AC) carriage bell. (6) (**hur*) A game in *mahjong*, a shout signifying completion of a set. (7) A surname.

V.i. & t. (1) (**huoh*) To mix, stir together, blend: 和麪, 和弄 *-miahn, -luhng*↓; 和味 to blend flavors; 和泥兒 *-nir'l*↓; 和羹 to blend into a soup, also (fig.) (LL) ministers who bring peace and unity to government. (2) (*heh) To "echo": 和詩, 和韻 to write a poem using same rhyme-words as the one written by another poet; 唱和 to write poems together (as litr. pastime), (of married couple) live in unison; 我唱你和 I sing and you join in; 一唱百和 response by crowd echoing the same idea; 隨聲附和 to follow the crowd. (3) (*hur) (Shanghai dial.) to complete a set in *mahjong*: 他和了 he has completed set.

Adj. (1) Gentle of disposition, mild: 温和, 和順 gentle, amiable; 和風 gentle breeze; 暖和 (*nuaan-'huo*) pleasantly warm (weather). (2) Harmonious, peaceful, calm, friendly: 和顏悦色 amiable manner; 和衷共濟 (of different factions) pull together for common cause; 君子和而不同 "a gentleman gets along with others, but not necessarily agrees with them"; see many compp.↓; 鸞鳳和鳴 (fig.) of happily married couple; 和平主義 pacifism.

Conj. (*her*; coll. *'han, *hair) And: 我和他兩人 I and he, we two.

Prep. With: (=vern. 跟, 同, LL 與): 我和你 (跟你, 同你) 去 I'll come with you; 她和我 she and I; 和他 (跟他, 同他) 説一聲 tell him, speak to him; 和衣而臥 sleep without undressing; 和盤托出 lay all the cards on the table, tell all.

和藹 *her-aai*, adj., peaceable, amiable, kindly (disposition, person).

和暢 *herchahng*, adj., gentle, relaxing (air, climate).

和氣 *herchih*, adj., placid, friendly, not given to disputes: 和和氣氣討論 let's discuss it calmly; 和氣生財 friendliness is conducive to business success.

和親 *her-chin*, v. i., (LL) (1) to be friendly with neighbors; (2) to cement friendly relationship with another country by a political marriage.

和服 *herfur*, n., Japanese dress.

和好 *herhaau*, adj., friendly: 和好如初 become reconciled.

和合 *herher*, adj., as in 夫婦和合 husband and wife live happily together (also 好合).

和緩 *herhuaan*, v. i. & adj., to conciliate, be conciliatory: 和緩之計 a strategy to play for time by conceding a little.

和姦 *herjian*, n. & v. i., adultery by consent.

和解 *herjiee*, v. i. & t., to reconcile (disputes), esp. settle out of court; be reconciled: 已經和解了.

和局 *herjyur*, n., (1) (chess or ball game) a tie, a draw; (2) outlook for a peaceful settlement.

和弄 *huoh'luhng, v. i. & t., (1) to stir together; (2) to stir up: 這個亂子都是他和弄起來的 this mess was stirred up by him.

和美 *hermeei*, adj., (1) soothing to the eye, harmonious; (2) friendly.

和麪 *huohmiahn, n., a kind of flour patties.

和睦 *hermuh*, adj., friendly (relations between countries, brothers).

和南 *hernarn*, v.i., (Budd.) to put palms together in greeting.

和鬧 *hernauh*, v. i., (MC) join in noisy display.

和泥兒 *huohnir'l, v. i., (coll.) to mediate: 給雙方和泥兒 mediate between the two parties.

和暖 *hernuaan*, adj., pleasantly warm (climate).

和平 *herpirng*, n. & adj., (1) peace, -ful, tranquil, -ity; 和平工作團 Peace Corps; 和平共處 (共存) peaceful coexistence; (2) peaceable (temper).

和善 *hershahn*, adj., kindly (disposition).

和尚 *her'shahng* (*-shahng*), n., a monk (also a term of polite address); 和尚菜 (bot.) a plant, *Adenocaulon bicolor*.

和聲 *hersheng*, n., (mus.) harmony; 和聲學 the science of harmony.

和絃 *hershiarn*, n., chord.

和協 *hershier*[1], v. i., to appease, to work together.

和諧 *hershier*[2], adj., harmonious, friendly.

和息 *her(')shir*, v. t., (MC) to reconcile, be reconciled.

和數 *hershuh*, n., (math.) sum of two or more numbers (also shortened as 和 see N. ↑).

和順 *hershuhn*, adj., gentle (disposition, conduct), understanding, accommodating.

和事老 (兒) *hershyh-laau('l)*, n., a person who often mediates troubles, mediator.

和頭 *her-tour*, n., the front end of coffin.

和菜 *hertsaih*, n., fixed or set menu in restaurant.

和音 *heryin*, n., (mus.) a chord.

和誘 *heryouh*, v. t., (law) seduce person by gentle methods (opp. 略誘).

和約 *heryue*, n., peace treaty.

§90A.41 (禾/図)

穡 90A.41-1

seh.

N. & v.i. (Do) farm work: 稼穡 ditto.

稽 90A.41

ji (*chii).

N. A surname.

V.i. & t. (1) Examine, investigate, study: 稽古 *-guu*, 稽核 *-her*, 稽查 *-char*[1], 稽察 *-char*[2], 稽考 *-kaau* ↓; 無稽 groundless, unfounded; 稽征 *-jeng* ↓. (2) To delay, hinder: 稽留 *-liour*, 稽遲 *-chyr*, 稽延 *-yarn* ↓; 稽時 procrastinate, protract. (3) Find fault with: 反脣相稽 to turn against another in mutual recrimination. (4) V. i., to kowtow: (*chii) 稽首 *-shoou*, 稽顙 *-saang* ↓.

稽查 *jichar*[1], v. t., to look into, to

find out the truth.
稽 察 *jichar*², v. t., ditto.
稽 遲 *jichyr*, v. i., delay, be late.
稽 古 *ji-guu*, v. i., make a study of ancient ways; (AC) in ancient days.
稽 核 *jiher*, (1) n., (accounting) an auditor, auditing; (2) v.t., examine carefully, (accounting) to audit.
稽 征 *jijeng*, v.t., examine (goods) and collect duty thereon.
稽 考 *jikaau*, v.t., investigate, examine.
稽 留 *jiliour*, v.i., to delay, be detained.
稽 顙 **chirsaang*, v.i., to kowtow.
稽 首 **chirshoou*, v.t., ditto.
稽 延 *jiyarn*, v.i., postpone, put off, be held up.

稭 90A.41-2

jie.

N. Stalks of rice or corn.

§90A.42 (禾/冈)

稍 90A.42-2

shau (also *shauh*).

Adv. Rather, just a little, slightly: 天氣稍冷 weather is rather cold; 稍有良心 (if only person) had a little conscience; 稍有誤會 had a slight misunderstanding; 稍有不愼 (if) there is some slight mistake; 稍可, 稍能 may slightly; (oft. court.) 稍表敬意 as a small token of my respect; 稍盡棉力 to do my humble best; 稍微, 稍稍 *-wei, -shau* ↓.

稍 秣 *shaumoh*, n., feed for horses.
稍 稍 *shaushau*, adv., just a little, slightly (too tight, too long): 稍稍高一點 move just a little higher.
稍 息 *shaushir*, n., (mil.) "at ease."
稍 微 *shauwei* (*-weir*), adv., see *-shau* ↑.

穤 90A.42-3

nuoh.
[Var. 糯 22C.42]

稠 90A.42-4

chour.

Adj. Dense (population, clouds), thick (gruel): 稠人廣衆 a dense crowd.

稠 糊 (兒) *chour'hu('l)*, adj., thick, pasty.
稠 濁 *chourjuor*, adj., crowded and mixed (gathering).
稠 密 *chourmih*, adj., close-woven (texture): 人煙稠密 densely populated.

稿 90A.42-6

gaau.
[Var. of 藁]

N. (1) Hay, the stalk of a rice plant. (2) A manuscript, a rough draft or copy: 文稿 draft or manuscript; 初稿 a first draft; 草稿 rough draft; 畫稿 a painter's sketch; 稿本 *-been*, 稿子 *-tz* ↓; 起稿 make a draft; 打稿 ditto; 腹稿 a general outline of an article in one's mind; 底稿 original copy of a published article.

V.i. & t. Discuss, engage in doing (cf. 搞 10A.42): 稿價兒 to bargain over prices; 稿酒 engage in a drinking bout; 稿拳 to play the finger game in which the loser has to drink a cup of wine.

稿 本 *gaaubeen*, n., manuscript copy.
稿 底 (兒) (子) *gaaudii('l)('tz)*, n., draft copy of an article, essay, etc.
稿 費 *gaaufeih*, n., payment for article published or accepted.
稿 件 *gaaujiahn*, n., manuscripts submitted to a periodical for publication.
稿 兒 *gaau'l*, n., a draft, a mental outline or plan: 起稿兒, 打稿兒 make a draft; 這事那有準稿兒 how can any definite plan be made for this matter?
稿 子 *gaautz*, n., a draft.

稱 90A.42-9

cheng (**chehng*, **chehn*).
[Pop. 称]

N. (1) Name: 名稱 name of person or thing; 稱號 term of addressing person's name and title. (2) (**chehng*) A weighing scale, steelyard (interch. 秤 90A.10).

V.i. & t. (1) To praise, extol: 稱讚, 稱許, etc. *-tzahn, -shyuu* ↓; to congratulate: 稱賀, 稱慶 *-heh, -chihng* ↓; 見稱於世 be well spoken of, well-known. (2) To declare, state officially: 稱述, 稱說, 稱道 *-shuh, -shuo, -dauh* ↓; 據稱 according to document mentioned (formula for giving contents); 稱兵 *-bing* ↓. (3) To declare oneself: 稱病 declare oneself sick; 稱王稱帝 declare oneself king or emperor; 稱霸, 稱雄 *-bah, -shyurng* ↓; 稱孤道寡 to call oneself king (孤 and 寡 being royal self-reference); 稱兄道弟 addressing each other in great familiarity. (4) (**chehng*) To weigh: 稱一稱 weigh it and see; 稱重量 find out thing's weight. (5) (*chehng) To fit: 衣服稱身 dress fits; 不相稱 do not fit well; 稱旨, 稱職 -jyy, -jyr ↓. (6) (*chehn) (Interch. 趁 11.83) to fulfill, satisfy: 稱心, 稱意, 稱願 -shin, -yih, -yuahn ↓.

稱霸 *cheng-bah*, v.i., (AC) assume hegemony of the warring states, usu. head of an alliance.
稱便 *cheng-biahn*, phr., is considered good and convenient.
稱兵 *cheng-bing*, phr., start war.
稱錢 **chehn-chiarn*, phr., make money (usu. 趁錢).
稱慶 *chengchihng*, v.i., to offer congratulations.
稱貸 *chengdaih*, v.i., to borrow money.
稱道 *chengdauh*, v.i., to declare; to praise.
稱號 *chenghauh*, n. & v.i., title, entitled.
稱賀 *chengheh*, v.i. & t., to congratulate.
稱呼 *cheng'hu*, n., way by which one is addressed: 怎麽稱呼 "how should I address you," i.e., what is your name?
稱制 *chengjyh*, v.i., (empress dowager) to assume throne (制 being imperial decree).
稱職 **chehng-jyr*, v.i., be competent in office.
稱旨 **chehng-jyy*, phr., approved by His Majesty.
稱快 *chengkuaih*, v.i., applaud: 拍手稱快 applaud with hand clap.
稱量 **chehngliarng*, v.t., to weigh (article).
稱亂 *cheng-luahn*, phr., to start rebellion.
稱美 *chengmeei*, v.t., to call good, to praise.
稱觴 *cheng-shang*, v.i., (LL) to raise the cup and give a toast.
稱身 **chehng-shen*, phr., (dress) to fit well.
稱羨 *chengshiahn*, v.t., to praise, admire.
稱謝 *cheng-shieh*, v.i., to give thanks.
稱心 **chehn-shin*, v.i., to have as one wishes.
稱述 *chengshuh*, v.t., to recount with admiration s.t. past.
稱說 *chengshuo*, v.i., to declare, announce (event, cause); to say (s.t.).
稱雄 *cheng-shyurng*, v.i., to be declared or considered leader.
稱許 *chengshyuu*, v.t., to praise, approve, esp. by superior.
稱頌 *chengsuhng*, v. t., to praise, adore.
稱讚 *chengtzahn*, v. t., to praise (good work).
稱字 *cheng-tzyh*, phr., to address person by his 字, literary or courtesy name, as dist. 名 registered name.
稱謂 *chengweih*, n., way of addressing person.
稱揚 *chengyarng*, n. & v. i. & t., praise, extol.
稱意 **chehn-yih*, (1) v. i., to do as one pleases; (2) adj., satisfactory.
稱引 *chengyiin*, v. t., to quote (from anc. sages or from others).
稱願 **chehn-yuahn*, v. i. & adj., satisfactory, have as one wishes (also wr. 趁).
稱譽 *chengyuh*, n. & v. t., a praise; to praise.

§ 90A.63 (禾/丶)

穮 90A.63–6

biau.

V.t. (AC) To till the field.

穐 90A.63–9

chiou.
[Arch. of 秋 90A.81]

§ 90A.70 (禾/乚)

秕 90A.70–2

bii.
[Var. 粃]

N. Empty rice husk, chaff; what is useless, riffraff.

Adj. Riffraff, see compp. ↓.

秕政 *biijehng*, n., bad government measures.
秕謬 *biimiouh*, adj., absurd, false (opinion).
秕滓 *birtzyy*, n., riffraff, scum.

秔 90A.70–6

geng (sp. pr. *jing*).
[Var. 稉; pop. 粳]

N. Non-glutinous rice: 秔米, 秔稻.

税 90A.70–8

shueih.

N. Taxes; taxation: 抽税 to levy tax; 課税 n. & v.t., tax; 税捐 -jyuan ↓; 納税 pay tax; 印花税 stamp duty; 營業税 business tax; 所得税 income tax; 利得税 tax on profits.

V.t. 税駕 (AC) to unharness horse, i.e., to stop and rest.

税契 *shueihchih*, n., title deed.
税單 *shueihdan*, n., tax receipt.
税額 *shueih-er*, n., amount of tax.
税法 *shueih-faa*, n., tariff, tax law.
税關 *shueih-guan*, n., customs (frontier, maritime).
税金 *shueih-jin*, n., tax dues.
税捐 *shueihjyuan*, n., taxes and levies.
税局(子) *shueih-jyur('tz)*, n., formerly, inland tax bureau.
税課 *shueihkeh*, n., tax, levy.
税款 *shueihkuaan*, n., tax dues.
税吏 *shueih-lih*, n., tax collector.
税率 *shueih-lyuh*, n., tax rate.

稅票 *shueihpiauh*, n., tax receipt, see *-dan* ↑.
稅收 *shueihshou*, n., revenue from tax.
稅則 *shueihtzer*, n., tariff, tax regulations.
稅務 *shueih-wuh*, n., customs administration; 稅務司 Commissioner of Customs.

§ 90A.71 (禾/七)

穢 90A.71-2

hueih (also *weih*).

N. Dirt, litter.

Adj. (1) Dirty, filthy: 污穢 garbage, filth; 穢物 dirt, refuse; 穢土 smudge, mud; 穢臭 smelly; 穢氣 foul air; 穢濁 unsanitary, polluted: (court. of self) base, unpresentable: 自慚形穢 ashamed of one's own unseemliness. (2) Immoral, lewd: 穢德, 穢行 immoral conduct; 穢史 salacious stories of a period.

秖 90A.71-9

jy.

Adv. (AC) only (cf. 秖; related modn. 祇).

§ 90A.72 (禾/心)

穗 90A.72-1

sueih.

N. (1) An ear of grain: 麥穗 an ear of wheat. (2) Tassel-like flowers of reed, etc. (3) Snuff of candle. (4) (*-tz*, *-'l*) Tassels (of hat, etc.).

秘 90A.72-6

mih (also *bih*).
[Pop. of 祕 63B.72]

稔 90A.72-8

reen.

N. The yearly rice crop, hence a year: 不及五稔 in less than five years.

V.i. & t. (1) V. i., (of rice) to ripen: 豐稔 a bumper harvest. (2) V. t., be intimate with: 稔知 know (s.o.) quite well; 稔悉 ditto; 熟稔 be on intimate terms with. (3) 稔亂 *-luahn* ↓.

稔亂 *reen-luahn*, v. i., (LL) sow the seeds of social discontent.
稔膩 *reennih*, adj., (MC) (of a woman) plump and smooth-skinned.
稔色 *reenseh*, (1) n., (MC) a beautiful woman, a pretty face; (2) v. i., be fond of feminine beauty.

穩 90A.72-9

ween.
[Dist. 隱 32A.72]

Adj. Stable, steady, safe: 穩當, 穩定 *-'dang*, *-dihng* ↓; 安穩 safe; 不穩 not reliable; 拿不穩 cannot be sure; 十拿九穩 ninety percent sure.

Adv. Surely: 穩贏, 穩輸 sure to win, to lose.

穩便 *weenbiahn*, adj., convenient and reliable (way).
穩當 *ween'dang*, adj., safe, reliable (plan, deposit, etc.).
穩定 *weendihng*, adj., stable (government, prices).
穩固 *weenguh*, adj., strong (foundation); strongly fortified.
穩健 *weenjiahn*, adj., solid, healthy (finance, health).
穩住 *ween'ju*, v.t., to keep back, hold ready (elements for attack).
穩重 *weenjuhng*, adj., steady (person), not flighty.
穩婆 *weenpor*, n., (1) midwife; (2) formerly, woman officer for examining women's corpses or prisoners.
穩下 *ween-shiah*, v.t., see *-'ju* ↑.
穩帖 *weentie*, adj., see *-'dang* ↑.
穩妥 *werntuoo*, adj., see *-'dang* ↑.

§ 90A.80 (禾/八)

積 90A.80-1

ji.

N. (1) (Math.) the product obtained by multiplication: 乘積 the product so obtained; 求積 find such product; 積數 *-shuh* ↓. (2) A measure of size: 體積 volume; 面積 surface area; 容積 capacity.

V.t. Amass, to store up: 堆積 to pile up; 聚積 accumulate, assemble together; 冲積 to form a delta; 積勞(憂)成疾 fall sick from overwork (excessive worry); 積羽沉舟 the awesome power of sheer numbers ("a heavy enough load of feathers can sink a boat"); 積少成多 from small increments comes abundance (cf. "take care of the pence and the pounds will take care of themselves").

Adj. Age-long, added bit by bit, made of small accretions, cumulative: 積弊 *-bih*, 積習 *-shir* ↓; 積重難返 old habits are difficult to get rid of; 積冰, 積雪, 積雨 accumulated ice, snow, rain water; 積久 *-jioou* ↓; 積善 habitual doing of good deeds: 積善之家 a family given to kindness and charity; 積惡 continual perpetration of evil deeds; 積威 accumulated power and prestige; 積怨, 積忿 pent-up grievances (grudges), anger.

積弊 *ji-bih*, n., age-old abuses or irregularities.

積德 *ji-der*, v. i., (1) be given to kindness and charity; (2) (sarcastic) behave oneself: 你多積點德吧! (admonition to be kind) please do not be so harsh, sharp, or cutting.

積犯 *jifahn*, phr., habitual criminal.

積分 *ji-fen*, n., (1) total number of credits a students has earned in school; (2) (math.) integral calculus.

積漸 *jijiahn*, adv., gradually, little by little, by degrees.

積久 *jijioou*, adj. & adv., over a long period.

積極 *jijir*, adj., (of a person's attitude or outlook) positive, energetic, affirmative, optimistic, resolute (opp. 消極 63A.42); 積極份子 activist.

積木 *ji-muh*, n., children's toy wooden blocks.

積年 *ji-niarn*, adv., for many years: 積年累月 for months and years.

積習 *ji-shir*, n., inveterate habits: 積習難改 ingrained habits can't be cast off overnight.

積數 *ji-shuh*, n., (math.) product.

積蓄 *jishyuh*, n., savings.

積儹 *ji'tzan*, n., (coll.) also wr. 積攢 see *-shyuh* ↑.

積作 *jitzuoh*, v. i., be kind and virtuous, also used in a sarcastic sense, see *-der* ↑.

積壓 *ji-ya*, v. t., put off, delay, postpone, defer: 積壓公文 accumulated and held up official documents.

穦 90A.80-2

jeen.

[Usu. wr. 稹]

V.t. (AC) to assemble.

Adj. U. f. 縝 93B.80; 穦密＝縝密 careful, well thought-out (plan).

---

§ 90A.81 (禾/人)

秩 90A.81-1

jyh.

N. (1) Order: 秩序 *-shyuh*² ↓. (2) Official rank: 品秩 ditto; 秩敍 *-shyuh*¹ ↓. (3) A decade: 八秩大壽 celebration of eightieth birthday.

秩祿 *jyhluh*, n., official salary.

秩然 *jyhrarn*, adj., orderly, neat.

秩敍 *jyhshyuh*¹, v. i., promote, appoint according to rank and qualifications.

秩序 *jyhshyuh*², n., order (in meeting, seating arrangements): 秩序大亂 (meeting) thrown into great disorder.

稬 90A.81-3

nuoh.

[Pop. 糯 22C.42]

秋 90A.81-9

chiou.

N. (1) The autumn season, the fall: 秋天 *-tian*↓; 秋老虎 very hot weather in autumn; 秋後 period after onset of autumn; 秋扇見捐 (woman) cast aside like the fan in autumn; 秋思 feeling of desolation; 秋風秋雨 disconsolate winds and rains; 秋士 old, forgotten scholar; 秋汎 autumn floods; 秋色 autumnal colors; 秋試, 秋闈 provincial test for 擧人 degree in civil examinations; 秋涼 the chill of autumn; 秋意 slight chill in the air, a "touch" of autumn; 秋季 autumn; 中秋 Mid-Autumn Festival (15th of the 8th lunar month); 晚秋 late autumn; 深秋 in deep autumn; 麥秋 harvest time; 春秋 Spring and Autumn, see 春 12.41. (2) Year: 千秋 a thousand years, (fig.) forever; 千秋萬歲 eternity. (3) Time, period: 多事之秋 troublous times; 危急存亡之秋 period of national crisis, a time when national existence hangs in the balance. (4) A surname.

秋波 *chioubo*, n., a girl's significant glance (compared to beauty of "autumn ripples"): 送秋波 to cast flirtatious looks at, make friendly gestures to (another).

秋成 *chioucherng*, n., harvest (season).

秋千 *chiouchian*, n., the swing (on which children and ladies play; var. of 鞦韆).

秋氣 *chiouchih*, n., the air, the chill of autumn; (fig.) air of desolation.

秋分 *chioufen*, n., the autumnal equinox (September 23 or 24).

秋風 *chioufeng*, n., (1) the autumnal winds: 秋風過耳 unheeded like a passing autumnal breeze; (2) 打秋風 get commission on errands, send birthday or wedding invitations indiscriminately to one and all with the hope of getting presents from them.

秋海棠 *chiouhaaitarng*, n., (bot.) the begonia, *Begonia evansiana*.

秋毫 *chiouhaur*, n., (lit.) autumn down on birds—very minute particle: 秋毫無犯 (of army) do not cause the slightest damage to the people (by looting, etc.).

秋節 *chioujier*, n., the Mid-Autumn Festival.

秋葵 *chioukueir*, n., (bot.) the hibiscus, *Abelmoschus esculentus*.

A

秋羅 *chiouluor*, n., a thin twill silk.

秋牡丹 *chioumuudan*, n., (bot.) Japanese anemone, *Anemone japonica*.

秋娘 *chiouniarng*, n., woman in the thirty-forties.

秋收 *chioushou*, n., the autumn harvest.

秋霜 *chioushuang*, n., frost in autumn, (fig.) of cold countenance, also of white hair on old man.

秋水 *chioushueei*, n., the autumn waters, (fig.) of woman's fluid glance, see *-bo* ↑; clear, bright look; sword flash.

秋事 *chioushyh*, n., harvest affairs.

秋汛 *chioushyuhn*, n., autumnal floods.

秋天 *chioutian*, n., autumn (days).

秧 90A.81-9

yang.

N. (1) Seedling of any plant nursery: 禾秧, 稻秧 rice seedling for transplanting; 松秧 pine seedling; 桑秧 mulberry seedling. (2) 魚秧 the fry in fish nursery.

V.t. To grow seedling, saplings: 秧幾棵花 grow saplings for flowers; 秧一盆魚 grow a basin of young fish.

秧歌 *yang'ge*, n., rice-transplantation song, accompanied by dance.

秧針 *yangjen*, n., first sprouts of rice seedlings.

秧雞 *yangji*, n., (zoo.) water rail, *Rallus aquaticus indicus*.

秧田 *yangtiarn*, n., paddy field, a farm where rice seedlings are raised waiting for transplanting.

秧子 *yangtz*, n., (1) seedling; (2) overprotected children of the rich who are easily deceived.

B

§ 90A.82 (禾/乂)

稜 90A.82-1

lerng.

[Anc. var. 棱]

N. (1) A square wooden block. (2) (*-tz*, *'l*) A corner, a raised angle: 觚稜, 柧稜 the turned-up corners of Chin. roofs; 稜角 *-jiaau* ↓. (3) (Math.) an edge.

稜縫兒 *lerng'fen'l*, n., a chance opening, a favorable opportunity.

稜睜 *lerngjeng*, adj., (1) rude, forbidding in manner, also 稜稜睜睜; (2) (*lerng'leng*) 稜稜著眼睛 stare in anger.

稜角 *lerngjiaau*, n., a raised or sharp angle; (coll.) person difficult to deal with.

稜稜 *lernglerng*, adj., (LL) extremely cold, see *-jeng* ↑.

穫 90A.82-2

huoh.

[Dist. 獲]

N. Harvest: 收穫 harvest; (fig.) results.

稷 90A.82-4

jih.

N. (1) (Bot.) panicled millet. (2) The God of Cereals: 社稷 the gods of the soil and cereals, together meaning "the state." (3) (AC) The minister of agriculture.

C

§ 90A.91 (禾/ノ)

秒 90A.91-2

miaau.

[Cf. 杪 10B.91; cogn. 渺 63A.91, 杳 10.41]

N. (1) The beard of corn or grain. (2) A second of time or of degree: 秒針 second hand of clock.

秒忽 *miaauhu*, n., infinitesimal amount.

穆 90A.91-9

muh.

N. (1) (AC) the right side position in ancestral temple, see 昭 left side, 41A.40. (2) A surname.

Adj. Reverent, majestic, serene, friendly (oft. used in posthumous titles).

穆罕默德 *Muhhaanmohder*, n., Mohammed.

§ 90A.93 (禾/く)

秐 90A.93-3

juung.

[Var. of 耘 90A.11]

私 90A.93-9

sy.

私 **N.** (LL) private parts, genitals: 私處 *-chuh*↓.

V.i. & t. (1) (AC, LL) to have sexual relations with (woman, man): 私通 *-tung*↓. (2) V. i., (AC) to urinate.

Adj. & adv. (1) Private, -ly, personal, -ly, opp. 公 public: 私產, 私房 *-chaan*, *-farng*↓; 私有 privately owned; 私見 (court.) my humble view, a selfish preconception; 私謁 see (person) in private; 私印 private, personal seal; 私地 private property; 私款 one's own money; 私函 personal letter. (2) Of the family, opp. public or government: 私家 *-jia*↓; 私祠 family temple; 私忌 death anniversary in the family; 私艱 (LL) death of parents. (3) Secret, confidential, -ly: 私語 *-yuu*↓; 私奔 *-ben*, 私下 *-shiah*, 私心, *-shin*, 私衷 *-jung*↓. (4) Illegal: 私貨, 私商, 私鹽 *-huoh*, *-shang*, *-yarn*↓; 私娼 *-chang*↓, 私相授受 illegal transfer of public or private property, offer and acceptance of bribes in secret, have underhand secret dealings. (5) Selfish: 自私 ditto; 私欲 *-yuh*↓; opp. 公 public-spirited or what is public; 大公無私 impartial, no personal or selfish consideration; 公私不分 do not distinguish what is one's own and what is public (money).

私奔 *syben*, v. i., to elope.
私弊 *sybih* (-'*bi*), n., corrupt practice.
私產 *sychaan*, n., private property.
私娼 *sychang*, n., private prostitute.
私錢 *sychiarn*, n., (1) formerly, illegal money, coins; (2) personal money.
私親 *sy-chin*, n., personal relative.
私情 *sy-chirng*, n., personal relations; personal feelings (for friends, family); illicit love.
私權 *sy-chuarn*, n., (law) personal rights.
私處 *sy-chuh*, n., private parts (of body), the genitals.
私曲 *sychyuu*, n., selfishness; selfish desires.
私德 *sy-der*, n., personal character.
私地 *sy-dih*^{1}, n., private property (land); adv., secretly.
私第 *sy-dih*^{2}, n., private residence.
私底下 *sy-dii'shia*, adv., privately, unknown to others.
私鬬 *sy-douh*, n., personal fights, quarrels; also clan fights.
私訪 *sy-faang*, v. t., see (person) unofficially, (formerly, of officials) make inspection trip incognito.
私販 *sy-fahn*, n. & v. t., a smuggler; to smuggle.
私坊 *sy'fang*, n., formerly, pederast; an establishment where pederasts are housed.
私房 *sy'farng* (-'*fang*), n., (1) private rooms; (2) (coll.) woman's private savings.
私館 *sy-guaan*, n., private residence.
私孩子 *sy-hair'tz*, n., illegitimate child.
私和 *sy-her*, v. i., (law) settle out of court.
私話(兒) *sy-huah*('*l*), n., strictly personal talk, not to be repeated.
私諱 *sy-hueih*, n., parents' personal names, tabooed in the family.
私貨 *sy-huoh*, n., smuggled goods.
私宅 *sy-jair*, n., private residence.
私家 *sy-jia*, n. & adj. & adv., (1) what concerns a person's private life; in private capacity; (2) (what one does) at home.
私見 *sy-jiahn*, n., personal views; (court.) my personal opinion.
私交 *syjiau*, n., a personal friend.
私計 *sy-jih*, n., personal plan; selfish plan.
私己 *syjii*, adj. & n., one's own (affairs); personal (benefits).
私酒 *sy-jioou*, n., bootleg, bootlegged liquor, moonshine.
私衷 *syjung*, n., (1) personal feeling; (2) (court.) my feeling on the matter.
私科子 *syketz*, n., (MC) private brothel.
私悃 *sy-kuun*, n., (LL) see *-jung*↑.
私累 *sy-leei*, n., (LL) family burden.
私立 *sylih*^{1}, adj., private (school, institution).
私利 *sylih*^{2}, n., private profit.
私門 *sy-mern*, n., (LL) private access to or connections with officials.
私面兒 *symiah'l*, n., parties to dispute in their private capacity.
私囊 *synarng*, n., a person's moneybag: 飽(入)私囊 embezzle public funds.
私暱 *synih*, v. t., be intimate with (person, a favorite).
私人 *sy-rern*, (1) adj., private, (in) private capacity, personal; 私人請求 private request; (2) n., personal friends or relatives, confident.
私商 *sy-shang*, n., smuggler.
私生子 *syshengtzyy*, n., illegitimate child.
私下 *sy-shiah* (-'*shia*), adv., privately, secretly: 私下裏 ditto.
私信 *sy-shihn*, n., personal letter.
私心 *syshin*, adj. & n., selfish, -ness: 私心話 confidential talk.
私刑 *syshirng*^{1}, n., illegal torture to extract confession.
私行 *syshirng*^{2}, (1) adv., secretly, on one's own initiative; (2) n., personal conduct.
私淑 *syshur*^{1}, v. t., (AC, LL) to study personally under (master).
私塾 *syshur*^{2}, n., private school; home school with private tutor.
私屬 *syshuu*, n., family relatives (children, etc.).
私事 *syshyh*^{1}, n., private, personal affairs.
私室 *syshyh*^{2}, n., private home.
私謚 *sy-shyh*^{3}, n., posthumous title conferred unofficially by people or relatives.
私史 *sy-shyy*, n., unofficial history, compiled by private persons.
私訴 *sysuh*, n., a lawsuit brought by parties concerned, opp. 公訴 public prosecution.
私帑 *sy-taang*, n., the king's private treasury.
私談 *sytarn*, v. i. & n., personal conversation, private chat.
私逃 *sy-taur*, v. i., (of criminal) to escape secretly.
私財 *sytsair*, n., person's financial possessions, personal property.

私通 *sytung*, v. t. & n., (1) (have) *liaison* between man and woman; (2) play traitor (with enemy).
私藏 *sytzahng*, (1) n., private treasury; (2) (*-tsarng*) v. t., keep (arms, etc.) illegally.
私債 *sy-tzaih*, n., personal debts.
私自 *sytzyh*, adv., (do it) alone, secretly, (depart, etc.) without proper authorization.
私窩子 *sywotz*, n., private brothel, see *-ketz*↑.
私務 *sy-wuh*, n., personal, private affairs.
私鹽 *syyarn*, n., smuggled salt, salt smuggling: 私鹽包 smuggled person or things.
私益 *syyih*, n., private profit.
私有 *syyoou*, v. t., own, possess; 私有物 private possession.
私願 *sy-yuahn*, n., personal wish.
私慾 *syyuh*, n., human passions, desires; (neo-Confucian) sinful desires, sin.
私運 *sy-yuhn*, v. i., illegally transport (arms, etc.).
私用 *sy-yuhng*, n., private use.
私語 *sy-yuu*, n., a whisper; intimate or confidential talk.

SECTION 90S

§90S.00 (ノ^{S}/亅)

刊 90S.00–2

kan.

[Usu. wr. 刋]

N. Publication, periodical: 刊物 *-wuh*^{1}↓; 月刊, 週刊 a monthly, a weekly; 季刊 a quarterly; 年刊 an annual; 副刊 (literary) supplement to dailies; 叢刊 a library of chosen books or articles.

V.t. (1) To print, publish: 刊版, 刊印, 刊行, 刊載 *-baan*, *-yihn*, *-shirng*, *-tzaih*↓; 刊出 publish. (2) To inscribe on stone or wood: 刊刻 inscribe; 刊石, 刊碑 inscribe on stone, monument. (3) To chop down branch, tree (var. 砍); to eradicate.

刊版 *kanbaan*, n., edition (of certain place, format); v. i., to set up printed edition, to print.
刊本 *kanbeen*, n., edition (of certain place, format).
刊登 *kandeng*, v. t., to publish (news, story).
刊落 *kanluoh*, v. t., to strike out, delete; (printer) to drop (certain words, lines).
刊行 *kanshirng*, v. t., to publish for sale.
刊頭 *kantour*, n., the masthead of newspaper or magazine.
刊載 *kantzaih*, v.t., publish, esp. in newspaper, magazine.
刊物 *kanwuh*^{1}(-*'wu*), n., publication: 定期刊物 periodical.
刊誤 *kanwuh*^{2}, n., (list of) errors and amendments: 刊誤表 errata.
刊印 *kanyihn*, v. t., to set up and print.

刮 90S.00–2

gua.

V.t. (1) Shave, pare off, scrape: 刮臉 shave one's face; 刮鬍子 shave one's whiskers, (coll.) rebuff, snub, criticize mercilessly; 刮頭 shave one's hair; 刮削 pare away; 刮痧 scrape certain parts of the body to obtain relief from nausea or sunstroke; 刮舌 scrape off the fur on the tongue; 刮平 to level down or up; 刮木 to plane wood; 精刮 (Shanghai dial.) cunning, esp. in monetary matters, foxy. (2) To "fleece" the people: 刮地皮 (of officials) fleece the country and get rich; 刮錢 amass money by illegal means. (3) Rub: 刮磨 scrape smooth; 刮目相待 regard (person) with special esteem; 士別三日, 刮目相待 after an absence of three days from a scholar, one "rubs one's eyes" and sees in him a changed man for the better. (4) (Of wind) to blow (=颳): 東風刮地 when the east wind swept over the land.

刮打 *gua'da*, v. t., to strike heavily: 刮打桌子 to pound the table.
刮拉 *guala*, v. t., verbally involve s. o.: 她好意勸你, 又刮拉上她 she has just tried to calm you down, but now you're also pulling her in; 刮拉拉 make a crashing sound.
刮刺 *gua'la*, v. t., in 刮刺上了 (MC) (of boys and girls) get hitched together.
刮皮 *guapir*, v. i. & adj., (dial.) (be) miserly.

剩 90S.00–2

shehng.

V.i. & t. To leave as remainder: 剩飯 rice leftover; 剩貨 leftovers, remainders of goods; 剩錢 money left; 剩下 to leave (so much after expenditure); 剩下三個人 three persons are left; 剩餘 *-yur* ↓.

剩飯手 *shehngfahn-shoou*, n., (sarc.) person of no ability, loafer at job.

剩餘 *shehngyur*, n., surplus, (math.) remainder: 剩餘價值 surplus value; 剩餘利潤 surplus profit; 剩餘法 (logic) method of residues.

劉 90S.00-2

liour.

[Abbr. 劉, 刘]

N. A surname.

劉海(兒) *liourhaii(-haa'l)*, n., bangs.

孵 90S.00-5

fu.

V.i. & t. (Of hens, birds.) to sit on eggs, to hatch: 孵卵 to hatch; 孵小雞 to hatch from eggs or spawn (of fish, insects).

孵化 *fu-huah*, v. i., to spawn or hatch from eggs.

掰 90S.00-8

bai.

V.t. To break (cake) open with hand: 掰開揉碎 phr., to give detailed and exhaustive exposition; 掰交情 break relationships; 掰文兒 to pick fault.

掎 90S.00-8

ger.

V.t. (Soochow dial.) hold with both hands.

§90S.02 (ノ^s/㇗)

舔 90S.02-9

tiaan.

V.t. To lick with tongue: 舔一舔 lick s.t. to see how it tastes; 舔乾淨 lick (a plate) clean.

§90S.10 (ノ^s/十)

拜 90S.10-3

baih.

V.i. & t. (1) To make a bow, obeisance; usu. perform gesture of respect, varying from simple bow, hands at side (鞠躬 *jyurgung*), or hands cupped one on top of the other (揖 *yih*), or palms together, fingers stretched (Budd. 合十 *hershyr*); to kowtow and worship on bended knees (跪拜 *gueihbaih*); usu. perform ceremonial forms in celebrations: 拜年, 拜節 make ceremonial calls on New Year, festival; 拜壽 *-shouh* ↓; 拜佛 worship Buddha at temple; 禮拜 (a) a week; (b) church service; 膜拜 (=跪拜) kowtow on knees. (2) To receive or confer government post: 拜相 to make or be made prime minister; 拜官, 拜爵 be conferred post, rank. (3) Formally establish or swear relationship: 拜老師 formally acknowledge (person) as master, teacher; 拜在門下, 拜門牆 ditto; 拜把子, 結拜, 拜兄弟 be sworn brothers.

Adv. As court. prefix esp. in letters: 拜啟, 拜覆 humbly communicate, reply; 拜謝 humbly thank; 拜懇, 拜禱 my humble request; 拜賜, 拜領 humbly receive (gifts, advice); 拜誦來札 I have read your letter; 你的新書已拜讀了 I have read your new book; 拜別 *-bier* ↓; 拜賀 *-heh* ↓.

拜拜 *baihbaih*, n., (in Taiwan) religious festival.

拜表 *baih-biaau*, v. i., send memorandum to emperor.

拜別 *bainbier*, v. i., take leave: 拜別以來 since I last saw you.

拜懺 *baih-chahn*, v. i., (Budd.) say mass for people.

拜茶 *baih-char*, v. i., (MC) ask guest to come in and have tea.

拜親 *baih-chin*, v. i., formally visit and be introduced to friend's parents.

拜訪 *baihfaang*, v. t., make calls on (person).

拜服 *baihfur* (=佩服), v.t., greatly admire.

拜跪 *baihgueih*, v.i., worship on knees.

拜賀 *baih-heh*, v.i., send greetings, felicitations.

拜會 *baih-hueih*, v.t., make official calls, esp. to make acquaintance.

拜火教 *baih-huoo-jiauh*, n., Zoroastrianism (fire-worship).

拜章 *baih-jang*, v.i., send emperor memorandum.

拜見 *baihjiahn*, v.t., (court.) visit, call on; 拜見禮(兒) *--lii (-lie'l)*, n., gift given on making formal calls.

拜教 *baih-jiauh*, v.i., (court.) receive instructions.

拜金主義 *baih-jin juuyih*, n., (facet.) cult of gold-worship.

拜桌 *baih-juo*, n., table for making and receiving ceremonial obeisance.

拜客 *baih-ker*, v.i., go on the round of calls on friends.

拜禮 *baihlii*, n., see *-jiahnlii* ↑.

拜門 *baih-mern*, v.i., pay thanks by personal visit.

拜命 *baih-mihng*, v.i., (1) receive

emperor's order; (2) (court.) receive or thank for receiving (message, advice).

拜掃 *baih-saau*, v.i., to make ceremonial visit at relative's tomb.

拜神 *baih-shern*, v.i., to worship diety or dieties.

拜壽 *baih-shouh*, v.i., to congratulate someone's birthday in person.

拜臺 *baih-tair*, n., see *-juo* ↑; esp. the stone altar at tombs.

拜堂 *baih-tarng*, v.i., perform formal bows by bride and groom in old custom.

拜天地 *baih-tian-dih*, v.i., (bride and groom) bow to heaven and earth as part of wedding ceremony.

拜託(托) *baihtuo*, v.t., request, entrust (service, favor) to (person): 這個事情拜托你了 I leave this matter in your hands.

拜望 *baihwahng*, v.i. & t., (court.) pay personal call (on person).

拜謁 *baihyeh*, v.i. & t. ditto.

釋 90S.10-4

shyh.

N. Buddhism: 釋迦, 釋教, 釋氏 *-jia, -jiauh, -shyh* ↓; 釋老 or 釋道 Buddhism and Taoism.

V.t. (1) To explain, elucidate: 解釋 explain, explanation; 註釋, 釋義, 釋言 exegesis, commentary on meaning of words, phrases; 釋疑 remove doubts, satisfy raised questions. (2) To release (restrictions), to pardon: 釋服, 釋褐 *-fur, -her* ↓; 釋縛 release tied-up person; 釋甲 doff armor—resume civilian life; 釋念 not to worry; 如釋重負 as if relieved from a big burden; 釋罪 pardon (s.o. or his crime); 開釋 to pardon, reprieve, also to allay fears, doubts. (3) To dissipate, dissolve (differences of opinion, hatreds, etc.): 釋恨, 釋憾 or 釋嫌 dissolve old grudge; 消釋, 冰釋 (doubts, differences) vanish, disappear.

釋部 *shyhbuh*, n., Buddhist sutras.

釋典 *shyhdiaan*, n., ditto.

釋奠 *shyhdiahn*, v. i., (AC) to pour libation.

釋放 *shyhfahng*, v. t., to release (prisoner).

釋服 *shyh-fur*, phr., to drop mourning.

釋褐 *shyh-her*, phr., to pass third degree 進士 and drop commoner's dress.

釋迦 *Shyhjia*, n., short for 釋迦牟尼 Sakyamuni, the founder of Buddhism; hence *-shyh, -jiauh* ↓.

釋教 *shyhjiauh*, n., Buddhism.

釋例 *shyhlih*, n., editorial notes on selection, omission, arrangement of book.

釋門 *shyhmern*, n., the Buddhist church.

釋然 *shyhrarn*, adj., (doubts) dissolved.

釋氏 *Shyhshyh*, n., see *-jia* ↑.

釋子 *Shyhtzyy*, n., Buddhist followers, monks.

辞 90S.10-6

tsyr.

[Pop. of 辭 ↓]

辤 90S.10-6

tsyr.

[Interch. 辭 ↓]

辭 90S.10-6

tsyr.

[Interch. 詞]

N. (1) A word, mono- or polysyllabic, see compp. of 詞 60A.50; 文辭 language of writing; 言辭 language of expression; 說辭 to speak, present a case; 遁辭 evasive talk; 詭辭 quibbling. (2) Literary phraseology, language in piece of writing: 辭達而已矣 (孔子) in the use of language the only aim is to express s. t.; 辭不達意 the language fails to express the idea. (3) U. f. 詞 in 詞訟, see 詞^4訟 60A.50. (4) An ancient form of poetic prose, as 楚辭 of 屈原, see 辭賦 *-fuh* ↓.

V.i. & t. (1) To take leave: 辭別, 辭行 *-bier, -shirng* ↓; 辭世, 辭歲 *-shyh, -sueih* ↓. (2) To resign: 辭退, 辭職 *-tueih, -jyr* ↓. (3) To concede, step back: 辭讓 *-rahng* ↓. (4) To evade, shirk: 不辭艱辛 do not shirk hardships.

辭別 *tsyrbier*, v. i. & t., to take leave, say good-bye.

辭氣 *tsyrchih*, n., manner or tone of speaking.

辭趣 *tsyrchyuh*, n., flavor of select language.

辭典 *tsyrdiaan*, n., a dictionary of words and phrases (also wr. 詞).

辭賦 *tsyrfuh*, n., a litr. form, sentimental or descriptive composition, oft. rhymed, esp. in Hahn and Weih Dyns.

辭活 *tsyr-huor*, v. i., (coll. of servants) resign from job.

辭章 *tsyrjang*, n., literary composition (also wr. 詞).

辭職 *tsyrjyr*, v. i., to resign office.

辭旨 *tsyrjyy*, n., main idea of speech or composition.

辭令 *tsyrlihng*, n., a person's command of language, ability to talk. [also 詞).

辭林 *tsyrlirn*, n., literary circles

辭靈 *tsyr-lirng*, v. i., (guests at funeral) bow to coffin before leaving.

辭命 *tsyrmihng*, v. i., see *-lihng* ↑.

辭讓 *tsyrrahng*, n. & v. i., (show) courtesy to others, self-abnegation.

辭色 *tsyrseh*, n., air of speaking, countenance (severe, embarrassed): 不假辭色 speak bluntly or harshly.
辭行 *tsyrshirng*, v. i., to take leave, say good-bye.
辭世 *tsyr-shyh*, v. i., to pass away.
辭歲 *tsyr-sueih*, v. i., celebrate New Year's Eve.
辭訟 *tsyrsuhng*, n., lawsuit.
辭退 *tsyrtueih*, v. t., to dismiss (person).

§90S.11 (ノ^{S}/土)

雞 90S.11-9

ji.

[Interch. 鷄; pop. 鸡]

N. Domestic fowls, chickens: 公雞 a cock; 母雞 a hen; 小雞 a chick; 火雞 a turkey; 雞貓子喊叫 shrill cries; 雞鳴狗盜之徒 a band of scoundrels, the riffraff, the dregs of society; 雞鳴五更天 at dawn ("as the cock crows"); 雞飛蛋打 come out empty-handed; 偷雞摸狗 do things stealthily; 雞蛋裏找骨頭 pick at, find fault with; 雞零狗碎 odds and ends, bits and pieces of things of little value; 寧爲鷄口, 勿爲牛後 would rather be leader anywhere than follower; 雞犬不寧 greatly upset like a poultry yard visited by a fox; 雞犬不留 utter extermination ("even chickens and dogs are not spared"); 雞犬不驚 complete peace and quiet; 一人得志, 雞犬升天 unashamed nepotism; 雞蟲得失 (fight over) trifles, inconsequential matters, trivialities; 雞鳴, 雞啼 cock's crow.

雞巴 *ji'ba*, n., (coll.) the penis.
雞棲 *jichi*, n., a hencoop, henhouse.
雞蛋 *jidahn*, n., hen's egg.
雞冠(子) *jiguan('tz)*, n., cock's comb; 雞冠花 (bot.) the cock's comb.
雞骨 *jiguu*, (1) n., chicken bones; (2) adj., skinny, emaciated.
雞姦 *jijian*, n., sodomy.
雞肋 *jileh*, n., chicken's ribs; anything insipid, uninteresting; (fig.) fragile.
雞卵 *jiluaan*, n., hen's egg, see *-dahn*↑.
雞毛 *jimaur*, n. & adj., chicken feathers; (fig.) trivial, insignificant, unimportant: 雞毛小事 trifles; 雞毛蒜皮 ditto; 雞毛當令箭 take seriously a casual word dropped by a superior; 雞毛帚 a duster made of chicken feathers.
雞鳴枕 *jimirng-jeen*, n., a pillow for the dead.
雞內金 *jineihjin*, n., the internal lining of a chicken gizzard, used as drug by herb doctors.
雞皮 *jipir*, n., (1) an old person's wrinkled face: 雞皮鶴髮 advanced in age ("wrinkled skin and white hair"); (2) 雞皮疙瘩 goose flesh.
雞舌香 *jishershiang*, n., (bot.) cloves (also 丁香).
雞心 *jishin*, n., a heart-shaped pendant.
雞黍 *ji-shuu*, n., dishes for guests ("fowl and millet").
雞頭 *jitour*, n., (1) (bot.) the foxnut, *Euryale ferox* (another name for 芡實); (2) a woman's teats; (3) 雞頭魚刺 a person of no consequence.
雞子兒 *jitzee'l*, n., hen's eggs.
雞尾酒 *jiweir-jioou*, n., cocktails: 雞尾酒會 cocktail party.
雞鶩 *ji-wuh*, n., petty or mean persons.
雞眼 *jiyaan*, n., corns (on the foot).
雞魚 *jiyur*, n., (zoo.) the grunt (fish).

§90S.22 (ノ^{S}/丨)

邱 90S.22-3

chiou.

[Interch. 丘 90.30]

N. (1) 邱婿 (AC) husband of deceased daughter (in the grave). (2) A surname.

邸 90S.22-3

dii.

N. (1) Official residence: 官邸 official residence; 京邸 residence at the capital. (2) A surname.

邸報 *diibauh*, n., formerly, court bulletin.
邸第 *diidih*, n., official residence.
邸舍 *diisheh*, n., (1) official residence; (2) inn.

郛 90S.22-3

fur.

N. Outer city: 郛郭 (fig.) outer defense of place.

郵 90S.22-3

your.

[Abbr. 邮]

N. (1) Courier system, post chaise. (2) Post office, the mail: 交郵, 付郵 to mail letter: 郵政, 郵票 *-jehng*, *-piauh*↓. (3) (AC rare) u. f. 尤. (4) A surname.

郵包兒 *yourbau'l*, n., postal parcel.
郵差 *yourchai*, n., mailman.
郵籤 *yourchian*, n., formerly, tallies used in courier system.
郵船 *your-chuarn*[1], n., mail boat, mail ship.
郵傳 *yourchuarn*[2], v. i., to send letters, deliver letters.
郵戳兒 *your-chuo'l*, n., postal cancellation, postmark.
郵袋 *your-daih*, n., a mailbag.

郵電 *your-diahn*, n., post and telegram.

郵遞 *yourdih*, n., postal delivery: 郵遞區 postal delivery zone; 郵遞區號 zip code.

郵費 *yourfeih*, n., postage.

郵館 *yourguaan*, n., (MC) an inn.

郵花 *yourhua*, n., see *-piauh*↓.

郵滙 *yourhueih*, n. & v. t., (send by) postal money order.

郵政 *yourjehng*, n., postal system: 郵政局 post office; 郵政管理局 postal administration.

郵件 *yourjiahn*, n., letters and parcels, mail.

郵寄 *yourjih*, v. t., to send by post.

郵局 *yourjyur*, n., post office.

郵吏 *your-lih*, n., courier clerk.

郵片 *yourpiahn*, n., post card (=明信片).

郵票 *yourpiauh*, n., postage stamp.

郵箱 *your-shiang*, n., postbox, mailbox, P.O.BOX. (Post Office Box).

郵亭 *your-tirng*, n., (1) resting station for ancient courier system; (2) (modn.) a post office booth.

郵筒 *yourturng*, n., (1) formerly, bamboo section for holding letters; (2) (*-tuung*) postbox.

郵資 *yourtzy*, n., postage.

郵務 *yourwuh*, n., postal affairs.

鄱 90S.22-3

por.

鄱陽 *Poryarng*, n., name of large lake in Kiangsi.

卬 90S.22-5

arng.

Pron. (AC) I—first person.

Adj. (Interch. 昂) high-priced.

印 90S.22-5

yihn.

N. (1) A seal: 印信, 印章 *-shihn*, *-jang*↓; 蓋印 to stamp seal on paper; 封印 formerly, the practice of "locking up the official seal" during the lunar New Year holidays. (2) Any mark, print: 腳印 footprint; 指印 fingerprint; 水印 watermark; 火印, 烙印 branding. (3) A surname.

V.t. (1) To print in publishing: 印刷 *-shua*↓; 重印 reprint; 複印 to make duplicates. (2) To make a perfect replica in thoughts: 心心相印 hearts and feelings find a perfect response.

印把子 *yihnbahtz*, n., official seal.

印本 *yihnbeen*, n., printed copy, dist. hand copy.

印第安人 *Yihndih-an-rern*, n., a red Indian.

印度 *Yihnduh*, n., India; 印度洋 the Indian Ocean.

印花 *yihnhua*, n., revenue stamp: 貼印花 stick revenue stamp on business paper to make it legal; 印花稅 stamp tax; 印花布 printed cotton.

印章 *yihnjang*, n., a seal: 私人印章 personal seal.

印證 *yihnjehng*, v.t., to corroborate: 互相印證 corroborate each other.

印鑑 *yihnjiahn*, n., copy of seal, used principally in lieu of signature and kept at bank, etc. for checking against seal in receipts, checks, etc.

印結 *yihnjier*, n., seal used in bureaucratic guarantee (結) to superiors concerning certain documents.

印可 *yihnkee*, v.t., (Budd.) approve.

印兒 *ye'l*, n., a trace, footprint, etc.

印模 *yihnmor*, n., metal dice used for marking trademarks, etc. on goods.

印尼 *Yihnnir*[1], n., Indonesia.

印泥 *yihnnir*[2], n., Chin. ink pad, containing cinnabar and oil.

印色 *yihn'se*, n., ditto.

印象 *yihnshiahng*, n., reactions or impressions (of a place, person, speech, trial, etc.): 印象派 n. & adj., impressionist(ic); 印象派主義 n., (art) impressionism.

印信 *yihnshihn*, n., official seal.

印行 *yihnshirng*, v.t., to publish (a book).

印刷 *yihnshua*, v.t., to print: 印刷廠 printing press; 印刷品, 印刷物 printed literature, brochures, etc.

印堂 *yihntarng*, n., (Chin. physiognomy) the top of the nose bridge connecting the eyebrows.

印子錢 *yihntzchiarn*, n., formerly, a form of usury loan, with interest daily compounded, recorded in an account book and stamped: 放印子 to lend such loan; 打印子 to contract such loan.

卯 90S.22-5

maau.

N. Number four of the duodecimal cycle; the two-hour period, 7:00–9:00 A.M.; hence 點卯 roll call, check-in time; 應卯 appear at morning session for work; 誤卯 be late; 卯簿 roll-call book; 卯飯 breakfast; 卯飲 drink in the morning (inappropriate).

卯勁(兒) *maaujihn(-jieh'l)*, n., extra energy.

卯子活 *maautz-huor*, n., work paid by the day.

卯眼 *mauryaan*, n., the concave end of joint to receive the convex or projecting part (筍頭).

卵 90S.22-5

luaan (**laan*).

N. (1) Egg, ovum, spawn: 雞卵, 鴨卵 a hen's egg, duck's egg: 卵翼 (v.t.) to mother and protect the young. (2) (**laan*) Human male testicles: 卵毛 male pubic hair, see 卵子 *-tz* ↓.

卵白 *luaanbair*, n., albumen, egg white.
卵胞子 *luaanbautz*, (bot.) oöspore, (zoo.) zygote.
卵巢 *luaanchaur*, n., ovary.
卵黃 *luaanhuarng*, n., egg yolk.
卵殼 *luaanker*, n., eggshell.
卵生 *luaansheng* (also **luoo-*), adj., oviparous, reproduced by egg.
卵細胞 *luaanshihbau*, n., ovum, ovary cell, egg; (bot.) oösphere.
卵形 *luaanshirng*, adj., oval-shaped.
卵胎生 *luaantaisheng*, adj., ovoviviparous.
卵子 *luaantzyy*, n., (1) (bot.) oöspore; (2) ovum; (3) (also pr. **laantz*) egg.

卿 90S.22-9

ching.

N. (1) (In anc. dyns.) high ministers of various ranks: 公卿 the dukes and high ministers; 卿大夫 high ministers and nobles; 六卿, 九卿 equivalent to "ministers." (2) Formerly, ruler's address to a minister. (3) (LL) husband's address to wife: 賢卿, 愛卿, 我卿 my dear wife; 卿卿我我 whispers of love, lovers' talk. (4) A surname.

卿雲 *chingyurn*, n., (LL) auspicious clouds: 卿雲歌 an ancient song of glory and peace.

所 90S.22-9

suoo.

N. adjunct. 一所房屋 a house.

N. (1) A place: 住所 where one lives, dwelling place; 得其所 has what one desires; 居無定所 without definite residence; 厠所, 便所 water closet. (2) An office, bureau, station: 公所 a civil office; 派出所 police station; 繳納所 bureau for receiving payments; 檢驗所 checking station, bureau of inspection; 衞生所 public health office; 診所 clinic.

Pron. (1) What, that which, all that, whatever (nearest thing to a Chin. relative pronoun, introducing a noun clause): 不知所當爲(當說) do not know what to do, what to say; 所不知者闕如 what one does not know should be left out; 有所不知 there are things which one does not know; 有所不及 there are things where one cannot compare with another; 無所不知 omniscient; 無所不爲 stop at nothing (i.e., cheating, lying, etc.); 大失所望 greatly disappoints one's hopes; 所見略同 share each other's views to a certain extent, agree mostly; 暢所欲言(欲爲) do (say) exactly as the mind dictates; 所爲何事 what are (you) here for? 所從出 where it comes from; 所憾 what one regrets; 所向披靡 ever triumphant, ever victorious. (2) Often expressing passive voice in "be＋agent＋所＋vb.": 爲匪所殺 was killed by bandits; 被水所淹 was drowned by water; 爲人所欺 was cheated by s. o.

所部 *suoo-buh*, n., see *-shuu* ↓.
所得 *suoo-der*, n., income, results: 毫無所得 without any results; 所得不償所失 gains cannot make up for losses; 所得稅 income tax.
所歡 *suoo-huan*, n., lover: 疑是所歡來 think her (his) lover has come.
所長 *suor-jaang*, (1) n., bureau chief; (2) (*suoo-charng*) n., what one is good at, strong points, specialty.
所知 *suoo-jy*, (1) phr., what one knows, the known; (2) n., an acquaintance.
所屬 *suor-shuu*, n., army units or staff under one's command.
所事 *suoo-shyh*[1], n., what one does or undertakes: 無所事事 do nothing all day.
所識 *suoo-shyh*[2], n., an acquaintance.
所司 *suoo-sy*[1], n., one's duties: 所司何事 isn't that part of your duties?
所思 *suoo-sy*[2], n., (LL) the person one loves and remembers; what one is thinking of: 若有所思 as if thinking of s.t.
所天 *suoo-tian*, n., (LL) husband ("what is heaven" to a wife); one's father, (AC) also the sovereign.
所在 *suootzaih*, (1) n., place: 忘其所在 forget the place; 那個所在 that place; (2) adv., everywhere: 所在都有 is found everywhere; 所在地 where a person, thing, is found or located.
所爲 *suoo-weih*[1], (1) n., reason, cause: 所爲何來 what do you come here for? (2) (*-weir*) what one does, (person's) conduct.
所謂 *suoo-weih*[2], adj., so-called: 所謂君子 so-called gentlemen.
所以 *suoryii*, conj., (1) therefore, reason why: 因爲…所以 because . . . therefore; 我所以不來 the reason I did not come; 所以不去 therefore I am not going, did not go; 所以敗了 therefore (s.o.) is defeated; 不知所以 do not know why; (2) whereby: 所以興懷 that by which one is moved; 所以然 the reason why: 知其然, 不知其所以然 know it is so, but do not know why it is so.
所有 *suor-yoou*, n., all one's possessions: 所有權 ownership; 財產所有權 property rights.

斵 90S.22-9

juor.

[Interch. 斲]

V.t. To chop, heck (wood): 斵樹 chop off tree; 斵雕爲樸 cut off embellishments and return to simplicity (uncarved state).

斲輪 *juorlurn*, phr., 斲輪老手 an old hand, a master (lit., "expert cartwright") at writing, etc.
斲喪 *juorsahng*, v. t., to injure vitality by dissipation.

斵 90S.22-9

juor.
[Pop. of 斲]

§90S.40 (ノ^s/口)

黏 90S.40-2

niarn.
[Var. 粘]

V.i. & t. (Lit.) to stick to, (fig.) to pester (s. o.) with requests for help or favors: 黏附, 黏住 stick to; 黏貼, 黏上去 stick s. t. up or on with glue; 黏著 pester (s. o.) with requests for help or favors, persistently dog another person's steps; 黏連 (of two things) be stuck together; 黏皮帶骨 (of conduct) insistent and unrelenting, (of things) involved, tangled.

Adj. (1) Sticky like glue: 黏性 sticky; 黏巴巴, 黏糊糊兒的, 黏得很 very sticky. (2) As in 黏叨叨, 絮叨叨 talking on and on, but not to the point; 黏涎 *-shiarn*↓.

黏著 *niarnje*, v.t., see V.i. & t.↑.
黏膜 *niarnmor*, n., (physiol.) mucous membrane.
黏涎 *niarnshiarn*, v.t., drag on (as of old sickness or interminable talk); 黏涎子 *--'tz*, n., saliva.
黏土 *niarntuu*, n., (geol.) clay.
黏液 *niarnyeh*, n., (physiol.) mucus.

谿 90S.40-8

shi (also *chi*).

N. A mountain stream; interch. 溪 river valley.

谿谷 *shi-guu*, n., river valley.
谿壑 *shi-huoh*, n., ravine.
谿澗 *shi-jiahn*, n., mountain brook.
谿刻 *shikeh*, adj., cutting, petty (criticism).

§90S.41 (ノ^s/図)

甜 90S.41-2

tiarn.

Adj. (1) Sweet, sweet-flavored: 甜津津, 甜蜜蜜, 甜絲絲 very sweet; 吃到人生的甜酸苦辣 taste all the flavors (bitterness, sweetness, etc.) of life; 甜言蜜語 sweet, honeyed (enticing) words; 甜麵醬 a sweet flour paste; 甜醬粥 a millet gruel, slightly sweet, served for breakfast. (2) Sweet in love, dreams, music: 甜睡 beautiful sleep; 甜笑 sweet smile; 長得很甜 possess a sweet look. (3) Sweet water: 甜水井 fresh water well, as against brackish water.

甜瓜 *tiarngua(-'gua)*, n., the muskmelon.
甜美 *tiarnmeei*, adj., sweet (music, dream, life).
甜蜜 *tiarnmih*, adj., sweet, loving: 甜蜜的婚姻, 家庭 a sweet marriage, home.
甜頭(兒) *tiarntour('l)*, n., a finger in the pie, a bait or lure: 給他一個甜頭吃 give him monetary lure; 吃到了甜頭 have had a taste of illegal money (bribe, etc.).
甜菜 *tiarntsaih*, n., various sweet-pickled vegetables; the leaf beet, *Beta vulgaris*.

釉 90S.41-2

youh.

N. (*-'l*, *-tz*) The glaze in pottery; enamel in porcelain: 彩釉 colored enamel.

§90S.50 (ノ^s/ㄱ)

翻 90S.50-5

fan.
[Var. 飜; cogn. 反]

V.i. & t. (1) Turn over, turn around, reverse: 翻過來 turn over; 翻來翻 (or 覆) 去 toss in bed, also change story, sides constantly; 翻餅 toss in bed, unable to sleep; 翻飛, 翻翔 circle, wheel about in the sky; 翻跟頭, 翻觔斗 (*-gendoou*), 翻金斗 turn somersault; 翻雲覆雨 break promise, change attitudes constantly; 翻口供 reverse story by accused; 翻案 *-ahn*↓; 翻舊卷 to pick on past deeds; 翻白眼 (兒) show white of eye (in pain, disappointment, etc.); 翻過兒 turn (things) upside down; 翻箱倒篋 turn over things in thorough search; 翻老底, 翻底牌 show trump card, show down. (2) Overturn: 翻車, 翻船 overturn car, boat or (v.i.) 車, 船翻了. (3) Rip off and repair: 翻蓋, 翻修 *-gaih*, *-shiou*↓. (4) Flip over: 翻書 flip over pages

斲 斵 黏 谿 甜 釉 翻

翻 動

of book; 翻閱 read over, look over (book, newspaper); 推翻 overthrow (government, theory); 打翻 knock down (table, glass). (5) Translate: 翻譯 *-yih*↓.

翻案 *fan-ahn*, v. i. & t., reverse verdict; reverse previously held theory; oft. 翻案文章, such essay or viewpoint.

翻版 *fanbaan*, n. & v. i., reprint.

翻本 *fanbeen*, v. i., recoup losses.

翻車魚 *fanche-yur*, n., the *Mola mola*, the ocean sunfish.

翻覆 *fanfuh*, v. i., change opinions, attitudes, frequently; break one's word: 翻覆無定 vacillating in attitude, policy; also 翻翻覆覆.

翻蓋 *fangaih*, v. i., renovate (building).

翻滾 *fanguun*, v. i., roll over and over.

翻悔 *fanhueei*, v. i., repent.

翻臉 *fan-liaan*, v. i., (1) break friendship as in 和人翻臉 with some one; (2) 翻臉不認人 pretend not to know old friend or colleague.

翻砂 *fan-sha*, v. i., make castings from sand mold.

翻梢 *fan-shau*, v. i., (1) recoup; (2) have one's luck turn.

翻身 *fanshen*, v. i., (1) turn on one's sides; (2) get up and fight again: 不得翻身 have no chance to rise again or recover.

翻戲 *fanshih*, v. i., a form of gamble.

翻修 *fanshiou*, v. i., renovate or repair (building).

翻騰 *fanterng*, v. i., upset, overturn everything; be a nuisance; toss about.

翻胃 *fan-weih*, v. i., turn the stomach.

翻譯 *fanyih*, n. & v. t., translate, -tion; also wr. 繙譯.

翻印 *fanyihn*, n. & v. t., reprint: 翻印必究 reproduction of book will be prosecuted.

動 90S.50-9

duhng.

N. Movement, action: 行動 activity, conduct; 擧動 a man's movements, deportment; 一擧一動 every movement (is watched, etc.); 運動 physical exercise, athletics, sports, (political, literary) movement; 波動 fluctuation (of prices), wave motion.

V.i. & t. (1) V.i., to move: 別動 don't move (before camera); 動不得 must not move, touch; 不能動 cannot move; 站立不動 stand still; 搖動 swing (as branch), falter (in opinion); 移動 move to another place; 流動 flux, flow; 震動 shake up, quake, vibrate, -tion. (2) V.t., to take up, usu. with idea of starting action: 動干戈, 動兵 take up arms, mobilize army; 動槍刀 fight with weapons; 動筷子 take up chopsticks, begin eating; 動刑 start to use torture; 動手 *-shoou*↓; 動手動脚 be fresh with girl, make motions to start a fight; 動兇, 動粗, 動武, 動土 *-shyung, -tsu, -wuu, -tuu*↓. (3) To move, stir, arouse, excite: 不爲所動 be not swayed (by speech) or attracted (by beauty); 無動於中 be completely indifferent; 感動 to inspire, feel touched or influenced; 動淫心 arouse sexual desire; 動疑心 arouse suspicion; 動起公憤 arouse public wrath; 動起念頭 put idea in one's head, start an idea; 動腦筋 do a lot of thinking; 動火, 動氣 *-huoo, -chih*↓.

Adj. Active, dynamic: 動的 dynamic; 動的美 dynamic beauty; 動態 *-taih*, 動力 *-lih*↓; 動人 attractive, touching, moving; 動目 good-looking, attractive, exciting in appearance.

動不動 *duhng-bur-duhng*, adv., at every move, on every occasion or pretext.

動產 *duhngchaan*, n., movable property, movables, opp. 不動產 real property.

動輒 *duhngcheh*, adv., at every move: 動輒得罪 (咎) blamed for every move.

動氣 *duhngchih*, v.i., get angry.

動情 *duhngchirng*, v.i., feel attracted, enamored.

動電 *duhngdiahn*, n., dynamic electricity.

動滑車 *duhng-huarche*, n., movable pulley.

動火 *duhng-huoo*, v. i., feel angry; start fighting.

動機 *duhngji*, n., motive (of action).

動靜 *duhng-jihng*, n., (1) news of action: 這事一直沒有動靜 no news of it so far; (2) noise, stir: 沒有絲毫動靜 not the slightest stir.

動量 *duhngliahng*, n., (phys.) momentum.

動力 *duhnglih*, n., motive power; 動力學 dynamics.

動亂 *duhngluahn*, n., social or political turmoil.

動(的)美 *duhng(dih)meei*, n., dynamic beauty.

動脈 *duhngmoh*, n., artery, opp. 靜脈 vein; 動脈硬化症 arteriosclerosis, hardening of the arteries; 動脈瘤 aneurysm.

動目 *duhng-muh*, adj., good to look at, attracting attention.

動能 *duhng-nerng*, n., kinetic energy.

動怒 *duhng-nuh*, v. i., be angry.

動人 *duhng-rern*, adj., very moving (play, story), touching.

動容 *duhng-rurng*, v. i., visibly touched; change countenance.

動身 *duhng-shen*, v. i., begin journey.

動向 *duhngshiahng*, n., trend, tendency, direction of movement.

動心 *duhng-shin*, v.i., be moved (by attractive offer), sexually aroused, excited.

動手 *duhng-shoou*, v. i., (1) start work; (2) raise hand to fight.

動兇 *duhng-shyung*, v.i. resort to violence.

動態 *duhngtaih*, n., general trend of affairs, general activities.

動彈 *duhng'tan*, v. i., move: 不能動彈 cannot move at all (sick person).

動聽 *duhngting*, adj., (speech) moving, persuasive.

動粗 *duhng-tsu*, v. i., resort to violence.

動詞 *duhngtsyr*, n., verb: 他動詞 transitive vb.; 自動詞 intransitive vb.; 助動詞 auxiliary vb.

動土 *duhng-tuu*, v. i., break ground.

動作 *duhngtzuoh*, n. & v. i., action; work, move: 不能動作 cannot work.

動問 *duhng-wehn*, v. i., proffer question.

動物 *duhngwuh*, n., animal: 動物界 animal kingdom; 動物園 zoological garden; 動物學 zoology.

動武 *duhngwuu*, v. i., resort to violence, fisticuffs.

動搖 *duhngyaur*, v. i., shake, falter in belief.

動議 *duhngyih*, v. i., to move (in assembly); n., such motion, suggestion.

動員 *duhngyuarn*, n. & v. i., mobilize, -ation.

動用 *duhngyuhng*, v. t., touch, draw upon (funds): 動用公款 (illegally) draw upon public funds.

鴟 90S.50–9

chy.

N. An owl; barn owl: 鴟視, 鴟顧 look at sides without turning head, like an owl; 鴟目 owl-like look.

鴟張 *chyjang*, adj., (people) fierce or ominous-looking.

鴟甍 *chy-merng*, n., roof tile with owl head.

鴟梟 *chyshiau*, adj. & n., ugly, intransigent or such person.

鴟尾 *chy-weei*, n., owl-like ornament on roof ridge.

鴟吻 *chy-ween*, n., owl-like ornament on roof corners.

鴟夷 *chyyir*, n., (AC) leather wine case.

鵝 90S.50–9

er.

[Var. 鵞]

N. A goose: 天鵝 the swan; 塘鵝 the pelican; 鵝行鴨步 to waddle (like goose); 鵝頸 goose's neck; 鵝掌 goose (webbed) claws; 鵝準 goose's crest; 鵝蛋 goose egg; 鵝酒禮 present of goose and wine at wedding; 鵝毛 goose down; 鵝毛片 large snowflakes.

鵝蛋臉兒 *erdahnliaa'l*, n., oval face.

鵝黃 *erhuarng*, adj., bright orange.

鵝掌風 *erjaangfen*, n., (med.) a disease of the palm.

鵝沾 *er'jan*, n., a stain (as with juice on dress).

鵝口瘡 *erkoouchuang*, n., (med.) thrush, a milky-white adhesion on mouth, (also horse's foot) with pus formation.

鵝漣 *er'lian*, n., see *-jan* ↑.

鵝梨角兒 *erlirjiaau'l*, n., an elongated oval coil on woman's hair.

鵝翎 *erlirng*, n., goose (wing) feather: 鵝翎扇 goose-feather fan; 鵝翎筆 goose-quill pen.

鵝卵石 *erluaan-shyr*, n., oval-shaped pebble.

鵝絨 *errurng*, n., goose down: 鵝絨被 goose-down quilt.

鷄 90S.50–9

ji.

[Var. of 雞 90S.11]

勳 90S.50–9

shyun.

[Var. 勛]

N. (1) Meritorious service: 功勳 ditto; 授勳, 贈勳 to award medal of honor for service. (2) Rank, nobility: 勳爵, 勳位, 勳貴 *-jyuer*, *-weih*, *-gueih* ↓; 勳附 those closely related to people of rank.

勳臣 *shyunchern*, n., an official with record of distinguished service to country.

勳閥 *shyunfar*, n., powerful family of general or politician.

勳官 *shyunguan*, n., a person with rank.

勳貴 *shyungueih*, n., the titled nobility.

勳功 *shyungung*, n., meritorious service, also 功勳.

勳章 *shyunjang*, n., medal of honor.

勳舊 *shyunjiouh*, n., formerly, person(s) with close connections with the emperor.

勳級 *shyunjir*, n., (ranking among men with) different degrees of meritorious service.

勳爵 *shyunjyuer*, n., titles of nobility conferred for meritorious service.

勳勞 *shyunlaur*, n., meritorious service.

勳位 *shyunweih*, n., rank.

勳業 *shyunyeh*, n., see *-laur* ↑.

勳庸 *shyunyung*, n., (LL) ditto.

§90S.70 (ノˢ/乚)

乳 90S.70–2

ruu.

N. (1) The breasts, nipples: 乳房 *-farng* ↓; 乳子 a sucking child; 布袋乳 pendulous breasts; 乳頭 *-tour* ↓; 乳癌 *-yarn* ↓; 石鐘乳 stalactites; 竹乳 tabashir. (2) Milk: 乳汁, 乳奶, 人乳 (human) milk; 牛乳 cow's milk; 乳酪 *-lauh* ↓; 乳油 butter; 喂乳 suckle (a baby); 斷乳 wean (a baby); 乳食 take nothing but milk as food.

V.t. (1) Suckle (babies): 乳牛 a

milch cow; 乳虎, 乳獸 a suckling tigress, animal; 乳母, 乳娘, 乳媼, 乳嫗 *-muu, -niarng, -aau, -yuh*↓. (2) Give birth to: 孳乳 (lit.) bear children, (fig.) reproduce and multiply; see 孳ᴬ乳 80.00.

Adj. Young, newly-born: 乳燕 squab; 乳兒 a sucking child; 乳名 *-mirng*↓.

乳媼 *rur-aau*, n., wet nurse.
乳瓣 *ruubahn*, n., (1) one of the constituent lobules of a woman's breasts; (2) mother's milk in the form of curds regurgitated by a sucking child.
乳餅 *rurbiing*, n., a baby feed.
乳鉢 *ruu-bo*, n., (MC) a mortar for grinding and pestle for grinding powder.
乳哺 *rurbuu*, v.i., feed child with prechewed food.
乳泣 *ruuchih*[1], v.i., (Chin. med.) (of pregnant woman) lactate before childbirth.
乳氣 *ruu-chih*[2], n., childishness.
乳泉 *ruu-chyuarn*, n., water dripping from stalactites.
乳齒 *rur-chyy*, n., baby teeth, milk teeth.
乳蛾 *ruu-er*, n., (Chin. med.) tonsils (also called 喉蛾).
乳房 *ruufarng*, n., the breasts.
乳柑 *ruugan*, n., (bot.) a kind of orange with thin peel and no seeds.
乳光 *ruuguang*, n., opalescence of certain precious stones.
乳核 *ruuher*, n., (med.) tubercle of the breast.
乳化 *ruuhuah*, v.i., emulsify.
乳膠 *ruujiau*, n., emulsion.
乳酒 *rurjioou*, n., milkwhite wine.
乳狀液 *ruujuahng-yeh*, n., milk-like liquid.
乳脂 *ruujy*, n., (LL) butter (now called 奶油, 黄油, 牛油).
乳橘 *ruu-jyur*, n., a kind of orange.
乳酪 *ruulauh*, n., (1) curds; (2) cheese (also called 乾酪).
乳栗 *ruulih*, n., (Chin. med.) =乳核 *ruuher*↑.
乳梨 *ruulir*, n., a large white juicy pear.
乳糜 *ruumir*, n., chyle.
乳名 *ruu-mirng*, n., a child's pet name.
乳母 *rurmuu*, n., wet nurse.
乳娘 *ruuniarng*, n., ditto.
乳腺 *ruu-shiahn*, n., the mammary glands.
乳臭 *ruu-shiouh*, n., childishness, puerility: 乳臭未乾 young and inexperienced.
乳樹 *ruu-shuh*, n., (bot.) *Galactodendron utile*.
乳懸 *ruu-shyuarn*, n., (Chin. med.) an abnormal elongation of a woman's breasts after childbirth.
乳酸 *ruu-suan*, n., lactic acid; 乳酸亞鐵 *--yahtiee*, n., ferrous lactate. ⌈lactose.
乳糖 *ruu-tarng*, n., milk sugar,
乳頭 *ruutour*, n., (1) nipples, teats; (2) any projection on the skin (as at hair root), the tongue or other parts of the body.
乳癌 *ruu-yarn*, n., (med.) cancer of the breast. ⌈poison.
乳藥 *ruuyauh*, v.i., (AC) take
乳嫗 *ruuyuh*, n., wet nurse.
乳癰 *ruuyung*, n., mastitis, abscess of the breast.

亂 90S.70-2

luahn.

[Abbr. 乱]

N. Confusion, state of chaos; revolt: 作亂 to revolt; see 亂子 *-tz*↓; 搗亂 to create trouble, break discipline.

V.t. (1) To confuse: 擾亂 (治安) disturb (law and order); 叛亂 revolt (n. & v.i.); 亂真, 亂離, 亂倫 *-jen, -lir, -lurn*↓. (2) (AC) v.t., commit incest with.

Adj. (1) Confused, disorderly, not peaceful: 雜亂 motley, not arranged or sorted out; 混亂 in state of confusion; 亂麻, 亂絲 snarled hemp, skein; 亂如麻 like tangled hemp; 亂烘烘 or 轟轟 tumultuous, in a big, noisy confusion; 亂騰騰, 亂紛紛 very disorderly; 亂鬆鬆 (of hair) dishevelled, fluffy; 亂邦, 亂國 chaotic country; 亂世 times of gen. chaos, upheaval. (2) Rebellious: 亂兵, 亂黨 rebellious troops, party; 亂民 rebels; 亂臣賊子 (AC) traitors and usurpers; 亂臣 (治亂之臣) (AC) able ministers.

Adv. Pell-mell, flurriedly, without order or restraint: 亂説, 胡説亂 (or 八) 道 talk without truth or restraint; 亂吃 eat anything without caution; 亂嚷, 亂叫 shout, scream madly; 亂跑 run about anywhere.

亂眞 *luahnjen*, phr., 足以亂眞 (of fake art) good enough to pass for genuine.
亂離 *luahnlir*, adj., separated by war: 亂離人 refugee, people so separated from homes.
亂倫 *luahnlurn*, n. & adj. & v.i., incest, -uous, commit incest.
亂視 *luahnshyh*, adj. & n., astigmatic, -tism.
亂彈 *luahntarn*, v.i. & n., (Chin. opera) play with mixed and unorthodox combination of instruments.
亂騰 *luahnteng*, adj., upset, agitated, unsettled: 亂騰騰 in great confusion; also 亂亂騰騰 *--tengteng*.
亂子 *luahntz*, n., trouble.

虢 90S.70-2

guor.

N. (1) Name of an ancient feudal land. (2) A surname.

飜 90S.70-3

fan.

[Var. 翻 90S.50]

魏 90S.70-9

weih.

N. (1) A surname. (2) Name of several states and dynasties in history: esp. 北魏 North Weih (386–532 A.D.); 魏 of Three Kingdoms (220–239 A.D.); also an ancient state (453–225 B.C.); see Dynasties and Reigns, Appendix D.

Adj. (*weir*) (AC) u. f. 巍 lofty: 魏魏.

§90S.71 (ノ^{s}/弋)

舐 90S.71-9

shyh.

V.t. To lick with tongue: 舐破紙窗 to wet a paper window by licking (for purpose of peeping); 舐犢 (mother cow) licks the calf, hence 舐犢情深 deep mother love.

§90S.72 (ノ^{s}/心)

馝 90S.72-6

bih.

馝馞 *bihbor*, adj., bursting with fragrance (var. 苾勃).

§90S.80 (ノ^{s}/八)

頎 90S.80-3

chir.

Adj. (AC) tall, stalwart: 頎長, 頎頎 (AC) ditto.

頽 90S.80-3

tueir.

V.i. & adj. (1) Decay, -ing, -ed: 頽廢, 頽唐, 頽喪 *-feih*, *-tarng*, *-sahng*↓; 頽齡 declining years; 頽壞, 頽敗 decaying, decadent; 頽俗, 頽風 degenerate manners, bad custom; 頽運 declining luck, bad times. (2) Collapse: 泰山其頽乎 the Taishan will perhaps collapse (Confucius' premonition of his own death).

頽放 *tueirfahng*, adj., dissolute, leading life of abandon.

頽廢 *tueirfeih*, adj., (person) downhearted, dispirited; (institutions) fallen into disuse.

頽圮 *tueirpii*, adj., (of institutions, laws, morals) in decay.

頽然 *tueirrarn*, adj., self-effacing; downhearted, downcast.

頽喪 *tueirsahng*, adj., decadent; disconcerted, gloomy.

頽唐 *tueirtarng*, adj., disconsolate; decadent, out of luck.

§90S.81 (ノ^{s}/人)

欣 90S.81-9

shin.

[Cogn. 忻]

Adj. Happy, joyful.

Adv. (LL) happily: 欣賀 joyfully congratulate; 欣羨, 欣欣, 欣然 *-shiahn*, *-shin*, *-rarn*↓; 欣企 happily hope; 欣敬, 欣戴 pay glad homage to.

欣忭 *shinbiahr*, adj., (LL) happy, glad.

欣然 *shinrarn*, adv., gladly (consent, etc.).

欣賞 *shinshaang*, v. t., to appreciate, like (good writing), enjoy (the moon, garden, etc.).

欣羨 *shinshiahn*, v. i., to envy (s. o.'s luck, wealth); adore (person).

欣喜 *shinshii*, v. i. & adj., glad: 欣喜若狂 in ruptures, jubilantly happy.

欣欣 *shinshin*, adv., (1) happily (take to journey): 欣欣自得 proud and self-satisfied; (2) 欣欣向榮 (vegetation, business) prosper, thrive.

欣慰 *shinweih*, adj., glad to hear news, read your letter.

欣躍 *shinyueh*, v. i., dance for joy.

歃 90S.81-9

shah.

V.t. 歃血為盟 (AC) smear mouth, bell with blood in an oath.

歟 90S.81-9

yur (also unaccented).

Fin. part. Interrogtive, used in counter-questioning or argument, esp. 抑…歟 or is it . . .? sometimes in exclamation: 猗歟盛哉 how great it is!

§90S.82 (ノ^{s}/乂)

段 90S.82-4

duahn.

段 殷 毀 馥 彩

[Dist. 㲉 52S.82]

N. & n. adjunct. (1) A section (road, cable); a paragraph, section (writing); a short piece (pencil); a division (arguments): 一段故事 a story, episode; 階段 stage of development; 手段 tactic, skill of procedure. (2) Official grade or class in jiujitsu, chess. (3) A surname.

段落 *duahnluoh*, n., conclusion of a part: 這事已告一段落 this matter has come to an end for the time being.

殷 90S.82-4

yin.

N. Name of dynasty: 殷朝, 殷代 also called 商朝, 商代; 殷商時代 the Shang period.

Adj. (1) Thriving, prosperous, substantial: 殷富, 殷實 *-fuh, -shyr* ↓. (2) (AC) great, big; numerous. (3) (**yiin*) (AC) rumbling: 殷其雷 thunder is rumbling.

殷勤 *yinchirn*, (1) adj., attentive (to duty, guest, lover); (2) n., as in 獻殷勤 to court, pay attention to (a lady), do things to please (office chief).

殷富 *yinfuh*, adj., rich, wealthy, substantial (family).

殷紅 *yinhurng*, adj., deep red, blood red.

殷鑑 *yinjiahn*, n., (allu. to Yin Dyn.) warning, example of disaster from the past.

殷實 *yinshyr* (-'*shy*), adj., substantial, well-to-do: 殷實舖保 shop guarantee, guarantee by reliable shop.

殷殷 *yinyin*, adj., (AC) (1) numerous; (2) sad: 憂心殷殷 my heart is sad.

殷憂 *yinyou*, n., cause for worry, concern.

毀 90S.82-4

hueei.

V.t. (1) To destroy: 毀壞, 毀傷, 毀損 *huaih, -shang, -suun* ↓; 打毀 destroy by force; 折毀 tear down (house, etc.); 撕毀 tear (book, cloth); 毀容 to disfigure one's face (in sorrow); 自毀前程 destroy one's own career; 毀家紓難 offer all one has to help in charity. (2) To slander: 毀謗 *-bahng* ↓; 詆毀, 謗毀 to slander, besmirch one's good name; 毀譽 *-yuh* ↓; 毀約 to tear up or violate treaty or agreement.

毀謗 *hueeibahng*, n. & v. t., slander, libel.

毀詆 *hueirdii*, v. t., to slander.

毀害 *hueeihaih*, v. t. & n., to destroy or damage (reputation), injure (life, person).

毀壞 *hueeihuaih*, v. t., to destroy (reputation, house, furniture); p.p., be destroyed.

毀滅 *hueeimieh*, v. t., to wipe out (tradition, institution, etc.); v. i., to vanish, perish.

毀人爐 *hueeirern-lur*, phr., sinks of iniquity (gambling places, opium dens, etc.).

毀傷 *hueeishang*, v. t., to hurt, injure (hand, foot, reputation, etc.).

毀損 *hueir suun*, v. t., to damage (property, name).

毀譽 *hueei-yuh*, phr., praise and blame: 毀譽參半 mixed reception; 不計毀譽 disregard praise or criticism.

馥 90S.82-9

fuh.

Adj. Rich in fragrance.

馥馥 *fuhfuh*, adj., descriptive of fragrance, sweet-scented.

馥郁 *fuhyuh*, adj., fragrant.

§90S.91 (ノ^{S}/ノ)

彩 90S.91-9

tsaai.

N. (1) Grace in art, gracefulness: 文彩 graceful beauty in wood grains, literary embellishments; 詞彩 stylistic brilliance. (2) Brilliance, lighted effect: 光彩 luster (of jade, etc.); 雲彩 brilliance of clouds; 大放異彩 strange luminescence in the skies, also (fig.) flowering of talent. (3) Variegated colors: 五彩, 十彩 different brilliant colors; 色彩 color and brilliance of precious stones. (4) Lottery prize: 彩票, 彩頭 *-piauh, -tour* ↓; 摸彩, 抽彩 draw lottery; 中彩 win lottery. (5) Special effects in Chin. theater: 血彩, 火彩 special effects symbolizing blood, fire. (6) Color festoons (interch. 綵): 結彩 hang colored silk festoons; 紅彩 red festoons for happy occasions; 無精打彩 listless (futile efforts at gayety); 多彩多姿 versatile. (7) Dress rehearsal: 彩排, 彩唱 *-pair, -chahng* ↓.

Adj. Colorful, of many colors: 彩衣, 彩旗 dress, flag of colored patterns; 彩色 *-seh* ↓; 精彩 brilliant (acting, writing).

彩唱 *tsaaichahng*, n., dress rehearsal in Chin. opera.

彩氣(兒) *tsaaichi(-chieh'l)*, n., luck, as in winning lottery.

彩球 *tssaichiour*, n., ball of colored silk.

彩旦 *tsaaidahn*, n., (Chin. opera) name of young female role.

彩轎 *tsaaijiauh*, n., bridal sedan chair.

彩禮 *tsairlii*, n., bridegroom's wedding gifts to bride's family.

彩排 *tsaaipair*, n., dress rehearsal.

彩票 *tsaaipiauh*, n., lottery ticket, raffles.

彩色 *tsaaiseh*, adj. & n., colored: 彩色照片, 影片, 電視 color photograph, cinema, television.

彩頭 *tsaaitour* (-'*tou*), n., good luck (in business, gambling).

SECTION 91

§91.00 (丿/亅)

身 91.00

shen.

N. adjunct. 一身衣服 one suit of clothing.

N. (1) Material human body: 身體, 身材, 身軀 *-tii, -tsair, -chyu* ↓; 身心 mind and body (relaxed, etc.); 身首異處 beheaded; 一身 whole body, also, all one's life; 周身, 全身, 渾身 the whole body (aches, shivers, is feverish, etc.); 終身 all one's life; 起身, 動身 to start (journey); 不克分身 cannot get away from present duties; 轉身 in a moment; 賣身 sell the body (prostitution); 稱身 (dress) fits the body. (2) Body of thing: 樹身 tree trunk; 船身 the hull; 河身 bed of river. (3) Self, personal character, status: 修身 "cultivate self"—moral culture; 立身 form certain principles of living; 身正不怕影兒斜 stand straight and never mind if shadow inclines; 身敗名裂 personal reputation is ruined; 己身 one's own self; 身家, 身世, 身分 *-jia, -shyh, -fehn* ↓; 身輕言微 (or 人微言輕) in my humble position, my word does not carry much weight. (4) Pregnancy: 有身 be pregnant; 身懷六甲, 身孕 ditto. (5) Life, incarnation: 前身, 後身 previous incarnation, later incarnation; 身後 *-houh* ↓; 身故, 身亡, 身死, 身逝 die.

Adv. Personally, bodily: 身歷其境 personally went through situation; 身當其衝 personally bear the brunt; 如同身受 would regard it as a personal favor to me (if you helped him).

身邊 *shenbian*, adv., at hand: 身邊沒錢 have no money on hand; nearby: 身邊沒人 no one nearby—living alone; 身邊人 (coll.) a mistress, i.e., concubine who attends to comfort.

身長 *shen-charng*, n. & adj., height: 身長六尺 stand six feet high.

身軀 *shenchyu*, n., the physical body; physical stature.

身底下 *shen-dii'shia*, adv., (1) under the body; (2) present place of living: 身底下那處房 that house where I am living.

身段 *shenduahn*, n., stature, body figure (of man or woman) including movement.

身法 *shenfaa*, n., boxer's or wrestler's skill.

身分 *shenfehn*, n., (1) person's social status; official or legal status: 身分不明 person's legal identity not clarified; 身分證 *--jehng*, n., legal card of identity; (2) material of cloth: 這布的身分很好 material of this cloth is good.

身故 *shenguh*, v.i., (LL) to die, pass away.

身後 *shen-houh*, phr., after person's death: 身後事 funeral arrangements; 身後蕭條 without money or progeny after person's death.

身家 *shen-jia*, n., (1) family origin: 身家清白 come of a decent family; (2) 身家性命 man's life and family possessions.

身價 *shenjiah*, n., (1) person's legal or social status (see *-fehn* ↑); (2) price for buying a girl, esp. singsong girl.

身己 *shenjii*, adj., (MC) one's own: 身己上的事 one's own affairs.

身框兒 *shen'kuang'l*, n., height and frame of body.

身兒 *shen'l*, n., the body: 稱身兒, 合身兒 (dress) fits the body.

身量(兒) *shen'liang('l)*, n., stature (height) of body.

身上 *shen-shahng*, (1) n., state of feeling: 身上不快 do not feel well; (2) adv., at hand, on hand: 身上沒錢 have (carry) no money with me.

身手 *shenshoou*, n., boxer's, wrestler's skill.

身世 *shenshyh*, n., life experience: 身世孤單 had a lonely life.

身體 *shentii*, n., person's body, bodily health.

身材 *shentsair*, n., see *-duahn* ↑.

身子 *shentz*, n., (1) bodily health: 身子不快 do not feel well; (2) pregnancy: 懷着身子 be pregnant.

身孕 *shenyuhn*, adj., pregnant.

豸 91.00

jyh.

N. (1) A radical (for beasts like 豺 "wolf"). (2) (AC) an "insect without legs": 蟲豸 insects in gen.; (AC) used as word of abuse, like "vermin."

§91.01 (丿/小)

豕 91.01

chiarn.

[Pop. of 錢 81A.71]

架 91.01

jiah.

N. adjunct. A constructed thing: 一架飛機 an airplane; 兩架照相機 two cameras; 三架電風扇 three electric fans.

N. (1) A frame, a stand, a rack: 衣架 dress hanger, clothes rack; 書架 bookcase; 帽架 hatrack, hatstand; 花架 a stand for flowerpots; 曬衣架 clothesline; 架子 *-'tz*↓. (2) Structure, composition, scaffold: 肩架 (Chin. callig.) proper positioning of corner strokes; a person's carriage.

V.i. & t. (1) V.i., to quarrel, fight: 打架 engage in fisticuffs; 吵架 pick a quarrel (with s.o.). (2) V.t., to lay on a frame, put up: 架橋 make a bridge; 架磚 lay bricks; 架牆 build a wall; 架屋頂 put up a ceiling. (3) Support with hands or arms, hold firmly, prop up, take forcibly: 架着他 (的膀子) help him walk, hold him by the arm(s); 架穩, 架住 fasten or stack firmly; 架走 carry away by force; 綁架 kidnap. (4) Sustain, bear the brunt of: 架不住 cannot bear; 招架 ward off (blows). (5) Falsify, fabricate: 架空 *-kung*↓.

架空 *jiahkung*, v.i., fabricate, create out of nothing, conjure up.

架弄 *jiah'nung*, v.t., (1) to fool (s.o.) by pretending to applaud him; (2) wear (s.t.) ill-befitting oneself.

架票(兒) *jiahpiauh'(l)*, v.t., kidnap.

架式 *jiah'shy*, n., form, structure, general shape.

架訟 *jiahsuhng*, v.i., urge s.o. to file a legal suit against another person.

架子 *jiah'tz*, n., (1) a supporting framework of or for things; (2) arrogance, haughtiness, insolence: 擺架子 self-important, officious, conceited; 臭架子 disgusting airs of importance; 官僚架子 bureaucratic snobbishness; 架子太大 too snobbish, unapproachable.

架秧子 *jiah-yangtz*, phr., to turn the head of a young man by feeding his vanity.

臬 91.01

nieh.

N. Standard: 圭臬 a pattern, model, or guidepost.

臬司 *niehsy*, n., a provincial judge in the Yuarn, Mirng, and Manchu Dyns.

臬臺 *niehtair*, n., (＝臬司↑).

臬兀 *niehwuh*, adj., uneasy, perturbed, anxious (also wr. 鯢卼).

梟 91.01

shiau.

N. (1) An owl (also wr. 鴞 40S.50, q.v.). (2) Smuggler: 鹽梟 salt smuggler; 私梟, 梟匪 smuggler; 梟首, 梟示 *-shoou, -shyh*↓.

Adj. Fierce, brave, vicious, see 梟雄, 梟騎 *-shyurng, -jih*↓.

梟將 *shiaujiahng*, n., a valiant general.

梟騎 *shiaujih*, n., brave, dauntless cavalry.

梟獍 *shiaujihng*, n., a beast reputed to eat its own mother.

梟盧 *shiau-lur*, n., gambling with dice (梟 or 么 pr. *yau*, standing for figure "1," and 盧 for "6.")

梟首 *shiaushoou*, v.i., to behead: 梟首示衆 (梟示) expose out-off head to public view as a warning to rebels.

梟示 *shiaushyh*, v.i., ditto.

梟雄 *shiaushyurng*, adj., fierce, dauntless.

集 91.01

jir.

N. (1) A collection of writings: 經史子集 Confucian classics, history, philosophy, and literature; 集部 *-buh*↓; 文集 a collection of essays; 詩集 a collection of poems. (2) A market: 市集 a country fair; 趕集 go to a country fair, which usu. takes place at regular intervals.

V.t. Assemble, gather together: 聚集 collect in one place; 集合 *-her*, 集中 *-jung*, 集體 *-tii*, 集會 *-hueih*↓; 集思廣益 to benefit by mutual discussion; 集腋成裘 (of fund-raising for charities) small contributions are equally welcome (lit., "make a garment by piercing together little bits of fur"); 集大成 the lifework of one who comes last and benefits by the labors of his predecessors, e.g., Confucius; 集股 form a stock company; 集資 collect capital for a business enterprise; 集句 poems composed of quotations from anc. poets.

集部 *jirbuh*, n., literary works as distinguished from the classics, history, and philosophy.

集成 *jircherng*, n., a grand compendium.

集權 *jirchyuarn*, v.t., centralize; 中央集權 centralization (opp. 地方分權 decentralization).

集合 *jirher*, v.i., assemble together, muster.

集會 *jirhueih*, v.i., hold a meeting: 集會結社權 the right of assembly and association.

集錦 *jirjiin*, n., collection of choice items of art or quotations.

集中 *jirjung*, v.t., concentrate, assemble together; 集中營 concentration camp.

集聚 *jirjyuh*, v.t., assemble in one place.

集市 *jirshyh*, n., a market, a country fair held at regular intervals.

集體 *jirtii*, adj., done by many people, collective: 集體創作 work done by many participants; 集體精神 ésprit de corps; 集體領導 collective leadership; 集體農場 collective farm; 集體安全 collective security.

集團 *jirtuarn*, n., (1) a group of persons or nations: 共產集團 the Communist bloc of nations; (2) group action: 集團結婚 mass wedding.

集議 *jiryih*, v.i., hold a meeting to exchange views.

集郵 *jiryour*, v.i., collect postal stamps: 集郵家 a philatelist; 集郵會 a philatelic society.

集約 *jiryue*, adj., done intensively; 集約農業 intensive farming; 勞力集約 labor-intensive; 資本集約 capital-intensive.

槃 91.01

parn.

N. (AC) Wooden tub or tray.

Adj. (AC) big: 槃才 great talent.

槃礴 *parnbor*, adj., expansive, untrammeled (art, art work), var. of 旁礴.
槃旋 *parnshyuarn*, adj., twisting (var. of 盤旋).
槃停 *parntirng*, v.i., (LL) to loiter, delay proceeding.

槩 91.01

gaih.
[Interch. 概 10B.70]

榮 91.01

rurng.

N. (1) A surname. (2) Honor, glory (opp. 辱 dishonor, humiliation, shame): 榮辱 honor versus dishonor; 榮恥 glory versus shame. (3) Flowers of grass.

Adj. (1) Prosperous, thriving, flourishing: 繁榮 growing vigorously, prosperous; 欣欣向榮 full of life and vigor, flourishing. (2) Honorable, glorious: 榮名 a good name; 榮問 reputation; 榮譽 *-yuh* ↓; 榮耀 *-yauh* ↓; 榮宗耀祖 redound to the glory of one's ancestors; 光榮 glorious, honorable; 引以爲榮 take it as a great honor; 榮幸 *-shihng* ↓; 殊榮 an extraordinary honor; 榮賜 rewards for distinguished services rendered; 榮典 honors conferred on individuals for outstanding contributions to the country; 榮歸 glorious homecoming, esp. of officials after retirement; 榮軍 soldiers deserving well of their country; 榮民 *-mirn* ↓.

Adv. Expressing congratulations: 榮升, 榮任, 榮調, 榮行, 榮旋 (best wishes for) your promotion, appointment, reassignment, departure, return.

榮哀錄 *rurngai-luh*, n., a collection of commemorative writings in honor of the deceased.
榮寵 *rurngchuung*, n., imperial favors shown to ministers of state; honors in gen.
榮光 *rurngguang*, n., (1) brilliance, splendor; (2) glory.
榮華 *rurnghuar*, (1) n., (of officials) holding of high positions in government: 榮華富貴 "glory, honor, and riches"; (2) adj., radiant with health.
榮枯 *rurng-ku*, n., (1) (of plants) growth and decay; (2) prosperity and adversity.
榮蘭 *rurnglarn*, n., (bot.) *Pandanus odoratissimus* (also 露兒樹).
榮民 *rurng-mirn*, n., war veterans; disabled soldiers.
榮幸 *rurngshihng*, adj., honored, fortunate; n., (it is an) honor.
榮侍 *rurng-shyh*, v.i., (LL) have both grandfather and father alive.
榮耀 *rurngyauh*, n., glory.
榮譽 *rurngyuh*, n., honor, renown, good name.

禦 91.01

yuh.

V.t. To resist (enemy), defy, defend against: 禦敵 resist enemy; 禦侮 resist enemy threats, etc.; 抵禦 to resist; 防禦 to defend (place, country), also provide against, prevent (thieves, etc.); 禦寒 provide against cold.

縈 91.01

yirng.

V.t. To entangle, coil around.

縈懷 *yirng-huair*, phr., to linger in one's heart.
縈廻 *yirnghueir*, v.i., to linger, swirl around in memory.
縈繞 *yirngrauh*, v.t., (of memories) to linger around.

§91.02 (丿/⺊)

泉 91.02

chyuarn.

N. (1) A spring (of water): 泉源, 泉水 *-yuarn, -shueei* ↓; 溫泉 hot springs; 噴泉 geyser. (2) The underground as symbolic of burial: 黃泉 under the burial ground; 泉下 *-shiah* ↓. (3) Coins (=錢): 古泉, 泉布 ancient coins (for collectors); 泉幣 *-bih* ↓.

泉幣 *chyuarnbih*, n., ancient coins (metal pieces in different shapes), also 泉布.
泉布 *chyuarnbuh*, n., see *-bih* ↑.
泉地 *chyuarndih*, n., oasis.
泉路 *chyuarnluh*, n., the nether world.
泉脈 *chyuarnmoh*, n., underground river.
泉壤 *chyuarnraang*, n., burial ground.

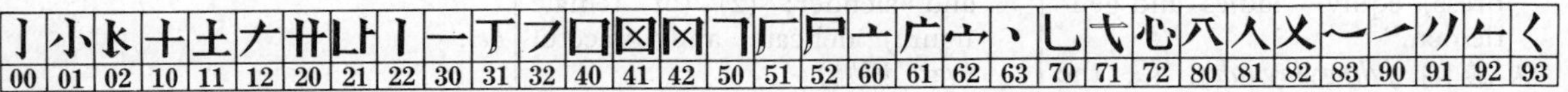

丨 小 ⺊ 十 土 ナ 廾 ㄴ 丨 一 丁 フ 口 図 冈 ㇆ 厂 尸 亠 广 宀 丶 乚 弋 心 八 人 乂 𠂉 一 丿 𠂊 く
00 01 02 10 11 12 20 21 22 30 31 32 40 41 42 50 51 52 60 61 62 63 70 71 72 80 81 82 83 90 91 92 93

泉下 *shyuarnshiah*, n., in the graveyard, (fig.) dwelling place of the dead (＝黃泉之下).

泉水 *chyuarn-shueei*, n., spring, spring water.

泉石 *chyuarn shyr*, phr., rocks and springs, as place for enjoying nature: 泉石之樂.

泉臺 *chyuarn-tair*, n., (LL) graveyard.

泉眼 *chyuarn'yan*, n., point in ground from which spring water issues.

泉源 *chyuarnyuarn*, n., springs, source of water.

衆 91.02

juhng.

[Var. 衆, 眾, pop. 众]

N. The multitudes: 民衆 the people, multitudes; 大衆 the masses; 觀衆, 聽衆 the audience; 公衆 the public; 示衆 exhibit (criminal) in disgrace to the public; 得衆, 失衆 win, lose, the public support.

Adj. (1) Of the people, the public: 衆怒難犯 an aroused public is difficult to tackle with; 衆志成城 a united people is like a city defense; 衆口爍金 a public clamor can melt metals; 衆擎易舉 what is supported by the people is easily accomplished; 衆望所歸 the people's hope (confidence) is centered on (one person); 衆矢之的 target of public criticism. (2) Numerous; 衆多 *-duo*↓; 衆寡 *-guaa*↓; 衆生 *-sheng*↓.

衆多 *juhngduo*, adj., numerous.

衆寡 *juhng-guaa*, phr., the comparative difference in numbers ("many and few"): 衆寡不敵 the few cannot fight the many.

衆生 *juhngsheng*, n., (Budd.) the myriad living things; (coll. & abusive) beast (＝畜[A]牲 60.41).

衆位 *juhngweih*, n., (in public address) equiv. "ladies and gentlemen."

衆議院 *juhngyihyuahn*, n., the House of Representatives; 衆議員 a congressman; a member of parliament.

滎 91.02

shirng (also *yirng*).

N. 滎陽 a county name in Honan.

袋 91.02

daih.

N. *(-tz)* Bag, sack, pocket: 衣袋, 口袋 pocket; 布袋, 蔴袋 calico, hemp, sack; 紙袋 paper bag; 錢袋 wallet; 煙袋 tobacco pouch.

袋鼠 *daihshuu*, n., the kangaroo.

袈 91.02

jia.

袈裟 *jiasha*, n., cassocks.

裊 91.02

niaau.

Adj. Curling upward; delicate and graceful.

裊裊 *niaurniaau*, adj., (1) curling up in the air like smoke: 香煙裊裊; (2) (interch. 嫋嫋) ditto; waving in the wind; (3) (of female figure) delicate and graceful: 裊裊婷婷, see 嫋 93A.50.

裊娜 *niaurnuoo*, adj., (1) delicate and slender; (2) (of female figure) delicate and graceful (var. 嫋娜).

§91.10 (ノ/十)

卆 91.10

tzur.

[Pop. of 卒 60.10]

皁 91.10

tzauh.

[Common var. 皂]

N. (1) Soap: 肥皁 ditto; 香皁 perfumed soap; 藥皁 carbolic soap; 皁粉 washing soda, detergent powder. (2) A menial servant: 皁隸 (AC) office boys, attendants. (3) A manger: 皁櫪 a stable; 皁棧 ditto.

Adj. Black: 皁白 *-bair*↓.

皁白 *tzauh-bair*, n. & adj., black and white, (fig.) right and wrong.

皁斗 *tzauh-doou*, n., the shell of an acorn.

皁纛 *tzauh-dur*, n., an army flag.

皁礬 *tzauh-farn*, n., sulphate of iron.

皁針 *tzauhjen*, n., see *-tsyh*↓.

皁莢 *tzauh-jiar*, n., (bot.) the pods of soap bean tree, *Gleditschia japonica.*

皁鞋 *tzauhshier*, n., a kind of slippers.

皁靴 *tzauhshyue*, n., (1) riding boots; (2) formerly, black boots as part of formal dress.

皁刺 *tzauhtsyh*, n., thorns on soap bean tree (see *-jiar*↑) used in Chin. medicine (also called 皁針).

卑 91.10

bei.

V.t. Disregard: 卑之無甚高論 regard it as beneath discussion; 卑躬屈節 to humble, humiliate oneself in serving master; 自卑 self-effacing; 自卑感 inferiority complex.

Adj. (1) Low, humble, inferior, of low rank: 卑官, 卑職 (court.) terms used by minor official in self-reference in addressing superiors, like "your humble servant"; 卑辭厚禮 with humble words and rich gifts, with unctuous subservience; 卑卑不足道 phr., beneath discussion or mention; 謙△卑, see 60A.22 humble. (2) Of lower generation: 比他卑一輩 is one generation lower (opp. 高一輩 higher); 卑親屬 relatives of younger generation.

卑鄙 *beibii*, n., of low character, mean; underhand, dishonorable (method, character): 卑鄙手段 hanky-panky tactics.
卑薄 *beibor*, n., bad, unproductive (land).
卑行 *bai-harng*, n., of lower generation (nephews, etc.).
卑賤 *beijiahn*., adj., lowly, menial (work, people).
卑劣 *beilyueh*, adj., bad, inferior in quality; dishonorable, mean (conduct).
卑讓 *bei-rahng*, adj., humble, courteous.
卑人 *bei-rern*, n., (MC) your humble servant.
卑下 *beishiah*, adj., low, lowly.
卑濕 *beishy*, adj., (of land, house) low and damp.
卑田院 *beitiarn yuahn*, n., institution for the poor (also wr. 悲田院).
卑污 *beiwu*, adj., mean, filthy, dishonorable (ways, conduct, character).

阜 91.10

fuh.

N. A mound; character for radical 阝 wr. on left (防); cf. 阝 wr. on right (邦), see 邑 40.70.

Adj. Abundant, big, wealthy: 物阜民康 goods overflow and the people are happy.

阜螽 *fuhjung*, n., (AC) grasshoppers.

隼 91.10

juun.

N. A small eagle.

皐 91.10

gau.

[Pop. of 臯]

N. (1) A marsh, the banks of a marsh: 江皐 a river bank. (2) A surname.

皐比 *gaubii*, n., (1) a tiger's skin; (2) (MC) a seat made of tiger's skin on which a schoolteacher sat, hence (LL) teacher's chair.
皐門 *gaumern*, n., (AC) the outermost one of five palace gates.

辠 91.10

tzueih.

[Anc. var. of 罪 41.22]

犖 91.10

luoh.

N. A brindled ox.

Adj. (1) Brindled in color. (2) Eminent, outstanding: 卓犖不羣 ditto; 犖犖大者 the most essential points.

鞶 91.10

parn.

N. Big leather belt.

聳 91.10

suung.

V.t. (1) To shock, see 聳動, 聳聽 *-duhng*, *-ting*↓. (2) To rise straight up: 高聳, 聳起 shoot high up (as skyscraper). (3) U.f. 悚 22A.01.

聳動 *suungduhng* (-'*dung*), v.t., to ruffle, shock, disturb the mind.
聳肩 *suung-jian*, v.i., to shrug shoulders.
聳懼 *suungjyuh*, adj., shocked (= 悚懼).
聳聽 *suung-ting*, phr., as in 危言聳聽 a startling statement creates a sensation.

§91.11 (丿/土)

皇 91.11

huarng.

N. (1) Emperor: 皇帝 *-dih*, 皇上 *-shahng*↓; 皇室 the imperial house; 皇儲 the crown prince;

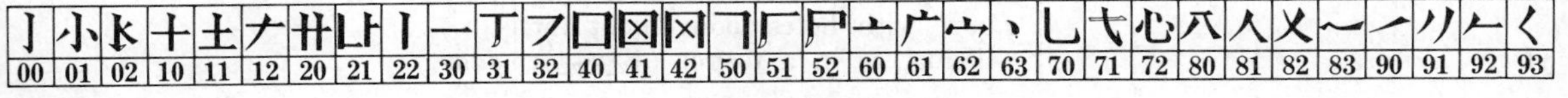

太上皇 emperor's father. (2) A surname.

Adj. (1) Honorific word for deceased ancestor used chiefly on tablets, tombstones: 皇考 my late illustrious father; 皇妣 my late illustrious mother. (2) Great, magnificent: (冠冕) 堂皇 impressive-looking. (3) Flurried, in a flutter: 倉皇, 皇皇 ditto (cf. 惶 22A.11).

皇帝 *huarngdih*, n., the emperor.
皇后 *huarnghouh*, n., empress.
皇皇 *huarnghuarng*, adj. & adv., (1) magnificent: 堂堂皇皇 open, -ly, in open view; (2) agitated: 倉倉皇皇 in a great flurry.
皇上 *huarngshahng*, n., Your Majesty; His Majesty.

堡 91.11

baau (also *puh*).

N. Fortress, small fort, walled village: 城堡 fortifications on city wall; 碉△堡 31B.42.

堡壘 *baurleei*, n., earthwork for defense; fortress: (lit. & fig.) 精神堡壘 spiritual fortress.

墾 91.11

keen.

V.t. To cultivate (land): 墾田 cultivate or till farm; 開墾 to colonize wild country.

墾荒 *keenhuang*, v.i., to reclaim wasteland.
墾殖 *keenjyr*, v. t., to cultivate, grow trees, vegetables.

塋 91.11

yirng.

N. Grave, cemetery: 塋地 ditto.

塋墳 *yirngfern*, n., a grave.
塋穴 *yirngshyuer*, n., ditto.

瑩 91.11

yirng.

N. Gem luster.

Adj. Lustrous: 晶瑩, 瑩潤 ditto; 瑩潔 pure and lustrous.

§91.20 (ノ/卄)

幷 91.20

bihng.

[Pop. 并; cogn. 並; interch 併]

N. Place name in 幷州 (*bing* or *bihng*): 幷州剪刀 famous scissors produced at Bingjou, also (fig.) highly efficient person.

V.t. To annex: 兼幷, 幷吞 annex and absorb (neighboring country), more commonly wr. 併; 幷日而食 (LL) to eat on alternate days.

鼻 91.20

bir.

N. (1) Usu. 鼻子 *-tz*↓ the nose: 大鼻子 big-nosed person, (coll.) Russians; 塌鼻子 snub-nosed person; 糟鼻子, 酒鼻鼻子, 紅糟鼻子 bottle-nosed; 牛鼻子, 牛鼻子老道 (facet.) old Taoist priest; 鷹鼻 hawk-nosed. (2) 鼻兒 *-'l*: the raised part of a cover or seal, usu. with holes, convenient for lifting, as in a teapot (茶壺兒); eye of needle 針鼻兒.

鼻腔 *birchiang*, n., nasal cavity; nasal twang.
鼻峯 *birfeng*, n., nasal bridge.
鼻加答兒 *birgadar'l*, n., nasal catarrh.
鼻骨 *birguu*, n., nasal bone.
鼻尖 *birjian*, n., the tip of nose.
鼻準 *birjuun*, n., nasal bridge.
鼻孔 *birkung*, n., the nose; the nostrils: 一鼻孔出氣 (two persons) echo one another's opinion.
鼻梁 *birliarng*, n., bridge of nose.
鼻衄 *birniouh*, n., (med.) nasal hemorrhage, epistaxis.
鼻牛兒 *birniour'l*, n., nose dirt, hardened mucus in nostrils.
鼻息 *birshir*, n., (1) breath: 仰人鼻息 phr., depend upon another's pleasure; (2) snore: 鼻息如雷 snore like thunder.
鼻涕 *birtih*, n., nasal discharge, (coll. *bir'ding*): 鼻涕嘎吧兒 *--gaba'l*, caked nasal discharge outside nostrils; 鼻涕眼淚的 adv., weeping and sniffling.
鼻頭 *birtour*, n., the nose.
鼻子 *birtz*, n., the nose; see N. 1↑.
鼻祖 *birtzuu*, n., the earliest ancestor; (fig.) the first person to do s.t., earliest founder.
鼻烟 *biryan*, n., snuff; 鼻烟壺 *--hur*, n., snuff bottle.
鼻咽喉 *biryanhouh*, n., (physiol.) nasopharynx.

§91.21 (ノ/乚)

岱 91.21

daih.

N. Var. for 泰山 Taishan.

島 91.21

daau.

[Anc. var. of 㿿 91.50]

罃 91.21

ying.

N. (AC) a long-necked, small-mouthed jar.

§91.22 (丿/丨)

彳 91.22

chyh.

彳亍 *chyhchuh*, (1) v.i., to walk (彳 explained as the left foot, and 亍 as the right—the two components forming 行 to walk); (2) n., symbol for "ch" before *a, e, o, u* sounds (not before *i, yu*) in Chin. phonetic alphabet; (3) a radical: as in 行, 街, index No. 91B.

片 91.22

piahn.

N. adjunct. Descriptive of things on a stretch, such as clouds, light, pervasive atmosphere: 一片好話 a stretch of sincere talk; 一片彩雲, 月亮 a stretch of colored clouds, moonlight; 一片時間, 時光 a stretch of time; 一片好意, 喜氣, 淒凉 an atmosphere of goodwill, hilarity, solitude, loneliness.

N. (1) Card, slice: oft. 片兒 *piah'l*, a slice: 切成一片一片兒 cut into slices; 卡片 card; 片目 card catalogue; 名片 name card, also 片子; 明信片 postcard; 雞片, 肉片, 魚片 chicken, pork, fish served in slices; 雪片 snowflakes; 花片 flower petals; 藥片 tablet of medicine. (2) Film: 膠片, 底片 photographic film; 相片 photograph; 影片 movie; 片名 name of movie; 片商 movie distributor; 片頭 the first part of movie, giving name of producer, etc., see 片子 *-tz* ↓.

Adj. Small in amount, small, thin: 片時 a short moment; 少留片刻 please remain for a little while; 片言折獄, 解紛 settle a case, dispute, with just a few words; 片言九鼎 (LL) a word from you carries great weight; 片紙隻字 just a short note, a scrap; 殺得片甲不留 completely destroy enemy, "not a piece of armor intact"; 片善 just a little good side (of character).

片段 *piahn-duahn*, n., incomplete section (taken out of context), or part.

片刻 *piahnkeh*, n., a short moment.

片兒湯 *piahn'l tang*, n., soup of flat noodles.

片面 *piahnmiahn*, adj., one-sided (talk).

片時 *piahnshyr*, n., a short moment.

片子 *piahn'tz*, n., movie film.

帛 91.22

bor.

N. (1) Silks: 衣帛 to dress in silks; 玉帛 (AC) jades and silks, oft. used as presents. (2) A surname.

§91.30 (丿/一)

血 91.30

shyueh (more common in litr. phrr.); **shiee* (more common in coll. phrr.).

N. Blood: 血脈, 血球, 血管, etc., *-moh, -chiour, -guaan* ↓; 熱血男兒 red-blooded patriots, (refers to idealism, enthusiasm); see 血氣, 血性 *-chih, -shihng* ↓; 冷血動物 cold-blooded animal, (fig.) an apathetic person; 浴血苦戰 a bloody battle, "bathed in blood"; 吸血鬼 blood-sucking vampire; 貧血症 anemia; 吐血 throw up blood; 血汗 blood and sweat: 血汗錢 hard-earned money, money earned with blood and sweat; 血淚 tears of blood; 含血噴人, 血口噴人 make unfounded, scurrilous attacks upon person; 流血標杵 (battlefield) strewn with blood, descriptive of a blood bath in war.

Adj. (1) Bloody color: 血紅. (2) Bloody: 血史 story of bloody battles; 血戰 bloody battle; 血淋淋, 血淥淥 血忽淋剌 dripping with blood, describing a bloody sight. (3) Related in blood: 血親, 血統, 血族 *-chin, -tuung, -tzur* ↓.

血案 *shyueh-ahn*, n., a murder case.

血本 *shyuehbeen*, n., capital investment which represents lifetime saving.

血崩 *shyuehbeng*, n., menorrhagia of the uterus.

血餅 *shyuehbiing*, n., cruor, (coagulated) blood clot.

血泊 *shyueh-bor*, phr., a pool of blood.

血腸 **shiee-charng*, n., blood sausage (of sheep intestines stuffed with blood).

血忱 *shyuehchern*, n., sincerity

from the heart.

血誠 *shyuehcherng*, n., ditto.

血氣 *shyuehchih*, n., animal spirits, vigor, oft. equiv. Eng. "guts"—courage, enthusiasm: 凡有血氣之人 all who have feeling (must feel aroused by the atrocities, etc.); 凡有血氣者莫不尊親 all who are endowed with breath ("blood") respect their parents; see *-shihng*↓; 血氣之勇 brute courage, as dist. moral courage; 血氣所使 slave to animal nature; 血氣未定 physical vigors of young people; 血氣虛弱 weak constitution, gen. debility.

血親 *shyuehchin*, n., blood kin.

血清 *shyuehching*, n., blood serum.

血球 *shyuehchiour*, n., blood corpuscles: 紅血球, 白血球 red, white corpuscles.

血栓症 *shyuehchuarn jehng*, n., thrombosis.

血赤素 *shyuehchyr-suh*, n., hemoglobin.

血道子 **shieedauh'tz*, n., scars of cuts on skin.

血管 *shyuehguaan*, n., blood vessels; arteries (動脈) and veins (靜脈); 血管硬化 arteriosclerosis.

血蠱 *shyueh-guu*, n., (Chin. med.) swelling in belly, described as due to clotting of blood from a fall or injury.

血海 *shyueh-haai*, n., (1) (Chin. med.) name of arterial focus point (經穴) on inner thigh; (2) 血海冤仇 a blood feud.

血汗 *shyueh-hahn*, n., hard toil (of sweat and blood).

血忽淋剌 *shyuehhulinla*, adj., shockingly bloody (appearance).

血花 *shyueh-hua*, n., sprays of spurting blood.

血活 **shieehuor*, adj., (coll.) frighteningly serious: 這點小事, 讓你說得那麼血活 you make this trifle sound terribly serious.

血紅 *shyueh-hurng*, adj., blood-red color.

血跡 *shyueh-ji*, n., blood stains.

血痂 *shyueh-jia*, n., a scab, clot of blood formed on wounds.

血漿 *shyuehjiang*, n., (blood) plasma.

血竭 *shyuehjier*, n., resin of certain palms, used as an herb (looking like "dried blood").

血忌 *shyueh-jih*, n., days when eating of meat or slaughter of animals is forbidden.

血晶 *shyuehjihng*, n., (min.) blood-red quartz crystal.

血櫧 *shyeh-ju*, n., the bitter acorn oak, *Quercus acuta.*

血痔 *shyueh-jyh*, n., bleeding piles.

血塊 *shyueh-kuaih*, n., coagulated blood clot; thrombus; 血塊子 (**shiee-*) blood clot.

血虧 *shyuehkuei*, n., anemia.

血庫 *shyueh-kuh*, n., blood bank.

血兒 **shiee'l*, n., commonly refers to blood oozing from surface cut.

血淚 **shiee-leih* (*shyueh-*), phr., blood and tears (from utter distress).

血料 **shieeliauh*, n., a paint mixture containing animal blood.

血淋 *shyuehlirn*, n., gonorrhea with traces of blood.

血輪 *shyuehlurn*, n., see *-chiour*↑.

血迷 *shyueh-mir*, n., a mother's swooning off due to excessive loss of blood during child delivery.

血脈 *shyuehmoh*, n., (1) blood circulation: 血脈流通; (2) the blood pulse; (3) blood relationship, see *-tuung*↓.

血沫子 **shiee-mohtz*, n., froth formed on stored blood.

血盆 *shyueh-pern*, n., (coll.) a big mouth, as 血盆的大口.

血珀 *shyueh-poh*, n., dark red amber.

血人兒 **shiee-re'l*, n., a person covered all over with blood.

血刃 *shyueh-rehn*, n., blood-stained knife.

血色 *shyueh-seh*, adj., blood-red color (血色兒 **shiershaa'l*); 血色素 haemoglobin.

血牲 *shyuehsheng*, n., animal sacrifice.

血小板 *shyueh-shiaur-baan*, n., blood platelets or thrombocyte.

血性 *shyuehshihng*, n., animal spirits, physical courage, guts.

血心 *shieh-shin*, n., sincerity of heart.

血腥氣 *shyuehshing-chih*, n., smell of fresh blood.

血型 *shyuehshirng*, n., blood type, blood group (considered in transfusion).

血行器 *shyuehshirng-chih*, n., blood circulatory system.

血書 *shyueh-shu*, n., letter written in blood (in some dramatic crisis).

血水 **shiershueei*, n., the blood as a fluid; water mixed with blood.

血屬 *shyuehshuu*, n., blood relative.

血食 *shyueh-shyr*, n., eating of sacrificial meat.

血虛 *shyuehshyu*, n., anemia.

血尿 *shyuehsuei*, n., blood in urine.

血絲(兒) **shieesy*(*-se'l*), n., fine capillaries; blood fibers.

血嗣 *shyuehsyh*, n., blood descendant.

血湯子 **shieetangtz*, n., see ⌈*-shueei*↑.

血統 *shyuehtuung*, n., blood relationship, consanguinity: 血統主義 *jus sanguinis*, law of certain countries which recognizes child's citizenship by its parents', irrespective of where it is born (opp. 屬地主義 *jus soli*).

血債 *shyueh-tzaih*, n., blood debt, a debt to be settled by blood.

血族 *shyuehtzur*, n., consanguine relation.

血污 *shyueh-wu*, n., blood stains.

血壓 *shyuehya*, n., blood pressure.

血癌 *shyueh-yarn*, n., leukemia.

血液 *shyuehyeh*, n., blood: 血液循環 blood circulation; 血液纖維素 fibrin, which helps coagulation of blood when exposed to air.

血印 **shieeyihn*, n., blood stains (on clothing, etc.).

血友病 *shyuehyoou-bihng*, n., hemophilia.

血緣 *shyueeh-yuarn*, n., see *-tuung*↑.

血玉髓 *shyuehyuhsueei*, n., (min). bloodstone.

血暈 **shieeyuhn*, n., see *-mir*↑.

血餘 *shyueh-yur*, n., (Chin. med.) human hair (used as medicine).

盎 90.30

ahng.

N. (1) A wine cup, a vessel. (2)

An ounce: 盎斯 *-sy*↓.

Adj. (1) (AC) standing up or out. (2) Vigorous, full of life: 盎然 *-rarn*↓.

盎盎 *ahngahng*, adj., (LL) vigorous, full of life.
盎然 *ahngrarn*, adj., (of portrait, description) full of life, interesting, alive.
盎斯 *ahngsy*, n., (translit.) an ounce.

暨 91.30

jih.

N. (1) Confines: 靡暨 (＝無旣) without limit; 大德無暨 (LL) your kindness (generosity) knows no bounds. (2) A surname.

Conj. And: 某某先生暨夫人 Mr. and Mrs. So and so.

暨今 *jihjin*, phr., (LL) up to the present, till now (＝至今).

盤 91.30

parn.
[Dist. 槃, 磐]

N. adjunct. 一盤生意 a business deal; 一盤棋 a game of chess.

N. A tray, plate, dish: 一盤菜 a dish at table; 冷盤, 涼盤 *hors d'oeuvres*; 拚盤 mixed *hors d'oeuvres*; usu. 盤子 *-tz*↓ or 盤兒 *par'l*: 臉盤兒 a person's face contour; anc. tub (cogn. modn. 盆); a plate-like object, like 棋ᐞ盤 chessboard, 10B.80; 算ᐞ盤 abacus, 92A.20; 打算盤 calculate cost and profit. (2) Market prices, quotations on stock market: 開盤, 收盤 opening, closing quotations. (3) A surname.

V.t. (1) To investigate: 盤賬 audit accounts; 盤庫, 盤貨 take inventory of stockpiles, goods; to cross-examine: 盤問, 盤究 *-wehn*, *-jiouh*↓. (2) To sell out shop: 盤店, 出盤 offer to sell. (3) To grind jade. (4) To cross, entwine, twist about: 盤膝, 盤腿兒 to cross legs; 盤起髮辮 coil up queue on the head; 盤根錯節 (of trees) with twisting roots and intercrossing branches.

盤剝 *parnbor*[1], v.t., practice usury; otherwise rob (person) of his property.
盤駁 *parnbor*[2], v.i. & t., cross-examine repeatedly.
盤礴 *parnbor*[3], adj., expansive, encompassing in space (also 旁ᐞ礴 see 60.50).
盤纏 *parn'chan*, n., money for travelling expenses.
盤查 *parnchar*, v.t., examine thoroughly (luggage at customs).
盤錢 *parnchiarn*, n., ditto.
盤川 *parnchuan*, n., see *-feih*↓.
盤曲 *parnchyu*, v.i. & adj., winding, twisting, having many turns (of roads).
盤費 *parnfeih*, n., money for travelling expenses; daily expenses.
盤槓子 *parn-gahngtz*, n., physical exercise at crossbars.
盤古 *Parnguu*[1], n., (Chin. myth.) person who created the universe.
盤骨 *parn-guu*[2], n., pelvis, also (骨盤).
盤桓 *parnhuarn*, v.i., loiter, linger around.
盤互 *parnhuh*, adj., crossing and recrossing.
盤獲 *parnhuoh*, v.t., find (smuggled goods, booty) after search.
盤結 *parnjier*, adj., intertwining (of branches).
盤究 *parnjiouh*, v.t., make thorough investigation.
盤轉 *parnjuaan*., v.i. & t., to pan.
盤踞 *parnjyuh*, v.t., occupy (要津 high posts, strategic posts).
盤弄 *parnluhng*, v.t., (＝撥弄), stir up trouble.
盤龍癖 *parnlurngpii*, n., gambling habit (allu. to anc. gambler, Liu Parnlurng).
盤尼西林 *parnnirshilirn*, n., (translit.) penicillin.
盤繞 *parnraur*, v.i. & t., surround, loiter around (person); fill (heart) with memories; fill (room) with incense, smoke.
盤香 *parnshiang*, n., incense coils.
盤旋 *parnshyuarn*, n. & v.i. & t., circle around (of roads); play diplomacy with person.
盤算 *parn'suan*, v.i., calculate.
盤飧 *parnsun*, n., see *-tsan*↓.
盤餐 *parntsan*, n., picnic; blue plate type of dinner.
盤陀 *parntuor*, (1) n., (AC) (poet.) saddle; (2) adj., rugged (of rocks).
盤子 *parntz*, n., (1) A plate, dinner plate; (2) vessel for grinding jade; (3) tips at singsong houses.
盤資 *parntzy*, n., see *-feih*↑.
盤問 *parnwehn*, v.t., interrogate (suspects, etc.).
盤渦 *parnwo*, n., whirlpool.
盤鴉 *parnya*, n., woman's coiled hairdo.
盤牙 *parnyar*, n., cogs on wheel.
盤鬱 *parnyuh*, adj., (of foliage) heavy and intertwining.
盤運 *parnyuhn*, n. & v.t., ship (goods).

§ 91.40 (ノ/口)

售 91.40

shouh.

V.i. & t. (1) To sell: 售貨 sell goods; 售出, 出售 to sell (land, house, goods); 零售 sell in retail; 廉售 sell at reduced price. (2) To sell (idea, plan) as in Eng.: 其

計不售 one's plan was not adopted; 得售 was adopted.

售價 *shouhjiah*, n., selling price.
售賣 *shouhmaih*, v.t., to sell; 售賣處 sales department, box office.
售品所 *shouhpirn-suoo*, n., sales counter or shop.

營 91.40

yirng.

N. (1) (Mil.) a battalion: 騎兵營 cavalry battalion; 營長 *-jaang* ↓. (2) Barracks, camp, encampment, army headquarters: 大本營 (mil.) general headquarters; 紮營 to encamp, pitch tent; 宿營 to camp out; 偷營 make surprise attack on enemy camp; 拔營 decamp; 營幕 *-muh* ↓; 夏令營 summer camp; 訓練營 training camp; 集中營 concentration camp.

V.t. (1) To run a business, to plan and manage: 經營 to run business; 營業 *-yeh* ↓; 營生, 營利, 營私 *-sheng, -lih, -sy* ↓; 國營, 民營 (business) run by state, by municipal government, by private capital. (2) To plan, build, construct: 營建, 營造 *-jiahn, -tzauh* ↓. (3) To nourish: 營養 *-yaang* ↓. (4) (AC, u.f. 縈) to entangle. (5) To seek measures, to try: 營救 *-jiouh* ↓; 營利 *-lih* ↓; 營福 seek good luck; 營餬 seek a living; 營療 seek cure.

Adj. U.f. 縈 perplexed.

營表 *yirngbiaau*, n., (AC) boundary lines drawn before construction.
營求 *yirngchiour*, v.t., (AC) to seek (help).
營奠 *yirngdiahn*, v.i., to offer sacrifices.
營地 *yirngdih*, n., encampment, camp ground.
營販 *yirngfahn*, v.i., to be pedlar; v.t., to peddle (food, etc.).
營房 *yirng-farng* (-'fang), n., a barracks.
營副 *yirngfuh*, n., second in command of a battalion.
營混子 *yirng-huhntz*, n., a veteran in soldiering of the ragged, undesirable type; an army ragamuffin.
營火 *yirnghuoo*, n., campfire: 營火會 a campfire (party).
營長 *yirngjaang*, n., battalion commander, a major.
營齋 *yirng-jai*, phr., to give feast to monks and have mass said for the departed.
營建 *yirngjiahn*, v.t., to construct (building).
營妓 *yirngjih*, n., whores supplied by the army.
營救 *yirngjiouh*, v.i., to try to rescue (man in water, etc.).
營治 *yirngjyh*, v.t., to build, construct.
營利 *yirng-lih*, v.i., to make money, to work for profit, see *-sy* ↓.
營亂 *yirngluahn*, adj., (AC, u.f. 熒亂) perplexing, -ed.
營幕 *yirngmuh*, n., a tent.
營盤 *yirngparn* (-'pan), n., a barracks; tent.
營繕 *yirngshahn*, v.i., (LL) to construct (buildings).
營生 *yirngsheng*, (1) v.i., to make a living; (2) n., a profession; 營生兒 business: 整天沒營生兒做 have no business to do the whole day.
營私 *yirngsy*, v.t., to make private profits: 營私舞弊 be corrupt in politics.
營田 *yirng-tiarn*, phr., (1) to till the farm; (2) to create settlement for unemployed.
營子 *yirngtz*, n., (Mongolian) village, or encampment.
營葬 *yirngtzahng*, v.i., to provide for proper burial; to manage funeral.
營造 *yirngtzauh*, v.i., to construct buildings: 營造廠 *--chaang*, n., firm for constructing buildings, architects; 營造尺 standard foot of Manchu Dyn.
營衞 *yirngweih*, n., nourishment, nutrition.
營養 *yirngyaang*, n., nutrition: 營養不足 malnutrition.
營業 *yirngyeh*, (1) v.i., to run business; (2) n., a business: 營業稅 business tax.
營營 *yirngyirng*, adj., hustling and bustling about.

磐 91.40

parn.

N. A big rock, foundation stone (磐石之安 safe as a rock).

磐礴 *parnbor*, adj., see 盤^礴 91.30.
磐牙 *parnyar*, adj., see 盤^牙 91.30.

諐 91.40

chian.

[Anc. var. of 愆 91.72]

§91.41 (ノ/図)

白 91.41

bair (sp. pr. *bair*; re. pr. **bor*; in certain phrr. marked ***bair*, or ***bor*, alternate pr. also used.)

N. (1) A surname. (2) The spoken parts of opera, such as dialogue: 說白, 道白 also 白口(兒) *-kou(e'l)* ↓; 獨白 soliloquy. (3) 浮一大白 (**bor*) have a strong drink, to celebrate (大白 name of goblet).

V.i. & t. (1) (LL) to present (case), clear up, lay before or confess to superior: 表白心跡 bare one's heart, true intentions; 自白 to explain oneself, confess; 無以自白 no chance to explain; 含冤莫白 suffer unjust accusation, with no chance to clear one's name; 眞相大白 the case is entirely cleared up. (2) Turn white: 白了少年

頭 hair turns white on a young head, from deep sorrow.

Adj. (1) White in color: 白頭, 白髮 white hair; 白頭偕老 (of married couple) reach old age together; 雪白 white as snow; 這丫頭生得白白淨淨的 this maid has a very fair complexion; 白茫茫 cloud-covered, mist-covered; 白晃晃, 白晰晰, 白皚皚, 白森森 dazzlingly white; 白生生 (of complexion) pale; 白鄧鄧 white with anger; 白眼 cold stare, cold disdainful look, showing white of eye: 遭人白眼 receive such stare; 白眼看人 giving such look; 白駒過隙 phr., life is short like white pony's shadow across a crevice; 白面書生 white-faced scholar, inexperienced in life; 白眉赤眼兒 phr., bare-faced (lie); 白色恐怖 white terror; 白雲蒼狗 (allu.) the vicissitudes of fortune, events (like changing cloud formations); 白雲親舍 phr., remembrance of parents (home) "from sight of white clouds"; the color of mourning: 穿白 wear white of mourning; hence 白事 (***bair*) funeral, contrasted with 紅事 wedding; hence 紅白 wedding and funeral gifts; part of many compp., as 白糖 *-tarng*, 白麪 *-miahn*↓. (2) Clear: 明白 clear, easy to understand; 不清不白, 不明不白 not clear, also not open, slightly underhand (of conduct). (3) Clean, pure, whole, plain, unmixed, unblemished, unused: 潔白 fresh and clean (skin, laundry); 一面白鏡子 has a clear face, or innocent heart; 白開水 plain boiled water; 白飯 rice without things to go with it, also white, polished rice; 白文 text without commentary; 白煮 boiled in plain water; 繳白卷 hand in blank examination paper; 白手 empty-handed; 白手成家 built up fortune from scratch, a selfmade man; 白璧微瑕 (***bor*) phr., slight flaw in a white jade, (fig.) blemish in man's good character.

Adv. (1) For no reason, in vain, without results, gain or compensation: 白等 wait in vain; 白忙 work in vain, waste efforts; 白費(脣舌, 金錢, 工夫) waste (words, money, efforts); 這話不是白說了麼 don't you think the words were completely wasted? 白死, 白活 die, live in vain; 白念, 白想 hope futilely; 白白的 without results; 白充數 just fill up the number without competency; 白效勞, 白勞神 labor in vain; 白得了 got it free; 白走了一趟 made a trip to no purpose; 白做了一天工夫 work a whole day without results; 白送, 白給 give away, give away foolishly; 白吃 eat without pay; 白地斷肝腸 (**bor*) vainly longing for loved one. (2) Simply, just: 叫了半天, 白不答應 knocked at the door for a long time, but just got no reply; 他今天不知怎的, 白不肯吃酒 he simply refused to drink today, I don't know why.

白鼻子 *bair-birtz*, n., a sly person.

白鉛 *bair-chian*, n., zinc.

白錢 *bair-chiarn*, n., (1) paper money for the dead; (2) (dial.) a pickpocket.

白鏹 ***bairchiarng*, n., silver.

白契 *bair-chih*, n., unregistered deed, contract, contrasted with 紅契.

白癡 **borchy*, n., idiot, mentally arrested person.

白屈菜 *bairchyu-tsaih*, n., a medical herb, *Chelidonium majus*.

白搭 *bairda*, adv., in vain.

白打 *bairdaa*, n. & v.i., (AC) game of shuttlecocks; (a hand) fight without weapons.

白帶 *hairdaih*, n., leucorrhoea.

白癜風 *bairdiahn-feng*, n., (med.) see 癜 61A. 82.

白丁 ***bair-ding*, n., illiterate person; (AC) common man, private.

白丁香 *bairdingshiang*, n., (bot.) white lilac; sparrow drippings used for treating wounds.

白豆 *bairdouh*, n., (bot.) white peas or beans.

白瓲 *bairduun*, n., kaolin, white clay used for porcelain.

白堊 ***bair-eh*[1], n., (min.) chalk; 白堊系 *--shih*, n., (geol.) cretaceous system.

白萼 *bair-eh*[2], n., (bot.)=玉簪, the tuberose, also *Hosta sieboldiana*.

白俄 *Bair Eh*[3], n., White Russian(s).

白礬 *bairfarn*, n., alum.

白附子 *bairfuhtzyy*, n., (bot.) a medical herb.

白乾(兒) *bairgan(-ga'l)*, n., strong liquor made from 高[Δ]粱 60.42 *gauliarng*.

白鴿 *bairge*, n., pigeon; 白鴿眼 look of disdain.

白圭 ***bor-guei*, (AC) allu., need for caution in speech (can grind off flaw in jade, but not undo damage of words).

白宮 *Bairgung*, n., the White House.

白果(兒) *bairguoo('l)*, n., (1) gingko tree, its fruits; 白果松 the gingko pine; (2) euphem. for hen's egg (to avoid the word "egg").

白骨 ***bair-guu*, n., bones of the dead.

白蒿 *bairhau*, n., (bot.) white rush, *Artemisia stelleriana*.

白喉 *bairhour*, n., diphtheria.

白花 *bair'hua*, n. & v.t., sweet words to console; *bair hua*, spend (time, money) without results.

白話 *bairhuah*, n., the vernacular: 白話文學 vernacular literature.

白化病 *bairhuah-bihng*, n., a plant disease, causing loss of colors in leaves.

白灰 *bairhuei*, n., lime.

白貨 *bairhuoh*, n., (coll.) heroin.

白虎 *bairhuu*, n., "White Tiger": (a) an evil spirit; (b) name of a star; (c) the right side; (d) a woman without pubic hair.

白齋 *bairjai*, n., vegetarian fast, excluding also salt, sauces.

白簡 ***bor-jiaan*, n., (LL) letter of impeachment.

白殭蠶 *bairjiang-tsarn*, n., silkworm which died from a certain disease, used as medicine.

白金 ***bair-jin*, n., platinum.

白
自

白酒 *bairjioou*, n., *-gan*↑.

白芨 ***bair-jir*, n., (bot.) mucilaginous root, used as medicine.

白晝 ***bor jouh*, n. & adv., (in) daytime.

白紵 **borjuh*, n., fine linen.

白濁 *bairjuor*, n., gonorrhea.

白朮 *bairjur*, n., see 朮 10.01.

白芷 *bairjyy*, n., (also wr. 白茝) (bot.) *Angelica anomala*, an aromatic herb.

白口(兒) *bairkou(e'l)*, n., dialogue spoken part in opera.

白蠟 *bairlah*[1], n., white wax: 白蠟蟲 (zoo.) *Flata limbata*, insect which exudes material for making wax.

白鑞 *bairlah*[2], n., solder.

白蘭地 *borlarndih*, n., brandy.

白蘞 ***bor-liahn*, n., (bot.) *Ampelopsis serjaniaefolia*.

白練 *bairliahn*, n., (LL) white silk; (fig.) waterfall.

白蓮教 *Bairliarnjiauh*, n., White Lotus Society, a secret sect.

白痢 *bairlih*, n., (med.) dysentery, *dysenteria alba*.

白領階級 *bair-liing jie-jir*, phr., white-collar workers.

白榴石 *bairliour-shyr*, n., (min.) a kind of marble.

白蛉子 *bairlirngtz* (*baai*--), n., a kind of gnat.

白露 ***bair-luh*[1], n., name of season in old calendar, about Sept. 8.

白鷺 *bairluh*[2], n., egret.

白螞蟻 *bair-maayih*, n., white ant (also 白蟻 *yih*).

白毛兒汗 *bairmaar'l hahn*, n., big sweat.

白麻 ***bair-mar*, n., (1) hemp; (2) (AC) imperial edict.

白茅 *bairmaur*, n., reed, *Imperata arundinacea*; 白茅千里 a stretch of monotony.

白煤 *bairmeir*[1], n., anthracite.

白黴 *bairmeir*[2], n., *Mucor stolonifer*, white mould on bread, etc.

白麪 *bairmiahn*, n., white wheat flour; 白麪兒 *-miah'l*, heroin.

白描 ***bormiaur*, v.i. & n., paint, sketch, chiefly contour lines without color.

白蜜 *bairmih*, n., white honey.

白民 ***bor-mirn*, n., (AC) common people＝白丁.

白墨 *bairmoh*[1], n., (dial.) chalk.

白膜 ***bair-moh*[2], n., (biol.) sclerotic coat in the eye.

白木耳 *bairmuh-eel*, n., edible, gelatinous white tree fungus.

白內障 *bair-neihjahng*, n., (med.) cataract.

白拈賊 *bairnian-tzeir*, n., a shoplifter.

白砒 *bairpi*, n.,＝砒霜 arsenic.

白皮書 *bairpir-shu*, n., a white paper issued by government.

白皮松 *bairpirsung*, n., white pine.

白熱 *bair-reh*, adj., white heat: 白熱化 adv., extreme state of passion; 白熱電燈 n., tungsten lamp.

白刃 **bor-rehn*, n., naked knives, swords: 白刃戰 (mil.) hand-to-hand combat, bayonet charge.

白人 *bair-rern*, n., white man.

白日 ***bair-ryh*, adv., in broad daylight: 白日見鬼 phr., (derog.) wild daydream, pure fantasy.

白砂 *bairsha*, n., silica or silex.

白沙糖 *bairshatarng*, n., refined cane sugar.

白墡 ***bair-shahn*[1], n., see *-eh*[1]↑.

白鱔 *bairshahn*[2], n., white eel.

白芍 *bairshaur*, n., (bot.) root of peony (芍藥 20A.50) used as medicine.

白鯗 ***bair-shiaang*, n., a kind of preserved fish (also 白首魚 *Seiaena schlegeli*).

白下 **Borshiah*, n., (MC) anc. name of Nanking.

白相 **borshiahng*, v.t., (Shanghai dial.) to loaf and seek pleasure: 白相人 (dial.) playboy.

白鮮 *bairshian*, n., (bot.) (also wr. 白羶, 白羊鮮) *Dictamnus albus*, a medicinal herb.

白鷴 (also 鷳) ***bair-shiarn*, n., (zoo.) a kind of pheasant, *Phasianus nyothemerus*.

白蛸 *bairshiau*, n., insect which blights rice plants.

白晳 ***bairshih*, (also 白晰), adj., (LL) pure white (complexion).

白錫 *bairshir*, n., pewter.

白首 ***bair-shoou*, adj., white-haired.

白薯 *bairshuu*, n., potato.

白四喜兒 *bair-shy-shie'l*, n., clown in opera, whose nose region is painted white.

白癬 *bairshyuan*, n., (med.) ringworm.

白血病 *bairshyueh-bihng*, n., leukemia.

白熊 *bair-shyurng*, n., the white bear.

白松 *bair-sung*, n., white pine.

白糖 *bairtarng*, n., refined sugar.

白藤 *bairterng*, n., rattan, cane plant.

白天 *bairtian*, n., daytime; adv., in daytime.

白鰷 *bairtiaur*, n., a fish (also 鰱魚 *Zucco platypus*).

白鐵 *bairtiee*, n., tin, tin plate.

白頭翁 *bairtourweng*, n., (zoo.) the grey starling, *Sturnus cineraceus*.

白菜 *bairtsaih*, n., cabbage.

白團扇 **bortuarnshaan*, n., white round silk fan.

白兔 **bor tuh*, n., the rabbit in the moon; the moon.

白銅 *bairturng*, n., white copper.

白字 *bairtzyh*, n., ＝別字 *bier-*, incorrect form of a character.

白薇 *bairweir*, n., (bot.) *Cynanchum atratum*.

白文 *bairwern*, n., text without commentary.

白雁 *boryahn*, n., the white goose.

白楊 *bairyarng*, n., the white poplar, *Populus balsamifera*.

白衣 **boryi*, n., (AC) common people; 白衣天使 "white angel," nurse in white; 白衣大士 the Goddess of Mercy (Kwanyin).

白蟻 *bairyih*, n., white ant.

白銀 *bairyirn*, n., silver dollar or ingot.

白芋 *bairyuh*, n., (bot.) small, white taro.

白魚 ***bair-yur*[1], n., (1) the white fish; (2) an insect (also 衣魚 *Lepisma sac-charina*) which eats into clothing, paper.

白榆 ***bair-yur*[2], n., (bot.) the white elm.

白雲母 *bairyurnmuu*, n., (min.) muscovite, of the mica group.

白雲石 *bairyurnshyr*, n., dolomite, a kind of white marble.

自 91.41

tzyh.

N. & Pron. Also used as adv. (as in self-), self, oneself: 自己

-jii↓; 自箇 oneself; 自身 *-shen* ↓; 自(己)個兒 (all by) oneself; 自家 ditto; 自家人, 自己人(兒) one's own people, kith and kin; 自己勁兒 intimacy between friends; 獨自 all alone, by oneself; 自己園兒 what's produced in one's own home; 自顧自 (be) selfish, self-regard(ing); 自寬 to comfort oneself; 自況 compare oneself to another; 自比 ditto; 自好 self-respect(ing); 自備 provide s.t. oneself; 自奉 spend on oneself (in food, clothing, etc.); 自費 at one's own cost (expense); 自暴自棄 give up hope in oneself, lose self-confidence (self-respect), self-degradation; 自甘墮落 ditto; 自私自利 (act) selfish(ly), self-seeking, egoistic; 自欺欺人 self-deceit (-deception), try to deceive others only to end in deceiving oneself; 自怨自艾 be contrite and reform oneself, regret one's past mistakes and try to do better in the future; 自鳴得意 be puffed up with pride, be self-satisfied; 自鳴清高 imagine oneself to be superior to others; 自本自立 depend on one's own resources and ability; 自命不凡 think of oneself as a superior being; 自誇 blow one's own trumpet, sing one's own praises; 自矜 ditto; 自任 take upon oneself; 自待 treat oneself to; 自持 assume a superior air, (exercise) self-control: 不能自持 cannot control one's passion; 以…自居 pretend to be…; 自謙 to humble oneself, be modest (humble); 自餒 have one's heart in one's boots, be greatly discouraged; 自掘墳墓 to dig one's own grave.

Adj. & adv. (1) Personal(ly), done by (to, for) oneself: 親自 do s.t. oneself; 自理 pay personal attention to, (of expenses) pay out of one's own pocket; 自行解決 settle a dispute by the parties concerned themselves or by oneself; 自決 self-determination; 自述(自陳) make a personal statement (explanation); 自問 ask oneself; 自反 self-examination; 自便 do as one pleases; 自專 arbitrarily decide to do this or that; 自肥 enrich oneself by unlawful means; 自薦 introduce oneself: 毛遂自薦 allu. to the story of Mao Sui who volunteered to serve as an emissary to the Kingdom of Chu; 自衒 brag about oneself, show off, be vainglorious; 自媒 (of a woman) marry a man without the help of a go-between; 自我介紹 introduce oneself to s.o.; 自伐 *-fa*[1]↓; 自戕 self-destruction, do things harmful to oneself; 自宮 castrate oneself; 自殺 *-sha*↓; 自盡 (commit) suicide; 自裁 ditto; 自縊 *-yih*↓; 自經 kill oneself; 自剄, 自刎 cut one's own throat; 自分必死 know oneself to be doomed; 自傷 hurt (cut, injure, grieve for) oneself; 自棄 despair of oneself; 自訟 *-suhng*↓; 自責 blame oneself; 自誤 it's all one's own fault; 何以自處 what shall one do (to extricate oneself from a predicament)? 自制 self-control, -discipline; 自首 *-shoou*↓; 自苦 deny oneself all the good things of life, bring trouble on one's own head: 何自苦乃爾 why should you be so hard on yourself? 自討苦吃 do s.t. which will only cause trouble to oneself; 自作自受 suffer the consequences of one's own action; 自作孽 sow the seeds of one's own ruin; 自討沒趣 invite ridicule (dislike, rebuff), make oneself unwelcome; 自遠遠人 to hold yourself aloof will only end in making others turn away from you; 自我陶醉 indulge in self-delusion as an escape from reality; 自我檢討 self-examination; 自救救人 do s.t. that will save both oneself and others; 自成一家 develop one's own style of writing (painting, calligraphy), found a new school of thought; 自我作古 do what others have never done before; 自出機杼 strike out a new path for oneself, originate an idea (method, fashion); 自作聰明 act on the strength of one's own imagined cleverness; 自告奮勇 volunteer one's services; 自投羅網 fall into a trap set for oneself by another; 自相矛盾 self-contradictory; 自相殘殺 mutual annihilation, internecine fight; 自相衝突 mutually conflicting; 自圓其說 give a satisfactory explanation of what one has said or done; self-justification: 不能自圓其說 unable to do that; 自顧不暇 unable even to fend for oneself; 自打嘴巴 contradict oneself ("slap one's own face"); 自言自語 murmur (talk) to oneself, keep on chattering though no one is listening, make unilateral declaration; 自瞞自欺 deceive oneself; 自遣 to solace oneself; 自娛 amuse oneself; 自飲(斟)自酌 enjoy a cup of wine all by oneself; 自得其樂 take delight in doing s.t. as a pleasurable occupation; 自奉 provide the necessities of life for oneself: 自奉甚薄 live very simply; 自給自足 self-sufficient, -cy; 自效 offer one's services to help; 自食其力 earn one's own living. (2) Natural(ly), spontaneous(ly): 自然 *-rarn*↓; 自然而然 come very naturally; 自當(悔改) will willingly (repent, mend one's ways); 自應 will of course. . . .

Prep. From, since: 自上而下 from top to bottom, come from above; 自今(而後) from now on; 自今天(年)起 beginning from today (this year); 自古以來 from time immemorial; 自天而降 descend from heaven, come from nowhere; 有朋自遠方來 have a friend coming from afar; 自從 *-tsurng*↓; 自打 *-daa*↓; 自茲 from this point on; 自後 *-houh*↓; 自此 *-tsyy*↓; 自淺入深 (of studies) advance step by step ("from the shallow to the deep"); 來自何處 where have you (they, has he, it) come from?

自愛 *tzyh-aih*, n. & adj., self-respect(ing).

自卑感 *tzyhbeigaan*, n., inferiority complex.

自白 *tzyh-bor*, v.i. & n., (make) a deposition or personal statement, clear oneself of all suspicion.

自

自稱 *tzyh-cheng*, v.t., to call oneself. . . .

自乘 *tzyh-cherng*, v.i., (math.) multiply a number by itself.

自強 *tzyh-chiarng*, v.i., (of a person or nation) make earnest efforts to stand on one's own feet.

自取 *tzyh-chyuu*, v.i., bring on oneself (punishment, etc.): 自取其辱 bring disgrace on one's own head.

自打 *tzyhdaa*, prep., since, from: 自打昨天就沒來 has (have) not come since yesterday.

自大 *tzyh-dah*, v.i., assume a superior air, look down upon all others, be self-assertive.

自得 *tzyh-der*, adj., (1) self-satisfied: 意氣揚揚, 甚自得也 proud and pleased with oneself; (2) be at peace with oneself, feeling perfectly happy: 俯仰自得 be contented and happy wherever one may be; 君子無入而不自得焉 a superior man is at peace with himself under any and every circumstance.

自動 *tzyh-duhng*, adj. & adv., (1) voluntary, -ily; (2) automatic, -ally: 自動電話 *--diahnhuah*, n., telephone by dialing.

自多 *tzyh-duo*, v.i. & adj., (be) self-satisfied or self-conceited.

自伐 *tzyh-fa*^{1} (*-far*), v.i., (1) do harm to oneself: 國必自伐而後人伐之 a country must destroy or weaken itself before others could destroy it, humiliate it; (2) be puffed up with pride: 不敢自伐 dare not be proud of oneself.

自發 *tzyh-fa*^{2}, (1) v.i., (of persons) do s.t. on one's own initiative, (of things) to start by itself; (2) adj., self-moving.

自封 *tzyh-feng*, v.i., isolate oneself: 故步自封 unwilling to move forward.

自負 *tzyh-fuh*, v.i., think highly of oneself.

自耕農 *tzyhgeng-nurng*, n., an owner-farmer.

自豪 *tzyh-haur*, adj., to be proud of.

自後 *tzyhhouh*, adv., thereafter, from then on, ever since.

自解 *tzyh-jiee*, v.i., (1) satisfy one's own conscience, rationalize; (2) extricate oneself from a bad fix.

自己 *tzyhjii*, (1) n., one's self; (2) close friends or relatives: 都是自己人, 何必客氣 we are close relatives or friends, why stand on ceremony? (3) (*-'ji*) adj., intimate: 彼此不拘束 we are so intimate, please just make yourselves at home.

自轉 *tzyh-juaan*, n. & v.i., (astron.) rotate, -ation.

自傳 *tzyh-juahn*, n., autobiography.

自助 *tzyh-juh*, n., self-help: 自助之人 one who depends upon himself; 自助餐 cafeteria, (self-service) buffet.

自重 *tzyh-juhng*, v.i., hold oneself with dignity, refrain from committing nuisance.

自主 *tzyhjuu*, v.i. & adj. & n., (be) independent, -ce, be one's own master.

自治 *tzyhjyh*, n. & adj., self-government, -ing: 自治領 (political science) a dominion, esp. of the British Commonwealth of Nations.

自絕 *tzyh-jyuer*^{1}, v.i., (1) become extinct; (2) invite one's own destruction, invite public contempt.

自覺 *tzyh-jyuer*^{2}, v.i. & adj. & n., (be) self-conscious, -ness; realize oneself.

自決 *tzyh-jyuer*^{3}, v.i., self-determine: n., 民族自決 national self-determination.

自來 *tzyhlair*, adv., from the very beginning: 自來白 a small moon-cake, esp. for the Mid-Autumn Festival (so-called from its white crust); 自來紅 ditto (so-called from its reddish-brown crust); 自來火 (a) matches; (b) a gas lamp; 自來水(兒) tap water, water supply; 自來水筆 a fountain pen.

自了 *tzyh-liaau*, v.i., deal with a situation by oneself; 自了漢 a self-centered person.

自量 *tzyh-liahng*, v.i., know one's own limits: 不知自量 undertake what is beyond one's power.

自力 *tzyh-lih*^{1}, v.i., do s.t. by one's own effort: 自力更生 rely on oneself, take fate in one's own hands.

自立 *tzyh-lih*^{2}, v.i. & adj., (be) independent (cf. 獨^{A}立 91C.50).

自律 *tzyh-lyuh*, v.i. & n., (exercise) self-control (self-discipline).

自鳴鐘 *tzyh-mirng-jung*, n., (old term for) a clock that strikes every quarter, half or full hour.

自然 *tzyhrarn*, adj. & adv., (1) natural(ly), spontaneous(ly), free(ly); by itself: 到時自然明白 when the time comes you will naturally understand; (2) of course, doubtless: 他唱的自然不好, 你也不見強 of course he can't sing very well, but you're not much better; (3) (*-'ran*) unconstrained, free from compulsion, flexible; (4) n., nature: 接近自然 live close to nature; 大自然 the great universe; 欣賞自然 enjoy nature; 征服自然 conquer nature; (5) adj., pertaining to nature: 自然哲學 natural philosophy; 自然界 the world of nature, Nature; 自然科學 the natural sciences; 自然力 natural forces (wind or water power); 自然美 the beauties of nature; 自然人 (law) a natural person (opp. 法人 legal person); 自然現象 natural phenomena, the phenomena of nature.

自恁 *tzyhrehn*, adv., (MC) freely (＝儘管): 自恁請你陪我來坐坐 please feel free to come and have a chat.

自若 *tzyhruoh*, adj., self-composed, serene, unruffled.

自如 *tzyhrur*, adj., ditto.

自殺 *tzyh-sha*, n. & v.i., (commit) suicide.

自傷 *tzyh-shang*, v.i., (1) hurt oneself; (2) feel sorry for oneself.

自身 *tzyhshen*, (1) n., (one's) self; (2) pron., oneself.

自信 *tzyh-shihn*, v.i. & n., self-confidence: 不敢自信 dare not trust my own opinion, etc.

自性 *tzyh-shihng*, n., (Budd.) one's original nature.

自省 *tzyh-shiing*, v.i. & n., introspect; self-examination, introspection.

自新 *tzyh-shin*, v.i., make a fresh start in life, cut off one's bad habits.

自修 *tzyh-shiou*, v.i., (1) review one's lessons; (2) to study by oneself without the benefit of teachers; (3) cultivate oneself, make oneself a better man.

自行車(兒) *tzyhshirng-che('l)*, n., a bicycle.

自首 *tzyh-shoou*, v.i., (of criminals) surrender oneself to the police.

自失 *tzyh-shy*, v.i., be at a loss as to what to do.

自是 *tzyh-shyh*, v.i. & adj. & adv., (1) (be) self-conceited; (2) henceforth, from then on.

自序 *tzyh-shyuh*, n., (1) an author's autobiographical sketch; (2) preface to one's book.

自敍式 *tzyhshyuh-shyh*, n., (a novel of) the autobiographical type.

自許 *tzyh-shyuu*, v.i., set a goal for oneself; permit nothing else but....

自訴 *tzyh-suh*, v.i., file a lawsuit against s.o.

自訟 *tzyh-suhng*, v.i., blame oneself.

自私 *tzyh-sy*, adj., selfish, egoistic.

自從 *tzyhtsurng*, adv., ever since (that time).

自此 *tzyhtsyy*, adv., from now on, from that time on.

自贊 *tzyh-tzahn*, v.i., (1) sing one's own praises; (2) introduce oneself.

自在 *tzyhtzaih*, adj., (1) able to do anything of one's own free will; (2) (also *-'tzai*) carefree, without the least worry; (3) (*-'tzai*) comfortable, pleasant; (4) (Budd.) (of the mind) free of delusion.

自尊 *tzyh-tzun*, n., self-respect; 自尊心 ditto.

自足 *tzyh-tzur*, adj., (1) self-sufficient; (2) self-satisfied.

自衞 *tzyh-weih*, n., self-defense.

自我 *tzyh-woo*, n., one's self, the ego: 自我陶醉 imagine oneself to be better than one really is; 自我宣傳(揚) blow one's own trumpet.

自縊 *tzyh-yih*, v.i., commit suicide by hanging.

自由 *tzyhyour*, (1) v.i., be free to act without restraint; (2) adj., free from control or outside interference: 自由人 a freeman (opp. 奴隸 a slave): 自由國家(人民) free nations (peoples); (3) n., liberty, freedom: 思想自由, 言論自由, 出版自由, 信仰自由, 集會結社自由 freedom of thought, speech, the press, belief, assembly and association; 公海自由 (international law) freedom of the seas; 自由主義(者) liberalism (a liberal); 自由黨 (Eng. history) the Liberal Party; 自由神像 Statue of Liberty; 自由港 a free port; 自由畫 freehand drawing; 自由教育 a liberal education; 自由競爭 free competition, system of free euterprise; 自由職業 the liberal professions; 自由戀愛 free love; 自由貿易 (econmics) free trade, freedom of trade; 自由日 Freedom Day (allu. to the release of prisoners of war by South Korea on January 23, 1954); 自由詩 free verse; 自由世界 the free world; 自由意志 free will.

自用 *tzyh-yuhng*, adj., self-willed to the point of foolishness: 愚而好自用 enterprising but ignorant, (person) ignorant without knowing it.

囟 91.41

shihn.

囟門 *shinhnmern*, n., the boneless opening in a baby's skull.

旮 91.41

ga.

旮旯(子)(兒) *galar(tz)('l)*, n., an out-of-the-way corner: 牆旮旯 a nook of the wall; 藏在旮旯 hidden in a secluded spot, in a cranny; 到處旮旯去找 search every nook and cranny, (possibly corruption from 角落).

囱 91.41

tsung.

N. Chimney: 煙囱.

凂 91.41

lirn.

[Abbr. of 臨 51S.40]

§91.42 (丿/冈)

向 91.42

shiahng.

N. (1) A surname. (2) Direction: 方向 ditto; 風向 direction of the wind; 定向 definite direction; 不知去向 do not know where (he, it) went; 傾向, 趨向 tendency, inclination, also v.t., incline toward; 歸向 the direction home; v.t., to turn toward (religion, ruling regime); direction of movement; ambition.

V.t. (1) To face, also facing (see also Prep.↓): 向東, 向西 face (or facing) east, west; 向後轉 about-face (mil.). (2) To aim, strive, develop in certain direction: 向上 develop, strive upwards; 向善 seek after the good; 欣欣向榮 (of plants) grow luxuriantly; see 向慕, 向化 *-muh, -huah*↓; 向風 *-feng*↓. (3) To side with, favor (person): 你老是向著他 you always take his side.

Adj. & adv. Past, earlier days: 向來, 向日 *-lair -ryh*↓; 向者 in former times; (also the past subjunctive) 向非戎事備 (LL) if the army had not been prepared in those days; 向使 if it had been.

Prep. Toward: 向明, 向晚 toward dawn, dusk; 向前, 向後 forward, backward; 向右轉 turn right; 向他説 speak to him; 向上帝祈求 pray to God; 奔向自由 flee to freedom; 向火取暖 warm oneself before the fire.

向背 *shiahng-beih*, n., "front and back"—inclination toward and away from: 人心的向背 the public attitude for or against (a regime); (callig.) the facing together or facing away of components of character.

向當兒 *shiahng'dang'l*, n., (coll.) means of livelihood, way out: 一點向當兒都沒有 don't know how to make a living, have no way out.

向風 *shiahng-feng*, (1) v.i., to flock toward, be attracted to; (2) adv., windward.

向後 *shiahnghouh*, adv., (1) backwards; (2) in the future: 向後怎麽辦呢 what of the future?

向化 *shiahnghuah*, v.i., to turn toward.

向著 *shiahng'je*, prep., facing.

向者 *shiahngjee*, adv., formerly.

向兒 *shiahng'l*, n., direction: 轉向兒 change direction.

向來 *shiahnglair*, adv., usually, so far: 向來是他出主意 usually he makes the decisions; 向來不請假 so far (he) never asked for leave.

向例 *shiahng-lih*, n., gen. practice, the usual rule.

向明 *shiang-mirng*, (1) adv., toward dawn; (2) n., the bright side of room.

向慕 *shiahngmuh*, v.t., to admire (person, also 嚮慕).

向內 *shiahng-neih*, adj., introvert.

向日 *shiahng-ryh*, adv., in former days; usually; 向日葵 the sunflower.

向曉 *shiahngshiau*, adv., see *-mirng*↑.

向心力 *shiahngshinlih*, n., (phys.) centripetal force; sense of cohesion in unit.

向晚 *shiahng-waan*, adv., toward evening.

向往 *shiahngwaang*, v.t., to be attracted toward, to crave for, admire (person) (also 嚮往).

向外 *shiahng-waih*, adv., (1) turning or orientated outward; (2) (MC) over and above (a number); (3) adj., extrovert.

向陽 *shiahng-yarng*, adj., "facing the sun"—(house) admitting sunlight freely.

向隅 *shiahng-yur*, v.i., "facing a corner or dead end"—be left out: 以免向隅 (hurry to buy) so that you will not miss the great chance.

甪 91.42

luh.

甪里 *Luhli*, n., a name of a place.

舟 91.42

jou.

N. (LL) a boat, usu. rowboat, sailboat (cf. modn. 船 91S.40): 小舟, 扁舟 a small rowboat; 漁舟 fishing boat; 舟車之苦 the hardships of a journey; 同舟共濟 those in the same boat (should) cooperate for the same aim.

V.t. (AC) 何以舟之 what shall one wear on the girdle?

舟楫 *joujir*, n., (1) boats, boat traffic; (2) (AC) (fig.) pilot to weather a storm—i.e., good minister.

舟人 *jourern*, n., boatman.

舟師 *joushy*, n., (1) see *-tzyy*↓; (2) anc. navy.

舟子 *joutzyy*, n., boatman.

脊 91.42

jii (jir).

N. The backbone, a ridge: 背脊 the spine; 脊梁 *-liarng*↓; 山脊 mountain ridge; 屋脊 the ridge of a house.

脊椎 *jiijuei*, n., (physiol.) the vertebrae: 脊椎動物 (zoo.) the vertebrates.

脊柱 *jiijuh*, n., the spinal column.

脊梁 *jiiliarng (-'liang, -'ning)*, n., the backbone, the spinal column. 「row.

脊髓 *jiisueei (-'suei)*, n., the mar-

脅 91.42

shier.

[Var. of 脇]

N. Ribs, flank; 脅下 *-shiah*↓.

V.t. (1) To intimidate, coerce: 脅迫, 脅制 *-poh, -jyh*↓. (2) To close: 脅肩諂笑 (of flatterer) shrug the shoulders and offer an ingratiating smile.

脅制 *shierjyh*, v.t., to coerce, control by force.

脅迫 *shierpoh*, v.t., coerce (s.o. into doing s.t.).

脅生 *shier-sheng*, v.i., give birth by Caesarian operation ("under the ribs").

脅下 *shier-shiah*, n., the armpit; under the ribs.

脅息 *shiershir*, v.i., (LL) gasp with fear.

脅從 *shiertzuhng*, n., person(s) forced into doing, obeying.

雋 91.42

*jyuhn (*jyuahn, *juh).*

N. (*jyuahn) A surname.

Adj. (1) (*juahn) Of lasting flavor; 雋永 *-yuung*↓. (2) Outstanding (also wr. 儁, 俊): 雋拔 *-bar*↓.

雋拔 *jyuhnbar*, adj., (of mountain peak) towering; (personality) distinguished, outstanding.

雋永 *jyuahnyuung, adj., (of speech or writing) of absorbing and enduring interest.

§ 91.50 (ノ/ㄱ)

粤 91.50

yueh.

N. Name for Kwangtung province: 粤人, 粤語 Cantonese (man, dialect); 粤菜 Cantonese food.

力 91.50

lih.

N. (1) Ability, capacity, mental power: 目力, 眼力 eyesight; 耳力 sense of hearing; 體力 bodily strength; 精力 mental energy; 生力, 生命力 vitality; 生殖力 virility, fecundity; 毅力 strength of purpose, perseverance; 能力 ability; 魄力 energy, strength of character; 魅力 magic power; 記憶力 memory; 智力 intelligence; 創造力 creativity; 才力 talent; 影響力 influence; 號召力 public appeal; 財力 financial power; 勢力 (範圍) (sphere of) influence; 國力 national power; 人力 manpower; 兵力 armed forces; 武力 military might; 盡力而爲 do one's utmost; 力不從心 lacking the ability to do what one would like to do; 力不勝任 without the required ability to undertake a given task; 力之所及 what lies in one's power to carry out. (2) (Phys.) force, energy, power: 張力 tension; 水力 hydraulic power; 電力 electric power; 火力 thermodynamic power; 動力 motive power; 向心力 centripetal force; 離心力 centrifugal force. (3) Muscular strength: 力大無比 without a match in physical prowess; 力氣 *-'chi*↓; 力氣活兒 work requiring physical exertions; 力量 *-liahng*↓; 力可拔山 so strong as to be able to lift a mountain; 筋疲力盡 utterly exhausted, dead tired; 力竭聲嘶 with voice hoarse and not an ounce of strength left; 膂力過人 physically stronger than other people. (4) Physical labor: 苦力 a coolie; 力伕, 力役 *-fu, -yih*↓. (5) A surname.

Adv. Energetically, vigorously, strenuously: 力求上進 strive vigorously to improve oneself, to do better; 力圖自強 (of nations) struggle to stand on one's own feet; 力耕 engage in farming; 力田 ditto; 力戰 fight with all one's might; 力請 to request most ardently; 力行不怠 do (s.t.) persistently without letup; 力爭上游 endeavor to gain the upper hand; 力疾從公 continue to attend to one's duties in spite of illness; 據理力爭 make utmost efforts to fight for one's point of view.

力巴 *lih'ba*, n., (northern dial.) a layman, an outsider, a person not in the trade (also 力把, 力巴頭, 力巴兒, 力笨兒).

力氣 *lih'chi*, n., strength, energy: 沒有力氣 weak physically.

力錢 *lihchiarn*, n., a tip, gratuity paid to bearer of gifts.

力伕 *lihfu*, n., a porter.

力量 *lihliahng*, n., strength, force, power: 感人的力量 power to inspire people.

力士 *lih-shyh*, n., a person of great physical strength, (boxing) a prize fighter; oft. 大力士.

力學 *lihshyuer*, n., (phys.) mechanics.

力役 *lihyih*, n., conscript labor, labor service.

办 91.50

bahn.

[Pop. of 辦 60S.10]

勞 91.50

laur (*lauh).

[Pop. 劳]

N. (1) Accomplishment, work: 功勞 merit, achievements. (2) A surname. (3) Worker, laborer: 勞方 the labor (opp. 資方 the management); 勞資糾紛 trouble between labor and management. (4) (Chin. med.) a wasting disease, any disease resulting from excessive physical weakening: 勞傷 *-shang*, 勞瘵 *-jaih*↓.

V.t. (1) Do manual work: 勞動 *-duhng*↓; 勞心, 勞力 mental and manual work(ers). (2) To trouble (s.o.) with (s.t.): 勞駕 *-jiah*↓; 勞人費馬 (of tasks) involve a lot of labor; 勞民 *-mirn*↓; 徒勞往返 made a trip in vain. (3) (*lauh) Bring gifts to fighting army, bring comfort to: 勞軍 *-jyun*↓; 慰勞 to comfort (victims of flood, etc.).

Adj. Hard, wearisome: 煩勞 troublesome; 疲勞 tiring, tiresome, tired.

勞保 *laurbaau*, n., labor insurance (short for 勞工保險).

勞步 *laurbuh*, v.t., (court.) (of friends) come to pay a visit: 昨天勞步, 還沒有回拜呢 I have not yet paid a return call on you for your call on me yesterday.

勞頓 *laurduhn*, adj., weary and tired.

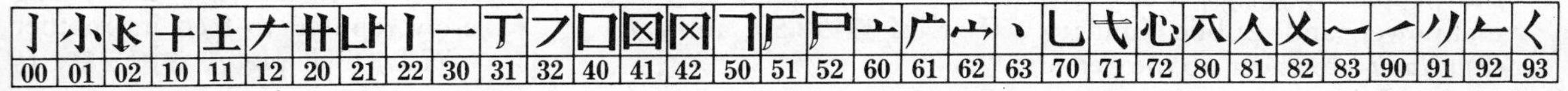

勞動 *laurduhng*, v.i., (1) do physical labor; 勞動者 workers, laborers; 勞動節 Labor Day; (2) (-*'dung*) (court.) to bother, trouble: 又得勞動您 sorry to trouble you again; 勞動大駕 please be good enough to do me a favor.

勞乏 *laurfar*, adj., physically exhausted.

勞煩 *laurfarn*, v.t., (court.) cause (s.o.) trouble: 勞煩你 may I trouble you?

勞費 *laurfeih*, v.t., cost trouble and expenses.

勞工 *laurgung*, n., labor, individual workers or as a class.

勞瘵 *laurjaih*, n., (med.) tuberculosis (＝肺癆).

勞症 *laurjehng*, n., ditto.

勞績 *laurji*, n., work done, accomplishment, merit.

勞駕 *laurjiah*, v.t., (usu. used in the second person) please do me a favor: 勞駕你一會兒 may I trouble you for a moment? 不敢勞您大駕 dare not trouble you; 勞駕! 勞駕! thank you so much!

勞金 *laurjin*, n., compensation for work, reward, fee.

勞倦 *laurjyuahn*, adj., tired out.

勞軍 **lauhjyun*, v.t., cheer up troops with gifts (also 勞師).

勞苦 *laurkuu*, (1) v.i., to work hard; (2) adj., having to work hard; (3) (**lauh-*) v.t., encourage, bring comfort to (s.o.).

勞來 **lauhlaih*, v.t., (also 勞徠) encourage (s.o.) to enlist or come over.

勞累 *laurleih*, v.t., to trouble, bother: 太勞累了 it's too much trouble; 勞累您了 sorry to have bothered you.

勞力 *laurlih*, n., manual labor: 勞力工作 physical or manual labor; 出賣勞力 sell one's labor for a living; 勞力所得 income from labor.

勞碌 *laurluh*, adj., hard-working: 奔忙勞碌 running about; 勞碌了一整天 have slaved for a whole day; 勞碌命 a person born to a hard lot, (joc.) a born slave.

勞民 *laurmirn*, v.t., (1) belabor the people: 勞民傷財 waste of manpower and public funds; (2) (**lauh-*) to cheer up the people by gift or message.

勞傷 *laurshang*, n., (Chin. med.) disease resulting from gen. weakening and exhaustion.

勞神 *laurshern*, v.t., bother (s.o. or oneself) with (s.t.); 勞神你 may I trouble you? please be so kind.

勞心 *laur-shin*, v.t., (1) do mental work: 勞心工作(者) white-collar work(er) opp. *-lih*↑; (2) to worry.

勞形 *laurshirng*, adj., tire body out (for living).

勞師 **lauh-shy*, v.t., comfort troops with gifts, see *-jyun*↑.

勞什子 *laurshyr'tz*, n., (＝牢什子) an eyesore, anything disagreeable or abominable.

勞瘁 *laurtsueih*, adj., wearied and worn.

勞作 *laurtzuoh*, n., (1) manual labor class in school; (2) manual labor.

勞資 *laur-tzy*, n., labor and management, labor and capital: 勞資關係 labor relations.

勞務 *laurwuh*, n., service.

勞燕 *lauryahn*, n., (LL) 伯勞 *Lanius bucephalus*, and swallows: 勞燕分飛 (LL) going in different ways, said of friends at time of departure.

勞役 *lauryih*, n., labor service, (criminal law) hard labor.

島 91.50

daau.

N. Island: 島嶼 island; 半島 peninsula; 羣島, 列島 archipelago, 孤島 lone island.

島國 *daau-guor*, n., island kingdom or country.

為 91.50

weir.

[Var. of 爲 90.50; abbr. 为]

駕 91·50

jiah.

N. (1) A carriage, cart: 車駕 formerly, imperial vehicles, hence, the emperor. (2) An honored presence, travel or arrival: 尊駕, 大駕, 臺駕 your good (honorable) self; 駕臨 your kind presence; 聖駕 His Majesty; 王駕 His Royal Highness; 御駕親征 (of the army) under the personal command of the emperor; 枉駕 thanks for calling; 候駕 wait for your arrival; 擋駕 polite refusal as one unworthy to receive a visitor, oft. as a matter of form; 返駕 return trip; 盼即命駕 please kindly come at once.

V.t. (1) To drive (a vehicle), sail (a ship), fly (an airplane): 駕車 drive a car; 駕船 pilot a ship; 駕飛機 fly an airplane; 駕駛 *-shyy*↓; 駕着一葉扁舟 row a small boat. (2) To mount (a horse): 駕馬 harness a horse, ride on horseback; (fig.) to control: 駕馭 *-yuh*↓; 駕輕就熟 follow the beaten path, do s.t. with ease through experience; 騰雲駕霧 (fairy tale) travel through space; 駕雲歸 to ride the clouds and come home.

駕崩 *jiah-beng*, v.i., (euphem.) die, said of a sovereign.

駕臨 *jiah-lirn*, n., (court.) your gracious presence, the pleasure of your company.

駕駛 *jiahshyy*, v.t., to drive (a car), pilot (a ship); 駕駛員 a pilot, driver; 駕駛艙 Command Module.

駕馭 *jiahyuh*, v.t., to control, govern (subordinates).

烏 91.50

wu.

N. (1) A crow: 烏哺 the young crow reputed to feed its mother—(LL) filial piety; 書經三寫, 烏

焉成馬 (anc. proverb) when a book is copied thrice, the characters 烏 and 焉 become 馬; 白烏頭 white-headed crow—an impossibility. (2) The sun (alleged to have a spot looking like a three-legged crow; cf. 兔 rabbit standing for the moon): hence 烏兔 (the crow and the rabbit) the sun and the moon; 金烏 the golden sun. (3) A surname.

Adj. Black: 烏黑 *-hei* ↓; 烏鬚 black beard; 烏木 black wood, ebony; 烏梅 black plums; 烏橄欖 black olives; 烏雲 dark clouds; 發烏 turn black.

Adv. How: 烏可, 烏能 how can? 烏有此事 how can such a thing be? no such thing! (also wr. 惡).

Excl. 烏乎 (u.f. 嗚呼) alas! (also wr. 烏虖).

烏豆 *wu-douh*, n., black beans.
烏龜 *wuguei*, n., tortoise (also a term of abuse).
烏骨雞 *wuguu ji*, n., the silky chicken with black bones—a delicacy.
烏黑(兒) *wuhei(-he'l)*, adj., jet black.
烏合 *wuher*, n., as in 烏合之衆 rabble troops.
烏喙 *wuhueih*, n., a poisonous plant of crowfoot family, monkshood, wolfsbane (also called 烏頭喙).
烏雞 *wu-ji*, n., see *-guu-ji* ↑.
烏巾 *wu-jin*[1], n., formerly, hat of black gauze, see *-sha* ↓.
烏金 *wu-jin*[2], n., copper and gold alloy.
烏韭 *wujioou*, n., (bot.) the rock fern.
烏臼 *wujouh*, n., (bot.) the tallow tree.
烏竹 *wujur*, n., black bamboo.
烏拉 *wula*, n., a moccasin used in 吉林 Kirin, northeast Manchuria, filled with 烏拉草 for warmth.
烏蘞莓 *wuliarnmeir*, n., (bot.) a vine, *Cissus japonica*.
烏龍茶 *wulurngchar*, n., oolong tea.
烏麥 *wumaih*, n., a kind of buckwheat.
烏木 *wumuh*, n., black wood.
烏紗 *wusha*, n., a hat of black gauze, generally known as official's cap, esp. since Tarng Dyn.
烏絲欄 *wusylarn*, n., thin black lines as ruling on paper or silk for paintings.
烏條蛇 *wutiiaur-sher*, n., a kind of snake.
烏頭 *wutour*, n., see *-hueih* ↑.
烏塗 *wu'tu*, adj. & n., (1) muddy; (2) half-boiled, warm (water); (3) var. of 糊塗 unclear, muddleheaded.
烏托邦 *Wutuobang*, n., Utopia.
烏雜 *wutzar*, adj., see *-her* ↑.
烏賊 *wutzer*, n., cuttlefish.
烏烏 *wuwu*, adj., descriptive of cry of pain, like Eng. "wow!"
烏鴉 *wuya*, n., the crow.
烏眼(兒)雞 *wuyaan(-yaa'l)ji*, n., "black-eyed chicken": 烏眼雞似的 venomous look of hatred.
烏芋 *wuyuh*, n., water chestnut.
烏魚 *wuyur*, n., black fish.
烏雲 *wuyurn*, n., (1) dark clouds; (2) woman's black hair.

鳥 91.50

niaau (**diaau*).

N. (1) Bird: 鳥類 all creatures of the bird family; 鳥語花香 singing birds and fragrant flowers; 鳥獸行 bestiality, beastly conduct; 鳥獸星散 (of human beings) scatter like birds and animals; 鳥盡弓藏 kick out (s.o.) after his services are no longer needed, (lit.) "the bow and arrows are stacked away when there are no more birds to shoot"; 鳥面鵠形 (of starving people) haggard, emaciated; 人爲財死, 鳥爲食亡 a man dies for money; a bird dies for food. (2) Male genital organ (var. 屌) **diaau*: 撮鳥 (MC) a curse word, oft. used in 水滸.

鳥巢 *niaauchaur*, n., a bird's nest.
鳥鎗 *niaauchiang*, n., fowling piece.
鳥銃 *niaauchuhng*, n., ditto.
鳥道 *niaau-dauh*, n., dangerously narrow hill path.
鳥篆 *niaau-juahn*, n., form of anc. script so called because it looked like birds' footprints.
鳥瞰 *niaaukahn*, (1) v.i., look down from above; (2) n., a bird's-eye view.
鳥窠 *niaauke*, n., see *-chaur* ↑.
鳥里 *niaur-lii*, n., (surveying) distance in miles "as the crow flies."
鳥媒 *niaaumeir*, n., a bird used as a decoy to catch other birds.
鳥信 *niaaushihn*, n., (鳥信風) seasonal wind occurring in the third month of the lunar calendar.

鴦 91.50

yang.

N. See 鴛^鴦 92.50.

鶯 91.50

ying.

N. The Chin. oriole: 鶯鶯燕燕 orioles and swallows—a bevy of young girls; 鶯簧, 鶯舌 chirping (as of orioles); 鶯谷 (LL, allu. of scholars) not yet well-known or officially successful.

鶯遷 *yingchian*, v.i., (LL allu.) (1) be promoted in office; (2) move into a new house.
鶯花 *ying-hua*, n., birds and flowers of spring.

§91.63 (丿/丶)

焦 91.63

jiau.

N. A surname.

Adj. (1) Burned, scorched: 焦頭爛額 utterly exhausted from overwork or anxiety; 燒焦了 scorched, charred; 烤焦了 burned in roasting or baking; 焦脆 *-tzueih* ↓; 焦味 taste of burned food; 焦臭 smell of s.t. burning; 焦灼 *-juor* ↓. (2) Anxious, uneasy, restless, worried: 焦急 *-jir*, 焦慮 *-lyuh*, 焦心 *-shin*, 焦躁 *-tzauh* ↓; 焦酸 sad at heart, distressed; 焦苦 miserable, wretched.

焦點 *jiaudiaan*, n., (lit. & fig.) focus, focal point.
焦黑 *jiauhei*, adj., burnt black.
焦黃 *jiauhuarng*, adj., yellowish brown, browned (food).
焦急 *jiaujir*, adj., extremely anxious and restless.
焦灼 *jiaujuor*, adj., (1) scorched by fire, burnt; (2) anxious, nervous, worried.
焦渴 *jiaukee*, adj., dying of thirst.
焦枯 *jiau-ku*, adj., withered by sun or heat.
焦雷 *jiau-leir*, n., a clap of thunder.
焦慮 *jiaulyuh*, adj., anxious, worried, apprehensive.
焦煤 *jiaumeir*, n., see *-tahn* ↓.
焦心 *jiaushin*, adj., distressing at heart.
焦思 *jiausy*, adj., anxious, worried, pensive.
焦炭 *jiautahn*, n., coke.
焦糖 *jiautarng*, n., caramel.
焦土 *jiautuu*, adj., scorched-earth: 一片焦土 with everything burned down and lying in ruins; 焦土政策 the scorched-earth policy.
焦躁 *jiautzauh*, adj., anxious and fretful.
焦脆 *jiautzueih*, adj., crisp.

黛 91.63

daih.

N. (1) Eyebrow black, used like eyebrow pencil. (2) In 粉黛 (powder and black) cosmetics, used to denote well-dressed (painted) ladies, or actresses.

Adj. The color black.

Section 91.70 (丿/乚)

皂 91.70

tzauh.
[Var. of 皁 91.10]

煢 91.70

chyurng.

Adj. The orphaned and widowed: 煢獨 orphaned, widowed; 煢煢 lonely.

九 91.70

jioou.

N. & adj. The number nine: 九月 September; 九一八事變 The Mukden Incident of September 18, 1931.

九成 *jioucherng*, n., (1) (mus.) nine movements; (2) ninety per cent: 九成新 90% new.
九竅 *jioouchiauh*, n., the orifices of the body.
九重 *jioou-churng*, n., (1) the sky (formerly, believed to be of nine strata, 九重天 being the highest); (2) the palace grounds.
九泉 *jioou-chyuarn*, n., Hades, the underworld.
九鼎 *jiour-diing*, n., the nine tripods which, according to legend, were cast by Emperor Yu and handed down from dynasty to dynasty as symbols of imperial authority.
九陔 *jioou-gai*, n., see *-tian* ↓.
九皐 *jioou-gau*, n., a marsh, swamp.
九歸 *jioou-guei*, n., (abacus) division by divisors not greater than "9".
九宮格 *jioougung-ger*, n., (callig.) squares into which each page of a copybook is divided (so called from the nine small squares forming a big one).
九廻腸 *jioou-hueircharng*, adj., (of lovers) pining after one another, wasting away through grief.
九九 *jiour-jioou*, n., (1) the period of eighty-one (9×9) days counting from the winter solstice; (2) (math.) multiplication of the numbers 1 to 9 by the same numbers seriatim; 九九表 the multiplication table up to nine times nine.
九連環 *jioou-liarnhuarn*, n., a toy consisting of nine interlocking links.
九流 *jioou-liour*, n., the nine schools of thought in anc. China.
九牛 *jioou niour*, n., as in 費盡九牛二虎之力 spent a tremendous amount of labor or money; 九牛一毛 a drop in the ocean.
九如 *jioou-rur*, n., birthday felicitations ("nine best wishes").
九霄 *jioou-shiau*, n., the farthest limits of the sky.
九死 *jioursyy*, phr., 九死一生 a ten percent chance to survive.
九天 *jioou-tian*, adj., high up in the heaven, sky-high.
九頭鳥 *jiooutour-niaau*, n., (1) an evil omen; (2) a tricky person.
九族 *jioou-tzur*, n., (1) the nine generations from great-great-grandfather down to one's great-great-grandson; (2) nine generations of paternal and maternal relatives.
九五 *jiour-wuu*, n., the royal pre-

rogative or position: 九五之尊.

九垠 *jioou-yirn*, n., the utmost limits of the sky.

九幽 *jioou-you*, n., the nether world, hell.

九淵 *jioou-yuan*, n., an abyss, a deep chasm.

九原 *jioou-yuarn*, n., a cemetery, graveyard.

丸 91.70

warn.

N. (-*tz*, -*'l*) A pill, a small ball: 魚丸 fish ball; 肉丸 pork ball.

V.t. (LL) to make pills: 使婢丸藥 ask a maid to roll pills.

丸藥 *warnyauh*, n., pill of medicine (cf. 丹 42.42, 散 20S.82).

旭 91.70

shyuh.

N. The rising sun.

旭日 *shyuh-ryh*, n., the morning sun.

旭旭 *shyuhshyuh*, adj., (1) bright, clear; (2) full of spirit.

馗 91.70

kueir.

[Var. 逵 11.83]

凭 91.70

pirng.

[Var. of 凴 63.72]

凫 91.70

fur.

N. A species of wild duck: 凫趨雀躍 wild ducks waddle and sparrows leap, i.e., leaps of joy; 凫乙 the difficulty of distinguishing different species of ducks in the distance.

V.i. Swim: 凫水＝浮水.

凫茨 *furtsy*, n., water chestnut, var. of 荸薺.

几 91.70

farn.

[Pop. of 凡 42.70]

鬼 91.70

gueei.

N. (1) A ghost, goblin: 鬼怪 evil spirits; 鬼物 phantoms; 鬼魅 demons; 疑神疑鬼 distrustful, suspicious (lit., "imagining seeing ghosts everywhere"); 鬼使神差 at the behest of supernatural powers; 鬼哭神(狼)號 terrifying cries; 鬼魂 disembodied spirits; 這屋子鬧鬼 the house is haunted. (2) A term of abuse for any ignoble character: 死鬼 you damn fool; 老鬼 an old fool; 冒失鬼 a daredevil; 餓鬼 a glutton; 鴉片鬼 an opium addict; 癆病鬼 a tuberculous person; 小器鬼 a mean miser; 勢利鬼 a bootlicker, toady; 窮鬼 a pauper, poor satyr, devil, church mouse; 色鬼 a satyr, sex maniac; 酒鬼, 醉鬼 a drunkard; 冤鬼 the ghost of a person whose violent death has yet to be avenged; 洋琴鬼 a player of pop music in night clubs. (3) A surname.

Adj. (1) Tricky, deceitful, mischievous: 鬼計多端 wily and mischievous; 鬼胎 -*tai* ↓; 鬼鬼祟祟 malicious, demonical, devilish; 鬼頭鬼腦 secretive, furtive, stealthy; 弄鬼 playing tricks; 搗鬼 instigate trouble. (2) Clever, crafty, artful: 鬼黠 -*shiar* ↓; 鬼機伶兒 devilishly clever; 鬼聰明 ditto; 鬼才 the devil of a genius, clever like a devil. (3) Unbelievable, false: 鬼話 outright lies.

鬼道 *gueei-dauh*, n., (1) witchcraft, sorcery; (2) (Budd.) the way of destiny of hungry ghosts.

鬼燈檠 *gueeidenchirng*, n., (bot.) edible tulip, *Tulipa edulis.*

鬼斧 *gueei-fuu*, adj., as in 鬼斧神工 extremely skillful or "divine" workmanship.

鬼混 *gueeihuhn*, v.i., (1) take a devil-may-care attitude; (2) make nuisance for others.

鬼火 *gueirhuoo*, n., a will-o'-the-wisp.

鬼節 *gueei-jier*, n., the ghost festival on the 15th day of the 7th lunar month (cf. All Souls' Day).

鬼臉(兒) *gueir-liaan*(-*liaa'l*), n., (1) grimaces: 做鬼臉 make grimaces; (2) a mask.

鬼錄 *gueeiluh*, n., a register of the names of the dead supposedly kept in the nether world.

鬼門關 *gueeimernguan*, n., (1) the Styx; (2) the jaws of death.

鬼黠 *gueeishiar*, adj., sly, crafty.

鬼市 *gueei-shyh*, n., (1) an unlighted night fair; (2) a marketplace where ghosts are said to congregate.

鬼祟 *gueeisueih*, (1) v.i., & adj., (of house) (be) haunted; (2) adj., (of conduct) dishonorable, tricky, intriguing.

鬼胎 *gueei-tai*, n., evil plots, dark schemes: 懷着鬼胎 fearful with a guilty conscience.

鬼頭 *gueei'tou*, adj., (of children or things) cute: 鬼頭鬼腦 secre-

九 丸 旭 馗 凭 凫 几 鬼

亅	小	⺊	十	土	ナ	卄	乚卜	丨	一	丁	フ	口	図	冈	㇕	厂	尸	亠	广	宀	丶	乚	弋	心	八	人	乂	一	一	丿丨	𠂉	く
00	01	02	10	11	12	20	21	22	30	31	32	40	41	42	50	51	52	60	61	62	63	70	71	72	80	81	82	83	90	91	92	93

tive, stealthy; 鬼頭刀 --*dau*, n., formerly, a sword for beheading persons sentenced to death. 鬼子 *gueeitz*, n., (abusive) a devil: 洋鬼子 a "foreign devil." 鬼影 *gueir-yiing*, n., an apparition: 正要找他，他鬼影也不見了 just as I wanted to see him, he had vanished without a trace. 鬼蜮 *gueei-yuh*, n. & adj., (a) scheming and malicious (person): 鬼蜮技(伎)倆 malicious intrigues, underhanded tricks.

魈 91.70

shiau.

N. A mythical mountain spirit or demon.

魅 91.70

meih.

N. See 魑^魅 91.70↓.

魃 91.70

bar.

N. Evil spirit causing drought.

魁 91.70

kueir.

N. (1) Leader, chief: 盜魁 bandits chief; 黨魁 party boss; 罪魁 chief culprit; 魁柄 the helm of state. (2) First in civil examinations: 魁元 -*yuarn*↓. (3) A constellation, var. of 奎^星 12.11.

Adj. Big of stature: see 魁梧, 魁偉 -*wuh*, -*weei*↓.

魁岸 *kueir-an*, adj., tall, stalwart.
魁蛤 *kueir-gar*, n., (zoo.) big clam.
魁首 *kueirshoou*, n., the leader, head of band or group.
魁偉 *kueirweei*, adj., tall and big in stature, strong in build.
魁梧 *kueirwuh*, adj., ditto.
魁元 *kueiryuarn*, n., the first in civil examinations.

魎 91.70

liaang.

N. See 魍^魎 91.70.

魍 91.70

waang.

魍魎 *wangliaang*, n., mountain spirits, demons.

魑 91.70

chy.

魑魅 *chymeih*, n., A goblin, banshee, evil mountain sprite.

魆 91.70

shyuh.

Adv. 黑魆魆 frightfully dark.

魋 91.70

tueir.

N. (AC) the brown bear, *Ursus arctos collaris* (also called 赤熊).

兆 91.70

jauh.

[See 22.70]

§91.72 (丿/心)

怹 91.72

tan.

Pron. Courtesy form of 他 (*ta*), he: 怹老人家, 怹老先生 (cf. 您 *nirn* for 你 *nii*).

恁 91.72

rehn (**nirn*).

Pron. (**nirn*) (MC=您) polite form of "you."

V.t. Consider, think of, take into account.

Adj. (1) (MC) that: 恁時 -*shyr*↓; 恁時節 at that time. (2) (MC) what (=modn. 甚麼): 有恁話吩咐 is there anything I can do for you?

Adv. (1) (MC) so, thus, in this way (=modn. 怎): 生死常有，如何恁怕怯 man being mortal, why should one be so afraid of death? 恁般 -*ban*↓; 恁的般 in such a way; 恁些 -*shie*↓. (2) (MC) why: 恁地 -*dih*¹↓.

恁般 *rehnban*, adj., (=modn. 怎般) such a kind of.
恁地 *rehndih*¹, adj. & adv., (MC) (1) such a (person, thing); (2) why, how: 恁地道他不是人? why do you say that he is a brute?
恁的 *rehndih*², adj. & adv., (MC) ditto.

A / B / C

恁來 *rehnlair*, adv., (MC) so, thus.

恁麼 *rehn'mo*, (MC) (1) adv., thus, so, in this way; (2) pron., what: 濟得恁麼事 what does it avail?

恁些 *rehnshie*, adj., (MC) these, so many, of this sort.

恁時 *rehnshyr*, adv., (MC) at that time.

息 91.72

shir.

N. (1) Children: 子息 one's children and children's wives (u.f. 媳): 息婦, 息男, 息女 *-fuh*, *-narn*, *-nyuu*↓. (2) Interest on loan: 年息, 月息, 日息 annual, monthly, daily interest; 起息期 day when capital bears interest; 付息 pay the interest; 股息 stock dividend; 出息 bear interest, (fig.) productive; 有出息 (of young men) will "bear fruit"—be of some use; 沒出息 of no use—will never amount to anything. (3) News: 消息 news, report. (4) Breath: 氣息, 鼻息 breathing; 屏息 hold one's breath in fear or rapt attention; 一息尚存 so long as this breath is left—alive; 喘息 gasp for breath; 瞬息 in a wink; 間不容息 in a split second; 息息相關 vitally interrelated; 歎息 a sigh, also to sigh; 太息, 長太息 draw a deep sigh.

V.i. & t. (1) To grow: 滋息, 蕃息 (of living things) grow and multiply. (2) To rest, stop, cease: 安息, 休息, 歇息, 憩息 to stop for rest; 事遂息 (LL) the matter was then closed, affair was settled. (3) V.t., to stop: 息交 drop friendship; 息兵, 息戰 stop war; 息爭 stop quarrel; 息怒 stop anger, be pacified; 息念頭 drop idea, usu. in pursuing lover, but also other schemes; 息謗 kill the rumor.

息錢 *shir-chiarn*, n., interest money.

息婦 *shirfuh*, n., daughter-in-law.

息耗 *shir-hauh*, n., news, esp. report of sickness, battle.

息肩 *shir-jian*, v.i., to lay down the burden ("ease the shoulder").

息借 *shir-jieh*, v.i., borrow with interest.

息款 *shir-kuaan*, n., interest from deposit.

息脈 *shirmoh*, n., pulse beat.

息男 *shirnarn*, n., one's own son.

息女 *shirnyuu*, n., one's own daughter.

息票 *shir-piauh*, n., interest coupon.

息壤 *shir-raang*, n., (AC) fertile soil.

息事 *shir-shyh*, v.i., to settle affair: 息事寧人 a policy of compromise to let everybody have peace.

息土 *shir-tuu*, n., (AC) see *-raang* ↑.

息影 *shir-yiing*, v.i., to retire from activities (in some place).

悤 91.72

tsung.

[Var. of 匆 92.83]

悠 91.72

you.

V.i. (1) To lift, hold above: 往上一悠, 就舉起來 with a heave, it was lifted up. (2) Do things in a leisurely way: 你老也得悠著來 you, sir, must take your time; 悠停 *-tirng*↓.

Adj. (1) Sad: 悠悠 *-you*↓. (2) Long past and gone, remote: 悠久 *-jioou*↓; 悠謬 *-miouh*↓; 悠遠 *-yuaan*↓.

悠忽 *youhu*, adj., fritter away one's time, energy.

悠久 *youjioou*, adj., long enduring.

悠邈 *youmiaau*, adj., faraway: 良朋悠邈 (friends) separated by long distance.

悠謬 *youmiouh*, adj., absurd (far off the mark).

悠然 *yourarn*, adv., naturally, without effort.

悠停 *you'tirng*, v.i., restrain oneself: 喝酒要悠停點兒, 過多就醉了 one must control oneself a little in drinking, not to get drunk.

悠揚 *youyarng*, adj., (melody) floating, lingering.

悠悠 *youyou*, adj., (1) (travel) long, far going or gone; (2) sad: 悠悠我思 sadly I remember; (3) restless, adrift: 悠悠蕩蕩 restless and drifting without direction; (4) 悠悠之談 abstruse, impractical discussion.

悠遠 *youyuaan*, adj., long, faraway (distance).

您 91.72

nirn.

Pron. (Polite form of address) you (second person singular)

愆 91.72

chian.

N. & adj. (1) Transgression, error, erroneous: 罪愆 sins of transgression or omission; 不愆不忘 (LL) neither err nor forget. (2) Upset: see 愆痾 *-ke*, 愆伏 *-fur*↓.

V.t. To transgress time limit: see 愆期 *-chir*↓.

愆期 *chianchir*, v.i., to transgress

愆慫憊懲懇𠔁貨賀

time limit, delay (in payment, etc.); (2) adj., passed time limit.

愆伏 *chian-fur*, phr., (from 愆陽伏陰) imbalance or upset of *yin* and *yang* principles.

愆滯 *chianjyh*, v.i., get blocked up, delayed.

愆痾 *chianke*, n., a disaster or epidemic, ascribed to imbalance of *yin* and *yang*, see *-fur* ↑.

愆面 *chian miahn*, phr., (LL) be separated (among friends).

愆序 *chianshyuh*, adj., (LL of weather) unseasonable (heat or cold).

愆忒 *chianteh*, n., (LL) sin, fault, transgression.

慫 91.72

suung.

慫動 *suungduhng* (-'*dung*), v.t., instigate to action.

慫恿 *surngyuung*, v.t., ditto.

憊 91.72

beih.

Adj. Tired, fatigued: usu. 疲憊 feel or look exhausted; 面有憊色 have a tired look.

憊賴 *beihlaih*, n., (coll.) a ne'er-do-well.

懲 91.72

cherng.

[Var. 懲]

V.t. (1) (LL) to punish: 懲罰 *-far* ↓; 懲治 *-jyh* ↓; 嚴懲, 重懲, punish sharply; 懲惡, 懲凶 punish the wicked; 懲一警百 punish one as warning to a hundred. (2) Take or give warning: 懲前毖後 take a lesson from the past and avoid future mistakes; 懲忿 guard against losing temper; 懲羹吹齏 once burnt by hot soup, blow at cold pickles—overcautious; 懲辦 to investigate and deal with.

懲創 *cherngchuahng*, v.i., see *-jieh* ↓.

懲處 *cherngchuu*, v.t., to punish, deal with.

懲勸 *cherngchyuahn*, v.t., to warn against transgressions.

懲罰 *cherngfar*, v.t., to deal out punishment.

懲戒 *cherngjieh*, v.t., to stop with warning.

懲治 *cherngjyh*, v.t., to punish.

懇 91.72

keen.

V.i. & t. To beg (person) sincerely or humbly: 懇求 *-chiour* ↓.

Adj. Earnest, sincere: 誠懇 sincere, see 懇切, 懇摯 *-chieh*, *-jyh* ↓.

Adv. Earnestly, sincerely: 懇請, 懇祈 earnestly beg (s. o.); 懇辭 try earnestly to beg off, decline; 懇謝 thank sincerely; 懇勸, 懇諫 earnestly persuade or admonish (s. o.).

懇切 *keenchieh*, adj., sincere, earnest (request, etc.).

懇親會 *keenchin-hueih*, n., meeting of group (clan, alumni) for social purposes.

懇求 *keenchiour*, v. t., to beg (s. o.) sincerely to.

懇摯 *keenjyh*, adj., earnest and warm (plea, words).

§ 91.80 (丿/八)

𠔁 91.80

shing.

[Abbr. of 興 90.80]

貨 91.80

huoh.

N. (1) Money: 貨幣 *-bih* ↓. (2) Goods, commodity: 來貨 incoming goods; 出貨 production of goods; 買貨, 賣貨 buy, sell, goods; 雜貨(店) dry goods (store); 百貨公司 department store; 貨車 freight car, boxcar, truck; 貨倉, 貨棧 a godown, warehouse, storehouse; 貨價 price of goods; 提貨單 bill of lading; 貨真價實 (comm. advertisement) honest prices and goods. (3) (AC) bribery. (4) A term of abuse of persons: 爛貨 louse; 笨貨 idiot, fathead; 賤貨 lout, (of woman) hussy; 不是好貨 is not decent person.

V.t. (LL) to sell: 貨物於市 sell things at the market.

貨幣 *huohbih*, n., currency, coins.

貨布 *huohbuh*, n., (AC) ditto.

貨泉 *huohchyuarn*, n., (AC) ditto.

貨殖 *hyohjyr*, n., (AC) trade and commerce.

貨郎 *huohlarng*, n., formerly, itinerant seller of trinkets, toys, etc.

貨品 *huohpiin*, n., goods, quality of product (scarce, high-class, cheap, etc.).

貨色 *huohseh*, n., kinds and quality of goods: 貨色繁多 many varieties of goods; 好貨色 fine quality of goods.

貨箱 *huohshiang*, n., container (also 箱櫃): 貨箱運輸 containerized shipping, containerization.

貨物 *huohwuh*, n., stock of goods.

貨運 *huohyuhn*, n., freight transportation.

賀 91.80

heh.

N. A surname.

V.i. & t. To congratulate: 慶賀 to celebrate; 道賀 to offer congratulations; 可喜可賀 you are to be congratulated; 祝賀, 恭賀新禧 Happy New Year! 賀客 friends who come to congratulate.

賀電 *heh-diahn*, n., a telegram of congratulations.
賀函 *heh-harn*, n., a letter of congratulations.
賀蘭 *Hehlarn*, n., a compound surname.
賀禮 *heh-lii*, n., present on some happy occasions.
賀年 *heh-niarn*, v.i., offer New Year congratulations; 賀年片 *--piahn*, n., New Year greeting card.
賀若 *Hehruoh*, n., a compound surname.
賀喜 *heh-shii*, v.t., to congratulate on happy occasion.
賀歲 *heh-sueih*, v.i., see *-niarn* ↑.
賀儀 *her-yir*, n., a present on happy occasion.

貸 91.80

daih.

V.i. & t. (1) To loan: 借貸 borrow; 貸出 lend; 貸入 borrow; 告貸 borrow; 賒貸 buy on credit. (2) Let off easily or pardon: 寬貸 forgive (person) for offense; let off easily; 貸減 reduce or convert sentence; 責無旁貸 responsibility for mistake cannot be blamed on others; 嚴究不貸 (offender) will be strictly prosecuted.

貸方 *daihfang*, n., (in balance sheet) the credit side, opp. 借方 debit.
貸借 *daihjieh*, n., lend.
貸主 *daihjuu*, n., creditor.
貸款 *daihkuaan*, n., money loan.

賃 91.80

lihn (re. pr. *rehn*).

V.i. & t. To hire (labor), rent (room, house): 賃房子, 賃屋 rent a room, a house; 房子出賃 house for rent; 賃工 hire(d) help.

賃金 *lihnjin*, n., rental, rent money.

---

§91.81 (ノ/人)

央 91.81

yang.

V.t. To beg: 央求, 央及, 央告 *-chiour*, *-'jir*, *-gauh* ↓; 央請 *-chiing* ↓; 央媒 to ask s.o. to act as matchmaker.

Adj. (1) Central: 中央; 中央政府 the central government. (2) Run out: 夜未央 the night is not spent yet.

央戧 *yang'chiang*, v.i., to drag on (of business, illness): 他的病也不過央戧一天是一天罷了 his illness is just a matter of dragging on from day to day; 這個買賣央戧着 this business is just dragging on (and may close any day).
央請 *yangchiing*, v.i. & t., to make a request; to request (a doctor, etc.).
央求 *yangchiour*, v.t., to beg (a person).
央告 *yanggauh*, v.t., make an earnest request of (s.o.).
央及 *yang'jir*, v.t., see *-chiour* ↑.
央央 *yangyang*, adj., (AC) (1) bright (flags); (2) tinkling, jangling (bells).

臾 91.81

yur.

N. & adv. See 須[A]臾 91S.80.

头 91.81

tour.

[Abbr. of 頭 30S.80]

臭 91.81

chouh (**shiouh*).

N. (1) (**shiouh*) Bad smell, stink, notoriety: 臭味相投 people of the same ilk like each other; 遺臭萬年 leave a name that stinks through the ages. (2) (**shiouh*) (AC) smell in gen.: 其臭如蘭 its smell is like that of the orchid.

V.i. & t. (1) To smell, emit a bad odor: 他往那兒臭到那兒 he smells everywhere he goes. (2) (**shiouh*) U.f. 嗅 to sniff at.

Adj. (1) Stinking, ill-smelling, odoriferous: 臭溝 stinking sewerage; 臭氣熏人 (person) stinks; 腥臭 emitting foul smell, having body odor or smell of raw meat; 臭名 *-mirng* ↓; as term of contempt: 臭女人 woman of bad reputation, hussy; 臭錢 filthy lucre. (2) Suffering decay, unwelcome: 他們本是好友, 近來忽然臭了 the two good friends have recently cooled off; 他在那裏弄得很臭 he has earned a bad name for himself there.

Adv. Severely, mercilessly: 臭打, 臭罵 to beat up, scold, mercilessly (cf. 醜 31S.70); 臭揍 give a severe beating; 臭死 *-syy* ↓.

臭橙 *chouhchern*, n., (bot.) a citrus fruit, *Citrus bigaradia*.

臭蟲 *chouhchurng*, n., bedbug.

臭豆腐 *chouh-douh'fu*, n., fermented bean curd.

臭感 **shiouhgaan*, n., (1) odor in gen.; (2) specific odor of certain minerals when heated or treated.

臭根 *chouhgen*, n., bad, incorrigible character.

臭嚼 *chouhjiaur*, v.i., (sarcastic) chatter nonsense.

臭爛 *chouhlahn*, v.i., to rot.

臭名 *chouh-mirng*, n., notorious reputation.

臭皮囊 *chouh-pirnarng*., n, (Budd.) a bag of stinking fluids, i.e., the human body.

臭事 *chouhshyh*, n., scandal (also 醜事).

臭死 *chouh-syy*, (1) v.i., stinks to heaven; (2) adv., terribly painful: 打了個臭死 beat one half dead.

臭蹄子 *chouhtir'tz*, n., (coll. contempt. or abusive) a hussy.

臭氧 *chouhyaang*, n., (chem.) ozone.

臭么 *chouhyau*, n., (MC) as in 裝煞臭么 put on airs.

奧 91.81

auh.

N. (1) (AC) southwest corner of house. (2) Mystery, see Adj.↓. (3) Hidden recesses, forbidden grounds: 禁奧 palace grounds. (4) Short for 奧地利 Austria: 奧國 Austria (dist. 澳洲 Australia).

Adj. Mysterious, profound: 奧妙 *-miauh*↓; 深奧, 玄奧 abstruse, difficult to understand: 奧旨, 奧義 profound meaning.

奧博 *auhbor*, adj., profound (scholarship, etc.); wealthy.

奧區 *auhchyu*, n., (AC) inland, heartland.

奧林比克 *Auhlirnpiikeh*, n., (translit.) Olympic.

奧妙 *auhmiauh*, adj., mysterious, wonderful, beyond one's understanding.

奧秘 *auhmih*, n., mystery =秘奧.

奧甜 *auhtiarn*, adj., (fruit) sweet and luscious.

奧賾 *auhtzer*, n., (LL) deep mystery.

奧衍 *auhyaan*, adj., deep, profound.

奧援 *auhyuarn*, n., ally, moral or material support during crisis.

火 91.81

huoo.

N. (1) Fire: 生火 light the fire; 點火 light lamp; 放火 set fire, arson; 失火 catch fire accidentally; 救火 to fight a fire; 着火 (*jaur-*) catch fire; 舉火 light fire for cooking meals; 武火, 文火 quick or slow fire in cooking; 火上加油 add fuel to the fire, (fig.) of trouble; 火燒眉毛 fire catches eyebrows—extremely urgent; 火燒了 burned by fire; 火燒心 overanxious, impatient ("heart is burning"); 火燒, 火燎 in flames, on fire, of scorching temperature; 火樹銀花 bonfires display or brilliantly lighted garden. (2) Anger, rage, fury, surge of emotions: 火氣 *-chih*[1]↓; 肝火 gall, anger; 動起肝火 arouse one's gall; 怒火冲天 a surge of great fury; 上火, 發火, 着火, flame up in anger; 他一聽了就上火 he flamed up as soon as he heard it; 無名火 a state of uncontrollable rage; 慾火 the fire of passion. (3) (Chin. med., of food) stimulant to the spleen, the gall, the heart (上火, 肝火, 心火). (4) (Mil.) firepower: 火力 *-lih*↓; 軍火 ammunition; 戰火 battle fire; 砲火 artillery fire; 烽火 signal fires, signs of war coming. (5) A surname.

V.i. & t. To get angry: 他火了, 火兒了 he became angry; 火上加油 add oil to fire, inflame one's anger.

Adj. Fiery: 火性 *-shihng*↓; 火辣辣 irritable, irascible.

火把 *huorbaa*, n., torch.

火伴(兒) *huoobahn(-bah'l)*, n., orig., comrade in arms, now (pop.) colleagues, companions in same establishment.

火棒 *huoobahng*, n., an acrobatic show with lighted torches.

火拔子 *huoobartz*, n., short funnel put over stove to make fire burn faster (also called 拔火罐兒).

火併 *huoobihng*, v.i. & n., open fight between two parties.

火玻璃 *huoobo'li*, n., fireproof glass.

火柴 *huoochair*, n., matches.

火車 *huooche*, n., a train: 火車站 railway station; 火車頭 locomotive.

火成岩 *huoocherngyarn*, n., igneous rocks.

火漆 *huoochi*, n., sealing wax.

火籤 *huoochian*, n., formerly, warrant for immediate presence at court.

火鉗 *huoochiarn*, n., fire tongs.

火氣 *huoochih*[1], (1) n., quick temper: 火氣太盛 very quick-tempered; (2) adj., (of art work) not mellow.

火器 *huoochih*[2], n., firearms.

火齊 *huoochir*, n., (1) (AC) see *-houh*↓; (2) jewelry or jewel-like thing.

火蟲(兒) *huoochurng('l)*, n., firefly, glowworm (coll. for 螢火).

火癉 *huoodan*, n., erysipelas (also called 丹毒).

火斗 *huordou*, n., a charcoal-burning pressing iron.

火房子 *huoofarngtz*, n., low-class resort for beggars and idlers.

火夫 *huoofu*, n., formerly, cook in army, etc.

火蓋 *huoogaih*, n., stove cover.

火鍋 *huooguo*, n., chafing dish.

火耗 *huoohauh*, n., wastage of metal in minting coins.

火候 *huoohouh* (-'*hou*), n., timing in cooking to get proper degree of softness; (fig.) depth of scholarship or thought.

火花 *huoohua*, n., sparks.

火化 *huoohuah*, v.i. & n., cremate, -tion.

火狐 *huoo-hur*, n., the red fox.

火宅 *huoojair*, n., (Budd.) the world of troubles of the senses ("house on fire"); 火宅僧 a married Buddhist monk.

火雞 *huooji*, n., a turkey.

火剪 *huorjiaan*, n., (1) fire tongs; (2) curling tongs, curling irons.

火箭 *huoojiahn*, n., a rocket, rocket missile: 減速火箭 retro-rocket; 掣動火箭 (astron.) braking rocket; 火箭炮 (mil.) *--pauh*, bazooka.

火教 *Huoojiauh*, n., Zoroastrianism, worship of fire.

火計 *huoojih*, n., an employee of a shop (usu. wr. 伙計, 夥計).

火警 *huorjiing*, n., fire alarm.

火酒 *huorjioou*, n., alcohol.

火磚 *huoojuan*, n., firebrick.

火燭(兒) *huoojur('l)*, n., candles and lamps in gen. as possible cause of fire (in Peking dial. also *-ju'l*).

火種 *huorjuung*, n., kindling, material for lighting fire.

火居道士 *huoojyu dauhshyh*, n., a married Taoist priest, cf. *-jair*↑.

火紙 *huorjyy*, n., a paper roll for lighting water pipe for tobacco.

火炕 *huookahng*, n., heated *kang* in North China, see 炕 91D.70.

火坑 *huookeng*, n., "fire-pit"—a place of misery, esp., the life of a prostitute: 落了火坑, 跳出火坑 fall into, get out of, prostitute's life.

火口 *huorkoou*, n., crater.

火筷子 *huookuaih'tz*, n., fire-tongs.

火兒 *huoo'l*, n., see *-chih*[1]↑.

火亮(兒) *huooliahng('l)*, adj., bright, illuminated.

火鐮 *huooliarn*, n., formerly, a flint cutter for getting sparks.

火力 *huoolih*, n., (mil.) firepower.

火籠 *huoo'lung*, adj., suffocated from heat: 花火籠了 flowers wilt from heat.

火爐 *huoolur*, n., a stove; fireplace.

火輪 *huoolurn*, n., (1) (LL) the sun; (2) a steamboat (also 火輪船).

火冒 *huoomauh*, adj., become enraged.

火綿 *huoomiarn*, n., guncotton.

火苗 *huoomiaur*, n., a flame (licking houses).

火泥 *huoonir*, n., fire clay.

火牌 *huoopair*, n., formerly, a military order to render service to imperial courier along the way.

火熱 *huoo-reh*, adj., very hot: 他倆兒打得火熱 they two are enamored.

火絨 *huoorurng*, n., tinder.

火傘 *huorsaan*, n., summer sunshine: 火傘高張 the sun is shining fiercely.

火色 *huooseh*, n., strength and condition of fire in stove; a person's ruddy complexion.

火山 *huooshan*, n., volcano.

火燒 *huooshau*, n., a fire disaster; 火燒雲 resplendent sunset.

火舌 *huoosher*, n., tongue of fire.

火繩 *huoosherng*, n., fuse.

火險 *huorshiaan*, n., fire insurance.

火線 *huooshiahn*, n., direct line of fire in battle.

火匣子 *huooshiartz*, n., (sl.) a cheap coffin.

火硝 *huooshiau*, n., saltpeter.

火性 *huooshihng*, n., (1) strength of fire; (2) fiery temper.

火星 *huooshing*, n., (1) the planet Mars; (2) sparks.

火石 *huooshyr*[1], n., flint.

火食 *huooshyr*[2], n., (1) daily meals, board: 火食不足 insufficient food at meals; 火食費 boarding fee; (2) (AC) eating cooked food instead of raw.

火速 *huoosuh*, adv., urgent: 火速送到 deliver immediately.

火田 *huootiarn*, v.i., (AC) to hunt by burning wooded area.

火頭 *huootour*, n., (1) formerly, the principal cook; (2) (AC) common footmen; (3) person responsible for causing a conflagration.

火彩兒 *huortsaa'l*, n., (Chin. theater) a device to represent appearance of a ghost by burning resin.

火腿 *huortueei*, n., ham.

火筒子 *huortuungtz*, n., a metal funnel or small chimney.

火葬 *huootzahng*, n., cremation.

火災 *huootzai*, n., fire accident, a conflagration.

火浣布 *huorwaanbuh*, n., asbestos cloth.

火網 *huorwaang*, n., (mil.) a crossfire; a barrage.

火眼 *huoryaan*, n., an eye inflammation.

火燄 *huooyahn*, n., flames.

火藥 *huooyauh*, n., gunpowder; 火藥庫 ammunition depot.

火曜日 *huooyauh ryh*, n., (LL) Tuesday.

火引子 *huoryiintz*, n., material for starting fire.

火油 *huooyour*, n., kerosene.

火魚 *huooyur*, n., (zoo.) a fish, *Lepidotrigla strauchi.*

炎 91.81

yarn.

[Related 焰 *yahn*, 91D.21]

N. (1) Inflammation: 氣管炎 bronchitis; 盲腸炎 appendicitis; 關節炎 arthritis; 肺炎 pneumonia; 腦炎 encephalitis; 腦膜炎 meningitis, etc. (2) Flame: 火炎.

Adj. Hot (weather): 炎熱 *-reh*↓; 炎日 hot sun.

炎方 *yarnfang*, n., (AC) the southern region.

炎腫 *yarnjuung*, n., inflammation with swelling.

炎涼 *yarn-liarng*, n., change of temperature; (fig.) change in attitude toward persons: 世態炎涼 change in warmth or coolness in attitude, following upon success or failure.

炎熱 *yarnreh*, adj., blazing hot, sweltering.

炎夏 *yarn-shiah*, n., hot summer.

炎暑 *yarn-shuu*, n., ditto.

炎天 *yarn-tian*, n., hot summer days.

炎炎 *yarnyarn*, adj., scorching, overpowering (influence).

炎陽 *yarn-yarng*, n., scorching sun.

熒 91.81

yirng.

V.i. To shimmer, flicker.

Adj. Shimmering; dazzling, -ed.

熒光 *yirngguang*, n., fluorescence: 熒光燈 fluorescent lamp (now called 日光燈).

熒惑 *yirnghuoh*, v.t., to dazzle, confuse, mislead; p.p., dazzled, perplexed.

熒石 *yirngshyr*, n., (min.) fluorite, fluorspar.

熒熒 *yirngyirng*, adj., shimmering, twinkling (stars), flickering (will-o'-the-wisp).

煲 91.81

bauh.

煲飯 *bauhfahn*, n., a Cantonese food, consisting of rice cooked with meat or sausage in same pot, the latter served separately; a casserole.

§91.82 (丿/乂)

史 91.82

shyy.

N. (1) History: 歷史 ditto; 青史 history in sense of record for posterity; 通史 general history; 野史, 外史 private or unofficial records of a period; 文學史 literary history; 思想史 history of thought; 哲學史 history of philosophy, etc.; 編年史 annals, chronological history; 史料, 史話 *-liauh*, *-huah*↓; 國史館 national archives; 史無前例 unprecedented in history. (2) An official: 御史 imperial censor; 令史, 典史 a government secretary. (3) A surname.

史筆 *shyrbii*, n., a habit of writers to hint at, rather than write explicitly (for reader to read between the lines).

史部 *shyybuh*, n., history as one of the four main divisions of Chin. libraries (經, 史, 子, 集, see 四^{A}部 41.41).

史館 *shyrguaan*, n., national archives, bureau in charge of writing and preserving historical records.

史官 *shyyguan*, n., a court historian.

史話 *shyyhuah*, n., historical narrative.

史料 *shyyliauh*, n., historical data.

史論 *shyy-luhn*, n., historical essay.

史評 *shyy-pirng*, n., historical criticism.

史乘 *shyyshehng*, n., histories, historical works.

史詩 *shyy-shy*, n., epic poetry, historical narrative poem.

史學 *shyyshyuer*, n., (1) the study of history; (2) the science of history, historiography.

史冊 *shyytseh*, n., anc. history books, historical works.

隻 91.82

jy.

N. adjunct. A piece of indeterminate character, usu. can be grabbed by hand; oft. of animal: 一隻雞, 一隻狗 a chicken, a dog, etc., also 一隻眼睛 an eye—not used of things which cannot be grasped or lifted by hand.

Adj. & adv. (1) Lone, alone: 隻手 single-handed, with a lone hand; 隻身 alone (steal into enemy ranks, etc.); 隻影 a lonely figure; 獨具隻眼 (of person) discern what others don't; 隻立 stand alone. (2) Very small number: 片言隻字 just a few words.

燮 91.82

shieh.

[Dist. 變 93.82]

Adj. Regulated, harmonious.

燮和 *shiehher*, adj., living in harmony.

燮理 *shiehlii*, adj., well-regulated: 陰陽燮理 the *yin* and the *yang* are in balance.

雙 91.82

shuang (**shuahng*).

[Pop. 双, 隻]

N. (1) (**shuahng*) A surname. (2) A pair (of chopsticks, hands, knees); a couple, male and female: 成雙成對 in pairs, female and male; 雙親 both parents, father and mother; 父母雙全 both parents living; 雙管齊下 writing with both hands simultaneously—do two things at the same time; 箭貫雙鵰 kill two birds with one stone; 雙杵 hull rice by two persons in alternation; 無雙 peerless, matchless.

Adj. (1) Double, both: 雙面, 雙邊 both sides, bilateral (treaty, etc.); 雙層 double layers; 雙十 *-shyr*↓. (2) Even (days): 雙日.

Adv. In pairs: 雙宿雙飛 (lovers) always keep each other's company, compared to birds flying and nestling together; 雙棲 (lovers) live together; amphibious: 雙棲動物.

雙棒兒 **shuahng-bahng'l*, n., (coll.) twin sons.

雙親 *shuang-chin*, n., both parents: 雙親大人 used in letters to both parents.

雙打 ˋ*shuang-daa*, phr., (tennis) play doubles.

雙方 *shuang-fang*, adv., both sides: 雙方同意 both parties agree.

雙分兒 *shuang-feh'l*, n., double portion.

雙峯駝 *shuangfeng-tuor*, n., two-humped camel.

雙幅(兒) *shuangfur('l)*, n., cloth of double width.

雙鉤 *shuanggou*, v.t., (callig.) trace contour of a stroke, leaving center hollow.

雙掛號 *shuang-guahhauh*, v.t., register a letter with demand for receiver's receipt.

雙關 *shuangguan*, adj., a pun, word with double meaning: 雙關語, 意義雙關 word with double meaning.

雙軌 *shuang-gueei*, n., double track; 雙軌鐵路 double-track railway.

雙宮 *shuang-gung*, n., cocoon with double covering.

雙簧 *shuanghuarng*, n., as in 唱雙簧 an act of entertainment, with one person making mouth gestures and another hidden behind making the voice; (fig.) two persons agree to say the same thing.

雙九 *shuang-jioou*, n., "double-nine"—families of bride and groom meet on 18th day after wedding.

雙立人兒 *shuanglihrer'l*, n., the radical "彳" (91B); index No. 91B, when on left side of character.

雙禮 *shuang-lii*, n., simultaneous bow by bride and groom to elders on wedding day.

雙陸 *shuangluh*, n., an anc. dice game (also wr. 雙六).

雙名 *shuang-mirng*, n., (MC) personal name with two characters.

雙生 *shuangsheng*[1], n., twins.

雙聲 *shuangsheng*[2], n., words with the same initial consonant, alliteration (like 彷彿 *faangfur*); such related words (like 寬, 濶 both beginning with *k*-, 亡, 無 beginning with *w*-).

雙身子 *shuang-shentz*, adj., (woman) being pregnant.

雙響兒 *shuang-shiang'l*, n., firecrackers with double explosions.

雙姓 *shuang-shihng*, n., a two-syllable surname.

雙喜 *shuang-shii*, n., "double happiness"—wedding.

雙雙 *shuangshuang*, adv., in pairs.

雙數(兒) *shuang-shuh('l)*, n., (math.) even numbers.

雙十(節) *shuangshyr(jie)*, n., a Chinese national holiday, on October 10, also called "Double Tenth."

雙石頭 *shuang-shyr'tou*, n., a bar with two stones on the ends for lifting weight.

雙套車 *shuangtauh-che*, n., carriage pulled by team of horses in front and behind (also called 二套車).

雙眼皮兒 *shuang-yaanpier'l*, n., double eyelid.

§91.83 (ノ/〜)

辵 91.83

chuoh.

N. A radical (var. 辶) seen in 道, 巡, etc.; appears as bottom stroke "83" in index system.

V.i. (AC) to walk, stroll.

迦 91.83

jia.

N. (1) 釋迦 (translit. from Sanskr.) Sakya, the clan or family of the Buddha. (2) 迦南 (Bible) Canaan.

迦藍 *jialarn*, n., a Buddhist temple (also 伽藍).

迦葉 *jiayeh*, n., Kasyapa Buddha (also wr. 迦攝).

迫 91.83

poh.

[Err. var. 廹; cogn. of 逼 *bi*, 30.83.]

V.t. To force, compel: 迫他投降 compel one to surrender; 迫死 persecute to death; 迫令 demand, compel by *force majeure* (person to); 迫上梁山 force to join the rebels; 迫從 compel compliance; 迫得 compel: 迫得無路可走 give (person) on choice but to (leave, etc.); 迫不得已 have no choice but; 迫於勢力 compelled by force or circumstances; 強迫 make s.o. do s.t. by force; 壓迫 to oppress.

Adj. Be very close, hard pressed, urgent: 迫不及待 cannot wait, time does not allow; 時間匆迫 in a rush; 局迫 hard pressed; 局勢危迫 situation is tense; 匆迫 compel; 窘迫 persecute.

迫切 *pohchie*, adj. & adv., urgent, -ly (request, etc.).

迫害 *pohhaih*, v.t., ruin, injure, persecute (person).

迫婚 *poh-hun*, v.i., force into marriage.

迫擊砲 *pohjir-pauh*, n., trench mortar.

迫脅 *pohshier*, v.t., compel by force or threat.

迥 91.83

jyuung.

[Pop. of 逈 42.83]

追 91.83

juei.

V.i. & t. (1) To chase after (lit. & fig., enemy, thief): 追女朋友 try

亅	小	⺊	十	土	ナ	廾	ㄴ	丨	一	丁	フ	口	囗	冂	ㄱ	厂	尸	亠	广	宀	丶	乚	弋	心	八	人	乂	〜	一	丿	𠂉	く
00	01	02	10	11	12	20	21	22	30	31	32	40	41	42	50	51	52	60	61	62	63	70	71	72	80	81	82	83	90	91	92	93

to woo a girl friend; 追趕 *-gaan*↓; 追蹤 *-tzung*↓; 追求 *-chiour*↓; 追隨 *-sheir*↓; 追風 said of horse's swiftness; 來者猶可追 (AC) the future can still be redeemed. (2) To trace: 追源, 追究, 追溯 *-yuarn*, *-jiouh*, *-suh*↓. (3) To hanker back, to reminisce, recall the past: 追悼 *-dauh*↓; 追憶, 追念, 追悔, 追想 think back, see *-yih*, *-niahn*, *-hueei*, *-shiaang*↓. (4) In some cases, to act retroactively: 追還舊債 demand payment of old debts; 追封, 追贈 give person posthumous rank; 追贓 recover thief's booty; 追加預算 to pass addition to budget; 追索積欠 demand repayment of past debt. (5) (**duei*) (AC) to carve.

追捕 *jueibuu*, v.t., search and arrest (escaped thief, prisoner).

追求 *jueichiour*, v.t., seek after (wisdom, progress, ideal girl friend).

追悼 *jueidauh*, v.t., to grieve for person's death; 追悼會 *--hueih*, n., memorial service for the dead.

追趕 *jueigaan*, v.t., to chase after: 追趕上去 hurry up, go forward to match s.o.

追歡 *jueihuan*, v.i., (LL) to enjoy oneself: 往歲追歡地 where one was having a good time last year.

追悔 *jueihueei*, v.i. & t., to regret.

追回 *jueihueir*, v.t., to recover (debt, lost property).

追徵 *jueijeng*, v.i., to demand payment of taxes owed.

追薦 *jueijiahn*, v.t., as in 追薦亡魂 to pray for blessing on the dead.

追究 *jueijiou*, v.t., to pursue investigation of origin, sources, cause of event, etc.

追科 *jueike*, v.i., see *-jeng*↑.

追念 *jueiniahn*, v.t., to remember with fond regret (anything past).

追陪 *jueipeir*, v.t., to keep company of an elder.

追認 *jueirehn*, v.t., to approve retroactively.

追想 *jueishiaang*, v.i. & t., to think back (upon old days, etc.).

追隨 *jueisueir*, v.t., to follow (a leader, master).

追溯 *jueisuh*, v.t., to trace back to the sources or early beginnings.

追蹤(踪) *jueitzung*, v.t., to imitate, emulate (anc. models).

追問 *jueiwehn*, v.t., to cross-examine, find out the bottom; to question one responsible for mistake.

追憶 *jueiyih*, v.t., think back (past events), to call up in reminiscence.

追影 *jueiyiing*, v.i., to paint portrait of one deceased.

追遠 *jueiyuaan*, v.i., as (AC) in 愼終追遠 to offer sacrifices to remote ancestors.

追源 *jueiyuarn*, v.t., see *-suh*↑.

追月 *juei-yueh*, n., the day after the full moon at Mid-Autumn Festival.

進 91.83

jihn.

N. (1) Personal ranking: 先進 seniors, persons of higher rank, better knowledge, more experience; (of countries) more advanced; 後進 juniors, persons of lower rank, poorer knowledge, less experience; 後學末進 I, your junior. (2) A courtyard: 前進, 後進 front, back, yard; 兩進院子 a building with a front and a back yard; 進深 *-shen*²↓.

V.i. & t. (1) Go ahead, move forward, advance (opp. 退 fall back, retreat): 前進 proceed, press on, go forth, make headway; 進行 *-shirng*, 進退 *-tueih*, 進逼 *-bi*, 進兵 *-bing*, 進攻 *-gung*, 進止 *jyy*↓; 進佔 (of troops) push on and occupy; 進發 to set out (on a journey); 長進 make progress, advance; 上進 try to do better, (of students) pursue further studies; 進步 *-buh*, 進取 *-chyuu*, 進益 *-yih*, 進展 *jaan*↓; 得寸進尺 the more one gets, the more one wants to have; 進一步 go a step further, furthermore, moreover; 不進則退 one either forges ahead or gradually falls behind. (2) Enter, come in, make way into (opp. 出 leave, go away, depart): 進來 *-'lai*, 進入 *-ruh*, 進口 *-koou*, 進去 *-chyuh*↓; 進京 go to the capital; 進學校 go to school, enroll as a student. (3) Introduce, recommend: 引進 introduce (new plants, varieties, breeds); 進賢 *-shiarn*↓. (4) To present: 進貢 *-guhng*, 進獻 *-shiahn*↓; 進呈 offer (presents) to superior; 進酒 fill up s.o.'s wine cup and toast him; 進香 go on pilgrimage, visit temple. (5) Receive (money payments): 進款 *-kuaan*, 進項 *-shiahng*, 進賬 *-jahng*↓.

進逼 *jihnbi*, v.t., to press hard.

進兵 *jihn-bing*, v.i., despatch troops, to order an attack on the enemy.

進步 *jihnbuh*, v.i. & n., (make) progress, advance(ment), improve(ment): 進步的 progressive.

進程 *jihncherng*, n., progress.

進錢 *jihn-chiarn*, n., cash received.

進出 *jihn-chu*, n., entrance and exit; receipt and expenditure; v.i., go out and in.

進去 *jihn-chyuh*, v.i., go in, enter.

進取 *jihnchyuu*, v.i., endeavor to improve one's lot or acquire more; adj., energetic, enterprising, aggressive (spirit).

進貢 *jihnguhng*, v.i., (of a vassal state) pay tribute to the suzerain.

進攻 *jihngung*, v.t., to mount an attack on (the enemy), (fig.) pursue (girl) with attentions.

進化 *jihnhuah*, (1) v.i., evolve, develop; (2) n., evolution: 進化論 theory of evolution.

進展 *jihnjaan*, v.i. & n., to advance, improve, make progress.

進賬 *jihnjahng*, n., money income, receipts; v.t., enter in account.

進見 *jihnjiahn*, v.t., to interview (s.o.).

進爵 *jihnjyuer*, v.t., promote to a higher rank.

進止 *jihn-jyy*, n., (1) manner of conducting oneself, personal carriage: 進止雍容 dignified in carriage; (2) decision to go forward or not: 取進止 formerly, wait for royal instructions.

進口 *jihn-koou*, n., (1) an entrance; (2) imports.
進款 *jihnkuaan*, n., income, revenue, receipts.
進來 *jihn'lai*, v.i., come in (into), enter.
進入 *jihn-ruh*, v.t., make way into, set foot in, penetrate, be admitted into.
進身 *jihn-shen*¹, v.i., gain entrance or be admitted into some exclusive circle: 進身之階 a steppingstone to such circle.
進深 *jihnshen*², n., (of a house) distance from entrance to the rear.
進獻 *jihnshiahn*, v.t., offer as present, pay tribute.
進項 *jihnshiahng*, n., =-*kuaan*↑.
進賢 *jihn-shiarn*, v.i., recommend properly qualified persons for service.
進修 *jihnshiou*, v.i., pursue further studies, take an advanced course in school or college.
進行 *jihnshirng*, v.i., proceed, go ahead, advance, carry on: 進行曲 a march.
進士 *jihnshyh*, n., formerly, a successful candidate in national examinations, the "third degree" (cf. 秀△才 90.50, 舉△人 90.00).
進學 *jihnshyuer*, v.i., go to school or college.
進退 *jihn-tueih*, n. & v.t., (decision) to do or not to do, go forward or not: 進退維谷 find oneself in a dilemma, between the devil and the deep sea; 進退兩難 equally difficult to go on or retreat.
進言 *jihn-yarn*, v.i., to offer suggestions, make recommendations.
進謁 *jihnyeh*, v.i., to interview (superior).
進益 *jihnyih*, n., progress, improvement (esp. in education).

遑 91.83

huarng.

N. Leisure, time: esp. 不遑 (LL) have no time for; 何遑 (LL) how can I have the time to.

Adv. (1) Hurrying, scurrying. (2) Nervous: 遑遑 -*huarng*↓.

遑遑 *huarnghuarng*, adv., in a hurry.
遑急 *huarngjir*, adj. & adv., urgent, in a great hurry: 遑急萬狀 great urgency.
遑遽 *huarngjyuh*, adj. & adv., hurriedly.

邀 91.83

yau.

V.i. & t. (1) To invite, request: 邀請, 邀集 -*chiing*, -*jir*↓; 邀宴 invite to dinner. (2) To receive (blessings of heaven, reward, award, etc.): 邀賞, 邀功 -*shaang*, -*gung*↓. (3) To stop over: 邀留 -*liour*↓. (4) (Coll.) to weigh: 把這包拿秤邀一邀 weigh this parcel on the scale.

邀請 *yauchiing*, v.t., to invite (professor, lecturer); invite (person to dinner, etc.).
邀功 *yau-gung*, v.i., to seek credit for another's accomplishment: 邀功圖賞.
邀集 *yau-jir*, v.t., to invite (person) to assembly.
邀勒 *yau-leh*, v.t., to force (person) to stay.
邀留 *yauliour*, v.i., invite to stop over.
邀買 *yaumaai*, v.t., as in 邀買人心 (politician) to buy popularity.
邀賞 *yaushaang*, v.i., try to please s.o. so as to win his favor and be rewarded.

邊 91.83

bian.

[Pop. 边]

N. (1) Border, edge, outer regions: 邊緣 border of dress, see -*yuarn*↓; 岸邊 near the bank; 河邊 river bank; 天邊海角 remote regions. (2) Near-by place, around, about: 身邊沒帶錢 do not carry money about person; 旁邊 at the side, near by: 這人旁邊 by this person. (3) Side, section: 左邊, 右邊, 裏邊, 外邊 the left, right side, inside, outside; 前邊, 後邊 the front, the back. (4) Border of a country, frontier: 邊省 border provinces; 邊陲, 邊隘, 邊塞 -*chueir*, -*aih*, -*saih*↓; 拓邊, 殖邊 expand, colonize frontiers; 邊防 frontier defense; 邊患 frontier troubles. (5) A surname.

Adv. Along, while: 邊坐邊談 sit and chat along, sit talking.

邊隘 *bian-aih*, n., frontier pass.
邊鄙 *bianbii*, n., (LL) frontiers, frontier region.
邊陲 *bianchueir*, n., frontier region.
邊幅 *bianfur*, n., (1) width of cloth, paper; (2) character, behavior of person: 不修邊幅 phr., loose, immoral conduct.
邊溝 *biangou*, n., roadside ditch.
邊疆 *bianjiang*, n., national border.
邊界 *bianjieh*, n., borderline.
邊際 *bianjih*, n., (1) border: 邊際效用, 成本, marginal utility, cost; (2) (Budd.) extremity of material universe; (3) clue, point in talk: 說話不着邊際 talk far off the mark or subject.
邊框 *bian-kuang*, n., frame (for pictures, etc.).
邊兒 *bia'l*, n., frequently used in 一邊兒 on one side; 這邊兒 on this side; approach: 摸不着邊兒 cannot find the approach.
邊爐 *bianlur*, n., (MC & dial.) chafing dish.
邊門 *bian-mern*, n., side door.
邊塞 *biansaih*, n., border pass, border region.

邊廂 *bianshiang*, n., side box in theater; (MC) side.
邊心 *bian-shin*, n., (LL) heart of traveller away from home.
邊式 *bianshy*, adj., (Peking dial.) smart, handsome.
邊頭風 *biantour-feng*, n., (med.) migraine.
邊緣 *bianyuarn*, n., hem (of dress, etc.); outskirts.

边 91.83

bian.
[Pop. of 邊↑]

逛 91.83

guahng.

V.i. & t. To stroll, saunter, wander about, visit: 逛逛 take a walk; 逛來逛去 to stroll aimlessly; 逛街 to stroll along the streets, go window-shopping; 逛燈 go and see the sights of the Lantern Festival on the 15th day of the first lunar month; 逛窰子 to visit brothels.

逖 91.83

tih.
[Var. 逷]

V.t. (AC) keep away from.

Adj. (AC) distant, faraway.

迩 91.83

eel.
[Var. of 邇 31.83]

邈 91.83

miaau.
[Cogn. 藐, 渺]

Adj. Distant and small.

邈邈 *miaurmiaau*, adj., distant.
邈然 *miaau-rarn*, adj., ditto.

§91.93 (ノ/く)

媻 91.93

parn.

媻媻 *parnparn*, adv., (AC) to and fro.
媻珊 *parnsan*, adj., stroll slowly (cogn. 婆娑 63.93, also wr. 盤珊).

么 91.93

yau.
[Pop. of 幺 93.93]

螌 91.93

ban.

螌蝥 *banmaur*, n., the Chin. cantharis, *Cicindela chinensis*, a poisonous fly (also 班蝥).

螢 91.93

yirng.

N. (1) A will-o'-the-wisp, glowworm. (2) U.f. 熒, see 91.81.

螢火蟲 *yirnghuoo-churng*, n., will-o'-the-wisp, glowworm.

蠺 91.93

tsarn.
[Common var. 蠶 51.93]

SECTION 91A

§91A.00 (亻/亅)

付 91A.00-1

fuh.

V.t. (1) To deliver (s.t. to s.o.): 付給某人 give to s.o.; 交付 deliver; 付郵 put in the mail; 付梓, 付印 *-tzyy, -yihn*↓. (2) Dismiss off the mind: 付之一笑 laugh and forget about it; 付之一炬 confine to the flames; 付之流水, 東流 throw to the winds, forget affair as s.t. past. (3) To pay: 付錢, 付現款 pay money, cash; 支付 pay out; 卽付 pay on demand; 見票卽付 demand draft, payable at sight; 預付 pay, -ment, in advance; 未付 unpaid; 付清, 付訖 all paid; 止付 stop payment; 代付 pay for another. (4) Entrust: 付托, 付管 *-tuo, -guaan*↓; 付以重任 entrust with important post.

付畀 *fuhbih*, v.t., entrust with responsibility.

付丙 *fuhbiing*, v.i., confine to the flames.

付管 *fuhguaan*, v.t., entrust to one's care.

付款 *fuhkuaan*, v.i., pay out: 分期付款 pay by instalment; 定期付款 pay on term, time payment; 貨到付款 cash on delivery (C.O.D.); 下定付款 cash with order (C.W.O.); 付款交單 documents against payment.

付託 *fuutuo*, v.t., entrust (person, affair).

付鋅 *furtzyy*, v.i., send to press.

付印 *fuhyihn*, v.i., ditto.

傅 91A.00-1

fuh.

N. (1) A surname. (2) Teacher: 師傅 (LL) teacher; 太傅, 太子太傅 Imperial Tutor to crown prince.

V.t. (1) Apply: 傅粉 apply face powder; 傅彩 add coat of colors, (cf. 敷 10S.82). (2) Add to, increase: 傅益 as rare var. of 附益.

傳 91A.00-1

*chuarn (*juahn).*

N. (1) (*juahn) Biography: 傳記 ditto; 列傳 section in dynastic histories, devoted to biographies of famous men; 外傳, 別傳 other than official biography; 小傳 a short biographical sketch; 自傳 autobiography; 立傳 to write a biography for s.o. (2) (*juahn) Anc. commentary: 傳注, 傳疏 *-juh, -shu*↓; 春秋三傳 the three records or elucidations relative to events covered in Confucius' *Spring and Autumn Annals.* (3) (*juahn) Courier system: 傳舍, 傳驛 *-sheh, -yih*↓. (4) (*chuarn*) Tradition: 眞傳 true oral tradition; 衣鉢眞傳 (Budd.) true teachings: 家傳 inherited in the family; 遺[△]傳 22.83.

V.i. & t. (1) To deliver, pass on, around or to posterity: 傳送, 傳遞 *-suhng, -dih*↓; 傳旨, 傳詔 deliver imperial decree; 傳信 deliver a letter; 傳檄 deliver a declaration of war; 傳閱, 傳視 circulate, pass round for perusal. (2) To spread: 名傳世界 name spreads over the world; 傳道 *-dauh*[1]↓; 宣傳 to publicize, do propaganda, also spread (doctrine, belief); 傳播(布), 傳染 *-boh (-buh), -raan*↓; 傳病 spread disease. (3) To bequeath: 傳子傳孫 bequeath to children and grandchildren; 傳家, 傳世 *-jia, -shyh*[2]↓. (4) To transmit: 傳聲, 傳熱 transmit sound, heat; 傳電 conduct electricity; 傳導 *-dauh*[2]↓. (5) To summon to court: 傳案, 傳訊 *-ahn, -shyuhn*↓.

傳案 *chuarn-ahn*, v.t., to summon to court.

傳播 *chuarnboh*, v.t., to spread (news, ideas, disease, etc.).

傳布 *chuarnbuh*, v.t., ditto.

傳奇 *chuarnchir*, n., (1) (Tarng, Suhng Dyns.) a short story; (2) (Yuarn Dyn.) a short play; (3) (Mirng Dyn.) a long play; 傳奇般 adj., like a story.

傳代 *chuarndaih*, v.i., to bequeath (throne, object) to future generations.

傳單 *chuarndan*, n., a billet, a handbill, a sheet circulated for publicity.

傳達 *chuarndar*, v.t., (1) to communicate (thoughts, ideas); (2) to transmit order from above.

傳道 *chuarndauh*[1], v.i., & t., to preach religion, teach disciples.

傳導 *chuarndauh*[2], v.t., to conduct (heat, electricity).

傳燈 *chuarndeng*, v.i., (Budd.) to pass the lamp of doctrine from master to pupil.

傳遞 *chuarndih*, v.t., to hand round (letter, message).

傳訛 *chuarn-er*, phr., 以訛傳訛 inherit and pass on wrong reports or errors.

傳發 *chuarnfa*, v.i., (LL) order to start on journey.

傳法 *chuarn-faa*, phr., (Budd.) to pass on teaching from master to disciple.

傳觀 *chuarnguan*, v.t., to circulate (object) for public inspection.

傳鼓 *chuarn-guu*, phr., to announce visitor by beating drum at funeral.

傳喚 *chuarnhuahn*, v.t., to summon (person) to court.

傳眞 *chuarnjen*, n., a portrait; portraiture.

傳家 *chuarn-jia*, v.i., bequeath to the family: 傳家之寶 art object kept as heirloom.

傳教 *chuarnjiauh*, v.i., to preach; 傳教士 *--shyh*, n., missionary.

傳記 **juahnjih*, n., a biographical sketch, biography.

亅	小	卜	十	土	ナ	廾	乚	丨	一	丁	フ	口	区	冈	冂	厂	尸	亠	广	宀	丶	乚	弋	心	八	人	乂	一	丿	丿	𠂉	く
00	01	02	10	11	12	20	21	22	30	31	32	40	41	42	50	51	52	60	61	62	63	70	71	72	80	81	82	83	90	91	92	93

傳經 *chuarn-jing*, phr., (1) to hand down the classics or sacred books; (2) (Chin. med.) (of disease) pass to different systems in the body.

傳注 **jyuahnjuh*, n., commentary on classic.

傳重 *chuarnjuhng*, phr., see 重^孫 90.11.

傳種 *chuarn-juung*, v.i., to reproduce own kind.

傳旨 *chuarnjyy*, v.i., to deliver imperial decree.

傳票 *chuarn-piauh*, n., (1) a court summons, subpoena; (2) (accounting) a voucher.

傳染 *chuarnraan*, v.t., to infect, communicate disease; 傳染病 communicable or infectious disease.

傳審 *chuarnsheen*, v.i., to summon for trial.

傳舍 **juahnsheh*, n., formerly, courier station.

傳神 *chuarn-shern*, v.i., to give expression in art work, esp. portraiture; see *-jen*↑.

傳寫 *chuarnshiee*, v.i., to make copies by hand.

傳信 *chuarn-shihn*, v.i., (1) to communicate (tradition, belief); 傳信錄 story of passing of teaching from master to disciple; (2) to deliver letters; 傳信鴿 homing pigeon.

傳薪 *chuarn-shin*, phr., (from 薪盡火傳——莊子) to pass on the torch of learning.

傳授 *chuarnshouh*, v.t., to teach, hand down (anc. teaching, esp. esoteric).

傳疏 **juahnshu*, n., commentary and further elucidation of said commentary.

傳説 *chuarnshuo*, v.i. & n., story that goes around: 民間傳説 folk tale; 傳説另一消息 I hear another piece of news.

傳示 *chuarnshyh*¹, v.i., to show around.

傳世 *chuarn-shyh*², v.i., to bequeath to posterity.

傳宣 *chuarnshyuan*, v.t., to summon to imperial audience.

傳訊 *chuarnshyuhn*, v.t., to summon for trial.

傳送 *chuarnsuhng*, v.t., to deliver (message, news).

傳統 *chuarntuung*, n., (1) tradition of ideas; orthodox tradition; (2) imperial succession.

傳贊 **juahntzahn*, n., brief moral comment (or eulogy) at end of biographical sketch.

傳宗 *chuarntzung*, v.i., see *-daih*↑.

傳聞 *chuarnwern*, phr., it is reported that, I hear that.

傳言 *chuarnyarn*, n., story circulated, a report.

傳揚 *chuarnyarng*, v.t., to spread (teaching, etc.).

傳夜 *chuarn-yeh*, v.i., to go round as night watchman.

傳驛 **juahnyih*, n., courier station.

傳疑 *chuarnyir*, v.i., to pass on (story, theory, etc.) with reservations as to authenticity.

侍 91A.00–1

shyh.

N. Attendant: 侍從, 侍者, 侍衛, etc. *-tzuhng*, *-jee*, *-weih*, etc.↓; 侍婢, 侍女, 侍兒 *-beih*, *-nyuu*, *-er*, etc.↓; 內侍, 常侍 palace attendant, official-in-waiting, (since Tarng Dyn.) eunuch.

V.t. To attend upon, to wait upon: 侍側, 隨侍 to wait upon; 服侍 to serve, look after (master, the aged, the sick); 侍奉 *-fehng*↓.

侍婢 *shyhbeih*, n., formerly, personal attendant maid or maid-slave.

侍讀 *shyhdur*, n., royal tutor, a rank varying in duties from one dynasty to another, including editorship.

侍兒 *shyh-er*, n., personal maid-servant.

侍奉 *shyhfehng*, v.i. & t., to attend upon (parents, ruler, etc.).

侍者 *shyhjee*, n., an attendant, a waiter.

侍講 *shyhjiaang*, n., imperial tutor, scholar-in-waiting, a Hanlin academician, varying from one dynasty to another.

侍郎 *shyhlarng*, n., formerly, official rank, with different status, including (Tarng) a minister of imperial secretariat; oft. equiv. vice-minister.

侍女 *shyhnyuu*, n., personal maid.

侍從 *shyhtzuhng*, n., royal retinue.

侍衛 *shyhweih*, n., retinue of bodyguards.

侍御 *shyhyuh*, n., royal attendants in gen.

儔 91A.00–1

chour.

N. Mate, companion, rival: 無儔 without rival.

儔類 *chourleih*, n., class, people of the same class.

儔匹 *chourpii*, n., rival.

倚 91A.00–1

yii.

[Closely related to and largely interch. 依 91A.02]

V.i. & t. (1) To lean on: 倚門而立 stand leaning by the door; 倚杖 lean on a cane, see 倚仗 *-jahng*²↓. (2) To rely on (wealth, powerful connections): 倚勢 *-shyh*²↓. (3) To lean heavily on (person) for help: 倚負 *-fuh*↓; 倚託, 倚賴 *-tuo*, *-laih*↓.

倚傍 *yiibahng*, v.i., to copy slavishly (anc. models), claim the prestige of schools and -isms.

倚畀 *yiibeih*, v.t., to rely on for advice, entrust moral responsibility to (person): 倚畀正殷 rely heavily on his advice.

倚薄 *yiibor*, v.t., (LL) to crowd together, pile on top of each other (such as one illness after another).

倚負 *yiifuh*, v.t., rely, depend on

for a living.

倚伏 *yiifur*, v.i., to be causally related: 禍福相倚伏 in fortune lies the seed of misfortune, and *vice versa*.

倚杖 *yii-jahng*[1], (1) phr., to lean on a cane; (2) v.t., 倚仗 to rely on (powerful connections, etc.), to rely for help.

倚仗 *yiijahng*[2], v.t., to rely on powerful connections (also 依).

倚著 *yiijuor*, (1) v.t., rely on support; (2) n., s.o. or s.t. to rely on.

倚靠 *yiikauh*, v.t., ditto (also 依「靠).

倚賴 *yiilaih*, v.t., to rely on (s.o.), not to stand on one's own feet (also 依); 倚賴性 lack of self-reliance, inability to stand on one's own feet, habit to depend on others.

倚閭 *yii-lyur*, phr., see *-mern*↓.

倚門 *yii-mern*, phr., (1) 倚門倚閭 said of mother waiting for son's return ("lean waiting by house door, and then by alley gate"); (2) 倚門賣笑 said of prostitutes standing by the door and smiling on passengers.

倚聲 *yii-sheng*, phr., to write 宋詞 *tsyr*, whose form is governed by the melody.

倚恃 *yii-shyh*[1], v.t., to depend on (also 依).

倚勢 (仗勢) *yii-shyh*[2], phr., to rely on powerful connections.

倚托 *yiituo*, v.t., to rely on s.o.'s support (also 依).

仃 91A.00-3

ding.

Adj. 伶仃 lonely, without relatives.

何 91A.00-3

her.

N. A surname.

Pron. What: 有何可說 what can I say? 有何不同 what is the difference? 爲何 for what reason? 何去何從 what should one do?

Adj. What: (LL also gen.)＝甚麽: 何益, 何害 what's the advantage? what's the harm? etc.; 何年, 何日 what year, day? 何人 who? 何處, 何地 what place? 何時 when? 何故, 何因, 何爲 why? for what reason? 是何道理 what is the explanation for this?

Adv. (1) How, why (interrogative): 何以這樣 how so? 何不這樣 why not this way? 何不先走 why don't (you) go first? 何樂而不爲 gladly, I don't see any reason why not; 何克臻此 (LL) how could it achieve this (without great persistence, etc.)? 幾何 (LL) how many? also geometry; 如何 how? 如何做法 how it is done? 奈何 (in remonstration) why (did he risk it)? etc.; 何苦 *-kuu*↓. (2) How (in exclamation): 哀音何動人 how touching! (3) Equiv. negative 不: 何敢＝不敢 how dare I, I dare not; 何堪＝不堪 how can I bear (to see s.t.); 何堪設想 dare not imagine; 何必這樣 (＝不必) why must it be so, it's too much trouble; 何須 (＝不須). Many of these constructions are extremely idiomatic, see below↓.

何必 *her bih*, phr., not necessary.

何不 *her buh*, phr., why not.

何嘗 *hercharng*, adv., never: 何嘗見過錢 never saw a cent; as a counter question: 我何嘗不知道 don't I know? (of course I know).

何期 *herchir*, adv., contrary to expectation: 何期有這樣結局 never thought it would end up like this (same usage with 何料＝不料).

何處 *herchuh*, adv., where, what place?

何啻 *herchyh*, phr., not different from, is the same as: 何啻天壤之別 the difference is like between heaven and earth; 何啻殺父 it's the same as if (s.o.) killed his own father.

何等 *herdeeng*, adv., (1) how (＝very): 何等快樂 how happy; 何等固執 how stubborn; (2) what kind: 何等人物 what kind of a person?

何得 *herder*, adv., how . . . can: 何得推開責任 how can one deny the responsibility?

何獨 *her dur*, phr., is it only (＝not only): 何獨問我 why question only me?

何妨 *her'fang*, adv., "what's the harm": 何妨試試 no harm trying; 何妨看一看 let's take a look.

何敢 *her gaan*, phr., how . . . dare (＝dare not).

何干 *her gan*, phr., 與你何干 what's that to you? has nothing to do with you.

何故 *herguh*, adv., for what reason? why (leave without permission, etc.)?

何者 *herjee*, adv., which one: 何者好, 何者不好 which one is good and which is bad.

何至 *herjyh*, adv., would not . . . to such extent: 何至一敗塗地 would not have suffered such crushing defeat (if, etc.)

何堪 *her kan*, phr., it's too much to bear: 何堪回首 (poet.) it's too sad to look back.

何況 *herkuahng*, adv., besides, furthermore.

何苦 *herkuu*, adv. phr., for what earthly reason? totally unnecessary: 你這是何苦 it's unnecessary to do this; 何苦來 why bring this trouble on yourself?

何乃 *her naai*, phr., why then?

何若 *herruoh*, adv., more literary than 何如 *-rur*↓.

何如 *herrur*, adv., (1) why not: 何如對他直講 why not talk to him directly; (2) how about: 再來一盤棋, 何如 how about another game of chess? (3) what do you think: 我比他何如 what do you think of me as compared with him?

何消 *hershiau*, adv., not necessary: 這何消你說 you don't have

亅	小	⺊	十	土	𠂇	卄	凵	丨	一	丁	𠃌	口	区	冈	冂	厂	尸	亠	广	亠	丶	乚	七	心	八	人	乂	乛	一	丿	𠂉	く
00	01	02	10	11	12	20	21	22	30	31	32	40	41	42	50	51	52	60	61	62	63	70	71	72	80	81	82	83	90	91	92	93

to tell me this.

何首烏 *hershoouwu*, n., (bot.) *Polygonum multiflorum*.

何事 *hershyh*, adv., (LL) for what reason: 何事令你如此煩惱 what makes you so worried? 干卿何事 (LL) what has that to do with you?

何時 *hershyr*, adv., when, at what time: 何時歸來 what time are you coming back?

何須 *hershyu*, adv., not necessary: 何須你自己去 you do not have to go yourself.

何許 *hershyuu*, adv., (LL) how many, so many; from what place: 不知何許人 his place of origin unknown.

何曾 *hertserng*, adv., see *-charng*↑.

何哉 *her tzai*, phr., (LL) why?

何在 *her tzaih*, phr., where is (s.t.): 那人何在 where is that person? 用意何在 what is the motive? 「rhet. question).

何則 *her'tzer*, phr., why? (a

何足 *hertzur*, phr., not worthy of: 何足掛齒 not worth bothering about. 「by . . .?

何謂 *her weih*, phr., what is meant

何爲 *her weir*, adv., (1) why (in rhet. question): 何爲捨此取彼 why choose this rather than that? 意欲何爲 what is (he) trying to do? (2) what is: 何爲五大洲 what are the Five Continents?

何以 *heryii*, adv., (1) why: 何以故 for what reason? 何以他要辭職 why does he want to resign? (2) how: 何以言之 how should one explain it? 何以交代 how to give a proper account? 何以自解 how can one justify oneself?

何有 *her youu*, phr., (LL) one would think nothing of, it's not difficult: 能以禮讓，爲國乎何有 (AC) if one taught good manners, it would be nothing difficult to rule a country.

何由 *heryour*, adv., how come: 何由見得 what makes you think so?

例 91A.00-3

lih.

N. (*tz*) (1) Example, precedent, s.t. analogous: 照例 according to usual practice; 舉例 give example, for instance; 援例 follow a set precedent; 前例, 先例 precedent; 示例 what is shown as example; 例如 for example; 例句 sentence as example; 常例, 慣例, 舊例, 成例 usual practice; 例案 regular practice and precedents; 例外 exception; 無例外 without exception; 破例 break a precedent or rule; 開一(惡)例 set a (bad) precedent. (2) Routine, what is regular: 例行公事 routine business; 例假 regular holiday. (3) Statutes, regulations, specific rules: 例規, 規例 regulations; 法例 legal statutes; 判例 a court decision serving as a precedent; 凡例, 例言, 總例 author's "general remarks" on selection, organization and points of detail about a book.

V.t. To compare: 以此例彼 compare one thing with another.

例證 *lihjehng*, n., (math.) proof of a given proposition or theorem.

例假 *lihjiah*, n., a legal holiday (also 例假日).

例如 *lihrur*, phr., for example, for instance, such as.

例外 *lihwaih*, n., an exception.

例言 *lihyarn*, n., gen. remarks on points of detail of a book.

倒 91A.00-3

daau (in sense of "fall down," "tumble down"), **dauh* (in sense of "reverse").

V.i. Fall down, lie down: 房子倒了 house tumbles down; 倒鳳顛鸞 or 顛鸞倒鳳 have sexual intercourse. (2) Take turns: 倒班兒 take turns; 倒不開 cannot meet the turnover in business. (3) Go bankrupt: 銀行倒了 the bank is bankrupt.

V.t. (**dauh*) Pour out: 倒茶, 倒水 pour tea, water; 倒拉圾 pour out garbage; 倒過來 put in reverse.

Vb. complement. Down: 推倒, 打倒 push down, overthrow(n); 跌倒, 摔倒, 栽倒 fall down; 辯倒 defeat by argument; 塌倒, 坍倒 or 倒塌, 倒坍 tumble down.

Adv. (1) (**dauh*) Back, in reverse order or wrong direction: 倒退 fall back; 倒流 flow back; 倒轉 turn in reverse; 倒敘 narrate from the end; 倒置, 倒裝 set upside down, set up wrong; 倒懸 hang upside down; 倒背着手 hands on the back; 倒賠, 倒欠 be in deficit; 太阿倒持 allow one's powers to fall into another's hands; 倒戈 *-ge*↓; 倒行逆施 (of government) exercise tyrannical rule; 倒抽一口氣 gasp inwards in surprise; 倒綳孩兒 "tie baby the wrong way," make mistakes in common things or when one assumes too much; 倒打鑼兒 orig. a woman's haircoil, "reversed gong," (fig.) everything upside down; 倒打一耙 blame on others while oneself is at fault.

Adv. conj. (**dauh*) Nevertheless, after all (＝到底): 他倒底說得不錯 what he said wasn't wrong after all; 這倒不要緊 after all, this is not so important; on the contrary (＝反而): 倒把事情弄僵了 on the contrary, contrary to what you think, the matter has been made worse; 這樣倒好辦 (＝反而好辦) as it is, the matter is so much simpler; 倒不如 rather: 倒不如死了乾淨 I'd rather die, it would seem better to die; but: 你說是他, 倒不是他 you think it is he, but it isn't; 倒是他太太拿錢出來 (he refused) but it was his wife who put up the money.

倒把 *daaubaa*, v.i., (1) back down, fall; (2) *daurbaa*, (coll.) buy stocks on margin.

倒包 *daaubau*, v.i., substitute one thing for another; give away gift received to s.o. else.

倒扁兒 *daurbiaa'l*, v.i., (coll.) run around to get cash or goods.

倒閉 *dauubih*, v.i., go bankrupt.

倒插 **dauhcha*, n., a literary technique of beginning at the middle of the story or mentioning s.t. to be expanded later.

倒欠 *dauhchiahn*, v.i., to owe instead of gaining.

倒蛋 *daaudahn*, v.i., make trouble, create mischief (also wr. 搗蛋).

倒斷 *daauduahn*, v.i., as in 無倒斷 (MC) without stop.

倒戈 **dauhge*, v.i. & n., mutiny; (of warlords) change sides (Peking coll. pr. *daauger*).

倒掛 **dauhguah*, n., (1) (zoo.) a kind of parakeet; (2) v.i., hang upside down.

倒好(兒) **dauhhaau('l)*, v.i., to hiss at performance (reverse applause).

倒換 *daauhuahn*, v.i. & t., replace.

倒價 *daaujiah*, n., selling-out price.

倒嚼 *daaujiauh*, v.i., chew the cud.

倒流刺 **dauhliourtsyh*, n., hangnail.

倒楣 *daaumeir*, adj., unlucky, run into bad luck.

倒嗓 *daursaang*, adj., having hoarse voice (of opera singers).

倒屣 **dauhshii*, v.i., in 倒屣相迎 hearty welcome (not waiting to put on slippers properly).

倒數 **dauhshuh*, n., (math.) reciprocal.

倒懸 **dauhshyuarn*, v.i., be hanged upside down; extreme oppression under tyranny.

倒許 **dauhshyuu*, adv., perhaps (=也許).

倒踏門 *dauh-tah-mern*, v.i., (of bridegroom) adopts wife's family name.

倒騰 *daau'teng*, v.i., turn upside down (also wr. 搗騰).

倒貼(兒) **dauhtie (-tie'l)*, v.i. & t., lose in bargain (like selling below cost); (sl.) (of a woman) pay her paramour instead of being paid.

倒替 *daautih*, v.i., substitute, replace.

倒頭 *daautour*, v.i., (1) lay down one's head to sleep; (2) die: 他剛一倒頭 the moment he dies; 倒頭飯, 倒頭兒, 倒頭紙 meal given, prayer said, paper money burned at death.

倒彩 **dauhtsaai*, n., as in 喝倒彩 to hiss a speaker or actor.

倒倉 *daautsang*, n., see *-saang* ↑.

倒曹 *daautsaur*, v.i., (coll.) "lose face."

倒栽葱 **dauhtzaitsung*, v.i., fall head down first.

倒竈 *daautzauh*, adj., see *-meir* ↑.

倒字(兒) *daautzyh (-tzeh'l)*, to mispronounce (in Peking opera).

倒影 **dauhyiing*, n., inverted image or reflection in water.

倒運 *daauyuhn*, n., bad luck; (**dauh*) reverse.

仔 91A.00–3

tzyy (**tzaai*, **tzy*).

N. (**tzaai*, *tzyy*) A very small thing, a kid: 豬仔 a piglet, a contemptible fellow, a victim of slave traffic; (Cantonese) s.t. small: 細蚊仔 *saimengtzaai*, a child; 牛仔褲 cowboy pants.

仔肩 **tzyjian (-tzyy)*, n., duties, responsibilities, official burdens.

仔密 *tzyy'mi*, adj., (of knitwear) close-knitted (of textiles) close-woven.

仔細 *tzyyshih*, v.i. & adj., (1) pay(ing) attention to every detail, do(ing) things carefully; (2) attentive, careful.

側 91A.00–4

tseh (also *tzeh*).

V.i. & t. (1) To slant, incline (ears), move sidewise (eyes): 側耳, 側目, 側聞 *-eel, -muh, -wern* ↓. (2) To incline forward: 側重 *-juhng* ↓.

Adj. (1) Side: 側面, 側室 *-miahn, -shyh* ↓; 側門 side door. (2) (AC) immoral, seductive: 側媚, 側豔, 側麗 enticing, seductive; 側慝 immoral.

側筆 *tseh-bii*, n., method of laying brush on paper at a slanting angle.

側柏 *tsehbor*, n., a species of cypress, the arborvitae, *Thuja orientalis*.

側耳 *tseh-eel*, v.i., to incline one's ears to listen.

側擊 *tsehjir*, v.t., to make flank attack: 旁敲側擊 make oblique references, innuendoes, sly injurious remarks.

側重 *tsehjuhng*, v.t., to lay special emphasis (on aspect).

側面 *tsehmiahn (-'mian)*, n., side view; side dimension; adv., from the side.

側目 *tseh-muh*, v.i., to look askance at.

側身 *tseh-shen*, v.i., to lean to one side; to occupy uneasy place in some group.

側室 *tsehshyh*, n., (1) concubine; (2) (AC) lineage of s.o. other than the eldest son.

側聽 *tsehting*, v.i., to listen on the side, to eavesdrop.

側聞 *tsehwern*, v.i., to learn on the side (news) from others.

們 91A.00–5

mern (usu. *'men*).

Pron. part. Plural particle for pron.: 我們, 你們, 他們 we, you, they; (now also more generally used for persons: 朋友們, 同胞們 friends, fellow citizens, but not for things like teacups, glasses).

停 91A.00–6

tirng.

停 俯 佇 偷

N. Ten per cent (＝成),...out of ten: 十停人家去了九停 nine out of ten families are gone.

V.i. & t. (1) To stop: 停住, 停著, 停下來 come to a stop; 停一會, 停停(兒) by and by, after a while; 不停的(動, 講, 跳) (move about, talk, jump) continuously; 停用 to stop using: 停駛 stop engine (of ship); 停刊 stop publication (of periodical); 停售 stop selling; 停戰 cease fire; 停妻再娶 divorce wife and remarry. (2) V.i., to bog down, remain inactive: 停頓, 停滯 *-duhn, -jyh*↓.

V.t. To fix or get ready: 停好了 (room, etc.) has been got ready; 調停 mediate, arbitrate (a dispute); (in participial use) 停當 got ready, all in proper place; 停當, 停妥, 停勻 *-dahng, -tuoo, -yurn*[1]↓.

停辦 *tirng-bahn*, v.t., give up, close up (business, project, school); v.i., close down.

停泊 *tirngbor*, v.i., to lie at anchor, lie alongshore.

停車 *tirng-che*, v.i., to stop driving, to park: 停車場 *--charng* (*--chaang*), a parking lot.

停牀 *tirng-chuarng*, v.i., lie on deathbed (cf. *-lirng*↓).

停當 *tirngdahng*, adj., all set, all arranged (of luggage, various arrangements for trip, etc.).

停頓 *tirngduhn* (*-'dun*), v.i., be at a standstill owing to difficulties, bog down.

停付 *tirng-fuh*, v.i., stop payment (of check, salaries).

停工 *tirng-gung*, v.i. & n., stop work, stoppage of work.

停戰 *tirng-jahn*, v.i. & n., to cease fire; a cease fire, armistice.

停滯 *tirngjyh*, v.i., be held up, delayed, not progress normally; be tied up, blocked up.

停止 *tingjyyr*, v.i. & t., gen. word for "stop" (of work, negotiations, clock).

停職 *tirngjyr*, v.i. & t., relieve of office, dismiss, suspend.

停刊 *tirng-kan*, v.i., cease publication (of periodical).

停課 *tirng-keh*, v.i., suspend classes in school.

停潦 *tirnglauh*, n., cesspool.

停留 *tirngliour*, v.i., stop over during journey, delay for rest, etc.

停靈 *tirng-lirng*, v.i., to keep coffin at certain place pending burial.

停水 *tirng-shueei*, (1) v.i., stop water supply; (2) n., still water.

停屍間 *tirng-shy-jian*, n., morgue.

停學 *tirng-shyuer*, v.i., give up schooling; suspend from school.

停訊 *tirng-shyuhn*, v.i., stop court proceedings.

停妥 *tirngtuoo*, adj., (of arrangements) all set.

停飲 *tirngyiin*, n., (med.) indigestion, form of stomach affection.

停勻 *tirngyurn*[1], adj., well blended or proportioned.

停雲 *tirngyurn*[2], phr., (allu.) thinking of absent friends or relatives.

俯 91A.00-6

fuu.

[Cogn. 伏 91A.81, 附 32A.00]

V.i. To bend down: 俯伏 prostrate; 俯首 bend one's head (in thinking, etc.); 俯首無言 bend one's head in silence; 俯首貼耳, 俯首傾耳 whisper, listen closely; 俯首順從, 就範 obey, submit "with bent head"; 俯拾 stoop and pick up; 俯拾即是 can find (s.t.) everywhere.

Adv. (Court.) design to, condescend to, prefixed to many vbb.: 俯允, 俯准 condescend to grant, approve (request); 俯念 kindly consider or remember; 俯察, 俯順輿情 (of superior) consider carefully, yield to public sentiment.

俯就 *fuujiouh*, v.i., (court.) deign to accept (post).

俯從 *fuutsurng*, v.i. & t., follow others' lead; deign to follow advice, request.

俯仰 *furyaang*, n., as in 俯仰之間 in but a short moment.

佇 91A.00-6

juh.

[Var. of 竚]

V.i. To stand waiting.

佇俟 *juhhouh*, v.i., to wait patiently or anxiously (for your reply 明教, etc.).

佇立 *juhlih*, v.t., to stand still.

佇盼 *juhpahn*, v.t., see *-houh*↑.

偷 91A.00-8

tou.

[Usu. printed 偸]

N. Burglar: 小偷兒 petty thief.

V.i. & t. (1) To steal (oft. forming words with nn. or vbb. like a prefix meaning secretly, stealthily): 偷東西 steal things (jewelry, etc.); 偷取, 偷來, 偷得 succeed in stealing; 我被偷了 I have been burglarized; 偷竊 *-chieh*↓; 偷雞摸狗 small burglar of the type of dog thieves and chicken thieves; 偷工減料 (contractors) save illegally on material and labor; 偷棺掘墓 break into tombs to rob the dead; 偷天換日 audacious scheme of cheating people; 偷龍轉鳳 secretly steal male child and substitute female child; 偷人, 偷漢子 (of women) have illicit relations with men; 偷香竊玉 (of men) have illicit relations with women; 偷情, 偷期 *-chirng, -chir*↓; 偷看, 偷窺, 偷眼兒 to keep, act like a Peeping Tom; 偷聽 eavesdrop; 偷嘴 steal food; 偷青 steal green crops, melons, fruit; 偷雨不偷雪, 偷風不偷月 thieves steal on rainy or windy nights, not on snowy or moonlight nights; 偷寒送暖 do everything to help, see to the comfort of (friends). (2) To attack by surprise or at night: 偷營 night attack on camp. (3) To do s.t. illegally: 偷稅 smuggle, evade tax. (4) To steal a moment of leisure, live on borrowed time: 苟且偷生 live on without ambition; 偷安 *-an*↓; 偷工夫 steal a moment; 偷空兒 (*-kuhng'l*) 來 manage to come at what spare moments possible; 偷閒 *-shiarn*↓.

Adj. (AC) lazy, mean: 則民不偷 then the people will not be lazy or deceitful; 偷薄 mean, decadent (customs).

Adv. Secretly: 偷往 go secretly; 偷着來 come secretly; 偷看書 read, consult books stealthily; 偷偷兒 *-tou'l*.

偷安 *tou-an*, v.i., have no higher ambition than just to get by.
偷巧 *touchiaau*, v.i., do s.t. not properly to save trouble.
偷竊 *touchieh*, v.t. & n., to steal; thievery, a thief.
偷期 *touchir*, v.i., (MC) see *-chirng*↓.
偷情 *tourchirng*, v.i., have illicit relations with men, women.
偷空(兒) *toukuhng('l)*, adv., when one can get away from duties (come for a visit, etc.).
偷兒 *tou'l*, n., a petty thief: 小偷兒.
偷懶(兒) *toulaan(-laa'l)*, v.i., to idle or be negligent at work.
偷冷的 *touleeng'de*, adv., (coll.) unexpectedly.
偷生 *tousheng*, v.i., live on without meaning or purpose.
偷閒 *toushiarn*, v.i., spare a few moments from work to do s.t. else.
偷襲 *toushir*, v.t., make a surprise attack on enemy (camp).
偷偷(兒) *toutou('l)*, adv., stealthily; also 偷偷摸摸的 *--moumou'de*.
偷嘴 *toutzueei*, v.i., steal food.
偷油兒 *touyour'l*, adj., slippery and lazy.

俐 91A.00-9

lih.

Adj. Smooth, active, sharp, intelligent, clever: 俐落 *-luoh*↓; 伶俐 skillful, clever (person).

俐亮 *lihliahng*, adj., simple and effective: 還是幹那舊營生俐亮 it would be much more comfortable to carry on my old trade.
俐落 *lihluoh*, adj., (=利落) well-executed: 這件事辦俐落了 this matter was skillfully handled; 乾淨俐落 smooth and clean (conclusion, deal).
俐索 *lih'suo*, adj., ditto.

俘 91A.00-9

fur.

N. Prisoner of war.

V.t. Take prisoner of war; take booty; see 俘獲 *-huoh*↓; 被俘 be taken prisoner.

俘馘 *furguor*, v.i., (AC) to cut off left ear of war prisoner or of corpse as sign of number of wounded or dead.
俘獲 *fur-huoh*, v.i., capture (booty).
俘虜 *furluu*, n., prisoner of war; 俘虜營 war prisoners' camp.
俘掠 *furlyueh*, v.t., ransack (city) and capture prisoners.

§91A.01 (亻/小)

休 91A.01-1

shiou.

N. Good times, luck: 休戚, 休咎 *-chi*^{1}, *-jiouh*↓.

V.i. (1) To rest: 休息, 休假 *-'shir*, *-jiah*↓; 休憩 to stop and rest; 不眠不休 go without sleep or rest. (2) To retire: 休老 retire from old age; 退休 retire from office. (3) To cease, give up: (LL) 休矣 time to stop or give up for failure: 君可休矣 would advise you to give up trying or time to retire for your good. (4) Do not (followed by vb.): 休想 do not think (I can help you any more, etc.); 休怪 do not take offense or be surprised (if I fail to do s.t.); 休要這樣 do not be like this; 休怕 do not be afraid; 休教他走了 do not let him get away.

V.t. To stop (s.t.): 休戰 armistice, cease fire; 休兵 stop war as policy; 休刊 stop publication (of magazine); 休會 close, adjourn meeting; 休業 close up business; 休學 *-shyuer*↓.

Adv. Off: 歸休 get off and retire; 罷休 let off, settle a quarrel.

休戚 *shiou-chi*^{1}, phr., happy and unhappy events, for better and worse: 休戚相關 mutually concerned in case of a good (休) or bad (戚) turn.
休妻 *shiou-chi*^{2}, v.i., to divorce wife.
休火山 *shiou-huooshan*, n., an extinct or dormant volcano.
休假 *shioujiah*, n., holiday.
休咎 *shiou-jiouh*, n., good or bad luck, see *-chi*^{1}↑.
休致 *shioujyh*, v.i., (LL) retire from office (致=致仕 retire).
休止符 *shioujyy-fur*, n., a rest in musical score.
休克 *shiouke*, n., (med.) shock.
休老 *shiou-laau*, v.i., retire from old age.
休烈 *shioulieh*, n., (AC) impressive achievements.
休沐 *shiou-muh*, v.i., a day of "rest and bath."
休暇 *shioushiah*, n., holiday, days of rest.

休閒 *shioushiarn*, (1) adj., free from work; enjoying leisure; (2) n., leisure.

休歇 *shioushie*, v.i. & n., to rest, relax.

休休 *shioushiou*, adj., (1) (AC) good at heart; (2) (MC) 休! 休! alas! 'tis enough!

休息 *shiou'shir*, v.i., to take a rest.

休書 *shioushu*, n., a letter by husband to wife announcing divorce.

休學 *shiou-shyuer*, v.i., to stop attending school: 勒令休學 expel from school.

休養 *shiouyaang*, v.i. & n., rest and recuperate, -tion.

侏 91A.01–1

ju.

侏儒 *jurur*, n., dwarf; also (AC) court jester.

倈 91A.01–1

lair (**laih*).
[Anc. form of 來]

V.t. (**laih*) Var. of 徠 91B.01.

倈子 *lairtzyy*, n., (MC) a prostitute (in Yuarn drama).

倷 91A.01–1

neih.

Pron. (Soochow dial.) you (singular).

僚 91A.01–1

liaur.

N. Companion, colleague: 同僚 colleague in government service; 官僚 official, usu. in derog. sense, bureaucrat: 官僚主義 bureaucracy; 幕^A僚 see 20A.22.

僚屬 *liaurshuu*, n., minor officials or staff under superior.

僚婿 *liaurshyuh*, n., husbands of sisters.

僚佐 *liaurtzuoo*, n., formerly, asisstants to high officials.

僚友 *liauryoou*, n., colleague and friend.

僄 91A.01–3

piauh.

Adj. Agile (body), smart-looking.

僄悍 *piauh-haan*, adj., ferocious, warlike.

保 91A.01–4

baau.

N. (1) Official in charge: 太子太保, 少保 Imperial Tutor in charge of upbringing of crown prince; 宮保 ditto; 太保 (coll.) juvenile delinquent; 酒保 wine shop owner or waiter. (2) Guarantor: 覓保, 鋪保 (find) guarantor (among shop owners); 承保 stand as guarantor, -tee.

V.t. (1) To keep, maintain in good condition with special meanings in compp.: 保持, 保養 *-chyr, -yaang*↓; 保健, 保固, 保育, etc. *-jiahn*[2], *-guh, -yuh*↓. (2) Guarantee, be responsible for safekeeping: 保不住 cannot guarantee; 保你沒錯 I guarantee it is okay; 難保 cannot guarantee . . . will not happen; 自身難保 cannot even be sure of one's own safety; 保證, 保管, 保險 *-jehng, -guaan, -shiaan*↓. (3) Recommend: 保薦, 保舉 *-jiahn*[1], *-jyuu*↓.

保安 *baau-an*, v.i. & n., public security; 保安隊 *--dueih*, n., security corps; 保安林 "national park" area where chopping down of trees is forbidden, protection forest.

保保 *baau'bau*, n., darling child (usu. wr. 寶寶).

保鏢 *baaubiau*, n., bodyguard, armed escort.

保持 *baauchyr*, v.t., maintain (road condition, temperature, etc.).

保全 *baauchyuarn*, v.t., protect (reputation, life, property).

保單 *baaudan*, n., certificate of guarantee; insurance policy.

保付支票 *baaufuh jypiauh*, n., guaranteed check.

保管 *baurguaan*, v.t., be in charge of (jewels, property, etc.): 保管庫 *--kuh*, n., safety vault; 保管人 custodian.

保固 *baauguh*, v.i., (of contractors) guarantee delivery in good shape within time limit.

保護 *baauhuh*, v.t., protect: 保護國 *--guor*, n., protectorate; 保護鳥 *--niaau*, n., birds protected under law against shooting; 保護人 *--rern*, n., guardian; 保護色 *--seh*, n., protective coloration.

保障 *baaujahng*, n. & v.t., protection (of civil rights, life, property).

保證 *baaujehng*, n. & v.t., guarantee: 保證人 *--rern*, n., guarantor; 保證書 *--shu*, n., guarantee certificate.

保駕 *baau-jiah*, v.t. & n., (be) emperor's escort, esp., in times of crisis.

保薦 *baaujiahn*[1], v.t., recommend (person) from responsible quarters.

保健 *baau-jiahn*[2], v.i. & n., (regimen, exercises for) physical health.

保結 *baaujier*, n., bail.

保重 *baaujuhng*, v.i. & t., (please) take good care of yourself: 保重身體 take care of health.

保准(兒) *baaujuun* (*-jue'l*), v.i., guarantee (in coll. sense): 保准你沒事 I guarantee nothing will

A

happen to you.

保舉 *baurjyuu*, v.t., recommend (person) for post with personal guarantee.

保兒 *baau'l*, n., guarantor for hired help.

保留 *baauliour*, v.t., (1) reserve: 保留權利 reserve rights; (2) defer discussion for future.

保母 *baurmuu*, n., nurse; (fig.) benefactor, good angel, godmother (also wr. 保姆 nursemaid).

保人 *baaurern*, n., guarantor.

保山 *baau-shan*, n., (euphem.) protector; (sometimes) go-betweener.

保險 *baurshiaan*, v.t. & n., (life, fire) insurance: 保險你無事, 他不敢來 guarantee nothing will happen, that he dare not come; 保險公司 insurance company; 保險金額 insured amount; 保險單 insurance policy; 保險費 premium; 保險剃刀 safety razor; 保險箱 safe-deposit box; 傷害保險 injury insurance; 火災保險 fire insurance; 人壽保險 life insurance; 財產保險 property insurance; 複保險 double insurance; 海上保險 marine insurance; 保險線 fuse.

保守 *baurshoou*, (1) v.t. & n., keep (secret, tradition, family property); (2) adj., conservative: 保守黨 Conservative Party; 保守主義 conservatism.

保釋 *baaushyh*, n. & v.i. & t., bail out.

保存 *baautsurn*, v.t., keep, preserve, guard from loss, harm: 保存國粹 preserve the national heritage; 保存古物 preserve historical treasures.

保溫瓶 *baauwen-pirng*, n., thermos bottle.

保養 *bauryaang*, v.t., take good care of (health): 保養身體.

保嬰堂 *baauyingtarng*, n., orphanage.

保佑 *baauyouh*, v.t., protect and bless (of God): 保佑平安 God give us peace and health.

保育 *baauyuh*, v.t., take care of and educate.

B

係 91A.01-9

shih.

V.t. (1) To tie up, (lit. & fig.) (＝繫): 係風捕影 to "tie up the winds and chase after shadows" (also 捕風捉影)—rely on rumors or speculations; 係頸 tie rope around neck; see 係臂, 係累 *-bih, -leei* ↓. (2) (Gen. LL & Cantonese coll.) be (＝是): 此係 this is; 確係 actually is; 委係 really is; 原係, 本係 originally was; 果係 if it is true that. (3) Involve, interrelate: 關係 connections, implications, consequences, see 關 52B.00; 所係非小 has grave implications or consequences.

係臂 *shihbih*, n., (LL) bracelet.

係踵 *shihijuung*, v.i., (LL) come in close succession (＝接踵).

係累 *shihleei*, n., burden, added responsibility.

係數 *shihshuh*, n., (math.) coefficient; 膨脹係數 (phys.) coefficient of expansion.

你 91A.01-9

nii.

Pron. You (singular); 你們 (*nii'men*) you (plural); 你老 (familiar but respectful) you venerable sir; 你是誰 who are you, sir? cf. 您 *nirn*, 91.72; 你瞧 look at that! 你好 how do you do?

條 91A.01-9

tiaur.

N. adjunct. A long piece, hard or soft: 一條線 a piece of thread; 兩條腿 two legs: 三條裙子, 褲子, 毛巾 three skirts, pairs of trousers, towels; 一條街 a street; 一條狗 one dog; 一條龍, 蛇, 魚 one dragon, snake, fish; 一條性命 (kill) one life; 幾條道理 several reasons, lines of reasoning, etc.

C

N. (1) A long piece, hard or soft: 麵條, 粉條 noodles, vermicelli; 鐵條 iron bar; 柳條 willow branch. (2) Thread or line of presentation, esp. 條理 *-lii* ↓: 條理分明, 有條有理 clear, orderly presentation; 有條不紊 orderly (reasoning, etc.); 條分縷析 point by point exposition. (3) Vein, wood grain: 條紋 *-wern*² ↓. (4) Item, clause, article of law or agreement: 第三條 article 3; 一條一條解釋 explain point by point; 條規, 條例 *-guei, -lih* ↓. (5) (*-tz, 'l*) A slip of paper, a short note: 便條, 字條兒 memo, scribbled note; 下條子 give written order (by superior).

Adj. Growing healthily (of plants): 條達, 條鬯, 條暢.

條陳 *tiaurchern* (-'*chen*), n., a memorandam, an official letter to superior containing proposals, requests: 上條陳.

條貫 *tiaurguahn*, n., continuity of thought, ideas.

條規 *tiaurguei*, n., regulations.

條件 *tiaurjiahn*, n., conditions (of agreement, approval); conditions or factors: 必要的條件 prerequisite.

條記 *tiaurjih*, n., formerly, official stamp on documents.

條款 *tiaurkuaan*, n., articles of agreement, treaty.

條例 *tiaurlih*, n., regulations, statutes, rules.

條理 *tiaurlii*, n., line of reasoning; orderly presentation: 很有條理 very clear, orderly.

條目 *tiaurmuh*, n., articles, items.

條子 *tiaur'tz*, n., see N. 5 ↑.

條文 *tiaurwern*¹, n., text of legal paper.

條紋 *tiaurwern*², n., lines, grain in wood, etc.

條約 *tiauryue*, n., treaty: 多邊條約 multilateral treaty; 共同防衛

保
係
你
條

條 絛 傑 傺 俅 俵 儂 儇 偎 倀 依

條約 mutual defense treaty; 互不侵略條約 treaty of non-aggression.

絛 91A.01-9

tau.
[Var. 縚]

N. Silk braid; 彩絛 colored silk braid.

絛蟲 *tauchurng*, n., a kind of tape-worm.

絛子 *tautz*, n., silk braid on border of gowns: 絛子辮子 silk braid in a queue.

傑 91A.01-9

jier.

N. & adj. Talented, extraordinary (person): 豪傑, 英傑, 人傑 a hero.

傑出 *jierchu*, adj., eminent, outstanding.

傑作 *jier-tzuoh*, n., a masterpiece.

傺 91A.01-9

chyh.

Adj. See 侘^A傺 91A.70.

§91A.02 (亻/k)

俅 91A.02-1

chiour.

俅俅 *chiourchiour*, adj., (AC) courteous.

俵 91A.02-1

biaau.

V.t. To distribute: 俵分 to divide; 俵散 to distribute.

儂 91A.02-2

nurng.

Pron. (1) (MC) I (first person). (2) (Dial.) 渠儂 he, she. (3) (Soochow dial.) you (singular).

儇 91A.02-4

shyuan.

儇薄 *shyuanbor*, adj., (LL) frivolous.

儇子 *shyuantzyy*, n., (LL) a frivolous person.

偎 91A.02-4

wei.

V.i. & t. To lean close to: 偎臉 put cheek and cheek together; 偎近 come close, esp. among lovers; 偎貼, 相偎 "necking"; 偎愛 hug, otherwise be close and familiar; (related 猥 *wei*, 91C.02); 偎冬兒 (of farmer) stay indoors to pass the winter.

倀 91A.02-5

chang.

N. Ghost of one devoured by tiger: 爲虎作倀 such ghost helps tiger to devour others—to assist tyrants.

依 91A.02-6

yi.

V.i. & t. (1) To consent, to obey a wish: 依着你 obey, accept your wish; 我要離婚, 她不依 I want a divorce, but she will not consent; 你依不依 will you do what I say, or won't you? 依着他的話罷 just do what he wants. (2) To rely on, to be based upon: 依賴, 依靠 *-laih, -kauh*↓; 依山靠水 (a city) based on the hill at the back and overlooking the river or sea; 依人籬下 to be dependent on s.o. for a living; 依草附木 orig. (of brigands) based on jungles and wild country, also (fig.) rely on powerful friends; also as n., 無依無靠 friendless and helpless; 憑依 s.o. or s.t. (friends, relatives) to rely on for help; 依書直說 go by the book. (3) (Coll.) to pardon: 不依不饒 will never pardon; 我必和你不依 I'll not let you go with this, see 饒 81B.70.

Prep. According to: 依我所見 according to my mind; 依他(所)說 according to what he says; 依律辦理 settle according to law; 依實招供 confess the truth at court.

依傍 *yibahng*, v.t., to rely on s.o. more powerful; to imitate slavishly anc. models in writing: 依傍古人.

依前 *yichiarn*, adv., as it used to be, as formerly, see *-jiouh*↓.

依戴 *yidaih*, v.t., (LL) to look up to (s.o.) with respect or gratitude.

依附 *yifuh*, v.t., to act as satellite (to s.o.), to join s.o.'s camp; to go to (relative) for a living.

依歸 *yiguei*, (1) v.t., to return to (place, person, faith); (2) n., an anchor, refuge: 無所依歸 drifting, without anchor or shelter.

A

依 仗 *yijahng*, v.t., to rely on (person, money, situation, personal connections).

依 照 *yijauh*, (1) prep., according to (your opinion, terms of contract, etc.); (2) v.t., to obey, accept, follow (path, instructions, wish, etc.).

依 舊 *yihjiouh*, adv., as it used to be, still . . . as usual: 依舊不改 still unrepentent; 依舊貧困 poor as usual.

依 據 *yijyuh*, (1) n., basis (for statement, belief, reasoning): 沒有依據 without basis; (2) v.t., to base oneself on: 依據這學説 according to this theory.

依 靠 *yikauh*, v.t. & n., to depend on (s.o.); dependence, support.

依 賴 *yilaih*, v.t., ditto.

依 戀 *yiliahn*, v.t., to continue to long for, to love.

依 慕 *yimuh*, v.t., to love, adore, long for (person).

依 然 *yirarn*, adv., still, as usual.

依 稀 *yishi*, adj., indistinct (shadows, image).

依 實 *yi-shyr*, adv., (report, confess) truthfully, according to fact.

依 隨 *yisueir*, v.t., to follow (person, wish).

依 從 *yitsurng*, v.i. & t., to accept, obey (opinion, command).

依 次 *yitsyh*, adv., according to proper order.

依 託 *yituo*, v.t., (1) to live with s.o. when in need; (2) to take anecdote in history as basis; to write fiction based on fact.

依 違 *yi-weir*, v.i., as in 依違兩可 be undecided, have no definite conviction of one's own.

依 樣 *yiyahng*, adv., according to model or pattern: 依樣畫葫蘆 do the routine thing without thinking, slavishly copy or imitate.

依 依 *yiyi*, adj., clinging, unable to part.

依 倚 *yiyii*, v.t., see *-kauh*↑.

依 約 *yi-yue*, (1) adj., see *-shi*↑; (2) phr., in accordance with promise.

B

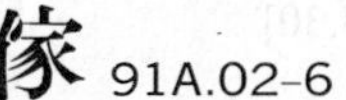

傢 91A.02–6

jia.

傢 伙 *jia'huo*, n., (1) furniture, utensils, tools, instruments; 吃飯傢伙 dining sets; 剃頭傢伙 razors and combs; (2) (sl.) pistols, knives, swords, etc.; (3) (contempt.) a man or boy: 這傢伙 this fellow; 壞傢伙 a bad egg; 好傢伙 what a guy! 小傢伙 a little imp.

傢 具 *jiajyuh*, n., furniture, household goods (also wr. 傢俱).

倀 91A.02–6

liarng.

Adj. Good and able: 倀工 skillful workman (=良工).

像 91A.02–9

shiahng.

N. An image, figure: 形像 appearance; 畫像 painted portrait; 像貌 *-mauh*↓; 遺像 portrait of deceased; 石像 statue; 照像 photograph; 想像 imagination.

V.t. To resemble: 兩人相像 the two resemble each other; 真像他 really resembles him; 像模像樣 with airs of importance; 像煞有介事 (Shanghai dial.) ditto.

V.i. To seem to, appear to (+vb.): 好像 or 像 or 像是 (as an independent phr.) it seems; 他像(好像)不大願意 he seems not very willing; 像 or 好像要下雨了 it looks like raining; 好像不在家 seems not be at home; 好像不聽見 seems not to hear; as if: 好像你不是我親生女兒 as if you were not my own daughter.

C

Adj. (Like the Eng. "like," this can be considered adj. or prep. because it takes an object—"like me," "like him," "like new," etc.) like, alike: 像這個, 像那個 like this, like that: 像我這個人 a person like me; 不大像 is not like (his doing); 太不像話 it's beyond the limit—going too far; it's preposterous.

像 姑 *shiahng-gu*, n., male prostitute or entertainer at banquet (=相公 10B.41).

像 話 *shiahng-huah*, phr., in 不像話 too much, beyond the limit.

像 兒 *shiahng'l*, n., (1) person's gen. appearance; (2) 給你一個像兒瞧 (a threat to punish) let you see what it is like.

像 貌 *shiahngmauh*, n., person's looks: 像貌非凡 a distinguished appearance (also 相貌).

像 片 *shiahngpian*, n., a photograph.

像 生 兒 *shianngsheng'l*, n., assumed airs: 不用做這些像生兒了 you don't need to put on this act.

像 是 *shiahng-shyh*, phr., it seems: 像是沒收到信 seems to have not yet received the letter.

像 似 *shiahng-syh*, phr., ditto.

像 贊 *shiahng-tzahn*, n., a verse of a few lines in praise of person who is subject of a portrait.

像 樣 兒 *shiahngyahng'l*, adj., proper in appearance: 穿得像樣兒 dress properly.

§ 91A.10 (亻/十)

什 91A.10–1

shyr (*tzar).

N. (1) (Anc. mil.) a file of ten soldiers. (2) U.f. "十", ten. (3) (AC) ten songs.

依
傢
倀
像
什

亅	小	k	十	土	ナ	廾	凵	丨	一	丅	フ	口	囟	冈	冂	厂	尸	亠	广	宀	丶	乚	弋	心	八	人	乂	乛	一	丿	㇀	く
00	01	02	10	11	12	20	21	22	30	31	32	40	41	42	50	51	52	60	61	62	63	70	71	72	80	81	82	83	90	91	92	93

Adj. (1) (*tzar*) Miscellaneous (= 雜): 什碎 chop suey, odds and ends; 牛什 odds and ends of beef. (2) U.f. 甚 in 什麽 *-mo* ↓.

什百 *shyrbor*, adj., (AC) tenfold or hundredfold.

什不閑兒 *shyrbushiar'l*, n., person in a variety show who sings to the accompaniment of musical instruments he himself plays.

什器 *shyrchih*, n., miscellaneous utensils.

什件(兒) *shyrjiaan(-jiaa'l)*, n., (1) a miscellany of objects; (2) entrails, tripe, gizzard, etc.

什錦 *shyrjiin*, adj., garnished with different ingredients (also wr. 十錦).

什麽 *shyrmo* (or *sher*, weak form *sh-*), adj., weak form of 甚麽 *shernmo*, what: 有什麽可吃 what is there to eat?

什閑兒 *shyrshiar'l*, adj., (coll.) quiet: 手脚沒個什閑兒 hands and feet never still for a moment.

什襲 *shyrshir*, adv., as in 什襲珍藏 carefully packed and preserved.

什物 *shyrwuh*, n., common everyday articles or objects.

什一 *shyr-yi*, n., (1) one tenth; (2) the tithe (tax).

件 91A.10–1

jiahn.

N. & n. adjunct. A unit or item of anything: 一件大事 a memorable (important) event; 一件案子 a lawsuit, an incident; 一件新聞 a piece of news; 一件衣服 a dress; 一件行李 a piece of luggage; 件件 each and every item, all items; 件數 number of items or pieces; 論件計酬 payment by the piece; 條件 a provision, condition; 物件 articles, things.

体 91A.10–1

tii.

[Pop. of 體 42B.30]

倖 91A.10–1

shihng.

Adj. & adv. (1) By luck or chance: 倖免 escape (punishment, etc.) by luck; 倖存 luckily survive; 倖進 be promoted by luck; 僥△倖 91A.82, by luck. (2) Sometimes err. var. of 幸 11.10.

俸 91A.10–1

fehng.

N. Salary: 薪俸 salary; 月俸 monthly pay.

俸錢 *fehngchiarn*, n., salary, pay.
俸給 *fehngjii*, n., salary, subsidies.
俸金 *fehngjin*, n., (LL) salary.
俸祿 *fehngluh*, n., salary of officials.
俸銀 *fehngyirn*, n., see *-jin* ↑.

倬 91A.10–2

juor.

Adj. (AC) awe-inspring.

伴 91A.10–2

bahn.

N. Companion: oft. 同伴, 伴侶; 終身伴侶 life companion; 旅伴 travelling companions.

V.t. Accompany (person at dinners, concerts, etc.).

伴當 *bahndang*, n., (MC) servant (also wr. 檔).

伴姑 *bahngu*, n., (MC) see *-niarng* ↓.

伴兒 *bah'l*, n., companion: 做伴兒 keep person company.

伴郎 *bahnlarng*, n., best man at wedding.

伴娘 *bahn-niarng*, n., bridesmaid.

伴食 *bahnshyr*, v.i., hold a sinecure.

伴宿 *bahnsuh*, v.i., keep vigil at funeral (also pr. *-shyur* in Peking dial.); pass night with person (of prostitute).

伴奏 *bahntzouh*, v.i. & t. & n., accompany (-niment) in musical performance.

偉 91A.10–2

weei.

Adj. Great, robust: 偉大, 偉人 *-dah*, *-rern* ↓; 雄偉 impressive-looking; 壯偉 robust; 偉丈夫 a husky fellow; 豐功偉業 great service to the country.

偉岸 *weei-ahn*, adj., tall and robust.

偉大 *weeidah*, adj., great (man, country, record).

偉人 *weeirern*, n., a great man.

伻 91A.10–3

beng.

N. & v.t. (AC, rare) emissary, send emissary to.

僻 91A.10–5

pih (*peih).

Adj. (1) Remote, seldom visited: 僻處, 僻地, 窮鄉僻壤 seldom visited place, remote village; 僻巷 out-of-the-way alley; 荒僻 (also *peih) desolate, remote and less civilized (place). (2) Devious, unorthodox: 偏僻, 邪僻 strange (teachings, conduct). (3) Rare: 僻字 rare character; 生僻 rarely seen (character).

僻道 *peihdauh, n., quiet bypath.
僻典 *pihdiaan*, n., rarely known allusion (in writing).
僻靜 *peihjihng, adj., quiet and out-of-the-way (place).
僻陋 *pihlouh*, n., rustic, uncultivated (person, place).
僻壤 *pihraang*, n., remote, little known region.
僻遠 *pihyuaan*, n., remote (place).

倅 91A.10-6

tsueih.

N. (AC) deputy, assistant, also v. i., act as assistant magistrate.

佯 91A.10-8

yarng.

V.i. & t. To pretend: 佯僞 pretend to be; 佯不知, 佯爲不知 pretend ignorance; 佯病, 佯狂, 佯死 pretend to be ill, to be mad, to be dead.

仟 91A.10-9

chian.

N. (1) "Capital" of 千 (thousand) in writing checks. (2) Var. of 阡 32A.10.

俾 91A.10-9

bih (beih).

Adv. conj. (1) (LL) So that, in order that: 俾得立刻進行 so that we may proceed at once; 俾得週知, 俾各懍遵 so that all may know, all may obey (the new law). (2) (Cogn. of 備) to serve for: (AC) 俾晝作夜 to make the day serve as night.

仵 91A.10-9

wuu.

N. A surname.

仵作 *wuutzuoh* (-'*tzuo*), n., formerly, medical examiner of dead or wounded bodies.

侔 91A.10-9

mour.

V.t. (AC) imitate: 侔色揣稱 (AC) try to match manner and appearance; 相侔 alike in appearance.

Adj. Equal, matching: 彼此相侔 matching each other.

§91A.11 (亻/土)

仕 91A.11-1

shyh.

V.i. To be official: 學而優則仕 "officialdom is the natural outlet for good scholars" (from *Analects*); 仕於齊 was official in *Chir*; 出仕 join government service; 致仕 resign from government; 仕進, 仕途, 仕宦 *-jihn*, *-tur*, *-huahn* ↓.

仕版 *shyh-baan*, n., court register of officials: 登仕版 enter government service.
仕宦 *shyhhuahn*, n., officials as a class, the gentry.
仕進 *shyh-jihn*, n., official career.
仕路 *shyh-luh*, n., ditto.
仕女 *shyh-nyuu*, n., men and women of supposedly educated class; 仕女畫 Chin. painting of human figures.
仕途 *shyhtur*, n., official career.

佳 91A.11-1

jia.

[Cf. 嘉 11.40, sometimes synonymous]

Adj. Good, nice, pleasing, beautiful: 佳節 a happy occasion, a joyful festival; 佳景 a lovely scene, a fascinating sight; 佳句 a well-turned phrase, celebrated verses of a poem; 佳作 an excellent piece of writing or art work; 佳婿 (euphem.) a son-in-law; 佳偶 a happily married couple; 佳對 ditto; 佳士 a cultured person; 佳子弟 worthy children; 佳況 (of persons) in fine or excellent condition; 佳味 dainty dishes; 佳肴 delicacies.

佳氣 *jiachih*[1], n., auspicious atmosphere or prospects.
佳器 *jiachih*[2], n., (LL) person of great potentialities.
佳期 *jia-chir*, n., wedding day, rendezvous between lovers.
佳趣 *jiachyuh*, n., high spirits, matters of intense interest, relish.
佳話 *jiahuah*, n., charming stories, anecdotes.

佳境 *jiajihng*, n., a desirable stage of affairs: 漸入佳境 getting more and more enjoyable (in drink, etc.).
佳麗 *jialih*, n., a beauty.
佳人 *jiarern*, n., a beauty, a pretty woman, a handsome young man.
佳音 *jiayin*, n., good tidings.

僅 91A.11-2

jiin (also *jihn*).

Adv. Only, solely, merely, just: 僅僅 *-jiin*↓; 不僅 not only; 僅可 may only; 僅能 can only; 僅够 barely enough; 僅只 only (in an emphatic sense); 僅此 only this and no more; 絕無僅有 s.t. very unique, rare.

僅僅 *jirnjiin*, (1) adj., only this and no other; (2) adv., only, barely, scarcely.

儺 91A.11-2

nuor.

N. & v.t. (AC) a festival to exorcize the devil causing any plague; to hold such a festival: 鄉人儺 (AC) the villagers were holding this festival.

Adj. 猗儺 (AC) soft and pliant; see 猗 91C.00.

催 91A.11-2

tsuei.

V.t. To urge, press for (payment of debt), request (doctor) urgently to come: 催促, 催逼 *-tsuh*, *-bi*↓; 催請 request urgently; 催歸 ask urgently to return home; 催辦 request s.t. be done quickly.

催逼 *tsueibi*, v.t., to press for s.t. to be done (payment of rent, etc.).
催請 *tsueichiing*, v.t., to request guest to come to dinner (formerly, make repeated requests as form of sincerity).
催青 *tsuei-ching*, v.i., hasten hatching of silkworms by heat.
催趕 *tsueigaan*, v.t., to hasten (s.o.) to come; to hasten to destination.
催化劑 *tsueihuahji*, n., (chem.) a catalyst (also called 觸媒).
催妝 *tsueijuang*, n., formerly, bridegroom's gift of cosmetics, etc. sent to bride on day before wedding; 催妝詩 poem written on day of friend's wedding.
催科 *tsuei-ke*, v.i., urge payment of taxes.
催淚彈 *tsueileih-dahn*, n., tear bomb.
催眠 *tsueimiarn*, v.t., to hypnotize; 催眠術 hypnotism; 催眠劑 soporific.
催命符 *tsuei-mihng-fur*, n., s.t. (such as bad news) which hasten person's death.
催迫 *tsueipoh*, v.t., to press for (payment, etc.).
催生 *tsueisheng*, (1) v.i., (Chin. med.) to hasten child delivery; (2) n., gift of maiden family to expectant mother one month before delivery.
催討 *tsueitaau*, v.i., to press for repayment of debt.
催促 *tsueitsuh*, v.t., to press for, ask for quick carrying out.

侄 91A.11-3

jyr.
[Pop. of 姪 93A.11]

儸 91A.11-4

luor.

N. See 僂⁴儸 91A.93↓.

俚 91A.11-4

lii.

N. Rustic songs.

Adj. Unpolished, rustic, vulgar: see 俚語 *-yuu*, 俚歌 *-ge*↓.

俚歌 *liige*, n., folk songs.
俚俗 *liisur*, adj., rustic, vulgar, unrefined.
俚言 *liiyarn*, n., vulgar speech, unrefined language.
俚語 *liryuu*, n., colloquial speech, colloquialisms, slang.

住 91A.11-6

juh.

V.i. (1) Reside, live at (place): 住所, 住宅 *-suoo*, *-jair*↓; 住家 *-jia*↓; 住處 where one stays; 居住 live, reside; 暫住, 久住 reside temporarily, for long; 住不下 house is too small for residence. (2) Lodge, stop for the night: 住了一夜 stop for one night; 住歇 stop for rest. (3) To stop (action): 住口, 住手 *-koou*, *-shoou*↓; 住嘴 (an order) shut up! 住了哭 stop crying; 住步 stop while walking. (4) Remain: 歌盡聲猶住 (LL) the song has stopped but the voice remains (lingers).

Adv. (Free suffix after many vbb.) fast as in "hold fast," indicating success in holding or obtaining: 抓住 have grasped (it)—succeeded in doing so; 拿住, 捉住 have grabbed or arrested; 綁住了 have (one) bound; 看住了 keep sharp watch (on person); 止不住 cannot stop (flow, etc.); 留不住 did not succeed in asking guest to stay longer; 忍不住 cannot help (protesting, laughing, etc.); 受不住 cannot bear (s.t.).

住持 *juhchyr*, n., abbot, business manager of monastery.

住戶 *juhhuh*, n., inhabitant; his house.
住宅 *juhjair*, n., residence, house.
住家 *juhjia*, v.i., (1) reside at home: 你在那裏住家 where do you live? (2) (of a married woman) live at maiden home.
住址 *juhjyy*, n., address (of person, office).
住口 *juh-koou*, v.i., (an order) shut up!
住手 *juh-shoou*, v.i., stop (an order to cease doing s.t.)!
住所 *juhsuoo*, n., place where one lives, accommodation.

隹 91A.11-6

juei.

N. Used as a radical, denoting generally birds and fowl (as in 雞 besides 鷄 hen, and 雉 pheasant).

僮 91A.11-6

turng.

N. (1) Page, boy servant: 家僮 boy servant: 書僮 page boy attending to studio. (2) Interch. 童 60.11.

僱 91A.11-6

guh.

[Var. of 雇]

V.t. Employ the services of: 僱工 *-gung* ↓; 僱車 hire a car; 僱不起 cannot afford to hire s.o.; 僱來的 a person employed for temporary service; 僱船 hire a boat.

僱工 *guhgung*, n., a hired hand.
僱主 *guhjuu*, n., an employer.
僱員 *guhyuarn*, n., an employee.
僱用 *guhyuhng*, v.t., engage (person, his services).
僱傭 *guhyurng*, n., a person employed by another: 僱傭關係 relationship between employer and employee.

任 91A.11-9

rehn (**rern*).

N. (1) One's duty, assignment, responsibility: 任務 *-wuh* ↓; 責任 official duties; 重任 heavy responsibility; 任重道遠 ability to carry heavy responsibilities through thick and thin. (2) An official post: 赴任 go to assume office; 卸任 step down from office; 到任 take up a post; 受任 receive an appointment to office; 接任 take office; 走馬上任 go to take office; 在任 during one's tenure of office; 前任, 後任 former, present incumbent; 新任, 舊任 new, old appointee; 原任 original officeholder; 歷任 successive officeholders; 薦任 (of section chiefs, secretaries, etc.) appoint on recommendation; 簡任 (of viceministers, counsellors, etc.) appoint by selection; 特任 (of Cabinet members, ambassador, etc.) appoint by special decree. (3) (*rern) U.f. 妊: pregnancy. (4) A surname.

V.t. (1) Appoint, assign: 任命 *-mihng* ↓; 任賢 select good men for service; 任免 *-miaan*, 任用 *-yuhng*, 任期 *-chir*, 任使 *-shyy* ↓; 委任 (of clerks, copyists, etc.) to appoint or commission; 聘任 (of teachers, professors, advisers, etc.) appoint by invitation; 調任 to transfer. (2) Be responsible for: 任勞 *-laur* ↓; 任怨 bear blame; 擔任 serve as, occupy the position of; 出任 assume the duties of; 專任 hold a full-time job; 兼任 serve concurrently as; 任內 during one's tenure of office; 初任 assume office for the first time; 勝任愉快 be fully qualified for work (duties, assignment); 連任 serve for a second term; 革職留任 be stripped of official title but not dismissed. (3) Let, allow: 任憑 *-pirng*, 任便 *-biahn* ↓; 任由 let it be; 任從 *-tsurng*, 任意 *-yih*, 任性 *-shihng* ↓; 任所欲爲 let him do as he pleases, give him a free hand. (4) To trust: 信任 entrust, have confidence in. (5) Let anyone: 任何人都不許進來 no one shall come in no matter who he is.

Adj. Any, no matter who, what, how: 任甚麼話都不聽 won't listen no matter what you say.

任便 *rehnbiahn*, phr., just as you (he) please(s), be free (at liberty) to.
任氣 *rehn-chih*, adj., hotheaded, quick-tempered, impetuous, rash.
任期 *rehn-chir*, n., tenure of office, a tour of duty.
任情 *rehn-chirng*, adj., (＝任性 *-shihng* ↓).
任達 *rehndar*, adj., easygoing, happy-go-lucky, free from worldly worries.
任何 *rehnher*, adj., any, whatever (person, place, thing).
任咎 *rehn-jiouh*, v.i., take upon oneself all the blame.
任勞 *rehn-laur*, v.i., bear responsibility for task, devote oneself wholeheartedly to duty.
任免 *rehnmiaan*, v.t. & n., appoint(ment) and dismiss(al).
任命 *rehnmihng*, v.t. & n., appoint(ment) to office.
任憑 *rehnpirng*, phr., (1) (＝任便 *-biahn* ↑); (2) no matter what, see Adj. ↑.
任人 **rernrern*, (1) n., (AC) a flatterer, a toady, a sycophant, a deceitful person (＝佞人); (2) adj., open to everybody.
任俠 *rehnshiar*, n., a gallant and chivalrous person.
任性 *rehnshihng*, (1) v.i., do as one pleases, follow one's na-

tural bent; (2) adj., intractable, refractory, recalcitrant: 不可任性 don't be self-willed.

任率 *rehnshuoh*, adj., ingenuous, artless, simple, natural.

任事 *rehn-shyh*[1], (1) v.i., to shoulder responsibility, discharge one's duties: 勇於任事 fulfill one's duties faithfully and energetically; (2) v.i., assign duties to (s.o.).

任是 *rehnshyh*[2], conj., even if.

任使 *rehnshyy*, v.t. & n., (1) (appoint to) service; (2) duties, responsibilities; (3) conj., even if.

任天 *rehn-tian*, v.i., leave everything to divine will.

任從 *rehntsurng*, phr., let s.o. do as he pleases.

任縱 *rehntzuhng*, adj., unrestrained.

任務 *rehnwuh*, n., an assigned task, duties, responsibilities.

任意 *rhehn-yih*, v.i., do as one pleases.

任用 *rehn-yuhng*, v.t., appoint to service.

§91A.20 (亻/卄)

併 91A.20-9

bihng.

[Interch. 幷]

V.t. (1) To combine (cases, treatments): 併合 *-her* ↓; 歸併一起 combine together; 併糧 to pool food together or combine two persons' food to keep one alive; 併案辦理 handle two matters, cases as one. (2) To annex (territory): 兼併 to annex; 併吞, 併滅 *-tun, -mieh* ↓.

Adj. & adv. (As var. of 並) to go side by side, take place at the same time or place: 齊頭併進 go forward together; 百花併放 all flowers bloom together; 諸病併發 different diseases break out at the same time.

併發 *bihngfa*, v.i., (of diseases) occur concurrently.

併骨 *bihngguu*, v.t., bury husband and wife in same grave.

併合 *bihngher*, v.t., combine (treatment), annex (territory); handle several cases in one.

併肩 *bihngjian*, adv., (fight, proceed) shoulder to shoulder.

併滅 *bihngmieh*, v.t., destroy (country).

併吞 *bihngtun*, v.t., annex and absorb (neighboring country).

§91A.21 (亻/乚)

仙 91A.21-2

shian.

N. (1) A fairy, (Taoist) immortal, a genie: 仙人 *-rern*, 仙公 *-gung* ↓; 神仙 a fairy; 神仙故事 a fairy tale; 大仙 a genie; 天仙 celestial fairy; 美若天仙 pretty as a fairy (oft. said of bride); 修仙 try to become an immortal by Taoist regimen; 成仙 become an immortal; 八$^{\Delta}$仙 80.80; 仙島 fairy island, fairies' abode, in mountains; 仙鄉, 仙界 fairyland; 仙洞 fairies' cave; 仙府 fairies' abode; 仙籍 register of names of immortals. (2) (Oft. used as modifier, in praise of) immortal, celestial talent or heavenly beauty: 仙才 ethereal poet (as 李白); 仙風道骨 (of person) sage-like type; 仙姿 a woman's ethereal beauty; 酒仙 great poetic drinkers; 詩仙 immortal poet. (3) N. modifier, having to do with Taoist, esoteric magic: 仙術, 仙法 fairy magic; 仙方, 仙藥 Taoist magic medicine; 仙丹 *-dan* ↓; 仙館 where a Taoist recluse lives; 仙去, 仙逝, 仙遊 pass away and ascend to heaven on a stork; 仙鶴 stork, a particular pet of Taoist.

仙班 *shian-ban*, n., the fairy retinue or staff.

仙禽 *shian-chirn*, n., a stork.

仙丹 *shiandan*, n., (1) pill of immortality; (2) (complim.) very excellent medicine.

仙方兒 *shianfang'l*, n., magical prescription, oft. given in temples in prayer to a god.

仙姑 *shiangu*, n., a female immortal: 何仙姑 one of the Eight Immortals.

仙公 *shiangung*, n., court. address for an immortal, also 仙翁, sometimes as fig. of speech for venerable old man.

仙鶴腿 *shianheh tueei*, phr., long, slender legs (of a person, like a stork's).

仙眞 *shianjen*, n., an immortal, a Taoist god.

仙家 *shian'jia*, n., see *-rern* ↓.

仙茅 *shianmaur*, n., (bot.) a grass, *Curculigo ensifolia*, whose root is used as medicine (also called "Brahmin ginseng" 婆羅門參).

仙女 *shiannyuu*, n., a fairy maiden; a very pretty girl.

仙人 *shianrern*, n., a fairy; 仙人拳 a kind of cactus, *Cereus multiplex*; 仙人擔 a bar with two big stones, used for exercise; 仙人掌 a kind of cactus, *Opuntia ficus*; 仙人跳 n., a confidence trick, using woman as decoy who then absconds with jewels and money.

仙術 *shianshuh*, n., magic formula.

仙逝 *shianshyh*, v.i., (euphem.) pass away.

仙壇 *shiantarn*, n., altar for use in planchette (扶乩) for invoking spirits.

仙桃 *shiantaur*, n., (poet.) peach.

仙才 *shiantsair*, n., a genius.

仙童 *shianturng*, n., boy servant of immortals: 仙童玉女 boy and girl servants in fairyland.

仙子 *shiantzyy*, n., (1) an immortal, genie; (2) pretty woman.

仙遊 *shianyour*, v.i., (euphem.) pass away.

佢 91A.21-5

chyur.

Pron. (Cantonese dial.) he (pr. nearly like *koer*), related 渠 63.01.

偃 91A.21-5

yaan.

N. (1) A surname. (2) U.f. 堰 earthen bank or dyke.

V.t. (1) To suppress, lay off, lay down: 偃兵 stop military preparations; 偃旗息鼓 (lit.) call off the army maneuvers, (fig.) stop all activities and lie low ("furl flag and silence the drums"); 偃武修文 to disband troops and attend to civilian affairs (after conquest). (2) To flop down, lie down on back: 偃臥, 偃仆 *-woh, -pu*↓.

偃蹇 *yarnjiaan,* (1) adj., winding up and down, undulating; (2) v.i., (AC) to sit idle, to idle about.
偃仆 *yaanpu,* v.i., to fall down.
偃鼠 *yarnshuu,* n., (AC) the mole.
偃臥 *yaanwoh,* v.i., to lie face up.
偃仰 *yarnyaang,* v.i., to bend and straighten up.
偃月 *yaan-yueh,* n., the crescent moon; 偃月刀 a curved sword or curving knife—an anc. weapon.

傴 91A.21-5

yuu.

Adj. Hunchbacked.

傴僂 *yuulour,* n., a hunchback.
傴人 *yuurern,* n., ditto.

倔 91A.21-5

jyuer (*jyueh*).

Adj. (1) Obstinate, stubborn: 倔強 *-jiahng*↓. (2) (*jyueh*) Rude in manner or speech: 脾氣倔 ill-tempered; 這人倔極了 this man is most impertinent; 倔巴棍子 a rude fellow.

倔強 *jyuerjiahng,* adj., obstinate, stubborn.

傜 91A.21-9

Yaur.

N. Name of aboriginal tribe in Southwest China.

§ 91A.22 (亻/丨)

佈 91A.22-1

buh.
[Interch. 布 in sense of "spread" "announce"]

V.t. To spread, publicize, announce, propagate: 散佈謠言 spread rumors; 傳佈命令 publish orders.

佈道 *buhdauh,* v.t. & n., spread (of) gospel.
佈防 *buhfarng,* v.i. & n., patrol, set up defense line with patrols or defense works.
佈告 *buhgauh,* n. & v.t., announce (-ment) (also wr. 布).
佈阱 *buh-jihng,* v.t. & n., to lay trap.
佈景 *buhjiing,* n. & v.i., (set) background, decorations (in garden, drama) (also wr. 布).
佈置 *buhjyh,* n. & v.t., arrange (-ment of) house interiors, dispose (troops); make arrangements for (uprising, any big event); set pieces in chess (also wr. 布).

仆 91A.22-2

pu (also *fuh*).

V.i. Fall to the ground, drop dead: 前仆後繼 others take up position as soldiers fall on the battlefield; heroic fighting.

仲 91A.22-2

juhng.

N. (1) A surname. (2) 昆仲 brothers.

Adj. No. 2: 仲春, 仲夏 second month in spring, summer, (second and fifth lunar month), cf. 孟 for 1st, and 季 for last or 3rd.

仲裁 *juhngtsair,* v.i. & n., mediation, arbitration: 仲裁者 or 人 mediator, arbitrator.
仲子 *juhngtzyy,* n., (AC) younger brother.

伸 91A.22-2

shen.

V.i. (1) To stretch: 伸出 stretch out: 伸手, 伸指 extend a hand, a finger; 伸大拇哥 raise a thumb in admiration; 伸舌頭 loll out tongue in surprise; 伸頸 crane one's neck; 伸頭探腦 poke one's head to peek at; 伸腿瞪眼 to fall dead. (2) To unbend, open up: 伸眉 lift an eyebrow to show satisfaction; 伸腰 to stretch oneself; 伸冤 *-yuan*↓; 伸開 open (one's arm);

能屈能伸 (a great man) can bend or unbend—can take temporary setbacks; 伸縮 *-suo* ↓.

伸欠 *shenchiahn*, v.i., to stretch and yawn (also 欠伸).
伸張 *shenjang*, v.i., to expand (power).
伸證 *shen-jehng*, n., (AC) evidence (of guilt).
伸志 *shen-jyh*, v.i., to have wish, ambition fulfilled.
伸開 *shen-kai*, v.i., to stretch open.
伸手 *shen-shoou*, v.i., to stretch one's hand: 伸手不見掌 (五指) pitch-dark; 伸手就辦 do s.t. at once.
伸縮 *shensuo*, v.i. & adj. & n., flexible, -bility; adjustment; range of change: 伸縮餘地 room for adjustment; 伸縮性 *--shihng*, n., flexibility, elasticity.
伸腰兒 *shen-yau'l*, v.i., to stretch oneself (after bending); (fig.) to hold one's head high: 不想今日咱們也伸腰兒了 never thought we would see this day of success.
伸冤 *shen-yuan*, v.i., to ask for redress of an injustice; to redress an injustice.

佛 91A.22-2

for (**bih*).

N. (1) (**bih*) 佛肸 Bihshi, AC proper name; (AC=弼) to assist. (2) Buddha, (*Sakyamuni* 釋迦牟尼, see 佛陀 *-tuor*) ↓; also various Buddhas, applied to those having attained Buddhahood; Buddhahood, state of holiness and wisdom, also different manifestations of Buddha; Buddhist religion, things having to do with Buddhist faith: 佛殿, 寺, 廟, 刹 Buddhist temple; 佛龕 niche for Buddha: 佛堂 hall with statue of Buddha; 佛國, 佛經 country of Buddha, Buddhist sutra; 佛會 Buddhist festival and activities; 禮佛, 拜佛 to worship Buddha; 念佛 repeat the name of Buddha; 佛誕日 Buddha's birthday, the 8th of 4th lunar month; 浴佛節 festival of bathing of Buddha, 8th of 4th lunar month; 放下屠刀, 立地成佛 "lay down the butcher's knife and become Buddha on the spot"—the Buddha nature being innate in man; 佛性 *-shihng* ↓; 佛眼相看 (MC) regard with mercy; 佛口蛇心 words of Buddha and heart of a serpent; 佛頭戴糞 desecration, sacrilege; 活佛 living Buddha; 阿彌陀佛 Amitabha, used like "Halleluya!" "God be praised," usu. fulfillment of a wish.

佛法 *forfaa*, n., power of Buddha; the law of Buddha.
佛果 *forguoo*, n., the attainment of Buddahood.
佛海 *forhaai*, n., the wide-open church of Buddhism.
佛家 *forjia*, n., Buddhist follower; school of philosophy.
佛甲草 *forjiar tsaau*, n., (bot.) *Sedum lineare*.
佛教 *forjiauh*, n., the Buddhist religion.
佛經 *forjing*, n., sutra.
佛老 *For-Laau*, n., Buddha and Laotse, their teachings oft. considered related in respect to life phenomena.
佛門 *formern*, n., the school of Buddhism: 佛門弟子 Buddhist followers.
佛桑 *Forsang*, n., place name=扶^△^桑 10A.81.
佛像 *forshiahng*, n., statue of Buddha.
佛性 *forshihng*, n., Buddha nature.
佛手 *forshoou*, n., an aromatic citrous fruit, with tip ending like fingers.
佛事 *forshyh*, n., Buddhist religious service: 做佛事 have mass, prayer said.
佛陀 *Fortuor*, n., translit. of term Buddha, quite exact in pronunciation of 600 A.D.
佛祖 *Fortzuu*, n., respectful address of Buddha.
佛子 *fortzyy*, n., Bodhisattva 菩^△^薩 20A.40; a Buddhist; a kind person.

俳 91A.22-2

pair.

[Dist. 排; var. 徘]

Adj. Prefix denoting comic, comedy.

俳賦 *pairfuh*, n., arch. form of light, ornate descriptive poetry of 4th–6th cen.
俳歌 *pairge*, n., (AC) comic songs, oft. satiric.
俳句 *pairjyuh*, n., a Japanese form of light poetry consisting of 17 words.
俳諢 *pairnyueh*, v.i. & adj., satiric, -ize.
俳諧 *pairshier*, adj., comic, satiric.
俳體詩 *pairtii-shy*, n., light, comic poetry.
俳優 *pairyou*, n., comedian.

侪 91A.22-6

chair.

[Abbr. of 儕 ↓]

儕 91A.22-6

chair.

[Abbr. 侪]

N. (LL) fellow, group: 吾儕 we; 儕輩, 儕類 fellows of the same class or group; 同儕 fellows, friends; 儕偶 companion.

价 91A.22-8

jieh.

N. (1) A male servant: 貴价 (court.) your messenger or boy; 尊价 ditto; 小价 a young attendant. (2) Pop. of 價 price.

仰 91A.22-9

yaang.

V.i. & t. (1) To face upward: 仰天長嘯 to make a long whistle or cry into the air; 仰面朝天 to fall down face up; 俯仰之間 in a short moment (of "facing up and down"). (2) To hope: 仰望 *-wahng*↓; 仰能合意 hope it is what you want. (3) To look up to (person): 敬仰 admire and respect; 仰慕 *-muh*↓; 久仰 short for 久仰大名 formula for first meeting of well-known person; 信仰 to believe in (God, s.t.). (4) (Documentary to subordinate official or common people) hope: 右仰知悉 hope you take note of the above; 仰即遵照 hope you will obey and do accordingly. (5) To rely on, depend on: 仰給, 仰賴 *-jii, -laih*↓; 仰人鼻息 depend on another's whims and pleasures ("snort and sneezes"); 仰食於人 to depend on another for living.

Adv. Up, upwards: 仰視, 仰觀 looking upwards.

仰八叉 *yaang-bacha*, v.i., to fall down on one's back with legs pointing up: 仰八腳兒(子) ditto.

仰毒 *yaang-dur*, phr., to take poison (drinking face up).

仰光 *Yaangguang*, n., Rangoon.

仰仗 *yaangjahng*, v.t., to rely on, see *-laih*↓.

仰角 *yarngjiaau*, n., (math.) angle of elevation.

仰給 *yarngjii*, v.t., to support (parents).

仰止 *yarngjyy*, v.t., to admire greatly (as one stops looking up at a peak).

仰賴 *yaanglaih*, v.t., to rely on (favor, support).

仰慕 *yaangmuh*, v.t., to admire (person).

仰攀 *yaangpan*, v.i., to climb up; (fig.) to climb socially.

仰望 *yaangwahng*, v.i. & t., hope.

仰藥 *yaang-yauh*, phr., to quaff medicine.

作 91A.22-9

tzuoh (**tzuo, *tzuor*).

N. A profession: 瓦作 mason, bricklayer; 木作 carpenter; 作坊 *-'fang*↓; 洗衣作 laundry.

V.i. & t. (1) V.i., arise, stand up: 聖人作 a sage arose; 客作而辭 the guest stood up to say good-bye. (2) V.t., do, make, work at (usu.) interch. 做, the vernacular form, except certain phrr. where 作 is preferred): 作工 do manual work (physical labor); 作事 to busy oneself with, be engaged in (employed at), work for a living; 作衣服(鞋子) make a dress (shoes).

作保 *tzuoh-baau*, v.t., stand guarantee, go security (bail) for (person): 作保見 be guarantor and witness.

作罷 *tzuohbah*, v.i., give up, dismiss as not worth more discussion.

作伴(兒) *tzuoh-bahn(-bah'l)*, v.t., serve as companion for (person), keep (s.o.) company.

作癟子 **tzuo-bieetz*, v.i., be embarrassed, condemned, reproached.

作別 *tzuohbier*, v.i., bid s.o. good-bye.

作弊 *tzuoh-bih*, v.i., practise irregularities (fraud); cheat (in examination, work).

作成 *tzuoh-cherng*, v.t., (1) have (s.t.) made or done; (2) help to do, make a success of; (3) play a trick on (person).

作情 *tzuoh'chin*, v.i. & t., (1) admire s.o. out of respect; (2) intercede, mediate; (3) make a pretense.

作輟 *tzuoh-chuoh*, v.i., (1) see *-bah*↑; (2) work and stop.

作曲 *tzuoh-chyuu*, v.i., write a song, set a song to music, compose melody: 作曲家 composer.

作歹 *tzuoh-daai*, v.i., as in 爲非作歹 do evil.

作抵 *tzuoh-dir*, v.t., offer (s.t.) as compensation.

作對 *tzuoh-dueih*, v.t., (1) to set against, be opposed to; (2) to match (person) with another in marriage.

作惡 *tzuoh-eh*, (1) v.i., see *-daai*↑; (2) adj., moody, melancholy; (3) v.i., vomit, see *-oou*↓.

作伐 *tzuoh-fa*, v.i., to act as a go-between in marriage.

作法 *tzuoh-faa*, (1) n., a method of making, preparing, manufacturing, cooking; procedure, course of action, step taken; (2) v.i., practise magic; (3) legislate, make laws: 作法自斃 caught by one's own laws or device.

作反 *tzuoh-faan*, v.i., to rebel, revolt, turn against.

作坊 **tzuo'fang*, n., a workshop.

作廢 *tzuohfeih*, v.t., annul, make null and void, declare invalid.

作風 *tzuohfeng*, n., way of doing things.

作佛事 *tzuoh-for'shy*, v.i., (Budd.) say mass.

作歌 *tzuoh-ge*, v.i., compose a song.

作梗 *tzuoh-geeng*, v.i., obstruct, impede, hamper, hinder.

作館 *tzuoh-guaan*, v.i., formerly, serve as a private tutor.

作怪 *tzuohguaih*, v.i., make trouble, play tricks, act in a strange way: 少和我作怪 don't play any of your dirty tricks on me.

作古 *tzuohguu*, v.i., (euphem.) (LL) pass away ("join the ancients").

作耗 *tzuohhauh*, v.i., (coll.) (1) take up arms in revolt; (2) make trouble: 生事作耗 instigate incidents and make trouble.

作活(兒) *tzuoh-huor('l)*, v.i., work to earn a living.

作戰 *tzuoh-jahn*, v.i., to fight, make war.

作證 *tzuoh-jehng*, v.i., serve as a witness in court.

作家 *tzuohjia*, (1) n., an author, writer; (2) v.i., (AC) take care of personal finance.

作假 *tzuohjiaa*, (1) v.i., pretend, present a false front; (2) v.t., to take, make an imitation copy.

作繭 *tzuoh-jiaan*, v.i., (of silk-

作 worm) to spin a cocoon; (fig.) tie oneself up with duties (like a cocoon): 作繭自縛 ditto.

作嫁 *tzuohjiah*[1], v.i., (of a woman) help another to get married ("make a trousseau for her"): 爲人作嫁 to busy oneself with helping other people.

作價 *tzuohjiah*[2], v.t., assess the value, set a price.

作踐 **tzuor'jian*, v.t., trample under foot, treat harshly.

作計 *tzuoh-jih*, v.t., intend, have in mind, aim at: 我本不爲卿作計 (LL) this was not done with you in mind.

作勁 *tzuoh-jihn*, v.t., render assistance to (s.o.): 他眞給你作勁 he went all out to help you.

作就 *tzuohjiouh*, v.i., get s.t. successfully done.

作急 *tzuohjir*, v.i., make haste, be snappy.

作主 *tzuoh-juu*, v.t., make the final decision (also 做主).

作客 *tzuoh-keh*, v.i., (1) be a guest at a friend's; (2) sojourn in a strange land.

作闊 *tzuohkuoh*, v.i., to show off, make a vain display.

作苦 *tzuohkuu*, v.i., to work at arduous task.

作樂 *tzuoh-leh*, v.i., (1) enjoy oneself, have a good time; (2) (*-yueh*) to play music; write scores.

作雷 **tzuoleir*, v.i., bring disaster on one's own head.

作料(兒) **tzuorliauh('l)*, n., (of food) seasoning.

作亂 *tzuoh-luahn*, v.i., rise in revolt, turn against the authorities.

作夢 *tzuoh-mehng*, v.i., to dream; give free rein to one's imagination.

作媒 *tzuoh-meir*, v.i., act as go-between in marriage (also 做).

作摩 **tzuor'mo*, v.i., make conjectures, try to figure s.t. out.

作麽 *tzuohmor*, adv., (MC) what for? why? what is one doing? (also 作麽生).

作幕 *tzuoh-muh*, v.i., (LL) serve as a secretary (assistant, adviser) to an official, be on his staff.

作難 *tzuoh-narn*, v.i., find oneself in a predicament, don't know what to do.

作孽 *tzuoh-nieh*, v.i., (abuse) do some cursed thing, be guilty of an act that will bring its own retribution.

作嘔 *tzuoh-oou*, v.i., (1) vomit, turn the stomach; (2) feel resentment, detest, loathe.

作派 *tzuoh'pai*, n., (1) gestures and movements of actors on stage; (2) affected manners.

作陪 *tzuoh-peir*, v.i., sit at the same table with the guest of honor.

作品 *tzuohpiin*, n., a literary or artistic work.

作人 *tzuoh-rern*, v.i., (1) behave oneself properly, maintain correct relations with other people; (2) help develop the capabilities of young talents.

作色 *tzuoh-seh*, v.i., to change color, as in anger.

作善 *tzuohshahn*, v.i., do good turns.

作聲 *tzuoh-sheng*, v.i., break silence, begin to speak.

作興 **tzuor'shing*, (1) v.t., hold in high regard: 着實作興這幾個人 (MC) set these few men on a pedestal; (2) vb. phr., might as well let: 作興女待詔做個媒人 might as well let the lady-in-waiting be the go-between; (3) adj., sanctioned by tradition: 大盜相傳有這個規矩，不作興害鏢局的 robbers are bound by a traditional rule not to attack those operating an escort service for travellers; (4) adv., perhaps, maybe: 看這天氣，作興要下雨 given such weather, maybe it's going to rain.

作耍 *tzuohshuaa*, v.i., (1) to joke, poke fun; (2) to play, make merry.

作述 *tzuohshuh*, v.i., make original contributions and be a transmitter of those of others.

作詩 *tzuoh-shy*, v.i., write poems, versify.

作勢 *tzuoh-shyh*, v.i., gesticulate: 舉手作勢 make a gesture with hands; 裝腔作勢 put on airs.

作酸 **tzuosuan*, v.i., (1) feel stomach acidity; (2) (*tzuoh-*) be jealous of husband, or wife.

作祟 *tzuoh-sueih*, v.i., (some evil spirit) cause trouble, make mischief.

作速 *tzuohsuh*, v.i., hurry up, make haste.

作死 **tzuosyy*, v.i., (abuse) dig one's own grave.

作態 *tzuohtaih*, v.i., (1) put on pretenses; (2) strike an attitude.

作痛 *tzuohtuhng*, v.i., to ache, cause pain.

作外 *tzuohwaih*, v.i., stand on ceremony (as "with outsiders"): 弟兄休作外 brothers don't need to stand on ceremony.

作爲 *tzuohweir* (-'*wei*), (1) n., conduct and actions; accomplishments, achievements; (2) vb. phr., regard as: 作爲罷論 let the matter be dropped ("regard as ended").

作文 *tzuoh-wern*, v.i. & n., (write) an essay, composition, article.

作物 *tzuohwuh*, n., (1) farm crop; (2) literary or artistic composition.

作押 *tzuoh-ya*, v.i., offer as security.

作眼 *tzuoh-yaan*, v.i., (1) serve as an informer; (2) (Chin. game of "go") make an encircling movement so as to occupy more space on the chessboard.

作癢 *tzuohyaang*, v.i., to itch.

作業 *tzuohyeh*, v.i. & n., (do) a school assignment, homework.

作揖 **tzuo-yi*, v.i., to make an obeisance.

作冤 **tzuoyuan*, v.i., fall into a trap set by oneself.

作用 *tzuohyuhng*, n., (1) essential function: 機器的作用在節省人力 it's the function of machines to save manpower; (2) underlying purpose: 那有甚麽作用 what purpose can it serve? (3) motive, reason: 他說那句話必有作用 he must have some good reason for saying so; (4) action produced by some natural force: 化學作用 chemical action; (5) effect: 這種藥發生了預期的作用 this drug has had the expected effect (on the patient).

作俑 *tzuoh-yuung*, phr., (AC) originate an immoral (vicious, wicked) practice: 始作俑者其無後乎 cursed be he who first introduced the practice of burying wooden images (and later living beings) with the dead (Mencius).

侨 91A.22-9

chiaur.
[Abbr. of 僑 91A.42]

§ 91A.30 (亻/一)

值 91A.30-1

jyr.
[Usu. printed 値]

N. Price, cost: 價值 value, price; 增值 increase in value; 貶值 devalue (currency).

V.i. & t. (1) Be one's turn, be on duty: 值日, 值班, 值勤 day or turn on duty; 輪值 take turns; 值事人 person on duty; 當值 take one's turn; 值星 one's turn on duty on Sunday. (2) Come upon, meet: 值天下雨 it happens to rain; 值他不在家 he happens to be not at home; 值此危急之秋 at such a critical time. (3) To cost or be worth (price): 值多少錢 how much does it cost? 價值千金 worth a thousand dollars: 值得, 值錢 *-'de, -chiarn*↓.

值錢 *jyr-chiarn*, adj., valuable, worth money: 不值錢 worthless.
值得 *jyr'de*, adj., worth it: 這件事值得費一番心 this matter is worth careful thinking; 值得研究 worth careful study; 眞值得 really worth it; 太不值得 not worth the trouble.

佐 91A.30-1

tzuoo.

N. An assistant: 佐雜 *-tzar*, 佐貳 *-ehl*↓; 警佐 deputy police officer; 巡佐 assistant police inspector.

V.t. Serve as an assistant to: 輔佐 serve as an assistant (adviser, minister) to s.o.

佐貳 *tzuoo-ehl*, n., deputy administrative officer.
佐證 *tzuoojehng*, n., evidence that serves to substantiate (a statement, charge).
佐車 *tzuoo-jyu*, n., (AC) a reserve carriage for use in an emergency.
佐理 *tzuorlii*, (1) v.t., assist s.o. in management; (2) n., assistant manager.
佐命 *tzuoo-mihng*, v.i., assist a prince to gain the throne and found a new dynasty.
佐雜 *tzuootzar*, n., gen. term for minor clerks and assistants.

儘 91A.30-2

jiin.
[Abbr. 侭]

V.i. & t. Be free, feel free to: 儘管 *-guaan*, 儘教 *-jiauh*, 儘自 *-tzyh*↓.

Adv. Particle used for emphasis or as a superlative: 儘底下 down to the lowest level, beginning from the very bottom; 儘上頭 up to the highest point, starting with the topmost; 儘量 *-liahng*, 儘够 *-gouh*, 儘先 *-shian*, 儘着 *-'je*↓; 儘可以 certainly may, be free to.

儘够 *jiingouh*, phr., more than enough (adequate, sufficient).
儘管 *jirnguaan*, adv., even if (= *-jiauh*↓).
儘着 *jiin'je*, phr., to the greatest possible extent: 儘着各人的能力做事 let each one do his best.
儘教 *jiinjiauh*, adv., with no restrictions imposed.
儘量 *jiinliahng*, adv., as much (many) as possible, to the fullest extent.
儘讓 *jiinrahng*, adv., be as humble and yielding as possible.
儘先 *jiinshian*, adv., as early (soon) as possible.
儘自 *jiintzyh*, phr., let s.o. do as he pleases.

仁 91A.30-3

rern.

N. (1) The core or kernel of fruits: 杏仁 almonds; 果仁 fruit kernels; 桃仁 peach kernels. (2) (=人) 同仁 colleagues, fellow workers. (3) Anything resembling a kernel: 瞳仁 the pupil of the eye; 蝦仁 shelled shrimps. (4) Love, benevolence, charity, humanity: 仁義 *-yih*↓; 仁愛 *-aih*↓; 仁慈 *-tsyr*↓. (5) A person of great virtue: 汎愛衆, 而親仁 love one's fellow men and associate with the virtuous; (Confu.) a true man as an ideal.

Adj. (1) Respectable, esteemed: 仁兄 *-shyung*↓; 仁弟 *-dih*↓; 仁公 *-gung*↓. (2) Sensitive to external stimuli: 麻木不仁 (lit.) insensitive, partially paralyzed, (fig.) unfeeling, apathetic, indifferent. (3) Humane, compassionate, humanitarian (policy, government), merciful (heart, character).

仁愛 *rern-aih*, n., love of one's fellow men.
仁德 *rernder*, n., love, kindheartedness, benevolence, humanity.
仁弟 *rerndih*, n., (1) (addressing a younger friend) "my dear

作 侨 值 佐 儘 仁

仁 仨 僵 伍 佂 伾 但

little brother"; (2) (addressing one's student) "my dear friend."

仁恩 *rernen*, n., kind and gracious acts, tender feelings.

仁風 *rernfeng*, n., pervading atmosphere of kindness and generosity.

仁公 *rerngung*, n., (court.) honored sir (used for venerable people).

仁厚 *rernhouh*, adj., kindhearted, charitable, considerate, sympathetic.

仁政 *rern-jehng*, n., (politics) policies for the good of the people; a humane government (Mencius).

仁兒 *rer'l*, n., the kernel of a fruit.

仁里 *rernlii*, n., a village (district, neighborhood) noted for good customs.

仁民 *rernmirn*, v.i., love the people; practice kindness to the people.

仁人 *rernrern*, n., a kindhearted (compassionate) person: 仁人君子 men of goodwill, philanthropists; (Confu.) ideal of true man.

仁聲 *rern-sheng*, n., (AC) the mellowing influence of classical music and poetry.

仁心 *rernshin*, n., kindheartedness, charity: 仁心仁聞 a good repute for kindness.

仁恕 *rernshuh*[1], adj., kind and forgiving.

仁術 *rernshuh*[2], n., (AC) acts of kindness, the ways of the kindhearted.

仁兄 *rernshyung*, n., (vocative) my good friend.

仁慈 *rerntsyr*, adj. & n., kindness, charity, love, tender mercy.

仁翁 *rernweng*, n., address of elderly person in letters, my esteemed sir.

仁言 *rernyarn*, n., (AC) precepts, moral teachings.

仁義 *rernyih*, (1) adj., kind and justice; (2) n., humanity and justice; (3) (**rern'yi*) well-behaved: 這個小孩子很仁義, 不淘氣 (coll.) this little boy has good manners and is never naughty.

仨 91A.30-3

sa.

N. (Vern. short for 三 *san*) three persons: 他們仨 *ta'm-sa*, they three.

僵 91A.30-3

jiang.

V.i. & t. (1) V.i., remain stiff and motionless: 僵仆 to fall, prostrate. (2) V.t., dare (s.o.), set on: 僵事 *-shyh*↓.

Adj. (1) Numb, stiff, motionless: 僵立, 僵卧 *-lih, -woh*↓; 僵直 stiff and rigid; 凍僵了 stiff with cold; 身體已經僵了 *rigor mortis* has set in; 僵硬 numb and rigid. (2) Deadlocked: 僵局 *-jyur*, 僵持 *-chyr*↓; 弄僵了, 鬧僵了 come to an impasse; 僵化 *-huah*↓.

僵持 *jiangchyr*, v.i., be deadlocked, stalemated.

僵化 *jianghuah*, v.i., come to a deadlock, reach an impasse.

僵局 *jiangjyur*, n., a deadlock, impasse, stalemate.

僵立 *jianglih*, v.i., stand motionless.

僵屍 *jiangshy*, n., vampire; a reported walking corpse.

僵事 *jiangshyh*, v.i., stir up trouble between others.

僵卧 *jiangwoh*, v.i., lie stiff and motionless.

伍 91A.30-3

wuu.

N. (1) (AC) a unit of five soldiers: 伍長 *-jaang*↓. (2) Troops, rank and file: 隊伍 ditto; 行伍出身 was originally in the army; 入伍, 退伍 join, retire from military service; 落伍 fail in examinations; 羞與爲伍 ashamed to be seen in the same company. (3) Used for "spelling out" the number "five" in checks, instead of 五.

伍長 *wurjaang*, n., (mil.) (roughly corresponds to) squad leader, now generally called 班長.

佂 91A.30-3

jeng.

[Cogn. 征 22A.30]

伾 91A.30-3

pi.

Adj. (AC) Moving (herd); powerful.

但 91A.30-4

dahn.

N. A surname.

Adj. (1) Only, just, merely: 但有一個 (=只有) there's only one; 但聽他吩咐 just follow what he says; 但坐無妨, 但說無妨 just sit down, just speak out what is on your mind; 但只一次 only this once; 但不過我們兩人知道 it's only between us two; 但須, 但要 only want; 但望 only hope; 不求有功, 但求無過 do not hope to distinguish myself, but only not to make mistakes; oft. used negatively in 不但, 豈但, 非但 not only; 不但如此 not only this.

Conj. But; vern. usu. 但是 LL 但 or 但係, see 但是 *-'shy*; if only: 但使 *-shyy*↓.

但凡 *dahnfarn*, conj. & adv., whoever, whenever, whatever, all:

但凡是人，都有個良心 all men have a conscience; 但凡不違法，都可以做 whatever is not against the law is permissible.

但只 *dahnjyy*, adv., only: 但只恨 I only regret.

但是 *dahn'shy*, (1) conj., but, nevertheless; (2) adv., only: 但是一個小孩子 it's only a child.

但使 *dahnshyy*, conj., only if: 衣沾不足惜，但使願無違 only if I could follow my wish, it does not matter that my dress is wet.

但願 *dahnyuahn*, v.i., wish, hope: 但願你能早到 hope that you can come early; 但願你成功 wish you success; 但願如此 I hope so.

位 91A.30-6

weih.

N. adjunct. 三位朋友，客人 three friends, visitors.

N. (1) Status, seat, position: 地位 a person's status or situation; 位卑，位尊 low, high status; 客位，主位 seat of guest, of host; 讓位 to play for giving higher seat to s.o. else, also to abdicate; 本位 a unit, basic unit. (2) Seat of authority; the throne, spirit tablet: 遜位，禪位 abdicate the throne; 退位 give up post of power; 神位，牌位 spirit tablet. (3) Person: 這位是誰 (more court. than 這個人) who is this gentleman? 諸位，列位 (term in public address) ladies and gentlemen; 好幾位 a good many persons; 第一位 number one person, also (gram.) first person; 第三位 third person; 三位一體 the Trinity.

V.t. (AC) to take its place: 天地位焉 things in the universe take their proper places; 位(於)東南 situated in southeast.

位分 *weih'fen*, n., proper status.

位號 *weihhauh*, n., seat numbering; (AC) official title.

位置 *weihjyh* (-'*jy*), (1) n., (a) situation, position, post; (b) place: 放在甚麽位置 where did you put it? (2) v.t., to place (a person) in some post.

位次 *weihtsyh*, n., order of seating.

位子 *weihtz*, n., a seat, a post.

位望 *weihwahng*, n., social status and prestige.

倥 91A.30-6

kung.

倥侗 *kungturng*, adj., (LL) as in phr., 倥侗無知 innocent like a child.

倥傯 *kurngtzuung*, adj., (AC) (1) hard pressed; (2) in a great hurry; (3) very much occupied.

§ 91A.32 (亻/フ)

侈 91A.32-9

chyy.

Adj. (1) Extravagant: 奢侈 ditto; 侈用 waste money; extravagant talk: 侈言，侈論，侈談 *-yarn*, *-luhn*, *-tarn* ↓. (2) Dissolute, immoral (邪侈). (3) Broad, open (vowels).

侈侈 *chyrchyy*, adv., (LL) extravagantly.

侈論 *chyy-luhn*, n., extravagant, high-sounding talk.

侈靡 *chyrmii*, adj., extravagant, wasteful.

侈談 *chyy-tarn*, n., see *-luhn* ↑.

侈言 *chyy-yarn*, v.i. & n., to exaggerate, swagger.

§ 91A.40 (亻/口)

估 91A.40-1

gu (also *guu*, **guh*).

V.t. Estimate, assess the value, see compp. ↓; 估堆兒 estimate value of whole lot; 預估 make a preliminary estimate; 擡估 put a higher value on things already assessed.

估單 *gudan* (*guu-*), n., an estimate of prices submitted to a prospective customer, a quotation.

估價 *gujiah* (*guu-*), v.t., (business) to quote the current price; estimate value (of jewels, etc.).

估計 *gujih* (*guu-*) n. & v.t., (make), an estimate (of costs).

估量 *gu'liahng* (*guu-*), v.t., (1) calculate (distance, conditions); (2) to estimate.

估摸 *gu'mo*, v.t. & n., (1) (make) a rough estimate; (2) (be on) guard against.

估衣 **guhyi*, n., secondhand clothes.

僖 91A.40-1

shi.

Adj. Happy: 僖樂 to enjoy oneself.

佑 91A.40-1

youh.

佑 **V.t.** To help: 庇佑, 保佑 (of God) to help, protect, bless (also wr. 祐).

偌 91A.40-2

ruoh.

Adv. So, to such an extent or degree: 偌大年紀 so old, so much advanced in age; 偌大房子 such a big house; 偌遠的到這裏來 have come from so far; 偌多 so much.

佔 91A.40-2

jahn.

V.t. (1) To occupy, esp. by force or illegally (also wr. 占): 佔據 *-jyuh*↓; 佔便宜 take advantage of situation; 佔上風 take advantageous position; 佔優勢 gain advantage, stand ahead, in contest; 侵佔, 霸佔 encroach on territory, take illegal possession of; 佔有 seize possession. (2) U.f. 覘 22S.70, to covet, watch.

佔奪 *jahnduor*, v.t., see *-liing*↓.
佔據 *jahnjyuh*, v.t., to occupy, esp. illegally.
佔領 *jahnliing*, v.t., to take possession by force.
佔先 *jahnshian*, v.i., to reach or occupy ahead of others.

侶 91A.40-4

lyuu.

N. Companion: 伴侶 companion; 情侶 lovers, sweetheart; 仙侶 companion in fairyland.

倨 91A.40-5

jyuh.

Adj. (1) Proud, haughty, arrogant: 倨傲 supercilious, conceited, puffed up. (2) Slightly bent.

信 91A.40-6

shihn.

N. (1) Mail, letter: 信件, 信箋, 信差, 信箱 *-jiahn*, *-jian*, *-chai*, *-shiang*, etc.↓; 來信 your letter, letter from s.o.; 去信 letter to s.o.; 快信 express letter; 回信 letter of reply; 信使往還 exchange of letters and messengers. (2) News, message, correspondence: 口信 oral message; 音信 letter, news; 通信(訊)社 news agency; 通信(訊)員 news correspondent. (3) Agreed signal: 信號 (war, naval) signal; 信牌 *-pair*↓; 憑信 document, evidence. (4) Regular periodical appearance: 月信, 信水 menstruation; 信風 seasonal winds; 潮信 tides. (5) (AC) messenger. (6) Sincerity; 失信 fail on promise; 背信 violate promise or agreement. (7) A surname.

V.i. & t. To believe, to trust: 相信 believe; 我相信 I believe; 將信將疑, 疑信參半 half believe and half doubt; 敢相信, 不敢相信 dare, dare not, believe; 信得, 信不得 believable, unbelievable; 信得及, 信不及, 信得來, 信不來 dare, dare not trust; 信得過, 信不過 can, cannot believe or trust, also trustworthy, not trustworthy; 自信 believe in oneself, self-confidence; 輕信 believe whatever one is told; 信奉, 信仰, 信徒, 信託, etc. *-fehng*, *-yaang*, *-tur*, *-tuo*, etc. ↓.

Adj. & adv. (1) (LL) true, truly, indeed: 信乎 is it true? 信有之矣 indeed there are such things; 信然 it is indeed true. (2) Honest: 信實 *-shyr*; 信史 *-shyy*[1]↓; 信賞必罰 awards and punishments rigorously carried out.

Prep. (Followed by nn. forming adv. phrr.) trusting, guided by: 信口, 信手, 信步 *-koou*, *-shoou*, *-buh*↓; 信筆, 信意兒 *-bii*, *-yeh'l*↓; 信馬由韁 ride with lax reins—(fig.) let things take their natural course.

信筆 *shihn-bii*, adv. phr., 信筆直書 write freely without too much hesitation or as fancy dictates.
信步 *shihn-buh*, adv. phr., 信步閒遊 roam about without definitive objective ("where the foot takes one").
信插 *shihn-cha*, n., mail rack.
信差 *shihn-chai*, n., mailman.
信臣 *shihn-chern*, n., (AC) emissary (＝使臣).
信牒 *shihn-dier*, n., (LL) official memos.
信底(兒)(子) *shihndii(-diee'l)(tz)*, n., original draft for a letter.
信幡 *shihnfan*, n., (1) (AC) a banner bearing title of commander; (2) (Budd.) banner of believer.
信奉 *shihnfehng*, v.t., to believe in and worship (God), to be member of (religion).
信封 *shihnfeng*[1], n., envelope.
信風 *shihn-feng*[2], phr., trade wind.
信服 *shihnfur*, v.t., see *-fehng*↑.
信鴿 *shihn-ge*, n., carrier pigeon.
信號 *shihnhauh*, n., military or naval signal: 信號砲 gun signal.
信滙 *shihn-hueih*, n., mail transfer.
信札 *shihnjar*, n., letters in gen.: 往來信札 exchange of correspondence.
信件 *shihnjiahn*, n., letters.
信箋 *shihn-jian*, n., letter paper, esp. artistic paper.
信局(子) *shihnjyur(tz)*, n., formerly, private firm for carrying mail before post office system was established.
信紙 *shihnjyy*, n., letter paper.
信靠 *shihnkauh*, v.t., to trust, rely on (God).
信口 *shihn-koou*, adv. phr., 信口開河 say whatever comes to one's mind, without proper consideration; 信口雌黃 criticize or make statements freely without careful thought (see 雌[A]黃 21S.11); 信口胡說 talk nonsense.
信念 *shihnniahn*, n., faith, esp.

A

religious.

信女 *shihn-nyuu*, n., female believer, usu. 善男信女 (Budd.) men and women believers.

信牌 *shihn-pair*, n., formerly, tally used in delivering official messages.

信砲 *shihn-pauh*, n., gun signal; formerly, also gun signal for daybreak (報曉砲) and noon (午砲) in some cities.

信片 *shihnpiahn*, n., postcard (also 明信片).

信皮 *shihnpir*, n., (vulg.) envelope.

信瓤兒 *shihnrarng'l*, n., (coll.) contents of an envelope.

信任 *shihnrehn*, v.i. & t., to trust, place confidence in (person): 太信任了 trust people too much; 信任投票 a vote of confidence; 信任狀 credentials.

信息 *shihn'shi*, n., news (=消息).

信箱 *shihn-shiang*, n., letter box, pillar box: 郵政信箱 post office box (P.O.B.).

信行兒 *shihn'shihng'l*, n., (coll.) promissory note, deed, certificate.

信心 *shihn-shin*, n., (1) faith, esp. religious; (2) confidence.

信手 *shihn-shoou*, adv. phr., do. s. t. without previous plan: 信手抽一本書 pick out a book at random.

信士 *shihn-shyh*[1], n., (1) believer, follower of religion; (2) an honest man.

信誓 *shihnshyh*[2], n., an oath, a pledge: 信誓旦旦 (AC) oath solemnly pledged.

信實 *shihnshyr*, adj., trustworthy, honest.

信史 *shihn-shyy*[1], phr., trustworthy historical record.

信使 *shihn-shyy*[2], n., messenger, emissary: 信使往還 exchange of correspondence and emissaries.

信宿 *shihnsuh*, adv., (LL) stay over for two consecutive nights.

信天翁 *shihntianweng*, n., (zoo.) the albatross.

信條 *shihntiaur*, n., creed; articles of creed.

信從 *shihntsurng*, v.t., to believe and obey (God, His teachings).

B

信託 *shihntuo*, (1) to trust, entrust; (2) a trust for managing funds: 信託基金 a trust fund; 信託局 a trust corporation; 信託銀行 a trust (bank).

信徒 *shihntur*, n., follower, believer (of religion).

信筒(子) *shihntuung(tz)* n., public post box for sending letters.

信子 *shihntz*, n., (pop. for 芯 lamp pith).

信物 *shihnwuh*, n., a token of promise, a ring, etc., as pledge, a keepsake.

信仰 *shihnyaang*, (1) n., faith, belief, esp. religious; (2) v.t., to believe in or worship (God, religion).

信意兒 *shihnyeh'l*, adv., (do things) impulsively, as one wishes.

信義 *shihnyih*, n., (1) honesty: 不守信義 do not keep promise; (2) justification by faith; 信義會 Evangelical Lutheran Church (religion).

信譽 *shihnyuh*, n., reputation for honesty, trustworthiness.

信用 *shihnyuhng*, n., (1) a man's trustworthiness, gen. reputation: 不守信用 do not keep one's words; (2) credit: 信用借款 credit loan; 信用交易 a business deal on credit; 信用合作社 a cooperative bank; 純信用狀 clean credit, also open credit; 信用評核 credit rating; 信用債券 debenture; 保兌信用狀 confirmed letter of credit; 現金信用狀 cash letter of credit.

倍 91A.40-6

beih.

N. Fold, multiple times: 三倍 three times; 五倍 five times; 百倍 a hundred fold; 加倍 double: 利錢加倍 double the interest; 加倍用工 double efforts (to study); 加倍小心 be twice as careful (extra careful).

C

V.t. (AC) synonymous with 背: 則民不倍 then the people do not turn their backs on (ruler).

Adj. & adv. Double, -bly: 倍增傷感 doubly grieved; 倍增, 倍加 doubly.

倍道 *beihdauh*, adv., (of travel) by day and night or by land and water, i.e., with best speed (dist. 背[Δ]道 22.42).

倍兒 *beh'l*, adv., (coll.) very, doubly: 倍兒亮 very bright and shining.

倍屣 *beihshii*, adv., double and redouble, (lit.) one to five times.

倍數 *beihshuh*, n., multiple.

倌 91A.40-6

guan.

N. (1) 堂倌 a boy in the employ of a teahouse, tavern or restaurant. (2) 倌人 *-rern*↓.

倌人 *guahrern*, n., (1) (AC) an officer in charge of royal chariots; (2) formerly, a euphemism for prostitutes or courtesans.

俗 91A.40-8

sur.

N. Social customs: 風俗, 慣俗, 俗慣, 習俗 ditto; 土俗, 俚俗 local customs; 流俗 common current customs; 世俗 the lay world, the common run of mankind.

Adj. (1) Vulgar, common, everyday, opp. 雅 *yaa*, elegant: 俗氣, 俗人 *-chih*, *-rern*↓; 俗事, 俗務 common, everyday business: 俗務纏身 tied down by everyday affairs; 俗累 business concerns, worries; 俗吏 average official or clerk; 俗目,

俗眼, 俗耳 mortal eyes, ears (what they see or hear); 俗不可耐 unbearably common; 未能免俗 have to do what others are doing; 俗套 *-tauh* ↓. (2) Secular (opp. religious), worldly, (what is) common and only human: 俗家, 俗父 *-jia, -fuh* ↓; 俗情, 俗欲 *-chirng, -yuh* ↓.

俗氣 *sur'chih*, adj., (1) vulgar, common; (2) tiresome: 這話我聽俗氣了 I am tired of this talk.

俗情 *surchirng*, n., common, human feelings. 「a monk.

俗父 *surfuh*, n., natural father of

俗骨 *surguu*, n., as in 凡胎俗骨 the body as heir to all mortal desires. 「saying.

俗話(兒) *surhuah('l)*, n., common

俗家 *surjia*, adj. & n., secular (dress); monk's blood kins.

俗例兒 *surlieh'l*, n., customary rules. 「of men.

俗流 *surliour*, n., the common run

俗人 *sur-rern*, n., vulgarian.

俗尚 *surshahng*, n., current fashions. 「common business.

俗事(兒) *surshyh(-sheh'l)*, n.,

俗態 *surtaih*, n., vulgar manner.

俗套(子) *surtauh(--tz)*, n., usual routine social activities (greetings, invitations, etc.); usual set of phrases, *clichés*.

俗字 *surtzyh*, n., popular form of character (as 战 for 戰).

俗文學 *sur-wernshyuer*, n., popular literature (ballads, songs, etc.).

俗物 *surwuh*, n., (contempt.) a vulgarian, philistine, a vulgar, unrefined person.

俗諺 *suryahn*, n., proverb.

俗緣 *suryuarn*, n., person's destiny in mortal world: 俗緣未了 the time has not yet come for entering monastery.

俗欲 *suryuh*, n., natural human desires; vulgar desires.

俗語(兒) *suryuu('l)*, n., proverb, popular saying.

佮 91A.40-8

sher.

[Var. of 啥 40A.40]

傖 91A.40-8

tsang (also *cherng*).

Adj. Vulgar: 傖父, 傖夫俗子 (LL contempt.) a vulgar person.

伽 91A.40-9

chier.

N. Word used in translit. of Sanskr. sound *ga* and *ka* (as also 迦), being also the Chin. pronunciation around 600 A.D. and in Fukien and Canton dialects today.

伽藍 *chierlarn*, n., (Budd.) temple; 伽藍鳥 the white pelican.

伽羅 *chierluor*, n., a Cambodian wood, prized for its perfume, eagle wood (also called 沉香).

伽南香 *chiernarnshiang*, n., a wood prized for its perfume; such perfume.

儋 91A.40-9

dan.

N. Name of county.

讐 91A.40-9

chour.

[Var. of 讎 91S.11]

§91A.41 (亻/図)

借 91A.41-2

jieh.

V.t. Borrow, lend, make use of, resort to, rely on: 暫借 temporarily use s.t. belonging to another; 借用 *-yuhng* ↓; 我借給他一些 I've lent him some (money); 好借好還 make it a point to return everything one has borrowed; 借錢, 借款 borrow money, funds; 借債 incur debt; 假借 borrow, make use of (oft. without due authorization), also use one character to serve for another of similar pronunciation ("u.f." in this dictionary): 假借他人名義 do s.t. in the name of s.o. else; 借風使船 (fig.) sail with the wind; 借刀殺人 do harm to s.o. through the hands of another; 借題發揮 give vent to one's pent-up feelings on some extraneous pretext; 借花獻佛 make presents provided by s.o. else; 借屍還魂 be reincarnated in s.o. else's body; 借故生端 pick a quarrel or fight on some flimsy pretext; 借光 *-guang*, 借火兒 *-huoo'l*, 借重 *-juhng* ↓.

Conj. If, supposing: 借如 *-rur* ↓.

借券 *jiehchyuahn*, n., a promissory note, an I.O.U.

借貸 *jieihdaih*, v.i., borrow money.

借道 *jieh-dauh*, v.i., (of thieves) pass through the premises of s.o. other than the person to be victimized; (mil.) carry war via neutral territory.

借端 *jieh-duan*, adv., on one pretext or another.

借方 *jieh-fang*, n., (accounting) the debit side.

借光 *jieh-guang*, v.i., (1) be indebted to s.o. for his kindness; (2) phr., "by your leave," "pardon me, please!" (used by driver to pass another car).

借火兒 *jieh-huoo'l*, v.i., borrow matches or a lighted cigarette.

借鑑 *jieh-jiahn*, v.i., to benefit by another person's past experience and avoid similar mistakes.

借鏡 *jieh-jihng*, v.i., ditto.

借助 *jiehjuh*[1], v.i., secure friendly assistance or support.

借住 *jiehjuh*[2], v.i., stay at a friend's for a day or two.

借箸 *jiehjuh*[3], v.i., (allu.) draw up a plan of action for others.
借重 *jiehjuhng*, v.t., rely on for help, enlist the services of.
借據 *jiehjyuh*, n., an I.O.U.
借名 *jiehmirng*, v.i., do s.t. on one pretext or another: 借名訛詐 extort money by false pretences.
借如 *jiehrur*, conj., in case, if, supposing (＝譬如).
借項 *jiehshiahng*, n., loan, debit: 借項通知 debit memo.
借孝 *jieh-shiauh*, v.i., (of people in bereavement) discard mourning garment in favor of ordinary dress on exceptional occasions.
借壽 *jieh-shouh*, v.i., offer in prayer to the gods to cut short one's own life to save that of one's parent or other close relative seriously ill.
借宿 *jiehsuh*, v.i., spend the night at another's.
借條 *jiehtiaur*, n., a promissory note, an I.O.U., see *-jyuh* ↑.
借字兒 *jiehtzeh'l*, n., ditto.
借問 *jiehwehn*, v.i., (court.) may I ask? 借問酒家何處有 "is there a tavern anywhere, pray?"
借因由兒 *jieh yin'you'l*, phr., on one pretext or another.
借喻 *jiehyuh*, v.i., use an analogy ＝比喻.
借用 *jiehyuhng*, v.t., borrow for temporary use.

偕 91A.41-2

jie.

Adv. Together: 偕老, 百年偕老 (of husband and wife) happily married and together reach old age; 偕行 go or walk together; 偕隱 retire together.

偪 91A.41-3

bi (also **bih*).
[Var. of 逼 30.83]

佰 91A.41-3

baai (sp. pr.), **bor* (re. pr.); **moh.*

N. & adj. (1) Var. of 百 hundred, used esp. in checks to avoid mistakes. (2) Centurion. (3) (**moh*) A hundred cash.

偭 91A.41-3

miaan.

V.t. (AC) violate: 偭規越矩 (AC) violate the rules.

倡 91A.41-4

chahng (**chang*).

N. (*chahng*) U.f. 娼 prostitute: 倡妓 ditto; 倡優 (LL) prostitutes and actors.

V.t. (*chahng*) To lead: 倡導, 倡言, 倡始 *-dauh, -yarn, -shyy* ↓; 首倡 the first to propose or lead (a movement), found (a theory); 提倡 to promote (simplified characters, Esperanto, etc.).

倡導 *chahngdauh*, v.t., to lead (a movement).
倡始 *chahngshyy*, v.t., to invent, found (theory, movement).
倡言 *chahngyarn*, v.t., be the first to propose, espouse, introduce (a doctrine) publicly.
倡議 *chahngyih*, v.t., to propose.

佃 91A.41-4

diahn.

V.i. & t. (1) To till field as tenant farmer. (2) (AC) to hunt.

佃戶 *diahnhuh*, n., tenant farmer.
佃農 *diahnnurng*, n., ditto.

偏 91A.41-4

leei.

N. A puppet: 傀△偏 91A.70.

個 91A.41-4

geh (**'ge*).
[Modn. form of 箇 92A.41]

儲 91A.41-6

chur (also *chuh*).

N. (1) Heir: 儲嗣, 儲君, 儲貳 *-syh, -jyun, -eh* ↓. (2) A surname.

V.t. To save, have savings, store up: 儲蓄 *-shyuh* ↓; 儲積, 儲藏 *-jir, -tsarng* ↓.

儲備 *churbeih*, v.i. & t. & n., (make) preparations, esp. for defense; to store up (food, etc.); reserve.
儲貳 *chureh*, n., crown prince.
儲宮 *churgung*, n., ditto.
儲積 *churjir*, v.i. & t., to store up, save up; to hoard (food).
儲君 *churjyun*, n., see *-eh* ↑.
儲胥 *churshyu*, n., (1) (AC) servants; (2) store of weapons, armory.
儲蓄 *churshyuh*, n. & v.t., savings; keep savings: 儲蓄銀行 savings bank; 儲蓄存戶 savings account.
儲嗣 *chursyh*, n., see *-eh* ↑.
儲藏 *churtsarng*, v.t. & n., to hoard, a hoard, accumulations; 儲藏室 storeroom.

僧 91A.41-8

seng.

N. A monk (from 僧伽 *-chier* ↓): 僧徒, 僧衆 monks; 僧院 *-yuahn* ↓; 高僧 monk of high renown; 僧尼 monk and nun.

僧伽 *sengchier*, n., (translit. of Sanskr. *sangha*) the monks, priests.
僧道 *sengdauh*, n., Buddhists and Taoists.
僧行 *sengharng*, n., (MC) the monks.
僧侶 *senglyuu*, n., *-tur* ↓.
僧人 *sengrern*, n., a monk.
僧俗 *seng-sur*, n., monks and laymen.
僧徒 *sengtur*, n., the monks as a group.
僧院 *sengyuahn*, n., monastery.

儈 91A.41-8

kuaih.

N. 市儈 (contempt.) common merchant, a broker.

伯 91A.41-9

bor (**baai*, **bah*).

N. (1) Elder brother of father: 伯父 *-fuh* ↓; dist. 叔 younger brother of father; 舅 maternal uncle; 姨丈 mother's sister's husband; coll. **baai*: 大伯子 address of first uncle. (2) (AC) first of brothers in 伯-仲-叔-季 series, now oft. used in personal names. (3) Term of address for husband's elder brother (the mother following children's address). (4) A count (a noble). (5) Term of honor, as in 詩伯 elderly poet. (6) (**bah*) (AC) leader of states: 五伯＝五霸[Δ] 31D.42. (7) A surname.

伯伯 *bo'bo*, n., address for elder brother of father; generally courtesy address for familiar friend of senior generation, like Eng. "uncle" (高伯伯 Uncle Gau).
伯道 *Bordauh*, n., virtuous person of Jihn Dyn. regretted to have no offspring, hence, 伯道之憂 (AC allu.) Bodauh's sorrow, i.e., having no children.
伯父 *borfuh*, n., father's elder brother.
伯仲 *borjuhng*, n., brothers, elder and younger: 不相伯仲 about equal.
伯勞 *borlaur*, n., the shrike.
伯樂 *Borleh*, n., (AC) famous trainer of horses.
伯氏 *bor'shy*, n., (AC) elder brother.

俻 91A.41-9

beih.
[Pop. of 備 ↓]

偺 91A.41-9

tzarn.
[Var. of 咱 40A.41]

僣 91A.41-9

jiahn.
[Dist. 僭]

V.t. Usurp, arrogate, encroach upon: 僣號 *-hauh*, 僣竊 *-chieh*, 僣越 *-yueh*, 僣位 *-weih* ↓: 僣國號 illegally assume the title of a reigning dynasty; 僣分 arrogate to oneself functions or rights belonging to another; 僣稱 assume an unlawful title.

僣竊 *jiahnchieh*, v.t., usurp (power, authority).
僣號 *jiahnhauh*, v.i., adopt an illegal title.
僣妄 *jiahnwahng*, adj., presumptuous, overbearing.
僣位 *jiahn-weih*, v.i., usurp the throne.
僣越 *jiahnyueh*, v.i., exceed one's authority, go beyond proper bounds.

§ 91A.42 (亻/冈)

倩 91A.42-1

chiahn (**chihng*).

N. (Also **chihng*) (LL) 妹倩 husband of younger sister (＝妹婿).

V.t. To ask or pay s.o. to act as substitute, see 倩代 *-daih* ↓.

Adj. Beautiful, pleasing.

倩倩 *chiahnchiahn*, adj., (LL) pleasing, attractive.
倩代 *chiahndaih*, v. t., (also **chihng*), to ask (related 請): 倩人代筆 ask s.o. to write or paint in name of another.
倩粧 *chiahn-juang*, n., beautiful make-up.

侑 91A.42-1

youh.

V.t. (1) To help. (2) To assist at: 侑觴, 侑酒 (professional girl) assist at drinking; 侑食 (AC) assist at dinner (＝modn. 陪宴).

備 91A.42-2

beih.

N. & v.t. (1) Prepare, provide

(preparation, provision), furnish, be furnished with: 備馬, 備食物 provide with horse, food. (2) Prepare for, provide against: 備考 prepare for examination, remark (also 備註); 以備不虞 provide against contingency; 備用 provide for use; 備文 prepare official document; 備戰 prepare for war. (3) Most commonly in combb.: 預備 prepare; 籌備 plan and provide (funds, plans); 準備 be prepared (to start, escape); 防備 provide against; 有備無患 with all precautions taken, one is safe; 軍備 armament.

Adv. All: 備悉 (in letters) I have noted all the contents; 備述詳情 detail all that has happened.

備案 *beih-ahn*, v.i. & n., communicate or register for the record.
備辦 *beihbahn*, v.t. & n., prepare, -ation (行裝 luggage, 筵席 celebration dinner, etc.).
備補 *beihbuu*, n., qualified candidate for office, waiting for opening.
備取 *beih-chyuu*, n., candidates on waiting list.
備細 *beihshih*, n., the details.
備忘錄 *beihwahngluh*, n., memo, official memo.
備位 *beih-weih*, v.i., (modest) fill the post.
備員 *beihyuarn*, n., one filling a post.

俏 91A.42-2

chiauh.

V.i. (Of prices) shoot up, firm up: 市價堅俏 prices firm up; 挺俏 go up sharply; 俏利 *-lih*[1]↓.

V.t. To resemble, be like: 俏似某人 resemble a certain person; 俏似一場空夢 just like a dream; also 俏如 ditto (cf. 恰[Δ]如, 恰[Δ]似 22A.40).

Adj. Handsome, beautiful (person): 俏女郎, 俏好女子, a pretty girl; 俏男子 a handsome man; 長得眞俏 has grown up very pretty; 俊俏 (of man) handsome; 依門賣俏 (or 笑) to flirt near the door with passengers; 俏生生的這兩條腿 (MC) such pretty legs; 俏蒨 (MC) handsome.

俏貨 *chiauh-huoh*, n., goods which could be picked up at low price and sold for profit.
俏利 *chiauh-lih*[1], phr., commanding good profits.
俏麗 *chiauhlih*[2], adj., beautiful, good-looking.
俏皮 *chiauhpir*, (1) adj., sarcastic, ironical: 俏皮話 sarcasm; (2) adj., handsome: 又年輕又俏皮 young and handsome; (3) v.t., to make sarcastic remarks at: 俏皮他兩句 make a few sarcastic remarks at him.
俏式 *chiauh'shy*, adj., handsome, pretty.
俏事 *chiauhshyh*, n., an "affair" (romance or illegal transaction).

倘 91A.42-2

taang.
[Var. 儻]

Conj. If, supposing that: 倘能如此 if this can be done; 倘蒙賜顧 (business) if we should have your patronage, if I should have your consideration or visit; 倘是事實 if it be true; 倘敢前來 if (he) dares to come; oft. used in bisyllabic compp. in spoken Chinese ↓.

The followings are used interchangeably: 倘使不肯, 倘若不肯, 倘如不肯, 倘是不肯, 倘然不肯, 倘或不肯 if (he) is unwilling:

倘或 *taanghuoh*, conj., if.
倘然 *taangrarn*, conj., if.
倘若 *taangreh*, conj., if.
倘如 *taangrur*, conj., if.
倘是 *taangshyh*, conj., if.
倘使 *taangshyy*, conj., if.

倆 91A.42-3

liaang.

N. (1) See 伎[Δ]倆 91A.82. (2) (*liaa*) Two persons: 他(們)倆 the two of them; 我倆, 我們倆 we two (habitually used in betrothal announcement); 姊妹倆 the two sisters.

儒 91A.42-3

rur.

N. (1) A scholar, a Confucianist: 儒者 a Confucian scholar; 儒士 a student, one well versed in one of the Confucian classics; 儒生 *-sheng*↓; 大儒 a great teacher; 名儒 a man of great learning; 宿儒 a savant; 寒儒 a poor scholar; 儒墨 Confucianists and Mohists (follower of Motse); 儒家 *-jia*↓; 儒宗 a teacher whom other scholars look up to for guidance; 儒門 *-mern*↓; 儒吏 a scholar-official; 儒醫 a scholar well read in the literature of herb medicine; 儒術 the way of the Confucian scholar; 儒道 Confucianism and Taoism; 儒典 the Confucian classics; 儒行 the conduct of a Confucian scholar; 儒素 the character of a Confucian scholar; 儒服 a scholar's dress; 儒冠 a scholar's headdress; 儒巾 ditto. (2) 侏儒 a pygmy, a dwarf.

Adj. Cowardly: 偷儒 (AC) lazy and spiritless.

儒兒 *rur-erl*, v.i., (LL) make a

forced smile (also 嚅唲).

儒緩 *rurhuaan*, adj., slow-witted, sluggish.

儒戶 *rur-huh*, n., a scholarly family.

儒家 *rur-jia*, n., Confucianism, -ists.

儒將 *rir-jiahng*, n., a soldier who is an equally accomplished man of letters.

儒教 *rurjiauh*, n., the teachings of Confucius.

儒林 *rur-lirn*, n., the scholars as a class.

儒門 *rur-mern*, n., (=儒家 *-jia* ↑).

儒儒 *rurrur*, adj., (LL) provincial, with a narrow outlook.

儒生 *rursheng*, n., (1) a young scholar; (2) a scholar well versed in one of the Confucian classics.

儒學 *rurshyuer*, n., (1) Confucian scholarship (also 儒學兒); (2) formerly, official instructors appointed by local governments.

儒雅 *ruryaa*, adj., genteel, refined, cultured.

俑 91A.42-3

yuung.

N. A wooden figure to bury with the dead (condemned by Confucius, probably on mistaken assumption that human sacrifice originated with use of figurines).

偶 91A.42-4

oou.

N. (1) Idol, wooden figure: 木偶 a wooden figure; 偶像 *-shiahng* ↓. (2) Mate, spouse: 良偶, 佳偶 good spouse; 喪偶, 失偶 lose one's wife or mate. (3) (AC) 曹偶 companions.

Adj. Even (number), opp. 奇 odd.

Adv. (1) By chance, accidentally, casually: 偶然 ditto; 偶見, 偶聞 happen to see, hear; 偶遇 meet accidentally. (2) Occasionally: 偶爾爲之 did it occasionally. (3) Together: 偶語 (AC) talk together; 偶視 (AC) look at each other.

偶爾 *our-eel*, adv., occasionally, not habitually.

偶或 *oouhuoh*, conj., if by chance.

偶然 *ourarn*, adj. & adv., accidental, not planned; also occasionally (meet person, etc.).

偶人 *oourern*, n., a clay or wooden idol.

偶像 *ooushiahng*, n., idol, image; (fig.) object of uncritical worship: 崇拜偶像 idolatry; 打倒偶像 iconoclasm.

偶戲 *ooushih*, n., marionette, puppet show.

偶性 *ooushihng*, n., (allowance for) the unforeseen, irregular, unexpected.

偶數 *oou-shuh*, n., even number.

偶影 *our-yiing*, phr., (LL) a person and his own shadow—loneliness.

佣 91A.42-4

yuhng.

N. Commission fee: 回佣 ditto.

佣錢 *yuhng'chian*, n., commission fee.

佣金 *yuhngjin*, n., ditto.

侗 91A.42-4

turng (**tung*).

N. Interch. 僮 91A.11, see 倥ᐞ侗 91A.30.

Adj. (**tung*) (AC) (1) Big. (2) Ignorant: 侗而不愿 ignorant but not simple. (3) 侗然 untrammeled, freely.

倜 91A.42-4

tih.

倜儻 *tihdaang*, adj., unconventional: 倜儻不羈 untrammeled, free, romantic (in character).

倜然 *tihrarn*, adj., (AC) aloof, unattached.

倜倜 *tihtih*, adj., ditto.

傭 91A.42-6

yurng (also *yung*).

N. Servant, attendant: 女傭 maidservant; 傭婦 woman servant.

V.t. To hire; p.p., be hired.

傭保 *yurngbaau*, n., hired labor.

傭兵 *yurngbing*, n., mercenary soldier.

傭工 *yurnggung*, n., hired labor or help.

傭書 *yurngshu*, v.i., to write letters, etc. for illiterate person.

傭作 *yurngtzuoh*, v.i., to work for hire.

偏 91A.42-6

pian.

[Dist. 徧 pr. *biahn*, 91B.42]

V.i. & t. (1) 偏了 to have eaten ahead of group dinner (modest exp.). (2) Incline to one side: 他偏過頭去 he turned his head.

Adj. (1) Slanting, slanted, favoring one or the other: 不偏不倚 impartial; 偏於某方 partial to one side; see 偏心, 偏愛, 偏頗, 偏見 *-shin*, *-aih*, *-po*, *-jiahn* and many common compp. ↓. (2) Special, on the side: 偏才 special aptitude, esp. apart from gen. studies, such as chess; 偏門 side door, side line.

Adv. (1) Against one's thinking or wish, in an unexpected and curious way, stubbornly: 他偏巧(不巧)來了 he turned up against expectations. (2) Conveying sense of stubborn opposition or emphasizing the opposite: 他偏不答應 he stubbornly refused; 你要去, 他偏不去 you want to go, but he insists on not going (on purpose); 你說他不會, 他偏會 you think he cannot do it but (to one's surprise) he can.

偏愛 *pian-aih*, n., special favorite, have fondness for (person, subject).
偏安 *pian-an*, v.i., rule a region (in times of national division).
偏差 *pian-cha*, n., deviation.
偏棲 *pianchi*, v.i., live life of widow, "roost alone."
偏情 *pian-chirng*, n., (Catholic) the passions.
偏殿 *piandiahn*, n., side temple.
偏方 *pianfang*, n., remote region; 偏方兒 --'*l*, (Chin. med.) special, not regular, prescription.
偏房 *pianfarng*, n., concubine (in gen. use).
偏廢 *pianfeih*, v.t., to neglect (some aspects).
偏鋒 *pianfeng*[1], n., term, in calligraphy and painting, signifying moving brush at a slant, cf. 中鋒.
偏風 *pianfeng*[2], n., semi-paralysis.
偏孤 *piangu*[1], adj., bereft of father, with mother living.
偏枯 *piangu*[2], n. & adj., semi-paralysis; (part) suffering from neglect.
偏好 *pianhauh*, n., hobby: 有所偏好 loves it specially.
偏諱 *pianhueih*, n., taboo against either of two characters in parent's or emperor's name.
偏護 *pianhuh*, v.t. & n., be partial to and support (one side, person).
偏角 *pianjiaau*, n., (astron.) declination of heavenly body from celestial equator.
偏見 *pianjiahn*, n., prejudice.
偏墜 *pianjueih*, n., one-sided hernia.
偏重 *pianjuhng*, n. & v.t., emphasis on one to the detriment of the other (subjects, aspects, etc.).
偏執 *pianjyr*, adj. & n., stubborn(ness); 偏執狂 monomania.
偏狂 *piankuarng*, n., special craze; monomania.
偏勞 *pianlaur*, v.i. & t., (court. of a person who) works harder than the group, also phr., thanking person for special effort: 偏勞了你.
偏盲 *pianmarng*, adj., blind in one eye.
偏旁 *pianparng*, n., the right and left parts of a character, but more esp. the right (phonetic) part, against the left (radical).
偏偏 *pianpian*, adv., stubbornly, against expectations, see Adv. 2↑.
偏僻 *pianpih*, adj., little known, out-of-the-way (place).
偏頗 *pianpo*, adj., biased (opinion).
偏衫 *pianshan*, n., monastic jacket.
偏生 *piansheng*, n., (MC) see Adv. 1↑.
偏向 *pianshiahng*, n. & v.t., angle, slanting or favored direction: 偏向某人 inclined toward person.
偏斜 *pianshier*, adj., slanted, not fair.
偏心 *pianshin*, adj. & n., favoritism, lack of impartiality.
偏蝕 *pianshyr*, n. & v.i., (astron.) partial eclipse.
偏私 *piansy*, n. & adj., selfish, favoring one's own.
偏袒 *piantaan*, v.t., unfairly partial to (person, side).
偏疼 *pianterng*, v.t., (of parents) love specially (a child).
偏頭痛 *piantourtuhng*, n., (med.) migraine.
偏才 *piantsair*, n., special aptitude.
偏災 *piantzai*, n., disaster caused by drought or flood.
偏倚 *pianyii*, adj., partial, not fair.

佾 91A.42–8

yih.

N. (AC) a dance squad: 八佾 a dance formation of 8 squads or 64 (8×8) persons.

倫 91A.42–8

lurn.

N. (1) 倫常(之道) Norm, normal human relations: 人倫 human relations, ethics; 倫理 -*lii*↓; 人倫大端 the main principles of human relationships; 五倫 the five cardinal relationships king-subject, father-son, husband-wife, between brothers, between friends. (2) Comparison, class: 荒謬絕倫 absurd without equal; 無與倫比 without compare, incomparable; 不倫不類 (argument, exhibitions, etc.) without sense or order, heterogeneous, jumbled; 語無倫次 (of arguments) rambling, inconsequential talk. (3) A surname.

倫比 *lurnbii*, n., comparable equal.
倫敦 *Lurndun*, n., London.
倫紀 *lurnjii*, n., moral order, social discipline.
倫理 *lurnlii*, n., ethics: 倫理學 ethics.
倫匹 *lurnpi*, n., equal, match.

僑 91A.42–9

chiaur.

N. A man living abroad: 華僑 Chinese overseas; 僑胞 -*bau*, 僑領 -*liing*↓; 僑民 those living abroad; 外僑 foreigners in China; 美僑 Americans in China or living abroad; 僑商, 僑資, 僑工 foreign

僑 佣 儁 脩 鵂 侉 俜 仍 偈 仞 伺

merchants, capital, labor; 僑務 (department of) overseas Chinese affairs; 僑居, 僑寓 to live, stay, abroad (as an alien).

僑胞 *chiaur-bau*, n., Chinese fellow-citizens abroad, overseas Chinese (from 同ᐞ胞 42.42).
僑居 *chiaur-jyu*, v.i., live abroad.
僑領 *chiaur-liing*, n., leaders of overseas Chinese.
僑民 *chiaurmirn*, n., overseas Chinese.
僑人 *chiaur-rern*, n., Chinese who moved down and settled near Shanghai, Nanking during northern invasion, 4th to 6th cen. A.D.
僑生 *chiaur-sheng*, n., children of overseas Chinese studying in China.

佣 91A.42-9

jou.

佣張 *joujang*, v.t., (AC) to deceive (also wr. 譸張).

儁 91A.42-9

jyuhn.

Adj. [U.f. 俊] (1) Talented, smart, bright. (2) Outstanding, conspicuous.

脩 91A.42-9

shiou.

N. Dried meat: (AC) dried meat or ham as gift to teacher in lieu of tuition, hence 脩金 *-jin*↓; 束脩 tuition, (AC) ham for tuition.

V.i. & t. Var. of 修 91A.91.

脩脯 *shioufuu*, n., dried meat.
脩金 *shioujin*, n., tuition fees.

§ 91A.50 (亻/ㄱ)

鵂 91A.50-1

shiou.

鵂鶹 *shiouliou*, n., (zoo.) a small Chin. owl, *Scops chinensis*.

侉 91A.50-1

kuaa.

Adj. (Coll.) stupid: 侉子 a fool, simpleton.

俜 91A.50-2

ping.

Adj. See 伶ᐞ俜 91A.63, lonely.

仍 91A.50-3

rerng.

Adv. (1) Still, yet: 仍舊 *-jiouh*↓; 仍舊貫 follow the beaten path (the old rut); 仍然 *-rarn*↓; 仍似 similar to, as before; 仍是 is still; 仍在 yet remains; 仍復如此 is still the same. (2) Again and again, over and over: 頻仍 often, repeatedly; 饑饉頻仍 famines occurred time and again.

仍舊 *rerngjiouh*, adv., yet, still, as of old.
仍然 *rerngrarn*, adv., as usual, as before.
仍仍 *rerngrerng*, adj., (AC) (1) a great many, a multitude of; (2) downcast, dejected.

偈 91A.50-4

jier.

N. A Buddhist chant or hymn, a Zen riddle in verse.

Adj. (1) (AC) brave, martial. (2) (AC) rushing past: 匪車偈兮 not that the carriage was running so fast. . . .

仞 91A.50-5

rehn.

N. An anc. measure of varying lengths: 壁立千仞 (of mountain cliffs) towering sky-high.

V.t. To fathom: 仞溝洫 (AC, interpreted as) to measure the depth of canals and ditches (to dredge).

伺 91A.50-5

syh (**tsyh*).

V.t. (1) To spy on, investigate: 偵伺 to spy on. (2) To wait for chance: 伺便, 伺隙 *-biahn*, *-shih*↓. (3) (**tsyh*) To wait upon (person): 伺候 *-'hou*↓.

伺便 *syh-biahn*, phr., wait for opportunity (to speak, etc.), when convenient.
伺察 *syhchar*, v.t., to spy on, investigate, trace secretly (movements).
伺諜 *syhdier*, n., a spy.
伺候 **tsyh'hou*, v.t., wait upon (person), attend upon.
伺隙 *syh-shih*, phr., wait for an opening (to attack).

伺探 *syhtahn*, v.t., to investigate secretly.

侷 91A.50-5

jyur.

侷促 *jyurtsuh*, adj., (1) narrow-minded; (2) 侷促不安 nervous, uneasy, agitated, discomfited.

仿 91A.50-6

faang.

[Interch. 倣]

V.t. Imitate, copy: 仿古 in the style of antique (painting, bronze, etc.); 摹仿 to copy (anc. picture, callig.); 仿宋 copy of Suhng Dyn. style of lettering, name of type.

仿圈 *faangchyuan*, n., brass or copper paper weight, used in copying calligraphy.

仿單 *faangdan*, n., (business) list of goods in stock and their prices.

仿佛 *faangfur*, adv., it seems like: 仿佛看見他 seem to have seen him, usu. wr. 彷彿.

仿照 *faangjauh*, v.t., follow, in accordance with: 仿照你的意思 in accordance with your instructions.

仿製 *faangjyh*, v. t., made or copied from anc. model.

仿紙 *farngjyy*, n., lettering sheets for children to practice calligraphy.

仿效 *faangshiauh*, v.t., to imitate, to copy, pattern after (model).

傍 91A.50-6

parng (**bang*, **bahng*).

V.t. (**bahng*) To be dependent on: 傍人門戶 to be dependent on person for living; esp. in 依傍 to be dependent on (person), to copy or imitate (masters); 傍花隨柳 enjoy flowers in spring outing.

Adj. & adv. Close to, by: 傍戶而立 standing close to the door.

份 91A.50-8

fehn.

[Commonly interch. 分 in all senses below, when 分 is pr. *fehn* 80.50]

N. (1) Part, portion, lot: 一份報 one copy of paper; 每一部份 every part; 股份 share of company; 成份 component, factor, proportion. (2) Duty: 本分, etc., see 分 80.50, N. 3.

份子 *fehntzyy*, n., (1) member, elements: 搗亂份子 troublesome elements (in school, etc.); (2) (*fehn'tz*) share in group contributions to wedding gifts, etc.: 隨份子 follow everybody in share of contributions.

僞 91A.50-9

weih.

[Var. 偽]

Adj. (1) False, imitation, fake, forged, not genuine: 虛僞 false, hypocritical; 僞裝, 僞造 *-juang*, *-tzauh* ↓; 僞本 forged edition; 僞書 spurious works; 僞證 false testimony; 作僞 to counterfeit; 僞鈔, 僞幣 *-chau*, *-bih* ↓. (2) A term applied to pretender to the throne or to a contending and therefore "illegal" state, opp. to legal; 僞政府 illegal government; 僞組織 illegal organization; 敵僞 the outlaw regime.

僞幣 *weihbih*, n., counterfeit money.

僞鈔 *weihchau*, n., ditto.

僞國 *weihguor*, n., illegal regime.

僞裝 *weihjuang*, v.i. & n., disguise.

僞君子 *weih-jyuntzyy*, n., a hypocrite.

僞善 *weishahn*, adj., hypocritical.

僞造 *weihtzauh*, v.t., to counterfeit.

仂 91A.50-9

leh.

N. A surplus or excess.

僗 91A.50-9

laur.

[Var. of 勞]

N. (North China) a term of abuse gen. used as a suffix: 囚僗 a jail-bird; 饞僗 a glutton; 呆僗 a damn fool.

佝 91A.50-9

kouh.

佝僂 *kouhlour*, n., (med.) rickets.

侮 91A.50-9

wuu.

V.t. (1) To humiliate, insult, slander: 侮慢, 侮辱 *-mahn*, *-ruh* ↓;

侮 㑳 傷 傷 儻

外侮 humiliation at the hand of foreign country. (2) To bully, harass: 欺侮 to browbeat or bully (s.o.).

侮慢 *wuumahn*, v.t. & adj., insult, -ing, haughty.
侮辱 *wuuruh*, v.t. & n., to humiliate; -tion.

㑳 91A.50–9

jouh.

Adj. (MC) handsome: 體態又㑳 has a handsome figure.

傷 91A.50–9

shiau.

傷然 *shiaurarn*, adj., & adv., silently, freely (＝蕭^△^然 20A.22).
傷傷 *shiaushiau*, adj., (1) (AC) bedraggled; (2) dispersed, thinning.

傷 91A.50–9

shang.

N. (1) A wound: 刀傷, 槍傷, 燙傷 knife wound, bullet wound, burn; 傷口, 傷痕 *-koou*, *-hern* ↓. (2) Harm: 無傷 no harm (doing s.t.); 何傷乎 (LL) what is the harm?

V.i. & t. (1) To hurt, wound: 傷感情, 傷和氣 hurt feelings among friends; 説話傷人 hurt (offend) people by one's words; 你把人都給傷了 you have offended so many people; 傷腦筋 (of problems, situations) take a great deal of thinking, similar to Eng. "is a headache." (2) To harm: 傷害, 傷身 *-haih*, *-shen* ↓; 損傷 cause damage (to property, life), to diminish or be harmed; 傷風敗俗 offensive to society's morals; 傷天害理 do things offensive to God and reason. (3) To be affected by, fall ill from: 傷風, 傷寒 *-feng*, *-harn* ↓; 傷酒, 傷食 *-jioou*, *-shyr* ↓; 傷水, 傷乳 *-shueei*, *-ruu* ↓; 傷弓之鳥 bird which has been hurt by arrow—person who learns to be cautious from having his finger burnt once. (4) To feel sad, be saddened: 傷心, 傷悲, 傷痛 *-shin*, *-bei*, *-tuhng* ↓; 哀傷, 悲傷 to grieve over; 傷春悲秋 to grieve over passing of spring or feel sad with autumn; 傷感 *-gaan* ↓.

Adv. Feeling surfeited, nauseated with: 這齣戲我都聽傷了 I have seen this play so often—am surfeited with it; 吃傷了 eat to harmful excess.

傷悲 *shangbei*, v.i. & adj., to regret, be regretful; to grieve over.
傷兵 *shang-bing*, n., wounded soldier.
傷氣 *shang-chih*, v.i., feel frustrated, upset (by some event).
傷處 *shangchuh*, n., wound, see *-koou* ↓.
傷悼 *shangdauh*, v.i., to grieve over (loss of dear one).
傷風 *shangfeng*, v.i., (1) to catch cold; (2) 傷風敗俗 or 有傷風化 harmful to society's morals.
傷感 *shanggaan*, adj., sentimental; sad: 傷感詩 sentimental poetry.
傷害 *shanghaih*, v.t., to do harm (to life, reputation, property, health).
傷寒 *shangharn*, n., typhoid; (Chin. med.) a variety of diseases with fever, including typhoid, paratyphoid, intestinal fever; 斑疹傷寒 typhus.
傷耗 *shang'hau*, v.t., to damage, waste away (esp. money, health), see *-haih* ↑.
傷痕 *shabghern*, n., scar.
傷酒 *shang-jioou*, v.i., get sick from too much drink.
傷科 *shangke*, n., (Chin. med.) branch dealing with knife cuts, external injury.
傷口(兒) *shangkoou* ('*l*), n., wound, open wound.
傷勞 *shanglaur*, n., (Chin. med.) ailment arising from overwork, oft. referring to tuberculosis, see 癆 61A.50.
傷乳 *shang-ruu*, v.i., (of baby) have stomach upset, ascribed to improper feeding or overfeeding at breast.
傷身 *shang-shen*, v.i. & t., to wound or to be wounded, to be injurious to health.
傷生 *shang-sheng*, phr., (1) to kill life; (2) to impair one's vitality.
傷神 *sheng-shern*, (1) v.i., to be grieved, disheartened; (2) adj., (of work) very fatiguing.
傷心 *shang-shin*, v.i. & adj., feel sad, brokenhearted; 傷心人 a sad person; 傷心事 a sad affair.
傷水 *shang-shueei*, v.i., get sick from drinking too much water.
傷事 *shang-shyh*[1], v.i., spoil things (by careless talk, etc.).
傷逝 *shang-shyh*[2], v.i., grieve over loss of person.
傷勢 *shang-shyh*[3], n., condition of the injured person.
傷食 *shang-shyr*, v.i., get sick from overeating; n., stomach catarrh.
傷損 *shangsuun*, v.t., to hurt, damage (reputation, property, etc.).
傷財 *shang-tsair*, v.i., suffer financial loss.
傷殘 *shangtsarn*, adj. & n., wounded and disabled.
傷痛 *shangtuhng*, v.i., (1) to feel painful, to ache; (2) to grieve over loss, feel greatly upset.
傷亡 *shang-warng*, n. & v.i., war casualties, the wounded and the killed in war; be killed in accident, disaster.
傷痍 *shang-yir*, n., (LL) the sufferings of the people from war.

§ 91A.63 (ㄔ/ㄟ)

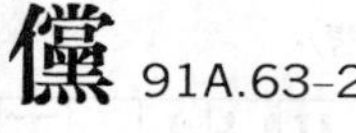

91A.63–2

taang.

Adj. (1) See 倜儻 91A.42. (2) 儻來之物 phr., s.t. come by accident (oft. referring to money, owned permanently by nobody).

Conj. Var. of 倘 see 91A.42↑.

伬 91A.63-5

jiin.

[Abbr. of 儘 91A.30↑]

伶 91A.63-8

lirng.

N. (1) Actor or actress: 優伶 (AC slightly contempt.) actor(s); 名伶, 紅伶 (LL) famous, popular actor, -tress; 伶人 (LL) actor, -tress; 女伶 actress. (2) A surname.

Adj. See compp.↓.

伶丁 *lirngding*, adj., as in 孤苦伶仃 alone (orphaned, widowed) and friendless; lonely, alone.
伶俐 *lirnglih*, adj., (of figure and character) clever, bright, clear-headed, quick in perception.
伶俜 *lirngping*, adj., see *-ding*↑.
伶透 *lirngtouh*, adj., see *-lih*↑.

佟 91A.63-9

turng.

N. A surname.

儵 91A.63-9

chour (also *tiaur*, *your*).

N. A long, slender white fish, *Zucco platypus* (also called 白條魚).

儵 91A.63-9

shuh.

[Anc. var. of 倏 91A.81]

§ 91A.70 (亻/乚)

僥 91A.70-1

jiaau.

Adj. Fortunate, lucky.

僥倖 *jaaushihng*, adj., obtain by sheer luck, luckily escape (danger) unscathed (also wr. 儌幸, 徼幸).

俺 91A.70-1

aan.

Pron. (MC) (1) I, the first person. (2) My: 俺爹, 俺大哥 my father, my eldest brother.

俺家 *aanjia*, pron., (MC) I; 俺家的 (MC) my husband.
俺每 *aan'mei*, pron., (MC) weak form of *-'men*↓.
俺們 *aan'men*, pron., (MC) we.
俺咱 *aantzar*, pron., (MC) we.

倦 91A.70-1

jyuahn.

Adj. Tired, weary: 疲倦 fatigued, sleepy, tired; 倦意 droopy, drowsy, also weary of exacting task; 倦極 overworked, dead tired; 厭倦 weary; 困倦 exhausted, tired out; 倦惰 *-duoh*, 倦怠 *-daih*↓.

倦勤 *jyuahnchirn*, v.i., be tired of work, weary of further efforts, (of politician) want to retire (withdraw from active life).
倦怠 *jyuahndaih*, adj., languid, sluggish, dull, slow.
倦惰 *jyuahnduoh*, adj., lazy, indolent, slothful.
倦飛 *jyuahn-fei*, v.i., (of official) retire, withdraw from active life.
倦游 *jyuahn-your*, v.i., (1) be tired of sightseeing (traveling); (2) (of official) weary of a public life.

仳 91A.70-2

pii.

仳離 *piilir*, adj., (LL) separated (of lovers, husband and wife, relatives).

化 91A.70-2

huah.

N. (1) Culture: 化行俗美 the spread of culture made for good manners, culture spread and the customs were good; 文化 culture; 風化 public morals, social customs; 化外 outside the pale of Chin. civilization. (2) Short for 化學 chemistry: 化工 chemical engineering; 理化 (=物理, 化學) physics and chemistry.

V.t. (1) To change, to convert, to

transform, to influence: 變化 to change; 化 . . . 爲 change into: 化敵爲友 convert enemy into friend; 化暗爲明 change dark into light, also legalize what was underground traffic; 化險爲夷 come out safely from danger, bring order and peace out of chaos and confusion; 化整爲零 break up whole into parts; 化腐朽爲神奇 transform the corruptible into mysterious life; 化干戈爲玉帛 "beat swords into ploughshares"—put an end to war and have peace; 春風化雨 the kindly influence of a good teacher. (2) To disguise: 化名 use an alias, to change one's name in disguise; 化服 change dress; 化裝 *-juang*[1] ↓. (3) To transform physically: 化氣 become gas; 化水 liquefy; 化成灰 become ashes; 分化 disintegrate; 溶化 to melt; 融化 to merge; 燒化, 焚化, 火化 to burn up (the dead as in cremation); 羽化 (Taoist) to go up to heaven as a fairy. (4) In many modn. terms=-ize: 歐化 Europeanize; 西化, 西洋化 westernize; 現代化 modernize; 形式化 become mere form, formalize; 合理化 rationalize (industrial management); 進化 to be progressive; 惡化 worsen, deteriorate, become worse; 表面化 bring to the surface. (5) To beg: 募化 (Budd.) solicit contributions; 叫化子 a beggar; see 化緣 *-yuarn* ↓.

化 除 *huahchur*, v.t., to abolish, remove (prejudices, bad customs).
化 度 *huahduh*, v.t., (Budd.) to convert to Buddhist way of life.
化 鶴 *huahheh*, phr., (Taoist & LL) to fly up bodily to heaven.
化 合 *huahher*, v.i. & n., (chem.) to combine in chemical process; 化合物 (chem.) compound.
化 境 *huahjihng*, n., in art, the ultimate highest state of becoming like nature itself.
化 裝 *hauhjuang*[1], v.i. & n., to dress in disguise.
化 妝 *hauhjuang*[2], v.i. & n., to apply make-up; 化妝品 cosmetics.
化 名 *huah-mirng*, v.t., to disguise one's name, adopt a pseudonym.
化 身 *huah-shen*, v.i., (1) (Budd.) transformation of Buddha in different manifestations; (2) (of persons) a personification (of love, piety).
化 生 *huahsheng*, v.i., (Budd.) the creation of life or animals; become s.t. from nothing.
化 香 樹 *huahshiang shuh*, n., (bot.) *Platycarya strobilacea*, a tree whose fruit is used for black dye.
化 石 *huahshyr*, (1) n., (geo.) fossil; (2) v.i., to fossilize.
化 學 *huahshyur*, n., chemistry; 化學式 chemical formula; 化學家 chemist.
化 驗 *huahyahn*, n., chemical analysis.
化 緣 *huahyuarn*, v.i., beg for alms.
化 育 *huahyuh*, n. & v.t., the growth and change of living things by nature.

他 91A.70–2

ta (re. pr. *tuo* from anc. 反切 system, but not gen.).
[Anc. var. 它 see 62.70; modn. var. 他 (he) 她 (she) and 牠 (it) are new, but not gen., except 她]

Pron. (1) (AC & LL) other: 此無他 no other cause but; 不疑有他 never suspected other motives; 王顧左右而言他 the king looked elsewhere and talked of other things. (2) He, she, it (third person in modn. Chinese —cf. 彼, 其, 之 in AC): 他們 *-men*, they; 他們的 their; 他們倆 *--liaa*, they two; 他的 his; 他那個人 (contempt.) that person; 別管他 don't pay any attention to him (or it); 非他莫屬 nobody else is worthy except him; 他媽的, 他奶奶的 (vulg. abusive) damn it (him)!

Adj. (1) Other, another: 他年, 他日 another year, day; 他人 another person, other person(s); 他事, 他用, 他故 another matter, use, cause; 其他 the others; 其他朋友 the other friends; 他國 another country; 他鄉, 他處 *-shiang*, *-chuh* ↓; 他山之石, 可以攻錯 (court.) my humble contribution may help to bring out better things from others, (fig.) the value of friendly counsel. (2) Different: 頓萌他志 suddenly had other (disloyal) ideas; 別無他圖 no ulterior motive or different plans.

Adv. Elsewhere: 他往 go elsewhere; 他就 accept another job.

他 處 *tachuh*, adv., elsewhere.
他 動 詞 *taduhng-tsyr*, n., transitive vb. (cf. 自動詞 v.i.).
他 方 *tafang*, n., another place; the other party.
他 家 *tajia*, n., (1) his home; (2) some other home or house; (3) he: 都爲他家害得人來病 fall lovesick because of him.
他 們 *ta'men*, n., they.
他 人 *tarern*, n., another, other person(s).
他 日 *taryh*, n., another day.
他 鄉 *ta-shiang*, phr., away from home: 他鄉遇故知 meet an old friend away from home.

佻 91A.70–2

tiaur (**tiau*).

V.t. (AC) steal (as cogn. of 偷): 佻天以爲己力 lay claim to what one has done nothing to deserve.

Adj. Frivolous, unsteady, see compp. ↓.

佻 薄 *tiaurbor*, adj., frivolous, impudent.
佻 巧 *tiaarchiaau*, adj., undependable.
佻 達 **tiautah*, adj., frivolous, loose.
佻 佻 公 子 *tiaurtiaur gungtzyy*, n., delicate, spoiled young gentleman.
佻 脫 *tiaurtuo*, adj., frivolous, undisciplined.

儷 91A.70–3

lih.

N. A pair, a couple: 伉儷 husband and wife.

Adj. Of a pair, parallel: 儷辭 phrases with parallel constructions; 儷影 a husband and wife appearing in public or in a photograph; 儷安 (in letters) wishing a couple's health; 駢儷 (of litr. style) characterized by parallel constructions.

僊 91A.70-3

shian.

[Var. of 仙 91A.21]

侃 91A.70-4

kaan.

Adj. Straightforward, self-possessed, open, see 侃侃 *-kaan* ↓.

侃侃 *karnkaan*, adv., openly and without sense of guilt; contentedly, at ease.

侃直 *kaanjyr*, adj., open, straightforward.

俔 91A.70-4

chiahn (**shiahn*).

V.i. (AC) (1) To look like. (2) (**shiahn*) To appear rarely: 俔俔, see 晛晛 41B.70.

佩 91A.70-4

peih.

N. Pendants, things worn on girdle (cf. 珮 31A.70).

V.t. (1) Carry in girdle, belt (knife, sword, ornaments). (2) Carry in heart, i.e., adore, as 敬佩 adore, respect and admire: see 佩服 *-fuh* ↓; 感佩 be grateful (to person) for kindness, favor.

佩帶 *peidaih*, v.i & t., to carry, to wear (as decorations, etc.)

佩服 *peihfuh*, v.t., admire from the heart, admit superiority (to person).

佩蘭 *peihlarn*, n., (bot.) a species of orchid.

佩弦 *peihshyarn*, phr., (AC) wear bowstring as memento to be alert.

佩韋 *peihweei*, phr., (AC) allu. to willingness to change character, (wearing leather 韋 as symbol of softness, and wearing bowstring 弦 as symbol of alertness).

伉 91A.70-6

kahng.

N. Matrimonial match, see 伉儷 *-lih* ↓.

V.t. (U.f. 抗 10A.70).

Adj. Strong, virile.

伉儷 *kahnglih*, n., married couple: 賢伉儷 (court.) you and your spouse; 伉儷情深 a married couple very much in love.

僦 91A.70-6

jiouh.

V.t. To rent: 僦居 live in a rented house; 僦屋 rent a room or house.

佗 91A.70-6

tuo (*tuor*).

[Var. 他 91A.70; interch. 它 62.70 (not current); var. 駝 51B.70]

佗佗 *tuortuor*, adj., (AC) as in 委委佗佗 easy, graceful in movement.

侘 91A.70-6

chah.

侘傺 *chahchyh*, adj., (LL) frustrated, disappointed, uneasy: 侘傺不安 uneasy.

倪 91A.70-9

nir.

N. (1) Child: 旄倪 the old and the young; 倪倪 *-nir* ↓; 倪子 (Soochow dial.) son. (2) Initial or embryonic stage: 端倪 the beginning or origin of (s.t.). (3) A surname.

Pron. (Soochow dial.) I, we: 倪搭 (Soochow dial.) our place, the place where we are.

倪倪 *nirnir*, n., (LL) the young and the helpless.

倪仉 *nirwuh*, adj., (also wr. 鯢甈) (LL) uneasy, perturbed, anxious.

仇 91A.70-9

chour (**chiour*).

N. (1) (**chiour*) A surname. (2)

(*chiour) (LL) a mate: 仇偶 -oou ↓. (3) Enemy: 仇人, 仇敵 -rern, -dir ↓; 冤仇 longstanding enemy; 恩仇 past favors and insults: 恩仇未報 have not settled old accounts (with person); 不共戴天之仇 sworn revenge for murder of parents ("will not share the same sky"); used as modifier: 仇視, 仇恨 -shyh, -hehn ↓.

仇敵 *chourdir*, n., enemy.
仇恨 *chourhehn*, n., old grudge, feud, hatred.
仇家 *chourjia*, n., personal enemy.
仇口兒 *chourkoou'l*, n., see -rern ↓.
仇偶 **chiour-oou*, n., rival.
仇人 *chourrern*, n., personal enemy.
仇隙 *chourshih*, n., old grudge.
仇視 *chourshyh*, v.t., to be hostile to.

傀 91A.70–9

kueei.

N. See 傀儡 -leei ↓.

傀儡 *kueirleei*, n., (lit. & fig.) a puppet.
傀偉 *kueirweei*, adj., great and imposing, stalwart (cf. 魁 91.70).
傀異 *kueeiyih*, adj., rare, strange.

仡 91A.70–9

yih.

Adj. Upright, see 屹 21B.70.

仡然 *yihrarn*, adj., (LL) standing upright.
仡仡 *yihyih*, adj., (AC) straight, tall.

俛 91A.70–9

fuu.

[Var. 俯 91A.00; also 勉 *miaan*, 92.70]

§ 91A.71 (亻/弋)

儎 91A.71–1

tzaih.

N. A load carried in boat or carriage.

代 91A.71–7

daih.

N. (1) Period, age: 古代 ancient age; 當代, 現代 contemporary age and modern age or period. (2) Generation: 這一代人 people of this generation; 下一代, 上一代 the next, preceding generation; 後代 posterity; 代代 generation after generation, every generation; 代有傳人 there were people who carried on in every generation. (3) Dynasty: 唐代, 明代, Tarng, Mirng Dyn.; 歷代 in the different dynasties or in the past. (4) Anc. kingdom. (5) A surname.

V.i. & t. (1) To act, do for others, to be substitute: 代人受過 take the blame for others; 請代我(代爲)致意, 致謝 please present my respects, or thank s.o. for me; 代爲傳達消息 to transmit news for person; 代拆代行 phr., (official) authorized to open letters and act during another's absence: 代墊 advance money for another; 替代 act for: 代理, 代表 -lii, -biaau ↓. (2) To replace, to succeed one another, take turns: 代換 take turns; 取而代之 to succeed in s.o.'s or s.t.'s place; 李代桃僵 (allu.) peach dies when neighboring pear is hurt by insects, (fig.) of changing lovers; 瓜代 (of officials) one taking the place of another when one's official term is up, (of soldiers) changing guards; 代謝 -shieh ↓.

代辦 *daihbahn*, n., *chargé d'affaires*; v.i., to act as deputy; 代辦商 commission agent.
代表 *daihbiaau*, n. & v.t., represent, -ative, delegate, deputy: 我代表他來 I come on his behalf; 你能不能代表他 are you authorized to represent him? 代表輿論 represent public opinion.
代筆 *daihbii*, v.i., to add a few words or write letters for another; to sign for another.
代步 *daih-buh*, v.i., take vehicle in place of walking.
代茶 *daih-char*, n., betrothal gift, in place of original present of tea.
代電 *daih-diahn*, n., public statement usu. published in place of telegram.
代換 *daihhuahn*, v.i., replace (each other).
代價 *daihjiah*, n., price one pays (for love, fame), some kind of sacrifice.
代理 *daihlii*, adj. & n. & v.i. & t., acting, deputy: 代理校長 acting president of school; 代理人 agent; v.i., 代理業務 act in such capacity in charge of business.
代名詞 *daihmirngtsyr*, n., (gram.) pronoun.
代謝 *daihshieh*, n., esp. in 新陳代謝 or 代謝作用 metabolism; 春秋代謝 seasonal changes, change from spring to autumn.
代席 *daihshir*, n., remuneration, "money in lieu of a feast."
代行 *daih-shirng*, v.i., to act for person: 代策代行 a deputy acting for his superior.
代書 *daihshu*, n. & v.i., (person who) writes letters, draws up contracts for others.
代數 *daihshuh*, n., algebra.
代序 *daihshyuh*, v.i., as in 春秋代序 see -shieh ↑.
代爲 *daihweir*, v.i., act for: 代爲辦理, 執行, 請求 to manage, act, request for another.
代議 *daihyih*, n., representative; 代議制度 parliamentary system;

代議政治 representative government.

伐 91A.71-7

far (also **fa*).

N. (AC) merit.

V.t. (1) To chop, cut: 伐冰 (AC) chop ice; 伐樹 chop (down) trees; oft. 砍伐 (fig.) 伐性之斧 sexual indulgence injures vitality. (2) (AC) to attack (country): oft. 討伐 send punitive expedition; 弔民伐罪 attack the tyrant and relieve the people of their sufferings; 口誅筆伐 (fig.) condemn by pen and word of mouth. (3) Boast: 伐善, 伐功, 矜伐 brag of one's own accomplishments.

伐柯 **fake*, v.i., (AC allu.) be matchmaker.

儀 91A.71-8

yir.

N. (1) Demeanor: 儀容, 儀表, 儀態 *-rurng, -biaau, -taih*↓; 威儀 dignified bearing; 芳儀 (woman's) gracious appearance. (2) Form of ceremony, rule: 禮儀 ditto; 司儀 master of ceremonies; 失儀 commit a breach of etiquette; 儀式 *-shyh*; 儀則 *-tzeh*↓. (3) Model: 儀範 *-fahn*↓. (4) Instrument: 儀器 *-chih*↓; 渾天儀 armillary sphere; 子午儀 transit instrument. (5) A present, gift: 壽儀, 賀儀 gifts for birthday, wedding presents.

V.t. To admire: 心儀其人 admire or respect that person.

儀表 *yirbiaau*, n., a man's personal appearance, looks.

儀器 *yirchih*, n., instrument (scientific, survey, etc.).

儀範 *yirfahn*, n., a person's character worthy of emulation; model of conduct.

儀仗 *yirjahng*, n., insignias of rank carried in procession.

儀狀 *yirjuahng*, n., see *-biaau*↑.

儀注 *yirjuh*, n., (1) (AC) rules of etiquette; program of ceremony; (2) (AC) rules and instructions on astronomical observation, about armillary sphere.

儀門 *yirmern*, n., the second gate of official court house leading to main hall.

儀容 *yirrurng*, n., demeanor, deportment.

儀型 *yirshirng*, n., model, pattern (AC also wr. 刑).

儀式 *yirshyh*, n., form of ceremony (as in wedding).

儀態 *yirtaih*, n., woman's charming ways and gestures: 儀態萬千(方) distinguished air of elegance and coquetry.

儀曹 *yirtsaur*, n., anc. bureau of ceremonies.

儀則 *yirtzeh*, n., model (of conduct, etc.).

低 91A.71-9

di.

V.i. & t. To lower, bend, bow: 低首 bend one's head; nod as consent; 低首無言 bend one's head, silent; 低首下心 be servile, submissive.

Adj. Low, opp. 高 high: 高低不平 uneven; 低價 low price; 低一格 one notch (class) lower: 低聲 low voice, whisper; 低音 bass, low octave; 低潮 low tide; 低原 low plain; 低三下四的 low, menial person or job; 低賤 *-jiahn*↓; low in grade, inferior: 低貨 inferior goods; 低級趣味 (of writing, entertainment) catering to cheap, lower tastes.

低昂 *di-arng*, v.i. & adj., (of singing, prices) swing up and down, soar and dip.

低沉 *dichern*, adj., deep and low (voice).

低回(徊) *dihueir*, v.i., loiter, linger, sunk in thought.

低賤 *dijiahn*, adj., cheap in price; low-class.

低空 *di-kung*, n., low altitude (flying).

低眉 *di-meir*, adj., looking downward in submission or (of Buddha) kindly.

低迷 *dimir*, adj., confused in thinking, dazed.

低能 *dinerng*, adj., stupid, incompetent: 低能兒 n., stupid person, an imbecile.

低聲 *di-sheng*, adj., soft-voiced, low-voiced.

低下 *dishiah*, adj., low, lowly.

低首 *di-shoou*, v.i., bend one's head.

低頭 *di-tour*, v.i., bend one's head (in thought, submission, in silence), also 低首 *-shoou*↑.

低窪 *diwa*, adj., low, low and damp (of place).

低微 *diweir*, adj., lowly, humble (birth, character); weak and small (voice).

低溫度 *di wenduh*, n., low temperature.

低啞 *diyaa*, adj., low and hoarse (voice), creaking noise of oars.

低音部記號 *diyinbuhjihhauh*, n., (mus.) F clef.

低音大提琴 *diyindahtirchirn*, n., contrabass; double bass.

俄 91A.71-9

er (also **eh*).

N. (Usu. *eh*) Russia: 俄國, 俄人 *-guor, -rern*↓, 蘇俄 Soviet Russia.

Adv. Soon, in a short moment.

代 伐 儀 低 俄

亅 00 | 小 01 | ⺊ 02 | 十 10 | 土 11 | ナ 12 | 廾 20 | 𠃊 21 | 丨 22 | 一 30 | 丁 31 | 𠃌 32 | 口 40 | 区 41 | 冈 42 | 乛 50 | 厂 51 | 尸 52 | 亠 60 | 广 61 | 宀 62 | 丶 63 | 乚 70 | 七 71 | 心 72 | 八 80 | 人 81 | 乂 82 | ⺈ 83 | 𠂉 90 | 丿 91 | 𠂆 92 | く 93

俄頃 *erchiing*, adv., in a short moment, very soon.
俄爾 *er-ee'l*, adv., ditto.
俄而 *er-er'l*, adv., and soon.
俄國 **Ehguor*, n., Russia.
俄羅斯 **Ehluorsy*, n., Russia.
俄然 *er-rarn*, adv., suddenly.
俄人 **Ehrern*, n., a Russian.
俄文 **Ehwern*, n., the Russian language.
俄延 *eryarn*, v.t., to prolong; to delay.

§ 91A.72 (亻/心)

偲 91A.72-4

sy.

Adj. 切切偲偲 (AC, of friends) meet and chat earnestly.

億 91A.72-6

yih.

N. (1) A hundred million (100, 000,000): 十億 one billion: 億兆 hundreds of millions, great number. (2) (AC) u.f. 臆 to conjecture, 42A.72.

伈 91A.72-6

shin.

伈伈 *shirnshiin*, adj., as in 伈伈俔俔 timid, timorous, easily worried.

偬 91A.72-9

tzuung.

Adv. 倥偬 Hurriedly, hastily.

§ 91A.80 (亻/八)

債 91A.80-1

jaih.

N. Debt, loan: 負債 owe debt; 躲債 evade payment of debt; 還債 repay debt; 舉債 raise a loan; 討債 press for payment of debt, also said of son who keeps on asking for money from parent, hence extravagant; 債臺高築 pile up debts; 債多不愁 when there are too many debts, one stops worrying about them; 公債 government or corporation bond; 外債 foreign loan.

債券 *jaihchuahn*, n., a bond.
債權 *jaihchyuarn*, n., legal right of bondholders and creditors; 債權人 creditor.
債戶 *jaih'huh*, n., debtor.
債家 *jaih'jia*, n., see *-juu* ↓.
債精(兒) *jaihjing('l)*, n., a person perpetually in debt.
債主 *jaihjuu*, n., creditor.
債票 *jaihpiauh*, n., see *-chuahn* ↑.
債務 *jaihwuh*, n., debts.

僨 91A.80-1

fehn.

V.i. & t. (1) To be defeated; fall down or over. (2) To spoil: 僨事 spoil matters (as by impetuousness).

儹 91A.80-1

tzaan.

[Cogn. 攢 10A.80]

供 91A.80-2

*gung (*guhng)*

N. (1) (**guhng*) Articles of sacrifice: 上供 offer sacrifice to the gods or spirits. (2) Testimonies of a prisoner: 口供 affidavit in court; 畫供 to sign one's affidavit. (3) Supplies: 供求 supply and demand: 供不應求 supply falling short of demand; 求過於供 demand exceeds supply.

V.i. & t. (1) (**guhng*) V.i., to offer sacrifices: 供佛 to worship the Buddha; 供奉 *-fehng*, 供桌 *-juo*, 供養 *-yaang*, 供碗 *-waan* ↓; 供祖宗, 供神 to sacrifice to the ancestors, to the gods. (2) V.i., (law) testify: 供述 make a deposition; 供狀 *-juahng*, 供認 *-rehn* ↓; 反供, 翻供 retract a statement. (3) V.t., to supply: 供應 *-yihng* ↓; 供不起 cannot supply what is demanded; 出錢供他讀書 give him financial support for his studies.

供奉 **guhngfehng*, n. & v.t., (1) to offer to, offerings; (2) formerly, a palace official, (Manchu Dyn.) actors who gave command performances.
供給 *gung'jii*, v.t., to supply, furnish, provide, equip.
供狀 *gungjuahng*, n., (law) a written deposition, affidavit.
供桌 **guhngjuo*, n., sacrificial altar.
供認 *gungrehn*, v.i. & t., to confess (theft, etc.); n., a confession.
供詞 *gungtsyr*, n., (law) verbal depositions.
供碗 **guhngwaan*, n., sacrificial vessel.
供養 *gungyaang*, v.t., (1) bring up, rear: 把這孩子供養大了 bring the child up to manhood; (2) care for: 供養父母 provide for the needs and comforts of one's parents; (3) (**guhng-*) offer sacrifice to (the gods).
供應 *gungyihng*, v.t., to supply, furnish, provide.

偵 91A.80-2

jen (also *jeng*).

V.t. To detect, spy, do espionage work, see compp. ↓.

偵查 *jenchar*[1], v.t., to investigate (murder, legal fraud, etc.).
偵察 *jenchar*[2], v.t., ditto: 偵察機 reconnaisance plane.
偵緝 *jenchih*, v.t., to search for (unapprehended criminal).
偵騎 *jen-jih*, n., formerly, cavalry on reconnaissance duty.
偵詢 *jenshyurn*, v.i., gather information in legal investigation.
偵探 *jentahn*, (1) v.t., to do detective work, spy; (2) n., a detective, espionage agent: 偵探小說 detective story.

傾 91A.80-2

ching (also *chirng*; **keng*).

V.i. (1) To incline to one side: 傾斜 *-shier* ↓; 左傾, 右傾分子 leftist, rightist elements; to tend toward: 傾向 *-shiahng* ↓. (2) To aspire, admire: 傾心, 傾佩 *-shin*, *-peih* ↓; 傾偈 phr., (Cantonese) to chat, to make conversation; to have a heart-to-heart talk. (3) To collapse or cause to collapse: 傾覆, 傾倒 *-fuh*, *-daau* ↓.

V.t. (1) To pour out, to flow over: 傾出 pour out; 傾溢 overflow; 傾筐倒篋 turn up lock, stock and barrel; 傾吐 pour out (one's sorrows, secret thoughts); 傾鎔 pour molten metal into ingots. (2) To use up, exhaust, all resources: 傾囊相助 "empty one's pocket," i.e., give one's all to help; 傾家蕩產 (also pr. **keng-jia*) spend one's entire fortune (to do s.t.), or to be broke. (3) (Also **keng* =坑) to ruin or destroy s.o.: 傾陷 *-shiahn* ↓.

傾城 *chingcherng*, n., as in 傾國傾城 allu. to a woman's great beauty (enough to "cause the downfall of a city or an entire country").
傾倒 (1) *chingdaau*, v.i., to prostrate; show extreme admiration or love of a person: 傾倒於她 fall in love with her; 十分傾倒 admire greatly (a person); (2) (*-dauh*) to pour out (feelings, etc.).
傾動 *chingduhng*, v.t., as in 傾動一時 powerfully affect the times or generation or have convulsive effect on one's mind.
傾耳 *ching-eel*, phr., incline one's ear, listen carefully.
傾覆 *chingfuh*, (1) v.i., to collapse; (2) v.t., overthrow (government), destroy (country).
傾蓋 *ching-gaih*, phr., (LL) to meet together among friends (as on a journey, the "wagon covers touch").
傾國 *chingguor*, phr., (1) see *-cherng* ↑; (2) the whole nation.
傾角 *chingjiaau*, n., (math.) angle of inclination.
傾襟 *ching-jin*, phr., pour out one's heart.
傾囊 *ching-narng*, phr., empty one's pocket—give all to help.
傾佩 *chingpeih*, v.t., to admire greatly.
傾盆 *ching-pern*, phr., 傾盆大雨 pouring rain, downpour.
傾圮 *chingpii*, v.i., (of buildings) collapse, in dilapidated condition.
傾人 **keng-rern*, phr., to frame to destroy person (=坑人).
傾陷 *chingshiahn*, v.t., to frame (a person) to destroy him.
傾向 *chingshiahng*, v.i., incline toward (person, belief); n., inclination, tendency.
傾銷 *chingshiau*, v.t. & n., to dump (goods); dumping.
傾斜 *chingshier*, v.i. & n., incline, inclination; (geol.) dip.
傾心 *chingshin*, v.i., to fall in love: 一見傾心 love at first sight; 傾心於他 fall in love with him.
傾世 *chingshyh*, v.i., (MC) to leave this world—to die.
傾訴 *chingsuh*, v.i. & t., get s.t. off one's chest.
傾聽 *chingting*, v.i., to listen attentively.
傾吐 *chingtuu*, v.t., to pour out (one's feelings).
傾座 *ching-tzuoh*, v.i., to take the audience by storm.
傾危 *chingweir*, adj., (1) dangerous; (2) (AC) crafty.
傾軋 *chingyah*, v.t., to jockey for position, to squeeze out: 互相傾軋 (of parties, cliques) have internal fight.

償 91A.80-2

charng.

N. Repayment: 報償 remuneration.

V.t. (1) To repay (debt): 償還 *-huarn* ↓; 償債 repay debt. (2) To fulfill a promise, pledge: 如願以償 have one's wish fulfilled; 償願 *-yuahn* ↓. (3) To repay in kind, indemnify: 抵償 repay with collateral; 賠償 to indemnify, an indemnity; 補償 make up deficit; 索償 demand for reimbursement or compensation; 得不償失 the game is not worth the candle; 償命 *-mihng* ↓.

償還 *charnghuarn*, v.t., to repay (debt).
償命 *charng-mihng*, v.i., to pay with life.
償願 *charngyuahn*, v.i., fulfill one's wish.

價 91A.80-3

jiah.

N. Price: 價錢 *-chiarn* ↓; 價廉物美 (of goods or services) cheap and fine; 價格 *-ger* ↓; 高價收購 offer to buy at attractive prices; 漲價 a price hike; 跌價 a drop in price; 無價之寶 a priceless treasure; 有價證券 negotiable instruments; 估價 (business) to quote prices; 估價單 a quotation; 討價還價 haggle, bargain; 半價 half price; 定價 the list price, fixed price; 市價 market price; 不二價 one-price system; 開價 offer to sell at a certain price; 索價 to ask or demand price; 時價 the current price.

價本 *jiahbeen*, n., business capital.
價錢 *jiahchiarn*, n., a thing's cost, price.
價格 *jiahger*, n., price.
價值 *jiah(')jyr*, n., (1) value; (2) cost; (3) worth.
價碼 *jiahmaa*, n., see *-muh*↓.
價目 *jiahmuh*, n., price: 價目表 price list.

俱 91A.80-4

jyu (also **jyuh*).

Adv. All: 俱備 all complete, nothing left out; 俱全 ditto; 俱已齊備 everything is ready; 俱盡 all finished, nothing left.

俱樂部 **jyuhlebuh* (*jyu--*), n., (translit.) club.

儐 91A.80-6

bihn (**bin*).

儐相 *bihnshiahng* (**bin-*), n., as in 女儐相 bridesmaid; 男儐相 best man at wedding.

§91A.81 (亻/人)

伏 91A.81-1

fur.

N. (1) Name of season: 三伏 or 三伏天 first, second and third ten days after summer solstice, considered the hottest season; 歇伏 summer vacation of this period. (2) A surname.

V.i. (1) To bend down, prostrate: 伏身 bend down; 伏案 bend over table (and sleep or work); 伏地 prostrate on the ground; 拜伏, 匍伏 to prostrate ceremoniously, (fig.) see Adv.↓. (2) To lie in concealment: 潛伏 lie in concealment, incubate (of virus, etc.); 埋伏, 隱伏 to ambush. (3) To admit defeat: 伏輸 (=服輸) *-shu*↓.

V.t. (1) To submit, cause to submit, +n.: 伏法, 伏誅 be executed; 伏罪 submit to punishment; 伏劍 kill oneself by sword. (2) To sit over (eggs): 伏卵.

Adj. Prostrate: 伏屍 prostrate dead bodies (on the battlefield); 伏兵 soldiers lying in ambush.

Adv. (Court. in correspondence) I pray, I beg, etc.: 伏祈, 伏乞 I pray; 伏維, 伏思 I believe (you are in good health); 伏念 remember, I think of (you).

伏辯 *furbiahn*, v.i., admit defeat in argument.
伏筆 *fur-bii*, n., (rhet.) a line throwing out a hint to be amplified later.
伏氣 *furchih*, v.i., esp. 不伏氣 not convinced of defeat (also wr. 服△氣 42A.82).
伏櫪 (歷) *fur-lih*, v.i., to be tied to stable post: 老驥伏櫪, 志在千里 the old horse in stable is yet dreaming of heroic exploits.
伏苓 *furlirng*, n., see 茯△苓 20A.81.
伏莽 *fur-maang*, v.i., (of bandits) hiding in jungles.
伏牛花 *furniour hua*, n., (bot.) *Berberis vulgaris*.
伏羲 *Furshi*, n., one of earliest legendary rulers 2852–2738 B.C., reputed to discover the 八△卦 *paguah*, 80.80, and invent writing.
伏輸 *fur-shu*, v.i., admit defeat (also wr. 服).
伏事 (侍) *furshyh*, v.t., to serve (person).
伏汛 *furshyuhn*, n., summer flood.
伏特 *furteh*, n., (translit.) volt.
伏天 *furtian*, n., see N. 1↑.
伏貼 *furtie*, adj., see 服△貼 42A.82.

伕 91A.81-1

fu.

N. Common laborer: 伕子, 伕役 see 夫△役 12.81, comp.

佚 91A.81-1

yih.

N. (AC) mistake.

V.i. & adj. (1) To indulge in pleasures: 淫佚 indulging in sensual pleasures (interch. 逸). (2) Missing, lost (anc. book): 遺佚 ditto (interch. 逸 92.83). (3) To transcend rules or the common run; to be distinguished.

佚蕩 *yihdahng*, adj., (1) indulgent in pleasure, debauched; (2) uninhibited, unconventional.
佚遊 *yihyour*, v.i., to fool around with women, spend one's time in sensual pleasures.

俠 91A.81-1

shiar.

N. A swordsman, an outlaw champion of the poor and oppressed, one who fights rather than submit to injustice—an ideal of chivalry and honor, popular in legend and novels: 豪俠 a hero, a man of honor and courage: 俠士, 劍俠, 俠客 practised swordsman; 游俠 a roaming swordsman; 武俠小說,影片 a novel, film, with lots of swordplay and dashing heroes.

Adj. Chivalrous: 俠骨 chivalrous frame of mind; 俠膽 fearlessness.

俠客 *shiarkeh*, n., an expert swordsman.
俠義 *shiaryih*, adj. & n., honor and gallantry.

僛 91A.81-2

chi.

V.i. (AC) to lean, incline to one side, (var. of 攲); 僛僛 (AC) to totter (as when drunk).

似 91A.81-2

syh.

V.i. Seem, appear, seem like: 似乎 -*'hu*↓; 似是而非 appears right but really wrong; 似此 like this; 似有似無 seems to exist and again not to exist; used oft. as aux. or as adv., apparently: 似可 it seems possible to; 似必 it seems one must; 似應, 似宜 it seems one should; 似非無因 it seems (s.t.) happens not without a reason—there is a reason.

Adj. Like, alike (Eng. "like" in "like this" is considered an unusual adj. which takes an object): 相似 alike; 似我 like me; 好似 (very common) is like; 好似沒見過 seem not to have seen (person) before; 宛似 just like; 類似 look like; 無似 lacking in courtesy (of speech, conduct); 似的 (used at the end of sentence: 好像沒見過似的 it looks like we have not met before.

Prep. (Used as a comparative) than: 一個高似一個 each is taller than another.

似的 *shy'de*, phr., see Adj.↑.
似價 *syh'ga*, phr., (dial.) used like -*'de*↑: 黑炭頭也似價的鬏角子 a side knot like a ball of charcoal.
似乎 *shy'hu*, adv., (commonly used in vern. in place of 似) apparently: 似乎太早 apparently too early; 似乎做不完 it seems not possible to finish it.
似續 *syhshyuh*, v.t., (AC) u.f. 嗣[Δ]續 40S.50 to continue ancestral line.

僕 91A.81-2

pur.

N. Servant: 男女僕人 man- and maidservants; 奴僕 formerly, slaves; 公僕 public servant.

Pron. (Court. used by man) "I," used like "your humble servant" in letters (cf. 妾 60.93).

V.i. (AC) to drive carriage.

僕夫 *purfu*, n., (AC) driver; manservant.
僕姑 *purgu*, n., (AC) arrow.
僕僕 *purpur*, adj. & adv., in a hustle: 僕僕長途 phr., after an arduous journey; 僕僕風塵 phr., endure the hardships of travel.
僕人 *pur-rern*, n., servant.
僕從 *purtzuhng*, n., retinue of servants and employees.
僕役 *puryih*, n., gen. term for servants.

侯 91A.81-3

hour.

[Dist. 候]

N. (1) A surname. (2) A marquis, a rank of nobility: 諸侯 the feudal princes of Confucius' times; 侯門(深)似海 a rich man's mansion is difficult of access. (3) (AC) shooting target. (4) Anc. var. of 何 and 維.

候 91A.81-3

houh.

[Dist. 侯]

N. (1) Season, weather: 氣候 weather, climate; 時候 time in gen.; 季候 season, the seasons. (2) Symptoms: 症候. (3) Timing: 火候 timing in cooking.

V.i. (1) To wait, to welcome: 等候 to wait; 迎候, 候駕, 候光, 候教 to wait to welcome (your presence at party, etc.). (2) To await: 候示, 候命 await your instructions; 候訊, 候審 to await court trial or cross-examination; 候補, 候選 -*buu*, -*shyuaan*↓. (3) To take care of the bill: 這賬我候了 I have paid the bill.

候補 *houhbuu*, v.i. & n., (be) a candidate: 候補知縣 a candidate for county magistrate's office.
候脈 *houhmoh*, v.t., (Peking, of physicians) to examine patient.
候鳥 *houhniaau*, n., a migratory bird which follows the seasons.
候選 *houhshyuaan*, v.i., be a candidate for election to office; 候選人 candidate.

儉 91A.81-8

jiaan (also *jiahn*).

Adj. (1) Frugal, economical, sparing: 節儉 thrifty; 儉樸 -*puu*↓; 儉省 -*sheeng*↓; 儉學 (of poor student) denying oneself all comforts to save money for studying; 勤儉 hardworking and thrifty; 儉用 frugal, provident, economizing; 儉約 *-yuei* ↓. (2) Wanting, lacking, short: 儉薄 *-bor* ↓; 儉腹 *-fuh* ↓.

儉薄 *jiaanbor*, adj., lacking the necessities of life.
儉腹 *jiaanfuh*, adj., scanty in knowledge, ignorant.
儉樸 *jiarnpuu*, adj., living a simple life.
儉省 *jiarnsheeng*, adj., frugal, economical.
儉約 *jiaanyuei*, adj., economical, thrifty, practising austerity.

伙 91A.81-9

huoo.

N. (1) 傢伙 furniture. (2) (AC) a squad of ten men was called 火, hence the derivatives 伙計, 伙伴 *-'ji*, *-bahn* ↓. (3) Short for 伙食 the meals: 包伙 board provided by the month, etc.; 搭伙 share board with others; 開伙, 停伙 begin, stop, providing of meals.

伙伴(兒) *huoobahn(-bah'l)*, n., (pop.) colleague, co-worker in shop (sharing meals, also wr. 火).
伙計 *huoo'ji*, n., employee, waiter.
伙食 *huoo'shy*, n., board, daily meals (also wr. 火).

倐 91A.81-9

shuh.
[Anc. var. 儵, 倏; pop. 倏]

Adv. Suddenly, abruptly: 倏然 *-rarn*, 倏忽 *-hu*, 倏爾 *-eel*, ditto.

倏 91A.81-9

shuh
[Pop. of 倐]

俟 91A.81-9

syh (**chir*).
[Var. 竢]

N. A comp. Tungusic (鮮卑) surname: 万俟 pr. **Mohchir*, also **Muhchir*.

V.i. & t. To wait, wait for (time, (person): 俟他來了 wait until he comes; 俟駕 (court.) wait for your arrival.

俟便 *syh-biahn*, phr., when convenient.
俟候 *syh-houh*, v.t., to wait for.
俟命 *syh-mihng*, phr., (AC) abide and wait for God's will.
俟時 *syh-shyr*, phr., when the time comes.

§ 91A.82 (亻/乂)

伎 91A.82-1

jih.

N. (1) (Interch. 技) skill, ability: 伎能 practical skill; 伎巧 dexterity; 伎倆 *-liaang* ↓; 伎癢 "itching" to show off one's ability. (2) (Interch. 妓) a female performer: 歌伎, 舞伎 a female singer, dancer.

伎倆 *jihliaang*, n., (1) cleverness; (2) special skill.
伎藝 *jihyih*, n., (1) mechanical arts; (2) expert skill.

做 91A.82-1

tzuoh.

V.t. (1) Do, make, work at: 做工 *-gung*, 做事 *-shyh* ↓; 做不(上)來 don't know how this is done; 做不了 unable to do (finish); 做惡(好)人 be bad (good) toward s.o., act the part of a villain (sympathizer); 做得很好 do a good job of; 做生意 do business, make a deal; 做買賣 keep a shop, be in trade; 做公務員 be in government service; 做菜 to cook; 做衣裳 make a dress; 做飯 *-fahn* ↓; 做賊心虛 have a guilty conscience. (2) Celebrate: 做生日 hold a birthday party; 做滿月, 做週歲 party marking a child's birth when he is one month (year) old; 做週年 commemorative service on the first anniversary of s.o.'s death; 做壽 give a party in honor of s.o. on his birthday. (3) Pretend, feign: 做派 *-'pai* ↓; 做好做歹(惡) pretend to be kindhearted or unfeeling, as the situation of the moment may require.

做愛 *tzuoh-aih*, v.t., to make love.
做親 *tzuoh-chin*, v.i., make marriage arrangements for one's child.
做情 *tzuoh'ching*, v.i. & t., (1) intercede, mediate: 兩方都不肯說價錢, 只好由我做情了 as neither party would make a (price) offer, I had to step in and set a figure for them; (2) make a pretense.
做大 *tzuoh-dah*, v.i., arrogate to oneself a position of superiority.
做得 *tzuoh'de*, adj., permissible, feasible, can be done.
做法 *tzuohfaa*, n., way of doing a thing.
做飯 *tzuohfahn*, v.i., prepare a meal ("cook rice").
做根兒 *tzuoge'l*, adv., from the very beginning, at first.
做官(兒) *tzuoh-guan(-gua'l)*, v.i., be an official, join government service.
做鬼兒 *tzuohguee'l*, v.i., practise tricks, irregularities.
做工(兒) *tzuohgung('l)*, v.i., do manual work.
做好事 *tzuoh-haau-shyh*, v.i., (1) do a good turn, help the needy, give to charity; (2) perform religious rites for the repose of a

dead person's soul.

做活(兒) *tzuohhuor('l)*, v.i., do manual labor for a living; 做活局子 gang up to cheat (deceive).

做腳 *tzuoh-jiaau*, v.i., serve to pass secret messages.

做計 *tzuoh-jih*, v.t., to plan, scheme, plot.

做主 *tzuoh-juu*, v.t., be master of, make the final decision on (question): 現在兒女的婚姻，父母不能做主了 nowadays parents have no control over the marriage of their children; 此事由你做主 this matter is up to you to decide.

做闊 *tzuohkuoh*, v.i., to show off, make a vain display of one's riches.

做臉(兒) *tzuoh-liaan (-liaa'l)*, phr., do s.t. for the sake of appearances.

做弄 *tzuohluhng*, v.t., manipulate (matter) for selfish ends, stir up dissension.

做面子 *tzuoh-miahntz*, phr., do s.t. for the sake of face.

做派 *tzuoh'pai*, n., (1) gestures and movements of actors on stage; (2) affected manners.

做人 *tzuohrern*, v.i., conduct oneself in society: 他很懂做人的道理 he knows how to get along with people; 做人情 v.i., do s.o. a special favor.

做聲 *tzuohsheng*, v.i., begin to speak, break silence.

做甚 *tzuoh shern*, phr., what for: 要他知做甚 why let him know (it)?

做小 *tzuoh-shiaau*, v.i., be s.o.'s concubine.

做線 *tzuoh-shiahn*, v.i., see *-jiaau*↑.

做壽 *tzuoh-shouh*, v.i., hold birthday celebrations.

做手腳 *tzuoh-shourjiaau*, phr., resort to irregular practices, make secret arrangements.

做事 *tzuohshyh*, v.i., to work: 他正在做事 he is busy at work.

做頭 *tzuoh'tou*, n., expected results, advantage to be gained from a certain course of action: 有甚麼做頭 what's to be gained?

做作 *tzuos'tzuo*, v.i., pretend, feign, affect; n., affectation.

做眼 *tzuoh-yaan*, v.i., gather intelligence: 再造兩處做眼酒店 let's build two more undercover taverns.

傲 91A.82-1

auh.

V.t. To defy: 傲霜枝 (of chrysanthemum) branches that defy the frost.

Adj. Proud, conceited, rude: 驕傲, 倨傲 ditto.

Adv. Haughtily: 傲視, 傲睨 *-shyh*[2], *-nih*↓.

傲岸 *auh-ahn*, adj., proud and independent.

傲氣 *auhchih*, n., pride.

傲骨 *auhguu*, n., naturally proud nature, innate pride.

傲慢 *auhmahn*, adj., haughty, impudent.

傲睨 *auhnih*, v.t., to look down upon, see *-shyh*[2]↓.

傲世 *auh-shyh*[1], adj., proud, lofty-minded.

傲視 *auh-shyh*[2], v.t., look down upon, treat lightly.

傲物 *auhwuh*, adj., proud, self-satisfied.

仗 91A.82-1

jahng.

N. (1) Weapons, warfare, a war: 打仗 to fight a war; a war; 內仗 civil war; 打勝仗, 打敗仗 to triumph, be defeated in war (also 勝陣, 敗陣); 接仗 join battle. (2) Weaponry on parade: 儀仗 parade of insignia of power.

V.t. (1) To rely on: 仰仗, 倚仗, 依仗, 憑仗 to rely on s.o.'s power or help; 仗著本事 rely on one's own skill or ability; 你仗著什麼 how dare you—relying on what (do you dare say such a thing)? 仗腰子, 仗腰眼子 to back up s.o.; 有人仗腰子 have s.o. back up (financially, etc.). (2) To take up: 仗劍 rest hand on sword. (3) To stand up in defense: 仗義, 仗氣 *-yih, -chih*↓.

仗氣 *jahng-chih*, v.i., to act on strength of impulse.

仗勢 *jahng-shyh*[1], v.i., as in 仗勢欺人 to rely on (relative's, friend's) power and bully people; 狗仗人勢 (abuse) a dog bites on strength of master's position.

仗恃 *jahngshyh*[2], v.i., to rely (on s.o.'s power).

仗衛 *jahngweih*, n., formal retinue and escort preceding official.

仗義 *jahngyih*, phr., 仗義疏財 be public-spirited, spend on a good cause; 仗義執言 to speak boldly in defense of justice.

使 91A.82-1

*shyy (*shyh).*

N. (**shyh*) (1) A messenger, servant: 來使 bearer, messenger; 專使 special envoy, (by) special messenger; 使婢, 使役 *-beih, -yih*↓. (2) (Usu. *shyy*) emissary, minister: 公使 minister accredited to foreign country; 大使 ambassador; 大使館 embassy.

V.i. & t. (1) Causative vb., make, let, allow (+vb. or n., pron., +vb.): 使(他)來, 使(他)去 make (him) come, go; 使(使得)高興, 使(得)憂鬱 make (person) pleased, depressed; 使不必來 tell him not to come; 使國亡 cause nation to perish. (2) To send, order: 使他去做 send him to do it; 差使 to send s.o.; 使喚 *-'huan*↓. (3) To use, employ, apply: 使用

做
傲
仗
使

-*yuhng*↓; 使不得 -*'bu'de*↓; 使不了 -*'buliaau*↓; 使信號 employ signals; 使武力 use force; 使勁 -*jihn*↓; 使手段, 使詭計 use strategy, tricks; 使乖弄巧 ditto. (4) To let go: 使脾氣, 使性子 vent anger, be temperamental; 使酒 -*jioou*↓. (5) (**shyh*) (LL) be sent abroad as minister: 使於楚 was minister to *Chuu*.

Conj. If: 設使, 假使 if; 縱使, 即使 even if, even though; 使有不虞 if s.t. untoward, unforeseen should happen.

使絆兒 *shyy-bah'l*, v.i. & n., (a boxing move, a rope) cause s.o. to stumble by catching his leg.

使婢 *shyybeih* (**shyh*-), n., maidservant.

使不得 *shyy'bu'de*, v.i., (utensil, person) cannot be used, will not do.

使不了 *shyy'buliaau*, v.i., (1) -*'bu'de*↑; (2) more than one needs: 使不了這麼許多 do not need this much.

使臣 **shyhchern*, n., representative of country abroad.

使氣 *shyy-chih*, v.i., act on impulse or in fit of anger.

使得 *shyy'de*, v.i., (1) (article, dress) will do; (2) see V.i. & t. 1↑.

使館 *shyrguaan* (**shyh*-), n., legation: 大使館 embassy.

使壞 *shyyhuaih*, v.t., (1) wilfully make (s.o.) suffer; (2) hurt, destroy: 給他使壞了 destroyed by him.

使喚 *shyy'huan*, v.t., to order (servants) about; 使喚人 a servant, attendant.

使者 **shyhjee*, n., messenger, royal messenger.

使節 **shyhjier*, n., ministership or official mission abroad.

使勁(兒) *shyyjihn*(-*jieh'l*), v.i., exert effort, put out strength, energy: 使勁兒讀書, 拔草 work, pull out weeds, with energy.

使酒 *shyr-jioou*, v.i., to shout, make a row on strength of alcohol.

使君 **shyhjyun*, n., (1) (LL) official sent to country; (2) (LL) (court. address) like Eng. "this gentleman."

使君子 *shyyjyuntzyy*, n., (bot.) the Rangoon creeper, *Quisqualis indica*.

使命 *shyymihng* (**shyh*-), n., official mission.

使女 **shyhnyuu*, n., maidservant.

使徒 *shyytur*, n., (Christ.) disciples.

使役 *shyyyih* (**shyh*-), n., servants, attendants.

使用 *shyyyuhng*, v.t., to employ, use (utensil, person).

儆 91A.82–2

jiing.

V.t. (Interch. 警) warn, admonish: 示儆 serve as a warning; 以儆效尤 so as to deter anyone from committing the same (mistake, sin, crime).

儆備 *jingbeih*, v.i., be prepared for emergencies, guard against all eventualities.

儆戒 *jiingjieh*, (1) v.i., hold oneself ready to meet enemy moves; (2) v.t., warn, caution.

俶 91A.82–2

chuh.

V.i. (1) (AC) to begin. (2) U.f. 束; 俶裝 (＝束裝) girdle up for journey.

傻 91A.82–2

shaa.

[Var. 儍]

Adj. & adv. Stupid, -ly, silly: 傻話 silly talk; 傻笑 silly smile; 傻樂 being happy in a silly manner; 傻小子 silly boy; 傻老爺們兒 silly old men; 傻子 -*tzyy*↓; 吓傻了 stunned, dumbfounded; 傻呵呵 stupid and honest.

傻氣 *shaa'chi*, n., unsophisticated or blind courage.

傻瓜 *shaagua*, n., (a curse) fool or damn(ed) fool, silly ass.

傻角 *sharjiaau*, n., a silly person.

傻子 *shaatz*, n., a fool, nincompoop.

佊 91A.82–2

bii.

[Dist. 彼]

Adj. (AC) erroneous (belief): 邪佊 *shier*-, (AC) erroneous (views).

便 91A.82–3

biahn (**piarn*).

N. (1) (**piarn*) A surname. (2) Convenience, ease: 得便 whenever convenient, when you have time; 便中 at your convenience; 順便 at a convenient occasion: 你到蔡家, 請順便帶這件給他 since you are going to the Tsai's, please bring this to him; 順便拿酒瓶下來, 省得我起來 bring me the bottle and save me from getting up; 就便 when convenient; 隨便 do what you like, disregard formalities, see 隨△便 32A.83. (3) Toilet, toilet functions: hence 便所 "place of convenience" = ladies' restroom, etc.; 小便 v.i. & n., relieve oneself, to urinate; 大便 v.i. & n., go to stool, ease bowels; 禁止小便 commit no nuisance; 便秘 -*bih*[1]↓.

Adj. (1) Convenient; 方便 convenient; 不便 inconvenient; 便利 -*lih*↓; 便當 -*dahng*↓; 便於 convenient for, so that: 便於進行 so that we may proceed. (2) Informal, at ease: 請便, 自便 do as you like, feel at home; 便衣, 便帽 -*yi*, -*mauh*↓; 便餐 -*chan*, etc.↓. (3)

Quick (route, etc.): 便徑, 便道. (4) (*piarn) Sycophant, flattering: 便佞, 便辟 -nihn, -pih ↓.

Adv. Then, just, simply, in that case (used much more than the Eng. "then"): 你愛她, 她不愛你, 便怎麼樣 (便如何) if you love her and she does not love you, then what? 寶玉聽見便說 when Baauyuh heard this, he (then) said; 這樣做去便是 (便罷, 便了) just do it like this; 那便不同 then it is different; 你不去, 我便得去, if you do not go, then I have to; 把蓋封好, 便可以收藏多日 keep it tightly covered, then it will keep a long time.

Conj. (1) Even if, even though: 便有不是, 也得原諒他 even if he is wrong, you can forgive him. (2) As soon as: 一進去, 便看見 as soon as you go in, you see (the) . . . .

便秘 *biahnbih*, n., constipation.
便嬖 **piarnbih*, n., (AC) favorite mistress.
便餐 *biahnchan*, n., informal, plain dinner, potluck.
便器 *biahn-chih*, n., urinal.
便當 *biahndahng*, (1) adj., easy and convenient; (2) n., lunch basket.
便道 *biahn-dauh*, n., (1) quick but small path; (2) then said.
便殿 *biahn-diahn*, n., emperor's rest room before or after audience.
便毒 *biahndur*, n., gonorrhea.
便飯 *biahnfahn*, n., potluck, simple meal.
便服 *bianfur*, n., informal dress, home gown, dist. from 禮服 official uniform.
便徑 *biahn-jihng*, n., quick route, small path.
便壺 *biahn-hur*, n., night pot.
便利 *biahnlih*, adj., & n., convenient, -ce: 很多便利 has many advantages.
便路 *biahn-luh*, n., bypath.
便爐 *biahn-lur*, n., see 邊△爐 91.83.
便帽 *biahn-mauh*, n., easy cap.
便溺 *biahn-niauh*, v.i. & n., urinate, urine; bowels.
便佞 **piarn-nihn*, adj., being a good talker, sycophant.
便辟 **piarnpih*, adj., sycophant, given to flattering.
便人 *biahn rern*, n., s.o. at hand (to do an errand).
便是 *biahnshyh*, (1) conj., even if; (2) see Adv. ↑.
便所 *biahnsuoo*, n., toilet.
便條 *biahntiaur*, n , memo, short note; 便條簿 --*buh*, n., note pad, scribble pad.
便桶 *biahntuung*, n., wooden pail for stool.
便衣 *biahn-yi*, n., ordinary dress; 便衣偵探 plain-clothes detective.
便宜 *biahnyir*, adv., (1) as in 便宜行事 use discretion; (2) (**piaryi*) (a) adj., cheap: 不便宜 expensive; 東西便宜 things are cheap; (b) v.t., as in 太便宜了他 he got it cheap (without due punishment); (c) n., advantage: 沒有什麼便宜 no advantage in that.

優 91A.82-3

you.

N. Actor: 優伶, 優人 -*lirng*, -*rern* ↓; 優孟衣冠 dress up as on stage (from allu. 優孟 a court jester); 俳優 actor, court jester (slightly contempt.).

Adj. (1) Excellent, superior: 優等, 優異 -*deeng*, -*yih* ↓; 優越 -*yueh* ↓; 優勝劣敗 survival of the fittest. (2) Ample, liberal: 優裕, 優渥 -*yuh*, -*woh* ↓. (3) Free, leisurely, easy: 優游, 優容 -*your*, -*rurng* ↓; 優柔 -*rour* ↓.

優長 *youcharng*, n., a person's strong points, specialty.
優缺 *youchyue*, n., an excellent job, position.
優待 *youdaih*, v.t. & n., give special treatment, privilege.
優等 *youdeeng*, n., special or excellent grade.
優點 *youdiaan*, n., strong points, where one excels.
優厚 *youhouh*, adj. & adv., liberal (compensation).
優假 *youjiaa*, v.t., (AC) give special pardon.
優獎 *youjiaang*, n. & v.t., special prize, award.
優良 *youliarng*, adj., excellent (character, etc.).
優劣 *you-lieh*, n., good and bad: 較優劣 determine who is better.
優禮 *youlii*, n., special kindness or favor.
優伶 *yourlirng*, n., actor, actress.
優美 *youmeei*, adj., beautiful (style, results).
優人 *yourern*, n., actor.
優柔 *yourour*, adj., (1) amiable; (2) leisurely; (3) weak in character: 優柔寡斷 incapable of taking strong decision.
優容 *yoururng*, v.t., to be generous, lenient toward (offending person).
優生學 *yousheng-shyuer*, n., eugenics.
優先權 *yourshian-chyuarn*, n., priority.
優先股 *yourshian-guu*, n., preferred stock.
優閒 *youshiarn*, adj., free and content.
優秀 *youshiouh*, adj., select (elements, students, etc.): 優秀份子 the elite.
優勢 *youshyh*, n., advantage in contest.
優曇華 *youtarn-hua*, n., see 曇△花 41.93.
優爲 *youweir*, adj., (LL) good at (s.t.).
優渥 *youwoh*, adj. & adv., liberal (compensation).
優異 *youyih*, adj. & adv., special, extra (treatment, consideration).
優優 *youyou*, adj., (AC) (1) amiable; (2) ample.
優游 *youyour*, adj., (1) free, unconstrained, at ease: 優游自在 (自得) completely free and at ease; (2) (AC) undecided; (3) resigning oneself to fate: 與一世而優游 (AC) spend one's life in resignation, not particular, to take what comes (also 優遊).

優越 *youyueh*, adj., superior, commendable: 優越感 sense of superiority.

優裕 *youyuh*, adj., ample (means), easy, well-to-do life.

儼 91A.82–4

yaan.

Adj. Impressive, solemn.

儼然 *yaanrarn*, adj., having the true appearance, like real: 儼然如見其人 looks indeed like seeing the real person.

儼若 *yaanruoh*, adj., ditto.

侵 91A.82–5

chin.

V.t. (1) To invade: 侵犯, 侵襲 *-fahn, -shir* ↓; (AC) 敵人來侵 the enemy came to attack; 侵入 invade into someone's territory. (2) To take, occupy by force, to rob, to infringe: 侵害, 侵呑, 侵略, 侵奪, 侵佔 *-haih, -tun, -lyueh*², *-duor, -jahn* ↓.

Adj. & adv. Gradual, -ly: 侵早, 侵晨 as day is breaking; 侵尋, 侵淫 *-shyurn, -yirn* ↓.

侵晨 *chinchern*, adv., at early dawn.

侵奪 *chinduor*, v.t., to violate, encroach: 侵奪權利 deprive of, violate rights.

侵犯 *chinfahn*, v.t., to encroach upon (territory), infringe upon (rights).

侵害 *chinhaih*, v.t., to violate (territory, rights).

侵佔 *chinjahn*, v.t., to occupy by force.

侵陵(凌) *chinlirng*, v.t., to browbeat and humiliate.

侵掠 *chinlyueh*¹, v.i., to break into, invade, to harass and loot.

侵略 *chinlyueh*², v.t., invade neighbor's territory.

侵擾 *chinraau*, v.t., to harass, molest.

侵曉 *chinshiaau*, adv., (LL) toward dawn.

侵襲 *chinshir*, v.t., to steal (territory), encroach upon, make a sneaking attack on.

侵蝕 *chinshyr*, (1) v.i., to deteriorate, fall off in value, to eat into gradually; (2) v.t., to misappropriate (public funds); erode.

侵尋 *chinshyurn*, adv., (LL) gradually (also wr. 浸尋).

侵呑 *chintun*, v.t., to embezzle (public funds); to annex, gobble up, absorb (neighbor's territory).

侵早 *chintzaau*, adv., early morning.

侵淫 *chinyirn*, adv., (LL) gradually.

假 91A.82–5

jiaa (**jiah*).

N. (1) A surname. (2) Falsehood, deception, opp. 眞 truth(fulness): 以假亂眞 pass fake imitations for genuine. (3) (**jiah*) Holiday, leave: 假期 *-chir*, 假日 *-ryh* ↓; 放假 public holiday; 告假, 請假 ask for a leave of absence; 例假 regular holiday; 公假 official leave; 病假 sick leave; 產假 maternity leave; 年假 New Year holidays; 暑假, 寒假 summer, winter vacation.

V.t. Borrow, permit, allow, make use of, take advantage of: 假借 *-jieh*, 假貸 *-daih*, 假托 *-tuo* ↓; 假道, 假途 go (come) by way of; 假公濟私 gain private ends in public cause or by public money; 假以顏色 put on a pleasant face; 假以時日 give(n) sufficient time; 天不假年 (his) life was unfortunately cut short; 狐假虎威 a fox put on tiger's skin—a bully with a coward's heart.

Adj. (1) False, fake, imitation: 假冒 *-mauh*, 假充 *-chung* ↓; 假(頭)髮 wig ("false hair"); 假髻 woman's wig; 假牙 denture; 假撇清 pretend to have nothing to do with, make hypocritical gestures; 假模, 假式(樣) (of things) imitation, (of persons) hypocritical; 假正經 hypocritical, dissembling ("pretend to be a saint"); 假老實 double-dealing, double-faced; 假仁假義 hypocritical ("pretend to be the paragon of virtue"); 假慈悲 pretending to be kindhearted. (2) Pretending: 假王, 假皇帝 a pretender king. (3) (Law) conditional, tentative: 假扣押 provisional seizure; 假處分 provisional measures; 假決議 tentative resolution; 假釋 conditional release.

Conj. If, supposing: 假定 *-dihng*, 假令 *-lihng*, 假使 *-shyy*, 假設 *-sheh*, 假如 *-rur*, 假若 *-ruoh* ↓.

假扮 *jiaabahn*, v.i., go in disguise, act the part of s.o. else.

假期 **jiahchir*, n., holidays, vacation.

假充 *jiaachung*, v.i. & t., pretend: 假充正經 put on as a gentlemen; 假充內行 pretend to know what one does not.

假貸 *jiaadaih*, v.t., (1) borrow (money, etc.); (2) 假貸顏色 tolerate, bear with, indulge.

假定 *jiaadihng*, (1) n. & v.t., suppose, -sition; (2) conj., supposing, if (it be granted).

假分數 *jiaa-fenshuh*, n., (math.) an improper fraction.

假父 *jiaa-fuh*, n., foster father.

假高眼 *jiaa-gauyaan*, phr., one who poses as an expert.

假招子 *jiaajautz*, phr., (make) hypocritical gestures.

假借 *jiaajieh*, v.t., (1) borrow (money, books, etc.); (2) use one Chin. character with similar pronunciation in place of another, used for (u.f.) in ancient works.

假裝(兒) *jiaajuang('l)*, v.i., disguise, simulate.

假柯子 *jiaa-ke'tz*, adj., hypocritical, dissembling.

假令 *jiaalihng*, conj., in case, in the event that.

假冒 *jiaamauh*, v.t., (of persons, things) pose as, pass for (the

genuine), counterfeit: 假冒爲善 be a hypocrite.
假寐 *jiaameih*, v.i. & n., (take) a nap, siesta.
假面 *jiaa-miahn*, n., a mask: 假面具 (a) a mask; (b) hypocrisy.
假母 *jiar-muu*, n., foster mother.
假若 *jiaaruoh*, conj., supposing (that).
假如 *jiaarur*, conj., ditto.
假日 **jiahryh*, n., see *-chir* ↑.
假山 *jiaashan*, n., a rock garden.
假設 *jiaasheh*, n. & conj., (1) n., hypothesis; (2) conj., supposing (that).
假想 *jiarshiaang*, n. & adj., & v.t., fancy: 假想敵 simulated enemy.
假象 *jiaashiahng*, n., (psych.) semblance, appearance.
假性 *jiaashihng*, adj., pseudo.
假惺惺 *jiaashingshing*, adj., hypocritical.
假手 *jiar-shoou*, v.t., do by proxy.
假釋 *jiaa-shy*, v.t., to free (a prisoner) on probation.
假使 *jiarshyy*, conj., if, in case.
假數 *jiarsuh*, n., (math.) mantissa, the decimal part of a logarithm.
假死 *jiarsyy*, (1) n., (med.) asphyxia; (2) v.i., pretend to be dead.
假托 *jiaatuo*, v.i. & n., (make) false pretenses, (tell) a white lie.
假子 *jiaa-tzyy*, n., (1) a foster son; (2) a stepson.
假意 *jiaa-yih*, adj. & adv., pretended friendship or cordiality.

佼 91A.82-6

jiaau.

Adj. Handsome, good-looking: 佼佼者 an outstanding (preeminent) person; 庸中佼佼 a giant among pigmies.

佼好 *jiaauhaau*, adj., pretty, pleasant, pleasing.
佼人 *jiaaurern*, n., a handsome young man, a beauty.
佼童 *jiaauturng*, n., a handsome lad.

倣 91A.82-6

faang.

[Var. of 仿 91A.50]

傚 91A.82-6

shiauh.

V.t. To copy, imitate: 倣傚 to copy style of a master.

仪 91A.82-8

yir.

[Abbr. of 儀 91A.71]

儌 91A.82-9

jiau (**jiaau*).

[Var. of 徼]

V.t. (1) Covet, crave, long for. (2) See comp. ↓.

儌幸 (1) **jiaaushihng*, adj., by luck; (2) (*jiau-*) (AC) 行險以儌幸 try for hazardous chance (also wr. 徼 91B.82).

攸 91A.82-9

you.

Adv. prefix. (1) Passing to, toward: 攸關, 攸歸 *-guan*, *-guei* ↓. (2) Past: 攸然 *-rarn* ↓ (cf. 悠▵然 91.72).

攸關 *youguan*, adj., connected: 名譽攸關 affects one's reputation.
攸歸 *youguei*, adj., connected, belonging: 罪有攸歸 responsibility for crime can be traced.
攸然 *yourarn*, adv., past: 攸然而逝 past and gone.

俊 91A.82-9

jyuhn (also *tzuhn*).

Adj. (1) Talented, smart, bright: 俊傑 *-jier* ↓. (2) Good-looking, handsome, personable: 英俊 handsome and smart; 俊俏 *-chiauh* ↓; 俊人物(兒) a charming person. (3) Great: 俊德 *-der* ↓.

俊俏 *jyuhnchiauh*, adj., graceful, elegant, lovely, charming; n., such persons.
俊德 *jyuhn-der*, n., great virtue.
俊傑 *jyuhnjier*, n., a person of extraordinary talent: 俊傑在位 with the most talented men in office.
俊秀 *jyuhnshiouh*, n., (1) handsome and talented men; (2) formerly, a Chin. scholar having no official qualifications during the Manchu Dyn.
俊雅 *jyuhnyaa*, adj., refined, elegant.
俊游 *jyuhnyour*, n., a congenial companion.

§ 91A.83 (亻/～)

㒓 91A.83-1

tah.

V.i. To flee.

假佼倣傚仪儌攸俊㒓

亅	小	卜	十	土	𠂇	廾	乚ト	丨	一	丅	フ	口	区	冈	乛	厂	尸	亠	广	宀	丶	乚	弋	心	八	人	乂	～	㇀	リ	𠂉	ㄑ
00	01	02	10	11	12	20	21	22	30	31	32	40	41	42	50	51	52	60	61	62	63	70	71	72	80	81	82	83	90	91	92	93

儗 91A.83-2

nii.

V.i. (Interch. 疑) compare with, draw an analogy between: 儗於不倫 the analogy is ill-drawn, the comparison is not apt.

健 91A.83-2

jiahn.

Adj. (1) Sound, healthy: 健康 *-kang*, 健全 *-chyuarn*, 健壯 *-juahng*, 健在 *-tzaih*↓; 積健爲雄 (LL) succeed through persistence; 天行健 (AC) keep on going without cease like the heavenly bodies; 健身 do exercises to keep fit; 健身操 calisthenics; 健身房 gymnasium. (2) Capable, talented: 穩健 dependable, reliable, mature and experienced; 健將 a person of great ability; 健兒 *-erl*↓; 健者 a man of action, one of high ambition, the bold and heroic type; 健僕 a faithful servant; 健卒 hard-fighting soldiers. (3) Good at, fond of: 健飯 have a good appetite; 健訟 fond of litigation; 健啖, 健飲 fond of eating, wine; 健談 *-tarn*↓; 健忘 *-wahng*[1]↓; 健羨 greedy, covetous, avaricious, admiring; 健筆 gifted with a ready pen.

健步 *jiahn-buh*, adj., swift-footed, vigorous in steps.

健全 *jiahnchyuarn*, adj., (1) sound and hale, in good health; (2) (of mental faculties) unimpaired.

健兒 *jiahnerl*, n., able-bodied persons, athletes, (euphem.) soldiers, heroes.

健壯 *jiahnjuahng*, adj., vigorous and healthy.

健康 *jiahnkang*, adj., healthy, sound, robust, hale, vigorous; 健康保險 health insurance.

健美 *jiahnmeei*, adj., (1) (of men) strongly built, muscular, brawny; (2) (of women) having a well-developed and graceful figure; (3) (facet.) stout, plump, corpulent.

健適 *jiahnshyh*, adj., in good health, sound and fit.

健談 *jiahntarn*, adj., talkative, be a good talker.

健在 *jiahntzaih*, adj., still living, going strong.

健忘 *jiahnwahng*[1], adj., forgetful, absent-minded.

健旺 *jiahnwahng*[2], adj., (of elderly person) in good health.

健胃 *jiahn-weih*, adj., (of drug) helping to stimulate appetite.

促 91A.83-4

tsuh.

V.i. & t. To hurry s.o. to do s.t.: 催促 ditto; to push forward: 促其成功, 實現 help make it a success, help to realize (a scheme); 督促 supervise (construction, etc.).

Adj. & adv. (1) Urgent: 急促, 忽促, 緊促 ditto. (2) 侷促 uneasy, cramped, restricted in space. (3) Closely: 促坐, 促席, 促膝 sitting closely on mat, knee touching knee, see 促膝 *-shi*, 促席 *-shir*↓.

促成 *tsuhcherng*, v.t., to facilitate, help realize (project, success).

促進 *tsuhjihn*, v.t., to promote (movement).

促織 *tsuhjy*, n., name for cricket 蟋蟀 ("urging to weave" from cricket's incessant cry).

促忙 *tsuhmarng*, adj., (MC) in a hurry.

促拍 *tsuhpoh*, n., (MC) quick tempo in music.

促膝 *tsuh-shi*, v.i., to sit with bended knees close together (sitting on mat): 促膝而談 have intimate chat together.

促狹 *tsuhshiar* (*-'shia*), adj., mean, spiteful; 促狹鬼 mean and spiteful fellow, a louse.

促席 *tsuh-shir*, adv., (AC) sitting closely on mat.

促促 *tsuhtsuh*, adj., fast closing (dusk).

§ 91A.91 (亻/丿)

伊 91A.91-5

yi.

N. (1) A surname. (2) First word in translation of some geographical names, like Iran, Iraq.

Pron. (AC and certain dial. & legal use) he, she: 伊人, 伊家 ditto; 伊等 they.

Adj. (LL) (1) That: 伊時, 伊日 that time, that day. (2) What, who: (AC) 伊誰, 伊何 *-shueir*, *-her*↓.

伊邇 *yi-eel*, adj., (AC) near.

伊何 *yiher*, adv., why? wherefor?

伊家 *yijia*, n., (coll. & legal) he, she.

伊人 *yirern*, n., (AC) that man, woman.

伊誰 *yishueir*, n., who?

伊始 *yishyy*, n., beginning.

伊吾 *yiwur*, adj., descriptive of sound of intoned reading (also wr. 咿唔).

伊伊 *yiyi*, adj., (LL) sound of creaking insects.

 91A.91-9

shiou.

V.i. & t. (1) To repair, keep in good condition, construct, build: 修改, 修補, 修訂 *-gaai*, *-buu*, *-dihng*↓; 修理 *-'lii*↓; 修路, 修橋 build road, bridge; 修房子 build a house; 修鉛筆 sharpen pencil; 修廟 build or rebuild temple; 重修 rebuild, also revise (book). (2) To trim nails, hair, etc.: 修容, 修指甲, 修面, 修腳 *-rurng*, *-jyrjiaa*, *-miahn*, *-jiaau*↓. (3) To cultivate (peace, good relationships, character etc.): 修和, 修好, 修身, 修福, 修行, etc. *-her*, haau, -shen, -fur^{2}, shihng↓; 修陰功 do secret good deeds; 不修邊幅 morally loose; 老不修 dissipated old man; 前^{4}修 80.00. (4) To study: 自修 study by oneself, free period in school for study; 進修 carry on further studies; 修業 study in school or for some profession. (5) To edit (history): 修府志 edit prefectural history; 修法令 edit code of laws; 編修 an editor.

Adj. (LL) long: 命之修短 the length ("long-short") of life; 修短不齊 uneven in length; 修竹 tall bamboo; 修眉 long eyebrows; 修齡 (LL) long life, old age.

修補 *shioubuu*, v.t. & n., to repair (house, roof, etc.).

修葺 *shiouchih*, v.t. & n., repair, renovate (house).

修齊 *shiou-chir*, phr., (1) cut even (hedge, etc.); (2) abbr. from 修身齊家 to cultive oneself and put family in order

修道 *shiou-dauh*, v.i., (1) to enter monastery; to go through religious regimen; (2) to cultivate the Way; 修道院 *--yuahn*, n., monastery.

修訂 *shioudihng*, v.t., to edit and revise; make or revise (treaties).

修短 *shiou-duaan*, phr., "long-short"—the length.

修髮 *shioufaa*, v.i., to trim the hair.

修復 *shioufur*^{1}, v.t., to renovate: 修復舊觀 restore (building, etc.) to original shape and appearance.

修福 *shiou-fur*^{2}, v.i., to "cultivate luck" by doing good deeds, philanthropy, etc.

修改 *shiougaai*, v.t., revise (script), renovate (house), revise (policy), see *-jehng*↓.

修蓋 *shiougaih*, v.t., build or rebuild (house, temple).

修好 *shiouhaau*, v.t., establish friendly relations, make allies.

修函 *shiou-harn*, v.i., compose a letter, see also *-shu*↓.

修和 *shiouher*, v.i., establish peace or friendly relations with neighbor countries.

修正 *shioujehng*, v.t., to revise (text, policy): 修正主義 revisionism.

修積 *shiou'ji*, v.i., see *-fur*^{2}↑.

修剪 *shioujiaan*, v.t., trim, cut, clip.

修腳 *shiou-jiaau*, v.i., pedicure.

修己 *shiou-jii*, v.i., to cultivate and constantly improve oneself.

修築 *shioujur*, v.t., to construct (road, bridge).

修治 *shioujyh*, v.i., to repair, adjust and regulate.

修指甲 *shiou-jyrjiaa*, v.i., manicure.

修濬 *shioujyuhn*, v.t., dredge (river) and build dykes.

修鍊 *shiouliahn*, v.i., go into religious self-discipline, esp. Buddist or Taoist control of mind and body.

修理 *shiou'lii*, v.t., repair (house, watch, etc.).

修羅場 *shiouluor-charng*, n., (Budd.) battlefield between giant demons, Asuras, and Indra—scene of bloody slaughter.

修面 *shioumiahn*, v.i., to shave (the face).

修名 *shiou-mirng*^{1}, v.i., cultivate a good name for posterity.

修明 *shioumirng*^{2}, adj., clean, enlightened, well-ordered (government).

修睦 *shioumuh*^{1}, v.i., cultivate friendship with neighbors.

修墓 *shiou-muh*^{2}, v.i., renovate or keep (ancestral grave) in good condition.

修女 *shiounyuu*, n., a nun; cf. *-shyh*^{1}↓.

修然 *shiourarn*, adj., (AC) trim, in good shape.

修容 *shiou-rurng*, v.i., make up hair and face: 修容室 beauty parlor.

修繕 *shioushahn*, v.t., see *-'lii*↑.

修身 *shiou-shen*, v.i. & n., cultivate oneself or improvement of the individual—Confucian basis of all social order.

修仙 *shiou-shian*, v.i., train by self-discipline to become an immortal.

修褉 *shiou-shih*, v.i., to hold the purification ceremony—see 褉 63C.81.

修省 *shioushiing*, v.i., to look after one's conduct by self-examination (from 修身自省).

修心 *shiou-shin*, v.i., to attend to spiritual things.

修行 *shioushing* (*-'shing*), (1) to practise moral teachings; (2) (*-shihng*) (Budd.) to practise Buddhist conduct.

修修 *shioushiou*, v.i., (AC) well-trimmed.

修書 *shiou-shu*, v.i., to compose a letter.

修士 *shioushyh*^{1}, n., a monk, see *-nyuu*↑.

修飾 *shioushyh*^{2}, v.t., to beautify, redecorate (room, house), refurbish.

修學 *shioushyuer*, v.i., to study, esp. in school.

修辭 *shioutsyr*, n., rhetoric, the use of proper words; 修辭學 rhetoric.

修造 *shioutzauh*, v.t., to build (house, road, bridge).

修阻 *shioutzuu*, adj., (roads, way) long and arduous.

修文 *shiou-wern*, v.i., to develop the cultural things (arts, literature, rites and ceremonies).

修養 *shiouyaang*, n., man's moral culture as the result of training: 他很有修養 he is very cultivated; 文學修養 wide reading in literature.

修業 *shiouyeh*, v.i., to go to school.

§91A.93 (亻/く)

傻 91A.93–2

lour.

N. A surname.

Adj. Hunchbacked: 背傻.

僂儸 *lourluor*, n., (also 嘍囉) (contempt.) followers of any leader: 小僂儸 riffraff followers.

佞 91A.93-6

nihng.

N. One given to flattery: 奸佞 ministers given to flattery, yes-men; 不佞 (litr., self-reference) I (an uncouth person).

V.t. To flatter: 佞佛 praise ("flatter") Buddha; (sarcastic) be devout Buddhist.

Adj. (AC) given to flattery; smooth-tongued, sycophant.

佞人 *nihngrern*, n., bootlicker.
佞幸 *nihngshihng*, n., flattering courtiers; favorite of king.

侩 91A.93-8

kuaih.

[Abbr. of 儈 91A.41]

倭 91A.93-9

weei (**wo*).

N. (1) A dwarf. (2) Formerly, used to refer to Japan: 倭寇 Japanese invaders.

Adj. (1) Dwarfish, short: 倭刀 *-dau*↓. (2) (**wei*) See 倭遲 *-chyr*↓.

倭遲 *weichyr*, adj., (AC) winding, circuitous (road).
倭刀 **wodau*, n., Japanese dagger, short sword.
倭瓜 **wogua* (*-'gua*), n., a kind of melon.

SECTION 91B

§ 91B.00 (彳/亅)

術 91B.00-1

shuh.

N. (1) A skill, an art, some special studies: 技術 technical skill, technique; 美術, 藝術 the fine arts; 手術 (a) skills; (b) surgical operation; 學術 learning, scholarship (of person, age, country), studies; 算術 arithmetic; 行述(術) biogarphical sketch; 道術 doctrine, school of philosophy; 邪術 evil doctrine, also black magic; 拳術 boxing; 劍術 swordsmanship; 妖術, 魔術 magic; 催眠術 hypnotism; 相術 fortunetelling. (2) Tactics, method: 戰術 military tactics; 權術 political strategy or maneuver; 仁術 the method of a kindhearted man; 心術 a calculating mind, heart of cunning; 妙術 admirable skill or method; 計術 strategy, plan to deceive.

術數 *shuhshuh*, n., art of prophecy based on interaction of *yin* and *yarng* (陰陽五行).
術士 *shuhshyh*, n., (AC) magician; political critics; Taoist, also (AC) Confucian scholar.
術語 *shuhyuu*, n., technical term.

衚 91B.00-1

hur.

衚衕(兒) *hurtuhng('l)*, n., a *hutung* or alleyway in Peking (also wr. 胡同).

待 91B.00-1

daih (**dai*).

V.t. (1) Receive (guests), treat (persons): 招待 or 款待客人, 待客 receive guests; 待上, 待下 deal with superiors, inferiors; 待人 act towards people (kindly, rudely); 待人接物 manner of dealing with people; 善待 treat kindly; 虐待 (usu. servants, etc.) treat badly; 優待 give special treatment, reception 厚待 treat generously; 慢待 treat coolly or ignore; 兩人相待 the two get along (well, ill); 看待 take care of. (2) To wait for, await: 待命 awaiting your command; 等待 wait for; 少待片刻 please wait a little while; 久待 wait for a long time; 待時而動 wait for the right time to take action; 坐以待斃 wait helplessly for the end; 待字, 待聘 *-tzyh*, *-pihn*↓; 待到, 待得 *-dauh*, *-der*↓. (3) (**dai*) V.i., tarry, delay, hang around: 我在家裏待一天 I have been hanging around at home the whole day; 待不了 cannot wait any longer; 待一會兒再來 come back after a while; 待了 *-liaau*↓. (4) (*daih*) Going to do: 待怎的 what about it? what do you propose to do? 待理(兒)不理(兒) listen to person half-heartedly, treat coolly.

待茶 *daihchar*, v.t., (MC) receive (guest) with tea.
待到 *daih-dauh*, prep., until: 待到那時候 until that time.
待等 *daihdeeng*, v.i., wait for.
待得 *daih-der*, conj., until: 待得不好意思 until one is embarrassed.
待詔 *daih-jauh*, n., (1) (MC) a junior secretary at court; (2) (MC) waiter; (3) (Peking dial.) a barber.
待了 **dai-liaau*, v.t., wait (a long time).
待漏 *daih-louh*, n., the hour (沙漏 hourglass) preparatory to going in for imperial audience.
待聘 *daih-pihn*, v.i., waiting for appointment to post; also not yet betrothed =*-tzyh*↓.

待罪 *daih-tzueih*, v.i., (court. at end of official letter) awaiting punishment (for statement of opinion): 待罪之身 (court.) my guilty self (said by person under investigation or impeachment).
待字 *daih-tzyh*, v.i., (of girl) waiting for right man to marry.
待遇 *daihyuh*, n., treatment, reception as visitor; pay, salary, emolument.

街 91B.00-1

jie.

N. A public thoroughfare: 大街小巷 streets and alleys; 市街 city street; 街市 *-shyh*↓; 十字街頭 (at) the crossroads; 街頭巷尾 street corners and alleys; 街談巷議 street gossips, rumors; 街里街坊 neighborly relations; 花街柳巷 red-light districts; 掃街 sweep the streets; 遊街 a procession or parade: 遊街示衆 to parade (a criminal) through streets; 逛街 go for a stroll, take a walk; 罵街 curse loudly in public.

街衢 *jiechyur*, n., a thoroughfare.
街道 *jiedauh*, n., a road, street.
街坊 *jiefang*, n., neighbors, neighborhood.
街門 *jiemern*, n., the front door facing the street.
街面兒 *jiemiah'l*, n., street, street scenes.
街上 *jie'shang*, phr., in the street.
街巷 *jieshiahng*, n., streets and lanes.
街市 *jieshyh*, n., business centers in cities, downtown district.

衖 91B.00-2

luhng.

N. (1) Var. for 弄 *nuhng*, alley. (2) Also var. for 巷 *shiahng*, alley.

衠 91B.00-2

jun.

Adv. (MC) really: (＝真) 妖嬈一團兒衠是嬌 her body soft and warm, really enticing.

衞 91B.00-2

weih.
[Pop. 衛]

N. (1) A guard: 衞兵, 衞隊 *-bing, -dueih*↓; 侍衞 bodyguard, personal guard; 守衞 guards. (2) A name for donkeys. (3) A surname. (4) Name of an anc. state.

V.t. (1) To defend, guard: 保衞 to protect (city, home); 守衞, 防衞 to defend; 自衞 self-defence. (2) To assist (ruler, regime): 衞君 assist the ruler; 衞政 assist in government.

衞兵 *weihbing*, n., guard(s).
衞隊 *weihdueih*, n., the guards, garrison.
衞仗 *weih-jahng*, n., insignia of authority on parade.
衞理公會 *Weihliigunghueih*, n., Methodist Church.
衞生 *weihsheng*, n. & adj., hygiene, -nic: 公共衞生 public sanitation; 衞生隊 sanitation squads; things of personal hygiene: 衞生帶 sanitation belt; 衞生紙 toilet paper; 衞生球 moth ball; 衞生丸(兒) moth ball, also (facet.) bullet which kills; 衞生衣 knitted underwear; 衞生巾 sanitary napkin.
衞星 *weihshing*, n., satellite: 人造衞星 man-made satellite; 衞星國 satellite country; 衞星轉播站 satellite earth station.
衞戍 *weihshuh*, n., guard, garrison.
衞士 *weihshyh*, n., (LL) bodyguard.

行 91B.00-3

shirng (**shihng, *harng*).

N. (1) 行書 the running script, half way between 楷書 formal script and 草書 cursive rapid script: 半行半草 midway between running and cursive script. (2) An anc. verse form usu. narrative and longer than the conventional four or eight lines of Tarng poetry. (3) (**shihng*) Conduct: 品行 person's conduct; 德行 personal character; 修行 (Budd.) follow the religious order; 苦行 life of abstinence, penance, etc.; 無行 (of person) a bad character; see 行狀, 行述 *-juahng, -shuh*↓. (4) 五行 the fundament five modes of movement (expansion, contraction, etc.): 金木水火土. (5) (**harng*) (a) A row, a column: 行列 *-lieh*↓; 八行書 standard letter-paper size for eight columns of characters; (b) (*harng*) lines: 寥寥數行 just a few lines; 雁行 cranes which fly in formation; (c) (**harng*) order of seniority in family: 行輩 generation; 兄弟行 status of brothers; 排行 sequence among brothers and sisters: 排行第二 number two. (6) (**harng*) A firm, a shop: 車行 a garage; 電料行 store for electrical supplies; 銀行 a bank; 批發行 wholesale dealer; 洋行 a foreign firm. (7) (**harng*) A line of business, a profession: 三百六十行 all the professions; 同行是冤家 same profession, natural rivals; 吃這行飯 live by this profession; 內行 n. & adj., professional; 外行 n. & adj., an amateur, amateurish; 在行 adj., professional (talk), knowing thoroughly; 當行, 本行 one's own profession; 改行 change profession; 隔行如隔山 difference in profession makes one feel worlds apart.

V.i. & t. (1) Go, proceed, including walking, sailing, flying, driving: 行路 to take walk, to walk; 行船

行 sail a boat; 船行 boat sails; 飛行 fly (by plane); 車行三十哩 the car goes 30 miles; 步行 go on foot; 航行 sail or fly in travel; 行走, 行程 *-tzoou*, *-cherng* ↓; 行期 date of departure; 旅行 travel; 開行 proceed (of train, car, ship); 行屍走肉 dead-alive person ("walking corpse"); 行雲流水 "floating clouds and flowing water"—freely flowing style of writing, casual, masterly, unconstrained. (2) Publish, circulate, prevail: 行世 (book) is published and known; 流行, 通行 be widely circulated or accepted; 風行 (book) popularly received; 發行 to issue (bank notes, bonds), publish (book, newspaper); 頒行 to publish order, statutes; 道行天下, 道不行 the right way (teaching) prevails, does not prevail. (3) To do, execute, carry out: 行不行 will that do? 行了 that will do; 不行 that won't do; 行得, 行不得 may, may not be done; 行得通, 行不得 can, cannot be carried out; 施行 put (law, regulations) into effect; 實行 carry out (teaching); 執行 carry out (punishment); 力行 proceed with determination. (4) To commit, practise some form of conduct: 行詐, 行騙 practise cheating, swindle; 行賄, 行劫, 行姦, 行兇 commit bribery, robbery, rape, violence; 行聘 go through with betrothal rites, to betroth; 行好事 do a good deed; 行樂 *-leh* ↓; 行人情 phr., to fulfill the social obligations (give gifts, etc.); 行孝 be a good dutiful son or daughter.

Adj. (1) Able, good, competent: 你眞行 you are really good (praise of efficiency or competence). (2) Enough: 行了, 吃不下了 it's enough, I can't eat any more, see V.i. & t. 3↑. (3) (**harng*) Bad, see 行貨, 行窳 *-huoh*, *-yuu* ↓.

Adv. (LL) soon: 行將出國 will go abroad soon; 行見天下太平 we shall soon see world peace.

行輩 **harngbeih*, n., seniority in family, usu. referring to generation.

行常 *shirngcharng*, adv., usually.

行程 *shirng-cherng*, n., schedule, route or distance of travel.

行篋 *shirngchieh*[1], n., luggage.

行竊 *shirng-chieh*[2], phr., commit burglary.

行乞 *shirng-chii*, phr., to beg as beggar.

行棋 *shirng-chir*, phr., to play chess.

行情 **harngchirng*, n., trade or market situation; current prices.

行船 *shirng-chyuarn*, v.i., be boatman as profession.

行當兒 **harng'da'l*, n., different arts and crafts: 手藝行當兒.

行道 *shirng-dauh*, phr., promote teachings (usu. Confucian); (2) practise medicine (＝行醫) (euphem. used by physicians); (3) go around the image of Buddha during worship.

行動 *shirngduhng*, n. & v.i., movement (to watch, be careful of); physical movement (slow, difficult for aged people, agile, free, etc.): 行動一致 unity of action, to act in unison.

行販 *shirng-fahn*, phr., be a small tradesman; to be pedlar: 行販兒 *-'fah'l*, a pedlar, small tradesman.

行房 *shirng-farng*, v.i., have sexual intercourse.

行規 **harng-guei*, n., rules observed among members of profession.

行宮 *shirnggung*, n., imperial palace or hostel away from capital.

行國 *shirngguor*, n., (AC) pastoral tribe.

行賈 *shirng-guu*, v.i., to carry on trade; n., a pedlar.

行好 *shirnghaau*, phr., to do good (＝行善).

行化 *shirng'hua*, v.i., (of food, medicine) be gradually absorbed by body.

行話 **harnghuah*, n., professional slang, argot.

行會 **harnghueih*, n., guild, association.

行貨 **harnghuoh*, (1) n., trade goods, esp. inferior goods; 行貨子 (a word of abuse) a harlot, a broad; (2) (*shirng-*) v.i., (a) (AC) to use bribery methods; (b) to trade.

行詐 *shirngjah*, v.i., to swindle.

行棧 **harngjahn*, n., storehouse.

行者 *shirngjee*, n., itinerant monk; attendant to abbot.

行政 *shirng-jehng*, v.i., to administer, execute: 行政人員 administrative staff; 行政院 the Executive Yuan of the central government; 辦行政 be charged with executive work (cf. 執行委員 member(s) of executive committee).

行鍼 *shirng-jen*, phr., practise acupuncture.

行家 **harngjia*, n., specialist, expert: 行家子 *--tz*, ditto.

行檢 *shirngjiaan*, n., decorum in conduct: 無行檢 dissolute.

行腳 *shirngjiaau*, n., an itinerant monk, who travels to increase knowledge.

行間 **harngjian*, n., (1) in army service (＝行伍間); (2) 字裏行間 (what one may read) between the lines.

行將 *shirng-jiang*, adv., will soon (be all destroyed, etc.).

行紀 **harngjih*, n., a broker.

行徑 *shirngjihng*, n., a man's gen. conduct or behavior; a path.

行經 (1) *shirng-jing*[1], v.i., menstruation comes; (2) (*shirng jing*) walk past (a place).

行旌 *shirngjing*[2], n., (court.) your travel or departure.

行酒 *shirng-jioou*, v.i., to serve wine to guests.

行狀 **shihngjuahng*, n., brief biographical sketch of deceased sometimes accompanying obituary notice.

行裝 *shirngjuang*, n., luggage; sometimes military uniform on expedition.

行軍 *shirng-jyun*, (1) n., moving troops; (2) v.i., command, lead or march an army, (Western reference) manner or strategy: 行軍敏速 march (one's) army with great speed.

行止 *shirngjyy*, n., (1) behavior, conduct (＝擧止): 行止不檢 dissolute in conduct; (2) person's movements: 行止不定 his movements are highly uncertain; (3) what to do: 等他來了, 再定行止 wait till he comes, then we'll decide what to do.

行客 *shirng-keh*, n., a traveller, a transient visitor: 行客拜坐客 it's up to the newcomer to call on his friends in town.

行款 **harngkuaan*, n., form and arrangement of lines in calligraphy.

行樂 *shirngleh*, v.i., enjoy oneself: 及時行樂 make merry while we can.

行列 **harnglieh*, n., a row in assembly, a column formation.

行令 *shirng-lihng*, v.i., to play wine game, with drinking as forfeit.

行李 *shirng'lii*, n., bagging, luggage.

行禮 *shirng-lii*, v.i., to salute (in various forms, such as bowing from the waist, etc.).

行旅 *shirnglyuu*, v.i., to travel.

行囊 *shirngnarng*, n., (LL) money or valuable carried during travel.

行內 *shirngneih*, phr., (AC) within the palace (＝行在之內 see *-tzaih*↓).

行年 *shirngniarn*, v.i., aged: 行年四十 aged forty.

行人 *shirngrern*, n., (1) pedestrian, passenger on street; 行人道 sidewalk, pedestrian's path; 行人免進 loiterers not admitted; (2) (AC) an emissary, envoy.

行色 *shirngseh*, n., style of travelling: 以壯行色 give money to help proper style of travelling.

行商 *shirng-shang*¹, v.i., be a travelling salesman.

行觴 *shirng-shang*², v.i., see *-jioou*↑.

行省 *shirngsheeng*, n., a province.

行香 *shirng-shiang*, v.i., hold or participate in prayer service at temple.

行銷 *shirngshiau*, v.i., (of goods) sell (well, etc.).

行星 *shirngshing*, n., a planet.

行息 *shirng-shir*, v.i., bear interest.

行刑 *shirng-shirng*, v.i., (1) to execute criminal; (2) to apply torture.

行書 *shirngshu*, n., (callig.) running script, see N. 1↑.

行述 **shihngshuh*, n., see *-juahng*↑.

行市 **harngshyh*, n., the fluctuating prices of a market.

行事 *shirngshyh*, v.i., (1) do s.t. planned, usu. secret: 決定半夜行事 decide to do it at midnight; (2) how one does things: 行事大方 act in generous manner; (3) how one runs things: 他眞會行事 he knows how to run things (such as dismissing an employee with as few words as possible); 不會行事 do not know when to act and when not to act.

行兇 *shirng-shyung*, v.i., commit assault, attempt to murder.

行使 *shirngshyy*¹, v.t., carry out (one's duties), make use of (one's legal power).

行駛 *shirngshyy*², v.i. & t., to sail (a boat), (boat) sails; to drive (a car); (car) drives (well, etc.): 行駛得法 drive or sail expertly.

行堂 *shirngtarng*, n., monks' bedroom in temple, room for visiting monks.

行頭 (1) *shirng'tou*, n., (a) actors' accoutrements (hats, shoes, etc.); (b) (MC): a form of football: 踢行頭 play football; (c) (MC) traveller's luggage; (2) (**harngtour*) (AC) a company officer.

行藏 *shirngtsarng*, n., a person's past, record of doings known and unknown.

行刺 *shirng-tsyh*, v.i., to attempt to assassinate.

行童 *shirngturng*, n., boy servant for running errands in monastery.

行在 *hsirngtzaih*, n., place of royal sojourn.

行走 *shirngtzoou*, v.i., (1) to run about; (2) (formerly, a form of appointment with privilege of entry but without specific work) 南書房行走 privilege to be attached to emperor's reading room.

行蹤 *shirngtzung*, n., person's whereabouts: 行蹤靡定 (LL) movements very uncertain; 行蹤詭秘 mysterious movements.

行資 *shirngtzy*, n., travelling expenses.

行爲 *shirngweir* (**shihng-*), n., (1) conduct; (2) (law) overt act; (3) (psych.) behavior, response to stimuli: 行爲論 behaviorism; 行爲科學 behavioral science.

行文 *shirng-wern*, v.i., (1) to write (beautifully, etc.); (2) to communicate officially.

行伍 **harngwuu*, n., military rank and file.

行業 **harngyeh*, n., a profession, a trade.

行醫 *shirng-yi*, v.i., to practise medicine.

行役 *shirng-yih*, v.i., (AC) go on a mission; serve as soldier away from home.

行營 *shirngyirng*, n., military camp, field headquarters.

行員 **harngyuarn*, n., staff member of business firm.

行轅 *shirngyuarn*, n., official residence of high officer or general during travel.

行窳 **harngyuu*, adj., (AC, of goods) flimsy, of shabby quality.

衎 91B.00-3

kahn.

Adj. & adv. (LL) contentedly, happily.

衙 91B.00-3

yar.

N. A government office, a magistrate's office: 衙門, 衙署 *-'men*, *-shuu*↓; 衙役 *-'yi*↓.

衙前 *yar-chiarn*, n., (MC) see *-'yi*↓.

衙集 *yar-jir*, v.i., (LL) to assemble.

衙吏 *yar-lih*, n., government clerk.

衙門 *yar'men*, n., "yamen," government office (cf. 牙^門 51.00).

衙內 *yarneih*, n., palace guard.

衙署 *yarshuu*, n., government office.

衙役 *yar'yi*, n., runners or servants of a government office, known for harassing the people.

得 91B.00-4

der (**deei*, **daai*).

Aux. vb. (1) (**deei*) Ought, should: 你也得想一想 you should think a little; 你得小心 you must be careful; 不得不 *burder'bu*, cannot but, have to: 不得不去一趟 have to go personally; 叫人不得不生氣 cannot help being angry. (2) (**deei*) Indicating continuous mood: 我(正)得做 I am (in the process of) doing. (3) (*der*) May, have the right to: 得申請重審 may ask for retrial; 得由常委解決之 may be decided by the Standing Committee. (4) (*der*) Able to, be enabled to: 接了來信，得悉(得知) I received your letter and was enabled to learn; 得聞 I learned; 復得相會 were able to meet again; 使得 enable to; 使得迅速了結 enable the matter to be closed quickly; see 得以 *-yii*[1]↓.

Part. (1) (*'de*) Particle (after vb.) introducing adv. or complement: 看得見 can see; 走得到 can reach by foot; 看得清楚 can see clearly; 病得利害 severely sick; 悶得慌 terribly bored; 來得巧 come at opportune moment; 虧得你來 luckily you have come; 說得過去 make sense; 說得天花亂墜 talk until the roof falls down. (2) (*'de*) As part of vb. or vb. complement with sense of "succeed in": 記得 remember: 記不得 cannot remember; 拿得，獲得，收得 receive; 聽得 hear. (3) (*der*) (After vb.) somewhat like "-able": 吃得嗎 is this eatable? 吃不得 not eatable; 說不得 can't talk about; 提不得 not to be mentioned; 禁不得 cannot help; 怪不得 not surprising that.

V.t. (1) Get, obtain, have: 得到 *der-dauh*, receive, get; 得不到，不着 *der-bur-dauh*, *--jaur*, could not get; 得彩，缺 get a lottery prize, a post; 得子 have a son born; 得病 become sick; 得益，得利 get benefit, profit; 得救，得生 be saved, be enabled to live; 得閒(閑)，得空兒，得暇 when you have time; 得便 whenever convenient; 得助 receive help; 得寸進尺 give an inch and he will take a foot; 得隴望蜀 the more one receives, the more one wants; 得魚忘筌 see 筌 92A.11. (2) To achieve in various senses: 得意，得志，得道，得勢 *-yih*, *-jyh*, *-dauh*, *-shyh*↓; to win: 得民心 win people's loyalty; 得天下 conquer the world; 相得 (friends) like each other; 相得益彰 benefit by association together. (3) (**daai*) Get suffer in: 得苦子 receive suffering.

得便 *derbiahn*, adv. phr., whenever convenient.

得竅 *derchiauh*, v.i., have the knack.

得寵 *derchuung*, v.i., be in ruler's or master's favor.

得當 *derdahng*, adj., proper: 辦事得當 do a thing properly.

得道 *derdauh*, v.i., achieve wisdom or sainthood.

得得 *derder*, adv., (MC) especially; descriptive of walking.

得法 *derfaa*, adv., all in proper form.

得非 *derfei*, adv., (MC) perhaps, it could be (＝莫非).

得過 *derguoh*, v.i., can pass: 得過且過 let well enough alone.

得計 *derjih*, v.i., succeed: 自以為得計 thinks he has succeeded in plan.

得勁(兒) *derjihn(-jieh'l)*, adv., smoothly, as one wished.

得救 *derjiouh*, v.i., be saved (from sin, drowning).

得及 *derjir*, vb. complement, in 來得及 still in time; 來不及 too late.

得中 *derjung*, adv., (1) just right, not overdone; (2) *-juhng*, win prize, get degrees.

得志 *derjyh*, v.i., attain one's ambition, enjoy success.

得了 (1) *der'le*, excl., well! well! it's enough! have done with it! (2) (*-liaau*) adv., in 不得了 cry or statement about s.t. disastrous, very, very upsetting; 怎麼得了 how will all this end? (Cf. 了不得 very good indeed).

得臉 *derliaan*, v.i., gain face or favor.

得力 *derlih*, adj., (1) reliable, efficient, most capable (assistant, friend); (2) v.i., benefit very much (from person, influence).

得人 *derrern*, adj., popular; having able assistants: 得人心 enjoying people's support.

得勝 *dersheng*, v.i., triumph at battle, contest.

得手 *dershoou*, adv., smoothly: 做事得手 work smoothly.

得數 *dershuh*, n., (math.) answer, solution.

得勢 *dershyh*, adj., in power, in advantageous position.

得時 *dershyr*[1], adj., in luck, riding the crest of fortune.

得失 *der-shyr*[2], n., (1) hits and misses, gains and losses: 所得不償所失 gains cannot offset losses; (2) mishaps: 有什麼得失 should anything go wrong.

得所 *dersuoo*, adj., have nice place or position, esp. 得其所.

得體 *dertii*, adj., in proper form or correct style (of writing, behavior).

得罪 *dertzueih*, (1) v.i., violate law; (2) v.t., to offend (s.o.); (3) 得罪得罪 phr., I apologize (for intrusion, etc.).

得樣(兒) *deryahng('l)*, adj., (coll.) attractive-looking (of woman).

得意 *deryih*, adj., proud, satisfied: 非常得意 very proud and satisfied; 得意揚揚 (or 洋洋) ditto.

得以 *deryii*[1], aux. vb., can, able to, so that one can: 得以安居樂業 be able to live happily.

得已 *deryii*[2], adv., in 不得已 against one's will.

得宜 *deryir*, adj. & adv., very proper, -ly, suitably arranged.

得用 *deryuhng*, adj., very usable.

衢 91B.00-4

chyur.

A

N. (LL) a thoroughfare, broad busy street: 通衢 broad avenue; 街衢 street in business section.

衢道 *chyurdauh*, n., a thoroughfare (also 衢塗).
衢路 *chyurluh*, n., ditto.
衢肆 *chyursyh*, n., (LL) shopping streets.

衕 91B.00-4

tuhng.

N. See 衚^衕 91B.00.

衒 91B.00-6

shyuahn.

[Largely interch. 炫 91D.93]

V.i. To show off, oft. with intent to deceive: 自衒 to show off; 衒賣, 衒鬻 (AC) show off one's wares for sale; 衒玉賈石 (AC) display as jade and sell stone; 衒俏 (AC) sell one's charms, to flirt (=賣俏).

Adj. Proud: 衒士, 衒學之士 proud or pedantic scholar.

衒弄 *shyuahnnuhng*, v.i. & t., to show off, be pedantic.
衒耀 *shyuahnyauh*, v.i., to show off.
衒異 *shyuahnyih*, v.i., to attract attention by novelty.

衍 91B.00-6

yaan.

[Related 演 development, 63A.80]

N. (AC) a bamboo basket.

B

Adj. (1) Sprawling, overflowing: 衍溢 (AC) spreading abroad; 豐衍 (AC) full, abundant; 曼衍, 繁衍 to multiply greatly; 敷^衍 10S.82; 平衍 stretching far and wide. (2) Redundant: 衍文 *-wern* ↓.

衍文 *yaan-wern*, n., passage that appears twice in same book.

銜 91B.00-8

shiarn.

[Related 含 *harn*]

N. (1) The bit in horse's mouth. (2) Official rank: 官銜, 職銜, 頭銜 ditto; 虛銜 an empty title.

V.t. (1) To bite, hold in mouth: see 銜枚, 銜環, etc. *-meir*, *-huarn* ↓; 銜尾 (animals) arrive in packs (snouts and tails together). (2) To carry (official order): 銜令, 銜命 ditto. (3) To harbor (hatred, grudge), to cherish (gratitude), nurse (sorrow).

銜璧 *shiarn-bih*, phr., (AC) to surrender by carrying a piece of jade in mouth as pledge.
銜泣 *shiarnchih*, v.i., to sob.
銜恩 *shiarn-en*, v.i., to cherish gratitude.
銜感 *shiarngaan*, v.i., ditto.
銜恨 *shiarn-hehn*, v.i., harbor a grudge.
銜環 *shiarn-huarn*, phr., (allu.) a bird returns with rings in its mouth thanking owner for freedom: 銜環以報 will repay with gratitude.
銜接 *shiarnjie*, v.i., (two sections) connect up: 不相銜接 do not connect up properly.
銜結 *shiarn jier*, phr., from 結草銜環, see *-huarn* ↑.
銜勒 *shiarnleh*, v.i., horse's bit and reins.
銜枚 *shiarn-meir*, phr., ancient custom of making soldiers march at night, biting a piece of wood in mouth, to prevent making noise; a custom of sending prisoner to execution gagged with piece of wood to prevent protesting innocence.

C

銜名 *shiarnmirng*, n., name and surname and rank of office, as shown on calling cards.
銜轡 *shiarn-peih*, n., bridle and reins.
銜恤 *shiarnshyuh*, v.i., (1) nurse a sorrow; (2) meet with death of parents.
銜冤 *shiarn-yuarn*, v.i., to suffer a miscarriage of justice: 銜冤而死 die with one's name uncleared.

衝 91B.00-9

chung (**chuhng*).

N. Strategic place: 要衝.

V.i. (1) To rush or dash forward: 直衝 ditto; 橫衝直撞 rush and swerve about madly; 衝撞 *-juahng* ↓; 衝進去 dash into (house). (2) To be in conflict with: 衝突 *-tur* ↓. (3) (**chuhng*) To fall asleep: 你別衝了 don't fall asleep; 衝盹兒 fall asleep. (4) (**chuhng*) In 衝著 happen, *-'je* ↓.

V.t. To strike: 衝陣 strike into enemy ranks; 衝鋒 *-feng* ↓.

Adj. (**chuhng*) (1) With full steam: 一股衝勁兒 full of spirit. (2) Rich, overflowing (style): 文氣很衝 ditto; 嗓子很衝 a rich, vibrant voice. (3) Straightforward: 口氣太衝 too blunt in speaking.

Prep. (**chuhng*) Toward: 衝你的面子 run smack up against you; 衝前走, 衝南走 go straight up, go south.

衝車 *chung-che*, n., (AC) a kind of

衢 衕 衒 衍 銜 衝

亅	小	⺊	十	土	ナ	卄	卜	丨	一	丅	フ	口	囗	冈	冂	厂	尸	亠	广	宀	丶	乚	弋	心	八	人	乂	冖	丆	丿	𠂉	く
00	01	02	10	11	12	20	21	22	30	31	32	40	41	42	50	51	52	60	61	62	63	70	71	72	80	81	82	83	90	91	92	93

chariot for breaking into enemy ranks.

衝動 *chungduhng*, (1) n., an impulse: 感情的衝動 an emotional impulse; (2) v.i. & t., to arouse, excite; to feel an impulse: 衝動起來 feel excited, aroused.

衝鋒 *chungfeng*, v.i., break into enemy ranks.

衝冠 *chung-guan*, phr., 怒髮衝冠 hairs stand on end with anger.

衝著 **chuhng'je*, phr., it happens, coincides: 衝著你來了 just at that moment you came in.

衝激 *chungji*, v.t., to dash against (rocks).

衝撞 *chungjuahng*, v.i. & t., to collide with (object); to rush against or about.

衝決 *chungjyuer*, v.i., break (dam), (dam) breaks; (troops) break out from siege.

衝尅 *chungkeh*, v.t., (of 五行 the five basic movements) to contradict or cancel out each other, to neutralize.

衝浪板 *chung-lahng-baan*, n., surf board.

衝力 *chunglih*, n., momentum.

衝陷 *chungshiahn*, v.t., to break into (enemy ranks); also 衝鋒陷陣 *-feng* ↑.

衝霄 *chung-shiau*, phr., to soar aloft (＝沖天).

衝突 *chungtur* (1) v.i., contradict: 互相衝突 contradict each other; (2) adj., contradictory: 衝突的; (3) n., conflict (of opinions, nations).

衝要 *chungyauh*, n., strategic point.

衡 91B.00-9

herng.

N. (1) Weighing scales: 權衡 the weight and beam in steelyard, a criterion. (2) Balance (of power): 平衡 equilibrium, stability; 爭衡 to match power, contend for mastery. (3) Cross yoke, cross bar in carriage (as var. of 横 10B.80). (4) A surname.

V.t. To weigh, judge, measure: 衡量 *-liarng* ↓; 權衡輕重 weigh importance; 衡之以新標準 to measure it by the new standard; 橫之以常情 judge it by common sense; 衡文 to grade examination essays; see 抗^A橫 10A.70.

Adj. Stable, balanced: 均衡, 平衡 balanced.

衡量 *herngliarng*, n. & v.t., a measure; to measure, to weigh.

衡山 *Herngshan*, n., the Heng Mountain in Hunan.

衡宇 *herngyuu*, n., the roof.

§91B.01 (彳/小)

徠 91B.01-1

laih.

V.t. Encourage (s.o.) to come over to one's side by showing him special favors: 勞徠 give gifts to (s.o.) to win his allegiance.

徐 91B.01-8

shyur.

N. A surname: 徐娘半老丰韻猶存 a charming woman in middle age.

Adj. & adv. Slow, -ly, leisurely: 徐行 walk slowly; 舒徐 leisurely; 徐顧 look about carefully.

徐步 *shyur-buh*, v.i., take a stroll.

徐緩 *shyurhuaan*, adj. & adv., slow, -ly.

徐徐 *shyurshyur*, adv., slowly, in a leisurely manner.

§91B.02 (彳/ㄗ)

很 91B.02-5

heen.

Adv. Very, much: 很多, 很好 very much (many), very good; 不很好 not very good; often in 得很 after adj. or vb.: 好得很, 快得很 very good, very fast; also before vbb.: 我很想去 I very much want to go, have a mind to; 很感謝你 thank you very much; 很對不起 very sorry for what happened; 很受打擊 received a heavy blow.

§91B.10 (彳/十)

律 91B.10-2

lyuh.

N. (1) Law, statute, regulation: 法律 law; 規律 regulations, rules; 軍律 military regulations, discipline; 刑律 criminal code; 校律 school discipline; 紀律 discipline. (2) Name of poetic form, see 律詩 *-shy*² ↓. (3) Standard pitch pipe, see 律呂 *-lyur* ↓.

V.t. To discipline, guide by principle: 律己甚嚴 guide his own conduct by severe rules; 律人 to measure others by certain standards; 律以重典 punish, deal with (person) by law against great crimes (such as treason).

律例 *lyuhlih*, n., statutes (litr. code and case law).

律令 *ltuhlihng*, n., command, order.

律呂 *lyuhlyur*, n., (AC) twelve standard pitch pipes of musical half-tones; musical scale in classical music.

律師 *lyuhshy*[1], n., lawyer, barrister, attorney.

律詩 *lyuhshy*[2], n., "standard" form of poetry, with strictly regulated tones and syllables, popular since Tarng Dynasty; 五律(七律) such poems of eight lines with five (seven) words each; 排律 standard poem with unlimited number of lines; see 絕$^{\Delta}$句 93B.70.

徉 91B.10-8

yarng.

V.i. See 徜$^{\Delta}$徉 91B.42.

§ 91B.11 (彳/土)

往 91B.11-6

waang (**wahng*).

V.i. Go: 往上海 go to Shanghai; 往返, 往來, 往復 *-faan, -lair, -fuh*↓.

Adj. Past: 往日, 往年, 往時 *-ryh, -niarn, -shyr*↓; 往景 past picture or situation; 往哲 sages of the past.

Prep. (Coll. also **wahng*) toward: 往上, 往下 up, upward, down, downward; 往東, 往西 (sp. pr. **wahng*) direction of car, etc., eastward, westward; 往前走 esp. (woman) to remarry ("pick up and go forward"); 往那兒去 where are you going?

往常 *waangcharng*, adv., usually, in the past, used to.

往初 *waangchu*, adv., formerly.

往返 *warngfaan*, adv., back and forth.

往復 *waangfuh*, adv., repeatedly, back and forth.

往古 *warngguu*, adj. & adv., in ancient times: 往古的事 ancient event.

往後 *waanghouh*, adv., (1) henceforth; (2) (*wahng-*) backward.

往還 *waanghuarn*, (1) adv., see *-fuh*↑; (2) v.i., to have social dealings with (person), see *-lair*↓.

往來 *waanglair*, v.i., (1) to have dealings with each other: 不相往來 have no dealings with each other; (2) visit and return visit.

往年 *waangniarn*, adv., in former year(s).

往日 *waangryh*, adv., in former days.

往昔 *waangshir*, adv., in early times.

往事 *waang-shyh*, n., things of the past.

往時 *waangshyr*, adv., formerly.

往往(兒) *warngwaang('l)*, adv., oftentimes, frequently (forget, etc.).

徨 91B.11-9

huarng.

Adj. Nervous, ill at ease; see 彷$^{\Delta}$徨 91B.50.

§ 91B.21 (彳/乚)

徭 91B.21-9

yaur.

N. Conscript labor: 徭役.

§ 91B.22 (彳/丨)

彿 91B.22-2

fur.

V.i. & t. See 彷$^{\Delta}$彿 91B.50.

徘 91B.22-2

pair.

[Dist. 俳, 排]

徘徊 *pairhueir*, v.i., to loiter around, linger around.

御 91B.22-9

yuh.

N. & adj. (1) His Majesty('s): 御前, 御駕, 御筆 *-chiarn, -jiah, -bii*↓. (2) Ladies-in-waiting at court: 嬪御. (3) A surname.

V.t. (1) To drive (a carriage), ride (horse), (var. 馭): 駕御 to control (person, machine), drive (horse, car, boat). (2) (LL) to "ride" a woman: 御女 sleep with woman; 進御 send lady in court to emperor's bedroom. (3) To handle affairs: 御世, 御事 *-shyh*[1,2]↓.

御寶 *yuh-baau*, n., imperial seal.

御筆 *yuh-bii*, n., imperial pen or handwriting.

御妻 *yuh-chi*, v.t., control the wife, "taming the shrew."

御前 *yuh-chiarn*, phr., in His Majesty's presence.

御風 *yuh-feng*, phr., (AC) to ride on the wind and fly.

御夫 *yuhfu*, v.t., control the husband.
御者 *yuh-jee*, n., (LL) a driver; (AC) retinue.
御駕 *yuh-jiah*, n., His Majesty's carriage or movements.
御街 *yuh-jie*, n., formerly, main highway in the capital.
御製 *yuh-jyh*, phr., (poem, composition) made by His Majesty, (porcelain, etc.) made by order of His Majesty.
御覽 *yuh-laan*, phr., seen or read by the emperor.
御林軍 *yuh-lirnjyun*, n., imperial guard.
御世 *yuh-shyh*^{1}, phr., to rule the empire.
御事 *yuh-shyh*^{2}, phr., to manage affairs.
御史 *yuhshyy*, n., formerly, the censor.
御賜 *yuh-tsyh (-syh)*, phr., given by the emperor.
御醫 *yuh-yi*, n., imperial physician.
御用 *yuh-yuhng*, phr., for the use of the emperor; employed by the emperor.
御宇 *yuh-yuu*, phr., government of the empire.

§ 91B.30 (彳/一)

征 91B.30-3

jeng.

N. A surname.

V.i. & t. (1) (AC & LL) to go on a journey, to travel: 征夫, 征途 *-fu, -tur*↓; 征雁 migratory geese; 征衣 travelling garment; 征帆 sailing boat; 征驂 riding horse on journey; 萬里長征 to go on a journey of thousands of miles; 征塵 the dust of journey. (2) To invade, to start a campaign: 征伐, 征討, 征服 *-far, -taau, -fur*↓; 遠征 a distant invasion. (3) To collect tax: 征稅 to tax, taxes; 征收 *-shou*↓.

征榷 *jengchyueh*, n., tax; (wine and tobacco) monopoly.
征伐 *jengfa (-far)*, v.t., to invade (country).
征夫 *jeng-fu*, n., (AC) a traveller.
征服 *jengfur*, v.t., to subdue (country, tribes).
征誅 *jengju*, v.t., to send out punitive expedition (against tyrant) with object of overthrowing his rule or against rebels.
征斂 *jengliahn*, v.t., to levy (taxes).
征旆 *jengpeih*, n., (LL) journey ("pennant" shown on missions).
征收 *jengshou*, v.t., to collect (tax).
征戍 *jengshuh*, v.i. & n., (sent on military) journey to frontier region.
征討 *jengtaau*, v.t., to campaign against (rebel, tyrant).
征途 *jeng-tur*, n., a long journey.

徑 91B.30-3

jihng.

N. (1) A narrow path: 曲徑 winding paths; 捷徑 a short cut; 小徑 a footpath; 徑路 *-luh*↓; 路徑 (lit. & fig.) a route, way, path; 行不由徑 don't take short cuts. (2) Diameter: 半徑 the radius; 徑三尺 three feet in diameter; 圓徑 diameter; 徑寸 one inch in diameter.

Adv. Straightforward, forthwith (interch. 逕): 徑行 *-shirng*↓.

徑路 *jihngluh*, n., a footpath.
徑賽 *jihngsaih*, n., (athletics) a track meet.
徑行 *jihngshirng*, v.i., act freely, impulsively.
徑庭 *jihngtirng*, adj., directly opposite, mutually incompatible: 大相徑庭 (AC) there is a vast difference between the two.

徂 91B.30-4

tsur.

V.i. (1) (AC) to go: 自東徂西 go from east to west. (2) U.f. 殂 to die, depart from life.

徂落 *tsurluoh*, v.i., (AC, of ruler) pass away.
徂謝 *tsurshieh*, v.i., (AC) to wither, die.
徂暑 *tsurshuu*, n., (AC) sixth lunar month, midsummer.

§ 91B.41 (彳/図)

徊 91B.41-4

huair (also *hueir*).

Adv. Back and forth: 徊翔 (of birds) wheel about in the sky; 徘徊 linger about; 低徊 linger buried deep in thought.

循 91B.41-9

shyurn.

V.t. (1) To follow (rules, precedents, customs): 循例 *-lih*^{2}↓; 循規蹈矩 obey the rules and regulations; 循俗 follow general practice; 循法 abide by the law. (2) To follow a course, an order, to trace: 循流而下 sail down the river, follow the river down; 循階而上 go up by the steps; 循路 follow the road; 循序 *-shyuh*↓; 循名責實 see that reality corresponds to claims or pretensions; 不循正道 (lit. & fig.) go astray, do not follow the regular teachings; 遵循 to follow instructions.

Adj. Law-abiding, upright (related 馴): 循吏 *-lih*^{1}↓; 循良 *-liarng*↓.

Prep. In the course of: 循月, 循日 after many months, days.

循便 *shyurnbiahn*, adv., (LL) at one's convenience.

循常 *shyurncharng*, adj. & adv., usual, -ly: 循常規矩 the usual customs or practices.

循分 *shyurn-fehn*, adv., according to one's duties.

循陔 *shyurngai*, v.i., (AC) to serve one's parents (from poem 南陔).

循環 *shyurnhuarn*, (1) adv., each in succession, by turns; continuously in a circle; (2) v.i., to revolve, circulate: 日月循環 the sun and moon follow their course; 循環小數 *--shiauushuh*, (math.) repeating decimal; 循環系統 *--shihtuung*, n., (physiol.) circulatory system; 血液循環 blood circulation; 商業循環 business cycle.

循良 *shyurnliarng*, adj., upright, law-abiding (officials).

循吏 *shyurnlih*[1], n., upright officials.

循例 *shyurnlih*[2], adv., according to rules.

循理 *shyurnlii*, adv., according to reason.

循行 *shyurnshirng*, v.i., go on a tour (also wr. 巡行).

循序 *shyurnshyuh*, adv., in proper order or sequence.

循循 *shyurnshyurn*, adj. & adv., gentle, -ly: 循循善誘 (AC & LL) (of a teacher) guide gently.

循俗 *shyurn-sur*, v.i., follow the customs.

循資 *shyurn-tzy*, adv., (LL, to promote) according to qualifications or seniority.

§ 91B.42 (彳/冈)

徜 91B.42-2

charng.

徜徉 *charngyarng*, v.i., to loiter.

徧 91B.42-6

biahn.

[Var. 遍 63D.83; dist. 偏 91A.42]

Adj. & adv. All, all around: 徧天下 all over the world; 徧地 everywhere on earth; 傳徧各地 spread all over the place; 走遍全國, 遊徧天下 travel all over the country, the world; 徧體鱗傷 whole body covered with wounds; 普徧 commonly known or seen.

§ 91B.50 (彳/冂)

彷 91B.50-6

parng (**faang*).

彷彿 **faangfu*, v.i. & t., (1) seem to: 彷彿是他 it seems to be he; 我彷彿記得 I seem to remember; 彷彿有這回事 have a vague idea that it did happen; (2) resemble: 他們兩人相彷彿 they resemble each other (also 髣髴).

彷徨 *parnghuarng*, v.i. & adj., to hesitate, hesitant.

彷徉 *parngyarng*, v.i., (AC) loiter.

徬 91B.50-6

parng (**bahng*).

V.i. (**bahng*) 徬行 run alongside.

徬徨 *parnghuarng*, v.i. & adj., to hesitate, be hesitant (also wr. 旁皇).

徇 91B.50-9

shyurn (**shyuhn*).

[Related 循, 巡, 殉 with different usage]

V.i. & t. (1) To give in to personal considerations: 徇私, 徇情 *-sy*, *-chirng* ↓; 徇義 *-yih* ↓. (2) (**shyuhn*) (AC) to parade: 徇行 (AC) to parade; 徇罰 to parade criminal. (3) (**shyuhn*) U.f. 殉 31S.50, to die a martyr for some cause.

Adv. (AC) all around: 徇通 *-tung* ↓.

徇情 **shyuhn-chirng*, phr., to give in to personal considerations.

徇私 *shyurn-sy*, phr., comply for personal or selfish motives, against law or justice.

徇通 *shyurntung*, adj., (AC) as in 思慮徇通 straight-thinking, clear-minded.

徇義 **shyuhn-yih*, phr., die for honor (also wr. 殉).

§ 91B.72 (彳/心)

德 91B.72-1

der.

N. (1) Virtue: 美德 beautiful virtues; power of Tao in action or Tao manifest in 道德經 *Dauhderjing*, book of Laotse 老子; particularly woman's virtue; 婦德 woman's virtue. (2) Moral character, personal character: 私德 private morals; 德行 moral conduct; 品德 a man's personal character; 德隆望重 of high character and great prestige; 進德修業 education in character and knowledge; 陰德 secret good

德 徯 微 徵

deeds, not for publicity; 公德 sense of social responsibility; 惡德 bad character; 喪德 wicked. (3) Act of kindness: 恩德 favor or act of kindness; 感恩戴德 feel debt of gratitude for some kind act.

V.t. 德之 (LL) feel grateful for some act.

Adj. 德政 good government; 德色 expression of pride or self-satisfaction.

德國 *Derguor*, n., Germany.
德化 *derhuah*, n., moral influence on the people.
德謨克拉西 *Dermorkehlashi*, n., (translit.) democracy.
德配 *derpeih*, n., (court.) (a person's) esteemed wife.
德性 *dershihng*[1], n., a man's moral character.
德行 *dershihng*[2], n., moral conduct.
德望 *derwahng*, n., a person's moral prestige.
德意志 *Deryihjyh*, n., Germany, translit. of Deutsch, -land.
德音 *deryin*, n., (court.) news from you.
德育 *deryuh*, n., moral education, cf. 智育, 體育 intellectual, physical education.

§91B.81 (彳/人)

徯 91B.81–9

shi.
[Related 蹊 40B.81]

§91B.82 (彳/乂)

微 91B.82–2

weir.

Adj. (1) Small, tiny, fine: 微小, 微妙 *-shiaau, -miauh*↓; 微忱 my little token of remembrance, etc.; 微菌 *-jyuhn*↓; 微不足道 insignificant, not worth mentioning. (2) Lowly, unnoticed: 卑微 low in social positive, humble (status); 微服, 微行 *-fur, -shirng*↓. (3) Roundabout: 微辭 *-tsyr*↓. (4) Declined: 衰微, (AC) 式微 (ruling house) on the decline.

Adv. A little: 稍微 a little (more, further, etc.).

Prep. But for: 微管仲 but for 管仲 (we would dress like barbarians); 微子之力 but for your help.

微波 *weir-bo*, n., (phy.) microwave.
微薄 *weirbor*, adj., meager (salary).
微分學 *weirfen-shyuer*, n., (math.) differential calculus, see *-jirfen*↓.
微服 *weir-fur*, v.i., to travel disguised as commoner, or in homely garment.
微賤 *weirjiahn*, adj., lowly (labor, people).
微晶 *weirjing*, n., (geol.) microlites; 微晶質 (geol.) microcrystalline.
微積分 *weirjirfen*, n., (math.) calculus.
微菌 *weirjyuhn*, n., bacteria (also 細菌, 微生物).
微旨 *weir-jyy*, n., profound meaning.
微粒子 *weirlihtzyy*, n., (zoo.) a tiny organism which destroys silkworms, *Glugea bombycis.*
微茫 *weirmarng*, adj., indistinct.
微眇 *weirmiaau*, adj., tiny; inscrutable.
微妙 *weirmiauh*, adj., excellent, mysterious, profound.
微弱 *weirruoh*, adj., weak, feeble (health).
微生物 *weirshengwuh*, n., see *-jyuhn*↑.
微小 *weirshiaau*, adj., small, little, insignificant.
微笑 *weirshiauh*, n. & v.i., give a wee smile.
微細 *weirshih*, adj., (1) very small; (2) extremely cautious, attentive to details.
微息 *weirshir*, adj., feeble; also phr., feeble breath, small profit, or interest.
微行 *weir-shirng*, v.i., travel in disguise.
微時 *weir-shyr*, adv., when one was small or unknown.
微血管 *weirshyuehguaan*, n., (biol.) capillaries.
微辭 *weir-tsyr*, n., covert criticism.
微言 *weir-yarn*, phr., 微言大義 the deeper political thoughts of Confucius, as expounded by 公羊.
微音器 *weiryinchih*, n., microphone.

徵 91B.82–2

jeng (**jyy*).

N. (1) (**jyy*) the note *sol* in pentatonic scale, see 五[4]音 31.30. (2) Evidence, proof, symbol: 象徵 characteristic, symbol (of progress, etc.); 徵兆, 徵驗 *-jauh*[2], *-yahn*↓; 明徵 clear evidence; 有徵 is supported by proof; 無徵之言 baseless talk; see V.t. 4↓.

V.t. (1) To enlist, recruit for government service: 徵兵 *-bing*↓; 徵募, 徵召 *-muh, -jauh*[1]↓; 徵才 call men to power. (2) To solicit, ask for (contributions, etc.): 徵稿 solicit articles for magazines; 徵文 ask for contributions of essays; 徵婚啓事 advertisement "marriage wanted"; 應徵, 徵答 answer to calls or requests. (3) To collect taxes: 徵稅 ditto; 徵斂, 徵收 *-liaan, -shou*↓. (4) To adduce or serve as evidence: 杞不足徵也 (AC) the city of Jii (杞) cannot provide adequate evidence (of the ancestral customs of 夏).

徵辟 *jengbih*, v.t., (AC) to appoint a scholar without degree or rank to office.
徵兵 *jeng-bing*, v.i., to recruit soldiers.
徵求 *jengchiour*, v.t., to ask for:

徵求同意 ask for consent; 徵求會員 canvass for new members; look for: 徵求材料 look for research material, etc.

徵調 *jengdiauh*, v.t., to recruit soldiers and requisition army supplies.

徵發 *jengfa*, v.t., ditto.

徵歌 *jeng-ge*, phr., call for sing-song girls to assist at dinners.

徵候 *jenghouh*, n., foreboding signs or indications.

徵召 *jengjauh*[1], v.t., to summon for imperial interview or appointment.

徵兆 *jengjauh*[2], n., omen, augury.

徵集 *jengjir*, v.t., to assemble, collect from the public (men, material, opinions).

徵逐 *jengjur*, v.i., to pursue after pleasures: 徵逐聲色 indulge in wine, song or with women, see *-ge* ↑.

徵斂 *jengliaan*, v.i., to collect (taxes).

徵募 *jenmuh*, v.t., to recruit (soldiers).

徵信 *jengshihn*, v.i., to show evidences, gain confidence: 不足徵信 credibility gap; 徵信錄 published account of receipts and expenditures; directory of credit information.

徵收 *jengshou*, v.t., to collect (dues, taxes).

徵士 *jeng-shyh*, n., formerly, scholars who have received emperor's call to service.

徵詢 *jengshyurn*, v.t., to gather or ask for: 徵詢意見, 同意 ask for opinion, consent.

徵驗 *jengyahn*, n., evidence, proof of results.

徵引 *jengyiin*, v.t., to quote from books, to adduce (proof).

徽 91B.82–2

huei.

N. (1) An insignia, emblem: 校徽 school emblem; 國徽 national emblem. (2) Flags of different commands. (3) A stop on a lute: 十三徽 thirteen stops. (4) Short for 安徽 Anhwei Province: 徽墨 Anhwei ink cake.

Adj. Excellent; beautiful.

徽號 *hueihauh*, n., (1) insignia on flags; (2) title of praise.

徽章 *hueijang*, n., a medal of honor; a medal (of school, organization).

徽音 *hueiyin*, n., (1) sound of lute or other string instruments; (2) (court.) your news.

黴 91B.82–2

meir.

N. (1) Short for 黴菌 *-jyuhn*↓. (2) Var. of 霉 31D.50.

黴毒 *meirdur*, n., as var. for 梅毒 syphilis.

黴菌 *meirjyuhn*, n., bacteria, virus.

彼 91B.82–2

bii.

Pron. (AC) (LL) he; him (equiv. vern. 他): 彼曰 he says; 彼哉, 彼哉 oh, that fellow! 彼亦人也, 我亦人也, 吾何畏彼哉 he is a man, I am also a man, why should I be afraid of him? 彼一時也, 此一時也 the times are different, not comparable; 彼蒼者天 phr., the sky as personified dispenser of justice.

Adj. (LL) that, the other: 彼時, 彼地 that time, that place; 彼人 that person (equiv. vern. 那); 彼此 *-tsyy*↓.

彼岸 *bii-ahn*, n., (Budd) the other shore of salvation, as contrasted with the bitter sea 苦海 of this sentient life.

彼得 *Biider*, n., Peter.

彼利時 *Biilihshyr*, n., Belgium.

彼此 *birtsyy*, adv., one another, each other: 彼此推讓, 和好 courteous, friendly to one another; 彼此懷恨 entertain hatred one for the other; 彼此之間 between the two of them; "彼此彼此" indulge in routine courteous remarks; 不分彼此 share together.

役 91B.82–4

yih.

N. (1) (LL) battle: 滑鐵盧之役 the Battle of Waterloo. (2) Labor, labor service, conscript labor: 勞役 labor service; 軍役, 兵役 military service; 于役 (AC) serve in army; 役戍 conscript labor in border regions; 現役軍人 soldier on military service. (3) Servant, worker: 差役 petty officer, office servant; 工役 laborer; 僕役 servant in gen.; 衙役 lictors, runners, underlings in *yamen* 衙門, magistrate's office; 役夫 worker in public works or army; 捕役 warrant officer in charge of arresting offenders.

V.i. (1) To serve labor at frontier. (2) To command or order s.o. as servant, be master of: 役使 *-shyy*↓; 以心爲形役 make the mind slave to the body's material needs; 役物, 不役於物 be master, and not slave, of material things.

役夫 *yihfur*, n., servant, laborer.

役人 *yihrern*, n., ditto.

役屬 *yihshuu*, v.t., (AC) to control as master.

役使 *yihshyy*, (1) n., servant, messenger; (2) v.t., to control and order about (s.o. to do).

役損 *yihsuun*, v.t., (MC) to weak-

亅	小	⺊	十	土	ナ	廾	ㄩ	丨	一	丁	フ	口	区	冈	冂	厂	尸	亠	广	宀	丶	乚	弋	心	八	人	乂	一	一	ノ	⺈	く
00	01	02	10	11	12	20	21	22	30	31	32	40	41	42	50	51	52	60	61	62	63	70	71	72	80	81	82	83	90	91	92	93

en through overwork or cause to weaken one's health.

役卒 *yihtzur*, n., petty officer; *yamen* servant.

役役 *yihyih*, (AC) (1) v.i., to belabor, overwork; (2) adj., servile.

徹 91B.82–6

cheh.

[Cf. 澈, 撤]

V.t. & adj. Penetrate, penetrating, through and through; thoroughgoing (usu. interch. 澈): 徹上徹下 up and down everywhere; 徹頭徹尾 from beginning to the end; 透徹(澈) very clear (exposition); 通徹 thorough.

徹底 *chehdii*, adv., thorough, -ly: 徹底查辦 get to the bottom (of illegal activities) also wr. 澈底.

徹骨 *chehguu*, adv., to the bones: 徹骨兒相思 deep longing in the blood; 徹骨貧 poor and bare to the bones.

徹夜 *chehyeh*, adv., all night (gambling, etc.).

儌 91B.82–9

jiauh (**jiaau*, **yau*).

N. The frontier or border: 邊儌 frontier areas; 儌外 lands across the border.

V.t. (1) Inspect: 儌巡 go on a tour of inspection. (2) (**yau*) Pray for: 儌福 ask the gods for blessing.

Adj. (**jiaau*) Lucky: 儌幸 *-shihng* ↓.

儌幸 **jiaaushihng* (*jiau-*), adv., by a lucky chance (escape, etc.) (also wr. 僥, 僥).

復 91B.82–9

fuh (**fouh*).

V.i. & t. (1) V.i., to revenge: 報復, 復仇 ditto. (2) To restore, return to+n.: 復業 re-establish business; 復職 resume post; 復工 return to work after stoppage; 而復其初 return to original nature; 恢復 restore; 反復 again and again; see 光△復, 22.70; 復古, 復旦, 復舊 *-guu*, *-dahn*, *-jiouh* ↓. (3) To reply: 答復, 回復 v.i. & t. & n., reply to letter; 照復 (formal) reply.

Adv. (1) (*fuh*, **fouh*) Again, repeatedly (LL for vern. 又): 復來了 come back again; 舊病復發 old disease again comes back; 復來相擾 came again to bother; 復歸於好 become reconciled; 故態復萌 old habits come back. (2) Next: 復言其不得已之故 next (continued to) say why he was forced to do this; 復思 then think (or thought).

復辟 *fuh-bih*, n. & v.i., restore monarchy.

復權 *fuhchyuarn*, n., restoration of right.

復旦 *fuh-dahn*, v.i., to restore former brilliance.

復古 *fuh-guu*, v.i., to restore ancient ways.

復合 *fuhher*, v.i., reunite.

復活 *fuhhuor*, n. & v.i., resurrection, revive; 復活節 Easter.

復健 *fuhjiahn*, n., rehabilitation.

復舊 *fuh-jiouh*, v.i., restore, return to old (condition, etc.).

復命 *fuh-mihng*, n. & v.i., report on completion of mission.

復信 *fuh-shihn*, n. & v.i., reply (letter).

復興 *fuhshing*, n. & v.i., renew, regain new strength, revive: 文化復興 cultural renaissance.

復又 *fuhyouh*, adv., again, see Adv. 1↑.

復原(元) *fuhyuarn*[1], n. & v.i., old pattern, restore to health.

復員 *fuhyuarn*[2], n. & v.i., demobilization of soldiers.

後 91B.82–9

houh.

N. (1) Posterity: 不孝有三, 無後爲大 "Of the three sins of lack of filial piety, the greatest is to have no sons"—a quotation from Mencius, later much used as justification for concubinage. (2) The back, backside: 後面, 後頭, 後邊兒 *-miahn*, *-'tour*, *-bia'l* ↓. (3) A surname.

Adj. & adv. (1) Behind back, rear, opp. 前: 瞻前顧後 watch in front and behind—cautious, also irresolute, wavering; 前後受敵 attacked by enemy in front and behind; 後排 the rear row; 後房 back room; where the concubines live; 後院, 後花園 back court, rear garden; 後門 back door; 後街 back street; 後牙 the back teeth; 後腿 hind leg; 後腰 the small of the back. (2) Afterward, later in time, opp. 先: 先後 in succession; 後半天, 後晌兒 afternoon; 後半晌兒 in late afternoon; 後半夜 time after midnight; 後妻 second wife; 後起之秀 the bright younger generation; 後輩, 後代, 後生, 後進, 後人 *-'beih*, *-daih*, *-sheng*, *-jihn*, *-rern* ↓; 以後, 然後 and then, later; 後命 a later order; 松柏後凋 evergreens (pine and cypress) survive winter best—reference to test of time in man's moral character. (3) Future: 後世, 後患 *-shyh*[2], *-huahn* ↓. (4) After next: 後天, 後日, 後兒 day after tomorrow; 後年 year after next. (5) Succeeding: 後任 successor.

後輩 *houh'beih*, n., the younger generation.

後備軍 *houhbeihjyun*, n., army reserves.

後邊兒 *houhbia'l*, n., the back, the rear.

後部 *houhbuh*, n., the rear part, the later part (of a novel, army, etc.).

後補 *houhbuu*, v.i. & t., (1) make amends; (2) replenish.

後塵 *houh-chern*, n., (LL) as in

A

步後塵 follow footsteps of predecessor (including mistakes).

後程 *houhcherng*, n., (1) formerly, reserve fund of a shop; (2) future prospect (＝前程); (3) durability: 看那單薄的沒後程的東西 such flimsy article.

後妻 *houh-chi*, n., second wife, see *-muu*↓.

後期 *houh-chir*, n., some future date; later period.

後勤 *houchirn*, n., (mil.) logistics.

後代 *houh-daih*, n., posterity, later generations.

後盾 *houhduhn*, n., backing, support.

後方 *houhfang*, n., (mil.) the rear (opp. the front), the people living in the rear during war.

後房 *houh-farng*, n., concubines in gen.

後夫 *houh-fu*, n., second husband.

後福 *houh-fur*, n., luck in later life.

後趕着 *houhgaan'je*, (1) v.i., to run after, to follow another in journey; (2) adv., (make a dress, etc.) at the last minute.

後鈎兒 *houhgou'l*, n., (1) loose ends, unfinished business; (2) (Chin. opera) lingering tone.

後顧 *houh-guh*, phr., 後顧之憂 cares at home, family considerations that cause delay in decision.

後宮 *houhgung*, n., royal harem; gen. term for queen and maids of different ranks.

後果 *houhguoo*, n., results, consequences: 前因後果 cause and effect in human life.

後患 *houh-huahn*, n., future trouble.

後悔 *houhhueei*, v.i., to repent, regret: 後悔莫及 too late to regret it; 後悔藥兒 "medicine for (increasing) regret"—things said to cause person to remember with deepened regret.

後婚兒 *houhhue'l*, n., a remarried woman.

後會 *houh-hueih*, phr., future reunion: 後會有期 we may meet again.

後罩房 *houhjauh-farng*, n., building just back of the living

B

court.

後繼 *houhjih*, n. & v.i., successor, to succeed.

後進 *houhjihn*, n., the younger generation (gen. of scholars); a backcourt.

後勁 *houhjihng*, n., (1) delayed effect of certain wines; (2) (mil.) a strong reserve force.

後脊梁 *houhjir'liang*, n., backbone.

後肢 *houh-jy*[1], n., (zoo.) hind legs; worm's legs near the tail end.

後知 *houh-jy*[2], n., as in 後知後覺 from 先知覺後知, 先覺覺後覺 those who believe and follow the seer (先覺 the forerunner of thought).

後兒 *houh'l*, n., (coll.) day after tomorrow.

後來 *houhlair*, adv., (1) later, later on; (2) come later: 後來居上 phr., successors excel the predecessor.

後臉兒 *houhliaa'l*, n., a man's back, backside: 看後臉兒好像某人 look like s.o. as seen from the back.

後路 *houhluh*, n., (mil.) back route: 抄後路 circumvent enemy (to attack from the rear); 後路兵到 troops come up from the back; 留後路 leave way of escape, room for retreat.

後媽 *houhma*, n., stepmother (also *-muu*).

後面(兒) *houh'mian(-'miah'l)*, n. & adv., back, at the back, behind: 走在你後面兒 walk behind you; 後面兒有人 there is s.o. behind.

後母 *houhmuu*, n., stepmother.

後腦杓子 *houh-naaushaur'tz*, n., back of the head.

後娘 *houhniarng*, n., stepmother (also *-muu*↑).

後人 *houhrern*, (1) n., posterity; (2) 不敢後人 phr., dare not fall behind others—must do my share.

後日 *houhryh*, adv., (1) day after tomorrow; (2) in later days.

後身 *houhshen*, n., (1) life in the next incarnation; (2) the back of dress; (3) the backside of a

C

street.

後生 *houhsheng*, (1) n., one of younger generation: 後生可畏 phr., commending a bright young man or scholar; (2) adj., (MC) young: 後生子 those of younger generation.

後項 *houhshiahng*, n., (algebra) the second term, the last term; the latter item.

後效 *houhshiauh*, n., after effect.

後心 *houhshin*, n., back of chest (in dress).

後手 *houhshoou*[1], n., (1) the successor (to a piece of property), or buyer who takes over; (2) ground for retreat: 做事須留後手兒 one must not push things (or opponent) too far, but provide for future contingency; (3) (chess) player who remains on the defensive (opp. 先手 one who takes the offensive).

後首 *houhshoou*[2], adv., later, afterwards (＝後來).

後市 *houhshyh*[1], n., (stock market) over the counter, business deals done in the afternoon.

後世 *houhshyh*[2], n., future generations.

後事 *houhshyh*[3], n., (1) funeral affairs: 料理後事 make arrangements for funeral; (2) later developments (as in a novel).

後學 *houhshyuer*, n., (1) (court. speaking of oneself to older scholar) a pupil or scholar of younger age; (2) scholars of later days: 後學兒 learned after school or independently.

後嗣 *houhsyh*, n., progeny.

後臺 *houhtair*, n., backstage, behind the curtains: 後臺老板 producer of play, etc., or one who gives financial support, director (of activities) behind the scenes.

後天 *houhtian*, n., day after tomorrow.

後庭 *houhtirng*, n., inner palace, backyard, backcourt: 隔江猶唱後庭花 (allu.) still live a gay life after one's country is lost.

後頭 *houh'tour*, n., back, back side; in time to come: 吃苦在後頭 will suffer in time to come.

後槽 *houh-tsaur*, n., stables,

horse's feeding trough; (MC) driver.

後圖 *houh-tur*, n., plans for the future.

後子 *houh-tzyy*, n., progeny.

後尾兒 *houhwee'l*, n. & adv., the end, at the end.

後衛 *houhweih*, n., (1) rearguard; (football) fullback, (basketball) guard.

後裔 *houhyih*, n., progeny, children and grandchildren of many generations.

後應 *houhyihng*, n., military support action from the rear or elsewhere.

後影兒 *houhyiing'l*, n., person's figure as seen from the back: 後影兒好像她 a figure looks like her, as seen from the back.

後援 *houhyuarn*, n., (mil.) reinforcements.

§ 91B.83 (彳/一)

徒 91B.83-1

tur.

[Dist. 徙 91B.83]

N. (1) Disciples: 門徒 disciples; 徒子徒孫 generations of followers of a school. (2) Followers of a group, gang: 教徒 followers of a religion; 叛徒 rebels; 酒徒 drunkards; 匪徒 bandits; 無賴之徒 group of ruffians.

Adj. Barehanded: 徒手 barehanded; 徒手致富 make a fortune starting from scratch; 徒步, 徒行 go on foot; 徒跣 (LL) barefoot(ed); 徒搏 fight barehanded; 徒杠 footbridge.

Adv. In vain, merely: 徒有其表 have good appearance only (of man); 徒有皮毛 superficial, without substance; 徒勞無功(無補, 無益) work in vain, wasted effort; 徒托空言 make empty promises; 徒喚奈何 regret in vain; 非徒 not only; 非徒無益, 而又害之 worse than useless; 非徒如此 not only this (=非但); 徒費脣舌 waste one's breath.

徒兵 *turbing*, n., foot soldier (=步兵).

徒步 *turbuh*, adv., on foot.

徒弟 *tur'di*, n., monk's or boxer's disciple; apprentice in trade, crafts.

徒然 *turrarn*(-*'ran*), adv., in vain: 徒然無功 in vain, without results.

徒刑 *turshirng*, n., (law) hard labor.

徒手 *turshoou*, adv., barehanded.

徙 91B.83-2

shii.

V.i. & t. (LL) to change sites, to move residence: 遷徙 to move home to a new place; 徙貫 change place of residence; 徙任 change to another post.

徙邊 *shii-bian*, v.i., to move population to a frontier region.

徙倚 *shiryii*, v.i., (MC) to linger in hesitation.

從 91B.83-8

tsurng (**tzung*, **tzuung*, **tzuhng*).

[Var. 从]

N. (1) (**tzuhng*) (LL) retinue, follower: 僕從 retinue; 隨從, 侍從 entourage, retinue officer; 從者 -*jee*↓. (2) (*tsurng*) (AC) 三從 three obediences of a woman: 從父, 從夫, 從子 follow father before marriage; follow husband after marriage; follow son when husband dies. (3) (**tzuhng*) Accessory (to crime): 首從 principal accessory. (4) (**tzung*) (In sense of verticle) u.f. 縱 93B.83.

V.t. (1) To follow: 跟從, 隨從 to follow (another); 依從 to comply with (s.o.'s wish); 順從 obey (wish, order); 從他意思, 命令 conform to his wish, obey his orders; 從其所欲 follow what he desires, let him have his way; 從其言 take his advice; 從其計 adopt his plan; 從衆議 abide by majority's opinion; 任從你辯, 求 however you argue, beg; 曲從其意 let him have his wish (against precedent, rules, other considerations); 天從人願 if God (Heaven) is willing, follows human wish; 從善如流 do good naturally and happily; 從一而終 (of wife) be faithful to husband unto death. (2) To take up as main work or profession: 從政, 從事, 從軍 -*jehng*, -*shyh*, -*jyun*↓.

Adj. (1) (**tzuhng*) Next in kin: 從父, 從母 uncle, aunt; 從兄弟 first cousin brothers; 從女, 從子 niece, nephew. (2) (**tzuhng*) Accessory to principal criminal: 從犯. (3) Assistant to superior: 從吏 staff member under official; 從祀 -*syh*↓.

Adv. (1) Ever, since: 從未, 從不, 從沒 never (seen it, etc.); 從未間斷 never stopped or interrupted (work); 自從 since (you arrived, etc.); 從來, 從頭 -*liar*, -*tour*↓. (2) And then proceed to: 從而責之 and then blame him for it; 從而取利 and then profit by it.

Prep. (1) From: 從上而下 from above down; 從天下來 come down from heaven; 從那兒來 where do you come from? 從今起 from now on; 從左至右 from left to right; 從頭 from the beginning, see -*tour*↓; 從小(兒)就這樣 was so from childhood; 從旁觀看 see it from the side; 從中取利 profit thereby, therefrom; 從另一方面講 to view it from another angle; 從頭到尾 from A to Z, from beginning to end. (2) Rather, leaning to (strictness, leniency, etc.): 從寬, 從嚴辦理 settle case (punishment, etc.) rather on the lenient, strict side; 從早, 從速 -*tzaau*, -*suh*↓; 從緩 -*huaan*↓; 從長 -*charng*↓; 從便 -*biahn*↓; 從豐, 從優 (give) as generously as possible; 從容 *-rurng*[2] ↓.

從便 *tsurngbiahn*, adv., whenever convenient.
從長 *tsurncharng*, adv., as in 從長計議 take more time to consider it.
從前 *tsurngchiarn*, adv., formerly.
從權 *tsurngchyuarn*, adv., allowing flexibility to rules, to suit exigency; opp. 經 basic principle.
從打 *tsurngdaa*, adv., (dial.) since (that day, etc.).
從犯 **tzuhngfahn*, n., accessory to crime: 事後從犯 accessory after the fact.
從風 *tsurng-feng*, v.i., to follow a trend of the moment.
從父 **tzuhngfuh*, n., uncle.
從官 **tzuhngguan*, n., staff officer.
從公 *tsurng-gung*, phr., 枵腹從公 attend office on an empty stomach (with inadequate pay).
從衡 **tzung-herng*, n., vertical and horizontal: 合從連橫 (AC) opposite theories of vertical (north-south) and horizontal (east-west) alliance of states with 秦 *chirn* as pivot.
從緩 *tsurnghuaan*, adv., rather slowly, not in a hurry, putting off to a later time.
從者 **tzuhngjee*, n., (AC) followers.
從政 *tsurngjehng*, v.i., to go into politics, join government service.
從嫁 *tsurngjiah*, n., formerly, a maidservant who follows her young mistress to bridegroom's home.
從價稅 *tsurngjiahshueih*, n., *ad valorem* duty.
從吉 *tsurng-jir*, phr., (AC) temporarily take off mourning to attend another's wedding.
從軍 *tsurngjyun*, v.i., to join the army.
從來 *tsurnglair*, adv., always: 從來不 never.
從良 *tsurngliarng*, v.i., (of prostitute) marry into a decent family, to come back to normal civic life.
從龍 *tsurng-lurng*, phr., follow one destined to become emperor.
從命 *tsurngmihng*, v.i., to obey orders, instructions.
從母 **tzuhngmuu*, n., aunt, mother's sister.
從女 **tzuhngnyuu*, n., niece.
從人 *tsurngrern*, n., staff officer.
從戎 *tsurngrurng*[1], v.i., see *-jyun* ↑.
從容 *tsurngrurng*[2], adv., slowly, leisurely.
從心 *tsurng-shin*[1], phr., following one's bent: 力不從心 be unable to do as well as one would wish to; 從心所欲 do as one pleases.
從新 *tsurngshin*[2], adv., once again, anew.
從事 *tsurng-shyh*, v.i., to follow, attend (to certain avocation); set to do.
從兄弟 **tzuhngshyungdih*, n., first cousins.
從速 *tsurng-suh*, adv., as quickly as possible.
從俗 *tsurng-sur*, v.i., follow the general customs.
從祀 *tsurngsyh*, v.i., (1) to be included among spirits to be worshipped at a temple; (2) to assist at sacrificial ceremony.
從頭 *tsurngtour*, adv., from the beginning; once again: 從頭做起 do it all over again.
從此 *tsurngtsyy*, adv., henceforth, from now on.
從早 *tsurngtzaau*, adv., early in the morning: 從早到晚 from morning until night.
從坐 *tsurngtzuoh*, v.i., be sentenced as accomplice, or sharing guilt.
從子 **tzuhngtzyy*, n., nephew.

SECTION 91C

§ 91C.00 (犭/亅)

猘 91C.00–1

jyh.

N. (-'*l*) A fierce dog.

猗 91C.00–1

yi (**ee*).

Adj. (1) See compp. ↓. (2) U.f. 旖 60S.00.

Excl. (A sigh of praise) O! Great! 猗歟盛哉 (LL) O, great!

猗儺 **eenuor*, adj., (AC) pliable, pleasantly soft (figure).
猗猗 *yiyi*, adj., (AC) thriving (vegetation).

狩 91C.00–6

shouh.

V.i. (1) (AC) orig. winter hunt; (LL) to hunt in gen. (2) Make an imperial visit in the country: 巡狩 ditto.

狩獵 *shouhlieh*, v.i., to hunt, go on a hunting expedition.

獰 91C.00–6

nirng.

獰 猁 猙 獉 獠 猱 猻 猿 猥 狠 狼

Adj. 猙獰 Hideous, repulsive: 獰笑 a hideous, hypocritical smile; 獰醜 hideous looks; 獰惡 hideous and wicked.

猁 91C.00–9

lih.

N. See 猞▵猁 91C.40.

猙 91C.00–9

jeng.

猙獰 *jengnihng*, adj., ferocious, vicious (beast).

§ 91C.01 (犭/小)

獉 91C.01–1

jen.

Adj. Aspect of primitive jungle, see 獰 91C.00↑.

獠 91C.01–1

liaur.

N. (1) Monster: 撲殺此獠 have the wicked rascal killed! (2) Night hunt.

Adj. Wicked, fiendish: 青面獠牙 (of monster) with green face and ferocious fangs.

猱 91C.01–3

naur.

N. A kind of monkey: 猱升 climb a tree as nimbly as a monkey.

V.t. (MC) (interch. 撓) scratch: 心癢難猱 it's impossible to scratch an itching heart.

猻 91C.01–3

sun.

N. See 猢▵猻 91C.42.

§ 91C.02 (犭/k)

猿 91C.02–1

yuarn.

N. An ape: 猿猴 ditto; 人猿, 人形猿 anthropoid ape.

猥 91C.02–4

weei.

Adj. (1) Trivial, cheap: 猥瑣 *-suoo*↓; 猥賤 *-jiahn*↓. (2) Numerous.

Adv. (Court.) unworthily: 猥蒙不棄 unworthily received your attention (cf. similar use 忝 90.02).

猥賤 *weeijiahn*, adj., cheap, lowly.

猥褻 *weeishieh*, adj., obscene, indecent.

猥瑣 *weeisuoo*, adj., trivial, unbearably detailed.

狠 91C.02–5

heen.

[Var. of 很]

Adj. Malicious, vindictive, cruel and ruthless: 凶狠 ferocious.

狠毒 *heendur*, adj., venomous.

狠狠的 *hernheen'de*, adv., forcefully, without compunction, mercilessly (thrash, kick, etc.).

狠命 *heenmihng*, adv., see above↑.

狠心 *heenshin*, adj., cruel, ruthless.

狼 91C.02–6

larng.

N. (1) (Zoo.) the wolf: 狼吞虎咽 voracious, gluttonous; 狼嗥鬼叫 howls; 黃鼠狼 the weasel; used as symbol of beastly cruelty, greed, etc.; 狼子野心 a wicked monster; 狼心狗肺 beastly, completely without conscience; 狼貪虎視 insatiably greedy like wolves and tigers. (2) (Astron.) the Sirius. (3) A surname.

V.t. Intimidate, cheat: 狼人 threaten or swindle people.

狼把草 *larngbartsaau*, n., (bot.) swamp beggar's ticks, water hemp, *Bidens tripartita.*

狼狽 *larngbeih*, adj., (1) helplessly dependent, distressing: 進退狼狽 not knowing what to do; 狼狽失據 helpless and with nothing to fall back upon; 狼狽不堪 totally helpless; 狼狽萬狀 placed in an extremely embarrassing situation; 狼狽極了, 狼狽得很 in most distressed, hard-pressed condition; (2) 狼狽爲奸 work in collusion for some evil purpose; (3) evil person.

狼瘡 *larngchuang*, n., (med.) *lupus*, an ugly skin disease.

狼犬 *larngchyuaan*, n., (zoo.) the German shepherd dog, a police dog.

狼癲 *larngdian*, n., (med.) lycanthropy, disease in which one imagines himself to be a wolf (also 狼狂).

狼毒 *larngdur*, (1) adj., merciless, savage; (2) n., (herb med.) the wolfsbane, a poisonous plant believed to be good for relieving deafness.

狼狗 *larnggoou*, n., see *-chyuaan* ↑.

狼顧 *larng-guh*, adj., suspicious and nervous for fear of attack from behind; accustomed to casting backward glances from time to time as the wolves do.

狼毫 *larng-haur*, n., (Chin. callig.) a writing brush made of the hair of the Chinese weasel or wolf's hair.

狼貛 *larnghuan*, n., (zoo.) the wolverine, glutton, *Gulo luscus*.

狼藉 *larngjir*, adj., disorderly, messy, untidy, dishonorable: 杯盤狼藉 with wine glasses and plates spread all over a dining-table; 聲名狼藉 with a bad, tattered reputation.

狼抗 *larng'kang*[1], adj., (1) wily, crafty, stubborn, unyielding; (2) voracious, gluttonous; (3) heavy and clumsy.

狼犺 *larng'kang*[2], adj., see *-kang* ↑.

狼戾 *larnglih*, adj., (1) lying here and there, scattered all around: 樂歲粒米狼戾 grains abound in a bumper year; 流涕狼戾 with tears all over the face; (2) ruthless: 狼戾不仁 ruthlessly cruel; 狼戾無親 without natural affection.

狼木 *larngmuh*, n., (bot.) *Viburnum furcatum*.

狼崽子 *larngtzaai'tz*, n., (abusive) a beastly cruel or ungrateful person.

狼子 *larngtzyy*, n., (1) a greedy and cruel person: 狼子野心 a person greedy and cruel and full of wild ambitions; (2) see *-yar* ↓.

狼尾草 *larngweeitsaau*, n., (bot.) the foxtail, *Pennisetum japonicum*.

狼烟 *larng yan*, n., a beacon, a signal fire: 狼烟四起 warning signals of approaching enemy forces are seen on all sides.

狼牙 *larng yar*, n., (1) (bot.) the Nippon cinquefoil, *Potentilla cryptotaeniae*; (2) a wolf's teeth, anything looking like such: 狼牙拍, 狼牙棒 a bat, club with teethlike edges.

§ 91C.10 (犭/十)

犴 91C.10-3

ahn (**hahn*).

N. (1) Prison. (2) (**hahn*) A fierce Mongolian dog.

猝 91C.10-6

tsuh.

Adv. (LL) Suddenly: 猝然 ditto; 猝斃 die suddenly; 猝不及防 be caught off guard.

獐 91C.10-6

jang.

[Var. of 麞 61.10]

狎 91C.10-9

bah.

N. (AC) a short-necked dog.

獬 91C.10-9

shieh.

N. (AC) an anc. goat, reputed to gore guilty person at court, see 獬豸 *-jyh* ↓.

獬叭狗 *shiehba-goou*, n., Pekingese dog (＝哈叭狗).

獬豸 *shiehjyh*, n., 獬豸冠 (AC) cap worn by judge, symbolizing justice; see N. ↑.

§ 91C.11 (犭/土)

狴 91C.11-2

bih.

狴犴 *bih-ahn*, n., (LL) name of anc. beast, now signifying prison.

狂 91C.11-3

kuarng.

N. A mania, insanity, madness: 瘋狂 ditto; 發狂 become mad, furious; 書狂, 酒狂 mania for books, wine; 狂熱 a craze (for s.t.).

Adj. & adv. (1) Violent, wild, raging, frenzied: 狂風 violent storm; 狂瀾 roaring waves; 狂歡, 狂喜 mad with joy; 狂怒 furious; 狂歌, 狂笑, 狂飲 sing, laugh, drink heartily; 狂呼 scream aloud; 狂奔 rush madly. (2) Mad, crazy, insane: 狂人 mad person; 狂態, 狂相 crazy, wild manner; 狂話, 狂語 crazy talk. (3) Proud, impetuous, unruly, unrestrained:

輕狂 incautious, frivolous; 狂思亂想 imagine all sorts of ideas, indulge in fantasy; 狂狷 the impetuous and the overcautious, two types described by Mencius; 狂生, 狂士 unconventional, singular person; see 狂想 *-shiaang*, 狂妄 *-wahng*, 狂蕩 *-dahng*, 狂恣 *-tzyh*↓.

狂傲 *kuarng-auh*, adj., self-conceited.
狂暴 *kuarngbauh*, adj., violent (person, storm).
狂悖 *kuarngbeih*, adj., licentious, abandoned, defiant of convention.
狂犬病 *kuarngchyuaan-bihng*, n., (med.) rabies, hydrophobia.
狂蕩 *kuarngdahng*, adj., highly unconventional (talk, conduct), unrestrained.
狂放 *kuarngfahng*, adj., ditto.
狂人 *kuarngrern*, n., (1) a demented person; (2) (contempt.) a "nut," mentally unsound person.
狂想 *kuarngshiaang*, n. & v.i., fantasy, entertain a wild hope; 狂想曲 a rhapsody.
狂相(兒) *kuarngshiahng('l)*, n., wild manners, ways.
狂士 *kuarngshyh*, n., a self-conceited scholar.
狂草 *kuarngtsaau*, n., (callig.) a highly cursive script.
狂童 *kuarngturng*, n., (AC) juvenile delinquent.
狂恣 *kuarngtzyh*, adj., bloated, self-opinionated, extravagant (person).
狂妄 *kuarngwahng*, adj., (thoughts, conduct) wild, wanton.

猩 91C.11–4

shing.

N. 猩猩 the chimpanzee.

Adj. Scarlet, blood-red.

猩紅 *shinghurng*, adj., scarlet: 猩紅氈 a small scarlet carpet; 猩紅熱 scarlet fever.
猩色 *shingseh*, adj., see *-hurng*↑.
猩猩 *shing'shing*, n., the chimpanzee.

狸 91C.11–4

lir.

[Pop. of 貍 91S.11]

§91C.22 (犭/丨)

狒 91C.22–2

feih.

狒狒 *feihfeih*, n., a kind of monkey, *Cynocephalus hamadryas.*

狎 91C.22–4

shiar.

V.i. (1) To indulge in flirtations or intimacies with (favorites, girls): 狎近, 狎昵 *-jihn*, *-nih*↓. (2) To disregard formalities, take liberties.

狎近 *shiarjihn*, v.t., take liberties with (person).
狎客 *shiar-keh*, n., (1) customers at brothels; (2) frivolous persons.
狎弄 *shiarluhng*, v.t., to treat (person) cheaply or without respect, from intimacy.
狎昵 *shiarnih*, v.t., be on intimacies with (woman, favorite).
狎邪 *shiarshier*, v.i., to visit houses of ill fame: 作狎邪遊 or 狎斜遊 ditto.
狎翫 *shiarwahn*, v.i., to regard familiarly and cheaply (also wr. 狎玩).
狎侮 *shiarwuu*, v.i., to take liberties with (person); treat disrespectfully.

獅 91C.22–9

shy.

N. (*-tz*) The lion: 獅吼, 河東獅吼 (a) lioness's roar, describing fear of henpecked husband; (b) the voice of Buddha (also 獅子吼).

獅子狗 *shytz-goou*, n., the Pekingese dog.
獅子國 *Shytz-guor*, n., (Budd.) Ceylon.
獅子貓 *shytz-mau*, n., a species of cat with long hair and bushy tail.
獅子頭 *shytztour*, n., a kind of meat ball.

§91C.30 (犭/一)

狉 91C.30–3

pi.

[Var. of 豾]

N. A small species of fox.

狉狉 *pipi*, adj., (LL) (place) alive with wild animals.

猛 91C.30–3

meeng.

Adv. (1) Fierce, valiant: 猛將, 猛士 valiant general, brave soldier; 猛火 hot fire; 猛藥 potent medicine; 勇猛 brave; 凶猛 fierce, ferocious, esp. appearance. (2) Fearful: 苛政猛於虎 Confucius: "A bad government is more fearful than a tiger."

Adv. (1) Suddenly: 猛省, 猛悟 realize suddenly, with a start. (2) Fiercely: 猛攻, 猛擊 launch a fierce attack; 突飛猛進 make remarkable progress.

猛禽 *meeng-chirn*, n., birds of prey.

猛孤丁(的) *meengguding(de)*, adv., suddenly.

猛汞 *merngguung*, n., bichloride of mercury.

猛可(裏)(的) *merngker (lii) (de)*, adv., (MC) in a sudden moment.

猛烈 *meenglieh*, adj., fierce (blow, attack, fire).

猛戾 *meenglih*[1], adj., intractable.

猛力 *meeng-lih*[2], adj. & adv., with great force.

猛然 *meeng-rarn*, adv., suddenly (realize, remember).

猛獸 *meeng-shouh*, n., beasts of prey.

猛子 *meeng'tz*, phr., 扎猛子 (coll.) take a dive, plunge.

狙 91C.30-4

jyu.

N. A monkey.

V.t. To watch for: 狙擊 *-jir*↓; 狙殺 assassinate; 狙伺 *-shy*↓.

狙擊 *jyujir*, v.t., attack by surprise: 狙擊手 a sniper; 狙擊兵 soldiers in ambush.

狙伺 *jyusyh*, v.t., lie in wait for.

狃 91C.30-5

nioou.

V.i. & adj. (be) accustomed to; (be) inured to: 狃於陋習 (be) accustomed to bad habits; 狃習 (be) inured to old habits.

§ 91C.40 (犭/口)

㹞 91C.40-6

yirn.

Adj. Descriptive of dog's barking.

猞 91C.40-8

sheh.

N. 猞猁猻 *shehlihsun*, n., a kind of small Asiatic monkey.

§ 91C.41 (犭/囟)

猪 91C.41-1

ju.

[Pop. of 豬 31S.41]

猫 91C.41-2

mau.

[Pop. of 貓 91S.41]

猖 91C.41-4

chang.

Adj. Unruly, dissolute, licentious; rash, reckless.

猖獗 *changjyuer*, v.i., (of bandits) grow bold; adj., on the rampage.

猖狂 *changkuarn*, adj., (1) unrestrained, defiant; (2) rash, reckless.

猖披 *changpi*, v.i., see *-jyuer*↑.

猶 91C.41-8

your.

[Var. 犹]

N. A surname.

Adj. Just like: 猶如, 猶似 *-rur*, *-syh*↓.

Adv. (LL=modn. 還) still (can walk, can be saved): 猶可 still can; 猶復 still again; giving a concession: 猶可說也 granting that s.t. is excusable (but not more extreme steps); denoting "even this": 猶不足以果腹 not enough even to stop hunger; 猶恐或失 lest one should fail to do enough (even within this small task).

Conj. As if: 猶緣木而求魚 as if to climb trees looking for fish.

猶古自 *yorguutzyh*, phr., (Yuarn Dyn. dial.) see *-wuhtzyh*↓.

猶之乎 *your-jy-hu*, phr., just like.

猶然 *yourrarn*, adj. & adv., (1) still; (2) (AC) happy, contented (also wr. 攸然, 悠然, 逌然).

猶若 *yourruoh*, conj., as if, like.

猶如 *yourrur*, conj., as if, like.

猶似 *yoursyh*, prep. & conj., just like.

猶太 *Yourtaih*, n., Judea; 猶太人 a Jew.

猶自 *yourtzyh*, adv., still.

猶子 *yourtzyy*, n., nephew ("like a son").

猶 獪 猜 猢 獳 獮 狷 猬 猾 獼 獢

猶兀自 *yourwuhtzyh*, adv., (Yuarn drama) still (=modn. 尚自).

猶疑 *your'yi*, v.i., to pause and hesitate.

猶猶 *youryour*, adj., (AC) leisurely.

猶豫 *youryuh*, v.i., to hesitate.

猶女 *yournyuu*, n., a niece ("like a daughter").

獪 91C.41–8

kuaih.

Adj. Cunning: 狡獪.

§91C.42 (犭/冈)

猜 91C.42–1

tsai.

V.i. & t. (1) To feel jealous, to envy, suspect: 猜疑, 猜忌 *-yir*, *-jih* ↓; 兩小無猜 innocence of childhood friends. (2) To guess, play game of guessing: 猜拳, 猜謎, 猜枚 *-chyuarn*, *-mir*, *-meir* ↓; 猜不著, 猜不出, 猜不透 cannot guess; 猜著, 猜中 (*-juhng*) guess right; 猜字兒謾兒 guess heads or tails of coin; 猜猜看 try and guess; 胡猜亂想 make blind and disorderly conjectures.

猜拳 *tsaichyuarn*, v.i., to play finger-guessing game, guessing at the total of fingers put out by self and opponent.

猜貳 *tsai-ehl*, v.t., to suspect (person).

猜忌 *tsaijih*, v.i. & t., to be jealous of (person).

猜懼 *tsaijyuh*, v.i., to be suspicious and afraid.

猜悶兒 *tsaimeh'l*, v.i., (1) to guess at riddles; (2) to be nonplussed.

猜枚 *tsaimeir*, v.i., to guess how many coins, etc., in an enclosed fist.

猜謎(兒) *tsaimir* (*-meh'l*), v.i., to guess at riddles.

猜破 *tsai-poh*, v.t., to penetrate to (hidden plan, etc.).

猜忍 *tsaireen*, adj., (AC) ruthless, cruel.

猜想 *tsaishiaang*, v.i., to imagine, wonder, conjecture.

猜嫌 *tsaishiarn*, v.i., to feel jealous, take a strong dislike to (person).

猜疑 *tsaiyir*, v.i. & t., to suspect (s.t. or s.o.).

猢 91C.42–1

hur.

猢猻 *hursun*, n., ape, monkey: 猢猻王 "king of monkeys"—schoolteacher.

獳 91C.42–3

nouh.

Adj. (AC) (of dogs) snarling.

獮 91C.42–3

shiaan.

N. (AC) autumn hunt.

V.t. (AC) to kill.

狷 91C.42–4

jyuahn.

Adj. (1) Impetuous, rash, impulsive: 狷急 *-jir* ↓; 狷忿 *-fehn* ↓; 狷狹 *-shiar* ↓. (2) High-minded, incorruptible: 狷介 *-jieh* ↓.

狷忿 *jyuahnfehn*, adj., irascible, quick-tempered.

狷介 *jyuahnjieh*, adj., incorruptible, upright, high-minded.

狷急 *jyuahnjir*, adj., straightforward, blunt, candid.

狷狹 *jyuahnshiar*, adj., narrow-minded, bigoted, prejudiced.

猬 91C.42–4

weih.

[Var. of 蝟 22D.42]

猾 91C.42–4

huar.

V.t. (AC) to harass: 蠻夷猾夏 the barbarians harassed China.

Adj. Cunning, deceitful: 狡猾, 奸猾 deceitful; 猾吏 crafty, wicked officials; 猾賊 cunning thief.

獼 91C.42–5

mir.

獼猴 *mirhour*, n., macaco monkey, common monkey in China.

獢 91C.42–9

shiau.

獢勇 *shiauyuung*, adj., stalwart, strong.

§ 91C.50 (ㄋ/ㄱ)

獨 91C.50-4

dur.

[Pop. 独]

N. (1) (AC) old person without children. (2) Solitude: 愼獨 a Confucian concept of being careful in thought when one is alone.

Adj. & adv. Single, -ly, alone, by oneself: 單獨一個人 by oneself, one person alone; 獨立, 坐, 處 stand, sit, live alone; 獨佔, 獨有 monopolize, possess singly; 獨斷獨行 decide and act alone (without advice from others); 獨享權利 enjoy privilege alone; 獨享其成 alone reap the benefit; 獨持異議 alone hold a different opinion, differ in view from all others; 獨步一時 be unequalled in one's generation; 獨具隻眼 (fig.) can see what others cannot; 獨樹一幟 create a separate school (in art, etc.); 獨往獨來 completely independent, not slavish follower of fashions; 獨出心裁, 獨創 be original, create new styles, fashions; 獨此一家 only authentic brand; 獨家經理 sole agent; 獨門, 獨院 house not sharing entrance with others; 獨力扶持 support single-handed; 獨當一面 be boss of one section, head of one department; 獨木不成林 one tree does not make a forest; 獨善其身 maintain personal integrity during chaotic times.

Prep. (1) Emphasizing interrogative: 獨不知 don't you know? 獨不聞 haven't you heard? 何獨 why particularly? (2) But, only: 豈獨 is it only; 不獨 not only.

獨白 *durbair*, n. & v.i., monologue, soliloquy; soliloquize.

獨唱 *durchahng*, n. & v.i., solo; 獨唱會 vocal recital.

獨夫 *durfu*, n., (AC) tyrant (concept that a king who has lost support is a "lone individual").

獨孤 *Durgu*, n., an anc. surname.

獨軌車 *durgueei-che*, n., monorail.

獨活 *durhuor*, n., (bot.) the angelica (also 羌活).

獨角仙 *durjiaaushian*, n., (zoo.) an insect, *Xylotrupos dichotomus*.

獨腳戲 *durjiaaushih*, n., a play acted by one person; (fig.) s.t. undertaken by one man alone, or without support.

獨止 *durjyy*, adv., only, only one.

獨立 *durlih*, adj. & n., independent, (-ce): 獨立意見, 精神 independent opinion, spirit; 獨立運動 movement for national independence; 獨立宣言 Declaration of Independence; 美國獨立宣言 (American) Declaration of Independence.

獨輪車 *durlurnche*, n., monocycle; (dial.) bicycle.

獨木舟 *durmuhjou*, n., canoe.

獨幕劇 *durmuhjyuh*, n., one-act play.

獨身 *durshen*, adj., living singly as bachelor; n., celibacy; 獨身者 celibate.

獨生 *dursheng*, n., as in 獨生子, 女 only son, daughter.

獨行 *durshirng* (*-shihng*), n. & v.i., walk alone: 特立獨行 personal independence of conduct.

獨特 *durteh*, adj., special, distinguished: 獨特見解 individual insight.

獨挑兒 *durtiaau'l*, v.i., (coll.) act on one's responsibility.

獨裁 *durtsair*, v.i. & n., dictate, -tor, -torship.

獨奏 *durtzouh*, n. & v.i., solo.

獨自 *durtzyh*, adj. & adv., alone, singly: 獨自一個人 a person alone.

獨子 *durtzyy*, n., only son.

獨眼龍 *duryaanlurng*, n., one-eyed goldfish or person.

狗 91C.50-9

goou.

N. A dog: 獵狗 the hound, a hunting dog; 哈吧狗 a Pekingese, a Peking poodle; 瘋狗 a dog infected with rabies; 癩狗 a mangy dog; 看門狗 a watchdog; 走狗 a person who does s.o.'s bidding, (lit., "a running dog"); 狗仗人勢 (contempt.) an underling gets haughty on the strength of an influential relative; 狗顛屁股兒 fawning, cringing; 狗苟蠅營 ingratiate oneself with s.o. to gain one's ends; 狗拿耗子 meddle in s.o. else's business; 狗咬呂洞賓 to mistake a good man for a bad one; 狗尾續貂 to write a deplorable sequel to a masterpiece (lit., "to patch up a sable coat with a dog's tail"); 雞鳴狗盜 (contempt.) the dregs of society, the lowest classes of people; 良心給狗吃了 be unscrupulous or without conscience; 喪家之狗 feeling lost like a stray dog; 他像瘋狗一樣亂咬人 he snarls at everyone like a mad dog; 踤了個狗吃屎 to stumble and fall on the ground face down.

V.t. To fawn or cringe: 這一般底下人專會狗着他 the people under him know only how to fawn on him.

Adj. (Contempt.) worthless, ignoble, despicable: 狗男女 sons of bitches; 狗東西 that son of a bitch; 狗頭 *-tour* ↓; 好大的狗膽 dare you do such a thing? 狗腿子 how running dog; 狗屁 *-pih* ↓; 狗屎文章 trash, potboiler; 狗眼看人低 (of uneducated people) look down upon everybody else.

狗寶 *gourbaau*, n., (herb med.) a gallstone taken from the body of a mangy dog and used for medical purposes, a bezoar from dogs.

狗氣 *goou-chih*, n., churlish manners of one who cringes before his superiors and is haughty towards his subordinates.

狗竇 *goudouh*, n., a hole in wall for a dog to go in and out.

狗豆子 *gooudouh'tz*, n., dog ticks.

狗貛 *goouhuan*, n., (zoo.) the badger.

狗脊 *gourjii*, n., (bot.) *Woodwardia radicans* var. *japonica*, the European chain fern.

狗鷲 *gooujiouh*, n., a vulture.

狗屁 *goupih*, n., (abusive) complete nonsense ("dog fart"): 放狗屁 "talk rot," say things worthless or nonsensical; 狗屁不通 (derog. of writing) dense trash.

狗蝨 *goushy*, n., (zoo.) dog ticks.

狗事 *gooushyh*, v., fawning or cringing behavior.

狗食 *gooushyr*, n., (1) (abusive) a despicable fellow; (2) dog's food.

狗熊 *gooushyurng*, n., (zoo.) a small black bear; (coll.) (contempt.) a minor, not a real hero.

狗屎 *gourshyy*, n., (1) dog's dung; (2) (abusive) anything as worthless or offensive.

狗頭 *gooutour*, n., (1) a dog's head; (2) a cur: 狗頭軍師 a good-for-nothing adviser.

狗才 *gooutsair*, n., (abusive) that "ass," a worthless fellow.

狗尾草 *goouweirtsaau*, n., (bot.) the green foxtail, bottle grass, *Setaria viridis*.

狗蠅 *goouyirng*, n., (zoo.) dog-flies, *Hippobosca capensis*.

狗 91C.50–9

shyuhn (*shyurn*).

[Pop. of 徇 91B.50]

§91C.70 (犭/ㄴ)

犹 91C.70–1

your.

[Var. 猶 91C.41]

猇 91C.70–2

shiau.

V.i. Roar as a tiger.

犯 91C.70–5

fahn.

N. Criminal: 犯人 *-rern*↓; 首犯, 從犯 chief criminal, accomplice; 獄犯, 囚犯 convict, prisoner; 兇犯 criminal (in murder case); 逃犯 escaped convict; 罪犯 convict; 疑犯 a suspect; 慣犯 habitual offender or criminal.

V.i. (1) (pr. *jaur*) 犯不著 it does not pay, or is below one's dignity; also 犯不上: 犯不著和這個人爭辯 it is not worth while to argue with him. (2) Clash: 相犯 clash in colors, composition.

V.t. (1) To violate (law, regulations): 犯規 *-guei*↓; 犯法 *-faa*↓; 犯禁, 犯戒 break into forbidden ground, break monk's vows, in gen. transgress; 犯案 be tried for law-breaking; 犯夜 go off bounds at night; 犯科, 犯款 break articles of law; 犯境, 犯界 poach into territory, (AC) invade country: 犯齊 attack Chir State, see 侵▵犯 91A.82. (2) Offend superiors, gods, taboos: 冒犯 incur (displeasure), violate (law); 犯上(作亂) be insubordinate; 犯闕 illegally break into royal palace; 犯顏力諫 talk to king in his face on matters of policy; 犯順 risk ruler's displeasure; 犯(忌)諱 break taboos; 犯土 offend god of soil or locality by buildings. (3) Touch, be touched by: 犯節氣 touched by the weather, contract seasonal illness; 犯病 catch illness, fall ill; 犯他的病 talk about something on which person talked to is sensitive or which he does not wish mentioned; 犯刺兒 pick fault; 犯怒 arouse anger; 犯死鼈兒 be obstinate; 犯脾氣 get angry; 犯疑心, 嫌疑 arouse, invite, suspicion; 犯疑 be suspect; 犯衆議 invite public criticism.

犯法 *fahn-faa*, v.i., break the law, regulations; adj., illegal: 犯法行爲 illegal conduct.

犯分 *fahn-fehn*, v.i., act above one's status.

犯規 *fahn-guei*, n. & v.t., (sports) foul.

犯難 *fahn-nahn*, v.i., risk (danger, difficulty).

犯人 *fahnrern*, n., convict.

犯聲 *fahnsheng*, v.i., discord, (in certain type of poem) break tone pattern prescribed.

犯舌 *fahnsher*, adj., talkative.

犯相 *fahn-shiahng*, (1) n., looks of a (potential) convict; (2) adj., incompatible between husband and wife as indicated by horoscope.

犯心 *fahn-shin*, v.i., get irritable with each other.

犯罪 *fahn-tzueih*, v.i. & n., transgress (-ion); be convicted: 犯死罪 incur death penalty.

犺 91C.70–6

kahng.

N. (AC) a powerful hound; an animal domesticated for hunting tigers, elephants, found in Thailand and Southwest China.

猄 91C.70–6

jihng.

N. (1) A legendary animal that eats its own mother. (2) An unfilial or beastly person.

猊 91C.70-9

nir.

N. (AC) a lion or wild horse: 狻猊 a fabulous beast, a lion cub.

獵 91C.70-9

lieh.

N. & v.i. & t. To hunt, a hunt: 打獵 hunt; 漁獵 hunting and fishing as a profession; 獵兔, 野豬 hunt hare, boar; (fig.) to hunt, search for good things: 獵其菁華 gather and select the best in writing; 獵取功名 try to win a degree in civil examinations.

獵槍 *liehchiang*, n., hunting gun, a fowling piece, shotgun.
獵犬 *liehchyuaan*, n., hound.
獵取 *liehchyuu*, v.t., try to get, hunt for, see V.i. & t.↑.
獵刀 *liehdau*, n., hunter's knife.
獵狗 *liehgoou*, n., hound.
獵戶 *liehhuh*, n., hunter.
獵裝 *lieh-juang*, n., hunting dress.
獵獵 *liehlieh*, adj., descriptive of sound of wind.
獵人 *liehrern*, n., hunter.
獵涉 *liehsheh*, v.i., (usu. 涉獵) to browse among books: 獵涉不精 read widely without intensive studies.
獵物 *liehwuh*, n., game or hunter's bag of animals.
獵豔 *liehyahn*, v.i., "hunt for beauties,"—philander with women.
獵鷹 *liehying*, n., falcon.

§91C.71 (犭/七)

狨 91C.71-7

rurng.

N. (1) (Zoo.) *Hapale jacchus.* (2) U.f. 絨 93B.71.

§91C.80 (犭/八)

獺 91C.80-1

tah (also *taa*).

N. Otter: 獺皮 otter skin; 水獺, 海獺, 旱獺 various breeds of otter, including beaver; 獺疫 a plague said communicated by beaver.

獺祭 *tahjih*, n., (contempt.) writer's empty parade of allusions and phrases passing for litr. composition (as otter spreads fish skeletons about).

狽 91C.80-4

beih.

N. See 狼^A狽 91C.02.

獷 91C.80-6

guaang.

Adj. Fierce, rude: 獷悍 ferocious; 獷俗 barbarous customs; 粗獷 crude and uncivilized.

§91C.81 (犭/人)

狹 91C.81-1

shiar.

N. (1) Narrow (alley, etc.): 狹路相逢 (old enemies) meet in a narrow path—inevitable revenge; 狹路曲巷 small, crooked alleyway. (2) Narrow-minded: 偏狹 stubborn, bigoted; 心地窄狹 insular, narrow-minded.

狹隘 *shiar-aih*, adj., narrow; narrow-minded, illiberal.
狹軌 *shiargueei*, n., narrow gauge: 狹軌鐵路 narrow-gauge railway.
狹窄 *shiarjaai*, adj., see *-aih*↑.
狹斜 *shiarshier*[1], adj., (a path, alleyway) crooked and narrow: 作狹斜遊 to visit brothels.
狹邪 *shiarshier*[2], adj., see *-shier*[1]↑.
狹義 *shiaryih*, n., in the narrow sense of word.
狹韻 *shiar-yuhn*, n., a rhyme "class" with few rhyming words in it, more difficult for writing verse.

獗 91C.81-5

jyuer.

Adj. 猖獗 rampant (bandits).

獄 91C.81-6

yuh.

N. (1) Prison, jail: 獄卒, 獄吏 *-tzur, -lih*↓; 下獄 put in prison; 入獄, 坐獄 sit in prison; 越獄 escape from prison. (2) Case in court: 斷獄, 折獄 (judge) decide a court case; 煉獄 to work on a prisoner by long cross-examinations or torture; (Cath.) purgatory. (3) Hell in 地獄.

獄囚 *yuh-chiour*, n., convict in prison.
獄犯 *yuh-fahn*, n., convict.
獄吏 *yuh-lih*, n., jailer.
獄訟 *yuh-suhng*, n., court trial.
獄卒 *yuh-tzur*, n., jailer.

狄 91C.81-9

dir.

N. (1) Term given to northern tribes: 夷狄 (AC) foreign tribes, barbarians in gen. (2) A surname.

猴 91C.81-9

hour.

N. (*-tz, 'l*) The monkey, ape: 猴戲, 耍猴 monkey show; 猴子 (derog. or facet.) a mischievous person who acts like a monkey; 猴兒 oft. used of children as term of endearment; 猴快 quick as a monkey; 猴頭猴腦 silly, silly-faced.

Adj. Monkey-like: 這孩子多猴啊 what a little darling!

猴精 *hourjing*, n., (derog.) a clever and mischievous person.
猴兒筋 *hour'ljin*, n., (coll.) rubber band.
猴賴 *hourlaih*, adj., mischievous.
猴熊 *hourshyurng*, n., a kind of bear.
猴猻 *hoursun*, n., monkey, ape; 猴猻王 "king of monkeys," oft. fig. of schoolteacher.
猴棗 *hourtzaau*, n., (1) a kind of persimmon; (2) (Chin. med.) bezoar from monkeys.

§91C.82 (犭/又)

獲 91C.82-2

huoh.
[Dist. 穫]

N. (AC) 臧獲 male and female slaves.

V.t. (1) To obtain, receive: usu. 獲得 *-der* ↓; 獲利 obtain profits; 獲罪 be punished for offense, to offend, receive punishment; 捕獲, 獵獲 to catch (game, turtle, etc.); 擒獲 to capture (enemy, thief). (2) Be able to: see 獲得 *-der* ↓; 不獲 (=不得) (LL) cannot: 不獲遵命 be unable to comply with your wish, to proceed as instructed; 不獲見諒 fail to have your sympathetic understanding, was not able to explain, i.e., was blamed (for s.t.); 不獲善終 was not able to die a natural death.

獲得 *huoh-der*, v.t., receive: 獲得消息 (榮獎) received news (award); 獲得免罪 received pardon.

狡 91C.82-6

jiaau.

Adj. (1) Crafty, cunning, tricky, wily: 奸狡 treacherous; see compp. ↓; 狡兔三窟 elude discovery, burrow oneself in secret hide-outs ("a rabbit with three burrows"); 狡計 a subterfuge, a ruse. (2) Superficial, without substance: 狡童 (AC) a good-looking but crafty boy, (now) juvenile delinquent.

狡辯 *jiaaubiahn*, v.i., use specious arguments to defend oneself, resort to sophistry.
狡猾 *jiaauhuar*, adj., untrustworthy, slippery.
狡詐 *jiaaujah*, adj., deceitful, cunning.
狡獪 *jiaaukuaih*, adj., treacherous, wily, deceitful.
狡賴 *jiaaulaih*, v.i., to lie, prevaricate, evade responsibility.
狡黠 *jiaaushiar*, adj., crafty, tricky, sly.

猨 91C.82-9

yuarn.
[Var. of 猿 monkey, 91C.02]

狻 91C.82-9

suan.

狻猊 *suannir*, n., (AC) interpreted as a lion puppy.

§91C.83 (犭/乛)

狐 91C.83-9

hur.

N. A fox: 狐貍 *-'li*; 狐皮 fox skin or fur; 狐尾巴 foxtail; 狐腿子 leg skin of fox; 狐脊 back fox-skin; 狐裘 robe of fox skin; 狐埋狐搰 suspicious and indecisive like a fox, constantly change plans—as fox changes holes; 狐假虎威 (fable) a fox makes himself feared by walking in tiger's company, (fig.) a man assuming self-importance by his connections; in comb. with 狗: 狐羣狗黨, 狐朋狗友 disreputable gang, rabble; 妖狐 a fox spirit oft. assuming form of a pretty girl; as symbol of suspicion: 狐疑 *-yir* ↓; as symbol of cunning, deceit and witchery: 狐貍精, 狐仙, 狐媚 *-lirjing, -shian, -meih* ↓.

狐臭 *hurchouh*, n., armpit odor.
狐狸 *hur'li*, n., the fox; (abusive) a bewitching woman, see *-meih* ↓; 狐狸精 *-lirjing*, n., a fox spirit; (abusive) a vixen.
狐媚 *hurmeih*, v.i. & t., to flatter, bewitch with feminine charms.
狐步舞 *hurpuh-wuu*, n., the fox trot (dance).
狐騷 *hursau*, adj., (1) n., see *-chouh* ↑; (2) sexy, flirtatious.
狐仙 *hurshian*, n., a fox spirit oft. appearing as old man gifted in fortunetelling.
狐疑 *huryir*, v.t., be suspicious, as a fox is reputed to be: 我狐疑他 I suspect him.

§ 91C.93 (犭/く)

独 91C.93–2

dur.
[Pop. of 獨 91C.50]

狯 91C.93–8

kuaih.
[Pop. of 獪 91C.41]

SECTION 91D

§ 91D.00 (火/丿)

灯 91D.00–3

deng.
[Pop. of 燈 91D.30]

焊 91D.00–5

shyurn.

V.t. (1) To singe (feathers). (2) To drop meat into boiling water to cook it.

焖 91D.00–5

mehn (or *men*).

V.t. Simmer over slow fire without allowing evaporation: 焖雞, 飯 chicken, rice so cooked.

爛 91D.00–5

lahn.

Adj. (1) (Of food) overdone, cooked soft or mushy: 肉煮爛了 the meat is boiled soft; 爛飯 rice cooked too long; 熟而不爛 thoroughly cooked but not mushy; 爛熟 *-shour* ↓; 糜爛 a state of utter confusion, a mess. (2) Rotten, decayed: 腐爛 putrefied; 爛水菓 spoiled fruits. (3) (AC) suffering from bruises or burns. (4) Bright, brilliant: 爛漫 *-mahn* ↓; 燦爛 brilliant, glistening; 爛爛 *-lahn*, 爛然 *-rarn* ↓. (5) Broken, torn to pieces, decayed: 爛紙 pieces of broken paper; 打爛 smashed; 碎爛 broken into pieces; 破爛 broken, tattered; 蛀爛 moth-eaten; 剁爛 mashed; 嚼爛 thoroughly chewed; 搗爛 well pounded, thoroughly mixed; 爛泥 quagmire. (6) Dissolute, messy: 爛賬 *-jahng* ↓; 爛賒惡討 indiscriminate borrowing; 爛好人 a goody-goody fellow; 爛小人 a mean fellow; 爛女人 a woman of loose morals; 爛東西 junk, trash; 爛貨 *-huoh* ↓.

爛糊 *lahn'hu*, n. & adj., mush, thoroughly cooked and easily digestible.
爛化 *lahn'hua*, adj., (of food) well-cooked and tender.
爛貨 *lahnhuoh*, n., (1) (abusive) a woman of easy virtue; (2) goods of poor quality.
爛賬 *lahnjahng*, n., (1) a bad debt; (2) a mess: 一本爛賬 it's a messy account.
爛爛 *lahnlahn*, adj., (1) shiningly bright; (2) well cooked: 粥要熬得爛爛兒的 the congee must be cooked soft and easy to swallow.
爛漫 *lahnmahn*, adj., (1) confused, scattered about; (2) glittering; (3) dissolute, given to dissipation; (4) fast asleep, sleeping soundly; (5) 天眞爛漫 ingenuous, naïve.
爛然 *lahnrarn*, adj., bright, brilliant.
爛熟 *lahnshour*, adj., (1) (of food) thoroughly cooked, well-done, (of fruit) thoroughly ripe; (2) (of sleep) sound; (3) fluent (in recitation, speech): 背得爛熟 can recite fluently from memory.
爛醉 *lahntzueih*, adj., dead drunk: 爛醉如泥 drunk like a fish.

爝 91D.00–9

jyuer.

爝 煉 燎 煤 燦 煠 煣 燥 烁 爍

N. A torch: 爝火不息 (AC) the torch kept on burning (in spite of sunshine).

§ 91D.01 (火/小)

煉 91D.01–1

liahn.

[Cf. 鍊 81A.01]

V.t. (1) To work on or refine metal: 煉鋼 make steel; shape metal by fire (interch. 鍊): 煉劍 forge a sword. (2) To refine, make by distilling or similar process: 煉蜜 make honey; 煉油 refine oil: 煉油廠 oil refinery; 煉藥 distill or concoct medicine; 提煉 extract by heat or other process; 煉乳 *-ruu*↓. (3) To train, form character by hardship: 鍛鍊 train character, learn experience like purging metal by fire; 熬煉 (lit., "stew over slow fire") learn experience, maturity, by hardships (cf. very similar use of 鍊 and 練).

煉焦 *liahnjiau*, n. & v.i., coke; to make coke.

煉乳 *liahnruu*, n., condensed milk.

煉獄 *liahnyuh*, n., purgatory.

燎 91D.01–1

liauh (**liaur*, **liaau*).

V.i. & t. (1) Set fire; (of fire) spread: 星星之火, 可以燎原 a little spark can cause a conflagration. (2) (**liaur*) To cause a burn on skin: 燎(爒)泡 blister caused by a burn. (3) (**liaau*) To scorch, singe: 燎毛 to singe hair; 燎毛之味 smell of singed hair.

Adj. Clearly discernible, bright, illumined; 燎燎 *-liauh*↓.

燎燎 *liauhliauh*, adj., brightly visible.

燎原 *liauhyuarn*, v.i. & n., (cause) a conflagration, a prairie fire.

煤 91D.01–2

meir.

N. Coal: 烟煤, 油煤 bituminous coal; 石煤, 白煤, 紅煤 anthracite; 煤渣兒 cinders, bits of coal; 煤屑 bits of coal.

煤氣 *meirchih*, n., coal gas; 煤氣燈 gas lamp; 煤氣炭 gas carbon.

煤球 *meirchiour*, n., coal ball, made with mixed earth, like bricket.

煤毒 *meirdur*, n., carbon monoxide, a poison gas.

煤黑子 *meirheitz*, n., (coll.) coal miner with blackened face.

煤焦 *meirjiau*, n., coke, coking coal, also 焦煤; 煤焦油 coal tar.

煤礦 *meir-kuahng*, n., coal mine.

煤爐 *meirlur*, n., coal heater or oven.

煤炭 *meirtahn*, n., coal (as fuel).

煤炱 *meirtair*, n., soot, lampblack.

煤田 *meir-tian*, n., coal field.

煤層 *meir-tserng*, n., coal veins.

煤烟 *meir-yan*, n., soot; coal smoke.

煤油 *meiryour*, n., kerosene.

燦 91D.01–2

tsahn.

Adj. Bright, illuminating.

燦爛 *tsahnlahn*, adj., bright, glorious, magnificent, splendid.

煠 91D.01–2

jar.

[Var. of 炸 91D.22]

煣 91D.01–3

roou.

V.t. (Of wood) apply heat to bend: 煣木爲耒 bend wood to make it into a plough.

燥 91D.01–4

tzauh.

Adj. Dry: 燥濕 dry and (or) wet; 燥熱 hot and dry; 燥渴 parched with thirst; 天氣發燥 the weather (air) is dry; 口燥 thirsty.

燥灼 *tzauhjuor*, adj., dreadfully anxious, worried.

燥脾 *tzauhpir*, adj., invigorating, refreshing, stimulating.

燥子 *tzauh'tz*, n., finely cut meat.

烁 91D.01–9

chiou.

[Anc. var. of 秋 90A.81]

爍 91D.01–9

shuoh.

V.i. (1) To flicker, shine: 閃爍 ditto. (2) Var. of 鑠 to melt, 81A.01; 衆口爍金 people's gossip is enough to melt metals—i.e., destroy anybody.

§ 91D.02 (火/卜)

爆 91D.02-4

bauh (**bor*).

V.t. (1) (*bauh*) Quick-fry, i.e., fry quickly in hot oil for crisp effect: 爆肚兒 quick-fried tripe. (2) (*bauh*) Explode. (3) (**bor*) To dry near fire; to broil.

爆發 *bauhfa*, v.i., (lit. & fig.) explode.

爆炸 *bauhjah*, v.i., explode like bombs; 爆炸物 *--wuh*, n., explosives.

爆仗 *bauhjahng*, n., firecrackers.

爆竹 *bauhjur*, n., ditto.

爆裂 *bauhlieh*, v.i., crack from heat.

煨 91D.02-4

wei.

N. Ashes: 煨燼.

V.t. To bake (potatoes), roast (chestnuts); to cook (chicken, pork) by slow fire.

烺 91D.02-6

laang.

Adj. Shiningly bright.

§ 91D.10 (火/十)

燁 91D.10-2

yeh.

Adj. Bright, flaming.

煒 91D.10-2

weei.

Adj. (AC) bright red.

燐 91D.10-2

lirn.

N. (Chem.) phosphorus (also 磷); phosphorescent lights.

燐光 *lirnguang*, n., phosphorescence.

燐火 *lirnhuoo*, n., firefly, will-o'-the-wisp.

焠 91D.10-6

tsueih.

V.i. (1) To burn. (2) Interch. 淬 63A.10.

煇 91D.10-6

huei.
[Var. of 輝 22S.10]

烊 91D.10-8

yarng.

V.t. Melt; 烊金 molten metal.

烽 91D.10-9

feng.

N. Ancient system of relaying war signals by series of fires from high stations: 烽火; 烽煙四起 uprisings of war everywhere.

烽火 *fenghuoo*, n., war signals: (fig.) 烽火連年 continuous wars.

§ 91D.11 (火/土)

灶 91D.11-1

tzauh.
[Pop. of 竈 62A.70]

煙 91D.11-3

yan.
[Var. of 烟 91D.41]

燿 91D.11-5

yauh.
[Pop. 耀]

灶 91D.11-6

juh.

N. adjunct. 一灶香 one incense-stick.

N. Lamp pith.

V.t. To burn (incense).

煌 91D.11-9

huarng.

Adj. Shining, brilliant: 輝煌的成就 brilliant achievement.

§91D.21 (火/ㄴ)

炬 91D.21-5

jyuh.

N. A torch: 火炬 a flambeau, a lighted torch; 蠟炬 a candle; 目光如炬 sparkling eyes.

焰 91D.21-9

yahn (yarn).
[Var. of 燄]

N. A flame: 火焰 flames of fire; 烈焰 hot, blazing flames; (fig.) excessive or domineering influence; 氣焰逼人 behave with unbearable insolence.

焰口 *yahn'kou*, n., (Budd.) hungry ghosts splitting fire; 放焰口 serve food to hungry ghosts.

§91D.22 (火/丨)

炘 91D.22-9

shin.

Adj. Bright and cheerful.

炸 91D.22-9

*jah (*jar).*

V.t. (1) (**jar*): To fry in deep oil; 炸丸子 fried meat ball; 炸醬 *-jiahng*↓; 油炸 fried in oil; 炸乾 fried crisp and served dry without sauce. (2) To bomb (place, railway, etc.): 炸彈 *-dahn*↓; 炸裂, 炸燬 *-lieh, -hueei*↓; 炸藥 *-yauh*↓; 轟炸 to bomb esp. from the air; 炸開 bomb open; 炸斷 bomb (bridge) in two; 炸死 bomb to death, kill by explosion.

V.i. (1) To explode in anger: 他聽見登時炸了 when he heard this, he exploded (at once). (2) To break up (meeting) in uproar: 炸獄 break jail and escape.

炸彈 *jahdahn*, n., a bomb.
炸燬 *jahhueei*, v.i., to bomb and burn out (house).
炸醬 **jarjiahng*, n., (1) 炸醬麵 a kind of noodles served with meat sauce; (2) v.t., (coll.) destroy beyond recognition: 我的幾本好書竟被他炸醬了 he has turned my few good books into mincemeat.
炸裂 *jah-lieh*, v.i., to explode in two.
炸妙 *jahmiauh*, v.i., (coll.) create a false scare (also wr. 炸廟).
炸窩 *jah-wo*, v.i., (of birds) flush out at noise of gun; (bees) rush out of beehive.
炸藥 *jahyauh*, n., explosive; dynamite.

§91D.30 (火/一)

爐 91D.30-2

lur.
[Pop. 炉]

N. Stove, furnace: 火爐 kitchen stove, or factory furnace; 煤爐 coal stove; 電爐 electric stove; 爐火純青 intense white flame when impurities disappear; (fig.) man's thoughts or ideas reach absolute clarity and purity.

爐坑 *lurkahng*, n., place in stove for ashes.
爐臺(兒)(子) *lurtair ('l) (tz)*, n., top of coal stove (for heating things).
爐條 *lurtiaur*, n., grill inside stove.
爐竈 *lurtzauh*, n., kitchen: 重起爐竈 begin another set-up in business or career, begin all over again.

燼 91D.30-2

jihn.

N. (1) Ashes, embers, cinder: 化爲灰燼 reduced to ashes; 燈燼 snuff on a wick. (2) Victims of disasters: 請收合餘燼 let's bring together the remnant troops and stage another fight.

烜 91D.30-3

shyuaan.

烜赫 *shyuaanheh*, adj., shining, impressive (reputation).

燈 91D.30-3

deng.
[Pop. 灯]

N. Lamp, light, lantern: 電燈 electric light; 油燈 oil lamp; 日光燈 sun lamp, fluorescent lamp, also neon light (also 霓虹燈); 宮燈 decorative ceiling light, usu. with hexagonal shade; 檯燈 desk lamp; 落地燈 floor lamp.

燈蛾 *deng-er*, n., moths that flit around lamp.
燈號 *denghauh*, n., flash signals.
燈花 *denghua*, n., the snuff of lamp wick.
燈火 *denghuoo*, n., lights in general: 小心燈火 be careful of the lights.
燈虎 *denghuu*, n., riddles pasted over lamps as party game (taken down by one who guesses right).
燈罩 *dengjauh*, n., lamp shade.
燈節(兒) *dengjier* (*-jier'l*), n., lantern festival, the 15th of first lunar month.
燈籠 *deng'lung*, n., lantern; 燈籠褲 baggy trousers.
燈謎 *dengmir*, n., see *-huu* ↑.
燈泡 *dengpauh*, n., electric globe, bulb.
燈心 *dengshin*, n., pith of certain plant used as wick in old-style oil lamps; 燈心草 n., (bot.) the common rush.
燈塔 *dengtaa*, n., lighthouse.
燈臺 *dengtair*, n., lamp stand.
燈頭 *dengtour*, n., (1) socket for electric light; (2) burning part of wick in oil lamp which can be adjusted for flame; (3) lamp.
燈語 *dengyuu*, n., message in code sent by flashing signals.

煜 91D.30-4

yuh.

N. Flame.

Adj. (1) Bright: 煜煜. (2) Shining, prosperous.

煊 91D.30-6

shyuan.

Adj. (1) Bright, shining (reputation). (2) Warm.

§91D.40 (火/口)

熺 91D.40-1

shi.
[Var. of 熹 11.63]

焐 91D.40-3

wuh.

V.i. To keep warm by contact.

炤 91D.40-5

jauh.
[Var. of 照]

焙 91D.40-6

beih.

V.t. To bake, to heat over slow fire, in pan or on tile, such as tea leaves, herbs.

熔 91D.40-6

rurng.
[Pop. of 鎔 81A.40]

熗 91D.40-8

chiahng.

V.t. To fry very quickly over hot fire (shrimp, celery, etc.).

烙 91D.40-9

luoh (sp. pr. *lauh*)

V.t. (1) To brand or press with hot iron: 烙鐵 hot irons; 烙印 to brand. (2) (*lauh*) 烙餅 baked wheat cake.

§91D.41 (火/囗)

烟 91D.41-4

yan.
[Var. of 煙]

N. (1) (*-'l*) Smoke: 吸烟, 抽烟 to smoke; 煤烟 coal smoke; 炊烟 chimney smoke; 烽烟, 狼烟 beacon-fire as war signal used in ancient times. (2) (*-tz*) Soot: 松烟 pine soot for making Chin. ink. (3) Tobacco (also wr. 菸): 烟草 *-tsaau* ↓; 香烟, 紙烟, 捲烟 cigarettes; 旱烟 pipe tobacco; 水烟 Chinese tobacco pipe where smoke is filtered through receptacle of water; 聞烟, 鼻烟 snuff. (4) Opium: 大烟 ditto; 烟土, 烟槍, 烟泡兒 *-tuu*, *-chiang*, *-pauh'l* ↓. (5) Mist, haze: 烟霧, 烟霞,

烟雲 -*wuh*, -*shiar*, -*yurn*↓.

烟靄 *yan-aai*, n., mist (over valley).

烟波 *yanbo*, n., the clouds and water, symbol of lake area or of fisherman's life.

烟塵 *yanchern*, n., the smoke of battle; smoke and dust in air.

烟槍 *yanchiang*, n., opium pipe.

烟袋 *yandaih*, n., usu. the Chin. tobacco pipe, also tobacco pouch; 旱烟袋 the common pipe; 水烟袋 pipe with water compartment for filtering tobacco; 烟袋桿子 the pipe stem; 烟袋鍋子 (or 兒) bowl for tobacco; 烟袋荷包 tobacco pouch; 烟袋嘴兒 mouthpiece in pipe; 烟袋油子 "goo," nicotine formation inside pipe.

烟燈 *yandeng*, n., lamp for roasting opium before smoking.

烟斗 *yandoou*, n., (1) opium pipe-bowl; (2) Western tobacco pipe.

烟膏(兒)(子) *yangau('l)(tz)*, n., prepared opium paste.

烟館 *yanguaan*, n., opium house.

烟鬼 *yangueei*, n., a habitual opium smoker, an opium addict.

烟花 *yanhua*, n., the world of wine and women; 烟花巷 formerly, red-light district.

烟灰 *yanhuei*, n., cigarette ashes; soot and ashes; 烟灰盤 ash tray; 烟灰缸 receptacle for ashes.

烟火 *yanhuoo*, n., (1) (-'*huo*) bonfires, fireworks display; (2) chimney smoke as sign of human habitation; (3) 不食烟火 (Taoist) stop eating cooked food (by taking nuts, fruit, water); 烟火氣 n., (of writing) vulgar air of plebeian thoughts and desires.

烟瘴 *yanjahng*, n., unhealthy air or noxious gas of swampy region.

烟傢伙 *yan jia'huo*, n., the paraphernalia that go with opium smoking.

烟禁 *yan-jihn*, n., ban on opium.

烟景 *yanjiing*, n., view of land and water, esp. of chimney smoke or haze on land.

烟捲兒 *yanjyuaa'l*, n., cigarette (also 香烟).

烟煤 *yanmeir*, n., bituminous coal.

烟苗 *yan-miaur*, n., opium poppies.

烟幕 *yanmuh*, n., smoke screen; 烟幕彈 shell for laying on smoke screen.

烟泡兒 *yanpauh'l*, n., the opium paste freshly roasted over the lamp.

烟霞 *yanshiar*, n., clouds and mist: 烟霞癖 love of natural scenery; (facet.) habit of smoking opium.

烟絲 *yansy*, n., cut tobacco.

烟臺 *Yantair*, n., Chefoo.

烟草 *yantsaau*, n., the tobacco plant, leaf tobacco.

烟囪 *yantsung*, n., chimney.

烟筒 *yan'tung*, n., a stovepipe; a chimney.

烟突 *yantur*, n., a chimney.

烟土 *yantuu*, n., opium.

烟嘴兒 *yantzuoo'l*, n., mouthpiece of tobacco pipe (sometimes of jade).

烟霧 *yanwuh*, n., vapor and mist.

烟癮 *yanyiin*, n., habitual desire for, or addiction to, opium or tobacco.

烟雲 *yanyurn*, n., clouds and mist; (fig.) a passing scene.

熠 91D.41–5

yih.

熠燿 *yihyauh*, adj., (AC) glistening. ⌈glistening.

熠熠 *yihyih*, adj., (AC) bright;

熷 91D.41–8

hueih.

V.t. To braise, a way of frying things with thick gravy added.

燔 91D.41–9

farn.

N. Roast, broiled meat: 燔祭 burnt offering.

V.t. To broil.

§91D.42 (火/冈)

炳 91D.42–3

biing.

V.t. Var. for 秉 in 炳燭: 炳燭夜遊 to celebrate night with candles in hand—enjoying the short span of life (also wr. 秉燭).

Adj. Shining (achievement): 彪炳事業 brilliant, glorious achievement.

炳然 *biingrarn*, adj., shining, manifest, clear for everybody to see.

炳耀 *biingyauh*, adj., shining, glorious, brilliant; v.i. to shine (of reputation).

炯 91D.42–4

jyung.

[Pop. 烱]

Adj. (1) Bright, brilliant: 炯炯 shining brightly, sparkling. (2) (Of fire) blazing.

熇 91D.42–6

huh.

Adj. Scorching hot.

㷍 91D.42–8

lurn.

N. (Chem.) old term for benzene, now rendered 苯 *been.*

§ 91D.50 (火/㇕)

烤 91D.50-1

kaau.

V.t. To roast, bake, heat near fire: 烤乾 roast dry, dry by keeping near fire; 烤熱 to heat near fire; 烤焦了 burn (toast); 烤糊了 roast into paste; 烤爛了 mushy, overdone; 烤肉 roast meat; 烤鴨 roast duck; 烤麵包 toast; 烤饅頭 toasted bun; 烤蕃薯 baked potato; 烤衣服 dry clothing near fire; 烤手, 烤脚 warm hands, feet near fire.

煬 91D.50-4

*yahng (*yarng).*

V.t. (**yarng*) Var. of 烊 to smelt metals.

Adj. Aflame.

燭 91D.50-4

jur.

[Pop. 烛]

N. Candle: 喜燭, 花燭 wedding candles; 壽燭 birthday candle; 蠟燭 wax candle.

V.i. (AC) to shine upon: 日月所燭 all that is illumined by the sun and moon.

燭光 *jurguang*, n., (1) candle power: 五十燭光 50 candle power; (2) candlelight.

燭花 *jurhua*, n., snuff of candle.

燭照 *jurjauh*, v.t., to illumine and discern (worthy from unworthy).

燭淚 *jurleih*, n., guttering of candle.

燭籠 *jurlurng*, n., lantern with candle.

燭穗 *jursueih*, n., see *-hua* ↑.

燭臺 *jurtair*, n., candlestick; candelabra.

煽 91D.50-6

shan.

V.t. To fan up (flame, revolt).

煽動 *shanduhng*, v.t., to instigate (mob, revolt).

煽惑 *shanhuoh*, v.t., to misguide (populace), to instigate: 煽惑人心 undermine popular morale by spreading unfounded rumors.

灼 91D.50-9

juor.

V.t. (1) To burn, broil. (2) To illumine, show penetrating insight: 灼見 *-jiahn* ↓; 火光灼天 the fire illumines the sky.

Adj. Shining bright: 灼爍, 灼然 *-shuoh, -rarn* ↓.

灼見 *juorjiahn*, n., as in 眞知灼見 personal, profound insight.

灼灼 *juorjuor*, adj., (1) (AC) in full bloom; (2) (LL) brightly shining.

灼然 *juorrarn*, adv., clearly.

灼爍 *juorshuoh*, adj., brightly colored, scintillating.

§ 91D.63 (火/丶)

烬 91D.63-5

jihn.

[Abbr. of 燼 91D.30]

燻 91D.63-9

shyun.

[Var. of 熏 90.63]

燋 91D.63-9

jiau.

N. (LL) a torch.

V.t. To burn, scorch.

燃 91D.63-9

rarn.

V.t. To burn, cause to shine: 燃燒 *-shau* ↓; 燃料 *-liauh* ↓; 燃眉 *-meir* ↓; 燃萁 discord between brothers leading to mutual destruction; 燃燈 to light lamps; 燃放 set off (firecrackers); 燃燭 to light candles; 點燃 to light up, put the lights on.

燃料 *rarn-liauh*, n., fuel, firewood; 燃料電池 fuel cell.

燃藜 *rarn-lir*, n., brambles used as a torch.

燃 眉 *rarn-meir*, adj., urgently critical ("eyebrows on fire").
燃 燒 *rarnshau*, (1) v.t., to burn, enkindle, set on fire; (2) n., combustion: 燃燒彈 napalm or incendiary bombs; 燃燒點 ignition point; 燃燒物 combustibles.

§ 91D.70 (火/乚)

燒 91D.70-1

shau.

N. Fever: 發燒 have fever; 高燒 high fever; 退燒 reduce fever.

V.i. & t. (1) To burn: 焚燒 ditto; 燒掉 burn away or down; 火燒房子 fire burns a house; (fig.) burn, splash money: 自從得了這筆小財,不知燒得怎樣才好 when he got this little fortune, he felt so hot that he didn't know what to do. (2) To cook: 燒飯, 燒菜 cook rice, vegetables: 燒水, 燒茶 boil water, tea; esp. to roast: 燒鴨, 燒豬 roast duck, pig; 燒餅 -(')*biing*↓; 燒冷竈 "heat up oven"—befriend s.o. when he is yet a nobody in the hope of winning his favor when he is rich or influential.

燒 杯 *shaubei*, n., a beaker.
燒 餅 *shau(')biing*, n., a baked wheat cake, usu. with sesame seeds on top; (AC) a wheat cake with mutton, onions.
燒 青 *shauching*, n., baked green (in *cloisonné*).
燒 刀 子 *shaudautz*, n., (sl.) strong liquor.
燒 點 *shaudiaan*, n., (phys.) ignition point, focus (also called 焦點).
燒 鍋 *shauguo*, n., vat for making liquor; formerly, brewery.
燒 化 *shauhuah*, v.t., to burn to ashes, to cremate.
燒 荒 *shau-huang*, n., (AC) to burn the prairie as a method of discouraging nomadic tribes.
燒 燬 *shauhueei*, v.t., to burn down.
燒 酒 *shaujioou*, n., strong liquor.
燒 紙 *shau(')jyy*, n., paper money burned for use of the dead; 燒紙引鬼 attract ghosts by burning spirit-money—stir up trouble where there was none.
燒 藍 *shaularn*, n., baked blue (*cloisonné*).
燒 煉 *shauliahn*, v.i., to practise alchemy.
燒 料 *shauliauh*, n., clouded or frosted imitation glass (made into lamps, etc.).
燒 賣 *shaumaih*, n., a stuffed dumpling, open and frilled on top.
燒 盤 兒 *shaupar'l*, v.i., (sl.) blush to the ears.
燒 瓶 *shaupirng*, n., a flask (in chem.).
燒 香 *shau-shiang*, v.i., to burn incense—to pray: 燒頭香 to be the first to light an incense on religious holiday.
燒 心 *shaushin*, v.i. & adj., agitate, -ing, -ed.
燒 石 膏 *shaushyrgau*, n., plaster of Paris powder.
燒 尾 宴 *shauweei-yahn*, n., a feast for successful candidates celebrated at end of civil examinations.
燒 夷 彈 *shauyir-dahn*, n., an incendiary bomb.

焜 91D.70-4

kun.

Adj. Bright, shining.

炕 91D.70-6

kahng.
[Dist. 坑]

N. A *kang* or earthen bed in North China, covered with bricks and mat, used for sitting and sleeping, heated from under during winter: 炕頭兒上 on the *kahng*; 炕裏頭 the inside of *kahng*; 炕沿(兒)(子) edge of the *kahng*; 炕頭子貨 rustic woman; 炕上地下 (coll.) a woman's household chores (needlework on the *kahng*, and sweeping floors and cooking on the floor); 炕單子 bedsheet for the *kahng*; 炕蓆 mat on the *kahng*; 炕桌兒, 炕琴(桌兒) low table on the *kahng*.

V.t. To broil.

Adj. Dry; 炕暴, 炕陽 -*bauh*, -*yarng*↓.

炕 暴 *kahngbauh*, adj., irascible, quick-tempered.
炕 洞 *kahngduhng*, n., hollow place beneath *kahng* for placing heating stove.
炕 陽 *kahngyarng*, adj., (1) dried up; (2) self-important.

爖 91D.70-6

lurng.

V.i. 爖火 To build up fire in stove or stir coal to help burning.

炮 91D.70-9

pauh (**paur*).

N. Firecrackers; artillery, see 砲 31B.70 for compp.

V.t. (**paur*) Roast in pan or with meat wrapped up: 炮肉 roast.

炮 火 *pauhhuoo*, n., gunfire, see under 砲 31B.70.
炮 製 **paurjyh*, v.t., (Chin. med.) treat herbs by slow fire: 如法炮製 make s.t. by old formula.
炮 煉 **paurliahn*, v.t., ditto.
炮 烙 **paurluoh*, n., (AC) form of punishment by embracing hot copper pillars recorded of ty-

rant king 紂 Jouh, 12th cen. B.C.

§91D.71 (火/弋)

熾 91D.71-6

chyh.

V.i. To burn, spread like fire.

Adj. Burning hot: (fig.) 盜賊猖熾 bandits spread like a flame; 朋黨熾結 (AC) political cliques spread about; 魚鼈熾殖 fish and turtle multiply.

熾烈 *chyhlieh*, adj., burning hot; (turmoil) spread like conflagration.

熾熱 *chyhreh*, adj., scorching hot.

§91D.72 (火/心)

熄 91D.72-9

shir.

V.i. & t. To extinguish (fire, lamp); (fire, lamp) is extinguished; (movements, influence) die out.

熄火器 *shir-huoo-chih*, n., fire extinguisher.

熄滅 *shir-mieh*, v.i., (of fire) be extinguished.

§91D.80 (火/八)

烘 91D.80-2

hung.

V.t. (1) To dry by heat: 烘衣服 to dry laundry by fire; 烘手 to warm hand by fire; 烘乾 to dry (s.t.) over fire. (2) To bake: 烘白薯 bake potato. (3) To set in contrast: 烘托, 烘襯 *-tuo, -chehn*↓.

烘襯 *hungchehn*, v.t., see *-tuo*↓.

烘烘 *hunghung*, adj. & adv., descriptive of warmth: 暖烘烘 cosily warm; 熱烘烘 steaming hot (meal), crowded, noisy (place, gathering).

烘暖 *hungnuaan*, v.t., to warm by fire.

烘托 *hungtuo*, v.t., to set off in contrast: 烘托作用 serve as contrast: 烘雲托月 "set off the moon with clouds"—litr. art of using contrasting effect.

煩 91D.80-3

farn.

[Cogn. 繁; oft. interch. in sense of confusing]

N. Trouble, bother: 不勝其煩 (LL) too much bother; 麻煩 trouble, troublesome; 不耐煩 impatient; 厭煩 bored.

V.t. Request, trouble (person to do thing): 敬煩 respectfully request; 勞煩, 敢煩 may I trouble you; 敢以此事奉煩 may I bother you with this; 煩請 I beg you; 煩交 I beg you to deliver.

Adj. (1) Troublesome, bothersome, confusing: 煩瑣, 煩碎 *-suoo, -sueih*↓. (2) Vexed, troubled: 心煩 feel vexed, uncomfortable; 煩死了 too much to deal with, too busy and bothered.

煩亂 *farnluahn*, adj., confusing, disorderly.

煩悶(懣) *farnmehn*, adj., uncomfortable, out of sorts; vexed, worried.

煩難 *farnnarn*, adj., (affair) difficult to deal with.

煩惱 *farnnaau*, n. & adj., worries, material worries; feel worried; confusing, vexing, cf. 惱 22A.41.

煩擾 *farnraau*, adj., confusing, bothersome, also 繁.

煩熱 *farnreh*, adj., feel irritable.

煩細 *farnshih*, adj., too detailed.

煩絮 *farnshyuh*, adj., repetitious, too wordy.

煩碎 *farnsueih*, adj., too detailed, bothersome, also 繁.

煩瑣 *farnsuoo*, adj., petty, trivial, too detailed, also 繁.

煩雜 *farntzar*, adj., confusing, also 繁.

煩躁 *farntzauh*, adj., irritable, -ting (affairs).

煩文 *farnwern*, n., empty forms, rigmarole, also 繁文.

煩言 *farnyarn*, n., complaints.

煩冤 *farnyuan*, adj., feel injured.

§91D.81 (火/人)

熯 91D.81-2

hahn.

V.t. (AC) to dry by fire.

焮 91D.81-9

shihn.

V.t. (1) To broil, radiate heat: 火氣焮天 rage to heaven. (2) To inflame: 焮腫 swollen from in-

炮 熾 熄 烘 煩 熯 焮

亅	小	⺊	十	土	ナ	卄	乚卜	丨	一	丅	フ	口	囟	冈	㇆	厂	尸	亠	广	宀	丶	乚	弋	心	八	人	乂	㇖	一	丿	⺊	く
00	01	02	10	11	12	20	21	22	30	31	32	40	41	42	50	51	52	60	61	62	63	70	71	72	80	81	82	83	90	91	92	93

燠 炊 焕 燉 煖 燬 煅 燧 炒 炉 烛

flammation.

燠 91D.81–9

yuh (**auh*).

Adj. (1) Warm. (2) (**auh*) 燠熱 very hot; 寒燠 heat and cold.

燠休 *yuhshyuu*, v.t., to comfort, soothe (the distressed, afflicted).

炊 91D.81–9

chuei.

N. & v.t. A meal; to cook a meal: 炊飯, 舉炊 ditto; 斷炊 go without meals (penniless); 巧婦難爲無米之炊 even a clever wife cannot prepare a meal without rice; 炊沙作飯 cook sand for meal—futile undertaking; 炊金饌玉 eat luxurious food.

炊餅 *chueibiing*, n., steamed wheat cake.

炊火 *chueihuoo*, n., see *-yan* ↓.

炊臼 *chuei-jiouh*, phr., to lose a wife (to "cook in mortar" in absence of cauldron (釜) *fuu*, a pun upon 婦 *fuh*, wife).

炊帚 *chuei'jou*, n., bamboo brush for cleaning frying pans.

炊事 *chueishyh*, n., the meals of a household.

炊煙 *chueiyan*, n., chimney smoke as indication of living resident.

焕 91D.81–9

huahn.

Adj. Shining, brilliant.

焕發 *huahnfa*, v.i. & adj., shine, shining: 精神焕發 in high spirits, fresh with energy; 容光焕發 radiating health, energetic-looking.

焕爛 *huahlahn*, adj., brightly lit, brilliant.

焕然 *huahnrarn*, adj., usu. in 焕然一新 having a bright, new look.

§91D.82 (火/乂)

燉 91D.82–6

duhn.

V.t. To boil in water over slow fire: 燉肉 boiled meat; 燉酒 to warm up wine; 燉藥 make concoction by simmering.

煖 91D.82–9

nuaan.

[Var. of 暖 41A.82]

燬 91D.82–9

hueei.

V.t. To destroy by fire, to burn down: 焚燬, 燒燬 ditto.

煅 91D.82–9

duahn.

[Var of 鍛 81A.82]

§91D.83 (火/一)

燧 91D.83–8

sueih.

V.t. To obtain fire by drilling wood or by flint: 陽燧 obtain fire from sun's heat; 木燧 by drilling wood: 燧人 *-rern* ↓.

N. (AC) a bonfire as war signal; a torch.

燧人(氏) *Sueihrern*, n., personification of age and tribe which discovered the use of fire.

燧石 *sueihshyr*, n., flint.

§91D.91 (火/ノ)

炒 91D.91–2

chaau.

[Dist. 吵]

V.t. To fry, stir-fry, quick-fry, pan-fry, sauté: 炒豆兒 fried beans, crackling noise like frying beans; 炒肉絲 fried pork slivers; 炒雞丁 fried chicken cubes; 清炒 fresh fried; 熱炒 fried and served hot; 糖炒 sweet fried.

炒飯 *chaaufahn*, n., fried rice.

炒米 *chaur-mii*, n., crisp fried rice, resembling popcorn.

炒勺 *chaaushaur*, n., a spatula used in sautéing or quick stirring of food being fried.

炉 91D.91–6

lur.

[Pop. of 爐 91D.30]

§91D.93 (火/く)

烛 91D.93–2

jur.

[Pop. of 燭 91D.50]

炫 91D.93-6

shyuahn.

V.i. To show off, to dazzle.

Adj. Radiant, glowing, dazzling.

炫怪 *shyuahnguaih*, adj., dazzlingly strange, shocking (tales, attitude).
炫惑 *shyuahnhuoh*, (1) adj., alluring, misleading. (2) v.t., to mislead by show-off.
炫目 *shyuahnmuh*, v.i. & adj., dazzle, -ling.
炫炫 *shyuahnshyuahn*, adj., dazzling.
炫耀 *shyuahnyuah*, adj., (1) dazzling, beaming; (2) v.i., to beam with pride, to show off, be pedantic.

烩 91D.93-8

hueih.

[Abbr. of 燴 91D.41]

SECTION 91S

§91S.00 (ノˢ/亅)

射 91S.00-1

sheh (*shyr*, **yeh*).

N. 僕射 (**puryeh*): (a) gen. officer in charge of royal household, chamberlain, steward; (b) a royal minister in Tarng Dyn.

V.i. & t. (1) To shoot with an arrow, rifle or injection: 射箭 shoot an arrow; 射擊 *-jir*↓; 注射 to inject, an injection. (2) To emit, radiate (rays), to jet: 射出, 發射, 放射 project (light, bullet); 射光 cast light; 射影 project image; 輻射 to radiate, -tion; 噴射 to cast a jet (of flame, fountain water, perfume); 噴射機 jet engine. (3) To "shoot" an answer to a riddle in a litr. game: 射覆 *-fuh*↓; 影ᐞ射 41S.91. (4) To aim at: 射利 aim at making profit.

射程 *sheh-cherng*, n., artillery range; trajectory.
射垛 *shehduoo*, n., archery target.
射覆 *shehfuh*, n., a literary and wine game, thus s.o. gives the combination "sky-jeans," the riddle is to find the middle common word which follows "sky" and precedes "jeans," namely, "sky-blue," "blue jeans."
射韝 *sheh-gou*, n., (AC) leather arm band worn on left arm of archer.
射侯 *shehhour*, n., archery target.
射擊 *shehjir*, v.i. & t., to shoot or shoot at with gun.
射獵 *shehlieh*, v.i. & t., to hunt.
射倖 *sheh-shihng*, v.i., to try one's luck at lottery, etc.
射帖 *shehtiee*, n., (LL) an archery target.
射策 *shehtseh*, n., (Hahn Dyn.) examination on current topics, later called 對策.

豺 91S.00-1

chair.

N. Wolf, short for 豺狼 *-larng*↓: 豺目, 豺聲 eyes, voice like a wolf's; 豺心 heart of a wild beast.

豺狼 *chairlarng*, n., wolf.

判 91S.00-2

pahn.

[Usu. wr. 刔]

V.t. (1) To separate. (2) To judge, hand down decision at court: 審判 to try at court; 判決 *-jyuer*↓; 判合 (court) decide against separation of couples; 判案, 裁判 to make decision; 批判 to comment on merits of cases, to judge case; 評判 to act as judge in contest; 評判員 such judge; 談判 negotiate.

Adj. Separate, disparate: 判若兩人 (behavior) different as if he were not the same person; 判若鴻溝 as if separated by a wide ditch, i.e., completely different.

N. A judge: 判官 *-guan*↓; 通ᐞ判 32.83.

判別 *pahnbier*, v.t., distinguish (right and wrong).
判斷 *pahnduahn*, n. & v.t., decide, decision; assessment of given situation: 錯誤判斷 wrong judgment of situation; 判斷力 ability for making judgment.
判牘 *pahn-dur*, n., document containing judge's decision.
判官 *pahnguan*, n., (1) (MC) chief of department; (2) a judge in Hades.

判
剡
劓
舸
皭
牒
躲
貅
緜

判決 *pahnjyuer*, v.t. & n., (make) court's decision, sentence (person); 判決書 judge's statement on decision; 判決之宣示 pronouncement of judgment.
判兒 *pah'l*, n., name given to sorcerer 鍾馗 *Junggueei*, reputed to catch and punish devils.
判例 *pahnlih*, n., (law) case law.
判袂 *pahn-meih*, v.i., (LL) (of friends on departure) to separate, part ways (lit., "separate sleeves").
判司 *pahn-sy*, n., (MC) (secretary in) department in charge of preparing court decisions.
判詞 *pahn-tsyr*, n., (law) text of court's decision.

剡 91S.00-2

yaan (**shahn*).

N. (**shahn*) Name of a river in Chekiang.

V.t. (AC) to chop, slice: 剡其脛 chop off his calf; 剡木爲矢 slice wood into arrows.

劓 91S.00-2

yih.

V.t. To cut off the nose—an anc. punishment.

舸 91S.00-3

gee.

N. Formerly, a big ship.

皭 91S.00-9

jiauh.

Adj. Pure white, clean: 皭然 (LL) maculate, unblemished.

§91S.01 (ノˢ/小)

牒 91S.01-1

dier.

N. Official communication, document: 牒狀 letter of complaint; 牒文, 牒呈 official letter; 訟牒 lawsuit, judicial complaint; 通牒 despatch; diplomatic note: 最後通牒 an ultimatum; 度ᐞ牒 61.82, cf. 諜 60A.01.

牒報 *dierbauh*, n., military intelligence, espionage report, (also wr. 諜).

躲 91S.01-4

duor.

V.i. & t. To hide, hide away from: 躲起來 avoid being seen; 躲雨 find shelter from rain; 躲難 (*-nahn*) escape from war or disaster, take refuge.

躲避 *duorbih*, v.t., avoid meeting (person, disaster).
躲開 *duor-kai*, v.i. & t., stay away, not to be involved: 躲開責任 shirk duty.
躲懶 *duorlaan*, v.i., try to get by without attending to work.
躲匿 *duornih*, v.i., to hide (in some place).
躲閃 *duorshaan*, v.i., avoid being seen.
躲藏 *duortsarng*, v.i., hide away: 躲躲藏藏 dare not show up openly.

貅 91S.01-9

shiou.

N. See 貔ᐞ貅 91S.70.

緜 91S.01-9

miarn.

[Var. 綿; dist. 棉]

N. (1) Cotton wad, wool (u.f. 棉). (2) Silk wool: 緜子 *-tz*↓. (3) A surname.

Adj. Soft, tensile, downy like cotton; long continuing: 緜緜, 緜延 *-miarn*, *-yarn*↓.

緜薄 *miarnbor*, n., (court.) my humble effort.
緜長 *miarncharng*, adj., extending far (of generations, dynasty).
緜芊 *miarnchian*, adj., luxuriant (plants).
緜紬 *miarnchour*, n., silk made from coarser threads of cocoons.
緜惙 *miarnchuoh*, adj., (LL) still hanging on and breathing (of dying person).
緜篤 *miarnduh*, adj., (LL) in critical prolonged illness.
緜頓 *miarnduhn*, adj., see *-duh*↑.
緜亙 *miarngehng*, adj., see *-charng*↑.
緜力 *miarnlih*, n., my humble effort: 竭盡緜力 do my best = *-bor*↑.
緜裏針 *miarnliijen*, n., needle in wool, dangerous person smooth in exterior.
緜蠻 *miarnmarn*, n., (AC) bird cry.
緜緜 *miarnmiarn*, adj., continuing, lingering on: 緜緜不絕 continuing for ever; 此恨緜緜無盡期 this lover's regret shall last for evermore.
緜密 *miarnmih*, adj., fine and careful (attention), well-meshed (system).
緜子 *miarntz*, n., silk wool in paper-thin sheets used in Chin. ink-pad, etc.
緜延 *miarnyarn*, v.i. & adj., con-

tinue (-ing) far or long (family tree, etc.).
緜羊 *miarnyarng*, n., sheep (cf. 山羊 goat).

§91S.02 (ノ^{s}/⺊)

齉 91S.02-1

nahng.

Adj. 齉鼻(子)(兒) nose blocked up.

艨 91S.02-2

merng.

艨衝 *merngchung*, n., anc. warships protected with cowhide (also wr. 蒙衝).
艨艟 *merngturng*, n., ditto.

衇 91S.02-9

moh.
[Interch. 脈 42A.02]

§91S.10 (ノ^{s}/十)

躰 91S.10-1

tii.
[Abbr. of 體 42B.30]

衅 91S.10-2

shihn.

N. (LL) a quarrel, dispute (var. 釁 90.50).

衈 91S.10-3

ehl.

V.t. (AC) to smear animal blood as pledge in signing treaties, by shaving off hair around animal's ear first.

鼾 91S.10-3

han.

V.i. To snore: 鼾睡 snore in sleep (cf. 齁 91S.50).

犴 91S.10-3

ahn (also *hahn*).

N. (AC) prison.

牌 91S.10-9

pair.

N. Tablet, signboard, usu. inscribed; playing card: 打牌 to play cards; 門牌號數 house number.

牌榜 *pairbaang*, n., notice board; signboard.
牌匾 *pairbiaan*, n., signboard over shop, hall or door; 牌匾兒 (*-biae'l*) one's prestige.
牌額 *pair-eh*, n., see *-biaan* ↑.
牌坊 *pair-fang*, n., memorial arch.
牌照 *pairjauh*, n., license, license plate.
牌九 *pairjioou*, n., game of dominoes.
牌局 *pairjyur*, n., gambling house or party, esp. at singsong house.
牌樓 *pairlour*, n., ornamental arch, archway.
牌示 *pairshyh*, n., public notice on signboard; v.i., give such notice.
牌子 *pairtz*, n., label, trademark; (fig.) a man's reputation: 他牌子眞大 enjoys a big name; name of song or theatrical selection, shown in theater.
牌位 *pairweih*, n., spirit tablet.

皞 91S.10-9

hauh.
[Pop. 皡; cf. 皓 91S.40]

§91S.11 (ノ^{s}/土)

貛 91S.11-2

huan.

N. The badger: 豬貛 badger; 狗貛 jackal.

貍 91S.11-4

lir.
[Pop. 狸]

N. (Zoo.) the fox, racoon, *Nyctereutes procyonoides*; see 狐⁴貍 91C.83; various animals of the feline family (usu. wr. 狸): 貍貓 *-mau* ↓; 香貍 the civet cat.

貍貓 *lirmau*, n., (zoo.) a kind of

亅	小	⺊	十	土	ナ	廾	㇗	丨	一	丁	フ	口	区	冈	㇆	厂	尸	亠	广	宀	丶	乚	七	心	八	人	乂	⺈	一	⺉	⺊	く
00	01	02	10	11	12	20	21	22	30	31	32	40	41	42	50	51	52	60	61	62	63	70	71	72	80	81	82	83	90	91	92	93

wild cat.

狸奴 *lirnur*, n., (LL) the cat.

狸藻 *lirtzaau*, n., (bot.) the common bladderwort, *Utricularia vulgaris*.

艟 91S.11–6

turng.

N. See 艨△艟 91S.02.

讎 91S.11–6

chour.
[Var. 讐]

N. (1) (=仇 91A.70) enemy: 報讎 to revenge. (2) (=儔) mate: 讎匹 rival. (3) (=酬) (AC) repayment; repartee. (4) Proofreading, to proofread; 校讎 comparison of texts.

讎校 *chourjiauh*, v.i., to proofread; compare texts.

§91S.21 (ノ^{s}/ㄴ)

舢 91S.21–2

shan.

舢板 *shanbaan*, n., a sampan.

軀 91S.21–5

chyu.

N. The human body: 肉軀 the flesh (physical body); 靈軀 the soul (spiritual body); 爲國捐軀 die for one's country.

軀殼 *chyuchiauh*, n., the physical body.

軀幹 *chyugahn*, n., (1) (physiol.) the trunk of animal; (2) stature: 軀幹雄偉 a tall stature.

軀體 *chyutii*, n., the human body.

牐 91S.21–9

jar.
[Var. of 閘 52B.00]

§91S.22 (ノ^{s}/丨)

帥 91S.22–2

shuaih (re. pr. *shuoh*, rare).
[Dist. 師 91S.22]

N. Commander in chief: 統帥, 主帥, 元帥 ditto; 主帥 polite address of commander; 將帥 commanders, generals, of the army.

V.t. (1) To command (army): 統帥 ditto: 帥師, 帥兵 command or lead troops. (2) (AC) u.f. 率, 帥(=率)由舊章△ 60.10.

Adj. Handsome, attractive (also wr. 率): 長得眞帥, 打扮得好帥 look handsome, dress handsomely.

帥領 *shauihliing*, v.t. & n., to command, commander.

師 91S.22–3

shy.

N. (1) Teacher: 老師 teacher (of any age or sex); 師父, 師傅 *-'fu*, *-fuh*↓; 師道 *-dauh*↓; 尊師 respect for teachers; 師生關係 relation of teacher and pupil; 師友 *-yoou*↓; 師範, 師資, 師表 *-fahn*, *-tzy*, *-biaau*↓. (2) Attached to term of address of various professional people: 醫師, 律師 doctor, lawyer; 牧師 clergyman, pastor; 工程師, 建築師 engineer, architect; 會計師 public accountant; 理髮師, 廚師 barber, cook. (3) (Mil.) a division: 師長 *-jaang*↓; 裝甲師 armored division; 步兵師 infantry division; 師團 *-tuarn*↓. (4) Gen. term for troops, army or navy: 雄師 a great army; 班師 recall troops; 水師 the navy, naval squadron; 師出無名 send army out without a righteous cause.

V.t. To imitate: 師其所長 learn from person his good points; 師古 to imitate the ancients; 師事, 師法 *-shyh*, *-faa*↓.

師保 *shybaau*, v.t., as in (AC) 師保萬民 to act as teacher and protector to the people.

師表 *shybiaau*, n., the model: 爲人師表 be model for others; 萬世師表 "the teacher for all ages" (title conferred upon Confucius).

師比 *shybii*, n., (AC) girdle hook.

師承 *shycherng*, n., the succession of teachings from master to disciples; 師承記 such record showing how oral tradition was handed down.

師道 *shydauh*, n., the teacher's status and position of respect.

師弟 *shydih*, n., (1) master and pupil; (2) formerly, address of a junior fellow student.

師法 *shyfaa*, (1) v.t., to imitate: 師法古人 imitate the ancients; (2) n., tradition, technique handed down by master; (3) (AC) strategy (=兵法).

師範 *shyfahn*, (1) n., the teacher as model for others; (2) adj., normal: 師範學校, 大學 normal school, teachers' college; (3) v.t., (LL) to take (s.o.) as model.

師父 *shy'fu*, n., (1) see *-fuh*↓; (2) address of respect to monks or nuns; (3) common address of certain professions, like "Master": 木匠師父, 廚師父 "master" carpenter, "master" cook.

師傅 *shyfuh*, n., (1) (LL) teacher, tutor, master; (2) (-*'fu*) ditto.

師輔 *shyfuu*, n., (LL) teachers and friends in learning.

師干 *shygan*, v.t., (AC) defense forces.

師姑 *shygu*, n., address of nun ("teacher-aunt").

師長 *shyjaang*, n., (1) division commander; (2) teachers and elders.

師姐 *shyjiee*, n., address of elder fellow girl student; teacher's daughter older than oneself.

師旅 *shylyuu*, n., troops in gen. ("divisions and brigades").

師妹 *shymeih*, n., address of younger fellow girl student; teacher's daughter younger than oneself.

師門 *shymern*, n., formerly, school of a private teacher or master (＝師之門下).

師母 *shymuu*, n., respectful address of teacher's wife or of wife of elderly friend.

師娘 *shyniarng*, n., (coll.) ditto.

師婆 *shypor*, n., priestess, sorceress.

師心 *shy-shin*, phr., 師心自用 not willing to listen to advice, act and show overconfidence in oneself.

師帥 *shyshuaih*, n., as in (AC) 民之師帥 guide and model for the people.

師事 *shyshyh*, v.t., to serve (s.o.) as master or teacher; to be taught by.

師兄 *shyshyung*, n., (1) address of fellow student, one's senior; (2) teacher's son older than oneself; (3) oft. address of one of younger generation, whose father is one's friend: 師兄幾位 how many sons have you? 師兄弟兒 --*dieh'l*, fellow students, students of same tutor (formerly, a closer relationship).

師太 *shytaih*, n., (sl.) teacher's wife, see -*muu* ↑.

師團 *shytuarn*, n., army corp.

師徒 *shy-tur*, n., teacher and pupil (relationship).

師資 *shytzy*, n., (1) standard and quality of teachers: 師資缺乏 lack of good teachers; (2) model and example: 善人者不善人之師也，不善者善人之資也（老子） the good are models for the bad, and the bad are examples (of warning) for the good.

師爺 *shyyer*, n., (1) formerly, teacher's teacher or teacher's father; (2) (-*'ye*) formerly, scholar or expert in law and bureaucratic matters in a magistrate's office: 紹興師爺 expert in legal briefs, usu. from 紹興 county.

師友 *shy-yoou*, n., teachers and friends.

郯 91S.22–3

tarn.

N. A surname.

郫 91S.22–3

pir.

N. Name of anc. county in Szechuan: 郫縣.

鄔 91S.22–3

wu.

N. A surname.

卹 91S.22–5

shyuh.

[Var. 恤; err. var. 䘏]

V.t. To comfort the afflicted or the bereaved, to relieve the poor, sick, those stricken with famine: 卹孤 comfort the orphan; 體卹 take pity on, have consideration for (the unfortunate); 撫卹孤兒 take care of orpahned child and bring him up.

卹典 *shyuhdiaan*, n., formerly, the elaborate funeral ceremonies of high officials.

卹荒 *shyuhhuang*, v.i. & n., (carry on) famine relief.

卹金 *shyuhjin*, n., grant of money for the bereaved, also 養卹金.

卽 91S.22–5

jir.

[Var. 即]

V.i. & t. (1) V.i., be: 卽此人也 it is he; 非其父兄，卽其子弟 if it's not his father or brother, it must be his children. (2) V.t., approach, go near to: 卽之也溫 (AC) when you go near him, you find him to be so gentle and kind. (3) Depart from: 卽世 -*shyh*¹↓. (4) Do, engage in, undertake, conduct: 不利卽戎 (AC) time not auspicious for going to war. (5) Assume (office), take (one's seat): 卽位 -*weih*↓

Adj. (1) The same (day, etc.), immediate: 卽日 -*ryh*, 卽期 -*chir*, 卽今 -*jin*↓. (2) Close together, nearby: 不卽不離 (of relations between persons) hold slightly aloof, neither accept nor reject (approach).

Adv. (1) As soon as: 黎明卽起 get up as soon as it dawns; 氣斷卽死 a person dies as soon as he ceases to breathe. (2) Then: 降卽免死 if you surrender, then your life will be spared; 無乃卽傷君王之所愛乎 won't you then give offense to the prince's beloved ones? (3) Quickly, at once: 當卽 right away; 卽刻 -*keh*↓; 立卽 immediately; 卽可使用 usable at once;

即將 soon, in no time; 即速 *-suh*↓.

Conj. Even if, even though: 即使 *-shyy*, 即令 *-lihng*↓; 即或 *-huoh*, 便 *-biahn*↓.

即便 *jirbiahn*, adv. phr., even if: 即便是你，也得處罰 even if it were you, you would be punished.
即期 *jirchir*, adj., as in 即期支票 a check payable on demand.
即或 *jirhuoh*, adv. phr., even though.
即眞 *jirjen*, v.i., (of officials) be formally appointed after a period of acting.
即漸 *jirjiahn*, adv., gradually, by slow steps.
即景 *jirjiing*, adj., (of poems) written with what one sees before one's eyes as subject matter.
即今 *jirjin*, adv., right now, at this very moment.
即吉 *jir-jir*, v.i., take off mourning garments.
即刻 *jirkeh*, adv., immediately, at once.
即令 *jirlihng*, conj. & v.t., even if; order immediately.
即如 *jirrur*, adv., as if.
即日 *jir-ryh*, adv., (1) this very day; (2) in the next few days.
即興 *jir-shihng*, adj., as in 即興賦詩, 即興表演 write poems, give a show on the spur of the moment.
即席 *jir-shir*, adj., in the course of a dinner party; on-the-spot.
即世 *jir-shyh*[1], v.i., (LL) depart from the world, pass away.
即事 *jir-shyh*[2], (1) v.i., assume office; (2) adv., with reference to conditions as they are.
即時 *jir-shyr*, adv., right away, immediately.
即使 *jirshyy*, conj., even if.
即速 *jirsuh*, adv., as soon as possible.
即此 *jirtsyy*, phr., that's it.
即早兒 *jirtzaau'l*, adv. phr., while it's early, at an early moment.
即位 *jir-weih*, v.i., (1) ascend the throne; (2) take seat.
即夜 *jir-yeh*, adv., the very night.

歸 91S.22-5

guei (**kueih*).

N. (1) Return (of persons or things borrowed). (2) (Math.) (calculation by the use of abacus) division: 九歸 division with a one-digit divisor. (3) A surname.

V.i. & t. (1) V.i., come back: 歸來 to return; 歸去來兮 I'm going home! 歸國 come back to one's homeland; 歸途 the return trip; 歸隊 (of soldiers) report for duty, (fig.) return to the fold; 衣錦榮歸 (of government officials) return home with high honors. (2) V.t., to return (s.t.) borrowed: 歸還 *-huarn*↓. (3) V.i., 于歸 (AC, of women) to marry. (4) V.i., submit, yield: 歸附 *-fuh*, 歸順 *-shuhn*↓; 歸降 to surrender; 歸化 *-huah*↓; 歸主 become a Christian. (5) V.t., put together, assemble in one place: 歸併 *-bihng*, 歸攏 *-luung*, 歸齊 *-chir*↓; 歸了包堆 calculate as a whole. (6) V.t., attribute to: 歸功 give (s.o.) credit for; 歸罪 blame (s.o.) for; 歸咎 *-jiouh*↓. (7) V.i., tend, come to an end: 歸宿 *-suh*↓; 殊途同歸 all roads lead to Rome; 同歸於盡 (of enemies, forlorn lovers, etc.) get killed at one and the same time; 歸根 *-gen*↓; 歸結 *-jier*↓. (8) (Var. 饋 **kueih*) v.t., (AC) give as present: 歸孔子豚 present Confucius with leg of pork.

歸案 *guei-ahn*, v.t., to bring back s.t. or s.o. to court, case or subject file.
歸併 *gueibihng*, v.t., annex (territory) by force; blend, mix, compound, reunite.
歸齊 *gueichir*, (1) v.t., to lump or put together; (2) adv., altogether, after all: 歸齊不到一個月 less than a month altogether; 說了歸齊，你還不成 won't you come round after all?
歸除 *gueichur*, n., (math.) (calculation by the use of abacus) division with a more than one-digit divisor.
歸附 *gueifuh*, v.i., pay allegiance to the rule of another, acknowledge sovereignty.
歸根(兒) *gueigen(-ge'l)*, (1) v.i., come to an end; (2) adv., in the end, at last, finally.
歸骨 *guei-guu*, v.i., have one's bones buried (usu. in one's native district).
歸化 *gueihuah*, v.i., (1) submit to Chin. rule; adopt Chin. customs; (2) (law) (be) naturalize(d).
歸還 *guei-huarn*, (1) v.i., come back; (2) v.t., return (things) borrowed.
歸趙 *guei-Jauh*, v.t., (allu.) to return (s.t.) to its rightful owner intact.
歸眞 *guei-jen*, v.i., (1) (Budd.) attain nirvana, pass away, die; (2) rediscover one's true self: 返樸歸眞 recover man's original simplicity.
歸家 *guei-jia*, v.i. & n., return home, home-coming.
歸結 *gueijier*, (1) v.i., come to a conclusion; (2) adv., in the end: 歸結落空 in the end get nothing.
歸咎 *guei-jiouh*, v.t., lay the blame on (s.o.).
歸著 *guei'juo*, v.t., fix up (room, clothing), put in order.
歸攏 *gueiluung*, v.t., collect, assemble together.
歸納 *gueinah*, v.t., (logic) infer by induction: 歸納法 (logic) the inductive method, *a posteriori* reasoning, induction (opp. 演繹法 *a priori* reasoning, deduction).
歸寧 *guei-nirng*, v.i., (of married women) go back to paternal home for a visit, (rarely of men) visit with one's parents.
歸西 *guei-shi*, v.i., die, pass away, (lit., "go west" or to the abode of the dead).
歸省 *gueishiing*, v.i., go home to pay respects to one's parents.
歸心 *gueishin*, v.t. & n., (1) v.t., pay allegiance to; (2) n., nostalgia for home: 歸心似箭 anxious to return home as soon as possible.
歸休 *gueishiou*, v.i., (1) retire and return home; (2) (AC) die, pass away, (lit., "go to one's rest").

歸 舴 皚 艫 舡 艋 衄 归 䶊 艦 皓 加

歸順 *gueishuhn*, v.i., to surrender, pay allegiance to.

歸宿 *gueisuh*, (1) v.i., (of persons) come to a (usu. happy) end; (2) n., a lasting or permanent in life: 找到歸宿 (of girls) be happily married.

歸天 *guei-tiarn*[1], v.i., (euphem.) die, pass away, (lit., "go up to heaven").

歸田 *guei-tiarn*[2], v.i., (of officials) resign from office and return home.

歸宗 *guei-tzung*, v.i., (of adopted children) return to one's own parents or clan.

歸依 *gueiyi*, v.i., become a Buddhist (also wr. 皈依).

舴 91S.22-9

tzer.

N. 舴艋 (LL) a small boat.

§91S.30 (ノ^{S}/一)

皚 91S.30-2

air.

Adj. (AC) dazzlingly white: 皚皚 ditto.

艫 91S.30-2

lur.

N. See 舳$^{\Delta}$艫 91S.41.

舡 91S.30-3

shiang.

N. A small boat.

艋 91S.30-3

meeng.

N. See 舴$^{\Delta}$艋 91S.22.

衄 91S.30-5

nyuh (also *niouh*).
[Var. 衂]

N. Bleeding from the nose; (med.) epistaxis.

V.i. & t. 敗衄 (of army) be defeated in battle.

归 91S.30-5

guei.
[Abbr. of 歸 91S.22]

䶊 91S.30-5

nyuh.
[Var. 衄]

N. Bleeding from the nose.

艦 91S.30-5

jiahn.

N. A warship: 艦隊 *-dueih*, 艦長 *-jaang*↓; 船艦, 艦艇 naval vessels; 主力艦 a battleship; 巡洋艦 a cruiser; 驅逐艦 a destroyer; 航空母艦 an aircraft carrier, a flattop; 戰艦 a man-of-war; 旗艦 the flagship; 砲艦 a gunboat; 軍艦 a warship.

艦隊 *jiahn-dueih*, n., a naval squadron, fleet.

艦長 *jiahn-jaang*, n., captain, commander, skipper (of a warship).

§91S.40 (ノ^{S}/口)

皓 91S.40-1

hauh.

Adj. Bright, hoary, brilliant white: 皓月當空 the bright moon in the sky; 明眸皓齒 clear eyes and white teeth; 童顏皓首 (of old man) ruddy complexion and hoary head.

皓皓 *hauhhauh*, adj., (1) shining white; (2) (AC) open-hearted and poised in character.

皓魄 *hauhpoh*, n., (LL) the moon.

加 91S.40-4

jia.

V.t. (1) Add to, increase: 加俸, 加薪 raise one's pay, pay-hike; 加增 *-tzeng*↓; 增加 add some more; 添加, 加多 to increase, augment; 加倍 *-beih*↓; 加工 (of raw materials) to process into a finished product; 加功 make redoubled efforts; 加餐 eat adequately; 加衣服穿 put on more clothes; 加勉

亅	小	⺊	十	土	ナ	廾	⺊	丨	一	丅	フ	口	囗	冈	丁	厂	尸	亠	广	宀	丶	乚	弋	心	八	人	乂	一	丆	丿	𠂉	く
00	01	02	10	11	12	20	21	22	30	31	32	40	41	42	50	51	52	60	61	62	63	70	71	72	80	81	82	83	90	91	92	93

加船貂艙貉艢

make greater exertions; 更加 more and more, all the more; 無以復加 the last word, the best (worst) of its kind; 罪加一等 doubly guilty; 加寫 insert words; 加印 to stamp or seal. (2) Confer, give, bestow: 加(之)於 give to, confer on; 加害 *-haih*↓; 加罪於他 blame it on him; 參加 be a party to, take part in; 加入 *-ruh*↓.

加班 *jia-ban*, v.i., to work overtime.
加倍 *jiabeih*, v.t., (1) to double (an amount); (2) redouble (efforts).
加法 *jiafaa*, n., (math.) addition.
加官 *jiaguan*, v.i., (1) hold a concurrent job; (2) formerly, be promoted to a higher position.
加害 *jiahaih*, v.t., intentionally hurt or injure, implicate, incriminate.
加號 *jiahauh*, n., (math.) the plus sign(＋).
加護 *jiahuh*, v.t., (of gods) bless, take special care of.
加重 *jiajuhng*, v.i. & t., (1) become or make heavier; (2) impose a heavier burden or severer penalty on s.o.
加料 *jia-liauh*, n., articles made of superior materials.
加禮 *jia-lii*, v.t., treat with exceptional civility.
加厘 *jialir*, n., (translit.) curry.
加侖 *jialurn*, n., (translit.) a gallon.
加盟 *jia-merng*, v.i., become a member of an alliance, a fraternity or a secret society.
加冕 *jia-miaan*, (1) v.t., to crown; (2) n., coronation.
加拿大 *Jianaadaih*, n., Canada.
加入 *jia-ruh*, v.t., join, enter, become a member of (a club, society, political party).
加數 *jiashuh*, n., (math.) a number to be added to another.
加速 *jiasuh*, v.i. & t., accelerate: 加速度 (phys.) acceleration; 加速力 (phys.) accelerated force.
加增 *jiatzeng*, v.t., to increase, raise, enhance, reinforce.
加言兒 *jiayar'l*[1], v.i., embellish reported speech with malicious falsifications.
加鹽兒 *jiayar'l*[2], v.i., ditto.
加一 *jiayi*, adj., ten per cent (extra, surcharge).
加意 *jiayih*, v.t., pay special attention to, heed.
加油(兒) *jiayour('l)*, v.i., to pep up, to cheer (game player).

船 91S.40-4

chuarn.

N. A boat, ship: 輪船, 汽船 steamboat; 漁船 fishing boat; 拖船, 駁船 tug boat; 划船 paddle boat; 飛船 airship, module; 太空船 spaceship; 上船, 下船 go aboard, disembark from ship; 坐船, 乘船 go by boat; 開船 boat sails.

船板 *chuarnbaan*, n., boat deck.
船幫 *chuarnbang*, n., hull of ship, ship's side.
船舶 *chuarnbor*, n., (oft. as collective n.) ships (on sea or harbor).
船埠 *chuarnbuh*, n., port of call.
船廠 *chuarnchaang*, n., shipyard.
船期 *chuarnchir*, n., sailing schedule.
船渠 *chuarnchyur*, n., *-wuh*↓.
船費 *chuarnfeih*, n., cost of boat ticket.
船夫 *chuarnfu*, n., boatman, boat hand.
船骨 *chuarnguu*, n., boat's beam.
船戶 *chuarnhuh*, n., boatman.
船長 *chuarnjaang*, n., ship's captain.
船家 *chuarnjia*, n., boatman or his family.
船脚 *chuarnjiaau*, n., cost of freight.
船籍 *chuarnjir*, n., nationality of ship's registration.
船主 *chuarnjuu*, n., (1) ship's captain; (2) shipowner.
船隻 *chuarnjy*, n., boats and ships in gen.: 往來船隻 the shipping traffic.
船面 *chuarnmiahn*, n., the deck.
船篷(子) *chuarnperng(tz)*, n., (1) matting cover for houseboats; (2) (LL) a sail (＝帆 22B.70).
船票 *chuarnpiauh*, n., boat ticket.
船梢 *chuarnshau*, n., bow of ship.
船舷 *chuarnshiarn*, n., gunwale.
船頭 *chuarntour*, n., ship's bow.
船艙 *chuarntsang*, n., berth, also ship's hold.
船尾 *chuarnweei*, n., stern.
船桅 *chuarnweir*, n., mast.
船塢 *chuarnwuh*, n., dock, dockyard.
船員 *chuarnyuarn*, n., seaman, sailor.
船運 *chuarnyuhn*, n., transportation by sea.

貂 91S.40-5

diau.

[Var. of 鼦]

N. Sable: 貂皮大衣 sable coat.

艙 91S.40-8

tsang.

N. A deck, a berth: 艙位 berth in ship; 頭等艙 firstclass berth; 客艙 passenger's berth; 艙面 the deck; 艙門 hatch; 艙底 ship's hold; 煤艙 the hold where coal is kept.

貉 91S.40-9

her (*moh, *haur).

N. (1) (Also **haur*) 貉子 a badger; 貉絨 badger skin. (2) (**moh*) 貉狄, 北貉 term for wild tribe in the north.

§91S.41 (ノS/図)

艢 91S.41-1

chiarng.

[Var. of 檣 10B.41]

舳 91S.41-2

jur (sp. pr. *jour*).

N. Helmsman's place.

舳艫 *jurlur*, n., formerly, broad-beamed and square-browed boat, used in sea battle.

貓 91S.41-2

mau.

N. (*-tz*, or *-'l*) Cat: 貓哭耗子 a cat crying at mouse's death, "crocodile tears"; 貓鼠同眠 thieves and police working together; 貓兒尿 (derisive of) bad wine ("cat's urine"); 貓兒溺 *-'lnih*, a personal secret that cannot be told.

貓兒眼 *mau'lyaan*, n., cat's-eye, a precious stone.
貓狸 *maulir*, n., wild cat, bobcat, lynx.
貓頭鷹 *mautour-ying*, n., owl.
貓眼石 *mauyaan-shyr*, n., see *-'lyaan*↑, also called 貓睛石 *-jing-shyr*.
貓魚 *mauyur*, n., small fish as cat's food.

貊 91S.41-3

moh.

N. Name of anc. northern tribe: 蠻貊之邦 country of barbarians.

皤 91S.41-9

por.

皤皤 *porpor*, adj., (AC) white (of hair, snow); big-bellied, paunchy.
皤然 *porrarn*, adj., (AC) white; paunchy.

舶 91S.41-9

bor.

N. Ship, usu. sea-going, usu. 船舶 sea-going ships.

舶來品 *borlair-piin*, n., goods from across the ocean, generally foreign goods.
舶物 *bor-wuh*, n., (MC) same as *-lair-piin*↑.

艪 91S.41-9

luu.

[Var. of 櫓 10B.41]

§91S.42 (ノ^{S}/冈)

艄 91S.42-2

shau.

N. The boat stern: 艄公 boatman, helmsman.

躺 91S.42-2

taang.

V.i. To lie down: 躺下, 躺下去 lie down; 躺在床上 lie in bed; 在這兒躺躺 lie down here a bit; 躺着歇歇 lie down for a little rest; 躺着談 talk lying down; 躺得渾身發痛 the body is sore from lying (a long time).

躺船 *taangchuarn*, n., a kind of boat with bed or space for lying down.
躺椅 *tarngyii*, n., deck chair; *chaise longue.*

貒 91S.42-2

tuan.

N. The badger, *Meles anakuma* (also known as 豬貛).

牖 91S.42-6

yoou.

N. (LL) window: 牖戶 doors and windows.

V.t. (AC) to enlighten (people).

§91S.50 (ノ^{S}/ㄱ)

艣 91S.50-2

luu.

[Var. of 櫓 10B.41]

躬 91S.50-5

gung.

N. The human body: 鞠躬 to bow (lit., "to bend the body"); 政躬違和 (of public men) be ill; 政躬

康泰 "best wishes for Your Excellency's health."

V.i. (Of the human body) bend: 躬身, 躬著身子 to bow with the body slightly bent, as a sign of respect.

Adv. Personally, in person: 反躬自問(省) self-introspection; 躬親 *-chin*↓; 躬行實踐 practice personally what one preaches; 躬耕 personally till the soil; 躬詣 pay a visit in person.

躬親 *gungchin*, v.i., do s.t. in person.

衂 91S.50-5

nyuh.

[Var. of 衄 91S.30]

翱 91S.50-5

aur.

翱翔 *aurshiarng*, v.i., (birds) to wheel about in the sky; to roam about.

舫 91S.50-6

faang.

N. Pleasure boat: 畫舫 painted pleasure boat.

牓 91S.50-6

baang.

[Var. of 榜]

的 91S.50-9

dih (**dir*, **'de*).

N. (*dih*) Target: 目的 goal, target; 目的地 destination; 鵠的 shooting target.

Adj. & adv. part. (*'de*) (1) Possessive particle: 我的, 你的, 李氏的: my, your, Mr. Li's. (2) Common adj. particle: 美麗的花 pretty flower; 無用的東西 useless thing. (3) Common adv. particle: 快快的走 go quickly; 慢慢的練習 practise slowly (some writers affect European style by writing 底 for 2 and 地 for 3 in place of 的).

Pron. part. (*'de*) Corresponding somewhat in meaning to "the one who (which)": 倒垃圾的 garbage collector (the one who . . .); 唱歌的, 跳舞的 those who sing, those who dance: 吃的穿的都有了 have food and dress (that for eating, that for clothing); 我要去的, 不去的 I am, am not going (among those who are, are not going). In this usage, 是 (不是) is added as vb. predicate: 這是外來的 this is made abroad; 這問題不容易解決 (without 是) this problem is not easy to solve, but 這問題是不容易解決的 this problem is not one which is easy to solve.

Vb. complement part. (**de*) For introducing vb. complement, used sometimes in place of 得 (also pr. *'de*): 唱的好 or 唱得好 sing well; 亂的 (or 得) 一場糊塗 confused (so that) all is in a mess; 看的(得)可憐 look pitiful.

Adj. (**dir*) True, definite: 的確, 的當, 的細 *-chyueh*, *-dahng*, *-shih*↓; 端⁴的 60S.42.

的確 **dirchyueh*, adv., truly, really: 的確走了 really gone; 的確不錯, 可靠 really very good, dependable, also 的的確確.

的當 **dirdahng*, adj., appropriate, suitable.

的細 **dirshih*, adj., detailed, fine.

豹 91S.50-9

bauh.

N. Leopard, panther, species of mountain cat, esp. 金錢豹 with ring-like spots; 豹死留皮 phr., leopard's skin survives the body (fig. of fame); 豹頭環眼 phr., round eyes and well-formed forehead.

豹變 *bauhbiahn*, n., rise to wealth from poverty.

豹略 *bauhlyueh*, n. strategic moves or plans.

豹隱 *bauhyiin*, v.i., live in retirement, obscurity, oft. voluntarily.

鳩 91S.50-9

jiou.

N. The pigeon, the turtledove: 班鳩 the rock pigeon; 雎鳩 the osprey; 鳩杖 *-jahng*↓; 鳩形鵠面 haggard, emaciated, skin and bone ("like a scarecrow").

V.t. Herd together: 鳩合 *-her*, 鳩集 *-jir*↓; 鳩工庀 (*pii*) 材 gather together workmen and construction materials.

鳩合 *jiouher*, v.t., (of birds, riffraff) gather together.

鳩杖 *jioujahng*, n., an old man's staff.

鳩集 *jioujir*, v.t., see *-her*↑.

鳩聚 *jioujyuh*, v.t., stack, pile up.

鳩槃荼 *jiouparntur*, n., (1) (Sanskr. *Kumbhanda*) a nightmare, incubus; (2) a hag.

鴆 91S.50-9

jehn.

N. (1) A secretary bird of prey

which feeds on snakes, reptiles; wine drained through its feathers is reputed to be poisonous, see 鴆酒 *-jioou*↓. (2) Poison, poisonous wine: 飲鴆 take poison; 飲鴆止渴 take poisonous drink to stop thirst—remedy worse than trouble.

V.t. To poison (person): 鴆殺, 鴆害 kill by poison.

鴆 毒 *jehndur*, n. & v.t., a poison; to poison.
鴆 酒 *jehnjioou*, n., poisonous wine.
鴆 媒 *jehnmeir*, n., venomous talk or gossip.

齁 91S.50–9

hou.

V.i. To snore: 齁聲, 齁齁 snoring noise.

Adj. Nauseating: 齁鹹, 齁苦 unbearably salty, bitter.

鶴 91S.50–9

heh (sp. pr. **haur*).

N. A stork, a crane: 鶴氅 a coat of stork feathers; (a) oft. a symbol of longevity: 鶴壽 long life; 童顏鶴髮 (of old people) with a ruddy complexion and white hair; (b) oft. a symbol of Taoist fairy: 騎鶴 riding on a stork through the sky; 鶴駕 a fairy's travel or whereabouts, also used of a prince's travel; 鶴馭 (LL) used at funeral of a woman's departure from life; (c) as a symbol of high office: 鶴俸 (LL) formerly, official's emoluments.

鶴頂紅 *hehdiinghurng*, n., the stork's red crest, alleged to be poisonous.
鶴 年 *heh-niarn*, n., long life.

鶺 91S.50–9

jir.

N. 鶺鴒 (zoo.) the pied wagtail.

鷦 91S.50–9

jiau.

N. 鷦鷯 (zoo.) the wren.

§91S.63 (ノˢ/丶)

皫 91S.63–6

piaau.

Adj. (AC) white in color.

舲 91S.63–8

lirng.

N. A small houseboat with lookout windows.

§91S.70 (ノˢ/乚)

既 91S.70–5

jih.

[Usu. wr. 既]

Adj. Complete, full: 日有食之既 (AC) there was a full eclipse; 蝕既 (AC) the moment of full eclipse; 既成事實 a *fait accompli*, an accomplished fact; 無既 limitless: 感荷無既 (LL) thank you ever so much ("no end of thanks").

Adv. (1) Already: 既往不咎 let bygones be bygones; 既成, 既遂 already done or committed. (2) Since: 既來之, 則安之 since we have come, let us stay and enjoy it. (3) Then, later on: 既而悔之 afterwards he repented of his promise. (4) 既...且 both . . . and: 既醉且飽 have had enough of both wine and food.

Conj. Since: see 既然 *-rarn*↓.

既 得 權 *jihder-chyuarn*, n., right of acquisition.
既 而 *jih-erl*, adv., then, soon thereafter, sometime later.
既 然 *jihrarn*, conj., since, as (it is so, etc.).
既 是 *jihshyh*, conj., ditto.
既 望 *jihwahng*, n., the 16th day of a lunar month ("day after 望, the full moon").

航 91S.70–6

harng.

N. A boat or ship.

V.i. (1) To navigate, to sail: 航海 航船 *-haai*, *-chuarn*↓. (2) To navigate the air: 航空, 航郵, 航運 *-kung*, *-your*, *-yuhn*↓.

航 程 *harngcherng*, n., distance by air or sea.
航 船 *harngchuarn*, n., ship in maritime trade; ship in gen.
航 權 *harngchyuarn*, n., right of navigation.

航 舵 皖 駝 胤 貌 貔 魄 皰 鮠 鼆 鱴

航道 *harngdauh*, n., navigation route.
航海 *harnghaai*, v.i., to sail across the sea: 航海曆 nautical almanac; 航海日誌 logbook.
航政 *harngjehng*, n., maritime administration.
航機 *harngji*, n., scheduled aircraft.
航空 *harngkung*, v.i. & n., to fly in airplane; aviation, aeronautics: 航空公司 airline company; 航空母艦 aircraft carrier.
航路 *harngluh*, n., air or navigation route.
航線 *harngshiahn*, n., ditto.
航行 *harngshirng*, v.i., to sail, navigate.
航業 *harngyeh*, n., the shipping trade or industry.
航郵 *harngyour*, n., airmail.
航運 *harngyuhn*, n., air freight, air transportation.

舵 91S.70-6

duoh.

N. Rudder: 掌舵 take the helm; 轉舵機 steering engine; 外舵 starboard the helm; 裏舵 port the helm.

舵把 *duohbaa*, n., tiller of boat; also 舵杆 *-gan.*
舵輪 *duohlurn*, n., steering wheel.
舵手 *duohshou*, n., helmsman; also 舵工 *-gung.*

皖 91S.70-6

waan.

N. Name for 安徽 Anhwei Province.

駝 91S.70-6

tuor.

N. 駝鳥 the ostrich (also wr. 鴕鳥).

胤 91S.70-9

yihn.

N. Progeny: 承胤 (of children) continue the family line.

貌 91S.70-9

mauh.

N. External appearance: 面貌, 容貌 facial appearance; 容貌端正 proper facial features; 貌寢 ugly in appearance; 美貌 pretty face, handsome looks; 貌似忠厚 appear to be honest; 不可以貌取人, 不可以貌相 cannot judge people by their looks; 貌合神離 friends in name or appearance only.

Adj. & adv. 貌接 (AC) treat correctly, receive formally; 王貌愛之 (AC) the king appeared to like her; 貌言 (AC) baseless talk.

貌似 *mauhsyh*, adj., resembling; appearing to be or like (s.o.).

貔 91S.70-9

pir.

貔虎 *pirhuu*, n., leopard and tigers, (fig.) brave generals or troops.
貔貅 *pirshiou*, n., fabulous wild beast like leopard, known for ferocity; (fig.) brave troops.

魄 91S.70-9

poh.

N. (Taoism) the baser animal spirits of man, contrasted with finer elements 魂 *huern* (三魂七魄 three finer spirits and seven animal spirits), the two together conceived as animating the human body; the dark portion of the moon in 旁$^{\Delta}$魄 60.50, 糟$^{\Delta}$魄 22C.41; 氣魄 energetic personality, great style of personality; 落魄 (of family, people) down and out.

魄力 *polih*, n., great vitality, energy (of man), force of character in carrying through.
魄門 *pohmern*, n., (AC) the anus.

皰 91S.70-9

bauh.

N. A pimple.

鮠 91S.70-9

nieh.

鮠卼 *niehwuh*, adj., uneasy, unhappy, vexed.

鼆 91S.70-9

wehng.

Adj. Blocked up (nose); (related 齆 60.70).

§91S.71 (ノ^{S}/乜)

鱴 91S.71-2

mieh.

N. (AC) dirty blood.

V.t. To smear (person's good name): 污䘏.

牋 91S.71-7

jian.
[Interch. 箋 92A.71]

艤 91S.71-8

yii.

V.t. To tie boat alongshore.

䳘 91S.71-9

er.
[Var. of 鵞 90.50]

§91S.72 (ノS/心)

勰 91S.72-4

shier.

Adj. (AC) peaceful (cf. 協, 諧).

牕 91S.72-9

chuang.
[Var. of 窗 62A.41]

§91S.80 (ノS/八)

牘 91S.80-1

dur.

N. Correspondence, documents: 文牘 correspondence; secretariat in charge of documents; 案牘 files, office records; 書牘, 尺牘 letter of correspondence.

頄 91S.80-3

chiour.

N. (AC) the cheekbone.

須 91S.80-3

shyu.

N. (1) Interch. 鬚 in 須眉 (=鬚Δ眉 51.80). (2) A surname.

Vb. aux. (1) Must (dist. 需 need): 必須 ditto; 須要, 須當, 須得 *-yauh, -dang, -der* ↓; 須知 (you) must know; 須是 must be (in sense of conjecture); 須不是 cannot be (conjecture): 這須不是我妬她, 是她自做出來的 this is not because of my jealousy, rather she brought it on herself; 須得 must have; 須用 must use; 須至 (formula at end of official communication) this goes to (addressee); 務須 please do, you certainly must (obey rules, etc.); 終須 in the end one has to. (2) (AC) wait: 何肯守此, 坐須老乎 (AC) are you going to sit here till old age? 須待, 須留 *-daih, -liour* ↓.

Adv. A little: 少須 (=少些) ditto; 須臾 *-yur* ↓.

須待 *shyudaih*, v.i., (1) must wait; (2) (AC) wait: 我有所須待也 I am expecting s.t. or s.o.
須當 *shyudang*, v.i., must: 須當如此 must do it like this.
須得 *shyuder*, v.i., must: 須得這樣做 must do it like this.
須著 *shyujuor*, v.i., (MC) must.
須留 *shyuliour*, v.i., wait a little, stay a while.
須彌山 *Shyumir-shan*, n., (Budd.) a fabulous mountain, abode of gods.
須索 *shyusuor*, v.i., (MC) must.
須要 *shyuyauh*, v.i., must: 須要趕快去 must go quickly (dist. 需要 need: 需要錢, 人 need money person).
須搖 *shyuyaur*, v.i., (AC) see *-yur* ↓.
須臾 *shyuyur*, n. & adv., a short moment.

顖 91S.80-3

shihn (also *shihng*).
[Arch. of 囟 91.41]

顦 91S.80-3

chiaur.
[Var. of 憔 in 憔Δ悴 22A.63]

§91S.81 (ノS/人)

欻 91S.81-9

hu (**shyuh*, **chua*).

Adj. (**chua*) Descriptive of sizzling sound: 欻的一聲, 欻拉

欻艘般皎皈叛版舨皦

(*chuala*) 一聲 (as water drops into boiling oil).

欻忽 *huhu* (**shyuh-*), adv., quickly (=忽忽 and 倏忽).
欻吸 *hushi* (**shyuh-*), adv., (MC) ditto.
欻欻 **shyuhshyuh*, adj., sound of wind's whistle.

§91S.82 (ノˢ/㐅)

艘 91S.82–2

sau (also *sou*).

N. adjunct. Used of boat: 三艘帆船, 巡洋艦 three sailboats, cruisers.

般 91S.82–4

ban (*parn*).

N. Class, type, way: 一般人 the average man, generally; 一般人所承認 is generally believed, considered; 多般, 百般 in many ways, by many means; 百般忍受, 勸導 use all forbearance, all ways of persuasion; 百般無賴 by all crooked means, wiles; 萬般皆下品, 惟有讀書高 to be a scholar is to be the top of society.

Adj. & adv. Alike in 一般: 一般(兒)大 of the same size; 一般模樣 look alike; 般大般小 of the same age.

般桓 **parnhuarn*, v.i., (AC) var. for 般恆, 盤ᐞ旋 91.30.
般樂 **parnleh*, v.i., (AC) to live steeped in pleasure.
般配 *banpeih*, adj., be well matched (as in marriage) (also wr. 班配).
般若 *banreh*, n., (Sanskr.) *prajna*, highest wisdom; v.t. to know, understand; 般若波羅密(多) *prajnaparamita*; 般若心經 the sutra of the heart of *prajna*.

皎 91S.82–6

jiaau.

Adj. White, bright, clear: 皎潔 clean, unsullied; 皎皎 shiningly bright, glistening white.

皈 91S.82–9

guei.

V.i. Be converted to Buddhism, become a Buddhist: 皈依 (=歸依).

叛 91S.82–9

pahn.

V.t. & i. To rebel: 衆叛親離 being isolated (of ruler), forsaken by friends and allies; 叛黨 to turn traitor to the party.

N. Rebellion: 反叛 ditto; 叛變 *-biahn*↓.

Adj. Rebellious: 叛軍 rebellious troops; 叛臣 minister who has switched loyalty to another ruler.

叛變 *pahnbiahn*, v.i. & n., revolt, rebellion; mutiny.
叛亂 *pahnluahn*, n., state of rebellion and confusion.
叛徒 *pahntur*, n., a rebel.

版 91S.82–9

baan.

[Cf. 板 10B.82]

N. (1) Wooden board. (2) Edition, oft. with reference to sequence or method of printing: 初版, 再版 first, second edition; 出版 publish; 絕版 out of print; 木版書 wood-block books; 活字版 edition from movable types; 鋅版 zinc plate; 石版 lithograph; 翻版 reprint edition; 盜版 pirated edition. (3) Memorial tablet: 奏版 see 笏 92A.50. (4) (AC) a unit of measurement =ancient eight feet.

版本 *barnbeen*, n., edition.
版權 *baanchyuarn*, n., copyright.
版籍 *baanjir*, n., a person's official district of origin.
版築 *baanjur*, n., a method of building walls by stamping earth between board frames.
版面 *baanmiahn*, n., layout of printed sheet.
版稅 *baanshueih*, n., an author's or artist's royalties.
版式 *baan shyh*, n., format in printing.
版圖 *baantur*, n., map or area of jurisdiction, national territory.
版位 *baanweih*, n., place of spirit tablet or ancestral tablet in temple.

舨 91S.82–9

baan.

N. 舢舨(板) *sanbaan*, sampan.

皦 91S.82–9

jiaau.

Adj. White, bright, shining, clear: 皦日 the bright sun: 有如皦日 (oath) let the sun be my witness! 皦皦 clear and bright, dazzling, also open, not deceiving.

A

§91S.83 (ノ^{s}/〜)

艇 91S.83-9

tiing.

N. (1) A pleasure boat, rowboat: 畫艇 painted houseboat; 遊艇 yacht, rowboat; 橡皮艇 rubber boat; 登陸艇 LST, landing barge. (2) A boat-like object: 魚雷艇 torpedo boat; 飛艇 airship, airplane; 潛水艇 submarine.

§91S.93 (ノ^{s}/く)

舷 91S.93-6

shiarn.

N. The hull, side of ship or boat: 左舷 port; 右舷 starboard.

舷邊 *shiarnbian*, n., gunwale.
舷窗 *shiarnchuang*, n., porthole.
舷弧 *shiarnhur*, n., sheer, curve of deck line.
舷門 *shiarnmern*, n., entrance and exit on ship for passengers.
舷梯 *shiarnti*, n., ship's ladder for boarding, gangway.

B

SECTION 92

§92.00 (𠂉/亅)

争 92.00

jeng.

[Err. var. of 爭 90.00]

§92.01 (𠂉/小)

桀 92.01

jier.

N. (1) A chicken roost. (2) Name of tyrant, last ruler of 夏 *Shiah* Dyn.: 桀紂 two typical tyrants; 桀犬吠堯 tyrant's dog barks at good ruler.

V.t. Carry on shoulder.

Adj. (1) Cruel, tyrannical, bloodthirsty. (2) (U.f. 傑) distinguished, outstanding.

桀驁 *jier-aur*, adj., brutal and arrogant: 桀驁不訓 wild and intractable.
桀黠 *jiershiar*, adj., cruel and crafty.

彙 92.01

hueih.

[Var. 彙]

V.t. To assemble and arrange (as in a report): 字彙 glossary, dictionary; 彙編, 彙集 collection of papers; 彙集 also to assemble; 彙報 collected reports.

C

条 92.01

tiaur.

[Pop. of 條 91A.01]

榘 92.01

jyuu.

[Var. of 矩 92S.21]

尔 92.01

eel.

[Abbr. of 爾 31.42]

祭 92.01

*jih (*jaih).*

N. (**jaih*) A surname.

V.t. To worship, sacrifice: 祭品 sacrificial offerings; 祭奠 *-diahn*, 祭祀 *-syh*↓; 祭告 to sacrifice to the gods in times of national crisis; 祭竈 to sacrifice to the kitchen god on the 23rd of the 12th lunar month.

祭典 *jihdiaan*, n., sacrificial rites.
祭奠 *jihdiahn*, n. & v. i., (to offer) sacrifices.
祭酒 *jihjioou*, n., (AC) the guest of honor at ceremonial dinners; (fig.) a leader in art or literature.
祭主 *jihjuu*, n., the master of ceremonies in religious sacrifices.

祭掃 *jihsaau*, v. i., to sacrifice at the ancestral tombs.

祭賽 *jihsaih*, n., a religious festival.

祭獻 *jihshiahn*, v.t., to sacrifice.

祭師 *jihshy*, n., a priest; one in charge of religious sacrifices; see *-sy*↓.

祭司 *jihsy*, n., (AC) a priest.

祭祀 *jihsyh* (*-'sy*), n. & v. i., (to offer) sacrifices.

祭文 *jihwern*, n., an elegiac essay usu. read aloud at a funeral service and burned as prayer.

繁 92.01

farn.

[Interch. 煩 in sense of confusing]

Adj. Complicated, difficult, numerous, in many compp. ↓: 繁星 an array of stars; 繁缺 difficult post.

繁多 *farnduo*, adj., undesirably numerous.

繁富 *farnfuh*[1], adj., thriving, rich (treasures, plantation).

繁複 *farnfuh*[2], adj., repetitions and overlapping.

繁華 *farnhuar*, (1) adj., flourishing, given to luxury: 繁華世界 affluent, rich society; (2) n., luxury, rich way of living.

繁重 *farnjuhng*, adj., (of duties) heavy.

繁殖 *farnjyr*, adj., proliferous, also 蕃殖.

繁劇 *farnjyuh*, adj., (duties) multifarious and heavy.

繁忙 *farnmang*, n. & adj., busily engaged.

繁難 *farnnarn*, adj., difficult to tackle (work, problem).

繁縟 *farnruh*, adj., variegated, with many details, see *-shih*↓.

繁榮 *farnrurng*, adj. & n., prosperous, -rity.

繁盛 *farnshehng*, adj., plenteous, thriving (progeny, plantation), thriving (city).

繁細 *farnshih*, adj., detailed and complicated, elaborate (rules, regulations).

繁碎 *farnsueih*, adj., ditto.

繁瑣 *farnsuoo*, adj., ditto.

繁雜 *farntzar*, adj., ditto.

繁文 *farnwern*, n., detailed forms, ritualistic formalities: 繁文縟節.

繁衍 *farnyaan*, adj. & n. & v. i., proliferous, -ation, multiply fast, also 蕃衍.

§ 92.02 (𠂉/ㄎ)

彔 92.02

luh.

彔彔 *luhluh*, adj., occupied with sundry affairs (cf. 栗△六, 栗△陸, 栗△碌 31B.02).

彖 92.02

tuahn.

[Dist. 篆 *juahn*, 92A.02]

N. 彖辭 the Tuahn commentary on meaning of different diagrams in 易經 (*Yiching*).

象 92.02

shiahng.

N. (1) The elephant: 巨象 a big elephant; 象齒焚身 an elephant is killed because of its ivory—warning against hoarding wealth. (2) A figure, image (interch. 像): 造象 statue; 肖象, 圖象, 畫象 (more commonly wr. 像) portrait. (3) Material form, atmosphere, appearance: 形象 shape, material form: 意象 idea, concept; 氣象 atmosphere; 莊嚴氣象 august atmosphere or appearance; 萬象 all the universe; 天象 meteorological phenomena; 觀象臺 observatory; 景象 gen. appearance or atmosphere; 太平景象 atmosphere of peace; 現象 phenomenon, -na, present conditions; 印象 impression (of person, country). (4) Ivory (used as n. modifier): 象箸 ivory chopsticks; 象簡 ivory tablets; 象床 ivory bed; 象環 ivory ring, etc., see 象牙 *-yar*↓.

象鼻蟲 *shiahngbir-churng*, n., the weevil, the snout beetle.

象棋 *shiahngchir*, n., Chin. chess.

象闕 *shiahng-chyueh*, n., (AC) palace gate.

象度 *shiahng-duh*, n., measurements of movements of heavenly bodies.

象服 *shiahng-fur*, n., (AC) ladies' formal dress.

象管 *shiahng-guaan*, n., ivory flute.

象笏 *shiahng-huh*, n., ivory memorial tablet held during imperial audience.

象徵 *shiahngjeng*, n., symbol; 象徵主義 symbolism in poetry, painting; 象徵的 symbolic.

象簡 *shiahng-jiaan*, n., see *-huh*↑.

象輦 *shiahng-niaan*, n., (AC) carriage of empress dowager drawn by elephant.

象皮病 *shiahngpir-bihng*, n., (med.) elephantiasis.

象人 *shiahng-rern*, n., (AC) idol, wooden image.

象限 *shiahngshiahn*, n., (geom.) quadrant.

象刑 *shiahng-shirng*[1], n., (AC) convict dress, a dress of disgrace.

象形 *shiahng-shirng*[2], n., in 象形文字 hieroglyphics, pictograph; one of the earliest principles of Chin. character creation, limited to picturing visible forms.

象數 *shiahng-shuh*, n., the study of the eight diagrams (八卦) in *Book of Changes* (易經); 象 the diagrams, and 數 position of strokes (upper, lower, etc.); see *-tsyr*↓.

象辭 *shiahng-tsyr*, n., one of the Comments in the *Book of Changes*, explaining meaning of combination of diagrams forming an oracle.

象眼 *shiahng-yaan*, n., as in 斜象眼兒 an oblong quadrangle.

象牙 *shiahngyar*, n., ivory: 象牙之塔 the ivory tower; 象牙筷子 ivory chopsticks; 象牙牀 ivory bed (shortened to 象 in AC, see N. 4↑); 狗嘴長不出象牙 you don't find ivory in a dog's mouth—contemptuous of person's filthy remarks; 象牙海岸 (Republic of) Ivory Coast; 象牙質 dentine.

象意 *shiahng-yih*¹, n., see 會△意 81.41, one of the principles of character formation.

象譯 *shiahng-yih*², n., (AC) interpreter of languages of South China.

§ 92.10 (⺈/十)

午 92.10

wuu.

N. (1) Number 7 in the duodecimal cycle (see Appendix A); 午時 *-shyr*↓. (2) Noon: 正午 midnoon; 上午 morning; 下午 afternoon; 午前, 午後 *-chiarn, -houh* ↓. (3) A horse (corresponding to No. 7 in duodecimal cycle): 典午 an official in charge of stables.

午前 *wuu-chiarn*, n., forenoon.

午後 *wuu-houh*, n., afternoon.

午門 *wuu-mern*, n., south gate of imperial palace.

午牌 *wuu-pair*, n., see *-shyr*↓.

午砲 *wuu-pauh*, n., gun fired at noon.

午時 *wuu-shyr*, n., (1) between 11:00 a.m. and 1.00 p.m.; (2) noontime.

午夜 *wuu-yeh*, n., midnight.

年 92.10

niarn.

N. (1) A year: 前年, 今年, 明年 last, this and next year; 年年 every year; 年內 within the year; 年首, 年末 beginning, end of year; 年來 in the last or last few years; 往年 in the year(s) gone by; 年根兒底下, 年終歲尾 toward the year's end; 多年往事 things of many years ago; 年久失修 has not been repaired for many years; 忘年之交 friendship between old and young people; 一年不如一年 every year gets worse; see 年代, 年度, 年俸 *-daih, -duh, -fehng*↓. (2) The New Year (新年): 拜年, 賀年 pay New Year calls; 過年 pass the New Year; 年夜 New Year's Eve; 過年活兒 things for New Year; see 年貨, 年紙 *-huoh, -jyy*↓. (3) Person's age: 少年 youth; 童年, 幼年 childhood; 成年 maturity; 壯年 prime of youth; 老年 old age; 年富力強 in the prime of life; 年高德劭 venerable in age and character; 以享天年 enjoy the last years of one's life; 流年 course of one's life in fortunetelling. (4) The times, condition of harvest: 豐年, 歉年 year of good, bad, crops; see 年頭, 年月 *-tour, -yueh*↓. (5) A surname.

年報 *niarnbauh*, n., yearbook; annual report.

年輩 *niarnbeih*, n., seniority according to age, see 輩 22.10.

年表 *niarnbiaau*, n., chronicle of events of a country or of person's life year by year.

年伯 *niarnbor*, n., formerly, a person of same class of graduates as one's father; father of a person of the same class of graduates.

年成 *niarn'cheng*, n., the condition of a year's harvest.

年期 *niarnchir*, n., (1) Age: 老年期 senility; 幼年期 childhood; (2) term of deposit: 二年期存款, 半年期 two-year fixed deposit, six-month deposit; (3) 更年期 (med.) menopause.

年歉 *niarn-chiahn*, n., crop failure, year of poor harvest.

年輕 *niarn-ching*, adj., young in age: 年輕輕兒的 (also wr. 年青).

年齒 *niarnchyy*, n., a person's age: 年齒尚幼 still young in age.

年代 *niarndaih*, n., an epoch, era or period: 三十年代 in the thirties.

年弟 *niarndih*, n., formerly, a person of the same class of graduation.

年底(下) *niarndii(shiah)*, n., year-end (also 年末).

年度 *niarnduh*, n., as in 會計年度 fiscal year; 學年度 school year; 下一年度 the next fiscal or school year.

年飯 *niarn-fahn*, n., New Year's Eve family dinner (also 年夜飯).

年分 *niarnfehn*, n., (of porcelain, wine, etc.) age or vintage.

年俸 *niarnfehng*, n., yearly stipend.

年豐 *niarn-feng*, n., a bumper year, a bumper harvest.

年糕 *niarngau*, n., New Year pudding made of glutinous rice flour.

年庚 *niarngeng*, n., a person's horoscope: 年庚八字 the hour, date, month, and year of one's birth.

年關 *niarnguan*, n., day for the settlement of accounts, on New Year's Eve: 過年關 settle such accounts.

年光 *niarnguang*, n., passage of time: 年光荏苒 the quick passing of time.

年功 *niarn-gung*, n., years of service: 年功加俸 pay hike with each additional year of service.

年穀 *niarn-guu*, n., the annual harvest, usu. of rice.

年號 *niarnhauh*, n., title of emperor's reign.

年畫(兒) *niarnhuah('l)*, n., ready-made painting sold during New Year's time, usu. depicting joyous scenes or showing good omen.

年華 *niarnhuar*, n., passage of time, age, esp. youth: 似水年華 time passes like flowing water; 二八年華 sweet sixteen.

年會 *niarnhueih*, n., annual convention.

年貨 *niarnhuoh*, n., food and other articles for use during the New Year season.

年長 *niarnjaang*, v. i. & adj., (become) older in age.

年家 *niarnjia*, n., formerly, a fellow graduate of the same class.

年假 *niarnjiah*, n., New Year holidays.

年鑑 *niarnjiahn*, n., yearbook, almanac.

年間 *niarnjian*, adv., during a certain era of period: 乾隆年間 during the reign of Chienlung.

年節 *niarnjier*, n., New Year festival.

年紀 *niarnjih*, n., a person's age: 年紀這麽大 now that you are so old; 小小年紀 one is yet so young; 多大年紀 how old are you? 年紀高不高 is he old or young?

年景(兒) *niarnjiing('l)*, n., (1) conditions at New Year's time; (2) harvest condition: 年景不好 this year's harvest (or business) is not good.

年金 *niarnjin*, n., annuity.

年級 *niarnjir*, n., class or grade in a school: 高年級 higher class; 低年級 lower class; 一, 二年級 first, second year in school.

年姪 *niarnjyr*, n., nephew in relation to 年伯 see *-bor* ↑.

年紙 *niarnjyy*, n., paper articles (such as scrolls, paper money for the dead) used at New Year.

年臘 *niarnlah*, n., the age of a Buddhist monk.

年力 *niarnlih*[1], n., one's mental or physical power at a certain age: 年力就衰 the physical or mental power on the decline.

年利 *niarnlih*[2], n., annual interest rate, interest per annum.

年例 *niarnlih*[3], n., annual custom.

年禮 *niarnlii*, n., New Year's gift.

年齡 *niarnlirng*, n., a person's age.

年輪 *niarn-lurn*, n., (bot.) annual rings of trees.

年邁 *niarn-maih*, adj., advanced in age: 壽高年邁.

年貌 *niarnmauh*, n., age and description (in registration, etc.).

年年(兒) *niarnniarn(-niar'l)*, adv., every year: 年年如意 New Year greetings.

年譜 *niarnpuu*, n., year by year chronicle of a person's history from birth to death—a litr. form.

年入 *niarn-ruh*, n., annual income.

年賞 *niarn-shaang*, n., New Year gifts to subordinates.

年少 *niarnshauh*, adj., young of age.

年限 *niarnshiahn*, n., a fixed number of years.

年禧 *niarn-shii*, n., Happy New Year: 恭祝年禧 best wishes for a happy New Year.

年壽 *niarnshouh*, n., the number of years one has lived.

年事 *niarnshyh*, n., a person's age: 年事已高 advanced in age.

年兄 *niarnshyung*, n., my elder brother, (court.) formerly, address to successful fellow students partaking in the same examination; see *-dih* ↑.

年歲 *niarnsueih*, n., (1) age: 這麽大年歲 now that you are so old; 多大年歲 how old are you? (2) see *-tour* ↓.

年所 *niarnsuoo*, n., (AC) the number of years that has expired.

年頭(兒) *niarntour('l)*, n., (1) condition of the times (good, bad); (2) condition of the harvest: 今年年頭兒很好 this year's harvest is pretty good.

年租 *niarn-tzu*, n., annual rental.

年祚 *niarn-tzuoh*, n., (1) the number of years of a dynasty or king's reign; (2) length of person's life.

年夜 *niarnyeh*, n., New Year's Eve (also 除夕).

年誼 *niarnyih*, n., formerly, friendship between persons of the same graduation class.

年月 *niarn-yueh*, n., condition of the times: 太平年月 peaceful times; 這種年月 such times!

舞 92.10

wuu.

N. Dance: 舞蹈 *-dauh* ↓; 舞女 *-nyuu* ↓; 跳舞 n. & v. i., dance; 歌舞 song and dance; 交際舞 social dancing; 脱衣舞 strip tease; 爵士舞 jazz; 探戈舞 tango; 扭擺舞 rock-and-roll; 草裙舞 hula-hula; 卻爾斯登舞 Charleston; 康康舞 can can; 康茄舞 conga; 方塊阿哥哥舞; square ago-go; 勃羅斯舞 blues; 扭扭舞 (扭腰舞) twist; 曼波舞 mambo; 恰恰舞 cha-cha; 吉特巴舞 jitterbug; 方塊舞 square dance; 森巴舞 samba; 狐步舞 fox trot; 輪擺舞 rumba; 華爾滋舞 waltz; 土風舞 folk dance; 靈魂舞 soul dance; 芭蕾舞 ballet; 茶舞 tea dance; 伴舞 to act as dance partner.

V.i. (1) To dance, see N. ↑; execute steps as if dancing: 鳳舞, 鶴舞 phoenix, stork, dances; 舞獅 lion's dance; 舞龍 dragon's dance; 鼓舞 to encourage. (2) To flourish, brandish (sword). (3) To play tricks with, to juggle: 舞弄 *-luhng*; 舞文 *-wern* ↓; 舞弊 *-bih* ↓.

舞伴 *wuu-bahn*, n., dancing partner, dancing hostess.

舞弊 *wuubih*, v. i., to juggle with the law: 營私舞弊 to engage in bribery, kick-backs and other illegal transfers of funds.

舞步 *wuu-buh*, n., dance step.

舞場 *wurchaang*, n., dance hall.

舞池 *wuuchyr*, n., dancing floor, space for dancing in night club.

舞曲 *wurchyuu*, n., a dance song.

舞蹈 *wuudauh*, n., a dance: 手舞足蹈 to dance for joy.

舞歌 *wuuge*, n., a dance song.

舞會 *wuuhueih*, n., dancing party.

舞弄 *wuuluhng*, v. i. & t., (1) make fun of (person); (2) 舞弄文墨, 舞文弄墨 show off literary skill, play with the pen; 舞文弄法 to juggle with the law, to quibble; (3) (*-nuhng*) take s. t. in hand and play with it, as in acrobatic show.

舞迷 *wuu-mir*, n., a habitual dancer or frequenter of dance hall.

舞男 *wuunarn*, n., gigolo.

舞女 *wurnyuu*, n., dancing hostess.

舞術 *wuushuh*, n., art of dancing.
舞臺 *wuutair*, n., the dancing stage; stage in gen.: 舞臺經驗 stage experience; 舞臺設計 stage setting.
舞廳 *wunting*, n., a dance hall.
舞文 *wuu-wern*, v.i., see *-luhng* ↑.

§92.11 (⺊/土)

玍 92.11

gaa.

玍古 *gaa'gu*, adj., eccentric, odd.
玍雜子 *gaatzartz*, n., (abusive) an eccentric, an odd fellow.

§92.20 (⺊/卄)

彝 92.20

yir.

N. (AC) (1) a wine vessel: 彝器 *-chih* ↓. (2) Cardinal principle: 國彝 a country's cardinal law, basis of order; 彝倫 *-lurn* ↓.

彝器 *yirchih*, n., sacrificial vessels.
彝倫 *yirlurn*, n., cardinal human relationships.

§92.21 (⺊/乚)

缶 92.21

foou.

N. (1) Earthen jar. (2) A radical, meaning earthenware, appearing in characters like 缸, 罐, 罋 (earthen pots and jars). (3) (AC) a clay musical instrument.

§92.22 (⺊/丨)

乍 92.22

jah.

V.t. Make bold: 乍着膽子 summon up courage (to do s. t.).

Adv. (1) Suddenly, abruptly: 乍冷乍熱 abruptly change from cold to hot; 乍晴乍雨 sudden changes from rain to shine; 乍見 saw suddenly; 乍聞 suddenly learn for the first time. (2) For the first time, newly: 新來乍到 has just arrived; 雨乍晴 the rain has just stopped; 乍富 newly rich; 乍乍的 *-jah'de* ↓.

乍乍的 *jahjah'de*, adv., (coll.) just now.
乍可 *jahkee*, adv., (MC) rather: 乍可沈爲香 rather sink as a perfume wood.
乍猛的 *jahmeeng'de*, adv., suddenly, abruptly: 他乍猛的一問我 he abruptly asked me.
乍然 *jahrarn*, adv., suddenly, unexpectedly: 乍然相逢 to meet unexpectedly.

§92.30 (⺊/一)

盝 92.30

luh.

N. A small casket (for cosmetics).

盌 92.30

waan.

[Pop. form 碗 31B.70]

§92.32 (⺊/フ)

夕 92.32

shih.

N. (1) (LL) night: 一夕 one night; 旦夕 morning and night, see 旦夕 41.30; 朝夕 morning and night; 除夕 New Year's Eve; 今夕何夕 Ah, what night is this? 七夕 the seventh day of the seventh lunar month. (2) Evening: 夕陽 the setting sun; 夕照 the reflected light of sunset.

多 92.32

duo (**duor*).

N. (1) Much, plenty: 三多 (多福, 多壽, 多男子) plenty of luck, children and a long life. (2) A surname.

V.i. Exceed a number: 多了三個 three more than listed or expected; come as surplus: 多下來, 多出(來), see 多餘 *-yur* ↓.

Adj. & adv. (1) Much or many (in Chin., not distinguished) opp. 少 *-shaau*: 多少 *-shaau* ↓; 好多, 很多, 許多 very many (much); 太多 too many (much); 多是, 多係 (as adv.) mostly are; 多有 mostly have; 多次 many times; 多年朋友

friend of many years; 多管閒事 like to meddle in affairs; 多愁善感 prone to illness and melancholy; 多災多難 dogged with misfortunes and mishaps; 好事多磨 the course of love (or other worthy projects) seldom runs smooth; 多聞多見 widely experienced; 多聞闕疑 (Confu.) be well-informed and suspend judgment on things in doubt; 多才多藝 versatile; 多財善賈 (pr. *guu*) it's easy to do business when you have the capital; 多此一舉 carry coal to Newcastle, superfluous action. (2) (AC) better: 孰多 which is better. (3) Demonstrably: 多見其不知量也 just shows how much he overrates himself.

Adv. (1) In 得多 after vb. or adj., much: 好得多 much better; 難得多 much more difficult; 病好多了 the sickness is much better. (2) (**duor*) How (as exclamation or question): 多大 how big? or how big! 多久, 多長, 多遠 how much time, how long, how far (? or !); 多沒出息 how useless (of person)! 多不要臉 how shameless; 多麽, 多會兒 *-'mo, -'hueih'l*↓.

多寶槅(兒) *duobaauger('l)*, n., curio stand with many sections.
多半 *duobahn*, adj. & adv., most, mostly, the greater half.
多般 *duoban*, adv., in so many ways.
多妻制 *duochijyh*, n., polygamy; cf. *-fujyh*↓.
多情 *duochirng*, adj., greatly enamored; warm (friend): 多情種子 a great lover.
多端 *duoduan*, adv., in many ways, on many occasions (create trouble).
多多 *duoduo*, adv., a great deal: 請你多多指教 I welcome a great deal of advice; 多多益善 the more, the better.
多方 *duofang*, adv., see *-duan*↑.
多夫制 *duofujyh*, n., polyandry.
多寡 *duoguaa*, n., number, frequency (LL for vern. 多少 *-shaau*↓): 戶口之多寡 density or number of population.
多故 *duoguh*, phr., (LL) 國家多故 many troubles, crises, in the nation.
多會兒 **duor'hueih'l*, adv., when, see *-'l, -'tzan*↓.
多角形 *duojiaaushirng*, n. & adj., polygon, -al.
多虧 *duokuei*, adv., luckily: 多虧他來了 luckily he came.
多兒 *duo'l*, adv., (1) how much: 多兒錢 how much does it cost? (2) in little while: 打多兒就要來看你 will soon come to see you, see *-'tzauwaa'l*↓.
多量 *duoliahng*, adv., in great quantities: 多量收入 great income.
多禮 *duolii*, adj., overcourteous.
多面體 *duomiahntii*, n., polyhedron, form with many angles or sides.
多麽 **duor'mo*, adv., how (exclam. or question): 多麽好 how good (? or !); 多麽難受, 可憐 how embarrassed, pitiful!
多少 *duoshaau*, adv. & adj. & n., (1) more or less: 多少有關係 more or less related; also 多多少少; (2) how much: 多少錢 how much does it cost? or how much money? 多少歲 how old (is a person); 剩了多少 how much is left? 不知埋沒多少英雄好漢 has prevented the emergence of I do not know how many heroes.
多神教 *duoshern-jiauh*, n., polytheism.
多相制 *duoshiahng-jyh*, n., (phys.) polyphase system of electric current.
多項式 *duoshiahngshyh*, n., (math.) polynomial or multinomial.
多嫌 *duoshiarn*, v. t., dislike (person).
多謝 *duoshieh*, phr., many thanks.
多心 *duoshin*, adj., distrustful, oversensitive (to remarks).
多數 *duoshuh*, n., most, greater part or number: 多數的人不贊成 the majority oppose it; 沉默的多數 the silent majority.
多事 *duoshyh*, adj., troublesome, meddling: 多事之秋 year of many troubles; meddlesome; 不必你多事, 你眞多事 you can well stay out.
多頭 *duotour*, n., usu. in 做多頭 (stock exchange) one who buys up stocks, a bull, bullish.
多采(彩)多姿 *duotsaai duotzy*, adj., magnificent, impressive, many-faceted (personality, performance).
多次 *duotsyh*, adv., many times.
多咱 **duor'tzan*, adv., when (can you finish, etc.?) (possibly short for 多早晚兒 *-'tzauwaa'l*↓), also wr. 多喒, 偺.
多早晚兒 **duor'tzauwaa'l*, adv., when (can you come, etc.?); soon, in a short time: 多早晚兒就來.
多嘴 *duotzueei*, v. i., talk too much or out of place.
多足類 *duotzurleih*, n., (zoo.) myriapod.
多疑 *duoyir*, adj., distrustful, prone to suspect.
多元論 *duoyuarnluhn*, n., pluralism.
多餘 *duoyur (-'yu)*, n. & adj., surplus, leftover, more than what is due: 你這話是多餘了 what you say is uncalled for or not necessary.

§ 92.40 (𠂉/口)

名 92.40

mirng.

N. adjunct. 一名犯人 one criminal; 錄取新生三名 three newly enrolled students.

N. (1) (*-'l*) Name, appellation: 姓名 surname and personal name; 人名, 地名 personal name, place name; legal personal name, dist. 字 literary name and 號 more poetic name; 名正言順 things called by their right names (Confucius); 混名 nickname; 乳名 name known in childhood; 筆名 *nom-de-plume*; see 諱 60A.10; 名稱, 名字 *-cheng, -tzyh*↓. (2) Number, order of selection: 他考第三名 he came out number three; 當選第二名 was elected number two. (3) Reputation: 久仰大名 heard of your great

名

reputation; 盛名之累 the penalties of being famous; 名不虛傳, 名副 (符) 其實, 名下無虛士 one's reputation is justified; 名滿天下 world-renowned; 名不符實 hollow reputation without basis; 名韁利鎖 the bondage of reputation and wealth; 名落孫山 phr., fail in civil examinations, really 孫山之外—allu. to 孫山, the last name of the successful candidates.

V.t. To name, describe: 莫以名之 (LL) do not know what to call it; 莫名其妙 phr., (derog.) queer, absurd, indescribable; 不名一文 not a cent to his name; 感激莫名 do not know how to thank you; 名世, 名於世 (LL) well-known to one's generation.

Adj. Famous, well-known: 名人 *-rern*↓; 名儒, 名宿 well-known scholar; 名士 *-shyh*[1]↓; 名著, 名作 famous work of author; 名醫, 匠, 影星 famous doctor, artisan, movie star; 名臣, 名相, 名將 famous official, prime minister, general; 名山大川 great mountains and rivers, objects of scholars' travel.

名簿 *mirngbuh*, n., book record of names.

名產 *mirng-chaan*, n., specialty, famous product (of place).

名場 *mirng-charng*, n., formerly, the civil examinations where one's success was determined.

名稱 *mirngcheng*, n., name by which person or thing is called.

名氣 *mirngchih*[1], n., reputation, prestige: 稍有名氣 enjoys some sort of reputation.

名器 *mirngchih*[2], n., (AC) an official's title and status.

名單 *mirngdan*, n., list of names.

名額 *mirng-er*, n., vacancies, number of students, candidates, etc.

名分 *mirngfehn*, n., (Confu.) a person's obligations, duties and respect due; a person's social status.

名貴 *mirnggueih*, adj., valuable, rare art objects.

名號 *mirnghauh*, n., name (of person, ship).

名花 *mirng-hua*, n., (1) famous courtesan; (2) famous flower.

名家 *mirng-jia*, n., (1) famous author, artist; (2) the School of Logicians of 墨子 Motse.

名腳(兒) *mirng-jiaau('l)*, n., famous actor, actress (also wr. 名角).

名教 *mirngjiauh*, n., Confucianism, the body of teachings on social relationships.

名節 *mirngjier*, n., moral integrity, honor.

名利 *mirng-lih*, n., fame and wealth.

名流 *mirngliour*, n., socially prominent person, esp. scholar: 社會名流 social leaders; V.I.P.; well-known leaders of society; people in social register.

名論 *mirng-luhn*, n., (1) famous opinion, essay; (2) (AC) reputation: 名論漸衰 their reputation gradually declined.

名門 *mirng-mern*, n., eminent family: 名門閨秀 daughter of such family; 名門之後 descendant of such family.

名目 *mirngmuh*, n., name, title esp. for drawing salaries: 巧立名目 create ingenious titles for padding pay or charging expense; 以什麼名目 in what capacity?

名片 *mirngpiahn*, n., name card.

名人 *mirng-rern*, n., a famous person.

名色 *mirngseh*, n., (1) famous beauty or courtesan; (2) see *-muh*↑.

名山 *mirng-shan*, n., famous mountain: 名山事業 author's works destined for posterity.

名勝 *mirngshehng*, n., famous sites, places of historic interest.

名聲 *mirngsheng*, n., fame.

名賢 *mirng-shiarn*, n., famous scholars (of a generation).

名手 *mirng-shoou*, n., distinguished expert, artist (at chess, opera, calligraphy, etc.).

名姝 *mirng-shu*, n., well-known beauty.

名數 *mirngshuh*, n., concrete number; (AC) population statistics.

名師 *mirng-shy*, n., famous master, teacher.

名士 *mirng-shyh*[1], n., esp. 名士派 scholar with unconventional ways, cranky scholar.

名氏 *mirngshyh*[2], n., a person's name and surname.

名實 *mirng-shyr*, n., (AC) name and solid accomplishments or characters; name and reality (agree, do not correspond).

名學 *mirng-shyuer*, n., (AC) the study of logic, esp. school of Motse.

名堂 *mirngtarng*, n., name, title, see *-muh*↑.

名帖 *mirngtiee*, n., (LL) name card.

名頭 *mirngtour*, n., (coll.) reputation.

名冊 *mirngtseh*, n., record of names (of members, etc.).

名刺 *mirngtsyh*, n., (LL) name card.

名詞 *mirngtsyr*, n., (1) word, term: 新名詞 new term; (2) (gram.) noun; 代名詞 pronoun.

名子 *mirngtz*, n., name; also *-'l*.

名字 *mirngtzyh*, n., person's name.

名望 *mirngwahng*, n., reputation: 有名望 enjoys a reputation.

名位 *mirngweih*, n., official rank.

名物 *mirngwuh*, n., things: 各種名物 different articles and things.

名言 *mirngyarn*, n., famous saying.

名義 *mirngyih*, n., official capacity: 假借名義 assume false official title; 名義上 in official capacity, as a matter of form.

名媛 *mirngyuarn*, n., debutante, daughter of rich family.

名譽 *mirngyuh*, (1) n., reputation: 破壞名譽 damage one's reputation; 名譽不好 have a bad reputation; 名譽擔保 on one's honor; (2) adj., honorary (doctor, president, chairman, etc.).

各 92.40

geh (**ger*).

Pron. & adj. Each, every(one), all: 各色各樣 all kinds of; 各式 every form, all forms; 各種 every kind, all kinds; 各類 every variety, all varieties; 各地 every locality, all localities; 各國 every nation, all nations; 各有千秋 each has its (his, her) merits; 各抱一角(兒) each doing his share; 各奔前程 each going his own way; 各自東西 ditto; 各行其是 each doing what he thinks is right; 各不相犯 each keeping within his sphere; 各爲己謀 everybody for himself; 各執己見 each holding fast to his own views; 各得其所 to the satisfaction of one and all; 各從其類 every item in its proper category; 各有所長 everyone has his own specialty; 各盡其力 everyone doing his best; 各個擊破 rout the enemy forces one by one; 各自各(箇)兒 each one by himself; 各人付各人的 go Dutch; 各人, 各自 *-rern, -tzyh* ↓.

各 別 *gehbier*, adj. & adv., (1) separate(ly): 各別叮囑 give instructions to each one separately; (2) different(ly): 他的脾氣很各別 his temper is rather peculiar; 各別另樣 of a different type.

各 各 *gehgeh*, pron., everyone, everybody.

各 扭 兒 *gehnioou'l*, n., differences of view: 他們兩人又鬧各扭兒了 the two are again having another dispute.

各 人 *gehrern* (**ger-*), pron., everyone, each one.

各 自 *gehtzyh* (**ger-*), (1) pron., each one himself: 他們倆各自幹各自的 the two are each doing what he likes; (2) (**ger-*) adj., eccentric, peculiar: 這個人脾氣很各自 this person has a most peculiar temper.

咎 92.40

jiouh.

N. (1) Fault, mistake, blame misconduct: 咎有應得 it's (s.o.'s) own fault; 咎由自取 (one) has only (oneself) to blame; 咎罪 *-tzueih*, 咎戾 *-leih* ↓; 引咎辭職 take the blame on oneself and resign; 咎無可辭 cannot escape blame, shirk responsibility; 難辭其咎 can hardly absolve oneself of all blame. (2) Misfortune, natural calamity (opp. 休 good fortune): 休咎 good and bad fortune; 咎徵 *-jeng* ↓; 災咎 a natural calamity; 天降之咎 Heaven calls down curses on his head.

V.t. To blame, censure, condemn, find fault with: 獲咎 incur displeasure, blame; 畏咎 to fear censure; 咎責 *-tzer* ↓.

咎 徵 *jiouhjeng*, n., portents of divine displeasure.

咎 戾 *jiouhleih*, n., fault, crime, misfortune, calamity.

咎 責 *jiouhtzer*, n., responsibility for sins of commission or omission.

咎 罪 *jiouhtzueih*, n., an offense, a crime.

詹 92.40

jan.

N. A surname.

V.i. (1) (AC var. of 瞻) to look at from afar. (2) (AC) arrive. (3) (Var. of 占) to fix a date; orig., fix by divination: 謹詹於某月某日 used in invitation to dinner.

詹 詹 *janjan*, adj., as in 小言詹詹 (莊子) petty words are argumentative.

詹 諸 *janju*, n., (AC of 蟾蜍) frog, toad.

詹 檀 *jantarn*, n., (var. of 旃檀) sandalwood.

詧 92.40

char.

[Var. of 察 62.01]

§ 92.41 (𠂉/図)

昝 92.41

tzaan.

N. A surname.

眢 92.41

yuan.

Adj. (AC) dried up (well); dull (eyes).

智 92.41

jyh.

N. (1) Wisdom, intelligence: 智慧, 智力 *-hueih, -lih*[1] ↓: 智育 intellectual education, dist. physical or moral education; 急智 quick wit; 智圓行方 (AC) to know all around but to act straight; 智勇雙全 good in astuteness and physical prowess; 足智多謀 very resourceful; 智, 仁, 勇 sagacity, charity and courage. (2) A surname.

Adj. Wise, clever, resourceful, astute: 上智下愚 the very wisest and the most stupid; 大智若愚 the wisest man is often stupid-looking.

智 巧 *jyhchiaau*, adj., clever.

智 齒 *jyhchyy*, n., wisdom tooth.

智 鬬 *jyhdouh*, v.i. (MC) vie in wisdom, strategy.

智 多 星 *jyhduoshing*, n., resourceful strategist.

智 慧 *jyhhueih*, n., wisdom; 智慧板 see 七$^{\Delta}$巧板 70.70; 智慧劍 (Budd.) the "sword of wisdom" to cut through mortal involvements.

智 者 *jyhjee*, n., a wise man.

智力 *jyhlih*[1], n., mental power; intelligence: 智力測驗 intelligence test.
智利 *Jyhlih*[2], n., Chile.
智謀 *jyhmour*, n., clever strategy.
智囊 *jyhnarng*, n., (LL) a bag of wisdom; a clever man; a presidential advisor; 智囊團 brain trust.
智能 *jyhnerng*, n., intellectual ability.
智識 *jyhshyh*, n., knowledge (also wr. 知識); 智識階級 the intelligentsia.

魯 92.41

luu.

N. Name of anc. city state of Confucius; (lit.) Shantung Province; 魯殿靈光 (allu. to 靈光殿 of a Hahn emperor) the only survivals; 魯男子 honest fellow, man not susceptible to female charms; 魯魚亥豕 printing mistakes owing to similar (ancient) forms of 魯 and 魚, 亥 and 豕.

Adj. Stupid, rash: 愚魯 uncouth, uneducated, ignorant; 粗魯 coarse (person).

魯仲連 *Luujuhngliarn*, n., (allu.) mediator: 你就爲他們的魯仲連吧 you'd better mediate for them.
魯莽 *lurmaang*, adj., reckless (also wr. 鹵莽).

§ 92.42 (⺈/冈)

角 92.42

jiaau (sp. pr.); **jyuer* (re. pr.).

N. adjunct. 一角公文 an official document.

N. (1) Horns of animals: 牛角, 羊角, 鹿角, 犀角 ox, sheep, deer, rhinoceros horns; 犄角之勢 (of troops) so deployed as to be able to come readily to one another's assistance. (2) A corner: 眼角, 嘴角 the corners of the eye, mouth; 躲在牆角 hidden in a wall corner; 坐在屋角 sit in a corner of the room; 海角 a promontory, headland, cape: 海角天涯 all corners of the earth; 好望角 Cape of Good Hope; 角落 *-luoh*↓; 拐角 (turn) the corner; 額角 the temples. (3) An angle: 三角 a triangle, trigonometry; 三角戀愛 the eternal (love) triangle; 多角形 a polygon, -al; 六角形 hexagon; 八角形 octagon; 對頂角 vertically opposite angles; 平角, 直角, 鋭角, 鈍角 straight, right, acute, obtuse angle; 角度 *-duh*↓. (4) Any point of the compass: 東南角 the southeast; 西北角 the northwest; 爆炸聲是從那一角來的 where has the explosion come from? (5) The third of the five notes (宮, 商, 角, 徵, 羽) of the anc. Chin. musical scale. (6) A coin: 一角錢 a dime; (銀)角子 a dime; 銅(角)子 a copper. (7) A dramatic role: 主角 the leading role, actor or actress; 男角, 女角 an actor, actress; 丑角 a clown; 配角 a supporting actor or actress. (8) A wind instrument: 號角 a bugle; 畫角 an anc. military bugle. (9) Tufts of hair left on center of child's head: 總角之交 childhood friends. (10) An anc. drinking vessel, an anc. measure of capacity.

V.i. Vie in feats of physical strength: 角力 *-lih*, 角觝 *-dii*↓.

角貝 *jiaaubeih*, n., (zoo.) the tooth shell, *Dentalium octoangulatum*.
角觝 **jyuerdii*, n., wrestling.
角度 *jiaauduh*, n., (1) (math.) an angle; (2) point of view: 從另一角度看 seen from a different angle.
角巾 **jyuerjin*, n., a kerchief worn by anc. hermits.
角逐 **jyuerjur*, v. t., contend for, compete with for mastery.
角兒 *jiaau'l*, n., (1) a corner, a point of the compass; (2) (**jyuer'l*) a dramatic actor.
角力 **jyuerlih*, v. i., engage in a physical contest, wrestle.
角樓 *jiaaulour*, n., a watchtower on a city wall.
角落 *jyuerluoh*, n., corners of a room: 每個角落 every nook and cranny.
角馬 *jyuermaa*, n., (1) a gnu, (African antelope); (2) an abnormality, a monstrosity.
角門 *jiaaumern*, n., a side gate.
角膜 *jiaaumor*, n., (physiol.) the cornea of the eye; 角膜炎 (med.) keratitis.
角色 **jyuerseh*, n., (1) a dramatic actor, a role in casting; (2) an outstanding actor or person in any walk of life.
角黍 **jyuershuu*, n., rice dumplings shaped like a pointed cylinder.
角鷹 **jyueryin*, n., (zoo.) the crested eagle.

胷 92.42

shyung.

[Var. of 胸 42A.50]

§ 92.50 (⺈/㇆)

每 92.50

meei.

Pron. (MC & dial.) plural ending of pronn: 你每, 他每＝你們, 他們.

Adj. Each, every: 每天, 每人, 每處

亅	小	⺊	十	土	ナ	廾	乚	丨	一	丅	乛	口	図	冈	㇆	厂	尸	亠	广	宀	丶	乚	弋	心	八	人	乂	乛	丿	丿丨	⺈	く
00	01	02	10	11	12	20	21	22	30	31	32	40	41	42	50	51	52	60	61	62	63	70	71	72	80	81	82	83	90	91	92	93

everyday, everybody, everywhere; 每一個人 each one; 每月 every month; 每次 every time; 每況愈下 or 每下愈況 phr., get worse every time.

Adv. Every: 每逢(値)星期一 every Monday; 每當他來的時候 every time he comes.

每常 *meeicharng*, adv., often.
每每 *meirmeei*, adv., often: 每每不在家 often not at home; 每每推故 often make some excuse.

鴛 92.50

yuan.

N. See 鴛鴦 *-yang* ↓.

鴛鴦 *yuanyang*, n., the mandarin ducks, which always go in pairs, symbol of lovers or marital harmony; hence 鴛侶, 鴛偶 lover, life mate; 鴛盟 lover's pledge; 鴛鴦劍 a pair of swords which match each other; 鴛鴦瓦 roof tiles, concave matching with convex.

匍 92.50

pur.

匍匐 *purfur*, v. i., crawl (AC var. 匍伏); 匍匐莖 (bot.) creeping plant, *Soboles*.

匎 92.50

eh.

N. 匎葉 (MC) woman's hair decoration.

芻 92.50

chur.

N. (1) Hay, fodder: 芻議, 芻言 *-yih*, *-yarn* ↓. (2) (AC) animal that feeds on grass: 芻豢 *-huahn* ↓.

V.t. (1) To pasture (sheep, cattle): 芻牧 *-muh* ↓. (2) (AC) to cut grass.

芻槀 *churgaau*, n., fodder.
芻狗 *churgoou*, n., a sacrificial straw dog, s.t. discarded after use: 天地不仁, 以萬物爲芻狗(老子) "Nature is unkind, it treats all things like straw dogs."
芻豢 *chur-huahn*, n., (AC) meat of animals that feed on grass (芻) and on flesh (豢).
芻糧 *churliarng*, n., fodder.
芻靈 *churlirng*, n., (AC) straw effigy of man or animal, buried to serve the dead (in place of real man, woman or horse).
芻秣 *churmoh*, n., fodder.
芻牧 *churmuh*, v.i., to pasture (sheep, cattle).
芻蕘 *churraur*, n., as in 芻蕘者 (AC) grass and woodcutter; (fig.) rustic, used in self-deprecation: 芻蕘之言 my rustic remarks.
芻言 *chur-yarn*, n., (self-deprecating) my rustic, humble words.
芻議 *churyih*, n., (self-deprecating) "a humble discussion"; (LL) an essay on some current topic.

匐 92.50

fur.

V.i. See 匍^Δ^匐 92.50, to crawl.

句 92.50

*jyuh (*gou, *gouh).*

N. (1) (Gram.) sentence: 句子; 句號 *-hauh*, 句點 *-diaan*, 句讀 *-douh* ↓; 句法 sentence construction; 造句 ditto; 一句話 a sentence, just a word, in short; 句句有理 every word sounds reasonable. (2) (*gou) (=勾) (U.f. 鉤) a hook. (3) (*gouh) (=勾) To bend, twist, fasten, catch: 句當 business, affairs, duties ("work which detains one"). (4) (*gou) A surname.

V.t. (U.f. 勾) 句引 entice, seduce; 句留 make a short stay; 句結 ally oneself with (s.o.) for some secret purpose; 句通 work in collusion with (another).

句點 *jyuhdiaan*, n., a period, full stop, see *-hauh* ↓.
句讀 *jyuhdouh*, n., (punctuation) periods and commas.
句號 *jyuhhauh*, n., (punctuation) a period, a full stop.

旬 92.50

shyurn.

N. (1) A period of ten days: 上旬, 中旬, 下旬 the first, middle and last ten days of a month; 旬刊 a ten-day periodical; 兼旬 about twenty days. (2) Ten years, used in counting birthdays: 六旬大壽 celebration of sixtieth birthday. (3) 旬月 a full month, also ten months.

甸 92.50

diahn.

N. (1) (AC) suburb: 畿甸 metropolitan suburbs. (2) (AC) farm products.

V.t. (AC) to govern (people, land).

勹 92.50

bau.

[Anc. form of 包 92.70]

N. A radical.

勺 92.50

shaur (re. pr. *shuoh*).

N. (1) (*-tz*, *'l*) A spoon, ladle, dipper: 飯勺 ladle for helping rice to bowl. (2) 燒勺 a cooking implement with dipper-shaped end for spreading food in stir-frying. (3) A hundredth part of a *sheng*, 升 90.20.

勺乎 *shaur'hu*, v.t., (sl.) to strike (a person).

勺口兒 *shaur'kou'l*, n., cooking skill of a cook: 嚐嚐新廚子的勺口兒怎樣 try the cooking skill of the new cook.

勺子 *shaurtz*, n., (1) a dipper, ladle; (2) the back part of human skull: 腦勺子.

匀 92.50

yurn.

V.t. (1) To share, divide (a piece of cake, etc.): 匀一點給他 give him a bit; 匀出, 匀分 *-chu*, *-fen* ↓. (2) To smooth out, even up (powder on face): 匀臉, 匀面 roll powder on face to make it even; apply powder on face.

Adj. Even, well divided, well balanced: 均匀 ditto; 停匀, 匀停 *-'ting* ↓.

匀稱 *yurnchehng*, adj., well-balanced (colors), well proportioned (figure).

匀出 *yurn-chu*, v. t., divide and share (a piece of land, cake).

匀兌 *yurn'duei*, v. t., divide and share.

匀分 *yurnfen*, v. t., divide equally.

匀淨 *yurn'jing*, adj., see *-chehng* ↑.

匀留(兒) *yurn'liou('l)*, adj., (thread) of the right size, texture; smooth.

匀調 *yurn'tiau*, adj., even.

匀停 *yurn'ting*, adj., ditto.

匀圓 *yurnyuarn*, adj., evenly round.

匃 92.50

gaih.

[Var. of 丐 31.50]

訇 92.50

hung.

N. A surname.

Adj. & adv. Loud, -ly.

匈 92.50

shyung.

[Arch. form of 胸]

匈奴 *shyungnur*, n., The Huns, Mongolian tribes in northeastern China and Mongolia, historically under various names (玁狁, 匈奴, 胡) 1000 B.C.—6th cen. A.D.

匈匈 *shyungshyung*, adj., clamorous, fierce (also wr. 詾).

匈牙利 *Shyungyarlih*, n., Hungary.

勾 92.50

gou (**gouh*).

N. (1) (Var. 鉤) a hook, barb, sickle. (2) (Var. 鉤) (callig.) a stroke with a hook. (3) (Math.) (AC) the base of a right triangle. (4) A surname.

V.t. (1) Strike out, cancel, delete: 勾消 (of debts, etc.) cancel: 一筆勾消 cancel with a stroke of the pen; 勾除 delete; 勾掉一句 strike out a sentence; 勾去了 have s. t. stricken out or canceled. (2) Delineate, paint: 勾臉 *-liaan*, 勾勒 *-leh* ↓. (3) To remind, be reminded of s.t. past, to induce state of mind: 勾上心事 remind s.o. of some unpleasant experience; 勾起一腔愁緒 arouse great sorrow. (4) To seduce, to induce or cooperate for evil purpose: 勾引, 勾搭, 勾情, 勾通, 勾串, 勾結 *-'yiin*, *-'da*, *-chirng*, *-tung*, *-chuahn*, *-jier* ↓; 她又勾上一個男人了 she has made another man fall for her; 勾人 seduce people; 勾生意 solicit business. (5) Add s. t. to soup to make it thicker: 勾芡 *-chiahn* ↓; 勾粥, 勾滷 to thicken congee, gravy. (6) (**gouh*) Grasp, take hold of, touch, reach: 勾到了最上一層 can reach the uppermost section; 勾取 lay one's hands on s. t.; 你勾得著那麼高嗎 can you reach so high?

勾芡 *gou-chiahn*, v. i., add thickening (e. g., corn starch) to soup (also 勾縴(兒)).

勾情 *gou-chirng*, v. i., flirt (with s.o.).

勾串 *gouchuahn*, v. i. & t., conspire.

勾除 *gou-chur*, v. t., delete, cancel, strike out, to mark with "√".

勾搭 *gou'da*, v. t., seduce (man, woman).

勾當 **gouh'dang*, n., (familiar, contempt.) business, affair: 幹這好勾當 do this dirty business.

勾股 *gouguu*, n., (math.) (AC) a right triangle: 勾股形.

勾魂 *gou-hurn*, v. i. & t., be seductive, seduce: 勾魂攝魄 (of women) have the power to make men crazy; 勾掉了魂 (of men) lose one's head under the seductive power of women.

亅	小	⺊	十	土	ナ	廾	丩	丨	一	丁	フ	口	囗	冂	⺄	厂	尸	亠	广	宀	丶	乚	弋	心	八	人	乂	乛	一	丿	⺊	く
00	01	02	10	11	12	20	21	22	30	31	32	40	41	42	50	51	52	60	61	62	63	70	71	72	80	81	82	83	90	91	92	93

勾 勿 匆 冬 炰 烰 魚

勾結 *goujier*, v. t., align oneself with (disreputable elements).
勾欄 *goularn*, n., (1) orig., a balustrade; (2) a house of ill fame: 勾欄中人, 勾欄女子 a prostitute.
勾勒 *gouleh*, v.i. & t., (painting) delineate the contour; n., contour lines.
勾臉(兒) *gou-liaan(-liaa'l)*, v. i., (Chin. opera) to paint masks.
勾連搭 *gouliarn'da*, n., (Peking coll.) a row of houses with easy intercommunication.
勾留 *gouliour*, v. i. & n., stop over, make a short stay. ⌈out.
勾消 *goushiau*, v. t., delete, strike
勾通 *goutung*, v. t., see *-chuahn*↑.
勾引 *gou'yiin*, v. t., seduce (women).

勿 92.50

wuh.

Vb. aux. Do not, do not be: 勿謂言之不早 don't say that I didn't warn you; 勿急 don't rush; 勿怒 don't be angry; 勿走 don't go away, don't run; 且勿 please do not for the moment; 萬勿 do not under any circumstances; 勿論 regardless, also let alone; 勿論其他 not to speak of others; 勿論新舊 regardless of new or old; 請勿 please don't; 切勿 absolutely not to.

勿勿 *wuhwuh*, adj. & adv., (1) in a hurry (now generally 匆匆 pr. *tsung*); (2) (AC) cautiously.

匆 92.50

tsung.
[Pop. var. of 悤, 怱]

Adv. Hurriedly.

匆遽 *tsungjyuh*, adv., see *-marng*↓.
匆忙 *tsungmarng*, adv., hurriedly.
匆匆 *tsungtsung*, adv., ditto.

§ 92.63 (𠂉/丶)

冬 92.63

dung.

N. The winter: 冬月 winter months; 冬日 winter days; 冬日可愛 welcome winter sun, (allu.) a man's kindly temperament, opp. 夏日可畏 oppressive summer sun; 冬藏, 冬儲 provisions of food for winter; 冬暖夏涼 cool in summer and warm in winter (of place); 冬溫夏凊 (pr. *jihng*) son's duty of keeping the parents warm in winter and cool in summer.

冬青 *dungching*, n., (bot.) long stalk holly, *Ilex pedunculosa*; 冬青科 (bot.) *aquifoliaceae*.
冬蟲夏草 *dungchurng-shiah-tsaau*, n., (bot.) a parasitic low-type fungus, *Cordyceps Robertii*, which spawns in insect's body, appearing in summer as part of plant—hence its name.
冬瓜 *dunggua*, n., Chin. wax gourd, winter melon.
冬烘 *dunghung*, adj., bigoted, pedantic: 冬烘秀才 shallow village schoolmaster, a pedant; hence 頭腦冬烘 badly read and extremely bigoted, die hard, ultraconservative.
冬節 *dungjier*, n., winter solstice.
冬季 *dungjih*, n., winter season.
冬至 *dungjyh*, n., winter solstice; 冬至線 the Tropic of Capricorn; 冬至點 winter solstice.
冬葵 *dungkueir*, n., (bot.) cluster mallow, *Malva verticillata*.
冬眠 *dungmiarn*, n., hibernation.
冬筍 *dungsuun*, n., an edible bamboo shoot.
冬天 *dungtian*, n., winter.
冬子月 *dungtzyueih*, n., eleventh month of lunar calendar.
冬芽 *dungyar*, n., winter bud in cold lands with protective tissue.

炰 92.63

paur.

V.i. (AC) to broil.

炰烋 *paurshiau*, adj., arrogant, overbearing; to rage and roar (var. of 咆哮 40A.70).

烰 92.63

foou.

V.t. Cook over slow fire.

魚 92.63

yur.

N. (1) Fish, reptile: 鯨魚 whale; 甲魚, 腳魚 turtle; 鱷魚 crocodile. (2) A surname.

V.t. U. f. 漁 to fish.

魚白 *yur-bair*, (1) adj., pale greenish white; (2) n., fish sperm.
魚鰾 *yur-biauh*, n., swimming bladder of fish.
魚叉 *yur-cha*, n., fish spear.
魚槍 *yur-chiang*, n., fishing gun.
魚契 *yur-chih*, n., a tally in the form of fish.
魚鰭 *yur-chir*, n., fish fins.
魚牀子 *yur-chuarngtz*, n., (Peking dial.) fish merchant.
魚翅 *yur-chyh*, n., shark's fins.
魚池 *yur-chyr*, n., fish pond.
魚毒 *yur-dur*, n., (bot.) *Daphne Genkwa*, a spice plant which when boiled and thrown into pond is said to kill the fish (also called 毒魚 or 芫花).
魚肚 *yur-duu*, n., fish maw; 魚肚白 see *-bair*↑.
魚餌 *yur-ehl*, n., fish bait.
魚販(子) *yur-fahn(tz)*, n., a fishmonger.

魚肥 *yur-feir*, n., fish meal, dried fish used as fertilizer.

魚符 *yur-fur*, n., see *-chih* ↑.

魚竿(兒)(子) *yur-gan(-ga'l)(tz)*, n., fishing rod.

魚缸 *yur-gang*, n., fish jar: 魚缸兒 a fish bowl.

魚肝油 *yurganyour*, n., cod-liver oil.

魚狗 *yur-goou*[1], n., a kind of fish hawk.

魚笱 *yur-goou*[2], n., fish trap.

魚鉤(兒) *yur-gou('l)*, n., fishing hook.

魚貫 *yur-guahn*, adv., file in, proceed in file.

魚罟 *yur-guu*[1], n., a fishing net.

魚鼓 *yur-guu*[2], n., wooden knocker at Buddhist temple, shaped like fish.

魚花 *yur-hua*, n., see *-miaur* ↓.

魚虎 *yur-huu*, n., (1) globefish; (2) a kind of fish hawk.

魚鮓 *yur-jaa*, n., salted fish.

魚繭 *yur-jiaan*, n., a fine-quality paper.

魚箋 *yur-jian*, n., (1) letter of correspondence (from allu.—a friend's letter found in belly of presented carp); (2) a special letter paper.

魚膠 *yur-jiau*, n., fish glue, isinglass, made from inner membrane of fish bladder.

魚坑 *yur-keng*, n., fishpond.

魚口 *yur-koou (-'ou)*, n., sores of venereal disease.

魚膾 *yur-kuaih*, n., sliced fish served with vegetable.

魚兒 *yue'l*, n., small fish.

魚爛 *yur-lahn*, n., (AC) decay or corruption from inside.

魚雷 *yurleir*, n., torpedo; 魚雷艇 torpedo boat.

魚鱗 *yurlirn*, n., fish scales, used as figure for serried roof tops; 魚鱗兒 scaly patterns; 魚鱗癬 fishskin disease, ichthyosis, or xeroderma, a skin disease with dry, hardened scabs; 魚鱗天兒 sky with clouds in scattered clusters, or of cirro-cumulus type.

魚簍 *yur-loou*, n., fish hamper.

魚卵石 *yur-luaan-shyr*, n., (geol.) oölite.

魚苗 *yur-miaur*, n., fish fry, minnows.

魚木 *yur-muh*, n., (bot.) a tropical brush, *Crataeva religiosa*, whose fruit can be used as fish bait.

魚片兒 *yur-piah'l*, n., sliced fillet of fish.

魚肉 *yur-rouh*, (1) v.i. & t., to victimize (from AC allu. 人爲刀俎, 我爲魚肉 "others are the chopping knife and board and me the fish and meat"): 魚肉鄉里 to victimize, oppress, the village people; (2) n., victims.

魚生粥 *yur-sheng-jou*, n., rice gruel with thin raw fish slices (Cantonese).

魚線 *yur-shiahn*, n., fishing line.

魚腥草 *yur-shing-tsaau*, n., a strong fishy-smelling grass, *Houttuynia cordata*.

魚水 *yur-shueei*, phr., esp. 如魚得水 like fish let into the water—happy in each other's company or in one's natural element; 魚水和諧 marital harmony.

魚蝨 *yur-shy*, n., a small parasite bug that destroys fish.

魚市 *yur-shyh*, n., fish market.

魚塘 *yur-tarng*, n., fishpond.

魚頭 *yur-tour*, n., difficult part of a job: 擇魚頭 choose the difficult part.

魚刺 *yur-tsyh*, n., fish bones.

魚藻 *yur-tzaau*, n., water cress and the like.

魚栽 *yur-tzai*, n., small fry raised in nursery.

魚子 *yur-tzyy*, n., roe of fish.

魚網 *yur-waang*, n., fishing net.

魚丸(子) *yur-warn(tz)*, n., fish balls.

魚眼 *yur-yaan*, n., bubbles when water begins to boil.

魚雁 *yur-yahn*, n., letter of correspondence ("fish and goose" from allu. see *-jian* ↑).

魚秧(子) *yur-yang(tz)*, n., see *-tzai* ↑.

魚鷹(子) *yur-ying(tz)*, n., a fish hawk, kingfisher.

魚油 *yur-your*, n., fish oil.

無 92.63

wur.

N. Nothing: 有生於無 being comes from not-being; 有無相助 those that have and those that have not help each other; 以有易無 exchange what one has for what one has not.

Adj. & adv. (1) No, not a, used oft. like Eng. "without" "-less": 無人 no man; 無錢 no money; 無底 bottomless; 無比 matchless; 無主 ownerless; 無法 helpless; 無線電 wireless; 無人飛機 unmanned aircraft; 無米之炊 cook a meal without rice; 無機 inorganic; 無病而死 died without any illness; 無病呻吟 to pine without cause, making a fuss about nothing; 無定性 capricious; 無可諱言 undeniable; oft. repeated 無...無: 無頭無腦 completely without clue; 無頭無尾 without head or tail, without beginning or end; 無上無下 regardless of above or below; 無緣無故 without any reason; 無拘無束 without any restraint; oft. 無不 all, without exception, or 無...不: 無微不至 without any detail not taken care of; 無孔不入 no opportunity overlooked, penetrates everywhere; see esp. 無奈, 無不, 無非 *-naih, -buh, -fei* ↓; 無論 *-luhn*; 無妨 *-farng* ↓; 無趣 out of humor, uninteresting, dejected; 無惡不作 stop at nothing; 無懈可擊 invulnerable, perfect; 無用 useless. (2) Regardless: 無少長皆斬之 behead them all, regardless of age; 無冬無夏 regardless of winter or summer; 無時無刻 every hour and moment; 無不 all, without exception.

無礙 *wur-aih*, adj. & adv., no harm (doing s.t.), does not prevent one from (doing), see *-farng* ↓.

無被花 *wur-beih-hua*, n., (bot.) flower without blossom or calyx.

A

無 無邊 *wur-bian*, adj. & adv., limitless.

無裨 *wur-bih*, phr., see *-buu*↓.

無比 *wur-bii*, adj., matchless.

無不 *wur-buh*, phr., all, no one but: 無不贊成 no one but approves.

無補 *wur-buu*, phr., of no help to (s.t.).

無產階級 *wurchaan jiejir*, n., the proletariat.

無常 *wurcharng*, adj., impermanent: 性命無常 life is inconstant, evanescent.

無腸公子 *wurcharng gungtzyy*, n., (litr.) the crab—"bowelless gentleman."

無前 *wur-chiarn*, adj., unprecedented.

無期徒刑 *wurchir turshirng*, phr., life labor (sentence).

無情 *wur-chirng*, adj., heartless.

無出 *wur-chu*, (1) adj., without pregnancy or heir; (2) phr., 無出其右 unexcelled.

無窮 *wur-chyurng*, adj., endless, limitless.

無恥 *wur-chyy*, adj., shameless: 無恥之徒 shameless scoundrels.

無定形 *wur-dihng-shirng*, n., amorphous.

無底洞 *wur-dii-duhng*, n., a bottomless pit.

無抵抗 *wur-dii-kahng*, n., nonresistance; 無抵抗主義 principle of non-resistance.

無敵 *wur-dir*, adj., matchless.

無端 *wur-duan*, adv., for no reason, see *-guh*↓.

無度 *wur-duh*, adv., excessively (drink, etc.).

無二鬼 *wur-ehl-gueei*, n., a mischievous rascal.

無妨 *wur-farng*, phr., it's no harm (to do), it's quite all right, no objection (to do): 這也無妨 this also will do.

無非 *wurfei*, phr., it's only, nothing but: 無非造事生非 (s.o.) does nothing but create troubles.

無風帶 *wur-feng-daih*, n., (geog.) calm zone.

無干 *wur-gan*, phr., "no relevance": 與你無干 has nothing to do with you.

無告 *wur-gauh*, adj., friendless, having nowhere to turn for help or redress.

B

無根水 *wur-gen-shueei*, n., (Chin. med.) rain water or well water that is free of sediments.

無鉤條蟲 *wurgou-tau-churng*, n., a kind of tape worm, *Taenia mediocanellata*.

無垢 *wur-gouh*, n., without stains on character.

無辜 *wur-gu*, adj. & n., innocent, guiltless; innocent people.

無怪 *wur-guaih*, phr., it's not surprising that; no wonder.

無關 *wur-guan*, phr., "no relations," irrelevant: 與你無關 has nothing to do with you; 無關緊要 unimportant; 無關宏旨 irrelevant.

無軌 *wur-gueei*, adj., trackless (streetcar).

無故 *wur-guh*, adv., for no reason.

無骨 *wur-guu*, adj., spineless, wishy-washy.

無害 *wur-haih*, adj., harmless.

無恆 *wur-herng*, adj., inconstant.

無後 *wur-houh*, phr., to have no sons—permission for taking concubine.

無花果 *wurhua-guoo*, n., the fig.

無患子 *wurhuahntz*, n., (bot.) bodhi seeds, *Sapindus Mukurosi*, whose seeds are used for rosary, beads.

無遮 *wur'je*, adj., (Budd.) as in 無遮大會 meeting open to all.

無政府主義 *wur-jehngfur juuyih*, n., anarchism.

無稽 *wur-ji*[1], adj., baseless: 無稽之談 baseless gossip.

無機 *wurji*[2], adj., inorganic: 無機酸 n., (chem.) inorganic acid; 無機化學 n., inorganic chemistry; 無機物 inorganic matter.

無價寶 *wur-jiah-baau*, n., priceless curio.

無間 *wur-jiahn*, adv., without interruption, directly after.

無際 *wur-jih*, n., limitless: 一望無際 (view) stretches to the horizon.

無幾 *wurjii (-ji)*, (1) adj., only a few (left, etc.); (2) adv., soon after.

無狀 *wur-juahng*, phr., (self-deprecation) have been delinquent, undutiful, etc.

無著 *wur-juor*, phr., (1) no visible progress; (2) no way to find (money).

無主物 *wur-juu-wuh*, n., lost property without claimant.

C

無知 *wur-jy*, adj., (1) ignorant, not educated or informed; (2) (contempt.) stupid (animal, etc.).

無賴 *wurlaih*, n., a ne'er-do-well, loafer, rascal (also 無賴子).

無兩 *wur-liaang*, phr., without equal, the one and only.

無量 *wur-liahng*, n., without limit; 無量壽佛 Amitabha, the Eternal Buddha; 無量光佛 Buddha of Infinite Light.

無良 *wur-liarng*, adj., (AC) immoral.

無聊 *wurliaur*, adj., bored, dull, boring; 無聊賴 phr., listless, without any occupation or distraction.

無理數 *wurlii-shuh*, n., (math.) irrational number, a surd; 無理式 (math.) irrational expression.

無論 *wurluhn*, (1) adj., regardless (of who wins, etc.): 無論如何 no matter what; (2) phr., not to speak of: 秦漢, 無論魏晉 never heard of Chirn and Hahn Dyns. let alone the Weih and Jihn (later) Dyns.

無慮 *wur-lyuu*, phr., (1) doubtless, it may well be: 無慮三千人 could be as many as three thousand people; (2) without worry.

無名 *wurmirng*, adj., anonymous: 無名腫毒 all kinds of unrecognized skin affections; 無名指 the fourth finger, the ring finger; 無名氏 anonymous; 無名異 (Chin. med.) ferrous oxide ores; 無名英雄 unknown hero; 無名小卒 a nobody.

無名骨 *wur-mirng-guu*, n., (physiol.) innominate bones.

無明火 *wur-mirng-huoo*, n., flame of anger.

無奈 *wurnaih*, (1) adj., helpless, feeling frustrated (oft. 無奈何 cannot do anything about it, see 奈[A]之何 12.01); (2) adv., unfortunately: 無奈他不聽話 unfortunately he would not listen.

無能 *wur-nerng*, (1) adj., (person) incapable, incompetent; (2) phr., cannot: 無能爲力 cannot do anything to help.

無寧 *wurnirng*, adv., rather (=寧可), it would be better to (throw it away, etc.).

A

無那 *wurnuoh*, adj. & phr., (MC) see *-naih* ↑.

無任 *wur-rehn*, adv., (LL) very, most: 無任感激 feel most grateful.

無如 *wur-rur*, adv., unfortunately: 無如天色已晚 unfortunately it is already getting late (cf. *-naih* (2) ↑).

無日 *wur-ryh*, adv., (1) not a day: 無日忘之 never forget it for one day; (2) very soon: 亡無日矣 the days are numbered.

無上 *wurshahng*, adj., highest (honor, happiness, etc.).

無傷 *wurshang*, (1) phr., it does not hurt: 無傷大體 it does not hurt the important essentials; 無傷大雅 (speech, conduct) permissible in polite society; (2) see *-farng* ↑.

無倫 *wurshar*, (1) adj., (Shanghai, also wr. 嘸啥, pr. *m-sa*; the indicated national pronunciation is never heard) fair, decent, not bad; (2) adv., nothing much: 無啥事體 nothing much to do.

無涉 *wur-sheh*, adj., irrelevant to, unrelated to: 與他人無涉 (matter) does not concern others (see *-gan* ↑).

無生代 *wur-sheng-daih*, n., (geol.) azoic era.

無神論 *wur-shern-luhn*, n., atheism; 無神論者 atheist.

無限 *wurshiahn*, adj. & adv., infinite, -ly, utmost (grateful, glory, etc.), see *-rehn* ↑: 無限級數 (math.) infinite series; 無限小數 (math.) infinite decimal; 無限公司 not a limited stock company; 無限責任 unlimited liability.

無線電 *wurshiahndiahn*, n., wireless, radio.

無瑕 *wur-shiar*, adj., spotless.

無效 *wur-shiauh*, adj., invalid.

無行 *wur-shihng*, adj., (person) immoral, without character.

無性生殖 *wurshihng-shengjyr*, n., (biol.) asexual reproduction.

無心 *wur-shin*, (1) adv., not intentional, without any intention, see *-yih*[1] ↓; (2) phr., have no mind to: 無心管事 have no mind to attend to business.

B

無形 *wur-shirng*, adj., invisible; 無形中 adv., invisibly; 無形資產 immaterial assets.

無殊 *wur-shu*, adj., just like, not different from.

無雙 *wur-shuang*, adj., matchless, peerless, one and only.

無水酸 *wur-shueei-suan*, n., (chem.) acid anhydrides.

無數 *wurshuh*, adj., numberless, innumerable; 無數字 (econ.) nil.

無視 *wur-shyh*, v.i., take no cognizance.

無事忙 *wurshyhmarng*, adj., bustle about without accomplishing anything.

無須 *wur-shyu*, vb. aux., need not.

無算 *wur-suahn*, adj., numberless, countless, also *-shuh* ↑.

無所 *wur-suoo*, pron., everything, whatever: 無所不能, 無所不知, 無所不在 omnipotent, omniscient, omnipresent; 無所不曉 understands every subject; 無所不會 can do everything; 無所不至 do everything to help; 無所爲 (person) do not regard as important, (thing) can be left out; 無所謂 it's not what is called, cannot be said to be (good, bad).

無似 *wursyh*, (1) adj., (court.) unworthy; (2) adv., extremely (used after vb.): 欽佩無似 admire intensely.

無頭案 *wur-tour-ahn*, n., a mystery case without clues.

無猜 *wur-tsai*, adj., innocent: 兩小無猜 two innocent children.

無措 *wur-tsuoh*, adj., see *-juor* ↑.

無存 *wur-tsurn*, adj., all used up, depleted.

無從 *wur-tsurng*, adj., unable: 無從知道 unable to find out; 無從說起 don't know where to begin telling a story.

無疵 *wur-tsy*, adj., spotless.

無他 *wur-tuo*, phr., (1) be not disloyal (=無他心): 有死無他 die loyally; (2) no other reason or nothing bad or unpleasant.

無罪 *wur-tzueih*, adj., innocent, not guilty.

無足類 *wurtzur-leih*, n., (zoo.) apoda.

C

無望 *wur-wahng*, (1) adj., hopeless (case); (2) phr., do not hope.

無味 *wur-weih*[1], adj., tasteless, flat.

無畏 *wur-weih*[2], adj., fearless.

無謂 *wur-weih*[3], adj., meaningless.

無爲 *wurweir*, phr. & n., (Taoist) *laissez-faire*, doctrine of non-interference in government, of leaving the people alone.

無恙 *wur-yahng*, adj., well, not sick.

無烟火藥 *wur-yan huooyauh*, n., smokeless gunpowder.

無烟煤 *wur-yan-meir*, n., anthracite coal.

無涯 *wuryar*, adj., infinite, limitless.

無意 *wuryih*[1], (1) adj., unintentional; be not interested: 無意進行 is not interested in proceeding further; (2) adv., as in 無意中 unintentionally; 無意識 stupid (act), unconscious (act).

無異 *wur-yih*[2], phr., just like, same as: 無異自殺 same as committing suicide; 無異投降 same as surrender; 無異議 no objection (to motion); no dissent.

無已 *wur-yii*, (1) adv., ceaselessly; (2) phr., (LL) if there is no alternative, one is forced to.

無因 *wur-yin*, phr., without any reason.

無疑 *wuryir*, adv., doubtless, -ly, certainly: 無疑是他 doubtless it is he.

無有 *wur-yoou*, v.t., do not have.

無由 *wur-your*, phr., without any cause.

無緣 *wur-yuarn*, (1) phr., have not had the pleasure or luck (to do); (2) phr., 兩人無緣 the two cannot get along.

無庸 *wuryung*, vb. aux., (LL and documentary) need not.

然 92.63

rarn.

V.i. & t. (1) To promise, pledge:

然 煞 鰵 鱻 乞

然諾 -*nuoh*↓. (2) To reply: 不然碴兒 make no reply to another person's remarks. (3) (U.f. 燃) (**raan*) to light (a fire, a lamp, a cigar, cigaret), burn.

Adj. (1) Right, correct: 雍之言然 Yung's words are right; 誠然 perfectly right; 甚然 quite correct. (2) Like, similar to: 無若宋人然 don't you be like the people of Suhng.

Particle. (1) Yes: 然, 有是言也 yes, it has been so said. (2) Serving as an affix or suffix to form adjj. and advv.: 天然 natural(ly); 自然 ditto, of course; 必然 certain(ly), sure(ly); 忽然 abrupt(ly), sudden(ly); 當然 (as a matter) of course; 既然 already, such being the case; 已然 ditto; 未然 not yet; 不然 if not, otherwise, no, not at all; 將然 about to; 所以然 why, wherefore; 果然 as a result, consequently, as expected; 淡然 nonchalant(ly), cool(ly), indifferent(ly); 斷然 firm(ly), resolute(ly); 悍然 with an iron hand, irrespective of all opposition, criticism or consequences; 巍巍然 dignified, stately, imposing(ly), majestic(ally); 飄飄然 pleasant(ly), joyful(ly), lighthearted(ly); 貿貿然 abrupt(ly), rough(ly), blunt(ly), unceremonious(ly); 惠然 kind(ly), gracious(ly); 斐然成章 well cultivated in the arts and manners; 其然, 豈其然乎 could it really be so? (3) Helping to form conjj.: 然則 -*tzer*↓; 然而 -*erl*↓; 然後 -*houh*↓; 雖然 though; 固然 even though; 縱然 even if. (4) Final particle: (=焉) 召而問然 summon s.o. and ask him.

然頃 *rarnchiing*, adv., in a short time, shortly, soon.

然而 *rarn-erl*, conj., but, however, nevertheless.

然否 *rarn-foou*, phr., yes or no? is it or isn't it so?

然後 *rarnhouh*, adv., then, thereafter, afterwards, subsequently, following that.

然納 *rarnnah*, v. t., endorse (views, suggestions, recommendations) and act accordingly.

然諾 *rarnnuoh*, v. i. & n., (make) a promise, (pledge) one's word of honor.

然信 *rarnshihn*, v. i., mutually agree on a common course of action, pledge to keep a promise.

然贊 *rarntzahn*, v. t., endorse, approve.

然則 *rarntzer* (-*'tze*), conj., but, but then.

然也 *rarnyee*, adv., certainly, surely, definitely, without doubt.

然疑 *rarn-yir*, phr., half believing half doubting.

煞 92.63

shah (**sha*).

N. (1) A noxious, evil spirit. (2) 回煞 41.41 return of soul of departed to residence.

V.i. & t. (1) To tighten, to put on the brake: 煞車 put on the brake; 煞腰帶 tighten the belt. (2) To lag, to end: 煞着步兒 to lag behind; 煞尾 -*weei*↓. (3) (**sha*) To take off, counteract: 煞濕氣 counteract damp weather (by eating garlic); 煞性子, 煞氣 -*shihngtz*, -*chih*↓; 煞風景 (phr.) throw a wet blanket.

Adv. (1) Very, exceedingly: 煞費事, 煞費苦心 takes a lot of troubles; 煞是難辦 very difficult to deal with; 煞札子白 deathly white. (2) Oft. used after vb. meaning "dead" (related 殺); 笑煞人 make one die with laughter; 釘煞 strike a nail dead fast; 收煞 to close up, come to an end.

煞白 *shahbair*, adj., deathly pale (complexion).

煞筆 *shah-bii*, v.i., to write this final line of a work.

煞車 **sha-che*, v. i., to put on the brake.

煞氣 *shahchih*, (1) n., a ferocious mien; (2) (**sha-*) v.i., to vent anger on s.o. else.

煞後兒 *shahhouh'l*, v. i., to lag behind.

煞賬 **sha-jahng*, v. i., to close the accounts.

煞腳 *shahjiaau*, v.i., draw up, stand still.

煞住 **sha-juh*, v. i., to draw up sharp, a cry "Stop!" (of a performance) to close; brake a car.

煞性子 **shashihngtz*, v. i., to vent anger, see -*chih*↑.

煞星 *shahshing*, n., unlucky star, evil star.

煞尾 *shahweei*, n., the end of song, story, play.

鰵 92.63

miin.

N. (Zoo.) the codfish; 鰵魚肝油 cod-liver oil.

鱻 92.63

shian.

[Anc. var. of 鮮 92C.10]

§ 92.70 (𠂉/乚)

乞 92.70

chii (**chih*).

N. A beggar: 乞丐, 乞兒 -*gaih*, -*erl*↓.

V.t. (1) To beg (for food, favor, pity, etc.); 乞食 beg for food; 乞借 beg to borrow; 乞求 to beg humbly; in letters, used like Eng. "beg"; 乞懇, 乞請 I beg you to; 乞休 beg to resign; 乞身, 乞骸骨 (ministers) beg for resignation (so as to be buried in native home);

乞假 request for leave; 乞師 beg for reinforcements or troops from ally; 乞救 ask for help; 乞和 sue for peace; 乞命 beg for life; 乞免 beg to be excused. (2) (*chih) 以墅乞汝 (AC) give you a villa.

乞巧 *chirchiaau*, n., the seventh day of seventh lunar month (see 七ᐞ夕 70.70) when young girls offer fruit in courtyard and beg for meeting right man.

乞貸 *chiidaih*, v. i. & t., to beg and borrow.

乞兒 *chii-erl*, n., a beggar.

乞丐 *chiigaih*, (1) n., a beggar; (2) v. t., to beg.

乞活 *chii-huor*, v. i., to wander about in search of a living.

乞假 *chii-jiah*, v. i., (1) to ask for leave; (2) see *-daih*↑.

乞鄰 *chii-lirn*, v. i., (LL allu.) to beg from neighbor.

乞靈 *chiilirng*, v. i., to beg for help from others (implying person himself is helpless).

乞盟 *chii-merng*, v. i., (1) ask for peace treaty; (2) take oath with blood at such treaty conference.

乞頭 *chii-tour*, n., commission for owner of gambling house.

乞養子 *chiiyarng-tzyy*, n., adopted son.

包 92.70

bau.

N. (1) Package, bag, any soft container: 一包米, 一包糖 a bag of rice, sugar (also *-'l*); 皮包, 錢包, 荷包 wallet; 書包 package of books; 紅包 gift for children, servants, etc., esp. gift for bribery; 門ᐞ包 52B.00 formerly, gift for gatekeeper; 包裹, 包袱 *-guoo*, *-'fu*↓. (2) A bun: 菜包 a bun stuffed with vegetables; 肉包 a bun stuffed with meat; 湯包 a bun with meat and gravy. (3) A surname.

V.t. (1) To wrap up: 包上, 包起來. (2) To include: 包這個在內 include this item, esp. 包括 *-guoh*↓. (3) To surround, esp. 包圍, 包抄 *-weir*, *-chau*↓; to shelter and protect: 包庇 *-bih*↓. (4) To cover and hide: 包藏禍心 entertain rebellious schemes in mind. (5) To pay an inclusive price for s.t., to hire for period of time: 包月 hire by the month; 包車, 船, 飛機 engage car, charter boat, airplane; 包妓 keep a prostitute as mistress for a period; 包飯 offer board at definite price for month, etc.; 包租 rent house with privilege of subletting; 包稅 pay sum for levies to government and then collect from taxpayers; 包攬 *-laan*↓. (6) To guarantee: 包換, 包退 guarantee change of article or refund if unsatisfactory; 包銷 guarantee purchase of specified amount; 包辦 *-bahn*↓; 包醫, 包治 guarantee cure.

包辦 *baubahn*, v. t., (1) take over, be responsible for, be entrusted with: 這事由我包辦 I will be responsible; 包辦筵席 cater to dinners; (2) to monopolize (opportunity, field of work).

包庇 *baubih*, v. t., shelter s. o. for wrongdoing.

包抄 *bauchau*, v. t., outflank (enemy) and attack.

包封 *baufeng*, v.t., to seal (package).

包袱 *bau'fu*, n., cloth bag containing clothing, etc. in travel; 掉包袱 *diauh--*, (communist phr.) cast away burden of past habits of thinking; 包袱底兒 n., the bottom of the bag: (a) a person's secrets; (b) the most precious, usu. untouched possession of the family (also 包袱皮兒); (c) 抖露包袱底兒 show one's best act in performance, usu. reserved for the last.

包管 *bauguaan*, v.i., guarantee, assure: 包管沒錯, 成功, 無事 I guarantee it's all right, it will succeed, there will be no trouble; 包管來回兒 (Peking coll.) guarantee satisfaction or exchange of article purchased.

包工 *baugung*, n., contract for labor; 包工制, 包工活 *--jyh*, *--huor*, piece-work basis, such contracted work.

包括 *bauguoh* (*-gua*), v.t., include.

包裹 *bauguoo*, v.t. & n., parcel.

包穀 *bauguu*, n., maize.

包含 *bauharn*[1], v.t., include.

包涵 *bauharn*[2], v.t., be lenient toward mistake (請你包涵); 包涵兒 *--'l*, n., (coll.) a small flaw: 只有家貧是個小包涵兒 my fault is that we are poor.

包荒 *bauhuang*, v.i., (LL, rare) shut eyes to filth, faults, i.e., be generous.

包活 *bauhuor*, n., see *-gung*↑.

包紮 *baujar*, v.t., to tie up (a bundle); to bandage.

包腳 *baujiaau*, v.i. & n., bind foot, footbinding (usu. 纏腳 *charn-jiaau*).

包莖 *baujihng*, n., prepuce.

包金 *baujin*, adj., covered with gold foil.

包裝 *baujuang*[1], n. & v.t., packing, to pack.

包莊 *baujuang*[2], v.i., to forfeit by paying for others' loss at cards.

包兒 *bau'l*, n., (1) a package; (2) ＝包子 bun, see N. 2↑; (3) 包兒米 *--mii*, n., maize.

包攬 *baulaan*, v.t., in 包攬詞訟 act as shyster.

包羅 *bauluor*, v.t., cover: 包羅萬象 (of great novel) cover and contain everything.

包票 *baupiauh*, n., certificate of guarantee.

包皮 *baupir*, n., outer skin, wrapper; prepuce: 包皮重量 chassis weight of car (also called 皮重).

包容 *baururng*, v.t., to forgive, pardon; see *-harn*[2]↑.

包廂 *baushiang*, n., box at theaters.

包探 *bautahn*, n., detective.

包頭 *bautour*, n., turban; head of contracted labor; 包頭的 *--de*, n., (a) female role played by actor (with turban for hair); (b) such hairdresser at theater; (c) name of city in Sueiyuan Province.

包圍 *bauweir*, v.t., (1) to surround (enemy) and attack; (2) to exert combined pressure on person.

包衣 *bauyi*, n., (Manchu) boy servant.

包銀 *bauyirn*, n., actor's monthly wages.

包圓兒 *bauyuar'l*, v.i., buy the whole lot.

包運 *bauyuhn*, v.i. & n., transport, -ation.

危 92.70

weir.

N. A surname.

V.t. To harm; to endanger: 危害 *-haih* ↓; 危身 to injure self, expose self to troubles; (AC) 危之 to threaten to destroy him.

Adj. (1) Dangerous, precarious in uncomfortably high position: 危險 *-shiaan* ↓; 危橋 shaky bridge; 危樓 high tower; 危崖 steep cliffside; 危冠 (AC) a tall hat; 臨危 upon deathbed; 居安思危 think of possible war when in peace; 危如累卵 precarious like a stack of eggs. (2) Cautious: 危言危行 (AC) cautious speech and conduct; 正襟危坐 sit solemnly, dress well buttoned (Confucian ethics).

危殆 *weirdaih*, adj., in danger.

危篤 *weirduu*, adj., critically ill.

危竿 *weir-gan*, n., acrobatic act, climbing on pole.

危害 *weirhaih*, v.t., to destroy, to plot to destroy (life), to endanger (society, country).

危機 *weirji*, n., a critical point, a crisis of danger.

危急 *weirjir*, adj., (1) critically ill; (2) urgent, critical (situation).

危懼 *weirjyuh*, v.i., to be in fear, be afraid and worried.

危難 *weirnahn*, n., calamity.

危險 *weirshiaan*, adj. & n., dangerous (place, step); danger.

危行 *weir-shihng*, n., cautious conduct, see Adj. 2 ↑.

危言 *weir-yarn*, n., as in 危言聳聽 shocking statement attracts attention; see also Adj. 2 ↑.

危語 *weir-yuu*, n., ditto.

色 92.70

seh (sp.pr. **shaai*).

N. (1) Color: 色彩, 色調 *-tsaai*, *-diauh* ↓; 五色, 彩色 many colors, multicolored; 英雄本色 true color of a hero; color as sensory image: 景色 the colors of a view, landscape (as of autumn); 色即是空 the sensory world is an illusion; 色, 香, 味 color, smell and taste--the three requisites of good cooking. (2) (**shaai*) Facial expression: 面色, 臉色 countenance; 氣色 facial complexion; 神色 air, looks (moody, spirited, etc.); 怒色, 喜色 anger, happiness on one's face; 變色 change countenance; 河山變色 situation of the land is greatly changed—usu. implying a change of dynasty; 失色, 作色 a startled look; 色厲內荏 appear severe, but weak inside; 和顏悅色 act or speak with a genial smile; 色養 *-yaang* ↓. (3) Sex, woman's charm: 女色 ditto; 色情, 色慾 *-chirng*, *-yuh* ↓; 色迷, 色鬼 *-mir*, *-gueei* ↓; 戒之在色 (during youth) avoid temptation of sex; 色衰 (woman) past her prime; 美色 feminine beauty; 好 (*hauh*) 色 be fond of female company, indulge in affairs with women. (4) Kinds: 各色人等 all kinds (classes) of people; 色色俱全 all kinds (of goods) are available; 清一色 pure, unadulterated, all of the same party or faith; 四色禮物 four kinds of gifts; 種色繁多 a great variety for one's choice. (5) Content of gold, silver: 成色 percentage of gold, silver; 足色 100% (gold, silver); 遜色 low-grade, inferior.

色情 *sehchirng*, n., sex: 色情小說 novels of sex; 色情狂 abnormal sexual desires, nymphomania or satyriasis.

色膽 (胆) *sehdaan*, n., as in 色膽天來大 (色膽包天) the extreme dangers to which one is willing to go for sex.

色調 *sehdiauh*, n., color of music, painting, textile, writing.

色鬼 *sehgueei*, n., a sex maniac, a satyr, a "wolf."

色狼 *sehlarng*, n., sexual maniac, "wolf."

色盲 *sehmarng*, n., color blindness; adj., color-blind.

色迷 *sehmir*, adj. & n., crazy about woman; sex mania.

色目 *sehmuh*, n., as in 各種色目 people of different professions, kinds and classes.

色色 *sehseh*, n., all kinds: 色色俱全 all kinds are available.

色相 *sehshiahng*, n., (Budd.) material appearance of things, sensory impressions; woman's sex appeal.

色笑 *sehshiauh*, phr., see *-yaang* 「↓.

色素 *sehsuh*, n., dye, pigment.

色彩 *sehtsaai*, n., the color (of paint, textile); quality (of actors); gayety (of entertainers).

色子 **shaaitz*, n., dice (also wr. 骰子).

色澤 *sehtzer*, n., luster (of jade, pearl); 色澤兒 extraneous remarks, descriptive additions: 說話別帶色澤兒, 直接了當多好 come straight to the point without the frostings.

色養 *sehyaang*, n., (Confu.) serve parents with a smile.

色樣 *sehyahng*, n., kind and quality (of wares, articles, people).

色藝 *sehyih*, n., (of entertainers) beauty and skill.

色慾 *sehyuh*, n., sexual desire.

免 92.70

miaan.

[Common var. of 免 50.70]

勉 92.70

miaan.

V.i. & t. (1) V.i., Make an effort to, endeavor to (do s. t.): 勉盡力量 do one's best; 勉爲其難 (persuade s. o.) to take up onerous work; 勤勉 work hard; 勉力 *-lih*[1]↓. (2) V. t., persuade s. o. to: 勸勉 ditto; 勉勵 *-lih*[2]↓.

勉強 *miarnchiaang*, (1) v. i., do under difficulty or against one's will: 勉強站起來 stand up with difficulty or unwillingly; 勉強一同去 be forced to go along; (2) v. t., force s. o. to do: 勉強他去 persuade or force one to; 不能勉強 cannot be forced; 不敢勉強 I dare not insist; also 勉勉強強 adv., unwillingly.

勉力 *miaanlih*[1], v.i., do one's best.

勉勵 *miaanlih*[2], v. t., persuade, urge by preaching.

彘 92.70

jyh.

N. (AC) pig, hog (modn. 豬): 彘肩 a shoulder of pork; 狗彘 dogs and pigs, expression of contempt.

龜 92.70

guei.

[Abbr. 亀]

N. (1) (Zoo.) the turtle, tortoise. (2) (Abusive) a cuckold: 烏龜.

龜版 *gueibaan*, n., tortoise shell, used in Chin. medicine.

龜坼 *guei-cheh*, n., (1) cracks in the fields caused by drought; (2) (AC) divination by observing crackings on tortoise-shell over fire.

龜鶴 *guei-heh*, phr., long-lived (like the turtle and the crane).

龜鑑 *guei-jiahn*, n., a past event or incident serving as an example or warning to future generations.

龜裂 *guei-lieh*, adj., (of fields) having cracks, (of hands) chapped.

龜齡 *guei-lirng*, adj., long-lived like the turtle.

龜紐 *guei-nioou*, n., turtle-shaped knob on a seal.

龜奴 *guei-nur*, n., (abusive) servant in a whorehouse.

龜婆 *gueipor*, n., woman in charge of prostitutes or brothel.

龜頭 *gueitour*, n., (physiol.) the glans penis.

氪 92.70

keh.

N. (Chem.) krypton.

氣 92.70

chih.

N. (1) Air, gas: 氣體 gas; 空氣 air, also atmosphere; 氧氣 oxygen; 氫氣 hydrogen; 天氣 weather, climate; 暖氣 warm air; 冷氣 cool air; 一氣讀完, 寫完 read in one sitting, write at one stretch; 氣候, 氣象 *-houh*, *-shiahng*↓. (2) Breath: 屛氣 hold one's breath; 斷氣, 氣絕 draw last breath; 出氣多, 入氣少 (patient about to die) feeble breath; 歎氣 sigh; 呵氣 blow breath (on cold hand, glass, etc.); 氣息 *-shir*↓. (3) Energy, force, vitality: 元氣 vital energy; 力氣 physical strength; 生氣 (勃勃) vitality; 氣虛 *-shyu*↓; (of writing) force: 文氣 force of writing; 行氣 (callig.) force or vitality of stroke; 大氣磅礴 great vitality; 傷氣 hurts one's spirit and energy. (4) Spirit, moral force: 志氣 ambition; 義氣 honor, integrity; 骨氣 backbone, integrity; 勇氣, 膽氣 courage; 俠氣, 豪氣 chivalry, generosity; 脾氣 temperament; 氣粗 (person) coarse temperament; 氣度, 氣概, 氣量 *-duh*, *-gaih*, *-liahng*↓; 英氣 brilliance; 氣格, 氣骨 *-ger*, *-guu*[1]↓. (5) Tone, atmosphere, manner: 習氣 habit, customs; 風氣, 流氣 atmosphere, (social, moral) fashion; 語氣, 口氣 tone of one's words; 士氣 morale, atmosphere of literary circles; 朝氣, 旺氣 atmosphere of growth and vitality; 暮氣, 衰氣 atmosphere of decay; 靈氣 vitality, moving spirit; 和氣 peaceable temper or atmosphere; 俗氣 vulgarity; 賤氣 cheap type, low and vulgar; 邪氣, 妖氣 evil, evil-minded; 陰陽怪氣 eccentric; 傻氣 dogged determination; 小氣 petty, mean; 小家氣 cheap, common, mean; 殺氣 blood-thirsty, terrorism, -stic; 晦氣 unlucky, misfortune. (6) Smell: 香氣 fragrance; 臭氣 bad odor, moldy odor. (7) Type: 氣派 type; 一氣 same type; 他們幾個人是一氣, 通同一氣 they are of the same group (acting together); 一鼻孔出氣 breathe, talk in the same way: 氣味 *-weih*↓.

V.i. & t. & adj. To fume, get angry; 生氣 get angry; 怒氣沖沖 enraged; 氣哼哼 fuming; to anger (person): 氣人 enrages people; 氣死我了 or 氣壞了 makes me boil with anger; 忍氣呑聲 swallow the humiliation and insult.

氣胞 *chih-bau*, n., (physiol.) air cell; respiratory hollow of plant.

氣槍 *chih-chiang*, n., air gun.

氣球 *chihchiour*, n., balloon.

氣喘 *chihchuaan*, v. i., to be short of breath, to gasp, suffer from asthma.

氣圈 *chihchyuan*, n., the air surrounding the earth.

氣道 *chihdauh*, n., (physiol.) respiratory circuit.

氣墊子 *chihdiahn'tz*, n., air cushion.

氣短 *chihduaan*, adj., disappointed, downcast: 英雄氣短 a good

氣 氙 氟 氬 氫

man caught in difficult circumstances; short of breath.

氣度 *chihduh*, n., generosity of spirit or appearance: 氣度非凡 impressive appearance; 氣度小 mean, spiteful.

氣忿 *chihfehn*[1], adj. & n., angry; anger.

氣憤 *chihfehn*[2], adj. & n., see *-fehn*[1] ↑.

氣氛 *chihfen*, n., atmosphere, esp. a laden atmosphere.

氣概 *chihgaih*, n., manner, spirit; heroic manner, see *-duh* ↑.

氣根 *chihgen*, n., (bot.) aerial root.

氣格 *chihger*, n., personal character; moral force or character.

氣管 *chihguaan*, n., (physiol.) the windpipe, trachea; the bronchial tubes; 氣管炎 bronchitis.

氣骨 *chihguu*[1], n., moral character, backbone of character.

氣鼓 *chihguu*[2], n., (Chin. med.) swelling ascribed to accumulation of gas.

氣恨 *chihhehn*, v. t., to hate.

氣候 *chihhouh*, n., (1) climate; (2) weather; (3) time of lunar year; 氣候帶 n., climatic zone; 氣候學 climatology.

氣化 *chihhuah*, v. i., to gasify, vaporize.

氣懷 *chihhuair*, v. i., (a baby) gets jealous seeing another baby in his mother's breast.

氣積 *chihji*, n., (Chin. med.) symptoms of indigestion.

氣界 *chihjieh*, n., see *-chyuan* ↑.

氣結 *chihjier*[1], (1) n., (Chin. med.) a distemper, block-up of circulatory system; (2) adj., miserable with suppressed sorrows or other emotions.

氣節 *chihjier*[2], n., moral integrity.

氣質 *chihjyr*, n., (1) natural endowment or inborn quality (of living things, persons); (2) a gaseous body; (3) temperament: 他的氣質太壞 his moral endowment is deficient.

氣絕 *chih-jyuer*, phr., draw last breath.

氣沮 *chih-jyuu*, phr., suffocate in spirit.

氣孔 *chihkuung*, n., stomata of plants or of lower animals.

氣累脖兒 *chihleeibor'l*, n., thyroglosaal cyst, (Chin. med.) a thyroid disease or malfunctioning (such as goiter).

氣類 *chihleih*, n., type of person.

氣量 *chihliahng*, n., as in 氣量大, 小 generosity or meanness.

氣力 *chihlih*, n., physical strength.

氣流 *chihliour*, n., current of air.

氣樓 *chihlour*, n., small tower for ventilation on top of granary.

氣籠 *chihlurng*, n., air tube of bamboo in granary to prevent moulding decay.

氣悶 *chihmehn*, adj., depressed.

氣門 *chihmern*, n., stomata of plants, (Chin. med.) pores in the skin.

氣惱 *chihnaau*, v. i., be angry.

氣囊 *chihnarng*, n., a bird's air sac.

氣逆 *chihnih*, adj., (Chin. med.) malfunction of regulatory system; shortness of breath.

氣派 *chih'pai*, n., style (of person).

氣魄 *chihpoh*, n., moral force, strength of purpose (big, small).

氣色 *chihseh*, n., complexion (good, bad, pale).

氣象 *chihshiahng*, n., (1) climatic phenomena; (2) see *-gaih* ↑; 氣象學 meteorology; 氣象臺 n., weather station, meteorological observatory.

氣性 *chihshihng*, n., person's temperament.

氣息 *chihshir*, n., (1) breath: 氣息尚存 person is still breathing, alive; (2) spirit of writing (文章氣息): 毫無氣息 totally lacking in spirit, insipid.

氣數 *chihshuh*, n., fate, destiny (as "reckoned" in divination).

氣虛 *chih-shyu*, n. & adj., (Chin. med.) debility; enervated, feeble in vitality.

氣死 *chih-syy*, v. t., to infuriate, drive (one) crazy; 氣死風 (coll.) storm lantern; 氣死貓 (coll.) wired food cabinet which frustrates cats.

氣體 *chihtii*, n., gaseous body.

氣層 *chihtserng*, n., strata of air.

氣筒(子) *chihtuung('tz)*, n., air pump for bicycle.

氣味 *chihweih*, n., (1) flavor, taste: 氣味相投 people of the same tastes, similar in inclinations, methods; (2) smell: 氣味難聞 (LL) stinks awfully.

氣溫 *chihwen*, n., air temperature.

氣壓 *chihya*, n., air pressure; 氣壓計 barometer.

氣眼 *chihyaan*, n., hole in hat or room for ventilation.

氣燄 *chihyahn*, n., flame of anger; person's arrogance: 氣燄逼人 insufferably haughty.

氣運 *chihyuhn*[1], n., luck (good, bad).

氣韻 *chihyuhn*[2], n., flavor (of writing), tone and atmosphere (of painting): 氣韻生動 (of painting) rhythmic vitality.

氣宇 *chihyuu*, n., inspiring looks, manner of a person's carriage.

氙 92.70

shian.

N. (Chem.) xenon.

氟 92.70

fur.

N. (Chem.) fluorine.

氬 92.70

yah.

N. (Chem.) argon.

氫 92.70

ching.

N. (Chem.) hydrogen: 氫彈 hydrogen bomb.

氫氯酸 *chinglyuh-suan*, n., hydrochloric acid.

氫氧化 *chingyaanghuah*, n., hydroxide: 氫氧化鈣 calcium hydroxide; 氫氧化鉀 potassium hydroxide; 氫氧化鈉 sodium hydroxide.

氫氧基 *chingyaangji*, n., hydroxyl.

氖 92.70

naai.

N. (Chem.) neon.

氤 92.70

yin.

氤氳 *yinyun*, adj., cloudy, misty.

氳 92.70

yun.

Adj. See 氤^氳 92.70 ↑.

氦 92.70

haih.

N. (Chem.) helium.

氨 92.70

an.

N. (Chem.) ammonia.

氛 92.70

fen.

N. Laden atmosphere: 氣氛 atmosphere of place, writing, assembly, etc.; 妖氛 obnoxious atmosphere, evil influence; 賊氛 evil influence of bandits conceived as burning flame.

氛氣 *fenchih*, n., obnoxious atmosphere (usu. 氣氛).
氛垢 *fengouh*, n., smog, noxious air.

氧 92.70

yaang.

N. (Chem.) oxygen.

氧氣 *yaangchih*, n., oxygen.
氧化 *yaanghuah*, v.t. & n., oxidize, oxidation; 氧化物 oxides; 氧化鈣 *--gaih*, n., calcium oxide; 氧化汞 *--guung*, n., mercuric oxide.

氝 92.70

neih.

N. (Chem.) neon (also 氖).

氮 92.70

dahn.

N. (Chem.) nitrogen; 氮肥 nitrogen fertilizer.

氯 92.70

lyuh (luh).

N. (Chem.) chlorine.

氯氣 *lyuhchih*, n., (chem.) chlorine gas; 氯氣砲 poison gas shell.
氯化物 *lyuhhuah-wuh*, n., (chem.) chloride: 氯化氫 hydrochloride; 氯化鈉 sodium chloride; 氯化鈣 calcium chloride; also 氯化鉀, 鋅, 鉛, 銀, 銅, 金, 鎂 chorides of potassium, zinc, lead, silver, copper, gold, magnesium.
氯水 *lyuhshueei*, n., (chem.) chlorine water.
氯酸 *lyuhsuan*, n., (chem.) chloric acid; 氯酸鉀 potassium chlorate.

氡 92.70

dung.

N. (Chem.) radon.

§ 92.72 (⺈/心)

忽 92.72

hu.

N. (1) One ten thousandth of a 分. (2) (Weight measure) one thousandth part of a *li* (釐), see Appendix C. (3) A surname.

V.t. To ignore, neglect, look down upon: 輕忽 to ignore or slight (s.o.); 疏忽 to be negligent toward (work, person); 忽略, 忽視 *-lyueh*, *-shyh* ↓.

Adv. Suddenly: 忽然, 忽地 *-rarn*, *-dih* ↓; 忽見 see suddenly; 忽有忽無 suddenly appear and disappear; 忽冷忽熱 fever alternates with chills; 忽發奇想 suddenly had an idea, inspiration.

忽地 *hudih*, adv., (MC & modn.)

氫 氖 氤 氳 氦 氨 氛 氧 氝 氮 氯 氡 忽

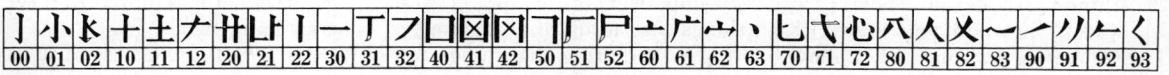

suddenly.

忽忽 *huhu*, (1) adv., with the quick passing of time: 忽忽一年 a year has so quickly gone by; (2) adj., feel or look lost, absent-minded: 忽忽若有所失 looking lost; 悠悠忽忽 misty, shadowy, uncertain (memory, image); not well thought out: 忽忽之謀 ill-conceived plan.

忽略 *hulyueh*, v. t., to neglect or slight (thing, person).

忽然 *hurarn*, adv., suddenly (disappear, arrive, etc.).

忽哨 *hushauh*, n. & v. i., whistle as a call.

忽視 *hushyh*, v. t., neglect, look down upon.

忽微 *huwei*, adj., minuscule, minimal.

怱 92.72

tsung.

[Var. of 匆 92.50]

怎 92.72

tzeen.

Adv. How, why: 怎麼 *-'me*, 怎樣 *-yahng* ↓; 怎好, 怎厲害 how good, how cruel (question and statement); 不知怎好 don't know what to do.

怎地 *tzeen'de*[1], adv., (1) why: 你等阻當我卻怎地 why are you barring my way? 你問我怎地 why are you asking me? (2) ＝怎的 (2) ↓.

怎的 *tzeen'de*[2], adv., (1) why: 和尚怎的不見 why isn't the monk here? ("why don't we see him?"); (2) how: 那人怎的打扮 how is the man dressed?

怎得 *tzeen-der*, phr. & adv., (1) phr., how could . . .: 怎得如此 how could you (he) do such a thing? (2) (*-'de*) adv., how: 你怎得知道 how do you know it?

怎敢 *tzern-gaan*, phr., (rhet.) how dare I (we)?

怎麼 *tzee'me* (*tzeen'me*), adv., (1) why: 你怎麼不來 why didn't you come? (2) how: 這怎麼好, 怎麼辦 what shall we (I) do? ("how to handle this?"); (3) however, whatever: 怎麼說他也不聽 he will not listen, however you speak to him, whatever you say; (4) excl., what! 怎麼, 你還在這兒麼 what! are you still here?

怎麼樣 *tzeen'meyahng*, phr., (1) how is (s.o., s. t.): 你看這枝筆怎麼樣 what do you think of this pen? 那個病人怎麼樣 how is that patient? (2) what's the matter: 你要怎麼樣 what's the matter with you? are you looking for trouble?

怎奈 *tzeen-naih*, phr., (1) except that, but for: 待不尋思, 怎奈心腸輭 I would not think of him any more, except that my heart would not allow me not to; (2) unfortunately: 怎奈他不聽話 unfortunately he will not listen.

怎能 *tzeen-nerng*, phr., how could (it be possible, one do such a thing)?

怎生 *tzeen-sheng*, adv., (MC) how.

怎樣 *tzeenyahng*, adv., see *-'meyahng* ↑.

急 92.72

jir.

V.i. Be zealous, warm-hearted: 急公好義 public-spirited; 急色 obsessed by sex; 急促 *-tsuh*, 急遽 *-jyuh*, 急切 *-chieh* ↓.

Adj. (1) Urgent, pressing, calling for immediate action: 急巴巴 very impatient; 急變 *-biahn*, 急迫 *-poh* ↓; 緊急 critical; 急電 an urgent telegram; 急驚風偏遇慢郎中 deferred action taken in cases requiring prompt attention; 急須, 急需 urgently necessary, needed; 急用 pressing need for money; 急於 impatient of or to; 急喳兒 things that admit of no delay; 急如星火 requiring lightning action, admitting of no delay. (2) Hard up: 窘急 in desperate straits; 急難 *-nahn* ↓. (3) Anxious, uneasy: 急躁 *-tzauh*; 急激 *-ji* ↓; 急煎煎 impatient with anxiety; 焦急, 着急 restless, worried, full of misgivings; 心急口快 outspoken; 急不的, 惱不的 one can neither cry nor laugh; 急赤白臉 face red or pale with too much anxiety; 急煞 (殺) worried to death; 急死人, 急得要命 ditto; 急三槍 (facet.) quick-tempered; 急甚麼 why the hurry? 急不得 don't worry, take it easy; 急出病來 get sick from excessive worries.

Adj. & adv. Hurried(ly), hast(il)y, rapid(ly): 急忙 *-marng*, 急急 *-jir* ↓; 急脈緩受 take tense situation calmly; 急流 *-liour* ↓; 急起直追 make amends while there is yet time ("up and be going").

急變 *jirbiahn*, n., emergency (in sickness, politics).

急病 *jir-bihng*, n., acute disease (also 急症 *-jehng* ↓).

急切 *jirchieh*, v. i. & adj., (be) excessively impatient, insistent or demanding.

急診 *jir-jeen*, n., (med.) emergency cases.

急症 *jir-jehng*, n., acute disease (also 急病 *-bihng* ↑).

急激 *jirji*, adj., easily wrought-up, excitable, temperamental.

急進 *jirjihn*, adj., progressive, radical (party).

急驚風 *jirjingfeng*, n., (med.) convulsion, generally of children.

急救 *jirjiouh*[1], n., (med.) first aid; 急救法 first-aid methods.

急就 *jirjiouh*[2], adj., (of programs, tasks) rush: 急就章 a work rushed through in the shortest possible time.

急急 *jirjir*, adv., hurriedly, feverishly: 急急趕來 come posthaste; 急急忙忙 hastily, in a rush; 急急如律令 (Taoist incantation) be it so quickly!

急抓 *jir-jua*, v. t., to scrape together what is required to meet emergency needs.

急智 *jirjyh*, n., quickness of wits.

急遽 *jirjyuh*, v.i. & adv., do things in a hurry.

急口令 *jirkoou-lihng*, n., a tongue twister.

急流 *jirliour*, n., rushing currents: 急流勇退 make a quick retreat before crisis, "slow down while riding high."

急忙 *jirmarng*, adj. & adv., in a great hurry.

急難 *jirnahn*, (1) n., in dire circumstances, (2) v.i., to help in a crisis.

急迫 *jirpoh*, adj. & adv., hasty, -ily.

急色兒 *jirseh'l*, n., a sex-starved person, a sex maniac (also 急色鬼).

急性 *jirshihng*, adj., (1) quick-tempered; (2) (of diseases) acute (opp. 慢性 chronic).

急行軍 *jirshirng-jyun*, n., troops in forced march.

急促 *jirtsuh*, v. i. & adj., (be) in a hurry.

急圖 *jirtur*, (1) n., urgent matters; (2) v. t., try quickly to (do): 急圖補救 work out immediate remedial measures.

急躁 *jirtzauh*, adj., impatient and quick-tempered, irritable, peevish.

急務 *jir-wuh*, n., urgent matter.

怨 92.72

yuahn.

N. Hatred, enmity: 結怨 become enemies; 懷怨, 抱怨 harbor hatred, resentment; 招怨 incur hostility; 報怨 to revenge, vengeance.

V.t. (1) To blame, put blame on: 怨他 (or 埋怨他) 不告訴我 blame him for not telling me; 怨不得 -*'bude*↓; 怨天尤人 blame God and others (not oneself). (2) To hate (person): 怨恨 -*'hehn*↓.

怨不得 *yuahn'bude*, phr., cannot blame (person).

怨氣 *yuahnchih*, n., hatred, resentment.

怨仇 *yuahnchour*, n., old enemy.

怨懟 *yuahndueih*, n., hatred, resentment.

怨毒 *yuahndur*, n., hatred, venom.

怨誹 *yuahnfeei*, v. i. & t., decry, disparage (person); n., disparagement.

怨忿 *yuahnfehn*, n., hatred.

怨府 *yuahn-fuu*, n., (AC, LL) target of public hatred or complaint.

怨鬼 *yuahn-gueei*, n., ghost of one who died of an injustice.

怨恨 *yuahn'hehn*, v.t. & n., to hate; hatred.

怨家 *yuahn-jia*, n., hated person, old enemy.

怨慕 *yuahnmuh*, v. i., (AC) to repine, regret, sorrow over alienated affection.

怨女 *yuahn-nyuu*, n., (AC, LL) old maid, spinster.

怨耦 *yuahn-oou*, n., hated spouse, estranged couple (also wr. 怨偶).

怨咨 *yuahntzy*, v. i., (LL) to repine, curse.

怨望 *yuahnwahng*, v. i., grumble against ruler.

怨言 *yuahnyarn*, n., complaints, murmurs.

§ 92.80 (⺊/八)

 92.80

yirn.

V.i. (AC) climb the official ladder: 螽緣 -*yuarn*↓.

螽夜 *yirnyeh*, n., deep night.

螽緣 *yirnyuarn*, v. i., to climb up on the basis of certain connections: 螽緣際會 to ride the crest of good luck.

負 92.80

fuh.

[Var. 頁 50.80]

§ 92.81 (⺊/人)

久 92.81

jioou.

Adj. (=舊) Old (opp. 新 new): 不忘久德 (AC) will not forget old kindnesses; 久要 -*yau*↓.

Adv. For a long time: 久違 -*weei*, 久仰 -*yaang*, 久遠 -*yuaan*↓; 久聞大名 I've heard of your name; 久別 long separation; 不能久留 sorry I can't stay longer; 久病成良醫 long illness makes the patient a good doctor; 好久, 許久, 長久 for a long time; 天長地久 everlasting, eternity; 由來久矣 it has been so for a long time; 耐久 enduring, lasting; 不久 soon; 多久 for a long time, how long?

久常 *jioucharng*, adj., lasting, enduring.

久視 *jiooushyh*, n., (Taoism) everlasting life.

久違 *jiourweei*, phr., (of s.o.) have not seen for a long time.

久仰 *jiouryaang*, phr., (of s.o. to whom one is being introduced) am glad to meet you whom I've always admired.

久要 *jioouyau*, n., (AC) an old promise.

久已 *jiouryii*, adv., long since, for a long time.

久遠 *jiouryuaan*, adv., for a very long time.

奐 92.81

huahn.

N. A surname.

Adj. Bright-colored, used only in phr. 美輪美奐 gorgeous, bright-colored.

欠 92.81

chiahn.

V.t. (1) To owe (debt, gratitude), to be in deficit: 欠缺, 欠款, 欠債, 欠賬 *-chyue*, *-kuaan*, *-jaih*, *-jahng*, etc.↓; 欠人五十元 owe s.o. fifty dollars; 不欠了 all paid now; 欠薪 salary in arrears; 前欠未還 have not paid the outstanding debts; 欠人情 owe gratitude to s. o. for his favor. (2) To need: 欠打, 欠罵 need a spanking, scolding. (3) To stretch and yawn: 欠伸, 欠身 *-shen*[1,2]↓.

Adj. Spiteful: 嘴欠 (person) likes to say mean things about people; 手欠 (person) tends to break or upset things.

Adv. Short of, short in, used like 不 (not) with a milder connotation: 欠妥 not very appropriate; 欠適 slightly unwell; 欠佳 not quite right (in composition); 欠聰明 not very bright (person); 欠考慮 rash, without due consideration.

欠安 *chiahn-an*, adj., not very well in health.

欠不 *chiahn buh*, adv. phr., almost: 他欠不花了兩千塊錢了 he has spent almost two thousand dollars.

欠錢 *chiahn-chiarn*, phr., owe money, need money.

欠情 *chiahn-chirng*, phr., to owe a debt of gratitude not yet repaid.

欠缺 *chiahnchyue*, (1) v. t., to need, be short of (money, friends); (2) n., a person's needs; shortcomings.

欠帳(賬) *chiahn-jahng*, v. i., to owe in accounts.

欠債 *chiahn-jaih*, v. i., to owe debts.

欠據 *chiahnjyuh*, n., I. O. U.

欠款 *chiahn-kuaan*, n., deficit; debt.

欠伸 *chiahnshen*[1], v. i., to yawn and stretch.

欠身 *chiahn-shen*[2], v. i., to make a gesture of rising from seat in greetings.

欠資 *chiahntzy*, phr., "postage due."

矢 92.81

shyy.

N. (1) An arrow: 矢石 arrows and rocks in anc. battles. (2) U.f. 屎 dung: 馬矢, 牛矢 horse dung, cow dung.

V.i. To swear: 矢以天日 swear by the sun and sky; 矢誓 swear an oath; 永矢勿諼 (AC) I swear never to forget; 矢志不移 swear will never change.

矢車菊 *shyyche-jyur*, n., (bot.) *Centaurea cyanus.*

矦 92.81

hour.

[Anc. var. of 侯 91A.81]

灸 92.81

jioou.

V.t. (Chin. med.) cauterize by burning moxa: 針灸 acupuncture.

炙 92.81

jyh.

V.t. & i. (1) To broil, to toast: 炙肉 broil (-ed) meat; 炙乾 to bake dry; 炙衣服 dry clothing over fire; 膾炙人口 (fig.) greatly relished (of popular books); 炙薰 to cook (fish, etc.) by smoking over open fire; 炙手可熱 (fig. of intense political power) burning to the touch; 焚炙 burn up. (2) To study directly under s. o. (receive the radiating influence of the teacher): 親炙. (3) To cauterize: 炙瘡 cauterize wound; 針炙 acupuncture (cf. 灸 *jioou*).

§ 92.82 (⺈/乂)

攵 92.82

pu (**wern*).

N. (1) A radical, see 攴 21A.82. (2) Pop. for 文 pr. **wern*, 60.82.

发 92.82

fa.

[Abbr. of 發 32.82]

敻 92.82

shyuhng.

Adj. (AC) (1) faraway: 敻古以來 since anc. times. (2) 敻敻 long.

§ 92.83 (⺈/乀)

迻 92.83

eel.

[Pop. of 邇 31.83]

迄 92.83

chih.

Prep. Up to: 迄今, 以迄於今 up to now; 迄至 up to (time, condition).

Adv. Yet, still (usu. negative): 迄無 (未) 成功 have still not succeeded; 迄未辦理 have not yet done it; 迄竟 still.

迤 92.83

yii

V.i. To wind (through, about): 迤邐 *-lii*↓; 迤西, 迤北 (mountain range, etc.) turn west, north; 逶迤 to circle around or about.

迤邐 *yirlii*, v.i., to wind, circle about.

迕 92.83

wuh.

V.t. (1) To defy, disobey (var. of 忤 22A.10). (2) (AC) to meet or welcome.

迮 92.83

tzer (also *tzuoh*).

N. A surname.

V.t. To press, push against: 鄰舍比里, 共相壓迮 houses in the neighborhood lean against one another.

Adv. Suddenly, all at once.

迻 92.83

yir.

V.t. (1) To move round (interch. 移). (2) 迻譯 to translate.

逄 92.83

parng.

N. (AC) a surname.

逢 92.83

ferng.

V.t. (1) Meet, find: 巧相逢 by chance meeting on the road; 喜相逢 happy meeting of friends, lovers. (2) Come upon (person, time, luck): 逢年過節 at the holidays and New Year; 生不逢時 born under a bad star, in wrong time; 逢處 everywhere; 每逢 every time it comes to be: 每逢星期六 every Saturday; 逢人便說 tell everybody one meets; 逢人說項 same meaning, but orig. allu. to praise person (項斯) before everybody; 逢凶化吉 (of person's luck in fortunetelling) turn every piece of bad luck into good; 絕路逢生 find rescue in desperate circumstances; 逢塲作戲 join in the spirit of the occasion, play along on rare occasions; 左右逢源 have material at fingertips, on hand within easy reach.

逢迎 *ferngyirng*, v. t., anticipate and meet person's every wish; bend every effort to please (person).

逯 92.83

luh.

N. A surname.

逯逯 *luhluh*, adj., incompetent, common (var. of 碌碌).
逯然 *luhrarn*, adv., (AC) abruptly.

逸 92.83

yih.

V.i. & t. (1) To flee, to break loose. (2) To excel: 超逸. (3) (AC) to let free (prisoner).

Adj. & adv. (1) Unconstrained, free, romantic, excellent, above common run: 逸品, 逸材 *-piin*, *-tsair*↓. (2) At ease, happy, retired from society: 隱逸 a recluse; 逸樂 *-leh*↓; 淫逸 licentious, given to sexual pleasures; 安逸 at ease, content; 逸居 live in content; 逸名 anonymous (author). (3) Fast: 逸足 fast-footed.

逸氣 *yih-chih*, n., romantic spirit, romantic or highly expressionistic style in painting or writing.
逸羣 *yih-chyurn*, adj., excellent, outstanding, surpassing (personality).
逸度 *yih-duh*, n., see *-chih*↑.
逸話 *yih-huah*, n., anecdote.
逸致 *yih-jyh*, phr., 閒情逸致 romantic or poetic fancy, see *-shihng*↓.
逸樂 *yihleh*, v.i. & n., live (life) in pleasure, be given to pleasures.
逸品 *yih-piin*, n., (art criticism) work of a romantic spirit.

逸聲 *yih-sheng*, n., licentious, lewd music.
逸想 *yih-shiaang*, n., fancy, whimsy.
逸興 *yih-shihng*, n., mood for relaxation (wine, poetry, chess); poetic fancy.
逸事 *yih-shyh*[1], n., anecdotes, usu. of a famous person (also wr. 軼事).
逸士 *yih-shyh*[2], n., retired scholar.
逸材 *yih-tsair*, n., spectacular talent (poet, etc.).
逸豫 *yihyuh*, v.i., (LL) live in idleness, spend one's time in pleasures of the flesh.

遙 92.83

yaur.

Adj. Faraway, long: 路遙 it is a long way; 遙夜 (LL) a long night.

Adv. From a distance: 遙領, 遙制 control (forces) from a distance; 遙望 look from a distance.

遙遙 *yauryau*, adv., far away: 遙遙無期 (a hope) far away and not within foreseeable future; 遙遙相對 (armies) face each other across a great distance.
遙遠 *yauryuaan*, adj., faraway, long (journey, etc.).

邂 92.83

shieh.

V.i. & t. (LL) to encounter by chance.

邂逅 *shiehhouh*, v. i., as in 邂逅相遇 to meet by chance.

処 92.83

chuu (**chuh*).

[Abbr. of 處 21A.83]

§ 92.93 (ㄧ/ㄑ)

螽 92.93

jung.

N. (AC) gen. term for grasshoppers, symbol of prolific offspring: 螽斯衍慶 a felicitation for having many children.

蟹 92.93

shieh (also *shiee*).

N. Crab: 蟹殼 crab shell; 蟹匡 back of crab; 蟹螯 crab's big claws; 蟹爪 crab's claws; 沒腳蟹 a crab without legs—helpless creature; 蟹厄 crab pest in fields; 蟹黃 *-huarng*↓.

蟹青 *shiehching*, n., greenish-grey color.
蟹臍 *shiechir*, n., the belly flap in the under part of crab, elongated in male, called 尖臍 and round in female, called 圓臍.
蟹斷 *shiehduahn*, n., a weir or stretch of bamboo stakes to intercept crabs.
蟹粉 *shiehfeen*, n., minced crab meat.
蟹黃 *shiehhuarng*, n., spawn or roe of crab.
蟹簾 *shiehliarn*, n., see *-duahn*↑.
蟹行 *shieh-shirng*, adj., as in 蟹行文字 writing which runs horizontally—English, Latin, etc.

蠡 92.93

lii (**lir*).

N. (1) A woodworm. (2) (**lir*) A gourd, a drinking cup, a dipper: 以蠡測海 take a very superficial view, to measure ocean with a dipper.

蠡實 *liishyr*, n., (bot.) the Chin. iris, *Iris ensata* var. *chinensis*.

蠭 92.93

feng.

N. Var. of 蜂; 蠭目豺聲 phr., (AC) eyes of a wasp and voice of a wolf, ferocious-looking.

SECTION 92A

§ 92A.00 (竹/丿)

等 92A.00-1

deeng.
[Abbr. 夸]

N. (1) Class, grade: 甲等, 乙等 "A" grade, "B" grade; 優等, 劣等 superior, inferior grade; 頭, 中, 下等 first, middle, low class; 同等 same class; 等而下之 from that (class) down; 何等 (excl.) how; 何等可恥, 美妙 how despicable, pretty! (2) People, group: 我等, 彼等 (LL) we, they; 一干人等 (such) group of people, such people; see Adj. 2↓.

V.i. & t. Wait, await: 等機會 wait for opportunity; 等人 wait for s. o.; 等時候 wait for time; 等(我)一會兒 wait (for me) a moment; 等會兒 or 等等兒 (再看) wait a while (and see); 等會兒給人瞧見 by and by s.o. may see you; oft. 等着 be waiting; 等着瞧 wait and see; 等着要 waiting for (s.t.); 等不着 *-buh-jaur*, cannot wait; 等不及 *-buh-jir*, ditto; see 等候, 等待 *-houh, -daih*↓.

Adj. (1) Equal to (等於): 等於白說 might as well not have said it at all; 相等 equal; 平等 equal, -ity, (in opportunity, law, status, treatment, etc.); 著作等身 one's works pile up as high as the writer himself, (of a writer) prolific, voluminous; 等量齊觀 to be regarded as equal (in value, merit). (2) Such, in phrr.: 等等 and such like, and so forth, "etc."; 南京, 上海等處 Nanking, Shanghai and such places; 等因, 等語 (end of quotation in official documents): 等因奉此 "whereas . . . therefore"—a phr., describing the conventional make-up of an official document; 等情, 等由 (end of narration) for these reasons.

Conj. When, till: 等他來了告訴他 I'll tell him when he comes; 等錢用光了 when money is all spent.

等邊 *deengbian*, adj., (geom.) equilateral: 等邊三角形 an equilateral triangle.
等比級數 *derngbii jirshuh*, n., (geom.) geometric progression; 等比中項 *--jungshiahng*, n., geometric mean.
等差 *deengcha*, n., gradations of difference: 愛有等差 (pr. *deengtsy*) there are gradations of love (Mencius, against "universal love" without distinctions); 等差級數 *--jirshuh*, arithmetic progression; 等差中項 arithmetic mean.
等傾線 *deengching-shiahn*, n., (geog.) isoclinic lines.
等待 *deengdaih*, (1) v. i. & t., wait: 等待好久 wait a long time; (2) conj., when: 等待太陽出來了 when the sun comes out.
等等 *derngdeeng*, phr., and so forth, see Adj. 2↑.
等第 *deengdih*, n., grade in examination; sequence.
等高線 *deenggau-shiahn*, n., (geog.) contour line in maps.
等號 *deenghauh*, n., sign of equality ("=").
等候 *deenghouh*, v.i. & t., to wait, to wait for (person, event).
等角線 *derngjiaau-shiahn*, n., (geom.) equiangular lines.
等級 *deengjir*, n., grade, gradation.
等距離 *deengjyuhlih*, adj., equidistant.
等力線 *deenglih-shiahn*, n., (phys.) isodynamic lines.
等閒 *deengshiarn*, adv., (1) (MC) by-and-by, in case: 等閒飛上別花枝 by-and-by it may fly up to another branch; (2) 等閒視之 regard it idly as of no importance.
等式 *deengshy*, n., (math.) equality, equation.
等時性 *deengshyr-shihng*, n., isochromism.
等速運動 *deengsuh yuhnduhng*, n., uniform motion; 等速度 equal velocity.
等次 *deengtsyh*, n., sequence.
等子 *deengtz*, n., small scales for medicine (=戥子).
等溫線 *deengwern-shiahn*, n., isotherm.
等壓線 *deengya-shiahn*, n., (geog.) isobars.
等韻 *deengyuhn*, n., science of classification of vowels or vowel groups according to qualities (back, front, with rounded lips, etc.), used in MC dictionaries.

籌 92A.00-1

chour.
[Abbr. 筹]

N. adjunct. (MC) 六籌好漢 six big fellows.

N. (1) Chips in gambling, token, tally for counting: 籌碼 *-maa*↓; 竹籌 bamboo chips; 算籌 chips used for counting. (2) 借箸代籌 (allu.) make use of chopsticks to stand as tokens to indicate position of army units (in military council); hence a plan, a move: 一籌莫展 couldn't suggest a move or do a thing; see V.i. & t.↓.

V.i. & t. (1) (In compp., 籌+vb.) to plan: 籌備, 籌畫 *-beih, -huah*↓. (2) To collect or prepare funds: 籌款, 籌措 *-kuaan, -tsuoh*↓.

籌辦 *chour bahn*, v. t., make plans to start (school, project).
籌備 *chourbeih*, v. i. & t., to make preparations: 籌備好了 all is prepared.
籌邊 *chour-bian*, v. i., make plans for frontier regions.
籌度 *chourduoh*, v. i., to reckon, calculate.
籌畫 *chourhuah*, v. i. & t., to

make plans for (future).

籌款 *chour-kuaan*, v. i., plan financing (of project), prepare necessary funds (for purpose).

籌略 *chourlyueh*, n., plan strategy.

籌馬(兒) *chour'maa* (-'*ma'l*[1]), n., chips (as in poker).

籌碼(兒) *chourmaa* (-'*ma'l*[2]), n. a debenture, voucher, certificate; gambling chips.

籌商 *chourshang*, v. i. & t., to discuss.

籌算 *choursuahn*, v. t., orig., to count with bamboo chips bearing notches, now to reckon in gen.

籌策 *chourtseh*, v. t., to plan (procedures, moves).

籌措 *chourtsuoh*, v. t., to raise necessary funds.

籌議 *chouryih*, v. i. & t., to discuss (in planning stage).

竽 92A.00-3

yur.

N. An anc. flute: 濫竽充數 (allu.) to fill a post without real qualification.

簡 92A.00-5

jiaan.

[Usu. wr. 简]

N. (1) A small bamboo or wooden strip used to write on: 簡冊 -*tseh*[1], 簡策 -*tseh*[2], 簡素 -*suh* ↓. (2) A written message: 書簡 written notes; 簡牘 -*dur*, 簡札 -*jar* ↓. (3) A surname.

V.t. (1) Select, appoint to office: 簡拔 -*bar*, 簡任 -*rehn* ↓. (2) Be rude to, treat with contempt: 簡慢 -*mahn*, 簡忽 -*hu* ↓.

Adj. Simple, brief, terse, concise: 簡筆字 -*biitzyh*, 簡體字 -*tiitzyh*, 簡字 -*tzyh* ↓; 簡明 -*mirng*, 簡練 -*liahn* ↓; 簡而言之 in fine, in short.

簡板 *jiarn-baan*, n., a musical instrument used in Chin. opera.

簡拔 *jiaanbar*, v. t., select (able and good men) for official posts.

簡便 *jiaanbiahn*, adj., simple and convenient, handy.

簡編 *jiaan-bian*, n., (1) books, written works; (2) an abridged compilation.

簡筆字 *jiarnbiitzyh*, n., a simpler form of writing with fewer strokes.

簡稱 *jiaancheng*, n. & v.t., abbreviated term, in short; to abbreviate.

簡單 *jiaandan*, adj., simple, easy (opp. 複雜 complex, difficult): 頭腦簡單 simple-minded; 這很簡單 that's easy.

簡短 *jiarnduaan*, adj., short, terse, brief.

簡牘 *jiaandur*, n., (1) written records; (2) letters, correspondence.

簡放 *jiaanfahng*, v. i., formerly, be appointed to a provincial post by imperial decree.

簡忽 *jiaanhu*, (1) adj., scanty, too brief; (2) v.t., to ignore, neglect (person, aspect).

簡化 *jiaanhuah*, v.t., to simplify; 簡單化 n., simplification.

簡章 *jiaanjang*, n., a set of simplified rules or regulations.

簡札 *jiaanjar*, n., a brief letter.

簡捷 *jiaanjier*[1], adj., short, to the point, simple and easily done.

簡潔 *jiaanjier*[2], adj., terse, concise.

簡直 *jiaanjyr*, (1) adj., outspoken, straightforward; (2) adv., simply, really, very much: 簡直是個大笑話 it's simply ridiculous; 簡直不堪想像 it's really unimaginable; 簡直像個流氓 he looks (acts) very much like a rascal.

簡括 *jiaankuoh*, adj., summary, concise, condensed: 簡括地 in brief.

簡練 *jiaanliahn*, adj., (of style of writing) concise, succinct and to the point.

簡陋 *jiaanlouh*, adj., humble, unpretentious, of modest pretensions, plain and simple.

簡略 *jiaanlyueh*, adj., simple, brief, terse, concise.

簡慢 *jiaanmahn*, v. t., to slight, treat as unimportant.

簡明 *jiaanmirng*, adj., simple and clear, concise.

簡任 *jiaanrehn*, v. t., appoint to government offices one grade below the ministerial rank.

簡素 *jiaansuh*, n., bamboo tablets and silk used to write on.

簡體字 *jiarntiitzyh*, n., see -*biitzyh* ↑.

簡冊 *jiaantseh*[1], n., (1) bamboo tablets for writing on in anc. times; (2) (AC, LL) books.

簡策 *jiaantseh*[2], n., ditto.

簡字 *jiaantzyh*, n., (1) a system of phonetic writing; (2) short for 簡體字, see -*tiitzyh* ↑.

簡要 *jiaanyauh*, adj., concise, brief and to the point.

簡易 *jiaanyih*, adj., simple and easy, easy to learn (understand), elementary.

簡約 *jiaanyue*, adj., brief, terse, concise.

簿 92A.00-6

buh (**bor*).

N. (1) Notebook, records, account books, oft. 簿子: 賬簿 account books; 練習簿 exercise book; 筆記簿 notebook; 日記簿 diary. (2) (**bor*) Var. of 箔 bamboo screen.

簿記 *buhjih*, n., notes; bookkeeping.

簿書 *buhshu*, n., official documents, papers, account records.

簿冊 *buhtseh*, n., ditto.

箭 92A.00-8

jiahn.

N. (1) An arrow: 箭靶 -*baa* ↓; 弓箭 bow and arrow; 火箭 a rocket; 毒箭 poisonous arrow; 箭頭子 -*tour'tz* ↓; 箭如雨下 arrows rained down thick and fast; 射箭 archery; 暗箭傷人 make sniping attacks, slander others behind their backs; 一箭之地 a bowshot, a short distance; 一箭貫雙鵰 kill two birds with one stone, marry two sisters. (2) A kind of bamboo: 箭竹 *-jur* ↓.

箭靶(子) *jiahn-baa(tz)*, n., a target for archery.
箭袋 *jiahn-daih*, n., a quiver.
箭垜子 *jiahn-duootz*, n., a target for archery.
箭豬 *jiahnju*, n., the porcupine.
箭竹 *jiahnjur*, n., a kind of bamboo, slender and tough, used for arrows.
箭翎子 *jiahnlirngtz*, n., arrow feather.
箭樓(子) *jiahnlour('tz)*, n., a watchtower in front of the city gate.
箭袖 *jiahnshiouh*, n., specially cut sleeves for archer's dress.
箭書 *jiahn-shu*, n., message sent by arrows.
箭頭子 *jiahntour'tz*, n., arrowhead: 箭頭子似的去了 he flashed past like an arrow.
箭鏃 *jiahn-tsuh*, n., metal barbs for arrows.
箭衣 *jiahn-yi*, n., archer's dress.

箣 92A.00-9

lir.
[Var. of 籬]

箣笓 *lirpir*, n., a bamboo fence or trap for catching shrimps (also wr. 笓箣, 藜笓).

箏 92A.00-9

jeng.

N. (1) A flat stringed instrument with (anc.) five and (later) thirteen strings. (2) 風箏 a kite.

符 92A.00-9

fur.

N. (1) Tally (with two halves, made of wood, bamboo, jade, metal): 符節 *-jie* ↓. (2) Marks, punctuation marks: 符號 *-hauh* ↓. (3) Taoist magic formulas, charms, curses, written in conglommerate and peculiar characters: 符籙, 符咒 *-luh, -jouh* ↓; 畫符 to draw Taoist magic characters; 護身符 amulet; 催命符 (fig.) death-warrant; 驅邪符 charm for driving away evil influences; 桃符 peachwood charm at New Year.

V.i. Fit in well, agree as in tally: 所言不符 their words do not tally; 言不符實 statement does not tally with the facts; 字跡不符 handwriting does not match; 定符下頌 may the future agree with my best wishes.

符板 *furbaan*, n., tally, check (a wooden piece).
符號 *furhauh*, n., marks; punctuation marks: 注音符號 pronunciation marks (such as 注音字母, 羅馬字母).
符合 *furher*, v. i., match, agree in substance, (facts) "check."
符節 *fur-jie*, n., tally.
符咒 *furjouh*, n., charm casting evil spell; curse.
符籙 *furluh*, n., Taoist books on magic.
符命 *furmihng*, n., supernatural omen showing Heaven's approval of s. o. becoming king.
符璽 *furshii*, n., emperor's seal.
符驗 *furyahn*, n., evidence of correctness of divination, prophecy.
符應 *furyihng*, n., fulfillment of prophecy.

§ 92A.01 (竹/小)

策 92A.01-1

tseh.

N. (1) Interch. 冊 42.42: 簡策＝簡冊; 策命, 策書 *-mihng, -shu* ↓. (2) A whip; a walking stick. (3) A plan, strategy: 計策 ditto; 策略 *-lyueh* ↓; 政策 policy; 良策 a good plan; 上策 the best plan; 失策 a plan that miscarried, a mistake in planning; 束手無策 fold one's hands helplessly; 對策 a countermeasure, personal interview with candidate in civil examinations, esp. on current topics; 策論 *-luhn* ↓.

V.i. & t. (1) To urge as with a horsewhip: 驅策, 鞭策 to lash and urge forward; 策勵, 策動 *-lih, -duhng* ↓. (2) To promote: 以策安全 so as not to run risks, in order to promote public safety. (3) To plan: 策畫 *-huah* ↓.

策動 *tsehduhng*, v. t., to incite to action, initiate (movements).
策反 *tsehfaan*, v.i. & t., to plan a counteroffensive.
策府 *tsehfuu*, v., see 冊^府 42.42.
策畫 *tseh-huah*, v.i. & t., to plan (procedure, strategy).
策杖 *tseh-jahng*, v. i., to go with cane in hand.
策勵 *tsehlih*, v. i., to urge oneself, to work intensively; v. t., to urge (students) to go forward, etc.
策論 *tsehluhn*, n., formerly, essay on current national topics in civil examinations.
策略 *tsehlyueh*, n., strategy, military and otherwise.
策命 *tsehmihng*, v. t., see 冊^命 42.42.
策名 *tseh-mirng*, v. i., (AC) to give formal writ, appointing person to office.

策書 *tsehshu*, n., writ of appointment or dismissal of officials in Hahn Dyn.
策士 *tsehshyh*, n., a strategist.
策勳 *tseh-shyun*, v. i., (AC) record on bamboo strips minister's service to country.
策應 *tsehyihng* (-*'ying*), v. t., (mil.) to make supporting movement to cut off enemy, etc.
策源地 *tsehyuarn-dih*, n., place of origin (of a revolutionary movement).

篥 92A.01-3

lih.

N. 觱篥 *bihlih*, Tartar horn or pipe, producing a mournful sound.

築 92A.01-3

jur.

N. A structure: 小築 a villa.

V.t. To build (bridge, house, pond, dam, road, etc.): 建築 to construct (building), a construction; 修築 to repair, also build (road, etc.); 版△築 91S.82; 築室道謀 one can never build a house by consulting every passer-by.

纂 92A.01-4

tzuaan (**tzuahn*).

N. (1) A red silk ribbon: 纂繡 -*shiouh* ↓. (2) (Of a woman's hair) a bun: 纂兒 *tzuaa'l* ↓.

V.t. (1) (**tzuahn*) Compile, edit: 編纂, 纂訂, 纂集 ditto; 纂修 -*shiou* ↓. (2) (Interch. 纘) succeed to (the throne): 纂臨 -*lirn* ↓.

纂兒 *tzuaa'l*, n., a woman's hair dressed in a bun.
纂臨 *tzuaanlirn*, v. i., succeed to the throne.
纂修 *tzuaanshiou*, v. t. & n., edit(or), compile(r).
纂繡 *tzuaanshiouh*, n., fabrics and embroidery.

§92A.02 (竹/卜)

簒 92A.02-4

juahn.

[Var. of 饌 81B.80]

簑 92A.02-6

suo.

[Var. of 蓑 20A.02]

簶 92A.02-8

luh.

N. See 圖△籙 41.41, 符△籙 92A.00.

篆 92A.02-9

juahn.

N. (1) Seal script: 大篆 "great" seal script, current generally 8th to 3rd cen. B.C.; 小篆 "smaller" or simplified seal script; invented by 李斯 end of 3rd cen., precursor of 隸書 *lihshu* of Hahn Dyn.; 篆刻 stone carving in *juahn* style; 篆額 horizontal hall sign on top of gate in this script. (2) (Court.) person's name; 名篆, 雅篆 your name. (3) Seal as symbol of office: 按篆 assume office; 卸篆 resign from office.

篆章 *juahnjang*, n., seal.
篆書 *juahnshu*, n., seal script.
篆字 *juahntzyh*, n., characters in *juahn* script.
篆文 *juahnwern*, n., ditto.

§92A.10 (竹/十)

笨 92A.10-1

behn.

Adj. (1) Stupid: 笨頭笨腦 stupid, blockhead; 愚笨 stupid. (2) Clumsy, awkward: 笨手笨腳 clumsy-handed; 粗笨 heavy, awkward to handle (of tools) or big and coarse (of person); 笨鳥先飛 phr., it's good to be careful, also modest expression of one's need for caution.

笨伯 *behnbor*, n., fool, clumsy fellow, slow wit.
笨車 *behnche*, n., heavy cart.
笨蛋 *behndahn*, n., (derog.) idiot, imbecile.
笨狗 *behngoou*, n., big mastiff.
笨漢 *behnhahn*, n., stupid person, fool.
笨貨 *behnhuoh*, n., -*hahn* ↑.
笨重 *behnjuhng*, adj., heavy (tool, luggage).
笨拙 *behnjuor*, adj., slow-witted.
笨牛 *behn-niour*, n., (derog.) stupid ox (said of person).

籜 92A.10-1

tuoh.

N. Sheaths of bamboo or bamboo shoot.

筆 92A.10-2

bii.

[Var. 笔]

N. (1) Writing brush (毛筆), also pen, pencil, stylus, in combb.: 鋼筆 pen, 鉛筆 pencil, 原子筆 ball pen; 臘紙筆 stylus; 粉筆 chalk; 眉筆 eyebrow pencil; 鐵筆 steel stylus for carving sealstones; 水筆 writing brush kept moist in cap; 排筆 multiple brush for painting. (2) Quality of writing, act of writing, writing as an art: 文筆 style of writing; 筆底下＝筆力 *-lih*↓; 筆鋒 *-feng*↓; 神來之筆 inspired passage or sentence; 筆生花, 生花妙筆 brilliant writing; 筆酣墨飽 joy of the brush; 刀筆 lawyer's skillful wording, cutting remarks; 潤筆 "brush moistener," i. e., fees for writing or painting; 動筆 start to write, commit to writing. (3) A stroke in callig.: 筆畫 brush strokes; 敗筆 a bad stroke.

V.t. Write: 筆之於書 write it down; see Adv. & adj.↓.

Adv. & adj. Done by writing, of writing: 筆談 talks on paper (in free, conversational style); 筆錄, 筆記 v.t., put down in writing, n., notes; see 筆記 *-jih*↓; 筆削 (court.) (please) correct (my) writing mistakes; 筆答 reply by writing in examination papers; 筆戰 controversy in current articles; 筆耕 make a living by writing.

筆牀 *biichuarng*, n., stack for holding brushes.
筆單 *biidan*, n., in 掛筆單 give author's, artist's, rates for remuneration (＝潤筆).
筆調 *biidiauh*, n., style of writing.
筆法 *birfaa*, n., (1) way, technique of forming a stroke; (2) technique of writing.
筆鋒 *biifeng*, n., power, sharpness of style; angle formations in calligraphy.
筆管(兒) *birguaan(-guaa'l)*, n., handle of brush.
筆會 *biihueih*, n., P.E.N., International Association of Poets, Playwrights, Editors, Essayists and Novelists.
筆札 *biijar*, n., stationery; things connected with writing; handwritten letter.
筆者 *birjee*, n., the present writer.
筆跡 *biiji*, n., handwriting (of persons).
筆架(兒) *biijiah('l)*, n., stack for holding brushes.
筆尖兒 *biijian(-jia'l)*, n., tip of brush.
筆記 *biijih*, n., notes of lectures, reading; "Notes," oft. name of a book.
筆直 *biijyr*, adj., straight (of street, etc.).
筆據 *biijyuh*, n., notes in writing (I. O. U., etc.) useful as legal proof.
筆力 *biilih*, n., power of style, or strokes.
筆路 *biiluh*, n., style, technique of calligraphy.
筆帽(兒) *biimauh('l)*, n., cap for brush.
筆名 *bii-mirng*, n., pen name.
筆墨 *biimoh*, n., stationery articles; 筆墨生涯 writing as a profession; 筆墨官司 controversy in writing.
筆下 *bii-shiah*, n., act or style of writing: 筆下留情 phr., spare person in critical attacks; 筆下超生 phr., asking judge to write a lenient sentence.
筆洗(子) *birshii(tz)*, n., small tray for washing brushes.
筆算 *biisuahn*, n., arithmetic (doing it on paper), as opposed to 珠算 (doing it by abacus).
筆套 *biitauh*, n., cap for brush.
筆筒 *birtuung*, n., container for brushes.
筆資 *biitzy*, n., fees for writing.
筆誤 *biiwuh*, n., mistake in writing, corresponding to "typographical error."
筆意 *biiyih*, n., charm of stroke; flow of thought in writing.
筆友 *bir-yoou*, n., friend by correspondence; pen pal.

竿 92A.10-3

gan.

N. Bamboo stem: 竹竿 a bamboo pole; 竿子 a rod or pole; 竿兒 ditto; 漁竿 a fishing rod; 撐竿 a supporting pole; 撐竿跳 (athletics) pole vault; 滑竿 an open chair carried on poles as a means of conveyance, pop. in Szechuan; 百尺竿頭, 更進一步 (court.) one should try to do still better after having achieved a fair degree of success.

簟 92A.10-3

diahn.

N. Bamboo mat.

簞 92A.10-4

dan.

N. Rice basket: 簞食 (*-syh*) a basket of rice: 簞食壺漿 allu. local population's welcome of soldiers with rice and soup; 一簞食, 一瓢飲 a basket of rice, a gourd dipper of drink—symbol of content in frugal living.

篳 92A.10-4

bih.

[Interch. 蓽]

箄 92A.10-9

pair.

N. A big raft, formed of banded bamboos (also wr. 簰, see↓).

A

簰 92A.10-9

pair.

[Var. 簰, 箄, 𥴦]

N. (1) Bamboo raft. (2) 藤簰 rattan shield for defence.

§ 92A.11 (竹/土)

笙 92A.11-1

sheng.

N. A gourd-shaped hand musical instrument with a row of reed pipes: 笙歌 the sound of music and song; 笙簧 reeds of the above.

籮 92A.11-4

luor.

N. (1) A kind of bamboo basket. (2) A sieve.

籊 92A.11-5

tih.

Adj. (AC) long and slender (fishing rod).

籬 92A.11-6

lir.

[Abbr. 篱]

N. A hedge or fence of bamboo or twigs: 籬笆 -*'ba* ↓; 竹籬 a bamboo fence.

B

籬笆 *lir'ba*, n., a hedge (also 籬笆障兒, 籬笆圈兒).

籬落 *lirluoh*, n., ditto.

筌 92A.11-8

chyuarn.

N. A bamboo trap for fish: 得魚忘筌 (AC) after catching fish, the trap can be forgotten—from 莊子's idea, after direct knowledge of Tao, the aids to devotion can be dispensed with.

箠 92A.11-9

chueir.

N. (1) A horsewhip. (2) A rod for caning: 箠楚 flogging.

篁 92A.11-9

huarng.

N. A bamboo grove.

§ 92A.20 (竹/廾)

筭 92A.20-3

suahn.

[U.f. 算↓]

筓 92A.20-3

ji.

N. A woman's large-sized pin for holding hair: 及筓之年 (AC) a girl's age of fifteen, the year in which a girl began to wear a pin for holding hair; 及筓 (AC) (of women) come of age.

C

筓冠 *ji-guahn*, n., (AC) a woman's coming of age at fifteen.

筓年 *ji-niarn*, n., (AC) the year in which a woman came of age.

算 92A.20-4

suahn.

[Var. 筭, 祘]

N. (1) Number: 活人無算 saved innumerable people's lives. (2) Accounting: 筆算 ordinary arithmetic; 珠算 arithmetic by abacus; 算術, 算數 -*shuh*[1], -*shuh*[2] ↓; 預算 budget; 結算 balance of accounts; 概算 rough estimate; 決算 final estimate.

V.t. (1) To count (sticks, etc.). (2) To plan, calculate, reckon: 籌算 ditto; 打算 plan, intend to (do s.t.); 計算 reckon, compute; 計算機 calculating machine; 盤算 ruminate in mind; 不如人算 not as one thought it would be; 暗算 plan to kill or injure (s.o.). (3) To grant in argument: 就算是他錯了 granted that he is wrong. (4) To count as, to call (it a failure, etc.): 算他福氣 call it his luck; 他算什麼東西 what is he anyway? (he does not count); 這算什麼 this is nothing (to worry, talk about); 這算誰的賬 who will pay for this? (on whose account will it be?); 他的話說了不算 his words do not count; 算數 -*shuh*[2] ↓; 算了 have done with it, call it quits or closed; 算不得, 算不了 -*'bu'de*, -*'buliaau* ↓.

Adv. Fairly (=還 *hair*): 算不錯 fairly good; 還算好 fairly good, could be worse.

算不得 *suahn'bu'de*, v.i., cannot be considered or reckoned as (unusual, rare, etc.).

算不了 *suahn'buliaau*, v.i., cannot be reckoned as, see *-bu'de* ↑: 算不了一回事, 不必介意 this is nothing, don't worry.
算器 *suahn-chih*, n., (AC) holder for chips in anc. shooting game.
算起來 *suahn-chii'lai*, phr., all considered: 算起來差不多 it's about the same, all considered.
算籌 *suahnchour*, n., chips or sticks used for counting.
算得 *suahn-der* (*-'de*), v.i., I reckon; it may be said (to be rare, etc.).
算法 *suahnfaa*, n., arithmetic.
算卦 *suahn-guah*, v.i., to practise divination by 八△卦 *baguah* 80.80; 算卦的 *--'de*, n., a practitioner of *baguah*.
算帳(賬) *suahnjahng*, v.i., (1) reckon accounts; ask for bill to pay; (2) even the score (for revenge): 回頭同你算帳 you'll pay for this or I will get even with you.
算計 *suahn'ji*, v.t., (1) to calculate, consider; (2) to plot ruin or injury of (s.o.): 受人算計 was ruined by s.o.; 算計兒 *--'l*, n., a plan.
算來 *suahn-lair*, phr., be considered, reckoned, after consideration: 算來不壞 is considered not bad; 算來第一 is reckoned first.
算了 *suahn'le*, phr., let it be, do not bother any more.
算命 *suahn-mihng*, v.i., to tell fortune: 算命的 *--'de*, n., a fortuneteller.
算盤 *suahnparn* (*-'pan*), n., the abacus: 打算盤 to calculate costs or benefits; 打如意算盤 indulge in wishful thinking; 算盤疙瘩 a string of rope knots; 算盤腦袋 a miser, a calculating person; 算盤手兒 a parsimonious person; 算盤子兒 a bead in abacus.
算上 *suahn'shang*, v.i., to include in list, bill: 今天請客也算上他 include him in today's dinner.
算術 *suahnshuh*[1], n., arithmetic.
算數(兒) *suahnshuh*[2]*('l)*, v.i., to count; (words) to be taken seriously: 你說的話算數兒不算 do you mean what you say?
算式 *suahnshyh*, n., an equation.
算學 *suahnshyuer*, n., mathematics, cf. 數△學 22S.82.
算題 *suahn-tir*, n., (math.) a problem.
算子 *suahn'tz*, n., (MC) fortuneteller.

箅 92A.20-4

bih.

N. Split-bamboo grill at bottom of double boiler.

§ 92A.21 (竹/乚)

箍 92A.21-1

gu.

N. A bamboo or metal hoop: 金箍, 銅箍 a gold, bronze hoop; 箍兒 a fillet, a band.

V.t. To bind (a cask, etc.) with hoops.

笸 92A.21-5

poo.

[Var. 箥]

笸籮 *pooluor*, n., wicker, wicker basket.

筐 92A.21-5

kuang.

N. (*-tz*, *'l*) A bamboo basket.

篋 92A.21-5

chieh.

N. A hamper, rattan box or suitcase: 行篋 such suitcase for luggage; 藤篋 rattan suitcase; 滿篋著作 a trunkful of manuscripts; 篋衍 (AC) bamboo box.

篋篋 *chiehchieh*, adj., (AC) slender and long.

篚 92A.21-5

feei.

N. A square bamboo vessel.

§ 92A.22 (竹/丨)

第 92A.22-2

tzyy.

N. A bed mat: 牀笫之私, 之言 intimate acts done, words said, in bed.

簫 92A.22-2

shiau.

N. A flute; anc. panpipes, a series of pipes banded together: 簫鼓 flutes and drums; festive music.

筇 92A.22-3

chyurng.

N. A kind of bamboo: 筇杖 bamboo cane (also wr. 邛), named after district.

第 92A.22-5

dih.

[Abbr. wr. form 第]

N. (1) House: 第宅, 宅第; 私第 private residence, home; 闔第光臨 the whole family is invited; see 門[A]第 52B.00. (2) Formerly, pass grade: 落第, 不第 fail in official examinations, i.e., not listed; 及第 pass, on the list. (3) Sequence: 次第 sequence; 等第 grade. (4) Number: 第一,二,三 Nos. 1, 2, 3; 第一,二,三人稱 (gram.) first, second, third person; 第一流人物 first-class person; 第一夫人 First Lady; 第三者 third party (damage, etc.); 第三國際 Third International; 第六感 sixth sense; 第二代 the next, lower, generation; 第五縱隊 fifth column(ist).

Adv. (LL) Only: 第求足用 only hope to have enough to live on; 第恐 I only fear.

箒 92A.22-5

joou.

N. A broom (also wr. 帚).

簾 92A.22-6

liarn.

N. (*-tz, 'l*) Screen of bamboo or cloth, curtain: 門簾, 窗簾 door, window curtain; 竹簾 bamboo screen; 布簾 cloth screen.

節 92A.22-9

jier.

[Pop. 莭; usu. wr. 節]

N. (1) (Bot.) knots, joints: 枝節 branches and joints: 枝節橫生 bristling with complications and difficulties; 竹節 bamboo joints; 節外(上)生枝 one complication leading to another; 節子 gnarls, nodules. (2) (Physiol.) joints: 關節 bodily joints, (fig.) underhanded deals: 暗通關節 make secret deals with s.o.; 節足動物 arthropoda; 脱節 (of bones) dislocated, -ion, (fig.) out of touch, out of joint; 骨節 joint between bones. (3) A segment, section, period of lesson in school: 章節 chapter and section of a book, chapter and verse of the Bible; 一節功課 one session of classroom work; 節節 *-jier*↓; 環節 links in a chain. (4) Moral integrity: 名節 honor and reputation; 志節 high aspirations; 節操 *-tsau*↓; 氣節 uprightness, loyalty, incorruptibility; 守節 (of married woman) refuse to remarry after husband's death, (of betrothed girl) refuse to marry another man after her fiance's death; 貞節 chastity (of girls, women); 節概 *-gaih*, 節義 *-yih*↓; 節婦, 節女 a chaste woman; 節烈 (of woman) dedicated to chastity even unto death; 失節 (of woman) compromise one's honor by adultery or remarrying after husband's death; 禮節 etiquet, formality, ceremony, rites; 小節 trifles, trivialities: 不拘小節 unconventional, unconstrained by formalities; 大節 a matter of principles. (5) Sequence of events, proceedings: 情節 circumstances, details of a case, event, incident: 情節重大 (of criminal offenses) of a serious nature; 節目 *-muh*, 節文 *-wern*↓; 細節 details of a thing, minutiae. (6) A period of time in a year, a festival: 時節 a season, time, juncture; 佳節 festival; 節令 *-lihng*, 節氣 *-chih*, 節序 *-shyuh*, 節禮 *-lii*, 節敬 *-jihng*↓; 中秋節 the Mid-Autumn Festival; 聖誕節 Christmas; 過節 observe a festival, generally by a dinner; 季節(性) a season, seasonal. (7) A tally or token, credentials: 符節 a token by which authority is conferred: 若合符節 (of two things) tally perfectly; 節鉞 *-yueh*↓; 使節 a diplomatic mission, a diplomat accredited to another country. (8) Rhythm: 節拍 *-pai*, 節奏 *-tzouh*↓; 擊節 (稱賞) to beat time, applaud enthusiastically (books, performance).

V.i. & t. (1) Save, economize: 節流 *-liour*, 節儉 *-jiaan*, 節省 *-sheeng*, 節約 *-yue*, 節錄 *-luh*, 節略 *-lyueh*, 節食 *-shyr*, 節用 *-yuhng*↓. (2) Regulate, restrict, restrain: 節勞 *-laur*, 節制 *-jyh*, 節哀 *-ai*, 節慾 *-yuh*[2], 節育 *-yuh*[1]↓.

節哀 *jier-ai*, v. i., restrain one's grief during bereavement.

節錢 *jier-chiarn*, n., tips to servants, or gifts to children, on festivals.

節氣 *jierchih*, n., (1) the 24 periods into which a year is divided; (2) seasonal changes, see Appendix B.

節概 *jiergaih*, n., nobility of character.

節儉 *jierjiaan*, adj. & n., frugal, -ity, thrifty, -iness.

節節 *jierjier*, (1) n., (AC) the cry of the phoenix; (2) adj. & adv., gradual(ly), step by step: 節節進攻 (of armies) push on relentlessly step by step; 節節勝利 scoring one victory after another; 節節高 rising higher and higher.

節敬 *jier-jihng*, n., money or other gifts presented to teacher on a festival.

節制 *jierjyh*, (1) adj., temperate, moderate, not going to excess; (2) v. t., keep (expenses, students) within bounds, put under control, exercise command over.

節勞 *jier-laur*, v. i., conserve energy, avoid overexertion.

節令 *jierlihng*, n., (1) the 24 periods into which a year is

divided; (2) seasonal changes; (3) a festive day, see Appendix B.

節禮 *jier-lii*, n., presents given on festivals to relatives or friends.

節流 *jier-liour*, v. i., reduce expenses: 開源節流 tap new sources of revenue and cut down expenditures.

節錄 *jierluh*, (1) v. t., summarize, make a digest of; (2) n., a summary, an abstract, a digest.

節略 *jierlyueh*, n., (1) an abstract; (2) a diplomatic note, an *aide-mémoire*.

節目 *jiermuh*, n., (1) a program of items of a performance or meeting; (2) what one intends to do: 你今天有甚麼節目嗎 do you have any plans (program) for today? (3) subheadings of a paragraph or section.

節拍 *jierpai*, n., musical rhythm, see *-tzouh* ↓.

節省 *jiersheeng*, (1) v. t., economize, save; (2) adj., thrifty, frugal, economical.

節下 *jiershiah*, n., (1) polite form of address to general (lit., "under your command"); (2) (*-'shia*) one of the major festivals of the year, such as the Dragon Boat Festival or the Mid-Autumn Festival.

節食 *jier-shyr*, v. i., go or be put on diet.

節序 *jiershyuh*, n., see *-chih* ↑.

節操 *jiertsau*, n., of honor, integrity of principle.

節奏 *jiertzouh*, n., musical rhythm, see *-pai* ↑.

節文 *jierwern*, n., ceremonial rites or forms.

節義 *jieryih*, n., chastity, purity, honor, fidelity.

節約 *jieryue*, v. i. & n., (practice) austerity.

節鉞 *jieryueh*, n., a battle-axe; formerly, symbol of authority military of commander.

節育 *jier-yuh*[1], v. i., practise birth control or planned parenthood.

節慾 *jier-yuh*[2], v. i., to curb one's passions or desires; practise continence.

節用 *jier-yuhng*, v. i., reduce expenses.

篩 92A.22-9

shai.

N. A sieve.

V.t. (1) To sift (rice, flour, etc.). (2) To strike gong: 篩鑼. (3) To warm a pot of wine over slow fire: 篩酒.

§92A.30 (竹/一)

篲 92A.30-1

hueih.

N. (AC) broomstick.

簴 92A.30-2

jyuh.

N. (AC) the poles of a rack on which musical stones were suspended.

竺 92A.30-3

jur.

N. (1) 天竺 anc. translit. of "Hindu"—India (also 身毒 Sindu). (2) A surname.

筮 92A.30-3

shyh.

N. Divination; divination stick.

笪 92A.30-4

dar.

N. (1) (AC & dial.) hemp rope for pulling boat; rough bamboo mat. (2) A surname.

簋 92A.30-5

gueei.

N. (AC) an anc. round bowl.

籃 92A.30-5

larn.

N. (*-tz*, *'l*) A bamboo or rattan basket: 菜籃 basket for groceries; 提籃 a hand basket; 網籃 a basket with netting to hold things together; 竹籃 a bamboo basket.

籃球 *larnchiour*, n., basketball.

籃輿 *larnyur*, n., a bamboo sedan chair.

笠 92A.30-6

lih.

N. A farmer's bamboo hat: 竹笠 a bamboo hat; 斗笠 ditto.

箜 92A.30-6

kung.

箜篌 *kunghour*, n., an anc. string instrument plucked with a wooden peg.

§ 92A.32 (竹/フ)

 92A.32-4

luor.

[Abbr. of 籮 92A.11]

 92A.32-9

yir.

N. A small connecting room between top apartments.

§ 92A.40 (竹/ロ)

箬 92A.40-2

ruoh.

N. A kind of bamboo; its cuticle ors heath: 箬竹 *-jur* ↓; 箬笠, 箬帽 a broad-rimmed hat made of bamboo splints and leaves; 箬帽芒鞋 the characteristic dress of a peasant, the ways of a hermit.

箬 竹 *ruohjur*, n., a kind of broad-leaved bamboo.

筥 92A.40-4

jyuu.

N. (AC) a bamboo basket for rice.

笤 92A.40-5

tiaur.

笤 帚 *tiaur'jou*, n., broom; 笤帚星 (also 掃帚星) comet.

管 92A.40-6

guaan.

N. (1) A wood-wind musical instrument: 管樂 *-yueh*[1] ↓; 管絃樂 *-shiarnyueh*, 管籥 *-yueh*[2] ↓. (2) A cylindrical tube: 自來水管, 油管, 橡皮管, 鋼管, 竹管, 汽管 water, oil, rubber, steel, bamboo, steam pipe; 喇叭管, 輸卵管 the oviduct; 吸管 a siphon; 滴管 a dropper; 食管 the esophagus; 氣管 the trachea, windpipe; 血管 blood vessels. (3) A tube-shaped thing: 筆管 a pen (holder); 握管揮毫 take up a pen to write. (4) A key: 管鑰 *-yueh*[3] ↓. (5) A surname.

V.t. (1) Be in charge of, supervise, take care of: 主管 be responsible for; 管理 *-lii*, 管事 *-shyh*, 管家 *-jia*, 管帶 *-daih*[2] ↓, 管賬的 *-jahng'de* ↓; 管轄 *-shiar* ↓; 管下 a subordinate; 保管 guarantee, also have in safekeeping; 託管 entrust to the care of; 託管地 entrusted territory; 代管 administer on behalf of; 看管 take care (of property), keep in custody; 管車的 person looking after cars; 管門的 a doorkeeper; 管飯 be responsible for the meals; 不管飯 do not provide the board. (2) Govern, manage: 管束 *-shuh*, 管教 *-jiauh* ↓; 管不了 beyond one's power to manage or care; 管不住 unmanageable or uncontrollable (child, etc.). (3) To interfere, to mind: 管閒事 poke one's nose into s. o. else's business; 你少管, 你不要多管, 你管你的罷 mind your own business! 管他呢 don't mind him! 管我什麼事 what does it matter to me? 不管他如何想法 no matter what he thinks; 只管說 just keep on talking; 儘管做 do without hesitation. (4) To guarantee, assure: 包管 it is guaranteed; 管保 *-baau* ↓; 管教你遂心所欲 you are assured of perfect satisfaction; 管退管換 (of goods) replacement of defective items guaranteed; 管飽 adequate food (provided in a mess) guaranteed.

Adj. Narrow, small, tiny: 管窺蠡測 take a narrow view of things, (lit., "to look at the sky through a peephole and measure the sea with a conchshell"); 管見 *-jiahn* ↓.

Prep. Used like 把 10A.70: 管他叫甚麼 what is he called?

管 保 *guarnbaau*, v. i., to guarantee.

管 待 *guaandaih*[1], v. t., entertain, play host to.

管 帶 *guaandaih*[2], n., formerly, a battalion commander.

管 賬 的 *guaanjahng'de*, n., a bookkeeper, a person in charge of accounts.

管 家 *guaanjia*, (1) v. i., have charge of domestic affairs; (2) (*-'jia*) n., also 管家的 *--'de*, one in charge of domestic affairs, formerly, a butler: 管家婆 a housewife, a woman who likes to interfere.

管 見 *guaanjiahn*, n., (court.) my humble view.

管 教 *guanjiauh*, v. t., (1) will certainly make or cause to: 管教他向你賠罪 will see that he apologizes to you; (2) (*-'jiau*) to take care of and supervise (children).

管 理 *guarnlii*, v. t., (1) manage; (2) (of schools) to counsel and discipline (students).

管 轄 *guaanshiar*, v. t., exercise control over: 管轄權 jurisdiction.

管 絃 *guaanshiarn*, n., musical instruments, both strings and wind; 管絃樂 *--yueh*, such music; 管絃樂法 orchestration.

管 束 *guaanshuh*, v. t., to control, supervise (children, students).

管 事 *guaanshyh*, (1) v. t., be in charge of; (2) (also *-'de*) n., a person in charge.

管 樂 *guaanyueh*[1], n., (mus.) the wood wind; 管樂器 orchestral wind instruments.

管 籥 *guaanyueh*[2], n., (mus.) the wind instruments (as flute panpipe) (also wr. 管鑰 *-yueh*[3] ↓).

管 鑰 *guaanyueh*[3], n., a key for a lock.

答 92A.40-8

dar (*da*).

[Interch. 荅, 畣]

N. & t. & v.i. (1) Reply: 問答 question and answer; 回答 reply; 你怎麼回答(他) how did you reply (to him)? 所答非所問 answer evades the question; 對答如流 quick in answer; 報答 to repay person for kindness or favor; 解答 explanation. (2) To consent: 答應 *-yihng* ↓.

答 案 *dar-ahn*, n., answer to question, solution of mathematical problem.

答 拜 *dar-baih*, v. i. & n., (pay) return call.

答 辯 *darbiahn*, v. i., reply in argument.

答 碴 兒 *darchar'l*, v. i., make answer to question; strike up conversation.

答 對 *dardueih*, v. i., make correct answer.

答 復 (覆) *darfuh*, v. i. & n., reply (to letter).

答 兒 *dar'l*, n., (MC) 這答兒, 那答兒 here, there.

答 禮 *dar-lii*[1], n., gift in return.

答 理 *darlii*[2], v. i., give proper answer; 不答理 ignore question.

答 聘 *dar-pihn*, v. i. & n., formal acknowledgement of betrothal gift; reply of acceptance to appointment.

答 謝 *darshieh*, v. i. & n., courtesy call or letter to thank s. o.

答 數 *darshuh*, n., correct number in math. question.

答 應 *daryihng*, v. i. & t., consent, promise: 他不答應 he refuses (request), will not consent; 答應要求 accept request or demand.

答 語 *daryuu*, n., reply, words of a reply.

笳 92A.40-9

jia.

N. An anc. reed musical instrument introduced from northwestern tribes.

簷 92A.40-9

yarn.

N. (1) The eaves: 簷下 under the eaves. (2) Projecting rim of hat, umbrella (帽簷, 傘簷).

簷 馬 *yarnmaa*, n., metal pieces under the eaves, clinking with the wind.

簷 牙 *yarnyar*, n., projecting fringe of roofs.

笞 92A.40-9

chy.

N. & v.t. A cane or bamboo splint for flogging; to cane, flog (pupil, prisoner); 笞刑 flogging as punishment; 笞背, 笞臀 flog the back, bottom.

---

§ 92A.41 (竹/図)

箝 92A.41-1

chiarn.

[Var. of 鉗]

N. (*-tz*) Pliers, pincers: 火箝 firetongs; 鬈箝 tweezers; 止血箝 (surgical) forceps.

V.t. To compress or hold closed by force: see compp. ↓.

箝 制 *chiarnjyh*, v. t., to suppress (movement, action).

箝 口 *chiarn-koou*, v. i., to shut up, stop talking, censor speech or writing: 箝口無言 to shut up; 箝口結舌 tongue-tied.

籒 92A.41-1

jouh.

[Commonly wr. 籀]

N. Style of script, approx. from 9th cen. B.C., called "Big Juahn" (大篆) before it was simplified as "small Juahn" (小 篆) at end of 3rd cen.: 籒文 *-wern*, 籒書 *-shu*, such script.

V.i. To draw conclusions: 內籒 (logic) by induction; 外籒 by deduction.

箱 92A.41-1

shiang.

N. (1) (*-tz*, *'l*) A trunk, box, case: 皮箱 leather case: 衣箱 trunk for clothing; 柳條箱 willow coffer; 保險箱 safety box, safe. (2) Enclosed space seating passengers in old-style carts: 車箱. (3) Incorrect var. of 廂 61.41.

箱 底 (兒) *shiangdii*(*-diee'l*), n., see 班[A]底 31A.11.

箱 運 *shiangyuhn*, n, containerized shipping.

亅	小	⺊	十	土	ナ	廾	㇄ト	丨	一	丅	フ	口	図	冈	㇆	厂	尸	亠	广	宀	丶	乚	弋	心	八	人	乂	㇀	乛	刂	⺈	く
00	01	02	10	11	12	20	21	22	30	31	32	40	41	42	50	51	52	60	61	62	63	70	71	72	80	81	82	83	90	91	92	93

籍 92A.41-1

jir.

N. (1) Written works: 書籍 books and publications; 圖籍 maps and books; 古籍 ancient works; 史籍 historical records; 典籍 books, records, esp. old. (2) Census records, nativity: 戶籍 the census; 籍貫 *-guahn*↓; 本籍, 原籍 native district; 祖籍 ancestral home; 國籍 nationality; 學籍 school in which a student is registered; 兵籍 military service obligations, such records. (3) A surname.

籍貫 *jirguahn*, n., one's native province or district.
籍籍 *jirjir*, adj., (1) disorderly, untidy, messy; (2) much spoken of, famous.
籍沒 *jirmoh*, v. t., confiscate.
籍甚 *jir-shehn*, adj., well-known: 名聲籍甚 renowned, widely known.

箸 92A.41-1

juh.

N. (*-tz*) Chopsticks (vern. 筷子 *kuaihtz*).

笛 92A.41-2

dir.

N. (*-tz, 'l*) (1) Flute; 吹笛子 play the flute. (2) Whistle: 口笛 a whistle; 汽笛 steam whistle; 羌笛 shepherd's flute; 簫笛 pipes; 軍笛 fife; 短笛 piccolo; 長笛 flute; 豎笛 clarinet.

簹 92A.41-2

dang.

N. See 篔^{A}簹 92A.80.

箇 92A.41-4

geh.

[個 preferable in modn. usage; abbr. 个]

N. adjunct. A piece: 一箇饅頭 one steamed bread; 十箇銅板 ten coppers.

N. A single unit, person or thing: 箇箇(兒) *-geh ('l)*↓; 箇的, 箇兒 everyone; 這箇, 那箇 (*'ge*) this, that one; 這些箇 (*'ge*) these ones; 箇位, 箇人, 箇體 *-weih, -rern, -tii*↓.

Adj. (1) One, single: 箇把 *-'baa*↓; 箇半月 one and a half months; 箇數來月 about one month; 箇月期程 ditto. (2) Belonging to or characteristic of an individual: 箇性 *-shihng*↓. (3) Indefinite article "a," this or that: 箇小兒 this or that child; 箇郎 this or that young man; 拿箇主意 make a decision; 打箇圓場 help settle a quarrel; 討箇吉利 ask for (s. t.) as a token of good omen; 有箇好處 get some benefit or advantage; 是箇奴才 is a slave, indeed! 箇中 *-jung*, 箇樣 *-yahng*, 箇般 *-ban*↓.

Adv. part. 眞箇是 truly is or are; 真箇像是 truly seem(s) to be; 說箇不停 keep on talking without cease.

箇案 *geh-ahn*, (1) n., (social work) individual cases as subject of study: 箇案研究 case study; (2) adj. & adv., see *-bier*↓.
箇把 *geh'baa*, adj., one or two, not many.
箇般 *gehban*, n., this way or manner (=這般).
箇別 *gehbier*, adv., individually, one by one: 箇別考試 individual tests.
箇箇(兒) *gehgeh('l)*, n., (1) every one; (2) each one.
箇中 *gehjung*, adj., inside: 箇中事 inside happenings; 箇中人 an insider, a person in the know; 箇中秘密 inside story.
箇兒 *geh'l*, n., (1) a person's stature: 大箇兒 a big fellow; 矮箇兒 a short fellow; (2) the size of a thing; (3) each one separately: 這梨論斤賣, 不論箇兒 the pears are sold by the catty and not by piece; (4) a match or peer: 他的力氣很大, 你可不是箇兒 he is so big and strong, and you are no match for him.
箇人 *gehrern*, n., (1) an individual: 箇人主義 individualism; 箇人本位 an individual as the basic unit of society and as the arbiter of values; (2) a speaker referring to himself: 箇人看來 as I see it; (3) another person: 豈可爲錢而誆箇人 how could you cheat another person for the sake of money?
箇性 *gehshihng*, n., individuality, individual traits.
箇體 *gehtii*, n., an entity.
箇頭兒 *gehtour'l*, n., the size of a thing: 箇頭兒不小 its size is by no means small.
箇子 *gehtz*, n., a person's stature: 高箇子, 小箇子 a tall, a little fellow.
箇位 *geh-weih*, n., a unit, digit.
箇樣 *gehyahng*, n., this or that way, fashion or style.

箘 92A.41-4

jyuhn.

N. Bamboo shoots (cf. 笋 92A.91).

箔 92A.41-6

bor.

N. (1) Foil: 金箔, 錫箔 gold leaf, tin foil. (2) Gold or silver-colored paper foil as offering for the dead (金箔, 銀箔). (3) Frame for silkworms. (4) Reed screen: 簾箔 (coll. *liarnbaur*).

簪 92A.41-9

tzan (*tzen*).

N. A hair clasp, used by men and women: 簪環首飾 hairpins and earrings; 簪子, 簪兒 a clasp for the hair; 銀簪, 玉簪 silver, jade clasp; 髮簪 hair clasp.

V.t. To stick in the hair, wear: 簪花 *-hua* ↓.

簪筆 *tzan-bii*, v. i., (AC) stick a pen in the hair for ready use.
簪紱 *tzan-fur*, n., (AC) hair clasp and sash, as a badge of nobility.
簪花 *tzan-hua*, v. i., wear flowers in the hair.
簪笏 *tzan-huh*, n., (AC) hair clasp and hand tablet, as a badge of officialdom.
簪裾 *tzan-jyu*, n., (AC) hair claps and flowing robe, as a badge of nobility.
簪纓 *tzan-ying*, n., anc. official headgear ("hair clasp and tassels").

§ 92A.42 (竹/冈)

箾 92A.42-1

shau.

N. (1) (AC) a rice basket; a basket for chopsticks. (2) (Coll.) 水箾 a water pail.

筩 92A.42-3

turng (*tuung*).
[Cogn. 桶]

N. (1) Var. of 筒. (2) Bamboo pipe. (3) A fishhook.

筒 92A.42-4

turng (coll. also *tuung*).
[Cogn. 桶, 筩 *tuung*]

N. A tube, tube-shaped container: 竹筒 a section of bamboo which can be used as container; 筆筒 container for writing brushes; 郵筒 mailbox; 煙筒 chimney, funnel.

篙 92A.42-6

gau.

N. A pole for punting boats.

篙工 *gaugung*, n., one who punts a boat with a pole. ⌈boatman.
篙師 *gaushy*, n., an experienced
篙子 *gautz*, n., a boat pole.

篱 92A.42-6

lir.
[Abbr. of 籬 92A.11]

篇 92A.42-6

pian.
[Wr. abbr. 萹]

N. adjunct. Used before a piece of writing or speech: 這篇演講 this speech; 一篇序文, 遊記 a (piece of) preface, article on a journey; 篇篇都好 every piece, chapter, is good; 頭三篇 the first three chapters or pieces.

N. An article, essay, chapter in a book: 三百篇 the *Book of Poetry*; 篇目 chapter heading; 篇次 order of chapters.

篇幅 *pianfur*, n., width or length of paper, cloth; canvass: 篇幅甚大 (lit. & fig.) on a wide canvass.
篇章 *pianjang*, n., literary piece; writings in gen.
篇籍 *pianjir*, n., (esp. anc.) books.
篇什 *pianshyr*, n., orig. each ten poems in the *Book of Poetry* taken as a unit (called "decade"), now generally used of poetry.

籥 92A.42-8

yueh.
[Interch. 龠 81.42]

§ 92A.50 (竹/ㄱ)

筠 92A.50-1

yurn.

N. The smooth hard skin of bamboo.

筋 92A.50-4

jin.

N. (1) Muscles, muscular strength; tendons: 筋肉 *-rouh*, 筋絡 *-luoh* ↓; 銅筋鐵骨 tough and strong as iron and steel; 抽筋 (have) convulsions, cramps; 筋疲力盡 (竭) utterly exhausted, dead tired. (2) Veins as seen from outside. (3) Fibers of plants.

筋斗 *jindoou*, n., a somersault (also 觔斗, 金斗, 跟頭): 翻筋斗 to turn a somersault; 栽筋斗 ditto, to trip, stumble, (fig.)

亅	小	⺊	十	土	ナ	廾	凵	丨	一	丁	フ	口	図	冈	ㄱ	厂	尸	亠	广	宀	丶	乚	弋	心	八	人	乂	⌒	一	ノ	𠂉	く
00	01	02	10	11	12	20	21	22	30	31	32	40	41	42	50	51	52	60	61	62	63	70	71	72	80	81	82	83	90	91	92	93

fail miserably in business, politics or any other pursuit ("fall from on high").

筋豆 *jindouh*, adj., (of food) tough and hard to chew.

筋疙瘩 *jinge'da*, n., scrofula.

筋骨 *jinguu*, n., a person's physique ("bones and sinews"): 他很有筋骨 he's tough, hardy; 筋骨疼 rheumatic pains.

筋節 *jinjier*, n., (1) muscles and joints; (2) (of compositions) proper arrangement of ideas and phrasing: 有筋節 forceful (writing): 筋節兒 *-'jie'l*, adv., just right, properly, fittingly: 這鍋炖肉是筋節兒了 this pot of stewed meat is well done; 這話正說到筋節兒上 you've hit the nail right on the head.

筋力 *jinlih*, n., manual work, physical labor.

筋絡 *jinluoh*, n., tendons and veins.

筋肉 *jinrouh*, n., muscles.

筋書 *jinshu*, n., a style of calligraphy characterized by sinuous strokes.

筋頭(巄腦) *jintour*, n., part of meat too tough to eat.

筋炎 *jinyarn*, n., neuritis, muscle tenderness.

筯 92A.50-4

juh.

[Dist. 筋↑]

N. (*-tz*) Chopsticks (var. 箸).

笥 92A.50-5

syh.

N. A wicker box (for books, sundries).

篤 92A.50-5

duu.

Adj. & adv. (1) Deep, -ly, sincere, -ly: 誠篤 sincere; 感情彌篤 have an ever deeper affection for each other; 篤愛 love deeply. (2) Deepened: 病篤 sickness becomes critical; 危篤 critical (condition).

篤厚 *duuhouh*, adj., sincere, solid (personality).

篤信 *duushihn*, v.i., believe sincerely.

篤行 *duushihng*, n., sincere conduct.

篤實 *duushyr*, adj., sincere (character), solid (scholarship).

篤學 *dushyuer*, adj., well-read, erudite.

竻 92A.50-9

leh.

N. (1) Bamboo roots. (2) 竻竹 a kind of tough and thorny bamboo.

笏 92A.50-9

huh.

N. A tablet of ivory, etc., held in two hands during audience with emperor, sometimes containing a memo of words to be said.

笱 92A.50-9

goou.

N. A basket trap for fish at the opening of a weir.

筍 92A.50-9

suun.

N. (1) Bamboo shoot. (2) A wooden joint (also wr. 榫): 接筍 joint in woodwork.

筍鞭 *suunbian*, n., a stick of bamboo root.

筍乾 *suungan*, n., dried bamboo shoot.

筍雞(兒) *suunji(-jie'l)*, n., (Peking dial.) young tender chicken.

筍尖 *suunjian*, n., dried and cut bamboo shoot.

筍皮 *suunpir*, n., sheath of bamboo shoot.

筍頭 *suuntour*, n., bamboo shoot.

筍輿 *suunyur*, n., a simple bamboo sedan, without sedan cover.

§ 92A.63 (竹/丶)

笭 92A.63-8

lirng.

笭箐 *lirngching*, n., a small basket.

§ 92A.70 (竹/乚)

笆 92A.70-1

par.

N. Hand rake.

範 92A.70-1

fahn.

N. (1) Model: 模範 model to be copied, ideal; 風範, 規範, 典範 model character, model of conduct; 師範大學 normal university. (2) Boundary: see 範圍 *-weir*↓; 閫範 formerly, rules of propriety for ladies and married girls; 示範 model, pilot (project); 示範農場 pilot or model farm.

範本 *fahnbeen*, n., text or painting to be copied. 範疇 *fahnchour*, n., categories of thought. 範圍 *fahnweir*, n., scope, range, confines: 越出範圍 beyond the scope.

笓 92A.70-2

pir.

笓箣 *pirlir*, n., a shrimp trap.

筑 92A.70-3

jur.

N. An anc. musical instrument with thirteen strings.

筧 92A.70-4

jiaan.

N. A conduit made of long bamboo poles.

簭 92A.70-4

jauhn.

[Var. of 撰 to compose, 10A.80; and 饌 food, 81B.80]

笆 92A.70-5

ba.

[Var. 芭 20A.70]

N. 笆籬 or 籬笆 a bamboo fence.

笆斗 *badouu*, n., wicker basket.

籠 92A.70-6

lurng (*luung*).

N. (*-tz*) (1) Round receptacle of bamboo or metal: 蒸籠 a steamer for steaming food; 竹籠 bamboo basket; 鐵絲籠 wire basket. (2) A pen, cage: 雞籠 chicken coop; 鳥籠 bird cage; 蛇籠 snake cage; 囚籠, 站籠 cage for prisoners. (3) Bamboo trunk or case.

V.t. To include, bring under shade or cover: 籠括, 籠罩 *-gua*, *-jauh* ↓.

籠括 *lurnggua*, v. t., encompass, to bring under rule: 籠括一切 encompass everything; 籠括天下 conquer the world (also 囊括).

籠罩 *lurngjauh*, v.i. & t., to cover as with mask, canopy, to coop up: 籠罩心頭 (despair, sorrow) to cast shadow over one's heart.

籠絡 *lurngluoh*, v. t., (lit.) to halter, harness horse; (fig.) to win control over: 籠絡人心 to cultivate popularity.

籠頭 *lurng'tou*, n., muzzle over horse's or cattle's mouth.

籠統 *lurngtuung*, adj., general, generalized, unspecified: 籠統的稱呼 general term of reference (as "chief," "boss").

籠子 *lurngtz*, n., cage in gen.

簏 92A.70-6

luh.

N. A woven trunk, a bamboo basket.

箲 92A.70-6

shiaan.

N. Scraper for cleaning pots.

笔 92A.70-9

bii.

[Var. for 筆 92A.10]

篪 92A.70-9

chyr.

N. An anc. musical pipe.

箆 92A.70-9

bih.

N. & v.t. Fine-toothed comb; comb with this.

篼 92A.70-9

dou.

N. Mountain sedan chair.

§ 92A.71 (竹/弋)

篾 92A.71-4

mieh.

N. Split bamboo, bamboo splint

with smooth outside on, used in weaving: 篾席 woven bamboo mat; 篾尺 flexible measure made of bamboo slat to measure tree circumference.

篾片 *mieh-piahn*, n., slat of bamboo; (fig.) a great flatterer (bends to shape).

筤 92A.71-5

miin.

N. (1) A small brush=抿子 10A.71. (2) Bamboo slat.

箋 92A.71-7

jian.
[Interch. 牋 91S.71]

N. (1) A written note: 箋牘 *-dur*, 箋札 *-jar* ↓; 寸箋 (self-derogatory) my letter. (2) Kind of high-quality paper: 箋紙 *-jyy* ↓. (3) An official memorandum.

V.t. Explain, analyze, interpret (the meanings of words, phrases): 箋注 *-juh* ↓; 箋疏 *-shu* ↓.

箋牘 *jiandur*, n., correspondence.
箋札 *jianjar*, n., a friendly letter.
箋注 *jianjuh*, v. t. & n., (make) commentary on anc. texts.
箋紙 *jianjyy*, n., high-quality note paper.
箋譜 *jianpuu*, n., collection of writing paper design.
箋疏 *jianshu*, n., exegesis, commentary on anc. texts.

箴 92A.71-7

jen.

N. Maxim, proverb; stern advice, rebuke.

V.i. & t. To admonish, give moral advice.

箴規 *jenguei*, n., (1) admonition; (2) rules and regulations.
箴諫 *jenjiahn*, v. i. & t., to admonish, warn against.
箴言 *jenyarn*, n., moral maxim.

籤 92A.71-8

chian.

N. (1) A slip of paper inserted or pasted in book: 書籤 (=簽). (2) A set of bamboo slips in a pot used in temple for divination; the one which falls out contains the oracle; 籤詩 such oracle in verse; 求籤問卜 to ask the gods for an oracle. (3) A slender chip used in gambling. (4) Any sharp pointed stick used for picking: 牙籤 a toothpick.

筏 92A.71-9

far.

N. (*-tz*) Bamboo or wooden raft: 竹筏, 木筏.

§ 92A.80 (竹/八)

簀 92A.80-1

tzer.

N. A bed mat: 易簀 (euphem.) die (allu. to the custom of changing the mat when a person was about to die).

籟 92A.80-1

laih.

N. (1) The flute. (2) Sound coming from any hollow or void: 天籟 sounds of nature (hurricane, etc.); 地籟 sounds coming from hollows or forests; 人籟 sounds made by man, such as song and music; 萬籟俱寂 all (the night) is quiet.

箕 92A.80-2

ji.

N. (1) A sieve. (2) A dustpan. (3) A surname.

箕張 *jichang*, v. i., to spread or fan out.
箕裘 *ji-chiour*, n., the art of making sieves and fur coats: 克紹箕裘 be a worthy son to an able father.
箕斗 *ji-doou*, n., lines and whorls on a person's finger, used in fingerprinting.
箕賦 *ji-fuh*, n., exorbitant taxes (lit., "collection of grains by basketfuls") (also *-liahn* ↓).
箕帚 *jijoou*, n., menial service ("dustpan and broom"): 侍奉箕帚 perform wifely duties.
箕踞 *jijyuh*, v. i., sit in a squatting position, like the Japanese.
箕斂 *ji-liahn*, n., see *-fuh* ↑.
箕坐 *jitzuoh*, v. i., =箕踞 *-jyuh* ↑.

簧 92A.80-2

huarng.

N. (1) A metal reed in wood-wind instruments: 簧風琴 reed organ; 簧鼓 "play reed pipes and drums" to stir up people—to make fine-sounding speeches; 簧片樂器 reed instruments. (2) A spring coil: 彈簧 spring (as in mattress).

簣 92A.80-2

kueih.

N. A basket for carrying earth, pebbles: see 功虧^Δ一簣 21S.50.

篔 92A.80-4

yuarn.

N. Species of tall bamboo.

籲 92A.80-8

yuh.

V.i. To cry, beg for help: 呼籲 make public appeal; 籲求, 籲請 beg for, make appeal.

§92A.81 (竹/人)

筴 92A.81-1

tseh.

[Var. of 策 92A.01]

簌 92A.81-1

suh.

N. A sieve.

Adj. & adv. Descriptive of (1) tears dropping: 簌地, 簌簌 (地) dropping fast; (2) of whistling wind.

筷 92A.81-2

kuaih.

N. (*-tz, 'l*) Chopsticks: 不動筷兒 did not move chopsticks (to take food).

簇 92A.81-6

tsuh.

V.i. To crowd together: 簇捧, 簇擁 *-peeng, -yuung* ↓.

N. (1) Arrowhead. (2) A bundle, a bouquet: 花團錦簇 bouquets of flowers and silks.

簇聚 *tsuhjyuh*, v. i., to crowd, huddle together.

簇捧 *tsuhpeeng*, v. t., (MC) to surround (person).

簇新 *tsuhshin*, adj., bright and new (atmosphere), mint new, (as if freshly minted), brand-new.

簇簇 *tsuhtsuh*, adj., in series, clumped together.

簇擁 *tsuhyuung*, v. t., to escort (bride, high official, etc.).

簽 92A.81-8

chian.

N. (1) A slip of paper, pasted on a page, containing notes and comments (簽註) or on book cover containing book title (題簽). (2) A lot in drawing lots: 抽簽, cf. 籤 92A.71.

V.i. To put signature on: 簽名 *-mirng* ↓; 簽到 sign arrival at meeting or office; 簽字蓋章 (also 簽蓋, 簽章) sign and put personal seal on.

簽呈 *chiancherng*, (1) n., a memorandum to one's superior; (2) v.t., (of document) signed and presented.

簽證 *chianjehng*, n. & v.t., visa (passport); endorse (document).

簽兒 *chia'l*, n., see *-tiaur* ↓.

簽名 *chianmirng*, v. t., to sign; n., signature.

簽署 *chianshuh*, v. t., to sign, esp. on book title.

簽條 *chiantiaur*, n., a slip of paper pasted or inserted in book; an office memo.

簽字 *chiantzyh*, v. t., to sign (treaty, etc.).

簽押 *chianyar*, v. t., to sign name or make any personal mark on document: 簽押房 n., formerly, a government bureau for registration or clerk's office.

簽印 *chianyihn*, v. t., to put signature and seal on (document).

笑 92A.81-9

shiauh.

V.i. & t. & n. (1) To laugh, smile: 笑一笑 give a laugh; 笑哈哈, 笑呵呵, 哈哈大笑 to roar with laughter; 笑嘻嘻, 笑瞇瞇 smile happily; 微笑 give a smile, give a wee smile; 狂笑 to guffaw, howl with laughter, a roaring laughter; 苦笑 give a wry smile; 笑語 a joke; 笑話 *-'huah* ↓ 笑臉, 笑顏 a smiling face; 笑納 please accept graciously. (2) To laugh at, sneer, snicker: 我笑你, 你笑我 I laugh at you and you laugh at me; 笑罵 to deride, mock and berate (person): 笑罵由人 let others say what they like: 恥笑 to mock; 笑死人 shame one (be mocked) to death; 嗤笑 snicker, sneer; 玩笑 make fun of; 譏笑 deride, disparage, make sarcastic remarks at; 笑掉大牙 extremely laughable ("laugh tooth off"); 笑裏藏刀 a smile of treachery; 笑傲 to defy the conventional; esp. in 笑傲山林 to wander and live with nature.

笑柄 *shiauh-biing*, n., butt or target of laughter.
笑氣 *shiauh-chih*, n., (chem.) laughing gas, N_2O.
笑話 *shiauh'huah*, (1) n., a joke, pleasantry; (2) s. t. laughable: 笑話, 笑話 (court. reply to appreciation of one's own gift or performance) such a little thing; 笑話兒 (Peking coll.) fairy tales, children's stories; (3) v. t., laugh at: 可別笑話 please do not laugh at (my gift or performance.).
笑林廣記 *Shiahlirn guaangjih*, n., famous collection of popular jokes.
笑面虎 *shiauhmiahn-huu*, n., a wicked person with a hypocritical smile.
笑容 *shiauhrurng*, n., a happy, smiling expression.
笑殺 *shiauh'sha*, v. t., make one laugh one's teeth off (also wr. 笑煞).
笑談 *shiauhtarn*, n., (1) s. t. to joke about; (2) comic stories.

篌 92A.81-9

hour.

N. See 箜篌 92A.30.

§ 92A.82 (竹/乂)

簸 92A.82-2

boo (**boh*).

[Cogn. 播 10A.41]

V.i. & t. To winnow rice; hence 簸揚 (also 颺) winnow grain and spread husk in the wind; cast, throw, see 簸錢 *-chiarn* ↓.

簸錢 *boochiarn*, n. & v.i., (MC) a game of throwing coins; to play such game.
簸盪 *boodahng*, v.i., to rock (of boat).
簸頓 *booduhn*, v.t., (MC) to dally with (statutes).
簸動 *booduhng*, v.i., (MC) as in 簸動金鑼 to strike gongs.
簸箕 **boh'ji* (*-'chi* in Peking dial.), n., a basket for dust or grain; sieve for shifting grain.
簸弄 *booluhng*, v.t., (=播弄) to spread rumors and cause trouble.

笈 92A.82-3

jir.

N. A travelling bamboo box, esp. for books: 負笈 travel to school.

筊 92A.82-6

jiaau.

N. Bamboo rope.

箥 92A.82-6

poo.

[Var. of 笸 92A.21]

筱 92A.82-9

shiaau.

N. (1) Pop. var. of 小 used in personal names. (2) Baby bamboo.

笯 92A.82-9

nur.

N. (AC) a bird cage.

§ 92A.83 (竹/〜)

箑 92A.83-1

shah (**shier*).

N. (AC) a fan.

簉 92A.83-1

tzauh (*chouh*).

N. 簉室 *-shyh*, (LL) a concubine.

籧 92A.83-2

chyur (**jyuh*).

N. (1) Coarse bamboo mat, see 籧篨 *-chur* ↓. (2) 籧筐 a frame for cultivating silkworms.

籧篨 *chyurchur* (**jyuh-*), n., (1) a coarse bamboo mat; (2) (AC) a hunchback.

笊 92A.83-9

jauh.

笊籬 *jauhlir*, n., a fisherman's rake for catching clams, etc.

筳 92A.83-9

tirng.

N. 筳子 (*-tz*) spindles (also called 錠子).

筵 92A.83-9

yarn.

N. (1) A feast, banquet. (2) A mat.

筵席 ***yarnshir***, n., a banquet, full dinner: 舖筵席 spread a banquet.

籩 92A.83-9

bian.

N. (AC) Split-bamboo food basket; 籩豆之事 (AC) things connected with offering sacrifices.

篷 92A.83-9

perng.
[Dist. 蓬]

N. (1) Woven, matting cover, esp. in a houseboat, as 船篷. (2) A sail, also (poet.) a boat: 扯篷, 落篷 hoist, drop sail.

V.t. Cover up, as cover up fireplace with coal dust.

篷拆 ***perngchai***, n. & adj., (coll.) rhythm of music.
篷窗 ***perngchuang***, n., window in houseboat matting.
篷船 ***perngchuarn***, n., houseboat, covered with bamboo matting for shelter.

§ 92A.91 (竹/ノ)

笋 92A.91-5

suun.
[Var. of 筍 92A.50]

§ 92A.93 (竹/く)

簍 92A.93-2

loou.

N. A container, basket: 竹簍(子)(兒) a bamboo basket; 炭簍 a charcoal basket; 紙簍 a wastepaper basket; 煤簍 a coal basket; 一簍, 十幾簍 one, over ten baskets.

篹 92A.93-4

tsuahn.

V.t. To usurp (throne, authority): 篹位, 篹權.

SECTION 92B

§ 92B.00 (角/亅)

觭 92B.00-1

ji.

Adj. (1) Uneven, unsymmetrical (like two horns one of which turns upward and the other downward). (2) Odd (opp. 偶 even): 觭偶 odd and even (＝奇偶).

§ 92B.01 (角/小)

觫 92B.01-1

suh.

Adj. See 觳觫 11S.82.

§ 92B.02 (角/⺊)

觩 92B.02-1

chiour.

Adj. (AC) curled up (horn), stretched tight (bow).

筳 筵 籩 篷 笋 簍 篹 觭 觫 觩

亅	小	⺊	十	土	ナ	卄	ㄴ卜	丨	一	丁	フ	口	区	冈	㇆	厂	尸	亠	广	宀	丶	乚	弋	心	八	人	乂	乛	一	丿	𠂉	く
00	01	02	10	11	12	20	21	22	30	31	32	40	41	42	50	51	52	60	61	62	63	70	71	72	80	81	82	83	90	91	92	93

§ 92B.10 (角/十)

斛 92B.10–1

hur.

N. (1) A grain measure, anciently =ten *doou* (斗), now=five *doou*. (2) An anc. surname.

觶 92B.10–4

jyh.

N. (AC) a wine goblet.

解 92B.10–5

jiee (**jieh*, **shieh*).

N. (1) Comprehension, understanding: 見解 interpretation, personal view; 別解 a different interpretation. (2) The bowels: 大解 go to stool; 小解 urinate. (3) (**shieh*) A surname.

V.t. (1) Cut open, untie, dissect, take off: 解剖 *-poou*, 解析 *-shi* ↓; 分解 to partition, divide. (2) Untie, unfasten: 解開 *-'kai* ↓; 解鈴繫鈴 let the mischief-maker undo the mischief ("only he who has tied the bell on the tiger's neck can untie it"); 解衣 take off clothing; 解民倒懸 relieve people of their sufferings. (3) Explain: 解答 *-dar*, 解勸 *-chyuahn*, 解釋 *-shyh*^{2}, 解說 *-shuo* ↓; 講解 explain in detail, to lecture; 何以自解 how can one justify oneself (for so doing)? 排解 mediate, act as an intermediary or conciliator; 曲解 misinterpret; 詳解 give a detailed explanation; 解夢 interpretation of dreams; 註解 explanatory notes. (4) Understand, comprehend, realize: 解事 *-shyh*^{1} ↓; 了解 understand, know thoroughly; 誤解 misunderstand, misinterpret; 不解 cannot comprehend; 解惑 dispel doubts, remove suspicions, answer queries; 解迷 solve a riddle; 求解 find a solution; 費解 hard to understand, inexplicable. (5) Dispel, dissolve: 解散 *-sahn*, 解悶兒 *-meh'l*, 解憂 *-you* ↓; 融解 melt by heat, to fuse; 溶解 become liquid, thaw; 解體 *-tii* ↓; 化解 dissolve, turn into liquid; 消解 melt, cause to disappear; 解凍 to defreeze; (banking) to receive a blocked account. (6) Put an end to, to free: 解放 *-fahng*, 解脫 *-tuo*, 解除 *-chur*, 解嚴 *-yarn*^{2} ↓; 解禁 lift an embargo, a blockade, a ban; 解約 *-yue* ↓; 解任 dismiss from office, fire; 解職 relieve of duty, resign a post; 解救 *-jiouh* ↓; 解危 deliver from peril, save from danger; 解圍 *-weir* ↓; 解急 help s.o. in his hour of need. (7) Eliminate waste matter from body: 解手兒 *-shoou'l* ↓; 解大便 move bowels; 解小便 to urinate. (8) (**jieh*) Send in custody to: 押解 send (prisoner) under guard; 解往法場 dispatch to execution grounds; 解差 send prisoner under escort; 解回 send back in custody; 解送 send under guard; 解餉, 解糧, 解犯 deliver funds, rice, prisoner under guard.

解嘲 *jiee-chaur*, v. i., justify one's action, answer criticism.

解氣 *jiee-chih*, v. i., mollify a person's anger.

解除 *jieechur*, v. t., (1) relieve of (duties, burdens, responsibilities, post); (2) get rid of, eliminate: 解除武裝 disarm (troops); (3) annul, rescind (an agreement, a contract).

解勸 *jieechyuahn*, v. t., exhort, persuade, pacify, calm down.

解答 *jieedar*, v. t., to answer (questions, inquiries), solve (problems).

解毒劑 *jieedurjih*, n., (med.) an antidote.

解放 *jieefahng*, v. t., liberate, set free: 解放黑奴 (U.S. history) emancipation of the Negro slaves.

解紛 *jiee-fen*, v. t., mediate (a quarrel, dispute).

解恨 *jiee-hehn*, v. i., get even with enemy.

解和 *jieeher*, v. t., conciliate, reconcile.

解救 *jieejiouh*, v. t., give relief to, save (from danger, starvation, oppression).

解決 *jieejyuer*, v. t., (1) settle (a question), solve (a problem); (2) put an end to (difficulties, disputes); (3) kill person off.

解開 *jiee'kai*, v. t., (1) untie (shoestrings, knots); (2) solve (a riddle); (3) dissolve, melt, disintegrate.

解渴 *jiee-kee*, v. i., slake thirst.

解扣兒 *jieekouh'l*, v. i., (1) untie a knot; (2) settle dispute.

解纜 *jiee-laan*, v. i., weigh anchor (lit., "untie the hawser").

解悶兒 *jiee-meh'l*, v. i., kill time, find distraction.

解囊 *jiee-narng*, v. i., donate money for worthy causes (lit., "loose the purse strings").

解剖 *jierpoou*, v. t., to cut open, dissect; 解剖學 anatomy.

解熱劑 *jieerehjih*, n., medicine for reducing fever (an antipyretic).

解人 *jiee-rern*, n., one who understands.

解散 *jieesahn*, v. t., (1) to part, scatter, break up, disperse; (2) dissolve (Parliament, a partnership, a contract).

解析 *jieeshi*, v. t., analyze: 解析幾何 analytic geometry.

解手兒 *jiershoou'l*, v. i., (also **jie-*) relieve oneself, urinate.

解說 *jieeshuo*, v. t. & n., explain; an explanation.

解事 *jieeshyh*^{1}, v. t., show understanding, can differentiate between right and wrong.

解釋 *jieeshyh*^{2}, (1) v. t., explain, clarify, expound: 解釋誤會 to clear away a misunderstanding; (2) n., explanation, clarification, exposition, statement: 解釋憲法 interpretation of the constitution.

解體 *jiertii*, v. i., disintegrate, fall into pieces.

解脫 *jieetuo*, (1) v. t., to set free; (2) v. t. & n., (Budd.) release, liberate from worldly cares.

解圍 *jiee-weir*, v. i., raise siege; (fig.) save s.o. from embarrassment, relieve s.o. in distress.

解悟 *jieewuh*, v. t., understand or realize all of a sudden.

A

解顏 *jiee-yarn*¹, v. i., feel happy and smile.

解嚴 *jiee-yarn*², v. i., to lift the curfew.

解衣 *jieeyi*, v. i., (1) to undress oneself; (2) be generous to those in need: 解衣推食 give food and clothing to the needy.

解頤 *jiee-yir*, v. i., to smile.

解憂 *jiee-you*, v. i., allay grief or sorrow.

解約 *jieeyue*, v. i., annul a contract, terminate an agreement.

§ 92B.42 (角/冈)

觽 92B.42–2

shi.

N. (AC) a horn bodkin for untying knots: 佩觽 (AC) bodkin worn on girdle by the young.

§ 92B.50 (角/ㄱ)

觸 92B.50–4

chuh.

V.t. (1) To buck against, to gore with horn: 觸藩 to butt the hedge; (fig.) to gainsay; 互相抵觸 contradict each other. (2) To contact, run into or against: 觸電 contact a live wire; 觸犯 *-fahn*↓; 觸礁 run into submerged rock. (3) To touch, arouse feeling: 觸目 (what) meets the eye; 觸目驚心 (s.t. which is) a ghastly sight; 觸景生情 a scene which recalls past memories; 觸動 *-duhng*↓; 觸怒 *-nuh*↓; 觸處 *-chuh*↓; 感觸 n., feeling, emotional reaction.

B

觸處 ***chuhchuh***, adv., everywhere: 觸處都是 is seen everywhere—i.e., in abundance.

觸動 ***chuhduhng***, v.i., to touch emotionally, to arouse: 觸動靈機 have an inspiration.

觸發 ***chuhfa***, v.t., ditto; also stmiulate, irritate.

觸犯 ***chuhfahn***, v.t., to violate (the law).

觸機 ***chuh-ji***, v.t., see *-duhng*↑.

觸角 ***chuhjiaau***, n., antenna, -nae, feelers of insects.

觸覺 ***chuhjyuer***, n., sense of touch.

觸媒 ***chuhmeir***, n., (chem.) catalyst.

觸目 ***chuh-muh***, adj., (object) conspicuous; attracting attention.

觸怒 ***chuh-nuh***, v.t., to offend, arouse wrath.

觸手 ***chuh-shoou***, n., (zoo.) tentacles.

觸鬚 ***chuh-shyu***, n., (zoo.) feelers.

觸突 ***chuhtur***, v.t., to run against (rules, etc.).

觸眼 ***chuh-yaan***, adj., see *-muh*↑.

觔 92B.50–9

jin.

N. (1) (Interch. 筋) physical strength: 觔骨 bones and sinews; 觔斗 *-doou*↓. (2) (Interch. 斤) a measure of weight equal to 16 taels (兩), a catty.

觔斗 *jindoou*, n., a somersault: 打觔斗 turn a somersault.

觴 92B.50–9

shang.

N. (LL) a wine cup; symbolic of drinking; 觴詠 to drink and sing; 稱觴 (LL) to propose a toast; 濫△

C

觴 63A.30.

§ 92B.70 (角/乚)

觥 92B.70–2

gung.

N. (LL) a wine cup made of horn: 觥籌交錯 wine cups made of horn and chopsticks lie about, phr. describing a dinner party at which wine flows freely.

§ 92B.71 (角/七)

觝 92B.71–9

dii.

[Var. of 牴 10C.71]

§ 92B.83 (角/〜)

觚 92B.83–9

gu.

N. (1) (AC) drinking cup. (2) An angle, ridge.

鰣 鰂 鱘 鱒 鮒 鰈 鰾 鯨 穌 鯀 鰥 鱗

SECTION 92C

§ 92C.00 (魚/丿)

鰣 92C.00-4

shyr.

N. The shad, *Ilisha elongata* (fish).

鰂 92C.00-4

tzer.

N. The cuttlefish.

鱘 92C.00-5

shyurn.
[Var. 鱏]

N. A giant fish (wr. in classics as 鱣 *jan*), *Acipenser mikadoi*; 鱘骨 edible cartilage from the head of this fish; 鱘鰉 a giant fish, akin to *Acipenser mikadoi*; cf. 鱏 92C.10.

鱒 92C.00-8

tzuhn.

N. (Zoo.) the trout.

鮒 92C.00-9

fuh.

N. Silver carp, *Carassicus auratus* (fish), usu. called 鯽 *jih.*

§ 92C.01 (魚/小)

鰈 92C.01-2

dier.

N. A kind of flounder: 鰈鶼 symbol of marital love (比目魚 and 比翼鳥).

鰾 92C.01-3

biauh.

N. Fish blubber.

鰾膠 *biauhjiau*, n., fish glue.

鯨 92C.01-6

jing (chirng).

N. A whale; a dolphin, a porpoise.

鯨波 *jingbo*, n., ocean waves.
鯨鯢 *jingnir*, n., (1) big fish that feed on small ones; (2) a wicked person; (3) persons condemned and executed.
鯨呑 *jingtun*, v. t., gobble up (territory belonging to another), annex: 鯨呑蠶食 take by force and encroach upon (land or territory).

穌 92C.01-9

su.

Adj. (1) Interch. 甦 31.83. (2) 耶穌 Jesus.

鯀 92C.01-9

guun.

N. (1) A great fish. (2) The name of Emperor Yu's (禹) father.

§ 92C.02 (魚/⺊)

鰥 92C.02-4

guan.

N. (1) A huge fish. (2) A widower, an unmarried man: 鰥夫 *-fu*↓; 鰥寡孤獨 widowers, widows, orphans and childless couples; 鰥棍子 *-guhntz*; 鰥棍兒 *-gueh'l*,↓. (3) A grass widower: 何人不鰥 who isn't sometimes a grass widower?

鰥夫 *guanfu*, n., a widower, a bachelor.
鰥棍兒 *guangueh'l*, n., (coll.) a single man (also 光棍兒).
鰥棍子 *guanguhntz*, n., ditto.

§ 92C.10 (魚/十)

鱗 92C.10-2

lirn.

N. Scales (of fish): 批逆鱗 scrape fish scales from underside, (fig.) offend powerful person by blunt criticism; 鱗族 the scaly tribe.

鱗爪 *lirnjaau*, n., remnants, like leftover "scales and claws" of feasts; tidbits, unimportant parts: 一鱗半爪 just a few

known details of a larger whole; 巴黎鱗爪 tidbits from Paris.
鱗甲 *lirnjiaa*, n., scales (of fish, reptiles).
鱗介 *lirnjieh*, n., "scales and shell"—fish and shellfish in gen.
鱗集 *lirnjir*, v. i., congregate (like school of fish).
鱗鱗 *lirnlirn*, adj., (MC) of scaly appearance, as ripples.
鱗傷 *lirnshang*, n., as in 徧體鱗傷 body covered with wounds.
鱗屑癬 *lirnshieh-shyuaan*, n., a kind of dry scaly skin disease.
鱗次 *lirntsyh*, adj., arranged in rows: 鱗次櫛比 in close order, such as houses in congested area.

鱏 92C.10-3

shyurn.

N. A giant fish, oft. identified with 鱘 92C.00.

鱓 92C.10-4

shahn.
[Var. of 鱔 92C.40]

鮮 92C.10-8

shian (**shiaan*).

N. (1) Fresh food: 海鮮 seafood (restaurant); 時鮮 fruit, vegetable or fish in season. (2) (AC) freshly-killed game.

Adj. (1) Fresh in flavor, tasty because of freshness: 鮮甜 fresh and sweet. (2) Fresh (flowers, fish, fruit): 新鮮 new and fresh (air); 鮮衣服 fresh clothing. (3) Brightly colored: 鮮紅 *-hurng*, 鮮豔 *-yahn*, 鮮麗 *-lih*↓. (4) (**shiaan*) (AC, LL) few, also adv., seldom: 鮮少, 鮮乏 *-shaau*, *-far*↓; 鮮矣仁 (AC) (flippant talkers) are seldom true men; 鮮覯, 鮮見 seldom seen, rare.

鮮卑 **Shiaanbei*, n., a Tungu (東胡) tribe in Southeast Mongolia.
鮮乏 **shiaanfar*, adj., scarce.
鮮活 *shianhuor*, adj., (1) fresh-looking; (2) (also -'*huo*) brightly colored.
鮮紅 *shianhurng*, adj., bright red.
鮮亮 *shianliahng*, adj., bright and shining.
鮮麗 *shianlih*, adj., resplendent, fresh-looking, and fair.
鮮美 *shianmeei*, adj., good and fresh (in color or taste).
鮮明 *shianmirng*, adj., bright and clear (printing, lettering, etc.).
鮮肉兒 *shianrouh'l*, n., exposed raw flesh in wounds.
鮮少 **shiarnshaau*, (1) adj., scarce; (2) adv., seldom: 鮮少有人來 rarely see visitors here.
鮮血 *shianshiee* (*-shyueh*), n., fresh blood.
鮮新 *shianshin*, adj., bright and new.
鮮食 *shianshyr*, n., (1) fresh food; (2) (AC) fresh game.
鮮翠 *shiantsueih*, adj., bright green (vegetation).
鮮味 *shianweih*, n., fresh sweet flavor.
鮮豔 *shianyahn*, adj., resplendent, dazzling (dress, beauty).

§92C.11 (魚/土)

鮭 92C.11-1

guei.

N. (Zoo.) the globefish, *Spheroides vermicularis*.

鯉 92C.11-4

lii.

N. (Zoo.) the carp: 雙鯉 (allu.) friend's letter; 鯉素 a letter from a friend; 鯉庭之訓 father's advice (allu., Confucius' son 鯉).

鰉 92C.11-9

huarng.

N. See 鱘^鰉 92C.00.

§92C.22 (魚/丨)

鱭 92C.22-6

jih.

N. (Zoo.) a fish, *Coilia nasus*.

鰜 92C.22-8

jian.

N. (AC) sole, flounder.

鯽 92C.22-9

jih.

N. (Zoo.) the silver carp, *Carassius auratus* (also known as 鮒): 過江之鯽 numerous like a school of silver carps moving down a stream.

鮓 92C.22-9

jaa.

N. Preserved fish of various kinds (salted, wined).

§ 92C.30 (魚/一)

鱸 92C.30-2

lur.

N. (Zoo.) the common perch.

鱧 92C.30-2

lii.

N. (Zoo.) the snakehead mullet (also wr. 鯇魚, pop. called 烏魚).

鱈 92C.30-3

shyuee.

N. Codfish (pop. called 繁).

鱷 92C.30-3

eh.
[Var. 鰐]

N. Crocodile.

鰛 92C.30-4

wen.

N. Sardine (now usu. called 沙丁).

鱣 92C.30-6

*jan (*shahn).*

N. (1) A giant sea fish, *Acipenser mikadoi*, (by some identified with 鱘鰉). (2) (**shahn*) U.f. 鱔 and 鱓 the eel.

§ 92C.40 (魚/口)

鮎 92C.40-2

niarn.

N. (Zoo.) *Parasilurus asota*, a fish known for its stickiness.

鱔 92C.40-8

shahn.
[Var. 鱓 92C.10]

N. The eel.

鮐 92C.40-9

tair.

N. Globefish: 鮐背 (AC) old man with wrinkled skin and rounded back.

§ 92C.41 (魚/囚)

鰭 92C.41-1

chir.

N. (Fish) fins: 脊鰭, 尾鰭, 胸鰭 dorsal, caudal, pectoral fins.

鰭棘 *chir-ji*, n., prickly points of fins.

鰭刺 *chir-tsyh*, n., base of fish fins, also called 鰭條.

鯧 92C.41-4

chang.

N. The pomfret fish.

鱠 92C.41-8

kuaih.
[Var. of 膾 42A.41]

§ 92C.42 (魚/冈)

鯖 92C.42-1

*ching (*jeng).*

N. (1) Mackerel. (2) (**jeng*) A kind of fish paste.

鮪 92C.42-1

weei.

N. (Zoo.) a giant sea fish, *Psephurus* (also called 鱣, 鱘鰉); sometimes identified as the sturgeon or tuna.

鯛 92C.42-4

diau.

N. The porgy, *pagrosomus major*; also known as 棘鬣魚.

鯿 92C.42-6

bian.

N. (Zoo.) a kind of bream.

§92C.50 (魚/ㄱ)

鰐 92C.50-4

eh.

[Var. 鱷]

N. Crocodile.

魴 92C.50-6

farng.

N. Bream (fish).

§92C.70 (魚/乚)

魷 92C.70-1

your.

N. Squid.

魟 92C.70-3

jer.

N. (AC) dried fish.

鯤 92C.70-4

kun.

N. (AC) a monster fish, leviathan.

鮀 92C.70-6

tuor.

N. A kind of small fish which burrows in the sand, (zoo.) *Acanthogobius flavimanus* (also 鯊鰕虎).

鯢 92C.70-9

nir.

N. (1) (Zoo.) the female whale. (2) (Zoo.) *Cryptobranchus japonicus.* (3) 鯢鮒, 鯢鰌 the loach (also 泥▵鰍 63A.70).

鮑 92C.70-9

bauh.

N. (1) A surname. (2) See comp. ↓.

鮑魚 *bauhyur*, n., abalone; (AC) dried fish: 如入鮑魚之肆 like the stink of fish market.

§92C.72 (魚/心)

鰓 92C.72-4

sai.

N. Fish gills.

§92C.81 (魚/人)

鱖 92C.81-5

jyuer (also *gueih*).

N. The mandarin perch.

鰍 92C.81-9

chiou.

N. (Zoo.) the loach: 泥鰍 a tiny fish that lives in mud.

§92C.82 (魚/乂)

鯪 92C.82-1

lirng.

N. (Zoo.) dace (a fish).

鯪鯉 *lirnglii*, n., (zoo.) anteater, an animal.

鯿 鰐 魴 魷 魟 鯤 鮀 鯢 鮑 鰓 鱖 鰍 鯪

亅	小	⺊	十	土	ナ	廾	𠃊	丨	一	丁	フ	口	区	冈	ㄱ	厂	尸	亠	广	亠	丶	乚	弋	心	八	人	乂	乛	乛	丿	ㄴ	く
00	01	02	10	11	12	20	21	22	30	31	32	40	41	42	50	51	52	60	61	62	63	70	71	72	80	81	82	83	90	91	92	93

鮁 92C.82-1

bar, por.

N. The bonito fish.

鯁 92C.82-3

geeng.
[Interch. 骾]

N. A fish bone.

V.i. Have a fish bone stuck in the throat.

Adj. Upright: 鯁直 honest, straightforward; 骨鯁之臣 an outspoken minister who gives unpleasant advice.

鯫 92C.82-3

tzou.

N. Small fish, fry.

Adj. Tiny, small.

鯫生 *tzousheng*, n., (1) (AC, LL) a contemptible fellow; (2) (self-derogatory) my humble self.

鱍 92C.82-3

bo.

鱍鱍 *bobo*, adj., (AC) splashing, flipping about (of fish).

鰻 92C.82-4

marn.

N. Eel: 河鰻 fresh-water eel; 海鰻 sea eel.

鮫 92C.82-6

jiau.

N. (Zoo.) (AC) the shark.

鲃 92C.82-9

baan.

N. Sole, flounder.

鰒 92C.82-9

fuh.

N. Anc. name for 鮑魚 abalone, a shellfish.

§ 92C.83 (魚/乀)

鰱 92C.83-1

liarn.

N. (Zoo.) the silver carp.

SECTION 92S

§ 92S.00 (⺈S/亅)

刎 92S.00-2

ween.

V.t. To cut throat: 自刎 commit suicide; 刎頸 cut one's throat; 刎頸交 friends sworn to death.

刨 92S.00-2

paur, bauh.
[Cogn. 鉋]

V.t. Uproot, dig up: 刨起來 dig up; 刨根(兒)問底(兒) to get to the root of the matter.

剝 92S.00-2

bo.

V.i. & t. To peel, peel off, shell (beans, water chestnuts, etc.): 剝皮 or 剝去皮 to skin, fleece; 剝下, 落, 去 peel off; rob: 剝衣服 strip off and rob clothing; 剝膚之痛 phr., what hurts closely (the pain of being skinned); 剝極必復 phr., turn of fortune after extremity; 剝蕉抽繭 phr., like peeling banana plant or unwinding cocoon, i. e., press inquiry step by step, investigate deeper and deeper; p.p., be stripped: 剝得精光 stripped of all belongings, stripped naked; 剝豬玀 to fleece a person; see 剝落 *-luoh*, 剝蝕 *-shyr* ↓.

剝剝 *bobo*, n., sound of pecking.
剝船 *bochuarn*, n., a lighter (vulg. var. of 駁船).

剝奪 *boduor*, v. t., deprive, strip: 剝奪權利 deprive person of rights; 剝奪財產 rob property.

剝落 *boluoh*, adj., (of paint, bark) peeling off; (of forest) shabby, jagged.

剝削 *boshiau*, v. t., chisel off (profits, property, rights as by taxes, intermediaries or illegal extortion).

剝蝕 *boshyr*, adj., faded, worn out.

劄 92S.00-2

jar.

[Interch. 札]

N. (1) A brief note. (2) Official communication from superior to inferior.

劄記 *jarjih*, n. & v. t., a literary notebook, a collection of sundry notes and comments; to make such notes.

劄子 *jartz*, n., orig. official communications in Tarng and Suhng Dyns.; later restricted to communication to official subordinate.

罅 92S.00-2

shiah.

N. Fissure, crack.

罅縫(兒) *shiahfehng('l)*, n., a fissure, a loose seam.

罅漏 *shiahlouh*, n., a leak.

劐 92S.00-2

charn.

V.t. To carve, chisel.

鐏 92S.00-8

tzun.

[Var. of 樽 10B.00]

竹 92S.00-9

jur.

N. (1) (*-tz*) Bamboo: 竹林 bamboo grove; 竹筒 bamboo section used as penholder, etc.; 勢如破竹 as easy as splitting bamboo—used of ease in slashing through enemy ranks; 胸有成竹 painter has image of bamboo in his mind before he paints it—of person ready to meet some situation; 竹報平安 (allu.) family letter reporting all is well; also used in New Year red scroll. (2) The flute, as one of the eight classes of music instruments (八音). (3) A radical: 竹字頭兒 the radical 竹.

竹帛 *jur-bor*, n., bamboo and silk; formerly, bamboo sticks and silk as writing material.

竹布 *jurbuh*, n., a kind of imported cotton cloth.

竹蜂 *jurfeng*, n., a kind of bee, *Osmia rufa.*

竹夫人 *jurfurern*, n., a woven oblong bamboo basket for resting legs in bed in place of cushion or pillow in summer.

竹槓 *jurgahng*, n., as in 敲竹槓, 敲他竹槓 force person to pay by deceit or blackmail; make friends pay or sponge on friends.

竹竿 *jurgan*, n., bamboo pole.

竹根青 *jurgenching*, n., bamboo green color.

竹工 *jurgung*, n., basket weaver; bamboo craft.

竹黃 *jurhuarng*, n., skin of bamboo below the green covering, used as powder in medicine; see *-rur* ↓.

竹雞 *jurji*, n., a kind of quail.

竹簡 *jurjiaan*, n., bamboo strips, used for writing before paper was invented.

竹節鞭 *jurjierbian*, n., iron whip made of sections (like bamboo).

竹紙 *jurjyy*, n., paper made from bamboo.

竹瀝 *jurlih*, n., liquid obtained from fumigating bamboo—a medicine for reducing fever.

竹馬 *jurmaa*, n., esp. in 青梅竹馬 (allu.) childhood games ("riding on a bamboo stick for a horse").

竹篾 *jurmieh*, n., bamboo splints, being outer layer of bamboo, used much in weaving for its smoothness.

竹米 *jurmii*, n., bamboo seeds (also called 竹實) made into flour, *Bambusa.*

竹批兒 *jurpie'l*, n., long pieces of split bamboo.

竹蕈 *jurruh*, n., edible mushroom, grown on old bamboo roots, like 木耳 (also called 竹肉), used also in medicine.

竹茹 *jurrur*, n., see *-huarng* ↑.

竹笘 *jurshan*, n., formerly, a kind of slate, made from bamboo and coated with white clay, for children's practice in writing.

竹鼠 *jurshuu*, n., a field mouse which feeds on bamboo roots.

竹實 *jurshyr*, n., wheat-like bamboo seeds, see *-mii* ↑.

竹筍 *jursuun*, n., bamboo shoots, a delicacy.

竹菜 *jurtsaih*, n., (bot.) edible plant, *Chamaele tenera.*

竹葉青 *juryehching*, n., (1) an old vintage Shauhshing 紹興 wine; (2) name of a snake, *Trimeresurus gramineus.*

竹輿 *juryur*, n., simple light mountain sedan chair with bamboo poles and seat.

繇飧舛缽鐔矬罐雉雒雛

§ 92S.01 (𠂉^s/小)

繇 92S.01-9

your (**yaur*).

[Var. of 由 22.41; var. of 徭 (**yaur*), 91B.21]

§ 92S.02 (𠂉^s/卜)

飧 92S.02-8

sun.

N. (AC) evening meal.

§ 92S.10 (𠂉^s/十)

舛 92S.10-1

chuaan.

Adj. & adv. Astray, mixed up.

舛駁 *chuaanbor*, adj., (teaching, thoughts, ideas) confused, disorganized.
舛逆 *chuaannih*, adj., (conduct, ideas) upside-down, disorderly, unruly.
舛錯 *chuaantsuoh*, (1) adj., uneven, mixed up; (2) (-'*tsuo*) n., mishap: 不會有什麽舛錯 there can't be any mishap (in competent hands).
舛雜 *chuaantzar*, adj., disorderly.
舛誤 *chuaanwuh*, n., mistake.

缽 92S.10-1

bo.

[Pop. of 鉢 81A.10]

N. A Buddhist monk's alms-bowl: 衣缽 a monk's robe and alms bowl; 衣缽眞傳 true teachings handed down from the Master.

鐔 92S.10-3

tarn.

[Var. of 壜 11A.93]

§ 92S.11 (𠂉^s/土)

矬 92S.11-2

tsuor.

Adj. (Coll.) short (person).

矬個兒 *tsuorgeh'l*, n., a "shorty" (person).
矬子 *tsuortz*, n., ditto.

罐 92S.11-2

guahn.

N. A jug, pitcher, jar, pot: 瓦罐 a clay pot: 罐子 a pot, jar or pitcher; 盆兒罐兒 an assortment of pots and jars; 茶罐 a tea-canister; 水罐 a water pitcher; 罐頭 *-tour* ↓.

罐頭 *guahntour*, n., canned goods; 罐頭刀 can opener.

雉 92S.11-9

jyh.

N. (1) Pheasant: 雉兔者 catchers of hares and pheasants. (2) (AC) a parapet section of city wall, 30 ft. high and 10 ft. long; 百雉之城 (AC) a city wall with a hundered parapets.

雉堞 *jyhdier*, n., parapet.
雉雞 *jyji*, n., the Tartar pheasant; 雉雞翎 pheasant's tail feather used on opera stage.
雉經 *jyhjing*, v. i., (LL) hang oneself.
雉鳩 *jyhjiou*, n., turtle dove, *Turtus orientalis*.
雉媒 *jyhmeir*, n., decoy pheasant.

雒 92S.11-9

luoh.

N. (1) (AC) black horse with white mane (cf. 駱 51B.40). (2) Var. of 洛 63A.40, place name. (3) A surname.

雛 92S.11-9

chur.

N. (1) A young chick; young of bird, fledgeling: 雛雞 ditto; 雛鴿 squab. (2) A baby, child.

Adj. Childish: 雛的很 still very childish, inexperienced.

雛鳳 *churfehng*, n., (LL, complim.) nice children.
雛菊 *churjur*, n., a miniature grass resembling chrysanthemum.
雛兒 *chur'l*, n., (1) (coll.) a young girl; an inexperienced young boy; (2) a teenage singsong girl.
雛形 *churshirng*, n., miniature model.

A | B | C

§92S.20 (ㄥ^{s}/卄)

絣 92S.20-8

pirng.

[Var. of 瓶 80S.70]

§92S.21 (ㄥ^{s}/ㄴ)

矩 92S.21-5

jyuu.

N. (1) A ruler for drawing squares or rectangles: 矩尺 *-chyy*↓; 規矩 regulations, social customs. (2) A rule, a pattern: 矩矱 *-huoh*↓.

矩尺 *jyurchyy*, n., a carpenter's square.

矩矱 *jyuuhuoh*, n., rules and regulations, standards to be followed.

矩形 *jyuushirng*, n. & adj., rectangle, -ular.

§92S.22 (ㄥ^{s}/丨)

外 92S.22-2

waih.

N. (1) (Chin. opera) an elderly man's role. (2) The outside, external side, foreign country: 對內對外 internal and external; 國外 outside the country; 出外 not at home, gone abroad; 世外 out of this world; 例外 exception to rule; 意外, 意料之外 unexpected happening; 話外之意 idea not expressed in words; 圈外 outside the circle; 校外 outside the school; 女主內, 男主外 woman takes care of the house, man the outside, hence 外子 *-tzyy*↓; 外強中乾 appear rich and successful, but actually in financial trouble; 見外, (court.) 不要見外 do not refuse my gift, invitation ("regard me as outside your circle of friends").

Adj. (1) External: 外面, 外邊 *-miahn, -bian*↓; 外表 *-biaau*↓; 外傷 external injury. (2) Foreign: 外交 *-jiau*, 外國 *-guor*, 外貨, 外賓 *-huoh, -bin*, etc.↓, 外邦人 the Gentiles (said by Jews). (3) On wife's or mother's side: 外公, 外婆, 外戚 *-gung, -por, -chi*↓.

Adv. Abroad: 外放 sent abroad as official; 外露 leak out; 外嫁 marry abroad or marry out; 外傳 (gossip) spread abroad.

外擺線 *waih-baai-shiahn*, n., (geom.) epicycloid.

外半徑 *waih-bahnjihng*, n., (geom.) circum-radius.

外表 *waihbiaau*, n., external appearance.

外邊 *waihbian*, n., outside (rumor, light, etc.); border region: 外邊兒 outside, also the outer edge of bed.

外賓 *waih-bin*, n., foreign guest or visitor.

外部 *waihbuh*, n., (1) outside (of body), outside part; (2) short for 外交部 *--jiaubuh*↓.

外塲 *waihchaang*, n., (1) outside area; 外塲人 man versed in social intercourse; (2) (baseball) outfielder: 外塲員.

外城 *waih-cherng*, n., the outer city.

外戚 *waih-chi*, n., wife's or mother's relatives.

外欠 *waihchiahn*, n., external debt.

外親 *waih-chin*, n., wife's or mother's relatives.

外勤 *waihchirn*, n., field work, work not inside office: 外勤記者 reporter.

外曲球 *waih-chyu-chiour*, n., (baseball) an outcurve ball.

外圈 *waihchyuan*, n., outer circle.

外旦 *waihdahn*, n., (Yuarn drama) a homely female role.

外道 *waihdauh*, (1) n., (Budd.) not orthodox teaching: 有了外道兒了 indulging in immoral conduct; (2) (-'*dau*) adj., standing on ceremonies, treating person as one of outer circles of friends.

外電路 *waih-diahn-luh*, n., external (electric) circuit; 外電阻 external (electric) resistance.

外動詞 *waih-duhng-tsyr*, n., transitive verb (v. t.).

外耳 *waih-eel*, n., external ear.

外方 *waihfang*, n., outside area, outside world.

外藩 *waihfarn*, n., a prince's domain in border province.

外分泌腺 *waih-fenmih-shiahn*, n., (biol.) external secretion glands.

外敷 *waihfu*, adj., (of med.) for external application.

外感 *waih-gaan*, n., (Chin. med.) effect of weather, heat or cold.

外姑 *waihgu*, n., (dial.) wife's mother.

外褂(子) *waihguah(tz)*, n., overjacket.

外官 *waih-guan*[1], n., official in the province.

外觀 *waihguan*[2], n., external appearance.

外光劇塲 *waih-guang jyuhchaang*, n., open air theater.

外公 *waihgung*, n., maternal grandfather.

外功(兒) *waihgung('l)*, n., bodily training in boxing skill, opp. 內$^{\Delta}$功 81.42.

外國 *waihguor*, n., a foreign country.

外行 *waihharng*, adj., being a layman, amateurish, not very familiar on subject.

外號兒 *waihhauh'l*, n., nickname, assumed name, alias.

外呼吸 *waih-hushi*, n., (biol.) external respiration.

外話 *waih-huah*, n., vulgar

絣 矩 外

丨	小	⺊	十	土	ナ	卄	ㄴ	丨	一	丁	フ	口	区	冈	ㄱ	厂	尸	亠	广	宀	丶	乚	弋	心	八	人	乂	乛	一	丿	ㄥ	く
00	01	02	10	11	12	20	21	22	30	31	32	40	41	42	50	51	52	60	61	62	63	70	71	72	80	81	82	83	90	91	92	93

A

外 speech.

外患 *waih-huahn*, n., external trouble of country.

外懷裏 *waihhuair'li*, n., outside seat.

外匯 *waihhueih*, n., foreign remittance, exchange..

外貨 *waihhuoh*, n., imported goods.

外找兒 *waihjaau'l*, n., formerly, extra incomes.

外債 *waih-jaih*, n., foreign debts.

外宅 *waih-jair*, n., outer house; (MC) a kept mistress living outside.

外罩(兒) *waihjauh('l)*, n., outer garment serving like overcoat.

外症 *waihjehng*, n., surface diseases.

外加 *waih-jia*^{1}, phr., in addition, additional (expense, etc.).

外家 *waihjia*^{2}, n., (1) wife's maiden home; (2) a kept mistress or her apartment.

外角 *waih-jiaau*, n., (math.) exterior angle.

外間 *waih'jian*, n., outside; 外間兒 *-jia'l*, court or rooms nearer the gate.

外交 *waihjiau*, n., diplomacy; 外交官 diplomat; 外交部 *--buh*, n., Ministry of Foreign Affairs.

外界 *waihjieh*, n., those not connected with a group: 外界人士 outside people, the public.

外淨 *waihjihng*, n., see 淨 63A.00.

外景 *waihjiing*, n., (cinema) outdoor shots; background of house.

外舅 *waihjiouh*, n., (dial.) wife's father.

外集 *waihjir*^{1}, n., later supplement to author's works.

外籍 *waihjir*^{2}, n., foreign nationality.

外中比 *waih-jung-bii*, n., (math.) extreme and mean ratio.

外種皮 *waih-juung-pir*, n., (bot.) hard outer covering of a seed, testa.

外痔 *waihjyh*, n., external piles.

外科 *waihke*, n., surgery; 外科醫生 a surgeon; 外科手術 a surgical operation; 美容外科 plastic surgery.

外客 *waihkeh*, n., a stranger, visitor; foreign visitor.

外快 *waihkuaih*, n., extra income besides salary.

B

外流 *waih-liour*, phr., outflow; 人才外流 brain drain.

外路 *waih'luh*, n., as in 外路客商 salesman or business representative from other cities.

外貌 *waihmauh*, n., outside appearance, looks.

外面 *waihmiahn*, n., outside; also 外面兒; 外面皮兒 the superficial look of things.

外膜 *waihmor*, n., (biol.) external membrane.

外男 *waihnarn*, n., nephew, see *-sheng* ↓.

外胚乳 *waihpeiruu*, n., (bot.) perisperm.

外胚葉 *waihpeiyeh*, n., (bot.) ectoblast, outer layer of embryo.

外撇子 *waihpieetz*, n., one considered an "outsider" in a group.

外婆 *waihpor*, n., maternal grandmother.

外人 *waihrern*, n., (1) outsider, one not regarded as a friend: 你我不是外人 we are friends; (2) foreigner.

外傷 *waihshang*, n., trauma.

外省 *waihsheeng*, n., another province: 外省人 person from another province.

外腎 *waihshehn*, n., the testicles.

外甥(兒) *waih'sheng('l)*, n., nephew.

外甥女 *waihshengnyuu*, n., niece.

外線 *waihshiahn*^{1}, n., person or persons making outside contact for a secret group; "front," see *-weir* ↓.

外縣 *waihshiahn*^{2}, n., another county.

外項 *waihshiahng*^{1}, n., (math.) extremes.

外相 *waihshiahng*^{2}, n., foreign minister.

外鄉 *waihshiang*, n., (from) another part of the country: 外鄉人兒 such person; 外鄉口音 foreign accent.

外銷 *waihshiau*, n., export (business, goods).

外姓 *waihshihng*, n., not of the same clan name.

外手 *waihshoou*, n., the outer side or edge (of bed, etc.).

外氏 *waih-shyh*^{1}, n., family of mother's relatives.

外室 *waihshyh*^{2}, n., a kept mistress living outside; see *-jair* ↑.

C

外四路兒 *waihshyhluh'l*, n., not close relatives, strangers to the family.

外旋神經 *waihshyuarn shernjing*, n., (physiol.) abducent nerves.

外史 *waihshyy*, n., unofficial history.

外祟 *waih'suei*, n., ghosts of strangers, not of one's own relatives; person who is a pest.

外孫(子) *waihsun (tz)* n., daughter's son; 外孫女(兒) n., daughter's daughter.

外套(兒) *waihtauh'l*, n., overcoat, outer garment.

外套膜 *waihtauhmor*, n., (zoo.) mantle.

外頭 *waih'tou*, n., outside.

外才 *waihtsair*, n., extrovert ability for meeting situations, business problems.

外族 *waihtzur*, n., foreign tribe or clan.

外祖母 *waihtzurmuu*, n., maternal grandmother.

外祖 *waihtzuu*, n., maternal grandfather.

外資 *waihtzy*, n., foreign capital.

外子 *waihtzyy*, n., woman's reference to her husband; opp. 內子 man's reference to wife.

外外 *waih'wai*, n., (dial.) nephew.

外圍 *waihweir*, n., outer circles, not inner core; Communist "front."

外翁 *waihweng*, n., maternal grandfather.

外務 *waihwuh*, n., (1) foreign affairs; (2) not one's own business.

外侮 *waih-wuu*, n., humiliations by foreign country.

外秧兒 *waihyang'l*, n., (sl.) outsider, not of one's group.

外延 *waihyarn*^{1}, n., (logic) extension.

外焰 *waihyarn*^{2}, n., (phys.) outer flame.

外洋 *waihyarng*, n., oceans outside China, foreign countries in gen.

外野手 *waihyer-shoou*, n., (baseball) outfielder, see *-chaang* ↑.

外援 *waihyuarn*, n., foreign aid.

外遇 *waihyuh*, n., lover outside marriage.

A

郇 92S.22-3

shyurn.

N. (1) A place name. (2) Translit. of Zion.

鄒 92S.22-3

tzou.

N. (1) Name of an anc. principality in modern Shantung. (2) A surname.

卸 92S.22-5

shieh.

V.t. To remove, strip off, lay down: 卸除 *-chur* ↓; 卸貨 unload goods; 卸牲口 take load from pack horses, etc.; 卸車 release pack animals from cart; 卸下責任 lay down the responsibility or burden.

卸除 *shieh-chur*, v. t., remove (burden, responsibility).
卸肩 *shieh-jian*, v. i., "free one's shoulders"—lay down burden.
卸妝 *shieh-juang*, v. i., (also wr. 卸粧) take off stage dress or formal dress, earrings, etc.; remove stage make-up.
卸任 *shieh-rehn*, v. i., quit office.
卸頭 *shiehtour*, v. i., (women) take off hair decorations.
卸載 *shieh-tzaih*, v. i., unload.
卸責 *shieh-tzer*, v. i., be removed of duty or responsibility.

矧 92S.22-5

sheen.

B

Conj. (AC, LL) Besides, not to speak of: 矧如伊人 not to speak of that man—i. e., much less he; 矧如是乎 how much less then in this case?

矫 92S.22-9

jiaau.

[Abbr. of 矯 92S.42]

§ 92S.30 (⺈^{S}/一)

罏 92S.30-2

lur.

[Dist. 爐]

N. A squat wine jar.

缸 92S.30-3

gang.

N. A jar, jug: 水缸 water jar; 醬缸 a soy sauce vat; 糖缸子 a sugar bowl; 醃菜缸 a vat for salted vegetables; 糞缸 receptacle for night soil.

缸瓦 *gangwaa*, n., earthenware with crude glaze.

短 92S.30-3

duaan.

N. Shortcoming: 護短, 揭短 cover up, expose, shortcomings; 勿道人之短 (or 短長) do not talk about

C

people's faults, foibles.

V.i. & t. (1) Lack: 不短什麼 do not lack anything; 短不了 cannot do without: 這會短不了他 this meeting cannot do without him; 我短不了往學校去 have to go to school (in the end); cf. 少 22.91. (2) Owe: 不短他錢 do not owe him money.

Adj. Short, brief: 短短的 short; 短橛橛 *-chyueichyuei*, very short; 短刀, 劍 short knife, sword; 短裝, 短打兒 in jacket, without long gown; 短襖 jacket; 短時間, 時期 short time, period; 簡短 brief (outline, speech); 截短 cut short. (2) Falling short, unwise, shortsighted: 短計 unwise move; 短處 weaknesses, shortcomings; 短見, 短路 *-jiahn*, *-luh* ↓. (3) Inadequate, insufficient: 短絀 *-chuh* ↓.

短波 *duaan-bo*, n., short-wave (electronics); 超短波 very high frequency (VHF).
短欠 *duaanchiahn*, v. i., fall short of proper amount, owe.
短氣 *duaanchih*, adj., short of breath; dispirited, downhearted.
短期 *duaan-chir*, adj., short-term: 短期借款, 公債 short-term loan, bond.
短處 *duaan'chuh*, n., shortcoming.
短絀 *duaanchuh*, adj., short, inadequate (means, rope).
短缺 *duaanchyue*, adj., missing, lacking.
短打(兒) *duarndaa('l)*, v. i., dress in jacket.
短工 *duaangung*, n., short time or piece-good worker.
短漢 *duaanhahn*, n., dwarf.
短折 *duaanjer*, v. i., die young.
短見 *duaanjiahn*, n., shortsighted opinion; 尋短見 seek the short way out—commit suicide.
短至 *duaanjyh*, n., winter solstice (＝冬至), the shortest day.
短兒 *duaa'l*, n., shortcoming: 說人的短兒 expose s. o.'s shortcomings (＝短處).

郇 鄒 卸 矧 矫 罏 缸 短

亅	小	⺊	十	土	ナ	廾	㇗	丨	一	丅	フ	口	⊠	冈	㇆	厂	尸	亠	广	宀	丶	乚	弋	心	八	人	乂	⌒	乛	丿	⺈	く
00	01	02	10	11	12	20	21	22	30	31	32	40	41	42	50	51	52	60	61	62	63	70	71	72	80	81	82	83	90	91	92	93

短路 *duaanluh*, n., irregular activities (banditry, etc.).

短命 *duaanmihng*, adj., & n. dying young—oft. a curse.

短篇 *duaanpian*, n., short piece; 短篇小説 short story.

短少 *duarnshaau*, v. i. & t., to lack, be short of proper amount: 短少十塊錢 ten dollars short; do without: 不能短少他 cannot do without him.

短小 *duarnshiaau*, adj., in 短小精幹 compact-built and capable.

短數 *duaanshuh*, n., what is short of proper amount.

短視 *duaanshyh*, adj., near-sighted.

短促 *duaantsuh*, adj., pressed for time: 時間短促.

§ 92S.32 (𠂉^s/フ)

够 92S.32-9

gouh.

[Var. of 夠 92S.50]

§ 92S.40 (𠂉^s/口)

知 92S.40-4

jy (**jyh*).

N. (1) Knowledge: 知識 *-shyh*[2] (also **jyh-*)↓; 無知 ignorant; 知難行易 (孫中山) knowledge is difficult, but action is easy; 知行合一 (王陽明) knowledge and action are one; knowledge is action, action is (true) knowledge. (2) (**jyh*) (AC)＝智 wisdom: 知不及人 wisdom cannot equal others; 大知若愚 great wisdom appears stupid (Taoist); 知者不惑 the wise man has no perplexity.

V.t. (1) To know: 你知不知道 do you know? 知道, 知悉 *-'dau, -shir*↓; 獲知, 探知 have found out that; 得知 know that or enabled to know that; 未知, 不知 do not know (未知 is more litr.); 深知 I realize, he really knows; 無所不知, 知古今兒 omniscient, know everything; 知無不言, 言無不盡 to say all that you know and say it without reserve; 一無所知 know nothing; 一知半解 have a superficial knowledge (of s. t.); 誰不知 who doesn't know; 明知故問 he asks, but already knows; 明知故犯, 知法犯法, deliberately flout the law; 知己知彼, 百戰百勝 to know one's own strength and the enemy's is the sure way to victory; 知錯 acknowledge one is wrong; 知白守黑 (老子) know and observe all but stay obscure; 知子莫若父 no one knows a man better than his own father; 知人知面不知心 we may know a man's exterior but not his heart; 若要人不知, 除非己莫爲 if you don't want people to know it, the best way is not to do it; 知根知底 know the bottom (of affair, about person); 知過, 知非, 知禮, 知恥 *-guoh, -fei, -lii, -chyy*↓; 知足 *-tzur*↓. (2) To feel, sense: 知覺 *-jyuer*↓; 先知 prophet; 先知先覺 those who think ahead of their generation, the seers, prophets; 後知後覺 those who learn in later generation; 不知不覺 unconsciously; 自知不如 know or feel one is not another's equal; 自知 know one's own weakness; 不自知 lack self-knowledge; 知疼着熱 feel for another person like oneself (as mother of child). (3) To be a bosom friend: 知己 *-jii*↓; 相知 (a) n., a close friend; (b) v.t., to know each other; 相知甚深 know each other for a long time; 知友, 知音, 知心 *-yoou, -yin, -shin*↓. (4) To recognize: 受知 be recognized for talent by superior; 見知於世 be recognized by society; 知遇 *-yuh*↓. (5) To be expert in subject: 知兵 expert in military science; 知醫 expert in medicine. (6) To communicate officially: 知會, 知照 *-hueih, -jauh*↓; 通知 (a) v. t., to inform, (b) n., a public notice; 示知 please let me know. (7) To be in charge of office: 知府, 知縣, 知事, 知州 *-fuu, -shiahn, -shyh*[1], *-jou*↓; 知客 *-keh*↓.

知情 *jy-chirng*, v. i., legal formula, like "with full knowledge of the facts": 實不知情 (affidavit) really have no knowledge (concerning s. t.); 知情自首 s. o. reports himself to justice on his involvement in case; 知情底保 offer guarantee with full knowledge of all the facts.

知趣 *jy-chyuh*, v. i., (1) appreciate (what is good or interesting, or what is fun); (2) 知趣兒 *-chyueh'l*, tactful, having a sense of the situation (and retire without being told, etc.).

知恥 *jy-chyy*, phr., have a sense of shame or of honor.

知單 *jydan*, n., notice of invitation with list of invited, on which the recipient signs the word 知, without commitment to attend.

知道 *jy'dau*, v. i. & t., regular vern. for 知: 不知道 do not know or realize; 知道了 phr., acknowledging receipt of communication or report, without saying "yes" or "no."

知方 *jy-fang*, phr., (AC) knowing what is right to do.

知非 *jy-fei*, phr., to know one's mistakes: 行年五十而後知四十九年之非 (AC) "at fifty I realize the mistakes of the forty-nine years," hence 知非之年 fifty years of age.

知風草 *jyfeng-tsaau*, n., (bot.) *Eragrostis ferruginea*.

知府 *jyfuu*, n., magistrate of a *fuu* or district.

知根兒 *jy-ge'l*, phr., know the bottom of things.

知更雀 *jygeng-chyueh*, n., (zoo.) a small bird, robin, *Erithacus namiyei*.

知過 *jyguoh*, v.i., realize one's mistake.

知會 *jyhueih*, v. i. & t., (1) to know, understand, appreciate; (2) to transmit official communication.

知照 *jyjauh*, v.t., officially inform, be informed.

知幾 *jyji*, phr., (AC) to sense

what is coming (also wr. 知機).

知己 *jyjii*, (1) n., a bosom friend; (2) phr., 知己知彼 to know one's and the enemy's situation or strength (to ensure victory).

知津 *jy-jin*, phr., (LL) know the way ("ferry").

知州 *jyjou*, n., magistrate of *jou* or prefecture.

知覺 *jyjyuer*, (1) v. i. & t., to perceive; to feel, realize: 知覺不對 feel s. t. is wrong; 不知不覺 unconscious, -ly; (2) n., conciousness, perception: 沒有知覺 have lost consciousness, (vb.) have not realized.

知止 *jy-jyy*, phr., (AC) knowing when (or where) to stop; knowing the goal or the faith to hold on to.

知客 *jykeh(-'ke)*, n., monk in charge of reception of visitors; 知客寮 (MC) reception room of monastery.

知了 *jyliaau*, n., (1) ("I know") another name of cicada from sound of its cry; (2) (-'*le*) I know.

知禮 *jy-lii*, adj., refined, conversant with proper manners or established customs.

知命 *jy-mihng*, phr., (1) know Heaven's will: 樂天知命 acceptance of Heaven's will and inner content; (2) 知命之年 (allu. Confucius) fifty years of age.

知名 *jy-mirng*, adj., well-known.

知母 *jymuu*, n., a grass, *Anemarrhena asphodeloides*.

知能 *jynerng*, n., consciousness, sense of perception.

知人 *jy-rern*, phr., 知人之明 capacity to judge person's qualities.

知曉 *jyshiaau*, v. i., (slightly litr. & MC) to know.

知縣 *jyshiahn*, n., magistrate of a *shiahn*, county.

知心 *jy-shin*, phr., 知心人 bosom friend; 知心話 heart-to-heart talk.

知悉 *jyshir*, v.i. & t., (LL esp., in letters) to know, have learned.

知事 *jyshyh*[1], n., 縣知事 see -*shiahn* ↑.

知識 **jyshyh*[2], n., knowledge; 知識豐富 having wide knowledge of subjects; 科學知識 scientific knowledge; 知識分子 or 階級 (**jyh*-) the intelligentsia.

知足 *jytzur*, adj. & n., content, -ed, -ment: 知足常樂 he who is contented is always happy; 不知足 discontented, (of person) never satisfied (cf. 知不足 knowing one's own limitations of knowledge).

知言 *jyy-yarn*, phr., to know what to say and when to say it.

知音 *jy-yin*, n., a good understanding friend.

知友 *jy-yoou*, n., a bosom friend.

知遇 *jy-yuh*, phr., in 受知遇 be recognized or discovered, receive help and encouragement by a superior; 知遇之恩 gratitude for such help.

§ 92S.41 (𠂉^{s}/区)

矰 92S.41-8

tzeng.

N. An arrow: 矰繳 an arrow with a silk streamer attached to it.

§ 92S.42 (𠂉^{s}/冈)

矯 92S.42-9

jiaau.

V.t. (1) To correct, rectify, improve upon: 矯正 -*jehng*, 矯世 -*shyh*[1] ↓; 矯枉過正 (of a reformer's efforts) overshoot one's mark. (2) Fabricate, falsify: 矯託 -*tuo* ↓; 矯命 issue unauthorized or faked orders; 矯詔 take unauthorized action in the name of the king; 矯誣 to accuse deceitfully or wilfully put blame on (person); 矯飾 -*shyh*[2] ↓; 矯揉 -*rour* ↓. (3) Lift up, raise: 矯首昂視 pass by with head high and eyebrows raised.

Adj. Strong, robust, sturdy: 矯矯 -*jiaau* ↓; 矯強 (of persons) tough, sinewy, firm, resolute.

矯情 *jiaauchirng*, v. i., (1) feign, affect, make a studied effort to show one is different; be inhuman, act against human nature; (2) (-'*ching*, Peking sp. pr. *jiaur'ching*) use specious arguments to justify oneself.

矯正 *jiaaujehng*, v. t., make corrections in, improve upon.

矯激 *jiaauji*, v. i., see -*chirng* ↑.

矯矯 *jiaurjiaau*, adj., (1) stalwart, brave and strong, chivalrous; (2) exalted, lofty, raised.

矯健 *jiaaujiahn*, adj., robust, vigorous.

矯亢 *jiaaukahng*, v. i., set oneself off by affectation.

矯揉 *jiaaurour*, v. t., (1) to bend, twist; (2) feign, pretend, counterfeit: 矯揉造作 try to deceive by covering up one's real purpose; (3) adj., artificial, made-up.

矯世 *jiaau-shyh*[1], v. i., make the world over in one's own image, be an uplifter.

矯飾 *jiaaushyh*[2], adj., pretending to be better than one is.

矯託 *jiaautuo*, v. t., falsify (requests, orders, statements), purposely misrepresent.

§ 92S.50 (𠂉^{s}/ㄱ)

劬 92S.50-9

chyur.

丨	小	⺊	十	土	ナ	卄	㔾	丨	一	丅	フ	口	区	冈	ㄱ	厂	尸	亠	广	宀	丶	乚	弋	心	八	人	乂	乛	ノ	刂	𠂉	く
00	01	02	10	11	12	20	21	22	30	31	32	40	41	42	50	51	52	60	61	62	63	70	71	72	80	81	82	83	90	91	92	93

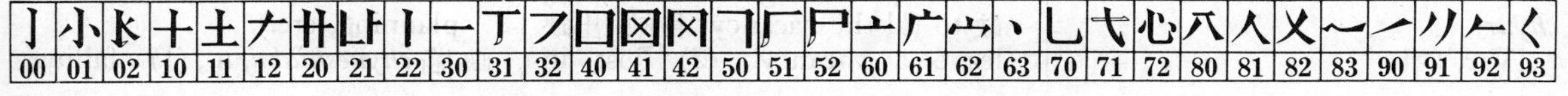

V.i. & adj. To labor incessantly: 劬劬, 劬碌 ditto; laborious and strenuous.

劬勞 *chyurlaur*, v. i., to labor hard (as parents for children).

夠 92S.50–9

gouh.

[Var. 够]

Adj. & adv. Enough, adequate(ly), sufficient(ly), to a high degree: 夠了 that's enough; 有夠 have enough; 沒夠, 不夠 not enough; 夠得很 more than sufficient; 夠朋友, 夠交情 good enough as a friend; 不夠朋友 do less than a friend should; 够面(子)(兒) enough of honor and respect ("face"); 够禮貌 be polite enough; 够客氣 be courteous enough; 够分兒 due honor; 夠數兒 adequate; 夠味兒 (of food) quite tasty, (of music, art or literature) highly pleasing and enjoyable, (of personal relations) pleasant enough; 夠狠 pretty hard-boiled, highhanded or exacting; 夠纏的 hard to deal with or get rid of; 夠壞 bad or wicked enough; 夠鬮兒 hardhearted enough; 夠吃 just enough to eat; 夠用 just enough to meet one's needs; 夠過兒 well-off enough in means; 够嚼裹兒 enough to eat and wear; 夠瞧的 (derog.) quite too much; 夠受 *-shouh*↓; 夠了, 夠了 enough! shut up! 我聽夠了 have heard enough.

夠本 *gouhbeen*, v.i., (1) be sufficient to cover the cost; (2) be worth the effort or money.

夠受 *gouhshouh*, v.t. & adj., (1) suffer enough; (2) more than enough to stand.

鴝 92S.50–9

chyur.

[Var. 鸜]

鴝鵒 *chyuryuh*, n., the mynah (coll. called 八哥).

鷂 92S.50–9

yauh.

N. (*-tz*) (1) The sparrow hawk: 鷂子翻身 do a somersault. (2) An eagle-shaped kite.

鷂鷹 *yauhying*, n., the sparrow hawk.

鷂魚 *yauhyur*, n., the ray (a fish).

§92S.70 (ㄥS/ㄴ)

飆 92S.70–4

yaur.

Adj. See 飄△飆 31S.70.

毓 92S.70–6

yuh.

[Var. of 育 60.42]

§92S.81 (ㄥS/人)

缺 92S.81–9

chyue.

N. (1) A vacancy, unoccupied post: 有缺, 沒缺 there is, is not, a vacancy; 空缺 a vacancy; 官缺 vacant post (in government); 補缺 to fill the vacancy; 開缺, 出缺 leave a vacancy. (2) Post in government: 肥缺, 美缺 a lucrative post; 閑缺 a sinecure, a post with nothing to do; 苦缺 poorly paid job. (3) A lack: 欠缺 shortcoming, s.t. wanting or lacking.

V.t. To be short of, to lack: 缺少 *-shaau*↓; 缺乏 *-far*↓; 缺錢, 缺食 lack money, food; 缺吃缺穿 have not enough for food and clothing; 缺穿, 缺戴 (of woman) not adequately dressed; 缺水 (of plants) need watering; 缺一門 short of one category; 缺三十塊錢 thirty dollars short or need thirty dollars to make an amount.

Adj. (1) Missing, cracked, crippled: 殘缺不全 (set of books) incomplete, (person) crippled; see 缺齒兒, 缺口 *-chee'l*, *-koou*↓. (2) Short in sense of shortcoming: 缺點, 缺憾, 缺陷 *-diaan*, *-hahn*, *-shiahn*↓. (3) (Of person) lacking in conscience: 這人眞缺, 他缺極了 this man is very unscrupulous (really short for 缺德 *-der*↓).

缺齒兒 *chyue-chee'l*, adj., with front teeth missing.

缺欠 *chyuechiahn*, v.t., to be short of (things, cash, etc.); to owe.

缺脣 *chyue-churn*, adj., harelipped.

缺德 *chyue-der*, adj., unscrupulous, wicked, without conscience.

缺點 *chyuediaan*, n., a shortcoming, a lack.

缺額 *chyue-er*, n., a vacancy.

缺乏 *chyuefar*, n. & v.t., a lack; to lack.

缺分 *chyue'fen*, n., a vacant post to be filled.

缺憾 *chyuehahn*, n., an imperfection.

缺刻葉 *chyueke-yeh*, n., (bot.) incised leaf.

缺課 *chyue-keh*, phr., to miss a class.

缺口 *chyuekoou*, adj., (1) (also 缺口兒) a crack (as in a teacup); (2) see *-tzueei*↓.

缺少 *chyueshaau*, n. & v.t. & adj., lack, lacking (in funds, talent, planning, etc.).

缺陷 *chyueshiahn*, n., (1) a failing;

(2) a shortcoming: 缺陷美 charm of some special characteristic or imperfection.

缺席 *chyue-shir*, v.i., to be absent at meeting.

缺嘴 *chyue-tzueei*, adj., (1) (child) never stops eating, loves eating; (2) harelipped; (3) (teapot) with a broken sprout.

餤 92S.81-9

yahn.

[Var. of 焰 91D.21]

§ 92S.82 (ᅩS/乂)

皺 92S.82-2

jouh.

[Cf. 縐 93B.50]

V.t. To wrinkle up, wrinkled: 皺眉 knit one's brow.

Adj. Knitted, wrinkled (face), crinkled up (dress); 皺紋 *-wern* ↓; 皺紙 crinkled paper; 皺皺巴巴 (of face, etc.) wrinkled, creased.

皺摺 *jouhjer*, n., crease (in dress, etc.).

皺胃 *jouhweih*, n., the maw (fourth stomach) of cud-chewing animal.

皺紋(兒) *jouhwern(-wer'l)*, n., crease (in face, dress).

矱 92S.82-2

huoh.

N. 榘矱 (AC) rule.

敂 92S.82-2

kouh.

[Var. of 叩 40S.22]

敏 92S.82-9

miin.

Adj. (1) Quick in understanding, feeling, response: 聰敏 bright, clever. (2) (AC) diligent: 敏以求之 work hard to get it (knowledge).

敏感 *miingan*, (1) n., allergy; (2) adj., very sensitive.

敏慧 *miinhueih*, adj., quick in understanding.

敏捷 *miinjier*, adj., quick in action or understanding, agile: 做事敏捷 quick and efficient.

§ 92S.93 (ᅩS/く)

矮 92S.93-9

aai.

N. A dwarf, a short person: 矮子 ditto: 矮人看(觀)場 a short person applauds or boos with audience in theatre although he cannot see the play—(fig.) lacking independent judgment, restricted in outlook.

Adj. Low (stool, house): 矮牆淺屋 a low or crowded house; 矮叭叭 *-baba*, 矮矬矬 *-tsuortsuor*, descriptive of shortness (of person, etc.); 矮顛顛兒的 *-diandia'l-de*, humble, self-effacing.

矮個(兒)(子) *aaigeh('l)('tz)*, n., a short person.

矮子 *aai'tz*, n., a dwarfish person.

SECTION 93

§ 93.00 (く/亅)

孥 93.00

nur.

N. (AC) collective term for one's children, or wife and children: 孥戮 punishment by the execution of all members of a family; 妻孥 wife and children.

拏 93.00

nar.

[Pop. var. 拿]

V.t. (1) (AC) drag, pull along. (2) To arrest: 拏問 arrest and interrogate, see 拿 81.00.

孿 93.00

lyuarn.

孿生 *lyuarnsheng*, n., twin: 孿生子 twin children; 孿生兄弟 twin brothers.

攣 93.00

lyuarn (liahn).

N. & adj. Bending, bent: 攣腰 bent back; 攣其手足 hands and feet bent—as with rheumatism; 拘攣 bent in disease; 痙攣 spasm of limbs.

缺 餤 皺 矱 敂 敏 矮 孥 拏 孿 攣

§ 93.01 (ㄑ/小)

枲 93.01

shii.

N. 枲麻 *shiimar*, (bot.) the male hemp, *Cannabis sativa*, as 苧麻 is the female hemp—species which produce marijuana.

巢 93.01

chaur.

N. (1) Bird nest: 鳥巢 ditto; 巢居 when people lived on trees—a stage of civilization in Chin. legend. (2) Thieves' lair or den.

巢窟 *chaurkuh*, n., thieves' den.
巢穴 *chaurshyueh*, n., ditto.

絮 93.01

shyuh.

N. A tassel-like cluster on certain plants: 柳絮 willow catkins; 棉絮 loose cotton; 棉絮被褥 cotton-padded quilt (and mattress); 蘆絮 rush flower.

Adj. Unending: 絮絮不休 a continuous endless talk, also v.i., to jabber continuously; 絮煩 *-'fan* ↓; 煩絮 tedious.

絮叨 *shyuh'dau*, v. i., to prattle, chatter, also 絮叨叨.
絮煩 *shyuh'fan*, adj., (1) tedious; (2) bored: 這齣戲我都聽絮煩了 I am bored with this opera.
絮聒 *shyuhgua*, v. i., to chatter endlessly; to bother (s. o.) with continuous pleas.
絮絮 *shyuhshyuh*, v. i. & adj., to babble, engage in a low-keyed continuous talk.
絮語 *shyuhyuu*, n., gossip, endless chatter.

樂 93.01

leh (happy; **yueh*, music; **yauh*, to like).

N. (1) (**yueh*) Music: 樂器, 樂譜 *-chih*, *-puu* ↓; 樂隊 *-dueih* ↓; 奏樂 play music; 交響樂 symphony; 室內樂 chamber music; 管絃樂 string and flute; 搖滾樂 rock-'n'-roll music; 爵士樂 jazz; 聲樂 vocal music; 器樂 instrumental music; 聖樂 sacred music; 教會音樂 church music. (2) (**yueh*) A surname. (3) Pleasure; enjoyment: 快樂, 安樂 ditto; 享樂 enjoy life; 取樂, 作樂 amuse oneself: 苦中作樂 try to be happy amidst adverse circumstances.

V.t. (1) (**yauh*, re. pr. of certain classic phrr.) To love (s.t.): 仁者樂山, 智者樂水 a true man loves the mountains, a wise man loves the sea; 樂羣 *-chyurn* ↓. (2) To love, enjoy: 樂善好施 love to do philanthropic work; 樂此不疲 love, enjoy doing s.t. without stop.

Adj. Happy, glad, enjoying oneself: 你樂不樂 are you happy? 我真樂 I am most happy; 小孩樂了 the child smiles; 安樂, 快樂, 歡樂 happy; 樂不可支 "unbearably," extremely happy; 樂不思蜀 phr., so happy as to forget home country; 樂極生悲 phr., joy gives place to sorrow; 樂天知命 phr., contented with one's lot; 樂觀 *-guan* ↓.

Adv. Gladly, happily, glad to, happy to: 樂於從命 most happy to obey; 樂於, 樂得 *-'yu*, *-'de* ↓; 樂助 glad to help, gladly help; 非我所樂聞 not what I would like to hear, i.e., I disapprove.

樂器 **yuehchih*, n., musical instrument.
樂處 *leh-chuh*, n., s.t. one enjoys, pleasure: 沒有樂處 no pleasure in it.
樂羣 **yauhchyurn* (*leh-*), phr., group play, group life as part of education.
樂曲 **yuehchyuu*, n., a melody, a musical composition.
樂得 *leh-der* (*-'de*), adj., happy to have the chance to: 樂得逍遙自在 happy to live one's own life; 樂得白吃 happy to eat without pay; 樂得作個順水人情 glad to do s.t. regarded as a favor without trouble to oneself.
樂典 **yuehdiaan*, n., musicological works.
樂隊 **yuehdueih*, n., orchestra: 軍樂隊 military band; 交響樂隊 symphony orchestra; 爵士樂隊 jazz band.
樂府 **yuehfuu*, n., anc. songs for court entertainment, esp. Hahn and Jihn Dyns.
樂觀 *lehguan*, n. & adj., optimism; optimistic.
樂國 *lehguor*, n., a paradise.
樂戶 **yuehhuh*, n., anc. singer or musician under government control, later professional musician, also professional prostitute.
樂章 **yuehjang*, n., a musical composition; a song composition.
樂境 *leh-jihng*, n., happy situation, surroundings.
樂兒 *leh'l*, n., (1) 招樂兒, 逗樂兒 try to win laughter of child or audience; (2) some kind of enjoyment: 找樂兒, 取樂兒 seek distraction; 這不是甚麼個樂兒 this is nothing to enjoy.
樂利 *leh-lih*, n., profit and pleasure.
樂理 **yueh-lii*, n., theory of music.
樂譜 **yueh-puu*, n., musical score, score sheets.
樂輸 *leh-shu*, v.t., volunteer to contribute (money, effort).
樂施 *leh-shy*, phr., philanthropic.
樂事 *leh-shyh*, n., a happy event; s.t. one enjoys.
樂天 *lehtian*, adj., as in 樂天知命 contented with one's lot; acceptance of fate and happy about it.

樂從 *leh-tsurng*, v.t., happily obey, follow.
樂土 *lehtuu*, n., a paradise.
樂紋兒 *lehwer'l*, n., a dimple.
樂業 *leh-yeh*, n., professional enthusiasm.
樂意 *lehyih*, v.t. & adj., willing, to like: 看你樂意不樂 see if you are willing, if you like it.
樂於 *leh'yu*, v.i., happy to (do).
樂園 *lehyuarn*, n., a paradise; 兒童樂園 children's playground.
樂育 *lehyuh*, n., education in games, recreation, healthy sports.

欒 93.01

luarn.

N. (1) Name of a tree. (2) Part of cornice above pillar. (3) A surname.

§93.02 (ㄑ/ㄎ)

叅 93.02

tsan.
[Pop. of 參 93.91]

饗 93.02

shiaang.
[Interch. 享 60.00]

V.i. & t. (1) To enjoy food; to give dinner to (people): 饗飲 enjoy offered food and drink; 以饗讀者 (fig.) to present to the readers. (2) To give sacrificial dinner (of spirits): 尚饗 (end of sacrificial prayer) hope you will deign to taste the sacrifices.

§93.10 (ㄑ/十)

牟 93.10

mour.

N. (1) A surname. (2) (AC) barley＝麰 10S.10.

V.i. & t. (1) Get: 牟利 try to earn profits＝謀利. (2) (MC) moo (of cows).

斚 93.10

jiaa.
[Var. of 斝 40.10]

§93.20 (ㄑ/廾)

弁 93.20

biahn.

N. (1) (AC) cap. (2) Non-commissioned officer: 武弁 (AC) patrol leader, sergeant.

Adj. (AC) trembling with fear.

弁髦 *biahnmaur*, n., (LL) worthless stuff; v. t., regard as worthless: 弁髦榮華 spurn worldly honors and comfort.
弁冕 *biahnmiaan*, n., (AC) formal cap; (fig.) the top (of scholars, etc.).
弁目 *biahnmuh*, n., (MC) patrol leader, sergeant.
弁言 *biahnyarn*, n., foreword.

§93.21 (ㄑ/ㄴ)

巒 93.21

luarn.

N. Mountain or hill range: 層巒疊嶂 multiple ranges of hills; 峯巒 number of peaks.

§93.22 (ㄑ/丨)

帑 93.22

nur (**taang*).

N. (1) AC var. of 孥 93.00. (2) (**taang*) Vault where public funds are kept; public funds: 帑藏 (*taangtsahng*) treasury; 耗費公帑 waste of public funds.

帤 93.22

rur.

N. (Archery) piece of supporting wood serving to tighten a bow.

§93.30 (ㄑ/一)

鑾 93.30

luarn.

N. (1) Bell on horse or carriage. (2) 鑾駕, 鑾輿 imperial carriage, sedan chair; 金鑾殿 an imperial palace; 鑾鈴 bell on imperial carriage.

§ 93.40 (ㄑ/口)

台 93.40

tair.

[Oft. used for phonetic value in place of 臺, such as 台灣 Taiwan]

N. (1) Term of respectful address in letters, equiv. 先生, in place of the more direct "you," "your": 台鑒, 台覽, 台照 your perusal (of this letter); 台察 your consideration; 兄台 (court.) you; 台教 your advice; 謹尊台命 obey your instructions; 台駕 your presence, arrival ("carriage"). (2) Common and gen. var. of 臺 11.11. (3) (*yir*) (AC) I, first person (＝予). (4) An erected structure: 地台 terrace; 月台, 講台 platform; 舞台 stage.

台步 *tair-buh*, n., prescribed gait, measured steps, in Chin. opera.
台端 *tairduan*, n., you, your esteemed self (chiefly in correspondence).
台風 *tairfeng*, n., stage manners.
台甫 *tairfuu*, n., (court.) your name.
台柱(子) *tairjuh(tz)*, n., important actor in troupe or cast.
台銜 *tairshiarn*, n., your rank.
台詞 *tair-tsyr*, n., stage dialogue; recitative.

砮 93.40

nuu.

N. Stone arrowhead.

轡 93.40

peih.

N. Reins and bridle.

§ 93.41 (ㄑ/図)

畚 93.41

been.

畚插 *beencha*, n., bin for soil, etc.
畚斗 *berndoou*, n., dustbin.
畚箕 *beenji*, n., flat basket for grain, etc.

響 93.41

shiaang.

[Pop. 响]

N. A sound.

V.i. & t. (1) To make a sound: 喇叭響了 the bugle call is sounded; 鐘響 the clock strikes the hour; 不聲不響 (person) does not make a sound, without revealing movement, or makes no reply. (2) To echo: 反△響 90.82 reponse; 影△響 41S.91 effect: 響應 *-yihng* ↓.

Adj. (1) Loud: 響亮 *-liahng* ↓: 響得很 it's very loud; 太響了 too loud; 響一點 make it louder. (2) Having effect: 他到那兒都叫得響 his name carries weight wherever he goes.

響器 *shiaang-chih*, n., musical instruments, like brass, cymbals, gongs, drums; 響器店 shop selling such.
響晴 *shiaangchirng*, adj., (sky) clear and bright.
響尺 *shiarng-chyy*, n., a wooden clapper keeping rhythm of steps for coffin carriers.
響動兒 *shiaang'dung'l*, n., noise of movement.
響房 *shiaang-farng*, n., a custom of having music and drums played in bridal chamber on wedding day before the wedding.
響喚 *shiaang'huan*, v. i., to call aloud.
響箭 *shiaang-jiahn*, n., a whistling arrow.
響炕 *shiaang-kang*, n., (North China) earthen bed (see 炕 91D.70) heated from outside and empty below.
響亮 *shiaangliahng*, adj., (1) loud and clear, vociferous; (2) forthright; 響亮人 (coll.) forthright person.
響鈴(兒) *shiaanglirng('l)*, n., a bell.
響螺 *shiaangluor*, n., conch shell, sometimes used in trumpet call.
響馬 *shiaangmaa*, n., (North China) bandits, who shoot whistling arrows to announce their coming.
響聲兒 *shiaangsheng'l*, n., a sound.
響鐵 *shiarngtiee*, n., good-quality iron.
響銅 *shiaangturng*, n., good quality copper or brass.
響尾蛇 *shiaangweei-sher*, n., rattlesnake.
響音兒 *shiaangye'l*, n., a sound.
響應 *shiaangyihng*, n. & v.t., response; to respond, do s.t. in response to.

§ 93.42 (ㄑ/冈)

嚮 93.42

shiaang.

V.t. To face; hence (prep.), facing, toward (see var. 向 91.42).

嚮晨 *shiaangchern*, adv., toward dawn.

嚮導 *shiaangdauh*, (1) v. t., to act as guide, to lead; (2) n., a guide.
嚮晦 *shiaanghueei*, adv., at dusk.
嚮明 *shiaangmirng*, adv., toward dawn.
嚮往 *shiarngwaang*, v. t., to yearn for, be attracted to, admire (person, the past).
嚮午 *shiarngwuu*, adv., toward noon.

臠 93.42

luarn (also *lyuarn*).

N. A slice of meat: 禁臠 forbidden slice of meat, inaccessible woman, object of unattainable desire (Eng. "forbidden fruit").

---

§ 93.50 (ㄑ/乛)

弩 93.50

nuu.

N. (1) A crossbow: 弩砲 stone-missiles released from a crossbow; 弩弓 a crossbow; 弩手, 弩牙 *-shoou, -yar* ↓; 劍拔弩張 with swords drawn and crossbows set, hence, ready to fight; 強弩之末 (lit. & fig.) be exhausted in strength. (2) (Chin. callig.) a downward stroke (generally wr. 努 93.50).

弩手 *nurshoou*, n., soldier with crossbow.
弩牙 *nuryar*, n., an attachment on string holding and releasing a crossbow.

努 93.50

nuu.

V.i. (1) To strive, make an effort: 努力 *-lih* ↓. (2) To pout: 努嘴 *-tzueei* ↓. (3) 努目 *-muh* ↓.

努勁兒 *nuujieh'l*, v.i., make an effort, strive hard.
努力 *nuulih*, v.i., strive, endeavor.
努目 *nuumuh*, v.i., to stare as if the eyes would pop out.
努嘴(兒) *nurtzueei(-tzuee'l)*, v.i., to signal with one's lips, usu. pointing to some object.

駑 93.50

nur.

Adj. Dull in intelligence: 駑鈍, 駑下 *-duhn, -shiah* ↓.

駑鈍 *nurduhn*, adj., dull and worthless, stupid.
駑馬 *nurmaa*, n., a nag, mediocre horse.
駑下 *nurshiah*, adj., dull (person).
駑駘 *nurtair*, n., ditto; (fig.) a good-for-nothing person.

彎 93.50

wan.

[Pop. 弯]

N. adjunct. 一彎新月 a new moon.

N. A bend (road, river); cf. 灣 63A.50.

V.i. & t. To bend (a bow, wire).

Adj. Bent.

彎曲 *wanchyu*, adj., bent, curving, -ed.
彎彎 *wanwan*, adj., as in 彎彎曲曲 see *-chyu* ↑.

鷥 93.50

sy.

N. See 鷺^鷥 40.50, the egret.

鸞 93.50

luarn.

N. (1) A fabulous bird, male phoenix: 鸞鳳和鳴 happy, harmonious marriage; 鸞鳳 married couple, also distingnished talents. (2) Interch. 鑾: 鸞輿 imperial sedan chair or carriage.

---

§ 93.63 (ㄑ/丶)

熊 93.63

shyurng.

N. A bear: 人熊 brown bear; 狗熊 small black bear; 白熊 white bear; 北極熊 arctic bear; 熊膽 gall of bear, used as medicine; 熊蹯, 熊掌 bear's paw, considered a delicacy; 熊虎之將 brave general.

熊貓 *shyurngmau*, n., (zoo.) panda.
熊羆 *shyurng-pir*, n., (AC) different kinds of bear, a phr. denoting great fighters.
熊熊 *shyurngshyurng*, adj., (of light, fire) flaming, scintillating.

熊丸 *shyurng-warn*, phr., (allu.) a pill of bear's paw used by a mother who made her son chew it during studies at night—hence a mother's instruction.

熊蟻 *shyurngyii*, n., a large ant, *Camponotus marginasus*.

§93.70 (ㄑ/乚)

允 93.70

yuun.

V.i. & t. Approve, give consent: 不允 will not give permission.

Adj. & adv. Just right, rightly: 允洽, 允當 *-shiar*, *-dahng*↓; 允文允武 both good in civil and in military affairs.

允當 *yuundahng*, adj., properly placed (words, decision), put just right: 是非允當 just appraisal of right and wrong.

允恭 *yuungung*, adj., honest and dutiful.

允准 *yurnjuun*, v. i., to grant permission.

允諾 *yuunnuoh*, v. i., to promise.

允洽 *yuunshiar*, adj., (decision, settlement) proper, fair, well settled.

允許 *yurnshyuu*, v. i., to give permission.

允從 *yuuntsurng*, v. t., promise to follow (suggestion).

邕 93.70

yung.

V.t. U. f. 雍 to block up.

Adj. Harmonious, peaceful: 邕邕.

§93.71 (ㄑ/七)

幾 93.71

ji (*jii).

N. (*ji*) Omen, auspices: 幾兆 *-jauh*↓; 幾微 *-weir*↓.

Adj. (1) (*jii) A few, how many: 幾何 *-her*; 幾許 *-shyuu*↓; 幾時 *-shyr*↓; 幾歲 only a few years old; 幾塊錢 a few dollars, how many dollars? 幾萬人 tens of thousands of people; 幾個 just a few; 幾點鐘 a few hours; 幾度 a few degrees. (2) (*ji*) 未幾 shortly thereafter; 無幾 not many, only a few; 幾希 *-shi*↓.

Adv. (1) Nearly, almost: 幾乎 *-(')hu*, 幾幾 *-ji*↓; 幾不欲生 almost despaired of living; 幾於 *-yur*↓; 庶幾 well-nigh, not far from. (2) Gently, softly: 幾諫 *-jiahn*↓.

幾殆 *jidaih*, adj., extremely precarious, dangerous.

幾頓 *jiduhn*, adj., (LL) in danger.

幾多 *jiiduo, adj., how much or many?

幾何 *jiiher, (1) n., (math.) short for geometry: 幾何學; (2) adj., how many?

幾乎 *ji(')hu*, adv., almost, nearly, within a trifle of.

幾兆 *jijauh*, n., premonition, portent, augury.

幾幾 *jiji*, adv., approximately, almost: 幾幾乎 within an ace of.

幾諫 *jijiahn*, v. t., gently remonstrate with one's parents.

幾兒 *jii'l, adv., when, what time: 你幾兒來 when are you coming?

幾希 *jishi*, (1) adj., a bit of, few, rare; (2) adv., nearly, by a narrow margin: 相去幾希 very nearly the same, little difference.

幾時 *jiishyr, adv., when?

幾許 *jirshyuu, adj., how many (are there)?

幾曾 *jiitserng, adv. phr., (rhet.) was it ever so? has it ever happened?

幾微 *jiweir*, n., (1) portent, omen; (2) niceties.

幾於 *jiyur*, adv., almost, at the point of, well-nigh, see *-(')hu*↑.

畿 93.71

ji (*chir*).

N. (1) The royal domain, the district in and around the royal capital: 近畿 in the vicinity of the royal capital; 京畿 the capital city; see compp.↓. (2) The threshold or the space inside.

畿甸 *jidiahn*, n., the royal domain, royal suburbs.

畿輔 *jifuu*, n., the royal capital and surrounding districts.

§93.72 (ㄑ/心)

怠 93.72

daih.

V.i. & adj. To idle, neglect (work); be idle, lazy, careless in work: 懈怠 ditto.

怠惰 *daihduoh*, v.i. & t., to slacken in work; adj., slack, idle.

怠工 *daih-gung*, n. & v.i., go-slow or sit-down strike.

怠忽 *daihhu*, v.t., neglect (duty).

怠慢 *daihmahn*, v.i. & t., receive guest without due attention: (court.) 怠慢, 怠慢 my apologies for lack of attention in my house (said to departing guest).

怒 93.72

nuh.

N. & adj. Angry, angered, anger: 忿怒, 憤怒, 狂怒, 暴怒, 盛怒, 大怒 great anger, fury; 怒容, 怒色 angry countenance; 怒目 angry look; 怒火中燒 burning with anger; 老羞成怒 lose temper from embarrassment; 發怒 be angered; 怒濤, 怒潮 angry waves, tides; 怒馬 spirited horse.

Adv. Madly: 怒號 scream aloud; 草木怒生 plants burst out in profusion; 心花怒放 mad with joy, elated.

怒氣 *nuhchih*, n., wrath, anger, rage, fury: 怒氣沖沖 in a great rage; 怒氣塡胸 filled with fury.

恕 93.72

shuh.

N. Consideration for others in moral conduct: 忠恕之道 the doctrine of loyalty and consideration for others; forgiveness; principle of reciprocity.

V.t. To forgive: 寬恕, 饒恕 ditto; 恕不奉陪 please pardon my inability to attend.

恕道 *shuh-dauh*, n., the principle of reciprocity, do unto others as you wish others to do unto you.
恕過 *shuh-guoh*, v. t., pardon the mistake.
恕罪 *shuh-tzueih*, v. i., to forgive offense, sin or crime: 請恕罪 please pardon the mistake.

態 93.72

taih.

N. (1) Attitude: 態度 *-duh*↓. (2) Form, demeanor: 體態 figure, demeanor: 體態輕盈 young, lissom figure; 儀態 personal appearance, charming deportment or expression: 姿態 outward looks, charm of figure. (3) Condition: 常態, 變態 normal, abnormal condition; 狀態 condition, situation, appearance; 動態 a state of flux, recent changes: 人口動態 population movements.

態度 *taihduh*, n., attitude (toward person, subject).

戀 93.72

liahn.

N. A surname.

N. & v.t. Love (s. o.), be enamored with: see 戀愛 *-aih*, 戀人 *-rern*, 戀歌 *-ge*, 戀情 *-chirng*↓; 戀舊 remember fondly the past; 戀家 long for home; 懷戀 think constantly of, remember fondly (home, country, parents); 戀戀不捨 very unwilling to part with (lover, friend); 熱戀, 癡戀 madly in love; 單戀 unrequited or one-sided love; 失戀 disappointed love.

戀愛 *liahn-aih*, n. & v. t., love, be in love with (s. o.): 戀愛故事 (小說) love story.
戀情 *liarnchirng*, n., love between man and woman.
戀歌 *liarnge*, n., love song.
戀棧 *liahn-jahn*, v. i., cling to official post when one should leave.
戀舊 *liahn-jiouh*, v. i., think constantly of old (country, home).
戀慕 *liahnmuh*, v. t., be enamored with, love at a distance or silently.
戀人 *liahnrern*, n., lover.

§ 93.80 (く/八)

貟 93.80

yuarn.

[Anc. var. of 員 40.80]

§ 93.81 (く/人)

矣 93.81

yii.

Fin. part. (LL) (1) has the force of exclamation, or of reinforcing a statement like Eng. "indeed": 吾老矣 I am really getting old; 甚矣吾衰也 ditto; 已矣 alas, it is finished! indeed: 鮮矣仁 (AC) indeed rarely are such people true men. (2) Has the sense of completion (=modn. 了 already): 離家十八年矣 it is already eighteen years since (he) left home; 吾必謂之學矣 I will say that he is already (really) educated (though he may not be able to read). (3) 而已矣, 耳矣 reinforcing 而已 and 耳 only, merely.

災 93.81

tzai.

N. Disaster, calamity: 災禍, 災患, 災殃 natural disaster; 災難 *-nahn*↓; 災害 *-haih*↓; 災變 portents of impending disaster; 災病, 災疫 a pestilence; 災情 damage done by natural disaster; 受災 be stricken by disaster; 多災多難 ill-starred, always dogged by misfortune; 災民, 災黎, 災胞 victims (of a disaster); 賑災, 救災 disaster relief; 消災 propitiate the gods, be generous to avoid trouble; 天災 natural calamity; 水災 floods; 火災, 風災 (destruction done by) fire, wind storm.

災區 *tzai-chyu*, n., disaster area.
災分(兒) *tzai'fen(-fe'l)*, n., a misfortune, mishap, unlucky accident.
災害 *tzai-haih*, n., (damage done by) natural disaster.
災荒 *tzai-huang*, n., crop failure due to drought or floods.
災難 *tzainahn*, n., misfortune, calamity, catastrophe, tribulations.
災祥 *tzaishiarng*, n., an omen of good or evil fortune.
災異 *tzaiyih*, n., visitations of nature, unusual astronomical phenomena.

炱 93.81

tair.

N. Soot: 烟炱.

§ 93.82 (ㄑ/ㄨ)

變 93.82

biahn.
[Pop. 変, 变]

N. (1) Change: as in 改變, 變更 change (of text, policy, goal, customs, etc.). (2) Rebellion, turmoil, disaster: 兵變, 譁變 mutiny, revolt; 民變, 叛變 people's revolt; 災變 natural disaster, strange natural phenomenon (earthquake, appearance of comet, etc.); 變亂不測 sudden disaster rises out of nowhere, changes unpredicated; 變亂, 變故 *-luahn, -guh* ↓. (3) Adaptation to circumstances: 機變 n. & adj., ability to adapt oneself, shrewdness; 隨機應變 change tactics, make decisions on the spot.

V.i. & t. (1) To change, become, grow, be transformed: 變好, 變壞, 變多, 變少, 變黃, 變白 grow, better, worse, more, less, yellow, white; oft. with vb. complements: 變成, 變爲, 變了 change into: 變成什麽 what has it become? 變爲飛蛾 transform into a moth; 變了樣子 change shape or attitude (as among friends), lose original shape; 變色 change countenance; 變志 change loyalty to state or lover; 她變心了 her heart has changed; 女人善變 a woman's heart is changeable. (2) To perform: 變魔術, 變戲法 perform magic.

變產 *biahn-chaan*, v. i., sell out estate.
變遷 *biahnchian*, v. i., change in trend, conditions.
變動 *biahnduhng*, n. & v. i., upset, fluid or drastic change, as 時代的變動 changes in the times; 變動權 right of alteration.
變法 *biahn-faa*, n. & v. i., political reform; to reform; 變法維新 reform of 1898; 變法兒 *-faa'l* think of other ways and means.
變更 *biahngeng*, n., change of course of action.
變革 *biahnger*, n. & v.i., change for the new (in system, policy).
變故 *biahnguh*, n., any untoward change or turn of events.
變宮 *biahn-gung*, n., (mus.) *do* sharp.
變化 *biahnhuah*, n. & v. i., changes in form or character, vicissitudes: 變化無常 constantly changing (tides and fortunes); 千變萬化 unending changes.
變價 *biahn-jiah*, v. i., sell out.
變節 *biahn-jier*, n. & v. i., change of loyalty; (of a widow) remarry, (of politician) switch loyalty.
變種 *biahn-juung*, n., (biol.) mutation.
變質 *biahn-jyr*, v. i., change in character, spoil, deteriorate (of medicine, contents, ideals).
變局 *biahn-jyur*, n., turn of events, such as political upheaval.
變徵 *biahn-jyy*, n., (mus.) *sol* flat.
變亂 *biahnluahn*, n., turmoil in country.
變賣 *biahnmaih*, n. & v.t., sell out (estate, store).
變弄 *biahn-nuhng*, v.i. & t., contrive to get (s. t.).
變色 *biahn-seh*, v. i., change countenance; change color.
變相 *baihn-shiahng*, n., & v. i., change in appearance or in essential character: 變相了 has changed greatly (for the worse).
變性 *biahn-shihng*, n. & v. i., change character; change sex; 變性(退化)的 adj., degenerative.
變形蟲 *biahnshirng-churng*, n., (zoo.) amoeba.
變數 *biahn-shuh*, n., (math.) variable.
變速運動 *biahnsuh yuhnduhng*, n., (phys.) variable motion.
變態 *biahn-taih*, n., change of character or attitude; (biol.) metamorphosis; adj., abnormal: 變態心理 abnormal psychology.
變天 *biahn-tian*, v. i., (weather) turn overcast, as 變天了.
變通 *biahntung*, v. i., change method: 變通辦理 do it another way, or by circumventing rules.
變造 *biahntzauh*, n., (law) change in value of property (checks) owing to alterations; v. t., to make such changes.
變壓器 *biahnya-chih*, n., transformer.
變樣 *biahn-yahng*, v. i., (of person) change attitude, grow bad.
變異 *biahnyih*, n., as in 突然變異 (biol.) mutation.

§ 93.83 (ㄑ/ㄧ)

巡 93.83

shyurn.
[Pop. 廵]

N. One round of drinks: 酒一巡.

V.i. & t. Mostly in compp. (1) To patrol: 巡邏, 巡警, 巡哨, 巡夜 *-luor*, *-jiing*, *-shauh*, *-yeh* ↓. (2) To go on circuit and inspect: 巡查, 巡視, etc. *-char*, *-shyh* ↓. (3) To pass around: 巡杯, 巡壺兒 *-bei*, *-hur'l* ↓; 巡指間 *-jyyjian* ↓.

巡按 *shyurn-ahn*, n., (in Manchu Dyn.) inspector-general of a province.

巡杯 *shyurn-bei*, v. i., to drink individually to guests around the table.

巡捕 *shyurnbuu*, n., (1) old term for police or sheriff officer; (2) formerly, police in foreign concessions; (3) v. t., (MC) to catch (thieves).

巡查 *shyurnchar*, v. i. & t., to patrol (an area).

巡緝 *shyurnchih*, v. i., to patrol against thieves and smugglers.

巡風 *shyurn-feng*, n., formerly, the look-out man of thieves during theft.

巡撫 *shyurnfuu*, n., (in Manchu Dyn.) provincial military governor; cf. 總△督 93B.72, governor, viceroy.

巡更 *shyurn-geng*, v. i., to keep watch.

巡官 *shyurn-guan*, n., police inspector.

巡功 *shyurn-gung*, v. i., formerly, (the emperor) makes a tour of inspection.

巡廻 *shyurnhueir*, v. i. & t., to go around (place); to patrol (area); make circuits of: 巡廻圖書館 a mobile library; 巡廻法庭 circuit court.

巡壺兒 *shyurn-hur'l*, v. i., to pass the wine pot around among guests.

巡靖 *shyurnjihng*, v. t., to pacify (area with rebel units).

巡警 *shyurnjiing*, (1) n., police; (2) v. t., (MC) to patrol, take alert measures.

巡指間 *shyurnjyyjian*, adv., (MC) at the snap of a finger, in a short moment: 巡指間春又秋 in a short time spring passes into autumn; cf. 旋△踵 60S.83.

巡禮 *shyurnlii*, n. & v. i., orig. to make a pilgrimage to holy place, now generally to make a tour; n., (somewhat rhet.) a survey.

巡邏 *shyurnluor*, n. & v.t., a patrol; to patrol (area), set up patrol.

巡哨 *shyurnshauh*, n., (mil.) sentry, sentinel.

巡幸 *shyurnshihng*, v. i. & t., formerly, (of an emperor) make a tour of visits of different places; cf. 幸 11.10; v. t., (emperor) visits.

巡錫 *shyurnshir*, v.i., (Buddhist monk) travel around (with 錫杖 pewter stick).

巡行 *shyurnshirng*, v. i., to go on circuit, to patrol.

巡狩 *shyurnshouh*, v. i., formerly, (of emperor) visit the different feudal states (euphem. called 狩 to go on a hunt).

巡視 *shyurnshyh*, v. t., to go around and inspect.

巡洋艦 *shyurnyarn-jiahn*, n., a cruiser.

巡夜 *shyurn-yeh*, v. i., to keep night watch.

迨 93.83

daih.

V.t. U.f. 逮 to arrest.

Prep. (LL) until: 迨後 until later; 迨於 (迨至) until today (also 逮 22.83); 迨冰未泮 (AC) before ice melts.

逡 93.83

chyun.

逡巡 *chyunshyurn*, v. i., to loiter about, to hang back (also wr. 逡循).

邋 93.83

lar (**lieh*).

邋邋 **lieh-lieh*, (of flags or banners) waving.

邋遢 *lar'ta*, adj., (1) dirty, untidy, slovenly; also 邋裏邋遢 *larlilar'ta*, ditto; (2) strolling along.

§ 93.91 (く/ノ)

參 93.91

tsan (**tsen*, **shen*, **chen*, **san*). [Abbr. 参]

N. (1) (**shen*) 人參 jinseng; 洋參 jinseng produced in America. (2) (**shen*) 海參 *bêche-de-mer*, sea cucumba, a delicacy. (3) (**shen*) Name of star: 參商 *-shang* ↓. (4) (**san*) Used in place of 三 in "capital" writing (checks) to avoid mistakes.

V.i. & t. (1) To take part in: 參加, 參預 (與) *-jia*, *-yuh* ↓; 參觀 *-guan* ↓. (2) To pay respects (to high officials only): 參拜, 參見, 參謁 *-baih*, *-jiahn*, *-yeh* ↓. (3) To soar aloft: 樹木參天, 參天古木 old trees that reach into the skies. (4) (Budd.) to penetrate (truth), to reach into the realm of understanding: 參悟, 參禪, 參透 *-wuh*, *-charn*, *-touh* ↓; 參破道理 see the truth; 參不破 (or 不透) cannot penetrate (a profundity). (5) To impeach (official): 參了他 impeached him; 參劾 *-her* ↓. (6) (MC) to recommend person to post: 參你作個教頭 recommended you as sergeant. (7) To study, examine: 參訂, 參考, 參驗 *-dihng*, *-kaau*, *-yahn* ↓.

Adj. (**tsen*) In 參差 *-tsy* ↓.

參
ㄙ
ㄠ
女

參半 *tsanbahn*, adj., half (of s.t.).
參拜 *tsanbaih*, v.t., to pay respects to (high official), worship (god).
參禪 *tsancharn*, v.i., to try to reach understanding of *Charn* (Zen); to practise meditation.
參訂 *tsandihng*, v.i., to revise text with editor's weighing of different versions or interpretations.
參膏 **shengau*, n., jinseng jelly, made from fibrous ends.
參觀 *tsanguan*, v.t., see as a tourist (famous places, museums, etc.), attend as observer (ceremonies, wedding, etc.).
參劾 *tsanher*, v.t., to impeach (person).
參政 *tsanjehng*, v.i., to participate in government (as people's delegates, councillor): 國民參政會 National Political Council; 參政權 suffrage; 婦女參政 women participate in government.
參加 *tsanjia*, v.t., to take part (in ceremonies, elections, any group action), contribute (opinion).
參見 *tsanjiahn*, v.t., see *-yeh* ↓.
參酌 *tsanjuor*, v.i. & t., to consult (persons, opinions), consult together.
參局 **shenjyur*, n., pharmacist specializing in jinseng, deer horns, etc.
參考 *tsankaau*, n. & v.t., reference (materials); to consult reference material: 參考資料 references for research; 作參考 for your reference.
參靈 *tsan-lirng*, n., ceremony of respect to the coffin before procession.
參謀 *tsanmour*, n., (mil.) staff officer: 參謀長 chief of staff.
參商 **shen-shang*, phr., the two stars Orion and Lucifer which never see each other; (fig.) (a) parting of friends for a long time; (b) (allu.) strife between brothers.
參透 *tsan-touh*, v.t., to penetrate, understand (mysteries, profundities).
參錯 *tsantsuoh* (**tsen-*), v.t. & adj., to shuffle about, shuffled, mixed-up, confusing, -ed; see *-wuu* ↓.
參差 **tsentsy*, adj., untrimmed, uneven in length; unsorted, mixed together.
參贊 *tsantzahn*, n., a councillor (in embassy, etc.); v.t., to act as advisor on project.
參佐 *tsantzuoo*, n., formerly, official advisors; v.t., to advise on matters.
參悟 *tsanwuh*, v.i., (Zen Budd.) to understand (mystery) from meditation, to see truth flash through the mind.
參伍 *tsanwuu*, v.t. & adj., as in 參伍錯綜 to shuffle together, shuffled, variegated.
參驗 *tsan yahn*, v.i., to verify (truth) by personal experience; to personally inspect.
參謁 *tsanyeh*, v.t., to pay respects to (high official, god).
參議 *tsanyih*, v.i., to partake in deliberations of policy; n., a senator; 參議院 the senate; 參議員 senator.
參預(與) *tsanyuh*, v.i. & t., to take part in (discussion, plan).

§ 93.93 (ㄑ/ㄑ)

ㄙ 93.93

sy (**moou*).

Adj. (1) Archaic for 私 90A.93, used as symbol for *s* in the phonetic script. (2) (**moou*) U.f. 某 a certain (person).

ㄠ 93.93

yau.

[Pop. 么]

N. (1) (Coll., esp. in dice games) the number "one": ㄠㄠ零三 1103. (2) A surname.

Adj. (AC, rare) small, insignificant: ㄠ麼 *-mor* ↓.

ㄠ二 *yau-eh*, n., term in dice games; a method of accounting in mahjong; (fig.) (Shanghai dial.) second-class prostitute.
ㄠ妹 *yaomeih*, n., the last born girl of same parents.
ㄠ麼 *yaumor*, adj., (AC) insignificant.

女 93.93

nyuu (**ruu*, **nyuh*).

Pron. (**ruu*) (AC) you (singular or plural, interch. 汝).

N. (1) (A member of) the female sex: 男女 men and women, of both sexes; attached freely to women of different profession: 女學生 girl student; 女記者 girl reporter; 女司機 a woman chauffeur or taxi driver; 女職員 a woman employee; 女朋友 girl friend; 女道士 a female Taoist priest; 女嬪相 bridesmaid; 女弟子 (LL) a female pupil; 女主人 hostess, mistress of home; 女侍 waitress; 女校書 (LL) singsong girl; 女作家 woman author; 女英雄 heroine; 女修士, 修女 a Catholic sister; 女光棍 a female gangster; 女扮男裝 girl dressed as boys (as on stage); 曠男怨女 men and women of marriageable age but unmarried; 烈女 a woman martyr, a married woman who commits suicide after the death of her husband or who dies in defense of her honor; 處女 a virgin; 美女 a beautiful girl; 少女 a young girl; 玉女 fairy damsel in heaven; 女青年會 Young Women's Christian Association (Y.W.C.A.). (2) A female child: 女兒 daughter; 子女 son and daughter; 長女 eldest daughter; 次女 second daughter; 養女 foster daughter; 義女 adopted daughter; 繼女 stepdaughter; 姪女 niece; 甥女 daughter of one's sister; 孫女 granddaughter.

V.t. (**nyuh*) (AC) to give one's daughter in marriage.

女伴 *nyuubahn*, n., a female companion.
女博士 *nyuu borshyh*, n., (1) a talented woman; (2) a woman with a doctor's degree.
女倩 *nyuuchiahn*, n., son-in-law (＝女婿).
女牆 *nyuuchiarng*, n., a parapet or battlements.
女氣 *nyuuchih*, n., femininity, effeminacy.
女權 *nyuuchyuarn*, n., woman's rights.
女弟 *nyuudih*, n., a younger sister; 女弟子 (LL) female disciple.
女兒 *nyuu-erl*, n., (1) girl; (2) daughter: 女兒寡 an unmarried girl or woman who chooses to remain single for life after the death of her fiancé; 女兒痨 tuberculosis believed to afflict an unmarried woman.
女夫 *nyuufu*, n., (LL) son-in-law (lit., daughter's husband).
女冠 *nyuu-guahn*, n., a female Taoist priest.
女官 *nyuu-guan*, n., formerly, a female court official.
女工 *nyuugung*, n., (1) a woman worker; (2) work such as sewing and embroidery, traditionally done by women (＝女紅).
女公子 *nyuu-gungtzyy*, n., (court.) your daughter, the daughter of distinguished parents.
女孩(兒)(子) *nyuuhair(-ar'l)(tz)*, n., a young girl, a daughter.
女花兒 *nyuuhua('l)*, n., (MC) a young girl (possibly a corruption of 孩兒 *hair'l* > *har'l* > *hua'l*).
女皇 *nyuuhuarng*, n., an empress, a queen.
女戶 *nyuuhuh*, n., a family composed of female members only.
女紅 *nyuuhurng*, n., see *-gung*↑.
女姪 *nyuujyr*, n., daughter of one's brother, niece.
女眷 *nyuujyuahn*, n., womenfolk of a family.
女科 *nyuuke*, n., (med.) gynecology, also called 婦科.
女郎 *nyuularng*, n., (litr.) a young girl.

女落子 *nyuulauhtz*, n., (coll.) variety show staged by women.
女流 *nyuuliour*, n., the fair sex, the womenfolk.
女伶 *nyuulirng*, n., an actress.
女蘿 *nyuulour*, n., (bot.) the dodder, also called 松蘿.
女奴 *nyuunur*, n., a female slave.
女僕 *nyurpuu*, n., a maidservant.
女人 *nyuurern*, n., (1) a woman; (2) (-'*ren*) wife; (3) (-'*ren*) (contempt.) a wench, dame.
女色 *nyuuseh*, n., feminine charms; women as sex: 貪女色 fond of women; 不近女色 sexually continent.
女生 *nyuusheng*, n., a girl student.
女神 *nyuushern*, n., a fairy, a goddess.
女校 *nyuushiauh*, n., a school for girls.
女性 *nyuushihng*, n., (a member of) the fair sex.
女士 *nyuushyh*, n., (1) an educated girl or woman; (2) a polite form of address for women or girls, used like Eng. "Miss," but not confined to unmarried girls or women.
女婿 *nyuushyuh*, n., son-in-law.
女兄 *nyuushyung*, n., (LL) an elder sister (＝姊).
女史 *nyuushyy*, n., LL for *-shyh*↑.
女孫 *nyuusun*, n., granddaughter.
女子 *nyurtzyy*, n., a girl or woman.
女菀 *nyurwaan*, n., (bot.) *Aster fastigiatus*.
女王 *nyuuwarng*, n., an empress, a queen.
女萎 *nyurweei*, n., (bot.) celery-leaved virgin's bower, *Clematis apiifolia*.
女巫 *nyuuwur*, n., a witch, a sorceress.
女優 *nyuuyou*, n., an actress (see *-lirng*↑.)
女垣 *nyuuyuarn*, n., see *-chiarng*↑.
女樂 *nyuuyueh*, n., (AC) a female singer or musician; female orchestra.

姦 93.93

jian.

[Interch. 奸 93A.10]

N. A wicked person, villain: 姦宄 *-gueei*↓; 姦細 *-shih*↓.

V.i. & t. Commit adultery, have illicit sexual relations (with): 姦淫 *-yirn*, 姦汚 *-wu*, 姦拐 *-guaai*↓; 姦通, 通姦 have illicit sexual relations with a man (woman); 強姦 to rape; 和姦 commit adultery by consent; 輪姦 take turns to rape a woman; 雞姦 commit sodomy; 姦夫 *-fu*, 姦婦 *-fuh*, 姦情 *-chirng*↓.

Adj. Villainous, wicked: 姦慝 *-teh*↓; 姦邪 *-shier*↓.

姦情 *jian-chirng*, n., adulterous relations, circumstances of adultery.
姦夫 *jianfu*, n., adulterer, see *-fuh*↓.
姦婦 *jianfuh*, n., adulteress.
姦拐 *jianguaai*, v. t., rape and kidnap.
姦宄 *jiangueei*, n., villains, scoundrels, traitors.
姦邪 *jianshier*, adj., wicked, vicious, immoral.
姦細 *jianshih*, n., a spy.
姦慝 *jianteh*, n. & adj., wicked (deeds).
姦汚 *jianwu*, v. t., violate a woman's honor, see *-yirn*↓.
姦淫 *jianyirn*, v. t., have illicit sexual relations with (woman).

孌 93.93

lyuaan (*luarn*).

孌童 *luarngturng*, n., a pederast, homosexual boy.

蠻 93.93

marn.

[Pop. 蛮]

蠻
好

N. Name for aboriginal tribes, esp. in south: 南蠻北狄 the *marns* in the south and *dirs* in the north.

Adj. Cross, unreasonable, overbearing: 蠻不講理 be unreasonable; 野蠻 savage, uncivilized.

Adv. (Soochow dial., now also gen.) very, fairly: 蠻好 fairly good, very good; 蠻有趣 quite interesting.

蠻橫 *marnhehng*, adj., arrogant, overbearing, unreasonable.

SECTION 93A

§ 93A.00 (ㄊ/ㄐ)

好 93A.00–3

haau (**hauh*).

Vb. suffix. Indicating the voice of completion, similar to perfect tense, esp. 好了: 好了沒有 have you finished? 做好了 have done; 穿好衣裳 have put on dress; 看好了電影 after seeing a movie; 弄好再走 we'll finish this before going.

V.i. & t. (**hauh*) Have special liking for (＋n. or adj.): 好酒, 好色 fond of wine and women; 好吃懶做 lazy and fond of food; 他所喜好 (愛好) what he especially likes; 嗜好 to be fond of, also fondness, weakness, hobby; 好強 -*chiarng*↓; 好高騖遠 idealistic, flighty.

Adj. (1) Good: 好人, 好馬 a good man, horse; 好戲 a good play; 好評 good opinion, favorable comments; 好人家兒的姑娘 girl from a decent family; 好手 (兒), 好身手 a good hand, an expert, good skill; 好天兒 a clear day; 好事多磨 the course of true love never runs smooth. (2) In good condition: 但願花常好 wish a flower could remain always so perfect; 他問你好 he is asking about your health, sends his greetings. (3) Like, good to, fond of (person): 兩人相好 the two are friends; 跟他要好 is fond of him; 和好, 友好 friendly; 買好, 討好 try to please (s. o.). (4) "Okay," used to ask or give consent, approval: 好不好 or 好嗎 will you approve? what do you think? 好! all right, "okay" (consent, resignation or threat); 叫好 applaud; 好啊, 好哇, 好呀! good! good! 只好不去 it's best (the only good way) not to go.

Adv. (1) Well: 做得好, 說得好, 唱得好 well done, well said, well sung; 這一巴掌打得好 that is a good slap. (2) Easy to: 好做, 好寫 easy to do, easy to write; 價錢好說 (in haggling) price can be discussed. (3) Good to: 好吃, 好看 good to eat, to look at; 好受 makes one feel good. (4) Very, how very: 好沒臉 how very embarrassed; 好久 very long time; 好半天 a good half-day; 好狠 how very cruel; 好高興 very excited; 好喜歡, 好快活 very happy; 好美 how pretty! 好討厭 very disgusting; 好難受, 好難過 feel very painful. (5) In certain idioms: 好容易 or 好不容易 with much difficulty (done finally); 好不應兒, 好不當兒 for no reason whatsoever: 好不應兒的生什麼氣 what on earth are you angry about? 好好的, 好端端的 for what (or no) reason: 好好的怎麼哭了 why are you crying? 好好的 -*haau'de*↓.

Conj. So that, so as: 你有個決定, 我好回(他) please decide, so that I can give a report (to my master); 你交代下來, 我好去叫他 give me the word, so that I can send for him; 書看完留着, 好送朋友 keep the book when you have finished, as you may find it convenient to give it to a friend.

Excl. Prefaced to phr. showing strong disapproval: 好傢伙, 好雜種 you bastard! 好一個不要臉的東西 what a shameless fellow! 你幹的這件好事 what a pretty mess you have made!

好辦 *haau-bahn*, phr., easy to do: 不好辦 difficult to do.
好辯 **hauh-biahn*, adj., fond of arguing, contentious.
好比 *haur-bii*, phr., as good as, suppose, it is as if: 好比說 it's like saying, for example; 我好比是你的父親 I am as good as a father to you; 好比他死了 suppose that he is dead.
好不 *haau buh*, adv. phr., very (oft. ＝好 but more emphatic): 好不傷心 (＝好傷心) how sad; 好不耐煩 how impatient, also

the reverse (好耐煩) how very patient; 好不容易 with great difficulty, also the reverse (好容易) very easy; 好不高興 very exciting (好高興), also the reverse (不高興) depressing.

好 強 *hauhchiarng, adj., stubborn, unwilling to play second fiddle, loving to excel others, self-confident.

好 奇 *hauhchir, adj., curious, inquisitive: 好奇心 curiosity, inquisitiveness.

好 處 haauchuh, n., good points, benefits, advantages.

好 歹 haurdaai, (1) adv., in any case (good or bad), regardless: 好歹你信先發了再說 anyway have the letter sent and then see; (2) referring to some contingency: 萬一有個好歹 if something should happen.

好 大 *hauhdah, adj., as in 好大喜功 flamboyant, ambitious for great achievements.

好 感 haur-gaan, phr., sympathy, good impression, friendly feeling: 給人一個好感 give people a good impression.

好 個 haauge, adj., good, wonderful (in praise): 好個太太 what a wonderful wife; 好個美人 what a beauty!

好 過 haauguoh, adj., (1) comfortable, nice, enjoyable: 心裏好過 feel good; (2) 日子好過 live comfortably.

好 好 的 haurhaau'de (sp. pr. haauhau'de), adv., (1) well: 好好的念書 study well; (2) for no reason suddenly: 好好的忽然辭職不幹 for no reason he suddenly resigned; 好好端端的 ditto; 好好先生 (haurhaau) a man who is always polite and never says no, a good fellow.

好 漢 haauhahn, n., a gallant, a stout-hearted, plucky fellow.

好 合 haau-her, v. i., live happily together: 夫婦好合 conjugal felicity, connubial happiness.

好 幾 haur'ji, adj., a good many (days, persons).

好 交 *hauhjiau, adj., sociable, gregarious, having many friends.

好 勁 haaujihn, excl., an exclamation of surprise.

好 久 haur jioou, adv. phr., a good long time.

好 轉 haur-juaan, v. i. & n., a turn for the better.

好 看 haaukahn, adj., good-looking, enjoyable to see: 這戲很好看 it's a delightful play.

好 兒 haau'l, n., a favor: 人家對偺們有個好兒 he has done us a good turn.

好 癩 haaulaih, adv., (coll.) regardless, good and bad, in any case (=好歹).

好 萊 塢 Haaulairwu, n., (translit.) Hollywood.

好 色 *hauh-seh, phr., fond of women.

好 尚 *hauhshahng, n. & v. t., personal hobbies, inclinations, what one values and loves.

好 勝 *hauhshehng, adj., loving to excel others, ambitious.

好 生 haausheng, adv., (1) carefully, well: 來，好生睡 be a good boy and go to sleep; 好生聽你爸爸的話 listen carefully to your father's advice; (2) very: 好生可憐 very pitiful; (3) (*hauhsheng) 上天好生之德 Heaven's (God's) care for every living thing.

好 像 haaushiahng, (1) conj., as though, as if: 好像是親生的一樣 as if the child were her own; 好像什麽大事情 as if it were some great event; (2) perhaps, seem to, look like: 好像有這麽一回事 I seem to remember the affair; 好像他不能來 it looks like he cannot come; 好像可能 seems possible; 好像已經走了 seems to have left.

好 笑 haaushiauh, adj., funny, laughable: 這事有什麽好笑 what is so funny about this?

好 些 haaushie, (1) adj., a good many (days, persons); (2) (-'shie) adj., a little better.

好 心 haaushin, adj., good-hearted.

好 受 haaushouh, adj., pleasurable, comfortable, feeling good, see -guoh ↑.

好 事 haau-shyh[1], phr., (1) good thing, a charitable act; (2) (Budd.) 作好事 say prayers, mass for the dead; (3) (*hauh-) adj., prone to take up things not strictly one's duty and perhaps get into trouble.

好 是 haau shyh[2], phr., very: 好是奇怪 is very strange.

好 學 *hauhshyuer, adj., fond of learning and scholarship.

好 使 haur shyy, phr., in order that: 寫一封信，好使他知道 write a letter in order that he may know about it.

好 死 haur-syy, phr., die a natural death: 不得好死 (he) will be punished for this, will die an unnatural death.

好 在 haau-tzaih, phr., the important thing is; luckily: 好在他不在車中 luckily he was not in the car (during the accident); 好在你還有三個兒子 the important thing is, you still have three sons left (don't feel too bad); 好在有許多朋友幫忙 fortunately you have so many friends to help you.

好 玩 haauwarn, adj., entertaining, playful, cute.

好 望 角 Haauwahngjiaau, n., Cape of Good Hope.

好 意 haau-yih, n., good intentions, friendly motive: 他來是好意 he came with good intentions; adv., cordially: 好意招待 welcome cordially.

好 音 haau-yin, phr., good news.

婀 93A.00-3

e (ee).

婀 娜 e-nuor (ee-), adj., gracefully slender (figure): 婀娜多姿 very pretty and charming.

嫺 93A.00-5

shiarn.

亅	小	⺊	十	土	ナ	卄	𠃊ト	丨	一	丅	フ	口	⊠	冈	㇆	厂	尸	亠	广	宀	丶	乚	弋	心	八	人	乂	㇀	丿	川	𠂉	く
00	01	02	10	11	12	20	21	22	30	31	32	40	41	42	50	51	52	60	61	62	63	70	71	72	80	81	82	83	90	91	92	93

[Var. of 嫻]

Adj. (1) Refined, elegant (of ladies) poised and quiet: 幽嫺 ditto. (2) Practised, expert.

嫺都 *shiarndu*, adj., beautiful and poised.

嫺靜 *shiarnjihng*, adj., quiet and refined (woman).

嫺習 *shiarnshir*, (1) adj., practiced, familiar: 嫺習文藝 well-read, familiar with literature and the arts; (2) v. t., to learn diligently: 嫺習武藝 skilled in boxing, fencing and the like.

嫺熟 *shiarnshur*, adj., expert, knowing thoroughly (classics, versification, etc.).

嫺雅 *shiarnyaa*, adj., refined.

婷 93A.00–6

tirng.

Adj. 婷婷, 娉婷 gracefully erect (of ladies' figure).

媮 93A.00–8

tou.

[Usu. printed 媮]

Adj. (1) Indolent: 因循媮惰 follow routine and do slipshod work (var. of 偷 91A.00). (2) (AC) cunning.

§93A.01 (女/小)

妹 93A.01–1

meih.

[Dist. 沬]

N. (1) Younger sister: 姊(姐)妹 sisters, see 姊 93A.22; 三妹, 四妹 3rd, 4th younger sister; 堂妹 cousin, younger sister on father's side; 表妹 ditto on mother's side (of different surname). (2) Oft. part of address attached to part of personal name (萱妹, etc.).

妹夫 *meih'fu*, n., husband of younger sister or cousin sister.

妹丈 *meihjahng* n., ditto.

妹妹 *meihmeih*, n., term of endearment for young daughter, also oft. among cousin lovers.

妹婿 *meihshyuh*, n., see -'*fu* ↑.

妹子 *meihtz*, n., (MC) term of address to or self-reference by younger sister or cousin sister.

姝 93A.01–1

shu.

Adj. (LL) beautiful girl: 麗姝 ditto.

媒 93A.01–2

meir.

N. Matchmaker, usu. 媒人, 做媒的, see 媒妁 -*shuoh* ↓: 做媒 act as go-between.

媒合 *mei-her*, v. t., arrange matrimonial match.

媒介 *meirjieh*, n., go-between; (fig.) transmitter (of disease, new ideas).

媒孽 *meirnieh*, v.t., as in (AC) 媒孽其短 point out his mistakes.

媒染劑 *meirraan-ji*, n., (chem.) mordant, substance used to fix dyeing colors.

媒人 *meir-rern*, n., matchmaker, go-between.

媒妁 *meirshuoh*, n., as in (LL) 父母之命, 媒妁之言 make match by parents' order and on matchmaker's word—old-fashioned marriage.

媟 93A.01–2

shieh.

Adj. Indecent, see compp. ↓.

媟黷 *shiehdur*, v. t., to flirt with, behave indecently.

媟慢 *shiehmahn*, v. t., treat cheaply or immodestly dally with.

媟狎 *shiehshiar*, v. i. & t., philander.

媟污 *shiehwu*, adj., indecent.

嫖 93A.01–3

piaur.

N. 嫖友 friend in visiting prostitutes; 嫖客 visitor of brothels.

V.i. & t. To visit prostitutes, to frequent brothels: used as v. t.: 嫖妓, 嫖娼, 嫖婊子 ditto; 嫖賭飲 frequenting brothels, gambling and drinking.

妳 93A.01–9

naai.

[Pop. of 嬭 93A.42]

§93A.02 (女/k)

婊 93A.02–1

biaau.

婊子 *biaautz*, n., prostitute, (derog.) harlot, strumpet.

A

嬛 93A.02-4

chyurng (**shyuan*, **huarn*).

N. (**huarn*) 嫏嬛 n. & adj., jangling sound of jade (also wr. 瑯環).

Adj. (1) (AC) lonely, orphaned, widowed (interch. 煢). (2) (**shyuan*) 嬛佞 (AC) sycophant, given to flattery.

娠 93A.02-5

shen (*jehn*).

V.i. Feel life of embryo in womb: 妊ᐞ娠 93A.11; be pregnant.

孃 93A.02-6

niarng.

[Var. of 娘↓]

嫁 93A·02-6

jiah.

V.i. & t. (1) (Of a girl) marry: 嫁人 *-rern*↓; 嫁雞隨雞, 嫁狗隨狗 advice to be contented with the man a woman has married; 婚嫁 marriage; 嫁娶 *-chyuu*↓; 女大當嫁 a girl should get married on coming of age; 出嫁 (of a girl) be married; 再嫁, 改嫁 remarry after husband's death or divorce; 陪嫁 dowry; 新嫁娘 a newlywed bride; 嫁女 marry off a daughter; 恨不相逢未嫁時 what a pity that we didn't meet before you and I were married! 嫁不出去 unmarriageable; 爲人作嫁 (衣裳) to slave for other people; 爲他人作嫁衣裳 make wedding dress for others—a woman's lament of being a bridesmaid and never a bride. (2) Transfer, shift, lay the blame on: 轉嫁 (public finance) shift the incidence of a tax; 嫁禍 *-huoh*↓.

嫁娶 *jiah-chyuu*, n., marriage ("marry a husband and take a wife").

嫁禍 *jiah-huoh*, v. t., put blame on others.

嫁妝 *jiahjuang*, n., a bride's dowry.

嫁人 *jiah-rern*, phr., (of a girl) get married.

娘 93A.02-6

niarng.

[Interch. 孃]

N. (1) Mother: 娘, 娘娘 mamma, mummy, see 娘娘 *-niarng*↓; 老娘 my old mother (occa. used as pron. by an elderly woman) I; 親娘 one's own mother; 乾娘 foster mother, mother of an adopted child; 後娘, 晚娘 stepmother; 過房娘 aunt adopted as mother; 爹娘 father and mother; 叫爹叫娘 (contempt.) cry "mamma" in distress; 娘兒 mother and child. (2) Elderly lady or lady of higher rank than oneself: 嬸娘 wife of one's paternal uncle; 姨娘 sister of one's mother; 舅娘 wife of one's mother's brother; 娘姨 maidservant, see 娘姨 *-yir*↓; 師娘 wife of one's teacher; 大娘 (vern.) "ma'am" as a polite form of address; 乳娘, 奶娘 a wet nurse; 喜娘 bride's advisor during ceremony. (3) A young girl or lady: 姑娘 miss, as a form of address; 李姑娘 Miss Li; 小嬌娘 a charming little lass; 伴娘 bridesmaid; 新娘 bride; 娘 oft. added to a girl's personal name as in 蕙娘.

娘親 *niarngchin*, n., (1) mother; (2) relatives on the maternal side.

娘家 *niarng'jia*, n., a married woman's maiden home.

娘舅 *niarngjiouh*, n., uncle on the maternal side.

娘兒 *niarng'l*, n., (Peking dial.) aunt: 娘兒們 *niar'lmen* (1) woman in gen.: 小娘兒們 cute little girls; 騷娘兒們 sexy girls; (2) mother and child(ren).

娘母子 *niarng'mutz*, n., (dial.) mother; also 娘母兒 *-'mu'l*, (MC) mother.

娘娘 *niarng'niarng*, n., (1) mother; (2) Her Majesty the Queen; (3) a goddess: 王母娘娘 Goddess the Queen Mother; 送子娘娘 Goddess of Fertility.

娘胎 *niarng-tai*, n., a mother's womb.

娘子 *niarngtz*, n., (1) (MC) one's own wife; (2) (dial.) one's own mother; (3) young women: 小娘子 (usu.) a married woman, (occa.) an unmarried girl; (4) a court lady.

娘姨 *niarngyir*, n., (1) sister of one's mother (same as 姨娘); (2) (Soochow dial.) maidservant.

§ 93A.10 (女/十)

婥 93A.10-2

chuoh.

婥約 *chuoyue*, adj., (woman) gracefully slender (also wr. 綽約).

奸 93A.10-3

jian.

N. Traitor, villain: 奸人 a villain;

漢奸 a Chin. traitor; 內奸 informer, renegade; 奸細 *-shih*↓; 奸黨 traitorous gang; 衆奸 villains and traitors; 奸賊 a scoundrel, secret plotter, conspirator; 奸宄 *-gueei*↓; 奸佞 double-faced courtiers, crafty persons; 奸雄 *-shyurng*↓.

Adj. (1) Treacherous, villainous, false, wicked: 奸謀, 奸計 conspiracy; 奸臣 a treacherous minister; 奸滑 *-huar*, 奸險 *-shiaan*, 奸詐 *-jah*↓; 奸刁 crafty, villainous, deceitful; 奸邪 *-shier*↓; 奸商 a dishonest trader, profiteer. (2) (Interch. 姦) lewd, lustful: 奸淫 *-yirn*↓; 奸夫 *-fu*, 奸婦 *-fuh*↓; 奸笑 treacherous smile.

V.i. & t. (Interch. 姦) commit adultery, have illicit sexual intercourse (with): 通奸 commit adultery; 強奸 to rape; 奸污 ditto.

奸臣 *jianchern*, n., treacherous minister of state.
奸夫 *jianfu*, n., an adulterer.
奸婦 *jianfuh*, n., an adultress.
奸宄 *jiangueei*, n., villains, scoundrels, traitors.
奸滑 *jianhuar*, adj., crafty, oily, unctuous.
奸詐 *jianjah*, adj., crafty.
奸險 *jianshiaan*, adj., crafty and dangerous.
奸邪 *jianshier*, adj. & n., traitorous, a traitor.
奸細 *jianshih*, n., (1) an intriguer; (2) a spy.
奸雄 *jianshyurng*, n., a master of political intrigues.
奸污 *jianwu*, v. t., to rape (woman).
奸淫 *jianyirn*, (1) v.t., have illicit relations with (women); (2) adj., lustful, lecherous.

嬋 93A.10-4

charn.

嬋娟 *charnjyuan*, (1) adj., lovely, graceful (girls); (2) v. i., to show clinging affection.

婢 93A.10-9

bih (*beih).

N. (1) Maidservant; formerly, slave girl: 奴婢 for servants of both sexes, whether slaves or not; 侍婢 attending maid; 婢學夫人 phr., imitate unsuccessfully or beyond one's station (maid acting as mistress of house). (2) (MC) "your slave," term of woman referring to herself (cf. 妾 60.93).

婢女 **beihnyuu*, n., maidservant; slave girl.
婢子 **beihtz*, n., (MC) maidservant referring to herself; maidservant.

§93A.11 (女/土)

姓 93A.11-1

shihng.

N. Surname, clan name: 同姓, 異姓 same, different clan surname; 貴姓 your surname; 敝姓 my surname; 百姓 the people; 姓名, 姓字 name and surname; 姓系 family line; 姓譜 genealogy; 姓氏 surname, cf. 氏 90.71.

娃 93A.11-1

war.

N. (1) A doll or pretty girl: 美娃 a pretty girl; 娃娃 *-war*↓. (2) (*-tz*, *'l*) A baby; (MC) a son.

娃娃 *warwar* (*-'wa*), n., a doll: 洋娃娃 a ("foreign") doll; 娃娃臉 a doll's face.

姪 93A.11-3

jyr.

[Pop. 侄]

N. (*-tz*, *'l*) A nephew: 姪女 niece; 姪輩 the nephews; 姪孫 grandnephew; 姪兒媳婦 nephew's wife; 姪女婿 or 姪婿 niece's husband.

娌 93A.11-4

lii.

N. See 妯^娌 93A.41.

妊 93A.11-9

rehn (*rern*).

V.i. Be pregnant: 妊娠 *-shen*↓; 妊婦 *-fuh*↓; 有妊, 懷妊 be expecting, *enceinte*.

妊婦 *rehnfuh*, n., a pregnant woman, an expectant mother.
妊娠 *rehnshen*, v. i., be with child.

§93A.20 (女/卄)

妍 93A.20-3

yarn.

Adj. (LL) pretty, beautiful: see 妍媸 *-chy*↓.

妍媸 *yarn-chy*, phr., beauty or ugliness.
妍麗 *yarnlih*, adj., beautiful, attractive (woman).

婩 93A.20-8

an.

婩婐 *an-o*, adj., hesitant.

姘 93A.20-9

pin.

V.i. Cohabit or have illicit relations between sexes.

姘夫 *pinfu*, n., man, one cohabits with, illegal husband.
姘婦 *pinfuh*, n., woman one cohabits with out of wedlock, mistress.
姘居 *pinjyu*, v. i., cohabit.
姘識 *pinshyh*, v.i., come to know (person) outside marriage, have illicit relations with (person).
姘頭 *ping'tour*, n., person who cohabits with member of opposite sex.

§ 93A.21 (女/乚)

姫 93A.21-5

ji.

N. (1) (Euphem. for) women: 仙姫 a goddess; 美姫 a belle; 豔姫 a charmer; 妖姫 an enchantress; 歌姫 a songstress; 舞姫 a professional female dancer. (2) Gen. term for concubines: 姫妾 concubines; 寵姫 a concubine in high favor; 愛姫 ditto; 小姫 a mistress, a kept woman. (3) A surname.

嫗 93A.21-5

yuh.

N. An old woman of lower class, a hag.

嫟 93A.21-5

nih.

[Var. of 暱 41A.21]

§ 93A.22 (女/丨)

奺 93A.22-2

niarng.

[Abbr. of 娘 93A.02]

姉 93A.22-2

jiee (sp. pr. *tzyy*).

N. Sister: 姉妹 *-meih*↓; 姉姉 *-'jie*↓; 大姉 eldest sister; 長姉 ditto; 表姉 elder maternal female cousin; 堂姉 elder paternal female cousin; 乾姉妹 foster sisters; 義姉 a foster elder sister.

姉夫 *jiee'fu*, n., elder sister's husband.
姉丈 *jieejahng*, n., ditto.
姉姉 *jiee'jie*, n., elder sister.
姉兒 *jiee'l*, n., (coll.) sisters: 你們姉兒幾個 how many sisters are there in your family? 姉兒倆 the two sisters.
姉們兒 *jiee'me'l*, n., (1) sisters old and young; (2) see *-'l*↑; (3) (coll.) sisters-in-law or intimate girl friends collectively.
姉妹 *jieemeih*, n., elder and younger sisters.

嫦 93A.22-2

charng.

嫦娥 *Charng-er*, n., name of the Lady in the Moon: 嫦娥奔月 (myth.) *Charng-er* flew to the moon with the elixir of life, chased by her famous archer-husband (orig. 姮娥 *Herng-er*, changed because of taboo in name of 漢文帝).

婣 93A.22-2

yin.

[Anc. wr. form of 姻 93A.41]

娜 93A.22-5

nuor (*nuoo*).

Adj. Delicate and gentle: 娜娜 pretty and delicate; 婀娜, 嬝娜, 嫋娜 (of female figure) delicate and graceful.

婦 93A.22-5

fuh.

N. (1) Womenfolk: usu. 婦女 *-nyuu*↓; 婦孺 women and children; 婦工 needlework, cuisine; 婦容 women's proper dress and appearance; 婦言 women's speech, esp. not to talk; 婦德 women's virtue, esp. as wife, mother, -in-law; 情婦 sweetheart; 淫婦, 蕩婦 woman of loose morals; 娼婦 prostitute; 妖

婦 娣 嫌 娇 娅 媪 姐 妞 嬗 妗

婦 vampire; 命婦 lady of rank. (2) Married woman: 新婦 bride; 少婦 young married woman; 寡婦 widow. (3) Wife: 夫婦 husband and wife; 媳婦 daughter-in-law.

婦道 *fuhdauh*, n., (1) women's proper conduct; (2) 婦道人家 *fuh'dauh'ren'jia*, womenfolk.
婦科 *fuhke*, n., gynecology.
婦女 *fuhnyuu*, n., women in gen.; 婦女節 *--jier*, Women's Day; 婦女會 *-hueih*, women's association, cf. 女 93.93.
婦人 *fuhrern*, n., women: 婦人之仁 petty kindness.

娣 93A.22-8

dih.

N. (AC) younger sister; wife of younger brother.

娣婦 *dihfuh*, n., wife of younger brother, generally wr. 弟婦.
娣姒 *dihsyh*, n., (AC) sisters-in-law.

嫌 93A.22-8

shiarn.

N. (1) Suspicion: 避嫌 avoid suspicion; 涉嫌 invite suspicion; 受嫌 under suspicion, receive blame; 兇嫌, 罪嫌 a criminal suspect. (2) Disapproval, see V.i. & t. 2↓. (3) Quarrel: 盡捐前嫌 forget all the past quarrel, ill will or enmity: 嫌怨, 嫌隙 *-yuahn*, *-shih*↓.

V.i. & t. (1) To suspect: 嫌疑 *-'yir*↓. (2) To criticize, disapprove, blame: 嫌他髒 dislike him for being so dirty; 嫌他小, 大 disapprove of it as too small, too large; 嫌老了一點 criticize (the fruit, meat) as too tough; 嫌多, 嫌少 criticise it as too much, too little; 嫌棄 *-chih*↓. (3) To quarrel, hate: 嫌恨, 嫌惡 *-hehn*, *-'wu*↓.

嫌棄 *shiarnchih*, v. t., to abandon (wife, lover).
嫌恨 *shiarnhehn*, v. i. & t., to harbor grudge against (person), be set against.
嫌忌 *shiarnjih*, v. t., keep away from (person) out of dislike.
嫌怕 *shiarnpah*, v. i. & t., dislike, fear (ugly person).
嫌隙 *shiarn-shih*, n., an old grudge, misunderstanding.
嫌疵 *shiarn'ts*, v. t., dislike, criticise: 嫌疵飯不好 dislike the meal. ⌈like heartily.
嫌憎 *shiarntzeng*, v. t., hate, dislike.
嫌惡 *shiarn'wu*, v. t., to loathe.
嫌厭 *shiarnyahn*, v. t., to dislike, loathe.
嫌疑 *shiarn'yir*, v. t. & n., cast suspicion on (person); suspicion: 避嫌疑 avoid suspicion; 嫌疑犯 a criminal suspect; 嫌疑行爲 suspicious conduct.
嫌怨 *shiarnyuahn*, n., an old quarrel (between two).

娇 93A.22-9

jiau.

[Abbr. of 嬌 93A.42]

§93A.30 (女/一)

娅 93A.30-3

yah.

N. Relation through marriage: 姻娅 ditto.

媪 93A.30-4

aau.

N. (LL) a lower-class woman; an old woman servant; mother.

姐 93A.30-4

jiee.

N. (1) Interch. 姊, elder sister. (2) A gen. term for women: 小姐 a girl, maiden, miss: 蘇小姐 Miss Su; 大姐 (court.) "my elder sister"; 姐兒 girls, women.

妞 93A.30-5

niou.

N. (Coll.) girl: 妞兒, 妞妞, 小妞(兒) a little girl.

嬗 93A.30-6

shahn.

V.i. To change in succession: 遞嬗 ditto.

嬗變 *shahnbiahn*, v. i., to change in succession (as historic periods).

§93A.32 (女/フ)

妗 93A.32-8

jihn.

N. The wife of mother's brother: 妗子 wife of wife's brother.

§93A.40 (女/口)

姑 93A.40-1

gu.

N. (1) Father's sister: 姑姑 -'*gu*, 姑母 -*muu*, 姑媽 -*ma*↓. (2) (LL) husband's mother: 翁姑 husband's parents. (3) Husband's sisters: 大姑, 小姑 elder, younger sister-in-law; 姑嫂 -*saau*↓. (4) An unmarried woman: 姑娘 -'*niang*↓; 小姑 husband's younger sister. (5) A member of the female sex: 道姑 a Taoist priestess; 尼姑 a Buddhist nun.

Adv. For the time being, with some hesitation or mental reservation: 姑且 -*chiee*↓; 姑念初犯 phr., pardon for first offense; 姑准 (as if with some mental reservation) the request is hereby temporarily approved; 姑妄言之, 姑妄聽之 (of tall tales, etc.) just let him talk and let's just listen.

姑表 *gubiaau*, n., cousins of either sex born of one's paternal aunt: 姑表兄弟 such male cousins; 姑表姊妹 such female cousins.

姑且 *guchiee*, adv., just for the time being or for the sake of trial or convenience; temporarily, see Adv.↑.

姑夫 *gu'fu*, n., paternal aunt's husband.

姑父 *gufuh*, n., ditto.

姑姑 *gu'gu*, n., an unmarried paternal aunt.

姑公 *gugung*, n., the husband of father's or mother's paternal aunt.

姑丈 *gujahng*, n., (=姑父) see -*fuh*↑.

姑老爺 *gulaau'ye*, n., (1) (court.) son-in-law; (2) the husband of mother's paternal aunt.

姑媽 *guma*, n., a married paternal elder sister.

姑母 *gumuu*, n., a married sister of father.

姑奶奶 *gunaai'nai*, n., (1) (court.) a young married daughter; (2) grandmother's sister; (3) (pop.) a Catholic sister.

姑娘 *gu'niang*, n., (1) an unmarried woman; (2) one's daughter; (3) the daughter of a friend; (4) a concubine; (5) formerly, a prostitute; (6) *guniarng*, a married sister of father.

姑婆 *gupor*, n., (1) husband's paternal aunt; (2) grandfather's sister.

姑嫂 *gusaau*, n., a married woman and her husband's sister.

姑息 *gushir*, v. t., (1) be too tolerant of, show excessive indulgence to: 姑息養奸 to be tolerant tends to breed traitors; (2) appease: 姑息政策 policy of appeasement; 姑息主義者 an appeaser.

姑太太 *gutaih'tai*, n., (court.) a married paternal aunt.

姑子 *gu'tz*, n., a Buddhist nun.

姑爺 *guyer*, n., (court.) son-in-law (also *gu'yie*).

姑爺爺 *guyer'ye*, n., father's paternal aunt's husband.

嬉 93A.40-1

shi.

V.i. (1) To play: 嬉戲 -*shih*↓; play as contrasted with work: 業精於勤荒於嬉 the progress of studies comes from hard work and is retarded by frivolities. (2) Var. of 嘻 40A.40.

嬉皮 *shipir*, n., hippies.

嬉笑 *shishiauh*, n. & v.i., mischievous smile.

嬉戲 *shishih*, v.i. & n., play about, make fun.

妬 93A.40-3

duh.

[Var. of 妒 93A.91]

如 93A.40-4

rur.

V.t. (1) Be like or similar to: 如花似玉 (of a woman) as beautiful as flowers and jades; 如湯沃雪 (of things) easy to do ("as easy as melting snow by pouring hot water on it"); 如荼如火 (of troops) massed together in splendid formation, (of things) growing vigorously; 如狼牧羊 (of magistrates) rule the people oppressively ("like a wolf shepherding sheep"); 如膠似漆 (of persons) love each other dearly ("be firmly attached to each other"); 如壎如篪 fraternal love; 如出一口 everyone says so; 如數家珍 can speak on a subject with great familiarity ("like telling off one's family treasures"); 如坐針氈 feel extremely uneasy ("like sitting on a pincushion"); 如臨大敵 be on one's guard for all possible dangers, be prepared for any eventualities ("as if facing a mortal enemy"); 如釋重負 heave a sigh of relief; 如魚得水 (of persons) get along with one another swimmingly ("like fish in water"); 如出一轍 (of actions) be identical or similar, (of ideas or plans) follow the same pattern ("as if made in the same mold"); 如兄如弟 act towards one another like brothers and sisters; 如喪考妣 be grief-stricken ("as if bereaved of parents"); 如影隨形 be a person's shadow, be a true reflection of what is, (of cause and effect) follow as a matter of course; 如鯁在喉 give vent to one's pent-up feelings ("like a fishbone stuck in the throat"); 有如 be similar to, such as, might be compared to; 猶如 ditto. (2) Measure up to, compare favorably with, be as good as: 自以爲不如 consider oneself inferior to another. (3) Visit, go to: 如厠 *-tseh* ↓.

Adj. In accordance with the convention or ritual: 如儀.

Prep. (1) According to: 如約 *-yue*, 如命 *-mihng*, 如期 *-chir*[1] ↓. (2) For: 例如 for example; 譬如 for instance.

Conj. If, supposing: 如若 *-ruoh* ↓; 如果 *-guoo* ↓.

Particle. (1) In special formation: 如之何 how, also what could be done? 如之奈何 what is there to do about it? (2) (AC, LL) serving as a vb. complement (=然): 海內晏如 peace reigns throughout the land; 恂恂如 truthfully, gently; 空空如也 entirely empty.

如常 *rurcharng*, (1) adj., commonplace, ordinary: 這個陣勢也只如常 this order of battle is rather commonplace; (2) adv., as usual.

如期 *rur-chir*[1], phr., according to schedule: 如期而至 come at the appointed time.

如其 *rurchir*[2], conj., if, supposing, in case.

如初 *rur-chu*, adv., as before, as of old.

如弟 *rur-dih*, n., a younger sworn brother.

如夫人 *rurfurern* (*-'ren*), n., a concubine.

如干 *rurgan*, adj., a certain number of; how many? (=若干).

如故 *rur-guh*, v.i. & adv., (1) v.i., be like old friends: 一見如故 strike a friendship with s.o. on first meeting him; (2) adv., as before, as in the good old days.

如果 *rurguoo*, conj., if (it should come to pass), supposing that.

如何 *rurher*, adv., (1) how? why? (2) at one's wits' end, at a loss as to what to do: 如何如何 what shall I do, what shall I do? (3) (if not) then what is: 聾啞非害國家如何也 if pretending to be deaf and dumb is not unpatriotic, then what is?

如或 *rurhuoh*, conj., if, perchance, in case.

如今 *rurjin*, adv., now(-adays), in these days, at the present time: 如今晚兒 *--waa'l*, ditto.

如舊 *rur-jiouh*, adj., as before, as of old.

如之何 *rurjyher*, adv., how: 如之何其可乎 how should this be best handled? what's the best way out? 將如之何 what are you (am I) going to do about it?

如來 *Rurlair*, n., (Budd.) the title for Sakyamuni.

如律令 *rur lyuhlihng*, phr., (1) strict and inviolate, (of laws) as hereby proclaimed; (2) (concluding phr. of charms, magic formulas) potent and binding.

如命 *rurmihng*, adv., (court.) according to your wish.

如若 *rurruoh*, conj., supposing, in case.

如如 *rurrur*, adv., as in 癢如如把心不定 (MC) itchy and restless.

如心 *rur-shin*[1], adj., pleased, gratified, satisfied, contented, delighted.

如馨 *rurshin*[2], adj. & adv., see 寧△馨 62.00.

如數(兒) *rur-shuh('l)*, adv., (of money) with the entire amount: 如數(兒)歸清 (of debts) all duly repaid.

如是 *rurshyh*[1], adv., (1) (Budd.) thus: 如是我聞 "thus have I heard (from the Buddha)"; (2) such, in this (that) way.

如適 *rurshyh*[2], adj., (AC) comfortable, contented, cheerful, happy, at ease.

如兄 *rur-shyung*, n., an elder sworn brother.

如許 *rurshyuu*, adj., (1) (LL) a certain amount (sum, quantity) of: 如許錢 so much money (cash); (2) (LL) such, of this (that) kind.

如斯 *rursy*, adj., like this (that), of this (that) kind.

如厠 *rur-tseh*, v. i., go to the toilet.

如此 *rurtsyy*, adj., so, such, like this (that).

如同 *rur(')turng*, adj., similar to, like.

如字 *rurtzyh*, adv., (of Chin. characters) according to the basic pronunciation: 讀如字 to be so read.

如一 *rur-yi*, adj., uniform, identical.

如意 *rur-yih*, (1) n., an ornamental piece made of bones, bamboo, wood, metals or jade; (2) adj., satisfied, pleased, happy, comfortable; 如意草 *--tsaau*, n., (1) (bot.) *Viola verecunda*; (2) the great burdock, *Arctium lappa*.

如有 *rur-yoou*, phr., if any.

如願 *rur-yuahn*, phr., (1) if willing; (2) as one wishes: 如願以償 have one's wish fulfilled.

如約 *ruryue* adv., as per agreement, according to appointment.

始 93A.40-9

shyy.

N. (1) A beginning: 事有始終 there is a sequence of beginning and end; 始終, 始末 *-jung*, *-moh* ↓; 有始有終, 全始全終 steadfast (finish what was started); 原始 the beginning, early days; 原始時代 primitive, primeval times; 原始動物 prehistoric animals; 開始 to start (work, fashion, etc.). (2) A surname.

V.i. 始自 date from (era, person).

Adv. (1) First: 始而哭, 繼而喊 first began to weep, then to scream. (2) Just, only then (=modn. 才): 始可出去 only then one may leave (room, school); 始能恢復原狀 (only after . . .) then it can be restored to original shape; 方始 only then; 未始 (=未嘗) never; 未始有錯 there was never a mistake; used in double negative: 未始不是好事 one cannot say it was not a good thing.

始期 *shyy-chir*, n., (1) beginning period; (2) (law) effective date.

始春 *shyy-chun*, n., beginning of spring in lunar calendar (＝立春) about Feb. 5–18.

始胥 *shyy-gau*, n., (Chin. med.) second month of embryo, see *-pei*, *-tai*↓.

始基 *shyy-ji*, n., foundation, beginning.

始終 *shyyjung*, (1) n., beginning to end, beginning and end; (2) adv., from the beginning to end: 始終不承認 never admitted; 始終沒來 never came.

始末 *shyy-moh*, n., beginning and end (of story).

始胚 *shyy-pei*, n., (Chin. med.) first month of embryo, see *-gau*↑, *-tai*↓.

始生代 *shyysheng-daih*, n., (geol.) Eozoic era; 始生界 Eozoic group.

始新世 *shyyshinshyh*, n., (geol.) Eocene period, 始新統 Eocene series.

始胎 *shyy-tai*, n., (Chin. med.) third month of embryo, see *-pei*↑.

始祖 *shyr-tzuu*, n., first ancestor.

始業式 *shyy-yeh-shyh*, n., ceremony for opening of school year.

始願 *shyy-yuahn*, n., original wish.

§ 93A.41 (女/図)

嬙 93A.41-1

chiarng.

N. Formerly, a lady-in-waiting: 嬪嬙.

妯 93A.41-2

jur (sp. pr. *jour*).

妯娌 *jour'li*, n., wives of brothers: 姊妹做妯娌 two sisters marry two brothers.

孀 93A.41-3

shuang.

N. Widow: 富孀 rich widow; 孀居 live the life of a widow.

孀婦 *shuangfuh*, n., a widow.

娼 93A.41-4

chang.

N. Prostitute: 娼妓 *-ji*↓; 逼良爲娼 force good family girl into prostitution; 私娼 private prostitute; 土娼 local prostitute; 流娼 streetwalker, prostitute in the white slave business.

娼婦 *changfuh*, n., (1) prostitute; (2) (term of abuse) harlot, strumpet, slut.

娼妓 *changji*, n., prostitute.

娼家 *changjia*, n., brothel keeper.

娼寮 *changliaur*, n., brothel.

娼門 *changmern*, n., house associated with prostitution.

媢 93A.41-4

mauh.

N. & v.t. (AC) 媢嫉 hatred, to hate.

姻 93A.41-4

yin.

N. Marital bond or relationship: 婚姻 wedding, marriage: 姻緣 *-yuarn*↓.

姻伯 *yin-bor*, n., an uncle by marriage.

姻戚 *yin-chih*, n., in-law relatives on wife's or mother's side.

姻親 *yin-chin*, n., a relative by marriage.

姻末 *yin-moh*, n., (court. self-reference) nephew-in-law.

姻母 *yin-muu*, n., an aunt by marriage.

姻兄弟 *yin-shyungdih*, n., cousin-in-law.

姻亞 *yin-yah*, n., relatives by marriage.

姻緣 *yinyuarn*, n., romance; romance as fated by heaven.

媚 93A.41-5

meih.

V.t. To flatter, toady, to get into the good graces of (person): 諂媚 flatter; 狐媚 (derog. of woman) seduce by attractive looks; 媚笑 bewitching smile; 媚世 court favor of public; 媚外 try to flatter foreigners.

Adj. Pleasing, attractive, feminine: 媚態, 媚氣 charming, seductive manner; 媚眼 seductive eyes; 嫵媚 (of woman) charmingly feminine.

媚人 *meih-rern*, adj., attractive, winsome (appearance, manner).

媚藥 *meih-yauh*, n., aphrodisiac.

嬸 93A.41-6

sheen.

N. (1) Wife of uncle who is

始 嬙 妯 孀 娼 媢 姻 媚 嬸

younger than father: also 嬸母, 嬸娘 ditto; 大嬸 auntie, as familiar address of woman of elder generation, not necessarily related. (2) 小嬸子(兒) younger brother's wife; (MC) 嬸子 ditto.

嬸母 *shernmuu*, n., see N. 1↑; also called 嬸兒, 嬸兒媽.
嬸娘 *sheenniarng*, n., see N. 1↑.
嬸婆 *sheenpor*, n., (1) wife of husband's uncle who is younger than his father; (2) familiar address of elder woman.
嬸嬸 *shernsheen*, n., see N. 1↑.
嬸子 *sheen'tz*, n., younger brother's wife.

婚 93A.41-9

hun.

N. & v.t. Wedding, marriage: 婚姻, 婚事 *-yin*, *-shyh*↓; 結婚 wedding; 未婚 not yet married; 婚配 to marry; 婚娶 to marry (a wife); 婚嫁 to marry (a man); 婚禮 *-lii*↓; 金婚, 銀婚 golden, silver, wedding anniversary.

婚期 *hun-chir*, n., wedding day.
婚媾 *hungouh*, n., (LL) marriage, wedding.
婚嫁 *hunjiah*, n., marriage: 婚嫁之事 the matter of marriage.
婚禮 *hunlii*, n., wedding ceremony.
婚書 *hunshu*, n., marriage certificate.
婚事 *hunshyh*, n., marriage, wedding, also betrothal.
婚姻 *hunyin*, n., marriage.
婚約 *hunyue*, n., engagement to marry.

§ 93A.42 (女/冈)

媾 93A.42-2

gouh.

V.i. (1) Marry: 婚媾 join in wedlock; 媒媾 serve as a go-between in marriage, (marry through) the good offices of a go-between. (2) Be on friendly terms: see 媾和 *-her*[2]↓. (3) Have sexual intercourse: 交媾, see 媾合 *-her*[1]↓.

媾合 *gouh-her*[1], v.i., to copulate.
媾和 *gouh-her*[2], v.i., make peace with a foreign country.

娚 93A.42-2

raan.

Adj. (Of woman) slender, delicate: 娚嫋 (of the feminine figure) tall and slender.

嬭 93A.42-3

naai.

[Var. of 奶 93A.50; pop. 妳]

婿 93A.42-3

shyuh.

[Var. 壻]

N. (1) Son-in-law: 女婿 ditto; 婿甥 ditto; 東牀佳婿, 乘龍快婿 proud or handsome son-in-law; 金龜婿 a rich son-in-law. (2) Husband, a male in-law from point of view of the family: 夫婿 husband; 孫婿 grandson-in-law; 甥婿 niece's husband.

娟 93A.42-4

jyuan.

Adj. Beautiful, graceful: 娟娟 *-jyuan*; 娟秀 *-shiouh*↓; 娟好 pretty, good-looking.

娟娟 *jyuanjyuan*, adj., (of person or thing) lovely, elegant, beautiful.
娟秀 *jyuanshiouh*, adj., graceful, exquisite.

姍 93A.42-4

shan.

姍姍 *shanshan*, adv., as in 姍姍來遲 (of lady's manner of walking) leisurely.
姍笑 *shanshiauh*, v. t., to laugh at (related 訕笑 60A.21).

媧 93A.42-4

wa.

N. 女媧 (Myth.) name of goddess who in her fight against another spirit caused a crack in the sky.

嫡 93A.42-6

dir.

N. Legal wife (opp. 妾 concubine): 嫡妻, 嫡配 *-chi*, *-peih*↓.

Adj. Of, born of, legal wife: 嫡子, 嫡嗣 son of legal wife: 嫡派, 嫡系 children of the legal wife; (in political parties) the rightful, correct successor, considered carrying on the orthodox policy; 嫡堂兄弟 cousins of the same grandfather by the direct line.

嫡妻 *dirchi*, n., legal wife.
嫡親 *dirchin*, n., blood relative; direct descendant.
嫡傳 *dirchuarn*, n., disciples of a master by direct line: 嫡傳弟子.

嫡母 *dirmuu* n., address of legal mother by children of concubines.

嫡配 *dirpeih*, n., legal spouse.

嬌 93A.42-9

jiau.

V.t. To love: 平生所嬌兒 the child I've most doted on.

Adj. Tender, delicate, dainty, lovely, charming: 嬌滴滴 delicate, radiating sweetness and charm; 嬌態 winsome, bewitching manner; 嬌聲 a sweet girlish voice; 嬌姿 delicate, charming manner; 嬌生慣養 brought up in easy circumstances by doting parents; 阿嬌 (LL) one's (lovely) children; 撒嬌 (of women or children) sulk or cry, act coquettishly or capriciously like spoiled children.

嬌妻 *jiau-chi*, n., a pretty young wife.

嬌氣 *jiau'chi*, adj., (of person) frail, delicate, weak.

嬌喘 *jiau-chuaan*, adj., (of young woman) panting from physical weakness.

嬌癡 *jiauchy*, adj., *ingénue*, guileless.

嬌兒 *jiauerl*, n., a darling son.

嬌哥兒 *jiauge'l*, n., a spoilt child.

嬌慣 *jiauguahn*, v. t., dote, spoil by doting; p.p., spoiled.

嬌貴 *jiaugueih*, adj., spoiled.

嬌憨 *jiauhan*, adj., see *-chy*↑.

嬌客 *jiau-keh*, n., a son-in-law.

嬌美 *jiaumeei*, adj., beautiful and graceful.

嬌媚 *jiaumeih*, adj., sweet and charming.

嬌嫩 *jiau'nen*, adj., young and delicate, soft and gentle.

嬌娘 *jiau-niarng*, n., a beautiful girl.

嬌娜 *jiaunuor*, adj., lovely, graceful.

嬌女 *jiau-nyuu*, n., a lovely daughter.

嬌嬈 *jiauraur*, adj., lovely, charming.

嬌小 *jiaushiaau*, adj., *petite*, dainty: 嬌小玲瓏 dainty and cute.

嬌羞 *jiaushiou*, adj., (of women) bashful, shy, blushing, modest and reserved.

嬌娃 *jiau-war*, n., a cute young girl, a charmer.

嬌養 *jiauyaang*, adj., reared by indulgent parents.

嬌豔 *jiauyahn*, adj., seductive, attractive (woman).

§93A.50 (女/ㄱ)

姱 93A.50-1

kua.

Adj. (AC) handsome.

娉 93A.50-2

ping.

娉婷 *pingtirng*, adj., attractive (of woman): 娉婷玉貌 slender, beautiful figure.

嫣 93A.50-3

yan.

Adj. & adv. Gay, merry.

嫣紅 *yanhurng*, adj., gorgeous red (flowers).

嫣然 *yanrarn*, adv., sweetly, merrily (smiling).

奶 93A.50-3

naai.

N. (1) A woman's breasts: 奶頭(兒) *-tour('l)*↓; 奶膀子 (coll. term for 乳房) nipples. (2) Milk: 牛奶 cow's milk; 奶子 *-'tz*↓.

V.t. To suckle: 奶孩子 feed the baby with milk; 奶着孩子 is suckling the baby.

奶瘡 *naaichuang*, n., (med.) breast abscess.

奶粉 *nairfeen*, n., powder milk.

奶糕 *naaigau*, n., a kind of food made of rice flour for infants.

奶公 *naaigung*, n., (court.) the husband of an infant's wet nurse.

奶罩 *naaijiauh*, n., brassiere.

奶媽(兒)(子) *naaima('l) (tz)*, n., a wet nurse; amah.

奶名(兒) *naaimirng('l)*, n., pet name given to a child.

奶母 *nairmuu*, n., a wet nurse.

奶奶 *naai'nai*, n., (1) grandmother; (2) polite form of address for young married women; 大奶奶, 二奶奶, 少奶奶 first, second, young daughter-in-law in house; (3) (among Manchus) mother.

奶娘 *naainiang*, n., (Soochow dial.) a wet nurse.

奶皮(子) *naaipir(tz)*, n., cream.

奶水 *nairshueei*, n., (1) canned milk; (2) woman's natural supply of milk; 奶水少 mother has insufficient milk.

奶頭(兒) *naaitour('l)*, n., the teats, nipples.

奶子 *naai'tz*, n., (1) mother's milk; (2) the teats; (3) a wet nurse.

奶牙 *naaiyar*, n., milk teeth, baby teeth.

奶油 *naaiyour*, n., cream.

姆 93A.50-4

*muu (*m).*

[Var. 姥 93A.70; cogn. 母 41.50]

N. 保姆 governess of child; 天姆 Mother of Heaven, Goddess Matsu.

姆媽 *m-ma*, n., (Shanghai dial.), term for mother.

姆姆 *murmuu*, n., (MC, obs.) wife of husband's elder brother.

嫋 93A.50-5

niaau.

[Interch. 裊, 嬝]

Adj. Slender and delicate.

嫋嫋 *niaurniaau*, adj., (1) delicate and graceful: 嫋嫋素女 delicate and graceful as a fairy; (2) waving in the wind: 春枝晨嫋嫋 the spring sprouts wave in the morning breeze; (3) curling up: 鑪香嫋嫋 incense smoke curls up from the burner; (4) (mus.) soft and lingering.

嫋娜 *niaurnuoo*, adj., (of female figure) delicate and graceful.

媽 93A.50-5

ma.

N. (1) Coll. short for "mamma" (cf. 爸 *pa* coll. for "papa"): 爸媽 father and mother (pop and mom); 乾媽 adopted mother. (2) Part of address for aunt: 姨媽 (on mother's side); 姑媽 (on father's side); 舅媽 (wife of mother's brother). (3) Part of address for maidservant or amah: 老媽子, 小老媽 maid, amah; 奶媽 wet nurse; 阿媽 amah, of different dialect usage.

媽的 *ma'de*, excl., vulgar curse word.

媽姐 *ma-jiee*, n., (Cantonese) maidservant; 媽姐裝 style of a maidservant's dress (Cantonese).

媽拉巴子 *malabatz*, excl., indecent curse word (see 巴△子 52.70).

媽媽 *ma'ma*, n., address for mother=mamma: 媽媽大全, 媽媽論兒 n., folklore, customs passed on by "old wives," including wisdom, superstition.

妨 93A.50-6

*farng (*fang).*

[Dist. 防 32A.50 guard against]

N. Objection in phrr. 何妨, 無妨 (also **fang*) what's the harm, no harm; 何妨, 無妨跟他說一說 there is no harm having a talk with him; 何妨擱一擱 no harm in letting the matter wait.

V.t. Interfere with: 不妨 no harm; 不妨試一試 no harm trying; 不妨事 do not matter, can go ahead; see 防礙, 防害 *-aih, -haih* ↓.

妨礙 *farng-aih*, v.t., interfere with, upset (discipline, friendly relations, etc.).

妨害 *farnghaih*, v.t., to harm, upset (public order, security, progress, etc.).

嫣 93A.50-9

guei.

N. An anc. surname.

妁 93A.50-9

shuoh.

N. See 媒△妁 93A.01.

§ 93A.63 (女/丶)

嫵 93A.63-9

wuu.

[Var. 娬 93A.71]

§ 93A.70 (女/ㄴ)

姥 93A.70-1

muu (laau).

N. (1) Old woman. (2) Var. of 姆 93A.50.

姥姥 **laurlaau*, n., (1) maternal grandmother; (2) gen. term for old woman, nurse: 劉姥姥 old peasant woman relative Liour.

嬈 93A.70-1

raur.

Adj. (1) Beautiful and charming: 嬌嬈 bewitching, enchanting, captivating. (2) Disturbing, troublesome: 嬈惱 worrisome: 無所嬈惱 nothing to worry about.

妣 93A.70-2

bii.

N. (LL) formal reference to deceased mother, as on tombstones: 先妣 my (our) deceased mother, see 考△妣 11.50.

她 93A.70-2

ta (*yi*).

Pron. She (an accepted modn. word, nonexistent in LL or AC; the pronunciation *yi* is purely theoretical, not current): 她們 female they; 他或她們 a modern pedantic, redundant circumlocution trying to indicate "they, male and female."

姚 93A.70-2

yaur.

N. A surname.

Adj. (1) U.f. 窕 charming (girl). (2) U.f. 遙 faraway.

妃 93A.70-5

fei.

N. (1) (AC) Imperial concubine, next to 后 queen or empress; oft. *-tz*; 妃嬪 gen. term for imperial concubines, or ladies-in-waiting, fixed in number by court protocol. (2) (AC) wife of a prince.

Adj. Light pink.

妮 93A.70-5

nir.

N. (1) A slave girl. (2) A cute little girl: 小妮子.

妮婢 *nirbih*, n., a maidservant.
妮子 *nirtzyy*, n., a young girl.

娓 93A.70-5

weei.

Adj. Pleasing.

娓娓 *weirweir*, adv., as in 娓娓而談 talk familiarly on and on.

姹 93A.70-6

chah.

Adj. (AC) 姹女 young maiden; 姹紫嫣紅 (LL) gaily dressed maidens.

婉 93A.70-6

waan.

Adj. (1) Soft, restrained, tactful: 婉轉 *-juaan*↓; 婉言相勸 plead with soft, tactful words; 婉容 soft manner; 和婉 easy to get along with; 委婉 tactfully; 婉約 *-yue*↓. (2) Charming, graceful: 婉麗 *-lih*↓.

Adv. Tactfully: 婉商 negotiate, discuss tactfully; 婉勸 explain tactfully.

婉轉 *warnjuaan*, adj. & adv., tactfully, gracefully (also wr. 宛轉).
婉麗 *waanlih*, adj., charming (manner).
婉孌 *warnlyuaan*, adj., (1) (AC) young and handsome; (2) blithe.
婉縟 *waanruh*, adj., (LL, of writing style) rich.
婉婉 *warnwaan*, adj. & adv., amiable, -y, graceful, -ly.
婉約 *waanyue*, adj., restrained, soft, plaintive (style of poetry).
婉愉 *waanyur*, adj., (LL) at ease, relaxed.

奼 93A.70-9

chah.
[Var. of 姹 93A.70↑]

婗 93A.70-9

nir.

N. (1) (=妮) A maidservant: 婗子, 妮子 ditto. (2) An infant girl: 嫛婗 (rare) a baby girl.

媿 93A.70-9

kueih.
[Var. of 愧 22A.70]

姽 93A.70-9

gueei.

Adj. Quiet and nice: 姽嫿 ditto.

娩 93A.70-9

waan.

N. Childbearing: 分娩 child delivery.

媲 93A.70-9

pih.

V.t. To match.

媲美 *pih-meei*, v. t., to match in excellence or beauty, to compare favorably with.

媲偶 *pih-oou*, v. i., to mate with, (var. of 配[A]偶 31C.70).

§ 93A.71 (女/弋)

娬 93A.71–7

wuu.

娬媚 *wuumeih*, adj., charming, enchanting (woman).

娥 93A.71–9

er.

N. (LL) a pretty lady: 宮娥 palace maid or lady.

娥娥 *er-er*, adj., (LL) pretty.
娥眉 *ermeir*, n., (LL) pretty eyebrows; (LL, fig.) a beautiful woman.

§ 93A.72 (女/心)

媳 93A.72–9

shir.

N. Daughter-in-law: 侄媳 nephew's wife; 兒媳 sons and daughters-in-law; 孫媳 grandson's wife.

媳婦 *shirfuh*, n., (1) daughter-in-law; (2) bride, wife (from the point of view of the family or parents): 討媳婦, 娶媳婦 marry a wife; 老黃的媳婦 old Huarng's wife (cf. 生孫 "give birth to a grandson"—really to a son).

§ 93A.80 (女/八)

嬾 93A.80–1

laan.
[Var. of 懶 22A.80]

媍 93A.80–5

fuh.
[Pop. of 婦 93A.22]

嬪 93A.80–6

pirn.

N. (1) (AC) palace maid: 嬪從, 嬪御 female retinue at court. (2) (AC) woman of virtue.

V.t. (AC) marry into.

嬪然 *pirnrarn*, adj., as in (AC) 嬪然成行 lined up in a row.

§ 93A.81 (女/人)

姨 93A.81–1

yir.

N. (1) Wife's sister: 大姨 wife's elder sister; 小姨(子) wife's younger sister. (2) Mother's sister: 姨母, 阿姨 ditto. (3) Concubine: 姨太太 *-taih'tai* ↓.

姨表 *yirbiaau*, n., female cousin on mother's side, opp. 姑表 on father's side.

姨爹 *yirdie*, n., (dial.) see *-jahng* ↓.

姨夫 *yirfuh*, n., (AC) see *-'fuh* ↓.

姨父 *yir(')fuh*, n., maternal aunt's husband.

姨丈 *yirjahng*, n., ditto.

姨姐 *yirjiee*, n., wife's elder sister; 姨姐妹 cousin sisters on mother's side.

姨兒 *yier'l*, n., (Peking dial.) maternal aunt.

姨媽 *yirma*, n., (1) see *-muu* ↓; (2) (dial.) amah, child's governess.

姨妹 *yirmeih*, n., wife's younger sister.

姨母 *yirmuu*, n., maternal aunt.

姨奶奶 *yirnaai'nai*, n., (formerly, respectful address to) concubine, mistress.

姨娘 *yir(')niarng*, n., (1) concubine; (2) stepmother.

姨婆 *yirpor*, n., grandaunt.

姨甥 *yirsheng*, n., (self-reference) niece on mother's side.

姨兄 *yirshyung*, n., elder cousin on mother's side.

姨兄弟 *yirshyungdih*, n., male cousins on mother's side.

姨太太 *yirtaih'tai*, n., (coll.) concubine.

姨姨 *yiryir*, n., (1) maternal aunt; (2) formerly, children's address of father's concubine.

姒 93A.81–2

syh.

N. (AC) (1) Wife of husband's elder brother. (2) (Of sisters who married same husband) the elder one (娣 the younger one): 娣姒 ditto, sisters-in-law. (3) A surname.

娛 93A.81–4

yur.

N. Enjoyment, amusement, relaxation, pleasure: 娛樂 *-leh*↓; 歡娛 joy, happiness.

V.t. To please (person, mind): 娛人 make one happy; 自娛 to amuse oneself; 娛目 to please the eye; 娛老 to amuse one in old age.

娛親 *yur-chin*, phr., do s. t. to please the parents.
娛樂 *yurleh*, n., amusements, pleasure, relaxation.
娛遊 *yuryour*, v. i., to travel for pleasure.
娛悅 *yuryueh*, (1) v. t., to please s. o.; (2) adj., pleased.

嫉 93A.81-6

jir.

V.t. (1) Be jealous of: 嫉妒 *-duh*↓; 嫉賢 envy s.o. better or abler than oneself. (2) Hate: 嫉惡如仇 abhor evils as deadly foes.

嫉妒 *jirduh*, v. t., to envy.

妖 93A.81-9

yau.

N. Evil spirit, demon, monster: 妖魔, 妖怪 *-mor, -'guaih*↓.

Adj. (1) Having to do with sorcery or the supernatural: 妖術, 妖邪 *-shuh, -shier*↓; 妖言惑衆 strange doctrines win a large following. (2) Seductive, bewitching, lewd: 妖冶, 妖豔, 妖媚 *-yee, -yahn, -meih*↓.

妖氣 *yau'chi*, n., witchery, lascivious air: 妖裏妖氣, 妖聲妖氣 ditto (said in disparagement).
妖道 *yau-dauh*, n., sorcery, witchcraft, black art.
妖調 *yaudiauh*, adv., lascivious, bewitching.
妖氛 *yau-fen*, n., ominous or pernicious atmosphere.
妖怪 *yau'guaih*, n., monster; goblin, phantom.
妖蠱 *yau-guu*, n., sorcery, black magic; witchery of woman's charm.
妖精 *yau'jing*, n., spirit transformed from a very old animal or tree, etc., as 狐狸精 fox spirit see *-'guaih*↑.
妖厲 *yaulih*, n., evil spirit, demon.
妖媚 *yaumeih*, adj., (woman) seductive, very charming, bewitching.
妖魔 *yaumor*, n., demon, devil, goblin.
妖孽 *yaunieh*, n., (1) a supernatural omen or event; (2) a person like a devil, a sexual pervert; (3) adj., perverse, evil.
妖嬈 *yauraur*, adj., flirtatious, charming, bewitching.
妖人 *yaurern*, n., person practising black art.
妖祥 *yau-shiarng*, n., bad (妖) and good (祥) omens.
妖邪 *yaushier*, adj. & n., leading one astray, heterodox; immoral; such doctrines.
妖星 *yaushing*, n., star of evil omen; comet.
妖術 *yau-shuh*, n., black magic or art.
妖災 *yautzai*, n., calamity ascribed to evil influence.
妖豔 *yauyahn*, adj., bewitchingly pretty.
妖言 *yau-yarn*, n., heterodox teachings, any irresponsible gossip.
妖冶 *yauyee*, adj., see *-yahn*↑.
妖異 *yauyih*, n., supernatural omen or event.

§93A.82 (女/乂)

妓 93A.82-1

jih.

N. (1) (AC) a female performer: 歌妓 a female singer; 舞妓 a female dancer; 藝妓 a geisha. (2) A prostitute: 妓女 *-nyuu*↓; 娼妓 a whore; 雛妓 a young prostitute.

妓女 *jihnyuu*, n., a prostitute, whore.
妓院 *jihyuahn*, n., a brothel, a singsong house.

嫩 93A.82-1

nehn (*nuhn*).

[Var. 嫰; pop. 嫩]

Adj. (1) Tender, delicate, soft: 嫩芽 a tender shoot; 嫩皮 soft skin, soft furs; 嫩嫩的 soft and tender; 嫩骨頭 cartilage, soft bones; 嫩豆腐 tender bean curd; 這肉很嫩 this piece of meat is very tender; 嬌嫩 (of woman) shy and delicate; 又白又嫩 (of face) fair and tender. (2) Initial, just beginning: 嫩晴, 嫩寒, 嫩涼 first days of fair, cold, cool weather. (3) Inexperienced, immature: 面皮嫩 (of a person's bearing or attitude) shy; 資格嫩 lacking experience or practice; 年紀嫩 young in years; 他還是嫩得很 he is still too immature. (4) Light-colored: 嫩黃 light yellow; 嫩綠 light green; 嫩色 pale-colored.

嬍 93A.82-2

meei.

[Interch. 美 80.81]

嫂 93A.82-2

saau.

N. Elder brother's wife: 嫂子, 嫂

嫂 ditto; used socially like the word 兄, in addressing a married woman: 嫂夫人 (litr. & court.) address of familiar friend's wife; 大嫂 eldest sister-in-law, also used socially of other women, esp. in rural class: 張大嫂=Mrs. Jang.

奴 93A.82-3

nur.

N. (1) Servant, slave, esp. 奴隸, 奴僕 *-lih, -puu*↓; 家奴 family slave; 農奴 serf; 奴戮 (of prisoners of war) slaughter or make slave; 奴顏婢膝 subservient like a slave; 奴脣婢舌 (of speech) loose-tongued like a slave or maid. (2) Formerly, "I," reference to self, used by servant or an official in relation to the master (like "your humble servant"); servant: 奴家, 奴才, *-jia, -tsair*↓. (3) Term of disparagement, slave: 倭奴 (derog.) the Japanese; 洋奴 Chinese in foreign employ or servile to foreigners; 守財奴 a miser (lit., "a slave to riches").

奴婢 *nurbih*, n., slaves and maid-servants.
奴家 *nurjia*, n., (MC) self-deprecating substitute for "I" (your slave).
奴隸 *nurlih*, n., slave.
奴僕 *nurpuu*, n., servant.
奴性 *nurshihng*, adj., slavish or servile character.
奴視 *nurshyh*, v. t., look down upon (s. o.) like a slave.
奴胎 *nurtai*, n., (derog.) a born slave: 不是這奴胎是誰 (MC) who else could it be but this born slave?
奴才 *nurtsair*, n., (1) (formerly, term of self-disparagement) your humble slave; (2) a mediocre person; (3) (contempt.) a morally despicable person; (4) (of a Manchu official in relation to the Emperor) your humble slave.
奴役 *nuryih*, v. t. & n., to enslave; slave labor, enslavement.

嫚 93A.82-4

mahn.

Adj. & adv. (1) Rude: 嫚罵 scold rudely (=慢 22A.82). (2) Graceful, -ly: 嫚嫚 (cf. 曼 41.82).

姣 93A.82-6

jiau (*jiaau*).

Adj. Good-looking, pretty, beautiful, handsome.

姣俏 *jiaauchiauh*, adj., pretty, handsome.
姣好 *jiaurhaau*, adj., ditto.
姣美 *jiaurmeei*, adj., ditto.
姣童 *jiaauturng*, n., handsome boy.

婈 93A.82-6

saau.

[Var. of 嫂↑]

媛 93A.82-9

yuahn (or *yuarn*).

N. A pretty girl, a young lady: 名媛 socially prominent young lady; 令媛 (court.) your daughter.

嬡 93A.82-9

aih.

N. (Court.) 令嬡 your daughter (also wr. 令愛).

§ 93A.91 (女/ノ)

妙 93A.91-2

miauh.

N. Mystery, charm; see 玄ᐞ妙 60.93.

Adj. Exquisite, wonderful, charming, subtle: 這事極妙, 妙不可言 this thing is extraordinary; 妙極了 wonderful! just what I had wished, most enjoyable (of play, story, writing, machine, etc.); 妙論 profound, utterly charming, unusual discourse; 妙語 charming remarks; 妙語如珠 sparkling discourse; 妙計 extraordinary plan, strategy; 妙品 art of a very high order; 妙藥 miraculous or unusual medicine.

妙訣 *miauh-jyuer*, n., valuable secret, formula.
妙麗 *miauhlih*, adj., (of lady) exquisite, beautiful.
妙理 *miauh-lii*, n., profound wisdom.
妙齡 *miauh-lirng*, n. & adj., young age, childhood.
妙曼(嫚) *miauhmahn*, adj., see *-lih*↑.
妙年 *miauh-niarn*, adj. & n., young, tender age.
妙想 *miaushiaang*, n., strange notions: 妙想天開 (having) some unheard-of, fantastic, idea.
妙手(回春) *miauh-shoou* (*hueir-chun*), phr., (of doctors) admirable skill in curing disease; 妙手空空 out of cash; clever at manipulating money, though destitute.
妙選 *miauh-shyuaan*, n. & adj., the elite, the pick of a group: 妙選人才 ditto.
妙悟 *miauh-wuh*, n., direct, intuitive comprehension; understanding of truth.
妙用 *miauh-yuhng*, n. & v. i., extraordinary power for bringing results; to exercise such power.

嫪 93A.91-5

lauh.

N. A surname.

V.t. Be enamored with, to lust for.

妒 93A.91-9

duh.
[Var. 妬]

N. & v.i. & t. & adj. Be jealous, jealousy: 相妒 jealous of each other; 妒某人 jealous of a certain person; 入宮見妒 ladies encounter jealousy in palace (or elsewhere); 同行 (*harng*) 相妒 professional jealousy.

妒忌 ***duhjih***, adj. & n., jealous, -y.
妒嫉 ***duhjir***, v. i., be jealous, hate with envy.
妒意 ***duhyih***, n., jealousy.

§ 93A.93 (女/く)

媸 93A.93-2

chy.

Adj. Ugly (woman), opp. 妍: 妍媸 whether one is handsome or not.

嫰 93A.93-3

nuhn (*nehn*).
[Var. of 嫩 93A.82]

嬷 93A.93-6

ma (usu. unaccented).

嬷嬷 ***ma'ma***, n., (1) mamma＝媽媽 93A.50; (2) court. address to wet nurse retained and respected in family; (3) old woman relative: 劉嬷嬷; 嬷嬷爹＝奶公 husband of old wet nurse.

SECTION 93B

§ 93B.00 (糸/亅)

紂 93B.00-1

jouh.

N. Name of tyrant, last emperor of Shang Dyn.

縛 93B.00-1

fur (*foh*).

V.t. To tie up: (lit. & fig.) 束縛 tie up; 縛縛 tie up with rope or cord; 反縛 hands tied behind the back.

綍 93B.00-1

fur.
[Var. of 紼 93B.22]

綺 93B.00-1

chii.

N. Fine, thin silk with slanting weave.

Adj. (1) (LL) beautiful, elegant: 綺麗, 綺靡 *-lih, -mii* ↓; 綺文 fine, elegant prose; 綺室 elegant house; 綺襦紈袴 arrayed in silk inner jackets and pants. (2) Young: 綺年 (LL) youth.

綺情 ***chiichirng***, n., beautiful love; beautiful or sentimental thoughts in writing.

綺麗 *chiilih*, adj., elegant, pretty.

綺靡 *chirmii*, adj., extravagant (house); exquisite, sentimental (prose).

綺思 *chiisy*, n., pretty thoughts in writing.

綺語 *chiryuu*, n., sentimental words; decorative prose.

紆 93B.00-3

yu.

Adj. (1) Roundabout (interch. 迂 31.83). (2) Dragging: 紆行 drag along slowly; 紆青拖紫 (LL) "trailing in green and purple"—the high officials.

紆曲 *yuchyu*, adj., roundabout (way), abstruse (opinion).

紆徐 *yushyur*, adj., sluggish.

紆鬱 *yuyuh*, adj., twisted, depressed.

紓 93B.00-3

shu.

V.t. To give relief to, untie, settle (difficulties): 紓難 ditto; 紓禍 relieve disaster.

縟 93B.00-5

ruh.

Adj. (1) Gay, elegant: 榮華紛縟 glorious and resplendent; 縟采 gorgeous, splendid. (2) Tediously cumbersome, involving much detail: 縟禮, 縟節 tiresome ceremonies; 繁文縟節 complicated rules and ceremonials; 繁縟 going into great detail; 縟細 tediously trivial.

紵 93B.00-6

juh.

[Var. of 苧 20A.01]

絎 93B.00-9

hehng (*harng*).

V.i. & n. (To sew with) long, loose stitches.

§ 93B.01 (糸/小)

練 93B.01-1

liahn.

[Cf. 煉, 鍊]

N. (1) Treated silk: 白練 white treated silk, sometimes fig. for waterfalls. (2) A surname.

V.t. (1) To treat, soften, whiten silk by boiling: 練熟絲 such fine silk. (2) To train, practise: 練習, 習練, 訓練, 教練 practice (lessons, games, singing, gymnastics, etc.); 練兵 *-bing* ↓; 練把式 practise, learn boxing postures; 練手兒 practise hand grip; 操練 to drill.

Adj. Skillful, well-trained: 熟練, 諳練 well-trained, thoroughly familiar; 練達 *-dar* ↓.

練兵 *liahnbing*, v. i., train soldiers to form an army.

練達 *liahndar*, adj., skilled, experienced (diplomat); steady and experienced.

練習 *liahnshir*, v. i. & t. & n., practise, -ice; 練習簿 exercise book; 練習生 apprentice, employee in training.

繚 93B.01-1

liaur.

繚亂 *liaurluahn*, adj., in confusion.

繚繞 *liaurraur*, v. i. & t., (of music, sounds, thoughts) encircle, linger in the air.

縹 93B.01-3

piaau.

Adj. Light green, pale green.

縹白 *piaaubor*, adj., clear white.

縹帙 *piaaujyh*, n., (LL) valuable volume, book (formerly, bound in pale green silk).

縹緲 *piaurmiaau*, adj., dimly discernible (of landscape).

縹囊 *piaaunaurng*, n., (LL) *-jyh* ↑.

縹縹 *piaurpiaau*, adj., ditto.

縹緗 *piaushiang*, n., (LL) see *-jyh* ↑.

縹瓦 *piaurwaa*, n., (LL) glazed tile (＝琉璃瓦).

繰 93B.01-4

tzaau (**sau*).

N. A kind of silk fabric.

V.t. (**sau*) (U.f. 繅) 繰絲 reel the silk thread off cocoons; 繰車 an apparatus for doing it.

縲 93B.01-4

leir.

N. A chain for binding criminals: 縲絏 *leirshieh*, n., (also 縲紲)

fetters, shackles.

綜 93B.01-6

tzuhng.

V.t. (1) Overlap: 錯綜 intertwined, variegated. (2) Combine, bring together: 綜括 *-gua* ↓.

綜括 *tzuhnggua*, (1) v. i., to sum up: 綜括一句 in a nutshell, in a word; (2) adj., all-inclusive, all-embracing.

綜合 *tzuhngher*¹, (1) v. t., integrate, synthesize (opp. 分析 analyze); (2) adj., synthetic (method, philosophy); comprehensive, miscellaneous.

綜核 *tzuhngher*², v. t., scrutinize carefully: 綜核(覈)名實 adoption of a policy of official accountability.

綜金字 *tzuhng-jintzyh*, n., characters cut out from wrinkled golden-colored paper.

綜理 *tzuhnglii*, v. t., exercise gen. supervision over, administer, direct, control.

綜析 *tzuhngshi*, v. t., synthesize and analyze.

綜綜 *tzuhng'tzung*, v. t., draw together: 綜綜着眉毛 knit the brows.

綵 93B.01-9

tsaai.

N. Silk festoon: 張燈結綵 hang lanterns and festoons; 剪綵 cut the ribbon (launching ship, etc.).

綵仗 *tsaaijahng*, n., official insignia, parasols, etc. on parade.

綵結 *tsaaijier*, n., a woman's hair decoration (=方[Δ]勝 60.50).

綵樓 *tsaailour*, n., decorative raised platform at festivals.

綵棚 *tsaiperng*, n., temporary booth hung with festoons.

綵勝 *tsaaishehng*, n., see *-jier* ↑.

緥 93B.01-9

baau.

[Var. of 褓, see 襁[Δ]褓 63C.93]

絲 93B.01-9

sy.

N. (1) Silk: 絲織品 silks, silk goods; 絲襪 silk stockings; 絲帶 silk ribbon; 絲巾 silk scarf; 抽絲, 抽繭剝絲 to reel silk from cocoon; 吐絲 (silkworm) spins silk; 生絲 raw silk. (2) Fine threads of many kinds: 蛛絲 gossamer; 蛛絲馬跡 clues to murder, mystery, etc.; 遊絲 flying gossamer; 鐵絲 wire; 銅絲 copper wire; 雨絲 fine drizzle; 藕絲 thread of arrowroot; 藕斷絲連 (love affair) not completely cut off; 肉絲 shredded meat; 命若懸絲 life hanging by a thread; 絲絲入扣 (story plot) intricately woven together. (3) (Poet.) u. f. 思 thread of thought: 愁絲 skein of sorrow; 情絲 longing of love. (4) One hundredth of 釐 *li* or one hundred thousandth of 兩 *liaang*; infinitesimal part: 絲毫, 絲髮, 絲忽 *-haur, -faa, -hu* ↓; 一絲不掛 stark naked. (5) Stringed instrument: 絲竹, 絲管 *-jur, -guaan* ↓; 絲絃 *-shiarn* ↓.

絲蟲 *sy-churng*, n., tapeworm.

絲髮 *syfaa*, n., (1) silky hair; (2) adv., very small, see *-haur* ↓.

絲瓜 *sygua* (*-'gua*), n., the loofah gourd.

絲管 *sy-guaan*, strings and woodwind instruments.

絲光棉 *syguang-miarn*, n., mercerized cotton.

絲毫 *syhaur*, n. & adv., the slightest (usu. used negatively) (10 絲 =1毫): 沒有絲毫不同 not the slightest difference; 絲毫不肯讓步 will not make the slightest concession.

絲忽 *syhu*, n., tiny, brief.

絲竹 *syjur*, n., music of string and flute.

絲兒 *se'l*, n., small, fine particles.

絲綹(兒) *sylioou*(*-liou'l*), n., tiny tuft (of s. t.).

絲蘿 *syluor*, n., (poet.) the bond of matrimony.

絲綸 *sylurn*, n., (AC) royal maukate, imperial decree.

絲棉 *symiarn*, n., silk wadding: 絲棉兒 silk quilted (dresses, etc.).

絲帕 *sypah*, n., silk shawl.

絲絨 *syrurng*, n., silk velvet.

絲紗 *sysha*, n., gauze.

絲線 *syshiahn*, n., silk thread.

絲絃 *syshiarn*, n., stringed instrument in gen.

絲絲 *sysy*, adj., in fine threads: 雨絲絲 it drizzles; 絲絲拉拉 (of disease) long drawn out.

絲桐 *syturng*, n., the lute.

絲子 *sytz*, n., filament, fiber, fine thread.

縧 93B.01-9

tau.

[Var. of 條 91A.01]

繅 93B.01-9

sau.

V.t. To reel the silk thread off cocoons: 繅絲 ditto.

§ 93B.02 (糸/ㄎ)

絿 93B.02-1

chiour.

Adj. 不競不絿 (AC) not tensed up in competition, not overanxious for honor or fame.

繯 93B.02-4

huarn.

N. & v.t. A noose: 投繯自盡 to hang oneself; 繯首 to hang as punishment.

縗 93B.02-6

tsuei.

N. Hemp covering over gown in severe mourning for parents.

線 93B.02-9

shiahn.
[Var. of 綫 93B.71]

N. (1) A thread: 針線 needlework; 棉線 cotton thread; 毛線 wool, woolen yarn; 絲線 silk thread; 鐵線 wire; 電線 wire (for electric power); 無線電 radio, wireless, etc. (2) A line: 直線 straight line; 平行線 parallel lines; 弧線 a curve; 界線 boundary line; 海岸線 coast line; 分水線 water shed. (3) Battle line: 前線 front line, front unit; 防線 defense line. (4) Route: 航線 navigation route; 路線 route in gen.; 幹線 main line; 支線 branch line. (5) Ray: 一線希望, 光明 a ray of hope, of light; 一線生機 a feeble thread of life, a ray of hope; 宇宙線 cosmic ray; X光線 X-ray; 紫外線 ultraviolet ray; 紅外線 infrared ray; 輻射線 radiation; 光線 light ray, beam. (6) Line of detection: 線索 *-suoo* ↓; 線人 *-rern* ↓.

線蟲 *shiahn-churng*, n., tapeworm and the like, *Nematoda*.
線圈 *shiahn-chyuan*, n., a coil.
線段 *shiahn-duahn*, n., section of line.
線桄(子)(兒) *shiahn-guahng(tz)('l)*, n., ball of thread; yarn.
線軸 *shiahn-jour*, n., spool for thread; bobbin.
線裝書 *shiahn-juang-shu*, n., books bound by stitches at back, gen. term for Chin. books of old-type binding.
線腳 *shiahn-jyuer* (*-jiaau*), n., the visible stitches.
線路 *shiahn-luh*, n., line of communication; circuit.
線民 *shiahn-mirn*, n., stool pigeon.
線人 *shiahn-rern*, n., see *-mirn* ↑.
線香 *shiahn-shiang*, n., coil incense.
線索 *shiahnsuoo*, n., line of story, clue to be followed in tracing crime.
線膛 *shiahn-tarng*, n., gun barrel with spiral lines inside.
線條 *shiahn-tiaur*, n., the line in drawing.
線頭兒 *shiahn-tour'l*, n., odd pieces of thread; (fig.) beginnings of things.

綠 93B.02-9

lyuh.
[Dist. 錄 81A.02]

N. & adj. (1) The green color, esp. of vegetation, or similar color: 綠草 green grass; 綠油油 dripping green; 青山綠水 green hills and blue waters; 綠茶 green tea; 墨綠 dark blue; 綠鬢朱顏 dark hair and ruddy complexion; 青綠 green; 碧綠 gen. blue (oft. of lake, pond); 綠野 green pastures, grassy plains; 綠茵 carpet of green lawn; 戴綠頭巾, 綠帽子 be a cuckold husband; 綠衣使者 mailman (usu. in green uniform); 綠葉成陰(子滿枝) (fig.) (girl become) young mother or many children; 綠林 *-lirn* ↓. (2) Chlorine (interch. 氯): 氯^Δ氣 92.70.

綠寶石 *lyuhbaaushyr*, n., see *-juhshyr* ↓.
綠豆 *lyuhdouh*, n., (bot.) green lentil: 綠豆糕, 粥, 湯 cake, gruel, soup of lentil.
綠礬 *lyuhfarn*, n., (min.) melanterite, green vitriol.
綠肥 *lyuhfeir*, n., (agriculture) green manure, compost of young plants.
綠洲 *lyuhjou*, n., oasis.
綠柱石 *lyuhjuhshyr*, n., (min.) beryl; 綠柱玉 emerald.
綠林 *lyuhlirn*, n., as in 綠林豪傑 (好漢) "heroes of greenwood" of Robin Hood type.
綠藻 *lyuhtzaau*, n., (bot.) any kind of floating waterweed, *Chlorophyceae*.
綠蔭 *lyuhyihn*, n., green shade; 「greenery.

緣 93B.02-9

yuarn (**yuahn*).

N. (1) Reason: 緣故, 緣由 *-guh*, *-your* ↓. (2) (**yuahn*) Hem, border (of sleeve, bed): 邊緣 ditto. (3) Affinity, sympathy, friendship: 姻緣 marriage. (4) Fate, predestination: 前緣 predestined in previous incarnation; 後緣 predestination in future; 夙緣, 宿緣 predestination from the past; 孽緣 fate as conditioned by person's past, *karma*. (5) Opportunity, luck: 良緣 good opportunity; 有緣 have the luck; 無緣 no luck or opportunity; 緣分 *-fehn* ↓. (6) (Budd.) contributions to temple, like "storing up treasures in heaven": 化緣 solicit contribution to Budd. church; 緣簿 book for recording contributions; 捐緣 make contributions to public cause.

A

V.t. To climb up: 緣木求魚 (AC) climb trees to look for fish—futile; 夤緣, 攀緣 climb up socially.

緣起 *yuarnchii*, n., (1) (a sketch of) origin of a work or society; (2) origin of events.
緣法(兒) *yuarn'fa('l)*, n., see -*fehn*↓.
緣分 *yuarnfehn*, n., (1) (Budd.) destiny, luck as conditioned by one's past; (2) good luck (to meet s.o.); (3) natural affinity among friends.
緣故 *yuarnguh*, n., reason, cause: 無緣無故 without any cause or reason.
緣何 *yuarn-her*, adv., wherefore, for what reason?
緣桑螺 *yuarnsang-luor*, n., (zoo.) a kind of snail, *Limnaea japonica*.
緣飾 *yuarnshyh*, v.t., (LL) to decorate up for show.
緣坐 *yuarntzuoh*, v.i., to be punished for complicity.
緣業 *yuarnyeh*, n., (Budd.) a man's fate as conditioned by his past.
緣因 *yuarnyin*, n., reason (for things), also wr. 原因.
緣由 *yuarnyour*, n., ditto, also wr. 原由.

§93B.10 (糸/十)

緙 93B.10-2

keh.

緙繡 *kehshiouh*, n., anc. "cut" embroidery.
緙絲 *kehsy*, n., anc. tapestry of cut silk.

B

綽 93B.10-2

chuoh.

V.t. (MC) u. f. 捉 to grasp: 把那箭一綽綽在手上 catch that (flying) arrow in one's hand.

Adj. (1) Graceful: 綽約 -*yue*↓. (2) Ample: 綽綽, 綽裕 -*chuoh*, -*yuh*↓; 寬綽 ample (gown, funds); 闊綽 have lots of money to throw around. (3) Nickname: 綽名, 綽號 -*mirng*, -*hauh*↓.

綽綽 *chuohchuoh*, adj., as in 綽綽有餘 more than enough to meet the needs.
綽號 *chuohhauh*, n., nickname.
綽名 *chuohmirng*, n., ditto.
綽約 *chuohyue*, adj., graceful (figure).
綽裕 *chuohyuh*, adj., ample (means).

絆 93B.10-2

bahn.
[Var. 靽]

N. Reins, a halter.

V.i. & t. (1) Be a hindrance: 絆住 successfully hinder movement; 給絆住了 so hindered. (2) To cause to trip: 把他絆倒 trip a person.

絆腳 *bahnjiaau*, v. i. & t., to trip, to tie up person's movements; 絆腳石 n., a stumbling block.
絆馬索 *bahnmarsuoo*, n., rope for tripping enemy's horse; 絆馬坑 --*keng*, n., horse trap.

緯 93B.10-2

weei.

C

N. (1) Woof, versus 經 warp: see 經[△]緯 93B.30. (2) Latitude, versus 經 longitude: 南緯, 北緯 southern, northern latitude(s).

緯度 *weeiduh*, n., degree of latitude.
緯線 *weeishiahn*, n., line of latitude.

緝 93B.10-4

chih (*chi).

V.t. (1) To weave hempen thread. (2) To hem clothing. (3) (Pr. *chi*) close stitching. (4) To search for (criminal) and arrest: 緝捕 -*buu*↓; 通緝 issue order for arrest of wanted criminal; 緝盜 search for thief or robber.

Adj. Bright, open, peaceful: 緝熙, 緝穆 -*shi*, -*muh*↓.

緝捕 *chihbuu*, (1) v. t., to warrant search and arrest; (2) n., formerly, officer in charge of catching thieves.
緝緝 *chihchih*, adv., (AC) as in 緝緝翩翩 make lisping noise.
緝獲 *chihhuoh*, v. t., succeed in arresting criminal or finding booty.
緝究 *chihjiouh*, v. t., investigate and prosecute.
緝理 *chihlii*, v. t., adjust, arrange.
緝穆 *chihmuh*, adj., (AC) in harmony.
緝拿 *chihnar*, v. t., arrest (criminal).
緝熙 *chihshi*, adj., (AC) bright and glorious.
緝私 *chih-sy*, v. i., search for smuggling, -er.

繹 93B.10-4

yih.

緣 緙 綽 絆 緯 緝 繹

亅	小	⺊	十	土	ナ	卄	凵	丨	一	丁	フ	口	囚	冈	冂	厂	尸	亠	广	宀	丶	乚	弋	心	八	人	乂	⌒	一	丿	⺊	く
00	01	02	10	11	12	20	21	22	30	31	32	40	41	42	50	51	52	60	61	62	63	70	71	72	80	81	82	83	90	91	92	93

繹 綷 綷 絳 經 絰 經 纏 紝 維

V.i. To unravel thread, reel the silk thread off cocoons: 絡繹 adj., continuous (coming and going); 演繹 (logic) to deduce, deductive, -tion; 抽繹 unravel (meaning).

綷 93B.10–6

tsueih.

V.i. (AC) to group together.

綷䌨 *tsuihtsaih*, n., rustling sound.

綷 93B.10–6

chiahn.

N. & v.t. To pull boat upstream with a rope by team of men walking on shore; such rope: 拉綷 to pull boat upstream; 綷夫, 綷戶 such boat hands.

絳 93B.10–9

jiahng.

N. & adj. Deep red (color): 絳色 deep crimson.

絳闕 *jiahngchyueh*, n., palace grounds.
絳帳 *jiahngjahng*, n., a teacher's seat—allu. to the story of Ma Rurng 馬融 of the Hahn Dyn.

§ 93B.11 (糸/土)

經 93B.11–3

jing.

[Abbr. of 經 93B.30]

絰 93B.11–3

dier.

N. (LL) hemp cloth of mourning: 衰絰 ditto.

經 93B.11–4

moh.

N. (AC) Double-strand rope.

纏 93B.11–6

charn (**tsair*).

V.t. (1) To bind, to encircle: 繞纏, 纏縛 *-rauh, -fur* ↓; 纏足, 纏腳 *-tzur, -jiaau* ↓; 腰纏, 盤纏 money carried in girdle, esp. for journey. (2) To tie up: 纏束 *-shuh* ↓; 俗務纏身 tied up with business affairs. (3) To bother, annoy, entangle: 糾纏 to tie up in a knot; (fig.) 休纏我 don't bother me; 纏來纏去 keep bothering, also drag around and around or get entangled. (4) (S.t.) difficult to handle: 她不好纏 she is difficult to cope with (better keep away from).

Adv. (**tsair*) Just, just now (also wr. 才): 剛纏 ditto; 纏在說話 was just talking a moment ago (see 才 10.00).

纏袋 *charndaih*[1], n., a wallet suspended on girdle.
纏帶 *charndaih*[2], n., girdle (usu. of cloth).
纏縛 *charnfur*, v.t., (lit. & fig.) tie up, bind (bundle, legs, etc.).
纏腳 *charnjiaau*, v. i., bind one's feet (foot binding), see *-tzur* ↓.
纏夾二 *charnjiar-erh*, n., (Shanghai) an annoying (muddle-headed) person, a pettifogger.
纏累 *charnleei*, v. t., to involve, implicate (another).
纏綿 *charnmiarn*, adj., sentimental: 纏綿悱惻 sad and sentimental (poem, letter).
纏磨 *charn'mo*, v. t., (1) to bother: 你別纏磨我 don't bother me; (2) to be tangled up with (girl, lover).
纏擾 *charnraau*, v. t., to annoy (person) by persistent pleading, etc.
纏繞 *charnrauh*, v. t., (of memories, longings) envelop (one's mind).
纏惹 *charnree*, v. t., to annoy.
纏身 *charn-shen*, v. t., to be entangled (with business).
纏聲 *charn-sheng*, n., (mus.) to prolong sound on string.
纏束 *charnshuh*, v. t. & n., to restrict by rules, to hamper; to tie up (girdle); girdle.
纏頭 *charntour*, n., formerly, gratuity given to singer in appreciation.
纏足 *charntzur*, v. i., to bind one's feet (foot binding).

紝 93B.11–9

rehn (*rern*).

V.t. Weave, esp. silken fabrics: 織紝 make by weaving.

維 93B.11–9

weir.

N. (1) A fish net, what holds together: 四維八德 the four anchors ("hawsers") and eight virtues, i.e., moral foundations of society. (2) Fiber: 纖維 fiber, plastic fiber.

V.i. & t. (1) To hold together, bind together, maintain: 維持, 維護 *-chyr* ↓, *-huh* ↓; 維繫 *-shih* ↓. (2) To think, ponder: 思維 ditto (also wr. 思惟). (3) (AC interch. 爲, 是, 以) to be: 其命維新 the mandate from Heaven is new; 進退維谷 only ravines——difficult to proceed or retreat; 時運維艱 the times are difficult; 維子之故 it is on account of you, see 惟 22A.11.

維持 *weirchyr*, v.t., to maintain, support, keep (order).
維護 *weirhuh*, v.t., support, uphold (faith, country).
維縶 *weirjyr*, v.t., to bind, hold together (people's loyalty, etc.); to restrain.
維生素 *weir-sheng-suh*, n., see *-tamihng* ↓; 維生系統 (astron.) life-support system.
維繫 *weirshih*, v.t., to tie, bind, keep from falling apart, support (faith, life).
維新 *weirshin*, v.i., to reform: 維新派 reformist in gen; 維新運動 Reformist Movement of 1898.
維他命 *weirtamihng*, n., (translit.) vitamin.

§93B.21 (糸/ㄴ)

絀 93B.21-2

chuh.

V.t. U. f. 黜 to downgrade.

Adj. Short of funds: 支絀, 短絀 ditto; 相形見絀 phr., inferior by comparison.

紲 93B.21-2

shieh.

N. Reins (interch. 絏 93A.70).

繼 93B.21-2

jih.

V.t. Continue, follow, come in the wake of: 繼續 *-shyuh* ↓; 相繼 come one after another; 繼承 *-cherng* ↓; 繼往開來 be a follower of past traditions and a trail blazer for future generations; 過繼 (of a child) adopt or be adopted.

Prep. Step-: 繼父, 繼母, 繼子 step-father, -mother, -son.

繼承 *jihcherng*, v. t., fall heir to, inherit: 繼承遺志 (of sons or political followers) carry on the unfinished lifework of the father or leader; 繼承財產 inherit property; 繼承權 right of inheritance; 繼承人 heir.
繼親 *jihchin*, v. i., (MC) become related by marriage, marry.
繼軌 *jih-gueei*, v. i., follow one after another.
繼踵 *jihjuung*, v. i., follow in the footsteps of another (踵＝heels).
繼志 *jihjyh*, v. i., carry on the unfinished work of one's father or predecessor.
繼配 *jihpeih*, n., the second wife.
繼任 *jihrehn*, v. i. & t., succeed (another) in office.
繼室 *jihshyh*, n., the second wife.
繼續 *jihshyuh*, (1) v. t., continue; (2) adj., continual, continuous: 繼續不斷 without a break.
繼嗣 *jih-syh*, n., an adopted son.
繼體 *jih-tii*, v. i., (LL) succeed to the throne.
繼統 *jih-tuung*, v. i., become king, ascend the throne.
繼武 *jihwuu*, v. i., follow the trail blazed by one's predecessor (武＝步武 footsteps).

綃 93B.21-9

tau.

[Var. of 絛 91A.01, and of 韜 20B.21]

§93B.22 (糸/丨)

綁 93B.22-1

baang.

V.t. Tie up; tie up with hands at the back, esp., to kidnap: 綁起來, 綁上 to tie up (person); 綁緊 tie up tight; 綁赴市曹 parade criminal on way to execution ground.

綁票 *baangpiauh*, v. t., kidnap person.
綁(裹)腿 *barng* (*guor*) *tueei*, n., leggings.

糾 93B.22-2

jiouh (*jioou*).

V.t. (1) Oversee, superintend: 糾察 *-char* ↓. (2) To correct, rectify, set right: 糾正 *-jehng* ↓. (3) Impeach, censure: 糾彈 *-tarn*, 糾舉 *-jyuu* ↓. (4) Join, band together, unite: 糾合 *-her*, 糾結 *-jier* ↓. (5) To stir up trouble: 糾纏 *-charn*, 糾紛 *-fen*, 糾葛 *-ger* ↓; 糾衆 incite people.

糾察 *jiouchar*, v. t., investigate, examine, probe.
糾纏 *jioucharn*, v. t., (1) entwine; (2) pester with unwanted attentions, persistent requests: 糾纏不清 (of problems) entangled, incapable of ready solution, (of persons) be a constant pest.
糾紛 *jioufen*, n., a dispute, conflicts.
糾葛 *jiouger*, n., entanglements,

維 絀 紲 繼 綃 綁 糾

亅	小	⺊	十	土	ナ	卄	ㄴ卜	丨	一	丅	フ	口	区	冈	㇆	𠂆	尸	亠	广	宀	丶	乚	弋	心	八	人	乂	⺄	一	丿丿	∠	く
00	01	02	10	11	12	20	21	22	30	31	32	40	41	42	50	51	52	60	61	62	63	70	71	72	80	81	82	83	90	91	92	93

disputes, complications.

糾合 *jiouher*, v. t., gather together, muster.

糾正 *jioujehng*, v. t., to correct (an error, mistake, misconduct).

糾結 *jioujier*, v. t., to band together, muster, rally.

糾糾 *jiourjioou*, adj., (1) interwoven, intertwining; (2) (=赳赳) valiant, gallant.

糾擧 *jioujyuu*, v. t., to censure, impeach (officials).

糾彈 *jioutarn*, v. t., impeach (corrupt officials).

紳 93B.22-2

shen.

N. (1) A girdle. (2) The gentry: 搢紳 ditto; 鄉紳 country gentry, usu. scholar out of employ and living by wits; 紳商 the gentry and the business people.

紳耆 *shenchir*, n., gentry and elders.

紳衿 *shenjin*, n., retired officials living in the country.

紳士 *shenshyh*, n., the gentry, esquires, gentlemen.

紼 93B.22-2

fur.

N. Big rope; cord guiding the hearse: 執紼 follow the coffin as bereaved son.

繡 93B.22-2

shiouh.

N. Embroidery.

V.t. To embroider; to cover with embroidery; hence (passive) embroidered (quilt cover, shoes).

Adj. Fine like embroidery: 錦繡河山 this beautiful land.

繡補 *shiouh-buu*, n., (Manchu Dyn.) square piece in chest and back of mandarin over-jacket, embroidered with different birds and animals indicating different ranks.

繡球 *shiouh-chiour*, n., (1) (bot.) hydrangea flower; (2) an embroidered ball: 拋繡球 throw an embroidered ball as a way of selecting a bridegroom (in stories).

繡墩 *shiouh-duhn*, n., a stool with embroidered cover.

繡房 *shiouhfarng*, n., formerly, a lady's bedroom, boudoir.

繡閣 *shiouhger*, n., formerly, a lady's private quarters.

繡工 *shiouhgung*, n., embroidery.

繡花 *shiouhhua*, adj., embroidered (pillowcase, shoes, etc.): 繡花(兒)枕頭 a person with good looks but empty-minded like an embroidered pillowcase.

繡戶 *shiouhhuh*, n., see *-ger* ↑.

繡貨 *shiouhhuoh*, n., embroidery goods.

繡活 *shiouhhuor*, n., see *-gung* ↑.

繡面 *shiouh-miahn*, n., (1) (aborigines) painted face of adult girl; (2) painted and powdered face in gen.

繡像 *shiouhshiahng*, n., (1) embroidered portrait; (2) fine-lined pen portrait: 繡像小說 a novel with illustrated portraits of heroes.

繡眼(兒) *shiouhyaan* (*-yaa'l*), n., (zoo.) a singing bird, *Zosterops.*

緋 93B.22-2

fei.

Adj. Deep red, dark red.

緋紅 *feeihurng*, adj., dark red, purplished pink: 兩頰緋紅 pink cheeks; flushed with shame, etc.

緋聞 *feeiwern*, n., sexy news.

締 93B.22-6

dih.

V.i. & t. Cement (wedlock, alliance): 締盟, 締約 form alliance, treaty; 締婚 unite in wedlock; 締交 cement friendship; 取^締 31S.82, prohibit, prosecute (person), suspend (rights).

締結 *dihjie*, v.t., form, unite: 締結邦交, 良緣 strengthen friendship between countries, form marital ties.

締造 *dihtzauh*, v.t., create (a republic).

綈 93B.22-8

tir.

N. A kind of heavy silk.

縑 93B.22-8

jian.

N. Fine silk: 縑素 white silk used for writing or painting; 零縑 odds and ends.

絺 93B.22-8

chy.

N. Fine linen: 絺綌 fine and coarse linen (綌).

緜 93B.22-9

miarn.

[Var. of 綿 91S.01]

§ 93B.30 (糸/一)

纑 93B.30-2

lur.

N. (1) A cloth cord. (2) Treated hemp; linen.

絚 93B.30-2

geng.

N. A hawser, cable.

繮 93B.30-3

jiang (gang).
[Var. of 韁 20B.30]

N. A bridle: 繮繩 reins.

紅 93B.30-3

*hurng (*gung).*

N. (1) Red apparel, festoon, etc.: 披紅 put on red robe (as bride, old lady on birthday, etc.); 掛紅 hang red festoons. (2) A bonus, an award: 分紅 distribute bonus, see 紅利 *-lih*¹↓. (3) (**gung*) In 女紅 women's needlework. (4) A surname.

V.t. To flush red, to blush red: 臉都紅了, 紅了臉 get red in the face from anger or shame; 發紅 to flush.

Adj. (1) Red in color (flowers, dress, ink): 淡紅, 桃紅 pink; 朱紅 vermilion; 紫紅 crimson; 鮮紅 fresh red color; 豔紅 a rich red; 紅光滿面 face glows with health; 紅紅綠綠 young men and women in holiday dress; 酒紅燈綠 bright wine banquet; 紅霞 red glow at sunset; 紅十字會 the Red Cross Society; 臉紅耳赤 flush red in the face; 紅顏 *-yarn*↓. (2) Red as Communist: 紅軍 the Red Army (cf. 赤 11.00). (3) Red as symbol of success, luck, happiness, popularity: 紅歌星 star singer at night clubs; 紅伶 popular actor or actress; 唱戲唱紅了 has become a star singer; 把她捧紅了 have, by popular acclaim, made her a star; 紅事 *-shyh*↓; 紅福 good luck: 紅運 *-yuhn*↓. (4) Red referring to women: 紅妝, 紅樓 *-juang, -lour*↓.

紅寶石 *hurng-baau-shyr*, n., ruby; jacinth (also called 紅玉).

紅八仙 *hurng bashian*, n., (bot.) hydrangea.

紅斑 *hurngban*, n., (med.) rash.

紅包 *hurngbau*, n., "red package"—(1) a gift of money to children, servants on holidays; (2) now generally a bribe with money.

紅璧璽 *hurngbihshii*, n., onyx.

紅茶 *hurng-char*, n., black tea.

紅潮 *hurng-chaur*, n., (1) menstruation; (2) flush on the face.

紅塵 *hurngchern*, n., (Budd.) the material or secular world.

紅契 *hurng-chih*, n., a deed with red stamp on it.

紅旗 *hurng-chir*, n., red flag denoting danger.

紅燈 *hurng-deng*, n., red light in traffic control: 紅燈區 n., red light district.

紅頂子 *hurngdiingtz*, n., a jewel button on top of official hat showing highest ranks in Manchu officialdom.

紅豆 *hurngdouh*, n., (1) red bean; (2) (=相思子) red seeds of *Abrus precatorius*, kept as souvenir of love.

紅番 *hurng-fan*, n., red Indians.

紅礬 *hurngfarn*, n., arsenic.

紅粉 *hurngfeen*, n., gaily dressed women.

紅倌兒 *hurngguа'l*, n., adult prostitute (also 渾倌兒) as contrasted with 清倌兒 singsong girls who are still virgins.

紅股 *hurng-guu*, n., bonus share in company given and not paid for.

紅鶴 *hurng-heh*, n., (zoo.) eastern ibis.

紅花 *hurnhua*, n., (1) a red flower; (2) the saffron (also 藏紅花); (3) 紅藍花 the safflower; (4) 大紅花 the red hibiscus.

紅貨 *hurnghuoh*, n., jewels, jade, etc.

紅鬍子 *Hurnghurtz*, n., (sl.) bandits in Manchuria.

紅疹子 *hurngjeentz*, n., scarlet fever (also 紅熱病).

紅教 *Hurngjiauh*, n., Red Lamaism.

紅淨 *hurng jihng*, n., (Peking opera) man's role wearing red (as 關公).

紅晶 *hurngjing*, n., rose quartz.

紅妝 *hurng-juang*, n., ladies' make-up and dress.

紅腫 *hurngjuung*, adj., red and swollen (parts of body).

紅軍 *hurng-jyun*, n., the Red Army.

紅藍花 *hurnglarn-hua*, n., (bot.) the safflower.

紅淚 *hnrng leih*, phr., (LL) tears of blood.

紅臉(兒) *hurngliaan(-liaa'l)*, adj., blushing out of shame or flushed with anger.

紅利 *hurnglih*¹, n., bonus; dividends.

紅痢 *hurnglih*², n., dysentery (with blood showing).

紅燐 *hurng-lirn*, n., (chem.) red phosphorus.

紅樓 *hurnglour*, n., "red tower"—ladies' apartments; 紅樓夢 "Red Chamber Dream," a famous novel.

紅鸞 *hurngluarn*, n., a lucky star of love.

紅蘿蔔 *hurngluo'bo*, n., carrots; radish.

紅瑪瑙 *hurng marnaau*, n., red agate; sardonyx.

紅毛 *hurng-maur*, n., formerly, a Britisher, Dutchman or foreigners (sl. in coastal provinces).
紅煤 *hurng-meir*, n., anthracite coal.
紅木 *hurngmuh*, n., teak; black wood, sometimes referred to as mahogany.
紅盤 *hurngparn*, n., business deal on 5th day of first lunar month, first day of New Year for doing business.
紅熱 *hurng-reh*, phr., (phys.) red heat.
紅人 *hurngrern*, n., person at the height of power, one whose services are much in demand.
紅色 *hurngseh*, adj., (1) red; (2) communist: 紅色恐怖 red terror; 紅色作品, etc., communist writings.
紅痧 *hurngsha*, n., scarlet fever (=猩紅熱).
紅生 *hurng sheng*, n., see *-jihng* ↑.
紅線 *hurng-shiahn*, n., (allu.) an invisible thread, tied by a spirit in heaven, to bind boy and girl together as man and wife.
紅事 *hurng-shyh*, n., happy occasion—weddings, birthdays, etc. (also called 喜事; cf. 白事 funeral); 紅白事 weddings and funerals—calls for social expenses.
紅血球 *hurngshyuehchiour*, n., red corpuscle.
紅絲疔 *hurngsy-ding*, n., a malignant boil which could be fatal, appearing as first as thin red streaks on skin.
紅糖 *hurngtarng*, n., brown sugar.
紅帖(子) *hurngtiee(tz)*, n., "red card"—card announcing a happy event (betrothal, birthday, etc.).
紅鐵礦 *hurntiee kuahng*, n., (min.) hematite.
紅土 *hurngtuu*, n., red clay; (min.) laterite.
紅棗 *hurngtzaau*[1], n., red dates.
紅藻 *hurngtzaau*[2], n., a kind of edible seaseed, dried and purple in color (also called 紫菜).
紅字 *hurngtzyh*, n., (1) red mark for failure in examination; (2) red-ink entry, "in the red"; (3) "The Scarlet Letter" by Nathaniel Hawthorne.
紅外線 *hurngwaih shiahn*, n., (phys.) infrared rays.
紅顏 *hurngyarn*, n., a beauty: 紅顏薄命 "a beautiful girl has (oft.) an unfortunate life."
紅葉 *hurng-yeh*, n., (poet.) maple leaf, usu. 楓葉.
紅玉 *hurngyuh*, n., ruby.
紅運 *hurng-yuhn*, n., good luck: 走紅運 in luck.

經 93B.30-3

jing.

N. (1) Classical works: 經書 *-shu* ↓; 五經, 十三經 the Five, Thirteen Confucian Classics; 經史子集 Classics, History, Philosophy, and Belles-lettres; 聖經 the Holy Bible; 可蘭經 the Koran; 佛經 Buddhist sutras; 念經 to chant the sutras; 講經 expound the teachings of Buddha or Confucius; 讀經 study the Confucian classics. (2) Immutable rules: 凡爲天下國家有九經 there are nine cardinal principles to be attended to in governing nations and empires. (3) The warp of a fabric, longitude (opp. 緯 the woof, latitude): 經緯 *-weei*, 經度 *-duh*, 經線 *-shiahn* ↓; 東經, 西經 east, west longitude. (4) Blood vessels: 經脈 *-moh*, 經絡 *-luoh* ↓. (5) Short for 月經, the menses: 經閉 *-bih*, 經水 *-shueei*, 經期 *-chir* ↓. (6) A surname.

V.i. & t. (1) V. i., die by hanging or strangulation: 自經 commit suicide by hanging. (2) V.t., manage, handle, engage in: 經理 *-lii* ↓; 經營 *-yirng*, 經略 *-lyueh* ↓; 經之營之 (AC) (of buildings) busily planning and designing; 經商 *-shang* ↓. (3) Go or pass through: 經過 *-guoh*, 經歷 *-lih* ↓; 流經, 行經 flow, go across; 經由 *-your* ↓; 經驗 *-yahn* ↓; 經年累月 for months and years on end; 身經百戰 battle-seasoned ("having seen action a hundred times").

Adv. Already: 已經, 曾經, 業經 previously, in the past.

經閉 *jingbih*, n., (physiol.) dysmenorrhea, stoppage of the menses.
經常費 *jingcharng-feih*, n., regular expenses (opp. 臨時費 extraordinary expenses).
經期 *jingchir*, n., period of menstruation.
經幢 *jing-chuarng*, n., a stone pillar with Buddhist inscriptions.
經典 *jingdiaan*, n., (1) classics; (2) religious works.
經度 *jingduh*, n., degrees of longitude.
經費 *jingfeih*, n., funds, expenditure, outlay.
經管 *jingguaan*, v. t., manage, administer.
經過 *jingguoh*, v. i. & t., (1) pass through; (2) have taken place; (3) extend over, cover.
經解 *jingjiee*, n., exegesis of the Confucian classics.
經界 *jingjieh*, n., (1) boundaries of farm lands; (2) national boundaries.
經紀 *jingjih*[1], n., (1) a business agent; (2) discipline.
經濟 *jingjih*[2], (1) adj., economic; (2) n., economy: 國民經濟 the national economy; (3) v.t., economize; 經濟學(家) economics, (-ist).
經今 *jingjin*, adv., up to the present, by now.
經久 *jingjioou*, adj., enduring, lasting, durable.
經籍 *jingjir*, n., (1) the Confucian classics; (2) books in gen.
經傳 *jingjuahn*, n., the Confucian classics and commentaries on them.
經練 *jing(')liahn*, v. i., to gain experience through practical work; n., such experience.
經歷 *jinglih*, (1) v. t., to experience; (2) pass or go through, extend over, cover; (3) n., a person's past career.
經理 *jinglii*, v. t. & n., manage(r); 經理人 agent, (mus.) impresario.
經絡 *jingluoh*, n., veins and arteries.
經綸 *jinglurn*, v. t., to rule, administer, govern: 經綸天下 to order and regulate the affairs of state.

經略 *jinglyueh*, (1) v. t., exercise gen. supervision over, pacify; (2) n., formerly, a High Commissioner, generally of border areas.

經脈 *jingmoh*, n., (Chin. med.) blood vessels.

經年 *jingniarn*, n. & adv., one year; all the year round.

經商 *jingshang*, v. i., go into business, engage in trading.

經線 *jingshiahn*, n., degrees of longitude.

經心 *jingshin*, v. t., pay close attention to, be heedful of: 偶不經心 inadvertently.

經手 *jingshoou*, v. t., to handle, take charge of, via a third party.

經售 *jingshouh*, v. t., sell, deal in (certain kinds of goods).

經書 *jingshu*, n., the Confucian classics.

經水 *jingshueei*, n., the menses.

經世 *jingshyh*, v. i., take an active interest in public affairs: 經世之學 studies on the at of government.

經學 *jingshyuer*, n., classical learning; 經學家 classical scholar, classicist.

經始 *jingshyy*, v. t., begin, lay the foundations of, initiate (an enterprise).

經藏 *jingtzahng*, n., (Budd.) the "sutra-pitaka," collection of sutras.

經緯 *jing-weei*, n., (1) the longitude and latitude of the earth; (2) perpendicular and horizontal lines; (3) any orderly and systematic arrangement: 經緯度 degrees of longitude and latitude; 經緯線 lines drawn on map showing degrees of longitude and latitude; 經緯儀 a theodolite.

經武 *jingwuu*, v. i., make military preparations: 整軍經武 build up the nation's defenses.

經驗 *jing(')yahn*, (1) v.t., have experience of; (2) n., practical experience.

經筵 *jingyarn*, n., a hall or assembly where, formerly, the emperor listened to lectures on the Confucian classics.

經意 *jingyih*[1], (1) v.t., see *-shin* ↑; (2) n., the meaning (of passages) of the Confucian classics.

經義 *jingyih*[2], n., see *-yih*[1] (2) ↑.

經營 *jingyirng*, v. t., (1) build, construct (a house, residence, mansion); (2) to draw up or carry out (a plan); (3) manage and operate (a business); 經營學 management science (Japanese).

經由 *jingyour*, v. i. & adv., (go) by way of.

緼 93B.30-4

yuhn (**yun*).

N. (AC) coarse hemp fiber: 緼袍 (AC) ragged garment filled with coarse hemp.

Adj. (1) Profound: 緼奥 ditto. (2) (**yun*) 絪縕 93B.41, misty.

組 93B.30-4

tzuu.

N. (1) Silk band or cord. (2) A group, section or unit. (3) A section or subdivision: 註冊組 the registrar's office; 醫務組 dispensary, clinic.

V.t. Organize: 組織 *-jy* ↓; 組閣 *-ger* ↓; 組合 unite, combine: 勞動(職工)組合 labor (trade) union; 組成 *-cherng* ↓; 重組 reorganize.

組成 *tzuu-cherng*, v. t., constitute, be composed of.

組閣 *tzuu-ger*, v. i., (political science) to form a Cabinet.

組織 *tzuujy*, v. t. & n., organize, -ation.

紐 93B.30-5

nioou.

N. (1) Handle, knob, part of utensil used in lifting: 壺紐 handle of a bottle; 杯紐 handle of a cup; 印紐 nose of a seal; 門紐 doorknob; 紐耳 a buttonhole. (2) Knot, button: 紐結 button; 紐襻 *-pahn* ↓; (also wr. 鈕) button in machine: 按紐 press a button.

紐扣 *niooukouh*, n., button.

紐襻 *nioоupahn*, n., cloth loops for buttons.

紐約 *Niooyue*, n., New York.

縊 93B.30-8

yih.

V.i. & t. To hang (person); to hang oneself: 自縊, 縊死 ditto.

§ 93B.40 (糸/口)

結 93B.40-1

jier (**jie*).

N. (1) A knot: 打結 to tie knots; 死結 a hard knot; 活結 a slipknot, a running knot; 雙結 a double knot; 蝴蝶結 a bowknot; 帶結 a knot of ribbon; 領結 necktie; 結繩 *-sherng* ↓. (2) A written statement binding the signer to do or refrain from doing certain things: 保結 a written bond offered as surety; 切結, 具結, 出結 a written promise to do or not to do certain things; 取結 take such a promise.

V.i. & t. (1) Unite, connect, join: 結縭 *-lir*, 結婚 *-hun*, 結合 *-her*[1], 結

親 *-chin*, 結拜 *-baih*, 結交 *-jiau*, 結契 *-chih*, 結識 *-shyh*, 結社 *-sheh*, 結義 *-yih* ↓; 巴結 fawn on, toady; 勾結 conspire, work in collusion with; 結嫌 *-shiarn*, 結仇 *-chour* ↓. (2) Congeal, coagulate: 結冰 *-bing*, 結力 *-lih* ↓; 凝結 congeal, coagulate, solidify; 聚結, 集結 adhere, assemble, group together; 結念 *-niahn* ↓. (3) Constitute, compose, form: 結構 *-gouh*, 結撰 *-juahn*, 結茅 *-maur*, 結廬 *-lur* ↓. (4) (Also **jie*) to bear fruit: 開花結果 to bloom and bear fruit. (5) Bind into a bundle: 結草 *-tsaau*, 結綵 *-tsaai* ↓. (6) Settle (accounts), wind up, sum up, conclude: 總結 render a final reckoning, summarize; 歸結 come to a conclusion, conclude; 結賬 *-jahng* ↓; 結案 to wind up a lawsuit; 收結, 了結 bring to an end, to end, put a stop to; 結論 *-luhn* ↓; 結果 *-guoo*, 結局 *-jyur* ↓.

Adv. 終結 finally, at last.

結 伴 *jier-bahn*, v. i., go in company with s.o.
結 拜 *jierbaih*, v. i., become sworn brothers or sisters.
結 冰 *jier-bing*, v. i., freeze.
結 腸 *jier-charng*, n., (physiol.) the colon.
結 欠 *jierchiahn*, phr., (accounting) debit balance in the red.
結 契 *jier-chih*, v. i., become fast friends, be on intimate terms with each other.
結 親 *jier-chin*, v. i., unite in marriage.
結 仇 *jier-chour*, v. t., become enemies with, invite the enmity of.
結 毒 *jier-dur*, n., syphilitic infection.
結 髮 *jier-faa*, n., (1) (AC) the coming of age; (2) first marriage: 結髮夫妻 husband and wife by the first marriage.
結 構 *jiergouh*, n., (1) construction, structure (of buildings); (2) composition, structure (of essay, novel); 結構主義 structuralism.
結 果 *jierguoo*, (1) n., outcome, result; (2) v. i., to bear fruit; (3) v. t., finish off, kill (person).
結 合 *jierher*[1], v. i., join together, be united, marry.
結 核 *jier-her*[2], n., (med.) tubercles: 肺結核, 腸結核 tuberculosis of the lungs, intestines.
結 滙 *jier-hueh*, v.i., to settle by a money transfer.
結 婚 *jier-hun*, v. i., marry: 結了婚 already married.
結 賬 *jier-jahng*, v. i., to clear or close accounts.
結 交 *jier-jiau*, v. t., become friends with, cultivate the goodwill or friendship of, befriend.
結 晶 *jierjihng*, (1) v. i., crystallize; (2) n., crystals, crystallization; (fig.) 結晶品 produce of crystallization.
結 撰 *jierjuahn*, v. t., (of litr. works) write, compose.
結 局 *jierjyur*, n., the final outcome, the last act, as of a drama.
結 力 *jierlih*, n., (phys.) cohesion.
結 縭 *jierlir*, v. i., marry, join in wedlock.
結 論 *jierluhn*, (1) v. t., to sum up, conclude; (2) n., summary, conclusion.
結 廬 *jier-lur*, v. i., build a house, hut, cottage.
結 茅 *jier-maur*, v. t., build (a hut) with straw.
結 膜 *jiermor*, n., (physiol.) the conjunctiva: 結膜炎 conjunctivitis.
結 念 *jierniahn*, v. t., be intent on, remember, constantly bear in mind.
結 社 *jier-sheh*, v. i., form a club.
結 舌 *jiersher*, adj., tongue-tied, speechless.
結 繩 *jiersherng*, phr., tie knots on cords as means of reckoning or record-keeping before invention of writing.
結 嫌 *jier-shiarn*, v. t., incur the displeasure of, fall out with through misunderstanding.
結 識 *jiershyh*, v. t., make the acquaintance of, become friends with.
結 實 *jiershyr*, (1) v.i., (of plant) bear fruit, fructify; (2) adj., (pr. *-'shy*) (of persons) strongly built, stout, robust, (of things) solid, firm, durable.
結 穴 *jiershyueih*, n., (1) the central theme, the dominant idea; (2) good site for a grave.
結 算 *jiersuahn*, v. i., see *-jahng* ↑.
結 束 *jiersuh*, v. t., to wind up, suspend (business), to end (war, debate, quarrel, etc.).
結 他 *jierta*, n., guitar.
結 綵 *jier-tsaai*, v. i., to festoon.
結 草 *jiertsaau*, phr., give expression of gratitude to one's benefactor.
結 存 *jiertsurn*, v. i. & n., the balance of a bank account.
結 子 *jiertz*, (1) n., small knots; (2) (**jie-tzyy*) v. i., bear fruit or seeds. ⌈-tion.
結 業 *jieryeh*, v. i. & n., graduate,
結 義 *jieryih*, v. i., see *-baih* ↑.
結 怨 *jier-yuahn*, v. i., see *-chour* ↑.
結 冤 *jier-yuan*, v. i., become deadly enemies.
結 緣 *jier-yuarn*, v. i., lay the basis for future relationship or intimacy.
結 約 *jier-yue*, v. i., sign a treaty or agreement.

紹 93B.40-5

shauh.

V.i. & t. (1) (LL) to continue, carry on: 紹述 carry on (old tradition); 克紹箕裘 carry on family tradition. (2) To put in contact: 介紹 to introduce (person); 紹介 *-jieh* ↓.

紹 介 *shauhjieh*, v. t., to introduce (person).
紹 酒 *shauhjioou*, n., see *-shing* ↓.
紹 興(酒) *Shauhshing(jioou)*, n., rice wine, named after district.

綰 93B.40-6

waan.

V.t. To tie up, to bind; to wind coils of hair.

繕 93B.40-8

shahn.

V.i. & t. (1) To repair: 修繕 renovate (building); 繕城郭 repair city walls for defense; 繕甲兵 keep army in good condition. (2) To make clean copy: 抄繕 ditto; 繕校 make copy and check (manuscript); 繕寫, 繕錄 *-shiee, -luh* ↓.

繕錄 *shahnluh*, v. t., to make hand copy.
繕生 *shahn-sheng*, v. i., (AC) to cultivate life and health.
繕寫 *shahnshiee*, v. i., to make hand copy.
繕性 *shahn-shihng*, v. i., (AC) cultivate man's original nature.

綌 93B.40-8

shih.

N. (AC) coarse linen.

給 93B.40-8

jii (re.pr.); **geei* (sp.pr.).

V.t. (1) To supply, furnish, provide: 供給 supply with things needed; 給養 *-yaang* ↓; 配給 to ration; 給與 *-yuu* ↓; 頒給 confer, bestow; 給獎 to award. (2) (**geei*) Give: 送給你, 給他 this is for you, for him; 把他給打了 he was beaten up ("given a beating"); 給錢 pay money; 給付 *-fuh* ↓; 交給他 hand to him.

Adj. Ample, sufficient: 自給, 自給自足 self-sufficient; 給足 *-tzur* ↓.

Prep. (1) (**geei*) By: 給人整慘了 was given the works or a good trouncing by others; 給汽車撞傷了 was knocked down by a car; 給騙子騙了 was gypped by a swindler. (2) (**geei*) For: 你給他洗洗傷口 please wash his wounds for him; 給我拿來 please bring it here for me.

給付 **geeifuh* (*jii-*), v. i., make payments.
給假 *jiijiah*, v. i., grant leave of absence.
給臉 **geirliaan*, v. i., show courtesy to s.o. who doesn't deserve it, save s.o.'s face: 給臉不要臉 prove oneself unworthy of such courtesy.
給水 *jirshueei*, n., water supply; 給水管 a water pipe; 給水量 the amount of water applied.
給足 *jiitzur*, adj., plentiful, abundant, copious, ample.
給養 *jiryaang*, n., provisions, maintenance, allowance.
給與 *jiryuu*, v. t., to present as a gift or favor.

絡 93B.40-9

luoh.

N. (1) Unbleached linen. (2) Net; halter. (3) 脈絡 vein, capillary network, also threads of thought, reasoning, fine fiber network in oranges, etc.

V.t. To enmesh: 籠絡 to secure allies, win friends with favors: 不爲所籠絡 will not be controlled in action ("put under halter"); 聯絡 affiliate, associate: 聯絡感情 cement friendship, feelings between parties.

絡新婦 *luohshinfuh*, n., a kind of spider.
絡石 *luohshyr*, n., (bot.) Chin. star jasmine.
絡絲娘 *luohsy-niarng*, n., (zoo.) an insect whose incessant cry suggests a spinning wheel (also called 莎雞).
絡緯 *luohweei*, n., ditto.
絡繹 *luohyih*, adv., as in 絡繹不絕 (of visitors, etc.) form a continuous stream.

絡 93B.40-9

lioou.

N. A skein (of silk), a tuft (of hair): 五絡鬚 goatee beard in five tufts.

V.i. (Of dress) form wrinkles: 衣服絡着 dress wrinkled up.

紿 93B.40-9

daih.

V.t. (AC) to cheat, to fool: 欺紿 deceive.

§ 93B.41 (糸/図)

緗 93B.41-1

shiang.

N. Pale yellow silk.

緗帙 *shiangjyh*, n., (1) silk casing for old Chin. books; (2) volumes filling shelves.
緗縹 *shiangpiaau*, n., ditto.
緗色 *shiangseh*, n., pale yellow.

緒 93B.41-1

shyuh.

N. (1) A thread, thread end. (2) A thread, line or order in affairs: 千頭萬緒 a thousand and one things to attend to; 頭緒, 端緒 orderly arrangement, outline, order: 弄個頭緒出來 put it into some kind of order; 一切就緒了 all in order. (3) Ancestral tradition, heritage: 緒業 *-yeh*↓; 統緒 the traditional pattern. (4) The skein of thought: 情緒不好 in an unhappy mood or state of mind.

緒論 *shyuhluhn*, n., introduction, preliminary remarks.
緒言 *shyuhyarn*, n., ditto.
緒業 *shyuhyeh*, n., the heritage of a royal house.
緒餘 *shyuhyur*, n., irrelevant details, thread ends; addenda.

紬 93B.41-2

chour (**chou*).

N. Silks (var. of 綢).

V.t. (**chou*) To select, draw out, (related 抽, see compp.↓).

紬績 **choujih*, v.t., to spin and weave (cloth).
紬次 **choutsyh*, v.t., (LL) to arrange in order.
紬繹 **chouyih*, v.t., to clarify meaning or line of thought.

紺 93B.41-2

gahn.

Adj. (AC) Purple, dark red.

緬 93B.41-3

miaan.

緬甸 *Miaandiahn*, n., Burma.
緬懷 *miaanhuair*, v. t., think of (past events, old friend).
緬邈 *miarnmiaau*, adj., faraway.

縉 93B.41-3

jihn.

N. Red silk.

縉紳 *jihnshen*, n., the officialdom, the gentry (also 搢紳).

細 93B.41-4

shih.

Adj. (1) Small: 細小 *-shiaau*↓; 細路 narrow path; 細流 small stream; 細水長流 a small but steady stream—small but steady income; 不分巨細 regardless of size ("big or small"); 細雨 drizzle, fine rain; 細聲 small voice. (2) Slender (waist, branch): 細裊裊 gracefully slender; 細高挑兒 (挑 pr. *tiaau*) tall and slender (person); 細柳 slender willows. (3) Fine, delicate, (cloth, porcelain): 精細 fine (carving, embroidery, etc.); 細密, 細膩, 細巧, 細緻 *-mih, -nih, -chiaau, -'jyh*↓; 細工, 細活 fine work, handicraft; 細針密縷 fine, close stitches—(fig.) very carefully prepared plot or composition. (4) Detailed, minute: 瑣細 trivial details, 苛細 to exacting (rules, taxes); 細則, 細故, 細情 *-tzer, -guh, -chirng*↓.

Adv. Carefully: 細問 question carefully; 細查, 細究, 細驗 examine carefully (accounts, goods at customs); 細談 have long talk, go over (subject) carefully; 細思, 細想 think carefully, ponder; 細味 ponder over meaning of words, or flavor of dish; 仔細, 詳細, 精細 careful, -ly, with attention to details.

細胞 *shihbau*, n., (biol.) cells; 細胞分裂 amitosis, cell division; 細胞學 cytology.
細部 *shihbuh*, n., minute parts.
細巧 *shihchiaau*, n., fine and delicate, dainty (watch, brooch, etc.).
細情 *shihchirng*, n., the details of a story.
細兒 *shih-erl*, n., young son.
細故 *shihguh*, n., the details, a small item, trivial happening.
細緻 *shih'jyh*, adj., see *-chiaau*↑.
細菌 *shihjyuhn*, n., bacteria; 細菌學 bacteriology.
細君 *shihjyun*, n., (AC) my wife.
細毛(兒) *shihmaur('l)*, n., (1) down, fine hair; (2) fur of fine quality.
細篾兒 *shihmieh'l*, n., fine bamboo splints (used in mats, fine baskets, etc.).
細密 *shihmih*, adj., close (stitches); delicate handling (of detective work or espionage).
細民 *shihmirn*, n., (AC) common people.
細目 *shihmuh*, n., items (of outline), clauses, specific details.
細嫩 *shihnehn*, adj., young tender (skin, sprout).
細娘 *shihniarng*, n., (MC) young girl.
細膩 *shihnih*, adj., dainty, beautiful (needlework, style, description).
細人 *shihrern*, n., (1) common people; (2) the mean and vulgar persons; (3) (MC) concubine: 叫我討個細人 asked me to find a concubine for him.
細輭 *shihruaan*, adj., as in 細輭物品 the valuables (jewels, silks, fragile things).
細弱 *shihruoh*, adj., young and helpless; n., young dependents.
細色 *shihseh*, n., (Budd.) handsome looks.
細小 *shihshiaau*, adj., small, trivial, unimportant (work, affair).
細細 *shihshih*, adj., small and soft (voice), fine, delicate, see Adj. 1 & 3↑; 細細的 adv., carefully.
細行 *shihshihng*, n., small questions of conduct: 不矜細行 is not rigidly puritanical.
細心 *shihshin*[1], adv., with quiet attention; with concentration: 細心的研究 study carefully.

A

細辛 *shihshin*², n., the wild ginger, *Asarum sieboldi*.
細說 *shih-shuo*, (1) v. t., to narrate at leisure; (2) n., (AC) gossip.
細事 *shihshyh*, n., small matters; circumstantial evidence.
細挑 *shih'tiau*, adj., slender (figure).
細崽 *shihtzaai*, n., a "boy" in employ of white foreign homes or firms (also 西崽).
細則 *shihtzer*, n., detailed regulations.
細作 *shihtzuoh*, n., a military spy.
細微 *shihweir*, adj., small, unimportant (matters).
細腰蜂 *shihyau-feng*, n., wasp.
細樂 *shihyueh*, n., Chin. stringed and woodwind music, equiv. chamber music type, without drums and gongs.
細勻 *shihyurn*, adj., smooth and delicate (skin).

絪 93B.41-4

yin.

N. (1) U.f. 茵 20A.41. (2) U.f. 氤 92.70.

綑 93B.41-4

kuun.
[Var. of 捆 10A.41]

緡 93B.41-5

mirn.

N. (AC) (1) A string of cash. (2) Fishing line.

縮 93B.41-6

suh (*suor).

B

V.i. & t. (sp. pr. **suor*) (1) To shrink: 縮小, 縮短 -*shiaau*, -*duaan* ↓; 伸縮 stretch and shrink; 伸縮性 flexibility; 緊縮 adj., tight, v.t., to retrench (economy): 緊縮政策 policy of retrenchment; 縮手縮腳 to shrink from doing s.t.; 縮頭縮腦 to hide from sight (as in peeping), to shrink away from situation. (2) To economize: 縮衣節食 to economize on food and clothing; 縮本 a condensed edition (of a book).

Adj. Short (of cash): 縮於財用 lacking in funds.

縮地 *suh-dih*, v.i., (myth.) magic of shortening distance, by calling forth a distant place at will.
縮短 *suhduaan* (sp.pr. *sour-*), v.t., to shorten (s.t.).
縮額 *suh-eh*, v.i., to knit the brows.
縮合 *suh'he*, v.i., (chem.) to condense.
縮酒 *suh jioou*, v.i., (AC) to pass wine through cloth as filter.
縮小 *suhshiaau* (sp. pr. **sour-*), v.i. & t., to shrink, condense.
縮寫 *suhshiee*, n., abbreviation.
縮手 *suh-shoou*, v.i., to fold one's hands (helplessly).
縮印 *suhyihn*, n. & v.t., to print (books, etc.) on a reduced scale; edition in reduced size.

緧 93B.41-8

chiou.
[Var. of 鞦 20B.81]

繒 93B.41-8

tzeng.

N. (1) Silk fabrics in gen. (2) A surname.

V.t. Fasten: 繒綳 fasten tight.

C

繪 93B.41-8

hueih.

V.i. & t. To draw pictures.

繪畫 *hueihhuah*, v. i. & n., draw (ing).
繪像 *hueihshiahng*, n. & v. i., a portrait; to draw portrait.
繪事 *hueihshyh*, n., (LL) drawing as an art.
繪圖 *hueihtur*, v. i. & n., to draw, drawing as a school subject.

繙 93B.41-9

fan.

V.t. Translate: 繙譯 -*yih*, also wr. 翻譯.

Adj. (AC) fluttering.

緇 93B.41-9

tzy.

Adj. Black: 緇衣 -*yi* ↓; 緇門 -*mern* ↓.

緇塵 *tzychern*, n., (AC) a dress soiled from too much exposure to the elements.
緇黃 *tzyhuarng*, n., monks and Taoist priests ("black and yellow robes").
緇流 *tzyliour*, n., monks.
緇門 *tzymern*, n., Buddhists (so called from the black robes they wear).
緇帷 *tzyweir*, adj., (AC, of forests) dense, overgrown with trees.
緇衣 *tzy-yi*, n., (AC) a black robe worn by a government official during off-duty hours.

綃 繃 繻 絹 絧 綢 綱

§ 93B.42 (糸/冈)

綃 93B.42–2

shiau.

N. A raw silk fabric.

綃鈔 *shiauchau*, n., hair scarf.
綃頭 *shiautour*, n., ditto.

繃 93B.42–2

beng (**beeng*, **behng*).

N. Swaddling clothes, baby wraps.

V.i. & t. (1) To strap: 繃孩子 strap baby on back as way of carrying. (2) Make rough stitches: 把這被面繃一繃 stitch up the bed sheets. (3) Cheat, see 繃騙 *-piahn*↓. (4) Stretch (cloth, drum skin) smooth on rack, or with underpinnings; maintain smooth appearance: 繃繃場面 help make good impression by showing up at occasions, parties. (5) Haggle price: 繃價 *-jiah*↓. (6) (**beeng*) Stifle temper, show long face: 繃着臉(兒) pull a grim face; 繃不住 cannot contain temper any more. (7) (**behng*) Burst open: 繃斷 snap from tension like bowstring.

繃帶 *bengdaih*, n., linen for binding up wounds, bandage.
繃弓(兒)(子) *beng-gung('l)* (*-tz*), n., device for preventing slamming of door.
繃簧 *benghuarng*, n., spring in machines.
繃針 *bengjen*, n., pin.
繃價 *beng-jiah*, v. i., to haggle.
繃騙 *bengpiahn*, v. t., to cheat.
繃子 *bengtz*, n., frame used for embroidery; 繃子手 *--shoou*, n., a professional cheat.

繻 93B.42–3

shyu (**rur*).

N. (1) (AC) fine, thin silk. (2) (**rur*) (LL) pyjama, jacket: 繻袴 silk pyjamas and trousers.

絹 93B.42–4

jyuahn.

N. A kind of fairly stiff silk, much used for painting or calligraphy: 絹綢 *-chour*↓; 絹子 *-tz*↓; 手絹兒 handkerchief; 絹布 lustring; 絹巾 a silk towel; 絹帶 a silk girdle (sash); 絹邊 a silk border (frame); 畫絹 stiff silk for painting on; 絹裱 silk mounting.

絹綢 *jyuahnchour*, n., heavy or stiff silk.
絹子 *jyuahntz*, n., a handkerchief.

絧 93B.42–4

jyuung.

N. An unlined outer garment.

綢 93B.42–4

chour.

N. Silks, silk goods: 綢緞 *-duahn*↓; 綢子 *-tz*↓; 綢衣服 silk dress; 彩綢 colored silks; 紡綢 pongee; 生綢 raw pongee; 熟綢 soft pongee.

綢緞 *chourduahn*, n., silk goods ("light silk and satin").
綢繆 *chourmour*, adj. & v.i., (1) very attentive, affectionate (to lovers, friends); (2) 未雨綢繆 take preventive measures ("fix doors and windows in anticipation of rain").
綢子 *chourtz*, n., silks in gen.

綱 93B.42–4

gang.

N. (1) The main rope of a net, a hawser. (2) Main threads, essential principles: 大綱 a general outline; 綱要 *-yauh*, 綱目 *-muh*, 綱領 *-liing*↓; 提綱挈領 to bring out the most essential points; 綱擧目張 a lucid exposition of outline; sharp definition of categories. (3) Discipline, morale: 綱常 *-charng*, 綱紀 *-jih*, 綱維 *-weir*↓. (4) Power, authority: 乾(*chiarn*)綱 the royal prerogatives, sovereign rights of a prince. (5) A batch of carts or boats going in a group for transporting goods: 鹽綱, 茶綱 transportation of salt, tea by such means; 綱運 *-yuhn*↓; 綱鹽 salt so transported; 綱商 a merchant in such group of transportation; 綱地 a place where goods are so transported; 綱岸 a port where goods are so transported; 到綱 arrival of goods so transported at their destination.

綱常 *gangcharng*, n., short for 三綱五常: 三綱(君臣, 父子, 夫婦) the proper relations between the prince and his ministers, between father and son, and between husband and wife; 五常 the five cardinal virtues of 仁義禮智信.
綱紀 *gangjih*, (1) n., discipline, morale, law and order; (2) formerly, a butler; (3) v. t., (AC) to rule, manage, oversee: 綱紀四方 to rule over the whole country.
綱領 *gangliing*, n., main headings.
綱目 *gangmuh*, n., a general outline (main and subdivisions).
綱維 *gangweir*, n., (1) cardinal principles underlying the morals of a nation; (2) (Budd.) a ruling priest.
綱要 *gangyauh*, n., essential

points, an outline (of a subject).
網運 *gangyuhn*, n., transportation of goods (e.g., salt or tea) by batches of carts or boats going in groups for mutual protection.

網 93B.42-4

waang.

N. (1) A net, netting: 漁網 fish net; 網羅 *-luor* ↓; 網開一面, 網開三面 a net open on one or three sides—purposely leave loopholes for escape from the law; 撒網 cast net; 設網 set trap; 布網 spread net; 漏網 escape being caught; (fig.) entanglements: 塵網 worldly entanglements; 法網 the encompassing laws. (2) Web, net-like structure: 蛛網 spider's web; 髮網 hair net; 鐵絲網 wire netting; barbed net. (3) Network: 通訊網 network of newspaper agencies; 鐵路網 network of railways, etc.

網版 *warngbaan*, n., (printing) copper plate.
網球 *waangchiour*, n., tennis.
網罟 *warngguu*, n., fishing net and traps.
網巾 *waangjin*, n., hair net, meshed shawl.
網狀脈 *waang-juahng-moh*, n., (bot.) netted veins.
網籃 *waanglarn*, n., a basket with net on top.
網羅 *waangluor*, v.t., to seek and collect (famous scholars, etc.).
網膜 *waangmor*, n., (physiol.) the retina.
網目 *waangmuh*, n., meshes.
網眼 *warngyaan*, n., meshes of net.

綳 93B.42-4

beng.

[Var. of 繃↑]

縞 93B.42-6

gaau.

N. White raw silk.

縞素 *gaausuh*, n., a mourning garment.

縭 93B.42-6

lir.
[Var. 褵]

N. Bridal veil, hence 結縭 be married.

V.t. Fasten, attach to.

編 93B.42-6

bian.

N. (1) (AC) a volume (orig. a string of written boards). (2) A surname.

V.t. (1) Weave (basket): 編織, 編結 make by weaving. (2) Make list, arrange in a list: 編號 give number to list of (persons, things); 編戶 register residents (for police records); 編名冊 record containing list of names; 編列 arrange; 編隊 organize troop units, form companies. (3) To edit: 編輯, 編訂 *-ji, -dihng* ↓; 重編 re-edit; 編集 edit by collecting pieces, make anthology or collected works; 編書, 編報 edit a book (dictionary, etc.), a paper. (4) To fictionize: 編造謊言 fabricate (rumors); 編派 *-paih* ↓.

編貝 *bian beih*, (AC phr.) teeth like row of shells.
編遣 *bianchiaan*, v.t., to disband (troops, personal) in breaking up unit, or for reassignment.
編訂 *biandihng*, v. t., edit (book) with idea of restoring correct version; establish (correct list of names, numbers).
編輯 *bienji*, v. t., edit (paper, magazine, anthology); n., editor; 總編輯 editor in chief.
編纂 *bianjuahn*, v. t., edit; n., editor.
編著 *bianjuh*, v.t. & n., to compile, -ation.
編制 *bianjyh*, v. t., organize (army, civilian unit); n., system, organization (of army).
編劇 *bian-jyuh*, v. i., write plays; n., script writer.
編類 *bian-leih*, v. i., classify; n., classification.
編年(史) *bian-niarn(shyy)*, n., form of history arranged by years and months; chronicles.
編派 *bianpaih*, v. i. & t., criticize, create stories about persons: 我就知道你是編派我的 I know you are criticizing me; 編派不是 put blame on (person).
編排 *bianpair*, v. t., arrange in order; n., writing and directing of play.
編審 *biansheen*, v. i., examine and approve, pass judgment on books, publications; n., such judges.
編譯 *bianyih*, v. t., edit and translate; n., editor and translator.

綸 93B.42-8

lurn (**guan*).

N. (1) Silk tassel, fishing line: 垂綸 let down the line in fishing. (2) A surname.

綸巾 **guanjin*, n., (AC) silk head dress (for man).
綸音 *lurnyin*, imperial edict.

納 93B.42-8

nah.

N. A surname.

V.t. (1) Receive, accept, welcome, take, be friends with: 納入 receive (a sum of money) and enter it in the ledger; 收納 receive (funds), give shelter to (s. o.); 接納 receive, welcome (a caller); 納賄 (also 受賄) accept bribes; 納妾 take a concubine; 納寵 ditto; 納諫 take advice, usu. from an inferior in status; 納交 become friends with (s. o.). (2) Pay, send, present, offer: 納貢 pay tribute; pay money to buy official title of; 貢生納款 make approaches to negotiate surrender; 納幣, 納采, 納徵 send precious gifts, silk presents to the bride's home at time of betrothal; 納稅人 taxpayer; 納糧 make tax payments in kind, usu. in rice; 出納 person in charge of cash receipts and payments, cashier; 繳納 make payments of any kind; 納賄 (also 行賄) offer bribes. (3) Calm down, restrain, keep under control: 納定性子 keep one's temper under control; 按納不住 cannot check or restrain. (4) Enjoy: 納福 enjoy the blessings of life; 納涼 cool oneself on a hot day, (lit.) enjoy the cool air. (5) Sew, stitch: 納鞋底 (var. of 衲), stitch layers of cloth to make cloth sole of shoes.

納罕(兒) *nahhaan(-haa'l)*, v. i., be surprised, admire (s. t.) as unusual.

納悶 *nahmehn*, v. i., be vexed or bored, moody: 獨自在家納悶 shut oneself up at home, gloomy and sullen; 納悶兒 being suspicious of s. t.

納粹 *nahtzueih*, n., Nazi (party); 納粹化 Nazification; 納粹主義 Nazism.

繑 93B.42-9

chiau.

V.i. To hem (clothing).

§ 93B.50 (糸/ㄱ)

絝 93B.50-1

kuh.

[Var. of 袴 63C.50]

紉 93B.50-5

rehn.

N. & v.i. & t. Sew(ing): 縫紉 (do) needlework; 紉緝 mend (clothes).

V.t. (1) To string (pearls, beads, etc.): 紉針 to thread a needle. (2) To esteem highly: 感紉 be grateful to; 紉佩 have admiration for.

紡 93B.50-6

faang.

N. & v.i. Reel, spin, spinning: 紡紗 spin cotton; 紡麻 spin hemp threads; 紡絲 spin silk threads; 紡織 spin and weave, see 紡織 *-jy* ↓.

紡車 *faangche*, n., spinning wheel.

紡織 *faangjy*, n. & v.i., gen. term for textile industry; 紡織機器 textile machinery; 紡織廠 textile mill; 紡織娘, a kind of cicada whose song reminds of incessant whirl of spinning wheel.

紛 93B.50-8

fen.

Adj. & adv. Confusing, tangled, profuse: 紛爭 confused wrangling; 雪片紛飛 snowflakes flutter about; 紛至沓來 (guests, etc.) come in a throng: 繽△紛 (flowers) 93B.80 in profusion.

紛歧 *fenchi*, v.i., (opinions) diverge in confusion: 意見紛歧 a confusing variety of opinions.

紛紛 *fenfen*, adj. & adv., profuse, -ly: 紛紛揚揚 profusely.

紛亂 *fenluahn*, adj., disorderly (assembly, program, furniture).

紛綸 *fenlurn*, adj., profuse, plenteous, filled full.

紛擾 *fenraau*, v.t. & adj. & n., confuse, -ing, -sion, annoyance, disturbance.

紛雜 *fentzar*, adj., disorderly (crowd, assortment of things).

紛紜 *fenyurn*, adj., profuse and confusing.

約 93B.50-9

yue.

N. A treaty, agreement, appointment: 條約 treaty; 盟約 treaty of alliance; 和約 peace treaty; 契約 commercial agreement; 婚約 marriage agreement; 聘約 appointment (to teach), also betrothal; 訂約, 立約 make an agreement, treaty; 締約 form agreement; 背約 break agreement or treaty; 解約, 退約 terminate agreement; 踐約 carry out terms of agreement; 爽約 fail to turn up; 赴約 go to appointment; 約期, 約會 *-chir*, *-hueih* ↓; 舊約, 新約 the Old, New Testament.

V.i. (1) To make an appointment: 約定 *-dihng* ↓; 邀約 invite. (2) To restrain, keep in control: 約束 *-shuh*^{1} ↓.

Adj. & adv. (1) Simple, -ly, brief, -ly: 簡約言之 to put it briefly. (2) Careful in spending: 節約, 儉約 ditto. (3) About, roughly: 約莫, 約略 *-'mo*, *-lyueh* ↓. (4)

Indistinct: 隱約, 隱隱約約 ditto.

約請 *yue-chiing*, v.t., to invite.
約期 *yuechir*, v.t. & n., (to make) appointment.
約迭 *yuedier*, adj., (MC) about (100 people, etc.).
約定 *yue-dihng*, v.t., to agree (on date, meeting).
約法 *yuefaa*, n., as in 約法三章 (AC) simple agreement with the people by new government.
約分 *yuefen*, n., (math.) common denominator.
約黃 *yue-huarng*, n., (MC) yellowish paint on ladies' temples.
約會 *yuehueih*, n., an appointment.
約計 *yuejih*, adv., in rough reckoning.
約據 *yuejyuh*, n., written agreement.
約指 *yuejyy*, n., ring finger.
約略 *yuelyueh*, adv., roughly (in estimate): 約略這個時候 about this time; 約略半月 about a fortnight.
約莫 *yue'mo*, adv., ditto.
約束 *yueshuh*¹, v.t., to restrain, control (children).
約數 *yueshuh*², n., (math.) divider, cf. 倍數 multiple.
約同 *yueturng*, adv., together with (a few friends, etc.).

絇 93B.50-9

shyuahn.

Adj. Effulgent, gleaming.

絇爛 *shyuahnlahn*, adj., flashing, brilliant with lighting and colors: 文章絇爛 writing sparkles.
絇練 *shyuahnliahn*, adj., ditto.

綯 93B.50-9

taur.

N. A twisted rope.

V.t. To twist rope: 綯索; 綯住 to tie up.

縐 93B.50-9

jouh.

N. (1) Crepe. (2) U. f. 皺 wrinkles, creases.

縐布 *jouhbuh*, n., crepe cloth.
縐絺 *jouhchy*, n., (AC) fine silk crepe.
縐紗 *jouhsha*, n., crepe silk.
縐紋(兒) *jouhwurn(-wer'l)*, n., creases (also wr. 皺).

綉 93B.50-9

shiouh.

[Pop. of 繡 93B.22]

§ 93B.63 (糸/丶)

終 93B.63-9

jung.

[Usu. printed as 終]

N. (1) End, ending, finish: 年終 year-end; 期終 end of semester; 終點 *-diaan* ↓; 告終 (a work) is finished, completed; 有始有終 once started, carry to the finish—steadfast to the end; 始終 adv., from the beginning to the end; 始終不說一句話 never said a single word; 終始 *-shyy* ↓. (2) Death: 臨終時候 before one expires; 臨終之言 dying advice or instructions; 壽終正寢 die peacefully; 送終 attend s. o.'s funeral. (3) A surname.

V.i. (1) To close a matter: 終了, 終結 *-liaau, -jier* ↓. (2) To die: 無疾而終 die without known cause; 終其天年 live to old age.

Adj. (1) Whole, entire: 終日, 終年, 終身, 終生 *-ryh, -niarn, -shen, -sheng* ↓; 終夜 the whole night. (2) (AC) lasting: 以永終譽 and win lasting fame.

Adv. In the end, after all: esp. 終於: 終於失敗 fail in the end; (with negative adv.) 終不悔改 never repent after all; 終非良計 after all it's not a good plan; 終不成 you are not going to . . . after all; (with aux.) 終須 after all must; 終須一走 after all, a trip cannot be avoided; 終必 after all must (fail, etc.); 終有一日 one day there will (happen); see compp. 終久, 終究, 終極 *-jioou, -jiouh, -jir* ↓.

Prep. Through: 終其一生 through his entire life.

終不成 *jung-buh-cherng*, phr., (a surmise) will not go so far as to: 終不成殺他兄弟 one cannot believe he will go so far as to kill his brother.
終場 *jungchaang*, n., (1) ending (of series of events); (2) the last series of examinations.
終點 *jungdiaan*, n., terminal point.
終歸 *jungguei*, adv., in the end: 終歸輸還給他 in the end lose it all back to him.
終古 *jungguu*, adv., in early times, since olden days: 終古紅顏多薄命 since olden times, beautiful women have suffered a harsh life.
終朝 *jungjau*, adv., (LL) all morning (rain).
終結 *jungjier*, adv. & n., the end, in the end; v. t., to wind up (matter).
終竟 *jungjihng*, adv. & n., the end, in the end.

終 純 繞 綣 紕 糺 絖 緄

終久 *jungjioou*, (1) adv., sooner or later, in the end; (2) v. i., last long: 不能終久 cannot last long.

終究 *jungjiouh* (-'*jiou*), adv., after all (he is your brother, etc.).

終極 *jungjir*, n., the extreme, the limit, the final outcome.

終竣 *jungjyuhn*, v. i., (LL) be completed.

終局 *jungjyur*, n., final upshot.

終止 *jungjyy*, (1) v. i., to stop, cease (work, etc.); (2) n., end: 沒有終止 without stop or end.

終了 *jungliaau*, v. i., be completed, finished.

終年 *jungniarn*, adv., the whole year round.

終日 *jungryh*, adv., all day.

終審 *jungsheen*, n., (law) the final court trial.

終身 *jungshen*, adv., the whole life.

終生 *jungsheng*, adv., ditto.

終食 *jungshyr*, n., (AC) the time of a meal, a short while.

終始 *jungshyy*, (1) v. i., as in 相終始 stick together from beginning to end; (2) adv., from beginning to end (=始終).

終天 *jungtian*, adv., all one's life: 抱恨終天 to regret forever.

終養 *jungyaang*, v. i., enjoy the privilege of serving parents in their old age.

§93B.70 (糸/ㄴ)

純 93B.70–1

churn (**juun*).

N. (**juun*) (AC) rim, braid.

Adj. & adv. (1) Pure, -ly, unadulterated: 純白, 純黑 solid white, black; 純粹 *-tsueih*↓; 純金, 純銀 pure gold, silver; 純品 pure, unadulterated product; 純種, 純血 pure breed; 純孝 completely filial (son); 純嘏 pure blessing. (2) Honest, sincere, loyal: 純正, 純良 *-jehng*, *-liarng*↓; 純臣 a loyal minister.

純篤 *churnduh*, adj., honest, devoted.

純厚 *churnhouh*, adj., ditto.

純正 *churnjehng*, adj., upright, honest.

純潔 *churnjier*, adj., pure (heart, water, character).

純淨 *churnjihng*, adj., ditto.

純良 *churnliarng*, adj., good, gentle (people.)

純利 *churn-lih*, n., net profit.

純樸 *churnpuu*, adj., simple and honest.

純如 *churnrur*, adj., (AC, mus.) harmonious.

純熟 *churnshur*, adj., well-learned (lesson), fluent (language).

純粹 *churntsueih*, adj. & adv., pure, -ly, clear, -ly, complete, -ly: 純粹是他不是 it is completely his mistake; 純粹是假造事實 it is a pure fabrication.

繞 93B.70–1

rauh.

V.t. (1) Entwine, intertwine: 纏繞 to wind round; 繞在一起 twine together; 繞起來 twist together, coil or wind up. (2) Revolve, encircle: 繞場一週 go round the stadium (or any enclosed area) once; 繞地球一週 revolve round the earth once; 圍繞 surround; 環繞 enclose, encircle; 繞過 by-pass; 繞道兒 *-dauh('l)*↓; 繞路 make a detour; 繞行 go in a roundabout way; 繞越 make a detour to bypass; 繞圈(彎)子 (lit. & fig.) go in a circle; 繞圈兒 ditto; 繞脖子 ditto; 繞彎兒 take a stroll; 繞月軌道 (astron.) lunar orbit.

繞道(兒) *rauh-dauh('l)*, v. i. & n., detour.

繞住 *rauh'ju*, adj., temporarily confused, perplexed, bewildered, nonplussed.

繞指柔 *rauhjyyrour*, phr., (of persons pliant or tractable ("can be twisted around the finger").

繞口令(兒) *rauhkoou-lihng('l)*, n., (1) a tongue twister; (2) roundabout talk.

繞梁 *rauh-liarng*, adj., (of music) reverberating: 繞樑三日 the tone lingered in the room for three days.

繞磨 *rauh'mo*, v. t., (1) set a trap for (s.o.); (2) to wind round.

繞嘴 *rauh-tzueei*, adj., difficult to pronounce or speak.

繞遠兒 *rauh-yuaa'l*, v. i., (lit. & fig.) go in a roundabout way.

綣 93B.70–1

chyuaan.

V.i. See 繾綣 93B.83.

紕 93B.70–2

pi (*pir*).

N. Border of dress.

V.t. Sew up (broken patches).

紕漏 *pilouh*, n., careless mistake, omission: 這件事出了紕漏 s.t. goes wrong with this matter.

紕繆 *pimiouh*, adj., erroneous (opinion, statement).

糺 93B.70–2

jioou (*jiou*).

V.i. To curl (of rope, beard).

絖 93B.70–2

kuahng.

[Var. of 纊 93B.80]

緄 93B.70–4

guun.

A

N. A cord; hemming.

V.t. Embroider, make hemming: 緄邊 embroidered border or dress.

繩 93B.70-4

sherng.

[Abbr. 縄]

N. (1) (*-tz*, *-'l*) A rope, cord, string: 蔴繩 hemp cord; 細繩, 繩子 a piece of string. (2) Rule of conduct, a guideline: 準繩 guideline, standard; 繩墨, 繩尺 *-moh*, *-chyy* ↓.

V.t. (LL) To guide, rectify, hold to the right standard: 繩之以法 punish s.o. according to law, to keep s.o. within line by punishments; 繩正 *-jehng* ↓.

繩 橋 *sherng-chiaur*, n., a rope bridge.

繩 牀 *sherng-chuarng*, n., a hammock.

繩 尺 *sherng-chyy*, n., (LL) correct guides to conduct, cf. 規^矩 91S.70.

繩 正 *sherng-jehng*, v. t., (LL) to correct s.o.'s mistake.

繩 伎 *sherng-jih*, n., tightrope walking.

繩 墨 *sherngmoh*, n., carpenter's guideline made by ink marking, (fig.) discipline, standard: 不拘繩墨 do not stick to usual formalities.

繩 繩 *sherngsherng*, adj., (AC) (1) continuous, unending; expansive; (2) cautious.

繩 戲 *sherngshih*, n., see *-jih* ↑.

繩 樞 *sherng-shu*, phr., 甕牖繩樞 (AC) using broken jars for windows and rope for fastening doors—living in extreme poverty.

繩 索 *sherngsuoo*, n., a rope.

B

紀 93B.70-5

jih (also *jii*).

N. (1) A year: 年紀 a person's age; 紀元 *-yuarn* ↓. (2) A period of years: 世紀 a century. (3) (AC) a period of twelve years. (4) (Geol.) a subdivision of a geological era. (5) Rules, regulations, laws: 紀律 *-lyuh*, 紀綱 *-gang* ↓; 綱紀 discipline, rules of conduct; 法紀 law and discipline. (6) A surname.

V.t. (1) To sort (silk threads). (2) To record in writing: 紀事 *-shyh*, 紀年 *-niarn*, 紀錄 *-luh* ↓.

紀 綱 *jihgang*, n., (1) legal institutions, legal and political order; (2) (AC) a servant.

紀 極 *jihjir*, n., the ultimate end (of things).

紀 錄 *jihluh*, (1) v. t., put down in writing; (2) n., the minutes of a meeting, written records; (3) (sports) the best record yet achieved.

紀 律 *jihlyuh*, n., discipline, morale.

紀 念 *jihniahn*, v. t., celebrate, commemorate: 紀念日 anniversaries of important events; 紀念門 a memorial arch; 紀念冊 a memento book; 紀念品 souvenir; 紀念碑 a memorial tablet, a cenotaph; 紀念郵票 a commemorative stamp.

紀 年 *jihniarn*, n., annals, yearly record of events.

紀 行 *jihshirng*, n., travel diary.

紀 事 *jihshyh*, (1) v. t., to chronicle; (2) n., chronicles, records.

紀 序 *jihshyuh*, n., order of precedence.

紀 元 *jihyuarn*, n., the beginning of a reign or an era: 紀元前 B.C.; 紀元後 A.D.

絕 93B.70-5

jyuer.

C

N. A poem with four lines to a stanza: 五絕 (七絕) such a poem with five (or seven) characters to one line; 絕句 *-jyuh* ↓.

V.i. (1) To end, cut short, break off: 絕命 *-mihng*, 絕交 *-jiau*, 絕跡 *-ji*, 絕種 *-juung* ↓; 絕罰 excommunication. (2) Cut off, isolated: 絕島 *-daau*[1], 絕境 *-jihng*, 絕路 *-luh* ↓.

Adj. (1) Lacking, wanting, devoid of: 絕乏 *-far* ↓. (2) Heirless: 絕後 *-houh*, 絕嗣 *-syh* ↓. (3) Extinct: 絕版 *-baan* ↓. (4) Absolute, extreme: 絕等 *-deeng* ↓; 絕頂 *-diing* ↓; 絕景 *-jiing* ↓.

Adv. (1) Very: 絕好, 絕佳 very good, excellent; 絕早 extremely early; 絕大多數 the great (overwhelming) majority. (2) Definitely: 絕對 *-dueih* ↓; 絕不 definitely not, never will; 絕無僅有 one and the only one.

絕 版 *jyuerbaan*, adj., (of books) out of print.

絕 壁 *jyuerbih*, n., an inaccessible precipice.

絕 筆 *jyuer-bii*, n., a person's last written words before his death.

絕 羣 *jyuerchyurn*, adj., matchless, peerless, unrivaled.

絕 島 *jyuerdaau*[1], n., a lone far-off island.

絕 倒 *jyuerdaau*[2], v.i., (1) laugh loudly: 哄堂絕倒 all broke into a loud laugh; (2) swoon from grief.

絕 代 *jyuerdaih*, (1) n., time immemorial; (2) adj., without a match, peerless: 絕代佳人 a matchless beauty.

絕 等 *jyuerdeeng*, adj., matchless, the highest (skill, products).

絕 地 *jyuerdih*, n., (1) a dangerous terrain; (2) a dead end, an impasse, a place of doom.

絕 頂 *jyuerdiing*, (1) n., the highest point, summit; (2) adv., extremely: 聰明絕頂 remarkably clever (intelligent).

絕 對 *jyuerdueih*, (1) adj., absolute

(opp. 相對 relative); (2) 絕對 or 絕對的 adv., definitely: 這件事絕對做不到 this matter is definitely impossible; 絕對是 absolutely right; 絕對可靠 absolutely reliable.

絕乏 *jyuerfar*, adj., completely short of goods.

絕港 *jyuer-gaang*, n., a harbor without access to rivers.

絕後 *jyuer-houh*, adj., (1) heirless, without issue; (2) 空前絕後 phr., unpredented and cannot be repeated.

絕戶 *jyuer-huh*, adj., heirless, without issue.

絕迹 *jyuerji*, v.i., (flies, mosquitoes, great art) completely disappear.

絕交 *jyuer-jiau*, v.i., break off friendly relations with (person, country).

絕技 *jyuerjih*, n., an incomparable skill.

絕境 *jyuerjihng*, n., (1) a place of doom: 陷於絕境 no hope for escape or recovery; (2) a secluded spot.

絕景 *jyuerjiing*, n., an incomparable scenery.

絕種 *jyuer-juung*, v.i., (of living organism) become extinct.

絕句 *jyuerjyuh*, n., a poem with four lines to a stanza, each line consisting of five or seven characters.

絕口 *jyuer-koou*, v.i., stop talking: 絕口不談 never mention it again.

絕糧 *jyuerliarng*, v.i., run short of food.

絕路 *jyuerluh*, n., dead end, no way out.

絕倫 *jyuerlurn*, adj., incomparable, matchless.

絕妙 *jyuermiauh*, adj., exquisite, most wonderful.

絕命 *jyuer-mihng*, v.i., about to die: 絕命書 last words written on one's deathbed.

絕品 *jyuerpiin*, n., a very rare work of art.

絕色 *jyuerseh*, n., a rare beauty.

絕響 *jyuer-shiaang*, v.i., (great work of art) be without followers.

絕世 *jyuer-shyh*, (1) adj., heirless, without issue; (2) peerless, without a match: 忠勇絕世 unrivaled in loyalty and courage; (3) v.i., die.

絕食 *jyuershyr*, v.i., (go on) a hunger strike.

絕學 *jyuershyuer*, (1) n., an anc. study lost to the modern world; (2) v.i., give up all studies: 絕學無憂 I would not be sorry if I should be ignorant.

絕緒 *jyuer-shyuh*, adj., see *-syh* ↓.

絕俗 *jyuersur*, v.i., (1) rise above the general run of people; (2) be free from worldly cares.

絕嗣 *jyuer-syh*, adj., heirless, without issue.

絕望 *jyuerwahng*, (1) adj., hopeless, in despair; (2) v.i., despair.

絕藝 *jyueryih*, n., see *-jih* ↑.

絕緣 *jyuer-yuarn*, (1) v.i., break off relations; (2) adj. & v.i., (phys.) insulate: 絕緣體 (phys.) an insulator.

絕域 *jyueryuh*, n., a distant and inaccessible region; (fig.) a hopeless situation.

纜 93B.70–5

lahn (*laan).

N. A rope, cable, hawser: 纜繩 cordage, thick ropes; 船纜 rope or cable by which a ship is anchored or towed, a towrope; 鋼纜 a steel cable; 電纜 telegraphic cable; 纜車 cable car.

統 93B.70–6

tuung.

N. Order, system: 系統, 統系 genealogical tree, lineage; (philosophic or administrative) system; 皇統 the imperial genealogical tree; 道統, 正統 orthodox tradition, explained as a continuous heritage from the ideal emperors 堯, 舜, 禹, 湯, 周公 and Confucius; 傳統 tradition; 體統 orderly appearance; 不成體統 unorthodox, disgraceful appearance; 總統 president of republic.

V.i. & t. (1) To unite: 統一 *-yi* ↓; 一統 to unite under one rule. (2) To command, lead: 統兵 command troops; 統轄, 總統 govern as the head; 統帥, 統領 *-shuaih*^{2}, *-liing*, etc. ↓.

Adj. & adv. All, entirely (interch. 通): 統通, 統共 *-tung*, *-guhng* ↓; 統盤 (通盤) 計劃 plan as a whole; 統籌 (通籌) 辦理 take charge and plan as a whole; 籠統 in an inexact, undefined slipshod manner.

統共 *tuungguhng*, adv., altogether, all counted (=通共), all in all.

統計 *tuungjih*, v. i. & t. & n., (compile) statistics: 統計起來; 人口統計 population statistics; 統計圖表 (數字) statistical charts (figures).

統制 *tuungjyh*^{1}, v. t., to govern (troops, territory).

統治 *tuungjyh*^{2}, v. t. & n., rule, govern; 統治權 right to rule; 統治階級 ruling class.

統括 *tuungkuoh*, (1) v. t., include altogether; (2) adj., all-inclusive.

統類 *tuungleih*, n., categories, species, kinds.

統例 *tuunglih*, n., general rules.

統領 *turngliing*, n., commander.

統收 *tuungshou*, n., centralized receipt: 統收統支 centralized bursary system.

統率 *tuungshuaih*^{1}, v. t., to command (troops).

統帥 *tuungshuaih*^{2}, v. t. & n., command; commander.

統緒 *tuungshyuh*, n., system of affairs, things.

統體 *turngtii*, n., whole body, the whole.

統廳 *tuungting*, n., hall connecting houses.

統艙 *tuungtsang*, n., steerage, deck, dist. cabins; 統艙客 steerage passenger.

統通 *tuungtung*, adv., see *-guhng* ↑.

統統 *turngtuung*, adv., entirely, all, altogether: 統統遺失 all lost (=通通).

統一 *tuungyi*, v. t., to unite, to bring under one system: 統一全國 (國語, 幣制) unite the country (national language, monetary system); p. p., united.

紽 93B.70-6

tuor.

N. Strand of silk.

紈 93B.70-9

warn.

N. White stiff silk; gauze.

紈袴 *warnkuh*, n., silk trousers; 紈袴子弟 rich men's sons ("in silk pyjamas").

紈扇 *warnshahn*, n., a flat, round fan with framed gauze.

紈素 *warnsuh*, n., white, fine gauze.

紇 93B.70-9

her (*ge).

N. Inferior silk.

紇縫(兒) **ge'da('l)*, n., a lump of thread, a knot.

絁 93B.70-9

shy.

N. A coarse silk fabric.

纔 93B.70-9

tsair.

[Pop. 才, dist. 讒 60A.70]

Adv. (1) Just, just now: 剛纔, 方纔 ditto; 纔待, 纔要 was just going to: 纔來 has just come; 這纔明白 now it has become clear, or now one understands. (2) Only: 纔不過 is only just (so much); 纔只, 纔有 there is only; 她纔十二歲 she is only twelve.

Conj. Then, only then: 考試完了, 纔可以玩 wait till after the examinations, then you can go and play.

---

§ 93B.71 (糸/弋)

織 93B.71-6

jy.

V.t. (1) To weave: 紡織 spin and weave, see 紡 93A.50; 毛織品 woolens, woolen fabrics; 棉織品 cotton goods; 絲織品 silks; 針織品 knitted goods; 織花 woven pattern; 織布 woven cloth, to weave; 編織 weave (a basket, etc.). (2) To organize: 組^A織 93B.30. (3) To frame up: 羅織成獄 frame up a crime.

織布娘 *jybuh-niarng*, n., name for cicada.

織補 *jybuu*, v. i. & t., mend clothing by experts to look like original.

織畫 *jyhuah*, n., hand-woven painting.

織毛衣 *jymauryi*, n., knitted woolens; sweater.

織女 *jynyuu*, n., the "Spinster Maid," a constellation celebrated in song and fable as lover of Cowboy 牛郎, another constellation, who are separated by the Milky Way and permitted to meet once a year.

織綉 *jyshiouh*, n., fine hand embroidery.

織紋 *jywern*, n., woven pattern; 織紋螺 n., a kind of snail.

絏 93B.71-7

shieh.

N. (1) (AC) Reins. (2) 縲^A絏 93B.01.

絨 93B.71-7

rurng.

N. Cotton, silk or woolen goods: 絨布 *-buh*↓; 絨花布 fine cotton fabrics; 絨毬兒 color woolen balls; 絨帽, 絨鞋, 絨襪, 絨毯子 felt cap, shoes, sock, blanket; 絨氈 blanket; 絨線 *-shiahn*↓; 絨繩(兒) yarn; 絨頭繩兒 yarn for tying hair; 絨線兒舖 store selling articles for sewing; 毛絨 woolen yarn; 團絨 woolen balls; 絲絨 silk velvet; 天鵝絨 velvet; 法蘭絨 flannel; 駱駝絨 camel-hair fabric.

絨蚑 *rurngbier*, n., (zoo.) *Mimela lucidula.*

絨布 *rurng-buh*, n., woolens, flannels.

絨花樹 *rurnghua-shuh*, n., (bot.) the silk tree, *Albizzia julibrissin* (also 絨樹).

絨線 *rurng-shiahn*, n., (1) silk threads; (2) woolen yarn.

絨鼠 *rurngshuu*, n., (zoo.) Chinchilla.

綫 93B.71-7

shiahn.

[Var. of 線 93B.02]

緘 93B.71-7

jian.

N. A letter: 緘札 *-jar*↓; 信緘, 書

緘 a note, message; 吉緘 a home letter; 玉緘 (court.) your kind favor.

V.t. To close, to seal: 緘口 *-koou*, 緘默 *-moh*, 緘密 *-mih* ↓.

緘札 *jianjar*, n., a written communication, note, letter.

緘口 *jiankoou*, v. i. & t., to seal up (a letter); keep mouth shut.

緘密 *jianmih*, adj., firmly sealed; kept secret.

緘默 *jianmoh*, v. i., keep silent and say nothing.

纖 93B.71-7

shian.

Adj. Minute, slender, fine: 纖指 slender finger; 纖腰 slender waist; 纖細, 纖小 *-shih*, *-shiaau* ↓.

Adv. In detail: 纖悉無遺 no detail escapes notice.

纖巧 *shianchiaau*, adj., exquisite (carving, needlework, lady's watch).

纖兒 *shian-er'l*, n., (AC) tender children.

纖毫 *shianhaur*, (1) n., minute particles; (2) adj., infinitesimal, tiny: 沒有纖毫差別 not the slightest difference.

纖介 *shianjieh*, n., tiny details (also wr. 芥).

纖毛 *shianmaur*, n., (zoo.) 纖毛蟲類 *Ciliata*.

纖柔 *shianrour*, adj., soft and smooth (hand).

纖弱 *shianruoh*, adj., fragile, tender (health); weak and small.

纖小 *shianshiaau*, adj., tiny, trivial, insignificant (detail).

纖纖 *shianshian*, adj., slender (hands); trivial: 纖纖細故 trivial events, details.

纖屑 *shianshieh*, adj., piddling, trivial, frothy (affairs).

纖細 *shianshih*, adj., slender (waist); microscopic, insignificant (detail).

纖微 *shianweir*¹, n. & adj., see *-haur* ↑.

纖維 *shianweir*², n., fibre, fibrous tissue: 纖維根 fibrous root; 纖維素 cellulose; 人造纖維 artificial fibre (nylon, etc.).

纖妍 *shianyarn*, adj., slender and pretty.

纖玉 *shianyuh*, n., (LL) lady's hand or fingers.

紙 93B.71-9

jyy.
[Var. of 帋]

N. Paper: 硬紙 thick paper, brown paper; 硬紙板 cardboard; 衞生紙 sanitary napkin; 紙巾 paper napkin; 吸墨紙 blotting paper; 複寫紙 carbon paper; 紙條 a slip of paper; 紙片 a card; 片紙隻字 just a note with writing on it; 紙杯 paper cup; 洛陽紙貴 sensational sale of a new book (causing paper shortage); 紙上談兵 be armchair strategist; 紙老虎 "paper tiger"—not to be feared; 紙包不住火 paper cannot wrap fire—futile effort to stop scandal.

紙版 *jyrbaan*, n., (1) cardboard; (2) *papier-mâché* for printing; matrix.

紙幣 *jyybih*, n., paper money.

紙錢兒 *jyychiar'l*, n., paper money burnt for the use of the departed spirits.

紙張 *jyyjang*, n., paper.

紙馬 *jyr-maa*, n., paper horse burned at funeral for use in the nether world.

紙媒(兒) *jyymeir*(*-mer'l*), n., a paper roll, shaped like drinking straw, used for lighting pipe.

紙捻兒 *jyrniaa'l*, n., ditto.

紙牌 *jyypair*, n., playing cards.

紙樣 *jyy-yahng*, n., paper pattern (tailoring).

紙烟 *jyyyan*, n., cigarette (also 捲烟, 烟捲兒).

紙鳶 *jyyyuan*, n., a kite.

紙魚 *jyyyur*, n., name for silver fish which eats into books.

§ 93B.72 (糸/心)

繐 93B.72-1

sueih.

N. Fine textured cloth: 繐帳 curtain hung around coffin.

緦 93B.72-4

sy.

N. Fine linen.

緦服 *sy-fur*, n., mourning for distant relatives (great-great-grandfathers, wife's parents, cousins of different surnames, etc.) limited to three months (called technically 小功).

總 93B.72-9

tzuung.
[Abbr. 総; err. var. 緫]

V.t. Collect, gather, assemble, add together.

Adj. General, chief, main, head: 總統 *-tuung*, 總裁 *-tsair* ↓; 老總 (coll.) the chief, the boss; 總經理 *-jinglii*, 總編輯 *-bianjih* ↓; 總公司 the head office (of company, firm); 總部 *-buh* ↓; 總攻擊令 an order to mount a general attack.

Adv. (1) Altogether: 總共 *-guhng* ↓; 總之 *-'jy* ↓; 總而言之 in fine, in a word, put in a nutshell. (2) At any rate, in any event, anyway, anyhow: 他總不肯讓步 in no event would he ever give in; 總有一天你會明白 there must be a day when you will understand.

總辦 *tzuungbahn*, n., director

general, superintendent.
總編輯 *tzuung-bianjih*, n., editor in chief.
總部 *tzuungbuh*, n., general headquarters (of army, navy, air force).
總得 *tzurng-deei*, vb. phr., (will) have to, have got to, must . . . anyway: 凡事總得三思而行 one has to think twice before doing anything; other phrr. similarly used are 總要, 總須.
總動員 *tzuung duhngyuarn*, n., (1) general mobilization of the armed forces; (2) mobilization of an entire group of people for a given task.
總髮 *tzurngfaa*, n., (LL) childhood.
總綱 *tzuunggang*, n., general outline.
總括 *tzuunggua*, v. t., to sum up, summarize, put in a nutshell: 總括一句 in a word; 總括起來 to summarize.
總丱 *tzuungguahn*, n., (LL) childhood.
總共 *tzuungguhng*, adv., altogether: 總共五百人 there are altogether 500 persons.
總行 *tzuungharng*, n., head office (of bank, company).
總號 *tzuunghauh*, n., (1) the head office (of business firm) (opp. 支店 branch office); (2) (punctuation) a colon.
總合 *tzuungher*[1], v. i., (of things) put together.
總和 *tzuungher*[2], n., (arithmetic) sum total, grand total.
總會 *tzuunghueih*[1], (1) v. i., gather or assemble together; (2) n., a club (-house): 夜總會 a night club; general headquarters of an association: 總工會 general (national) labor union.
總匯 *tzuunghueih*[2], v. i. & n., to flow or flock together; confluence, concourse.
總長 *tzurngjaang*, n., formerly, a Cabinet minister.
總帳 *tzuungjahng*, n., general ledger (of business firm).
總結 *tzuungjier*, (1) n., summary, conclusion; (2) v. t., to sum up, summarize, recapitulate.
總機關 *tzuung-jiguan*, n., (1) headquarters; (2) the head switchboard.
總計 *tzuungjih*, phr., amount to a total of.
總經理 *tzuung-jinglii*, n., general manager.
總集 *tzuungjir*, n., an anthology of works of certain period or category.
總角 *tzuungjuer*, n., childhood.
總主筆 *tzuung-jurbii*, n., chief editorial writer, editor in chief.
總之 *tzuung'jy*, adv., in a word, in fine, in short, in a nutshell.
總指揮 *tzurng-jyyhuei*, n., commanding general, commander (of a sector, area, front-line troops).
總理 *tzurnglii*, (1) director general (of bank, political party); (2) the prime minister.
總論 *tzuungluhn*, n., a general introduction to a subject.
總目 *tzuungmuh*, n., a general index, table of contents.
總數 *tzuungshuh*, n., total amount, sum total.
總算 *tzuungsuahn*, adv., on the whole, by and large, considering everything: 他功課總算不錯 on the whole he is a fairly good student in school.
總司令 *tzuung-sy-lihng*, n., commander in chief (of army, navy, air force).
總裁 *tzuungtsair*, n., (1) director general (of political party); (2) governor (of bank).
總統 *tzurngtuung*, n., (1) the president (of a country); (2) formerly, a commanding officer (of army).
總總 *tzurngtzuung*, adj., numerous, abundant, teeming: 林林總總 in great abundance.
總務 *tzuungwuh*, n., general affairs, business department; business manager.

§ 93B.80 (糸/八)

總 績 纘 續

績 93B.80-1

ji.

N. Deeds, any work done: 業績 accomplishments; 功績 meritorious acts; 勳績 outstanding achievements of a statesman, soldier, etc.; 考績 year-end review of an employee's efficiency and performance; 成績 achievements, scholastic record; 績效 *-shiauh*↓.

V.i. (1) Spin thread, join threads: 績麻 to twist threads; 績女 *-nyuu*↓; 績紡 to wind, spin. (2) To study: 績學 *-shyuer*↓.

績女 *jinyuu*, n., a woman who spins thread.
績效 *jishiauh*, n., results, effects.
績學 *jishyuer*, adj., erudite: 績學之士 an erudite scholar.
績用 *jiyuhng*, n., practical utility.

纘 93B.80-1

tzuaan.

V.i. Succeed to (position), continue to do (predecessor's work): 纘緒 *-shyuh*, 纘繼 *-jih*↓.

纘繼 *tzuaanjih*, v. i., carry on ancestral work.
纘緒 *tzuaanshyuh*, v. i., ditto.

續 93B.80-1

shyuh.
[Abbr. 続]

N. A surname.

亅	小	⺊	十	土	ナ	卄	ㄴ卜	丨	一	丁	フ	口	区	冈	㇕	厂	尸	亠	广	宀	丶	乚	弋	心	八	人	乂	乛	一	ノ	𠂉	く
00	01	02	10	11	12	20	21	22	30	31	32	40	41	42	50	51	52	60	61	62	63	70	71	72	80	81	82	83	90	91	92	93

續 縝 績 纊 繽 続 綾 紱 繖 綆 緅

V.i. & t. (1) To continue: 繼續, 連續, 接續, 延續 ditto; 斷續, 斷斷續續 continue from time to time, continue off and on (to give money, borrow money); 續談 continue the talk; 續假 extend the holiday leave; 補續, 續補 complete, write supplement to unfinished work. (2) To replace: 續絃 *-shiarn*↓; 續娶 *-chyuu*↓; 狗尾續貂 a sable coat with a dog's tail—(in disparagement) make an unworthy continuation of a great work.

Adj. & adv. Continued (installment): 續稿 supplement to manuscript; 續集, 續篇, 續版 *-jir*, *-pian*, *-baan*↓; 連續 continuously.

續版 *shyuhbaan*, n., later edition.
續補 *shyuhbuu*, v. t., to continue unfinished work or write sequel or supplement (to work).
續娶 *shyuh-chyuu*, v. t., to remarry.
續鳧 *shyuh-fur*, phr., (allu.) try to add length to duck's eggs, which would displease the duck (as trying to shorten crane's neck would displease the crane).
續後 *shyuhhouh*, adv., (MC) later.
續集 *shyuhjir*, n., supplement(s) in author's works.
續命湯 *shyuhmihng tang*, n., medicine to continue patient's life.
續母 *shyuhmuu*, n., stepmother (usu. 繼母).
續篇 *shyuh pian*, n., sequel to some essay or collection of essays.
續絃 *shyuh-shiarn*, phr., (man) to remarry, "replace string" on music instrument.
續續 *shyuhshyuh*, adv., continuously.
續添 *shyuhtian*, v. t., to keep on adding (a son, coal to the fire).
續約 *shyuh-yue*, v.i., renew tready or contract.

縝 93B.80–2

jeen.

Adj. See 縝密 *-mih*↓.

縝密 *jeenmih*, adj., closely woven, carefully thought-out (plan).

績 93B.80–2

hueih.

N. (1) (AC) colored silk. (2) Var. of 繪 93B.41.

纊 93B.80–6

kuahng.

N. (AC) silks.

繽 93B.80–6

bin.

Adj. In profusion, variegated.

繽繽 *binbin*, adj., (LL) numerous (guests, leaves, etc.).
繽紛 *binfen*, adj., (LL) in rich variety or confusion.
繽亂 *binluahn*, adj., (LL) in confusion.

§ 93B.81 (糸/人)

続 93B.81–1

shyuh.

[Abbr. of 續 93B.80]

§ 93B.82 (糸/乂)

綾 93B.82–1

lirng.

N. (*-tz*) Damask; a kind of thin but fairly stiff silk.

綾錦 *lirngjiin*, n., silk brocade.
綾絹 *lirngjyuahn*, n., fairly stiff silk.
綾羅 *lirngluor*, n., see 羅 41D.11.

紱 93B.82–1

fur.

N. (AC) silk cord for holding jade seal through its nose; 紱冕 (fig.) referring to officialdom.

繖 93B.82–2

saan.

[Anc. var. of 傘 81.10]

綆 93B.82–3

geeng.

N. A well rope: 綆短汲深 (self-deprecatory) unequal to a given task (lit., "my rope is so short but the well is so deep").

緅 93B.82–3

tzou.

N. (AC) a dark, purplish color.

緻 93B.82-3

jyh.

N. Fine woven silk.

Adj. Fine, close-woven: 精緻, 細緻 delicate (carving, etc.); 雅緻 elegant (all can be wr. with 致).

緻密 *jyhmih*, adj., fine (mesh), closely woven (cloth, plot of novel).

級 93B.82-3

jir.

N. (1) Rank(ing): 上級, 下級 higher, lower rank; 一級上將 a full general. (2) Grade or quality: 低級貨物 inferior goods; 高級品 high-quality articles; 甲級, 乙級 first, second grade. (3) Class in school: 班級 classes into which students are divided; 年級 ditto; 級會 class meeting; 級友 classmates; 同級生 fellow students of the same class. (4) Short for 首級: 斬首級數千 cut off thousands of enemy heads.

級俸 *jirfehng*, n., salary scale.
級任 *jir-rehn*, n., a class tutor.
級數 *jir-shuh*, n., (math.) a series.

綴 93B.82-3

jueih.

V.t. To tie separate pieces together: 連綴起來 tie up or string up together; 補綴 make additions, insertions (to text, garment); 綴上, 綴著 patch up, make patches (on clothing); 服上綴滿了珠子 the garment is studded with pearls; 綴輯 collate different versions; 綴句成章 put (ornate) sentences together in composition; 綴編, 編綴成書 make different excerpts, passages, into a book.

綴宅 *jueihjeh*, n., (AC) the physical human body.
綴旒 *jueihliour*, n., knotted tassels.
綴術 *jueihshuh*, n., an anc. method of astronomical calculation.

縵 93B.82-4

mahn.

N. Plain thin silk: 縵布.

Adj. 縵縵 Slow-moving (clouds); 縵立 (LL) stand waiting.

綅 93B.82-5

*chin (*shian).*

N. (1) (AC) tassels on armor. (2) (**shian*) (AC) black-and-white textile.

紋 93B.82-6

wern.

N. (-'*l*) Natural lines of object: 花紋 curving and irregular lines in stone, texture, veins on petals, leaves, patterns on cloth, etc.; 裂紋 crack, fissures; 波紋 ripples; 縐紋 wrinkles; 紋絲兒不動 not a wrinkle was touched.

紋章 *wern-jang*, n., crest.
紋理 *wernlii*, n., threads in texture.
紋縷兒 *wernlyuu'l*, n., ditto.
紋銀 *wernyirn*, n., silver ingots (also called 馬蹄銀 from its shape like horse's hoof).

絞 93B.82-6

jiaau.

V.t. (1) To twist, entwine, interweave: 絞盤 *-parn*↓; 絞臉 *-liaan* ↓; 心痛如絞 have an excruciating pain in the chest; 絞緊 (of ropes of threads) to wind tight. (2) Strangle to death: 絞刑 *-shirng*↓; 絞死, 絞決 put (criminal) to death by strangulation; 絞立決 such punishment to be carried out as soon as the sentence was handed down; 絞監候 formerly, such punishment not to be carried out pending imperial review.

絞臉 *jiaurliaan*, v. i., (formerly, of women) remove fine hair from face by the interweaving action of two threads held close to the skin.
絞盤 *jiaauparn*, n., a capstan, a 「windlass.
絞刑 *jiaaushirng*, v. t. & n., (put to death by) strangulation.

綬 93B.82-9

shouh.

N. A ribbon, cord, sash: 印綬 cord attached to official seal; hence 解綬而去 return the office seal and resign.

緞 93B.82-9

duahn.

N. Satin.

緩 93B.82–9

huaan.

V.i. & t. To delay: 暫緩一天 delay one day; 緩徵, 緩召 to hold up temporarily calling up reserves; 緩兵之計 a strategy to stall off immediate attack by enemy; 一切從緩 go slow in everything; 延緩 to delay, postpone time limit; 緩一天再說 wait a day and then see; 緩一口氣 get a breathing space; 刻不容緩 urgent, (attend to) immediately.

Adj. & adv. Slow, -ly: 緩緩的說 speak slowly; 緩行 go slowly; 緩步 take a stroll; 舒緩, 遲緩 slow (mail, etc.); opp. to 急 (urgent); 緩不濟急 delayed or retarded help cannot meet the urgent need; see 緩急 *-jir*↓.

緩期 *huaanchir*, n., delayed schedule.

緩衝 *huaanchung*, v. i., to slow down attack; 緩衝方法 a way to play for time; 緩衝區域 a buffer zone.

緩和 *huaanher*, v. i., to appease, pacify.

緩緩 *huarnhuaan*, adj. & adv., slow, -ly.

緩頰 *huaanjiar*, v. i., to speak for s. o. and calm down the anger of the one spoken to ("save from a slap on the face").

緩急 *huaan-jir*, n., emergency: 緩急相助 help each other in case of need.

緩慢 *huaanmahn*, adj., slow-moving.

緩限 *huaanshiahn*, v. i., to postpone time limit.

緩刑 *huaanshirng*, v. i., to stay sentence of punishment.

緶 93B.82–9

biahn (*piarn).

N. A plait, braid (cogn. of 辮 60S.10).

V.t. (*piarn) To sew up; to braid together (loose hemp fibres) into a rope.

繳 93B.82–9

jiaau.

V.t. To hand over, deliver to: 繳納 *-nah*↓; 繳款 effect money payment; 繳稅 pay tax; 繳還 to hand back; 繳交 deliver to; 繳械 *-shieh*↓.

繳納 *jiaaunah*, v. t., pay (taxes, fees, dues).

繳械 *jiaau-shieh*, v. t., disarm (troops).

---

§ 93B.83 (糸/〜)

繨 93B.83–1

'da.

N. See 紇^繨 93B.70.

繾 93B.83–2

chiaan.

繾綣 *chiarnchuaan*, v. i., to be solicitous for a guest's comfort; show the greatest attention (to lover): 繾綣情意 the beautiful relations between lovers or friends.

緹 93B.83–4

tir.

N. (AC) brown earth; brown silk.

Adj. (AC) brown in color.

綻 93B.83–6

jahn.

N. A loose stitch: 綻裂 *-lieh* ditto; (fig.) a flaw in argument: 破綻 ditto.

V.i. (1) To have a loose stitch: 綻了縫. (2) To split, to break open as flower: 綻開 blossom opens; 綻出了微笑 (face) breaks out in a smile.

縋 93B.83–9

jueih.

V.i. & t. To scale down wall or send articles down from top floor by rope.

縱 93B.83–9

tzuhng (*tzung).

V.i. & t. (1) V. t., indulge, give oneself up to: 縱性 *-shihng*, 縱慾 *-yuh*↓; 縱情 indulge one's passions; 縱酒 be given to alcoholic liquors; 縱飲 drink wine to excess; 縱慣 to spoil (a child). (2) Let go, set free: 縱囚 to free prisoners; 縱釋 release, discharge, set free. (3) Shoot (arrow): 縱送 *-suhng*↓. (4) V. i., jump up: 縱身 *-shen*↓.

Adj. Vertical, from north to south: 縱橫 *-herng*, 縱線 *-shiahn*, 縱貫 *-guahn*↓.

Conj. Though, even if: 縱使 *-shyy*, 縱然 *-rarn*, 縱令 *-lihng*, 縱或 *-huoh*↓.

縱隊 *tzuhngdueih*, n., (armed

forces) a column of troops or ships.

縱貫 *tzuhngguahn*, adj., vertical, from north (top) to south (bottom): 縱貫鐵路 a north-south railway line.

縱觀 *tzuhngguan*, v. t., take a panoramic view of.

縱橫 *tzuhngherng* (**tzung-*) (1) adv., vertically and horizontally, lengthwise and crosswise; (2) n., (also 縱衡); 縱橫家 an ancient school of thought specializing in political alliances and strategies.

縱或 *tzuhnghuoh*, conj., though, even if.

縱火 *tzuhng-huoo*, v. t., set on fire.

縱覽 *tzuhnglaan*, v. t., see *-guan* ↑.

縱浪 *tzuhnglahng*, v. i., indulge oneself.

縱令 *tzuhnglihng*, conj., even if (though).

縱目 *tzuhngmuh*, v. t., to survey all that is spread before one.

縱然 *tzuhngrarn*, conj., even if.

縱容 *tzuhngrurng* (*-'rung*), v. t., permit (s.o.) to do as he pleases, connive at, tolerate.

縱身 *tzuhng-shen*, v. i., (of a person) to jump up.

縱線 *tzuhngshiahn*, n., north-south line or railway line, vertical line.

縱性 *tzuhng-shihng*, v. i., do as one pleases, be guided by one's whims.

縱使 *tzuhngshyy*, conj., even if.

縱送 *tzuhngsuhng*, v. t., (hunting) shoot and pursue (game).

縱談 *tzuhng-tarn*, v. i., converse freely.

縱恣 *tzuhngtzyh*, v. i., give free rein to one's passions.

縱養 *tzuhngyaang*, v. t., to spoil (a child).

縱言 *tzuhng-yarn*, v. i., carry on an informal and free conversation with friends.

縱慾 *tzuhng-yuh*, v. i., indulge in sensual pleasures (also wr. 縱欲).

縫 93B.83-9

ferng (**fehng*).

N. **fehng* (*feh'l*) Crack, slit, open seam (*-'l*): 小縫兒 a little slit; 門縫兒 slight opening in door panel; 天衣無縫 perfect work of art, like seamless garment, without artifice; 漏縫 a leak; 裂縫 a crack.

V.i. & t. (1) To sew: 縫合 sew up; 縫傷口 sew up wound; 密密縫 close stitch. (2) To make dress: 縫衣裳 sew, make a dress; 縫工 sewing man or woman; 裁縫 tailor ("cut and sew"); 縫紉 *-rehn* ↓; 縫綴 sew and patch up; 彌縫差錯, 缺憾 patch up mistakes.

縫窮的 *ferngchyurng-de*, n., former term for poor sewing woman.

縫縫連連 *ferngferng-liarnliarn*, adv., descriptive of sewing work.

縫紉 *ferngrehn*, v. i. & n., dressmaking; 縫紉機 sewing machine, see *-yi-ji* ↓.

縫子 **fehng'tz*, 縫兒 **fehng'l*, n., flaws in argument.

縫衣機 *ferngyi-ji*, n., sewing machine.

§93B.91 (糸/ノ)

紗 93B.91-2

sha.

N. (1) Gauze, a fine, sheer cloth of silk, cotton or linen. (2) Cotton: 紗廠 *-chaang* ↓.

紗布 *shabuh*, n., textiles; 紗布業 textile industry.

紗廠 *shachaang*, n., cotton mill.

紗窗 *shachuang*, n., screen window.

紗櫥 *shachur*, n., curtained cabinet; anc. style bed with posts, cabinets and curtains.

紗錠 *shadihng*, n., cotton spindles.

紗罩(兒) *shajauh('l)*, n., (1) screen cover, as for food on table; (2) gas mantle for burner.

紗帽 *shamauh*, n., formerly, a cone-shaped hat of an official or a scholar of first degree (秀才).

緲 93B.91-4

miaau.

Adj. See 縹△緲 93B.01.

繆 93B.91-5

miauh (with var.).

[*muh*, as var. of 穆 90A.91; *miouh*, as var. of 謬 60A.91; *mour*, see 綢△繆 93B.42]

N. (*miauh*) A surname.

紾 93B.91-8

jeen.

V.t. To twist: 紾兄之臂 (AC) do arm-twisting to elder brother.

§93B.93 (糸/く)

紘 93B.93-1

hurng.

紘 縷 紜 纓 繈 紭 絵 綏 緌 剿 雝 部 鄙 鄉

Adj. (AC) broad.

縷 93B.93-2

lyuu.

N. A fine thread: 萬縷青絲 a mass of black hair; 金縷衣 jacket of gold threads.

Adv. Finely, in fine detail: 條分縷析 analyze point by point; 縷陳, 縷述 to narrate in detail, point by point.

縷縷 *lyurlyuu*, adv., (1) in detail: 縷縷陳述 to narrate in detail; 不盡縷縷 (in conclusion of letters) I need not detail all that I feel; (2) continuously.
縷續 *lyuushyuh*, adv., (also 縷縷續續) continuously, (narrate) in snatches, on and off, (related to 陸續 *luhshyuh*).

紜 93B.93-3

yurn.

Adj. Confused: 紛紜 ditto.

纓 93B.93-4

ying.

N. (*-tz*, *-'l*) Hat or cap tassels; tassels on spears: 請纓 (allu.) to volunteer or offer service to army.

V.t. To surround, bother.

纓絡 *yingluoh*, n., hat or cap tassels.

繈 93B.93-5

chiaang.

N. (1) A string of copper coins. (2) Swaddling clothes, see 襁^Δ褓 63C.93.

紭 93B.93-6

shiarn.

[Anc. var. 弦 50A.93]

絵 93B.93-8

hueih.

[Abbr. of 繪 93B.41]

綏 93B.93-9

suei (also **sueir*).

N. (1) (LL, greeting in letters) health and happiness: 公綏, 日綏, 福綏 best wishes (interch. 安). (2) (AC) a pennant; sashes.

V.t. To pacify (rebels, area).

綏憮 *sueifuu*, v. t., to pacify (area, people).
綏靖 *sueijihng*, v. t., ditto.
綏遠 *Sueiyuaan*, n., a province in Northwest China.

緌 93B.93-9

rueir.

N. (AC) tassels hanging from hat or cap.

SECTION 93S

§ 93S.00 (ㄑ^s/ㄐ)

剿 93S.00-2

jiaau.

V.t. To exterminate, wipe out rebels (interch. 勦 93S.50).

§ 93S.11 (ㄑ^s/土)

雝 93S.11-9

yung.

[Var. wr. form 雍 60.11]

§ 93S.22 (ㄑ^s/ㄧ)

部 93S.22-3

tair.

N. A surname.

鄙 93S.22-3

bii.

[Pop. of 鄙 40S.22]

鄉 93S.22-9

shiang (**shiahng*).

N. (1) Village 鄉村 *-tsun*, 鄉下 *-shiah*↓. (2) Native place or district: 鄉里, 鄉井 *-lii*, *-jiing*↓; 故鄉, 家鄉 home district; 鄉親, 老鄉, 同鄉 person from the same home district; 衣 (*yih*) 錦還鄉 return of the home town boy who made good; 離鄉(背井) go abroad from native place (cf. 鄉井 *-jiing*↓); 本鄉本土 home town. (3) District, region: 他鄉, 異鄉, 客鄉 place away from home, foreign place or country; 入鄉隨俗 when in Rome, do as the Romans do.

V.i. (*shiahng) As rare var. of 嚮 and 向 to face, facing, in 鄉壁虛構, 鄉方 (AC) (=向壁, 向方).

鄉親 *shiang'chin*, n., fellow citizen of the same district.

鄉愁 *shiangchour*, n., nostalgia.

鄉曲 *shiangchyuu*, n., village; 鄉曲之士 a village schoolmaster, a man of narrow culture.

鄉黨 *shiangdaang*, n., village people.

鄉弟 *shiang-dih*, n., (1) younger person of same district; (2) (self-reference) your younger brother of the same district.

鄉貫 *shiang-guahn*, n., person's nativity.

鄉關 *shiang-guan*, n., home town.

鄉國 *shiang-guor*, n., home district.

鄉宦 *shiang-huahn*, n., village gentry who has held official position.

鄉戶 *shiang-huh*, n., village resident; village population.

鄉長 *shiangjaang*, n., (1) village elder; (2) administrative chief of village.

鄉鎮 *shiangjehn*, n., a hamlet.

鄉井 *shiangjiing*, n., "village and well"—home town.

鄉姪 *shiangjyr*, n., a member of younger generation from same district; oft. used in self-reference.

鄉聚 *shiang-jyuh*, n., (AC) village, hamlet.

鄉老兒 *shianglaau'l*, n., see *-shiahlaau'l*↓.

鄉里 *shianglii*, n., (1) village; (2) village people.

鄉民 *shiangmirn*, n., villagers, peasants, rustic people.

鄉末 *shiang-moh*, n., (court. self-reference) a person of same home town.

鄉評 *shiang-pirng*, phr., gen. reputation of person in home town—a method for selection of officials in 3rd-5th cen. A.D.

鄉人 *shiangrern*, n., (1) a villager; (2) people of the same district.

鄉紳 *shiangshen*, n., local gentry.

鄉下 *shiangshiah*, n., the countryside; 鄉下人, 鄉下老兒 (*--laau'l*) a country bumpkin.

鄉賢 *shiang-shiarn*, n., an honored and respected gentleman of the town or village.

鄉塾 *shiang-shur*, n., private village school.

鄉試 *shiangshyh*, n., formerly, triennial examination in each province for the second degree of 舉人.

鄉俗 *shiangsur*, n., local customs.

鄉談 *shiangtarn*, n., local patois.

鄉村 *shiangtsun*, n., village, hamlet; rustic area.

鄉望 *shiang-wahng*, n., public esteem enjoyed in home town.

鄉味 *shiang-weih*, n., home-grown product.

鄉誼 *shiang-yih*, n., relationship of being from same town or village.

鄉音 *shiangyin*, n., local accent.

鄉愿 *shiangyuahn*, n., (AC) the correctly behaved hypocrite; local conformist.

鄉愚 *shiang-yur*, phr., the ignorant rustics.

§ 93S.50 (ㄑ^s/ㄱ)

幻 93S.50–5

huahn.

Adj. Illusive, chimerical, like a figment of imagination: 變幻無常 constantly changing shapes; 夢幻 an insubstantial daydream, a mirage, fantasy; 虛幻 unreal, insubstantial, like an air castle.

幻變 *huahnbiahn*, v. i., to change kaleidoscopically.

幻燈 *huahndeng*, n., projector; a lantern for showing slides; 彩色幻燈片 color slides.

幻化 *huahnhuah*, v. i., (1) to change and disappear; (2) (LL) to pass away.

幻境 *huahnjihng*, n., a phantasmagoria of dim, unreal shapes.

幻覺 *huahnjyuer*, n., a creature of the imagination, a vagary, an illusion.

幻滅 *huahnmieh*, v. i., to melt into nothingness.

幻泡 *huahnpauh*, phr., from 夢幻泡影 (human life is) like a vanishing dream, a bursting bubble.

幻想 *huahnshiaang*, n., fantasy, illusion, imagination; v. i., to imagine, daydream, fancy.

幻象 *huahnshiahng*, n., a mirage, unreal shapes.

幻術 *huahnshuh*, n., magic, sleight of hand.

勦 93S.50–5

jiaau.

[Var. of 剿 93S.00]

幼 93S.50–9

youh.

V.t. (AC, rare) 幼吾幼 to be kind to one's own young.

Adj. Young, in childhood: 幼年, 幼小, 幼稚 *-niarn*, *-shiaau*, *-jyh*↓.

幼兒 *youh-erl*, n., a young child.

幼稚(穉) *youhjyh*, adj., young, immature; infantile (mentally); 幼稚病 infantilism; 幼稚園 kindergarten.

幼年 *youhniarn*, n., childhood, childhood years.

幼僧 *youhseng*, n., another term for nuns.

幼小 *youhshiaau*, adj., young and still needing help, of young childhood.

幼子 *youhtzyy*, n., young child; youngest child.

幼芽 *youhyar*, n., (bot.) tender sprout.

勦 93S.50-9

jiaau (**chaur*).

V.t. Exterminate, annihilate, extirpate: 勦匪 to wage a war of extermination against rebels; 清勦 annihilate (roving bands of bandits, rebels).

§ 93S.63 (ㄑ^{s}/丶)

絲 93S.63-9

sy.

[Pop. of 絲 93B.01]

§ 93S.70 (ㄑ^{s}/ㄴ)

能 93S.70-2

nerng.

N. (i) Ability, capability, an able person: 才能 talent; 能幹(兒) *-gahn*(-*'gah'l*)↓; 能力 *-lih*↓; 能耐 *-naih*↓; 何德何能 (rhet.) what virtues or abilities (have I?); 技能 technical skill; 能者多勞 phr., the able ones always have calls upon their time; 能事 *-shyh*↓; 能手 *-shoou*↓; 能人 *-rern*↓; 能爲 *-weir*↓; 選賢與能 select the good and the capable for public service. (2) (Phys.) power, energy: 電能 electric power; 動能 motive power; 熱能 thermodynamic power; 原子能 atomic energy; 日光能 solar energy.

Vb. aux. (1) Can, be able to: 能夠 (vern.) *-gouh*↓; 能得 be able to; 能不 (rhet.) can one help?＝cannot help; 能不依依 can I not help thinking of you? 不能不 cannot help; 能無(原因嗎) can there be no (reason for it)? 能以 can; 全能 omnipotent; 不能 cannot, be unable to; 可能 possible. (2) Be good at: 能說會道 be a good talker; 能吃能喝 be healthy enough to enjoy food and drinks; 能寫能算 be good at the three R's. (3) Tolerate: 積不相能 cannot tolerate one another.

Adv. Rather: 能可 would rather (corrupt. for 寧可 *nirngkee* 62.01).

能幹(兒) *nernggahn*(-*gah'l*), n., ability to have things done; adj., able: 他很能幹 he is very able.

能夠 *nernggouh*, aux. vb., (vern.) can.

能量 *nernghiahng*, n., physical capacity.

能力 *nernglih*, n., potentiality, ability: 他很有能力 he has great ability.

能率 *nernglyuh*, n., efficiency.

能耐 *nerngnaih*, n., patience, endurance.

能人 *nerng-rern*, n., an able person: 能人背後有能人 no one can boast of being superior to all others (lit., "back of an able person is an abler person").

能手 *nerng-shoou*, n., expert: 個中能手 an expert in a given field.

能事 *nerngshyh*, n., one's specialty, what one can do best.

能爲 *nerngweir*, adj., able, resourceful.

毵 93S.70-9

san.

Adj. Scraggy.

§ 93S.81 (ㄑ^{s}/人)

欸 93S.81-9

eih (**ai*, **aai*).

Excl. (1) (Affirmation) yea, yes! (2) (**aai*) A sighing sound.

欸乃 **airnaai*, n., (LL & poet.) sound of swishing and cracking of boat sweeps in water.

§ 93S.82 (ㄑ^{s}/乂)

皴 93S.82-2

tsun.

N. (1) A wrinkle (on face, skin), also dirt accumulated on wrinkles: 一脖子皴 sooty lines on neck. (2) Surface lines (of hills, rocks) in Chin. painting—a cultivated technique.

V.t. To make surface lines on rocks and hills: 皴法 such technique.

Adj. Wrinkled.

APPENDIX A

The Sexagenary Cycle

The very ancient sexagenary cycle of sixty years or days consists of permutation of the Decimal Cycle and the Duodecimal Cycle. Five of the Duodecimal Cycle (5×12) or six of the Decimal Cycle (6×10) make a complete cycle of sixty years. This is the Jiahtzyy 甲子 system, otherwise known as Ganjy 干支.

The Decimal Cycle is in common use serving like A, B, C, D in numbering grades or any series. The Duodecimal Cycle is usually used in designating hour periods.

The Decimal Cycle

甲	jiah	己	jii
乙	yir	庚	geng
丙	biing	辛	shin
丁	ding	壬	rern
戊	wuh	癸	gueei

The Duodecimal Cycle

Branches	Animals	Zodiac	Hours
子 Tzyy	Rat	Aries	11–1 a.m.
丑 Choou	Ox	Taurus	1–3
寅 Yirn	Tiger	Gemini	3–5
卯 Maau	Hare	Cancer	5–7
辰 Chern	Dragon	Leo	7–9
巳 Syh	Serpent	Virgo	9–11
午 Wuu	Horse	Libra	11–1 p.m.
未 Weih	Sheep	Scorpio	1–3
申 Shen	Monkey	Sagittarius	3–5
酉 Yoou	Cock	Capricorn	5–7
戌 Shyu	Dog	Aquarius	7–9
亥 Haih	Pig	Pisces	9–11

A GROUP OF FOUR CYCLES 1804–2043 A.D.

鼠 *shuu*	rat	甲 1804 1864 子 1924 1984	丙 1816 1876 子 1936 1996	戊 1828 1888 子 1948 2008	庚 1840 1900 子 1960 2020	壬 1852 1912 子 1972 2032
牛 *niur*	ox	乙 1805 1865 丑 1925 1985	丁 1817 1877 丑 1937 1997	己 1829 1889 丑 1949 2009	辛 1841 1901 丑 1961 2021	癸 1853 1913 丑 1973 2033
虎 *huu*	tiger	丙 1806 1866 寅 1926 1986	戊 1818 1878 寅 1938 1998	庚 1830 1890 寅 1950 2010	壬 1842 1902 寅 1962 2022	甲 1854 1914 寅 1974 2034

兎 *tuh*	hare	丁 1807 1867 卯 1927 1987	己 1819 1879 卯 1939 1999	辛 1831 1891 卯 1951 2011	癸 1843 1903 卯 1963 2023	乙 1855 1915 卯 1975 2035
龍 *lurng*	dragon	戊 1808 1868 辰 1928 1988	庚 1820 1880 辰 1940 2000	壬 1832 1892 辰 1952 2012	甲 1844 1904 辰 1964 2024	丙 1856 1916 辰 1976 2036
蛇 *sher*	serpent	己 1809 1869 巳 1929 1989	辛 1821 1881 巳 1941 2001	癸 1833 1893 巳 1953 2013	乙 1845 1905 巳 1965 2025	丁 1857 1917 巳 1977 2037
馬 *maa*	horse	庚 1810 1870 午 1930 1990	壬 1822 1882 午 1942 2002	甲 1834 1894 午 1954 2014	丙 1846 1906 午 1966 2026	戊 1858 1918 午 1978 2038
羊 *yarng*	sheep	辛 1811 1871 未 1931 1991	癸 1823 1883 未 1943 2003	乙 1835 1895 未 1955 2015	丁 1847 1907 未 1967 2027	己 1859 1919 未 1979 2039
猴 *hour*	monkey	壬 1812 1872 申 1932 1992	甲 1824 1884 申 1944 2004	丙 1836 1896 申 1956 2016	戊 1848 1908 申 1968 2028	庚 1860 1920 申 1980 2040
雞 *ji*	cock	癸 1813 1873 酉 1933 1993	乙 1825 1885 酉 1945 2005	丁 1837 1897 酉 1957 2017	己 1849 1909 酉 1969 2029	辛 1861 1921 酉 1981 2041
狗 *goou*	dog	甲 1814 1874 戌 1834 1994	丙 1826 1886 戌 1946 2006	戊 1838 1898 戌 1958 2018	庚 1850 1910 戌 1970 2030	壬 1862 1922 戌 1982 2042
豬 *ju*	pig	乙 1815 1875 亥 1935 1995	丁 1827 1887 亥 1947 2007	己 1839 1899 亥 1959 2019	辛 1851 1911 亥 1971 2031	癸 1863 1923 亥 1983 2043

APPENDIX B

In the "farmers' calendar" 農曆, the "Solar terms," fluctuating from year to year in lunar terms, are nevertheless calculated to correspond with dates of the Gregorian calendar.

The 24 Solar Terms

Approximate dates			
February	5	立　春	Spring begins.
,,	19	雨　水	The rains.
March	5	驚　蟄	Insects awaken.
,,	20	春　分	Vernal Equinox.
April	5	清　明	Clear and bright.
,,	20	穀　雨	Grain rain.
May	5	立　夏	Summer begins.

Approximate dates			
May	21	小 满	Grain buds.
June	6	芒 種	Grain in ear.
,,	21	夏 至	Summer Solstice.
July	7	小 暑	Slight heat.
,,	23	大 暑	Great heat.
August	7	立 秋	Autumn begins.
,,	23	處 暑	Stopping of heat.
September	8	白 露	White dews.
,,	23	秋 分	Autumnal Equinox.
October	8	寒 露	Cold dews.
,,	23	霜 降	Hoar frost falls.
November	7	立 冬	Winter begins.
,,	22	小 雪	Light snow.
December	7	大 雪	Heavy snow.
,,	21	冬 至	Winter Solstice.
January	6	小 寒	Slight cold.
,,	21	大 寒	Great cold.

APPENDIX C

WEIGHTS, MEASURES AND NUMERALS

(1) Simple Weights and Measures

Avoirdupois: A 斤 (lb.) consists of 16 兩 (ounces); below the 兩 in decimals follow 錢, 分, 釐, 毫, 絲, 忽, 微.

Corn measure: A 石 (*dahn*) has 10 斗 (bushels); a 斗 has 10 升 (pints), and in decimals follow 合, 勺, 抄, 撮, 圭, and 6 粟 make a 圭.

Measure of distance: 10 分 (lines) make a 寸 (inch), 10 寸 a 尺 (foot), 5 尺 a 步, (pace) 2 步 (or 10 尺) a 丈, 180 丈 a 里 *lii* (one third of mile). English: 吋 inch, 呎 foot, 碼 yard, 哩 mile.

Square measure: 100 方寸 make a 方尺, 25 方尺 a 方步, 4 方步 (or 100 方尺) a 方丈, 6 方丈 a 分, 10 分 a 畝 (Chinese acre), 100 畝 a 頃, 540 畝 a 方里.

Cubic measure: 1,000 立方寸 make a 立方尺, 125 立方尺 a 立方步, 8 立方步, a 立方丈.

Time measure: 15 分 (minutes) make a 刻 (quarter hour), 8 刻 a 時辰 (Chinese hour), 12 時辰 a 日 (day), 29 or 30 日 a 月, 12 月 (13 when there is an intercalary month 閏月) a year. Or, 60 秒 (seconds) make a 分, 60 分 (minutes) a 點 (hour), 24 點 a 日 (day).

(2) The Metric System

Length

原 名	Millimétre (Mm.)	Centimétre (Cm.)	Métre (m.)	Kilométre (Km.)
譯 名	毫 米	厘米 (公分)	米 (公 尺)	千米 (公里)
等 數		10 毫 米	100 厘 米	1,000 米

Area

原　名	Milliméti re Carré (Mm.²)	Centimétre Carré (Cm.²)	Métre Carré (M.²)	Kilométre Carré (Km.²)
譯　名	方毫米	方厘米	方　米	方公里(千米)
等　數		100方毫米	10,000方厘米	1,000,000方米

原　名	Centiare (Ca.)	Are (a.)	Hectare (Ha.)	Kilométre Carré (Km.²)
譯　名	公厘(即方米)	公　畝	公　頃	方公里
等　數		100公厘	100公畝	100公頃

Liquid Measure

原　名	Millilitre (mL.)	Centilitre (cL.)	Décilitre (dL.)	Litre (L.)	Décalitre (DL.)	Hectolitre (HL.)	Kilolitre (KL.)
譯　名	公撮(𥫃)	公勺(竘)	公合(竤)	公升(竔)	公斗(竨)	公石(竡)	公秉(竦)
等　數		10公撮	10公勺	10公合	10公升	10公斗	10公石

Weight

原　名	Milligramme (mg.)	Centigramme (cg.)	Gramme (G.)	Kilogramme (Kg.)	Tonne (T.)
譯　名	毫　克	厘　克	克	千克(公斤)	公噸(𠗆)
等　數		10毫克	100厘克	1,000克	1,000公斤

(3) The Chinese Numerals

	Ordinary style	Style in check to avoid mistakes	Numerals in accounts
1	一	弌 壹	〡
2	二	弍 貳	〢
3	三	弎 叁	〣
4	四	肆	〤
5	五	伍	〥
6	六	陸	〦
7	七	柒	〧
8	八	捌	〨
9	九	玖	〩
10	十	拾 什	
100	百	佰	
1,000	千	仟	
10,000	萬 (万)		
100,000	十萬		
1,000,000	百萬		
10,000,000	千萬		
100,000,000	一億		
1,000,000,000	十億		

APPENDIX D

Chinese Dynasties

In common Wade spellings, followed by *Guoryuu* spellings in *italics*.

Furshi (伏羲)		2852 B.C.
Shernnurng (神農)		2737 B.C.
Huarngdih (黃帝)		2697 B.C.
Shauhhauh (少昊)		2597 B.C.
Chuanshyuh (顓頊)		2513 B.C.
Yaur (帝堯)		2356 B.C.
Shuhn (帝舜)		2255 B.C.
Hsia (*Shiah*)	夏	2205–1766 B.C.
Shang or Yin (*Shang*)	商殷	1766–1123 B.C.
Chou (*Jou*)	周	1122– 249 B.C.
[Ch'un Ch'iu 春秋 722–481/480 B.C.]		
[Warring Kingdoms 戰國 403–221 B.C.]		
Ch'in (*Chirn*)	秦	221–207 B.C.
Western or Earlier Han (*Hahn*)	漢	206 B.C.–A.D. 7
Eastern or Later Han (*Hahn*)	後漢	25–220
Three Kingdoms	三國	220–265
Shu (*Shuu*) 蜀 221–264		
Wei (*Weih*) 魏 220–265		
Wu (*Wur*) 吳 222–280		
Western Chin (*Jihn*)	晉	265–317
Southern Dynasties 南朝 (合隋又名六朝)		
Eastern Chin (*Jihn*)	東晉	317–420
Former Sung [Liu] (*Suhng*)	宋 (劉)	420–479
Southern Ch'i (*Chir*)	南齊	479–502
Southern Liang (*Liarng*)	南梁	502–557
Southern Ch'ên (*Chern*)	南陳	557–589
Northern Dynasties 北朝		
Northern Wei (*Weih*)	北魏	386–535
Eastern Wei (*Weih*)	東魏	534–550
Western Wei (*Weih*)	西魏	535–556
Northern Ch'i (*Chir*)	北齊	550–577
Northern Chou (*Jou*)	北周	557–581
Sui (*Sueir*)	隋	590–618
T'ang (*Tarng*)	唐	618–906
Five dynasties 五代		907–960
Later Liang (*Liarng*) 後梁 907–923		
Later T'ang (*Tarng*) 後唐 923–936		
Later Chin (*Jihn*) 後晉 936–947		
Later Han (*Hahn*) 後漢 947–950		
Later Chou (*Jou*) 後周 951–960		
Liao (*Liaur*)	遼	907–1125
Northern Sung (*Suhng*)	宋	960–1126
Hsi-hsia (*Shishiah*)	西夏	990–1227

Southern Sung (*Suhng*)	南宋	1127–1279
Chin (*Jin*)	金	1115–1234
Yüan (*Yuarn*) (Mongol)	元	1260–1368
Ming (*Mirng*)	明	1368–1644
Ch'ing (*Ching*) (Manshu)	清	1644–1912
The Republic of China	中華民國	1912–

APPENDIX E

GEOGRAPHICAL NAMES

(1) **The Provinces**

with Archaic Names and Capital (in established Wade rendering)

	Modern name		Archaic names	Capital	
1	河北	Hopei	冀, 幽燕	天津	Tientsin
2	山東	Shantung	魯, 山左	濟南	Tsinan
3	山西	Shansi	晋, 山右	太原	T'aiyüan
4	河南	Honan	豫, 中州	開封	K'aifeng
5	江蘇	Kiangsu	吳	南京	Nanking
6	安徽	Anhwei	皖	安慶	Anching
7	江西	Kiangsi	贛, 豫章	南昌	Nanch'ang
8	浙江	Chekiang	越, 浙	杭州	Hangchow
9	福建	Fukien	閩	福州	Foochow
10	湖北	Hupeh	鄂	武昌	Wuch'ang
11	湖南	Hunan	湘	長沙	Ch'angsha
12	廣東	Kwangtung	粵, 粵東	廣州	Canton
13	廣西	Kwangsi	桂, 粵西	桂林	Kweilin
14	雲南	Yünnan	滇	昆明	K'unming
15	貴州	Kweichow	黔	貴陽	Kweiyang
16	四川	Szechwan	蜀	成都	Ch'engtu
17	陝西	Shensi	秦, 關中	長安	Ch'angan (Sian)
18	甘肅	Kansu	隴	蘭州	Lanchow
19	臺灣	Taiwan		臺中	Taichung
20	西康	Sikang		康定	Kangting
21	寧夏	Ningsia		銀川	Yinchuan
22	綏遠	Suiyuan		歸綏	Kueisui
23	察哈爾	Chahar		張垣 (張家口)	Kalgan
24	新疆	Sinkiang		迪化	Urumchi (Tihua)
25	熱河	Jehol		承德	Chengteh
26	青海	Tsinghai		西寧	Hsining
27	遼寧	Liaoning		瀋陽	Mukden (Shenyang)
28	遼北	Liaopei		遼源	Liaoyuan
29	吉林	Kirin		吉林	Kirin
30	黑龍江	Heilungkiang		北安	Peian
31	興安	Hsingan		海拉爾	Hailar
32	嫩江	Nunkiang		齊齊哈爾	Tsitsihar

	Modern name		Archaic names	Capital	
33	松江	Sungkiang		牡丹江	Mutankiang
34	合江	Hokiang		佳木斯	Kiamusze
35	安東	Antung		通化	Tunghua
36	西藏 (特別行政區)	Tibet		拉薩	Lhasa

(2) Some Common English Names

(Wade)		(Guoryuu)
Aden	亞丁	Yahding
Afghanistan	阿富汗	Afuhhahn
Africa	阿非利加 (非洲)	Afeilihjia (Feijou)
Alaska	阿拉斯加	Alasyjia
Albania	阿爾巴尼亞	A-eelbaniryah
Algeria	阿爾及利亞	A-eeljilihyah
America	美利堅 (美國)	Meeilihjian (Meeiguor)
Amman	安曼	Anmahn
Amsterdam	阿姆斯特丹	Amuusytehdan
Andorra	安道爾	Andauh-eel
Angkor	安哥	Ange
Ankara	安哥拉	Angela
Antarctica	南極洲	Narnjirjou
Arctic Ocean	北極海	Beeijirhaai
Argentina	阿根廷	Agentirng
Asia	亞細亞 (亞洲)	Yahshiyah (Yahjou); also pr. *yaa-*
Athens	雅典	Yardiaan
Atlantic Ocean	大西洋	Dahshiyarng
Australia	澳大利亞 (澳洲)	Auhdahlihyah (Auhjou)
Austria	奧地利 (奧國)	Auhdihlia (Auhguor)
Bagdad	巴格達	Bagedar
Baguio	碧瑤	Bihyaur
Barbados	巴貝多	Babeihduo
Bandung	萬隆	Wahnlurng
Bangkok	曼谷	Mahnguu
Beirut	貝魯特	Beihluuteh
Belgium	比利時	Biilihshyr
Berlin	柏林	Berlirn
Bermuda	百慕達	Baaimuhdar
Bethlehem	伯利恆	Berlihherng
Bhutan	不丹	Buhdan
Bolivia	玻利維亞	Belihweiryah
Bombay	孟買	Mehngmaai
Bonn	波昂	Bo-arng
Brazil	巴西	Bashi

(Wade)		(Guoryuu)
Brussels	布魯塞爾	Buhluuseh-eel
Budapest	布達佩斯	Buhdarpeihsy
Buenos Aires	布宜諾斯艾利斯	Buhyirnuohsy-aihlihsy
Bulgaria	保加利亞	Baaujialihyah
Burma	緬甸	Miaandiahn
Cairo	開羅	Kailuor
Calcutta	加爾各答	Jia-eelgedar
Cambodia	柬埔寨	Jiarnpuujaih
Cameroon	喀麥隆	Kamohlurng
Canada	加拿大	Jianardah
Canberra	坎培拉	Kaanpeirla
Caucasia	高加索	Gaujiasuoo
Ceylon	錫蘭	Shilarn
Chicago	芝加哥	Jyjiage
Chile	智利	Jyhlih
Colombia	哥倫比亞	Gelurnbiiyah
Colombo	可倫坡	Keelurnpo
Congo	剛果	Gangguoo
Copenhagen	哥本哈根	Gebeenhagen
Costa Rica	哥斯大黎加	Gesydahlirjia
Cuba	古巴	Guuba
Cyprus	塞浦路斯	Saihpuuluhsy
Czechoslovakia	捷克	Jierkeh
Dahomey	達荷美	Darhermeei
Damascus	大馬士革	Dahmaashyhger
Denmark	丹麥	Danmaih
Dominica	多明尼加	Duomirngnirjia
Dublin	都伯林	Duberlirn
Ecuador	厄瓜多爾	Erguaduo-eel
Egypt	埃及	Aijir
England	英格蘭	Yinggelarn
Estonia	愛沙尼亞	Aihshaniryah
Ethiopia	衣索比亞	Yisuobiiyah
Europe	歐羅巴 (歐洲)	Ouluorba (Oujou)
Finland	芬蘭	Fenlan
France	法蘭西 (法國)	Fahlarnshi (Fahguor) or Faa-
Fujiyama	富士山	Fuhshyhshan
Geneva	日內瓦	Ryhneihwaa

(Wade)		(Guoryuu)	(Wade)		(Guoryuu)
Germany	德國	Derguor	Lebanon	黎巴嫩	Lirbanehn
Ghana	迦納	Jianah	Leningrad	列寧格勒	Liehnirnggerleh
Gibraltar	直布羅陀	Jybuhluortuor	Liberia	賴比瑞亞	Laihbiirueihyah
Great Britain	大不列顛	Dah Burliehdian	Libya	利比亞	Lihbiiyah
Greece	希臘	Shilah	Lisbon	里斯本	Liisybeen
Greenland	格陵蘭	Gerlirnglarn	Lithuania	立陶宛	Lihtaurwaan
Guam Island	關島	Guandaau	Liverpool	利物浦	Lihwuhpuu
Guinea	幾內亞	Jiineihyah	London	倫敦	Lurndun
Guatemala	瓜地馬拉	Guadihmaala	Los Angeles	洛杉磯	Luohshanji
Hague	海牙	Haaiyar	Luxemburg	盧森堡	Lursenbaau
Haiti	海地	Haaidih	Luzon	呂宋	Lyuusuhng
Hamburg	漢堡	Hahnbaau	Madrid	馬德里	Maaderlii
Hanoi	河內	Herneih	Malaysia	馬來西亞	Maalairshiyah
Havana	哈瓦那	Hawaanah	Malta	馬爾他	Mar-eelta
Hawaii	夏威夷	Shiahweiyir	Manila	馬尼拉	Maanirla
Helsinki	赫爾辛基	Heh-eelshinji	Marseille	馬賽	Maasaih
Hiroshima	廣島	Guarngdaau	Mecca	麥加	Maihjia
Hokkaido	北海道	Beirhaaidauh	Mexico	墨西哥	Mohshige
Hollywood	好萊塢	Haaulairwu	Monaco	摩納哥	Mornahge
Honduras	宏都拉斯	Hurngdulasy	Monte Carlo	蒙地卡羅	Merngdihkaaluor
Honolulu	檀香山	Tarnshiangshan	Montreal	蒙特婁	Merngtehlour
Honshu	本州	Beenchou	Morocco	摩洛哥	Morluohge
Hué	順化	Shuhnhuah	Moscow	莫斯科	Morsyke
Hungary	匈牙利	Shyungyarlih	Munich	慕尼黑	Muhnirhei
Iceland	冰島	Bingdaau	Nagasaki	長崎	Charngchir
Inchon	仁川	Rernchuan	Nagoya	名古屋	Mirngguuwu
India	印度	Yihnduh	Naples	那不勒斯	Naabuhlehsy
Indonesia	印尼	Yihnnir	Nepal	尼泊爾	Nirpoh-eel
Iran	伊朗	Yilarng	Netherland	荷蘭	Herlarn
Iraq	伊拉克	Yilake	New Delhi	新德里	Shinderlii
Ireland	愛爾蘭	Aih-eellarn	New Guinea	新幾內亞	Shinjiineihyah
Israel	以色列	Yiisehlieh	New Foundland	紐芬蘭	Nioufenlarn
Italy	義大利	Yihdahlih	New York	紐約	Nioouyue
Jakarta	雅加達	Yaajiadar	New Zealand	紐西蘭	Niooushilarn
Jamaica	牙買加	Yarmaaijia	Nicaragua	尼加拉瓜	Nirjialagua
Japan	日本	Ryhbeen	Nigeria	奈及利亞	Naihjirlihyah
Java	爪哇	Jaauwa	North America	北美州	Beirmeeijou
Jerusalem	耶路撒冷	Yerluhsaleeng	Norway	挪威	Nuorwei
Jordan	約旦	Yuedahn	Oceania	大洋洲	Dahyarngjou
Kabul	喀布爾	Kebuh-eel	Okinawa	冲繩	Chungsherng
Karachi	喀喇蚩	Kelachy	Oman	阿曼	Ahmahn
Katmandu	加德滿都	Jiadermaandu	Osaka	大阪	Dahbaan
Kazakh	哈薩克	Hasakeh	Oslo	奧斯陸	Auhsyluh
Kiev	基輔	Jifuu	Ottawa	渥太華	Wutaihhuar
Korea	韓國	Harnguor	Pacific Ocean	太平洋	Taihpirngyarng
Kuala Lumpur	吉隆坡	Jilurngpo	Pakistan	巴基斯坦	Bajisytaan
Kyoto	京都	Jingdu	Palestine	巴勒斯坦	Balehsytaan
Kyushu	九州	Jiooujou	Panama	巴拿馬	Banarmaa
Laos	寮國	Liaurguor	Panmunjom	板門店	Baanmerndiahn
Latvia	拉脫維亞	Latuoweiryah	Paraguay	巴拉圭	Balaguei

(Wade)		(Guoryuu)
Paris	巴黎	Balir
Peru	秘魯	Mihluu
Philippines	菲律賓	Feilyuhbin
Pnompenh	金邊	Jinbian
Poland	波蘭	Polarn
Portugal	葡萄牙	Purtauryar
Prague	布拉格	Buhlager
Pusan	釜山	Fuushan
Pyongyang	平壤	Pirngraang
Rangoon	仰光	Yaangguang
Rio de Janeiro	里約熱內盧	Liiyuerehneihlur
Romania	羅馬尼亞	Luormaaniryah
Rome	羅馬	Luormaa
Russia	蘇俄(俄國)	Su-eh (Eh-guor)
Ryukyu	琉球	Liourchiour
Saigon	西貢	Shiguhng
Sakhalin	庫頁島	Kuhyehdaau
Salvador	薩爾瓦多	Sa-erwaaduo
San Francisco	舊金山	Jiouhjinshan
Santiago	聖地牙哥	Shehngdihyarge
Saudi Arabia	沙烏地阿拉伯	Shawudih Ahlabor
Scotland	蘇格蘭	Sugerlarn
Seattle	西雅圖	Shiyaatur
Seoul	漢城	Hahncherng
Siberia	西伯利亞	Shiborlihyah
Sicily	西西里	Shishilii
Sikkim	錫金	Shijin
Singapore	星加坡	Shingjiapo
Somalia	索馬利亞	Suormaalihyah
South America	南美洲	Narnmeeijou
Spain	西班牙	Shibanyar
Stockholm	斯德哥爾摩	Syderge-eelmor
Sudan	蘇丹	Sudan
Suez	蘇彝士	Suyirshyh

(Wade)		(Guoryuu)
Sumatra	蘇門答臘	Sumerndarlah
Surabaja	泗水	Syshueei
Sweden	瑞典	Rueihdiaan
Switzerland	瑞士	Rueihshyh
Sydney	雪黎	Shyueelir
Syria	叙利亞	Shyuhlihyah
Tahiti	大溪地	Dahshirdih
Tehran(Teheran)	德黑蘭	Derheilarn
Tel Aviv	台拉維夫	Tairlaweirfu
Thailand	泰國	Taihguor
Tokyo	東京	Dungjing
Trinidad	千里達	Chianliidar
Tunisia	突尼西亞	Tunirshiyah
Turkey	土耳其	Tur-eelchir
Ukraine	烏克蘭	Wukelarn
United Kingdom	聯合王國	Liarnher Warngguor
Uraguay	烏拉圭	Wulaguei
Vancouver	温哥華	Wengehuar
Vatican	梵蒂岡	Farntihgang
Venezuela	委內瑞拉	Weeineihrueihla
Venice	威尼斯	Weinirsy
Vienna	維也納	Weiryeenah
Vientiane	永珍	Yuungjen
Vietnam	越南	Yuehnarn
Vladivostok	海參崴	Haaishenwei
Wales	威爾斯	Wei-eelsy
Warsaw	華沙	Huarsha
Washington	華盛頓	Huarshehngduhn
White Russia	白俄羅斯	Bair-Ehluorsy
Yemen	葉門	Yehmern
Yokohama	横濱	Herngbin
Yugoslavia	南斯拉夫	Narnsylafu
Zurich	蘇黎世	Sulirshyh

(3) Some Common Chinese Names

(Guoryuu)		(Wade)
Anhuei	安 徽	Anhwei
Andung	安 東	Antung
Boryarnghur	鄱陽湖	Poyang Lake
Beei-an	北 安	Peian
Beeipirng	北 平	Peiping
Charhaeel	察哈爾	Chahar
Charngcherng	長 城	The Great Wall
Charngchun	長 春	Changchun
Charngjiang	長 江	Yangtze River
Charngsha	長 沙	Changsha
Cherngder	承 德	Chengteh

(Guoryuu)		(Wade)
Cherngdu	成 都	Chengtu
Chingdaau	青 島	Tsingtao
Chinghaai	青 海	Tsinghai
Chingyuahn	清 苑	Tsingyuan
Churngchihng	重 慶	Chungking
Chyuufuh	曲 阜	Chufu
Dahliarn	大 連	Dairen
Dahnshueei	淡 水	Tamsui
Dirhuah	廸 化	Urumchi
Duhngtirnghur	洞庭湖	Tungting Lake
Furjiahn	福 建	Fukien

(Guoryuu)		(Wade)
Furjou	福州	Foochow
Gansuh	甘肅	Kansu
Gaushyurng	高雄	Kaohsiung
Guaangdung	廣東	Kwangtung
Guaangjou	廣州	Canton (Kwangchow)
Guaangshi	廣西	Kwangsi
Gueihjou	貴州	Kweichow
Gueihlirn	桂林	Kweilin
Gueihyarng	貴陽	Kweiyang
Ha-eelbin	哈爾濱	Harbin
Hahnkoou	漢口	Hankow
Harngjou	杭州	Hangchow
Heilurngjiang	黑龍江	Amur River
Herbeei	河北	Hopeh
Herfeir	合肥	Hofei
Hernarn	河南	Honan
Huarngher	黃河	Yellow River (Hwang Ho)
Hurbeei	湖北	Hupeh
Hurnarn	湖南	Hunan
Jangjiakoou	張家口	Kalgan
Jehjiang	浙江	Chekiang
Jehnjiang	鎮江	Chinkiang
Jiangshi	江西	Kiangsi
Jiangsu	江蘇	Kiangsu
Jihnarn	濟南	Tsinan
Jilirn	吉林	Kirin
Jilurng	基隆	Keelung
Jinmern	金門	Quemoy
Jiooulurng	九龍	Kowloon
Kaifeng	開封	Kaifeng
Kunmirng	昆明	Kunming
Lasah	拉薩	Lhasa
Larnjou	蘭州	Lanchow
Liaurbeei	遼北	Liaopei
Liaurnirng	遼寧	Liaoning
Maanjou	滿州	Manchuria

(Guoryuu)		(Wade)
Martzuu	馬祖	Matsu
Mengguu	蒙古	Mongolia
Narnchang	南昌	Nanchang
Narnjing	南京	Nanking
Nirngpo	寧波	Ningpo
Nirngshiah	寧夏	Ningsia
Pernghur	澎湖	Pescadores
Rehher	熱河	Jehol
Shaanshi	陝西	Shensi
Shahtour	汕頭	Swatow
Shahnghaai	上海	Shanghai
Shandung	山東	Shantung
Shanshi	山西	Shansi
Sheenyarng	瀋陽	Mukden
Shiahmern	廈門	Amoy
Shi-an	西安	Sian
Shianggaang	香港	Hong Kong
Shikang	西康	Sikong
Shitzahng	西藏	Tibet
Shinjiang	新疆	Sinkiang
Sujou	蘇州	Soochow
Sueiyuaan	綏遠	Suiyuan
Syhchuan	四川	Szechwan
Taihyuarn	太原	Taiyuan
Tairbeei	台北	Taipei
Tairdung	台東	Taitung
Taijung	台中	Taichung
Tairnarn	台南	Tainan
Taiwan	台灣	Taiwan
Tarnggu	塘沽	Tangku
Tianjin	天津	Tientsin
Wuuchang	武昌	Wuchang
Yantair	烟台	Cheefoo
Yaluhjiang	鴨綠江	Yalu River
Yurnanarn	雲南	Yunnan
Yuhnniarngho	運糧河	The Grand Canal

APPENDIX F

LIST OF CHEMICAL ELEMENTS

原子序	中名	讀音	英名	符號
1	氫	ching	Hydrogen	H
2	氦	haih	Helium	He
3	鋰	lii	Lithium	Li
4	鈹	pi	Beryllium	Be
5	硼	perng	Boron	B
6	碳	tahn	Carbon	C
7	氮	dahn	Nitrogen	N
8	氧	yanng	Oxygen	O
9	氟	fur	Fluorine	F
10	氖	naai	Neon	Ne
11	鈉	nah	Sodium	Na
12	鎂	meei	Magnesium	Mg
13	鋁	lyuu	Aluminium	Al
14	矽(硅)	shih	Silicon	Si
15	磷	lirn	Phosphorus	P
16	硫	liour	Sulfur	S
17	氯	lyuh (luh)	Chlorine	Cl
18	氬	yah	Argon	A (Ar)
19	鉀	jiaa	Potassium	K
20	鈣	gaih	Calcium	Ca
21	鈧	keng	Scandium	Sc
22	鈦	taih	Titanium	Ti
23	釩	farn	Vanadium	V
24	鉻	geh	Chromium	Cr
25	錳	meeng	Manganese	Mn
26	鐵	tiee	Iron	Fe
27	鈷	gu	Cobalt	Co
28	鎳	nieh	Nickel	Ni
29	銅	turng	Copper	Cu
30	鋅	shin	Zinc	Zn
31	鎵	jia	Gallium	Ga
32	鍺	jee	Germanium	Ge
33	砷	shen	Arsenic	As
34	硒	shi	Selenium	Se
35	溴	shiouh	Bromine	Br
36	氪	keh	Krypton	Kr
37	銣	rur	Rubidium	Rb
38	鍶	sy	Strontium	Sr
39	釔	yii	Yttrium	Y
40	鋯	gauh	Zirconium	Zr
41	鈮(鈳)	nir	Niobium	Nb(Cb)
42	鉬	muh	Molybdenum	Mo
43	鎝(鍀)	taa	Technetium	Tc
44	釕	liaau	Ruthenium	Ru
45	銠	laau	Rhodium	Rh
46	鈀	baa	Palladium	Pd
47	銀	yirn	Silver	Ag
48	鎘	ger	Cadmium	Cd
49	銦	yin	Indium	In
50	錫	shir	Tin	Sn
51	銻	tih	Antimony	Sb
52	鍗(碲)	dih	Tellurium	Te
53	碘	diaan	Iodine	I (J)
54	氙	shian	Xenon	Xe
55	銫	seh	Cesium	Cs
56	鋇	beih	Barium	Ba
57	鑭	larn	Lanthanum	La
58	鈰	shyh	Cerium	Ce
59	鐠	puu	Praseodymium	Pr
60	釹(釢)	nyuu	Neodymium	Nd
61	鉕	poo	Promethium	Pm
62	釤	san	Samarium	Sm
63	銪	yioou	Europium	Eu
64	釓	gar	Gadolinium	Gd
65	鋱	teh	Terbium	Tb
66	鏑	di	Dysprosium	Dy
67	鈥	huoo	Holmium	Ho
68	鉺	eel	Erbium	Er
69	銩	diou	Thulium	Tm(Tu)
70	鐿	yih	Ytterbium	Yb
71	鎦	liour	Lutecium	Lu
72	鉿	her	Hafnium	Hf
73	鉭	dahn	Tantalum	Ta
74	鎢	wuh	Tungsten	W
75	錸	lair	Rhenium	Re
76	鋨	er	Osmium	Os
77	銥	yi	Iridium	Ir
78	鉑	bor	Platinum	Pt
79	金	jin	Gold	Au
80	汞	guung	Mercury	Hg

原子序	中名	讀音	英名	符號	原子序	中名	讀音	英名	符號
81	鉈	ta	Thallium	Tl	93	錼(鎿)	naih	Neptunium	Np
82	鉛	chian	Lead	Pb	94	鈽(鈈)	buh	Plutonium	Pu
83	鉍	bih	Bismuth	Bi	95	鋂(鎇)	meei	Americium	Am
84	釙	pur	Polonium	Po	96	鋦	jyur	Curium	Cm
85	砈(鈘)	eh	Astatine	At	97	鉳(錇)	beei	Berkelium	Bk
86	氡	dung	Radon	Rn	98	鉲(鐦)	kaa	Californium	Cf
87	鍅(鈁)	faa	Francium	Fr	99	鑀(鎄,鍝)	aih	Einsteinium	E (An)
88	鐳(銧)	leir	Radium	Ra	100	鐨(鉦)	feih	Fermium	Fm (Ct)
89	錒	ah	Actinium	Ac	101	鍆	mern	Mendelevium	Mv
90	釷	tur	Thorium	Th	102	鍩	ruoh	Nobelium	No
91	鏷	pur	Protactinium	Pa	103	鐒	laur	Lawrencium	Lw
92	鈾	your	Uranium	U					

APPENDIX G

THE 214 RADICALS

Strokes

1

1 一
2 丨
3 丶
4 丿
5 乙
6 亅

2

7 二
8 亠
9 人, 亻
10 儿
11 入
12 八
13 冂
14 冖
15 冫
16 几
17 凵
18 刀, 刂
19 力
20 勹
21 匕
22 匚
23 匸
24 十
25 卜
26 卩, 㔾
27 厂
28 厶
29 又

3

30 口
31 囗
32 土
33 士
34 夂
35 夊
36 夕
37 大
38 女
39 子
40 宀
41 寸
42 小
43 尢, 兀, 尣
44 尸
45 屮
46 山
47 巛, 川, 巜
48 工
49 己
50 巾
51 干
52 幺
53 广
54 廴
55 廾
56 弋
57 弓
58 彐, 彑
59 彡
60 彳

4

61 心, 忄, ⺗
62 戈
63 戶
64 手, 扌
65 支
66 攴, 攵
67 文
68 斗
69 斤
70 方
71 无, 旡
72 日
73 曰
74 月
75 木
76 欠
77 止
78 歹, 歺
79 殳
80 毋
81 比
82 毛
83 氏
84 气
85 水, 氵
86 火, 灬
87 爪, 爫
88 父
89 爻
90 爿
91 片
92 牙
93 牛, 牜
94 犬, 犭

5

95 玄
96 玉, ⺩, 王
97 瓜
98 瓦
99 甘
100 生
101 用
102 田
103 疋
104 疒
105 癶
106 白
107 皮
108 皿
109 目, 罒
110 矛
111 矢
112 石
113 示, 礻
114 禸
115 禾
116 穴
117 立

6

118 竹, ⺮
119 米
120 糸, 糹
121 缶
122 网, 罒, 㓁
123 羊
124 羽
125 老
126 而
127 耒
128 耳
129 聿
130 肉, ⺼
131 臣
132 自
133 至
134 臼
135 舌
136 舛
137 舟
138 艮
139 色
140 艸, 艹
141 虍
142 虫
143 血
144 行
145 衣, 衤
146 襾, 覀

7

147 見
148 角
149 言
150 谷
151 豆
152 豕
153 豸
154 貝
155 赤
156 走
157 足
158 身
159 車
160 辛
161 辰
162 辵, 辶
163 邑, 阝(右旁)
164 酉
165 釆
166 里

8

167 金
168 長, 镸
169 門
170 阜, 阝(左旁)
171 隶
172 隹
173 雨, ⻗
174 青
175 非

9

176 面
177 革
178 韋
179 韭
180 音
181 頁
182 風
183 飛
184 食
185 首
186 香

10

187 馬
188 骨
189 高
190 髟
191 鬥
192 鬯
193 鬲
194 鬼

11

195 魚
196 鳥
197 鹵
198 鹿
199 麥
200 麻

12

201 黃
202 黍
203 黑
204 黹

13

205 黽
206 鼎
207 鼓
208 鼠

14

209 鼻
210 齊

15

211 齒

16

212 龍
213 龜

17

214 龠

APPENDICES H

LIST OF REGULAR AND SIMPLIFIED CHARACTERS

a. Regular to Simplified 繁體簡體對照表

（七劃）

車 车 10.10
夾 夹 12.81
貝 贝 41.80
見 见 41.70
壯 壮 21S.11
妝 妆 21S.93

（八劃）

長 长 51.02
亞 亚 31.30
軋 轧 10D.70
東 东 10.01
兩 两 31.42
協 协 10S.50
來 来 10.01
戔 戋 71.71
門 门 52B.00
岡 冈 42.42
兒 儿 90.70
狀 状 21S.81
糾 纠 93B.22

（九劃）

剋 克 10.70
軌 轨 10D.70
頁 页 31.80
勁 劲 31S.50
貞 贞 21A.80
則 则 41C.00
閂 闩 52B.00
迴 回 41.83
俠 侠 91A.81
係 系 91A.01
皃 皃 91.70
帥 帅 91S.22
後 后 91B.82
釓 钆 81A.70
負 负 92.80
風 风 42.70
訂 订 60A.00
計 计 60A.10
訃 讣 60A.22
軍 军 62.10
祇 只 63B.71
陣 阵 32A.10
韋 韦 22.10
陝 陕 32A.81
陘 陉 32A.30
飛 飞 32.70
紆 纡 93B.00
紅 红 93B.30
紂 纣 93B.00
紈 纨 93B.70
級 级 93B.82
約 约 93B.50
紇 纥 93B.70
紀 纪 93B.70
紉 纫 93B.50

（拾劃）

馬 马 51.50
挾 挟 10A.81
貢 贡 31.80
華 华 20A.10
莢 荚 20A.81
莖 茎 20A.30
莧 苋 20A.70
莊 庄 20A.11
軒 轩 10D.10
連 连 10.83
軔 轫 10D.50
剗 刬 71S.00
鬥 斗 52B.00
時 时 41A.00
畢 毕 41.10
財 财 41C.00
閃 闪 52B.00
唄 呗 40A.80
員 员 40.80
豈 岂 21.30
峽 峡 21B.81
剛 刚 42S.00
剮 剐 42S.00
氣 气 92.70
郵 邮 90S.22
倀 伥 91A.02
倆 俩 91A.42
條 条 91A.01
們 们 91A.00
個 个 91A.41
倫 伦 91A.42
隻 只 91.82
島 岛 91.50
烏 乌 91.50
師 师 91S.22
徑 径 91B.30
釘 钉 81A.00
針 针 81A.10
釗 钊 81A.00
釙 钋 81A.22
釕 钌 81A.00
殺 杀 82S.82
倉 仓 81.40
脅 胁 91.42
狹 狭 91C.81
狽 狈 91C.80
芻 刍 92.50
訐 讦 60A.10
討 讨 60A.00
訌 讧 60A.30
訕 讪 60A.21
訖 讫 60A.70
訓 训 60A.22
這 这 60.83
訊 讯 60A.70
記 记 60A.70
凍 冻 63A.01
畝 亩 60S.81
庫 库 61.10
浹 浃 63A.81
涇 泾 63A.30
書 书 22.41
陸 陆 32A.11
陳 陈 32A.01
孫 孙 32S.01
陰 阴 32A.93
務 务 32S.50
紜 纭 93B.93
純 纯 93B.70
紕 纰 93B.70
紗 纱 93B.91
納 纳 93B.42
紝 纴 93B.11
紛 纷 93B.50
紙 纸 93B.71
紋 纹 93B.82
紡 纺 93B.50
紐 纽 93B.30
紓 纾 93B.00

（拾一劃）

責 责 10.80
現 现 31A.70
甌 瓯 51.21
規 规 12S.70
殼 壳 11S.82
捨 舍 10A.40
捫 扪 10A.00
頂 顶 31S.80
掄 抡 10A.42
執 执 11S.70
捲 卷 10A.70
掃 扫 10A.22
堊 垩 31.11
萊 莱 20A.01
萵 莴 20A.42
乾 干 10S.70
軛 轭 10D.70
斬 斩 10D.22
軟 软 10D.81
專 专 10.00
區 区 51.21
堅 坚 51.11
帶 带 22.22
厠 厕 51A.00
硃 朱 31B.01
麥 麦 10.32
頃 顷 21S.80
鹵 卤 21A.41
處 处 21A.83
敗 败 41C.82
販 贩 41C.82
貶 贬 41C.83
啞 哑 40A.30
掗 挜 10A.30
閉 闭 52B.00
問 问 52B.00
婁 娄 22.93
國 国 41.41
喎 㖞 40A.42
帳 帐 22B.02
崍 崃 21B.81
崗 岗 21.42
圇 囵 41.41
過 过 42.83

氫 氢 92.70
動 动 90S.50
偵 侦 91A.80
側 侧 91A.00
貨 货 91.80
進 进 91.83
梟 枭 91.01
鳥 鸟 91.50
偉 伟 91A.22
徠 徕 91B.01
術 术 91B.00
從 从 91B.83
釷 钍 81A.11
釧 钏 81A.22
釤 钐 81A.91
釣 钓 81A.50
釩 钒 81A.70
鈤 铵 81A.93
釵 钗 81A.82
貪 贪 81.80
覓 觅 90.70
貧 贫 80.80
脛 胫 42A.30
魚 鱼 92.63
詎 讵 60A.21
訝 讶 60A.00
訥 讷 60A.42
許 许 60A.10
訛 讹 60A.70
訴 诉 60A.22
訩 讻 60A.21
訟 讼 60A.93
設 设 60A.82
訪 访 60A.50

訣 诀 60A.81
產 产 60.11
牽 牵 60.10
淺 浅 63A.71
渦 涡 63A.42
淪 沦 63A.42
悵 怅 22A.02
鄆 郓 62S.22
啓 启 63.40
視 视 63B.70
將 将 21S.00
晝 昼 22.30
張 张 50A.02
階 阶 32A.41
陽 阳 32A.50
隊 队 32A.02
婭 娅 93A.30
媧 娲 93A.42
婦 妇 93A.22
習 习 50.41
參 参 93.91
紱 绂 93B.82
組 组 93B.30
紳 绅 93B.22
紬 䌷 93B.41
細 细 93B.41
終 终 93B.63
絆 绊 93B.10
紼 绋 93B.22
絀 绌 93B.21
紹 绍 93B.40
紿 绐 93B.40
貫 贯 41.80
鄉 乡 93S.22

（拾二劃）

貳 贰 71.71
預 预 31S.80
堯 尧 11.70
揀 拣 10A.01
馭 驭 51B.82
項 项 31S.80
賁 贲 10.80
場 场 11A.50
揚 扬 10A.50
塊 块 11A.70
達 达 11.83
報 报 11S.82
揮 挥 10A.10
壺 壶 11.30
惡 恶 31.72
葉 叶 20A.01
棖 枨 10B.02
萬 万 20A.42
葷 荤 20A.10
喪 丧 10.02
葦 苇 20A.10
葒 荭 20A.30
棟 栋 10B.01
棧 栈 10B.71
極 极 10B.30
軻 轲 10D.00
軸 轴 10D.41
軼 轶 10D.81
軫 轸 10D.91
軺 轺 10D.40
畫 画 22.30
腎 肾 51.42

棗 枣 10.01
硤 硖 31B.81
硯 砚 31B.70
殘 残 31S.70
雲 云 31D.93
覘 觇 21S.70
睏 困 41B.41
貼 贴 41C.40
貺 贶 41C.70
貯 贮 41C.00
貽 贻 41C.40
閏 闰 52B.00
開 开 52B.00
閑 闲 52B.00
間 间 52B.00
閔 闵 52B.00
悶 闷 52B.00
貴 贵 22.80
勛 勋 40S.50
單 单 40.10
喲 哟 40A.50
買 买 41D.80
剴 剀 21S.00
凱 凯 21S.70
幀 帧 22B.80
嵐 岚 21.70
幃 帏 22B.10
圍 围 41.41
無 无 92.63
氬 氩 92.70
喬 乔 90.42
筆 笔 92A.10
備 备 91A.42
貸 贷 91.80

順 顺 22S.80
傖 伧 91A.40
㑳 㑇 91A.50
傢 家 91A.02
鄔 邬 91S.22
衆 众 91.02
復 复 91B.82
須 须 91S.80
鈣 钙 81A.50
鈈 钚 81A.22
鈦 钛 81A.81
鈍 钝 81A.70
鈔 钞 81A.91
鈉 钠 81A.42
鈐 钤 81A.32
欽 钦 81A.81
鈞 钧 81A.50
鈎 钩 81A.50
鈧 钪 81A.70
鈁 钫 81A.50
鈥 钬 81A.81
鈕 钮 81A.30
鈀 钯 81A.70
傘 伞 81.10
爺 爷 80.22
創 创 81S.00
飩 饨 81B.70
飫 饫 81B.81
飭 饬 81B.50
飯 饭 81B.82
飲 饮 81B.81
爲 为 90.50
脹 胀 42A.02
腡 脶 42A.42

勝 胜 42A.50
貿 贸 90.80
鄒 邹 92S.22
詁 诂 60A.40
訶 诃 60A.00
評 评 60A.10
詛 诅 60A.30
詗 诇 60A.42
詐 诈 60A.22
訴 诉 60A.22
診 诊 60A.91
詆 诋 60A.71
詞 词 60A.50
詘 诎 60A.21
詔 诏 60A.40
詒 诒 60A.40
馮 冯 63A.50
痙 痉 61A.30
勞 劳 91.50
詼 诙 60A.80
測 测 63A.00
湯 汤 63A.50
淵 渊 63A.22
渾 浑 63A.10
愜 惬 22A.21
惻 恻 22A.00
惲 恽 22A.10
惱 恼 22A.41
運 运 62.83
補 补 63C.42
禍 祸 63B.42
尋 寻 50.00
費 费 22.80
違 违 22.83

靭 韧 22S.50
隕 陨 32A.80
賀 贺 91.80
發 发 32.82
綁 绑 93B.22
絨 绒 93B.71
結 结 93B.40
絝 绔 93B.50
絰 绖 93B.11
絎 绗 93B.00
給 给 93B.40
絢 绚 93B.50
絳 绛 93B.10
絡 络 93B.40
絞 绞 93B.82
統 统 93B.70
絶 绝 93B.70
絲 丝 93B.01
幾 几 93.71

(**拾三劃**)

項 项 31A.80
瑋 玮 31A.10
頑 顽 30S.80
載 载 11.71
馱 驮 51B.81
馴 驯 51B.22
馳 驰 51B.70
塒 埘 11A.00
損 损 10A.80
遠 远 11.83
塏 垲 11A.30
勢 势 11.50
搶 抢 10A.40
搗 捣 10A.50
塢 坞 11A.50
壺 壶 11.30
聖 圣 31.11
蓋 盖 20A.30
蓮 莲 20A.83
蒔 莳 20A.00
蓽 荜 20A.10
夢 梦 20A.32
蒼 苍 20A.40
幹 干 10S.10
蓀 荪 20A.01
蔭 荫 20A.93
蒓 莼 20A.70
楨 桢 10B.80
楊 杨 10B.50
嗇 啬 10.41
楓 枫 10B.70
軾 轼 10D.71
輊 轾 10D.11
輅 辂 10D.40
較 较 10D.82
竪 竖 51.30
賈 贾 31.80
匯 汇 51.21
電 电 31D.70
頓 顿 10S.80
盞 盏 71.30
歲 岁 21A.71
虜 虏 21A.50
業 业 22.01
當 当 22.41
睞 睐 41B.01
賊 贼 41C.71
賄 贿 41C.42
賂 赂 41C.40
賅 赅 41C.81
嗎 吗 40A.50
嘩 哗 40A.10
暘 旸 41A.50
閘 闸 52B.00
黽 黾 42.70
暈 晕 41.10
號 号 40S.70
園 园 41.41
蛺 蛱 22D.81
蜆 蚬 22D.70
農 农 22.02
嗩 唢 40A.80
嗶 哔 40A.10
鳴 鸣 40A.50
嗆 呛 40A.40
圓 圆 41.41
骯 肮 42B.70
筧 笕 92A.70
節 节 92A.22
與 与 90.80
債 债 91A.80
僅 仅 91A.11
傳 传 91A.00
傴 伛 91A.21
傾 倾 91A.80
僂 偻 91A.93
賃 赁 91.80
傷 伤 91A.50
傭 佣 91A.42
梟 枭 91.02
頎 颀 90S.80
鈺 钰 81A.11
鉦 钲 81A.30
鉗 钳 81A.41
鈷 钴 81A.40
鉢 钵 81A.10
鉅 钜 81A.21
鈳 钶 81A.00
鈸 钹 81A.82
鉞 钺 81A.71
鉬 钼 81A.41
鉭 钽 81A.30
鉀 钾 81A.22
鈾 铀 81A.41
鈿 钿 81A.41
鉑 铂 81A.41
鈴 铃 81A.63
鉛 铅 81A.40
鉈 铊 81A.70
鉍 铋 81A.72
鈮 铌 81A.70
鈹 铍 81A.82
僉 佥 81.81
會 会 81.41
亂 乱 90S.70
愛 爱 90.82
飾 饰 81B.22
飽 饱 81B.70
飼 饲 81B.50
飿 饳 81B.21
飴 饴 81B.40
頒 颁 80S.80
頌 颂 80S.80
腸 肠 42A.50
腫 肿 42A.11
腦 脑 42A.41
像 象 91A.02
鳩 鸠 91S.50
獅 狮 91C.22
猻 狲 91C.01
詎 讵 60A.21
誄 诔 60A.01
試 试 60A.71
註 注 60A.11
詩 诗 60A.00
詰 诘 60A.40
誇 诗 60A.50
詼 诙 60A.81
誠 诚 60A.71
誅 诛 60A.01
話 话 60A.40
誕 诞 60A.83
詬 诟 60A.40
詮 诠 60A.11
詭 诡 60A.70
詢 询 60A.50
詣 诣 60A.41
諍 诤 60A.00
該 该 60A.81
詳 详 60A.10
詫 诧 60A.70
詡 诩 60A.50
裏 里 60.02
準 准 63.10
頏 颃 60S.80
資 资 63.80
義 义 80.71
煉 炼 91D.01
煩 烦 91D.80
煬 炀 91D.50
塋 茔 91.11
煢 茕 91.70
煒 炜 91D.10
遞 递 90.83
溝 沟 63A.42
漣 涟 63A.83
滅 灭 63A.71
滌 涤 63A.01
塗 涂 63.11
滄 沧 63A.40
愷 恺 22A.30
愾 忾 22A.70
愴 怆 22A.40
窩 窝 62A.42
禎 祯 63B.80
肅 肃 22.22
裝 装 21.02
遜 逊 32.83
際 际 32A.01
媽 妈 93A.50
預 预 32S.80
疊 迭 32.30
綆 绠 93B.82
經 经 93B.30
綃 绡 93B.42
絹 绢 93B.42
綉 绣 93B.50
綏 绥 93B.93
綈 绨 93B.22
彙 汇 92.01

(**拾四劃**)

瑪 玛 31A.50

瑣 琐	31A.80	碩 硕	31B.80	嶇 岖	21B.21	鉸 铰	81A.82	塵 尘	61.11	寢 寝	62.82
瑲 玱	31A.40	碭 砀	31B.50	罰 罚	41D.00	銥 铱	81A.02	颯 飒	60S.70	實 实	62.80
駁 驳	51B.82	奩 奁	12.21	幗 帼	22B.41	銃 铳	81A.70	適 适	60.83	皺 皱	62S.82
摶 抟	10A.00	爾 尔	31.42	圖 图	41.41	銀 银	81A.02	齊 齐	60.22	複 复	63C.82
摳 抠	10A.21	奪 夺	12.00	製 制	10.02	銣 铷	81A.40	養 养	80.02	盡 尽	22.30
趙 赵	11.83	殞 殒	31S.80	種 种	90A.11	餞 饯	81S.71	鄰 邻	22S.22	屢 屡	52A.93
趕 赶	11.83	鳶 鸢	71.50	稱 称	90A.42	餌 饵	81B.10	鄭 郑	80S.22	獎 奖	21.81
摟 搂	10A.93	對 对	22S.00	箋 笺	92A.71	蝕 蚀	81B.93	燁 烨	91D.10	墮 堕	32.11
摑 掴	10A.41	幣 币	22.22	僥 侥	91A.70	餉 饷	81B.42	熗 炝	91D.40	隨 随	32A.83
臺 台	11.11	彆 别	22.50	僨 偾	91A.80	餃 饺	81B.82	榮 荣	91.01	墜 坠	32.11
撾 挝	10A.83	嘗 尝	22.41	僕 仆	91A.81	餅 饼	81B.20	滎 荥	91.02	嫗 妪	93A.21
墊 垫	11.11	嘖 啧	40A.80	僑 侨	91A.42	領 领	81S.80	犖 荦	91.10	頗 颇	22S.80
壽 寿	11.00	曄 晔	41A.10	僞 伪	91A.50	鳳 凤	42.70	熒 荧	91.81	態 态	93.72
摺 折	10A.41	夥 伙	41S.32	銜 衔	91B.00	颱 台	42.70	漬 渍	63A.80	鄧 邓	32S.22
摻 掺	10A.91	賑 赈	41C.02	鉶 铏	81A.00	獄 狱	91C.81	漢 汉	63A.81	緒 绪	93B.41
摜 掼	10A.80	賒 赊	41C.01	銬 铐	81A.50	誡 诫	60A.71	漸 渐	63A.22	綾 绫	93B.82
蔞 蒌	20A.93	嘆 叹	40A.81	銠 铑	81A.70	誣 诬	60A.30	漚 沤	63A.21	綺 绮	93B.00
蔦 茑	20A.50	暢 畅	22S.50	鉺 铒	81A.10	語 语	60A.40	滯 滞	63A.22	綫 线	93B.71
蔔 卜	20A.50	閨 闺	52B.00	鋩 铓	81A.21	誚 诮	60A.42	滷 卤	63A.41	緋 绯	93B.22
蔣 蒋	20A.00	聞 闻	52B.00	銪 铕	81A.42	誤 误	60A.81	漁 渔	63A.63	綽 绰	93B.10
薌 芗	20A.22	閩 闽	52B.00	鋁 铝	81A.40	誥 诰	60A.40	滸 浒	63A.10	緄 绲	93B.70
構 构	10B.42	閭 闾	52B.00	銅 铜	81A.42	誘 诱	60A.50	滬 沪	63A.70	綱 纲	93B.42
樺 桦	10B.10	閥 阀	52B.00	銦 铟	81A.41	誨 诲	60A.50	漲 涨	63A.02	網 网	93B.42
覡 觋	31S.70	閤 𬮤	52B.00	銖 铢	81A.01	誑 诳	60A.11	滲 渗	63A.91	維 维	93B.11
槍 枪	10B.40	閣 阁	52B.00	銑 铣	81A.70	說 说	60A.70	慚 惭	22A.22	綿 绵	93B.22
輒 辄	10D.70	閡 阂	52B.00	銛 铦	81A.93	認 认	60A.72	慪 怄	22A.21	綸 纶	93B.42
輔 辅	10D.42	嘔 呕	40A.21	鋌 铤	81A.83	誦 诵	60A.42	慳 悭	22A.11	綬 绶	93B.82
輕 轻	10D.30	蝸 蜗	22D.42	銓 铨	81A.11	誒 诶	60A.81	慟 恸	22A.50	綳 绷	93B.42
塹 堑	10.11	團 团	41.41	鉿 铪	81A.40	廣 广	61.80	慘 惨	22A.91	綢 绸	93B.42
匱 匮	51.21	嘍 喽	40A.93	銚 铫	81A.70	麼 么	61.93	慣 惯	22A.80	綹 绺	93B.40
監 监	51.30	鄲 郸	40S.22	銘 铭	81A.40	廎 庼	61.80	寬 宽	62.70	綣 绻	93B.70
緊 紧	51.01	鳴 鸣	40A.50	鉻 铬	81A.40	瘧 疟	61A.21	賓 宾	62.80	綜 综	93B.01
厲 厉	51A.42	幘 帻	22B.80	錚 铮	81A.00	瘍 疡	61A.50	窪 洼	62A.11	綻 绽	93B.83
厭 厌	51A.81	嶄 崭	21.22	銫 铯	81A.70	瘋 疯	61A.70	寧 宁	62.00	綰 绾	93B.40

綠 绿 93B.02	撥 拨 10A.82	遼 辽 12.83	嶔 嵚 21.81	鋃 锒 81A.02	諂 谄 60A.21
綴 缀 93B.82	蕘 荛 20A.70	殤 殇 31S.50	幟 帜 22B.71	鋟 锓 81A.82	諒 谅 60A.01
緇 缁 93B.41	蕆 蒇 20A.71	鴉 鸦 51S.50	篋 箧 92A.21	鋼 锕 81A.00	諄 谆 60A.00
	蕓 芸 20A.93	輩 辈 22.10	範 范 92A.70	鍋 锅 81A.50	誶 谇 60A.10
（拾五劃）	邁 迈 20A.83	劌 刿 21S.00	價 价 91A.80	劍 剑 81S.00	談 谈 60A.81
鬧 闹 52B.00	蕢 蒉 20A.80	齒 齿 21A.21	儂 侬 91A.02	劊 刽 81S.00	誼 谊 60A.30
靚 靓 10S.70	蕪 芜 20A.63	劇 剧 21S.00	儉 俭 91A.81	鄶 郐 81S.22	廟 庙 61.42
輂 [illegible] 12.10	蕎 荞 20A.42	膚 肤 21A.42	儈 侩 91A.41	餑 饽 81B.00	廠 厂 61.82
髮 发 51.82	蕕 莸 20A.41	慮 虑 21A.72	億 亿 91A.72	餓 饿 81B.71	廡 庑 61.63
撓 挠 10A.70	蕩 荡 20A.50	鄴 邺 22S.22	儀 仪 91A.71	餘 余 81B.01	瘞 瘗 61A.11
墳 坟 11A.80	蕁 荨 20A.00	輝 辉 22S.10	皚 皑 91S.30	餒 馁 81B.93	瘡 疮 61A.40
撻 挞 10A.83	樁 桩 10B.21	賞 赏 22.80	樂 乐 93.01	膞 䏝 42A.00	賡 赓 61.80
駔 驵 51B.30	樞 枢 10B.21	賦 赋 41C.71	質 质 90.80	膠 胶 42A.91	慶 庆 61.82
駛 驶 51B.82	標 标 10B.01	賬 账 41C.02	徵 征 91B.82	鴇 鸨 21S.50	廢 废 61.82
駟 驷 51B.41	樓 楼 10B.93	賭 赌 41C.41	衝 冲 91B.00	魷 鱿 92C.70	敵 敌 60S.82
駙 驸 51B.00	樅 枞 10B.83	賤 贱 41C.71	慫 怂 91.72	魯 鲁 92.41	頦 颏 60S.80
駒 驹 51B.50	麩 麸 10S.83	賜 赐 41C.50	徹 彻 91B.82	魴 鲂 92C.50	導 导 80.00
駐 驻 51B.11	樣 样 10B.02	賙 赒 41C.42	衛 卫 91B.00	潁 颍 21S.80	瑩 莹 91.11
駝 驼 51B.70	橢 椭 10B.42	賠 赔 41C.40	盤 盘 91.30	颳 刮 42.70	潔 洁 63A.01
駘 骀 51B.40	輛 辆 10D.42	嘵 哓 40A.70	鋪 铺 81A.42	劉 刘 90S.00	澆 浇 63A.70
撲 扑 10A.81	槧 椠 10.01	噴 喷 40A.80	鋏 铗 81A.81	皺 皱 92S.82	潤 润 63A.00
頡 颉 11S.80	暫 暂 10.41	闐 阗 52B.00	鉽 铽 81A.71	請 请 60A.42	澗 涧 63A.00
撣 掸 10A.10	輪 轮 10D.42	閱 阅 52B.00	銷 销 81A.42	諸 诸 60A.41	潰 溃 63A.80
賣 卖 11.80	輟 辍 10D.82	閬 阆 52B.00	鋥 锃 81A.11	諏 诹 60A.82	澇 涝 63A.50
撫 抚 10A.63	輜 辎 10D.41	數 数 22S.82	鋇 钡 81A.80	諾 诺 60A.40	潯 浔 63A.00
撟 挢 10A.42	甌 瓯 51S.70	踐 践 40B.71	鋤 锄 81A.50	諑 诼 60A.02	潑 泼 63A.82
擻 擞 10A.81	歐 欧 51S.81	遺 遗 22.83	鋯 锆 81A.40	誹 诽 60A.22	憤 愤 22A.80
熱 热 11.63	毆 殴 51S.82	蝦 虾 22D.82	鋨 锇 81A.71	課 课 60A.01	憫 悯 22A.00
鞏 巩 31.10	賢 贤 51.80	嘸 呒 40A.63	銹 锈 81A.50	諉 诿 60A.93	憒 愦 22A.80
摯 挚 11.00	遷 迁 31.83	嘮 唠 40A.50	銼 锉 81A.11	諛 谀 60A.81	憚 惮 22A.10
撈 捞 10A.50	憂 忧 31.82	嘰 叽 40A.71	鋒 锋 81A.10	誰 谁 60A.11	憮 怃 22A.63
穀 谷 11S.82	碼 码 31B.50	嶢 峣 21B.70	鋅 锌 81A.10	論 论 60A.42	憐 怜 22A.10
慤 悫 11.72	確 确 31B.11	罷 罢 41D.70	銳 锐 81A.70	諗 谂 60A.72	寫 写 62.50
撏 挦 10A.00	賚 赉 10.80	嶠 峤 21B.42	銻 锑 81A.22	調 调 60A.42	審 审 62.41

竆 穷	62A.50	編 编	93B.42	機 机	10B.71	曇 昙	41.93	錯 错	81A.41	鮓 鲊	92C.22
褳 裢	63C.83	緡 缗	93B.41	輳 辏	10D.81	噸 吨	40A.80	鍩 锘	81A.40	穌 稣	92C.01
褲 裤	63C.10	緯 纬	93B.10	輻 辐	10D.41	鴞 鸮	40S.50	錨 锚	81A.41	鮒 鲋	92C.00
鴆 鸩	91S.50	緣 缘	93B.02	輯 辑	10D.10	踴 踊	40B.50	錛 锛	81A.20	鮑 鲍	92C.70
遲 迟	52A.83			輸 输	10D.00	螞 蚂	22D.50	錸 铼	81A.01	鮐 鲐	92C.40
層 层	52A.41	（拾六劃）		賴 赖	10S.80	螄 蛳	22D.22	錢 钱	81A.71	鴝 鸲	92S.50
彈 弹	50A.10	璣 玑	31A.71	頭 头	30S.80	噹 当	40A.41	鍀 锝	81A.00	獲 获	91C.82
選 选	52.83	墻 墙	11A.41	醞 酝	31C.30	罵 骂	41D.50	錁 锞	81A.01	穎 颖	21S.80
漿 浆	21.02	駱 骆	51B.40	醜 丑	31C.70	噥 哝	40A.02	錫 锡	81A.50	獨 独	91C.50
槳 桨	21.01	駭 骇	51B.81	勵 励	51S.50	戰 战	40S.71	錮 锢	81A.41	獫 猃	91C.41
險 险	32A.81	駢 骈	51B.20	磧 碛	31B.80	噲 哙	40A.41	鋼 钢	81A.42	鴛 鸳	92.50
嬈 娆	93A.70	攄 摅	10A.21	磚 砖	31B.00	鴦 鸯	91.50	鍋 锅	81A.42	謀 谋	60A.01
嫻 娴	93A.00	擄 掳	10A.50	磣 碜	31B.91	噯 嗳	40A.82	錘 锤	81A.11	諶 谌	60A.21
駕 驾	91.50	擋 挡	10A.41	歷 历	51A.30	嘯 啸	40A.22	錐 锥	81A.11	諜 谍	60A.01
嬋 婵	93A.10	擇 择	10A.10	曆 历	51A.41	還 还	41D.83	錦 锦	81A.22	謊 谎	60A.70
嫵 妩	93A.63	撿 捡	10A.81	奮 奋	12.41	嶼 屿	21B.80	錇 锫	81A.40	諫 谏	60A.01
嬌 娇	93A.42	擔 担	10A.40	頰 颊	12S.80	積 积	90A.80	錠 锭	81A.83	諧 谐	60A.41
媯 妫	93A.50	壇 坛	11A.30	殫 殚	31S.10	頹 颓	90S.80	鍵 键	81A.83	謔 谑	60A.21
駑 驽	93.50	擁 拥	10A.11	頸 颈	31S.80	篤 笃	92A.50	鋸 锯	81A.40	謁 谒	60A.50
翬 翚	50.10	據 据	10A.02	頻 频	21S.80	築 筑	92A.01	錳 锰	81A.30	謂 谓	60A.42
毿 毵	93S.70	薔 蔷	20A.41	盧 卢	21A.30	篳 筚	92A.10	錙 锱	81A.41	諤 谔	60A.50
緙 缂	93B.10	薑 姜	20A.30	曉 晓	41A.70	篩 筛	92A.22	覦 觎	81S.70	諭 谕	60A.00
緗 缃	93B.41	薈 荟	20A.41	瞞 瞒	41B.42	舉 举	90.00	墾 垦	91.11	諼 谖	60A.82
練 练	93B.01	薊 蓟	20A.00	縣 县	41S.01	興 兴	90.80	餞 饯	81B.71	諷 讽	60A.70
緘 缄	93B.71	薦 荐	20A.50	瞘 眍	41B.21	學 学	90.00	餜 馃	81B.01	諮 谘	60A.40
緬 缅	93B.41	蕭 萧	20A.22	瞜 䁖	41B.93	儔 俦	91A.00	餛 馄	81B.70	諳 谙	60A.41
緹 缇	93B.83	頤 颐	51S.80	瞶 瞆	41C.41	憊 惫	91.72	餡 馅	81B.21	諺 谚	60A.91
緲 缈	93B.91	鴣 鸪	10S.50	鴨 鸭	41S.50	儕 侪	91A.22	館 馆	81B.40	諦 谛	60A.22
緝 缉	93B.10	薩 萨	20A.11	閾 阈	52B.00	儐 傧	91A.80	頷 颔	81S.80	謎 谜	60A.83
縕 缊	93B.30	蕷 蓣	20A.80	閹 阉	52B.00	儘 尽	91A.30	鴒 鸰	81S.50	諢 诨	60A.10
緞 缎	93B.82	橈 桡	10B.70	閶 阊	52B.00	鴕 鸵	91S.70	膩 腻	42A.71	諞 谝	60A.42
縋 缒	93B.83	樹 树	10B.00	閽 阍	52B.00	艙 舱	91S.40	鴟 鸱	90S.50	諱 讳	60A.10
緩 缓	93B.82	樸 朴	10B.81	閻 阎	52B.00	錶 表	81A.02	鮁 鲅	92C.82	諝 谞	60A.42
締 缔	93B.22	橋 桥	10B.42	閼 阏	52B.00	鍺 锗	81A.41	鮎 鲇	92C.40	憑 凭	63.72

鄺 邝 61S.22
瘻 瘘 61A.93
親 亲 60S.70
辦 办 60S.10
龍 龙 60S.70
劑 剂 60S.00
燒 烧 91D.70
燜 焖 91D.00
熾 炽 91D.71
螢 萤 91.93
營 营 91.40
縈 萦 91.01
燈 灯 91D.30
濛 蒙 63A.02
燙 烫 63.81
澠 渑 63A.70
濃 浓 63A.02
澤 泽 63A.10
濁 浊 63A.50
澮 浍 63A.41
澱 淀 63A.82
懌 怿 22A.10
憶 忆 22A.72
憲 宪 62.72
窺 窥 62A.70
窶 窭 62A.93
褸 褛 63C.93
禪 禅 63B.10
隱 隐 32A.72
嬙 嫱 93A.41
嬡 嫒 93A.82
縉 缙 93B.41
縝 缜 93B.80
縛 缚 93B.00
縟 缛 93B.00
緻 致 93B.82
縧 绦 93B.01
縫 缝 93B.83
縐 绉 93B.50
縗 缞 93B.02
縞 缟 93B.42
縭 缡 93B.42
縑 缣 93B.22
縊 缢 93B.30

（拾七劃）

耬 耧 10S.93
環 环 31A.02
贅 赘 10.80
璦 瑷 31A.82
覯 觏 20S.70
幫 帮 11.22
騁 骋 51B.50
駸 骎 51B.82
駿 骏 51B.82
趨 趋 11.83
擱 搁 10A.00
擬 拟 10A.83
擴 扩 10A.80
壙 圹 11A.80
擠 挤 10A.22
蟄 蛰 11.93
縶 絷 11.01
擲 掷 10A.22
擯 摈 10A.80
擰 拧 10A.00
轂 毂 11S.82
聲 声 11.10
聰 聪 31S.72
聯 联 31S.22
艱 艰 20S.02
藍 蓝 20A.30
舊 旧 20A.21
薺 荠 20A.22
韓 韩 10S.10
隸 隶 10S.02
檉 柽 10B.11
檣 樯 10B.41
檔 档 10B.41
櫛 栉 10B.22
檢 检 10B.81
檜 桧 10B.41
麯 曲 10S.41
轅 辕 10D.02
轄 辖 10D.40
輾 辗 10D.02
擊 击 10.00
臨 临 51S.40
磽 硗 31B.70
壓 压 51A.11
磯 矶 31B.71
邇 迩 31.83
尷 尴 12.70
殮 殓 31S.81
齔 龀 21S.70
戲 戏 21S.71
虧 亏 21S.50
斃 毙 22.70
瞭 了 41B.01
顆 颗 41S.80
購 购 41C.42
嬰 婴 41.93
賺 赚 41C.22
嚇 吓 40A.00
闌 阑 52B.00
闆 闆 52B.00
闊 阔 52B.00
闈 闱 52B.00
闋 阕 52B.00
曖 暧 41A.82
蹕 跸 40B.10
蹌 跄 40B.40
螻 蝼 22D.93
蟈 蝈 22D.41
雖 虽 40S.11
嚀 咛 40A.00
覬 觊 21S.70
嶺 岭 21.80
嶸 嵘 21B.01
點 点 41S.40
矯 矫 92S.42
簍 篓 92A.93
輿 舆 90.80
歟 欤 90S.81
鵂 鸺 91A.50
龜 龟 92.70
優 优 91A.82
償 偿 91A.80
儲 储 91A.41
魎 魉 91.70
禦 御 91.01
聳 耸 91.10
鍥 锲 81A.81
鍇 锴 81A.41
鍘 铡 81A.00
鍚 钖 81A.50
鍶 锶 81A.72
鍔 锷 81A.50
鍾 钟 81A.11
鍛 锻 81A.82
鍬 锹 81A.81
鍰 锾 81A.82
鎄 锿 81A.02
鍍 镀 81A.82
鎂 镁 81A.81
鎡 镃 81A.93
鎇 镅 81A.41
懇 恳 91.72
餳 饧 81B.50
斂 敛 81S.82
鴿 鸽 81S.50
膿 脓 42A.02
臉 脸 42A.81
膾 脍 42A.41
膽 胆 42A.40
謄 誊 42A.40
鮭 鲑 92C.11
鮪 鲔 92C.42
鮫 鲛 92C.82
鮮 鲜 92C.10
颶 飓 42.70
獷 犷 91C.80
獰 狞 91C.00
講 讲 60A.42
謨 谟 60A.81
謖 谡 60A.82
謝 谢 60A.00
謠 谣 60A.21
謅 诌 60A.50
謗 谤 60A.50
謚 谥 60A.30
謙 谦 60A.22
謐 谧 60A.30
褻 亵 60.02
氈 毡 60S.70
應 应 61.72
癘 疠 61A.42
療 疗 61A.01
癇 痫 61A.00
癉 瘅 61A.10
癆 痨 61A.50
齋 斋 60.22
糞 粪 22.80
糝 糁 22C.91
燦 灿 91D.01
燭 烛 91D.50
燴 烩 91D.41
鴻 鸿 63A.50
濤 涛 63A.00
濫 滥 63A.30
濕 湿 63A.63
濟 济 63A.22
濱 滨 63A.80
濘 泞 63A.00
澀 涩 63A.30
懨 恹 22A.81
賽 赛 62.80
襇 裥 63C.00
𧞫 䙌 63C.80
襖 袄 63C.81
禮 礼 63B.30
屨 屦 52A.93
彌 弥 50A.42
嬪 嫔 93A.80

績 绩 93B.80
縹 缥 93B.01
縷 缕 93B.93
縵 缦 93B.82
縲 缧 93B.01
總 总 93B.72
縱 纵 93B.83
縴 纤 93B.10
縮 缩 93B.41
繆 缪 93B.91
繅 缫 93B.01
嚮 向 93.42

（拾八劃）

閱 阅 52B.00
瓊 琼 31A.82
撻 挞 10A.10
鬆 松 51.93
翹 翘 11.70
擷 撷 10A.80
擾 扰 10A.82
騏 骐 51B.80
騎 骑 51B.00
騍 骒 51B.01
騅 骓 51B.11
擻 擞 10A.82
鼕 冬 11.63
擺 摆 10A.70
贄 贽 11.80
燾 焘 11.63
聶 聂 31.10
職 职 31S.71
藝 艺 20A.93
覲 觐 20S.70
鞦 秋 20B.81
藪 薮 20A.82
蠆 虿 20A.93
繭 茧 20A.42
藥 药 20A.01
藭 䓖 20A.50
賾 赜 51S.80
蘊 蕴 20A.30
檯 枱 10B.11
櫃 柜 10B.21
檻 槛 10B.30
櫚 榈 10B.00
檳 槟 10B.80
檸 柠 10B.00
鶇 鸫 10S.50
轉 转 10D.00
轆 辘 10D.70
覆 复 31.82
醫 医 51.41
礎 础 31B.83
殯 殡 31S.80
霧 雾 31D.50
豐 丰 21.30
懟 怼 22.72
叢 丛 22.82
矇 蒙 41B.02
題 题 41.83
韙 韪 41.83
闖 闯 52B.00
闔 阖 52B.00
闐 阗 52B.00
闓 闿 52B.00
闕 阙 52B.00
顒 颙 41S.80
曠 旷 41A.80
蹣 蹒 40B.42
嚙 啮 40A.21
壘 垒 41.11
蟯 蛲 22D.70
蟲 虫 22.93
蟬 蝉 22D.10
蟣 虮 22D.71
鵑 鹃 40S.50
嚕 噜 40A.41
顓 颛 21S.80
鵠 鹄 10S.50
鵝 鹅 90S.50
穡 穑 90A.41
穢 秽 90A.71
簡 简 92A.00
簣 篑 92A.80
簞 箪 92A.10
雙 双 91.82
軀 躯 91S.21
邊 边 91.83
歸 归 91S.22
鎮 镇 81A.80
鏈 链 81A.83
鎘 镉 81A.42
鎖 锁 81A.80
鎧 铠 81A.30
鎳 镍 81A.01
鎢 钨 81A.50
鎩 铩 81A.82
鎿 镎 81A.00
鎦 镏 81A.41
鎬 镐 81A.42
鎊 镑 81A.50
鎰 镒 81A.30
鎵 镓 81A.02
鵒 鹆 80S.50
餺 馎 81B.00
餼 饩 81B.70
餾 馏 81B.41
饈 馐 81B.30
臍 脐 42A.22
鯁 鲠 92C.82
鯉 鲤 92C.11
鯀 鲧 92C.01
鯽 鲫 92C.22
颼 飕 42.70
觴 觞 92B.50
獵 猎 91C.70
雛 雏 92S.11
臏 膑 42A.80
謹 谨 60A.11
謳 讴 60A.21
謾 谩 60A.82
謫 谪 60A.42
謬 谬 60A.91
癤 疖 61A.22
雜 杂 60S.11
離 离 60S.11
顏 颜 60S.80
糧 粮 22C.11
燼 烬 91D.30
鵜 鹈 80S.50
瀆 渎 63A.80
瀅 滢 63.72
濾 滤 63A.72
鯊 鲨 63.63
濺 溅 63A.71
瀏 浏 63A.00
瀉 泻 63A.50
瀋 沈 63A.41
竄 窜 62A.70
竅 窍 62A.82
額 额 62S.80
襠 裆 63C.41
襝 裣 63C.81
禱 祷 63B.00
醬 酱 21.41
隴 陇 32A.70
嬸 婶 93A.41
繞 绕 93B.70
繚 缭 93B.01
織 织 93B.71
繕 缮 93B.40
繒 缯 93B.41
斷 断 21S.22

（拾九劃）

鵡 鹉 71S.50
鬍 胡 51.42
騙 骗 51B.42
騷 骚 51B.93
壚 垆 11A.30
壞 坏 11A.02
攏 拢 10A.70
攆 撵 20A.10
難 难 20S.11
鵲 鹊 20S.50
蘋 苹 20A.80
蘆 芦 20A.30
藺 蔺 20A.00
躉 趸 20A.93
蘄 蕲 20A.22
勸 劝 20S.50
蘇 苏 20A.01
藹 蔼 20A.50
蘢 茏 20A.70
顛 颠 21S.80
櫝 椟 10B.80
櫟 栎 10B.01
櫓 橹 10B.41
櫧 槠 10B.41
轎 轿 10D.42
鏨 錾 10.30
轍 辙 10D.82
轔 辚 10D.10
繫 系 10.01
麗 丽 30.70
礪 砺 31B.42
礙 碍 31B.83
礦 矿 31B.80
贗 赝 51A.80
願 愿 51S.80
鶴 鹌 12S.50
璽 玺 31.30
贈 赠 41C.41
闞 阚 52B.00
關 关 52B.00
嚦 呖 40A.30
疇 畴 41S.00
蹺 跷 40B.70
蠅 蝇 22D.70
蟻 蚁 22D.71
嚴 严 40.82
獸 兽 40S.81
嚨 咙 40A.70

羆 罴 41D.63
羅 罗 41D.11
氌 氇 90.70
犢 犊 10C.80
贊 赞 10.80
穩 稳 90A.72
簽 签 92A.81
簾 帘 92A.22
簫 箫 92A.22
牘 牍 91S.80
懲 惩 91.72
鏗 铿 81A.11
鏢 镖 81A.01
鏜 镗 81A.11
鏤 镂 81A.93
鏝 镘 81A.82
鏰 镚 81A.42
鏞 镛 81A.42
鏡 镜 81A.70
鏟 铲 81A.11
鏑 镝 81A.42
鏃 镞 81A.81
鏘 锵 81A.00
辭 辞 90S.10
饉 馑 81B.11
饅 馒 81B.82
鵬 鹏 42A.50
臘 腊 42A.70
鯖 鲭 92C.42
鯪 鲮 92C.82
鯫 鲰 92C.82
鯤 鲲 92C.70
鯧 鲳 92C.41
鯢 鲵 92C.70

鯛 鲷 92C.42
鯨 鲸 92C.01
獺 獭 91C.80
譚 谭 60A.10
譖 谮 60A.41
譙 谯 60A.63
識 识 60A.71
譜 谱 60A.41
證 证 60A.30
譎 谲 60A.42
譏 讥 60A.71
廬 庐 61.30
癢 痒 61A.02
龐 庞 61.70
壟 垄 60.11
鶉 鹑 61S.50
類 类 22S.80
爍 烁 91D.01
瀟 潇 63A.22
瀨 濑 63A.80
瀝 沥 63A.30
瀕 濒 63A.80
瀘 泸 63A.30
瀧 泷 63A.70
懶 懒 22A.80
懷 怀 22A.02
寵 宠 62.70
襪 袜 63C.71
襤 褴 63C.30
韜 韬 22S.21
騭 骘 32.50
騖 骛 32.50
顙 颡 32S.80
繮 缰 93B.30

繩 绳 93B.70
繾 缱 93B.83
繰 缲 93B.01
繹 绎 93B.10
繯 缳 93B.02
繳 缴 93B.82
繪 绘 93B.41

（二拾劃）

瓏 珑 31A.70
驁 骜 10.50
驊 骅 51B.10
騮 骝 51B.41
騶 驺 51B.50
騸 骟 51B.50
攖 撄 10A.93
攔 拦 10A.00
攙 搀 10A.70
顢 颟 20S.80
驀 蓦 20A.50
蘚 藓 20A.10
鶘 鹕 10S.50
飄 飘 31S.70
櫪 枥 10B.30
櫨 栌 10B.30
櫸 榉 10B.10
礬 矾 10.40
麵 面 10S.41
櫬 榇 10B.70
櫳 栊 10B.70
礫 砾 31B.01
鹹 咸 21S.71
齠 龆 21S.30
齡 龄 21S.63

齣 出 21S.50
獻 献 21S.81
黨 党 22.63
懸 悬 41.72
罌 罂 41.21
贍 赡 41C.40
闥 闼 52B.00
闡 阐 52B.00
曨 昽 41A.70
蠣 蛎 22D.42
蠐 蛴 22D.22
嚶 嘤 40A.93
鶚 鹗 40S.50
髏 髅 42B.93
犧 牺 10C.71
鶖 鹙 90.50
籌 筹 92A.00
籃 篮 92A.30
譽 誉 90.40
覺 觉 90.70
嚳 喾 90.40
衊 蔑 91S.71
艦 舰 91S.30
鐃 铙 81A.70
鐐 镣 81A.01
鏷 镤 81A.81
鐦 锎 81A.00
鐧 锏 81A.00
鐘 钟 81A.11
鐒 铹 81A.50
鐠 镨 81A.93
鐙 镫 81A.30
釋 释 90S.10
饒 饶 81B.70

饋 馈 81B.80
饌 馔 81B.80
饑 饥 81B.71
臚 胪 42A.30
朧 胧 42A.70
騰 腾 42A.50
鰈 鲽 92C.01
鰂 鲗 92C.00
鰛 鳁 92C.30
鰓 鳃 92C.72
鰍 鳅 92C.81
鰒 鳆 92C.82
鰉 鳇 92C.11
鯿 鳊 92C.42
獼 猕 91C.42
觸 触 92B.50
護 护 60A.82
譴 谴 60A.83
譯 译 60A.10
譫 谵 60A.40
議 议 60A.71
癥 症 61A.82
辮 辫 60S.10
競 竞 60S.70
贏 赢 60.70
糲 粝 22C.42
糰 团 22C.41
鶿 鹚 80S.50
爐 炉 91D.30
瀾 澜 63A.00
瀲 潋 63A.82
瀰 沵 63A.42
懺 忏 22A.71
寶 宝 62.80

騫 骞 62.50
竇 窦 62A.80
襬 摆 63C.70
鶩 鹜 32.50
纊 纩 93B.80
繽 缤 93B.80
繼 继 93B.21
饗 飨 93.02

（廿一劃）

瓔 璎 31A.93
鰲 鳌 10.63
攝 摄 10A.10
騾 骡 51B.01
驅 驱 51B.21
驃 骠 51B.01
驄 骢 51B.72
驂 骖 51B.91
擼 撸 10A.70
歡 欢 20S.81
權 权 10B.11
櫻 樱 10B.93
轟 轰 10.10
覽 览 51.70
酈 郦 30S.22
飆 飙 12S.70
殲 歼 31S.71
齜 龇 21S.70
齦 龈 21S.02
贐 赆 41C.30
囁 嗫 40A.10
囈 呓 40A.93
闢 辟 52B.00
囀 啭 40A.00

顥 颢 41S.80
躊 踌 40B.00
躋 跻 40B.22
躑 踯 40B.22
躍 跃 40B.11
纍 累 41.01
蠟 蜡 22D.70
囂 嚣 40.40
巋 岿 21.22
髒 脏 42B.20
儺 傩 91A.11
儷 俪 91A.70
儼 俨 91A.82
鐵 铁 81A.71
鑊 镬 81A.82
鐳 镭 81A.41
鐺 铛 81A.41
鐸 铎 81A.10
鐶 镮 81A.02
鐲 镯 81A.50
鐿 镱 81A.72
鶻 鹘 91S.50
鷂 鹞 92S.50
雞 鸡 90S.11
臟 脏 42A.71
鰭 鳍 92C.41
鰱 鲢 92C.83
鰣 鲥 92C.00
鰥 鳏 92C.02
鰜 鳒 92C.22
癩 癞 61A.80
癧 疬 61A.30
癮 瘾 61A.72
孄 𡢃 60S.00

辯 辩 60S.10
礱 砻 60.40
鶼 鹣 80S.50
爛 烂 91D.00
鶯 莺 91.50
灃 沣 63A.30
懾 慑 22A.10
懼 惧 22A.11
竈 灶 62A.70
顧 顾 63S.80
襯 衬 63C.70
鶴 鹤 91S.50
屬 属 52A.50
纈 缬 93B.80
續 续 93B.80
纏 缠 93B.11

（廿二劃）

驍 骁 51B.70
驕 骄 51B.42
攤 摊 10A.11
覿 觌 11S.70
攢 攒 10A.80
鷙 鸷 11.50
聽 听 31S.72
蘿 萝 20A.11
驚 惊 20.50
轢 轹 10D.01
鷗 鸥 51S.50
鑒 鉴 51.30
邐 逦 30.83
霽 霁 31D.22
齬 龉 21S.40
齪 龊 21S.83

鱉 鳖 22.63
贖 赎 41C.80
躓 踬 40B.80
囌 苏 40A.01
囉 罗 40A.11
囅 冁 40S.02
巔 巅 21.80
邏 逻 41D.83
體 体 42B.30
籜 箨 92A.10
籟 籁 92A.80
籙 箓 92A.02
籠 笼 92A.70
鼈 鳖 92.63
儻 傥 91A.63
艫 舻 91S.30
鑄 铸 81A.00
鑌 镔 81A.80
鑔 镲 81A.01
龕 龛 81.70
糴 籴 81S.11
鰳 鳓 92C.50
鰾 鳔 92C.01
鱈 鳕 92C.30
鰻 鳗 92C.82
讀 读 60A.80
讅 谉 60A.41
巒 峦 93.21
彎 弯 93.50
孿 孪 93.00
孌 娈 93.93
顫 颤 60S.80
鷓 鹧 61S.50
癭 瘿 61A.93

癬 癣 61A.10
聾 聋 60.10
龔 龚 60.80
襲 袭 60.02
灘 滩 63A.11
灑 𬇙 63A.70
竊 窃 62A.42
轡 辔 93.40

（廿三劃）

瓚 瓒 31A.80
驛 驿 51B.10
驗 验 51B.81
攪 搅 10A.70
欏 椤 10B.11
轤 轳 10D.30
黶 黡 51A.41
魘 魇 51A.70
饜 餍 51A.02
鶉 鹑 12S.50
曬 晒 41A.70
鷳 鹇 52S.50
顯 显 41S.80
蠱 蛊 22.30
髕 髌 42B.80
籤 签 92A.71
雔 雔 91S.11
鵻 𬷕 91S.50
黴 霉 91B.82
鑠 铄 81A.01
鑕 锧 81A.80
鑞 镴 81A.70
臢 臜 42A.80
鱖 鳜 92C.81

鱔 鳝 92C.40
鱗 鳞 92C.10
鱒 鳟 92C.00
鱘 鲟 92C.00
讌 䜩 60A.63
欒 栾 93.01
攣 挛 93.00
變 变 93.82
戀 恋 93.72
鷲 鹫 60.50
癰 痈 61A.11
齏 齑 60.22
鷸 鹬 32S.50
纓 缨 93B.93
纖 纤 93B.71
纔 才 93B.70
鷥 鸶 93.50

（廿四劃）

鬢 鬓 51.80
攬 揽 10A.70
驟 骤 51B.02
壩 坝 11A.42
韆 靬 20B.83
觀 观 20S.70
鹽 盐 51.30
釀 酿 31C.02
靂 雳 31D.30
靈 灵 31D.30
靄 霭 31D.50
蠶 蚕 51.93
艷 艳 21S.70
豔 搕 21S.30
齲 龋 21S.42

齷 龌 21S.11
䶬 [illegible] 21S.81
贓 赃 41C.71
鷺 鹭 40.50
囑 嘱 40A.50
羈 羁 41D.50
籩 笾 92A.83
籬 篱 92A.11
黌 黉 90.80
黨 党 90.63
鱧 鳢 92C.30
鱠 鲙 92C.41
鱣 鳣 92C.30
讕 谰 60A.00
讖 谶 60A.71
讒 谗 60A.70
讓 让 60A.02
鸇 鹯 60S.50
鷹 鹰 61.50
癱 瘫 61A.11
癲 癫 61A.80
贛 赣 60S.80
灝 灏 63A.80

（廿五劃）

韉 鞯 20B.50
欖 榄 10B.70
靉 叆 31S.82
顱 颅 21S.80
躡 蹑 40B.10
躥 蹿 40B.70
鼉 鼍 40.70
籮 箩 92A.11
鑭 镧 81A.00

b. Simplified to Regular 簡體繁體對照表

(二劃)	专 專	丑 醜	们 們	辽 遼	压 壓	迁 遷	壮 壯	设 設	驰 馳
厂 廠	云 雲	队 隊	仪 儀	边 邊	厌 厭	乔 喬	冲 衝	访 訪	纫 紉
卜 蔔	艺 藝	办 辦	丛 叢	出 齣	页 頁	伟 偉	妆 妝	诀 訣	
儿 兒	厅 廳	邓 鄧	尔 爾	发 發	夸 誇	传 傳	庄 莊	寻 尋	(七劃)
几 幾	历 歷	劝 勸	乐 樂	发 髮	夺 奪	伛 傴	庆 慶	尽 盡	寿 壽
了 瞭	历 曆	双 雙	处 處	圣 聖	达 達	优 優	刘 劉	尽 儘	麦 麥
	区 區	书 書	冬 鼕	对 對	夹 夾	伤 傷	齐 齊	导 導	玛 瑪
(三劃)	车 車		鸟 鳥	台 臺	轨 軌	伥 倀	产 產	孙 孫	进 進
干 乾	冈 岡	(五劃)	务 務	纠 糾	尧 堯	价 價	闭 閉	阵 陣	远 遠
亏 虧	贝 貝	击 擊	刍 芻	驭 馭	迈 邁	伦 倫	问 問	阳 陽	违 違
才 纔	见 見	戋 戔	饥 饑	丝 絲	毕 畢	伧 傖	闯 闖	阶 階	韧 韌
万 萬	气 氣	扑 撲	邝 鄺		贞 貞	华 華	关 關	阴 陰	刬 剗
与 與	长 長	节 節	冯 馮		师 師	伙 夥	灯 燈	妇 婦	运 運
千 韆	仆 僕	术 術	闪 閃	(六劃)	当 當	伪 僞	汤 湯	妈 媽	抚 撫
亿 億	币 幣	龙 龍	汇 匯	玑 璣	当 噹	向 嚮	忏 讖	戏 戲	坛 壇
个 個	从 從	厉 厲	汇 彙	动 動	尘 塵	后 後	兴 興	观 觀	抟 摶
么 麼	仑 侖	灭 滅	头 頭	执 執	吁 籲	会 會	讲 構	欢 歡	坏 壞
广 廣	仓 倉	东 東	汉 漢	巩 鞏	吓 嚇	杀 殺	讳 諱	买 買	抠 摳
门 門	风 風	轧 軋	宁 寧	圹 壙	虫 蟲	合 閤	讴 謳	纡 紆	坜 壢
义 義	仅 僅	卢 盧	讦 訐	扩 擴	团 團	众 衆	军 軍	红 紅	扰 擾
卫 衞	凤 鳳	业 業	讧 訌	扪 捫	吗 嗎	爷 爺	讵 詎	纣 紂	坝 壩
飞 飛	乌 烏	旧 舊	讨 討	扫 掃	屿 嶼	伞 傘	讶 訝	驮 馱	贡 貢
习 習	闩 閂	帅 帥	写 寫	扬 揚	岁 歲	创 創	讷 訥	纤 縴	掴 摑
马 馬	为 爲	归 歸	让 讓	场 場	回 迴	杂 雜	许 許	纤 纖	折 摺
乡 鄉	斗 鬬	叶 葉	礼 禮	亚 亞	岂 豈	负 負	讹 訛	纥 紇	抡 掄
	忆 憶	号 號	讪 訕	芗 薌	则 則	犷 獷	䜣 訢	驯 馴	抢 搶
(四劃)	订 訂	电 電	讫 訖	朴 樸	刚 剛	犸 獁	论 論	纨 紈	坞 塢
丰 豐	计 計	只 隻	训 訓	机 機	网 網	凫 鳧	讻 訩	约 約	坟 墳
开 開	讣 訃	只 祇	议 議	权 權	钆 釓	邬 鄔	讼 訟	级 級	护 護
无 無	认 認	叽 嘰	讯 訊	过 過	钇 釔	饪 飪	讽 諷	纩 纊	壳 殼
韦 韋	讥 譏	叹 嘆	记 記	协 協	朱 硃	饧 餳	农 農	纪 紀	块 塊

声 聲	县 縣	彻 徹	闲 閑	诉 訴	驳 駁	范 範	轭 軛	钓 釣	胀 脹
报 報	里 裏	余 餘	间 間	诊 診	纵 縱	茔 塋	斩 斬	钒 釩	肮 骯
拟 擬	呓 囈	佥 僉	闵 閔	诋 詆	纷 紛	茕 煢	轮 輪	钔 鍆	胁 脅
芜 蕪	呕 嘔	谷 穀	闷 悶	诌 謅	纸 紙	茎 莖	软 軟	钕 釹	迩 邇
苇 葦	园 園	邻 鄰	灿 燦	词 詞	纹 紋	枢 樞	鸢 鳶	钖 鍚	鱼 魚
芸 蕓	呖 嚦	肠 腸	灶 竈	诎 詘	纺 紡	枥 櫪	齿 齒	钗 釵	狞 獰
苋 莧	旷 曠	龟 龜	炀 煬	诏 詔	驴 驢	柜 櫃	虏 虜	制 製	备 備
苍 蒼	围 圍	犹 猶	沣 灃	译 譯	纼 紖	㭎 棡	肾 腎	迭 疊	枭 梟
严 嚴	吨 噸	狈 狽	沤 漚	诒 詒	纽 紐	枨 棖	贤 賢	刮 颳	饯 餞
芦 蘆	旸 暘	鸠 鳩	沥 瀝	灵 靈	纾 紓	板 闆	昙 曇	侠 俠	饰 飾
劳 勞	邮 郵	条 條	沦 淪	层 層		枞 樅	国 國	侥 僥	饱 飽
克 剋	困 睏	岛 島	沧 滄	迟 遲	**（八劃）**	松 鬆	畅 暢	侦 偵	饲 飼
苏 蘇	员 員	邹 鄒	沟 溝	张 張	玮 瑋	枪 槍	咙 嚨	侧 側	饳 飿
极 極	呗 唄	饨 飩	沩 溈	际 際	环 環	枫 楓	虮 蟣	凭 憑	饴 飴
杨 楊	听 聽	饩 餼	沪 滬	陆 陸	责 責	构 構	黾 黽	侨 僑	变 變
两 兩	呛 嗆	饪 飪	沈 瀋	陇 隴	现 現	丧 喪	鸣 鳴	侩 儈	庞 龐
丽 麗	呜 嗚	饫 飫	怃 憮	陈 陳	表 錶	画 畫	咛 嚀	货 貨	庙 廟
医 醫	别 彆	饬 飭	怀 懷	坠 墜	玱 瑲	枣 棗	罗 羅	侪 儕	疟 瘧
励 勵	财 財	饭 飯	怄 慪	陉 陘	规 規	卖 賣	岿 巋	侬 儂	疠 癘
还 還	囵 圇	饮 飲	忧 憂	妪 嫗	匦 匭	郁 鬱	帜 幟	质 質	疡 瘍
矶 磯	帏 幃	系 係	忾 愾	妩 嫵	拢 攏	矾 礬	岭 嶺	征 徵	剂 劑
奁 奩	岖 嶇	系 繫	怅 悵	妫 媯	拣 揀	矿 礦	刿 劌	径 徑	废 廢
歼 殲	岗 崗	冻 凍	怆 愴	刭 剄	垆 壚	砀 碭	剀 剴	舍 捨	闸 閘
来 來	帐 帳	状 狀	穷 窮	劲 勁	担 擔	码 碼	凯 凱	刽 劊	闹 鬧
欤 歟	岚 嵐	亩 畝	证 證	鸡 雞	顶 頂	厕 廁	败 敗	郐 鄶	郑 鄭
轩 軒	针 針	庑 廡	诂 詁	纬 緯	拥 擁	奋 奮	账 賬	怂 慫	卷 捲
连 連	钉 釘	库 庫	诃 訶	纭 紜	势 勢	态 態	贩 販	籴 糴	单 單
轫 軔	钊 釗	疖 癤	启 啓	驱 驅	𢫬 𢹭	瓯 甌	贬 貶	觅 覓	炜 煒
卤 鹵	钋 釙	疗 療	评 評	纯 純	拧 擰	欧 歐	贮 貯	贪 貪	炝 熗
卤 滷	钌 釕	应 應	补 補	纰 紕	拨 撥	殴 毆	图 圖	贫 貧	炉 爐
邺 鄴	乱 亂	这 這	诅 詛	纱 紗	择 擇	垄 壟	购 購	戗 戧	浅 淺
坚 堅	体 體	庐 廬	识 識	纲 綱	茏 蘢	轰 轟	钍 釷	肤 膚	泷 瀧
时 時	佣 傭	闰 閏	诇 詗	纳 納	苹 蘋	顷 頃	钏 釧	䏝 膞	泸 瀘
呒 嘸	㑇 㑳	闱 闈	诈 詐	纴 紝	茑 蔦	转 轉	钐 釤	肿 腫	泞 濘

泻瀉
泼潑
泽澤
泾涇
怜憐
怿懌
学學
宝寶
宠寵
审審
帘簾
实實
诓誆
诔誄
试試
诗詩
诘詰
诙詼
诚誠
郓鄆
衬襯
视視
诛誅
话話
诞誕
诟詬
诠詮
诡詭
询詢
诣詣
诤諍
该該
详詳
诧詫

诨諢
诩詡
肃肅
隶隸
录錄
弥彌
陕陝
驽駑
驾駕
参參
艰艱
线綫
绀紺
绁紲
绂紱
练練
组組
驵駔
绅紳
䌷紬
细細
驶駛
驸駙
驷駟
驹駒
终終
织織
驺騶
绉縐
驻駐
绊絆
驼駝
绋紼
绌絀

绍紹
驿驛
绎繹
经經
骀駘
绐紿
贯貫

（九劃）

贰貳
帮幫
珑瓏
顸頇
挜掗
挝撾
项項
挞撻
挟挾
挠撓
赵趙
贲賁
挡擋
垲塏
挢撟
垫墊
挤擠
挥揮
挦撏
荐薦
荚莢
贳貰
荛蕘
荜蓽
带帶

茧繭
荞蕎
荟薈
荠薺
荡蕩
垩堊
荣榮
荤葷
荥滎
荦犖
荧熒
荨蕁
胡鬍
荩藎
荪蓀
荫蔭
荭葒
药藥
标標
栈棧
栉櫛
栊櫳
栋棟
栌櫨
栎櫟
柠檸
柽檉
树樹
郦酈
咸鹹
砖磚
砚硯
面麵
牵牽

鸥鷗
龚龔
残殘
殇殤
轲軻
轳轤
轴軸
轶軼
轸軫
轹轢
轺軺
轻輕
鸦鴉
虿蠆
战戰
觇覘
点點
临臨
览覽
坚堅
竖豎
尝嘗
眍瞘
昽曨
哑啞
显顯
哓嘵
哔嗶
贵貴
虾蝦
蚁蟻
蚂螞
虽雖
骂罵

剐剮
勋勛
哗嘩
响響
哙噲
哝噥
哟喲
峡峽
峣嶢
帧幀
罚罰
峤嶠
贱賤
贴貼
贶貺
贻貽
钘鈃
钚鈈
钛鈦
钝鈍
钞鈔
钟鍾
钟鐘
钡鋇
钢鋼
钠鈉
钥鑰
钦欽
钧鈞
钤鈐
钨鎢
钩鈎
钪鈧
钫鈁

钬鈥
钮鈕
钯鈀
毡氈
氢氫
选選
适適
种種
秋鞦
复復
复複
复覆
笃篤
俦儔
俨儼
俩倆
俪儷
贷貸
顺順
俭儉
剑劍
须鬚
胧朧
胪臚
胆膽
胜勝
胫脛
鸨鴇
狭狹
狮獅
独獨
狯獪
狱獄
狲猻

贸貿
饵餌
饶饒
蚀蝕
饷餉
饺餃
饼餅
峦巒
弯彎
孪孿
娈孌
将將
奖獎
疬癧
疮瘡
疯瘋
亲親
飒颯
闺閨
闻聞
闼闥
闽閩
闾閭
闿闓
阀閥
阁閣
阂閡
养養
姜薑
类類
娄婁
总總
炼煉
炽熾

烁爍
烃烴
洼窪
洁潔
洒灑
浃浹
浇澆
浈湞
浊濁
测測
浍澮
浏瀏
济濟
浑渾
浒滸
浓濃
浔潯
浕濜
恸慟
恹懨
恺愷
恻惻
恼惱
恽惲
举舉
觉覺
宪憲
窃竊
诫誡
诬誣
语語
袄襖
诮誚
祢禰

误誤
诰誥
诱誘
诲誨
诳誑
鸩鴆
说說
诵誦
诶誒
垦墾
昼晝
费費
逊遜
陨隕
险險
贺賀
怼懟
垒壘
娅婭
娆嬈
娇嬌
绑綁
绒絨
结結
绔絝
骁驍
绕繞
绖絰
骄驕
骅驊
绘繪
骆駱
骈駢
绞絞

恶惡
哑啞
䓖藭
莹瑩
莺鶯
鸪鴣
莼蒓
桡橈
桢楨
档檔
桥橋
桦樺
桧檜
桩樁
样樣
贾賈
逦邐
砺礪
砾礫
础礎
砻礱
顾顧
轼軾
轾輊
轿轎
辂輅
较較
顿頓
趸躉
毙斃
致緻
龀齔
鸬鸕
虑慮

监監
紧緊
党黨
唛嘜
晒曬
晓曉
唠嘮
鸭鴨
晔曄
晕暈
鸮鴞
唝嗊
㖞喎
蚬蜆
鸯鴦
罢罷
圆圓
觊覬
贼賊
贿賄
赂賂
赃贜
赅賅
赆贐
钰鈺
钱錢
钲鉦
钳鉗
钴鈷
钵鉢
钶鈳
钷鉕
钹鈸
钺鉞

钻鑽
钼鉬
钽鉭
钾鉀
铀鈾
钿鈿
铁鐵
铂鉑
铃鈴
铅鉛
铈鈰
铊鉈
铋鉍
铌鈮
铍鈹
铎鐸
氩氬
牺犧
敌敵
积積
称稱
笕筧
笔筆
债債
倾傾
赁賃
颀頎
徕徠
舰艦
舱艙
耸聳
爱愛
鸰鴒
颁頒

颂頌
脍膾
脏臟
脐臍
脑腦
胶膠
脓膿
鸱鴟
玺璽
鸲鴝
鸵鴕
袅裊
鸳鴛
皱皺
饽餑
饿餓
馁餒
栾欒
挛攣
恋戀
桨槳
浆漿
症癥
痈癰
斋齋
痉痙
准準
离離
颃頏
资資
竞競
阃閫
阄鬮
阅閱

阎閻
郸鄲
烦煩
烧燒
烛燭
烨燁
烩燴
烬燼
递遞
涛濤
涝澇
涞淶
涟漣
涡渦
涂塗
涤滌
润潤
涧澗
涨漲
烫燙
涩澀
悭慳
悯憫
宽寬
家傢
宾賓
窍竅
鸢鳶
请請
诸諸
诹諏
诺諾
诼諑
读讀

诽誹
袜襪
祯禎
课課
诿諉
谁誰
谂諗
调調
谄諂
谅諒
谆諄
谇誶
谈談
谊誼
谉讅
恳懇
剧劇
娲媧
娴嫻
难難
预預
绠綆
骊驪
绡綃
骋騁
绢絹
绣綉
验驗
绥綏
绦縧
继繼
绨綈
骎駸
骏駿

鸶鷥

（拾一劃）

焘燾
琐瑣
麸麩
掳擄
掴摑
鸷鷙
掷擲
掸撣
壸壼
悫愨
据據
掺摻
掼摜
职職
萚蘀
勚勩
萝蘿
萤螢
营營
萦縈
萧蕭
萨薩
梦夢
觋覡
检檢
啬嗇
匮匱
酝醞
硕碩
硖硤
硗磽

聋聾
龚龔
袭襲
殒殞
殓殮
赍賚
辄輒
辅輔
辆輛
堑塹
颅顱
啧嘖
悬懸
啭囀
跃躍
啮嚙
跄蹌
蛎蠣
蛊蠱
蛏蟶
累纍
啸嘯
帻幘
崭嶄
逻邏
帼幗
赈賑
婴嬰
赊賒
铏鉶
铐銬
铑銠
铒鉺
铓鋩

铕銪
铗鋏
铙鐃
铛鐺
铝鋁
铜銅
铟銦
铠鎧
铡鍘
铢銖
铣銑
铥銩
铤鋌
铨銓
铩鎩
铪鉿
铫銚
铭銘
铬鉻
铮錚
铯銫
铰鉸
铱銥
铲鏟
铳銃
铵銨
银銀
铷銣
矫矯
秽穢
笺箋
笼籠
笾籩
偾僨

鸺 鵂
偿 償
偻 僂
躯 軀
皑 皚
衅 釁
衔 銜
舻 艫
盘 盤
龛 龕
鸽 鴿
领 領
腘 膕
脸 臉
象 像
猎 獵
猕 獼
馃 餜
馄 餛
馅 餡
馆 館
鸾 鸞
庼 廎
痒 癢
旋 鏇
阈 閾
阉 閹
阊 閶
阅 閱
阇 闍
阎 閻
阏 閼
阐 闡
羟 羥

盖 蓋
粝 糲
断 斷
兽 獸
焖 燜
渍 漬
鸿 鴻
渎 瀆
渐 漸
渑 澠
渊 淵
渔 漁
淀 澱
渗 滲
惬 愜
惭 慚
惧 懼
惊 驚
惮 憚
惨 慘
惯 慣
祷 禱
谌 諶
谋 謀
谍 諜
谎 謊
谏 諫
皲 皸
谐 諧
谑 謔
裆 襠
祸 禍
谒 謁
谓 謂

谔 諤
谕 諭
谖 諼
谗 讒
谘 諮
谙 諳
谚 諺
谛 諦
谜 謎
谝 諞
谞 諝
弹 彈
堕 墮
随 隨
粜 糶
隐 隱
婵 嬋
婶 嬸
颇 頗
颈 頸
绩 績
绪 緒
绫 綾
骐 騏
续 續
绮 綺
骑 騎
绯 緋
绰 綽
绲 緄
绳 繩
骓 騅
维 維
绵 綿

绶 綬
绷 繃
绸 綢
绺 綹
绻 綣
综 綜
绽 綻
绾 綰
绿 綠
骖 驂
缀 綴
缁 緇

(拾二劃)

靓 靚
琼 瓊
辇 輦
鼋 黿
趋 趨
揽 攬
颉 頡
揿 撳
搀 攙
蛰 蟄
絷 縶
搁 擱
搂 摟
搅 攪
联 聯
蒇 蕆
蒉 蕢
蒋 蔣
蒌 蔞
韩 韓

椟 櫝
椤 欏
赍 賫
椭 橢
鹁 鵓
鹂 鸝
觌 覿
硷 鹼
确 確
殚 殫
颊 頰
雳 靂
椠 槧
暂 暫
辍 輟
辎 輜
翘 翹
辈 輩
凿 鑿
辉 輝
赏 賞
睐 睞
喷 噴
畴 疇
践 踐
遗 遺
蛱 蛺
蛲 蟯
蛳 螄
蛴 蠐
鹃 鵑
喽 嘍
嵘 嶸
嵚 嶔

赋 賦
赌 賭
赎 贖
赐 賜
赒 賙
赔 賠
铸 鑄
铹 鐒
铺 鋪
铼 錸
铽 鋱
链 鏈
铿 鏗
销 銷
锁 鎖
锃 鋥
锄 鋤
锂 鋰
锅 鍋
锆 鋯
锇 鋨
锈 銹
锉 銼
锋 鋒
锌 鋅
锎 鐦
锏 鐧
锐 銳
锑 銻
锒 鋃
锓 鋟
锔 鋦
锕 錒
犊 犢

鹄 鵠
鹅 鵝
筑 築
筚 篳
筛 篩
牍 牘
傥 儻
傧 儐
储 儲
傩 儺
惩 懲
御 禦
颌 頜
释 釋
鸧 鶬
腊 臘
鱿 魷
鲁 魯
鲂 魴
颍 潁
飓 颶
觞 觴
惫 憊
馈 饋
馊 餿
馋 饞
亵 褻
装 裝
蛮 蠻
脔 臠
痨 癆
痫 癇
赓 賡
颏 頦

鹇 鷳
阑 闌
阔 闊
阕 闋
粪 糞
鹈 鵜
窜 竄
窝 窩
喾 嚳
愤 憤
愦 憒
滞 滯
湿 濕
溃 潰
溅 濺
溇 漊
湾 灣
谟 謨
裢 褳
裣 襝
裤 褲
裥 襉
禅 禪
谠 讜
谡 謖
谢 謝
谣 謠
谤 謗
谥 謚
谦 謙
谧 謐
属 屬
屡 屢
骘 騭

毵 毿
翚 翬
骛 騖
缂 緙
缃 緗
缄 緘
缅 緬
缆 纜
缇 緹
缉 緝
缊 緼
缌 緦
缎 緞
缓 緩
缒 縋
缔 締
缕 縷
骗 騙
编 編
骚 騷
缘 緣
飨 饗

(拾三劃)

耢 耮
鹉 鵡
韫 韞
骜 驁
摄 攝
摆 擺
䙓 襬
摈 擯
毂 轂
摊 攤

鹊 鵲
蓝 藍
蓦 驀
蓟 薊
蒙 矇
蒙 濛
颐 頤
献 獻
蓣 蕷
榄 欖
榇 櫬
榈 櫚
楼 樓
榉 櫸
赖 賴
碛 磧
碍 礙
碜 磣
鹌 鵪
尴 尷
殨 殨
雾 霧
辏 輳
辐 輻
辑 輯
输 輸
频 頻
龃 齟
龄 齡
龅 齙
鉴 鑒
韪 韙
嗫 囁
跸 蹕

跷蹺
跻躋
跹躚
蜗蝸
嗳噯
睸睸
锗鍺
错錯
锘鍩
锚錨
锛錛
锝鍀
锞錁
锡錫
锢錮
锣鑼
锤錘
锥錐
锦錦
锧鑕
锫錇
锭錠
键鍵
锯鋸
锰錳
锱錙
辞辭
颓頹
筹籌
签簽
签籤
简簡
觎覦
颔頷
腻膩
鹏鵬
腾騰
鲅鮁
鲇鮎
鲈鱸
鲊鮓
稣穌
鲋鮒
鲍鮑
鲐鮐
颖穎
飕颼
触觸
雏雛
馎餺
馍饃
馏餾
馐饈
酱醬
鹑鶉
瘅癉
鹕鶘
阖闔
阗闐
阙闕
誊謄
粮糧
数數
滟灩
满滿
滤濾
滥濫
滨濱
滩灘
慑懾
誉譽
鲎鱟
骞騫
窥窺
窦竇
谨謹
谩謾
谪謫
谬謬
辟闢
嫒嬡
嫔嬪
缙縉
缜縝
缚縛
缛縟
辔轡
缝縫
骝騮
缞縗
缟縞
缠纏
缡縭
缢縊
缤繽
骟騸

(拾四劃)

赘贅
觏覯
韬韜
叆靉
墙墻
撄攖
蔷薔
蔑衊
蔹蘞
蔺藺
蔼藹
鹕鶘
槚檟
槛檻
槟檳
槠櫧
酽釅
酿釀
霁霽
愿願
殡殯
辕轅
辖轄
辗輾
龇齜
龈齦
颗顆
䁖瞜
暧曖
踌躊
踊踴
蜡蠟
蝈蟈
蝇蠅
蝉蟬
鹗鶚
嘤嚶
罴羆
赙賻
罂罌
赚賺
锲鍥
锴鍇
锶鍶
锷鍔
锹鍬
锸鍤
锻鍛
锾鍰
锵鏘
锿鎄
镀鍍
镁鎂
镂鏤
镄鐨
镅鎇
鹙鶖
稳穩
箦簀
箧篋
箨籜
箩籮
箪簞
箓籙
箫簫
舆輿
膑臏
鲑鮭
鲔鮪
鲗鰂
鲙鱠
鲚鱭
鲛鮫
鲜鮮
鲟鱘
馑饉
馒饅
銮鑾
瘗瘞
瘘瘻
阚闞
鲞鯗
糁糝
鹚鷀
潇瀟
潋瀲
赛賽
窭窶
谭譚
谮譖
褛褸
谯譙
谰讕
谱譜
谲譎
嫱嬙
鹜鶩
缥縹
骠驃
缦縵
骡騾
缧縲
缨纓
骢驄
缩縮
缪繆
缫繅

(拾五劃)

耧耬
璎瓔
撵攆
撷擷
撺攛
聩聵
聪聰
觐覲
蕲蘄
赜賾
蕴蘊
樯檣
樱櫻
飘飄
靥靨
魇魘
餍饜
霉黴
辘轆
龉齬
龊齪
觑覷
瞒瞞
题題
颙顒
踬躓
踯躑
蝼螻
噜嚕
嘱囑
颛顓
镊鑷
镉鎘
镴鑞
镍鎳
镎鎿
镏鎦
镐鎬
镑鎊
镒鎰
镓鎵
镔鑌
篑簣
篓簍
鹆鵒
鹞鷂
鲠鯁
鲢鰱
鲥鰣
鲤鯉
鲧鯀
鲫鯽
馔饌
瘪癟
瘫癱
齑齏
颜顏
鹈鵜
鲨鯊
澜瀾
额額
谳讞
褴襤
谴譴
鹤鶴
谵譫
屦屨
缭繚
缮繕
缯繒

(拾六劃)

擞擻
颞顳
颟顢
薮藪
颠顛
橹櫓
赝贗
飙飆
錾鏨
辙轍
辚轔
鹦鸚
赠贈
镖鏢
镗鏜
镘鏝
镛鏞
镜鏡
镝鏑
镞鏃
氇氌
赞贊
穑穡
篮籃
篱籬
魉魎
鲭鯖
鲮鯪
鲰鯫
鲲鯤
鲳鯧
鲵鯢
鲷鯛
鲸鯨
獭獺
鹧鷓
瘿癭
瘾癮
斓斕
辫辮
濑瀨
濒瀕
懒懶
黉黌
鹨鷚
颡顙
缰繮
缱繾
缲繰
缳繯
缴繳

(拾七劃)

藓蘚
鹩鷯
龋齲
龌齷
瞩矚
蹒蹣

蹑 躡
羁 羈
赡 贍
镣 鐐
镤 鏷
镧 鑭
镩 鑹
镪 鏹
镫 鐙
鹧 鷓
鲽 鰈
鳃 鰓
鳁 鰮
鳄 鱷
鳅 鰍
鳆 鰒
鳊 鯿
鹫 鷲
辫 辮
赢 贏
懑 懣
鹬 鷸
骤 驟

(拾八劃)
鳌 鰲
鞯 韉
黡 黶
颢 顥
鹭 鷺
嚣 囂
髅 髏
镬 鑊
镭 鐳
镮 鐶
镯 鐲
镰 鐮
镱 鐿
雠 讎
鳍 鰭
鳏 鰥
鳒 鰜
鹯 鸇
鹰 鷹
癞 癩
冁 囅
谳 讞

(拾九劃)
攒 攢
霭 靄
鳖 鱉
巅 巔
髌 髕
镲 鑔
籁 籟
鳘 鰵
鳔 鰾
鳕 鱈
鳗 鰻
颤 顫
癣 癬
谶 讖
骥 驥
缵 纘

(二拾劃)
瓒 瓚
鬓 鬢
鼍 鼉
黩 黷
镳 鑣
错 鑞
臜 臢
鳜 鱖
鳝 鱔
鳞 鱗
鳟 鱒
骧 驤

(廿一劃)
颦 顰
躏 躪
鳢 鱧
鳣 鱣
癫 癲
赣 贛
灏 灝

(廿二劃)
鹳 鸛
镶 鑲

(廿三劃)
趱 趲
颧 顴
躜 躦

(廿五劃)
戆 戇

ROMANIZED INDEX

Chinese characters often have several alternative pronunciations which are fully given in the Dictionary. This Romanized Index can only give one most common pronunciation, sometimes two. The variants and abbreviated forms of the same character are given in parenthesis.

漢字每有「破音」字，在字典中詳細分別指出，但爲讀者便利，在本索引中僅擧其最常讀音，括號內卽異體及簡筆字。

灞 63A.42 995
罷 41D.70 683
罢 41D.93 684
垻 11A.80 206
猈 91C.10 1299

ㄅㄞ **BAI** (bai)
掰 90S.00 1188

ㄅㄞˊ (bair)
白 91.41 1208

ㄅㄞˇ (baai)
擺 10A.70 87
摆 10A.93 107
襬 63C.70 1040
百 31.41 463
栢 10B.41 126
捭 10A.10 55
柏 10B.41 128

ㄅㄞˋ (baih)
唄 40A.80 600
敗 41C.82 678
粺 22C.10 406
稗 90A.10 1177
拜 90S.10 1188

ㄅㄢ **BAN** (ban)
般 91S.82 1330
搬 10A.82 103
瘢 61A.82 911
螌 91.93 1230
班 31A.11 485
斑 31A.11 485
癍 61A.11 904
扳 10A.82 102
媥 60S.42 875
頒 80S.80 1082

ㄅㄢˇ (baan)
板 10B.82 142
坂 11A.82 207
岅 21B.82 333
阪 32A.82 560
版 91S.82 1330
舨 91S.82 1330
鈑 92C.82 1382
闆 52B.00 794

ㄅㄢˋ (bahn)
半 22.10 352
拌 10A.10 53
靽 20B.10 294
伴 91A.10 1242
絆 93B.10 1423
辦 60S.10 871
(办)
瓣 60S.10 870
扮 10A.50 83

ㄅㄤ **BANG** (bang)
[illegible] 11.10 171
幇 11.22 174
幫 11.22 174
梆 10B.22 119
帮 90.22 1152
幚 90.22 1152
邦 10S.22 160
[illegible] 20B.50 295
浜 63A.80 1015

ㄅㄤˇ (baang)
榜 10B.50 131
膀 42A.50 714
髈 42B.50 725
牓 91S.50 1326
綁 93B.22 1425

ㄅㄤˋ (bahng)
蒡 20A.50 277
磅 31B.50 497
謗 60A.50 856
鎊 81A.50 1117
棒 10B.10 114
蚌 22D.10 412

ㄅㄠ **BAU** (bau)
包 92.70 1347
苞 20A.70 285
齙 21S.70 340
胞 42A.70 717
褒 60.02 810
襃 60.02 810
勹 92.50 1341

ㄅㄠˊ (baur)
鞄 20B.70 296

ㄅㄠˇ (baau)
宝 62.11 921
寚 62.21 922
寶 62.80 934
保 91A.01 1238
葆 20A.01 252
褓 63C.01 1035
堡 91.11 1204
緥 93B.01 1421
鴇 21S.50 338
飽 81B.70 1131

ㄅㄠˋ (bauh)
抱 10A.70 91
菢 20A.70 280
鉋 81A.70 1120
[illegible] 91S.70 1328
鮑 92C.70 1381
趵 40B.50 613

豹 91S.50 1326
暴 41.02 623
爆 91D.02 1309
報 11S.82 213
(报)
煲 91.81 1226

ㄅㄟ **BEI** (bei)
卑 91.10 1202
椑 10B.10 115
碑 31B.10 493
杯 10B.22 119
桮 10B.40 124
盃 31.30 461
悲 22.72 373

ㄅㄟˇ (beei)
北 22.70 371
鈚 81A.70 1119
錇 81A.40 1112

ㄅㄟˋ (beih)
貝 41.80 651
鋇 81A.80 1123
狽 91C.80 1305
蓓 20A.40 269
倍 91A.40 1255
焙 91D.40 1311
鞴 20B.42 295
糒 22C.42 409
僃 91.72 1222
備 91A.42 1258
背 22.42 369
褙 63C.42 1039
孛 10.00 3
悖 22A.00 382
輩 22.10 353
被 63C.82 1041

俻 91A.41 1258

ㄅㄣ **BEN** (ben)
奔 12.20 219
(犇)
錛 81A.20 1108
賁 10.80 36

ㄅㄣˇ (been)
本 10.10 15
畚 93.41 1394

ㄅㄣˋ (behn)
坌 80.11 1061
笨 92A.10 1360
逩 12.83 234

ㄅㄥ **BENG** (beng)
崩 21.42 314
弸 50A.42 736
痭 61A.42 907
繃 93B.42 1434
綳 93B.42 1435
伻 91A.10 1242

ㄅㄥˊ (berng)
甭 31.42 468

ㄅㄥˇ (beeng)
琫 31A.10 483

ㄅㄥˋ (behng)
堋 11A.42 201
蹦 40B.42 612
搒 10A.50 82
泵 31.02 443
迸 80.83 1075

ㄅㄧ **BI** (bi)
逼 30.83 436
偪 91A.41 1257
屄 52A.80 786

ㄅㄧˊ (bir)		
荸	20A.00	246
鼻	91.20	1204
ㄅㄧˇ (bii)		
匕	21A.70	326
比	21S.70	339
粃	22C.70	410
秕	90A.70	1182
妣	93A.70	1414
佊	91A.82	1276
彼	91B.82	1293
啚	40.41	572
鄙	40S.22	619
(鄙)		
筆	92A.10	1360
笔	92A.70	1371
ㄅㄧˋ (bih)		
必	72.72	1057
苾	20A.72	287
毖	21A.72	327
閟	52B.00	799
泌	63A.72	1013
鉍	81A.72	1122
飶	81B.72	1131
秘	90S.72	1197
蓖	20A.70	284
陛	32A.11	552
庇	61.70	896
狴	91C.11	1299
篦	92A.70	1371
萆	20A.10	257
睥	41B.10	667
髀	42B.10	723
庳	61.10	889
痺	61A.10	903
裨	63C.10	1036
俾	91A.10	1243
婢	93A.10	1406
畀	41.22	628
痹	61A.22	904
箅	92A.20	1363
敝	22S.82	428
蔽	20A.82	290
弊	22.20	355
幣	22.22	360
斃	22.70	373
辟	52S.10	802
薜	20A.10	257
躃	40B.10	608
襞	52.02	772
壁	52.11	773
璧	52.11	773
臂	52.42	774
避	52.83	779
躄	52.83	780
嬖	52.93	780
髲	42B.82	725
詖	60A.82	866
賁	10.80	36
贔	41.80	652
畢	41.10	625
蓽	20A.10	257
嗶	40A.10	581
蹕	40B.10	608
篳	92A.10	1361
愊	22A.41	392
腷	42A.41	711
愎	22A.82	401
碧	31.40	463
弼	50A.50	737
閉	52B.00	788
觱	71.42	1048
ㄅㄧㄢ **BIAN** (bian)		
邊	91.83	1229
(边)		
籩	92A.83	1375
蝙	22D.42	417
鯿	92C.42	1381
編	93B.42	1435
鞭	20B.82	297
砭	31B.83	502
ㄅㄧㄢˇ (biaan)		
扁	63D.42	1044
萹	20A.42	276
匾	51.21	747
褊	63C.42	1039
貶	41C.83	679
窆	62A.83	949
ㄅㄧㄢˋ (biahn)		
卞	60.22	816
抃	10A.22	64
忭	22A.22	389
汴	63A.22	978
遍	63D.83	1045
徧	91B.42	1291
辨	60S.10	870
辯	60S.10	870
辮	60S.10	871
便	91A.82	1276
緶	93B.82	1444
弁	93.20	1393
變	93.82	1398
(变)		
ㄅㄧㄠ **BIAU** (biau)		
臕	42A.63	715
鑣	81A.63	1118
穮	90A.63	1182
猋	12.81	229
飆	12S.70	236
飈	42.70	701
摽	10A.01	49
標	10B.01	112
鏢	81A.01	1104
彪	21A.70	327
ㄅㄧㄠˇ (biaau)		
表	10.02	13
褾	63C.02	1035
錶	81A.02	1104
俵	91A.02	1240
婊	93A.02	1404
ㄅㄧㄠˋ (biauh)		
鰾	92C.01	1378
ㄅㄧㄝ **BIE** (bie)		
鱉	22.63	371
鼈	22.70	373
憋	22.72	374
ㄅㄧㄝˊ (bier)		
別	40S.00	618
别	40S.00	618
蹩	22.83	380
(蹩)		
ㄅㄧㄝˇ (biee)		
癟	61A.42	908
ㄅㄧㄝˋ (bieh)		
彆	22.50	370
ㄅㄧㄣ **BIN** (bin)		
賓	62.80	934
檳	10B.80	138
蠙	22D.80	420
濱	63A.80	1014
鑌	81A.80	1123
繽	93B.80	1444
彬	10B.91	143
豳	21.21	310
斌	60S.71	881
瀕	63A.80	1014
邠	80S.22	1080
ㄅㄧㄣˋ (bihn)		
擯	10A.80	94
殯	31S.80	528
臏	42A.80	719
髕	42B.80	725
鬢	51.80	753
儐	91A.80	1272
髩	51.50	751
ㄅㄧㄥ **BING** (bing)		
冰	22.02	352
氷	63A.02	967
兵	90.80	1164
ㄅㄧㄥˇ (biing)		
丙	31.42	467
昺	41.42	642
炳	91D.42	1312
稟	60.01	805
禀	60.01	805
餅	81B.20	1127
秉	90.01	1146
ㄅㄧㄥˋ (bihng)		
幷	91.20	1204
(并)		
摒	10A.20	58
併	91A.20	1246
並	80.30	1063
竝	80.30	1063
柄	10B.42	129

病 61A.42 906
竝 60S.30 874
ㄅㄛ **BO** (bo)
菠 20A.82 290
玻 31A.82 490
啵 40A.82 604
波 63A.82 1019
鉢 81A.10 1106
缽 92S.10 1384
撥 10A.82 100
鱍 92C.82 1382
盋 12.30 220
嶓 21B.41 331
癶 32S.83 567
餑 81B.00 1126
剝 92S.00 1382
ㄅㄛˊ (bor)
泊 63A.41 990
鉑 81A.41 1114
帛 91.22 1205
伯 91A.41 1258
舶 91S.41 1325
箔 92A.41 1368
孛 10.00 3
桲 10B.00 109
勃 10S.50 163
鵓 10S.50 163
葧 20A.50 276
脖 42A.00 704
浡 63A.00 958
渤 63A.50 997
搏 10A.00 44
欂 10B.00 110
博 10S.00 156
薄 20A.00 248
膊 42A.00 704
髆 42B.00 723
鑮 81A.00 1102
鎛 81A.00 1102
餺 81B.00 1126
雹 31D.70 516
骲 42B.70 725
僰 10.81 38
蔔 20A.50 279
菔 20A.82 290
踣 40B.40 610
駁 51B.82 767
檗 52.01 772
襮 63C.02 1035
襏 63C.82 1042
餢 81B.22 1128
佰 91A.41 1257
ㄅㄛˇ (boo)
跛 40B.82 617
簸 92A.82 1374
ㄅㄛˋ (boh)
蘗 20A.01 250
擘 52.00 772
檗 52.01 772
播 10A.41 78
亳 60.70 826
ㄅㄨ **BU** (bu)
逋 10.83 40
晡 41A.42 660
餔 81B.42 1129
不 31.22 451
ㄅㄨˊ (bur)
醭 31C.81 508
ㄅㄨˇ (buu)
捕 10A.42 78
埔 11A.42 201
哺 40A.42 591
補 63C.42 1038
卜 22.22 356
ㄅㄨˋ (buh)
布 12.22 219
怖 22A.22 389
鈽 81A.22 1109
佈 91A.22 1247
埠 11A.10 197
步 21A.91 329
部 60S.22 873
鈈 81A.22 1109
簿 92A.00 1358
ㄔ, ㄑ C
ㄔㄚ **CHA** (cha)
叉 32.82 542
扠 10A.82 100
杈 10B.82 141
臿 90.21 1151
插 10A.21 60
挿 10A.22 66
喳 40A.30 585
差 80.30 1063
ㄔㄚˊ (char)
查 10.30 23
楂 10B.30 121
碴 31B.30 495
茶 20A.01 251
搽 10A.01 49
察 62.01 917
詧 92.40 1338
槎 10B.30 123
垞 11A.70 205
鍤 81A.21 1109
ㄔㄚˇ (chaa)
蹅 40B.30 610
鑔 81A.01 1104
ㄔㄚˋ (chah)
汊 63A.82 1019
衩 63C.82 1042
詫 60A.70 858
侘 91A.70 1267
奼 93A.70 1415
姹 93A.70 1415
岔 80.21 1061
剎 82S.00 1139
ㄔㄞ **CHAI** (chai)
釵 81A.82 1124
ㄔㄞˊ (chair)
侪 91A.22 1248
儕 91A.22 1248
柴 21A.01 317
豺 91S.00 1317
ㄔㄞˋ (chaih)
蠆 20A.93 293
瘥 61A.30 905
ㄔㄢ **CHAN** (chan)
幨 22B.40 403
襜 63C.40 1037
攙 10A.70 91
摻 10A.91 106
ㄔㄢˊ (charn)
孱 52A.00 780
潺 63A.00 960
蟬 22D.10 412
襌 63B.10 1027
嬋 93A.10 1406
廛 61.11 890
躔 40B.11 609
纏 93B.11 1424
巉 21B.70 332
讒 60A.70 861
鑱 81A.70 1120
饞 81B.70 1131
劖 92S.00 1383
蟾 22D.40 415
澶 63A.30 981
ㄔㄢˇ (chaan)
產 60.11 814
剷 60S.00 869
鏟 81A.11 1107
囅 40S.02 619
闡 52B.00 794
蕆 20A.71 285
諂 60A.21 845
(讇)
刬 71S.00 1054
ㄔㄢˋ (chahn)
懺 22A.71 398
羼 52A.10 781
ㄔㄤ **CHANG** (chang)
昌 41.41 631
菖 20A.41 271
閶 52B.00 795
猖 91C.41 1301
鯧 92C.41 1380
娼 93A.41 1411
倀 91A.02 1240
ㄔㄤˊ (charng)
裳 22.02 352
常 22.22 359
嘗 22.41 365
嚐 40A.41 589
(甞)(尝)

償 91A.80 1271
徜 91B.42 1291
嫦 93A.22 1407
場 11A.50 202
腸 42A.50 714
長 51.02 743
长 10.93 42

ㄔㄤˇ (chaang)

敞 22S.82 428
氅 22.70 373
廠 61.82 900
(厰)
昶 63.83 957

ㄔㄤˋ (chahng)

唱 40A.41 590
倡 91A.41 1257
鬯 21.70 314
悵 22A.02 384
暢 22S.50 425

ㄔㄠ **CHAU** (chau)

抄 10A.91 106
鈔 81A.91 1126
超 11.83 190

ㄔㄠˊ (chaur)

晁 41.70 647
鼂 41.70 647
朝 10S.42 161
潮 63A.42 992
巢 93.01 1392

ㄔㄠˇ (chaau)

吵 40A.91 605
炒 91D.91 1316

ㄔㄜ **CHE** (che)

車 10.10 17

ㄔㄜˇ (chee)

扯 10A.30 66

ㄔㄜˋ (cheh)

撤 10A.82 98
轍 10D.82 155
澈 63A.82 1020
徹 91B.82 1294
掣 10.00 4
拆 10A.22 66
呫 40A.40 588

ㄔㄣ **CHEN** (chen)

嗔 40A.80 600
瞋 41B.80 671
抻 10A.80 93
琛 31A.01 482

ㄔㄣˊ (chern)

辰 51A.02 756
晨 41.02 624
宸 62.02 919
陳 32A.01 549
蔯 20A.01 250
忱 22A.70 397
沈 63A.70 1010
沉 63A.70 1009
梣 10B.32 123
臣 51.21 745
諶 60A.21 845
塵 61.11 890

ㄔㄣˇ (cheen)

硶 31B.32 496
磣 31B.91 502

ㄔㄣˋ (chehn)

櫬 10B.70 134
襯 63C.70 1040
趁 11.83 193

齔 21S.70 340
讖 60A.71 862

ㄔㄥ **CHENG** (cheng)

樘 10B.11 117
蟶 22D.11 413
撐 10A.00 44
琤 31A.00 481
噌 40A.41 590
瞠 41B.11 667
稱 90A.42 1181
(称)

ㄔㄥˊ (cherng)

成 71.71 1051
城 11A.71 205
誠 60A.71 862
丞 32.30 538
承 32.00 536
呈 40.11 569
裎 63C.11 1036
程 90A.11 1177
橙 10B.30 122
澄 63A.30 979
澂 63A.82 1019
懲 91.72 1222
棖 10B.02 113
乘 90.01 1147
塖 11A.11 197
塍 42A.11 707

ㄔㄥˇ (cheeng)

逞 40.83 575
騁 51B.50 765

ㄔㄥˋ (chehng)

秤 90A.10 1177

ㄑㄧ **CHI** (chi)

妻 10.93 42
棲 10B.93 143
郪 10S.22 160
萋 20A.93 293
悽 22A.93 401
淒 63A.93 1024
欺 20S.81 302
僛 91A.81 1273
七 10.70 31
柒 63.01 951
戚 71.71 1053
慽 22A.71 398
嘁 40A.71 599
慼 71·72 1054
桼 10.02 13
漆 63A.02 966
栖 10B.41 126
攲 12S.82 237
沏 63A.50 997

ㄑㄧˊ (chir)

歧 21S.82 344
岐 21B.82 333
蚑 22D.82 421
跂 40B.82 616
圻 11A.22 198
蘄 20A.22 261
旂 60S.22 873
祈 63B.22 1029
頎 90S.80 1197
其 20.80 243
棋 10B.80 137
(棊)(碁)
綦 20.01 238
萁 20A.80 287
期 20S.42 299
蜞 22D.80 420
琪 31A.80 490
騏 51B.80 766
旗 60S.80 882
麒 61S.80 913
淇 63A.80 1013
祺 63B.80 1034
奇 12.00 215
崎 21B.00 330
琦 31A.00 481
騎 51B.00 761
錡 81A.00 1102
芪 20A.71 286
祇 63B.71 1033
衹 63C.71 1041
耆 11.41 177
鰭 92C.41 1380
齊 60.22 816
懠 22A.22 389
蠐 22D.22 414
臍 42A.22 708

ㄑㄧˇ (chii)

杞 10B.70 134
起 11.83 191
芑 20A.70 281
玘 31A.70 489
棨 63.01 951
綮 63.01 952
啓 63D.40 1043
啟 63S.82 1046
(啓)
豈 21.30 312
(岂)
祁 63B.22 1029
乞 92.70 1346
綺 93B.00 1419

ㄑㄧㄣˊ (chirn)
秦 12.01 217
螓 22D.01 411
勤 20S.50 300
懃 20.72 243
禽 81.42 1094
擒 10A.42 81
檎 10B.42 130
噙 40A.42 593
芩 20A.32 265
琴 31.32 461
捦 10A.30 70
芹 20A.22 262
琹 31.01 443
ㄑㄧㄣˇ (chiin)
寑 62.82 937
ㄑㄧㄣˋ (chihn)
沁 63A.72 1013
搇 10A.02 52
撳 10A.81 96
唚 40A.82 604
ㄑㄧㄥ **CHING** (ching)
青 10.42 28
蜻 22D.42 416
圊 41.41 635
清 63A.42 990
鯖 92C.42 1380
頃 21S.80 341
傾 91A.80 1271
輕 10D.30 150
氫 92.70 1350
卿 90S.22 1192
ㄑㄧㄥˊ (chirng)
黥 41S.01 686
剠 60S.00 869
勍 60S.50 876
情 22A.42 393
晴 41A.42 660
擎 20.00 237
檠 20.01 238
ㄑㄧㄥˇ (chiing)
請 60A.42 851
廎 61.80 899
ㄑㄧㄥˋ (chihng)
罄 11.21 174
磬 11.40 176
謦 11.40 176
慶 61.82 900
ㄑㄧㄡ **CHIOU** (chiou)
丘 90.30 1152
坵 11A.30 199
蚯 22D.30 415
邱 90S.22 1190
秋 90A.81 1184
(龝)(秌)
萩 20A.81 288
鞦 20B.81 296
鶖 90.50 1159
鰍 92C.81 1381
鞧 20B.41 295
緧 93B.41 1433
ㄑㄧㄡˊ (chiour)
囚 41.41 640
泅 63A.41 988
求 10.02 12
裘 10.02 14
逑 10.83 41
球 31A.02 482
賕 41C.02 674
毬 90.70 1162
俅 91A.02 1240
觩 92B.02 1375
絿 93B.02 1422
酋 80.41 1067
蝤 22D.41 416
遒 80.83 1077
虯 22D.22 414
(虬)
璆 31A.91 491
頄 91S.80 1329
ㄑㄧㄡˇ (chioou)
糗 22C.81 410
ㄔㄡ **CHOU** (chou)
抽 10A.41 76
搐 10A.41 78
搊 10A.50 84
瘳 61A.91 912
ㄔㄡˊ (chour)
惆 22A.42 395
稠 90A.42 1181
綢 93B.42 1434
躊 40B.00 606
疇 41S.00 685
儔 91A.00 1232
籌 92A.00 1357
圳 11A.22 198
酬 31C.22 505
(酧)
愁 90.72 1164
儵 91A.63 1265
仇 91A.70 1267
讎 91S.11 1320
(讐)
紬 93B.41 1432
ㄔㄡˇ (choou)
醜 31C.70 508
瞅 41B.81 672
丑 50.30 729
ㄔㄡˋ (chouh)
臭 91.81 1223
ㄔㄨ **CHU** (chu)
出 21.21 307
齣 21S.50 338
初 63C.50 1039
ㄔㄨˊ (chur)
蜍 22D.01 412
除 32A.01 549
芻 92.50 1340
雛 92S.11 1384
耡 10S.50 162
鉏 81A.30 1110
鋤 81A.50 1117
厨 51A.00 754
廚 61.00 887
櫥 10B.00 110
躕 40B.00 607
躇 40B.41 611
儲 91A.41 1257
ㄔㄨˇ (chuu)
楮 10B.41 125
褚 63C.41 1037
楚 10.83 39
礎 31B.83 501
杵 10B.10 115
ㄔㄨˋ (chuh)
畜 60.41 820
搐 10A.41 78
黜 41S.21 687
絀 93B.21 1425
矗 10.30 23
處 21A.83 328
(処)
怵 22A.01 383
亍 30.00 429
俶 91A.82 1276
觸 92B.50 1377
ㄔㄨㄞ **CHUAI** (chuai)
搋 10A.70 90
ㄔㄨㄞˊ (chuair)
膗 42A.11 707
ㄔㄨㄞˇ (chuaai)
揣 10A.42 79
ㄔㄨㄞˋ (chuaih)
嘬 40A.82 604
膪 42A.40 710
ㄔㄨㄢ **CHUAN** (chuan)
穿 62A.00 941
川 22.22 361
ㄔㄨㄢˊ (chuarn)
椽 10B.02 114
遄 21.83 316
傳 91A.00 1231
船 91S.40 1324
ㄔㄨㄢˇ (chuaan)
喘 40A.42 592
舛 92S.10 1384
ㄔㄨㄢˋ (chuahn)
串 22.22 358
釧 81A.22 1109
ㄔㄨㄤ **CHUANG** (chuang)
窗 62A.41 945
(窓)

窻 62A.72 948
牕 91S.72 1329
瘡 61A.40 906

ㄔㄨㄤˊ (chuarng)

牀 21S.01 335
(床)
幢 22B.11 403

ㄔㄨㄤˇ (chuaang)

闖 52B.00 797

ㄔㄨㄤˋ (chuahng)

愴 22A.40 391
創 80S.00 1134
刱 80S.50 1081

ㄔㄨㄟ **CHUEI** (chuei)

吹 40A.81 602
(龡)
炊 91D.81 1316

ㄔㄨㄟˊ (chueir)

垂 90.11 1149
(埀)
捶 10A.11 57
棰 10B.11 117
陲 32A.11 552
錘 81A.11 1108
箠 92A.11 1362
搥 10A.83 106
槌 10B.83 142
鎚 81A.83 1126

ㄔㄨㄣ **CHUN** (chun)

春 12.41 221
(旾)
椿 10B.41 125

ㄔㄨㄣˊ (churn)

純 93B.70 1438
蒓 20A.70 285
醇 31C.00 503
(醕)
鶉 60S.50 876
淳 63A.00 960
(湻)
蓴 20A.00 246
脣 51A.42 759
(唇)

ㄔㄨㄣˇ (chuun)

惷 12.72 226
蠢 12.93 234

ㄔㄨㄥ **CHUNG** (chung)

忡 22A.22 389
沖 63A.22 976
舂 12.21 219
摏 10A.21 59
憧 22A.11 388
充 60.70 826
衝 91B.00 1287

ㄔㄨㄥˊ (churng)

崇 21.01 305
蟲 22.93 382

ㄔㄨㄥˇ (chuung)

寵 62.70 932

ㄔㄨㄥˋ (chuhng)

銃 81A.70 1119

ㄔㄨㄛ **CHUO** (chuo)

戳 50S.71 741

ㄔㄨㄛˋ (chuoh)

輟 10D.82 155
惙 22A.82 400
醊 31C.82 508
啜 40A.82 603
婥 93A.10 1405
綽 93B.10 1423
齪 21S.83 345
辵 91.83 1227

ㄔ **CHY** (chy)

蚩 21.93 316
嗤 40A.93 605
媸 93A.93 1419
欷 82S.22 1139
絺 93B.22 1426
摛 10A.42 80
螭 22D.42 417
魑 91.70 1220
吃 40A.70 597
喫 40A.81 601
眵 41B.32 668
痴 61A.40 906
癡 61A.83 911
鴟 90S.50 1195
笞 92A.40 1367

ㄔˊ (chyr)

馳 51B.70 765
池 63A.70 1005
墀 11A.10 196
遲 52A.83 787
持 10A.00 43
坻 11A.71 206
踟 40B.40 611
匙 41.83 654
篪 92A.70 1371

ㄔˇ (chyy)

齒 21A.21 318
恥 31S.30 522
豉 30S.82 440
耻 31S.72 527
尺 52A.83 787
褫 63C.70 1040
侈 91A.32 1253

ㄔˋ (chyh)

勅 10S.50 163
飭 81B.50 1130
翅 10.83 39
翄 10.83 39
敕 10S.82 168
赤 11.00 170
叱 40A.70 596
眙 41B.40 669
啻 60.40 819
懘 63.72 956
斥 90.22 1152
彳 91.22 1205
傺 91A.01 1240
熾 91D.71 1315

ㄑㄩ **CHYU** (chyu)

呿 40A.93 605
胠 42A.93 722
袪 63B.93 1034
祛 63C.93 1043
區 51.21 746
嶇 21B.21 330
驅 51B.21 762
(駈)
軀 91S.21 1320
屈 52A.21 782
詘 60A.21 845
趍 11.83 194
趨 11.83 194
曲 22.41 368
蛆 22D.30 415
瞿 41.11 627

ㄑㄩˊ (chyur)

蕖 20A.01 250
渠 63.01 951
佢 91A.21 1246
朐 42A.50 714
劬 92S.50 1389
鴝 92S.50 1390
蘧 20A.83 291
璩 31A.02 482
籧 92A.83 1374
鸜 41S.50 689
氍 41S.70 690
臞 42A.11 708
癯 61A.11 904
衢 91B.00 1286
麴 10S.50 163
(麯)
蛐 22D.41 415

ㄑㄩˇ (chyuu)

取 31S.82 529
娶 31.93 481
齲 21S.42 338

ㄑㄩˋ (chyuh)

趣 11.83 189
去 11.93 194
覷 21S.70 340
闃 52B.00 800

ㄑㄩㄢ **CHYUAN** (chyuan)

棬 10B.70 133
圈 41.41 635
悛 22A.82 401

ㄑㄩㄢˊ (chyuarn)

全 81.11 1085
輇 10D.11 150

荃 20A.11 259
醛 31C.11 504
詮 60A.11 844
痊 61A.11 904
銓 81A.11 1108
筌 92A.11 1362
惓 22A.70 396
蜷 22D.70 418
踡 40B.70 614
鬈 51.70 752
權(权) 10B.11 116
顴 20S.80 302
拳 12.00 216
泉 91.02 1201

ㄑㄩㄢˇ (chyuaan)
犬 12.81 226
畎 41S.81 691
綣 93B.70 1438

ㄑㄩㄢˋ (chyuahn)
券 12.50 224
勸(劝) 12S.50 300

ㄑㄩㄝ **CHYUE** (chyue)
缺 92S.81 1390
闕 52B.00 800

ㄑㄩㄝˊ (chyuer)
瘸 61A.42 907

ㄑㄩㄝˋ (chyueh)
怯 22A.93 402
恪(愙) 22A.40 392
卻(却) 80S.22 1080

埆 11A.42 201
确 31B.42 497
雀 22.11 355
殼(壳) 11S.82 212
慤 11.72 186
搉 10A.11 57
榷 10B.11 118
確 31B.11 494
鵲 20S.50 301
闋 52B.00 793
礐 90.40 1154

ㄑㄩㄣ **CHYUN** (chyun)
逡 93.83 1399

ㄑㄩㄣˊ (chyurn)
羣(群) 52.10 772
宭 62.40 926
裙 63C.40 1037

ㄑㄩㄥ **CHYUNG** (chyung)
芎 20A.50 277
穹 62A.50 946

ㄑㄩㄥˊ (chyurng)
邛 31S.22 520
笻 92A.22 1364
跫 31.83 479
蛩 31.93 481
藭 20A.50 278
窮 62A.50 946
惸 22A.00 383
瓊 31A.82 491
煢 91.70 1218
嬛 93A.02 1405

ㄑㄩㄥˇ (chyuung)
熲 21S.80 342

ㄉ D

ㄉㄚ **DA** (da)
搭 10A.40 70
褡 63C.40 1037
耷 12.10 218

ㄉㄚˊ (dar)
怛 22A.30 390
笪 92A.30 1365
達 11.83 186
答(荅)([illegible]) 92A.40 1367

ㄉㄚˇ (daa)
打 10A.00 44

ㄉㄚˋ (dah)
大 12.81 226

ㄉㄚ ('da)
瘩 61A.40 905
繨 93B.83 1446
吋 40A.00 576

ㄉㄞ **DAI**

ㄉㄞˇ (daai)
歹 31.32 461

ㄉㄞˋ (daih)
代 91A.71 1268
玳(瑇) 31A.71 489
袋 91.02 1202
岱 91.21 1204
黛 91.63 1218
貸 91.80 1223
殆 31S.40 522
怠 93.72 1396
迨 93.83 1399
紿 93B.40 1431
戴 11.71 184
帶 22.22 360
逮 22.83 379
待 91B.00 1282

ㄉㄢ **DAN** (dan)
單 40.10 568
殫 31S.10 520
簞 92A.10 1361
擔(担) 10A.40 74
儋 91A.40 1256
酖 31C.70 508
耽 31S.70 525
眈 41B.70 671
聃 31S.42 522
丹 42.42 694

ㄉㄢˇ (daan)
撢 10A.10 53
撣 10A.10 53
膽(胆) 42A.40 710
疸 61A.30 905

ㄉㄢˋ (dahn)
旦 41.30 629
鉭 81A.30 1110
但 91A.30 1252
啖(啗) 40A.81 602
淡 63A.81 1017
氮 92.70 1351
憚 22A.10 385
彈 50A.10 735
癉 61A.10 903
萏 20A.21 260
蛋 32.93 546
噉 40A.82 603
誕 60A.83 867
擔 10A.41 74
澹 63A.40 985

ㄉㄤ **DANG** (dang)
當(当) 22.41 366
璫 31A.41 486
噹 40A.41 590
襠 63C.41 1038
鐺 81A.41 1113
簹 92A.41 1368

ㄉㄤˇ (daang)
黨 22.63 370
攩 10A.63 84
讜 60A.63 857

ㄉㄤˋ (dahng)
蕩 20A.50 278
碭 31B.50 497
盪 63.30 954
擋(挡) 10A.41 77
檔 10B.41 126
宕 62.40 924

ㄉㄠ **DAU** (dau)
刀 50.50 730
忉 22A.50 396

ㄉㄠˊ (daur)
捯 10A.00 44

ㄉㄠˇ (daau)
島(㠀) 91.50 1216
搗 10A.50 83
擣 10A.00 44

檮 63B.00 1026
(梼)
倒 91A.00 1234
ㄉㄠˋ (dauh)
道 80.83 1076
導 80.00 1059
蹈 40B.21 609
稻 90A.21 1178
纛 10.01 12
悼 22A.10 385
幬 22B.00 402
到 31S.00 518
盜 63.30 954
ㄉㄜ **DE** (de)
嘚 40A.00 578
ㄉㄜˊ (der)
得 91B.00 1286
鍀 81A.00 1103
德 91B.72 1291
ㄉㄥ **DENG** (deng)
登 32.30 539
燈 91D.30 1311
(灯)
ㄉㄥˇ (deeng)
等 92A.00 1357
(䒭)
ㄉㄥˋ (dehng)
嶝 21B.30 330
磴 31B.30 495
凳 32.70 541
(櫈)
鄧 32S.22 564
蹬 40B.30 610
瞪 41B.30 668
鐙 81A.30 1110

ㄉㄧ **DI** (di)
羝 80S.71 1082
低 91A.71 1269
滴 63A.42 997
ㄉㄧˊ (dir)
迪 22.83 378
笛 92A.41 1368
狄 91C.81 1306
荻 20A.81 289
⿰口狄 40A.81 602
敵 60S.82 885
鏑 81A.42 1116
嫡 93A.42 1412
覿 11S.70 210
滌 63A.01 966
糴 81S.11 1135
ㄉㄧˇ (dii)
抵 10A.71 92
柢 10B.71 136
牴 10C.71 147
砥 31B.71 499
骶 42B.71 725
詆 60A.71 862
底 61.71 897
邸 90S.22 1190
觝 92B.71 1377
ㄉㄧˋ (dih)
弟 80.22 1062
睇 41B.22 668
第 92A.22 1364
(苐)
娣 93A.22 1408
帝 60.22 816
蒂 20A.22 262
諦 60A.22 846

鍗 81A.22 1109
(碲)
締 93B.22 1426
棣 10B.02 113
杕 10B.81 138
地 11A.70 203
踶 40B.83 617
遞 90.83 1173
的 91S.50 1326
ㄉㄧㄢ **DIAN** (dian)
顛 10S.80 166
巔 21.80 315
癲 61A.80 910
掂 10A.40 73
敁 21S.82 344
滇 63A.80 1013
ㄉㄧㄢˇ (diaan)
典 22.80 374
碘 31B.80 499
點 41S.40 687
(点)
ㄉㄧㄢˋ (diahn)
鈿 81A.41 1113
佃 91A.41 1257
甸 92.50 1340
惦 22A.40 391
玷 31A.40 486
阽 32A.40 554
店 61.40 893
痁 61A.40 905
殿 52S.82 803
癜 61A.82 911
澱 63A.82 1020
靛 10S.83 168
淀 63A.83 1022

墊 11.11 173
電 31D.70 515
奠 80.81 1073
簟 92A.10 1361
ㄉㄧㄠ **DIAU** (diau)
刁 50.50 730
叼 40A.50 594
琱 31A.42 487
碉 31B.42 497
雕 42S.11 726
鵰 42S.50 727
彫 42S.91 727
凋 63A.42 995
鯛 92C.42 1380
貂 91S.40 1324
(鼦)
ㄉㄧㄠˇ (diaau)
屌 52A.22 783
ㄉㄧㄠˋ (diauh)
掉 10A.10 52
弔 50.22 728
(吊)
窵 62A.50 947
釣 81A.50 1117
ㄉㄧㄝ **DIE** (die)
爹 80.32 1065
ㄉㄧㄝˊ (dier)
堞 11A.01 196
蝶 22D.01 411
(蜨)
碟 31B.01 492
喋 40A.01 579
蹀 40B.01 607
諜 60A.01 840
牒 91S.01 1318

鰈 92C.01 1378
迭 12.83 234
跌 40B.81 616
耋 11.11 174
垤 11A.11 197
絰 93B.11 1424
疊 41.30 629
(叠)
ㄉㄧㄥ **DING** (ding)
丁 31.00 440
靪 20B.00 294
玎 31A.00 481
叮 40A.00 576
疔 61A.00 902
釘 81A.00 1102
仃 91A.00 1233
ㄉㄧㄥˇ (diing) 503
酊 31C.00 527
頂 31S.80 629
鼎 41.22
ㄉㄧㄥˋ (dihng)
定 62.83 938
碇 31B.83 502
腚 42A.83 722
錠 81A.83 1125
訂 60A.00 838
ㄉㄧㄡ **DIOU** (diou)
丟 90.93 1174
銩 81A.93 1126
ㄉㄡ **DOU** (dou)
兜 90.70 1163
篼 92A.70 1371
唗 40A.83 604
ㄉㄡˇ (doou)
斗 63.10 953

抖	10A.10	52
蚪	22D.10	412
陡	32A.83	560
ㄉㄡˋ	(douh)	
豆	30.30	435
荳	20A.30	264
逗	30.83	436
痘	61A.30	905
餖	81B.30	1128
鬥	52B.00	797
鬭	52B.00	794
(鬦)(鬪)		
竇	62A.80	948
ㄉㄨ	**DU** (du)	
都	11S.22	209
嘟	40A.22	584
督	21A.41	325
ㄉㄨˊ	(dur)	
櫝	10B.80	137
犢	10C.80	147
殰	31S.80	527
黷	41S.80	690
匵	51.21	745
讀	60A.80	864
瀆	63A.80	1013
瀆	63A.80	1013
牘	91S.80	1329
髑	42B.50	725
獨	91C.50	1303
(独)		
毒	10.50	30
碡	31B.50	497
ㄉㄨˇ	(duu)	
堵	11A.41	200
覩	11S.70	210
(睹)		
賭	41C.41	675
篤	92A.50	1370
ㄉㄨˋ	(duh)	
杜	10B.11	115
肚	42A.11	707
度	61.82	899
渡	63A.82	1020
鍍	81A.82	1125
蠹	10.93	43
(蠧)		
妒	93A.91	1419
(妬)		
ㄉㄨㄢ	**DUAN** (duan)	
端	60S.42	875
ㄉㄨㄢˇ	(duaan)	
短	92S.30	1387
ㄉㄨㄢˋ	(duahn)	
段	90S.82	1197
鍛	81A.82	1125
煅	91D.82	1316
緞	93B.82	1445
斷	21S.22	336
(断)		
ㄉㄨㄟ	**DUEI** (duei)	
堆	11A.11	197
ㄉㄨㄟˋ	(dueih)	
對	22S.00	422
(对)		
懟	22.70	374
憝	60.72	829
譈	60A.82	867
碓	31B.11	494
隊	32A.02	551
兌	80.70	1070
ㄉㄨㄣ	**DUN** (dun)	
墩	11A.82	207
惇	22A.00	383
敦	60S.82	885
蹲	40B.00	607
ㄉㄨㄣˇ	(duun)	
躉	20A.83	292
盹	41B.70	670
ㄉㄨㄣˋ	(duhn)	
頓	10S.80	166
噸	40A.80	600
囤	41.41	634
沌	63A.70	1004
鈍	81A.70	1118
遯	42.83	704
遁	90.83	1173
燉	91D.82	1316
ㄉㄨㄥ	**DUNG** (dung)	
冬	92.63	1342
鼕	11.63	179
咚	40A.63	596
氡	92.70	1351
東	10.01	8
ㄉㄨㄥˇ	(duung)	
董	20A.11	259
懂	22A.11	387
ㄉㄨㄥˋ	(duhng)	
胴	42A.42	712
洞	63A.42	995
棟	10B.01	111
凍	63A.01	963
動	90S.50	1194
ㄉㄨㄛ	**DUO** (duo)	
多	92.32	1335
哆	40A.32	587
ㄉㄨㄛˊ	(duor)	
掇	10A.82	100
剟	32S.00	563
敠	32S.82	566
裰	63C.82	1042
奪	12.00	216
鐸	81A.10	1106
ㄉㄨㄛˇ	(duoo)	
朵	32.01	536
垛	11A.01	196
躲	91S.01	1318
埵	11A.11	197
ㄉㄨㄛˋ	(duoh)	
柁	10B.70	134
舵	91S.70	1328
剁	32S.00	563
跺	40B.01	607
惰	22A.42	394
墮	32.11	538
柮	10B.21	118
咄	40A.21	583
飿	81B.21	1128
踱	40B.82	617
ㄜ	E	
ㄜ	**E** (e)	
阿	32A.00	547
屙	52A.00	780
疴	61A.00	902
痾	61A.00	902
婀	93A.00	1403
ㄜˊ	(er)	
吪	40A.70	597
囮	41.41	642
訛	60A.70	860
莪	20A.71	286
峨	21B.71	332
(峩)		
蛾	22D.71	420
哦	40A.71	599
鵞	90.50	1159
鵝	90S.50	1195
(䳘)		
俄	91A.71	1269
娥	93A.71	1416
譌	60A.50	856
額	62S.80	950
ㄜˋ	(eh)	
厄	51A.70	759
扼	10A.70	88
軛	10D.70	154
阨	32A.70	557
呃	40A.70	597
蕚	20A.50	276
愕	22A.50	395
鄂	40S.22	619
鶚	40S.50	620
顎	40S.80	621
腭	42A.50	714
(噩)		
諤	60A.50	855
鍔	81A.50	1116
鰐	92C.50	1381
齶	21S.50	338
堊	31.11	450
惡	31.72	472
噩	31.30	461
鱷	92C.30	1380
搕	10A.30	70
遏	41.83	653
閼	52B.00	799

餓 81B.71 1131
匋 92.50 1340

ㄝ È

ㄝ **È**

ㄝˊ (er)
鋨 81A.71 1121

ㄝˋ (eh)
砨 31B.70 498
誒 60A.81 865

ㄟ **EI**

ㄟˇ (eei)
吪 40A.70 596

ㄟˋ (eih)
欸 93S.81 1450

ㄦ **EL**

ㄦˊ (erl)
而 31.42 466
洏 63A.42 994
兒 90.70 1160

ㄦˇ (eel)
耳 31.10 446
珥 31A.10 483
洱 63A.10 970
鉺 81A.10 1106
餌 81B.10 1127
爾 31.42 468
(尒)
邇 31.83 479
(迩)

ㄦˋ (ehl)
二 30.30 431
弍 71.71 1048
貳 71.71 1050
則 31S.00 518
鮞 91S.10 1319

ㄣ **EN** (en)
恩 41.72 648

ㄣˋ (ehn)
摁 10A.72 93

ㄈ F

ㄈㄚ **FA** (fa)
發 32.82 543
(发)
伐 91A.72 1269

ㄈㄚˊ (far)
砝 31B.93 502
法 63A.93 1025
(灋)
閥 52B.00 800
筏 92A.71 1372
罰 41D.00 679
乏 90.83 1170

ㄈㄚˇ (faa)
髮 51.82 753
鈁 81A.50 1117
鍅 81A.93 1126
(法)

ㄈㄚˋ (fah)
珐 31A.93 492

ㄈㄢ **FAN** (fan)
番 90.41 1157
幡 22B.41 404
旛 60S.41 875
翻 90S.50 1193
(飜)
繙 93B.41 1433

ㄈㄢˊ (farn)
凡 42.70 698
(凢)
帆 22B.70 404
釩 81A.70 1119
墦 11A.41 201
蕃 20A.41 273
藩 20A.41 272
蹯 40B.41 612
膰 42A.41 711
燔 91D.41 1312
礬 10.40 27
樊 10.81 37
煩 91D.80 1315
繁 92.01 1332

ㄈㄢˇ (faan)
反 90.82 1167
返 90.83 1171

ㄈㄢˋ (fahn)
販 41C.82 678
飯 81B.82 1132
(飰)
梵 10.70 34
汎 63A.70 1007
范 20A.70 282
氾 63A.70 1007
犯 91C.70 1304
範 92A.70 1370
泛 63A.83 1022

ㄈㄤ **FANG** (fang)
方 60.50 823
枋 10B.50 131
坊 11A.50 202
芳 20A.50 277
鈁 81A.50 1117

ㄈㄤˊ (farng)
防 32A.50 556
肪 42A.50 714
房 63D.50 1044
魴 92C.50 1381
妨 93A.50 1414

ㄈㄤˇ (faang)
昉 41A.50 661
髣 51.50 751
訪 60A.50 856
仿 91A.50 1263
倣 91A.82 1279
舫 91S.50 1326
紡 93B.50 1436

ㄈㄤˋ (fahng)
放 60S.82 883

ㄈㄟ **FEI** (fei)
非 22.22 361
霏 31D.22 511
啡 40A.22 584
騑 51B.22 763
扉 63D.22 1043
緋 93B.22 1426
飛 32.70 541
妃 93A.70 1415

ㄈㄟˊ (feir)
肥 42A.70 716
蜰 42.93 704
淝 63A.70 1007
腓 42A.22 708

ㄈㄟˇ (feei)
榧 10B.21 118
菲 20A.22 261
翡 22.50 370
斐 22.82 377
蜚 22.93 382
悱 22A.22 389
匪 51.21 746
誹 60A.22 846
篚 92A.21 1363
朏 42A.21 708

ㄈㄟˋ (feih)
費 22.80 375
疿 61A.22 904
沸 63A.22 977
鐨 81A.80 1123
狒 91C.22 1300
芾 20A.22 262
肺 42A.22 708
廢 61.82 900
(废)
癈 61A.82 911
吠 40A.82 601
痱 61A.22 904

ㄈㄣ **FEN** (fen)
分 80.50 1067
棻 20A.01 251
芬 20A.50 278
雰 31D.50 514
吩 40A.50 595
氛 92.70 1351
紛 93B.50 1436

ㄈㄣˊ (fern)
棼 10.50 30
枌 10B.50 132
蚡 22D.50 417
汾 63A.50 1000
鼢 90.70 1163
墳 11A.80 206
蕡 20A.80 287
焚 10.81 38

ㄈㄣˇ (feen)
粉 22C.50 409

ㄈㄣˋ (fehn)
忿 80.72 1071
份 91A.50 1263
憤 22A.80 398
僨 91A.80 1270
奮 12.41 222
糞 22.80 375
ㄈㄥ **FENG** (feng)
丰 10.10 16
峯 21.10 306
(峰)
蜂 22D.10 413
鋒 81A.10 1107
烽 91D.10 1309
蠭 92.93 1356
風 42.70 699
(凨)
楓 10B.70 134
瘋 61A.70 908
封 11S.00 208
葑 20A.00 246
豐 21.30 312
酆 21S.22 336
灃 63A.30 979
ㄈㄥˊ (ferng)
逢 92.83 1355
縫 93B.83 1447
馮 63A.50 999
ㄈㄥˇ (feeng)
唪 40A.10 581
ㄈㄥˋ (fehng)
奉 12.10 217
俸 91A.10 1242
賵 41C.41 676
鳳 42.70 699
(风)
諷 60A.70 858
ㄈㄛ **FO**
ㄈㄛˊ (for)
佛 91A.22 1248
ㄈㄡ **FOU**
ㄈㄡˊ (four)
芣 20A.22 261
ㄈㄡˇ (foou)
缶 92.21 1335
缹 92.63 1342
否 31.40 461
ㄈㄨ **FU** (fu)
夫 12.81 229
麩 10.83 42
麸 10S.81 166
趺 40B.81 616
鈇 81A.81 1123
伕 91A.81 1272
跗 40B.00 607
胕 42A.00 705
枹 10B.70 135
敷 10S.82 168
膚 21A.42 326
鄜 61S.22 913
孵 90S.00 1188
ㄈㄨˊ (fur)
扶 10A.81 95
芙 20A.81 287
蚨 22D.81 420
苻 20A.00 248
符 92A.00 1359
孚 90.00 1144
桴 10B.00 111
莩 20A.00 248
蜉 22D.00 411
罘 41D.00 680
浮 63A.00 961
郛 90S.22 1190
俘 91A.00 1237
弗 22.22 362
拂 10A.22 62
茀 20A.22 261
怫 22A.22 389
艴 22S.70 426
髴 51.22 748
彿 91B.22 1289
氟 92.70 1350
紼 93B.22 1426
(綍)
茯 20A.81 289
洑 63A.81 1017
袱 63C.81 1041
伏 91A.81 1272
服 42A.82 720
菔 20A.82 290
黻 22S.82 427
祓 63B.82 1034
紱 93B.82 1444
輻 10D.41 152
葍 20A.41 271
幅 22B.41 403
蝠 22D.41 416
福 63B.41 1031
匐 92.50 1340
罘 41D.22 681
涪 63A.40 983
鳧 91.70 1219
縛 93B.00 1419
ㄈㄨˇ (fuu)
拊 10A.00 48
腑 42A.00 705
府 61.00 887
腐 61.42 894
俯 91A.00 1236
斧 80.22 1062
釜 80.30 1064
甫 10.42 28
輔 10D.42 152
黼 22S.42 425
脯 42A.42 712
撫 10A.63 85
俛 91A.70 1268
ㄈㄨˋ (fuh)
付 91A.00 1231
坿 11A.00 196
附 32A.00 548
咐 40A.00 578
駙 51B.00 761
鮒 92C.00 1378
赴 11.83 189
訃 60A.22 846
副 30S.00 437
富 62.41 927
賻 41C.00 673
傅 91A.00 1231
蝮 22D.82 421
覆 31.82 477
腹 42A.82 721
複 63C.82 1042
馥 90S.82 1198
復 91B.82 1294
鰒 92C.82 1382
賦 41C.71 677
負 50.80 733
(負)
父 80.80 1074
阜 91.10 1203
婦 93A.22 1407
(媍)
ㄍ G
ㄍㄚ **GA** (ga)
嘎 40A.71 599
旮 91.41 1213
ㄍㄚˊ (gar)
噶 40A.50 593
釓 81A.70 1119
ㄍㄚˇ (gaa)
玍 92.11 1335
ㄍㄚˇㄇ (gaam)
咁 40A.41 590
ㄍㄚˋ (gah)
尬 12.70 225
ㄍㄞ **GAI** (gai)
垓 11A.81 207
賅 41C.81 678
該 60A.81 864
ㄍㄞˇ (gaai)
改 52S.82 803
ㄍㄞˋ (gaih)
概 10B.70 135
(槩)
溉 63A.10 1010
丐 31.50 469
(匄)
鈣 81A.50 1116
蓋 20A.30 263
(盖)
戤 32S.71 566

ㄍㄢ **GAN** (gan)
干 31.10 444
杆 10B.10 114
玕 31A.10 483
肝 42A.10 706
竿 92A.10 1361
甘 20.41 240
柑 10B.41 125
坩 11A.41 200
泔 63A.41 986
疳 61A.41 906
乾 10S.70 164
尷 12.70 225
ㄍㄢˇ (gaan)
桿 10B.10 114
趕 11.83 190
稈 90A.10 1177
敢 31S.82 532
橄 10B.82 141
擀 10A.10 52
感 71.71 1053
ㄍㄢˋ (gahn)
榦 10S.01 158
幹 10S.10 159
贛 60S.80 882
灨 63A.80 1014
淦 63A.30 981
紺 93B.41 1432
ㄍㄤ **GANG** (gang)
扛 10A.30 67
杠 10B.30 121
肛 42A.30 709
疘 61A.30 905
缸 92S.30 1387
岡 42.42 698
崗 21.42 313
剛 42S.00 726
鋼 81A.42 1115
綱 93B.42 1434
罡 41D.30 681
ㄍㄤˇ (gaang)
港 63A.70 1005
ㄍㄤˋ (gahng)
槓 10B.80 138
ㄍㄠ **GAU** (gau)
羔 80.63 1069
糕 22C.63 410
(餻)
高 60.42 821
膏 60.42 820
篙 92A.42 1369
櫜 10.01 10
皋 91.10 1203
睪 41D.10 680
(睾)
ㄍㄠˇ (gaau)
搞 10A.42 80
槁 10B.42 130
槀 60.01 806
鎬 81A.42 1116
稿 90A.42 1181
(藁)
縞 93B.42 1435
ㄍㄠˋ (gauh)
告 10.40 26
誥 60A.40 848
鋯 81A.40 1111
ㄍㄜ **GE** (ge)
哥 31.00 442
歌 31S.81 529
(謌)
肐 42A.70 717
疙 61A.70 909
擱 10A.00 47
咯 40A.10 589
胳 42A.40 710
割 62S.00 949
戈 71.71 1048
鴿 81S.50 1136
ㄍㄜˊ (ger)
格 10B.40 124
茖 20A.40 269
骼 42B.40 724
閣 52B.00 800
蛤 22D.40 415
閤 52B.00 800
翮 90S.00 1188
槅 10B.42 129
隔 32A.42 555
嗝 40A.42 592
膈 42A.42 712
鎘 81A.42 1115
革 20.10 238
葛 20A.50 276
ㄍㄜˇ (gee)
舸 91S.00 1318
ㄍㄜˋ (geh)
各 92.40 1338
硌 31B.40 496
鉻 81A.40 1112
虼 22D.70 419
個 91A.41 1257
(个)
箇 92A.41 1368
ㄍㄣ **GEN** (gen)
根 10B.02 113
跟 40B.02 608
ㄍㄣˊ (gern)
哏 40A.02 580
ㄍㄣˋ (gehn)
艮 52.02 772
茛 20A.02 254
亙 31.30 458
ㄍㄥ **GENG** (geng)
庚 61.80 899
賡 61.80 899
鶊 61S.50 913
耕 10S.20 159
更 31.82 476
羹 80.81 1074
秔 90A.70 1182
緪 93B.30 1427
ㄍㄥˇ (geeng)
梗 10B.82 141
埂 11A.82 207
哽 40A.82 603
骾 42B.82 725
鯁 92C.82 1382
綆 93B.82 1444
耿 31S.81 529
ㄍㄡ **GOU** (gou)
勾 92.50 1341
鉤 81A.50 1118
(鈎)
溝 63A.42 993
ㄍㄡˇ (goou)
枸 10B.50 132
耇 11.50 178
苟 20A.50 279
狗 91C.50 1303
笱 92A.50 1370
ㄍㄡˋ (gouh)
垢 11A.40 200
詬 60A.40 850
搆 10A.42 79
構 10B.42 128
遘 20.83 377
覯 20S.70 301
購 41C.42 676
媾 93A.42 1412
彀 11S.82 212
夠 92S.50 1390
(够)
ㄍㄨ **GU** (gu)
辜 10.10 18
鴣 10S.50 163
菇 20A.40 269
蛄 22D.40 415
酤 31C.40 506
咕 40A.40 587
沽 63A.40 982
鈷 81A.40 1111
估 91A.40 1253
姑 93A.40 1409
菰 20A.83 291
孤 32S.83 567
呱 40A.83 605
觚 92B.83 1377
箍 92A.21 1363
ㄍㄨˇ (guu)
古 10.40 25
盬 10.30 24
牯 10C.40 146
嘏 10S.82 167

罟 41D.40 682
盬 51.30 749
詁 60A.40 848
鼓 11S.82 212
瞽 11.41 177
臌 42A.82 720
穀 11S.82 212
轂 11S.82 212
股 42A.82 720
羖 80S.82 1083
蠱 22.30 364
骨 42.42 694
汩 63A.41 988
谷 80.40 1065

ㄍㄨˋ (guh)

固 41.41 634
痼 61A.41 906
錮 81A.41 1114
雇 63D.11 1043
顧 63S.80 1046
僱 91A.11 1245
梏 10B.40 123
故 10S.82 167

ㄍㄨㄚ **GUA** (gua)

括 10A.40 74
栝 10B.40 124
聒 31S.40 522
颳 42.70 702
适 90.83 1173
刮 90S.00 1187
蝸 22D.42 417
瓜 90.83 1170

ㄍㄨㄚˇ (guaa)

剮 42S.00 726
寡 62.50 929

ㄍㄨㄚˋ (guah)

卦 11S.22 209
掛 10A.22 61
褂 63C.22 1036
罣 41D.11 680

ㄍㄨㄞ **GUAI** (guai)

乖 90.22 1152

ㄍㄨㄞˇ (guaai)

拐 10A.50 81
柺 10B.50 131

ㄍㄨㄞˋ (guaih)

怪 22A.11 387

ㄍㄨㄢ **GUAN** (guan)

官 62.40 924
棺 10B.40 124
倌 91A.41 1255
瘝 61A.02 903
鰥 92C.02 1378
觀 20S.70 301
關 52B.00 801
(関)
冠 62.70 931

ㄍㄨㄢˇ (guaan)

館 81B.40 1128
(舘)
管 92A.40 1366
脘 42A.70 716

ㄍㄨㄢˋ (guahn)

毌 41.41 633
摜 10A.80 94
慣 22A.80 399
貫 41.80 652
鸛 20S.50 301
灌 63A.11 972
鑵 81A.11 1107
罐 92S.11 1384
丱 22.22 361
丱 22.22 361
盥 90.30 1153

ㄍㄨㄤ **GUANG** (guang)

光 22.70 372
桄 10B.70 133
胱 42A.70 715
銧 81A.70 1118

ㄍㄨㄤˇ (guaang)

廣 61.80 898
獷 91C.80 1305

ㄍㄨㄤˋ (guahng)

逛 91.83 1230

ㄍㄨㄟ **GUEI** (guei)

圭 11.11 173
珪 31A.11 483
閨 52B.00 789
鮭 92C.11 1379
規 12S.70 236
瓌 31A.02 483
瑰 31A.70 489
歸 91S.22 1322
(帰)(逯)(归)
皈 91S.82 1330
龜 92.70 1349
嬀 93A.50 1414

ㄍㄨㄟˇ (gueei)

垝 11A.70 205
詭 60A.70 860
姽 93A.70 1415
軌 10D.70 154
匭 51.21 745
宄 62.70 933
癸 32.81 542
晷 41.40 630
鬼 91.70 1219
簋 92A.30 1365

ㄍㄨㄟˋ (gueih)

貴 22.80 375
櫃 10B.21 118
瞶 41B.80 671
桂 10B.11 115
劌 21S.00 334
跪 40B.70 615

ㄍㄨㄣ **GUN**

ㄍㄨㄣˇ (guun)

衮 60.02 809
滾 63A.02 968
鯀 92C.01 1378
緄 93B.70 1438

ㄍㄨㄣˋ (guhn)

棍 10B.70 134

ㄍㄨㄥ **GUNG** (gung)

工 31.30 456
功 31S.50 523
攻 31S.82 530
公 80.93 1077
蚣 22D.93 422
弓 50.50 731
躬 91S.50 1325
恭 20.02 238
龔 60.80 830
供 91A.80 1270
肱 42A.93 722
宮 62.40 925
觥 92B.70 1377

ㄍㄨㄥˇ (guung)

汞 31.02 443
鞏 31.10 446
拱 10A.80 93

ㄍㄨㄥˋ (guhng)

共 20.80 243
貢 31.80 473

ㄍㄨㄛ **GUO** (guo)

蟈 22D.41 416
嘓 40A.41 590
郭 60S.22 873
鍋 81A.42 1115

ㄍㄨㄛˊ (guor)

國 41.41 638
摑 10A.41 77
幗 22B.41 404
馘 80S.71 1082
虢 90S.70 1196

ㄍㄨㄛˇ (guoo)

果 41.01 622
菓 20A.01 250
蜾 22D.01 412
裹 60.02 809
餜 81B.01 1126
椁 10B.22 119

ㄍㄨㄛˋ (guoh)

過 42.83 702

ㄏ H

ㄏㄚ **HA** (ha)

哈 40A.40 588

ㄏㄞ **HAI** (hai)

咍 40A.40 589
嗨 40A.50 594

ㄏㄞˊ (hair)

孩 32S.81 566
骸 42B.81 725
頦 60S.80 881

ㄏㄞˇ (haai)
醢 31C.30 505
海 63A.50 1000
ㄏㄞˋ (haih)
亥 60.81 830
駭 51B.81 766
氦 92.70 1351
害 62.40 923
嗐 40A.40 588
ㄏㄢ **HAN** (han)
頇 31S.80 528
鼾 91S.10 1319
蚶 22D.41 415
酣 31C.41 506
憨 31.72 473
唅 40A.40 589
ㄏㄢˊ (harn)
函 31.21 451
(圅)
涵 63A.21 975
韓 10S.10 159
邯 20S.22 299
邗 31S.22 520
寒 62.63 930
含 81.40 1090
ㄏㄢˇ (haan)
蔊 20A.10 257
喊 40A.71 599
罕 62.10 921
ㄏㄢˋ (hahn)
扞 10A.10 53
閈 52B.00 790
汗 63A.10 970
旱 41.10 625
捍 10A.10 53
悍 22A.10 386
銲 81A.10 1106
暵 41A.81 663
漢 63A.81 1015
熯 91D.81 1315
翰 10S.50 162
瀚 63A.50 997
琀 31A.40 486
頷 81S.80 1137
撼 10A.72 93
憾 22A.72 398
菡 20A.21 260
ㄏㄤ **HANG** (hang)
夯 12.50 224
ㄏㄤˊ (harng)
杭 10B.70 134
吭 40A.70 597
頏 60S.80 881
沆 63A.70 1008
航 91S.70 1327
ㄏㄠ **HAU** (hau)
蒿 20A.42 275
嚆 40A.42 592
薅 20A.00 249
ㄏㄠˊ (haur)
豪 60.02 806
壕 11A.02 196
蠔 22D.02 412
嚎 40A.02 580
濠 63A.02 968
嗥 40A.10 581
毫 60.70 826
ㄏㄠˇ (haau)
郝 11S.22 209
好 93A.00 1402
ㄏㄠˋ (hauh)
号 40.50 572
號 40S.70 620
浩 63A.40 982
皓 91S.40 1323
顥 41S.80 690
灝 63A.80 1014
耗 10S.70 164
昊 41.81 652
皞 91S.10 1319
ㄏㄜ **HE** (he)
呵 40A.00 576
訶 60A.00 838
喝 40A.50 593
ㄏㄜˊ (her)
禾 90.01 1146
和 90A.40 1179
龢 81S.01 1134
荷 20A.00 248
河 63A.00 959
何 91A.00 1233
合 81.40 1089
盒 81.30 1089
鉿 81A.40 1112
核 10B.81 139
閡 52B.00 798
劾 60S.50 876
齕 21S.70 340
紇 93B.70 1441
曷 41.50 644
鞨 20B.50 295
褐 63C.50 1039
盇 11.30 174
闔 52B.00 789
覈 31.82 477
礉 31B.82 501
盍 12.30 220
翮 30S.50 438
涸 63A.41 988
貉 91S.40 1324
ㄏㄜˋ (heh)
赫 11S.00 208
嚇 40A.00 576
賀 91.80 1222
鶴 91S.50 1327
ㄏㄟ **HEI** (hei)
黑 41.63 644
ㄏㄣ **HEN**
ㄏㄣˊ (hern)
痕 61A.02 903
ㄏㄣˇ (heen)
很 91B.02 1288
狠 91C.02 1298
ㄏㄣˋ (hehn)
恨 22A.02 384
ㄏㄥ **HENG** (heng)
亨 60.00 804
哼 40A.00 577
ㄏㄥˊ (herng)
桁 10B.00 111
蘅 20A.00 249
珩 31A.00 481
衡 91B.00 1288
橫 10B.80 137
恆 22A.30 390
ㄏㄥˋ (hehng)
絎 93B.00 1420
ㄏㄇ **HM** (hm)
噷 40A.81 601
ㄏㄫ **HNG** (hng)
哼 40A.00 577
ㄏㄡ **HOU** (hou)
齁 91S.50 1327
ㄏㄡˊ (hour)
侯 91A.81 1273
(矦)
喉 40A.81 602
瘊 61A.81 910
餱 81B.81 1132
猴 91C.81 1306
篌 92A.81 1374
ㄏㄡˇ (hoou)
吼 40A.70 596
ㄏㄡˋ (houh)
后 90.40 1153
逅 90.83 1173
候 91A.81 1273
堠 11A.81 207
厚 51A.00 755
鱟 90.63 1160
後 91B.82 1294
ㄏㄨ **HU** (hu)
乎 90.00 1143
虖 21A.00 317
呼 40A.00 577
嘑 40A.00 576
忽 92.72 1351
惚 22A.72 398
唿 40A.72 599
欻 91S.81 1329
ㄏㄨˊ (hur)
胡 10S.42 160
鶘 10S.50 162
葫 20A.42 273

嘒 40A.30 585
篲 92A.30 1365
恵 10.72 34
蕙 20A.72 286
蟪 22D.72 420
會 81.41 1091
薈 20A.41 272
燴 91D.41 1312
(烩)
繪 93B.41 1433
(絵)
闠 52B.00 790
繢 93B.80 1444
卉 10.20 22
恚 11.72 186
頮 22S.80 427
喙 40A.02 580
賄 41C.42 676
匯 51.21 747
(滙)
諱 60A.10 842
穢 90A.71 1183
彙 92.01 1331
(彚)(彙)

ㄏㄨㄣ **HUN** (hun)
昏 90.41 1154
(昬)
惛 22A.41 393
閽 52B.00 800
婚 93A.41 1412
葷 20A.10 257

ㄏㄨㄣˊ (hurn)
魂 30S.70 438
(䰟)
渾 63A.10 971
餛 81B.70 1130

ㄏㄨㄣˋ (huhn)
圂 41.41 636
溷 63A.41 988
慁 41.72 649
(㥵)
諢 60A.10 843
混 63A.70 1006

ㄏㄨㄥ **HUNG** (hung)
哄 40A.80 600
烘 91D.80 1315
訇 92.50 1341
輷 10D.50 153
轟 10.10 18
薨 20A.70 281
吽 40A.10 580

ㄏㄨㄥˊ (hurng)
紅 93B.30 1427
葒 20A.30 265
虹 22D.30 414
訌 60A.30 847
鴻 63A.50 998
弘 50A.93 738
泓 63A.93 1025
翃 12S.50 236
閎 52B.00 789
竑 60S.93 886
宏 62.93 939
紘 93B.93 1447
洪 63A.80 1013
黌 90.80 1167

ㄏㄨㄥˋ (huhng)
蕻 20A.80 287
閧 52B.00 790
(鬨)

ㄏㄨㄛ **HUO** (huo)
劐 20S.00 298
豁 62S.40 950

ㄏㄨㄛˊ (huor)
活 63A.40 984

ㄏㄨㄛˇ (huoo)
火 91.81 1224
鈥 81A.81 1124
伙 91A.81 1274
夥 41S.32 687

ㄏㄨㄛˋ (huoh)
或 71.71 1049
惑 71.72 1054
砉 10.40 27
剨 10S.00 158
騞 51B.40 763
湱 63A.40 982
霍 31D.11 510
攉 10A.11 56
藿 20A.11 258
矐 41B.11 668
濩 63A.82 1018
穫 90A.82 1185
獲 91C.82 1306
蠖 22D.82 421
嚄 40A.82 603
臒 42S.82 727
鑊 81A.82 1124
矱 92S.82 1391
壑 21A.11 318
禍 63B.42 1032
貨 91.80 1222

ㄓ ㄐ J

ㄓㄚ **JA** (ja)
揸 10A.30 66
楂 10B.30 121
渣 63A.30 978
扎 10A.70 86
樝 10B.30 121
奓 12.32 221
皻 21S.82 344

ㄓㄚˊ (jar)
紮 10.01 12
紥 10.01 12
札 10B.70 133
剳 20S.00 297
劄 92S.00 1383
閘 52B.00 795
鍘 81A.00 1103
煠 91D.01 1308
牐 91S.21 1320

ㄓㄚˇ (jaa)
眨 41B.83 672
鮓 92C.22 1380

ㄓㄚˋ (jah)
乍 92.22 1335
蚱 22D.22 414
砟 31B.22 495
咋 40A.22 585
詐 60A.22 847
痄 61A.22 905
炸 91D.22 1310
蛇 22D.70 419
吒 40A.70 597
咤 40A.70 597
蜡 22D.41 415
䄍 63B.41 1031
搾 10A.22 64
榨 10B.22 120
醡 31C.22 505
柵 10B.42 130

ㄓㄞ **JAI** (jai)
齋 60.22 817
(斎)

ㄓㄞˊ (jair)
翟 50.11 728
宅 62.70 932

ㄓㄞˇ (jaai)
窄 62A.22 943

ㄓㄞˋ (jaih)
瘵 61A.01 902
寨 62.01 916
債 91A.80 1270

ㄓㄢ **JAN** (jan)
占 21A.40 324
覘 21S.70 340
霑 31D.40 512
呫 40A.40 588
沾 63A.40 982
栴 10B.42 130
旃 60S.42 875
旜 60S.30 874
鸇 60S.50 876
氈 60S.70 881
(氊)
饘 81B.30 1128
鱣 92C.30 1380
詹 92.40 1338
瞻 41B.40 669
譫 60A.40 850

ㄓㄢˇ (jaan)
展 52A.02 781
搌 10A.02 51
輾 10D.02 149
蹍 40B.02 608

Character	Code	Page
琖	31A.71	489
盞	71.30	1048
斬	10D.22	150
嶄	21.22	312
(嶃)		
颭	42.70	701
皻	60S.82	883
ㄓㄢˋ (jahn)		
棧	10B.71	136
戰	40S.71	620
(战)		
站	60S.40	874
佔	91A.40	1254
暫	10.41	27
蘸	20A.63	279
顫	60S.80	881
湛	63A.21	975
綻	93B.83	1446
ㄓㄤ **JANG** (jang)		
粻	22C.02	405
張	50A.02	734
餦	81B.02	1127
章	60.10	810
樟	10B.10	115
璋	31A.10	483
彰	60S.91	886
麞	61.10	889
漳	63A.10	971
獐	91C.10	1299
ㄓㄤˇ (jaang)		
掌	22.00	345
ㄓㄤˋ (jahng)		
丈	12.82	233
杖	10B.82	140
仗	91A.82	1275
帳	22B.02	402
賬	41C.02	674
脹	42A.02	706
漲	63A.02	967
嶂	21B.10	330
幛	22B.10	402
障	32A.10	551
瘴	61A.10	903
ㄓㄠ **JAU** (jau)		
招	10A.40	71
昭	41A.40	659
朝	10S.42	161
嘲	40A.42	591
釗	81A.00	1102
ㄓㄠˇ (jaau)		
找	10A.71	92
沼	63A.40	983
爪	90.83	1170
ㄓㄠˋ (jauh)		
召	50.40	729
照	41.63	645
詔	60A.40	849
炤	91D.40	1311
兆	22.70	371
旐	60S.70	880
櫂	10B.11	117
趙	11.83	189
罩	41D.10	680
肇	63.10	953
笊	92A.83	1374
ㄓㄜ **JE** (je)		
螫	11.93	195
遮	61.83	901
ㄓㄜˊ (jer)		
折	10A.22	65
哲	10.40	26
蜇	10.93	43
輒	10D.70	154
(輙)		
鮿	92C.70	1381
摺	10A.41	77
慴	22A.41	392
褶	63C.41	1038
摘	10A.42	80
謫	60A.42	854
讁	60A.83	867
喆	11S.40	209
懾	22A.10	385
磔	31B.01	492
ㄓㄜˇ (jee)		
者	11.41	176
赭	11S.41	210
鍺	81A.41	1112
ㄓㄜˋ (jeh)		
蔗	20A.63	280
嗻	40A.63	596
鷓	61S.50	913
柘	10B.40	123
這	60.83	834
宅	62.70	932
浙	63A.22	976
ㄓㄣ **JEN** (jen)		
珍	31A.91	491
(珎)		
胗	42A.91	722
貞	21A.80	327
楨	10B.80	138
遉	21A.83	329
湞	63A.80	1014
禎	63B.80	1034
偵	91A.80	1271
真	10.80	35
眞	21.80	315
禛	63B.80	1033
榛	10B.01	112
蓁	20A.01	249
臻	31S.01	520
溱	63A.01	964
獉	91C.01	1298
椹	10B.21	118
斟	20S.10	298
碪	31B.21	494
瑊	31A.71	489
鍼	81A.71	1121
箴	92A.71	1372
砧	31B.40	496
甄	31S.70	524
針	81A.10	1106
ㄓㄣˇ (jeen)		
畛	10D.91	156
眕	41S.91	692
診	60A.91	868
疹	61A.91	912
袗	63C.91	1042
紾	93B.91	1447
鬒	51.80	753
稹	90A.80	1184
縝	93B.80	1444
枕	10B.70	135
ㄓㄣˋ (jehn)		
振	10A.02	51
震	31D.02	510
賑	41C.02	674
朕	42A.81	719
揕	10A.21	59
陣	32A.10	551
鎮	81A.80	1122
鴆	91S.50	1326
ㄓㄥ **JENG** (jeng)		
怔	22A.30	390
鉦	81A.30	1110
佂	91A.30	1252
征	91B.30	1290
爭	90.00	1143
(争)		
掙	10A.00	48
崢	21B.00	330
睜	41B.00	665
鬇	51.00	742
諍	60A.00	839
錚	81A.00	1103
猙	91C.00	1298
箏	92A.00	1359
烝	32.63	540
蒸	20A.63	280
徵	91B.82	1292
癥	61A.82	911
ㄓㄥˇ (jeeng)		
整	10.30	24
拯	10A.30	67
ㄓㄥˋ (jehng)		
正	31.30	458
政	31S.82	531
証	60A.30	847
症	61A.30	905
幀	22B.80	404
鄭	80S.22	1080
證	60A.30	847
ㄐㄧ **JI** (ji)		
肌	42A.70	715

飢 81B.70 1130
基 20.11 238
朞 20.42 241
箕 92A.80 1372
犄 10C.00 145
剞 12S.00 235
羇 41D.00 679
(覉)
羈 41D.50 682
(覊)
畸 41S.00 685
觭 92B.00 1375
幾 93.71 1396
機 10B.71 136
璣 31A.71 489
磯 31B.71 499
嘰 40A.71 599
譏 60A.71 862
禨 63B.71 1033
饑 81B.71 1131
畿 93.71 1396
虀 20A.30 264
隮 32A.22 553
躋 40B.22 610
齎 60.22 817
(賫)
齏 60.22 817
勣 10S.50 163
蹟 40B.80 616
積 90A.80 1183
績 93B.80 1443
嵇 90A.21 1178
稽 90A.41 1180
乩 21S.70 340
咭 40A.40 588
屐 52A.82 786
迹 60.83 834
跡 40B.00 607
激 63A.82 1021
雞 90S.11 1190
(鸡)(鷄)
笄 92A.20 1362
姬 93A.21 1407
ㄐㄧˊ (jir)
及 32.82 542
圾 11A.82 207
芨 20A.82 290
岌 21.82 316
汲 63A.82 1019
笈 92A.82 1374
級 93B.82 1445
亟 32.30 538
極 10B.30 121
殛 31S.30 522
卽 91S.22 1321
(即)
唧 40A.22 585
瘠 61A.42 907
鶺 91S.50 1327
疾 61A.81 910
蒺 20A.81 288
嫉 93A.81 1417
楫 10B.10 114
輯 10D.10 150
蕺 20A.71 285
戢 40S.71 620
擊 10.00 4
棘 10S.01 158
吉 11.40 175
寂 62.82 936
集 91.01 1200
急 92.72 1352
籍 92A.41 1368
ㄐㄧˇ (jii)
几 42.70 698
麂 61.70 896
掎 10A.00 44
踦 40B.00 606
幾 93.71 1396
蟣 22D.71 420
擠 10A.22 64
戟 10S.71 165
己 52.70 775
庋 61.82 899
泲 63A.22 977
脊 91.42 1214
給 93B.40 1431
ㄐㄧˋ (jih)
旣 91S.70 1327
(既)
暨 91.30 1207
技 10A.82 98
伎 91A.82 1274
妓 93A.82 1417
跽 40B.72 615
忌 50.72 732
記 60A.70 858
紀 93B.70 1439
季 90.00 1144
悸 22A.00 383
祭 92.01 1331
際 32A.01 550
漈 63A.01 966
薺 20A.22 262
霽 31D.22 511
劑 60S.00 869
濟 63A.22 978
鱭 92C.22 1379
冀 22.80 374
驥 51B.80 766
薊 20A.00 249
覬 21S.70 340
罽 41D.00 679
髻 51.40 749
計 60A.10 842
寄 62.00 914
洎 63A.41 990
稷 90A.82 1185
鯽 92C.22 1379
繼 93B.21 1425
ㄐㄧㄚ **JIA** (jia)
加 91S.40 1323
枷 10B.40 124
嘉 11.40 176
跏 40B.40 611
痂 61A.40 906
袈 91.02 1202
迦 91.83 1227
笳 92A.40 1367
家 62.02 918
鎵 81A.02 1105
傢 91A.02 1241
葭 20A.82 290
豭 31S.82 530
佳 91A.11 1243
ㄐㄧㄚˊ (jiar)
夾 12.81 231
頰 12S.80 237
莢 20A.81 288
蛺 22D.81 421
浹 63A.81 1015
裌 63C.81 1041
鋏 81A.81 1123
恝 10.72 34
戛 31.71 472
袷 63C.40 1037
ㄐㄧㄚˇ (jiaa)
瘕 61A.82 911
假 91A.82 1278
甲 41.22 628
岬 21B.22 330
胛 42A.22 708
鉀 81A.22 1109
賈 31.80 473
斝 40.10 568
(斚)
ㄐㄧㄚˋ (jiah)
架 91.01 1199
駕 91.50 1216
稼 90A.02 1176
嫁 93A.02 1405
價 91A.80 1271
ㄐㄧㄢ **JIAN** (jian)
戔 71.71 1050
殘 91S.71 1329
箋 92A.71 1372
鬋 51.00 742
湔 63A.00 961
煎 80.63 1069
兼 80.22 1062
(兼)
搛 10A.22 64
蒹 20A.22 262
鶼 80S.50 1081
鰜 92C.22 1379

羯 80S.50 1081
偈 91A.50 1262
絜 10.01 12
潔 63A.01 963
杰 10.63 30
截 11.71 185
劫 11S.50 210
(刦)
孑 32.00 534
訐 60A.10 842

ㄐㄧㄝˇ (jiee)
解 92B.10 1376
姊 93A.22 1407
姐 93A.30 1408

ㄐㄧㄝˋ (jieh)
介 81.22 1086
芥 20A.22 262
蚧 22D.22 414
界 41.22 628
疥 61A.22 904
价 91A.22 1248
戒 71.71 1049
誡 60A.71 862
藉 20A.41 270
借 91A.41 1256
屆 52A.21 782
(届)
廨 61.10 889
(廨)
褯 63C.22 1036

ㄐㄧㄣ **JIN** (jin)
今 81.32 1089
矜 32S.32 564
衿 63C.32 1037
筋 92A.50 1369
觔 92B.50 1377
巾 22.22 356
津 63A.10 969
襟 63C.01 1035
金 81.30 1087
斤 90.22 1151

ㄐㄧㄣˇ (jiin)
堇 20.11 239
菫 20A.11 258
槿 10B.11 116
覲 20S.70 301
瑾 31A.11 484
殣 31S.11 520
謹 60A.11 844
廑 61.11 889
(厪)
饉 81B.11 1127
僅 91A.11 1244
卺 32.70 541
緊 51.01 742
錦 81A.22 1109
儘 91A.30 1251
(侭)

ㄐㄧㄣˋ (jihn)
晉 31.41 464
搢 10A.41 77
縉 93B.41 1432
盡 22.30 363
(尽)
藎 20A.30 264
贐 41C.30 674
(賮)
燼 91D.30 1310
(烬)
浸 63A.82 1020
寢 62.82 937
禁 10.01 10
噤 40A.01 579
靳 20B.22 295
近 90.83 1172
進 91.83 1228
妗 93A.32 1408

ㄐㄧㄥ **JING** (jing)
京 60.01 805
鯨 92C.01 1378
菁 20A.42 273
精 22C.42 408
睛 41B.42 669
莖 20A.30 264
涇 63A.30 979
經 93B.30 1428
(経)
兢 10S.70 164
驚 20.50 241
荊 20S.00 297
晶 41.41 631
旌 60S.11 871

ㄐㄧㄥˇ (jiing)
井 20.20 239
阱 32A.20 553
穽 62A.20 942
剄 31S.00 519
頸 31S.80 528
景 41.01 623
憬 22A.01 384
璟 31A.01 482
警 20.40 240
儆 91A.82 1276

ㄐㄧㄥˋ (jihng)
逕 31.83 478
勁 31S.50 524
踁 40B.30 610
脛 42A.30 709
痙 61A.30 905
徑 91B.30 1290
靚 10S.70 164
靖 60S.42 875
清 63A.42 992
竟 60.70 827
境 11A.70 205
鏡 81A.70 1119
獍 91C.70 1304
靜 10S.00 158
淨 63A.00 962
敬 20S.82 304
競 60S.70 880

ㄐㄧㄡ **JIOU** (jiou)
揪 10A.81 97
湫 63A.81 1016
轇 10D.91 156
鬮 51S.00 801
(䦰)
鳩 91S.50 1326
糾 93B.22 1425
糺 93B.70 1438

ㄐㄧㄡˇ (jioou)
久 92.81 1353
玖 31A.81 490
灸 92.81 1354
赳 11.83 189
韭 22.30 362
(韮)
酒 63A.41 987
九 91.70 1218

ㄐㄧㄡˋ (jiouh)
臼 90.21 1151
桕 10B.21 119
舊 20A.21 260
(旧)
舅 90.50 1158
柩 10B.21 118
疚 61A.81 910
捄 10A.02 51
救 10S.82 168
就 60S.70 877
鷲 60.50 825
僦 91A.70 1267
廄 61.70 897
(廏)
究 62A.70 948
咎 92.40 1338

ㄓㄡ **JOU** (jou)
州 22.22 361
洲 63A.22 977
舟 91.42 1214
輈 10D.42 153
侜 91A.42 1262
周 42.42 697
啁 40A.42 593
賙 41C.42 676
週 42.83 702
盩 11.30 175
譸 60A.00 838

ㄓㄡˇ (joou)
帚 50.22 729
箒 92A.22 1364
肘 42A.00 704

ㄓㄡˋ (jouh)
咒 40.70 573

呪 40A.70 596
胄 22.42 369
宙 62.41 927
酎 31C.00 503
紂 93B.00 1419
僽 91A.50 1264
皺 92S.82 1391
縐 93B.50 1437
晝(昼) 22.30 362
噣 40A.50 594
甃 90.70 1160
籀 92A.41 1367

ㄓㄨ **JU** (ju)
朱 10.01 5
株 10B.01 111
茱 20A.01 249
蛛 22D.01 411
珠 31A.01 481
硃 31B.01 492
誅 60A.01 840
洙 63A.01 963
銖 81A.01 1103
侏 91A.01 1238
諸 60A.41 850
櫧 10B.41 128
藷 20A.41 272
櫫 31.01 443
豬 31S.41 522
瀦 63A.41 988
猪 91C.41 1301

ㄓㄨˊ (jur)
竹 92S.00 1383
竺 92A.30 1365
軸 10D.41 152
舳 91S.41 1325
妯 93A.41 1411
蓫 20A.83 291
逐 31.83 478
瘃 61A.02 903
筑 92A.70 1371
築 92A.01 1360
蠋 22D.50 417
躅 40B.50 613
燭(烛) 91D.50 1313
朮 10.01 4

ㄓㄨˇ (juu)
主 60.11 812
拄 10A.11 56
麈 61.11 890
煮 11.63 178
渚 63A.41 986
囑(嘱) 40A.50 594
矚 41B.50 670
貯 41C.00 673

ㄓㄨˋ (juh)
苧 20A.00 248
竚 60S.00 869
佇 91A.00 1236
紵 93B.00 1420
助 41S.50 688
筯 92A.50 1370
柱 10B.11 117
蛀 22D.11 413
駐 51B.11 762
註 60A.11 844
注 63A.11 973
住 91A.11 1244
炷 91D.11 1310
翥 11.50 178
著 20A.41 270
箸 92A.41 1368
柷 10B.70 133
祝 63B.70 1032
杼 10B.00 110
粥 50A.50 737
鑄 81A.00 1102

ㄓㄨㄚ **JUA** (jua)
抓 10A.83 105
撾 10A.83 105

ㄓㄨㄞ **JUAI**

ㄓㄨㄞˇ (juaai)
跩 40B.71 615

ㄓㄨㄞˋ (juaih)
拽 10A.71 92

ㄓㄨㄢ **JUAN** (juan)
專 10.00 2
甎 10S.70 164
磚 31B.00 492
膞 42A.00 705
耑 21.42 313
顓 21S.80 342

ㄓㄨㄢˇ (juaan)
轉 10D.00 148
囀 40A.00 576

ㄓㄨㄢˋ (juahn)
撰 10A.80 94
譔 60A.80 864
饌 81B.80 1132
籑 92A.02 1360
篹 92A.70 1371
賺 41C.22 674
篆 92A.02 1360

ㄓㄨㄤ **JUANG** (juang)
庄 61.11 889
粧 22C.11 406
莊 20A.11 258
裝 21.02 305
樁 10B.21 118
妝 21S.93 345
粧 22C.93 411

ㄓㄨㄤˋ (juahng)
壯(壮) 21S.11 335
狀 21S.81 342
撞 10A.11 56
戇 60.72 829

ㄓㄨㄟ **JUEI** (juei)
隹 91A.11 1245
椎 10B.11 117
騅 51B.11 762
錐 81A.11 1108
追 91.83 1227

ㄓㄨㄟˋ (jueih)
贅 10.80 36
惴 22A.42 394
墜 32.11 538
綴 93B.82 1445
縋 93B.83 1446

ㄓㄨㄣ **JUN** (jun)
迍 10.83 39
肫 42A.70 715
窀 62A.70 947
諄 60A.00 839
衠 91B.00 1283

ㄓㄨㄣˇ (juun)
準 63.10 953
准 63A.11 974
隼 91.10 1203

ㄓㄨㄥ **JUNG** (jung)
中 22.22 356
盅 22.30 363
忠 22.72 373
衷 60.02 808
螽 92.93 1356
終 93B.63 1437
忪 22A.93 402
鍾 81A.11 1108
鐘(鈡) 81A.11 1107

ㄓㄨㄥˇ (juung)
踵 40B.11 609
腫 42A.11 708
種(秐) 90A.11 1177
冢 62.02 919

ㄓㄨㄥˋ (juhng)
眾 41D.02 680
衆(乑) 91.02 1202
众 81.81 1101
重 90.11 1149
仲 91A.22 1247

ㄓㄨㄛ **JUO** (juo)
棹 10B.10 114
桌 21A.01 317
捉 10A.83 104
涿 63A.02 967

ㄓㄨㄛˊ (juor)
酌 31C.50 507
灼 91D.50 1313
卓 21A.10 318

趠	40B.10	608
倬	91A.10	1242
拙	10A.21	59
茁	20A.21	260
琢	31A.02	483
啄	40A.02	580
諑	60A.02	841
濁	63A.50	999
鐲	81A.50	1117
擢	10A.11	56
鸐	50S.50	740
濯	63A.11	973
斮	20S.22	299
棁	10B.70	134
斫	31B.22	495
着	80.41	1067
斲	90S.22	1192
(斵)		
ㄓ	**JY** (jy)	
之	63.83	957
芝	20A.83	292
支	10.82	38
枝	10B.82	140
鳷	10S.50	163
肢	42A.82	720
疷	61A.71	909
秖	90A.71	1183
卮	90.70	1160
梔	10B.70	134
知	92S.40	1388
蜘	22D.40	415
胝	42A.71	718
祗	63B.71	1033
搘	10A.41	75
脂	42A.41	711
汁	63A.10	969
隻	91.82	1226
織	93B.71	1441
ㄓˊ	(jyr)	
侄	91A.11	1244
姪	93A.11	1406
直	10.30	22
植	10B.30	121
埴	11A.30	198
殖	31S.30	521
値	91A.30	1251
執	11S.70	210
(执)		
縶	11.01	170
蟄	11.93	195
摯	10.93	43
摭	10A.63	84
蹠	40B.63	613
擲	10A.22	64
躑	40B.22	610
職	31S.71	525
跖	40B.40	610
質	90.80	1166
ㄓˇ	(jyy)	
止	21A.30	322
址	11A.30	199
芷	20A.30	263
阯	32A.30	554
趾	40B.30	610
沚	63A.30	979
祉	63B.30	1030
只	40.80	573
枳	10B.80	138
咫	52A.83	787
扺	10A.71	92
紙	93B.71	1442
(帋)		
旨	21A.41	324
指	10A.41	75
黹	22.42	370
ㄓˋ	(jyh)	
至	31.11	449
桎	10B.11	117
輊	10D.11	150
蛭	22D.11	413
郅	31S.22	520
致	31S.82	531
膣	42A.11	708
窒	62A.11	942
緻	93B.82	1445
志	11.72	150
誌	60A.72	863
痣	61A.72	909
制	10S.00	157
製	10.02	14
猘	91C.00	1297
峙	21B.00	330
痔	61A.00	902
稚	90A.11	1178
雉	92S.11	1384
摯	11.00	170
鷙	11.50	178
贄	11.80	186
疐	10.83	39
懥	22A.83	401
躓	40B.80	616
鑕	81A.80	1123
帙	22B.81	404
袠	60.02	809
秩	90A.81	1184
陟	32A.91	561
騭	32.50	540
忮	22A.82	400
幟	22B.71	404
置	41D.30	681
廌	61.50	894
寘	62.80	934
滯	63A.22	977
治	63A.40	985
豸	91.00	1199
穉	90A.10	1177
智	92.41	1338
彘	92.70	1349
炙	92.81	1354
觶	92B.10	1376
ㄐㄩ	**JYU** (jyu)	
趄	11.83	190
苴	20A.30	264
菹	20A.30	265
疽	61A.30	905
沮	63A.30	980
狙	91C.30	1301
雎	41S.11	687
居	52A.40	783
据	10A.40	73
裾	63C.40	1037
拘	10A.50	83
駒	51B.50	765
痀	61A.50	908
車	10.10	17
俱	91A.80	1272
ㄐㄩˊ	(jyur)	
局	52A.50	785
跼	42B.50	613
鋦	81A.50	1117
侷	91A.50	1263
掬	10A.50	84
椈	10B.50	132
菊	20A.50	279
鞠	20B.50	296
橘	10B.42	129
鞫	20B.50	296
ㄐㄩˇ	(jyuu)	
柜	10B.21	118
榘	92.01	1331
矩	92S.21	1385
莒	20A.40	267
筥	92A.40	1366
擧	90.00	1142
(舉)		
櫸	10B.10	115
蒟	20A.50	277
齟	21S.30	337
咀	40A.30	586
踽	40B.42	612
ㄐㄩˋ	(jyuh)	
巨	51.21	746
拒	10A.21	59
苣	20A.21	260
岠	21S.21	336
距	40B.21	609
詎	60A.21	845
鉅	81A.21	1108
炬	91D.21	1310
具	41.80	650
惧	22A.80	399
颶	42.70	702
踞	40B.40	610
鋸	81A.40	1111
倨	91A.40	1254

據 10A.02 51
(攄)
遽 21A.83 329
劇 21S.00 333
醵 31C.02 504
鐻 81A.02 1104
屨 52A.93 788
窶 62A.93 949
懼 22A.11 388
聚 31.02 444
句 92.50 1340
簴 92A.30 1365

ㄐㄩㄢ **JYUAN** (jyuan)
捐 10A.42 79
鵑 40S.50 620
涓 63A.42 995
娟 93A.42 1412
朘 42A.82 721
蠲 80S.50 1081
鐫 81A.42 1116

ㄐㄩㄢˇ (jyuaan)
捲 10A.70 86

ㄐㄩㄢˋ (jyuahn)
卷 12.70 225
倦 91A.70 1265
悁 22A.42 395
狷 91C.42 1302
絹 93B.42 1434
眷 12.41 222

ㄐㄩㄝ **JYUE** (jyue)
撅 10A.81 96
噘 40A.81 601
撧 10A.70 92

ㄐㄩㄝˊ (jyuer)
抉 10A.81 97
玦 31A.81 490
趹 40B.81 616
訣 60A.81 865
決 63A.81 1016
掘 10A.21 59
崛 21B.21 330
倔 91A.21 1247
厥 51A.81 760
橛 10B.81 139
蕨 20A.81 288
蹶 40B.81 616
劂 51S.00 768
獗 91C.81 1305
鱖 92C.81 1381
譎 60A.42 853
鐍 81A.42 1115
爵 90.00 1145
嚼 40A.00 578
爝 91D.00 1307
矍 41.82 653
攫 10A.82 101
玨 31A.11 484
孓 32.00 534
噱 40A.02 580
覺 90.70 1161
(覐)
絕 93B.70 1439

ㄐㄩㄣ **JYUN** (jyun)
均 11A.50 202
鈞 81A.50 1117
軍 62.10 920
皸 62S.82 950
君 52.40 773

ㄐㄩㄣˋ (jyuhn)
峻 21B.82 333
晙 41S.82 692
駿 51B.82 767
竣 60S.82 885
浚 63A.82 1022
餕 81B.82 1133
俊 91A.82 1279
捃 10A.40 73
郡 52S.22 803
菌 20A.41 272
箘 92A.41 1368
麕 61.41 893
攟 10A.41 78
雋 91.42 1214
寯 62.42 929
儁 91A.42 1262
濬 63A.41 986

ㄐㄩㄥ **JYUNG** (jyung)
埛 11A.42 201
駉 51B.42 764
扃 63D.42 1044

ㄐㄩㄥˇ (jyuung)
迥 42.83 702
(逈)
泂 63A.42 995
炯 91D.42 1312
絅 93B.42 1434
窘 62A.40 944

ㄎ K

ㄎㄚ **KA** (ka)
咖 40A.40 589

ㄎㄚˇ (kaa)
卡 21A.22 319
鉲 81A.22 1109
咯 40A.40 589

ㄎㄚˋ (kah)
喀 40A.40 588
髂 42B.40 724

ㄎㄞ **KAI** (kai)
開 52B.00 790
鐦 81A.00 1103
揩 10A.41 76

ㄎㄞˇ (kaai)
塏 11A.30 199
剴 21S.00 333
凱 21S.70 340
愷 22A.30 390
闓 52B.00 790
鎧 81A.30 1110
楷 10B.41 126
鍇 81A.41 1113
慨 22A.70 397
嘅 40A.70 597

ㄎㄞˋ (kaih)
愾 22A.70 398

ㄎㄢ **KAN** (kan)
堪 11A.21 198
戡 20S.71 302
嵁 21B.21 330
龕 81.70 1095
刊 90S.00 1187

ㄎㄢˇ (kaan)
坎 11A.81 207
砍 31B.81 500
轗 10D.72 154
壈 11A.72 206
埳 11A.21 198
侃 91A.70 1267

ㄎㄢˋ (kahn)
墈 11A.50 201
勘 20S.50 300
磡 31B.21 494
矙 41B.00 665
瞰 41B.82 672
闞 52B.00 793
看 90.41 1155
衎 91B.00 1285

ㄎㄤ **KANG** (kang)
康 61.02 889
慷 22A.02 385
糠 22C.02 405
穅 90A.02 1176
忼 22A.70 397

ㄎㄤˋ (kahng)
亢 60.70 826
抗 10A.70 89
匟 51.21 747
伉 91A.70 1267
犺 91C.70 1304
炕 91D.70 1314

ㄎㄠ **KAU** (kau)
尻 52A.70 786

ㄎㄠˇ (kaau)
考 11.50 177
(攷)
拷 10A.50 81
栲 10B.50 130
烤 91D.50 1313

ㄎㄠˋ (kauh)
靠 10.22 22
犒 10C.42 146
銬 81A.50 1116

ㄎㄜ **KE** (ke)
科 90A.10 1176
蝌 22D.10 413
柯 10B.00 110
軻 10D.00 148
苛 20A.00 246
珂 31A.00 481
鈳 81A.00 1103
棵 10B.01 112
顆 41S.80 690
髁 42B.01 723
窠 62A.01 942
稞 90A.01 1176
搕 10A.30 66
磕 31B.30 495
瞌 41B.30 668

ㄎㄜˊ (ker)
揢 10A.40 73
咳 40A.81 601
欬 60S.81 882

ㄎㄜˇ (kee)
可 31.00 441
坷 11A.00 195
渴 63A.50 998

ㄎㄜˋ (keh)
課 60A.01 840
錁 81A.01 1104
克 10.70 33
剋 10.70 33
氪 92.70 1349
客 62.40 926
恪 22A.40 392
榼 10B.30 121
嗑 40A.30 586
溘 63A.30 978
刻 60S.00 868
緙 93B.10 1423

ㄎㄣ **KEN**

ㄎㄣˇ (keen)
肯 21A.42 325
啃 40A.42 591
墾 91.11 1204
懇 91.72 1222

ㄎㄣˋ (kehn)
掯 10A.42 79
褃 63C.42 1038
裉 63C.02 1035

ㄎㄥ **KENG** (keng)
坑 11A.70 204
(阬)
鈧 81A.70 1119
牼 10C.30 146
硜 31B.30 495
鏗 81A.11 1107

ㄎㄡ **KOU** (kou)
摳 10A.21 59
瞘 41B.21 668
彄 50A.21 735

ㄎㄡˇ (koou)
口 40.40 569

ㄎㄡˋ (kouh)
扣 10A.40 71
叩 40A.22 584
釦 81A.40 1111
佝 91A.50 1263
敂 92S.82 1391
寇 62.70 932
蔻 20A.70 282
鷇 11S.82 213

ㄎㄨ **KU** (ku)
枯 10B.40 123
骷 42B.40 724
堀 11A.21 198
窟 62A.21 942
刳 12S.00 235
哭 40.81 574

ㄎㄨˇ (kuu)
苦 20A.40 265

ㄎㄨˋ (kuh)
庫 61.10 889
褲 63C.10 1036
酷 31C.40 506
嚳 90.40 1154
矻 31B.70 498
袴 63C.50 1039
(絝)

ㄎㄨㄚ **KUA** (kua)
夸 12.50 224
誇 60A.50 855
姱 93A.50 1413

ㄎㄨㄚˇ (kuaa)
垮 11A.50 201
咵 40A.50 593
侉 91A.50 1262

ㄎㄨㄚˋ (kuah)
跨 40B.50 612
胯 42A.50 713
骻 42B.50 724

ㄎㄨㄞ **KUAI** (kuai)
咼 42.42 698
喎 40A.42 593

ㄎㄨㄞˇ (kuaai)
擓 10A.21 59
蒯 20S.00 297

ㄎㄨㄞˋ (kuaih)
快 22A.81 400
筷 92A.81 1373
檜 10B.41 128
噲 40A.41 590
膾 42A.41 711
澮 63A.41 989
劊 81S.00 1134
鄶 81S.22 1135
儈 91A.41 1258
(侩)
獪 91C.41 1302
鱠 92C.41 1380
塊 11A.70 205
(块)

ㄎㄨㄢ **KUAN** (kuan)
寬 62.70 930

ㄎㄨㄢˇ (kuaan)
款 11S.81 211
(歀)(欵)
窾 62A.81 948

ㄎㄨㄤ **KUANG** (kuang)
匡 51.21 746
恇 22A.21 388
劻 51S.50 770
誆 60A.21 845
筐 92A.21 1363

ㄎㄨㄤˊ (kuarng)
狂 91C.11 1299
誑 60A.11 845

ㄎㄨㄤˋ (kuahng)
貺 41C.70 677
況 63A.70 1006
况 63A.70 1006
框 10B.21 118
眶 41B.21 668
壙 11A.80 206
礦 31B.80 499
曠 41A.80 663
(旷)
鄺 61S.22 913
鑛 81A.80 1123
纊 93B.80 1444
卝 22.22 361
絖 93B.70 1438

ㄎㄨㄟ **KUEI** (kuei)
闚 52B.00 790
窺 62A.70 947
刲 11S.00 209
盔 12.30 220
巋 21.22 312
虧 21S.50 338
(亏)

ㄎㄨㄟˊ (kueir)
揆 10A.81 96
葵 20A.81 288
暌 41A.81 664
睽 41B.81 671
逵 11.83 186
奎 12.11 219
夔 20A.82 290
馗 91.70 1219
魁 91S.70 1220

ㄎㄨㄟˇ (kueei)
跬 40B.11 609
傀 91A.70 1268

ㄎㄨㄟˋ (kueih)
愧 22A.70 397
(媿)

餽 81B.70 1130
蕢 20A.80 287
憒 22A.80 399
璝 31S.80 527
膭 41B.80 671
匱 51.21 745
潰 63A.80 1014
饋 81B.80 1132
簣 92A.80 1373
喟 40A.42 593

ㄎㄨㄣ **KUN** (kun)

昆 41.70 647
崑 21.70 314
(崐)
琨 31A.70 488
裩 63C.70 1040
焜 91D.70 1314
鯤 92C.70 1387
坤 11A.22 198
髡 51.70 752
堃 60.11 814
褌 63C.10 1036

ㄎㄨㄣˇ (kuun)

捆 10A.41 77
梱 10B.41 128
悃 22A.41 392
閫 52B.00 795
綑 93B.41 1433
壼 11.30 175

ㄎㄨㄣˋ (kuhn)

困 41.41 633
睏 41B.41 669

ㄎㄨㄥ **KUNG** (kung)

空 62A.30 943
崆 21B.30 331
悾 22A.30 391
涳 63A.30 981
倥 91A.30 1253
箜 92A.30 1365

ㄎㄨㄥˇ (kuung)

恐 31.72 472
孔 32S.70 565

ㄎㄨㄥˋ (kuhng)

控 10A.30 69

ㄎㄨㄛ **KUO**

ㄎㄨㄛˋ (kuoh)

擴 10A.80 94
(扩)
彍 50A.80 737
闊 52B.00 799
廓 61.22 891

ㄌ L

ㄌㄚ **LA** (la)

拉 10A.30 68
啦 40A.30 585

ㄌㄚˊ (lar)

旯 41.70 646
邋 93.83 1399

ㄌㄚˇ (laa)

喇 40A.00 576

ㄌㄚˋ (lah)

剌 10S.00 157
蝲 22D.00 411
鬎 51.00 742
辣 60S.01 870
瘌 61A.00 902
蠟 22D.70 419
臘 42A.70 717
鑞 81A.70 1120

ㄌㄞ **LAI**

ㄌㄞˊ (lair)

來 10.01 6
萊 20A.01 249
錸 81A.01 1104
倈 91A.01 1238

ㄌㄞˋ (laih)

賚 10.80 36
睞 41B.01 665
徠 91B.01 1288
賴 10S.80 166
癩 61A.80 909
瀨 63A.80 1013
籟 92A.80 1372

ㄌㄢ **LAN**

ㄌㄢˊ (larn)

闌 52B.00 789
攔 10A.00 47
欄 10B.00 110
蘭 20A.00 247
㘓 40A.00 577
斕 60S.00 869
讕 60A.00 839
瀾 63A.00 960
襴 63C.00 1034
鑭 81A.00 1103
藍 20A.30 264
襤 63C.30 1036
籃 92A.30 1365
婪 10.93 43
嵐 21.70 314

ㄌㄢˇ (laan)

覽 51.70 752
攬 10A.70 88
(擥)
欖 10B.70 134
懶 22A.80 398
嬾 93A.80 1416

ㄌㄢˋ (lahn)

爛 91D.00 1307
濫 63A.30 980
纜 93B.70 1440

ㄌㄤ **LANG** (lang)

啷 40A.22 585

ㄌㄤˊ (larng)

莨 20A.02 254
蜋 22D.02 412
琅 31A.02 483
硠 31B.02 493
踉 40B.02 608
鋃 81A.02 1105
稂 90A.02 1176
狼 91C.02 1298
郎 63S.22 1045
榔 10B.22 120
螂 22D.22 414
瑯 31A.22 486
廊 61.22 891

ㄌㄤˇ (laang)

閬 52B.00 799
朗 63S.42 1046
烺 91D.02 1309

ㄌㄤˋ (lahng)

浪 63A.02 968

ㄌㄠ **LAU**

ㄌㄠˊ (laur)

勞 91.50 1215
(劳)
撈 10A.50 84
嘮 40A.50 595
癆 61A.50 908
鐒 81A.50 1118
僗 91A.50 1263
醪 31C.91 509
牢 62.10 920

ㄌㄠˇ (laau)

老 11.70 180
栳 10B.70 132
銠 81A.70 1118

ㄌㄠˋ (lauh)

潦 63A.01 964
澇 63A.50 1000
嫪 93A.91 1419

ㄌㄜ **LE**

ㄌㄜˋ (leh)

勒 20B.50 295
肋 42A.50 714
泐 63A.50 998
仂 91A.50 1263
竻 92A.50 1370
扐 10A.00 47
埒 11A.00 195
垃 11A.30 199
樂 93.01 1392
(乐)

·ㄌㄜ ('le)

嘞 40A.50 593

ㄌㄟ **LEI**

ㄌㄟˊ (leir)

雷 31D.41 513
擂 10A.41 77
檑 10B.41 126
鐳 81A.41 1113
櫐 41.01 623
罍 41.21 628

縲	93B.01	1420
羸	60.70	828
ㄌㄟˇ (leei)		
耒	10.01	6
誄	60A.01	840
蕾	20A.41	271
累	41.01	622
壘	41.11	627
儡	91A.41	1257
磊	31.40	463
ㄌㄟˋ (leih)		
類	22S.80	427
纇	22S.80	427
礌	31B.41	496
酹	31C.00	503
淚	63A.81	1016
(泪)		
ㄌㄥ **LENG**		
ㄌㄥˊ (lerng)		
薐	20A.82	291
崚	21B.82	333
稜	90A.82	1185
楞	10B.50	131
ㄌㄥˇ (leeng)		
冷	63A.63	1002
ㄌㄥˋ (lehng)		
愣	22A.50	395
ㄌㄧ **LI** (li)		
哩	40A.11	582
ㄌㄧˊ (lir)		
蜊	22D.00	411
筣	92A.00	1359
藜	20A.02	254
棃	90.01	1146
黎	90.02	1148
犂	90.10	1148
黧	90.63	1159
璃	31A.42	487
(瓈)		
離	60S.11	872
(离)		
漓	63A.42	996
籬	92A.11	1362
(篱)		
縭	93B.42	1435
(褵)		
漦	10.02	13
犛	10.10	19
釐	10.11	21
㔏	10.50	30
氂	10.70	34
([illegible])		
嫠	10.93	43
鸝	30S.50	438
驪	51B.70	765
罹	41D.11	680
狸	91C.11	1300
(貍)		
ㄌㄧˇ (lii)		
里	41.11	625
理	31A.11	484
裏	60.02	809
(裡)		
鋰	81A.11	1107
俚	91A.11	1244
鯉	92C.11	1379
娌	93A.11	1406
醴	31C.30	505
澧	63A.30	979
禮	63B.30	1030
(礼)		
鱧	92C.30	1380
李	10.00	3
邐	30.83	436
蠡	92.93	1356
ㄌㄧˋ (lih)		
栵	10B.00	110
㾐	61A.00	902
例	91A.00	1234
利	90A.00	1175
莉	20A.00	248
悧	22A.00	383
鬁	51.00	742
痢	61A.00	902
俐	91A.00	1237
猁	91C.00	1298
莅	20A.30	265
涖	63A.30	982
戾	63D.81	1045
唳	40A.81	601
厲	51A.42	758
(厉)		
蠣	22D.42	417
糲	22C.42	409
礪	31B.42	497
勵	51S.50	770
癘	61A.42	906
麗	30.70	436
(丽)		
酈	30S.22	437
儷	91A.70	1266
立	60.30	817
粒	22C.30	407
笠	92A.30	1365
栗	31.01	442
慄	22A.01	384
凓	63A.01	964
溧	63A.01	964
篥	92A.01	1360
歷	51A.30	757
櫪	10B.30	122
轣	10D.30	151
靂	31D.30	512
嚦	40A.30	586
癧	61A.30	905
瀝	63A.30	981
櫟	10B.01	112
轢	10D.01	149
礫	31B.01	493
隸	10S.02	158
(隷)		
吏	12.82	233
荔	20A.50	278
鬲	30.42	435
(鬲)		
詈	41D.40	682
曆	51A.41	758
沴	63A.91	1024
力	91.50	1215
ㄌㄧㄢ **LIAN**		
ㄌㄧㄢˊ (liarn)		
連	10.83	41
蓮	20A.83	291
漣	63A.83	1022
褳	63C.83	1042
鰱	92C.83	1382
廉	61.22	891
(亷)		
濂	63A.22	978
鐮	81A.22	1109
簾	92A.22	1364
憐	22A.10	385
聯	31S.22	521
(联)(聮)(聫)		
匳	51.21	747
(奩)		
帘	62A.22	943
ㄌㄧㄢˇ (liaan)		
臉	42A.81	719
ㄌㄧㄢˋ (liahn)		
楝	10B.01	112
鍊	81A.01	1103
煉	91D.01	1308
練	93B.01	1420
殮	31S.81	528
瀲	63A.82	1021
襝	63C.81	1041
斂	81S.82	1138
鏈	81A.83	1125
戀	93.72	1397
(恋)		
ㄌㄧㄤ **LIANG**		
ㄌㄧㄤˊ (liarng)		
良	63.02	952
俍	91A.02	1241
梁	63.01	951
粱	63.01	951
糧	22C.11	406
(粮)		
涼	63A.01	964
ㄌㄧㄤˇ (liaang)		
兩	31.42	468
魎	91.70	1220
倆	91A.42	1259

ㄌㄧㄤˋ (liahng)
亮 60.70 827
喨 40A.70 597
晾 41A.01 657
諒 60A.01 841
輛 10D.42 152
悢 22A.02 385
量 41.11 626

ㄌㄧㄠ **LIAU**

ㄌㄧㄠˊ (liaur)
憀 22A.91 401
寥 62.91 939
漻 63A.91 1024
撩 10A.01 48
遼 12.83 234
鷯 12S.50 236
嘹 40A.01 579
屪 52A.01 781
療 61A.01 902
寮 62.01 916
鐐 81A.01 1104
僚 91A.01 1238
獠 91C.01 1298
繚 93B.01 1420
聊 31S.22 520

ㄌㄧㄠˇ (liaau)
了 32.00 533
釕 81A.00 1102
蓼 20A.91 292
瞭 41B.01 665

ㄌㄧㄠˋ (liauh)
撂 10A.40 71
尥 12.70 226
料 22C.10 405
廖 61.91 901
燎 91D.01 1308

ㄌㄧㄝ **LIE** (lie)
咧 40A.00 577

ㄌㄧㄝˋ (lieh)
列 31S.00 517
趔 11.83 189
裂 31.02 444
烈 31.63 469
洌 63A.00 959
冽 63A.00 959
鬣 51.70 752
躐 40B.70 615
獵 91C.70 1305
捩 10A.81 96
劣 22.50 370

ㄌㄧㄣ **LIN**

ㄌㄧㄣˊ (lirn)
轔 10D.10 149
嶙 21B.10 330
鄰 22S.22 425
(隣)
遴 22.83 380
璘 31A.10 483
磷 31B.10 493
瞵 41B.10 667
麟 61S.10 913
潾 63A.10 970
燐 91D.10 1309
鱗 92C.10 1378
林 10B.01 111
琳 31A.01 481
霖 31D.01 510
痳 61A.01 902
淋 63A.01 963
臨 51S.40 770
(临)
廪 61.40 893

ㄌㄧㄣˇ (liin)
檁 10B.01 112
懍 22A.01 384
廩 61.01 888
凜 63A.01 965
澟 63A.01 965

ㄌㄧㄣˋ (lihn)
藺 20A.00 248
躪 40B.00 606
吝 60.40 819
賃 91.80 1223

ㄌㄧㄥ **LING** (ling)
拎 10A.63 84

ㄌㄧㄥˊ (lirng)
苓 20A.63 280
齡 21S.63 339
(龄)
蛉 22D.63 418
玲 31A.63 487
零 31D.63 514
聆 31S.63 524
囹 41·41 640
泠 63A.63 1002
羚 80S.63 1081
鈴 81A.63 1118
翎 81S.50 1135
鴒 81S.50 1135
瓴 81S.70 1136
伶 91A.63 1265
舲 91S.63 1327
笭 92A.63 1370
菱 20A.82 289
㥄 22A.82 400
陵 32A.82 559
凌 63A.82 1018
鯪 92C.82 1381
綾 93B.82 1444
霝 31D.40 512
櫺 10B.40 124
醽 31C.40 506
靈 31D.30 511
(霛)
灵 50.81 733

ㄌㄧㄥˇ (liing)
領 81S.80 1136
嶺 21.80 315

ㄌㄧㄥˋ (lihng)
令 81.63 1095
另 40.50 572

ㄌㄧㄡ **LIOU** (liou)
溜 63A.41 989

ㄌㄧㄡˊ (liour)
琉 31A.70 489
(瑠)
硫 31B.70 498
旒 60S.70 881
流 63A.70 1008
(𣲽)
留 90.41 1156
(畱)(畄)
榴 10B.41 128
罶 41D.41 682
騮 51B.41 764
(駵)
瘤 61A.41 906
鎦 81A.41 1114
遛 90.83 1174
劉 90S.00 1188
(刘)
瀏 63A.00 962

ㄌㄧㄡˇ (lioou)
柳 10B.22 120
綹 93B.40 1431

ㄌㄧㄡˋ (liouh)
餾 81B.41 1129
六 60.80 829

ㄌㄡ **LOU** (lou)
膢 41B.93 672

ㄌㄡˊ (lour)
婁 22.93 382
摟 10A.93 107
樓 10B.93 143
耬 10S.93 168
蔞 20A.93 293
螻 22D.93 422
嘍 40A.93 605
髏 42B.93 726
僂 91A.93 1281

ㄌㄡˇ (loou)
簍 92A.93 1375

ㄌㄡˋ (louh)
瘺 61A.42 907
瘻 61A.93 912
漏 63A.42 996
鏤 81A.93 1126
陋 32A.21 553

ㄌㄨ **LU** (lu)
嚕 40A.41 591

ㄌㄨˊ (lur)
盧 21A.30 324
櫨 10B.30 121
轤 10D.30 150
壚 11A.30 199

蘆	20A.30	263
(芦)		
鸕	21S.50	338
顱	21S.80	342
臚	42A.30	709
廬	61.30	892
瀘	63A.30	979
鑪	81A.30	1110
爐	91D.30	1310
(炉)		
艫	91S.30	1323
鱸	92C.30	1380
罏	92S.30	1387
纑	93B.30	1427
ㄌㄨˇ (luu)		
鹵	21A.41	325
樐	10B.41	126
磠	31B.41	496
滷	63A.41	986
虜	21A.50	326
擄	10A.50	81
艣	91S.50	1325
魯	92.41	1339
櫓	10B.41	128
氌	90.70	1162
艪	91S.41	1325
ㄌㄨˋ (luh)		
路	40B.40	611
璐	31A.40	486
露	31D.40	512
鷺	40.50	572
輅	10D.40	152
賂	41C.40	675
陸	32A.11	552
稑	90A.11	1177
彔	92.02	1332
菉	20A.02	254
碌	31B.02	493
醁	31C.02	504
睩	41B.02	667
淥	63A.02	969
祿	63B.02	1027
錄	81A.02	1105
盝	92.30	1335
逯	92.83	1355
籙	92A.02	1360
鹿	61.70	896
麓	10.70	34
轆	10D.70	154
漉	63A.70	1009
簏	92A.70	1371
戮	50S.71	741
甪	91.42	1214
ㄌㄨㄢ **LUAN**		
ㄌㄨㄢˊ (luarn)		
圞	41.41	642
欒	93.01	1393
(栾)		
巒	93.21	1393
(峦)		
鑾	93.30	1393
(銮)		
臠	93.42	1395
(脔)		
鸞	93.50	1395
(鸾)		
ㄌㄨㄢˇ (luaan)		
卵	90S.22	1192
ㄌㄨㄢˋ (luahn)		
亂	90S.70	1196
ㄌㄨㄣ **LUN**		
ㄌㄨㄣˊ (lurn)		
掄	10A.42	81
輪	10D.42	153
崙	21.42	313
圇	41.41	640
淪	63A.42	997
倫	91A.42	1261
㷍	91D.42	1312
綸	93B.42	1435
ㄌㄨㄣˋ (luhn)		
論	60A.42	854
ㄌㄨㄥ **LUNG**		
ㄌㄨㄥˊ (lurng)		
隆	32A.11	552
癃	61A.11	904
窿	62A.11	942
龍	60S.70	878
櫳	10B.70	134
蘢	20A.70	282
瓏	31A.70	489
嚨	40A.70	597
曨	41A.70	662
矓	41B.70	671
朧	42A.70	716
聾	60.10	812
礱	60.40	819
瀧	63A.70	1009
爖	91D.70	1314
籠	92A.70	1371
ㄌㄨㄥˇ (luung)		
攏	10A.70	89
壠	11A.70	205
隴	32A.70	557
壟	60.11	815
ㄌㄨㄥˋ (luhng)		
弄	31.20	450
哢	40A.20	583
衖	91B.00	1283
ㄌㄨㄛ **LUO** (luo)		
攞	10A.11	56
ㄌㄨㄛˊ (luor)		
螺	22D.01	412
騾	51B.01	761
羅	41D.11	680
(罗)		
欏	10B.11	117
蘿	20A.11	258
(萝)		
囉	40A.11	582
(啰)		
邏	41.D83	684
鑼	81A.11	1107
(锣)		
儸	91A.11	1244
籮	92A.11	1362
(箩)		
覼	31S.70	525
腡	42A.42	712
ㄌㄨㄛˇ (luoo)		
蓏	20A.83	292
瘰	61A.01	902
裸	63C.01	1035
ㄌㄨㄛˋ (luoh)		
落	20A.40	268
珞	31A.40	486
酪	31C.40	506
駱	51B.40	764
洛	63A.40	984
烙	91D.40	1311
雒	92S.11	1384
絡	93B.40	1431
躒	40B.01	607
犖	91.10	1203
ㄌㄩ **LYU**		
ㄌㄩˊ (lyur)		
閭	52B.00	794
櫚	10B.00	110
驢	51B.30	763
(馿)		
ㄌㄩˇ (lyuu)		
呂	40.40	570
梠	10B.40	124
鋁	81A.40	1111
侶	91A.40	1254
旅	60S.02	870
膂	60.42	820
[illegible]	60.50	825
屢	52A.93	788
褸	63C.93	1043
縷	93B.93	1448
履	52A.82	787
ㄌㄩˋ (lyuh)		
慮	21A.72	327
濾	63A.72	1012
鑢	81A.72	1122
律	91B.10	1288
葎	20A.10	257
嵂	21.10	306
菉	20A.02	254
氯	92.70	1351
綠	93B.02	1422
ㄌㄩㄢ **LYUAN**		
ㄌㄩㄢˊ (lyuarn)		
孿	93.00	1391

孿 93.00 1391
(孪)
ㄌㄩㄢˇ (lyuaan)
孌 93.93 1401
(娈)
ㄌㄩㄝ **LYUE**
ㄌㄩㄝˋ (lyueh)
掠 10A.01 50
剠 60S.00 869
略 41S.40 688
(畧)
ㄇ M
ㄇ **M** (m)
呣 40A.50 594
ㄇˊ (mr)
唔 40A.40 588
嘸 40A.63 596
ㄇㄚ **MA** (ma)
媽 93A.50 1414
嬤 93A.93 1419
ㄇㄚˊ (mar)
麻 61.01 888
蔴 20A.01 250
痲 61A.01 902
蟆 22D.81 421
ㄇㄚˇ (maa)
馬 51.50 750
螞 22D.50 417
瑪 31A.50 487
碼 31B.50 497
ㄇㄚˋ (mah)
罵 41D.50 682
禡 63B.50 1032
·ㄇㄚ ('ma)
嘛 40A.01 579
嗎 40A.50 594
ㄇㄞ **MAI**
ㄇㄞˊ (mair)
埋 11A.11 197
薶 20A.11 259
霾 31D.11 510
ㄇㄞˇ (maai)
買 41D.80 683
ㄇㄞˋ (maih)
賣 11.80 186
(卖)
邁 20A.83 292
勱 20S.50 300
麥 10.32 24
(麦)
ㄇㄢ **MAN**
ㄇㄢˊ (marn)
顢 20S.80 302
蹣 40B.42 612
瞞 41B.42 670
鬘 51.82 753
謾 60A.82 866
饅 81B.82 1132
鰻 92C.82 1382
鞔 20B.70 296
蠻 93.93 1401
(蛮)
ㄇㄢˇ (maan)
滿 63A.42 993
ㄇㄢˋ (mahn)
曼 41.82 652
(⿱日男)
墁 11A.82 207
蔓 20A.82 290
慢 22A.82 400
幔 22B.82 405
謾 60A.82 866
漫 63A.82 1020
鏝 81A.82 1124
嫚 93A.82 1418
縵 93B.82 1445
ㄇㄤ **MANG**
ㄇㄤˊ (marng)
芒 20A.21 260
茫 20A.21 260
忙 22A.21 388
盲 60.41 819
蝱 60.93 837
(虻)
鋩 81A.21 1108
牻 10C.70 146
ㄇㄤˇ (maang)
⿰木莽 10B.20 118
莽 20A.20 259
蟒 22D.20 414
漭 63A.20 975
ㄇㄠ **MAU** (mau)
貓 91S.41 1325
(猫)
ㄇㄠˊ (maur)
毛 90.70 1161
髦 51.70 751
⿸广毛 60S.70 880
矛 32.00 534
茅 20A.00 246
蟊 32.93 547
蝥 32.93 547
錨 81A.41 1113
ㄇㄠˇ (maau)
卯 90S.22 1191
茆 20A.22 263
ㄇㄠˋ (mauh)
冒 41.41 631
帽 22B.41 403
媢 93A.41 1411
耄 11.70 183
芼 20A.70 282
眊 41B.70 671
懋 10.72 35
瞀 32.41 539
袤 60.02 808
茂 20A.71 285
貿 90.80 1166
貌 91S.70 1328
ㄇㄟ **MEI**
ㄇㄟˊ (meir)
枚 10B.82 142
玫 31A.82 491
黴 91B.82 1293
眉 52.41 774
楣 10B.41 128
湄 63A.41 988
鎇 81A.41 1114
禖 63B.01 1026
煤 91D.01 1308
媒 93A.01 1404
梅 10B.50 132
(槑)
苺 20A.50 276
莓 20A.50 278
霉 31D.50 514
沒 63A.82 1021
ㄇㄟˇ (meei)
美 80.81 1073
(美)
渼 63A.81 1016
鎂 81A.81 1124
每 92.50 1339
鋂 81A.50 1118
浼 63A.70 1011
媺 93A.82 1417
ㄇㄟˋ (meih)
昧 41A.01 657
眛 41B.01 665
寐 62.01 916
沬 63A.01 963
魅 91.70 1220
妹 93A.01 1404
瑁 31A.41 486
痗 61A.50 908
袂 63C.81 1041
媚 93A.41 1411
ㄇㄣ **MEN**
ㄇㄣˊ (mern)
門 52B.00 796
(门)
捫 10A.00 46
鍆 81A.00 1103
們 91A.00 1235
ㄇㄣˋ (mehn)
悶 52B.00 799
燜 91D.00 1307
懣 63.72 956
ㄇㄥ **MENG**
ㄇㄥˊ (merng)
蒙 20A.02 254
檬 10B.02 112
懞 22B.02 402
曚 41A.02 657
矇 41B.02 666

朦 42A.02 705
濛 63A.02 966
艨 91S.02 1319
瞢 20A.41 271
甍 20A.70 281
萌 20A.42 274
盟 41.30 629
虻 22D.21 414
氓 60S.71 881
雺 31D.00 510

ㄇㄥˇ (meeng)
蜢 22D.30 414
錳 81A.30 1110
猛 91C.30 1300
艋 91S.30 1323
懵 22A.41 392
蠓 22D.02 412

ㄇㄥˋ (mehng)
夢 20A.32 265
(梦)
孟 32.30 538

ㄇㄧ **MI** (mi)
咪 40A.01 579
瞇 41B.83 672

ㄇㄧˊ (mir)
迷 22.83 378
謎 60A.83 867
麋 61.01 888
糜 61.01 888
彌 50A.42 736
(弥)
瀰 63A.42 996
獼 91C.42 1302
蘼 20A.22 262
縻 61.01 888
醾 31C.01 503
醿 31C.22 505

ㄇㄧˇ (mii)
米 22.01 348
敉 22C.82 410
眯 41B.01 665
弭 50A.10 735
靡 61.22 890

ㄇㄧˋ (mih)
謐 60A.30 848
密 62.21 922
宓 62.72 933
蜜 62.93 939
泌 63A.72 1013
祕 63B.72 1033
(秘)
塓 11A.80 206
幂 62.22 922
(幎)(羃)
冪 62.22 922
覓 90.70 1161
(覔)

ㄇㄧㄢ **MIAN**

ㄇㄧㄢˊ (miarn)
棉 10B.22 120
緜 91S.01 1318
(綿)
眠 41B.71 671

ㄇㄧㄢˇ (miaan)
免 92.70 1348
(兎)
冕 41.70 647
勉 92.70 1348
愐 22A.41 392
勔 31S.50 524
腼 42A.41 711
湎 63A.41 988
偭 91A.41 1257
緬 93B.41 1432
眄 41B.50 670
沔 63A.50 998

ㄇㄧㄢˋ (miahn)
面 31.41 465
麵 10S.41 160
(麺)
麫 10S.50 161
(麪)

ㄇㄧㄠ **MIAU** (miau)
喵 40A.41 589

ㄇㄧㄠˊ (miaur)
描 10A.41 75
苗 20A.41 271
瞄 41B.41 669

ㄇㄧㄠˇ (miaau)
杪 10B.91 143
眇 41B.91 672
渺 63A.91 1024
秒 90A.91 1185
緲 93B.91 1447
藐 20A.70 282
邈 91.83 1230
淼 22.02 352

ㄇㄧㄠˋ (miauh)
廟 61.42 893
(庙)
妙 93A.91 1418
(玅)

ㄇㄧㄝ **MIE** (mie)
芈 20A.10 254
乜 22.70 371

ㄇㄧㄝˋ (mieh)
蔑 20A.71 285
蠛 22D.71 420
衊 91S.71 1328
篾 92A.71 1371
滅 63A.71 1012

ㄇㄧㄣ **MIN**

ㄇㄧㄣˊ (mirn)
民 52.71 776
岷 21B.71 332
珉 31A.71 489
緡 93B.41 1433
旻 41.82 652
閩 52B.00 790

ㄇㄧㄣˇ (miin)
敏 92S.82 1391
鰵 92.63 1346
抿 10A.71 92
暋 52.41 774
愍 52.72 777
泯 63A.71 1011
笢 92A.71 1372
閔 52B.00 798
憫 22A.00 383
黽 42.70 699
(黾)
澠 63A.70 1007
皿 42.30 693

ㄇㄧㄥ **MING**

ㄇㄧㄥˊ (mirng)
名 92.40 1336
茗 20A.40 269
酩 31C.40 506
銘 81A.40 1112
冥 62.80 935
(冥)
螟 22D.80 420
暝 41A.80 663
瞑 41B.80 671
溟 63A.80 1014
鳴 40A.50 595
明 41A.42 660
(朙)

ㄇㄧㄥˋ (mihng)
命 81.22 1086

ㄇㄧㄡ **MIOU**

ㄇㄧㄡˋ (miouh)
謬 60A.91 867

ㄇㄛ **MO** (mo)
摸 10A.81 95

ㄇㄛˊ (mor)
模 10B.81 138
摹 20A.00 246
糢 22C.81 410
謨 60A.81 864
饃 81B.81 1132
蘑 20A.40 267
摩 61.00 886
磨 61.40 892
魔 61.70 895
麼 61.93 901
(広)
劘 61S.00 913
饝 81B.40 1128

ㄇㄛˇ (moo)
抹 10A.01 48

ㄇㄛˋ (moh)
末 10.01 5
茉 20A.01 249
靺 20B.01 294

沫 63A.01 963
秣 90A.01 1176
莫 20A.81 288
驀 20A.50 276
膜 42A.81 719
瘼 61A.10 910
寞 62.81 936
漠 63A.81 1015
墨 41.11 627
嚜 40A.11 582
纆 93B.11 1424
霢 31D.02 510
脈 41B.02 667
脈 42A.02 706
(脉)(衇)
陌 32A.41 555
貊 91S.41 1325
歿 31S.82 530
默 41S.81 691

ㄇㄡ **MOU**

ㄇㄡˊ (mour)
牟 93.10 1393
蛑 22D.10 413
眸 41B.10 667
侔 91A.10 1243
鍪 32.30 539
謀 60A.01 840
繆 93B.91 1447

ㄇㄡˇ (moou)
有 12.41 223
某 20.01 237

ㄇㄨ **MU**

ㄇㄨˇ (muu)
母 41.50 643
拇 10A.C0 82
姆 93A.50 1413
牡 10C.11 145
畝 60S.81 882
(畆)
姥 93A.70 1414

ㄇㄨˋ (muh)
慕 20A.02 253
墓 20A.11 258
幕 20A.22 261
暮 20A.41 271
募 20A.50 276
木 10.01 9
沐 63A.01 963
目 41.41 632
苜 20A.41 271
睦 41B.11 667
鉬 81A.41 1114
牧 10C.82 147
穆 90A.91 1185

ㄋ N

ㄋ **N**

ㄋˋ (nh)
⿰口五 40A.30 586

ㄋㄚ **NA**

ㄋㄚˊ (nar)
拿 81.00 1083
鎿 81A.00 1103
拏 93.00 1391

ㄋㄚˇ (naa)
哪 40A.22 584

ㄋㄚˋ (nah)
吶 40A.42 593
肭 42A.42 713
訥 60A.42 855
衲 63C.42 1039
鈉 81A.42 1116
納 93B.42 1436
捺 10A.01 48
那 50S.22 739

ㄋㄞ **NAI**

ㄋㄞˇ (naai)
乃 32.50 540
釢 81A.50 1116
氖 92.70 1351
奶 93A.50 1413
迺 31.83 478
(廼)
嬭 93A.42 1412
(妳)

ㄋㄞˋ (naih)
奈 12.01 216
錼 81A.01 1104
柰 10.01 10
耐 31S.00 517
鼐 32.22 538
褦 63C.70 1040

ㄋㄢ **NAN** (nan)
囝 41.41 636
囡 41.41 642

ㄋㄢˊ (narn)
南 10.42 29
楠 10B.42 128
喃 40A.42 591
諵 60A.42 851
難 20S.11 298
(难)
男 41.50 643

ㄋㄢˇ (naan)
蝻 22D.42 416
腩 42A.42 712
赧 11S.82 213
戁 20.72 243

ㄋㄤ **NANG**

ㄋㄤˊ (narng)
囊 10.02 15

ㄋㄤˇ (naang)
攮 10A.02 51
曩 41.02 624

ㄋㄤˋ (nahng)
齉 91S.02 1319

·ㄋㄤ ('nang)
囔 40A.02 580

ㄋㄠ **NAU**

ㄋㄠˊ (naur)
撓 10A.70 85
橈 10B.70 132
譊 60A.70 857
鐃 81A.70 1118
怓 22A.82 401
呶 40A.82 604
(詉)
硇 31B.41 496
猱 91C.01 1298

ㄋㄠˇ (naau)
惱 22A.41 393
瑙 31A.41 486
腦 42A.41 711

ㄋㄠˋ (nauh)
鬧 52B.00 798
淖 63A.10 969

ㄋㄜ, ㄋㄟ **NEI**

ㄋㄜˋ (neih)
倷 91A.01 1238

ㄋㄟˇ (neei)
餒 81B.93 1133

ㄋㄟˋ (neih)
內 81.42 1092
氝 92.70 1351

ㄋㄣ **NEN**

ㄋㄣˋ (nehn)
嫩 93A.82 1417

ㄋㄥ **NENG**

ㄋㄥˊ (nerng)
能 93S.70 1450

ㄋㄧ **NI**

ㄋㄧˊ (nir)
尼 52A.70 786
怩 22A.70 397
呢 40A.70 597
泥 63A.70 1007
鈮 81A.70 1119
妮 93A.70 1415
輗 10D.70 154
堄 11A.70 205
齯 21S.70 340
蜺 22D.70 419
霓 31D.70 516
麑 61.70 896
倪 91A.70 1267
猊 91C.70 1305
鯢 92C.70 1381
婗 93A.70 1415

ㄋㄧˇ (nii)
擬 10A.83 103
(拟)
薿 20A.83 291
儗 91A.83 1280
旎 60S.70 880
禰 63B.42 1031
你 91A.01 1239

ㄋㄧˋ (nih)
匿 51.21 745
暱 41A.21 658
惄 21A.72 327
昵 41A.70 662
睨 41B.70 671
膩 42A.71 718
溺 63A.50 999
衵 63C.41 1038
逆 80.83 1075

ㄋㄧㄢ **NIAN** (nian)
蔫 20A.50 276

ㄋㄧㄢˊ (niarn)
拈 10A.40 71
粘 22C.40 407
黏 90S.40 1193
鮎 92C.40 1380
年 92.10 1333
(秊)

ㄋㄧㄢˇ (niaan)
輦 12.10 218
攆 10A.10 52
捻 10A.72 93
淰 63A.72 1013
撚 10A.63 85
碾 31B.02 493

ㄋㄧㄢˋ (niahn)
念 81.72 1095
埝 11A.72 206
唸 40A.72 599
廿 20.21 239

ㄋㄧㄤ **NIANG**
ㄋㄧㄤˊ (niarng)
娘 93A.02 1405
(㚷)
孃 93A.02 1405

ㄋㄧㄤˋ (niahng)
釀 31C.02 504

ㄋㄧㄠ **NIAU**
ㄋㄧㄠˇ (niaau)
鳥 91.50 1217
蔦 20A.50 278
裊 91.02 1202
嬲 41S.50 689
褭 60.02 809
嫋 93A.50 1414

ㄋㄧㄠˋ (niauh)
尿 52A.02 781

ㄋㄧㄝ **NIE** (nie)
捏 10A.30 67

ㄋㄧㄝˊ (nier)
苶 20A.01 250

ㄋㄧㄝˋ (nieh)
涅 63A.11 973
湼 63A.30 982
臬 91.01 1200
鎳 81A.01 1104
[illegible] 91S.70 1328
孽 20A.00 249
(孼)
蘖 20A.01 252
(櫱)
糵 20A.01 252
(糱)
聶 31.10 447
囁 40A.10 581
躡 40B.10 608
鑷 81A.10 1106
齧 10.21 22
(囓)
不 31.22 451
痆 61A.70 909

ㄋㄧㄣ **NIN**
ㄋㄧㄣˊ (nirn)
您 91.72 1221

ㄋㄧㄥ **NING**
ㄋㄧㄥˊ (nirng)
寧 62.00 916
擰 10A.00 47
檸 10B.00 110
嚀 40A.00 577
鬡 51.00 742
獰 91C.00 1297
凝 63A.83 1022

ㄋㄧㄥˋ (nihng)
甯 62.42 929
濘 63A.00 961
佞 91A.93 1282

ㄋㄧㄡ **NIOU** (niou)
妞 93A.30 1408

ㄋㄧㄡˊ (niour)
牛 10.10 18

ㄋㄧㄡˇ (nioou)
扭 10A.30 67
鈕 81A.30 1110
狃 91C.30 1301
紐 93B.30 1429

ㄋㄡ **NOU**
ㄋㄡˋ (nouh)
耨 10S.00 158
獳 91C.42 1302

ㄋㄨ **NU**
ㄋㄨˊ (nur)
奴 93A.82 1418
笯 92A.82 1374
孥 93.00 1391
帑 93.22 1393
駑 93.50 1395

ㄋㄨˇ (nuu)
砮 93.40 1394
努 93.50 1395
弩 93.50 1395

ㄋㄨˋ (nuh)
怒 93.72 1396

ㄋㄨㄢ **NUAN**
ㄋㄨㄢˇ (nuaan)
暖 41A.82 664
(暝)(煖)

ㄋㄨㄥ **NUNG**
ㄋㄨㄥˊ (nurng)
農 22.02 352
(辳)
醲 31C.02 504
噥 40A.02 580
膿 42A.02 705
濃 63A.02 966
襛 63C.02 1035
穠 90A.02 1176
儂 91A.02 1240

ㄋㄨㄛ **NUO**
ㄋㄨㄛˊ (nuor)
挪 10A.22 63
娜 93A.22 1407
挼 10A.93 108
捼 10A.93 108
儺 91A.11 1244

ㄋㄨㄛˋ (nuoh)
懦 22A.42 395
糯 22C.42 409
(穤)(稬)
掿 10A.40 70
諾 60A.40 848
搦 10A.50 82

ㄋㄩ **NYU**
ㄋㄩˇ (nyuu)
女 93.93 1400
釹 81A.93 1126

ㄋㄩˋ (nyuh)
忸 22A.30 390
衄 91S.30 1323
䶊 91S.30 1323
衂 91S.50 1326
恧 31.72 472

ㄋㄩㄝ **NYUE**
ㄋㄩㄝˋ (nyueh)
虐 21A.21 318
謔 60A.21 845
瘧 61A.21 904

ㄛ O
ㄛ **O** (o)
喔 40A.11 582

ㄛˇ (oo)
嚄 40A.82 603

ㄡ OU
ㄡ **OU** (ou)
鷗 51S.50 771
甌 51S.70 771
歐 51S.81 772
毆 51S.82 772
敺 51S.82 772
謳 60A.21 845

ㄡˇ (oou)
耦 10S.42 161
藕 20A.42 273
偶 91A.42 1260

嘔	40A.21	583
ㄡˋ	(ouh)	
慪	22A.21	388
漚	63A.21	975
ㄆ	P	
ㄆㄚ	PA (pa)	
葩	20A.70	284
啪	40A.41	591
趴	40B.80	616
ㄆㄚˊ	(par)	
杷	10B.70	134
耙	10S.70	164
琶	31.70	470
爬	90.83	1170
筢	92A.70	1370
扒	10A.80	94
ㄆㄚˋ	(pah)	
怕	22A.41	393
帕	22B.41	404
汃	63A.80	1014
ㄆㄞ	PAI (pai)	
拍	10A.41	78
ㄆㄞˊ	(pair)	
排	10A.22	62
俳	91A.22	1248
徘	91B.22	1289
牌	91S.10	1319
簰	92A.10	1362
箄	92A.10	1361
ㄆㄞˋ	(paih)	
派	63A.02	969
湃	63A.10	972
ㄆㄢ	PAN (pan)	
攀	10.00	4
潘	63A.41	990
ㄆㄢˊ	(parn)	
槃	91.01	1201
鞶	91.10	1203
盤	91.30	1207
磐	91.40	1208
媻	91.93	1230
蟠	22D.41	416
磻	31B.41	469
ㄆㄢˋ	(pahn)	
畔	41S.10	686
泮	63A.10	969
判	91S.00	1317
叛	91S.82	1330
拚	10A.20	58
盼	41B.50	670
襻	63C.00	1034
ㄆㄤ	PANG (pang)	
乓	90.63	1159
滂	63A.50	999
ㄆㄤˊ	(parng)	
旁	60.50	824
螃	22D.50	417
霶	31D.50	514
傍	91A.50	1263
徬	91B.50	1291
雱	31D.50	514
彷	91B.50	1291
龎	51A.70	759
龐	61.70	896
尨	12.70	225
厖	51A.70	759
庬	61.70	896
逄	92.83	1355
ㄆㄤˇ	(paang)	
耪	10S.50	162
嗙	40A.50	594
ㄆㄤˋ	(pahng)	
胖	42A.10	706
ㄆㄠ	PAU (pau)	
拋	10A.70	85
(抛)		
脬	42A.00	705
ㄆㄠˊ	(paur)	
匏	12S.70	237
咆	40A.70	598
庖	61.70	896
麅	61.70	896
袍	63C.70	1040
炮	91D.70	1314
炰	92.63	1342
刨	92S.00	1382
麃	61.63	895
ㄆㄠˇ	(paau)	
跑	40B.70	615
ㄆㄠˋ	(pauh)	
炮	22S.70	426
砲	31B.70	498
疱	61A.70	909
泡	63A.70	1011
礮	31B.82	501
(礟)		
ㄆㄟ	PEI (pei)	
坯	11A.30	199
呸	40A.30	586
胚	42A.30	709
披	10A.83	99
醅	31C.40	506
ㄆㄟˊ	(peir)	
培	11A.40	200
陪	32A.40	554
賠	41C.40	675
坏	11A.22	198
邳	31S.22	520
裴	22.02	352
ㄆㄟˋ	(peih)	
珮	31A.70	489
佩	91A.70	1267
霈	31D.22	511
旆	60S.22	873
沛	63A.22	978
帔	22B.82	405
配	31C.70	507
轡	93.40	1394
ㄆㄣ	PEN (pen)	
歕	10S.81	167
噴	40A.80	600
ㄆㄣˊ	(pern)	
盆	80.30	1064
湓	63A.30	981
ㄆㄥ	PENG (peng)	
抨	10A.10	53
怦	22A.10	385
砰	31B.10	493
烹	60.63	825
澎	63A.91	1023
ㄆㄥˊ	(perng)	
朋	42A.42	712
棚	10B.42	130
硼	31B.42	497
鵬	42A.50	714
鬅	51.42	750
彭	11S.91	214
蟛	22D.91	422
膨	42A.91	722
蓬	20A.83	292
篷	92A.83	1375
芃	20A.70	281
ㄆㄥˇ	(peeng)	
捧	10A.10	52
ㄆㄥˋ	(pehng)	
碰	31B.30	495
ㄆㄧ	PI (pi)	
批	10A.70	86
砒	31B.70	498
紕	93B.70	1438
丕	31.30	458
伾	91A.30	1252
狉	91C.30	1300
霹	31D.10	510
劈	52.50	775
披	10A.82	99
ㄆㄧˊ	(pir)	
皮	22.82	376
疲	61A.82	910
鼙	11.10	171
埤	11A.10	196
陴	32A.10	551
啤	40A.10	581
脾	42A.10	707
郫	91S.22	1321
枇	10B.70	133
蚍	22D.70	418
琵	31.70	470
毗	41S.70	689
(毘)		
貔	91S.70	1328
笓	92A.70	1371
羆	41D.63	683
ㄆㄧˇ	(pii)	
嚭	11S.40	209

痞 61A.40 905
庀 61.70 896
仳 91A.70 1265
圮 11A.70 204
疋 32.83 544
匹 51.21 747
癖 61A.10 903

ㄆㄧˋ (pih)
屁 52A.70 786
媲 93A.70 1415
擗 10A.10 54
譬 52.40 774
鷿 52.50 775
甓 52.70 776
闢 52B.00 797
澼 63A.10 970
鈹 81A.82 1124
僻 91A.10 1242
濞 63A.20 975

ㄆㄧㄢ **PIAN** (pian)
萹 20A.42 275
翩 63S.50 1046
偏 91A.42 1260
篇 92A.42 1369

ㄆㄧㄢˊ (piarn)
胼 42A.20 708
駢 51B.20 762
蹁 40B.42 612
諞 60A.42 854
楩 10B.82 142

ㄆㄧㄢˋ (piahn)
騙 51B.42 764
片 91.22 1205

ㄆㄧㄠ **PIAU** (piau)
螵 22D.01 411
飄 31S.70 525
彯 31S.91 533
嘌 40A.01 579
漂 63A.01 964

ㄆㄧㄠˊ (piaur)
瓢 31S.83 532
嫖 93A.01 1404

ㄆㄧㄠˇ (piaau)
醥 31C.01 503
瞟 41B.01 665
縹 93B.01 1420
殍 31S.00 519
皫 91S.63 1327

ㄆㄧㄠˋ (piauh)
票 31.01 443
剽 31S.00 519
驃 51B.01 761
僄 91A.01 1238

ㄆㄧㄝ **PIE** (pie)
撇 10A.82 100
瞥 22.41 366

ㄆㄧㄝˇ (piee)
苤 20A.30 264

ㄆㄧㄣ **PIN** (pin)
拼 10A.20 58
姘 93A.20 1407

ㄆㄧㄣˊ (pirn)
頻 21S.80 342
蘋 20A.80 287
顰 21A.10 318
矉 41B.80 671
嬪 93A.80 1416
貧 80.80 1072

ㄆㄧㄣˇ (piin)
品 40.40 571

ㄆㄧㄣˋ (pihn)
朩 10.01 4
牝 10C.70 147
聘 31S.50 522

ㄆㄧㄥ **PING** (ping)
俜 91A.50 1262
娉 93A.50 1413
乒 90.01 1174

ㄆㄧㄥˊ (pirng)
平 31.10 445
枰 10B.10 114
坪 11A.10 196
苹 20A.10 255
萍 20A.10 257
評 60A.10 842
秤 90A.10 1177
軿 10D.20 150
帡 22B.20 403
屏 52A.20 782
洴 63A.20 975
瓶 80S.70 1082
憑 63.72 955
(凴)
凭 91.70 1219

ㄆㄛ **PO** (po)
坡 11A.82 207
頗 22S.80 427
陂 32A.82 560
潑 63A.82 1019

ㄆㄛˊ (por)
鄱 90S.22 1191
皤 91S.41 1325
婆 63.93 958

ㄆㄛˇ (poo)
叵 51.21 746
鉕 81A.21 1108
笸 92A.21 1363
頗 22S.80 427
箥 92A.82 1374

ㄆㄛˋ (poh)
粕 22C.41 408
珀 31A.41 486
迫 91.83 1227
魄 91S.70 1328
朴 10B.22 119
破 31B.82 500
醱 31C.82 508

ㄆㄡ **POU**

ㄆㄡˊ (pour)
抔 10A.22 63
掊 10A.40 73
裒 60.02 809

ㄆㄡˇ (poou)
剖 60S.00 869
瓿 60S.70 878

ㄆㄨ **PU** (pu)
痡 61A.42 906
鋪 81A.42 1114
舖 81S.42 1135
撲 10A.81 96
噗 40A.81 601
扑 10A.22 62
仆 91A.22 1247
攴 21A.82 328
攵 92.82 1354

ㄆㄨˊ (pur)
蒱 20A.42 273
蒲 20A.42 275
葡 20A.50 279
酺 31C.42 507
匍 92.50 1340
樸 10B.81 139
幞 22B.81 405
璞 31A.81 490
蹼 40B.81 616
濮 63A.81 1018
襆 63C.81 1041
鏷 81A.81 1123
僕 91A.81 1273
菩 20A.40 267
釙 81A.22 1109

ㄆㄨˇ (puu)
圃 41.41 634
溥 63A.00 958
浦 63A.42 992
普 80.41 1067
譜 60A.41 851
鐠 81A.41 1114
氆 90.70 1162

ㄆㄨˋ (puh)
曝 41A.02 657
瀑 63A.02 967
舖 81S.42 1135

ㄖ R

ㄖㄢ **RAN**

ㄖㄢˊ (rarn)
然 92.63 1345
燃 91D.62 1313
蚺 22D.42 416
髯 51.42 750

ㄖㄢˇ (raan)
冉 22.42 369
苒 20A.42 273
姌 93A.42 1412
染 63.01 951

ㄖㄤ **RANG**
ㄖㄤˊ (rarng)
蘘 20A.02 254
勷 60S.50 876
瓤 60S.83 886
瀼 63A.02 968
禳 63B.02 1026
穰 90A.02 1176
ㄖㄤˇ (raang)
攘 10A.02 51
壤 11A.02 196
嚷 40A.02 580
ㄖㄤˋ (rahng)
讓 60A.02 841
ㄖㄠ **RAU**
ㄖㄠˊ (raur)
蕘 20A.70 281
蟯 22D.70 418
饒 81B.70 1130
嬈 93A.70 1414
ㄖㄠˇ (raau)
擾 10A.82 100
ㄖㄠˋ (rauh)
遶 11.83 188
繞 93B.70 1438
ㄖㄜ **RE**
ㄖㄜˇ (ree)
惹 20A.72 286
喏 40A.40 588
ㄖㄜˋ (reh)
熱 11.63 178
(热)
ㄖㄣ **REN**
ㄖㄣˊ (rern)
人 81.81 1096
壬 90.11 1149
仁 91A.30 1251
ㄖㄣˇ (reen)
荏 20A.11 259
忍 50.72 732
稔 91A.72 1183
ㄖㄣˋ (rehn)
刃 50.50 731
杒 10C.50 146
軔 10D.50 153
韌 22S.50 425
(靭)
訒 60A.50 855
認 60A.72 863
仞 91A.50 1262
紉 93B.50 1436
衽 63C.11 1036
飪 81B.11 1127
恁 91.72 1220
任 91A.11 1245
妊 93A.11 1406
紝 93B.11 1424
ㄖㄥ **RENG** (reng)
扔 10A.50 81
ㄖㄥˊ (rerng)
仍 91A.50 1262
ㄖㄡ **ROU**
ㄖㄡˊ (rour)
柔 32.01 537
揉 10A.01 49
輮 10D.01 149
蹂 40B.01 607
ㄖㄡˇ (roou)
糅 22C.01 405
煣 91D.01 1308
ㄖㄡˋ (rouh)
肉 81.42 1093
ㄖㄨ **RU**
ㄖㄨˊ (rur)
如 93A.40 1409
茹 20A.40 269
銣 81A.40 1112
帤 93.22 1393
薷 20A.42 274
[illegible] 32S.42 564
嚅 40A.42 592
濡 63A.42 994
襦 63C.42 1039
儒 91A.42 1259
ㄖㄨˇ (ruu)
汝 63A.93 1026
乳 90S.70 1195
ㄖㄨˋ (ruh)
洳 63A.40 985
辱 51A.00 754
蓐 20A.00 247
溽 63A.00 960
褥 63C.00 1034
縟 93B.00 1420
擩 10A.42 79
入 81.81 1099
ㄖㄨㄢ **RUAN**
ㄖㄨㄢˊ (ruarn)
撋 10A.00 47
堧 11A.93 208
壖 11A.42 201
ㄖㄨㄢˇ (ruaan)
耎 31.81 476
愞 22A.81 399
蝡 22D.81 421
軟 10D.81 155
蠕 22D.42 416
阮 32A.70 557
ㄖㄨㄟ **RUEI**
ㄖㄨㄟˊ (rueir)
蕤 20A.83 291
緌 93B.93 1448
ㄖㄨㄟˇ (rueei)
蕊 20A.72 286
(蕋)
蘂 20A.01 250
桵 10B.93 144
ㄖㄨㄟˋ (rueih)
枘 10B.42 130
芮 20A.42 275
蚋 22D.42 417
汭 63A.42 997
睿 21A.41 325
叡 21S.82 344
瑞 31A.42 487
銳 81A.70 1119
ㄖㄨㄣ **RUN**
ㄖㄨㄣˋ (ruhn)
閏 52B.00 790
潤 63A.00 960
ㄖㄨㄥ **RUNG**
ㄖㄨㄥˊ (rurng)
戎 71.71 1048
羢 80S.71 1082
毧 90.70 1162
狨 91C.71 1305
絨 93B.71 1441
容 62.40 926
榕 10B.40 124
蓉 20A.40 268
溶 63A.40 983
鎔 81A.40 1112
(熔)
榮 91.01 1201
(荣)
嶸 21B.01 330
茸 20A.10 255
融 30S.93 440
ㄖㄨㄥˇ (ruung)
氄 32S.70 565
宂 62.70 933
ㄖㄨㄛ **RUO**
ㄖㄨㄛˋ (ruoh)
若 20A.40 266
鍩 81A.40 1111
偌 91A.40 1254
箬 92A.40 1366
弱 50S.50 740
蒻 20A.50 277
爇 20A.63 279
ㄖ **RY**
ㄖˋ (ryh)
日 41.41 630
馹 51B.41 764
ㄙ S
ㄒ, ㄕ SH
ㄙㄚ **SA** (sa)
仨 91A.30 1252
ㄙㄚˇ (saa)
撒 10A.82 98
洒 63A.41 987
灑 63A.70 1005
ㄙㄚˋ (sah)
摋 10A.82 102
薩 20A.11 258

卅 22.22 361
趿 40B.82 617
颯 60S.70 879

ㄙㄞ **SAI** (sai)

揌 10A.72 93
顋 41S.80 690
腮 42A.72 718
鰓 92C.72 1381
㙞 11A.11 197
㩙 10A.11 57

ㄙㄞˋ (saih)

賽 62.80 934

ㄙㄢ **SAN** (san)

叄 93.91 1399
毿 93S.70 1450
三 30.30 433
釤 81A.91 1126

ㄙㄢˇ (saan)

糝 22C.91 411
傘 81.10 1085
繖 93B.82 1444

ㄙㄢˋ (sahn)

散 20S.82 303

ㄙㄤ **SANG** (sang)

喪 10.02 14
桑 32.01 537

ㄙㄤˇ (saang)

搡 10A.01 49
磉 31B.01 492
顙 32S.80 566
嗓 40A.01 579

ㄙㄤˋ (sahng)

喪 10.02 14

ㄙㄠ **SAU** (sau)

搔 10A.93 107
騷 51B.93 767
臊 42A.01 705
艘 91S.82 1330
繅 93B.01 1421

ㄙㄠˇ (saau)

掃 10A.22 63
(埽)
嫂 93A.82 1417
㛮 93A.82 1418

ㄙㄜ **SE**

ㄙㄜˋ (seh)

色 92.70 1348
銫 81A.70 1120
嗇 10.41 27
穡 90A.41 1180
瑟 31.72 473
塞 62.11 921
澀 63A.30 980

ㄙㄣ **SEN** (sen)

森 10.01 9

ㄙㄥ **SENG** (seng)

僧 91A.41 1258

ㄕㄚ **SHA** (sha)

砂 31B.91 502
紗 93B.91 1447
沙 63A.91 1023
吵 40A.91 605
痧 61.A91 912
裟 63.02 953
鯊 63.63 955
殺 82S.82 1139
鎩 81A.82 1125

ㄕㄚˊ (shar)

啥 40A.40 589
(倽)

ㄕㄚˇ (shaa)

傻 91A.82 1276

ㄕㄚˋ (shah)

霎 31D.93 517
唼 40A.93 606
翣 50.93 734
喢 40A.21 584
歃 90S.81 1197
啑 40A.83 604
箑 92A.83 1374
嗄 40A.82 603
煞 92.63 1346

ㄕㄞ **SHAI** (shai)

篩 92A.22 1365

ㄕㄞˇ (shaai)

骰 42B.82 725

ㄕㄞˋ (shaih)

晒 41A.41 659
曬 41A.70 662

ㄕㄢ **SHAN** (shan)

山 21.21 306
舢 91S.21 1320
珊 31A.42 487
跚 40B.42 612
刪 42S.00 726
姍 93A.42 1412
搧 10A.50 83
煽 91D.50 1313
杉 10B.91 143
衫 63C.91 1042
摻 10A.91 106
苫 20A.40 267
芟 20A.82 290
潸 63A.42 992
羶 80S.30 1081
(膻)

ㄕㄢˇ (shaan)

陝 32A.81 559
閃 52B.00 800

ㄕㄢˋ (shahn)

訕 60A.21 845
疝 61A.21 904
汕 63A.21 975
扇 63D.50 1044
騸 51B.50 765
善 80.40 1065
蟮 22D.40 415
膳 42A.40 710
鄯 80S.22 1080
鐥 81B.40 1129
鱔 92C.40 1380
繕 93B.40 1431
擅 10A.30 69
(抎)
嬗 93A.30 1408
贍 41C.40 675
鱓 92C.10 1379

ㄕㄤ **SHANG** (shang)

殤 31S.50 524
傷 91A.50 1264
觴 92B.50 1377
商 60.42 822

ㄕㄤˇ (shaang)

賞 22.80 376
晌 41A.42 661

ㄕㄤˋ (shahng)

上 21A.30 319
尚 22.42 370

ㄕㄠ **SHAU** (shau)

捎 10A.42 79
梢 10B.42 129
稍 90A.42 1181
艄 91S.42 1325
筲 92A.42 1369
燒 91D.70 1314

ㄕㄠˊ (shaur)

勺 92.50 1341
杓 10B.50 132
芍 20A.50 279
韶 60S.40 875

ㄕㄠˇ (shaau)

少 22.91 381

ㄕㄠˋ (shauh)

邵 50S.22 739
劭 50S.50 740
紹 93B.40 1430
哨 40A.42 591

ㄕㄜ **SHE** (she)

佘 81.01 1084
賒 41C.01 674
奢 12.41 222

ㄕㄜˊ (sher)

蛇 22D.70 418
(虵)
舌 90.40 1153

ㄕㄜˇ (shee)

捨 10A.40 74

ㄕㄜˋ (sheh)

舍 81.40 1091
猞 91C.40 1301
射 91S.00 1317
麝 61.00 887
攝 10A.10 53
赦 11S.82 214
設 60A.81 866

涉 63A.91 1023
社 63B.11 1027

ㄕㄣ **SHEN** (shen)

申 22.22 359
砷 31B.22 495
呻 40A.22 584
伸 91A.22 1247
紳 93B.22 1426
甡 10S.11 159
莘 20A.10 257
詵 60A.70 857
深 63A.01 965
身 91.00 1199
娠 93A.02 1405

ㄕㄣˊ (shern)

神 63B.22 1028

ㄕㄣˇ (sheen)

審 62.41 928
讅 60A.41 851
瀋 63A.41 989
嬸 93A.41 1411
哂 40A.41 590
諗 60A.72 863
矧 92S.22 1387

ㄕㄣˋ (shehn)

甚 20.21 239
(乜)
葚 20A.21 259
抻 10A.22 62
慎 22A.80 398
(昚)
腎 51.42 749
脤 51A.93 760
滲 63A.91 1024

ㄕㄥ **SHENG** (sheng)

升 90.20 1151
陞 32A.11 552
昇 41.20 627
生 10.11 19
牲 10C.11 145
甥 10S.50 162
笙 92A.11 1362
聲 11.10 171
(声)

ㄕㄥˊ (sherng)

繩 93B.70 1439

ㄕㄥˇ (sheeng)

眚 10.41 27
省 22.41 366

ㄕㄥˋ (shehng)

晟 41.71 647
盛 71.30 1048
乘 90.01 1147
嵊 21B.01 330
剩 90S.00 1187
聖 31.11 450
勝 42A.50 713
賸 42A.80 719

ㄒㄧ **SHI** (shi)

兮 80.50 1068
醯 31C.30 506
西 31.41 464
栖 10B.41 126
恓 22A.41 392
希 82.22 1138
悕 22A.22 390
豨 31S.22 520
唏 40A.22 585
晞 41A.22 658
欷 82S.81 1139
稀 90A.22 1178
奚 90.81 1167
蹊 40B.81 616
溪 63A.81 1016
鼷 90.70 1163
谿 90S.40 1193
徯 91B.81 1292
犀 52A.10 781
樨 10B.10 115
熹 11.63 179
嘻 40A.40 588
禧 63B.40 1031
僖 91A.40 1253
熺 91D.40 1311
嬉 93A.40 1409
巇 21B.71 332
嚱 40A.71 598
羲 80.71 1071
犧 10C.71 147
曦 41A.71 663
攜 10A.42 79
(携)
觿 92B.42 1377
析 10B.22 120
晳 10.41 27
皙 10.41 27
蜥 22D.22 414
晰 41A.22 658
淅 63A.22 976
悉 90.72 1164
蟋 22D.72 420
醯 31C.30 506
噏 40A.50 595
吸 40A.82 603
畦 41S.11 686
膝 42A.02 705
熙 51.63 751

ㄒㄧˊ (shir)

昔 20.41 241
惜 22A.41 392
腊 42A.41 711
息 91.72 1221
熄 91D.72 1315
媳 93A.72 1416
席 61.22 891
蓆 20A.22 262
裼 63C.50 1039
錫 81A.50 1116
檄 10B.82 142
覡 31S.70 525
隰 32A.63 557
習 50.41 729
襲 60.02 806

ㄒㄧˇ (shii)

徙 91B.83 1296
蓰 20A.83 292
屣 52A.83 788
(蹝)
喜 11.40 175
葸 20A.72 286
璽 31.11 450
洗 63A.70 1004
枲 93.01 1392

ㄒㄧˋ (shih)

系 90.01 1146
繫 10.01 12
係 91A.01 1239
夕 92.32 1335
矽 31B.32 496
穸 62A.32 944
汐 63A.32 982
翕 81.50 1095
歙 81S.81 1137
舄 90.50 1158
潟 63A.50 1000
扢 10A.70 90
戲 21S.71 341
(戏)
卌 22.22 361
隙 32A.01 549
咥 40A.11 582
盻 41B.50 670
肸 42A.10 707
(肹)
鬩 52B.00 800
屭 52A.80 786
禊 63B.81 1034
郤 80S.22 1080
餼 81B.80 1131
郄 82S.22 1139
綌 93B.40 1431
細 93B.41 1432

ㄒㄧㄚ **SHIA** (shia)

蝦 22D.82 421
(虾)
瞎 41B.40 669

ㄒㄧㄚˊ (shair)

瑕 31A.82 491
霞 31D.82 516
遐 52.83 778
柙 10B.22 119
呷 40A.22 584
匣 51.21 746
狎 91C.22 1300

Character	Code	Page
峽	21B.81	332
硤	31B.81	500
陝	32A.81	559
俠	91A.81	1272
狹	91C.81	1305
轄	10D.40	152
黠	41S.40	687
洽	63A.40	983
ㄒㄧㄚˋ (shiah)		
夏	31.82	477
厦	51A.82	760
廈	61.82	900
下	31.22	454
吓	40A.22	584
暇	41A.82	664
諕	60A.70	857
罅	92S.00	1383
ㄒㄧㄢ **SHIAN** (shian)		
秈	90A.21	1178
仙	91A.21	1246
氙	92.70	1350
先	10.70	32
掀	10A.81	97
暹	41.83	654
祆	63B.81	1034
銛	81A.40	1112
躚	40B.70	614
僊	91A.70	1267
鱻	92.63	1346
鮮	92C.10	1379
纖	93B.71	1442
ㄒㄧㄢˊ (shiarn)		
弦	50A.93	737
痃	61A.93	912
舷	91S.93	1331
絃	93B.93	1448
閑	52B.00	795
嫻	93A.00	1403
鷴	52S.50	803
癇	61A.00	902
咸	71.71	1052
鹹	21S.71	341
醎	31C.71	508
啣	40A.22	585
賢	51.80	752
([illegible])		
閑	52B.00	789
涎	63A.83	1023
銜	91B.00	1287
嫌	93A.22	1408
ㄒㄧㄢˇ (shiaan)		
跣	40B.70	613
銑	81A.70	1118
箲	92A.70	1371
蘚	20A.10	257
癬	61A.10	903
嶮	21B.81	332
險	32A.81	559
蜆	22D.70	418
燹	31.81	476
尟	41.83	654
(尠)		
顯	41S.80	690
獮	91C.42	1302
ㄒㄧㄢˋ (shiahn)		
莧	20A.70	281
現	31A.70	488
睍	41B.70	671
腺	42A.02	706
線	93B.02	1422
献	10S.81	167
獻	21S.81	343
陷	32A.21	553
餡	81B.21	1128
霰	31D.82	516
限	32A.02	550
縣	41S.01	686
(県)(县)		
憲	62.72	933
羨	80.81	1074
綫	93B.71	1441
ㄒㄧㄤ **SHIANG** (shiang)		
鄉	93S.22	1448
薌	20A.22	263
相	10B.41	126
廂	61.41	893
湘	63A.41	986
箱	92A.41	1367
緗	93B.41	1431
襄	60.02	809
驤	51B.02	761
鑲	81A.02	1105
香	90.41	1154
舡	91S.30	1323
ㄒㄧㄤˊ (shiarng)		
詳	60A.10	843
庠	61.00	889
祥	63B.10	1027
翔	80S.50	1081
ㄒㄧㄤˇ (shiaang)		
响	40A.42	593
餉	81B.42	1129
饗	93.02	1393
響	93.41	1394
嚮	93.42	1394
想	10.72	34
享	60.00	804
鮝	80.63	1069
ㄒㄧㄤˋ (shiahng)		
向	91.42	1213
象	92.02	1332
橡	10B.02	114
像	91A.02	1241
巷	20.70	242
項	31S.80	528
ㄒㄧㄠ **SHIAU** (shiau)		
枵	10B.50	131
鴞	40S.50	619
逍	22.83	379
硝	31B.42	496
霄	31D.42	513
宵	62.42	929
消	63A.42	993
銷	81A.42	1114
魈	91.70	1220
綃	93B.42	1434
嘵	40A.70	596
髐	42B.70	725
驍	51B.70	765
蕭	20A.20	261
瀟	63A.20	976
簫	92A.22	1363
囂	40.40	572
哮	40A.00	576
嘐	40A.91	605
梟	91.01	1200
翛	91A.50	1264
獢	91C.42	1302
猇	91C.70	1304
ㄒㄧㄠˇ (shiaau)		
小	22.01	346
曉	41A.70	662
筱	92A.82	1374
ㄒㄧㄠˋ (shiauh)		
孝	11.00	169
酵	31C.00	503
校	10B.82	141
效	60S.82	884
(効)		
傚	91A.82	1279
肖	22.42	368
嘯	40A.22	584
笑	92A.81	1373
(咲)(关)		
ㄒㄧㄝ **SHIE** (shie)		
蝎	22D.50	417
蠍	22D.81	421
歇	41S.81	691
揳	10A.81	95
些	21A.30	322
ㄒㄧㄝˊ (shier)		
協	10S.50	163
(恊)		
脇	42A.50	714
脅	91.42	1214
勰	91S.72	1329
頡	11S.80	211
擷	10A.80	93
挾	10A.81	95
鞋	20B.11	294
叶	40A.10	580
邪	51S.22	769
諧	60A.41	850
斜	81S.10	1134

曙	41A.41	659
戍	71.71	1051
恕	93.72	1397
ㄕㄨㄚ **SHUA** (shua)		
刷	52S.00	802
ㄕㄨㄚˇ (shuaa)		
耍	31.93	479
ㄕㄨㄞ **SHUAI** (shuai)		
摔	10A.10	54
衰	60.02	808
ㄕㄨㄞˇ (shuaai)		
甩	42.70	698
ㄕㄨㄞˋ (shuaih)		
率	60.10	811
蟀	22D.70	413
帥	91S.22	1320
ㄕㄨㄢ **SHUAN** (shuan)		
拴	10A.11	57
栓	10B.11	117
閂	52B.00	790
ㄕㄨㄢˋ (shuahn)		
踹	40B.42	612
涮	63A.00	960
ㄕㄨㄤ **SHUANG** (shuang)		
霜	31D.41	512
孀	93A.41	1411
双	32S.22	566
雙 (雙)	91.82	1226
ㄕㄨㄤˇ (shuaang)		
爽	12.81	232
塽	11A.81	206
ㄕㄨㄟ **SHUEI**		
ㄕㄨㄟˊ (shueir)		
誰	60A.11	844
ㄕㄨㄟˇ (shueei)		
水	22.01	349
ㄕㄨㄟˋ (shueih)		
帨	22B.70	404
蛻	22D.70	419
稅	90A.70	1182
睡	41B.11	668
ㄕㄨㄣ **SHUN**		
ㄕㄨㄣˇ (shuun)		
盾	90.41	1156
楯	10B.41	128
吮	40A.70	598
ㄕㄨㄣˋ (shuhn)		
舜	90.10	1149
瞬	41B.10	667
順	22S.80	426
ㄕㄨㄛ **SHUO** (shuo)		
說	60A.70	858
ㄕㄨㄛˋ (shuoh)		
朔	80S.42	1081
搠	10A.42	80
蒴	20A.42	276
槊	80.01	1060
鑠	81A.01	1104
爍	91D.01	1308
妁	93A.50	1414
ㄕ **SHY** (shy)		
尸	52.91	780
屍	52A.70	786
鳲	52S.50	803
施	60S.70	880
絁	93B.70	1441
師	91S.22	1320
蒒	20A.22	263
獅	91C.22	1300
失	12.81	230
蓍	20A.41	271
虱	32.70	541
蝨	32.93	547
詩	60A.00	838
濕 (溼)	63A.63	1002
ㄕˊ (shyr)		
時 (旹)(时)	41A.00	656
塒	11A.00	195
蒔	20A.00	246
鰣	92C.00	1378
十	10.10	15
什	91A.10	1241
石	31.40	462
碩	31B.80	499
鼫	90.70	1163
食	81.02	1084
蝕	81B.93	1133
拾	10A.40	73
實 (实)	62.80	935
ㄕˇ (shyy)		
史	91.82	1226
駛	51B.82	767
使	91A.82	1275
豕	31.02	443
弛	50A.70	737
屎	52A.01	780
矢	92.81	1354
始	93A.40	1410
ㄕˋ (shyh)		
士	11.11	173
仕	91A.11	1243
氏	90.71	1163
舐	90S.71	1197
市	60.22	816
柿	10B.22	119
鈰	81A.22	1109
示	30.01	429
視 (眎)	63B.70	1032
世 (丗)	21.21	310
貰	21.80	315
是	41.83	654
諟	60A.83	867
誓	10.40	26
逝	10.83	40
式	71·71	1049
拭	10A.71	92
軾	10D.71	154
試	60A.71	861
弒	82S.71	1139
恃	22A.00	383
侍	91A.00	1232
筮	92A.30	1365
噬	40A.30	587
事	10.00	1
勢	11.50	178
螫	11.93	195
奭	12.81	232
豉	30S.82	440
嗜	40A.41	589
適	60.83	835
謚	60A.30	848
識	60A.71	861
室	62.11	921
飾	81B.22	1128
釋	90S.10	1189
ㄒㄩ **SHYU** (shyu)		
吁	40A.00	576
盱	41B.00	665
訏	60A.00	838
虛 (虚)	21A.30	323
墟	11A.30	199
歔	21S.81	344
噓	40A.30	586
須 (湏)	91S.80	1329
鬚	51.80	753
需	31D.42	514
繻	93B.42	1434
胥	32.42	539
戌	71.71	1051
ㄒㄩˊ (shyur)		
徐	91B.01	1288
ㄒㄩˇ (shyuu)		
呴	40.63	572
煦	41.63	645
栩	10B.50	131
詡	60A.50	856
糈	22C.42	409
諝	60A.42	853
許	60A.10	843
ㄒㄩˋ (shyuh)		
壻	11A.42	201
婿	93A.42	1412
恤	22A.30	391
賉	41C.30	674

洫 63A.30 981
(淢)
卹 91S.22 1321
勗 41.50 643
勖 41S.50 689
蓄 20A.41 272
頊 31A.80 490
酗 31C.21 505
序 61.00 887
叙 81S.82 1137
(敍)
旭 91.70 1219
魆 91.70 1220
絮 93.01 1392
緒 93B.41 1431
續 93B.80 1443
(続)

ㄒㄩㄢ **SHYUAN** (shyuan)
宣 63.30 922
揎 10A.30 69
萱 20A.30 264
喧 40A.30 586
暄 41A.30 659
諠 60A.30 848
煊 91D.30 1311
儇 91A.02 1240
嬛 93A.02 1405
軒 10D.10 149
諼 60A.82 867

ㄒㄩㄢˊ (shyuarn)
旋 60S.83 885
璇 31A.83 491
漩 63A.83 1022
璿 31A.41 486
懸 41.72 649
玄 60.93 836

ㄒㄇㄢˇ (shyuaan)
咺 40A.30 586
烜 91D.30 1310
選 52.83 779
(选)

ㄒㄩㄢˋ (shyuahn)
眩 41B.93 672
泫 63A.93 1025
衒 91B.00 1287
炫 91D.93 1317
楦 10B.30 123
(楥)
渲 63A.30 981
鏇 81A.83 1125
絢 93B.50 1437

ㄒㄩㄝ **SHYUE** (shyue)
薛 20A.10 257
靴 20B.70 296

ㄒㄩㄝˊ (shyuer)
學 90.00 1144
([illegible])(斈)(学)
鷽 90.50 1159
踅 10.83 39

ㄒㄩㄝˇ (shyuee)
雪 31D.30 511
鱈 92C.30 1380

ㄒㄩㄝˋ (shyueh)
削 22S.00 424
穴 62.80 936
血 91.30 1205

ㄒㄩㄣ **SHYUN** (shyun)
熏 90.63 1159
壎 11A.63 203
薰 20A.63 280
醺 31C.63 507
曛 41A.63 662
勳 90S.50 1195
(勛)
燻 91D.63 1313

ㄒㄩㄣˊ (shyurn)
旬 92.50 1340
栒 10B.50 132
荀 20A.50 279
峋 21B.50 332
恂 22A.50 396
詢 60A.50 856
洵 63A.50 1000
郇 92S.22 1387
尋 50.00 727
撏 10A.00 46
蕁 20A.00 247
潯 63A.00 960
燖 91D.00 1307
鱘 92C.00 1378
馴 51B.22 763
循 91B.41 1290
鱏 92C.10 1379
巡 93.83 1398

ㄒㄩㄣˋ (shyuhn)
迅 32.83 544
訊 60A.70 857
汛 63A.70 1005
殉 31S.50 524
徇 91B.50 1291
(狥)
蕈 20A.10 255
遜 32.83 546
巽 52.80 777
訓 60A.22 846

ㄒㄩㄥ **SHYUNG** (shyung)
凶 21.21 311
兇 21.70 314
胸 42A.50 714
(胷)
詾 60A.50 857
洶 63A.50 1000
匈 92.50 1341
兄 40.70 572

ㄒㄩㄥˊ (shyurng)
雄 12S.11 235
熊 93.63 1395

ㄒㄩㄥˋ (shyuhng)
詗 60A.42 853
敻 92.82 1354

ㄙㄡ **SOU** (sou)
搜 10A.82 99
颼 42.70 701
廋 61.82 900
溲 63A.82 1019
餿 81B.82 1132
蒐 20A.70 284

ㄙㄡˇ (soou)
擻 10A.82 100
藪 20A.82 290
叟 22.82 377
(叜)
嗾 40A.81 601

ㄙㄡˋ (souh)
嗽 40A.81 600
漱 63A.81 1015

ㄙㄨ **SU** (su)
穌 92C.01 1378
蘇 20A.01 252
(苏)
囌 40A.01 579
甦 31.83 479
酥 31C.01 503

ㄙㄨˊ (sur)
俗 91A.40 1255

ㄙㄨˋ (suh)
素 10.01 11
愫 22A.01 384
嗉 40A.01 579
膆 42A.01 705
溯 63A.42 997
塑 80.11 1061
愬 80.72 1072
遡 80.83 1075
速 10.83 40
蔌 20A.81 287
餗 81B.01 1126
簌 92A.81 1373
觫 92B.01 1375
宿 62.41 928
蓿 20A.41 272
縮 93B.41 1433
肅 22.22 359
鷫 22S.50 426
驌 51B.22 763
粟 31.01 443
夙 42.70 699
訴 60A.22 847
謖 60A.82 866
窣 62A.10 942

ㄙㄨㄢ **SUAN** (suan)
酸 31C.82 509
痠 61A.82 911
狻 91C.82 1306

ㄙㄨㄢˋ (suahn)
祘 30S.01 437
蒜 20A.01 250
筭 92A.20 1362
算 92A.20 1362

ㄙㄨㄟ **SUEI** (suei)
荽 20A.93 294
綏 93B.93 1448
雖 40S.11 619
(虽)
睢 41B.11 668

ㄙㄨㄟˊ (sueir)
隋 32A.42 555
隨 32A.83 560

ㄙㄨㄟˇ (sueei)
髓 42B.83 725

ㄙㄨㄟˋ (sueih)
遂 80.83 1076
隧 32A.83 561
邃 62A.83 949
燧 91D.83 1316
碎 31B.10 493
睟 41B.10 667
誶 60A.10 843
穗 90A.72 1183
繐 93B.72 1442
祟 21.01 304
歲 21A.71 327

ㄙㄨㄣ **SUN** (sun)
孫 32S.01 563
搎 10A.01 49
蓀 20A.01 250
猻 91C.01 1298
飧 31S.02 520
(飱)

ㄙㄨㄣˇ (suun)
損 10A.80 93
榫 10B.10 115
筍 92A.50 1370
笋 92A.91 1375

ㄙㄨㄥ **SUNG** (sung)
松 10B.93 144
菘 20A.93 293
崧 21.93 316
鬆 51.93 753
淞 63A.93 1024
嵩 21.42 314

ㄙㄨㄥˊ (surng)
㞞 52A.83 788

ㄙㄨㄥˇ (suung)
悚 22A.01 384
竦 60S.01 869
聳 91.10 1203
慫 91.72 1222

ㄙㄨㄥˋ (suhng)
訟 60A.93 868
頌 80S.80 1082
誦 60A.42 853
宋 60.01 916
送 80.83 1074

ㄙㄨㄛ **SUO** (suo)
梭 10B.82 142
唆 40A.82 604
挱 10A.91 106
桫 10A.91 143
莎 20A.91 293
挲 63.00 951
娑 63.93 958
蓑 20A.02 254
簑 92A.02 1360
嗦 40A.01 579

ㄙㄨㄛˇ (suoo)
瑣 31A.80 490
嗩 40A.80 600
鎖 81A.80 1122
索 10.01 10
璅 31A.01 482
所 90S.22 1192
(㪽)

ㄙ **SY** (sy)
ㄙ 93.93 1400
私 90A.93 1185
思 41.72 648
鍶 81A.72 1122
偲 91A.72 1270
緦 93B.72 1442
斯 20S.22 299
撕 10A.22 16
嘶 40A.22 584
廝 61.22 891
(厮)
澌 63A.22 976
凘 63A.22 976
絲 93B.01 1421
(絲)
鷥 93.50 1395
螄 22D.22 414
司 50.50 731

ㄙˇ (syy)
死 31.70 470

ㄙˋ (shy)
巳 52.70 775
汜 63A.70 1007
祀 63B.70 1033
四 41.41 640
駟 51B.41 764
泗 63A.41 988
似 91A.81 1273
姒 93A.81 1416
嗣 40S.50 619
飼 81B.50 1130
伺 91A.50 1262
笥 92A.50 1370
竢 60S.81 883
涘 63A.81 1018
俟 91A.81 1274
耜 10S.40 160
寺 11.00 169
賜 41C.50 676
兕 40.70 573
肆 51S.10 768

ㄊ T
ㄘ TS
ㄗ TZ

ㄊㄚ **TA** (ta)
塌 11A.50 202
溻 63C.50 1039
靸 20B.82 297
鉈 81A.70 1119
他 91A.70 1266
她 93A.70 1415

ㄊㄚˇ (taa)
塔 11A.40 199
鎝 81A.40 1111

ㄊㄚˋ (tah)
沓 22.41 364
踏 40B.41 611
搨 10A.50 82
榻 10B.50 131
蹋 40B.50 613
遢 41.83 653
闒 52B.00 795
撻 10A.83 103
躂 40B.83 617
闥 52B.00 789
㒓 91A.83 1279
嗒 40A.40 588
遝 41D.83 684
獺 91C.80 1305

ㄊㄞ **TAI** (tai)
胎 42A.40 710

ㄊㄞˊ (tair)
台 93.40 1394
苔 20A.40 269
颱 42.70 702
駘 51B.40 764
鮐 92D.40 1380
炱 93.81 1398
邰 93S.22 1448
臺 11.11 173
擡 10A.11 55
(抬)
檯 10B.11 116
(枱)
薹 20A.11 258

ㄊㄞˋ (taih)
太 12.81 228
汰 63A.81 1015
鈦 81A.81 1123

泰 12.02 217
態 93.72 1397

ㄊㄢ **TAN** (tan)

攤 10A.11 55
癱 61A.11 904
灘 63A.11 972
坍 11A.42 201
貪 81.80 1096
怹 91.72 1220

ㄊㄢˊ (tarn)

談 60A.81 865
痰 61A.81 910
郯 91S.22 1321
覃 31.01 446
蟫 22D.10 412
醰 31C.10 504
譚 60A.10 843
潭 63A.10 970
檀 10B.30 122
(枟)
壇 11A.30 199
(坛)
曇 41.93 655
壜 11A.93 208
(罈)

ㄊㄢˇ (taan)

坦 11A.30 199
袒 63C.30 1036
忐 21A.72 327
黮 41S.21 687
毯 90.70 1162

ㄊㄢˋ (tahn)

炭 21.81 315
碳 31B.81 500
探 10A.01 50
歎 20S.81 302
(嘆)

ㄊㄤ **TANG** (tang)

鞺 20B.11 294
蹚 40B.11 609
鏜 81A.11 1107
湯 63A.50 998

ㄊㄤˊ (tarng)

唐 61.40 893
搪 10A.40 73
塘 11A.40 200
赯 11S.40 209
糖 22C.40 407
螗 22D.40 415
溏 63A.40 983
堂 22.11 355
螳 22D.11 413
膛 42A.11 707
棠 22.01 348

ㄊㄤˇ (taang)

惝 22A.42 395
淌 63A.42 994
倘 91A.42 1259
躺 91S.42 1325
鎲 81A.63 1118
儻 91A.63 1264

ㄊㄤˋ (tahng)

趟 11.83 189
燙 63.81 956

ㄊㄠ **TAU** (tau)

搯 10A.21 60
槄 10B.21 119
慆 22A.21 389
韜 22S.21 425
謟 60A.21 845
滔 63A.21 976
縚 93B.21 1425
掏 10A.50 84
饕 40.02 568
叨 40A.50 594
弢 50A.82 737
絛 91A.01 1240
(縧)

ㄊㄠˊ (taur)

桃 10B.70 133
鼗 22.82 377
(鞉)
逃 22.83 377
咷 40A.70 596
洮 63A.70 1005
萄 20A.50 279
陶 32A.50 557
啕 40A.50 595
淘 63A.50 1000
綯 93B.50 1437
檮 10B.00 110
燾 11.63 179
濤 63A.00 958

ㄊㄠˇ (taau)

討 60A.00 837

ㄊㄠˋ (tauh)

套 12.93 234

ㄊㄜ **TE**

ㄊㄜˋ (teh)

忒 71.71 1050
鋱 81A.71 1121
特 10C.00 145
忑 31.72 472
螣 42A.93 723
慝 51.72 752

ㄊㄥ **TENG**

ㄊㄥˊ (terng)

滕 42A.02 705
藤 20A.02 253
縢 42A.01 705
謄 42A.40 710
騰 40A.50 713
疼 61A.63 908

ㄊㄧ **TI** (ti)

踢 40B.50 613
剔 41.00 685
梯 10B.22 120

ㄊㄧˊ (tir)

提 10A.83 104
醍 31C.83 509
隄 32A.83 561
(堤)
題 41.83 654
鶗 41.83 655
緹 93B.83 1446
啼 40A.22 584
(嗁)
蹄 40B.22 610
(蹏)
鵜 80S.50 1081
稊 90A.22 1178
綈 93B.22 1426
荑 20A.81 288

ㄊㄧˇ (tii)

體 42B.30 724
(躰)
体 91A.10 1242

ㄊㄧˋ (tih)

悌 22A.22 389
涕 63A.22 978
剃 80S.00 1080
(鬀)
銻 81A.22 1109
鬄 51.50 751
髢 51.70 751
趯 11.83 191
籊 92A.11 1362
替 12.41 222
薙 20A.11 259
惕 22A.50 396
殢 31S.22 520
嚏 40A.83 604
屜 52A.21 783
逖 91.83 1230
(逷)
倜 91A.42 1260

ㄊㄧㄢ **TIAN** (tian)

天 31.81 473
添 63A.02 969

ㄊㄧㄢˊ (tiarn)

田 41.41 632
畋 41S.82 692
恬 22A.40 391
甜 90S.41 1193
填 11A.80 206
闐 52B.00 790
滇 63A.80 1013
菾 20A.02 254

ㄊㄧㄢˇ (tiaan)

忝 90.02 1147
餂 81B.40 1129
舔 90S.02 1188
㥏 22A.80 399
覥 22S.70 426
腆 42A.80 719

洟 63A.80 1013
靦 31S.70 525
殄 31S.91 532
ㄊㄧㄢˋ (tiahn)
掭 10A.02 52
瑱 31A.80 490
ㄊㄧㄠ TIAU (tiau)
挑 10A.70 87
恌 22A.70 397
祧 63B.70 1032
ㄊㄧㄠˊ (tiaur)
苕 20A.40 267
岧 21.40 313
齠 21S.40 337
迢 50.83 734
髫 51.40 749
笤 92A.40 1366
蜩 22D.42 417
調 60A.42 853
條 91A.01 1239
(条)
佻 91A.70 1266
ㄊㄧㄠˇ (tiaau)
窕 62A.70 948
ㄊㄧㄠˋ (tiauh)
跳 40B.70 614
眺 41B.70 671
糶 21S.11 335
ㄊㄧㄝ TIE (tie)
怗 22A.40 391
帖 22B.40 403
貼 41C.40 674
ㄊㄧㄝˇ (tiee)
帖 22B.40 403
鐵 81A.71 1120
(銕)(鉄)
ㄊㄧㄝˋ (tieh)
餮 31.02 444
ㄊㄧㄥ TING (ting)
聽 31S.72 526
廳 61.72 897
(廰)(听)
桯 10B.11 117
鞓 20B.11 294
汀 63A.00 958
ㄊㄧㄥˊ (tirng)
廷 90.83 1171
莛 20A.83 292
蜓 22D.83 422
霆 31D.83 516
庭 61.83 901
筳 92A.83 1375
亭 60.00 805
楟 10B.00 110
葶 20A.00 248
停 91A.00 1235
婷 93A.00 1404
ㄊㄧㄥˇ (tiing)
挺 10A.83 106
梃 10B.83 142
鋌 81A.83 1125
艇 91S.83 1331
町 41S.00 685
ㄊㄡ TOU (tou)
鍮 81A.00 1103
偷 91A.00 1236
媮 93A.00 1404
ㄊㄡˊ (tour)
投 10A.82 101
酘 31C.82 508
頭 30S.80 438
(头)
ㄊㄡˋ (touh)
透 90.83 1173
ㄘㄚ TSA (tsa)
搽 10A.01 49
擦 10A.01 50
ㄘㄞ TSAI (tsai)
猜 91C.42 1302
ㄘㄞˊ (tsair)
才 10.00 1
材 10B.00 109
財 41C.00 673
裁 11.71 184
纔 93B.70 1441
ㄘㄞˇ (tsaai)
采 90.01 1146
採 10A.01 50
睬 41B.01 665
寀 62.01 917
彩 90S.91 1198
綵 93B.01 1421
跴 40B.41 611
ㄘㄞˋ (tsaih)
菜 20A.01 251
蔡 20A.01 252
ㄘㄢ TSAN (tsan)
參 93.91 1399
(叅)
驂 51B.91 767
餐 21A.02 318
(湌)(飡)
ㄘㄢˊ (tsarn)
慙 10.72 35
慚 22A.22 389
殘 31S.71 526
蠶 51.93 754
(蠺)(蚕)
ㄘㄢˇ (tsaan)
慘 22A.91 401
黲 41S.91 692
ㄘㄢˋ (tsahn)
粲 21A.01 317
璨 31A.01 482
燦 91D.01 1308
ㄘㄤ TSANG (tsang)
倉 81.40 1091
蒼 20A.40 269
滄 63A.40 984
傖 91A.40 1256
艙 91S.40 1324
ㄘㄤˊ (tsarng)
藏 20A.71 285
ㄘㄠ TSAU (tsau)
操 10A.01 49
糙 22C.83 410
ㄘㄠˊ (tsaur)
曹 20.41 241
(曺)
槽 10B.41 125
螬 22D.41 415
嘈 40A.41 589
漕 63A.41 986
ㄘㄠˇ (tsaau)
草 20A.10 256
艸 22.22 361
ㄘㄠˋ (tsauh)
肏 81.42 1094
ㄘㄜ TSE
ㄘㄜˋ (tseh)
惻 22A.00 383
測 63A.00 959
側 91A.00 1235
冊 42.42 695
策 92A.01 1359
(筞)
ㄘㄣ TSEN
ㄘㄣˊ (tsern)
岑 21.32 313
涔 63A.32 982
ㄘㄥ TSENG
ㄘㄥˊ (tserng)
嶒 21B.41 331
層 51A.41 784
ㄘㄥˋ (tsehng)
蹭 40B.41 612
ㄘㄡ TSOU
ㄘㄡˋ (tsouh)
輳 10D.81 155
腠 42A.81 719
湊 63A.81 1015
ㄘㄨ TSU (tsu)
粗 22C.30 406
麤 61.70 896
ㄘㄨˊ (tsur)
殂 31S.30 522
徂 91B.30 1290
ㄘㄨˋ (tsuahn)
蹙 71.83 1054
顣 71S.80 1055
蔟 20A.81 288
簇 92A.81 1373
醋 31C.41 506

蹴 40B.70 614
(蹵)
踧 40B.82 617
促 91A.83 1280
猝 91C.10 1299

ㄘㄨㄢ **TSUAN** (tsuan)
攛 10A.70 89
躥 40B.70 614
汆 81.02 1084

ㄘㄨㄢˋ (tsuahn)
竄 62A.70 948
鑹 81A.70 1119
爨 90.81 1167
篡 92A.93 1375

ㄘㄨㄟ **TSUEI** (tsuei)
崔 21.11 306
摧 10A.11 56
催 91A.11 1244
縗 93B.02 1422

ㄘㄨㄟˇ (tsueei)
璀 31A.11 484

ㄘㄨㄟˋ (tsueih)
萃 20A.10 257
悴 22A.10 386
粹 22C.10 406
啐 40A.10 581
膵 42A.10 706
翠 50.10 728
瘁 61A.10 903
淬 63A.10 971
倅 91A.10 1243
焠 91D.10 1309
綷 93B.10 1424
毳 90.70 1162
橇 10B.70 135

脆 42A.70 717
(脃)

ㄘㄨㄣ **TSUN** (tsun)
村 10B.00 109
皴 93S.82 1450
邨 10S.22 160

ㄘㄨㄣˊ (tsurn)
存 12.00 215

ㄘㄨㄣˇ (tsuun)
忖 22A.00 382

ㄘㄨㄣˋ (tsuhn)
寸 10.00 2

ㄘㄨㄥ **TSUNG** (tsung)
匆 92.50 1342
怱 92.72 1352
葱 20A.72 287
囱 91.41 1213
悤 91.72 1221
(忩)
璁 31A.72 490
聰 31S.72 527
驄 51B.72 766
樅 10B.83 142
瑽 31A.83 491

ㄘㄨㄥˊ (tsurng)
叢 22.82 377
(菆)(藂)
淙 63A.01 965
從 91B.83 1296
从 81S.81 1137

ㄘㄨㄛ **TSUO** (tsuo)
搓 10A.30 70
磋 31B.30 496
蹉 40B.30 610

撮 10A.82 101

ㄘㄨㄛˊ (tsuor)
嵯 21B.30 331
矬 92S.11 1384

ㄘㄨㄛˇ (tsuoo)
瑳 31A.30 486
脞 42A.11 707

ㄘㄨㄛˋ (tsuoh)
挫 10A.11 55
剉 22S.00 424
銼 81A.11 1107
措 10A.41 75
厝 51A.41 758
錯 81A.41 1113

ㄘ **TSY** (tsy)
雌 21S.11 336
呲 40A.70 596
疵 61A.70 908

ㄘˊ (tsyr)
詞 60A.50 855
祠 63B.50 1032
茨 20A.81 288
瓷 63.70 955
糍 22C.93 411
磁 31B.93 502
鶿 80.50 1069
甆 80.70 1070
慈 80.72 1071
鷀 80S.50 1081
辤 90S.10 1189
辞 90S.10 1189
辭 90S.10 1189

ㄘˇ (tsyy)
此 21S.70 339
跐 40B.70 614

泚 63A.70 1005

ㄘˋ (tsyh)
厠 51A.00 755
廁 61.00 887
刺 10S.00 157
次 63A.81 1018

ㄊㄨ **TU** (tu)
禿 90.70 1160

ㄊㄨˊ (tur)
荼 20A.01 251
酴 31C.01 503
途 81.83 1101
涂 63A.01 966
塗 63.11 954
屠 52A.41 784
瘏 61A.41 906
凸 40.40 570
圖 41.41 638
(图)
突 62A.81 948
釷 81A.11 1107
徒 91B.83 1296

ㄊㄨˇ (tuu)
土 11.11 172
吐 40A.11 582

ㄊㄨˋ (tuh)
兔 50.70 732
(兎)
堍 11A.70 204
菟 20A.70 281

ㄊㄨㄢ **TUAN** (tuan)
湍 63A.42 993
貒 91S.42 1325

ㄊㄨㄢˊ (tuarn)
摶 10A.00 44
慱 22A.00 383
團 41.41 635
糰 22C.41 408

ㄊㄨㄢˋ (tuahn)
彖 92.02 1332

ㄊㄨㄟ **TUEI** (tuei)
推 10A.11 57

ㄊㄨㄟˊ (tueir)
隤 32A.80 559
頹 90S.80 1197
魋 91.70 1220

ㄊㄨㄟˇ (tueei)
腿 42A.83 721

ㄊㄨㄟˋ (tueih)
退 52.83 778

ㄊㄨㄣ **TUN** (tun)
啍 40A.00 577
暾 41A.82 664
呑 90.40 1153

ㄊㄨㄣˊ (turn)
屯 10.70 32
飩 81B.70 1130
豚 42A.02 706
臀 52.42 774

ㄊㄨㄣˋ (tuhn)
褪 63C.83 1042

ㄊㄨㄥ **TUNG** (tung)
恫 22A.42 395
痌 61A.42 907
通 32.83 544

ㄊㄨㄥˊ (turng)
同 42.42 696
桐 10B.42 129
茼 20A.42 275
峒 21B.42 331

銅 81A.42 1115
侗 91A.42 1260
筒 92A.42 1369
童 60.11 814
橦 10B.11 117
曈 41A.11 658
瞳 41B.11 668
潼 63A.11 974
僮 91A.11 1245
艟 91S.11 1320
彤 42S.91 727
仝 81.30 1087
佟 91A.63 1265
筩 92A.42 1369

ㄊㄨㄥˇ (tuung)
捅 10A.42 79
桶 10B.42 129
統 93B.70 1440

ㄊㄨㄥˋ (tuhng)
慟 22A.50 396
痛 61A.42 907
衕 91B.00 1287

ㄊㄨㄛ **TUO** (tuo)
它 62.70 931
佗 91A.70 1267
拖 10A.70 90
牠 10C.70 147
托 10A.70 90
託 60A.70 860
脫 42A.70 716

ㄊㄨㄛˊ (tuor)
坨 11A.70 205
酡 31C.70 508
陀 32A.70 557
跎 40B.70 614
駝 51B.70 765
沱 63A.70 1009
鼧 90.70 1163
鴕 91S.70 1328
鮀 92C.70 1381
紽 93B.70 1441
橐 10.01 10
(槖)
鼉 40.70 573
馱 51B.81 766

ㄊㄨㄛˇ (tuoo)
橢 10B.42 129
妥 90.93 1174

ㄊㄨㄛˋ (tuoh)
蘀 20A.10 255
籜 92A.10 1360
拓 10A.40 71
柝 10B.22 120
唾 40A.11 583

ㄗㄚ **TZA** (tza)
匝 51.21 745
咂 40A.21 583
唼 40A.93 606

ㄗㄚˊ (tzar)
拶 10A.32 70
桚 10B.32 123
雜 60S.11 871
襍 63C.01 1035
砸 31B.21 494

ㄗㄞ **TZAI** (tzai)
灾 62.81 936
災 93.81 1397
哉 11.71 184
栽 11.71 183
烖 11.71 185

ㄗㄞˇ (tzaai)
崽 21.72 315
宰 62.10 921

ㄗㄞˋ (tzaih)
載 11.71 184
儎 91A.71 1268
在 12.11 218
再 31.42 467

ㄗㄢ **TZAN** (tzan)
簪 92A.41 1369

ㄗㄢˊ (tzarn)
糌 22C.41 408
喒 40A.41 591
偺 91A.41 1258
咱 40A.41 591

ㄗㄢˇ (tzaan)
攢 10A.80 93
趲 11.83 189
儹 91A.80 1270
噆 40A.41 590
寁 62.83 937
昝 92.41 1338

ㄗㄢˋ (tzahn)
贊 10.80 37
(賛)
瓚 31A.80 490
囋 40A.80 600
讚 60A.80 864
鏨 10.30 24

ㄗㄤ **TZANG** (tzang)
臧 71.71 1053
贓 41C.71 678
牂 21S.10 335
賍 41C.11 674
臢 42A.80 718
髒 42B.20 724

ㄗㄤˇ (tzaang)
駔 51B.30 763

ㄗㄤˋ (tzahng)
塟 20A.11 258
葬 20A.20 259
奘 21.81 315
臟 42A.71 718

ㄗㄠ **TZAU** (tzau)
遭 20.83 245
糟 22C.41 407
蹧 40B.41 611

ㄗㄠˇ (tzaau)
澡 63A.01 964
藻 20A.01 250
璪 31A.01 482
繰 93B.01 1420
棗 10.01 8
蚤 32.93 546
早 41.10 624

ㄗㄠˋ (tzauh)
皂 91.70 1218
唣 40A.70 597
皁 91.10 1202
造 10.83 40
慥 22A.83 401
簉 92A.83 1374
趮 11.83 190
噪 40A.01 579
躁 40B.01 607
譟 60A.01 840
燥 91D.01 1308
竈 62A.70 947
灶 91D.11 1309

ㄗㄜ **TZE**

ㄗㄜˊ (tzer)
舴 91S.22 1323
迮 92.83 1355
則 41C.00 673
鰂 92C.00 1378
責 10.80 36
幘 22B.80 404
嘖 40A.80 600
賾 51S.80 771
簀 92A.80 1372
擇 10A.10 54
澤 63A.10 970

ㄗㄜˋ (tzeh)
仄 51A.81 760
昃 41.81 652

ㄗㄟ **TZEI**

ㄗㄟˊ (tzeir)
賊 41C.71 677

ㄗㄣ **TZEN**

ㄗㄣˇ (tzeen)
怎 92.72 1352

ㄗㄣˋ (tzehn)
譖 60A.41 851

ㄗㄥ **TZENG** (tzeng)
曾 80.41 1067
增 11A.41 200
憎 22A.41 393
罾 41D.41 682
矰 92S.41 1389
繒 93B.41 1433

ㄗㄥˋ (tzehng)
贈 41C.41 676
甑 80S.70 1082

ㄗㄡ **TZOU** (tzou)
陬 32A.82 560
諏 60A.82 866
鯫 92C.82 1382
緅 93B.82 1444
騶 51B.50 765
謅 60A.50 857
鄒 92S.22 1387

ㄗㄡˇ (tzoou)
走 11.83 188

ㄗㄡˋ (tzouh)
奏 12.81 233
揍 10A.81 95
驟 51B.02 761

ㄗㄨ **TZU** (tzu)
租 90A.30 1178

ㄗㄨˊ (tzur)
卒 60.10 810
(卆)
捽 10A.10 54
崒 21.10 306
族 60S.81 882
鏃 81A.81 1124
槭 10B.71 136
足 40.83 574

ㄗㄨˇ (tzuu)
阻 32A.30 554
詛 60A.30 848
祖 63B.30 1030
俎 81S.30 1135
組 93B.30 1429

ㄗㄨㄢ **TZUAN** (tzuan)
躦 40B.80 616
鑽 81A.80 1122

ㄗㄨㄢˇ (tzuaan)
纂 92A.01 1360
纘 93B.80 1443

ㄗㄨㄢˋ (tzuahn)
攥 10A.01 50
揝 10A.41 78

ㄗㄨㄟ **TZUEI**

ㄗㄨㄟˇ (tzueei)
嘴 40A.42 592

ㄗㄨㄟˋ (tzueih)
最 41.83 652
蕞 20A.82 290
冣 62.82 937
醉 31C.10 504
晬 41A.10 658
檇 10B.42 130
罪 41D.22 681
辠 91.10 1203

ㄗㄨㄣ **TZUN** (tzun)
尊 80.00 1058
樽 10B.00 111
遵 80.83 1077
鐏 81A.00 1103
鷷 92S.00 1383

ㄗㄨㄣˇ (tzuun)
撙 10A.00 47

ㄗㄨㄣˋ (tzuhn)
鱒 92C.00 1378

ㄗㄨㄥ **TZUNG** (tzung)
宗 62.01 916
棕 10B.01 112
踪 40B.01 607
鬃 51.01 742
椶 10B.82 141
蹤 40B.83 617

ㄗㄨㄥˇ (tzuung)
偬 91A.72 1270
總 93B.72 1442

ㄗㄨㄥˋ (tzuhng)
粽 22C.01 405
綜 93B.01 1421
糉 22C.82 410
縱 93B.83 1446

ㄗㄨㄛ **TZUO**

ㄗㄨㄛˊ (tzuor)
昨 41A.22 658

ㄗㄨㄛˇ (tzuoo)
左 12.30 220
佐 91A.30 1251

ㄗㄨㄛˋ (tzuoh)
坐 22.11 353
座 61.11 890
銼 81A.11 1107
柞 10B.22 121
怍 22A.22 390
酢 31C.22 505
阼 32A.22 353
胙 42A.22 709
祚 63B.22 1030
作 91A.22 1249
鑿 22.30 364
做 91A.82 1274

ㄗ **TZY** (tzy)
孖 32S.00 563
孜 32S.82 567
仔 91A.00 1235
咨 63.40 954
諮 60A.40 849
趑 11.83 193
粢 63.01 952
資 63.80 956
姿 63.93 958
茲 20A.93 294
(兹)([illegible])
孳 20A.00 1059
嵫 21B.93 333
滋 63A.93 1026
鎡 81A.93 1126
輜 10D.41 152
菑 20A.41 273
淄 63A.41 990
錙 81A.41 1114
緇 93B.41 1433
貲 21A.80 328
齜 21S.70 340
髭 51.70 752
鼒 10.22 22
吱 40A.82 603

ㄗˇ (tzyy)
子 32.00 534
耔 10S.00 158
籽 22C.00 465
仔 91A.00 1235
胏 42A.22 708
秭 90A.22 1178
笫 92A.22 1363
紫 21A.01 317
訾 21A.40 324
梓 10B.10 115
滓 63A.10 971

ㄗˋ (tzyh)
眥 21A.41 325
(眦)
胔 21A.42 326
胾 11.71 185
字 62.00 915
恣 63.72 955
漬 63A.80 1013
自 91.41 1210

ㄨ U

ㄨ WU

ㄨㄚ **WA** (wa)
蛙 22D.11 413
哇 40A.11 582
窪 62A.11 942
挖 10A.70 89
媧 93A.42 1412

ㄨㄚˊ (war)
娃 93A.11 1406

ㄨㄚˇ (waa)
瓦 31.70 469

ㄨㄚˋ (wah)
嗢 40A.30 586
膃 42A.30 709
襪 63C.71 1041
(韤)(韈)(袜)

ㄨㄞ **WAI** (wai)
歪 31.30 460

ㄨㄞˋ (waih)
外 92S.22 1385

ㄨㄢ **WAN** (wan)
蜿 22D.70 419
豌 30S.70 438
剜 62S.00 949
彎 93.50 1395
(弯)
灣 63A.50 1002

ㄨㄢˊ (warn)
丸 91.70 1219
芄 20A.70 284

汍 63A.70 1009
紈 93B.70 1441
刓 30S.00 437
頑 30S.80 438
完 62.70 931
ㄨㄢˇ (waan)
宛 62.70 933
琬 31A.70 489
碗 31B.70 498
(椀)(盌)
畹 41S.70 690
婉 93A.70 1415
莞 20A.70 282
皖 91S.70 1328
挽 10A.70 91
輓 10D.70 154
晚 41A.70 662
娩 93A.70 1415
綰 93B.40 1430
ㄨㄢˋ (wahn)
玩 31A.70 488
翫 50S.70 740
惋 22A.70 397
腕 42A.70 716
萬 20A.42 274
万 31.50 469
卍 50.21 728
ㄨㄤ **WANG** (wang)
汪 63A.11 973
尪 80.70 1070
(尫)
ㄨㄤˊ (warng)
王 31.11 447
亡 60.21 815
(亾)

ㄨㄤˇ (waang)
罔 42.42 698
惘 22A.42 395
蝄 22D.42 417
魍 91.70 1220
網 93B.42 1435
枉 10B.11 116
网 42.42 696
往 91B.11 1289
ㄨㄤˋ (wahng)
望 60.11 813
忘 60.72 828
妄 60.93 836
旺 41A.11 658
ㄨㄟ **WEI** (wei)
萎 20A.93 294
逶 90.83 1173
威 71.71 1052
葳 20A.71 285
崴 21.71 314
隈 32A.02 550
偎 91A.02 1240
煨 91D.02 1309
ㄨㄟˊ (weir)
危 92.70 1348
桅 10B.70 135
韋 22.10 353
違 22.83 379
幃 22B.10 402
圍 41.41 636
闈 52B.00 790
惟 22A.11 388
帷 22B.11 403
唯 40A.11 583
維 93B.11 1424

微 91B.82 1292
薇 20A.82 291
嵬 21.70 314
巍 21.70 314
囗 40.40 570
爲 90.50 1158
(為)
ㄨㄟˇ (weei)
尾 52A.70 786
娓 93A.70 1415
委 90.93 1174
諉 60A.93 868
痿 61A.93 912
洧 63A.42 992
鮪 92C.42 1380
葦 20A.10 255
韡 22S.10 424
瑋 31A.10 483
韙 41.83 654
偉 91A.10 1242
煒 91D.10 1309
緯 93B.10 1423
隗 32A.70 558
骫 42B.70 725
亹 60.30 818
猥 91C.02 1298
ㄨㄟˋ (weih)
未 10.01 4
味 40A.01 578
畏 41.02 624
喂 40A.02 580
餵 81B.02 1127
(餧)
胃 41.42 642
蝟 22D.42 416

(猬)
謂 60A.42 853
尉 52S.00 802
蔚 20A.00 247
慰 52.72 777
魏 90S.70 1196
位 91A.30 1253
僞 91A.50 1263
衛 91B.00 1283
ㄨㄣ **WEN** (wen)
榅 10B.30 122
瘟 61A.30 905
溫 63A.30 979
鰛 92C.30 1380
ㄨㄣˊ (wern)
文 60.82 830
蚊 22D.82 421
(螡)
雯 31D.82 516
紋 93B.82 1445
聞 52B.00 793
ㄨㄣˇ (ween)
吻 40A.50 595
脗 42A.40 710
刎 92S.00 1382
穩 90A.72 1183
ㄨㄣˋ (wehn)
抆 10A.82 102
紊 60.01 806
汶 63A.82 1020
搵 10A.30 67
問 52B.00 793
ㄨㄥ **WENG** (weng)
翁 80.50 1068
嗡 40A.50 595

ㄨㄥˇ (weeng)
蓊 20A.50 278
滃 63A.50 1000
ㄨㄥˋ (wehng)
罋 60.21 816
甕 60.70 826
(瓮)
齆 91S.70 1328
ㄨㄛ **WO** (wo)
萵 20A.42 275
窩 62A.42 945
渦 63A.42 995
倭 91A.93 1282
ㄨㄛˇ (woon)
我 90.71 1164
ㄨㄛˋ (woh)
握 10A.11 56
齷 21S.11 336
幄 22B.11 403
喔 40A.11 582
渥 63A.11 973
斡 10S.10 159
臥 51S.22 769
(卧)
沃 63A.81 1016
ㄨ **WU** (wu)
圬 11A.50 201
汚 63A.50 997
(污)
烏 91.50 1216
嗚 40A.50 595
鄔 91S.22 1321
屋 52A.11 782
汙 63A.00 959

Character	Code	Page
ㄨˊ	(wur)	
巫	31.30	460
誣	60A.30	847
吳	40.81	574
蜈	22D.81	421
吾	31.40	462
梧	10B.40	124
唔	40A.40	588
鼯	90.70	1163
無	92.63	1343
蕪	20A.63	280
无	31.70	469
毋	41.50	642
ㄨˇ	(wuu)	
五	31.30	457
牾	10C.40	146
伍	91A.30	1252
午	92.10	1333
忤	22A.10	386
仵	91A.10	1243
武	71.71	1050
鵡	71S.50	1054
娬	93A.71	1416
憮	22A.63	396
廡	61.63	895
舞	92.10	1334
嫵	93A.63	1414
摀	10A.50	83
侮	91A.50	1263
ㄨˋ	(wuh)	
悟	22A.40	391
晤	41A.40	659
寤	62.40	924
焐	91D.40	1311
悞	22A.81	399
誤	60A.81	864
霧	31D.50	514
鶩	32.50	540
騖	32.50	540
婺	32.93	546
務	32S.50	564
塢	11A.50	202
(隝)		
鎢	81A.50	1117
兀	31.70	470
杌	10B.70	133
勿	92.50	1342
物	10C.50	146
戊	71.71	1050
迕	92.83	1355
ㄧ, ㄩㄚ		
ㄧ	YI	
ㄩ	YU	
ㄧㄚ	**YA** (ya)	
呀	40A.00	577
鴉	51S.50	771
押	10A.22	63
鴨	41S.50	689
椏	10B.30	121
壓	51A.11	756
丫	80.22	1062
ㄧㄚˊ	(yar)	
牙	51.00	741
枒	10B.00	110
芽	20A.00	247
蚜	22D.00	411
涯	63A.11	973
衙	91B.00	1285
ㄧㄚˇ	(yaa)	
啞	40A.30	586
雅	51S.11	768
ㄧㄚˋ	(yah)	
砑	31B.00	492
迓	51.83	753
訝	60A.00	839
亞	31.30	460
掗	10A.30	67
氬	92.70	1350
婭	93A.30	1408
揠	10A.21	59
軋	10D.70	153
ㄚㄞ	**YAI**	
ㄧㄞˊ	(yair)	
厓	51A.11	756
崖	21.11	306
睚	41B.11	668
ㄧㄢ	**YAN** (yan)	
咽	40A.41	590
胭	42A.41	711
烟	91D.41	1311
焉	31.50	469
鄢	31S.22	520
嫣	93A.50	1413
崦	21B.70	332
醃	31C.70	507
閹	52B.00	789
淹	63A.70	1004
菸	20A.63	280
懨	22A.81	399
臙	42A.63	715
煙	91D.11	1309
ㄧㄢˊ	(yarn)	
延	90.83	1171
埏	11A.83	208
蜒	22D.83	422
筵	92A.83	1375
研	31B.20	494
妍	93A.20	1406
嵒	40.21	569
碞	40.40	571
癌	61A.21	904
檐	10B.40	125
簷	92A.40	1367
嚴	40.82	574
巖	21·82	316
岩	21.40	313
鹽	51.30	749
(塩)(圤)		
閻	52B.00	801
言	60.40	818
顏	60S.80	881
沿	63A.40	983
炎	91.81	1225
ㄧㄢˇ	(yaan)	
郾	51S.22	770
鼴	90.70	1163
偃	91A.21	1247
巘	21B.81	332
甗	21S.70	340
奄	12.70	225
掩	10A.70	85
罨	41D.70	683
黶	51A.63	759
魘	51A.70	759
揜	10A.20	58
眼	41B.02	666
兗	60.70	827
演	63A.80	1014
儼	91A.32	1278
衍	91B.00	1287
剡	91S.00	1318
ㄧㄢˋ	(yahn)	
彥	60.91	836
喭	40A.91	605
諺	60A.91	867
堰	11A.21	198
晏	41.93	655
鷃	41S.50	689
宴	62.93	939
燕	20.63	242
嚥	40A.63	596
讌	60A.63	857
厭	51A.81	759
饜	51A.02	756
豔	21S.30	337
(艷)(艳)		
灩	63A.30	979
(灧)		
雁	51A.11	757
(鴈)		
贗	51A.80	759
硯	31B.70	498
釅	31C.82	508
唁	40A.40	588
騐	51B.72	766
驗	51B.81	766
讞	60A.81	864
焰	91D.21	1310
(燄)		
ㄧㄤ	**YANG** (yang)	
央	91.81	1223
殃	31S.81	529
泱	63A.81	1017
秧	90A.81	1185
鴦	91.50	1217

憶 22A.72 398
臆 40A.72 718
(肊)
鐿 81A.72 1122
億 91A.72 1270
羿 50.20 728
翌 50.30 729
翊 60S.50 876
異 41.80 650
(异)
翼 50.80 733
藝 20A.93 293
囈 40A.93 605
益 80.30 1065
嗌 40A.30 587
溢 63A.30 981
鎰 81A.30 1110
縊 93B.30 1429
懿 11S.72 211
殪 31S.30 522
曀 41A.30 659
瞖 51.41 749
翳 51.50 751
屹 21B.70 332
阣 32A.70 558
仡 91A.70 1268
亦 60.00 804
弈 60.20 815
奕 60.81 830
軼 10D.81 154
佚 91A.81 1272
邑 40.70 572
挹 10A.70 87
悒 22A.70 397
裛 60.02 809
浥 63A.70 1006
毅 60S.82 883
疫 61A.82 911
役 91B.82 1293
掖 10A.83 105
腋 42A.83 722
懌 22A.10 386
斁 41S.82 692
驛 51B.10 762
譯 60A.10 843
繹 93B.10 1423
抑 10A.22 64
肄 21S.10 335
勩 21S.50 338
裔 60.42 823
誼 60A.30 848
詣 60A.41 850
瘞 61A.11 903
弋 71.71 1048
曳 71.71 1050
佾 91A.42 1261
熠 91D.41 1312
劓 91S.00 1318
逸 92.83 1355

丨ㄣ **YIN** (yin)
因 41.41 633
茵 20A.41 272
裀 63C.41 1038
銦 81A.41 1114
氤 92.70 1351
姻 93A.41 1411
(婣)
絪 93B.41 1433
殷 90S.82 1198
慇 90.72 1164
堙 11A.11 197
(陻)
湮 63A.11 973
禋 63B.11 1028
音 60.41 819
愔 22A.41 392
喑 40A.41 590
瘖 61A.41 906
陰 32A.93 561

丨ㄣˊ (yirn)
誾 52B.00 798
狺 91C.40 1301
垠 11A.02 196
齦 21S.02 335
銀 81A.02 1104
寅 62.80 934
夤 92.80 1353
斷 21S.22 337
釿 81A.22 1109
淫 63A.11 974
霪 31D.11 510
鄞 20S.22 299
嚚 40.40 571
唫 40A.30 587
吟 40A.32 587

丨ㄣˇ (yiin)
引 50A.22 735
靷 20B.22 294
蚓 22D.22 414
隱 32.01 537
隱 32A.72 558
讔 60A.72 863
癮 61A.72 909
尹 52.91 780
飲 81B.81 1132

丨ㄣˋ (yihn)
蔭 20A.93 293
癊 61.93 901
窨 62A.41 944
印 90S.22 1191
胤 91S.70 1328

丨ㄥ **YING** (ying)
英 20A.81 288
瑛 31A.81 490
霙 31D.81 516
罃 91.21 1205
鶯 91.50 1217
膺 61.42 894
鷹 61.50 894
應 61.72 897
(应)
嬰 41.93 655
攖 10A.93 107
櫻 10B.93 144
瓔 31A.93 492
嚶 40A.93 606
鸚 41S.50 689
纓 93B.93 1448
罌 41.21 628
甖 41.70 647

丨ㄥˊ (yirng)
盈 32.30 538
楹 10B.30 122
瑩 91.11 1204
瀅 63A.11 975
縈 91.01 1201
瀠 63A.01 966
瑩 91.11 1204
營 91.40 1208
(营)
熒 91.81 1226
螢 91.93 1230
贏 60.70 828
嬴 60.70 828
瀛 63A.70 1009
蠅 22D.70 418
迎 90.83 1172
(迊)

丨ㄥˇ (yiing)
潁 21S.80 341
穎 21S.80 342
郢 40S.22 619
影 41S.91 692
癭 61A.93 912

丨ㄥˋ (yihng)
硬 31B.82 501
映 41A.81 664
媵 42A.93 723
應 61.72 897
(应)

丨ㄛ **YO** (yo)
唷 40A.42 593

丨ㄡ **YOU** (you)
攸 91A.82 1279
悠 91.72 1221
憂 31.82 477
耰 10S.82 167
優 91A.82 1277
幽 21.21 310
呦 40A.50 595
麀 61.70 896

丨ㄡˊ (your)
尤 12.70 225
疣 61A.70 908
魷 92C.70 1381

由	22.41	367
蚰	22D.41	415
油	63A.41	986
鈾	81A.41	1113
蝣	22D.00	411
遊	60.83	835
(遊)		
游	63A.00	961
猶	91C.41	1301
(犹)		
蕕	20A.41	273
猷	80S.81	1082
逌	21A.83	329
郵	90S.22	1190
繇	92S.01	1384
ㄧㄡˇ	(yoou)	
有	12.42	223
銪	81A.42	1114
友	12.82	233
莠	20A.50	278
卣	21A.41	325
酉	31.41	465
黝	41S.50	689
牖	91S.42	1325
ㄧㄡˋ	(youh)	
右	12.40	221
祐	63B.40	1031
佑	91A.40	1253
囿	41.41	634
宥	62.42	928
侑	91A.42	1258
柚	10B.41	126
鼬	90.70	1163
釉	90S.41	1193
又	32.82	542

褎	60.02	810
誘	60A.50	856
幼	93S.50	1449
ㄩ	**YU** (yu)	
迂	31.83	478
紆	93B.00	1420
瘀	61A.63	908
淤	63A.63	1002
ㄩˊ	(yur)	
于	31.00	441
杅	10B.00	110
圩	11A.00	195
盂	31.00	461
竽	92A.00	1358
余	81.01	1084
畬	81.41	1091
餘	81B.01	1126
臾	91.81	1223
萸	20A.81	289
腴	42A.81	720
諛	60A.81	865
舁	90.20	1151
禺	41.42	642
嵎	21B.42	331
齵	21S.42	338
隅	32A.42	555
愚	41.72	649
俞	81.00	1083
揄	10A.00	47
榆	10B.00	111
愉	22A.00	383
瑜	31A.00	481
隃	32A.00	548
(隃)		
踰	40B.00	607

窬	62A.00	942
渝	63A.00	961
毹	90.70	1162
兪	81.93	1102
楡	10B.93	144
愉	22A.93	402
瑜	31A.93	492
踰	40B.93	618
窬	62A.93	949
渝	63A.93	1026
逾	81.83	1101
覦	81S.70	1136
歈	81S.81	1137
虞	21A.81	328
娛	93A.81	1416
魚	92.63	1342
漁	63A.63	1003
璵	31A.80	490
歟	90S.81	1197
(欤)		
雩	31D.50	514
予	32.00	534
於	60S.63	876
(扵)		
輿	90.80	1166
ㄩˇ	(yuu)	
齬	21S.40	337
圄	41.41	636
語	60A.40	848
庾	61.81	899
瘐	61A.81	910
與	90.80	1165
(与)		
嶼	21B.80	332
雨	31.42	467

圉	41.41	634
羽	50S.50	740
宇	62.00	915
窳	62A.83	949
禹	90.42	1157
傴	91A.21	1247
ㄩˋ	(yuh)	
遇	41.83	653
庽	61.42	894
寓	62.42	929
喩	40A.00	577
諭	60A.00	839
瘉	61A.00	902
癒	61A.72	909
喻	40A.93	606
諭	60A.93	868
瘉	61A.93	912
愈	81.72	1096
御	91B.22	1289
禦	91.01	1201
預	32S.80	566
蕷	20A.80	287
豫	32S.02	563
龥	81S.80	1137
籲	92A.80	1373
玉	31.11	448
鈺	81A.11	1107
峪	21B.40	331
浴	63A.40	983
裕	63C.40	1037
鵒	80S.50	1081
昱	41.30	629
煜	91D.30	1311
域	11A.71	206
蜮	22D.71	420

閾	52B.00	799
彧	71.71	1049
欲	80S.81	1082
慾	80.72	1071
矞	32.42	540
鷸	32S.50	564
隩	32A.81	559
燠	91D.81	1316
鬱	10.91	42
郁	12S.22	236
芋	20A.00	246
聿	22.10	353
鬻	50.42	730
馭	51B.82	767
育	60.42	820
飫	81B.81	1132
譽	90.40	1154
(誉)		
獄	91C.81	1305
毓	92S.70	1390
嫗	93A.21	1407
ㄩㄢ	**YUAN** (yuan)	
眢	92.41	1338
鴛	92.50	1340
冤	62.70	932
(寃)		
淵	63A.22	977
鳶	71.50	1048
ㄩㄢˊ	(yuarn)	
元	30.70	435
芫	20A.70	281
黿	30.70	436
沅	63A.70	1005
爰	90.82	1169
援	10A.82	103

湲 63A.82 1021
猨 91C.82 1306
原 51A.01 755
源 63A.01 964
袁 11.02 170
轅 10D.02 149
園 41.41 635
猿 91C.02 1298
員 40.80 573
(貟)
圓 41.41 637
垣 11A.30 199
圜 41.41 638
緣 93B.02 1422
ㄩㄢˇ (yuaan)
遠 11.83 187
(远)
ㄩㄢˋ (yuahn)
苑 20A.70 285
怨 92.72 1353
愿 51A.72 759
願 51S.80 771
掾 10A.02 52
櫞 10B.02 114
院 32A.70 557
媛 93A.82 1418
ㄩㄝ **YUE** (yue)
曰 41.41 631
約 93B.50 1436
ㄩㄝˋ (yueh)
月 42.42 693
刖 42A.00 705
越 11.83 193
鉞 81A.71 1121
悅 22A.70 397
閱 52B.00 799
龠 81.42 1095
瀹 63A.42 997
鑰 81A.42 1116
籥 92A.42 1369
軏 10D.70 153
嶽 21.81 316
躍 40B.11 609
岳 90.21 1151
粵 91.50 1215
樂 93.01 1392
ㄩㄣ **YUN** (yun)
暈 41.10 625
氳 92.70 1351
ㄩㄣˊ (yurn)
云 30.93 437
耘 10S.93 168
芸 20A.93 293
紜 93B.93 1448
雲 31D.93 516
蕓 20A.93 293
匀 92.50 1341
昀 41S.50 689
筠 92A.50 1369
篔 92A.80 1373
ㄩㄣˇ (yuun)
殞 31S.80 528
隕 32A.80 559
允 93.70 1396
ㄩㄣˋ (yuhn)
惲 22A.10 386
運 62.83 937
鄆 62S.22 950
緼 93B.30 1429
蘊 20A.30 265
慍 22A.30 390
韞 22S.30 425
醞 31C.30 506
孕 32.00 536
熨 52.81 777
韵 60S.50 876
韻 60S.80 881
ㄩㄥ **YUNG** (yung)
庸 61.42 894
墉 11A.42 201
慵 22A.42 395
鄘 61S.22 913
鏞 81A.42 1116
傭 91A.42 1260
雍 60.11 815
蕹 20A.11 258
饔 60.02 807
邕 93.70 1396
灉 61A.11 904
雝 93S.11 1448
ㄩㄥˊ (yurng)
喁 40A.42 593
顒 41S.80 690
ㄩㄥˇ (yuung)
永 63.02 952
咏 40A.02 580
詠 60A.02 841
泳 63A.02 968
甬 32.42 539
蛹 22D.42 416
勇 32.50 540
恿 32.72 541
踊 40B.42 612
踴 40B.50 613
慂 63.72 955
涌 63A.42 995
湧 63A.50 998
俑 91A.42 1260
擁 10A.11 56
臃 42A.11 708
壅 60.11 815
(𡒊)
ㄩㄥˋ (yuhng)
用 42.42 695
佣 91A.42 1260

ENGLISH INDEX

B

C

D

E

F

G

H

M

N

Q

R

T

W

X

Y

Ref
PL
1455
L75

Lin, Yutang, 1895–
Chinese-English dictionary of modern usage. [Hong Kong] Chinese University of Hong Kong [distributed by McGraw-Hill, New York] 1972.

lxvi, 1720 p. 27 cm.

1. Chinese language—Dictionaries—English. I. Title.

268514 PL1455.L67 495.1'3'21 72-3899
ISBN 0-07-099695-4 MARC

Library of Congress 73 [4]